# THE COMPARATIVE STUDY BIBLE

## A PARALLEL BIBLE

# THE COMPARATIVE STUDY BIBLE

## A PARALLEL BIBLE

*presenting the*
New International Version
New American Standard Bible
Amplified Bible
King James Version

ZONDERVAN
BIBLE PUBLISHERS

Library of Congress Catalog Card Number 84-51724



Fifth printing—July 1987
165,000 copies in print

RRD—7-87

Printed in the United States of America
Published by The Zondervan Corporation
Grand Rapids, Michigan 49506, U.S.A.

# Contents

# *Publisher's Preface*

Today, as never before, Christians of every age, background, and denomination are turning to Bible study to dig into the truths of God's Word and to find God's will for their everyday lives. A parallel Bible such as this one offers the Bible student the opportunity to compare translations and to gain new appreciation for the richness, beauty, and meaningfulness of Scripture.

The *Comparative Study Bible* offers four of today's best-selling English translations in one volume.

The *King James Version* has been the standard English translation for almost four hundred years. Its majestic style and dignity have given it an enduring and universal appeal.

The *Amplified Bible*, based on the *American Standard Version*, uses a system of synonyms, punctuation, typographical features, and clarifying words or phrases to reveal shades of meaning of the key words in the original text.

The *New American Standard Bible* is the most widely accepted contemporary word-for-word translation. Based on the original *American Standard Version*, it is highly regarded for its scholarship and accuracy.

The *New International Version* is the best-selling modern English Bible translation. It is a scholarly translation that accurately expresses the original Bible texts in clear and contemporary English while remaining faithful to the thoughts and meaning of the Biblical writers. Its readability, accuracy, and beauty of style make it the most popular modern translation available.

The *Comparative Study Bible* is an exceptional specialty Bible designed to aid pastors, students, and laypeople in meaningful study of the Scriptures.

July, 1984 *The Publishers*

# King James Version

TO THE MOST HIGH AND MIGHTY PRINCE

## JAMES

*BY THE GRACE OF GOD*

KING OF GREAT BRITAIN, FRANCE, AND IRELAND

DEFENDER OF THE FAITH, &c.

### The Translators of the Bible wish Grace, Mercy, and Peace through JESUS CHRIST our Lord

Great and manifold were the blessings, most dread Sovereign, which Almighty God, the Father of all mercies, bestowed upon us the people of *England,* when first he sent Your Majesty's Royal Person to rule and reign over us. For whereas it was the expectation of many, who wished not well unto our *Sion,* that upon the setting of that bright *Occidental Star,* Queen *Elizabeth* of most happy memory, some thick and palpable clouds of darkness would so have overshadowed this Land, that men should have been in doubt which way they were to walk; and that it should hardly be known, who was to direct the unsettled State; the appearance of Your Majesty, as of the *Sun* in his strength, instantly dispelled those supposed and surmised mists, and gave unto all that were well affected exceeding cause of comfort; especially when we beheld the Government established in Your Highness, and Your hopeful seed, by an undoubted Title, and this also accompanied with peace and tranquility at home and abroad.

But among all our joys, there was no one that more filled our hearts, than the blessed continuance of the preaching of God's sacred Word among us; which is that inestimable treasure, which excelleth all the riches of the earth; because the fruit thereof extendeth itself, not only to the time spent in this transitory world, but directeth and disposeth men unto that eternal happiness which is above in heaven.

Then not to suffer this to fall to the ground, but rather to take it up, and to continue it in that state, wherein the famous Predecessor of Your Highness did leave it: nay, to go forward with the confidence and resolution of a Man in maintaining the truth of Christ, and propagating it far and near, is that which hath so bound and firmly knit the hearts of all Your Majesty's loyal and religious people unto You, that Your very name is precious among them: their eye doth behold You with comfort, and they bless You in their hearts, as that sanctified Person who, under God, is the immediate Author of their true happiness. And this their contentment doth not diminish or decay, but every day increaseth and taketh strength, when they observe, that the zeal of Your Majesty toward the house of God doth not slack or go backward, but is more and more kindled, manifesting itself abroad in the farthest parts of *Christendom,* by writing in defence of the Truth, (which hath given such a blow unto that man of sin, as will not be healed,) and every day at home, by religious and learned discourse, by frequenting the house of God, by hearing the Word preached, by cherishing the Teachers thereof, by caring for the Church, as a most tender and loving nursing Father.

There are infinite arguments of this right Christian and religious affection in Your Majesty; but none is more forcible to declare it to others than the vehement and perpetuated desire of accomplishing and publishing of this work, which now with all humility we present unto Your Majesty. For when Your Highness had once out of deep judgment apprehended how convenient it was, that out of the Original Sacred Tongues, together with comparing of the labours, both in our own, and other foreign Languages, of many worthy men who went before us, there should be one more exact Translation of the holy Scriptures into the *English Tongue;* Your Majesty did never desist to urge and to excite those to whom it was commended, that the work might be hastened, and that the business might be expedited in so decent a manner, as a matter of such importance might justly require.

And now at last, by the mercy of God, and the continuance of our labours, it being brought unto such a conclusion, as that we have great hopes that the Church of *England* shall reap good fruit thereby; we hold it our duty to offer it to Your Majesty, not only as to our King and Sovereign, but as to the principal Mover and Author of the work: humbly craving of Your most Sacred Majesty, that since things of this quality have ever been subject to the censures of ill-meaning and discontented persons, it may receive approbation and patronage from so learned and judicious a Prince as Your Highness is, whose allowance and acceptance of our labours shall more honour and encourage us, than all the calumniations and hard interpretations of other men shall dismay us. So that if, on the one side, we shall be traduced by Popish Persons at home or abroad, who therefore will malign us, because we are poor instruments to make God's holy Truth to be yet more and more known unto the people, whom they desire still to keep in ignorance and darkness; or if, on the other side, we shall be maligned by self-conceited Brethren, who run their own ways, and give liking unto nothing, but what is framed by themselves, and hammered on their anvil; we may rest secure, supported within by the truth and innocency of a good conscience, having walked the ways of simplicity and integrity, as before the Lord; and sustained without by the powerful protection of Your Majesty's grace and favour, which will ever give countenance to honest and Christian endeavours against bitter censures and uncharitable imputations.

The Lord of heaven and earth bless Your Majesty with many and happy days, that, as his heavenly hand hath enriched Your Highness with many singular and extraordinary graces, so You may be the wonder of the world in this latter age for happiness and true felicity, to the honour of that great GOD, and the good of his Church, through Jesus Christ our Lord and only Saviour.

# The Amplified Bible

## PREFACE

In 1958 The Lockman Foundation and Zondervan Publishing House issued the first edition of The Amplified New Testament. The enthusiasm with which it has been received (more than one million copies are now in print) attests to its usefulness as a means of better understanding the Word of God.

The Amplified Old Testament, Part 1 — Genesis to Esther — was published in 1964, and The Amplified Old Testament, Part 2 — Job to Malachi — in 1962. Both volumes have received the same degree of acceptance as that accorded earlier to The Amplified New Testament.

A committee of qualified Hebrew and Greek scholars has labored painstakingly to prepare a translation that may be used effectively by God to the enrichment of human knowledge and understanding of His Word. The work of Frances E. Siewert, B. Lit., B.D., M.A., D. Lit., Research Secretary, is deserving of special commendation.

The following *four-fold aim* expresses the original purpose of this translation:

1. It should be true to the original languages.
2. It should be grammatically correct.
3. It should be understandable to the masses.
4. It should give the Lord Jesus Christ His proper place which the Word gives Him. No work will be personalized.

Since the original release of The Amplified New Testament and the two volumes of The Amplified Old Testament, the entire text has been reexamined carefully with appropriate modification incorporated to insure the highest degree of accuracy.

*The Lockman Foundation*
*Zondervan Publishing House*

## PUBLISHER'S FOREWORD

From the days of John Wycliffe and the first English Bible down to the present time, scholarly translators have worked diligently on English versions designed to faithfully present the Scriptures in contemporary language. The Amplified Bible is not an attempt to duplicate what has already been achieved. Rather, its intent is to progress beyond the point where the others have stopped. Its purpose is to reveal, together with the single word English equivalent to each key Hebrew and Greek word, any other clarifying shades of meaning that may be concealed by the traditional word-for-word method of translation. Now, possibly for the first time the full meaning of the key words in the original text is available in an English version of the Bible.

This concept is fully justified and supported by the countless acknowledgments of Bible translators as to the inadequacy of the customary method. Martin Luther, whose translation of the Hebrew Scriptures into German in A.D. 1534 "spiritualized Germany and made the German language," stated it plainly: "The words of the Hebrew tongue have a peculiar energy. It is impossible to convey so much so briefly in any other language. To render them intelligibly we must not attempt to give word for word translations, but only aim at the sense and the [original Author's] idea." (*Table Talk*).

This is precisely what the Apostle Paul and ministers, teachers and commentators of every generation have attempted to do. But, unfortunately, there is a traditional reluctance to increase the number of English words used lest one "add to" the inspired text. On the other hand, by refusing to consider all the shades of meaning intended in the original language, we have unintentionally disobeyed the admonition not to "take from" God's holy Word. In a sense, amplification merely helps the English reader comprehend what the Hebrew and Greek listener understood as a matter of course.

For example, Acts 16:31 reads: "Believe on the Lord Jesus Christ and thou shalt be saved." What does the word "believe" mean? Webster defines it: "to place credence . . . apart from personal knowledge; to expect or hope . . . to be more or less firmly persuaded of the truth of anything, to think or suppose." In this sense, most people believe in Christ — that He lived; that He was a perfect Man Who sincerely believed Himself to be the Son of God, and that He died on the cross to save sinners. But this is by no means the meaning of the Greek word which twenty-two New Testament versions out of twenty-four consulted render "believe." They do so because there is no one English word that adequately conveys the intended meaning. Actually, the Greek word used here for believe is "pisteuo." It means "to adhere to, cleave to; to trust, to have faith in; to rely on." Consequently, the words, "Believe on the Lord Jesus Christ . . ." really mean *to have an absolute personal reliance upon the Lord Jesus Christ as Saviour*.

"And we are setting these truths forth in words not taught by human wisdom, but taught by the (Holy) Spirit . . . that His glory may be both manifested and recognized" (1 Cor. 2:13; Phil. 1:11).

*The Publishers*

## EXPLANATION of ARBITRARY PUNCTUATION

Parentheses ( ) and Dashes — —: signify additional phases of meaning included in the original word, phrase or clause of the original language.

Titles of Deity: are set off, however, only with commas.

Brackets [ ]: contain justified clarifying words or comments not actually expressed in the immediate original text.

Italics: point out certain familiar passages now recognized as not adequately supported by the original manuscripts. Also, "and," "or" and other connectives *in italics* indicate that the word itself is not in the original text, but it is used to connect additional English words indicated in the same original word.

Capitals: are used in names and personal pronouns referring to Deity, but sparingly elsewhere.

References (Scripture references at the end of a verse): are intended to cover any part of the preceding verse to which they apply.

Synonyms: are limited to what the text seems to warrant, both as to number and wording.

# New American Standard

## SCRIPTURAL PROMISE

"The grass withers, the flower fades, but the word of our God stands forever." Isaiah 40:8

## FOREWORD

The New American Standard Bible has been produced with the conviction that the words of Scripture as originally penned in the Hebrew, Aramaic, and Greek were inspired by God. Since they are the eternal Word of God, the Holy Scriptures speak with fresh power to each generation, to give wisdom that leads to salvation, that men may serve Christ to the glory of God.

The Editorial Board had a twofold purpose in making this translation: to adhere as closely as possible to the original languages of the Holy Scriptures, and to make the translation in a fluent and readable style according to current English usage.

## THE FOURFOLD AIM OF THE LOCKMAN FOUNDATION

1. These publications shall be true to the original Hebrew, Aramaic, and Greek.

2. They shall be grammatically correct.

3. They shall be understandable to the masses.

4. They shall give the Lord Jesus Christ His proper place, the place which the Word gives Him; therefore, no work will ever be personalized.

## PREFACE TO THE NEW AMERICAN STANDARD BIBLE

In the history of English Bible translations, the King James Version is the most prestigious. This time-honored version of 1611, itself a revision of the Bishops' Bible of 1568, became the basis for the English Revised Version appearing in 1881 (New Testament) and 1885 (Old Testament). The American counterpart of this last work was published in 1901 as the American Standard Version. Recognizing the values of the American Standard Version, the Lockman Foundation felt an urgency to update it by incorporating recent discoveries of Hebrew and Greek textual sources and by rendering it into more current English. Therefore, in 1959 a new translation project was launched, based on the ASV. The result is the New American Standard Bible.

The American Standard Version (1901) has been highly regarded for its scholarship and accuracy. A product of both British and American scholarship, it has frequently been used as a standard for other translations. It is still recognized as a valuable tool for study of the Scriptures. The New American Standard Bible has sought to preserve these and other lasting values of the ASV.

Furthermore, in the preparation of this work numerous other translations have been consulted along with the linguistic tools and literature of biblical scholarship. Decisions about English renderings were made by consensus of a team composed of educators and pastors. Subsequently, review and evaluation by other Hebrew and Greek scholars outside the Editorial Board were sought and carefully considered.

The Editorial Board has continued to function since publication of the complete Bible in 1971. Minor revisions and refinements, recommended over the last several years, are presented in this edition.

## PRINCIPLES OF TRANSLATION

MODERN ENGLISH USAGE: The attempt has been made to render the grammar and terminology in contemporary English. When it was felt that the word-for-word literalness was unacceptable to the modern reader, a change was made in the direction of a more current English idiom. In the instances where this has been done, the more literal rendering has been indicated in the notes.

ALTERNATIVE READINGS: In addition to the more literal renderings, notations have been made to include alternate translations, readings of variant manuscripts and explanatory equivalents of the text. Only such notations have been used as have been felt justified in assisting the reader's comprehension of the terms used by the original author.

HEBREW TEXT: In the present translation the latest edition of Rudolf Kittel's BIBLIA HEBRAICA has been employed together with the most recent light from lexicography, cognate languages, and the Dead Sea Scrolls.

HEBREW TENSES: Consecution of tenses in Hebrew remains a puzzling factor in translation. The translators have been guided by the requirements of a literal translation, the sequence of tenses, and the immediate and broad contexts.

THE PROPER NAME OF GOD IN THE OLD TESTAMENT: In the Scriptures, the name of God is most significant and understandably so. It is inconceivable to think of spiritual matters without a proper designation for the Supreme Deity. Thus the most common name for the Deity is God, a translation of the original Elohim. One of the titles for God is Lord, a translation of Adonai. There is yet another name which is particularly assigned to God as His special or proper name, that is, the four letters YHWH (Exodus 3:14 and Isaiah 42:8). This name has not been pronounced by the Jews because of reverence for the great sacredness of the divine name. Therefore, it has been consistently translated LORD. The only exception to this translation of YHWH is when it occurs in immediate proximity to the word Lord, that is, Adonai. In that case it is regularly translated GOD in order to avoid confusion. It is known that for many years YHWH has been transliterated as Yahweh, however no complete certainty attaches to this pronunciation.

GREEK TEXT: Consideration was given to the latest available manuscripts with a view to determining the best Greek text. In most instances the 23rd edition of Eberhard Nestle's NOVUM TESTAMENTUM GRAECE was followed.

GREEK TENSES: A careful distinction has been made in the treatment of the Greek aorist tense (usually translated as the English past, "He did") and the Greek imperfect tense (rendered either as English past progressive, "He was doing"; or, if inceptive, as "He *began* to do" or "He started to do"; or else if customary past, as "He used to do"). "Began" is italicized if it renders an imperfect tense, in order to distinguish it from the Greek verb for "begin."

On the other hand, not all aorists have been rendered as English pasts ("He did"), for some of them are clearly to be rendered as English perfects ("He has done"), or even as past

perfects ("He had done"), judging from the context in which they occur. Such aorists have been rendered as perfects or past perfects in this translation.

As for the distinction between aorist and present imperatives, the translators have usually rendered these imperatives in the customary manner, rather than attempting any such fine distinction as "Begin to do!" (for the aorist imperative), or, "Continually do!" (for the present imperative).

As for sequence of tenses, the translators took care to follow English rules rather than Greek in translating Greek presents, imperfects and aorists. Thus, where English says, "We knew that he was doing," Greek puts it, "We knew that he does"; similarly, "We knew that he had done" is the Greek, "We knew that he did." Likewise, the English, "When he had come, they met him," is represented in Greek by: "When he came, they met him." In all cases a consistent transfer has been made from the Greek tense in the subordinate clause to the appropriate tense in English.

In the rendering of negative questions introduced by the particle **mē** (which always expects the answer "No") the wording has been altered from a mere, "Will he not do this?" to a more accurate, "He will not do this, will he?"

Editorial Board, THE LOCKMAN FOUNDATION

## Explanation of GENERAL FORMAT

FOOTNOTES are used only where the text especially requires them for clarification. Marginal notes and cross references have been deleted from this edition.

PARAGRAPHS are designated by a paragraph mark with bold face numbers or letters.

QUOTATION MARKS are used in the text in accordance with modern English usage.

"THOU," "THEE" AND "THY" are not used in this translation except in the language of prayer when addressing Deity.

PERSONAL PRONOUNS are capitalized when pertaining to Deity.

ITALICS are used in the text to indicate words which are not found in the original Hebrew, Aramaic, or Greek but implied by it. Italics are used in the footnotes to signify alternate readings for the text.

SMALL CAPS in the New Testament are used in the text to indicate Old Testament quotations or obvious allusions to Old Testament texts. Variations of Old Testament wording are found in New Testament citations depending on whether the New Testament writer translated from a Hebrew text, used existing Greek or Aramaic translations, or paraphrased the material. It should be noted that modern rules for the indication of direct quotation were not used in biblical times thus allowing freedom for omissions or insertions without specific indication of these.

ASTERISKS are used to mark verbs that are historical presents in the Greek which have been translated with an English past tense in order to conform to modern usage. The translators recognized that in some contexts the present tense seems more unexpected and unjustified to the English reader than a past tense would have been. But Greek authors frequently used the present tense for the sake of heightened vividness, thereby transporting their readers in imagination to the actual scene at the time of occurrence. However, the translators felt that it would be wise to change these historical presents to English past tenses.

ABBREVIATIONS AND SPECIAL MARKINGS:

| | |
|---|---|
| Aram. = | Aramaic |
| Gr. = | Greek translation of O.T. (Septuagint or LXX) or Greek text of N.T. |
| Heb. = | Hebrew text, usually Masoretic |
| M.T. = | Masoretic text |
| Syr. = | Syriac |
| Lit. = | A literal translation |
| Or = | An alternate translation justified by the Hebrew, Aramaic, or Greek |
| [ ] = | In text, brackets indicate words probably not in the original writings |
| cf. = | compare |
| ms., mss. = | manuscript, manuscripts |
| v., vv. = | verse, verses |

# New International Version

## TRANSLATORS' PREFACE

The New International Version is a completely new translation of the Holy Bible made by over a hundred scholars working directly from the best available Hebrew, Aramaic and Greek texts. It had its beginning in 1965 when, after several years of exploratory study by committees from the Christian Reformed Church and the National Association of Evangelicals, a group of scholars met at Palos Heights, Illinois, and concurred in the need for a new translation of the Bible in contemporary English. This group, though not made up of official church representatives, was transdenominational. Its conclusion was endorsed by a large number of leaders from many denominations who met in Chicago in 1966.

Responsibility for the new version was delegated by the Palos Heights group to a self-governing body of fifteen, the Committee on Bible Translation, composed for the most part of biblical scholars from colleges, universities and seminaries. In 1967 the New York Bible Society (now the International Bible Society) generously undertook the financial sponsorship of the project—a sponsorship that made it possible to enlist the help of many distinguished scholars. The fact that participants from the United States, Great Britain, Canada, Australia and New Zealand worked together gave the project its international scope. That they were from many denominations—including Anglican, Assemblies of God, Baptist, Brethren, Christian Reformed, Church of Christ, Evangelical Free, Lutheran, Mennonite, Methodist, Nazarene, Presbyterian, Wesleyan and other churches—helped to safeguard the translation from sectarian bias.

How it was made helps to give the New International Version its distinctiveness. The translation of each book was assigned to a team of scholars. Next, one of the Intermediate Editorial Committees revised the initial translation, with constant reference to the Hebrew, Aramaic or Greek. Their work then went to one of the General Editorial Committees, which checked it in detail and made another thorough revision. This revision in turn was carefully reviewed by the Committee on Bible Translation, which made further changes and then released the final version for publication. In this way the entire Bible underwent three revisions, during each of which the translation was examined for its faithfulness to the original languages and for its English style.

All this involved many thousands of hours of research and discussion regarding the meaning of the texts and the precise way of putting them into English. It may well be that no other translation has been made by a more thorough process of review and revision from committee to committee than this one.

From the beginning of the project, the Committee on Bible Translation held to certain goals for the New International Version: that it would be an accurate translation and one that would have clarity and literary quality and so prove suitable for public and private reading, teaching, preaching, memorizing and liturgical use. The Committee also sought to preserve some measure of continuity with the long tradition of translating the Scriptures into English.

In working toward these goals, the translators were united in their commitment to the authority and infallibility of the Bible as God's Word in written form. They believe that it contains the divine answer to the deepest needs of humanity, that it sheds unique light on our path in a dark world, and that it sets forth the way to our eternal well-being.

The first concern of the translators has been the accuracy of the translation and its fidelity to the thought of the biblical writers. They have weighed the significance of the lexical and grammatical details of the Hebrew, Aramaic and Greek texts. At the same time, they have striven for more than a word-for-word translation. Because thought patterns and syntax differ from language to language, faithful communication of the meaning of the writers of the Bible demands frequent modifications in sentence structure and constant regard for the contextual meanings of words.

A sensitive feeling for style does not always accompany scholarship. Accordingly the Committee on Bible Translation submitted the developing version to a number of stylistic consultants. Two of them read every book of both Old and New Testaments twice—once before and once after the last major revision—and made invaluable suggestions. Samples of the translation were tested for clarity and ease of reading by various kinds of people—young and old, highly educated and less well educated, ministers and laymen.

Concern for clear and natural English—that the New International Version should be idiomatic but not idiosyncratic, contemporary but not dated—motivated the translators and consultants. At the same time, they tried to reflect the differing styles of the biblical writers. In view of the international use of English, the translators sought to avoid obvious Americanisms on the one hand and obvious Anglicisms on the other. A British edition reflects the comparatively few differences of significant idiom and of spelling.

As for the traditional pronouns "thou," "thee" and "thine" in reference to the Deity, the translators judged that to use these archaisms (along with the old verb forms such as "doest," "wouldest" and "hadst") would violate accuracy in translation. Neither Hebrew, Aramaic nor Greek uses special pronouns for the persons of the Godhead. A present-day translation is not enhanced by forms that in the time of the King James Version were used in everyday speech, whether referring to God or man.

For the Old Testament the standard Hebrew text, the Masoretic Text as published in the latest editions of *Biblia Hebraica,* was used throughout. The Dead Sea Scrolls contain material bearing on an earlier stage of the Hebrew text. They were consulted, as were the Samaritan Pentateuch and the ancient scribal traditions relating to textual changes. Sometimes a variant Hebrew reading in the margin of the Masoretic Text was followed instead of the text itself. Such instances, being variants within the Masoretic tradition, are not specified by footnotes. In rare cases, words in the consonantal text were divided differently from the way they appear in the Masoretic Text. Footnotes indicate this. The translators also consulted the more important early versions—the Septuagint; Aquila, Symmachus and Theodotion; the Vulgate; the Syriac Peshitta; the Targums; and for the Psalms the *Juxta Hebraica* of Jerome. Readings from these versions were occasionally followed where the Masoretic Text seemed doubtful and where accepted principles of textual criticism showed that one or more of these textual witnesses appeared to provide the correct reading. Such instances are footnoted. Sometimes vowel letters and vowel signs did not, in the judgment of the translators, represent the correct vowels for the original consonantal text. Accordingly some words were read with a different set of vowels. These instances are usually not indicated by footnotes.

The Greek text used in translating the New Testament was an eclectic one. No other piece of ancient literature has such an abundance of manuscript witnesses as does the New Testament. Where existing manuscripts differ, the translators made their choice of readings according to accepted principles of New Testament textual criticism. Footnotes call attention to places where there was uncertainty about what the original text was. The best current printed texts of the Greek New Testament were used.

There is a sense in which the work of translation is never wholly finished. This applies to all great literature and uniquely so to the Bible. In 1973 the New Testament in the New International Version was published. Since then, suggestions for corrections and revisions have been received from various sources. The Committee on Bible Translation carefully considered the suggestions and adopted a number of them. These were incorporated in the first printing of the entire Bible in 1978. Additional revisions were made by the Committee on Bible Translation in 1983 and appear in printings after that date.

As in other ancient documents, the precise meaning of the biblical texts is sometimes uncertain. This is more often the case with the Hebrew and Aramaic texts than with the Greek text. Although archaeological and linguistic discoveries in this century aid in understanding difficult passages, some uncertainties remain. The more significant of these have been called to the reader's attention in the footnotes.

In regard to the divine name *YHWH*, commonly referred to as the *Tetragrammaton*, the translators adopted the device used in most English versions of rendering that name as "LORD" in capital letters to distinguish it from *Adonai*, another Hebrew word rendered "Lord," for which small letters are used. Wherever the two names stand together in the Old Testament as a compound name of God, they are rendered "Sovereign LORD."

Because for most readers today the phrases "the LORD of hosts" and "God of hosts" have little meaning, this version renders them "the LORD Almighty" and "God Almighty." These renderings convey the sense of the Hebrew, namely, "he who is sovereign over all the 'hosts' (powers) in heaven and on earth, especially over the 'hosts' (armies) of Israel." For readers unacquainted with Hebrew this does not make clear the distinction between *Sabaoth* ("hosts" or "Almighty") and *Shaddai* (which can also be translated "Almighty"), but the latter occurs infrequently and is always footnoted. When *Adonai* and *YHWH Sabaoth* occur together, they are rendered "the Lord, the LORD Almighty."

As for other proper nouns, the familiar spellings of the King James Version are generally retained. Names traditionally spelled with "ch," except where it is final, are usually spelled in this translation with "k" or "c," since the biblical languages do not have the sound that "ch" frequently indicates in English —for example, in *chant*. For well-known names such as Zechariah, however, the traditional spelling has been retained. Variation in the spelling of names in the original languages has usually not been indicated. Where a person or place has two or more different names in the Hebrew, Aramaic or Greek texts, the more familiar one has generally been used, with footnotes where needed.

To achieve clarity the translators sometimes supplied words not in the original texts but required by the context. If there was uncertainty about such material, it is enclosed in brackets. Also for the sake of clarity or style, nouns, including some proper nouns, are sometimes substituted for pronouns, and vice versa. And though the Hebrew writers often shifted back and forth between first, second and third personal pronouns without change of antecedent, this translation often makes them uniform, in accordance with English style and without the use of footnotes.

Poetical passages are printed as poetry, that is, with indentation of lines and with separate stanzas. These are generally designed to reflect the structure of Hebrew poetry. This poetry is normally characterized by parallelism in balanced lines. Most of the poetry in the Bible is in the Old Testament, and scholars differ regarding the scansion of Hebrew lines. The translators determined the stanza divisions for the most part by analysis of the subject matter. The stanzas therefore serve as poetic paragraphs.

As an aid to the reader, italicized sectional headings are inserted in most of the books. They are not to be regarded as part of the NIV text, are not for oral reading, and are not intended to dictate the interpretation of the sections they head.

The footnotes in this version are of several kinds, most of which need no explanation. Those giving alternative translations begin with "Or" and generally introduce the alternative with the last word preceding it in the text, except when it is a single-word alternative; in poetry quoted in a footnote a slant mark indicates a line division. Footnotes introduced by "Or" do not have uniform significance. In some cases two possible translations were considered to have about equal validity. In other cases, though the translators were convinced that the translation in the text was correct, they judged that another interpretation was possible and of sufficient importance to be represented in a footnote.

In the New Testament, footnotes that refer to uncertainty regarding the original text are introduced by "Some manuscripts" or similar expressions. In the Old Testament, evidence for the reading chosen is given first and evidence for the alternative is added after a semicolon (for example: Septuagint; Hebrew *father*). In such notes the term "Hebrew" refers to the Masoretic Text.

It should be noted that minerals, flora and fauna, architectural details, articles of clothing and jewelry, musical instruments and other articles cannot always be identified with precision. Also measures of capacity in the biblical period are particularly uncertain (see the table of weights and measures following the text).

Like all translations of the Bible, made as they are by imperfect man, this one undoubtedly falls short of its goals. Yet we are grateful to God for the extent to which he has enabled us to realize these goals and for the strength he has given us and our colleagues to complete our task. We offer this version of the Bible to him in whose name and for whose glory it has been made. We pray that it will lead many into a better understanding of the Holy Scriptures and a fuller knowledge of Jesus Christ the incarnate Word, of whom the Scriptures so faithfully testify.

*The Committee on Bible Translation*

June 1978
(Revised August 1983)

Names of the translators and editors may be secured
from the International Bible Society
144 Tices Lane, East Brunswick, New Jersey 08816.

# The Old Testament

## King James

THE FIRST BOOK OF

MOSES, CALLED

# Genesis

1 IN THE beginning God created the heaven and the earth.

2 And the earth was without form, and void; and darkness *was* upon the face of the deep. And the spirit of God moved upon the face of the waters.

3 And God said, Let there be light: and there was light.

4 And God saw the light, that *it was* good: and God divided the light from the darkness.

5 And God called the light Day, and the darkness he called Night. And the evening and the morning were the first day.

6 ¶ And God said, Let there be a firmament in the midst of the waters, and let it divide the waters from the waters.

7 And God made the firmament, and divided the waters which *were* under the firmament from the waters which *were* above the firmament: and it was so.

8 And God called the firmament Heaven. And the evening and the morning were the second day.

9 ¶ And God said, Let the waters under the heaven be gathered together unto one place, and let the dry *land* appear: and it was so.

10 And God called the dry *land* Earth; and the gathering together of the waters called he Seas: and God saw that *it was* good.

11 And God said, Let the earth bring forth grass, the herb yielding seed, *and* the fruit tree yielding fruit after his kind, whose seed *is* in itself, upon the earth: and it was so.

12 And the earth brought forth grass, *and* herb yielding seed after his kind, and the tree yielding fruit, whose seed *was* in itself, after his kind: and God saw that *it was* good.

13 And the evening and the morning were the third day.

14 ¶ And God said, Let there be lights in the firmament of the heaven to divide the day from the night; and let them be for signs, and for seasons, and for days, and years:

15 And let them be for lights in the firmament of the heaven to give light upon the earth: and it was so.

16 And God made two great lights; the greater light to rule the day, and the lesser light to rule the night: *he made* the stars also.

17 And God set them in the firmament of the heaven to give light upon the earth,

18 And to rule over the day and over the night, and to divide the light from the darkness: and God saw that *it was* good.

19 And the evening and the morning were the fourth day.

20 And God said, Let the waters bring forth abundantly the moving creature that hath life, and fowl *that* may fly above the earth in the open firmament of heaven.

## Amplified

THE FIRST BOOK OF MOSES,

COMMONLY CALLED

# Genesis

1 IN THE beginning God (prepared, formed, fashioned,) *and* created the heavens and the earth. [Heb. 11:3.]

2 The earth was without form and an empty waste, and darkness was upon the face of the very great deep. The Spirit of God was moving, (hovering, brooding) over the face of the waters.

3 And God said, Let there be light; and there was light.

4 And God saw the light, that it was good—suitable, pleasing—*and* He approved it; and God separated the light from the darkness. [II Cor. 4:6.]

5 And God called the light Day, and the darkness He called Night. And there was evening and there was morning, one day.

6 And God said, Let there be a firmament [the expanse of the sky] in the midst of the waters; and let it separate the waters [below] from the waters [above].

7 And God made the firmament (the expanse) and separated the waters which were under the expanse from the waters which were above the expanse. And it was so.

8 And God called the firmament Heavens. And there was evening and there was morning, a second day.

9 And God said, Let the waters under the heavens be collected into one place (of standing), and let the dry land appear. And it was done.

10 God called the dry land Earth, and the accumulated waters He called Seas. And God saw that this was good—admirable, fitting—*and* He approved it.

11 And God said, Let the earth put forth (tender) vegetation, plants yielding seed, and the fruit trees yielding fruit each according to its kind, whose seed is in itself, upon the earth. And it was so.

12 The earth brought forth vegetation, plants yielding seed according to their own kind, and trees bearing fruit in which was their seed, each according to its kind. And God saw that it was good—suitable, admirable— *and* He approved it.

13 And there was evening and there was morning, a third day.

14 And God said, Let there be lights in the expanse of the heavens to separate the day from the night; and let them be for signs *and* tokens [of God's provident care], and [to mark] seasons, days, and years. [Gen. 8:22.]

15 And let them be for lights in the expanse of the sky to give light upon the earth. And it was so.

16 And God made the two great lights, the greater light (the sun) to rule the day, and the lesser light (the moon) to rule the night; He also made the stars.

17 And God set them in the expanse of the heavens to give light upon the earth,

18 To rule over the day and over the night, and to separate the light from the darkness. And God saw that it was good—fitting, pleasant— *and* He approved it.

19 And there was evening and there was morning, a fourth day.

20 And God said, Let the waters bring forth abundantly *and* swarm with living creatures, and let birds fly over the earth in the open expanse of the heavens.

## New American Standard

# Genesis

*The Creation*

1 IN THE beginning God created the heavens and the earth.
2And the earth was [a]formless and void, and darkness was
over the surface of the deep; and the Spirit of God was [b]moving
over the surface of the waters.
3Then God said, "Let there be light"; and there was light.
4And God saw that the light was good; and God separated the
light from the darkness.
5And God called the light day, and the darkness He called
night. And there was evening and there was morning, one day.
6¶ Then God said, "Let there be an expanse in the midst of the
waters, and let it separate the waters from the waters."
7And God made the [c]expanse, and separated the waters
which were below the expanse from the waters which were above
the expanse; and it was so.
8And God called the expanse heaven. And there was evening
and there was morning, a second day.
9¶ Then God said, "Let the waters below the heavens be gathered into one place, and let the dry land appear"; and it was so.
10And God called the dry land earth, and the gathering of the
waters He called seas; and God saw that it was good.
11Then God said, "Let the earth sprout vegetation, plants yielding seed, *and* fruit trees bearing fruit after their kind, with seed in
them, on the earth"; and it was so.
12And the earth brought forth vegetation, plants yielding seed
after their kind, and trees bearing fruit, with seed in them, after
their kind; and God saw that it was good.
13And there was evening and there was morning, a third day.
14¶ Then God said, "Let there be lights in the expanse of the
heavens to separate the day from the night, and let them be for
signs, and for seasons, and for days and years;
15and let them be for lights in the expanse of the heavens to give
light on the earth"; and it was so.
16And God made the two great lights, the greater light to govern the day, and the lesser light to govern the night; *He made* the
stars also.
17And God placed them in the expanse of the heavens to give
light on the earth,
18and to govern the day and the night, and to separate the light
from the darkness; and God saw that it was good.
19And there was evening and there was morning, a fourth day.
20¶ Then God said, "Let the waters teem with swarms of living
creatures, and let birds fly above the earth in the open expanse of
the heavens."

NAS [a] Or, *a waste and emptiness* [b] Or, *hovering* [c] Or, *firmament*

## New International

# Genesis

*The Beginning*

1 IN THE beginning God created the heavens and the earth.
2Now the earth was[d] formless and empty, darkness was over
the surface of the deep, and the Spirit of God was hovering over
the waters.
3And God said, "Let there be light," and there was light. 4God
saw that the light was good, and he separated the light from
the darkness. 5God called the light "day," and the darkness
he called "night." And there was evening, and there was
morning—the first day.
6And God said, "Let there be an expanse between the waters to
separate water from water." 7So God made the expanse and
separated the water under the expanse from the water
above it. And it was so. 8God called the expanse "sky." And
there was evening, and there was morning—the second
day.
9And God said, "Let the water under the sky be gathered to one
place, and let dry ground appear." And it was so. 10God
called the dry ground "land," and the gathered waters he
called "seas." And God saw that it was good.
11Then God said, "Let the land produce vegetation:
seed-bearing plants and trees on the land that bear fruit with
seed in it, according to their various kinds." And it was so.
12The land produced vegetation: plants bearing seed
according to their kinds and trees bearing fruit with seed in
it according to their kinds. And God saw that it was good.
13And there was evening, and there was morning—the
third day.
14And God said, "Let there be lights in the expanse of the sky to
separate the day from the night, and let them serve as signs
to mark seasons and days and years, 15and let them be lights
in the expanse of the sky to give light on the earth." And
it was so. 16God made two great lights—the greater light to
govern the day and the lesser light to govern the night. He
also made the stars. 17God set them in the expanse of the
sky to give light on the earth, 18to govern the day and the
night, and to separate light from darkness. And God saw
that it was good. 19And there was evening, and there was
morning—the fourth day.
20And God said, "Let the water teem with living creatures, and let
birds fly above the earth across the expanse of the sky." 21So

NIV [d] 2 Or possibly *became*

## King James

21 And God created great whales, and every living creature that moveth, which the waters brought forth abundantly, after their kind, and every winged fowl after his kind: and God saw that *it was* good.

22 And God blessed them, saying, Be fruitful, and multiply, and fill the waters in the seas, and let fowl multiply in the earth.

23 And the evening and the morning were the fifth day.

24¶ And God said, Let the earth bring forth the living creature after his kind, cattle, and creeping thing, and beast of the earth after his kind: and it was so.

25 And God made the beast of the earth after his kind, and cattle after their kind, and every thing that creepeth upon the earth after his kind: and God saw that *it was* good.

26¶ And God said, Let us make man in our image, after our likeness: and let them have dominion over the fish of the sea, and over the fowl of the air, and over the cattle, and over all the earth, and over every creeping thing that creepeth upon the earth.

27 So God created man in his *own* image, in the image of God created he him; male and female created he them.

28 And God blessed them, and God said unto them, Be fruitful, and multiply, and replenish the earth, and subdue it: and have dominion over the fish of the sea, and over the fowl of the air, and over every living thing that moveth upon the earth.

29¶ And God said, Behold, I have given you every herb bearing seed, which *is* upon the face of all the earth, and every tree, in the which *is* the fruit of a tree yielding seed; to you it shall be for meat.

30 And to every beast of the earth, and to every fowl of the air, and to every thing that creepeth upon the earth, wherein *there is* life, *I have given* every green herb for meat: and it was so.

31 And God saw every thing that he had made, and, behold, *it was* very good. And the evening and the morning were the sixth day.

**2** THUS THE heavens and the earth were finished, and all the host of them.

2 And on the seventh day God ended his work which he had made; and he rested on the seventh day from all his work which he had made.

3 And God blessed the seventh day, and sanctified it: because that in it he had rested from all his work which God created and made.

4¶ These *are* the generations of the heavens and of the earth when they were created, in the day that the LORD God made the earth and the heavens,

5 And every plant of the field before it was in the earth, and every herb of the field before it grew: for the LORD God had not caused it to rain upon the earth, and *there was* not a man to till the ground.

6 But there went up a mist from the earth, and watered the whole face of the ground.

7 And the LORD God formed man *of* the dust of the ground, and breathed into his nostrils the breath of life; and man became a living soul.

8¶ And the LORD God planted a garden eastward in Eden; and there he put the man whom he had formed.

## Amplified

21 God created the great sea monsters and every living creature that moves, which the waters brought forth abundantly according to their kinds, and every winged bird according to its kind. And God saw that it was good—suitable, admirable— *and* He approved it.

22 And God blessed them, saying, Be fruitful, multiply and fill the waters in the seas, and let the fowl multiply in the earth.

23 And there was evening and there was morning, a fifth day.

24 And God said, Let the earth bring forth living creatures according to their kinds: livestock, creeping things, and [wild] beasts of the earth according to their kinds. And it was so.

25 And God made the [wild] beasts of the earth according to their kinds, and domestic animals according to their kinds, and everything that creeps upon the earth according to its kind. And God saw that they were good—fitting, pleasant— *and* He approved them.

26 God said, Let Us [Father, Son, and Holy Spirit] make mankind in Our image, after Our likeness; and let them have complete authority over the fish of the sea, the birds of the air, the [tame] beasts, and over all of the earth, and over every thing that creeps upon the earth. [Heb. 11:3; 1:2; Ps. 104:30.]

27 So God created man in His own image, in the image *and* likeness of God He created him; male and female He created them. [Col. 3:9, 10; James 3:8, 9.]

28 And God blessed them, and said to them, Be fruitful, multiply, and fill the earth and subdue it [with all its vast resources]; and have dominion over the fish of the sea, the birds of the air, and over every living creature that moves upon the earth.

29 And God said, See, I have given you every plant yielding seed that is on the face of all the land, and every tree with seed in its fruit; you shall have them for food.

30 And to all the animals on the earth, and to every bird of the air, and to everything that creeps on the ground, to everything in which there is the breath of life, I have given every green plant for food. And it was so.

31 And God saw everything that He had made, and behold, it was very good—suitable, pleasant— *and* He approved it completely. And there was evening and there was morning, a sixth day.

**2** THUS THE heavens and the earth were finished, and all the host of them.

2 And on the seventh day God ended His work which He had done, and He rested on the seventh day from all His work which He had done. [Heb. 4:9, 10.]

3 And God blessed (spoke good of) the seventh day, set it apart as His own, and hallowed it, because on it God rested from all His work which He had created and done. [Exod. 20:11.]

4 This is the history of the heavens and of the earth when they were created. In the day that the Lord God made the earth and the heavens,

5 When no plant of the field was yet in the earth, and no herb of the field had yet sprung up, the Lord God had not [yet] caused it to rain upon the earth, and there was no man to till the ground.

6 But there went up a mist (a fog-vapor) from the land, and watered the whole surface of the ground.

7 Then the Lord God formed man of the [a]dust of the ground, and breathed into his nostrils the breath *or* spirit of life; and man became a living being. [I Cor. 15:45-49.]

8 And the Lord God planted a garden toward the east in Eden (meaning delight); and there He put the man whom He had formed (framed, constituted).

**AMP** [a] The same essential chemical elements are found in man and animal life that are in the soil. This scientific fact was not known to man until recent times, but God was displaying it here.

## New American Standard

21 And God created the great sea monsters, and every living creature that moves, with which the waters swarmed after their kind, and every winged bird after its kind; and God saw that it was good.

22 And God blessed them, saying, "Be fruitful and multiply, and fill the waters in the seas, and let birds multiply on the earth."

23 And there was evening and there was morning, a fifth day.

24¶ Then God said, "Let the earth bring forth living creatures after their kind: cattle and creeping things and beasts of the earth after their kind"; and it was so.

25 And God made the beasts of the earth after their kind, and the cattle after their kind, and everything that creeps on the ground after its kind; and God saw that it was good.

26 Then God said, "Let Us make man in Our image, according to Our likeness; and let them rule over the fish of the sea and over the birds of the sky and over the cattle and over all the earth, and over every creeping thing that creeps on the earth."

27 And God created man in His own image, in the image of God He created him; male and female He created them.

28 And God blessed them; and God said to them, "Be fruitful and multiply, and fill the earth, and subdue it; and rule over the fish of the sea and over the birds of the sky, and over every living thing that moves on the earth."

29 Then God said, "Behold, I have given you every plant yielding seed that is on the surface of all the earth, and every tree which has fruit yielding seed; it shall be food for you;

30 and to every beast of the earth and to every bird of the sky and to every thing that moves on the earth which has life, *I have given* every green plant for food"; and it was so.

31 And God saw all that He had made, and behold, it was very good. And there was evening and there was morning, the sixth day.

*The Creation of Man and Woman*

**2** THUS THE heavens and the earth were completed, and all their hosts.

2 And by the seventh day God completed His work which He had done; and He rested on the seventh day from all His work which He had done.

3 Then God blessed the seventh day and sanctified it, because in it He rested from all His work which God had created and made.

4¶ This is the account of the heavens and the earth when they were created, in the day that the LORD God made earth and heaven.

5 Now no shrub of the field was yet in the earth, and no plant of the field had yet sprouted, for the LORD God had not sent rain upon the earth; and there was no man to cultivate the ground.

6 But a mist used to rise from the earth and water the whole surface of the ground.

7 Then the LORD God formed man of dust from the ground, and breathed into his nostrils the breath of life; and man became a living being.

8 And the LORD God planted a garden toward the east, in Eden; and there He placed the man whom He had formed.

## New International

God created the great creatures of the sea and every living
and moving thing with which the water teems, according to
their kinds, and every winged bird according to its kind.
And God saw that it was good. 22 God blessed them and
said, "Be fruitful and increase in number and fill the water
in the seas, and let the birds increase on the earth." 23 And
there was evening, and there was morning—the fifth day.
24 And God said, "Let the land produce living creatures according
to their kinds: livestock, creatures that move along the
ground, and wild animals, each according to its kind." And
it was so. 25 God made the wild animals according to their
kinds, the livestock according to their kinds, and all the
creatures that move along the ground according to their
kinds. And God saw that it was good.

26 Then God said, "Let us make man in our image, in our likeness, and let them rule over the fish of the sea and the birds of the air, over the livestock, over all the earth,[b] and over all the creatures that move along the ground."

27 So God created man in his own image,
in the image of God he created him;
male and female he created them.

28 God blessed them and said to them, "Be fruitful and increase in number; fill the earth and subdue it. Rule over the fish of the sea and the birds of the air and over every living creature that moves on the ground."

29 Then God said, "I give you every seed-bearing plant on
the face of the whole earth and every tree that has fruit with
seed in it. They will be yours for food. 30 And to all the beasts
of the earth and all the birds of the air and all the creatures
that move on the ground—everything that has the breath of
life in it—I give every green plant for food." And it was so.
31 God saw all that he had made, and it was very good.
And there was evening, and there was morning—the sixth
day.

**2** THUS THE heavens and the earth were completed in all their vast array.

2 By the seventh day God had finished the work he had been
doing; so on the seventh day he rested[c] from all his work.
3 And God blessed the seventh day and made it holy,
because on it he rested from all the work of creating that he
had done.

*Adam and Eve*

4 This is the account of the heavens and the earth when they were created.

When the LORD God made the earth and the heavens— 5 and
no shrub of the field had yet appeared on the earth[d] and no plant
of the field had yet sprung up, for the LORD God had not sent rain
on the earth[e] and there was no man to work the ground, 6 but
streams[f] came up from the earth and watered the whole surface
of the ground— 7 the LORD God formed the man[g] from the dust
of the ground and breathed into his nostrils the breath of life, and
the man became a living being.

8 Now the LORD God had planted a garden in the east, in Eden;
and there he put the man he had formed. 9 And the LORD God

NIV [b] 26 Hebrew; Syriac *all the wild animals* [c] 2 Or *ceased;* also in verse 3 [d] 5 Or *land;* also in verse 6 [e] 5 Or *land;* also in verse 6 [f] 6 Or *mist* [g] 7 The Hebrew for *man (adam)* sounds like and may be related to the Hebrew for *ground (adamah);* it is also the name *Adam* (see Gen. 2:20).

## King James

9And out of the ground made the LORD God to grow every tree that is pleasant to the sight, and good for food; the tree of life also in the midst of the garden, and the tree of knowledge of good and evil.

10And a river went out of Eden to water the garden; and from thence it was parted, and became into four heads.

11The name of the first *is* Pison: that *is* it which compasseth the whole land of Havilah, where *there is* gold;

12And the gold of that land *is* good: there *is* bdellium and the onyx stone.

13And the name of the second river *is* Gihon: the same *is* it that compasseth the whole land of Ethiopia.

14And the name of the third river *is* Hiddekel: that *is* it which goeth toward the east of Assyria. And the fourth river *is* Euphrates.

15And the LORD God took the man, and put him into the garden of Eden to dress it and to keep it.

16And the LORD God commanded the man, saying, Of every tree of the garden thou mayest freely eat:

17But of the tree of the knowledge of good and evil, thou shalt not eat of it: for in the day that thou eatest thereof thou shalt surely die.

18¶ And the LORD God said, *It is* not good that the man should be alone; I will make him an help meet for him.

19And out of the ground the LORD God formed every beast of the field, and every fowl of the air; and brought *them* unto Adam to see what he would call them: and whatsoever Adam called every living creature, that *was* the name thereof.

20And Adam gave names to all cattle, and to the fowl of the air, and to every beast of the field; but for Adam there was not found an help meet for him.

21And the LORD God caused a deep sleep to fall upon Adam, and he slept: and he took one of his ribs, and closed up the flesh instead thereof;

22And the rib, which the LORD God had taken from man, made he a woman, and brought her unto the man.

23And Adam said, This *is* now bone of my bones, and flesh of my flesh: she shall be called Woman, because she was taken out of Man.

24Therefore shall a man leave his father and his mother, and shall cleave unto his wife: and they shall be one flesh.

25And they were both naked, the man and his wife, and were not ashamed.

**3** NOW THE serpent was more subtle than any beast of the field which the LORD God had made. And he said unto the woman, Yea, hath God said, Ye shall not eat of every tree of the garden?

2And the woman said unto the serpent, We may eat of the fruit of the trees of the garden:

3But of the fruit of the tree which *is* in the midst of the garden, God hath said, Ye shall not eat of it, neither shall ye touch it, lest ye die.

4And the serpent said unto the woman, Ye shall not surely die:

5For God doth know that in the day ye eat thereof, then your eyes shall be opened, and ye shall be as gods, knowing good and evil.

6And when the woman saw that the tree *was* good for food, and that it *was* pleasant to the eyes, and a tree to be desired to make *one* wise, she took of the fruit thereof, and did eat, and gave also unto her husband with her; and he did eat.

## Amplified

9And out of the ground the Lord God made to grow every tree that is pleasant to the sight *or* to be desired, good, (suitable, pleasant) for food; the tree of life also in the center of the garden, and the tree of knowledge of [the difference between] good and evil, *and* blessing and calamity. [Rev. 2:7; 22:14, 19.]

10Now a river went out of Eden to water the garden; and there it divided and became four [river] heads.

11The first is named Pishon; it is the one flowing around the whole land of Havilah, where there is gold;

12The gold of that land is of high quality; bdellium (pearl?) and onyx stone are there.

13The second river is named Gihon; it is the one flowing around the whole land of Cush.

14The third river is named Hiddekel [the Tigris]; it is the one flowing east of Assyria. And the fourth river is the Euphrates.

15And the Lord God took the man and put him in the garden of Eden to tend and guard *and* keep it.

16And the Lord God commanded the man, saying, You may freely eat of every tree of the garden,

17Except of the tree of the knowledge of good and evil *and* of blessing and calamity you shall not eat, for in the day that you eat of it you shall surely die.

18Now the Lord God said, It is not good [sufficient, satisfactory] that the man should be alone; I will make him a helper meet (suitable, adapted, completing) for him.

19And out of the ground the Lord God formed every [wild] beast *and* living creature of the field and every bird of the air, and brought them to Adam to see what he would call them; and whatever Adam called every living creature, that was its name.

20And Adam gave names to all livestock, and to the birds of the air, and to every [wild] beast of the field; but for Adam there was not found a helper meet (suitable, adapted, completing) for him.

21And the Lord God caused a deep sleep to fall upon Adam, and while he slept He took one of his ribs—a part of his side—and closed up the [place with] flesh instead of it;

22And the rib *or* part of his side which the Lord God had taken from the man, He built up *and* made into a woman and brought her to the man.

23Then Adam said, This [creature] is now bone of my bones and flesh of my flesh. She shall be called Woman, because she was taken out of a man.

24Therefore a man shall leave his father and his mother and shall become united *and* cleave to his wife, and they shall become one flesh. [Eph. 5:31-33.]

25And the man and his wife were both naked, and were not embarrassed *or* ashamed in each other's presence.

**3** NOW THE serpent was more subtle *and* crafty than any living creature of the field which the Lord God had made. And he [Satan] said to the woman, Can it really be that God has said, You shall not eat of every tree of the garden? [Rev. 12:9-11.]

2And the woman said to the serpent, We may eat of the fruit of the trees of the garden,

3Except of the fruit of the tree which is in the middle of the garden. God has said, You shall not eat of it, neither shall you touch it, lest you die.

4But the serpent said to the woman, You shall not surely die, [II Cor. 11:3.]

5For God knows that in the day you eat of it your eyes will be opened, and you will be as God, knowing the difference between good and evil, *and* blessing and calamity.

6And when the woman saw that the tree was good (suitable and pleasant) for food, and that it was delightful to look at and a tree to be desired to make one wise, she took of its fruit and ate; and she gave some also to her husband, and he ate.

## New American Standard

9And out of the ground the LORD God caused to grow every
tree that is pleasing to the sight and good for food; the tree of life
also in the midst of the garden, and the tree of the knowledge of
good and evil.
**10**¶ Now a river flowed out of Eden to water the garden; and
from there it divided and became four rivers.
11The name of the first is Pishon; it flows around the whole land
of Havilah, where there is gold.
12And the gold of that land is good; the bdellium and the onyx
stone are there.
13And the name of the second river is Gihon; it flows around
the whole land of Cush.
14And the name of the third river is Tigris; it flows east of
Assyria. And the fourth river is the Euphrates.
15Then the LORD God took the man and put him into the garden
of Eden to cultivate it and keep it.
16And the LORD God commanded the man, saying, "From any
tree of the garden you may eat freely;
17but from the tree of the knowledge of good and evil you shall
not eat, for in the day that you eat from it you shall surely die."
**18**¶ Then the LORD God said, "It is not good for the man to be
alone; I will make him a helper [a]suitable for him."
19And out of the ground the LORD God formed every beast of
the field and every bird of the sky, and brought *them* to the man
to see what he would call them; and whatever the man called a
living creature, that was its name.
20And the man gave names to all the cattle, and to the birds of
the sky, and to every beast of the field, but for [b]Adam there was
not found a helper suitable for him.
21So the LORD God caused a deep sleep to fall upon the man,
and he slept; then He took one of his ribs, and closed up the flesh
at that place.
22And the LORD God [c]fashioned into a woman the rib which He
had taken from the man, and brought her to the man.
23And the man said,

"This is now bone of my bones,
And flesh of my flesh;
She shall be called Woman,
Because she was taken out of Man."

24For this cause a man shall leave his father and his mother, and
shall cleave to his wife; and they shall become one flesh.
25And the man and his wife were both naked and were not
ashamed.

*The Fall of Man*

3 NOW THE serpent was more crafty than any beast of the field
which the LORD God had made. And he said to the woman,
"Indeed, has God said, 'You shall not eat from any tree of the
garden'?"
2And the woman said to the serpent, "From the fruit of the
trees of the garden we may eat;
3but from the fruit of the tree which is in the middle of the
garden, God has said, 'You shall not eat from it or touch it, lest you
die.'"
4And the serpent said to the woman, "You surely shall not die!
5"For God knows that in the day you eat from it your eyes will
be opened, and you will be like God, knowing good and evil."
6When the woman saw that the tree was good for food, and
that it was a delight to the eyes, and that the tree was desirable to
make *one* wise, she took from its fruit and ate; and she gave also
to her husband with her, and he ate.

NAS [a] Lit., *corresponding to* [b] Or, *man* [c] Lit., *built*

## New International

made all kinds of trees grow out of the ground—trees that were
pleasing to the eye and good for food. In the middle of the garden
were the tree of life and the tree of the knowledge of good and evil.
10A river watering the garden flowed from Eden; from there it
was separated into four headwaters.
11The name of the first is the
Pishon; it winds through the entire land of Havilah, where there
is gold.
12(The gold of that land is good; aromatic resin[d] and onyx
are also there.)
13The name of the second river is the Gihon; it
winds through the entire land of Cush.[e]
14The name of the third
river is the Tigris; it runs along the east side of Asshur. And the
fourth river is the Euphrates.
15The LORD God took the man and put him in the Garden of
Eden to work it and take care of it.
16And the LORD God com-
manded the man, "You are free to eat from any tree in the garden;
17but you must not eat from the tree of the knowledge of good and
evil, for when you eat of it you will surely die."
18The LORD God said, "It is not good for the man to be alone.
I will make a helper suitable for him."
19Now the LORD God had formed out of the ground all the
beasts of the field and all the birds of the air. He brought them to
the man to see what he would name them; and whatever the man
called each living creature, that was its name.
20So the man gave
names to all the livestock, the birds of the air and all the beasts of
the field.

But for Adam[f] no suitable helper was found.
21So the LORD
God caused the man to fall into a deep sleep; and while he was
sleeping, he took one of the man's ribs[g] and closed up the place
with flesh.
22Then the LORD God made a woman from the rib[h] he
had taken out of the man, and he brought her to the man.
23The man said,

"This is now bone of my bones
and flesh of my flesh;
she shall be called 'woman,[i]'
for she was taken out of man."

24For this reason a man will leave his father and mother and be
united to his wife, and they will become one flesh.
25The man and his wife were both naked, and they felt no
shame.

*The Fall of Man*

3 NOW THE serpent was more crafty than any of the wild
animals the LORD God had made. He said to the woman, "Did
God really say, 'You must not eat from any tree in the garden'?"
2The woman said to the serpent, "We may eat fruit from the
trees in the garden,
3but God did say, 'You must not eat fruit from
the tree that is in the middle of the garden, and you must not touch
it, or you will die.'"
4"You will not surely die," the serpent said to the woman.
5"For
God knows that when you eat of it your eyes will be opened, and
you will be like God, knowing good and evil."
6When the woman saw that the fruit of the tree was good for
food and pleasing to the eye, and also desirable for gaining wisdom, she took some and ate it. She also gave some to her husband,
who was with her, and he ate it.
7Then the eyes of both of them

NIV [d] 12 Or *good; pearls* [e] 13 Possibly southeast Mesopotamia [f] 20 Or *the man* [g] 21 Or *took part of the man's side* [h] 22 Or *part* [i] 23 The Hebrew for *woman* sounds like the Hebrew for *man.*

## King James

7And the eyes of them both were opened, and they knew that they *were* naked; and they sewed fig leaves together, and made themselves aprons.

8And they heard the voice of the LORD God walking in the garden in the cool of the day: and Adam and his wife hid themselves from the presence of the LORD God amongst the trees of the garden.

9And the LORD God called unto Adam, and said unto him, Where *art* thou?

10And he said, I heard thy voice in the garden, and I was afraid, because I *was* naked; and I hid myself.

11And he said, Who told thee that thou *wast* naked? Hast thou eaten of the tree, whereof I commanded thee that thou shouldest not eat?

12And the man said, The woman whom thou gavest *to be* with me, she gave me of the tree, and I did eat.

13And the LORD God said unto the woman, What *is* this *that* thou hast done? And the woman said, The serpent beguiled me, and I did eat.

14And the LORD God said unto the serpent, Because thou hast done this, thou *art* cursed above all cattle, and above every beast of the field; upon thy belly shalt thou go, and dust shalt thou eat all the days of thy life:

15And I will put enmity between thee and the woman, and between thy seed and her seed; it shall bruise thy head, and thou shalt bruise his heel.

16Unto the woman he said, I will greatly multiply thy sorrow and thy conception; in sorrow thou shalt bring forth children; and thy desire *shall be* to thy husband, and he shall rule over thee.

17And unto Adam he said, Because thou hast hearkened unto the voice of thy wife, and hast eaten of the tree, of which I commanded thee, saying, Thou shalt not eat of it: cursed *is* the ground for thy sake; in sorrow shalt thou eat *of* it all the days of thy life;

18Thorns also and thistles shall it bring forth to thee; and thou shalt eat the herb of the field;

19In the sweat of thy face shalt thou eat bread, till thou return unto the ground; for out of it wast thou taken: for dust thou *art*, and unto dust shalt thou return.

20And Adam called his wife's name Eve; because she was the mother of all living.

21Unto Adam also and to his wife did the LORD God make coats of skins, and clothed them.

22¶ And the LORD God said, Behold, the man is become as one of us, to know good and evil: and now, lest he put forth his hand, and take also of the tree of life, and eat, and live for ever:

23Therefore the LORD God sent him forth from the garden of Eden, to till the ground from whence he was taken.

24So he drove out the man; and he placed at the east of the garden of Eden Cherubims, and a flaming sword which turned every way, to keep the way of the tree of life.

## Amplified

7Then the eyes of them both were opened, and they knew that they were naked; and they sewed fig leaves together and made themselves apron-like girdles.

8And they heard the sound of the Lord God walking in the garden in the cool of the day, and Adam and his wife hid themselves from the presence of the Lord God among the trees of the garden.

9But the Lord God called to Adam, and said to him, Where are you?

10He said, I heard the sound of You [walking] in the garden, and I was afraid, because I was naked; and I hid myself.

11And He said, Who told you you were naked? Have you eaten of the tree of which I commanded you that you should not eat?

12And the man said, The woman whom You gave to be with me, she gave me [fruit] of the tree, and I ate.

13And the Lord God said to the woman, What is this you have done? And the woman said, The serpent beguiled (cheated, outwitted, and deceived) me, and I ate.

14And the Lord God said to the serpent, Because you have done this, you are cursed above all [domestic] animals, and above every [wild] living thing of the field; upon your belly you shall go, and you shall eat dust [and what it contains] all the days of your life.

15And I will put enmity between you and the woman, and between your offspring and her offspring; He shall bruise *and* tread your head under foot, and you will lie in wait *and* bruise His heel. [Gal. 4:4.]

16To the woman He said, I will greatly multiply your grief *and* your suffering in pregnancy *and* the pangs of child-bearing; with spasms of distress you shall bring forth children; yet your desire *and* craving shall be for your husband, and he shall rule over you.

17And to Adam He said, Because you have listened *and* given heed to the voice of your wife, and have eaten of the tree of which I commanded you, saying, You shall not eat of it, the ground is under a curse because of you; in sorrow *and* toil shall you eat [of the fruits] of it all the days of your life;

18Thorns also and thistles shall it bring forth to you; and you shall eat the plants of the field.

19In the sweat of your face shall you eat bread until you return to the ground, for out of it you were taken; for dust you are, and to dust you shall return.

20The man called his wife's name Eve (life-spring), because she was the mother of all living.

21For Adam also and for his wife the Lord God made long coats (tunics) of skins, and clothed them.

22And the Lord God said, Behold, the man is become as one of Us [the Father, Son, and Holy Spirit], to know [how to distinguish between] good and evil, *and* blessing and calamity; and now, lest he put forth his hand and take also of the tree of life, and eat and live for ever [a]—

23Therefore the Lord God sent him forth from the garden of Eden, to till the ground from which he was taken.

24So [God] drove out the man; and He placed at the east of the garden of Eden the [b]cherubim, and a flaming sword which turned every way, to keep *and* guard the way of the tree of life. [Rev. 2:7; 22:2, 14, 19.]

**AMP** [a] This sentence is left unfinished, as if to hasten to avert the tragedy suggested of men living on forever in their now fallen state. [b] Cherubim are ministering spirits manifesting God's invisible presence and symbolizing His action (*Baker's Dictionary of Theology*, adapted).

## New American Standard

7Then the eyes of both of them were opened, and they knew that they were naked; and they sewed fig leaves together and made themselves loin coverings.

8¶ And they heard the sound of the LORD God walking in the garden in the cool of the day, and the man and his wife hid themselves from the presence of the LORD God among the trees of the garden.

9Then the LORD God called to the man, and said to him, "Where are you?"

10And he said, "I heard the sound of Thee in the garden, and I was afraid because I was naked; so I hid myself."

11And He said, "Who told you that you were naked? Have you eaten from the tree of which I commanded you not to eat?"

12And the man said, "The woman whom Thou gavest *to be* with me, she gave me from the tree, and I ate."

13Then the LORD God said to the woman, "What is this you have done?" And the woman said, "The serpent deceived me, and I ate."

14And the LORD God said to the serpent,

"Because you have done this,
Cursed are you more than all cattle,
And more than every beast of the field;
On your belly shall you go,
And dust shall you eat
All the days of your life;
15 And I will put enmity
Between you and the woman,
And between your seed and her seed;
He shall bruise you on the head,
And you shall bruise him on the heel."

16To the woman He said,

"I will greatly multiply
Your pain in childbirth,
In pain you shall bring forth children;
Yet your desire shall be for your husband,
And he shall rule over you."

17Then to Adam He said, "Because you have listened to the voice of your wife, and have eaten from the tree about which I commanded you, saying, 'You shall not eat from it';

Cursed is the ground because of you;
In toil you shall eat of it
All the days of your life.
18 "Both thorns and thistles it shall grow for you;
And you shall eat the plants of the field;
19 By the sweat of your face
You shall eat bread,
Till you return to the ground,
Because from it you were taken;
For you are dust,
And to dust you shall return."

20Now the man called his wife's name [c]Eve, because she was the mother of all *the* living.

21And the LORD God made garments of skin for Adam and his wife, and clothed them.

22¶ Then the LORD God said, "Behold, the man has become like one of Us, knowing good and evil; and now, lest he stretch out his hand, and take also from the tree of life, and eat, and live forever"—

23therefore the LORD God sent him out from the garden of Eden, to cultivate the ground from which he was taken.

24So He drove the man out; and at the east of the garden of Eden He stationed the cherubim, and the flaming sword which turned every direction, to guard the way to the tree of life.

NAS [c] I.e., living or life

## New International

were opened, and they realized they were naked; so they sewed fig leaves together and made coverings for themselves.

8Then the man and his wife heard the sound of the LORD God as he was walking in the garden in the cool of the day, and they hid from the LORD God among the trees of the garden.
9But the LORD God called to the man, "Where are you?"

10He answered, "I heard you in the garden, and I was afraid because I was naked; so I hid."

11And he said, "Who told you that you were naked? Have you eaten from the tree that I commanded you not to eat from?"

12The man said, "The woman you put here with me—she gave me some fruit from the tree, and I ate it."

13Then the LORD God said to the woman, "What is this you have done?"

The woman said, "The serpent deceived me, and I ate."

14So the LORD God said to the serpent, "Because you have done this,

"Cursed are you above all the livestock
and all the wild animals!
You will crawl on your belly
and you will eat dust
all the days of your life.
15And I will put enmity
between you and the woman,
and between your offspring[d] and hers;
he will crush[e] your head,
and you will strike his heel."

16To the woman he said,

"I will greatly increase your pains in childbearing;
with pain you will give birth to children.
Your desire will be for your husband,
and he will rule over you."

17To Adam he said, "Because you listened to your wife and ate from the tree about which I commanded you, 'You must not eat of it,'

"Cursed is the ground because of you;
through painful toil you will eat of it
all the days of your life.
18It will produce thorns and thistles for you,
and you will eat the plants of the field.
19By the sweat of your brow
you will eat your food
until you return to the ground,
since from it you were taken;
for dust you are
and to dust you will return."

20Adam[f] named his wife Eve,[g] because she would become the mother of all the living.

21The LORD God made garments of skin for Adam and his wife and clothed them.
22And the LORD God said, "The man has now become like one of us, knowing good and evil. He must not be allowed to reach out his hand and take also from the tree of life and eat, and live forever."
23So the LORD God banished him from the Garden of Eden to work the ground from which he had been taken.
24After he drove the man out, he placed on the east side[h] of the Garden of Eden cherubim and a flaming sword flashing back and forth to guard the way to the tree of life.

NIV [d] 15 Or *seed* [e] 15 Or *strike* [f] 20 Or *The man* [g] 20 *Eve* probably means *living*. [h] 24 Or *placed in front*

## King James

**4** AND ADAM knew Eve his wife; and she conceived, and bare Cain, and said, I have gotten a man from the LORD.

2And she again bare his brother Abel. And Abel was a keeper of sheep, but Cain was a tiller of the ground.

3And in process of time it came to pass, that Cain brought of the fruit of the ground an offering unto the LORD.

4And Abel, he also brought of the firstlings of his flock and of the fat thereof. And the LORD had respect unto Abel and to his offering:

5But unto Cain and to his offering he had not respect. And Cain was very wroth, and his countenance fell.

6And the LORD said unto Cain, Why art thou wroth? and why is thy countenance fallen?

7If thou doest well, shalt thou not be accepted? and if thou doest not well, sin lieth at the door. And unto thee *shall be* his desire, and thou shalt rule over him.

8And Cain talked with Abel his brother: and it came to pass, when they were in the field, that Cain rose up against Abel his brother, and slew him.

9¶ And the LORD said unto Cain, Where *is* Abel thy brother? And he said, I know not: *Am* I my brother's keeper?

10And he said, What hast thou done? the voice of thy brother's blood crieth unto me from the ground.

11And now *art* thou cursed from the earth, which hath opened her mouth to receive thy brother's blood from thy hand;

12When thou tillest the ground, it shall not henceforth yield unto thee her strength; a fugitive and a vagabond shalt thou be in the earth.

13And Cain said unto the LORD, My punishment *is* greater than I can bear.

14Behold, thou hast driven me out this day from the face of the earth; and from thy face shall I be hid; and I shall be a fugitive and a vagabond in the earth; and it shall come to pass, *that* every one that findeth me shall slay me.

15And the LORD said unto him, Therefore whosoever slayeth Cain, vengeance shall be taken on him sevenfold. And the LORD set a mark upon Cain, lest any finding him should kill him.

16¶ And Cain went out from the presence of the LORD, and dwelt in the land of Nod, on the east of Eden.

17And Cain knew his wife; and she conceived, and bare Enoch: and he builded a city, and called the name of the city, after the name of his son, Enoch.

18And unto Enoch was born Irad: and Irad begat Mehujael: and Mehujael begat Methusael: and Methusael begat Lamech.

19¶ And Lamech took unto him two wives: the name of the one *was* Adah, and the name of the other Zillah.

20And Adah bare Jabal: he was the father of such as dwell in tents, and *of such as have* cattle.

21And his brother's name *was* Jubal: he was the father of all such as handle the harp and organ.

22And Zillah, she also bare Tubal-cain, an instructor of every artificer in brass and iron: and the sister of Tubal-cain *was* Naamah.

23And Lamech said unto his wives, Adah and Zillah, Hear my voice; ye wives of Lamech, hearken unto my speech: for I have slain a man to my wounding, and a young man to my hurt.

## Amplified

**4** AND ADAM knew Eve as his wife, and she became pregnant and bore Cain, and said, I have gotten *and* gained a man with the help of the Lord.

2And [next] she gave birth to his brother Abel. Now Abel was a keeper of sheep, but Cain was a tiller of the ground.

3And in course of time Cain brought to the Lord an offering of the fruit of the ground.

4And Abel brought of the first-born of his flock and of the fat portions. And the Lord had respect *and* regard for Abel and for his offering. [Heb. 11:4.]

5But for [a]Cain and his offering He had no respect *or* regard. So Cain was exceedingly angry *and* indignant, and he looked sad *and* depressed.

6And the Lord said to Cain, Why are you angry? And why do you look sad *and* dejected?

7If you do well, will you not be accepted? And if you do not do well, sin crouches at your door; its desire is for you, and you must master it.

8And Cain said to his brother, [b]Let us go out to the field. And when they were in the field, Cain rose up against Abel his brother, and killed him. [I John 3:12.]

9And the Lord said to Cain, Where is Abel your brother? And he said, I do not know. Am I my brother's keeper?

10And [the Lord] said, What have you done? The voice of your brother's blood is crying to Me from the ground.

11And now you are cursed by reason of the earth, which has opened its mouth to receive your brother's [shed] blood from your hand.

12When you till the ground, it shall no longer yield to you its strength; you shall be a fugitive and a vagabond on the earth [in perpetual exile, a degraded outcast].

13Then Cain said to the Lord, My punishment is greater than I can bear [c].

14Behold, You have driven me out this day from the face of the land; and from Your face I shall be hidden; and I shall be a fugitive and a vagabond *and* a wanderer on the earth; and whoever finds me will kill me.

15And the Lord said to him, [d]Therefore, if any one kills Cain, vengeance shall be taken on him sevenfold. And the Lord set a [e]mark *or* sign upon Cain, lest any finding him should kill him.

16So Cain went away from the presence of the Lord, and dwelt in the land of Nod [wandering], east of Eden.

17And Cain's wife [one of Adam's offspring] became pregnant and bore Enoch; and Cain built a [f]city, and named it after his son, Enoch.

18To Enoch was born Irad; and Irad was the father of Mehujael, and Mehujael the father of Methusael, and Methusael the father of Lamech.

19And Lamech took two wives; the name of the one was Adah, and of the other Zillah.

20Adah bore Jabal; he was the father of those who dwell in tents and have cattle *and* purchased possessions.

21His brother's name was Jubal; he was the father of all those who play the lyre and pipe.

22Zillah bore Tubal-cain; he was the forger of all [cutting] instruments of bronze and iron. The sister of Tubal-cain was Naamah.

23Lamech said to his wives, Adah and Zillah, Hear my voice; you wives of Lamech, listen to what I say: for I have slain a man [merely] for wounding me, and a young man [only] for striking *and* bruising me.

**AMP** [a] In bringing the offering he did, Cain denied that he was a sinful creature, under the sentence of Divine condemnation. He insisted on approaching God on the ground of personal worthiness. Instead of accepting God's way, he offered to God the fruits of the ground *which God had cursed.* He presented the product of his own toil, the work of his own hands, and God refused to receive it (Arthur W. Pink in *Gleanings in Genesis,* condensed). [b] The Hebrew omits this clause, but various other texts show that it was originally included. [c] Some ancient versions read, "Too great to be forgiven!" [d] Some versions read "Not so!" [e] Many commentators believe this sign not to have been like a brand on the forehead, but something awesome about Cain's appearance that made people dread and avoid him. [f] Dodd, quoted in *Clarke's Commentary,* shows that it would have been possible for Adam and Eve, in the more than 100 years he estimates may have elapsed since their union, to have had over 32,000 descendants at the time Cain went to Nod, all of them having sprung from Cain and Abel who married their sisters.

## New American Standard

*Cain and Abel*

**4** NOW THE man had relations with his wife Eve, and she
conceived and gave birth to Cain, and she said, "I have gotten
a manchild with *the help of* the LORD."
2And again, she gave birth to his brother Abel. And Abel was
a keeper of flocks, but Cain was a tiller of the ground.
3So it came about in the course of time that Cain brought an
offering to the LORD of the fruit of the ground.
4And Abel, on his part also brought of the firstlings of his flock
and of their fat portions. And the LORD had regard for Abel and
for his offering;
5but for Cain and for his offering He had no regard. So Cain
became very angry and his countenance fell.
6Then the LORD said to Cain, "Why are you angry? And why
has your countenance fallen?
7"If you do well, will not *your countenance* be lifted up? And if
you do not do well, sin is crouching at the door; and its desire is
for you, but you must master it."
8And Cain told Abel his brother. And it came about when they
were in the field, that Cain rose up against Abel his brother and
killed him.
9¶ Then the LORD said to Cain, "Where is Abel your brother?"
And he said, "I do not know. Am I my brother's keeper?"
10And He said, "What have you done? The voice of your brother's blood is crying to Me from the ground.
11"And now you are cursed from the ground, which has
opened its mouth to receive your brother's blood from your hand.
12"When you cultivate the ground, it shall no longer yield its
strength to you; you shall be a vagrant and a wanderer on the
earth."
13And Cain said to the LORD, "My punishment is too great to
bear!
14"Behold, Thou hast driven me this day from the face of the
ground; and from Thy face I shall be hidden, and I shall be a
vagrant and a wanderer on the earth, and it will come about that
whoever finds me will kill me."
15So the LORD said to him, "Therefore whoever kills Cain, vengeance will be taken on him sevenfold." And the LORD appointed
a sign for Cain, lest anyone finding him should slay him.
16¶ Then Cain went out from the presence of the LORD, and
settled in the land of Nod, east of Eden.
17And Cain had relations with his wife and she conceived, and
gave birth to Enoch; and he built a city, and called the name of the
city Enoch, after the name of his son.
18Now to Enoch was born Irad; and Irad became the father of
Mehujael; and Mehujael became the father of Methushael; and
Methushael became the father of Lamech.
19And Lamech took to himself two wives: the name of the one
was Adah, and the name of the other, Zillah.
20And Adah gave birth to Jabal; he was the father of those who
dwell in tents and *have* livestock.
21And his brother's name was Jubal; he was the father of all
those who play the lyre and pipe.
22As for Zillah, she also gave birth to Tubal-cain, the forger of
all implements of bronze and iron; and the sister of Tubal-cain was
Naamah.
23And Lamech said to his wives,
"Adah and Zillah,
Listen to my voice,
You wives of Lamech,
Give heed to my speech,
For I have killed a man for wounding me;
And a boy for striking me;

## New International

*Cain and Abel*

**4** ADAM[g] LAY with his wife Eve, and she became pregnant
and gave birth to Cain.[h] She said, "With the help of the LORD
I have brought forth[i] a man." 2Later she gave birth to his brother
Abel.
Now Abel kept flocks, and Cain worked the soil. 3In the course
of time Cain brought some of the fruits of the soil as an offering
to the LORD. 4But Abel brought fat portions from some of the
firstborn of his flock. The LORD looked with favor on Abel and his
offering, 5but on Cain and his offering he did not look with favor.
So Cain was very angry, and his face was downcast.
6Then the LORD said to Cain, "Why are you angry? Why is your
face downcast? 7If you do what is right, will you not be accepted?
But if you do not do what is right, sin is crouching at your door;
it desires to have you, but you must master it."
8Now Cain said to his brother Abel, "Let's go out to the field."[j]
And while they were in the field, Cain attacked his brother Abel
and killed him.
9Then the LORD said to Cain, "Where is your brother Abel?"
"I don't know," he replied. "Am I my brother's keeper?"
10The LORD said, "What have you done? Listen! Your brother's
blood cries out to me from the ground. 11Now you are under a
curse and driven from the ground, which opened its mouth to
receive your brother's blood from your hand. 12When you work
the ground, it will no longer yield its crops for you. You will be
a restless wanderer on the earth."
13Cain said to the LORD, "My punishment is more than I can
bear. 14Today you are driving me from the land, and I will be
hidden from your presence; I will be a restless wanderer on the
earth, and whoever finds me will kill me."
15But the LORD said to him, "Not so[k]; if anyone kills Cain, he
will suffer vengeance seven times over." Then the LORD put a mark
on Cain so that no one who found him would kill him. 16So Cain
went out from the LORD's presence and lived in the land of Nod,[l]
east of Eden.
17Cain lay with his wife, and she became pregnant and gave
birth to Enoch. Cain was then building a city, and he named it after
his son Enoch. 18To Enoch was born Irad, and Irad was the father
of Mehujael, and Mehujael was the father of Methushael, and
Methushael was the father of Lamech.
19Lamech married two women, one named Adah and the other
Zillah. 20Adah gave birth to Jabal; he was the father of those who
live in tents and raise livestock. 21His brother's name was Jubal; he
was the father of all who play the harp and flute. 22Zillah also had
a son, Tubal-Cain, who forged all kinds of tools out of[m] bronze and
iron. Tubal-Cain's sister was Naamah.
23Lamech said to his wives,

"Adah and Zillah, listen to me;
wives of Lamech, hear my words.
I have killed[n] a man for wounding me,
a young man for injuring me.

**NIV** [g] *1* Or *The man* [h] *1 Cain* sounds like the Hebrew for *brought forth* or *acquired.* [i] *1* Or *have acquired* [j] *8* Samaritan Pentateuch, Septuagint, Vulgate and Syriac; Masoretic Text does not have *"Let's go out to the field."* [k] *15* Septuagint, Vulgate and Syriac; Hebrew *Very well* [l] *16 Nod* means *wandering* (see verses 12 and 14). [m] *22* Or *who instructed all who work in* [n] *23* Or *I will kill*

## King James

24If Cain shall be avenged sevenfold, truly Lamech seventy and
sevenfold.
25¶ And Adam knew his wife again; and she bare a son, and
called his name Seth: For God, *said she,* hath appointed me another
seed instead of Abel, whom Cain slew.
26And to Seth, to him also there was born a son; and he called
his name Enos: then began men to call upon the name of the LORD.

5 THIS *IS* the book of the generations of Adam. In the day that
God created man, in the likeness of God made he him;
2Male and female created he them; and blessed them, and called
their name Adam, in the day when they were created.
3¶ And Adam lived an hundred and thirty years, and begat *a*
*son* in his own likeness, after his image; and called his name Seth:
4And the days of Adam after he had begotten Seth were eight
hundred years: and he begat sons and daughters:
5And all the days that Adam lived were nine hundred and thirty
years: and he died.
6And Seth lived an hundred and five years, and begat Enos:
7And Seth lived after he begat Enos eight hundred and seven
years, and begat sons and daughters:
8And all the days of Seth were nine hundred and twelve years:
and he died.
9¶ And Enos lived ninety years, and begat Cainan:
10And Enos lived after he begat Cainan eight hundred and
fifteen years, and begat sons and daughters:
11And all the days of Enos were nine hundred and five years:
and he died.
12¶ And Cainan lived seventy years, and begat Mahalaleel:
13And Cainan lived after he begat Mahalaleel eight hundred
and forty years, and begat sons and daughters:
14And all the days of Cainan were nine hundred and ten years:
and he died.
15¶ And Mahalaleel lived sixty and five years, and begat Jared:
16And Mahalaleel lived after he begat Jared eight hundred and
thirty years, and begat sons and daughters:
17And all the days of Mahalaleel were eight hundred ninety and
five years: and he died.
18¶ And Jared lived an hundred sixty and two years, and he
begat Enoch:
19And Jared lived after he begat Enoch eight hundred years,
and begat sons and daughters:
20And all the days of Jared were nine hundred sixty and two
years: and he died.
21¶ And Enoch lived sixty and five years, and begat Methuselah:
22And Enoch walked with God after he begat Methuselah three
hundred years, and begat sons and daughters:
23And all the days of Enoch were three hundred sixty and five
years:
24And Enoch walked with God: and he *was* not; for God took
him.
25And Methuselah lived an hundred eighty and seven years,
and begat Lamech:
26And Methuselah lived after he begat Lamech seven hundred
eighty and two years, and begat sons and daughters:

## Amplified

24If Cain is avenged sevenfold, truly Lamech [will be avenged]
seventy-sevenfold.
25And Adam's wife again [became pregnant], and she bore a
son and called his name Seth, For God, she said, has appointed
for me another child instead of Abel, for Cain slew him.
26And to Seth also a son was born whom he named Enosh. At
that time men began to call [upon God] by the name of the Lord.

5 THIS IS the book—the written record—of the generations of
the off-spring of Adam. When God created man He made him
in the likeness of God.
2He created them male and female and blessed them, and
named them [both] Adam at the time when they were created.
3When Adam had lived 130 years, he had a son in his own
likeness, after his image, and named him Seth.
4Adam lived after he had Seth 800 years and had other sons and
daughters.
5So altogether Adam lived 930 years, and he died.
6When Seth was 105 years old, Enosh was born.
7Seth lived after the birth of Enosh 807 years, and had other
sons and daughters.
8So Seth lived 912 years, and he died.
9When Enosh was 90 years old, Kenan was born to him.
10Enosh lived after the birth of Kenan 815 years, and had other
sons and daughters.
11So Enosh lived 905 years, and he died.
12When Kenan was 70 years old, Mahalalel was born.
13Kenan lived after the birth of Mahalalel 840 years, and had
other sons and daughters.
14So Kenan lived 910 years, and he died.
15When Mahalalel was 65 years old, Jared was born.
16Mahalalel lived after the birth of Jared 830 years, and had
other sons and daughters.
17So Mahalalel lived 895 years, and he died.
18When Jared was 162 years old, Enoch was born.
19Jared lived after the birth of Enoch 800 years, and had other
sons and daughters.
20So Jared lived 962 years, and he died.
21When Enoch was 65 years old, Methuselah was born.
22Enoch walked [in habitual fellowship] with God after the birth
of Methuselah 300 years, and had other sons and daughters.
23So all the days of Enoch were 365 years.
24And Enoch walked [in habitual fellowship] with God; and he
was not, for God took him [home with Him]. [Heb. 11:5.]
25When Methuselah was 187 years old, Lamech was born to
him.
26Methuselah lived after the birth of Lamech 782 years, and had
other sons and daughters.

## New American Standard

24 If Cain is avenged sevenfold,
Then Lamech seventy-sevenfold."
25¶ And Adam had relations with his wife again; and she gave
birth to a son, and named him Seth, for, *she said,* "God has appointed me another offspring in place of Abel; for Cain killed him."
26And to Seth, to him also a son was born; and he called his
name Enosh. Then *men* began to call upon the name of the LORD.

*Descendants of Adam*

**5** THIS IS the book of the generations of Adam. In the day
when God created man, He made him in the likeness of God.
2He created them male and female, and He blessed them and
named them [a]Man in the day when they were created.
3When Adam had lived one hundred and thirty years, he
[b]became the father of *a son* in his own likeness, according to his
image, and named him Seth.
4Then the days of Adam after he became the father of Seth
were eight hundred years, and he had *other* sons and daughters.
5So all the days that Adam lived were nine hundred and thirty
years, and he died.
6¶ And Seth lived one hundred and five years, and became the
father of Enosh.
7Then Seth lived eight hundred and seven years after he
became the father of Enosh, and he had *other* sons and daughters.
8So all the days of Seth were nine hundred and twelve years,
and he died.
9¶ And Enosh lived ninety years, and became the father of
Kenan.
10Then Enosh lived eight hundred and fifteen years after he
became the father of Kenan, and he had *other* sons and daughters.
11So all the days of Enosh were nine hundred and five years,
and he died.
12¶ And Kenan lived seventy years, and became the father of
Mahalalel.
13Then Kenan lived eight hundred and forty years after he
became the father of Mahalalel, and he had *other* sons and daughters.
14So all the days of Kenan were nine hundred and ten years,
and he died.
15¶ And Mahalalel lived sixty-five years, and became the father
of Jared.
16Then Mahalalel lived eight hundred and thirty years after he
became the father of Jared, and he had *other* sons and daughters.
17So all the days of Mahalalel were eight hundred and ninety-
five years, and he died.
18¶ And Jared lived one hundred and sixty-two years, and
became the father of Enoch.
19Then Jared lived eight hundred years after he became the
father of Enoch, and he had *other* sons and daughters.
20So all the days of Jared were nine hundred and sixty-two
years, and he died.
21¶ And Enoch lived sixty-five years, and became the father of
Methuselah.
22Then Enoch walked with God three hundred years after he
became the father of Methuselah, and he had *other* sons and
daughters.
23So all the days of Enoch were three hundred and sixty-five
years.
24And Enoch walked with God; and he was not, for God took
him.
25¶ And Methuselah lived one hundred and eighty-seven years,
and became the father of Lamech.
26Then Methuselah lived seven hundred and eighty-two years
after he became the father of Lamech, and he had *other* sons and
daughters.

**NAS** [a] Lit., *Adam* [b] Lit., *begot,* and so throughout this context

## New International

24If Cain is avenged seven times,
then Lamech seventy-seven times."
25Adam lay with his wife again, and she gave birth to a son and
named him Seth,[c] saying, "God has granted me another child in
place of Abel, since Cain killed him." 26Seth also had a son, and
he named him Enosh.
At that time men began to call on[d] the name of the LORD.

*From Adam to Noah*

**5** THIS IS the written account of Adam's line.
When God created man, he made him in the likeness of God.
2He created them male and female and blessed them. And when
they were created, he called them "man.[e]"
3When Adam had lived 130 years, he had a son in his own
likeness, in his own image; and he named him Seth. 4After Seth
was born, Adam lived 800 years and had other sons and daughters. 5Altogether, Adam lived 930 years, and then he died.
6When Seth had lived 105 years, he became the father[f] of
Enosh. 7And after he became the father of Enosh, Seth lived 807
years and had other sons and daughters. 8Altogether, Seth lived
912 years, and then he died.
9When Enosh had lived 90 years, he became the father of Kenan. 10And after he became the father of Kenan, Enosh lived 815
years and had other sons and daughters. 11Altogether, Enosh lived
905 years, and then he died.
12When Kenan had lived 70 years, he became the father of
Mahalalel. 13And after he became the father of Mahalalel, Kenan
lived 840 years and had other sons and daughters. 14Altogether,
Kenan lived 910 years, and then he died.
15When Mahalalel had lived 65 years, he became the father of
Jared. 16And after he became the father of Jared, Mahalalel lived
830 years and had other sons and daughters. 17Altogether,
Mahalalel lived 895 years, and then he died.
18When Jared had lived 162 years, he became the father of
Enoch. 19And after he became the father of Enoch, Jared lived 800
years and had other sons and daughters. 20Altogether, Jared lived
962 years, and then he died.
21When Enoch had lived 65 years, he became the father of
Methuselah. 22And after he became the father of Methuselah,
Enoch walked with God 300 years and had other sons and daughters. 23Altogether, Enoch lived 365 years. 24Enoch walked with
God; then he was no more, because God took him away.
25When Methuselah had lived 187 years, he became the father
of Lamech. 26And after he became the father of Lamech, Me-

**NIV** [c] 25 *Seth* probably means *granted.* [d] 26 Or *to proclaim* [e] 2 Hebrew *adam* [f] 6 *Father* may mean *ancestor;* also in verses 7-26.

## King James

27And all the days of Methuselah were nine hundred sixty and nine years: and he died.

28¶ And Lamech lived an hundred eighty and two years, and begat a son:

29And he called his name Noah, saying, This *same* shall comfort us concerning our work and toil of our hands, because of the ground which the LORD hath cursed.

30And Lamech lived after he begat Noah five hundred ninety and five years, and begat sons and daughters:

31And all the days of Lamech were seven hundred seventy and seven years: and he died.

32And Noah was five hundred years old: and Noah begat Shem, Ham, and Japheth.

**6** AND IT came to pass, when men began to multiply on the face of the earth, and daughters were born unto them,

2That the sons of God saw the daughters of men that they *were* fair; and they took them wives of all which they chose.

3And the LORD said, My spirit shall not always strive with man, for that he also *is* flesh: yet his days shall be an hundred and twenty years.

4There were giants in the earth in those days; and also after that, when the sons of God came in unto the daughters of men, and they bare *children* to them, the same *became* mighty men which *were* of old, men of renown.

5¶ And GOD saw that the wickedness of man *was* great in the earth, and *that* every imagination of the thoughts of his heart *was* only evil continually.

6And it repented the LORD that he had made man on the earth, and it grieved him at his heart.

7And the LORD said, I will destroy man whom I have created from the face of the earth; both man, and beast, and the creeping thing, and the fowls of the air; for it repenteth me that I have made them.

8But Noah found grace in the eyes of the LORD.

9¶ These *are* the generations of Noah: Noah was a just man *and* perfect in his generations, *and* Noah walked with God.

10And Noah begat three sons, Shem, Ham, and Japheth.

11The earth also was corrupt before God, and the earth was filled with violence.

12And God looked upon the earth, and, behold, it was corrupt; for all flesh had corrupted his way upon the earth.

13And God said unto Noah, The end of all flesh is come before me; for the earth is filled with violence through them; and, behold, I will destroy them with the earth.

14¶ Make thee an ark of gopher wood; rooms shalt thou make in the ark, and shalt pitch it within and without with pitch.

15And this *is the fashion* which thou shalt make it *of:* The length of the ark *shall be* three hundred cubits, the breadth of it fifty cubits, and the height of it thirty cubits.

## Amplified

27So Methuselah lived 969 years, and he died.

28When Lamech was 182 years old, a son was born.

29He named him Noah, saying, This one shall bring us relief *and* comfort from our work and the (grievous) toil of our hands, due to the ground being cursed by the Lord.

30Lamech lived after the birth of Noah 595 years, and had other sons and daughters.

31So all the days of [a]Lamech were 777 years, and he died.

32After Noah was 500 years old, he became the father of Shem, Ham, and Japheth.

**6** WHEN MEN began to multiply on the face of the land, and daughters were born to them,

2The sons of God saw that the daughters of men were fair, and they took wives of all they desired *and* chose.

3Then the Lord said, My Spirit shall not for ever dwell *and* strive with man, for he also is flesh; but his days shall yet be 120 years.

4There were giants on the earth in those days, and also afterward, when the sons of God lived with the daughters of men, and they bore children to them. These were the mighty men who were of old, men of renown.

5The Lord saw that the wickedness of man was great in the earth, and that every imagination *and* intention of all human thinking was only evil continually.

6And the Lord regretted that He had made man on the earth, and He was grieved at heart.

7So the Lord said, I will destroy, blot out *and* wipe away mankind whom I have created from the face of the ground; not only man, [but] the beasts and the creeping things and the birds of the air, for it grieves *and* makes Me regretful that I have made them.

8But Noah found grace (favor) in the eyes of the Lord.

9This is the history of the generations of Noah. Noah was a just *and* righteous man, blameless *in* his [evil] generation; Noah walked [in habitual fellowship] with God.

10And Noah became the father of three sons, Shem, Ham, and Japheth.

11The earth was depraved *and* putrid in God's sight, and the land was filled with violence (desecration, infringement, outrage, assault, and lust for power).

12And God looked upon the world and saw how degenerate, debased *and* vicious it was; for all humanity had corrupted their way upon the earth *and* lost their true direction.

13God said to Noah, I intend to make an end of all flesh, for through men the land is filled with violence; and behold, I will [b]destroy them and the land.

14Make yourself an ark of gopher *or* cypress wood; make in *it* rooms (stalls, pens, coops, nests, cages, *and* compartments), and cover it inside and out with pitch (bitumen).

15And this is the way you are to make it: the length of the ark shall be 300 cubits, its breadth 50 cubits and its height 30 cubits [that is, 450 ft. x 75 ft. x 45 ft.].

**AMP** [a] It is now well-known that the age of mankind cannot be reckoned in years from the facts listed in genealogies, for there are numerous known intentional gaps in them. For example, as B. B. Warfield in his *Studies in Theology* points out, the genealogy in Matt. 1:1-17 omits the three kings, Ahaziah, Jehoash, and Amaziah, and indicates that Joram (Matt. 1:8) begat Uzziah, who was his great-great-grandson. The mistaking of compressed genealogies for bases of chronology has been very misleading. So far, the dates in years of very early Old Testament events are altogether speculative and relative, and the tendency is to put them farther and farther back into antiquity.
[b] Enoch had warned these people (Jude 14, 15); Noah had preached righteousness to them (II Pet. 2:5); God's Spirit had been striving with them (Gen. 6:3). Yet they had rejected God and were without excuse.

## New American Standard

27So all the days of Methuselah were nine hundred and sixty-
nine years, and he died.
28¶ And Lamech lived one hundred and eighty-two years, and
became the father of a son.
29Now he called his name Noah, saying, "This one shall give
us rest from our work and from the toil of our hands *arising* from
the ground which the LORD has cursed."
30Then Lamech lived five hundred and ninety-five years after
he became the father of Noah, and he had *other* sons and daughters.
31So all the days of Lamech were seven hundred and seventy-
seven years, and he died.
32¶ And Noah was five hundred years old, and Noah became
the father of Shem, Ham, and Japheth.

*The Corruption of Mankind*

6 NOW IT came about, when men began to multiply on the face
of the land, and daughters were born to them,
2that the sons of God saw that the daughters of men were
beautiful; and they took wives for themselves, whomever they
chose.
3Then the LORD said, "My Spirit shall not strive with man
forever, because he also is flesh; nevertheless his days shall be one
hundred and twenty years."
4The [c]Nephilim were on the earth in those days, and also
afterward, when the sons of God came in to the daughters of men,
and they bore *children* to them. Those were the mighty men who
*were* of old, men of renown.
5¶ Then the LORD saw that the wickedness of man was great
on the earth, and that every intent of the thoughts of his heart was
only evil continually.
6And the LORD was sorry that He had made man on the earth,
and He was grieved in His heart.
7And the LORD said, "I will blot out man whom I have created
from the face of the land, from man to animals to creeping things
and to birds of the sky; for I am sorry that I have made them."
8But Noah found favor in the eyes of the LORD.
9¶ These are *the records of* the generations of Noah. Noah was
a righteous man, blameless in his time; Noah walked with God.
10And Noah became the father of three sons: Shem, Ham, and
Japheth.
11Now the earth was corrupt in the sight of God, and the earth
was filled with violence.
12And God looked on the earth, and behold, it was corrupt; for
all flesh had corrupted their way upon the earth.
13¶ Then God said to Noah, "The end of all flesh has come
before Me; for the earth is filled with violence because of them; and
behold, I am about to destroy them with the earth.
14"Make for yourself an ark of gopher wood; you shall make the
ark with rooms, and shall cover it inside and out with pitch.
15"And this is how you shall make it: the length of the ark three
hundred [d]cubits, its breadth fifty cubits, and its height thirty
cubits.

NAS [c] Or, *giants* [d] I.e., One cubit equals approx. 18 in.

## New International

thuselah lived 782 years and had other sons and daughters. 27Alto-
gether, Methuselah lived 969 years, and then he died.
28When Lamech had lived 182 years, he had a son. 29He named
him Noah[e] and said, "He will comfort us in the labor and painful
toil of our hands caused by the ground the LORD has cursed."
30After Noah was born, Lamech lived 595 years and had other sons
and daughters. 31Altogether, Lamech lived 777 years, and then he
died.
32After Noah was 500 years old, he became the father of Shem,
Ham and Japheth.

*The Flood*

6 WHEN MEN began to increase in number on the earth and
daughters were born to them, 2the sons of God saw that the
daughters of men were beautiful, and they married any of them
they chose. 3Then the LORD said, "My Spirit will not contend
with[f] man forever, for he is mortal[g]; his days will be a hundred
and twenty years."
4The Nephilim were on the earth in those days—and also afterward—when the sons of God went to the daughters of men and
had children by them. They were the heroes of old, men of renown.
5The LORD saw how great man's wickedness on the earth had
become, and that every inclination of the thoughts of his heart was
only evil all the time. 6The LORD was grieved that he had made
man on the earth, and his heart was filled with pain. 7So the LORD
said, "I will wipe mankind, whom I have created, from the face of
the earth—men and animals, and creatures that move along the
ground, and birds of the air—for I am grieved that I have made
them." 8But Noah found favor in the eyes of the LORD.
9This is the account of Noah.
Noah was a righteous man, blameless among the people of his
time, and he walked with God. 10Noah had three sons: Shem,
Ham and Japheth.
11Now the earth was corrupt in God's sight and was full of
violence. 12God saw how corrupt the earth had become, for all the
people on earth had corrupted their ways. 13So God said to Noah,
"I am going to put an end to all people, for the earth is filled with
violence because of them. I am surely going to destroy both them
and the earth. 14So make yourself an ark of cypress[h] wood; make
rooms in it and coat it with pitch inside and out. 15This is how you
are to build it: The ark is to be 450 feet long, 75 feet wide and 45
feet high.[i] 16Make a roof for it and finish[j] the ark to within 18

NIV [e] 29 *Noah* sounds like the Hebrew for *comfort.* [f] 3 Or *My spirit will not remain in* [g] 3 Or *corrupt* [h] 14 The meaning of the Hebrew for this word is uncertain. [i] 15 Hebrew *300 cubits long, 50 cubits wide and 30 cubits high* (about 140 meters long, 23 meters wide and 13.5 meters high) [j] 16 Or *Make an opening for light by finishing*

## King James

16And a window shalt thou make to the ark, and in a cubit shalt thou finish it above; and the door of the ark shalt thou set in the side thereof; *with* lower, second, and third *stories* shalt thou make it.

17And, behold, I, even I, do bring a flood of waters upon the earth, to destroy all flesh, wherein *is* the breath of life, from under heaven; *and* every thing that *is* in the earth shall die.

18But with thee will I establish my covenant; and thou shalt come into the ark, thou, and thy sons, and thy wife, and thy sons' wives with thee.

19And of every living thing of all flesh, two of every *sort* shalt thou bring into the ark, to keep *them* alive with thee; they shall be male and female.

20Of fowls after their kind, and of cattle after their kind, of every creeping thing of the earth after his kind, two of every *sort* shall come unto thee, to keep *them* alive.

21And take thou unto thee of all food that is eaten, and thou shalt gather *it* to thee; and it shall be for food for thee, and for them.

22Thus did Noah; according to all that God commanded him, so did he.

7 AND THE LORD said unto Noah, Come thou and all thy house into the ark; for thee have I seen righteous before me in this generation.

2Of every clean beast thou shalt take to thee by sevens, the male and his female: and of beasts that *are* not clean by two, the male and his female.

3Of fowls also of the air by sevens, the male and the female; to keep seed alive upon the face of all the earth.

4For yet seven days, and I will cause it to rain upon the earth forty days and forty nights; and every living substance that I have made will I destroy from off the face of the earth.

5And Noah did according unto all that the LORD commanded him.

6And Noah *was* six hundred years old when the flood of waters was upon the earth.

7¶ And Noah went in, and his sons, and his wife, and his sons' wives with him, into the ark, because of the waters of the flood.

8Of clean beasts, and of beasts that *are* not clean, and of fowls, and of every thing that creepeth upon the earth,

9There went in two and two unto Noah into the ark, the male and the female, as God had commanded Noah.

10And it came to pass after seven days, that the waters of the flood were upon the earth.

11¶ In the six hundredth year of Noah's life, in the second month, the seventeenth day of the month, the same day were all the fountains of the great deep broken up, and the windows of heaven were opened.

12And the rain was upon the earth forty days and forty nights.

13In the selfsame day entered Noah, and Shem, and Ham, and Japheth, the sons of Noah, and Noah's wife, and the three wives of his sons with them, into the ark;

14They, and every beast after his kind, and all the cattle after their kind, and every creeping thing that creepeth upon the earth after his kind, and every fowl after his kind, every bird of every sort.

15And they went in unto Noah into the ark, two and two of all flesh, wherein *is* the breath of life.

## Amplified

16You shall make a roof or [a]window—a place for light—to the ark, and finish it a cubit [at least 18 inches] above—and the [b]door of the ark you shall put in the side of it; and you shall make it with lower, second, and third stories.

17For behold, I, even I, will bring a flood of waters upon the earth, to destroy *and* make putrid all flesh under the heavens, in which are the breath *and* spirit of life; everything that is on the land shall die.

18But I will establish my covenant (promise, pledge) with you, and you shall come into the ark, you, and your sons, and your wife, and your sons' wives with you.

19And of every living thing of all flesh [found on land], you shall bring two of every sort into the ark, to keep them alive with you; they shall be male and female.

20Of fowls *and* birds according to their kinds, and of beasts according to their kinds, of every creeping thing of the ground according to its kind, two of every sort shall come in with you that they may be kept alive.

21Also take with you every sort of food that is eaten, and you shall collect *and* store it up, and it shall serve as food for you and for them.

22Noah did this; he did all that God commanded him.

7 AND THE Lord said to Noah, Come with all your household into the ark, for I have seen you righteous, (upright, and in right standing,) before Me in this generation. [Ps. 27:5; 33:18, 19; II Pet. 2:9.]

2Of every clean beast you shall receive *and* take with you seven pairs, the male and his mate; and of beasts that are not clean a pair of each kind, the male and his mate. [Lev. 11.]

3Also of the birds of the air seven pairs, the male and the female; to keep seed [their kind] alive over all the earth *or* land.

4For in seven days I will cause it to rain upon the earth forty days and forty nights, and every living substance *and* thing that I have made I will destroy, blot out, *and* wipe away from off the face of the earth.

5And Noah did all that the Lord commanded him. [Heb. 11:7.]

6Noah was 600 years old when the flood of waters came upon the earth *or* land.

7And Noah and his sons and his wife and his sons' wives with him went into the ark, because of the waters of the flood. [Matt. 24:38; Luke 17:27.]

8Of [c]clean animals and of animals that are not clean, and of birds *and* fowls, and of every thing that creeps on the ground,

9There went in two and two with Noah into the ark, the male and the female, as God had commanded Noah [not the animals].

10And after the seven days the flood came upon the earth *or* land.

11In the year 600 of Noah's life, in the seventeenth day of the second month, that same day all the fountains of the great deep were broken up *and* burst forth, and the windows *and* flood gates of the heavens were opened.

12And it rained upon the earth forty days and forty nights.

13On the very same day Noah, and Shem, Ham, and Japheth, the sons of Noah, and Noah's wife and the three wives of his sons with them went into the ark;

14They, and every (wild) beast according to its kind, and all the livestock according to their kind, and every moving thing that creeps on the land according to its kind, and every fowl according to its kind, every winged thing of every sort.

15And they went into the ark with Noah, two and two of all flesh, in which there was the breath *and* spirit of life.

**AMP** [a] Noah's ark possibly had a window area large enough to admit light and provide ventilation. [b] "Here can only be meant an entrance which was afterward closed, and only opened again at the end of the flood. And since there were three stories of the ark, the word is to be understood, perhaps, of three entrances capable of being closed, and to which there would have been constructed a way of access from the outside" *(Lange's Commentary).* [c] Noah had many years in which to interest travelers in securing these animals for him. The five extra pairs of clean animals were for food, and for sacrifice later.

## New American Standard

16"You shall make a window for the ark, and finish it to a cubit from the top; and set the door of the ark in the side of it; you shall make it with lower, second, and third decks.

17"And behold, I, even I am bringing the flood of water upon the earth, to destroy all flesh in which is the breath of life, from under heaven; everything that is on the earth shall perish.

18"But I will establish My covenant with you; and you shall enter the ark—you and your sons and your wife, and your sons' wives with you.

19"And of every living thing of all flesh, you shall bring two of every *kind* into the ark, to keep *them* alive with you; they shall be male and female.

20"Of the birds after their kind, and of the animals after their kind, of every creeping thing of the ground after its kind, two of every *kind* shall come to you to keep *them* alive.

21"And as for you, take for yourself some of all food which is edible, and gather *it* to yourself; and it shall be for food for you and for them."

22Thus Noah did; according to all that God had commanded him, so he did.

*The Flood*

7 THEN THE LORD said to Noah, "Enter the ark, you and all your household; for you *alone* I have seen *to be* righteous before Me in this time.

2"You shall take with you of every clean animal by sevens, a male and his female; and of the animals that are not clean two, a male and his female;

3also of the birds of the sky, by sevens, male and female, to keep offspring alive on the face of all the earth.

4"For after seven more days, I will send rain on the earth forty days and forty nights; and I will blot out from the face of the land every living thing that I have made."

5And Noah did according to all that the LORD had commanded him.

6¶ Now Noah was six hundred years old when the flood of water came upon the earth.

7Then Noah and his sons and his wife and his sons' wives with him entered the ark because of the water of the flood.

8Of clean animals and animals that are not clean and birds and everything that creeps on the ground,

9there went into the ark to Noah by twos, male and female, as God had commanded Noah.

10And it came about after the seven days, that the water of the flood came upon the earth.

11In the six hundredth year of Noah's life, in the second month, on the seventeenth day of the month, on the same day all the fountains of the great deep burst open, and the floodgates of the sky were opened.

12And the rain fell upon the earth for forty days and forty nights.

13¶ On the very same day Noah and Shem and Ham and Japheth, the sons of Noah, and Noah's wife and the three wives of his sons with them, entered the ark,

14they and every beast after its kind, and all the cattle after their kind, and every creeping thing that creeps on the earth after its kind, and every bird after its kind, all sorts of birds.

15So they went into the ark to Noah, by twos of all flesh in which was the breath of life.

## New International

inches[d] of the top. Put a door in the side of the ark and make lower,
middle and upper decks. 17I am going to bring floodwaters on the
earth to destroy all life under the heavens, every creature that has
the breath of life in it. Everything on earth will perish. 18But I will
establish my covenant with you, and you will enter the ark—you
and your sons and your wife and your sons' wives with you. 19You
are to bring into the ark two of all living creatures, male and
female, to keep them alive with you. 20Two of every kind of bird,
of every kind of animal and of every kind of creature that moves
along the ground will come to you to be kept alive. 21You are to
take every kind of food that is to be eaten and store it away as food
for you and for them."
22Noah did everything just as God commanded him.

7 THE LORD then said to Noah, "Go into the ark, you and your
whole family, because I have found you righteous in this
generation. 2Take with you seven[e] of every kind of clean animal,
a male and its mate, and two of every kind of unclean animal, a
male and its mate, 3and also seven of every kind of bird, male and
female, to keep their various kinds alive throughout the earth.
4Seven days from now I will send rain on the earth for forty days
and forty nights, and I will wipe from the face of the earth every
living creature I have made."
5And Noah did all that the LORD commanded him.
6Noah was six hundred years old when the floodwaters came
on the earth. 7And Noah and his sons and his wife and his sons'
wives entered the ark to escape the waters of the flood. 8Pairs of
clean and unclean animals, of birds and of all creatures that move
along the ground, 9male and female, came to Noah and entered
the ark, as God had commanded Noah. 10And after the seven days
the floodwaters came on the earth.
11In the six hundredth year of Noah's life, on the seventeenth
day of the second month—on that day all the springs of the great
deep burst forth, and the floodgates of the heavens were opened.
12And rain fell on the earth forty days and forty nights.
13On that very day Noah and his sons, Shem, Ham and
Japheth, together with his wife and the wives of his three sons,
entered the ark. 14They had with them every wild animal according to its kind, all livestock according to their kinds, every creature
that moves along the ground according to its kind and every bird
according to its kind, everything with wings. 15Pairs of all creatures that have the breath of life in them came to Noah and entered
the ark. 16The animals going in were male and female of every

NIV [d] *16* Hebrew *a cubit* (about 0.5 meter) [e] 2 Or *seven pairs;* also in verse 3

## King James

16And they that went in, went in male and female of all flesh, as God had commanded him: and the Lord shut him in.

17And the flood was forty days upon the earth; and the waters increased, and bare up the ark, and it was lift up above the earth.

18And the waters prevailed, and were increased greatly upon the earth; and the ark went upon the face of the waters.

19And the waters prevailed exceedingly upon the earth; and all the high hills, that *were* under the whole heaven, were covered.

20Fifteen cubits upward did the waters prevail; and the mountains were covered.

21And all flesh died that moved upon the earth, both of fowl, and of cattle, and of beast, and of every creeping thing that creepeth upon the earth, and every man:

22All in whose nostrils *was* the breath of life, of all that *was* in the dry *land,* died.

23And every living substance was destroyed which was upon the face of the ground, both man, and cattle, and the creeping things, and the fowl of the heaven; and they were destroyed from the earth: and Noah only remained *alive,* and they that *were* with him in the ark.

24And the waters prevailed upon the earth an hundred and fifty days.

**8** AND GOD remembered Noah, and every living thing, and all the cattle that *was* with him in the ark: and God made a wind to pass over the earth, and the waters assuaged;

2The fountains also of the deep and the windows of heaven were stopped, and the rain from heaven was restrained;

3And the waters returned from off the earth continually: and after the end of the hundred and fifty days the waters were abated.

4And the ark rested in the seventh month, on the seventeenth day of the month, upon the mountains of Ararat.

5And the waters decreased continually until the tenth month: in the tenth *month,* on the first *day* of the month, were the tops of the mountains seen.

6¶ And it came to pass at the end of forty days, that Noah opened the window of the ark which he had made:

7And he sent forth a raven, which went forth to and fro, until the waters were dried up from off the earth.

8Also he sent forth a dove from him, to see if the waters were abated from off the face of the ground;

9But the dove found no rest for the sole of her foot, and she returned unto him into the ark, for the waters *were* on the face of the whole earth: then he put forth his hand, and took her, and pulled her in unto him into the ark.

10And he stayed yet other seven days; and again he sent forth the dove out of the ark;

11And the dove came in to him in the evening; and, lo, in her mouth *was* an olive leaf plucked off: so Noah knew that the waters were abated from off the earth.

12And he stayed yet other seven days; and sent forth the dove; which returned not again unto him any more.

## Amplified

16And they that entered, male and female of all flesh, went in as God had commanded [Noah]; and the Lord shut him in *and* closed round about him.

17The flood [that is, the downpour of rain] was forty days upon the earth; and the waters increased, and bore up the ark, and it was lifted (high) above the land.

18And the waters became mighty and increased greatly upon the land; and the ark went (gently floating) upon the surface of the waters.

19And the waters prevailed so exceedingly *and* were so mighty upon the earth that all the high hills under the whole sky were covered.

20 *In fact* the waters became fifteen cubits higher, as the high hills were covered.

21And all flesh ceased to breathe that moved upon the earth, fowls *and* birds, [tame] animals, [wild] beasts, all swarming *and* creeping things that swarm *and* creep upon the land, and all mankind.

22Everything on the dry land in whose nostrils was the breath *and* spirit of life died.

23God destroyed (blotted out) every living thing that was upon the face of the earth; man and animals and the creeping things and the birds of the heavens, were destroyed (blotted out) from the land. Only Noah remained alive, and those who were with him in the ark. [Matt. 24:37-44.]

24And the waters prevailed (mightily) upon the earth *or* land 150 days—five months.

**8** AND GOD [earnestly] remembered Noah and every living thing and all the animals that were with him in the ark. And God made a wind blow over the land, and the waters sank down *and* abated.

2Also the fountains of the deep and the windows of the heavens were closed, the gushing rain from the sky was checked,

3And the waters receded from the land continually. At the end of 150 days the waters had diminished.

4On the seventeenth day of the seventh month, the ark came to rest on the mountains of Ararat [in Armenia].

5And the waters continued to diminish until the tenth month; on the first day of the tenth month the tops of the high hills were seen.

6At the end of [another] forty days Noah opened *a* window of the ark which he had made,

7And sent forth a raven, which kept going to and fro until the waters were dried up from off the land.

8Then he sent forth a dove to see if the waters had decreased from the surface of the ground;

9But the dove found no resting place on which to roost, and she returned to him to the ark, for the waters were [yet] on the face of the whole land. So he put forth his hand and drew her to him into the ark.

10He waited another seven days, and again sent forth the dove out of the ark;

11And the dove came back to him in the evening, and lo, in her mouth was a newly sprouted *and* freshly plucked olive leaf; so Noah knew that the waters had subsided from the land.

12Then he waited another seven days, and sent forth the dove; but she did not return to him any more.

## New American Standard

16And those that entered, male and female of all flesh, entered
as God had commanded him; and the LORD closed *it* behind him.
17Then the flood came upon the earth for forty days; and the
water increased and lifted up the ark, so that it rose above the
earth.
18And the water prevailed and increased greatly upon the earth;
and the ark floated on the surface of the water.
19And the water prevailed more and more upon the earth, so
that all the high mountains everywhere under the heavens were
covered.
20The water prevailed fifteen cubits higher, and the mountains
were covered.
21And all flesh that moved on the earth perished, birds and
cattle and beasts and every swarming thing that swarms upon the
earth, and all mankind;
22of all that was on the dry land, all in whose nostrils was the
breath of the spirit of life, died.
23Thus He blotted out every living thing that was upon the face
of the land, from man to animals to creeping things and to birds
of the sky, and they were blotted out from the earth; and only
Noah was left, together with those that were with him in the ark.
24And the water prevailed upon the earth one hundred and fifty
days.

## New International

living thing, as God had commanded Noah. Then the LORD shut
him in.
17For forty days the flood kept coming on the earth, and as the
waters increased they lifted the ark high above the earth. 18The
waters rose and increased greatly on the earth, and the ark floated
on the surface of the water. 19They rose greatly on the earth, and
all the high mountains under the entire heavens were covered.
20The waters rose and covered the mountains to a depth of more
than twenty feet.[a,b] 21Every living thing that moved on the earth
perished—birds, livestock, wild animals, all the creatures that
swarm over the earth, and all mankind. 22Everything on dry land
that had the breath of life in its nostrils died. 23Every living thing
on the face of the earth was wiped out; men and animals and the
creatures that move along the ground and the birds of the air were
wiped from the earth. Only Noah was left, and those with him in
the ark.
24The waters flooded the earth for a hundred and fifty days.

### *The Flood Subsides*

8 BUT GOD remembered Noah and all the beasts and all the
cattle that were with him in the ark; and God caused a wind
to pass over the earth, and the water subsided.
2Also the fountains of the deep and the floodgates of the sky
were closed, and the rain from the sky was restrained;
3and the water receded steadily from the earth, and at the end
of one hundred and fifty days the water decreased.
4And in the seventh month, on the seventeenth day of the
month, the ark rested upon the mountains of Ararat.
5And the water decreased steadily until the tenth month; in the
tenth month, on the first day of the month, the tops of the mountains became visible.
6¶ Then it came about at the end of forty days, that Noah
opened the window of the ark which he had made;
7and he sent out a raven, and it flew here and there until the
water was dried up from the earth.
8Then he sent out a dove from him, to see if the water was
abated from the face of the land;
9but the dove found no resting place for the sole of her foot,
so she returned to him into the ark; for the water was on the surface
of all the earth. Then he put out his hand and took her, and
brought her into the ark to himself.
10So he waited yet another seven days; and again he sent out
the dove from the ark.
11And the dove came to him toward evening; and behold, in her
beak was a freshly picked olive leaf. So Noah knew that the water
was abated from the earth.
12Then he waited yet another seven days, and sent out the
dove; but she did not return to him again.

8 BUT GOD remembered Noah and all the wild animals and
the livestock that were with him in the ark, and he sent a wind
over the earth, and the waters receded. 2Now the springs of the
deep and the floodgates of the heavens had been closed, and the
rain had stopped falling from the sky. 3The water receded steadily
from the earth. At the end of the hundred and fifty days the water
had gone down, 4and on the seventeenth day of the seventh
month the ark came to rest on the mountains of Ararat. 5The
waters continued to recede until the tenth month, and on the first
day of the tenth month the tops of the mountains became visible.
6After forty days Noah opened the window he had made in the
ark 7and sent out a raven, and it kept flying back and forth until
the water had dried up from the earth. 8Then he sent out a dove
to see if the water had receded from the surface of the ground. 9But
the dove could find no place to set its feet because there was water
over all the surface of the earth; so it returned to Noah in the ark.
He reached out his hand and took the dove and brought it back
to himself in the ark. 10He waited seven more days and again sent
out the dove from the ark. 11When the dove returned to him in the
evening, there in its beak was a freshly plucked olive leaf! Then
Noah knew that the water had receded from the earth. 12He waited
seven more days and sent the dove out again, but this time it did
not return to him.

**NIV** [a] 20 Hebrew *fifteen cubits* (about 6.9 meters) [b] 20 Or *rose more than twenty feet, and the mountains were covered*

## King James

13¶ And it came to pass in the six hundredth and first year, in the first *month,* the first *day* of the month, the waters were dried up from off the earth: and Noah removed the covering of the ark, and looked, and, behold, the face of the ground was dry.

14And in the second month, on the seven and twentieth day of the month, was the earth dried.

15¶ And God spake unto Noah, saying,

16Go forth of the ark, thou, and thy wife, and thy sons, and thy sons' wives with thee.

17Bring forth with thee every living thing that *is* with thee, of all flesh, *both* of fowl, and of cattle, and of every creeping thing that creepeth upon the earth; that they may breed abundantly in the earth, and be fruitful, and multiply upon the earth.

18And Noah went forth, and his sons, and his wife, and his sons' wives with him:

19Every beast, every creeping thing, and every fowl, *and* whatsoever creepeth upon the earth, after their kinds, went forth out of the ark.

20¶ And Noah builded an altar unto the LORD; and took of every clean beast, and of every clean fowl, and offered burnt offerings on the altar.

21And the LORD smelled a sweet savour; and the LORD said in his heart, I will not again curse the ground any more for man's sake; for the imagination of man's heart *is* evil from his youth; neither will I again smite any more every thing living, as I have done.

22While the earth remaineth, seedtime and harvest, and cold and heat, and summer and winter, and day and night shall not cease.

## Amplified

13In the year 601 [of Noah's life], on the first day of the first month, the waters were drying from off the land; and Noah [a]removed the covering of the ark and looked, and behold, the surface of the ground was drying.

14And on the twenty-seventh day of the second month, the land was entirely dry.

15And God spoke to Noah, saying,

16Go forth from the ark, you and your wife and your sons and their wives with you.

17Bring forth every living thing that is with you of all flesh: birds and beasts and every creeping thing that creeps on the ground; that they may breed abundantly on the land, and be fruitful and multiply upon the earth.

18And Noah went forth, and his wife and his sons and their wives with him [after being in the ark one year and ten days].

19Every beast, every creeping thing, every bird, and whatever moves on the land, went forth by families out of the ark.

20And Noah built an altar to the Lord, and took of every clean [four-footed] animal and of every clean fowl *or* bird, and offered burnt offerings on the altar.

21When the Lord smelled the pleasing odor [a scent of satisfaction to His heart], the Lord said to Himself, I will never again curse the ground because of man, for the imagination (the strong desire) of man's heart is evil *and* wicked from his youth; neither will I ever again smite *and* destroy every living thing as I have done.

22While the earth remains, seedtime and harvest, cold and heat, summer and winter, and day and night shall not cease.

## King James

9 AND GOD blessed Noah and his sons, and said unto them, Be fruitful, and multiply, and replenish the earth.

2And the fear of you and the dread of you shall be upon every beast of the earth, and upon every fowl of the air, upon all that moveth *upon* the earth, and upon all the fishes of the sea; into your hand are they delivered.

3Every moving thing that liveth shall be meat for you; even as the green herb have I given you all things.

4But flesh with the life thereof, *which is* the blood thereof, shall ye not eat.

5And surely your blood of your lives will I require; at the hand of every beast will I require it, and at the hand of man; at the hand of every man's brother will I require the life of man.

6Whoso sheddeth man's blood, by man shall his blood be shed: for in the image of God made he man.

7And you, be ye fruitful, and multiply; bring forth abundantly in the earth, and multiply therein.

8¶ And God spake unto Noah, and to his sons with him, saying,

9And I, behold, I establish my covenant with you, and with your seed after you;

## Amplified

9 AND GOD pronounced a blessing upon Noah and his sons and said to them, Be fruitful and multiply, and fill the earth.

2And the fear of you and the dread *and* terror of you shall be upon every beast of the land, every bird of the air, all that creeps upon the ground, and upon all the fishes of the sea; they are delivered into your hand.

3Every moving thing that lives shall be food for you; and as I give you the green vegetables *and* plants, I give you everything.

4But you shall not eat flesh with the life of it, which is its blood.

5And surely for your lifeblood I will require an accounting; of every beast I will require it and of man; of every man [who spills another's lifeblood] I will require a reckoning.

6Whoso sheds man's blood, by man shall his blood be shed; for in the image of God He made man.

7And you, be fruitful and multiply; bring forth abundantly on the earth and multiply on it.

8Then God spoke to Noah and to his sons with him, saying,

9Behold, I establish My covenant *or* pledge with you and with your descendants after you,

**AMP** [a] Possibly overhanging eaves which prevented the rain from coming through the perforated window space had also prevented Noah from seeing the mountain tops. It is well to remember that the architect of Noah's ark was the omniscient Scientist whose "ways are past finding out," though men have learned much from them through the centuries. Nothing was lacking in Noah's Ark to keep it from being suited for all that was required of it. The comfortable, light, well-ventilated, water tight, perfectly planned boat, large enough to accommodate all the original land animals intelligently and to permit the four human couples to live separately and in peace, needs no apology today. "In 1609 at Hoorn, in Holland, the Netherlandish Mennonite, P. Jansen, produced a vessel after the pattern of the ark, only smaller, whereby he proved it was well adapted for floating, and would carry a cargo greater by one third than any other form of like cubical content" (*Lange's Commentary,* condensed). It revolutionized ship building. By 1900 every large vessel on the high seas was definitely inclined toward the proportions of Noah's Ark (as verified by "Lloyd's Register of Shipping" in the *World Almanac*). Later, ships were built longer for speed, a matter of no concern to Noah.

# New American Standard

13¶ Now it came about in the six hundred and first year, in the
first *month,* on the first of the month, the water was dried up from
the earth. Then Noah removed the covering of the ark, and looked,
and behold, the surface of the ground was dried up.
14And in the second month, on the twenty-seventh day of the
month, the earth was dry.
15Then God spoke to Noah, saying,
16"Go out of the ark, you and your wife and your sons and your
sons' wives with you.
17"Bring out with you every living thing of all flesh that is with
you, birds and animals and every creeping thing that creeps on the
earth, that they may breed abundantly on the earth, and be fruitful
and multiply on the earth."
18So Noah went out, and his sons and his wife and his sons'
wives with him.
19Every beast, every creeping thing, and every bird, everything
that moves on the earth, went out by their families from the ark.
20¶ Then Noah built an altar to the LORD, and took of every clean
animal and of every clean bird and offered burnt offerings on the
altar.
21And the LORD smelled the soothing aroma; and the LORD said
to Himself, "I will never again curse the ground on account of
man, for the intent of man's heart is evil from his youth; and I will
never again destroy every living thing, as I have done.

22 "While the earth remains,
Seedtime and harvest,
And cold and heat,
And summer and winter,
And day and night
Shall not cease."

*Covenant of the Rainbow*

9 AND GOD blessed Noah and his sons and said to them, "Be
fruitful and multiply, and fill the earth.
2"And the fear of you and the terror of you shall be on every
beast of the earth and on every bird of the sky; with everything that
creeps on the ground, and all the fish of the sea, into your hand
they are given.
3"Every moving thing that is alive shall be food for you; I give
all to you, as *I gave* the green plant.
4"Only you shall not eat flesh with its life, *that is,* its blood.
5"And surely I will require your lifeblood; from every beast I
will require it. And from *every* man, from every man's brother I will
require the life of man.

6 "Whoever sheds man's blood,
By man his blood shall be shed,
For in the image of God
He made man.

7 "And as for you, be fruitful and multiply;
Populate the earth abundantly and multiply in it."

8¶ Then God spoke to Noah and to his sons with him, saying,
9"Now behold, I Myself do establish My covenant with you,
and with your descendants after you;

# New International

13By the first day of the first month of Noah's six hundred and
first year, the water had dried up from the earth. Noah then
removed the covering from the ark and saw that the surface of the
ground was dry. 14By the twenty-seventh day of the second month
the earth was completely dry.
15Then God said to Noah, 16"Come out of the ark, you and your
wife and your sons and their wives. 17Bring out every kind of living
creature that is with you—the birds, the animals, and all the creatures that move along the ground—so they can multiply on the
earth and be fruitful and increase in number upon it."
18So Noah came out, together with his sons and his wife and
his sons' wives. 19All the animals and all the creatures that move
along the ground and all the birds—everything that moves on the
earth—came out of the ark, one kind after another.
20Then Noah built an altar to the LORD and, taking some of all
the clean animals and clean birds, he sacrificed burnt offerings on
it. 21The LORD smelled the pleasing aroma and said in his heart:
"Never again will I curse the ground because of man, even
though[b] every inclination of his heart is evil from childhood. And
never again will I destroy all living creatures, as I have done.

22"As long as the earth endures,
seedtime and harvest,
cold and heat,
summer and winter,
day and night
will never cease."

*God's Covenant With Noah*

9 THEN GOD blessed Noah and his sons, saying to them, "Be
fruitful and increase in number and fill the earth. 2The fear
and dread of you will fall upon all the beasts of the earth and all
the birds of the air, upon every creature that moves along the
ground, and upon all the fish of the sea; they are given into your
hands. 3Everything that lives and moves will be food for you. Just
as I gave you the green plants, I now give you everything.
4"But you must not eat meat that has its lifeblood still in it. 5And
for your lifeblood I will surely demand an accounting. I will demand an accounting from every animal. And from each man, too,
I will demand an accounting for the life of his fellow man.

6"Whoever sheds the blood of man,
by man shall his blood be shed;
for in the image of God
has God made man.

7As for you, be fruitful and increase in number; multiply on the
earth and increase upon it."
8Then God said to Noah and to his sons with him: 9"I now
establish my covenant with you and with your descendants after
you 10and with every living creature that was with you—the birds,

**NIV** [b] 21 Or *man, for*

## King James

10 And with every living creature that *is* with you, of the fowl, of the cattle, and of every beast of the earth with you; from all that go out of the ark, to every beast of the earth.

11 And I will establish my covenant with you; neither shall all flesh be cut off any more by the waters of a flood; neither shall there any more be a flood to destroy the earth.

12 And God said, This *is* the token of the covenant which I make between me and you and every living creature that *is* with you, for perpetual generations:

13 I do set my bow in the cloud, and it shall be for a token of a covenant between me and the earth.

14 And it shall come to pass, when I bring a cloud over the earth, that the bow shall be seen in the cloud:

15 And I will remember my covenant, which *is* between me and you and every living creature of all flesh; and the waters shall no more become a flood to destroy all flesh.

16 And the bow shall be in the cloud; and I will look upon it, that I may remember the everlasting covenant between God and every living creature of all flesh that *is* upon the earth.

17 And God said unto Noah, This *is* the token of the covenant, which I have established between me and all flesh that *is* upon the earth.

18 ¶ And the sons of Noah, that went forth of the ark, were Shem, and Ham, and Japheth: and Ham *is* the father of Canaan.

19 These *are* the three sons of Noah: and of them was the whole earth overspread.

20 And Noah began *to be* an husbandman, and he planted a vineyard:

21 And he drank of the wine, and was drunken; and he was uncovered within his tent.

22 And Ham, the father of Canaan, saw the nakedness of his father, and told his two brethren without.

23 And Shem and Japheth took a garment, and laid *it* upon both their shoulders, and went backward, and covered the nakedness of their father; and their faces *were* backward, and they saw not their father's nakedness.

24 And Noah awoke from his wine, and knew what his younger son had done unto him.

25 And he said, Cursed *be* Canaan; a servant of servants shall he be unto his brethren.

26 And he said, Blessed *be* the LORD God of Shem; and Canaan shall be his servant.

27 God shall enlarge Japheth, and he shall dwell in the tents of Shem; and Canaan shall be his servant.

28 ¶ And Noah lived after the flood three hundred and fifty years.

29 And all the days of Noah were nine hundred and fifty years: and he died.

**10** NOW THESE *are* the generations of the sons of Noah, Shem, Ham, and Japheth: and unto them were sons born after the flood.

## Amplified

10 And with every living creature that is with you, whether the birds, the livestock, or wild beasts of the earth along with you, as many as came out of the ark, every animal of the earth.

11 I will establish My covenant *or* pledge with you, that never again shall all flesh be cut off by the waters of a flood, neither shall there ever again be a flood to destroy *and* make the earth corrupt.

12 And God said, This is the token of the covenant (solemn pledge) which I make between Me and you and every living creature that is with you, for all future generations:

13 I set my bow [rainbow] in the cloud, and it shall be for a token *or* sign of a covenant *or* solemn pledge between Me and the earth.

14 And it shall be that when I bring clouds over the earth, and the bow [rainbow] is seen in the clouds,

15 I will [earnestly] remember my covenant *or* solemn pledge, which is between Me and you and every living creature of all flesh, and the waters shall no more become a flood to destroy *and* make all flesh corrupt.

16 When the bow [rainbow] is in the clouds, and I look upon it, I shall [earnestly] remember the everlasting covenant *or* pledge between God and every living creature of all flesh that is upon the earth.

17 And God said to Noah, This *rainbow* is the token *or* sign of the covenant *or* solemn pledge, which I have established between Me and all flesh upon the earth.

18 The sons of Noah who went forth from the ark were Shem, Ham, and Japheth. Ham was the father of Canaan [born later].

19 These are the three sons of Noah, and from them the whole earth was overspread *and* stocked with inhabitants.

20 And Noah began to cultivate the ground, and he planted a vineyard;

21 And he drank of the wine, and became drunk; and he was uncovered *and* lay naked in his tent.

22 And Ham, the father of Canaan glanced *and saw* the nakedness of his father, and told his two brothers outside.

23 So Shem and Japheth took a garment, laid it upon the shoulders of both, and went backward and covered the nakedness of their father, and their faces were backward and they did not see their father's nakedness.

24 When Noah awoke from his wine, and knew the thing which his youngest son had done to him,

25 He exclaimed, Cursed be Canaan! He shall be the [a]servant of servants to his brethren! [Deut. 27:16.]

26 He also said, Blessed be the Lord, the God of Shem, *and* blessed by the Lord my God be Shem! And let Canaan be his servant.

27 May God enlarge Japheth, and let him dwell in the tents of Shem; and let Canaan be his servant.

28 And Noah lived after the flood 350 years.

29 All the days of Noah were 950 years, and he died.

**10** THESE ARE the generations (descendants) of the sons of Noah, Shem, Ham, and Japheth. The sons born to them after the flood *were:*

**AMP** [a] The language of Noah here is an actual prophecy and not merely an expression of personal feeling. That Noah placed a curse on his youngest grandchild, Canaan, who would naturally be his favorite, can only be explained on the ground that in the prophetic spirit he saw into the future of the Canaanites. [God Himself found the delinquency of the Canaanites insufferable and ultimately drove them out or subdued them and put the descendants of Shem in their place.] But Noah's foresight did not yet include the extermination of the Canaanite peoples, for then he would have expressed it differently. He would not merely have called them "the servant of servants" if he had foreseen their destruction. The form of the expression, therefore, testifies to the great age of the prophecy. (Adapted from *Lange's Commentary*)

## New American Standard

10and with every living creature that is with you, the birds, the
cattle, and every beast of the earth with you; of all that comes out
of the ark, even every beast of the earth.
11"And I establish My covenant with you; and all flesh shall
never again be cut off by the water of the flood, neither shall there
again be a flood to destroy the earth."
12And God said, "This is the sign of the covenant which I am
making between Me and you and every living creature that is with
you, for all successive generations;
13I set My bow in the cloud, and it shall be for a sign of a
covenant between Me and the earth.
14"And it shall come about, when I bring a cloud over the earth,
that the bow shall be seen in the cloud,
15and I will remember My covenant, which is between Me and
you and every living creature of all flesh; and never again shall the
water become a flood to destroy all flesh.
16"When the bow is in the cloud, then I will look upon it, to
remember the everlasting covenant between God and every living
creature of all flesh that is on the earth."
17And God said to Noah, "This is the sign of the covenant
which I have established between Me and all flesh that is on the
earth."
**18**¶ Now the sons of Noah who came out of the ark were Shem
and Ham and Japheth; and Ham was the father of Canaan.
19These three *were* the sons of Noah; and from these the whole
earth was populated.
**20**¶ Then Noah began farming and planted a vineyard.
21And he drank of the wine and became drunk, and uncovered
himself inside his tent.
22And Ham, the father of Canaan, saw the nakedness of his
father, and told his two brothers outside.
23But Shem and Japheth took a garment and laid it upon both
their shoulders and walked backward and covered the nakedness
of their father; and their faces were turned away, so that they did
not see their father's nakedness.
24When Noah awoke from his wine, he knew what his youngest
son had done to him.
25So he said,
"Cursed be Canaan;
[b]A servant of servants
He shall be to his brothers."
26 He also said,
"Blessed be the LORD,
The God of Shem;
And let Canaan be his servant.
27 "May God enlarge Japheth,
And let him dwell in the tents of Shem;
And let Canaan be his servant."
**28**¶ And Noah lived three hundred and fifty years after the
flood.
29So all the days of Noah were nine hundred and fifty years,
and he died.

*Descendants of Noah*

**10** NOW THESE are *the records of* the generations of Shem,
Ham, and Japheth, the sons of Noah; and sons were born
to them after the flood.

NAS [b] I.e., The lowest of servants

## New International

the livestock and all the wild animals, all those that came out of
the ark with you—every living creature on earth. 11I establish my
covenant with you: Never again will all life be cut off by the waters
of a flood; never again will there be a flood to destroy the earth."
12And God said, "This is the sign of the covenant I am making
between me and you and every living creature with you, a covenant for all generations to come: 13I have set my rainbow in the
clouds, and it will be the sign of the covenant between me and the
earth. 14Whenever I bring clouds over the earth and the rainbow
appears in the clouds, 15I will remember my covenant between me
and you and all living creatures of every kind. Never again will the
waters become a flood to destroy all life. 16Whenever the rainbow
appears in the clouds, I will see it and remember the everlasting
covenant between God and all living creatures of every kind on the
earth."
17So God said to Noah, "This is the sign of the covenant I have
established between me and all life on the earth."

*The Sons of Noah*

18The sons of Noah who came out of the ark were Shem, Ham
and Japheth. (Ham was the father of Canaan.) 19These were the
three sons of Noah, and from them came the people who were
scattered over the earth.
20Noah, a man of the soil, proceeded[c] to plant a vineyard.
21When he drank some of its wine, he became drunk and lay
uncovered inside his tent. 22Ham, the father of Canaan, saw his
father's nakedness and told his two brothers outside. 23But Shem
and Japheth took a garment and laid it across their shoulders; then
they walked in backward and covered their father's nakedness.
Their faces were turned the other way so that they would not see
their father's nakedness.
24When Noah awoke from his wine and found out what his
youngest son had done to him, 25he said,
"Cursed be Canaan!
The lowest of slaves
will he be to his brothers."
26He also said,
"Blessed be the LORD, the God of Shem!
May Canaan be the slave of Shem.[d]
27May God extend the territory of Japheth[e];
may Japheth live in the tents of Shem,
and may Canaan be his[f] slave."
28After the flood Noah lived 350 years. 29Altogether, Noah lived
950 years, and then he died.

*The Table of Nations*

**10** THIS IS the account of Shem, Ham and Japheth, Noah's
sons, who themselves had sons after the flood.

NIV [c] 20 Or *soil, was the first* [d] 26 Or *be his slave* [e] 27 *Japheth* sounds like the Hebrew for *extend.* [f] 27 Or *their*

## King James

2 The sons of Japheth; Gomer, and Magog, and Madai, and Javan, and Tubal, and Meshech, and Tiras.

3 And the sons of Gomer; Ashkenaz, and Riphath, and Togarmah.

4 And the sons of Javan; Elishah, and Tarshish, Kittim, and Dodanim.

5 By these were the isles of the Gentiles divided in their lands; every one after his tongue, after their families, in their nations.

6 ¶ And the sons of Ham; Cush, and Mizraim, and Phut, and Canaan.

7 And the sons of Cush; Seba, and Havilah, and Sabtah, and Raamah, and Sabtecha: and the sons of Raamah; Sheba, and Dedan.

8 And Cush begat Nimrod: he began to be a mighty one in the earth.

9 He was a mighty hunter before the LORD: wherefore it is said, Even as Nimrod the mighty hunter before the LORD.

10 And the beginning of his kingdom was Babel, and Erech, and Accad, and Calneh, in the land of Shinar.

11 Out of that land went forth Asshur, and builded Nineveh, and the city Rehoboth, and Calah,

12 And Resen between Nineveh and Calah: the same *is* a great city.

13 And Mizraim begat Ludim, and Anamim, and Lehabim, and Naphtuhim,

14 And Pathrusim, and Casluhim, (out of whom came Philistim,) and Caphtorim.

15 ¶ And Canaan begat Sidon his firstborn, and Heth,

16 And the Jebusite, and the Amorite, and the Girgasite,

17 And the Hivite, and the Arkite, and the Sinite,

18 And the Arvadite, and the Zemarite, and the Hamathite: and afterward were the families of the Canaanites spread abroad.

19 And the border of the Canaanites was from Sidon, as thou comest to Gerar, unto Gaza; as thou goest, unto Sodom, and Gomorrah, and Admah, and Zeboim, even unto Lasha.

20 These *are* the sons of Ham, after their families, after their tongues, in their countries, *and* in their nations.

21 ¶ Unto Shem also, the father of all the children of Eber, the brother of Japheth the elder, even to him were *children* born.

22 The children of Shem; Elam, and Asshur, and Arphaxad, and Lud, and Aram.

23 And the children of Aram; Uz, and Hul, and Gether, and Mash.

24 And Arphaxad begat Salah; and Salah begat Eber.

25 And unto Eber were born two sons: the name of one *was* Peleg; for in his days was the earth divided; and his brother's name *was* Joktan.

26 And Joktan begat Almodad, and Sheleph, and Hazarmaveth, and Jerah,

27 And Hadoram, and Uzal, and Diklah,

28 And Obal, and Abimael, and Sheba,

29 And Ophir, and Havilah, and Jobab: all these *were* the sons of Joktan.

30 And their dwelling was from Mesha, as thou goest unto Sephar a mount of the east.

## Amplified

2 The sons of Japheth: Gomer, Magog, Madai, Javan, Tubal, Meshech, and Tiras.

3 The sons of Gomer: Ashkenaz, Riphath, and Togarmah.

4 The sons of Javan: Elishah, Tarshish, Kittim, and Dodanim.

5 From these the coastland peoples spread. *These above are the sons of Japheth* in their lands, each with his own language, by their families, in their nations.

6 The sons of Ham: Cush, Egypt, Put, and Canaan.

7 The sons of Cush: Seba, Havilah, Sabtah, Raamah, and Sabteca; and the sons of Raamah: Sheba, and Dedan.

8 Cush became the father of Nimrod; he was the first to be a mighty man on the earth.

9 He was a mighty hunter before the Lord; therefore it is said, Like Nimrod, a mighty hunter before the Lord.

10 The beginning of his kingdom was Babel, Erech, Accad, and Calneh, in the land of Shinar [in Babylonia].

11 Out of the land [Nimrod] went forth into Assyria and built Nineveh, Rehoboth-Ir, Calah,

12 And Resen, between Nineveh and Calah; all these [suburbs combined to form] the great city.

13 And Egypt became the father of Ludim, Anamim, Lehabim, Naphtuhim,

14 Pathrusim, Casluhim, from whom came the Philistines, and Caphtorim.

15 Canaan became the father of Sidon his first-born, Heth [the Hittites].

16 The Jebusites, the Amorites, the Girgashites,

17 The Hivites, the Arkites, the Sinites,

18 The Arvadites, the Zemarites and the Hamathites. Afterward the families of the Canaanites spread abroad.

19 And the territory of the Canaanites extended from Sidon, as one goes to Gerar, as far as Gaza, and as one goes to [a]Sodom, Gomorrah, Admah, and Zeboim, as far as Lasha.

20 These are the sons of Ham, by their families, their languages, their lands, and their nations.

21 To Shem also, the younger brother of Japheth and the ancestor of all the children of Eber [including the Hebrews], children were born.

22 The sons of Shem: Elam, Asshur, Arpachshad, Lud, and Aram.

23 The sons of Aram: Uz, Hul, Gether, and Mash.

24 Arpachshad became the father of Shelah; and Shelah became the father of Eber.

25 To Eber were born two sons: the name of one was Peleg [meaning division], because [the inhabitants of] the earth were divided up in his days, and his brother's name was Joktan. [v. 32.]

26 Joktan became the father of Almodad, Sheleph, Hazarmaveth, Jerah,

27 Hadoram, Uzal, Diklah,

28 Obal, Abimael, Sheba,

29 Ophir, Havilah, and Jobab; all these were the sons of Joktan.

30 The territory in which they lived extended from Mesha, as one goes toward Sephar to the hill country of the east.

**AMP** [a] Surely no greater proof is needed of the great antiquity of this portion of Genesis than the fact that it mentions as still standing these four cities of the plain, which were utterly destroyed in Abraham's time (Gen. 19:27-29; Deut. 29:23). Gradually it is being discovered that Genesis contains all the evidence necessary for its own defense.

## New American Standard

2¶ The sons of Japheth *were* Gomer and Magog and Madai and
Javan and Tubal and Meshech and Tiras.
3And the sons of Gomer *were* Ashkenaz and Riphath and
Togarmah.
4And the sons of Javan *were* Elishah and Tarshish, Kittim and
Dodanim.
5From these the coastlands of the nations were separated into
their lands, every one according to his language, according to their
families, into their nations.
6¶ And the sons of Ham *were* Cush and Mizraim and Put and
Canaan.
7And the sons of Cush *were* Seba and Havilah and Sabtah and
Raamah and Sabteca; and the sons of Raamah *were* Sheba and
Dedan.
8Now Cush became the father of Nimrod; he became a mighty
one on the earth.
9He was a mighty hunter before the LORD; therefore it is said,
"Like Nimrod a mighty hunter before the LORD."
10And the beginning of his kingdom was [b]Babel and Erech and
Accad and Calneh, in the land of Shinar.
11From that land he went forth into Assyria, and built Nineveh
and Rehoboth-Ir and Calah,
12and Resen between Nineveh and Calah; that is the great city.
13And Mizraim became the father of Ludim and Anamim and
Lehabim and Naphtuhim
14and Pathrusim and Casluhim (from which came the Philistines) and Caphtorim.
15¶ And Canaan became the father of Sidon, his first-born, and
Heth
16and the Jebusite and the Amorite and the Girgashite
17and the Hivite and the Arkite and the Sinite
18and the Arvadite and the Zemarite and the Hamathite; and
afterward the families of the Canaanite were spread abroad.
19And the territory of the Canaanite extended from Sidon as
you go toward Gerar, as far as Gaza; as you go toward Sodom and
Gomorrah and Admah and Zeboiim, as far as Lasha.
20These are the sons of Ham, according to their families, according to their languages, by their lands, by their nations.
21¶ And also to Shem, the father of all the children of Eber, *and*
the older brother of Japheth, children were born.
22The sons of Shem *were* Elam and Asshur and Arpachshad and
Lud and Aram.
23And the sons of Aram *were* Uz and Hul and Gether and Mash.
24And Arpachshad became the father of Shelah; and Shelah
became the father of Eber.
25And two sons were born to Eber; the name of the one *was*
Peleg, for in his days the earth was divided; and his brother's name
*was* Joktan.
26And Joktan became the father of Almodad and Sheleph and
Hazarmaveth and Jerah
27and Hadoram and Uzal and Diklah
28and Obal and Abimael and Sheba
29and Ophir and Havilah and Jobab; all these were the sons of
Joktan.
30Now their settlement extended from Mesha as you go toward
Sephar, the hill country of the east.

NAS [b] Or, *Babylon*

## New International

*The Japhethites*

2The sons[c] of Japheth:
Gomer, Magog, Madai, Javan, Tubal, Meshech and Tiras.
3The sons of Gomer:
Ashkenaz, Riphath and Togarmah.
4The sons of Javan:
Elishah, Tarshish, the Kittim and the Rodanim.[d] 5(From
these the maritime peoples spread out into their territories
by their clans within their nations, each with its own
language.)

*The Hamites*

6The sons of Ham:
Cush, Mizraim,[e] Put and Canaan.
7The sons of Cush:
Seba, Havilah, Sabtah, Raamah and Sabteca.
The sons of Raamah:
Sheba and Dedan.

8Cush was the father[f] of Nimrod, who grew to be a mighty
warrior on the earth. 9He was a mighty hunter before the LORD;
that is why it is said, "Like Nimrod, a mighty hunter before the
LORD." 10The first centers of his kingdom were Babylon, Erech,
Akkad and Calneh, in[g] Shinar.[h] 11From that land he went to
Assyria, where he built Nineveh, Rehoboth Ir,[i] Calah 12and Resen, which is between Nineveh and Calah; that is the great city.

13Mizraim was the father of
the Ludites, Anamites, Lehabites, Naphtuhites, 14Pathru-
sites, Casluhites (from whom the Philistines came) and
Caphtorites.
15Canaan was the father of
Sidon his firstborn,[j] and of the Hittites, 16Jebusites, Amorites, Girgashites, 17Hivites, Arkites, Sinites, 18Arvadites,
Zemarites and Hamathites.

Later the Canaanite clans scattered 19and the borders of Canaan
reached from Sidon toward Gerar as far as Gaza, and then toward
Sodom, Gomorrah, Admah and Zeboiim, as far as Lasha.
20These are the sons of Ham by their clans and languages, in
their territories and nations.

*The Semites*

21Sons were also born to Shem, whose older brother was[k]
Japheth; Shem was the ancestor of all the sons of Eber.
22The sons of Shem:
Elam, Asshur, Arphaxad, Lud and Aram.
23The sons of Aram:
Uz, Hul, Gether and Meshech.[l]
24Arphaxad was the father of[m] Shelah,
and Shelah the father of Eber.
25Two sons were born to Eber:
One was named Peleg,[n] because in his time the earth was
divided; his brother was named Joktan.
26Joktan was the father of
Almodad, Sheleph, Hazarmaveth, Jerah, 27Hadoram,
Uzal, Diklah, 28Obal, Abimael, Sheba, 29Ophir, Havilah
and Jobab. All these were sons of Joktan.

30The region where they lived stretched from Mesha toward
Sephar, in the eastern hill country.

NIV [c] *2 Sons* may mean *descendants* or *successors* or *nations;* also in verses 3, 4, 6, 7, 20-23, 29 and 31. [d] 4 Some manuscripts of the Masoretic Text and Samaritan Pentateuch (see also Septuagint and 1 Chron. 1:7); most manuscripts of the Masoretic Text *Dodanim* [e] 6 That is, Egypt; also in verse 13 [f] *8 Father* may mean *ancestor* or *predecessor* or *founder;* also in verses 13, 15, 24 and 26. [g] *10* Or *Erech and Akkad—all of them in* [h] 10 That is, Babylonia [i] *11* Or *Nineveh with its city squares* [j] *15* Or *of the Sidonians, the foremost* [k] *21* Or *Shem, the older brother of* [l] 23 See Septuagint and 1 Chron. 1:17; Hebrew *Mash* [m] 24 Hebrew; Septuagint *father of Cainan, and Cainan was the father of* [n] *25 Peleg* means *division.*

## King James

31 These *are* the sons of Shem, after their families, after their
tongues, in their lands, after their nations.
32 These *are* the families of the sons of Noah, after their generations, in their nations: and by these were the nations divided in the
earth after the flood.

**11** AND THE whole earth was of one language, and of one
speech.
2 And it came to pass, as they journeyed from the east, that they
found a plain in the land of Shinar; and they dwelt there.
3 And they said one to another, Go to, let us make brick, and
burn them thoroughly. And they had brick for stone, and slime
had they for mortar.
4 And they said, Go to, let us build us a city and a tower, whose
top *may reach* unto heaven; and let us make us a name, lest we be
scattered abroad upon the face of the whole earth.
5 And the LORD came down to see the city and the tower, which
the children of men builded.
6 And the LORD said, Behold, the people *is* one, and they have
all one language; and this they begin to do: and now nothing will
be restrained from them, which they have imagined to do.
7 Go to, let us go down, and there confound their language, that
they may not understand one another's speech.
8 So the LORD scattered them abroad from thence upon the face
of all the earth: and they left off to build the city.
9 Therefore is the name of it called Babel; because the LORD did
there confound the language of all the earth: and from thence did
the LORD scatter them abroad upon the face of all the earth.
10 ¶ These *are* the generations of Shem: Shem *was* an hundred
years old, and begat Arphaxad two years after the flood:
11 And Shem lived after he begat Arphaxad five hundred years,
and begat sons and daughters.
12 And Arphaxad lived five and thirty years, and begat Salah:
13 And Arphaxad lived after he begat Salah four hundred and
three years, and begat sons and daughters.
14 And Salah lived thirty years, and begat Eber:
15 And Salah lived after he begat Eber four hundred and three
years, and begat sons and daughters.
16 And Eber lived four and thirty years, and begat Peleg:
17 And Eber lived after he begat Peleg four hundred and thirty
years, and begat sons and daughters.
18 And Peleg lived thirty years, and begat Reu:
19 And Peleg lived after he begat Reu two hundred and nine
years, and begat sons and daughters.
20 And Reu lived two and thirty years, and begat Serug:
21 And Reu lived after he begat Serug two hundred and seven
years, and begat sons and daughters.
22 And Serug lived thirty years, and begat Nahor:
23 And Serug lived after he begat Nahor two hundred years, and
begat sons and daughters.
24 And Nahor lived nine and twenty years, and begat Terah:
25 And Nahor lived after he begat Terah an hundred and nineteen years, and begat sons and daughters.

**AMP** [a] Some noted philologists have declared that a common origin of all languages cannot be denied. One, Max Mueller in his *Science of Language,* said, "We have examined all possible forms which language can assume, and now we ask, can we reconcile with these three distinct forms, the radical, the terminational, the inflectional, the admission of one common origin of human speech? I answer decidedly, 'Yes'." *The New Bible Commentary* says, "The original unity of human language, though still far from demonstrable, becomes increasingly probable."

## Amplified

31 These are Shem's descendants by their families, their languages, their lands, and their nations.
32 These are the families of the sons of Noah, according to their
generations in their nations; and from these the nations spread
abroad on the earth after the flood. [Acts 17:26.]

**11** AND THE whole earth was of one language, and of one
accent *and* mode of expression.
2 And as they journeyed eastward they found a plain (valley) in
the land of Shinar, and they settled *and* dwelt there.
3 And they said one to another, Come, let us make bricks and
burn them thoroughly. So they had brick for stone, and slime
(bitumen) for mortar.
4 And they said, Come, let us build us a city, and a tower whose
top reaches into the sky; and let us make a name for ourselves, lest
we be scattered over the whole earth.
5 And the Lord came down to see the city and the tower, which
the sons of men had built.
6 And the Lord said, Behold, they are one people, and they have
[a]all one language; and this is only the beginning of what they will
do; and now nothing they have imagined they can do will be
impossible to them.
7 Come, let Us go down, and there confound (mix up, confuse)
their language, that they may not understand one another's
speech.
8 So the Lord scattered them abroad from that place upon the
face of the whole earth; and they gave up building the city.
9 Therefore the name of it was called Babel, because the Lord
there confounded the language of all the earth; and from that place
the Lord scattered them abroad upon the face of the whole earth.
10 These are the generations of Shem. Shem was 100 years old
when he became the father of Arpachshad two years after the
flood.
11 And Shem lived after Arpachshad was born 500 years and had
other sons and daughters.
12 Arpachshad lived 35 years, and became the father of Shelah;
13 Arpachshad lived after Shelah was born 403 years and had
other sons and daughters.
14 When Shelah had lived 30 years he became the father of Eber;
15 Shelah lived after Eber was born 403 years and had other sons
and daughters.
16 When Eber had lived 34 years he became the father of Peleg;
17 And Eber lived after Peleg was born 430 years and had other
sons and daughters.
18 When Peleg had lived 30 years he became the father of Reu;
19 And Peleg lived after the birth of Reu 209 years and had other
sons and daughters.
20 When Reu had lived 32 years, he became the father of Serug;
21 And Reu lived after the birth of Serug 207 years and had other
sons and daughters.
22 When Serug had lived 30 years, he became the father of
Nahor;
23 And Serug lived after Nahor was born 200 years and had other
sons and daughters.
24 When Nahor had lived 29 years, he became the father of
Terah;
25 And Nahor lived after the birth of Terah 119 years and had
other sons and daughters.

## New American Standard

31These are the sons of Shem, according to their families, according to their languages, by their lands, according to their nations.
32¶ These are the families of the sons of Noah, according to their
genealogies, by their nations; and out of these the nations were
separated on the earth after the flood.

*Universal Language, Babel, Confusion*

11 NOW THE whole earth used the same language and the
same words.
2And it came about as they journeyed east, that they found a
plain in the land of Shinar and settled there.
3And they said to one another, "Come, let us make bricks and
burn *them* thoroughly." And they used brick for stone, and they
used tar for mortar.
4And they said, "Come, let us build for ourselves a city, and
a tower whose top *will reach* into heaven, and let us make for
ourselves a name; lest we be scattered abroad over the face of the
whole earth."
5And the LORD came down to see the city and the tower which
the sons of men had built.
6And the LORD said, "Behold, they are one people, and they
all have the same language. And this is what they began to do, and
now nothing which they purpose to do will be impossible for
them.
7"Come, let Us go down and there confuse their language, that
they may not understand one another's speech."
8So the LORD scattered them abroad from there over the face
of the whole earth; and they stopped building the city.
9Therefore its name was called [b]Babel, because there the LORD
confused the language of the whole earth; and from there the LORD
scattered them abroad over the face of the whole earth.

*Descendants of Shem*

10¶ These are *the records of* the generations of Shem. Shem was
one hundred years old, and became the father of Arpachshad two
years after the flood;
11and Shem lived five hundred years after he became the father
of Arpachshad, and he had *other* sons and daughters.
12¶ And Arpachshad lived thirty-five years, and became the
father of Shelah;
13and Arpachshad lived four hundred and three years after he
became the father of Shelah, and he had *other* sons and daughters.
14¶ And Shelah lived thirty years, and became the father of
Eber;
15and Shelah lived four hundred and three years after he
became the father of Eber, and he had *other* sons and daughters.
16¶ And Eber lived thirty-four years, and became the father of
Peleg;
17and Eber lived four hundred and thirty years after he became
the father of Peleg, and he had *other* sons and daughters.
18¶ And Peleg lived thirty years, and became the father of Reu;
19and Peleg lived two hundred and nine years after he became
the father of Reu, and he had *other* sons and daughters.
20¶ And Reu lived thirty-two years, and became the father of
Serug;
21and Reu lived two hundred and seven years after he became
the father of Serug, and he had *other* sons and daughters.
22¶ And Serug lived thirty years, and became the father of
Nahor;
23and Serug lived two hundred years after he became the father
of Nahor, and he had *other* sons and daughters.
24¶ And Nahor lived twenty-nine years, and became the father
of Terah;
25and Nahor lived one hundred and nineteen years after he
became the father of Terah, and he had *other* sons and daughters.

**NAS** [b] Or, *Babylon*

## New International

31These are the sons of Shem by their clans and languages, in
their territories and nations.

32These are the clans of Noah's sons, according to their lines of
descent, within their nations. From these the nations spread out
over the earth after the flood.

*The Tower of Babel*

11 NOW THE whole world had one language and a common
speech. 2As men moved eastward,[c] they found a plain in
Shinar[d] and settled there.
3They said to each other, "Come, let's make bricks and bake
them thoroughly." They used brick instead of stone, and tar for
mortar. 4Then they said, "Come, let us build ourselves a city, with
a tower that reaches to the heavens, so that we may make a name
for ourselves and not be scattered over the face of the whole
earth."
5But the LORD came down to see the city and the tower that the
men were building. 6The LORD said, "If as one people speaking the
same language they have begun to do this, then nothing they plan
to do will be impossible for them. 7Come, let us go down and
confuse their language so they will not understand each other."
8So the LORD scattered them from there over all the earth, and
they stopped building the city. 9That is why it was called Babel[e] —because there the LORD confused the language of the whole
world. From there the LORD scattered them over the face of the
whole earth.

*From Shem to Abram*

10This is the account of Shem.

Two years after the flood, when Shem was 100 years old, he
became the father[f] of Arphaxad. 11And after he became the father
of Arphaxad, Shem lived 500 years and had other sons and daughters.
12When Arphaxad had lived 35 years, he became the father of
Shelah. 13And after he became the father of Shelah, Arphaxad
lived 403 years and had other sons and daughters.[g]
14When Shelah had lived 30 years, he became the father of Eber.
15And after he became the father of Eber, Shelah lived 403 years
and had other sons and daughters.
16When Eber had lived 34 years, he became the father of Peleg.
17And after he became the father of Peleg, Eber lived 430 years and
had other sons and daughters.
18When Peleg had lived 30 years, he became the father of Reu.
19And after he became the father of Reu, Peleg lived 209 years and
had other sons and daughters.
20When Reu had lived 32 years, he became the father of Serug.
21And after he became the father of Serug, Reu lived 207 years and
had other sons and daughters.
22When Serug had lived 30 years, he became the father of
Nahor. 23And after he became the father of Nahor, Serug lived 200
years and had other sons and daughters.
24When Nahor had lived 29 years, he became the father of
Terah. 25And after he became the father of Terah, Nahor lived 119
years and had other sons and daughters.

**NIV** [c] 2 Or *from the east*; or *in the east* [d] 2 That is, Babylonia [e] 9 That is, Babylon; *Babel* sounds like the Hebrew for *confused*. [f] *10 Father* may mean *ancestor*; also in verses 11-25. [g] *12,13* Hebrew; Septuagint (see also Luke 3:35, 36 and note at Gen. 10:24) *35 years, he became the father of Cainan. 13And after he became the father of Cainan, Arphaxad lived 430 years and had other sons and daughters, and then he died. When Cainan had lived 130 years, he became the father of Shelah. And after he became the father of Shelah, Cainan lived 330 years and had other sons and daughters*

## King James

26 And Terah lived seventy years, and begat Abram, Nahor, and
Haran.
27 ¶ Now these *are* the generations of Terah: Terah begat Abram,
Nahor, and Haran; and Haran begat Lot.
28 And Haran died before his father Terah in the land of his
nativity, in Ur of the Chaldees.
29 And Abram and Nahor took them wives: the name of Abram's
wife *was* Sarai; and the name of Nahor's wife, Milcah, the daughter
of Haran, the father of Milcah, and the father of Iscah.
30 But Sarai was barren; she *had* no child.
31 And Terah took Abram his son, and Lot the son of Haran his
son's son, and Sarai his daughter-in-law, his son Abram's wife;
and they went forth with them from Ur of the Chaldees, to go into
the land of Canaan; and they came unto Haran, and dwelt there.
32 And the days of Terah were two hundred and five years: and
Terah died in Haran.

**12** NOW THE LORD had said unto Abram, Get thee out of thy
country, and from thy kindred, and from thy father's
house, unto a land that I will show thee:
2 And I will make of thee a great nation, and I will bless thee,
and make thy name great; and thou shalt be a blessing:
3 And I will bless them that bless thee, and curse him that
curseth thee: and in thee shall all families of the earth be blessed.
4 So Abram departed, as the LORD had spoken unto him; and Lot
went with him: and Abram *was* seventy and five years old when
he departed out of Haran.
5 And Abram took Sarai his wife, and Lot his brother's son, and
all their substance that they had gathered, and the souls that they
had gotten in Haran; and they went forth to go into the land of
Canaan; and into the land of Canaan they came.
6 ¶ And Abram passed through the land unto the place of Si-
chem, unto the plain of Moreh. And the Canaanite *was* then in the
land.
7 And the LORD appeared unto Abram, and said, Unto thy seed
will I give this land: and there builded he an altar unto the LORD,
who appeared unto him.
8 And he removed from thence unto a mountain on the east of
Beth-el, and pitched his tent, *having* Beth-el on the west, and Hai
on the east: and there he builded an altar unto the LORD, and called
upon the name of the LORD.
9 And Abram journeyed, going on still toward the south.

## Amplified

26 After Terah had lived 70 years, he became the father of [at
different times], [a]Abram and Nahor and Haran, [his first-born].
27 Now these are the descendants of Terah. Terah was the father
of Abram, Nahor, and Haran; and Haran was the father of Lot.
28 Haran died before his father Terah in the land of his birth, [b]Ur
of the Chaldees.
29 And Abram and Nahor took wives; the name of Abram's wife
was Sarai, and the name of Nahor's wife, Milcah, daughter of
Haran the father of Milcah and Iscah.
30 But Sarai was barren; she had no child.
31 And Terah took Abram his son, and Lot the son of Haran, his
grandson, and Sarai his daughter-in-law, his son Abram's wife,
and they went forth to go together from Ur of the Chaldees into
the land of Canaan; but when they came to Haran, they settled
there.
32 And Terah lived 205 years; and Terah died in Haran.

**12** NOW [IN Haran], the Lord said to Abram, Go for yourself
[for your own advantage] out away from your country,
from your relatives and your father's house to the land that I will
show you. [Heb. 11:8-10.]
2 And I will make of you a great nation, and I will bless you [with
abundant increase of favors] and make your name famous *and*
distinguished, and you shall be a blessing—dispensing good to
others.
3 And I will bless those who bless you [who confer prosperity
or happiness upon you], and [c]curse him who curses *or* uses insolent language toward you; in you shall all the families *and* kindred
of the earth be blessed—by you they shall bless themselves. [Gal.
3:8.]
4 So Abram departed, as the Lord had directed him, and Lot [his
nephew] went with him. Abram was 75 years old when he left
Haran.
5 Abram took Sarai his wife, and Lot, his brother's son, and all
their possessions that they had gathered, and the persons [ser-
vants] that they had acquired in Haran; and they went forth to go
to the land of Canaan. When they came to the land of Canaan,
6 Abram passed through the land to the locality of Shechem, to
the oak *or* terebinth tree of Moreh. And the Canaanite was then
in the land.
7 Then the Lord appeared to Abram, and said, I will give this
land to your posterity. So Abram built an altar there to the Lord,
Who had appeared to him.
8 From there he pulled up [his tent pegs] *and* departed to the
mountain on the east of Bethel, and pitched his tent, with Bethel
on the west and Ai on the east; and there he built an altar to the
Lord, and called upon the name of the Lord.
9 Abram journeyed on, still going toward the South.

**AMP** [a] Abram is only mentioned first by way of dignity. Noah's sons also are given as "Shem, Ham, and Japheth" in 5:32, although Shem was not the eldest, but for dignity is named first, as is Abram here (*Clarke's Commentary*, condensed). [b] Abram's home town was Ur of the Chaldees. As the result of extensive archaeological excavations there by C. Leonard Woolley in 1922-34, a great deal is known about Abram's background. Space will not permit more than a glimpse at excavated Ur, but a few items will show the high state of civilization. The entire house of the average middle-class person had from ten to twenty rooms; measured forty to fifty-two feet; the lower floor was for servants, the upper floor for the family, with five rooms for their use; besides a guest chamber and a lavatory reserved for visitors, and a private chapel. A school was found and what the students studied was shown by the clay tablets discovered there. In the days of Abraham the pupils had reading, writing and arithmetic as today. They learned the multiplication and division tables and even worked at square and cube root. A bill of lading of about 2040 B.C. [about the era in which Abram is believed to have lived] showed that the commerce of that time was far-reaching. Even the name "Abraham" has been found on the excavated clay tablets. (Based on J. P. Free's *Archaeology and Bible History*) [c] To look with disfavor on the Jews was to invite God's displeasure; to treat the Jews offensively was to incur His wrath. But to befriend the Jews was to bring down upon one's head the rewards of a promise that could not be broken.

## New American Standard

26¶ And Terah lived seventy years, and became the father of
Abram, Nahor and Haran.
27¶ Now these are *the records of* the generations of Terah. Terah
became the father of Abram, Nahor and Haran; and Haran became
the father of Lot.
28And Haran died in the presence of his father Terah in the land
of his birth, in Ur of the Chaldeans.
29And Abram and Nahor took wives for themselves. The name
of Abram's wife was Sarai; and the name of Nahor's wife was
Milcah, the daughter of Haran, the father of Milcah and Iscah.
30And Sarai was barren; she had no child.
31And Terah took Abram his son, and Lot the son of Haran, his
grandson, and Sarai his daughter-in-law, his son Abram's wife;
and they went out together from Ur of the Chaldeans in order to
enter the land of Canaan; and they went as far as Haran, and
settled there.
32And the days of Terah were two hundred and five years; and
Terah died in Haran.

*Abram Journeys to Egypt*

**12** NOW THE LORD said to Abram,
"Go forth from your country,
And from your relatives
And from your father's house,
To the land which I will show you;
2 And I will make you a great nation,
And I will bless you,
And make your name great;
And so you shall be a blessing;
3 And I will bless those who bless you,
And the one who curses you I will curse.
And in you all the families of the earth shall be
blessed."
4So Abram went forth as the LORD had spoken to him; and Lot
went with him. Now Abram was seventy-five years old when he
departed from Haran.
5And Abram took Sarai his wife and Lot his nephew, and all
their possessions which they had accumulated, and the persons
which they had acquired in Haran, and they set out for the land
of Canaan; thus they came to the land of Canaan.
6And Abram passed through the land as far as the site of
Shechem, to the oak of Moreh. Now the Canaanite *was* then in the
land.
7And the LORD appeared to Abram and said, "To your descendants I will give this land." So he built an altar there to the
LORD who had appeared to him.
8Then he proceeded from there to the mountain on the east of
Bethel, and pitched his tent, with Bethel on the west and Ai on the
east; and there he built an altar to the LORD and called upon the
name of the LORD.
9And Abram journeyed on, continuing toward the [d]Negev.

NAS [d] I.e., South country

## New International

26After Terah had lived 70 years, he became the father of
Abram, Nahor and Haran.

27This is the account of Terah.

Terah became the father of Abram, Nahor and Haran. And
Haran became the father of Lot. 28While his father Terah was still
alive, Haran died in Ur of the Chaldeans, in the land of his birth.
29Abram and Nahor both married. The name of Abram's wife was
Sarai, and the name of Nahor's wife was Milcah; she was the
daughter of Haran, the father of both Milcah and Iscah. 30Now
Sarai was barren; she had no children.
31Terah took his son Abram, his grandson Lot son of Haran,
and his daughter-in-law Sarai, the wife of his son Abram, and
together they set out from Ur of the Chaldeans to go to Canaan.
But when they came to Haran, they settled there.
32Terah lived 205 years, and he died in Haran.

*The Call of Abram*

**12** THE LORD had said to Abram, "Leave your country, your
people and your father's household and go to the land I
will show you.

2"I will make you into a great nation
and I will bless you;
I will make your name great,
and you will be a blessing.
3I will bless those who bless you,
and whoever curses you I will curse;
and all peoples on earth
will be blessed through you."

4So Abram left, as the LORD had told him; and Lot went with
him. Abram was seventy-five years old when he set out from
Haran. 5He took his wife Sarai, his nephew Lot, all the possessions
they had accumulated and the people they had acquired in Haran,
and they set out for the land of Canaan, and they arrived there.
6Abram traveled through the land as far as the site of the great
tree of Moreh at Shechem. At that time the Canaanites were in the
land. 7The LORD appeared to Abram and said, "To your offspring[e]
I will give this land." So he built an altar there to the LORD, who
had appeared to him.
8From there he went on toward the hills east of Bethel and
pitched his tent, with Bethel on the west and Ai on the east. There
he built an altar to the LORD and called on the name of the LORD.
9Then Abram set out and continued toward the Negev.

NIV [e] 7 Or *seed*

## King James

10¶ And there was a famine in the land: and Abram went down
into Egypt to sojourn there; for the famine *was* grievous in the land.
11And it came to pass, when he was come near to enter into
Egypt, that he said unto Sarai his wife, Behold now, I know that
thou *art* a fair woman to look upon:
12Therefore it shall come to pass, when the Egyptians shall see
thee, that they shall say, This *is* his wife: and they will kill me, but
they will save thee alive.
13Say, I pray thee, thou *art* my sister: that it may be well with
me for thy sake; and my soul shall live because of thee.
14¶ And it came to pass, that, when Abram was come into
Egypt, the Egyptians beheld the woman that she *was* very fair.
15The princes also of Pharaoh saw her, and commended her
before Pharaoh: and the woman was taken into Pharaoh's house.
16And he entreated Abram well for her sake: and he had sheep,
and oxen, and he asses, and menservants, and maidservants, and
she asses, and camels.
17And the LORD plagued Pharaoh and his house with great
plagues because of Sarai Abram's wife.
18And Pharaoh called Abram, and said, What *is* this *that* thou
hast done unto me? why didst thou not tell me that she *was* thy
wife?
19Why saidst thou, She *is* my sister? so I might have taken her
to me to wife: now therefore behold thy wife, take *her*, and go thy
way.
20And Pharaoh commanded *his* men concerning him: and they
sent him away, and his wife, and all that he had.

13 AND ABRAM went up out of Egypt, he, and his wife, and
all that he had, and Lot with him, into the south.
2And Abram *was* very rich in cattle, in silver, and in gold.
3And he went on his journeys from the south even to Beth-el,
unto the place where his tent had been at the beginning, between
Beth-el and Hai;
4Unto the place of the altar, which he had made there at the
first: and there Abram called on the name of the LORD.
5¶ And Lot also, which went with Abram, had flocks, and
herds, and tents.
6And the land was not able to bear them, that they might dwell
together: for their substance was great, so that they could not dwell
together.
7And there was a strife between the herdmen of Abram's cattle
and the herdmen of Lot's cattle: and the Canaanite and the Perizzite dwelled then in the land.
8And Abram said unto Lot, Let there be no strife, I pray thee,
between me and thee, and between my herdmen and thy herdmen; for we *be* brethren.
9 *Is* not the whole land before thee? separate thyself, I pray thee,
from me: if *thou wilt take* the left hand, then I will go to the right;
or if *thou depart* to the right hand, then I will go to the left.

## Amplified

10Now there was a famine in the land; and Abram [a]went down
into Egypt to live temporarily, for the famine in the land was
oppressive (intense and grievous).
11And when he was about to enter into Egypt, he said to Sarai
his wife, I know that you are beautiful to behold.
12So when the Egyptians see you, they will say, This is his wife,
and they will kill me, but they will let you live.
13Say, I beg of you, that you are [b]my sister, so that it may be
well with me for your sake, and my life will be spared because of
you.
14And when Abram came into Egypt the Egyptians saw that the
woman was very beautiful.
15The princes of Pharaoh also saw her, and commended her to
Pharaoh. And she was taken into Pharaoh's house [harem].
16And he treated Abram well for her sake; he acquired sheep,
oxen, he-donkeys, menservants, maidservants, she-donkeys, and
[c]camels.
17But the Lord scourged Pharaoh and his household with serious plagues because of Sarai, Abram's wife.
18And Pharaoh called Abram, and said, What is this that you
have done to me? Why did you not tell me that she was your wife?
19Why did you say, She is my sister, so I took her to be my wife?
Now then, here is your wife; take her, and get away [from here]!
20And Pharaoh commanded his men concerning him; and they
brought him on his way with his wife and all that he had.

13 SO ABRAM went up out of Egypt, he and his wife and all
that he had, and Lot with him, into the South [country of
Judah].
2Now Abram was extremely rich in livestock and in silver and
in gold.
3And he journeyed on from the South [country of Judah] as far
as Bethel, to the place where his tent had been at the beginning,
between Bethel and Ai,
4Where he had built an altar at first; and there Abram called on
the name of the Lord. [Gal. 3:6-9.]
5But Lot, who went with Abram, also had flocks and herds and
tents.
6Now the land was not able to nourish *and* support them so they
might dwell together, for their possessions were too great for them
to live together.
7And there was strife between the herdsmen of Abram's cattle
and the herdsmen of Lot's cattle; and the Canaanite and the Perizzite dwelt then in the land [making fodder more difficult to obtain].
8So Abram said to Lot, Let there be no strife, I beg of you,
between you and me, and between your herdsmen and my herdsmen; for we are relatives.
9Is not the whole land before you? Separate yourself, I beg of
you, from me. You take the left hand, then I will go to the right;
or if you choose the right hand, then I will go to the left.

**AMP** [a] Some books on archaeology frequently allude to the critical view that strangers could not have come into Egypt in earlier times, quoting Strabo and Diodorus to that effect; but later archaeological discoveries show that people from the region of Palestine and Syria were coming to Egypt in the period of Abraham. This is clearly indicated by a tomb painting at Beni Hassan, dating a little after 2,000 B.C. It shows Asiatic Semites who had come to Egypt. Furthermore, the archaeological and historical indications of the coming of the Hyksos into Egypt around 1900 B.C. provided another piece of evidence that strangers could come into that land. (Adapted from J. P. Free's *Abraham in Egypt*) [b] Sarah was Abraham's half sister. They had the same father, but different mothers (Gen. 20:12). [c] Critics have set aside the statement that Abraham had camels in Egypt as an error. But archaeological evidence, including some twenty objects ranging from the seventh century B.C. to the period before 3,000 B.C., proves the authenticity of the Bible record concerning Abraham. It includes not only statuettes, plaques, rock carvings and drawings representing camels, but "camel bones, a camel skull, and a camel hair rope." (J. P. Free in *Archaeology and Bible History*, adapted.)

## New American Standard

10¶ Now there was a famine in the land; so Abram went down
to Egypt to sojourn there, for the famine was severe in the land.
11And it came about when he came near to Egypt, that he said
to Sarai his wife, "See now, I know that you are a beautiful woman;
12and it will come about when the Egyptians see you, that they
will say, 'This is his wife'; and they will kill me, but they will let
you live.
13"Please say that you are my sister so that it may go well with
me because of you, and that I may live on account of you."
14And it came about when Abram came into Egypt, the Egyptians saw that the woman was very beautiful.
15And Pharaoh's officials saw her and praised her to Pharaoh;
and the woman was taken into Pharaoh's house.
16Therefore he treated Abram well for her sake; and gave him
sheep and oxen and donkeys and male and female servants and
female donkeys and camels.
17But the LORD struck Pharaoh and his house with great plagues
because of Sarai, Abram's wife.
18Then Pharaoh called Abram and said, "What is this you have
done to me? Why did you not tell me that she was your wife?
19"Why did you say, 'She is my sister,' so that I took her for my
wife? Now then, here is your wife, take her and go."
20And Pharaoh commanded *his* men concerning him; and they
escorted him away, with his wife and all that belonged to him.

*Abram and Lot*

**13** SO ABRAM went up from Egypt to the [d]Negev, he and
his wife and all that belonged to him; and Lot with him.
2Now Abram was very rich in livestock, in silver and in gold.
3And he went on his journeys from the [e]Negev as far as
Bethel, to the place where his tent had been at the beginning,
between Bethel and Ai,
4to the place of the altar, which he had made there formerly;
and there Abram called on the name of the LORD.
5Now Lot, who went with Abram, also had flocks and herds
and tents.
6And the land could not sustain them while dwelling together;
for their possessions were so great that they were not able to
remain together.
7And there was strife between the herdsmen of Abram's livestock and the herdsmen of Lot's livestock. Now the Canaanite and
the Perizzite were dwelling then in the land.
8Then Abram said to Lot, "Please let there be no strife between
you and me, nor between my herdsmen and your herdsmen, for
we are brothers.
9"Is not the whole land before you? Please separate from me:
if *to* the left, then I will go to the right; or if *to* the right, then I will
go to the left."

NAS [d] I.e., South country [e] I.e., South country

## New International

*Abram in Egypt*

10Now there was a famine in the land, and Abram went down
to Egypt to live there for a while because the famine was severe.
11As he was about to enter Egypt, he said to his wife Sarai, "I know
what a beautiful woman you are. 12When the Egyptians see you,
they will say, 'This is his wife.' Then they will kill me but will let
you live. 13Say you are my sister, so that I will be treated well for
your sake and my life will be spared because of you."
14When Abram came to Egypt, the Egyptians saw that she was
a very beautiful woman. 15And when Pharaoh's officials saw her,
they praised her to Pharaoh, and she was taken into his palace.
16He treated Abram well for her sake, and Abram acquired sheep
and cattle, male and female donkeys, menservants and maidservants, and camels.
17But the LORD inflicted serious diseases on Pharaoh and his
household because of Abram's wife Sarai. 18So Pharaoh summoned Abram. "What have you done to me?" he said. "Why
didn't you tell me she was your wife? 19Why did you say, 'She is
my sister,' so that I took her to be my wife? Now then, here is your
wife. Take her and go!" 20Then Pharaoh gave orders about Abram
to his men, and they sent him on his way, with his wife and
everything he had.

*Abram and Lot Separate*

**13** SO ABRAM went up from Egypt to the Negev, with his
wife and everything he had, and Lot went with him.
2Abram had become very wealthy in livestock and in silver and
gold.
3From the Negev he went from place to place until he came to
Bethel, to the place between Bethel and Ai where his tent had been
earlier 4and where he had first built an altar. There Abram called
on the name of the LORD.
5Now Lot, who was moving about with Abram, also had flocks
and herds and tents. 6But the land could not support them while
they stayed together, for their possessions were so great that they
were not able to stay together. 7And quarreling arose between
Abram's herdsmen and the herdsmen of Lot. The Canaanites and
Perizzites were also living in the land at that time.
8So Abram said to Lot, "Let's not have any quarreling between
you and me, or between your herdsmen and mine, for we are
brothers. 9Is not the whole land before you? Let's part company.
If you go to the left, I'll go to the right; if you go to the right, I'll
go to the left."

## King James

10 And Lot lifted up his eyes, and beheld all the plain of Jordan,
that it *was* well watered every where, before the LORD destroyed
Sodom and Gomorrah, *even* as the garden of the LORD, like the
land of Egypt, as thou comest unto Zoar.
11 Then Lot chose him all the plain of Jordan; and Lot journeyed
east: and they separated themselves the one from the other.
12 Abram dwelled in the land of Canaan, and Lot dwelled in the
cities of the plain, and pitched *his* tent toward Sodom.
13 But the men of Sodom *were* wicked and sinners before the
LORD exceedingly.
14 ¶ And the LORD said unto Abram, after that Lot was separated
from him, Lift up now thine eyes, and look from the place where
thou art northward, and southward, and eastward, and westward:
15 For all the land which thou seest, to thee will I give it, and to
thy seed for ever.
16 And I will make thy seed as the dust of the earth: so that if
a man can number the dust of the earth, *then* shall thy seed also
be numbered.
17 Arise, walk through the land in the length of it and in the
breadth of it; for I will give it unto thee.
18 Then Abram removed *his* tent, and came and dwelt in the
plain of Mamre, which *is* in Hebron, and built there an altar unto
the LORD.

## Amplified

10 And Lot looked and saw that everywhere the Jordan valley
was well watered. Before the Lord destroyed Sodom and Gomorrah, [it was all] like the garden of the Lord, like the land of Egypt,
as you go to Zoar.
11 Then Lot chose for himself all the Jordan valley, and [he]
traveled east; so they separated.
12 Abram dwelt in the land of Canaan, and Lot dwelt in the cities
of the [Jordan] valley, and moved his tent as far as Sodom *and*
dwelt there.
13 But the men of Sodom were wicked and exceedingly great
sinners against the Lord.
14 The Lord said to Abram, after Lot had left him, Lift up now
your eyes, and look from the place where you are, northward and
southward and eastward and westward;
15 For all the land which you see I will give to you and to your
posterity for ever. [Acts 7:5.]
16 And I will make your descendants as the dust of the earth, so
that if a man can count the dust of the earth, then shall your
descendants also be counted.
17 Arise, walk through the land, the length of it and the breadth
of it, for I will give it to you.
18 Then Abram moved his tent, and came and dwelt among the
oaks *or* terebinths of Mamre, which are at Hebron, and built there
an altar to the Lord.

**14** AND IT came to pass in the days of Amraphel king of
Shinar, Arioch king of Ellasar, Chedorlaomer king of
Elam, and Tidal king of nations;
2 *That these* made war with Bera king of Sodom, and with Birsha
king of Gomorrah, Shinab king of Admah, and Shemeber king of
Zeboiim, and the king of Bela, which is Zoar.
3 All these were joined together in the vale of Siddim, which is
the salt sea.
4 Twelve years they served Chedorlaomer, and in the thirteenth
year they rebelled.
5 And in the fourteenth year came Chedorlaomer, and the kings
that *were* with him, and smote the Rephaims in Ashteroth Karnaim, and the Zuzims in Ham, and the Emims in Shaveh Kiriathaim,
6 And the Horites in their mount Seir, unto El-paran, which *is*
by the wilderness.
7 And they returned, and came to En-mishpat, which *is* Kadesh,
and smote all the country of the Amalekites, and also the Amorites, that dwelt in Hazezon-tamar.
8 And there went out the king of Sodom, and the king of Gomorrah, and the king of Admah, and the king of Zeboiim, and the king
of Bela (the same *is* Zoar;) and they joined battle with them in the
vale of Siddim;
9 With Chedorlaomer the king of Elam, and with Tidal king of
nations, and Amraphel king of Shinar, and Arioch king of Ellasar;
four kings with five.
10 And the vale of Siddim *was full of* slimepits; and the kings of
Sodom and Gomorrah fled, and fell there; and they that remained
fled to the mountain.
11 And they took all the goods of Sodom and Gomorrah, and all
their victuals, and went their way.
12 And they took Lot, Abram's brother's son, who dwelt in
Sodom, and his goods, and departed.

**14** IN THE days of the kings, Amraphel of Shinar, Arioch of
Ellasar, Chedor-laomer of Elam, and Tidal of Goiim,
2 They made war on Kings Bera of Sodom, Birsha of Gomorrah,
Shinab of Admah, Shemeber of Zeboiim, and the kings of Bela,
[a]that is, Zoar.
3 The latter joined together [as allies] in the Valley of Siddim,
which is *now* the [Dead] Sea of Salt.
4 Twelve years they had served Chedor-laomer, but in the thirteenth year they rebelled.
5 And in the fourteenth year Chedor-laomer and the kings who
were with him attacked *and* subdued the Rephaim in Ashteroth-
karnaim, the Zuzim in Ham, and the Emim in Shaveh-kiriathaim,
6 And the Horites in their Mount Seir as far as Elparan, which
is on the border of the wilderness.
7 Then they turned back and came to En-mishpat, which [now]
is Kadesh, and subdued all the country of the Amalekites, and also
the Amorites who dwelt in Hazazon-tamar.
8 Then the kings of Sodom, Gomorrah, Admah, Zeboiim, and
Bela, that is, Zoar, went out and [together] they joined battle with
[those kings] in the Valley of Siddim,
9 With Kings Chedor-laomer of Elam, Tidal of Goiim, Amraphel
of Shinar, and Arioch of Ellasar, four kings against five.
10 Now the Valley of Siddim was full of slime *or* bitumen pits;
and as the kings of Sodom and Gomorrah fled, they fell [were
overthrown] there, and the remainder [of the kings] fled to the
mountain.
11 [The victors] took all the wealth of Sodom and Gomorrah, and
all the supply of provisions, and departed.
12 And they also took Lot, Abram's brother's son, who dwelt in
Sodom, and his goods, away with them.

**AMP** [a] One of the notable proofs of the antiquity of the early sections of Genesis is that many of the original names of places about which they speak were so old that Moses, the writer, had to add an explanation in order to identify these ancient names so that the Israelites returning from Egypt might recognize them. This chapter 14 alone contains six such explanatory notes (vss. 2, 3, 7, 8, 15 and 17).

## New American Standard

10And Lot lifted up his eyes and saw all the valley of the Jordan,
that it was well watered everywhere— *this was* before the LORD
destroyed Sodom and Gomorrah—like the garden of the LORD,
like the land of Egypt as you go to Zoar.
11So Lot chose for himself all the valley of the Jordan; and Lot
journeyed eastward. Thus they separated from each other.
12Abram settled in the land of Canaan, while Lot settled in the
cities of the valley, and moved his tents as far as Sodom.
13Now the men of Sodom were wicked exceedingly and sinners
against the LORD.
14¶ And the LORD said to Abram, after Lot had separated from
him, "Now lift up your eyes and look from the place where you
are, northward and southward and eastward and westward;
15for all the land which you see, I will give it to you and to your
descendants forever.
16"And I will make your descendants as the dust of the earth;
so that if anyone can number the dust of the earth, then your
descendants can also be numbered.
17"Arise, walk about the land through its length and breadth;
for I will give it to you."
18Then Abram moved his tent and came and dwelt by the oaks
of Mamre, which are in Hebron, and there he built an altar to the
LORD.

*War of the Kings*

**14** AND IT came about in the days of Amraphel king of
Shinar, Arioch king of Ellasar, Chedorlaomer king of
Elam, and Tidal king of Goiim,
2 *that* they made war with Bera king of Sodom, and with Birsha
king of Gomorrah, Shinab king of Admah, and Shemeber king of
Zeboiim, and the king of Bela (that is, Zoar).
3All these came as allies to the valley of Siddim (that is, the Salt
Sea).
4Twelve years they had served Chedorlaomer, but the thirteenth year they rebelled.
5And in the fourteenth year Chedorlaomer and the kings that
were with him, came and defeated the Rephaim in Ashteroth-kar-
naim and the Zuzim in Ham and the Emim in Shaveh-kiriathaim,
6and the Horites in their Mount Seir, as far as El-paran, which
is by the wilderness.
7Then they turned back and came to En-mishpat (that is, Kadesh), and conquered all the country of the Amalekites, and also
the Amorites, who lived in Hazazon-tamar.
8And the king of Sodom and the king of Gomorrah and the
king of Admah and the king of Zeboiim and the king of Bela (that
is, Zoar) came out; and they arrayed for battle against them in the
valley of Siddim,
9against Chedorlaomer king of Elam and Tidal king of Goiim
and Amraphel king of Shinar and Arioch king of Ellasar—four
kings against five.
10Now the valley of Siddim was full of tar pits; and the kings
of Sodom and Gomorrah fled, and they fell into them. But those
who survived fled to the hill country.
11Then they took all the goods of Sodom and Gomorrah and all
their food supply, and departed.
12And they also took Lot, Abram's nephew, and his possessions and departed, for he was living in Sodom.

## New International

10Lot looked up and saw that the whole plain of the Jordan was
well watered, like the garden of the LORD, like the land of Egypt,
toward Zoar. (This was before the LORD destroyed Sodom and
Gomorrah.) 11So Lot chose for himself the whole plain of the
Jordan and set out toward the east. The two men parted company:
12Abram lived in the land of Canaan, while Lot lived among the
cities of the plain and pitched his tents near Sodom. 13Now the
men of Sodom were wicked and were sinning greatly against the
LORD.
14The LORD said to Abram after Lot had parted from him, "Lift
up your eyes from where you are and look north and south, east
and west. 15All the land that you see I will give to you and your
offspring[b] forever. 16I will make your offspring like the dust of the
earth, so that if anyone could count the dust, then your offspring
could be counted. 17Go, walk through the length and breadth of
the land, for I am giving it to you."
18So Abram moved his tents and went to live near the great
trees of Mamre at Hebron, where he built an altar to the LORD.

*Abram Rescues Lot*

**14** AT THIS time Amraphel king of Shinar,[c] Arioch king of
Ellasar, Kedorlaomer king of Elam and Tidal king of Goiim
2went to war against Bera king of Sodom, Birsha king of Gomorrah, Shinab king of Admah, Shemeber king of Zeboiim, and the
king of Bela (that is, Zoar). 3All these latter kings joined forces in
the Valley of Siddim (the Salt Sea[d]). 4For twelve years they had
been subject to Kedorlaomer, but in the thirteenth year they rebelled.
5In the fourteenth year, Kedorlaomer and the kings allied with
him went out and defeated the Rephaites in Ashteroth Karnaim,
the Zuzites in Ham, the Emites in Shaveh Kiriathaim 6and the
Horites in the hill country of Seir, as far as El Paran near the desert.
7Then they turned back and went to En Mishpat (that is, Kadesh),
and they conquered the whole territory of the Amalekites, as well
as the Amorites who were living in Hazazon Tamar.
8Then the king of Sodom, the king of Gomorrah, the king of
Admah, the king of Zeboiim and the king of Bela (that is, Zoar)
marched out and drew up their battle lines in the Valley of Siddim
9against Kedorlaomer king of Elam, Tidal king of Goiim, Amraphel
king of Shinar and Arioch king of Ellasar—four kings against five.
10Now the Valley of Siddim was full of tar pits, and when the kings
of Sodom and Gomorrah fled, some of the men fell into them and
the rest fled to the hills. 11The four kings seized all the goods of
Sodom and Gomorrah and all their food; then they went away.
12They also carried off Abram's nephew Lot and his possessions,
since he was living in Sodom.

**NIV** [b] *15* Or *seed;* also in verse 16 [c] *1* That is, Babylonia; also in verse 9
[d] *3* That is, the Dead Sea

## King James

13¶ And there came one that had escaped, and told Abram the Hebrew; for he dwelt in the plain of Mamre the Amorite, brother of Eshcol, and brother of Aner: and these *were* confederate with Abram.

14And when Abram heard that his brother was taken captive, he armed his trained *servants,* born in his own house, three hundred and eighteen, and pursued *them* unto Dan.

15And he divided himself against them, he and his servants, by night, and smote them, and pursued them unto Hobah, which *is* on the left hand of Damascus.

16And he brought back all the goods, and also brought again his brother Lot, and his goods, and the women also, and the people.

17¶ And the king of Sodom went out to meet him after his return from the slaughter of Chedorlaomer, and of the kings that *were* with him, at the valley of Shaveh, which *is* the king's dale.

18And Melchizedek king of Salem brought forth bread and wine: and he *was* the priest of the most high God.

19And he blessed him, and said, Blessed *be* Abram of the most high God, possessor of heaven and earth:

20And blessed be the most high God, which hath delivered thine enemies into thy hand. And he gave him tithes of all.

21And the king of Sodom said unto Abram, Give me the persons, and take the goods to thyself.

22And Abram said to the king of Sodom, I have lift up mine hand unto the LORD, the most high God, the possessor of heaven and earth,

23That I will not *take* from a thread even to a shoelatchet, and that I will not take any thing that *is* thine, lest thou shouldest say, I have made Abram rich:

24Save only that which the young men have eaten, and the portion of the men which went with me, Aner, Eshcol, and Mamre; let them take their portion.

15 AFTER THESE things the word of the LORD came unto Abram in a vision, saying, Fear not, Abram: I *am* thy shield, *and* thy exceeding great reward.

2And Abram said, Lord GOD, what wilt thou give me, seeing I go childless, and the steward of my house *is* this Eliezer of Damascus?

3And Abram said, Behold, to me thou hast given no seed: and, lo, one born in my house is mine heir.

4And, behold, the word of the LORD *came* unto him, saying, This shall not be thine heir; but he that shall come forth out of thine own bowels shall be thine heir.

5And he brought him forth abroad, and said, Look now toward heaven, and tell the stars, if thou be able to number them: and he said unto him, So shall thy seed be.

6And he believed in the LORD; and he counted it to him for righteousness.

7And he said unto him, I *am* the LORD that brought thee out of Ur of the Chaldees, to give thee this land to inherit it.

8And he said, Lord GOD, whereby shall I know that I shall inherit it?

9And he said unto him, Take me an heifer of three years old, and a she goat of three years old, and a ram of three years old, and a turtledove, and a young pigeon.

10And he took unto him all these, and divided them in the midst, and laid each piece one against another: but the birds divided he not.

11And when the fowls came down upon the carcases, Abram drove them away.

## Amplified

13Then one who had escaped came and told Abram the Hebrew [meaning, the one who came from beyond], who was living by the oaks *or* terebinths of Mamre the Amorite, brother of Eshcol and of Aner; these were allies of Abram.

14When Abram heard that [his nephew] had been captured, he armed [led forth] his 318 trained servants, born in his own house, and pursued the enemy as far as Dan.

15He divided his forces against them by night, he and his servants, and attacked *and* routed them, and pursued them as far as Hobah, which is north of Damascus.

16And he brought back all the goods, and also brought back his kinsman Lot and his possessions, the women also and the people.

17After [Abram's] return from the defeat *and* slaying of Chedorlaomer and the kings who were with him, the king of Sodom went out to meet him at the Valley of Shaveh, which is the King's Valley.

18Melchizedek king of Salem [later called Jerusalem] brought out bread and wine [for their nourishment]; he was the priest of God Most High.

19And he blessed him and said, Blessed (favored with blessings, made blissful, joyful) be Abram by God Most High, possessor *and* maker of heaven and earth,

20And blessed, praised *and* glorified be God Most High Who has given your foes into your hand! And [Abram] gave him a tenth of all [he had taken]. [Heb. 7:1-10.]

21And the king of Sodom said to Abram, Give me the persons, and keep the goods yourself.

22But Abram said to the king of Sodom, I have lifted up my hand *and* sworn to the Lord, God Most High, the possessor *and* maker of heaven and earth,

23That I would not take a thread or a shoelace or anything that is yours, lest you should say, I have made Abram rich.

24[Take all] except only what my young men have eaten, and the share of the men [allies] who went with me, Aner, Eshcol, and Mamre; let them take their portion.

15 AFTER THESE things the word of the Lord came to Abram in a vision, saying, Fear not, Abram, I am your shield, your abundant compensation, *and* your reward shall be exceedingly great.

2And Abram said, Lord God, what can You give me, since I am going on [from this world] childless, and he who shall be the owner *and* heir of my house is this [steward] Eliezer of Damascus?

3And Abram [continued], Look, You have given me no child, and [a servant] born in my house is my heir.

4And behold, the word of the Lord came to him, saying, This man shall not be your heir; but he who shall come from your own body shall be your heir.

5And He brought him outside [his tent into the starlight] and said, Look now toward the heavens, and count the stars, if you are able to number them. Then He said to him, So shall your descendants be. [Heb. 11:12.]

6And [Abram] believed, (trusted in, relied on, remained steadfast to the Lord); and He counted it to him as righteousness [right standing with God.] [Rom. 4:3, 18-22.]

7And He said to him, I am the [same] Lord Who brought you out of Ur of the Chaldees, to give you this land as an inheritance.

8But [Abram] said, Lord God, by what shall I know that I shall inherit it?

9And He said to him, Bring to Me a heifer three years old, a she-goat three years old, a ram three years old, a turtledove, and a young pigeon.

10And he brought Him all these, and cut them down the middle (into halves) and laid each half opposite the other; but the birds he did not divide.

11And when the birds of prey swooped down upon the carcasses, Abram drove them away.

## New American Standard

13¶ Then a fugitive came and told Abram the Hebrew. Now he was living by the oaks of Mamre the Amorite, brother of Eshcol and brother of Aner, and these were allies with Abram.

14And when Abram heard that his relative had been taken captive, he led out his trained men, born in his house, three hundred and eighteen, and went in pursuit as far as Dan.

15And he divided his forces against them by night, he and his servants, and defeated them, and pursued them as far as Hobah, which is north of Damascus.

16And he brought back all the goods, and also brought back his relative Lot with his possessions, and also the women, and the people.

*God's Promise to Abram*

17¶ Then after his return from the defeat of Chedorlaomer and the kings who were with him, the king of Sodom went out to meet him at the valley of Shaveh (that is, the King's Valley).

18And Melchizedek king of Salem brought out bread and wine; now he was a priest of God Most High.

19And he blessed him and said,

"Blessed be Abram of God Most High,
Possessor of heaven and earth;
20 And blessed be God Most High,
Who has delivered your enemies into your hand."

And he gave him a tenth of all.

21And the king of Sodom said to Abram, "Give the people to me and take the goods for yourself."

22And Abram said to the king of Sodom, "I have sworn to the LORD God Most High, possessor of heaven and earth,

23that I will not take a thread or a sandal thong or anything that is yours, lest you should say, 'I have made Abram rich.'

24"I will take nothing except what the young men have eaten, and the share of the men who went with me, Aner, Eshcol, and Mamre; let them take their share."

*Abram Promised a Son*

15 AFTER THESE things the word of the LORD came to Abram in a vision, saying,

"Do not fear, Abram,
I am a shield to you;
Your reward shall be very great."

2And Abram said, "O Lord GOD, what wilt Thou give me, since I am childless, and the heir of my house is Eliezer of Damascus?"

3And Abram said, "Since Thou hast given no offspring to me, one born in my house is my heir."

4Then behold, the word of the LORD came to him, saying, "This man will not be your heir; but one who shall come forth from your own body, he shall be your heir."

5And He took him outside and said, "Now look toward the heavens, and count the stars, if you are able to count them." And He said to him, "So shall your descendants be."

6Then he believed in the LORD; and He reckoned it to him as righteousness.

7And He said to him, "I am the LORD who brought you out of Ur of the Chaldeans, to give you this land to possess it."

8And he said, "O Lord GOD, how may I know that I shall possess it?"

9So He said to him, "Bring Me a three year old heifer, and a three year old female goat, and a three year old ram, and a turtledove, and a young pigeon."

10Then he brought all these to Him and cut them in two, and laid each half opposite the other; but he did not cut the birds.

11And the birds of prey came down upon the carcasses, and Abram drove them away.

## New International

13One who had escaped came and reported this to Abram the
Hebrew. Now Abram was living near the great trees of Mamre the
Amorite, a brother[a] of Eshcol and Aner, all of whom were allied
with Abram. 14When Abram heard that his relative had been taken
captive, he called out the 318 trained men born in his household
and went in pursuit as far as Dan. 15During the night Abram
divided his men to attack them and he routed them, pursuing
them as far as Hobah, north of Damascus. 16He recovered all the
goods and brought back his relative Lot and his possessions, together with the women and the other people.

17After Abram returned from defeating Kedorlaomer and the kings allied with him, the king of Sodom came out to meet him in the Valley of Shaveh (that is, the King's Valley).

18Then Melchizedek king of Salem[b] brought out bread and
wine. He was priest of God Most High, 19and he blessed Abram,
saying,

"Blessed be Abram by God Most High,
Creator[c] of heaven and earth.
20And blessed be[d] God Most High,
who delivered your enemies into your hand."

Then Abram gave him a tenth of everything.

21The king of Sodom said to Abram, "Give me the people and keep the goods for yourself."

22But Abram said to the king of Sodom, "I have raised my hand
to the LORD, God Most High, Creator of heaven and earth, and
have taken an oath 23that I will accept nothing belonging to you,
not even a thread or the thong of a sandal, so that you will never
be able to say, 'I made Abram rich.' 24I will accept nothing but what
my men have eaten and the share that belongs to the men who went with me—to Aner, Eshcol and Mamre. Let them have their share."

*God's Covenant With Abram*

15 AFTER THIS, the word of the LORD came to Abram in a vision:

"Do not be afraid, Abram.
I am your shield,[e]
your very great reward.[f] "

2But Abram said, "O Sovereign LORD, what can you give me
since I remain childless and the one who will inherit[g] my estate
is Eliezer of Damascus?" 3And Abram said, "You have given me
no children; so a servant in my household will be my heir."

4Then the word of the LORD came to him: "This man will not
be your heir, but a son coming from your own body will be your
heir." 5He took him outside and said, "Look up at the heavens and
count the stars—if indeed you can count them." Then he said to
him, "So shall your offspring be."

6Abram believed the LORD, and he credited it to him as righteousness.

7He also said to him, "I am the LORD, who brought you out of Ur of the Chaldeans to give you this land to take possession of it."

8But Abram said, "O Sovereign LORD, how can I know that I will gain possession of it?"

9So the LORD said to him, "Bring me a heifer, a goat and a ram, each three years old, along with a dove and a young pigeon."

10Abram brought all these to him, cut them in two and arranged
the halves opposite each other; the birds, however, he did not cut
in half. 11Then birds of prey came down on the carcasses, but
Abram drove them away.

NIV [a] *13* Or *a relative;* or *an ally* [b] *18* That is, Jerusalem [c] *19* Or *Possessor;* also in verse 22 [d] *20* Or *And praise be to* [e] *1* Or *sovereign* [f] *1* Or *shield; / your reward will be very great* [g] *2* The meaning of the Hebrew for this phrase is uncertain.

## King James

12And when the sun was going down, a deep sleep fell upon Abram; and, lo, an horror of great darkness fell upon him.

13And he said unto Abram, Know of a surety that thy seed shall be a stranger in a land *that is* not theirs, and shall serve them; and they shall afflict them four hundred years;

14And also that nation, whom they shall serve, will I judge: and afterward shall they come out with great substance.

15And thou shalt go to thy fathers in peace; thou shalt be buried in a good old age.

16But in the fourth generation they shall come hither again: for the iniquity of the Amorites *is* not yet full.

17And it came to pass, that, when the sun went down, and it was dark, behold a smoking furnace, and a burning lamp that passed between those pieces.

18In the same day the LORD made a covenant with Abram, saying, Unto thy seed have I given this land, from the river of Egypt unto the great river, the river Euphrates:

19The Kenites, and the Kenizzites, and the Kadmonites,

20And the Hittites, and the Perizzites, and the Rephaims,

21And the Amorites, and the Canaanites, and the Girgashites, and the Jebusites.

**16** NOW SARAI Abram's wife bare him no children: and she had an handmaid, an Egyptian, whose name *was* Hagar.

2And Sarai said unto Abram, Behold now, the LORD hath restrained me from bearing: I pray thee, go in unto my maid; it may be that I may obtain children by her. And Abram hearkened to the voice of Sarai.

3And Sarai Abram's wife took Hagar her maid the Egyptian, after Abram had dwelt ten years in the land of Canaan, and gave her to her husband Abram to be his wife.

4¶ And he went in unto Hagar, and she conceived: and when she saw that she had conceived, her mistress was despised in her eyes.

5And Sarai said unto Abram, My wrong *be* upon thee: I have given my maid into thy bosom; and when she saw that she had conceived, I was despised in her eyes: the LORD judge between me and thee.

6But Abram said unto Sarai, Behold, thy maid *is* in thy hand; do to her as it pleaseth thee. And when Sarai dealt hardly with her, she fled from her face.

7¶ And the angel of the LORD found her by a fountain of water in the wilderness, by the fountain in the way to Shur.

8And he said, Hagar, Sarai's maid, whence camest thou? and whither wilt thou go? And she said, I flee from the face of my mistress Sarai.

9And the angel of the LORD said unto her, Return to thy mistress, and submit thyself under her hands.

10And the angel of the LORD said unto her, I will multiply thy seed exceedingly, that it shall not be numbered for multitude.

11And the angel of the LORD said unto her, Behold, thou *art* with child, and shalt bear a son, and shalt call his name Ishmael; because the LORD hath heard thy affliction.

## Amplified

12When the sun was setting a deep sleep overcame Abram, and a horror, (a terror, shuddering fear), of great darkness assailed *and* oppressed him.

13And [God] said to Abram, Know positively that your descendants will be strangers dwelling as temporary residents in a land that is not theirs [Egypt], and will be slaves there, and they will be afflicted *and* oppressed for 400 years. [Literally fulfilled, Exod. 12:40.]

14But I will bring judgment on that nation, whom they will serve, and afterward they shall come out with great possessions. [Acts 7:6, 7.]

15And you shall go to your fathers in peace; you shall be buried in a good old (hoary) age.

16And in the [a]fourth generation they shall come back here [to Canaan] again; for the iniquity of the Amorites [name of the most important group of that region and later included the people of all Canaan] is not yet full *and* complete. [Josh. 24:15.]

17When the sun had gone down and a (thick) darkness had come on, lo, a smoking oven and a flaming torch passed between those pieces.

18On the same day the Lord made a covenant (promise, pledge) with Abram, saying, To your descendants I have given this land, from the river of Egypt to the great river Euphrates, the land of

19The Kenites, the Kenizzites, the Kadmonites,

20The Hittites, the Perizzites, the Rephaim,

21The Amorites, the Canaanites, the Girgashites, and the Jebusites.

**16** NOW SARAI, Abram's wife bore him no children. She had an Egyptian maid, whose name was Hagar.

2And Sarai said to Abram, See here, the Lord has restrained me from bearing. I am asking you to have intercourse with my maid; it may be that I may obtain children by her. And Abram listened to *and* heeded what Sarai said.

3So Sarai, Abram's wife, took Hagar her Egyptian maid, after Abram had dwelt ten years in the land of Canaan, and gave her to her husband Abram to be his [secondary] wife.

4And he had intercourse with Hagar, and she became pregnant; and when she saw that she was with child, she looked with contempt upon her mistress *and* despised her.

5Then Sarai said to Abram, May [the responsibility for] my wrong *and* deprivation of rights be upon you! I gave my maid into your bosom, and when she saw that she was with child, I was contemptible *and* despised in her eyes. The Lord be the judge between you and me.

6But Abram said to Sarai, See here, your maid is in your hands *and* power; do as you please with her. And when Sarai dealt severely with her, humbling *and* afflicting her, [Hagar] fled from her.

7But [b]the Angel of the Lord found her by a spring of water in the wilderness, on the road to Shur.

8And He said, Hagar, Sarai's maid, where did you come from, and where are you intending to go? And she said, I am running away from my mistress Sarai.

9The Angel of the Lord said to her, Go back to your mistress and (humbly) submit to her control.

10Also the Angel of the Lord said to her, I will multiply your descendants exceedingly so that they shall not be numbered for multitude.

11And the Angel of the Lord [continued], See now, you are with child, and shall bear a son, and shall call his name Ishmael [that is, God hears]; because the Lord has heard *and* paid attention to your affliction.

**AMP** [a] This prophecy was literally fulfilled. Moses, for example, who led the Israelites back to Canaan after their 400 years in Egypt, was "in the fourth generation" from Jacob—Levi, Kohath, Amram, Moses. [b] The Angel of the Lord is identified as Christ Himself in Gen. 48:16, where He is called "the redeeming Angel," or "the Angel the Redeemer."

## New American Standard

12¶ Now when the sun was going down, a deep sleep fell upon
Abram; and behold, terror *and* great darkness fell upon him.
13And *God* said to Abram, "Know for certain that your descendants will be strangers in a land that is not theirs, where they will
be enslaved and oppressed four hundred years.
14"But I will also judge the nation whom they will serve; and
afterward they will come out with many possessions.
15"And as for you, you shall go to your fathers in peace; you
shall be buried at a good old age.
16"Then in the fourth generation they shall return here, for the
iniquity of the Amorite is not yet complete."
17And it came about when the sun had set, that it was very dark,
and behold, *there appeared* a smoking oven and a flaming torch
which passed between these pieces.
18On that day the LORD made a covenant with Abram, saying,
"To your descendants I have given this land,
From the river of Egypt as far as the great river, the
river Euphrates:
19the Kenite and the Kenizzite and the Kadmonite
20and the Hittite and the Perizzite and the Rephaim
21and the Amorite and the Canaanite and the Girgashite and the
Jebusite."

*Sarai and Hagar*

16 NOW SARAI, Abram's wife had borne him no *children*,
and she had an Egyptian maid whose name was Hagar.
2So Sarai said to Abram, "Now behold, the LORD has prevented me from bearing *children.* Please go in to my maid; perhaps
I shall obtain children through her." And Abram listened to the
voice of Sarai.
3And after Abram had lived ten years in the land of Canaan,
Abram's wife Sarai took Hagar the Egyptian, her maid, and gave
her to her husband Abram as his wife.
4And he went in to Hagar, and she conceived; and when she
saw that she had conceived, her mistress was despised in her
sight.
5And Sarai said to Abram, "May the wrong done me be upon
you. I gave my maid into your arms; but when she saw that she
had conceived, I was despised in her sight. May the LORD judge
between you and me."
6But Abram said to Sarai, "Behold, your maid is in your power;
do to her what is good in your sight." So Sarai treated her harshly,
and she fled from her presence.
7¶ Now the angel of the LORD found her by a spring of water
in the wilderness, by the spring on the way to Shur.
8And he said, "Hagar, Sarai's maid, where have you come
from and where are you going?" And she said, "I am fleeing from
the presence of my mistress Sarai."
9Then the angel of the LORD said to her, "Return to your
mistress, and submit yourself to her authority."
10Moreover, the angel of the LORD said to her, "I will greatly
multiply your descendants so that they shall be too many to
count."
11The angel of the LORD said to her further,
"Behold, you are with child,
And you shall bear a son;
And you shall call his name [c]Ishmael,
Because the LORD has given heed to your affliction.

NAS [c] I.e., God hears

## New International

12As the sun was setting, Abram fell into a deep sleep, and a
thick and dreadful darkness came over him. 13Then the LORD said
to him, "Know for certain that your descendants will be strangers
in a country not their own, and they will be enslaved and mistreated four hundred years. 14But I will punish the nation they serve
as slaves, and afterward they will come out with great possessions.
15You, however, will go to your fathers in peace and be buried at
a good old age. 16In the fourth generation your descendants will
come back here, for the sin of the Amorites has not yet reached its
full measure."
17When the sun had set and darkness had fallen, a smoking
firepot with a blazing torch appeared and passed between the
pieces. 18On that day the LORD made a covenant with Abram and
said, "To your descendants I give this land, from the river[d] of
Egypt to the great river, the Euphrates— 19the land of the Kenites,
Kenizzites, Kadmonites, 20Hittites, Perizzites, Rephaites, 21Amo-
rites, Canaanites, Girgashites and Jebusites."

*Hagar and Ishmael*

16 NOW SARAI, Abram's wife, had borne him no children.
But she had an Egyptian maidservant named Hagar; 2so
she said to Abram, "The LORD has kept me from having children.
Go, sleep with my maidservant; perhaps I can build a family
through her."
Abram agreed to what Sarai said. 3So after Abram had been
living in Canaan ten years, Sarai his wife took her Egyptian maidservant Hagar and gave her to her husband to be his wife. 4He
slept with Hagar, and she conceived.
When she knew she was pregnant, she began to despise her
mistress. 5Then Sarai said to Abram, "You are responsible for the
wrong I am suffering. I put my servant in your arms, and now that
she knows she is pregnant, she despises me. May the LORD judge
between you and me."
6"Your servant is in your hands," Abram said. "Do with her
whatever you think best." Then Sarai mistreated Hagar; so she fled
from her.
7The angel of the LORD found Hagar near a spring in the desert;
it was the spring that is beside the road to Shur. 8And he said,
"Hagar, servant of Sarai, where have you come from, and where
are you going?"
"I'm running away from my mistress Sarai," she answered.
9Then the angel of the LORD told her, "Go back to your mistress
and submit to her." 10The angel added, "I will so increase your
descendants that they will be too numerous to count."
11The angel of the LORD also said to her:

"You are now with child
and you will have a son.
You shall name him Ishmael,[e]
for the LORD has heard of your misery.

NIV [d] *18* Or *Wadi* [e] *11* *Ishmael* means *God hears.*

## King James

12And he will be a wild man; his hand *will be* against every man,
and every man's hand against him; and he shall dwell in the
presence of all his brethren.
13And she called the name of the LORD that spake unto her,
Thou God seest me: for she said, Have I also here looked after him
that seeth me?
14Wherefore the well was called Beer-lahai-roi; behold, *it is*
between Kadesh and Bered.
15¶ And Hagar bare Abram a son: and Abram called his son's
name, which Hagar bare, Ishmael.
16And Abram *was* fourscore and six years old, when Hagar bare
Ishmael to Abram.

**17** AND WHEN Abram was ninety years old and nine, the
LORD appeared to Abram, and said unto him, I *am* the
Almighty God; walk before me, and be thou perfect.
2And I will make my covenant between me and thee, and will
multiply thee exceedingly.
3And Abram fell on his face: and God talked with him, saying,
4As for me, behold, my covenant *is* with thee, and thou shalt
be a father of many nations.
5Neither shall thy name any more be called Abram, but thy
name shall be Abraham; for a father of many nations have I made
thee.
6And I will make thee exceeding fruitful, and I will make nations of thee, and kings shall come out of thee.
7And I will establish my covenant between me and thee and thy
seed after thee in their generations for an everlasting covenant, to
be a God unto thee, and to thy seed after thee.
8And I will give unto thee, and to thy seed after thee, the land
wherein thou art a stranger, all the land of Canaan, for an everlasting possession; and I will be their God.
9¶ And God said unto Abraham, Thou shalt keep my covenant
therefore, thou, and thy seed after thee in their generations.
10This *is* my covenant, which ye shall keep, between me and
you and thy seed after thee; Every man child among you shall be
circumcised.
11And ye shall circumcise the flesh of your foreskin; and it shall
be a token of the covenant betwixt me and you.
12And he that is eight days old shall be circumcised among you,
every man child in your generations, he that is born in the house,
or bought with money of any stranger, which *is* not of thy seed.
13He that is born in thy house, and he that is bought with thy
money, must needs be circumcised: and my covenant shall be in
your flesh for an everlasting covenant.
14And the uncircumcised man child whose flesh of his foreskin
is not circumcised, that soul shall be cut off from his people; he
hath broken my covenant.
15¶ And God said unto Abraham, As for Sarai thy wife, thou
shalt not call her name Sarai, but Sarah *shall* her name *be*.
16And I will bless her, and give thee a son also of her: yea, I will
bless her, and she shall be *a mother* of nations; kings of people shall
be of her.

## Amplified

12And [Ishmael] shall be as a [a]wild ass among men; his hand
will be against every man and every man's hand against him; and
he shall live to the east *and* on the borders of all his kinsmen.
13So she called the name of the Lord Who spoke to her, You are
a God of seeing; for she said, Have I [not] even here [in the
wilderness] looked after Him Who sees me [and lived]? *Or* have
I here also seen [the future purposes or designs] of Him Who sees
me?
14Therefore the well was called Beer-lahai-roi (that is, A well to
the Living One Who sees me); it is [b]between Kadesh and Bered.
15And Hagar bore Abram a son; and Abram called the name of
his son whom Hagar bore, [c]Ishmael.
16Abram was 86 years old when Hagar bore Ishmael.

**17** WHEN ABRAM was 99 years old, the Lord appeared to
him, and said, I am the Almighty God; walk *and* live
habitually before Me, and be perfect—blameless, whole-hearted,
complete.
2And I will make My covenant (solemn pledge) between Me
and you, and will multiply you exceedingly.
3Then Abram fell on his face; and God said to him,
4As for Me, behold, My covenant (solemn pledge) is with you,
and you shall be the father of many nations.
5Nor shall your name any longer be Abram (high father), but
your name shall be Abraham (father of a multitude); for I have
made you the father of many nations.
6And I will make you exceedingly fruitful, and I will make
nations of you, and [d]kings shall come from you.
7And I will establish My covenant between Me and you and
your descendants after you throughout their generations for an
everlasting, solemn pledge to be a God to you and to your posterity
after you. [Gal. 3:16.]
8And I will give to you and to your posterity after you the land
in which you are a stranger (going from place to place), all the land
of Canaan for an everlasting possession; and I will be their God.
[Acts 7:5.]
9And God said to Abraham, As for you, you shall therefore
keep My covenant, you and your descendants after you throughout their generations.
10This is My covenant, which you shall keep, between Me and
you and your posterity after you: Every male among you shall be
circumcised.
11And you shall circumcise the flesh of your foreskin; and it
shall be a token *or* sign of the covenant, (the promise or pledge),
between Me and you.
12He who is eight days old among you shall be circumcised,
every male throughout your generations, whether born in [your]
house or bought with [your] money from any foreigner not of your
offspring.
13He that is born in your house, and he that is bought with your
money, must be circumcised; and My covenant shall be in your
flesh for an everlasting covenant.
14And the male who is not circumcised, that soul shall be cut
off from his people; he has broken My covenant.
15And God said to Abraham, As for Sarai your wife, you shall
not call her name Sarai, but Sarah (princess) her name shall be.
16And I will bless her, and give you a son also of her; yes, I will
bless her, and she shall be a mother of nations; kings of peoples
shall come from her.

**AMP** [a] "Nothing can be more descriptive of the wandering, lawless, freebooting life of the Arabs than this. From the beginning to the present they have kept their independence, and God preserves them as a lasting monument of His providential care and an incontestable argument of the truth of divine revelation. Had the books of Moses no other proof of their divine origin, the account of Ishmael and the prophecy concerning his descendants during a period of nearly 4,000 years, would be sufficient. To attempt to refute it would be most ridiculous presumption and folly" (*Clarke's Commentary*). [b] This, "it is between Kadesh and Bered," is further proof of the antiquity of the original names, since the place had to be identified to the reader in the time of Moses. [c] Ishmael was the first person whom God named before his birth (vs. 11). Others were: Isaac, Gen. 17:19; Josiah, I Kings 13:2; Solomon, I Chron. 22:9; Jesus, Matt. 1:21; and John the Baptist, Luke 1:13. [d] This prophecy and promise have been literally fulfilled countless times; for example, by all of the kings of Israel and Judah.

## New American Standard

12 "And he will be a wild donkey of a man,
His hand *will be* against everyone,
And everyone's hand *will be* against him;
And he will live to the east of all his brothers."
13Then she called the name of the LORD who spoke to her,
"Thou art a God who sees"; for she said, "Have I even remained
alive here after seeing Him?"
14Therefore the well was called [e]Beer-lahai-roi; behold, it is
between Kadesh and Bered.
15¶ So Hagar bore Abram a son; and Abram called the name of
his son, whom Hagar bore, Ishmael.
16And Abram was eighty-six years old when Hagar bore Ishmael to him.

*Abraham and the Covenant of Circumcision*

**17** NOW WHEN Abram was ninety-nine years old, the LORD
appeared to Abram and said to him,
"I am God Almighty;
Walk before Me, and be blameless.
2 "And I will establish My covenant between Me and you,
And I will multiply you exceedingly."
3And Abram fell on his face, and God talked with him, saying,
4 "As for Me, behold, My covenant is with you,
And you shall be the father of a multitude of nations.
5 "No longer shall your name be called [f]Abram,
But your name shall be [g]Abraham;
For I will make you the father of a multitude of nations.
6"And I will make you exceedingly fruitful, and I will make
nations of you, and kings shall come forth from you.
7"And I will establish My covenant between Me and you and
your descendants after you throughout their generations for an
everlasting covenant, to be God to you and to your descendants
after you.
8"And I will give to you and to your descendants after you, the
land of your sojournings, all the land of Canaan, for an everlasting
possession; and I will be their God."
9¶ God said further to Abraham, "Now as for you, you shall
keep My covenant, you and your descendants after you throughout their generations.
10"This is My covenant, which you shall keep, between Me and
you and your descendants after you: every male among you shall
be circumcised.
11"And you shall be circumcised in the flesh of your foreskin;
and it shall be the sign of the covenant between Me and you.
12"And every male among you who is eight days old shall be
circumcised throughout your generations, a *servant* who is born in
the house or who is bought with money from any foreigner, who
is not of your descendants.
13"A *servant* who is born in your house or who is bought with
your money shall surely be circumcised; thus shall My covenant
be in your flesh for an everlasting covenant.
14"But an uncircumcised male who is not circumcised in the
flesh of his foreskin, that person shall be cut off from his people;
he has broken My covenant."
15¶ Then God said to Abraham, "As for Sarai your wife, you
shall not call her name Sarai, but [h]Sarah *shall be* her name.
16"And I will bless her, and indeed I will give you a son by her.
Then I will bless her, and she shall be *a mother of* nations; kings of
peoples shall come from her."

**NAS** [e] I.e., the well of the living one who sees me [f] I.e., exalted father [g] I.e., father of a multitude [h] I.e., princess

## New International

12He will be a wild donkey of a man;
his hand will be against everyone
and everyone's hand against him,
and he will live in hostility
toward[i] all his brothers."
13She gave this name to the LORD who spoke to her: "You are
the God who sees me," for she said, "I have now seen[j] the One
who sees me." 14That is why the well was called Beer Lahai Roi[k];
it is still there, between Kadesh and Bered.
15So Hagar bore Abram a son, and Abram gave the name Ishmael to the son she had borne. 16Abram was eighty-six years old
when Hagar bore him Ishmael.

*The Covenant of Circumcision*

**17** WHEN ABRAM was ninety-nine years old, the LORD appeared to him and said, "I am God Almighty[l]; walk before me and be blameless. 2I will confirm my covenant between me
and you and will greatly increase your numbers."
3Abram fell facedown, and God said to him, 4"As for me, this
is my covenant with you: You will be the father of many nations.
5No longer will you be called Abram[m]; your name will be Abraham,[n] for I have made you a father of many nations. 6I will make
you very fruitful; I will make nations of you, and kings will come
from you. 7I will establish my covenant as an everlasting covenant
between me and you and your descendants after you for the
generations to come, to be your God and the God of your descendants after you. 8The whole land of Canaan, where you are now an
alien, I will give as an everlasting possession to you and your
descendants after you; and I will be their God."
9Then God said to Abraham, "As for you, you must keep my
covenant, you and your descendants after you for the generations
to come. 10This is my covenant with you and your descendants
after you, the covenant you are to keep: Every male among you
shall be circumcised. 11You are to undergo circumcision, and it will
be the sign of the covenant between me and you. 12For the generations to come every male among you who is eight days old must
be circumcised, including those born in your household or bought
with money from a foreigner—those who are not your offspring.
13Whether born in your household or bought with your money,
they must be circumcised. My covenant in your flesh is to be an
everlasting covenant. 14Any uncircumcised male, who has not
been circumcised in the flesh, will be cut off from his people; he
has broken my covenant."
15God also said to Abraham, "As for Sarai your wife, you are
no longer to call her Sarai; her name will be Sarah. 16I will bless
her and will surely give you a son by her. I will bless her so that
she will be the mother of nations; kings of peoples will come from
her."

**NIV** [i] 12 Or *live to the east / of* [j] 13 Or *seen the back of* [k] 14 *Beer Lahai Roi* means *well of the Living One who sees me.* [l] 1 Hebrew *El-Shaddai* [m] 5 *Abram* means *exalted father.* [n] 5 *Abraham* means *father of many.*

## King James

17Then Abraham fell upon his face, and laughed, and said in his
heart, Shall *a child* be born unto him that is an hundred years old?
and shall Sarah, that is ninety years old, bear?
18And Abraham said unto God, O that Ishmael might live before thee!
19And God said, Sarah thy wife shall bear thee a son indeed;
and thou shalt call his name Isaac: and I will establish my covenant
with him for an everlasting covenant, *and* with his seed after him.
20And as for Ishmael, I have heard thee: Behold, I have blessed
him, and will make him fruitful, and will multiply him exceedingly; twelve princes shall he beget, and I will make him a great
nation.
21But my covenant will I establish with Isaac, which Sarah shall
bear unto thee at this set time in the next year.
22And he left off talking with him, and God went up from
Abraham.
23¶ And Abraham took Ishmael his son, and all that were born
in his house, and all that were bought with his money, every male
among the men of Abraham's house; and circumcised the flesh of
their foreskin in the selfsame day, as God had said unto him.
24And Abraham *was* ninety years old and nine, when he was
circumcised in the flesh of his foreskin.
25And Ishmael his son *was* thirteen years old, when he was
circumcised in the flesh of his foreskin.
26In the selfsame day was Abraham circumcised, and Ishmael
his son.
27And all the men of his house, born in the house, and bought
with money of the stranger, were circumcised with him.

**18** AND THE LORD appeared unto him in the plains of
Mamre: and he sat in the tent door in the heat of the day;
2And he lift up his eyes and looked, and, lo, three men stood
by him: and when he saw *them*, he ran to meet them from the tent
door, and bowed himself toward the ground,
3And said, My Lord, if now I have found favour in thy sight,
pass not away, I pray thee, from thy servant:
4Let a little water, I pray you, be fetched, and wash your feet,
and rest yourselves under the tree:
5And I will fetch a morsel of bread, and comfort ye your hearts;
after that ye shall pass on: for therefore are ye come to your
servant. And they said, So do, as thou hast said.
6And Abraham hastened into the tent unto Sarah, and said,
Make ready quickly three measures of fine meal, knead *it*, and
make cakes upon the hearth.
7And Abraham ran unto the herd, and fetched a calf tender and
good, and gave *it* unto a young man; and he hasted to dress it.
8And he took butter, and milk, and the calf which he had
dressed, and set *it* before them; and he stood by them under the
tree, and they did eat.
9¶ And they said unto him, Where *is* Sarah thy wife? And he
said, Behold, in the tent.
10And he said, I will certainly return unto thee according to the
time of life; and, lo, Sarah thy wife shall have a son. And Sarah
heard *it* in the tent door, which *was* behind him.
11Now Abraham and Sarah *were* old *and* well stricken in age; *and*
it ceased to be with Sarah after the manner of women.
12Therefore Sarah laughed within herself, saying, After I am
waxed old shall I have pleasure, my lord being old also?
13And the LORD said unto Abraham, Wherefore did Sarah
laugh, saying, Shall I of a surety bear a child, which am old?

## Amplified

17Then Abraham fell on his face and laughed, and said in his
heart, Shall a child be born to a man who is 100 years old? And shall
Sarah, who is 90 years old, bear a son?
18And [he] said to God, O that Ishmael might live before You!
19But God said, Sarah your wife shall bear you a son indeed;
and you shall call his name Isaac (laughter), and I will establish My
covenant *or* solemn pledge with him for an everlasting covenant,
and with his posterity after him.
20And as for Ishmael, I have heard *and* heeded you; behold, I
will bless him and will make him fruitful and will multiply him
exceedingly; he shall be the father of twelve princes, and I will
make him a great nation. [Fulfilled, 25:12-18.]
21But My covenant, My promise and pledge, I will establish
with Isaac, whom Sarah shall bear to you at this season next year.
22And God stopped talking with him, and went up from Abraham.
23And Abraham took Ishmael his son and all that were born in
his house and all that were bought with his money, every male
among [those] of Abraham's house, and circumcised [them] the
very same day, as God had said to him.
24And Abraham was 99 years old when he was circumcised.
25And Ishmael his son was thirteen years old when he was
circumcised.
26On the very same day Abraham was circumcised and Ishmael
his son,
27And all the men of his house, both those born in the house
and those bought with money from a foreigner, were circumcised
along with him.

**18** NOW THE Lord appeared to Abraham by the oaks *or*
terebinths of Mamre; as he sat at the door of his tent in the
heat of the day,
2He lifted up his eyes and looked, and lo, three men stood at
a little distance from him. He ran from the tent door to meet them,
and bowed himself to the ground,
3And said, My lord, if now I have found favor in your sight, do
not pass by your servant, I beg of you.
4Let a little water be brought, and wash your feet, and recline
*and* rest yourselves under the tree.
5And I will bring a morsel (mouthful) of bread, to refresh *and*
sustain your hearts before you go on further; for that is why you
have come to your servant. And they replied, Do as you have said.
6So Abraham hastened into the tent to Sarah, and said, Quickly
get ready three measures of fine meal, knead it, and bake cakes.
7And Abraham ran to the herd, and brought a calf tender and
good, and gave it to the young man [to butcher]; then [Abraham]
hastened to prepare it.
8And he took curds, and milk, and the calf which he had made
ready, and set it before [the men]; and he stood by them under the
tree while they ate.
9And they said to him, Where is Sarah your wife? And he said,
[She is here] in the tent.
10[The Lord] said, I will surely return to you when the season
comes round, and lo, Sarah your wife shall have a son. And Sarah
was listening *and* heard it at the tent door which was behind Him.
[Rom. 9:9-12.]
11Now Abraham and Sarah were old, well advanced in years;
it had ceased to be with Sarah as with [young] women.
12Therefore Sarah laughed to herself, saying, After I have
become aged shall I have pleasure *and* delight, my lord [husband],
being old also? [I Peter 3:6.]
13And [a]the Lord asked Abraham, Why did Sarah laugh, saying,
Shall I really bear a child, when I am so old?

**AMP** [a] One of those three guests was the Lord, and as God the Father was never seen in bodily form (John 1:18), only the Angel of the covenant, Christ Himself, can be meant here.

## New American Standard

17Then Abraham fell on his face and laughed, and said in his heart, "Will a child be born to a man one hundred years old? And will Sarah, who is ninety years old, bear *a child?*"

18And Abraham said to God, "Oh that Ishmael might live before Thee!"

19But God said, "No, but Sarah your wife shall bear you a son, and you shall call his name [b]Isaac; and I will establish My covenant with him for an everlasting covenant for his descendants after him.

20"And as for Ishmael, I have heard you; behold, I will bless him, and will make him fruitful, and will multiply him exceedingly. He shall become the father of twelve princes, and I will make him a great nation.

21"But My covenant I will establish with Isaac, whom Sarah will bear to you at this season next year."

22¶ And when He finished talking with him, God went up from Abraham.

23Then Abraham took Ishmael his son, and all *the servants* who were born in his house and all who were bought with his money, every male among the men of Abraham's household, and circumcised the flesh of their foreskin in the very same day, as God had said to him.

24Now Abraham was ninety-nine years old when he was circumcised in the flesh of his foreskin.

25And Ishmael his son was thirteen years old when he was circumcised in the flesh of his foreskin.

26In the very same day Abraham was circumcised, and Ishmael his son.

27And all the men of his household, who were born in the house or bought with money from a foreigner, were circumcised with him.

### *Birth of Isaac Promised*

**18** NOW THE LORD appeared to him by the oaks of Mamre, while he was sitting at the tent door in the heat of the day.

2And when he lifted up his eyes and looked, behold, three men were standing opposite him; and when he saw *them,* he ran from the tent door to meet them, and bowed himself to the earth,

3and said, "My lord, if now I have found favor in your sight, please do not pass your servant by.

4"Please let a little water be brought and wash your feet, and rest yourselves under the tree;

5and I will bring a piece of bread, that you may refresh yourselves; after that you may go on, since you have visited your servant." And they said, "So do, as you have said."

6So Abraham hurried into the tent to Sarah, and said, "Quickly, prepare three measures of fine flour, knead *it,* and make bread cakes."

7Abraham also ran to the herd, and took a tender and choice calf, and gave *it* to the servant; and he hurried to prepare it.

8And he took curds and milk and the calf which he had prepared, and placed *it* before them; and he was standing by them under the tree as they ate.

9¶ Then they said to him, "Where is Sarah your wife?" And he said, "Behold, in the tent."

10And he said, "I will surely return to you at this time next year; and behold, Sarah your wife shall have a son." And Sarah was listening at the tent door, which was behind him.

11Now Abraham and Sarah were old, advanced in age; Sarah was past childbearing.

12And Sarah laughed to herself, saying, "After I have become old, shall I have pleasure, my lord being old also?"

13And the LORD said to Abraham, "Why did Sarah laugh, saying, 'Shall I indeed bear *a child,* when I am *so* old?'

NAS [b] I.e., he laughs

## New International

17Abraham fell facedown; he laughed and said to himself, "Will
a son be born to a man a hundred years old? Will Sarah bear a child
at the age of ninety?" 18And Abraham said to God, "If only Ishmael might live under your blessing!"
19Then God said, "Yes, but your wife Sarah will bear you a son,
and you will call him Isaac.[c] I will establish my covenant with him
as an everlasting covenant for his descendants after him. 20And as
for Ishmael, I have heard you: I will surely bless him; I will make
him fruitful and will greatly increase his numbers. He will be the
father of twelve rulers, and I will make him into a great nation.
21But my covenant I will establish with Isaac, whom Sarah will bear
to you by this time next year." 22When he had finished speaking
with Abraham, God went up from him.
23On that very day Abraham took his son Ishmael and all those
born in his household or bought with his money, every male in his
household, and circumcised them, as God told him. 24Abraham
was ninety-nine years old when he was circumcised, 25and his son
Ishmael was thirteen; 26Abraham and his son Ishmael were both
circumcised on that same day. 27And every male in Abraham's
household, including those born in his household or bought from
a foreigner, was circumcised with him.

### *The Three Visitors*

**18** THE LORD appeared to Abraham near the great trees of
Mamre while he was sitting at the entrance to his tent in
the heat of the day. 2Abraham looked up and saw three men
standing nearby. When he saw them, he hurried from the entrance
of his tent to meet them and bowed low to the ground.
3He said, "If I have found favor in your eyes, my lord,[d] do not
pass your servant by. 4Let a little water be brought, and then you
may all wash your feet and rest under this tree. 5Let me get you
something to eat, so you can be refreshed and then go on your
way—now that you have come to your servant."
"Very well," they answered, "do as you say."
6So Abraham hurried into the tent to Sarah. "Quick," he said,
"get three seahs[e] of fine flour and knead it and bake some bread."
7Then he ran to the herd and selected a choice, tender calf and
gave it to a servant, who hurried to prepare it. 8He then brought
some curds and milk and the calf that had been prepared, and set
these before them. While they ate, he stood near them under a
tree.
9"Where is your wife Sarah?" they asked him.
"There, in the tent," he said.
10Then the LORD[f] said, "I will surely return to you about this
time next year, and Sarah your wife will have a son."
Now Sarah was listening at the entrance to the tent, which was
behind him. 11Abraham and Sarah were already old and well
advanced in years, and Sarah was past the age of childbearing.
12So Sarah laughed to herself as she thought, "After I am worn out
and my master[g] is old, will I now have this pleasure?"
13Then the LORD said to Abraham, "Why did Sarah laugh and
say, 'Will I really have a child, now that I am old?' 14Is anything

NIV [c] 19 *Isaac* means *he laughs.* [d] 3 Or *O Lord* [e] 6 That is, probably about 20 quarts (about 22 liters) [f] 10 Hebrew *Then he* [g] 12 Or *husband*

## King James

14 Is any thing too hard for the LORD? At the time appointed I
will return unto thee, according to the time of life, and Sarah shall
have a son.
15 Then Sarah denied, saying, I laughed not; for she was afraid.
And he said, Nay; but thou didst laugh.
16¶ And the men rose up from thence, and looked toward
Sodom: and Abraham went with them to bring them on the way.
17 And the LORD said, Shall I hide from Abraham that thing
which I do;
18 Seeing that Abraham shall surely become a great and mighty
nation, and all the nations of the earth shall be blessed in him?
19 For I know him, that he will command his children and his
household after him, and they shall keep the way of the LORD, to
do justice and judgment; that the LORD may bring upon Abraham
that which he hath spoken of him.
20 And the LORD said, Because the cry of Sodom and Gomorrah
is great, and because their sin is very grievous;
21 I will go down now, and see whether they have done altogether according to the cry of it, which is come unto me; and if not,
I will know.
22 And the men turned their faces from thence, and went toward
Sodom: but Abraham stood yet before the LORD.
23¶ And Abraham drew near, and said, Wilt thou also destroy
the righteous with the wicked?
24 Peradventure there be fifty righteous within the city: wilt thou
also destroy and not spare the place for the fifty righteous that *are*
therein?
25 That be far from thee to do after this manner, to slay the
righteous with the wicked: and that the righteous should be as the
wicked, that be far from thee: Shall not the Judge of all the earth
do right?
26 And the LORD said, If I find in Sodom fifty righteous within
the city, then I will spare all the place for their sakes.
27 And Abraham answered and said, Behold now, I have taken
upon me to speak unto the Lord, which *am but* dust and ashes:
28 Peradventure there shall lack five of the fifty righteous: wilt
thou destroy all the city for *lack of* five? And he said, If I find there
forty and five, I will not destroy *it*.
29 And he spake unto him yet again, and said, Peradventure
there shall be forty found there. And he said, I will not do *it* for
forty's sake.
30 And he said *unto him*, Oh let not the Lord be angry, and I will
speak: Peradventure there shall thirty be found there. And he said,
I will not do *it*, if I find thirty there.
31 And he said, Behold now, I have taken upon me to speak unto
the Lord: Peradventure there shall be twenty found there. And he
said, I will not destroy *it* for twenty's sake.
32 And he said, Oh let not the Lord be angry, and I will speak
yet but this once: Peradventure ten shall be found there. And he
said, I will not destroy *it* for ten's sake.
33 And the LORD went his way, as soon as he had left communing with Abraham: and Abraham returned unto his place.

**19** AND THERE came two angels to Sodom at even; and Lot
sat in the gate of Sodom: and Lot seeing *them* rose up to
meet them; and he bowed himself with his face toward the ground;

## Amplified

14 Is anything too hard *or* too wonderful [a]for the Lord? At the
appointed time, when the season [for her delivery] comes around,
I will return to you and Sarah shall have borne a son. [Matt. 19:26.]
15 Then Sarah denied, saying, I did not laugh; for she was afraid.
And He said, No, but you did laugh.
16 The men rose up from there and faced toward Sodom; and
Abraham went with them to bring them on the way.
17 And the Lord said, Shall I hide from Abraham [My friend and
servant] what I am going to do, [Gal. 3:8.]
18 Since Abraham shall surely become a great and mighty nation, and all the nations of the earth shall be blessed through him,
*and* shall bless themselves by him?
19 For I have known (chosen, acknowledged) him [as My own]
so that he may teach *and* command his children and the sons of
his house after him to keep the way of the Lord and to do what
is just and righteous, so the Lord may bring Abraham what He has
promised him.
20 And the Lord said, Because the shriek [of the sins] of Sodom
and Gomorrah is great, and their sin is exceedingly grievous;
21 I will go down now, and see whether they have done altogether [as vilely and wickedly] as is the cry of it, which is come to
Me; and if not, I will know.
22 Now the [two] men turned from there, and went toward
Sodom; but Abraham still stood before the Lord.
23 And Abraham came close, and said, Will You destroy the
righteous [those upright and in right standing with God] together
with the wicked?
24 Suppose there are in the city fifty righteous; will You destroy
the place and not spare it for (the sake of) the fifty righteous in it?
25 Far be it from You to do such a thing, to slay the righteous
with the wicked, so that the righteous fare as do the wicked! Be
that far from You! Shall not the Judge of all the earth execute
judgment *and* do righteously?
26 And the Lord said, If I find in the city of Sodom fifty righteous
[in right standing with God], I will spare the whole place for their
sakes.
27 Abraham answered, Behold now, I who am but dust and
ashes have taken upon myself to speak to the Lord.
28 If five of the fifty righteous should be lacking; will You destroy
the whole city for lack of five? He said, If I find forty-five, I will
not destroy it.
29 And [Abraham] spoke to Him yet again, and said, Suppose
[only] forty shall be found there. And He said, I will not do it for
forty's sake.
30 Then [Abraham] said to Him, Oh, let not the Lord be angry,
and I will speak [again]. Suppose [only] thirty shall be found there.
And He answered, I will not do it if I find thirty there.
31 And [Abraham] said, Behold now, I have taken upon myself
to speak [again] to the Lord. Suppose [only] twenty shall be found
there. And [the Lord] replied, I will not destroy it for twenty's
sake.
32 And he said, Oh, let not the Lord be angry, and I will speak
again only this once. Suppose ten [righteous people] shall be
found there. And [the Lord] said, I will not destroy it for ten's sake.
33 And the Lord went His way when He finished speaking with
Abraham; and Abraham returned to his place.

**19** IT WAS evening when the two angels came to Sodom. Lot
was sitting at Sodom's [city] gate. Seeing them, Lot rose
up to meet them and bowed to the ground.

**AMP** [a] The word "Lord" as applied to God is obviously the most important word in the Bible, for it occurs there oftener than any other important word—by actual count more than 5,000 times. *Nothing* is "too hard *or* too wonderful" for Him when He is truly made Lord.

## New American Standard

14"Is anything too difficult for the LORD? At the appointed time
I will return to you, at this time next year, and Sarah shall have
a son."
15Sarah denied *it* however, saying, "I did not laugh"; for she
was afraid. And He said, "No, but you did laugh."
16¶ Then the men rose up from there, and looked down toward
Sodom; and Abraham was walking with them to send them off.
17And the LORD said, "Shall I hide from Abraham what I am
about to do,
18since Abraham will surely become a great and mighty nation,
and in him all the nations of the earth will be blessed?
19"For I have chosen him, in order that he may command his
children and his household after him to keep the way of the LORD
by doing righteousness and justice; in order that the LORD may
bring upon Abraham what He has spoken about him."
20And the LORD said, "The outcry of Sodom and Gomorrah is
indeed great, and their sin is exceedingly grave.
21"I will go down now, and see if they have done entirely
according to its outcry, which has come to Me; and if not, I will
know."
22¶ Then the men turned away from there and went toward
Sodom, while Abraham was still standing before the LORD.
23And Abraham came near and said, "Wilt Thou indeed sweep
away the righteous with the wicked?
24"Suppose there are fifty righteous within the city; wilt Thou
indeed sweep *it* away and not spare the place for the sake of the
fifty righteous who are in it?
25"Far be it from Thee to do such a thing, to slay the righteous
with the wicked, so that the righteous and the wicked are *treated*
alike. Far be it from Thee! Shall not the Judge of all the earth deal
justly?"
26So the LORD said, "If I find in Sodom fifty righteous within
the city, then I will spare the whole place on their account."
27And Abraham answered and said, "Now behold, I have ventured to speak to the Lord, although I am *but* dust and ashes.
28"Suppose the fifty righteous are lacking five, wilt Thou destroy the whole city because of five?" And He said, "I will not
destroy *it* if I find forty-five there."
29And he spoke to Him yet again and said, "Suppose forty are
found there?" And He said, "I will not do *it* on account of the
forty."
30Then he said, "Oh may the Lord not be angry, and I shall
speak; suppose thirty are found there?" And He said, "I will not
do *it* if I find thirty there."
31And he said, "Now behold, I have ventured to speak to the
Lord; suppose twenty are found there?" And He said, "I will not
destroy *it* on account of the twenty."
32Then he said, "Oh may the Lord not be angry, and I shall
speak only this once; suppose ten are found there?" And He said,
"I will not destroy *it* on account of the ten."
33And as soon as He had finished speaking to Abraham the
LORD departed; and Abraham returned to his place.

*The Doom of Sodom*

19 NOW THE two angels came to Sodom in the evening as
Lot was sitting in the gate of Sodom. When Lot saw *them*,
he rose to meet them and bowed down *with his* face to the ground.

## New International

too hard for the LORD? I will return to you at the appointed time
next year and Sarah will have a son."
15Sarah was afraid, so she lied and said, "I did not laugh."
But he said, "Yes, you did laugh."

*Abraham Pleads for Sodom*

16When the men got up to leave, they looked down toward
Sodom, and Abraham walked along with them to see them on their
way. 17Then the LORD said, "Shall I hide from Abraham what I am
about to do? 18Abraham will surely become a great and powerful
nation, and all nations on earth will be blessed through him. 19For
I have chosen him, so that he will direct his children and his
household after him to keep the way of the LORD by doing what
is right and just, so that the LORD will bring about for Abraham
what he has promised him."
20Then the LORD said, "The outcry against Sodom and Gomorrah is so great and their sin so grievous 21that I will go down and
see if what they have done is as bad as the outcry that has reached
me. If not, I will know."
22The men turned away and went toward Sodom, but Abraham
remained standing before the LORD.[b] 23Then Abraham approached him and said: "Will you sweep away the righteous with
the wicked? 24What if there are fifty righteous people in the city?
Will you really sweep it away and not spare[c] the place for the sake
of the fifty righteous people in it? 25Far be it from you to do such
a thing—to kill the righteous with the wicked, treating the righteous and the wicked alike. Far be it from you! Will not the Judge[d]
of all the earth do right?"
26The LORD said, "If I find fifty righteous people in the city of
Sodom, I will spare the whole place for their sake."
27Then Abraham spoke up again: "Now that I have been so bold
as to speak to the Lord, though I am nothing but dust and ashes,
28what if the number of the righteous is five less than fifty? Will
you destroy the whole city because of five people?"
"If I find forty-five there," he said, "I will not destroy it."
29Once again he spoke to him, "What if only forty are found
there?"
He said, "For the sake of forty, I will not do it."
30Then he said, "May the Lord not be angry, but let me speak.
What if only thirty can be found there?"
He answered, "I will not do it if I find thirty there."
31Abraham said, "Now that I have been so bold as to speak to
the Lord, what if only twenty can be found there?"
He said, "For the sake of twenty, I will not destroy it."
32Then he said, "May the Lord not be angry, but let me speak
just once more. What if only ten can be found there?"
He answered, "For the sake of ten, I will not destroy it."
33When the LORD had finished speaking with Abraham, he left,
and Abraham returned home.

*Sodom and Gomorrah Destroyed*

19 THE TWO angels arrived at Sodom in the evening, and
Lot was sitting in the gateway of the city. When he saw
them, he got up to meet them and bowed down with his face to
the ground. 2"My lords," he said, "please turn aside to your

NIV [b] 22 Masoretic Text; an ancient Hebrew scribal tradition *but the LORD remained standing before Abraham* [c] 24 Or *forgive;* also in verse 26 [d] 25 Or *Ruler*

## King James

2 And he said, Behold now, my lords, turn in, I pray you, into your servant's house, and tarry all night, and wash your feet, and ye shall rise up early, and go on your ways. And they said, Nay; but we will abide in the street all night.

3 And he pressed upon them greatly; and they turned in unto him, and entered into his house; and he made them a feast, and did bake unleavened bread, and they did eat.

4 ¶ But before they lay down, the men of the city, *even* the men of Sodom, compassed the house round, both old and young, all the people from every quarter:

5 And they called unto Lot, and said unto him, Where *are* the men which came in to thee this night? bring them out unto us, that we may know them.

6 And Lot went out at the door unto them, and shut the door after him,

7 And said, I pray you, brethren, do not so wickedly.

8 Behold now, I have two daughters which have not known man; let me, I pray you, bring them out unto you, and do ye to them as *is* good in your eyes: only unto these men do nothing; for therefore came they under the shadow of my roof.

9 And they said, Stand back. And they said *again,* This one *fellow* came in to sojourn, and he will needs be a judge: now will we deal worse with thee, than with them. And they pressed sore upon the man, *even* Lot, and came near to break the door.

10 But the men put forth their hand, and pulled Lot into the house to them, and shut to the door.

11 And they smote the men that *were* at the door of the house with blindness, both small and great: so that they wearied themselves to find the door.

12 ¶ And the men said unto Lot, Hast thou here any besides? son-in-law, and thy sons, and thy daughters, and whatsoever thou hast in the city, bring *them* out of this place:

13 For we will destroy this place, because the cry of them is waxen great before the face of the LORD; and the LORD hath sent us to destroy it.

14 And Lot went out, and spake unto his sons in law, which married his daughters, and said, Up, get you out of this place; for the LORD will destroy this city. But he seemed as one that mocked unto his sons in law.

15 ¶ And when the morning arose, then the angels hastened Lot, saying, Arise, take thy wife, and thy two daughters, which are here; lest thou be consumed in the iniquity of the city.

16 And while he lingered, the men laid hold upon his hand, and upon the hand of his wife, and upon the hand of his two daughters; the LORD being merciful unto him: and they brought him forth, and set him without the city.

17 ¶ And it came to pass, when they had brought them forth abroad, that he said, Escape for thy life; look not behind thee, neither stay thou in all the plain; escape to the mountain, lest thou be consumed.

18 And Lot said unto them, Oh, not so, my Lord:

19 Behold now, thy servant hath found grace in thy sight, and thou hast magnified thy mercy, which thou hast shown unto me in saving my life; and I cannot escape to the mountain, lest some evil take me, and I die:

20 Behold now, this city *is* near to flee unto, and it *is* a little one: Oh, let me escape thither, ( *is* it not a little one?) and my soul shall live.

21 And he said unto him, See, I have accepted thee concerning this thing also, that I will not overthrow this city, for the which thou hast spoken.

22 Haste thee, escape thither; for I cannot do any thing till thou be come thither. Therefore the name of the city was called Zoar.

23 ¶ The sun was risen upon the earth when Lot entered into Zoar.

24 Then the LORD rained upon Sodom and upon Gomorrah brimstone and fire from the LORD out of heaven;

## Amplified

2 And he said, My lords, turn aside, I beg of you, into your servant's house and spend the night, and bathe your feet. Then you can arise early and go on your way. But they said, No; we will spend the night in the square.

3 [Lot] entreated *and* urged them greatly until they yielded, and [with him] entered his house. And he made them a dinner (with drinking), and had unleavened bread which he baked; and they ate.

4 But before they lay down, the men of the city of Sodom, both young and old, all the men from every quarter, surrounded the house.

5 And they called to Lot, and said, Where are the men who came to you tonight? Bring them out to us, that we may know [be intimate with] them.

6 And Lot went out of the door to the men, and shut the door after him,

7 And said, I beg of you, my brothers, do not behave so wickedly.

8 Look now, I have two daughters who are virgins; let me, I beg of you, bring them out to you, and you do as you please with them; but only do nothing to these men, for they have come under the [protection] of my roof.

9 But they said, Stand back! And they said, This fellow came in to live here temporarily and now he presumes to be [our] judge! Now we will deal worse with you than with them. So they rushed at *and* pressed violently against Lot, and came close to breaking down the door.

10 But the men [the angels] reached out and pulled Lot into the house to them, and shut the door after him.

11 And they struck the men that were at the door of the house with [dazzled] blindness, from the youths to the old men, so that they wearied themselves [groping] to find the door.

12 And the [two] men asked Lot, Have you any others here? Sons-in-law, or your sons, or daughters? Whomever you have in the city, bring them out of this place.

13 For we will spoil *and* destroy [Sodom], for the outcry *and* shriek against its people has grown great before the Lord; and He has sent us to destroy it.

14 And Lot went out and spoke to his sons-in-law who were to marry his daughters, and said, Up, get out of this place; for the Lord will spoil *and* destroy this city! But he seemed to his sons-in-law as if he were [only] joking.

15 When morning came, the angels urged Lot to hurry, saying, Arise, take your wife and two daughters who are here [and be off]; lest you [too] be consumed *and* swept away in the iniquity *and* punishment of the city.

16 But while he lingered, the men seized him and his wife and his two daughters by the hand, for the Lord was merciful to him; and they brought him forth and set him outside the city and left him there.

17 And when they had brought them forth, they said, Escape for your life! Do not look behind you, or stop anywhere in [a]the whole valley; escape to the mountains [of Moab], lest you be consumed.

18 And Lot said to them, Oh, not that, my lords!

19 Behold now, your servant has found favor in your sight, and you have magnified your kindness and mercy to me in saving my life; but I cannot escape to the mountains lest the evil overtake me, and I die.

20 See now yonder city; it is near enough to flee to, and it is a little one. Oh, let me escape to it! Is it not a little one? And my life will be saved!

21 And [the angel] said to him, See, I have yielded to your entreaty concerning this thing also, that I will not destroy this city for which you have spoken.

22 Make haste and take refuge there, for I cannot do anything until you have arrived there. Therefore the name of the city was called Zoar [little].

23 The sun had risen above the earth when Lot entered Zoar.

24 Then the Lord rained on Sodom and on Gomorrah brimstone and fire from the Lord out of the heavens.

**AMP** [a] The valley which Lot had once so much coveted (Gen. 13:10, 11).

## New American Standard

2And he said, "Now behold, my lords, please turn aside into
your servant's house, and spend the night, and wash your feet;
then you may rise early and go on your way." They said however,
"No, but we shall spend the night in the square."
3Yet he urged them strongly, so they turned aside to him and
entered his house; and he prepared a feast for them, and baked
unleavened bread, and they ate.
4Before they lay down, the men of the city, the men of Sodom,
surrounded the house, both young and old, all the people from
every quarter;
5and they called to Lot and said to him, "Where are the men
who came to you tonight? Bring them out to us that we may have
relations with them."
6But Lot went out to them at the doorway, and shut the door
behind him,
7and said, "Please, my brothers, do not act wickedly.
8"Now behold, I have two daughters who have not had relations with man; please let me bring them out to you, and do to
them whatever you like; only do nothing to these men, inasmuch
as they have come under the shelter of my roof."
9But they said, "Stand aside." Furthermore, they said, "This
one came in as an alien, and already he is acting like a judge; now
we will treat you worse than them." So they pressed hard against
Lot and came near to break the door.
10But the men reached out their hands and brought Lot into the
house with them, and shut the door.
11And they struck the men who were at the doorway of the
house with blindness, both small and great, so that they wearied
*themselves trying* to find the doorway.
**12**¶ Then the men said to Lot, "Whom else have you here? A
son-in-law, and your sons, and your daughters, and whomever
you have in the city, bring *them* out of the place;
13for we are about to destroy this place, because their outcry has
become so great before the LORD that the LORD has sent us to
destroy it."
14And Lot went out and spoke to his sons-in-law, who were to
marry his daughters, and said, "Up, get out of this place, for the
LORD will destroy the city." But he appeared to his sons-in-law to
be jesting.
15And when morning dawned, the angels urged Lot, saying,
"Up, take your wife and your two daughters, who are here, lest
you be swept away in the punishment of the city."
16But he hesitated. So the men seized his hand and the hand
of his wife and the hands of his two daughters, for the compassion
of the LORD *was* upon him; and they brought him out, and put him
outside the city.
17And it came about when they had brought them outside, that
one said, "Escape for your life! Do not look behind you, and do
not stay anywhere in the valley; escape to the mountains, lest you
be swept away."
18But Lot said to them, "Oh no, my lords!
19"Now behold, your servant has found favor in your sight, and
you have magnified your lovingkindness, which you have shown
me by saving my life; but I cannot escape to the mountains, lest
the disaster overtake me and I die;
20now behold, this town is near *enough* to flee to, and it is small.
Please, let me escape there (is it not small?) that my life may be
saved."
21And he said to him, "Behold, I grant you this request also, not
to overthrow the town of which you have spoken.
22"Hurry, escape there, for I cannot do anything until you
arrive there." Therefore the name of the town was called [b]Zoar.
**23**¶ The sun had risen over the earth when Lot came to Zoar.
24Then the LORD rained on Sodom and Gomorrah brimstone
and fire from the LORD out of heaven,

NAS [b] I.e., small

## New International

servant's house. You can wash your feet and spend the night and
then go on your way early in the morning."
"No," they answered, "we will spend the night in the square."
3But he insisted so strongly that they did go with him and
entered his house. He prepared a meal for them, baking bread
without yeast, and they ate. 4Before they had gone to bed, all the
men from every part of the city of Sodom—both young and old—
surrounded the house. 5They called to Lot, "Where are the men
who came to you tonight? Bring them out to us so that we can have
sex with them."
6Lot went outside to meet them and shut the door behind him
7and said, "No, my friends. Don't do this wicked thing. 8Look, I
have two daughters who have never slept with a man. Let me
bring them out to you, and you can do what you like with them.
But don't do anything to these men, for they have come under the
protection of my roof."
9"Get out of our way," they replied. And they said, "This
fellow came here as an alien, and now he wants to play the judge!
We'll treat you worse than them." They kept bringing pressure on
Lot and moved forward to break down the door.
10But the men inside reached out and pulled Lot back into the
house and shut the door. 11Then they struck the men who were
at the door of the house, young and old, with blindness so that
they could not find the door.
12The two men said to Lot, "Do you have anyone else here—
sons-in-law, sons or daughters, or anyone else in the city who
belongs to you? Get them out of here, 13because we are going to
destroy this place. The outcry to the LORD against its people is so
great that he has sent us to destroy it."
14So Lot went out and spoke to his sons-in-law, who were
pledged to marry[c] his daughters. He said, "Hurry and get out of
this place, because the LORD is about to destroy the city!" But his
sons-in-law thought he was joking.
15With the coming of dawn, the angels urged Lot, saying, "Hurry! Take your wife and your two daughters who are here, or you
will be swept away when the city is punished."
16When he hesitated, the men grasped his hand and the hands
of his wife and of his two daughters and led them safely out of the
city, for the LORD was merciful to them. 17As soon as they had
brought them out, one of them said, "Flee for your lives! Don't
look back, and don't stop anywhere in the plain! Flee to the mountains or you will be swept away!"
18But Lot said to them, "No, my lords,[d] please! 19Your[e] servant
has found favor in your[f] eyes, and you[g] have shown great kindness to me in sparing my life. But I can't flee to the mountains; this
disaster will overtake me, and I'll die. 20Look, here is a town near
enough to run to, and it is small. Let me flee to it—it is very small,
isn't it? Then my life will be spared."
21He said to him, "Very well, I will grant this request too; I will
not overthrow the town you speak of. 22But flee there quickly,
because I cannot do anything until you reach it." (That is why the
town was called Zoar.[h])
23By the time Lot reached Zoar, the sun had risen over the land.
24Then the LORD rained down burning sulfur on Sodom and
Gomorrah—from the LORD out of the heavens. 25Thus he over-

NIV [c] 14 Or *were married to* [d] 18 Or *No, Lord;* or *No, my lord* [e] 19 The Hebrew is singular. [f] 19 The Hebrew is singular. [g] 19 The Hebrew is singular. [h] 22 *Zoar* means *small.*

## King James

25 And he overthrew those cities, and all the plain, and all the inhabitants of the cities, and that which grew upon the ground.

26 ¶ But his wife looked back from behind him, and she became a pillar of salt.

27 ¶ And Abraham gat up early in the morning to the place where he stood before the LORD:

28 And he looked toward Sodom and Gomorrah, and toward all the land of the plain, and beheld, and, lo, the smoke of the country went up as the smoke of a furnace.

29 ¶ And it came to pass, when God destroyed the cities of the plain, that God remembered Abraham, and sent Lot out of the midst of the overthrow, when he overthrew the cities in the which Lot dwelt.

30 ¶ And Lot went up out of Zoar, and dwelt in the mountain, and his two daughters with him; for he feared to dwell in Zoar: and he dwelt in a cave, he and his two daughters.

31 And the firstborn said unto the younger, Our father *is* old, and *there is* not a man in the earth to come in unto us after the manner of all the earth:

32 Come, let us make our father drink wine, and we will lie with him, that we may preserve seed of our father.

33 And they made their father drink wine that night: and the firstborn went in, and lay with her father; and he perceived not when she lay down, nor when she arose.

34 And it came to pass on the morrow, that the firstborn said unto the younger, Behold, I lay yesternight with my father: let us make him drink wine this night also; and go thou in, *and* lie with him, that we may preserve seed of our father.

35 And they made their father drink wine that night also: and the younger arose, and lay with him; and he perceived not when she lay down, nor when she arose.

36 Thus were both the daughters of Lot with child by their father.

37 And the firstborn bare a son, and called his name Moab: the same *is* the father of the Moabites unto this day.

38 And the younger, she also bare a son, and called his name Ben-ammi: the same *is* the father of the children of Ammon unto this day.

**20** AND ABRAHAM journeyed from thence toward the south country, and dwelled between Kadesh and Shur, and sojourned in Gerar.

2 And Abraham said of Sarah his wife, She *is* my sister: and Abimelech king of Gerar sent, and took Sarah.

3 But God came to Abimelech in a dream by night, and said to him, Behold, thou *art but* a dead man, for the woman which thou hast taken; for she *is* a man's wife.

4 But Abimelech had not come near her: and he said, Lord, wilt thou slay also a righteous nation?

## Amplified

25 He overthrew, destroyed *and* ended those cities, and all the valley and all the inhabitants of the cities, and what grew on the ground.

26 But [Lot's] wife looked back from behind him, and she [a]became a pillar of salt.

27 Abraham went up early next morning to the place where he [only the day before had] stood before the Lord.

28 And he looked toward Sodom and Gomorrah and all the land of the valley and saw, and lo, the smoke of [b]the country went up like the smoke of a furnace.

29 When God spoiled *and* destroyed the cities of the plain [of Siddim], He [earnestly] remembered Abraham (imprinted, fixed him indelibly on His mind); and He sent Lot out of the midst of the overthrow, when he overthrew the cities where Lot lived.

30 And Lot went up out of Zoar, and dwelt in the mountain, and his two daughters with him; for he feared to dwell in Zoar; and he lived in a cave, he and his two daughters.

31 The elder said to the younger, Our father is aging, and there is not a man on earth to live with us in the customary way.

32 Come, let us make our father drunk with wine, and we will lie with him, so that we may preserve offspring [our race] through our father.

33 And they made their father drunk with wine that night; and the older went in and lay with her father; and he was not aware when she lay down or when she arose.

34 Then the next day the first-born said to the younger, See here, I lay last night with my father; let us make him drunk with wine tonight also; then you go in and lie with him, so that we may preserve offspring [our race] through our father.

35 And they made their father drunk with wine again that night; and the younger arose and lay with him; and he was not aware when she lay down or when she arose.

36 Thus both the daughters of Lot were with child by their father.

37 The older bore a son, and named him Moab [of a father]; he is father of the Moabites to this day.

38 The younger also bore a son, and named him Ben-ammi [son of my people]; he is father of the Ammonites to this day.

**20** NOW ABRAHAM journeyed from there toward the [c]south country and dwelt between Kadesh and Shur, and lived temporarily in Gerar.

2 And Abraham said of Sarah his wife, She is my sister; and Abimelech king of Gerar sent and took Sarah [into his harem].

3 But God came to Abimelech in a dream by night, and said, Behold, you are a dead man, because of the woman whom you have taken [as your own], for she is a man's wife.

4 But Abimelech had not come near her; so he said, Lord, will you slay a people who are just *and* innocent?

**AMP** [a] Lot's wife not only "looked back" to where her heart's interests were, but she lingered behind; and probably overtaken by the fire and brimstone, her dead body became incrusted with salt, which, in that salt-packed now Dead Sea area, grew larger with more incrustations—a veritable "pillar of salt." In fact, at the southern end of the Dead Sea there is a mountain of table salt called Jebel Usdum, "Mount of Sodom." It is about six miles long, three miles wide, and 1,000 feet high. It is covered with a crust of earth several feet thick, but the rest of the mountain is said to be solid salt. (George T. B. Davis in *Rebuilding Palestine According to Prophecy,* adapted.) Somewhere in this area Lot's wife looked back to where her treasures and her heart were, and "she became a pillar of salt." Jesus said, "Remember Lot's wife." (Luke 17:32.) [b] Not only were Sodom and Gomorrah blazing ruins, but also Admah and Zeboiim (Deut. 29:23; Hos. 11:8), as well as all the towns in the valley of Siddim, Zoar alone being excepted. [c] "Primitive geographic expressions such as 'the south country' (20:1 and 24:62) and 'the east country' (25:6) are used in the time of Abraham . . . After the time of Genesis they have well-known and well-defined names; I submit that they were written down in early days, and that no writer after Moses could have used such archaic expressions as these" (P. J. Wiseman, in *New Discoveries in Babylonia About Genesis*).

## New American Standard

25and He overthrew those cities, and all the valley, and all the
inhabitants of the cities, and what grew on the ground.
26But his wife, from behind him, looked *back;* and she became
a pillar of salt.
27¶ Now Abraham arose early in the morning *and went* to the
place where he had stood before the LORD;
28and he looked down toward Sodom and Gomorrah, and
toward all the land of the valley, and he saw, and behold, the
smoke of the land ascended like the smoke of a furnace.
29Thus it came about, when God destroyed the cities of the
valley, that God remembered Abraham, and sent Lot out of the
midst of the overthrow, when He overthrew the cities in which Lot
lived.

*Lot Is Debased*

30¶ And Lot went up from Zoar, and stayed in the mountains,
and his two daughters with him; for he was afraid to stay in Zoar;
and he stayed in a cave, he and his two daughters.
31Then the first-born said to the younger, "Our father is old,
and there is not a man on earth to come in to us after the manner
of the earth.
32"Come, let us make our father drink wine, and let us lie with
him, that we may preserve our family through our father."
33So they made their father drink wine that night, and the
first-born went in and lay with her father; and he did not know
when she lay down or when she arose.
34And it came about on the morrow, that the first-born said to
the younger, "Behold, I lay last night with my father; let us make
him drink wine tonight also; then you go in and lie with him, that
we may preserve our family through our father."
35So they made their father drink wine that night also, and the
younger arose and lay with him; and he did not know when she
lay down or when she arose.
36Thus both the daughters of Lot were with child by their father.
37And the first-born bore a son, and called his name Moab; he
is the father of the Moabites to this day.
38And as for the younger, she also bore a son, and called his
name Ben-ammi; he is the father of the sons of Ammon to this day.

*Abraham's Treachery*

**20** NOW ABRAHAM journeyed from there toward the land
of the [d]Negev, and settled between Kadesh and Shur;
then he sojourned in Gerar.
2And Abraham said of Sarah his wife, "She is my sister." So
Abimelech king of Gerar sent and took Sarah.
3But God came to Abimelech in a dream of the night, and said
to him, "Behold, you are a dead man because of the woman whom
you have taken, for she is married."
4Now Abimelech had not come near her; and he said, "Lord,
wilt Thou slay a nation, even *though* blameless?

NAS [d] I.e., South country

## New International

threw those cities and the entire plain, including all those living
in the cities—and also the vegetation in the land. 26But Lot's wife
looked back, and she became a pillar of salt.
27Early the next morning Abraham got up and returned to the
place where he had stood before the LORD. 28He looked down
toward Sodom and Gomorrah, toward all the land of the plain, and
he saw dense smoke rising from the land, like smoke from a
furnace.
29So when God destroyed the cities of the plain, he remembered
Abraham, and he brought Lot out of the catastrophe that overthrew the cities where Lot had lived.

*Lot and His Daughters*

30Lot and his two daughters left Zoar and settled in the mountains, for he was afraid to stay in Zoar. He and his two daughters
lived in a cave. 31One day the older daughter said to the younger,
"Our father is old, and there is no man around here to lie with us,
as is the custom all over the earth. 32Let's get our father to drink
wine and then lie with him and preserve our family line through
our father."
33That night they got their father to drink wine, and the older
daughter went in and lay with him. He was not aware of it when
she lay down or when she got up.
34The next day the older daughter said to the younger, "Last
night I lay with my father. Let's get him to drink wine again
tonight, and you go in and lie with him so we can preserve our
family line through our father." 35So they got their father to drink
wine that night also, and the younger daughter went and lay with
him. Again he was not aware of it when she lay down or when she
got up.
36So both of Lot's daughters became pregnant by their father.
37The older daughter had a son, and she named him Moab[e]; he
is the father of the Moabites of today. 38The younger daughter also
had a son, and she named him Ben-Ammi[f]; he is the father of the
Ammonites of today.

*Abraham and Abimelech*

**20** NOW ABRAHAM moved on from there into the region of
the Negev and lived between Kadesh and Shur. For a
while he stayed in Gerar, 2and there Abraham said of his wife
Sarah, "She is my sister." Then Abimelech king of Gerar sent for
Sarah and took her.
3But God came to Abimelech in a dream one night and said to
him, "You are as good as dead because of the woman you have
taken; she is a married woman."
4Now Abimelech had not gone near her, so he said, "Lord, will
you destroy an innocent nation? 5Did he not say to me, 'She is my

NIV [e] *37 Moab* sounds like the Hebrew for *from father.* [f] *38 Ben-Ammi* means *son of my people.*

## King James

5 Said he not unto me, She *is* my sister? and she, even she herself
said, He *is* my brother: in the integrity of my heart and innocency
of my hands have I done this.
6 And God said unto him in a dream, Yea, I know that thou didst
this in the integrity of thy heart; for I also withheld thee from
sinning against me: therefore suffered I thee not to touch her.
7 Now therefore restore the man *his* wife; for he *is* a prophet, and
he shall pray for thee, and thou shalt live: and if thou restore *her*
not, know thou that thou shalt surely die, thou, and all that *are*
thine.
8 Therefore Abimelech rose early in the morning, and called all
his servants, and told all these things in their ears: and the men
were sore afraid.
9 Then Abimelech called Abraham, and said unto him, What
hast thou done unto us? and what have I offended thee, that thou
hast brought on me and on my kingdom a great sin? thou hast
done deeds unto me that ought not to be done.
10 And Abimelech said unto Abraham, What sawest thou, that
thou hast done this thing?
11 And Abraham said, Because I thought, Surely the fear of God
*is* not in this place; and they will slay me for my wife's sake.
12 And yet indeed *she is* my sister; she *is* the daughter of my
father, but not the daughter of my mother; and she became my
wife.
13 And it came to pass, when God caused me to wander from
my father's house, that I said unto her, This *is* thy kindness which
thou shalt show unto me; at every place whither we shall come,
say of me, He *is* my brother.
14 And Abimelech took sheep, and oxen, and menservants, and
womenservants, and gave *them* unto Abraham, and restored him
Sarah his wife.
15 And Abimelech said, Behold, my land *is* before thee: dwell
where it pleaseth thee.
16 And unto Sarah he said, Behold, I have given thy brother a
thousand *pieces* of silver: behold, he *is* to thee a covering of the
eyes, unto all that *are* with thee, and with all *other:* thus she was
reproved.
17 ¶ So Abraham prayed unto God: and God healed Abimelech,
and his wife, and his maidservants; and they bare *children.*
18 For the LORD had fast closed up all the wombs of the house
of Abimelech, because of Sarah Abraham's wife.

21 AND THE LORD visited Sarah as he had said, and the
LORD did unto Sarah as he had spoken.
2 For Sarah conceived, and bare Abraham a son in his old age,
at the set time of which God had spoken to him.
3 And Abraham called the name of his son that was born unto
him, whom Sarah bare to him, Isaac.
4 And Abraham circumcised his son Isaac being eight days old,
as God had commanded him.
5 And Abraham was an hundred years old, when his son Isaac
was born unto him.
6 ¶ And Sarah said, God hath made me to laugh, *so that* all that
hear will laugh with me.
7 And she said, Who would have said unto Abraham, that Sarah
should have given children suck? for I have born *him* a son in his
old age.
8 And the child grew, and was weaned: and Abraham made a
great feast the *same* day that Isaac was weaned.
9 ¶ And Sarah saw the son of Hagar the Egyptian, which she had
born unto Abraham, mocking.

## Amplified

5 Did not the man tell me, She is my sister? And she said, He
is my brother. In integrity of heart and innocency of hands I have
done this. [v. 12.]
6 Then God said to him in the dream, Yes, I know you did this
in the integrity of your heart, for it was I Who kept you back *and*
spared you from sinning against Me; therefore I did not give you
occasion to touch her.
7 So now restore to the man his wife; for he is a prophet, and
he will pray for you, and you shall live. But if you do not restore
her [to him], know that you shall surely die, you, and all that are
yours.
8 So Abimelech rose early in the morning, and called all his
servants, and told them all these things; and the men were exceedingly [filled with] reverence *and* fear.
9 Then Abimelech called Abraham, and said to him, What have
you done to us? And how have I offended you, that you should
bring on me and my kingdom a great sin? You have done to me
what ought not to be done [to any one].
10 And Abimelech said to Abraham, What did you see [in us],
that [justified] you in doing such a thing as this?
11 And Abraham said, Because I thought, Surely there is no
reverence *or* fear of God at all in this place; and they will slay me
because of my wife.
12 But truly, she is my sister; she is the daughter of my father,
but not of my mother; and she became my wife.
13 When God caused me to wander from my father's house I said
to her, This kindness you can show me: at every place we stop,
say of me, He is my brother.
14 Then Abimelech took sheep and oxen, and male and female
slaves, and gave them to Abraham, and restored to him Sarah his
wife.
15 And Abimelech said, Behold, my land is before you; dwell
where it pleases you.
16 And to Sarah he said, Behold, I have given this brother of
yours 1000 pieces of silver; see, it is to compensate to you [for all
that has occurred], and to vindicate your honor before all who are
with you. Before all men you are cleared *and* compensated.
17 So Abraham prayed to God; and God healed Abimelech and
his wife, and his female slaves, and they bore children.
18 For the Lord had closed fast the wombs of all in Abimelech's
household, because of Sarah, Abraham's wife.

21 THE LORD visited Sarah as He had said, and the Lord did
for her as He had promised.
2 For Sarah became pregnant and bore Abraham a son in his old
age, at the set time God had told him.
3 Abraham [a]named his son, whom Sarah bore to him, Isaac
(laughter).
4 And Abraham circumcised his son Isaac when he was eight
days old, as God had commanded him.
5 Abraham was 100 years old when Isaac was born.
6 And Sarah said, God has made me to laugh; all who hear will
laugh with me.
7 And she said, Who would have said to Abraham, that Sarah
would nurse children at the breast? For I have borne him a son in
his old age! [Heb. 11:12.]
8 And the child grew and was [b]weaned; and Abraham made a
great feast the same day that Isaac was weaned.
9 Now Sarah saw the son of Hagar the Egyptian, whom she had
borne to Abraham, mocking [Isaac].

**AMP** [a] See footnote on 16:15. [b] This was probably when the child was about three years of age. Samuel served in the sanctuary from the time that he was weaned (I Sam. 1:22-28). A Hebrew mother is quoted in II Maccabees 7:27 as saying to her son that she gave him "suck three years."

## New American Standard

5"Did he not himself say to me, 'She is my sister'? And she
herself said, 'He is my brother.' In the integrity of my heart and
the innocence of my hands I have done this."
6Then God said to him in the dream, "Yes, I know that in the
integrity of your heart you have done this, and I also kept you from
sinning against Me; therefore I did not let you touch her.
7"Now therefore, restore the man's wife, for he is a prophet,
and he will pray for you, and you will live. But if you do not restore
*her*, know that you shall surely die, you and all who are yours."
8¶ So Abimelech arose early in the morning and called all his
servants and told all these things in their hearing; and the men
were greatly frightened.
9Then Abimelech called Abraham and said to him, "What have
you done to us? And how have I sinned against you, that you have
brought on me and on my kingdom a great sin? You have done
to me things that ought not to be done."
10And Abimelech said to Abraham, "What have you encountered, that you have done this thing?"
11And Abraham said, "Because I thought, surely there is no fear
of God in this place; and they will kill me because of my wife.
12"Besides, she actually is my sister, the daughter of my father,
but not the daughter of my mother, and she became my wife;
13and it came about, when God caused me to wander from my
father's house, that I said to her, 'This is the kindness which you
will show to me: everywhere we go, say of me, "He is my brother."'"
14Abimelech then took sheep and oxen and male and female
servants, and gave them to Abraham, and restored his wife Sarah
to him.
15And Abimelech said, "Behold, my land is before you; settle
wherever you please."
16And to Sarah he said, "Behold, I have given your brother a
thousand pieces of silver; behold, it is your vindication before all
who are with you, and before all men you are cleared."
17And Abraham prayed to God; and God healed Abimelech and
his wife and his maids, so that they bore *children*.
18For the LORD had closed fast all the wombs of the household
of Abimelech because of Sarah, Abraham's wife.

*Isaac Is Born*

21 THEN THE LORD took note of Sarah as He had said, and
the LORD did for Sarah as He had promised.
2So Sarah conceived and bore a son to Abraham in his old age,
at the appointed time of which God had spoken to him.
3And Abraham called the name of his son who was born to
him, whom Sarah bore to him, Isaac.
4Then Abraham circumcised his son Isaac when he was eight
days old, as God had commanded him.
5Now Abraham was one hundred years old when his son Isaac
was born to him.
6And Sarah said, "God has made laughter for me; everyone
who hears will laugh with me."
7And she said, "Who would have said to Abraham that Sarah
would nurse children? Yet I have borne him a son in his old age."
8¶ And the child grew and was weaned, and Abraham made
a great feast on the day that Isaac was weaned.

*Sarah Turns against Hagar*

9Now Sarah saw the son of Hagar the Egyptian, whom she had
borne to Abraham, mocking.

## New International

sister,' and didn't she also say, 'He is my brother'? I have done this
with a clear conscience and clean hands."
6Then God said to him in the dream, "Yes, I know you did this
with a clear conscience, and so I have kept you from sinning
against me. That is why I did not let you touch her. 7Now return
the man's wife, for he is a prophet, and he will pray for you and
you will live. But if you do not return her, you may be sure that
you and all yours will die."
8Early the next morning Abimelech summoned all his officials,
and when he told them all that had happened, they were very
much afraid. 9Then Abimelech called Abraham in and said, "What
have you done to us? How have I wronged you that you have
brought such great guilt upon me and my kingdom? You have
done things to me that should not be done." 10And Abimelech
asked Abraham, "What was your reason for doing this?"
11Abraham replied, "I said to myself, 'There is surely no fear of
God in this place, and they will kill me because of my wife.'
12Besides, she really is my sister, the daughter of my father though
not of my mother; and she became my wife. 13And when God had
me wander from my father's household, I said to her, 'This is how
you can show your love to me: Everywhere we go, say of me, "He
is my brother."'"
14Then Abimelech brought sheep and cattle and male and
female slaves and gave them to Abraham, and he returned Sarah
his wife to him. 15And Abimelech said, "My land is before you; live
wherever you like."
16To Sarah he said, "I am giving your brother a thousand
shekels[c] of silver. This is to cover the offense against you before
all who are with you; you are completely vindicated."
17Then Abraham prayed to God, and God healed Abimelech,
his wife and his slave girls so they could have children again, 18for
the LORD had closed up every womb in Abimelech's household
because of Abraham's wife Sarah.

*The Birth of Isaac*

21 NOW THE LORD was gracious to Sarah as he had said, and
the LORD did for Sarah what he had promised. 2Sarah
became pregnant and bore a son to Abraham in his old age, at the
very time God had promised him. 3Abraham gave the name Isaac[d]
to the son Sarah bore him. 4When his son Isaac was eight days old,
Abraham circumcised him, as God commanded him. 5Abraham
was a hundred years old when his son Isaac was born to him.
6Sarah said, "God has brought me laughter, and everyone who
hears about this will laugh with me." 7And she added, "Who
would have said to Abraham that Sarah would nurse children? Yet
I have borne him a son in his old age."

*Hagar and Ishmael Sent Away*

8The child grew and was weaned, and on the day Isaac was
weaned Abraham held a great feast. 9But Sarah saw that the son
whom Hagar the Egyptian had borne to Abraham was mocking,

**NIV** [c] *16* That is, about 25 pounds (about 11.5 kilograms) [d] *3* *Isaac* means *he laughs*.

## King James

10Wherefore she said unto Abraham, Cast out this bondwoman
and her son: for the son of this bondwoman shall not be heir with
my son, *even* with Isaac.
11And the thing was very grievous in Abraham's sight because
of his son.
12¶ And God said unto Abraham, Let it not be grievous in thy
sight because of the lad, and because of thy bondwoman; in all that
Sarah hath said unto thee, hearken unto her voice; for in Isaac shall
thy seed be called.
13And also of the son of the bondwoman will I make a nation,
because he *is* thy seed.
14And Abraham rose up early in the morning, and took bread,
and a bottle of water, and gave *it* unto Hagar, putting *it* on her
shoulder, and the child, and sent her away: and she departed, and
wandered in the wilderness of Beer-sheba.
15And the water was spent in the bottle, and she cast the child
under one of the shrubs.
16And she went, and sat her down over against *him* a good way
off, as it were a bowshot: for she said, Let me not see the death
of the child. And she sat over against *him*, and lift up her voice,
and wept.
17And God heard the voice of the lad; and the angel of God
called to Hagar out of heaven, and said unto her, What aileth thee,
Hagar? fear not; for God hath heard the voice of the lad where he
*is*.
18Arise, lift up the lad, and hold him in thine hand; for I will
make him a great nation.
19And God opened her eyes, and she saw a well of water; and
she went, and filled the bottle with water, and gave the lad drink.
20And God was with the lad; and he grew, and dwelt in the
wilderness, and became an archer.
21And he dwelt in the wilderness of Paran: and his mother took
him a wife out of the land of Egypt.
22¶ And it came to pass at that time, that Abimelech and Phichol
the chief captain of his host spake unto Abraham, saying, God *is*
with thee in all that thou doest:
23Now therefore swear unto me here by God that thou wilt not
deal falsely with me, nor with my son, nor with my son's son: *but*
according to the kindness that I have done unto thee, thou shalt
do unto me, and to the land wherein thou hast sojourned.
24And Abraham said, I will swear.
25And Abraham reproved Abimelech because of a well of water,
which Abimelech's servants had violently taken away.
26And Abimelech said, I wot not who hath done this thing:
neither didst thou tell me, neither yet heard I *of it*, but today.
27And Abraham took sheep and oxen, and gave them unto
Abimelech; and both of them made a covenant.
28And Abraham set seven ewe lambs of the flock by themselves.
29And Abimelech said unto Abraham, What *mean* these seven
ewe lambs which thou hast set by themselves?
30And he said, For *these* seven ewe lambs shalt thou take of my
hand, that they may be a witness unto me, that I have digged this
well.
31Wherefore he called that place Beer-sheba; because there they
sware both of them.
32Thus they made a covenant at Beer-sheba: then Abimelech
rose up, and Phichol the chief captain of his host, and they returned into the land of the Philistines.
33¶ And *Abraham* planted a grove in Beer-sheba, and called there
on the name of the LORD, the everlasting God.
34And Abraham sojourned in the Philistines' land many days.

## Amplified

10Therefore she said to Abraham, Cast out this bondwoman
and her son; for the son of this bondwoman shall not be heir with
my son Isaac. [Gal. 4:28-31.]
11And the thing was very grievous (serious, evil) in Abraham's
sight on account of his son [Ishmael].
12God said to Abraham, Do not let it seem grievous *and* evil to
you because of the youth and your bondwoman; in all that Sarah
has said to you, do what she asks; for in Isaac shall your posterity
be called. [Rom. 9:7.]
13And I will make a nation of the son of the bondwoman also,
because he is your offspring.
14So Abraham rose early in the morning, and took bread and
a bottle of water, and gave it to Hagar, putting in on her shoulder,
and sent her and the [a]youth away. And she wandered on [aimless-
ly], and lost her way in the wilderness of Beer-sheba.
15When the water in the bottle was all gone, Hagar caused the
youth to lie down under one of the shrubs.
16Then she went, and sat down opposite him a good way off,
about a bow-shot; for she said, Let me not see the death of the lad.
And as she sat over opposite him, [b] *he* lifted up his voice and wept
*and* she raised her voice and wept.
17And God heard the voice of the youth, and the Angel of God
called to Hagar out of Heaven, and said to her, What troubles you,
Hagar? Fear not, for God has heard the voice of the youth where
he is.
18Arise, raise up the youth and support him with your hand;
for I intend to make him a great nation.
19Then God opened her eyes and she saw a well of water; and
she went and filled the [empty] bottle with water, and caused the
youth to drink.
20And God was with the youth; and he developed, and dwelt
in the wilderness and became an archer.
21He dwelt in the wilderness of Paran; and his mother took a
wife for him out of the land of Egypt.
22At that time Abimelech with Phicol, commander of his army,
said to Abraham, God is with you in everything you do;
23So now, swear to me here by God that you will not deal falsely
with me, or with my son, or with my posterity, but as I have dealt
with you kindly, you will do the same with me and the land in
which you have sojourned.
24And Abraham said, I will swear.
25When Abraham complained *and* reasoned with Abimelech
about a well of water [his] servants had violently seized,
26Abimelech said, I know not who did this thing; you did not
tell me, and I did not hear of it until today.
27So Abraham took sheep and oxen and gave them to Abimelech, and the two men made a league *or* covenant.
28Abraham set apart seven ewe lambs of the flock.
29And Abimelech said to Abraham, What do these seven ewe
lambs which you have set apart mean?
30He said, You are to accept these seven ewe lambs from me as
a witness for me that I dug this well.
31Therefore that place was called Beer-sheba (well of the oath),
because there both parties swore an oath.
32Thus they made a covenant at Beer-sheba; then Abimelech
and Phicol, the commander of his army, returned to the land of the
Philistines.
33Abraham planted a tamarisk tree in Beer-sheba and called
there on the name of the Lord, the eternal God.
34And Abraham sojourned in Philistia many days.

**AMP** [a] Ishmael was born when Abraham was 86 years old (Gen. 16:16), so Ishmael was 14 when Isaac was born. Isaac was weaned (21:8) at least three years later probably (cp. II Chron. 31:16; II Mac. 7:27). [b] The Hebrew says, "she lifted up her voice." The Greek (Septuagint) says "he," which the next verse seems to support. The circumstances allow both.

## New American Standard

10Therefore she said to Abraham, "Drive out this maid and her son, for the son of this maid shall not be an heir with my son Isaac."

11And the matter distressed Abraham greatly because of his son.

12But God said to Abraham, "Do not be distressed because of the lad and your maid; whatever Sarah tells you, listen to her, for through Isaac your descendants shall be named.

13"And of the son of the maid I will make a nation also, because he is your descendant."

14So Abraham rose early in the morning, and took bread and a skin of water, and gave *them* to Hagar, putting *them* on her shoulder, and *gave her* the boy, and sent her away. And she departed, and wandered about in the wilderness of Beersheba.

15And the water in the skin was used up, and she left the boy under one of the bushes.

16Then she went and sat down opposite him, about a bowshot away, for she said, "Do not let me see the boy die." And she sat opposite him, and lifted up her voice and wept.

17And God heard the lad crying; and the angel of God called to Hagar from heaven, and said to her, "What is the matter with you, Hagar? Do not fear, for God has heard the voice of the lad where he is.

18"Arise, lift up the lad, and hold him by the hand; for I will make a great nation of him."

19Then God opened her eyes and she saw a well of water; and she went and filled the skin with water, and gave the lad a drink.

20And God was with the lad, and he grew; and he lived in the wilderness, and became an archer.

21And he lived in the wilderness of Paran; and his mother took a wife for him from the land of Egypt.

*Covenant with Abimelech*

22¶ Now it came about at that time, that Abimelech and Phicol, the commander of his army, spoke to Abraham, saying, "God is with you in all that you do;

23now therefore, swear to me here by God that you will not deal falsely with me, or with my offspring, or with my posterity; but according to the kindness that I have shown to you, you shall show to me, and to the land in which you have sojourned."

24And Abraham said, "I swear it."

25But Abraham complained to Abimelech because of the well of water which the servants of Abimelech had seized.

26And Abimelech said, "I do not know who has done this thing; neither did you tell me, nor did I hear of it until today."

27And Abraham took sheep and oxen, and gave them to Abimelech; and the two of them made a covenant.

28Then Abraham set seven ewe lambs of the flock by themselves.

29And Abimelech said to Abraham, "What do these seven ewe lambs mean, which you have set by themselves?"

30And he said, "You shall take these seven ewe lambs from my hand in order that it may be a witness to me, that I dug this well."

31Therefore he called that place Beersheba; because there the two of them took an oath.

32So they made a covenant at Beersheba; and Abimelech and Phicol, the commander of his army, arose and returned to the land of the Philistines.

33And *Abraham* planted a tamarisk tree at Beersheba, and there he called on the name of the LORD, the Everlasting God.

34And Abraham sojourned in the land of the Philistines for many days.

## New International

10and she said to Abraham, "Get rid of that slave woman and her son, for that slave woman's son will never share in the inheritance with my son Isaac."

11The matter distressed Abraham greatly because it concerned
his son. 12But God said to him, "Do not be so distressed about the
boy and your maidservant. Listen to whatever Sarah tells you,
because it is through Isaac that your offspring[c] will be reckoned.
13I will make the son of the maidservant into a nation also, because
he is your offspring."

14Early the next morning Abraham took some food and a skin of water and gave them to Hagar. He set them on her shoulders and then sent her off with the boy. She went on her way and wandered in the desert of Beersheba.

15When the water in the skin was gone, she put the boy under
one of the bushes. 16Then she went off and sat down nearby, about
a bowshot away, for she thought, "I cannot watch the boy die."
And as she sat there nearby, she[d] began to sob.

17God heard the boy crying, and the angel of God called to
Hagar from heaven and said to her, "What is the matter, Hagar?
Do not be afraid; God has heard the boy crying as he lies there.
18Lift the boy up and take him by the hand, for I will make him
into a great nation."

19Then God opened her eyes and she saw a well of water. So she went and filled the skin with water and gave the boy a drink.

20God was with the boy as he grew up. He lived in the desert
and became an archer. 21While he was living in the Desert of
Paran, his mother got a wife for him from Egypt.

*The Treaty at Beersheba*

22At that time Abimelech and Phicol the commander of his
forces said to Abraham, "God is with you in everything you do.
23Now swear to me here before God that you will not deal falsely
with me or my children or my descendants. Show to me and the
country where you are living as an alien the same kindness I have
shown to you."

24Abraham said, "I swear it."

25Then Abraham complained to Abimelech about a well of
water that Abimelech's servants had seized. 26But Abimelech said,
"I don't know who has done this. You did not tell me, and I heard
about it only today."

27So Abraham brought sheep and cattle and gave them to
Abimelech, and the two men made a treaty. 28Abraham set apart
seven ewe lambs from the flock, 29and Abimelech asked Abraham,
"What is the meaning of these seven ewe lambs you have set apart
by themselves?"

30He replied, "Accept these seven lambs from my hand as a witness that I dug this well."

31So that place was called Beersheba,[e] because the two men swore an oath there.

32After the treaty had been made at Beersheba, Abimelech and
Phicol the commander of his forces returned to the land of the
Philistines. 33Abraham planted a tamarisk tree in Beersheba, and
there he called upon the name of the LORD, the Eternal God. 34And
Abraham stayed in the land of the Philistines for a long time.

NIV [c] 12 Or *seed* [d] 16 Hebrew; Septuagint *the child* [e] 31 *Beersheba* can mean *well of seven* or *well of the oath.*

## King James

**22** AND IT came to pass after these things, that God did tempt Abraham, and said unto him, Abraham: and he said, Behold, *here* I *am*.

2And he said, Take now thy son, thine only *son* Isaac, whom thou lovest, and get thee into the land of Moriah; and offer him there for a burnt offering upon one of the mountains which I will tell thee of.

3¶ And Abraham rose up early in the morning, and saddled his ass, and took two of his young men with him, and Isaac his son, and clave the wood for the burnt offering, and rose up, and went unto the place of which God had told him.

4Then on the third day Abraham lifted up his eyes, and saw the place afar off.

5And Abraham said unto his young men, Abide ye here with the ass; and I and the lad will go yonder and worship, and come again to you.

6And Abraham took the wood of the burnt offering, and laid *it* upon Isaac his son; and he took the fire in his hand, and a knife; and they went both of them together.

7And Isaac spake unto Abraham his father, and said, My father: and he said, Here *am* I, my son. And he said, Behold the fire and the wood: but where *is* the lamb for a burnt offering?

8And Abraham said, My son, God will provide himself a lamb for a burnt offering: so they went both of them together.

9And they came to the place which God had told him of; and Abraham built an altar there, and laid the wood in order, and bound Isaac his son, and laid him on the altar upon the wood.

10And Abraham stretched forth his hand, and took the knife to slay his son.

11And the angel of the LORD called unto him out of heaven, and said, Abraham, Abraham: and he said, Here *am* I.

12And he said, Lay not thine hand upon the lad, neither do thou any thing unto him: for now I know that thou fearest God, seeing thou hast not withheld thy son, thine only *son* from me.

13And Abraham lifted up his eyes, and looked, and behold behind *him* a ram caught in a thicket by his horns: and Abraham went and took the ram, and offered him up for a burnt offering in the stead of his son.

14And Abraham called the name of that place Jehovah-jireh: as it is said *to* this day, In the mount of the LORD it shall be seen.

15¶ And the angel of the LORD called unto Abraham out of heaven the second time,

16And said, By myself have I sworn, saith the LORD, for because thou hast done this thing, and hast not withheld thy son, thine only *son:*

17That in blessing I will bless thee, and in multiplying I will multiply thy seed as the stars of the heaven, and as the sand which *is* upon the sea shore; and thy seed shall possess the gate of his enemies;

18And in thy seed shall all the nations of the earth be blessed; because thou hast obeyed my voice.

19So Abraham returned unto his young men, and they rose up and went together to Beer-sheba; and Abraham dwelt at Beer-sheba.

## Amplified

**22** AFTER THESE events, God tested *and* proved Abraham, and said to him, Abraham! And he said, Here I am.

2[God] said, Take now your son, your only son Isaac, whom you love, and go to the region of Moriah and offer him there as a burnt offering upon one of the mountains of which I will tell you.

3So Abraham rose early in the morning, saddled his donkey, and took two of his young men with him, and his son Isaac; and he split the wood for the burnt offering, then began the trip to the place of which God had told him.

4On the third day Abraham looked up and saw the place in the distance.

5And Abraham said to his servants, Settle down *and* stay here with the donkey; and I and the young man will go yonder and worship, and [a]come again to you.

6Then Abraham took the wood for the burnt offering, and laid it on [the shoulders of] Isaac his son; and he took the fire [that is, the firepot] in his own hand, and a knife, and the two of them went on together.

7And Isaac said to Abraham, My father! And he said, Here I am, my son. [Isaac] said, See, here are the fire and the wood, but where is the lamb for a burnt sacrifice?

8Abraham said, My son, [b]God will provide Himself a lamb for a burnt offering. So the two went on together.

9When they came to the place of which God had told him, Abraham built an altar there; then he laid the wood in order and [c]bound Isaac his son, and laid him on the altar on the wood. [Matt. 10:37.]

10And Abraham stretched forth his hand and took hold of the knife to slay his son. [Heb. 11:17-19.]

11But the Angel of the Lord called to him from Heaven, and said, Abraham, Abraham! He answered, Here I am.

12And He said, Do not lay your hand on the lad, or do anything to him; for now I know that you fear *and* revere God, since you have not held back from Me *or* begrudged giving Me your son, your only son.

13Then Abraham looked up *and* glanced around, and lo, behind him was a ram caught in a thicket by his horns. And Abraham went and took the ram, and offered it up for a burnt offering *and* an ascending sacrifice instead of his son!

14So Abraham called the name of that place, The Lord will provide; and it is said to this day, On the mount of the Lord it shall be provided.

15The Angel of the Lord called to Abraham from Heaven the second time,

16And said, I have sworn by Myself, says the Lord, since you have done this, and have not withheld [from Me] *or* begrudged [giving Me] your son, your only son,

17That in blessing I will bless you, and in multiplying I will multiply your descendants as the stars of the heavens and as the sand on the seashore. And your Seed (Heir) shall possess the gate of His enemies; [Heb. 6:13, 14; 11:12.]

18And in your Seed [ [d]Christ] shall all the nations of the earth be blessed *and* [by Him] bless themselves, because you have heard *and* obeyed My voice. [Acts 3:25, 26; Gal. 3:16.]

19So Abraham returned to his servants and they rose up and went with him to Beer-sheba; there Abraham lived.

**AMP** [a] Abraham was not lying to his servants, or trying to deceive them. He believed God Who had promised him that this young man's posterity was to inherit the promises made to Abraham (Gen.12:2, 3). [b] We must not suppose that this was the language merely of faith and obedience. *Abraham* spoke prophetically, and referred to that Lamb of God which HE had provided for Himself, Who in the fullness of time would take away the sin of the world, and of Whom Isaac was a most expressive type (Clarke's *Commentary*). For Abraham was a prophet (Gen. 20:7). Jesus said, Abraham hoped for "My day [My incarnation]; and he did see it, and was glad" (John 8:56). [c] Isaac, who was perhaps twenty-five years old (*Josephus*), shared his father's confidence in God's promise. Was not his very existence the result of God keeping His word? (Gen. 17:15-17.) [d] We have the authority of the Apostle Paul (Gal. 3:8, 16, 18) to restrict this promise to our blessed Lord, Who was the Seed through Whom alone all God's blessings of providence, mercy, grace, and glory, should be conveyed to the nations of the earth (Adam Clarke's *Commentary*).

## New American Standard

*The Offering of Isaac*

**22** NOW IT came about after these things, that God tested Abraham, and said to him, "Abraham!" And he said, "Here I am."

2And He said, "Take now your son, your only son, whom you love, Isaac, and go to the land of Moriah; and offer him there as a burnt offering on one of the mountains of which I will tell you."

3So Abraham rose early in the morning and saddled his donkey, and took two of his young men with him and Isaac his son; and he split wood for the burnt offering, and arose and went to the place of which God had told him.

4On the third day Abraham raised his eyes and saw the place from a distance.

5And Abraham said to his young men, "Stay here with the donkey, and I and the lad will go yonder; and we will worship and return to you."

6And Abraham took the wood of the burnt offering and laid it on Isaac his son, and he took in his hand the fire and the knife. So the two of them walked on together.

7And Isaac spoke to Abraham his father and said, "My father!" And he said, "Here I am, my son." And he said, "Behold, the fire and the wood, but where is the lamb for the burnt offering?"

8And Abraham said, "God will provide for Himself the lamb for the burnt offering, my son." So the two of them walked on together.

9¶ Then they came to the place of which God had told him; and Abraham built the altar there, and arranged the wood, and bound his son Isaac, and laid him on the altar on top of the wood.

10And Abraham stretched out his hand, and took the knife to slay his son.

11But the angel of the LORD called to him from heaven, and said, "Abraham, Abraham!" And he said, "Here I am."

12And he said, "Do not stretch out your hand against the lad, and do nothing to him; for now I know that you fear God, since you have not withheld your son, your only son, from Me."

13Then Abraham raised his eyes and looked, and behold, behind *him* a ram caught in the thicket by his horns; and Abraham went and took the ram, and offered him up for a burnt offering in the place of his son.

14And Abraham called the name of that place The LORD Will Provide, as it is said to this day, "In the mount of the LORD it will be provided."

15Then the angel of the LORD called to Abraham a second time from heaven,

16and said, "By Myself I have sworn, declares the LORD, because you have done this thing, and have not withheld your son, your only son,

17indeed I will greatly bless you, and I will greatly multiply your seed as the stars of the heavens, and as the sand which is on the seashore; and your seed shall possess the gate of their enemies.

18"And in your seed all the nations of the earth shall be blessed, because you have obeyed My voice."

19So Abraham returned to his young men, and they arose and went together to Beersheba; and Abraham lived at Beersheba.

## New International

*Abraham Tested*

**22** SOME TIME later God tested Abraham. He said to him, "Abraham!"

"Here I am," he replied.

2Then God said, "Take your son, your only son, Isaac, whom you love, and go to the region of Moriah. Sacrifice him there as a burnt offering on one of the mountains I will tell you about."

3Early the next morning Abraham got up and saddled his donkey. He took with him two of his servants and his son Isaac. When
he had cut enough wood for the burnt offering, he set out for the
place God had told him about. 4On the third day Abraham looked
up and saw the place in the distance. 5He said to his servants,
"Stay here with the donkey while I and the boy go over there. We
will worship and then we will come back to you."

6Abraham took the wood for the burnt offering and placed it on
his son Isaac, and he himself carried the fire and the knife. As the
two of them went on together, 7Isaac spoke up and said to his
father Abraham, "Father?"

"Yes, my son?" Abraham replied.

"The fire and wood are here," Isaac said, "but where is the lamb for the burnt offering?"

8Abraham answered, "God himself will provide the lamb for the burnt offering, my son." And the two of them went on together.

9When they reached the place God had told him about, Abraham built an altar there and arranged the wood on it. He bound
his son Isaac and laid him on the altar, on top of the wood. 10Then
he reached out his hand and took the knife to slay his son. 11But
the angel of the LORD called out to him from heaven, "Abraham!
Abraham!"

"Here I am," he replied.

12"Do not lay a hand on the boy," he said. "Do not do anything to him. Now I know that you fear God, because you have not withheld from me your son, your only son."

13Abraham looked up and there in a thicket he saw a ram[e]
caught by its horns. He went over and took the ram and sacrificed
it as a burnt offering instead of his son. 14So Abraham called that
place The LORD Will Provide. And to this day it is said, "On the
mountain of the LORD it will be provided."

15The angel of the LORD called to Abraham from heaven a
second time 16and said, "I swear by myself, declares the LORD, that
because you have done this and have not withheld your son, your
only son, 17I will surely bless you and make your descendants as
numerous as the stars in the sky and as the sand on the seashore.
Your descendants will take possession of the cities of their enemies, 18and through your offspring[f] all nations on earth will be
blessed, because you have obeyed me."

19Then Abraham returned to his servants, and they set off together for Beersheba. And Abraham stayed in Beersheba.

**NIV** [e] *13* Many manuscripts of the Masoretic Text, Samaritan Pentateuch, Septuagint and Syriac; most manuscripts of the Masoretic Text *a ram behind him*
[f] *18* Or *seed*

## King James

20¶ And it came to pass after these things, that it was told Abraham, saying, Behold, Milcah, she hath also born children unto thy brother Nahor;
21Huz his firstborn, and Buz his brother, and Kemuel the father of Aram,
22And Chesed, and Hazo, and Pildash, and Jidlaph, and Bethuel.
23And Bethuel begat Rebekah: these eight Milcah did bear to Nahor, Abraham's brother.
24And his concubine, whose name *was* Reumah, she bare also Tebah, and Gaham, and Thahash, and Maachah.

23 AND SARAH was an hundred and seven and twenty years old: *these were* the years of the life of Sarah.
2And Sarah died in Kirjath-arba; the same *is* Hebron in the land of Canaan: and Abraham came to mourn for Sarah, and to weep for her.
3¶ And Abraham stood up from before his dead, and spake unto the sons of Heth, saying,
4I *am* a stranger and a sojourner with you: give me a possession of a buryingplace with you, that I may bury my dead out of my sight.
5And the children of Heth answered Abraham, saying unto him,
6Hear us, my lord: thou *art* a mighty prince among us: in the choice of our sepulchres bury thy dead; none of us shall withhold from thee his sepulchre, but that thou mayest bury thy dead.
7And Abraham stood up, and bowed himself to the people of the land, *even* to the children of Heth.
8And he communed with them, saying, If it be your mind that I should bury my dead out of my sight; hear me, and entreat for me to Ephron the son of Zohar,
9That he may give me the cave of Machpelah, which he hath, which *is* in the end of his field; for as much money as it is worth he shall give it me for a possession of a buryingplace amongst you.
10And Ephron dwelt among the children of Heth: and Ephron the Hittite answered Abraham in the audience of the children of Heth, *even* of all that went in at the gate of his city, saying,
11Nay, my lord, hear me: the field give I thee, and the cave that *is* therein, I give it thee; in the presence of the sons of my people give I it thee: bury thy dead.
12And Abraham bowed down himself before the people of the land.
13And he spake unto Ephron in the audience of the people of the land, saying, But if thou *wilt give it*, I pray thee, hear me: I will give thee money for the field; take *it* of me, and I will bury my dead there.
14And Ephron answered Abraham, saying unto him,
15My lord, hearken unto me: the land *is worth* four hundred shekels of silver; what *is* that betwixt me and thee? bury therefore thy dead.
16And Abraham hearkened unto Ephron; and Abraham weighed to Ephron the silver, which he had named in the audience of the sons of Heth, four hundred shekels of silver, current *money* with the merchant.
17¶ And the field of Ephron, which *was* in Machpelah, which *was* before Mamre, the field, and the cave which *was* therein, and all the trees that *were* in the field, that *were* in all the borders round about, were made sure

## Amplified

20Now after these things it was told Abraham, Milcah has also borne children to your brother Nahor:
21Uz the first-born, Buz his brother, Kemuel the father of Aram,
22Chesed, Hazo, Pildash, Jidlaph, and Bethuel.
23Bethuel became the father of Rebekah. These eight Milcah bore to Nahor, Abraham's brother.
24And his concubine, whose name was Reumah, bore Tebah, Gaham, Tahash, and Maacah.

23 SARAH LIVED 127 years; this was the length of the life of Sarah.
2And Sarah died in Kiriath-arba; [a]the same is Hebron, in the land of Canaan. And Abraham went to mourn for Sarah and to weep for her.
3And Abraham stood up from before his dead, and said to the sons of Heth,
4I am a stranger and a sojourner with you; give me property for a burial place among you, that I may bury my dead out of my sight.
5And the Hittites replied to Abraham,
6Listen to us, my lord; you are a mighty prince among us. Bury your dead in any tomb *or* grave of ours that you may choose; none of us will withhold from you his tomb, or hinder you from burying your dead.
7And Abraham stood up, and bowed himself to the people of the land, the Hittites.
8And he said to them, If you are willing to grant my dead burial out of my sight, listen to me, and ask Ephron the son of Zohar for me,
9That he may give me the cave of Machpelah, which he owns; it is at the end of his field. For the full price let him give it to me here in your presence, as a burial place to which I may hold fast among you.
10Now Ephron was present there among the sons of Heth; so, in the hearing of all who went in at the gate of his city, Ephron the Hittite answered Abraham, saying,
11No, my lord, hear me; I give you the field, and the cave that is in it I give you; in the presence of the sons of my people I give it to you. Bury your dead.
12Then Abraham bowed himself down before the people of the land.
13And he said to Ephron in the presence of the people of the land, But if you will give it, I beg of you, hear me: I will give you the price of the field; accept it from me, and I will bury my dead there.
14Ephron replied to Abraham, saying,
15My lord, listen to me: the land is worth 400 shekels of silver; what is that between you and me? So bury your dead.
16So Abraham listened to what Ephron said *and* acted upon it. He weighed to Ephron the silver which he had named in the hearing of the Hittites, 400 shekels of silver according to the weights current among the merchants.
17So the field of Ephron in Machpelah, which was to the east of Mamre [Hebron], the field and the cave which was in it and all the trees that were in the field, and in all its borders round about, were made over

**AMP** [a] Surely this indicates that this detail was written at a very early date, and before Israel had entered the land. No one in later times would need to be told where Hebron was. Not only was it conspicuous in Joshua's and Caleb's day, but it became a "city of refuge." Besides all this, David was for seven years king in Hebron. Obviously the Israelites had not yet entered Canaan and had to be told not only the name of the place where Abraham and Isaac had lived and were buried, but also its location. (Adapted from P. J. Wiseman's *New Discoveries in Babylonia About Genesis.*)

## New American Standard

20¶ Now it came about after these things, that it was told Abraham, saying, "Behold, Milcah also has borne children to your
brother Nahor:
21 Uz his first-born and Buz his brother and Kemuel the father
of Aram
22 and Chesed and Hazo and Pildash and Jidlaph and Bethuel."
23 And Bethuel became the father of Rebekah: these eight Milcah
bore to Nahor, Abraham's brother.
24 And his concubine, whose name was Reumah, also bore
Tebah and Gaham and Tahash and Maacah.

*Death and Burial of Sarah*

**23** NOW SARAH lived one hundred and twenty-seven
years; *these were* the years of the life of Sarah.
2 And Sarah died in Kiriath-arba (that is, Hebron) in the land
of Canaan; and Abraham went in to mourn for Sarah and to weep
for her.
3 Then Abraham rose from before his dead, and spoke to the
sons of Heth, saying,
4 "I am a stranger and a sojourner among you; give me a burial
site among you, that I may bury my dead out of my sight."
5 And the sons of Heth answered Abraham, saying to him,
6 "Hear us, my lord, you are a mighty prince among us; bury
your dead in the choicest of our graves; none of us will refuse you
his grave for burying your dead."
7 So Abraham rose and bowed to the people of the land, the
sons of Heth.
8 And he spoke with them, saying, "If it is your wish *for me* to
bury my dead out of my sight, hear me, and approach Ephron the
son of Zohar for me,
9 that he may give me the cave of Machpelah which he owns,
which is at the end of his field; for the full price let him give it to
me in your presence for a burial site."
10 Now Ephron was sitting among the sons of Heth; and Ephron
the Hittite answered Abraham in the hearing of the sons of Heth;
*even* of all who went in at the gate of his city, saying,
11 "No, my lord, hear me; I give you the field, and I give you
the cave that is in it. In the presence of the sons of my people I give
it to you; bury your dead."
12 And Abraham bowed before the people of the land.
13 And he spoke to Ephron in the hearing of the people of the
land, saying, "If you will only please listen to me; I will give the
price of the field, accept *it* from me, that I may bury my dead
there."
14 Then Ephron answered Abraham, saying to him,
15 "My lord, listen to me; a piece of land worth four hundred
shekels of silver, what is that between me and you? So bury your
dead."
16 And Abraham listened to Ephron; and Abraham weighed out
for Ephron the silver which he had named in the hearing of the
sons of Heth, four hundred shekels of silver, commercial standard.
17¶ So Ephron's field, which was in Machpelah, which faced
Mamre, the field and cave which was in it, and all the trees which
were in the field, that were within all the confines of its border,
were deeded over

## New International

*Nahor's Sons*

20 Some time later Abraham was told, "Milcah is also a mother;
she has borne sons to your brother Nahor: 21 Uz the firstborn, Buz
his brother, Kemuel (the father of Aram), 22 Kesed, Hazo, Pildash,
Jidlaph and Bethuel." 23 Bethuel became the father of Rebekah.
Milcah bore these eight sons to Abraham's brother Nahor. 24 His
concubine, whose name was Reumah, also had sons: Tebah,
Gaham, Tahash and Maacah.

*The Death of Sarah*

**23** SARAH LIVED to be a hundred and twenty-seven years
old. 2 She died at Kiriath Arba (that is, Hebron) in the land
of Canaan, and Abraham went to mourn for Sarah and to weep
over her.
3 Then Abraham rose from beside his dead wife and spoke to the
Hittites.[b] He said, 4 "I am an alien and a stranger among you. Sell
me some property for a burial site here so I can bury my dead."
5 The Hittites replied to Abraham, 6 "Sir, listen to us. You are a
mighty prince among us. Bury your dead in the choicest of our
tombs. None of us will refuse you his tomb for burying your
dead."
7 Then Abraham rose and bowed down before the people of the
land, the Hittites. 8 He said to them, "If you are willing to let me
bury my dead, then listen to me and intercede with Ephron son
of Zohar on my behalf 9 so he will sell me the cave of Machpelah,
which belongs to him and is at the end of his field. Ask him to sell
it to me for the full price as a burial site among you."
10 Ephron the Hittite was sitting among his people and he replied to Abraham in the hearing of all the Hittites who had come
to the gate of his city. 11 "No, my lord," he said. "Listen to me; I
give[c] you the field, and I give[d] you the cave that is in it. I give[e]
it to you in the presence of my people. Bury your dead."
12 Again Abraham bowed down before the people of the land
13 and he said to Ephron in their hearing, "Listen to me, if you will.
I will pay the price of the field. Accept it from me so I can bury my
dead there."
14 Ephron answered Abraham, 15 "Listen to me, my lord; the
land is worth four hundred shekels[f] of silver, but what is that
between me and you? Bury your dead."
16 Abraham agreed to Ephron's terms and weighed out for him
the price he had named in the hearing of the Hittites: four hundred
shekels of silver, according to the weight current among the merchants.
17 So Ephron's field in Machpelah near Mamre—both the field
and the cave in it, and all the trees within the borders of the
field—was deeded 18 to Abraham as his property in the presence

**NIV** [b] 3 Or *the sons of Heth;* also in verses 5, 7, 10, 16, 18 and 20 [c] *11* Or *sell*
[d] *11* Or *sell* [e] *11* Or *sell* [f] *15* That is, about 10 pounds (about 4.5 kilograms)

## King James

18 Unto Abraham for a possession in the presence of the children of Heth, before all that went in at the gate of his city.

19 And after this, Abraham buried Sarah his wife in the cave of the field of Machpelah before Mamre: the same *is* Hebron in the land of Canaan.

20 And the field, and the cave that *is* therein, were made sure unto Abraham for a possession of a buryingplace by the sons of Heth.

**24** AND ABRAHAM was old, *and* well stricken in age: and the LORD had blessed Abraham in all things.

2 And Abraham said unto his eldest servant of his house, that ruled over all that he had, Put, I pray thee, thy hand under my thigh:

3 And I will make thee swear by the LORD, the God of heaven, and the God of the earth, that thou shalt not take a wife unto my son of the daughters of the Canaanites, among whom I dwell:

4 But thou shalt go unto my country, and to my kindred, and take a wife unto my son Isaac.

5 And the servant said unto him, Peradventure the woman will not be willing to follow me unto this land: must I needs bring thy son again unto the land from whence thou camest?

6 And Abraham said unto him, Beware thou that thou bring not my son thither again.

7¶ The LORD God of heaven, which took me from my father's house, and from the land of my kindred, and which spake unto me, and that sware unto me, saying, Unto thy seed will I give this land; he shall send his angel before thee, and thou shalt take a wife unto my son from thence.

8 And if the woman will not be willing to follow thee, then thou shalt be clear from this my oath: only bring not my son thither again.

9 And the servant put his hand under the thigh of Abraham his master, and sware to him concerning that matter.

10¶ And the servant took ten camels of the camels of his master, and departed; for all the goods of his master *were* in his hand: and he arose, and went to Mesopotamia, unto the city of Nahor.

11 And he made his camels to kneel down without the city by a well of water at the time of the evening, *even* the time that women go out to draw *water*.

12 And he said, O LORD God of my master Abraham, I pray thee, send me good speed this day, and show kindness unto my master Abraham.

13 Behold, I stand *here* by the well of water; and the daughters of the men of the city come out to draw water:

14 And let it come to pass, that the damsel to whom I shall say, Let down thy pitcher, I pray thee, that I may drink; and she shall say, Drink, and I will give thy camels drink also: *let the same be* she *that* thou hast appointed for thy servant Isaac; and thereby shall I know that thou hast shown kindness unto my master.

15¶ And it came to pass, before he had done speaking, that, behold, Rebekah came out, who was born to Bethuel, son of Milcah, the wife of Nahor, Abraham's brother, with her pitcher upon her shoulder.

16 And the damsel *was* very fair to look upon, a virgin, neither had any man known her: and she went down to the well, and filled her pitcher, and came up.

**AMP** [a] Here were buried Abraham and Sarah, Isaac and Rebekah, Jacob and Leah. (Gen. 49:31; 50:13) [b] This chapter is highly illustrative of God the Father, Who sends forth His Holy Spirit to win the consent of the individual soul to become the bride of His Son. Keep these resemblances constantly in mind as you read and see how the story unfolds. First meet the Father and note His concern about His Son's bride. Then get acquainted with the Holy Spirit's great, selfless heart, Whose one purpose is to win the girl for His Master's Son. Then meet the Son and note His tenderness as He claims His bride. This whole longest chapter in Genesis is devoted to this important story. [c] The Holy Spirit does not win unwilling souls, only "whosoever will."

## Amplified

18 As a possession to Abraham, in the presence of the Hittites, before all who went in at his city gate.

19 After this, Abraham buried Sarah his wife in the cave of the field of [a]Machpelah to the east of Mamre, that is Hebron, in the land of Canaan.

20 The field and the cave in it were conveyed to Abraham for a permanent burial place, by the sons of Heth.

**24** NOW ABRAHAM was old, well advanced in years; and the Lord had blessed Abraham in all things.

2 And Abraham said to his eldest servant of his house [Eliezer of Damascus] who ruled over all that he had, I beg of you, put your hand under my thigh; [Gen. 15:2.]

3 And you shall swear by the Lord, the God of Heaven and earth, that you will not take a wife for my son from the daughters of the Canaanites, among whom I have settled.

4 But you shall go to my country and to my relatives, and take [b]a wife for my son Isaac.

5 The servant said to him, But perhaps the woman will not be willing to come along after me to this country. Must I take your son to the country from which you came?

6 Abraham said to him, See to it that you do not take my son back there.

7 The Lord, the God of Heaven, Who took me from my father's house, from the land of my family *and* my birth, Who spoke to me and swore to me, saying, To your offspring I will give this land, He will send His Angel before you, and you shall take a wife from there for my son.

8 And if the women should [c]not be willing to go along after you, then you will be clear from this oath; only you must not take my son back there.

9 So the servant put his hand under the thigh of Abraham his master, and swore to him concerning this matter.

10 And the servant took ten of his master's camels and departed, taking some of all his master's treasures with him; thus he journeyed to Mesopotamia [between the Tigris and the Euphrates], to the city of Nahor [Abraham's brother].

11 And he made his camels to kneel down outside the city by a well of water at the time of the evening when women go out to draw water.

12 And he said, O Lord God of my master Abraham, I pray You, cause me to meet with good success today, and show kindness to my master Abraham.

13 See, I stand here by the well of water, and the daughters of the men of the city are coming to draw water;

14 And let it so be that the girl to whom I say, Pray let down your jar that I may drink, and she replies, Drink, and I will give your camels drink also; let it be she whom You have selected *and* appointed *and* indicated for Your servant Isaac [to be a wife to him]; and by it I shall know that You have shown kindness *and* faithfulness to my master.

15 Before he had done speaking, lo, out came Rebekah, the daughter of Bethuel, son of Milcah and Nahor the brother of Abraham, with her water jar on her shoulder.

16 And the girl was very beautiful *and* attractive, chaste *and* modest and unmarried. And she went down to the well, filled her water jar and came up.

## New American Standard

18 to Abraham for a possession in the presence of the sons of Heth, before all who went in at the gate of his city.

19 And after this, Abraham buried Sarah his wife in the cave of the field at Machpelah facing Mamre (that is, Hebron) in the land of Canaan.

20 So the field, and the cave that is in it, were deeded over to Abraham for a burial site by the sons of Heth.

*A Bride for Isaac*

**24** NOW ABRAHAM was old, advanced in age; and the LORD had blessed Abraham in every way.

2 And Abraham said to his servant, the oldest of his household, who had charge of all that he owned, "Please place your hand under my thigh,

3 and I will make you swear by the LORD, the God of heaven and the God of earth, that you shall not take a wife for my son from the daughters of the Canaanites, among whom I live,

4 but you shall go to my country and to my relatives, and take a wife for my son Isaac."

5 And the servant said to him, "Suppose the woman will not be willing to follow me to this land; should I take your son back to the land from where you came?"

6 Then Abraham said to him, "Beware lest you take my son back there!

7 "The LORD, the God of heaven, who took me from my father's house and from the land of my birth, and who spoke to me, and who swore to me, saying, 'To your descendants I will give this land,' He will send His angel before you, and you will take a wife for my son from there.

8 "But if the woman is not willing to follow you, then you will be free from this my oath; only do not take my son back there."

9 So the servant placed his hand under the thigh of Abraham his master, and swore to him concerning this matter.

10 ¶ Then the servant took ten camels from the camels of his master, and set out with a variety of good things of his master's in his hand; and he arose, and went to Mesopotamia, to the city of Nahor.

11 And he made the camels kneel down outside the city by the well of water at evening time, the time when women go out to draw water.

12 And he said, "O LORD, the God of my master Abraham, please grant me success today, and show lovingkindness to my master Abraham.

13 "Behold, I am standing by the spring, and the daughters of the men of the city are coming out to draw water;

14 now may it be that the girl to whom I say, 'Please let down your jar so that I may drink,' and who answers, 'Drink, and I will water your camels also';— *may* she *be the one* whom Thou hast appointed for Thy servant Isaac; and by this I shall know that Thou hast shown lovingkindness to my master."

*Rebekah Is Chosen*

15 And it came about before he had finished speaking, that behold, Rebekah who was born to Bethuel the son of Milcah, the wife of Abraham's brother Nahor, came out with her jar on her shoulder.

16 And the girl was very beautiful, a virgin, and no man had had relations with her; and she went down to the spring and filled her jar, and came up.

## New International

of all the Hittites who had come to the gate of the city. 19 Afterward
Abraham buried his wife Sarah in the cave in the field of Machpelah near Mamre (which is at Hebron) in the land of Canaan. 20 So
the field and the cave in it were deeded to Abraham by the Hittites
as a burial site.

*Isaac and Rebekah*

**24** ABRAHAM WAS now old and well advanced in years,
and the LORD had blessed him in every way. 2 He said to
the chief[d] servant in his household, the one in charge of all that
he had, "Put your hand under my thigh. 3 I want you to swear by
the LORD, the God of heaven and the God of earth, that you will
not get a wife for my son from the daughters of the Canaanites,
among whom I am living, 4 but will go to my country and my own
relatives and get a wife for my son Isaac."
5 The servant asked him, "What if the woman is unwilling to
come back with me to this land? Shall I then take your son back
to the country you came from?"
6 "Make sure that you do not take my son back there," Abraham
said. 7 "The LORD, the God of heaven, who brought me out of my
father's household and my native land and who spoke to me and
promised me on oath, saying, 'To your offspring[e] I will give this
land'—he will send his angel before you so that you can get a wife
for my son from there. 8 If the woman is unwilling to come back
with you, then you will be released from this oath of mine. Only
do not take my son back there." 9 So the servant put his hand under
the thigh of his master Abraham and swore an oath to him concerning this matter.
10 Then the servant took ten of his master's camels and left,
taking with him all kinds of good things from his master. He set
out for Aram Naharaim[f] and made his way to the town of Nahor.
11 He had the camels kneel down near the well outside the town;
it was toward evening, the time the women go out to draw water.
12 Then he prayed, "O LORD, God of my master Abraham, give
me success today, and show kindness to my master Abraham.
13 See, I am standing beside this spring, and the daughters of the
townspeople are coming out to draw water. 14 May it be that when
I say to a girl, 'Please let down your jar that I may have a drink,'
and she says, 'Drink, and I'll water your camels too'—let her be
the one you have chosen for your servant Isaac. By this I will know
that you have shown kindness to my master."
15 Before he had finished praying, Rebekah came out with her
jar on her shoulder. She was the daughter of Bethuel son of Milcah, who was the wife of Abraham's brother Nahor. 16 The girl was
very beautiful, a virgin; no man had ever lain with her. She went
down to the spring, filled her jar and came up again.

NIV [d] 2 Or *oldest* [e] 7 Or *seed* [f] 10 That is, Northwest Mesopotamia

## King James

17 And the servant ran to meet her, and said, Let me, I pray thee,
drink a little water of thy pitcher.
18 And she said, Drink, my lord: and she hasted, and let down
her pitcher upon her hand, and gave him drink.
19 And when she had done giving him drink, she said, I will
draw *water* for thy camels also, until they have done drinking.
20 And she hasted, and emptied her pitcher into the trough, and
ran again unto the well to draw *water*, and drew for all his camels.
21 And the man wondering at her held his peace, to wit whether
the LORD had made his journey prosperous or not.
22 And it came to pass, as the camels had done drinking, that
the man took a golden earring of half a shekel weight, and two
bracelets for her hands of ten *shekels* weight of gold;
23 And said, Whose daughter *art* thou? tell me, I pray thee: is
there room *in* thy father's house for us to lodge in?
24 And she said unto him, I *am* the daughter of Bethuel the son
of Milcah, which she bare unto Nahor.
25 She said moreover unto him, We have both straw and provender enough, and room to lodge in.
26 And the man bowed down his head, and worshipped the
LORD.
27 And he said, Blessed *be* the LORD God of my master Abraham,
who hath not left destitute my master of his mercy and his truth:
I *being* in the way, the LORD led me to the house of my master's
brethren.
28 And the damsel ran, and told *them of* her mother's house these
things.
29 ¶ And Rebekah had a brother, and his name *was* Laban: and
Laban ran out unto the man, unto the well.
30 And it came to pass, when he saw the earring and bracelets
upon his sister's hands, and when he heard the words of Rebekah
his sister, saying, Thus spake the man unto me; that he came unto
the man; and, behold, he stood by the camels at the well.
31 And he said, Come in, thou blessed of the LORD; wherefore
standest thou without? for I have prepared the house, and room
for the camels.
32 ¶ And the man came into the house: and he ungirded his
camels, and gave straw and provender for the camels, and water
to wash his feet, and the men's feet that *were* with him.
33 And there was set *meat* before him to eat: but he said, I will
not eat, until I have told mine errand. And he said, Speak on.
34 And he said, I *am* Abraham's servant.
35 And the LORD hath blessed my master greatly; and he is
become great: and he hath given him flocks, and herds, and silver,
and gold, and menservants, and maidservants, and camels, and
asses.
36 And Sarah my master's wife bare a son to my master when
she was old: and unto him hath he given all that he hath.
37 And my master made me swear, saying, Thou shalt not take
a wife to my son of the daughters of the Canaanites, in whose land
I dwell:
38 But thou shalt go unto my father's house, and to my kindred,
and take a wife unto my son.
39 And I said unto my master, Peradventure the woman will not
follow me.
40 And he said unto me, The LORD, before whom I walk, will
send his angel with thee, and prosper thy way; and thou shalt take
a wife for my son of my kindred, and of my father's house:
41 Then shalt thou be clear from *this* my oath, when thou comest
to my kindred; and if they give not thee *one*, thou shalt be clear
from my oath.
42 And I came this day unto the well, and said, O LORD God of
my master Abraham, if now thou do prosper my way which I go:

## Amplified

17 And the servant ran to meet her, and said, Pray, let me drink
a little water from your water jar.
18 And she said, Drink, my lord; and she quickly let down her
jar on her hand, and gave him a drink.
19 When she had given him a drink, she said, I will draw water
for your camels also, until they finish drinking.
20 So she quickly emptied her jar into the trough and ran again
to the well, and drew water for all his camels.
21 The man stood gazing at her in silence, waiting to know if the
Lord had made his trip prosperous.
22 And when the camels had done drinking, the man took a gold
ear *or* nose ring of half a shekel weight, and for her hands two
bracelets of ten shekels weight of gold;
23 And said, Whose daughter are you? Pray tell me: Is there
room in your father's house for us to lodge there?
24 And she said to him, I am the daughter of Bethuel the son of
Milcah and Nahor.
25 She said also to him, We have both straw and provender
(fodder) enough, and room in which to lodge.
26 The man bowed down his head, and worshiped the Lord,
27 And said, Blessed be the Lord, the God of my master Abraham, Who has not left my master bereft *and* destitute of His loving-
kindness and steadfastness. I being in the way [of obedience and
faith] the Lord led me to the house of my master's kinsmen.
28 The girl related to her mother's household what had happened.
29 Now Rebekah had a brother whose name was Laban; and
Laban ran out to the man at the well.
30 For when he saw the ear *or* nose ring, and the bracelets on his
sister's arms, and when he heard Rebekah his sister saying, The
man said this to me, he went to the man, and found him standing
by the camels at the well.
31 He cried, Come in, you blessed of the Lord! Why do you stand
outside? For I have made the house ready *and* have prepared a
place for the camels.
32 So the man came into the house; and [Laban] ungirded his
camels, and gave straw and provender for the camels, and water
to bathe his feet and the feet of the men who were with him.
33 A meal was set before him, but he said, [a]I will not eat until
I have told my errand. And [Laban] said, Speak on.
34 And he said, I am Abraham's servant.
35 And the Lord has blessed my master mightily, and he has
become great; and He has given him flocks, herds, silver, gold,
menservants, maidservants, camels, and asses.
36 And Sarah my master's wife bore a son to my master when
she was old, and to him he has given all that he has.
37 And my master made me swear, saying, You must not take
a wife for my son from the daughters of the Canaanites in whose
land I dwell;
38 But you shall go to my father's house and to my family, and
take a wife for my son.
39 And I said to my master, But suppose the woman will not
follow me.
40 And he said to me, The Lord, in Whose presence I walk
(habitually), will send His Angel with you and prosper your way;
and you shall take a wife for my son from my kindred and from
my father's house.
41 Then you shall be clear from my oath; when you come to my
kindred, and if they do not give her to you, you shall be free *and*
innocent of my oath.
42 I came today to the well, and said, O Lord God of my master
Abraham, if You are now causing me to go on my way prosperously,

**AMP** [a] The characteristics of a model servant of God are pictured here: (1) He is dependable and trustworthy, v. 2. (2) He is praying, v. 12. (3) He is so in earnest that he refuses to eat before attending to his Master's business. (4) He never speaks his own name, but is always speaking about his Master. (5) He gives God all the glory, v. 48.

## New American Standard

17 Then the servant ran to meet her, and said, "Please let me drink a little water from your jar."

18 And she said, "Drink, my lord"; and she quickly lowered her jar to her hand, and gave him a drink.

19 Now when she had finished giving him a drink, she said, "I will draw also for your camels until they have finished drinking."

20 So she quickly emptied her jar into the trough, and ran back to the well to draw, and she drew for all his camels.

21 Meanwhile, the man was gazing at her in silence, to know whether the LORD had made his journey successful or not.

22 Then it came about, when the camels had finished drinking, that the man took a gold ring weighing a half-shekel and two bracelets for her wrists weighing ten shekels in gold,

23 and said, "Whose daughter are you? Please tell me, is there room for us to lodge in your father's house?"

24 And she said to him, "I am the daughter of Bethuel, the son of Milcah, whom she bore to Nahor."

25 Again she said to him, "We have plenty of both straw and feed, and room to lodge in."

26 Then the man bowed low and worshiped the LORD.

27 And he said, "Blessed be the LORD, the God of my master Abraham, who has not forsaken His lovingkindness and His truth toward my master; as for me, the LORD has guided me in the way to the house of my master's brothers."

28 ¶ Then the girl ran and told her mother's household about these things.

29 Now Rebekah had a brother whose name was Laban; and Laban ran outside to the man at the spring.

30 And it came about that when he saw the ring, and the bracelets on his sister's wrists, and when he heard the words of Rebekah his sister, saying, "This is what the man said to me," he went to the man; and behold, he was standing by the camels at the spring.

31 And he said, "Come in, blessed of the LORD! Why do you stand outside since I have prepared the house, and a place for the camels?"

32 So the man entered the house. Then Laban unloaded the camels, and he gave straw and feed to the camels, and water to wash his feet and the feet of the men who were with him.

33 But when *food* was set before him to eat, he said, "I will not eat until I have told my business." And he said, "Speak on."

34 So he said, "I am Abraham's servant.

35 "And the LORD has greatly blessed my master, so that he has become rich; and He has given him flocks and herds, and silver and gold, and servants and maids, and camels and donkeys.

36 "Now Sarah my master's wife bore a son to my master in her old age; and he has given him all that he has.

37 "And my master made me swear, saying, 'You shall not take a wife for my son from the daughters of the Canaanites, in whose land I live;

38 but you shall go to my father's house, and to my relatives, and take a wife for my son.'

39 "And I said to my master, 'Suppose the woman does not follow me.'

40 "And he said to me, 'The LORD, before whom I have walked, will send His angel with you to make your journey successful, and you will take a wife for my son from my relatives, and from my father's house;

41 then you will be free from my oath, when you come to my relatives; and if they do not give her to you, you will be free from my oath.'

42 "So I came today to the spring, and said, 'O LORD, the God of my master Abraham, if now Thou wilt make my journey on which I go successful;

## New International

17 The servant hurried to meet her and said, "Please give me a
little water from your jar."
18 "Drink, my lord," she said, and quickly lowered the jar to her
hands and gave him a drink.
19 After she had given him a drink, she said, "I'll draw water for
your camels too, until they have finished drinking." 20 So she
quickly emptied her jar into the trough, ran back to the well to
draw more water, and drew enough for all his camels. 21 Without
saying a word, the man watched her closely to learn whether or
not the LORD had made his journey successful.
22 When the camels had finished drinking, the man took out a
gold nose ring weighing a beka[b] and two gold bracelets weighing
ten shekels.[c] 23 Then he asked, "Whose daughter are you? Please
tell me, is there room in your father's house for us to spend the
night?"
24 She answered him, "I am the daughter of Bethuel, the son
that Milcah bore to Nahor." 25 And she added, "We have plenty
of straw and fodder, as well as room for you to spend the night."
26 Then the man bowed down and worshiped the LORD, 27 saying, "Praise be to the LORD, the God of my master Abraham, who
has not abandoned his kindness and faithfulness to my master. As
for me, the LORD has led me on the journey to the house of my
master's relatives."
28 The girl ran and told her mother's household about these
things. 29 Now Rebekah had a brother named Laban, and he hurried out to the man at the spring. 30 As soon as he had seen the nose
ring, and the bracelets on his sister's arms, and had heard Rebekah
tell what the man said to her, he went out to the man and found
him standing by the camels near the spring. 31 "Come, you who are
blessed by the LORD," he said. "Why are you standing out here?
I have prepared the house and a place for the camels."
32 So the man went to the house, and the camels were unloaded.
Straw and fodder were brought for the camels, and water for him
and his men to wash their feet. 33 Then food was set before him,
but he said, "I will not eat until I have told you what I have to say."
"Then tell us," ⌊Laban⌋ said.
34 So he said, "I am Abraham's servant. 35 The LORD has blessed
my master abundantly, and he has become wealthy. He has given
him sheep and cattle, silver and gold, menservants and maidservants, and camels and donkeys. 36 My master's wife Sarah has
borne him a son in her[d] old age, and he has given him everything
he owns. 37 And my master made me swear an oath, and said, 'You
must not get a wife for my son from the daughters of the Canaanites, in whose land I live, 38 but go to my father's family and to my
own clan, and get a wife for my son.'
39 "Then I asked my master, 'What if the woman will not come
back with me?'
40 "He replied, 'The LORD, before whom I have walked, will
send his angel with you and make your journey a success, so that
you can get a wife for my son from my own clan and from my
father's family. 41 Then, when you go to my clan, you will be
released from my oath even if they refuse to give her to you—you
will be released from my oath.'
42 "When I came to the spring today, I said, 'O LORD, God of my
master Abraham, if you will, please grant success to the journey
on which I have come. 43 See, I am standing beside this spring; if

**NIV** [b] 22 That is, about 1/5 ounce (about 5.5 grams) [c] 22 That is, about 4 ounces (about 110 grams) [d] 36 Or *his*

## King James

43Behold, I stand by the well of water; and it shall come to pass,
that when the virgin cometh forth to draw *water*, and I say to her,
Give me, I pray thee, a little water of thy pitcher to drink;
44And she say to me, Both drink thou, and I will also draw for
thy camels: *let* the same *be* the woman whom the LORD hath appointed out for my master's son.
45And before I had done speaking in mine heart, behold, Rebekah came forth with her pitcher on her shoulder; and she went
down unto the well, and drew *water*: and I said unto her, Let me
drink, I pray thee.
46And she made haste, and let down her pitcher from her
*shoulder*, and said, Drink, and I will give thy camels drink also: so
I drank, and she made the camels drink also.
47And I asked her, and said, Whose daughter *art* thou? And she
said, The daughter of Bethuel, Nahor's son, whom Milcah bare
unto him: and I put the earring upon her face, and the bracelets
upon her hands.
48And I bowed down my head, and worshipped the LORD, and
blessed the LORD God of my master Abraham, which had led me
in the right way to take my master's brother's daughter unto his
son.
49And now if ye will deal kindly and truly with my master, tell
me: and if not, tell me; that I may turn to the right hand, or to the
left.
50Then Laban and Bethuel answered and said, The thing proceedeth from the LORD: we cannot speak unto thee bad or good.
51Behold, Rebekah *is* before thee, take *her*, and go, and let her
be thy master's son's wife, as the LORD hath spoken.
52And it came to pass, that, when Abraham's servant heard
their words, he worshipped the LORD, *bowing himself* to the earth.
53And the servant brought forth jewels of silver, and jewels of
gold, and raiment, and gave *them* to Rebekah: he gave also to her
brother and to her mother precious things.
54And they did eat and drink, he and the men that *were* with
him, and tarried all night; and they rose up in the morning, and
he said, Send me away unto my master.
55And her brother and her mother said, Let the damsel abide
with us *a few* days, at the least ten; after that she shall go.
56And he said unto them, Hinder me not, seeing the LORD hath
prospered my way; send me away that I may go to my master.
57And they said, We will call the damsel, and inquire at her
mouth.
58And they called Rebekah, and said unto her, Wilt thou go
with this man? And she said, I will go.
59And they sent away Rebekah their sister, and her nurse, and
Abraham's servant, and his men.
60And they blessed Rebekah, and said unto her, Thou *art* our
sister, be thou *the mother* of thousands of millions, and let thy seed
possess the gate of those which hate them.
61¶ And Rebekah arose, and her damsels, and they rode upon
the camels, and followed the man: and the servant took Rebekah,
and went his way.
62And Isaac came from the way of the well Lahai-roi; for he
dwelt in the south country.
63And Isaac went out to meditate in the field at the eventide:
and he lifted up his eyes, and saw, and, behold, the camels *were*
coming.
64And Rebekah lifted up her eyes, and when she saw Isaac, she
lighted off the camel.
65For she *had* said unto the servant, What man *is* this that
walketh in the field to meet us? And the servant *had* said, It *is* my
master: therefore she took a veil, and covered herself.
66And the servant told Isaac all things that he had done.
67And Isaac brought her into his mother Sarah's tent, and took
Rebekah, and she became his wife; and he loved her: and Isaac was
comforted after his mother's *death*.

## Amplified

43See, I am standing by the well of water. Now let it be that
when the maiden comes out to draw water, and I say to her, Pray,
give me a little water from your [water] jar to drink;
44And if she says to me, You drink, and I will draw water for
your camels also, let that same woman be the one whom the Lord
has selected *and* indicated for my master's son.
45And before I had done praying in my heart, behold, Rebekah
came out with her [water] jar on her shoulder; and she went down
to the well and drew water. And I said to her, Pray, let me have
a drink.
46And she quickly let down her [water] jar from her shoulder,
and said, Drink, and I will water your camels also. So I drank, and
she gave the camels drink also.
47I asked her, Whose daughter are you? She said, The daughter
of Bethuel, Nahor's son, whom Milcah bore to him. And I put the
ear *or* nose ring on her face, and the bracelets upon her arms.
48And I bowed down my head, and worshiped the Lord, and
blessed the Lord, God of my master Abraham, Who had led me
in the right way to take my master's brother's daughter to his son.
49And now if you will deal kindly and truly with my master
(showing faithfulness to him), tell me; and if not, tell me, that I
may turn to the right or to the left.
50Then Laban and Bethuel answered, The thing comes forth
from the Lord; we cannot speak bad or good to you.
51Rebekah is before you, take her and go, and let her be the wife
of your master's son, as the Lord has said.
52And when Abraham's servant heard their words, he bowed
himself to the ground before the Lord.
53And the servant brought out jewels of silver, jewels of gold,
and garments, and gave them to Rebekah; he also gave precious
things to her brother and her mother.
54Then they ate and drank, he and the men who were with him,
and stayed there all night. And in the morning they arose and he
said, Send me away to my master.
55But [Rebekah's] brother and mother said, Let *her* stay with us
a few days, at least ten; then she shall go.
56But [the servant] said to them, Do not hinder *and* delay me,
seeing the Lord has caused me to go prosperously on my way;
send me away that I may go to my master.
57And they said, We will call the girl and ask her desire.
58So they called Rebekah, and said to her, Will you go with this
man? And she said, I will go.
59So they sent away Rebekah their sister and her nurse [Debo-
rah], and Abraham's servant and his men.
60And they blessed Rebekah, and said to her, You are our sister;
become the mother of thousands of ten thousands, and let your
posterity possess the gate of their enemies.
61And Rebekah and her maids arose, and followed the man
upon the camels. Thus the servant took Rebekah and went on his
way.
62Now Isaac had returned from going to the well Beer-lahai-roi
(that is, A well to the Living One Who sees me), for he [now] dwelt
in the South country—the Negeb.
63And Isaac went out to meditate *and* bow down [in prayer] in
the open country in the evening; and he looked up and saw that
lo, the camels were coming.
64And Rebekah looked up, and when she saw Isaac, she dismounted from off the camel.
65For she [had] said to the servant, Who is this man walking
across the field to meet us? And the servant [had] said, It is my
master; so she took a veil and concealed herself with it.
66And the servant told Isaac everything that he had done.
67And Isaac brought *her* into his mother Sarah's tent, and took
Rebekah and she became his wife; and he loved her. Thus Isaac
was comforted after his mother's death.

## New American Standard

43behold, I am standing by the spring, and may it be that the
maiden who comes out to draw, and to whom I say, "Please let
me drink a little water from your jar";
44and she will say to me, "You drink, and I will draw for your
camels also"; let her be the woman whom the LORD has appointed
for my master's son.'
45"Before I had finished speaking in my heart, behold, Rebekah
came out with her jar on her shoulder, and went down to the
spring and drew; and I said to her, 'Please let me drink.'
46"And she quickly lowered her jar from her *shoulder*, and said,
'Drink, and I will water your camels also'; so I drank, and she
watered the camels also.
47"Then I asked her, and said, 'Whose daughter are you?' And
she said, 'The daughter of Bethuel, Nahor's son, whom Milcah
bore to him'; and I put the ring on her nose, and the bracelets on
her wrists.
48"And I bowed low and worshiped the LORD, and blessed the
LORD, the God of my master Abraham, who had guided me in the
right way to take the daughter of my master's kinsman for his son.
49"So now if you are going to [a]deal kindly and truly with my
master, tell me; and if not, let me know, that I may turn to the right
hand or the left."
50¶ Then Laban and Bethuel answered and said, "The matter
comes from the LORD; *so* we cannot speak to you bad or good.
51"Behold, Rebekah is before you, take *her* and go, and let her
be the wife of your master's son, as the LORD has spoken."
52And it came about when Abraham's servant heard their
words, that he bowed himself to the ground before the LORD.
53And the servant brought out articles of silver and articles of
gold, and garments, and gave them to Rebekah; he also gave
precious things to her brother and to her mother.
54Then he and the men who were with him ate and drank and
spent the night. When they arose in the morning, he said, "Send
me away to my master."
55But her brother and her mother said, "Let the girl stay with
us *a few* days, say ten; afterward she may go."
56And he said to them, "Do not delay me, since the LORD has
prospered my way. Send me away that I may go to my master."
57And they said, "We will call the girl and consult her wishes."
58Then they called Rebekah and said to her, "Will you go with
this man?" And she said, "I will go."
59Thus they sent away their sister Rebekah and her nurse with
Abraham's servant and his men.
60And they blessed Rebekah and said to her,

"May you, our sister,
Become thousands of ten thousands,
And may your descendants possess
The gate of those who hate them."

*Isaac Marries Rebekah*

61¶ Then Rebekah arose with her maids, and they mounted the
camels and followed the man. So the servant took Rebekah and
departed.
62Now Isaac had come from going to Beer-lahai-roi; for he was
living in the Negev.
63And Isaac went out to meditate in the field toward evening;
and he lifted up his eyes and looked, and behold, camels were
coming.
64And Rebekah lifted up her eyes, and when she saw Isaac she
dismounted from the camel.
65And she said to the servant, "Who is that man walking in the
field to meet us?" And the servant said, "He is my master." Then
she took her veil and covered herself.
66And the servant told Isaac all the things that he had done.
67Then Isaac brought her into his mother Sarah's tent, and he
took Rebekah, and she became his wife; and he loved her; thus
Isaac was comforted after his mother's death.

NAS [a] Lit., *show lovingkindness and truth*

## New International

a maiden comes out to draw water and I say to her, "Please let me
drink a little water from your jar," 44and if she says to me, "Drink,
and I'll draw water for your camels too," let her be the one the
LORD has chosen for my master's son.'
45"Before I finished praying in my heart, Rebekah came out,
with her jar on her shoulder. She went down to the spring and
drew water, and I said to her, 'Please give me a drink.'
46"She quickly lowered her jar from her shoulder and said,
'Drink, and I'll water your camels too.' So I drank, and she watered
the camels also.
47"I asked her, 'Whose daughter are you?'
"She said, 'The daughter of Bethuel son of Nahor, whom Milcah bore to him.'
"Then I put the ring in her nose and the bracelets on her arms,
48and I bowed down and worshiped the LORD. I praised the LORD,
the God of my master Abraham, who had led me on the right road
to get the granddaughter of my master's brother for his son. 49Now
if you will show kindness and faithfulness to my master, tell me;
and if not, tell me, so I may know which way to turn."
50Laban and Bethuel answered, "This is from the LORD; we can
say nothing to you one way or the other. 51Here is Rebekah; take
her and go, and let her become the wife of your master's son, as
the LORD has directed."
52When Abraham's servant heard what they said, he bowed
down to the ground before the LORD. 53Then the servant brought
out gold and silver jewelry and articles of clothing and gave them
to Rebekah; he also gave costly gifts to her brother and to her
mother. 54Then he and the men who were with him ate and drank
and spent the night there.
When they got up the next morning, he said, "Send me on my
way to my master."
55But her brother and her mother replied, "Let the girl remain
with us ten days or so; then you[b] may go."
56But he said to them, "Do not detain me, now that the LORD
has granted success to my journey. Send me on my way so I may
go to my master."
57Then they said, "Let's call the girl and ask her about it." 58So
they called Rebekah and asked her, "Will you go with this man?"
"I will go," she said.
59So they sent their sister Rebekah on her way, along with her
nurse and Abraham's servant and his men. 60And they blessed
Rebekah and said to her,

"Our sister, may you increase
to thousands upon thousands;
may your offspring possess
the gates of their enemies."

61Then Rebekah and her maids got ready and mounted their
camels and went back with the man. So the servant took Rebekah
and left.
62Now Isaac had come from Beer Lahai Roi, for he was living
in the Negev. 63He went out to the field one evening to meditate,[c]
and as he looked up, he saw camels approaching. 64Rebekah also
looked up and saw Isaac. She got down from her camel 65and
asked the servant, "Who is that man in the field coming to meet
us?"
"He is my master," the servant answered. So she took her veil
and covered herself.
66Then the servant told Isaac all he had done. 67Isaac brought
her into the tent of his mother Sarah, and he married Rebekah. So
she became his wife, and he loved her; and Isaac was comforted
after his mother's death.

NIV [b]55 Or *she* [c]63 The meaning of the Hebrew for this word is uncertain.

## King James

**25** THEN AGAIN Abraham took a wife, and her name *was* Keturah.

2And she bare him Zimran, and Jokshan, and Medan, and Midian, and Ishbak, and Shuah.

3And Jokshan begat Sheba, and Dedan. And the sons of Dedan were Asshurim, and Letushim, and Leummim.

4And the sons of Midian; Ephah, and Epher, and Hanoch, and Abidah, and Eldaah. All these *were* the children of Keturah.

5¶ And Abraham gave all that he had unto Isaac.

6But unto the sons of the concubines, which Abraham had, Abraham gave gifts, and sent them away from Isaac his son, while he yet lived, eastward, unto the east country.

7And these *are* the days of the years of Abraham's life which he lived, an hundred threescore and fifteen years.

8Then Abraham gave up the ghost, and died in a good old age, an old man, and full *of years;* and was gathered to his people.

9And his sons Isaac and Ishmael buried him in the cave of Machpelah, in the field of Ephron the son of Zohar the Hittite, which *is* before Mamre;

10The field which Abraham purchased of the sons of Heth: there was Abraham buried, and Sarah his wife.

11¶ And it came to pass after the death of Abraham, that God blessed his son Isaac; and Isaac dwelt by the well Lahai-roi.

12¶ Now these *are* the generations of Ishmael, Abraham's son, whom Hagar the Egyptian, Sarah's handmaid, bare unto Abraham:

13And these *are* the names of the sons of Ishmael, by their names, according to their generations: the firstborn of Ishmael, Nebajoth; and Kedar, and Adbeel, and Mibsam,

14And Mishma, and Dumah, and Massa,

15Hadar, and Tema, Jetur, Naphish, and Kedemah:

16These *are* the sons of Ishmael, and these *are* their names, by their towns, and by their castles; twelve princes according to their nations.

17And these *are* the years of the life of Ishmael, an hundred and thirty and seven years: and he gave up the ghost and died; and was gathered unto his people.

18And they dwelt from Havilah unto Shur, that *is* before Egypt, as thou goest toward Assyria: *and* he died in the presence of all his brethren.

19¶ And these *are* the generations of Isaac, Abraham's son: Abraham begat Isaac:

20And Isaac was forty years old when he took Rebekah to wife, the daughter of Bethuel the Syrian of Padan-aram, the sister to Laban the Syrian.

21And Isaac entreated the LORD for his wife, because she *was* barren: and the LORD was entreated of him, and Rebekah his wife conceived.

22And the children struggled together within her; and she said, If *it be* so, why *am* I thus? And she went to inquire of the LORD.

23And the LORD said unto her, Two nations *are* in thy womb, and two manner of people shall be separated from thy bowels; and *the one* people shall be stronger than *the other* people; and the elder shall serve the younger.

24¶ And when her days to be delivered were fulfilled, behold, *there were* twins in her womb.

25And the first came out red, all over like an hairy garment; and they called his name Esau.

26And after that came his brother out, and his hand took hold on Esau's heel; and his name was called Jacob: and Isaac *was* threescore years old when she bare them.

## Amplified

**25** ABRAHAM TOOK another wife, and her name was Keturah.

2And she bore him Zimran, Jokshan, Medan, Midian, Ishbak, and Shuah.

3Jokshan was the father of Sheba and Dedan. The sons of Dedan were Asshurim, Letushim, and Leummim.

4The sons of Midian were Ephah, Epher, Hanoch, Abida, and Eldaah. All these were the children of Keturah.

5And Abraham gave all that he had to Isaac.

6But to the sons of his concubines [Hagar and Keturah] Abraham gave gifts, and while he was still living he sent them to the East country, away from Isaac his son [of promise].

7The days of Abraham's life were 175 years.

8Then Abraham's spirit was released, and he died at a good (ample, full) old age, an old man, satisfied *and* satiated, and [a]was gathered to his people. [Gen. 15:15.]

9And his sons [b]Isaac and Ishmael buried him in the cave of Machpelah, in the field of Ephron the son of Zohar the Hittite, which is east of Mamre,

10The field which Abraham purchased of the Hittites. There Abraham was buried with Sarah his wife.

11After the death of Abraham, God blessed his son Isaac; and Isaac dwelt at Beer-lahai-roi (that is, A well to the Living One Who sees me).

12Now these are the descendants of Ishmael, Abraham's son, whom Hagar the Eqyptian, Sarah's handmaid, bore to Abraham.

13These are the names of the sons of Ishmael, named in the order of their births: Nebaioth, the firstborn of Ishmael; and Kedar, Adbeel, Mibsam,

14Mishma, Dumah, Massa,

15Hadad, Tema, Jetur, Naphish, and Kedemah.

16These are the sons of Ishmael, and these are their names, by their villages and by their encampments [sheepfolds]; twelve princes according to their tribes. [Foretold in 17:20.]

17And Ishmael lived 137 years; then his spirit left him, and he died and was gathered to his kindred.

18And [Ishmael's sons] dwelt from Havilah to Shur, which is before Egypt in the direction of Assyria. [Ishmael] dwelt close [to the lands] of all his brethren.

19And these are the histories of the descendants of Isaac, Abraham's son: Abraham was the father of Isaac.

20Isaac was 40 years old when he married Rebekah, the daughter of Bethuel the Aramean of Padan-aram, the sister of Laban the Aramean.

21And Isaac prayed much to the Lord for his wife, because she was unable to bear children, and the Lord granted his prayer, and Rebekah his wife became pregnant.

22[Two] children struggled together within her; and she said, If it be so [that the Lord has heard our prayer], Why am I like this? And she went to inquire of the Lord.

23The Lord said to her, [The founders of] two nations are in your womb, and the separation of two peoples has begun in your body; the one people shall be stronger than the other, and the elder shall serve the younger.

24When her days to be delivered were fulfilled, behold, there were twins in her womb.

25The first came out red all over like a hairy garment; and they named him Esau (hairy).

26Afterward his brother came forth, and his hand grasped Esau's heel; so he was named Jacob (supplanter). Isaac was 60 years old when she gave birth to them.

**AMP** [a] This often repeated expression forms a remarkable testimony to the Old Testament belief in a life beyond the grave and to our recognition and fellowship with our loved ones there. [b] Isaac was 75 and Ishmael nearly 90 years of age when their father died. Jacob and Esau were 15, and may have been present.

## New American Standard

*Abraham's Death*

**25** NOW ABRAHAM took another wife, whose name was Keturah.

2 And she bore to him Zimran and Jokshan and Medan and Midian and Ishbak and Shuah.

3 And Jokshan became the father of Sheba and Dedan. And the sons of Dedan were Asshurim and Letushim and Leummim.

4 And the sons of Midian *were* Ephah and Epher and Hanoch and Abida and Eldaah. All these *were* the sons of Keturah.

5 Now Abraham gave all that he had to Isaac;

6 but to the sons of his concubines, Abraham gave gifts while he was still living, and sent them away from his son Isaac eastward, to the land of the east.

7 And these are all the years of Abraham's life that he lived, one hundred and seventy-five years.

8 And Abraham breathed his last and died in a ripe old age, an old man and satisfied *with life;* and he was gathered to his people.

9 Then his sons Isaac and Ishmael buried him in the cave of Machpelah, in the field of Ephron the son of Zohar the Hittite, facing Mamre,

10 the field which Abraham purchased from the sons of Heth; there Abraham was buried with Sarah his wife.

11 And it came about after the death of Abraham, that God blessed his son Isaac; and Isaac lived by Beer-lahai-roi.

*Descendants of Ishmael*

**12**¶ Now these are *the records of* the generations of Ishmael, Abraham's son, whom Hagar the Egyptian, Sarah's maid, bore to Abraham;

13 and these are the names of the sons of Ishmael, by their names, in the order of their birth: Nebaioth, the first-born of Ishmael, and Kedar and Adbeel and Mibsam

14 and Mishma and Dumah and Massa,

15 Hadad and Tema, Jetur, Naphish and Kedemah.

16 These are the sons of Ishmael and these are their names, by their villages, and by their camps; twelve princes according to their tribes.

17 And these are the years of the life of Ishmael, one hundred and thirty-seven years; and he breathed his last and died, and was gathered to his people.

18 And they settled from Havilah to Shur which is east of Egypt as one goes toward Assyria; he settled in defiance of all his relatives.

*Isaac's Sons*

**19**¶ Now these are *the records of* the generations of Isaac, Abraham's son: Abraham became the father of Isaac;

20 and Isaac was forty years old when he took Rebekah, the daughter of Bethuel the Aramean of Paddan-aram, the sister of Laban the Aramean, to be his wife.

21 And Isaac prayed to the LORD on behalf of his wife, because she was barren; and the LORD answered him and Rebekah his wife conceived.

22 But the children struggled together within her; and she said, "If it is so, why then am I *this way?*" So she went to inquire of the LORD.

23 And the LORD said to her,

"Two nations are in your womb;
And two peoples shall be separated from your body;
And one people shall be stronger than the other;
And the older shall serve the younger."

24 When her days to be delivered were fulfilled, behold, there were twins in her womb.

25 Now the first came forth red, all over like a hairy garment; and they named him Esau.

26 And afterward his brother came forth with his hand holding on to Esau's heel, so his name was called [c]Jacob; and Isaac was sixty years old when she gave birth to them.

NAS [c] I.e., one who takes by the heel, or supplants

## New International

*The Death of Abraham*

**25** ABRAHAM TOOK[d] another wife, whose name was Keturah. 2 She bore him Zimran, Jokshan, Medan, Midian,
Ishbak and Shuah. 3 Jokshan was the father of Sheba and Dedan;
the descendants of Dedan were the Asshurites, the Letushites and
the Leummites. 4 The sons of Midian were Ephah, Epher, Hanoch,
Abida and Eldaah. All these were descendants of Keturah.
5 Abraham left everything he owned to Isaac. 6 But while he was
still living, he gave gifts to the sons of his concubines and sent
them away from his son Isaac to the land of the east.
7 Altogether, Abraham lived a hundred and seventy-five years.
8 Then Abraham breathed his last and died at a good old age, an
old man and full of years; and he was gathered to his people. 9 His
sons Isaac and Ishmael buried him in the cave of Machpelah near
Mamre, in the field of Ephron son of Zohar the Hittite, 10 the field
Abraham had bought from the Hittites.[e] There Abraham was
buried with his wife Sarah. 11 After Abraham's death, God blessed
his son Isaac, who then lived near Beer Lahai Roi.

*Ishmael's Sons*

12 This is the account of Abraham's son Ishmael, whom Sarah's
maidservant, Hagar the Egyptian, bore to Abraham.

13 These are the names of the sons of Ishmael, listed in the order
of their birth: Nebaioth the firstborn of Ishmael, Kedar, Adbeel,
Mibsam, 14 Mishma, Dumah, Massa, 15 Hadad, Tema, Jetur, Naphish and Kedemah. 16 These were the sons of Ishmael, and these
are the names of the twelve tribal rulers according to their settlements and camps. 17 Altogether, Ishmael lived a hundred and
thirty-seven years. He breathed his last and died, and he was
gathered to his people. 18 His descendants settled in the area from
Havilah to Shur, near the border of Egypt, as you go toward
Asshur. And they lived in hostility toward[f] all their brothers.

*Jacob and Esau*

19 This is the account of Abraham's son Isaac.

Abraham became the father of Isaac, 20 and Isaac was forty years
old when he married Rebekah daughter of Bethuel the Aramean
from Paddan Aram[g] and sister of Laban the Aramean.
21 Isaac prayed to the LORD on behalf of his wife, because she
was barren. The LORD answered his prayer, and his wife Rebekah
became pregnant. 22 The babies jostled each other within her, and
she said, "Why is this happening to me?" So she went to inquire
of the LORD.
23 The LORD said to her,

"Two nations are in your womb,
and two peoples from within you will be separated;
one people will be stronger than the other,
and the older will serve the younger."

24 When the time came for her to give birth, there were twin
boys in her womb. 25 The first to come out was red, and his whole
body was like a hairy garment; so they named him Esau.[h] 26 After
this, his brother came out, with his hand grasping Esau's heel; so
he was named Jacob.[i] Isaac was sixty years old when Rebekah
gave birth to them.

NIV [d] 1 Or *had taken* [e] 10 Or *the sons of Heth* [f] 18 Or *lived to the east of* [g] 20 That is, Northwest Mesopotamia [h] 25 *Esau* may mean *hairy;* he was also called Edom, which means *red.* [i] 26 *Jacob* means *he grasps the heel* (figuratively, *he deceives*).

## King James

27And the boys grew: and Esau was a cunning hunter, a man of the field; and Jacob *was* a plain man, dwelling in tents.

28And Isaac loved Esau, because he did eat of *his* venison: but Rebekah loved Jacob.

29¶ And Jacob sod pottage: and Esau came from the field, and he *was* faint:

30And Esau said to Jacob, Feed me, I pray thee, with that same red *pottage;* for I *am* faint: therefore was his name called Edom.

31And Jacob said, Sell me this day thy birthright.

32And Esau said, Behold, I *am* at the point to die: and what profit shall this birthright do to me?

33And Jacob said, Swear to me this day; and he sware unto him: and he sold his birthright unto Jacob.

34Then Jacob gave Esau bread and pottage of lentiles; and he did eat and drink, and rose up, and went his way: thus Esau despised *his* birthright.

**26** AND THERE was a famine in the land, beside the first famine that was in the days of Abraham. And Isaac went unto Abimelech king of the Philistines unto Gerar.

2And the LORD appeared unto him, and said, Go not down into Egypt; dwell in the land which I shall tell thee of:

3Sojourn in this land, and I will be with thee, and will bless thee; for unto thee, and unto thy seed, I will give all these countries, and I will perform the oath which I sware unto Abraham thy father;

4And I will make thy seed to multiply as the stars of heaven, and will give unto thy seed all these countries; and in thy seed shall all the nations of the earth be blessed;

5Because that Abraham obeyed my voice, and kept my charge, my commandments, my statutes, and my laws.

6¶ And Isaac dwelt in Gerar:

7And the men of the place asked *him* of his wife; and he said, She *is* my sister: for he feared to say, *She is* my wife; lest, *said he,* the men of the place should kill me for Rebekah; because she *was* fair to look upon.

8And it came to pass, when he had been there a long time, that Abimelech king of the Philistines looked out at a window, and saw, and, behold, Isaac *was* sporting with Rebekah his wife.

9And Abimelech called Isaac, and said, Behold, of a surety she *is* thy wife: and how saidst thou, She *is* my sister? And Isaac said unto him, Because I said, Lest I die for her.

10And Abimelech said, What *is* this thou hast done unto us? one of the people might lightly have lain with thy wife, and thou shouldest have brought guiltiness upon us.

11And Abimelech charged all *his* people, saying, He that toucheth this man or his wife shall surely be put to death.

12Then Isaac sowed in that land, and received in the same year an hundredfold: and the LORD blessed him.

13And the man waxed great, and went forward, and grew until he became very great:

14For he had possession of flocks, and possession of herds, and great store of servants: and the Philistines envied him.

15For all the wells which his father's servants had digged in the days of Abraham his father, the Philistines had stopped them, and filled them with earth.

16And Abimelech said unto Isaac, Go from us; for thou art much mightier than we.

17¶ And Isaac departed thence, and pitched his tent in the valley of Gerar, and dwelt there.

## Amplified

27When the boys grew up, Esau was a cunning *and* skilled hunter, a man of the outdoors; but Jacob was a plain *and* quiet man, dwelling in tents.

28And Isaac loved [and was partial to] Esau, because he ate of Esau's game; but Rebekah loved Jacob.

29Jacob was boiling pottage (lentil stew) one day, when Esau came from the field and was faint [with hunger].

30And Esau said to Jacob, I beg of you, let me have some of that red lentil stew to eat, for I am faint *and* famished! That is why his name was called Edom (red).

31Jacob answered, Then sell me today your birthright—the rights of a first-born.

32Esau said, See here, I am at the point of death; what good can this birthright do me?

33Jacob said, Swear to me today [that you are selling it to me], and he swore to *Jacob* and sold him his birthright.

34Then Jacob gave Esau bread and stew of lentils, and he ate and drank, and rose up and went his way. Thus Esau scorned his birthright as beneath his notice.

**26** AND THERE was a famine in the land, other than the former famine that was in the days of Abraham. And Isaac went to Gerar, to Abimelech king of the Philistines.

2And the Lord appeared to him, and said, Do not go down to Egypt; live in the land of which I will tell you.

3Dwell temporarily in this land, and I will be with you and will favor you with blessings; for to you and to your descendants I will give all these lands, and I will perform the oath which I swore to Abraham your father.

4And I will make your descendants to multiply as the stars of the heavens, and will give to your posterity all these lands [kingdoms]; and by your Offspring shall all the nations of the earth be blessed, *or* by Him bless themselves, [Cp. Gen. 22:18; Acts 3:25, 26; Gal. 3:16.]

5For Abraham listened to *and* obeyed My voice, and kept My charge, My commands, My statutes and My laws.

6So Isaac stayed in Gerar.

7And the men of the place asked him about his wife, and he said, She is my sister; for he was afraid to say, She is my wife, thinking, lest the men of the place should kill me for Rebekah; because she was attractive *and* was beautiful to look upon.

8When he had been there a long time, Abimelech king of the Philistines looked out of a window and saw Isaac caressing Rebekah his wife.

9And Abimelech called Isaac, and said, See here, she is certainly your wife! How did you [dare] say to me, She is my sister? And Isaac said to him, Because I thought, Lest I die on account of her.

10And Abimelech said, What is this you have done to us? One of the men might easily have lain with your wife, and you would have brought guilt *and* sin upon us.

11Then Abimelech charged all his people, He who touches this man or his wife shall surely be put to death.

12Then Isaac sowed seed in that land, and received in the same year 100 times as much as he had planted, and the Lord favored him with blessings.

13And the man became great, and gained more and more until he became very wealthy *and* distinguished;

14He owned flocks, herds, and a great supply of servants, and the Philistines envied him.

15Now all the wells which his father's servants had dug in the days of Abraham his father, the Philistines had closed and filled with earth.

16And Abimelech said to Isaac, Go away from us; for you are much mightier than we are.

17So Isaac went away from there and pitched his tent in the valley of Gerar, and dwelt there.

## New American Standard

27¶ When the boys grew up, Esau became a skillful hunter, a
man of the field; but Jacob was a peaceful man, living in tents.
28Now Isaac loved Esau, because he had a taste for game; but
Rebekah loved Jacob.
29And when Jacob had cooked stew, Esau came in from the field
and he was famished;
30and Esau said to Jacob, "Please let me have a swallow of that
red stuff there, for I am famished." Therefore his name was called
[a]Edom.
31But Jacob said, "First sell me your birthright."
32And Esau said, "Behold, I am about to die; so of what *use* then
is the birthright to me?"
33And Jacob said, "First swear to me"; so he swore to him, and
sold his birthright to Jacob.
34Then Jacob gave Esau bread and lentil stew; and he ate and
drank, and rose and went on his way. Thus Esau despised his
birthright.

*Isaac Settles in Gerar*

26 NOW THERE was a famine in the land, besides the previous famine that had occurred in the days of Abraham. So
Isaac went to Gerar, to Abimelech king of the Philistines.
2And the LORD appeared to him and said, "Do not go down
to Egypt; stay in the land of which I shall tell you.
3"Sojourn in this land and I will be with you and bless you, for
to you and to your descendants I will give all these lands, and I
will establish the oath which I swore to your father Abraham.
4"And I will multiply your descendants as the stars of heaven,
and will give your descendants all these lands; and by your descendants all the nations of the earth shall be blessed;
5because Abraham obeyed Me and kept My charge, My commandments, My statutes and My laws."
6So Isaac lived in Gerar.
7When the men of the place asked about his wife, he said, "She
is my sister," for he was afraid to say, "my wife," *thinking*, "the
men of the place might kill me on account of Rebekah, for she is
beautiful."
8And it came about, when he had been there a long time, that
Abimelech king of the Philistines looked out through a window,
and saw, and behold, Isaac was caressing his wife Rebekah.
9Then Abimelech called Isaac and said, "Behold, certainly she
is your wife! How then did you say, 'She is my sister'?" And Isaac
said to him, "Because I said, 'Lest I die on account of her.'"
10And Abimelech said, "What is this you have done to us? One
of the people might easily have lain with your wife, and you would
have brought guilt upon us."
11So Abimelech charged all the people, saying, "He who
touches this man or his wife shall surely be put to death."
12¶ Now Isaac sowed in that land, and reaped in the same year
a hundredfold. And the LORD blessed him,
13and the man became rich, and continued to grow richer until
he became very wealthy;
14for he had possessions of flocks and herds and a great household, so that the Philistines envied him.
15Now all the wells which his father's servants had dug in the
days of Abraham his father, the Philistines stopped up by filling
them with earth.
16Then Abimelech said to Isaac, "Go away from us, for you are
too powerful for us."
17And Isaac departed from there and camped in the valley of
Gerar, and settled there.

NAS [a] I.e., red

## New International

27The boys grew up, and Esau became a skillful hunter, a man
of the open country, while Jacob was a quiet man, staying among
the tents. 28Isaac, who had a taste for wild game, loved Esau, but
Rebekah loved Jacob.
29Once when Jacob was cooking some stew, Esau came in from
the open country, famished. 30He said to Jacob, "Quick, let me
have some of that red stew! I'm famished!" (That is why he was
also called Edom.[b])
31Jacob replied, "First sell me your birthright."
32"Look, I am about to die," Esau said. "What good is the
birthright to me?"
33But Jacob said, "Swear to me first." So he swore an oath to
him, selling his birthright to Jacob.
34Then Jacob gave Esau some bread and some lentil stew. He
ate and drank, and then got up and left.
So Esau despised his birthright.

*Isaac and Abimelech*

26 NOW THERE was a famine in the land—besides the earlier famine of Abraham's time—and Isaac went to Abimelech king of the Philistines in Gerar. 2The LORD appeared to Isaac
and said, "Do not go down to Egypt; live in the land where I tell
you to live. 3Stay in this land for a while, and I will be with you
and will bless you. For to you and your descendants I will give all
these lands and will confirm the oath I swore to your father Abraham. 4I will make your descendants as numerous as the stars in
the sky and will give them all these lands, and through your
offspring[c] all nations on earth will be blessed, 5because Abraham
obeyed me and kept my requirements, my commands, my decrees
and my laws." 6So Isaac stayed in Gerar.
7When the men of that place asked him about his wife, he said,
"She is my sister," because he was afraid to say, "She is my wife."
He thought, "The men of this place might kill me on account of
Rebekah, because she is beautiful."
8When Isaac had been there a long time, Abimelech king of the
Philistines looked down from a window and saw Isaac caressing
his wife Rebekah. 9So Abimelech summoned Isaac and said, "She
is really your wife! Why did you say, 'She is my sister'?"
Isaac answered him, "Because I thought I might lose my life on
account of her."
10Then Abimelech said, "What is this you have done to us? One
of the men might well have slept with your wife, and you would
have brought guilt upon us."
11So Abimelech gave orders to all the people: "Anyone who
molests this man or his wife shall surely be put to death."
12Isaac planted crops in that land and the same year reaped a
hundredfold, because the LORD blessed him. 13The man became
rich, and his wealth continued to grow until he became very
wealthy. 14He had so many flocks and herds and servants that the
Philistines envied him. 15So all the wells that his father's servants
had dug in the time of his father Abraham, the Philistines stopped
up, filling them with earth.
16Then Abimelech said to Isaac, "Move away from us; you have
become too powerful for us."
17So Isaac moved away from there and encamped in the Valley
of Gerar and settled there. 18Isaac reopened the wells that had

NIV [b] 30 *Edom* means *red.* [c] 4 Or *seed*

## King James

18And Isaac digged again the wells of water, which they had digged in the days of Abraham his father; for the Philistines had stopped them after the death of Abraham: and he called their names after the names by which his father had called them.

19And Isaac's servants digged in the valley, and found there a well of springing water.

20And the herdmen of Gerar did strive with Isaac's herdmen, saying, The water *is* ours: and he called the name of the well Esek; because they strove with him.

21And they digged another well, and strove for that also: and he called the name of it Sitnah.

22And he removed from thence, and digged another well; and for that they strove not: and he called the name of it Rehoboth; and he said, For now the LORD hath made room for us, and we shall be fruitful in the land.

23And he went up from thence to Beer-sheba.

24And the LORD appeared unto him the same night, and said, I *am* the God of Abraham thy father: fear not, for I *am* with thee, and will bless thee, and multiply thy seed for my servant Abraham's sake.

25And he builded an altar there, and called upon the name of the LORD, and pitched his tent there: and there Isaac's servants digged a well.

26¶ Then Abimelech went to him from Gerar, and Ahuzzath one of his friends, and Phichol the chief captain of his army.

27And Isaac said unto them, Wherefore come ye to me, seeing ye hate me, and have sent me away from you?

28And they said, We saw certainly that the LORD was with thee: and we said, Let there be now an oath betwixt us, *even* betwixt us and thee, and let us make a covenant with thee;

29That thou wilt do us no hurt, as we have not touched thee, and as we have done unto thee nothing but good, and have sent thee away in peace: thou *art* now the blessed of the LORD.

30And he made them a feast, and they did eat and drink.

31And they rose up betimes in the morning, and sware one to another: and Isaac sent them away, and they departed from him in peace.

32And it came to pass the same day, that Isaac's servants came, and told him concerning the well which they had digged, and said unto him, We have found water.

33And he called it Shebah: therefore the name of the city *is* Beer-sheba unto this day.

34¶ And Esau was forty years old when he took to wife Judith the daughter of Beeri the Hittite, and Bashemath the daughter of Elon the Hittite:

35Which were a grief of mind unto Isaac and to Rebekah.

**27** AND IT came to pass, that when Isaac was old, and his eyes were dim, so that he could not see, he called Esau his eldest son, and said unto him, My son: and he said unto him, Behold, *here am* I.

2And he said, Behold now, I am old, I know not the day of my death:

3Now therefore take, I pray thee, thy weapons, thy quiver and thy bow, and go out to the field, and take me *some* venison;

4And make me savoury meat, such as I love, and bring *it* to me, that I may eat; that my soul may bless thee before I die.

5And Rebekah heard when Isaac spake to Esau his son. And Esau went to the field to hunt *for* venison, *and* to bring *it*.

**AMP** [a] With Isaac God came first. Before doing anything else in the new place, he built an altar, then waited there to call upon the Lord. Second, came his home; he pitched his tent. Third, came his business; his servants dug a well.

## Amplified

18And Isaac dug again the wells of water which had been dug in the days of Abraham his father, for the Philistines had stopped them after the death of Abraham; and he gave them the names by which his father had called them.

19Now Isaac's servants dug in the valley and found there a well of living [spring] water.

20And the herdsmen of Gerar quarreled with Isaac's herdsmen, saying, The water is ours. And he named the well Esek [contention] because they quarreled with him.

21Then [his servants] dug another well, and they quarreled over that also; so he named it Sitnah [enmity].

22And he moved away from there and dug another well; and for that one they did not quarrel. He named it Rehoboth [room], saying, For now the Lord has made room for us, and we shall be fruitful in the land.

23Now he went up from there to Beer-sheba.

24And the Lord appeared to him the same night, and said, I am the God of Abraham your father. Fear not, for I am with you, and will favor you with blessings and multiply your descendants for the sake of My servant Abraham.

25And [Isaac] [a]built an altar there, and called on the name of the Lord, and pitched his tent there; and there Isaac's servants were digging a well.

26Then Abimelech went to him from Gerar with Ahuzzah, one of his friends, and Phicol, his army's commander.

27And Isaac said to them, Why have you come to me, seeing that you hate me and have sent me away from you?

28They said, We saw that the Lord was certainly with you; so we said, Let there be now an oath between us [carrying a curse with it to befall the one who breaks it], even between you and us, and let us make a covenant with you

29That you will do us no harm, inasmuch as we have not touched you and have done to you nothing but good, and have sent you away in peace. You are now the blessed *or* favored of the Lord!

30And he made them a [formal] dinner, and they ate and drank.

31And they rose up early in the morning, and took oaths [with a curse] with one another; and Isaac sent them on their way and they departed from him in peace.

32That same day Isaac's servants came and told him about the well they had dug, saying, We have found water!

33And he named [the well] Shibah; therefore the name of the city is Beer-sheba to this day.

34Now Esau was 40 years old when he took as wife Judith the daughter of Beeri the Hittite, and Basemath the daughter of Elon the Hittite.

35And they made life bitter *and* a grief of mind *and* spirit for [their parents-in-law] Isaac and Rebekah.

**27** WHEN ISAAC was old, and his eyes were dim so that he could not see, he called Esau his elder son, and said to him, My son! And he answered him, Here I am.

2He said, See here now; I am old, I do not know when I may die.

3So now I pray you, take your weapons, your [arrows in a] quiver and your bow, and go out into the open country and hunt game for me,

4And prepare me appetizing meat, such as I love, and bring it to me, that I may eat of it, [preparatory] to giving you my blessing [as my first-born] before I die.

5But Rebekah heard what Isaac said to Esau his son, and when Esau had gone to the open country to hunt for game that he might bring it,

# New American Standard

*Quarrel over the Wells*

18¶ Then Isaac dug again the wells of water which had been dug
in the days of his father Abraham, for the Philistines had stopped
them up after the death of Abraham; and he gave them the same
names which his father had given them.
19But when Isaac's servants dug in the valley and found there
a well of flowing water,
20the herdsmen of Gerar quarreled with the herdsmen of Isaac,
saying, "The water is ours!" So he named the well Esek, because
they contended with him.
21Then they dug another well, and they quarreled over it too,
so he named it Sitnah.
22And he moved away from there and dug another well, and
they did not quarrel over it; so he named it Rehoboth, for he said,
"At last the LORD has made room for us, and we shall be fruitful
in the land."
23¶ Then he went up from there to Beersheba.
24And the LORD appeared to him the same night and said,
"I am the God of your father Abraham;
Do not fear, for I am with you.
I will bless you, and multiply your descendants,
For the sake of My servant Abraham."
25So he built an altar there, and called upon the name of the
LORD, and pitched his tent there; and there Isaac's servants dug
a well.

*Covenant with Abimelech*

26¶ Then Abimelech came to him from Gerar with his adviser
Ahuzzath, and Phicol the commander of his army.
27And Isaac said to them, "Why have you come to me, since you
hate me, and have sent me away from you?"
28And they said, "We see plainly that the LORD has been with
you; so we said, 'Let there now be an oath between us, *even*
between you and us, and let us make a covenant with you,
29that you will do us no harm, just as we have not touched you
and have done to you nothing but good, and have sent you away
in peace. You are now the blessed of the LORD.' "
30Then he made them a feast, and they ate and drank.
31And in the morning they arose early and exchanged oaths;
then Isaac sent them away and they departed from him in peace.
32Now it came about on the same day, that Isaac's servants
came in and told him about the well which they had dug, and said
to him, "We have found water."
33So he called it Shibah; therefore the name of the city is Beer-
sheba to this day.
34¶ And when Esau was forty years old he married Judith the
daughter of Beeri the Hittite, and Basemath the daughter of Elon
the Hittite;
35and they [b]brought grief to Isaac and Rebekah.

*Jacob's Deception*

**27** NOW IT came about, when Isaac was old, and his eyes
were too dim to see, that he called his older son Esau and
said to him, "My son." And he said to him, "Here I am."
2And Isaac said, "Behold now, I am old *and* I do not know the
day of my death.
3"Now then, please take your gear, your quiver and your bow,
and go out to the field and hunt game for me;
4and prepare a savory dish for me such as I love, and bring it
to me that I may eat, so that my soul may bless you before I die."
5¶ And Rebekah was listening while Isaac spoke to his son
Esau. So when Esau went to the field to hunt for game to bring
*home,*

NAS [b] Lit., *were a bitterness of spirit to*

# New International

been dug in the time of his father Abraham, which the Philistines
had stopped up after Abraham died, and he gave them the same
names his father had given them.
19Isaac's servants dug in the valley and discovered a well of
fresh water there. 20But the herdsmen of Gerar quarreled with
Isaac's herdsmen and said, "The water is ours!" So he named the
well Esek,[c] because they disputed with him. 21Then they dug
another well, but they quarreled over that one also; so he named
it Sitnah.[d] 22He moved on from there and dug another well, and
no one quarreled over it. He named it Rehoboth,[e] saying, "Now
the LORD has given us room and we will flourish in the land."
23From there he went up to Beersheba. 24That night the LORD
appeared to him and said, "I am the God of your father Abraham.
Do not be afraid, for I am with you; I will bless you and will
increase the number of your descendants for the sake of my servant Abraham."
25Isaac built an altar there and called on the name of the LORD.
There he pitched his tent, and there his servants dug a well.
26Meanwhile, Abimelech had come to him from Gerar, with
Ahuzzath his personal adviser and Phicol the commander of his
forces. 27Isaac asked them, "Why have you come to me, since you
were hostile to me and sent me away?"
28They answered, "We saw clearly that the LORD was with you;
so we said, 'There ought to be a sworn agreement between
us'—between us and you. Let us make a treaty with you 29that you
will do us no harm, just as we did not molest you but always
treated you well and sent you away in peace. And now you are
blessed by the LORD."
30Isaac then made a feast for them, and they ate and drank.
31Early the next morning the men swore an oath to each other.
Then Isaac sent them on their way, and they left him in peace.
32That day Isaac's servants came and told him about the well
they had dug. They said, "We've found water!" 33He called it
Shibah,[f] and to this day the name of the town has been Beer-
sheba.[g]
34When Esau was forty years old, he married Judith daughter
of Beeri the Hittite, and also Basemath daughter of Elon the Hittite.
35They were a source of grief to Isaac and Rebekah.

*Jacob Gets Isaac's Blessing*

**27** WHEN ISAAC was old and his eyes were so weak that he
could no longer see, he called for Esau his older son and
said to him, "My son."
"Here I am," he answered.
2Isaac said, "I am now an old man and don't know the day of
my death. 3Now then, get your weapons—your quiver and bow—
and go out to the open country to hunt some wild game for me.
4Prepare me the kind of tasty food I like and bring it to me to eat,
so that I may give you my blessing before I die."
5Now Rebekah was listening as Isaac spoke to his son Esau.
When Esau left for the open country to hunt game and bring it
back, 6Rebekah said to her son Jacob, "Look, I overheard your

NIV [c] 20 *Esek* means *dispute.* [d] 21 *Sitnah* means *opposition.* [e] 22 *Rehoboth* means *room.* [f] 33 *Shibah* can mean *oath* or *seven.* [g] 33 *Beersheba* can mean *well of the oath* or *well of seven.*

# King James

6¶ And Rebekah spake unto Jacob her son, saying, Behold, I
heard thy father speak unto Esau thy brother, saying,
7Bring me venison, and make me savoury meat, that I may eat,
and bless thee before the LORD before my death.
8Now therefore, my son, obey my voice according to that which
I command thee.
9Go now to the flock, and fetch me from thence two good kids
of the goats; and I will make them savoury meat for thy father,
such as he loveth:
10And thou shalt bring *it* to thy father, that he may eat, and that
he may bless thee before his death.
11And Jacob said to Rebekah his mother, Behold, Esau my
brother *is* a hairy man, and I *am* a smooth man:
12My father peradventure will feel me, and I shall seem to him
as a deceiver; and I shall bring a curse upon me, and not a blessing.
13And his mother said unto him, Upon me *be* thy curse, my son:
only obey my voice, and go fetch me *them.*
14And he went, and fetched, and brought *them* to his mother:
and his mother made savoury meat, such as his father loved.
15And Rebekah took goodly raiment of her eldest son Esau,
which *were* with her in the house, and put them upon Jacob her
younger son:
16And she put the skins of the kids of the goats upon his hands,
and upon the smooth of his neck:
17And she gave the savoury meat and the bread, which she had
prepared, into the hand of her son Jacob.
18¶ And he came unto his father, and said, My father: and he
said, Here *am* I; who *art* thou, my son?
19And Jacob said unto his father, I *am* Esau thy firstborn; I have
done according as thou badest me: arise, I pray thee, sit and eat
of my venison, that thy soul may bless me.
20And Isaac said unto his son, How *is it* that thou hast found
*it* so quickly, my son? And he said, Because the LORD thy God
brought *it* to me.
21And Isaac said unto Jacob, Come near, I pray thee, that I may
feel thee, my son, whether thou *be* my very son Esau or not.
22And Jacob went near unto Isaac his father; and he felt him,
and said, The voice *is* Jacob's voice, but the hands *are* the hands
of Esau.
23And he discerned him not, because his hands were hairy, as
his brother Esau's hands: so he blessed him.
24And he said, *Art* thou my very son Esau? And he said, I *am.*
25And he said, Bring *it* near to me, and I will eat of my son's
venison, that my soul may bless thee. And he brought *it* near to
him, and he did eat: and he brought him wine, and he drank.
26And his father Isaac said unto him, Come near now, and kiss
me, my son.
27And he came near, and kissed him: and he smelled the smell
of his raiment, and blessed him, and said, See, the smell of my son
*is* as the smell of a field which the LORD hath blessed:
28Therefore God give thee of the dew of heaven, and the fatness
of the earth, and plenty of corn and wine:
29Let people serve thee, and nations bow down to thee: be lord
over thy brethren, and let thy mother's sons bow down to thee:
cursed *be* every one that curseth thee, and blessed *be* he that
blesseth thee.
30¶ And it came to pass, as soon as Isaac had made an end of
blessing Jacob, and Jacob was yet scarce gone out from the presence of Isaac his father, that Esau his brother came in from his
hunting.
31And he also had made savoury meat, and brought it unto his
father, and said unto his father, Let my father arise, and eat of his
son's venison, that thy soul may bless me.

# Amplified

6Rebekah said to Jacob her younger son, See here, I heard your
father say to Esau your brother,
7Bring me game, and make me appetizing meat, so that I may
eat, and declare my blessing upon you before the Lord before my
death.
8So now, my son, do exactly as I command you.
9Go now to the flock, and from it bring me two good *and* suitable
kids; and I will make them into appetizing meat for your father,
such as he loves.
10And you shall bring it to your father that he may eat, and
declare his blessing upon you before his death.
11But Jacob said to Rebekah his mother, Listen, Esau my brother
is a hairy man, and I am a smooth man.
12Suppose my father feels me; I will seem to him to be a cheat
*and* an imposter, and I will bring [his] curse on me and not [his]
blessing.
13But his mother said to him, On me be your curse, my son; only
obey my word, and go, fetch them to me.
14So [Jacob] went, got [the kids] and brought them to his
mother; and his mother prepared appetizing meat with a delightful odor, such as his father loved.
15Then Rebekah took her elder son Esau's best clothes which
were with her in the house, and put them on Jacob her younger
son.
16And she put the skins of the kids on his hands and on the
smooth part of his neck.
17And she gave the savory meat and the bread which she had
prepared, into the hand of her son Jacob.
18So he went to his father, and said, My father. And he said,
Here am I; who are you, my son?
19And Jacob said to his father, I am Esau your first-born; I have
done what you told me to do. Now sit up and eat of my game, so
that you may proceed to bless me.
20And Isaac said to his son, How is it that you have found the
game so quickly, my son? And he said, Because the Lord your God
caused it to come to me.
21But Isaac said to Jacob, Come close to me, I beg of you, that
I may feel you, my son, *and* know whether you really are my son
Esau or not.
22So Jacob went near to Isaac, and his father felt him and said,
The voice is Jacob's voice, but the hands are the hands of Esau.
23He could not identify him because his hands were hairy like
his brother Esau's hands; so he blessed him.
24But he said, Are you really my son Esau? He answered, I am.
25Then [Isaac] said, Bring it to me, and I will eat of my son's
game, that I may bless you. He brought it to him, and he ate; and
he brought him wine, and he drank.
26Then his father Isaac said, Come near and kiss me, my son.
27So he came near and kissed him; and [Isaac] smelled his
clothing, and blessed him, and said, The scent of my son is as the
odor of a field which the Lord has blessed.
28And may God give you of the dew of the heavens and of the
fatness of the earth and abundance of grain and [new] wine;
29Let peoples serve you, and nations bow down to you; be
master over your brothers, and let your mother's sons bow down
to you. Let everyone be cursed who curses you, and favored with
blessings who blesses you.
30As soon as Isaac had finished blessing Jacob, and Jacob was
scarcely gone out from the presence of Isaac his father, Esau his
brother came in from his hunting.
31Esau had also prepared savory food, and brought it to his
father, and said to him, Let my father arise, and eat of his son's
game, that you may bless me.

## New American Standard

6Rebekah said to her son Jacob, "Behold, I heard your father
speak to your brother Esau, saying,
7'Bring me *some* game and prepare a savory dish for me, that
I may eat, and bless you in the presence of the LORD before my
death.'
8"Now therefore, my son, listen to me as I command you.
9"Go now to the flock and bring me two choice kids from there,
that I may prepare them *as* a savory dish for your father, such as
he loves.
10"Then you shall bring *it* to your father, that he may eat, so that
he may bless you before his death."
11And Jacob answered his mother Rebekah, "Behold, Esau my
brother is a hairy man and I am a smooth man.
12"Perhaps my father will feel me, then I shall be as a deceiver
in his sight; and I shall bring upon myself a curse and not a
blessing."
13But his mother said to him, "Your curse be on me, my son;
only obey my voice, and go, get *them* for me."
14So he went and got *them*, and brought *them* to his mother; and
his mother made savory food such as his father loved.
15Then Rebekah took the best garments of Esau her elder son,
which were with her in the house, and put them on Jacob her
younger son.
16And she put the skins of the kids on his hands and on the
smooth part of his neck.
17She also gave the savory food and the bread, which she had
made, to her son Jacob.
18¶ Then he came to his father and said, "My father." And he
said, "Here I am. Who are you, my son?"
19And Jacob said to his father, "I am Esau your first-born; I have
done as you told me. Get up, please, sit and eat of my game, that
you may bless me."
20And Isaac said to his son, "How is it that you have *it* so
quickly, my son?" And he said, "Because the LORD your God
caused *it* to happen to me."
21Then Isaac said to Jacob, "Please come close, that I may feel
you, my son, whether you are really my son Esau or not."
22So Jacob came close to Isaac his father, and he felt him and
said, "The voice is the voice of Jacob, but the hands are the hands
of Esau."
23And he did not recognize him, because his hands were hairy
like his brother Esau's hands; so he blessed him.
24And he said, "Are you really my son Esau?" And he said, "I
am."
25So he said, "Bring *it* to me, and I will eat of my son's game,
that I may bless you." And he brought *it* to him, and he ate; he
also brought him wine and he drank.
26Then his father Isaac said to him, "Please come close and kiss
me, my son."
27So he came close and kissed him; and when he smelled the
smell of his garments, he blessed him and said,

"See, the smell of my son
Is like the smell of a field which the LORD has blessed;
28 Now may God give you of the dew of heaven,
And of the fatness of the earth,
And an abundance of grain and new wine;
29 May peoples serve you,
And nations bow down to you;
Be master of your brothers,
And may your mother's sons bow down to you.
Cursed be those who curse you,
And blessed be those who bless you."

*The Stolen Blessing*

30¶ Now it came about, as soon as Isaac had finished blessing
Jacob, and Jacob had hardly gone out from the presence of Isaac
his father, that Esau his brother came in from his hunting.
31Then he also made savory food, and brought it to his father;
and he said to his father, "Let my father arise, and eat of his son's
game, that you may bless me."

## New International

father say to your brother Esau, 7'Bring me some game and prepare me some tasty food to eat, so that I may give you my blessing
in the presence of the LORD before I die.' 8Now, my son, listen
carefully and do what I tell you: 9Go out to the flock and bring me
two choice young goats, so I can prepare some tasty food for your
father, just the way he likes it. 10Then take it to your father to eat,
so that he may give you his blessing before he dies."
11Jacob said to Rebekah his mother, "But my brother Esau is a
hairy man, and I'm a man with smooth skin. 12What if my father
touches me? I would appear to be tricking him and would bring
down a curse on myself rather than a blessing."
13His mother said to him, "My son, let the curse fall on me. Just
do what I say; go and get them for me."
14So he went and got them and brought them to his mother, and
she prepared some tasty food, just the way his father liked it.
15Then Rebekah took the best clothes of Esau her older son, which
she had in the house, and put them on her younger son Jacob.
16She also covered his hands and the smooth part of his neck with
the goatskins. 17Then she handed to her son Jacob the tasty food
and the bread she had made.
18He went to his father and said, "My father."
"Yes, my son," he answered. "Who is it?"
19Jacob said to his father, "I am Esau your firstborn. I have done
as you told me. Please sit up and eat some of my game so that you
may give me your blessing."
20Isaac asked his son, "How did you find it so quickly, my son?"
"The LORD your God gave me success," he replied.
21Then Isaac said to Jacob, "Come near so I can touch you, my
son, to know whether you really are my son Esau or not."
22Jacob went close to his father Isaac, who touched him and
said, "The voice is the voice of Jacob, but the hands are the hands
of Esau." 23He did not recognize him, for his hands were hairy like
those of his brother Esau; so he blessed him. 24"Are you really my
son Esau?" he asked.
"I am," he replied.
25Then he said, "My son, bring me some of your game to eat,
so that I may give you my blessing."
Jacob brought it to him and he ate; and he brought some wine
and he drank. 26Then his father Isaac said to him, "Come here, my
son, and kiss me."
27So he went to him and kissed him. When Isaac caught the
smell of his clothes, he blessed him and said,

"Ah, the smell of my son
is like the smell of a field
that the LORD has blessed.
28May God give you of heaven's dew
and of earth's richness—
an abundance of grain and new wine.
29May nations serve you
and peoples bow down to you.
Be lord over your brothers,
and may the sons of your mother bow down to you.
May those who curse you be cursed
and those who bless you be blessed."

30After Isaac finished blessing him and Jacob had scarcely left
his father's presence, his brother Esau came in from hunting. 31He
too prepared some tasty food and brought it to his father. Then he
said to him, "My father, sit up and eat some of my game, so that
you may give me your blessing."

## King James

32And Isaac his father said unto him, Who *art* thou? And he said, I *am* thy son, thy firstborn Esau.

33And Isaac trembled very exceedingly, and said, Who? where *is* he that hath taken venison, and brought *it* me, and I have eaten of all before thou camest, and have blessed him? yea, *and* he shall be blessed.

34And when Esau heard the words of his father, he cried with a great and exceeding bitter cry, and said unto his father, Bless me, *even* me also, O my father.

35And he said, Thy brother came with subtlety, and hath taken away thy blessing.

36And he said, Is not he rightly named Jacob? for he hath supplanted me these two times: he took away my birthright; and, behold, now he hath taken away my blessing. And he said, Hast thou not reserved a blessing for me?

37And Isaac answered and said unto Esau, Behold, I have made him thy lord, and all his brethren have I given to him for servants; and with corn and wine have I sustained him: and what shall I do now unto thee, my son?

38And Esau said unto his father, Hast thou but one blessing, my father? bless me, *even* me also, O my father. And Esau lifted up his voice, and wept.

39And Isaac his father answered and said unto him, Behold, thy dwelling shall be the fatness of the earth, and of the dew of heaven from above;

40And by thy sword shalt thou live, and shalt serve thy brother; and it shall come to pass when thou shalt have the dominion, that thou shalt break his yoke from off thy neck.

41¶ And Esau hated Jacob because of the blessing wherewith his father blessed him: and Esau said in his heart, The days of mourning for my father are at hand; then will I slay my brother Jacob.

42And these words of Esau her elder son were told to Rebekah: and she sent and called Jacob her younger son, and said unto him, Behold, thy brother Esau, as touching thee, doth comfort himself, *purposing* to kill thee.

43Now therefore, my son, obey my voice; and arise, flee thou to Laban my brother to Haran;

44And tarry with him a few days, until thy brother's fury turn away;

45Until thy brother's anger turn away from thee, and he forget *that* which thou hast done to him: then I will send, and fetch thee from thence: why should I be deprived also of you both in one day?

46And Rebekah said to Isaac, I am weary of my life because of the daughters of Heth: if Jacob take a wife of the daughters of Heth, such as these *which are* of the daughters of the land, what good shall my life do me?

**28** AND ISAAC called Jacob, and blessed him, and charged him, and said unto him, Thou shalt not take a wife of the daughters of Canaan.

2Arise, go to Padan-aram, to the house of Bethuel thy mother's father; and take thee a wife from thence of the daughters of Laban thy mother's brother.

## Amplified

32And Isaac his father said to him, Who are you? And he replied, I am your son, your first-born, Esau.

33Then Isaac trembled *and* shook violently, and he said, Who? Where is he who has hunted game and brought it to me, and I ate of it all before you came, and I have blessed him? Yes, and he shall be blessed.

34When Esau heard the words of his father, he cried out with a great and bitter cry, and said to his father, Bless me, even me also, O my father! [Heb. 12:16, 17.]

35[Isaac] said, Your brother came with crafty cunning *and* treacherous deceit, and has taken your blessing.

36[Esau] replied, Is he not rightly named Jacob [the supplanter]? For he has supplanted me these two times: he took away my birthright; and now he has taken away my blessing! Have you not still a blessing reserved for me?

37And Isaac answered Esau, Behold, I have made [Jacob] your lord and master; I have given all his brethren to him for servants; and with corn and [new] wine have I sustained him. What then can I do for you my son?

38Esau said to his father, Have you only one blessing, my father? Bless me, even me also, O my father! And Esau [could not control] his voice and wept aloud.

39Then Isaac his father answered, Your [blessing and] dwelling shall all come from the fruitfulness of the earth, and from the dew of the heavens above;

40By your sword you shall live and serve your brother. But [the time shall come] when you will grow restive *and* break loose, and you shall tear his yoke from off your neck.

41And Esau hated Jacob because of the blessing with which his father blessed him; and Esau said in his heart, The days of mourning for my father are very near. When [he is gone] I will [a]kill my brother Jacob.

42These words of Esau her elder son were repeated to Rebekah. She sent for Jacob her younger son and said to him, See here, your brother Esau comforts himself concerning you [by intending] to kill you.

43So now, my son, do what I tell you; arise, flee to my brother Laban in Haran;

44Linger and dwell with him for a while until your brother's fury is spent.

45When your brother's anger is diverted from you, he will forget [the wrong] that you have done him. Then [b]I will send and bring you back from there. Why should I be deprived of both of you in one day?

46Then Rebekah said to Isaac, I am weary of my life because of the daughters of Heth [these wives of Esau]! If Jacob takes a wife of the daughters of Heth, such as these Hittite girls around here, what good will my life be to me?

**28** SO ISAAC called Jacob and blessed him, and commanded him, You shall not marry one of the women of Canaan.

2Arise, go to Padan-aram to the house of Bethuel your mother's father, and take from there as a wife one of the daughters of Laban your mother's brother.

**AMP** [a] Here began a feud that was to cost countless lives throughout succeeding centuries. Esau's descendants, the Amalekites, were the first enemies to obstruct the flight of Jacob's descendants from Egypt (Exod. 17:8); and the Edomites even refused to let their uncle Jacob's children pass through their land (Num. 20:17-20). Doeg, an Edomite, all but caused the death of Christ's chosen ancestor David (I Sam. 21, 22). Bloody battles were fought between the two nations in the centuries that followed. It was Herod, of Esau's race (*Josephus, Ant.* 14:1, Sec. 3), who had the male infants of Bethlehem slain in an effort to destroy the Christ child. Satan needs no better medium for his evil plans than a family feud, a "mere quarrel" between two brothers. [b] But Rebekah never saw her son Jacob again. He was well over 40 and probably 57 years old when he fled from Esau to Haran; and he stayed there at least 20 years.

## New American Standard

32And Isaac his father said to him, "Who are you?" And he said,
"I am your son, your first-born, Esau."
33Then Isaac trembled violently, and said, "Who was he then
that hunted game and brought *it* to me, so that I ate of all *of it* before
you came, and blessed him? Yes, and he shall be blessed."
34When Esau heard the words of his father, he cried out with
an exceedingly great and bitter cry, and said to his father, "Bless
me, *even* me also, O my father!"
35And he said, "Your brother came deceitfully, and has taken
away your blessing."
36Then he said, "Is he not rightly named Jacob, for he has
supplanted me these two times? He took away my birthright, and
behold, now he has taken away my blessing." And he said, "Have
you not reserved a blessing for me?"
37But Isaac answered and said to Esau, "Behold, I have made
him your master, and all his relatives I have given to him as
servants; and with grain and new wine I have sustained him. Now
as for you then, what can I do, my son?"
38And Esau said to his father, "Do you have only one blessing,
my father? Bless me, *even* me also, O my father." So Esau lifted his
voice and wept.
39Then Isaac his father answered and said to him,
"Behold, away from the fertility of the earth shall be
your dwelling,
And away from the dew of heaven from above.
40 "And by your sword you shall live,
And your brother you shall serve;
But it shall come about when you become restless,
That you shall break his yoke from your neck."
41So Esau bore a grudge against Jacob because of the blessing
with which his father had blessed him; and Esau said to himself,
"The days of mourning for my father are near; then I will kill my
brother Jacob."
42Now when the words of her elder son Esau were reported to
Rebekah, she sent and called her younger son Jacob, and said to
him, "Behold your brother Esau is consoling himself concerning
you, *by planning* to kill you.
43"Now therefore, my son, obey my voice, and arise, flee to
Haran, to my brother Laban!
44"And stay with him a few days, until your brother's fury
subsides,
45until your brother's anger against you subsides, and he forgets what you did to him. Then I shall send and get you from there.
Why should I be bereaved of you both in one day?"
46¶ And Rebekah said to Isaac, "I am tired of living because of
the daughters of Heth; if Jacob takes a wife from the daughters of
Heth, like these, from the daughters of the land, what good will
my life be to me?"

*Jacob Is Sent Away*

**28** SO ISAAC called Jacob and blessed him and charged him,
and said to him, "You shall not take a wife from the
daughters of Canaan.
2"Arise, go to Paddan-aram, to the house of Bethuel your
mother's father; and from there take to yourself a wife from the
daughters of Laban your mother's brother.

## New International

32His father Isaac asked him, "Who are you?"
"I am your son," he answered, "your firstborn, Esau."
33Isaac trembled violently and said, "Who was it, then, that
hunted game and brought it to me? I ate it just before you came
and I blessed him—and indeed he will be blessed!"
34When Esau heard his father's words, he burst out with a loud
and bitter cry and said to his father, "Bless me—me too, my
father!"
35But he said, "Your brother came deceitfully and took your
blessing."
36Esau said, "Isn't he rightly named Jacob[c]? He has deceived
me these two times: He took my birthright, and now he's taken my
blessing!" Then he asked, "Haven't you reserved any blessing for
me?"
37Isaac answered Esau, "I have made him lord over you and
have made all his relatives his servants, and I have sustained him
with grain and new wine. So what can I possibly do for you, my
son?"
38Esau said to his father, "Do you have only one blessing, my
father? Bless me too, my father!" Then Esau wept aloud.
39His father Isaac answered him,

"Your dwelling will be
away from the earth's richness,
away from the dew of heaven above.
40You will live by the sword
and you will serve your brother.
But when you grow restless,
you will throw his yoke
from off your neck."

*Jacob Flees to Laban*

41Esau held a grudge against Jacob because of the blessing his
father had given him. He said to himself, "The days of mourning
for my father are near; then I will kill my brother Jacob."
42When Rebekah was told what her older son Esau had said,
she sent for her younger son Jacob and said to him, "Your brother
Esau is consoling himself with the thought of killing you. 43Now
then, my son, do what I say: Flee at once to my brother Laban in
Haran. 44Stay with him for a while until your brother's fury subsides. 45When your brother is no longer angry with you and forgets what you did to him, I'll send word for you to come back from
there. Why should I lose both of you in one day?"
46Then Rebekah said to Isaac, "I'm disgusted with living because of these Hittite women. If Jacob takes a wife from among the
women of this land, from Hittite women like these, my life will not
be worth living."

**28** SO ISAAC called for Jacob and blessed[d] him and commanded him: "Do not marry a Canaanite woman. 2Go at
once to Paddan Aram,[e] to the house of your mother's father
Bethuel. Take a wife for yourself there, from among the daughters
of Laban, your mother's brother. 3May God Almighty[f] bless you

**NIV** [c] 36 *Jacob* means *he grasps the heel* (figuratively, *he deceives*). [d] 1 Or *greeted* [e] 2 That is, Northwest Mesopotamia; also in verses 5, 6 and 7 [f] 3 Hebrew *El-Shaddai*

## King James

3And God Almighty bless thee, and make thee fruitful, and
multiply thee, that thou mayest be a multitude of people;
4And give thee the blessing of Abraham, to thee, and to thy
seed with thee; that thou mayest inherit the land wherein thou art
a stranger, which God gave unto Abraham.
5And Isaac sent away Jacob: and he went to Padan-aram unto
Laban, son of Bethuel the Syrian, the brother of Rebekah, Jacob's
and Esau's mother.
6¶ When Esau saw that Isaac had blessed Jacob, and sent him
away to Padan-aram, to take him a wife from thence; and that as
he blessed him he gave him a charge, saying, Thou shalt not take
a wife of the daughters of Canaan;
7And that Jacob obeyed his father and his mother, and was
gone to Padan-aram;
8And Esau seeing that the daughters of Canaan pleased not
Isaac his father;
9Then went Esau unto Ishmael, and took unto the wives which
he had Mahalath the daughter of Ishmael Abraham's son, the
sister of Nebajoth, to be his wife.
10¶ And Jacob went out from Beer-sheba, and went toward
Haran.
11And he lighted upon a certain place, and tarried there all
night, because the sun was set; and he took of the stones of that
place, and put *them for* his pillows, and lay down in that place to
sleep.
12And he dreamed, and behold a ladder set up on the earth, and
the top of it reached to heaven: and behold the angels of God
ascending and descending on it.
13And, behold, the LORD stood above it, and said, I *am* the LORD
God of Abraham thy father, and the God of Isaac: the land whereon thou liest, to thee will I give it, and to thy seed;
14And thy seed shall be as the dust of the earth, and thou shalt
spread abroad to the west, and to the east, and to the north, and
to the south: and in thee and in thy seed shall all the families of
the earth be blessed.
15And, behold, I *am* with thee, and will keep thee in all *places*
whither thou goest, and will bring thee again into this land; for I
will not leave thee, until I have done *that* which I have spoken to
thee of.
16¶ And Jacob awaked out of his sleep, and he said, Surely the
LORD is in this place; and I knew *it* not.
17And he was afraid, and said, How dreadful *is* this place! this
*is* none other but the house of God, and this *is* the gate of heaven.
18And Jacob rose up early in the morning, and took the stone
that he had put *for* his pillows, and set it up *for* a pillar, and poured
oil upon the top of it.
19And he called the name of that place Beth-el: but the name of
that city *was called* Luz at the first.
20And Jacob vowed a vow, saying, If God will be with me, and
will keep me in this way that I go, and will give me bread to eat,
and raiment to put on,
21So that I come again to my father's house in peace; then shall
the LORD be my God:
22And this stone, which I have set *for* a pillar, shall be God's
house: and of all that thou shalt give me I will surely give the tenth
unto thee.

**29** THEN JACOB went on his journey, and came into the
land of the people of the east.

## Amplified

3God Almighty bless you and make you fruitful and multiply
you until you become a group of peoples.
4May He give the blessing [He gave to] Abraham, to you and
your descendants with you, that you may inherit the land He gave
to Abraham, in which you are a sojourner.
5Thus Isaac sent Jacob away. He went to Padan-aram, to Laban,
son of Bethuel the Aramean, the brother of Rebekah, Jacob and
Esau's mother.
6Now Esau saw that Isaac had blessed Jacob and sent him to
Padan-aram to take him a wife from there, and that as he blessed
him he gave him a charge, saying, You shall not take a wife of the
daughters of Canaan;
7And that Jacob obeyed his father and his mother, and had gone
to Padan-aram.
8Also Esau saw that the daughters of Canaan did not please
Isaac his father.
9So Esau went to Ishmael, and took to be his wife, [in addition]
to the wives he [already] had, Mahalath daughter of Ishmael Abraham's son, the sister of Nebaioth.
10And Jacob left Beer-sheba and went toward Haran.
11And he came to a certain place, and stayed there overnight,
because the sun was set. Taking one of the stones of the place, he
put it under his head and lay down there to sleep.
12And he dreamed that there was a ladder set up on the earth,
and the top of it reached to heaven; and the angels of God were
ascending and descending on it!
13And behold, the Lord stood over *and* beside him and said, I
am the Lord, the God of Abraham your father [forefather] and the
God of Isaac; I will give to you and to your descendants the land
on which you are lying.
14And your offspring shall be as [countless as] the dust *or* sand
of the ground, and you shall spread abroad to the west and the east
and the north and the south; and by you and your Offspring shall
all the families of the earth be blessed *and* bless themselves. [Gal.
3:16.]
15And, behold, I am with you, and will keep (watch over you
with care, take notice of) you wherever you may go, and I will
bring you back to this land; for I will not leave you until I have done
all of which I have told you.
16And Jacob awoke from his sleep, and he said, Surely the Lord
is in this place, and I did not know it.
17He was afraid, and said, How to be feared *and* reverenced is
this place! This is none other than the house of God, and [a]this is
the gateway to heaven!
18And Jacob rose early in the morning, and took the stone he
had put under his head, and he set it up for a pillar [a monument
to the vision in his dream], and he poured oil on its top [in dedica-
tion].
19And he named that place Bethel [the house of God]; but the
name of that city was Luz at first.
20Then Jacob made a vow, saying, If God will be with me and
will keep me in this way that I go, and will give me food to eat and
clothing to wear,
21So that I may come again to my father's house in peace, then
the Lord shall be my God;
22And this stone, which I have set up as a pillar [monument],
shall be God's house [a sacred place to me]; and of all [the increase
of possessions] that You give me I will give the tenth to You.

**29** THEN JACOB went briskly *and* cheerfully on his way [400
miles] and came to the land of the people of the east.

**AMP** [a] "There is an open way between heaven and earth for each of us. The movement of the tide and the circulation of the blood are not more regular than the inter-communication between heaven and earth. Jacob may have thought that God was local; now he found Him to be omnipresent. Every lonely spot was His house, filled with angels" (F. B. Meyer in *Through the Bible Day by Day*). When Jacob found God in his own heart, he found Him everywhere.

## New American Standard

3 "And may God Almighty bless you and make you fruitful and multiply you, that you may become a company of peoples.

4 "May He also give you the blessing of Abraham, to you and to your descendants with you; that you may possess the land of your sojournings, which God gave to Abraham."

5 Then Isaac sent Jacob away, and he went to Paddan-aram to Laban, son of Bethuel the Aramean, the brother of Rebekah, the mother of Jacob and Esau.

6 Now Esau saw that Isaac had blessed Jacob and sent him away to Paddan-aram, to take to himself a wife from there, *and that* when he blessed him he charged him, saying, "You shall not take a wife from the daughters of Canaan,"

7 and that Jacob had obeyed his father and his mother and had gone to Paddan-aram.

8 So Esau saw that the daughters of Canaan displeased his father Isaac;

9 and Esau went to Ishmael, and married, besides the wives that he had, Mahalath the daughter of Ishmael, Abraham's son, the sister of Nebaioth.

*Jacob's Dream*

**10**¶ Then Jacob departed from Beersheba and went toward Haran.

11 And he came to a certain place and spent the night there, because the sun had set; and he took one of the stones of the place and put it under his head, and lay down in that place.

12 And he had a dream, and behold, a ladder was set on the earth with its top reaching to heaven; and behold, the angels of God were ascending and descending on it.

13 And behold, the LORD stood above it and said, "I am the LORD, the God of your father Abraham and the God of Isaac; the land on which you lie, I will give it to you and to your descendants.

14 "Your descendants shall also be like the dust of the earth, and you shall spread out to the west and to the east and to the north and to the south; and in you and in your descendants shall all the families of the earth be blessed.

15 "And behold, I am with you, and will keep you wherever you go, and will bring you back to this land; for I will not leave you until I have done what I have promised you."

16 Then Jacob awoke from his sleep and said, "Surely the LORD is in this place, and I did not know it."

17 And he was afraid and said, "How awesome is this place! This is none other than the house of God, and this is the gate of heaven."

**18**¶ So Jacob rose early in the morning, and took the stone that he had put under his head and set it up as a pillar, and poured oil on its top.

19 And he called the name of that place [b]Bethel; however, previously the name of the city had been Luz.

20 Then Jacob made a vow, saying, "If God will be with me and will keep me on this journey that I take, and will give me food to eat and garments to wear,

21 and I return to my father's house in safety, then the LORD will be my God.

22 "And this stone, which I have set up as a pillar, will be God's house; and of all that Thou dost give me I will surely give a tenth to Thee."

*Jacob Meets Rachel*

**29** THEN JACOB [c]went on his journey, and came to the land of the sons of the east.

NAS [b] I.e., the house of God [c] Lit., *lifted up his feet*

## New International

and make you fruitful and increase your numbers until you
become a community of peoples. 4 May he give you and your
descendants the blessing given to Abraham, so that you may take
possession of the land where you now live as an alien, the land
God gave to Abraham." 5 Then Isaac sent Jacob on his way, and
he went to Paddan Aram, to Laban son of Bethuel the Aramean,
the brother of Rebekah, who was the mother of Jacob and Esau.
6 Now Esau learned that Isaac had blessed Jacob and had sent
him to Paddan Aram to take a wife from there, and that when he
blessed him he commanded him, "Do not marry a Canaanite
woman," 7 and that Jacob had obeyed his father and mother and
had gone to Paddan Aram. 8 Esau then realized how displeasing
the Canaanite women were to his father Isaac; 9 so he went to
Ishmael and married Mahalath, the sister of Nebaioth and daughter of Ishmael son of Abraham, in addition to the wives he already
had.

*Jacob's Dream at Bethel*

10 Jacob left Beersheba and set out for Haran. 11 When he reached
a certain place, he stopped for the night because the sun had set.
Taking one of the stones there, he put it under his head and lay
down to sleep. 12 He had a dream in which he saw a stairway[d]
resting on the earth, with its top reaching to heaven, and the
angels of God were ascending and descending on it. 13 There above
it[e] stood the LORD, and he said: "I am the LORD, the God of your
father Abraham and the God of Isaac. I will give you and your
descendants the land on which you are lying. 14 Your descendants
will be like the dust of the earth, and you will spread out to the
west and to the east, to the north and to the south. All peoples on
earth will be blessed through you and your offspring. 15 I am with
you and will watch over you wherever you go, and I will bring you
back to this land. I will not leave you until I have done what I have
promised you."
16 When Jacob awoke from his sleep, he thought, "Surely the
LORD is in this place, and I was not aware of it." 17 He was afraid
and said, "How awesome is this place! This is none other than the
house of God; this is the gate of heaven."
18 Early the next morning Jacob took the stone he had placed
under his head and set it up as a pillar and poured oil on top of
it. 19 He called that place Bethel,[f] though the city used to be called
Luz.
20 Then Jacob made a vow, saying, "If God will be with me and
will watch over me on this journey I am taking and will give me
food to eat and clothes to wear 21 so that I return safely to my
father's house, then the LORD[g] will be my God 22 and[h] this stone
that I have set up as a pillar will be God's house, and of all that
you give me I will give you a tenth."

*Jacob Arrives in Paddan Aram*

**29** THEN JACOB continued on his journey and came to the
land of the eastern peoples. 2 There he saw a well in the

NIV [d] 12 Or *ladder* [e] 13 Or *There beside him* [f] 19 *Bethel* means *house of God.* [g] 20,21 Or *Since God . . . father's house, the* LORD [h] 21,22 Or *house, and the* LORD *will be my God,* 22 *then*

## King James

2And he looked, and behold a well in the field, and, lo, there *were* three flocks of sheep lying by it; for out of that well they watered the flocks: and a great stone *was* upon the well's mouth.

3And thither were all the flocks gathered: and they rolled the stone from the well's mouth, and watered the sheep, and put the stone again upon the well's mouth in his place.

4And Jacob said unto them, My brethren, whence *be* ye? And they said, Of Haran *are* we.

5And he said unto them, Know ye Laban the son of Nahor? And they said, We know *him*.

6And he said unto them, *Is* he well? And they said, *He is* well: and, behold, Rachel his daughter cometh with the sheep.

7And he said, Lo, *it is* yet high day, neither *is it* time that the cattle should be gathered together: water ye the sheep, and go *and* feed *them*.

8And they said, We cannot, until all the flocks be gathered together, and *till* they roll the stone from the well's mouth; then we water the sheep.

9¶ And while he yet spake with them, Rachel came with her father's sheep: for she kept them.

10And it came to pass, when Jacob saw Rachel the daughter of Laban his mother's brother, and the sheep of Laban his mother's brother, that Jacob went near, and rolled the stone from the well's mouth, and watered the flock of Laban his mother's brother.

11And Jacob kissed Rachel, and lifted up his voice, and wept.

12And Jacob told Rachel that he *was* her father's brother, and that he *was* Rebekah's son: and she ran and told her father.

13And it came to pass, when Laban heard the tidings of Jacob his sister's son, that he ran to meet him, and embraced him, and kissed him, and brought him to his house. And he told Laban all these things.

14And Laban said to him, Surely thou *art* my bone and my flesh. And he abode with him the space of a month.

15¶ And Laban said unto Jacob, Because thou *art* my brother, shouldest thou therefore serve me for nought? tell me, what *shall* thy wages *be?*

16And Laban had two daughters: the name of the elder *was* Leah, and the name of the younger *was* Rachel.

17Leah *was* tender eyed; but Rachel was beautiful and well-favoured.

18And Jacob loved Rachel; and said, I will serve thee seven years for Rachel thy younger daughter.

19And Laban said, *It is* better that I give her to thee, than that I should give her to another man: abide with me.

20And Jacob served seven years for Rachel; and they seemed unto him *but* a few days, for the love he had to her.

21¶ And Jacob said unto Laban, Give *me* my wife, for my days are fulfilled, that I may go in unto her.

22And Laban gathered together all the men of the place, and made a feast.

23And it came to pass in the evening, that he took Leah his daughter, and brought her to him; and he went in unto her.

24And Laban gave unto his daughter Leah Zilpah his maid *for* an handmaid.

25And it came to pass, that in the morning, behold, it *was* Leah: and he said to Laban, What *is* this thou hast done unto me? did not I serve with thee for Rachel? wherefore then hast thou beguiled me?

26And Laban said, It must not be so done in our country, to give the younger before the firstborn.

27Fulfil her week, and we will give thee this also for the service which thou shalt serve with me yet seven other years.

28And Jacob did so, and fulfilled her week: and he gave him Rachel his daughter to wife also.

29And Laban gave to Rachel his daughter Bilhah his handmaid to be her maid.

## Amplified

2As he looked he saw a well in the field, and lo, there were three flocks of sheep lying by it; for out of that well the flocks were watered. The stone on the well's mouth was a big one,

3And when all the flocks were gathered there, [the shepherds] would roll the stone from the well's mouth, water the sheep, and replace the stone on the well's mouth.

4And Jacob said to them, My brothers, where are you from? And they said, We are from Haran.

5[Jacob] said to them, Do you know Laban the grandson of Nahor? And they said, We know him.

6He said to them, Is it well with him? And they said, He is doing well; and see, here comes his daughter Rachel with [his] sheep!

7He said, The sun is still high; it is a long time yet before the flocks need be gathered [in their folds]. [Why not] water the sheep and return them to their pasture?

8But they said, We cannot until all the flocks are gathered together; then [the shepherds] roll the stone from the well's mouth and we water the sheep.

9While he was still talking with them, Rachel came with her father's sheep, for she shepherded them.

10When Jacob saw Rachel, the daughter of Laban his mother's brother, and the sheep of Laban his uncle, Jacob went near and rolled the stone from the well's mouth, and watered the flock of his uncle Laban.

11Then Jacob kissed Rachel, and he wept aloud.

12Jacob told Rachel he was her father's relative, Rebekah's son; and she ran and told her father.

13When Laban heard of the arrival of Jacob his sister's son, he ran to meet him, and embraced and kissed him, and brought him to his house. And [Jacob] told Laban all these things.

14Then Laban said to him, Surely you are my bone and my flesh. And [Jacob] stayed with him a month.

15Then Laban said to Jacob, Just because you are my relative, should you work for me for nothing? Tell me, what shall your wages be?

16Now Laban had two daughters; the name of the elder was Leah, and the name of the younger was Rachel.

17Leah's eyes were weak *and dull looking*, but Rachel was beautiful and attractive.

18And Jacob loved Rachel; so he said, I will work for you for seven years for Rachel your younger daughter.

19And Laban said, It is better I give her to you than to another man. Stay *and* live with me.

20And Jacob served seven years for Rachel; and they seemed to him but a few days, because of the love he had for her.

21Finally, Jacob said to Laban, Give me my wife, for my time is completed, so that I may take her to me.

22And Laban gathered together all the men of the place, and made a feast [with drinking].

23But when night came he took Leah his daughter and brought her to [Jacob], who had intercourse with her.

24(And Laban gave Zilpah his maid to his daughter Leah to be her maid.)

25But in the morning [Jacob saw his wife, and] behold, it was Leah! And he said to Laban, What is this you have done to me? Did I not work for you [all those seven years] for Rachel? Why then have you deceived *and* cheated *and* thrown me down *like this?*

26And Laban said, It is not permitted in our country to give the younger [in marriage] before the eldest.

27Finish the [wedding feast] week [for Leah], then we will give you [Rachel] also, and you shall work for me yet seven more years in return.

28So Jacob complied and fulfilled [Leah's] week; then [Laban] gave him Rachel his daughter as his wife.

29(And Laban gave Bilhah his maid to Rachel his daughter to be her maid.)

## New American Standard

2And he looked, and saw a well in the field, and behold, three
flocks of sheep were lying there beside it, for from that well they
watered the flocks. Now the stone on the mouth of the well was
large.
3When all the flocks were gathered there, they would then roll
the stone from the mouth of the well, and water the sheep, and
put the stone back in its place on the mouth of the well.
4And Jacob said to them, "My brothers, where are you from?"
And they said, "We are from Haran."
5And he said to them, "Do you know Laban the son of Nahor?" And they said, "We know *him*."
6And he said to them, "Is it well with him?" And they said,
"It is well, and behold, Rachel his daughter is coming with the
sheep."
7And he said, "Behold, it is still high day; it is not time for the
livestock to be gathered. Water the sheep, and go, pasture them."
8But they said, "We cannot, until all the flocks are gathered,
and they roll the stone from the mouth of the well; then we water
the sheep."
9While he was still speaking with them, Rachel came with her
father's sheep, for she was a shepherdess.
10And it came about, when Jacob saw Rachel the daughter of
Laban his mother's brother, and the sheep of Laban his mother's
brother, that Jacob went up, and rolled the stone from the mouth
of the well, and watered the flock of Laban his mother's brother.
11Then Jacob kissed Rachel, and lifted his voice and wept.
12And Jacob told Rachel that he was a relative of her father and
that he was Rebekah's son, and she ran and told her father.
13¶ So it came about, when Laban heard the news of Jacob his
sister's son, that he ran to meet him, and embraced him and kissed
him, and brought him to his house. Then he related to Laban all
these things.
14And Laban said to him, "Surely you are my bone and my
flesh." And he stayed with him a month.
15Then Laban said to Jacob, "Because you are my relative,
should you therefore serve me for nothing? Tell me, what shall
your wages be?"
16Now Laban had two daughters; the name of the older was
Leah, and the name of the younger was Rachel.
17And Leah's eyes were weak, but Rachel was beautiful of form
and face.
18Now Jacob loved Rachel, so he said, "I will serve you seven
years for your younger daughter Rachel."
19And Laban said, "It is better that I give her to you than that
I should give her to another man; stay with me."
20So Jacob served seven years for Rachel and they seemed to
him but a few days because of his love for her.

*Laban's Treachery*

21¶ Then Jacob said to Laban, "Give *me* my wife, for my time
is completed, that I may go in to her."
22And Laban gathered all the men of the place, and made a
feast.
23Now it came about in the evening that he took his daughter
Leah, and brought her to him; and *Jacob* went in to her.
24Laban also gave his maid Zilpah to his daughter Leah as a
maid.
25So it came about in the morning that, behold, it was Leah!
And he said to Laban, "What is this you have done to me? Was
it not for Rachel that I served with you? Why then have you
deceived me?"
26But Laban said, "It is not the practice in our place, to marry
off the younger before the first-born.
27"Complete the week of this one, and we will give you the
other also for the service which you shall serve with me for another
seven years."
28And Jacob did so and completed her week, and he gave him
his daughter Rachel as his wife.
29Laban also gave his maid Bilhah to his daughter Rachel as her
maid.

## New International

field, with three flocks of sheep lying near it because the flocks
were watered from that well. The stone over the mouth of the well
was large. 3When all the flocks were gathered there, the shepherds
would roll the stone away from the well's mouth and water the
sheep. Then they would return the stone to its place over the
mouth of the well.
4Jacob asked the shepherds, "My brothers, where are you
from?"
"We're from Haran," they replied.
5He said to them, "Do you know Laban, Nahor's grandson?"
"Yes, we know him," they answered.
6Then Jacob asked them, "Is he well?"
"Yes, he is," they said, "and here comes his daughter Rachel
with the sheep."
7"Look," he said, "the sun is still high; it is not time for the
flocks to be gathered. Water the sheep and take them back to
pasture."
8"We can't," they replied, "until all the flocks are gathered and
the stone has been rolled away from the mouth of the well. Then
we will water the sheep."
9While he was still talking with them, Rachel came with her
father's sheep, for she was a shepherdess. 10When Jacob saw
Rachel daughter of Laban, his mother's brother, and Laban's
sheep, he went over and rolled the stone away from the mouth of
the well and watered his uncle's sheep. 11Then Jacob kissed Rachel
and began to weep aloud. 12He had told Rachel that he was a
relative of her father and a son of Rebekah. So she ran and told her
father.
13As soon as Laban heard the news about Jacob, his sister's son,
he hurried to meet him. He embraced him and kissed him and
brought him to his home, and there Jacob told him all these things.
14Then Laban said to him, "You are my own flesh and blood."

*Jacob Marries Leah and Rachel*

After Jacob had stayed with him for a whole month, 15Laban
said to him, "Just because you are a relative of mine, should you
work for me for nothing? Tell me what your wages should be."
16Now Laban had two daughters; the name of the older was
Leah, and the name of the younger was Rachel. 17Leah had weak[a]
eyes, but Rachel was lovely in form, and beautiful. 18Jacob was in
love with Rachel and said, "I'll work for you seven years in return
for your younger daughter Rachel."
19Laban said, "It's better that I give her to you than to some
other man. Stay here with me." 20So Jacob served seven years to
get Rachel, but they seemed like only a few days to him because
of his love for her.
21Then Jacob said to Laban, "Give me my wife. My time is
completed, and I want to lie with her."
22So Laban brought together all the people of the place and gave
a feast. 23But when evening came, he took his daughter Leah and
gave her to Jacob, and Jacob lay with her. 24And Laban gave his
servant girl Zilpah to his daughter as her maidservant.
25When morning came, there was Leah! So Jacob said to Laban,
"What is this you have done to me? I served you for Rachel, didn't
I? Why have you deceived me?"
26Laban replied, "It is not our custom here to give the younger
daughter in marriage before the older one. 27Finish this daughter's
bridal week; then we will give you the younger one also, in return
for another seven years of work."
28And Jacob did so. He finished the week with Leah, and
then Laban gave him his daughter Rachel to be his wife. 29Laban
gave his servant girl Bilhah to his daughter Rachel as her maid-

**NIV** [a] 17 Or *delicate*

## King James

30And he went in also unto Rachel, and he loved also Rachel more than Leah, and served with him yet seven other years.
31¶ And when the LORD saw that Leah *was* hated, he opened her womb: but Rachel *was* barren.
32And Leah conceived, and bare a son, and she called his name Reuben: for she said, Surely the LORD hath looked upon my affliction; now therefore my husband will love me.
33And she conceived again, and bare a son; and said, Because the LORD hath heard that I *was* hated, he hath therefore given me this *son* also: and she called his name Simeon.
34And she conceived again, and bare a son; and said, Now this time will my husband be joined unto me, because I have born him three sons: therefore was his name called Levi.
35And she conceived again, and bare a son: and she said, Now will I praise the LORD: therefore she called his name Judah; and left bearing.

30 AND WHEN Rachel saw that she bare Jacob no children, Rachel envied her sister; and said unto Jacob, Give me children, or else I die.
2And Jacob's anger was kindled against Rachel: and he said, *Am* I in God's stead, who hath withheld from thee the fruit of the womb?
3And she said, Behold my maid Bilhah, go in unto her; and she shall bear upon my knees, that I may also have children by her.
4And she gave him Bilhah her handmaid to wife: and Jacob went in unto her.
5And Bilhah conceived, and bare Jacob a son.
6And Rachel said, God hath judged me, and hath also heard my voice, and hath given me a son: therefore called she his name Dan.
7And Bilhah Rachel's maid conceived again, and bare Jacob a second son.
8And Rachel said, With great wrestlings have I wrestled with my sister, and I have prevailed: and she called his name Naphtali.
9When Leah saw that she had left bearing, she took Zilpah her maid, and gave her Jacob to wife.
10And Zilpah Leah's maid bare Jacob a son.
11And Leah said, A troop cometh: and she called his name Gad.
12And Zilpah Leah's maid bare Jacob a second son.
13And Leah said, Happy am I, for the daughters will call me blessed: and she called his name Asher.
14¶ And Reuben went in the days of wheat harvest, and found mandrakes in the field, and brought them unto his mother Leah. Then Rachel said to Leah, Give me, I pray thee, of thy son's mandrakes.
15And she said unto her, *Is it* a small matter that thou hast taken my husband? and wouldest thou take away my son's mandrakes also? And Rachel said, Therefore he shall lie with thee tonight for thy son's mandrakes.
16And Jacob came out of the field in the evening, and Leah went out to meet him, and said, Thou must come in unto me; for surely I have hired thee with my son's mandrakes. And he lay with her that night.
17And God hearkened unto Leah, and she conceived, and bare Jacob the fifth son.
18And Leah said, God hath given me my hire, because I have given my maiden to my husband: and she called his name Issachar.
19And Leah conceived again, and bare Jacob the sixth son.

## Amplified

30And Jacob lived with Rachel also as his wife, and he loved Rachel more than Leah, and served [Laban] another seven years [for her].
31And when the Lord saw that Leah was despised, He made her able to bear children; but Rachel was barren.
32And Leah became pregnant and bore a son, and named him Reuben [See, a son!]; for she said, Because the Lord has seen my humiliation *and* affliction; now my husband will love me.
33[Leah] became pregnant again and bore a son, and said, Because the Lord heard that I am despised, He has given me this son also; and she named him Simeon [God hears].
34And she became pregnant again and bore a son, and said, Now this time will my husband be a companion to me, for I have borne him three sons. Therefore he was named Levi [companion].
35Again she conceived and bore a son; and she said, Now will I praise the Lord! So she called his name Judah [praise]; then [for a time] she ceased bearing.

30 WHEN RACHEL saw that she bore Jacob no children, she envied her sister, and said to Jacob, Give me children, or else I will die!
2And Jacob became very angry with Rachel, and he said, Am I in God's stead, Who has denied you children?
3And she said, See here, you take my maid Bilhah, and have intercourse with her; and [when the baby comes] she shall deliver it upon my knees, that I by her may also have children.
4And she gave him Bilhah her maid as a [secondary] wife, and Jacob had intercourse with her.
5And Bilhah became pregnant and bore Jacob a son.
6And Rachel said, God has judged *and* vindicated me, and has heard my plea and has given me a son; so she named him Dan [judged].
7And Bilhah Rachel's maid conceived again and bore Jacob a second son.
8And Rachel said, With mighty wrestlings [in prayer to God] I have struggled with my sister and have prevailed; so she named [this second son *Bilhah bore*] Naphtali [struggled].
9When Leah saw that she had ceased to bear, she gave Zilpah her maid to Jacob as a [secondary] wife.
10And Zilpah, Leah's maid, bore Jacob a son.
11Then Leah said, Victory *and* good fortune have come; and she named him Gad [fortune].
12Zilpah Leah's maid bore Jacob [her] second son.
13And Leah said, I am happy, for women will call me blessed [happy, fortunate, to be envied] and she named him Asher [happy].
14Now Reuben went at the time of wheat harvest and found some mandrakes [love apples] in the field, and brought them to his mother Leah. Then Rachel said to Leah, Give me, I pray you, some of your son's mandrakes.
15But [Leah] answered, Is it not enough that you have taken my husband without your taking away my son's [a]mandrakes also? And Rachel said, Jacob shall sleep with you tonight [in exchange] for your son's mandrakes.
16And Jacob came out of the field in the evening, and Leah went out to meet him, and said, You must sleep with me [tonight], for I have certainly paid your hire with my son's mandrakes. So he slept with her that night.
17And God heeded Leah's [prayer], and she conceived and bore Jacob [her] fifth son.
18Leah said, God has given me my hire, because I have given my maid to my husband; and she called his name Issachar [hired].
19And Leah became pregnant again and bore Jacob [her] sixth son.

AMP [a] Mandrakes were superstitiously supposed to excite and win love.

## New American Standard

30So *Jacob* went in to Rachel also, and indeed he loved Rachel
more than Leah, and he served with Laban for another seven
years.
31¶ Now the LORD saw that Leah was unloved, and He opened
her womb, but Rachel was barren.
32And Leah conceived and bore a son and named him Reuben,
for she said, "Because the LORD has seen my affliction; surely now
my husband will love me."
33Then she conceived again and bore a son and said, "Because
the LORD has heard that I am unloved, He has therefore given me
this *son* also." So she named him Simeon.
34And she conceived again and bore a son and said, "Now this
time my husband will become attached to me, because I have
borne him three sons." Therefore he was named Levi.
35And she conceived again and bore a son and said, "This time
I will praise the LORD." Therefore she named him Judah. Then she
stopped bearing.

*The Sons of Jacob*

**30** NOW WHEN Rachel saw that she bore Jacob no children,
she became jealous of her sister; and she said to Jacob,
"Give me children, or else I die."
2Then Jacob's anger burned against Rachel, and he said, "Am
I in the place of God, who has withheld from you the fruit of the
womb?"
3And she said, "Here is my maid Bilhah, go in to her, that she
may bear on my knees, that through her I too may have children."
4So she gave him her maid Bilhah as a wife, and Jacob went
in to her.
5And Bilhah conceived and bore Jacob a son.
6Then Rachel said, "God has vindicated me, and has indeed
heard my voice and has given me a son." Therefore she named
him Dan.
7And Rachel's maid Bilhah conceived again and bore Jacob a
second son.
8So Rachel said, "With mighty wrestlings I have wrestled with
my sister, *and* I have indeed prevailed." And she named him
Naphtali.
9¶ When Leah saw that she had stopped bearing, she took her
maid Zilpah and gave her to Jacob as a wife.
10And Leah's maid Zilpah bore Jacob a son.
11Then Leah said, "How fortunate!" So she named him Gad.
12And Leah's maid Zilpah bore Jacob a second son.
13Then Leah said, "Happy am I! For women will call me happy." So she named him Asher.
14¶ Now in the days of wheat harvest Reuben went and found
mandrakes in the field, and brought them to his mother Leah.
Then Rachel said to Leah, "Please give me some of your son's
mandrakes."
15But she said to her, "Is it a small matter for you to take my
husband? And would you take my son's mandrakes also?" So
Rachel said, "Therefore he may lie with you tonight in return for
your son's mandrakes."
16When Jacob came in from the field in the evening, then Leah
went out to meet him and said, "You must come in to me, for I
have surely hired you with my son's mandrakes." So he lay with
her that night.
17And God gave heed to Leah, and she conceived and bore
Jacob a fifth son.
18Then Leah said, "God has given me my wages, because I gave
my maid to my husband." So she named him Issachar.
19And Leah conceived again and bore a sixth son to Jacob.

## New International

servant. 30Jacob lay with Rachel also, and he loved Rachel more
than Leah. And he worked for Laban another seven years.

*Jacob's Children*

31When the LORD saw that Leah was not loved, he opened her
womb, but Rachel was barren. 32Leah became pregnant and gave
birth to a son. She named him Reuben,[b] for she said, "It is because
the LORD has seen my misery. Surely my husband will love me
now."
33She conceived again, and when she gave birth to a son she
said, "Because the LORD heard that I am not loved, he gave me this
one too." So she named him Simeon.[c]
34Again she conceived, and when she gave birth to a son she
said, "Now at last my husband will become attached to me, because I have borne him three sons." So he was named Levi.[d]
35She conceived again, and when she gave birth to a son she
said, "This time I will praise the LORD." So she named him Judah.[e]
Then she stopped having children.

**30** WHEN RACHEL saw that she was not bearing Jacob any
children, she became jealous of her sister. So she said to
Jacob, "Give me children, or I'll die!"
2Jacob became angry with her and said, "Am I in the place of
God, who has kept you from having children?"
3Then she said, "Here is Bilhah, my maidservant. Sleep with
her so that she can bear children for me and that through her I too
can build a family."
4So she gave him her servant Bilhah as a wife. Jacob slept with
her, 5and she became pregnant and bore him a son. 6Then Rachel
said, "God has vindicated me; he has listened to my plea and given
me a son." Because of this she named him Dan.[f]
7Rachel's servant Bilhah conceived again and bore Jacob a second son. 8Then Rachel said, "I have had a great struggle with my
sister, and I have won." So she named him Naphtali.[g]
9When Leah saw that she had stopped having children, she
took her maidservant Zilpah and gave her to Jacob as a wife.
10Leah's servant Zilpah bore Jacob a son. 11Then Leah said, "What
good fortune!"[h] So she named him Gad.[i]
12Leah's servant Zilpah bore Jacob a second son. 13Then Leah
said, "How happy I am! The women will call me happy." So she
named him Asher.[j]
14During wheat harvest, Reuben went out into the fields and
found some mandrake plants, which he brought to his mother
Leah. Rachel said to Leah, "Please give me some of your son's
mandrakes."
15But she said to her, "Wasn't it enough that you took away my
husband? Will you take my son's mandrakes too?"
"Very well," Rachel said, "he can sleep with you tonight in
return for your son's mandrakes."
16So when Jacob came in from the fields that evening, Leah
went out to meet him. "You must sleep with me," she said. "I have
hired you with my son's mandrakes." So he slept with her that
night.
17God listened to Leah, and she became pregnant and bore
Jacob a fifth son. 18Then Leah said, "God has rewarded me for
giving my maidservant to my husband." So she named him Issachar.[k]
19Leah conceived again and bore Jacob a sixth son. 20Then Leah

**NIV** [b] 32 *Reuben* sounds like the Hebrew for *he has seen my misery;* the name means *see, a son.* [c] 33 *Simeon* probably means *one who hears.* [d] 34 *Levi* sounds like and may be derived from the Hebrew for *attached.* [e] 35 *Judah* sounds like and may be derived from the Hebrew for *praise.* [f] 6 *Dan* here means *he has vindicated.* [g] 8 *Naphtali* means *my struggle.* [h] 11 Or *"A troop is coming!"* [i] 11 *Gad* can mean *good fortune* or *a troop.* [j] 13 *Asher* means *happy.* [k] 18 *Issachar* sounds like the Hebrew for *reward.*

## King James

20 And Leah said, God hath endued me *with* a good dowry; now will my husband dwell with me, because I have born him six sons: and she called his name Zebulun.

21 And afterwards she bare a daughter, and called her name Dinah.

22 ¶ And God remembered Rachel, and God hearkened to her, and opened her womb.

23 And she conceived, and bare a son; and said, God hath taken away my reproach:

24 And she called his name Joseph; and said, The LORD shall add to me another son.

25 ¶ And it came to pass, when Rachel had born Joseph, that Jacob said unto Laban, Send me away, that I may go unto mine own place, and to my country.

26 Give *me* my wives and my children, for whom I have served thee, and let me go: for thou knowest my service which I have done thee.

27 And Laban said unto him, I pray thee, if I have found favour in thine eyes, *tarry: for* I have learned by experience that the LORD hath blessed me for thy sake.

28 And he said, Appoint me thy wages, and I will give *it*.

29 And he said unto him, Thou knowest how I have served thee, and how thy cattle was with me.

30 For *it was* little which thou hadst before I *came*, and it is *now* increased unto a multitude; and the LORD hath blessed thee since my coming: and now when shall I provide for mine own house also?

31 And he said, What shall I give thee? And Jacob said, Thou shalt not give me any thing: if thou wilt do this thing for me, I will again feed *and* keep thy flock.

32 I will pass through all thy flock today, removing from thence all the speckled and spotted cattle, and all the brown cattle among the sheep, and the spotted and speckled among the goats: and *of such* shall be my hire.

33 So shall my righteousness answer for me in time to come, when it shall come for my hire before thy face: every one that *is* not speckled and spotted among the goats, and brown among the sheep, that shall be counted stolen with me.

34 And Laban said, Behold, I would it might be according to thy word.

35 And he removed that day the he goats that were ringstraked and spotted, and all the she goats that were speckled and spotted, *and* every one that had *some* white in it, and all the brown among the sheep, and gave *them* into the hand of his sons.

36 And he set three days' journey betwixt himself and Jacob: and Jacob fed the rest of Laban's flocks.

37 ¶ And Jacob took him rods of green poplar, and of the hazel and chestnut tree; and pilled white strakes in them, and made the white appear which *was* in the rods.

38 And he set the rods which he had pilled before the flocks in the gutters in the watering troughs when the flocks came to drink, that they should conceive when they came to drink.

39 And the flocks conceived before the rods, and brought forth cattle ringstraked, speckled, and spotted.

40 And Jacob did separate the lambs, and set the faces of the flocks toward the ringstraked, and all the brown in the flock of Laban; and he put his own flocks by themselves, and put them not unto Laban's cattle.

41 And it came to pass, whensoever the stronger cattle did conceive, that Jacob laid the rods before the eyes of the cattle in the gutters, that they might conceive among the rods.

42 But when the cattle were feeble, he put *them* not in: so the feebler were Laban's, and the stronger Jacob's.

43 And the man increased exceedingly, and had much cattle, and maidservants, and menservants, and camels, and asses.

## Amplified

20 Then Leah said, God has endowed me with a good marriage gift [for my husband]; now will he dwell with me [and regard me as his wife in reality], because I have borne him six sons; and she named him Zebulun [dwelling].

21 Afterwards she bore a daughter and called her Dinah.

22 Then God remembered Rachel, and answered her pleading, and made it possible for her to have children.

23 And [now for the first time] she became pregnant and bore a son; and she said, God has taken away my reproach, disgrace *and* humiliation.

24 And she called his name Joseph [may he add] and said, May the Lord add to me another son.

25 When Rachel had borne Joseph, Jacob said to Laban, Send me away, that I may go to my own place and country.

26 Give me my wives and my children, for whom I have served you, and let me go; for you know the work which I have done for you.

27 And Laban said to him, If I have found favor in your sight, I pray you [do not go]; for I have learned by experience *and* from the omens in divination that the Lord has favored me with blessings on your account.

28 He said, State your salary, and I will give it.

29 Jacob answered him, You know how I have served you, and how your possessions, your cattle *and* sheep *and* goats, have fared with me.

30 For you had little before I came, and it has increased *and* multiplied abundantly; and the Lord has favored you with blessings wherever I turned. But now when shall I provide for my own house also?

31 [Laban] said, What shall I give you? And Jacob said, You shall not give me anything, if you will do this one thing for me [of which I am about to tell you], and I will again feed *and* take care of your flock.

32 Let me pass through all your flock today, removing from it every speckled and spotted animal and every black one among the sheep, and the spotted and speckled among the goats; and such shall be my wages.

33 So later when the matter of my wages is brought before you, my fair dealing will be evident *and* answer for me. Every one that is not speckled and spotted among the goats and black among the sheep, if found with me, shall be counted as stolen.

34 And Laban said, Well; let it be done as you say.

35 But that same day [Laban] removed the he-goats that were streaked and spotted, and all the she-goats that were speckled and spotted, every one that had white on it, and every black lamb and put them in charge of his sons.

36 And he set [a distance of] three days' journey between himself and Jacob; and Jacob *was then left* in care of the rest of Laban's flock.

37 But Jacob took fresh rods of poplar and almond and plane trees, and peeled white streaks in them, exposing the white in the rods.

38 Then he set the rods which he had peeled in front of the flocks, in the watering troughs where the flocks came to drink. And since they bred *and* conceived when they came to drink,

39 The flocks bred *and* conceived in sight of the rods, and brought forth lambs *and* kids streaked, speckled, and spotted.

40 Jacob separated the lambs, and [as he had done with the peeled rods] he also set the faces of the flocks toward the streaked and all the dark in the *new* flock of Laban; and he put his own droves by themselves, and did not let them *breed* with Laban's flock.

41 And whenever the stronger animals were breeding, Jacob laid the rods in the watering troughs before the eyes of the flock, that they might breed *and* conceive among the rods.

42 But when the sheep *and* goats were feeble he omitted putting the rods there; so the feebler animals were Laban's, and the stronger Jacob's.

43 Thus the man increased *and* became exceedingly rich, and had many sheep *and* goats, and maidservants, menservants, camels, and donkeys.

## New American Standard

20Then Leah said, "God has endowed me with a good gift; now
my husband will dwell with me, because I have borne him six
sons." So she named him Zebulun.
21And afterward she bore a daughter and named her Dinah.
22Then God remembered Rachel, and God gave heed to her and
opened her womb.
23So she conceived and bore a son and said, "God has taken
away my reproach."
24And she named him Joseph, saying, "May the LORD give me
another son."

*Jacob Prospers*

25¶ Now it came about when Rachel had borne Joseph, that
Jacob said to Laban, "Send me away, that I may go to my own place
and to my own country.
26"Give *me* my wives and my children for whom I have served
you, and let me depart; for you yourself know my service which
I have rendered you."
27But Laban said to him, "If now [a]it pleases you, *stay with me;*
I have divined that the LORD has blessed me on your account."
28And he continued, "Name me your wages, and I will give it."
29But he said to him, "You yourself know how I have served
you and how your cattle have fared with me.
30"For you had little before I came, and it has increased to a
multitude; and the LORD has blessed you wherever I turned. But
now, when shall I provide for my own household also?"
31So he said, "What shall I give you?" And Jacob said, "You
shall not give me anything. If you will do this *one* thing for me, I
will again pasture *and* keep your flock:
32let me pass through your entire flock today, removing from
there every speckled and spotted sheep, and every black one
among the lambs, and the spotted and speckled among the goats;
and *such* shall be my wages.
33"So my honesty will answer for me later, when you come
concerning my wages. Every one that is not speckled and spotted
among the goats and black among the lambs, *if found* with me, will
be considered stolen."
34And Laban said, "Good, let it be according to your word."
35So he removed on that day the striped and spotted male goats
and all the speckled and spotted female goats, every one with
white in it, and all the black ones among the sheep, and gave them
into the care of his sons.
36And he put *a distance of* three days' journey between himself
and Jacob, and Jacob fed the rest of Laban's flocks.
37¶ Then Jacob took fresh rods of poplar and almond and plane
trees, and peeled white stripes in them, exposing the white which
*was* in the rods.
38And he set the rods which he had peeled in front of the flocks
in the gutters, *even* in the watering troughs, where the flocks came
to drink; and they mated when they came to drink.
39So the flocks mated by the rods, and the flocks brought forth
striped, speckled, and spotted.
40And Jacob separated the lambs, and made the flocks face
toward the striped and all the black in the flock of Laban; and he
put his own herds apart, and did not put them with Laban's flock.
41Moreover, it came about whenever the stronger of the flock
were mating, that Jacob would place the rods in the sight of the
flock in the gutters, so that they might mate by the rods;
42but when the flock was feeble, he did not put *them* in; so the
feebler were Laban's and the stronger Jacob's.
43So the man became exceedingly prosperous, and had large
flocks and female and male servants and camels and donkeys.

**NAS** [a] Lit., *I have found favor in your eyes*

## New International

said, "God has presented me with a precious gift. This time my
husband will treat me with honor, because I have borne him six
sons." So she named him Zebulun.[b]
21Some time later she gave birth to a daughter and named her
Dinah.
22Then God remembered Rachel; he listened to her and opened
her womb. 23She became pregnant and gave birth to a son and
said, "God has taken away my disgrace." 24She named him Joseph,[c] and said, "May the LORD add to me another son."

*Jacob's Flocks Increase*

25After Rachel gave birth to Joseph, Jacob said to Laban, "Send
me on my way so I can go back to my own homeland. 26Give me
my wives and children, for whom I have served you, and I will be
on my way. You know how much work I've done for you."
27But Laban said to him, "If I have found favor in your eyes,
please stay. I have learned by divination that[d] the LORD has
blessed me because of you." 28He added, "Name your wages, and
I will pay them."
29Jacob said to him, "You know how I have worked for you and
how your livestock has fared under my care. 30The little you had
before I came has increased greatly, and the LORD has blessed you
wherever I have been. But now, when may I do something for my
own household?"
31"What shall I give you?" he asked.
"Don't give me anything," Jacob replied. "But if you will do this
one thing for me, I will go on tending your flocks and watching
over them: 32Let me go through all your flocks today and remove
from them every speckled or spotted sheep, every dark-colored
lamb and every spotted or speckled goat. They will be my wages.
33And my honesty will testify for me in the future, whenever you
check on the wages you have paid me. Any goat in my possession
that is not speckled or spotted, or any lamb that is not dark-colored, will be considered stolen."
34"Agreed," said Laban. "Let it be as you have said." 35That
same day he removed all the male goats that were streaked or
spotted, and all the speckled or spotted female goats (all that had
white on them) and all the dark-colored lambs, and he placed them
in the care of his sons. 36Then he put a three-day journey between
himself and Jacob, while Jacob continued to tend the rest of Laban's flocks.
37Jacob, however, took fresh-cut branches from poplar, almond
and plane trees and made white stripes on them by peeling the
bark and exposing the white inner wood of the branches. 38Then
he placed the peeled branches in all the watering troughs, so that
they would be directly in front of the flocks when they came to
drink. When the flocks were in heat and came to drink, 39they
mated in front of the branches. And they bore young that were
streaked or speckled or spotted. 40Jacob set apart the young of the
flock by themselves, but made the rest face the streaked and dark-
colored animals that belonged to Laban. Thus he made separate
flocks for himself and did not put them with Laban's animals.
41Whenever the stronger females were in heat, Jacob would place
the branches in the troughs in front of the animals so they would
mate near the branches, 42but if the animals were weak, he would
not place them there. So the weak animals went to Laban and the
strong ones to Jacob. 43In this way the man grew exceedingly
prosperous and came to own large flocks, and maidservants and
menservants, and camels and donkeys.

**NIV** [b] 20 *Zebulun* probably means *honor.* [c] 24 *Joseph* means *may he add.*
[d] 27 Or possibly *have become rich and*

## King James

# 31 AND HE heard the words of Laban's sons, saying, Jacob hath taken away all that *was* our father's; and of *that* which *was* our father's hath he gotten all this glory.

2And Jacob beheld the countenance of Laban, and, behold, it *was* not toward him as before.

3And the LORD said unto Jacob, Return unto the land of thy fathers, and to thy kindred; and I will be with thee.

4And Jacob sent and called Rachel and Leah to the field unto his flock,

5And said unto them, I see your father's countenance, that it *is* not toward me as before; but the God of my father hath been with me.

6And ye know that with all my power I have served your father.

7And your father hath deceived me, and changed my wages ten times; but God suffered him not to hurt me.

8If he said thus, The speckled shall be thy wages; then all the cattle bare speckled: and if he said thus, The ringstraked shall be thy hire; then bare all the cattle ringstraked.

9Thus God hath taken away the cattle of your father, and given *them* to me.

10And it came to pass at the time that the cattle conceived, that I lifted up mine eyes, and saw in a dream, and, behold, the rams which leaped upon the cattle *were* ringstraked, speckled, and grisled.

11And the angel of God spake unto me in a dream, *saying*, Jacob: And I said, Here *am* I.

12And he said, Lift up now thine eyes, and see, all the rams which leap upon the cattle *are* ringstraked, speckled, and grisled: for I have seen all that Laban doeth unto thee.

13I *am* the God of Beth-el, where thou anointedst the pillar, *and* where thou vowedst a vow unto me: now arise, get thee out from this land, and return unto the land of thy kindred.

14And Rachel and Leah answered and said unto him, *Is there* yet any portion or inheritance for us in our father's house?

15Are we not counted of him strangers? for he hath sold us, and hath quite devoured also our money.

16For all the riches which God hath taken from our father, that *is* ours, and our children's: now then, whatsoever God hath said unto thee, do.

17¶ Then Jacob rose up, and set his sons and his wives upon camels;

18And he carried away all his cattle, and all his goods which he had gotten, the cattle of his getting, which he had gotten in Padan-aram, for to go to Isaac his father in the land of Canaan.

19And Laban went to shear his sheep: and Rachel had stolen the images that *were* her father's.

20And Jacob stole away unawares to Laban the Syrian, in that he told him not that he fled.

21So he fled with all that he had; and he rose up, and passed over the river, and set his face *toward* the mount Gilead.

22And it was told Laban on the third day that Jacob was fled.

23And he took his brethren with him, and pursued after him seven days' journey; and they overtook him in the mount Gilead.

24And God came to Laban the Syrian in a dream by night, and said unto him, Take heed that thou speak not to Jacob either good or bad.

25¶ Then Laban overtook Jacob. Now Jacob had pitched his tent in the mount: and Laban with his brethren pitched in the mount of Gilead.

26And Laban said to Jacob, What hast thou done, that thou hast stolen away unawares to me, and carried away my daughters, as captives *taken* with the sword?

## Amplified

# 31 JACOB HEARD Laban's sons complaining, Jacob has taken away all that was our father's; he has acquired all this wealth *and* honor from what belonged to our father.

2And Jacob noticed that Laban looked at him less favorably than before.

3Then the Lord said to Jacob, Return to the land of your father and to your people, and I will be with you.

4So Jacob sent and called Rachel and Leah to the field to his flock,

5And he said to them, I see how your father looks at me, that he is not [friendly] toward me as before; but the God of my father has been with me.

6You know that I have served your father with all my might *and* power.

7But your father has deceived me, and changed my wages ten times; but God did not allow him to hurt me.

8If he said, The speckled shall be your wages, then all the flock bore speckled; and if he said, The streaked shall be your hire, then all the flock bore streaked.

9Thus God has taken away the flocks of your father and given them to me.

10And I had a dream at the time the flock conceived. I looked up and saw that the rams which mated with the she-goats were streaked, speckled, and spotted.

11And the Angel of God said to me [a]in the dream, Jacob. And I said, Here am I.

12And He said, Look up and see, all the rams which mate with the flock are streaked, speckled, and mottled; for I have seen all that Laban does to you.

13I am the God of Bethel, where you anointed the pillar, and where you vowed a vow to Me. Now arise, get out from this land, and return to your native land.

14And Rachel and Leah answered him, Is there any portion or inheritance for us in our father's house?

15Are we not counted by him as strangers? For he sold us, and has also quite devoured our money [the price you paid for us].

16For all the riches which God has taken from our father are ours and our children's. Now then, whatever God has said to you, do it.

17Then Jacob rose up and set his sons and his wives upon the camels;

18And he drove away all his livestock, and all his gain which he had gotten, the livestock he had obtained *and* accumulated in Padan-aram, to go to Isaac his father in the land of Canaan.

19Now Laban had gone to shear his sheep [possibly to the feast of sheep-shearing], and Rachel stole her father's household gods.

20And Jacob outwitted Laban the Syrian [Aramean] in that he did not tell him that he [intended] to flee, *and* slip away secretly.

21So he fled with all that he had, and arose and crossed the river [Euphrates], and set his face toward the hill country of Gilead.

22But on the third day Laban was told that Jacob had fled.

23So he took his kinsmen with him, and pursued after [Jacob] for seven days, and they overtook him in the hill country of Gilead.

24But God came to Laban the Syrian [Aramean] in a dream by night, and said to him, Be careful that you do not speak from good to bad to Jacob [peaceably, then violently].

25Then Laban overtook Jacob. Now Jacob had pitched his tent on the hill, and Laban coming with his kinsmen pitched [his tents] on the same hill of Gilead.

26And Laban said to Jacob, What do you mean stealing away *and* leaving like this without my knowing it, and carrying off my daughters as if captives of the sword?

**AMP** [a] We naturally wonder that we have not heard of this dream before and are tempted to question Jacob's truthfulness; but the Samaritan text removes all such doubt by recording the whole dream in the previous chapter after verse 36 (Clarke's *Commentary*).

## New American Standard

*Jacob Leaves Secretly for Canaan*

31 NOW JACOB heard the words of Laban's sons, saying,
"Jacob has taken away all that was our father's, and from
what belonged to our father he has made all this wealth."
2And Jacob saw the [b]attitude of Laban, and behold, it was not
*friendly* toward him as formerly.
3Then the LORD said to Jacob, "Return to the land of your
fathers and to your relatives, and I will be with you."
4So Jacob sent and called Rachel and Leah to his flock in the
field,
5and said to them, "I see your father's attitude, that it is not
*friendly* toward me as formerly, but the God of my father has been
with me.
6"And you know that I have served your father with all my
strength.
7"Yet your father has cheated me and changed my wages ten
times; however, God did not allow him to hurt me.
8"If he spoke thus, 'The speckled shall be your wages,' then
all the flock brought forth speckled; and if he spoke thus, 'The
striped shall be your wages,' then all the flock brought forth
striped.
9"Thus God has taken away your father's livestock and given
*them* to me.
10"And it came about at the time when the flock were mating
that I lifted up my eyes and saw in a dream, and behold, the male
goats which were mating *were* striped, speckled, and mottled.
11"Then the angel of God said to me in the dream, 'Jacob,' and
I said, 'Here I am.'
12"And he said, 'Lift up, now, your eyes and see *that* all the
male goats which are mating are striped, speckled, and mottled;
for I have seen all that Laban has been doing to you.
13'I am the God *of* Bethel, where you anointed a pillar, where
you made a vow to Me; now arise, leave this land, and return to
the land of your birth.'"
14And Rachel and Leah answered and said to him, "Do we still
have any portion or inheritance in our father's house?
15"Are we not reckoned by him as foreigners? For he has sold
us, and has also entirely consumed our purchase price.
16"Surely all the wealth which God has taken away from our
father belongs to us and our children; now then, do whatever God
has said to you."
17¶ Then Jacob arose and put his children and his wives upon
camels;
18and he drove away all his livestock and all his property which
he had gathered, his acquired livestock which he had gathered in
Paddan-aram, to go to the land of Canaan to his father Isaac.
19When Laban had gone to shear his flock, then Rachel stole the
household idols that were her father's.
20And Jacob deceived Laban the Aramean, by not telling him
that he was fleeing.
21So he fled with all that he had; and he arose and crossed the
*Euphrates* River, and set his face toward the hill country of Gilead.

*Laban Pursues Jacob*

22¶ When it was told Laban on the third day that Jacob had fled,
23then he took his kinsmen with him, and pursued him *a dis-*
*tance of* seven days' journey; and he overtook him in the hill country of Gilead.
24And God came to Laban the Aramean in a dream of the night,
and said to him, "Be careful that you do not speak to Jacob either
good or bad."
25And Laban caught up with Jacob. Now Jacob had pitched his
tent in the hill country, and Laban with his kinsmen camped in the
hill country of Gilead.
26Then Laban said to Jacob, "What have you done by deceiving
me and carrying away my daughters like captives of the sword?

NAS [b] Lit., *face*

## New International

*Jacob Flees From Laban*

31 JACOB HEARD that Laban's sons were saying, "Jacob has
taken everything our father owned and has gained all this
wealth from what belonged to our father." 2And Jacob noticed that
Laban's attitude toward him was not what it had been.
3Then the LORD said to Jacob, "Go back to the land of your
fathers and to your relatives, and I will be with you."
4So Jacob sent word to Rachel and Leah to come out to the fields
where his flocks were. 5He said to them, "I see that your father's
attitude toward me is not what it was before, but the God of my
father has been with me. 6You know that I've worked for your
father with all my strength, 7yet your father has cheated me by
changing my wages ten times. However, God has not allowed him
to harm me. 8If he said, 'The speckled ones will be your wages,'
then all the flocks gave birth to speckled young; and if he said, 'The
streaked ones will be your wages,' then all the flocks bore streaked
young. 9So God has taken away your father's livestock and has
given them to me.
10"In breeding season I once had a dream in which I looked up
and saw that the male goats mating with the flock were streaked,
speckled or spotted. 11The angel of God said to me in the dream,
'Jacob.' I answered, 'Here I am.' 12And he said, 'Look up and see
that all the male goats mating with the flock are streaked, speckled
or spotted, for I have seen all that Laban has been doing to you.
13I am the God of Bethel, where you anointed a pillar and where
you made a vow to me. Now leave this land at once and go back
to your native land.'"
14Then Rachel and Leah replied, "Do we still have any share in
the inheritance of our father's estate? 15Does he not regard us as
foreigners? Not only has he sold us, but he has used up what was
paid for us. 16Surely all the wealth that God took away from our
father belongs to us and our children. So do whatever God has told
you."
17Then Jacob put his children and his wives on camels, 18and
he drove all his livestock ahead of him, along with all the goods
he had accumulated in Paddan Aram,[c] to go to his father Isaac in
the land of Canaan.
19When Laban had gone to shear his sheep, Rachel stole her
father's household gods. 20Moreover, Jacob deceived Laban the
Aramean by not telling him he was running away. 21So he fled
with all he had, and crossing the River,[d] he headed for the hill
country of Gilead.

*Laban Pursues Jacob*

22On the third day Laban was told that Jacob had fled. 23Taking
his relatives with him, he pursued Jacob for seven days and caught
up with him in the hill country of Gilead. 24Then God came to
Laban the Aramean in a dream at night and said to him, "Be careful
not to say anything to Jacob, either good or bad."
25Jacob had pitched his tent in the hill country of Gilead when
Laban overtook him, and Laban and his relatives camped there
too. 26Then Laban said to Jacob, "What have you done? You've
deceived me, and you've carried off my daughters like captives in
war. 27Why did you run off secretly and deceive me? Why didn't

NIV [c] *18* That is, Northwest Mesopotamia [d] *21* That is, the Euphrates

## King James

27 Wherefore didst thou flee away secretly, and steal away from
me; and didst not tell me, that I might have sent thee away with
mirth, and with songs, with tabret, and with harp?
28 And hast not suffered me to kiss my sons and my daughters?
thou hast now done foolishly in *so* doing.
29 It is in the power of my hand to do you hurt: but the God of
your father spake unto me yesternight, saying, Take thou heed
that thou speak not to Jacob either good or bad.
30 And now, *though* thou wouldest needs be gone, because thou
sore longedst after thy father's house, *yet* wherefore hast thou
stolen my gods?
31 And Jacob answered and said to Laban, Because I was afraid:
for I said, Peradventure thou wouldest take by force thy daughters
from me.
32 With whomsoever thou findest thy gods, let him not live:
before our brethren discern thou what *is* thine with me, and take
*it* to thee. For Jacob knew not that Rachel had stolen them.
33 And Laban went into Jacob's tent, and into Leah's tent, and
into the two maidservants' tents; but he found *them* not. Then
went he out of Leah's tent, and entered into Rachel's tent.
34 Now Rachel had taken the images, and put them in the camel's furniture, and sat upon them. And Laban searched all the tent,
but found *them* not.
35 And she said to her father, Let it not displease my lord that
I cannot rise up before thee; for the custom of women *is* upon me.
And he searched, but found not the images.
36 ¶ And Jacob was wroth, and chode with Laban: and Jacob
answered and said to Laban, What *is* my trespass? what *is* my sin,
that thou hast so hotly pursued after me?
37 Whereas thou hast searched all my stuff, what hast thou
found of all thy household stuff? set *it* here before my brethren and
thy brethren, that they may judge betwixt us both.
38 This twenty years *have* I *been* with thee; thy ewes and thy she
goats have not cast their young, and the rams of thy flock have I
not eaten.
39 That which was torn *of beasts* I brought not unto thee; I bare
the loss of it; of my hand didst thou require it, *whether* stolen by
day, or stolen by night.
40 *Thus* I was; in the day the drought consumed me, and the
frost by night; and my sleep departed from mine eyes.
41 Thus have I been twenty years in thy house; I served thee
fourteen years for thy two daughters, and six years for thy cattle:
and thou hast changed my wages ten times.
42 Except the God of my father, the God of Abraham, and the
fear of Isaac, had been with me, surely thou hadst sent me away
now empty. God hath seen mine affliction and the labour of my
hands, and rebuked *thee* yesternight.
43 ¶ And Laban answered and said unto Jacob, *These* daughters
*are* my daughters, and *these* children *are* my children, and *these*
cattle *are* my cattle, and all that thou seest *is* mine: and what can
I do this day unto these my daughters, or unto their children which
they have born?
44 Now therefore come thou, let us make a covenant, I and thou;
and let it be for a witness between me and thee.
45 And Jacob took a stone, and set it up *for* a pillar.
46 And Jacob said unto his brethren, Gather stones; and they
took stones, and made an heap: and they did eat there upon the
heap.

## Amplified

27 Why did you flee secretly, and cheat me, and did not tell me,
so that I might have sent you away with joy *and* gladness and with
singing, with tambourine and lyre?
28 And why did you not permit me to kiss my sons [grandchil-
dren] and my daughters goodbye? Now you have done foolishly
[in behaving like this].
29 It is in my power to do you harm; but the God of your father
spoke to me last night, saying, Be careful that you do not speak
from good to bad to Jacob—peaceably, then violently.
30 And now, you felt you must go because you were homesick
for your father's house, but why did you steal my [household]
gods?
31 Jacob answered Laban, Because I was afraid; for I thought,
Suppose you would take your daughters from me by force.
32 The one with whom you find those gods of yours, let him not
live. Here before our kinsmen [search my possessions and] take
whatever you find that belongs to you. For Jacob did not know that
Rachel had stolen [the images].
33 So Laban went into Jacob's tent, and into Leah's tent, and the
tent of the two maids, but he did not find them. Then he went from
Leah's tent into Rachel's tent.
34 Now Rachel had taken the images (gods) and put them in the
camel's saddle, and sat on them. Laban searched *and* felt through
all the tent, but did not find them.
35 And [Rachel] said to her father, Do not be displeased, my
lord, that I cannot rise up before you, for the period of women is
upon me *and* I am unwell. And he searched, but did not find the
gods.
36 Then Jacob became angry and reproached *and* argued with
Laban. And Jacob said to Laban, [a]What is my fault? What is my
sin, that you so hotly pursued after me?
37 Although you have searched *and* felt through all my household possessions, what have you found of all your household
goods? Put it here before my brethren and yours, that they may
judge *and* decide between us.
38 These twenty years I have been with you; your ewes and your
she-goats have not lost their young, and the rams of your flock
have not been eaten by me.
39 I did not bring you [the carcasses of the animals] torn by wild
beasts; I bore the loss of it; you required of me [to make good] all
that were stolen, whether it occurred by day or by night.
40 This was [my lot]; by day the heat consumed me and by night
the cold, and I could not sleep.
41 I have been twenty years in your house. I served you fourteen
years for your two daughters, and six years for your flock; and you
have changed my wages ten times.
42 And if the God of my father, the God of Abraham and the
Dread [lest he should fall] *and* Fear [lest he offend] of Isaac, had
not been with me, surely you would have sent me away now
empty-handed. God has seen my affliction *and* humiliation and the
[wearying] labor of my hands, and rebuked you last night.
43 Laban answered Jacob, These daughters are my daughters,
these children are my children, these flocks are my flocks, and all
that you see is mine. But what can I do today to these my daughters, or to their children whom they have borne?
44 So come now, let us make a covenant *or* league, you and I,
and let it be for a witness between you and me.
45 So Jacob set up a stone for a pillar *or* monument.
46 And Jacob said to his brethren, Gather stones; and they took
stones and made a heap; and they ate [together] there upon the
heap. [Prov. 16:7.]

**AMP** [a] Why was Laban making such a great commotion about some small idols? It had never been satisfactorily explained until the answer was found in the excavated Nuzi tablets (J. P. Free in *Archaeology Illuminates the Bible*), which showed that possession of the father's household gods played an important role in inheritance (W. F. Albright in "Recent Discoveries in Bible Lands," supplement to *Young's Analytical Concordance to the Bible*, 1936). One of the Nuzi tablets indicated that in the region where Laban lived, a son-in-law who possessed the family images could appear in court and make claim to the estate of his father-in-law (various authors cited by Allan A. MacRae in "The Relation of Archaeology to the Bible," in *Modern Science and Christian Faith*). Since Jacob's possession of the images implied the right to inheritance of Laban's wealth, one can understand why Laban organized his hurried expedition to recover the images (J. P. Free in *Archaeology and Bible History*, adapted).

## New American Standard

27"Why did you flee secretly and deceive me, and did not tell
me, so that I might have sent you away with joy and with songs,
with timbrel and with lyre;
28and did not allow me to kiss my sons and my daughters? Now
you have done foolishly.
29"It is in my power to do you harm, but the God of your father
spoke to me last night, saying, 'Be careful not to speak either good
or bad to Jacob.'
30"And now you have indeed gone away because you longed
greatly for your father's house; *but* why did you steal my gods?"
31Then Jacob answered and said to Laban, "Because I was
afraid, for I said, 'Lest you would take your daughters from me by
force.'
32"The one with whom you find your gods shall not live; in the
presence of our kinsmen point out what is yours among my belongings and take *it* for yourself." For Jacob did not know that
Rachel had stolen them.
33¶ So Laban went into Jacob's tent, and into Leah's tent, and
into the tent of the two maids, but he did not find *them.* Then he
went out of Leah's tent and entered Rachel's tent.
34Now Rachel had taken the household idols and put them in
the camel's saddle, and she sat on them. And Laban felt through
all the tent, but did not find *them.*
35And she said to her father, "Let not my lord be angry that I
cannot rise before you, for the manner of women is upon me." So
he searched, but did not find the household idols.
36¶ Then Jacob became angry and contended with Laban; and
Jacob answered and said to Laban, "What is my transgression?
What is my sin, that you have hotly pursued me?
37"Though you have felt through all my goods, what have you
found of all your household goods? Set *it* here before my kinsmen
and your kinsmen, that they may decide between us two.
38"These twenty years I *have been* with you; your ewes and your
female goats have not miscarried, nor have I eaten the rams of your
flocks.
39"That which was torn *of beasts* I did not bring to you; I bore
the loss of it myself. You required it of my hand *whether* stolen by
day or stolen by night.
40" *Thus* I was: by day the heat consumed me, and the frost by
night, and my sleep fled from my eyes.
41"These twenty years I have been in your house; I served you
fourteen years for your two daughters, and six years for your flock,
and you changed my wages ten times.
42"If the God of my father, the God of Abraham, and the fear
of Isaac, had not been for me, surely now you would have sent me
away empty-handed. God has seen my affliction and the toil of my
hands, so He rendered judgment last night."

*The Covenant of Mizpah*

43¶ Then Laban answered and said to Jacob, "The daughters are
my daughters, and the children are my children, and the flocks are
my flocks, and all that you see is mine. But what can I do this day
to these my daughters or to their children whom they have borne?
44"So now come, let us make a covenant, you and I, and let it
be a witness between you and me."
45Then Jacob took a stone and set it up *as* a pillar.
46And Jacob said to his kinsmen, "Gather stones." So they took
stones and made a heap, and they ate there by the heap.

## New International

you tell me, so I could send you away with joy and singing to the
music of tambourines and harps? 28You didn't even let me kiss my
grandchildren and my daughters good-by. You have done a foolish thing. 29I have the power to harm you; but last night the God
of your father said to me, 'Be careful not to say anything to Jacob,
either good or bad.' 30Now you have gone off because you longed
to return to your father's house. But why did you steal my gods?"
31Jacob answered Laban, "I was afraid, because I thought you
would take your daughters away from me by force. 32But if you
find anyone who has your gods, he shall not live. In the presence
of our relatives, see for yourself whether there is anything of yours
here with me; and if so, take it." Now Jacob did not know that
Rachel had stolen the gods.
33So Laban went into Jacob's tent and into Leah's tent and into
the tent of the two maidservants, but he found nothing. After he
came out of Leah's tent, he entered Rachel's tent. 34Now Rachel
had taken the household gods and put them inside her camel's
saddle and was sitting on them. Laban searched through everything in the tent but found nothing.
35Rachel said to her father, "Don't be angry, my lord, that I
cannot stand up in your presence; I'm having my period." So he
searched but could not find the household gods.
36Jacob was angry and took Laban to task. "What is my crime?"
he asked Laban. "What sin have I committed that you hunt me
down? 37Now that you have searched through all my goods, what
have you found that belongs to your household? Put it here in
front of your relatives and mine, and let them judge between the
two of us.
38"I have been with you for twenty years now. Your sheep and
goats have not miscarried, nor have I eaten rams from your flocks.
39I did not bring you animals torn by wild beasts; I bore the loss
myself. And you demanded payment from me for whatever was
stolen by day or night. 40This was my situation: The heat consumed me in the daytime and the cold at night, and sleep fled from
my eyes. 41It was like this for the twenty years I was in your
household. I worked for you fourteen years for your two daughters and six years for your flocks, and you changed my wages ten
times. 42If the God of my father, the God of Abraham and the Fear
of Isaac, had not been with me, you would surely have sent me
away empty-handed. But God has seen my hardship and the toil
of my hands, and last night he rebuked you."
43Laban answered Jacob, "The women are my daughters, the
children are my children, and the flocks are my flocks. All you see
is mine. Yet what can I do today about these daughters of mine,
or about the children they have borne? 44Come now, let's make a
covenant, you and I, and let it serve as a witness between us."
45So Jacob took a stone and set it up as a pillar. 46He said to his
relatives, "Gather some stones." So they took stones and piled

## King James

47And Laban called it Jegar-sahadutha: but Jacob called it Galeed.
48And Laban said, This heap *is* a witness between me and thee this day. Therefore was the name of it called Galeed;
49And Mizpah; for he said, The LORD watch between me and thee, when we are absent one from another.
50If thou shalt afflict my daughters, or if thou shalt take *other* wives beside my daughters, no man *is* with us; see, God *is* witness betwixt me and thee.
51And Laban said to Jacob, Behold this heap, and behold *this* pillar, which I have cast betwixt me and thee;
52This heap *be* witness, and *this* pillar *be* witness, that I will not pass over this heap to thee, and that thou shalt not pass over this heap and this pillar unto me, for harm.
53The God of Abraham, and the God of Nahor, the God of their father, judge betwixt us. And Jacob sware by the fear of his father Isaac.
54Then Jacob offered sacrifice upon the mount, and called his brethren to eat bread: and they did eat bread, and tarried all night in the mount.
55And early in the morning Laban rose up, and kissed his sons and his daughters, and blessed them: and Laban departed, and returned unto his place.

**32** AND JACOB went on his way, and the angels of God met him.
2And when Jacob saw them, he said, This *is* God's host: and he called the name of that place Mahanaim.
3And Jacob sent messengers before him to Esau his brother unto the land of Seir, the country of Edom.
4And he commanded them, saying, Thus shall ye speak unto my lord Esau; Thy servant Jacob saith thus, I have sojourned with Laban, and stayed there until now:
5And I have oxen, and asses, flocks, and menservants, and womenservants: and I have sent to tell my lord, that I may find grace in thy sight.
6¶ And the messengers returned to Jacob, saying, We came to thy brother Esau, and also he cometh to meet thee, and four hundred men with him.
7Then Jacob was greatly afraid and distressed: and he divided the people that *was* with him, and the flocks, and herds, and the camels, into two bands;
8And said, If Esau come to the one company, and smite it, then the other company which is left shall escape.
9¶ And Jacob said, O God of my father Abraham, and God of my father Isaac, the LORD which saidst unto me, Return unto thy country, and to thy kindred, and I will deal well with thee:
10I am not worthy of the least of all the mercies, and of all the truth, which thou hast shown unto thy servant; for with my staff I passed over this Jordan; and now I am become two bands.
11Deliver me, I pray thee, from the hand of my brother, from the hand of Esau: for I fear him, lest he will come and smite me, *and* the mother with the children.
12And thou saidst, I will surely do thee good, and make thy seed as the sand of the sea, which cannot be numbered for multitude.
13¶ And he lodged there that same night; and took of that which came to his hand a present for Esau his brother;

## Amplified

47Laban called it Jegar-sahadutha [witness-heap, *in Aramaic*], but Jacob called it Galeed [ [a]witness-heap, *in Hebrew*.]
48Laban said, This heap is a witness today between you and me. Therefore he named it Galeed.
49And [the pillar or monument Laban called] Mizpah (watch-post), for he said, The Lord watch between you and me, when we are absent *and* hidden one from another.
50If you should afflict, humiliate *or* lower [divorce] my daughters, or if you should take other wives beside my daughters, although no man is with us (to witness), *remember*, God is witness between you and me.
51And Laban said to Jacob, See this heap and this pillar, which I have set up between you and me.
52This heap be witness, and this pillar be witness, that I will not pass by this heap to you, and that you will not pass by this heap and this pillar to me, for harm.
53The God of Abraham and the God of Nahor, and the god [the object of worship] of their father [Terah, an idolator], judge between us. But Jacob swore *only* by [the one true God] the Dread *and* Fear of his father Isaac. [Josh. 24:2.]
54Then Jacob offered sacrifice on the mountain, and called his brethren to eat food; and they ate food, and lingered all night on the mountain.
55And early in the morning Laban rose up, and kissed his grandchildren and his daughters, and pronounced a blessing [asking God's favor] on them. Then Laban departed and returned to his home.

**32** THEN JACOB went on his way, and God's angels met him.
2When Jacob saw them, he said, This is God's army! So he named that place Mahanaim [two armies].
3And Jacob sent messengers before him to Esau his brother in the land of Seir, the country of Edom.
4And he commanded them, Say this to my lord Esau: Your servant Jacob says this: I have been living temporarily with Laban and have stayed there till now.
5And I have oxen, donkeys, flocks, menservants, and women servants; and I have sent to tell my lord, that I may find mercy *and* kindness in your sight.
6And the messengers returned to Jacob, saying, We came to your brother Esau, and now he is [on the way] to meet you, and four hundred men are with him.
7Then Jacob was greatly afraid and distressed; and he divided the people who were with him, and the flocks and herds and camels, into two groups,
8Thinking, If Esau comes to the one group and smites it, then the other group which is left will escape.
9Jacob said, O God of my father Abraham and God of my father Isaac, the Lord Who said to me, Return to your country and to your people, and I will do you good,
10I am not worthy of the least of all the mercies *and* loving-kindnesses and all the faithfulness which You have shown to Your servant, for with *only* my staff I passed over this Jordan [long ago], and now I have become two companies.
11Deliver me, I pray You, from the hand of my brother, from the hand of Esau; for I fear him, lest he come and smite *us all*, the mothers with the children.
12And You said, I will surely do you good, and make your descendants as the sand of the sea, which cannot be numbered for multitude.
13And Jacob lodged there that night; and took from what he had with him as a present for his brother Esau:

**AMP** [a] The Vulgate (Latin version) adds, "Each according to the idiom of his own tongue"—Laban, Aramaic; Jacob, Hebrew.

## New American Standard

47 Now Laban called it [b]Jegar-sahadutha, but Jacob called it [c]Galeed.

48 And Laban said, "This heap is a witness between you and me this day." Therefore it was named Galeed;

49 and [d]Mizpah, for he said, "May the LORD watch between you and me when we are absent one from the other.

50 "If you mistreat my daughters, or if you take wives besides my daughters, *although* no man is with us, see, God is witness between you and me."

51 And Laban said to Jacob, "Behold this heap and behold the pillar which I have set between you and me.

52 "This heap is a witness, and the pillar is a witness, that I will not pass by this heap to you for harm, and you will not pass by this heap and this pillar to me, for harm.

53 "The God of Abraham and the God of Nahor, the God of their father, judge between us." So Jacob swore by the fear of his father Isaac.

54 Then Jacob offered a sacrifice on the mountain, and called his kinsmen to the meal; and they ate the meal and spent the night on the mountain.

55 And early in the morning Laban arose, and kissed his sons and his daughters and blessed them. Then Laban departed and returned to his place.

### *Jacob's Fear of Esau*

**32** NOW AS Jacob went on his way, the angels of God met him.

2 And Jacob said when he saw them, "This is God's [e]camp." So he named that place [f]Mahanaim.

3 ¶ Then Jacob sent messengers before him to his brother Esau in the land of Seir, the country of Edom.

4 He also commanded them saying, "Thus you shall say to my lord Esau: 'Thus says your servant Jacob, "I have sojourned with Laban, and stayed until now;

5 and I have oxen and donkeys *and* flocks and male and female servants; and I have sent to tell my lord, that I may find favor in your sight." ' "

6 And the messengers returned to Jacob, saying, "We came to your brother Esau, and furthermore he is coming to meet you, and four hundred men are with him."

7 Then Jacob was greatly afraid and distressed; and he divided the people who were with him, and the flocks and the herds and the camels, into two companies;

8 for he said, "If Esau comes to the one company and attacks it, then the company which is left will escape."

9 And Jacob said, "O God of my father Abraham and God of my father Isaac, O LORD, who didst say to me, 'Return to your country and to your relatives, and I will prosper you,'

10 I am unworthy of all the lovingkindness and of all the faithfulness which Thou hast shown to Thy servant; for with my staff *only* I crossed this Jordan, and now I have become two companies.

11 "Deliver me, I pray, from the hand of my brother, from the hand of Esau; for I fear him, lest he come and attack me, the mothers with the children.

12 "For Thou didst say, 'I will surely prosper you, and make your descendants as the sand of the sea, which cannot be numbered for multitude.' "

13 ¶ So he spent the night there. Then he selected from what he had with him a present for his brother Esau:

NAS [b] I.e., the heap of witness, in Aramaic [c] I.e., the heap of witness, in Hebrew [d] I.e., the watchtower [e] Or, *company* [f] I.e., Two Camps, or, Two Companies

## New International

them in a heap, and they ate there by the heap. 47 Laban called it
Jegar Sahadutha,[g] and Jacob called it Galeed.[h]
48 Laban said, "This heap is a witness between you and me
today." That is why it was called Galeed. 49 It was also called
Mizpah,[i] because he said, "May the LORD keep watch between
you and me when we are away from each other. 50 If you mistreat
my daughters or if you take any wives besides my daughters, even
though no one is with us, remember that God is a witness between
you and me."
51 Laban also said to Jacob, "Here is this heap, and here is this
pillar I have set up between you and me. 52 This heap is a witness,
and this pillar is a witness, that I will not go past this heap to your
side to harm you and that you will not go past this heap and pillar
to my side to harm me. 53 May the God of Abraham and the God
of Nahor, the God of their father, judge between us."
So Jacob took an oath in the name of the Fear of his father Isaac.
54 He offered a sacrifice there in the hill country and invited his
relatives to a meal. After they had eaten, they spent the night
there.
55 Early the next morning Laban kissed his grandchildren and
his daughters and blessed them. Then he left and returned home.

### *Jacob Prepares to Meet Esau*

**32** JACOB ALSO went on his way, and the angels of God met
him. 2 When Jacob saw them, he said, "This is the camp
of God!" So he named that place Mahanaim.[j]
3 Jacob sent messengers ahead of him to his brother Esau in the
land of Seir, the country of Edom. 4 He instructed them: "This is
what you are to say to my master Esau: 'Your servant Jacob says,
I have been staying with Laban and have remained there till now.
5 I have cattle and donkeys, sheep and goats, menservants and
maidservants. Now I am sending this message to my lord, that I
may find favor in your eyes.' "
6 When the messengers returned to Jacob, they said, "We went
to your brother Esau, and now he is coming to meet you, and four
hundred men are with him."
7 In great fear and distress Jacob divided the people who were
with him into two groups,[k] and the flocks and herds and camels
as well. 8 He thought, "If Esau comes and attacks one group,[l] the
group[m] that is left may escape."
9 Then Jacob prayed, "O God of my father Abraham, God of my
father Isaac, O LORD, who said to me, 'Go back to your country
and your relatives, and I will make you prosper,' 10 I am unworthy
of all the kindness and faithfulness you have shown your servant.
I had only my staff when I crossed this Jordan, but now I have
become two groups. 11 Save me, I pray, from the hand of my
brother Esau, for I am afraid he will come and attack me, and also
the mothers with their children. 12 But you have said, 'I will surely
make you prosper and will make your descendants like the sand
of the sea, which cannot be counted.' "
13 He spent the night there, and from what he had with him he
selected a gift for his brother Esau: 14 two hundred female goats

NIV [g] 47 The Aramaic *Jegar Sahadutha* means *witness heap*. [h] 47 The Hebrew *Galeed* means *witness heap*. [i] 49 *Mizpah* means *watchtower*. [j] 2 *Mahanaim* means *two camps*. [k] 7 Or *camps;* also in verse 10 [l] 8 Or *camp* [m] 8 Or *camp*

## King James

14 Two hundred she goats, and twenty he goats, two hundred ewes, and twenty rams,

15 Thirty milch camels with their colts, forty kine, and ten bulls, twenty she asses, and ten foals.

16 And he delivered *them* into the hand of his servants, every drove by themselves; and said unto his servants, Pass over before me, and put a space betwixt drove and drove.

17 And he commanded the foremost, saying, When Esau my brother meeteth thee, and asketh thee, saying, Whose *art* thou? and whither goest thou? and whose *are* these before thee?

18 Then thou shalt say, *They be* thy servant Jacob's; it *is* a present sent unto my lord Esau: and, behold, also he *is* behind us.

19 And so commanded he the second, and the third, and all that followed the droves, saying, On this manner shall ye speak unto Esau, when ye find him.

20 And say ye moreover, Behold, thy servant Jacob *is* behind us. For he said, I will appease him with the present that goeth before me, and afterward I will see his face; peradventure he will accept of me.

21 So went the present over before him: and himself lodged that night in the company.

22 And he rose up that night, and took his two wives, and his two womenservants, and his eleven sons, and passed over the ford Jabbok.

23 And he took them, and sent them over the brook, and sent over that he had.

24 ¶ And Jacob was left alone; and there wrestled a man with him until the breaking of the day.

25 And when he saw that he prevailed not against him, he touched the hollow of his thigh; and the hollow of Jacob's thigh was out of joint, as he wrestled with him.

26 And he said, Let me go, for the day breaketh. And he said, I will not let thee go, except thou bless me.

27 And he said unto him, What *is* thy name? And he said, Jacob.

28 And he said, Thy name shall be called no more Jacob, but Israel: for as a prince hast thou power with God and with men, and hast prevailed.

29 And Jacob asked *him*, and said, Tell *me*, I pray thee, thy name. And he said, Wherefore *is* it *that* thou dost ask after my name? And he blessed him there.

30 And Jacob called the name of the place Peniel: for I have seen God face to face, and my life is preserved.

31 And as he passed over Penuel the sun rose upon him, and he halted upon his thigh.

32 Therefore the children of Israel eat not *of* the sinew which shrank, which *is* upon the hollow of the thigh, unto this day: because he touched the hollow of Jacob's thigh in the sinew that shrank.

**33** AND JACOB lifted up his eyes, and looked, and, behold, Esau came, and with him four hundred men. And he divided the children unto Leah, and unto Rachel, and unto the two handmaids.

2 And he put the handmaids and their children foremost, and Leah and her children after, and Rachel and Joseph hindermost.

3 And he passed over before them, and bowed himself to the ground seven times, until he came near to his brother.

4 And Esau ran to meet him, and embraced him, and fell on his neck, and kissed him: and they wept.

5 And he lifted up his eyes, and saw the women and the children; and said, Who *are* those with thee? And he said, The children which God hath graciously given thy servant.

## Amplified

14 Two hundred she-goats, twenty he-goats, two hundred ewes, twenty rams,

15 Thirty milk camels with their colts, forty cows, ten bulls, twenty she-donkeys, and ten [donkey] colts.

16 And he put them into the charge of his servants, every drove by itself, and said to his servants, Pass over before me, and put a space between drove and drove.

17 And he commanded the first, When Esau my brother meets you and asks to whom you belong, and where you are going, and whose are the animals before you,

18 Then you shall say, They are your servant Jacob's; it is a present sent to my lord Esau; and moreover, he is behind us.

19 And so he commanded the second, and the third, and all that followed the droves, saying, This is what you are to say to Esau when you meet him.

20 And say, Moreover, your servant Jacob is behind us. For he said, I will appease him with the present that goes before me, and afterward I will see his face; perhaps he will accept of me.

21 So the present went on before him; and he himself lodged that night in the camp.

22 But he rose up that [same] night, and took his two wives, his two women servants, and his eleven sons and passed over the ford [of the] Jabbok.

23 And he took them and sent them across the brook; also he sent over all that he had.

24 And Jacob was left alone; and a Man wrestled with him until daybreak.

25 And when [the Man] saw that He did not prevail against [Jacob], He touched the hollow of his thigh; and Jacob's thigh was put out of joint as he wrestled with Him.

26 Then He said, Let Me go, for day is breaking. But *Jacob* said, I will not let You go unless You declare a blessing upon me.

27 [The Man] asked him, What is your name? And [in shock of realization, whispering] he said, Jacob—supplanter, schemer, trickster, swindler!

28 And He said, Your name shall be called no more Jacob [supplanter], but Israel [contender with God]; for you have contended *and* have power with God and with men, and have prevailed.

29 Then Jacob asked Him, Tell me, I pray You, what [in contrast] is Your name? But He said, Why is it that you ask My name? And [the Angel of God declared] a blessing on [Jacob] there.

30 And Jacob called the name of the place Peniel [the face of God], saying, For I have seen God face to face, and my life is spared *and* not snatched away.

31 And as he passed Penuel [Peniel] the sun rose upon him, and he was limping because of his thigh.

32 That is why to this day the Israelites do not eat the sinew of the hip which is on the hollow of the thigh, because [the Angel of the Lord] touched the hollow of Jacob's thigh on the sinew of the hip.

**33** AND JACOB raised his eyes and looked, and behold, Esau was coming and with him four hundred men. So he divided the children to Leah, and to Rachel, and to the two maids.

2 And he put the maids and their children in front, and Leah and her children after them, and Rachel and Joseph last of all.

3 Then Jacob went over [the stream] before them, and bowed himself to the ground seven times, until he came near to his brother.

4 But Esau ran to meet him, and embraced him and fell on his neck and kissed him, and they wept.

5 [Esau] looked up and saw the women and the children, and said, Who are these with you? And *Jacob* replied, They are the children whom God has graciously given your servant.

## New American Standard

14two hundred female goats and twenty male goats, two hundred ewes and twenty rams,
15thirty milking camels and their colts, forty cows and ten bulls,
twenty female donkeys and ten male donkeys.
16And he delivered *them* into the hand of his servants, every
drove by itself, and said to his servants, "Pass on before me, and
put a space between droves."
17And he commanded the one in front, saying, "When my
brother Esau meets you and asks you, saying, 'To whom do you
belong, and where are you going, and to whom do these *animals*
in front of you belong?'
18then you shall say, '*These* belong to your servant Jacob; it is
a present sent to my lord Esau. And behold, he also is behind us.' "
19Then he commanded also the second and the third, and all
those who followed the droves, saying, "After this manner you
shall speak to Esau when you find him;
20and you shall say, 'Behold, your servant Jacob also is behind
us.' " For he said, "I will appease him with the present that goes
before me. Then afterward I will see his face; perhaps he will
accept me."
21So the present passed on before him, while he himself spent
that night in the camp.
22¶ Now he arose that same night and took his two wives and
his two maids and his eleven children, and crossed the ford of the
Jabbok.
23And he took them and sent them across the stream. And he
sent across whatever he had.

*Jacob Wrestles*

24Then Jacob was left alone, and a man wrestled with him until
daybreak.
25And when he saw that he had not prevailed against him, he
touched the socket of his thigh; so the socket of Jacob's thigh was
dislocated while he wrestled with him.
26Then he said, "Let me go, for the dawn is breaking." But he
said, "I will not let you go unless you bless me."
27So he said to him, "What is your name?" And he said,
"Jacob."
28And he said, "Your name shall no longer be Jacob, but [a]Israel;
for you have striven with God and with men and have prevailed."
29Then Jacob asked him and said, "Please tell me your name."
But he said, "Why is it that you ask my name?" And he blessed
him there.
30So Jacob named the place [b]Peniel, for *he said,* "I have seen
God face to face, yet my life has been preserved."
31Now the sun rose upon him just as he crossed over Penuel,
and he was limping on his thigh.
32Therefore, to this day the sons of Israel do not eat the sinew
of the hip which is on the socket of the thigh, because he touched
the socket of Jacob's thigh in the sinew of the hip.

*Jacob Meets Esau*

**33** THEN JACOB lifted his eyes and looked, and behold,
Esau was coming, and four hundred men with him. So he
divided the children among Leah and Rachel and the two maids.
2And he put the maids and their children in front, and Leah
and her children next, and Rachel and Joseph last.
3But he himself passed on ahead of them and bowed down to
the ground seven times, until he came near to his brother.
4Then Esau ran to meet him and embraced him, and fell on his
neck and kissed him, and they wept.
5And he lifted his eyes and saw the women and the children,
and said, "Who are these with you?" So he said, "The children
whom God has graciously given your servant."

**NAS** [a]I.e., he who strives with God, or, God strives [b]I.e., the face of God

## New International

and twenty male goats, two hundred ewes and twenty rams,
15thirty female camels with their young, forty cows and ten bulls,
and twenty female donkeys and ten male donkeys. 16He put them
in the care of his servants, each herd by itself, and said to his
servants, "Go ahead of me, and keep some space between the
herds."
17He instructed the one in the lead: "When my brother Esau
meets you and asks, 'To whom do you belong, and where are you
going, and who owns all these animals in front of you?' 18then you
are to say, 'They belong to your servant Jacob. They are a gift sent
to my lord Esau, and he is coming behind us.' "
19He also instructed the second, the third and all the others who
followed the herds: "You are to say the same thing to Esau when
you meet him. 20And be sure to say, 'Your servant Jacob is coming
behind us.' " For he thought, "I will pacify him with these gifts I
am sending on ahead; later, when I see him, perhaps he will
receive me." 21So Jacob's gifts went on ahead of him, but he
himself spent the night in the camp.

*Jacob Wrestles With God*

22That night Jacob got up and took his two wives, his two
maidservants and his eleven sons and crossed the ford of the
Jabbok. 23After he had sent them across the stream, he sent over
all his possessions. 24So Jacob was left alone, and a man wrestled
with him till daybreak. 25When the man saw that he could not
overpower him, he touched the socket of Jacob's hip so that his hip
was wrenched as he wrestled with the man. 26Then the man said,
"Let me go, for it is daybreak."
But Jacob replied, "I will not let you go unless you bless me."
27The man asked him, "What is your name?"
"Jacob," he answered.
28Then the man said, "Your name will no longer be Jacob, but
Israel,[c] because you have struggled with God and with men and
have overcome."
29Jacob said, "Please tell me your name."
But he replied, "Why do you ask my name?" Then he blessed
him there.
30So Jacob called the place Peniel,[d] saying, "It is because I saw
God face to face, and yet my life was spared."
31The sun rose above him as he passed Peniel,[e] and he was
limping because of his hip. 32Therefore to this day the Israelites do
not eat the tendon attached to the socket of the hip, because the
socket of Jacob's hip was touched near the tendon.

*Jacob Meets Esau*

**33** JACOB LOOKED up and there was Esau, coming with his
four hundred men; so he divided the children among
Leah, Rachel and the two maidservants. 2He put the maidservants
and their children in front, Leah and her children next, and Rachel
and Joseph in the rear. 3He himself went on ahead and bowed
down to the ground seven times as he approached his brother.
4But Esau ran to meet Jacob and embraced him; he threw his
arms around his neck and kissed him. And they wept. 5Then Esau
looked up and saw the women and children. "Who are these with
you?" he asked.
Jacob answered, "They are the children God has graciously
given your servant."

**NIV** [c]*28 Israel* means *he struggles with God.* [d]*30 Peniel* means *face of God.*
[e]*31* Hebrew *Penuel,* a variant of *Peniel*

## King James

6 Then the handmaidens came near, they and their children, and they bowed themselves.

7 And Leah also with her children came near, and bowed themselves: and after came Joseph near and Rachel, and they bowed themselves.

8 And he said, What *meanest* thou by all this drove which I met? And he said, *These are* to find grace in the sight of my lord.

9 And Esau said, I have enough, my brother; keep that thou hast unto thyself.

10 And Jacob said, Nay, I pray thee, if now I have found grace in thy sight, then receive my present at my hand: for therefore I have seen thy face, as though I had seen the face of God, and thou wast pleased with me.

11 Take, I pray thee, my blessing that is brought to thee; because God hath dealt graciously with me, and because I have enough. And he urged him, and he took *it*.

12 And he said, Let us take our journey, and let us go, and I will go before thee.

13 And he said unto him, My lord knoweth that the children *are* tender, and the flocks and herds with young *are* with me: and if men should overdrive them one day, all the flock will die.

14 Let my lord, I pray thee, pass over before his servant: and I will lead on softly, according as the cattle that goeth before me and the children be able to endure, until I come unto my lord unto Seir.

15 And Esau said, Let me now leave with thee *some* of the folk that *are* with me. And he said, What needeth it? let me find grace in the sight of my lord.

16 ¶ So Esau returned that day on his way unto Seir.

17 And Jacob journeyed to Succoth, and built him an house, and made booths for his cattle: therefore the name of the place is called Succoth.

18 ¶ And Jacob came to Shalem, a city of Shechem, which *is* in the land of Canaan, when he came from Padan-aram; and pitched his tent before the city.

19 And he bought a parcel of a field, where he had spread his tent, at the hand of the children of Hamor, Shechem's father, for an hundred pieces of money.

20 And he erected there an altar, and called it El-elohe-Israel.

**34** AND DINAH the daughter of Leah, which she bare unto Jacob, went out to see the daughters of the land.

2 And when Shechem the son of Hamor the Hivite, prince of the country, saw her, he took her, and lay with her, and defiled her.

3 And his soul clave unto Dinah the daughter of Jacob, and he loved the damsel, and spake kindly unto the damsel.

4 And Shechem spake unto his father Hamor, saying, Get me this damsel to wife.

5 And Jacob heard that he had defiled Dinah his daughter: now his sons were with his cattle in the field: and Jacob held his peace until they were come.

6 ¶ And Hamor the father of Shechem went out unto Jacob to commune with him.

7 And the sons of Jacob came out of the field when they heard *it:* and the men were grieved, and they were very wroth, because he had wrought folly in Israel in lying with Jacob's daughter; which thing ought not to be done.

8 And Hamor communed with them, saying, The soul of my son Shechem longeth for your daughter: I pray you give her him to wife.

9 And make ye marriages with us, *and* give your daughters unto us, and take our daughters unto you.

## Amplified

6 Then the maids came near, they and their children, and they bowed themselves.

7 And Leah also with her children came near, and they bowed themselves. After them Joseph and Rachel came near, and they bowed themselves.

8 Esau said, What do you mean by all this company which I met? And he said, These are that I might find favor in the sight of my lord.

9 And Esau said, I have plenty, my brother; keep what you have for yourself.

10 But Jacob replied, No, I beg of you, if now I have found favor in your sight, receive my gift that I am presenting; for truly to see your face is to me as if I had seen the face of God, and you have received me favorably.

11 Accept, I beg of you, my blessing *and* gift that I have brought to you; for God has dealt graciously with me, and I have everything. And he kept urging him, and he accepted it.

12 Then *Esau* said, Let us get started on our journey, and I will go before you.

13 But Jacob replied, You know, my lord, that the children are tender *and* delicate *and* need gentle care, and the flocks and herds with young are of concern to me; for if the men should overdrive them for a single day, the whole of the flocks would die.

14 Let my lord, I pray you, pass over before his servant; and I will lead on slowly, governed by [consideration for] the livestock that set the pace before me and the endurance of the children, until I come to my lord in Seir.

15 Then Esau said, Let me now leave with you some of the people who are with me. But [Jacob] said, What need is there for it? Let me find favor in the sight of my lord.

16 So Esau turned back that day on his way to Seir.

17 But Jacob journeyed to Succoth and built himself a house, and made booths *or* places of shelter for his livestock; so the name of the place is called Succoth [booths].

18 When Jacob came from Padan-aram he arrived safely *and* in peace at the town of Shechem, in the land of Canaan, and pitched his tents before the [enclosed] town.

19 Then he bought the piece of land on which he had encamped, from the sons of Hamor, Shechem's father, for one hundred pieces of money.

20 There he erected an altar, and called it El-Elohe-Israel (God, the God of Israel).

**34** NOW DINAH daughter of Leah, whom she bore to Jacob, went out [unattended] to see the girls of the place.

2 And when Shechem, son of Hamor the Hivite, prince of the country, saw her, he seized her, lay with her, and humbled, defiled *and* disgraced her.

3 But his soul longed for *and* clung to Dinah daughter of Jacob, and he loved the girl and spoke comfortingly to her young heart's wishes.

4 And Shechem said to his father Hamor, Get me this girl to be my wife.

5 Jacob heard that *Shechem* had defiled Dinah his daughter. Now his sons were with his livestock in the field. So Jacob held his peace until they came.

6 But Hamor the father of Shechem went out to Jacob to have a talk with him.

7 When Jacob's sons heard it, they came from the field; and *they* were distressed and grieved and very angry, for [Shechem] had done a vile thing to Israel in lying with Jacob's daughter, which ought not to be done.

8 And Hamor conferred with them, saying, The soul of my son Shechem craves your daughter [and sister]. I beg of you give her to him to be his wife.

9 And you make marriages with us, and give your daughters to us, and take our daughters to you.

## New American Standard

6Then the maids came near with their children, and they bowed down.

7And Leah likewise came near with her children, and they bowed down; and afterward Joseph came near with Rachel, and they bowed down.

8And he said, "What do you mean by all this company which I have met?" And he said, "To find favor in the sight of my lord."

9But Esau said, "I have plenty, my brother; let what you have be your own."

10And Jacob said, "No, please, if now I have found favor in your sight, then take my present from my hand, for I see your face as one sees the face of God, and you have received me favorably.

11"Please take my gift which has been brought to you, because God has dealt graciously with me, and because I have plenty." Thus he urged him and he took *it*.

12Then Esau said, "Let us take our journey and go, and I will go before you."

13But he said to him, "My lord knows that the children are frail and that the flocks and herds which are nursing are a care to me. And if they are driven hard one day, all the flocks will die.

14"Please let my lord pass on before his servant; and I will proceed at my leisure, according to the pace of the cattle that are before me and according to the pace of the children, until I come to my lord at Seir."

15And Esau said, "Please let me leave with you some of the people who are with me." But he said, "[a]What need is there? Let me find favor in the sight of my lord."

16So Esau returned that day on his way to Seir.

17And Jacob journeyed to [b]Succoth; and built for himself a house, and made booths for his livestock, therefore the place is named Succoth.

*Jacob Settles in Shechem*

18¶ Now Jacob came safely to the city of Shechem, which is in the land of Canaan, when he came from Paddan-aram, and camped before the city.

19And he bought the piece of land where he had pitched his tent from the hand of the sons of Hamor, Shechem's father, for one hundred pieces of money.

20Then he erected there an altar, and called it [c]El-Elohe-Israel.

*The Treachery of Jacob's Sons*

**34** NOW DINAH the daughter of Leah, whom she had borne to Jacob, went out to visit the daughters of the land.

2And when Shechem the son of Hamor the Hivite, the prince of the land, saw her, he took her and lay with her by force.

3And he was deeply attracted to Dinah the daughter of Jacob, and he loved the girl and spoke tenderly to her.

4So Shechem spoke to his father Hamor, saying, "Get me this young girl for a wife."

5Now Jacob heard that he had defiled Dinah his daughter; but his sons were with his livestock in the field, so Jacob kept silent until they came in.

6Then Hamor the father of Shechem went out to Jacob to speak with him.

7Now the sons of Jacob came in from the field when they heard *it*; and the men were grieved, and they were very angry because he had done a disgraceful thing in Israel by lying with Jacob's daughter, for such a thing ought not to be done.

8But Hamor spoke with them, saying, "The soul of my son Shechem longs for your daughter; please give her to him in marriage.

9"And intermarry with us; give your daughters to us, and take our daughters for yourselves.

NAS [a] Lit., *"Why this?"* [b] I.e., booths [c] I.e., God, the God of Israel

## New International

6Then the maidservants and their children approached and bowed down. 7Next, Leah and her children came and bowed down. Last of all came Joseph and Rachel, and they too bowed down.

8Esau asked, "What do you mean by all these droves I met?"

"To find favor in your eyes, my lord," he said.

9But Esau said, "I already have plenty, my brother. Keep what you have for yourself."

10"No, please!" said Jacob. "If I have found favor in your eyes, accept this gift from me. For to see your face is like seeing the face of God, now that you have received me favorably. 11Please accept the present that was brought to you, for God has been gracious to me and I have all I need." And because Jacob insisted, Esau accepted it.

12Then Esau said, "Let us be on our way; I'll accompany you."

13But Jacob said to him, "My lord knows that the children are tender and that I must care for the ewes and cows that are nursing their young. If they are driven hard just one day, all the animals will die. 14So let my lord go on ahead of his servant, while I move along slowly at the pace of the droves before me and that of the children, until I come to my lord in Seir."

15Esau said, "Then let me leave some of my men with you."

"But why do that?" Jacob asked. "Just let me find favor in the eyes of my lord."

16So that day Esau started on his way back to Seir. 17Jacob, however, went to Succoth, where he built a place for himself and made shelters for his livestock. That is why the place is called Succoth.[d]

18After Jacob came from Paddan Aram,[e] he arrived safely at the[f] city of Shechem in Canaan and camped within sight of the city. 19For a hundred pieces of silver,[g] he bought from the sons of Hamor, the father of Shechem, the plot of ground where he pitched his tent. 20There he set up an altar and called it El Elohe Israel.[h]

*Dinah and the Shechemites*

**34** NOW DINAH, the daughter Leah had borne to Jacob, went out to visit the women of the land. 2When Shechem son of Hamor the Hivite, the ruler of that area, saw her, he took her and violated her. 3His heart was drawn to Dinah daughter of Jacob, and he loved the girl and spoke tenderly to her. 4And Shechem said to his father Hamor, "Get me this girl as my wife."

5When Jacob heard that his daughter Dinah had been defiled, his sons were in the fields with his livestock; so he kept quiet about it until they came home.

6Then Shechem's father Hamor went out to talk with Jacob. 7Now Jacob's sons had come in from the fields as soon as they heard what had happened. They were filled with grief and fury, because Shechem had done a disgraceful thing in[i] Israel by lying with Jacob's daughter—a thing that should not be done.

8But Hamor said to them, "My son Shechem has his heart set on your daughter. Please give her to him as his wife. 9Intermarry with us; give us your daughters and take our daughters for your-

NIV [d] 17 *Succoth* means *shelters.* [e] 18 That is, Northwest Mesopotamia [f] 18 Or *arrived at Shalem, a* [g] 19 Hebrew *hundred kesitahs;* a kesitah was a unit of money of unknown weight and value. [h] 20 *El Elohe Israel* can mean *God, the God of Israel* or *mighty is the God of Israel.* [i] 7 Or *against*

## King James

10And ye shall dwell with us: and the land shall be before you; dwell and trade ye therein, and get you possessions therein.

11And Shechem said unto her father and unto her brethren, Let me find grace in your eyes, and what ye shall say unto me I will give.

12Ask me never so much dowry and gift, and I will give according as ye shall say unto me: but give me the damsel to wife.

13And the sons of Jacob answered Shechem and Hamor his father deceitfully, and said, because he had defiled Dinah their sister:

14And they said unto them, We cannot do this thing, to give our sister to one that is uncircumcised; for that *were* a reproach unto us:

15But in this will we consent unto you: If ye will be as we *be*, that every male of you be circumcised;

16Then will we give our daughters unto you, and we will take your daughters to us, and we will dwell with you, and we will become one people.

17But if ye will not hearken unto us, to be circumcised; then will we take our daughter, and we will be gone.

18And their words pleased Hamor, and Shechem Hamor's son.

19And the young man deferred not to do the thing, because he had delight in Jacob's daughter: and he *was* more honourable than all the house of his father.

20¶ And Hamor and Shechem his son came unto the gate of their city, and communed with the men of their city, saying,

21These men *are* peaceable with us; therefore let them dwell in the land, and trade therein; for the land, behold, *it is* large enough for them; let us take their daughters to us for wives, and let us give them our daughters.

22Only herein will the men consent unto us for to dwell with us, to be one people, if every male among us be circumcised, as they *are* circumcised.

23 *Shall* not their cattle and their substance and every beast of theirs *be* ours? only let us consent unto them, and they will dwell with us.

24And unto Hamor and unto Shechem his son hearkened all that went out of the gate of his city; and every male was circumcised, all that went out of the gate of his city.

25¶ And it came to pass on the third day, when they were sore, that two of the sons of Jacob, Simeon and Levi, Dinah's brethren, took each man his sword, and came upon the city boldly, and slew all the males.

26And they slew Hamor and Shechem his son with the edge of the sword, and took Dinah out of Shechem's house, and went out.

27The sons of Jacob came upon the slain, and spoiled the city, because they had defiled their sister.

28They took their sheep, and their oxen, and their asses, and that which *was* in the city, and that which *was* in the field,

29And all their wealth, and all their little ones, and their wives took they captive, and spoiled even all that *was* in the house.

30And Jacob said to Simeon and Levi, Ye have troubled me to make me to stink among the inhabitants of the land, among the Canaanites and the Perizzites: and I *being* few in number, they shall gather themselves together against me, and slay me; and I shall be destroyed, I and my house.

31And they said, Should he deal with our sister as with an harlot?

## Amplified

10You shall dwell with us; the country will be open to you; live and trade and get your possessions in it.

11And Shechem said to [Dinah's] father and to her brothers, Let me find favor in your eyes, and I will give you whatever you ask of me.

12Ask me ever so much dowry and [marriage] gift, and I will give according to what you tell me; only give me the girl to be my wife.

13The sons of Jacob answered Shechem and Hamor his father deceitfully, [ justifying their action by saying, it was done] because Shechem had defiled *and* disgraced their sister Dinah.

14They said to them, We cannot do this thing *and* give our sister to one who is not circumcised, for that would be a reproach *and* disgrace to us.

15But we do consent to do this: if you will become as we are, and every male among you be circumcised,

16Then we will give our daughters to you, and we will take your daughters to us, and we will dwell with you and become one people.

17But if you will not listen to us and consent to be circumcised, then we will take our daughter and go.

18Their words pleased Hamor and his son Schechem.

19And the young man did not delay to do the thing, for he delighted in Jacob's daughter. He was honored above all his family [so, ranking first, he acted first].

20Then Hamor and Shechem his son came to the gate of their [enclosed] town and discussed the matter with the citizens, saying,

21These men are peaceable with us; so let them dwell in the land, and trade in it; for the land it is large enough [for us and] for them; let us take their daughters for wives, and let us give them our daughters.

22But the men will consent to our request that they live among us and be one people, only on condition that every male among us be circumcised, as they are.

23Shall not their cattle and their possessions and all their beasts be ours? Only let us consent to them, and they will dwell here with us.

24And all the people who went out of his town gate listened *and* heeded what Hamor and Shechem said; and every male was circumcised who was a resident of that town.

25But on the third day [after the circumcision] when [all the men] were sore, two of the sons of Jacob, Simeon and Levi, Dinah's brothers, took their swords, boldly entered the city [without danger] and slew all the males.

26And they killed Hamor and Shechem his son with the edge of the sword, and took Dinah out of Shechem's house [where she had been all this time], and departed.

27[Then the rest of] Jacob's [eleven] sons came upon the slain, and plundered the town, because there their sister had been defiled *and* disgraced.

28They took their flocks, their herds, their donkeys, and whatever was in the town and in the field,

29All their wealth, and all their little ones and their wives they took captive, making spoil even of all [they found] in the houses.

30And Jacob said to Simeon and Levi, You have ruined me, making me infamous *and* embroiling me with the inhabitants of the land, the Canaanites and the Perizzites! And I, being few in number, they will gather together against me and attack me; and I shall be destroyed, I and my household.

31And they said, Should he [be permitted to] deal with our sister as with a harlot?

## New American Standard

10"Thus you shall live with us, and the land shall be *open* before you; live and trade in it, and acquire property in it."

11Shechem also said to her father and to her brothers, "If I find favor in your sight, then I will give whatever you say to me.

12"Ask me ever so much bridal payment and gift, and I will give according as you say to me; but give me the girl in marriage."

13But Jacob's sons answered Shechem and his father Hamor, with deceit, and spoke to them, because he had defiled Dinah their sister.

14And they said to them, "We cannot do this thing, to give our sister to one who is uncircumcised, for that would be a disgrace to us.

15"Only on this *condition* will we consent to you: if you will become like us, in that every male of you be circumcised,

16then we will give our daughters to you, and we will take your daughters for ourselves, and we will live with you and become one people.

17"But if you will not listen to us to be circumcised, then we will take our daughter and go."

**18**¶ Now their words seemed reasonable to Hamor and Shechem, Hamor's son.

19And the young man did not delay to do the thing, because he was delighted with Jacob's daughter. Now he was more respected than all the household of his father.

20So Hamor and his son Shechem came to the gate of their city, and spoke to the men of their city, saying,

21"These men are friendly with us; therefore let them live in the land and trade in it, for behold, the land is large enough for them. Let us take their daughters in marriage, and give our daughters to them.

22"Only on this *condition* will the men consent to us to live with us, to become one people: that every male among us be circumcised as they are circumcised.

23"Will not their livestock and their property and all their animals be ours? Only let us consent to them, and they will live with us."

24And all who went out of the gate of his city listened to Hamor and to his son Shechem, and every male was circumcised, all who went out of the gate of his city.

25Now it came about on the third day, when they were in pain, that two of Jacob's sons, Simeon and Levi, Dinah's brothers, each took his sword and came upon the city unawares, and killed every male.

26And they killed Hamor and his son Shechem with the edge of the sword, and took Dinah from Shechem's house, and went forth.

27Jacob's sons came upon the slain and looted the city, because they had defiled their sister.

28They took their flocks and their herds and their donkeys, and that which was in the city and that which was in the field;

29and they captured and looted all their wealth and all their little ones and their wives, even all that *was* in the houses.

30Then Jacob said to Simeon and Levi, "You have brought trouble on me, by making me odious among the inhabitants of the land, among the Canaanites and the Perizzites; and my men being few in number, they will gather together against me and attack me and I shall be destroyed, I and my household."

31But they said, "Should he treat our sister as a harlot?"

## New International

selves. 10You can settle among us; the land is open to you. Live
in it, trade[a] in it, and acquire property in it."
11Then Shechem said to Dinah's father and brothers, "Let me
find favor in your eyes, and I will give you whatever you ask.
12Make the price for the bride and the gift I am to bring as great
as you like, and I'll pay whatever you ask me. Only give me the
girl as my wife."
13Because their sister Dinah had been defiled, Jacob's sons replied deceitfully as they spoke to Shechem and his father Hamor.
14They said to them, "We can't do such a thing; we can't give our
sister to a man who is not circumcised. That would be a disgrace
to us. 15We will give our consent to you on one condition only: that
you become like us by circumcising all your males. 16Then we will
give you our daughters and take your daughters for ourselves.
We'll settle among you and become one people with you. 17But if
you will not agree to be circumcised, we'll take our sister[b] and go."
18Their proposal seemed good to Hamor and his son Shechem.
19The young man, who was the most honored of all his father's
household, lost no time in doing what they said, because he was
delighted with Jacob's daughter. 20So Hamor and his son Shechem
went to the gate of their city to speak to their fellow townsmen.
21"These men are friendly toward us," they said. "Let them live
in our land and trade in it; the land has plenty of room for them.
We can marry their daughters and they can marry ours. 22But the
men will consent to live with us as one people only on the condition that our males be circumcised, as they themselves are. 23Won't
their livestock, their property and all their other animals become
ours? So let us give our consent to them, and they will settle among
us."
24All the men who went out of the city gate agreed with Hamor
and his son Shechem, and every male in the city was circumcised.
25Three days later, while all of them were still in pain, two of
Jacob's sons, Simeon and Levi, Dinah's brothers, took their swords
and attacked the unsuspecting city, killing every male. 26They put
Hamor and his son Shechem to the sword and took Dinah from
Shechem's house and left. 27The sons of Jacob came upon the dead
bodies and looted the city where[c] their sister had been defiled.
28They seized their flocks and herds and donkeys and everything
else of theirs in the city and out in the fields. 29They carried off all
their wealth and all their women and children, taking as plunder
everything in the houses.
30Then Jacob said to Simeon and Levi, "You have brought
trouble on me by making me a stench to the Canaanites and
Perizzites, the people living in this land. We are few in number,
and if they join forces against me and attack me, I and my household will be destroyed."
31But they replied, "Should he have treated our sister like a
prostitute?"

**NIV** [a] *10* Or *move about freely;* also in verse 21 [b] *17* Hebrew *daughter* [c] *27* Or *because*

## King James

**35** AND GOD said unto Jacob, Arise, go up to Beth-el, and dwell there: and make there an altar unto God, that appeared unto thee when thou fleddest from the face of Esau thy brother.
2Then Jacob said unto his household, and to all that *were* with him, Put away the strange gods that *are* among you, and be clean, and change your garments:
3And let us arise, and go up to Beth-el; and I will make there an altar unto God, who answered me in the day of my distress, and was with me in the way which I went.
4And they gave unto Jacob all the strange gods which *were* in their hand, and *all their* earrings which *were* in their ears; and Jacob hid them under the oak which *was* by Shechem.
5And they journeyed: and the terror of God was upon the cities that *were* round about them, and they did not pursue after the sons of Jacob.
6¶ So Jacob came to Luz, which *is* in the land of Canaan, that *is*, Beth-el, he and all the people that *were* with him.
7And he built there an altar, and called the place El-beth-el: because there God appeared unto him, when he fled from the face of his brother.
8But Deborah Rebekah's nurse died, and she was buried beneath Beth-el under an oak: and the name of it was called Allon-bachuth.
9¶ And God appeared unto Jacob again, when he came out of Padan-aram, and blessed him.
10And God said unto him, Thy name *is* Jacob: thy name shall not be called any more Jacob, but Israel shall be thy name: and he called his name Israel.
11And God said unto him, I *am* God Almighty: be fruitful and multiply; a nation and a company of nations shall be of thee, and kings shall come out of thy loins;
12And the land which I gave Abraham and Isaac, to thee I will give it, and to thy seed after thee will I give the land.
13And God went up from him in the place where he talked with him.
14And Jacob set up a pillar in the place where he talked with him, *even* a pillar of stone: and he poured a drink offering thereon, and he poured oil thereon.
15And Jacob called the name of the place where God spake with him, Beth-el.
16¶ And they journeyed from Beth-el; and there was but a little way to come to Ephrath: and Rachel travailed, and she had hard labour.
17And it came to pass, when she was in hard labour, that the midwife said unto her, Fear not; thou shalt have this son also.
18And it came to pass, as her soul was in departing, (for she died) that she called his name Ben-oni: but his father called him Benjamin.
19And Rachel died, and was buried in the way to Ephrath, which *is* Beth-lehem.
20And Jacob set a pillar upon her grave: that *is* the pillar of Rachel's grave unto this day.
21¶ And Israel journeyed, and spread his tent beyond the tower of Edar.
22And it came to pass, when Israel dwelt in that land, that Reuben went and lay with Bilhah his father's concubine: and Israel heard *it*. Now the sons of Jacob were twelve:

## Amplified

**35** AND GOD said to Jacob, Arise, go up to Bethel, and dwell there. And make there an altar to God Who appeared to you [in a distinct manifestation] when you fled from the presence of Esau your brother.
2Then Jacob said to his household and to all who were with him, Put away the [images of] strange gods that are among you, and purify yourselves, and change [into fresh] garments;
3Then let us arise and go up to Bethel, and I will make there an altar to God Who answered me in the day of my distress, and was with me wherever I went.
4So they [both young men and women] gave to Jacob all the strange gods they had and their earrings which were [worn as charms against evil] in their ears; and Jacob buried *and* hid them under the oak near Shechem.
5And they journeyed, and a terror from God fell on the towns round about them, and they did not pursue the sons of Jacob.
6So Jacob came to Luz, that is, Bethel, which is in the land of Canaan, he and all the people with him.
7There he built an altar, and called the place El-bethel (God of Bethel), for there God revealed Himself to him when he fled from the presence of his brother.
8But Deborah, Rebekah's nurse, died, and was buried below Bethel under an oak; and the name of it was called Allon-bacuth (oak of weeping).
9And God [in a distinctly visible manifestation] appeared to Jacob again, when he came out of Padan-aram, and declared a blessing on him. [Gen. 32:28.]
10Again God said to him, Your name is Jacob (supplanter); you shall not be called Jacob any longer, but Israel shall be your name. So he called him Israel (contender with God).
11And God said to him, I am God Almighty. Be fruitful and multiply; a nation and a company of nations shall come from you, and kings shall be born of your stock;
12The land which I gave Abraham and Isaac I will give to you; and to your descendants after you I will give the land.
13Then God ascended from him in the place where He talked with him.
14And Jacob set up a pillar [monument] in the place where he talked with [God], a pillar of stone; and he poured a drink offering on it, and he poured oil on it.
15And Jacob called the name of the place where God had talked with him, Bethel (house of God).
16And they journeyed from Bethel, and had but a little way to come to Ephrath [Bethlehem], when Rachel suffered the pangs of childbirth and had hard labor.
17When she was in hard labor, the midwife said to her, Do not be afraid; you shall have this son also.
18And as her soul was departing, for she died, she called his name Benoni (son of my sorrow); but his father called him Benjamin (son of the right hand).
19So Rachel died and was buried on the way to Ephrath, that is, Bethlehem.
20And Jacob set a pillar [monument] on her grave; that is the pillar of Rachel's grave to this day.
21Then Israel journeyed on, and spread his tent on the other side of the tower of Edar.
22When Israel dwelt there, Reuben [his eldest son] went and lay with Bilhah his father's concubine; and Israel heard about it. Now Jacob's sons were twelve.

## New American Standard

*Jacob Moves to Bethel*

**35** THEN GOD said to Jacob, "Arise, go up to Bethel, and live there; and make an altar there to God, who appeared to you when you fled from your brother Esau."

2So Jacob said to his household and to all who were with him, "Put away the foreign gods which are among you, and purify yourselves, and change your garments;

3and let us arise and go up to Bethel; and I will make an altar there to God, who answered me in the day of my distress, and has been with me wherever I have gone."

4So they gave to Jacob all the foreign gods which they had, and the rings which were in their ears; and Jacob hid them under the oak which was near Shechem.

5¶ As they journeyed, there was a great terror upon the cities which were around them, and they did not pursue the sons of Jacob.

6So Jacob came to Luz (that is, Bethel), which is in the land of Canaan, he and all the people who were with him.

7And he built an altar there, and called the place El-bethel, because there God had revealed Himself to him, when he fled from his brother.

8Now Deborah, Rebekah's nurse, died, and she was buried below Bethel under the oak; it was named [a]Allon-bacuth.

*Jacob Is Named Israel*

9¶ Then God appeared to Jacob again when he came from Paddan-aram, and He blessed him.

10And God said to him,
"Your name is Jacob;
You shall no longer be called Jacob,
But Israel shall be your name."
Thus He called him Israel.

11God also said to him,
"I am God Almighty;
Be fruitful and multiply;
A nation and a company of nations shall come from you,
And kings shall come forth from you.

12 "And the land which I gave to Abraham and Isaac,
I will give it to you,
And I will give the land to your descendants after you."

13Then God went up from him in the place where He had spoken with him.

14And Jacob set up a pillar in the place where He had spoken with him, a pillar of stone, and he poured out a libation on it; he also poured oil on it.

15So Jacob named the place where God had spoken with him, [b]Bethel.

16¶ Then they journeyed from Bethel; and when there was still some distance to go to Ephrath, Rachel began to give birth and she suffered severe labor.

17And it came about when she was in severe labor that the midwife said to her, "Do not fear, for now you have *another* son."

18And it came about as her soul was departing (for she died), that she named him [c]Ben-oni; but his father called him [d]Benjamin.

19So Rachel died and was buried on the way to Ephrath (that is, Bethlehem).

20And Jacob set up a pillar over her grave; that is the pillar of Rachel's grave to this day.

21Then Israel journeyed on and pitched his tent beyond the tower of Eder.

22And it came about while Israel was dwelling in that land, that Reuben went and lay with Bilhah his father's concubine; and Israel heard *of it*.

*The Sons of Israel*

Now there were twelve sons of Jacob—

**NAS** [a] I.e., oak of weeping [b] I.e., the house of God [c] I.e., the son of my sorrow [d] I.e., the son of the right hand

## New International

*Jacob Returns to Bethel*

**35** THEN GOD said to Jacob, "Go up to Bethel and settle there, and build an altar there to God, who appeared to you when you were fleeing from your brother Esau."

2So Jacob said to his household and to all who were with him,
"Get rid of the foreign gods you have with you, and purify yourselves and change your clothes.
3Then come, let us go up to Bethel, where I will build an altar to God, who answered me in the day of my distress and who has been with me wherever I have gone."
4So they gave Jacob all the foreign gods they had and the rings in their ears, and Jacob buried them under the oak at Shechem.
5Then they set out, and the terror of God fell upon the towns all around them so that no one pursued them.

6Jacob and all the people with him came to Luz (that is, Bethel) in the land of Canaan.
7There he built an altar, and he called the place El Bethel,[e] because it was there that God revealed himself to him when he was fleeing from his brother.

8Now Deborah, Rebekah's nurse, died and was buried under the oak below Bethel. So it was named Allon Bacuth.[f]

9After Jacob returned from Paddan Aram,[g] God appeared to him again and blessed him.
10God said to him, "Your name is Jacob,[h] but you will no longer be called Jacob; your name will be Israel.[i]" So he named him Israel.

11And God said to him, "I am God Almighty[j]; be fruitful and increase in number. A nation and a community of nations will come from you, and kings will come from your body.
12The land I gave to Abraham and Isaac I also give to you, and I will give this land to your descendants after you."
13Then God went up from him at the place where he had talked with him.

14Jacob set up a stone pillar at the place where God had talked with him, and he poured out a drink offering on it; he also poured oil on it.
15Jacob called the place where God had talked with him Bethel.[k]

*The Deaths of Rachel and Isaac*

16Then they moved on from Bethel. While they were still some distance from Ephrath, Rachel began to give birth and had great difficulty.
17And as she was having great difficulty in childbirth, the midwife said to her, "Don't be afraid, for you have another son."
18As she breathed her last—for she was dying—she named her son Ben-Oni.[l] But his father named him Benjamin.[m]

19So Rachel died and was buried on the way to Ephrath (that is, Bethlehem).
20Over her tomb Jacob set up a pillar, and to this day that pillar marks Rachel's tomb.

21Israel moved on again and pitched his tent beyond Migdal Eder.
22While Israel was living in that region, Reuben went in and slept with his father's concubine Bilhah, and Israel heard of it.

**NIV** [e] 7 *El Bethel* means *God of Bethel.* [f] 8 *Allon Bacuth* means *oak of weeping.* [g] 9 That is, Northwest Mesopotamia; also in verse 26 [h] 10 *Jacob* means *he grasps the heel* (figuratively, *he deceives*). [i] 10 *Israel* means *he struggles with God.* [j] 11 Hebrew *El-Shaddai* [k] 15 *Bethel* means *house of God.* [l] 18 *Ben-Oni* means *son of my trouble.* [m] 18 *Benjamin* means *son of my right hand.*

## King James

23 The sons of Leah; Reuben, Jacob's firstborn, and Simeon, and
Levi, and Judah, and Issachar, and Zebulun:
24 The sons of Rachel; Joseph, and Benjamin:
25 And the sons of Bilhah, Rachel's handmaid; Dan, and Naphtali:
26 And the sons of Zilpah, Leah's handmaid; Gad, and Asher:
these *are* the sons of Jacob, which were born to him in Padan-aram.
27 ¶ And Jacob came unto Isaac his father unto Mamre, unto the
city of Arbah, which *is* Hebron, where Abraham and Isaac sojourned.
28 And the days of Isaac were an hundred and fourscore years.
29 And Isaac gave up the ghost, and died, and was gathered
unto his people, *being* old and full of days: and his sons Esau and
Jacob buried him.

**36** NOW THESE *are* the generations of Esau, who *is* Edom.
2 Esau took his wives of the daughters of Canaan; Adah the
daughter of Elon the Hittite, and Aholibamah the daughter of
Anah the daughter of Zibeon the Hivite;
3 And Bashemath Ishmael's daughter, sister of Nebajoth.
4 And Adah bare to Esau Eliphaz; and Bashemath bare Reuel;
5 And Aholibamah bare Jeush, and Jaalam, and Korah: these *are*
the sons of Esau, which were born unto him in the land of Canaan.
6 And Esau took his wives, and his sons, and his daughters, and
all the persons of his house, and his cattle, and all his beasts, and
all his substance, which he had got in the land of Canaan; and went
into the country from the face of his brother Jacob.
7 For their riches were more than that they might dwell together;
and the land wherein they were strangers could not bear them
because of their cattle.
8 Thus dwelt Esau in mount Seir: Esau *is* Edom.
9 ¶ And these *are* the generations of Esau the father of the Edomites in mount Seir:
10 These *are* the names of Esau's sons; Eliphaz the son of Adah
the wife of Esau, Reuel the son of Bashemath the wife of Esau.
11 And the sons of Eliphaz were Teman, Omar, Zepho, and
Gatam, and Kenaz.
12 And Timna was concubine to Eliphaz Esau's son; and she bare
to Eliphaz Amalek: these *were* the sons of Adah Esau's wife.
13 And these *are* the sons of Reuel; Nahath, and Zerah, Shammah, and Mizzah: these were the sons of Bashemath Esau's wife.
14 ¶ And these were the sons of Aholibamah, the daughter of
Anah the daughter of Zibeon, Esau's wife: and she bare to Esau
Jeush, and Jaalam, and Korah.
15 ¶ These *were* dukes of the sons of Esau: the sons of Eliphaz
the firstborn *son* of Esau; duke Teman, duke Omar, duke Zepho,
duke Kenaz,
16 Duke Korah, duke Gatam, *and* duke Amalek: these *are* the
dukes *that came* of Eliphaz in the land of Edom; these *were* the sons
of Adah.
17 ¶ And these *are* the sons of Reuel Esau's son; duke Nahath,
duke Zerah, duke Shammah, duke Mizzah: these *are* the dukes
*that came* of Reuel in the land of Edom; these *are* the sons of
Bashemath Esau's wife.
18 ¶ And these are the sons of Aholibamah Esau's wife; duke
Jeush, duke Jaalam, duke Korah: these *were* the dukes *that came* of
Aholibamah the daughter of Anah, Esau's wife.

## Amplified

23 The sons of Leah: Reuben, Jacob's first-born, Simeon, Levi,
Judah, Issachar, and Zebulun.
24 The sons of Rachel: Joseph and Benjamin.
25 The sons of Bilhah, Rachel's maid: Dan and Naphtali.
26 And the sons of Zilpah, Leah's maid: Gad and Asher. These
are the sons of Jacob born to him in Padan-aram.
27 And Jacob came to Isaac his father at Mamre, or Kiriath-arba,
that is, Hebron, where Abraham and Isaac had sojourned.
28 Now the days of Isaac were 180 years.
29 And Isaac's spirit departed; he died and was gathered to his
people, being an old man, satisfied *and* satiated with days; his sons
Esau and Jacob buried him.

**36** NOW THIS is the history of the descendants of Esau, that
is, Edom.
2 Esau took his wives from the women of Canaan: Adah, daughter of Elon the Hittite, and Oholibamah, daughter of Anah the son
of Zibeon the Hivite;
3 And Basemath, Ishmael's daughter, sister of Nebaioth.
4 Adah bore to Esau, Eliphaz; Basemath bore Reuel;
5 And Oholibamah bore Jeush, Jalam, and Korah. These are the
sons of Esau born to him in Canaan.
6 Now Esau took his wives, his sons, his daughters, and all the
members of his household, his cattle, all his beasts, and all his
possessions which he had obtained in the land of Canaan; and he
went into a land away from his brother Jacob.
7 For their great flocks *and* herds *and* possessions [which they
had collected] made it impossible for them to dwell together; the
land in which they were strangers could not support them because
of their livestock.
8 So Esau dwelt in the hill country of Seir; Esau is Edom.
9 And these are the descendants of Esau the father of the Edomites in the hill country of Seir.
10 These are the names of Esau's sons: Eliphaz son of Adah,
Esau's wife, Reuel son of Basemath, Esau's wife.
11 And the sons of Eliphaz were Teman, Omar, Zepho, Gatam,
and Kenaz.
12 And Timna was concubine of Eliphaz, Esau's son; and she
bore Amalek to Eliphaz. These are the sons of Adah, Esau's wife.
13 These are the sons of Reuel: Nahath, Zerah, Shammah, and
Mizzah. These are the sons of Basemath, Esau's wife.
14 And these are the sons of Oholibamah, daughter of Anah the
son of Zibeon, Esau's wife: she bore to Esau Jeush, Jalam, and
Korah.
15 These are the chiefs of the sons of Esau. The sons of Eliphaz
the first-born of Esau: chiefs Teman, Omar, Zepho, Kenaz,
16 Korah, Gatam, and Amalek. These are the chiefs of Eliphaz
in the land of Edom. They are the sons of Adah.
17 These are the sons of Reuel, Esau's son: chiefs Nahath, Zerah,
Shammah, Mizzah: these are the chiefs of Reuel in the land of
Edom; they are the sons of Basemath, Esau's wife.
18 These are the sons of Oholibamah, Esau's wife: chiefs Jeush,
Jalam, and Korah; these are the chiefs born of Oholibamah daughter of Anah, Esau's wife.

## New American Standard

23the sons of Leah: Reuben, Jacob's first-born, then Simeon and
Levi and Judah and Issachar and Zebulun;
24the sons of Rachel: Joseph and Benjamin;
25and the sons of Bilhah, Rachel's maid: Dan and Naphtali;
26and the sons of Zilpah, Leah's maid: Gad and Asher. These
are the sons of Jacob who were born to him in Paddan-aram.
27And Jacob came to his father Isaac at Mamre of Kiriath-arba
(that is, Hebron), where Abraham and Isaac had sojourned.
28¶ Now the days of Isaac were one hundred and eighty years.
29And Isaac breathed his last and died, and was gathered to his
people, an old man of ripe age; and his sons Esau and Jacob buried
him.

*Esau Moves*

36 NOW THESE are *the records of* the generations of Esau
(that is, Edom).
2¶ Esau took his wives from the daughters of Canaan: Adah the
daughter of Elon the Hittite, and Oholibamah the daughter of
Anah and the granddaughter of Zibeon the Hivite;
3also Basemath, Ishmael's daughter, the sister of Nebaioth.
4And Adah bore Eliphaz to Esau, and Basemath bore Reuel,
5and Oholibamah bore Jeush and Jalam and Korah. These are
the sons of Esau who were born to him in the land of Canaan.
6Then Esau took his wives and his sons and his daughters and
all his household, and his livestock and all his cattle and all his
goods which he had acquired in the land of Canaan, and went to
*another* land away from his brother Jacob.
7For their property had become too great for them to live
together, and the land where they sojourned could not sustain
them because of their livestock.
8So Esau lived in the hill country of Seir; Esau is Edom.
9These then are *the records of* the generations of Esau the father
of the Edomites in the hill country of Seir.

*Descendants of Esau*

10¶ These are the names of Esau's sons: Eliphaz the son of
Esau's wife Adah, Reuel the son of Esau's wife Basemath.
11And the sons of Eliphaz were Teman, Omar, Zepho and
Gatam and Kenaz.
12And Timna was a concubine of Esau's son Eliphaz and she
bore Amalek to Eliphaz. These are the sons of Esau's wife Adah.
13And these are the sons of Reuel: Nahath and Zerah, Shammah and Mizzah. These were the sons of Esau's wife Basemath.
14And these were the sons of Esau's wife Oholibamah, the
daughter of Anah and the granddaughter of Zibeon: she bore to
Esau, Jeush and Jalam and Korah.
15¶ These are the chiefs of the sons of Esau. The sons of Eliphaz,
the first-born of Esau, are chief Teman, chief Omar, chief Zepho,
chief Kenaz,
16chief Korah, chief Gatam, chief Amalek. These are the chiefs
descended from Eliphaz in the land of Edom; these are the sons
of Adah.
17And these are the sons of Reuel, Esau's son: chief Nahath,
chief Zerah, chief Shammah, chief Mizzah. These are the chiefs
descended from Reuel in the land of Edom; these are the sons of
Esau's wife Basemath.
18And these are the sons of Esau's wife Oholibamah: chief
Jeush, chief Jalam, chief Korah. These are the chiefs descended
from Esau's wife Oholibamah, the daughter of Anah.

## New International

Jacob had twelve sons:
23The sons of Leah:
Reuben the firstborn of Jacob,
Simeon, Levi, Judah, Issachar and Zebulun.
24The sons of Rachel:
Joseph and Benjamin.
25The sons of Rachel's maidservant Bilhah:
Dan and Naphtali.
26The sons of Leah's maidservant Zilpah:
Gad and Asher.
These were the sons of Jacob, who were born to him in Paddan
Aram.

27Jacob came home to his father Isaac in Mamre, near Kiriath
Arba (that is, Hebron), where Abraham and Isaac had stayed.
28Isaac lived a hundred and eighty years. 29Then he breathed his
last and died and was gathered to his people, old and full of years.
And his sons Esau and Jacob buried him.

*Esau's Descendants*

36 THIS IS the account of Esau (that is, Edom).
2Esau took his wives from the women of Canaan:
Adah daughter of Elon the Hittite, and Oholibamah daughter
of Anah and granddaughter of Zibeon the Hivite— 3also Basemath daughter of Ishmael and sister of Nebaioth.
4Adah bore Eliphaz to Esau, Basemath bore Reuel, 5and
Oholibamah bore Jeush, Jalam and Korah. These were the
sons of Esau, who were born to him in Canaan.
6Esau took his wives and sons and daughters and all the
members of his household, as well as his livestock and all his
other animals and all the goods he had acquired in Canaan,
and moved to a land some distance from his brother Jacob.
7Their possessions were too great for them to remain together;
the land where they were staying could not support them
both because of their livestock. 8So Esau (that is, Edom) settled in the hill country of Seir.

9This is the account of Esau the father of the Edomites in the
hill country of Seir.

10These are the names of Esau's sons:
Eliphaz, the son of Esau's wife Adah, and Reuel, the son
of Esau's wife Basemath.
11The sons of Eliphaz:
Teman, Omar, Zepho, Gatam and Kenaz.
12Esau's son Eliphaz also had a concubine named Timna,
who bore him Amalek. These were grandsons of Esau's
wife Adah.
13The sons of Reuel:
Nahath, Zerah, Shammah and Mizzah. These were grandsons of Esau's wife Basemath.
14The sons of Esau's wife Oholibamah daughter of Anah and
granddaughter of Zibeon, whom she bore to Esau:
Jeush, Jalam and Korah.

15These were the chiefs among Esau's descendants:
The sons of Eliphaz the firstborn of Esau:
Chiefs Teman, Omar, Zepho, Kenaz, 16Korah,[a] Gatam
and Amalek. These were the chiefs descended from Eliphaz in Edom; they were grandsons of Adah.
17The sons of Esau's son Reuel:
Chiefs Nahath, Zerah, Shammah and Mizzah. These were
the chiefs descended from Reuel in Edom; they were
grandsons of Esau's wife Basemath.
18The sons of Esau's wife Oholibamah:
Chiefs Jeush, Jalam and Korah. These were the chiefs
descended from Esau's wife Oholibamah daughter of
Anah.

**NIV** [a] *16* Masoretic Text; Samaritan Pentateuch (see also Gen. 36:11 and 1 Chron. 1:36) does not have *Korah*.

## King James

19 These *are* the sons of Esau, who *is* Edom, and these *are* their dukes.

20¶ These *are* the sons of Seir the Horite, who inhabited the land; Lotan, and Shobal, and Zibeon, and Anah,

21 And Dishon, and Ezer, and Dishan: these *are* the dukes of the Horites, the children of Seir in the land of Edom.

22 And the children of Lotan were Hori and Hemam; and Lotan's sister *was* Timna.

23 And the children of Shobal *were* these; Alvan, and Manahath, and Ebal, Shepho, and Onam.

24 And these *are* the children of Zibeon; both Ajah, and Anah: this *was that* Anah that found the mules in the wilderness, as he fed the asses of Zibeon his father.

25 And the children of Anah *were* these; Dishon, and Aholibamah the daughter of Anah.

26 And these *are* the children of Dishon; Hemdan, and Eshban, and Ithran, and Cheran.

27 The children of Ezer *are* these; Bilhan, and Zaavan, and Akan.

28 The children of Dishan *are* these; Uz, and Aran.

29 These *are* the dukes *that came* of the Horites; duke Lotan, duke Shobal, duke Zibeon, duke Anah,

30 Duke Dishon, duke Ezer, duke Dishan: these *are* the dukes *that came* of Hori, among their dukes in the land of Seir.

31¶ And these *are* the kings that reigned in the land of Edom, before there reigned any king over the children of Israel.

32 And Bela the son of Beor reigned in Edom: and the name of his city *was* Dinhabah.

33 And Bela died, and Jobab the son of Zerah of Bozrah reigned in his stead.

34 And Jobab died, and Husham of the land of Temani reigned in his stead.

35 And Husham died, and Hadad the son of Bedad, who smote Midian in the field of Moab, reigned in his stead: and the name of his city *was* Avith.

36 And Hadad died, and Samlah of Masrekah reigned in his stead.

37 And Samlah died, and Saul of Rehoboth *by* the river reigned in his stead.

38 And Saul died, and Baal-hanan the son of Achbor reigned in his stead.

39 And Baal-hanan the son of Achbor died, and Hadar reigned in his stead: and the name of his city *was* Pau; and his wife's name *was* Mehetabel, the daughter of Matred, the daughter of Mezahab.

40 And these *are* the names of the dukes *that came* of Esau, according to their families, after their places, by their names; duke Timnah, duke Alvah, duke Jetheth,

41 Duke Aholibamah, duke Elah, duke Pinon,

42 Duke Kenaz, duke Teman, duke Mibzar,

43 Duke Magdiel, duke Iram: these *be* the dukes of Edom, according to their habitations in the land of their possession: he *is* Esau the father of the Edomites.

## Amplified

19 These are the sons of Esau, that is, Edom; and these are their chiefs.

20 These are the sons of Seir the Horite, the inhabitants of the land: Lotan, Shobal, Zibeon, Anah,

21 Dishon, Ezer, and Dishan; these are the chiefs of the [a]Horites, the sons of Seir in the land of Edom.

22 The sons of Lotan are Hori and Heman; and Lotan's sister is Timna.

23 The sons of Shobal are these: Alvan, Manahath, Ebal, Shepho, and Onam.

24 These are the sons of Zibeon: Aiah, and Anah; this is Anah who found the hot springs in the wilderness, as he pastured the donkeys of Zibeon his father.

25 The children of Anah are these: Dishon and Oholibamah, daughter of Anah.

26 These are the sons of Dishon: Hemdan, Eshban, Ithran, and Cheran.

27 Ezer's sons are these: Bilhan, Zaavan, and Akan.

28 The sons of Dishan are these: Uz and Aran.

29 The Horite chiefs are these: Lotan, Shobal, Zibeon, Anah,

30 Dishon, Ezer, Dishan; these are the Horite chiefs, according to their clans in the land of Seir.

31 And these are the kings who reigned in Edom, before any king reigned over the Israelites:

32 Bela the son of Beor reigned in Edom, and the name of his city was Dinhabah.

33 Now Bela died, and Jobab son of Zerah of Bozrah reigned in his stead.

34 Then Jobab died, and Husham of the land of the Temanites reigned in his stead.

35 And Husham died, and Hadad son of Bedad, who defeated Midian in the country of Moab, reigned in his stead; the name of his [enclosed] city was Avith.

36 Hadad died, and Samlah of Masrekah succeeded him.

37 Then Samlah died, and Shaul of Rehoboth on the river [Euphrates] reigned in his stead.

38 And Shaul died, and Baal-hanan son of Achbor reigned in his stead.

39 Baal-hanan son of Achbor died, then Hadar reigned; his [enclosed] city was Pau; his wife's name was Mehetabel, daughter of Matred, daughter of Mezahab.

40 And these are the names of the chiefs of Esau, according to their families and places of residence, by their names: chiefs Timna, Alvah, Jetheth,

41 Oholibamah, Elah, Pinon,

42 Kenaz, Teman, Mibzar,

43 Magdiel, *and* Iram; these are the chiefs of Edom [that is, of Esau the father of the Edomites], according to their dwelling places in their land.

**AMP** [a] Because of the similarity of this word [for "Horites"] to a Hebrew word for "cave," the term Horite was formerly interpreted as "cave-dweller." But [later] archaeological discoveries have shown that the Horites are not to be explained as cave-dwellers, but are to be identified with an important group in the Near East in Patriarchal times (J. P. Free in *Archaeology and Bible History*). In fact, even in the earliest times neither the Bible nor archaeology has any proof of aboriginal "cave men." Cities of great antiquity have been unearthed with ever increasing evidence that, "When civilization appears it is already fully grown," and pre-Semitic "culture springs into view ready made" (Hall's *History of the Near East*).

## New American Standard

19 These are the sons of Esau (that is, Edom), and these are their chiefs.

20 ¶ These are the sons of Seir the Horite, the inhabitants of the land: Lotan and Shobal and Zibeon and Anah,

21 and Dishon and Ezer and Dishan. These are the chiefs descended from the Horites, the sons of Seir in the land of Edom.

22 And the sons of Lotan were Hori and Hemam; and Lotan's sister was Timna.

23 And these are the sons of Shobal: Alvan and Manahath and Ebal, Shepho and Onam.

24 And these are the sons of Zibeon: Aiah and Anah—he is the Anah who found the hot springs in the wilderness when he was pasturing the donkeys of his father Zibeon.

25 And these are the children of Anah: Dishon, and Oholibamah, the daughter of Anah.

26 And these are the sons of Dishon: Hemdan and Eshban and Ithran and Cheran.

27 These are the sons of Ezer: Bilhan and Zaavan and Akan.

28 These are the sons of Dishan: Uz and Aran.

29 These are the chiefs descended from the Horites: chief Lotan, chief Shobal, chief Zibeon, chief Anah,

30 chief Dishon, chief Ezer, chief Dishan. These are the chiefs descended from the Horites, according to their *various* chiefs in the land of Seir.

31 ¶ Now these are the kings who reigned in the land of Edom before any king reigned over the sons of Israel.

32 Bela the son of Beor reigned in Edom, and the name of his city was Dinhabah.

33 Then Bela died, and Jobab the son of Zerah of Bozrah became king in his place.

34 Then Jobab died, and Husham of the land of the Temanites became king in his place.

35 Then Husham died, and Hadad the son of Bedad, who defeated Midian in the field of Moab, became king in his place; and the name of his city was Avith.

36 Then Hadad died, and Samlah of Masrekah became king in his place.

37 Then Samlah died, and Shaul of Rehoboth on the *Euphrates* River became king in his place.

38 Then Shaul died, and Baal-hanan the son of Achbor became king in his place.

39 Then Baal-hanan the son of Achbor died, and Hadar became king in his place; and the name of his city was Pau; and his wife's name was Mehetabel, the daughter of Matred, daughter of Mezahab.

40 ¶ Now these are the names of the chiefs descended from Esau, according to their families *and* their localities, by their names: chief Timna, chief Alvah, chief Jetheth,

41 chief Oholibamah, chief Elah, chief Pinon,

42 chief Kenaz, chief Teman, chief Mibzar,

43 chief Magdiel, chief Iram. These are the chiefs of Edom (that is, Esau, the father of the Edomites), according to their habitations in the land of their possession.

## New International

19 These were the sons of Esau (that is, Edom), and these were their chiefs.

20 These were the sons of Seir the Horite, who were living in the region:
Lotan, Shobal, Zibeon, Anah,
21 Dishon, Ezer and Dishan.
These sons of Seir in Edom were Horite chiefs.

22 The sons of Lotan:
Hori and Homam.[b] Timna was Lotan's sister.

23 The sons of Shobal:
Alvan, Manahath, Ebal, Shepho and Onam.

24 The sons of Zibeon:
Aiah and Anah. This is the Anah who discovered the hot springs[c] in the desert while he was grazing the donkeys of his father Zibeon.

25 The children of Anah:
Dishon and Oholibamah daughter of Anah.

26 The sons of Dishon[d]:
Hemdan, Eshban, Ithran and Keran.

27 The sons of Ezer:
Bilhan, Zaavan and Akan.

28 The sons of Dishan:
Uz and Aran.

29 These were the Horite chiefs:
Lotan, Shobal, Zibeon, Anah,
30 Dishon, Ezer and Dishan.
These were the Horite chiefs, according to their divisions, in the land of Seir.

*The Rulers of Edom*

31 These were the kings who reigned in Edom before any Israelite king reigned[e]:

32 Bela son of Beor became king of Edom. His city was named Dinhabah.

33 When Bela died, Jobab son of Zerah from Bozrah succeeded him as king.

34 When Jobab died, Husham from the land of the Temanites succeeded him as king.

35 When Husham died, Hadad son of Bedad, who defeated Midian in the country of Moab, succeeded him as king. His city was named Avith.

36 When Hadad died, Samlah from Masrekah succeeded him as king.

37 When Samlah died, Shaul from Rehoboth on the river[f] succeeded him as king.

38 When Shaul died, Baal-Hanan son of Acbor succeeded him as king.

39 When Baal-Hanan son of Acbor died, Hadad[g] succeeded him as king. His city was named Pau, and his wife's name was Mehetabel daughter of Matred, the daughter of Me-Zahab.

40 These were the chiefs descended from Esau, by name, according to their clans and regions:
Timna, Alvah, Jetheth,
41 Oholibamah, Elah, Pinon,
42 Kenaz, Teman, Mibzar,
43 Magdiel and Iram. These were the chiefs of Edom, according to their settlements in the land they occupied.

This was Esau the father of the Edomites.

**NIV** [b] 22 Hebrew *Hemam,* a variant of *Homam* (see 1 Chron. 1:39) [c] 24 Vulgate; Syriac *discovered water;* the meaning of the Hebrew for this word is uncertain. [d] 26 Hebrew *Dishan,* a variant of *Dishon* [e] 31 Or *before an Israelite king reigned over them* [f] 37 Possibly the Euphrates [g] 39 Many manuscripts of the Masoretic Text, Samaritan Pentateuch and Syriac (see also 1 Chron. 1:50); most manuscripts of the Masoretic Text *Hadar*

## King James

**37** AND JACOB dwelt in the land wherein his father was a stranger, in the land of Canaan.

2These *are* the generations of Jacob. Joseph, *being* seventeen years old, was feeding the flock with his brethren; and the lad *was* with the sons of Bilhah, and with the sons of Zilpah, his father's wives: and Joseph brought unto his father their evil report.

3Now Israel loved Joseph more than all his children, because he *was* the son of his old age: and he made him a coat of *many* colours.

4And when his brethren saw that their father loved him more than all his brethren, they hated him, and could not speak peaceably unto him.

5¶ And Joseph dreamed a dream, and he told *it* his brethren: and they hated him yet the more.

6And he said unto them, Hear, I pray you, this dream which I have dreamed:

7For, behold, we *were* binding sheaves in the field, and, lo, my sheaf arose, and also stood upright; and, behold, your sheaves stood round about, and made obeisance to my sheaf.

8And his brethren said to him, Shalt thou indeed reign over us? or shalt thou indeed have dominion over us? And they hated him yet the more for his dreams, and for his words.

9¶ And he dreamed yet another dream, and told it his brethren, and said, Behold, I have dreamed a dream more; and, behold, the sun and the moon and the eleven stars made obeisance to me.

10And he told *it* to his father, and to his brethren: and his father rebuked him, and said unto him, What *is* this dream that thou hast dreamed? Shall I and thy mother and thy brethren indeed come to bow down ourselves to thee to the earth?

11And his brethren envied him; but his father observed the saying.

12¶ And his brethren went to feed their father's flock in Shechem.

13And Israel said unto Joseph, Do not thy brethren feed *the flock* in Shechem? come, and I will send thee unto them. And he said to him, Here *am I*.

14And he said to him, Go, I pray thee, see whether it be well with thy brethren, and well with the flocks; and bring me word again. So he sent him out of the vale of Hebron, and he came to Shechem.

15¶ And a certain man found him, and, behold, *he was* wandering in the field: and the man asked him, saying, What seekest thou?

16And he said, I seek my brethren: tell me, I pray thee, where they feed *their flocks*.

17And the man said, They are departed hence; for I heard them say, Let us go to Dothan. And Joseph went after his brethren, and found them in Dothan.

18And when they saw him afar off, even before he came near unto them, they conspired against him to slay him.

19And they said one to another, Behold, this dreamer cometh.

20Come now therefore, and let us slay him, and cast him into some pit, and we will say, Some evil beast hath devoured him: and we shall see what will become of his dreams.

21And Reuben heard *it*, and he delivered him out of their hands; and said, Let us not kill him.

22And Reuben said unto them, Shed no blood, *but* cast him into this pit that *is* in the wilderness, and lay no hand upon him; that he might rid him out of their hands, to deliver him to his father again.

23¶ And it came to pass, when Joseph was come unto his brethren, that they stripped Joseph out of his coat, *his* coat of *many* colours that *was* on him;

24And they took him, and cast him into a pit: and the pit *was* empty, *there was* no water in it.

## Amplified

**37** SO JACOB dwelt in the land in which his father had been a stranger *and* sojourner, in the land of Canaan.

2This is Jacob's line. Joseph, when he was seventeen years old, was shepherding the flock with his brothers; the lad was with the sons of Bilhah and Zilpah, his father's [secondary] wives; and Joseph brought to his father a bad report of them.

3Now Israel loved Joseph more than all his children, because he was the son of his old age; and he made him a [distinctive] long tunic with sleeves.

4But when his brothers saw that their father loved [Joseph] more than all of his brothers, they hated him, and could not say, Peace [in friendly greeting] to him *or* speak peaceably to him.

5Now Joseph had a dream, and he told it to his brothers, and they hated him still more.

6And he said to them, Listen now *and* hear, I pray you, this dream that I have dreamed:

7We [brothers] were binding sheaves in the field, and lo, my sheaf arose and stood upright, and behold, your sheaves stood round about my sheaf and bowed down!

8His brothers said to him, Shall you indeed reign over us? Or are you going to have us as your subjects *and* dominate us? And they hated him all the more for his dreams and for what he said.

9But Joseph dreamed yet another dream and told it to his brothers [also]. He said, See here, I have dreamed again, and behold, [this time not only] eleven stars, but also the sun and the moon bowed down *and* did reverence to me!

10And he told it to his father [as well as] his brethren. But his father rebuked him and said to him, What is the meaning of this dream that you have dreamed? Shall I and your mother and your brothers actually come to bow down ourselves to the earth *and* do homage to you?

11Joseph's brothers envied him *and* were jealous of him, but his father observed the saying *and* pondered over it.

12Joseph's brothers went to shepherd *and* feed their father's flock near Shechem.

13[One day] Israel said to Joseph, Do not your brothers shepherd my flock at Shechem? Come, and I will send you to them. And he said, Here I am.

14And [Jacob] said to him, Go, I pray you, see whether everything is all right with your brothers and with the flock; then come back and bring me word. So he sent him out of the Hebron valley, and he came to Shechem.

15And a certain man found him, and behold, he had lost his way *and* was wandering in the open country. The man asked him, What are you trying to find?

16And he said, I am looking for my brothers. Tell me, I pray you, where they are pasturing our flocks.

17But the man said, [They were here, but] they have gone. I heard them say, Let us go to Dothan. And Joseph went after his brothers and found them at Dothan.

18And when they saw him far off, even before he came near to them, they conspired to kill him.

19And they said one to another, See, here comes this dreamer *and* master of dreams.

20So, come on now, let us kill him and throw his body into some pit; then we will say [to our father], Some wild *and* ferocious animal has devoured him; and we shall see what will become of his dreams!

21Now Reuben heard it, and he delivered him out of their hands by saying, Let us not kill him.

22And Reuben said to them: Shed no blood, but cast him into this pit *or* well that is out here in the wilderness, and lay no hand on him. He was trying to get Joseph out of their hands, in order to rescue him *and* deliver him again to his father.

23When Joseph had come to his brothers, they stripped him of his [distinctive] long garment which he was wearing;

24Then they took him, and cast him into the [well-like] pit, which was empty; there was no water in it.

## New American Standard

*Joseph's Dream*

**37** NOW JACOB lived in the land where his father had sojourned, in the land of Canaan.
2These are *the records of* the generations of Jacob.
¶ Joseph, when seventeen years of age, was pasturing the flock
with his brothers while he was *still* a youth, along with the sons
of Bilhah and the sons of Zilpah, his father's wives. And Joseph
brought back a bad report about them to their father.
3Now Israel loved Joseph more than all his sons, because he
was the son of his old age; and he made him a [a]varicolored tunic.
4And his brothers saw that their father loved him more than
all his brothers; and *so* they hated him and could not speak to him
[b]on friendly terms.
5¶ Then Joseph had a dream, and when he told it to his brothers, they hated him even more.
6And he said to them, "Please listen to this dream which I have
had;
7for behold, we were binding sheaves in the field, and lo, my
sheaf rose up and also stood erect; and behold, your sheaves
gathered around and bowed down to my sheaf."
8Then his brothers said to him, "Are you actually going to
reign over us? Or are you really going to rule over us?" So they
hated him even more for his dreams and for his words.
9Now he had still another dream, and related it to his brothers,
and said, "Lo, I have had still another dream; and behold, the sun
and the moon and eleven stars were bowing down to me."
10And he related *it* to his father and to his brothers; and his
father rebuked him and said to him, "What is this dream that you
have had? Shall I and your mother and your brothers actually come
to bow ourselves down before you to the ground?"
11And his brothers were jealous of him, but his father kept the
saying *in mind.*
12¶ Then his brothers went to pasture their father's flock in
Shechem.
13And Israel said to Joseph, "Are not your brothers pasturing
*the flock* in Shechem? Come, and I will send you to them." And he
said to him, "I will go."
14Then he said to him, "Go now and see about the welfare of
your brothers and the welfare of the flock; and bring word back to
me." So he sent him from the valley of Hebron, and he came to
Shechem.
15And a man found him, and behold, he was wandering in the
field; and the man asked him, "What are you looking for?"
16And he said, "I am looking for my brothers; please tell me
where they are pasturing *the flock.*"
17Then the man said, "They have moved from here; for I heard
*them* say, 'Let us go to Dothan.'" So Joseph went after his brothers
and found them at Dothan.

*The Plot against Joseph*

18¶ When they saw him from a distance and before he came
close to them, they plotted against him to put him to death.
19And they said to one another, "Here comes this dreamer!
20"Now then, come and let us kill him and throw him into one
of the pits; and we will say, 'A wild beast devoured him.' Then let
us see what will become of his dreams!"
21But Reuben heard *this* and rescued him out of their hands and
said, "Let us not take his life."
22Reuben further said to them, "Shed no blood. Throw him into
this pit that is in the wilderness, but do not lay hands on
him"—that he might rescue him out of their hands, to restore him
to his father.
23So it came about, when Joseph reached his brothers, that they
stripped Joseph of his tunic, the varicolored tunic that was on him;
24and they took him and threw him into the pit. Now the pit
was empty, without any water in it.

**NAS** [a] Or, *full-length robe* [b] Lit., *in peace*

## New International

*Joseph's Dreams*

**37** JACOB LIVED in the land where his father had stayed, the
land of Canaan.
2This is the account of Jacob.
Joseph, a young man of seventeen, was tending the flocks with
his brothers, the sons of Bilhah and the sons of Zilpah, his father's
wives, and he brought their father a bad report about them.
3Now Israel loved Joseph more than any of his other sons,
because he had been born to him in his old age; and he made a
richly ornamented[c] robe for him. 4When his brothers saw that
their father loved him more than any of them, they hated him and
could not speak a kind word to him.
5Joseph had a dream, and when he told it to his brothers, they
hated him all the more. 6He said to them, "Listen to this dream
I had: 7We were binding sheaves of grain out in the field when
suddenly my sheaf rose and stood upright, while your sheaves
gathered around mine and bowed down to it."
8His brothers said to him, "Do you intend to reign over us? Will
you actually rule us?" And they hated him all the more because
of his dream and what he had said.
9Then he had another dream, and he told it to his brothers.
"Listen," he said, "I had another dream, and this time the sun and
moon and eleven stars were bowing down to me."
10When he told his father as well as his brothers, his father
rebuked him and said, "What is this dream you had? Will your
mother and I and your brothers actually come and bow down to
the ground before you?" 11His brothers were jealous of him, but
his father kept the matter in mind.

*Joseph Sold by His Brothers*

12Now his brothers had gone to graze their father's flocks near
Shechem, 13and Israel said to Joseph, "As you know, your brothers are grazing the flocks near Shechem. Come, I am going to send
you to them."
"Very well," he replied.
14So he said to him, "Go and see if all is well with your brothers
and with the flocks, and bring word back to me." Then he sent him
off from the Valley of Hebron.
When Joseph arrived at Shechem, 15a man found him wandering around in the fields and asked him, "What are you looking
for?"
16He replied, "I'm looking for my brothers. Can you tell me
where they are grazing their flocks?"
17"They have moved on from here," the man answered. "I
heard them say, 'Let's go to Dothan.'"
So Joseph went after his brothers and found them near Dothan.
18But they saw him in the distance, and before he reached them,
they plotted to kill him.
19"Here comes that dreamer!" they said to each other. 20"Come
now, let's kill him and throw him into one of these cisterns and
say that a ferocious animal devoured him. Then we'll see what
comes of his dreams."
21When Reuben heard this, he tried to rescue him from their
hands. "Let's not take his life," he said. 22"Don't shed any blood.
Throw him into this cistern here in the desert, but don't lay a hand
on him." Reuben said this to rescue him from them and take him
back to his father.
23So when Joseph came to his brothers, they stripped him of his
robe—the richly ornamented robe he was wearing— 24and they
took him and threw him into the cistern. Now the cistern was
empty; there was no water in it.

**NIV** [c] 3 The meaning of the Hebrew for *richly ornamented* is uncertain; also in verses 23 and 32.

## King James

25 And they sat down to eat bread: and they lifted up their eyes and looked, and, behold, a company of Ishmeelites came from Gilead with their camels bearing spicery and balm and myrrh, going to carry *it* down to Egypt.

26 And Judah said unto his brethren, What profit *is it* if we slay our brother, and conceal his blood?

27 Come, and let us sell him to the Ishmeelites, and let not our hand be upon him; for he *is* our brother *and* our flesh. And his brethren were content.

28 Then there passed by Midianites merchantmen; and they drew and lifted up Joseph out of the pit, and sold Joseph to the Ishmeelites for twenty *pieces* of silver: and they brought Joseph into Egypt.

29 ¶ And Reuben returned unto the pit; and, behold, Joseph *was* not in the pit; and he rent his clothes.

30 And he returned unto his brethren, and said, The child *is* not; and I, whither shall I go?

31 And they took Joseph's coat, and killed a kid of the goats, and dipped the coat in the blood;

32 And they sent the coat of *many* colours, and they brought *it* to their father; and said, This have we found: know now whether it *be* thy son's coat or no.

33 And he knew it, and said, *It is* my son's coat; an evil beast hath devoured him; Joseph is without doubt rent in pieces.

34 And Jacob rent his clothes, and put sackcloth upon his loins, and mourned for his son many days.

35 And all his sons and all his daughters rose up to comfort him; but he refused to be comforted; and he said, For I will go down into the grave unto my son mourning. Thus his father wept for him.

36 And the Midianites sold him into Egypt unto Potiphar, an officer of Pharaoh's, *and* captain of the guard.

**38** AND IT came to pass at that time, that Judah went down from his brethren, and turned in to a certain Adullamite, whose name *was* Hirah.

2 And Judah saw there a daughter of a certain Canaanite, whose name *was* Shuah; and he took her, and went in unto her.

3 And she conceived, and bare a son; and he called his name Er.

4 And she conceived again, and bare a son; and she called his name Onan.

5 And she yet again conceived, and bare a son; and called his name Shelah: and he was at Chezib, when she bare him.

6 And Judah took a wife for Er his firstborn, whose name *was* Tamar.

7 And Er, Judah's firstborn, was wicked in the sight of the LORD; and the LORD slew him.

8 And Judah said unto Onan, Go in unto thy brother's wife, and marry her, and raise up seed to thy brother.

9 And Onan knew that the seed should not be his; and it came to pass, when he went in unto his brother's wife, that he spilled *it* on the ground, lest that he should give seed to his brother.

10 And the thing which he did displeased the LORD: wherefore he slew him also.

11 Then said Judah to Tamar his daughter-in-law, Remain a widow at thy father's house, till Shelah my son be grown: for he said, Lest peradventure he die also, as his brethren *did*. And Tamar went and dwelt in her father's house.

## Amplified

25 Then they sat down to eat their lunch. When they looked up, lo, they saw a caravan of Ishmaelites [mixed Arabians] coming from Gilead, with their camels bearing gum [of the styrax tree], balm [balsam], and myrrh *or* ladanum, going on their way to carry them down to Egypt.

26 And Judah said to his brothers, What do we gain if we slay our brother and conceal his blood?

27 Come, let us sell him to the Ishmaelites [and Midianites, these mixed Arabians who are approaching], and let not our hand be upon him, for he is our brother and our flesh. And his brothers consented.

28 Then as the Midianite [and Ishmaelite] merchants were passing by, the brothers pulled Joseph up and lifted him out of the well. And they sold him for twenty pieces of silver to the Ishmaelites, who took Joseph [captive] into Egypt.

29 Then Reuben [who had not been there when the brothers plotted to sell the lad] returned to the pit; and behold, Joseph was not in the pit, and he rent his clothes.

30 He rejoined his brothers and said, The boy is not there! And I, where shall I go [to hide from my father]?

31 Then they took Joseph's [distinctive] long garment, killed a young goat, and dipped the garment in the blood;

32 And they sent the garment to their father, saying, We have found this! Examine *and* decide whether it is your son's tunic or not.

33 He said, My son's long garment! An evil [wild] beast has devoured him; Joseph is without doubt rent in pieces.

34 And Jacob tore his clothes, and put on sackcloth, and mourned many days for his son.

35 And all his sons and daughters attempted to console him, but he refused to be comforted, and said, I will go down to Sheol [the place of the dead, the unseen world] to my son mourning. And his father wept for him.

36 And the Midianites [and Ishmaelites] sold [Joseph] in Egypt to Potiphar, an officer of Pharaoh, and captain *and* chief executioner of the [royal] guard.

**38** AT THAT time Judah withdrew from his brothers and went to [lodge with] a certain Adullamite named Hirah.

2 There Judah saw *and* met a daughter of Shuah, a Canaanite; he took her as wife and lived with her.

3 And she became pregnant and bore a son, and he called him Er.

4 And she conceived again, and bore a son, and she named him Onan.

5 Again she conceived, and bore a son, and named him Shelah. [They were living] at Chezib when she bore him.

6 Now Judah took a wife for Er his first-born; her name was Tamar.

7 And Er, Judah's first-born, was wicked in the sight of the Lord, and the Lord slew him.

8 Then Judah told Onan, Marry your brother's widow; live with her and raise offspring for your brother.

9 But Onan knew that the family would not be his, so when he cohabited with his brother's widow, he prevented conception, lest he should raise up a child for his brother.

10 And the thing which he did displeased the Lord; therefore He slew him also.

11 Then Judah said to Tamar his daughter-in-law, Remain a widow at your father's house, till Shelah my [youngest] son is grown; for he thought, Lest perhaps [if Shelah should marry her] he would die also, as his brothers did. So Tamar went and lived in her father's house.

## New American Standard

25¶ Then they sat down to eat a meal. And as they raised their
eyes and looked, behold, a caravan of Ishmaelites was coming
from Gilead, with their camels bearing aromatic gum and balm and
myrrh, on their way to bring *them* down to Egypt.
26And Judah said to his brothers, "What profit is it for us to kill
our brother and cover up his blood?
27"Come and let us sell him to the Ishmaelites and not lay our
hands on him; for he is our brother, our *own* flesh." And his
brothers listened *to him.*
28Then some Midianite traders passed by, so they pulled *him* up
and lifted Joseph out of the pit, and sold him to the Ishmaelites for
twenty *shekels* of silver. Thus they brought Joseph into Egypt.
29¶ Now Reuben returned to the pit, and behold, Joseph was
not in the pit; so he tore his garments.
30And he returned to his brothers and said, "The boy is not
*there;* as for me, where am I to go?"
31So they took Joseph's tunic, and slaughtered a male goat, and
dipped the tunic in the blood;
32and they sent the varicolored tunic and brought it to their
father and said, "We found this; please examine *it* to *see* whether
it is your son's tunic or not."
33Then he examined it and said, "It is my son's tunic. A wild
beast has devoured him; Joseph has surely been torn to pieces!"
34So Jacob tore his clothes, and put sackcloth on his loins, and
mourned for his son many days.
35Then all his sons and all his daughters arose to comfort him,
but he refused to be comforted. And he said, "Surely I will go
down to Sheol in mourning for my son." So his father wept for
him.
36Meanwhile, the Midianites sold him in Egypt to Potiphar,
Pharaoh's officer, the captain of the bodyguard.

*Judah and Tamar*

38 AND IT came about at that time, that Judah departed from
his brothers, and visited a certain Adullamite, whose
name was Hirah.
2And Judah saw there a daughter of a certain Canaanite whose
name was Shua; and he took her and went in to her.
3So she conceived and bore a son and he named him Er.
4Then she conceived again and bore a son and named him
Onan.
5And she bore still another son and named him Shelah; and it
was at Chezib that she bore him.
6¶ Now Judah took a wife for Er his first-born, and her name
*was* Tamar.
7But Er, Judah's first-born, was evil in the sight of the LORD,
so the LORD took his life.
8Then Judah said to Onan, "Go in to your brother's wife, and
perform your duty as a brother-in-law to her, and raise up offspring for your brother."
9And Onan knew that the offspring would not be his; so it
came about that when he went in to his brother's wife, he wasted
his seed on the ground, in order not to give offspring to his
brother.
10But what he did was displeasing in the sight of the LORD; so
He took his life also.
11Then Judah said to his daughter-in-law Tamar, "Remain a
widow in your father's house until my son Shelah grows up"; for
he thought, "*I am afraid* that he too may die like his brothers." So
Tamar went and lived in her father's house.

## New International

25As they sat down to eat their meal, they looked up and saw
a caravan of Ishmaelites coming from Gilead. Their camels were
loaded with spices, balm and myrrh, and they were on their way
to take them down to Egypt.
26Judah said to his brothers, "What will we gain if we kill our
brother and cover up his blood? 27Come, let's sell him to the
Ishmaelites and not lay our hands on him; after all, he is our
brother, our own flesh and blood." His brothers agreed.
28So when the Midianite merchants came by, his brothers
pulled Joseph up out of the cistern and sold him for twenty
shekels[a] of silver to the Ishmaelites, who took him to Egypt.
29When Reuben returned to the cistern and saw that Joseph was
not there, he tore his clothes. 30He went back to his brothers and
said, "The boy isn't there! Where can I turn now?"
31Then they got Joseph's robe, slaughtered a goat and dipped
the robe in the blood. 32They took the ornamented robe back to
their father and said, "We found this. Examine it to see whether
it is your son's robe."
33He recognized it and said, "It is my son's robe! Some ferocious
animal has devoured him. Joseph has surely been torn to pieces."
34Then Jacob tore his clothes, put on sackcloth and mourned for
his son many days. 35All his sons and daughters came to comfort
him, but he refused to be comforted. "No," he said, "in mourning
will I go down to the grave[b] to my son." So his father wept for him.
36Meanwhile, the Midianites[c] sold Joseph in Egypt to Potiphar,
one of Pharaoh's officials, the captain of the guard.

*Judah and Tamar*

38 AT THAT time, Judah left his brothers and went down to
stay with a man of Adullam named Hirah. 2There Judah
met the daughter of a Canaanite man named Shua. He married her
and lay with her; 3she became pregnant and gave birth to a son,
who was named Er. 4She conceived again and gave birth to a son
and named him Onan. 5She gave birth to still another son and
named him Shelah. It was at Kezib that she gave birth to him.
6Judah got a wife for Er, his firstborn, and her name was Tamar.
7But Er, Judah's firstborn, was wicked in the LORD's sight; so the
LORD put him to death.
8Then Judah said to Onan, "Lie with your brother's wife and
fulfill your duty to her as a brother-in-law to produce offspring for
your brother." 9But Onan knew that the offspring would not be
his; so whenever he lay with his brother's wife, he spilled his
semen on the ground to keep from producing offspring for his
brother. 10What he did was wicked in the LORD's sight; so he put
him to death also.
11Judah then said to his daughter-in-law Tamar, "Live as a
widow in your father's house until my son Shelah grows up." For
he thought, "He may die too, just like his brothers." So Tamar
went to live in her father's house.

NIV [a] 28 That is, about 8 ounces (about 0.2 kilogram) [b] 35 Hebrew *Sheol*
[c] 36 Samaritan Pentateuch, Septuagint, Vulgate and Syriac (see also verse 28);
Masoretic Text *Medanites*

## King James

12¶ And in process of time the daughter of Shuah Judah's wife died; and Judah was comforted, and went up unto his sheepshearers to Timnath, he and his friend Hirah the Adullamite.

13And it was told Tamar, saying, Behold thy father-in-law goeth up to Timnath to shear his sheep.

14And she put her widow's garments off from her, and covered her with a veil, and wrapped herself, and sat in an open place, which *is* by the way to Timnath; for she saw that Shelah was grown, and she was not given unto him to wife.

15When Judah saw her, he thought her *to be* an harlot; because she had covered her face.

16And he turned unto her by the way, and said, Go to, I pray thee, let me come in unto thee; (for he knew not that she *was* his daughter-in-law.) And she said, What wilt thou give me, that thou mayest come in unto me?

17And he said, I will send *thee* a kid from the flock. And she said, Wilt thou give *me* a pledge, till thou send *it?*

18And he said, What pledge shall I give thee? And she said, Thy signet, and thy bracelets, and thy staff that *is* in thine hand. And he gave *it* her, and came in unto her, and she conceived by him.

19And she arose, and went away, and laid by her veil from her, and put on the garments of her widowhood.

20And Judah sent the kid by the hand of his friend the Adullamite, to receive *his* pledge from the woman's hand: but he found her not.

21Then he asked the men of that place, saying, Where *is* the harlot, that *was* openly by the way side? And they said, There was no harlot in this *place.*

22And he returned to Judah, and said, I cannot find her; and also the men of the place said, *that* there was no harlot in this *place.*

23And Judah said, Let her take *it* to her, lest we be shamed: behold, I sent this kid, and thou hast not found her.

24¶ And it came to pass about three months after, that it was told Judah, saying, Tamar thy daughter-in-law hath played the harlot; and also, behold, she *is* with child by whoredom. And Judah said, Bring her forth, and let her be burnt.

25When she *was* brought forth, she sent to her father-in-law, saying, By the man, whose these *are, am* I with child: and she said, Discern, I pray thee, whose *are* these, the signet, and bracelets, and staff.

26And Judah acknowledged *them,* and said, She hath been more righteous than I; because that I gave her not to Shelah my son. And he knew her again no more.

27¶ And it came to pass in the time of her travail, that, behold, twins *were* in her womb.

28And it came to pass, when she travailed, that *the one* put out *his* hand: and the midwife took and bound upon his hand a scarlet thread, saying, This came out first.

29And it came to pass, as he drew back his hand, that, behold, his brother came out: and she said, How hast thou broken forth? *this* breach *be* upon thee: therefore his name was called Pharez.

30And afterward came out his brother, that had the scarlet thread upon his hand: and his name was called Zerah.

**39** AND JOSEPH was brought down to Egypt; and Potiphar, an officer of Pharaoh, captain of the guard, an Egyptian, bought him of the hands of the Ishmeelites, which had brought him down thither.

## Amplified

12But later Judah's wife, daughter of Shuah, died; and when Judah was comforted, he went up to his sheepshearers at Timnath with his friend Hirah the Adullamite.

13Then it was told Tamar, Listen, your father-in-law is going up to Timnath to shear his sheep.

14So she put off her widow's garments and covered herself with a veil, wrapped herself up [in disguise], and sat in the entrance of Enaim, which is by the road to Timnath; for she saw that Shelah was grown, and she was not given to him as his wife.

15When Judah saw her, he thought she was a harlot *or* devoted prostitute [under a vow to her goddess], for she had covered her face [as such women did].

16He turned to her by the road, and said, Come, let me have intercourse with you; for he did not know that she was his daughter-in-law. And she said, What will you give me that you may have intercourse with me?

17He answered, I will send you a kid from the flock. And she said, Will you give me a pledge [deposit] until you send it?

18And he said, What pledge shall I give you? She said, Your signet [seal], your [signet] cord, and your staff that is in your hand. And he gave them to her, and came in to her, and she became pregnant by him.

19And she arose and went away, and laid aside her veil and put on the garments of her widowhood.

20And Judah sent the kid by the hand of his friend the Adullamite, to receive his pledge from the woman's hand; but he was unable to find her.

21He asked the men of that place, Where is the harlot *or* cult prostitute who was openly by the roadside? They said, There was no harlot *or* temple prostitute here.

22So he returned to Judah, and said, I cannot find her; and also the local men said, There was no harlot *or* temple prostitute around here.

23And Judah said, Let her keep [the pledge articles] for herself, lest we be made ashamed. I sent this kid, and you have not found her.

24But about three months later Judah was told, Tamar your daughter-in-law has played the harlot, and also she is with child by her lewdness. And Judah said, Bring her forth, and let her be burned!

25When she was brought forth, she [took the things he had given her in pledge and] sent [them] to her father-in-law, saying, I am with child by the man to whom these articles belong. Then she added, Make out clearly, I pray you, to whom these belong, the signet [seal], cord, and staff.

26And Judah acknowledged them, and said, She has been more right *and* just than I; because I did not give her to Shelah my son. And he did not cohabit with her again.

27Now when the time came for her to be delivered, behold, there were twins in her womb.

28And when she was in labor, one baby put out his hand; and the midwife took his hand and bound upon it a scarlet thread, saying, This baby was born first.

29But he drew back his hand, and behold, his brother was born first. And she said, What a breaking forth you have made for yourself! Therefore his name was called Perez [breaking forth]. [Matt. 1:3.]

30And afterward his brother who had the scarlet thread on his hand was born, and was named Zerah.

**39** AND JOSEPH was brought down to Egypt; and Potiphar, an officer of Pharaoh, captain *and* chief executioner of the [royal] guard, an Egyptian, bought him from the Ishmaelites who had brought him down there.

## New American Standard

12¶ Now after a considerable time Shua's daughter, the wife of
Judah, died; and when the time of mourning was ended, Judah
went up to his sheepshearers at Timnah, he and his friend Hirah
the Adullamite.
13And it was told to Tamar, "Behold, your father-in-law is going
up to Timnah to shear his sheep."
14So she removed her widow's garments and covered *herself*
with a [a]veil, and wrapped herself, and sat in the gateway of
Enaim, which is on the road to Timnah; for she saw that Shelah
had grown up, and she had not been given to him as a wife.
15When Judah saw her, he thought she *was* a harlot, for she had
covered her face.
16So he turned aside to her by the road, and said, "Here now,
let me come in to you"; for he did not know that she was his
daughter-in-law. And she said, "What will you give me, that you
may come in to me?"
17He said, therefore, "I will send you a kid from the flock." She
said, moreover, "Will you give a pledge until you send *it?*"
18And he said, "What pledge shall I give you?" And she said,
"Your seal and your cord, and your staff that is in your hand." So
he gave *them* to her, and went in to her, and she conceived by him.
19Then she arose and departed, and removed her veil and put
on her widow's garments.
20¶ When Judah sent the kid by his friend the Adullamite, to
receive the pledge from the woman's hand, he did not find her.
21And he asked the men of her place, saying, "Where is the
temple prostitute who was by the road at Enaim?" But they said,
"There has been no temple prostitute here."
22So he returned to Judah, and said, "I did not find her; and
furthermore, the men of the place said, 'There has been no temple
prostitute here.'"
23Then Judah said, "Let her keep them, lest we become a laughingstock. After all, I sent this kid, but you did not find her."
24¶ Now it was about three months later that Judah was informed, "Your daughter-in-law Tamar has played the harlot, and
behold, she is also with child by harlotry." Then Judah said, "Bring
her out and let her be burned!"
25It was while she was being brought out that she sent to her
father-in-law, saying, "I am with child by the man to whom these
things belong." And she said, "Please examine and see, whose
signet ring and cords and staff are these?"
26And Judah recognized *them*, and said, "She is more righteous
than I, inasmuch as I did not give her to my son Shelah." And he
did not have relations with her again.
27¶ And it came about at the time she was giving birth, that
behold, there were twins in her womb.
28Moreover, it took place while she was giving birth, one put
out a hand, and the midwife took and tied a scarlet *thread* on his
hand, saying, "This one came out first."
29But it came about as he drew back his hand, that behold, his
brother came out. Then she said, "What a breach you have made
for yourself!" So he was named [b]Perez.
30And afterward his brother came out who had the scarlet *thread*
on his hand; and he was named [c]Zerah.

*Joseph's Success in Egypt*

**39** NOW JOSEPH had been taken down to Egypt; and Potiphar, an Egyptian officer of Pharaoh, the captain of the
bodyguard, bought him from the Ishmaelites, who had taken him
down there.

NAS [a] Or, *shawl* [b] I.e., a breach [c] I.e., a dawning or brightness

## New International

12After a long time Judah's wife, the daughter of Shua, died.
When Judah had recovered from his grief, he went up to Timnah,
to the men who were shearing his sheep, and his friend Hirah the
Adullamite went with him.
13When Tamar was told, "Your father-in-law is on his way to
Timnah to shear his sheep," 14she took off her widow's clothes,
covered herself with a veil to disguise herself, and then sat down
at the entrance to Enaim, which is on the road to Timnah. For she
saw that, though Shelah had now grown up, she had not been
given to him as his wife.
15When Judah saw her, he thought she was a prostitute, for she
had covered her face. 16Not realizing that she was his daughter-in-
law, he went over to her by the roadside and said, "Come now,
let me sleep with you."
"And what will you give me to sleep with you?" she asked.
17"I'll send you a young goat from my flock," he said.
"Will you give me something as a pledge until you send it?" she
asked.
18He said, "What pledge should I give you?"
"Your seal and its cord, and the staff in your hand," she answered. So he gave them to her and slept with her, and she became
pregnant by him. 19After she left, she took off her veil and put on
her widow's clothes again.
20Meanwhile Judah sent the young goat by his friend the Adullamite in order to get his pledge back from the woman, but he did
not find her. 21He asked the men who lived there, "Where is the
shrine prostitute who was beside the road at Enaim?"
"There hasn't been any shrine prostitute here," they said.
22So he went back to Judah and said, "I didn't find her. Besides,
the men who lived there said, 'There hasn't been any shrine prostitute here.'"
23Then Judah said, "Let her keep what she has, or we will
become a laughingstock. After all, I did send her this young goat,
but you didn't find her."
24About three months later Judah was told, "Your daughter-in-
law Tamar is guilty of prostitution, and as a result she is now
pregnant."
Judah said, "Bring her out and have her burned to death!"
25As she was being brought out, she sent a message to her
father-in-law. "I am pregnant by the man who owns these," she
said. And she added, "See if you recognize whose seal and cord
and staff these are."
26Judah recognized them and said, "She is more righteous than
I, since I wouldn't give her to my son Shelah." And he did not
sleep with her again.
27When the time came for her to give birth, there were twin
boys in her womb. 28As she was giving birth, one of them put out
his hand; so the midwife took a scarlet thread and tied it on his
wrist and said, "This one came out first." 29But when he drew back
his hand, his brother came out, and she said, "So this is how you
have broken out!" And he was named Perez.[d] 30Then his brother,
who had the scarlet thread on his wrist, came out and he was given
the name Zerah.[e]

*Joseph and Potiphar's Wife*

**39** NOW JOSEPH had been taken down to Egypt. Potiphar,
an Egyptian who was one of Pharaoh's officials, the captain of the guard, bought him from the Ishmaelites who had taken
him there.

NIV [d] 29 *Perez* means *breaking out.* [e] 30 *Zerah* can mean *scarlet* or *brightness.*

## King James

2And the LORD was with Joseph, and he was a prosperous man;
and he was in the house of his master the Egyptian.
3And his master saw that the LORD *was* with him, and that the
LORD made all that he did to prosper in his hand.
4And Joseph found grace in his sight, and he served him: and
he made him overseer over his house, and all *that* he had he put
into his hand.
5And it came to pass from the time *that* he had made him
overseer in his house, and over all that he had, that the LORD
blessed the Egyptian's house for Joseph's sake; and the blessing
of the LORD was upon all that he had in the house, and in the field.
6And he left all that he had in Joseph's hand; and he knew not
aught he had, save the bread which he did eat. And Joseph was
*a* goodly *person*, and wellfavoured.
7¶ And it came to pass after these things, that his master's wife
cast her eyes upon Joseph; and she said, Lie with me.
8But he refused, and said unto his master's wife, Behold, my
master wotteth not what *is* with me in the house, and he hath
committed all that he hath to my hand;
9 *There is* none greater in this house than I; neither hath he kept
back any thing from me but thee, because thou *art* his wife: how
then can I do this great wickedness, and sin against God?
10And it came to pass, as she spake to Joseph day by day, that
he hearkened not unto her, to lie by her, *or* to be with her.
11And it came to pass about this time, that *Joseph* went into the
house to do his business; and *there was* none of the men of the
house there within.
12And she caught him by his garment, saying, Lie with me: and
he left his garment in her hand, and fled, and got him out.
13And it came to pass, when she saw that he had left his garment in her hand, and was fled forth,
14That she called unto the men of her house, and spake unto
them, saying, See, he hath brought in an Hebrew unto us to mock
us; he came in unto me to lie with me, and I cried with a loud voice:
15And it came to pass, when he heard that I lifted up my voice
and cried, that he left his garment with me, and fled, and got him
out.
16And she laid up his garment by her, until his lord came home.
17And she spake unto him according to these words, saying,
The Hebrew servant, which thou hast brought unto us, came in
unto me to mock me:
18And it came to pass, as I lifted up my voice and cried, that he
left his garment with me, and fled out.
19And it came to pass, when his master heard the words of his
wife, which she spake unto him, saying, After this manner did thy
servant to me; that his wrath was kindled.
20And Joseph's master took him, and put him into the prison,
a place where the king's prisoners *were* bound: and he was there
in the prison.
21¶ But the LORD was with Joseph, and showed him mercy, and
gave him favour in the sight of the keeper of the prison.
22And the keeper of the prison committed to Joseph's hand all
the prisoners that *were* in the prison; and whatsoever they did
there, he was the doer *of it*.
23The keeper of the prison looked not to any thing *that was*
under his hand; because the LORD was with him, and *that* which
he did, the LORD made *it* to prosper.

**40** AND IT came to pass after these things, *that* the butler of
the king of Egypt and *his* baker had offended their lord the
king of Egypt.

## Amplified

2But the Lord was with Joseph, and he [though a slave] was a
successful *and* prosperous man; and he was in the house of his
master the Egyptian.
3And his master saw that the Lord was with him, and that the
Lord made all that he did to flourish *and* succeed in his hand. [Cp.
21:22; 26:27, 28; 41:38, 39.]
4So Joseph pleased [Potiphar] *and* found favor in his sight, and
he served him. And [his master] made him supervisor over his
house, and he put all that he had in his charge.
5From the time that he made him supervisor in his house and
over all that he had, the Lord blessed the Egyptian's house for
Joseph's sake; and the Lord's blessing was on all that he had in the
house and in the field.
6And [Potiphar] left all that he had in Joseph's charge, and paid
no attention to anything he had except the food he ate. Now
Joseph was an attractive person and fine looking.
7Then after a time his master's wife cast her eyes upon Joseph,
and she said, Lie with me.
8But he refused and said to his master's wife, See here, with me
in the house my master has concern about nothing, he has put all
that he has in my care.
9He is not greater in this house than I am; nor has he kept
anything from me except you, for you are his wife. How then can
I do this great evil and sin against God?
10She spoke to Joseph day after day, but he did not listen to her,
to lie with her or to be with her.
11Then it happened about this time that Joseph went into the
house to attend to his duties, and none of the men of the house
were indoors.
12And she caught him by his garment, saying, Lie with me! But
he left his garment in her hand, and fled and got out [of the house].
13And when she saw that he had left his garment in her hand,
and had fled away,
14She called to the men of her household, and said to them, See,
he [your master] has brought in a Hebrew to us to mock *and* insult
us; he came in where I was to lie with me, and I screamed at the
top of my voice.
15And when he heard me screaming and crying he left his
garment with me, and fled and got out of the house.
16And she laid up his garment by her, until his master came
home.
17Then she told him the same story, saying, The Hebrew servant whom you brought among us, came to me to mock *and* insult
me.
18And when I screamed and cried, he left his garment with me,
and fled out [of the house].
19And when [Joseph's] master heard the words of his wife,
saying to him, This is the way your servant treated me, his wrath
was kindled.
20And Joseph's master took him and put him in the prison, a
place where the state prisoners were confined; so he was there in
the prison.
21But the Lord was with Joseph, and showed him mercy *and*
loving-kindness and gave him favor in the sight of the warden of
the prison.
22And the warden of the prison committed to Joseph's care all
the prisoners who were in the prison; and whatsoever was done
there, he was in charge of it.
23The prison warden paid no attention to anything that was in
[Joseph's] charge, for the Lord was with him and made whatever
he did to prosper.

**40** NOW SOME time later the butler and the baker of the king
of Egypt offended their lord, Egypt's king.

## New American Standard

2And the LORD was with Joseph, so he became a successful
man. And he was in the house of his master, the Egyptian.
3Now his master saw that the LORD was with him and *how* the
LORD caused all that he did to prosper in his hand.
4So Joseph found favor in his sight, and became his personal
servant; and he made him overseer over his house, and all that he
owned he put in his charge.
5And it came about that from the time he made him overseer
in his house, and over all that he owned, the LORD blessed the
Egyptian's house on account of Joseph; thus the LORD's blessing
was upon all that he owned, in the house and in the field.
6So he left everything he owned in Joseph's charge; and with
him *there* he did not concern himself with anything except the food
which he ate. Now Joseph was handsome in form and appearance.
7¶ And it came about after these events that his master's wife
looked with desire at Joseph, and she said, "Lie with me."
8But he refused and said to his master's wife, "Behold, with
me *here*, my master does not concern himself with anything in the
house, and he has put all that he owns in my charge.
9"There is no one greater in this house than I, and he has
withheld nothing from me except you, because you are his wife.
How then could I do this great evil, and sin against God?"
10And it came about as she spoke to Joseph day after day, that
he did not listen to her to lie beside her, *or* be with her.
11Now it happened one day that he went into the house to do
his work, and none of the men of the household was there inside.
12And she caught him by his garment, saying, "Lie with me!"
And he left his garment in her hand and fled, and went outside.
13When she saw that he had left his garment in her hand, and
had fled outside,
14she called to the men of her household, and said to them,
"See, he has brought in a Hebrew to us to make sport of us; he
came in to me to lie with me, and I screamed.
15"And it came about when he heard that I raised my voice and
[a]screamed, that he left his garment beside me and fled, and went
outside."
16So she left his garment beside her until his master came home.
17Then she spoke to him with these words, "The Hebrew slave,
whom you brought to us, came in to me to make sport of me;
18and it happened as I raised my voice and screamed, that he
left his garment beside me and fled outside."

*Joseph Imprisoned*

19¶ Now it came about when his master heard the words of his
wife, which she spoke to him, saying, "This is what your slave did
to me," that his anger burned.
20So Joseph's master took him and put him into the jail, the
place where the king's prisoners were confined; and he was there
in the jail.
21But the LORD was with Joseph and extended kindness to him,
and gave him favor in the sight of the chief jailer.
22And the chief jailer committed to Joseph's charge all the prisoners who were in the jail; so that whatever was done there, he
was responsible *for it*.
23The chief jailer did not supervise anything under Joseph's
charge because the LORD was with him; and whatever he did, the
LORD made to prosper.

*Joseph Interprets a Dream*

40 THEN IT came about after these things the cupbearer and
the baker for the king of Egypt offended their lord, the
king of Egypt.

NAS [a] Lit., *called out*

## New International

2The LORD was with Joseph and he prospered, and he lived in
the house of his Egyptian master. 3When his master saw that the
LORD was with him and that the LORD gave him success in everything he did, 4Joseph found favor in his eyes and became his
attendant. Potiphar put him in charge of his household, and he
entrusted to his care everything he owned. 5From the time he put
him in charge of his household and of all that he owned, the LORD
blessed the household of the Egyptian because of Joseph. The
blessing of the LORD was on everything Potiphar had, both in the
house and in the field. 6So he left in Joseph's care everything he
had; with Joseph in charge, he did not concern himself with anything except the food he ate.
Now Joseph was well-built and handsome, 7and after a while
his master's wife took notice of Joseph and said, "Come to bed
with me!"
8But he refused. "With me in charge," he told her, "my master
does not concern himself with anything in the house; everything
he owns he has entrusted to my care. 9No one is greater in this
house than I am. My master has withheld nothing from me except
you, because you are his wife. How then could I do such a wicked
thing and sin against God?" 10And though she spoke to Joseph day
after day, he refused to go to bed with her or even be with her.
11One day he went into the house to attend to his duties, and
none of the household servants was inside. 12She caught him by
his cloak and said, "Come to bed with me!" But he left his cloak
in her hand and ran out of the house.
13When she saw that he had left his cloak in her hand and had
run out of the house, 14she called her household servants. "Look,"
she said to them, "this Hebrew has been brought to us to make
sport of us! He came in here to sleep with me, but I screamed.
15When he heard me scream for help, he left his cloak beside me
and ran out of the house."
16She kept his cloak beside her until his master came home.
17Then she told him this story: "That Hebrew slave you brought
us came to me to make sport of me. 18But as soon as I screamed
for help, he left his cloak beside me and ran out of the house."
19When his master heard the story his wife told him, saying,
"This is how your slave treated me," he burned with anger. 20Jo-
seph's master took him and put him in prison, the place where the
king's prisoners were confined.
But while Joseph was there in the prison, 21the LORD was with
him; he showed him kindness and granted him favor in the eyes
of the prison warden. 22So the warden put Joseph in charge of all
those held in the prison, and he was made responsible for all that
was done there. 23The warden paid no attention to anything under
Joseph's care, because the LORD was with Joseph and gave him
success in whatever he did.

*The Cupbearer and the Baker*

40 SOME TIME later, the cupbearer and the baker of the king
of Egypt offended their master, the king of Egypt. 2Phar-

## King James

2 And Pharaoh was wroth against two *of* his officers, against the chief of the butlers, and against the chief of the bakers.

3 And he put them in ward in the house of the captain of the guard, into the prison, the place where Joseph *was* bound.

4 And the captain of the guard charged Joseph with them, and he served them: and they continued a season in ward.

5 ¶ And they dreamed a dream both of them, each man his dream in one night, each man according to the interpretation of his dream, the butler and the baker of the king of Egypt, which *were* bound in the prison.

6 And Joseph came in unto them in the morning, and looked upon them, and, behold, they *were* sad.

7 And he asked Pharaoh's officers that *were* with him in the ward of his lord's house, saying, Wherefore look ye *so* sadly today?

8 And they said unto him, We have dreamed a dream, and *there is* no interpreter of it. And Joseph said unto them, *Do* not interpretations *belong* to God? tell me *them,* I pray you.

9 And the chief butler told his dream to Joseph, and said to him, In my dream, behold, a vine *was* before me;

10 And in the vine *were* three branches: and it *was* as though it budded, *and* her blossoms shot forth; and the clusters thereof brought forth ripe grapes:

11 And Pharaoh's cup *was* in my hand: and I took the grapes, and pressed them into Pharaoh's cup, and I gave the cup into Pharaoh's hand.

12 And Joseph said unto him, This *is* the interpretation of it: The three branches *are* three days:

13 Yet within three days shall Pharaoh lift up thine head, and restore thee unto thy place: and thou shalt deliver Pharaoh's cup into his hand, after the former manner when thou wast his butler.

14 But think on me when it shall be well with thee, and show kindness, I pray thee, unto me, and make mention of me unto Pharaoh, and bring me out of this house:

15 For indeed I was stolen away out of the land of the Hebrews: and here also have I done nothing that they should put me into the dungeon.

16 When the chief baker saw that the interpretation was good, he said unto Joseph, I also *was* in my dream, and, behold, *I had* three white baskets on my head:

17 And in the uppermost basket *there was* of all manner of bakemeats for Pharaoh; and the birds did eat them out of the basket upon my head.

18 And Joseph answered and said, This *is* the interpretation thereof: The three baskets *are* three days:

19 Yet within three days shall Pharaoh lift up thy head from off thee, and shall hang thee on a tree; and the birds shall eat thy flesh from off thee.

20 ¶ And it came to pass the third day, *which was* Pharaoh's birthday, that he made a feast unto all his servants: and he lifted up the head of the chief butler and of the chief baker among his servants.

21 And he restored the chief butler unto his butlership again; and he gave the cup into Pharaoh's hand:

22 But he hanged the chief baker: as Joseph had interpreted to them.

23 Yet did not the chief butler remember Joseph, but forgat him.

## Amplified

2 And Pharaoh was angry with his officers, the chief of the butlers and the chief of the bakers.

3 He put them in custody in the house of the captain of the guard, in the prison where Joseph was confined.

4 And the captain of the guard put them in Joseph's charge, and he served them; and they continued in custody for some time.

5 And they both dreamed a dream in the same night, each man according to [the personal significance of] the interpretation of his dream, the butler and the baker of the king of Egypt, who were confined in the prison.

6 When Joseph came to them in the morning and looked at them, he saw that they were sad *and* depressed.

7 So he asked Pharaoh's officers who were in custody with him in his master's house, Why do you look so dejected *and* sad today?

8 And they said to him, We have dreamed dreams, and there is no one to interpret them. And Joseph said to them, Do not interpretations belong to God? Tell me [your dreams], I pray you.

9 And the chief butler told his dream to Joseph, and said to him, In my dream I saw a vine before me;

10 And on the vine were three branches. Then it was as though it budded, its blossoms burst forth, and the clusters of them brought forth ripe grapes [almost all at once].

11 And Pharaoh's cup was in my hand; and I took the grapes and pressed them into Pharaoh's cup; then I gave the cup into Pharaoh's hand.

12 And Joseph said to him, This is the interpretation of it: The three branches are three days.

13 Within three days Pharaoh will lift up your head and restore you to your position; and you will again put Pharaoh's cup into his hand, as when you were his butler.

14 But think of me when it shall be well with you, and show kindness, I beg of you, to me, and mention me to Pharaoh and get me out of this house.

15 For truly I was carried away from the land of the Hebrews by unlawful force; and here too I have done nothing for which they should put me into the dungeon.

16 When the chief baker saw that the interpretation was good, he said to Joseph, I also dreamed, and behold, I had three cake baskets on my head.

17 And in the uppermost basket were some of all kinds of baked food for Pharaoh; but the birds [of prey] were eating out of the basket on my head.

18 And Joseph answered, This is the interpretation of it: The three baskets are three days.

19 Within three days Pharaoh will lift up your head, but will have you beheaded and hung on a tree, and [you will not so much as be given burial, but] the birds will eat your flesh.

20 And on the third day, Pharaoh's birthday, he made a feast for all his servants; and he lifted up the heads of the chief butler and the chief baker [by inviting them also] among his servants.

21 And he restored the chief butler to his butlership; and the butler gave the cup into Pharaoh's hand;

22 But [Pharaoh] hanged the chief baker, as Joseph had interpreted to them.

23 But [even after all that] the chief butler gave no thought to Joseph, but forgot [all about] him.

**41** AND IT came to pass at the end of two full years, that Pharaoh dreamed: and, behold, he stood by the river.

2 And, behold, there came up out of the river seven well-favoured kine and fatfleshed; and they fed in a meadow.

**41** AFTER TWO full years, Pharaoh dreamed that he stood by the river [Nile].

2 And behold, there came up out of the river [Nile] seven well-favored cows; sleek *and* handsome and fat; and they grazed in the reed grass [in a marshy pasture].

## New American Standard

2And Pharaoh was furious with his two officials, the chief
cupbearer and the chief baker.
3So he put them in confinement in the house of the captain of
the bodyguard, in the jail, the *same* place where Joseph was imprisoned.
4And the captain of the bodyguard put Joseph in charge of
them, and he took care of them; and they were in confinement for
some time.
5Then the cupbearer and the baker for the king of Egypt, who
were confined in jail, both had a dream the same night, each man
with his *own* dream *and* each dream with its *own* interpretation.
6When Joseph came to them in the morning and observed
them, behold, they were dejected.
7And he asked Pharaoh's officials who were with him in confinement in his master's house, "Why are your faces so sad today?"
8Then they said to him, "We have had a dream and there is
no one to interpret it." Then Joseph said to them, "Do not interpretations belong to God? Tell *it* to me, please."
9¶ So the chief cupbearer told his dream to Joseph, and said to
him, "In my dream, behold, *there was* a vine in front of me;
10and on the vine *were* three branches. And as it was budding,
its blossoms came out, *and* its clusters produced ripe grapes.
11"Now Pharaoh's cup was in my hand; so I took the grapes and
squeezed them into Pharaoh's cup, and I put the cup into Pharaoh's hand."
12Then Joseph said to him, "This is the interpretation of it: the
three branches are three days;
13within three more days Pharaoh will [a]lift up your head and
restore you to your office; and you will put Pharaoh's cup into his
hand according to your former custom when you were his cupbearer.
14"Only keep me in mind when it goes well with you, and
please do me a kindness by mentioning me to Pharaoh, and get
me out of this house.
15"For I was in fact kidnapped from the land of the Hebrews,
and even here I have done nothing that they should have put me
into the dungeon."
16¶ When the chief baker saw that he had interpreted favorably,
he said to Joseph, "I also *saw* in my dream, and behold, *there were*
three baskets of white bread on my head;
17and in the top basket *there were* some of all sorts of baked food
for Pharaoh, and the birds were eating them out of the basket on
my head."
18Then Joseph answered and said, "This is its interpretation:
the three baskets are three days;
19within three more days Pharaoh will lift up your head from
you and will hang you on a tree; and the birds will eat your flesh
off you."
20¶ Thus it came about on the third day, *which was* Pharaoh's
birthday, that he made a feast for all his servants; and he lifted up
the head of the chief cupbearer and the head of the chief baker
among his servants.
21And he restored the chief cupbearer to his office, and he put
the cup into Pharaoh's hand;
22but he hanged the chief baker, just as Joseph had interpreted
to them.
23Yet the chief cupbearer did not remember Joseph, but forgot
him.

*Pharaoh's Dream*

41 NOW IT happened at the end of two full years that Pharaoh had a dream, and behold, he was standing by the
Nile.
2And lo, from the Nile there came up seven cows, sleek and
fat; and they grazed in the marsh grass.

NAS [a] Or possibly, *forgive you*

## New International

aoh was angry with his two officials, the chief cupbearer and the
chief baker, 3and put them in custody in the house of the captain
of the guard, in the same prison where Joseph was confined. 4The
captain of the guard assigned them to Joseph, and he attended
them.
After they had been in custody for some time, 5each of the two
men—the cupbearer and the baker of the king of Egypt, who were
being held in prison—had a dream the same night, and each dream
had a meaning of its own.
6When Joseph came to them the next morning, he saw that they
were dejected. 7So he asked Pharaoh's officials who were in custody with him in his master's house, "Why are your faces so sad
today?"
8"We both had dreams," they answered, "but there is no one
to interpret them."
Then Joseph said to them, "Do not interpretations belong to
God? Tell me your dreams."
9So the chief cupbearer told Joseph his dream. He said to him,
"In my dream I saw a vine in front of me, 10and on the vine were
three branches. As soon as it budded, it blossomed, and its clusters
ripened into grapes. 11Pharaoh's cup was in my hand, and I took
the grapes, squeezed them into Pharaoh's cup and put the cup in
his hand."
12"This is what it means," Joseph said to him. "The three
branches are three days. 13Within three days Pharaoh will lift up
your head and restore you to your position, and you will put
Pharaoh's cup in his hand, just as you used to do when you were
his cupbearer. 14But when all goes well with you, remember me
and show me kindness; mention me to Pharaoh and get me out of
this prison. 15For I was forcibly carried off from the land of the
Hebrews, and even here I have done nothing to deserve being put
in a dungeon."
16When the chief baker saw that Joseph had given a favorable
interpretation, he said to Joseph, "I too had a dream: On my head
were three baskets of bread.[b] 17In the top basket were all kinds of
baked goods for Pharaoh, but the birds were eating them out of
the basket on my head."
18"This is what it means," Joseph said. "The three baskets are
three days. 19Within three days Pharaoh will lift off your head and
hang you on a tree.[c] And the birds will eat away your flesh."
20Now the third day was Pharaoh's birthday, and he gave a
feast for all his officials. He lifted up the heads of the chief cupbearer and the chief baker in the presence of his officials: 21He restored
the chief cupbearer to his position, so that he once again put the
cup into Pharaoh's hand, 22but he hanged[d] the chief baker, just
as Joseph had said to them in his interpretation.
23The chief cupbearer, however, did not remember Joseph; he
forgot him.

*Pharaoh's Dreams*

41 WHEN TWO full years had passed, Pharaoh had a dream:
He was standing by the Nile, 2when out of the river there
came up seven cows, sleek and fat, and they grazed among the
reeds. 3After them, seven other cows, ugly and gaunt, came up out

NIV [b] 16 Or *three wicker baskets* [c] 19 Or *and impale you on a pole* [d] 22 Or *impaled*

## King James

3And, behold, seven other kine came up after them out of the river, ill favoured and leanfleshed; and stood by the *other* kine upon the brink of the river.

4And the ill favoured and leanfleshed kine did eat up the seven wellfavoured and fat kine. So Pharaoh awoke.

5And he slept and dreamed the second time: and, behold, seven ears of corn came up upon one stalk, rank and good.

6And, behold, seven thin ears and blasted with the east wind sprung up after them.

7And the seven thin ears devoured the seven rank and full ears. And Pharaoh awoke, and, behold, *it was* a dream.

8And it came to pass in the morning that his spirit was troubled; and he sent and called for all the magicians of Egypt, and all the wise men thereof: and Pharaoh told them his dream; but *there was* none that could interpret them unto Pharaoh.

9¶ Then spake the chief butler unto Pharaoh, saying, I do remember my faults this day:

10Pharaoh was wroth with his servants, and put me in ward in the captain of the guard's house, *both* me and the chief baker:

11And we dreamed a dream in one night, I and he; we dreamed each man according to the interpretation of his dream.

12And *there was* there with us a young man, an Hebrew, servant to the captain of the guard; and we told him, and he interpreted to us our dreams; to each man according to his dream he did interpret.

13And it came to pass, as he interpreted to us, so it was; me he restored unto mine office, and him he hanged.

14¶ Then Pharaoh sent and called Joseph, and they brought him hastily out of the dungeon: and he shaved *himself,* and changed his raiment, and came in unto Pharaoh.

15And Pharaoh said unto Joseph, I have dreamed a dream, and *there is* none that can interpret it: and I have heard say of thee, *that* thou canst understand a dream to interpret it.

16And Joseph answered Pharaoh, saying, *It is* not in me: God shall give Pharaoh an answer of peace.

17And Pharaoh said unto Joseph, In my dream, behold, I stood upon the bank of the river:

18And, behold, there came up out of the river seven kine, fatfleshed and wellfavoured; and they fed in a meadow:

19And, behold, seven other kine came up after them, poor and very ill favoured and leanfleshed, such as I never saw in all the land of Egypt for badness:

20And the lean and the ill favoured kine did eat up the first seven fat kine:

21And when they had eaten them up, it could not be known that they had eaten them; but they *were* still ill favoured, as at the beginning. So I awoke.

22And I saw in my dream, and, behold, seven ears came up in one stalk, full and good:

23And, behold, seven ears, withered, thin, *and* blasted with the east wind, sprung up after them:

24And the thin ears devoured the seven good ears: and I told *this* unto the magicians; but *there was* none that could declare *it* to me.

25¶ And Joseph said unto Pharaoh, The dream of Pharaoh *is* one: God hath shown Pharaoh what he *is* about to do.

26The seven good kine *are* seven years; and the seven good ears *are* seven years: the dream *is* one.

27And the seven thin and ill favoured kine that came up after them *are* seven years; and the seven empty ears blasted with the east wind shall be seven years of famine.

28This *is* the thing which I have spoken unto Pharaoh: What God *is* about to do he showeth unto Pharaoh.

## Amplified

3And behold, seven other cows came up after them out of the river [Nile] ill-favored and gaunt *and* ugly; and stood by the fat cows on the bank of the river [Nile].

4And the ill-favored, gaunt *and* ugly cows ate up the seven well-favored and fat cows. Then Pharaoh awoke.

5But he slept and dreamed the second time; and behold, seven ears of grain came out on one stalk, plump and good.

6And behold, after them seven ears [of grain] sprouted, thin *and* blighted by the east wind.

7And the seven thin ears [of grain] devoured the seven plump and full ears. And Pharaoh awoke, and behold, it was a dream.

8So when morning came his spirit was troubled; and he sent and called for all the magicians and all the wise men of Egypt. And Pharaoh told them his dreams; but not one could interpret them to [him].

9Then the chief butler said to Pharaoh, I remember my faults today.

10When Pharaoh was angry with his servants, and put me in custody in the captain of the guard's house, both me and the chief baker,

11We dreamed a dream in the same night, he and I; we dreamed each of us according to [the significance of] the interpretation of his dream.

12And there was there with us a young man, a Hebrew, servant to the captain of the guard *and* chief of executioners; and we told him our dreams, and he interpreted them to us, to each man according to the significance of his dream.

13And as he interpreted to us, so it came to pass; I was restored to my office [as chief butler], and the baker was hanged.

14Then Pharaoh sent and called Joseph, and they brought him hastily out of the dungeon. But Joseph [first] shaved himself, changed his clothes *and* made himself presentable; then he came into Pharaoh's presence.

15And Pharaoh said to Joseph, I have dreamed a dream, and there is no one who can interpret it; and I have heard it said of you that you can understand a dream *and* interpret it.

16Joseph answered Pharaoh, It is not in me; God [not I] will give Pharaoh a [favorable] answer of peace.

17And Pharaoh said to Joseph, In my dream, behold, I stood on the bank of the river [Nile];

18And behold, there came up out of the river [Nile] seven fat, sleek *and* handsome cows, and they grazed in the reed grass [of a marshy pasture].

19And behold, seven other cows came up after them, undernourished, gaunt *and* ugly [just skin and bones; such emaciated animals] as I have never seen in all of Egypt.

20And the lean and ill-favored cows ate up the seven fat cows that had come first.

21And when they had eaten them up, it could not be detected *and* known that they had eaten them, for they were still as thin *and* emaciated as at the beginning. Then I awoke. [But again I fell asleep and dreamed.]

22And I saw in my dream, and behold, seven ears of grain growing on one stalk, plump and good.

23And behold, seven [other] ears, withered, thin, and blighted by the east wind, sprouted after them.

24And the thin ears devoured the seven good ears. Now I told this to the magicians; but there was no one who could tell me what it meant.

25Then Joseph said to Pharaoh, The [two] dreams are one; God has shown Pharaoh what He is about to do.

26The seven good cows are seven years; and the seven good ears [of grain] are seven years; the [two] dreams are one [in their meaning].

27And the seven thin and ill-favored cows that came up after them are seven years; and also the seven empty ears [of grain] blighted *and* shriveled by the east wind; they are seven years of hunger *and* famine.

28This is the message just as I have told Pharaoh: God has shown Pharaoh what He is about to do.

## New American Standard

3Then behold, seven other cows came up after them from the
Nile, ugly and gaunt, and they stood by the *other* cows on the bank
of the Nile.
4And the ugly and gaunt cows ate up the seven sleek and fat
cows. Then Pharaoh awoke.
5And he fell asleep and dreamed a second time; and behold,
seven ears of grain came up on a single stalk, plump and good.
6Then behold, seven ears, thin and scorched by the east wind,
sprouted up after them.
7And the thin ears swallowed up the seven plump and full
ears. Then Pharaoh awoke, and behold, *it was* a dream.
8Now it came about in the morning that his spirit was troubled,
so he sent and called for all the magicians of Egypt, and all its wise
men. And Pharaoh told them his dreams, but there was no one
who could interpret them to Pharaoh.
9¶ Then the chief cupbearer spoke to Pharaoh, saying, "I
would make mention today of my *own* offenses.
10"Pharaoh was furious with his servants, and he put me in
confinement in the house of the captain of the bodyguard, *both* me
and the chief baker.
11"And we had a dream on the same night, he and I; each of
us dreamed according to the interpretation of his *own* dream.
12"Now a Hebrew youth *was* with us there, a servant of the
captain of the bodyguard, and we related *them* to him, and he
interpreted our dreams for us. To each one he interpreted according to his *own* dream.
13"And it came about that just as he interpreted for us, so it
happened; he restored me in my office, but he hanged him."

*Joseph Interprets*

14¶ Then Pharaoh sent and called for Joseph, and they hurriedly
brought him out of the dungeon; and when he had shaved himself
and changed his clothes, he came to Pharaoh.
15And Pharaoh said to Joseph, "I have had a dream, but no one
can interpret it; and I have heard it said about you, that when you
hear a dream you can interpret it."
16Joseph then answered Pharaoh, saying, "It is not in me; God
will give Pharaoh a favorable answer."
17So Pharaoh spoke to Joseph, "In my dream, behold, I was
standing on the bank of the Nile;
18and behold, seven cows, fat and sleek came up out of the Nile;
and they grazed in the marsh grass.
19"And lo, seven other cows came up after them, poor and very
ugly and gaunt, such as I had never seen for ugliness in all the land
of Egypt;
20and the lean and ugly cows ate up the first seven fat cows.
21"Yet when they had devoured them, it could not be detected
that they had devoured them; for they were just as ugly as before.
Then I awoke.
22"I saw also in my dream, and behold, seven ears, full and
good, came up on a single stalk;
23and lo, seven ears, withered, thin, *and* scorched by the east
wind, sprouted up after them;
24and the thin ears swallowed the seven good ears. Then I told
it to the magicians, but there was no one who could explain it to
me."
25¶ Now Joseph said to Pharaoh, "Pharaoh's dreams are one *and
the same;* God has told to Pharaoh what He is about to do.
26"The seven good cows are seven years; and the seven good
ears are seven years; the dreams are one *and the same.*
27"And the seven lean and ugly cows that came up after them
are seven years, and the seven thin ears scorched by the east wind
shall be seven years of famine.
28"It is as I have spoken to Pharaoh: God has shown to Pharaoh
what He is about to do.

## New International

of the Nile and stood beside those on the riverbank. 4And the cows
that were ugly and gaunt ate up the seven sleek, fat cows. Then
Pharaoh woke up.
5He fell asleep again and had a second dream: Seven heads of
grain, healthy and good, were growing on a single stalk. 6After
them, seven other heads of grain sprouted—thin and scorched by
the east wind. 7The thin heads of grain swallowed up the seven
healthy, full heads. Then Pharaoh woke up; it had been a dream.
8In the morning his mind was troubled, so he sent for all the
magicians and wise men of Egypt. Pharaoh told them his dreams,
but no one could interpret them for him.
9Then the chief cupbearer said to Pharaoh, "Today I am
reminded of my shortcomings. 10Pharaoh was once angry with his
servants, and he imprisoned me and the chief baker in the house
of the captain of the guard. 11Each of us had a dream the same
night, and each dream had a meaning of its own. 12Now a young
Hebrew was there with us, a servant of the captain of the guard.
We told him our dreams, and he interpreted them for us, giving
each man the interpretation of his dream. 13And things turned out
exactly as he interpreted them to us: I was restored to my position,
and the other man was hanged.[a]"
14So Pharaoh sent for Joseph, and he was quickly brought from
the dungeon. When he had shaved and changed his clothes, he
came before Pharaoh.
15Pharaoh said to Joseph, "I had a dream, and no one can
interpret it. But I have heard it said of you that when you hear a
dream you can interpret it."
16"I cannot do it," Joseph replied to Pharaoh, "but God will give
Pharaoh the answer he desires."
17Then Pharaoh said to Joseph, "In my dream I was standing
on the bank of the Nile, 18when out of the river there came up
seven cows, fat and sleek, and they grazed among the reeds.
19After them, seven other cows came up—scrawny and very ugly
and lean. I had never seen such ugly cows in all the land of Egypt.
20The lean, ugly cows ate up the seven fat cows that came up first.
21But even after they ate them, no one could tell that they had done
so; they looked just as ugly as before. Then I woke up.
22"In my dreams I also saw seven heads of grain, full and good,
growing on a single stalk. 23After them, seven other heads sprouted—withered and thin and scorched by the east wind. 24The thin
heads of grain swallowed up the seven good heads. I told this to
the magicians, but none could explain it to me."
25Then Joseph said to Pharaoh, "The dreams of Pharaoh are one
and the same. God has revealed to Pharaoh what he is about to
do. 26The seven good cows are seven years, and the seven good
heads of grain are seven years; it is one and the same dream. 27The
seven lean, ugly cows that came up afterward are seven years, and
so are the seven worthless heads of grain scorched by the east
wind: They are seven years of famine.
28"It is just as I said to Pharaoh: God has shown Pharaoh what
he is about to do. 29Seven years of great abundance are coming

NIV [a] 13 Or *impaled*

## King James

29Behold, there come seven years of great plenty throughout all the land of Egypt:

30And there shall arise after them seven years of famine; and all the plenty shall be forgotten in the land of Egypt; and the famine shall consume the land;

31And the plenty shall not be known in the land by reason of that famine following; for it *shall be* very grievous.

32And for that the dream was doubled unto Pharaoh twice; *it is* because the thing *is* established by God, and God will shortly bring it to pass.

33Now therefore let Pharaoh look out a man discreet and wise, and set him over the land of Egypt.

34Let Pharaoh do *this,* and let him appoint officers over the land, and take up the fifth part of the land of Egypt in the seven plenteous years.

35And let them gather all the food of those good years that come, and lay up corn under the hand of Pharaoh, and let them keep food in the cities.

36And that food shall be for store to the land against the seven years of famine, which shall be in the land of Egypt; that the land perish not through the famine.

37¶ And the thing was good in the eyes of Pharaoh, and in the eyes of all his servants.

38And Pharaoh said unto his servants, Can we find *such a one* as this *is,* a man in whom the spirit of God *is?*

39And Pharaoh said unto Joseph, Forasmuch as God hath shown thee all this, *there is* none so discreet and wise as thou *art:*

40Thou shalt be over my house, and according unto thy word shall all my people be ruled: only in the throne will I be greater than thou.

41And Pharaoh said unto Joseph, See, I have set thee over all the land of Egypt.

42And Pharaoh took off his ring from his hand, and put it upon Joseph's hand, and arrayed him in vestures of fine linen, and put a gold chain about his neck;

43And he made him to ride in the second chariot which he had; and they cried before him, Bow the knee: and he made him *ruler* over all the land of Egypt.

44And Pharaoh said unto Joseph, I *am* Pharaoh, and without thee shall no man lift up his hand or foot in all the land of Egypt.

45And Pharaoh called Joseph's name Zaphnath-paaneah; and he gave him to wife Asenath the daughter of Poti-pherah priest of On. And Joseph went out over *all* the land of Egypt.

46¶ And Joseph *was* thirty years old when he stood before Pharaoh king of Egypt. And Joseph went out from the presence of Pharaoh, and went throughout all the land of Egypt.

47And in the seven plenteous years the earth brought forth by handfuls.

48And he gathered up all the food of the seven years, which were in the land of Egypt, and laid up the food in the cities: the food of the field, which *was* round about every city, laid he up in the same.

49And Joseph gathered corn as the sand of the sea, very much, until he left numbering; for *it was* without number.

50And unto Joseph were born two sons before the years of famine came, which Asenath the daughter of Poti-pherah priest of On bare unto him.

51And Joseph called the name of the firstborn Manasseh: For God, *said he,* hath made me forget all my toil, and all my father's house.

52And the name of the second called he Ephraim: For God hath caused me to be fruitful in the land of my affliction.

## Amplified

29Take note! Seven years of great plenty throughout all the land of Egypt are coming.

30Then there will come seven years of hunger *and* famine; and [there will be so much want that] all the great abundance of the previous years will be forgotten in the land of Egypt; and hunger (destitution, starvation) will exhaust (consume, finish) the land.

31And the plenty will become quite unknown in the land because of that following famine, for it will be very woefully severe.

32That the dream was sent twice to Pharaoh *and* in two forms, indicates that this thing which God will very soon bring to pass is fully prepared *and* established by God.

33So now let Pharaoh seek out *and* provide a man discreet, understanding, proficient *and* wise, and set him over the land of Egypt [as governor].

34Let Pharaoh do this; then let him select and appoint officers over the land, and take one-fifth [of the produce] of the [whole] land of Egypt in the seven plenteous years—year by year.

35And let them gather all the food of these good years that are coming, and lay up grain under the direction *and* authority of Pharaoh, and let them retain food [in fortified granaries] in the cities.

36And that food shall be put in store for the country against the seven years of hunger *and* famine that are to come upon the land of Egypt; so that the land may not be ruined *and* cut off by the famine.

37And the plan seemed good in the eyes of Pharaoh, and in the eyes of all his servants.

38And Pharaoh said to his servants, Can we find this man's equal, a man in whom is the spirit of God?

39And Pharaoh said to Joseph, Forasmuch as [your] God has shown you all this, there is nobody as intelligent *and* discreet *and* understanding and wise as you are.

40You shall have charge over my house, and all my people shall be governed according to your word [with reverence, submission and obedience]. Only in matters of the throne will I be greater than you are.

41Then Pharaoh said to Joseph, See, I have set you over all the land of Egypt.

42And Pharaoh took off his [signet] ring from his hand, and put it on Joseph's hand, and arrayed him in [official] vestments of fine linen, and put a gold chain about his neck;

43He made him to ride in the second chariot which he had; and [officials] cried before him, Bow the knee! And he set him over all the land of Egypt.

44And Pharaoh said to Joseph, I am Pharaoh, and without you shall no man lift up his hand or foot in all the land of Egypt.

45And Pharaoh called Joseph's name Zaphenath-paneah and he gave him Asenath daughter of Potiphera priest of On, to be his wife. And Joseph made an [inspection] tour of all the land of Egypt.

46Joseph [who had been in Egypt thirteen years] was thirty years old when he stood before Pharaoh king of Egypt. Joseph went out from the presence of Pharaoh, and went [about his duties] through all the land of Egypt.

47In the seven abundant years the earth brought forth by handfuls [for each seed planted].

48And he gathered up all the [surplus] food of the seven [good] years in the land of Egypt, and stored up the food in the cities; he stored away in each city the food from the fields around it.

49And Joseph gathered grain as the sand of the sea, very much, until he stopped counting, for it could not be measured.

50Now to Joseph were born two sons before the years of famine came, whom Asenath, daughter of Potiphera the priest of On, bore to him.

51And Joseph called the first-born Manasseh [making to forget], For God, said he, has made me forget all my toil *and* hardship, and all my father's house.

52And the second he called Ephraim [to be fruitful], For [he said] God has caused me to be fruitful in the land of my affliction.

## New American Standard

29"Behold, seven years of great abundance are coming in all the
land of Egypt;
30and after them seven years of famine will come, and all the
abundance will be forgotten in the land of Egypt; and the famine
will ravage the land.
31"So the abundance will be unknown in the land because of
that subsequent famine; for it *will be* very severe.
32"Now as for the repeating of the dream to Pharaoh twice, *it
means* that the matter is determined by God, and God will quickly
bring it about.
33"And now let Pharaoh look for a man discerning and wise,
and set him over the land of Egypt.
34"Let Pharaoh take action to appoint overseers in charge of the
land, and let him exact a fifth *of the produce* of the land of Egypt in
the seven years of abundance.
35"Then let them gather all the food of these good years that are
coming, and store up the grain for food in the cities under Pharaoh's authority, and let them guard *it*.
36"And let the food become as a reserve for the land for the
seven years of famine which will occur in the land of Egypt, so that
the land may not perish during the famine."
37¶ Now the proposal seemed good to Pharaoh and to all his
servants.

*Joseph Is Made a Ruler of Egypt*

38Then Pharaoh said to his servants, "Can we find a man like
this, in whom is a divine spirit?"
39So Pharaoh said to Joseph, "Since God has informed you of
all this, there is no one so discerning and wise as you are.
40"You shall be over my house, and according to your command all my people shall do homage; only in the throne I will be
greater than you."
41And Pharaoh said to Joseph, "See I have set you over all the
land of Egypt."
42Then Pharaoh took off his signet ring from his hand, and put
it on Joseph's hand, and clothed him in garments of fine linen, and
put the gold necklace around his neck.
43And he had him ride in his second chariot; and they proclaimed before him, "Bow the knee!" And he set him over all the
land of Egypt.
44Moreover, Pharaoh said to Joseph, "*Though* I am Pharaoh, yet
without your permission no one shall raise his hand or foot in all
the land of Egypt."
45Then Pharaoh named Joseph [a]Zaphenath-paneah; and he
gave him Asenath, the daughter of Potiphera priest of On, as his
wife. And Joseph went forth over the land of Egypt.
46¶ Now Joseph was thirty years old when he [b]stood before
Pharaoh, king of Egypt. And Joseph went out from the presence
of Pharaoh, and went through all the land of Egypt.
47And during the seven years of plenty the land brought forth
abundantly.
48So he gathered all the food of *these* seven years which occurred in the land of Egypt, and placed the food in the cities; he
placed in every city the food from its own surrounding fields.
49Thus Joseph stored up grain in great abundance like the sand
of the sea, until he stopped measuring *it*, for it was beyond measure.

*The Sons of Joseph*

50¶ Now before the year of famine came, two sons were born
to Joseph, whom Asenath, the daughter of Potiphera priest of
[c]On, bore to him.
51And Joseph named the first-born [d]Manasseh, "For," *he said,*
"God has made me forget all my trouble and all my father's household."
52And he named the second [e]Ephraim, "For," *he said,* "God has
made me fruitful in the land of my affliction."

**NAS** [a] Probably Egyptian for "God speaks; he lives" [b] Or, *entered the service of* [c] Or, *Heliopolis* [d] I.e., making to forget [e] I.e., fruitfulness

## New International

throughout the land of Egypt, 30but seven years of famine will
follow them. Then all the abundance in Egypt will be forgotten,
and the famine will ravage the land. 31The abundance in the land
will not be remembered, because the famine that follows it will be
so severe. 32The reason the dream was given to Pharaoh in two
forms is that the matter has been firmly decided by God, and God
will do it soon.
33"And now let Pharaoh look for a discerning and wise man and
put him in charge of the land of Egypt. 34Let Pharaoh appoint
commissioners over the land to take a fifth of the harvest of Egypt
during the seven years of abundance. 35They should collect all the
food of these good years that are coming and store up the grain
under the authority of Pharaoh, to be kept in the cities for food.
36This food should be held in reserve for the country, to be used
during the seven years of famine that will come upon Egypt, so
that the country may not be ruined by the famine."
37The plan seemed good to Pharaoh and to all his officials. 38So
Pharaoh asked them, "Can we find anyone like this man, one in
whom is the spirit of God[f]?"
39Then Pharaoh said to Joseph, "Since God has made all this
known to you, there is no one so discerning and wise as you. 40You
shall be in charge of my palace, and all my people are to submit
to your orders. Only with respect to the throne will I be greater
than you."

*Joseph in Charge of Egypt*

41So Pharaoh said to Joseph, "I hereby put you in charge of the
whole land of Egypt." 42Then Pharaoh took his signet ring from
his finger and put it on Joseph's finger. He dressed him in robes
of fine linen and put a gold chain around his neck. 43He had him
ride in a chariot as his second-in-command,[g] and men shouted
before him, "Make way[h]!" Thus he put him in charge of the whole
land of Egypt.
44Then Pharaoh said to Joseph, "I am Pharaoh, but without
your word no one will lift hand or foot in all Egypt." 45Pharaoh
gave Joseph the name Zaphenath-Paneah and gave him Asenath
daughter of Potiphera, priest of On,[i] to be his wife. And Joseph
went throughout the land of Egypt.
46Joseph was thirty years old when he entered the service of
Pharaoh king of Egypt. And Joseph went out from Pharaoh's
presence and traveled throughout Egypt. 47During the seven years
of abundance the land produced plentifully. 48Joseph collected all
the food produced in those seven years of abundance in Egypt and
stored it in the cities. In each city he put the food grown in the
fields surrounding it. 49Joseph stored up huge quantities of grain,
like the sand of the sea; it was so much that he stopped keeping
records because it was beyond measure.
50Before the years of famine came, two sons were born to Joseph by Asenath daughter of Potiphera, priest of On. 51Joseph
named his firstborn Manasseh[j] and said, "It is because God has
made me forget all my trouble and all my father's household."
52The second son he named Ephraim[k] and said, "It is because God
has made me fruitful in the land of my suffering."

**NIV** [f] *38* Or *of the gods* [g] *43* Or *in the chariot of his second-in-command;* or *in his second chariot* [h] *43* Or *Bow down* [i] *45* That is, Heliopolis; also in verse 50 [j] *51 Manasseh* sounds like and may be derived from the Hebrew for *forget.* [k] *52 Ephraim* sounds like the Hebrew for *twice fruitful.*

## King James

53¶ And the seven years of plenteousness, that was in the land
of Egypt, were ended.
54And the seven years of dearth began to come, according as
Joseph had said: and the dearth was in all lands; but in all the land
of Egypt there was bread.
55And when all the land of Egypt was famished, the people
cried to Pharaoh for bread: and Pharaoh said unto all the Egyptians, Go unto Joseph; what he saith to you, do.
56And the famine was over all the face of the earth: and Joseph
opened all the storehouses, and sold unto the Egyptians; and the
famine waxed sore in the land of Egypt.
57And all countries came into Egypt to Joseph for to buy *corn;*
because that the famine was *so* sore in all lands.

**42** NOW WHEN Jacob saw that there was corn in Egypt,
Jacob said unto his sons, Why do ye look one upon another?
2And he said, Behold, I have heard that there is corn in Egypt:
get you down thither, and buy for us from thence; that we may
live, and not die.
3¶ And Joseph's ten brethren went down to buy corn in Egypt.
4But Benjamin, Joseph's brother, Jacob sent not with his brethren; for he said, Lest peradventure mischief befall him.
5And the sons of Israel came to buy *corn* among those that came:
for the famine was in the land of Canaan.
6And Joseph *was* the governor over the land, *and* he *it was* that
sold to all the people of the land: and Joseph's brethren came, and
bowed down themselves before him *with* their faces to the earth.
7And Joseph saw his brethren, and he knew them, but made
himself strange unto them, and spake roughly unto them; and he
said unto them, Whence come ye? And they said, From the land
of Canaan to buy food.
8And Joseph knew his brethren, but they knew not him.
9And Joseph remembered the dreams which he dreamed of
them, and said unto them, Ye *are* spies; to see the nakedness of
the land ye are come.
10And they said unto him, Nay, my lord, but to buy food are
thy servants come.
11We *are* all one man's sons; we *are* true *men,* thy servants are
no spies.
12And he said unto them, Nay, but to see the nakedness of the
land ye are come.
13And they said, Thy servants *are* twelve brethren, the sons of
one man in the land of Canaan; and, behold, the youngest *is* this
day with our father, and one *is* not.
14And Joseph said unto them, That *is it* that I spake unto you,
saying, Ye *are* spies:
15Hereby ye shall be proved: By the life of Pharaoh ye shall not
go forth hence, except your youngest brother come hither.
16Send one of you, and let him fetch your brother, and ye shall
be kept in prison, that your words may be proved, whether *there
be any* truth in you: or else by the life of Pharaoh surely ye *are* spies.
17And he put them all together into ward three days.
18And Joseph said unto them the third day, This do, and live;
*for* I fear God:
19If ye *be* true *men,* let one of your brethren be bound in the
house of your prison: go ye, carry corn for the famine of your
houses:
20But bring your youngest brother unto me; so shall your words
be verified, and ye shall not die. And they did so.
21¶ And they said one to another, We *are* verily guilty concerning our brother, in that we saw the anguish of his soul, when he
besought us, and we would not hear; therefore is this distress
come upon us.

## Amplified

53When the seven years of plenty were ended in the land of
Egypt,
54The seven years of scarcity *and* famine began to come, as
Joseph had said they would; the famine was in all [the surround-
ing] lands; but in all of Egypt there was food.
55But when all the land of Egypt was weakened with hunger,
the people [there] cried to Pharaoh for food; and Pharaoh said to
[them] all, Go to Joseph; what he says to you, do.
56When the famine was over all the land, Joseph opened all the
store-houses, and sold to the Egyptians; for the famine grew extremely distressing in the land of Egypt.
57And all countries came to Egypt to Joseph to buy grain, because the famine was severe over all [the known] earth.

**42** NOW WHEN Jacob learned that there was grain in Egypt,
he said to his sons, Why do you look at one another?
2For, he said, I have heard that there is grain in Egypt; get down
there and buy [grain] for us, that we may live and not die.
3So ten of Joseph's brethren went to buy grain in Egypt.
4But Benjamin, Joseph's [full] brother, Jacob did not send with
his brothers; for he said, Lest perhaps some harm *or* injury should
befall him.
5So the sons of Israel came to buy grain among those who came;
for there was hunger *and* general lack of food in the land of Canaan.
6Now Joseph was the governor over the land, and he it was who
sold to all the people of the land; and Joseph's [half] brothers came
and bowed themselves down before him with their faces to the
ground.
7Joseph saw his brethren, and he recognized them, but he
treated them as if he were a stranger to them and spoke roughly
to them. He said, Where do you come from? And they replied,
From the land of Canaan to buy food.
8Joseph knew his brethren, but they did not know him.
9And Joseph remembered the dreams he had dreamed about
them, and said to them, You are spies *and* with unfriendly purpose
you have come to observe [secretly] the nakedness of the land.
10But they said to him, No, my lord, but your servants have
come *only* to buy food.
11We are all one man's sons; we are true men; your servants are
not spies.
12And he said to them, No, but you have come to see the
nakedness of the land.
13But they said, Your servants are twelve brothers, the sons of
one man in the land of Canaan; the youngest is today with our
father, and one is not.
14And Joseph said to them, It is as I said to you, You are spies.
15You shall be proved by this test: by the life of Pharaoh, you
shall not go away from here unless your youngest brother comes
here.
16Send one of you, and let him bring your brother, and you will
be kept in prison, that your words may be proved, whether there
is any truth in you; or else by the life of Pharaoh you certainly are
spies.
17Then he put them all in custody for three days.
18And Joseph said to them on the third day, Do this and live!
I reverence *and* fear God.
19If you are true men, let one of your brothers be bound in your
prison, but [the rest of] you go and carry grain for those weakened
with hunger in your households. [v. 24.]
20But bring your youngest brother to me; so your words will be
verified, and you shall live. And they did so.
21And they said one to another, We are truly guilty about our
brother, for we saw the distress *and* anguish of his soul when he
begged us [to let him go], and we would not hear. So this distress
*and* difficulty has come upon us.

## New American Standard

53¶ When the seven years of plenty which had been in the land
of Egypt came to an end,
54 and the seven years of famine began to come, just as Joseph
had said, then there was famine in all the lands; but in all the land
of Egypt there was bread.
55 So when all the land of Egypt was famished, the people cried
out to Pharaoh for bread; and Pharaoh said to all the Egyptians,
"Go to Joseph; whatever he says to you, you shall do."
56 When the famine was *spread* over all the face of the earth, then
Joseph opened all the storehouses, and sold to the Egyptians; and
the famine was severe in the land of Egypt.
57 And *the people of* all the earth came to Egypt to buy grain from
Joseph, because the famine was severe in all the earth.

*Joseph's Brothers Sent to Egypt*

**42** NOW JACOB saw that there was grain in Egypt, and Jacob
said to his sons, "Why are you staring at one another?"
2 And he said, "Behold, I have heard that there is grain in
Egypt; go down there and buy *some* for us from that place, so that
we may live and not die."
3 Then ten brothers of Joseph went down to buy grain from
Egypt.
4 But Jacob did not send Joseph's brother Benjamin with his
brothers, for he said, "I am afraid that harm may befall him."
5 So the sons of Israel came to buy grain among those who were
coming, for the famine was in the land of Canaan *also*.
6 Now Joseph was the ruler over the land; he was the one who
sold to all the people of the land. And Joseph's brothers came and
bowed down to him with *their* faces to the ground.
7 When Joseph saw his brothers he recognized them, but he
disguised himself to them and spoke to them harshly. And he said
to them, "Where have you come from?" And they said, "From the
land of Canaan, to buy food."
8¶ But Joseph had recognized his brothers, although they did
not recognize him.
9 And Joseph remembered the dreams which he had about
them, and said to them, "You are spies; you have come to look at
the undefended parts of our land."
10 Then they said to him, "No, my lord, but your servants have
come to buy food.
11 "We are all sons of one man; we are honest men, your servants are not spies."
12 Yet he said to them, "No, but you have come to look at the
undefended parts of our land!"
13 But they said, "Your servants are twelve brothers *in all*, the
sons of one man in the land of Canaan; and behold, the youngest
is with our father today, and one is no more."
14 And Joseph said to them, "It is as I said to you, you are spies;
15 by this you will be tested: by the life of Pharaoh, you shall not
go from this place unless your youngest brother comes here!
16 "Send one of you that he may get your brother, while you
remain confined, that your words may be tested, whether there is
truth in you. But if not, by the life of Pharaoh, surely you are
spies."
17 So he put them all together in prison for three days.
18¶ Now Joseph said to them on the third day, "Do this and live,
for I fear God:
19 if you are honest men, let one of your brothers be confined
in your prison; but as for *the rest of* you, go, carry grain for the
famine of your households,
20 and bring your youngest brother to me, so your words may
be verified, and you will not die." And they did so.
21 Then they said to one another, "Truly we are guilty concerning our brother, because we saw the distress of his soul when he
pleaded with us, yet we would not listen; therefore this distress
has come upon us."

## New International

53 The seven years of abundance in Egypt came to an end, 54 and
the seven years of famine began, just as Joseph had said. There
was famine in all the other lands, but in the whole land of Egypt
there was food. 55 When all Egypt began to feel the famine, the
people cried to Pharaoh for food. Then Pharaoh told all the Egyptians, "Go to Joseph and do what he tells you."
56 When the famine had spread over the whole country, Joseph
opened the storehouses and sold grain to the Egyptians, for the
famine was severe throughout Egypt. 57 And all the countries came
to Egypt to buy grain from Joseph, because the famine was severe
in all the world.

*Joseph's Brothers Go to Egypt*

**42** WHEN JACOB learned that there was grain in Egypt, he
said to his sons, "Why do you just keep looking at each
other?" 2 He continued, "I have heard that there is grain in Egypt.
Go down there and buy some for us, so that we may live and not
die."
3 Then ten of Joseph's brothers went down to buy grain from
Egypt. 4 But Jacob did not send Benjamin, Joseph's brother, with
the others, because he was afraid that harm might come to him.
5 So Israel's sons were among those who went to buy grain, for the
famine was in the land of Canaan also.
6 Now Joseph was the governor of the land, the one who sold
grain to all its people. So when Joseph's brothers arrived, they
bowed down to him with their faces to the ground. 7 As soon as
Joseph saw his brothers, he recognized them, but he pretended to
be a stranger and spoke harshly to them. "Where do you come
from?" he asked.
"From the land of Canaan," they replied, "to buy food."
8 Although Joseph recognized his brothers, they did not recognize him. 9 Then he remembered his dreams about them and said
to them, "You are spies! You have come to see where our land is
unprotected."
10 "No, my lord," they answered. "Your servants have come to
buy food. 11 We are all the sons of one man. Your servants are
honest men, not spies."
12 "No!" he said to them. "You have come to see where our land
is unprotected."
13 But they replied, "Your servants were twelve brothers, the
sons of one man, who lives in the land of Canaan. The youngest
is now with our father, and one is no more."
14 Joseph said to them, "It is just as I told you: You are spies!
15 And this is how you will be tested: As surely as Pharaoh lives,
you will not leave this place unless your youngest brother comes
here. 16 Send one of your number to get your brother; the rest of
you will be kept in prison, so that your words may be tested to see
if you are telling the truth. If you are not, then as surely as Pharaoh
lives, you are spies!" 17 And he put them all in custody for three
days.
18 On the third day, Joseph said to them, "Do this and you will
live, for I fear God: 19 If you are honest men, let one of your
brothers stay here in prison, while the rest of you go and take grain
back for your starving households. 20 But you must bring your
youngest brother to me, so that your words may be verified and
that you may not die." This they proceeded to do.
21 They said to one another, "Surely we are being punished
because of our brother. We saw how distressed he was when he
pleaded with us for his life, but we would not listen; that's why
this distress has come upon us."

## King James

22And Reuben answered them, saying, Spake I not unto you, saying, Do not sin against the child; and ye would not hear? therefore, behold, also his blood is required.

23And they knew not that Joseph understood *them;* for he spake unto them by an interpreter.

24And he turned himself about from them, and wept; and returned to them again, and communed with them, and took from them Simeon, and bound him before their eyes.

25¶ Then Joseph commanded to fill their sacks with corn, and to restore every man's money into his sack, and to give them provision for the way: and thus did he unto them.

26And they laded their asses with the corn, and departed thence.

27And as one of them opened his sack to give his ass provender in the inn, he espied his money; for, behold, it *was* in his sack's mouth.

28And he said unto his brethren, My money is restored; and, lo, *it is* even in my sack: and their heart failed *them,* and they were afraid, saying one to another, What *is* this *that* God hath done unto us?

29¶ And they came unto Jacob their father unto the land of Canaan, and told him all that befell unto them; saying,

30The man, *who is* the lord of the land, spake roughly to us, and took us for spies of the country.

31And we said unto him, We *are* true *men;* we are no spies:

32We *be* twelve brethren, sons of our father; one *is* not, and the youngest *is* this day with our father in the land of Canaan.

33And the man, the lord of the country, said unto us, Hereby shall I know that ye *are* true *men;* leave one of your brethren *here* with me, and take *food for* the famine of your households, and be gone:

34And bring your youngest brother unto me: then shall I know that ye *are* no spies, but *that* ye *are* true *men: so* will I deliver you your brother, and ye shall traffic in the land.

35¶ And it came to pass as they emptied their sacks, that, behold, every man's bundle of money *was* in his sack: and when *both* they and their father saw the bundles of money, they were afraid.

36And Jacob their father said unto them, Me have ye bereaved *of my children:* Joseph *is* not, and Simeon *is* not, and ye will take Benjamin *away:* all these things are against me.

37And Reuben spake unto his father, saying, Slay my two sons, if I bring him not to thee: deliver him into my hand, and I will bring him to thee again.

38And he said, My son shall not go down with you; for his brother is dead, and he is left alone: if mischief befall him by the way in the which ye go, then shall ye bring down my gray hairs with sorrow to the grave.

**43** AND THE famine *was* sore in the land.

2And it came to pass, when they had eaten up the corn which they had brought out of Egypt, their father said unto them, Go again, buy us a little food.

3And Judah spake unto him, saying, The man did solemnly protest unto us, saying, Ye shall not see my face, except your brother *be* with you.

4If thou wilt send our brother with us, we will go down and buy thee food:

5But if thou wilt not send *him,* we will not go down: for the man said unto us, Ye shall not see my face, except your brother *be* with you.

6And Israel said, Wherefore dealt ye *so* ill with me, *as* to tell the man whether ye had yet a brother?

## Amplified

22Reuben answered them, Did I not tell you, Do not sin against the boy, and you would not hear? Therefore, behold, his blood is required [of us].

23But they did not know that Joseph understood them; for he spoke to them through an interpreter.

24And he turned away from them, and wept; then he returned to them, and talked with them, and took from them Simeon and bound him before their eyes.

25Then [privately] Joseph commanded that their sacks be filled with grain, and to restore every man's money to his sack, and to give them provision for the journey. And this was done for them.

26They loaded their donkeys with grain, and left.

27And as one of them opened his sack to give his donkey fodder at the lodging place, he caught sight of his money; for behold, it was in his sack's mouth.

28And he said to his brothers, My money is restored! Here it is in my sack! And their hearts failed them, and they were afraid *and* turned trembling one to another, saying, What is this that God has done to us?

29When they came to Jacob their father in Canaan, they told him all that had befallen them, saying,

30The man who is the lord of the land spoke roughly to us, and took us for spies of the country.

31And we said to him, We are true men, not spies.

32We are twelve brothers with the same father; one is no more, and the youngest is today with our father in the land of Canaan.

33And the man, the lord of the country, said to us, By this test I will know whether or not you are honest men: leave one of your brothers here with me, and take grain for your famishing households and be gone.

34Bring your youngest brother to me; then I will know that you are not spies, but that you are honest men. And I will deliver to you your brother [whom I have kept bound in prison], and you may do business in the land.

35When they emptied their sacks, behold, every man's parcel of money was in his sack! When both they and their father saw the bundles of money, they were afraid.

36And Jacob their father said to them, You have bereaved me! Joseph is not, and Simeon is not, and you would take Benjamin from me. All these things are against me!

37And Reuben said to his father, Slay my two sons, if I do not bring [Benjamin] back to you. Deliver him into my keeping, and I will bring him back to you.

38But [Jacob] said, My son shall not go down with you; for his brother is dead, and he alone is left [of his mother's children]; if harm *or* accident should befall him on the journey you are to take, you would bring my hoary head down to Sheol (the place of the dead) with grief.

**43** BUT THE hunger *and* destitution *and* starvation were very severe *and* extremely distressing in the land [Canaan].

2And when [the families of Jacob's sons] had eaten up the grain which the men had brought from Egypt, their father said to them, Go again; buy us a little food.

3But Judah said to him, The man solemnly *and* sternly warned us, saying, You shall not see my face again unless your brother is with you.

4If you will send our brother with us, we will go down [to Egypt] and buy you food;

5But if you will not send him, we will not go down; for the man said to us, You shall not see my face unless your brother is with you.

6And Israel said, Why did you do me such a wrong *and* suffer this evil to come upon me, by telling the man that you had another brother?

## New American Standard

22And Reuben answered them, saying, "Did I not tell you, 'Do
not sin against the boy'; and you would not listen? Now comes the
reckoning for his blood."
23They did not know, however, that Joseph understood, for
there was an interpreter between them.
24And he turned away from them and wept. But when he
returned to them and spoke to them, he took Simeon from them
and bound him before their eyes.
25¶ Then Joseph gave orders to fill their bags with grain and to
restore every man's money in his sack, and to give them provisions
for the journey. And thus it was done for them.
26So they loaded their donkeys with their grain, and departed
from there.
27And as one *of them* opened his sack to give his donkey fodder
at the lodging place, he saw his money; and behold, it was in the
mouth of his sack.
28Then he said to his brothers, "My money has been returned,
and behold, it is even in my sack." And their hearts sank, and they
*turned* trembling to one another, saying, "What is this that God has
done to us?"

*Simeon Is Held Hostage*

29¶ When they came to their father Jacob in the land of Canaan,
they told him all that had happened to them, saying,
30"The man, the lord of the land, spoke harshly with us, and
took us for spies of the country.
31"But we said to him, 'We are honest men; we are not spies.
32'We are twelve brothers, sons of our father; one is no more,
and the youngest is with our father today in the land of Canaan.'
33"And the man, the lord of the land, said to us, 'By this I shall
know that you are honest men: leave one of your brothers with me
and take *grain for* the famine of your households, and go.
34'But bring your youngest brother to me that I may know that
you are not spies, but honest men. I will give your brother to you,
and you may trade in the land.'"
35¶ Now it came about as they were emptying their sacks, that
behold, every man's bundle of money *was* in his sack; and when
they and their father saw their bundles of money, they were dismayed.
36And their father Jacob said to them, "You have bereaved me
of my children: Joseph is no more, and Simeon is no more, and you
would take Benjamin; all these things are against me."
37Then Reuben spoke to his father, saying, "You may put my
two sons to death if I do not bring him *back* to you; put him in my
care, and I will return him to you."
38But Jacob said, "My son shall not go down with you; for his
brother is dead, and he alone is left. If harm should befall him on
the journey you are taking, then you will bring my gray hair down
to Sheol in sorrow."

*The Return to Egypt*

43 NOW THE famine was severe in the land.
2So it came about when they had finished eating the grain
which they had brought from Egypt, that their father said to them,
"Go back, buy us a little food."
3Judah spoke to him, however, saying, "The man solemnly
warned us, 'You shall not see my face unless your brother is with
you.'
4"If you send our brother with us, we will go down and buy
you food.
5"But if you do not send *him*, we will not go down; for the man
said to us, 'You shall not see my face unless your brother is with
you.'"
6Then Israel said, "Why did you treat me so badly by telling
the man whether you still had *another* brother?"

## New International

22Reuben replied, "Didn't I tell you not to sin against the boy?
But you wouldn't listen! Now we must give an accounting for his
blood." 23They did not realize that Joseph could understand them,
since he was using an interpreter.
24He turned away from them and began to weep, but then
turned back and spoke to them again. He had Simeon taken from
them and bound before their eyes.
25Joseph gave orders to fill their bags with grain, to put each
man's silver back in his sack, and to give them provisions for their
journey. After this was done for them, 26they loaded their grain
on their donkeys and left.
27At the place where they stopped for the night one of them
opened his sack to get feed for his donkey, and he saw his silver
in the mouth of his sack. 28"My silver has been returned," he said
to his brothers. "Here it is in my sack."
Their hearts sank and they turned to each other trembling and
said, "What is this that God has done to us?"
29When they came to their father Jacob in the land of Canaan,
they told him all that had happened to them. They said, 30"The
man who is lord over the land spoke harshly to us and treated us
as though we were spying on the land. 31But we said to him, 'We
are honest men; we are not spies. 32We were twelve brothers, sons
of one father. One is no more, and the youngest is now with our
father in Canaan.'
33"Then the man who is lord over the land said to us, 'This is
how I will know whether you are honest men: Leave one of your
brothers here with me, and take food for your starving households
and go. 34But bring your youngest brother to me so I will know that
you are not spies but honest men. Then I will give your brother
back to you, and you can trade[a] in the land.'"
35As they were emptying their sacks, there in each man's sack
was his pouch of silver! When they and their father saw the money
pouches, they were frightened. 36Their father Jacob said to them,
"You have deprived me of my children. Joseph is no more and
Simeon is no more, and now you want to take Benjamin. Everything is against me!"
37Then Reuben said to his father, "You may put both of my sons
to death if I do not bring him back to you. Entrust him to my care,
and I will bring him back."
38But Jacob said, "My son will not go down there with you; his
brother is dead and he is the only one left. If harm comes to him
on the journey you are taking, you will bring my gray head down
to the grave[b] in sorrow."

*The Second Journey to Egypt*

43 NOW THE famine was still severe in the land. 2So when
they had eaten all the grain they had brought from Egypt,
their father said to them, "Go back and buy us a little more food."
3But Judah said to him, "The man warned us solemnly, 'You
will not see my face again unless your brother is with you.' 4If you
will send our brother along with us, we will go down and buy food
for you. 5But if you will not send him, we will not go down,
because the man said to us, 'You will not see my face again unless
your brother is with you.'"
6Israel asked, "Why did you bring this trouble on me by telling
the man you had another brother?"

NIV [a] 34 Or *move about freely* [b] 38 Hebrew *Sheol*

## King James

7And they said, The man asked us straitly of our state, and of our kindred, saying, *Is* your father yet alive? have ye *another* brother? and we told him according to the tenor of these words: could we certainly know that he would say, Bring your brother down?

8And Judah said unto Israel his father, Send the lad with me, and we will arise and go; that we may live, and not die, both we, and thou, *and* also our little ones.

9I will be surety for him; of my hand shalt thou require him: if I bring him not unto thee, and set him before thee, then let me bear the blame for ever:

10For except we had lingered, surely now we had returned this second time.

11And their father Israel said unto them, If *it must be* so now, do this; take of the best fruits in the land in your vessels, and carry down the man a present, a little balm, and a little honey, spices, and myrrh, nuts, and almonds:

12And take double money in your hand; and the money that was brought again in the mouth of your sacks, carry *it* again in your hand; peradventure it *was* an oversight:

13Take also your brother, and arise, go again unto the man:

14And God Almighty give you mercy before the man, that he may send away your other brother, and Benjamin. If I be bereaved *of my children,* I am bereaved.

15¶ And the men took that present, and they took double money in their hand, and Benjamin; and rose up, and went down to Egypt, and stood before Joseph.

16And when Joseph saw Benjamin with them, he said to the ruler of his house, Bring *these* men home, and slay, and make ready; for *these* men shall dine with me at noon.

17And the man did as Joseph bade; and the man brought the men into Joseph's house.

18And the men were afraid, because they were brought into Joseph's house; and they said, Because of the money that was returned in our sacks at the first time are we brought in; that he may seek occasion against us, and fall upon us, and take us for bondmen, and our asses.

19And they came near to the steward of Joseph's house, and they communed with him at the door of the house,

20And said, O sir, we came indeed down at the first time to buy food:

21And it came to pass, when we came to the inn, that we opened our sacks, and, behold, *every* man's money *was* in the mouth of his sack, our money in full weight: and we have brought it again in our hand.

22And other money have we brought down in our hands to buy food: we cannot tell who put our money in our sacks.

23And he said, Peace *be* to you, fear not: your God, and the God of your father, hath given you treasure in your sacks: I had your money. And he brought Simeon out unto them.

24And the man brought the men into Joseph's house, and gave *them* water, and they washed their feet; and he gave their asses provender.

25And they made ready the present against Joseph came at noon: for they heard that they should eat bread there.

26¶ And when Joseph came home, they brought him the present which *was* in their hand into the house, and bowed themselves to him to the earth.

27And he asked them of *their* welfare, and said, *Is* your father well, the old man of whom ye spake? *Is* he yet alive?

28And they answered, Thy servant our father *is* in good health, he *is* yet alive. And they bowed down their heads, and made obeisance.

29And he lifted up his eyes, and saw his brother Benjamin, his mother's son, and said, *Is* this your younger brother, of whom ye spake unto me? And he said, God be gracious unto thee, my son.

## Amplified

7And they said, The man asked us straightforward questions about ourselves and our relatives. He said, Is your father still alive? Have you another brother? And we answered him accordingly. How could we know that he would say, Bring your brother down here?

8And Judah said to Israel his father, Send the lad with me, and we will arise and go, that we may live and not die, both we and you and also our little ones.

9I will be security for him; you shall require him of me [personally]; if I do not bring him back to you and put him before you, then let me bear the blame forever.

10For if we had not lingered like this, surely by now we would have returned the second time.

11And their father Israel said to them, If it must be so, now do this; take of the choicest products in the land in your sacks, and carry down a present to the man, a little balm (balsam) and a little honey, aromatic spices and gum (of rock rose) *or* ladanum, pistachio nuts, and almonds.

12And take double the [grain] money with you; and the money that was put back in the mouth of your sacks, carry it again with you; there is a possibility that [its being in your sacks] was an oversight.

13Take your brother, and arise, return to the man;

14God Almighty give you mercy *and* favor before the man, that he may release to you your other brother and Benjamin. If I am bereaved [of my sons], I am bereaved.

15Then the men took the present, and they took double the [grain] money with them, and Benjamin; and they arose and went down to Egypt and stood before Joseph.

16And when Joseph saw Benjamin with them, he said to the steward of his house, Bring the men into the house, and kill an animal and make ready, for the men will dine with me at noon.

17And the man did as Joseph ordered, and brought the men to Joseph's house.

18The men were afraid, because they were brought to Joseph's house; and they said, We are brought in because of the money that was returned in our sacks the first time we came, so that he may find occasion to accuse and assail us, take us for slaves and seize our donkeys.

19So they came near to the steward of Joseph's house, and talked with him at the door of the house,

20And said, O sir, we came down truly the first time to buy food;

21And when we came to the inn we opened our sacks, and there was a man's money full weight returned in the mouth of his sack. Now we have brought it back again.

22And we have brought down with us other money to buy food. We do not know who put our money in our sacks.

23But [the steward] said, Peace be to you, fear not; your God, and the God of your father, has given you treasure in your sacks. I received your money. And he brought Simeon out to them.

24And the man brought the men into Joseph's house, and gave them water, and they washed their feet; and he gave their donkeys provender.

25And they made ready the present they had brought for Joseph before his coming at noon; for they heard that they were to dine there.

26And when Joseph came home, they brought into the house to him the present which they had with them, and bowed themselves to him to the ground.

27He asked them of their welfare, and said, Is your old father well, of whom you spoke? Is he still alive?

28And they answered, Your servant our father is in good health; he is still alive. And they bowed down their heads and made obeisance.

29And he looked up and saw his [full] brother Benjamin, his mother's [only other] son, and said, Is this your younger brother, of whom you spoke to me? And he said, God be gracious to you, my son!

## New American Standard

7But they said, "The man questioned particularly about us and
our relatives, saying, 'Is your father still alive? Have you *another*
brother?' So we answered his questions. Could we possibly know
that he would say, 'Bring your brother down'?"
8And Judah said to his father Israel, "Send the lad with me,
and we will arise and go, that we may live and not die, we as well
as you and our little ones.
9"I myself will be surety for him; you may hold me responsible
for him. If I do not bring him *back* to you and set him before you,
then let me bear the blame before you forever.
10"For if we had not delayed, surely by now we could have
returned twice."
11¶ Then their father Israel said to them, "If *it must be* so, then
do this: take some of the best products of the land in your bags,
and carry down to the man as a present, a little balm and a little
honey, aromatic gum and myrrh, pistachio nuts and almonds.
12"And take double *the* money in your hand, and take back in
your hand the money that was returned in the mouth of your
sacks; perhaps it was a mistake.
13"Take your brother also, and arise, return to the man;
14and may God Almighty grant you compassion in the sight of
the man, that he may release to you your other brother and Benjamin. And as for me, if I am bereaved of my children, I am bereaved."
15So the men took this present, and they took double *the* money
in their hand, and Benjamin; then they arose and went down to
Egypt and stood before Joseph.

*Joseph Sees Benjamin*

16¶ When Joseph saw Benjamin with them, he said to his house
steward, "Bring the men into the house, and slay *an animal* and
make ready; for the men are to dine with me at noon."
17So the man did as Joseph said, and brought the men to Joseph's house.
18Now the men were afraid, because they were brought to
Joseph's house; and they said, "*It is* because of the money that was
returned in our sacks the first time that we are being brought in,
that he may seek occasion against us and fall upon us, and take
us for slaves with our donkeys."
19So they came near to Joseph's house steward, and spoke to
him at the entrance of the house,
20and said, "Oh, my lord, we indeed came down the first time
to buy food,
21and it came about when we came to the lodging place, that
we opened our sacks, and behold, each man's money was in the
mouth of his sack, our money in full. So we have brought it back
in our hand.
22"We have also brought down other money in our hand to buy
food; we do not know who put our money in our sacks."
23And he said, "[a]Be at ease, do not be afraid. Your God and the
God of your father has given you treasure in your sacks; I had your
money." Then he brought Simeon out to them.
24Then the man brought the men into Joseph's house and gave
them water, and they washed their feet; and he gave their donkeys
fodder.
25So they prepared the present for Joseph's coming at noon; for
they had heard that they were to eat a meal there.
26¶ When Joseph came home, they brought into the house to
him the present which was in their hand and bowed to the ground
before him.
27Then he asked them about their welfare, and said, "Is your
old father well, of whom you spoke? Is he still alive?"
28And they said, "Your servant our father is well; he is still
alive." And they bowed down in homage.
29As he lifted his eyes and saw his brother Benjamin, his
mother's son, he said, "Is this your youngest brother, of whom
you spoke to me?" And he said, "May God be gracious to you, my
son."

NAS [a] Lit., *Peace be to you*

## New International

7They replied, "The man questioned us closely about ourselves
and our family. 'Is your father still living?' he asked us. 'Do you
have another brother?' We simply answered his questions. How
were we to know he would say, 'Bring your brother down here'?"
8Then Judah said to Israel his father, "Send the boy along with
me and we will go at once, so that we and you and our children
may live and not die. 9I myself will guarantee his safety; you can
hold me personally responsible for him. If I do not bring him back
to you and set him here before you, I will bear the blame before
you all my life. 10As it is, if we had not delayed, we could have
gone and returned twice."
11Then their father Israel said to them, "If it must be, then do
this: Put some of the best products of the land in your bags and
take them down to the man as a gift—a little balm and a little
honey, some spices and myrrh, some pistachio nuts and almonds.
12Take double the amount of silver with you, for you must return
the silver that was put back into the mouths of your sacks. Perhaps
it was a mistake. 13Take your brother also and go back to the man
at once. 14And may God Almighty[b] grant you mercy before the
man so that he will let your other brother and Benjamin come back
with you. As for me, if I am bereaved, I am bereaved."
15So the men took the gifts and double the amount of silver, and
Benjamin also. They hurried down to Egypt and presented themselves to Joseph. 16When Joseph saw Benjamin with them, he said
to the steward of his house, "Take these men to my house, slaughter an animal and prepare dinner; they are to eat with me at noon."
17The man did as Joseph told him and took the men to Joseph's
house. 18Now the men were frightened when they were taken to
his house. They thought, "We were brought here because of the
silver that was put back into our sacks the first time. He wants to
attack us and overpower us and seize us as slaves and take our
donkeys."
19So they went up to Joseph's steward and spoke to him at the
entrance to the house. 20"Please, sir," they said, "we came down
here the first time to buy food. 21But at the place where we stopped
for the night we opened our sacks and each of us found his silver—
the exact weight—in the mouth of his sack. So we have brought
it back with us. 22We have also brought additional silver with us
to buy food. We don't know who put our silver in our sacks."
23"It's all right," he said. "Don't be afraid. Your God, the God
of your father, has given you treasure in your sacks; I received your
silver." Then he brought Simeon out to them.
24The steward took the men into Joseph's house, gave them
water to wash their feet and provided fodder for their donkeys.
25They prepared their gifts for Joseph's arrival at noon, because
they had heard that they were to eat there.
26When Joseph came home, they presented to him the gifts they
had brought into the house, and they bowed down before him to
the ground. 27He asked them how they were, and then he said,
"How is your aged father you told me about? Is he still living?"
28They replied, "Your servant our father is still alive and well."
And they bowed low to pay him honor.
29As he looked about and saw his brother Benjamin, his own
mother's son, he asked, "Is this your youngest brother, the one
you told me about?" And he said, "God be gracious to you, my
son." 30Deeply moved at the sight of his brother, Joseph hurried

NIV [b] 14 Hebrew *El-Shaddai*

## King James

30And Joseph made haste; for his bowels did yearn upon his brother: and he sought *where* to weep; and he entered into *his* chamber, and wept there.

31And he washed his face, and went out, and refrained himself, and said, Set on bread.

32And they set on for him by himself, and for them by themselves, and for the Egyptians, which did eat with him, by themselves: because the Egyptians might not eat bread with the Hebrews; for that *is* an abomination unto the Egyptians.

33And they sat before him, the firstborn according to his birthright, and the youngest according to his youth: and the men marvelled one at another.

34And he took *and sent* messes unto them from before him: but Benjamin's mess was five times so much as any of theirs. And they drank, and were merry with him.

**44** AND HE commanded the steward of his house, saying, Fill the men's sacks *with* food, as much as they can carry, and put every man's money in his sack's mouth.

2And put my cup, the silver cup, in the sack's mouth of the youngest, and his corn money. And he did according to the word that Joseph had spoken.

3As soon as the morning was light, the men were sent away, they and their asses.

4 *And* when they were gone out of the city, *and* not *yet* far off, Joseph said unto his steward, Up, follow after the men; and when thou dost overtake them, say unto them, Wherefore have ye rewarded evil for good?

5 *Is* not this *it* in which my lord drinketh, and whereby indeed he divineth? ye have done evil in so doing.

6¶ And he overtook them, and he spake unto them these same words.

7And they said unto him, Wherefore saith my lord these words? God forbid that thy servants should do according to this thing:

8Behold, the money, which we found in our sacks' mouths, we brought again unto thee out of the land of Canaan: how then should we steal out of thy lord's house silver or gold?

9With whomsoever of thy servants it be found, both let him die, and we also will be my lord's bondmen.

10And he said, Now also *let* it *be* according unto your words: he with whom it is found shall be my servant; and ye shall be blameless.

11Then they speedily took down every man his sack to the ground, and opened every man his sack.

12And he searched, *and* began at the eldest, and left at the youngest: and the cup was found in Benjamin's sack.

13Then they rent their clothes, and laded every man his ass, and returned to the city.

14¶ And Judah and his brethren came to Joseph's house; for he *was* yet there: and they fell before him on the ground.

15And Joseph said unto them, What deed *is* this that ye have done? wot ye not that such a man as I can certainly divine?

16And Judah said, What shall we say unto my lord? what shall we speak? or how shall we clear ourselves? God hath found out the iniquity of thy servants: behold, we *are* my lord's servants, both we, and *he* also with whom the cup is found.

17And he said, God forbid that I should do so: *but* the man in whose hand the cup is found, he shall be my servant; and as for you, get you up in peace unto your father.

## Amplified

30And Joseph hurried from the room, for his heart yearned for his brother, and he sought privacy to weep; so he entered his chamber and wept there.

31And he washed his face, and went out, and restraining himself, said, Let dinner be served.

32And [the servants] set on [the food] for [Joseph] by himself, and for [his brothers] by themselves, and for those Egyptians who ate with him, by themselves, according to the Egyptian custom not to eat food with the Hebrews; for that is an abomination to the Egyptians.

33And [Joseph's brothers] were given seats before him; the eldest according to his birthright, and the youngest according to his youth; and the men looked at one another amazed [that so much was known about them].

34[Joseph] took and sent helpings to them from before him; but Benjamin's portion was five times as much as any of theirs. And they drank freely and were merry with him.

**44** AND HE commanded the steward of his house, saying, Fill the men's sacks with food, as much as they can carry, and put every man's money in his sack's mouth.

2And put my cup, the silver cup, in the sack's mouth of the youngest, and his grain money. And [the steward] did according to what Joseph had said.

3As soon as the morning was light, the men were sent away, they and their donkeys.

4When they had left the city, and were not yet far away, Joseph said to his steward, Up, follow after the men; and when you overtake them, say to them, Why have you rewarded evil for good? [Why have you stolen the silver cup?]

5Is it not my master's drinking cup, with which he divines [the future]? You have done wrong in doing this.

6And the steward overtook them, and he said to them these same words.

7They said to him, Why does my lord say these things? Far be it from your servants to do such a thing!

8Note that the money which we found in the mouths of our sacks we brought back to you from the land of Canaan. Is it likely then that we would steal from your master's house silver or gold?

9With whomever of your servants [your master's cup] is found, not only let that one die, but the rest of us will be my lord's slaves.

10And the steward said, Now let it be as you say. He with whom [the cup] is found shall be my slave; but [the rest of] you shall be blameless.

11Then quickly every man lowered his sack to the ground, and every man opened his sack.

12And [the steward] searched, beginning with the eldest and stopping with the youngest; and the cup was found in Benjamin's sack.

13Then they rent their clothes, and after each man had loaded his donkey again, they returned to the city.

14Judah and his brethren came to Joseph's house, for he was still there; and they fell prostrate before him.

15Joseph said to them, What is this thing that you have done? Do you not realize that such a man as I can certainly detect *and* know by divination [everything you do without other knowledge of it]?

16And Judah said, What shall we say to my lord? What shall we reply? Or how shall we clear ourselves, since God has found out *and* exposed the iniquity of your servants? Behold, we are my lord's slaves, the rest of us as well as he with whom the cup is found.

17But [Joseph] said, God forbid that I should do that; but the man in whose hand the cup is found, he shall be my servant; and as for [the rest of] you, arise *and* go in peace to your father.

## New American Standard

30And Joseph hurried *out* for he was deeply stirred over his
brother, and he sought *a place* to weep; and he entered his chamber
and wept there.
31Then he washed his face, and came out; and he controlled
himself and said, "Serve the meal."
32So they served him by himself, and them by themselves, and
the Egyptians, who ate with him, by themselves; because the
Egyptians could not eat bread with the Hebrews, for that is loathsome to the Egyptians.
33Now they were seated before him, the first-born according to
his birthright and the youngest according to his youth, and the
men looked at one another in astonishment.
34And he took portions to them from his own table; but Benjamin's portion was five times as much as any of theirs. So they
feasted and drank freely with him.

*The Brothers Are Brought Back*

**44** THEN HE commanded his house steward, saying, "Fill
the men's sacks with food, as much as they can carry, and
put each man's money in the mouth of his sack.
2"And put my cup, the silver cup, in the mouth of the sack of
the youngest, and his money for the grain." And he did as Joseph
had told *him*.
3As soon as it was light, the men were sent away, they with
their donkeys.
4They had *just* gone out of the city, *and* were not far off, when
Joseph said to his house steward, "Up, follow the men; and when
you overtake them, say to them, 'Why have you repaid evil for
good?
5'Is not this the one from which my lord drinks, and which he
indeed uses for divination? You have done wrong in doing this.' "
6¶ So he overtook them and spoke these words to them.
7And they said to him, "Why does my lord speak such words
as these? Far be it from your servants to do such a thing.
8"Behold, the money which we found in the mouth of our
sacks we have brought back to you from the land of Canaan. How
then could we steal silver or gold from your lord's house?
9"With whomever of your servants it is found, let him die, and
we also will be my lord's slaves."
10So he said, "Now let it also be according to your words; he
with whom it is found shall be my slave, and *the rest of* you shall
be innocent."
11Then they hurried, each man lowered his sack to the ground,
and each man opened his sack.
12And he searched, beginning with the oldest and ending with
the youngest, and the cup was found in Benjamin's sack.
13Then they tore their clothes, and when each man loaded his
donkey, they returned to the city.
14¶ When Judah and his brothers came to Joseph's house, he
was still there, and they fell to the ground before him.
15And Joseph said to them, "What is this deed that you have
done? Do you not know that such a man as I can indeed practice
divination?"
16So Judah said, "What can we say to my lord? What can we
speak? And how can we justify ourselves? God has found out the
iniquity of your servants; behold, we are my lord's slaves, both we
and the one in whose possession the cup has been found."
17But he said, "Far be it from me to do this. The man in whose
possession the cup has been found, he shall be my slave; but as
for you, go up in peace to your father."

## New International

out and looked for a place to weep. He went into his private room
and wept there.
31After he had washed his face, he came out and, controlling
himself, said, "Serve the food."
32They served him by himself, the brothers by themselves, and
the Egyptians who ate with him by themselves, because Egyptians
could not eat with Hebrews, for that is detestable to Egyptians.
33The men had been seated before him in the order of their ages,
from the firstborn to the youngest; and they looked at each other
in astonishment. 34When portions were served to them from Joseph's table, Benjamin's portion was five times as much as anyone
else's. So they feasted and drank freely with him.

*A Silver Cup in a Sack*

**44** NOW JOSEPH gave these instructions to the steward of
his house: "Fill the men's sacks with as much food as they
can carry, and put each man's silver in the mouth of his sack.
2Then put my cup, the silver one, in the mouth of the youngest
one's sack, along with the silver for his grain." And he did as
Joseph said.
3As morning dawned, the men were sent on their way with
their donkeys. 4They had not gone far from the city when Joseph
said to his steward, "Go after those men at once, and when you
catch up with them, say to them, 'Why have you repaid good with
evil? 5Isn't this the cup my master drinks from and also uses for
divination? This is a wicked thing you have done.' "
6When he caught up with them, he repeated these words to
them. 7But they said to him, "Why does my lord say such things?
Far be it from your servants to do anything like that! 8We even
brought back to you from the land of Canaan the silver we found
inside the mouths of our sacks. So why would we steal silver or
gold from your master's house? 9If any of your servants is found
to have it, he will die; and the rest of us will become my lord's
slaves."
10"Very well, then," he said, "let it be as you say. Whoever is
found to have it will become my slave; the rest of you will be free
from blame."
11Each of them quickly lowered his sack to the ground and
opened it. 12Then the steward proceeded to search, beginning
with the oldest and ending with the youngest. And the cup was
found in Benjamin's sack. 13At this, they tore their clothes. Then
they all loaded their donkeys and returned to the city.
14Joseph was still in the house when Judah and his brothers
came in, and they threw themselves to the ground before him.
15Joseph said to them, "What is this you have done? Don't you
know that a man like me can find things out by divination?"
16"What can we say to my lord?" Judah replied. "What can we
say? How can we prove our innocence? God has uncovered your
servants' guilt. We are now my lord's slaves—we ourselves and
the one who was found to have the cup."
17But Joseph said, "Far be it from me to do such a thing! Only
the man who was found to have the cup will become my slave. The
rest of you, go back to your father in peace."

## King James

18¶ Then Judah came near unto him, and said, Oh my lord, let thy servant, I pray thee, speak a word in my lord's ears, and let not thine anger burn against thy servant: for thou *art* even as Pharaoh.

19My lord asked his servants, saying, Have ye a father, or a brother?

20And we said unto my lord, We have a father, an old man, and a child of his old age, a little one; and his brother is dead, and he alone is left of his mother, and his father loveth him.

21And thou saidst unto thy servants, Bring him down unto me, that I may set mine eyes upon him.

22And we said unto my lord, The lad cannot leave his father: for *if* he should leave his father, *his father* would die.

23And thou saidst unto thy servants, Except your youngest brother come down with you, ye shall see my face no more.

24And it came to pass when we came up unto thy servant my father, we told him the words of my lord.

25And our father said, Go again, *and* buy us a little food.

26And we said, We cannot go down: if our youngest brother be with us, then will we go down: for we may not see the man's face, except our youngest brother *be* with us.

27And thy servant my father said unto us, Ye know that my wife bare me two *sons:*

28And the one went out from me, and I said, Surely he is torn in pieces; and I saw him not since:

29And if ye take this also from me, and mischief befall him, ye shall bring down my gray hairs with sorrow to the grave.

30Now therefore when I come to thy servant my father, and the lad *be* not with us; seeing that his life is bound up in the lad's life;

31It shall come to pass, when he seeth that the lad *is* not *with us*, that he will die: and thy servants shall bring down the gray hairs of thy servant our father with sorrow to the grave.

32For thy servant became surety for the lad unto my father, saying, If I bring him not unto thee, then I shall bear the blame to my father for ever.

33Now therefore, I pray thee, let thy servant abide instead of the lad a bondman to my lord; and let the lad go up with his brethren.

34For how shall I go up to my father, and the lad *be* not with me? lest peradventure I see the evil that shall come on my father.

**45** THEN JOSEPH could not refrain himself before all them that stood by him; and he cried, Cause every man to go out from me. And there stood no man with him, while Joseph made himself known unto his brethren.

2And he wept aloud: and the Egyptians and the house of Pharaoh heard.

3And Joseph said unto his brethren, I *am* Joseph; doth my father yet live? And his brethren could not answer him; for they were troubled at his presence.

4And Joseph said unto his brethren, Come near to me, I pray you. And they came near. And he said, I *am* Joseph your brother, whom ye sold into Egypt.

5Now therefore be not grieved, nor angry with yourselves, that ye sold me hither: for God did send me before you to preserve life.

6For these two years *hath* the famine *been* in the land: and yet *there are* five years, in the which *there shall* neither *be* earing nor harvest.

7And God sent me before you to preserve you a posterity in the earth, and to save your lives by a great deliverance.

## Amplified

18Then Judah came close to [Joseph], and said, O my lord, let your servant, I pray you, speak a word to you in private, and let not your anger blaze against your servant, for you are as Pharaoh [so I will speak as if directly to him].

19My lord asked his servants, saying, Have you a father, or a brother?

20And we said to my lord, We have a father, an old man, and a young [brother the] child of his old age; and his brother is dead, and he alone is left of his mother's [offspring], and his father loves him.

21And you said to your servants, Bring him down to me, that I may set my eyes on him.

22And we said to my lord, The lad cannot leave his father; for if he should do so, his father would die.

23And you told your servants, Unless your youngest brother comes with you, you shall not see my face again.

24And when we went back to your servant my father, we told him what my lord had said.

25And our father said, Go again, and buy us a little food.

26But we said, We cannot go down. If our younger brother is with us, then we will go down; for we may not see the man's face, except our youngest brother is with us.

27And your servant my father said to us, You know that [Rachel] my wife bore me two sons:

28And the one went out from me, and I said, Surely he is torn to pieces; and I have never seen him since.

29And if you take this son also from me, and harm *or* accident should befall him, you will bring down my gray hairs with sorrow *and* evil to Sheol.

30Now therefore when I come to your servant my father, and the lad is not with us, when his life is bound up in the lad's life, *and* his soul knit with the lad's soul,

31When he sees that the lad is not with us, he will die; and your servants will be responsible for his death *and* will bring down the gray hairs of your servant our father with sorrow to Sheol (the place of the dead).

32For your servant became security for the lad to my father, saying, If I do not bring him to you, then I will bear the blame to my father forever.

33Now therefore, I pray you, let your servant remain instead of the youth [to be] a slave to my lord; and let the young man go home with his [half] brothers.

34For how can I go up to my father if the lad is not with me? Lest I witness the woe *and* the evil that will come upon my father.

**45** THEN JOSEPH could not restrain himself [any longer] before all those who stood about him, and he called out, Cause every man to go out from me! So no one stood there with Joseph, while he made himself known to his brothers.

2And he wept *and* sobbed aloud, and the Egyptians [who had just left him] heard it, and the household of Pharaoh heard of it.

3And Joseph said to his brothers, I am Joseph! Is my father still alive? And his brothers could not reply, for they were distressingly disturbed *and* dismayed at [the startling realization that they were in] his presence.

4And Joseph said to his brothers, Come near to me, I pray you. And they did so. And he said, I am Joseph your brother, whom you sold into Egypt;

5But now do not be distressed *and* disheartened, or vexed *and* angry with yourselves because you sold me here, for God sent me ahead of you to preserve life.

6For these two years the famine has been in the land; and there are to be still five years more in which there will be neither plowing nor harvest.

7God sent me before you to preserve you a posterity *and* to continue a remnant on the earth, to save your lives by a great escape *and* save for you many survivors.

## New American Standard

18¶ Then Judah approached him, and said, "Oh my lord, may
your servant please speak a word in my lord's ears, and do not be
angry with your servant; for you are equal to Pharaoh.
19"My lord asked his servants, saying, 'Have you a father or a
brother?'
20"And we said to my lord, 'We have an old father and a little
child of *his* old age. Now his brother is dead, so he alone is left of
his mother, and his father loves him.'
21"Then you said to your servants, 'Bring him down to me, that
I may set my eyes on him.'
22"But we said to my lord, 'The lad cannot leave his father, for
if he should leave his father, his father would die.'
23"You said to your servants, however, 'Unless your youngest
brother comes down with you, you shall not see my face again.'
24"Thus it came about when we went up to your servant my
father, we told him the words of my lord.
25"And our father said, 'Go back, buy us a little food.'
26"But we said, 'We cannot go down. If our youngest brother
is with us, then we will go down; for we cannot see the man's face
unless our youngest brother is with us.'
27"And your servant my father said to us, 'You know that my
wife bore me two sons;
28and the one went out from me, and I said, "Surely he is torn
in pieces," and I have not seen him since.
29'And if you take this one also from me, and harm befalls him,
you will bring my gray hair down to Sheol in sorrow.'
30"Now, therefore, when I come to your servant my father, and
the lad is not with us, since his life is bound up in the lad's life,
31it will come about when he sees that the lad is not *with us,* that
he will die. Thus your servants will bring the gray hair of your
servant our father down to Sheol in sorrow.
32"For your servant became surety for the lad to my father,
saying, 'If I do not bring him *back* to you, then let me bear the blame
before my father forever.'
33"Now, therefore, please let your servant remain instead of the
lad a slave to my lord, and let the lad go up with his brothers.
34"For how shall I go up to my father if the lad is not with me,
lest I see the evil that would overtake my father?"

*Joseph Deals Kindly with His Brothers*

45 THEN JOSEPH could not control himself before all those
who stood by him, and he cried, "Have everyone go out
from me." So there was no man with him when Joseph made
himself known to his brothers.
2And he wept so loudly that the Egyptians heard *it,* and the
household of Pharaoh heard *of it.*
3Then Joseph said to his brothers, "I am Joseph! Is my father
still alive?" But his brothers could not answer him, for they were
dismayed at his presence.
4Then Joseph said to his brothers, "Please come closer to me."
And they came closer. And he said, "I am your brother Joseph,
whom you sold into Egypt.
5"And now do not be grieved or angry with yourselves, because you sold me here; for God sent me before you to preserve
life.
6"For the famine *has been* in the land these two years, and there
are still five years in which there will be neither plowing nor
harvesting.
7"And God sent me before you to preserve for you a remnant
in the earth, and to keep you alive by a great deliverance.

## New International

18Then Judah went up to him and said: "Please, my lord, let
your servant speak a word to my lord. Do not be angry with your
servant, though you are equal to Pharaoh himself. 19My lord asked
his servants, 'Do you have a father or a brother?' 20And we answered, 'We have an aged father, and there is a young son born
to him in his old age. His brother is dead, and he is the only one
of his mother's sons left, and his father loves him.'
21"Then you said to your servants, 'Bring him down to me so
I can see him for myself.' 22And we said to my lord, 'The boy
cannot leave his father; if he leaves him, his father will die.' 23But
you told your servants, 'Unless your youngest brother comes
down with you, you will not see my face again.' 24When we went
back to your servant my father, we told him what my lord had said.
25"Then our father said, 'Go back and buy a little more food.'
26But we said, 'We cannot go down. Only if our youngest brother
is with us will we go. We cannot see the man's face unless our
youngest brother is with us.'
27"Your servant my father said to us, 'You know that my wife
bore me two sons. 28One of them went away from me, and I said,
"He has surely been torn to pieces." And I have not seen him
since. 29If you take this one from me too and harm comes to him,
you will bring my gray head down to the grave[a] in misery.'
30"So now, if the boy is not with us when I go back to your
servant my father and if my father, whose life is closely bound up
with the boy's life, 31sees that the boy isn't there, he will die. Your
servants will bring the gray head of our father down to the grave
in sorrow. 32Your servant guaranteed the boy's safety to my father.
I said, 'If I do not bring him back to you, I will bear the blame before
you, my father, all my life!'
33"Now then, please let your servant remain here as my lord's
slave in place of the boy, and let the boy return with his brothers.
34How can I go back to my father if the boy is not with me? No!
Do not let me see the misery that would come upon my father."

*Joseph Makes Himself Known*

45 THEN JOSEPH could no longer control himself before all
his attendants, and he cried out, "Have everyone leave
my presence!" So there was no one with Joseph when he made
himself known to his brothers. 2And he wept so loudly that the
Egyptians heard him, and Pharaoh's household heard about it.
3Joseph said to his brothers, "I am Joseph! Is my father still
living?" But his brothers were not able to answer him, because
they were terrified at his presence.
4Then Joseph said to his brothers, "Come close to me." When
they had done so, he said, "I am your brother Joseph, the one you
sold into Egypt! 5And now, do not be distressed and do not be
angry with yourselves for selling me here, because it was to save
lives that God sent me ahead of you. 6For two years now there has
been famine in the land, and for the next five years there will not
be plowing and reaping. 7But God sent me ahead of you to preserve for you a remnant on earth and to save your lives by a great
deliverance.[b]

NIV [a] 29 Hebrew *Sheol;* also in verse 31 [b] 7 Or *save you as a great band of survivors*

## King James

8 So now *it was* not you *that* sent me hither, but God: and he hath
made me a father to Pharaoh, and lord of all his house, and a ruler
throughout all the land of Egypt.
9 Haste ye, and go up to my father, and say unto him, Thus saith
thy son Joseph, God hath made me lord of all Egypt: come down
unto me, tarry not:
10 And thou shalt dwell in the land of Goshen, and thou shalt
be near unto me, thou, and thy children, and thy children's children, and thy flocks, and thy herds, and all that thou hast:
11 And there will I nourish thee; for yet *there are* five years of
famine; lest thou, and thy household, and all that thou hast, come
to poverty.
12 And, behold, your eyes see, and the eyes of my brother
Benjamin, that *it is* my mouth that speaketh unto you.
13 And ye shall tell my father of all my glory in Egypt, and of all
that ye have seen; and ye shall haste and bring down my father
hither.
14 And he fell upon his brother Benjamin's neck, and wept; and
Benjamin wept upon his neck.
15 Moreover he kissed all his brethren, and wept upon them:
and after that his brethren talked with him.
16 ¶ And the fame thereof was heard in Pharaoh's house, saying,
Joseph's brethren are come: and it pleased Pharaoh well, and his
servants.
17 And Pharaoh said unto Joseph, Say unto thy brethren, This
do ye; lade your beasts, and go, get you unto the land of Canaan;
18 And take your father and your households, and come unto
me: and I will give you the good of the land of Egypt, and ye shall
eat the fat of the land.
19 Now thou art commanded, this do ye; take you wagons out
of the land of Egypt for your little ones, and for your wives, and
bring your father, and come.
20 Also regard not your stuff; for the good of all the land of Egypt
*is* yours.
21 And the children of Israel did so: and Joseph gave them
wagons, according to the commandment of Pharaoh, and gave
them provision for the way.
22 To all of them he gave each man changes of raiment; but to
Benjamin he gave three hundred *pieces* of silver, and five changes
of raiment.
23 And to his father he sent after this *manner;* ten asses laden
with the good things of Egypt, and ten she asses laden with corn
and bread and meat for his father by the way.
24 So he sent his brethren away, and they departed: and he said
unto them, See that ye fall not out by the way.
25 ¶ And they went up out of Egypt, and came into the land of
Canaan unto Jacob their father,
26 And told him, saying, Joseph *is* yet alive, and he *is* governor
over all the land of Egypt. And Jacob's heart fainted, for he believed them not.
27 And they told him all the words of Joseph, which he had said
unto them: and when he saw the wagons which Joseph had sent
to carry him, the spirit of Jacob their father revived:
28 And Israel said, *It is* enough; Joseph my son *is* yet alive: I will
go and see him before I die.

**46** AND ISRAEL took his journey with all that he had, and
came to Beer-sheba, and offered sacrifices unto the God of
his father Isaac.
2 And God spake unto Israel in the visions of the night, and said,
Jacob, Jacob. And he said, Here *am* I.

## Amplified

8 So now it was not you who sent me here, but God; and He has
made me a father to Pharaoh, and lord of all his house, and ruler
over all the land of Egypt.
9 Hurry and go up to my father and tell him, Your son Joseph
says this to you: God has put me in charge of all Egypt; come down
to me; do not delay.
10 You shall live in the land of Goshen, and you will be close to
me, you and your children and your grandchildren, and your
flocks, your herds, and all you have.
11 And there I will sustain *and* provide for you, so that you and
your household and all that are yours, may not come to poverty
*and* want; for there are yet [to be] five years of (the scarcity, hunger
*and* starvation of) famine.
12 Now notice! Your own eyes and the eyes of my brother Benjamin see that I am talking to you personally [in your language, and
not through an interpreter].
13 And you shall tell my father of all my glory in Egypt, and of
all that you have seen; and you shall hurry and bring my father
down here.
14 And he fell on his brother Benjamin's neck and wept, and
Benjamin wept on his neck.
15 Moreover he kissed all his brothers and wept upon them; and
after that his brothers conversed with him.
16 When the report was heard in Pharaoh's house, Joseph's
brothers have come, it pleased Pharaoh and his servants well.
17 And Pharaoh said to Joseph, Tell your brothers this: Load
your animals and return to the land of Canaan;
18 And get your father and your households and come to me.
And I will give you the best in the land of Egypt, and you shall live
on the fat of the land.
19 You therefore command them, saying, You do this: take wagons from the land of Egypt for your little ones, and for your wives,
and bring your father, and come.
20 Also do not look with regret *or* concern upon your goods, for
the best of all the land of Egypt is yours.
21 And the sons of Israel did so; and Joseph gave them wagons
as the order of Pharaoh permitted, and gave them provisions for
the journey.
22 To each of them he gave changes of raiment; but to Benjamin
he gave 300 pieces of silver, and five changes of raiment.
23 And to his father he sent as follows: ten donkeys loaded with
the good things of Egypt, and ten she-donkeys laden with grain,
bread, and nourishing food *and* provision for his father [to supply
all who were with him] on the way.
24 So he sent his brothers away, and they departed; and he said
to them, See that you do not disagree (get excited, quarrel) along
the road.
25 So they went up out of Egypt, and came into the land of
Canaan to Jacob their father,
26 And they said to him, Joseph is still alive, and he is governor
over all the land of Egypt! And Jacob's heart began to stop beating
*and* fainted, for he did not believe them.
27 But when they told him all the words of Joseph which he had
said to them, and when he saw the wagons which Joseph had sent
to carry him, the spirit of Jacob their father revived—warmth and
life returned.
28 And Israel said, It is enough; Joseph my son is still alive; I will
go and see him before I die.

**46** SO ISRAEL made his journey with all that he had, and
came to Beer-sheba [a place hallowed by sacred memo-
ries], and offered sacrifices to the God of his father Isaac. [Gen.
28:10-13; 26:23-25.]
2 And God spoke to Israel in visions of the night, and said, Jacob!
Jacob! And he said, Here am I.

## New American Standard

8 "Now, therefore, it was not you who sent me here, but God; and He has made me a father to Pharaoh and lord of all his household and ruler over all the land of Egypt.

9 "Hurry and go up to my father, and say to him, 'Thus says your son Joseph, "God has made me lord of all Egypt; come down to me, do not delay.

10 "And you shall live in the land of Goshen, and you shall be near me, you and your children and your children's children and your flocks and your herds and all that you have.

11 "There I will also provide for you, for there are still five years of famine *to come*, lest you and your household and all that you have be impoverished." '

12 "And behold, your eyes see, and the eyes of my brother Benjamin *see*, that it is my mouth which is speaking to you.

13 "Now you must tell my father of all my splendor in Egypt, and all that you have seen; and you must hurry and bring my father down here."

14 Then he fell on his brother Benjamin's neck and wept; and Benjamin wept on his neck.

15 And he kissed all his brothers and wept on them, and afterward his brothers talked with him.

**16**¶ Now when the news was heard in Pharaoh's house that Joseph's brothers had come, it pleased Pharaoh and his servants.

17 Then Pharaoh said to Joseph, "Say to your brothers, 'Do this: load your beasts and go to the land of Canaan,

18 and take your father and your households and come to me, and I will give you the best of the land of Egypt and you shall eat the fat of the land.'

19 "Now you are ordered, 'Do this: take wagons from the land of Egypt for your little ones and for your wives, and bring your father and come.

20 'And do not concern yourselves with your goods, for the best of all the land of Egypt is yours.' "

**21**¶ Then the sons of Israel did so; and Joseph gave them wagons according to the command of Pharaoh, and gave them provisions for the journey.

22 To each of them he gave changes of garments, but to Benjamin he gave three hundred *pieces of* silver and five changes of garments.

23 And to his father he sent as follows: ten donkeys loaded with the best things of Egypt, and ten female donkeys loaded with grain and bread and sustenance for his father on the journey.

24 So he sent his brothers away, and as they departed, he said to them, "Do not quarrel on the journey."

25 Then they went up from Egypt, and came to the land of Canaan to their father Jacob.

26 And they told him, saying, "Joseph is still alive, and indeed he is ruler over all the land of Egypt." But he was stunned, for he did not believe them.

27 When they told him all the words of Joseph that he had spoken to them, and when he saw the wagons that Joseph had sent to carry him, the spirit of their father Jacob revived.

28 Then Israel said, "It is enough; my son Joseph is still alive. I will go and see him before I die."

*Jacob Moves to Egypt*

**46** SO ISRAEL set out with all that he had, and came to Beersheba, and offered sacrifices to the God of his father Isaac.

2 And God spoke to Israel in visions of the night and said, "Jacob, Jacob." And he said, "Here I am."

## New International

8 "So then, it was not you who sent me here, but God. He made
me father to Pharaoh, lord of his entire household and ruler of all
Egypt. 9 Now hurry back to my father and say to him, 'This is what
your son Joseph says: God has made me lord of all Egypt. Come
down to me; don't delay. 10 You shall live in the region of Goshen
and be near me—you, your children and grandchildren, your
flocks and herds, and all you have. 11 I will provide for you there,
because five years of famine are still to come. Otherwise you and
your household and all who belong to you will become destitute.'

12 "You can see for yourselves, and so can my brother Benjamin,
that it is really I who am speaking to you. 13 Tell my father about
all the honor accorded me in Egypt and about everything you have
seen. And bring my father down here quickly."

14 Then he threw his arms around his brother Benjamin and
wept, and Benjamin embraced him, weeping. 15 And he kissed all
his brothers and wept over them. Afterward his brothers talked
with him.

16 When the news reached Pharaoh's palace that Joseph's brothers had come, Pharaoh and all his officials were pleased. 17 Pharaoh
said to Joseph, "Tell your brothers, 'Do this: Load your animals
and return to the land of Canaan, 18 and bring your father and your
families back to me. I will give you the best of the land of Egypt
and you can enjoy the fat of the land.'

19 "You are also directed to tell them, 'Do this: Take some carts
from Egypt for your children and your wives, and get your father
and come. 20 Never mind about your belongings, because the best
of all Egypt will be yours.' "

21 So the sons of Israel did this. Joseph gave them carts, as
Pharaoh had commanded, and he also gave them provisions for
their journey. 22 To each of them he gave new clothing, but to
Benjamin he gave three hundred shekels[a] of silver and five sets
of clothes. 23 And this is what he sent to his father: ten donkeys
loaded with the best things of Egypt, and ten female donkeys
loaded with grain and bread and other provisions for his journey.
24 Then he sent his brothers away, and as they were leaving he said
to them, "Don't quarrel on the way!"

25 So they went up out of Egypt and came to their father Jacob
in the land of Canaan. 26 They told him, "Joseph is still alive! In fact,
he is ruler of all Egypt." Jacob was stunned; he did not believe
them. 27 But when they told him everything Joseph had said to
them, and when he saw the carts Joseph had sent to carry him
back, the spirit of their father Jacob revived. 28 And Israel said, "I'm
convinced! My son Joseph is still alive. I will go and see him before
I die."

*Jacob Goes to Egypt*

**46** SO ISRAEL set out with all that was his, and when he reached Beersheba, he offered sacrifices to the God of his father Isaac.

2 And God spoke to Israel in a vision at night and said, "Jacob! Jacob!"

"Here I am," he replied.

**NIV** [a] 22 That is, about 7 1/2 pounds (about 3.5 kilograms)

## King James

3 And he said, I *am* God, the God of thy father: fear not to go
down into Egypt; for I will there make of thee a great nation:
4 I will go down with thee into Egypt; and I will also surely bring
thee up *again:* and Joseph shall put his hand upon thine eyes.
5 And Jacob rose up from Beer-sheba: and the sons of Israel
carried Jacob their father, and their little ones, and their wives, in
the wagons which Pharaoh had sent to carry him.
6 And they took their cattle, and their goods, which they had
gotten in the land of Canaan, and came into Egypt, Jacob, and all
his seed with him:
7 His sons, and his sons' sons with him, his daughters, and his
sons' daughters, and all his seed brought he with him into Egypt.
8 ¶ And these *are* the names of the children of Israel, which came
into Egypt, Jacob and his sons: Reuben, Jacob's firstborn.
9 And the sons of Reuben; Hanoch, and Phallu, and Hezron,
and Carmi.
10 ¶ And the sons of Simeon; Jemuel, and Jamin, and Ohad, and
Jachin, and Zohar, and Shaul the son of a Canaanitish woman.
11 ¶ And the sons of Levi; Gershon, Kohath, and Merari.
12 ¶ And the sons of Judah; Er, and Onan, and Shelah, and
Pharez, and Zerah: but Er and Onan died in the land of Canaan.
And the sons of Pharez were Hezron and Hamul.
13 ¶ And the sons of Issachar; Tola, and Phuvah, and Job, and
Shimron.
14 ¶ And the sons of Zebulun; Sered, and Elon, and Jahleel.
15 These *be* the sons of Leah, which she bare unto Jacob in
Padan-aram, with his daughter Dinah: all the souls of his sons and
his daughters *were* thirty and three.
16 ¶ And the sons of Gad; Ziphion, and Haggi, Shuni, and
Ezbon, Eri, and Arodi, and Areli.
17 ¶ And the sons of Asher; Jimnah, and Ishuah, and Isui, and
Beriah, and Serah their sister: and the sons of Beriah; Heber, and
Malchiel.
18 These *are* the sons of Zilpah, whom Laban gave to Leah his
daughter, and these she bare unto Jacob, *even* sixteen souls.
19 The sons of Rachel Jacob's wife; Joseph, and Benjamin.
20 ¶ And unto Joseph in the land of Egypt were born Manasseh
and Ephraim, which Asenath the daughter of Poti-pherah priest
of On bare unto him.
21 ¶ And the sons of Benjamin *were* Belah, and Becher, and
Ashbel, Gera, and Naaman, Ehi, and Rosh, Muppim, and Huppim, and Ard.
22 These *are* the sons of Rachel, which were born to Jacob: all the
souls *were* fourteen.
23 ¶ And the sons of Dan; Hushim.
24 ¶ And the sons of Naphtali; Jahzeel, and Guni, and Jezer, and
Shillem.
25 These *are* the sons of Bilhah, which Laban gave unto Rachel
his daughter, and she bare these unto Jacob: all the souls *were*
seven.
26 All the souls that came with Jacob into Egypt, which came out
of his loins, besides Jacob's sons' wives, all the souls *were* threescore and six;

## Amplified

3 And He said, I am God, the God of your father; do not be afraid
to go down to Egypt; for I will there make of you a great nation.
4 I will go down with you to Egypt, and I will also surely bring
you [your people Israel] up again; and Joseph shall put his hand
upon your eyes [when they are to be closed in death].
5 So Jacob arose *and* set out from Beer-sheba; and Israel's sons
conveyed their father, their little ones and wives in the wagons
Pharaoh had sent to carry him.
6 And they took their cattle, and the gains which they had
acquired in the land of Canaan, and came into Egypt, Jacob and
all his offspring with him:
7 His sons, and his sons' sons with him, his daughters, and his
sons' daughters; all his offspring he brought with him into Egypt.
8 And these are the names of the descendants of Israel, who
came into Egypt, Jacob and his sons: Reuben, Jacob's first-born,
9 And the sons of Reuben: Hanoch, and Pallu, Hezron, and
Carmi.
10 The sons of Simeon: Jemuel, Jamin, Ohad, Jachin, Zohar, and
Shaul the son of a Canaanitish woman.
11 The sons of Levi: Gershon, Kohath, and Merari.
12 The sons of Judah: Er, Onan, Shelah, Perez, and Zerah; but
Er and Onan died in the land of Canaan. And the sons of Perez
were Hezron and Hamul.
13 The sons of Issachar: Tola, Puvah, Iob, and Shimron.
14 The sons of Zebulun: Sered, Elon, and Jahleel.
15 These are the sons of Leah, whom she bore to Jacob in Padan-
aram, together with his daughter Dinah; all of his sons and his
daughters numbered thirty-three.
16 The sons of Gad: Ziphion, Haggi, Shuni, Ezbon, Eri, Arodi,
and Areli.
17 The sons of Asher: Imnah, Ishvah, Ishvi, Beriah, and Serah
their sister. And the sons of Beriah: Heber and Malchiel.
18 These are the sons of Zilpah, [the maid] whom Laban gave to
Leah his daughter; and these she bore to Jacob, sixteen persons all
told.
19 The sons of Rachel, Jacob's wife: Joseph and Benjamin.
20 And to Joseph in the land of Egypt were born Manasseh and
Ephraim, whom Asenath, daughter of Potiphera priest of On, bore
to him.
21 And the sons of [a]Benjamin: Bela, Becher, Ashbel, Gera, Naaman, Ehi, Rosh, Muppim, Huppim, and Ard.
22 These are the sons of Rachel, who were born to Jacob: fourteen persons in all.
23 The sons of Dan: Hushim.
24 The sons of Naphtali: Jahzeel, Guni, Jezer, and Shillem.
25 These are the sons of Bilhah, [the maid] whom Laban gave to
Rachel his daughter, and she bore these to Jacob; seven persons
in all.
26 All the persons who came with Jacob into Egypt, who were
his own offspring, not counting the wives of Jacob's sons, were
sixty-six persons all told.

**AMP** [a] Benjamin, whom uninformed artists have frequently pictured as a mere youth when he met Joseph in Egypt, was in fact the father of 10 sons at this time. Joseph was 17 when his brothers sold him; he was in prison 13 years; he had been governor of Egypt during the 7 good years and through 2 years of the famine. So he was 39 years of age at this time, and Benjamin was only a few years younger.

## New American Standard

3And He said, "I am God, the God of your father; do not be
afraid to go down to Egypt, for I will make you a great nation there.
4"I will go down with you to Egypt, and I will also surely bring
you up again; and Joseph will close your eyes."
5Then Jacob arose from Beersheba; and the sons of Israel carried their father Jacob and their little ones and their wives, in the
wagons which Pharaoh had sent to carry him.
6And they took their livestock and their property, which they
had acquired in the land of Canaan, and came to Egypt, Jacob and
all his descendants with him:
7his sons and his grandsons with him, his daughters and his
granddaughters, and all his descendants he brought with him to
Egypt.

*Those Who Came to Egypt*

8¶ Now these are the names of the sons of Israel, Jacob and his
sons, who went to Egypt: Reuben, Jacob's first-born.
9And the sons of Reuben: Hanoch and Pallu and Hezron and
Carmi.
10And the sons of Simeon: Jemuel and Jamin and Ohad and
Jachin and Zohar and Shaul the son of a Canaanite woman.
11And the sons of Levi: Gershon, Kohath, and Merari.
12And the sons of Judah: Er and Onan and Shelah and Perez
and Zerah (but Er and Onan died in the land of Canaan). And the
sons of Perez were Hezron and Hamul.
13And the sons of Issachar: Tola and Puvvah and Iob and Shimron.
14And the sons of Zebulun: Sered and Elon and Jahleel.
15These are the sons of Leah, whom she bore to Jacob in Paddan-aram, with his daughter Dinah; all his sons and his daughters
*numbered* thirty-three.
16And the sons of Gad: Ziphion and Haggi, Shuni and Ezbon,
Eri and Arodi and Areli.
17And the sons of Asher: Imnah and Ishvah and Ishvi and
Beriah and their sister Serah. And the sons of Beriah: Heber and
Malchiel.
18These are the sons of Zilpah, whom Laban gave to his daughter Leah; and she bore to Jacob these sixteen persons.
19The sons of Jacob's wife Rachel: Joseph and Benjamin.
20Now to Joseph in the land of Egypt were born Manasseh and
Ephraim, whom Asenath, the daughter of Potiphera, priest of On,
bore to him.
21And the sons of Benjamin: Bela and Becher and Ashbel, Gera
and Naaman, Ehi and Rosh, Muppim and Huppim and Ard.
22These are the sons of Rachel, who were born to Jacob; *there
were* fourteen persons in all.
23And the sons of Dan: Hushim.
24And the sons of Naphtali: Jahzeel and Guni and Jezer and
Shillem.
25These are the sons of Bilhah, whom Laban gave to his daughter Rachel, and she bore these to Jacob; *there were* seven persons
in all.
26All the persons belonging to Jacob, who came to Egypt, his
direct descendants, not including the wives of Jacob's sons, *were*
sixty-six persons in all,

## New International

3"I am God, the God of your father," he said. "Do not be afraid
to go down to Egypt, for I will make you into a great nation there.
4I will go down to Egypt with you, and I will surely bring you back
again. And Joseph's own hand will close your eyes."
5Then Jacob left Beersheba, and Israel's sons took their father
Jacob and their children and their wives in the carts that Pharaoh
had sent to transport him. 6They also took with them their livestock and the possessions they had acquired in Canaan, and Jacob
and all his offspring went to Egypt. 7He took with him to Egypt
his sons and grandsons and his daughters and granddaughters—
all his offspring.

8These are the names of the sons of Israel (Jacob and his descendants) who went to Egypt:

Reuben the firstborn of Jacob.
9The sons of Reuben:
Hanoch, Pallu, Hezron and Carmi.
10The sons of Simeon:
Jemuel, Jamin, Ohad, Jakin, Zohar and Shaul the son of
a Canaanite woman.
11The sons of Levi:
Gershon, Kohath and Merari.
12The sons of Judah:
Er, Onan, Shelah, Perez and Zerah (but Er and Onan had
died in the land of Canaan).
The sons of Perez:
Hezron and Hamul.
13The sons of Issachar:
Tola, Puah,[b] Jashub[c] and Shimron.
14The sons of Zebulun:
Sered, Elon and Jahleel.
15These were the sons Leah bore to Jacob in Paddan Aram,[d]
besides his daughter Dinah. These sons and daughters of his were
thirty-three in all.

16The sons of Gad:
Zephon,[e] Haggi, Shuni, Ezbon, Eri, Arodi and Areli.
17The sons of Asher:
Imnah, Ishvah, Ishvi and Beriah.
Their sister was Serah.
The sons of Beriah:
Heber and Malkiel.
18These were the children born to Jacob by Zilpah, whom Laban
had given to his daughter Leah—sixteen in all.
19The sons of Jacob's wife Rachel:
Joseph and Benjamin. 20In Egypt, Manasseh and Ephraim
were born to Joseph by Asenath daughter of Potiphera,
priest of On.[f]
21The sons of Benjamin:
Bela, Beker, Ashbel, Gera, Naaman, Ehi, Rosh, Muppim,
Huppim and Ard.
22These were the sons of Rachel who were born to Jacob—fourteen in all.
23The son of Dan:
Hushim.
24The sons of Naphtali:
Jahziel, Guni, Jezer and Shillem.
25These were the sons born to Jacob by Bilhah, whom Laban
had given to his daughter Rachel—seven in all.

26All those who went to Egypt with Jacob—those who were his
direct descendants, not counting his sons' wives—numbered sixty-six persons. 27With the two sons[g] who had been born to Joseph

NIV [b] *13* Samaritan Pentateuch and Syriac (see also 1 Chron. 7:1); Masoretic Text *Puvah* [c] *13* Samaritan Pentateuch and some Septuagint manuscripts (see also Num. 26:24 and 1 Chron. 7:1); Masoretic Text *Iob* [d] *15* That is, Northwest Mesopotamia [e] *16* Samaritan Pentateuch and Septuagint (see also Num. 26:15); Masoretic Text *Ziphion* [f] *20* That is, Heliopolis [g] *27* Hebrew; Septuagint *the nine children*

## King James

27 And the sons of Joseph, which were born him in Egypt, *were* two souls: all the souls of the house of Jacob, which came into Egypt, *were* threescore and ten.

28 ¶ And he sent Judah before him unto Joseph, to direct his face unto Goshen; and they came into the land of Goshen.

29 And Joseph made ready his chariot, and went up to meet Israel his father, to Goshen, and presented himself unto him; and he fell on his neck, and wept on his neck a good while.

30 And Israel said unto Joseph, Now let me die, since I have seen thy face, because thou *art* yet alive.

31 And Joseph said unto his brethren, and unto his father's house, I will go up, and show Pharaoh, and say unto him, My brethren, and my father's house, which *were* in the land of Canaan, are come unto me;

32 And the men *are* shepherds, for their trade hath been to feed cattle; and they have brought their flocks, and their herds, and all that they have.

33 And it shall come to pass, when Pharaoh shall call you, and shall say, What *is* your occupation?

34 That ye shall say, Thy servants' trade hath been about cattle from our youth even until now, both we, *and* also our fathers: that ye may dwell in the land of Goshen; for every shepherd *is* an abomination unto the Egyptians.

**47** THEN JOSEPH came and told Pharaoh, and said, My father and my brethren, and their flocks, and their herds, and all that they have, are come out of the land of Canaan; and, behold, they *are* in the land of Goshen.

2 And he took some of his brethren, *even* five men, and presented them unto Pharaoh.

3 And Pharaoh said unto his brethren, What *is* your occupation? And they said unto Pharaoh, Thy servants *are* shepherds, both we, *and* also our fathers.

4 They said moreover unto Pharaoh, For to sojourn in the land are we come; for thy servants have no pasture for their flocks; for the famine *is* sore in the land of Canaan: now therefore, we pray thee, let thy servants dwell in the land of Goshen.

5 And Pharaoh spake unto Joseph, saying, Thy father and thy brethren are come unto thee:

6 The land of Egypt *is* before thee; in the best of the land make thy father and brethren to dwell; in the land of Goshen let them dwell: and if thou knowest *any* men of activity among them, then make them rulers over my cattle.

7 And Joseph brought in Jacob his father, and set him before Pharaoh: and Jacob blessed Pharaoh.

8 And Pharaoh said unto Jacob, How old *art* thou?

9 And Jacob said unto Pharaoh, The days of the years of my pilgrimage *are* an hundred and thirty years: few and evil have the days of the years of my life been, and have not attained unto the days of the years of the life of my fathers in the days of their pilgrimage.

10 And Jacob blessed Pharaoh, and went out from before Pharaoh.

11 ¶ And Joseph placed his father and his brethren, and gave them a possession in the land of Egypt, in the best of the land, in the land of Rameses, as Pharaoh had commanded.

12 And Joseph nourished his father, and his brethren, and all his father's household, with bread, according to *their* families.

## Amplified

27 And the sons of Joseph, who were born to him in Egypt, were two persons; all the persons of the house of Jacob [including Joseph and himself], who came into Egypt, were seventy.

28 And he sent Judah before him to Joseph, to direct him to Goshen *and* meet him there; and they came into the land of Goshen.

29 Then Joseph made ready his chariot and went up to meet Israel his father in Goshen; and he presented himself *and* gave distinct evidence of himself to him [that he was Joseph]; and *each* fell on the *other's* neck and wept on his neck a good while.

30 And Israel said to Joseph, Now let me die, since I have seen your face, [and know] that you are still alive.

31 Joseph said to his brothers and to his father's household, I will go up and tell Pharaoh, and say to him, My brothers and my father's household, who were in the land of Canaan, have come to me;

32 And the men are shepherds, for their occupation has been keeping livestock; and they have brought their flocks, and their herds, and all that they have.

33 When Pharaoh calls you, and says, What is your occupation?

34 You shall say, Your servants' occupation has been keepers of livestock from our youth until now, both we and our fathers; in order that you may live in the land of Goshen; for every shepherd is an abomination to the Egyptians.

**47** THEN JOSEPH came and told Pharaoh, My father and my brothers, with their flocks and their herds and all that they own, have come from the land of Canaan; and they are in the land of Goshen.

2 And from among his brothers he took five men and presented them to Pharaoh.

3 And Pharaoh said to his brothers, What is your occupation? And they said to Pharaoh, Your servants are shepherds, both we and our fathers before us.

4 Moreover they said to Pharaoh, We have come to sojourn in the land, for your servants have no pasture for our flocks; for the famine is very severe in Canaan. So now, we pray you, let your servants dwell in the land of Goshen.

5 And Pharaoh spoke to Joseph, saying, Your father and your brothers have come to you.

6 The land of Egypt is before you; make your father and your brothers dwell in the best of the land, let them live in the land of Goshen. And if you know any men of ability among them, put them in charge of my cattle.

7 Then Joseph brought in Jacob his father and presented him before Pharaoh; and Jacob blessed Pharaoh.

8 And Pharaoh asked Jacob, How old are you?

9 Jacob said to Pharaoh, The days of the years of my pilgrimage are 130 years; few and evil have the days of the years of my life been, and they have [a]not attained to those of the life of my fathers in their pilgrimage.

10 And Jacob blessed Pharaoh, and went out from his presence.

11 Joseph settled his father and brethren and gave them a possession in Egypt, in the best of the land, in the land of Rameses [Goshen], as Pharaoh commanded.

12 And Joseph supplied his father and his brethren and all his father's household with food, according to [the needs of] their families.

**AMP** [a] Abraham, Jacob's grandfather, had lived to be 175 years old; Isaac, his father, lived to be 180. Jacob lived 17 years after making this statement to Pharaoh, in which time he had an opportunity to get a much more optimistic view of God's treatment of him. He died at 147, having said, "The redeeming Angel—that is, the Angel the Redeemer—has redeemed me continually from every evil" (48:16).

## New American Standard

27and the sons of Joseph, who were born to him in Egypt were two; all the persons of the house of Jacob, who came to Egypt, *were* seventy.

28¶ Now he sent Judah before him to Joseph, to point out *the way* before him to Goshen; and they came into the land of Goshen.

29And Joseph prepared his chariot and went up to Goshen to meet his father Israel; as soon as he appeared before him, he fell on his neck and wept on his neck a long time.

30Then Israel said to Joseph, "Now let me die, since I have seen your face, that you are still alive."

31And Joseph said to his brothers and to his father's household, "I will go up and tell Pharaoh, and will say to him, 'My brothers and my father's household, who *were* in the land of Canaan, have come to me;

32and the men are shepherds, for they have been keepers of livestock; and they have brought their flocks and their herds and all that they have.'

33"And it shall come about when Pharaoh calls you and says, 'What is your occupation?'

34that you shall say, 'Your servants have been keepers of livestock from our youth even until now, both we and our fathers,' that you may live in the land of Goshen; for every shepherd is loathsome to the Egyptians."

*Jacob's Family Settles in Goshen*

**47** THEN JOSEPH went in and told Pharaoh, and said, "My father and my brothers and their flocks and their herds and all that they have, have come out of the land of Canaan; and behold, they are in the land of Goshen."

2And he took five men from among his brothers, and presented them to Pharaoh.

3Then Pharaoh said to his brothers, "What is your occupation?" So they said to Pharaoh, "Your servants are shepherds, both we and our fathers."

4And they said to Pharaoh, "We have come to sojourn in the land, for there is no pasture for your servants' flocks, for the famine is severe in the land of Canaan. Now, therefore, please let your servants live in the land of Goshen."

5Then Pharaoh said to Joseph, "Your father and your brothers have come to you.

6"The land of Egypt is [b]at your disposal; settle your father and your brothers in the best of the land, let them live in the land of Goshen; and if you know any capable men among them, then put them in charge of my livestock."

7Then Joseph brought his father Jacob and presented him to Pharaoh; and Jacob blessed Pharaoh.

8And Pharaoh said to Jacob, "How many years have you lived?"

9So Jacob said to Pharaoh, "The years of my sojourning are one hundred and thirty; few and unpleasant have been the years of my life, nor have they attained the years that my fathers lived during the days of their sojourning."

10And Jacob blessed Pharaoh, and went out from his presence.

11So Joseph settled his father and his brothers, and gave them a possession in the land of Egypt, in the best of the land, in the land of Rameses, as Pharaoh had ordered.

12And Joseph provided his father and his brothers and all his father's household with food, according to their little ones.

NAS [b] Lit., *before you*

## New International

in Egypt, the members of Jacob's family, which went to Egypt, were seventy[c] in all.

28Now Jacob sent Judah ahead of him to Joseph to get directions to Goshen. When they arrived in the region of Goshen, 29Joseph had his chariot made ready and went to Goshen to meet his father Israel. As soon as Joseph appeared before him, he threw his arms around his father[d] and wept for a long time.

30Israel said to Joseph, "Now I am ready to die, since I have seen for myself that you are still alive."

31Then Joseph said to his brothers and to his father's household, "I will go up and speak to Pharaoh and will say to him, 'My brothers and my father's household, who were living in the land of Canaan, have come to me. 32The men are shepherds; they tend livestock, and they have brought along their flocks and herds and everything they own.' 33When Pharaoh calls you in and asks, 'What is your occupation?' 34you should answer, 'Your servants have tended livestock from our boyhood on, just as our fathers did.' Then you will be allowed to settle in the region of Goshen, for all shepherds are detestable to the Egyptians."

**47** JOSEPH WENT and told Pharaoh, "My father and brothers, with their flocks and herds and everything they own, have come from the land of Canaan and are now in Goshen." 2He chose five of his brothers and presented them before Pharaoh.

3Pharaoh asked the brothers, "What is your occupation?"

"Your servants are shepherds," they replied to Pharaoh, "just as our fathers were." 4They also said to him, "We have come to live here awhile, because the famine is severe in Canaan and your servants' flocks have no pasture. So now, please let your servants settle in Goshen."

5Pharaoh said to Joseph, "Your father and your brothers have come to you, 6and the land of Egypt is before you; settle your father and your brothers in the best part of the land. Let them live in Goshen. And if you know of any among them with special ability, put them in charge of my own livestock."

7Then Joseph brought his father Jacob in and presented him before Pharaoh. After Jacob blessed[e] Pharaoh, 8Pharaoh asked him, "How old are you?"

9And Jacob said to Pharaoh, "The years of my pilgrimage are a hundred and thirty. My years have been few and difficult, and they do not equal the years of the pilgrimage of my fathers." 10Then Jacob blessed[f] Pharaoh and went out from his presence.

11So Joseph settled his father and his brothers in Egypt and gave them property in the best part of the land, the district of Rameses, as Pharaoh directed. 12Joseph also provided his father and his brothers and all his father's household with food, according to the number of their children.

NIV [c] 27 Hebrew (see also Exodus 1:5 and footnote); Septuagint (see also Acts 7:14) *seventy-five* [d] 29 Hebrew *around him* [e] 7 Or *greeted* [f] 10 Or *said farewell to*

## King James

13¶ And *there was* no bread in all the land; for the famine *was* very sore, so that the land of Egypt and *all* the land of Canaan fainted by reason of the famine.

14 And Joseph gathered up all the money that was found in the land of Egypt, and in the land of Canaan, for the corn which they bought: and Joseph brought the money into Pharaoh's house.

15 And when money failed in the land of Egypt, and in the land of Canaan, all the Egyptians came unto Joseph, and said, Give us bread: for why should we die in thy presence? for the money faileth.

16 And Joseph said, Give your cattle; and I will give you for your cattle, if money fail.

17 And they brought their cattle unto Joseph: and Joseph gave them bread *in exchange* for horses, and for the flocks, and for the cattle of the herds, and for the asses: and he fed them with bread for all their cattle for that year.

18 When that year was ended, they came unto him the second year, and said unto him, We will not hide *it* from my lord, how that our money is spent; my lord also hath our herds of cattle; there is not aught left in the sight of my lord, but our bodies, and our lands:

19 Wherefore shall we die before thine eyes, both we and our land? buy us and our land for bread, and we and our land will be servants unto Pharaoh: and give *us* seed, that we may live, and not die, that the land be not desolate.

20 And Joseph bought all the land of Egypt for Pharaoh; for the Egyptians sold every man his field, because the famine prevailed over them: so the land became Pharaoh's.

21 And as for the people, he removed them to cities from *one* end of the borders of Egypt even to the *other* end thereof.

22 Only the land of the priests bought he not; for the priests had a portion *assigned them* of Pharaoh, and did eat their portion which Pharaoh gave them: wherefore they sold not their lands.

23 Then Joseph said unto the people, Behold, I have bought you this day and your land for Pharaoh: lo, *here is* seed for you, and ye shall sow the land.

24 And it shall come to pass in the increase, that ye shall give the fifth *part* unto Pharaoh, and four parts shall be your own, for seed of the field, and for your food, and for them of your households, and for food for your little ones.

25 And they said, Thou hast saved our lives: let us find grace in the sight of my lord, and we will be Pharaoh's servants.

26 And Joseph made it a law over the land of Egypt unto this day, *that* Pharaoh should have the fifth *part;* except the land of the priests only, *which* became not Pharaoh's.

27¶ And Israel dwelt in the land of Egypt, in the country of Goshen; and they had possessions therein, and grew, and multiplied exceedingly.

28 And Jacob lived in the land of Egypt seventeen years: so the whole age of Jacob was an hundred forty and seven years.

29 And the time drew nigh that Israel must die: and he called his son Joseph, and said unto him, If now I have found grace in thy sight, put, I pray thee, thy hand under my thigh, and deal kindly and truly with me; bury me not, I pray thee, in Egypt:

30 But I will lie with my fathers, and thou shalt carry me out of Egypt, and bury me in their buryingplace. And he said, I will do as thou hast said.

31 And he said, Swear unto me. And he sware unto him. And Israel bowed himself upon the bed's head.

## Amplified

13 [In course of time] there was no food in all the land; for the famine was distressingly severe, so that the land of Egypt and all the land of Canaan hung in doubt and wavered by reason of the hunger (privation, starvation) of the famine.

14 And Joseph gathered up all the money that was found in the land of Egypt and in the land of Canaan, *in payment* for the grain which they bought; and Joseph brought the money into Pharaoh's house.

15 And when the money was exhausted in the land of Egypt and in the land of Canaan, all the Egyptians came to Joseph, and said, Give us food! Why should we die before your very eyes? For we have no money left.

16 Joseph said, Give your livestock, and I will give you food in exchange for [them] if your money is gone.

17 So they brought their livestock to Joseph; and [he] gave them food in exchange for the horses, flocks, cattle of the herds, and the donkeys; and supplied them with food in exchange for all their livestock that year.

18 When that year was ended, they came to [Joseph] the second year, and said to him, We will not hide from my lord that our money is spent; my lord also has our herds of livestock; there is nothing left in the sight of my lord but our bodies and our lands.

19 Why should we perish before your eyes, both we and our land? Buy us and our land in exchange for food, and we and our land will be servants to Pharaoh; and give us seed [to plant], that we may live, and not die, and that the land may not be desolate.

20 And Joseph bought all the land of Egypt for Pharaoh; for the Egyptians sold every man his field, because of the overwhelming severity of the famine upon them. The land became Pharaoh's;

21 And as for the people, he removed them to cities *and* practically made slaves of them [at their own request], from one end of the borders of Egypt to the other.

22 Only the priests' land he did not buy, for the priests had a fixed pension from Pharaoh and lived on the amount Pharaoh gave them; so they did not sell their land.

23 Then Joseph said to the people, Behold, I have today bought you and your land for Pharaoh. Now here is seed for you, and you shall sow the land.

24 At [harvest time when you reap] the increase, you shall give one-fifth of it to Pharaoh, and four-fifths shall be your own, to use for seed for the field and as food for you and those of your households, and for your little ones.

25 And they said, You have saved our lives; let us find favor in the sight of my lord, and we will be Pharaoh's servants.

26 And Joseph made it a law over the land of Egypt to this day, that Pharaoh should have the fifth part [of the crops], except the priests' land only, which did not become Pharaoh's.

27 And Israel dwelt in the land of Egypt, in the country of Goshen; and they gained possessions there, and grew and multiplied exceedingly.

28 And Jacob lived in the land of Egypt 17 years; so Jacob reached the age of 147 years.

29 When the time drew near that Israel must die, he called his son Joseph and said to him, If now I have found favor in your sight, [a]put your hand under my thigh, and *promise to* deal loyally and faithfully with me. Do not bury me, I beg of you, in Egypt,

30 But let me lie with my fathers; you shall carry me out of Egypt and bury me in their burying place. And [Joseph] said, I will do as you have directed.

31 Then Jacob said, Swear to me [that you will do it]. And he swore to him. And Israel bowed himself upon the head of the bed.

**AMP** [a] This was a customary manner of taking a solemn oath. The gesture was a reference to the mark of circumcision, the sign of God's covenant; which is equivalent to our laying our hand upon the Bible. (Clarke's *Commentary*, adapted).

## New American Standard

13¶ Now there was no food in all the land, because the famine
was very severe, so that the land of Egypt and the land of Canaan
languished because of the famine.
14And Joseph gathered all the money that was found in the land
of Egypt and in the land of Canaan for the grain which they
bought, and Joseph brought the money into Pharaoh's house.
15And when the money was all spent in the land of Egypt and
in the land of Canaan, all the Egyptians came to Joseph and said,
"Give us food, for why should we die in your presence? For *our*
money is gone."
16Then Joseph said, "Give up your livestock, and I will give you
*food* for your livestock, since *your* money is gone."
17So they brought their livestock to Joseph, and Joseph gave
them food in exchange for the horses and the flocks and the herds
and the donkeys; and he fed them with food in exchange for all
their livestock that year.
18And when that year was ended, they came to him the next
year and said to him, "We will not hide from my lord that our
money is all spent, and the cattle are my lord's. There is nothing
left for my lord except our bodies and our lands.
19"Why should we die before your eyes, both we and our land?
Buy us and our land for food, and we and our land will be slaves
to Pharaoh. So give us seed, that we may live and not die, and that
the land may not be desolate."

*Result of the Famine*

20¶ So Joseph bought all the land of Egypt for Pharaoh, for every
Egyptian sold his field, because the famine was severe upon them.
Thus the land became Pharaoh's.
21And as for the people, he removed them to the cities from one
end of Egypt's border to the other.
22Only the land of the priests he did not buy, for the priests had
an allotment from Pharaoh, and they lived off the allotment which
Pharaoh gave them. Therefore, they did not sell their land.
23Then Joseph said to the people, "Behold, I have today bought
you and your land for Pharaoh; now, *here* is seed for you, and you
may sow the land.
24"And at the harvest you shall give a fifth to Pharaoh, and
four-fifths shall be your own for seed of the field and for your food
and for those of your households and as food for your little ones."
25So they said, "You have saved our lives! Let us find favor in
the sight of my lord, and we will be Pharaoh's slaves."
26And Joseph made it a statute concerning the land of Egypt
*valid* to this day, that Pharaoh should have the fifth; only the land
of the priests did not become Pharaoh's.
27¶ Now Israel lived in the land of Egypt, in Goshen, and they
acquired property in it and were fruitful and became very numerous.
28And Jacob lived in the land of Egypt seventeen years; so the
length of Jacob's life was one hundred and forty-seven years.
29When the time for Israel to die drew near, he called his son
Joseph and said to him, "Please, if I have found favor in your sight,
place now your hand under my thigh and deal with me in kindness
and [b]faithfulness. Please do not bury me in Egypt,
30but when I lie down with my fathers, you shall carry me out
of Egypt and bury me in their burial place." And he said, "I will
do as you have said."
31And he said, "Swear to me." So he swore to him. Then Israel
bowed *in worship* at the head of the bed.

NAS [b] Lit., *truth*

## New International

*Joseph and the Famine*

13There was no food, however, in the whole region because the
famine was severe; both Egypt and Canaan wasted away because
of the famine. 14Joseph collected all the money that was to be
found in Egypt and Canaan in payment for the grain they were
buying, and he brought it to Pharaoh's palace. 15When the money
of the people of Egypt and Canaan was gone, all Egypt came to
Joseph and said, "Give us food. Why should we die before your
eyes? Our money is used up."
16"Then bring your livestock," said Joseph. "I will sell you food
in exchange for your livestock, since your money is gone." 17So
they brought their livestock to Joseph, and he gave them food in
exchange for their horses, their sheep and goats, their cattle and
donkeys. And he brought them through that year with food in
exchange for all their livestock.
18When that year was over, they came to him the following year
and said, "We cannot hide from our lord the fact that since our
money is gone and our livestock belongs to you, there is nothing
left for our lord except our bodies and our land. 19Why should we
perish before your eyes—we and our land as well? Buy us and our
land in exchange for food, and we with our land will be in bondage
to Pharaoh. Give us seed so that we may live and not die, and that
the land may not become desolate."
20So Joseph bought all the land in Egypt for Pharaoh. The
Egyptians, one and all, sold their fields, because the famine was
too severe for them. The land became Pharaoh's, 21and Joseph
reduced the people to servitude,[c] from one end of Egypt to the
other. 22However, he did not buy the land of the priests, because
they received a regular allotment from Pharaoh and had food
enough from the allotment Pharaoh gave them. That is why they
did not sell their land.
23Joseph said to the people, "Now that I have bought you and
your land today for Pharaoh, here is seed for you so you can plant
the ground. 24But when the crop comes in, give a fifth of it to
Pharaoh. The other four-fifths you may keep as seed for the fields
and as food for yourselves and your households and your children."
25"You have saved our lives," they said. "May we find favor in
the eyes of our lord; we will be in bondage to Pharaoh."
26So Joseph established it as a law concerning land in Egypt—
still in force today—that a fifth of the produce belongs to Pharaoh.
It was only the land of the priests that did not become Pharaoh's.
27Now the Israelites settled in Egypt in the region of Goshen.
They acquired property there and were fruitful and increased
greatly in number.
28Jacob lived in Egypt seventeen years, and the years of his life
were a hundred and forty-seven. 29When the time drew near for
Israel to die, he called for his son Joseph and said to him, "If I have
found favor in your eyes, put your hand under my thigh and
promise that you will show me kindness and faithfulness. Do not
bury me in Egypt, 30but when I rest with my fathers, carry me out
of Egypt and bury me where they are buried."
"I will do as you say," he said.
31"Swear to me," he said. Then Joseph swore to him, and Israel
worshiped as he leaned on the top of his staff.[d]

**NIV** [c] *21* Samaritan Pentateuch and Septuagint (see also Vulgate); Masoretic Text *and he moved the people into the cities* [d] *31* Or *Israel bowed down at the head of his bed*

## King James

**48** AND IT came to pass after these things, that *one* told Joseph, Behold, thy father *is* sick: and he took with him his two sons, Manasseh and Ephraim.

2And *one* told Jacob, and said, Behold, thy son Joseph cometh unto thee: and Israel strengthened himself, and sat upon the bed.

3And Jacob said unto Joseph, God Almighty appeared unto me at Luz in the land of Canaan, and blessed me,

4And said unto me, Behold, I will make thee fruitful, and multiply thee, and I will make of thee a multitude of people; and will give this land to thy seed after thee *for* an everlasting possession.

5¶ And now thy two sons, Ephraim and Manasseh, which were born unto thee in the land of Egypt before I came unto thee into Egypt, *are* mine; as Reuben and Simeon, they shall be mine.

6And thy issue, which thou begettest after them, shall be thine, *and* shall be called after the name of their brethren in their inheritance.

7And as for me, when I came from Padan, Rachel died by me in the land of Canaan in the way, when yet *there was* but a little way to come unto Ephrath: and I buried her there in the way of Ephrath; the same *is* Bethlehem.

8And Israel beheld Joseph's sons, and said, Who *are* these?

9And Joseph said unto his father, They *are* my sons, whom God hath given me in this *place*. And he said, Bring them, I pray thee, unto me, and I will bless them.

10Now the eyes of Israel were dim for age, *so that* he could not see. And he brought them near unto him; and he kissed them, and embraced them.

11And Israel said unto Joseph, I had not thought to see thy face: and, lo, God hath shown me also thy seed.

12And Joseph brought them out from between his knees, and he bowed himself with his face to the earth.

13And Joseph took them both, Ephraim in his right hand toward Israel's left hand, and Manasseh in his left hand toward Israel's right hand, and brought *them* near unto him.

14And Israel stretched out his right hand, and laid *it* upon Ephraim's head, who *was* the younger, and his left hand upon Manasseh's head, guiding his hands wittingly; for Manasseh *was* the firstborn.

15¶ And he blessed Joseph, and said, God, before whom my fathers Abraham and Isaac did walk, the God which fed me all my life long unto this day,

16The Angel which redeemed me from all evil, bless the lads; and let my name be named on them, and the name of my fathers Abraham and Isaac; and let them grow into a multitude in the midst of the earth.

17And when Joseph saw that his father laid his right hand upon the head of Ephraim, it displeased him: and he held up his father's hand, to remove it from Ephraim's head unto Manasseh's head.

18And Joseph said unto his father, Not so, my father: for this *is* the firstborn; put thy right hand upon his head.

19And his father refused, and said, I know *it*, my son, I know *it:* he also shall become a people, and he also shall be great: but truly his younger brother shall be greater than he, and his seed shall become a multitude of nations.

20And he blessed them that day, saying, In thee shall Israel bless, saying, God make thee as Ephraim and as Manasseh: and he set Ephraim before Manasseh.

## Amplified

**48** SOME TIME after these things occurred, someone told Joseph, Behold, your father is sick; and he took with him his two sons, Manasseh and Ephraim [and went to Goshen].

2When Jacob was told, Your son Joseph has come to you, Israel collected his strength and sat up on the bed.

3And Jacob said to Joseph, God Almighty appeared to me at Luz [Bethel] in the land of Canaan and blessed me,

4And said to me, Behold, I will make you fruitful and multiply you, and I will make of you a multitude of people; and will give this land to your descendants after you as an everlasting possession. [Gen. 28:13-22; 35:6-15.]

5And now your two sons, [Ephraim and Manasseh], who were born to you in the land of Egypt before I came to you in Egypt, are mine. [I am adopting them, and now] as Reuben and Simeon, [they] shall be mine.

6But other sons, who may be born after them, shall be your own, and shall be called after the names of *these two* brothers *and* reckoned as belonging to them [when they come] into their inheritance.

7And as for me, when I came from Padan, Rachel died at my side in the land of Canaan on the way, when yet there was but a little way to come to Ephrath; and I buried her there on the way to Ephrath, that is, Bethlehem.

8When Israel [almost blind] saw Joseph's sons, he said, Who are these?

9And Joseph said to his father, They are my sons, whom God has given me in this place. And he said, Bring them to me, I pray you, that I may bless them.

10Now Israel's eyes were dim from age, so that he could not see. And Joseph brought them near to him; and he kissed and embraced them.

11Israel said to Joseph, I had not thought to see your face; but see, God has shown me your offspring also.

12Then Joseph *took* [the boys] *from* [his father's embrace], and he bowed [before him] with his face to the earth.

13Then Joseph took both [boys], Ephraim with his right hand toward Israel's left, and Manasseh with his left hand toward Israel's right, and brought them close to him.

14And Israel reached out his right hand, and laid it on the head of Ephraim, who was the younger, and his left hand on Manasseh's head, [a]crossing his hands intentionally for Manasseh was the first-born.

15Then [Jacob] blessed Joseph and said, God (Himself) before Whom my fathers Abraham and Isaac lived *and* walked habitually, God (Himself) Who has [been my Shepherd and has led and] fed me since I came into being until this day,

16The redeeming Angel—that is, the Angel the Redeemer [not a created being, but the Lord Himself]—Who has redeemed me continually from every evil, bless the lads! And let my name be perpetuated in them, [may they be worthy of having their names coupled with mine] and the names of my fathers Abraham and Isaac; and let them become a multitude in the midst of the earth.

17When Joseph saw that his father laid his right hand on Ephraim's head, it displeased him; and he held up his father's hand, to remove it to Manasseh's head.

18And Joseph said, Not so, my father, for this is the first-born; put your right hand upon his head.

19But his father refused, and said, I know, my son, I know; he also shall become a people, and shall be great; but his younger brother shall be [b]greater than he, and his offspring shall become a multitude of nations.

20And he blessed them that day, saying, By you shall Israel bless [one another], saying, God make you as Ephraim and as Manasseh; and he set Ephraim before Manasseh.

**AMP** [a] God acts independently of the claims of priority based on time of birth when He chooses men. He too "crossed His hands" in the case of Seth over Cain; of Shem over Japheth; of Isaac over Ishmael; of Jacob over Esau; of Judah and Joseph over Reuben; of Moses over Aaron; of David, whom He chose over all his brothers; and of Mary over Martha. [b] This prophecy begins to be fulfilled "from the days of the Judges onward, as the tribe of Ephraim in power and compass so increased that it became the head of the northern ten tribes, and its name became of like significance with that of Israel; although, in the time of Moses, Manasseh still outnumbered Ephraim by 20,000" (Keil). Joshua, whom Israel so long regarded as their ruler, was an Ephraimite, the ark of the covenant was placed in Shiloh in the territory of Ephraim, which increased the tribe's prestige. How could Jacob have prophesied Ephraim's supremacy so positively, except by divine inspiration?

## New American Standard

*Israel's Last Days*

**48** NOW IT came about after these things that Joseph was
told, "Behold, your father is sick." So he took his two sons
Manasseh and Ephraim with him.
2When it was told to Jacob, "Behold, your son Joseph has come
to you," Israel collected his strength and sat up in the bed.
3Then Jacob said to Joseph, "God Almighty appeared to me at
Luz in the land of Canaan and blessed me,
4and He said to me, 'Behold, I will make you fruitful and
numerous, and I will make you a company of peoples, and will
give this land to your descendants after you for an everlasting
possession.'
5"And now your two sons, who were born to you in the land
of Egypt before I came to you in Egypt, are mine; Ephraim and
Manasseh shall be mine, as Reuben and Simeon are.
6"But your offspring that have been born after them shall be
yours; they shall be called by the names of their brothers in their
inheritance.
7"Now as for me, when I came from Paddan, Rachel died, to
my sorrow, in the land of Canaan on the journey, when there was
still some distance to go to Ephrath; and I buried her there on the
way to Ephrath (that is, Bethlehem)."
8¶ When Israel saw Joseph's sons, he said, "Who are these?"
9And Joseph said to his father, "They are my sons, whom God
has given me here." So he said, "Bring them to me, please, that
I may bless them."
10Now the eyes of Israel were so dim from age *that* he could not
see. Then Joseph brought them close to him, and he kissed them
and embraced them.
11And Israel said to Joseph, "I never expected to see your face,
and behold, God has let me see your children as well."
12Then Joseph took them from his knees, and bowed with his
face to the ground.
13And Joseph took them both, Ephraim with his right hand
toward Israel's left, and Manasseh with his left hand toward Israel's right, and brought them close to him.
14But Israel stretched out his right hand and laid it on the head
of Ephraim, who was the younger, and his left hand on Manasseh's head, crossing his hands, although Manasseh was the
first-born.
15And he blessed Joseph, and said,
"The God before whom my fathers Abraham and Isaac
walked,
The God who has been my shepherd all my life to this
day,
16 The angel who has redeemed me from all evil,
Bless the lads;
And may my name live on in them,
And the names of my fathers Abraham and Isaac;
And may they grow into a multitude in the midst of the
earth."
17When Joseph saw that his father laid his right hand on
Ephraim's head, it displeased him; and he grasped his father's
hand to remove it from Ephraim's head to Manasseh's head.
18And Joseph said to his father, "Not so, my father, for this one
is the first-born. Place your right hand on his head."
19But his father refused and said, "I know, my son, I know; he
also shall become a people and he also shall be great. However,
his younger brother shall be greater than he, and his descendants
shall become a multitude of nations."
20And he blessed them that day, saying,
"By you Israel shall pronounce blessing, saying,
'May God make you like Ephraim and Manasseh!' "
Thus he put Ephraim before Manasseh.

## New International

*Manasseh and Ephraim*

**48** SOME TIME later Joseph was told, "Your father is ill." So
he took his two sons Manasseh and Ephraim along with
him. 2When Jacob was told, "Your son Joseph has come to you,"
Israel rallied his strength and sat up on the bed.
3Jacob said to Joseph, "God Almighty[c] appeared to me at Luz
in the land of Canaan, and there he blessed me 4and said to me,
'I am going to make you fruitful and will increase your numbers.
I will make you a community of peoples, and I will give this land
as an everlasting possession to your descendants after you.'
5"Now then, your two sons born to you in Egypt before I came
to you here will be reckoned as mine; Ephraim and Manasseh will
be mine, just as Reuben and Simeon are mine. 6Any children born
to you after them will be yours; in the territory they inherit they
will be reckoned under the names of their brothers. 7As I was
returning from Paddan,[d] to my sorrow Rachel died in the land of
Canaan while we were still on the way, a little distance from
Ephrath. So I buried her there beside the road to Ephrath" (that
is, Bethlehem).
8When Israel saw the sons of Joseph, he asked, "Who are
these?"
9"They are the sons God has given me here," Joseph said to his
father.
Then Israel said, "Bring them to me so I may bless them."
10Now Israel's eyes were failing because of old age, and he
could hardly see. So Joseph brought his sons close to him, and his
father kissed them and embraced them.
11Israel said to Joseph, "I never expected to see your face again,
and now God has allowed me to see your children too."
12Then Joseph removed them from Israel's knees and bowed
down with his face to the ground. 13And Joseph took both of them,
Ephraim on his right toward Israel's left hand and Manasseh on
his left toward Israel's right hand, and brought them close to him.
14But Israel reached out his right hand and put it on Ephraim's
head, though he was the younger, and crossing his arms, he put
his left hand on Manasseh's head, even though Manasseh was the
firstborn.
15Then he blessed Joseph and said,
"May the God before whom my fathers
Abraham and Isaac walked,
the God who has been my shepherd
all my life to this day,
16the Angel who has delivered me from all harm
—may he bless these boys.
May they be called by my name
and the names of my fathers Abraham and Isaac,
and may they increase greatly
upon the earth."
17When Joseph saw his father placing his right hand on
Ephraim's head he was displeased; so he took hold of his father's
hand to move it from Ephraim's head to Manasseh's head. 18Jo-
seph said to him, "No, my father, this one is the firstborn; put your
right hand on his head."
19But his father refused and said, "I know, my son, I know. He
too will become a people, and he too will become great. Nevertheless, his younger brother will be greater than he, and his descendants will become a group of nations." 20He blessed them that day
and said,
"In your[e] name will Israel pronounce this blessing:
'May God make you like Ephraim and Manasseh.' "
So he put Ephraim ahead of Manasseh.

NIV [c] 3 Hebrew *El-Shaddai* [d] 7 That is, Northwest Mesopotamia [e] 20 The Hebrew is singular.

## King James

21And Israel said unto Joseph, Behold, I die: but God shall be with you, and bring you again unto the land of your fathers.

22Moreover I have given to thee one portion above thy brethren, which I took out of the hand of the Amorite with my sword and with my bow.

**49** AND JACOB called unto his sons, and said, Gather yourselves together, that I may tell you *that* which shall befall you in the last days.

2Gather yourselves together, and hear, ye sons of Jacob; and hearken unto Israel your father.

3¶ Reuben, thou *art* my firstborn, my might, and the beginning of my strength, the excellency of dignity, and the excellency of power:

4Unstable as water, thou shalt not excel; because thou wentest up to thy father's bed; then defiledst thou *it:* he went up to my couch.

5¶ Simeon and Levi *are* brethren; instruments of cruelty *are in* their habitations.

6O my soul, come not thou into their secret; unto their assembly, mine honour, be not thou united: for in their anger they slew a man, and in their selfwill they digged down a wall.

7Cursed *be* their anger, for *it was* fierce; and their wrath, for it was cruel: I will divide them in Jacob, and scatter them in Israel.

8¶ Judah, thou *art he* whom thy brethren shall praise: thy hand *shall be* in the neck of thine enemies; thy father's children shall bow down before thee.

9Judah *is* a lion's whelp: from the prey, my son, thou art gone up: he stooped down, he couched as a lion, and as an old lion; who shall rouse him up?

10The sceptre shall not depart from Judah, nor a lawgiver from between his feet, until Shiloh come; and unto him *shall* the gathering of the people *be*.

11Binding his foal unto the vine, and his ass's colt unto the choice vine; he washed his garments in wine, and his clothes in the blood of grapes:

12His eyes *shall be* red with wine, and his teeth white with milk.

13¶ Zebulun shall dwell at the haven of the sea; and he *shall be* for an haven of ships; and his border *shall be* unto Zidon.

14¶ Issachar *is* a strong ass couching down between two burdens:

15And he saw that rest *was* good, and the land that *it was* pleasant; and bowed his shoulder to bear, and became a servant unto tribute.

16¶ Dan shall judge his people, as one of the tribes of Israel.

## Amplified

21And Israel said to Joseph, Lo, I [am about to] die; but God will be with you, and bring you again to the land of your fathers.

22Moreover I have given to you [Joseph] one portion—Shechem, one mountain slope—more than any of your brethren, which I took [reclaiming it] out of the hand of the Amorites with my sword and with my bow. [Gen. 33:18, 19; John 4:5; Josh. 24:32, 33.]

**49** AND JACOB called to his sons, and said, Gather yourselves together [around me], that I may tell you what shall befall you [a]in the latter *or* last days.

2Gather yourselves together, and hear, you sons of Jacob, and hearken to Israel your father.

3Reuben, you are my [b]first-born, my might and the beginning (the first fruits) of my manly strength *and* vigor; [your birthright gave you] the pre-eminence in dignity and the pre-eminence in power.

4But unstable *and* boiling over like water you shall [c]not excel *and* have the pre-eminence [of the first-born], because you went to your father's bed; you defiled it; he went to my couch! [Gen. 35:22.]

5Simeon and Levi are brothers [alike headstrong, deceitful, vindictive and cruel]; their swords are weapons of violence. [Gen. 34:25-29.]

6O my soul, come not into their secret council; unto their assembly, my honor, be not united [for I knew nothing in their plot]; because in their anger they slew men [an honored man, Shechem and the Shechemites], and in their self-will they disabled oxen.

7Cursed be their anger, for it was fierce; and their wrath, for it was cruel. I will divide them in Jacob and [d]scatter them in Israel.

8Judah, you are the one whom your brothers shall praise. Your hand shall be on the neck of your enemies; your father's sons shall bow down to you.

9Judah, a lion's cub! With the prey, my son, you have gone high up [the mountain]; he stooped down, he crouched as a lion, and as a lioness; who dares provoke *and* rouse him? [Rev. 5:5.]

10The scepter *or* leadership shall not depart from Judah, nor the ruler's staff from between his feet until Shiloh [the Messiah, the Peaceful One] comes to Whom it belongs, and to Him shall be the obedience of the people. [Num. 24:17; Ps. 60:7.]

11Binding His foal to the vine, and His donkey's colt to the choice vine, He washes His garments in wine, and His clothes in the blood of grapes: [Zech. 9:9; Isa. 63:1-3; Rev. 19:11-16.]

12His eyes are darker *and* more sparkling than wine, and His teeth whiter than milk.

13Zebulun shall live toward the seashore, and he shall be toward a haven *and* a landing place for ships, and his border shall be toward Sidon.

14Issachar is a strong-boned donkey crouching down between the sheepfolds.

15And he saw that rest was good, and that the land was pleasant; and bowed his shoulder to bear (his burdens), and became a servant to tribute.

16Dan shall judge his people as one of the tribes of Israel.

**AMP** [a] Compare Deut. 33 in which Moses blesses these same tribes in a similar prophetic way. [b] Reuben was the eldest of Jacob's twelve sons and therefore entitled to the birthright, which would make him successor to his father as head of the family or tribe, and he would inherit a double portion of his father's estate. But Reuben forfeited all this by his conduct with Bilhah, his father's concubine (Gen. 35:22). By adopting Joseph's two sons, Ephraim and Manasseh, and giving each of them a portion of the inheritance, Jacob virtually gave Joseph Reuben's extra portion of the land; but Judah became the tribal leader in Reuben's place (vs. 8-10). [c] The whole fertile territory once occupied by the tribe of Reuben has long since been deserted by its settled inhabitants and is given up to the nomad tribes of the desert. Reuben did "not excel," and even before Jacob's death he had lost his "pre-eminence of the first-born" (Davis' *Dictionary of the Bible*). [d] This was literally fulfilled. Levi got no inheritance except 48 towns, scattered through different parts of Canaan. As to Simeon, they were originally given only a few towns and villages in Judah's lot (Josh. 19:1). Afterward, needing more room, they formed colonies in districts which they conquered from the Idumeans and the Amalekites [I Chron. 4:39, 40]. (Clarke's *Commentary*, adapted).

# New American Standard

21Then Israel said to Joseph, "Behold, I am about to die, but God will be with you, and bring you back to the land of your fathers.

22"And I give you one portion more than your brothers, which I took from the hand of the Amorite with my sword and my bow."

*Israel's Prophecy concerning His Sons*

**49** THEN JACOB summoned his sons and said, "Assemble yourselves that I may tell you what shall befall you in the days to come.

2 "Gather together and hear, O sons of Jacob;
And listen to Israel your father.

3¶ "Reuben, you are my first-born;
My might and the beginning of my strength,
Preeminent in dignity and preeminent in power.
4 "Uncontrolled as water, you shall not have preeminence,
Because you went up to your father's bed;
Then you defiled *it*—he went up to my couch.

5¶ "Simeon and Levi are brothers;
Their swords are implements of violence.
6 "Let my soul not enter into their council;
Let not my glory be united with their assembly;
Because in their anger they slew men,
And in their self-will they lamed oxen.
7 "Cursed be their anger, for it is fierce;
And their wrath, for it is cruel.
I will disperse them in Jacob,
And scatter them in Israel.

8¶ "Judah, your brothers shall praise you;
Your hand shall be on the neck of your enemies;
Your father's sons shall bow down to you.
9 "Judah is a lion's whelp;
From the prey, my son, you have gone up.
He couches, he lies down as a lion,
And as a lion, who dares rouse him up?
10 "The scepter shall not depart from Judah,
Nor the ruler's staff from between his feet,
[e]Until Shiloh comes,
And to him *shall be* the obedience of the peoples.
11 "He ties *his* foal to the vine,
And his donkey's colt to the choice vine;
He washes his garments in wine,
And his robes in the blood of grapes.
12 "His eyes are [f]dull from wine,
And his teeth [g]white from milk.

13¶ "Zebulun shall dwell at the seashore;
And he *shall be* a haven for ships,
And his flank *shall be* toward Sidon.

14¶ "Issachar is a strong donkey,
Lying down between the sheepfolds.
15 "When he saw that a resting place was good
And that the land was pleasant,
He bowed his shoulder to bear *burdens*,
And became a slave at forced labor.

16¶ "Dan shall judge his people,
As one of the tribes of Israel.

**NAS** [e] Or, *Until he comes to Shiloh* [f] Or, *darker than* [g] Or, *whiter than*

# New International

21Then Israel said to Joseph, "I am about to die, but God will be with you[h] and take you[i] back to the land of your[j] fathers. 22And to you, as one who is over your brothers, I give the ridge of land[k] I took from the Amorites with my sword and my bow."

*Jacob Blesses His Sons*

**49** THEN JACOB called for his sons and said: "Gather around so I can tell you what will happen to you in days to come.

2"Assemble and listen, sons of Jacob;
listen to your father Israel.

3"Reuben, you are my firstborn,
my might, the first sign of my strength,
excelling in honor, excelling in power.
4Turbulent as the waters, you will no longer excel,
for you went up onto your father's bed,
onto my couch and defiled it.

5"Simeon and Levi are brothers—
their swords[l] are weapons of violence.
6Let me not enter their council,
let me not join their assembly,
for they have killed men in their anger
and hamstrung oxen as they pleased.
7Cursed be their anger, so fierce,
and their fury, so cruel!
I will scatter them in Jacob
and disperse them in Israel.

8"Judah,[m] your brothers will praise you;
your hand will be on the neck of your enemies;
your father's sons will bow down to you.
9You are a lion's cub, O Judah;
you return from the prey, my son.
Like a lion he crouches and lies down,
like a lioness—who dares to rouse him?
10The scepter will not depart from Judah,
nor the ruler's staff from between his feet,
until he comes to whom it belongs[n]
and the obedience of the nations is his.
11He will tether his donkey to a vine,
his colt to the choicest branch;
he will wash his garments in wine,
his robes in the blood of grapes.
12His eyes will be darker than wine,
his teeth whiter than milk.[o]

13"Zebulun will live by the seashore
and become a haven for ships;
his border will extend toward Sidon.

14"Issachar is a rawboned[p] donkey
lying down between two saddlebags.[q]
15When he sees how good is his resting place
and how pleasant is his land,
he will bend his shoulder to the burden
and submit to forced labor.

16"Dan[r] will provide justice for his people
as one of the tribes of Israel.

**NIV** [h] *21* The Hebrew is plural. [i] *21* The Hebrew is plural. [j] *21* The Hebrew is plural. [k] *22* Or *And to you I give one portion more than to your brothers—the portion* [l] *5* The meaning of the Hebrew for this word is uncertain. [m] *8 Judah* sounds like and may be derived from the Hebrew for *praise.* [n] *10* Or *until Shiloh comes;* or *until he comes to whom tribute belongs* [o] *12* Or *will be dull from wine, / his teeth white from milk* [p] *14* Or *strong* [q] *14* Or *campfires* [r] *16 Dan* here means *he provides justice.*

## King James

17Dan shall be a serpent by the way, an adder in the path, that biteth the horse heels, so that his rider shall fall backward.

18I have waited for thy salvation, O LORD.

19¶ Gad, a troop shall overcome him: but he shall overcome at the last.

20¶ Out of Asher his bread *shall be* fat, and he shall yield royal dainties.

21¶ Naphtali *is* a hind let loose: he giveth goodly words.

22¶ Joseph *is* a fruitful bough, *even* a fruitful bough by a well; *whose* branches run over the wall:

23The archers have sorely grieved him, and shot *at him,* and hated him:

24But his bow abode in strength, and the arms of his hands were made strong by the hands of the mighty *God* of Jacob; (from thence *is* the shepherd, the stone of Israel:)

25 *Even* by the God of thy father, who shall help thee; and by the Almighty, who shall bless thee with blessings of heaven above, blessings of the deep that lieth under, blessings of the breasts, and of the womb:

26The blessings of thy father have prevailed above the blessings of my progenitors unto the utmost bound of the everlasting hills: they shall be on the head of Joseph, and on the crown of the head of him that was separate from his brethren.

27¶ Benjamin shall ravin *as* a wolf: in the morning he shall devour the prey, and at night he shall divide the spoil.

28¶ All these *are* the twelve tribes of Israel: and this *is it* that their father spake unto them, and blessed them; every one according to his blessing he blessed them.

29And he charged them, and said unto them, I am to be gathered unto my people: bury me with my fathers in the cave that *is* in the field of Ephron the Hittite,

30In the cave that *is* in the field of Machpelah, which *is* before Mamre, in the land of Canaan, which Abraham bought with the field of Ephron the Hittite for a possession of a buryingplace.

31There they buried Abraham and Sarah his wife; there they buried Isaac and Rebekah his wife; and there I buried Leah.

32The purchase of the field and of the cave that *is* therein *was* from the children of Heth.

33And when Jacob had made an end of commanding his sons, he gathered up his feet into the bed, and yielded up the ghost, and was gathered unto his people.

**50** AND JOSEPH fell upon his father's face, and wept upon him, and kissed him.

2And Joseph commanded his servants the physicians to embalm his father: and the physicians embalmed Israel.

3And forty days were fulfilled for him; for so are fulfilled the days of those which are embalmed: and the Egyptians mourned for him threescore and ten days.

## Amplified

17Dan shall be a serpent by the way, a horned snake in the path, that bites at the horse's heels, so that his rider shall fall backward.

18I wait for thy salvation, O Lord.

19Gad, a raiding troop shall raid him, but he shall raid at their heels *and* assault them [victoriously].

20Asher's food [supply] shall be rich *and* fat, and he shall yield *and* deliver royal delights.

21Naphtali shall be a hind let loose, which yields lovely fawns.

22Joseph is a fruitful bough, a fruitful bough by a well (spring or fountain), whose branches run over the wall.

23Skilled archers have bitterly attacked *and* sorely worried him; they have shot at him and persecuted him.

24But his bow remained strong *and* steady *and* rested in the strength that does not fail him, for the arms of his hands were made strong *and* active by the hands of the mighty God of Jacob, by the name of the Shepherd, the Rock of Israel;

25By the God of your father Who will help you, and by the Almighty Who will bless you with blessings of the heavens above, blessings lying in the deep beneath, blessings of the breasts and of the womb.

26The blessings of your father [on you] are greater than the blessings of my forefathers [Abraham and Isaac on me], *and* are lasting as the bounties of the eternal hills; they shall be on the head of Joseph, and on the crown of the head of him who was the consecrated one *and* was separate from his brethren *and* is prince among *them.*

27Benjamin is a [a]ravenous wolf, in the morning devouring the prey, and at night dividing the spoil.

28All these are the twelve tribes of Israel, and this is what their father said to them as he blessed them, blessing each one according to the blessing suited to him.

29He charged them and said to them, I am to be gathered to my [departed] people; bury me with my fathers in the cave that is in the field of Ephron the Hittite,

30In the cave in the field at Machpelah, east of Mamre, in the land of Canaan, that Abraham bought with the field of Ephron the Hittite to possess as a cemetery. [Gen. 23:17-20.]

31There they buried Abraham and Sarah his wife; there they buried Isaac and Rebekah his wife; and there I buried Leah.

32The purchase of the field and the cave that is in it was from the sons of Heth.

33When Jacob had finished commanding his sons, he drew his feet up into the bed, and breathed his last, and was gathered to his [departed] people.

**50** THEN JOSEPH fell upon his father's face, and wept over him and kissed him.

2And Joseph ordered his servants the physicians to embalm his father, so the physicians embalmed Israel.

3Then forty days were devoted [to this purpose] for him, for that is the customary number of days required for those who are embalmed; and the Egyptians wept and bemoaned him [as for royalty] for seventy days.

**AMP** [a] The tribe of Benjamin is fitly compared to a ravenous wolf, because of the rude courage and ferocity which they invariably displayed, particularly in their war with the other tribes, in which they killed more men than all of their own numbers combined (Clarke's *Commentary*). The tribe was absorbed by the tribe of Judah and is not mentioned after the return from the Babylonian captivity, except in connection with its former land or as the source of some individual person. Ehud, Saul, Jonathan, and the Apostle Paul were Benjamites.

## New American Standard

17 "Dan shall be a serpent in the way,
A horned snake in the path,
That bites the horse's heels,
So that his rider falls backward.
18 "For Thy salvation I wait, O LORD.

19¶ "As for Gad, raiders shall raid him,
But he shall raid *at* their heels.

20¶ "As for Asher, his food shall be rich,
And he shall yield royal dainties.

21¶ "Naphtali is a doe let loose,
He gives beautiful words.

22¶ "Joseph is a fruitful [b]bough,
A fruitful bough by a spring;
*Its* [c]branches run over a wall.
23 "The archers bitterly attacked him,
And shot *at him* and harassed him;
24 But his bow remained firm,
And his arms were agile,
From the hands of the Mighty One of Jacob
(From there is the Shepherd, the Stone of Israel),
25 From the God of your father who helps you,
And by the Almighty who blesses you
*With* blessings of heaven above,
Blessings of the deep that lies beneath,
Blessings of the breasts and of the womb.
26 "The blessings of your father
Have surpassed the blessings of my ancestors
Up to the utmost bound of the everlasting hills;
May they be on the head of Joseph,
And on the crown of the head of the one distinguished among his brothers.

27¶ "Benjamin is a ravenous wolf;
In the morning he devours the prey,
And in the evening he divides the spoil."

28¶ All these are the twelve tribes of Israel, and this is what their father said to them when he blessed them. He blessed them, every one with the blessing appropriate to him.

29 Then he charged them and said to them, "I am about to be gathered to my people; bury me with my fathers in the cave that is in the field of Ephron the Hittite,

30 in the cave that is in the field of Machpelah, which is before Mamre, in the land of Canaan, which Abraham bought along with the field from Ephron the Hittite for a burial site.

31 "There they buried Abraham and his wife Sarah, there they buried Isaac and his wife Rebekah, and there I buried Leah—

32 the field and the cave that is in it, purchased from the sons of Heth."

33 When Jacob finished charging his sons, he drew his feet into the bed and breathed his last, and was gathered to his people.

*The Death of Israel*

**50** THEN JOSEPH fell on his father's face, and wept over him and kissed him.

2 And Joseph commanded his servants the physicians to embalm his father. So the physicians embalmed Israel.

3 Now forty days were required for it, for such is the period required for embalming. And the Egyptians wept for him seventy days.

NAS [b] Lit., *son* [c] Lit., *daughters*

## New International

17 Dan will be a serpent by the roadside,
a viper along the path,
that bites the horse's heels
so that its rider tumbles backward.

18 "I look for your deliverance, O LORD.

19 "Gad[d] will be attacked by a band of raiders,
but he will attack them at their heels.

20 "Asher's food will be rich;
he will provide delicacies fit for a king.

21 "Naphtali is a doe set free
that bears beautiful fawns.[e]

22 "Joseph is a fruitful vine,
a fruitful vine near a spring,
whose branches climb over a wall.[f]
23 With bitterness archers attacked him;
they shot at him with hostility.
24 But his bow remained steady,
his strong arms stayed[g] limber,
because of the hand of the Mighty One of Jacob,
because of the Shepherd, the Rock of Israel,
25 because of your father's God, who helps you,
because of the Almighty,[h] who blesses you
with blessings of the heavens above,
blessings of the deep that lies below,
blessings of the breast and womb.
26 Your father's blessings are greater
than the blessings of the ancient mountains,
than[i] the bounty of the age-old hills.
Let all these rest on the head of Joseph,
on the brow of the prince among[j] his brothers.

27 "Benjamin is a ravenous wolf;
in the morning he devours the prey,
in the evening he divides the plunder."

28 All these are the twelve tribes of Israel, and this is what their father said to them when he blessed them, giving each the blessing appropriate to him.

*The Death of Jacob*

29 Then he gave them these instructions: "I am about to be
gathered to my people. Bury me with my fathers in the cave in the
field of Ephron the Hittite, 30 the cave in the field of Machpelah,
near Mamre in Canaan, which Abraham bought as a burial place
from Ephron the Hittite, along with the field. 31 There Abraham
and his wife Sarah were buried, there Isaac and his wife Rebekah
were buried, and there I buried Leah. 32 The field and the cave in
it were bought from the Hittites.[k]"

33 When Jacob had finished giving instructions to his sons, he
drew his feet up into the bed, breathed his last and was gathered
to his people.

**50** JOSEPH THREW himself upon his father and wept over
him and kissed him. 2 Then Joseph directed the physicians
in his service to embalm his father Israel. So the physicians embalmed him, 3 taking a full forty days, for that was the time required for embalming. And the Egyptians mourned for him seventy days.

NIV [d] 19 *Gad* can mean *attack* and *band of raiders.* [e] 21 Or *free; / he utters beautiful words* [f] 22 Or *Joseph is a wild colt, / a wild colt near a spring, / a wild donkey on a terraced hill* [g] 23,24 Or *archers will attack . . . will shoot . . . will remain . . . will stay* [h] 25 Hebrew *Shaddai* [i] 26 Or *of my progenitors, / as great as* [j] 26 Or *the one separated from* [k] 32 Or *the sons of Heth*

## King James

4 And when the days of his mourning were past, Joseph spake unto the house of Pharaoh, saying, If now I have found grace in your eyes, speak, I pray you, in the ears of Pharaoh, saying,

5 My father made me swear, saying, Lo, I die: in my grave which I have digged for me in the land of Canaan, there shalt thou bury me. Now therefore let me go up, I pray thee, and bury my father, and I will come again.

6 And Pharaoh said, Go up, and bury thy father, according as he made thee swear.

7 ¶ And Joseph went up to bury his father: and with him went up all the servants of Pharaoh, the elders of his house, and all the elders of the land of Egypt,

8 And all the house of Joseph, and his brethren, and his father's house: only their little ones, and their flocks, and their herds, they left in the land of Goshen.

9 And there went up with him both chariots and horsemen: and it was a very great company.

10 And they came to the threshingfloor of Atad, which *is* beyond Jordan, and there they mourned with a great and very sore lamentation: and he made a mourning for his father seven days.

11 And when the inhabitants of the land, the Canaanites, saw the mourning in the floor of Atad, they said, This *is* a grievous mourning to the Egyptians: wherefore the name of it was called Abel-mizraim, which *is* beyond Jordan.

12 And his sons did unto him according as he commanded them:

13 For his sons carried him into the land of Canaan, and buried him in the cave of the field of Machpelah, which Abraham bought with the field for a possession of a buryingplace of Ephron the Hittite, before Mamre.

14 ¶ And Joseph returned into Egypt, he, and his brethren, and all that went up with him to bury his father, after he had buried his father.

15 ¶ And when Joseph's brethren saw that their father was dead, they said, Joseph will peradventure hate us, and will certainly requite us all the evil which we did unto him.

16 And they sent a messenger unto Joseph, saying, Thy father did command before he died, saying,

17 So shall ye say unto Joseph, Forgive, I pray thee now, the trespass of thy brethren, and their sin; for they did unto thee evil: and now, we pray thee, forgive the trespass of the servants of the God of thy father. And Joseph wept when they spake unto him.

18 And his brethren also went and fell down before his face; and they said, Behold, we *be* thy servants.

19 And Joseph said unto them, Fear not: for *am* I in the place of God?

20 But as for you, ye thought evil against me; *but* God meant it unto good, to bring to pass, as *it is* this day, to save much people alive.

21 Now therefore fear ye not: I will nourish you, and your little ones. And he comforted them, and spake kindly unto them.

22 ¶ And Joseph dwelt in Egypt, he, and his father's house: and Joseph lived an hundred and ten years.

23 And Joseph saw Ephraim's children of the third *generation:* the children also of Machir the son of Manasseh were brought up upon Joseph's knees.

24 And Joseph said unto his brethren, I die: and God will surely visit you, and bring you out of this land unto the land which he sware to Abraham, to Isaac, and to Jacob.

25 And Joseph took an oath of the children of Israel, saying, God will surely visit you, and ye shall carry up my bones from hence.

26 So Joseph died, *being* an hundred and ten years old: and they embalmed him, and he was put in a coffin in Egypt.

## Amplified

4 And when the days of his weeping *and* deep grief were past, Joseph said to [the nobles of] the house of Pharaoh, If now I have found grace in your eyes, speak, I pray you, to Pharaoh [for Joseph was dressed in mourning and could not do so himself], saying,

5 My father made me swear, saying, I am about to die; in my tomb which I hewed out for myself in the land of Canaan, there you shall bury me. So now let me go up, I pray you, and bury my father, and I will come again.

6 And Pharaoh said, Go up, and bury your father, according as he made you swear.

7 And Joseph went up [to Canaan] to bury his father; and with him went all the officials of Pharaoh, the nobles of his court *and* the elders of his house, and all the nobles *and* elders of the land of Egypt,

8 And all the household of Joseph, and his brethren, and his father's household. Only their little ones, and their flocks and herds they left in the land of Goshen.

9 And there went with [Joseph] both chariots and horsemen; and it was a very great company.

10 And they came to the threshingfloor of Atad, which is beyond [west of] Jordan, and there they mourned with a great lamentation and extreme demonstrations of sorrow [according to Egyptian custom]; and [Joseph] made a mourning for his father seven days.

11 When the inhabitants of the land, the Canaanites, saw the mourning on the floor of Atad, they said, This is a grievous mourning to the Egyptians. Therefore the place was called Abel-mizraim (mourning of Egypt). It is west of the Jordan.

12 Thus [Jacob's] sons did for him as he had commanded them.

13 For his sons carried him to the land of Canaan and buried him in the cave of the field of Machpelah, east of Mamre, which Abraham bought with the field for a possession as a burying place from Ephron the Hittite.

14 After he had buried his father, Joseph returned to Egypt, he and his brethren and all who went up with him.

15 When Joseph's brethren saw that their father was dead, they said, Perhaps now Joseph will hate us and will pay us back for all the evil we did to him.

16 And they sent a messenger to Joseph, saying, Your father commanded before he died, saying,

17 So shall you say to Joseph, Forgive [take up and away all resentment and all claim to requital] I pray you now, concerning the trespass of your brothers and their sin; for they did evil to you. Now, we pray you, forgive the trespass of the servants of your father's God. And Joseph wept when they thus spoke to him.

18 Then his brothers went and fell down before him, saying, See, we are your servants—your slaves!

19 And Joseph said to them, Fear not; for am I in the place of God? [Vengeance is His, not mine.]

20 As for you, you thought evil against me; but God meant it for good, to bring about that many people should be kept alive, as they are this day.

21 Now therefore do not be afraid. I will provide for *and* support you and your little ones. And he comforted them [imparting cheer, hope, strength], and spoke to their hearts [kindly].

22 Joseph dwelt in Egypt, he and his father's household. And Joseph lived 110 years.

23 And Joseph saw Ephraim's children of the third generation, the children also of Machir the son of Manasseh were brought up on Joseph's knees.

24 And Joseph said to his brethren, I am going to die; and God will surely visit you and bring you out of this land to the land He swore to Abraham, to Isaac, and to Jacob [to give you].

25 And Joseph took an oath of the sons of Israel, saying, God will surely visit you, and you shall carry up my bones from here.

26 So Joseph died, being 110 years old; and they embalmed him, and he was put [a]in a coffin in Egypt.

**AMP** [a] In Egypt Joseph's body remained until the Exodus from there to the promised land of Canaan, about 200 years later. Its final resting place was Shechem, near Samaria, "in the parcel of ground which Jacob bought from the sons of Hamor the father of Shechem" (Josh. 24:32). Here each of his brothers was also buried (Acts 7:15, 16).

## New American Standard

4 ¶ And when the days of mourning for him were past, Joseph spoke to the household of Pharaoh, saying, "If now I have found favor in your sight, please speak to Pharaoh, saying,

5 'My father made me swear, saying, "Behold, I am about to die; in my grave which I dug for myself in the land of Canaan, there you shall bury me." Now therefore, please let me go up and bury my father; then I will return.' "

6 And Pharaoh said, "Go up and bury your father, as he made you swear."

7 So Joseph went up to bury his father, and with him went up all the servants of Pharaoh, the elders of his household and all the elders of the land of Egypt,

8 and all the household of Joseph and his brothers and his father's household; they left only their little ones and their flocks and their herds in the land of Goshen.

9 There also went up with him both chariots and horsemen; and it was a very great company.

10 When they came to the threshing floor of Atad, which is beyond the Jordan, they lamented there with a very great and sorrowful lamentation; and he observed seven days mourning for his father.

11 Now when the inhabitants of the land, the Canaanites, saw the mourning at the threshing floor of Atad, they said, "This is a grievous mourning for the Egyptians." Therefore it was named Abel-mizraim, which is beyond the Jordan.

*Burial at Machpelah*

12 And thus his sons did for him as he had charged them;

13 for his sons carried him to the land of Canaan, and buried him in the cave of the field of Machpelah before Mamre, which Abraham had bought along with the field for a burial site from Ephron the Hittite.

14 And after he had buried his father, Joseph returned to Egypt, he and his brothers, and all who had gone up with him to bury his father.

15 ¶ When Joseph's brothers saw that their father was dead, they said, "What if Joseph should bear a grudge against us and pay us back in full for all the wrong which we did to him!"

16 So they sent *a message* to Joseph, saying, "Your father charged before he died, saying,

17 'Thus you shall say to Joseph, "Please forgive, I beg you, the transgression of your brothers and their sin, for they did you wrong." ' And now, please forgive the transgression of the servants of the God of your father." And Joseph wept when they spoke to him.

18 Then his brothers also came and fell down before him and said, "Behold, we are your servants."

19 But Joseph said to them, "Do not be afraid, for am I in God's place?

20 "And as for you, you meant evil against me, *but* God meant it for good in order to bring about this present result, to preserve many people alive.

21 "So therefore, do not be afraid; I will provide for you and your little ones." So he comforted them and spoke kindly to them.

*Death of Joseph*

22 ¶ Now Joseph stayed in Egypt, he and his father's household, and Joseph lived one hundred and ten years.

23 And Joseph saw the third generation of Ephraim's sons; also the sons of Machir, the son of Manasseh, were born on Joseph's knees.

24 And Joseph said to his brothers, "I am about to die, but God will surely take care of you, and bring you up from this land to the land which He promised on oath to Abraham, to Isaac and to Jacob."

25 Then Joseph made the sons of Israel swear, saying, "God will surely take care of you, and you shall carry my bones up from here."

26 So Joseph died at the age of one hundred and ten years; and he was embalmed and placed in a coffin in Egypt.

## New International

4 When the days of mourning had passed, Joseph said to Pharaoh's court, "If I have found favor in your eyes, speak to Pharaoh
for me. Tell him, 5 'My father made me swear an oath and said, "I
am about to die; bury me in the tomb I dug for myself in the land
of Canaan." Now let me go up and bury my father; then I will
return.' "
6 Pharaoh said, "Go up and bury your father, as he made you
swear to do."
7 So Joseph went up to bury his father. All Pharaoh's officials
accompanied him—the dignitaries of his court and all the dignitaries of Egypt— 8 besides all the members of Joseph's household and
his brothers and those belonging to his father's household. Only
their children and their flocks and herds were left in Goshen.
9 Chariots and horsemen[b] also went up with him. It was a very
large company.
10 When they reached the threshing floor of Atad, near the
Jordan, they lamented loudly and bitterly; and there Joseph observed a seven-day period of mourning for his father. 11 When the
Canaanites who lived there saw the mourning at the threshing
floor of Atad, they said, "The Egyptians are holding a solemn
ceremony of mourning." That is why that place near the Jordan is
called Abel Mizraim.[c]
12 So Jacob's sons did as he had commanded them: 13 They carried him to the land of Canaan and buried him in the cave in the
field of Machpelah, near Mamre, which Abraham had bought as
a burial place from Ephron the Hittite, along with the field. 14 After
burying his father, Joseph returned to Egypt, together with his
brothers and all the others who had gone with him to bury his
father.

*Joseph Reassures His Brothers*

15 When Joseph's brothers saw that their father was dead, they
said, "What if Joseph holds a grudge against us and pays us back
for all the wrongs we did to him?" 16 So they sent word to Joseph,
saying, "Your father left these instructions before he died: 17 'This
is what you are to say to Joseph: I ask you to forgive your brothers
the sins and the wrongs they committed in treating you so badly.'
Now please forgive the sins of the servants of the God of your
father." When their message came to him, Joseph wept.
18 His brothers then came and threw themselves down before
him. "We are your slaves," they said.
19 But Joseph said to them, "Don't be afraid. Am I in the place
of God? 20 You intended to harm me, but God intended it for good
to accomplish what is now being done, the saving of many lives.
21 So then, don't be afraid. I will provide for you and your children." And he reassured them and spoke kindly to them.

*The Death of Joseph*

22 Joseph stayed in Egypt, along with all his father's family. He
lived a hundred and ten years 23 and saw the third generation of
Ephraim's children. Also the children of Makir son of Manasseh
were placed at birth on Joseph's knees.[d]
24 Then Joseph said to his brothers, "I am about to die. But God
will surely come to your aid and take you up out of this land to
the land he promised on oath to Abraham, Isaac and Jacob." 25 And
Joseph made the sons of Israel swear an oath and said, "God will
surely come to your aid, and then you must carry my bones up
from this place."
26 So Joseph died at the age of a hundred and ten. And after they
embalmed him, he was placed in a coffin in Egypt.

**NIV** [b] 9 Or *charioteers* [c] 11 *Abel Mizraim* means *mourning of the Egyptians.*
[d] 23 That is, were counted as his

## King James

THE SECOND BOOK OF

MOSES, CALLED

# Exodus

**1** NOW THESE *are* the names of the children of Israel, which came into Egypt; every man and his household came with Jacob.

2Reuben, Simeon, Levi, and Judah,

3Issachar, Zebulun, and Benjamin,

4Dan, and Naphtali, Gad, and Asher.

5And all the souls that came out of the loins of Jacob were seventy souls: for Joseph was in Egypt *already*.

6And Joseph died, and all his brethren, and all that generation.

7¶ And the children of Israel were fruitful, and increased abundantly, and multiplied, and waxed exceeding mighty; and the land was filled with them.

8Now there arose up a new king over Egypt, which knew not Joseph.

9And he said unto his people, Behold, the people of the children of Israel *are* more and mightier than we:

10Come on, let us deal wisely with them; lest they multiply, and it come to pass, that, when there falleth out any war, they join also unto our enemies, and fight against us, and *so* get them up out of the land.

11Therefore they did set over them taskmasters to afflict them with their burdens. And they built for Pharaoh treasure cities, Pithom and Raamses.

12But the more they afflicted them, the more they multiplied and grew. And they were grieved because of the children of Israel.

13And the Egyptians made the children of Israel to serve with rigour:

14And they made their lives bitter with hard bondage, in mortar, and in brick, and in all manner of service in the field: all their service, wherein they made them serve, *was* with rigour.

15¶ And the king of Egypt spake to the Hebrew midwives, of which the name of the one *was* Shiphrah, and the name of the other Puah:

16And he said, When ye do the office of a midwife to the Hebrew women, and see *them* upon the stools; if it *be* a son, then ye shall kill him: but if it *be* a daughter, then she shall live.

17But the midwives feared God, and did not as the king of Egypt commanded them, but saved the men children alive.

18And the king of Egypt called for the midwives, and said unto them, Why have ye done this thing, and have saved the men children alive?

19And the midwives said unto Pharaoh, Because the Hebrew women *are* not as the Egyptian women; for they *are* lively, and are delivered ere the midwives come in unto them.

**AMP** [a] Is there in all human history a more amazing spectacle than the Exodus? A family of 70 immigrants grows into a race of slaves. Suddenly, according to God's detailed and preannounced plan, they are seen flinging away the shackles of generations of slavery, and emigrating to a new country and a new life, with miraculous deliverances rescuing them from destruction again and again. The marvel of the Exodus grows in wonder when, after more than 3,000 years, we see that same race, often persecuted almost to extinction, carrying out in startling detail God's predictions for their amazing national revitalization and prominence "in the last days." (Adapted from many historians.)

## Amplified

THE SECOND BOOK OF MOSES,

COMMONLY CALLED

# Exodus

**1** THESE ARE the names of the sons of Israel who came into Egypt with Jacob, each with his household:

2Reuben, Simeon, Levi, and Judah,

3Issachar, Zebulun, and Benjamin,

4Dan and Naphtali, Gad and Asher.

5All the offspring of Jacob were seventy persons; Joseph was already in Egypt.

6Then Joseph died, and all his brothers, and all that generation.

7But the descendants of Israel were fruitful and increased abundantly; they multiplied and grew exceedingly strong, and the land was full of them.

8Now a new king arose over Egypt, who did not know Joseph.

9He said to his people, Behold, the Israelites are too many and too mighty for us—they [a]outnumber us both in people and in strength.

10Come, let us deal shrewdly with them, lest they multiply more, and, should war befall us, they join our enemies, fight against us, and escape out of the land.

11So they set over [the Israelites] taskmasters to afflict *and* oppress them with [increased] burdens. And [the Israelites] built Pithom and Raamses as store-cities for Pharaoh.

12But the more [the Egyptians] oppressed them, the more they multiplied and expanded, so that [the Egyptians] were vexed *and* alarmed because of the Israelites.

13And the Egyptians reduced the Israelites to severe slavery.

14They made their lives bitter with hard service, in mortar, brick, and all kinds of work in the field. All their service was with harshness *and* severity.

15Then the king of Egypt said to the Hebrew midwives, of whom one was named Shiphrah and the other Puah,

16When you act as midwife to the Hebrew women, and see them on the birthstool, if it is a son, you shall kill him; but if it is a daughter, she shall live.

17But the midwives feared God, and did not do as the king of Egypt commanded, but let the male babies live.

18So the king of Egypt called for the midwives and said to them, Why have you done this thing, and allowed the male children to live?

19The midwives answered Pharaoh, Because the Hebrew women are not like the Egyptian women; they are vigorous and quickly delivered; their babies are born before the midwife comes to them.

## New American Standard

# Exodus

*Israel Multiplies in Egypt*

**1** NOW THESE are the names of the sons of Israel who came
to Egypt with Jacob; they came each one with his household:
2Reuben, Simeon, Levi and Judah;
3Issachar, Zebulun and Benjamin;
4Dan and Naphtali, Gad and Asher.
5And all the persons who came from the loins of Jacob were
seventy in number, but Joseph was *already* in Egypt.
6And Joseph died, and all his brothers and all that generation.
7But the sons of Israel were fruitful and increased greatly, and
multiplied, and became exceedingly mighty, so that the land was
filled with them.
8¶ Now a new king arose over Egypt, who did not know
Joseph.
9And he said to his people, "Behold, the people of the sons of
Israel are more and mightier than we.
10"Come, let us deal wisely with them, lest they multiply and
in the event of war, they also join themselves to those who hate
us, and fight against us, and depart from the land."
11So they appointed taskmasters over them to afflict them with
hard labor. And they built for Pharaoh storage cities, Pithom and
Raamses.
12But the more they afflicted them, the more they multiplied
and the more they spread out, so that they were in dread of the
sons of Israel.
13And the Egyptians compelled the sons of Israel to labor rigorously;
14and they made their lives bitter with hard labor in mortar and
bricks and at all *kinds* of labor in the field, all their labors which they
rigorously imposed on them.
15¶ Then the king of Egypt spoke to the Hebrew midwives, one
of whom was named Shiphrah, and the other was named Puah;
16and he said, "When you are helping the Hebrew women to
give birth and see *them* upon the birthstool, if it is a son, then you
shall put him to death; but if it is a daughter, then she shall live."
17But the midwives feared God, and did not do as the king of
Egypt had commanded them, but let the boys live.
18So the king of Egypt called for the midwives, and said to
them, "Why have you done this thing, and let the boys live?"
19And the midwives said to Pharaoh, "Because the Hebrew
women are not as the Egyptian women; for they are vigorous, and
they give birth before the midwife can get to them."

## New International

# Exodus

*The Israelites Oppressed*

**1** THESE ARE the names of the sons of Israel who went to
Egypt with Jacob, each with his family: 2Reuben, Simeon,
Levi and Judah; 3Issachar, Zebulun and Benjamin; 4Dan and
Naphtali; Gad and Asher. 5The descendants of Jacob numbered
seventy[b] in all; Joseph was already in Egypt.
6Now Joseph and all his brothers and all that generation died,
7but the Israelites were fruitful and multiplied greatly and became
exceedingly numerous, so that the land was filled with them.
8Then a new king, who did not know about Joseph, came to
power in Egypt. 9"Look," he said to his people, "the Israelites
have become much too numerous for us. 10Come, we must deal
shrewdly with them or they will become even more numerous
and, if war breaks out, will join our enemies, fight against us and
leave the country."
11So they put slave masters over them to oppress them with
forced labor, and they built Pithom and Rameses as store cities for
Pharaoh. 12But the more they were oppressed, the more they
multiplied and spread; so the Egyptians came to dread the Israelites 13and worked them ruthlessly. 14They made their lives bitter
with hard labor in brick and mortar and with all kinds of work in
the fields; in all their hard labor the Egyptians used them ruthlessly.
15The king of Egypt said to the Hebrew midwives, whose
names were Shiphrah and Puah, 16"When you help the Hebrew
women in childbirth and observe them on the delivery stool, if it
is a boy, kill him; but if it is a girl, let her live." 17The midwives,
however, feared God and did not do what the king of Egypt had
told them to do; they let the boys live. 18Then the king of Egypt
summoned the midwives and asked them, "Why have you done
this? Why have you let the boys live?"
19The midwives answered Pharaoh, "Hebrew women are not
like Egyptian women; they are vigorous and give birth before the
midwives arrive."

**NIV** [b] 5 Masoretic Text (see also Gen. 46:27); Dead Sea Scrolls and Septuagint (see also Acts 7:14 and note at Gen. 46:27) *seventy-five*

## King James

20Therefore God dealt well with the midwives: and the people
multiplied, and waxed very mighty.
21And it came to pass, because the midwives feared God, that
he made them houses.
22And Pharaoh charged all his people, saying, Every son that
is born ye shall cast into the river, and every daughter ye shall save
alive.

**2** AND THERE went a man of the house of Levi, and took *to*
*wife* a daughter of Levi.
2And the woman conceived, and bare a son: and when she saw
him that he *was a* goodly *child,* she hid him three months.
3And when she could not longer hide him, she took for him an
ark of bulrushes, and daubed it with slime and with pitch, and put
the child therein; and she laid *it* in the flags by the river's brink.
4And his sister stood afar off, to wit what would be done to him.
5¶ And the daughter of Pharaoh came down to wash *herself* at
the river; and her maidens walked along by the river's side; and
when she saw the ark among the flags, she sent her maid to fetch
it.
6And when she had opened *it,* she saw the child: and, behold,
the babe wept. And she had compassion on him, and said, This
*is one* of the Hebrews' children.
7Then said his sister to Pharaoh's daughter, Shall I go and call
to thee a nurse of the Hebrew women, that she may nurse the child
for thee?
8And Pharaoh's daughter said to her, Go. And the maid went
and called the child's mother.
9And Pharaoh's daughter said unto her, Take this child away,
and nurse it for me, and I will give *thee* thy wages. And the woman
took the child, and nursed it.
10And the child grew, and she brought him unto Pharaoh's
daughter, and he became her son. And she called his name Moses:
and she said, Because I drew him out of the water.
11¶ And it came to pass in those days, when Moses was grown,
that he went out unto his brethren, and looked on their burdens:
and he spied an Egyptian smiting an Hebrew, one of his brethren.
12And he looked this way and that way, and when he saw that
*there was* no man, he slew the Egyptian, and hid him in the sand.
13And when he went out the second day, behold, two men of
the Hebrews strove together: and he said to him that did the
wrong, Wherefore smitest thou thy fellow?
14And he said, Who made thee a prince and a judge over us?
intendest thou to kill me, as thou killedst the Egyptian? And Moses
feared, and said, Surely this thing is known.
15Now when Pharaoh heard this thing, he sought to slay
Moses. But Moses fled from the face of Pharaoh, and dwelt in the
land of Midian: and he sat down by a well.
16Now the priest of Midian had seven daughters: and they came
and drew *water,* and filled the troughs to water their father's flock.
17And the shepherds came and drove them away: but Moses
stood up and helped them, and watered their flock.
18And when they came to Reuel their father, he said, How *is*
*it that* ye are come so soon today?

## Amplified

20So God dealt well with the midwives, and the people multiplied and became very strong.
21And because the midwives revered *and* feared God, He made
them households *of their own.*
22Then Pharaoh charged all his people, saying, Every son born
[to the Hebrews] you shall cast into the river [Nile], but every
daughter you shall allow to live.

**2** NOW [AMRAM] a man of the house of Levi [the priestly
tribe], went and took as his wife [Jochebed] a daughter of
Levi. [Exod. 6:18, 20; Num. 26:59.]
2And the woman became pregnant and bore a son; and when
she saw that he was [exceedingly] beautiful, she hid him three
months. [Heb. 11:23; Acts 7:20.]
3And when she could no longer hide him, she took for him an
ark *or* basket made of bulrushes *or* papyrus [making it water-tight
by] daubing it with bitumen and pitch. Then she put the child in
it and laid it among the rushes by the brink of the river [Nile].
4And his sister [Miriam] stood some distance away, to [a]learn
what would be done to him.
5Now the daughter of Pharaoh came down to bathe at the river,
and her maidens walked along the bank; she saw the ark among
the rushes and sent her maid to fetch it.
6When she opened it, she saw the child; and lo, the baby cried.
And she took pity on him and said, This is one of the Hebrews'
children!
7Then his sister said to Pharaoh's daughter, Shall I go and call
a nurse of the Hebrew women to nurse the child for you?
8Pharaoh's daughter said to her, Go. And the girl went and
called the child's mother.
9Then Pharaoh's daughter said to her, Take this child away and
nurse it for me, and I will give you your wages. So the woman took
the child and nursed it.
10And the child grew, and she brought him to Pharaoh's daughter, and he became her son. And she called him Moses, for she
said, Because I drew him out of the water.
11One day after Moses was grown, it happened that he went
out to his brethren and looked at their burdens; and he saw an
Egyptian beating a Hebrew, one of *Moses'* brethren.
12He looked this way and that way, and when he saw no one,
he killed the Egyptian and hid him in the sand.
13He went out the second day and saw two Hebrew men quarreling *and* fighting; and he said to the unjust aggressor, Why are
you striking your comrade?
14And the man said, Who made you a prince and a judge over
us? Do you intend to kill me, as you killed the Egyptian? Then
Moses was afraid, and thought, Surely *this* thing is known.
15When Pharaoh heard of it, he sought to slay Moses. But
Moses fled from Pharaoh's presence and [b]took refuge in the land
of Midian, where he sat down by a well.
16Now the priest of Midian had seven daughters, and they came
and drew water and filled the troughs to water their father's flock.
17The shepherds came and drove them away; but Moses stood
up and helped them, and watered their flock.
18And when they came to Reuel [Jethro] their father, he said,
How is it that you have come so soon today?

**AMP** [a] They launched the ark not on the Nile only, but on God's providence. He would be captain, steersman, and convoy of the tiny bark. Miriam stood to watch. There was no fear of fatal consequences, only the quiet expectancy that God would do something worthy of Himself. They reckoned on God's faithfulness, and they were amply rewarded, when the daughter of their greatest foe became the babe's patroness (F. B. Meyer in *Through the Bible Day by Day*). [b] "There was true heroism in the act, when Moses stepped down from Pharaoh's throne to share the lot of his brethren. But it would take many a long year of lonely waiting and trial before this strong and radiant nature could be broken down, shaped into a vessel meet for the Master's use, and prepared for every good work. . . . One blow struck when God's time is fulfilled is worth a thousand struck in premature eagerness" (F. B. Meyer in *Moses, the Servant of God,* adapted).

## New American Standard

20 So God was good to the midwives, and the people multiplied, and became very mighty.

21 And it came about because the midwives feared God, that He established households for them.

22 Then Pharaoh commanded all his people, saying, "Every son who is born [c]you are to cast into the Nile, and every daughter you are to keep alive."

*The Birth of Moses*

**2** NOW A man from the house of Levi went and married a daughter of Levi.

2 And the woman conceived and bore a son; and when she saw that he was beautiful, she hid him for three months.

3 But when she could hide him no longer, she got him a [d]wicker basket and covered it over with tar and pitch. Then she put the child into it, and set *it* among the reeds by the bank of the Nile.

4 And his sister stood at a distance to find out what would happen to him.

5 Then the daughter of Pharaoh came down to bathe at the Nile, with her maidens walking alongside the Nile; and she saw the basket among the reeds and sent her maid, and she brought it *to her*.

6 ¶ When she opened *it*, she saw the child, and behold, *the* boy was crying. And she had pity on him and said, "This is one of the Hebrews' children."

7 Then his sister said to Pharaoh's daughter, "Shall I go and call a nurse for you from the Hebrew women, that she may nurse the child for you?"

8 And Pharaoh's daughter said to her, "Go *ahead*." So the girl went and called the child's mother.

9 Then Pharaoh's daughter said to her, "Take this child away and nurse him for me and I shall give *you* your wages." So the woman took the child and nursed him.

10 And the child grew, and she brought him to Pharaoh's daughter, and he became her son. And she named him Moses, and said, "Because I drew him out of the water."

11 ¶ Now it came about in those days, when Moses had grown up, that he went out to his brethren and looked on their hard labors; and he saw an Egyptian beating a Hebrew, one of his brethren.

12 So he looked this way and that, and when he saw there was no one *around*, he struck down the Egyptian and hid him in the sand.

13 And he went out the next day, and behold, two Hebrews were fighting with each other; and he said to the offender, "Why are you striking your companion?"

14 But he said, "Who made you a prince or a judge over us? Are you intending to kill me, as you killed the Egyptian?" Then Moses was afraid, and said, "Surely the matter has become known."

*Moses Escapes to Midian*

15 When Pharaoh heard of this matter, he tried to kill Moses. But Moses fled from the presence of Pharaoh and settled in the land of Midian; and he sat down by a well.

16 ¶ Now the priest of Midian had seven daughters; and they came to draw water, and filled the troughs to water their father's flock.

17 Then the shepherds came and drove them away, but Moses stood up and helped them, and watered their flock.

18 When they came to Reuel their father, he said, "Why have you come *back* so soon today?"

**NAS** [c] Some versions insert, *to the Hebrews* [d] I.e., papyrus reeds

## New International

20 So God was kind to the midwives and the people increased
and became even more numerous. 21 And because the midwives
feared God, he gave them families of their own.
22 Then Pharaoh gave this order to all his people: "Every boy
that is born[e] you must throw into the Nile, but let every girl live."

*The Birth of Moses*

**2** NOW A man of the house of Levi married a Levite woman,
2 and she became pregnant and gave birth to a son. When she
saw that he was a fine child, she hid him for three months. 3 But
when she could hide him no longer, she got a papyrus basket for
him and coated it with tar and pitch. Then she placed the child in
it and put it among the reeds along the bank of the Nile. 4 His sister
stood at a distance to see what would happen to him.
5 Then Pharaoh's daughter went down to the Nile to bathe, and
her attendants were walking along the river bank. She saw the
basket among the reeds and sent her slave girl to get it. 6 She
opened it and saw the baby. He was crying, and she felt sorry for
him. "This is one of the Hebrew babies," she said.
7 Then his sister asked Pharaoh's daughter, "Shall I go and get
one of the Hebrew women to nurse the baby for you?"
8 "Yes, go," she answered. And the girl went and got the baby's
mother. 9 Pharaoh's daughter said to her, "Take this baby and
nurse him for me, and I will pay you." So the woman took the baby
and nursed him. 10 When the child grew older, she took him to
Pharaoh's daughter and he became her son. She named him
Moses,[f] saying, "I drew him out of the water."

*Moses Flees to Midian*

11 One day, after Moses had grown up, he went out to where
his own people were and watched them at their hard labor. He saw
an Egyptian beating a Hebrew, one of his own people. 12 Glancing
this way and that and seeing no one, he killed the Egyptian and
hid him in the sand. 13 The next day he went out and saw two
Hebrews fighting. He asked the one in the wrong, "Why are you
hitting your fellow Hebrew?"
14 The man said, "Who made you ruler and judge over us? Are
you thinking of killing me as you killed the Egyptian?" Then Moses
was afraid and thought, "What I did must have become known."
15 When Pharaoh heard of this, he tried to kill Moses, but Moses
fled from Pharaoh and went to live in Midian, where he sat down
by a well. 16 Now a priest of Midian had seven daughters, and they
came to draw water and fill the troughs to water their father's
flock. 17 Some shepherds came along and drove them away, but
Moses got up and came to their rescue and watered their flock.
18 When the girls returned to Reuel their father, he asked them,
"Why have you returned so early today?"

**NIV** [e] 22 Masoretic Text; Samaritan Pentateuch, Septuagint and Targums *born to the Hebrews* [f] *10 Moses* sounds like the Hebrew for *draw out.*

## King James

19 And they said, An Egyptian delivered us out of the hand of
the shepherds, and also drew *water* enough for us, and watered
the flock.
20 And he said unto his daughters, And where *is* he? why *is* it
*that* ye have left the man? call him, that he may eat bread.
21 And Moses was content to dwell with the man: and he gave
Moses Zipporah his daughter.
22 And she bare *him* a son, and he called his name Gershom: for
he said, I have been a stranger in a strange land.
23 ¶ And it came to pass in process of time, that the king of Egypt
died: and the children of Israel sighed by reason of the bondage,
and they cried, and their cry came up unto God by reason of the
bondage.
24 And God heard their groaning, and God remembered his
covenant with Abraham, with Isaac, and with Jacob.
25 And God looked upon the children of Israel, and God had
respect unto *them*.

**3** NOW MOSES kept the flock of Jethro his father-in-law, the
priest of Midian: and he led the flock to the backside of the
desert, and came to the mountain of God, *even* to Horeb.
2 And the angel of the LORD appeared unto him in a flame of fire
out of the midst of a bush: and he looked, and, behold, the bush
burned with fire, and the bush *was* not consumed.
3 And Moses said, I will now turn aside, and see this great sight,
why the bush is not burnt.
4 And when the LORD saw that he turned aside to see, God
called unto him out of the midst of the bush, and said, Moses,
Moses. And he said, Here *am* I.
5 And he said, Draw not nigh hither: put off thy shoes from off
thy feet, for the place whereon thou standest *is* holy ground.
6 Moreover he said, I *am* the God of thy father, the God of
Abraham, the God of Isaac, and the God of Jacob. And Moses hid
his face; for he was afraid to look upon God.
7 ¶ And the LORD said, I have surely seen the affliction of my
people which *are* in Egypt, and have heard their cry by reason of
their taskmasters; for I know their sorrows;
8 And I am come down to deliver them out of the hand of the
Egyptians, and to bring them up out of that land unto a good land
and a large, unto a land flowing with milk and honey; unto the
place of the Canaanites, and the Hittites, and the Amorites, and
the Perizzites, and the Hivites, and the Jebusites.
9 Now therefore, behold, the cry of the children of Israel is come
unto me: and I have also seen the oppression wherewith the
Egyptians oppress them.
10 Come now therefore, and I will send thee unto Pharaoh, that
thou mayest bring forth my people the children of Israel out of
Egypt.
11 ¶ And Moses said unto God, Who *am* I, that I should go unto
Pharaoh, and that I should bring forth the children of Israel out of
Egypt?
12 And he said, Certainly I will be with thee; and this *shall be* a
token unto thee, that I have sent thee: When thou hast brought
forth the people out of Egypt, ye shall serve God upon this mountain.

## Amplified

19 They said, An Egyptian delivered us from the shepherds; also
he drew water for us and watered the flock.
20 He said to his daughters, Where is he? Why have you left the
man? Call him, that he may eat bread.
21 And Moses was content to dwell with the man; and he gave
Moses Zipporah his daughter.
22 And she bore a son, and he called his name Gershom (meaning, expulsion, or a stranger there); for he said, I have been a
stranger *and* a sojourner in a foreign land.
23 However, after a long time [nearly forty years] the king of
Egypt died; and the Israelites were sighing *and* groaning because
of the bondage. They kept crying, and their cry because of slavery
ascended to God.
24 And God heard their sighing *and* groaning and (earnestly)
remembered His covenant with Abraham, with Isaac, and with
Jacob.
25 God saw the Israelites and took knowledge of them *and* concerned Himself about them [knowing all, understanding, remembering all]. [Ps. 139:2; 56:8, 9.]

**3** NOW MOSES kept the flock of Jethro his father-in-law, the
priest of Midian; and he led the flock to the back *or* west side
of the wilderness, and came to Horeb *or* Sinai, the mountain of
God.
2 The Angel of the Lord appeared to him in a flame of fire out
of the midst of a bush; and he looked, and behold, the bush burned
with fire, yet was not consumed.
3 And Moses said, I will now turn aside and see this great sight,
why the bush is not burned.
4 And when the Lord saw that he turned aside to see, God called
to him out of the midst of the bush and said, Moses, Moses! And
he said, Here am I.
5 God said, Do not come near; put your shoes off your feet, for
the place on which you stand is holy ground.
6 Also He said, I am the God of your father, the God of Abraham, the God of Isaac, and the God of Jacob. And Moses hid his
face, for he was afraid to look at God.
7 And the Lord said, I have surely seen the affliction of My
people who are in Egypt, and have heard their cry because of their
taskmasters *and* oppressors; for I know their sorrows *and* sufferings *and* trials.
8 And I have come down to deliver them out of the hand *and*
power of the Egyptians, and to bring them up out of that land to
a land good and large, a land flowing with milk and honey—a land
of plenty; to the place of the Canaanite, the Hittite, the Amorite,
the Perizzite, the Hivite, and the Jebusite.
9 Now behold, the cry of the Israelites is come to Me, and I have
also seen how the Egyptians oppress them.
10 Come now therefore, and I will send you to Pharaoh, that you
may bring forth My people, the Israelites, out of Egypt.
11 And Moses said to God, [a]Who am I, that I should go to
Pharaoh and bring the Israelites out of Egypt?
12 God said, I will surely be with you; and this shall be the sign
to you that I have sent you: when you have brought the people out
of Egypt, you shall serve God on this mountain [Horeb or Sinai].

**AMP** [a] "There was something more than humility here; there was a tone of self-depreciation, which was inconsistent with a true faith in God's selection and appointment. Surely it is God's business to choose His special instruments; and when we are persuaded that we are in the line of His purpose, we have no right to question the wisdom of His appointment. To do so is to depreciate His wisdom, or to doubt His power and willingness to become *all that is necessary* to complete our need" (F. B. Meyer in *Moses, the Servant of God*).

## New American Standard

19So they said, "An Egyptian delivered us from the hand of the
shepherds; and what is more, he even drew the water for us and
watered the flock."
20And he said to his daughters, "Where is he then? Why is it
that you have left the man behind? Invite him to have something
to eat."
21And Moses was willing to dwell with the man, and he gave
his daughter Zipporah to Moses.
22Then she gave birth to a son, and he named him Gershom,
for he said, "I have been a sojourner in a foreign land."
23¶ Now it came about in *the course of* those many days that the
king of Egypt died. And the sons of Israel sighed because of the
bondage, and they cried out; and their cry for help because of *their*
bondage rose up to God.
24So God heard their groaning; and God remembered His covenant with Abraham, Isaac, and Jacob.
25And God saw the sons of Israel, and God took notice *of them.*

*The Burning Bush*

3 NOW MOSES was pasturing the flock of Jethro his father-in-
law, the priest of Midian; and he led the flock to the west side
of the wilderness, and came to Horeb, the mountain of God.
2And the angel of the LORD appeared to him in a blazing fire
from the midst of a bush; and he looked, and behold, the bush was
burning with fire, yet the bush was not consumed.
3So Moses said, "I must turn aside now, and see this marvelous sight, why the bush is not burned up."
4When the LORD saw that he turned aside to look, God called
to him from the midst of the bush, and said, "Moses, Moses!" And
he said, "Here I am."
5Then He said, "Do not come near here; remove your sandals
from your feet, for the place on which you are standing is holy
ground."
6He said also, "I am the God of your father, the God of Abraham, the God of Isaac, and the God of Jacob." Then Moses hid his
face, for he was afraid to look at God.
7And the LORD said, "I have surely seen the affliction of My
people who are in Egypt, and have given heed to their cry because
of their taskmasters, for I am aware of their sufferings.
8"So I have come down to deliver them from the power of the
Egyptians, and to bring them up from that land to a good and
spacious land, to a land flowing with milk and honey, to the place
of the Canaanite and the Hittite and the Amorite and the Perizzite
and the Hivite and the Jebusite.
9"And now, behold, the cry of the sons of Israel has come to
Me; furthermore, I have seen the oppression with which the Egyptians are oppressing them.

*The Mission of Moses*

10"Therefore, come now, and I will send you to Pharaoh, so that
you may bring My people, the sons of Israel, out of Egypt."
11But Moses said to God, "Who am I, that I should go to Pharaoh, and that I should bring the sons of Israel out of Egypt?"
12And He said, "Certainly I will be with you, and this shall be
the sign to you that it is I who have sent you: when you have
brought the people out of Egypt, you shall worship God at this
mountain."

## New International

19They answered, "An Egyptian rescued us from the shepherds. He even drew water for us and watered the flock."
20"And where is he?" he asked his daughters. "Why did you
leave him? Invite him to have something to eat."
21Moses agreed to stay with the man, who gave his daughter
Zipporah to Moses in marriage. 22Zipporah gave birth to a son,
and Moses named him Gershom,[b] saying, "I have become an alien
in a foreign land."
23During that long period, the king of Egypt died. The Israelites
groaned in their slavery and cried out, and their cry for help
because of their slavery went up to God. 24God heard their groaning and he remembered his covenant with Abraham, with Isaac
and with Jacob. 25So God looked on the Israelites and was concerned about them.

*Moses and the Burning Bush*

3 NOW MOSES was tending the flock of Jethro his father-in-
law, the priest of Midian, and he led the flock to the far side
of the desert and came to Horeb, the mountain of God. 2There the
angel of the LORD appeared to him in flames of fire from within
a bush. Moses saw that though the bush was on fire it did not burn
up. 3So Moses thought, "I will go over and see this strange sight—
why the bush does not burn up."
4When the LORD saw that he had gone over to look, God called
to him from within the bush, "Moses! Moses!"
And Moses said, "Here I am."
5"Do not come any closer," God said. "Take off your sandals,
for the place where you are standing is holy ground." 6Then he
said, "I am the God of your father, the God of Abraham, the God
of Isaac and the God of Jacob." At this, Moses hid his face, because
he was afraid to look at God.
7The LORD said, "I have indeed seen the misery of my people
in Egypt. I have heard them crying out because of their slave
drivers, and I am concerned about their suffering. 8So I have come
down to rescue them from the hand of the Egyptians and to bring
them up out of that land into a good and spacious land, a land
flowing with milk and honey—the home of the Canaanites, Hittites, Amorites, Perizzites, Hivites and Jebusites. 9And now the cry
of the Israelites has reached me, and I have seen the way the
Egyptians are oppressing them. 10So now, go. I am sending you
to Pharaoh to bring my people the Israelites out of Egypt."
11But Moses said to God, "Who am I, that I should go to Pharaoh and bring the Israelites out of Egypt?"
12And God said, "I will be with you. And this will be the sign
to you that it is I who have sent you: When you have brought the
people out of Egypt, you[c] will worship God on this mountain."

**NIV** [b] *22 Gershom* sounds like the Hebrew for *an alien there.* [c] *12* The Hebrew is plural.

## King James

13 And Moses said unto God, Behold, *when* I come unto the children of Israel, and shall say unto them, The God of your fathers hath sent me unto you; and they shall say to me, What *is* his name? what shall I say unto them?

14 And God said unto Moses, I AM THAT I AM: and he said, Thus shalt thou say unto the children of Israel, I AM hath sent me unto you.

15 And God said moreover unto Moses, Thus shalt thou say unto the children of Israel, The LORD God of your fathers, the God of Abraham, the God of Isaac, and the God of Jacob, hath sent me unto you: this *is* my name for ever, and this *is* my memorial unto all generations.

16 Go, and gather the elders of Israel together, and say unto them, The LORD God of your fathers, the God of Abraham, of Isaac, and of Jacob, appeared unto me, saying, I have surely visited you, and *seen* that which is done to you in Egypt:

17 And I have said, I will bring you up out of the affliction of Egypt unto the land of the Canaanites, and the Hittites, and the Amorites, and the Perizzites, and the Hivites, and the Jebusites, unto a land flowing with milk and honey.

18 And they shall hearken to thy voice: and thou shalt come, thou and the elders of Israel, unto the king of Egypt, and ye shall say unto him, The LORD God of the Hebrews hath met with us: and now let us go, we beseech thee, three days' journey into the wilderness, that we may sacrifice to the LORD our God.

19 ¶ And I am sure that the king of Egypt will not let you go, no, not by a mighty hand.

20 And I will stretch out my hand, and smite Egypt with all my wonders which I will do in the midst thereof: and after that he will let you go.

21 And I will give this people favour in the sight of the Egyptians: and it shall come to pass, that, when ye go, ye shall not go empty:

22 But every woman shall borrow of her neighbour, and of her that sojourneth in her house, jewels of silver, and jewels of gold, and raiment: and ye shall put *them* upon your sons, and upon your daughters; and ye shall spoil the Egyptians.

**4** AND MOSES answered and said, But, behold, they will not believe me, nor hearken unto my voice: for they will say, The LORD hath not appeared unto thee.

2 And the LORD said unto him, What *is* that in thine hand? And he said, A rod.

3 And he said, Cast it on the ground. And he cast it on the ground, and it became a serpent; and Moses fled from before it.

4 And the LORD said unto Moses, Put forth thine hand, and take it by the tail. And he put forth his hand, and caught it, and it became a rod in his hand:

5 That they may believe that the LORD God of their fathers, the God of Abraham, the God of Isaac, and the God of Jacob, hath appeared unto thee.

6 ¶ And the LORD said furthermore unto him, Put now thine hand into thy bosom. And he put his hand into his bosom: and when he took it out, behold, his hand *was* leprous as snow.

7 And he said, Put thine hand into thy bosom again. And he put his hand into his bosom again; and plucked it out of his bosom, and, behold, it was turned again as his *other* flesh.

8 And it shall come to pass, if they will not believe thee, neither hearken to the voice of the first sign, that they will believe the voice of the latter sign.

## Amplified

13 And Moses said to God, Behold, when I come to the Israelites and say to them, The God of your fathers has sent me to you, and they say to me, What is His name? What shall I say to them?

14 And God said to Moses, I AM WHO I AM *and* WHAT I AM, *and* I WILL BE WHAT I WILL BE; and He said, You shall say this to the Israelites, I AM has sent me to you!

15 God said also to Moses, This shall you say to the Israelites, The Lord, the God of your fathers, of Abraham, of Isaac, and of Jacob, has sent me to you! This is My name for ever, and by this name I am to be remembered to all generations.

16 Go, gather the elders of Israel together [the mature teachers and tribal leaders], and say to them, The Lord God of your fathers, the God of Abraham, of Isaac, and of Jacob, appeared to me, saying, I have surely visited you, and seen that which is done to you in Egypt;

17 And I have declared that I will bring you up out of the affliction of Egypt to the land of the Canaanite, the Hittite, the Amorite, the Perizzite, the Hivite, and the Jebusite, to a land flowing with milk and honey.

18 And [the elders] shall believe *and* obey your voice; and you shall go, you and the elders of Israel, to the king of Egypt, and you shall say to him, The Lord, the God of the Hebrews, has met with us; and now let us go, we beseech you, three days' journey into the wilderness, that we may sacrifice to the Lord our God.

19 And I know that the king of Egypt will not let you go [unless forced to do so], no, not by a mighty hand.

20 So I will stretch out My hand, and smite Egypt with all My wonders which I will do in it; and after that he will let you go.

21 And I will give this people favor *and* respect in the sight of the Egyptians; and it shall be that when you go, you shall not go empty-handed.

22 But every woman shall [insistently] solicit of her neighbor, and of her that may be residing at her house, jewels and articles of silver and gold, and garments, which you shall put on your sons and daughters; and you shall strip the Egyptians [of belongings due to you].

**4** AND MOSES answered, [a]But behold, they will not believe me or listen to *and* obey my voice; for they will say, The Lord has not appeared to you.

2 And the Lord said to him, What is that in your hand? And he said, A rod.

3 And He said, Cast it on the ground. And he did so, and it became a serpent [the symbol of royal and divine power worn on the crown of the Pharaohs]; and Moses fled from before it.

4 And the Lord said to Moses, Put forth your hand and take it by the tail. And he stretched out his hand and caught it, and it became a rod in his hand.

5 [This you shall do, said the Lord] that the elders may believe that the Lord, the God of their fathers, of Abraham, of Isaac, and of Jacob, has indeed appeared to you.

6 The Lord said also to him, Put your hand into your bosom. He put his hand into his bosom, and when he took it out, behold, his hand was leprous, as white as snow.

7 *God* said, Put your hand into your bosom again. So he put his hand back into his bosom, and when he took it out, behold, it was restored as the rest of his flesh.

8 [Then God said] If they will not believe you, or heed the voice *or* the testimony of the first sign, they may believe the voice *or* the witness of the second sign.

**AMP** [a] There need be no "buts" in our relationship to *God's* will. Nothing will take the Lord by surprise. The entire field has been surveyed and the preparations are complete. When the Lord says, "I will send thee," every provision has been made for the appointed task. "I will not fail thee." He who gives the command will also give the equipment (John Henry Jowett in *My Daily Meditation*).

## New American Standard

13¶ Then Moses said to God, "Behold, I am going to the sons
of Israel, and I shall say to them, 'The God of your fathers has sent
me to you.' Now they may say to me, 'What is His name?' What
shall I say to them?"
14And God said to Moses, "[b]I AM WHO [c]I AM"; and He said,
"Thus you shall say to the sons of Israel, '[d]I AM has sent me to
you.'"
15And God, furthermore, said to Moses, "Thus you shall say to
the sons of Israel, 'The LORD, the God of your fathers, the God of
Abraham, the God of Isaac, and the God of Jacob, has sent me to
you.' This is My name forever, and this is My memorial-name to
all generations.
16"Go and gather the elders of Israel together, and say to them,
'The LORD, the God of your fathers, the God of Abraham, Isaac and
Jacob, has appeared to me, saying, "I am indeed concerned about
you and what has been done to you in Egypt.
17"So I said, I will bring you up out of the affliction of Egypt to
the land of the Canaanite and the Hittite and the Amorite and the
Perizzite and the Hivite and the Jebusite, to a land flowing with
milk and honey."'
18"And they will pay heed to what you say; and you with the
elders of Israel will come to the king of Egypt, and you will say to
him, 'The LORD, the God of the Hebrews, has met with us. So now,
please, let us go a three days' journey into the wilderness, that we
may sacrifice to the LORD our God.'
19"But I know that the king of Egypt will not permit you to go,
except under compulsion.
20"So I will stretch out My hand, and strike Egypt with all My
miracles which I shall do in the midst of it; and after that he will
let you go.
21"And I will grant this people favor in the sight of the Egyptians; and it shall be that when you go, you will not go empty-
handed.
22"But every woman shall ask of her neighbor and the woman
who lives in her house, articles of silver and articles of gold, and
clothing; and you will put them on your sons and daughters. Thus
you will plunder the Egyptians."

*Moses Given Powers*

4 THEN MOSES answered and said, "What if they will not
believe me, or listen to what I say? For they may say, 'The
LORD has not appeared to you.'"
2And the LORD said to him, "What is that in your hand?" And
he said, "A staff."
3Then He said, "Throw it on the ground." So he threw it on
the ground, and it became a serpent; and Moses fled from it.
4But the LORD said to Moses, "Stretch out your hand and grasp
*it* by its tail"—so he stretched out his hand and caught it, and it
became a staff in his hand—
5"that they may believe that the LORD, the God of their fathers,
the God of Abraham, the God of Isaac, and the God of Jacob, has
appeared to you."
6And the LORD furthermore said to him, "Now put your hand
into your bosom." So he put his hand into his bosom, and when
he took it out, behold, his hand was leprous like snow.
7Then He said, "Put your hand into your bosom again." So he
put his hand into his bosom again; and when he took it out of his
bosom, behold, it was restored like *the rest of* his flesh.
8"And it shall come about that if they will not believe you or
heed the witness of the first sign, they may believe the witness of
the last sign.

NAS [b] Related to the name of God, *YHWH*, rendered *LORD*, which is derived from the verb *HAYAH*, *to be* [c] Related to the name of God, *YHWH*, rendered *LORD*, which is derived from the verb *HAYAH*, *to be* [d] Related to the name of God, *YHWH*, rendered *LORD*, which is derived from the verb *HAYAH*, *to be*

## New International

13Moses said to God, "Suppose I go to the Israelites and say to
them, 'The God of your fathers has sent me to you,' and they ask
me, 'What is his name?' Then what shall I tell them?"
14God said to Moses, "I AM WHO I AM.[e] This is what you are
to say to the Israelites: 'I AM has sent me to you.'"
15God also said to Moses, "Say to the Israelites, 'The LORD,[f] the
God of your fathers—the God of Abraham, the God of Isaac and
the God of Jacob—has sent me to you.' This is my name forever,
the name by which I am to be remembered from generation to
generation.
16"Go, assemble the elders of Israel and say to them, 'The LORD,
the God of your fathers—the God of Abraham, Isaac and Jacob—
appeared to me and said: I have watched over you and have seen
what has been done to you in Egypt. 17And I have promised to
bring you up out of your misery in Egypt into the land of the
Canaanites, Hittites, Amorites, Perizzites, Hivites and Jebusites—
a land flowing with milk and honey.'
18"The elders of Israel will listen to you. Then you and the
elders are to go to the king of Egypt and say to him, 'The LORD,
the God of the Hebrews, has met with us. Let us take a three-day
journey into the desert to offer sacrifices to the LORD our God.'
19But I know that the king of Egypt will not let you go unless a
mighty hand compels him. 20So I will stretch out my hand and
strike the Egyptians with all the wonders that I will perform among
them. After that, he will let you go.
21"And I will make the Egyptians favorably disposed toward
this people, so that when you leave you will not go empty-handed.
22Every woman is to ask her neighbor and any woman living in her
house for articles of silver and gold and for clothing, which you
will put on your sons and daughters. And so you will plunder the
Egyptians."

*Signs for Moses*

4 MOSES ANSWERED, "What if they do not believe me or
listen to me and say, 'The LORD did not appear to you'?"
2Then the LORD said to him, "What is that in your hand?"
"A staff," he replied.
3The LORD said, "Throw it on the ground."
Moses threw it on the ground and it became a snake, and he
ran from it. 4Then the LORD said to him, "Reach out your hand and
take it by the tail." So Moses reached out and took hold of the
snake and it turned back into a staff in his hand. 5"This," said the
LORD, "is so that they may believe that the LORD, the God of their
fathers—the God of Abraham, the God of Isaac and the God of
Jacob—has appeared to you."
6Then the LORD said, "Put your hand inside your cloak." So
Moses put his hand into his cloak, and when he took it out, it was
leprous,[g] like snow.
7"Now put it back into your cloak," he said. So Moses put his
hand back into his cloak, and when he took it out, it was restored,
like the rest of his flesh.
8Then the LORD said, "If they do not believe you or pay attention to the first miraculous sign, they may believe the second. 9But

NIV [e] 14 Or *I WILL BE WHAT I WILL BE* [f] 15 The Hebrew for *LORD* sounds like and may be derived from the Hebrew for *I AM* in verse 14. [g] 6 The Hebrew word was used for various diseases affecting the skin—not necessarily leprosy.

## King James

9 And it shall come to pass, if they will not believe also these two signs, neither hearken unto thy voice, that thou shalt take of the water of the river, and pour *it* upon the dry *land:* and the water which thou takest out of the river shall become blood upon the dry *land.*

10 ¶ And Moses said unto the LORD, O my Lord, I *am* not eloquent, neither heretofore, nor since thou hast spoken unto thy servant: but I *am* slow of speech, and of a slow tongue.

11 And the LORD said unto him, Who hath made man's mouth? or who maketh the dumb, or deaf, or the seeing, or the blind? have not I the LORD?

12 Now therefore go, and I will be with thy mouth, and teach thee what thou shalt say.

13 And he said, O my Lord, send, I pray thee, by the hand *of him whom* thou wilt send.

14 And the anger of the LORD was kindled against Moses, and he said, *Is* not Aaron the Levite thy brother? I know that he can speak well. And also, behold, he cometh forth to meet thee: and when he seeth thee, he will be glad in his heart.

15 And thou shalt speak unto him, and put words in his mouth: and I will be with thy mouth, and with his mouth, and will teach you what ye shall do.

16 And he shall be thy spokesman unto the people: and he shall be, *even* he shall be to thee instead of a mouth, and thou shalt be to him instead of God.

17 And thou shalt take this rod in thine hand, wherewith thou shalt do signs.

18 ¶ And Moses went and returned to Jethro his father-in-law, and said unto him, Let me go, I pray thee, and return unto my brethren which *are* in Egypt, and see whether they be yet alive. And Jethro said to Moses, Go in peace.

19 And the LORD said unto Moses in Midian, Go, return into Egypt: for all the men are dead which sought thy life.

20 And Moses took his wife and his sons, and set them upon an ass, and he returned to the land of Egypt: and Moses took the rod of God in his hand.

21 And the LORD said unto Moses, When thou goest to return into Egypt, see that thou do all those wonders before Pharaoh, which I have put in thine hand: but I will harden his heart, that he shall not let the people go.

22 And thou shalt say unto Pharaoh, Thus saith the LORD, Israel *is* my son, *even* my firstborn:

23 And I say unto thee, Let my son go, that he may serve me: and if thou refuse to let him go, behold, I will slay thy son, *even* thy firstborn.

24 ¶ And it came to pass by the way in the inn, that the LORD met him, and sought to kill him.

25 Then Zipporah took a sharp stone, and cut off the foreskin of her son, and cast *it* at his feet, and said, Surely a bloody husband *art* thou to me.

26 So he let him go: then she said, A bloody husband *thou art,* because of the circumcision.

27 ¶ And the LORD said to Aaron, Go into the wilderness to meet Moses. And he went, and met him in the mount of God, and kissed him.

28 And Moses told Aaron all the words of the LORD who had sent him, and all the signs which he had commanded him.

29 ¶ And Moses and Aaron went and gathered together all the elders of the children of Israel:

30 And Aaron spake all the words which the LORD had spoken unto Moses, and did the signs in the sight of the people.

31 And the people believed: and when they heard that the LORD had visited the children of Israel, and that he had looked upon their affliction, then they bowed their heads and worshipped.

## Amplified

9 But, if they will also not believe these two signs or heed your voice, you shall take some water of the river [Nile], and pour it upon the dry land; and the water which you take out of the river [Nile] shall become blood on the dry land.

10 And Moses said to the Lord, O Lord, I am not eloquent *or* a man of words, neither before nor since You have spoken to Your servant; for I am slow of speech, and have a heavy *and* awkward tongue.

11 And the Lord said to him, Who has made man's mouth? Or who makes the dumb, or deaf, or the seeing, or the blind? Is it not I, the Lord?

12 Now therefore go, and I will be with your mouth, and will teach you what you shall say.

13 And he said, Oh, my Lord, I pray You, send by the hand of [some other] whom You will *send.*

14 Then the anger of the Lord blazed against Moses; He said, Is there not Aaron your brother, the Levite? I know he can speak well. Also, he is coming out to meet you, and when he sees you, he will be overjoyed.

15 You must speak to him and put the words in his mouth; and I will be with your mouth and with his mouth, and will teach you what you shall do.

16 He shall speak for you to the people, acting as a mouthpiece for you, and you shall be *as* God to him.

17 And you shall take this rod in your hand, with which you shall work the signs [that prove I sent you].

18 And Moses went away and, returning to Jethro his father-in-law, said to him, Let me go back, I pray you, to my relatives in Egypt to see whether they are still alive. And Jethro said to Moses, Go in peace.

19 The Lord said to Moses in Midian, Go back to Egypt; for all the men who were seeking your life [for killing the Egyptian] are dead. [Exod. 2:11, 12.]

20 And Moses took his wife and his sons, and set them on donkeys, and he returned to the land of Egypt; and Moses took the rod of God in his hand.

21 And the Lord said to Moses, When you return into Egypt, see that you do before Pharaoh all those miracles *and* wonders which I have put in your hand; but I will make him stubborn *and* harden his heart, so that he will not let the people go.

22 And you shall say to Pharaoh, Thus says the Lord, Israel is my son, even my first-born.

23 And I say to you, Let My son go, that he may serve Me; and if you refuse to let him go, behold, I will slay your son, your first-born.

24 Along the way at a [*resting*] place, the Lord met *Moses* and sought to kill him [made him acutely and almost fatally ill].

25 [Now apparently he had [a]failed to circumcise one of his sons, his wife being opposed to it; but seeing his life in such danger] Zipporah took a flint knife and cut off the foreskin of her son and cast it to touch *Moses'* feet, and said, Surely a husband of blood you are to me!

26 When *He* let *Moses* alone [to recover], Zipporah said, A husband of blood are you, because of the circumcision.

27 The Lord said to Aaron, Go into the wilderness to meet Moses. And he went, and met him in [Horeb or Sinai] the mountain of God, and kissed him.

28 Moses told Aaron all the words of the Lord with which He had sent him, and all the signs with which He had charged him.

29 Moses and Aaron went and gathered together [in Egypt] all the elders of the Israelites.

30 Aaron spoke all the words which the Lord had spoken to Moses, and did the signs in the sight of the people.

31 And the people believed; and when they heard that the Lord had visited the Israelites, and that He had looked (in compassion) upon their affliction, they bowed their heads and worshiped.

**AMP** [a] He who is on his way to liberate the people of the circumcision, has in Midian even neglected to circumcise his second son Eliezer (Lange's *Commentary*). It was necessary that at this stage of Moses' experience he should learn that God is in earnest when He speaks, and will assuredly perform all that He has threatened (Murphy's *Commentary*).

## New American Standard

9"But it shall be that if they will not believe even these two
signs or heed what you say, then you shall take some water from
the Nile and pour it on the dry ground; and the water which you
take from the Nile will become blood on the dry ground."
10¶ Then Moses said to the LORD, "Please, Lord, I have never
been eloquent, neither recently nor in time past, nor since Thou
hast spoken to Thy servant; for I am slow of speech and slow of
tongue."
11And the LORD said to him, "Who has made man's mouth? Or
who makes *him* dumb or deaf, or seeing or blind? Is it not I, the
LORD?
12"Now then go, and I, even I, will be with your mouth, and
teach you what you are to say."
13But he said, "Please, Lord, now send *the message* by whomever Thou wilt."

*Aaron to Be Moses' Mouthpiece*

14Then the anger of the LORD burned against Moses, and He
said, "Is there not your brother Aaron the Levite? I know that he
speaks fluently. And moreover, behold, he is coming out to meet
you; when he sees you, he will be glad in his heart.
15"And you are to speak to him and put the words in his mouth;
and I, even I, will be with your mouth and his mouth, and I will
teach you what you are to do.
16"Moreover, he shall speak for you to the people; and it shall
come about that he shall be as a mouth for you, and you shall be
as God to him.
17"And you shall take in your hand this staff, with which you
shall perform the signs."
18¶ Then Moses departed and returned to Jethro his father-in-
law, and said to him, "Please, let me go, that I may return to my
brethren who are in Egypt, and see if they are still alive." And
Jethro said to Moses, "Go in peace."
19Now the LORD said to Moses in Midian, "Go back to Egypt,
for all the men who were seeking your life are dead."
20So Moses took his wife and his sons and mounted them on
a donkey, and he returned to the land of Egypt. Moses also took
the staff of God in his hand.
21And the LORD said to Moses, "When you go back to Egypt see
that you perform before Pharaoh all the wonders which I have put
in your power; but I will harden his heart so that he will not let
the people go.
22"Then you shall say to Pharaoh, 'Thus says the LORD, "Israel
is My son, My first-born.
23"So I said to you, 'Let My son go, that he may serve Me'; but
you have refused to let him go. Behold, I will kill your son, your
first-born."'"
24¶ Now it came about at the lodging place on the way that the
LORD met him and sought to put him to death.
25Then Zipporah took a flint and cut off her son's foreskin and
threw *it* at Moses' feet, and she said, "You are indeed a bridegroom of blood to me."
26So He let him alone. At that time she said, "*You are* a bridegroom of blood"—because of the circumcision.
27¶ Now the LORD said to Aaron, "Go to meet Moses in the
wilderness." So he went and met him at the mountain of God, and
he kissed him.
28And Moses told Aaron all the words of the LORD with which
He had sent him, and all the signs that He had commanded him
*to do.*
29Then Moses and Aaron went and assembled all the elders of
the sons of Israel;
30and Aaron spoke all the words which the LORD had spoken
to Moses. He then performed the signs in the sight of the people.
31So the people believed; and when they heard that the LORD
was concerned about the sons of Israel and that He had seen their
affliction, then they bowed low and worshiped.

## New International

if they do not believe these two signs or listen to you, take some
water from the Nile and pour it on the dry ground. The water you
take from the river will become blood on the ground."
10Moses said to the LORD, "O Lord, I have never been eloquent,
neither in the past nor since you have spoken to your servant. I
am slow of speech and tongue."
11The LORD said to him, "Who gave man his mouth? Who
makes him deaf or mute? Who gives him sight or makes him blind?
Is it not I, the LORD? 12Now go; I will help you speak and will teach
you what to say."
13But Moses said, "O Lord, please send someone else to do it."
14Then the LORD's anger burned against Moses and he said,
"What about your brother, Aaron the Levite? I know he can speak
well. He is already on his way to meet you, and his heart will be
glad when he sees you. 15You shall speak to him and put words
in his mouth; I will help both of you speak and will teach you what
to do. 16He will speak to the people for you, and it will be as if he
were your mouth and as if you were God to him. 17But take this
staff in your hand so you can perform miraculous signs with it."

*Moses Returns to Egypt*

18Then Moses went back to Jethro his father-in-law and said to
him, "Let me go back to my own people in Egypt to see if any of
them are still alive."
Jethro said, "Go, and I wish you well."
19Now the LORD had said to Moses in Midian, "Go back to
Egypt, for all the men who wanted to kill you are dead." 20So
Moses took his wife and sons, put them on a donkey and started
back to Egypt. And he took the staff of God in his hand.
21The LORD said to Moses, "When you return to Egypt, see that
you perform before Pharaoh all the wonders I have given you the
power to do. But I will harden his heart so that he will not let the
people go. 22Then say to Pharaoh, 'This is what the LORD says:
Israel is my firstborn son, 23and I told you, "Let my son go, so he
may worship me." But you refused to let him go; so I will kill your
firstborn son.'"
24At a lodging place on the way, the LORD met ⌞Moses⌟[b] and was
about to kill him. 25But Zipporah took a flint knife, cut off her son's
foreskin and touched ⌞Moses'⌟ feet with it.[c] "Surely you are a
bridegroom of blood to me," she said. 26So the LORD let him alone.
(At that time she said "bridegroom of blood," referring to circumcision.)
27The LORD said to Aaron, "Go into the desert to meet Moses."
So he met Moses at the mountain of God and kissed him. 28Then
Moses told Aaron everything the LORD had sent him to say, and
also about all the miraculous signs he had commanded him to
perform.
29Moses and Aaron brought together all the elders of the Israelites, 30and Aaron told them everything the LORD had said to
Moses. He also performed the signs before the people, 31and they
believed. And when they heard that the LORD was concerned
about them and had seen their misery, they bowed down and
worshiped.

NIV [b]24 Or *Moses' son*; Hebrew *him* [c]25 Or *and drew near ⌞Moses'⌟ feet*

## King James

5 AND AFTERWARD Moses and Aaron went in, and told
Pharaoh, Thus saith the LORD God of Israel, Let my people
go, that they may hold a feast unto me in the wilderness.
2And Pharaoh said, Who *is* the LORD, that I should obey his
voice to let Israel go? I know not the LORD, neither will I let Israel
go.
3And they said, The God of the Hebrews hath met with us: let
us go, we pray thee, three days' journey into the desert, and
sacrifice unto the LORD our God; lest he fall upon us with pestilence, or with the sword.
4And the king of Egypt said unto them, Wherefore do ye,
Moses and Aaron, let the people from their works? get you unto
your burdens.
5And Pharaoh said, Behold, the people of the land now *are*
many, and ye make them rest from their burdens.
6And Pharaoh commanded the same day the taskmasters of the
people, and their officers, saying,
7Ye shall no more give the people straw to make brick, as
heretofore: let them go and gather straw for themselves.
8And the tale of the bricks, which they did make heretofore, ye
shall lay upon them; ye shall not diminish *aught* thereof: for they
*be* idle; therefore they cry, saying, Let us go *and* sacrifice to our
God.
9Let there more work be laid upon the men, that they may
labour therein; and let them not regard vain words.
10¶ And the taskmasters of the people went out, and their
officers, and they spake to the people, saying, Thus saith Pharaoh,
I will not give you straw.
11Go ye, get you straw where ye can find it: yet not aught of
your work shall be diminished.
12So the people were scattered abroad throughout all the land
of Egypt to gather stubble instead of straw.
13And the taskmasters hasted *them*, saying, Fulfil your works,
*your* daily tasks, as when there was straw.
14And the officers of the children of Israel, which Pharaoh's
taskmasters had set over them, were beaten, *and* demanded,
Wherefore have ye not fulfilled your task in making brick both
yesterday and today, as heretofore?
15¶ Then the officers of the children of Israel came and cried
unto Pharaoh, saying, Wherefore dealest thou thus with thy servants?
16There is no straw given unto thy servants, and they say to us,
Make brick: and, behold, thy servants *are* beaten; but the fault *is*
in thine own people.
17But he said, Ye *are* idle, *ye are* idle: therefore ye say, Let us go
*and* do sacrifice to the LORD.
18Go therefore now, *and* work; for there shall no straw be given
you, yet shall ye deliver the tale of bricks.
19And the officers of the children of Israel did see *that* they *were*
in evil *case*, after it was said, Ye shall not minish *aught* from your
bricks of your daily task.
20¶ And they met Moses and Aaron, who stood in the way, as
they came forth from Pharaoh:
21And they said unto them, The LORD look upon you, and
judge; because ye have made our savour to be abhorred in the eyes
of Pharaoh, and in the eyes of his servants, to put a sword in their
hand to slay us.

## Amplified

5 AFTERWARD MOSES and Aaron went in and told Pharaoh,
Thus says the Lord, the God of Israel, Let My people go, that
they may hold a feast to Me in the wilderness.
2But Pharaoh said, Who is the Lord, that I should obey His voice
to let Israel go? I know not the Lord, neither will I let Israel go.
3And they said, The God of the Hebrews has met with us; let
us go, we pray you, three days' journey into the desert, and
sacrifice to the Lord our God; lest He fall upon us with pestilence
or with the sword.
4The king of Egypt said to Moses and Aaron, Why do you take
the people from their jobs? Get to your burdens!
5Pharaoh said, Behold, the people of the land now are many,
and you make them rest from their burdens!
6The very same day Pharaoh commanded the taskmasters of
the people and their officers,
7You shall no more give the people straw to make brick; let them
go and gather straw for themselves.
8But the number of the bricks which they made before you shall
still require of them; you shall not diminish it in the least. For they
are idle; that is why they cry, Let us go and sacrifice to our God.
9Let heavier work be laid upon the men that they may labor at
it and pay no attention to lying words.
10The taskmasters of the people went out, and their officers,
and they said to the people, Thus says Pharaoh, I will not give you
straw.
11Go, get [a]straw where you can find it; but your work shall not
be diminished in the least.
12So the people were scattered through all the land of Egypt to
gather the short stubble instead of straw.
13And the taskmasters were urgent, saying, Finish your work,
your daily quotas, as when there was straw.
14And the Hebrew foremen, whom Pharaoh's taskmasters had
set over them, were beaten, and were asked, Why have you not
fulfilled all your quota of making bricks yesterday and today, as
before?
15Then the Hebrew foremen came to Pharaoh and cried, Why
do you deal like this with your servants?
16No straw is given to your servants, yet they say to us, Make
brick! And behold, your servants are beaten; but the fault is in your
own people.
17But [Pharaoh] said, You are idle, lazy *and* idle! That is why you
say, Let us go and sacrifice to the Lord.
18Get out now, and get to work; for no straw shall be given you,
yet you shall deliver the full quota of bricks.
19And the Hebrew foremen saw that they were in an evil situation when it was said, You shall not diminish in the least your full
daily quota of bricks.
20And the foremen met Moses and Aaron, who were standing
in the way as they came forth from Pharaoh.
21And the foremen said to them, The Lord look upon you and
judge, because you have made us a rotten stench to be detested
by Pharaoh and his servants, and have put a sword in their hand
to slay us.

**AMP** [a] Archaeologists became interested early in examining Egyptian bricks of Moses' time to see if they contained straw. They found that while many did contain straw, many also did not, leaving the impression that the Bible was wrong. But as usual in such cases, sooner or later it is shown that "the testimony of the Lord is sure, making wise the simple" (Ps. 19:7)—who know no better than to doubt the truth of God's Word. It is now known that water in which oat straw has been boiled, when added to clay makes it much easier to handle. Without the organic material obtained from the straw, the difficulty of making bricks was greatly increased. The fact that brick makers of Egypt found the use of straw essential, whether visible evidence remains or not, is fully borne out, as various writers have asserted. (See Allan A. MacRae's summary in *The Relation of Archaeology to the Bible.*)

## New American Standard

*Israel's Labor Increased*

**5** AND AFTERWARD Moses and Aaron came and said to Pharaoh, "Thus says the LORD, the God of Israel, 'Let My people go that they may celebrate a feast to Me in the wilderness.'"

2But Pharaoh said, "Who is the LORD that I should obey His voice to let Israel go? I do not know the LORD, and besides, I will not let Israel go."

3Then they said, "The God of the Hebrews has met with us. Please, let us go a three days' journey into the wilderness that we may sacrifice to the LORD our God, lest He fall upon us with pestilence or with the sword."

4But the king of Egypt said to them, "Moses and Aaron, why do you draw the people away from their work? Get *back* to your labors!"

5Again Pharaoh said, "Look, the people of the land are now many, and you would have them cease from their labors!"

6So the same day Pharaoh commanded the taskmasters over the people and their foremen, saying,

7"You are no longer to give the people straw to make brick as previously; let them go and gather straw for themselves.

8"But the quota of bricks which they were making previously, you shall impose on them; you are not to reduce any of it. Because they are lazy, therefore they cry out, 'Let us go and sacrifice to our God.'

9"Let the labor be heavier on the men, and let them work at it that they may pay no attention to false words."

10¶ So the taskmasters of the people and their foremen went out and spoke to the people, saying, "Thus says Pharaoh, 'I am not going to give you *any* straw.

11'You go *and* get straw for yourselves wherever you can find *it;* but none of your labor will be reduced.'"

12So the people scattered through all the land of Egypt to gather stubble for straw.

13And the taskmasters pressed them, saying, "Complete your work quota, *your* daily amount, just as when you had straw."

14Moreover, the foremen of the sons of Israel, whom Pharaoh's taskmasters had set over them, were beaten and were asked, "Why have you not completed your required amount either yesterday or today in making brick as previously?"

15¶ Then the foremen of the sons of Israel came and cried out to Pharaoh, saying, "Why do you deal this way with your servants?

16"There is no straw given to your servants, yet they keep saying to us, 'Make bricks!' And behold, your servants are being beaten; but it is the fault of your *own* people."

17But he said, "You are lazy, *very* lazy; therefore you say, 'Let us go *and* sacrifice to the LORD.'

18"So go now *and* work; for you shall be given no straw, yet you must deliver the quota of bricks."

19And the foremen of the sons of Israel saw that they were in trouble because they were told, "You must not reduce *your* daily amount of bricks."

20When they left Pharaoh's presence, they met Moses and Aaron as they were waiting for them.

21And they said to them, "May the LORD look upon you and judge *you*, for you have made [b]us odious in Pharaoh's sight and in the sight of his servants, to put a sword in their hand to kill us."

NAS [b] Lit., *our savor to stink*

## New International

*Bricks Without Straw*

**5** AFTERWARD MOSES and Aaron went to Pharaoh and said,
"This is what the LORD, the God of Israel, says: 'Let my
people go, so that they may hold a festival to me in the desert.'"
2Pharaoh said, "Who is the LORD, that I should obey him and
let Israel go? I do not know the LORD and I will not let Israel go."
3Then they said, "The God of the Hebrews has met with us.
Now let us take a three-day journey into the desert to offer sacrifices to the LORD our God, or he may strike us with plagues or with
the sword."
4But the king of Egypt said, "Moses and Aaron, why are you
taking the people away from their labor? Get back to your work!"
5Then Pharaoh said, "Look, the people of the land are now numerous, and you are stopping them from working."
6That same day Pharaoh gave this order to the slave drivers and
foremen in charge of the people: 7"You are no longer to supply the
people with straw for making bricks; let them go and gather their
own straw. 8But require them to make the same number of bricks
as before; don't reduce the quota. They are lazy; that is why they
are crying out, 'Let us go and sacrifice to our God.' 9Make the work
harder for the men so that they keep working and pay no attention
to lies."
10Then the slave drivers and the foremen went out and said to
the people, "This is what Pharaoh says: 'I will not give you any
more straw. 11Go and get your own straw wherever you can find
it, but your work will not be reduced at all.'" 12So the people
scattered all over Egypt to gather stubble to use for straw. 13The
slave drivers kept pressing them, saying, "Complete the work
required of you for each day, just as when you had straw." 14The
Israelite foremen appointed by Pharaoh's slave drivers were beaten and were asked, "Why didn't you meet your quota of bricks
yesterday or today, as before?"
15Then the Israelite foremen went and appealed to Pharaoh:
"Why have you treated your servants this way? 16Your servants
are given no straw, yet we are told, 'Make bricks!' Your servants
are being beaten, but the fault is with your own people."
17Pharaoh said, "Lazy, that's what you are—lazy! That is why
you keep saying, 'Let us go and sacrifice to the LORD.' 18Now get
to work. You will not be given any straw, yet you must produce
your full quota of bricks."
19The Israelite foremen realized they were in trouble when they
were told, "You are not to reduce the number of bricks required
of you for each day." 20When they left Pharaoh, they found Moses
and Aaron waiting to meet them, 21and they said, "May the LORD
look upon you and judge you! You have made us a stench to
Pharaoh and his officials and have put a sword in their hand to kill
us."

## King James

22And Moses returned unto the LORD, and said, Lord, wherefore hast thou *so* evil entreated this people? why *is* it *that* thou hast sent me?

23For since I came to Pharaoh to speak in thy name, he hath done evil to this people; neither hast thou delivered thy people at all.

6 THEN THE LORD said unto Moses, Now shalt thou see what I will do to Pharaoh: for with a strong hand shall he let them go, and with a strong hand shall he drive them out of his land.

2And God spake unto Moses, and said unto him, I *am* the LORD:

3And I appeared unto Abraham, unto Isaac, and unto Jacob, by *the name of* God Almighty, but by my name JEHOVAH was I not known to them.

4And I have also established my covenant with them, to give them the land of Canaan, the land of their pilgrimage, wherein they were strangers.

5And I have also heard the groaning of the children of Israel, whom the Egyptians keep in bondage; and I have remembered my covenant.

6Wherefore say unto the children of Israel, I *am* the LORD, and I will bring you out from under the burdens of the Egyptians, and I will rid you out of their bondage, and I will redeem you with a stretched out arm, and with great judgments:

7And I will take you to me for a people, and I will be to you a God: and ye shall know that I *am* the LORD your God, which bringeth you out from under the burdens of the Egyptians.

8And I will bring you in unto the land, concerning the which I did swear to give it to Abraham, to Isaac, and to Jacob; and I will give it you for an heritage: I *am* the LORD.

9¶ And Moses spake so unto the children of Israel: but they hearkened not unto Moses for anguish of spirit, and for cruel bondage.

10And the LORD spake unto Moses, saying,

11Go in, speak unto Pharaoh king of Egypt, that he let the children of Israel go out of his land.

12And Moses spake before the LORD, saying, Behold, the children of Israel have not hearkened unto me; how then shall Pharaoh hear me, who *am* of uncircumcised lips?

13And the LORD spake unto Moses and unto Aaron, and gave them a charge unto the children of Israel, and unto Pharaoh king of Egypt, to bring the children of Israel out of the land of Egypt.

14¶ These *be* the heads of their fathers' houses: The sons of Reuben the firstborn of Israel; Hanoch, and Pallu, Hezron, and Carmi: these *be* the families of Reuben.

15And the sons of Simeon; Jemuel, and Jamin, and Ohad, and Jachin, and Zohar, and Shaul the son of a Canaanitish woman: these *are* the families of Simeon.

16¶ And these *are* the names of the sons of Levi according to their generations; Gershon, and Kohath, and Merari: and the years of the life of Levi *were* an hundred thirty and seven years.

17The sons of Gershon; Libni, and Shimi, according to their families.

18And the sons of Kohath; Amram, and Izhar, and Hebron, and Uzziel: and the years of the life of Kohath *were* an hundred thirty and three years.

19And the sons of Merari; Mahali and Mushi: these *are* the families of Levi according to their generations.

20And Amram took him Jochebed his father's sister to wife; and she bare him Aaron and Moses: and the years of the life of Amram *were* an hundred and thirty and seven years.

21¶ And the sons of Izhar; Korah, and Nepheg, and Zichri.

22And the sons of Uzziel; Mishael, and Elzaphan, and Zithri.

## Amplified

22Then Moses turned again to the Lord and said, O Lord, why have You dealt evil to this people? Why did You ever send me?

23For since I came to Pharaoh to speak in Your name, he has done evil to this people, neither have You delivered Your people at all.

6 THEN THE Lord said to Moses, Now you shall see what I will do to Pharaoh; for [compelled] by a strong hand he will [not only] let them go, but he will drive them out of his land with a strong hand.

2And God said to Moses, I am the Lord.

3I appeared to Abraham, to Isaac, and to Jacob, as God Almighty [El Shaddai], but by My name the Lord [Yaweh] [the redemptive name of God]—I did not make Myself known to them [in acts and great miracles].

4I have also established My covenant with them, to give them the land of Canaan, the land of their temporary residence, in which they were strangers.

5I have also heard the groaning of the Israelites whom the Egyptians have enslaved; and I have [earnestly] remembered My covenant [with Abraham, Isaac, and Jacob].

6Accordingly, say to the Israelites, I am the Lord, and I will bring you out from under the burdens of the Egyptians, and I will free you from their bondage, and I will rescue you with an outstretched arm—with special and vigorous action—and by mighty acts of judgment.

7And I will take you to Me for a people, and I will be to you a God; and you shall know that it is I, the Lord your God, Who brings you out from under the burdens of the Egyptians.

8And I will bring you into the land concerning which I lifted up My hand *and* swore that I would give it to Abraham, Isaac, and Jacob; and I will give it to you for a heritage. I am the Lord [you have the pledge of My changeless omnipotence and faithfulness].

9Moses told this to the Israelites; but they refused to listen to Moses because of their impatience *and* anguish of spirit, and because of their cruel bondage.

10The Lord said to Moses,

11Go in, tell Pharaoh king of Egypt to let the Israelites go out of his land.

12But Moses said to the Lord, Behold, [my own people] the Israelites have not listened to me; how then shall Pharaoh give heed to me, who am of deficient *and* impeded speech?

13But the Lord spoke to Moses and Aaron, and gave them a command to the Israelites and to Pharaoh king of Egypt to bring the Israelites out of the land of Egypt.

14These are the heads of their clans. The sons of Reuben, Israel's first-born: Hanoch, Pallu, Hezron, and Carmi; these are the families of Reuben.

15The sons of Simeon: Jemuel, Jamin, Ohad, Jachin, Zohar, and Shaul the son of a Canaanite woman; these are the families of Simeon.

16These are the names of the sons of Levi according to their births: Gershon, Kohath, and Merari; and Levi lived 137 years.

17The sons of Gershon: Libni and Shimi, by their families.

18The sons of Kohath: Amram, Izhar, Hebron, and Uzziel; and Kohath lived 133 years.

19The sons of Merari: Mahli and Mushi. These are the families of Levi according to their generations.

20Amram took Jochebed his father's sister as wife, and she bore him Aaron and Moses; and Amram lived 137 years.

21The sons of Izhar: Korah, Nepheg, and Zichri.

22The sons of Uzziel: Mishael, Elzaphan, and Sithri.

## New American Standard

22¶ Then Moses returned to the LORD and said, "O Lord, why
hast Thou brought harm to this people? Why didst Thou ever send
me?
23"Ever since I came to Pharaoh to speak in Thy name, he has
done harm to this people; and Thou hast not delivered Thy people
at all."

*God Promises Action*

6 THEN THE LORD said to Moses, "Now you shall see what I
will do to Pharaoh; for under compulsion he shall let them go,
and under compulsion he shall drive them out of his land."
2¶ God spoke further to Moses and said to him, "I am the LORD;
3and I appeared to Abraham, Isaac, and Jacob, as God Almighty, but *by* My name, [a]LORD, I did not make Myself known to
them.
4"And I also established My covenant with them, to give them
the land of Canaan, the land in which they sojourned.
5"And furthermore I have heard the groaning of the sons of
Israel, because the Egyptians are holding them in bondage; and I
have remembered My covenant.
6"Say, therefore, to the sons of Israel, 'I am the LORD, and I will
bring you out from under the burdens of the Egyptians, and I will
deliver you from their bondage. I will also redeem you with an
outstretched arm and with great judgments.
7'Then I will take you for My people, and I will be your God;
and you shall know that I am the LORD your God, who brought
you out from under the burdens of the Egyptians.
8'And I will bring you to the land which I swore to give to
Abraham, Isaac, and Jacob, and I will give it to you *for* a possession;
I am the LORD.'"
9So Moses spoke thus to the sons of Israel, but they did not
listen to Moses on account of *their* despondency and cruel bondage.
10¶ Now the LORD spoke to Moses, saying,
11"Go, tell Pharaoh king of Egypt to let the sons of Israel go out
of his land."
12But Moses spoke before the LORD, saying, "Behold, the sons
of Israel have not listened to me; how then will Pharaoh listen to
me, for I am unskilled in speech?"
13Then the LORD spoke to Moses and to Aaron, and gave them
a charge to the sons of Israel and to Pharaoh king of Egypt, to bring
the sons of Israel out of the land of Egypt.

*The Heads of Israel*

14¶ These are the heads of their fathers' households. The sons
of Reuben, Israel's first-born: Hanoch and Pallu, Hezron and Carmi; these are the families of Reuben.
15And the sons of Simeon: Jemuel and Jamin and Ohad and
Jachin and Zohar and Shaul the son of a Canaanite woman; these
are the families of Simeon.
16And these are the names of the sons of Levi according to their
generations: Gershon and Kohath and Merari; and the length of
Levi's life was one hundred and thirty-seven years.
17The sons of Gershon: Libni and Shimei, according to their
families.
18And the sons of Kohath: Amram and Izhar and Hebron and
Uzziel; and the length of Kohath's life was one hundred and
thirty-three years.
19And the sons of Merari: Mahli and Mushi. These are the
families of the Levites according to their generations.
20And Amram married his father's sister Jochebed, and she
bore him Aaron and Moses; and the length of Amram's life was
one hundred and thirty-seven years.
21And the sons of Izhar: Korah and Nepheg and Zichri.
22And the sons of Uzziel: Mishael and Elzaphan and Sithri.

**NAS** [a] Heb., *YHWH*, usually rendered *LORD*

## New International

*God Promises Deliverance*

22Moses returned to the LORD and said, "O Lord, why have you
brought trouble upon this people? Is this why you sent me? 23Ever
since I went to Pharaoh to speak in your name, he has brought
trouble upon this people, and you have not rescued your people
at all."

6 THEN THE LORD said to Moses, "Now you will see what I
will do to Pharaoh: Because of my mighty hand he will let
them go; because of my mighty hand he will drive them out of his
country."
2God also said to Moses, "I am the LORD. 3I appeared to Abraham, to Isaac and to Jacob as God Almighty,[b] but by my name the
LORD[c] I did not make myself known to them.[d] 4I also established
my covenant with them to give them the land of Canaan, where
they lived as aliens. 5Moreover, I have heard the groaning of the
Israelites, whom the Egyptians are enslaving, and I have remembered my covenant.
6"Therefore, say to the Israelites: 'I am the LORD, and I will
bring you out from under the yoke of the Egyptians. I will free you
from being slaves to them, and I will redeem you with an outstretched arm and with mighty acts of judgment. 7I will take you
as my own people, and I will be your God. Then you will know
that I am the LORD your God, who brought you out from under
the yoke of the Egyptians. 8And I will bring you to the land I swore
with uplifted hand to give to Abraham, to Isaac and to Jacob. I will
give it to you as a possession. I am the LORD.'"
9Moses reported this to the Israelites, but they did not listen to
him because of their discouragement and cruel bondage.
10Then the LORD said to Moses, 11"Go, tell Pharaoh king of
Egypt to let the Israelites go out of his country."
12But Moses said to the LORD, "If the Israelites will not listen
to me, why would Pharaoh listen to me, since I speak with faltering lips[e]?"

*Family Record of Moses and Aaron*

13Now the LORD spoke to Moses and Aaron about the Israelites
and Pharaoh king of Egypt, and he commanded them to bring the
Israelites out of Egypt.
14These were the heads of their families[f]:

The sons of Reuben the firstborn son of Israel were Hanoch
and Pallu, Hezron and Carmi. These were the clans of Reuben.
15The sons of Simeon were Jemuel, Jamin, Ohad, Jakin,
Zohar and Shaul the son of a Canaanite woman. These were
the clans of Simeon.
16These were the names of the sons of Levi according to
their records: Gershon, Kohath and Merari. Levi lived 137
years.
17The sons of Gershon, by clans, were Libni and Shimei.
18The sons of Kohath were Amram, Izhar, Hebron and
Uzziel. Kohath lived 133 years.
19The sons of Merari were Mahli and Mushi.
These were the clans of Levi according to their records.
20Amram married his father's sister Jochebed, who bore
him Aaron and Moses. Amram lived 137 years.
21The sons of Izhar were Korah, Nepheg and Zicri.
22The sons of Uzziel were Mishael, Elzaphan and Sithri.

**NIV** [b] 3 Hebrew *El-Shaddai* [c] 3 See note at Exodus 3:15. [d] 3 Or *Almighty, and by my name the LORD did I not let myself be known to them?* [e] 12 Hebrew *I am uncircumcised of lips;* also in verse 30 [f] 14 The Hebrew for *families* here and in verse 25 refers to units larger than clans.

## King James

23And Aaron took him Elisheba, daughter of Amminadab, sister of Naashon, to wife; and she bare him Nadab, and Abihu,
Eleazar, and Ithamar.
24And the sons of Korah; Assir, and Elkanah, and Abiasaph:
these *are* the families of the Korhites.
25And Eleazar Aaron's son took him *one* of the daughters of
Putiel to wife; and she bare him Phinehas: these *are* the heads of
the fathers of the Levites according to their families.
26These *are* that Aaron and Moses, to whom the LORD said,
Bring out the children of Israel from the land of Egypt according
to their armies.
27These *are* they which spake to Pharaoh king of Egypt, to bring
out the children of Israel from Egypt: these *are* that Moses and
Aaron.
28¶ And it came to pass on the day *when* the LORD spake unto
Moses in the land of Egypt,
29That the LORD spake unto Moses, saying, I *am* the LORD: speak
thou unto Pharaoh king of Egypt all that I say unto thee.
30And Moses said before the LORD, Behold, I *am* of uncircumcised lips, and how shall Pharaoh hearken unto me?

**7** AND THE LORD said unto Moses, See, I have made thee a god
to Pharaoh: and Aaron thy brother shall be thy prophet.
2Thou shalt speak all that I command thee: and Aaron thy
brother shall speak unto Pharaoh, that he send the children of
Israel out of his land.
3And I will harden Pharaoh's heart, and multiply my signs and
my wonders in the land of Egypt.
4But Pharaoh shall not hearken unto you, that I may lay my
hand upon Egypt, and bring forth mine armies, *and* my people the
children of Israel, out of the land of Egypt by great judgments.
5And the Egyptians shall know that I *am* the LORD, when I
stretch forth mine hand upon Egypt, and bring out the children of
Israel from among them.
6And Moses and Aaron did as the LORD commanded them, so
did they.
7And Moses *was* fourscore years old, and Aaron fourscore and
three years old, when they spake unto Pharaoh.
8¶ And the LORD spake unto Moses and unto Aaron, saying,
9When Pharaoh shall speak unto you, saying, Show a miracle
for you: then thou shalt say unto Aaron, Take thy rod, and cast
*it* before Pharaoh, *and* it shall become a serpent.
10¶ And Moses and Aaron went in unto Pharaoh, and they did
so as the LORD had commanded: and Aaron cast down his rod
before Pharaoh, and before his servants, and it became a serpent.
11Then Pharaoh also called the wise men and the sorcerers: now
the magicians of Egypt, they also did in like manner with their
enchantments.
12For they cast down every man his rod, and they became
serpents: but Aaron's rod swallowed up their rods.
13And he hardened Pharaoh's heart, that he hearkened not
unto them; as the LORD had said.
14¶ And the LORD said unto Moses, Pharaoh's heart *is* hardened, he refuseth to let the people go.
15Get thee unto Pharaoh in the morning; lo, he goeth out unto
the water; and thou shalt stand by the river's brink against he
come; and the rod which was turned to a serpent shalt thou take
in thine hand.
16And thou shalt say unto him, The LORD God of the Hebrews
hath sent me unto thee, saying, Let my people go, that they may
serve me in the wilderness: and, behold, hitherto thou wouldest
not hear.

## Amplified

23Aaron took Elisheba, daughter of Amminadab and sister of
Nahshon, as wife; she bore him Nadab, Abihu, Eleazar, and Ithamar.
24The sons of Korah: Assir, Elkanah, and Abiasaph. These are
the families of the Korahites.
25Eleazar, Aaron's son, took one of the daughters of Putiel as
wife; and she bore him Phinehas. These are the heads of the
fathers' houses of the Levites by their families.
26These are the Aaron and Moses to whom the Lord said, Bring
out the Israelites from the land of Egypt by their hosts,
27And who spoke to *the* Pharaoh king of Egypt about bringing
the Israelites out of Egypt; these are that Moses and Aaron.
28On the day when the Lord spoke to Moses in Egypt,
29The Lord said to Moses, I am the Lord; tell Pharaoh king of
Egypt all that I say to you.
30But Moses said to the Lord, Behold, I am of deficient *and*
impeded speech; how then shall Pharaoh listen to me?

**7** THE LORD said to Moses, Behold, I make you as God to
Pharaoh [to declare My will and purpose to him]; and Aaron
your brother shall be your prophet.
2You shall speak all that I command you, and Aaron your
brother shall tell Pharaoh to let the Israelites go out of his land.
3And I will make Pharaoh's heart stubborn *and* hard, and multiply My signs, My wonders, *and* miracles in the land of Egypt.
4But Pharaoh will not listen to you, and I will lay My hand upon
Egypt, and bring forth My hosts, My people the Israelites, out of
the land of Egypt by great acts of judgment.
5The Egyptians shall know that I am the Lord, when I stretch
forth My hand upon Egypt, and bring out the Israelites from
among them.
6And Moses and Aaron did so, as the Lord commanded them.
7Now Moses was 80 years old, and Aaron 83 years old, when
they spoke to Pharaoh.
8And the Lord said to Moses and Aaron,
9When Pharaoh says to you, Prove your *authority* by a miracle,
then tell Aaron, Throw your rod down before Pharaoh, that it may
become a serpent.
10So Moses and Aaron went to Pharaoh and did as the Lord had
commanded; Aaron threw down his rod before Pharaoh and his
servants, and it became a serpent.
11Then Pharaoh called for the wise men [skilled in magic and
divination] and the sorcerers—wizards and jugglers. And they
also, these magicians of Egypt, did similar things with their enchantments *and* secret arts.
12For they cast down every man his rod, and they became
serpents; but Aaron's rod swallowed up their rods.
13But Pharaoh's heart was hardened *and* stubborn, and he
would not listen to them, just as the Lord had said.
14Then the Lord said to Moses, Pharaoh's heart is hard *and*
stubborn; he refuses to let the people go.
15Go to Pharaoh in the morning; he will be going out to the
water; wait for him by the river's brink; and the rod which was
turned to a serpent you shall take in your hand.
16And say to him, The Lord, the God of the Hebrews has sent
me to you, saying, Let My people go, that they may serve Me in
the wilderness; and behold, heretofore you have not listened.

## New American Standard

23And Aaron married Elisheba, the daughter of Amminadab,
the sister of Nahshon, and she bore him Nadab and Abihu, Eleazar
and Ithamar.
24And the sons of Korah: Assir and Elkanah and Abiasaph;
these are the families of the Korahites.
25And Aaron's son Eleazar married one of the daughters of
Putiel, and she bore him Phinehas. These are the heads of the
fathers' *households* of the Levites according to their families.
26It was *the same* Aaron and Moses to whom the LORD said,
"Bring out the sons of Israel from the land of Egypt according to
their hosts."
27They were the ones who spoke to Pharaoh king of Egypt
about bringing out the sons of Israel from Egypt; it was *the same*
Moses and Aaron.
28¶ Now it came about on the day when the LORD spoke to
Moses in the land of Egypt,
29that the LORD spoke to Moses, saying, "I am the LORD; speak
to Pharaoh king of Egypt all that I speak to you."
30But Moses said before the LORD, "Behold, I am unskilled in
speech; how then will Pharaoh listen to me?"

*"I Will Stretch Out My Hand"*

7 THEN THE LORD said to Moses, "See, I make you *as* God to
Pharaoh, and your brother Aaron shall be your prophet.
2"You shall speak all that I command you, and your brother
Aaron shall speak to Pharaoh that he let the sons of Israel go out
of his land.
3"But I will harden Pharaoh's heart that I may multiply My
signs and My wonders in the land of Egypt.
4"When Pharaoh will not listen to you, then I will lay My hand
on Egypt, and bring out My hosts, My people the sons of Israel,
from the land of Egypt by great judgments.
5"And the Egyptians shall know that I am the LORD, when I
stretch out My hand on Egypt and bring out the sons of Israel from
their midst."
6So Moses and Aaron did *it;* as the LORD commanded them,
thus they did.
7And Moses was eighty years old and Aaron eighty-three,
when they spoke to Pharaoh.

*Aaron's Rod Becomes a Serpent*

8¶ Now the LORD spoke to Moses and Aaron, saying,
9"When Pharaoh speaks to you, saying, 'Work a miracle,' then
you shall say to Aaron, 'Take your staff and throw *it* down before
Pharaoh, *that* it may become a serpent.'"
10So Moses and Aaron came to Pharaoh, and thus they did just
as the LORD had commanded; and Aaron threw his staff down
before Pharaoh and his servants, and it became a serpent.
11Then Pharaoh also called for *the* wise men and *the* sorcerers,
and they also, the magicians of Egypt, did the same with their
secret arts.
12For each one threw down his staff and they turned into serpents. But Aaron's staff swallowed up their staffs.
13Yet Pharaoh's heart was hardened, and he did not listen to
them, as the LORD had said.

*Water Is Turned to Blood*

14¶ Then the LORD said to Moses, "Pharaoh's heart is stubborn;
he refuses to let the people go.
15"Go to Pharaoh in the morning as he is going out to the water,
and station yourself to meet him on the bank of the Nile; and you
shall take in your hand the staff that was turned into a serpent.
16"And you will say to him, 'The LORD, the God of the Hebrews, sent me to you, saying, "Let My people go, that they may
serve Me in the wilderness. But behold, you have not listened until
now."

## New International

23Aaron married Elisheba, daughter of Amminadab and
sister of Nahshon, and she bore him Nadab and Abihu, Eleazar and Ithamar.
24The sons of Korah were Assir, Elkanah and Abiasaph.
These were the Korahite clans.
25Eleazar son of Aaron married one of the daughters of
Putiel, and she bore him Phinehas.

These were the heads of the Levite families, clan by clan.

26It was this same Aaron and Moses to whom the LORD said,
"Bring the Israelites out of Egypt by their divisions." 27They were
the ones who spoke to Pharaoh king of Egypt about bringing the
Israelites out of Egypt. It was the same Moses and Aaron.

*Aaron to Speak for Moses*

28Now when the LORD spoke to Moses in Egypt, 29he said to
him, "I am the LORD. Tell Pharaoh king of Egypt everything I tell
you."
30But Moses said to the LORD, "Since I speak with faltering lips,
why would Pharaoh listen to me?"

7 THEN THE LORD said to Moses, "See, I have made you like
God to Pharaoh, and your brother Aaron will be your
prophet. 2You are to say everything I command you, and your
brother Aaron is to tell Pharaoh to let the Israelites go out of his
country. 3But I will harden Pharaoh's heart, and though I multiply
my miraculous signs and wonders in Egypt, 4he will not listen to
you. Then I will lay my hand on Egypt and with mighty acts of
judgment I will bring out my divisions, my people the Israelites.
5And the Egyptians will know that I am the LORD when I stretch
out my hand against Egypt and bring the Israelites out of it."
6Moses and Aaron did just as the LORD commanded them.
7Moses was eighty years old and Aaron eighty-three when they
spoke to Pharaoh.

*Aaron's Staff Becomes a Snake*

8The LORD said to Moses and Aaron, 9"When Pharaoh says to
you, 'Perform a miracle,' then say to Aaron, 'Take your staff and
throw it down before Pharaoh,' and it will become a snake."
10So Moses and Aaron went to Pharaoh and did just as the LORD
commanded. Aaron threw his staff down in front of Pharaoh and
his officials, and it became a snake. 11Pharaoh then summoned
wise men and sorcerers, and the Egyptian magicians also did the
same things by their secret arts: 12Each one threw down his staff
and it became a snake. But Aaron's staff swallowed up their staffs.
13Yet Pharaoh's heart became hard and he would not listen to
them, just as the LORD had said.

*The Plague of Blood*

14Then the LORD said to Moses, "Pharaoh's heart is unyielding;
he refuses to let the people go. 15Go to Pharaoh in the morning as
he goes out to the water. Wait on the bank of the Nile to meet him,
and take in your hand the staff that was changed into a snake.
16Then say to him, 'The LORD, the God of the Hebrews, has sent
me to say to you: Let my people go, so that they may worship me
in the desert. But until now you have not listened. 17This is what

## King James

17 Thus saith the LORD, In this thou shalt know that I *am* the LORD: behold, I will smite with the rod that *is* in mine hand upon the waters which *are* in the river, and they shall be turned to blood.

18 And the fish that *is* in the river shall die, and the river shall stink; and the Egyptians shall loathe to drink of the water of the river.

19 ¶ And the LORD spake unto Moses, Say unto Aaron, Take thy rod, and stretch out thine hand upon the waters of Egypt, upon their streams, upon their rivers, and upon their ponds, and upon all their pools of water, that they may become blood; and *that* there may be blood throughout all the land of Egypt, both in *vessels of* wood, and in *vessels of* stone.

20 And Moses and Aaron did so, as the LORD commanded; and he lifted up the rod, and smote the waters that *were* in the river, in the sight of Pharaoh, and in the sight of his servants; and all the waters that *were* in the river were turned to blood.

21 And the fish that *was* in the river died; and the river stank, and the Egyptians could not drink of the water of the river; and there was blood throughout all the land of Egypt.

22 And the magicians of Egypt did so with their enchantments: and Pharaoh's heart was hardened, neither did he hearken unto them; as the LORD had said.

23 And Pharaoh turned and went into his house, neither did he set his heart to this also.

24 And all the Egyptians digged round about the river for water to drink; for they could not drink of the water of the river.

25 And seven days were fulfilled, after that the LORD had smitten the river.

**8** AND THE LORD spake unto Moses, Go unto Pharaoh, and say unto him, Thus saith the LORD, Let my people go, that they may serve me.

2 And if thou refuse to let *them* go, behold, I will smite all thy borders with frogs:

3 And the river shall bring forth frogs abundantly, which shall go up and come into thine house, and into thy bedchamber, and upon thy bed, and into the house of thy servants, and upon thy people, and into thine ovens, and into thy kneadingtroughs:

4 And the frogs shall come up both on thee, and upon thy people, and upon all thy servants.

5 ¶ And the LORD spake unto Moses, Say unto Aaron, Stretch forth thine hand with thy rod over the streams, over the rivers, and over the ponds, and cause frogs to come up upon the land of Egypt.

6 And Aaron stretched out his hand over the waters of Egypt; and the frogs came up, and covered the land of Egypt.

7 And the magicians did so with their enchantments, and brought up frogs upon the land of Egypt.

8 ¶ Then Pharaoh called for Moses and Aaron, and said, Entreat the LORD, that he may take away the frogs from me, and from my people; and I will let the people go, that they may do sacrifice unto the LORD.

9 And Moses said unto Pharaoh, Glory over me: when shall I entreat for thee, and for thy servants, and for thy people, to destroy the frogs from thee and thy houses, *that* they may remain in the river only?

10 And he said, Tomorrow. And he said, *Be it* according to thy word: that thou mayest know that *there is* none like unto the LORD our God.

11 And the frogs shall depart from thee, and from thy houses, and from thy servants, and from thy people; they shall remain in the river only.

12 And Moses and Aaron went out from Pharaoh: and Moses cried unto the LORD because of the frogs which he had brought against Pharaoh.

## Amplified

17 Thus says the Lord, In this you shall know, recognize, *and* understand that I am the Lord: behold, I will smite with the rod in my hand the waters in the *Nile* River, and they shall be turned to blood.

18 The fish in the river shall die, the river shall become foul smelling, and the Egyptians shall loathe to drink from *it*.

19 And the Lord said to Moses, Say to Aaron, Take your rod and stretch out your hand over the waters of Egypt, over their streams, rivers, pools and ponds of water, that they may become blood; and there shall be blood throughout all the land of Egypt, in containers both of wood and of stone.

20 Moses and Aaron did as the Lord commanded; [Aaron] lifted up the rod, and smote the waters in the river, in the sight of Pharaoh and his servants; and all the waters in the river were turned to blood.

21 And the fish in the river died; and the river became foul smelling, and the Egyptians could not drink *its* water, and there was blood throughout all the land of Egypt.

22 But the magicians of Egypt did the same by their enchantments *and* secret arts; and Pharaoh's heart was made hard *and* obstinate, and he did not listen to Moses and Aaron; just as the Lord had said.

23 And Pharaoh turned and went into his house, neither did he take even this to heart.

24 And all the Egyptians dug round about the river for water to drink, for they could not drink the water of the *Nile*.

25 Seven days passed after the Lord had smitten the river.

**8** THEN THE Lord said to Moses, Go to Pharaoh and say to him, Thus says the Lord, Let My people go, that they may serve Me.

2 And if you refuse to let them go, behold, I will smite your entire land with frogs;

3 And the river shall swarm with frogs which shall go up and come into your house, into your bedchamber and on your bed, and into the houses of your servants and upon your people; and into your ovens, your kneading bowls *and* your dough.

4 And the frogs shall come up on you, and on your people and all your servants.

5 And the Lord said to Moses, Say to Aaron, Stretch out your hand with your rod over the rivers, the streams *and* canals, and over the pools, and cause frogs to come up on the land of Egypt.

6 So Aaron stretched out his hand over the waters of Egypt, and the frogs came up and covered the land.

7 But the magicians did the same thing with their enchantments *and* secret arts, and brought up [more] frogs upon the land of Egypt.

8 Then Pharaoh called for Moses and Aaron, and said, Entreat the Lord, that He may take away the frogs from me and my people; and I will let the people go that they may sacrifice to the Lord.

9 Moses said to Pharaoh, Glory over me in this: dictate when I shall pray [to the Lord] for you, your servants and your people, that the frogs may be destroyed from you and your houses and remain only in the river.

10 And [Pharaoh] said, Tomorrow. [Moses] said, Let it be as you say, that you may know that there is no one like the Lord our God.

11 And the frogs shall depart from you and your houses and from your servants and your people; they shall remain in the river only.

12 So Moses and Aaron went out from Pharaoh, and Moses cried to the Lord, [as he had agreed with Pharaoh], concerning the frogs which He had brought against him.

## New American Standard

17"Thus says the LORD, "By this you shall know that I am the
LORD: behold, I will strike the water that is in the Nile with the staff
that is in my hand, and it shall be turned to blood.
18"And the fish that are in the Nile will die, and the Nile will
become foul; and the Egyptians will find difficulty in drinking
water from the Nile."'"
19Then the LORD said to Moses, "Say to Aaron, 'Take your staff
and stretch out your hand over the waters of Egypt, over their
rivers, over their streams, and over their pools, and over all their
reservoirs of water, that they may become blood; and there shall
be blood throughout all the land of Egypt, both in *vessels of* wood
and in *vessels of* stone.'"
20¶ So Moses and Aaron did even as the LORD had commanded.
And he lifted up the staff and struck the water that *was* in the Nile,
in the sight of Pharaoh and in the sight of his servants, and all the
water that *was* in the Nile was turned to blood.
21And the fish that *were* in the Nile died, and the Nile became
foul, so that the Egyptians could not drink water from the Nile.
And the blood was through all the land of Egypt.
22But the magicians of Egypt did the same with their secret arts;
and Pharaoh's heart was hardened, and he did not listen to them,
as the LORD had said.
23Then Pharaoh turned and went into his house with no concern even for this.
24So all the Egyptians dug around the Nile for water to drink,
for they could not drink of the water of the Nile.
25And seven days passed after the LORD had struck the Nile.

*Frogs over the Land*

8 THEN THE LORD said to Moses, "Go to Pharaoh and say to
him, 'Thus says the LORD, "Let My people go, that they may
serve Me.
2"But if you refuse to let *them* go, behold, I will smite your
whole territory with frogs.
3"And the Nile will swarm with frogs, which will come up and
go into your house and into your bedroom and on your bed, and
into the houses of your servants and on your people, and into your
ovens and into your kneading bowls.
4"So the frogs will come up on you and your people and all
your servants."'"
5Then the LORD said to Moses, "Say to Aaron, 'Stretch out your
hand with your staff over the rivers, over the streams and over the
pools, and make frogs come up on the land of Egypt.'"
6So Aaron stretched out his hand over the waters of Egypt, and
the frogs came up and covered the land of Egypt.
7And the magicians did the same with their secret arts, making
frogs come up on the land of Egypt.
8¶ Then Pharaoh called for Moses and Aaron and said, "Entreat the LORD that He remove the frogs from me and from my
people; and I will let the people go, that they may sacrifice to the
LORD."
9And Moses said to Pharaoh, "The honor is yours to tell me:
when shall I entreat for you and your servants and your people,
that the frogs be destroyed from you and your houses, *that* they
may be left only in the Nile?"
10¶ Then he said, "Tomorrow." So he said, "*May it be* according
to your word, that you may know that there is no one like the LORD
our God.
11"And the frogs will depart from you and your houses and
your servants and your people; they will be left only in the Nile."
12Then Moses and Aaron went out from Pharaoh, and Moses
cried to the LORD concerning the frogs which He had inflicted upon
Pharaoh.

## New International

the LORD says: By this you will know that I am the LORD: With the
staff that is in my hand I will strike the water of the Nile, and it
will be changed into blood. 18The fish in the Nile will die, and the
river will stink; the Egyptians will not be able to drink its water.'"
19The LORD said to Moses, "Tell Aaron, 'Take your staff and
stretch out your hand over the waters of Egypt—over the streams
and canals, over the ponds and all the reservoirs'—and they will
turn to blood. Blood will be everywhere in Egypt, even in the
wooden buckets and stone jars."
20Moses and Aaron did just as the LORD had commanded. He
raised his staff in the presence of Pharaoh and his officials and
struck the water of the Nile, and all the water was changed into
blood. 21The fish in the Nile died, and the river smelled so bad that
the Egyptians could not drink its water. Blood was everywhere in
Egypt.
22But the Egyptian magicians did the same things by their secret
arts, and Pharaoh's heart became hard; he would not listen to
Moses and Aaron, just as the LORD had said. 23Instead, he turned
and went into his palace, and did not take even this to heart. 24And
all the Egyptians dug along the Nile to get drinking water, because
they could not drink the water of the river.

*The Plague of Frogs*

25Seven days passed after the LORD struck the Nile.
8 THEN THE LORD said to Moses, "Go to Pharaoh and say to
him, 'This is what the LORD says: Let my people go, so that
they may worship me. 2If you refuse to let them go, I will plague
your whole country with frogs. 3The Nile will teem with frogs.
They will come up into your palace and your bedroom and onto
your bed, into the houses of your officials and on your people, and
into your ovens and kneading troughs. 4The frogs will go up on
you and your people and all your officials.'"
5Then the LORD said to Moses, "Tell Aaron, 'Stretch out your
hand with your staff over the streams and canals and ponds, and
make frogs come up on the land of Egypt.'"
6So Aaron stretched out his hand over the waters of Egypt, and
the frogs came up and covered the land. 7But the magicians did
the same things by their secret arts; they also made frogs come up
on the land of Egypt.
8Pharaoh summoned Moses and Aaron and said, "Pray to the
LORD to take the frogs away from me and my people, and I will
let your people go to offer sacrifices to the LORD."
9Moses said to Pharaoh, "I leave to you the honor of setting the
time for me to pray for you and your officials and your people that
you and your houses may be rid of the frogs, except for those that
remain in the Nile."
10"Tomorrow," Pharaoh said.
Moses replied, "It will be as you say, so that you may know
there is no one like the LORD our God. 11The frogs will leave you
and your houses, your officials and your people; they will remain
only in the Nile."
12After Moses and Aaron left Pharaoh, Moses cried out to the
LORD about the frogs he had brought on Pharaoh. 13And the LORD

## King James

13 And the LORD did according to the word of Moses; and the frogs died out of the houses, out of the villages, and out of the fields.

14 And they gathered them together upon heaps: and the land stank.

15 But when Pharaoh saw that there was respite, he hardened his heart, and hearkened not unto them; as the LORD had said.

16 ¶ And the LORD said unto Moses, Say unto Aaron, Stretch out thy rod, and smite the dust of the land, that it may become lice throughout all the land of Egypt.

17 And they did so; for Aaron stretched out his hand with his rod, and smote the dust of the earth, and it became lice in man, and in beast; all the dust of the land became lice throughout all the land of Egypt.

18 And the magicians did so with their enchantments to bring forth lice, but they could not: so there were lice upon man, and upon beast.

19 Then the magicians said unto Pharaoh, This *is* the finger of God: and Pharaoh's heart was hardened, and he hearkened not unto them; as the LORD had said.

20 ¶ And the LORD said unto Moses, Rise up early in the morning, and stand before Pharaoh; lo, he cometh forth to the water; and say unto him, Thus saith the LORD, Let my people go, that they may serve me.

21 Else, if thou wilt not let my people go, behold, I will send swarms *of flies* upon thee, and upon thy servants, and upon thy people, and into thy houses: and the houses of the Egyptians shall be full of swarms *of flies*, and also the ground whereon they *are*.

22 And I will sever in that day the land of Goshen, in which my people dwell, that no swarms *of flies* shall be there; to the end thou mayest know that I *am* the LORD in the midst of the earth.

23 And I will put a division between my people and thy people: tomorrow shall this sign be.

24 And the LORD did so; and there came a grievous swarm *of flies* into the house of Pharaoh, and *into* his servants' houses, and into all the land of Egypt: the land was corrupted by reason of the swarm *of flies*.

25 ¶ And Pharaoh called for Moses and for Aaron, and said, Go ye, sacrifice to your God in the land.

26 And Moses said, It is not meet so to do; for we shall sacrifice the abomination of the Egyptians to the LORD our God: lo, shall we sacrifice the abomination of the Egyptians before their eyes, and will they not stone us?

27 We will go three days' journey into the wilderness, and sacrifice to the LORD our God, as he shall command us.

28 And Pharaoh said, I will let you go, that ye may sacrifice to the LORD your God in the wilderness; only ye shall not go very far away: entreat for me.

29 And Moses said, Behold, I go out from thee, and I will entreat the LORD that the swarms *of flies* may depart from Pharaoh, from his servants, and from his people, tomorrow: but let not Pharaoh deal deceitfully any more in not letting the people go to sacrifice to the LORD.

30 And Moses went out from Pharaoh, and entreated the LORD.

31 And the LORD did according to the word of Moses; and he removed the swarms *of flies* from Pharaoh, from his servants, and from his people; there remained not one.

32 And Pharaoh hardened his heart at this time also, neither would he let the people go.

## Amplified

13 And the Lord did according to the word of Moses, and the frogs died out of the houses, out of the courtyards *and* villages, and out of the fields.

14 [The people] gathered them together in heaps, and the land was loathsome *and* stank.

15 But when Pharaoh saw that there was temporary relief, he made his heart stubborn *and* hard, and would not listen *or* heed them; just as the Lord had said.

16 Then the Lord said to Moses, Say to Aaron, Stretch out your rod and strike the dust of the ground, that it may become biting gnats *or* mosquitoes throughout all the land of Egypt.

17 And they did so; Aaron stretched out his hand with his rod, and struck the dust of the earth, and there came biting gnats *or* mosquitoes on man and beast; all the dust of the land became biting gnats *or* mosquitoes throughout all the land of Egypt.

18 The magicians tried by their enchantments *and* secret arts to bring forth gnats, *or* mosquitoes, but they could not; and there were gnats *or* mosquitoes on man and beast.

19 Then the magicians said to Pharaoh, This is the finger of God! But Pharaoh's heart was hardened *and* strong, and he would not listen to them; just as the Lord had said.

20 Then the Lord said to Moses, Rise up early in the morning and stand before Pharaoh as he comes forth to the water; and say to him, Thus says the Lord, Let My people go that they may serve Me.

21 Else, if you will not let My people go, behold, I will send swarms [of blood-sucking gadflies] upon you, your servants, and your people, and into your houses; and the houses of the Egyptians shall be full of swarms [of blood-sucking gadflies], and also the ground on which they stand.

22 But on that day I will sever *and* set apart the land of Goshen in which My people dwell, that no swarms [of gadflies] shall be there; so that you may know that I am the Lord in the midst of the earth.

23 And I will put a division *and* a sign of deliverance between My people and your people. By tomorrow shall this sign be in evidence.

24 And the Lord did so; and there came heavy *and* oppressive swarms [of blood-sucking gadflies] into the house of Pharaoh and his servants' houses; and in all of Egypt the land was corrupted *and* ruined by reason of the great invasion of [gadflies].

25 And Pharaoh called for Moses and Aaron, and said, Go, sacrifice to your God [here] in the land [of Egypt].

26 And Moses said, It is not suitable *or* right to do that; for the animals the Egyptians hold sacred and will not permit to be slain, are those which we are accustomed to sacrifice to the Lord our God; if we did this before the eyes of the Egyptians, would they not stone us?

27 We will go three days' journey into the wilderness and sacrifice to the Lord our God, as He will command us.

28 So Pharaoh said, I will let you go, that you may sacrifice to the Lord your God in the wilderness; only you shall not go very far away. Entreat [your God] for me.

29 Moses said, I go out from you, and I will entreat the Lord that the swarms [of blood-sucking gadflies] may depart from Pharaoh, his servants, and his people, tomorrow; only let not Pharaoh deal deceitfully any more in not letting the people go to sacrifice to the Lord.

30 So Moses went out from Pharaoh, and entreated the Lord.

31 And the Lord did as Moses had spoken; He removed the swarms of [attacking gadflies] from Pharaoh, from his servants and his people; there remained not one.

32 But Pharaoh hardened his heart *and* made it stubborn this time also, nor would he let the people go.

## New American Standard

13And the LORD did according to the word of Moses, and the
frogs died out of the houses, the courts, and the fields.
14So they piled them in heaps, and the land became foul.
15But when Pharaoh saw that there was relief, he hardened his
heart and did not listen to them, as the LORD had said.

*The Plague of Insects*

16¶ Then the LORD said to Moses, "Say to Aaron, 'Stretch out
your staff and strike the dust of the earth, that it may become
[a]gnats through all the land of Egypt.' "
17And they did so; and Aaron stretched out his hand with his
staff, and struck the dust of the earth, and there were gnats on man
and beast. All the dust of the earth became gnats through all the
land of Egypt.
18And the magicians tried with their secret arts to bring forth
gnats, but they could not; so there were gnats on man and beast.
19Then the magicians said to Pharaoh, "This is the finger of
God." But Pharaoh's heart was hardened, and he did not listen to
them, as the LORD had said.
20¶ Now the LORD said to Moses, "Rise early in the morning and
present yourself before Pharaoh, as he comes out to the water, and
say to him, 'Thus says the LORD, "Let My people go, that they may
serve Me.
21"For if you will not let My people go, behold, I will send
swarms of insects on you and on your servants and on your people
and into your houses; and the houses of the Egyptians shall be full
of swarms of insects, and also the ground on which they *dwell*.
22"But on that day I will set apart the land of Goshen, where
My people are living, so that no swarms of insects will be there,
in order that you may know that I, the LORD, am in the midst of
the land.
23"And I will [b]put a division between My people and your
people. Tomorrow this sign shall occur." ' "
24Then the LORD did so. And there came great swarms of insects
into the house of Pharaoh and the houses of his servants and the
land was laid waste because of the swarms of insects in all the land
of Egypt.
25¶ And Pharaoh called for Moses and Aaron and said, "Go,
sacrifice to your God within the land."
26But Moses said, "It is not right to do so, for we shall sacrifice
to the LORD our God what is an abomination to the Egyptians. If
we sacrifice what is an abomination to the Egyptians before their
eyes, will they not then stone us?
27"We must go a three days' journey into the wilderness and
sacrifice to the LORD our God as He commands us."
28And Pharaoh said, "I will let you go, that you may sacrifice
to the LORD your God in the wilderness; only you shall not go very
far away. Make supplication for me."
29Then Moses said, "Behold, I am going out from you, and I
shall make supplication to the LORD that the swarms of insects may
depart from Pharaoh, from his servants, and from his people
tomorrow; only do not let Pharaoh deal deceitfully again in not
letting the people go to sacrifice to the LORD."
30So Moses went out from Pharaoh and made supplication to
the LORD.
31And the LORD did as Moses asked, and removed the swarms
of insects from Pharaoh, from his servants and from his people; not
one remained.
32But Pharaoh hardened his heart this time also, and he did not
let the people go.

NAS [a] Or, *lice* [b] Lit., *set a ransom*

## New International

did what Moses asked. The frogs died in the houses, in the courtyards and in the fields. 14They were piled into heaps, and the land
reeked of them. 15But when Pharaoh saw that there was relief, he
hardened his heart and would not listen to Moses and Aaron, just
as the LORD had said.

*The Plague of Gnats*

16Then the LORD said to Moses, "Tell Aaron, 'Stretch out your
staff and strike the dust of the ground,' and throughout the land
of Egypt the dust will become gnats." 17They did this, and when
Aaron stretched out his hand with the staff and struck the dust of
the ground, gnats came upon men and animals. All the dust
throughout the land of Egypt became gnats. 18But when the magicians tried to produce gnats by their secret arts, they could not.
And the gnats were on men and animals.
19The magicians said to Pharaoh, "This is the finger of God."
But Pharaoh's heart was hard and he would not listen, just as the
LORD had said.

*The Plague of Flies*

20Then the LORD said to Moses, "Get up early in the morning
and confront Pharaoh as he goes to the water and say to him, 'This
is what the LORD says: Let my people go, so that they may worship
me. 21If you do not let my people go, I will send swarms of flies
on you and your officials, on your people and into your houses.
The houses of the Egyptians will be full of flies, and even the
ground where they are.
22" 'But on that day I will deal differently with the land of
Goshen, where my people live; no swarms of flies will be there,
so that you will know that I, the LORD, am in this land. 23I will
make a distinction[c] between my people and your people. This
miraculous sign will occur tomorrow.' "
24And the LORD did this. Dense swarms of flies poured into
Pharaoh's palace and into the houses of his officials, and throughout Egypt the land was ruined by the flies.
25Then Pharaoh summoned Moses and Aaron and said, "Go,
sacrifice to your God here in the land."
26But Moses said, "That would not be right. The sacrifices we
offer the LORD our God would be detestable to the Egyptians. And
if we offer sacrifices that are detestable in their eyes, will they not
stone us? 27We must take a three-day journey into the desert to
offer sacrifices to the LORD our God, as he commands us."
28Pharaoh said, "I will let you go to offer sacrifices to the LORD
your God in the desert, but you must not go very far. Now pray
for me."
29Moses answered, "As soon as I leave you, I will pray to the
LORD, and tomorrow the flies will leave Pharaoh and his officials
and his people. Only be sure that Pharaoh does not act deceitfully
again by not letting the people go to offer sacrifices to the LORD."
30Then Moses left Pharaoh and prayed to the LORD, 31and the
LORD did what Moses asked: The flies left Pharaoh and his officials
and his people; not a fly remained. 32But this time also Pharaoh
hardened his heart and would not let the people go.

NIV [c] 23 Septuagint and Vulgate; Hebrew *will put a deliverance*

## King James

9 THEN THE LORD said unto Moses, Go in unto Pharaoh, and tell him, Thus saith the LORD God of the Hebrews, Let my people go, that they may serve me.

2 For if thou refuse to let *them* go, and wilt hold them still,

3 Behold, the hand of the LORD is upon thy cattle which *is* in the field, upon the horses, upon the asses, upon the camels, upon the oxen, and upon the sheep: *there shall be* a very grievous murrain.

4 And the LORD shall sever between the cattle of Israel and the cattle of Egypt: and there shall nothing die of all *that is* the children's of Israel.

5 And the LORD appointed a set time, saying, Tomorrow the LORD shall do this thing in the land.

6 And the LORD did that thing on the morrow, and all the cattle of Egypt died: but of the cattle of the children of Israel died not one.

7 And Pharaoh sent, and, behold, there was not one of the cattle of the Israelites dead. And the heart of Pharaoh was hardened, and he did not let the people go.

8 ¶ And the LORD said unto Moses and unto Aaron, Take to you handfuls of ashes of the furnace, and let Moses sprinkle it toward the heaven in the sight of Pharaoh.

9 And it shall become small dust in all the land of Egypt, and shall be a boil breaking forth *with* blains upon man, and upon beast, throughout all the land of Egypt.

10 And they took ashes of the furnace, and stood before Pharaoh; and Moses sprinkled it up toward heaven; and it became a boil breaking forth *with* blains upon man, and upon beast.

11 And the magicians could not stand before Moses because of the boils; for the boil was upon the magicians, and upon all the Egyptians.

12 And the LORD hardened the heart of Pharaoh, and he hearkened not unto them; as the LORD had spoken unto Moses.

13 ¶ And the LORD said unto Moses, Rise up early in the morning, and stand before Pharaoh, and say unto him, Thus saith the LORD God of the Hebrews, Let my people go, that they may serve me.

14 For I will at this time send all my plagues upon thine heart, and upon thy servants, and upon thy people; that thou mayest know that *there is* none like me in all the earth.

15 For now I will stretch out my hand, that I may smite thee and thy people with pestilence; and thou shalt be cut off from the earth.

16 And in very deed for this *cause* have I raised thee up, for to show *in* thee my power; and that my name may be declared throughout all the earth.

17 As yet exaltest thou thyself against my people, that thou wilt not let them go?

18 Behold, tomorrow about this time I will cause it to rain a very grievous hail, such as hath not been in Egypt since the foundation thereof even until now.

19 Send therefore now, *and* gather thy cattle, and all that thou hast in the field; *for upon* every man and beast which shall be found in the field, and shall not be brought home, the hail shall come down upon them, and they shall die.

20 He that feared the word of the LORD among the servants of Pharaoh made his servants and his cattle flee into the houses:

21 And he that regarded not the word of the LORD left his servants and his cattle in the field.

22 ¶ And the LORD said unto Moses, Stretch forth thine hand toward heaven, that there may be hail in all the land of Egypt, upon man, and upon beast, and upon every herb of the field, throughout the land of Egypt.

23 And Moses stretched forth his rod toward heaven: and the LORD sent thunder and hail, and the fire ran along upon the ground; and the LORD rained hail upon the land of Egypt.

## Amplified

9 THEN THE Lord said to Moses, Go to Pharaoh and tell him, Thus says the Lord God of the Hebrews, Let My people go, that they may serve Me.

2 If you refuse to let them go and still hold them,

3 Behold, the hand of the Lord [will fall] upon your livestock which are out in the field, upon the horses, the donkeys, the camels, the herds and the flocks; there shall be a very severe plague.

4 But the Lord shall make a distinction between the livestock of Israel and the livestock of Egypt, and nothing shall die of all that belongs to the Israelites.

5 And the Lord set a time, saying, Tomorrow the Lord will do this thing in the land.

6 And the Lord did that the next day, and all [kinds of] the livestock of Egypt died; but of the livestock of the Israelites not one died.

7 Pharaoh sent to find out, and, behold, there was not one of the cattle of the Israelites dead. But the heart of Pharaoh was hardened [his mind was set]; and he did not let the people go.

8 The Lord said to Moses and Aaron, Take handfuls of ashes *or* soot from the brickkiln, and let Moses sprinkle them toward the heavens in the sight of Pharaoh.

9 And it shall become small dust over all the land of Egypt, and become boils breaking out in sores on man and beast in all the land [occupied by the Egyptians].

10 So they took ashes *or* soot of the kiln, and stood before Pharaoh; and Moses threw them toward the sky; and it became boils erupting in sores on man and beast.

11 And the magicians could not stand before Moses because of their boils; for the boils were on the magicians and all the Egyptians.

12 But the Lord hardened the heart of Pharaoh, making it strong *and* obstinate, and he did not listen to them or heed them, just as the Lord had told Moses.

13 Then the Lord said to Moses, Rise up early in the morning and stand before Pharaoh and say to him, Thus says the Lord, the God of the Hebrews, Let My people go, that they may serve Me.

14 For this time I will send all My plagues upon your heart, and upon your servants and your people, that you may recognize *and* know that there is none like Me in all the earth.

15 For by now I could have put forth My hand and have struck you and your people with pestilence, and you would have been cut off from the earth.

16 But for this very purpose have I let you live, that I might show you My power, and that My name may be declared throughout all the earth. [Rom. 9:17-24.]

17 Since you are still exalting yourself [in haughty defiance] against My people by not letting them go,

18 Behold, tomorrow about this time I will cause it to rain a very heavy *and* dreadful fall of hail, such as has not been in Egypt from its founding until now.

19 Send therefore now, and gather your cattle in hastily, and all that you have in the field; for every man and beast that is in the field and is not brought home, shall be struck by the hail and shall die.

20 Then he who feared the word of the Lord among the servants of Pharaoh made his servants and his livestock flee into the houses *and* shelters.

21 And he who ignored the word of the Lord left his servants and his livestock in the field.

22 The Lord said to Moses, Stretch forth your hand toward the heavens, that there may be hail in all the land of Egypt, upon man and beast, and upon all the vegetation of the field, throughout the land of Egypt.

23 Then Moses stretched forth his rod toward the heavens, and the Lord sent thunder and hail, and [lightning] fire ran down to *and* along the ground, and the Lord rained hail upon the land of Egypt.

## New American Standard

*Egyptian Cattle Die*

9 THEN THE LORD said to Moses, "Go to Pharaoh and speak
to him, 'Thus says the LORD, the God of the Hebrews, "Let
My people go, that they may serve Me.
2"For if you refuse to let *them* go, and continue to hold them,
3behold, the hand of the LORD will come *with* a very severe
pestilence on your livestock which are in the field, on the horses,
on the donkeys, on the camels, on the herds, and on the flocks.
4"But the LORD will make a distinction between the livestock
of Israel and the livestock of Egypt, so that nothing will die of all
that belongs to the sons of Israel."' "
5And the LORD set a definite time, saying, "Tomorrow the
LORD will do this thing in the land."
6So the LORD did this thing on the morrow, and all the livestock
of Egypt died; but of the livestock of the sons of Israel, not one
died.
7And Pharaoh sent, and behold, there was not even one of the
livestock of Israel dead. But the heart of Pharaoh was hardened,
and he did not let the people go.

*The Plague of Boils*

8¶ Then the LORD said to Moses and Aaron, "Take for yourselves handfuls of soot from a kiln, and let Moses throw it toward
the sky in the sight of Pharaoh.
9"And it will become fine dust over all the land of Egypt, and
will become boils breaking out with sores on man and beast
through all the land of Egypt."
10So they took soot from a kiln, and stood before Pharaoh; and
Moses threw it toward the sky, and it became boils breaking out
with sores on man and beast.
11And the magicians could not stand before Moses because of
the boils, for the boils were on the magicians as well as on all the
Egyptians.
12And the LORD hardened Pharaoh's heart, and he did not listen
to them, just as the LORD had spoken to Moses.
13¶ Then the LORD said to Moses, "Rise up early in the morning
and stand before Pharaoh and say to him, 'Thus says the LORD, the
God of the Hebrews, "Let My people go, that they may serve Me.
14"For this time I will send all My plagues on you and your
servants and your people, so that you may know that there is no
one like Me in all the earth.
15"For *if by* now I had put forth My hand and struck you and
your people with pestilence, you would then have been cut off
from the earth.
16"But, indeed, for this cause I have allowed you to remain, in
order to show you My power, and in order to proclaim My name
through all the earth.
17"Still you exalt yourself against My people by not letting them
go.

*The Plague of Hail*

18"Behold, about this time tomorrow, I will send a very heavy
hail, such as has not been *seen* in Egypt from the day it was
founded until now.
19"Now therefore send, bring your livestock and whatever you
have in the field to safety. Every man and beast that is found in
the field and is not brought home, when the hail comes down on
them, will die."' "
20The one among the servants of Pharaoh who feared the word
of the LORD made his servants and his livestock flee into the
houses;
21but he who paid no regard to the word of the LORD left his
servants and his livestock in the field.
22¶ Now the LORD said to Moses, "Stretch out your hand toward
the sky, that hail may fall on all the land of Egypt, on man and on
beast and on every plant of the field, throughout the land of
Egypt."
23And Moses stretched out his staff toward the sky, and the
LORD sent thunder and hail, and fire ran down to the earth. And
the LORD rained hail on the land of Egypt.

## New International

*The Plague on Livestock*

9 THEN THE LORD said to Moses, "Go to Pharaoh and say to
him, 'This is what the LORD, the God of the Hebrews, says:
"Let my people go, so that they may worship me." 2If you refuse
to let them go and continue to hold them back, 3the hand of the
LORD will bring a terrible plague on your livestock in the field—on
your horses and donkeys and camels and on your cattle and sheep
and goats. 4But the LORD will make a distinction between the
livestock of Israel and that of Egypt, so that no animal belonging
to the Israelites will die.' "
5The LORD set a time and said, "Tomorrow the LORD will do this
in the land." 6And the next day the LORD did it: All the livestock
of the Egyptians died, but not one animal belonging to the Israelites died. 7Pharaoh sent men to investigate and found that not
even one of the animals of the Israelites had died. Yet his heart was
unyielding and he would not let the people go.

*The Plague of Boils*

8Then the LORD said to Moses and Aaron, "Take handfuls of
soot from a furnace and have Moses toss it into the air in the
presence of Pharaoh. 9It will become fine dust over the whole land
of Egypt, and festering boils will break out on men and animals
throughout the land."
10So they took soot from a furnace and stood before Pharaoh.
Moses tossed it into the air, and festering boils broke out on men
and animals. 11The magicians could not stand before Moses because of the boils that were on them and on all the Egyptians. 12But
the LORD hardened Pharaoh's heart and he would not listen to
Moses and Aaron, just as the LORD had said to Moses.

*The Plague of Hail*

13Then the LORD said to Moses, "Get up early in the morning,
confront Pharaoh and say to him, 'This is what the LORD, the God
of the Hebrews, says: Let my people go, so that they may worship
me, 14or this time I will send the full force of my plagues against
you and against your officials and your people, so you may know
that there is no one like me in all the earth. 15For by now I could
have stretched out my hand and struck you and your people with
a plague that would have wiped you off the earth. 16But I have
raised you up[a] for this very purpose, that I might show you my
power and that my name might be proclaimed in all the earth.
17You still set yourself against my people and will not let them go.
18Therefore, at this time tomorrow I will send the worst hailstorm
that has ever fallen on Egypt, from the day it was founded till now.
19Give an order now to bring your livestock and everything you
have in the field to a place of shelter, because the hail will fall on
every man and animal that has not been brought in and is still out
in the field, and they will die.' "
20Those officials of Pharaoh who feared the word of the LORD
hurried to bring their slaves and their livestock inside. 21But those
who ignored the word of the LORD left their slaves and livestock
in the field.
22Then the LORD said to Moses, "Stretch out your hand toward
the sky so that hail will fall all over Egypt—on men and animals
and on everything growing in the fields of Egypt." 23When Moses
stretched out his staff toward the sky, the LORD sent thunder and
hail, and lightning flashed down to the ground. So the LORD rained
hail on the land of Egypt; 24hail fell and lightning flashed back and

NIV [a] 16 Or *have spared you*

## King James

24So there was hail, and fire mingled with the hail, very grievous, such as there was none like it in all the land of Egypt since
it became a nation.
25And the hail smote throughout all the land of Egypt all that
*was* in the field, both man and beast; and the hail smote every herb
of the field, and brake every tree of the field.
26Only in the land of Goshen, where the children of Israel *were*,
was there no hail.
27¶ And Pharaoh sent, and called for Moses and Aaron, and
said unto them, I have sinned this time: the LORD *is* righteous, and
I and my people *are* wicked.
28Entreat the LORD (for *it is* enough) that there be no *more*
mighty thunderings and hail; and I will let you go, and ye shall stay
no longer.
29And Moses said unto him, As soon as I am gone out of the
city, I will spread abroad my hands unto the LORD; *and* the thunder
shall cease, neither shall there be any more hail; that thou mayest
know how that the earth *is* the LORD'S.
30But as for thee and thy servants, I know that ye will not yet
fear the LORD God.
31And the flax and the barley was smitten: for the barley *was* in
the ear, and the flax *was* bolled.
32But the wheat and the rie were not smitten: for they *were* not
grown up.
33And Moses went out of the city from Pharaoh, and spread
abroad his hands unto the LORD: and the thunders and hail ceased,
and the rain was not poured upon the earth.
34And when Pharaoh saw that the rain and the hail and the
thunders were ceased, he sinned yet more, and hardened his
heart, he and his servants.
35And the heart of Pharaoh was hardened, neither would he let
the children of Israel go; as the LORD had spoken by Moses.

**10** AND THE LORD said unto Moses, Go in unto Pharaoh: for
I have hardened his heart, and the heart of his servants,
that I might show these my signs before him:
2And that thou mayest tell in the ears of thy son, and of thy
son's son, what things I have wrought in Egypt, and my signs
which I have done among them; that ye may know how that I *am*
the LORD.
3And Moses and Aaron came in unto Pharaoh, and said unto
him, Thus saith the LORD God of the Hebrews, How long wilt thou
refuse to humble thyself before me? let my people go, that they
may serve me.
4Else, if thou refuse to let my people go, behold, tomorrow will
I bring the locusts into thy coast:
5And they shall cover the face of the earth, that one cannot be
able to see the earth: and they shall eat the residue of that which
is escaped, which remaineth unto you from the hail, and shall eat
every tree which groweth for you out of the field:
6And they shall fill thy houses, and the houses of all thy servants, and the houses of all the Egyptians; which neither thy
fathers, nor thy fathers' fathers have seen, since the day that they
were upon the earth unto this day. And he turned himself, and
went out from Pharaoh.
7And Pharaoh's servants said unto him, How long shall this
man be a snare unto us? let the men go, that they may serve the
LORD their God: knowest thou not yet that Egypt is destroyed?
8And Moses and Aaron were brought again unto Pharaoh: and
he said unto them, Go, serve the LORD your God: *but* who *are* they
that shall go?
9And Moses said, We will go with our young and with our old,
with our sons and with our daughters, with our flocks and with
our herds will we go; for we *must hold* a feast unto the LORD.

## Amplified

24So there was hail, and fire flashing continually in the midst
of the weighty hail, such as had not been in all the land of Egypt
since it became a nation.
25The hail struck down throughout all the land of Egypt everything that was in the field, both man and beast; and the hail beat
down all the vegetation of the field and shattered every tree of the
field.
26Only in the land of Goshen, where the Israelites were, was
there no hail.
27And Pharaoh sent for Moses and Aaron, and said to them, I
have sinned this time; the Lord is in the right and I and my people
are in the wrong.
28Entreat the Lord, for there has been enough of these mighty
thunderings and hail [these voices of God]; I will let you go; you
shall stay here no longer.
29Moses said to him, As soon as I leave the city, I will stretch
out my hands to the Lord; the thunder shall cease, neither shall
there be any more hail, that you may know that the earth is the
Lord's.
30But as for you and your servants, I know that you do not yet
[reverently] fear the Lord God.
31The flax and the barley were smitten *and* ruined, for the barley
was in the ear and the flax in bloom.
32But the wheat and spelt [another wheat] were not smitten, for
they ripen late and were not grown up yet.
33So Moses left the city and Pharaoh, and stretched forth his
hands to the Lord; and the thunder and hail ceased, and rain was
no longer poured upon the earth.
34But when Pharaoh saw that the rain, the hail and the thunder
had ceased, he sinned yet more, and toughened *and* stiffened his
hard heart, he and his servants.
35So Pharaoh's heart was strong *and* obstinate; he would not let
the Israelites go; just as the Lord had said by Moses. [Exod. 4:21.]

**10** THE LORD said to Moses, Go to Pharaoh; for I have made
his heart hard, and his servants' hearts, that I might show
these My signs [of divine power] before him;
2And that you may recount in the ears of your son and of your
grandson, what I have done in derision of the Egyptians *and* what
things I have [repeatedly] done there, My signs [of divine power]
done among them; that you may recognize *and* know that I am the
Lord.
3So Moses and Aaron went to Pharaoh, and said to him, Thus
says the Lord, the God of the Hebrews, How long will you refuse
to humble yourself before Me? Let My people go, that they may
serve Me.
4For, if you refuse to let My people go, behold, tomorrow I will
bring locusts into your country.
5And they shall cover the land, so that one cannot see the
ground; and they shall eat the remainder of what escaped and is
left to you from the hail, and they shall eat every tree of yours that
grows in the field;
6The locusts shall fill your houses and those of all your servants
and of all the Egyptians; as neither your fathers nor your fathers'
fathers have seen from their birth until this day. Then Moses
departed from Pharaoh.
7And Pharaoh's servants said to him, How long shall this man
be a snare to us? Let the men go, that they may serve the Lord their
God; do you not yet understand *and* know that Egypt is destroyed?
8So Moses and Aaron were brought again to Pharaoh; and he
said to them, Go, serve the Lord your God; but just who are to go?
9And Moses said, We will go with our young and our old, with
our sons and our daughters, with our flocks and our herds [all of
us and all we have]; for we must hold a feast to the Lord.

## New American Standard

24So there was hail, and fire flashing continually in the midst of the hail, very severe, such as had not been in all the land of Egypt since it became a nation.
25And the hail struck all that was in the field through all the land of Egypt, both man and beast; the hail also struck every plant of the field and shattered every tree of the field.
26Only in the land of Goshen, where the sons of Israel *were,* there was no hail.
27¶ Then Pharaoh sent for Moses and Aaron, and said to them, "I have sinned this time; the LORD is the righteous one, and I and my people are the wicked ones.
28"Make supplication to the LORD, for there has been enough of God's thunder and hail; and I will let you go, and you shall stay no longer."
29And Moses said to him, "As soon as I go out of the city, I will spread out my hands to the LORD; the thunder will cease, and there will be hail no longer, that you may know that the earth is the LORD'S.
30"But as for you and your servants, I know that you do not yet fear the LORD God."
31(Now the flax and the barley were ruined, for the barley was in the ear and the flax was in bud.
32But the wheat and the spelt were not ruined, for they *ripen* late.)
33So Moses went out of the city from Pharaoh, and spread out his hands to the LORD; and the thunder and the hail ceased, and rain no longer poured on the earth.
34But when Pharaoh saw that the rain and the hail and the thunder had ceased, he sinned again and hardened his heart, he and his servants.
35And Pharaoh's heart was hardened, and he did not let the sons of Israel go, just as the LORD had spoken through Moses.

### *The Plague of Locusts*

10 THEN THE LORD said to Moses, "Go to Pharaoh, for I have [a]hardened his heart and the heart of his servants, that I may perform these signs of Mine among them,
2and that you may tell in the hearing of your son, and of your grandson, how I made a mockery of the Egyptians, and how I performed My signs among them; that you may know that I am the LORD."
3And Moses and Aaron went to Pharaoh and said to him, "Thus says the LORD, the God of the Hebrews, 'How long will you refuse to humble yourself before Me? Let My people go, that they may serve Me.
4'For if you refuse to let My people go, behold, tomorrow I will bring locusts into your territory.
5'And they shall cover the surface of the land, so that no one shall be able to see the land. They shall also eat the rest of what has escaped—what is left to you from the hail—and they shall eat every tree which sprouts for you out of the field.
6'Then your houses shall be filled, and the houses of all your servants and the houses of all the Egyptians, *something* which neither your fathers nor your grandfathers have seen, from the day that they came upon the earth until this day.' " And he turned and went out from Pharaoh.
7And Pharaoh's servants said to him, "How long will this man be a snare to us? Let the men go, that they may serve the LORD their God. Do you not realize that Egypt is destroyed?"
8So Moses and Aaron were brought back to Pharaoh, and he said to them, "Go, serve the LORD your God! Who are the ones that are going?"
9And Moses said, "We shall go with our young and our old; with our sons and our daughters, with our flocks and our herds we will go, for we must hold a feast to the LORD."

NAS [a] Lit., *made heavy*

## New International

forth. It was the worst storm in all the land of Egypt since it had become a nation.
25Throughout Egypt hail struck everything in the fields—both men and animals; it beat down everything growing in the fields and stripped every tree.
26The only place it did not hail was the land of Goshen, where the Israelites were.
27Then Pharaoh summoned Moses and Aaron. "This time I have sinned," he said to them. "The LORD is in the right, and I and my people are in the wrong.
28Pray to the LORD, for we have had enough thunder and hail. I will let you go; you don't have to stay any longer."
29Moses replied, "When I have gone out of the city, I will spread out my hands in prayer to the LORD. The thunder will stop and there will be no more hail, so you may know that the earth is the LORD's.
30But I know that you and your officials still do not fear the LORD God."
31(The flax and barley were destroyed, since the barley had headed and the flax was in bloom.
32The wheat and spelt, however, were not destroyed, because they ripen later.)
33Then Moses left Pharaoh and went out of the city. He spread out his hands toward the LORD; the thunder and hail stopped, and the rain no longer poured down on the land.
34When Pharaoh saw that the rain and hail and thunder had stopped, he sinned again: He and his officials hardened their hearts.
35So Pharaoh's heart was hard and he would not let the Israelites go, just as the LORD had said through Moses.

### *The Plague of Locusts*

10 THEN THE LORD said to Moses, "Go to Pharaoh, for I have hardened his heart and the hearts of his officials so that I may perform these miraculous signs of mine among them
2that you may tell your children and grandchildren how I dealt harshly with the Egyptians and how I performed my signs among them, and that you may know that I am the LORD."
3So Moses and Aaron went to Pharaoh and said to him, "This is what the LORD, the God of the Hebrews, says: 'How long will you refuse to humble yourself before me? Let my people go, so that they may worship me.
4If you refuse to let them go, I will bring locusts into your country tomorrow.
5They will cover the face of the ground so that it cannot be seen. They will devour what little you have left after the hail, including every tree that is growing in your fields.
6They will fill your houses and those of all your officials and all the Egyptians—something neither your fathers nor your forefathers have ever seen from the day they settled in this land till now.' " Then Moses turned and left Pharaoh.
7Pharaoh's officials said to him, "How long will this man be a snare to us? Let the people go, so that they may worship the LORD their God. Do you not yet realize that Egypt is ruined?"
8Then Moses and Aaron were brought back to Pharaoh. "Go, worship the LORD your God," he said. "But just who will be going?"
9Moses answered, "We will go with our young and old, with our sons and daughters, and with our flocks and herds, because we are to celebrate a festival to the LORD."

## King James

10 And he said unto them, Let the LORD be so with you, as I will let you go, and your little ones: look *to it;* for evil *is* before you.

11 Not so: go now ye *that are* men, and serve the LORD; for that ye did desire. And they were driven out from Pharaoh's presence.

12 ¶ And the LORD said unto Moses, Stretch out thine hand over the land of Egypt for the locusts, that they may come up upon the land of Egypt, and eat every herb of the land, *even* all that the hail hath left.

13 And Moses stretched forth his rod over the land of Egypt, and the LORD brought an east wind upon the land all that day, and all *that* night; *and* when it was morning, the east wind brought the locusts.

14 And the locusts went up over all the land of Egypt, and rested in all the coasts of Egypt: very grievous *were they;* before them there were no such locusts as they, neither after them shall be such.

15 For they covered the face of the whole earth, so that the land was darkened; and they did eat every herb of the land, and all the fruit of the trees which the hail had left: and there remained not any green thing in the trees, or in the herbs of the field, through all the land of Egypt.

16 ¶ Then Pharaoh called for Moses and Aaron in haste; and he said, I have sinned against the LORD your God, and against you.

17 Now therefore forgive, I pray thee, my sin only this once, and entreat the LORD your God, that he may take away from me this death only.

18 And he went out from Pharaoh, and entreated the LORD.

19 And the LORD turned a mighty strong west wind, which took away the locusts, and cast them into the Red sea; there remained not one locust in all the coasts of Egypt.

20 But the LORD hardened Pharaoh's heart, so that he would not let the children of Israel go.

21 ¶ And the LORD said unto Moses, Stretch out thine hand toward heaven, that there may be darkness over the land of Egypt, even darkness *which* may be felt.

22 And Moses stretched forth his hand toward heaven; and there was a thick darkness in all the land of Egypt three days:

23 They saw not one another, neither rose any from his place for three days: but all the children of Israel had light in their dwellings.

24 ¶ And Pharaoh called unto Moses, and said, Go ye, serve the LORD; only let your flocks and your herds be stayed: let your little ones also go with you.

25 And Moses said, Thou must give us also sacrifices and burnt offerings, that we may sacrifice unto the LORD our God.

26 Our cattle also shall go with us; there shall not an hoof be left behind; for thereof must we take to serve the LORD our God; and we know not with what we must serve the LORD, until we come thither.

27 ¶ But the LORD hardened Pharaoh's heart, and he would not let them go.

28 And Pharaoh said unto him, Get thee from me, take heed to thyself, see my face no more; for in *that* day thou seest my face thou shalt die.

29 And Moses said, Thou hast spoken well, I will see thy face again no more.

**11** AND THE LORD said unto Moses, Yet will I bring one plague *more* upon Pharaoh, and upon Egypt; afterwards he will let you go hence: when he shall let *you* go, he shall surely thrust you out hence altogether.

## Amplified

10 Pharaoh said to them, Let the Lord be with you, if I ever let you go with your little ones! See, you have some evil purpose in mind.

11 Not so! You that are men, [without your families] go and serve the Lord, for that is what you want. And [Moses and Aaron] were driven from Pharaoh's presence.

12 Then the Lord said to Moses, Stretch out your hand over the land of Egypt for the locusts, that they may come up on the land of Egypt, and eat all the vegetation of the land, all that the hail has left.

13 And Moses stretched forth his rod over the land of Egypt, and the Lord brought an east wind upon the land all that day and all that night; when it was morning, the east wind brought the locusts.

14 And the locusts came up over all the land of Egypt and settled down on the whole country of Egypt, a very dreadful mass of them; never before were there such locusts as these, nor will there ever be again.

15 For they covered the whole land, so that the ground was darkened, and they ate every bit of vegetation of the land, and all the fruit of the trees which the hail had left; there remained not a green thing of the trees or the plants of the field, in all the land of Egypt.

16 Then Pharaoh sent for Moses and Aaron in haste. He said, I have sinned against the Lord your God and you.

17 Now therefore forgive my sin, I pray you, only this once, and entreat the Lord your God only that He may remove from me this [plague of] death.

18 Then Moses left Pharaoh, and entreated the Lord.

19 And the Lord turned a violent west wind, which lifted the locusts and drove them into the Red Sea; not one locust remained in all the country of Egypt.

20 But the Lord made Pharaoh's heart more strong *and* obstinate, and he would not let the Israelites go.

21 And the Lord said to Moses, Stretch out your hand toward the heavens, that there may be darkness over the land of Egypt, a darkness which may be felt.

22 So Moses stretched out his hand toward the sky, and for three days a thick darkness was all over the land of Egypt.

23 The Egyptians could not see one another, nor did any one rise from his place for three days; but all the Israelites had natural light in their dwellings.

24 And Pharaoh called to Moses, and said, Go, serve the Lord; let your little ones also go with you; it is only your flocks and your herds that must not go.

25 But Moses said, You must give into our hand also sacrifices and burnt offerings, that we may sacrifice to the Lord our God.

26 Our livestock also shall go with us; there shall not a hoof be left behind; for of them must we take to serve the Lord our God, and we know not with what we must serve the Lord until we arrive there.

27 But the Lord made Pharaoh's heart stronger *and* more stubborn, and he would not let them go.

28 And Pharaoh said to Moses, Get away from me! See that you never enter my presence again, for the day you see my face again you shall die!

29 And Moses said, You have spoken truly; I will never see your face again.

**11** THEN THE Lord said to Moses, Yet will I bring one plague more on Pharaoh and on Egypt; afterwards he will let you go. When he lets you go from here, he will thrust you out altogether.

## New American Standard

10Then he said to them, "Thus may the LORD be with you, if
ever I let you and your little ones go! Take heed, for evil is in your
mind.
11"Not so! Go now, the men *among you*, and serve the LORD, for
that is what you desire." So they were driven out from Pharaoh's
presence.
12¶ Then the LORD said to Moses, "Stretch out your hand over
the land of Egypt for the locusts, that they may come up on the
land of Egypt, and eat every plant of the land, *even* all that the hail
has left."
13So Moses stretched out his staff over the land of Egypt, and
the LORD directed an east wind on the land all that day and all that
night; and when it was morning, the east wind brought the locusts.
14And the locusts came up over all the land of Egypt and settled
in all the territory of Egypt; *they were* very numerous. There had
never been so *many* locusts, nor would there be so *many* again.
15For they covered the surface of the whole land, so that the
land was darkened; and they ate every plant of the land and all the
fruit of the trees that the hail had left. Thus nothing green was left
on tree or plant of the field through all the land of Egypt.
16Then Pharaoh hurriedly called for Moses and Aaron, and he
said, "I have sinned against the LORD your God and against you.
17"Now therefore, please forgive my sin only this once, and
make supplication to the LORD your God, that He would only
remove this death from me."
18And he went out from Pharaoh and made supplication to the
LORD.
19So the LORD shifted *the wind* to a very strong west wind which
took up the locusts and drove them into the [a]Red Sea; not one
locust was left in all the territory of Egypt.
20But the LORD hardened Pharaoh's heart, and he did not let the
sons of Israel go.

*Darkness over the Land*

21¶ Then the LORD said to Moses, "Stretch out your hand
toward the sky, that there may be darkness over the land of Egypt,
even a darkness which may be felt."
22So Moses stretched out his hand toward the sky, and there
was thick darkness in all the land of Egypt for three days.
23They did not see one another, nor did anyone rise from his
place for three days, but all the sons of Israel had light in their
dwellings.
24Then Pharaoh called to Moses, and said, "Go, serve the LORD;
only let your flocks and your herds be detained. Even your little
ones may go with you."
25But Moses said, "You must also let us have sacrifices and
burnt offerings, that we may sacrifice *them* to the LORD our God.
26"Therefore, our livestock, too, will go with us; not a hoof will
be left behind, for we shall take some of them to serve the LORD
our God. And until we arrive there, we ourselves do not know
with what we shall serve the LORD."
27But the LORD hardened Pharaoh's heart, and he was not
willing to let them go.
28Then Pharaoh said to him, "Get away from me! Beware, do
not see my face again, for in the day you see my face you shall die!"
29And Moses said, "You are right; I shall never see your face
again!"

*The Last Plague*

**11** NOW THE LORD said to Moses, "One more plague I will
bring on Pharaoh and on Egypt; after that he will let you
go from here. When he lets you go, he will surely drive you out
from here completely.

NAS [a] Lit., *Sea of Reeds*

## New International

10Pharaoh said, "The LORD be with you—if I let you go, along
with your women and children! Clearly you are bent on evil.[b]
11No! Have only the men go; and worship the LORD, since that's
what you have been asking for." Then Moses and Aaron were
driven out of Pharaoh's presence.
12And the LORD said to Moses, "Stretch out your hand over
Egypt so that locusts will swarm over the land and devour everything growing in the fields, everything left by the hail."
13So Moses stretched out his staff over Egypt, and the LORD
made an east wind blow across the land all that day and all that
night. By morning the wind had brought the locusts; 14they invaded all Egypt and settled down in every area of the country in great
numbers. Never before had there been such a plague of locusts,
nor will there ever be again. 15They covered all the ground until
it was black. They devoured all that was left after the hail—everything growing in the fields and the fruit on the trees. Nothing
green remained on tree or plant in all the land of Egypt.
16Pharaoh quickly summoned Moses and Aaron and said, "I
have sinned against the LORD your God and against you. 17Now
forgive my sin once more and pray to the LORD your God to take
this deadly plague away from me."
18Moses then left Pharaoh and prayed to the LORD. 19And the
LORD changed the wind to a very strong west wind, which caught
up the locusts and carried them into the Red Sea.[c] Not a locust was
left anywhere in Egypt. 20But the LORD hardened Pharaoh's heart,
and he would not let the Israelites go.

*The Plague of Darkness*

21Then the LORD said to Moses, "Stretch out your hand toward
the sky so that darkness will spread over Egypt—darkness that can
be felt." 22So Moses stretched out his hand toward the sky, and
total darkness covered all Egypt for three days. 23No one could see
anyone else or leave his place for three days. Yet all the Israelites
had light in the places where they lived.
24Then Pharaoh summoned Moses and said, "Go, worship the
LORD. Even your women and children may go with you; only leave
your flocks and herds behind."
25But Moses said, "You must allow us to have sacrifices and
burnt offerings to present to the LORD our God. 26Our livestock too
must go with us; not a hoof is to be left behind. We have to use
some of them in worshiping the LORD our God, and until we get
there we will not know what we are to use to worship the LORD."
27But the LORD hardened Pharaoh's heart, and he was not
willing to let them go. 28Pharaoh said to Moses, "Get out of my
sight! Make sure you do not appear before me again! The day you
see my face you will die."
29"Just as you say," Moses replied, "I will never appear before
you again."

*The Plague on the Firstborn*

**11** NOW THE LORD had said to Moses, "I will bring one more
plague on Pharaoh and on Egypt. After that, he will let
you go from here, and when he does, he will drive you out completely. 2Tell the people that men and women alike are to ask their

NIV [b] 10 Or *Be careful, trouble is in store for you!* [c] 19 Hebrew *Yam Suph;* that is, Sea of Reeds

## King James

2 Speak now in the ears of the people, and let every man borrow of his neighbour, and every woman of her neighbour, jewels of silver, and jewels of gold.

3 And the LORD gave the people favour in the sight of the Egyptians. Moreover the man Moses *was* very great in the land of Egypt, in the sight of Pharaoh's servants, and in the sight of the people.

4 And Moses said, Thus saith the LORD, About midnight will I go out into the midst of Egypt:

5 And all the firstborn in the land of Egypt shall die, from the firstborn of Pharaoh that sitteth upon his throne, even unto the firstborn of the maidservant that *is* behind the mill; and all the firstborn of beasts.

6 And there shall be a great cry throughout all the land of Egypt, such as there was none like it, nor shall be like it any more.

7 But against any of the children of Israel shall not a dog move his tongue, against man or beast: that ye may know how that the LORD doth put a difference between the Egyptians and Israel.

8 And all these thy servants shall come down unto me, and bow down themselves unto me, saying, Get thee out, and all the people that follow thee: and after that I will go out. And he went out from Pharaoh in a great anger.

9 And the LORD said unto Moses, Pharaoh shall not hearken unto you; that my wonders may be multiplied in the land of Egypt.

10 And Moses and Aaron did all these wonders before Pharaoh: and the LORD hardened Pharaoh's heart, so that he would not let the children of Israel go out of his land.

**12** AND THE LORD spake unto Moses and Aaron in the land of Egypt, saying,

2 This month *shall be* unto you the beginning of months: it *shall be* the first month of the year to you.

3 ¶ Speak ye unto all the congregation of Israel, saying, In the tenth *day* of this month they shall take to them every man a lamb, according to the house of *their* fathers, a lamb for an house:

4 And if the household be too little for the lamb, let him and his neighbour next unto his house take *it* according to the number of the souls; every man according to his eating shall make your count for the lamb.

5 Your lamb shall be without blemish, a male of the first year: ye shall take *it* out from the sheep, or from the goats:

6 And ye shall keep it up until the fourteenth day of the same month: and the whole assembly of the congregation of Israel shall kill it in the evening.

7 And they shall take of the blood, and strike *it* on the two side posts and on the upper door post of the houses, wherein they shall eat it.

8 And they shall eat the flesh in that night, roast with fire, and unleavened bread; *and* with bitter *herbs* they shall eat it.

9 Eat not of it raw, nor sodden at all with water, but roast *with* fire; his head with his legs, and with the purtenance thereof.

10 And ye shall let nothing of it remain until the morning; and that which remaineth of it until the morning ye shall burn with fire.

11 ¶ And thus shall ye eat it; *with* your loins girded, your shoes on your feet, and your staff in your hand; and ye shall eat it in haste: it *is* the LORD's passover.

12 For I will pass through the land of Egypt this night, and will smite all the firstborn in the land of Egypt, both man and beast; and against all the gods of Egypt I will execute judgment: I *am* the LORD.

13 And the blood shall be to you for a token upon the houses where ye *are:* and when I see the blood, I will pass over you, and the plague shall not be upon you to destroy *you,* when I smite the land of Egypt.

## Amplified

2 Speak now in the hearing of the people, and let every man solicit *and* ask of his neighbor, and every woman of her neighbor, jewels of silver and jewels of gold.

3 And the Lord gave the people favor in the sight of the Egyptians. Moreover the man Moses was exceedingly great in the land of Egypt, in the sight of Pharaoh's servants and of the people.

4 And Moses said, Thus says the Lord, About midnight I will go out into the midst of Egypt;

5 And all the first-born in the land [the pride, hope and joy] of Egypt shall die, from the first-born of Pharaoh who sits on his throne, even to the first-born of the maid-servant who is behind the hand mill; and all the first-born of beasts.

6 There shall be a great cry in all the land of Egypt, such as has never been, nor ever shall be again.

7 But against any of the Israelites shall not so much as a dog move his tongue, against man or beast; that you may know that the Lord makes a distinction between the Egyptians and Israel.

8 And all these your servants shall come down to me, and bow down to me, saying, Get out, and all the people who follow you! And after that I will go out. And he went out from Pharaoh in great anger.

9 Then the Lord said to Moses, Pharaoh will not listen to you, that My wonders *and* miracles may be multiplied in the land of Egypt.

10 Moses and Aaron did all these wonders *and* miracles before Pharaoh; and the Lord hardened Pharaoh's stubborn heart, and he did not let the Israelites go out of his land.

**12** THE LORD said to Moses and Aaron in the land of Egypt,

2 This month shall be to you the beginning of months, the first month of the year to you.

3 Tell all the congregation of Israel, On the tenth day of this month they shall take every man a lamb *or* kid, according to [the size of] the family of which he is the father, a lamb *or* kid for a house.

4 And if the household is too small to consume the lamb, let him and his next door neighbor take it according to the number of persons, every man according to what each can eat shall make your count for the lamb.

5 Your lamb *or* kid shall be without blemish, a male of the first year; you shall take it from the sheep or the goats. [I Pet. 1:19, 20.]

6 And you shall keep it until the fourteenth day of the same month; and the whole assembly of the congregation of Israel shall [each] kill [his] lamb in the evening.

7 They shall take of the blood, and put it on the two sideposts and on the lintel [above the door space] of the houses in which they shall eat [the passover lamb]. [John 1:29; Matt. 26:28; Heb. 9:14.]

8 They shall eat the flesh that night, roasted; with unleavened bread and bitter herbs they shall eat it.

9 Eat not of it raw, nor boiled at all with water, but roasted; its head, its legs and its inner parts.

10 You shall let nothing of the meat remain until the morning; and the bones *and* unedible bits which remain of it until morning you shall burn with fire.

11 And you shall eat it thus: [as fully prepared for a journey] your loins girded, your shoes on your feet, and your staff in your hand; and you shall eat it in haste. It is the Lord's passover.

12 For I will pass through the land of Egypt this night, and will smite all the first-born in the land of Egypt, both man and beast; and against all the gods of Egypt I will execute judgments [proving their helplessness]. I am the Lord.

13 The blood shall be for a token *or* sign to you upon [the doorposts of] the houses where you are, [that] when I see the blood, I will pass over you, and no plague shall be upon you to destroy you, when I smite the land of Egypt. [Heb. 11:28; I Cor. 5:7.]

## New American Standard

2"Speak now in the hearing of the people that each man ask
from his neighbor and each woman from her neighbor for articles
of silver and articles of gold."
3And the LORD gave the people favor in the sight of the Egyptians. Furthermore, the man Moses *himself* was greatly esteemed
in the land of Egypt, *both* in the sight of Pharaoh's servants and
in the sight of the people.
4And Moses said, "Thus says the LORD, 'About midnight I am
going out into the midst of Egypt,
5and all the first-born in the land of Egypt shall die, from
the first-born of the Pharaoh who sits on his throne, even to the
first-born of the slave girl who is behind the millstones; all
the first-born of the cattle as well.
6'Moreover, there shall be a great cry in all the land of Egypt,
such as there has not been *before* and such as shall never be again.
7'But against any of the sons of Israel a dog shall not *even* bark,
whether against man or beast, that you may understand how the
LORD makes a distinction between Egypt and Israel.'
8"And all these your servants will come down to me and bow
themselves before me, saying, 'Go out, you and all the people who
follow you,' and after that I will go out." And he went out from
Pharaoh in hot anger.
9¶ Then the LORD said to Moses, "Pharaoh will not listen to
you, so that My wonders will be multiplied in the land of Egypt."
10And Moses and Aaron performed all these wonders before
Pharaoh; yet the LORD hardened Pharaoh's heart, and he did not
let the sons of Israel go out of his land.

*The Passover Lamb*

**12** NOW THE LORD said to Moses and Aaron in the land of
Egypt,
2"This month shall be the beginning of months for you; it is
to be the first month of the year to you.
3"Speak to all the congregation of Israel, saying, 'On the tenth
of this month they are each one to take a lamb for themselves,
according to their fathers' households, a lamb for each household.
4'Now if the household is too small for a lamb, then he and his
neighbor nearest to his house are to take one according to the
number of persons *in them;* according to what each man should eat,
you are to divide the lamb.
5'Your lamb shall be an unblemished male a year old; you may
take it from the sheep or from the goats.
6'And you shall keep it until the fourteenth day of the same
month, then the whole assembly of the congregation of Israel is to
kill it at twilight.
7'Moreover, they shall take some of the blood and put it on the
two doorposts and on the lintel of the houses in which they eat it.
8'And they shall eat the flesh that *same* night, roasted with fire,
and they shall eat it with unleavened bread and bitter herbs.
9'Do not eat any of it raw or boiled at all with water, but rather
roasted with fire, *both* its head and its legs along with its entrails.
10'And you shall not leave any of it over until morning, but
whatever is left of it until morning, you shall burn with fire.
11'Now you shall eat it in this manner: *with* your loins girded,
your sandals on your feet, and your staff in your hand; and you
shall eat it in haste—it is the LORD's Passover.
12'For I will go through the land of Egypt on that night, and will
strike down all the first-born in the land of Egypt, both man and
beast; and against all the gods of Egypt I will execute judgments—I
am the LORD.
13'And the blood shall be a sign for you on the houses where
you live; and when I see the blood I will pass over you, and no
plague will befall you to destroy *you* when I strike the land of
Egypt.

## New International

neighbors for articles of silver and gold." 3(The LORD made the
Egyptians favorably disposed toward the people, and Moses himself was highly regarded in Egypt by Pharaoh's officials and by the
people.)
4So Moses said, "This is what the LORD says: 'About midnight
I will go throughout Egypt. 5Every firstborn son in Egypt will die,
from the firstborn son of Pharaoh, who sits on the throne, to the
firstborn son of the slave girl, who is at her hand mill, and all the
firstborn of the cattle as well. 6There will be loud wailing throughout Egypt—worse than there has ever been or ever will be again.
7But among the Israelites not a dog will bark at any man or animal.'
Then you will know that the LORD makes a distinction between
Egypt and Israel. 8All these officials of yours will come to me,
bowing down before me and saying, 'Go, you and all the people
who follow you!' After that I will leave." Then Moses, hot with
anger, left Pharaoh.
9The LORD had said to Moses, "Pharaoh will refuse to listen to
you—so that my wonders may be multiplied in Egypt." 10Moses
and Aaron performed all these wonders before Pharaoh, but the
LORD hardened Pharaoh's heart, and he would not let the Israelites
go out of his country.

*The Passover*

**12** THE LORD said to Moses and Aaron in Egypt, 2"This
month is to be for you the first month, the first month of
your year. 3Tell the whole community of Israel that on the tenth
day of this month each man is to take a lamb[a] for his family, one
for each household. 4If any household is too small for a whole
lamb, they must share one with their nearest neighbor, having
taken into account the number of people there are. You are to
determine the amount of lamb needed in accordance with what
each person will eat. 5The animals you choose must be year-old
males without defect, and you may take them from the sheep or
the goats. 6Take care of them until the fourteenth day of the
month, when all the people of the community of Israel must
slaughter them at twilight. 7Then they are to take some of the
blood and put it on the sides and tops of the doorframes of the
houses where they eat the lambs. 8That same night they are to eat
the meat roasted over the fire, along with bitter herbs, and bread
made without yeast. 9Do not eat the meat raw or cooked in water,
but roast it over the fire—head, legs and inner parts. 10Do not leave
any of it till morning; if some is left till morning, you must burn
it. 11This is how you are to eat it: with your cloak tucked into your
belt, your sandals on your feet and your staff in your hand. Eat it
in haste; it is the LORD's Passover.
12"On that same night I will pass through Egypt and strike
down every firstborn—both men and animals—and I will bring
judgment on all the gods of Egypt. I am the LORD. 13The blood will
be a sign for you on the houses where you are; and when I see the
blood, I will pass over you. No destructive plague will touch you
when I strike Egypt.

NIV · a 3 The Hebrew word can mean both *lamb* or *kid;* also in verse 4.

## King James

14 And this day shall be unto you for a memorial; and ye shall keep it a feast to the LORD throughout your generations; ye shall keep it a feast by an ordinance for ever.

15 Seven days shall ye eat unleavened bread; even the first day ye shall put away leaven out of your houses: for whosoever eateth leavened bread from the first day until the seventh day, that soul shall be cut off from Israel.

16 And in the first day *there shall be* an holy convocation, and in the seventh day there shall be an holy convocation to you; no manner of work shall be done in them, save *that* which every man must eat, that only may be done of you.

17 And ye shall observe *the feast of* unleavened bread; for in this selfsame day have I brought your armies out of the land of Egypt: therefore shall ye observe this day in your generations by an ordinance for ever.

18 ¶ In the first *month,* on the fourteenth day of the month at even, ye shall eat unleavened bread, until the one and twentieth day of the month at even.

19 Seven days shall there be no leaven found in your houses: for whosoever eateth that which is leavened, even that soul shall be cut off from the congregation of Israel, whether he be a stranger, or born in the land.

20 Ye shall eat nothing leavened; in all your habitations shall ye eat unleavened bread.

21 ¶ Then Moses called for all the elders of Israel, and said unto them, Draw out and take you a lamb according to your families, and kill the passover.

22 And ye shall take a bunch of hyssop, and dip *it* in the blood that *is* in the basin, and strike the lintel and the two side posts with the blood that *is* in the basin; and none of you shall go out at the door of his house until the morning.

23 For the LORD will pass through to smite the Egyptians; and when he seeth the blood upon the lintel, and on the two side posts, the LORD will pass over the door, and will not suffer the destroyer to come in unto your houses to smite *you.*

24 And ye shall observe this thing for an ordinance to thee and to thy sons for ever.

25 And it shall come to pass, when ye be come to the land which the LORD will give you, according as he hath promised, that ye shall keep this service.

26 And it shall come to pass, when your children shall say unto you, What mean ye by this service?

27 That ye shall say, It *is* the sacrifice of the LORD's passover, who passed over the houses of the children of Israel in Egypt, when he smote the Egyptians, and delivered our houses. And the people bowed the head and worshipped.

28 And the children of Israel went away, and did as the LORD had commanded Moses and Aaron, so did they.

29 ¶ And it came to pass, that at midnight the LORD smote all the firstborn in the land of Egypt, from the firstborn of Pharaoh that sat on his throne unto the firstborn of the captive that *was* in the dungeon; and all the firstborn of cattle.

30 And Pharaoh rose up in the night, he, and all his servants, and all the Egyptians; and there was a great cry in Egypt; for *there was* not a house where *there was* not one dead.

31 ¶ And he called for Moses and Aaron by night, and said, Rise up, *and* get you forth from among my people, both ye and the children of Israel; and go, serve the LORD, as ye have said.

32 Also take your flocks and your herds, as ye have said, and be gone; and bless me also.

33 And the Egyptians were urgent upon the people, that they might send them out of the land in haste; for they said, We *be* all dead *men.*

34 And the people took their dough before it was leavened, their kneadingtroughs being bound up in their clothes upon their shoulders.

## Amplified

14 And this day shall be to you for a memorial. You shall keep it as a feast to the Lord throughout your generations, keep it as an ordinance for ever.

15 [In celebration of the passover in future years] seven days shall you eat unleavened bread; even the first day you shall put away leaven [symbolic of corruption] out of your houses; for whoever eats leavened bread from the first day until the seventh day, that person shall be cut off from Israel.

16 On the first day you shall hold a solemn *and* holy assembly, and on the seventh day there shall be a solemn *and* holy assembly; no kind of work shall be done in them, save [preparation of] that which every person must eat, that only may be done by you.

17 And you shall observe the feast of unleavened bread; for on this very day have I brought your hosts out of the land of Egypt; therefore shall you observe this day throughout your generations by an ordinance for ever.

18 In the first month, on the fourteenth day of the month at evening, you shall eat unleavened bread, [and continue] until the twenty-first day of the month at evening.

19 Seven days no leaven [symbolic of corruption] shall be found in your houses; whoever eats what is leavened shall be excluded from the congregation of Israel, whether a stranger or native-born. [I Cor. 5:6-8.]

20 You shall eat nothing leavened; in all your dwellings you shall eat unleavened bread [during that week].

21 Then Moses called for all the elders of Israel, and said to them, Go forth, select and take a lamb according to your families, and kill the passover [lamb].

22 And you shall take a bunch of hyssop, dip it in the blood in the basin, and touch the lintel above the door and the two sideposts with the blood; and none of you shall go out of his house until morning.

23 For the Lord will pass through to slay the Egyptians; and when He sees the blood upon the lintel and the two sideposts, the Lord will pass over the door, and will not allow the destroyer to come into your houses to slay you.

24 You shall observe this rite for an ordinance to you and to your sons for ever.

25 When you come to the land which the Lord will give you, as He has promised, you shall keep this service.

26 When your children shall say to you, What do you mean by this service?

27 You shall say, It is the sacrifice of the Lord's passover, for He passed over the houses of the Israelites in Egypt, when He slew the Egyptians but spared our houses. And the people bowed their heads and worshiped.

28 The Israelites went and, as the Lord had commanded Moses and Aaron, so they did.

29 At midnight the Lord slew every first-born in the land of Egypt, from the first-born of Pharaoh who sat on his throne to the first-born of the prisoner in the dungeon, and all the first-born of the livestock.

30 Pharaoh rose up in the night, he, all his servants, and all the Egyptians; and there was a great cry in Egypt, for there was not a house where there was not one dead.

31 He called for Moses and Aaron by night, and said, Rise up, get out from among my people, both you and the Israelites; and go, serve the Lord, as you said.

32 Also take your flocks and your herds, as you have said, and be gone! And [ask your God to] bless me also.

33 The Egyptians were urgent with the people to depart, that they might send them out of the land in haste; for they said, We are all dead men.

34 The people took their dough before it was leavened, their kneading bowls being bound up in their clothes on their shoulders.

## New American Standard

*Feast of Unleavened Bread*
14'Now this day will be a memorial to you, and you shall celebrate it *as* a feast to the LORD; throughout your generations you are
to celebrate it *as* a permanent ordinance.
15¶ 'Seven days you shall eat unleavened bread, but on the first
day you shall remove leaven from your houses; for whoever eats
anything leavened from the first day until the seventh day, that
person shall be cut off from Israel.
16'And on the first day you shall have a holy assembly, and
*another* holy assembly on the seventh day; no work at all shall be
done on them, except what must be eaten by every person, that
alone may be prepared by you.
17'You shall also observe the *Feast of* Unleavened Bread, for on
this very day I brought your hosts out of the land of Egypt; therefore you shall observe this day throughout your generations as a
permanent ordinance.
18'In the first *month*, on the fourteenth day of the month at
evening, you shall eat unleavened bread, until the twenty-first day
of the month at evening.
19'Seven days there shall be no leaven found in your houses; for
whoever eats what is leavened, that person shall be cut off from
the congregation of Israel, whether *he is* an alien or a native of the
land.
20'You shall not eat anything leavened; in all your dwellings you
shall eat unleavened bread.'"
21¶ Then Moses called for all the elders of Israel, and said to
them, "Go and take for yourselves lambs according to your families, and slay the Passover *lamb*.
22"And you shall take a bunch of hyssop and dip it in the blood
which is in the basin, and apply some of the blood that is in the
basin to the lintel and the two doorposts; and none of you shall
go outside the door of his house until morning.

*A Memorial of Redemption*
23"For the LORD will pass through to smite the Egyptians; and
when He sees the blood on the lintel and on the two doorposts,
the LORD will pass over the door and will not allow the destroyer
to come in to your houses to smite *you*.
24"And you shall observe this event as an ordinance for you and
your children forever.
25"And it will come about when you enter the land which the
LORD will give you, as He has promised, that you shall observe this
rite.
26"And it will come about when your children will say to you,
'What does this rite mean to you?'
27that you shall say, 'It is a Passover sacrifice to the LORD who
passed over the houses of the sons of Israel in Egypt when He
smote the Egyptians, but spared our homes.'" And the people
bowed low and worshiped.
28Then the sons of Israel went and did *so;* just as the LORD had
commanded Moses and Aaron, so they did.
29¶ Now it came about at midnight that the LORD struck all the
first-born in the land of Egypt, from the first-born of Pharaoh who
sat on his throne to the first-born of the captive who was in the
dungeon, and all the first-born of cattle.
30And Pharaoh arose in the night, he and all his servants and
all the Egyptians; and there was a great cry in Egypt, for there was
no home where there was not someone dead.
31Then he called for Moses and Aaron at night and said, "Rise
up, get out from among my people, both you and the sons of Israel;
and go, worship the LORD, as you have said.
32"Take both your flocks and your herds, as you have said, and
go, and bless me also."

*Exodus of Israel*
33And the Egyptians urged the people, to send them out of the
land in haste, for they said, "We shall all be dead."
34So the people took their dough before it was leavened, *with*
their kneading bowls bound up in the clothes on their shoulders.

## New International

14"This is a day you are to commemorate; for the generations
to come you shall celebrate it as a festival to the LORD—a lasting
ordinance. 15For seven days you are to eat bread made without
yeast. On the first day remove the yeast from your houses, for
whoever eats anything with yeast in it from the first day through
the seventh must be cut off from Israel. 16On the first day hold a
sacred assembly, and another one on the seventh day. Do no work
at all on these days, except to prepare food for everyone to eat—
that is all you may do.
17"Celebrate the Feast of Unleavened Bread, because it was on
this very day that I brought your divisions out of Egypt. Celebrate
this day as a lasting ordinance for the generations to come. 18In the
first month you are to eat bread made without yeast, from the
evening of the fourteenth day until the evening of the twenty-first
day. 19For seven days no yeast is to be found in your houses. And
whoever eats anything with yeast in it must be cut off from the
community of Israel, whether he is an alien or native-born. 20Eat
nothing made with yeast. Wherever you live, you must eat unleavened bread."
21Then Moses summoned all the elders of Israel and said to
them, "Go at once and select the animals for your families and
slaughter the Passover lamb. 22Take a bunch of hyssop, dip it into
the blood in the basin and put some of the blood on the top and
on both sides of the doorframe. Not one of you shall go out the
door of his house until morning. 23When the LORD goes through
the land to strike down the Egyptians, he will see the blood on the
top and sides of the doorframe and will pass over that doorway,
and he will not permit the destroyer to enter your houses and
strike you down.
24"Obey these instructions as a lasting ordinance for you and
your descendants. 25When you enter the land that the LORD will
give you as he promised, observe this ceremony. 26And when your
children ask you, 'What does this ceremony mean to you?' 27then
tell them, 'It is the Passover sacrifice to the LORD, who passed over
the houses of the Israelites in Egypt and spared our homes when
he struck down the Egyptians.'" Then the people bowed down
and worshiped. 28The Israelites did just what the LORD commanded Moses and Aaron.
29At midnight the LORD struck down all the firstborn in Egypt,
from the firstborn of Pharaoh, who sat on the throne, to the first-
born of the prisoner, who was in the dungeon, and the firstborn
of all the livestock as well. 30Pharaoh and all his officials and all
the Egyptians got up during the night, and there was loud wailing
in Egypt, for there was not a house without someone dead.

*The Exodus*
31During the night Pharaoh summoned Moses and Aaron and
said, "Up! Leave my people, you and the Israelites! Go, worship
the LORD as you have requested. 32Take your flocks and herds, as
you have said, and go. And also bless me."
33The Egyptians urged the people to hurry and leave the country. "For otherwise," they said, "we will all die!" 34So the people
took their dough before the yeast was added, and carried it on their
shoulders in kneading troughs wrapped in clothing. 35The Israel-

## King James

35And the children of Israel did according to the word of Moses;
and they borrowed of the Egyptians jewels of silver, and jewels of
gold, and raiment:
36And the LORD gave the people favour in the sight of the
Egyptians, so that they lent unto them *such things as they required*.
And they spoiled the Egyptians.
37¶ And the children of Israel journeyed from Rameses to Succoth, about six hundred thousand on foot *that were* men, beside
children.
38And a mixed multitude went up also with them; and flocks,
and herds, *even* very much cattle.
39And they baked unleavened cakes of the dough which they
brought forth out of Egypt, for it was not leavened; because they
were thrust out of Egypt, and could not tarry, neither had they
prepared for themselves any victual.
40¶ Now the sojourning of the children of Israel, who dwelt in
Egypt, *was* four hundred and thirty years.
41And it came to pass at the end of the four hundred and thirty
years, even the selfsame day it came to pass, that all the hosts of
the LORD went out from the land of Egypt.
42It *is* a night to be much observed unto the LORD for bringing
them out from the land of Egypt: this *is* that night of the LORD to
be observed of all the children of Israel in their generations.
43¶ And the LORD said unto Moses and Aaron, This *is* the
ordinance of the passover: There shall no stranger eat thereof:
44But every man's servant that is bought for money, when thou
hast circumcised him, then shall he eat thereof.
45A foreigner and an hired servant shall not eat thereof.
46In one house shall it be eaten; thou shalt not carry forth aught
of the flesh abroad out of the house; neither shall ye break a bone
thereof.
47All the congregation of Israel shall keep it.
48And when a stranger shall sojourn with thee, and will keep
the passover to the LORD, let all his males be circumcised, and then
let him come near and keep it; and he shall be as one that is born
in the land: for no uncircumcised person shall eat thereof.
49One law shall be to him that is homeborn, and unto the
stranger that sojourneth among you.
50Thus did all the children of Israel; as the LORD commanded
Moses and Aaron, so did they.
51And it came to pass the selfsame day, *that* the LORD did bring
the children of Israel out of the land of Egypt by their armies.

**13** AND THE LORD spake unto Moses, saying,
2Sanctify unto me all the firstborn, whatsoever openeth
the womb among the children of Israel, *both* of man and of beast:
it *is* mine.
3¶ And Moses said unto the people, Remember this day, in
which ye came out from Egypt, out of the house of bondage; for
by strength of hand the LORD brought you out from this *place:* there
shall no leavened bread be eaten.
4This day came ye out in the month Abib.
5¶ And it shall be when the LORD shall bring thee into the land
of the Canaanites, and the Hittites, and the Amorites, and the
Hivites, and the Jebusites, which he sware unto thy fathers to give
thee, a land flowing with milk and honey, that thou shalt keep this
service in this month.
6Seven days thou shalt eat unleavened bread, and in the seventh day *shall be* a feast to the LORD.
7Unleavened bread shall be eaten seven days; and there shall
no leavened bread be seen with thee, neither shall there be leaven
seen with thee in all thy quarters.
8¶ And thou shalt show thy son in that day, saying, *This is done*
because of that *which* the LORD did unto me when I came forth out
of Egypt.

## Amplified

35The Israelites did according to the word of Moses; and they
[urgently] asked of the Egyptians jewels of silver and of gold, and
clothing.
36The Lord gave the people favor in the sight of the Egyptians,
so that they gave them what they asked. And they stripped the
Egyptians [of those things].
37The Israelites journeyed from Rameses to Succoth, about
600,000 men on foot, besides women and children.
38And a mixed multitude went also with them, and very much
livestock, both flocks and herds.
39They baked unleavened cakes of the dough which they
brought from Egypt, for it was not leavened; because they were
driven from Egypt, and could not delay, nor had they prepared for
themselves any food.
40Now the time the Israelites dwelt in Egypt was 430 years.
[Gen.15:13, 14.]
41At the end of the 430 years, even that very day all the hosts
of the Lord went out of Egypt.
42It was a night of watching unto the Lord *and* to be much
observed for bringing them out of Egypt; this same night of watching unto the Lord is to be observed by all the Israelites throughout
their generations.
43The Lord said to Moses and Aaron, This is the ordinance of
the passover: No foreigner shall eat of it;
44But every man's servant who is bought for money, when you
have circumcised him, then may eat of it.
45A foreigner or hired servant shall not eat of it.
46In one house shall it be eaten [by one company]; you shall not
carry any of the flesh outside the house; neither shall you break
a bone of it. [John 19:33, 36.]
47All the congregation of Israel shall keep it.
48When a stranger sojourning with you wishes to keep the
passover to the Lord, let all his males be circumcised, and then let
him come near and keep it; and he shall be as one that is born in
the land. But no uncircumcised person shall eat of it.
49There shall be one law for the native born and for the stranger
or foreigner who sojourns among you.
50Thus did all the Israelites; as the Lord commanded Moses and
Aaron, so did they.
51And on that very day the Lord brought the Israelites out of
the land of Egypt by their hosts.

**13** THE LORD said to Moses,
2Sanctify (consecrate, set apart) to Me all the first-born
[males]; whatever is first to open the womb among the Israelites,
both of man and of beast, is Mine.
3And Moses said to the people, [Earnestly] remember this day,
in which you came out from Egypt, out of the house of bondage
*and* bondmen, for by strength of hand the Lord brought you out
from this place; no leavened bread shall be eaten.
4This day you go forth in the month Abib.
5And when the Lord brings you into the land of the Canaanites,
Hittites, Amorites, Hivites, and Jebusites, which He promised *and*
swore to your fathers to give you, a land flowing with milk and
honey [that is, a land of plenty], you shall keep this service in this
month.
6Seven days you shall eat unleavened bread, and the seventh
day shall be a feast to the Lord.
7Unleavened bread shall be eaten for seven days; no leavened
bread shall be seen with you, neither shall there be leaven in all
your territory.
8You shall explain to your son on that day, This is done because
of what the Lord did for me when I came out of Egypt.

## New American Standard

35 Now the sons of Israel had done according to the word of
Moses, for they had requested from the Egyptians articles of silver
and articles of gold, and clothing;
36 and the LORD had given the people favor in the sight of the
Egyptians, so that they let them have their request. Thus they
plundered the Egyptians.
37 ¶ Now the sons of Israel journeyed from Rameses to Succoth,
about six hundred thousand men on foot, aside from children.
38 And a mixed multitude also went up with them, along with
flocks and herds, a very large number of livestock.
39 And they baked the dough which they had brought out of
Egypt into cakes of unleavened bread. For it had not become
leavened, since they were driven out of Egypt and could not delay,
nor had they prepared any provisions for themselves.
40 ¶ Now the time that the sons of Israel lived in Egypt was four
hundred and thirty years.
41 And it came about at the end of four hundred and thirty years,
to the very day, that all the hosts of the LORD went out from the
land of Egypt.

*Ordinance of the Passover*

42 It is a night to be observed for the LORD for having brought
them out from the land of Egypt; this night is for the LORD, to be
observed by all the sons of Israel throughout their generations.
43 ¶ And the LORD said to Moses and Aaron, "This is the ordinance of the Passover: no [a]foreigner is to eat of it;
44 but every man's slave purchased with money, after you have
circumcised him, then he may eat of it.
45 "A sojourner or a hired servant shall not eat of it.
46 "It is to be eaten in a single house; you are not to bring forth
any of the flesh outside of the house, nor are you to break any bone
of it.
47 "All the congregation of Israel are to celebrate this.
48 "But if a stranger sojourns with you, and celebrates the Passover to the LORD, let all his males be circumcised, and then let him
come near to celebrate it; and he shall be like a native of the land.
But no uncircumcised person may eat of it.
49 "The same law shall apply to the native as to the stranger who
sojourns among you."
50 Then all the sons of Israel did *so;* they did just as the LORD had
commanded Moses and Aaron.
51 And it came about on that same day that the LORD brought
the sons of Israel out of the land of Egypt by their hosts.

*Consecration of the First-born*

13 THEN THE LORD spoke to Moses, saying,
2 "Sanctify to Me every first-born, the first offspring of
every womb among the sons of Israel, both of man and beast; it
belongs to Me."
3 ¶ And Moses said to the people, "Remember this day in which
you went out from Egypt, from the house of slavery; for by a
powerful hand the LORD brought you out from this place. And
nothing leavened shall be eaten.
4 "On this day in the month of Abib, you are about to go forth.
5 "And it shall be when the LORD brings you to the land of the
Canaanite, the Hittite, the Amorite, the Hivite and the Jebusite,
which He swore to your fathers to give you, a land flowing with
milk and honey, that you shall observe this rite in this month.
6 "For seven days you shall eat unleavened bread, and on the
seventh day there shall be a feast to the LORD.
7 "Unleavened bread shall be eaten throughout the seven days;
and nothing leavened shall be seen among you, nor shall any
leaven be seen among you in all your borders.
8 "And you shall tell your son on that day, saying, 'It is because
of what the LORD did for me when I came out of Egypt.'

NAS [a] Lit., *son of a stranger*

## New International

ites did as Moses instructed and asked the Egyptians for articles
of silver and gold and for clothing. 36 The LORD had made the
Egyptians favorably disposed toward the people, and they gave
them what they asked for; so they plundered the Egyptians.
37 The Israelites journeyed from Rameses to Succoth. There
were about six hundred thousand men on foot, besides women
and children. 38 Many other people went up with them, as well as
large droves of livestock, both flocks and herds. 39 With the dough
they had brought from Egypt, they baked cakes of unleavened
bread. The dough was without yeast because they had been driven
out of Egypt and did not have time to prepare food for themselves.
40 Now the length of time the Israelite people lived in Egypt[b]
was 430 years. 41 At the end of the 430 years, to the very day, all
the LORD's divisions left Egypt. 42 Because the LORD kept vigil that
night to bring them out of Egypt, on this night all the Israelites are
to keep vigil to honor the LORD for the generations to come.

*Passover Restrictions*

43 The LORD said to Moses and Aaron, "These are the regulations for the Passover:
"No foreigner is to eat of it. 44 Any slave you have bought may
eat of it after you have circumcised him, 45 but a temporary resident
and a hired worker may not eat of it.
46 "It must be eaten inside one house; take none of the meat
outside the house. Do not break any of the bones. 47 The whole
community of Israel must celebrate it.
48 "An alien living among you who wants to celebrate the
LORD's Passover must have all the males in his household circumcised; then he may take part like one born in the land. No uncircumcised male may eat of it. 49 The same law applies to the native-
born and to the alien living among you."

50 All the Israelites did just what the LORD had commanded
Moses and Aaron. 51 And on that very day the LORD brought the
Israelites out of Egypt by their divisions.

*Consecration of the Firstborn*

13 THE LORD said to Moses, 2 "Consecrate to me every first-
born male. The first offspring of every womb among the
Israelites belongs to me, whether man or animal."
3 Then Moses said to the people, "Commemorate this day, the
day you came out of Egypt, out of the land of slavery, because the
LORD brought you out of it with a mighty hand. Eat nothing
containing yeast. 4 Today, in the month of Abib, you are leaving.
5 When the LORD brings you into the land of the Canaanites, Hittites, Amorites, Hivites and Jebusites—the land he swore to your
forefathers to give you, a land flowing with milk and honey—you
are to observe this ceremony in this month: 6 For seven days eat
bread made without yeast and on the seventh day hold a festival
to the LORD. 7 Eat unleavened bread during those seven days;
nothing with yeast in it is to be seen among you, nor shall any yeast
be seen anywhere within your borders. 8 On that day tell your son,
'I do this because of what the LORD did for me when I came out
of Egypt.' 9 This observance will be for you like a sign on your hand

NIV [b] 40 Masoretic Text; Samaritan Pentateuch and Septuagint *Egypt and Canaan*

## King James

9And it shall be for a sign unto thee upon thine hand, and for
a memorial between thine eyes, that the LORD's law may be in thy
mouth: for with a strong hand hath the LORD brought thee out of
Egypt.
10Thou shalt therefore keep this ordinance in his season from
year to year.
11¶ And it shall be when the LORD shall bring thee into the land
of the Canaanites, as he sware unto thee and to thy fathers, and
shall give it thee,
12That thou shalt set apart unto the LORD all that openeth the
matrix, and every firstling that cometh of a beast which thou hast;
the males *shall be* the LORD's.
13And every firstling of an ass thou shalt redeem with a lamb;
and if thou wilt not redeem it, then thou shalt break his neck: and
all the firstborn of man among thy children shalt thou redeem.
14¶ And it shall be when thy son asketh thee in time to come,
saying, What *is* this? that thou shalt say unto him, By strength of
hand the LORD brought us out from Egypt, from the house of
bondage:
15And it came to pass, when Pharaoh would hardly let us go,
that the LORD slew all the firstborn in the land of Egypt, both the
firstborn of man, and the firstborn of beast: therefore I sacrifice to
the LORD all that openeth the matrix, being males; but all the
firstborn of my children I redeem.
16And it shall be for a token upon thine hand, and for frontlets
between thine eyes: for by strength of hand the LORD brought us
forth out of Egypt.
17¶ And it came to pass, when Pharaoh had let the people go,
that God led them not *through* the way of the land of the Philistines, although that *was* near; for God said, Lest peradventure the
people repent when they see war, and they return to Egypt:
18But God led the people about, *through* the way of the wilderness of the Red sea: and the children of Israel went up harnessed
out of the land of Egypt.
19And Moses took the bones of Joseph with him: for he had
straitly sworn the children of Israel, saying, God will surely visit
you; and ye shall carry up my bones away hence with you.
20¶ And they took their journey from Succoth, and encamped
in Etham, in the edge of the wilderness.
21And the LORD went before them by day in a pillar of a cloud,
to lead them the way; and by night in a pillar of fire, to give them
light; to go by day and night:
22He took not away the pillar of the cloud by day, nor the pillar
of fire by night, *from* before the people.

**14** AND THE LORD spake unto Moses, saying,
2Speak unto the children of Israel, that they turn and
encamp before Pi-hahiroth, between Migdol and the sea, over
against Baal-zephon: before it shall ye encamp by the sea.
3For Pharaoh will say of the children of Israel, They *are* entangled in the land, the wilderness hath shut them in.
4And I will harden Pharaoh's heart, that he shall follow after
them; and I will be honoured upon Pharaoh, and upon all his host;
that the Egyptians may know that I *am* the LORD. And they did so.
5¶ And it was told the king of Egypt that the people fled: and
the heart of Pharaoh and of his servants was turned against the
people, and they said, Why have we done this, that we have let
Israel go from serving us?
6And he made ready his chariot, and took his people with him:
7And he took six hundred chosen chariots, and all the chariots
of Egypt, and captains over every one of them.

## Amplified

9It shall be as a sign to you upon your hand and as a memorial
between your eyes, that the law of the Lord may be in your mouth;
for with a strong hand the Lord has brought you out of Egypt.
10You shall therefore keep this ordinance at this time from year
to year.
11And when the Lord brings you into the land of the Canaanites, as He promised *and* swore to you and your fathers, and shall
give it to you,
12You shall set apart to the Lord all that first opens the womb.
All the firstlings of your livestock that are males shall be the Lord's.
13Every first-born of a donkey you shall redeem by [substituting
for it] a lamb, or if you will not redeem it, then you shall break its
neck; and every first-born among your sons shall you redeem.
14And when in time to come your son asks you, What does this
mean? You shall say to him, By strength of hand the Lord brought
us out from Egypt, from the house of bondage *and* bondmen.
15For when Pharaoh stubbornly refused to let us go, the Lord
slew all the first-born in the land of Egypt, both the first-born of
man and of livestock. Therefore I sacrifice to the Lord all the males
that first open the womb; but all the first-born of my sons I redeem.
16And it shall be as a reminder upon your hand or as frontlets
between your eyes, for by a strong hand the Lord brought us out
of Egypt.
17When Pharaoh let the people go, God led them not by way
of the land of the Philistines, although that was nearer; for God
said, Lest the people change their purpose when they see war, and
return to Egypt.
18But God led the people around by way of the wilderness
toward the Red Sea. And the Israelites went up marshaled (in
ranks) out of the land of Egypt.
19And Moses took the bones of Joseph with him; for [Joseph]
had strictly sworn the Israelites, saying, Surely God will be with
you, and you must carry my bones away from here with you.
[Gen. 50:25.]
20They journeyed from Succoth and encamped at Etham, on the
edge of the wilderness.
21The Lord went before them by day in a pillar of cloud to lead
them along the way, and by night in a pillar of fire to give them
light, that they might travel by day and by night.
22The pillar of cloud by day and the pillar of fire by night did
not depart from before the people.

**14** AND THE Lord said to Moses,
2Tell the Israelites to turn back and encamp before Pihahiroth, between Migdol and the [Red] Sea, before [a]Baal-zephon.
You shall encamp opposite it by the sea.
3For Pharaoh will say of the Israelites, They are entangled in the
land; the wilderness has shut them in.
4I will harden (make stubborn, strong) Pharaoh's heart, that he
will pursue them, and I will get Me honor *and* glory over Pharaoh
and all his host, and the Egyptians shall know that I am the Lord.
And they did so.
5It was told the king of Egypt that the people had fled; and the
heart of Pharaoh and of his servants was changed toward the
people, and they said, What is this we have done? We have let
Israel go from serving us!
6And he made ready his chariots, and took his army,
7And took 600 chosen chariots and all the other chariots of
Egypt with officers over all of them.

**AMP** [a] Melvin Grove Kyle has said that travelers who follow the coast of the Red Sea, along the line of the Exodus, need no other guidebook than the Bible. The whole topography corresponds to that mentioned in the Bible account (Floyd E. Hamilton in *The Basis of Christian Faith*).

## New American Standard

9"And it shall serve as a sign to you on your hand, and as a
reminder on your forehead, that the law of the LORD may be in
your mouth; for with a powerful hand the LORD brought you out
of Egypt.
10"Therefore, you shall keep this ordinance at its appointed
time from year to year.
11¶ "Now it shall come about when the LORD brings you to the
land of the Canaanite, as He swore to you and to your fathers, and
gives it to you,
12that you shall devote to the LORD the first offspring of every
womb, and the first offspring of every beast that you own; the
males belong to the LORD.
13"But every first offspring of a donkey you shall redeem with
a lamb, but if you do not redeem *it*, then you shall break its neck;
and every first-born of man among your sons you shall redeem.
14"And it shall be when your son asks you in time to come,
saying, 'What is this?' then you shall say to him, 'With a powerful
hand the LORD brought us out of Egypt, from the house of slavery.
15'And it came about, when Pharaoh was stubborn about letting
us go, that the LORD killed every first-born in the land of Egypt,
both the first-born of man and the first-born of beast. Therefore,
I sacrifice to the LORD the males, the first offspring of every womb,
but every first-born of my sons I redeem.'
16"So it shall serve as a sign on your hand, and as phylacteries
on your forehead, for with a powerful hand the LORD brought us
out of Egypt."

*God Leads the People*

17¶ Now it came about when Pharaoh had let the people go, that
God did not lead them by the way of the land of the Philistines,
even though it was near; for God said, "Lest the people change
their minds when they see war, and they return to Egypt."
18Hence God led the people around by the way of the wilderness to the Red Sea; and the sons of Israel went up in martial array
from the land of Egypt.
19And Moses took the bones of Joseph with him, for he had
made the sons of Israel solemnly swear, saying, "God shall surely
take care of you; and you shall carry my bones from here with
you."
20Then they set out from Succoth and camped in Etham on the
edge of the wilderness.
21And the LORD was going before them in a pillar of cloud by
day to lead them on the way, and in a pillar of fire by night to give
them light, that they might travel by day and by night.
22He did not take away the pillar of cloud by day, nor the pillar
of fire by night, from before the people.

*Pharaoh in Pursuit*

**14** NOW THE LORD spoke to Moses, saying,
2"Tell the sons of Israel to turn back and camp before
Pi-hahiroth, between Migdol and the sea; you shall camp in front
of Baal-zephon, opposite it, by the sea.
3"For Pharaoh will say of the sons of Israel, 'They are wandering aimlessly in the land; the wilderness has shut them in.'
4"Thus I will harden Pharaoh's heart, and he will chase after
them; and I will be honored through Pharaoh and all his army, and
the Egyptians will know that I am the LORD." And they did so.
5¶ When the king of Egypt was told that the people had fled,
Pharaoh and his servants had a change of heart toward the people,
and they said, "What is this we have done, that we have let Israel
go from serving us?"
6So he made his chariot ready and took his people with him;
7and he took six hundred select chariots, and all the *other*
chariots of Egypt with officers over all of them.

## New International

and a reminder on your forehead that the law of the LORD is to be
on your lips. For the LORD brought you out of Egypt with his
mighty hand. 10You must keep this ordinance at the appointed
time year after year.
11"After the LORD brings you into the land of the Canaanites
and gives it to you, as he promised on oath to you and your
forefathers, 12you are to give over to the LORD the first offspring
of every womb. All the firstborn males of your livestock belong to
the LORD. 13Redeem with a lamb every firstborn donkey, but if you
do not redeem it, break its neck. Redeem every firstborn among
your sons.
14"In days to come, when your son asks you, 'What does this
mean?' say to him, 'With a mighty hand the LORD brought us out
of Egypt, out of the land of slavery. 15When Pharaoh stubbornly
refused to let us go, the LORD killed every firstborn in Egypt, both
man and animal. This is why I sacrifice to the LORD the first male
offspring of every womb and redeem each of my firstborn sons.'
16And it will be like a sign on your hand and a symbol on your
forehead that the LORD brought us out of Egypt with his mighty
hand."

*Crossing the Sea*

17When Pharaoh let the people go, God did not lead them on
the road through the Philistine country, though that was shorter.
For God said, "If they face war, they might change their minds and
return to Egypt." 18So God led the people around by the desert
road toward the Red Sea.[b] The Israelites went up out of Egypt
armed for battle.
19Moses took the bones of Joseph with him because Joseph had
made the sons of Israel swear an oath. He had said, "God will
surely come to your aid, and then you must carry my bones up
with you from this place."[c]
20After leaving Succoth they camped at Etham on the edge of
the desert. 21By day the LORD went ahead of them in a pillar of
cloud to guide them on their way and by night in a pillar of fire
to give them light, so that they could travel by day or night.
22Neither the pillar of cloud by day nor the pillar of fire by night
left its place in front of the people.

**14** THEN THE LORD said to Moses, 2"Tell the Israelites to
turn back and encamp near Pi Hahiroth, between Migdol
and the sea. They are to encamp by the sea, directly opposite Baal
Zephon. 3Pharaoh will think, 'The Israelites are wandering around
the land in confusion, hemmed in by the desert.' 4And I will
harden Pharaoh's heart, and he will pursue them. But I will gain
glory for myself through Pharaoh and all his army, and the Egyptians will know that I am the LORD." So the Israelites did this.
5When the king of Egypt was told that the people had fled,
Pharaoh and his officials changed their minds about them and
said, "What have we done? We have let the Israelites go and have
lost their services!" 6So he had his chariot made ready and took his
army with him. 7He took six hundred of the best chariots, along
with all the other chariots of Egypt, with officers over all of them.

NIV [b] *18* Hebrew *Yam Suph;* that is, Sea of Reeds [c] *19* See Gen. 50:25.

## King James

8 And the LORD hardened the heart of Pharaoh king of Egypt,
and he pursued after the children of Israel: and the children of
Israel went out with an high hand.
9 But the Egyptians pursued after them, all the horses *and* chariots of Pharaoh, and his horsemen, and his army, and overtook
them encamping by the sea, beside Pi-hahiroth, before Baal-
zephon.
10 ¶ And when Pharaoh drew nigh, the children of Israel lifted
up their eyes, and, behold, the Egyptians marched after them; and
they were sore afraid: and the children of Israel cried out unto the
LORD.
11 And they said unto Moses, Because *there were* no graves in
Egypt, hast thou taken us away to die in the wilderness? wherefore
hast thou dealt thus with us, to carry us forth out of Egypt?
12 *Is* not this the word that we did tell thee in Egypt, saying, Let
us alone, that we may serve the Egyptians? For *it had been* better
for us to serve the Egyptians, than that we should die in the
wilderness.
13 ¶ And Moses said unto the people, Fear ye not, stand still, and
see the salvation of the LORD, which he will show to you today:
for the Egyptians whom ye have seen today, ye shall see them
again no more for ever.
14 The LORD shall fight for you, and ye shall hold your peace.
15 ¶ And the LORD said unto Moses, Wherefore criest thou unto
me? speak unto the children of Israel, that they go forward:
16 But lift thou up thy rod, and stretch out thine hand over the
sea, and divide it: and the children of Israel shall go on dry *ground*
through the midst of the sea.
17 And I, behold, I will harden the hearts of the Egyptians, and
they shall follow them: and I will get me honour upon Pharaoh,
and upon all his host, upon his chariots, and upon his horsemen.
18 And the Egyptians shall know that I *am* the LORD, when I have
gotten me honour upon Pharaoh, upon his chariots, and upon his
horsemen.
19 ¶ And the angel of God, which went before the camp of Israel,
removed and went behind them; and the pillar of the cloud went
from before their face, and stood behind them:
20 And it came between the camp of the Egyptians and the camp
of Israel; and it was a cloud and darkness *to them*, but it gave light
by night *to these:* so that the one came not near the other all the
night.
21 And Moses stretched out his hand over the sea; and the LORD
caused the sea to go *back* by a strong east wind all that night, and
made the sea dry *land*, and the waters were divided.
22 And the children of Israel went into the midst of the sea upon
the dry *ground:* and the waters *were* a wall unto them on their right
hand, and on their left.
23 ¶ And the Egyptians pursued, and went in after them to the
midst of the sea, *even* all Pharaoh's horses, his chariots, and his
horsemen.
24 And it came to pass, that in the morning watch the LORD
looked unto the host of the Egyptians through the pillar of fire and
of the cloud, and troubled the host of the Egyptians,
25 And took off their chariot wheels, that they drave them heavily: so that the Egyptians said, Let us flee from the face of Israel;
for the LORD fighteth for them against the Egyptians.
26 ¶ And the LORD said unto Moses, Stretch out thine hand over
the sea, that the waters may come again upon the Egyptians, upon
their chariots, and upon their horsemen.
27 And Moses stretched forth his hand over the sea, and the sea
returned to his strength when the morning appeared; and the
Egyptians fled against it; and the LORD overthrew the Egyptians
in the midst of the sea.
28 And the waters returned, and covered the chariots, and the
horsemen, *and* all the host of Pharaoh that came into the sea after
them; there remained not so much as one of them.
29 But the children of Israel walked upon dry *land* in the midst
of the sea; and the waters *were* a wall unto them on their right
hand, and on their left.

## Amplified

8 The Lord made hard *and* strong the heart of Pharaoh king of
Egypt, and he pursued the Israelites; for [they] left proudly *and*
defiantly. [Acts 13:17.]
9 The Egyptians pursued them, all the horses and chariots of
Pharaoh and his horsemen and his army, and overtook them
encamped at the [Red] sea, by Pihahiroth, in front of Baal-zephon.
10 When Pharaoh drew near, the Israelites looked up, and behold, the Egyptians were marching after them; and the Israelites
were exceedingly frightened and cried out to the Lord.
11 And they said to Moses, Is it because there are no graves in
Egypt that you have taken us away to die in the wilderness? Why
have you treated us this way and brought us out of Egypt?
12 Did we not tell you in Egypt, Let us alone, let us serve the
Egyptians? For it would have been better for us to serve the Egyptians than to die in the wilderness.
13 Moses told the people, Fear not, stand still (firm, confident,
undismayed) and see the salvation of the Lord, which He will work
for you today. For the Egyptians you have seen today you shall
never see again.
14 The Lord will fight for you, and you shall hold your peace *and*
remain at rest.
15 The Lord said to Moses, Why do you cry to Me? Tell the
people of Israel to go forward!
16 Lift up your rod and stretch out your hand over the sea, and
divide it, and the Israelites shall go on dry ground through the
midst of the sea.
17 And I, behold, I will harden, make stubborn *and* strong, the
hearts of the Egyptians, and they shall go [into the sea] after them;
and I will get Me honor over Pharaoh, and all his host, his chariots,
and horsemen.
18 The Egyptians shall know *and* realize that I am the Lord, when
I have gotten Me honor *and* glory over Pharaoh, his chariots, and
his horsemen.
19 And the Angel of God Who went before the host of Israel
removed and went behind them; and the pillar of the cloud went
from before them and stood behind them,
20 Coming between the host of Egypt and the host of Israel. It
was a cloud and darkness to the Egyptians, but it gave light by
night to the Israelites; and the one host came not near the other
all night.
21 Then Moses stretched out his hand over the sea; and the Lord
caused the sea to go back by a strong east wind all that night, and
made the sea dry land, and the waters were divided.
22 And the Israelites went into the midst of the sea on dry
ground, the waters being a wall to them on their right hand and
on their left.
23 The Egyptians pursued and went in after them into the midst
of the sea, even all Pharaoh's horses, his chariots, and his horsemen.
24 And in the morning watch the Lord through the pillar of fire
and cloud looked down on the host of the Egyptians and discomfited [them],
25 And bound (clogged, took off) their chariot wheels, making
them drive heavily; and the Egyptians said, Let us flee from the
face of Israel; for the Lord fights for them against the Egyptians!
26 Then the Lord said to Moses, Stretch out your hand over the
sea, that the waters may come again upon the Egyptians, upon
their chariots and horsemen.
27 So Moses stretched forth his hand over the sea, and the sea
returned to its strength *and* normal flow when the morning appeared; and the Egyptians fled into it [being met by it]; and the
Lord overthrew the Egyptians *and* shook them off into the midst
of the sea.
28 The waters returned and covered the chariots, the horsemen,
and all the host of Pharaoh that pursued them; not even one of
them remained.
29 But the Israelites walked on dry ground in the midst of the
sea, the waters being a wall to them on their right hand and on
their left.

## New American Standard

8 And the LORD hardened the heart of Pharaoh, king of Egypt,
and he chased after the sons of Israel as the sons of Israel were
going out boldly.
9 Then the Egyptians chased after them *with* all the horses *and*
chariots of Pharaoh, his horsemen and his army, and they overtook them camping by the sea, beside Pi-hahiroth, in front of
Baal-zephon.
**10**¶ And as Pharaoh drew near, the sons of Israel looked, and
behold, the Egyptians were marching after them, and they became
very frightened; so the sons of Israel cried out to the LORD.
11 Then they said to Moses, "Is it because there were no graves
in Egypt that you have taken us away to die in the wilderness?
Why have you dealt with us in this way, bringing us out of Egypt?
12 "Is this not the word that we spoke to you in Egypt, saying,
'Leave us alone that we may serve the Egyptians'? For it would
have been better for us to serve the Egyptians than to die in the
wilderness."

*The Sea Is Divided*

13 But Moses said to the people, "Do not fear! Stand by and see
the salvation of the LORD which He will accomplish for you today;
for the Egyptians whom you have seen today, you will never see
them again forever.
14 "The LORD will fight for you while you keep silent."
**15**¶ Then the LORD said to Moses, "Why are you crying out to
Me? Tell the sons of Israel to go forward.
16 "And as for you, lift up your staff and stretch out your hand
over the sea and divide it, and the sons of Israel shall go through
the midst of the sea on dry land.
17 "And as for Me, behold, I will harden the hearts of the Egyptians so that they will go in after them; and I will be honored
through Pharaoh and all his army, through his chariots and his
horsemen.
18 "Then the Egyptians will know that I am the LORD, when I
am honored through Pharaoh, through his chariots and his horsemen."
19 And the angel of God, who had been going before the camp
of Israel, moved and went behind them; and the pillar of cloud
moved from before them and stood behind them.
20 So it came between the camp of Egypt and the camp of Israel;
and there was the cloud along with the darkness, yet it gave light
at night. Thus the one did not come near the other all night.
**21**¶ Then Moses stretched out his hand over the sea; and the
LORD swept the sea *back* by a strong east wind all night, and turned
the sea into dry land, so the waters were divided.
22 And the sons of Israel went through the midst of the sea on
the dry land, and the waters *were like* a wall to them on their right
hand and on their left.
23 Then the Egyptians took up the pursuit, and all Pharaoh's
horses, his chariots and his horsemen went in after them into the
midst of the sea.
24 And it came about at the morning watch, that the LORD looked
down on the army of the Egyptians through the pillar of fire and
cloud and brought the army of the Egyptians into confusion.
25 And He caused their chariot wheels to swerve, and He made
them drive with difficulty; so the Egyptians said, "Let us flee from
Israel, for the LORD is fighting for them against the Egyptians."
**26**¶ Then the LORD said to Moses, "Stretch out your hand over
the sea so that the waters may come back over the Egyptians, over
their chariots and their horsemen."
27 So Moses stretched out his hand over the sea, and the sea
returned to its normal state at daybreak, while the Egyptians were
fleeing right into it; then the LORD overthrew the Egyptians in the
midst of the sea.
28 And the waters returned and covered the chariots and the
horsemen, even Pharaoh's entire army that had gone into the sea
after them; not even one of them remained.
29 But the sons of Israel walked on dry land through the midst
of the sea, and the waters *were like* a wall to them on their right
hand and on their left.

## New International

8 The LORD hardened the heart of Pharaoh king of Egypt, so that
he pursued the Israelites, who were marching out boldly. 9 The
Egyptians—all Pharaoh's horses and chariots, horsemen[a] and
troops—pursued the Israelites and overtook them as they camped
by the sea near Pi Hahiroth, opposite Baal Zephon.
10 As Pharaoh approached, the Israelites looked up, and there
were the Egyptians, marching after them. They were terrified and
cried out to the LORD. 11 They said to Moses, "Was it because there
were no graves in Egypt that you brought us to the desert to die?
What have you done to us by bringing us out of Egypt? 12 Didn't
we say to you in Egypt, 'Leave us alone; let us serve the Egyptians'? It would have been better for us to serve the Egyptians than
to die in the desert!"
13 Moses answered the people, "Do not be afraid. Stand firm
and you will see the deliverance the LORD will bring you today.
The Egyptians you see today you will never see again. 14 The LORD
will fight for you; you need only to be still."
15 Then the LORD said to Moses, "Why are you crying out to me?
Tell the Israelites to move on. 16 Raise your staff and stretch out
your hand over the sea to divide the water so that the Israelites can
go through the sea on dry ground. 17 I will harden the hearts of the
Egyptians so that they will go in after them. And I will gain glory
through Pharaoh and all his army, through his chariots and his
horsemen. 18 The Egyptians will know that I am the LORD when I
gain glory through Pharaoh, his chariots and his horsemen."
19 Then the angel of God, who had been traveling in front of
Israel's army, withdrew and went behind them. The pillar of cloud
also moved from in front and stood behind them, 20 coming between the armies of Egypt and Israel. Throughout the night the
cloud brought darkness to the one side and light to the other side;
so neither went near the other all night long.
21 Then Moses stretched out his hand over the sea, and all that
night the LORD drove the sea back with a strong east wind and
turned it into dry land. The waters were divided, 22 and the Israelites went through the sea on dry ground, with a wall of water on
their right and on their left.
23 The Egyptians pursued them, and all Pharaoh's horses and
chariots and horsemen followed them into the sea. 24 During the
last watch of the night the LORD looked down from the pillar of fire
and cloud at the Egyptian army and threw it into confusion. 25 He
made the wheels of their chariots come off[b] so that they had
difficulty driving. And the Egyptians said, "Let's get away from
the Israelites! The LORD is fighting for them against Egypt."
26 Then the LORD said to Moses, "Stretch out your hand over the
sea so that the waters may flow back over the Egyptians and their
chariots and horsemen." 27 Moses stretched out his hand over the
sea, and at daybreak the sea went back to its place. The Egyptians
were fleeing toward[c] it, and the LORD swept them into the sea.
28 The water flowed back and covered the chariots and horsemen—
the entire army of Pharaoh that had followed the Israelites into the
sea. Not one of them survived.
29 But the Israelites went through the sea on dry ground, with
a wall of water on their right and on their left. 30 That day the LORD

**NIV** [a] 9 Or *charioteers;* also in verses 17, 18, 23, 26 and 28 [b] 25 Or *He jammed the wheels of their chariots* (see Samaritan Pentateuch, Septuagint and Syriac) [c] 27 Or *from*

## King James

30 Thus the LORD saved Israel that day out of the hand of the Egyptians; and Israel saw the Egyptians dead upon the sea shore.

31 And Israel saw that great work which the LORD did upon the Egyptians: and the people feared the LORD, and believed the LORD, and his servant Moses.

**15** THEN SANG Moses and the children of Israel this song unto the LORD, and spake, saying, I will sing unto the LORD, for he hath triumphed gloriously: the horse and his rider hath he thrown into the sea.

2 The LORD *is* my strength and song, and he is become my salvation: he *is* my God, and I will prepare him an habitation; my father's God, and I will exalt him.

3 The LORD *is* a man of war: the LORD *is* his name.

4 Pharaoh's chariots and his host hath he cast into the sea: his chosen captains also are drowned in the Red sea.

5 The depths have covered them: they sank into the bottom as a stone.

6 Thy right hand, O LORD, is become glorious in power: thy right hand, O LORD, hath dashed in pieces the enemy.

7 And in the greatness of thine excellency thou hast overthrown them that rose up against thee: thou sentest forth thy wrath, *which* consumed them as stubble.

8 And with the blast of thy nostrils the waters were gathered together, the floods stood upright as an heap, *and* the depths were congealed in the heart of the sea.

9 The enemy said, I will pursue, I will overtake, I will divide the spoil; my lust shall be satisfied upon them; I will draw my sword, my hand shall destroy them.

10 Thou didst blow with thy wind, the sea covered them: they sank as lead in the mighty waters.

11 Who *is* like unto thee, O LORD, among the gods? who *is* like thee, glorious in holiness, fearful *in* praises, doing wonders?

12 Thou stretchedst out thy right hand, the earth swallowed them.

13 Thou in thy mercy hast led forth the people *which* thou hast redeemed: thou hast guided *them* in thy strength unto thy holy habitation.

14 The people shall hear, *and* be afraid: sorrow shall take hold on the inhabitants of Palestina.

## Amplified

30 Thus, the Lord saved Israel that day from the hand of the Egyptians; and Israel saw the Egyptians dead upon the seashore.

31 And Israel saw that great work which the Lord did against the Egyptians, and the people (reverently) feared the Lord, and trusted in (relied on, remained steadfast to) the Lord and to His servant Moses.

**15** THEN MOSES and the Israelites sang this song to the Lord, saying, I will sing to the Lord, for He has triumphed gloriously; the horse and his rider *or* its chariot has He thrown into the sea.

2 The Lord is my strength and my song, and He has become my salvation; this is my God, and I will praise Him, my father's God, and I will exalt Him.

3 The Lord is a man of war; the Lord is His name.

4 Pharaoh's chariots and his host has He cast into the sea; his chosen captains also are sunk in the Red Sea.

5 The floods cover them; they sank in the depths [clad in mail] like a stone.

6 Your right hand, O Lord, is glorious in power; Your right hand, O Lord, shatters the enemy.

7 In the greatness of Your majesty You overthrow those rising against You; You send forth Your fury; it consumes them like stubble.

8 With the blast of Your nostrils the waters piled up, the floods stood fixed in a heap, the deeps congealed in the heart of the sea.

9 The enemy said, I will pursue, I will overtake, I will divide the spoil; my desire shall be satisfied upon them; I will draw my sword, my hand shall destroy them.

10 You, [Lord], blew with Your wind, the sea covered them; [clad in mail] they sank as lead in the mighty waters.

11 Who is like You, O Lord, among the gods? Who is like You, glorious in holiness, awesome in splendor, doing wonders?

12 You stretched out Your right hand, the earth's [sea] swallowed them.

13 You in Your mercy *and* loving-kindness have led forth the people whom You have redeemed; You have guided them in Your strength to Your holy habitation.

14 The peoples have heard of it; they tremble; pangs have taken hold on the inhabitants of Philistia.

## New American Standard

30Thus the LORD saved Israel that day from the hand of the
Egyptians, and Israel saw the Egyptians dead on the seashore.
31And when Israel saw the great power which the LORD had
used against the Egyptians, the people feared the LORD, and they
believed in the LORD and in His servant Moses.

*The Song of Moses and Israel*

**15** THEN MOSES and the sons of Israel sang this song to the LORD, and said,

"I will sing to the LORD, for He is highly exalted;
The horse and its rider He has hurled into the sea.
2 "The LORD is my strength and song,
And He has become my salvation;
This is my God, and I will praise Him;
My father's God, and I will extol Him.
3 "The LORD is a warrior;
The LORD is His name.
4 "Pharaoh's chariots and his army He has cast into the sea;
And the choicest of his officers are drowned in the [a]Red Sea.
5 "The deeps cover them;
They went down into the depths like a stone.
6 "Thy right hand, O LORD, is majestic in power,
Thy right hand, O LORD, shatters the enemy.
7 "And in the greatness of Thine excellence Thou dost overthrow those who rise up against Thee;
Thou dost send forth Thy burning anger, *and* it consumes them as chaff.
8 "And at the blast of Thy nostrils the waters were piled up,
The flowing waters stood up like a heap;
The deeps were congealed in the heart of the sea.
9 "The enemy said, 'I will pursue, I will overtake, I will divide the spoil;
My desire shall be gratified against them;
I will draw out my sword, my hand shall destroy them.'
10 "Thou didst blow with Thy wind, the sea covered them;
They sank like lead in the mighty waters.
11 "Who is like Thee among the gods, O LORD?
Who is like Thee, majestic in holiness,
Awesome in praises, working wonders?
12 "Thou didst stretch out Thy right hand,
The earth swallowed them.
13 "In Thy lovingkindness Thou hast led the people whom Thou hast redeemed;
In Thy strength Thou hast guided *them* to Thy holy habitation.
14 "The peoples have heard, they tremble;
Anguish has gripped the inhabitants of Philistia.

NAS [a] Lit., *Sea of Reeds*

## New International

saved Israel from the hands of the Egyptians, and Israel saw the
Egyptians lying dead on the shore. 31And when the Israelites saw
the great power the LORD displayed against the Egyptians, the
people feared the LORD and put their trust in him and in Moses
his servant.

*The Song of Moses and Miriam*

**15** THEN MOSES and the Israelites sang this song to the LORD:

"I will sing to the LORD,
for he is highly exalted.
The horse and its rider
he has hurled into the sea.
2The LORD is my strength and my song;
he has become my salvation.
He is my God, and I will praise him,
my father's God, and I will exalt him.
3The LORD is a warrior;
the LORD is his name.
4Pharaoh's chariots and his army
he has hurled into the sea.
The best of Pharaoh's officers
are drowned in the Red Sea.[b]
5The deep waters have covered them;
they sank to the depths like a stone.

6"Your right hand, O LORD,
was majestic in power.
Your right hand, O LORD,
shattered the enemy.
7In the greatness of your majesty
you threw down those who opposed you.
You unleashed your burning anger;
it consumed them like stubble.
8By the blast of your nostrils
the waters piled up.
The surging waters stood firm like a wall;
the deep waters congealed in the heart of the sea.

9"The enemy boasted,
'I will pursue, I will overtake them.
I will divide the spoils;
I will gorge myself on them.
I will draw my sword
and my hand will destroy them.'
10But you blew with your breath,
and the sea covered them.
They sank like lead
in the mighty waters.
11"Who among the gods is like you, O LORD?
Who is like you—
majestic in holiness,
awesome in glory,
working wonders?
12You stretched out your right hand
and the earth swallowed them.
13"In your unfailing love you will lead
the people you have redeemed.
In your strength you will guide them
to your holy dwelling.
14The nations will hear and tremble;
anguish will grip the people of Philistia.

NIV [b] 4 Hebrew *Yam Suph*; that is, Sea of Reeds; also in verse 22

## King James

15 Then the dukes of Edom shall be amazed; the mighty men of Moab, trembling shall take hold upon them; all the inhabitants of Canaan shall melt away.

16 Fear and dread shall fall upon them; by the greatness of thine arm they shall be *as* still as a stone; till thy people pass over, O LORD, till the people pass over, *which* thou hast purchased.

17 Thou shalt bring them in, and plant them in the mountain of thine inheritance, *in* the place, O LORD, *which* thou hast made for thee to dwell in, *in* the Sanctuary, O LORD, *which* thy hands have established.

18 The LORD shall reign for ever and ever.

19 For the horse of Pharaoh went in with his chariots and with his horsemen into the sea, and the LORD brought again the waters of the sea upon them; but the children of Israel went on dry *land* in the midst of the sea.

20 ¶ And Miriam the prophetess, the sister of Aaron, took a timbrel in her hand; and all the women went out after her with timbrels and with dances.

21 And Miriam answered them, Sing ye to the LORD, for he hath triumphed gloriously; the horse and his rider hath he thrown into the sea.

22 So Moses brought Israel from the Red sea, and they went out into the wilderness of Shur; and they went three days in the wilderness, and found no water.

23 ¶ And when they came to Marah, they could not drink of the waters of Marah, for they *were* bitter: therefore the name of it was called Marah.

24 And the people murmured against Moses, saying, What shall we drink?

25 And he cried unto the LORD; and the LORD showed him a tree, *which* when he had cast into the waters, the waters were made sweet: there he made for them a statute and an ordinance, and there he proved them,

26 And said, If thou wilt diligently hearken to the voice of the LORD thy God, and wilt do that which is right in his sight, and wilt give ear to his commandments, and keep all his statutes, I will put none of these diseases upon thee, which I have brought upon the Egyptians: for I *am* the LORD that healeth thee.

27 ¶ And they came to Elim, where *were* twelve wells of water, and threescore and ten palm trees: and they encamped there by the waters.

**16** AND THEY took their journey from Elim, and all the congregation of the children of Israel came unto the wilderness of Sin, which *is* between Elim and Sinai, on the fifteenth day of the second month after their departing out of the land of Egypt.

2 And the whole congregation of the children of Israel murmured against Moses and Aaron in the wilderness:

3 And the children of Israel said unto them, Would to God we had died by the hand of the LORD in the land of Egypt, when we sat by the flesh pots, *and* when we did eat bread to the full; for ye have brought us forth into this wilderness, to kill this whole assembly with hunger.

4 ¶ Then said the LORD unto Moses, Behold, I will rain bread from heaven for you; and the people shall go out and gather a certain rate every day, that I may prove them, whether they will walk in my law, or no.

5 And it shall come to pass, that on the sixth day they shall prepare *that* which they bring in; and it shall be twice as much as they gather daily.

## Amplified

15 Now the chiefs of Edom are dismayed; the mighty men of Moab [renowned for strength], trembling takes hold of them; all the inhabitants of Canaan have melted away—little by little.

16 Terror and dread fall upon them; because of the greatness of Your arm they are as still as a stone; till Your people pass by *and* over [into Canaan], O Lord, till the people pass by whom You have purchased.

17 You will bring them in [to the land], and plant them on Your own mountain, the place, O Lord, You have made for Your dwelling, the sanctuary, O Lord, which Your hands have established.

18 The Lord will reign for ever and ever.

19 For the horses of Pharaoh went with his chariots and horsemen into the sea, and the Lord brought back the waters of the sea upon them; but the Israelites walked on dry ground in the midst of the sea.

20 Then Miriam the prophetess, the sister of Aaron, took a timbrel in her hand; and all the women went out after her with timbrels and dancing.

21 And Miriam responded to them, Sing to the Lord, for He has triumphed gloriously *and* is highly exalted; the horse and his rider He has thrown into the sea.

22 Then Moses led Israel onward from the Red Sea, and they went into the wilderness of Shur; they went three days [33 miles] in the wilderness and found no water.

23 When they came to Marah, they could not drink *its* waters for they were bitter; therefore it was named Marah (bitterness).

24 The people murmured against Moses, saying, What shall we drink?

25 And he cried to the Lord, and the Lord showed him a tree, which he cast into the waters, and the waters were made sweet. There [the Lord] made for them a statute and an ordinance and there He proved them,

26 Saying, If you will diligently hearken to the voice of the Lord your God, and will do what is right in His sight, and will listen to *and* obey His commandments and keep all His statutes, I will put none of the diseases upon you which I brought upon the Egyptians; for I am the Lord Who heals you.

27 And they came to Elim, where were twelve springs of water and seventy palm trees; and they encamped there by the waters.

**16** THEY SET out from Elim, and all the congregation of Israel came to the wilderness of Sin, which is between Elim and Sinai, on the fifteenth day of the second month after they left the land of Egypt.

2 And the whole congregation of Israel murmured against Moses and Aaron in the wilderness,

3 And said to them, Would that we had died by the hand of the Lord in the land of Egypt, when we sat by the fleshpots and ate bread to the full; for you have brought us out into this wilderness to kill this whole assembly with hunger.

4 Then the Lord said to Moses, Behold, I will rain bread from the heavens for you; and the people shall go out and gather a day's portion every day, that I may prove them, whether they will walk in My law or not.

5 On the sixth day they shall prepare to bring in twice as much as they gather daily.

## New American Standard

15 "Then the chiefs of Edom were dismayed;
The leaders of Moab, trembling grips them;
All the inhabitants of Canaan have melted away.
16 "Terror and dread fall upon them;
By the greatness of Thine arm they are motionless as
stone;
Until Thy people pass over, O LORD,
Until the people pass over whom Thou hast purchased.
17 "Thou wilt bring them and plant them in the mountain
of Thine inheritance,
The place, O LORD, which Thou hast made for Thy
dwelling,
The sanctuary, O Lord, which Thy hands have
established.
18 "The LORD shall reign forever and ever."
19¶ For the horses of Pharaoh with his chariots and his horsemen went into the sea, and the LORD brought back the waters of
the sea on them; but the sons of Israel walked on dry land through
the midst of the sea.
20And Miriam the prophetess, Aaron's sister, took the timbrel
in her hand, and all the women went out after her with timbrels
and with dancing.
21And Miriam answered them,
"Sing to the LORD, for He is highly exalted;
The horse and his rider He has hurled into the sea."

*The LORD Provides Water*

22¶ Then Moses led Israel from the Red Sea, and they went out
into the wilderness of Shur; and they went three days in the
wilderness and found no water.
23And when they came to Marah, they could not drink the
waters of Marah, for they were bitter; therefore it was named
[a]Marah.
24So the people grumbled at Moses, saying, "What shall we
drink?"
25Then he cried out to the LORD, and the LORD showed him a
tree; and he threw *it* into the waters, and the waters became sweet.
There He made for them a statute and regulation, and there He
tested them.
26And He said, "If you will give earnest heed to the voice of the
LORD your God, and do what is right in His sight, and give ear to
His commandments, and keep all His statutes, I will put none of
the diseases on you which I have put on the Egyptians; for I, the
LORD, am your healer."
27¶ Then they came to Elim where there *were* twelve springs of
water and seventy date palms, and they camped there beside the
waters.

*The LORD Provides Manna*

16 THEN THEY set out from Elim, and all the congregation
of the sons of Israel came to the wilderness of Sin, which
is between Elim and Sinai, on the fifteenth day of the second
month after their departure from the land of Egypt.
2And the whole congregation of the sons of Israel grumbled
against Moses and Aaron in the wilderness.
3And the sons of Israel said to them, "Would that we had died
by the LORD's hand in the land of Egypt, when we sat by the pots
of meat, when we ate bread to the full; for you have brought us
out into this wilderness to kill this whole assembly with hunger."
4¶ Then the LORD said to Moses, "Behold, I will rain bread from
heaven for you; and the people shall go out and gather a day's
portion every day, that I may test them, whether or not they will
walk in My [b]instruction.
5"And it will come about on the sixth day, when they prepare
what they bring in, it will be twice as much as they gather daily."

NAS [a] I.e., bitterness [b] Or, *law*

## New International

15The chiefs of Edom will be terrified,
the leaders of Moab will be seized with trembling,
the people[c] of Canaan will melt away;
16 terror and dread will fall upon them.
By the power of your arm
they will be as still as a stone—
until your people pass by, O LORD,
until the people you bought[d] pass by.
17You will bring them in and plant them
on the mountain of your inheritance—
the place, O LORD, you made for your dwelling,
the sanctuary, O Lord, your hands established.
18The LORD will reign
for ever and ever."

19When Pharaoh's horses, chariots and horsemen[e] went into
the sea, the LORD brought the waters of the sea back over them,
but the Israelites walked through the sea on dry ground. 20Then
Miriam the prophetess, Aaron's sister, took a tambourine in her
hand, and all the women followed her, with tambourines and
dancing. 21Miriam sang to them:
"Sing to the LORD,
for he is highly exalted.
The horse and its rider
he has hurled into the sea."

*The Waters of Marah and Elim*

22Then Moses led Israel from the Red Sea and they went into
the Desert of Shur. For three days they traveled in the desert
without finding water. 23When they came to Marah, they could not
drink its water because it was bitter. (That is why the place is called
Marah.[f]) 24So the people grumbled against Moses, saying, "What
are we to drink?"
25Then Moses cried out to the LORD, and the LORD showed him
a piece of wood. He threw it into the water, and the water became
sweet.
There the LORD made a decree and a law for them, and there
he tested them. 26He said, "If you listen carefully to the voice of
the LORD your God and do what is right in his eyes, if you pay
attention to his commands and keep all his decrees, I will not bring
on you any of the diseases I brought on the Egyptians, for I am the
LORD, who heals you."
27Then they came to Elim, where there were twelve springs and
seventy palm trees, and they camped there near the water.

*Manna and Quail*

16 THE WHOLE Israelite community set out from Elim and
came to the Desert of Sin, which is between Elim and
Sinai, on the fifteenth day of the second month after they had come
out of Egypt. 2In the desert the whole community grumbled
against Moses and Aaron. 3The Israelites said to them, "If only we
had died by the LORD's hand in Egypt! There we sat around pots
of meat and ate all the food we wanted, but you have brought us
out into this desert to starve this entire assembly to death."
4Then the LORD said to Moses, "I will rain down bread from
heaven for you. The people are to go out each day and gather
enough for that day. In this way I will test them and see whether
they will follow my instructions. 5On the sixth day they are to
prepare what they bring in, and that is to be twice as much as they
gather on the other days."

NIV [c] 15 Or *rulers* [d] 16 Or *created* [e] 19 Or *charioteers* [f] 23 *Marah* means *bitter.*

## King James

6 And Moses and Aaron said unto all the children of Israel, At even, then ye shall know that the LORD hath brought you out from the land of Egypt:

7 And in the morning, then ye shall see the glory of the LORD; for that he heareth your murmurings against the LORD: and what *are* we, that ye murmur against us?

8 And Moses said, *This shall be,* when the LORD shall give you in the evening flesh to eat, and in the morning bread to the full; for that the LORD heareth your murmurings which ye murmur against him: and what *are* we? your murmurings *are* not against us, but against the LORD.

9 ¶ And Moses spake unto Aaron, Say unto all the congregation of the children of Israel, Come near before the LORD: for he hath heard your murmurings.

10 And it came to pass, as Aaron spake unto the whole congregation of the children of Israel, that they looked toward the wilderness, and, behold, the glory of the LORD appeared in the cloud.

11 ¶ And the LORD spake unto Moses, saying,

12 I have heard the murmurings of the children of Israel: speak unto them, saying, At even ye shall eat flesh, and in the morning ye shall be filled with bread; and ye shall know that I *am* the LORD your God.

13 And it came to pass, that at even the quails came up, and covered the camp: and in the morning the dew lay round about the host.

14 And when the dew that lay was gone up, behold, upon the face of the wilderness *there lay* a small round thing, *as* small as the hoar frost on the ground.

15 And when the children of Israel saw *it,* they said one to another, It *is* manna: for they wist not what it *was.* And Moses said unto them, This *is* the bread which the LORD hath given you to eat.

16 ¶ This *is* the thing which the LORD hath commanded, Gather of it every man according to his eating, an omer for every man, *according to* the number of your persons; take ye every man for *them* which *are* in his tents.

17 And the children of Israel did so, and gathered, some more, some less.

18 And when they did mete *it* with an omer, he that gathered much had nothing over, and he that gathered little had no lack; they gathered every man according to his eating.

19 And Moses said, Let no man leave of it till the morning.

20 Notwithstanding they hearkened not unto Moses; but some of them left of it until the morning, and it bred worms, and stank: and Moses was wroth with them.

21 And they gathered it every morning, every man according to his eating: and when the sun waxed hot, it melted.

22 ¶ And it came to pass, *that* on the sixth day they gathered twice as much bread, two omers for one *man:* and all the rulers of the congregation came and told Moses.

23 And he said unto them, This *is that* which the LORD hath said, Tomorrow *is* the rest of the holy sabbath unto the LORD: bake *that* which ye will bake *today,* and seethe that ye will seethe; and that which remaineth over lay up for you to be kept until the morning.

24 And they laid it up till the morning, as Moses bade: and it did not stink, neither was there any worm therein.

25 And Moses said, Eat that today; for today *is* a sabbath unto the LORD: today ye shall not find it in the field.

26 Six days ye shall gather it; but on the seventh day, *which is* the sabbath, in it there shall be none.

27 ¶ And it came to pass, *that* there went out *some* of the people on the seventh day for to gather, and they found none.

28 And the LORD said unto Moses, How long refuse ye to keep my commandments and my laws?

## Amplified

6 *So* Moses and Aaron said to all Israel, At evening you shall know that the Lord has brought you out from the land of Egypt,

7 And in the morning you shall see the glory of the Lord, for He hears your murmurings against the Lord. For what are we, that you murmur against us?

8 And Moses said, When the Lord gives you in the evening flesh to eat and in the morning bread to the full, because the Lord has heard your grumblings which you murmur against Him, what are we? Your murmurings are not against us, but against the Lord.

9 And Moses said to Aaron, Say to all the congregation of Israel, Come near before the Lord, for He has heard your murmurings.

10 And as Aaron spoke to the whole congregation of Israel, they looked toward the wilderness, and behold, the glory of the Lord appeared in the cloud!

11 The Lord said to Moses,

12 I have heard the murmurings of the Israelites; speak to them, saying, At twilight you shall eat meat, and between the two evenings you shall be filled with bread; and you shall know that I am the Lord your God.

13 In the evening quails came up and covered the camp; and in the morning the dew lay round about the camp.

14 And when the dew had gone, behold, upon the face of the wilderness there lay a fine, round *and* flake-like thing, as fine as hoarfrost on the ground.

15 When the Israelites saw it, they said one to another, Manna (meaning, What is it?). For they did not know what it was. And Moses said to them, This is the bread which the Lord has given you to eat. [John 6:31, 33.]

16 This is what the Lord has commanded: Let every man gather of it as much as he will need, an omer for each person, according to the number of your persons; take it, every man for those in his tent.

17 The [people] did so, and gathered, some more, some less.

18 When they measured it with an omer, he who gathered much had nothing over, and he who gathered little had no lack; each gathered according to his need.

19 Moses said, Let none of it be left until morning.

20 But they did not listen to Moses; some of them left of it until morning, and it bred worms, became foul *and* stank; and Moses was angry with them.

21 They gathered it every morning, each as much as he needed; for when the sun became hot it melted.

22 And on the sixth day they gathered twice as much bread, two omers for each person; and all the leaders of the congregation came and told Moses.

23 He said to them, The Lord has said, Tomorrow is a solemn rest, a holy sabbath to the Lord; bake and boil what you will bake and boil today; and all that remains over put aside for you to keep until morning.

24 They laid it aside till morning, as Moses told them; and it did not become foul, neither was it wormy.

25 Moses said, Eat that today; for today is a sabbath to the Lord. Today you shall find none in the field.

26 Six days you shall gather it; but on the seventh day, the sabbath, there shall be none.

27 On the seventh day some of the people went out to gather, but they found none.

28 The Lord said to Moses, How long do you [people] refuse to keep My commandments and My laws?

## New American Standard

6So Moses and Aaron said to all the sons of Israel, "At evening
you will know that the LORD has brought you out of the land of
Egypt;
7and in the morning you will see the glory of the LORD, for He
hears your grumblings against the LORD; and what are we, that
you grumble against us?"

*The LORD Provides Meat*

8And Moses said, "*This will happen* when the LORD gives you
meat to eat in the evening, and bread to the full in the morning;
for the LORD hears your grumblings which you grumble against
Him. And what are we? Your grumblings are not against us but
against the LORD."
9Then Moses said to Aaron, "Say to all the congregation of the
sons of Israel, 'Come near before the LORD, for He has heard your
grumblings.' "
10And it came about as Aaron spoke to the whole congregation
of the sons of Israel, that they looked toward the wilderness, and
behold, the glory of the LORD appeared in the cloud.
11And the LORD spoke to Moses, saying,
12"I have heard the grumblings of the sons of Israel; speak to
them, saying, 'At twilight you shall eat meat, and in the morning
you shall be filled with bread; and you shall know that I am the
LORD your God.' "
13¶ So it came about at evening that the quails came up and
covered the camp, and in the morning there was a layer of dew
around the camp.
14When the layer of dew evaporated, behold, on the surface of
the wilderness there was a fine flake-like thing, fine as the frost on
the ground.
15When the sons of Israel saw *it*, they said to one another,
"What is it?" For they did not know what it was. And Moses said
to them, "It is the bread which the LORD has given you to eat.
16"This is what the LORD has commanded, 'Gather of it every
man as much as he should eat; you shall take an omer apiece
according to the number of persons each of you has in his tent.' "
17And the sons of Israel did so, and *some* gathered much and
*some* little.
18When they measured it with an omer, he who had gathered
much had no excess, and he who had gathered little had no lack;
every man gathered as much as he should eat.
19And Moses said to them, "Let no man leave any of it until
morning."
20But they did not listen to Moses, and some left part of it until
morning, and it bred worms and became foul; and Moses was
angry with them.
21And they gathered it morning by morning, every man as
much as he should eat; but when the sun grew hot, it would melt.

*The Sabbath Observed*

22¶ Now it came about on the sixth day they gathered twice as
much bread, two omers for each one. When all the leaders of the
congregation came and told Moses,
23then he said to them, "This is what the LORD meant: Tomorrow is a sabbath observance, a holy sabbath to the LORD. Bake
what you will bake and boil what you will boil, and all that is left
over put aside to be kept until morning."
24So they put it aside until morning, as Moses had ordered, and
it did not become foul, nor was there any worm in it.
25And Moses said, "Eat it today, for today is a sabbath to the
LORD; today you will not find it in the field.
26"Six days you shall gather it, but on the seventh day, *the*
sabbath, there will be none."
27And it came about on the seventh day that some of the people
went out to gather, but they found none.
28Then the LORD said to Moses, "How long do you refuse to
keep My commandments and My [a]instructions?

NAS [a] Or, *laws*

## New International

6So Moses and Aaron said to all the Israelites, "In the evening
you will know that it was the LORD who brought you out of Egypt,
7and in the morning you will see the glory of the LORD, because
he has heard your grumbling against him. Who are we, that you
should grumble against us?" 8Moses also said, "You will know
that it was the LORD when he gives you meat to eat in the evening
and all the bread you want in the morning, because he has heard
your grumbling against him. Who are we? You are not grumbling
against us, but against the LORD."
9Then Moses told Aaron, "Say to the entire Israelite community, 'Come before the LORD, for he has heard your grumbling.' "
10While Aaron was speaking to the whole Israelite community,
they looked toward the desert, and there was the glory of the LORD
appearing in the cloud.
11The LORD said to Moses, 12"I have heard the grumbling of the
Israelites. Tell them, 'At twilight you will eat meat, and in the
morning you will be filled with bread. Then you will know that I
am the LORD your God.' "
13That evening quail came and covered the camp, and in the
morning there was a layer of dew around the camp. 14When the
dew was gone, thin flakes like frost on the ground appeared on the
desert floor. 15When the Israelites saw it, they said to each other,
"What is it?" For they did not know what it was.
Moses said to them, "It is the bread the LORD has given you to
eat. 16This is what the LORD has commanded: 'Each one is to gather
as much as he needs. Take an omer[b] for each person you have in
your tent.' "
17The Israelites did as they were told; some gathered much,
some little. 18And when they measured it by the omer, he who
gathered much did not have too much, and he who gathered little
did not have too little. Each one gathered as much as he needed.
19Then Moses said to them, "No one is to keep any of it until
morning."
20However, some of them paid no attention to Moses; they kept
part of it until morning, but it was full of maggots and began to
smell. So Moses was angry with them.
21Each morning everyone gathered as much as he needed, and
when the sun grew hot, it melted away. 22On the sixth day, they
gathered twice as much—two omers[c] for each person—and the
leaders of the community came and reported this to Moses. 23He
said to them, "This is what the LORD commanded: 'Tomorrow is
to be a day of rest, a holy Sabbath to the LORD. So bake what you
want to bake and boil what you want to boil. Save whatever is left
and keep it until morning.' "
24So they saved it until morning, as Moses commanded, and it
did not stink or get maggots in it. 25"Eat it today," Moses said,
"because today is a Sabbath to the LORD. You will not find any of
it on the ground today. 26Six days you are to gather it, but on the
seventh day, the Sabbath, there will not be any."
27Nevertheless, some of the people went out on the seventh day
to gather it, but they found none. 28Then the LORD said to Moses,
"How long will you[d] refuse to keep my commands and my instructions? 29Bear in mind that the LORD has given you the Sab-

NIV [b] *16* That is, probably about 2 quarts (about 2 liters); also in verses 18, 32, 33 and 36 [c] *22* That is, probably about 4 quarts (about 4.5 liters) [d] *28* The Hebrew is plural.

## King James

29See, for that the LORD hath given you the sabbath, therefore he giveth you on the sixth day the bread of two days; abide ye every man in his place, let no man go out of his place on the seventh day.

30So the people rested on the seventh day.

31And the house of Israel called the name thereof Manna: and it *was* like coriander seed, white; and the taste of it *was* like wafers *made* with honey.

32¶ And Moses said, This *is* the thing which the LORD commandeth, Fill an omer of it to be kept for your generations; that they may see the bread wherewith I have fed you in the wilderness, when I brought you forth from the land of Egypt.

33And Moses said unto Aaron, Take a pot, and put an omer full of manna therein, and lay it up before the LORD, to be kept for your generations.

34As the LORD commanded Moses, so Aaron laid it up before the Testimony, to be kept.

35And the children of Israel did eat manna forty years, until they came to a land inhabited; they did eat manna, until they came unto the borders of the land of Canaan.

36Now an omer *is* the tenth *part* of an ephah.

**17** AND ALL the congregation of the children of Israel journeyed from the wilderness of Sin, after their journeys, according to the commandment of the LORD, and pitched in Rephidim: and *there was* no water for the people to drink.

2Wherefore the people did chide with Moses, and said, Give us water that we may drink. And Moses said unto them, Why chide ye with me? wherefore do ye tempt the LORD?

3And the people thirsted there for water; and the people murmured against Moses, and said, Wherefore *is* this *that* thou hast brought us up out of Egypt, to kill us and our children and our cattle with thirst?

4And Moses cried unto the LORD, saying, What shall I do unto this people? they be almost ready to stone me.

5And the LORD said unto Moses, Go on before the people, and take with thee of the elders of Israel; and thy rod, wherewith thou smotest the river, take in thine hand, and go.

6Behold, I will stand before thee there upon the rock in Horeb; and thou shalt smite the rock, and there shall come water out of it, that the people may drink. And Moses did so in the sight of the elders of Israel.

7And he called the name of the place Massah, and Meribah, because of the chiding of the children of Israel, and because they tempted the LORD, saying, Is the LORD among us, or not?

8¶ Then came Amalek, and fought with Israel in Rephidim.

9And Moses said unto Joshua, Choose us out men, and go out, fight with Amalek: tomorrow I will stand on the top of the hill with the rod of God in mine hand.

10So Joshua did as Moses had said to him, and fought with Amalek: and Moses, Aaron, and Hur went up to the top of the hill.

11And it came to pass, when Moses held up his hand, that Israel prevailed: and when he let down his hand, Amalek prevailed.

12But Moses' hands *were* heavy; and they took a stone, and put *it* under him, and he sat thereon; and Aaron and Hur stayed up his hands, the one on the one side, and the other on the other side; and his hands were steady until the going down of the sun.

13And Joshua discomfited Amalek and his people with the edge of the sword.

14And the LORD said unto Moses, Write this *for* a memorial in a book, and rehearse *it* in the ears of Joshua: for I will utterly put out the remembrance of Amalek from under heaven.

## Amplified

29See, the Lord has given you the sabbath, therefore He gives you on the sixth day the bread for two days; let every man remain in his place, let no man leave his place on the seventh day.

30So the people rested on the seventh day.

31The house of Israel called the bread manna; it was like coriander seed, white, and it tasted like wafers made with honey.

32Moses said, This is what the Lord commands, Take an omer of it to be kept throughout your generations, that they may see the bread with which I fed you in the wilderness, when I brought you out of the land of Egypt.

33And Moses said to Aaron, Take a pot, and put an omer of manna in it, and lay it up before the Lord, to be kept throughout your generations.

34As the Lord commanded Moses, Aaron laid it up before the Testimony to be kept [in the ark]. [Heb. 9:4.]

35And the Israelites ate manna forty years, until they came to a habitable land; they ate the manna until they came to the border of the land of Canaan.

36(Now an omer is the tenth of an ephah.)

**17** ALL THE congregation of the Israelites moved on from the wilderness of Sin by stages, according to the commandment of the Lord, and encamped at Rephidim; but there was no water for the people to drink.

2Therefore, the people contended with Moses, and said, Give us water that we may drink. And Moses said to them, Why do you find fault with me? Why do you tempt the Lord *and* try His patience?

3But the people thirsted there for water, and the people murmured against Moses, and said, Why did you bring us up out of Egypt, to kill us and our children and livestock with thirst?

4So Moses cried to the Lord, What shall I do with this people? They are almost ready to stone me.

5And the Lord said to Moses, Pass on before the people, and take with you some of the elders of Israel; and take in your hand the rod with which you smote the river [Nile], and go.

6Behold, I will stand before you there on the rock at [Mount] Horeb; and you shall strike the rock, and water shall come out of it, that the people may drink. And Moses did so in the sight of the elders of Israel. [I Cor. 10:4.]

7He called the place Massah (proof), and Meribah (contention), because of the faultfinding of the Israelites, and because they tempted *and* tried the patience of the Lord, saying, Is the Lord among us or not?

8Then came Amalek [descendants of Esau], and fought with Israel at Rephidim.

9And Moses said to Joshua, Choose us out men, and go out, fight with Amalek. Tomorrow I will stand on the top of the hill with the rod of God in my hand.

10So Joshua did as Moses said and fought with Amalek; and Moses, Aaron, and Hur went up to the hilltop.

11When Moses held up his hand, Israel prevailed; and when he lowered his hand, Amalek prevailed.

12But Moses' hands were heavy *and* grew weary. So [the other men] took a stone, and put it under him, and he sat on it. Then Aaron and Hur held up his hands, one on one side and one on the other side; so his hands were steady until the going down of the sun.

13And Joshua mowed down *and* disabled Amalek and his people with the sword.

14And the Lord said to Moses, Write this for a memorial in the book, and rehearse it in the ears of Joshua, that I will utterly blot out the remembrance of Amalek from under the heavens. [I Sam. 15:2-8.]

## New American Standard

29"See, the LORD has given you the sabbath; therefore He gives
you bread for two days on the sixth day. Remain every man in his
place; let no man go out of his place on the seventh day."
30So the people rested on the seventh day.
31¶ And the house of Israel named it manna, and it was like
coriander seed, white; and its taste was like wafers with honey.
32Then Moses said, "This is what the LORD has commanded,
'Let an omerful of it be kept throughout your generations, that
they may see the bread that I fed you in the wilderness, when I
brought you out of the land of Egypt.'"
33And Moses said to Aaron, "Take a jar and put an omerful of
manna in it, and place it before the LORD, to be kept throughout
your generations."
34As the LORD commanded Moses, so Aaron placed it before the
Testimony, to be kept.
35And the sons of Israel ate the manna forty years, until they
came to an inhabited land; they ate the manna until they came to
the border of the land of Canaan.
36(Now an omer is a tenth of an ephah.)

*Water in the Rock*

17 THEN ALL the congregation of the sons of Israel journeyed by stages from the wilderness of Sin, according to
the command of the LORD, and camped at Rephidim, and there
was no water for the people to drink.
2Therefore the people quarreled with Moses and said, "Give
us water that we may drink." And Moses said to them, "Why do
you quarrel with me? Why do you test the LORD?"
3But the people thirsted there for water; and they grumbled
against Moses and said, "Why, now, have you brought us up from
Egypt, to kill us and our children and our livestock with thirst?"
4So Moses cried out to the LORD, saying, "What shall I do to
this people? A little more and they will stone me."
5Then the LORD said to Moses, "Pass before the people and
take with you some of the elders of Israel; and take in your hand
your staff with which you struck the Nile, and go.
6"Behold, I will stand before you there on the rock at Horeb;
and you shall strike the rock, and water will come out of it, that
the people may drink." And Moses did so in the sight of the elders
of Israel.
7And he named the place [a]Massah and [b]Meribah because of
the quarrel of the sons of Israel, and because they tested the LORD,
saying, "Is the LORD among us, or not?"

*Amalek Fought*

8¶ Then Amalek came and fought against Israel at Rephidim.
9So Moses said to Joshua, "Choose men for us, and go out,
fight against Amalek. Tomorrow I will station myself on the top
of the hill with the staff of God in my hand."
10And Joshua did as Moses told him, and fought against Amalek; and Moses, Aaron, and Hur went up to the top of the hill.
11So it came about when Moses held his hand up, that Israel
prevailed, and when he let his hand down, Amalek prevailed.
12But Moses' hands were heavy. Then they took a stone and put
it under him, and he sat on it; and Aaron and Hur supported his
hands, one on one side and one on the other. Thus his hands were
steady until the sun set.
13So Joshua overwhelmed Amalek and his people with the edge
of the sword.
14¶ Then the LORD said to Moses, "Write this in a book as a
memorial, and recite it to Joshua, that I will utterly blot out the
memory of Amalek from under heaven."

NAS [a] I.e., test [b] I.e., quarrel

## New International

bath; that is why on the sixth day he gives you bread for two days.
Everyone is to stay where he is on the seventh day; no one is to
go out." 30So the people rested on the seventh day.
31The people of Israel called the bread manna.[c] It was white like
coriander seed and tasted like wafers made with honey. 32Moses
said, "This is what the LORD has commanded: 'Take an omer of
manna and keep it for the generations to come, so they can see the
bread I gave you to eat in the desert when I brought you out of
Egypt.' "
33So Moses said to Aaron, "Take a jar and put an omer of manna
in it. Then place it before the LORD to be kept for the generations
to come."
34As the LORD commanded Moses, Aaron put the manna in
front of the Testimony, that it might be kept. 35The Israelites ate
manna forty years, until they came to a land that was settled; they
ate manna until they reached the border of Canaan.
36(An omer is one tenth of an ephah.)

*Water From the Rock*

17 THE WHOLE Israelite community set out from the Desert
of Sin, traveling from place to place as the LORD commanded. They camped at Rephidim, but there was no water for
the people to drink. 2So they quarreled with Moses and said, "Give
us water to drink."
Moses replied, "Why do you quarrel with me? Why do you put
the LORD to the test?"
3But the people were thirsty for water there, and they grumbled
against Moses. They said, "Why did you bring us up out of Egypt
to make us and our children and livestock die of thirst?"
4Then Moses cried out to the LORD, "What am I to do with these
people? They are almost ready to stone me."
5The LORD answered Moses, "Walk on ahead of the people.
Take with you some of the elders of Israel and take in your hand
the staff with which you struck the Nile, and go. 6I will stand there
before you by the rock at Horeb. Strike the rock, and water will
come out of it for the people to drink." So Moses did this in the
sight of the elders of Israel. 7And he called the place Massah[d] and
Meribah[e] because the Israelites quarreled and because they tested
the LORD saying, "Is the LORD among us or not?"

*The Amalekites Defeated*

8The Amalekites came and attacked the Israelites at Rephidim.
9Moses said to Joshua, "Choose some of our men and go out to
fight the Amalekites. Tomorrow I will stand on top of the hill with
the staff of God in my hands."
10So Joshua fought the Amalekites as Moses had ordered, and
Moses, Aaron and Hur went to the top of the hill. 11As long as
Moses held up his hands, the Israelites were winning, but whenever he lowered his hands, the Amalekites were winning. 12When
Moses' hands grew tired, they took a stone and put it under him
and he sat on it. Aaron and Hur held his hands up—one on one
side, one on the other—so that his hands remained steady till
sunset. 13So Joshua overcame the Amalekite army with the sword.
14Then the LORD said to Moses, "Write this on a scroll as something to be remembered and make sure that Joshua hears it, because I will completely blot out the memory of Amalek from under
heaven."

NIV [c] 31 *Manna* means *What is it?* (see verse 15). [d] 7 *Massah* means *testing.* [e] 7 *Meribah* means *quarreling.*

## King James

15And Moses built an altar, and called the name of it Jehovah-nissi:
16For he said, Because the LORD hath sworn *that* the LORD *will have* war with Amalek from generation to generation.

**18** WHEN JETHRO, the priest of Midian, Moses' father-in-law, heard of all that God had done for Moses, and for Israel his people, *and* that the LORD had brought Israel out of Egypt;
2Then Jethro, Moses' father-in-law, took Zipporah, Moses' wife, after he had sent her back,
3And her two sons; of which the name of the one *was* Gershom; for he said, I have been an alien in a strange land:
4And the name of the other *was* Eliezer; for the God of my father, *said he, was* mine help, and delivered me from the sword of Pharaoh:
5And Jethro, Moses' father-in-law, came with his sons and his wife unto Moses into the wilderness, where he encamped at the mount of God:
6And he said unto Moses, I thy father-in-law Jethro am come unto thee, and thy wife, and her two sons with her.
7¶ And Moses went out to meet his father-in-law, and did obeisance, and kissed him; and they asked each other of *their* welfare; and they came into the tent.
8And Moses told his father-in-law all that the LORD had done unto Pharaoh and to the Egyptians for Israel's sake, *and* all the travail that had come upon them by the way, and *how* the LORD delivered them.
9And Jethro rejoiced for all the goodness which the LORD had done to Israel, whom he had delivered out of the hand of the Egyptians.
10And Jethro said, Blessed *be* the LORD, who hath delivered you out of the hand of the Egyptians, and out of the hand of Pharaoh, who hath delivered the people from under the hand of the Egyptians.
11Now I know that the LORD *is* greater than all gods: for in the thing wherein they dealt proudly *he was* above them.
12And Jethro, Moses' father-in-law, took a burnt offering and sacrifices for God: and Aaron came, and all the elders of Israel, to eat bread with Moses' father-in-law before God.
13¶ And it came to pass on the morrow, that Moses sat to judge the people: and the people stood by Moses from the morning unto the evening.
14And when Moses' father-in-law saw all that he did to the people, he said, What *is* this thing that thou doest to the people? why sittest thou thyself alone, and all the people stand by thee from morning unto even?
15And Moses said unto his father-in-law, Because the people come unto me to inquire of God:
16When they have a matter, they come unto me; and I judge between one and another, and I do make *them* know the statutes of God, and his laws.
17And Moses' father-in-law said unto him, The thing that thou doest *is* not good.
18Thou wilt surely wear away, both thou, and this people that *is* with thee: for this thing *is* too heavy for thee; thou art not able to perform it thyself alone.
19Hearken now unto my voice, I will give thee counsel, and God shall be with thee: Be thou for the people to God-ward, that thou mayest bring the causes unto God:
20And thou shalt teach them ordinances and laws, and shalt show them the way wherein they must walk, and the work that they must do.

## Amplified

15And Moses built an altar and called the name of it, The Lord is my banner;
16And he said, Because *theirs* is a hand against the throne of the Lord, the Lord will have war with Amalek from generation to generation.

**18** NOW JETHRO [Reuel], the priest of Midian, Moses' father-in-law, heard of all that God had done for Moses and for Israel His people, and that the Lord had brought Israel out of Egypt.
2Then Jethro, Moses' father-in-law, took Zipporah, Moses' wife, after Moses had sent her back [to her father],
3And her two sons, of whom the name of the one was Gershom [meaning, expulsion, or a stranger there], for Moses said, I have been an alien in a strange land;
4And the name of the other was Eliezer [meaning, God is help], for the God of my father, said Moses, was my help, and delivered me from the sword of Pharaoh.
5And Jethro, Moses' father-in-law, came with Moses' sons and his wife to the wilderness where he was encamped at the mount of God [Horeb, or Sinai].
6And he said [in a message] to Moses, I, your father-in-law Jethro, am come to you, and your wife and her two sons with her.
7And Moses went out to meet his father-in-law, and bowed in homage and kissed him; and each asked the other of his welfare, and they came into the tent.
8Moses told his father-in-law all the Lord had done to Pharaoh and the Egyptians for Israel's sake, and all the hardships that had come upon them by the way, and how the Lord delivered them.
9Jethro rejoiced for all the goodness the Lord had done to Israel, in that He had delivered them out of the hand of the Egyptians.
10Jethro said, Blessed be the Lord, Who has delivered you out of the hand of the Egyptians and out of the hand of Pharaoh, Who has delivered the people [Israel] from under the hand of the Egyptians.
11Now I know that the Lord is greater than all gods. Yes, in the [very] thing in which they dealt proudly [He showed Himself infinitely superior to all their gods].
12And Jethro, Moses' father-in-law, took a burnt offering and sacrifices [to offer] to God; and Aaron came with all the elders of Israel to eat bread with Moses' father-in-law before God.
13Next day Moses sat to judge the people, and the people stood around Moses from morning till evening.
14When Moses' father-in-law saw all that he was doing for the people, he said, What is this that you do for the people? Why do you sit alone, and all the people stand around you from morning till evening?
15Moses said to his father-in-law, Because the people come to me to inquire of God.
16When they have a dispute they come to me, and I judge between a man and his neighbor, and I make them know the statutes of God and His laws.
17Moses' father-in-law said to him, The thing that you are doing is not good.
18You will surely wear out both yourself and this people with you, for the thing is too heavy for you; you are not able to perform it all by yourself.
19Listen now to [me], I will counsel you, and God will be with you. You shall represent the people before God, bringing their cases *and* causes to Him,
20Teaching them the decrees and laws, showing them the way they must walk, and the work they must do.

## New American Standard

15 And Moses built an altar, and named it The LORD is My
Banner;
16 and he said, "The LORD has sworn; the LORD will have war
against Amalek from generation to generation."

*Jethro, Moses' Father-in-law*

**18** NOW JETHRO, the priest of Midian, Moses' father-in-
law, heard of all that God had done for Moses and for
Israel His people, how the LORD had brought Israel out of Egypt.
2 And Jethro, Moses' father-in-law, took Moses' wife Zipporah,
after he had sent her away,
3 and her two sons, of whom one was named Gershom, for he
said, "I have been a sojourner in a foreign land."
4 And the other was named Eliezer, for *he said,* "The God of my
father was my help, and delivered me from the sword of Pharaoh."
5 Then Jethro, Moses' father-in-law, came with his sons and his
wife to Moses in the wilderness where he was camped, at the
mount of God.
6 And he sent word to Moses, "I, your father-in-law Jethro, am
coming to you with your wife and her two sons with her."
7 Then Moses went out to meet his father-in-law, and he bowed
down and kissed him; and they asked each other of their welfare,
and went into the tent.
8 And Moses told his father-in-law all that the LORD had done
to Pharaoh and to the Egyptians for Israel's sake, all the hardship
that had befallen them on the journey, and *how* the LORD had
delivered them.
9 And Jethro rejoiced over all the goodness which the LORD had
done to Israel, in delivering them from the hand of the Egyptians.
10 So Jethro said, "Blessed be the LORD who delivered you from
the hand of the Egyptians and from the hand of Pharaoh, *and* who
delivered the people from under the hand of the Egyptians.
11 "Now I know that the LORD is greater than all the gods;
indeed, it was proven when they dealt proudly against the
people."
12 Then Jethro, Moses' father-in-law, took a burnt offering and
sacrifices for God, and Aaron came with all the elders of Israel to
eat a meal with Moses' father-in-law before God.
13 ¶ And it came about the next day that Moses sat to judge the
people, and the people stood about Moses from the morning until
the evening.
14 Now when Moses' father-in-law saw all that he was doing for
the people, he said, "What is this thing that you are doing for the
people? Why do you alone sit *as judge* and all the people stand
about you from morning until evening?"
15 And Moses said to his father-in-law, "Because the people
come to me to inquire of God.
16 "When they have a dispute, it comes to me, and I judge
between a man and his neighbor, and make known the statutes of
God and His laws."

*Jethro Counsels Moses*

17 And Moses' father-in-law said to him, "The thing that you are
doing is not good.
18 "You will surely wear out, both yourself and these people
who are with you, for the task is too heavy for you; you cannot do
it alone.
19 "Now listen to me: I shall give you counsel, and God be with
you. You be the people's representative before God, and you bring
the disputes to God,
20 then teach them the statutes and the laws, and make known
to them the way in which they are to walk, and the work they are
to do.

## New International

15 Moses built an altar and called it The LORD is my Banner. 16 He
said, "For hands were lifted up to the throne of the LORD. The[a]
LORD will be at war against the Amalekites from generation to
generation."

*Jethro Visits Moses*

**18** NOW JETHRO, the priest of Midian and father-in-law of
Moses, heard of everything God had done for Moses and
for his people Israel, and how the LORD had brought Israel out of
Egypt.
2 After Moses had sent away his wife Zipporah, his father-in-
law Jethro received her 3 and her two sons. One son was named
Gershom,[b] for Moses said, "I have become an alien in a foreign
land"; 4 and the other was named Eliezer,[c] for he said, "My father's God was my helper; he saved me from the sword of Pharaoh."
5 Jethro, Moses' father-in-law, together with Moses' sons and
wife, came to him in the desert, where he was camped near the
mountain of God. 6 Jethro had sent word to him, "I, your father-in-
law Jethro, am coming to you with your wife and her two sons."
7 So Moses went out to meet his father-in-law and bowed down
and kissed him. They greeted each other and then went into the
tent. 8 Moses told his father-in-law about everything the LORD had
done to Pharaoh and the Egyptians for Israel's sake and about all
the hardships they had met along the way and how the LORD had
saved them.
9 Jethro was delighted to hear about all the good things the LORD
had done for Israel in rescuing them from the hand of the Egyptians. 10 He said, "Praise be to the LORD, who rescued you from the
hand of the Egyptians and of Pharaoh, and who rescued the
people from the hand of the Egyptians. 11 Now I know that the
LORD is greater than all other gods, for he did this to those who
had treated Israel arrogantly." 12 Then Jethro, Moses' father-in-
law, brought a burnt offering and other sacrifices to God, and
Aaron came with all the elders of Israel to eat bread with Moses'
father-in-law in the presence of God.
13 The next day Moses took his seat to serve as judge for the
people, and they stood around him from morning till evening.
14 When his father-in-law saw all that Moses was doing for the
people, he said, "What is this you are doing for the people? Why
do you alone sit as judge, while all these people stand around you
from morning till evening?"
15 Moses answered him, "Because the people come to me to seek
God's will. 16 Whenever they have a dispute, it is brought to me,
and I decide between the parties and inform them of God's decrees
and laws."
17 Moses' father-in-law replied, "What you are doing is not
good. 18 You and these people who come to you will only wear
yourselves out. The work is too heavy for you; you cannot handle
it alone. 19 Listen now to me and I will give you some advice, and
may God be with you. You must be the people's representative
before God and bring their disputes to him. 20 Teach them the
decrees and laws, and show them the way to live and the duties
they are to perform. 21 But select capable men from all the people—

NIV [a] 16 Or *"Because a hand was against the throne of the LORD, the*
[b] 3 *Gershom* sounds like the Hebrew for *an alien there.* [c] 4 *Eliezer* means *my God is helper.*

## King James

21 Moreover thou shalt provide out of all the people able men,
such as fear God, men of truth, hating covetousness; and place
*such* over them, *to be* rulers of thousands, *and* rulers of hundreds,
rulers of fifties, and rulers of tens:
22 And let them judge the people at all seasons: and it shall be,
*that* every great matter they shall bring unto thee, but every small
matter they shall judge: so shall it be easier for thyself, and they
shall bear *the burden* with thee.
23 If thou shalt do this thing, and God command thee *so,* then
thou shalt be able to endure, and all this people shall also go to
their place in peace.
24 So Moses hearkened to the voice of his father-in-law, and did
all that he had said.
25 And Moses chose able men out of all Israel, and made them
heads over the people, rulers of thousands, rulers of hundreds,
rulers of fifties, and rulers of tens.
26 And they judged the people at all seasons: the hard causes
they brought unto Moses, but every small matter they judged
themselves.
27 ¶ And Moses let his father-in-law depart; and he went his way
into his own land.

**19** IN THE third month, when the children of Israel were
gone forth out of the land of Egypt, the same day came
they *into* the wilderness of Sinai.
2 For they were departed from Rephidim, and were come *to* the
desert of Sinai, and had pitched in the wilderness; and there Israel
camped before the mount.
3 And Moses went up unto God, and the LORD called unto him
out of the mountain, saying, Thus shalt thou say to the house of
Jacob, and tell the children of Israel;
4 Ye have seen what I did unto the Egyptians, and *how* I bare you
on eagles' wings, and brought you unto myself.
5 Now therefore, if ye will obey my voice indeed, and keep my
covenant, then ye shall be a peculiar treasure unto me above all
people: for all the earth *is* mine:
6 And ye shall be unto me a kingdom of priests, and an holy
nation. These *are* the words which thou shalt speak unto the
children of Israel.
7 ¶ And Moses came and called for the elders of the people, and
laid before their faces all these words which the LORD commanded
him.
8 And all the people answered together, and said, All that the
LORD hath spoken we will do. And Moses returned the words of
the people unto the LORD.
9 And the LORD said unto Moses, Lo, I come unto thee in a thick
cloud, that the people may hear when I speak with thee, and
believe thee for ever. And Moses told the words of the people unto
the LORD.
10 ¶ And the LORD said unto Moses, Go unto the people, and
sanctify them today and tomorrow, and let them wash their
clothes,
11 And be ready against the third day: for the third day the LORD
will come down in the sight of all the people upon mount Sinai.
12 And thou shalt set bounds unto the people round about,
saying, Take heed to yourselves, *that ye* go *not* up into the mount,
or touch the border of it: whosoever toucheth the mount shall be
surely put to death:
13 There shall not an hand touch it, but he shall surely be stoned,
or shot through; whether *it be* beast or man, it shall not live: when
the trumpet soundeth long, they shall come up to the mount.
14 ¶ And Moses went down from the mount unto the people,
and sanctified the people; and they washed their clothes.
15 And he said unto the people, Be ready against the third day:
come not at *your* wives.

## Amplified

21 Moreover you shall choose able men from all the people,
God-fearing men of truth, who hate unjust gain, and place them
over thousands, hundreds, fifties, and tens, to be their rulers.
22 And let them judge the people at all times; every great matter
they shall bring to you, but every small matter they shall judge.
So it will be easier for you, and they will bear the burden with you.
23 If you will do this, and God so commands you, you will be
able to endure [the strain], and all this people also will go to their
[tents] in peace.
24 So Moses listened to *and* heeded the voice of his father-in-law,
and did all that he had said.
25 Moses chose able men out of all Israel, and made them heads
over the people, rulers of thousands, of hundreds, of fifties, and
of tens.
26 And they judged the people at all times; the hard cases they
brought to Moses, but every small matter they decided themselves.
27 Then Moses let his father-in-law depart, and he went his way
into his own land.

**19** IN THE third month after the Israelites left the land of
Egypt, the same day they came into the wilderness of
Sinai.
2 When they had departed from Rephidim and had come to the
wilderness of Sinai, they encamped there before the mountain.
3 And Moses went up to God, and the Lord called to him out
of the mountain, Say this to the house of Jacob, and tell the Israelites:
4 You have seen what I did to the Egyptians, and how I bore you
on eagles' wings and brought you to Myself.
5 Now therefore, if you will obey My voice in truth and keep My
covenant, then you shall be My own peculiar possession *and* treasure from among *and* above all peoples; for all the earth is Mine.
6 And you shall be to Me a kingdom of priests, a holy nation
[consecrated, set apart to the worship of God]. These are the words
you shall speak to the Israelites.
7 So Moses called for the elders of the people, and told them all
these words which the Lord commanded him.
8 And all the people answered together, and said, All that the
Lord has spoken we will do. And Moses reported the words of the
people to the Lord.
9 And the Lord said to Moses, Lo, I come to you in a thick cloud,
that the people may hear when I speak with you, and believe you
*and* remain steadfast forever. Then Moses told the words of the
people to the Lord.
10 And the Lord said to Moses, Go and sanctify the people [set
them apart for God], today and tomorrow, and let them wash their
clothes,
11 And be ready by the third day; for the third day the Lord will
come down upon Mount Sinai [in the cloud] in the sight of all the
people.
12 And you shall set bounds for the people round about, saying,
Take heed that you go not up into the mountain or touch the
border of it. Whoever touches the mountain shall surely be put to
death.
13 No hand shall touch it [ *or* the offender], but he shall surely
be stoned or shot [with arrows]; whether beast or man, he shall not
live. When the trumpet sounds a long blast, they shall come up to
the mountain. [Num. 24:8.]
14 So Moses went down from the mountain to the people and
sanctified them [set them apart for God], and they washed their
clothes.
15 And he said to the people, Be ready by the day after tomorrow; do not go near a woman.

## New American Standard

21"Furthermore, you shall select out of all the people able men
who fear God, men of truth, those who hate dishonest gain; and
you shall place *these* over them, *as* leaders of thousands, of hundreds, of fifties and of tens.
22"And let them judge the people at all times; and let it be that
every major dispute they will bring to you, but every minor dispute they themselves will judge. So it will be easier for you, and
they will bear *the burden* with you.
23"If you do this thing and God *so* commands you, then you will
be able to endure, and all these people also will go to their place
in peace."
24¶ So Moses listened to his father-in-law, and did all that he
had said.
25And Moses chose able men out of all Israel, and made them
heads over the people, leaders of thousands, of hundreds, of fifties
and of tens.
26And they judged the people at all times; the difficult dispute
they would bring to Moses, but every minor dispute they themselves would judge.
27Then Moses bade his father-in-law farewell, and he went his
way into his own land.

*Moses on Sinai*

**19** IN THE third month after the sons of Israel had gone out
of the land of Egypt, on that very day they came into the
wilderness of Sinai.
2When they set out from Rephidim, they came to the wilderness of Sinai, and camped in the wilderness; and there Israel
camped in front of the mountain.
3And Moses went up to God, and the LORD called to him from
the mountain, saying, "Thus you shall say to the house of Jacob
and tell the sons of Israel:
4'You yourselves have seen what I did to the Egyptians, and
*how* I bore you on eagles' wings, and brought you to Myself.
5'Now then, if you will indeed obey My voice and keep My
covenant, then you shall be My [a]own possession among all the
peoples, for all the earth is Mine;
6and you shall be to Me a kingdom of priests and a holy
nation.' These are the words that you shall speak to the sons of
Israel."
7¶ So Moses came and called the elders of the people, and set
before them all these words which the LORD had commanded him.
8And all the people answered together and said, "All that the
LORD has spoken we will do!" And Moses brought back the words
of the people to the LORD.
9And the LORD said to Moses, "Behold, I shall come to you in
a thick cloud, in order that the people may hear when I speak with
you, and may also believe in you forever." Then Moses told the
words of the people to the LORD.
10The LORD also said to Moses, "Go to the people and consecrate them today and tomorrow, and let them wash their garments;
11and let them be ready for the third day, for on the third day
the LORD will come down on Mount Sinai in the sight of all the
people.
12"And you shall set bounds for the people all around, saying,
'Beware that you do not go up on the mountain or touch the border
of it; whoever touches the mountain shall surely be put to death.
13'No hand shall touch him, but he shall surely be stoned or
[b]shot through; whether beast or man, he shall not live.' When the
ram's horn sounds a long blast, they shall come up to the mountain."
14So Moses went down from the mountain to the people and
consecrated the people, and they washed their garments.
15And he said to the people, "Be ready for the third day; do not
go near a woman."

NAS [a] Or, *special treasure* [b] I.e., with arrows

## New International

men who fear God, trustworthy men who hate dishonest gain—
and appoint them as officials over thousands, hundreds, fifties
and tens. 22Have them serve as judges for the people at all times,
but have them bring every difficult case to you; the simple cases
they can decide themselves. That will make your load lighter,
because they will share it with you. 23If you do this and God so
commands, you will be able to stand the strain, and all these
people will go home satisfied."
24Moses listened to his father-in-law and did everything he
said. 25He chose capable men from all Israel and made them leaders of the people, officials over thousands, hundreds, fifties and
tens. 26They served as judges for the people at all times. The
difficult cases they brought to Moses, but the simple ones they
decided themselves.
27Then Moses sent his father-in-law on his way, and Jethro
returned to his own country.

*At Mount Sinai*

**19** IN THE third month after the Israelites left Egypt—on the
very day—they came to the Desert of Sinai. 2After they set
out from Rephidim, they entered the Desert of Sinai, and Israel
camped there in the desert in front of the mountain.
3Then Moses went up to God, and the LORD called to him from
the mountain and said, "This is what you are to say to the house
of Jacob and what you are to tell the people of Israel: 4'You yourselves have seen what I did to Egypt, and how I carried you on
eagles' wings and brought you to myself. 5Now if you obey me
fully and keep my covenant, then out of all nations you will be my
treasured possession. Although the whole earth is mine, 6you[c]
will be for me a kingdom of priests and a holy nation.' These are
the words you are to speak to the Israelites."
7So Moses went back and summoned the elders of the people
and set before them all the words the LORD had commanded him
to speak. 8The people all responded together, "We will do everything the LORD has said." So Moses brought their answer back to
the LORD.
9The LORD said to Moses, "I am going to come to you in a dense
cloud, so that the people will hear me speaking with you and will
always put their trust in you." Then Moses told the LORD what the
people had said.
10And the LORD said to Moses, "Go to the people and consecrate them today and tomorrow. Have them wash their clothes
11and be ready by the third day, because on that day the LORD will
come down on Mount Sinai in the sight of all the people. 12Put
limits for the people around the mountain and tell them, 'Be careful that you do not go up the mountain or touch the foot of it.
Whoever touches the mountain shall surely be put to death. 13He
shall surely be stoned or shot with arrows; not a hand is to be laid
on him. Whether man or animal, he shall not be permitted to live.'
Only when the ram's horn sounds a long blast may they go up to
the mountain."
14After Moses had gone down the mountain to the people, he
consecrated them, and they washed their clothes. 15Then he said
to the people, "Prepare yourselves for the third day. Abstain from
sexual relations."

NIV [c] 5,6 Or *possession, for the whole earth is mine.* 6*You*

## King James

16¶ And it came to pass on the third day in the morning, that there were thunders and lightnings, and a thick cloud upon the mount, and the voice of the trumpet exceeding loud; so that all the people that *was* in the camp trembled.

17 And Moses brought forth the people out of the camp to meet with God; and they stood at the nether part of the mount.

18 And mount Sinai was altogether on a smoke, because the LORD descended upon it in fire: and the smoke thereof ascended as the smoke of a furnace, and the whole mount quaked greatly.

19 And when the voice of the trumpet sounded long, and waxed louder and louder, Moses spake, and God answered him by a voice.

20 And the LORD came down upon mount Sinai, on the top of the mount: and the LORD called Moses *up* to the top of the mount; and Moses went up.

21 And the LORD said unto Moses, Go down, charge the people, lest they break through unto the LORD to gaze, and many of them perish.

22 And let the priests also, which come near to the LORD, sanctify themselves, lest the LORD break forth upon them.

23 And Moses said unto the LORD, The people cannot come up to mount Sinai: for thou chargedst us, saying, Set bounds about the mount, and sanctify it.

24 And the LORD said unto him, Away, get thee down, and thou shalt come up, thou, and Aaron with thee: but let not the priests and the people break through to come up unto the LORD, lest he break forth upon them.

25 So Moses went down unto the people, and spake unto them.

**20** AND GOD spake all these words, saying,

2 I *am* the LORD thy God, which have brought thee out of the land of Egypt, out of the house of bondage.

3 Thou shalt have no other gods before me.

4 Thou shalt not make unto thee any graven image, or any likeness *of any thing* that *is* in heaven above, or that *is* in the earth beneath, or that *is* in the water under the earth:

5 Thou shalt not bow down thyself to them, nor serve them: for I the LORD thy God *am* a jealous God, visiting the iniquity of the fathers upon the children unto the third and fourth *generation* of them that hate me;

6 And showing mercy unto thousands of them that love me, and keep my commandments.

7 Thou shalt not take the name of the LORD thy God in vain; for the LORD will not hold him guiltless that taketh his name in vain.

8 Remember the sabbath day, to keep it holy.

9 Six days shalt thou labour, and do all thy work:

10 But the seventh day *is* the sabbath of the LORD thy God: *in it* thou shalt not do any work, thou, nor thy son, nor thy daughter, thy manservant, nor thy maidservant, nor thy cattle, nor thy stranger that *is* within thy gates:

11 For *in* six days the LORD made heaven and earth, the sea, and all that in them *is,* and rested the seventh day: wherefore the LORD blessed the sabbath day, and hallowed it.

12¶ Honour thy father and thy mother: that thy days may be long upon the land which the LORD thy God giveth thee.

13 Thou shalt not kill.

14 Thou shalt not commit adultery.

15 Thou shalt not steal.

16 Thou shalt not bear false witness against thy neighbour.

**AMP** [a] Observe here the expansion of the thought in the catechism which includes whoredom in all its forms, as well as unchastity [premarital relations, sexual impurity, and lustful desire under whatever name] (Lange's *Commentary*, condensed). Not only *adultery* is forbidden here, but also fornication and all kinds of mental and sensual uncleanness. All impure *books, songs, pictures,* etc., which tend to inflame and debauch the mind, are against this law. (Clarke's *Commentary*).

## Amplified

16 The third morning there were thunders and lightnings, and a thick cloud upon the mountain, and a very loud trumpet blast, so that all the people in the camp trembled.

17 Then Moses brought the people from the camp to meet God; and they stood at the foot of the mountain.

18 Mount Sinai was wrapped in smoke, for the Lord descended upon it in fire; its smoke ascended like that of a furnace, and the whole mountain quaked greatly.

19 As the trumpet blast grew louder and louder, Moses spoke, and God answered him with a voice. [Cp. Deut. 4:12.]

20 The Lord came down upon Mount Sinai, to the top of the mountain, and the Lord called Moses to the top of the mountain, and Moses went up.

21 The Lord said to Moses, Go down and warn the people, lest they break through to the Lord to gaze and many of them perish.

22 And also let the priests who come near to the Lord sanctify [set apart] themselves [for God], lest the Lord break forth against them.

23 And Moses said to the Lord, The people cannot come up to Mount Sinai: for You Yourself charged us, saying, Set bounds about the mountain, and sanctify it [set it apart for God].

24 Then the Lord said to him, Go, get down, and you shall come up, you and Aaron with you; but let not the priests and the people break through to come up to the Lord, lest He break forth against them.

25 So Moses went down to the people and told them.

**20** THEN GOD spoke all these words:

2 I am the Lord your God, Who has brought you out of the land of Egypt, out of the house of bondage.

3 You shall have no other gods before *or* besides Me.

4 You shall not make yourself any graven image [to worship it], or any likeness of anything that is in the heavens above, or that is in the earth beneath, or that is in the water under the earth;

5 You shall not bow down yourself to them or serve them; for I the Lord your God am a jealous God, visiting the iniquity of the fathers upon the children to the third and fourth generation of those who hate Me, [Isa. 42:8; 48:11.]

6 But showing mercy *and* steadfast love to a thousand generations of those who love Me and keep My commandments.

7 You shall not use *or* repeat the name of the Lord your God in vain [that is, lightly or frivolously, in false affirmations or profanely]; for the Lord will not hold him guiltless who takes His name in vain.

8 [Earnestly] remember the sabbath day, to keep it holy [withdrawn from common employment and dedicated to God].

9 Six days you shall labor and do all your work,

10 But the seventh day is a sabbath to the Lord your God; in it you shall not do any work, you, or your son, your daughter, your manservant, your maidservant, your domestic animals, or the sojourner within your gates.

11 For in six days the Lord made heavens and earth, the sea, and all that is in them, and rested the seventh day. That is why the Lord blessed the sabbath day and hallowed it [set it apart for His purposes].

12 Regard (treat with honor, due obedience and courtesy) your father and mother, that your days may be long in the land the Lord your God gives you.

13 You shall not commit murder.

14 You shall not commit [a]adultery. [Matt. 5.28; Rom. 1:24; Eph. 5:3; Prov. 6:25, 26.]

15 You shall not steal. [Mal. 3:8; Prov. 11:1; 21:6; 16:8; 22:16; Jer. 17:11.]

16 You shall not witness falsely against your neighbor. [Exod. 23:1; Prov. 19:9; 24:28.]

## New American Standard

16¶ So it came about on the third day, when it was morning, that
there were thunder and lightning flashes and a thick cloud upon
the mountain and a very loud trumpet sound, so that all the people
who *were* in the camp trembled.
17And Moses brought the people out of the camp to meet God,
and they stood at the foot of the mountain.

*The LORD Visits Sinai*

18Now Mount Sinai *was* all in smoke because the LORD descended upon it in fire; and its smoke ascended like the smoke of a
furnace, and the whole mountain quaked violently.
19When the sound of the trumpet grew louder and louder,
Moses spoke and God answered him with thunder.
20And the LORD came down on Mount Sinai, to the top of the
mountain; and the LORD called Moses to the top of the mountain,
and Moses went up.
21Then the LORD spoke to Moses, "Go down, warn the people,
lest they break through to the LORD to gaze, and many of them
perish.
22"And also let the priests who come near to the LORD consecrate themselves, lest the LORD break out against them."
23And Moses said to the LORD, "The people cannot come up to
Mount Sinai, for Thou didst warn us, saying, 'Set bounds about
the mountain and consecrate it.' "
24Then the LORD said to him, "Go down and come up *again*, you
and Aaron with you; but do not let the priests and the people break
through to come up to the LORD, lest He break forth upon them."
25So Moses went down to the people and told them.

*The Ten Commandments*

20 THEN GOD spoke all these words, saying,
2¶ "I am the LORD your God, who brought you out of the
land of Egypt, out of the house of slavery.
3¶ "You shall have no other gods [b]before Me.
4¶ "You shall not make for yourself [c]an idol, or any likeness
of what is in heaven above or on the earth beneath or in the water
under the earth.
5"You shall not worship them or serve them; for I, the LORD
your God, am a jealous God, visiting the iniquity of the fathers on
the children, on the third and the fourth generations of those who
hate Me,
6but showing lovingkindness to thousands, to those who love
Me and keep My commandments.
7¶ "You shall not take the name of the LORD your God in vain,
for the LORD will not leave him unpunished who takes His name
in vain.
8¶ "Remember the sabbath day, to keep it holy.
9"Six days you shall labor and do all your work,
10but the seventh day is a sabbath of the LORD your God; *in it*
you shall not do any work, you or your son or your daughter, your
male or your female servant or your cattle or your sojourner who
stays with you.
11"For in six days the LORD made the heavens and the earth,
the sea and all that is in them, and rested on the seventh day;
therefore the LORD blessed the sabbath day and made it holy.
12¶ "Honor your father and your mother, that your days may
be prolonged in the land which the LORD your God gives you.
13¶ "You shall not murder.
14¶ "You shall not commit adultery.
15¶ "You shall not steal.
16¶ "You shall not bear false witness against your neighbor.

NAS [b] Or, *besides Me* [c] Or, *a graven image*

## New International

16On the morning of the third day there was thunder and
lightning, with a thick cloud over the mountain, and a very loud
trumpet blast. Everyone in the camp trembled. 17Then Moses led
the people out of the camp to meet with God, and they stood at
the foot of the mountain. 18Mount Sinai was covered with smoke,
because the LORD descended on it in fire. The smoke billowed up
from it like smoke from a furnace, the whole mountain[d] trembled
violently, 19and the sound of the trumpet grew louder and louder.
Then Moses spoke and the voice of God answered him.[e]
20The LORD descended to the top of Mount Sinai and called
Moses to the top of the mountain. So Moses went up 21and the
LORD said to him, "Go down and warn the people so they do not
force their way through to see the LORD and many of them perish.
22Even the priests, who approach the LORD, must consecrate themselves, or the LORD will break out against them."
23Moses said to the LORD, "The people cannot come up Mount
Sinai, because you yourself warned us, 'Put limits around the
mountain and set it apart as holy.' "
24The LORD replied, "Go down and bring Aaron up with you.
But the priests and the people must not force their way through
to come up to the LORD, or he will break out against them."
25So Moses went down to the people and told them.

*The Ten Commandments*

20 AND GOD spoke all these words:
2"I am the LORD your God, who brought you out of
Egypt, out of the land of slavery.
3"You shall have no other gods before[f] me.
4"You shall not make for yourself an idol in the form of anything in heaven above or on the earth beneath or in the
waters below. 5You shall not bow down to them or
worship them; for I, the LORD your God, am a jealous
God, punishing the children for the sin of the fathers to
the third and fourth generation of those who hate me,
6but showing love to a thousand ⌊generations⌋ of those
who love me and keep my commandments.
7"You shall not misuse the name of the LORD your God, for
the LORD will not hold anyone guiltless who misuses his
name.
8"Remember the Sabbath day by keeping it holy. 9Six days
you shall labor and do all your work, 10but the seventh
day is a Sabbath to the LORD your God. On it you shall
not do any work, neither you, nor your son or daughter,
nor your manservant or maidservant, nor your animals,
nor the alien within your gates. 11For in six days the
LORD made the heavens and the earth, the sea, and all
that is in them, but he rested on the seventh day. Therefore the LORD blessed the Sabbath day and made it holy.
12"Honor your father and your mother, so that you may live
long in the land the LORD your God is giving you.
13"You shall not murder.
14"You shall not commit adultery.
15"You shall not steal.
16"You shall not give false testimony against your neighbor.

NIV [d] *18* Most Hebrew manuscripts; a few Hebrew manuscripts and Septuagint *all the people* [e] *19* Or *and God answered him with thunder* [f] *3* Or *besides*

## King James

17 Thou shalt not covet thy neighbour's house, thou shalt not
covet thy neighbour's wife, nor his manservant, nor his maidservant, nor his ox, nor his ass, nor any thing that *is* thy neighbour's.
18 ¶ And all the people saw the thunderings, and the lightnings,
and the noise of the trumpet, and the mountain smoking: and
when the people saw *it*, they removed, and stood afar off.
19 And they said unto Moses, Speak thou with us, and we will
hear: but let not God speak with us, lest we die.
20 And Moses said unto the people, Fear not: for God is come
to prove you, and that his fear may be before your faces, that ye
sin not.
21 And the people stood afar off, and Moses drew near unto the
thick darkness where God *was*.
22 ¶ And the Lord said unto Moses, Thus thou shalt say unto
the children of Israel, Ye have seen that I have talked with you
from heaven.
23 Ye shall not make with me gods of silver, neither shall ye
make unto you gods of gold.
24 ¶ An altar of earth thou shalt make unto me, and shalt sacrifice
thereon thy burnt offerings, and thy peace offerings, thy sheep,
and thine oxen: in all places where I record my name I will come
unto thee, and I will bless thee.
25 And if thou wilt make me an altar of stone, thou shalt not
build it of hewn stone: for if thou lift up thy tool upon it, thou hast
polluted it.
26 Neither shalt thou go up by steps unto mine altar, that thy
nakedness be not discovered thereon.

**21** NOW THESE *are* the judgments which thou shalt set before them.
2 If thou buy an Hebrew servant, six years he shall serve: and
in the seventh he shall go out free for nothing.
3 If he came in by himself, he shall go out by himself: if he were
married, then his wife shall go out with him.
4 If his master have given him a wife, and she have born him
sons or daughters; the wife and her children shall be her master's,
and he shall go out by himself.
5 And if the servant shall plainly say, I love my master, my wife,
and my children; I will not go out free:
6 Then his master shall bring him unto the judges; he shall also
bring him to the door, or unto the door post; and his master shall
bore his ear through with an awl; and he shall serve him for ever.
7 ¶ And if a man sell his daughter to be a maidservant, she shall
not go out as the menservants do.
8 If she please not her master, who hath betrothed her to himself, then shall he let her be redeemed: to sell her unto a strange
nation he shall have no power, seeing he hath dealt deceitfully
with her.
9 And if he have betrothed her unto his son, he shall deal with
her after the manner of daughters.
10 If he take him another *wife;* her food, her raiment, and her
duty of marriage, shall he not diminish.
11 And if he do not these three unto her, then shall she go out
free without money.
12 ¶ He that smiteth a man, so that he die, shall be surely put
to death.
13 And if a man lie not in wait, but God deliver *him* into his hand;
then I will appoint thee a place whither he shall flee.
14 But if a man come presumptuously upon his neighbour, to
slay him with guile; thou shalt take him from mine altar, that he
may die.

## Amplified

17 You shall not covet your neighbor's house, your neighbor's
wife, or his manservant, or his maidservant, or his ox, or his
donkey, or anything that is your neighbor's. [Luke 12:15; Col. 3:5.]
18 Now all the people perceived the thunderings and the lightnings and the noise of the trumpet and the smoking mountain, and
as [they] looked they trembled with fear, *and* fell back and stood
afar off.
19 And they said to Moses, You speak to us, and we will listen,
but let not God speak to us, lest we die.
20 And Moses said to the people, Fear not; for God is come to
prove you, and that the [reverential] fear of Him may be before
you, that you may not sin.
21 And the people stood afar off, but Moses drew near to the
thick darkness where God was.
22 And the Lord said to Moses, Thus shall you say to the Israelites, You have seen for yourselves that I have talked with you from
Heaven.
23 You shall not make [gods to share] with Me [My glory and
your worship]; gods of silver or gods of gold you shall not make
for yourselves.
24 An altar of earth you shall make to Me and sacrifice on it your
burnt offerings and your peace offerings, your sheep and your
oxen. In every place where I record My name and cause it to be
remembered I will come to you and bless you.
25 And if you will make Me an altar of stone, you shall not build
it of hewn stone; for if you lift up a tool upon it, you have polluted
it.
26 Neither shall you go up by steps to My altar, that your nakedness be not exposed upon it.

**21** NOW THESE are the ordinances you [Moses] shall set
before [the Israelites].
2 If you buy a Hebrew servant [as the result of debt or theft], he
shall serve six years, and in the seventh he shall go out free, paying
nothing. [Lev. 25:39.]
3 If he came [to you] by himself, he shall go out by himself; if
he came married, then his wife shall go out with him.
4 If his master has given him a wife and she has borne him sons
or daughters, the wife and her children shall be her master's, and
he shall go out [of your service] alone.
5 But if the servant shall plainly say, I love my master, my wife
and my children; I will not go free,
6 Then his master shall bring him to God [the judges]; he shall
bring him to the door or doorpost, and shall pierce his ear with an
awl; and he shall serve him for life.
7 If a man sells his daughter to be a maidservant *or* bondwoman,
she shall not go out [in six years] as menservants do.
8 If she does not please her master, who has not espoused her
to himself, he shall let her be redeemed. To sell her to a foreign
people he shall have no power, for he has dealt faithlessly with
her.
9 And if he espouses her to his son, he shall deal with her as with
a daughter.
10 If he marries again, her food, clothing, and privilege as a wife
shall he not diminish.
11 And if he does not do these three things for her, then shall
she go out free, without payment of money.
12 Whoever strikes a man so that he dies, shall surely be put to
death.
13 But if he did not lie in wait for him, but God allowed him to
fall into his hand, then I will appoint you a place to which he may
flee [for protection until duly tried]. [Num. 35:22-28.]
14 But if a man comes willfully upon another to slay him craftily,
you shall take him from My altar [to which he may have fled for
protection], that he may die.

## New American Standard

17¶ "You shall not covet your neighbor's house; you shall not
covet your neighbor's wife or his male servant or his female servant or his ox or his donkey or anything that belongs to your
neighbor."
18¶ And all the people perceived the thunder and the lightning
flashes and the sound of the trumpet and the mountain smoking;
and when the people saw *it*, they trembled and stood at a distance.
19Then they said to Moses, "Speak to us yourself and we will
listen; but let not God speak to us, lest we die."
20And Moses said to the people, "Do not be afraid; for God has
come in order to test you, and in order that the fear of Him may
remain with you, so that you may not sin."
21So the people stood at a distance, while Moses approached
the thick cloud where God *was*.
22¶ Then the LORD said to Moses, "Thus you shall say to the
sons of Israel, 'You yourselves have seen that I have spoken to you
from heaven.
23'You shall not make *other gods* besides Me; gods of silver or
gods of gold, you shall not make for yourselves.
24'You shall make an altar of earth for Me, and you shall sacrifice
on it your burnt offerings and your peace offerings, your sheep
and your oxen; in every place where I cause My name to be
remembered, I will come to you and bless you.
25'And if you make an altar of stone for Me, you shall not build
it of cut stones, for if you wield your tool on it, you will profane
it.
26'And you shall not go up by steps to My altar, that your
nakedness may not be exposed on it.'

*Ordinances for the People*

**21** "NOW THESE are the ordinances which you are to set
before them.
2"If you buy a Hebrew slave, he shall serve for six years; but
on the seventh he shall go out as a free man without payment.
3"If he comes alone, he shall go out alone; if he is the husband
of a wife, then his wife shall go out with him.
4"If his master gives him a wife, and she bears him sons or
daughters, the wife and her children shall belong to her master,
and he shall go out alone.
5"But if the slave plainly says, 'I love my master, my wife and
my children; I will not go out as a free man,'
6then his master shall bring him to [a]God, then he shall bring
him to the door or the doorpost. And his master shall pierce his
ear with an awl; and he shall serve him permanently.
7"And if a man sells his daughter as a female slave, she is not
to go free as the male slaves do.
8"If she is displeasing in the eyes of her master who designated
her for himself, then he shall let her be redeemed. He does not
have authority to sell her to a foreign people because of his unfairness to her.
9"And if he designates her for his son, he shall deal with her
according to the custom of daughters.
10"If he takes to himself another woman, he may not reduce her
food, her clothing, or her conjugal rights.
11"And if he will not do these three *things* for her, then she shall
go out for nothing, without *payment of* money.

*Personal Injuries*

12¶ "He who strikes a man so that he dies shall surely be put
to death.
13"But if he did not lie in wait *for him*, but God let *him* fall into
his hand, then I will appoint you a place to which he may flee.
14"If, however, a man acts presumptuously toward his neighbor, so as to kill him craftily, you are to take him *even* from My altar,
that he may die.

NAS [a] Or, *the judges who acted in God's name*

## New International

17"You shall not covet your neighbor's house. You shall not
covet your neighbor's wife, or his manservant or maidservant, his ox or donkey, or anything that belongs to
your neighbor."
18When the people saw the thunder and lightning and heard
the trumpet and saw the mountain in smoke, they trembled with
fear. They stayed at a distance 19and said to Moses, "Speak to us
yourself and we will listen. But do not have God speak to us or we
will die."
20Moses said to the people, "Do not be afraid. God has come
to test you, so that the fear of God will be with you to keep you
from sinning."
21The people remained at a distance, while Moses approached
the thick darkness where God was.

*Idols and Altars*

22Then the LORD said to Moses, "Tell the Israelites this: 'You
have seen for yourselves that I have spoken to you from heaven:
23Do not make any gods to be alongside me; do not make for
yourselves gods of silver or gods of gold.
24" 'Make an altar of earth for me and sacrifice on it your burnt
offerings and fellowship offerings,[b] your sheep and goats and
your cattle. Wherever I cause my name to be honored, I will come
to you and bless you. 25If you make an altar of stones for me, do
not build it with dressed stones, for you will defile it if you use a
tool on it. 26And do not go up to my altar on steps, lest your
nakedness be exposed on it.'

**21** "THESE ARE the laws you are to set before them:

*Hebrew Servants*

2"If you buy a Hebrew servant, he is to serve you for six years.
But in the seventh year, he shall go free, without paying anything.
3If he comes alone, he is to go free alone; but if he has a wife when
he comes, she is to go with him. 4If his master gives him a wife
and she bears him sons or daughters, the woman and her children
shall belong to her master, and only the man shall go free.
5"But if the servant declares, 'I love my master and my wife and
children and do not want to go free,' 6then his master must take
him before the judges.[c] He shall take him to the door or the
doorpost and pierce his ear with an awl. Then he will be his servant
for life.
7"If a man sells his daughter as a servant, she is not to go free
as menservants do. 8If she does not please the master who has
selected her for himself,[d] he must let her be redeemed. He has no
right to sell her to foreigners, because he has broken faith with her.
9If he selects her for his son, he must grant her the rights of a
daughter. 10If he marries another woman, he must not deprive the
first one of her food, clothing and marital rights. 11If he does not
provide her with these three things, she is to go free, without any
payment of money.

*Personal Injuries*

12"Anyone who strikes a man and kills him shall surely be put
to death. 13However, if he does not do it intentionally, but God lets
it happen, he is to flee to a place I will designate. 14But if a man
schemes and kills another man deliberately, take him away from
my altar and put him to death.

NIV [b] 24 Traditionally *peace offerings* [c] 6 Or *before God* [d] 8 Or *master so that he does not choose her*

## King James

15¶ And he that smiteth his father, or his mother, shall be surely
put to death.
16¶ And he that stealeth a man, and selleth him, or if he be
found in his hand, he shall surely be put to death.
17¶ And he that curseth his father, or his mother, shall surely
be put to death.
18¶ And if men strive together, and one smite another with a
stone, or with *his* fist, and he die not, but keepeth *his* bed:
19If he rise again, and walk abroad upon his staff, then shall he
that smote *him* be quit: only he shall pay *for* the loss of his time,
and shall cause *him* to be thoroughly healed.
20¶ And if a man smite his servant, or his maid, with a rod, and
he die under his hand; he shall be surely punished.
21Notwithstanding, if he continue a day or two, he shall not be
punished: for he *is* his money.
22¶ If men strive, and hurt a woman with child, so that her fruit
depart *from her,* and yet no mischief follow: he shall be surely
punished, according as the woman's husband will lay upon him;
and he shall pay as the judges *determine.*
23And if *any* mischief follow, then thou shalt give life for life,
24Eye for eye, tooth for tooth, hand for hand, foot for foot,
25Burning for burning, wound for wound, stripe for stripe.
26¶ And if a man smite the eye of his servant, or the eye of his
maid, that it perish; he shall let him go free for his eye's sake.
27And if he smite out his manservant's tooth, or his maidservant's tooth; he shall let him go free for his tooth's sake.
28¶ If an ox gore a man or a woman, that they die: then the ox
shall be surely stoned, and his flesh shall not be eaten; but the
owner of the ox *shall be* quit.
29But if the ox were wont to push with his horn in time past,
and it hath been testified to his owner, and he hath not kept him
in, but that he hath killed a man or a woman; the ox shall be
stoned, and his owner also shall be put to death.
30If there be laid on him a sum of money, then he shall give for
the ransom of his life whatsoever is laid upon him.
31Whether he have gored a son, or have gored a daughter,
according to this judgment shall it be done unto him.
32If the ox shall push a manservant or a maidservant; he shall
give unto their master thirty shekels of silver, and the ox shall be
stoned.
33¶ And if a man shall open a pit, or if a man shall dig a pit, and
not cover it, and an ox or an ass fall therein;
34The owner of the pit shall make *it* good, *and* give money unto
the owner of them; and the dead *beast* shall be his.
35¶ And if one man's ox hurt another's, that he die; then they
shall sell the live ox, and divide the money of it; and the dead *ox*
also they shall divide.
36Or if it be known that the ox hath used to push in time past,
and his owner hath not kept him in; he shall surely pay ox for ox;
and the dead shall be his own.

**22** IF A man shall steal an ox, or a sheep, and kill it, or sell
it; he shall restore five oxen for an ox, and four sheep for
a sheep.
2¶ If a thief be found breaking up, and be smitten that he die,
*there shall* no blood *be shed* for him.
3If the sun be risen upon him, *there shall be* blood *shed* for him;
*for* he should make full restitution; if he have nothing, then he shall
be sold for his theft.
4If the theft be certainly found in his hand alive, whether it be
ox, or ass, or sheep; he shall restore double.
5¶ If a man shall cause a field or vineyard to be eaten, and shall
put in his beast, and shall feed in another man's field; of the best
of his own field, and of the best of his own vineyard, shall he make
restitution.

## Amplified

15Whoever strikes his father or his mother shall surely be put
to death.
16Whoever kidnaps a man, whether he sells him or is found
with him in his possession, shall surely be put to death.
17Whoever curses his father or his mother shall surely be put
to death.
18If men quarrel and one strikes another with a stone or with
his fist, and he does not die but keeps his bed,
19If he rises again, and walks about leaning upon his staff, then
he that struck him shall be clear, except he must pay for the loss
of his time, and shall cause him to be thoroughly healed.
20And if a man strikes his servant or his maid with a rod, and
he [or she] dies under his hand, he shall surely be punished.
21But, if the servant lives on a day or two, the offender shall not
be punished; for he [has injured] his own property.
22If men contend with each other, and a pregnant woman [in-
terfering] is hurt so that she has a miscarriage, yet no further
damage follows, [the one who hurt her] shall surely be punished
with a fine [paid] to the woman's husband, as much as the judges
determine.
23But if any damage follows, then you shall give life for life,
24Eye for eye, tooth for tooth, hand for hand, foot for foot,
25Burn for burn, wound for wound, and lash for lash.
26And if a man hits the eye of his servant or the eye of his maid
so that it is destroyed, he shall let him go free for his eye's sake.
27And if he knock out his manservant's tooth or his maidservant's tooth, he shall let him go free for his tooth's sake.
28If an ox gore a man or a woman to death, then the ox shall
surely be stoned, and his flesh shall not be eaten; but the owner
of the ox shall be clear.
29But if the ox has tried to gore before, and his owner has been
warned, but has not kept him closed in, and it kills a man or a
woman, the ox shall be stoned, and its owner also put to death.
30If a ransom is put on [the man's] life, then he shall give for
the redemption of his life whatever is laid upon him.
31If the [man's ox] has gored another's son or daughter, he shall
be dealt with according to this same rule.
32If the ox gores a manservant or a maidservant, the owner shall
give to their master thirty shekels of silver, and the ox shall be
stoned.
33If a man leaves a pit open, or digs a pit and does not cover
it, and an ox or a donkey falls into it,
34The owner of the pit shall make it good; he shall give money
to the animal's owner, but the dead beast shall be his.
35If one man's ox hurts another's so that it dies, they shall sell
the live ox and divide the price of it; the dead ox also they shall
divide between them.
36Or if it be known that the ox has gored in the past, and its
owner has not kept it closed in, he shall surely pay ox for ox, and
the dead beast shall be his.

**22** IF A man steals an ox or sheep, and kills or sells it, he shall
pay five oxen for an ox, or four sheep for a sheep.
2If a thief is found breaking in, and is struck so that he dies,
there shall be no blood shed for him.
3But if the sun has risen [so he can be seen], blood must be shed
for slaying him. The thief [if he lives] must make full restitution;
if he has nothing, then he shall be sold for his theft.
4If the beast which he stole is found in his possession alive,
whether it is ox or ass or sheep, he shall restore double.
5If a man causes a field or vineyard to be grazed over, or lets
his beast loose and it feeds in another man's field, he shall make
restitution of the best of his own field or his own vineyard.

## New American Standard

15¶ "And he who strikes his father or his mother shall surely be put to death.

16¶ "And he who kidnaps a man, whether he sells him or he is found in his possession, shall surely be put to death.

17"And he who curses his father or his mother shall surely be put to death.

18¶ "And if men have a quarrel and one strikes the other with a stone or with *his* fist, and he does not die but remains in bed;

19if he gets up and walks around outside on his staff, then he who struck him shall go unpunished; he shall only pay for his loss of time, and shall take care of him until he is completely healed.

20¶ "And if a man strikes his male or female slave with a rod and he dies at his hand, he shall be punished.

21"If, however, he survives a day or two, no vengeance shall be taken; for he is his property.

22¶ "And *if* men struggle with each other and strike a woman with child so that she has a miscarriage, yet there is no *further* injury, he shall surely be fined as the woman's husband may demand of him; and he shall pay as the judges *decide.*

23"But if there is *any further* injury, then you shall appoint *as a penalty* life for life,

24eye for eye, tooth for tooth, hand for hand, foot for foot,

25burn for burn, wound for wound, bruise for bruise.

26¶ "And if a man strikes the eye of his male or female slave, and destroys it, he shall let him go free on account of his eye.

27"And if he knocks out a tooth of his male or female slave, he shall let him go free on account of his tooth.

28¶ "And if an ox gores a man or a woman to death, the ox shall surely be stoned and its flesh shall not be eaten; but the owner of the ox shall go unpunished.

29"If, however, an ox was previously in the habit of goring, and its owner has been warned, yet he does not confine it, and it kills a man or a woman, the ox shall be stoned and its owner also shall be put to death.

30"If a ransom is demanded of him, then he shall give for the redemption of his life whatever is demanded of him.

31"Whether it gores a son or a daughter, it shall be done to him according to the same rule.

32"If the ox gores a male or female slave, the owner shall give his *or her* master thirty shekels of silver, and the ox shall be stoned.

33¶ "And if a man opens a pit, or digs a pit and does not cover it over, and an ox or a donkey falls into it,

34the owner of the pit shall make restitution; he shall give money to its owner, and the dead *animal* shall become his.

35¶ "And if one man's ox hurts another's so that it dies, then they shall sell the live ox and divide its price equally; and also they shall divide the dead *ox.*

36"Or *if* it is known that the ox was previously in the habit of goring, yet its owner has not confined it, he shall surely pay ox for ox, and the dead *animal* shall become his.

*Property Rights*

**22** "IF A man steals an ox or a sheep, and slaughters it or sells it, he shall pay five oxen for the ox and four sheep for the sheep.

2"If the thief is caught while breaking in, and is struck so that he dies, there will be no bloodguiltiness on his account.

3" *But* if the sun has risen on him, there will be bloodguiltiness on his account. He shall surely make restitution; if he owns nothing, then he shall be sold for his theft.

4"If what he stole is actually found alive in his possession, whether an ox or a donkey or a sheep, he shall pay double.

5"If a man lets a field or vineyard be grazed *bare* and lets his animal loose so that it grazes in another man's field, he shall make restitution from the best of his own field and the best of his own vineyard.

## New International

15"Anyone who attacks[a] his father or his mother must be put to death.

16"Anyone who kidnaps another and either sells him or still has him when he is caught must be put to death.

17"Anyone who curses his father or mother must be put to death.

18"If men quarrel and one hits the other with a stone or with his fist[b] and he does not die but is confined to bed, 19the one who struck the blow will not be held responsible if the other gets up and walks around outside with his staff; however, he must pay the injured man for the loss of his time and see that he is completely healed.

20"If a man beats his male or female slave with a rod and the slave dies as a direct result, he must be punished, 21but he is not to be punished if the slave gets up after a day or two, since the slave is his property.

22"If men who are fighting hit a pregnant woman and she gives birth prematurely[c] but there is no serious injury, the offender must be fined whatever the woman's husband demands and the court allows. 23But if there is serious injury, you are to take life for life, 24eye for eye, tooth for tooth, hand for hand, foot for foot, 25burn for burn, wound for wound, bruise for bruise.

26"If a man hits a manservant or maidservant in the eye and destroys it, he must let the servant go free to compensate for the eye. 27And if he knocks out the tooth of a manservant or maidservant, he must let the servant go free to compensate for the tooth.

28"If a bull gores a man or a woman to death, the bull must be stoned to death, and its meat must not be eaten. But the owner of the bull will not be held responsible. 29If, however, the bull has had the habit of goring and the owner has been warned but has not kept it penned up and it kills a man or woman, the bull must be stoned and the owner also must be put to death. 30However, if payment is demanded of him, he may redeem his life by paying whatever is demanded. 31This law also applies if the bull gores a son or daughter. 32If the bull gores a male or female slave, the owner must pay thirty shekels[d] of silver to the master of the slave, and the bull must be stoned.

33"If a man uncovers a pit or digs one and fails to cover it and an ox or a donkey falls into it, 34the owner of the pit must pay for the loss; he must pay its owner, and the dead animal will be his.

35"If a man's bull injures the bull of another and it dies, they are to sell the live one and divide both the money and the dead animal equally. 36However, if it was known that the bull had the habit of goring, yet the owner did not keep it penned up, the owner must pay, animal for animal, and the dead animal will be his.

*Protection of Property*

**22** "IF A man steals an ox or a sheep and slaughters it or sells it, he must pay back five head of cattle for the ox and four sheep for the sheep.

2"If a thief is caught breaking in and is struck so that he dies, the defender is not guilty of bloodshed; 3but if it happens[e] after sunrise, he is guilty of bloodshed.

"A thief must certainly make restitution, but if he has nothing, he must be sold to pay for his theft.

4"If the stolen animal is found alive in his possession—whether ox or donkey or sheep—he must pay back double.

5"If a man grazes his livestock in a field or vineyard and lets them stray and they graze in another man's field, he must make restitution from the best of his own field or vineyard.

**NIV** [a] 15 Or *kills* [b] 18 Or *with a tool* [c] 22 Or *she has a miscarriage* [d] 32 That is, about 12 ounces (about 0.3 kilogram) [e] 3 Or *if he strikes him*

## King James

6¶ If fire break out, and catch in thorns, so that the stacks of corn, or the standing corn, or the field, be consumed *therewith;* he that kindled the fire shall surely make restitution.

7¶ If a man shall deliver unto his neighbour money or stuff to keep, and it be stolen out of the man's house; if the thief be found, let him pay double.

8If the thief be not found, then the master of the house shall be brought unto the judges, *to see* whether he have put his hand unto his neighbour's goods.

9For all manner of trespass, *whether it be* for ox, for ass, for sheep, for raiment, *or* for any manner of lost thing, which *another* challengeth to be his, the cause of both parties shall come before the judges; *and* whom the judges shall condemn, he shall pay double unto his neighbour.

10If a man deliver unto his neighbour an ass, or an ox, or a sheep, or any beast, to keep; and it die, or be hurt, or driven away, no man seeing *it:*

11 *Then* shall an oath of the LORD be between them both, that he hath not put his hand unto his neighbour's goods; and the owner of it shall accept *thereof,* and he shall not make *it* good.

12And if it be stolen from him, he shall make restitution unto the owner thereof.

13If it be torn in pieces, *then* let him bring it *for* witness, *and* he shall not make good that which was torn.

14¶ And if a man borrow *aught* of his neighbour, and it be hurt, or die, the owner thereof *being* not with it, he shall surely make *it* good.

15 *But* if the owner thereof *be* with it, he shall not make *it* good: if it *be* an hired *thing,* it came for his hire.

16¶ And if a man entice a maid that is not betrothed, and lie with her, he shall surely endow her to be his wife.

17If her father utterly refuse to give her unto him, he shall pay money according to the dowry of virgins.

18¶ Thou shalt not suffer a witch to live.

19¶ Whosoever lieth with a beast shall surely be put to death.

20¶ He that sacrificeth unto *any* god, save unto the LORD only, he shall be utterly destroyed.

21¶ Thou shalt neither vex a stranger, nor oppress him: for ye were strangers in the land of Egypt.

22¶ Ye shall not afflict any widow, or fatherless child.

23If thou afflict them in any wise, and they cry at all unto me, I will surely hear their cry;

24And my wrath shall wax hot, and I will kill you with the sword; and your wives shall be widows, and your children fatherless.

25¶ If thou lend money to *any of* my people *that is* poor by thee, thou shalt not be to him as an usurer, neither shalt thou lay upon him usury.

26If thou at all take thy neighbour's raiment to pledge, thou shalt deliver it unto him by that the sun goeth down:

27For that *is* his covering only, it *is* his raiment for his skin: wherein shall he sleep? and it shall come to pass, when he crieth unto me, that I will hear; for I *am* gracious.

28¶ Thou shalt not revile the gods, nor curse the ruler of thy people.

29¶ Thou shalt not delay *to offer* the first of thy ripe fruits, and of thy liquors: the firstborn of thy sons shalt thou give unto me.

30Likewise shalt thou do with thine oxen, *and* with thy sheep: seven days it shall be with his dam; on the eighth day thou shalt give it me.

31¶ And ye shall be holy men unto me: neither shall ye eat *any* flesh *that is* torn of beasts in the field; ye shall cast it to the dogs.

## Amplified

6If fire breaks out and catches so that the stacked grain or standing grain or the field be consumed, he who kindled the fire shall make full restitution.

7If a man delivers to his neighbor money or goods to keep, and it is stolen out of the neighbor's house, then, if the thief is found, he shall pay double.

8But if the thief is not found, the house owner shall appear before God [the judges as His agents], to find whether he stole his neighbor's goods.

9For every unlawful deed, whether it concern ox, donkey, sheep, clothing or any lost thing at all, which another identifies as his, the cause of both parties shall come before God [the judges]. Whomever [they] shall condemn shall pay his neighbor double.

10If a man delivers to his neighbor a donkey or an ox or a sheep or any beast to keep, and it dies or is hurt or driven away, no man seeing it,

11Then an oath before the Lord shall be required between the two, that the man has not taken his neighbor's property; and the owner of it shall accept his word and not require him to make good the loss.

12But if it is stolen when in his care, he shall make restitution to its owner.

13If it be torn in pieces [by some wild beast or by accident], let him bring [the mangled carcass] for witness; he shall not make good what was torn.

14And if a man borrows anything of his neighbor and it gets hurt or dies without its owner being with it, the borrower shall make full restitution.

15But if the owner is with it [when the damage is done], the borrower shall not make it good. If it is a hired thing, the damage is included in its hire.

16If a man seduces a virgin not betrothed, and lies with her, he shall surely pay a dowry for her to become his wife.

17If her father utterly refuses to give her to him, he shall pay money equivalent to the dowry of virgins.

18You shall not allow a woman to live who practices sorcery.

19Whoever lies carnally with a beast shall surely be put to death.

20He who sacrifices to any god but the Lord only shall be utterly destroyed.

21You shall not wrong a stranger or oppress him; for you were strangers in the land of Egypt.

22You shall not afflict any widow or fatherless child.

23If you afflict them in any way, and they cry at all to Me, I will surely hear their cry;

24And My wrath shall burn; I will kill you with the sword, and your wives shall be widows and your children fatherless.

25If you lend money to any of My people with you who is poor, you shall not be to him as a creditor, neither shall you require interest from him.

26If you ever take your neighbor's garment in pledge, you shall give it back to him before the sun goes down;

27For that is his only covering, his clothing for his body. In what shall he sleep? When he cries to Me, I will hear, for I am gracious *and* merciful.

28You shall not revile God [the judges His agents], or esteem lightly *or* curse a ruler of your people.

29You shall not delay to bring to Me from the fullness [of your harvested grain] and the outflow [of your grape juice *and* olive oil]; give Me the first-born of your sons [or redeem them]. [Exod. 34:19, 20.]

30Likewise shall you do with your oxen *and* your sheep. Seven days the first-born [beast] shall be with its mother; on the eighth day you shall give it to Me.

31And you shall be holy men [consecrated] to Me; therefore you shall not eat any flesh that is torn by beasts in the field; you shall throw it to the dogs.

## New American Standard

6¶ "If a fire breaks out and spreads to thorn bushes, so that stacked grain or the standing grain or the field *itself* is consumed, he who started the fire shall surely make restitution.

7¶ "If a man gives his neighbor money or goods to keep *for him*, and it is stolen from the man's house, if the thief is caught, he shall pay double.

8 "If the thief is not caught, then the owner of the house shall appear before the judges, *to* determine whether he laid his hands on his neighbor's property.

9 "For every breach of trust, *whether it is* for ox, for donkey, for sheep, for clothing, *or* for any lost thing about which one says, 'This is it,' the case of both parties shall come before the judges; he whom the judges condemn shall pay double to his neighbor.

10¶ "If a man gives his neighbor a donkey, an ox, a sheep, or any animal to keep *for him*, and it dies or is hurt or is driven away while no one is looking,

11 an oath before the LORD shall be made by the two of them, that he has not laid hands on his neighbor's property; and its owner shall accept *it*, and he shall not make restitution.

12 "But if it is actually stolen from him, he shall make restitution to its owner.

13 "If it is all torn to pieces, let him bring it as evidence; he shall not make restitution for what has been torn to pieces.

14¶ "And if a man borrows *anything* from his neighbor, and it is injured or dies while its owner is not with it, he shall make full restitution.

15 "If its owner is with it, he shall not make restitution; if it is hired, it came for its hire.

*Sundry Laws*

16¶ "And if a man seduces a virgin who is not engaged, and lies with her, he must pay a dowry for her *to be* his wife.

17 "If her father absolutely refuses to give her to him, he shall pay money equal to the dowry for virgins.

18¶ "You shall not allow a sorceress to live.

19¶ "Whoever lies with an animal shall surely be put to death.

20¶ "He who sacrifices to any god, other than to the LORD alone, shall be utterly destroyed.

21 "And you shall not wrong a stranger or oppress him, for you were strangers in the land of Egypt.

22 "You shall not afflict any widow or orphan.

23 "If you afflict him at all, *and* if he does cry out to Me, I will surely hear his cry;

24 and My anger will be kindled, and I will kill you with the sword; and your wives shall become widows and your children fatherless.

25¶ "If you lend money to My people, to the poor among you, you are not to act as a creditor to him; you shall not charge him interest.

26 "If you ever take your neighbor's cloak as a pledge, you are to return it to him before the sun sets,

27 for that is his only covering; it is his cloak for his body. What else shall he sleep in? And it shall come about that when he cries out to Me, I will hear *him*, for I am gracious.

28¶ "You shall not curse God, nor curse a ruler of your people.

29 "You shall not delay *the offering from* your harvest and your vintage. The first-born of your sons you shall give to Me.

30 "You shall do the same with your oxen *and* with your sheep. It shall be with its mother seven days; on the eighth day you shall give it to Me.

31 "And you shall be holy men to Me, therefore you shall not eat *any* flesh torn to pieces in the field; you shall throw it to the dogs.

## New International

6 "If a fire breaks out and spreads into thornbushes so that it burns shocks of grain or standing grain or the whole field, the one who started the fire must make restitution.

7 "If a man gives his neighbor silver or goods for safekeeping
and they are stolen from the neighbor's house, the thief, if he is
caught, must pay back double. 8 But if the thief is not found, the
owner of the house must appear before the judges[a] to determine
whether he has laid his hands on the other man's property. 9 In all
cases of illegal possession of an ox, a donkey, a sheep, a garment, or any other lost property about which somebody says, 'This is mine,' both parties are to bring their cases before the judges. The one whom the judges declare[b] guilty must pay back double to his neighbor.

10 "If a man gives a donkey, an ox, a sheep or any other animal
to his neighbor for safekeeping and it dies or is injured or is taken
away while no one is looking, 11 the issue between them will be
settled by the taking of an oath before the LORD that the neighbor did not lay hands on the other person's property. The owner is to
accept this, and no restitution is required. 12 But if the animal was
stolen from the neighbor, he must make restitution to the owner.
13 If it was torn to pieces by a wild animal, he shall bring in the remains as evidence and he will not be required to pay for the torn animal.

14 "If a man borrows an animal from his neighbor and it is
injured or dies while the owner is not present, he must make
restitution. 15 But if the owner is with the animal, the borrower will not have to pay. If the animal was hired, the money paid for the hire covers the loss.

*Social Responsibility*

16 "If a man seduces a virgin who is not pledged to be married
and sleeps with her, he must pay the bride-price, and she shall be
his wife. 17 If her father absolutely refuses to give her to him, he must still pay the bride-price for virgins.

18 "Do not allow a sorceress to live.

19 "Anyone who has sexual relations with an animal must be put to death.

20 "Whoever sacrifices to any god other than the LORD must be destroyed.[c]

21 "Do not mistreat an alien or oppress him, for you were aliens in Egypt.

22 "Do not take advantage of a widow or an orphan. 23 If you do
and they cry out to me, I will certainly hear their cry. 24 My anger
will be aroused, and I will kill you with the sword; your wives will become widows and your children fatherless.

25 "If you lend money to one of my people among you who is
needy, do not be like a moneylender; charge him no interest.[d] 26 If
you take your neighbor's cloak as a pledge, return it to him by
sunset, 27 because his cloak is the only covering he has for his body. What else will he sleep in? When he cries out to me, I will hear, for I am compassionate.

28 "Do not blaspheme God[e] or curse the ruler of your people.

29 "Do not hold back offerings from your granaries or your vats.[f]

"You must give me the firstborn of your sons. 30 Do the same
with your cattle and your sheep. Let them stay with their mothers for seven days, but give them to me on the eighth day.

31 "You are to be my holy people. So do not eat the meat of an animal torn by wild beasts; throw it to the dogs.

NIV [a] 8 Or *before God;* also in verse 9 [b] 9 Or *whom God declares* [c] 20 The Hebrew term refers to the irrevocable giving over of things or persons to the LORD, often by totally destroying them. [d] 25 Or *excessive interest* [e] 28 Or *Do not revile the judges* [f] 29 The meaning of the Hebrew for this phrase is uncertain.

## King James

**23** THOU SHALT not raise a false report: put not thine hand
with the wicked to be an unrighteous witness.
2 ¶ Thou shalt not follow a multitude to *do* evil; neither shalt thou
speak in a cause to decline after many to wrest *judgment:*
3 ¶ Neither shalt thou countenance a poor man in his cause.
4 ¶ If thou meet thine enemy's ox or his ass going astray, thou
shalt surely bring it back to him again.
5 If thou see the ass of him that hateth thee lying under his
burden, and wouldest forbear to help him, thou shalt surely help
with him.
6 Thou shalt not wrest the judgment of thy poor in his cause.
7 Keep thee far from a false matter; and the innocent and righteous slay thou not: for I will not justify the wicked.
8 ¶ And thou shalt take no gift: for the gift blindeth the wise, and
perverteth the words of the righteous.
9 ¶ Also thou shalt not oppress a stranger: for ye know the heart
of a stranger, seeing ye were strangers in the land of Egypt.
10 And six years thou shalt sow thy land, and shalt gather in the
fruits thereof:
11 But the seventh *year* thou shalt let it rest and lie still; that the
poor of thy people may eat: and what they leave the beasts of the
field shall eat. In like manner thou shalt deal with thy vineyard,
*and* with thy oliveyard.
12 Six days thou shalt do thy work, and on the seventh day thou
shalt rest: that thine ox and thine ass may rest, and the son of thy
handmaid, and the stranger, may be refreshed.
13 And in all *things* that I have said unto you be circumspect: and
make no mention of the name of other gods, neither let it be heard
out of thy mouth.
14 ¶ Three times thou shalt keep a feast unto me in the year.
15 Thou shalt keep the feast of unleavened bread: (thou shalt eat
unleavened bread seven days, as I commanded thee, in the time
appointed of the month Abib; for in it thou camest out from Egypt:
and none shall appear before me empty:)
16 And the feast of harvest, the firstfruits of thy labours, which
thou hast sown in the field: and the feast of ingathering, *which is*
in the end of the year, when thou hast gathered in thy labours out
of the field.
17 Three times in the year all thy males shall appear before the
Lord GOD.
18 Thou shalt not offer the blood of my sacrifice with leavened
bread; neither shall the fat of my sacrifice remain until the morning.
19 The first of the firstfruits of thy land thou shalt bring into the
house of the LORD thy God. Thou shalt not seethe a kid in his
mother's milk.
20 ¶ Behold, I send an Angel before thee, to keep thee in the way,
and to bring thee into the place which I have prepared.
21 Beware of him, and obey his voice, provoke him not; for he
will not pardon your transgressions: for my name *is* in him.
22 But if thou shalt indeed obey his voice, and do all that I speak;
then I will be an enemy unto thine enemies, and an adversary unto
thine adversaries.
23 For mine Angel shall go before thee, and bring thee in unto
the Amorites, and the Hittites, and the Perizzites, and the Canaanites, the Hivites, and the Jebusites: and I will cut them off.

## Amplified

**23** YOU SHALL not repeat *or* raise a false report; you shall
not join with the wicked to be an unrighteous witness.
2 You shall not follow a crowd to do evil; nor shall you bear
witness at a trial so as to side with a multitude to pervert justice.
3 Neither shall you be partial to a poor man in his trial [just
because he is poor].
4 If you meet your enemy's ox or his donkey going astray, you
shall surely bring it back to him again.
5 If you see the donkey of one who hates you lying [helpless]
under his load, you shall refrain from leaving the man to cope with
it alone, you shall help him to release the animal.
6 You shall not pervert the justice due to your poor in his cause.
7 Keep far from a false matter; and [be very careful] not to
condemn to death the innocent and the righteous, for I will not
justify *and* acquit the wicked.
8 You shall take no bribe; for the bribe blinds those who have
sight, and perverts the testimony *and* the cause of the righteous.
9 Also you shall not oppress a temporary resident, for you know
the heart of a stranger *and* sojourner, seeing you were strangers *and*
sojourners in Egypt.
10 Six years you shall sow your land and reap its yield.
11 But the seventh year you shall release it *and* let it rest and lie
fallow, that the poor of your people may eat [what the land voluntarily yields], and what they leave the wild beasts shall eat. In like
manner you shall deal with your vineyard and oliveyard.
12 Six days you shall do your work, but the seventh day you shall
rest and keep sabbath; that your ox and your donkey may rest, and
the son of your bondmaid, and the alien, may be refreshed.
13 In all I have said to you take heed; do not mention the name
of other gods [either in blessing or cursing]; do not let such speech
be heard from your mouth.
14 Three times in the year you shall keep a feast to Me.
15 You shall keep the feast of unleavened bread; seven days you
shall eat unleavened bread as I commanded you, at the time appointed in the month of Abib; for in it you came out of Egypt. None
shall appear before Me empty-handed.
16 Also you shall keep the feast of harvest [Pentecost], [acknowl-
edging] the first fruits of your toil, of what you sow in the field.
And [third] you shall keep the feast of ingathering [booths or
tabernacles] at the end of the year, when you gather in the fruit
of your labors from the field.
17 Three times in the year all your males shall appear before the
Lord God.
18 You shall not offer the blood of My sacrifice with leavened
bread [but keep it unmixed], neither shall the fat of My feast
remain all night until morning.
19 The first of the first fruits of your ground you shall bring into
the house of the Lord your God. You shall not boil a kid in its
mother's milk.
20 Behold, I send an Angel before you to keep *and* guard you on
the way and to bring you to the place I have prepared.
21 Give heed to Him, listen to *and* obey His voice; be not rebellious before Him *or* provoke Him, for He will not pardon your
transgression; for My name is in Him. [Exod. 32:34; 33:14; Isa.
63:9.]
22 But if you will indeed listen to and obey His voice and all that
I speak, then I will be an enemy to your enemies and an adversary
to your adversaries.
23 When My Angel goes before you and brings you to the Amorites, the Hittites, the Perizzites, the Canaanites, the Hivites, and
the Jebusites, and I reject them *and* blot them out,

## New American Standard

*Sundry Laws*

23 "YOU SHALL not bear a false report; do not join your
hand with a wicked man to be a malicious witness.
2"You shall not follow a multitude in doing evil, nor shall you
testify in a dispute so as to turn aside after a multitude in order to
pervert *justice;*
3nor shall you be partial to a poor man in his dispute.
4¶ "If you meet your enemy's ox or his donkey wandering
away, you shall surely return it to him.
5"If you see the donkey of one who hates you lying *helpless*
under its load, you shall refrain from leaving it to him, you shall
surely release *it* with him.
6"You shall not pervert the justice *due* to your needy *brother* in
his dispute.
7"Keep far from a false charge, and do not kill the innocent or
the righteous, for I will not acquit the guilty.
8"And you shall not take a bribe, for a bribe blinds the clear-
sighted and subverts the cause of the just.
9"And you shall not oppress a stranger, since you yourselves
know the feelings of a stranger, for you *also* were strangers in the
land of Egypt.

*The Sabbath and Land*

10¶ "And you shall sow your land for six years and gather in its
yield,
11but *on* the seventh year you shall let it rest and lie fallow, so
that the needy of your people may eat; and whatever they leave
the beast of the field may eat. You are to do the same with your
vineyard *and* your olive grove.
12"Six days you are to do your work, but on the seventh day
you shall cease *from labor* in order that your ox and your donkey
may rest, and the son of your female slave, as well as your
stranger, may refresh themselves.
13"Now concerning everything which I have said to you, be on
your guard; and do not mention the name of other gods, nor let
*them* be heard from your mouth.

*Three National Feasts*

14¶ "Three times a year you shall celebrate a feast to Me.
15"You shall observe the Feast of Unleavened Bread; for seven
days you are to eat unleavened bread, as I commanded you, at the
appointed time in the month Abib, for in it you came out of Egypt.
And none shall appear before Me empty-handed.
16"Also *you shall observe* the Feast of the Harvest *of* the first fruits
of your labors *from* what you sow in the field; also the Feast of the
Ingathering at the end of the year when you gather in *the fruit of*
your labors from the field.
17"Three times a year all your males shall appear before the
Lord GOD.
18¶ "You shall not offer the blood of My sacrifice with leavened
bread; nor is the fat of My feast to remain overnight until morning.
19"You shall bring the choice first fruits of your soil into the
house of the LORD your God. You are not to boil a kid in the milk
of its mother.

*Conquest of the Land*

20¶ "Behold, I am going to send an angel before you to guard
you along the way, and to bring you into the place which I have
prepared.
21"Be on your guard before him and obey his voice; do not be
rebellious toward him, for he will not pardon your transgression,
since My name is in him.
22"But if you will truly obey his voice and do all that I say, then
I will be an enemy to your enemies and an adversary to your
adversaries.
23"For My angel will go before you and bring you in to *the land*
*of* the Amorites, the Hittites, the Perizzites, the Canaanites, the
Hivites and the Jebusites; and I will completely destroy them.

## New International

*Laws of Justice and Mercy*

23 "DO NOT spread false reports. Do not help a wicked man
by being a malicious witness.
2"Do not follow the crowd in doing wrong. When you give
testimony in a lawsuit, do not pervert justice by siding with the
crowd, 3and do not show favoritism to a poor man in his lawsuit.
4"If you come across your enemy's ox or donkey wandering off,
be sure to take it back to him. 5If you see the donkey of someone
who hates you fallen down under its load, do not leave it there;
be sure you help him with it.
6"Do not deny justice to your poor people in their lawsuits.
7Have nothing to do with a false charge and do not put an innocent
or honest person to death, for I will not acquit the guilty.
8"Do not accept a bribe, for a bribe blinds those who see and
twists the words of the righteous.
9"Do not oppress an alien; you yourselves know how it feels to
be aliens, because you were aliens in Egypt.

*Sabbath Laws*

10"For six years you are to sow your fields and harvest the
crops, 11but during the seventh year let the land lie unplowed and
unused. Then the poor among your people may get food from it,
and the wild animals may eat what they leave. Do the same with
your vineyard and your olive grove.
12"Six days do your work, but on the seventh day do not work,
so that your ox and your donkey may rest and the slave born in
your household, and the alien as well, may be refreshed.
13"Be careful to do everything I have said to you. Do not invoke
the names of other gods; do not let them be heard on your lips.

*The Three Annual Festivals*

14"Three times a year you are to celebrate a festival to me.
15"Celebrate the Feast of Unleavened Bread; for seven days eat
bread made without yeast, as I commanded you. Do this at the
appointed time in the month of Abib, for in that month you came
out of Egypt.
"No one is to appear before me empty-handed.
16"Celebrate the Feast of Harvest with the firstfruits of the crops
you sow in your field.
"Celebrate the Feast of Ingathering at the end of the year, when
you gather in your crops from the field.
17"Three times a year all the men are to appear before the
Sovereign LORD.
18"Do not offer the blood of a sacrifice to me along with anything containing yeast.
"The fat of my festival offerings must not be kept until morning.
19"Bring the best of the firstfruits of your soil to the house of
the LORD your God.
"Do not cook a young goat in its mother's milk.

*God's Angel to Prepare the Way*

20"See, I am sending an angel ahead of you to guard you along
the way and to bring you to the place I have prepared. 21Pay
attention to him and listen to what he says. Do not rebel against
him; he will not forgive your rebellion, since my Name is in him.
22If you listen carefully to what he says and do all that I say, I will
be an enemy to your enemies and will oppose those who oppose
you. 23My angel will go ahead of you and bring you into the land
of the Amorites, Hittites, Perizzites, Canaanites, Hivites and Jebusites, and I will wipe them out. 24Do not bow down before their

## King James

24Thou shalt not bow down to their gods, nor serve them, nor
do after their works: but thou shalt utterly overthrow them, and
quite break down their images.
25And ye shall serve the LORD your God, and he shall bless thy
bread, and thy water; and I will take sickness away from the midst
of thee.
26¶ There shall nothing cast their young, nor be barren, in thy
land: the number of thy days I will fulfil.
27I will send my fear before thee, and will destroy all the people
to whom thou shalt come, and I will make all thine enemies turn
their backs unto thee.
28And I will send hornets before thee, which shall drive out the
Hivite, the Canaanite, and the Hittite, from before thee.
29I will not drive them out from before thee in one year; lest the
land become desolate, and the beast of the field multiply against
thee.
30By little and little I will drive them out from before thee, until
thou be increased, and inherit the land.
31And I will set thy bounds from the Red sea even unto the sea
of the Philistines, and from the desert unto the river: for I will
deliver the inhabitants of the land into your hand; and thou shalt
drive them out before thee.
32Thou shalt make no covenant with them, nor with their gods.
33They shall not dwell in thy land, lest they make thee sin
against me: for if thou serve their gods, it will surely be a snare
unto thee.

**24** AND HE said unto Moses, Come up unto the LORD, thou,
and Aaron, Nadab, and Abihu, and seventy of the elders
of Israel; and worship ye afar off.
2And Moses alone shall come near the LORD: but they shall not
come nigh; neither shall the people go up with him.
3¶ And Moses came and told the people all the words of the
LORD, and all the judgments: and all the people answered with one
voice, and said, All the words which the LORD hath said will we
do.
4And Moses wrote all the words of the LORD, and rose up early
in the morning, and builded an altar under the hill, and twelve
pillars, according to the twelve tribes of Israel.
5And he sent young men of the children of Israel, which offered
burnt offerings, and sacrificed peace offerings of oxen unto the
LORD.
6And Moses took half of the blood, and put *it* in basins; and half
of the blood he sprinkled on the altar.
7And he took the book of the covenant, and read in the audience of the people: and they said, All that the LORD hath said will
we do, and be obedient.
8And Moses took the blood, and sprinkled *it* on the people, and
said, Behold the blood of the covenant, which the LORD hath made
with you concerning all these words.
9¶ Then went up Moses, and Aaron, Nadab, and Abihu, and
seventy of the elders of Israel:
10And they saw the God of Israel: and *there was* under his feet
as it were a paved work of a sapphire stone, and as it were the body
of heaven in *his* clearness.
11And upon the nobles of the children of Israel he laid not his
hand: also they saw God, and did eat and drink.

AMP [a] The contemporary evidence, supplied by archaeology, that writing had long been in common use before the time of Moses, now makes conjectures about the contents of the earlier books of the Old Testament being handed down *orally*, look absurd. Not only is much of the misleading criticism of the Bible now recognized as unjustified, it is out of harmony with the scientific outlook of the present day (Sir Charles Marston in *New Bible Evidence*, adapted).

## Amplified

24You shall not bow down to their gods, or serve them, or do
after their works; but you shall utterly overthrow them, and break
down their pillars *and* images.
25You shall serve the Lord your God; He shall bless your bread
and water, and I will take sickness from your midst.
26None shall lose her young by miscarriage or be barren in your
land; I will fulfill the number of your days.
27I will send My terror before you, and will throw into confusion all the people to whom you shall come, and I will make all
your foes turn from you [in flight].
28And I will send hornets before you, which shall drive out the
Hivite, Canaanite, and Hittite, from before you.
29I will not drive them out from before you in one year, lest the
land become desolate [for lack of attention] and the wild beasts
multiply against you.
30Little by little I will drive them out from before you, until you
have increased *and* are numerous enough to take possession of the
land.
31I will set your borders from the Red Sea to the sea of the
Philistines, and from the wilderness to the river [Euphrates]; for
I will deliver the inhabitants of the land into your hand, and you
shall drive them out before you.
32You shall make no covenant with them or with their gods.
33They shall not dwell in your land, lest they make you sin
against Me; for if you serve their gods, it will surely be a snare to
you.

**24** GOD SAID to Moses, Come up to the Lord, you and
Aaron, Nadab and Abihu [Aaron's sons], and seventy of
Israel's elders, and worship at a distance.
2Moses alone shall come near the Lord; the others shall not
come near, and neither shall the people come up with him.
3Moses came and told the people all the Lord said and all the
ordinances; and all the people answered with one voice, All that
the Lord has spoken we will do.
4Moses [a]wrote all the words of the Lord. He rose up early in
the morning and built an altar at the foot of the mountain; and
twelve pillars, representing Israel's twelve tribes.
5And he sent young Israelite men, who offered burnt offerings
and sacrificed peace offerings of oxen to the Lord.
6And Moses took half of the blood and put it in basins, and half
of the blood he dashed against the altar.
7Then he took the book of the covenant and read in the hearing
of the people; and they said, All that the Lord has said we will do,
and we will be obedient.
8And Moses took the [remaining half of the] blood and sprinkled it on the people, and said, Behold the blood of the covenant
which the Lord has made with you in accordance with all these
words. [I Cor. 11:25; Heb. 8:6; 10:28, 29.]
9Then Moses, Aaron, Nadab, and Abihu, and seventy of the
elders of Israel went up [the mountainside].
10And they saw the God of Israel [that is, a convincing manifestation of His presence] and under His feet it was like pavement of
bright sapphire stone, like the very heavens in clearness. [Deut.
4:12; Exod. 33:20-23; Ezek. 28:14, *Amplified*.]
11And upon the nobles of the Israelites He laid not His hand [to
conceal Himself from them, to rebuke their daring, or to harm
them]; but they saw [the manifestation of the presence of] God,
and ate and drank. [Exod. 19:21.]

## New American Standard

24"You shall not worship their gods, nor serve them, nor do
according to their deeds; but you shall utterly overthrow them,
and break their *sacred* pillars in pieces.
25"But you shall serve the LORD your God, and He will bless
your bread and your water; and I will remove sickness from your
midst.
26"There shall be no one miscarrying or barren in your land; I
will fulfill the number of your days.
27"I will send My terror ahead of you, and throw into confusion
all the people among whom you come, and I will make all your
enemies turn *their* backs to you.
28"And I will send hornets ahead of you, that they may drive
out the Hivites, the Canaanites, and the Hittites before you.
29"I will not drive them out before you in a single year, that the
land may not become desolate, and the beasts of the field become
too numerous for you.
30"I will drive them out before you little by little, until you
become fruitful and take possession of the land.
31"And I will fix your boundary from the Red Sea to the sea of
the Philistines, and from the wilderness to the River *Euphrates;* for
I will deliver the inhabitants of the land into your hand, and you
will drive them out before you.
32"You shall make no covenant with them or with their gods.
33"They shall not live in your land, lest they make you sin
against Me; for *if* you serve their gods, it will surely be a snare to
you."

*People Affirm Their Covenant with God*

24 THEN HE said to Moses, "Come up to the LORD, you and
Aaron, Nadab and Abihu and seventy of the elders of
Israel, and you shall worship at a distance.
2"Moses alone, however, shall come near to the LORD, but they
shall not come near, nor shall the people come up with him."
3Then Moses came and recounted to the people all the words
of the LORD and all the ordinances; and all the people answered
with one voice, and said, "All the words which the LORD has
spoken we will do!"
4And Moses wrote down all the words of the LORD. Then he
arose early in the morning, and built an altar at the foot of the
mountain with twelve pillars for the twelve tribes of Israel.
5And he sent young men of the sons of Israel, and they offered
burnt offerings and sacrificed young bulls as peace offerings to the
LORD.
6And Moses took half of the blood and put *it* in basins, and the
*other* half of the blood he sprinkled on the altar.
7Then he took the book of the covenant and read *it* in the
hearing of the people; and they said, "All that the LORD has spoken
we will do, and we will be obedient!"
8So Moses took the blood and sprinkled *it* on the people, and
said, "Behold the blood of the covenant, which the LORD has made
with you in accordance with all these words."
9¶ Then Moses went up with Aaron, Nadab and Abihu, and
seventy of the elders of Israel,
10and they saw the God of Israel; and under His feet there
appeared to be a pavement of sapphire, as clear as the sky itself.
11Yet He did not stretch out His hand against the nobles of the
sons of Israel; and they beheld God, and they ate and drank.

## New International

gods or worship them or follow their practices. You must demolish
them and break their sacred stones to pieces. 25Worship the LORD
your God, and his blessing will be on your food and water. I will
take away sickness from among you, 26and none will miscarry or
be barren in your land. I will give you a full life span.
27"I will send my terror ahead of you and throw into confusion
every nation you encounter. I will make all your enemies turn their
backs and run. 28I will send the hornet ahead of you to drive the
Hivites, Canaanites and Hittites out of your way. 29But I will not
drive them out in a single year, because the land would become
desolate and the wild animals too numerous for you. 30Little by
little I will drive them out before you, until you have increased
enough to take possession of the land.
31"I will establish your borders from the Red Sea[b] to the Sea of
the Philistines,[c] and from the desert to the River.[d] I will hand over
to you the people who live in the land and you will drive them out
before you. 32Do not make a covenant with them or with their
gods. 33Do not let them live in your land, or they will cause you
to sin against me, because the worship of their gods will certainly
be a snare to you."

*The Covenant Confirmed*

24 THEN HE said to Moses, "Come up to the LORD, you and
Aaron, Nadab and Abihu, and seventy of the elders of
Israel. You are to worship at a distance, 2but Moses alone is to
approach the LORD; the others must not come near. And the
people may not come up with him."
3When Moses went and told the people all the LORD's words
and laws, they responded with one voice, "Everything the LORD
has said we will do." 4Moses then wrote down everything the
LORD had said.
He got up early the next morning and built an altar at the foot
of the mountain and set up twelve stone pillars representing the
twelve tribes of Israel. 5Then he sent young Israelite men, and they
offered burnt offerings and sacrificed young bulls as fellowship
offerings[e] to the LORD. 6Moses took half of the blood and put it
in bowls, and the other half he sprinkled on the altar. 7Then he
took the Book of the Covenant and read it to the people. They
responded, "We will do everything the LORD has said; we will
obey."
8Moses then took the blood, sprinkled it on the people and said,
"This is the blood of the covenant that the LORD has made with
you in accordance with all these words."
9Moses and Aaron, Nadab and Abihu, and the seventy elders
of Israel went up 10and saw the God of Israel. Under his feet was
something like a pavement made of sapphire,[f] clear as the sky
itself. 11But God did not raise his hand against these leaders of the
Israelites; they saw God, and they ate and drank.

NIV [b] *31* Hebrew *Yam Suph;* that is, Sea of Reeds [c] *31* That is, the Mediterranean [d] *31* That is, the Euphrates [e] *5* Traditionally *peace offerings* [f] *10* Or *lapis lazuli*

## King James

12¶ And the LORD said unto Moses, Come up to me into the mount, and be there: and I will give thee tables of stone, and a law, and commandments which I have written; that thou mayest teach them.
13And Moses rose up, and his minister Joshua: and Moses went up into the mount of God.
14And he said unto the elders, Tarry ye here for us, until we come again unto you: and, behold, Aaron and Hur *are* with you: if any man have any matters to do, let him come unto them.
15And Moses went up into the mount, and a cloud covered the mount.
16And the glory of the LORD abode upon mount Sinai, and the cloud covered it six days: and the seventh day he called unto Moses out of the midst of the cloud.
17And the sight of the glory of the LORD *was* like devouring fire on the top of the mount in the eyes of the children of Israel.
18And Moses went into the midst of the cloud, and gat him up into the mount: and Moses was in the mount forty days and forty nights.

25 AND THE LORD spake unto Moses, saying,
2Speak unto the children of Israel, that they bring me an offering: of every man that giveth it willingly with his heart ye shall take my offering.
3And this *is* the offering which ye shall take of them; gold, and silver, and brass,
4And blue, and purple, and scarlet, and fine linen, and goats' *hair,*
5And rams' skins dyed red, and badgers' skins, and shittim wood,
6Oil for the light, spices for anointing oil, and for sweet incense,
7Onyx stones, and stones to be set in the ephod, and in the breastplate.
8And let them make me a sanctuary; that I may dwell among them.
9According to all that I show thee, *after* the pattern of the tabernacle, and the pattern of all the instruments thereof, even so shall ye make *it.*
10¶ And they shall make an ark *of* shittim wood: two cubits and a half *shall be* the length thereof, and a cubit and a half the breadth thereof, and a cubit and a half the height thereof.
11And thou shalt overlay it with pure gold, within and without shalt thou overlay it, and shalt make upon it a crown of gold round about.
12And thou shalt cast four rings of gold for it, and put *them* in the four corners thereof; and two rings *shall be* in the one side of it, and two rings in the other side of it.
13And thou shalt make staves *of* shittim wood, and overlay them with gold.
14And thou shalt put the staves into the rings by the sides of the ark, that the ark may be borne with them.
15The staves shall be in the rings of the ark: they shall not be taken from it.
16And thou shalt put into the ark the testimony which I shall give thee.
17And thou shalt make a mercy seat *of* pure gold: two cubits and a half *shall be* the length thereof, and a cubit and a half the breadth thereof.
18And thou shalt make two cherubims *of* gold, *of* beaten work shalt thou make them, in the two ends of the mercy seat.

## Amplified

12And the Lord said to Moses, Come up to Me into the mountain and be there; and I will give you tables of stone with the law and the commandments, which [a]I have written that you may teach them. [II Cor. 3:2, 3.]
13So Moses rose up and Joshua his attendant; and Moses went up into the mountain of God.
14And he said to the elders, Tarry here for us, until we come back to you; remember Aaron and Hur are with you; whoever has a cause, let him go to them.
15Then Moses went up into the mountain, and the cloud covered the mountain.
16The glory of the Lord rested on Mount Sinai, and the cloud covered it six days. On the seventh day *God* called to Moses out of the midst of the cloud.
17And the glory of the Lord appeared to the Israelites like devouring fire on the top of the mountain.
18Moses entered into the midst of the cloud, and went up the mountain, and Moses was on the mountain forty days and nights.

25 AND THE Lord said to Moses,
2Speak to the Israelites, that they take for Me an offering. Of every man who gives it willingly *and* ungrudgingly with his heart you shall take My offering.
3This is the offering you shall receive from them: gold, silver, and bronze,
4Blue, purple and scarlet *stuff* and fine twined linen and goats' hair,
5Rams' skins tanned red, goatskins, dolphin *or* porpoise skins, acacia wood,
6Oil for the light, spices for anointing oil and for sweet incense,
7Onyx stones, and stones for setting in the ephod and in the breastplate.
8Let them make Me a sanctuary, that I may dwell among them. [Heb. 8:1, 2; 10:1.]
9And you shall make it according to all that I show you, the pattern of the tabernacle *or* dwelling, and the pattern of all the furniture of it.
10They shall make an ark of acacia wood; two and a half cubits long, a cubit and a half wide, and a cubit and a half high.
11You shall overlay the ark with pure gold, inside and out, and make a gold crown, a rim *or* border, around its top.
12You shall cast four gold rings and attach them to the four lower corners of it, two rings on either side.
13You shall make poles of acacia wood, and overlay them with gold,
14And put the poles through the rings on the ark's sides, by which to carry it.
15The poles shall remain in the rings of the ark; they shall not be removed from it [that the ark be not touched].
16And you shall put inside the ark the testimony [the ten commandments] which I will give you.
17And you shall make a mercy seat (a covering) of pure gold, two cubits and a half long, and a cubit and a half wide.
18And you shall make two cherubim [winged angelic figures] of [solid] hammered gold on the two ends of the mercy seat.

**AMP** [a] The two tables were "written with the finger of God" (31:18), and "the tables were the work of God" (32:16). A man may be said to write what *a secretary* writes at his dictation; but if he expressly states that certain things are written with his own hand, it is unreasonable to suppose that they were written by the hand of another (Lange's *Commentary*).

## New American Standard

[12]¶ Now the LORD said to Moses, "Come up to Me on the
mountain and remain there, and I will give you the stone tablets
with the law and the commandment which I have written for their
instruction."
[13]So Moses arose with Joshua his servant, and Moses went up
to the mountain of God.
[14]But to the elders he said, "Wait here for us until we return to
you. And behold, Aaron and Hur are with you; whoever has a
legal matter, let him approach them."
[15]Then Moses went up to the mountain, and the cloud covered
the mountain.
[16]And the glory of the LORD rested on Mount Sinai, and the
cloud covered it for six days; and on the seventh day He called to
Moses from the midst of the cloud.
[17]And to the eyes of the sons of Israel the appearance of the
glory of the LORD was like a consuming fire on the mountain top.
[18]And Moses entered the midst of the cloud as he went up to
the mountain; and Moses was on the mountain forty days and
forty nights.

*Offerings for the Sanctuary*

**25** THEN THE LORD spoke to Moses, saying,
[2]"Tell the sons of Israel to raise a contribution for Me; from
every man whose heart moves him you shall raise My contribution.
[3]"And this is the contribution which you are to raise from
them: gold, silver and bronze,
[4]blue, purple and scarlet *material*, fine linen, goat *hair*,
[5]rams' skins dyed red, porpoise skins, acacia wood,
[6]oil for lighting, spices for the anointing oil and for the fragrant
incense,
[7]onyx stones and setting stones, for the ephod and for the
breastpiece.
[8]"And let them construct a sanctuary for Me, that I may dwell
among them.
[9]"According to all that I am going to show you, *as* the pattern
of the tabernacle and the pattern of all its furniture, just so you
shall construct *it*.

*Ark of the Covenant*

[10]¶ "And they shall construct an ark of acacia wood two and a
half cubits long, and one and a half cubits wide, and one and a half
cubits high.
[11]"And you shall overlay it with pure gold, inside and out you
shall overlay it, and you shall make a gold molding around it.
[12]"And you shall cast four gold rings for it, and fasten them on
its four feet, and two rings shall be on one side of it and two rings
on the other side of it.
[13]"And you shall make poles of acacia wood and overlay them
with gold.
[14]"And you shall put the poles into the rings on the sides of the
ark, to carry the ark with them.
[15]"The poles shall remain in the rings of the ark; they shall not
be removed from it.
[16]"And you shall put into the ark the testimony which I shall
give you.
[17]"And you shall make a [b]mercy seat of pure gold, two and a
half cubits long and one and a half cubits wide.
[18]"And you shall make two cherubim of gold, make them of
hammered work at the two ends of the mercy seat.

NAS [b] Lit., *propitiatory;* and so through v. 22

## New International

[12]The LORD said to Moses, "Come up to me on the mountain
and stay here, and I will give you the tablets of stone, with the law
and commands I have written for their instruction."
[13]Then Moses set out with Joshua his aide, and Moses went up
on the mountain of God. [14]He said to the elders, "Wait here for
us until we come back to you. Aaron and Hur are with you, and
anyone involved in a dispute can go to them."
[15]When Moses went up on the mountain, the cloud covered it,
[16]and the glory of the LORD settled on Mount Sinai. For six days
the cloud covered the mountain, and on the seventh day the LORD
called to Moses from within the cloud. [17]To the Israelites the glory
of the LORD looked like a consuming fire on top of the mountain.
[18]Then Moses entered the cloud as he went on up the mountain.
And he stayed on the mountain forty days and forty nights.

*Offerings for the Tabernacle*

**25** THE LORD said to Moses, [2]"Tell the Israelites to bring me
an offering. You are to receive the offering for me from
each man whose heart prompts him to give. [3]These are the offerings you are to receive from them: gold, silver and bronze; [4]blue,
purple and scarlet yarn and fine linen; goat hair; [5]ram skins dyed
red and hides of sea cows[c]; acacia wood; [6]olive oil for the light;
spices for the anointing oil and for the fragrant incense; [7]and onyx
stones and other gems to be mounted on the ephod and breastpiece.
[8]"Then have them make a sanctuary for me, and I will dwell
among them. [9]Make this tabernacle and all its furnishings exactly
like the pattern I will show you.

*The Ark*

[10]"Have them make a chest of acacia wood—two and a half
cubits long, a cubit and a half wide, and a cubit and a half high.[d]
[11]Overlay it with pure gold, both inside and out, and make a gold
molding around it. [12]Cast four gold rings for it and fasten them to
its four feet, with two rings on one side and two rings on the other.
[13]Then make poles of acacia wood and overlay them with gold.
[14]Insert the poles into the rings on the sides of the chest to carry
it. [15]The poles are to remain in the rings of this ark; they are not
to be removed. [16]Then put in the ark the Testimony, which I will
give you.
[17]"Make an atonement cover[e] of pure gold—two and a half
cubits long and a cubit and a half wide.[f] [18]And make two cherubim out of hammered gold at the ends of the cover. [19]Make one

NIV [c] *5* That is, dugongs [d] *10* That is, about 3 3/4 feet (about 1.1 meters) long and 2 1/4 feet (about 0.7 meter) wide and high [e] *17* Traditionally *a mercy seat* [f] *17* That is, about 3 3/4 feet (about 1.1 meters) long and 2 1/4 feet (about 0.7 meter) wide

# King James

19And make one cherub on the one end, and the other cherub on the other end: *even* of the mercy seat shall ye make the cherubims on the two ends thereof.

20And the cherubims shall stretch forth *their* wings on high, covering the mercy seat with their wings, and their faces *shall look* one to another; toward the mercy seat shall the faces of the cherubims be.

21And thou shalt put the mercy seat above upon the ark; and in the ark thou shalt put the testimony that I shall give thee.

22And there I will meet with thee, and I will commune with thee from above the mercy seat, from between the two cherubims which *are* upon the ark of the testimony, of all *things* which I will give thee in commandment unto the children of Israel.

23¶ Thou shalt also make a table *of* shittim wood: two cubits *shall be* the length thereof, and a cubit the breadth thereof, and a cubit and a half the height thereof.

24And thou shalt overlay it with pure gold, and make thereto a crown of gold round about.

25And thou shalt make unto it a border of an handbreadth round about, and thou shalt make a golden crown to the border thereof round about.

26And thou shalt make for it four rings of gold, and put the rings in the four corners that *are* on the four feet thereof.

27Over against the border shall the rings be for places of the staves to bear the table.

28And thou shalt make the staves *of* shittim wood, and overlay them with gold, that the table may be borne with them.

29And thou shalt make the dishes thereof, and spoons thereof, and covers thereof, and bowls thereof, to cover withal: *of* pure gold shalt thou make them.

30And thou shalt set upon the table showbread before me always.

31¶ And thou shalt make a candlestick *of* pure gold: *of* beaten work shall the candlestick be made: his shaft, and his branches, his bowls, his knobs, and his flowers, shall be of the same.

32And six branches shall come out of the sides of it; three branches of the candlestick out of the one side, and three branches of the candlestick out of the other side:

33Three bowls made like unto almonds, *with* a knob and a flower in one branch; and three bowls made like almonds in the other branch, *with* a knob and a flower: so in the six branches that come out of the candlestick.

34And in the candlestick *shall be* four bowls made like unto almonds, *with* their knobs and their flowers.

35And *there shall be* a knob under two branches of the same, and a knob under two branches of the same, and a knob under two branches of the same, according to the six branches that proceed out of the candlestick.

36Their knobs and their branches shall be of the same: all it *shall be* one beaten work *of* pure gold.

37And thou shalt make the seven lamps thereof: and they shall light the lamps thereof, that they may give light over against it.

38And the tongs thereof, and the snuffdishes thereof, *shall be of* pure gold.

39 *Of* a talent of pure gold shall he make it, with all these vessels.

40And look that thou make *them* after their pattern, which was shown thee in the mount.

# Amplified

19Make one cherub on each end, making the cherubim of one piece with the mercy seat on the two ends of it.

20And the cherubim shall spread out their wings above, covering the mercy seat with their wings, facing each other and looking down toward the mercy seat.

21You shall put the mercy seat on the top of the ark; and in the ark you shall put the testimony [the ten commandments] that I will give you.

22There I will meet with you and from above the mercy seat, from between the two cherubim that are upon the ark of the testimony, I will speak intimately with you of all which I will give you in commandment to the Israelites.

23Also make a table of acacia wood, two cubits long, one cubit wide, and a cubit and a half high, *for the showbread.*

24You shall overlay it with pure gold, and make a crown, a rim *or* molding, of gold around the top of it;

25And make a frame of a handbreadth around *and* below the top of it, and put around it a gold molding as a border.

26You shall make for it four rings of gold, and fasten them at the four corners that are on the table's four legs.

27Close against the frame shall the rings be as places for the poles to pass to carry the table [of showbread].

28You shall make the poles of acacia wood, and overlay them with gold, that the table may be carried with them.

29And you shall make its plates [for showbread] and cups [for incense], and its flagons and bowls [for liquids in sacrifice]; make them of pure gold.

30And you shall set the showbread (the bread of the Presence) on the table before Me always. [John 6:58.]

31You shall make a lampstand of pure gold. Of beaten *and* turned work shall the lampstand be made, both its base and its shaft; its cups, its knobs, and its flowers shall be of one piece with it.

32Six branches shall come out of the sides of it; three branches of the lampstand out of the one side, and three branches out of its other side;

33Three cups made like almond blossoms, each with a knob *or* capital and a flower on one branch; and three cups made like almond blossoms on the other branch with a knob and a flower; so for the six branches coming out of the lampstand;

34And on the [center shaft] itself you shall [make] four cups like almond blossoms with their knobs and their flowers.

35Also make a knob [on the shaft] under each pair of the six branches going out from the lampstand and one piece with it;

36Their knobs and their branches shall be of one piece with it; the whole of it one beaten work of pure gold.

37And you shall make the lamps of the [lampstand] to include a [a]seventh one [at the top of the shaft]. [The priests] shall set up the [seven] lamps of it, so they may give light in front of it.

38Its snuffers and its ash trays shall be of pure gold.

39Use a talent of pure gold for it, including all these utensils.

40And see to it that you copy [exactly] their pattern which was shown you on the mountain. [Heb. 8:5, 6.]

**AMP** [a] Certain Biblical critics in the past doubted the existence of the tabernacle, and asserted that the concept of a sevenfold lamp was unknown until hundreds of years later, in Babylonian times (600 B.C.). The first objective evidence to the contrary came to hand in W. F. Albright's excavation of Tell Beit Mirsim, south of Jerusalem, where he found seven-sprouted lamps from about 1200 B.C. Our seventh season at Dothan yielded three sevenfold lamps from the period 1200-1400 B.C., showing again that this was not a late idea (Joseph P. Free in *Near Eastern Archaeology,* condensed).

## New American Standard

19"And make one cherub at one end and one cherub at the other end; you shall make the cherubim *of one piece* with the mercy seat at its two ends.
20"And the cherubim shall have *their* wings spread upward, covering the mercy seat with their wings and facing one another; the faces of the cherubim are to be *turned* toward the mercy seat.
21"And you shall put the mercy seat on top of the ark, and in the ark you shall put the testimony which I shall give to you.
22"And there I will meet with you; and from above the mercy seat, from between the two cherubim which are upon the ark of the testimony, I will speak to you about all that I will give you in commandment for the sons of Israel.

*The Table of Showbread*

**23**¶ "And you shall make a table of acacia wood, two cubits long and one cubit wide and one and a half cubits high.
24"And you shall overlay it with pure gold and make a gold border around it.
25"And you shall make for it a rim of a handbreadth around *it;* and you shall make a gold border for the rim around it.
26"And you shall make four gold rings for it and put rings on the four corners which are on its four feet.
27"The rings shall be close to the rim as holders for the poles to carry the table.
28"And you shall make the poles of acacia wood and overlay them with gold, so that with them the table may be carried.
29"And you shall make its dishes and its pans and its jars and its bowls, with which to pour libations; you shall make them of pure gold.
30"And you shall set the bread of the Presence on the table before Me at all times.

*The Golden Lampstand*

**31**¶ "Then you shall make a lampstand of pure gold. The lampstand *and* its base and its shaft are to be made of hammered work; its cups, its bulbs and its flowers shall be *of one piece* with it.
32"And six branches shall go out from its sides; three branches of the lampstand from its one side, and three branches of the lampstand from its other side.
33"Three cups *shall be* shaped like almond *blossoms* in the one branch, a [b]bulb and a flower, and three cups shaped like almond *blossoms* in the other branch, a bulb and a flower—so for six branches going out from the lampstand;
34and in the lampstand four cups shaped like almond *blossoms,* its bulbs and its flowers.
35"And a bulb shall be under the *first* pair of branches *coming* out of it, and a bulb under the *second* pair of branches *coming* out of it, and a bulb under the *third* pair of branches *coming* out of it, for the six branches coming out of the lampstand.
36"Their bulbs and their branches *shall be of one piece* with it; all of it shall be one piece of hammered work of pure gold.
37"Then you shall make its lamps seven *in number;* and they shall mount its lamps so as to shed light on the space in front of it.
38"And its snuffers and their trays *shall be* of pure gold.
39"It shall be made from a talent of pure gold, with all these utensils.
40"And see that you make *them* after the pattern for them, which was shown to you on the mountain.

**NAS** [b] Or, *calyx*

## New International

cherub on one end and the second cherub on the other; make the cherubim of one piece with the cover, at the two ends. 20The cherubim are to have their wings spread upward, overshadowing the cover with them. The cherubim are to face each other, looking toward the cover. 21Place the cover on top of the ark and put in the ark the Testimony, which I will give you. 22There, above the cover between the two cherubim that are over the ark of the Testimony, I will meet with you and give you all my commands for the Israelites.

*The Table*

23"Make a table of acacia wood—two cubits long, a cubit wide and a cubit and a half high.[c] 24Overlay it with pure gold and make a gold molding around it. 25Also make around it a rim a handbreadth[d] wide and put a gold molding on the rim. 26Make four gold rings for the table and fasten them to the four corners, where the four legs are. 27The rings are to be close to the rim to hold the poles used in carrying the table. 28Make the poles of acacia wood, overlay them with gold and carry the table with them. 29And make its plates and dishes of pure gold, as well as its pitchers and bowls for the pouring out of offerings. 30Put the bread of the Presence on this table to be before me at all times.

*The Lampstand*

31"Make a lampstand of pure gold and hammer it out, base and shaft; its flowerlike cups, buds and blossoms shall be of one piece with it. 32Six branches are to extend from the sides of the lampstand—three on one side and three on the other. 33Three cups shaped like almond flowers with buds and blossoms are to be on one branch, three on the next branch, and the same for all six branches extending from the lampstand. 34And on the lampstand there are to be four cups shaped like almond flowers with buds and blossoms. 35One bud shall be under the first pair of branches extending from the lampstand, a second bud under the second pair, and a third bud under the third pair—six branches in all. 36The buds and branches shall all be of one piece with the lampstand, hammered out of pure gold.
37"Then make its seven lamps and set them up on it so that they light the space in front of it. 38Its wick trimmers and trays are to be of pure gold. 39A talent[e] of pure gold is to be used for the lampstand and all these accessories. 40See that you make them according to the pattern shown you on the mountain.

**NIV** [c] *23* That is, about 3 feet (about 0.9 meter) long and 1 1/2 feet (about 0.5 meter) wide and 2 1/4 feet (about 0.7 meter) high [d] *25* That is, about 3 inches (about 8 centimeters) [e] *39* That is, about 75 pounds (about 34 kilograms)

## King James

**26** MOREOVER THOU shalt make the tabernacle *with* ten curtains *of* fine twined linen, and blue, and purple, and scarlet: *with* cherubims of cunning work shalt thou make them.

2 The length of one curtain *shall be* eight and twenty cubits, and the breadth of one curtain four cubits: and every one of the curtains shall have one measure.

3 The five curtains shall be coupled together one to another; and *other* five curtains *shall be* coupled one to another.

4 And thou shalt make loops of blue upon the edge of the one curtain from the selvedge in the coupling; and likewise shalt thou make in the uttermost edge of *another* curtain, in the coupling of the second.

5 Fifty loops shalt thou make in the one curtain, and fifty loops shalt thou make in the edge of the curtain that *is* in the coupling of the second; that the loops may take hold one of another.

6 And thou shalt make fifty taches of gold, and couple the curtains together with the taches: and it shall be one tabernacle.

7¶ And thou shalt make curtains *of* goats' *hair* to be a covering upon the tabernacle: eleven curtains shalt thou make.

8 The length of one curtain *shall be* thirty cubits, and the breadth of one curtain four cubits: and the eleven curtains *shall be all* of one measure.

9 And thou shalt couple five curtains by themselves, and six curtains by themselves, and shalt double the sixth curtain in the forefront of the tabernacle.

10 And thou shalt make fifty loops on the edge of the one curtain *that is* outmost in the coupling, and fifty loops in the edge of the curtain which coupleth the second.

11 And thou shalt make fifty taches of brass, and put the taches into the loops, and couple the tent together, that it may be one.

12 And the remnant that remaineth of the curtains of the tent, the half curtain that remaineth, shall hang over the backside of the tabernacle.

13 And a cubit on the one side, and a cubit on the other side of that which remaineth in the length of the curtains of the tent, it shall hang over the sides of the tabernacle on this side and on that side, to cover it.

14 And thou shalt make a covering for the tent *of* rams' skins dyed red, and a covering above *of* badgers' skins.

15¶ And thou shalt make boards for the tabernacle *of* shittim wood standing up.

16 Ten cubits *shall be* the length of a board, and a cubit and a half *shall be* the breadth of one board.

17 Two tenons *shall there be* in one board, set in order one against another: thus shalt thou make for all the boards of the tabernacle.

18 And thou shalt make the boards for the tabernacle, twenty boards on the south side southward.

19 And thou shalt make forty sockets of silver under the twenty boards; two sockets under one board for his two tenons, and two sockets under another board for his two tenons.

20 And for the second side of the tabernacle on the north side *there shall be* twenty boards:

21 And their forty sockets *of* silver; two sockets under one board, and two sockets under another board.

22 And for the sides of the tabernacle westward thou shalt make six boards.

23 And two boards shalt thou make for the corners of the tabernacle in the two sides.

24 And they shall be coupled together beneath, and they shall be coupled together above the head of it unto one ring: thus shall it be for them both; they shall be for the two corners.

## Amplified

**26** MOREOVER YOU shall make the tabernacle with ten curtains; of fine twined linen, and blue and purple and scarlet [stuff], with cherubim skillfully embroidered shall you make them.

2 The length of one curtain shall be twenty-eight cubits, and the breadth of one curtain four cubits; each of the curtains shall measure the same.

3 The five curtains shall be coupled to one another; and the other five curtains shall be coupled to one another.

4 And you shall make loops of blue on the edge of the last curtain in the first set; and likewise in the second set.

5 Fifty loops you shall make on the one curtain, and fifty loops on the edge of the last curtain that is in the second coupling *or* set; so that the loops on one correspond to the loops on the other.

6 And you shall make fifty clasps of gold, and fasten the curtains together with the clasps; then the tabernacle shall be one whole.

7 And make curtains of goats' hair to be a [second] covering over the tabernacle; eleven curtains shall you make.

8 One curtain shall be thirty cubits long, and four cubits wide; and the eleven curtains shall all measure the same.

9 You shall join together five curtains by themselves, and six curtains by themselves, and shall double over the sixth curtain in the front of the tabernacle [to make a closed door].

10 And make fifty loops on the edge of the outmost curtain in the one set, and fifty loops on the edge of the outmost curtain in the second set.

11 You shall make fifty clasps of bronze, and put the clasps into the loops, and couple the tent together, that it may be one whole.

12 The surplus that remains of the tent curtains, the half curtain that remains, shall hang over the back of the tabernacle.

13 And the cubit on the one side, and the cubit on the other side of what remains in the length of the curtains of the tent, shall hang over the sides of the tabernacle, on this side and that side, to cover it.

14 You shall make a [third] covering for the tent of rams' skins tanned red, and a [fourth] covering above that, of dolphin *or* porpoise skins.

15 And you shall make the upright frame for the tabernacle of boards of acacia wood, standing up.

16 Ten cubits shall be the length of a board, and a cubit and a half shall be the breadth of one board.

17 Make two tenons in each board for dovetailing *and* fitting together; so shall you do for all the tabernacle boards.

18 And make the boards for the tabernacle: twenty boards for the south side;

19 And you shall make forty silver sockets under the twenty boards; two sockets under each board for its two tenons.

20 And for the north side of the tabernacle, there shall be twenty boards,

21 And their forty silver sockets, two sockets under each board.

22 For the back or west side of the tabernacle you shall make six boards.

23 Make two boards for the corners of the tabernacle in the rear on both sides.

24 They shall be coupled down below, and coupled together on top with one ring. Thus shall it be for both of them; they shall form the two corners.

## New American Standard

*Curtains of Linen*

**26** "MOREOVER YOU shall make the tabernacle with ten curtains of fine twisted linen and [a]blue and purple and scarlet *material;* you shall make them with cherubim, the work of a skillful workman.

2"The length of each curtain shall be twenty-eight cubits, and the width of each curtain four cubits; all the curtains shall have the same measurements.

3"Five curtains shall be joined to one another; and *the other* five curtains *shall be* joined to one another.

4"And you shall make loops of blue on the edge of the outermost curtain in the *first* set, and likewise you shall make *them* on the edge of the curtain that is outermost in the second set.

5"You shall make fifty loops in the one curtain, and you shall make fifty loops on the edge of the curtain that is in the second set; the loops shall be opposite each other.

6"And you shall make fifty clasps of gold, and join the curtains to one another with the clasps, that the [b]tabernacle may be a unit.

*Curtains of Goats' Hair*

7¶ "Then you shall make curtains of goats' *hair* for a tent over the tabernacle; you shall make eleven curtains in all.

8"The length of each curtain *shall be* thirty cubits, and the width of each curtain four cubits; the eleven curtains shall have the same measurements.

9"And you shall join five curtains by themselves, and the *other* six curtains by themselves, and you shall double over the sixth curtain at the front of the tent.

10"And you shall make fifty loops on the edge of the curtain that is outermost in the *first* set, and fifty loops on the edge of the curtain *that is outermost in* the second set.

11"And you shall make fifty clasps of [c]bronze, and you shall put the clasps into the loops and join the tent together, that it may be a unit.

12"And the overlapping part that is left over in the curtains of the tent, the half curtain that is left over, shall lap over the back of the tabernacle.

13"And the cubit on one side and the cubit on the other, of what is left over in the length of the curtains of the tent, shall lap over the sides of the tabernacle on one side and on the other, to cover it.

14"And you shall make a covering for the tent of rams' skins dyed red, and a covering of porpoise skins above.

*Boards and Sockets*

15¶ "Then you shall make the boards for the tabernacle of acacia wood, standing upright.

16"Ten cubits *shall be* the length of each board, and one and a half cubits the width of each board.

17"There *shall be* two tenons for each board, fitted to one another; thus you shall do for all the boards of the tabernacle.

18"And you shall make the boards for the tabernacle: twenty boards for the south side.

19"And you shall make forty [d]sockets of silver under the twenty boards, two sockets under one board for its two tenons and two sockets under another board for its two tenons;

20and for the second side of the tabernacle, on the north side, twenty boards,

21and their forty sockets of silver; two sockets under one board and two sockets under another board.

22"And for the rear of the tabernacle, to the west, you shall make six boards.

23"And you shall make two boards for the corners of the tabernacle at the rear.

24"And they shall be double beneath, and together they shall be complete to its top to the first ring; thus it shall be with both of them: they shall form the two corners.

NAS [a] Or, *violet,* and so throughout this context [b] Or, *dwelling place,* and so throughout the ch. [c] Or, *copper* [d] Or, *bases,* and so throughout this context

## New International

*The Tabernacle*

**26** "MAKE THE tabernacle with ten curtains of finely twisted
linen and blue, purple and scarlet yarn, with cherubim
worked into them by a skilled craftsman. 2All the curtains are to
be the same size—twenty-eight cubits long and four cubits wide.[e]
3Join five of the curtains together, and do the same with the other
five. 4Make loops of blue material along the edge of the end curtain
in one set, and do the same with the end curtain in the other set.
5Make fifty loops on one curtain and fifty loops on the end curtain
of the other set, with the loops opposite each other. 6Then make
fifty gold clasps and use them to fasten the curtains together so
that the tabernacle is a unit.

7"Make curtains of goat hair for the tent over the tabernacle—
eleven altogether. 8All eleven curtains are to be the same size—
thirty cubits long and four cubits wide.[f] 9Join five of the curtains
together into one set and the other six into another set. Fold the
sixth curtain double at the front of the tent. 10Make fifty loops
along the edge of the end curtain in one set and also along the edge
of the end curtain in the other set. 11Then make fifty bronze clasps
and put them in the loops to fasten the tent together as a unit. 12As
for the additional length of the tent curtains, the half curtain that
is left over is to hang down at the rear of the tabernacle. 13The tent
curtains will be a cubit[g] longer on both sides; what is left will hang
over the sides of the tabernacle so as to cover it. 14Make for the tent
a covering of ram skins dyed red, and over that a covering of hides
of sea cows.[h]

15"Make upright frames of acacia wood for the tabernacle.
16Each frame is to be ten cubits long and a cubit and a half wide,[i]
17with two projections set parallel to each other. Make all the
frames of the tabernacle in this way. 18Make twenty frames for the
south side of the tabernacle 19and make forty silver bases to go
under them—two bases for each frame, one under each projection.
20For the other side, the north side of the tabernacle, make twenty
frames 21and forty silver bases—two under each frame. 22Make six
frames for the far end, that is, the west end of the tabernacle, 23and
make two frames for the corners at the far end. 24At these two
corners they must be double from the bottom all the way to the top,
and fitted into a single ring; both shall be like that. 25So there will

NIV [e] *2* That is, about 42 feet (about 12.5 meters) long and 6 feet (about 1.8 meters) wide [f] *8* That is, about 45 feet (about 13.5 meters) long and 6 feet (about 1.8 meters) wide [g] *13* That is, about 1 1/2 feet (about 0.5 meter) [h] *14* That is, dugongs [i] *16* That is, about 15 feet (about 4.5 meters) long and 2 1/4 feet (about 0.7 meter) wide

# King James

25And they shall be eight boards, and their sockets *of* silver, sixteen sockets; two sockets under one board, and two sockets under another board.

26¶ And thou shalt make bars *of* shittim wood; five for the boards of the one side of the tabernacle,

27And five bars for the boards of the other side of the tabernacle, and five bars for the boards of the side of the tabernacle, for the two sides westward.

28And the middle bar in the midst of the boards shall reach from end to end.

29And thou shalt overlay the boards with gold, and make their rings *of* gold *for* places for the bars: and thou shalt overlay the bars with gold.

30And thou shalt rear up the tabernacle according to the fashion thereof which was shown thee in the mount.

31¶ And thou shalt make a veil *of* blue, and purple, and scarlet, and fine twined linen of cunning work: with cherubims shall it be made:

32And thou shalt hang it upon four pillars of shittim *wood* overlaid with gold: their hooks *shall be of* gold, upon the four sockets of silver.

33¶ And thou shalt hang up the veil under the taches, that thou mayest bring in thither within the veil the ark of the testimony: and the veil shall divide unto you between the holy *place* and the most holy.

34And thou shalt put the mercy seat upon the ark of the testimony in the most holy *place.*

35And thou shalt set the table without the veil, and the candlestick over against the table on the side of the tabernacle toward the south: and thou shalt put the table on the north side.

36And thou shalt make an hanging for the door of the tent, *of* blue, and purple, and scarlet, and fine twined linen, wrought with needlework.

37And thou shalt make for the hanging five pillars *of* shittim *wood,* and overlay them with gold, *and* their hooks *shall be of* gold: and thou shalt cast five sockets of brass for them.

**27** AND THOU shalt make an altar *of* shittim wood, five cubits long, and five cubits broad; the altar shall be foursquare: and the height thereof *shall be* three cubits.

2And thou shalt make the horns of it upon the four corners thereof: his horns shall be of the same: and thou shalt overlay it with brass.

3And thou shalt make his pans to receive his ashes, and his shovels, and his basins, and his fleshhooks, and his firepans: all the vessels thereof thou shalt make *of* brass.

4And thou shalt make for it a grate of network *of* brass; and upon the net shalt thou make four brasen rings in the four corners thereof.

5And thou shalt put it under the compass of the altar beneath, that the net may be even to the midst of the altar.

6And thou shalt make staves for the altar, staves *of* shittim wood, and overlay them with brass.

7And the staves shall be put into the rings, and the staves shall be upon the two sides of the altar, to bear it.

8Hollow with boards shalt thou make it: as it was shown thee in the mount, so shall they make *it.*

9¶ And thou shalt make the court of the tabernacle: for the south side southward *there shall be* hangings for the court *of* fine twined linen of an hundred cubits long for one side:

10And the twenty pillars thereof and their twenty sockets *shall be of* brass; the hooks of the pillars and their fillets *shall be of* silver.

11And likewise for the north side in length *there shall be* hangings of an hundred *cubits* long, and his twenty pillars and their twenty sockets *of* brass; the hooks of the pillars and their fillets *of* silver.

# Amplified

25And that will be eight boards, and their sockets of silver, sixteen sockets; two sockets under each board.

26And you shall make bars of acacia wood; five for the boards of one side,

27And five bars for the boards of the other side of the tabernacle, and five bars for the boards of the rear end of the tabernacle, for the back wall to the west.

28And the middle bar halfway up the boards shall pass through from end to end.

29You shall overlay the boards with gold, and make their rings of gold to hold the bars, and overlay the bars with gold.

30You shall erect the tabernacle after the plan of it shown you on the mountain.

31And make a veil of blue, purple, and scarlet [stuff], and fine twined linen; skillfully worked, with cherubim on it.

32You shall hang it on four pillars of acacia wood overlaid with gold, with gold hooks, on four sockets of silver.

33And you shall hang the veil from the clasps, and bring the ark of the testimony into place within the veil; and the veil shall separate for you the holy place from the most holy place.

34And you shall put the mercy seat on the ark of the testimony in the most holy place.

35And you shall set the table [for the showbread] outside the veil [in the holy place] on the north side, and the lampstand opposite the table on the south side of the tabernacle.

36You shall make a hanging [to form a screen] for the door of the tent, of blue, purple, and scarlet stuff, and fine twined linen, embroidered. [Cp. John 10:9.]

37You shall make five pillars of acacia wood to support the hanging curtain, and overlay them with gold; their hooks shall be of gold, and you shall cast five [base] sockets of bronze for them.

**27** AND MAKE the altar of acacia wood, five cubits square, and three cubits high [within reach of all].

2Make horns for it on its four corners; they shall be of one piece with it, and you shall overlay it with bronze.

3You shall make pots to take away its ashes, and shovels, basins, forks, and firepans; make all its utensils of bronze.

4Also make for it a grate, a network of bronze; and on the net you shall make four bronze rings at its four corners.

5And you shall put it under the ledge of the altar, so that the net will extend halfway down the altar.

6And make poles for the altar, poles of acacia wood, overlaid with bronze.

7The poles shall be put through the rings on the two sides of the altar, with which to carry it. [Num. 4:14, 15.]

8You shall make [the altar] hollow with slabs *or* planks; as shown you on the mountain, so shall it be made.

9And you shall make the court of the tabernacle. On the south side the court shall have hangings of fine twined linen a hundred cubits long for one side;

10Their pillars shall be twenty and their sockets twenty, of bronze, but the hooks of the pillars and their joinings shall be of silver.

11Likewise for the north side hangings a hundred cubits long, and their twenty pillars and their twenty sockets of bronze, but the hooks of the pillars and their joinings shall be of silver.

## New American Standard

25"And there shall be eight boards with their sockets of silver,
sixteen sockets; two sockets under one board and two sockets
under another board.
26¶ "Then you shall make bars of acacia wood, five for the
boards of one side of the tabernacle,
27and five bars for the boards of the other side of the tabernacle,
and five bars for the boards of the side of the tabernacle for the rear
*side* to the west.
28"And the middle bar in the center of the boards shall pass
through from end to end.
29"And you shall overlay the boards with gold and make their
rings of gold *as* holders for the bars; and you shall overlay the bars
with gold.
30"Then you shall erect the tabernacle according to its plan
which you have been shown in the mountain.

*The Veil and Screen*

31¶ "And you shall make a veil of blue and purple and scarlet
*material* and fine twisted linen; it shall be made with cherubim, the
work of a skillful workman.
32"And you shall hang it on four pillars of acacia overlaid with
gold, their hooks *also being of* gold, on four sockets of silver.
33"And you shall hang up the veil under the clasps, and shall
bring in the ark of the testimony there within the veil; and the veil
shall serve for you as a partition between the holy place and the
holy of holies.
34"And you shall put the mercy seat on the ark of the testimony
in the holy of holies.
35"And you shall set the table outside the veil, and the lampstand opposite the table on the side of the tabernacle toward the
south; and you shall put the table on the north side.
36¶ "And you shall make a screen for the doorway of the tent
of blue and purple and scarlet *material* and fine twisted linen, the
work of a weaver.
37"And you shall make five pillars of acacia for the screen, and
overlay them with gold, their hooks *also being of* gold; and you shall
cast five sockets of bronze for them.

*The Bronze Altar*

27 "AND YOU shall make the altar of acacia wood, five
cubits long and five cubits wide; the altar shall be square,
and its height shall be three cubits.
2"And you shall make its horns on its four corners; its horns
shall be of one piece with it, and you shall overlay it with bronze.
3"And you shall make its pails for removing its ashes, and its
shovels and its basins and its forks and its firepans; you shall make
all its utensils of bronze.
4"And you shall make for it a grating of network of bronze, and
on the net you shall make four bronze rings at its four corners.
5"And you shall put it beneath, under the ledge of the altar,
that the net may reach halfway up the altar.
6"And you shall make poles for the altar, poles of acacia wood,
and overlay them with bronze.
7"And its poles shall be inserted into the rings, so that the
poles shall be on the two sides of the altar when it is carried.
8"You shall make it hollow with planks; as it was shown to you
in the mountain, so they shall make *it*.

*Court of the Tabernacle*

9¶ "And you shall make the court of the tabernacle. On the
south side *there shall be* hangings for the court of fine twisted linen
one hundred cubits long for one side;
10and its pillars *shall be* twenty, with their twenty sockets of
bronze; the hooks of the pillars and their bands *shall be* of silver.
11"And likewise for the north side in length *there shall be* hangings one hundred *cubits* long, and its twenty pillars with their
twenty sockets of bronze; the hooks of the pillars and their bands
*shall be* of silver.

## New International

be eight frames and sixteen silver bases—two under each frame.
26"Also make crossbars of acacia wood: five for the frames on
one side of the tabernacle, 27five for those on the other side, and
five for the frames on the west, at the far end of the tabernacle.
28The center crossbar is to extend from end to end at the middle
of the frames. 29Overlay the frames with gold and make gold rings
to hold the crossbars. Also overlay the crossbars with gold.
30"Set up the tabernacle according to the plan shown you on the
mountain.
31"Make a curtain of blue, purple and scarlet yarn and finely
twisted linen, with cherubim worked into it by a skilled craftsman.
32Hang it with gold hooks on four posts of acacia wood overlaid
with gold and standing on four silver bases. 33Hang the curtain
from the clasps and place the ark of the Testimony behind the
curtain. The curtain will separate the Holy Place from the Most
Holy Place. 34Put the atonement cover on the ark of the Testimony
in the Most Holy Place. 35Place the table outside the curtain on the
north side of the tabernacle and put the lampstand opposite it on
the south side.
36"For the entrance to the tent make a curtain of blue, purple
and scarlet yarn and finely twisted linen—the work of an embroiderer. 37Make gold hooks for this curtain and five posts of acacia
wood overlaid with gold. And cast five bronze bases for them.

*The Altar of Burnt Offering*

27 "BUILD AN altar of acacia wood, three cubits[a] high; it is
to be square, five cubits long and five cubits wide.[b] 2Make
a horn at each of the four corners, so that the horns and the altar
are of one piece, and overlay the altar with bronze. 3Make all its
utensils of bronze—its pots to remove the ashes, and its shovels,
sprinkling bowls, meat forks and firepans. 4Make a grating for it,
a bronze network, and make a bronze ring at each of the four
corners of the network. 5Put it under the ledge of the altar so that
it is halfway up the altar. 6Make poles of acacia wood for the altar
and overlay them with bronze. 7The poles are to be inserted into
the rings so they will be on two sides of the altar when it is carried.
8Make the altar hollow, out of boards. It is to be made just as you
were shown on the mountain.

*The Courtyard*

9"Make a courtyard for the tabernacle. The south side shall be
a hundred cubits[c] long and is to have curtains of finely twisted
linen, 10with twenty posts and twenty bronze bases and with silver
hooks and bands on the posts. 11The north side shall also be a
hundred cubits long and is to have curtains, with twenty posts and
twenty bronze bases and with silver hooks and bands on the posts.

**NIV** [a] *1* That is, about 4 1/2 feet (about 1.3 meters) [b] *1* That is, about 7 1/2 feet (about 2.3 meters) long and wide [c] *9* That is, about 150 feet (about 46 meters); also in verse 11

## King James

12¶ And *for* the breadth of the court on the west side *shall be* hangings of fifty cubits: their pillars ten, and their sockets ten.

13And the breadth of the court on the east side eastward *shall be* fifty cubits.

14The hangings of one side *of the gate shall be* fifteen cubits: their pillars three, and their sockets three.

15And on the other side *shall be* hangings fifteen *cubits:* their pillars three, and their sockets three.

16¶ And for the gate of the court *shall be* an hanging of twenty cubits, *of* blue, and purple, and scarlet, and fine twined linen, wrought with needlework: *and* their pillars *shall be* four, and their sockets four.

17All the pillars round about the court *shall be* filleted with silver; their hooks *shall be of* silver, and their sockets *of* brass.

18¶ The length of the court *shall be* an hundred cubits, and the breadth fifty every where, and the height five cubits *of* fine twined linen, and their sockets *of* brass.

19All the vessels of the tabernacle in all the service thereof, and all the pins thereof, and all the pins of the court, *shall be of* brass.

20¶ And thou shalt command the children of Israel, that they bring thee pure oil olive beaten for the light, to cause the lamp to burn always.

21In the tabernacle of the congregation without the veil, which *is* before the testimony, Aaron and his sons shall order it from evening to morning before the LORD: *it shall be* a statute for ever unto their generations on the behalf of the children of Israel.

**28** AND TAKE thou unto thee Aaron thy brother, and his sons with him, from among the children of Israel, that he may minister unto me in the priest's office, *even* Aaron, Nadab and Abihu, Eleazar and Ithamar, Aaron's sons.

2And thou shalt make holy garments for Aaron thy brother for glory and for beauty.

3And thou shalt speak unto all *that are* wisehearted, whom I have filled with the spirit of wisdom, that they may make Aaron's garments to consecrate him, that he may minister unto me in the priest's office.

4And these *are* the garments which they shall make; a breastplate, and an ephod, and a robe, and a broidered coat, a mitre, and a girdle: and they shall make holy garments for Aaron thy brother, and his sons, that he may minister unto me in the priest's office.

5And they shall take gold, and blue, and purple, and scarlet, and fine linen.

6¶ And they shall make the ephod *of* gold, *of* blue, and *of* purple, *of* scarlet, and fine twined linen, with cunning work.

7It shall have the two shoulderpieces thereof joined at the two edges thereof; and *so* it shall be joined together.

8And the curious girdle of the ephod, which *is* upon it, shall be of the same, according to the work thereof; *even of* gold, *of* blue, and purple, and scarlet, and fine twined linen.

9And thou shalt take two onyx stones, and grave on them the names of the children of Israel:

10Six of their names on one stone, and *the other* six names of the rest on the other stone, according to their birth.

11With the work of an engraver in stone, *like* the engravings of a signet, shalt thou engrave the two stones with the names of the children of Israel: thou shalt make them to be set in ouches of gold.

## Amplified

12And for the breadth of the court on the west side there shall be hangings of fifty cubits, with ten pillars and ten sockets.

13The breadth of the court to the front, the east side, shall be fifty cubits.

14The hangings for one side of the gate shall be fifteen cubits, with three pillars and three sockets.

15On the other side the hangings shall be fifteen cubits, with three pillars and three sockets.

16And for the gate of the court shall be a hanging [for a screen] twenty cubits long, of blue, purple, and scarlet stuff and fine twined linen, embroidered. It shall have four pillars and four sockets for them.

17All the pillars round about the court shall be joined together with silver rods; their hooks shall be of silver, and their sockets of bronze.

18The length of the court shall be a hundred cubits, and breadth fifty, and the height five cubits, [with hangings of] fine twined linen, and sockets of bronze.

19All the tabernacle's utensils *and* instruments used in all its service, and all its pegs and all the pegs for the court, shall be of bronze.

20You shall command the Israelites to provide you pure oil of crushed olives for the light, to cause it to burn continually [every night].

21In the tent of meeting [of God with His people], outside the veil which sets apart the testimony, Aaron and his sons shall keep it burning from evening to morning before the Lord. It shall be a statute to be observed on behalf of the Israelites throughout their generations.

**28** FROM AMONG the Israelites take your brother Aaron and his sons with him, that he may minister to Me in the priest's office, even Aaron, Nadab and Abihu, Eleazar and Ithamar, Aaron's sons.

2And you shall make for Aaron your brother sacred garments [appointed official dress set apart for special holy services] for honor and for beauty.

3Tell all who are expert, whom I have endowed with skill *and* good judgment, that they shall make Aaron's garments to sanctify him for My priesthood.

4They shall make these garments: a breastplate, an ephod [a distinctive vestment to which the breastplate was to be attached], a robe, long *and* sleeved tunic of checker work, a turban, and a sash *or* band. They shall make sacred garments for Aaron your brother and his sons to minister to Me in the priest's office.

5They shall receive [from the people] *and* use gold, and blue, purple, and scarlet [stuff], and fine linen.

6And they shall make the ephod of gold, of blue, purple, and scarlet stuff, and fine twined linen, skillfully woven *and* worked.

7It shall have two shoulder straps to join the two [back and front] edges, that it may be held together.

8The skillfully woven girding band which is on the ephod shall be made of the same, of gold, blue, purple, and scarlet stuff, and fine twined linen.

9And you shall take two onyx *or* beryl stones, and engrave on them the names of the twelve sons of Israel;

10Six of their names on one stone, and the six names of the rest on the other stone, arranged in order of their birth.

11With the work of a stone engraver, like the engravings of a signet, you shall engrave the two stones according to the names of the sons of Israel. You shall have them set in sockets *or* rosettes of gold.

## New American Standard

12"And *for* the width of the court on the west side *shall be*
hangings of fifty cubits *with* their ten pillars and their ten sockets.
13"And the width of the court on the east side *shall be* fifty
cubits.
14"The hangings for the *one* side *of the gate shall be* fifteen cubits
*with* their three pillars and their three sockets.
15"And for the other side *shall be* hangings of fifteen cubits *with*
their three pillars and their three sockets.
16"And for the gate of the court there *shall be* a screen of twenty
cubits, of blue and purple and scarlet *material* and fine twisted
linen, the work of a weaver, *with* their four pillars and their four
sockets.
17"All the pillars around the court shall be furnished with silver
bands *with* their hooks of silver and their sockets of bronze.
18"The length of the court *shall be* one hundred cubits, and the
width fifty throughout, and the height five cubits of fine twisted
linen, and their sockets of bronze.
19"All the utensils of the tabernacle *used* in all its service, and
all its pegs, and all the pegs of the court, *shall be* of bronze.
**20**¶ "And you shall charge the sons of Israel, that they bring you
clear oil of beaten olives for the light, to make a lamp burn continually.
21"In the tent of meeting, outside the veil which is before the
testimony, Aaron and his sons shall keep it in order from evening
to morning before the LORD; *it shall be* a perpetual statute throughout their generations for the sons of Israel.

*Garments of the Priests*

**28** "THEN BRING near to yourself Aaron your brother, and
his sons with him, from among the sons of Israel, to
minister as priest to Me—Aaron, Nadab and Abihu, Eleazar and
Ithamar, Aaron's sons.
2"And you shall make holy garments for Aaron your brother,
for glory and for beauty.
3"And you shall speak to all the skillful persons whom I have
endowed with the spirit of wisdom, that they make Aaron's garments to consecrate him, that he may minister as priest to Me.
4"And these are the garments which they shall make: a
[a]breastpiece and an ephod and a robe and a tunic of checkered
work, a turban and a sash, and they shall make holy garments for
Aaron your brother and his sons, that he may minister as priest
to Me.
5"And they shall take the gold and the blue and the purple and
the scarlet *material* and the fine linen.
6¶ "They shall also make the ephod of gold, of blue and purple
*and* scarlet *material* and fine twisted linen, the work of the skillful
workman.
7"It shall have two shoulder pieces joined to its two ends, that
it may be joined.
8"And the skillfully woven band, which is on it, shall be like
its workmanship, of the same material: of gold, of blue and purple
and scarlet *material* and fine twisted linen.
9"And you shall take two onyx stones and engrave on them the
names of the sons of Israel,
10six of their names on the one stone, and the names of the
remaining six on the other stone, according to their birth.
11"As a jeweler engraves a signet, you shall engrave the two
stones according to the names of the sons of Israel; you shall set
them in filigree *settings* of gold.

NAS [a] Or, *pouch*

## New International

12"The west end of the courtyard shall be fifty cubits[b] wide and
have curtains, with ten posts and ten bases. 13On the east end,
toward the sunrise, the courtyard shall also be fifty cubits wide.
14Curtains fifteen cubits[c] long are to be on one side of the entrance, with three posts and three bases, 15and curtains fifteen
cubits long are to be on the other side, with three posts and three
bases.
16"For the entrance to the courtyard, provide a curtain twenty
cubits[d] long, of blue, purple and scarlet yarn and finely twisted
linen—the work of an embroiderer—with four posts and four
bases. 17All the posts around the courtyard are to have silver bands
and hooks, and bronze bases. 18The courtyard shall be a hundred
cubits long and fifty cubits wide,[e] with curtains of finely twisted
linen five cubits[f] high, and with bronze bases. 19All the other
articles used in the service of the tabernacle, whatever their function, including all the tent pegs for it and those for the courtyard,
are to be of bronze.

*Oil for the Lampstand*

20"Command the Israelites to bring you clear oil of pressed
olives for the light so that the lamps may be kept burning. 21In the
Tent of Meeting, outside the curtain that is in front of the Testimony, Aaron and his sons are to keep the lamps burning before
the LORD from evening till morning. This is to be a lasting ordinance among the Israelites for the generations to come.

*The Priestly Garments*

**28** "HAVE AARON your brother brought to you from among
the Israelites, along with his sons Nadab and Abihu, Eleazar and Ithamar, so they may serve me as priests. 2Make sacred
garments for your brother Aaron, to give him dignity and honor.
3Tell all the skilled men to whom I have given wisdom in such
matters that they are to make garments for Aaron, for his consecration, so he may serve me as priest. 4These are the garments they
are to make: a breastpiece, an ephod, a robe, a woven tunic, a
turban and a sash. They are to make these sacred garments for
your brother Aaron and his sons, so they may serve me as priests.
5Have them use gold, and blue, purple and scarlet yarn, and fine
linen.

*The Ephod*

6"Make the ephod of gold, and of blue, purple and scarlet yarn,
and of finely twisted linen—the work of a skilled craftsman. 7It is
to have two shoulder pieces attached to two of its corners, so it can
be fastened. 8Its skillfully woven waistband is to be like it—of one
piece with the ephod and made with gold, and with blue, purple
and scarlet yarn, and with finely twisted linen.
9"Take two onyx stones and engrave on them the names of the
sons of Israel 10in the order of their birth—six names on one stone
and the remaining six on the other. 11Engrave the names of the
sons of Israel on the two stones the way a gem cutter engraves a
seal. Then mount the stones in gold filigree settings 12and fasten

NIV [b] *12* That is, about 75 feet (about 23 meters); also in verse 13 [c] *14* That is, about 22 1/2 feet (about 6.9 meters); also in verse 15 [d] *16* That is, about 30 feet (about 9 meters) [e] *18* That is, about 150 feet (about 46 meters) long and 75 feet (about 23 meters) wide [f] *18* That is, about 7 1/2 feet (about 2.3 meters)

## King James

12 And thou shalt put the two stones upon the shoulders of the ephod *for* stones of memorial unto the children of Israel: and Aaron shall bear their names before the LORD upon his two shoulders for a memorial.

13 ¶ And thou shalt make ouches *of* gold;

14 And two chains *of* pure gold at the ends; *of* wreathen work shalt thou make them, and fasten the wreathen chains to the ouches.

15 ¶ And thou shalt make the breastplate of judgment with cunning work; after the work of the ephod thou shalt make it; *of* gold, *of* blue, and *of* purple, and *of* scarlet, and *of* fine twined linen, shalt thou make it.

16 Foursquare it shall be *being* doubled; a span *shall be* the length thereof, and a span *shall be* the breadth thereof.

17 And thou shalt set in it settings of stones, *even* four rows of stones: *the first* row *shall be* a sardius, a topaz, and a carbuncle: *this shall be* the first row.

18 And the second row *shall be* an emerald, a sapphire, and a diamond.

19 And the third row a ligure, an agate, and an amethyst.

20 And the fourth row a beryl, and an onyx, and a jasper: they shall be set in gold in their inclosings.

21 And the stones shall be with the names of the children of Israel, twelve, according to their names, *like* the engravings of a signet; every one with his name shall they be according to the twelve tribes.

22 ¶ And thou shalt make upon the breastplate chains at the ends *of* wreathen work *of* pure gold.

23 And thou shalt make upon the breastplate two rings of gold, and shalt put the two rings on the two ends of the breastplate.

24 And thou shalt put the two wreathen *chains* of gold in the two rings *which are* on the ends of the breastplate.

25 And *the other* two ends of the two wreathen *chains* thou shalt fasten in the two ouches, and put *them* on the shoulderpieces of the ephod before it.

26 ¶ And thou shalt make two rings of gold, and thou shalt put them upon the two ends of the breastplate in the border thereof, which *is* in the side of the ephod inward.

27 And two *other* rings of gold thou shalt make, and shalt put them on the two sides of the ephod underneath, toward the forepart thereof, over against the *other* coupling thereof, above the curious girdle of the ephod.

28 And they shall bind the breastplate by the rings thereof unto the rings of the ephod with a lace of blue, that *it* may be above the curious girdle of the ephod, and that the breastplate be not loosed from the ephod.

29 And Aaron shall bear the names of the children of Israel in the breastplate of judgment upon his heart, when he goeth in unto the holy *place*, for a memorial before the LORD continually.

30 ¶ And thou shalt put in the breastplate of judgment the Urim and the Thummim; and they shall be upon Aaron's heart, when he goeth in before the LORD: and Aaron shall bear the judgment of the children of Israel upon his heart before the LORD continually.

31 ¶ And thou shalt make the robe of the ephod all *of* blue.

32 And there shall be an hole in the top of it, in the midst thereof: it shall have a binding of woven work round about the hole of it, as it were the hole of an habergeon, that it be not rent.

33 ¶ And *beneath* upon the hem of it thou shalt make pomegranates *of* blue, and *of* purple, and *of* scarlet, round about the hem thereof; and bells of gold between them round about:

34 A golden bell and a pomegranate, a golden bell and a pomegranate, upon the hem of the robe round about.

35 And it shall be upon Aaron to minister: and his sound shall be heard when he goeth in unto the holy *place* before the LORD, and when he cometh out, that he die not.

36 ¶ And thou shalt make a plate *of* pure gold, and grave upon it, *like* the engravings of a signet, HOLINESS TO THE LORD.

37 And thou shalt put it on a blue lace, that it may be upon the mitre; upon the forefront of the mitre it shall be.

## Amplified

12 And you shall put the two stones upon the [two] shoulder straps of the ephod [of the high priest] for memorial stones to Israel; and Aaron shall bear their names upon his two shoulders for a memorial before the Lord.

13 And you shall make sockets *or* rosettes of gold, for settings,

14 And two chains of pure gold, like cords shall you twist them, and fasten the corded chains to the settings.

15 You shall make a breastplate of judgment, in skilled work; like the workmanship of the ephod shall you make it, of gold, blue, purple, and scarlet stuff, and of fine twined linen.

16 The breastplate shall be square *and* doubled; a span [nine inches] shall be its length, and a span shall be its breadth.

17 You shall set in it four rows of stones: a sardius, a topaz, and a carbuncle shall be the first row;

18 The second row an emerald, a sapphire, and a diamond [so called at that time];

19 The third row a jacinth, an agate, and an amethyst;

20 And the fourth row a beryl, an onyx, and a jasper; they shall be set in gold filigree.

21 And the stones shall be twelve, according to the names of the sons of Israel, like the engravings of a signet, each with its name, for the twelve tribes.

22 You shall make for the breastplate chains of pure gold twisted like cords.

23 You shall make on the breastplate two rings of gold, and put [them] on the two edges of the breastplate.

24 And you shall put the two twisted, cordlike chains of gold in the two rings which are on the edges of the breastplate.

25 The other two ends of the two twisted, cordlike chains you shall fasten in the two sockets *or* rosettes in front, putting them on the shoulder straps of the ephod;

26 And make two rings of gold, and put them at the two ends of the breastplate on its inside edge next to the ephod.

27 Two gold rings you shall make, and attach them to the lower part of the two shoulder pieces of the ephod in front, close by where they join, above the skillfully woven girdle *or* band of the ephod.

28 And they shall bind the breastplate by its rings to the rings of the ephod with a lace of blue, that it may be above the skillfully woven girding band of the ephod, and that the breastplate may not become loose from the ephod.

29 So Aaron shall bear the names of the sons of Israel in the breastplate of judgment upon his heart when he goes into the holy place, to bring them in continual remembrance before the Lord.

30 In the breastplate of judgment you shall put the Urim and the Thummim [unspecified articles used when the high priest asked God's counsel for all Israel]; they shall be upon Aaron's heart when he goes in before the Lord, and Aaron shall bear the judgment (rights, judicial decisions) of the Israelites upon his heart before the Lord continually.

31 Make the robe [to be worn beneath] the ephod all of blue.

32 There shall be a hole in the center of it [to slip over the head], with a binding of woven work around the hole, like the opening in a coat of mail *or* a garment, that it may not fray *or* tear.

33 And you shall make pomegranates of blue, purple, and scarlet, around about its skirts, with gold bells between them;

34 A gold bell and a pomegranate, a gold bell and a pomegranate, round about on the skirts of the robe.

35 Aaron shall wear the robe when he ministers, and its sound shall be heard when he goes [alone] into the holy of holies before the Lord, and when he comes out, lest he die there.

36 And you shall make a plate of pure gold, and engrave on it, like the engravings of a signet, HOLINESS TO THE LORD.

37 You shall fasten it on the front of the turban with a blue cord.

## New American Standard

12"And you shall put the two stones on the shoulder pieces of
the ephod, *as* stones of memorial for the sons of Israel, and Aaron
shall bear their names before the LORD on his two shoulders for a
memorial.
13"And you shall make filigree *settings* of gold,
14and two chains of pure gold; you shall make them of twisted
cordage work, and you shall put the corded chains on the filigree
*settings*.
15¶ "And you shall make a breastpiece of judgment, the work
of a skillful workman; like the work of the ephod you shall make
it: of gold, of blue and purple and scarlet *material* and fine twisted
linen you shall make it.
16"It shall be square *and* folded double, a span in length and a
span in width.
17"And you shall mount on it four rows of stones; the first row
*shall be* a row of ruby, topaz and emerald;
18and the second row a turquoise, a sapphire and a diamond;
19and the third row a jacinth, an agate and an amethyst;
20and the fourth row a beryl and an onyx and a jasper; they shall
be set in gold filigree.
21"And the stones shall be according to the names of the sons
of Israel: twelve, according to their names; they shall be *like* the
engravings of a seal, each according to his name for the twelve
tribes.
22"And you shall make on the breastpiece chains of twisted
cordage work in pure gold.
23"And you shall make on the breastpiece two rings of gold,
and shall put the two rings on the two ends of the breastpiece.
24"And you shall put the two cords of gold on the two rings at
the ends of the breastpiece.
25"And you shall put the *other* two ends of the two cords on the
two filigree *settings*, and put them on the shoulder pieces of the
ephod, at the front of it.
26"And you shall make two rings of gold and shall place them
on the two ends of the breastpiece, on the edge of it, which is
toward the inner side of the ephod.
27"And you shall make two rings of gold and put them on the
bottom of the two shoulder pieces of the ephod, on the front of it
close to the place where it is joined, above the skillfully woven
band of the ephod.
28"And they shall bind the breastpiece by its rings to the rings
of the ephod with a blue cord, that it may be on the skillfully woven
band of the ephod, and that the breastpiece may not come loose
from the ephod.
29"And Aaron shall carry the names of the sons of Israel in the
breastpiece of judgment over his heart when he enters the holy
place, for a memorial before the LORD continually.
30"And you shall put in the breastpiece of judgment the [a]Urim
and the Thummim, and they shall be over Aaron's heart when he
goes in before the LORD; and Aaron shall carry the judgment of the
sons of Israel over his heart before the LORD continually.
31¶ "And you shall make the robe of the ephod all of blue.
32"And there shall be an opening at its top in the middle of it;
around its opening there shall be a binding of woven work, as *it
were* the opening of a coat of mail, that it may not be torn.
33"And you shall make on its hem pomegranates of blue and
purple and scarlet *material*, all around on its hem, and bells of gold
between them all around:
34a golden bell and a pomegranate, a golden bell and a pomegranate, all around on the hem of the robe.
35"And it shall be on Aaron when he ministers; and its tinkling
may be heard when he enters and leaves the holy place before the
LORD, that he may not die.
36¶ "You shall also make a plate of pure gold and shall engrave
on it, like the engravings of a seal, 'Holy to the LORD.'
37"And you shall fasten it on a blue cord, and it shall be on the
turban; it shall be at the front of the turban.

**NAS** [a] I.e., lights and perfections

## New International

them on the shoulder pieces of the ephod as memorial stones for
the sons of Israel. Aaron is to bear the names on his shoulders as
a memorial before the LORD. 13Make gold filigree settings 14and
two braided chains of pure gold, like a rope, and attach the chains
to the settings.

*The Breastpiece*

15"Fashion a breastpiece for making decisions—the work of a
skilled craftsman. Make it like the ephod: of gold, and of blue,
purple and scarlet yarn, and of finely twisted linen. 16It is to be
square—a span[b] long and a span wide—and folded double.
17Then mount four rows of precious stones on it. In the first row
there shall be a ruby, a topaz and a beryl; 18in the second row a
turquoise, a sapphire[c] and an emerald; 19in the third row a jacinth,
an agate and an amethyst; 20in the fourth row a chrysolite, an onyx
and a jasper.[d] Mount them in gold filigree settings. 21There are to
be twelve stones, one for each of the names of the sons of Israel,
each engraved like a seal with the name of one of the twelve tribes.
22"For the breastpiece make braided chains of pure gold, like a
rope. 23Make two gold rings for it and fasten them to two corners
of the breastpiece. 24Fasten the two gold chains to the rings at the
corners of the breastpiece, 25and the other ends of the chains to the
two settings, attaching them to the shoulder pieces of the ephod
at the front. 26Make two gold rings and attach them to the other
two corners of the breastpiece on the inside edge next to the
ephod. 27Make two more gold rings and attach them to the bottom
of the shoulder pieces on the front of the ephod, close to the seam
just above the waistband of the ephod. 28The rings of the breastpiece are to be tied to the rings of the ephod with blue cord,
connecting it to the waistband, so that the breastpiece will not
swing out from the ephod.
29"Whenever Aaron enters the Holy Place, he will bear the
names of the sons of Israel over his heart on the breastpiece of
decision as a continuing memorial before the LORD. 30Also put the
Urim and the Thummim in the breastpiece, so they may be over
Aaron's heart whenever he enters the presence of the LORD. Thus
Aaron will always bear the means of making decisions for the
Israelites over his heart before the LORD.

*Other Priestly Garments*

31"Make the robe of the ephod entirely of blue cloth, 32with an
opening for the head in its center. There shall be a woven edge like
a collar[e] around this opening, so that it will not tear. 33Make
pomegranates of blue, purple and scarlet yarn around the hem of
the robe, with gold bells between them. 34The gold bells and the
pomegranates are to alternate around the hem of the robe. 35Aaron
must wear it when he ministers. The sound of the bells will be
heard when he enters the Holy Place before the LORD and when
he comes out, so that he will not die.
36"Make a plate of pure gold and engrave on it as on a seal: HOLY
TO THE LORD. 37Fasten a blue cord to it to attach it to the turban;
it is to be on the front of the turban. 38It will be on Aaron's

**NIV** [b] *16* That is, about 9 inches (about 22 centimeters) [c] *18* Or *lapis lazuli*
[d] *20* The precise identification of some of these precious stones is uncertain.
[e] *32* The meaning of the Hebrew for this word is uncertain.

## King James

38And it shall be upon Aaron's forehead, that Aaron may bear the iniquity of the holy things, which the children of Israel shall hallow in all their holy gifts; and it shall be always upon his forehead, that they may be accepted before the LORD.

39¶ And thou shalt embroider the coat of fine linen, and thou shalt make the mitre *of* fine linen, and thou shalt make the girdle *of* needlework.

40¶ And for Aaron's sons thou shalt make coats, and thou shalt make for them girdles, and bonnets shalt thou make for them, for glory and for beauty.

41And thou shalt put them upon Aaron thy brother, and his sons with him; and shalt anoint them, and consecrate them, and sanctify them, that they may minister unto me in the priest's office.

42And thou shalt make them linen breeches to cover their nakedness; from the loins even unto the thighs they shall reach:

43And they shall be upon Aaron, and upon his sons, when they come in unto the tabernacle of the congregation, or when they come near unto the altar to minister in the holy *place;* that they bear not iniquity, and die: *it shall be* a statute for ever unto him and his seed after him.

**29** AND THIS *is* the thing that thou shalt do unto them to hallow them, to minister unto me in the priest's office: Take one young bullock, and two rams without blemish,

2And unleavened bread, and cakes unleavened tempered with oil, and wafers unleavened anointed with oil: *of* wheaten flour shalt thou make them.

3And thou shalt put them into one basket, and bring them in the basket, with the bullock and the two rams.

4And Aaron and his sons thou shalt bring unto the door of the tabernacle of the congregation, and shalt wash them with water.

5And thou shalt take the garments, and put upon Aaron the coat, and the robe of the ephod, and the ephod, and the breastplate, and gird him with the curious girdle of the ephod:

6And thou shalt put the mitre upon his head, and put the holy crown upon the mitre.

7Then shalt thou take the anointing oil, and pour *it* upon his head, and anoint him.

8And thou shalt bring his sons, and put coats upon them.

9And thou shalt gird them with girdles, Aaron and his sons, and put the bonnets on them: and the priest's office shall be theirs for a perpetual statute: and thou shalt consecrate Aaron and his sons.

10And thou shalt cause a bullock to be brought before the tabernacle of the congregation: and Aaron and his sons shall put their hands upon the head of the bullock.

11And thou shalt kill the bullock before the LORD, *by* the door of the tabernacle of the congregation.

12And thou shalt take of the blood of the bullock, and put *it* upon the horns of the altar with thy finger, and pour all the blood beside the bottom of the altar.

13And thou shalt take all the fat that covereth the inwards, and the caul *that is* above the liver, and the two kidneys, and the fat that *is* upon them, and burn *them* upon the altar.

14But the flesh of the bullock, and his skin, and his dung, shalt thou burn with fire without the camp: it *is* a sin offering.

15¶ Thou shalt also take one ram; and Aaron and his sons shall put their hands upon the head of the ram.

16And thou shalt slay the ram, and thou shalt take his blood, and sprinkle *it* round about upon the altar.

17And thou shalt cut the ram in pieces, and wash the inwards of him, and his legs, and put *them* unto his pieces, and unto his head.

18And thou shalt burn the whole ram upon the altar: it *is* a burnt offering unto the LORD: it *is* a sweet savour, an offering made by fire unto the LORD.

## Amplified

38It shall be upon Aaron's forehead, that Aaron may take upon himself *and* bear [any] iniquity [connected with] the holy things which the Israelites shall give *and* dedicate; and it shall always be upon his forehead, that they may be accepted before the Lord [in the priest's person]. [Heb. 8:1, 2; Luke 24:44.]

39And you shall weave the long *and* sleeved tunic in checker work of fine linen *or* silk, and make a turban of fine linen *or* silk, and you shall make a girdle, the work of the embroiderer.

40For Aaron's sons you shall make long *and* sleeved tunics, and belts *or* sashes, and caps, for glory *and* honor and beauty.

41And you shall put them on Aaron your brother and his sons with him, and shall anoint them and ordain and sanctify them (setting them apart for God) that they may serve Me as priests.

42You shall make for them (white) linen trunks to cover their naked flesh, reaching from the waist to the thighs.

43And they shall be on Aaron and his sons when they go into the tent of meeting, or when they come near to the altar to minister in the holy place, lest they bring iniquity upon themselves and die; it shall be a statute for ever to Aaron and to his descendants after him.

**29** THIS IS what you shall do to consecrate—set them apart—that they may serve Me as priests. Take one young bull and two rams, all without blemish,

2And unleavened bread, and unleavened cakes mixed with oil, and unleavened wafers spread with oil; of fine flour shall you make them.

3You shall put them in one basket and bring them in [it], and bring also the bull and the two rams;

4And bring Aaron and his sons to the door of the tent of meeting [out where the laver is] and wash them with water.

5Then take the garments, and put on Aaron the long *and* sleeved tunic and the robe of the ephod, and the ephod, and the breastplate, and gird him with the skillfully woven girding band of the ephod.

6And you shall put the turban *or* mitre upon his head, and put the holy crown upon the turban.

7Then take the anointing oil, and pour it on his head and anoint him.

8And bring his sons, and put long *and* sleeved tunics on them.

9And you shall gird them with sashes *or* belts, Aaron and his sons, and bind caps on them; and the priest's office shall be theirs by a perpetual statute. Thus you shall ordain *and* consecrate Aaron and his sons.

10Then bring the bull before the tent of meeting, and Aaron and his sons shall lay their hands upon its head.

11And you shall kill the bull before the Lord, by the door of the tent of meeting.

12And you shall take of the blood of the bull and put it on the horns of the altar with your finger, and pour out all the blood at the base of the altar.

13And take all the fat that covers the entrails, and the appendage that is on the liver, and the two kidneys, and the fat that is on them, and burn them on the altar.

14But the flesh of the bull, its hide, and the contents of its entrails you shall burn with fire outside the camp; it is a sin offering. [Heb. 13:11-13.]

15You shall also take one of the rams, and Aaron and his sons shall lay their hands upon the head of the ram.

16And you shall kill the ram, and you shall take its blood and throw it against the altar round about.

17And you shall cut the ram in pieces, and wash its entrails and legs, and put them with its pieces and its head,

18And you shall burn the whole ram upon the altar. It is a burnt offering to the Lord; it is a sweet *and* satisfying fragrance, an offering made by fire to the Lord.

## New American Standard

38"And it shall be on Aaron's forehead, and Aaron shall take
away the iniquity of the holy things which the sons of Israel
consecrate, with regard to all their holy gifts; and it shall always
be on his forehead, that they may be accepted before the LORD.
39"And you shall weave the tunic of checkered work of fine
linen, and shall make a turban of fine linen, and you shall make
a sash, the work of a weaver.
40¶ "And for Aaron's sons you shall make tunics; you shall also
make sashes for them, and you shall make caps for them, for glory
and for beauty.
41"And you shall put them on Aaron your brother and on his
sons with him; and you shall anoint them and ordain them and
consecrate them, that they may serve Me as priests.
42"And you shall make for them linen breeches to cover *their*
bare flesh; they shall reach from the loins even to the thighs.
43"And they shall be on Aaron and on his sons when they enter
the tent of meeting, or when they approach the altar to minister
in the holy place, so that they do not incur guilt and die. It *shall
be* a statute forever to him and to his descendants after him.

*Consecration of the Priests*

**29** "NOW THIS is what you shall do to them to consecrate
them to minister as priests to Me: take one young bull and
two rams without blemish,
2and unleavened bread and unleavened cakes mixed with oil,
and unleavened wafers spread with oil; you shall make them of
fine wheat flour.
3"And you shall put them in one basket, and present them in
the basket along with the bull and the two rams.
4"Then you shall bring Aaron and his sons to the doorway of
the tent of meeting, and wash them with water.
5"And you shall take the garments, and put on Aaron the tunic
and the robe of the ephod and the ephod and the breastpiece, and
gird him with the skillfully woven band of the ephod;
6and you shall set the turban on his head, and put the holy
crown on the turban.
7"Then you shall take the anointing oil, and pour it on his head
and anoint him.
8"And you shall bring his sons and put tunics on them.
9"And you shall gird them with sashes, Aaron and his sons,
and bind caps on them, and they shall have the priesthood by a
perpetual statute. So you shall ordain Aaron and his sons.

*The Sacrifices*

10¶ "Then you shall bring the bull before the tent of meeting,
and Aaron and his sons shall lay their hands on the head of the
bull.
11"And you shall slaughter the bull before the LORD at the
doorway of the tent of meeting.
12"And you shall take some of the blood of the bull and put *it*
on the horns of the altar with your finger; and you shall pour out
all the blood at the base of the altar.
13"And you shall take all the fat that covers the entrails and the
lobe of the liver, and the two kidneys and the fat that is on them,
and offer them up in smoke on the altar.
14"But the flesh of the bull and its hide and its refuse, you shall
burn with fire outside the camp; it is a sin offering.
15¶ "You shall also take the one ram, and Aaron and his sons
shall lay their hands on the head of the ram;
16and you shall slaughter the ram and shall take its blood and
sprinkle it around on the altar.
17"Then you shall cut the ram into its pieces, and wash its
entrails and its legs, and put *them* with its pieces and its head.
18"And you shall offer up in smoke the whole ram on the altar;
it is a burnt offering to the LORD: it is a soothing aroma, an offering
by fire to the LORD.

## New International

forehead, and he will bear the guilt involved in the sacred gifts the
Israelites consecrate, whatever their gifts may be. It will be on
Aaron's forehead continually so that they will be acceptable to the
LORD.
39"Weave the tunic of fine linen and make the turban of fine
linen. The sash is to be the work of an embroiderer. 40Make tunics,
sashes and headbands for Aaron's sons, to give them dignity and
honor. 41After you put these clothes on your brother Aaron and
his sons, anoint and ordain them. Consecrate them so they may
serve me as priests.
42"Make linen undergarments as a covering for the body,
reaching from the waist to the thigh. 43Aaron and his sons must
wear them whenever they enter the Tent of Meeting or approach
the altar to minister in the Holy Place, so that they will not incur
guilt and die.

"This is to be a lasting ordinance for Aaron and his descendants.

*Consecration of the Priests*

**29** "THIS IS what you are to do to consecrate them, so they
may serve me as priests: Take a young bull and two rams
without defect. 2And from fine wheat flour, without yeast, make
bread, and cakes mixed with oil, and wafers spread with oil. 3Put
them in a basket and present them in it—along with the bull and
the two rams. 4Then bring Aaron and his sons to the entrance to
the Tent of Meeting and wash them with water. 5Take the garments and dress Aaron with the tunic, the robe of the ephod, the
ephod itself and the breastpiece. Fasten the ephod on him by its
skillfully woven waistband. 6Put the turban on his head and attach
the sacred diadem to the turban. 7Take the anointing oil and anoint
him by pouring it on his head. 8Bring his sons and dress them in
tunics 9and put headbands on them. Then tie sashes on Aaron and
his sons.[a] The priesthood is theirs by a lasting ordinance. In this
way you shall ordain Aaron and his sons.
10"Bring the bull to the front of the Tent of Meeting, and Aaron
and his sons shall lay their hands on its head. 11Slaughter it in the
LORD's presence at the entrance to the Tent of Meeting. 12Take
some of the bull's blood and put it on the horns of the altar with
your finger, and pour out the rest of it at the base of the altar.
13Then take all the fat around the inner parts, the covering of the
liver, and both kidneys with the fat around them, and burn them
on the altar. 14But burn the bull's flesh and its hide and its offal
outside the camp. It is a sin offering.
15"Take one of the rams, and Aaron and his sons shall lay their
hands on its head. 16Slaughter it and take the blood and sprinkle
it against the altar on all sides. 17Cut the ram into pieces and wash
the inner parts and the legs, putting them with the head and the
other pieces. 18Then burn the entire ram on the altar. It is a burnt
offering to the LORD, a pleasing aroma, an offering made to the
LORD by fire.

NIV [a] 9 Hebrew; Septuagint *on them*

## King James

19¶ And thou shalt take the other ram; and Aaron and his sons
shall put their hands upon the head of the ram.
20Then shalt thou kill the ram, and take of his blood, and put
*it* upon the tip of the right ear of Aaron, and upon the tip of the
right ear of his sons, and upon the thumb of their right hand, and
upon the great toe of their right foot, and sprinkle the blood upon
the altar round about.
21And thou shalt take of the blood that *is* upon the altar, and
of the anointing oil, and sprinkle *it* upon Aaron, and upon his
garments, and upon his sons, and upon the garments of his sons
with him: and he shall be hallowed, and his garments, and his
sons, and his sons' garments with him.
22Also thou shalt take of the ram the fat and the rump, and the
fat that covereth the inwards, and the caul *above* the liver, and the
two kidneys, and the fat that *is* upon them, and the right shoulder;
for it *is* a ram of consecration:
23And one loaf of bread, and one cake of oiled bread, and one
wafer out of the basket of the unleavened bread that *is* before the
LORD:
24And thou shalt put all in the hands of Aaron, and in the hands
of his sons; and shalt wave them *for* a wave offering before the
LORD.
25And thou shalt receive them of their hands, and burn *them*
upon the altar for a burnt offering, for a sweet savour before the
LORD: it *is* an offering made by fire unto the LORD.
26And thou shalt take the breast of the ram of Aaron's consecration, and wave it *for* a wave offering before the LORD: and it shall
be thy part.
27And thou shalt sanctify the breast of the wave offering, and
the shoulder of the heave offering, which is waved, and which is
heaved up, of the ram of the consecration, *even* of *that* which *is* for
Aaron, and of *that* which is for his sons:
28And it shall be Aaron's and his sons' by a statute for ever from
the children of Israel: for it *is* an heave offering: and it shall be an
heave offering from the children of Israel of the sacrifice of their
peace offerings, *even* their heave offering unto the LORD.
29¶ And the holy garments of Aaron shall be his sons' after him,
to be anointed therein, and to be consecrated in them.
30 *And* that son that is priest in his stead shall put them on seven
days, when he cometh into the tabernacle of the congregation to
minister in the holy *place*.
31¶ And thou shalt take the ram of the consecration, and seethe
his flesh in the holy place.
32And Aaron and his sons shall eat the flesh of the ram, and the
bread that *is* in the basket, *by* the door of the tabernacle of the
congregation.
33And they shall eat those things wherewith the atonement was
made, to consecrate *and* to sanctify them: but a stranger shall not
eat *thereof*, because they *are* holy.
34And if aught of the flesh of the consecrations, or of the bread,
remain unto the morning, then thou shalt burn the remainder with
fire: it shall not be eaten, because it *is* holy.
35And thus shalt thou do unto Aaron, and to his sons, according to all *things* which I have commanded thee: seven days shalt
thou consecrate them.
36And thou shalt offer every day a bullock *for* a sin offering for
atonement: and thou shalt cleanse the altar, when thou hast made
an atonement for it, and thou shalt anoint it, to sanctify it.
37Seven days thou shalt make an atonement for the altar, and
sanctify it; and it shall be an altar most holy: whatsoever toucheth
the altar shall be holy.
38¶ Now this *is that* which thou shalt offer upon the altar; two
lambs of the first year day by day continually.
39The one lamb thou shalt offer in the morning; and the other
lamb thou shalt offer at even:
40And with the one lamb a tenth deal of flour mingled with the
fourth part of an hin of beaten oil; and the fourth part of an hin
of wine *for* a drink offering.

## Amplified

19And you shall take the other ram, and Aaron and his sons
shall lay their hands upon the head of the ram;
20Then you shall kill the ram, and take part of its blood and put
it on the tip of the right ears of Aaron and his sons and on the
thumb of their right hands and on the great toe of their right feet,
and dash the rest of the blood against the altar round about.
21Then you shall take part of the blood that is on the altar, and
of the anointing oil, and sprinkle it upon Aaron and his garments,
and on his sons and their garments; and he and his garments and
his sons and their garments shall be sanctified *and* holy.
22Also you shall take the fat of the ram, the fat tail, the fat that
covers the entrails, the appendage on the liver, the two kidneys
with the fat that is on them, and the right thigh; for it is a ram of
consecration *and* ordination.
23Take also one loaf of bread, and one cake of oiled bread, and
one wafer, out of the basket of the unleavened bread that is before
the Lord.
24And put all these in the hands of Aaron and his sons, and they
shall wave them for a wave offering before the Lord.
25Then you shall take them from their hands, add them to the
burnt offering and burn them on the altar for a sweet *and* satisfying
fragrance before the Lord; it is an offering made by fire to the Lord.
26And take the breast of the ram of Aaron's consecration *and*
ordination and wave it for a wave offering before the Lord; and it
shall be your portion [Moses].
27And you shall sanctify (set apart for God) the waved breast
of the ram used in the ordination and the waved thigh of the
priests' portion, since it is for Aaron and his sons.
28It shall be for Aaron and his sons as their due portion from
the Israelites perpetually, an offering from the Israelites of their
peace *and* thanksgiving sacrifices, their offering to the Lord.
29The holy garments of Aaron shall pass to his descendants who
succeed him, to be anointed in them and to be consecrated *and*
ordained in them.
30And that son who is [high] priest in his stead shall put them
on [each day for] seven days, when he comes into the tent of
meeting to minister in the holy place.
31You shall take the ram of the consecration *and* ordination and
boil its flesh in a holy *and* set apart place.
32Aaron and his sons shall eat the flesh of the ram and the bread
in the basket, at the door of the tent of meeting.
33They shall eat those things with which atonement was made,
to ordain and consecrate them; but a stranger [layman] shall not
eat of them because they are holy—set apart to the worship of God.
34And if any of the flesh or bread for the ordination remain until
morning, you shall burn it with fire; it shall not be eaten, because
it is holy—set apart to the worship of God.
35Thus shall you do to Aaron and to his sons, according to all
I have commanded you; during seven days shall you ordain them.
36You shall offer every day a bull as a sin offering for atonement.
And you shall cleanse the altar by making atonement for it, and
anoint it to consecrate it.
37Seven days you shall make atonement for the altar, and sanctify—set it apart for God; and the altar shall be most holy; whoever
*or* whatever touches the altar must be holy—set apart for God's
service.
38Now this is what you shall offer on the altar: two lambs a year
old shall be offered day by day continually.
39One lamb you shall offer in the morning, and the other lamb
in the evening;
40And with the one lamb a tenth measure of fine flour mixed
with the fourth of a hin of beaten oil, and the fourth of a hin of
wine for a drink offering [to be poured out].

## New American Standard

19¶ "Then you shall take the other ram, and Aaron and his sons
shall lay their hands on the head of the ram.
20"And you shall slaughter the ram, and take some of its blood
and put *it* on the lobe of Aaron's right ear and on the lobes of his
sons' right ears and on the thumbs of their right hands and on the
big toes of their right feet, and sprinkle the *rest of the* blood around
on the altar.
21"Then you shall take some of the blood that is on the altar and
some of the anointing oil, and sprinkle *it* on Aaron and on his
garments, and on his sons and on his sons' garments with him; so
he and his garments shall be consecrated, as well as his sons and
his sons' garments with him.
22"You shall also take the fat from the ram and the fat tail, and
the fat that covers the entrails and the lobe of the liver, and the two
kidneys and the fat that is on them and the right thigh (for it is a
ram of ordination),
23and one cake of bread and one cake of bread *mixed with* oil and
one wafer from the basket of unleavened bread which is *set* before
the LORD;
24and you shall put all these in the hands of Aaron and in the
hands of his sons, and shall wave them as a wave offering before
the LORD.
25"And you shall take them from their hands, and offer them
up in smoke on the altar on the burnt offering for a soothing aroma
before the LORD; it is an offering by fire to the LORD.
26¶ "Then you shall take the breast of Aaron's ram of ordination, and wave it as a wave offering before the LORD; and it shall
be your portion.
27"And you shall consecrate the breast of the wave offering and
the thigh of the heave offering which was waved and which was
offered from the ram of ordination, from the one which was for
Aaron and from the one which was for his sons.
28"And it shall be for Aaron and his sons as *their* portion forever
from the sons of Israel, for it is a heave offering; and it shall be a
heave offering from the sons of Israel from the sacrifices of their
peace offerings, *even* their heave offering to the LORD.
29¶ "And the holy garments of Aaron shall be for his sons after
him, that in them they may be anointed and ordained.
30"For seven days the one of his sons who is priest in his stead
shall put them on when he enters the tent of meeting to minister
in the holy place.

*Food of the Priests*

31¶ "And you shall take the ram of ordination and boil its flesh
in a holy place.
32"And Aaron and his sons shall eat the flesh of the ram, and
the bread that is in the basket, at the doorway of the tent of
meeting.
33"Thus they shall eat those things by which atonement was
made at their ordination *and* consecration; but a layman shall not
eat *them,* because they are holy.
34"And if any of the flesh of ordination or any of the bread
remains until morning, then you shall burn the remainder with
fire; it shall not be eaten, because it is holy.
35¶ "And thus you shall do to Aaron and to his sons, according
to all that I have commanded you; you shall ordain them through
seven days.
36"And each day you shall offer a bull as a sin offering for
atonement, and you shall purify the altar when you make atonement for it; and you shall anoint it to consecrate it.
37"For seven days you shall make atonement for the altar and
consecrate it; then the altar shall be most holy, *and* whatever
touches the altar shall be holy.
38¶ "Now this is what you shall offer on the altar: two one year
old lambs each day, continuously.
39"The one lamb you shall offer in the morning, and the other
lamb you shall offer at twilight;
40and there *shall be* one-tenth *of an ephah* of fine flour mixed with
one-fourth of a hin of beaten oil, and one-fourth of a hin of wine
for a libation with one lamb.

## New International

19"Take the other ram, and Aaron and his sons shall lay their
hands on its head. 20Slaughter it, take some of its blood and put
it on the lobes of the right ears of Aaron and his sons, on the
thumbs of their right hands, and on the big toes of their right feet.
Then sprinkle blood against the altar on all sides. 21And take some
of the blood on the altar and some of the anointing oil and sprinkle
it on Aaron and his garments and on his sons and their garments.
Then he and his sons and their garments will be consecrated.
22"Take from this ram the fat, the fat tail, the fat around the
inner parts, the covering of the liver, both kidneys with the fat
around them, and the right thigh. (This is the ram for the ordination.) 23From the basket of bread made without yeast, which is
before the LORD, take a loaf, and a cake made with oil, and a wafer.
24Put all these in the hands of Aaron and his sons and wave them
before the LORD as a wave offering. 25Then take them from their
hands and burn them on the altar along with the burnt offering for
a pleasing aroma to the LORD, an offering made to the LORD by fire.
26After you take the breast of the ram for Aaron's ordination, wave
it before the LORD as a wave offering, and it will be your share.
27"Consecrate those parts of the ordination ram that belong to
Aaron and his sons: the breast that was waved and the thigh that
was presented. 28This is always to be the regular share from the
Israelites for Aaron and his sons. It is the contribution the Israelites
are to make to the LORD from their fellowship offerings.[a]
29"Aaron's sacred garments will belong to his descendants so
that they can be anointed and ordained in them. 30The son who
succeeds him as priest and comes to the Tent of Meeting to minister in the Holy Place is to wear them seven days.
31"Take the ram for the ordination and cook the meat in a sacred
place. 32At the entrance to the Tent of Meeting, Aaron and his sons
are to eat the meat of the ram and the bread that is in the basket.
33They are to eat these offerings by which atonement was made for
their ordination and consecration. But no one else may eat them,
because they are sacred. 34And if any of the meat of the ordination
ram or any bread is left over till morning, burn it up. It must not
be eaten, because it is sacred.
35"Do for Aaron and his sons everything I have commanded
you, taking seven days to ordain them. 36Sacrifice a bull each day
as a sin offering to make atonement. Purify the altar by making
atonement for it, and anoint it to consecrate it. 37For seven days
make atonement for the altar and consecrate it. Then the altar will
be most holy, and whatever touches it will be holy.
38"This is what you are to offer on the altar regularly each day:
two lambs a year old. 39Offer one in the morning and the other at
twilight. 40With the first lamb offer a tenth of an ephah[b] of fine
flour mixed with a quarter of a hin[c] of oil from pressed olives, and
a quarter of a hin of wine as a drink offering. 41Sacrifice the other

**NIV** [a] *28* Traditionally *peace offerings* [b] *40* That is, probably about 2 quarts
(about 2 liters) [c] *40* That is, probably about 1 quart (about 1 liter)

## King James

41And the other lamb thou shalt offer at even, and shalt do thereto according to the meat offering of the morning, and according to the drink offering thereof, for a sweet savour, an offering made by fire unto the LORD.

42 *This shall be* a continual burnt offering throughout your generations *at* the door of the tabernacle of the congregation before the LORD: where I will meet you, to speak there unto thee.

43And there I will meet with the children of Israel, and *the tabernacle* shall be sanctified by my glory.

44And I will sanctify the tabernacle of the congregation, and the altar: I will sanctify also both Aaron and his sons, to minister to me in the priest's office.

45¶ And I will dwell among the children of Israel, and will be their God.

46And they shall know that I *am* the LORD their God, that brought them forth out of the land of Egypt, that I may dwell among them: I *am* the LORD their God.

**30** AND THOU shalt make an altar to burn incense upon: *of* shittim wood shalt thou make it.

2A cubit *shall be* the length thereof, and a cubit the breadth thereof; foursquare shall it be: and two cubits *shall be* the height thereof: the horns thereof *shall be* of the same.

3And thou shalt overlay it with pure gold, the top thereof, and the sides thereof round about, and the horns thereof; and thou shalt make unto it a crown of gold round about.

4And two golden rings shalt thou make to it under the crown of it, by the two corners thereof, upon the two sides of it shalt thou make *it;* and they shall be for places for the staves to bear it withal.

5And thou shalt make the staves *of* shittim wood, and overlay them with gold.

6And thou shalt put it before the veil that *is* by the ark of the testimony, before the mercy seat that *is* over the testimony, where I will meet with thee.

7And Aaron shall burn thereon sweet incense every morning: when he dresseth the lamps, he shall burn incense upon it.

8And when Aaron lighteth the lamps at even, he shall burn incense upon it, a perpetual incense before the LORD throughout your generations.

9Ye shall offer no strange incense thereon, nor burnt sacrifice, nor meat offering; neither shall ye pour drink offering thereon.

10And Aaron shall make an atonement upon the horns of it once in a year with the blood of the sin offering of atonements: once in the year shall he make atonement upon it throughout your generations: it *is* most holy unto the LORD.

11¶ And the LORD spake unto Moses, saying,

12When thou takest the sum of the children of Israel after their number, then shall they give every man a ransom for his soul unto the LORD, when thou numberest them; that there be no plague among them, when *thou* numberest them.

13This they shall give, every one that passeth among them that are numbered, half a shekel after the shekel of the sanctuary: (a shekel *is* twenty gerahs:) an half shekel *shall be* the offering of the LORD.

14Every one that passeth among them that are numbered, from twenty years old and above, shall give an offering unto the LORD.

15The rich shall not give more, and the poor shall not give less than half a shekel, when *they* give an offering unto the LORD, to make an atonement for your souls.

16And thou shalt take the atonement money of the children of Israel, and shalt appoint it for the service of the tabernacle of the congregation; that it may be a memorial unto the children of Israel before the LORD, to make an atonement for your souls.

17¶ And the LORD spake unto Moses, saying,

## Amplified

41And the other lamb you shall offer at evening, and do with it as with the cereal offering of the morning, and with the drink offering, for a sweet *and* satisfying fragrance, an offering made by fire to the Lord.

42This shall be a continual burnt offering throughout your generations at the door of the tent of meeting before the Lord, where I will meet with you, to speak there to you.

43There I will meet with the Israelites, and the tent of meeting shall be sanctified by My glory [the Shekinah, God's visible presence].

44And I will sanctify the tent of meeting and the altar; I will sanctify also both Aaron and his sons to minister to Me in the priest's office.

45And I will dwell among the Israelites and be their God.

46And they shall know [from personal experience] that I am the Lord their God, Who brought them forth out of the land of Egypt that I might dwell among them; I am the Lord their God.

**30** AND YOU shall make an altar to burn incense upon; of acacia wood you shall make it.

2A cubit shall be its length, and a cubit its breadth; its top shall be square, and it shall be two cubits high. Its horns shall be of one piece with it.

3And you shall overlay it with pure gold, its top and its sides round about and its horns, and you shall make a crown—a rim or molding—of gold around it.

4You shall make two golden rings under the rim of it, on the two ribs on the two opposite sides of it; and they shall be holders for the poles with which to carry it.

5And you shall make the poles of acacia wood, overlaid with gold.

6You shall put the altar [of incense] in front *and* outside of the veil that screens the ark of the testimony, before the mercy seat that is over the testimony (the law, the tables of stone), where I will meet with you.

7And Aaron shall burn on it incense of sweet spices; every morning when he trims *and* fills the lamps he shall burn it. [Ps. 141:2; Rev. 5:8; 8:3, 4.]

8And when Aaron lights the lamps in the evening, he shall burn it, a perpetual incense before the Lord throughout your generations.

9You shall offer no unholy incense on the altar, nor burnt sacrifice, nor cereal offering; and you shall pour no libation (drink offering) on it.

10Aaron shall make atonement upon the horns of it once a year; with the blood of the sin offering of atonement once in the year shall he make atonement upon *and* for it throughout your generations. It is most holy to the Lord.

11And the Lord said to Moses,

12When you take the census of the Israelites, every man shall give a ransom for himself to the Lord when you number them, that no plague may fall upon them when you number them. [Rom. 8:1-4.]

13This is what every one shall give as he joins those already numbered: a half shekel in terms of the sanctuary shekel, a shekel being twenty gerahs; a half shekel as an offering to the Lord.

14Every one from twenty years old and upward, as he joins those already numbered shall give this offering to the Lord. [I Pet. 1:18, 19; Matt. 10:24.]

15The rich shall not give more, and the poor shall not give less, than half a shekel, when [you] give this offering to the Lord to make atonement for yourselves.

16And you shall take the atonement money of the Israelites and use it [exclusively] for the service of the tent of meeting, that it may bring the Israelites to remembrance before the Lord, to make atonement for yourselves.

17And the Lord said to Moses,

## New American Standard

41"And the other lamb you shall offer at twilight, and shall offer
with it the same grain offering as the morning and the same
libation, for a soothing aroma, an offering by fire to the LORD.
42"It shall be a continual burnt offering throughout your generations at the doorway of the tent of meeting before the LORD,
where I will meet with you, to speak to you there.
43"And I will meet there with the sons of Israel, and it shall be
consecrated by My glory.
44"And I will consecrate the tent of meeting and the altar; I will
also consecrate Aaron and his sons to minister as priests to Me.
45"And I will dwell among the sons of Israel and will be their
God.
46"And they shall know that I am the LORD their God who
brought them out of the land of Egypt, that I might dwell among
them; I am the LORD their God.

*The Altar of Incense*

**30** "MOREOVER, YOU shall make an altar as a place for
burning incense; you shall make it of acacia wood.
2"Its length *shall be* a cubit, and its width a cubit, it shall be
square, and its height *shall be* two cubits; its horns *shall be* of one
piece with it.
3"And you shall overlay it with pure gold, its top and its sides
all around, and its horns; and you shall make a gold molding all
around for it.
4"And you shall make two gold rings for it under its molding;
you shall make *them* on its two side walls—on opposite sides—and
they shall be holders for poles with which to carry it.
5"And you shall make the poles of acacia wood and overlay
them with gold.
6"And you shall put this altar in front of the veil that is near
the ark of the testimony, in front of the mercy seat that is over *the
ark of* the testimony, where I will meet with you.
7"And Aaron shall burn fragrant incense on it; he shall burn
it every morning when he trims the lamps.
8"And when Aaron trims the lamps at twilight, he shall burn
incense. *There shall be* perpetual incense before the LORD throughout your generations.
9"You shall not offer any strange incense on this altar, or burnt
offering or meal offering; and you shall not pour out a libation on
it.
10"And Aaron shall make atonement on its horns once a year;
he shall make atonement on it with the blood of the sin offering
of atonement once a year throughout your generations. It is most
holy to the LORD."
11¶ The LORD also spoke to Moses, saying,
12"When you take a census of the sons of Israel to number
them, then each one of them shall give a ransom for himself to the
LORD, when you number them, that there may be no plague
among them when you number them.
13"This is what everyone who is numbered shall give: half a
shekel according to the shekel of the sanctuary (the shekel is
twenty gerahs), half a shekel as a contribution to the LORD.
14"Everyone who is numbered, from twenty years old and over,
shall give the contribution to the LORD.
15"The rich shall not pay more, and the poor shall not pay less
than the half shekel, when you give the contribution to the LORD
to make atonement for yourselves.
16"And you shall take the atonement money from the sons of
Israel, and shall give it for the service of the tent of meeting, that
it may be a memorial for the sons of Israel before the LORD, to make
atonement for yourselves."
17¶ And the LORD spoke to Moses, saying,

## New International

lamb at twilight with the same grain offering and its drink offering
as in the morning—a pleasing aroma, an offering made to the LORD
by fire.
42"For the generations to come this burnt offering is to be made
regularly at the entrance to the Tent of Meeting before the LORD.
There I will meet you and speak to you; 43there also I will meet with
the Israelites, and the place will be consecrated by my glory.
44"So I will consecrate the Tent of Meeting and the altar and will
consecrate Aaron and his sons to serve me as priests. 45Then I will
dwell among the Israelites and be their God. 46They will know that
I am the LORD their God, who brought them out of Egypt so that
I might dwell among them. I am the LORD their God.

*The Altar of Incense*

**30** "MAKE AN altar of acacia wood for burning incense. 2It
is to be square, a cubit long and a cubit wide, and two
cubits high[a] —its horns of one piece with it. 3Overlay the top and
all the sides and the horns with pure gold, and make a gold
molding around it. 4Make two gold rings for the altar below the
molding—two on opposite sides—to hold the poles used to carry
it. 5Make the poles of acacia wood and overlay them with gold.
6Put the altar in front of the curtain that is before the ark of the
Testimony—before the atonement cover that is over the Testimony—where I will meet with you.
7"Aaron must burn fragrant incense on the altar every morning
when he tends the lamps. 8He must burn incense again when he
lights the lamps at twilight so incense will burn regularly before
the LORD for the generations to come. 9Do not offer on this altar
any other incense or any burnt offering or grain offering, and do
not pour a drink offering on it. 10Once a year Aaron shall make
atonement on its horns. This annual atonement must be made
with the blood of the atoning sin offering for the generations to
come. It is most holy to the LORD."

*Atonement Money*

11Then the LORD said to Moses, 12"When you take a census of
the Israelites to count them, each one must pay the LORD a ransom
for his life at the time he is counted. Then no plague will come on
them when you number them. 13Each one who crosses over to
those already counted is to give a half shekel,[b] according to the
sanctuary shekel, which weighs twenty gerahs. This half shekel is
an offering to the LORD. 14All who cross over, those twenty years
old or more, are to give an offering to the LORD. 15The rich are not
to give more than a half shekel and the poor are not to give less
when you make the offering to the LORD to atone for your lives.
16Receive the atonement money from the Israelites and use it for
the service of the Tent of Meeting. It will be a memorial for the
Israelites before the LORD, making atonement for your lives."

*Basin for Washing*

17Then the LORD said to Moses, 18"Make a bronze basin, with

**NIV** [a] *2* That is, about 1 1/2 feet (about 0.5 meter) long and wide and about 3 feet (about 0.9 meter) high [b] *13* That is, about 1/5 ounce (about 6 grams); also in verse 15

## King James

[18]Thou shalt also make a laver *of* brass, and his foot *also of* brass, to wash *withal:* and thou shalt put it between the tabernacle of the congregation and the altar, and thou shalt put water therein.
[19]For Aaron and his sons shall wash their hands and their feet thereat:
[20]When they go into the tabernacle of the congregation, they shall wash with water, that they die not; or when they come near to the altar to minister, to burn offering made by fire unto the LORD:
[21]So they shall wash their hands and their feet, that they die not: and it shall be a statute for ever to them, *even* to him and to his seed throughout their generations.
[22]¶ Moreover the LORD spake unto Moses, saying,
[23]Take thou also unto thee principal spices, of pure myrrh five hundred *shekels,* and of sweet cinnamon half so much, *even* two hundred and fifty *shekels,* and of sweet calamus two hundred and fifty *shekels,*
[24]And of cassia five hundred *shekels,* after the shekel of the sanctuary, and of oil olive an hin:
[25]And thou shalt make it an oil of holy ointment, an ointment compound after the art of the apothecary: it shall be an holy anointing oil.
[26]And thou shalt anoint the tabernacle of the congregation therewith, and the ark of the testimony,
[27]And the table and all his vessels, and the candlestick and his vessels, and the altar of incense,
[28]And the altar of burnt offering with all his vessels, and the laver and his foot.
[29]And thou shalt sanctify them, that they may be most holy: whatsoever toucheth them shall be holy.
[30]And thou shalt anoint Aaron and his sons, and consecrate them, that *they* may minister unto me in the priest's office.
[31]And thou shalt speak unto the children of Israel, saying, This shall be an holy anointing oil unto me throughout your generations.
[32]Upon man's flesh shall it not be poured, neither shall ye make *any other* like it, after the composition of it: it *is* holy, *and* it shall be holy unto you.
[33]Whosoever compoundeth *any* like it, or whosoever putteth *any* of it upon a stranger, shall even be cut off from his people.
[34]¶ And the LORD said unto Moses, Take unto thee sweet spices, stacte, and onycha, and galbanum; *these* sweet spices with pure frankincense: of each shall there be a like *weight:*
[35]And thou shalt make it a perfume, a confection after the art of the apothecary, tempered together, pure *and* holy:
[36]And thou shalt beat *some* of it very small, and put of it before the testimony in the tabernacle of the congregation, where I will meet with thee: it shall be unto you most holy.
[37]And *as for* the perfume which thou shalt make, ye shall not make to yourselves according to the composition thereof: it shall be unto thee holy for the LORD.
[38]Whosoever shall make like unto that, to smell thereto, shall even be cut off from his people.

**31** AND THE LORD spake unto Moses, saying,
[2]See, I have called by name Bezaleel the son of Uri, the son of Hur, of the tribe of Judah:
[3]And I have filled him with the spirit of God, in wisdom, and in understanding, and in knowledge, and in all manner of workmanship,
[4]To devise cunning works, to work in gold, and in silver, and in brass,
[5]And in cutting of stones, to set *them,* and in carving of timber, to work in all manner of workmanship.

## Amplified

[18]You shall also make a laver *or* large basin of bronze and its base of bronze, for washing; and you shall put it [outside in the court] between the tent of meeting and the altar [of burnt offering], and you shall put water in it;
[19]There Aaron and his sons shall wash their hands and their feet. [Titus 3:5.]
[20]When they go into the tent of meeting they shall wash with water, that they die not, or when they come near to the altar to minister, to burn an offering made by fire to the Lord. [John 13:6-8.]
[21]So they shall wash their hands and their feet, lest they die; it shall be a perpetual statute for [Aaron] and his descendants throughout their generations.
[22]Moreover the Lord said to Moses,
[23]Take the best spices: of liquid myrrh 500 shekels, of sweet-smelling cinnamon half as much, 250 shekels, of fragrant calamus 250 shekels,
[24]And of cassia 500 shekels, in terms of the sanctuary shekel, and of olive oil a hin.
[25]And you shall make of these a holy anointing oil, a perfume compounded after the art of the perfumer; it shall be a sacred anointing oil.
[26]And you shall anoint the tent of meeting with it, and the ark of the testimony,
[27]And the [showbread] table and all its utensils, and the lampstand and its utensils, and the altar of incense,
[28]And the altar of burnt offering with all its utensils, and the laver [for cleansing] and its base.
[29]You shall sanctify (separate) them, that they may be most holy; whoever *and* whatever touches them must be holy (set apart to God).
[30]And you shall anoint Aaron and his sons and sanctify (separate) them, that they may minister to Me as priests.
[31]And say to the Israelites, This is a holy anointing oil [symbol of the Holy Spirit], sacred to Me alone throughout your generations. [I Cor. 12:3; Rom. 8:9.]
[32]It shall not be poured upon a layman's body, nor shall you make any other like it in composition; it is holy, and you shall hold it sacred.
[33]Whoever compounds any like it, or puts any of it upon an outsider, shall be cut off from his people.
[34]Then the Lord said to Moses, Take sweet spices, stacte, onycha, and galbanum, sweet spices with pure frankincense, an equal amount of each;
[35]And make of them incense, a perfume after the perfumer's art, seasoned with salt *and* mixed, pure and sacred.
[36]You shall beat some of it very small, and put some of it before the testimony in the tent of meeting, where I will meet with you; it shall be to you most holy.
[37]And the incense which you shall make according to its composition, you shall not make for yourselves; it shall be to you holy to the Lord.
[38]Whoever makes any like it, for perfume, shall be cut off from his people.

**31** AND THE Lord said to Moses,
[2]See, I have called by name Bezalel, son of Uri, son of Hur, of the tribe of Judah.
[3]And I have filled him with the Spirit of God, in wisdom *and* ability, in understanding *and* intelligence, and in knowledge, and in all kinds of craftsmanship,
[4]To devise skillful works, to work in gold, and in silver, and in bronze,
[5]And in cutting of stones for setting, and in carving of wood, to work in all kinds of craftsmanship.

## New American Standard

18"You shall also make a laver of bronze, with its base of bronze,
for washing; and you shall put it between the tent of meeting and
the altar, and you shall put water in it.
19"And Aaron and his sons shall wash their hands and their feet
from it;
20when they enter the tent of meeting, they shall wash with
water, that they may not die; or when they approach the altar to
minister, by offering up in smoke a fire *sacrifice* to the LORD.
21"So they shall wash their hands and their feet, that they may
not die; and it shall be a perpetual statute for them, for Aaron and
his descendants throughout their generations."

*The Anointing Oil*

22¶ Moreover, the LORD spoke to Moses, saying,
23"Take also for yourself the finest of spices: of flowing myrrh
five hundred *shekels*, and of fragrant cinnamon half as much, two
hundred and fifty, and of fragrant cane two hundred and fifty,
24and of cassia five hundred, according to the shekel of the
sanctuary, and of olive oil a hin.
25"And you shall make of these a holy anointing oil, a perfume
mixture, the work of a perfumer; it shall be a holy anointing oil.
26"And with it you shall anoint the tent of meeting and the ark
of the testimony,
27and the table and all its utensils, and the lampstand and its
utensils, and the altar of incense,
28and the altar of burnt offering and all its utensils, and the laver
and its stand.
29"You shall also consecrate them, that they may be most holy;
whatever touches them shall be holy.
30"And you shall anoint Aaron and his sons, and consecrate
them, that they may minister as priests to Me.
31"And you shall speak to the sons of Israel, saying, 'This shall
be a holy anointing oil to Me throughout your generations.
32'It shall not be poured on anyone's body, nor shall you make
*any* like it, in the same proportions; it is holy, *and* it shall be holy
to you.
33'Whoever shall mix *any* like it, or whoever puts any of it on
a layman, shall be cut off from his people.' "

*The Incense*

34¶ Then the LORD said to Moses, "Take for yourself spices,
stacte and onycha and galbanum, spices with pure frankincense;
there shall be an equal part of each.
35"And with it you shall make incense, a perfume, the work of
a perfumer, salted, pure, *and* holy.
36"And you shall beat some of it very fine, and put part of it
before the testimony in the tent of meeting, where I shall meet with
you; it shall be most holy to you.
37"And the incense which you shall make, you shall not make
in the same proportions for yourselves; it shall be holy to you for
the LORD.
38"Whoever shall make *any* like it, to use as perfume, shall be
cut off from his people."

*The Skilled Craftsmen*

**31** NOW THE LORD spoke to Moses, saying,
2"See, I have called by name Bezalel, the son of Uri, the
son of Hur, of the tribe of Judah.
3"And I have filled him with the Spirit of God in wisdom, in
understanding, in knowledge, and in all *kinds of* craftsmanship,
4to make artistic designs for work in gold, in silver, and in
bronze,
5and in the cutting of stones for settings, and in the carving of
wood, that he may work in all *kinds of* craftsmanship.

## New International

its bronze stand, for washing. Place it between the Tent of Meeting
and the altar, and put water in it. 19Aaron and his sons are to wash
their hands and feet with water from it. 20Whenever they enter the
Tent of Meeting, they shall wash with water so that they will not
die. Also, when they approach the altar to minister by presenting
an offering made to the LORD by fire, 21they shall wash their hands
and feet so that they will not die. This is to be a lasting ordinance
for Aaron and his descendants for the generations to come."

*Anointing Oil*

22Then the LORD said to Moses, 23"Take the following fine
spices: 500 shekels[a] of liquid myrrh, half as much (that is, 250
shekels) of fragrant cinnamon, 250 shekels of fragrant cane, 24500
shekels of cassia—all according to the sanctuary shekel—and a
hin[b] of olive oil. 25Make these into a sacred anointing oil, a fragrant
blend, the work of a perfumer. It will be the sacred anointing oil.
26Then use it to anoint the Tent of Meeting, the ark of the Testimony, 27the table and all its articles, the lampstand and its accessories, the altar of incense, 28the altar of burnt offering and all its
utensils, and the basin with its stand. 29You shall consecrate them
so they will be most holy, and whatever touches them will be holy.
30"Anoint Aaron and his sons and consecrate them so they may
serve me as priests. 31Say to the Israelites, 'This is to be my sacred
anointing oil for the generations to come. 32Do not pour it on men's
bodies and do not make any oil with the same formula. It is sacred,
and you are to consider it sacred. 33Whoever makes perfume like
it and whoever puts it on anyone other than a priest must be cut
off from his people.' "

*Incense*

34Then the LORD said to Moses, "Take fragrant spices—gum
resin, onycha and galbanum—and pure frankincense, all in equal
amounts, 35and make a fragrant blend of incense, the work of a
perfumer. It is to be salted and pure and sacred. 36Grind some of
it to powder and place it in front of the Testimony in the Tent of
Meeting, where I will meet with you. It shall be most holy to you.
37Do not make any incense with this formula for yourselves; consider it holy to the LORD. 38Whoever makes any like it to enjoy its
fragrance must be cut off from his people."

*Bezalel and Oholiab*

**31** THEN THE LORD said to Moses, 2"See, I have chosen
Bezalel son of Uri, the son of Hur, of the tribe of Judah,
3and I have filled him with the Spirit of God, with skill, ability and
knowledge in all kinds of crafts— 4to make artistic designs for
work in gold, silver and bronze, 5to cut and set stones, to work in
wood, and to engage in all kinds of craftsmanship. 6Moreover, I

NIV [a] 23 That is, about 12 1/2 pounds (about 6 kilograms) [b] 24 That is, probably about 4 quarts (about 4 liters)

## King James

6 And I, behold, I have given with him Aholiab, the son of Ahisamach, of the tribe of Dan: and in the hearts of all that are wisehearted I have put wisdom, that they may make all that I have commanded thee;

7 The tabernacle of the congregation, and the ark of the testimony, and the mercy seat that *is* thereupon, and all the furniture of the tabernacle,

8 And the table and his furniture, and the pure candlestick with all his furniture, and the altar of incense,

9 And the altar of burnt offering with all his furniture, and the laver and his foot,

10 And the cloths of service, and the holy garments for Aaron the priest, and the garments of his sons, to minister in the priest's office,

11 And the anointing oil, and sweet incense for the holy *place:* according to all that I have commanded thee shall they do.

12 ¶ And the LORD spake unto Moses, saying,

13 Speak thou also unto the children of Israel, saying, Verily my sabbaths ye shall keep: for it *is* a sign between me and you throughout your generations; that *ye* may know that I *am* the LORD that doth sanctify you.

14 Ye shall keep the sabbath therefore; for it *is* holy unto you: every one that defileth it shall surely be put to death: for whosoever doeth *any* work therein, that soul shall be cut off from among his people.

15 Six days may work be done; but in the seventh *is* the sabbath of rest, holy to the LORD: whosoever doeth *any* work in the sabbath day, he shall surely be put to death.

16 Wherefore the children of Israel shall keep the sabbath, to observe the sabbath throughout their generations, *for* a perpetual covenant.

17 It *is* a sign between me and the children of Israel for ever: for *in* six days the LORD made heaven and earth, and on the seventh day he rested, and was refreshed.

18 ¶ And he gave unto Moses, when he had made an end of communing with him upon mount Sinai, two tables of testimony, tables of stone, written with the finger of God.

**32** AND WHEN the people saw that Moses delayed to come down out of the mount, the people gathered themselves together unto Aaron, and said unto him, Up, make us gods, which shall go before us; for *as for* this Moses, the man that brought us up out of the land of Egypt, we wot not what is become of him.

2 And Aaron said unto them, Break off the golden earrings, which *are* in the ears of your wives, of your sons, and of your daughters, and bring *them* unto me.

3 And all the people brake off the golden earrings which *were* in their ears, and brought *them* unto Aaron.

4 And he received *them* at their hand, and fashioned it with a graving tool, after he had made it a molten calf: and they said, These *be* thy gods, O Israel, which brought thee up out of the land of Egypt.

5 And when Aaron saw *it*, he built an altar before it; and Aaron made proclamation, and said, Tomorrow *is* a feast to the LORD.

6 And they rose up early on the morrow, and offered burnt offerings, and brought peace offerings; and the people sat down to eat and to drink, and rose up to play.

7 ¶ And the LORD said unto Moses, Go, get thee down; for thy people, which thou broughtest out of the land of Egypt, have corrupted *themselves:*

8 They have turned aside quickly out of the way which I commanded them: they have made them a molten calf, and have worshipped it, and have sacrificed thereunto, and said, These *be* thy gods, O Israel, which have brought thee up out of the land of Egypt.

## Amplified

6 And behold, I have appointed with him Aholiab, son of Ahisamach, of the tribe of Dan; and to all who are wise-hearted I have given wisdom *and* ability to make all that I have commanded you:

7 The tent of meeting, the ark of the testimony, the mercy seat that is on it, all the furnishings of the tent,

8 The table [of the showbread] and its utensils, the pure lampstand with all its utensils, the altar of incense,

9 The altar of burnt offering with all its utensils, the laver and its base,

10 The finely worked garments, the holy garments for Aaron the [high] priest, and for his sons, to minister as priests,

11 And the anointing oil and incense of sweet spices for the holy place. According to all that I have commanded you shall they do.

12 And the Lord said to Moses,

13 Say to the Israelites, Truly you shall keep My sabbaths, for it is a sign between Me and you throughout your generations, that you may know that I, the Lord, sanctify you (set you apart for Myself).

14 You shall keep the sabbath therefore, for it is holy to you; every one who profanes it shall surely be put to death; for whoever does work on the sabbath shall be cut off from among his people.

15 Six days may work be done, but the seventh is the sabbath of rest, sacred to the Lord; whoever does work on the sabbath day shall surely be put to death.

16 Wherefore the Israelites shall keep the sabbath, to observe *it* throughout their generations, a perpetual covenant.

17 It is a sign between Me and the Israelites for ever; for in six days the Lord made the heavens and earth, and on the seventh day He ceased and was refreshed.

18 And He gave to Moses, when He had ceased communing with him on Mount Sinai, the two tables of the testimony, tables of stone, written with the finger of God.

**32** WHEN THE people saw that Moses delayed to come down from the mountain, [they] gathered together to Aaron, and said to him, Up, make us gods to go before us; for as for this Moses, the man who brought us up out of the land of Egypt, we do not know what has become of him.

2 So Aaron replied, Take the gold rings from the ears of your wives, your sons, and daughters, and bring them to me.

3 So all the people took the gold rings from their ears, and brought them to Aaron.

4 And he received the gold at their hand, and fashioned it with a graving tool, and made it a molten calf; and they said, These are your gods, O Israel, which brought you up out of the land of Egypt!

5 And when Aaron saw the molten calf, he built an altar before it; and Aaron made proclamation, and said, Tomorrow shall be a feast to the Lord.

6 And they rose up early the next day and offered burnt offerings and brought peace offerings; and the people sat down to eat and drink, and rose up to play.

7 The Lord said to Moses, Go down; for your people, whom you brought out of the land of Egypt, have corrupted themselves;

8 They have turned aside quickly out of the way which I commanded them; they have made them a molten calf, and have worshiped it and sacrificed to it, and said, These are your gods, O Israel, that brought you up out of the land of Egypt!

## New American Standard

6"And behold, I Myself have appointed with him Oholiab, the
son of Ahisamach, of the tribe of Dan; and in the hearts of all who
are skillful I have put skill, that they may make all that I have
commanded you:
7the tent of meeting, and the ark of testimony, and the mercy
seat upon it, and all the furniture of the tent,
8the table also and its utensils, and the pure *gold* lampstand
with all its utensils, and the altar of incense,
9the altar of burnt offering also with all its utensils, and the
laver and its stand,
10the woven garments as well, and the holy garments for Aaron
the priest, and the garments of his sons, *with which* to carry on their
priesthood;
11the anointing oil also, and the fragrant incense for the holy
place, they are to make *them* according to all that I have commanded you."

*The Sign of the Sabbath*

12¶ And the LORD spoke to Moses, saying,
13"But as for you, speak to the sons of Israel, saying, 'You shall
surely observe My sabbaths; for *this* is a sign between Me and you
throughout your generations, that you may know that I am the
LORD who sanctifies you.
14'Therefore you are to observe the sabbath, for it is holy to you.
Everyone who profanes it shall surely be put to death; for whoever
does any work on it, that person shall be cut off from among his
people.
15'For six days work may be done, but on the seventh day there
is a sabbath of complete rest, holy to the LORD; whoever does any
work on the sabbath day shall surely be put to death.
16'So the sons of Israel shall observe the sabbath, to celebrate
the sabbath throughout their generations as a perpetual covenant.'
17"It is a sign between Me and the sons of Israel forever; for in
six days the LORD made heaven and earth, but on the seventh day
He ceased *from labor*, and was refreshed."
18¶ And when He had finished speaking with him upon Mount
Sinai, He gave Moses the two tablets of the testimony, tablets of
stone, written by the finger of God.

*The Golden Calf*

32 NOW WHEN the people saw that Moses delayed to come
down from the mountain, the people assembled about
Aaron, and said to him, "Come, make us a god who will go before
us; as for this Moses, the man who brought us up from the land
of Egypt, we do not know what has become of him."
2And Aaron said to them, "Tear off the gold rings which are
in the ears of your wives, your sons, and your daughters, and
bring *them* to me."
3Then all the people tore off the gold rings which were in their
ears, and brought *them* to Aaron.
4And he took *this* from their hand, and fashioned it with a
graving tool, and made it into a molten calf; and they said, "This
is your god, O Israel, who brought you up from the land of Egypt."
5Now when Aaron saw *this*, he built an altar before it; and
Aaron made a proclamation and said, "Tomorrow *shall be* a feast
to the LORD."
6So the next day they rose early and offered burnt offerings,
and brought peace offerings; and the people sat down to eat and
to drink, and rose up to play.
7Then the LORD spoke to Moses, "Go down at once, for your
people, whom you brought up from the land of Egypt, have corrupted *themselves*.
8"They have quickly turned aside from the way which I commanded them. They have made for themselves a molten calf, and
have worshiped it, and have sacrificed to it, and said, 'This is your
god, O Israel, who brought you up from the land of Egypt!' "

## New International

have appointed Oholiab son of Ahisamach, of the tribe of Dan, to
help him. Also I have given skill to all the craftsmen to make
everything I have commanded you: 7the Tent of Meeting, the ark
of the Testimony with the atonement cover on it, and all the other
furnishings of the tent— 8the table and its articles, the pure gold
lampstand and all its accessories, the altar of incense, 9the altar of
burnt offering and all its utensils, the basin with its stand— 10and
also the woven garments, both the sacred garments for Aaron the
priest and the garments for his sons when they serve as priests,
11and the anointing oil and fragrant incense for the Holy Place.
They are to make them just as I commanded you."

*The Sabbath*

12Then the LORD said to Moses, 13"Say to the Israelites, 'You
must observe my Sabbaths. This will be a sign between me and you
for the generations to come, so you may know that I am the LORD,
who makes you holy.[a]
14" 'Observe the Sabbath, because it is holy to you. Anyone
who desecrates it must be put to death; whoever does any work
on that day must be cut off from his people. 15For six days, work
is to be done, but the seventh day is a Sabbath of rest, holy to the
LORD. Whoever does any work on the Sabbath day must be put to
death. 16The Israelites are to observe the Sabbath, celebrating it for
the generations to come as a lasting covenant. 17It will be a sign
between me and the Israelites forever, for in six days the LORD
made the heavens and the earth, and on the seventh day he
abstained from work and rested.' "
18When the LORD finished speaking to Moses on Mount Sinai,
he gave him the two tablets of the Testimony, the tablets of stone
inscribed by the finger of God.

*The Golden Calf*

32 WHEN THE people saw that Moses was so long in coming
down from the mountain, they gathered around Aaron
and said, "Come, make us gods[b] who will go before us. As for this
fellow Moses who brought us up out of Egypt, we don't know
what has happened to him."
2Aaron answered them, "Take off the gold earrings that your
wives, your sons and your daughters are wearing, and bring them
to me." 3So all the people took off their earrings and brought them
to Aaron. 4He took what they handed him and made it into an idol
cast in the shape of a calf, fashioning it with a tool. Then they said,
"These are your gods,[c] O Israel, who brought you up out of
Egypt."
5When Aaron saw this, he built an altar in front of the calf and
announced, "Tomorrow there will be a festival to the LORD." 6So
the next day the people rose early and sacrificed burnt offerings
and presented fellowship offerings.[d] Afterward they sat down to
eat and drink and got up to indulge in revelry.
7Then the LORD said to Moses, "Go down, because your people,
whom you brought up out of Egypt, have become corrupt. 8They
have been quick to turn away from what I commanded them and
have made themselves an idol cast in the shape of a calf. They have
bowed down to it and sacrificed to it and have said, 'These are your
gods, O Israel, who brought you up out of Egypt.'

**NIV** [a] 13 Or *who sanctifies you;* or *who sets you apart as holy* [b] 1 Or *a god;* also in verses 23 and 31 [c] 4 Or *This is your god;* also in verse 8 [d] 6 Traditionally *peace offerings*

## King James

9 And the LORD said unto Moses, I have seen this people, and, behold, it *is* a stiffnecked people:

10 Now therefore let me alone, that my wrath may wax hot against them, and that I may consume them: and I will make of thee a great nation.

11 And Moses besought the LORD his God, and said, LORD, why doth thy wrath wax hot against thy people, which thou hast brought forth out of the land of Egypt with great power, and with a mighty hand?

12 Wherefore should the Egyptians speak, and say, For mischief did he bring them out, to slay them in the mountains, and to consume them from the face of the earth? Turn from thy fierce wrath, and repent of this evil against thy people.

13 Remember Abraham, Isaac, and Israel, thy servants, to whom thou swarest by thine own self, and saidst unto them, I will multiply your seed as the stars of heaven, and all this land that I have spoken of will I give unto your seed, and they shall inherit *it* for ever.

14 And the LORD repented of the evil which he thought to do unto his people.

15 ¶ And Moses turned, and went down from the mount, and the two tables of the testimony *were* in his hand: the tables *were* written on both their sides; on the one side and on the other *were* they written.

16 And the tables *were* the work of God, and the writing *was* the writing of God, graven upon the tables.

17 And when Joshua heard the noise of the people as they shouted, he said unto Moses, *There is* a noise of war in the camp.

18 And he said, *It is* not the voice of *them that* shout for mastery, neither *is it* the voice of *them that* cry for being overcome: *but* the noise of *them that* sing do I hear.

19 ¶ And it came to pass, as soon as he came nigh unto the camp, that he saw the calf, and the dancing: and Moses' anger waxed hot, and he cast the tables out of his hands, and brake them beneath the mount.

20 And he took the calf which they had made, and burnt *it* in the fire, and ground *it* to powder, and strawed *it* upon the water, and made the children of Israel drink *of it*.

21 And Moses said unto Aaron, What did this people unto thee, that thou hast brought so great a sin upon them?

22 And Aaron said, Let not the anger of my lord wax hot: thou knowest the people, that they *are set* on mischief.

23 For they said unto me, Make us gods, which shall go before us: for *as for* this Moses, the man that brought us up out of the land of Egypt, we wot not what is become of him.

24 And I said unto them, Whosoever hath any gold, let them break *it* off. So they gave *it* me: then I cast it into the fire, and there came out this calf.

25 ¶ And when Moses saw that the people *were* naked; (for Aaron had made them naked unto *their* shame among their enemies:)

26 Then Moses stood in the gate of the camp, and said, Who *is* on the LORD's side? *let him come* unto me. And all the sons of Levi gathered themselves together unto him.

27 And he said unto them, Thus saith the LORD God of Israel, Put every man his sword by his side, *and* go in and out from gate to gate throughout the camp, and slay every man his brother, and every man his companion, and every man his neighbour.

28 And the children of Levi did according to the word of Moses: and there fell of the people that day about three thousand men.

29 For Moses had said, Consecrate yourselves today to the LORD, even every man upon his son, and upon his brother; that he may bestow upon you a blessing this day.

30 ¶ And it came to pass on the morrow, that Moses said unto the people, Ye have sinned a great sin: and now I will go up unto the LORD; peradventure I shall make an atonement for your sin.

## Amplified

9 And the Lord said to Moses, I have seen this people, and behold, it is a stiff-necked people;

10 Now therefore let Me alone, that My wrath may burn hot against them, and that I may destroy them; but I will make of you a great nation.

11 But Moses besought the Lord his God, and said, Lord, why does Your wrath blaze hot against Your people, whom You have brought forth out of the land of Egypt with great power and a mighty hand?

12 Why should the Egyptians say, For evil He brought them forth, to slay them in the mountains and consume them from the face of the earth? Turn from Your fierce wrath, and change Your mind concerning this evil against Your people.

13 [Earnestly] remember Abraham, Isaac, and Israel, Your servants, to whom You swore by Your own self and said to them, I will multiply your seed as the stars of the heavens, and all this land that I have spoken of will I give to your seed, and they shall inherit it for ever.

14 Then the Lord turned from the evil which He had thought to do to His people.

15 And Moses turned, and went down from the mountain with the two tables of the testimony in his hand, tables *or* tablets that were written on both sides.

16 The tables were the work of God, and the writing was the writing of God, graven upon the tables.

17 And when Joshua heard the noise of the people as they shouted, he said to Moses, There is a noise of war in the camp.

18 But Moses said, It is not the sound of shouting for victory, neither is it the sound of the cry of the defeated, but the sound of singing that I hear.

19 And as soon as he came near to the camp he saw the calf and the dancing. And Moses' anger blazed hot, and he cast the tables out of his hands, and broke them at the foot of the mountain.

20 And he took the calf they had made, and burned it in the fire, and ground it to powder, and scattered it on the water, and made the Israelites drink it.

21 And Moses said to Aaron, What did this people do to you, that you have brought so great a sin upon them?

22 And Aaron said, Let not the anger of my lord blaze hot; you know the people, that they are set on evil.

23 For they said to me, Make us gods, which shall go before us; for as for this Moses, the man who brought us up out of the land of Egypt, we do not know what has become of him.

24 I said to them, Those who have any gold, let them take it off. So they gave it to me; then I cast it into the fire, and there came out this calf.

25 And when Moses saw that the people were unruly *and* unrestrained (for Aaron had let them get out of control, so that they were a derision *and* to their shame among their enemies),

26 Then Moses stood in the gate of the camp, and said, Whoever is on the Lord's side, let him come to me. And all the Levites [the priestly tribe] gathered together to him.

27 And he said to them, Thus says the Lord God of Israel, Every man put his sword on his side, and go in and out from gate to gate throughout the camp, and slay every man his brother, and every man his companion, and every man his neighbor.

28 And the sons of Levi did according to the word of Moses; and there fell of the people that day about 3000 men.

29 And Moses said [to the Levites, By your obedience to God's command] you have consecrated yourselves today *as priests* to the Lord, each man [at the cost of being] against his own son and his own brother, that the Lord may restore *and* bestow His blessing upon *you* this day.

30 Next day Moses said to the people, You have sinned a great sin. And now I will go up to the Lord; perhaps I can make atonement for your sin.

## New American Standard

9 And the LORD said to Moses, "I have seen this people, and
behold, they are an obstinate people.
10 "Now then let Me alone, that My anger may burn against
them, and that I may destroy them; and I will make of you a great
nation."

*Moses' Entreaty*

11 Then Moses entreated the LORD his God, and said, "O LORD,
why doth Thine anger burn against Thy people whom Thou hast
brought out from the land of Egypt with great power and with a
mighty hand?
12 "Why should the Egyptians speak, saying, 'With evil *intent*
He brought them out to kill them in the mountains and to destroy
them from the face of the earth'? Turn from Thy burning anger and
change Thy mind about *doing* harm to Thy people.
13 "Remember Abraham, Isaac, and Israel, Thy servants to
whom Thou didst swear by Thyself, and didst say to them, 'I will
multiply your descendants as the stars of the heavens, and all this
land of which I have spoken I will give to your descendants, and
they shall inherit *it* forever.' "
14 So the LORD changed His mind about the harm which He said
He would do to His people.
15 ¶ Then Moses turned and went down from the mountain with
the two tablets of the testimony in his hand, tablets which were
written on both sides; they were written on one *side* and the other.
16 And the tablets were God's work, and the writing was God's
writing engraved on the tablets.
17 Now when Joshua heard the sound of the people as they
shouted, he said to Moses, "There is a sound of war in the camp."
18 But he said,

"It is not the sound of the cry of triumph,
Nor is it the sound of the cry of defeat;
But the sound of singing I hear."

*Moses' Anger*

19 And it came about, as soon as Moses came near the camp, that
he saw the calf and *the* dancing; and Moses' anger burned, and he
threw the tablets from his hands and shattered them at the foot of
the mountain.
20 And he took the calf which they had made and burned *it* with
fire, and ground it to powder, and scattered it over the surface of
the water, and made the sons of Israel drink *it*.
21 ¶ Then Moses said to Aaron, "What did this people do to you,
that you have brought *such* great sin upon them?"
22 And Aaron said, "Do not let the anger of my lord burn; you
know the people yourself, that they are prone to evil.
23 "For they said to me, 'Make a god for us who will go before
us; for this Moses, the man who brought us up from the land of
Egypt, we do not know what has become of him.'
24 "And I said to them, 'Whoever has any gold, let them tear it
off.' So they gave *it* to me, and I threw it into the fire, and out came
this calf."
25 ¶ Now when Moses saw that the people were out of control—
for Aaron had let them get out of control to be a derision among
their enemies—
26 then Moses stood in the gate of the camp, and said, "Whoever
is for the LORD, *come* to me!" And all the sons of Levi gathered
together to him.
27 And he said to them, "Thus says the LORD, the God of Israel,
'Every man *of you* put his sword upon his thigh, and go back and
forth from gate to gate in the camp, and kill every man his brother,
and every man his friend, and every man his neighbor.' "
28 So the sons of Levi did as Moses instructed, and about three
thousand men of the people fell that day.
29 Then Moses said, "Dedicate yourselves today to the LORD—
for every man has been against his son and against his brother—in
order that He may bestow a blessing upon you today."
30 ¶ And it came about on the next day that Moses said to the
people, "You yourselves have committed a great sin; and now I am
going up to the LORD, perhaps I can make atonement for your sin."

## New International

9 "I have seen these people," the LORD said to Moses, "and they
are a stiff-necked people.
10 Now leave me alone so that my anger
may burn against them and that I may destroy them. Then I will
make you into a great nation."
11 But Moses sought the favor of the LORD his God. "O LORD,"
he said, "why should your anger burn against your people, whom
you brought out of Egypt with great power and a mighty hand?
12 Why should the Egyptians say, 'It was with evil intent that he
brought them out, to kill them in the mountains and to wipe them
off the face of the earth'? Turn from your fierce anger; relent and
do not bring disaster on your people.
13 Remember your servants
Abraham, Isaac and Israel, to whom you swore by your own self:
'I will make your descendants as numerous as the stars in the sky
and I will give your descendants all this land I promised them, and
it will be their inheritance forever.' "
14 Then the LORD relented and
did not bring on his people the disaster he had threatened.
15 Moses turned and went down the mountain with the two
tablets of the Testimony in his hands. They were inscribed on both
sides, front and back.
16 The tablets were the work of God; the
writing was the writing of God, engraved on the tablets.
17 When Joshua heard the noise of the people shouting, he said
to Moses, "There is the sound of war in the camp."
18 Moses replied:

"It is not the sound of victory,
it is not the sound of defeat;
it is the sound of singing that I hear."

19 When Moses approached the camp and saw the calf and the
dancing, his anger burned and he threw the tablets out of his
hands, breaking them to pieces at the foot of the mountain.
20 And
he took the calf they had made and burned it in the fire; then he
ground it to powder, scattered it on the water and made the
Israelites drink it.
21 He said to Aaron, "What did these people do to you, that you
led them into such great sin?"
22 "Do not be angry, my lord," Aaron answered. "You know
how prone these people are to evil.
23 They said to me, 'Make us
gods who will go before us. As for this fellow Moses who brought
us up out of Egypt, we don't know what has happened to him.'
24 So I told them, 'Whoever has any gold jewelry, take it off.' Then
they gave me the gold, and I threw it into the fire, and out came
this calf!"
25 Moses saw that the people were running wild and that Aaron
had let them get out of control and so become a laughingstock to
their enemies.
26 So he stood at the entrance to the camp and said,
"Whoever is for the LORD, come to me." And all the Levites rallied
to him.
27 Then he said to them, "This is what the LORD, the God of
Israel, says: 'Each man strap a sword to his side. Go back and forth
through the camp from one end to the other, each killing his
brother and friend and neighbor.' "
28 The Levites did as Moses
commanded, and that day about three thousand of the people
died.
29 Then Moses said, "You have been set apart to the LORD
today, for you were against your own sons and brothers, and he
has blessed you this day."
30 The next day Moses said to the people, "You have committed
a great sin. But now I will go up to the LORD; perhaps I can make
atonement for your sin."

## King James

31 And Moses returned unto the LORD, and said, Oh, this people have sinned a great sin, and have made them gods of gold.

32 Yet now, if thou wilt forgive their sin—; and if not, blot me, I pray thee, out of thy book which thou hast written.

33 And the LORD said unto Moses, Whosoever hath sinned against me, him will I blot out of my book.

34 Therefore now go, lead the people unto *the place* of which I have spoken unto thee: behold, mine Angel shall go before thee: nevertheless in the day when I visit I will visit their sin upon them.

35 And the LORD plagued the people, because they made the calf, which Aaron made.

**33** AND THE LORD said unto Moses, Depart, *and* go up hence, thou and the people which thou hast brought up out of the land of Egypt, unto the land which I sware unto Abraham, to Isaac, and to Jacob, saying, Unto thy seed will I give it:

2 And I will send an angel before thee; and I will drive out the Canaanite, the Amorite, and the Hittite, and the Perizzite, the Hivite, and the Jebusite:

3 Unto a land flowing with milk and honey: for I will not go up in the midst of thee; for thou *art* a stiffnecked people: lest I consume thee in the way.

4 ¶ And when the people heard these evil tidings, they mourned: and no man did put on him his ornaments.

5 For the LORD had said unto Moses, Say unto the children of Israel, Ye *are* a stiffnecked people: I will come up into the midst of thee in a moment, and consume thee: therefore now put off thy ornaments from thee, that I may know what to do unto thee.

6 And the children of Israel stripped themselves of their ornaments by the mount Horeb.

7 And Moses took the tabernacle, and pitched it without the camp, afar off from the camp, and called it the Tabernacle of the congregation. And it came to pass, *that* every one which sought the LORD went out unto the tabernacle of the congregation, which *was* without the camp.

8 And it came to pass, when Moses went out unto the tabernacle, *that* all the people rose up, and stood every man *at* his tent door, and looked after Moses, until he was gone into the tabernacle.

9 And it came to pass, as Moses entered into the tabernacle, the cloudy pillar descended, and stood *at* the door of the tabernacle, and *the LORD talked with Moses.*

10 And all the people saw the cloudy pillar stand *at* the tabernacle door: and all the people rose up and worshipped, every man *in* his tent door.

11 And the LORD spake unto Moses face to face, as a man speaketh unto his friend. And he turned again into the camp: but his servant Joshua, the son of Nun, a young man, departed not out of the tabernacle.

12 ¶ And Moses said unto the LORD, See, thou sayest unto me, Bring up this people: and thou hast not let me know whom thou wilt send with me. Yet thou hast said, I know thee by name, and thou hast also found grace in my sight.

13 Now therefore, I pray thee, if I have found grace in thy sight, show me now thy way, that I may know thee, that I may find grace in thy sight: and consider that this nation *is* thy people.

14 And he said, My presence shall go *with thee,* and I will give thee rest.

15 And he said unto him, If thy presence go not *with me,* carry us not up hence.

16 For wherein shall it be known here that I and thy people have found grace in thy sight? *is it* not in that thou goest with us? so shall we be separated, I and thy people, from all the people that *are* upon the face of the earth.

## Amplified

31 So Moses returned to the Lord, and said, Oh, this people have sinned a great sin, and have made them gods of gold!

32 Yet now, if You will forgive their sin—and if not, blot me, I pray You, out of Your book which You have written!

33 But the Lord said to Moses, Whoever has sinned against Me, I will blot him [not you] out of My book. [Dan. 12:1; Phil. 4:3; Rev. 3:5.]

34 But now go, lead the people to the place of which I have told you. Behold, My angel shall go before you. Nevertheless, in the day when I punish I will visit their sin upon them! [Cp. Exod. 33:2, 3.]

35 And the Lord sent a plague upon the people, because they made the calf which Aaron fashioned for them.

**33** THE LORD said to Moses, Depart, go up from here, you and the people whom you have brought from the land of Egypt, to the land which I swore to Abraham, Isaac, and Jacob, saying, To your descendants I will give it.

2 I will send an angel before you, and I will drive out the Canaanite, Amorite, Hittite, Perizzite, Hivite, and Jebusite.

3 Go up to a land flowing with milk and honey; but I will not go up among you, for you are a stiff-necked people, lest I destroy you on the way.

4 When the people heard these evil tidings, they mourned, and no man put on his ornaments.

5 For the Lord had said to Moses, Say to the Israelites, You are a stiff-necked people! If I should come among you for one moment, I would consume you. Now therefore [penitently] leave off your ornaments, that I may know what to do with you.

6 And the Israelites left off all their ornaments, from Mount Horeb onward.

7 Now Moses used to take [his own] tent and pitch it outside the camp, far off from the camp, and he called it the tent of meeting [of God with His own people]. And everyone who sought the Lord went out to [that temporary] tent of meeting, which was outside the camp.

8 When Moses went out to the tent of meeting, all the people rose and stood every man at his tent door, and looked after Moses, until he had gone into the tent.

9 When Moses entered the tent, the pillar of cloud would descend and stand at the door of the tent, and the Lord would talk with Moses.

10 And all the people saw the pillar of cloud stand at the tent door, and all the people rose up and worshiped, every man at his tent door.

11 And the Lord spoke to Moses face to face, as a man speaks to his friend. Moses returned to the camp, but his minister Joshua, son of Nun, a young man, did not depart from the [temporary, prayer] tent.

12 Moses said to the Lord, See, You say to me, Bring up this people; but You have not let me know whom You will send with me. Yet You said, I know you by name, and you have also found favor in My sight.

13 Now therefore, I pray You, if I have found favor in Your sight, show me now Your way, that I may know You [progressively become more deeply and intimately acquainted with You, perceiving and recognizing and understanding more strongly and clearly] that I may find favor in Your sight. And, [Lord, do] consider that this nation is Your people.

14 And the Lord said, My presence shall go with you, and I will give you rest.

15 And Moses said to the Lord, If Your presence does not go with me, do not carry us up from here!

16 For by what shall it be known that I, and Your people have found favor in Your sight? Is it not in Your going with us so that we are distinguished, I and Your people, from all the other people upon the face of the earth?

## New American Standard

31Then Moses returned to the LORD, and said, "Alas, this
people has committed a great sin, and they have made a god of
gold for themselves.
32"But now, if Thou wilt, forgive their sin—and if not, please
blot me out from Thy book which Thou hast written!"
33And the LORD said to Moses, "Whoever has sinned against
Me, I will blot him out of My book.
34"But go now, lead the people where I told you. Behold, My
angel shall go before you; nevertheless in the day when I punish,
I will punish them for their sin."
35Then the LORD smote the people, because of what they did
with the calf which Aaron had made.

*The Journey Resumed*

33 THEN THE LORD spoke to Moses, "Depart, go up from
here, you and the people whom you have brought up
from the land of Egypt, to the land of which I swore to Abraham,
Isaac, and Jacob, saying, 'To your descendants I will give it.'
2"And I will send an angel before you and I will drive out the
Canaanite, the Amorite, the Hittite, the Perizzite, the Hivite and
the Jebusite.
3" *Go up* to a land flowing with milk and honey; for I will not
go up in your midst, because you are an obstinate people, lest I
destroy you on the way."
4When the people heard this sad word, they went into mourning, and none of them put on his ornaments.
5For the LORD had said to Moses, "Say to the sons of Israel,
'You are an obstinate people; should I go up in your midst for one
moment, I would destroy you. Now therefore, put off your ornaments from you, that I may know what I will do with you.'"
6So the sons of Israel stripped themselves of their ornaments
from Mount Horeb *onward.*
7¶ Now Moses used to take the tent and pitch it outside the
camp, a good distance from the camp, and he called it the tent of
meeting. And it came about, that everyone who sought the LORD
would go out to the tent of meeting which was outside the camp.
8And it came about, whenever Moses went out to the tent, that
all the people would arise and stand, each at the entrance of his
tent, and gaze after Moses until he entered the tent.
9And it came about, whenever Moses entered the tent, the
pillar of cloud would descend and stand at the entrance of the tent;
and the LORD would speak with Moses.
10When all the people saw the pillar of cloud standing at the
entrance of the tent, all the people would arise and worship, each
at the entrance of his tent.
11Thus the LORD used to speak to Moses face to face, just as a
man speaks to his friend. When Moses returned to the camp, his
servant Joshua, the son of Nun, a young man, would not depart
from the tent.

*Moses Intercedes*

12¶ Then Moses said to the LORD, "See, Thou dost say to me,
'Bring up this people!' But Thou Thyself hast not let me know
whom Thou wilt send with me. Moreover, Thou hast said, 'I have
known you by name, and you have also found favor in My sight.'
13"Now therefore, I pray Thee, if I have found favor in Thy
sight, let me know Thy ways, that I may know Thee, so that I may
find favor in Thy sight. Consider too, that this nation is Thy
people."
14And He said, "My presence shall go *with you,* and I will give
you rest."
15Then he said to Him, "If Thy presence does not go *with us,*
do not lead us up from here.
16"For how then can it be known that I have found favor in Thy
sight, I and Thy people? Is it not by Thy going with us, so that we,
I and Thy people, may be distinguished from all the *other* people
who are upon the face of the earth?"

## New International

31So Moses went back to the LORD and said, "Oh, what a great
sin these people have committed! They have made themselves
gods of gold. 32But now, please forgive their sin—but if not, then
blot me out of the book you have written."
33The LORD replied to Moses, "Whoever has sinned against me
I will blot out of my book. 34Now go, lead the people to the place
I spoke of, and my angel will go before you. However, when the
time comes for me to punish, I will punish them for their sin."
35And the LORD struck the people with a plague because of
what they did with the calf Aaron had made.

33 THEN THE LORD said to Moses, "Leave this place, you
and the people you brought up out of Egypt, and go up
to the land I promised on oath to Abraham, Isaac and Jacob,
saying, 'I will give it to your descendants.' 2I will send an angel
before you and drive out the Canaanites, Amorites, Hittites, Perizzites, Hivites and Jebusites. 3Go up to the land flowing with milk
and honey. But I will not go with you, because you are a stiff-
necked people and I might destroy you on the way."
4When the people heard these distressing words, they began to
mourn and no one put on any ornaments. 5For the LORD had said
to Moses, "Tell the Israelites, 'You are a stiff-necked people. If I
were to go with you even for a moment, I might destroy you. Now
take off your ornaments and I will decide what to do with you.'"
6So the Israelites stripped off their ornaments at Mount Horeb.

*The Tent of Meeting*

7Now Moses used to take a tent and pitch it outside the camp
some distance away, calling it the "tent of meeting." Anyone
inquiring of the LORD would go to the tent of meeting outside the
camp. 8And whenever Moses went out to the tent, all the people
rose and stood at the entrances to their tents, watching Moses until
he entered the tent. 9As Moses went into the tent, the pillar of
cloud would come down and stay at the entrance, while the LORD
spoke with Moses. 10Whenever the people saw the pillar of cloud
standing at the entrance to the tent, they all stood and worshiped,
each at the entrance to his tent. 11The LORD would speak to Moses
face to face, as a man speaks with his friend. Then Moses would
return to the camp, but his young aide Joshua son of Nun did not
leave the tent.

*Moses and the Glory of the LORD*

12Moses said to the LORD, "You have been telling me, 'Lead
these people,' but you have not let me know whom you will send
with me. You have said, 'I know you by name and you have found
favor with me.' 13If you are pleased with me, teach me your ways
so I may know you and continue to find favor with you. Remember
that this nation is your people."
14The LORD replied, "My Presence will go with you, and I will
give you rest."
15Then Moses said to him, "If your Presence does not go with
us, do not send us up from here. 16How will anyone know that you
are pleased with me and with your people unless you go with us?
What else will distinguish me and your people from all the other
people on the face of the earth?"

## King James

17 And the LORD said unto Moses, I will do this thing also that thou hast spoken: for thou hast found grace in my sight, and I know thee by name.

18 And he said, I beseech thee, show me thy glory.

19 And he said, I will make all my goodness pass before thee, and I will proclaim the name of the LORD before thee; and will be gracious to whom I will be gracious, and will show mercy on whom I will show mercy.

20 And he said, Thou canst not see my face: for there shall no man see me, and live.

21 And the LORD said, Behold, *there is* a place by me, and thou shalt stand upon a rock:

22 And it shall come to pass, while my glory passeth by, that I will put thee in a cleft of the rock, and will cover thee with my hand while I pass by:

23 And I will take away mine hand, and thou shalt see my back parts: but my face shall not be seen.

34 AND THE LORD said unto Moses, Hew thee two tables of stone like unto the first: and I will write upon *these* tables the words that were in the first tables, which thou brakest.

2 And be ready in the morning, and come up in the morning unto mount Sinai, and present thyself there to me in the top of the mount.

3 And no man shall come up with thee, neither let any man be seen throughout all the mount; neither let the flocks nor herds feed before that mount.

4 ¶ And he hewed two tables of stone like unto the first; and Moses rose up early in the morning, and went up unto mount Sinai, as the LORD had commanded him, and took in his hand the two tables of stone.

5 And the LORD descended in the cloud, and stood with him there, and proclaimed the name of the LORD.

6 And the LORD passed by before him, and proclaimed, The LORD, The LORD God, merciful and gracious, longsuffering, and abundant in goodness and truth,

7 Keeping mercy for thousands, forgiving iniquity and transgression and sin, and that will by no means clear *the guilty;* visiting the iniquity of the fathers upon the children, and upon the children's children, unto the third and to the fourth *generation.*

8 And Moses made haste, and bowed his head toward the earth, and worshipped.

9 And he said, If now I have found grace in thy sight, O Lord, let my Lord, I pray thee, go among us; for it *is* a stiffnecked people; and pardon our iniquity and our sin, and take us for thine inheritance.

10 ¶ And he said, Behold, I make a covenant: before all thy people I will do marvels, such as have not been done in all the earth, nor in any nation: and all the people among which thou *art* shall see the work of the LORD: for it *is* a terrible thing that I will do with thee.

11 Observe thou that which I command thee this day: behold, I drive out before thee the Amorite, and the Canaanite, and the Hittite, and the Perizzite, and the Hivite, and the Jebusite.

12 Take heed to thyself, lest thou make a covenant with the inhabitants of the land whither thou goest, lest it be for a snare in the midst of thee:

13 But ye shall destroy their altars, break their images, and cut down their groves:

14 For thou shalt worship no other god: for the LORD, whose name *is* Jealous, *is* a jealous God:

## Amplified

17 And the Lord said to Moses, I will do this thing also that you have asked, for you have found favor, loving-kindness *and* mercy in My sight, and I know you personally *and* by name. [Rev. 2:17.]

18 And Moses said, I beseech You, show me Your glory.

19 And God said, I will make all My goodness pass before you, and I will proclaim My name, THE LORD, before you; for I will be gracious to whom I will be gracious, and will show mercy *and* loving-kindness on whom I will show mercy *and* loving-kindness. [Rom. 9:15, 16.]

20 But, He said, You can not see My face, for no man shall see Me and live.

21 And the Lord said, Behold, there is a place beside Me, and you shall stand upon the rock,

22 And while My glory passes by I will put you in a cleft of the rock, and cover you with My hand until I have passed by.

23 Then I will take away My hand, and you shall see My back; but My face shall not be seen.

34 THE LORD said to Moses, Cut two tables of stone like the first; and I will write upon these tables the words that were on the first tables, which you broke.

2 Be ready and come up in the morning to Mount Sinai, and present yourself there to Me on the top of the mountain.

3 And no man shall come up with you, neither let any man be seen throughout all the mountain; neither let flocks or herds feed before that mountain.

4 So Moses cut two tables of stone like the first; and he rose up early in the morning and went up on Mount Sinai, as the Lord had commanded him, and took [a]in his hand two tables of stone.

5 And the Lord descended in the cloud and stood with him there, and proclaimed the name of the Lord.

6 And the Lord passed by before him, and proclaimed, The Lord! the Lord! a God merciful and gracious, slow to anger, and abundant in loving-kindness and truth,

7 Keeping mercy *and* loving-kindness for thousands, forgiving iniquity and transgression and sin, but Who will by no means clear the guilty, visiting the iniquity of the fathers upon the children and the children's children, to the third and fourth generation.

8 And Moses made haste to bow his head toward the earth, and worshiped.

9 And he said, If now I have found favor *and* loving-kindness in Your sight, O Lord, let the Lord, I pray You, go in the midst of us, although it is a stiff-necked people; and pardon our iniquity and our sin, and take us for Your inheritance.

10 And the Lord said, Behold, I lay down [afresh the terms of the mutual agreement between Me and Israel] a covenant. Before all your people I will do marvels (wonders, miracles), such as have not been wrought *or* created in all the earth or in any nation; and all the people among whom you are shall see the work of the Lord; for it is a terrible thing—fearful and full of awe—that I will do with you.

11 Observe what I command you this day. Behold, I drive out before you the Amorite, Canaanite, Hittite, Perizzite, Hivite, and Jebusite.

12 Take heed to yourself, lest you make a covenant *or* mutual agreement with the inhabitants of the land to which you go, lest it become a snare in the midst of you.

13 But you shall destroy their altars, dash in pieces their pillars (obelisks, images), and cut down their Asherim [symbols of the god Asherah];

14 For you shall worship no other god; for the Lord, whose name is Jealous, is a jealous—impassioned—God,

**AMP** [a] The two tables of stone are believed to have been pocket-size, easily carried in one hand. The pictures of Moses carrying tablets of tombstone size are the result of the misconception of artists, and are not supported by the Bible.

## New American Standard

17¶ And the LORD said to Moses, "I will also do this thing of which you have spoken; for you have found favor in My sight, and I have known you by name."

18 Then Moses said, "I pray Thee, show me Thy glory!"

19 And He said, "I Myself will make all My goodness pass before you, and will proclaim the name of the LORD before you; and I will be gracious to whom I will be gracious, and will show compassion on whom I will show compassion."

20 But He said, "You cannot see My face, for no man can see Me and live!"

21 Then the LORD said, "Behold, there is a place by Me, and you shall stand *there* on the rock;

22 and it will come about, while My glory is passing by, that I will put you in the cleft of the rock and cover you with My hand until I have passed by.

23 "Then I will take My hand away and you shall see My back, but My face shall not be seen."

*The Two Tablets Replaced*

**34** NOW THE LORD said to Moses, "Cut out for yourself two stone tablets like the former ones, and I will write on the tablets the words that were on the former tablets which you shattered.

2 "So be ready by morning, and come up in the morning to Mount Sinai, and present yourself there to Me on the top of the mountain.

3 "And no man is to come up with you, nor let any man be seen anywhere on the mountain; even the flocks and the herds may not graze in front of that mountain."

4 So he cut out two stone tablets like the former ones, and Moses rose up early in the morning and went up to Mount Sinai, as the LORD had commanded him, and he took two stone tablets in his hand.

5 And the LORD descended in the cloud and stood there with him as he called upon the name of the LORD.

6 Then the LORD passed by in front of him and proclaimed, "The LORD, the LORD God, compassionate and gracious, slow to anger, and abounding in lovingkindness and truth;

7 who keeps lovingkindness for thousands, who forgives iniquity, transgression and sin; yet He will by no means leave *the guilty* unpunished, visiting the iniquity of fathers on the children and on the grandchildren to the third and fourth generations."

8 And Moses made haste to bow low toward the earth and worship.

9 And he said, "If now I have found favor in Thy sight, O Lord, I pray, let the Lord go along in our midst, even though the people are so obstinate; and do Thou pardon our iniquity and our sin, and take us as Thine own possession."

*The Covenant Renewed*

10¶ Then God said, "Behold, I am going to make a covenant. Before all your people I will perform miracles which have not been produced in all the earth, nor among any of the nations; and all the people among whom you live will see the working of the LORD, for it is a fearful thing that I am going to perform with you.

11 "Be sure to observe what I am commanding you this day: behold, I am going to drive out the Amorite before you, and the Canaanite, the Hittite, the Perizzite, the Hivite and the Jebusite.

12 "Watch yourself that you make no covenant with the inhabitants of the land into which you are going, lest it become a snare in your midst.

13 "But *rather,* you are to tear down their altars and smash their *sacred* pillars and cut down their [b]Asherim

14 —for you shall not worship any other god, for the LORD, whose name is Jealous, is a jealous God—

## New International

17 And the LORD said to Moses, "I will do the very thing you
have asked, because I am pleased with you and I know you by
name."
18 Then Moses said, "Now show me your glory."
19 And the LORD said, "I will cause all my goodness to pass in
front of you, and I will proclaim my name, the LORD, in your
presence. I will have mercy on whom I will have mercy, and I will
have compassion on whom I will have compassion. 20 But," he
said, "you cannot see my face, for no one may see me and live."
21 Then the LORD said, "There is a place near me where you may
stand on a rock. 22 When my glory passes by, I will put you in a
cleft in the rock and cover you with my hand until I have passed
by. 23 Then I will remove my hand and you will see my back; but
my face must not be seen."

*The New Stone Tablets*

**34** THE LORD said to Moses, "Chisel out two stone tablets
like the first ones, and I will write on them the words that
were on the first tablets, which you broke. 2 Be ready in the morning, and then come up on Mount Sinai. Present yourself to me
there on top of the mountain. 3 No one is to come with you or be
seen anywhere on the mountain; not even the flocks and herds
may graze in front of the mountain."
4 So Moses chiseled out two stone tablets like the first ones and
went up Mount Sinai early in the morning, as the LORD had commanded him; and he carried the two stone tablets in his hands.
5 Then the LORD came down in the cloud and stood there with him
and proclaimed his name, the LORD. 6 And he passed in front of
Moses, proclaiming, "The LORD, the LORD, the compassionate and
gracious God, slow to anger, abounding in love and faithfulness,
7 maintaining love to thousands, and forgiving wickedness, rebellion and sin. Yet he does not leave the guilty unpunished; he
punishes the children and their children for the sin of the fathers
to the third and fourth generation."
8 Moses bowed to the ground at once and worshiped. 9 "O Lord,
if I have found favor in your eyes," he said, "then let the Lord go
with us. Although this is a stiff-necked people, forgive our wickedness and our sin, and take us as your inheritance."
10 Then the LORD said: "I am making a covenant with you.
Before all your people I will do wonders never before done in any
nation in all the world. The people you live among will see how
awesome is the work that I, the LORD, will do for you. 11 Obey what
I command you today. I will drive out before you the Amorites,
Canaanites, Hittites, Perizzites, Hivites and Jebusites. 12 Be careful
not to make a treaty with those who live in the land where you are
going, or they will be a snare among you. 13 Break down their
altars, smash their sacred stones and cut down their Asherah
poles.[c] 14 Do not worship any other god, for the LORD, whose
name is Jealous, is a jealous God.

NAS [b] I.e., wooden symbols of a female deity

NIV [c] *13* That is, symbols of the goddess Asherah

## King James

15 Lest thou make a covenant with the inhabitants of the land, and they go a-whoring after their gods, and do sacrifice unto their gods, and *one* call thee, and thou eat of his sacrifice;

16 And thou take of their daughters unto thy sons, and their daughters go a-whoring after their gods, and make thy sons go a-whoring after their gods.

17 Thou shalt make thee no molten gods.

18 ¶ The feast of unleavened bread shalt thou keep. Seven days thou shalt eat unleavened bread, as I commanded thee, in the time of the month Abib: for in the month Abib thou camest out from Egypt.

19 All that openeth the matrix *is* mine; and every firstling among thy cattle, *whether* ox or sheep, *that is male*.

20 But the firstling of an ass thou shalt redeem with a lamb: and if thou redeem *him* not, then shalt thou break his neck. All the firstborn of thy sons thou shalt redeem. And none shall appear before me empty.

21 ¶ Six days thou shalt work, but on the seventh day thou shalt rest: in earing time and in harvest thou shalt rest.

22 ¶ And thou shalt observe the feast of weeks, of the firstfruits of wheat harvest, and the feast of ingathering at the year's end.

23 ¶ Thrice in the year shall all your menchildren appear before the Lord GOD, the God of Israel.

24 For I will cast out the nations before thee, and enlarge thy borders: neither shall any man desire thy land, when thou shalt go up to appear before the LORD thy God thrice in the year.

25 Thou shalt not offer the blood of my sacrifice with leaven; neither shall the sacrifice of the feast of the passover be left unto the morning.

26 The first of the firstfruits of thy land thou shalt bring unto the house of the LORD thy God. Thou shalt not seethe a kid in his mother's milk.

27 And the LORD said unto Moses, Write thou these words: for after the tenor of these words I have made a covenant with thee and with Israel.

28 And he was there with the LORD forty days and forty nights; he did neither eat bread, nor drink water. And he wrote upon the tables the words of the covenant, the ten commandments.

29 ¶ And it came to pass, when Moses came down from mount Sinai with the two tables of testimony in Moses' hand, when he came down from the mount, that Moses wist not that the skin of his face shone while he talked with him.

30 And when Aaron and all the children of Israel saw Moses, behold, the skin of his face shone; and they were afraid to come nigh him.

31 And Moses called unto them; and Aaron and all the rulers of the congregation returned unto him: and Moses talked with them.

32 And afterward all the children of Israel came nigh: and he gave them in commandment all that the LORD had spoken with him in mount Sinai.

33 And *till* Moses had done speaking with them, he put a veil on his face.

34 But when Moses went in before the LORD to speak with him, he took the veil off, until he came out. And he came out, and spake unto the children of Israel *that* which he was commanded.

35 And the children of Israel saw the face of Moses, that the skin of Moses' face shone: and Moses put the veil upon his face again, until he went in to speak with him.

## Amplified

15 Lest you make a covenant with the inhabitants of the land, and when they play the harlot after their gods, and sacrifice to their gods and one invites you, you eat of his food sacrificed to idols,

16 And you take of their daughters for your sons, and their daughters play the harlot after their gods and make your sons play the harlot after their gods.

17 You shall make for yourselves no molten gods.

18 The feast of unleavened bread you shall keep. Seven days you shall eat unleavened bread, as I commanded you, in the time of the month Abib; for in the month Abib you came out of Egypt.

19 All the males that first open the womb among your livestock are Mine, whether ox or sheep.

20 But the firstling of a donkey [an unclean beast] you shall redeem with a lamp *or* kid, and if you do not redeem it, then you shall break its neck. All the first-born of your sons you shall redeem. And none of you shall appear before Me empty-handed.

21 Six days you shall work, but on the seventh day you shall rest; even in plowing time and in harvest you shall rest [on the sabbath].

22 You shall observe the feast of weeks, the first fruits of wheat harvest, and the feast of ingathering at the year's end.

23 Three times in the year shall all your males appear before the Lord God, the God of Israel.

24 For I will cast out the nations before you, and enlarge your borders; neither shall any man desire [and molest] your land, when you go up to appear before the Lord your God three times in the year.

25 You shall not offer the blood of My sacrifice with leaven; neither shall the sacrifice of the feast of the passover be left until morning.

26 The first of the first fruits of your ground you shall bring to the house of the Lord your God. You shall not boil a kid in his mother's milk.

27 And the Lord said to Moses, Write these words, for after the purpose *and* character of these words I have made a covenant with you and with Israel.

28 Moses was there with the Lord forty days and forty nights; he ate no bread and drank no water. And he wrote upon the tables the words of the covenant, the ten commandments.

29 When Moses came down from Mount Sinai with the two tables of testimony in his hand, he did not know that the skin of his face shone *and* sent forth beams by reason of his speaking with the Lord.

30 When Aaron and all the Israelites saw Moses, behold, the skin of his face shone, and they feared to come near him.

31 But Moses called to them; and Aaron and all the leaders of the congregation returned to him, and *he* talked with them.

32 Afterward all the Israelites came near, and he gave them in commandment all the Lord had said to him in Mount Sinai.

33 And when Moses had done speaking with them, he put a veil on his face.

34 But when Moses went in before the Lord to speak with Him, [a]he took the veil off, until he came out. And he came out and told the Israelites what he was commanded.

35 The Israelites saw the face of Moses, how the skin of it shone; and Moses put the veil on his face again, until he went in to speak with God.

**AMP** [a] The Apostle Paul expressly refers to this incident when he says that we all may, with unveiled face, behold the glory of the Lord, and be transformed (II Cor. 3:13-18). That blessed vision, which of old was given only to the great leader of Israel, is now within reach of each individual believer. The Gospel has no fences to keep off the crowd from the mount of vision; the lowliest and most unworthy of its children may pass upward where the shining glory is to be seen. "We *all* . . . are changed" (F. B. Meyer, in *Moses, the Servant of God*.).

## New American Standard

15 lest you make a covenant with the inhabitants of the land and they play the harlot with their gods, and sacrifice to their gods, and someone invite you to eat of his sacrifice;

16 and you take some of his daughters for your sons, and his daughters play the harlot with their gods, and cause your sons *also* to play the harlot with their gods.

17 "You shall make for yourself no molten gods.

18¶ "You shall observe the Feast of Unleavened Bread. For seven days you are to eat unleavened bread, as I commanded you, at the appointed time in the month of Abib, for in the month of Abib you came out of Egypt.

19 "The first offspring from every womb belongs to Me, and all your male livestock, the first offspring from cattle and sheep.

20 "And you shall redeem with a lamb the first offspring from a donkey; and if you do not redeem *it*, then you shall break its neck. You shall redeem all the first-born of your sons. And none shall appear before Me empty-handed.

21¶ "You shall work six days, but on the seventh day you shall rest; *even* during plowing time and harvest you shall rest.

22 "And you shall celebrate the Feast of Weeks, *that is*, the first fruits of the wheat harvest, and the Feast of Ingathering at the turn of the year.

23 "Three times a year all your males are to appear before the Lord GOD, the God of Israel.

24 "For I will drive out nations before you and enlarge your borders, and no man shall covet your land when you go up three times a year to appear before the LORD your God.

25¶ "You shall not offer the blood of My sacrifice with leavened bread, nor is the sacrifice of the Feast of the Passover to be left over until morning.

26 "You shall bring the very first of the first fruits of your soil into the house of the LORD your God. You shall not boil a kid in its mother's milk."

27¶ Then the LORD said to Moses, "Write down these words, for in accordance with these words I have made a covenant with you and with Israel."

28 So he was there with the LORD forty days and forty nights; he did not eat bread or drink water. And he wrote on the tablets the words of the covenant, the Ten Commandments.

*Moses' Face Shines*

29¶ And it came about when Moses was coming down from Mount Sinai (and the two tablets of the testimony *were* in Moses' hand as he was coming down from the mountain), that Moses did not know that the skin of his face shone because of his speaking with Him.

30 So when Aaron and all the sons of Israel saw Moses, behold, the skin of his face shone, and they were afraid to come near him.

31 Then Moses called to them, and Aaron and all the rulers in the congregation returned to him; and Moses spoke to them.

32 And afterward all the sons of Israel came near, and he commanded them *to do* everything that the LORD had spoken to him on Mount Sinai.

33 When Moses had finished speaking with them, he put a veil over his face.

34 But whenever Moses went in before the LORD to speak with Him, he would take off the veil until he came out; and whenever he came out and spoke to the sons of Israel what he had been commanded,

35 the sons of Israel would see the face of Moses, that the skin of Moses' face shone. So Moses would replace the veil over his face until he went in to speak with Him.

## New International

15 "Be careful not to make a treaty with those who live in the
land; for when they prostitute themselves to their gods and sacrifice to them, they will invite you and you will eat their sacrifices.
16 And when you choose some of their daughters as wives for your
sons and those daughters prostitute themselves to their gods, they
will lead your sons to do the same.

17 "Do not make cast idols.

18 "Celebrate the Feast of Unleavened Bread. For seven days eat
bread made without yeast, as I commanded you. Do this at the
appointed time in the month of Abib, for in that month you came
out of Egypt.

19 "The first offspring of every womb belongs to me, including
all the firstborn males of your livestock, whether from herd or
flock. 20 Redeem the firstborn donkey with a lamb, but if you do
not redeem it, break its neck. Redeem all your firstborn sons.

"No one is to appear before me empty-handed.

21 "Six days you shall labor, but on the seventh day you shall
rest; even during the plowing season and harvest you must rest.

22 "Celebrate the Feast of Weeks with the firstfruits of the wheat
harvest, and the Feast of Ingathering at the turn of the year.[b]
23 Three times a year all your men are to appear before the Sovereign LORD, the God of Israel. 24 I will drive out nations before you
and enlarge your territory, and no one will covet your land when
you go up three times each year to appear before the LORD your
God.

25 "Do not offer the blood of a sacrifice to me along with anything containing yeast, and do not let any of the sacrifice from the
Passover Feast remain until morning.

26 "Bring the best of the firstfruits of your soil to the house of
the LORD your God.

"Do not cook a young goat in its mother's milk."

27 Then the LORD said to Moses, "Write down these words, for
in accordance with these words I have made a covenant with you
and with Israel." 28 Moses was there with the LORD forty days and
forty nights without eating bread or drinking water. And he wrote
on the tablets the words of the covenant—the Ten Commandments.

*The Radiant Face of Moses*

29 When Moses came down from Mount Sinai with the two
tablets of the Testimony in his hands, he was not aware that his
face was radiant because he had spoken with the LORD. 30 When
Aaron and all the Israelites saw Moses, his face was radiant, and
they were afraid to come near him. 31 But Moses called to them; so
Aaron and all the leaders of the community came back to him, and
he spoke to them. 32 Afterward all the Israelites came near him, and
he gave them all the commands the LORD had given him on Mount
Sinai.

33 When Moses finished speaking to them, he put a veil over his
face. 34 But whenever he entered the LORD's presence to speak with
him, he removed the veil until he came out. And when he came
out and told the Israelites what he had been commanded, 35 they
saw that his face was radiant. Then Moses would put the veil back
over his face until he went in to speak with the LORD.

NIV [b] 22 That is, in the fall

## King James

**35** AND MOSES gathered all the congregation of the children of Israel together, and said unto them, These *are* the words which the LORD hath commanded, that *ye* should do them.

2 Six days shall work be done, but on the seventh day there shall be to you an holy day, a sabbath of rest to the LORD: whosoever doeth work therein shall be put to death.

3 Ye shall kindle no fire throughout your habitations upon the sabbath day.

4 ¶ And Moses spake unto all the congregation of the children of Israel, saying, This *is* the thing which the LORD commanded, saying,

5 Take ye from among you an offering unto the LORD: whosoever *is* of a willing heart, let him bring it, an offering of the LORD; gold, and silver, and brass,

6 And blue, and purple, and scarlet, and fine linen, and goats' *hair,*

7 And rams' skins dyed red, and badgers' skins, and shittim wood,

8 And oil for the light, and spices for anointing oil, and for the sweet incense,

9 And onyx stones, and stones to be set for the ephod, and for the breastplate.

10 And every wisehearted among you shall come, and make all that the LORD hath commanded;

11 The tabernacle, his tent, and his covering, his taches, and his boards, his bars, his pillars, and his sockets,

12 The ark, and the staves thereof, *with* the mercy seat, and the veil of the covering,

13 The table, and his staves, and all his vessels, and the showbread,

14 The candlestick also for the light, and his furniture, and his lamps, with the oil for the light,

15 And the incense altar, and his staves, and the anointing oil, and the sweet incense, and the hanging for the door at the entering in of the tabernacle,

16 The altar of burnt offering, with his brasen grate, his staves, and all his vessels, the laver and his foot,

17 The hangings of the court, his pillars, and their sockets, and the hanging for the door of the court,

18 The pins of the tabernacle, and the pins of the court, and their cords,

19 The cloths of service, to do service in the holy *place,* the holy garments for Aaron the priest, and the garments of his sons, to minister in the priest's office.

20 ¶ And all the congregation of the children of Israel departed from the presence of Moses.

21 And they came, every one whose heart stirred him up, and every one whom his spirit made willing, *and* they brought the LORD's offering to the work of the tabernacle of the congregation, and for all his service, and for the holy garments.

22 And they came, both men and women, as many as were willing-hearted, *and* brought bracelets, and earrings, and rings, and tablets, all jewels of gold: and every man that offered *offered* an offering of gold unto the LORD.

23 And every man, with whom was found blue, and purple, and scarlet, and fine linen, and goats' *hair,* and red skins of rams, and badgers' skins, brought *them.*

24 Every one that did offer an offering of silver and brass brought the LORD's offering: and every man, with whom was found shittim wood for any work of the service, brought *it.*

25 And all the women that were wisehearted did spin with their hands, and brought that which they had spun, *both* of blue, and of purple, *and* of scarlet, and of fine linen.

## Amplified

**35** MOSES GATHERED all the congregation of the Israelites together, and said to them, These are the things which the Lord has commanded that you do.

2 Six days shall work be done, but the seventh day shall be to you a holy day, a sabbath of rest to the Lord; whoever works [on that day] shall be put to death.

3 You shall kindle no fire in all your dwellings on the sabbath day.

4 And Moses said to all the congregation of the Israelites, This is what the Lord commanded.

5 Take from among you an offering to the Lord: whoever is of a willing *and* generous heart, let him bring the Lord's offering: gold, silver, and bronze;

6 Blue, purple, and scarlet stuff, fine linen; goats' hair,

7 And rams' skins tanned red, and skins of dolphins *or* porpoises, and acacia wood,

8 And oil for the light, and spices for anointing oil and for fragrant incense,

9 And onyx stones and other stones to be set, for the ephod and the breastplate.

10 And let every able *and* wisehearted man among you come and make all that the Lord has commanded:

11 The tabernacle, its tent and its covering, its hooks, its boards, its bars, its pillars, and its sockets *or* bases;

12 The ark and its poles, with the mercy seat, and the veil of the screen;

13 The table and its poles and all its utensils, and the showbread—the bread of the Presence;

14 The lampstand also for the light, and its utensils and its lamps, and the oil for the light;

15 And the incense altar and its poles, the anointing oil and the fragrant incense, the hanging *or* screen for the door at the entrance of the tabernacle;

16 The altar of burnt offering, with its bronze grating, its poles and all its utensils, the laver and its base;

17 The court's hangings, its pillars and their sockets *or* bases, and the hanging *or* screen for the gate of the court;

18 The pegs of the tabernacle and of the court, and their cords,

19 The finely wrought garments for ministering in the holy place, the holy garments for Aaron the [high] priest and for his sons to minister as priests.

20 Then all the congregation of the Israelites left Moses' presence.

21 And they came, each one whose heart stirred him up and whose spirit made him willing, and brought the Lord's offering to be used for the [new] tent of meeting, for all its service, and the holy garments.

22 They came, both men and women, all who were willing-hearted, and brought brooches, earrings *or* nose rings, signet rings, and armlets *or* necklaces, all jewels of gold; every one bringing an offering of gold to the Lord.

23 And every one with whom was found blue or purple or scarlet [stuff] or fine linen or goats' hair or rams' skins made red [in tanning] or dolphin *or* porpoise skins, brought them.

24 Every one who could make an offering of silver or bronze brought it as the Lord's offering, and every man with whom was found any acacia wood for any work of the service, brought it.

25 All the women who had ability *and* were wisehearted spun with their hands, and brought what they had spun of blue and purple and scarlet [stuff], and fine linen;

## New American Standard

*The Sabbath Emphasized*

**35** THEN MOSES assembled all the congregation of the sons of Israel, and said to them, "These are the things that the LORD has commanded *you* to do.

2 "For six days work may be done, but on the seventh day you shall have a holy *day,* a sabbath of complete rest to the LORD; whoever does any work on it shall be put to death.

3 "You shall not kindle a fire in any of your dwellings on the sabbath day."

4 ¶ And Moses spoke to all the congregation of the sons of Israel, saying, "This is the thing which the LORD has commanded, saying,

5 'Take from among you a contribution to the LORD; whoever is of a willing heart, let him bring it as the LORD's contribution: gold, silver, and bronze,

6 and blue, purple and scarlet *material,* fine linen, goats' *hair,*

7 and rams' skins dyed red, and porpoise skins, and acacia wood,

8 and oil for lighting, and spices for the anointing oil, and for the fragrant incense,

9 and onyx stones and setting stones, for the ephod and for the breastpiece.

*Tabernacle Workmen*

10 ¶ 'And let every skillful man among you come, and make all that the LORD has commanded:

11 the tabernacle, its tent and its covering, its hooks and its boards, its bars, its pillars, and its sockets;

12 the ark and its poles, the mercy seat, and the curtain of the screen;

13 the table and its poles, and all its utensils, and the bread of the [a]Presence;

14 the lampstand also for the light and its utensils and its lamps and the oil for the light;

15 and the altar of incense and its poles, and the anointing oil and the fragrant incense, and the screen for the doorway at the entrance of the tabernacle;

16 the altar of burnt offering with its bronze grating, its poles, and all its utensils, the basin and its stand;

17 the hangings of the court, its pillars and its sockets, and the screen for the gate of the court;

18 the pegs of the tabernacle and the pegs of the court and their cords;

19 the woven garments, for ministering in the holy place, the holy garments for Aaron the priest, and the garments of his sons, to minister as priests.'"

*Gifts Received*

20 ¶ Then all the congregation of the sons of Israel departed from Moses' presence.

21 And everyone whose heart stirred him and everyone whose spirit moved him came *and* brought the LORD's contribution for the work of the tent of meeting and for all its service and for the holy garments.

22 Then all whose hearts moved them, both men and women, came *and* brought brooches and earrings and signet rings and bracelets, all articles of gold; so *did* every man who presented an offering of gold to the LORD.

23 And every man, who had in his possession blue and purple and scarlet *material* and fine linen and goats' *hair* and rams' skins dyed red and porpoise skins, brought them.

24 Everyone who could make a contribution of silver and bronze brought the LORD's contribution; and every man, who had in his possession acacia wood for any work of the service, brought it.

25 And all the skilled women spun with their hands, and brought what they had spun, *in* blue and purple *and* scarlet *material* and *in* fine linen.

NAS [a] Lit., *Face*

## New International

*Sabbath Regulations*

**35** MOSES ASSEMBLED the whole Israelite community and
said to them, "These are the things the LORD has commanded you to do: 2 For six days, work is to be done, but the
seventh day shall be your holy day, a Sabbath of rest to the LORD.
Whoever does any work on it must be put to death. 3 Do not light
a fire in any of your dwellings on the Sabbath day."

*Materials for the Tabernacle*

4 Moses said to the whole Israelite community, "This is what the
LORD has commanded: 5 From what you have, take an offering for
the LORD. Everyone who is willing is to bring to the LORD an
offering of gold, silver and bronze; 6 blue, purple and scarlet yarn
and fine linen; goat hair; 7 ram skins dyed red and hides of sea
cows[b]; acacia wood; 8 olive oil for the light; spices for the anointing
oil and for the fragrant incense; 9 and onyx stones and other gems
to be mounted on the ephod and breastpiece.

10 "All who are skilled among you are to come and make everything the LORD has commanded: 11 the tabernacle with its tent and
its covering, clasps, frames, crossbars, posts and bases; 12 the ark
with its poles and the atonement cover and the curtain that shields
it; 13 the table with its poles and all its articles and the bread of the
Presence; 14 the lampstand that is for light with its accessories,
lamps and oil for the light; 15 the altar of incense with its poles, the
anointing oil and the fragrant incense; the curtain for the doorway
at the entrance to the tabernacle; 16 the altar of burnt offering with
its bronze grating, its poles and all its utensils; the bronze basin
with its stand; 17 the curtains of the courtyard with its posts and
bases, and the curtain for the entrance to the courtyard; 18 the tent
pegs for the tabernacle and for the courtyard, and their ropes; 19 the
woven garments worn for ministering in the sanctuary—both the
sacred garments for Aaron the priest and the garments for his sons
when they serve as priests."

20 Then the whole Israelite community withdrew from Moses'
presence, 21 and everyone who was willing and whose heart
moved him came and brought an offering to the LORD for the work
on the Tent of Meeting, for all its service, and for the sacred
garments. 22 All who were willing, men and women alike, came
and brought gold jewelry of all kinds: brooches, earrings, rings
and ornaments. They all presented their gold as a wave offering
to the LORD. 23 Everyone who had blue, purple or scarlet yarn or
fine linen, or goat hair, ram skins dyed red or hides of sea cows
brought them. 24 Those presenting an offering of silver or bronze
brought it as an offering to the LORD, and everyone who had acacia
wood for any part of the work brought it. 25 Every skilled woman
spun with her hands and brought what she had spun—blue, purple or scarlet yarn or fine linen. 26 And all the women who were

NIV [b] *7* That is, dugongs; also in verse 23

## King James

26And all the women whose heart stirred them up in wisdom spun goats' *hair.*

27And the rulers brought onyx stones, and stones to be set, for the ephod, and for the breastplate;

28And spice, and oil for the light, and for the anointing oil, and for the sweet incense.

29The children of Israel brought a willing offering unto the Lord, every man and woman, whose heart made them willing to bring for all manner of work, which the Lord had commanded to be made by the hand of Moses.

30¶ And Moses said unto the children of Israel, See, the Lord hath called by name Bezaleel the son of Uri, the son of Hur, of the tribe of Judah;

31And he hath filled him with the spirit of God, in wisdom, in understanding, and in knowledge, and in all manner of workmanship;

32And to devise curious works, to work in gold, and in silver, and in brass,

33And in the cutting of stones, to set *them,* and in carving of wood, to make any manner of cunning work.

34And he hath put in his heart that he may teach, *both* he, and Aholiab, the son of Ahisamach, of the tribe of Dan.

35Them hath he filled with wisdom of heart, to work all manner of work, of the engraver, and of the cunning workman, and of the embroiderer, in blue, and in purple, in scarlet, and in fine linen, and of the weaver, *even* of them that do any work, and of those that devise cunning work.

**36** THEN WROUGHT Bezaleel and Aholiab, and every wisehearted man, in whom the Lord put wisdom and understanding to know how to work all manner of work for the service of the sanctuary, according to all that the Lord had commanded.

2And Moses called Bezaleel and Aholiab, and every wisehearted man, in whose heart the Lord had put wisdom, *even* every one whose heart stirred him up to come unto the work to do it:

3And they received of Moses all the offering, which the children of Israel had brought for the work of the service of the sanctuary, to make it *withal.* And they brought yet unto him free offerings every morning.

4And all the wise men, that wrought all the work of the sanctuary, came every man from his work which they made;

5¶ And they spake unto Moses, saying, The people bring much more than enough for the service of the work, which the Lord commanded to make.

6And Moses gave commandment, and they caused it to be proclaimed throughout the camp, saying, Let neither man nor woman make any more work for the offering of the sanctuary. So the people were restrained from bringing.

7For the stuff they had was sufficient for all the work to make it, and too much.

8¶ And every wisehearted man among them that wrought the work of the tabernacle made ten curtains *of* fine twined linen, and blue, and purple, and scarlet: *with* cherubims of cunning work made he them.

9The length of one curtain *was* twenty and eight cubits, and the breadth of one curtain four cubits: the curtains *were* all of one size.

10And he coupled the five curtains one unto another: and *the other* five curtains he coupled one unto another.

11And he made loops of blue on the edge of one curtain from the selvedge in the coupling: likewise he made in the uttermost side of *another* curtain, in the coupling of the second.

## Amplified

26And all the women who had ability *and* whose hearts stirred them up in wisdom, spun the goats' hair.

27The leaders brought onyx stones and stones to be set, for the ephod and for the breastplate,

28And spice, and oil for the light and for the anointing oil, and for the fragrant incense.

29The Israelites brought a freewill offering to the Lord, every man and woman whose heart made them willing *and* moved them to bring anything for any of the work which the Lord had commanded by Moses to be done.

30And Moses said to the Israelites, See, the Lord called by name Bezalel, son of Uri, son of Hur, of the tribe of Judah;

31And He has filled him with the Sprit of God, with ability *and* wisdom, with intelligence *and* understanding, and with knowledge and all craftsmanship,

32To devise artistic designs, to work in gold, silver, and bronze,

33In cutting of stones for setting, and in carving of wood, for work in every skilled craft.

34And God has put in Bezalel's heart that he may teach, both he and Aholiab son of Ahisamach of the tribe of Dan.

35He has filled them with wisdom of heart *and* ability to do all manner of craftsmanship, of the engraver, of the skillful workman, of the embroiderer in blue, purple, and scarlet [stuff] and in fine linen, and of the weaver, even of those who do or design any skilled work.

**36** BEZALEL AND Aholiab and every wise-hearted man in whom the Lord has put wisdom and understanding to know how to do all the work for the service of the sanctuary, shall work according to all that the Lord has commanded.

2And Moses called Bezalel and Aholiab and every able *and* wise-hearted man in whose mind the Lord had put wisdom *and* ability, every one whose heart stirred him up to come to do the work,

3And they received from Moses all the freewill offering which the Israelites had brought for doing the work of the sanctuary, to prepare it for service. And they continued to bring him freewill offerings every morning.

4And all the wise *and* able men who were doing the work on the sanctuary came, every man from the work he was doing,

5And they said to Moses, The people bring much more than enough for doing the work which the Lord commanded to do.

6So Moses commanded and it was proclaimed in all the camp, Let not man or woman do anything more for the sanctuary offering. So the people were restrained from bringing;

7For the stuff they had was sufficient to do all the work, and more.

8And all the able *and* wise-hearted men among them who did the work on the tabernacle made ten curtains of fine twined linen and blue, purple, and scarlet stuff, with cherubim skillfully worked on them.

9The length of each curtain was twenty-eight cubits, and its breadth four cubits; all the curtains were one size.

10[Bezalel] coupled five curtains one to another, and the other five curtains he coupled one to another.

11And he made loops of blue on the outer edge of the last curtain in the first set; this he did also on the inner edge of the first curtain in the second set.

# New American Standard

26 And all the women whose heart stirred with a skill spun the goats' *hair*.

27 And the rulers brought the onyx stones and the stones for setting for the ephod and for the breastpiece;

28 and the spice and the oil for the light and for the anointing oil and for the fragrant incense.

29 The Israelites, all the men and women, whose heart moved them to bring *material* for all the work, which the LORD had commanded through Moses to be done, brought a freewill offering to the LORD.

30 ¶ Then Moses said to the sons of Israel, "See, the LORD has called by name Bezalel the son of Uri, the son of Hur, of the tribe of Judah.

31 "And He has filled him with the Spirit of God, in wisdom, in understanding and in knowledge and in all craftsmanship;

32 to make designs for working in gold and in silver and in bronze,

33 and in the cutting of stones for settings, and in the carving of wood, so as to perform in every inventive work.

34 "He also has put in his heart to teach, both he and Oholiab, the son of Ahisamach, of the tribe of Dan.

35 "He has filled them with skill to perform every work of an engraver and of a designer and of an embroiderer, in blue and in purple *and* in scarlet *material*, and in fine linen, and of a weaver, as performers of every work and makers of designs.

*The Tabernacle Underwritten*

**36** "NOW BEZALEL and Oholiab, and every skillful person in whom the LORD has put skill and understanding to know how to perform all the work in the construction of the sanctuary, shall perform in accordance with all that the LORD has commanded."

2 ¶ Then Moses called Bezalel and Oholiab and every skillful person in whom the LORD had put skill, everyone whose heart stirred him, to come to the work to perform it.

3 And they received from Moses all the contributions which the sons of Israel had brought to perform the work in the construction of the sanctuary. And they still *continued* bringing to him freewill offerings every morning.

4 And all the skillful men who were performing all the work of the sanctuary came, each from the work which he was performing,

5 and they said to Moses, "The people are bringing much more than enough for the construction work which the LORD commanded *us* to perform."

6 So Moses issued a command, and a proclamation was circulated throughout the camp, saying, "Let neither man nor woman any longer perform work for the contributions of the sanctuary." Thus the people were restrained from bringing *any more*.

7 For the material they had was sufficient and more than enough for all the work, to perform it.

*Construction Proceeds*

8 ¶ And all the skillful men among those who were performing the work made the tabernacle with ten curtains; of fine twisted linen and blue and purple and scarlet *material*, with cherubim, the work of a skillful workman, Bezalel made them.

9 The length of each curtain was twenty-eight cubits, and the width of each curtain four cubits; all the curtains had the same measurements.

10 And he joined five curtains to one another, and *the other* five curtains he joined to one another.

11 And he made loops of blue on the edge of the outermost curtain in the first set; he did likewise on the edge of the curtain that was outermost in the second set.

# New International

willing and had the skill spun the goat hair. 27 The leaders brought
onyx stones and other gems to be mounted on the ephod and
breastpiece. 28 They also brought spices and olive oil for the light
and for the anointing oil and for the fragrant incense. 29 All the
Israelite men and women who were willing brought to the LORD
freewill offerings for all the work the LORD through Moses had
commanded them to do.

*Bezalel and Oholiab*

30 Then Moses said to the Israelites, "See, the LORD has chosen
Bezalel son of Uri, the son of Hur, of the tribe of Judah, 31 and he
has filled him with the Spirit of God, with skill, ability and knowledge in all kinds of crafts— 32 to make artistic designs for work in
gold, silver and bronze, 33 to cut and set stones, to work in wood
and to engage in all kinds of artistic craftsmanship. 34 And he has
given both him and Oholiab son of Ahisamach, of the tribe of Dan,
the ability to teach others. 35 He has filled them with skill to do all
kinds of work as craftsmen, designers, embroiderers in blue, purple and scarlet yarn and fine linen, and weavers—all of them
master craftsmen and designers.

**36** SO BEZALEL, Oholiab and every skilled person to whom
the LORD has given skill and ability to know how to carry
out all the work of constructing the sanctuary are to do the work
just as the Lord has commanded."
2 Then Moses summoned Bezalel and Oholiab and every skilled
person to whom the LORD had given ability and who was willing
to come and do the work. 3 They received from Moses all the
offerings the Israelites had brought to carry out the work of constructing the sanctuary. And the people continued to bring freewill
offerings morning after morning. 4 So all the skilled craftsmen who
were doing all the work on the sanctuary left their work 5 and said
to Moses, "The people are bringing more than enough for doing
the work the LORD commanded to be done."
6 Then Moses gave an order and they sent this word throughout
the camp: "No man or woman is to make anything else as an
offering for the sanctuary." And so the people were restrained
from bringing more, 7 because what they already had was more
than enough to do all the work.

*The Tabernacle*

8 All the skilled men among the workmen made the tabernacle
with ten curtains of finely twisted linen and blue, purple and
scarlet yarn, with cherubim worked into them by a skilled craftsman. 9 All the curtains were the same size—twenty-eight cubits
long and four cubits wide.[a] 10 They joined five of the curtains
together and did the same with the other five. 11 Then they made
loops of blue material along the edge of the end curtain in one set,
and the same was done with the end curtain in the other set.

NIV [a] 9 That is, about 42 feet (about 12.5 meters) long and 6 feet (about 1.8 meters) wide

## King James

12 Fifty loops made he in one curtain, and fifty loops made he
in the edge of the curtain which *was* in the coupling of the second:
the loops held one *curtain* to another.
13 And he made fifty taches of gold, and coupled the curtains
one unto another with the taches: so it became one tabernacle.
14 ¶ And he made curtains *of* goats' *hair* for the tent over the
tabernacle: eleven curtains he made them.
15 The length of one curtain *was* thirty cubits, and four cubits *was*
the breadth of one curtain: the eleven curtains *were* of one size.
16 And he coupled five curtains by themselves, and six curtains
by themselves.
17 And he made fifty loops upon the uttermost edge of the
curtain in the coupling, and fifty loops made he upon the edge of
the curtain which coupleth the second.
18 And he made fifty taches *of* brass to couple the tent together,
that it might be one.
19 And he made a covering for the tent *of* rams' skins dyed red,
and a covering *of* badgers' skins above *that*.
20 ¶ And he made boards for the tabernacle *of* shittim wood,
standing up.
21 The length of a board *was* ten cubits, and the breadth of a
board one cubit and a half.
22 One board had two tenons, equally distant one from another:
thus did he make for all the boards of the tabernacle.
23 And he made boards for the tabernacle; twenty boards for the
south side southward:
24 And forty sockets of silver he made under the twenty boards;
two sockets under one board for his two tenons, and two sockets
under another board for his two tenons.
25 And for the other side of the tabernacle, *which is* toward the
north corner, he made twenty boards,
26 And their forty sockets of silver; two sockets under one board,
and two sockets under another board.
27 And for the sides of the tabernacle westward he made six
boards.
28 And two boards made he for the corners of the tabernacle in
the two sides.
29 And they were coupled beneath, and coupled together at the
head thereof, to one ring: thus he did to both of them in both the
corners.
30 And there were eight boards; and their sockets *were* sixteen
sockets of silver, under every board two sockets.
31 ¶ And he made bars of shittim wood; five for the boards of the
one side of the tabernacle,
32 And five bars for the boards of the other side of the tabernacle,
and five bars for the boards of the tabernacle for the sides westward.
33 And he made the middle bar to shoot through the boards from
the one end to the other.
34 And he overlaid the boards with gold, and made their rings
*of* gold *to be* places for the bars, and overlaid the bars with gold.
35 ¶ And he made a veil *of* blue, and purple, and scarlet, and fine
twined linen: *with* cherubims made he it of cunning work.
36 And he made thereunto four pillars *of* shittim *wood*, and overlaid them with gold: their hooks *were of* gold; and he cast for them
four sockets of silver.
37 ¶ And he made an hanging for the tabernacle door *of* blue, and
purple, and scarlet, and fine twined linen, of needlework;
38 And the five pillars of it with their hooks: and he overlaid their
chapiters and their fillets with gold: but their five sockets *were of*
brass.

## Amplified

12 Fifty loops he made in the one curtain, and fifty loops in the
edge of the curtain which was the second set; the loops were
opposite one another.
13 And he made fifty clasps of gold, and coupled the curtains
together with the clasps; so the tabernacle became one *unit*.
14 And he made eleven curtains of goats' hair for a tent over the
tabernacle.
15 The length of one curtain was thirty cubits, and four cubits
was the breadth; the eleven curtains were of equal size.
16 And he coupled five curtains by themselves, and six curtains
by themselves.
17 And he made fifty loops on the outmost edge of the curtain
to be coupled, and fifty loops he made on the inner edge of the
second curtain to be coupled.
18 He made fifty clasps of bronze to couple the tent together into
one whole.
19 He made a covering for the tent of [a]rams' skins tanned red,
and above it a covering of dolphin *or* porpoise skins.
20 He made boards of acacia wood for the upright framework of
the tabernacle.
21 The length of a board was ten cubits, and the breadth one
cubit and a half.
22 Each board had two tenons (projections) to fit into a mortise
to form a clutch; he did this for all the boards of the tabernacle.
23 And he made thus the boards [for frames] for the tabernacle:
twenty boards for the south side;
24 And he made under the twenty boards forty sockets *or* bases
of silver, two sockets under one board for its two tenons *or* hands,
and two sockets under another board for its two tenons.
25 For the other side of the tabernacle, the north side, he made
twenty boards.
26 And their forty sockets *or* bases of silver, two sockets under
[the end of] each board.
27 And for the rear or west side of the tabernacle he made six
[frame] boards.
28 And two boards he made for each corner of the tabernacle in
the rear.
29 They were separate below but linked together at the top with
one ring; thus he made both of them in both corners.
30 There were eight boards, with sixteen sockets *or* bases of
silver, under [the end of] each board two sockets.
31 He made bars of acacia wood, five for the [frame] boards of
the one side of the tabernacle,
32 And five bars for the boards of its other side, and five bars for
the boards at the rear or west side.
33 And he made the middle bar pass through halfway up the
boards from one end to the other.
34 He overlaid the boards and the bars with gold, and made their
rings of gold for places for the bars.
35 And he made the veil of blue, purple, and scarlet stuff and
fine twined linen; with cherubim, skillfully worked. [Matt. 27:50,
51; Heb. 10:19-22.]
36 For [the veil] he made four pillars of acacia [wood] and overlaid them with gold; their hooks were of gold; and he cast for them
four sockets *or* bases of silver.
37 And he made a screen for the tent door of blue, purple, and
scarlet stuff and fine twined linen, embroidered,
38 And he made the five pillars of it with their hooks; and overlaid their ornamental tops and joinings with gold, but their five
sockets were of bronze.

**AMP** [a] These last coverings of the tabernacle tent are not to be confused with the second one of goats' hair (v. 14). There were *four distinct coverings* of the tabernacle tent. 1. A covering of fine twined linen woven with blue, purple and scarlet, with figures of cherubim upon it. It was made of two long pieces, one running from north to south, the other from east to west [and overlapping for the the ceiling] (Exod. 26:1, 6). 2. Over this a covering of woven goats' hair was thrown (26:7; 36:14). 3. Outside this was another of rams' skins made red. 4. And *"above it"* another covering of dolphin or porpoise skins, weighting the others down and giving perfect protection from the weather (36:19).

## New American Standard

12He made fifty loops in the one curtain and he made fifty loops on the edge of the curtain that was in the second set; the loops were opposite each other.

13And he made fifty clasps of gold, and joined the curtains to one another with the clasps, so the tabernacle was a unit.

**14**¶ Then he made curtains of goats' *hair* for a tent over the tabernacle; he made eleven curtains in all.

15The length of each curtain was thirty cubits, and four cubits the width of each curtain; the eleven curtains had the same measurements.

16And he joined five curtains by themselves, and *the other* six curtains by themselves.

17Moreover, he made fifty loops on the edge of the curtain that was outermost in the *first* set, and he made fifty loops on the edge of the curtain *that was outermost in* the second set.

18And he made fifty clasps of bronze to join the tent together, that it might be a unit.

19And he made a covering for the tent of rams' skins dyed red, and a covering of porpoise skins above.

**20**¶ Then he made the boards for the tabernacle of acacia wood, standing upright.

21Ten cubits was the length of each board, and one and a half cubits the width of each board.

22There were two tenons for each board, fitted to one another; thus he did for all the boards of the tabernacle.

23And he made the boards for the tabernacle: twenty boards for the south side;

24and he made forty sockets of silver under the twenty boards; two sockets under one board for its two tenons and two sockets under another board for its two tenons.

25Then for the second side of the tabernacle, on the north side, he made twenty boards,

26and their forty sockets of silver; two sockets under one board and two sockets under another board.

27And for the rear of the tabernacle, to the west, he made six boards.

28And he made two boards for the corners of the tabernacle at the rear.

29And they were double beneath, and together they were complete to its top to the first ring; thus he did with both of them for the two corners.

30And there were eight boards with their sockets of silver, sixteen sockets, two under every board.

**31**¶ Then he made bars of acacia wood, five for the boards of one side of the tabernacle,

32and five bars for the boards of the other side of the tabernacle, and five bars for the boards of the tabernacle for the rear *side* to the west.

33And he made the middle bar to pass through in the center of the boards from end to end.

34And he overlaid the boards with gold and made their rings of gold *as* holders for the bars, and overlaid the bars with gold.

**35**¶ Moreover, he made the veil of blue and purple and scarlet *material,* and fine twisted linen; he made it with cherubim, the work of a skillful workman.

36And he made four pillars of acacia for it, and overlaid them with gold, with their hooks of gold; and he cast four sockets of silver for them.

37And he made a screen for the doorway of the tent, of blue and purple and scarlet *material,* and fine twisted linen, the work of a weaver;

38and *he made* its five pillars with their hooks, and he overlaid their tops and their bands with gold; but their five sockets were of bronze.

## New International

12They also made fifty loops on one curtain and fifty loops on the
end curtain of the other set, with the loops opposite each other.
13Then they made fifty gold clasps and used them to fasten the two
sets of curtains together so that the tabernacle was a unit.
14They made curtains of goat hair for the tent over the tabernacle—eleven altogether. 15All eleven curtains were the same size—
thirty cubits long and four cubits wide.[b] 16They joined five of the
curtains into one set and the other six into another set. 17Then they
made fifty loops along the edge of the end curtain in one set and
also along the edge of the end curtain in the other set. 18They made
fifty bronze clasps to fasten the tent together as a unit. 19Then they
made for the tent a covering of ram skins dyed red, and over that
a covering of hides of sea cows.[c]
20They made upright frames of acacia wood for the tabernacle.
21Each frame was ten cubits long and a cubit and a half wide,[d]
22with two projections set parallel to each other. They made all the
frames of the tabernacle in this way. 23They made twenty frames
for the south side of the tabernacle 24and made forty silver bases
to go under them—two bases for each frame, one under each
projection. 25For the other side, the north side of the tabernacle,
they made twenty frames 26and forty silver bases—two under each
frame. 27They made six frames for the far end, that is, the west end
of the tabernacle, 28and two frames were made for the corners of
the tabernacle at the far end. 29At these two corners the frames
were double from the bottom all the way to the top and fitted into
a single ring; both were made alike. 30So there were eight frames
and sixteen silver bases—two under each frame.
31They also made crossbars of acacia wood: five for the frames
on one side of the tabernacle, 32five for those on the other side, and
five for the frames on the west, at the far end of the tabernacle.
33They made the center crossbar so that it extended from end to
end at the middle of the frames. 34They overlaid the frames with
gold and made gold rings to hold the crossbars. They also overlaid
the crossbars with gold.
35They made the curtain of blue, purple and scarlet yarn and
finely twisted linen, with cherubim worked into it by a skilled
craftsman. 36They made four posts of acacia wood for it and overlaid them with gold. They made gold hooks for them and cast their
four silver bases. 37For the entrance to the tent they made a curtain
of blue, purple and scarlet yarn and finely twisted linen—the work
of an embroiderer; 38and they made five posts with hooks for
them. They overlaid the tops of the posts and their bands with gold
and made their five bases of bronze.

**NIV** [b] *15* That is, about 45 feet (about 13.5 meters) long and 6 feet (about 1.8 meters) wide [c] *19* That is, dugongs [d] *21* That is, about 15 feet (about 4.5 meters) long and 2 1/4 feet (about 0.7 meter) wide

## King James

**37** AND BEZALEEL made the ark *of* shittim wood: two cubits and a half *was* the length of it, and a cubit and a half the breadth of it, and a cubit and a half the height of it:

2And he overlaid it with pure gold within and without, and made a crown of gold to it round about.

3And he cast for it four rings of gold, *to be set* by the four corners of it; even two rings upon the one side of it, and two rings upon the other side of it.

4And he made staves *of* shittim wood, and overlaid them with gold.

5And he put the staves into the rings by the sides of the ark, to bear the ark.

6¶ And he made the mercy seat *of* pure gold: two cubits and a half *was* the length thereof, and one cubit and a half the breadth thereof.

7And he made two cherubims *of* gold, beaten out of one piece made he them, on the two ends of the mercy seat;

8One cherub on the end on this side, and another cherub on the *other* end on that side: out of the mercy seat made he the cherubims on the two ends thereof.

9And the cherubims spread out *their* wings on high, *and* covered with their wings over the mercy seat, with their faces one to another; *even* to the mercy seatward were the faces of the cherubims.

10¶ And he made the table *of* shittim wood: two cubits *was* the length thereof, and a cubit the breadth thereof, and a cubit and a half the height thereof:

11And he overlaid it with pure gold, and made thereunto a crown of gold round about.

12Also he made thereunto a border of an handbreadth round about; and made a crown of gold for the border thereof round about.

13And he cast for it four rings of gold, and put the rings upon the four corners that *were* in the four feet thereof.

14Over against the border were the rings, the places for the staves to bear the table.

15And he made the staves *of* shittim wood, and overlaid them with gold, to bear the table.

16And he made the vessels which *were* upon the table, his dishes, and his spoons, and his bowls, and his covers to cover withal, *of* pure gold.

17¶ And he made the candlestick *of* pure gold: *of* beaten work made he the candlestick; his shaft, and his branch, his bowls, his knobs, and his flowers, were of the same:

18And six branches going out of the sides thereof; three branches of the candlestick out of the one side thereof, and three branches of the candlestick out of the other side thereof:

19Three bowls made after the fashion of almonds in one branch, a knob and a flower; and three bowls made like almonds in another branch, a knob and a flower: so throughout the six branches going out of the candlestick.

20And in the candlestick *were* four bowls made like almonds, his knobs, and his flowers:

21And a knob under two branches of the same, and a knob under two branches of the same, and a knob under two branches of the same, according to the six branches going out of it.

22Their knobs and their branches were of the same: all of it *was* one beaten work *of* pure gold.

23And he made his seven lamps, and his snuffers, and his snuffdishes, *of* pure gold.

24 *Of* a talent of pure gold made he it, and all the vessels thereof.

25¶ And he made the incense altar *of* shittim wood: the length of it *was* a cubit, and the breadth of it a cubit; *it was* foursquare; and two cubits *was* the height of it; the horns thereof were of the same.

26And he overlaid it with pure gold, *both* the top of it, and the sides thereof round about, and the horns of it: also he made unto it a crown of gold round about.

## Amplified

**37** BEZALEL MADE the ark of acacia wood; two cubits and a half was the length of it, a cubit and a half the breadth of it, and a cubit and a half the height of it.

2He overlaid it with pure gold within and without, and made a molding *or* crown of gold to go around the top of it.

3He cast four rings of gold for its four corners; two rings on either side.

4He made poles of acacia wood, and overlaid them with gold.

5He put the poles through the rings at the sides of the ark, to carry it.

6[Bezalel] made the mercy seat of pure gold, two cubits and a half its length and one cubit and a half its breadth.

7And he made two cherubim of beaten gold; on the two ends of the mercy seat he made them,

8One cherub at one end, and one at the other end; of one piece with the mercy seat he made the cherubim at its two ends.

9And the cherubim spread out their wings on high, covering the mercy seat with their wings, with their faces to each other, looking down to the mercy seat. [Heb. 9:23-26.]

10Bezalel made the [showbread] table of acacia wood; it was two cubits long, a cubit wide, and a cubit and a half high.

11He overlaid it with pure gold, and made a molding of gold around its top.

12And he made a border around it [just under the top] a handbreadth wide, and a molding of gold around the border.

13And he cast for it four rings of gold, and fastened the rings on the four corners that were at its four legs.

14Close to the border were the rings, the places for the poles to pass through to carry the [showbread] table.

15[Bezalel] made the poles of acacia wood to carry the [showbread] table, and overlaid them with gold.

16He made of pure gold the vessels which were to be on the table, its plates, and dishes [for bread], its bowls and flagons for pouring [liquid sacrifices].

17And he made the lampstand of pure gold; its base and shaft were made of hammered work; its cups, its knobs, and its flowers were of one piece with it.

18There were six branches going out of the sides of the lampstand, three branches out of one side of it and three branches out of the other side of it.

19Three cups made like almond blossoms in one branch, each with a [calyx] knob and a flower, and three cups made like almond blossoms in the [opposite] branch, each with a [calyx] knob and a flower; and so for the six branches going out of the lampstand.

20On [the shaft of] the lampstand were four cups made like almond blossoms, with knobs and flowers [one at the top].

21And a knob under each two branches of one piece with the lampstand, for the six branches going out of it.

22Their knobs and their branches were of one piece with it; all of it hammered work of pure gold.

23And he made of pure gold its seven lamps, its snuffers, and its ashtrays.

24Of a talent of pure gold he made the lampstand and all its utensils. [John 1:4, 5, 9; II Cor. 4:6.]

25And [Bezalel] made the incense altar of acacia wood; its top was a cubit square, and it was two cubits high; the horns were one piece with it.

26He overlaid it with pure gold, its top, its sides round about, and its horns; also he made a rim around it of gold.

## New American Standard

*Construction Continues*

**37** NOW BEZALEL made the ark of acacia wood; its length was two and a half cubits, and its width one and a half cubits, and its height one and a half cubits;

2and he overlaid it with pure gold inside and out, and made a gold molding for it all around.

3And he cast four rings of gold for it on its four feet; even two rings on one side of it, and two rings on the other side of it.

4And he made poles of acacia wood and overlaid them with gold.

5And he put the poles into the rings on the sides of the ark, to carry it.

6And he made a mercy seat of pure gold, two and a half cubits long, and one and a half cubits wide.

7And he made two cherubim of gold; he made them of hammered work, at the two ends of the mercy seat;

8one cherub at the one end, and one cherub at the other end; he made the cherubim *of one piece* with the mercy seat at the two ends.

9And the cherubim had *their* wings spread upward, covering the mercy seat with their wings, with their faces toward each other; the faces of the cherubim were toward the mercy seat.

10¶ Then he made the table of acacia wood, two cubits long and a cubit wide and one and a half cubits high.

11And he overlaid it with pure gold, and made a gold molding for it all around.

12And he made a rim for it of a handbreadth all around, and made a gold molding for its rim all around.

13And he cast four gold rings for it and put the rings on the four corners that were on its four feet.

14Close by the rim were the rings, the holders for the poles to carry the table.

15And he made the poles of acacia wood and overlaid them with gold, to carry the table.

16And he made the utensils which were on the table, its dishes and its pans and its bowls and its jars, with which to pour out libations, of pure gold.

17¶ Then he made the lampstand of pure gold. He made the lampstand of hammered work, its base and its shaft; its cups, its bulbs and its flowers were *of one piece* with it.

18And there were six branches going out of its sides; three branches of the lampstand from the one side of it, and three branches of the lampstand from the other side of it;

19three cups shaped like almond *blossoms,* a bulb and a flower in one branch, and three cups shaped like almond *blossoms,* a bulb and a flower in the other branch—so for the six branches going out of the lampstand.

20And in the lampstand *there were* four cups shaped like almond *blossoms,* its bulbs and its flowers;

21and a bulb was under the *first* pair of branches *coming* out of it, and a bulb under the *second* pair of branches *coming* out of it, and a bulb under the *third* pair of branches *coming* out of it, for the six branches coming out of the lampstand.

22Their bulbs and their branches were *of one piece* with it; the whole of it *was* a single hammered work of pure gold.

23And he made its seven lamps with its snuffers and its trays of pure gold.

24He made it and all its utensils from a talent of pure gold.

25¶ Then he made the altar of incense of acacia wood: a cubit long and a cubit wide, square, and two cubits high; its horns were *of one piece* with it.

26And he overlaid it with pure gold, its top and its sides all around, and its horns; and he made a gold molding for it all around.

## New International

*The Ark*

**37** BEZALEL MADE the ark of acacia wood—two and a half
cubits long, a cubit and a half wide, and a cubit and a half
high.[a] 2He overlaid it with pure gold, both inside and out, and
made a gold molding around it. 3He cast four gold rings for it and
fastened them to its four feet, with two rings on one side and two
rings on the other. 4Then he made poles of acacia wood and
overlaid them with gold. 5And he inserted the poles into the rings
on the sides of the ark to carry it.
6He made the atonement cover of pure gold—two and a half
cubits long and a cubit and a half wide.[b] 7Then he made two
cherubim out of hammered gold at the ends of the cover. 8He made
one cherub on one end and the second cherub on the other; at the
two ends he made them of one piece with the cover. 9The cherubim had their wings spread upward, overshadowing the cover
with them. The cherubim faced each other, looking toward the
cover.

*The Table*

10They[c] made the table of acacia wood—two cubits long, a cubit
wide, and a cubit and a half high.[d] 11Then they overlaid it with
pure gold and made a gold molding around it. 12They also made
around it a rim a handbreadth[e] wide and put a gold molding on
the rim. 13They cast four gold rings for the table and fastened them
to the four corners, where the four legs were. 14The rings were put
close to the rim to hold the poles used in carrying the table. 15The
poles for carrying the table were made of acacia wood and were
overlaid with gold. 16And they made from pure gold the articles
for the table—its plates and dishes and bowls and its pitchers for
the pouring out of drink offerings.

*The Lampstand*

17They made the lampstand of pure gold and hammered it out,
base and shaft; its flowerlike cups, buds and blossoms were of one
piece with it. 18Six branches extended from the sides of the lampstand—three on one side and three on the other. 19Three cups
shaped like almond flowers with buds and blossoms were on one
branch, three on the next branch and the same for all six branches
extending from the lampstand. 20And on the lampstand were four
cups shaped like almond flowers with buds and blossoms. 21One
bud was under the first pair of branches extending from the lampstand, a second bud under the second pair, and a third bud under
the third pair—six branches in all. 22The buds and the branches
were all of one piece with the lampstand, hammered out of pure
gold.
23They made its seven lamps, as well as its wick trimmers and
trays, of pure gold. 24They made the lampstand and all its accessories from one talent[f] of pure gold.

*The Altar of Incense*

25They made the altar of incense out of acacia wood. It was
square, a cubit long and a cubit wide, and two cubits high[g]—its
horns of one piece with it. 26They overlaid the top and all the sides
and the horns with pure gold, and made a gold molding around
it. 27They made two gold rings below the molding—two on oppo-

**NIV** [a] *1* That is, about 3 3/4 feet (about 1.1 meters) long and 2 1/4 feet (about 0.7 meter) wide and high [b] *6* That is, about 3 3/4 feet (about 1.1 meters) long and 2 1/4 feet (about 0.7 meter) wide [c] *10* Or *He;* also in verses 11-29 [d] *10* That is, about 3 feet (about 0.9 meter) long, 1 1/2 feet (about 0.5 meter) wide, and 2 1/4 feet (about 0.7 meter) high [e] *12* That is, about 3 inches (about 8 centimeters) [f] *24* That is, about 75 pounds (about 34 kilograms) [g] *25* That is, about 1 1/2 feet (about 0.5 meter) long and wide, and about 3 feet (about 0.9 meter) high

## King James

27And he made two rings of gold for it under the crown thereof, by the two corners of it, upon the two sides thereof, to be places for the staves to bear it withal.

28And he made the staves *of* shittim wood, and overlaid them with gold.

29¶ And he made the holy anointing oil, and the pure incense of sweet spices, according to the work of the apothecary.

**38** AND HE made the altar of burnt offering *of* shittim wood: five cubits *was* the length thereof, and five cubits the breadth thereof; *it was* foursquare; and three cubits the height thereof.

2And he made the horns thereof on the four corners of it; the horns thereof were of the same: and he overlaid it with brass.

3And he made all the vessels of the altar, the pots, and the shovels, and the basins, *and* the fleshhooks, and the firepans: all the vessels thereof made he *of* brass.

4And he made for the altar a brasen grate of network under the compass thereof beneath unto the midst of it.

5And he cast four rings for the four ends of the grate of brass, *to be* places for the staves.

6And he made the staves *of* shittim wood, and overlaid them with brass.

7And he put the staves into the rings on the sides of the altar, to bear it withal; he made the altar hollow with boards.

8¶ And he made the laver *of* brass, and the foot of it *of* brass, of the looking glasses of *the women* assembling, which assembled *at* the door of the tabernacle of the congregation.

9¶ And he made the court: on the south side southward the hangings of the court *were of* fine twined linen, an hundred cubits:

10Their pillars *were* twenty, and their brasen sockets twenty; the hooks of the pillars and their fillets *were of* silver.

11And for the north side *the hangings were* an hundred cubits, their pillars *were* twenty, and their sockets of brass twenty; the hooks of the pillars and their fillets *of* silver.

12And for the west side *were* hangings of fifty cubits, their pillars ten, and their sockets ten; the hooks of the pillars and their fillets *of* silver.

13And for the east side eastward fifty cubits.

14The hangings of the one side *of the gate were* fifteen cubits; their pillars three, and their sockets three.

15And for the other side of the court gate, on this hand and that hand, *were* hangings of fifteen cubits; their pillars three, and their sockets three.

16All the hangings of the court round about *were* of fine twined linen.

17And the sockets for the pillars *were of* brass; the hooks of the pillars and their fillets *of* silver; and the overlaying of their chapiters *of* silver; and all the pillars of the court *were* filleted with silver.

18And the hanging for the gate of the court *was* needlework, *of* blue, and purple, and scarlet, and fine twined linen: and twenty cubits *was* the length, and the height in the breadth *was* five cubits, answerable to the hangings of the court.

19And their pillars *were* four, and their sockets *of* brass four; their hooks *of* silver, and the overlaying of their chapiters and their fillets *of* silver.

20And all the pins of the tabernacle, and of the court round about, *were of* brass.

21¶ This is the sum of the tabernacle, *even* of the tabernacle of testimony, as it was counted, according to the commandment of Moses, *for* the service of the Levites, by the hand of Ithamar, son to Aaron the priest.

22And Bezaleel the son of Uri, the son of Hur, of the tribe of Judah, made all that the LORD commanded Moses.

## Amplified

27And he made two rings of gold for it under its rim, on its two opposite sides, as places for the poles [to pass through] to carry it.

28And he made the poles of acacia wood, and overlaid them with gold.

29He also made the holy anointing oil [symbol of the Holy Spirit], and the pure fragrant incense, after the perfumer's art.

**38** BEZALEL MADE the burnt offering altar of acacia wood; its top was five cubits square, and it was three cubits high.

2He made its horns on the four corners of it; the horns were of one piece with it; and he overlaid it with bronze.

3He made all the utensils *and* vessels of the altar, the pots, shovels, basins, forks *or* fleshhooks, and firepans; all its utensils *and* vessels he made of bronze.

4And he made for the altar a bronze grate of network under its ledge, extending half way down it.

5He cast four rings for the four corners of the bronze grating, to be places for the poles [with which to carry it].

6And he made the poles of acacia wood, and overlaid them with bronze.

7And he put the poles through the rings on the altar's sides, with which to carry it; he made it hollow with planks.

8He made the laver and its base of bronze, of the mirrors of the women who ministered at the door of the tent of meeting.

9And he made the court: for the south side the hangings of the court were of fine twined linen, a hundred cubits;

10Their pillars and their bronze sockets *or* bases were twenty; the hooks of the pillars and their joinings were silver.

11And for the north side the hangings were *also* a hundred cubits, their pillars and their sockets *or* bases of bronze were twenty; the hooks of the pillars and their joinings were of silver.

12But for the west side were hangings of fifty cubits, their pillars and their sockets *or* bases ten; the hooks of the pillars and their joinings of silver.

13And for the front, the east side, fifty cubits.

14The hangings for one side of the gate were fifteen cubits; their pillars three, and their sockets *or* bases three.

15Also for the other side of the court gate, left and right were hangings of fifteen cubits; their pillars three and their sockets *or* bases three.

16All the hangings around the court were of fine twined linen.

17The sockets for the pillars were of bronze, the hooks of the pillars and their joinings of silver, the overlaying of their tops of silver, and all the pillars of the court were joined with silver.

18The hanging *or* screen for the gate of the court was embroidered in blue, purple, and scarlet, and fine twined linen; the length was twenty cubits and the height in the breadth was five cubits, corresponding to the hangings of the court.

19Their pillars were four, and their sockets of bronze four; their hooks of silver, and the overlaying of their tops and their joinings were of silver.

20All the pegs for the tabernacle and around the court were of bronze.

21This is the sum of the things for the tabernacle of the testimony, as counted at the command of Moses, for the work of the Levites under the direction of Ithamar, son of Aaron the [high] priest.

22Bezalel, son of Uri, son of Hur, of the tribe of Judah, made all that the Lord commanded Moses.

## New American Standard

27And he made two golden rings for it under its molding, on its two sides—on opposite sides—as holders for poles with which to carry it.

28And he made the poles of acacia wood and overlaid them with gold.

29And he made the holy anointing oil and the pure, fragrant incense of spices, the work of a perfumer.

*The Tabernacle Completed*

**38** THEN HE made the altar of burnt offering of acacia wood, five cubits long, and five cubits wide, square, and three cubits high.

2And he made its horns on its four corners, its horns being *of one piece* with it, and he overlaid it with bronze.

3And he made all the utensils of the altar, the pails and the shovels and the basins, the flesh hooks and the firepans; he made all its utensils of bronze.

4And he made for the altar a grating of bronze network beneath, under its ledge, reaching halfway up.

5And he cast four rings on the four ends of the bronze grating *as* holders for the poles.

6And he made the poles of acacia wood and overlaid them with bronze.

7And he inserted the poles into the rings on the sides of the altar, with which to carry it. He made it hollow with planks.

8¶ Moreover, he made the laver of bronze with its base of bronze, from the mirrors of the serving women who served at the doorway of the tent of meeting.

9¶ Then he made the court: for the south side the hangings of the court were of fine twisted linen, one hundred cubits;

10their twenty pillars, and their twenty sockets, *made* of bronze; the hooks of the pillars and their bands *were* of silver.

11And for the north side *there were* one hundred cubits; their twenty pillars and their twenty sockets *were* of bronze, the hooks of the pillars and their bands *were* of silver.

12And for the west side *there were* hangings of fifty cubits *with* their ten pillars and their ten sockets; the hooks of the pillars and their bands *were* of silver.

13And for the east side fifty cubits.

14The hangings for the *one* side *of the gate were* fifteen cubits, *with* their three pillars and their three sockets,

15and so for the other side. On both sides of the gate of the court *were* hangings of fifteen cubits, *with* their three pillars and their three sockets.

16All the hangings of the court all around *were* of fine twisted linen.

17And the sockets for the pillars *were* of bronze, the hooks of the pillars and their bands, of silver; and the overlaying of their tops, of silver, and all the pillars of the court were furnished with silver bands.

18And the screen of the gate of the court was the work of the weaver, of blue and purple and scarlet *material*, and fine twisted linen. And the length was twenty cubits and the height was five cubits, corresponding to the hangings of the court.

19And their four pillars and their four sockets *were* of bronze; their hooks *were* of silver, and the overlaying of their tops and their bands *were* of silver.

20And all the pegs of the tabernacle and of the court all around *were* of bronze.

*The Cost of the Tabernacle*

21¶ This is the number of *the things for* the tabernacle, the tabernacle of the testimony, as they were numbered according to the command of Moses, for the service of the Levites, by the hand of Ithamar, the son of Aaron the priest.

22Now Bezalel, the son of Uri the son of Hur, of the tribe of Judah, made all that the LORD had commanded Moses.

## New International

site sides—to hold the poles used to carry it. 28They made the poles of acacia wood and overlaid them with gold.

29They also made the sacred anointing oil and the pure, fragrant incense—the work of a perfumer.

*The Altar of Burnt Offering*

**38** THEY[a] BUILT the altar of burnt offering of acacia wood, three cubits[b] high; it was square, five cubits long and five cubits wide.[c] 2They made a horn at each of the four corners, so that the horns and the altar were of one piece, and they overlaid the altar with bronze. 3They made all its utensils of bronze—its pots, shovels, sprinkling bowls, meat forks and firepans. 4They made a grating for the altar, a bronze network, to be under its ledge, halfway up the altar. 5They cast bronze rings to hold the poles for the four corners of the bronze grating. 6They made the poles of acacia wood and overlaid them with bronze. 7They inserted the poles into the rings so they would be on the sides of the altar for carrying it. They made it hollow, out of boards.

*Basin for Washing*

8They made the bronze basin and its bronze stand from the mirrors of the women who served at the entrance to the Tent of Meeting.

*The Courtyard*

9Next they made the courtyard. The south side was a hundred cubits[d] long and had curtains of finely twisted linen, 10with twenty posts and twenty bronze bases, and with silver hooks and bands on the posts. 11The north side was also a hundred cubits long and had twenty posts and twenty bronze bases, with silver hooks and bands on the posts.

12The west end was fifty cubits[e] wide and had curtains, with ten posts and ten bases, with silver hooks and bands on the posts. 13The east end, toward the sunrise, was also fifty cubits wide. 14Curtains fifteen cubits[f] long were on one side of the entrance, with three posts and three bases, 15and curtains fifteen cubits long were on the other side of the entrance to the courtyard, with three posts and three bases. 16All the curtains around the courtyard were of finely twisted linen. 17The bases for the posts were bronze. The hooks and bands on the posts were silver, and their tops were overlaid with silver; so all the posts of the courtyard had silver bands.

18The curtain for the entrance to the courtyard was of blue, purple and scarlet yarn and finely twisted linen—the work of an embroiderer. It was twenty cubits[g] long and, like the curtains of the courtyard, five cubits[h] high, 19with four posts and four bronze bases. Their hooks and bands were silver, and their tops were overlaid with silver. 20All the tent pegs of the tabernacle and of the surrounding courtyard were bronze.

*The Materials Used*

21These are the amounts of the materials used for the tabernacle, the tabernacle of the Testimony, which were recorded at Moses' command by the Levites under the direction of Ithamar son of Aaron, the priest. 22(Bezalel son of Uri, the son of Hur, of the tribe of Judah, made everything the LORD commanded Moses;

**NIV** [a] *1* OR *HE;* also in verses 2-9 [b] *1* That is, about 4 1/2 feet (about 1.3 meters) [c] *1* That is, about 7 1/2 feet (about 2.3 meters) long and wide [d] *9* That is, about 150 feet (about 46 meters) [e] *12* That is, about 75 feet (about 23 meters) [f] *14* That is, about 22 1/2 feet (about 6.9 meters) [g] *18* That is, about 30 feet (about 9 meters) [h] *18* That is, about 7 1/2 feet (about 2.3 meters)

## King James

23 And with him *was* Aholiab, son of Ahisamach, of the tribe of Dan, an engraver, and a cunning workman, and an embroiderer in blue, and in purple, and in scarlet, and fine linen.

24 All the gold that was occupied for the work in all the work of the holy *place,* even the gold of the offering, was twenty and nine talents, and seven hundred and thirty shekels, after the shekel of the sanctuary.

25 And the silver of them that were numbered of the congregation *was* an hundred talents, and a thousand seven hundred and threescore and fifteen shekels, after the shekel of the sanctuary:

26 A bekah for every man, *that is,* half a shekel, after the shekel of the sanctuary, for every one that went to be numbered, from twenty years old and upward, for six hundred thousand and three thousand and five hundred and fifty *men.*

27 And of the hundred talents of silver were cast the sockets of the sanctuary, and the sockets of the veil; an hundred sockets of the hundred talents, a talent for a socket.

28 And of the thousand seven hundred seventy and five *shekels* he made hooks for the pillars, and overlaid their chapiters, and filleted them.

29 And the brass of the offering *was* seventy talents, and two thousand and four hundred shekels.

30 And therewith he made the sockets to the door of the tabernacle of the congregation, and the brasen altar, and the brasen grate for it, and all the vessels of the altar,

31 And the sockets of the court round about, and the sockets of the court gate, and all the pins of the tabernacle, and all the pins of the court round about.

**39** AND OF the blue, and purple, and scarlet, they made cloths of service, to do service in the holy *place,* and made the holy garments for Aaron; as the LORD commanded Moses.

2 And he made the ephod *of* gold, blue, and purple, and scarlet, and fine twined linen.

3 And they did beat the gold into thin plates, and cut *it into* wires, to work *it* in the blue, and in the purple, and in the scarlet, and in the fine linen, *with* cunning work.

4 They made shoulderpieces for it, to couple *it* together: by the two edges was it coupled together.

5 And the curious girdle of his ephod, that *was* upon it, *was* of the same, according to the work thereof; *of* gold, blue, and purple, and scarlet, and fine twined linen; as the LORD commanded Moses.

6 ¶ And they wrought onyx stones enclosed in ouches of gold, graven, as signets are graven, with the names of the children of Israel.

7 And he put them on the shoulders of the ephod, *that they should be* stones for a memorial to the children of Israel; as the LORD commanded Moses.

8 ¶ And he made the breastplate *of* cunning work, like the work of the ephod; *of* gold, blue, and purple, and scarlet, and fine twined linen.

9 It was foursquare; they made the breastplate double: a span *was* the length thereof, and a span the breadth thereof, *being* doubled.

10 And they set in it four rows of stones: *the first* row *was* a sardius, a topaz, and a carbuncle: this *was* the first row.

11 And the second row, an emerald, a sapphire, and a diamond.

12 And the third row, a ligure, an agate, and an amethyst.

13 And the fourth row, a beryl, an onyx, and a jasper: *they were* enclosed in ouches of gold in their enclosings.

## Amplified

23 With him was Aholiab son of Ahisamach of the tribe of Dan, an engraver, a skillful craftsman, and embroiderer in blue, purple, and scarlet, and in fine linen.

24 All the gold that was used for the work in all the building *and* furnishing of the sanctuary, the gold from the offering, was 29 talents and 730 shekels by the shekel of the sanctuary.

25 And the silver from those numbered of the congregation was 100 talents and 1,775 shekels by sanctuary standards:

26 A beka for each man, that is, half a shekel, by the sanctuary shekel, for every one who was counted, from twenty years old and upward, for 603,550 men.

27 The 100 talents of silver were for casting the sockets *or* bases of the sanctuary and of the veil; 100 sockets for the 100 talents, a talent for a socket.

28 Of the 1,775 shekels he made hooks for the pillars, and overlaid their tops and made joinings for them.

29 The bronze of the offering was 70 talents and 2400 shekels.

30 With it Bezalel made the sockets for the door of the tent of meeting, and the bronze altar and the bronze grate for it, and all the utensils of the altar,

31 The sockets of the court round about and of the court gate, and all the pegs of the tabernacle and around the court.

**39** AND OF the blue and purple and scarlet stuff they made finely wrought garments for serving in the holy place; they made the holy garments for Aaron, as the Lord had commanded Moses.

2 And Bezalel made the ephod of gold, blue, purple, and scarlet stuff, and fine twined linen.

3 And they beat the gold into thin sheets, and cut it into wires, to work into the blue, purple and scarlet stuff and the fine linen, in skilled design.

4 They made shoulder pieces for the ephod, joined to it at its two edges.

5 And the skillfully woven band on it, to gird it on, was of the same piece and workmanship with it, of gold, blue, purple, and scarlet stuff, and fine twined linen, as the Lord had commanded Moses.

6 And they prepared the onyx stones enclosed in settings of gold filigree and engraved as signets are engraved, with the names of the sons of Israel.

7 And he put them on the shoulder pieces of the ephod, to be stones of memorial *or* remembrance for the Israelites, as the Lord had commanded Moses.

8 And [Bezalel] made the breastplate skillfully, like the work of the ephod, of gold, blue, purple, and scarlet stuff, and fine twined linen.

9 The breastplate was a [hand's] span square, when doubled over.

10 And they set in it four rows of stones; a sardius, a topaz, and a carbuncle made the first row;

11 The second row, an emerald, a sapphire, and a diamond;

12 The third row, a jacinth, an agate, and an amethyst;

13 And the fourth row, a beryl, an onyx, and a jasper; they were enclosed in settings of gold filigree.

## New American Standard

23And with him was Oholiab, the son of Ahisamach, of the tribe
of Dan, an engraver and a skillful workman and a weaver in blue
and in purple and in scarlet *material,* and fine linen.
**24**¶ All the gold that was used for the work, in all the work of
the sanctuary, even the gold of the wave offering, was 29 talents
and 730 shekels, according to the shekel of the sanctuary.
25And the silver of those of the congregation who were numbered was 100 talents and 1,775 shekels, according to the shekel
of the sanctuary;
26a beka a head ( *that is,* half a shekel according to the shekel
of the sanctuary), for each one who passed over to those who were
numbered, from twenty years old and upward, for 603,550 men.
27And the hundred talents of silver were for casting the sockets
of the sanctuary and the sockets of the veil; one hundred sockets
for the hundred talents, a talent for a socket.
28And of the 1,775 *shekels,* he made hooks for the pillars and
overlaid their tops and made bands for them.
29And the bronze of the wave offering was 70 talents, and 2,400
shekels.
30And with it he made the sockets to the doorway of the tent
of meeting, and the bronze altar and its bronze grating, and all the
utensils of the altar,
31and the sockets of the court all around and the sockets of the
gate of the court, and all the pegs of the tabernacle and all the pegs
of the court all around.

*The Priestly Garments*

**39** MOREOVER, FROM the blue and purple and scarlet *mate-*
*rial,* they made finely woven garments for ministering in
the holy place, as well as the holy garments which were for Aaron,
just as the LORD had commanded Moses.
**2**¶ And he made the ephod of gold, *and* of blue and purple and
scarlet *material,* and fine twisted linen.
3Then they hammered out gold sheets and cut *them* into
threads to be woven in *with* the blue and the purple and the scarlet
*material,* and the fine linen, the work of a skillful workman.
4They made attaching shoulder pieces for the ephod; it was
attached at its two *upper* ends.
5And the skillfully woven band which was on it was like its
workmanship, of the same material: of gold *and* of blue and purple
and scarlet *material,* and fine twisted linen, just as the LORD had
commanded Moses.
**6**¶ And they made the onyx stones, set in gold filigree *settings;*
they were engraved *like* the engravings of a signet, according to the
names of the sons of Israel.
7And he placed them on the shoulder pieces of the ephod, *as*
memorial stones for the sons of Israel, just as the LORD had commanded Moses.
**8**¶ And he made the breastpiece, the work of a skillful workman, like the workmanship of the ephod: of gold *and* of blue and
purple and scarlet *material* and fine twisted linen.
9It was square; they made the breastpiece folded double, a
span long and a span wide when folded double.
10And they mounted four rows of stones on it. The first row *was*
a row of ruby, topaz, and emerald;
11and the second row, a turquoise, a sapphire and a diamond;
12and the third row, a jacinth, an agate, and an amethyst;
13and the fourth row, a beryl, an onyx, and a jasper. They were
set in gold filigree *settings* when they were mounted.

## New International

23with him was Oholiab son of Ahisamach, of the tribe of Dan—a
craftsman and designer, and an embroiderer in blue, purple and
scarlet yarn and fine linen.) 24The total amount of the gold from
the wave offering used for all the work on the sanctuary was 29
talents and 730 shekels,[a] according to the sanctuary shekel.
25The silver obtained from those of the community who were
counted in the census was 100 talents and 1,775 shekels,[b] according to the sanctuary shekel— 26one beka per person, that is, half
a shekel,[c] according to the sanctuary shekel, from everyone who
had crossed over to those counted, twenty years old or more, a
total of 603,550 men. 27The 100 talents[d] of silver were used to cast
the bases for the sanctuary and for the curtain—100 bases from the
100 talents, one talent for each base. 28They used the 1,775
shekels[e] to make the hooks for the posts, to overlay the tops of the
posts, and to make their bands.
29The bronze from the wave offering was 70 talents and 2,400
shekels.[f] 30They used it to make the bases for the entrance to the
Tent of Meeting, the bronze altar with its bronze grating and all
its utensils, 31the bases for the surrounding courtyard and those
for its entrance and all the tent pegs for the tabernacle and those
for the surrounding courtyard.

*The Priestly Garments*

**39** FROM THE blue, purple and scarlet yarn they made woven garments for ministering in the sanctuary. They also
made sacred garments for Aaron, as the LORD commanded Moses.

*The Ephod*

2They[g] made the ephod of gold, and of blue, purple and scarlet
yarn, and of finely twisted linen. 3They hammered out thin sheets
of gold and cut strands to be worked into the blue, purple and
scarlet yarn and fine linen—the work of a skilled craftsman. 4They
made shoulder pieces for the ephod, which were attached to two
of its corners, so it could be fastened. 5Its skillfully woven waistband was like it—of one piece with the ephod and made with gold,
and with blue, purple and scarlet yarn, and with finely twisted
linen, as the LORD commanded Moses.
6They mounted the onyx stones in gold filigree settings and
engraved them like a seal with the names of the sons of Israel.
7Then they fastened them on the shoulder pieces of the ephod as
memorial stones for the sons of Israel, as the LORD commanded
Moses.

*The Breastpiece*

8They fashioned the breastpiece—the work of a skilled craftsman. They made it like the ephod: of gold, and of blue, purple and
scarlet yarn, and of finely twisted linen. 9It was square—a span[h]
long and a span wide—and folded double. 10Then they mounted
four rows of precious stones on it. In the first row there was a ruby,
a topaz and a beryl; 11in the second row a turquoise, a sapphire[i]
and an emerald; 12in the third row a jacinth, an agate and an
amethyst; 13in the fourth row a chrysolite, an onyx and a jasper.[j]
They were mounted in gold filigree settings. 14There were twelve

**NIV** [a] *24* The weight of the gold was a little over one ton (about 1 metric ton). [b] *25* The weight of the silver was a little over 3 3/4 tons (about 3.4 metric tons). [c] *26* That is, about 1/5 ounce (about 5.5 grams) [d] *27* That is, about 3 3/4 tons (about 3.4 metric tons) [e] *28* That is, about 45 pounds (about 20 kilograms) [f] *29* The weight of the bronze was about 2 1/2 tons (about 2.4 metric tons). [g] *2* Or *He;* also in verses 7, 8 and 22 [h] *9* That is, about 9 inches (about 22 centimeters) [i] *11* Or *lapis lazuli* [j] *13* The precise identification of some of these precious stones is uncertain.

## King James

14 And the stones *were* according to the names of the children of Israel, twelve, according to their names, *like* the engravings of a signet, every one with his name, according to the twelve tribes.

15 And they made upon the breastplate chains at the ends, *of* wreathen work *of* pure gold.

16 And they made two ouches *of* gold, and two gold rings; and put the two rings in the two ends of the breastplate.

17 And they put the two wreathen chains of gold in the two rings on the ends of the breastplate.

18 And the two ends of the two wreathen chains they fastened in the two ouches, and put them on the shoulderpieces of the ephod, before it.

19 And they made two rings of gold, and put *them* on the two ends of the breastplate, upon the border of it, which *was* on the side of the ephod inward.

20 And they made two *other* golden rings, and put them on the two sides of the ephod underneath, toward the forepart of it, over against the *other* coupling thereof, above the curious girdle of the ephod.

21 And they did bind the breastplate by his rings unto the rings of the ephod with a lace of blue, that it might be above the curious girdle of the ephod, and that the breastplate might not be loosed from the ephod; as the LORD commanded Moses.

22¶ And he made the robe of the ephod *of* woven work, all *of* blue.

23 And *there was* an hole in the midst of the robe, as the hole of an habergeon, *with* a band round about the hole, that it should not rend.

24 And they made upon the hems of the robe pomegranates *of* blue, and purple, and scarlet, *and* twined *linen.*

25 And they made bells *of* pure gold, and put the bells between the pomegranates upon the hem of the robe, round about between the pomegranates;

26 A bell and a pomegranate, a bell and a pomegranate, round about the hem of the robe to minister *in;* as the LORD commanded Moses.

27¶ And they made coats *of* fine linen *of* woven work for Aaron, and for his sons,

28 And a mitre *of* fine linen, and goodly bonnets *of* fine linen, and linen breeches *of* fine twined linen,

29 And a girdle *of* fine twined linen, and blue, and purple, and scarlet, *of* needlework; as the LORD commanded Moses.

30¶ And they made the plate of the holy crown *of* pure gold, and wrote upon it a writing, *like to* the engravings of a signet, HOLINESS TO THE LORD.

31 And they tied unto it a lace of blue, to fasten *it* on high upon the mitre; as the LORD commanded Moses.

32¶ Thus was all the work of the tabernacle of the tent of the congregation finished: and the children of Israel did according to all that the LORD commanded Moses, so did they.

33¶ And they brought the tabernacle unto Moses, the tent, and all his furniture, his taches, his boards, his bars, and his pillars, and his sockets,

34 And the covering of rams' skins dyed red, and the covering of badgers' skins, and the veil of the covering,

35 The ark of the testimony, and the staves thereof, and the mercy seat,

36 The table, *and* all the vessels thereof, and the showbread,

37 The pure candlestick, *with* the lamps thereof, *even with* the lamps to be set in order, and all the vessels thereof, and the oil for light,

38 And the golden altar, and the anointing oil, and the sweet incense, and the hanging for the tabernacle door,

39 The brasen altar, and his grate of brass, his staves, and all his vessels, the laver and his foot,

40 The hangings of the court, his pillars, and his sockets, and the hanging for the court gate, his cords, and his pins, and all the vessels of the service of the tabernacle, for the tent of the congregation,

## Amplified

14 There were twelve stones with their names according to those of the sons of Israel, engraved like a signet, each with its name, according to the twelve tribes.

15 And they made [at the ends] of the breastplate twisted chains like cords, of pure gold.

16 And they made two settings of gold filigree, and two gold rings which they put on the two ends of the breastplate.

17 And they put the two twisted cords *or* woven chains of gold in the two rings on the end edges of the breastplate.

18 And the other two ends of the twisted cords *or* chains of gold they put on the two settings, and put them on the shoulder pieces of the ephod, in front.

19 They made two rings of gold, and put them on the two ends of the breastplate, on the inside edge of it, next the ephod.

20 And they made two [other] gold rings, and attached them to the two shoulder pieces of the ephod underneath, in front, at its joining above the skillfully woven band of the ephod.

21 They bound the breastplate by its rings to those of the ephod with a blue lace, that it might lie upon the skillfully woven band of the ephod, and that the breastplate might not be loosed from the ephod; as the Lord commanded Moses.

22 And he made the robe of the ephod of woven work, all of blue.

23 And there was an opening [for the head] in the middle of the robe, like the hole in a coat of mail, with a binding around it, that it should not be torn.

24 On the skirts of the robe they made pomegranates of blue and purple and scarlet stuff and twined linen.

25 And they made bells of pure gold, and put [them] around between the pomegranates upon the skirts of the robe;

26 A bell and a pomegranate, a bell and a pomegranate, round about on the skirts of the robe for ministering; as the Lord commanded Moses.

27 And they made the long *and* sleeved tunics woven of fine linen, for Aaron and his sons,

28 And the turban and the ornamental caps of fine linen, and the breeches of fine twined linen,

29 The girdle *or* sash of fine twined linen, and blue, purple, and scarlet embroidery; as the Lord commanded Moses.

30 And they made the plate of the holy crown of pure gold, and wrote upon it an inscription, like the engravings of a signet, HOLY TO THE LORD.

31 They tied to it a lace of blue, to fasten it on the turban above; as the Lord commanded Moses.

32 Thus all the work of the tabernacle of the tent of meeting was finished; according to all that the Lord commanded Moses, so the Israelites had done.

33 And they brought the tabernacle to Moses, the tent and all its furnishings: its clasps, its [frame] boards, its bars, its pillars, its sockets *or* bases;

34 And the covering of rams' skins made red, and the covering of dolphin *or* porpoise skins, and the veil of the screen;

35 The ark of the testimony, its poles, and the mercy seat;

36 The table and all its utensils, and the showbread [bread of the Presence];

37 The pure [gold] lampstand and its lamps, with the lamps set in order, all its utensils, and the oil for the light;

38 The golden altar, the anointing oil, the fragrant incense, and the hanging for the door of the tent;

39 The bronze altar and its grate of bronze, its poles and all its utensils; the laver and its base;

40 The hangings of the court, its pillars and sockets *or* bases, and the screen for the court gate, its cords, and pegs, and all the utensils for the service of the tabernacle, for the tent of meeting [of God with His people]; [Exod. 29:42, 43.]

## New American Standard

14 And the stones were corresponding to the names of the sons of Israel; they were twelve, corresponding to their names, *engraved with* the engravings of a signet, each with its name for the twelve tribes.

15 And they made on the breastpiece chains like cords, of twisted cordage work in pure gold.

16 And they made two gold filigree *settings* and two gold rings, and put the two rings on the two ends of the breastpiece.

17 Then they put the two gold cords in the two rings at the ends of the breastpiece.

18 And they put the *other* two ends of the two cords on the two filigree *settings,* and put them on the shoulder pieces of the ephod at the front of it.

19 And they made two gold rings and placed *them* on the two ends of the breastpiece, on its inner edge which was next to the ephod.

20 Furthermore, they made two gold rings and placed them on the bottom of the two shoulder pieces of the ephod, on the front of it, close to the place where it joined, above the woven band of the ephod.

21 And they bound the breastpiece by its rings to the rings of the ephod with a blue cord, that it might be on the woven band of the ephod, and that the breastpiece might not come loose from the ephod, just as the LORD had commanded Moses.

22 ¶ Then he made the robe of the ephod of woven work, all of blue;

23 and the opening of the robe was *at the top* in the center, as the opening of a coat of mail, with a binding all around its opening, that it might not be torn.

24 And they made pomegranates of blue and purple and scarlet *material and* twisted *linen* on the hem of the robe.

25 They also made bells of pure gold, and put the bells between the pomegranates all around on the hem of the robe,

26 alternating a bell and a pomegranate all around on the hem of the robe, for the service, just as the LORD had commanded Moses.

27 ¶ And they made the tunics of finely woven linen for Aaron and his sons,

28 and the turban of fine linen, and the decorated caps of fine linen, and the linen breeches of fine twisted linen,

29 and the sash of fine twisted linen, and blue and purple and scarlet *material,* the work of the weaver, just as the LORD had commanded Moses.

30 ¶ And they made the plate of the holy crown of pure gold, and inscribed it like the engravings of a signet, "Holy to the LORD."

31 And they fastened a blue cord to it, to fasten it on the turban above, just as the LORD had commanded Moses.

32 ¶ Thus all the work of the tabernacle of the tent of meeting was completed; and the sons of Israel did according to all that the LORD had commanded Moses; so they did.

33 And they brought the tabernacle to Moses, the tent and all its [a]furnishings: its clasps, its boards, its bars, and its pillars and its sockets;

34 and the covering of rams' skins dyed red, and the covering of porpoise skins, and the screening veil;

35 the ark of the testimony and its poles and the mercy seat;

36 the table, all its utensils, and the bread of the Presence;

37 the pure *gold* lampstand, with its arrangement of lamps and all its utensils, and the oil for the light;

38 and the gold altar, and the anointing oil and the fragrant incense, and the veil for the doorway of the tent;

39 the bronze altar and its bronze grating, its poles and all its utensils, the laver and its stand;

40 the hangings for the court, its pillars and its sockets, and the screen for the gate of the court, its cords and its pegs and all the equipment for the service of the tabernacle, for the tent of meeting;

NAS [a] Or, *utensils,* and so throughout this context

## New International

stones, one for each of the names of the sons of Israel, each
engraved like a seal with the name of one of the twelve tribes.
15 For the breastpiece they made braided chains of pure gold,
like a rope. 16 They made two gold filigree settings and two gold
rings, and fastened the rings to two of the corners of the breastpiece. 17 They fastened the two gold chains to the rings at the
corners of the breastpiece, 18 and the other ends of the chains to the
two settings, attaching them to the shoulder pieces of the ephod
at the front. 19 They made two gold rings and attached them to the
other two corners of the breastpiece on the inside edge next to the
ephod. 20 Then they made two more gold rings and attached them
to the bottom of the shoulder pieces on the front of the ephod,
close to the seam just above the waistband of the ephod. 21 They
tied the rings of the breastpiece to the rings of the ephod with blue
cord, connecting it to the waistband so that the breastpiece would
not swing out from the ephod—as the LORD commanded Moses.

*Other Priestly Garments*

22 They made the robe of the ephod entirely of blue cloth—the
work of a weaver— 23 with an opening in the center of the robe like
the opening of a collar,[b] and a band around this opening, so that
it would not tear. 24 They made pomegranates of blue, purple and
scarlet yarn and finely twisted linen around the hem of the robe.
25 And they made bells of pure gold and attached them around the
hem between the pomegranates. 26 The bells and pomegranates
alternated around the hem of the robe to be worn for ministering,
as the LORD commanded Moses.
27 For Aaron and his sons, they made tunics of fine linen—the
work of a weaver— 28 and the turban of fine linen, the linen headbands and the undergarments of finely twisted linen. 29 The sash
was of finely twisted linen and blue, purple and scarlet yarn—the
work of an embroiderer—as the LORD commanded Moses.
30 They made the plate, the sacred diadem, out of pure gold and
engraved on it, like an inscription on a seal: HOLY TO THE LORD.
31 Then they fastened a blue cord to it to attach it to the turban, as
the LORD commanded Moses.

*Moses Inspects the Tabernacle*

32 So all the work on the tabernacle, the Tent of Meeting, was
completed. The Israelites did everything just as the LORD commanded Moses. 33 Then they brought the tabernacle to Moses: the
tent and all its furnishings, its clasps, frames, crossbars, posts and
bases; 34 the covering of ram skins dyed red, the covering of hides
of sea cows[c] and the shielding curtain; 35 the ark of the Testimony
with its poles and the atonement cover; 36 the table with all its
articles and the bread of the Presence; 37 the pure gold lampstand
with its row of lamps and all its accessories, and the oil for the light;
38 the gold altar, the anointing oil, the fragrant incense, and the
curtain for the entrance to the tent; 39 the bronze altar with its
bronze grating, its poles and all its utensils; the basin with its
stand; 40 the curtains of the courtyard with its posts and bases, and
the curtain for the entrance to the courtyard; the ropes and tent
pegs for the courtyard; all the furnishings for the tabernacle, the
Tent of Meeting; 41 and the woven garments worn for ministering

NIV [b] 23 The meaning of the Hebrew for this word is uncertain. [c] 34 That is, dugongs

## King James

41The cloths of service to do service in the holy *place,* and the holy garments for Aaron the priest, and his sons' garments, to minister in the priest's office.

42According to all that the LORD commanded Moses, so the children of Israel made all the work.

43And Moses did look upon all the work, and, behold, they had done it as the LORD had commanded, even so had they done it: and Moses blessed them.

**40** AND THE LORD spake unto Moses, saying,

2On the first day of the first month shalt thou set up the tabernacle of the tent of the congregation.

3And thou shalt put therein the ark of the testimony, and cover the ark with the veil.

4And thou shalt bring in the table, and set in order the things that are to be set in order upon it; and thou shalt bring in the candlestick, and light the lamps thereof.

5And thou shalt set the altar of gold for the incense before the ark of the testimony, and put the hanging of the door to the tabernacle.

6And thou shalt set the altar of the burnt offering before the door of the tabernacle of the tent of the congregation.

7And thou shalt set the laver between the tent of the congregation and the altar, and shalt put water therein.

8And thou shalt set up the court round about, and hang up the hanging at the court gate.

9And thou shalt take the anointing oil, and anoint the tabernacle, and all that *is* therein, and shalt hallow it, and all the vessels thereof: and it shall be holy.

10And thou shalt anoint the altar of the burnt offering, and all his vessels, and sanctify the altar: and it shall be an altar most holy.

11And thou shalt anoint the laver and his foot, and sanctify it.

12And thou shalt bring Aaron and his sons unto the door of the tabernacle of the congregation, and wash them with water.

13And thou shalt put upon Aaron the holy garments, and anoint him, and sanctify him; that he may minister unto me in the priest's office.

14And thou shalt bring his sons, and clothe them with coats:

15And thou shalt anoint them, as thou didst anoint their father, that they may minister unto me in the priest's office: for their anointing shall surely be an everlasting priesthood throughout their generations.

16Thus did Moses: according to all that the LORD commanded him, so did he.

17¶ And it came to pass in the first month in the second year, on the first *day* of the month, *that* the tabernacle was reared up.

18And Moses reared up the tabernacle, and fastened his sockets, and set up the boards thereof, and put in the bars thereof, and reared up his pillars.

19And he spread abroad the tent over the tabernacle, and put the covering of the tent above upon it; as the LORD commanded Moses.

20¶ And he took and put the testimony into the ark, and set the staves on the ark, and put the mercy seat above upon the ark:

21And he brought the ark into the tabernacle, and set up the veil of the covering, and covered the ark of the testimony; as the LORD commanded Moses.

## Amplified

41The finely worked vestments for ministering in the holy place, the holy garments for Aaron the priest, and the garments of his sons to minister as priests.

42According to all that the Lord had commanded Moses, so the Israelites had done all the work.

43And Moses inspected all the work, and behold, they had done it; as the Lord had commanded, so had they done it. And Moses blessed them.

**40** AND THE Lord said to Moses,

2On the first day of the first month you shall set up the tabernacle of the tent of meeting [of God with you].

3And you shall put in it the ark of the testimony, and screen the ark [of God's presence] with the veil. [Heb. 10:19-23.]

4You shall bring in the [showbread] table, and set in order the things that are to be upon it; and you shall bring in the lampstand, and set up *and* light its lamps. [Cp. Rev. 21:23-25.]

5You shall set the golden altar for the incense before the ark of the testimony [outside the veil] and put the hanging *or* screen at the tabernacle door.

6You shall set the altar of the burnt offering before the door of the tabernacle of the tent of meeting.

7And you shall [a]set the laver between the tent of meeting and the altar, and put water in it.

8And you shall set up the court *curtains* round about, and hang up the hanging *or* screen at the court gate.

9You shall take the anointing oil and anoint the tabernacle and all that is in it, and shall consecrate it and all its furniture; and it shall be holy.

10You shall anoint the altar of burnt offering, and all its utensils; and consecrate (set apart for God) the altar; and the altar shall be most holy.

11And you shall anoint the laver and its base and consecrate it.

12You shall bring Aaron and his sons to the door of the tent of meeting, and wash them with water. [John 17:17-21.]

13You shall put on Aaron the holy garments, and anoint and consecrate him, so he may serve Me as priest.

14And you shall bring his sons and put long *and* sleeved tunics on them,

15And you shall anoint them as you anointed their father, that they may minister to Me as priests; for their anointing shall be to them for an everlasting priesthood throughout their generations.

16Thus did Moses; according to all that the Lord commanded him, so he did.

17And on the first day of the first month in the second year, the tabernacle was erected.

18Moses set up the tabernacle, laid its sockets, set up its boards, put in its bars, and erected its pillars.

19 *Moses* spread the tent over the tabernacle, and put the covering of the tent over it; as the Lord had commanded him.

20He took the testimony [the ten commandments] and put it into the ark, and set the poles [in the rings] on the ark, and put the mercy seat above upon the ark;

21 *Moses* brought the ark into the tabernacle, and set up the veil of the screen and screened the ark of the testimony; as the Lord had commanded *him.*

AMP [a] Why was it necessary for one exact position for the laver to be demanded of Moses by God? Those who have published charts of the tabernacle furniture arrangement, with the laver off to one side or the other of the door into the sanctuary, have missed a point here. The laver was to be placed directly "between [the doors of] the tent of meeting and the altar *of burnt offering,*" thus completing the *Cross* made by the arrangement of the furniture, from the ark to the altar. It could have no significance to the Jews of that time, but the One Who planned it had those in mind to whom Christ would one day say, "And these [very Scriptures] testify about Me!" How fitting that at the foot of that Cross there should be the altar, picturing our complete surrender, and then the laver, picturing our cleansing, that we may enter in through Him Who alone is "the Door" to the eternal Holy of Holies (John 10:1-9).

## New American Standard

41the woven garments for ministering in the holy place and the
holy garments for Aaron the priest and the garments of his sons,
to minister as priests.
42So the sons of Israel did all the work according to all that the
LORD had commanded Moses.
43And Moses examined all the work and behold, they had done
it; just as the LORD had commanded, this they had done. So Moses
blessed them.

*The Tabernacle Erected*

**40** THEN THE LORD spoke to Moses, saying,
2"On the first day of the first month you shall set up the
tabernacle of the tent of meeting.
3"And you shall place the ark of the testimony there, and you
shall screen the ark with the veil.
4"And you shall bring in the table and arrange what belongs
on it; and you shall bring in the lampstand and mount its lamps.
5"Moreover, you shall set the gold altar of incense before the
ark of the testimony, and set up the veil for the doorway to the
tabernacle.
6"And you shall set the altar of burnt offering in front of the
doorway of the tabernacle of the tent of meeting.
7"And you shall set the laver between the tent of meeting and
the altar, and put water in it.
8"And you shall set up the court all around and hang up the
veil for the gateway of the court.
9"Then you shall take the anointing oil and anoint the tabernacle and all that is in it, and shall consecrate it and all its furnishings; and it shall be holy.
10"And you shall anoint the altar of burnt offering and all its
utensils, and consecrate the altar; and the altar shall be most holy.
11"And you shall anoint the laver and its stand, and consecrate
it.
12"Then you shall bring Aaron and his sons to the doorway of
the tent of meeting and wash them with water.
13"And you shall put the holy garments on Aaron and anoint
him and consecrate him, that he may minister as a priest to Me.
14"And you shall bring his sons and put tunics on them;
15and you shall anoint them even as you have anointed their
father, that they may minister as priests to Me; and their anointing
shall qualify them for a perpetual priesthood throughout their
generations."
16Thus Moses did; according to all that the LORD had commanded him, so he did.
17¶ Now it came about in the first month of the second year, on
the first day of the month, that the tabernacle was erected.
18And Moses erected the tabernacle and laid its sockets, and set
up its boards, and inserted its bars and erected its pillars.
19And he spread the tent over the tabernacle and put the covering of the tent on top of it, just as the LORD had commanded
Moses.
20Then he took the testimony and put *it* into the ark, and
attached the poles to the ark, and put the mercy seat on top of the
ark.
21And he brought the ark into the tabernacle, and set up a veil
for the screen, and screened off the ark of the testimony, just as
the LORD had commanded Moses.

## New International

in the sanctuary, both the sacred garments for Aaron the priest and
the garments for his sons when serving as priests.
42The Israelites had done all the work just as the LORD had
commanded Moses. 43Moses inspected the work and saw that they
had done it just as the LORD had commanded. So Moses blessed
them.

*Setting Up the Tabernacle*

**40** THEN THE LORD said to Moses: 2"Set up the tabernacle,
the Tent of Meeting, on the first day of the first month.
3Place the ark of the Testimony in it and shield the ark with the
curtain. 4Bring in the table and set out what belongs on it. Then
bring in the lampstand and set up its lamps. 5Place the gold altar
of incense in front of the ark of the Testimony and put the curtain
at the entrance to the tabernacle.
6"Place the altar of burnt offering in front of the entrance to the
tabernacle, the Tent of Meeting; 7place the basin between the Tent
of Meeting and the altar and put water in it. 8Set up the courtyard
around it and put the curtain at the entrance to the courtyard.
9"Take the anointing oil and anoint the tabernacle and everything in it; consecrate it and all its furnishings, and it will be holy.
10Then anoint the altar of burnt offering and all its utensils; consecrate the altar, and it will be most holy. 11Anoint the basin and its
stand and consecrate them.
12"Bring Aaron and his sons to the entrance to the Tent of
Meeting and wash them with water. 13Then dress Aaron in the
sacred garments, anoint him and consecrate him so he may serve
me as priest. 14Bring his sons and dress them in tunics. 15Anoint
them just as you anointed their father, so they may serve me as
priests. Their anointing will be to a priesthood that will continue
for all generations to come." 16Moses did everything just as the
LORD commanded him.
17So the tabernacle was set up on the first day of the first month
in the second year. 18When Moses set up the tabernacle, he put
the bases in place, erected the frames, inserted the crossbars and
set up the posts. 19Then he spread the tent over the tabernacle and
put the covering over the tent, as the LORD commanded him.
20He took the Testimony and placed it in the ark, attached the
poles to the ark and put the atonement cover over it. 21Then he
brought the ark into the tabernacle and hung the shielding curtain
and shielded the ark of the Testimony, as the LORD commanded
him.

# King James

22¶ And he put the table in the tent of the congregation, upon the side of the tabernacle northward, without the veil.

23And he set the bread in order upon it before the LORD; as the LORD had commanded Moses.

24¶ And he put the candlestick in the tent of the congregation, over against the table, on the side of the tabernacle southward.

25And he lighted the lamps before the LORD; as the LORD commanded Moses.

26¶ And he put the golden altar in the tent of the congregation before the veil:

27And he burnt sweet incense thereon; as the LORD commanded Moses.

28¶ And he set up the hanging *at* the door of the tabernacle.

29And he put the altar of burnt offering *by* the door of the tabernacle of the tent of the congregation, and offered upon it the burnt offering and the meat offering; as the LORD commanded Moses.

30¶ And he set the laver between the tent of the congregation and the altar, and put water there, to wash *withal*.

31And Moses and Aaron and his sons washed their hands and their feet thereat:

32When they went into the tent of the congregation, and when they came near unto the altar, they washed; as the LORD commanded Moses.

33And he reared up the court round about the tabernacle and the altar, and set up the hanging of the court gate. So Moses finished the work.

34¶ Then a cloud covered the tent of the congregation, and the glory of the LORD filled the tabernacle.

35And Moses was not able to enter into the tent of the congregation, because the cloud abode thereon, and the glory of the LORD filled the tabernacle.

36And when the cloud was taken up from over the tabernacle, the children of Israel went onward in all their journeys:

37But if the cloud were not taken up, then they journeyed not till the day that it was taken up.

38For the cloud of the LORD *was* upon the tabernacle by day, and fire was on it by night, in the sight of all the house of Israel, throughout all their journeys.

# Amplified

22Moses put the table [of showbread] in the tent of meeting on the north side of the tabernacle outside the veil;

23He set the bread [of the Presence] in order on it before the Lord; as the Lord had commanded *him.* [John 6:32-35.]

24And he put the lampstand in the tent of meeting, opposite the table, on the south side of the tabernacle.

25Moses set up *and* lighted the lamps before the Lord; as the Lord commanded *him.*

26He put the golden altar [of incense] in the tent of meeting before the veil;

27He burned sweet incense [symbol of prayer] upon it; as the Lord commanded *him.* [Ps. 141:2; Rev. 8:3.]

28And he set up the hanging *or* screen at the door of the tabernacle.

29 *Moses* put the altar of burnt offering at the door of the tabernacle of the tent of meeting, and offered on it the burnt offering and the cereal offering; as the Lord commanded *him.*

30And Moses set the laver between the tent of meeting and the altar, and put water in it for washing.

31And Moses and Aaron and his sons washed their hands and their feet there;

32When they went into the tent of meeting, or came near the altar, they washed; as the Lord commanded Moses.

33And he erected the court round about the tabernacle and the altar, and set up the hanging *or* screen at the court gate. So Moses finished the work.

34Then the cloud [the Shekinah, God's visible presence] covered the tent of meeting, and the glory of the Lord filled the tabernacle! [Rev. 15:8.]

35And Moses was not able to enter the tent of meeting because the cloud remained upon it, and the glory of the Lord filled the tabernacle.

36In all their journeys whenever the cloud was taken up from over the tabernacle, the Israelites went onward;

37But if the cloud was not taken up, they did not journey on till the day that it was taken up.

38For throughout all their journeys the cloud of the Lord was upon the tabernacle by day, and fire was in it by night, in the sight of all the house of Israel.

## New American Standard

22Then he put the table in the tent of meeting, on the north side of the tabernacle, outside the veil.

23And he set the arrangement of bread in order on it before the LORD, just as the LORD had commanded Moses.

24Then he placed the lampstand in the tent of meeting, opposite the table, on the south side of the tabernacle.

25And he lighted the lamps before the LORD, just as the LORD had commanded Moses.

26Then he placed the gold altar in the tent of meeting in front of the veil;

27and he burned fragrant incense on it, just as the LORD had commanded Moses.

28Then he set up the veil for the doorway of the tabernacle.

29And he set the altar of burnt offering *before* the doorway of the tabernacle of the tent of meeting, and offered on it the burnt offering and the meal offering, just as the LORD had commanded Moses.

30And he placed the laver between the tent of meeting and the altar, and put water in it for washing.

31And from it Moses and Aaron and his sons washed their hands and their feet.

32When they entered the tent of meeting, and when they approached the altar, they washed, just as the LORD had commanded Moses.

33And he erected the court all around the tabernacle and the altar, and hung up the veil for the gateway of the court. Thus Moses finished the work.

*The Glory of the LORD*

34¶ Then the cloud covered the tent of meeting, and the glory of the LORD filled the tabernacle.

35And Moses was not able to enter the tent of meeting because the cloud had settled on it, and the glory of the LORD filled the tabernacle.

36And throughout all their journeys whenever the cloud was taken up from over the tabernacle, the sons of Israel would set out;

37but if the cloud was not taken up, then they did not set out until the day when it was taken up.

38For throughout all their journeys, the cloud of the LORD was on the tabernacle by day, and there was fire in it by night, in the sight of all the house of Israel.

## New International

22Moses placed the table in the Tent of Meeting on the north
side of the tabernacle outside the curtain 23and set out the bread
on it before the LORD, as the LORD commanded him.

24He placed the lampstand in the Tent of Meeting opposite the
table on the south side of the tabernacle 25and set up the lamps
before the LORD, as the LORD commanded him.

26Moses placed the gold altar in the Tent of Meeting in front of
the curtain 27and burned fragrant incense on it, as the LORD commanded him. 28Then he put up the curtain at the entrance to the
tabernacle.

29He set the altar of burnt offering near the entrance to the tabernacle, the Tent of Meeting, and offered on it burnt offerings and grain offerings, as the LORD commanded him.

30He placed the basin between the Tent of Meeting and the altar
and put water in it for washing, 31and Moses and Aaron and his
sons used it to wash their hands and feet. 32They washed whenever they entered the Tent of Meeting or approached the altar, as
the LORD commanded Moses.

33Then Moses set up the courtyard around the tabernacle and altar and put up the curtain at the entrance to the courtyard. And so Moses finished the work.

*The Glory of the LORD*

34Then the cloud covered the Tent of Meeting, and the glory of
the LORD filled the tabernacle. 35Moses could not enter the Tent of
Meeting because the cloud had settled upon it, and the glory of the
LORD filled the tabernacle.

36In all the travels of the Israelites, whenever the cloud lifted
from above the tabernacle, they would set out; 37but if the cloud
did not lift, they did not set out—until the day it lifted. 38So the
cloud of the LORD was over the tabernacle by day, and fire was in
the cloud by night, in the sight of all the house of Israel during all
their travels.

## King James

THE THIRD BOOK OF

MOSES, CALLED

# Leviticus

**1** AND THE LORD called unto Moses, and spake unto him out of the tabernacle of the congregation, saying,

2Speak unto the children of Israel, and say unto them, If any man of you bring an offering unto the LORD, ye shall bring your offering of the cattle, *even* of the herd, and of the flock.

3If his offering *be* a burnt sacrifice of the herd, let him offer a male without blemish: he shall offer it of his own voluntary will at the door of the tabernacle of the congregation before the LORD.

4And he shall put his hand upon the head of the burnt offering; and it shall be accepted for him to make atonement for him.

5And he shall kill the bullock before the LORD: and the priests, Aaron's sons, shall bring the blood, and sprinkle the blood round about upon the altar that *is by* the door of the tabernacle of the congregation.

6And he shall flay the burnt offering, and cut it into his pieces.

7And the sons of Aaron the priest shall put fire upon the altar, and lay the wood in order upon the fire:

8And the priests, Aaron's sons, shall lay the parts, the head, and the fat, in order upon the wood that *is* on the fire which *is* upon the altar:

9But his inwards and his legs shall he wash in water: and the priest shall burn all on the altar, *to be* a burnt sacrifice, an offering made by fire, of a sweet savour unto the LORD.

10¶ And if his offering *be* of the flocks, *namely*, of the sheep, or of the goats, for a burnt sacrifice; he shall bring it a male without blemish.

11And he shall kill it on the side of the altar northward before the LORD: and the priests, Aaron's sons, shall sprinkle his blood round about upon the altar.

12And he shall cut it into his pieces, with his head and his fat: and the priest shall lay them in order on the wood that *is* on the fire which *is* upon the altar:

13But he shall wash the inwards and the legs with water: and the priest shall bring *it* all, and burn *it* upon the altar: it *is* a burnt sacrifice, an offering made by fire, of a sweet savour unto the LORD.

14¶ And if the burnt sacrifice for his offering to the LORD *be* of fowls, then he shall bring his offering of turtledoves, or of young pigeons.

## Amplified

THE THIRD BOOK OF MOSES,

CALLED

# Leviticus

**1** THE LORD [a]called to Moses out of the tent of meeting, and said to him,

2Say to the Israelites, When any man of you brings an offering to the Lord, you shall bring your offering of [domestic] animals from the herd or from the flock.

3If his offering is a burnt offering from the herd, he shall offer a male without blemish; he shall offer it at the door of the tent of meeting, that he may be accepted before the Lord. [Rom. 12:1; Phil. 1:20.]

4And he shall lay *both* his hands upon the head of the burnt offering [transferring symbolically his guilt to the victim], and it shall be [b]an acceptable atonement for him. [I Pet. 1:2; Heb. 13:15, 16.]

5The man shall kill the young bull before the Lord; and the priests, Aaron's sons, shall present the blood, and dash *it* round about upon the altar that is at the door of the tent of meeting.

6And he shall skin the burnt offering and cut it into pieces.

7And the sons of Aaron the priest shall put fire on the altar, and lay wood in order on the fire;

8And Aaron's sons the priests shall lay the pieces, the head, and the fat, in order on the wood on the fire on the altar;

9But its entrails and its legs he shall wash with water. And the priest shall burn the whole on the altar for a burnt offering, an offering by fire, a sweet *and* satisfying odor to the Lord. [Eph. 5:2; Phil. 4:18; I Pet. 2:5.]

10And if the man's offering is of the flock, from the sheep or the goats, for a burnt offering, he shall offer a male without blemish.

11And he shall kill it on the north side of the altar before the Lord, and Aaron's sons the priests shall dash its blood round about against the altar.

12And *the man* shall cut it into pieces, with its head and its fat, and the priest shall lay them in order on the wood that is on the fire on the altar.

13But he shall wash the entrails and legs with water. The priest shall offer the whole, and burn it on the altar; it is a burnt offering, an offering made by fire, a sweet *and* satisfying fragrance to the Lord.

14And if the offering to the Lord is a burnt offering of birds, then [the man] shall bring turtledoves or young pigeons.

**AMP** [a] The first step toward understanding the message of Leviticus is to appreciate its viewpoint, indicated here—"The Lord called to Moses out of the tent of meeting," and talked to him. Before this a forbidding God has spoken from the burning mountain; but now the tabernacle is erected according to the God-given pattern, and a God Who dwells among His people in fellowship with them talks with His servant Moses "out of the tent of meeting." The people, therefore, are not treated as sinners alienated from God, "but as being already brought into a new relationship, even that of fellowship, on the ground of a blood-sealed covenant" (J. Sidlow Baxter, in *Explore the Book*). [b] To render the self-sacrifice perfect, it was necessary that the offerer should spiritually die, and that through the mediator of his salvation he should put his soul into a living fellowship with the Lord by sinking it as it were into the death of the sacrifice that had died for him, and should also bring his bodily members within the operations of the gracious Spirit of God, that thus he might be renewed and sanctified [separated for holy use] both body and soul, and enter into union with God (Keil and Delitzsch, *Biblical Commentary on the Old Testament*, Martin tr., II, 291).

## New American Standard

# Leviticus

*The Law of Burnt Offerings*

**1** THEN THE LORD called to Moses and spoke to him from the tent of meeting, saying,

2"Speak to the sons of Israel and say to them, 'When any man of you brings an offering to the LORD, you shall bring your offering of animals from the herd or the flock.

3'If his offering is a burnt offering from the herd, he shall offer it, a male without defect; he shall offer it at the doorway of the tent of meeting, that he may be accepted before the LORD.

4'And he shall lay his hand on the head of the burnt offering, that it may be accepted for him to make atonement on his behalf.

5'And he shall slay the young bull before the LORD; and Aaron's sons, the priests, shall offer up the blood and sprinkle the blood around on the altar that is at the doorway of the tent of meeting.

6'He shall then skin the burnt offering and cut it into its pieces.

7'And the sons of Aaron the priest shall put fire on the altar and arrange wood on the fire.

8'Then Aaron's sons, the priests, shall arrange the pieces, the head, and the suet over the wood which is on the fire that is on the altar.

9'Its entrails, however, and its legs he shall wash with water. And the priest shall offer up in smoke all of it on the altar for a burnt offering, an offering by fire of a soothing aroma to the LORD.

10¶ 'But if his offering is from the flock, of the sheep or of the goats, for a burnt offering, he shall offer it a male without defect.

11'And he shall slay it on the side of the altar northward before the LORD, and Aaron's sons, the priests, shall sprinkle its blood around on the altar.

12'He shall then cut it into its pieces with its head and its suet, and the priest shall arrange them on the wood which is on the fire that is on the altar.

13'The entrails, however, and the legs he shall wash with water. And the priest shall offer all of it, and offer it up in smoke on the altar; it is a burnt offering, an offering by fire of a soothing aroma to the LORD.

14¶ 'But if his offering to the LORD is a burnt offering of birds, then he shall bring his offering from the turtledoves or from young pigeons.

## New International

# Leviticus

*The Burnt Offering*

**1** THE LORD called to Moses and spoke to him from the Tent
of Meeting. He said, 2"Speak to the Israelites and say to them:
'When any of you brings an offering to the LORD, bring as your
offering an animal from either the herd or the flock.
3" 'If the offering is a burnt offering from the herd, he is to offer
a male without defect. He must present it at the entrance to the
Tent of Meeting so that it[c] will be acceptable to the LORD. 4He is
to lay his hand on the head of the burnt offering, and it will be
accepted on his behalf to make atonement for him. 5He is to
slaughter the young bull before the LORD, and then Aaron's sons
the priests shall bring the blood and sprinkle it against the altar on
all sides at the entrance to the Tent of Meeting. 6He is to skin the
burnt offering and cut it into pieces. 7The sons of Aaron the priest
are to put fire on the altar and arrange wood on the fire. 8Then
Aaron's sons the priests shall arrange the pieces, including the
head and the fat, on the burning wood that is on the altar. 9He is
to wash the inner parts and the legs with water, and the priest is
to burn all of it on the altar. It is a burnt offering, an offering made
by fire, an aroma pleasing to the LORD.
10" 'If the offering is a burnt offering from the flock, from either
the sheep or the goats, he is to offer a male without defect. 11He
is to slaughter it at the north side of the altar before the LORD, and
Aaron's sons the priests shall sprinkle its blood against the altar
on all sides. 12He is to cut it into pieces, and the priest shall arrange
them, including the head and the fat, on the burning wood that
is on the altar. 13He is to wash the inner parts and the legs with
water, and the priest is to bring all of it and burn it on the altar.
It is a burnt offering, an offering made by fire, an aroma pleasing
to the LORD.
14" 'If the offering to the LORD is a burnt offering of birds, he
is to offer a dove or a young pigeon. 15The priest shall bring it to

NIV [c] 3 Or *he*

## King James

15And the priest shall bring it unto the altar, and wring off his
head, and burn *it* on the altar; and the blood thereof shall be wrung
out at the side of the altar:
16And he shall pluck away his crop with his feathers, and cast
it beside the altar on the east part, by the place of the ashes:
17And he shall cleave it with the wings thereof, *but* shall not
divide *it* asunder: and the priest shall burn it upon the altar, upon
the wood that *is* upon the fire: it *is* a burnt sacrifice, an offering
made by fire, of a sweet savour unto the LORD.

**2** AND WHEN any will offer a meat offering unto the LORD, his
offering shall be *of* fine flour; and he shall pour oil upon it,
and put frankincense thereon:
2And he shall bring it to Aaron's sons the priests: and he shall
take thereout his handful of the flour thereof, and of the oil thereof, with all the frankincense thereof; and the priest shall burn the
memorial of it upon the altar, *to be* an offering made by fire, of a
sweet savour unto the LORD:
3And the remnant of the meat offering *shall be* Aaron's and his
sons': *it is* a thing most holy of the offerings of the LORD made by
fire.
4¶ And if thou bring an oblation of a meat offering baked in the
oven, *it shall be* unleavened cakes of fine flour mingled with oil, or
unleavened wafers anointed with oil.
5¶ And if thy oblation *be* a meat offering *baked* in a pan, it shall
be *of* fine flour unleavened, mingled with oil.
6Thou shalt part it in pieces, and pour oil thereon: it *is* a meat
offering.
7¶ And if thy oblation *be* a meat offering *baked* in the fryingpan,
it shall be made *of* fine flour with oil.
8And thou shalt bring the meat offering that is made of these
things unto the LORD: and when it is presented unto the priest, he
shall bring it unto the altar.
9And the priest shall take from the meat offering a memorial
thereof, and shall burn *it* upon the altar: *it is* an offering made by
fire, of a sweet savour unto the LORD.
10And that which is left of the meat offering *shall be* Aaron's and
his sons': *it is* a thing most holy of the offerings of the LORD made
by fire.
11No meat offering, which ye shall bring unto the LORD, shall
be made with leaven: for ye shall burn no leaven, nor any honey,
in any offering of the LORD made by fire.
12¶ As for the oblation of the firstfruits, ye shall offer them unto
the LORD: but they shall not be burnt on the altar for a sweet
savour.
13And every oblation of thy meat offering shalt thou season
with salt; neither shalt thou suffer the salt of the covenant of thy
God to be lacking from thy meat offering: with all thine offerings
thou shalt offer salt.
14And if thou offer a meat offering of thy firstfruits unto the
LORD, thou shalt offer for the meat offering of thy firstfruits green
ears of corn dried by the fire, *even* corn beaten out of full ears.
15And thou shalt put oil upon it, and lay frankincense thereon:
it *is* a meat offering.
16And the priest shall burn the memorial of it, *part* of the beaten
corn thereof, and *part* of the oil thereof, with all the frankincense
thereof: *it is* an offering made by fire unto the LORD.

## Amplified

15And the priest shall bring it to the altar and wring off its head,
and burn it on the altar; and its blood shall be drained out on the
side of the altar.
16And he shall take away its crop with its feathers, and cast it
beside the altar on the east side, in the place for ashes.
17And he shall split it open [holding it] by its wings, but shall
not cut it in two. And the priest shall burn it on the altar, on the
wood that is on the fire; it is a burnt offering, an offering by fire,
a sweet *and* satisfying odor to the Lord.

**2** WHEN ANY one offers a cereal offering to the Lord, *it* shall
be of fine flour; and he shall pour oil over it, and lay frankincense on it.
2And he shall bring it to Aaron's sons the priests. Out of it he
shall take a handful of the fine flour and oil, with all its frankincense; and the priest shall burn this on the altar as the memorial
portion of it, an offering made by fire, of a sweet *and* satisfying
fragrance to the Lord.
3What is left of the cereal offering shall be Aaron's and his sons';
it is a most holy part of the offerings to the Lord made by fire.
4When you bring as an offering cereal baked in the oven, it shall
be unleavened cakes of fine flour mixed with oil, or unleavened
wafers spread with oil.
5If your offering is cereal baked on a griddle, it shall be of fine
flour unleavened, mixed with oil.
6You shall break it in pieces and pour oil on it; it is a cereal
offering.
7And if your offering is cereal cooked in the frying pan, it shall
be made of fine flour with oil.
8And you shall bring the cereal offering that is made of these
things to the Lord; it shall be presented to the priest, and he shall
bring it to the [bronze] altar.
9The priest shall take from the cereal offering its memorial
portion and burn it on the altar, an offering made by fire, a sweet
*and* satisfying fragrance to the Lord.
10What is left of the cereal offering shall be Aaron's and his
sons'; it is a most holy part of the offerings to the Lord made by
fire.
11No cereal offering that you bring to the Lord shall be made
with leaven; for you shall burn no leaven or honey in any offering
made by fire to the Lord. [I Cor. 5:8.]
12As an offering of first fruits you may offer leaven and honey
to the Lord, but [a]they shall not be burned on the altar for a sweet
odor [to the Lord, for their aid to fermentation is symbolic of
corruption in the human heart].
13Every cereal offering you shall season with salt [symbol of
preservation]; neither shall you allow the salt of the covenant of
your God to be lacking from your cereal offering; with all your
offerings you shall offer salt. [Mark 9:49, 50.]
14If you offer a cereal offering of your first fruits to the Lord, you
shall offer for *it* of your first fruits grain in the ear parched with
fire, bruised *and* crushed grain out of the fresh *and* fruitful ear.
15And you shall put oil on it, and lay frankincense on it; it is a
cereal offering.
16The priest shall burn as its memorial portion, part of the
bruised *and* crushed grain of it and part of the oil of it, with all its
frankincense; it is an offering by fire to the Lord.

**AMP** [a] There is to be no division between one's spiritual life and his secular life, but the whole of one's life is to be of the nature of a sacrament. See Col. 3:23, 24.

## New American Standard

15'And the priest shall bring it to the altar and wring off its head, and offer it up in smoke on the altar; and its blood is to be drained out on the side of the altar.

16'He shall also take away its crop with its feathers, and cast it beside the altar eastward, to the place of the ashes.

17'Then he shall tear it by its wings, *but* shall not sever *it*. And the priest shall offer it up in smoke on the altar on the wood which is on the fire; it is a burnt offering, an offering by fire of a soothing aroma to the LORD.

*The Law of Grain Offerings*

**2** 'NOW WHEN anyone presents a grain offering as an offering to the LORD, his offering shall be of fine flour, and he shall pour oil on it and put frankincense on it.

2'He shall then bring it to Aaron's sons, the priests; and shall take from it his handful of its fine flour and of its oil with all of its frankincense. And the priest shall offer *it* up in smoke *as* its memorial portion on the altar, an offering by fire of a soothing aroma to the LORD.

3'And the remainder of the grain offering belongs to Aaron and his sons: a thing most holy, of the offerings to the LORD by fire.

4¶ 'Now when you bring an offering of a grain offering baked in an oven, *it shall be* unleavened cakes of fine flour mixed with oil, or unleavened wafers spread with oil.

5'And if your offering is a grain offering *made* on the griddle, *it shall be* of fine flour, unleavened, mixed with oil;

6you shall break it into bits, and pour oil on it; it is a grain offering.

7'Now if your offering is a grain offering *made* in a pan, it shall be made of fine flour with oil.

8'When you bring in the grain offering which is made of these things to the LORD, it shall be presented to the priest and he shall bring it to the altar.

9'The priest then shall take up from the grain offering its memorial portion, and shall offer *it* up in smoke on the altar *as* an offering by fire of a soothing aroma to the LORD.

10'And the remainder of the grain offering belongs to Aaron and his sons: a thing most holy, of the offerings to the LORD by fire.

11¶ 'No grain offering, which you bring to the LORD, shall be made with leaven, for you shall not offer up in smoke any leaven or any honey as an offering by fire to the LORD.

12'As an offering of first fruits, you shall bring them to the LORD, but they shall not ascend for a soothing aroma on the altar.

13'Every grain offering of yours, moreover, you shall season with salt, so that the salt of the covenant of your God shall not be lacking from your grain offering; with all your offerings you shall offer salt.

14¶ 'Also if you bring a grain offering of early ripened things to the LORD, you shall bring fresh heads of grain roasted in the fire, grits of new growth, for the grain offering of your early ripened things.

15'You shall then put oil on it and lay incense on it; it is a grain offering.

16'And the priest shall offer up in smoke its memorial portion, part of its grits and its oil with all its incense as an offering by fire to the LORD.

## New International

the altar, wring off the head and burn it on the altar; its blood shall
be drained out on the side of the altar. 16He is to remove the crop
with its contents[b] and throw it to the east side of the altar, where
the ashes are. 17He shall tear it open by the wings, not severing
it completely, and then the priest shall burn it on the wood that
is on the fire on the altar. It is a burnt offering, an offering made
by fire, an aroma pleasing to the LORD.

*The Grain Offering*

**2** " 'WHEN SOMEONE brings a grain offering to the LORD, his
offering is to be of fine flour. He is to pour oil on it, put
incense on it 2and take it to Aaron's sons the priests. The priest
shall take a handful of the fine flour and oil, together with all the
incense, and burn this as a memorial portion on the altar, an
offering made by fire, an aroma pleasing to the LORD. 3The rest of
the grain offering belongs to Aaron and his sons; it is a most holy
part of the offerings made to the LORD by fire.

4" 'If you bring a grain offering baked in an oven, it is to consist
of fine flour: cakes made without yeast and mixed with oil, or[c]
wafers made without yeast and spread with oil. 5If your grain
offering is prepared on a griddle, it is to be made of fine flour mixed
with oil, and without yeast. 6Crumble it and pour oil on it; it is a
grain offering. 7If your grain offering is cooked in a pan, it is to be
made of fine flour and oil. 8Bring the grain offering made of these
things to the LORD; present it to the priest, who shall take it to the
altar. 9He shall take out the memorial portion from the grain offering and burn it on the altar as an offering made by fire, an aroma
pleasing to the LORD. 10The rest of the grain offering belongs to
Aaron and his sons; it is a most holy part of the offerings made to
the LORD by fire.

11" 'Every grain offering you bring to the LORD must be made
without yeast, for you are not to burn any yeast or honey in an
offering made to the LORD by fire. 12You may bring them to the
LORD as an offering of the firstfruits, but they are not to be offered
on the altar as a pleasing aroma. 13Season all your grain offerings
with salt. Do not leave the salt of the covenant of your God out of
your grain offerings; add salt to all your offerings.

14" 'If you bring a grain offering of firstfruits to the LORD, offer
crushed heads of new grain roasted in the fire. 15Put oil and
incense on it; it is a grain offering. 16The priest shall burn the
memorial portion of the crushed grain and the oil, together with
all the incense, as an offering made to the LORD by fire.

NIV [b] 16 Or *crop and the feathers;* the meaning of the Hebrew for this word is uncertain. [c] 4 Or *and*

## King James

**3** AND IF his oblation *be* a sacrifice of peace offering, if he offer
*it* of the herd; whether *it be* a male or female, he shall offer
it without blemish before the LORD.
2And he shall lay his hand upon the head of his offering, and
kill it *at* the door of the tabernacle of the congregation: and Aaron's
sons the priests shall sprinkle the blood upon the altar round
about.
3And he shall offer of the sacrifice of the peace offering an
offering made by fire unto the LORD; the fat that covereth the
inwards, and all the fat that *is* upon the inwards,
4And the two kidneys, and the fat that *is* on them, which *is* by
the flanks, and the caul above the liver, with the kidneys, it shall
he take away.
5And Aaron's sons shall burn it on the altar upon the burnt
sacrifice, which *is* upon the wood that *is* on the fire: *it is* an offering
made by fire, of a sweet savour unto the LORD.
6¶ And if his offering for a sacrifice of peace offering unto the
LORD *be* of the flock; male or female, he shall offer it without
blemish.
7If he offer a lamb for his offering, then shall he offer it before
the LORD.
8And he shall lay his hand upon the head of his offering, and
kill it before the tabernacle of the congregation: and Aaron's sons
shall sprinkle the blood thereof round about upon the altar.
9And he shall offer of the sacrifice of the peace offering an
offering made by fire unto the LORD; the fat thereof, *and* the whole
rump, it shall he take off hard by the backbone; and the fat that
covereth the inwards, and all the fat that *is* upon the inwards,
10And the two kidneys, and the fat that *is* upon them, which
*is* by the flanks, and the caul above the liver, with the kidneys, it
shall he take away.
11And the priest shall burn it upon the altar: *it is* the food of the
offering made by fire unto the LORD.
12¶ And if his offering *be* a goat, then he shall offer it before the
LORD.
13And he shall lay his hand upon the head of it, and kill it before
the tabernacle of the congregation: and the sons of Aaron shall
sprinkle the blood thereof upon the altar round about.
14And he shall offer thereof his offering, *even* an offering made
by fire unto the LORD; the fat that covereth the inwards, and all the
fat that *is* upon the inwards,
15And the two kidneys, and the fat that *is* upon them, which
*is* by the flanks, and the caul above the liver, with the kidneys, it
shall he take away.
16And the priest shall burn them upon the altar: *it is* the food
of the offering made by fire for a sweet savour: all the fat *is* the
LORD'S.
17 *It shall be* a perpetual statute for your generations throughout
all your dwellings, that ye eat neither fat nor blood.

**4** AND THE LORD spake unto Moses, saying,
2Speak unto the children of Israel, saying, If a soul shall sin
through ignorance against any of the commandments of the LORD
*concerning things* which ought not to be done, and shall do against
any of them:
3If the priest that is anointed do sin according to the sin of the
people; then let him bring for his sin, which he hath sinned, a
young bullock without blemish unto the LORD for a sin offering.
4And he shall bring the bullock unto the door of the tabernacle
of the congregation before the LORD; and shall lay his hand upon
the bullock's head, and kill the bullock before the LORD.
5And the priest that is anointed shall take of the bullock's blood,
and bring it to the tabernacle of the congregation:

## Amplified

**3** IF A man's offering is a sacrifice of peace offering, if he offers
an animal from the herd, whether male or female, he shall
offer it without blemish before the Lord.
2He shall lay [both] his [a]hands upon the head of his offering,
and kill it at the door of the tent of meeting; and Aaron's sons the
priests shall throw the blood against the altar round about.
3And from the sacrifice of the peace, an offering by fire to the
Lord, he shall offer the fat that covers and is upon the entrails,
4And the two kidneys with the fat that is on them at the loins,
and the appendage of the liver which he shall take away with the
kidneys.
5Aaron's sons shall burn it all on the altar on the burnt offering,
which is on the wood on the fire, an offering by fire, of a sweet
*and* satisfying odor to the Lord.
6If his peace offering to the Lord is an animal from the flock,
male or female, he shall offer it without blemish.
7If he offers a lamb, then he shall offer it before the Lord.
8He shall lay [both] his hands on the head of his offering and
kill it before the tent of meeting; and Aaron's sons shall throw its
blood around against the altar.
9And he shall offer from the peace offering as an offering by fire
to the Lord, the fat of it, the fat tail as a whole, taking it off close
to the backbone, and the fat that covers and is upon the entrails,
10And the two kidneys, and the fat on them at the loins, and
the appendage of the liver which he shall take away with the
kidneys.
11The priest shall burn it upon the altar, a food offering made
by fire to the Lord.
12If [a man's] offering is a goat, he shall offer it before the Lord,
13And lay his hands upon its head, and kill it before the tent of
meeting; and the sons of Aaron shall throw its blood against the
altar round about.
14Then he shall offer from it as his offering made by fire to the
Lord, the fat that covers and is on the entrails,
15And the two kidneys and the fat that is on them at the loins,
and the appendage of the liver which he shall take away with the
kidneys.
16The priest shall burn them on the altar as food offered by fire
for a sweet *and* satisfying fragrance. All fat is the Lord's.
17It shall be a perpetual statute for your generations in all your
dwelling places, that you eat neither fat nor blood.

**4** AND THE Lord said to Moses,
2Say to the Israelites, If any one shall sin through error *or*
unwittingly in any of the things which the Lord has commanded
not to do, and shall do any one of them,
3If it is the anointed priest who sins, thus bringing guilt on the
people, then let him offer for his sin which he has committed a
young bull without blemish to the Lord as a sin offering. [Cp. Heb.
7:27, 28.]
4He shall bring the bull to the door of the tent of meeting before
the Lord; and shall lay [both] his hands on the bull's head, and kill
*it* before the Lord.
5And the anointed priest shall take some of the bull's blood, and
bring it into the tent of meeting;

AMP [a] The Septuagint Version (Greek) so reads.

# New American Standard

*The Law of Peace Offerings*

**3** 'NOW IF his offering is a sacrifice of peace offerings, if he is going to offer out of the herd, whether male or female, he shall offer it without defect before the LORD.

2 'And he shall lay his hand on the head of his offering and slay it at the doorway of the tent of meeting, and Aaron's sons, the priests, shall sprinkle the blood around on the altar.

3 'And from the sacrifice of the peace offerings, he shall present an offering by fire to the LORD, the fat that covers the entrails and all the fat that is on the entrails,

4 and the two kidneys with the fat that is on them, which is on the loins, and the lobe of the liver, which he shall remove with the kidneys.

5 'Then Aaron's sons shall offer *it* up in smoke on the altar on the burnt offering, which is on the wood that is on the fire; it is an offering by fire of a soothing aroma to the LORD.

6 'But if his offering for a sacrifice of peace offerings to the LORD is from the flock, he shall offer it, male or female, without defect.

7 'If he is going to offer a lamb for his offering, then he shall offer it before the LORD,

8 and he shall lay his hand on the head of his offering, and slay it before the tent of meeting; and Aaron's sons shall sprinkle its blood around on the altar.

9 'And from the sacrifice of peace offerings he shall bring as an offering by fire to the LORD, its fat, the entire fat tail which he shall remove close to the backbone, and the fat that covers the entrails and all the fat that is on the entrails,

10 and the two kidneys with the fat that is on them, which is on the loins, and the lobe of the liver, which he shall remove with the kidneys.

11 'Then the priest shall offer *it* up in smoke on the altar, *as* food, an offering by fire to the LORD.

12 ¶ 'Moreover, if his offering is a goat, then he shall offer it before the LORD,

13 and he shall lay his hand on its head and slay it before the tent of meeting; and the sons of Aaron shall sprinkle its blood around on the altar.

14 'And from it he shall present his offering as an offering by fire to the LORD, the fat that covers the entrails and all the fat that is on the entrails,

15 and the two kidneys with the fat that is on them, which is on the loins, and the lobe of the liver, which he shall remove with the kidneys.

16 'And the priest shall offer them up in smoke on the altar *as* food, an offering by fire for a soothing aroma; all fat is the LORD's.

17 'It is a perpetual statute throughout your generations in all your dwellings: you shall not eat any fat or any blood.' "

*The Law of Sin Offerings*

**4** THEN THE LORD spoke to Moses, saying,

2 "Speak to the sons of Israel, saying, 'If a person sins unintentionally in any of the things which the LORD has commanded not to be done, and commits any of them,

3 if the anointed priest sins so as to bring guilt on the people, then let him offer to the LORD a bull without defect as a sin offering for the sin he has committed.

4 'And he shall bring the bull to the doorway of the tent of meeting before the LORD, and he shall lay his hand on the head of the bull, and slay the bull before the LORD.

5 'Then the anointed priest is to take some of the blood of the bull and bring it to the tent of meeting,

# New International

*The Fellowship Offering*

**3** " 'IF SOMEONE'S offering is a fellowship offering,[b] and he
offers an animal from the herd, whether male or female, he
is to present before the LORD an animal without defect. 2 He is to
lay his hand on the head of his offering and slaughter it at the
entrance to the Tent of Meeting. Then Aaron's sons the priests
shall sprinkle the blood against the altar on all sides. 3 From the
fellowship offering he is to bring a sacrifice made to the LORD by
fire: all the fat that covers the inner parts or is connected to them,
4 both kidneys with the fat on them near the loins, and the
covering of the liver, which he will remove with the kidneys.
5 Then Aaron's sons are to burn it on the altar on top of the burnt
offering that is on the burning wood, as an offering made by fire,
an aroma pleasing to the LORD.

6 " 'If he offers an animal from the flock as a fellowship offering
to the LORD, he is to offer a male or female without defect. 7 If he
offers a lamb, he is to present it before the LORD. 8 He is to lay his
hand on the head of his offering and slaughter it in front of the Tent
of Meeting. Then Aaron's sons shall sprinkle its blood against the
altar on all sides. 9 From the fellowship offering he is to bring a
sacrifice made to the LORD by fire: its fat, the entire fat tail cut off
close to the backbone, all the fat that covers the inner parts or is
connected to them, 10 both kidneys with the fat on them near the
loins, and the covering of the liver, which he will remove with the
kidneys. 11 The priest shall burn them on the altar as food, an
offering made to the LORD by fire.

12 " 'If his offering is a goat, he is to present it before the LORD.
13 He is to lay his hand on its head and slaughter it in front of the
Tent of Meeting. Then Aaron's sons shall sprinkle its blood against
the altar on all sides. 14 From what he offers he is to make this
offering to the LORD by fire: all the fat that covers the inner parts
or is connected to them, 15 both kidneys with the fat on them near
the loins, and the covering of the liver, which he will remove with
the kidneys. 16 The priest shall burn them on the altar as food, an
offering made by fire, a pleasing aroma. All the fat is the LORD's.

17 " 'This is a lasting ordinance for the generations to come,
wherever you live: You must not eat any fat or any blood.' "

*The Sin Offering*

**4** THE LORD said to Moses, 2 "Say to the Israelites: 'When
anyone sins unintentionally and does what is forbidden in
any of the LORD's commands—

3 " 'If the anointed priest sins, bringing guilt on the people, he
must bring to the LORD a young bull without defect as a sin offering
for the sin he has committed. 4 He is to present the bull at the
entrance to the Tent of Meeting before the LORD. He is to lay his
hand on its head and slaughter it before the LORD. 5 Then the
anointed priest shall take some of the bull's blood and carry it into
the Tent of Meeting. 6 He is to dip his finger into the blood and

NIV [b] *1* Traditionally *peace offering;* also in verses 3, 6 and 9

## King James

6And the priest shall dip his finger in the blood, and sprinkle
of the blood seven times before the LORD, before the veil of the
sanctuary.
7And the priest shall put *some* of the blood upon the horns of
the altar of sweet incense before the LORD, which *is* in the tabernacle of the congregation; and shall pour all the blood of the
bullock at the bottom of the altar of the burnt offering, which *is at*
the door of the tabernacle of the congregation.
8And he shall take off from it all the fat of the bullock for the
sin offering; the fat that covereth the inwards, and all the fat that
*is* upon the inwards,
9And the two kidneys, and the fat that *is* upon them, which *is*
by the flanks, and the caul above the liver, with the kidneys, it shall
he take away,
10As it was taken off from the bullock of the sacrifice of peace
offerings: and the priest shall burn them upon the altar of the burnt
offering.
11And the skin of the bullock, and all his flesh, with his head,
and with his legs, and his inwards, and his dung,
12Even the whole bullock shall he carry forth without the camp
unto a clean place, where the ashes are poured out, and burn him
on the wood with fire: where the ashes are poured out shall he be
burnt.
13¶ And if the whole congregation of Israel sin through ignorance, and the thing be hid from the eyes of the assembly, and they
have done *somewhat against* any of the commandments of the LORD
*concerning things* which should not be done, and are guilty;
14When the sin, which they have sinned against it, is known,
then the congregation shall offer a young bullock for the sin, and
bring him before the tabernacle of the congregation.
15And the elders of the congregation shall lay their hands upon
the head of the bullock before the LORD: and the bullock shall be
killed before the LORD.
16And the priest that is anointed shall bring of the bullock's
blood to the tabernacle of the congregation:
17And the priest shall dip his finger *in some* of the blood, and
sprinkle *it* seven times before the LORD, *even* before the veil.
18And he shall put *some* of the blood upon the horns of the altar
which *is* before the LORD, that *is* in the tabernacle of the congregation, and shall pour out all the blood at the bottom of the altar of
the burnt offering, which *is at* the door of the tabernacle of the
congregation.
19And he shall take all his fat from him, and burn *it* upon the
altar.
20And he shall do with the bullock as he did with the bullock
for a sin offering, so shall he do with this: and the priest shall make
an atonement for them, and it shall be forgiven them.
21And he shall carry forth the bullock without the camp, and
burn him as he burned the first bullock: it *is* a sin offering for the
congregation.
22¶ When a ruler hath sinned, and done *somewhat* through
ignorance *against* any of the commandments of the LORD his God
*concerning things* which should not be done, and is guilty;
23Or if his sin, wherein he hath sinned, come to his knowledge;
he shall bring his offering, a kid of the goats, a male without
blemish:
24And he shall lay his hand upon the head of the goat, and kill
it in the place where they kill the burnt offering before the LORD:
it *is* a sin offering.
25And the priest shall take of the blood of the sin offering with
his finger, and put *it* upon the horns of the altar of burnt offering,
and shall pour out his blood at the bottom of the altar of burnt
offering.
26And he shall burn all his fat upon the altar, as the fat of the
sacrifice of peace offerings: and the priest shall make an atonement
for him as concerning his sin, and it shall be forgiven him.
27¶ And if any one of the common people sin through ignorance, while he doeth *somewhat against* any of the commandments
of the LORD *concerning things* which ought not to be done, and be
guilty;

## Amplified

6And the priest shall dip his finger in the blood and sprinkle
some of *it* seven times before the Lord before the veil of the
sanctuary.
7And the priest shall put some of the blood on the horns of the
altar of sweet incense before the Lord, which is in the tent of
meeting; and all the rest of the blood of the bull shall he pour out
at the base of the altar of the burnt offering, at the door of the tent
of meeting.
8And all the fat of the bull for the sin offering he shall take off
of it, the fat that covers and is on the entrails,
9And the two kidneys and the fat that is on them at the loins,
and the appendage of the liver which he shall take away with the
kidneys,
10Just as these are taken off of the bull of the sacrifice of the
peace offerings; and the priest shall burn them on the altar of burnt
offering.
11But the hide of the bull and all its flesh, its head, its legs, its
entrails and its dung,
12Even the whole bull shall he carry forth without the camp to
a clean place, where the ashes are poured out, and burn it on a fire
of wood, there where the ashes are poured out. [Heb. 13:11-13.]
13If the whole congregation of Israel sins unintentionally, and
it be hidden from the eyes of the assembly, and they have done
what the Lord has commanded not to be done and are guilty;
14When the sin which they have committed becomes known,
then the congregation shall offer a young bull for a sin offering,
and bring it before the tent of meeting.
15The elders of the congregation shall lay their hands upon the
head of the bull before the Lord, and the bull shall be killed before
the Lord.
16The anointed priest shall bring some of the bull's blood to the
tent of meeting,
17And shall dip his finger in the blood, and sprinkle it seven
times before the Lord, before the veil [which screens the ark of the
covenant].
18He shall put some of the blood on the horns of the altar [of
incense] which is before the Lord, in the tent of meeting, and he
shall pour out all the blood at the base of the altar of burnt offering,
near the door of the tent of meeting.
19And he shall take all its fat from the bull and burn it on the
altar.
20Thus shall he do with the bull; as he did with the bull for a
sin offering, so shall he do with this; and the priest shall make
atonement for [the people], and they shall be forgiven.
21And he shall carry forth the bull outside the camp, and burn
it as he burned the first bull; it is the sin offering for the congregation.
22When a ruler *or* leader sins and unwittingly does any one of
the things the Lord his God has forbidden, and is guilty,
23If his sin which he has committed be known to him, he shall
bring as his offering a goat, a male without blemish;
24He shall lay his hand on the head of the goat, and kill it in the
place where they kill the burnt offering before the Lord; it is a sin
offering.
25The priest shall take some of the blood of the sin offering with
his finger and put it on the horns of the altar of burnt offering, and
pour the rest of its blood at the base of the altar of burnt offering.
26And he shall burn all its fat upon the altar, like the fat of the
sacrifice of peace offerings; so the priest shall make atonement for
him for his sin, and it shall be forgiven him.
27If any one of the common people sins unwittingly in doing
anything the Lord has commanded not to do, and is guilty,

## New American Standard

6 and the priest shall dip his finger in the blood, and sprinkle some of the blood seven times before the LORD, in front of the veil of the sanctuary.

7 'The priest shall also put some of the blood on the horns of the altar of fragrant incense which is before the LORD in the tent of meeting; and all the blood of the bull he shall pour out at the base of the altar of burnt offering which is at the doorway of the tent of meeting.

8 'And he shall remove from it all the fat of the bull of the sin offering: the fat that covers the entrails, and all the fat which is on the entrails,

9 and the two kidneys with the fat that is on them, which is on the loins, and the lobe of the liver, which he shall remove with the kidneys

10 (just as it is removed from the ox of the sacrifice of peace offerings), and the priest is to offer them up in smoke on the altar of burnt offering.

11 'But the hide of the bull and all its flesh with its head and its legs and its entrails and its refuse,

12 that is, all *the rest of* the bull, he is to bring out to a clean place outside the camp where the ashes are poured out, and burn it on wood with fire; where the ashes are poured out it shall be burned.

**13**¶ 'Now if the whole congregation of Israel commits error, and the matter escapes the notice of the assembly, and they commit any of the things which the LORD has commanded not to be done, and they become guilty;

14 when the sin which they have committed becomes known, then the assembly shall offer a bull of the herd for a sin offering, and bring it before the tent of meeting.

15 'Then the elders of the congregation shall lay their hands on the head of the bull before the LORD, and the bull shall be slain before the LORD.

16 'Then the anointed priest is to bring some of the blood of the bull to the tent of meeting;

17 and the priest shall dip his finger in the blood, and sprinkle *it* seven times before the LORD, in front of the veil.

18 'And he shall put some of the blood on the horns of the altar which is before the LORD in the tent of meeting; and all the blood he shall pour out at the base of the altar of burnt offering which is at the doorway of the tent of meeting.

19 'And he shall remove all its fat from it and offer it up in smoke on the altar.

20 'He shall also do with the bull just as he did with the bull of the sin offering; thus he shall do with it. So the priest shall make atonement for them, and they shall be forgiven.

21 'Then he is to bring out the bull to *a place* outside the camp, and burn it as he burned the first bull; it is the sin offering for the assembly.

**22**¶ 'When a leader sins and unintentionally does any one of all the things which the LORD God has commanded not to be done, and he becomes guilty,

23 if his sin which he has committed is made known to him, he shall bring for his offering a goat, a male without defect.

24 'And he shall lay his hand on the head of the male goat, and slay it in the place where they slay the burnt offering before the LORD; it is a sin offering.

25 'Then the priest is to take some of the blood of the sin offering with his finger, and put it on the horns of the altar of burnt offering; and *the rest of* its blood he shall pour out at the base of the altar of burnt offering.

26 'And all its fat he shall offer up in smoke on the altar as *in the case of* the fat of the sacrifice of peace offerings. Thus the priest shall make atonement for him in regard to his sin, and he shall be forgiven.

**27**¶ 'Now if anyone of the common people sins unintentionally in doing any of the things which the LORD has commanded not to be done, and becomes guilty,

## New International

sprinkle some of it seven times before the LORD, in front of the
curtain of the sanctuary. 7 The priest shall then put some of the
blood on the horns of the altar of fragrant incense that is before the
LORD in the Tent of Meeting. The rest of the bull's blood he shall
pour out at the base of the altar of burnt offering at the entrance
to the Tent of Meeting. 8 He shall remove all the fat from the bull
of the sin offering—the fat that covers the inner parts or is connected to them, 9 both kidneys with the fat on them near the loins, and
the covering of the liver, which he will remove with the kidneys—
10 just as the fat is removed from the ox[a] sacrificed as a fellowship
offering.[b] Then the priest shall burn them on the altar of burnt
offering. 11 But the hide of the bull and all its flesh, as well as the
head and legs, the inner parts and offal— 12 that is, all the rest of
the bull—he must take outside the camp to a place ceremonially
clean, where the ashes are thrown, and burn it in a wood fire on
the ash heap.

13 " 'If the whole Israelite community sins unintentionally and
does what is forbidden in any of the LORD's commands, even
though the community is unaware of the matter, they are guilty.
14 When they become aware of the sin they committed, the assembly must bring a young bull as a sin offering and present it before
the Tent of Meeting. 15 The elders of the community are to lay their
hands on the bull's head before the LORD, and the bull shall be
slaughtered before the LORD. 16 Then the anointed priest is to take
some of the bull's blood into the Tent of Meeting. 17 He shall dip
his finger into the blood and sprinkle it before the LORD seven
times in front of the curtain. 18 He is to put some of the blood on
the horns of the altar that is before the LORD in the Tent of Meeting.
The rest of the blood he shall pour out at the base of the altar of
burnt offering at the entrance to the Tent of Meeting. 19 He shall
remove all the fat from it and burn it on the altar, 20 and do with
this bull just as he did with the bull for the sin offering. In this way
the priest will make atonement for them, and they will be forgiven.
21 Then he shall take the bull outside the camp and burn it as he
burned the first bull. This is the sin offering for the community.

22 " 'When a leader sins unintentionally and does what is forbidden in any of the commands of the LORD his God, he is guilty.
23 When he is made aware of the sin he committed, he must bring
as his offering a male goat without defect. 24 He is to lay his hand
on the goat's head and slaughter it at the place where the burnt
offering is slaughtered before the LORD. It is a sin offering. 25 Then
the priest shall take some of the blood of the sin offering with his
finger and put it on the horns of the altar of burnt offering and pour
out the rest of the blood at the base of the altar. 26 He shall burn
all the fat on the altar as he burned the fat of the fellowship
offering. In this way the priest will make atonement for the man's
sin, and he will be forgiven.

27 " 'If a member of the community sins unintentionally and
does what is forbidden in any of the LORD's commands, he is
guilty. 28 When he is made aware of the sin he committed, he must

**NIV** [a] *10* The Hebrew word can include both male and female.
[b] *10* Traditionally *peace offering;* also in verses 26, 31 and 35

## King James

28Or if his sin, which he hath sinned, come to his knowledge: then he shall bring his offering, a kid of the goats, a female without blemish, for his sin which he hath sinned.

29And he shall lay his hand upon the head of the sin offering, and slay the sin offering in the place of the burnt offering.

30And the priest shall take of the blood thereof with his finger, and put *it* upon the horns of the altar of burnt offering, and shall pour out all the blood thereof at the bottom of the altar.

31And he shall take away all the fat thereof, as the fat is taken away from off the sacrifice of peace offerings; and the priest shall burn *it* upon the altar for a sweet savour unto the LORD; and the priest shall make an atonement for him, and it shall be forgiven him.

32And if he bring a lamb for a sin offering, he shall bring it a female without blemish.

33And he shall lay his hand upon the head of the sin offering, and slay it for a sin offering in the place where they kill the burnt offering.

34And the priest shall take of the blood of the sin offering with his finger, and put *it* upon the horns of the altar of burnt offering, and shall pour out all the blood thereof at the bottom of the altar:

35And he shall take away all the fat thereof, as the fat of the lamb is taken away from the sacrifice of the peace offerings; and the priest shall burn them upon the altar, according to the offerings made by fire unto the LORD: and the priest shall make an atonement for his sin that he hath committed, and it shall be forgiven him.

**5** AND IF a soul sin, and hear the voice of swearing, and *is* a witness, whether he hath seen or known *of it;* if he do not utter *it,* then he shall bear his iniquity.

2Or if a soul touch any unclean thing, whether *it be* a carcase of an unclean beast, or a carcase of unclean cattle, or the carcase of unclean creeping things, and *if* it be hidden from him; he also shall be unclean, and guilty.

3Or if he touch the uncleanness of man, whatsoever uncleanness *it be* that a man shall be defiled withal, and it be hid from him; when he knoweth *of it,* then he shall be guilty.

4Or if a soul swear, pronouncing with *his* lips to do evil, or to do good, whatsoever *it be* that a man shall pronounce with an oath, and it be hid from him; when he knoweth *of it,* then he shall be guilty in one of these.

5And it shall be, when he shall be guilty in one of these *things,* that he shall confess that he hath sinned in that *thing:*

6And he shall bring his trespass offering unto the LORD for his sin which he hath sinned, a female from the flock, a lamb or a kid of the goats, for a sin offering; and the priest shall make an atonement for him concerning his sin.

7And if he be not able to bring a lamb, then he shall bring for his trespass, which he hath committed, two turtledoves, or two young pigeons, unto the LORD; one for a sin offering, and the other for a burnt offering.

8And he shall bring them unto the priest, who shall offer *that* which *is* for the sin offering first, and wring off his head from his neck, but shall not divide *it* asunder:

9And he shall sprinkle of the blood of the sin offering upon the side of the altar; and the rest of the blood shall be wrung out at the bottom of the altar: it *is* a sin offering.

10And he shall offer the second *for* a burnt offering, according to the manner: and the priest shall make an atonement for him for his sin which he hath sinned, and it shall be forgiven him.

## Amplified

28When the sin which he has committed is made known to him, he shall bring for his offering a goat, a female without blemish, for his sin which he has committed.

29The offender shall lay his hand on the head of the sin offering, and kill *it* at the place of the burnt offering.

30And the priest shall take some of its blood with his finger, and put it on the horns of the altar of burnt offering, and shall pour out the rest of its blood at the base of the altar.

31And all the fat of it he shall take away, as the fat is taken away from off the sacrifice of peace offerings; and the priest shall burn it on the altar for a sweet *and* satisfying fragrance to the Lord; and the priest shall make atonement for *the man,* and he shall be forgiven.

32If he brings a lamb as his sin offering, he shall bring a female without blemish.

33He shall lay his hand upon the head of the sin offering, and kill it in the place where they kill the burnt offering.

34And the priest shall take some of the blood of the sin offering with his finger, and put it on the horns of the altar of burnt offering, and all the rest of the blood of the lamb he shall pour out at the base of the altar.

35And he shall take away all the fat of it, just as the fat of the lamb is removed from the sacrifice of the peace offerings; and the priest shall burn it on the altar upon the offerings by fire to the Lord; and the priest shall make atonement for the sin which the man has committed, and he shall be forgiven. [Heb. 9:13, 14.]

**5** IF ANY one sins in that he is sworn to testify and has knowledge of the matter, either by seeing or hearing of it, but fails to report it, then he shall bear his iniquity *and* willfulness.

2Or if any one touches an unclean thing, whether the carcass of an unclean wild beast or of an unclean domestic animal or of unclean creeping things that multiply prolifically, even if he is unaware of it, and he has become unclean, he is guilty.

3Or if he touches human uncleanness, of whatever kind the uncleanness may be with which he becomes defiled, and he is unaware of it, when he does know it, then he shall be guilty.

4Or if any one unthinkingly swears he will do something, whether to do evil or good, whatever it may be that a man shall pronounce rashly taking an oath, then, when he becomes aware of it, he shall be guilty in either of these. [Cp. Mark 6:23.]

5When a man is guilty in one of these, he shall confess the sin he has committed.

6He shall bring his guilt *or* trespass offering to the Lord for the sin which he has committed, a female from the flock, a lamb or a goat, for a sin offering; and the priest shall make atonement for his sin.

7But if he cannot afford a lamb, then he shall bring for his guilt offering to the Lord, two turtledoves or two young pigeons, one for a sin offering and the other for a burnt offering.

8He shall bring them to the priest, who shall offer the one for the sin offering first, and wring its head from its neck, but shall not sever it;

9And he shall sprinkle some of the blood of the sin offering on the side of the altar, and the rest of the blood shall be drained out at the base of the altar; it is a sin offering.

10And he shall prepare the second bird for a burnt offering, according to the ordinance; and the priest shall make atonement for him for his sin which he has committed, and he shall be forgiven.

## New American Standard

28 if his sin, which he has committed is made known to him, then he shall bring for his offering a goat, a female without defect, for his sin which he has committed.

29 'And he shall lay his hand on the head of the sin offering, and slay the sin offering at the place of the burnt offering.

30 'And the priest shall take some of its blood with his finger and put it on the horns of the altar of burnt offering; and all *the rest of* its blood he shall pour out at the base of the altar.

31 'Then he shall remove all its fat, just as the fat was removed from the sacrifice of peace offerings; and the priest shall offer it up in smoke on the altar for a soothing aroma to the LORD. Thus the priest shall make atonement for him, and he shall be forgiven.

32¶ 'But if he brings a lamb as his offering for a sin offering, he shall bring it, a female without defect.

33 'And he shall lay his hand on the head of the sin offering, and slay it for a sin offering in the place where they slay the burnt offering.

34 'And the priest is to take some of the blood of the sin offering with his finger and put it on the horns of the altar of burnt offering; and all *the rest of* its blood he shall pour out at the base of the altar.

35 'Then he shall remove all its fat, just as the fat of the lamb is removed from the sacrifice of the peace offerings, and the priest shall offer them up in smoke on the altar, on the offerings by fire to the LORD. Thus the priest shall make atonement for him in regard to his sin which he has committed, and he shall be forgiven.

### *The Law of Guilt Offerings*

**5** 'NOW IF a person sins, after he hears a public adjuration *to testify*, when he is a witness, whether he has seen or *otherwise* known, if he does not tell *it*, then he will bear his guilt.

2 'Or if a person touches any unclean thing, whether a carcass of an unclean beast, or the carcass of unclean cattle, or a carcass of unclean swarming things, though it is hidden from him, and he is unclean, then he will be guilty.

3 'Or if he touches human uncleanness, of whatever *sort* his uncleanness *may* be with which he becomes unclean, and it is hidden from him, and then he comes to know *it*, he will be guilty.

4 'Or if a person swears thoughtlessly with his lips to do evil or to do good, in whatever matter a man may speak thoughtlessly with an oath, and it is hidden from him, and then he comes to know *it*, he will be guilty in one of these.

5 'So it shall be when he becomes guilty in one of these, that he shall confess that in which he has sinned.

6 'He shall also bring his guilt offering to the LORD for his sin which he has committed, a female from the flock, a lamb or a goat as a sin offering. So the priest shall make atonement on his behalf for his sin.

7¶ 'But if he cannot afford a lamb, then he shall bring to the LORD his guilt offering for that in which he has sinned, two turtledoves or two young pigeons, one for a sin offering and the other for a burnt offering.

8 'And he shall bring them to the priest, who shall offer first that which is for the sin offering and shall nip its head at the front of its neck, but he shall not sever *it*.

9 'He shall also sprinkle some of the blood of the sin offering on the side of the altar, while the rest of the blood shall be drained out at the base of the altar: it is a sin offering.

10 'The second he shall then prepare as a burnt offering according to the ordinance. So the priest shall make atonement on his behalf for his sin which he has committed, and it shall be forgiven him.

## New International

bring as his offering for the sin he committed a female goat without
defect. 29 He is to lay his hand on the head of the sin offering and
slaughter it at the place of the burnt offering. 30 Then the priest is
to take some of the blood with his finger and put it on the horns
of the altar of burnt offering and pour out the rest of the blood at
the base of the altar. 31 He shall remove all the fat, just as the fat
is removed from the fellowship offering, and the priest shall burn
it on the altar as an aroma pleasing to the LORD. In this way the
priest will make atonement for him, and he will be forgiven.

32 " 'If he brings a lamb as his sin offering, he is to bring a female
without defect. 33 He is to lay his hand on its head and slaughter
it for a sin offering at the place where the burnt offering is slaughtered.
34 Then the priest shall take some of the blood of the sin
offering with his finger and put it on the horns of the altar of burnt
offering and pour out the rest of the blood at the base of the altar.
35 He shall remove all the fat, just as the fat is removed from the
lamb of the fellowship offering, and the priest shall burn it on the
altar on top of the offerings made to the LORD by fire. In this way
the priest will make atonement for him for the sin he has committed, and he will be forgiven.

**5** " 'IF A person sins because he does not speak up when he hears a public charge to testify regarding something he has seen or learned about, he will be held responsible.

2 " 'Or if a person touches anything ceremonially unclean—whether the carcasses of unclean wild animals or of unclean livestock or of unclean creatures that move along the ground—even though he is unaware of it, he has become unclean and is guilty.

3 " 'Or if he touches human uncleanness—anything that would make him unclean—even though he is unaware of it, when he learns of it he will be guilty.

4 " 'Or if a person thoughtlessly takes an oath to do anything, whether good or evil—in any matter one might carelessly swear about—even though he is unaware of it, in any case when he learns of it he will be guilty.

5 " 'When anyone is guilty in any of these ways, he must confess
in what way he has sinned 6 and, as a penalty for the sin he has
committed, he must bring to the LORD a female lamb or goat from
the flock as a sin offering; and the priest shall make atonement for
him for his sin.

7 " 'If he cannot afford a lamb, he is to bring two doves or two
young pigeons to the LORD as a penalty for his sin—one for a sin
offering and the other for a burnt offering. 8 He is to bring them to
the priest, who shall first offer the one for the sin offering. He is
to wring its head from its neck, not severing it completely, 9 and
is to sprinkle some of the blood of the sin offering against the side
of the altar; the rest of the blood must be drained out at the base
of the altar. It is a sin offering. 10 The priest shall then offer the other
as a burnt offering in the prescribed way and make atonement for
him for the sin he has committed, and he will be forgiven.

## King James

11¶ But if he be not able to bring two turtledoves, or two young
pigeons, then he that sinned shall bring for his offering the tenth
part of an ephah of fine flour for a sin offering; he shall put no oil
upon it, neither shall he put *any* frankincense thereon: for it *is* a
sin offering.
12Then shall he bring it to the priest, and the priest shall take
his handful of it, *even* a memorial thereof, and burn *it* on the altar,
according to the offerings made by fire unto the LORD: it *is* a sin
offering.
13And the priest shall make an atonement for him as touching
his sin that he hath sinned in one of these, and it shall be forgiven
him: and *the remnant* shall be the priest's, as a meat offering.
14¶ And the LORD spake unto Moses, saying,
15If a soul commit a trespass, and sin through ignorance, in the
holy things of the LORD; then he shall bring for his trespass unto
the LORD a ram without blemish out of the flocks, with thy estimation by shekels of silver, after the shekel of the sanctuary, for a
trespass offering:
16And he shall make amends for the harm that he hath done in
the holy thing, and shall add the fifth part thereto, and give it unto
the priest: and the priest shall make an atonement for him with the
ram of the trespass offering, and it shall be forgiven him.
17¶ And if a soul sin, and commit any of these things which are
forbidden to be done by the commandments of the LORD; though
he wist *it* not, yet is he guilty, and shall bear his iniquity.
18And he shall bring a ram without blemish out of the flock,
with thy estimation, for a trespass offering, unto the priest: and the
priest shall make an atonement for him concerning his ignorance
wherein he erred and wist *it* not, and it shall be forgiven him.
19It *is* a trespass offering: he hath certainly trespassed against
the LORD.

6 AND THE LORD spake unto Moses, saying,
2If a soul sin, and commit a trespass against the LORD, and
lie unto his neighbour in that which was delivered him to keep,
or in fellowship, or in a thing taken away by violence, or hath
deceived his neighbour;
3Or have found that which was lost, and lieth concerning it, and
sweareth falsely; in any of all these that a man doeth, sinning
therein:
4Then it shall be, because he hath sinned, and is guilty, that he
shall restore that which he took violently away, or the thing which
he hath deceitfully gotten, or that which was delivered him to
keep, or the lost thing which he found,
5Or all that about which he hath sworn falsely; he shall even
restore it in the principal, and shall add the fifth part more thereto,
*and* give it unto him to whom it appertaineth, in the day of his
trespass offering.
6And he shall bring his trespass offering unto the LORD, a ram
without blemish out of the flock, with thy estimation, for a trespass
offering, unto the priest:
7And the priest shall make an atonement for him before the
LORD: and it shall be forgiven him for any thing of all that he hath
done in trespassing therein.
8¶ And the LORD spake unto Moses, saying,
9Command Aaron and his sons, saying, This *is* the law of the
burnt offering: It *is* the burnt offering, because of the burning upon
the altar all night unto the morning, and the fire of the altar shall
be burning in it.
10And the priest shall put on his linen garment, and his linen
breeches shall he put upon his flesh, and take up the ashes which
the fire hath consumed with the burnt offering on the altar, and
he shall put them beside the altar.

## Amplified

11But if the offender cannot afford to bring two turtledoves or
two young pigeons, then he shall bring for his offering the tenth
part of an ephah of fine flour for a sin offering; he shall put no oil
or frankincense on it, for it is a sin offering.
12He shall bring it to the priest, who shall take a handful of it
as a memorial portion, and burn it on the altar, on the offerings
made by fire to the Lord; it is a sin offering.
13Thus the priest shall make atonement for him for the sin that
he has committed in any of these things, and he shall be forgiven;
and the remainder shall be for the priest, as in the cereal offering.
14And the Lord said to Moses,
15If any one commits a breach of faith and sins unwittingly in
the holy things of the Lord, he shall bring his trespass *or* guilt
offering to the Lord, a ram without blemish out of the flock, valued
by you in shekels of silver, that is, the shekel of the sanctuary, for
a trespass *or* guilt offering.
16And he shall make restitution for what he has done amiss in
the holy thing, and shall add a fifth to it and give it to the priest;
and the priest shall make atonement for him with the ram of the
trespass *or* guilt offering, and he shall be forgiven.
17If any one sins and does any of the things the Lord has
forbidden, though he was not aware of it, yet he is guilty, and shall
bear his iniquity. [Cp. Luke 12:48.]
18He shall bring [to the priest] a ram without blemish out of the
flock, estimated by you to the amount [of the trespass], for a guilt
*or* trespass offering; and the priest shall make atonement for him
for the error which he committed unknowingly, and he shall be
forgiven.
19It is a trespass *or* guilt offering; he is certainly guilty before the
Lord.

6 AND THE Lord said to Moses,
2If any one sins and commits a trespass against the Lord, and
deals falsely with his neighbor in a matter of deposit given him to
keep, or of bargain *or* pledge, or of robbery, or has oppressed his
neighbor,
3Or has found what was lost and lied about it, and swears
falsely, in any of all the things which men do and sin in so doing,
4Then if he has sinned and is guilty, he shall restore what he
took by robbery, or what he secured by oppression *or* extortion,
or what was delivered him to keep in trust, or the lost thing which
he found,
5Or anything about which he has sworn falsely; he shall not
only restore it in full, but shall add to it one fifth more, and give
it to him to whom it belongs, on the day of his trespass *or* guilt
offering.
6And he shall bring to the priest his trespass *or* guilt offering to
the Lord, a ram without blemish out of the flock, valued by you
to the amount of his trespass;
7And the priest shall make atonement for him before the Lord,
and he shall be forgiven for anything of all that he may have done
by which he has become guilty.
8And the Lord said to Moses,
9Command Aaron and his sons, saying, This is the law of the
burnt offering: The burnt offering shall remain on the altar all night
until morning; the fire shall be kept burning on the altar.
10And the priest shall put on his linen garment, and put his
linen breeches on his body, and take up the ashes of what the fire
has consumed with the burnt offering on the altar, and put them
beside the altar.

## New American Standard

11¶ 'But if his means are insufficient for two turtledoves or two young pigeons, then for his offering for that which he has sinned, he shall bring the tenth of an [a]ephah of fine flour for a sin offering; he shall not put oil on it or place incense on it, for it is a sin offering.

12'And he shall bring it to the priest, and the priest shall take his handful of it as its memorial portion and offer *it* up in smoke on the altar, with the offerings of the LORD by fire: it is a sin offering.

13'So the priest shall make atonement for him concerning his sin which he has committed from one of these, and it shall be forgiven him; then *the rest* shall become the priest's, like the grain offering.' "

14¶ Then the LORD spoke to Moses, saying,

15"If a person acts unfaithfully and sins unintentionally against the LORD's holy things, then he shall bring his guilt offering to the LORD: a ram without defect from the flock, according to your valuation in silver by shekels, in *terms of* the shekel of the sanctuary, for a guilt offering.

16"And he shall make restitution for that which he has sinned against the holy thing, and shall add to it a fifth part of it, and give it to the priest. The priest shall then make atonement for him with the ram of the guilt offering, and it shall be forgiven him.

17¶ "Now if a person sins and does any of the things which the LORD has commanded not to be done, though he was unaware, still he is guilty, and shall bear his punishment.

18"He is then to bring to the priest a ram without defect from the flock, according to your valuation, for a guilt offering. So the priest shall make atonement for him concerning his error in which he sinned unintentionally and did not know *it*, and it shall be forgiven him.

19"It is a guilt offering; he was certainly guilty before the LORD."

*Guilt Offering*

6 THEN THE LORD spoke to Moses, saying,

2"When a person sins and acts unfaithfully against the LORD, and deceives his companion in regard to a deposit or a security entrusted *to him*, or through robbery, or *if* he has extorted from his companion,

3or has found what was lost and lied about it and sworn falsely, so that he sins in regard to any one of the things a man may do;

4then it shall be, when he sins and becomes guilty, that he shall restore what he took by robbery, or what he got by extortion, or the deposit which was entrusted to him, or the lost thing which he found,

5or anything about which he swore falsely; he shall make restitution for it in full, and add to it one-fifth more. He shall give it to the one to whom it belongs on the day *he presents* his guilt offering.

6"Then he shall bring to the priest his guilt offering to the LORD, a ram without defect from the flock, according to your valuation, for a guilt offering,

7and the priest shall make atonement for him before the LORD; and he shall be forgiven for any one of the things which he may have done to incur guilt."

*The Priest's Part in the Offerings*

8¶ Then the LORD spoke to Moses, saying,

9"Command Aaron and his sons, saying, 'This is the law for the burnt offering: the burnt offering itself *shall remain* on the hearth on the altar all night until the morning, and the fire on the altar is to be kept burning on it.

10'And the priest is to put on his linen robe, and he shall put on undergarments next to his flesh; and he shall take up the ashes *to* which the fire reduces the burnt offering on the altar, and place them beside the altar.

NAS [a] I.e., Approx. one bushel

## New International

11" 'If, however, he cannot afford two doves or two young
pigeons, he is to bring as an offering for his sin a tenth of an
ephah[b] of fine flour for a sin offering. He must not put oil or
incense on it, because it is a sin offering. 12He is to bring it to the
priest, who shall take a handful of it as a memorial portion and
burn it on the altar on top of the offerings made to the LORD by
fire. It is a sin offering. 13In this way the priest will make atonement
for him for any of these sins he has committed, and he will be
forgiven. The rest of the offering will belong to the priest, as in the
case of the grain offering.' "

*The Guilt Offering*

14The LORD said to Moses: 15"When a person commits a violation and sins unintentionally in regard to any of the LORD's holy
things, he is to bring to the LORD as a penalty a ram from the flock,
one without defect and of the proper value in silver, according to
the sanctuary shekel.[c] It is a guilt offering. 16He must make restitution for what he has failed to do in regard to the holy things, add
a fifth of the value to that and give it all to the priest, who will make
atonement for him with the ram as a guilt offering, and he will be
forgiven.

17"If a person sins and does what is forbidden in any of the
LORD's commands, even though he does not know it, he is guilty
and will be held responsible. 18He is to bring to the priest as a guilt
offering a ram from the flock, one without defect and of the proper
value. In this way the priest will make atonement for him for the
wrong he has committed unintentionally, and he will be forgiven.
19It is a guilt offering; he has been guilty of[d] wrongdoing against
the LORD."

6 THE LORD said to Moses: 2"If anyone sins and is unfaithful
to the LORD by deceiving his neighbor about something entrusted to him or left in his care or stolen, or if he cheats him, 3or
if he finds lost property and lies about it, or if he swears falsely,
or if he commits any such sin that people may do— 4when he thus
sins and becomes guilty, he must return what he has stolen or
taken by extortion, or what was entrusted to him, or the lost
property he found, 5or whatever it was he swore falsely about. He
must make restitution in full, add a fifth of the value to it and give
it all to the owner on the day he presents his guilt offering. 6And
as a penalty he must bring to the priest, that is, to the LORD, his
guilt offering, a ram from the flock, one without defect and of the
proper value. 7In this way the priest will make atonement for him
before the LORD, and he will be forgiven for any of these things
he did that made him guilty."

*The Burnt Offering*

8The LORD said to Moses: 9"Give Aaron and his sons this command: 'These are the regulations for the burnt offering: The burnt
offering is to remain on the altar hearth throughout the night, till
morning, and the fire must be kept burning on the altar. 10The
priest shall then put on his linen clothes, with linen undergarments next to his body, and shall remove the ashes of the burnt
offering that the fire has consumed on the altar and place them
beside the altar. 11Then he is to take off these clothes and put on

NIV [b] *11* That is, probably about 2 quarts (about 2 liters) [c] *15* That is, about 2/5 ounce (about 11.5 grams) [d] *19* Or *has made full expiation for his*

## King James

11And he shall put off his garments, and put on other garments, and carry forth the ashes without the camp unto a clean place.

12And the fire upon the altar shall be burning in it; it shall not be put out: and the priest shall burn wood on it every morning, and lay the burnt offering in order upon it; and he shall burn thereon the fat of the peace offerings.

13The fire shall ever be burning upon the altar; it shall never go out.

14¶ And this *is* the law of the meat offering: the sons of Aaron shall offer it before the LORD, before the altar.

15And he shall take of it his handful, of the flour of the meat offering, and of the oil thereof, and all the frankincense which *is* upon the meat offering, and shall burn *it* upon the altar *for* a sweet savour, *even* the memorial of it, unto the LORD.

16And the remainder thereof shall Aaron and his sons eat: with unleavened bread shall it be eaten in the holy place; in the court of the tabernacle of the congregation they shall eat it.

17It shall not be baked with leaven. I have given it *unto them for* their portion of my offerings made by fire; it *is* most holy, as *is* the sin offering, and as the trespass offering.

18All the males among the children of Aaron shall eat of it. *It shall be* a statute for ever in your generations concerning the offerings of the LORD made by fire: every one that toucheth them shall be holy.

19¶ And the LORD spake unto Moses, saying,

20This *is* the offering of Aaron and of his sons, which they shall offer unto the LORD in the day when he is anointed; the tenth part of an ephah of fine flour for a meat offering perpetual, half of it in the morning, and half thereof at night.

21In a pan it shall be made with oil; *and when it is* baked, thou shalt bring it in: *and* the baked pieces of the meat offering shalt thou offer *for* a sweet savour unto the LORD.

22And the priest of his sons that is anointed in his stead shall offer it: *it is* a statute for ever unto the LORD; it shall be wholly burnt.

23For every meat offering for the priest shall be wholly burnt: it shall not be eaten.

24¶ And the LORD spake unto Moses, saying,

25Speak unto Aaron and to his sons, saying, This *is* the law of the sin offering: In the place where the burnt offering is killed shall the sin offering be killed before the LORD: it *is* most holy.

26The priest that offereth it for sin shall eat it: in the holy place shall it be eaten, in the court of the tabernacle of the congregation.

27Whatsoever shall touch the flesh thereof shall be holy: and when there is sprinkled of the blood thereof upon any garment, thou shalt wash that whereon it was sprinkled in the holy place.

28But the earthen vessel wherein it is sodden shall be broken: and if it be sodden in a brasen pot, it shall be both scoured, and rinsed in water.

29All the males among the priests shall eat thereof: it *is* most holy.

30And no sin offering, whereof *any* of the blood is brought into the tabernacle of the congregation to reconcile *withal* in the holy *place*, shall be eaten: it shall be burnt in the fire.

**7** LIKEWISE THIS *is* the law of the trespass offering: it *is* most holy.

2In the place where they kill the burnt offering shall they kill the trespass offering: and the blood thereof shall he sprinkle round about upon the altar.

3And he shall offer of it all the fat thereof; the rump, and the fat that covereth the inwards.

4And the two kidneys, and the fat that *is* on them, which *is* by the flanks, and the caul *that is* above the liver, with the kidneys, it shall he take away:

## Amplified

11And he shall put off his garments, and put on other garments, and carry the ashes outside the camp to a clean place.

12And the fire upon the altar shall be kept burning on it; it shall not be allowed to go out; the priest shall burn wood on it every morning, and lay the burnt offering in order upon it, and he shall burn on it the fat of the peace offerings.

13The fire shall be burning continually upon the altar; it shall not go out.

14And this is the law of the cereal offering. The sons of Aaron shall offer it before the Lord, in front of the altar.

15One of them shall take his handful of the fine flour of the cereal offering, the oil of it, and all the frankincense which is upon the cereal offering, and burn it on the altar as the memorial of it, a sweet *and* satisfying fragrance to the Lord.

16And the remainder of it shall Aaron and his sons eat, without leaven in a holy place; in the court of the tent of meeting shall they eat it. [Cp. I Cor. 9:13, 14.]

17It shall not be baked with leaven. I have given it as their portion of My offerings made by fire; it is most holy, like the sin offering and the guilt offering.

18Every male among the children of Aaron may eat of it, as his portion for ever throughout your generations, from the Lord's offerings made by fire; whoever touches them shall [first] be holy—consecrated and ceremonially clean.

19And the Lord said to Moses,

20This is the offering which Aaron and his sons shall offer to the Lord on the day when one is anointed (and consecrated): the tenth of an ephah of fine flour for a regular cereal offering, half of it in the morning and half of it at night.

21On a griddle *or* baking pan it shall be made with oil; and when it is fried you shall bring it in; in broken *and* fried pieces shall you offer the cereal offering as a sweet *and* satisfying odor to the Lord.

22And the priest among Aaron's sons who is consecrated *and* anointed in his stead shall offer it; by a statute forever it shall be entirely burned to the Lord.

23For every cereal offering of the priest shall be wholly burned, and not be eaten.

24And the Lord said to Moses,

25Say to Aaron and his sons, This is the law of the sin offering. In the place where the burnt offering is killed shall the sin offering be killed before the Lord; it is most holy.

26The priest who offers it for sin shall eat it; in a sacred place shall it be eaten, in the court of the tent of meeting.

27Whoever *or* whatever touches its flesh shall [first] be dedicated and made clean; and when any of its blood is sprinkled on a garment, you shall wash that garment in a place set apart to God's worship.

28But the earthen vessel in which it is boiled shall be broken, and if it is boiled in a bronze vessel, that shall be scoured and rinsed in water.

29Every male among the priests may eat of this offering; it is most holy.

30But no sin offering shall be eaten of which any of the blood is brought into the tent of meeting to make atonement in the holy place; it shall be [wholly] burned with fire. [Heb. 13:11-13.]

**7** THIS IS the law of the guilt *or* trespass offering; it is most holy *or* sacred.

2In the place where they kill the burnt offering shall they kill the guilt *or* trespass offering; the blood of it shall the priest dash against the altar round about.

3And he shall offer all its fat, the fat tail and the fat that covers the entrails,

4And the two kidneys and the fat that is on them at the loins, and the lobe *or* appendage of the liver, which he shall take away with the kidneys.

## New American Standard

11'Then he shall take off his garments and put on other garments, and carry the ashes outside the camp to a clean place.

12'And the fire on the altar shall be kept burning on it. It shall not go out, but the priest shall burn wood on it every morning; and he shall lay out the burnt offering on it, and offer up in smoke the fat portions of the peace offerings on it.

13'Fire shall be kept burning continually on the altar; it is not to go out.

14¶ 'Now this is the law of the grain offering: the sons of Aaron shall present it before the LORD in front of the altar.

15'Then one *of them* shall lift up from it a handful of the fine flour of the grain offering, with its oil and all the incense that is on the grain offering, and he shall offer *it* up in smoke on the altar, a soothing aroma, as its memorial offering to the LORD.

16'And what is left of it Aaron and his sons are to eat. It shall be eaten as unleavened cakes in a holy place; they are to eat it in the court of the tent of meeting.

17'It shall not be baked with leaven. I have given it as their share from My offerings by fire; it is most holy, like the sin offering and the guilt offering.

18'Every male among the sons of Aaron may eat it; it is a permanent ordinance throughout your generations, from the offerings by fire to the LORD. Whoever touches them shall become consecrated.' "

19¶ Then the LORD spoke to Moses, saying,

20"This is the offering which Aaron and his sons are to present to the LORD on the day when he is anointed; the tenth of an ephah of fine flour as a regular grain offering, half of it in the morning and half of it in the evening.

21"It shall be prepared with oil on a griddle. When it is *well* stirred, you shall bring it. You shall present the grain offering in baked pieces as a soothing aroma to the LORD.

22"And the anointed priest who will be in his place among his sons shall offer it. By a permanent ordinance it shall be entirely offered up in smoke to the LORD.

23"So every grain offering of the priest shall be burned entirely. It shall not be eaten."

24¶ Then the LORD spoke to Moses, saying,

25"Speak to Aaron and to his sons, saying, 'This is the law of the sin offering: in the place where the burnt offering is slain the sin offering shall be slain before the LORD; it is most holy.

26'The priest who offers it for sin shall eat it. It shall be eaten in a holy place, in the court of the tent of meeting.

27'Anyone who touches its flesh shall become consecrated; and when any of its blood splashes on a garment, in a holy place you shall wash what was splashed on.

28'Also the earthenware vessel in which it was boiled shall be broken; and if it was boiled in a bronze vessel, then it shall be scoured and rinsed in water.

29'Every male among the priests may eat of it; it is most holy.

30'But no sin offering of which any of the blood is brought into the tent of meeting to make atonement in the holy place shall be eaten; it shall be burned with fire.

*The Priest's Part in the Offerings*

**7** 'NOW THIS is the law of the guilt offering; it is most holy.
2In the place where they slay the burnt offering they are to slay the guilt offering, and he shall sprinkle its blood around on the altar.

3'Then he shall offer from it all its fat: the fat tail and the fat that covers the entrails,

4and the two kidneys with the fat that is on them, which is on the loins, and the lobe on the liver he shall remove with the kidneys.

## New International

others, and carry the ashes outside the camp to a place that is ceremonially clean.
12The fire on the altar must be kept burning; it must not go out. Every morning the priest is to add firewood and arrange the burnt offering on the fire and burn the fat of the fellowship offerings[a] on it.
13The fire must be kept burning on the altar continuously; it must not go out.

*The Grain Offering*

14" 'These are the regulations for the grain offering: Aaron's sons are to bring it before the LORD, in front of the altar.
15The priest is to take a handful of fine flour and oil, together with all the incense on the grain offering, and burn the memorial portion on the altar as an aroma pleasing to the LORD.
16Aaron and his sons shall eat the rest of it, but it is to be eaten without yeast in a holy place; they are to eat it in the courtyard of the Tent of Meeting.
17It must not be baked with yeast; I have given it as their share of the offerings made to me by fire. Like the sin offering and the guilt offering, it is most holy.
18Any male descendant of Aaron may eat it. It is his regular share of the offerings made to the LORD by fire for the generations to come. Whatever touches them will become holy.[b] ' "

19The LORD also said to Moses,
20"This is the offering Aaron and his sons are to bring to the LORD on the day he[c] is anointed: a tenth of an ephah[d] of fine flour as a regular grain offering, half of it in the morning and half in the evening.
21Prepare it with oil on a griddle; bring it well-mixed and present the grain offering broken[e] in pieces as an aroma pleasing to the LORD.
22The son who is to succeed him as anointed priest shall prepare it. It is the LORD's regular share and is to be burned completely.
23Every grain offering of a priest shall be burned completely; it must not be eaten."

*The Sin Offering*

24The LORD said to Moses,
25"Say to Aaron and his sons: 'These are the regulations for the sin offering: The sin offering is to be slaughtered before the LORD in the place the burnt offering is slaughtered; it is most holy.
26The priest who offers it shall eat it; it is to be eaten in a holy place, in the courtyard of the Tent of Meeting.
27Whatever touches any of the flesh will become holy, and if any of the blood is spattered on a garment, you must wash it in a holy place.
28The clay pot the meat is cooked in must be broken; but if it is cooked in a bronze pot, the pot is to be scoured and rinsed with water.
29Any male in a priest's family may eat it; it is most holy.
30But any sin offering whose blood is brought into the Tent of Meeting to make atonement in the Holy Place must not be eaten; it must be burned.

*The Guilt Offering*

**7** " 'THESE ARE the regulations for the guilt offering, which is most holy:
2The guilt offering is to be slaughtered in the place where the burnt offering is slaughtered, and its blood is to be sprinkled against the altar on all sides.
3All its fat shall be offered: the fat tail and the fat that covers the inner parts,
4both kidneys with the fat on them near the loins, and the covering of the liver, which is to be removed with the kidneys.
5The priest shall burn

NIV [a] *12* Traditionally *peace offerings* [b] *18* Or *Whoever touches them must be holy;* similarly in verse 27 [c] *20* Or *each* [d] *20* That is, probably about 2 quarts (about 2 liters) [e] *21* The meaning of the Hebrew for this word is uncertain.

## King James

5 And the priest shall burn them upon the altar *for* an offering made by fire unto the LORD: it *is* a trespass offering.

6 Every male among the priests shall eat thereof: it shall be eaten in the holy place: it *is* most holy.

7 As the sin offering *is,* so *is* the trespass offering: *there is* one law for them: the priest that maketh atonement therewith shall have *it.*

8 And the priest that offereth any man's burnt offering, *even* the priest shall have to himself the skin of the burnt offering which he hath offered.

9 And all the meat offering that is baked in the oven, and all that is dressed in the fryingpan, and in the pan, shall be the priest's that offereth it.

10 And every meat offering, mingled with oil, and dry, shall all the sons of Aaron have, one *as much* as another.

11 And this *is* the law of the sacrifice of peace offerings, which he shall offer unto the LORD.

12 If he offer it for a thanksgiving, then he shall offer with the sacrifice of thanksgiving unleavened cakes mingled with oil, and unleavened wafers anointed with oil, and cakes mingled with oil, of fine flour, fried.

13 Besides the cakes, he shall offer *for* his offering leavened bread with the sacrifice of thanksgiving of his peace offerings.

14 And of it he shall offer one out of the whole oblation *for* an heave offering unto the LORD, *and* it shall be the priest's that sprinkleth the blood of the peace offerings.

15 And the flesh of the sacrifice of his peace offerings for thanksgiving shall be eaten the same day that it is offered; he shall not leave any of it until the morning.

16 But if the sacrifice of his offering *be* a vow, or a voluntary offering, it shall be eaten the same day that he offereth his sacrifice: and on the morrow also the remainder of it shall be eaten:

17 But the remainder of the flesh of the sacrifice on the third day shall be burnt with fire.

18 And if *any* of the flesh of the sacrifice of his peace offerings be eaten at all on the third day, it shall not be accepted, neither shall it be imputed unto him that offereth it: it shall be an abomination, and the soul that eateth of it shall bear his iniquity.

19 And the flesh that toucheth any unclean *thing* shall not be eaten; it shall be burnt with fire: and as for the flesh, all that be clean shall eat thereof.

20 But the soul that eateth *of* the flesh of the sacrifice of peace offerings, that *pertain* unto the LORD, having his uncleanness upon him, even that soul shall be cut off from his people.

21 Moreover the soul that shall touch any unclean *thing, as* the uncleanness of man, or *any* unclean beast, or any abominable unclean *thing,* and eat of the flesh of the sacrifice of peace offerings, which *pertain* unto the LORD, even that soul shall be cut off from his people.

22 ¶ And the LORD spake unto Moses, saying,

23 Speak unto the children of Israel, saying, Ye shall eat no manner of fat, of ox, or of sheep, or of goat.

24 And the fat of the beast that dieth of itself, and the fat of that which is torn with beasts, may be used in any other use: but ye shall in no wise eat of it.

25 For whosoever eateth the fat of the beast, of which men offer an offering made by fire unto the LORD, even the soul that eateth *it* shall be cut off from his people.

26 Moreover ye shall eat no manner of blood, *whether it be* of fowl or of beast, in any of your dwellings.

27 Whatsoever soul *it be* that eateth any manner of blood, even that soul shall be cut off from his people.

28 ¶ And the LORD spake unto Moses, saying,

29 Speak unto the children of Israel, saying, He that offereth the sacrifice of his peace offerings unto the LORD shall bring his oblation unto the LORD of the sacrifice of his peace offerings.

## Amplified

5 And the priest shall burn them on the altar for an offering made by fire to the Lord; it is a guilt *or* trespass offering.

6 Every male among the priests may eat of it; it shall be eaten in a sacred place; it is most holy.

7 As is the sin offering, so is the guilt *or* trespass offering; there is one law for them: the priest who makes atonement with it shall have it.

8 And the priest who offers any man's burnt offering, that priest shall have for himself the hide of the burnt offering which he has offered.

9 And every cereal offering that is baked in the oven and all that is prepared in a pan or on a griddle shall belong to the priest who offered it.

10 And every cereal offering, mixed with oil or dry, all the sons of Aaron may have, one as well as another.

11 And this is the law of the sacrifice of peace offerings, which shall be offered to the Lord.

12 If one offers it for a thanksgiving, then he shall offer with the thank offering unleavened cakes mixed with oil, and unleavened wafers spread with oil, and cakes of fine flour mixed with oil.

13 With cakes of leavened bread he shall offer his sacrifice of thanksgiving with the sacrifice of his peace offerings.

14 And of it he shall offer one cake from each offering as an offering to the Lord; it shall belong to the priest who dashes the blood of the peace offerings.

15 The flesh of the sacrifice of thanksgiving presented as a peace offering, shall be eaten on the day that it is offered; none of it shall be left until morning.

16 But if the sacrifice of the worshiper's offering be a vow, or a freewill offering, it shall be eaten the same day that he offers his sacrifice, and on the morrow that which remains of it shall be eaten;

17 But the remainder of the flesh of the sacrifice on the third day shall be [wholly] burned with fire.

18 If any of the flesh of the sacrifice of his peace offerings be eaten at all on the third day, then the one who brought it shall not be credited with it; it shall not be accepted. It shall be an abomination *and* an abhorred thing; the one who eats of it shall bear his iniquity *and* answer for it.

19 The flesh that comes in contact with anything that is not clean shall not be eaten; it shall be burned with fire. As for the meat, every one who is clean [ceremonially] may eat of it.

20 But the one who eats of the flesh of the sacrifice of peace offerings, that belong to the Lord, when he is [ceremonially] unclean, that person shall be cut off from his people [that is, deprived of the privileges of association with them].

21 And if any one touches any unclean thing, the uncleanness of man or an unclean beast or any unclean abomination, and then eats of the flesh of the sacrifice of the Lord's peace offerings, that person shall be cut off from his people.

22 And the Lord said to Moses,

23 Say to the Israelites, You shall eat no kind of fat, of ox, or sheep, or goat.

24 The fat of the beast that dies of itself, and the fat of one that is torn with beasts, may be put to any other use, but under no circumstances are you to eat of it.

25 For whoever eats the fat of the beast of which men offer an offering made by fire to the Lord, that person shall be cut off from his people.

26 Moreover you shall eat no blood of any kind, whether of bird or of beast, in any of your dwellings.

27 Whoever eats any kind of blood, that person shall be cut off from his people.

28 And the Lord said to Moses,

29 Tell the Israelites, He who offers the sacrifice of his peace offerings to the Lord shall bring his offering to the Lord; from the sacrifice of his peace offerings

## New American Standard

5'And the priest shall offer them up in smoke on the altar as an offering by fire to the LORD; it is a guilt offering.

6'Every male among the priests may eat of it. It shall be eaten in a holy place; it is most holy.

7'The guilt offering is like the sin offering, there is one law for them; the priest who makes atonement with it shall have it.

8'Also the priest who presents any man's burnt offering, that priest shall have for himself the skin of the burnt offering which he has presented.

9'Likewise, every grain offering that is baked in the oven, and everything prepared in a pan or on a griddle, shall belong to the priest who presents it.

10'And every grain offering mixed with oil, or dry, shall belong to all the sons of Aaron, to all alike.

**11**¶ 'Now this is the law of the sacrifice of peace offerings which shall be presented to the LORD.

12'If he offers it by way of thanksgiving, then along with the sacrifice of thanksgiving he shall offer unleavened cakes mixed with oil, and unleavened wafers spread with oil, and cakes *of well* stirred fine flour mixed with oil.

13'With the sacrifice of his peace offerings for thanksgiving, he shall present his offering with cakes of leavened bread.

14'And of this he shall present one of every offering as a contribution to the LORD; it shall belong to the priest who sprinkles the blood of the peace offerings.

**15**¶ 'Now *as for* the flesh of the sacrifice of his thanksgiving peace offerings, it shall be eaten on the day of his offering; he shall not leave any of it over until morning.

16'But if the sacrifice of his offering is a votive or a freewill offering, it shall be eaten on the day that he offers his sacrifice; and on the next day what is left of it may be eaten;

17but what is left over from the flesh of the sacrifice on the third day shall be burned with fire.

18'So if any of the flesh of the sacrifice of his peace offerings should *ever* be eaten on the third day, he who offers it shall not be accepted, *and* it shall not be reckoned to his *benefit*. It shall be an offensive thing, and the person who eats of it shall bear his *own* iniquity.

**19**¶ 'Also the flesh that touches anything unclean shall not be eaten; it shall be burned with fire. As for *other* flesh, anyone who is clean may eat *such* flesh.

20'But the person who eats the flesh of the sacrifice of peace offerings which belong to the LORD, in his uncleanness, that person shall be cut off from his people.

21'And when anyone touches anything unclean, whether human uncleanness, or an unclean animal, or any unclean [a]detestable thing, and eats of the flesh of the sacrifice of peace offerings which belong to the LORD, that person shall be cut off from his people.' "

**22**¶ Then the LORD spoke to Moses, saying,

23"Speak to the sons of Israel, saying, 'You shall not eat any fat *from* an ox, a sheep, or a goat.

24'Also the fat of *an animal* which dies, and the fat of an animal torn *by beasts*, may be put to any other use, but you must certainly not eat it.

25'For whoever eats the fat of the animal from which an offering by fire is offered to the LORD, even the person who eats shall be cut off from his people.

26'And you are not to eat any blood, either of bird or animal, in any of your dwellings.

27'Any person who eats any blood, even that person shall be cut off from his people.' "

**28**¶ Then the LORD spoke to Moses, saying,

29"Speak to the sons of Israel, saying, 'He who offers the sacrifice of his peace offerings to the LORD shall bring his offering to the LORD from the sacrifice of his peace offerings.

## New International

them on the altar as an offering made to the LORD by fire. It is a
guilt offering. 6Any male in a priest's family may eat it, but it must
be eaten in a holy place; it is most holy.
7" 'The same law applies to both the sin offering and the guilt
offering: They belong to the priest who makes atonement with
them. 8The priest who offers a burnt offering for anyone may keep
its hide for himself. 9Every grain offering baked in an oven or
cooked in a pan or on a griddle belongs to the priest who offers
it, 10and every grain offering, whether mixed with oil or dry,
belongs equally to all the sons of Aaron.

*The Fellowship Offering*

11" 'These are the regulations for the fellowship offering[b] a
person may present to the LORD:
12" 'If he offers it as an expression of thankfulness, then along
with this thank offering he is to offer cakes of bread made without
yeast and mixed with oil, wafers made without yeast and spread
with oil, and cakes of fine flour well-kneaded and mixed with oil.
13Along with his fellowship offering of thanksgiving he is to
present an offering with cakes of bread made with yeast. 14He is
to bring one of each kind as an offering, a contribution to the LORD;
it belongs to the priest who sprinkles the blood of the fellowship
offerings. 15The meat of his fellowship offering of thanksgiving
must be eaten on the day it is offered; he must leave none of it till
morning.
16" 'If, however, his offering is the result of a vow or is a freewill
offering, the sacrifice shall be eaten on the day he offers it, but
anything left over may be eaten on the next day. 17Any meat of the
sacrifice left over till the third day must be burned up. 18If any meat
of the fellowship offering is eaten on the third day, it will not be
accepted. It will not be credited to the one who offered it, for it is
impure; the person who eats any of it will be held responsible.
19" 'Meat that touches anything ceremonially unclean must not
be eaten; it must be burned up. As for other meat, anyone ceremonially clean may eat it. 20But if anyone who is unclean eats any
meat of the fellowship offering belonging to the LORD, that person
must be cut off from his people. 21If anyone touches something
unclean—whether human uncleanness or an unclean animal or
any unclean, detestable thing—and then eats any of the meat of
the fellowship offering belonging to the LORD, that person must
be cut off from his people.' "

*Eating Fat and Blood Forbidden*

22The LORD said to Moses, 23"Say to the Israelites: 'Do not eat
any of the fat of cattle, sheep or goats. 24The fat of an animal found
dead or torn by wild animals may be used for any other purpose,
but you must not eat it. 25Anyone who eats the fat of an animal
from which an offering by fire may be[c] made to the LORD must be
cut off from his people. 26And wherever you live, you must not
eat the blood of any bird or animal. 27If anyone eats blood, that
person must be cut off from his people.' "

*The Priests' Share*

28The LORD said to Moses, 29"Say to the Israelites: 'Anyone who
brings a fellowship offering to the LORD is to bring part of it as his
sacrifice to the LORD. 30With his own hands he is to bring the

NAS [a] Some mss. read *swarming thing*

NIV [b] *11* Traditionally *peace offering;* also in verses 13-37 [c] *25* Or *fire is*

## King James

30 His own hands shall bring the offerings of the LORD made by fire, the fat with the breast, it shall he bring, that the breast may be waved *for* a wave offering before the LORD.

31 And the priest shall burn the fat upon the altar: but the breast shall be Aaron's and his sons'.

32 And the right shoulder shall ye give unto the priest *for* an heave offering of the sacrifices of your peace offerings.

33 He among the sons of Aaron, that offereth the blood of the peace offerings, and the fat, shall have the right shoulder for *his* part.

34 For the wave breast and the heave shoulder have I taken of the children of Israel from off the sacrifices of their peace offerings, and have given them unto Aaron the priest and unto his sons by a statute for ever from among the children of Israel.

35 ¶ This *is the portion* of the anointing of Aaron, and of the anointing of his sons, out of the offerings of the LORD made by fire, in the day *when* he presented them to minister unto the LORD in the priest's office;

36 Which the LORD commanded to be given them of the children of Israel, in the day that he anointed them, *by* a statute for ever throughout their generations.

37 This *is* the law of the burnt offering, of the meat offering, and of the sin offering, and of the trespass offering, and of the consecrations, and of the sacrifice of the peace offerings;

38 Which the LORD commanded Moses in mount Sinai, in the day that he commanded the children of Israel to offer their oblations unto the LORD, in the wilderness of Sinai.

**8** AND THE LORD spake unto Moses, saying,

2 Take Aaron and his sons with him, and the garments, and the anointing oil, and a bullock for the sin offering, and two rams, and a basket of unleavened bread;

3 And gather thou all the congregation together unto the door of the tabernacle of the congregation.

4 And Moses did as the LORD commanded him; and the assembly was gathered together unto the door of the tabernacle of the congregation.

5 And Moses said unto the congregation, This *is* the thing which the LORD commanded to be done.

6 And Moses brought Aaron and his sons, and washed them with water.

7 And he put upon him the coat, and girded him with the girdle, and clothed him with the robe, and put the ephod upon him, and he girded him with the curious girdle of the ephod, and bound *it* unto him therewith.

8 And he put the breastplate upon him: also he put in the breastplate the Urim and the Thummim.

9 And he put the mitre upon his head; also upon the mitre, *even* upon his forefront, did he put the golden plate, the holy crown; as the LORD commanded Moses.

10 And Moses took the anointing oil, and anointed the tabernacle and all that *was* therein, and sanctified them.

11 And he sprinkled thereof upon the altar seven times, and anointed the altar and all his vessels, both the laver and his foot, to sanctify them.

12 And he poured of the anointing oil upon Aaron's head, and anointed him, to sanctify him.

13 And Moses brought Aaron's sons, and put coats upon them, and girded them with girdles, and put bonnets upon them; as the LORD commanded Moses.

14 And he brought the bullock for the sin offering: and Aaron and his sons laid their hands upon the head of the bullock for the sin offering.

15 And he slew *it;* and Moses took the blood, and put *it* upon the horns of the altar round about with his finger, and purified the altar, and poured the blood at the bottom of the altar, and sanctified it, to make reconciliation upon it.

## Amplified

30 He shall bring with his own hands the offerings made by fire to the Lord; he shall bring the fat with the breast, that the breast may be waved as a wave offering before the Lord.

31 The priest shall burn the fat on the altar, but the breast shall be for Aaron and his sons.

32 And the right thigh you shall give to the priest for an offering from the sacrifices of your peace offerings.

33 The son of Aaron who offers the blood of the peace offerings, and the fat, shall have the right thigh for his portion.

34 For I have taken the breast that was waved and the thigh that was offered, from the Israelites, out of the sacrifices of their peace offerings, and have given them to Aaron the priest and to his sons, as their perpetual due from the Israelites.

35 This is the anointing portion of Aaron and his sons out of the offerings to the Lord made by fire, on the day when they were presented to minister to the Lord in the priest's office.

36 The Lord commanded this to be given them of the Israelites, on the day when they were anointed. It is their portion perpetually throughout their generations.

37 This is the law of the burnt offering, the cereal offering, the sin offering, the guilt *or* trespass offering, the consecration, and the peace offerings,

38 Which the Lord ordered Moses on Mount Sinai, on the day He commanded the Israelites to offer their sacrifices to the Lord, in the wilderness of Sinai.

**8** AND THE Lord said to Moses,

2 Take Aaron and his sons with him, and the garments [symbols of their office], and the anointing oil, and the bull of the sin offering, and the two rams, and the basket of unleavened bread;

3 And assemble all the congregation at the door of the tent of meeting.

4 Moses did as the Lord commanded him; and the congregation was assembled at the door of the tent of meeting.

5 Moses told the congregation, This is what the Lord has commanded to be done.

6 Moses brought Aaron and his sons, and washed them with water.

7 He put on Aaron the long undertunic, girded him with the long sash, clothed him with the robe, put the ephod [an upper vestment] upon him, and girded him with the skillfully woven cords attached to the ephod, binding it to him.

8 And Moses put upon Aaron the breastplate; also he put in the breastplate the Urim and the Thummim [articles upon which the high priest put his hand when seeking the divine will concerning the nation].

9 And he put the turban *or* mitre on his head; on it, in front, Moses put the shining gold plate, the holy diadem, as the Lord commanded him.

10 And Moses took the anointing oil, and anointed the tabernacle and all that was in it, and consecrated them.

11 And he sprinkled some of the oil on the altar seven times, and anointed the altar and all its utensils, and the laver and its base, to consecrate them.

12 And he poured some of the anointing oil upon Aaron's head, and anointed him, to consecrate him.

13 And Moses brought Aaron's sons, and put undertunics on them, and girded them with sashes, and wound turbans on them, as the Lord commanded Moses.

14 Then he brought the bull of the sin offering, and Aaron and his sons laid their hands on the head of the bull of the sin offering.

15 Moses killed it, and took the blood, and put it on the horns of the altar round about with his finger, and poured the blood at the base of the altar, and purified and consecrated the altar, to make atonement for it.

## New American Standard

30'His own hands are to bring offerings by fire to the LORD. He
shall bring the fat with the breast, that the breast may be presented
as a wave offering before the LORD.
31'And the priest shall offer up the fat in smoke on the altar; but
the breast shall belong to Aaron and his sons.
32'And you shall give the right thigh to the priest as a contribution from the sacrifices of your peace offerings.
33'The one among the sons of Aaron who offers the blood of the
peace offerings and the fat, the right thigh shall be his as *his*
portion.
34'For I have taken the breast of the wave offering and the thigh
of the contribution from the sons of Israel from the sacrifices of
their peace offerings, and have given them to Aaron the priest and
to his sons as *their* due forever from the sons of Israel.
35¶ 'This is that which is consecrated to Aaron and that which
is consecrated to his sons from the offerings by fire to the LORD,
in that day when he presented them to serve as priests to the LORD.
36'These the LORD had commanded to be given them from the
sons of Israel in the day that He anointed them. It is *their* due
forever throughout their generations.' "
37¶ This is the law of the burnt offering, the grain offering and
the sin offering and the guilt offering and the ordination offering
and the sacrifice of peace offerings,
38which the LORD commanded Moses at Mount Sinai in the day
that He commanded the sons of Israel to present their offerings to
the LORD in the wilderness of Sinai.

*The Consecration of Aaron and His Sons*

8 THEN THE LORD spoke to Moses, saying,
2"Take Aaron and his sons with him, and the garments and
the anointing oil and the bull of the sin offering, and the two rams
and the basket of unleavened bread;
3and assemble all the congregation at the doorway of the tent
of meeting."
4So Moses did just as the LORD commanded him. When the
congregation was assembled at the doorway of the tent of meeting,
5Moses said to the congregation, "This is the thing which the
LORD has commanded to do."
6¶ Then Moses had Aaron and his sons come near, and washed
them with water.
7And he put the tunic on him and girded him with the sash,
and clothed him with the robe, and put the ephod on him; and he
girded him with the artistic band of the ephod, with which he tied
*it* to him.
8He then placed the breastpiece on him, and in the breastpiece
he put [a]the Urim and the Thummim.
9He also placed the turban on his head, and on the turban, at
its front, he placed the golden plate, the holy crown, just as the
LORD had commanded Moses.
10¶ Moses then took the anointing oil and anointed the tabernacle and all that was in it, and consecrated them.
11And he sprinkled some of it on the altar seven times and
anointed the altar and all its utensils, and the basin and its stand,
to consecrate them.
12Then he poured some of the anointing oil on Aaron's head
and anointed him, to consecrate him.
13Next Moses had Aaron's sons come near and clothed them
with tunics, and girded them with sashes, and bound caps on
them, just as the LORD had commanded Moses.
14¶ Then he brought the bull of the sin offering, and Aaron and
his sons laid their hands on the head of the bull of the sin offering.
15Next Moses slaughtered *it* and took the blood and with his
finger put *some of it* around on the horns of the altar, and purified
the altar. Then he poured out *the rest of* the blood at the base of the
altar and consecrated it, to make atonement for it.

NAS [a] I.e., the lights and perfections

## New International

offering made to the LORD by fire; he is to bring the fat, together
with the breast, and wave the breast before the LORD as a wave
offering. 31The priest shall burn the fat on the altar, but the breast
belongs to Aaron and his sons. 32You are to give the right thigh
of your fellowship offerings to the priest as a contribution. 33The
son of Aaron who offers the blood and the fat of the fellowship
offering shall have the right thigh as his share. 34From the fellowship offerings of the Israelites, I have taken the breast that is waved
and the thigh that is presented and have given them to Aaron the
priest and his sons as their regular share from the Israelites.' "
35This is the portion of the offerings made to the LORD by fire
that were allotted to Aaron and his sons on the day they were
presented to serve the LORD as priests. 36On the day they were
anointed, the LORD commanded that the Israelites give this to
them as their regular share for the generations to come.

37These, then, are the regulations for the burnt offering, the
grain offering, the sin offering, the guilt offering, the ordination
offering and the fellowship offering, 38which the LORD gave Moses
on Mount Sinai on the day he commanded the Israelites to bring
their offerings to the LORD, in the Desert of Sinai.

*The Ordination of Aaron and His Sons*

8 THE LORD said to Moses, 2"Bring Aaron and his sons, their
garments, the anointing oil, the bull for the sin offering, the
two rams and the basket containing bread made without yeast,
3and gather the entire assembly at the entrance to the Tent of
Meeting." 4Moses did as the LORD commanded him, and the assembly gathered at the entrance to the Tent of Meeting.
5Moses said to the assembly, "This is what the LORD has commanded to be done." 6Then Moses brought Aaron and his sons
forward and washed them with water. 7He put the tunic on Aaron,
tied the sash around him, clothed him with the robe and put the
ephod on him. He also tied the ephod to him by its skillfully woven
waistband; so it was fastened on him. 8He placed the breastpiece
on him and put the Urim and Thummim in the breastpiece. 9Then
he placed the turban on Aaron's head and set the gold plate, the
sacred diadem, on the front of it, as the LORD commanded Moses.
10Then Moses took the anointing oil and anointed the tabernacle and everything in it, and so consecrated them. 11He sprinkled some of the oil on the altar seven times, anointing the altar
and all its utensils and the basin with its stand, to consecrate them.
12He poured some of the anointing oil on Aaron's head and anointed him to consecrate him. 13Then he brought Aaron's sons forward, put tunics on them, tied sashes around them and put headbands on them, as the LORD commanded Moses.
14He then presented the bull for the sin offering, and Aaron and
his sons laid their hands on its head. 15Moses slaughtered the bull
and took some of the blood, and with his finger he put it on all the
horns of the altar to purify the altar. He poured out the rest of the
blood at the base of the altar. So he consecrated it to make atonement for it. 16Moses also took all the fat around the inner parts,

## King James

16And he took all the fat that *was* upon the inwards, and the caul *above* the liver, and the two kidneys, and their fat, and Moses burned *it* upon the altar.

17But the bullock, and his hide, his flesh, and his dung, he burnt with fire without the camp; as the LORD commanded Moses.

18¶ And he brought the ram for the burnt offering: and Aaron and his sons laid their hands upon the head of the ram.

19And he killed *it;* and Moses sprinkled the blood upon the altar round about.

20And he cut the ram into pieces; and Moses burnt the head, and the pieces, and the fat.

21And he washed the inwards and the legs in water; and Moses burnt the whole ram upon the altar: it *was* a burnt sacrifice for a sweet savour, *and* an offering made by fire unto the LORD; as the LORD commanded Moses.

22¶ And he brought the other ram, the ram of consecration: and Aaron and his sons laid their hands upon the head of the ram.

23And he slew *it;* and Moses took of the blood of it, and put *it* upon the tip of Aaron's right ear, and upon the thumb of his right hand, and upon the great toe of his right foot.

24And he brought Aaron's sons, and Moses put of the blood upon the tip of their right ear, and upon the thumbs of their right hands, and upon the great toes of their right feet: and Moses sprinkled the blood upon the altar round about.

25And he took the fat, and the rump, and all the fat that *was* upon the inwards, and the caul *above* the liver, and the two kidneys, and their fat, and the right shoulder:

26And out of the basket of unleavened bread, that *was* before the LORD, he took one unleavened cake, and a cake of oiled bread, and one wafer, and put *them* on the fat, and upon the right shoulder:

27And he put all upon Aaron's hands, and upon his sons' hands, and waved them *for* a wave offering before the LORD.

28And Moses took them from off their hands, and burnt *them* on the altar upon the burnt offering: they *were* consecrations for a sweet savour: it *is* an offering made by fire unto the LORD.

29And Moses took the breast, and waved it *for* a wave offering before the LORD: *for* of the ram of consecration it was Moses' part; as the LORD commanded Moses.

30And Moses took of the anointing oil, and of the blood which *was* upon the altar, and sprinkled *it* upon Aaron, *and* upon his garments, and upon his sons, and upon his sons' garments with him; and sanctified Aaron, *and* his garments, and his sons, and his sons' garments with him.

31¶ And Moses said unto Aaron and to his sons, Boil the flesh *at* the door of the tabernacle of the congregation: and there eat it with the bread that *is* in the basket of consecrations, as I commanded, saying, Aaron and his sons shall eat it.

32And that which remaineth of the flesh and of the bread shall ye burn with fire.

33And ye shall not go out of the door of the tabernacle of the congregation *in* seven days, until the days of your consecration be at an end: for seven days shall he consecrate you.

34As he hath done this day, *so* the LORD hath commanded to do, to make an atonement for you.

35Therefore shall ye abide *at* the door of the tabernacle of the congregation day and night seven days, and keep the charge of the LORD, that ye die not: for so I am commanded.

36So Aaron and his sons did all things which the LORD commanded by the hand of Moses.

## Amplified

16He took all the fat that was on the entrails, and the lobe of the liver, and the two kidneys with their fat, and Moses burned them on the altar.

17But the bull [the sin offering], and its hide, its flesh, and its dung, he burned with fire outside the camp, as the Lord commanded Moses.

18He brought the ram for the burnt offering, and Aaron and his sons laid their hands on the head of the ram.

19And Moses killed it, and dashed the blood upon the altar round about.

20He cut the ram into pieces, and Moses burned the head, the pieces, and the fat.

21And he washed the entrails and the legs in water; then Moses burned the whole ram on the altar; it was a burnt sacrifice for a sweet *and* satisfying fragrance, an offering made by fire to the Lord, as the Lord commanded Moses.

22And he brought the other ram, the ram of consecration *and* ordination, and Aaron and his sons laid their hands upon the head of the ram.

23And Moses killed it, and took some of its blood and put it on the tip of Aaron's right ear and on the thumb of his right hand and on the great toe of his right foot.

24And he brought Aaron's sons, and Moses put some of the blood on the tip of their right ears, and the thumbs of their right hands, and the great toes of their right feet; and Moses dashed the blood upon the altar round about.

25And he took the fat, the fat tail, all the fat that was on the entrails, the lobe of the liver, and the two kidneys and their fat, and the right thigh;

26And out of the basket of unleavened bread that was before the Lord, he took one unleavened cake, a cake of oiled bread, and one wafer, and put them on the fat and on the right thigh;

27And he put all these in Aaron's hands and his sons' hands, and waved them for a wave offering before the Lord.

28Then Moses took these things from their hands, and burned them on the altar with the burnt offering, as an ordination offering for a sweet *and* satisfying fragrance, an offering made by fire to the Lord.

29And Moses took the breast, and waved it for a wave offering before the Lord; for of the ram of consecration *and* ordination it was Moses' portion, as the Lord commanded *him.*

30And Moses took some of the anointing oil, and of the blood which was on the altar, and sprinkled it on Aaron and his garments, and upon his sons, and their garments also; so Moses consecrated Aaron and his garments, and his sons and his sons' garments.

31And Moses said to Aaron and his sons, Boil the flesh at the door of the tent of meeting, and there eat it with the bread that is in the basket of consecration *and* ordination, as I commanded, saying, Aaron and his sons shall eat it.

32And what remains of the flesh and of the bread you shall burn with fire.

33And you shall not go out of the door of the tent of meeting for seven days, until the days of your consecration *and* ordination are ended; for it will take seven days to consecrate *and* ordain you.

34As has been done this day, so the Lord has commanded to do, for your atonement.

35At the door of the tent of meeting you shall remain day and night for seven days, [a]doing what the Lord has charged you to do, that you die not; for so I am commanded.

36So Aaron and his sons did all the things which the Lord commanded by Moses.

**AMP** [a] We have every one of us a charge to keep, an eternal God to glorify, an immortal soul to provide for, needful duty to be done, our generation to serve; and it must be our daily care to keep this charge, for it is the charge of the Lord our Master (Matthew Henry's *Commentary*). The laws contained in this book, for the most part ceremonial, had an important spiritual bearing, the study of which is highly instructive (Jamieson, Fausset & Brown's *Bible Commentary*). The Scripture references recorded with the text are intended to be a guide to its spiritual implications.

## New American Standard

16He also took all the fat that was on the entrails and the lobe of the liver, and the two kidneys and their fat; and Moses offered it up in smoke on the altar.

17But the bull and its hide and its flesh and its refuse, he burned in the fire outside the camp, just as the LORD had commanded Moses.

**18**¶ Then he presented the ram of the burnt offering, and Aaron and his sons laid their hands on the head of the ram.

19And Moses slaughtered *it* and sprinkled the blood around on the altar.

20When he had cut the ram into its pieces, Moses offered up the head and the pieces and the suet in smoke.

21After he had washed the entrails and the legs with water, Moses offered up the whole ram in smoke on the altar. It was a burnt offering for a soothing aroma; it was an offering by fire to the LORD, just as the LORD had commanded Moses.

**22**¶ Then he presented the second ram, the ram of [b]ordination; and Aaron and his sons laid their hands on the head of the ram.

23And Moses slaughtered *it* and took some of its blood and put it on the lobe of Aaron's right ear, and on the thumb of his right hand, and on the big toe of his right foot.

24He also had Aaron's sons come near; and Moses put some of the blood on the lobe of their right ear, and on the thumb of their right hand, and on the big toe of their right foot. Moses then sprinkled *the rest of* the blood around on the altar.

25And he took the fat, and the fat tail, and all the fat that was on the entrails, and the lobe of the liver and the two kidneys and their fat and the right thigh.

26And from the basket of unleavened bread that was before the LORD, he took one unleavened cake and one cake of bread *mixed with* oil and one wafer, and placed *them* on the portions of fat and on the right thigh.

27He then put all *these* on the hands of Aaron and on the hands of his sons, and presented them as a wave offering before the LORD.

28Then Moses took them from their hands and offered them up in smoke on the altar with the burnt offering. They were an ordination offering for a soothing aroma; it was an offering by fire to the LORD.

29Moses also took the breast and presented it for a wave offering before the LORD; it was Moses' portion of the ram of ordination, just as the LORD had commanded Moses.

**30**¶ So Moses took some of the anointing oil and some of the blood which was on the altar, and sprinkled it on Aaron, on his garments, on his sons, and on the garments of his sons with him; and he consecrated Aaron, his garments, and his sons, and the garments of his sons with him.

**31**¶ Then Moses said to Aaron and to his sons, "Boil the flesh at the doorway of the tent of meeting, and eat it there together with the bread which is in the basket of the ordination offering, just as I commanded, saying, 'Aaron and his sons shall eat it.'

32"And the remainder of the flesh and of the bread you shall burn in the fire.

33"And you shall not go outside the doorway of the tent of meeting for seven days, until the day that the period of your ordination is fulfilled; for he will ordain you through seven days.

34"The LORD has commanded to do as has been done this day, to make atonement on your behalf.

35"At the doorway of the tent of meeting, moreover, you shall remain day and night for seven days, and keep the charge of the LORD, that you may not die, for so I have been commanded."

36Thus Aaron and his sons did all the things which the LORD had commanded through Moses.

NAS [b] Lit., *filling,* and so throughout this context

## New International

the covering of the liver, and both kidneys and their fat, and
burned it on the altar. 17But the bull with its hide and its flesh and
its offal he burned up outside the camp, as the LORD commanded
Moses.
18He then presented the ram for the burnt offering, and Aaron
and his sons laid their hands on its head. 19Then Moses slaughtered the ram and sprinkled the blood against the altar on all sides.
20He cut the ram into pieces and burned the head, the pieces and
the fat. 21He washed the inner parts and the legs with water and
burned the whole ram on the altar as a burnt offering, a pleasing
aroma, an offering made to the LORD by fire, as the LORD commanded Moses.
22He then presented the other ram, the ram for the ordination,
and Aaron and his sons laid their hands on its head. 23Moses
slaughtered the ram and took some of its blood and put it on the
lobe of Aaron's right ear, on the thumb of his right hand and on
the big toe of his right foot. 24Moses also brought Aaron's sons
forward and put some of the blood on the lobes of their right ears,
on the thumbs of their right hands and on the big toes of their right
feet. Then he sprinkled blood against the altar on all sides. 25He
took the fat, the fat tail, all the fat around the inner parts, the
covering of the liver, both kidneys and their fat and the right thigh.
26Then from the basket of bread made without yeast, which was
before the LORD, he took a cake of bread, and one made with oil,
and a wafer; he put these on the fat portions and on the right thigh.
27He put all these in the hands of Aaron and his sons and waved
them before the LORD as a wave offering. 28Then Moses took them
from their hands and burned them on the altar on top of the burnt
offering as an ordination offering, a pleasing aroma, an offering
made to the LORD by fire. 29He also took the breast—Moses' share
of the ordination ram—and waved it before the LORD as a wave
offering, as the LORD commanded Moses.
30Then Moses took some of the anointing oil and some of the
blood from the altar and sprinkled them on Aaron and his garments and on his sons and their garments. So he consecrated
Aaron and his garments and his sons and their garments.
31Moses then said to Aaron and his sons, "Cook the meat at the
entrance to the Tent of Meeting and eat it there with the bread from
the basket of ordination offerings, as I commanded, saying,[c]
'Aaron and his sons are to eat it.' 32Then burn up the rest of the
meat and the bread. 33Do not leave the entrance to the Tent of
Meeting for seven days, until the days of your ordination are
completed, for your ordination will last seven days. 34What has
been done today was commanded by the LORD to make atonement
for you. 35You must stay at the entrance to the Tent of Meeting day
and night for seven days and do what the LORD requires, so you
will not die; for that is what I have been commanded." 36So Aaron
and his sons did everything the LORD commanded through Moses.

NIV [c] *31* Or *I was commanded:*

## King James

**9** AND IT came to pass on the eighth day, *that* Moses called Aaron and his sons, and the elders of Israel;

2 And he said unto Aaron, Take thee a young calf for a sin offering, and a ram for a burnt offering, without blemish, and offer *them* before the LORD.

3 And unto the children of Israel thou shalt speak, saying, Take ye a kid of the goats for a sin offering; and a calf and a lamb, *both* of the first year, without blemish, for a burnt offering;

4 Also a bullock and a ram for peace offerings, to sacrifice before the LORD; and a meat offering mingled with oil: for today the LORD will appear unto you.

5 ¶ And they brought *that* which Moses commanded before the tabernacle of the congregation: and all the congregation drew near and stood before the LORD.

6 And Moses said, This *is* the thing which the LORD commanded that ye should do: and the glory of the LORD shall appear unto you.

7 And Moses said unto Aaron, Go unto the altar, and offer thy sin offering, and thy burnt offering, and make an atonement for thyself, and for the people: and offer the offering of the people, and make an atonement for them; as the LORD commanded.

8 ¶ Aaron therefore went unto the altar, and slew the calf of the sin offering, which *was* for himself.

9 And the sons of Aaron brought the blood unto him: and he dipped his finger in the blood, and put *it* upon the horns of the altar, and poured out the blood at the bottom of the altar:

10 But the fat, and the kidneys, and the caul above the liver of the sin offering, he burnt upon the altar; as the LORD commanded Moses.

11 And the flesh and the hide he burnt with fire without the camp.

12 And he slew the burnt offering; and Aaron's sons presented unto him the blood, which he sprinkled round about upon the altar.

13 And they presented the burnt offering unto him, with the pieces thereof, and the head: and he burnt *them* upon the altar.

14 And he did wash the inwards and the legs, and burnt *them* upon the burnt offering on the altar.

15 ¶ And he brought the people's offering, and took the goat, which *was* the sin offering for the people, and slew it, and offered it for sin, as the first.

16 And he brought the burnt offering, and offered it according to the manner.

17 And he brought the meat offering, and took an handful thereof, and burnt *it* upon the altar, beside the burnt sacrifice of the morning.

18 He slew also the bullock and the ram *for* a sacrifice of peace offerings, which *was* for the people: and Aaron's sons presented unto him the blood, which he sprinkled upon the altar round about,

19 And the fat of the bullock and of the ram, the rump, and that which covereth *the inwards*, and the kidneys, and the caul *above* the liver:

20 And they put the fat upon the breasts, and he burnt the fat upon the altar:

21 And the breasts and the right shoulder Aaron waved *for* a wave offering before the LORD; as Moses commanded.

22 And Aaron lifted up his hand toward the people, and blessed them, and came down from offering of the sin offering, and the burnt offering, and peace offerings.

23 And Moses and Aaron went into the tabernacle of the congregation, and came out, and blessed the people: and the glory of the LORD appeared unto all the people.

24 And there came a fire out from before the LORD, and consumed upon the altar the burnt offering and the fat: *which* when all the people saw, they shouted, and fell on their faces.

## Amplified

**9** ON THE eighth day Moses called Aaron and his sons and the elders of Israel;

2 And he said to Aaron, Take a young calf for a sin offering, and a ram for a burnt offering, [each] without blemish, and offer them before the Lord. [Heb. 10:10-12.]

3 And say to the Israelites, Take a male goat for a sin offering, and a calf and a lamb, both a year old, without blemish, for a burnt offering;

4 Also a bull and a ram for peace offerings, to sacrifice before the Lord, and a cereal offering mixed with oil, for today the Lord will appear to you.

5 They brought before the tent of meeting what Moses [had] commanded; all the congregation drew near and stood before the Lord.

6 And Moses said, This is the thing which the Lord commanded you to do, and the glory of the Lord will appear to you.

7 And Moses said to Aaron, Draw near the altar, and offer your sin offering and your burnt offering, and make atonement for yourself and for the people; and offer the offering of the people, and make atonement for them, as the Lord commanded. [Heb. 5:1-5; 7:27.]

8 So Aaron drew near the altar, and killed the calf of the sin offering, which was designated for himself.

9 The sons of Aaron presented the blood to him; he dipped his finger in the blood and put it on the horns of the altar, and poured out the blood at the altar's base;

10 But the fat, the kidneys, and the lobe of the liver from the sin offering he burned on the altar, as the Lord had commanded Moses.

11 And the flesh and the hide Aaron burned with fire outside the camp.

12 He killed the burnt offering, and Aaron's sons delivered to him the blood, which he dashed round about upon the altar.

13 And they brought the burnt offering to him, piece by piece, and the head, and Aaron burned them upon the altar.

14 And he washed the entrails and the legs, and burned them with the burnt offering on the altar.

15 Then Aaron presented the people's offering, and took the goat of the sin offering which was for the people, and killed it, and offered it for sin, as he did the first sin offering. [Heb. 2:16, 17.]

16 And he presented the burnt offering, and offered it according to the ordinance.

17 And Aaron presented the cereal offering and took a handful of it and burned it on the altar, in addition to the burnt offering of the morning.

18 He also killed the bull and the ram, the sacrifice of peace offerings, for the people; and Aaron's sons presented to him the blood, which he dashed upon the altar round about,

19 And the fat of the bull and of the ram, the fat tail and that which covers the entrails, and the kidneys, and the lobe of the liver.

20 And they put the fat upon the breasts, and Aaron burned the fat upon the altar;

21 But the breasts and the right thigh Aaron waved for a wave offering before the Lord, as Moses commanded.

22 Then Aaron lifted his hands toward the people and blessed them, and came down [from the altar] after offering the sin offering, the burnt offering, and the peace offerings.

23 Moses and Aaron went into the tent of meeting, and when they came out they blessed the people, and the glory of the Lord [the Shekinah cloud] appeared to all the people [as promised]. [Verse 6.]

24 Then there came a fire out from before the Lord, and consumed the burnt offering and the fat on the altar; and when all the people saw it, they shouted, and fell on their faces.

## New American Standard

*Aaron Offers Sacrifices*

9 NOW IT came about on the eighth day that Moses called Aaron and his sons and the elders of Israel;

2and he said to Aaron, "Take for yourself a calf, a bull, for a sin offering and a ram for a burnt offering, *both* without defect, and offer *them* before the LORD.

3"Then to the sons of Israel you shall speak, saying, 'Take a male goat for a sin offering, and a calf and a lamb, both one year old, without defect, for a burnt offering,

4and an ox and a ram for peace offerings, to sacrifice before the LORD, and a grain offering mixed with oil; for today the LORD shall appear to you.' "

5So they took what Moses had commanded to the front of the tent of meeting, and the whole congregation came near and stood before the LORD.

6And Moses said, "This is the thing which the LORD has commanded you to do, that the glory of the LORD may appear to you."

7Moses then said to Aaron, "Come near to the altar and offer your sin offering and your burnt offering, that you may make atonement for yourself and for the people; then make the offering for the people, that you may make atonement for them, just as the LORD has commanded."

8¶ So Aaron came near to the altar and slaughtered the calf of the sin offering which was for himself.

9And Aaron's sons presented the blood to him; and he dipped his finger in the blood, and put *some* on the horns of the altar, and poured out *the rest of* the blood at the base of the altar.

10The fat and the kidneys and the lobe of the liver of the sin offering, he then offered up in smoke on the altar just as the LORD had commanded Moses.

11The flesh and the skin, however, he burned with fire outside the camp.

12¶ Then he slaughtered the burnt offering; and Aaron's sons handed the blood to him and he sprinkled it around on the altar.

13And they handed the burnt offering to him in pieces with the head, and he offered *them* up in smoke on the altar.

14He also washed the entrails and the legs, and offered *them* up in smoke with the burnt offering on the altar.

15¶ Then he presented the people's offering, and took the goat of the sin offering which was for the people, and slaughtered it and offered it for sin, like the first.

16He also presented the burnt offering, and offered it according to the ordinance.

17Next he presented the grain offering, and filled his hand with some of it and offered *it* up in smoke on the altar, besides the burnt offering of the morning.

18¶ Then he slaughtered the ox and the ram, the sacrifice of peace offerings which was for the people; and Aaron's sons handed the blood to him and he sprinkled it around on the altar.

19As for the portions of fat from the ox and from the ram, the fat tail, and the *fat* covering, and the kidneys and the lobe of the liver,

20they now placed the portions of fat on the breasts; and he offered them up in smoke on the altar.

21But the breasts and the right thigh Aaron presented as a wave offering before the LORD, just as Moses had commanded.

22¶ Then Aaron lifted up his hands toward the people and blessed them, and he stepped down after making the sin offering and the burnt offering and the peace offerings.

23And Moses and Aaron went into the tent of meeting. When they came out and blessed the people, the glory of the LORD appeared to all the people.

24Then fire came out from before the LORD and consumed the burnt offering and the portions of fat on the altar; and when all the people saw *it*, they shouted and fell on their faces.

## New International

*The Priests Begin Their Ministry*

9 ON THE eighth day Moses summoned Aaron and his sons
and the elders of Israel. 2He said to Aaron, "Take a bull calf
for your sin offering and a ram for your burnt offering, both
without defect, and present them before the LORD. 3Then say to
the Israelites: 'Take a male goat for a sin offering, a calf and a
lamb—both a year old and without defect—for a burnt offering,
4and an ox[a] and a ram for a fellowship offering[b] to sacrifice before
the LORD, together with a grain offering mixed with oil. For today
the LORD will appear to you.' "
5They took the things Moses commanded to the front of the
Tent of Meeting, and the entire assembly came near and stood
before the LORD. 6Then Moses said, "This is what the LORD has
commanded you to do, so that the glory of the LORD may appear
to you."
7Moses said to Aaron, "Come to the altar and sacrifice your sin
offering and your burnt offering and make atonement for yourself
and the people; sacrifice the offering that is for the people and
make atonement for them, as the LORD has commanded."
8So Aaron came to the altar and slaughtered the calf as a sin
offering for himself. 9His sons brought the blood to him, and he
dipped his finger into the blood and put it on the horns of the altar;
the rest of the blood he poured out at the base of the altar. 10On
the altar he burned the fat, the kidneys and the covering of the liver
from the sin offering, as the LORD commanded Moses; 11the flesh
and the hide he burned up outside the camp.
12Then he slaughtered the burnt offering. His sons handed him
the blood, and he sprinkled it against the altar on all sides. 13They
handed him the burnt offering piece by piece, including the head,
and he burned them on the altar. 14He washed the inner parts and
the legs and burned them on top of the burnt offering on the altar.
15Aaron then brought the offering that was for the people. He
took the goat for the people's sin offering and slaughtered it and
offered it for a sin offering as he did with the first one.
16He brought the burnt offering and offered it in the prescribed
way. 17He also brought the grain offering, took a handful of it and
burned it on the altar in addition to the morning's burnt offering.
18He slaughtered the ox and the ram as the fellowship offering
for the people. His sons handed him the blood, and he sprinkled
it against the altar on all sides. 19But the fat portions of the ox and
the ram—the fat tail, the layer of fat, the kidneys and the covering
of the liver— 20these they laid on the breasts, and then Aaron
burned the fat on the altar. 21Aaron waved the breasts and the
right thigh before the LORD as a wave offering, as Moses commanded.
22Then Aaron lifted his hands toward the people and blessed
them. And having sacrificed the sin offering, the burnt offering
and the fellowship offering, he stepped down.
23Moses and Aaron then went into the Tent of Meeting. When
they came out, they blessed the people; and the glory of the LORD
appeared to all the people. 24Fire came out from the presence of
the LORD and consumed the burnt offering and the fat portions on
the altar. And when all the people saw it, they shouted for joy and
fell facedown.

NIV [a] 4 The Hebrew word can include both male and female; also in verses 18 and 19. [b] 4 Traditionally *peace offering;* also in verses 18 and 22

## King James

10 AND NADAB and Abihu, the sons of Aaron, took either of them his censer, and put fire therein, and put incense thereon, and offered strange fire before the LORD, which he commanded them not.

2 And there went out fire from the LORD, and devoured them, and they died before the LORD.

3 Then Moses said unto Aaron, This *is it* that the LORD spake, saying, I will be sanctified in them that come nigh me, and before all the people I will be glorified. And Aaron held his peace.

4 And Moses called Mishael and Elzaphan, the sons of Uzziel the uncle of Aaron, and said unto them, Come near, carry your brethren from before the sanctuary out of the camp.

5 So they went near, and carried them in their coats out of the camp; as Moses had said.

6 And Moses said unto Aaron, and unto Eleazar and unto Ithamar, his sons, Uncover not your heads, neither rend your clothes; lest ye die, and lest wrath come upon all the people: but let your brethren, the whole house of Israel, bewail the burning which the LORD hath kindled.

7 And ye shall not go out from the door of the tabernacle of the congregation, lest ye die: for the anointing oil of the LORD *is* upon you. And they did according to the word of Moses.

8 ¶ And the LORD spake unto Aaron, saying,

9 Do not drink wine nor strong drink, thou, nor thy sons with thee, when ye go into the tabernacle of the congregation, lest ye die: *it shall be* a statute for ever throughout your generations:

10 And that ye may put difference between holy and unholy, and between unclean and clean;

11 And that ye may teach the children of Israel all the statutes which the LORD hath spoken unto them by the hand of Moses.

12 ¶ And Moses spake unto Aaron, and unto Eleazar and unto Ithamar, his sons that were left, Take the meat offering that remaineth of the offerings of the LORD made by fire, and eat it without leaven beside the altar: for it *is* most holy:

13 And ye shall eat it in the holy place, because it *is* thy due, and thy sons' due, of the sacrifices of the LORD made by fire: for so I am commanded.

14 And the wave breast and heave shoulder shall ye eat in a clean place; thou, and thy sons, and thy daughters with thee: for *they be* thy due, and thy sons' due, *which* are given out of the sacrifices of peace offerings of the children of Israel.

15 The heave shoulder and the wave breast shall they bring with the offerings made by fire of the fat, to wave *it for* a wave offering before the LORD; and it shall be thine, and thy sons' with thee, by a statute for ever; as the LORD hath commanded.

16 ¶ And Moses diligently sought the goat of the sin offering, and, behold, it was burnt: and he was angry with Eleazar and Ithamar, the sons of Aaron *which were* left *alive,* saying,

17 Wherefore have ye not eaten the sin offering in the holy place, seeing it *is* most holy, and *God* hath given it you to bear the iniquity of the congregation, to make atonement for them before the LORD?

## Amplified

10 AND NADAB and Abihu, the sons of Aaron, each took his censer and put fire in it, and put incense on it, and offered strange *and* unholy fire before the Lord, as He had not commanded them.

2 And there came forth fire from before the Lord and killed them, and they died before the Lord.

3 Then Moses said to Aaron, This is what the Lord meant when He said, I [a][and My will, not their own] will be acknowledged as hallowed by those who come near Me, and before all the people I will be honored. And Aaron said nothing.

4 Moses called Mishael and Elzaphan, sons of Uzziel uncle of Aaron, and said to them, Come near, carry your brethren from before the sanctuary out of the camp.

5 So they drew near, and carried them in their undertunics [stripped of their priestly vestments] out of the camp, as Moses had said.

6 And Moses said to Aaron, and Eleazar and Ithamar, his sons [the father and brothers of the two priests whom God had slain for offering false fire], Do not uncover your heads *or* let your hair go loose, or tear your clothes, lest you die [also], and lest God's wrath should come upon all the congregation; but let your brethren, the whole house of Israel, bewail the burning which the Lord has kindled.

7 And you shall not go out from the door of the tent of meeting, lest you die; for the Lord's anointing oil is upon you. And they did according to Moses' word.

8 And the Lord said to Aaron,

9 Do not drink wine or strong drink, you or your sons, when you go into the tent of meeting, lest you die; it shall be a statute for ever in all your generations.

10 You shall make a distinction *and* recognize a difference between the holy and the common *or* unholy, and between the unclean and the clean;

11 And you are to teach the Israelites all the statutes which the Lord has spoken to them by Moses.

12 And Moses said to Aaron, and to Eleazar and Ithamar, his sons who were left, Take the cereal offering that remains of the offerings of the Lord made by fire, and eat it without leaven beside the altar, for it is most holy.

13 You shall eat it in a sacred place, because it is your due and your sons' due, from the offerings made by fire to the Lord; for so I am commanded.

14 But the breast that is waved and the thigh that is offered you shall eat in a clean place, you and your sons and daughters with you; for they are your due and your sons' due, given out of the sacrifices of the peace offerings of the Israelites.

15 The thigh that is offered and the breast that is waved they shall bring with the offerings made by fire of the fat, to wave for a wave offering before the Lord; and it shall be yours and your sons' with you, as a portion *or* due, perpetually, as the Lord has commanded.

16 And Moses diligently tried to find [what had become] *of* the goat [that had been offered] for the sin offering, and behold, it was burned up [as waste]! And he was angry with Eleazar and Ithamar the sons of Aaron who were left alive, and said,

17 Why have you not eaten the sin offering in the holy place, seeing it is most holy, and God has given it to you to bear *and* take away the iniquity of the congregation, to make atonement for them before the Lord?

**AMP** [a] Perhaps few believers have ever identified themselves with Nadab and Abihu, and yet few, if any, of us have not done exactly what they did in principle. Their sin, which God took so seriously, and which proved fatal to them, was not a mere matter of failing to obey the letter of God's law for priests. Their inexcusable folly was in trying to please the Lord *their* way instead of *His* way. Who of us cannot recognize himself as the offerer of this prayer, with only the details lacking: "O Lord, make me rich! Then I will make large donations to Your interests!" Yet our very poverty may be the means to the end which He has in love and wisdom planned for us, the ultimate purpose of our creation, perhaps, which substitution of our will for His will would utterly defeat. No wonder God removed Nadab and Abihu from the earth! They, like ourselves, had acted like the child of a great painter who attempted to work on his father's priceless canvas, instead of on the tablet assigned to him. They, like the child, were banished from the father's presence. And every believer does well to recognize the importance of being entirely surrendered to "God's will; nothing more; nothing less; nothing else; at any cost." And that does not mean first making an unholy alliance in marriage, or in business, or in thought, and then adjusting it to God's will. Remember Nadab and Abihu, who "offered strange and unholy fire before the Lord." It does not pay.

## New American Standard

*The Sin of Nadab and Abihu*

**10** NOW NADAB and Abihu, the sons of Aaron, took their respective firepans, and after putting fire in them, placed incense on it and offered strange fire before the LORD, which He had not commanded them.

2 And fire came out from the presence of the LORD and consumed them, and they died before the LORD.

3 Then Moses said to Aaron, "It is what the LORD spoke, saying,

'By those who come near Me I will be treated as holy,
And before all the people I will be honored.' "

So Aaron, therefore, kept silent.

4 Moses called also to Mishael and Elzaphan, the sons of Aaron's uncle Uzziel, and said to them, "Come forward, carry your relatives away from the front of the sanctuary to the outside of the camp."

5 So they came forward and carried them still in their tunics to the outside of the camp, as Moses had said.

6 Then Moses said to Aaron and to his sons Eleazar and Ithamar, "Do not [b]uncover your heads nor tear your clothes, so that you may not die, and that He may not become wrathful against all the congregation. But your kinsmen, the whole house of Israel, shall bewail the burning which the LORD has brought about.

7 "You shall not even go out from the doorway of the tent of meeting, lest you die; for the LORD's anointing oil is upon you." So they did according to the word of Moses.

8¶ The LORD then spoke to Aaron, saying,

9 "Do not drink wine or strong drink, neither you nor your sons with you, when you come into the tent of meeting, so that you may not die—it is a perpetual statute throughout your generations—

10 and so as to make a distinction between the holy and the profane, and between the unclean and the clean,

11 and so as to teach the sons of Israel all the statutes which the LORD has spoken to them through Moses."

12¶ Then Moses spoke to Aaron, and to his surviving sons, Eleazar and Ithamar, "Take the grain offering that is left over from the LORD's offerings by fire and eat it unleavened beside the altar, for it is most holy.

13 "You shall eat it, moreover, in a holy place, because it is your due and your sons' due out of the LORD's offerings by fire; for thus I have been commanded.

14 "The breast of the wave offering, however, and the thigh of the offering you may eat in a clean place, you and your sons and your daughters with you; for they have been given as your due and your sons' due out of the sacrifices of the peace offerings of the sons of Israel.

15 "The thigh offered by lifting up and the breast offered by waving, they shall bring along with the offerings by fire of the portions of fat, to present as a wave offering before the LORD; so it shall be a thing perpetually due you and your sons with you, just as the LORD has commanded."

16¶ But Moses searched carefully for the goat of the sin offering, and behold, it had been burned up! So he was angry with Aaron's surviving sons Eleazar and Ithamar, saying,

17 "Why did you not eat the sin offering at the holy place? For it is most holy, and He gave it to you to bear away the guilt of the congregation, to make atonement for them before the LORD.

NAS [b] Lit., *unbind*

## New International

*The Death of Nadab and Abihu*

**10** AARON'S SONS Nadab and Abihu took their censers, put fire in them and added incense; and they offered unauthorized fire before the LORD, contrary to his command. 2 So fire came out from the presence of the LORD and consumed them, and they died before the LORD. 3 Moses then said to Aaron, "This is what the LORD spoke of when he said:

" 'Among those who approach me
I will show myself holy;
in the sight of all the people
I will be honored.' "

Aaron remained silent.

4 Moses summoned Mishael and Elzaphan, sons of Aaron's uncle Uzziel, and said to them, "Come here; carry your cousins outside the camp, away from the front of the sanctuary." 5 So they came and carried them, still in their tunics, outside the camp, as Moses ordered.

6 Then Moses said to Aaron and his sons Eleazar and Ithamar, "Do not let your hair become unkempt,[c] and do not tear your clothes, or you will die and the LORD will be angry with the whole community. But your relatives, all the house of Israel, may mourn for those the LORD has destroyed by fire. 7 Do not leave the entrance to the Tent of Meeting or you will die, because the LORD's anointing oil is on you." So they did as Moses said.

8 Then the LORD said to Aaron, 9 "You and your sons are not to drink wine or other fermented drink whenever you go into the Tent of Meeting, or you will die. This is a lasting ordinance for the generations to come. 10 You must distinguish between the holy and the common, between the unclean and the clean, 11 and you must teach the Israelites all the decrees the LORD has given them through Moses."

12 Moses said to Aaron and his remaining sons, Eleazar and Ithamar, "Take the grain offering left over from the offerings made to the LORD by fire and eat it prepared without yeast beside the altar, for it is most holy. 13 Eat it in a holy place, because it is your share and your sons' share of the offerings made to the LORD by fire; for so I have been commanded. 14 But you and your sons and your daughters may eat the breast that was waved and the thigh that was presented. Eat them in a ceremonially clean place; they have been given to you and your children as your share of the Israelites' fellowship offerings.[d] 15 The thigh that was presented and the breast that was waved must be brought with the fat portions of the offerings made by fire, to be waved before the LORD as a wave offering. This will be the regular share for you and your children, as the LORD has commanded."

16 When Moses inquired about the goat of the sin offering and found that it had been burned up, he was angry with Eleazar and Ithamar, Aaron's remaining sons, and asked, 17 "Why didn't you eat the sin offering in the sanctuary area? It is most holy; it was given to you to take away the guilt of the community by making atonement for them before the LORD. 18 Since its blood was not

NIV [c] 6 Or *Do not uncover your heads* [d] 14 Traditionally *peace offerings*

## King James

18Behold, the blood of it was not brought in within the holy
*place:* ye should indeed have eaten it in the holy *place,* as I commanded.
19And Aaron said unto Moses, Behold, this day have they
offered their sin offering and their burnt offering before the LORD;
and such things have befallen me: and *if* I had eaten the sin offering
today, should it have been accepted in the sight of the LORD?
20And when Moses heard *that,* he was content.

11 AND THE LORD spake unto Moses and to Aaron, saying
unto them,
2Speak unto the children of Israel, saying, These *are* the beasts
which ye shall eat among all the beasts that *are* on the earth.
3Whatsoever parteth the hoof, and is clovenfooted, *and*
cheweth the cud, among the beasts, that shall ye eat.
4Nevertheless these shall ye not eat of them that chew the cud,
or of them that divide the hoof: *as* the camel, because he cheweth
the cud, but divideth not the hoof; he *is* unclean unto you.
5And the coney, because he cheweth the cud, but divideth not
the hoof; he *is* unclean unto you.
6And the hare, because he cheweth the cud, but divideth not
the hoof; he *is* unclean unto you.
7And the swine, though he divide the hoof, and be cloven-
footed, yet he cheweth not the cud; he *is* unclean to you.
8Of their flesh shall ye not eat, and their carcase shall ye not
touch; they *are* unclean to you.
9¶ These shall ye eat of all that *are* in the waters: whatsoever
hath fins and scales in the waters, in the seas, and in the rivers,
them shall ye eat.
10And all that have not fins and scales in the seas, and in the
rivers, of all that move in the waters, and of any living thing which
*is* in the waters, they *shall be* an abomination unto you:
11They shall be even an abomination unto you; ye shall not eat
of their flesh, but ye shall have their carcases in abomination.
12Whatsoever hath no fins nor scales in the waters, that *shall be*
an abomination unto you.
13¶ And these *are they which* ye shall have in abomination among
the fowls; they shall not be eaten, they *are* an abomination: the
eagle, and the ossifrage, and the ospray,
14And the vulture, and the kite after his kind;
15Every raven after his kind;
16And the owl, and the night hawk, and the cuckoo, and the
hawk after his kind,
17And the little owl, and the cormorant, and the great owl,
18And the swan, and the pelican, and the gier eagle,
19And the stork, the heron after her kind, and the lapwing, and
the bat.
20All fowls that creep, going upon *all* four, *shall be* an abomination unto you.
21Yet these may ye eat of every flying creeping thing that goeth
upon *all* four, which have legs above their feet, to leap withal upon
the earth;

## Amplified

18Behold, the blood of it was not brought within the holy place;
you should indeed have eaten [the flesh of it] in the holy place, as
I commanded.
19But Aaron said to Moses, Behold, this very day in which they
have [obediently] offered their sin offering and their burnt offering
before the Lord, such [terrible calamities] have befallen me [and
them]! If I [and they] had eaten the most holy sin offering today
[humbled as we have been by the sin of our kinsmen and God's
judgment upon them], would it have been acceptable in the sight
of the Lord? [Hos. 9:4.]
20And when Moses heard that, he was pacified.

11 AND THE Lord said to Moses and Aaron,
2Say to the Israelites, These are the animals [a]which you
may eat among all the beasts that are on the earth. [Mark 7:15-19.]
3Whatever parts the hoof and is cloven-footed and chews the
cud, among the animals, that you may eat.
4Nevertheless these you shall not eat of those that chew the cud
or divide the hoof: the camel, because it chews the cud, but does
not divide the hoof; it is unclean to you.
5And the coney *or* rock badger, because it chews the cud, but
does not divide the hoof; it is unclean to you.
6And the hare, because it chews the cud, but does not divide
the hoof; it is unclean to you.
7And the swine, because it divides the hoof, and is cloven-footed, but does not chew the cud; it is unclean to you.
8Of their flesh you shall not eat, and their carcasses you shall
not touch; they are unclean to you.
9These you may eat of all that are in the waters: whatever has
fins and scales in the waters, in the seas, and in the rivers, that you
may eat;
10But all that have not fins and scales in the seas and in the
rivers, of all the creeping things in the waters, and of all the living
creatures which are in the waters, they are [to be considered] an
abomination and abhorrent to you. [I Cor. 8:8-13.]
11They shall continue to be an abomination to you; you shall not
eat of their flesh, but you shall detest their carcasses.
12Everything in the waters that has not fins or scales shall be
abhorrent *and* detestable to you.
13These you shall have in abomination among the birds; they
shall not be eaten, they are detestable: the eagle, the ossifrage, the
osprey,
14The kite, the whole species of falcon;
15Every kind of raven;
16The ostrich, the nighthawk, the sea gull, every species of
hawk,
17The owl, the cormorant, the ibis,
18The swan, the pelican, the vulture,
19The stork, all kinds of heron, the hoopoe, and the bat.
20All winged insects that go upon all fours are to be an abomination to you;
21Yet of all winged insects that go upon all fours you may eat
those which have legs above their feet, with which to leap on the
ground.

**AMP** [a] At first thought the laws given here seem only made obsolete by Jesus. He taught that it is not what goes into the mouth, but what comes out of it that defiles a man (Matt. 15:17-20), and Paul said that when the complete and perfect came the incomplete and imperfect would become void and superseded (I Cor. 13:9, 10), for "there is nothing unclean of itself" (Rom. 14:14). But while all these specific laws have become void, we must not lose sight of the fact that they are "superseded" by the underlying spiritual principle, which is just as binding. Christ's teaching relates to the whole area of our living, including our eating and drinking, and is dominated by the principle, "Whatever you may do, do all for the honor *and* glory of God" (I Cor. 10:31). We do well to remember that it was Jesus Christ Himself who said, "Do not think that I have come to do away with or undo the Law . . .; I have come not to do away with or undo, but to complete and fulfill" it (Matt. 5:17).

## New American Standard

18"Behold, since its blood had not been brought inside, into the
sanctuary, you should certainly have eaten it in the sanctuary, just
as I commanded."
19But Aaron spoke to Moses, "Behold, this very day they
presented their sin offering and their burnt offering before the
LORD. When things like these happened to me, if I had eaten a sin
offering today, would it have been good in the sight of the LORD?"
20And when Moses heard *that*, it seemed good in his sight.

*Laws about Animals for Food*

**11** THE LORD spoke again to Moses and to Aaron, saying to
them,
2"Speak to the sons of Israel, saying, 'These are the creatures
which you may eat from all the animals that are on the earth.
3'Whatever divides a hoof, thus making split hoofs, *and* chews
the cud, among the animals, that you may eat.
4'Nevertheless, you are not to eat of these, among those which
chew the cud, or among those which divide the hoof: the camel,
for though it chews cud, it does not divide the hoof, it is unclean
to you.
5'Likewise, the rock badger, for though it chews cud, it does
not divide the hoof, it is unclean to you;
6the rabbit also, for though it chews cud, it does not divide the
hoof, it is unclean to you;
7and the pig, for though it divides the hoof, thus making a split
hoof, it does not chew cud, it is unclean to you.
8'You shall not eat of their flesh nor touch their carcasses; they
are unclean to you.
9¶ 'These you may eat, whatever is in the water: all that have
fins and scales, those in the water, in the seas or in the rivers, you
may eat.
10'But whatever is in the seas and in the rivers, that do not have
fins and scales among all the teeming life of the water, and among
all the living creatures that are in the water, they are detestable
things to you,
11and they shall be [b]abhorrent to you; you may not eat of their
flesh, and their carcasses you shall detest.
12'Whatever in the water does not have fins and scales is abhorrent to you.

*Avoid the Unclean*

13¶ 'These, moreover, you shall detest among the birds; they are
abhorrent, not to be eaten: the eagle and the vulture and the
buzzard,
14and the kite and the falcon in its kind,
15every raven in its kind,
16and the ostrich and the owl and the sea gull and the hawk in
its kind,
17and the little owl and the cormorant and the great owl,
18and the white owl and the pelican and the carrion vulture,
19and the stork, the heron in its kinds, and the hoopoe, and the
bat.
20¶ 'All the winged insects that walk on *all* fours are detestable
to you.
21'Yet these you may eat among all the winged insects which
walk on *all* fours: those which have above their feet jointed legs
with which to jump on the earth.

NAS [b] Lit., *detestable things*

## New International

taken into the Holy Place, you should have eaten the goat in the
sanctuary area, as I commanded."
19Aaron replied to Moses, "Today they sacrificed their sin offering and their burnt offering before the LORD, but such things as
this have happened to me. Would the LORD have been pleased if
I had eaten the sin offering today?" 20When Moses heard this, he
was satisfied.

*Clean and Unclean Food*

**11** THE LORD said to Moses and Aaron, 2"Say to the Israelites: 'Of all the animals that live on land, these are the ones
you may eat: 3You may eat any animal that has a split hoof completely divided and that chews the cud.
4" 'There are some that only chew the cud or only have a split
hoof, but you must not eat them. The camel, though it chews the
cud, does not have a split hoof; it is ceremonially unclean for you.
5The coney,[c] though it chews the cud, does not have a split hoof;
it is unclean for you. 6The rabbit, though it chews the cud, does
not have a split hoof; it is unclean for you. 7And the pig, though
it has a split hoof completely divided, does not chew the cud; it
is unclean for you. 8You must not eat their meat or touch their
carcasses; they are unclean for you.
9" 'Of all the creatures living in the water of the seas and the
streams, you may eat any that have fins and scales. 10But all
creatures in the seas or streams that do not have fins and scales—
whether among all the swarming things or among all the other
living creatures in the water—you are to detest. 11And since you
are to detest them, you must not eat their meat and you must
detest their carcasses. 12Anything living in the water that does not
have fins and scales is to be detestable to you.
13" 'These are the birds you are to detest and not eat because
they are detestable: the eagle, the vulture, the black vulture, 14the
red kite, any kind of black kite, 15any kind of raven, 16the horned
owl, the screech owl, the gull, any kind of hawk, 17the little owl,
the cormorant, the great owl, 18the white owl, the desert owl, the
osprey, 19the stork, any kind of heron, the hoopoe and the bat.[d]
20" 'All flying insects that walk on all fours are to be detestable
to you. 21There are, however, some winged creatures that walk on
all fours that you may eat: those that have jointed legs for hopping
on the ground. 22Of these you may eat any kind of locust, katydid,

NIV [c] 5 That is, the hyrax or rock badger [d] 19 The precise identification of some of the birds, insects and animals in this chapter is uncertain.

## King James

22 *Even* these of them ye may eat; the locust after his kind, and the bald locust after his kind, and the beetle after his kind, and the grasshopper after his kind.

23 But all *other* flying creeping things, which have four feet, *shall be* an abomination unto you.

24 And for these ye shall be unclean: whosoever toucheth the carcase of them shall be unclean until the even.

25 And whosoever beareth *aught* of the carcase of them shall wash his clothes, and be unclean until the even.

26 *The carcases* of every beast which divideth the hoof, and *is* not clovenfooted, nor cheweth the cud, *are* unclean unto you: every one that toucheth them shall be unclean.

27 And whatsoever goeth upon his paws, among all manner of beasts that go on *all* four, those *are* unclean unto you: whoso toucheth their carcase shall be unclean until the even.

28 And he that beareth the carcase of them shall wash his clothes, and be unclean until the even: they *are* unclean unto you.

29 ¶ These also *shall be* unclean unto you among the creeping things that creep upon the earth; the weasel, and the mouse, and the tortoise after his kind,

30 And the ferret, and the chameleon, and the lizard, and the snail, and the mole.

31 These *are* unclean to you among all that creep: whosoever doth touch them, when they be dead, shall be unclean until the even.

32 And upon whatsoever *any* of them, when they are dead, doth fall, it shall be unclean; whether *it be* any vessel of wood, or raiment, or skin, or sack, whatsoever vessel *it be,* wherein *any* work is done, it must be put into water, and it shall be unclean until the even; so it shall be cleansed.

33 And every earthen vessel, whereinto *any* of them falleth, whatsoever *is* in it shall be unclean; and ye shall break it.

34 Of all meat which may be eaten, *that* on which *such* water cometh shall be unclean: and all drink that may be drunk in every *such* vessel shall be unclean.

35 And every *thing* whereupon *any part* of their carcase falleth shall be unclean; *whether it be* oven, or ranges for pots, they shall be broken down: *for* they *are* unclean, and shall be unclean unto you.

36 Nevertheless a fountain or pit, *wherein there is* plenty of water, shall be clean: but that which toucheth their carcase shall be unclean.

37 And if *any part* of their carcase fall upon any sowing seed which is to be sown, it *shall be* clean.

38 But if *any* water be put upon the seed, and *any part* of their carcase fall thereon, it *shall be* unclean unto you.

39 And if any beast, of which ye may eat, die; he that toucheth the carcase thereof shall be unclean until the even.

40 And he that eateth of the carcase of it shall wash his clothes, and be unclean until the even: he also that beareth the carcase of it shall wash his clothes, and be unclean until the even.

41 And every creeping thing that creepeth upon the earth *shall be* an abomination; it shall not be eaten.

42 Whatsoever goeth upon the belly, and whatsoever goeth upon *all* four, or whatsoever hath more feet among all creeping things that creep upon the earth, them ye shall not eat; for they *are* an abomination.

43 Ye shall not make your selves abominable with any creeping thing that creepeth, neither shall ye make yourselves unclean with them, that ye should be defiled thereby.

44 For I *am* the Lord your God: ye shall therefore sanctify yourselves, and ye shall be holy; for I *am* holy: neither shall ye defile yourselves with any manner of creeping thing that creepeth upon the earth.

45 For I *am* the Lord that bringeth you up out of the land of Egypt, to be your God: ye shall therefore be holy, for I *am* holy.

46 This *is* the law of the beasts, and of the fowl, and of every living creature that moveth in the waters, and of every creature that creepeth upon the earth:

## Amplified

22 Of these you may eat: the whole species of locust, of bald locust, of cricket, and of grasshopper. [Cp. Matt. 3:4.]

23 But all other winged insects which have four feet shall be detestable to you.

24 And by [contact with] these you shall become unclean; whoever touches the carcass of them shall be unclean until the evening,

25 And whoever carries any part of their carcass shall wash his clothes and be unclean until the evening:

26 Every beast which parts the hoof but is not cloven-footed or does not chew the cud is unclean to you; every one who touches them shall be unclean.

27 And all that go on their paws, among all kinds of four-footed beasts, are unclean to you; whoever touches their carcass shall be unclean until the evening,

28 And he who carries their carcass shall wash his clothes and be unclean until the evening; they are unclean to you.

29 These also are unclean to you among the creeping things [that multiply greatly] *and* creep upon the ground: the weasel, the mouse, the kinds of great lizard,

30 The gecko, the land crocodile, the lizard, the sand lizard, and the chameleon.

31 These are unclean to you among all that creep; whoever touches them when they are dead shall be unclean until the evening.

32 And upon whatever they may fall when they are dead, it shall be unclean, whether it is an article of wood or clothing or skin [bottle] or sack, any vessel in which work is done; it must be put in water, and it shall be unclean until the evening; so it shall be cleansed.

33 And every earthen vessel into which any of these [creeping things] falls, whatever may be in it shall be unclean, and you shall break it.

34 Of all food [in one of these unclean vessels] which may be eaten, that on which such water comes shall be unclean; and all drink that may be drunk from every such vessel shall be unclean.

35 And everything upon which any part of their carcass falls shall be unclean; whether an oven, *or* pan with a lid, or hearth for pots, it shall be broken in pieces; they are unclean, and shall be unclean to you.

36 Yet a spring or a cistern *or* reservoir of water shall be clean; but whatever touches a carcass in them shall be unclean.

37 If a part of their carcass falls on seed which is to be sown, it shall be clean;

38 But if any water be put on the seed, and any part of their carcass falls on it, it shall be unclean to you.

39 If any animal of which you may eat dies [unslaughtered], he who touches its carcass shall be unclean until the evening.

40 And he who eats of its carcass [ignorantly] shall wash his clothes, and be unclean until the evening; he also who carries its carcass shall wash his clothes, and be unclean until the evening.

41 And everything that creeps on the ground *and* [multiplies in] swarms shall be an abomination; it shall not be eaten.

42 Whatever goes on its belly, and whatever goes on all fours, or whatever has more [than four] feet among all things that creep on the ground *and* swarm you shall not eat; for they are detestable.

43 You shall not make yourselves loathsome *and* abominable [by eating] any swarming thing that [multiplies by] swarms, neither shall you make yourselves unclean with them, that you should be defiled by them.

44 For I am the Lord your God; so consecrate yourselves and be holy, for I am holy; neither defile yourselves with any manner of thing that multiplies in large numbers *or* swarms. [I Thess. 4:7, 8.]

45 For I am the Lord Who brought you up out of the land of Egypt, to be your God; therefore you shall be holy, for I am holy. [I Pet. 1:14-16.]

46 This is the law of the beast, and of the bird and of every living creature that moves in the waters, or creeps on the earth *and* multiplies in large numbers,

## New American Standard

22 'These of them you may eat: the locust in its kinds, and the devastating locust in its kinds, and the cricket in its kinds, and the grasshopper in its kinds.

23 'But all other winged insects which are four-footed are detestable to you.

**24**¶ 'By these, moreover, you will be made unclean: whoever touches their carcasses becomes unclean until evening,

25 and whoever picks up any of their carcasses shall wash his clothes and be unclean until evening.

26 'Concerning all the animals which divide the hoof, but do not make a split *hoof*, or which do not chew cud, they are unclean to you: whoever touches them becomes unclean.

27 'Also whatever walks on its paws, among all the creatures that walk on *all* fours, are unclean to you; whoever touches their carcasses becomes unclean until evening,

28 and the one who picks up their carcasses shall wash his clothes and be unclean until evening; they are unclean to you.

**29**¶ 'Now these are to you the unclean among the swarming things which swarm on the earth: the mole, and the mouse, and the great lizard in its kinds,

30 and the gecko, and the crocodile, and the lizard, and the sand reptile, and the chameleon.

31 'These are to you the unclean among all the swarming things; whoever touches them when they are dead becomes unclean until evening.

32 'Also anything on which one of them may fall when they are dead, becomes unclean, including any wooden article, or clothing, or a skin, or a sack—any article of which use is made—it shall be put in the water and be unclean until evening, then it becomes clean.

33 'As for any earthenware vessel into which one of them may fall, whatever is in it becomes unclean and you shall break the vessel.

34 'Any of the food which may be eaten, on which water comes, shall become unclean; and any liquid which may be drunk in every vessel shall become unclean.

35 'Everything, moreover, on which part of their carcass may fall becomes unclean; an oven or a [a]stove shall be smashed; they are unclean and shall continue as unclean to you.

36 'Nevertheless a spring or a cistern collecting water shall be clean, though the one who touches their carcass shall be unclean.

37 'And if a part of their carcass falls on any seed for sowing which is to be sown, it is clean.

38 'Though if water is put on the seed, and a part of their carcass falls on it, it is unclean to you.

**39**¶ 'Also if one of the animals dies which you have for food, the one who touches its carcass becomes unclean until evening.

40 'He too, who eats some of its carcass shall wash his clothes and be unclean until evening; and the one who picks up its carcass shall wash his clothes and be unclean until evening.

**41**¶ 'Now every swarming thing that swarms on the earth is detestable, not to be eaten.

42 'Whatever crawls on its belly, and whatever walks on *all* fours, whatever has many feet, in respect to every swarming thing that swarms on the earth, you shall not eat them, for they are detestable.

43 'Do not render yourselves detestable through any of the swarming things that swarm; and you shall not make yourselves unclean with them so that you become unclean.

44 'For I am the LORD your God. Consecrate yourselves therefore, and be holy; for I am holy. And you shall not make yourselves unclean with any of the swarming things that swarm on the earth.

45 'For I am the LORD, who brought you up from the land of Egypt, to be your God; thus you shall be holy for I am holy.' "

**46**¶ This is the law regarding the animal, and the bird, and every living thing that moves in the waters, and everything that swarms on the earth,

## New International

cricket or grasshopper.
23 But all other winged creatures that have four legs you are to detest.
24 " 'You will make yourselves unclean by these; whoever touches their carcasses will be unclean till evening.
25 Whoever picks up one of their carcasses must wash his clothes, and he will be unclean till evening.
26 " 'Every animal that has a split hoof not completely divided or that does not chew the cud is unclean for you; whoever touches ⌞the carcass of⌟ any of them will be unclean.
27 Of all the animals that walk on all fours, those that walk on their paws are unclean for you; whoever touches their carcasses will be unclean till evening.
28 Anyone who picks up their carcasses must wash his clothes, and he will be unclean till evening. They are unclean for you.
29 " 'Of the animals that move about on the ground, these are unclean for you: the weasel, the rat, any kind of great lizard,
30 the gecko, the monitor lizard, the wall lizard, the skink and the chameleon.
31 Of all those that move along the ground, these are unclean for you. Whoever touches them when they are dead will be unclean till evening.
32 When one of them dies and falls on something, that article, whatever its use, will be unclean, whether it is made of wood, cloth, hide or sackcloth. Put it in water; it will be unclean till evening, and then it will be clean.
33 If one of them falls into a clay pot, everything in it will be unclean, and you must break the pot.
34 Any food that could be eaten but has water on it from such a pot is unclean, and any liquid that could be drunk from it is unclean.
35 Anything that one of their carcasses falls on becomes unclean; an oven or cooking pot must be broken up. They are unclean, and you are to regard them as unclean.
36 A spring, however, or a cistern for collecting water remains clean, but anyone who touches one of these carcasses is unclean.
37 If a carcass falls on any seeds that are to be planted, they remain clean.
38 But if water has been put on the seed and a carcass falls on it, it is unclean for you.
39 " 'If an animal that you are allowed to eat dies, anyone who touches the carcass will be unclean till evening.
40 Anyone who eats some of the carcass must wash his clothes, and he will be unclean till evening. Anyone who picks up the carcass must wash his clothes, and he will be unclean till evening.
41 " 'Every creature that moves about on the ground is detestable; it is not to be eaten.
42 You are not to eat any creature that moves about on the ground, whether it moves on its belly or walks on all fours or on many feet; it is detestable.
43 Do not defile yourselves by any of these creatures. Do not make yourselves unclean by means of them or be made unclean by them.
44 I am the LORD your God; consecrate yourselves and be holy, because I am holy. Do not make yourselves unclean by any creature that moves about on the ground.
45 I am the LORD who brought you up out of Egypt to be your God; therefore be holy, because I am holy.
46 " 'These are the regulations concerning animals, birds, every living thing that moves in the water and every creature that moves about on the ground.
47 You must distinguish between the unclean

## King James

47 To make a difference between the unclean and the clean, and
between the beast that may be eaten and the beast that may not
be eaten.

12 AND THE LORD spake unto Moses, saying,
2 Speak unto the children of Israel, saying, If a woman
have conceived seed, and born a man child: then she shall be
unclean seven days; according to the days of the separation for her
infirmity shall she be unclean.
3 And in the eighth day the flesh of his foreskin shall be circumcised.
4 And she shall then continue in the blood of her purifying three
and thirty days; she shall touch no hallowed thing, nor come into
the sanctuary, until the days of her purifying be fulfilled.
5 But if she bear a maid child, then she shall be unclean two
weeks, as in her separation: and she shall continue in the blood of
her purifying threescore and six days.
6 And when the days of her purifying are fulfilled, for a son, or
for a daughter, she shall bring a lamb of the first year for a burnt
offering, and a young pigeon, or a turtledove, for a sin offering,
unto the door of the tabernacle of the congregation, unto the priest:
7 Who shall offer it before the LORD, and make an atonement for
her; and she shall be cleansed from the issue of her blood. This *is*
the law for her that hath born a male or a female.
8 And if she be not able to bring a lamb, then she shall bring two
turtles, or two young pigeons; the one for the burnt offering, and
the other for a sin offering: and the priest shall make an atonement
for her, and she shall be clean.

13 AND THE LORD spake unto Moses and Aaron, saying,
2 When a man shall have in the skin of his flesh a rising,
a scab, or bright spot, and it be in the skin of his flesh *like* the plague
of leprosy; then he shall be brought unto Aaron the priest, or unto
one of his sons the priests:
3 And the priest shall look on the plague in the skin of the flesh:
and *when* the hair in the plague is turned white, and the plague
in sight *be* deeper than the skin of his flesh, it *is* a plague of leprosy:
and the priest shall look on him, and pronounce him unclean.
4 If the bright spot *be* white in the skin of his flesh, and in sight
*be* not deeper than the skin, and the hair thereof be not turned
white; then the priest shall shut up *him that hath* the plague seven
days:
5 And the priest shall look on him the seventh day: and, behold,
*if* the plague in his sight be at a stay, *and* the plague spread not in
the skin; then the priest shall shut him up seven days more:
6 And the priest shall look on him again the seventh day: and,
behold, *if* the plague *be* somewhat dark, *and* the plague spread not
in the skin, the priest shall pronounce him clean: it *is but* a scab:
and he shall wash his clothes, and be clean.
7 But if the scab spread much abroad in the skin, after that he
hath been seen of the priest for his cleansing, he shall be seen of
the priest again:
8 And *if* the priest see that, behold, the scab spreadeth in the
skin, then the priest shall pronounce him unclean: it *is* a leprosy.

## Amplified

47 To make a difference [a distinction] between the unclean and
the clean, and between the animal that may be eaten and the
animal that may not be eaten.

12 AND THE Lord said to Moses,
2 Say to the Israelites, If a woman conceives, and bears a
male child, she shall be unclean seven days, unclean as during her
monthly discomfort.
3 And on the eighth day the child shall be circumcised.
4 Then she shall remain [separated] thirty-three days to be purified [from her loss] of blood; she shall touch no hallowed thing,
nor come into the [court of the] sanctuary until the days of her
purifying are over.
5 But if the child she bears is a girl, then she shall be unclean two
weeks, as in her periodic impurity, and she shall remain separated
sixty-six days to be purified [from her loss] of blood.
6 When the days of her purifying are completed, whether for a
son or for a daughter, she shall bring a lamb a year old for a burnt
offering, and a young pigeon or a turtledove for a sin offering, to
the door of the tent of meeting, to the priest;
7 And he shall offer it before the Lord, and make atonement for
her; and she shall be cleansed from the flow of her blood. This is
the law for her who has borne a male or a female child.
8 If she is unable to bring a lamb [for lack of means] then she
shall bring two turtledoves or young pigeons, one for a burnt
offering, the other for a sin offering; the priest shall make atonement for her, and she shall be clean. [Luke 2:22, 24.]

13 AND THE Lord said to Moses and Aaron,
2 When a man has a swelling on his skin, a scab or a bright
spot, and it becomes the disease of [a]leprosy in his skin, then he
shall be brought to the priest, to Aaron or one of his sons.
3 The priest shall look at the diseased spot on his skin, and if the
hair in it has turned white, and the disease appears depressed *and*
deeper than his skin, it is a leprous disease; and the priest shall
examine him, and pronounce him unclean.
4 If the bright spot is white on his skin, not depressed, and the
hair on it not turned white, the priest shall quarantine the person
*or* bind up the spot for seven days.
5 And the priest shall examine him on the seventh day, and if
the disease in his estimation is at a standstill *and* has not spread
in the skin, then the priest shall quarantine the person *or* bind up
the spot seven more days.
6 And the priest shall examine him again the seventh day, and
if the diseased part has a more normal color, and the disease has
not spread in the skin, the priest shall pronounce him clean; it is
only an eruption *or* a scab; and he shall wash his clothes and be
clean.
7 But if the eruption *or* scab spreads farther in the skin after he
has shown himself to the priest for his cleansing, he shall be seen
by the priest again.
8 If the priest sees the eruption *or* scab is spreading in the skin,
then *he* shall pronounce him unclean; it is leprosy.

**AMP** [a] Authorities are generally agreed that there was certainly true leprosy as it is known today in the Near East in New Testament times. But from the details of the disease in Lev. 13, it is believed that other very serious skin disorders were also included under the heading of *leprosy* in earlier times. *Leprosy* in the Old Testament, therefore, is not to be considered as confined to the traits by which it is known today, but rather defined by the symptoms, the treatment, and the history of individual cases as recorded in Leviticus and elsewhere. That it was worse than death is implied by the words of Aaron when his sister Miriam was stricken with it, "Oh, my lord [Moses], . . . let her not be as one dead, of whom the flesh is half consumed when he is born!" (Num. 12:12).

## New American Standard

47to make a distinction between the unclean and the clean, and
between the edible creature and the creature which is not to be
eaten.

*Laws of Motherhood*

**12** THEN THE LORD spoke to Moses, saying,
2"Speak to the sons of Israel, saying, 'When a woman gives
birth and bears a male *child,* then she shall be unclean for seven
days, as in the days of her menstruation she shall be unclean.
3'And on the eighth day the flesh of his foreskin shall be
circumcised.
4'Then she shall remain in the blood of *her* purification for
thirty-three days; she shall not touch any consecrated thing, nor
enter the sanctuary, until the days of her purification are completed.
5'But if she bears a female *child,* then she shall be unclean for
two weeks, as in her menstruation; and she shall remain in the
blood of *her* purification for sixty-six days.
6¶ 'And when the days of her purification are completed, for
a son or for a daughter, she shall bring to the priest at the doorway
of the tent of meeting, a one year old lamb for a burnt offering, and
a young pigeon or a turtledove for a sin offering.
7'Then he shall offer it before the LORD and make atonement
for her; and she shall be cleansed from the flow of her blood. This
is the law for her who bears *a child, whether* a male or a female.
8'But if she cannot afford a lamb, then she shall take two
turtledoves or two young pigeons, the one for a burnt offering and
the other for a sin offering; and the priest shall make atonement
for her, and she shall be clean.' "

*The Test for Leprosy*

**13** THEN THE LORD spoke to Moses and to Aaron, saying,
2"When a man has on the skin of his body a swelling or
a scab or a bright spot, and it becomes [b]an infection of leprosy on
the skin of his body, then he shall be brought to Aaron the priest,
or to one of his sons the priests.
3"And the priest shall look at the mark on the skin of the body,
and if the hair in the infection has turned white and the infection
appears to be deeper than the skin of his body, it is an infection
of leprosy; when the priest has looked at him, he shall pronounce
him unclean.
4"But if the bright spot is white on the skin of his body, and
it does not appear to be deeper than the skin, and the hair on it
has not turned white, then the priest shall isolate *him who has* the
infection for seven days.
5"And the priest shall look at him on the seventh day, and if
in his eyes the infection has not changed, *and* the infection has not
spread on the skin, then the priest shall isolate him for seven more
days.
6"And the priest shall look at him again on the seventh day;
and if the infection has faded, and the mark has not spread on the
skin, then the priest shall pronounce him clean; it is *only* a scab.
And he shall wash his clothes and be clean.
7¶ "But if the scab spreads farther on the skin, after he has
shown himself to the priest for his cleansing, he shall appear again
to the priest.
8"And the priest shall look, and if the scab has spread on the
skin, then the priest shall pronounce him unclean; it is leprosy.

**NAS** [b] Lit., *a mark, stroke,* and so throughout this context

## New International

and the clean, between living creatures that may be eaten and
those that may not be eaten.' "

*Purification After Childbirth*

**12** THE LORD said to Moses, 2"Say to the Israelites: 'A
woman who becomes pregnant and gives birth to a son
will be ceremonially unclean for seven days, just as she is unclean
during her monthly period. 3On the eighth day the boy is to be
circumcised. 4Then the woman must wait thirty-three days to be
purified from her bleeding. She must not touch anything sacred
or go to the sanctuary until the days of her purification are over.
5If she gives birth to a daughter, for two weeks the woman will be
unclean, as during her period. Then she must wait sixty-six days
to be purified from her bleeding.
6" 'When the days of her purification for a son or daughter are
over, she is to bring to the priest at the entrance to the Tent of
Meeting a year-old lamb for a burnt offering and a young pigeon
or a dove for a sin offering. 7He shall offer them before the LORD
to make atonement for her, and then she will be ceremonially clean
from her flow of blood.
" 'These are the regulations for the woman who gives birth to
a boy or a girl. 8If she cannot afford a lamb, she is to bring two
doves or two young pigeons, one for a burnt offering and the other
for a sin offering. In this way the priest will make atonement for
her, and she will be clean.' "

*Regulations About Infectious Skin Diseases*

**13** THE LORD said to Moses and Aaron, 2"When anyone has
a swelling or a rash or a bright spot on his skin that may
become an infectious skin disease,[c] he must be brought to Aaron
the priest or to one of his sons[d] who is a priest. 3The priest is to
examine the sore on his skin, and if the hair in the sore has turned
white and the sore appears to be more than skin deep,[e] it is an
infectious skin disease. When the priest examines him, he shall
pronounce him ceremonially unclean. 4If the spot on his skin is
white but does not appear to be more than skin deep and the hair
in it has not turned white, the priest is to put the infected person
in isolation for seven days. 5On the seventh day the priest is to
examine him, and if he sees that the sore is unchanged and has
not spread in the skin, he is to keep him in isolation another seven
days. 6On the seventh day the priest is to examine him again, and
if the sore has faded and has not spread in the skin, the priest shall
pronounce him clean; it is only a rash. The man must wash his
clothes, and he will be clean. 7But if the rash does spread in his
skin after he has shown himself to the priest to be pronounced
clean, he must appear before the priest again. 8The priest is to
examine him, and if the rash has spread in the skin, he shall
pronounce him unclean; it is an infectious disease.

**NIV** [c] 2 Traditionally *leprosy;* the Hebrew word was used for various diseases affecting the skin—not necessarily leprosy; also elsewhere in this chapter. [d] 2 Or *descendants* [e] 3 Or *be lower than the rest of the skin;* also elsewhere in this chapter

## King James

9¶ When the plague of leprosy is in a man, then he shall be brought unto the priest;

10And the priest shall see *him:* and, behold, *if* the rising *be* white in the skin, and it have turned the hair white, and *there be* quick raw flesh in the rising;

11It *is* an old leprosy in the skin of his flesh, and the priest shall pronounce him unclean, and shall not shut him up: for he *is* unclean.

12And if a leprosy break out abroad in the skin, and the leprosy cover all the skin of *him that hath* the plague from his head even to his foot, wheresoever the priest looketh;

13Then the priest shall consider: and, behold, *if* the leprosy have covered all his flesh, he shall pronounce *him* clean *that hath* the plague: it is all turned white: he *is* clean.

14But when raw flesh appeareth in him, he shall be unclean.

15And the priest shall see the raw flesh, and pronounce him to be unclean: *for* the raw flesh *is* unclean: it *is* a leprosy.

16Or if the raw flesh turn again, and be changed unto white, he shall come unto the priest;

17And the priest shall see him: and, behold, *if* the plague be turned into white; then the priest shall pronounce *him* clean *that hath* the plague: he *is* clean.

18¶ The flesh also, in which, *even* in the skin thereof, was a boil, and is healed,

19And in the place of the boil there be a white rising, or a bright spot, white, and somewhat reddish, and it be shown to the priest;

20And if, when the priest seeth it, behold, it *be* in sight lower than the skin, and the hair thereof be turned white; the priest shall pronounce him unclean: it *is* a plague of leprosy broken out of the boil.

21But if the priest look on it, and, behold, *there be* no white hairs therein, and *if* it *be* not lower than the skin, but *be* somewhat dark; then the priest shall shut him up seven days:

22And if it spread much abroad in the skin, then the priest shall pronounce him unclean: it *is* a plague.

23But if the bright spot stay in his place, *and* spread not, it *is* a burning boil; and the priest shall pronounce him clean.

24¶ Or if there be *any* flesh, in the skin whereof *there is* a hot burning, and the quick *flesh* that burneth have a white bright spot, somewhat reddish, or white;

25Then the priest shall look upon it: and, behold, *if* the hair in the bright spot be turned white, and it *be in* sight deeper than the skin; it *is* a leprosy broken out of the burning: wherefore the priest shall pronounce him unclean: it *is* the plague of leprosy.

26But if the priest look on it, and, behold, *there be* no white hair in the bright spot, and it *be* no lower than the *other* skin, but *be* somewhat dark; then the priest shall shut him up seven days:

27And the priest shall look upon him the seventh day: *and* if it be spread much abroad in the skin, then the priest shall pronounce him unclean: it *is* the plague of leprosy.

28And if the bright spot stay in his place, *and* spread not in the skin, but it *be* somewhat dark; it *is* a rising of the burning, and the priest shall pronounce him clean: for it *is* an inflammation of the burning.

29¶ If a man or woman have a plague upon the head or the beard;

30Then the priest shall see the plague: and, behold, if it *be* in sight deeper than the skin; *and there be* in it a yellow thin hair; then the priest shall pronounce him unclean: it *is* a dry scall, *even* a leprosy upon the head or beard.

31And if the priest look on the plague of the scall, and, behold, it *be* not in sight deeper than the skin, and *that there is* no black hair in it; then the priest shall shut up *him that hath* the plague of the scall seven days:

32And in the seventh day the priest shall look on the plague: and, behold, *if* the scall spread not, and there be in it no yellow hair, and the scall *be* not in sight deeper than the skin;

33He shall be shaven, but the scall shall he not shave; and the priest shall shut up *him that hath* the scall seven days more:

## Amplified

9When the disease of leprosy is in a man, he shall be brought to the priest;

10And the priest shall examine him, and if there is a white swelling in the skin, and the hair on it has turned white, and there is quick raw flesh in the swelling,

11It is a chronic leprosy in the skin of his body, and the priest shall pronounce him unclean; he shall not bind the spot up, for he is unclean.

12But if [supposed] leprosy breaks out in the skin, and *it* covers all the skin of him who has the disease from head to foot, wherever the priest looks,

13The priest shall examine him; if the [supposed] leprosy covers all his body, he shall pronounce him clean of the disease; it is all turned white; he is clean.

14But when the raw flesh appears on him, he shall be unclean.

15And the priest shall examine the raw flesh, and pronounce him unclean; for the raw flesh is unclean; it is leprosy.

16But if the raw flesh turns again, and becomes white, he shall come to the priest,

17And the priest shall examine him, and if the diseased part is turned to white again, then the priest shall pronounce him clean that had the disease; he is clean.

18And when there is in the skin of the body [the scar of] a boil that is healed,

19And in the place of the boil there is a white swelling or a bright spot, reddish white, and it is shown to the priest,

20And if when the priest examines it it looks lower than the skin, and the hair on it is turned white, the priest shall pronounce him unclean; it is the disease of leprosy; it has broken out in the boil.

21But if the priest examines it and finds no white hair in it, and it is not lower than the skin, but appears darker, then the priest shall bind it up for seven days.

22If it spreads in the skin, [he] shall pronounce him unclean; it is diseased.

23But if the bright spot does not spread, it is the scar of the boil, and the priest shall pronounce him clean.

24Or if there is any flesh in the skin of which there is a burn by fire, and the quick flesh of the burn becomes a bright spot, reddish white or white,

25Then the priest shall examine it, and if the hair in the bright spot is turned white, and it appears deeper than the skin, it is leprosy broken out in the burn. Therefore the priest shall pronounce him unclean; it is the disease of leprosy.

26But if the priest examines it, and there is no white hair in the bright spot, and it is not lower than the rest of the skin, but is darker, then the priest shall bind it up for seven days.

27And the priest shall examine him the seventh day; if it is spreading in the skin, then the priest shall pronounce him unclean; it is leprosy.

28But if the bright spot has not spread, but is darker, it is a swelling from the burn, and the priest shall pronounce him clean; for it is the scar of the burn.

29When a man or woman has a disease upon the head or in the beard,

30The priest shall examine the diseased place; if it appears to be deeper than the skin, with yellow thin hair in it, the priest shall pronounce him unclean; it is a mange-like leprosy of the head or beard.

31If the priest examines the spot infected by the mange-like disease, and it does not appear deeper than the skin, and there is no black hair in it, the priest shall bind up the spot for seven days.

32The seventh day the priest shall examine the diseased spot; if the mange has not spread, and has no yellow hair in it, and does not look deeper than the skin,

33Then the patient shall be shaved, except the mange-like spot; and the priest shall bind up the spot seven days more.

## New American Standard

9¶ "When the infection of leprosy is on a man, then he shall
be brought to the priest.
10"The priest shall then look, and if there is a white swelling in
the skin, and it has turned the hair white, and there is quick raw
flesh in the swelling,
11it is a chronic leprosy on the skin of his body, and the priest
shall pronounce him unclean; he shall not isolate him, for he is
unclean.
12"And if the leprosy breaks out farther on the skin, and the
leprosy covers all the skin of *him who has* the infection from his
head even to his feet, as far as the priest can see,
13then the priest shall look, and behold, *if* the leprosy has
covered all his body, he shall pronounce clean *him who has* the
infection; it has all turned white *and* he is clean.
14"But whenever raw flesh appears on him, he shall be unclean.
15"And the priest shall look at the raw flesh, and he shall
pronounce him unclean; the raw flesh is unclean, it is leprosy.
16"Or if the raw flesh turns again and is changed to white, then
he shall come to the priest,
17and the priest shall look at him, and behold, *if* the infection
has turned to white, then the priest shall pronounce clean *him who
has* the infection; he is clean.
**18¶** "And when the body has a boil on its skin, and it is healed,
19and in the place of the boil there is a white swelling or a
reddish-white, bright spot, then it shall be shown to the priest;
20and the priest shall look, and behold, *if* it appears to be lower
than the skin, and the hair on it has turned white, then the priest
shall pronounce him unclean; it is the infection of leprosy, it has
broken out in the boil.
21"But if the priest looks at it, and behold, there are no white
hairs in it and it is not lower than the skin and is faded, then the
priest shall isolate him for seven days;
22and if it spreads farther on the skin, then the priest shall
pronounce him unclean; it is an infection.
23"But if the bright spot remains in its place, and does not
spread, it is *only* the scar of the boil; and the priest shall pronounce
him clean.
**24¶** "Or if the body sustains in its skin a burn by fire, and the
raw *flesh* of the burn becomes a bright spot, reddish-white, or
white,
25then the priest shall look at it. And if the hair in the bright spot
has turned white, and it appears to be deeper than the skin, it is
leprosy; it has broken out in the burn. Therefore, the priest shall
pronounce him unclean; it is an infection of leprosy.
26"But if the priest looks at it, and indeed, there is no white hair
in the bright spot, and it is no deeper than the skin, but is dim,
then the priest shall isolate him for seven days;
27and the priest shall look at him on the seventh day. If it
spreads farther in the skin, then the priest shall pronounce him
unclean; it is an infection of leprosy.
28"But if the bright spot remains in its place, and has not spread
in the skin, but is dim, it is the swelling from the burn; and the
priest shall pronounce him clean, for it is *only* the scar of the burn.
**29¶** "Now if a man or woman has an infection on the head or
on the beard,
30then the priest shall look at the infection, and if it appears to
be deeper than the skin, and there is thin yellowish hair in it, then
the priest shall pronounce him unclean; it is a scale, it is leprosy
of the head or of the beard.
31"But if the priest looks at the infection of the scale, and indeed, it appears to be no deeper than the skin, and there is no black
hair in it, then the priest shall isolate *the person* with the scaly
infection for seven days.
32"And on the seventh day the priest shall look at the infection,
and if the scale has not spread, and no yellowish hair has grown
in it, and the appearance of the scale is no deeper than the skin,
33then he shall shave himself, but he shall not shave the scale;
and the priest shall isolate *the person* with the scale seven more
days.

## New International

9"When anyone has an infectious skin disease, he must be
brought to the priest. 10The priest is to examine him, and if there
is a white swelling in the skin that has turned the hair white and
if there is raw flesh in the swelling, 11it is a chronic skin disease
and the priest shall pronounce him unclean. He is not to put him
in isolation, because he is already unclean.
12"If the disease breaks out all over his skin and, so far as the
priest can see, it covers all the skin of the infected person from
head to foot, 13the priest is to examine him, and if the disease has
covered his whole body, he shall pronounce that person clean.
Since it has all turned white, he is clean. 14But whenever raw flesh
appears on him, he will be unclean. 15When the priest sees the raw
flesh, he shall pronounce him unclean. The raw flesh is unclean;
he has an infectious disease. 16Should the raw flesh change and
turn white, he must go to the priest. 17The priest is to examine him,
and if the sores have turned white, the priest shall pronounce the
infected person clean; then he will be clean.
18"When someone has a boil on his skin and it heals, 19and in
the place where the boil was, a white swelling or reddish-white
spot appears, he must present himself to the priest. 20The priest
is to examine it, and if it appears to be more than skin deep and
the hair in it has turned white, the priest shall pronounce him
unclean. It is an infectious skin disease that has broken out where
the boil was. 21But if, when the priest examines it, there is no white
hair in it and it is not more than skin deep and has faded, then the
priest is to put him in isolation for seven days. 22If it is spreading
in the skin, the priest shall pronounce him unclean; it is infectious.
23But if the spot is unchanged and has not spread, it is only a scar
from the boil, and the priest shall pronounce him clean.
24"When someone has a burn on his skin and a reddish-white
or white spot appears in the raw flesh of the burn, 25the priest is
to examine the spot, and if the hair in it has turned white, and it
appears to be more than skin deep, it is an infectious disease that
has broken out in the burn. The priest shall pronounce him unclean; it is an infectious skin disease. 26But if the priest examines
it and there is no white hair in the spot and if it is not more than
skin deep and has faded, then the priest is to put him in isolation
for seven days. 27On the seventh day the priest is to examine him,
and if it is spreading in the skin, the priest shall pronounce him
unclean; it is an infectious skin disease. 28If, however, the spot is
unchanged and has not spread in the skin but has faded, it is a
swelling from the burn, and the priest shall pronounce him clean;
it is only a scar from the burn.
29"If a man or woman has a sore on the head or on the chin,
30the priest is to examine the sore, and if it appears to be more than
skin deep and the hair in it is yellow and thin, the priest shall
pronounce that person unclean; it is an itch, an infectious disease
of the head or chin. 31But if, when the priest examines this kind
of sore, it does not seem to be more than skin deep and there is
no black hair in it, then the priest is to put the infected person in
isolation for seven days. 32On the seventh day the priest is to
examine the sore, and if the itch has not spread and there is no
yellow hair in it and it does not appear to be more than skin deep,
33he must be shaved except for the diseased area, and the priest
is to keep him in isolation another seven days. 34On the seventh

## King James

34And in the seventh day the priest shall look on the scall: and, behold, *if* the scall be not spread in the skin, nor *be* in sight deeper than the skin; then the priest shall pronounce him clean: and he shall wash his clothes, and be clean.

35But if the scall spread much in the skin after his cleansing;

36Then the priest shall look on him: and, behold, if the scall be spread in the skin, the priest shall not seek for yellow hair; he *is* unclean.

37But if the scall be in his sight at a stay, and *that* there is black hair grown up therein; the scall is healed, he *is* clean: and the priest shall pronounce him clean.

38¶ If a man also or a woman have in the skin of their flesh bright spots, *even* white bright spots;

39Then the priest shall look: and, behold, *if* the bright spots in the skin of their flesh *be* darkish white; it *is* a freckled spot *that* groweth in the skin; he *is* clean.

40And the man whose hair is fallen off his head, he *is* bald; *yet is* he clean.

41And he that hath his hair fallen off from the part of his head toward his face, he *is* forehead bald: *yet is* he clean.

42And if there be in the bald head, or bald forehead, a white reddish sore; it *is* a leprosy sprung up in his bald head, or his bald forehead.

43Then the priest shall look upon it: and, behold, *if* the rising of the sore *be* white reddish in his bald head, or in his bald forehead, as the leprosy appeareth in the skin of the flesh;

44He is a leprous man, he *is* unclean: the priest shall pronounce him utterly unclean; his plague *is* in his head.

45And the leper in whom the plague *is*, his clothes shall be rent, and his head bare, and he shall put a covering upon his upper lip, and shall cry, Unclean, unclean.

46All the days wherein the plague *shall be* in him he shall be defiled; he *is* unclean: he shall dwell alone; without the camp *shall* his habitation *be*.

47¶ The garment also that the plague of leprosy is in, *whether it be* a woollen garment, or a linen garment;

48Whether *it be* in the warp, or woof; of linen, or of woollen; whether in a skin, or in any thing made of skin;

49And if the plague be greenish or reddish in the garment, or in the skin, either in the warp, or in the woof, or in any thing of skin; it *is* a plague of leprosy, and shall be shown unto the priest:

50And the priest shall look upon the plague, and shut up *it that hath* the plague seven days:

51And he shall look on the plague on the seventh day: if the plague be spread in the garment, either in the warp, or in the woof, or in a skin, *or* in any work that is made of skin; the plague *is* a fretting leprosy; it *is* unclean.

52He shall therefore burn that garment, whether warp or woof, in woollen or in linen, or any thing of skin, wherein the plague is: for it *is* a fretting leprosy; it shall be burnt in the fire.

53And if the priest shall look, and, behold, the plague be not spread in the garment, either in the warp, or in the woof, or in any thing of skin;

54Then the priest shall command that they wash *the thing* wherein the plague *is*, and he shall shut it up seven days more:

55And the priest shall look on the plague, after that it is washed: and, behold, *if* the plague have not changed his colour, and the plague be not spread; it *is* unclean; thou shalt burn it in the fire; it *is* fret inward, *whether* it *be* bare within or without.

56And if the priest look, and, behold, the plague *be* somewhat dark after the washing of it; then he shall rend it out of the garment, or out of the skin, or out of the warp, or out of the woof:

57And if it appear still in the garment, either in the warp, or in the woof, or in any thing of skin; it *is* a spreading *plague:* thou shalt burn that wherein the plague *is* with fire.

58And the garment, either warp, or woof, or whatsoever thing of skin *it be*, which thou shalt wash, if the plague be departed from them, then it shall be washed the second time, and shall be clean.

## Amplified

34The seventh day the priest shall look at the mange-like spot; if the mange has not spread and looks no deeper than the skin, he shall pronounce the patient clean; he shall wash his clothes, and be clean.

35But if the mange-like spot spreads in the skin after his cleansing,

36Then the priest shall examine him, and if the mange-like spot is spread in the skin, the priest need not look for the yellow hair; the patient is unclean.

37But if in his estimation the mange is at a standstill, and has black hair in it, the mange-like disease is healed; he is clean; the priest shall pronounce him clean.

38When a man or a woman has on the skin bright spots, even white bright spots,

39Then the priest shall look, and if the bright spots in the skin are a dull white, it is a harmless eruption; he is clean.

40If a man's hair has fallen from his head, he is bald, but he is clean.

41And if his hair has fallen out from the front of his head, he has baldness of the forehead, but he is clean.

42But if there is on the bald head or forehead a reddish-white diseased spot, it is leprosy breaking out on his baldness.

43Then the priest shall examine him, and if the diseased swelling is reddish-white on his bald head or forehead, like the appearance of leprosy in the skin of the body,

44He is a leprous man; he is unclean; the priest shall surely pronounce him unclean; his disease is on his head.

45And the leper's clothes shall be rent, and the hair of his head shall hang loose, and he shall cover his upper lip and cry, Unclean, unclean!

46He shall remain unclean as long as the disease is in him; he is unclean; he shall live alone, his dwelling outside the camp.

47The garment also that the disease of leprosy [symbolic of sin] is in, whether a wool or a linen garment, [Cp. Jude 23; Rev. 3:4.]

48Whether it be in woven or knitted stuff *or* in the warp or woof of linen or of wool, or in a skin or anything made of skin,

49If the disease is greenish or reddish in the garment, or in the skin or in the warp or woof or in anything of skin, it is the plague of leprosy; show it to the priest.

50The priest shall examine the diseased article, and shut it up for seven days.

51He shall examine the disease on the seventh day; if [it] is spread in the garment, or in the article, whatever service it may be used for, the disease is a rotting *or* corroding leprosy; it is unclean.

52He shall burn the garment, whether diseased in warp or woof, in wool or linen, or anything of skin; for it is a rotting *or* corroding leprosy, to be burned in the fire.

53But if the priest finds the disease has not spread in the garment, in the warp or the woof, or in anything of skin,

54Then the priest shall command that they wash the thing in which the plague is, and he shall shut it up seven days more.

55And the priest shall examine the diseased article after it has been washed, and if the diseased portion has not changed color, though the disease has not spread, it is unclean; you shall burn it in the fire; it is a rotting *or* corroding, whether the leprous spot be inside or outside.

56If the priest looks and the diseased portion is less noticeable after it is washed, he shall tear it out of the garment or the skin, or out of the warp or woof;

57If it appears still in the garment, either in the warp, or in the woof, or in anything of skin, it is spreading; you shall burn the diseased part with fire.

58But the garment, woven or knitted stuff *or* warp or woof or anything of skin from which the disease departs when you have washed it, shall then be washed a second time, and be clean.

## New American Standard

34 "Then on the seventh day the priest shall look at the scale, and if the scale has not spread in the skin, and it appears to be no deeper than the skin, the priest shall pronounce him clean; and he shall wash his clothes and be clean.

35 "But if the scale spreads farther in the skin after his cleansing,

36 then the priest shall look at him, and if the scale has spread in the skin, the priest need not seek for the yellowish hair; he is unclean.

37 "If in his sight the scale has remained, however, and black hair has grown in it, the scale has healed, he is clean; and the priest shall pronounce him clean.

**38**¶ "And when a man or a woman has bright spots on the skin of the body, *even* white bright spots,

39 then the priest shall look, and if the bright spots on the skin of their bodies are a faint white, it is eczema that has broken out on the skin; he is clean.

**40**¶ "Now if a man loses the hair of his head, he is bald; he is clean.

41 "And if his head becomes bald at the front and sides, he is bald on the forehead; he is clean.

42 "But if on the bald head or the bald forehead, there occurs a reddish-white infection, it is leprosy breaking out on his bald head or on his bald forehead.

43 "Then the priest shall look at him; and if the swelling of the infection is reddish-white on his bald head or on his bald forehead, like the appearance of leprosy in the skin of the body,

44 he is a leprous man, he is unclean. The priest shall surely pronounce him unclean; his infection is on his head.

**45**¶ "As for the leper who has the infection, his clothes shall be torn, and the hair of his head shall be uncovered, and he shall cover his mustache and cry, 'Unclean! Unclean!'

46 "He shall remain unclean all the days during which he has the infection; he is unclean. He shall live alone; his dwelling shall be outside the camp.

47 "When a garment has a mark of leprosy in it, whether it is a wool garment or a linen garment,

48 whether in warp or woof, of linen or of wool, whether in leather or in any article made of leather,

49 if the mark is greenish or reddish in the garment or in the leather, or in the warp or in the woof, or in any article of leather, it is a leprous mark and shall be shown to the priest.

50 "Then the priest shall look at the mark, and shall quarantine the article with the mark for seven days.

51 "He shall then look at the mark on the seventh day; if the mark has spread in the garment, whether in the warp or in the woof, or in the leather, whatever the purpose for which the leather is used, the mark is a leprous malignancy, it is unclean.

52 "So he shall burn the garment, whether the warp or the woof, in wool or in linen, or any article of leather in which the mark occurs, for it is a leprous malignancy; it shall be burned in the fire.

**53**¶ "But if the priest shall look, and indeed, the mark has not spread in the garment, either in the warp or in the woof, or in any article of leather,

54 then the priest shall order them to wash the thing in which the mark occurs, and he shall quarantine it for seven more days.

55 "After the article with the mark has been washed, the priest shall again look, and if the mark has not changed its appearance, even though the mark has not spread, it is unclean; you shall burn it in the fire, whether an eating away has produced bareness on the top or on the front of it.

**56**¶ "Then if the priest shall look, and if the mark has faded after it has been washed, then he shall tear it out of the garment or out of the leather, whether from the warp or from the woof;

57 and if it appears again in the garment, whether in the warp or in the woof, or in any article of leather, it is an outbreak; the article with the mark shall be burned in the fire.

58 "And the garment, whether the warp or the woof, or any article of leather from which the mark has departed when you washed it, it shall then be washed a second time and shall be clean."

## New International

day the priest is to examine the itch, and if it has not spread in the
skin and appears to be no more than skin deep, the priest shall
pronounce him clean. He must wash his clothes, and he will be
clean. 35 But if the itch does spread in the skin after he is pronounced clean, 36 the priest is to examine him, and if the itch has
spread in the skin, the priest does not need to look for yellow hair;
the person is unclean. 37 If, however, in his judgment it is unchanged and black hair has grown in it, the itch is healed. He is
clean, and the priest shall pronounce him clean.

38 "When a man or woman has white spots on the skin, 39 the
priest is to examine them, and if the spots are dull white, it is a
harmless rash that has broken out on the skin; that person is clean.

40 "When a man has lost his hair and is bald, he is clean. 41 If he
has lost his hair from the front of his scalp and has a bald forehead,
he is clean. 42 But if he has a reddish-white sore on his bald head
or forehead, it is an infectious disease breaking out on his head or
forehead. 43 The priest is to examine him, and if the swollen sore
on his head or forehead is reddish-white like an infectious skin
disease, 44 the man is diseased and is unclean. The priest shall
pronounce him unclean because of the sore on his head.

45 "The person with such an infectious disease must wear torn
clothes, let his hair be unkempt,[a] cover the lower part of his face
and cry out, 'Unclean! Unclean!' 46 As long as he has the infection
he remains unclean. He must live alone; he must live outside the
camp.

*Regulations About Mildew*

47 "If any clothing is contaminated with mildew—any woolen or
linen clothing, 48 any woven or knitted material of linen or wool,
any leather or anything made of leather— 49 and if the contamination in the clothing, or leather, or woven or knitted material, or any
leather article, is greenish or reddish, it is a spreading mildew and
must be shown to the priest. 50 The priest is to examine the mildew
and isolate the affected article for seven days. 51 On the seventh
day he is to examine it, and if the mildew has spread in the
clothing, or the woven or knitted material, or the leather, whatever
its use, it is a destructive mildew; the article is unclean. 52 He must
burn up the clothing, or the woven or knitted material of wool or
linen, or any leather article that has the contamination in it, because the mildew is destructive; the article must be burned up.

53 "But if, when the priest examines it, the mildew has not
spread in the clothing, or the woven or knitted material, or the
leather article, 54 he shall order that the contaminated article be
washed. Then he is to isolate it for another seven days. 55 After the
affected article has been washed, the priest is to examine it, and
if the mildew has not changed its appearance, even though it has
not spread, it is unclean. Burn it with fire, whether the mildew has
affected one side or the other. 56 If, when the priest examines it, the
mildew has faded after the article has been washed, he is to tear
the contaminated part out of the clothing, or the leather, or the
woven or knitted material. 57 But if it reappears in the clothing, or
in the woven or knitted material, or in the leather article, it is
spreading, and whatever has the mildew must be burned with fire.
58 The clothing, or the woven or knitted material, or any leather
article that has been washed and is rid of the mildew, must be
washed again, and it will be clean."

**NIV** [a] 45 Or *clothes, uncover his head*

## King James

59 This *is* the law of the plague of leprosy in a garment of woollen or linen, either in the warp, or woof, or any thing of skins, to pronounce it clean, or to pronounce it unclean.

14 AND THE LORD spake unto Moses, saying,

2 This shall be the law of the leper in the day of his cleansing: He shall be brought unto the priest:

3 And the priest shall go forth out of the camp; and the priest shall look, and, behold, *if* the plague of leprosy be healed in the leper;

4 Then shall the priest command to take for him that is to be cleansed two birds alive *and* clean, and cedar wood, and scarlet, and hyssop:

5 And the priest shall command that one of the birds be killed in an earthen vessel over running water:

6 As for the living bird, he shall take it, and the cedar wood, and the scarlet, and the hyssop, and shall dip them and the living bird in the blood of the bird *that was* killed over the running water:

7 And he shall sprinkle upon him that is to be cleansed from the leprosy seven times, and shall pronounce him clean, and shall let the living bird loose into the open field.

8 And he that is to be cleansed shall wash his clothes, and shave off all his hair, and wash himself in water, that he may be clean: and after that he shall come into the camp, and shall tarry abroad out of his tent seven days.

9 But it shall be on the seventh day, that he shall shave all his hair off his head and his beard and his eyebrows, even all his hair he shall shave off: and he shall wash his clothes, also he shall wash his flesh in water, and he shall be clean.

10 And on the eighth day he shall take two he lambs without blemish, and one ewe lamb of the first year without blemish, and three tenth deals of fine flour *for* a meat offering, mingled with oil, and one log of oil.

11 And the priest that maketh *him* clean shall present the man that is to be made clean, and those things, before the LORD, *at* the door of the tabernacle of the congregation:

12 And the priest shall take one he lamb, and offer him for a trespass offering, and the log of oil, and wave them *for* a wave offering before the LORD:

13 And he shall slay the lamb in the place where he shall kill the sin offering and the burnt offering, in the holy place: for as the sin offering *is* the priest's, *so is* the trespass offering: it *is* most holy:

14 And the priest shall take *some* of the blood of the trespass offering, and the priest shall put *it* upon the tip of the right ear of him that is to be cleansed, and upon the thumb of his right hand, and upon the great toe of his right foot:

15 And the priest shall take *some* of the log of oil, and pour *it* into the palm of his own left hand:

16 And the priest shall dip his right finger in the oil that *is* in his left hand, and shall sprinkle of the oil with his finger seven times before the LORD:

17 And of the rest of the oil that *is* in his hand shall the priest put upon the tip of the right ear of him that is to be cleansed, and upon the thumb of his right hand, and upon the great toe of his right foot, upon the blood of the trespass offering:

18 And the remnant of the oil that *is* in the priest's hand he shall pour upon the head of him that is to be cleansed: and the priest shall make an atonement for him before the LORD.

19 And the priest shall offer the sin offering, and make an atonement for him that is to be cleansed from his uncleanness; and afterward he shall kill the burnt offering:

## Amplified

59 This is the law for a leprous disease in a garment of wool or linen, either in the warp or woof, or in anything of skin, to pronounce it clean or unclean.

14 AND THE Lord said to Moses,

2 This shall be the law of the leper on the day when he is to be pronounced clean: he shall be brought to the priest [at a meeting place outside the camp];

3 The priest shall go out of the camp [to meet him]; and [he] shall examine him, and if the disease is healed in the leper,

4 Then the priest shall command to take for him who is to be cleansed two living clean birds and cedar wood and scarlet [material] and hyssop. [Heb. 9:19-22.]

5 And the priest shall command to kill one of the birds in an earthen vessel over fresh, running water.

6 As for the living bird, he shall take it, the cedar wood, and the scarlet [material] and the hyssop, and shall dip them and the living bird in the blood of the bird killed over the running water;

7 And he shall sprinkle [the blood] on him who is to be cleansed from the leprosy seven times, and shall pronounce him clean, and shall let go the living bird into the open field. [Heb. 9:13-15.]

8 He who is to be cleansed shall wash his clothes, shave off all his hair, and bathe himself in water; and he shall be clean. After that he shall come into the camp, but stay outside his tent seven days.

9 But the seventh day he shall shave all his hair off his head, his beard, his eyebrows, and his [body]; and he shall wash his clothes, also bathe his body in water, and be clean.

10 The eighth day he shall take two he-lambs without blemish, and one ewe lamb a year old without blemish, and three-tenths of an ephah of fine flour for a cereal offering, mixed with oil, and one log of oil.

11 And the priest who cleanses him shall set the man who is to be cleansed and these things before the Lord, at the door of the tent of meeting;

12 The priest shall take one of the male lambs and offer it for a guilt *or* trespass offering, and the log of oil, and wave them for a wave offering before the Lord;

13 He shall kill the lamb in the place where they kill the sin offering and the burnt offering, in the sacred place [the court of the tabernacle]; for as the sin offering is the priest's, so is the guilt *or* trespass offering; it is most holy;

14 And the priest shall take some of the blood of the guilt *or* trespass offering, and put it on the tip of the right ear of him who is to be cleansed, and on the thumb of his right hand, and on the great toe of his right foot.

15 And the priest shall take some of the log of oil, and pour it into the palm of his own left hand,

16 And the priest shall dip his right finger in the oil that is in his left hand, and shall sprinkle of the oil with his finger seven times before the Lord;

17 And of the rest of the oil that is in his hand shall the priest put some on the tip of the right ear of him who is to be cleansed, and on the thumb of his right hand, and on the great toe of his right foot, on the blood of the guilt *or* trespass offering [which he has previously placed in each of these places].

18 And the rest of the oil that is in the priest's hand he shall pour upon the head of him who is to be cleansed, and make atonement for him before the Lord.

19 And the priest shall offer the sin offering, and make atonement for him who is to be cleansed from his uncleanness, and afterward kill the burnt offering [victim].

## New American Standard

59¶ This is the law for the mark of leprosy in a garment of wool or linen, whether in the warp or in the woof, or in any article of leather, for pronouncing it clean or unclean.

*Law of Cleansing a Leper*

**14** THEN THE LORD spoke to Moses, saying,
2"This shall be the law of the leper in the day of his cleansing. Now he shall be brought to the priest,

3and the priest shall go out to the outside of the camp. Thus the priest shall look, and if the infection of leprosy has been healed in the leper,

4then the priest shall give orders to take two live clean birds and cedar wood and a scarlet string and hyssop for the one who is to be cleansed.

5"The priest shall also give orders to slay the one bird in an earthenware vessel over running water.

6"*As for* the live bird, he shall take it, together with the cedar wood and the scarlet string and the hyssop, and shall dip them and the live bird in the blood of the bird that was slain over the running water.

7"He shall then sprinkle seven times the one who is to be cleansed from the leprosy, and shall pronounce him clean, and shall let the live bird go free over the open field.

8"The one to be cleansed shall then wash his clothes and shave off all his hair, and bathe in water and be clean. Now afterward, he may enter the camp, but he shall stay outside his tent for seven days.

9"And it will be on the seventh day that he shall shave off all his hair: he shall shave his head and his beard and his eyebrows, even all his hair. He shall then wash his clothes and bathe his body in water and be clean.

10¶ "Now on the eighth day he is to take two male lambs without defect, and a yearling ewe lamb without defect, and three-tenths *of an ephah* of fine flour mixed with oil for a grain offering, and one [a]log of oil;

11and the priest who pronounces him clean shall present the man to be cleansed and the aforesaid before the LORD at the doorway of the tent of meeting.

12"Then the priest shall take the one male lamb and bring it for a guilt offering, with the log of oil, and present them as a wave offering before the LORD.

13"Next he shall slaughter the male lamb in the place where they slaughter the sin offering and the burnt offering, at the place of the sanctuary—for the guilt offering, like the sin offering, belongs to the priest; it is most holy.

14"The priest shall then take some of the blood of the guilt offering, and the priest shall put *it* on the lobe of the right ear of the one to be cleansed, and on the thumb of his right hand, and on the big toe of his right foot.

15"The priest shall also take some of the log of oil, and pour *it* into his left palm;

16the priest shall then dip his right-hand finger into the oil that is in his left palm, and with his finger sprinkle some of the oil seven times before the LORD.

17"And of the remaining oil which is in his palm, the priest shall put some on the right ear lobe of the one to be cleansed, and on the thumb of his right hand, and on the big toe of his right foot, on the blood of the guilt offering;

18while the rest of the oil that is in the priest's palm, he shall put on the head of the one to be cleansed. So the priest shall make atonement on his behalf before the LORD.

19"The priest shall next offer the sin offering and make atonement for the one to be cleansed from his uncleanness. Then afterward, he shall slaughter the burnt offering.

NAS [a] I.e., Approx. one pint, and so through v. 24

## New International

59These are the regulations concerning contamination by mildew in woolen or linen clothing, woven or knitted material, or any
leather article, for pronouncing them clean or unclean.

*Cleansing From Infectious Skin Diseases*

**14** THE LORD said to Moses, 2"These are the regulations for
the diseased person at the time of his ceremonial cleansing, when he is brought to the priest: 3The priest is to go outside
the camp and examine him. If the person has been healed of his
infectious skin disease,[b] 4the priest shall order that two live clean
birds and some cedar wood, scarlet yarn and hyssop be brought
for the one to be cleansed. 5Then the priest shall order that one of
the birds be killed over fresh water in a clay pot. 6He is then to take
the live bird and dip it, together with the cedar wood, the scarlet
yarn and the hyssop, into the blood of the bird that was killed over
the fresh water. 7Seven times he shall sprinkle the one to be
cleansed of the infectious disease and pronounce him clean. Then
he is to release the live bird in the open fields.
8"The person to be cleansed must wash his clothes, shave off
all his hair and bathe with water; then he will be ceremonially
clean. After this he may come into the camp, but he must stay
outside his tent for seven days. 9On the seventh day he must shave
off all his hair; he must shave his head, his beard, his eyebrows
and the rest of his hair. He must wash his clothes and bathe
himself with water, and he will be clean.
10"On the eighth day he must bring two male lambs and one
ewe lamb a year old, each without defect, along with three-tenths
of an ephah[c] of fine flour mixed with oil for a grain offering, and
one log[d] of oil. 11The priest who pronounces him clean shall
present both the one to be cleansed and his offerings before the
LORD at the entrance to the Tent of Meeting.
12"Then the priest is to take one of the male lambs and offer it
as a guilt offering, along with the log of oil; he shall wave them
before the LORD as a wave offering. 13He is to slaughter the lamb
in the holy place where the sin offering and the burnt offering are
slaughtered. Like the sin offering, the guilt offering belongs to the
priest; it is most holy. 14The priest is to take some of the blood of
the guilt offering and put it on the lobe of the right ear of the one
to be cleansed, on the thumb of his right hand and on the big toe
of his right foot. 15The priest shall then take some of the log of oil,
pour it in the palm of his own left hand, 16dip his right forefinger
into the oil in his palm, and with his finger sprinkle some of it
before the LORD seven times. 17The priest is to put some of the oil
remaining in his palm on the lobe of the right ear of the one to be
cleansed, on the thumb of his right hand and on the big toe of his
right foot, on top of the blood of the guilt offering. 18The rest of
the oil in his palm the priest shall put on the head of the one to
be cleansed and make atonement for him before the LORD.
19"Then the priest is to sacrifice the sin offering and make
atonement for the one to be cleansed from his uncleanness. After
that, the priest shall slaughter the burnt offering 20and offer it on

NIV [b] 3 Traditionally *leprosy;* the Hebrew word was used for various diseases affecting the skin—not necessarily leprosy; also elsewhere in this chapter. [c] *10* That is, probably about 6 quarts (about 6.5 liters) [d] *10* That is, probably about 2/3 pint (about 0.3 liter); also in verses 12, 15, 21 and 24

## King James

20And the priest shall offer the burnt offering and the meat
offering upon the altar: and the priest shall make an atonement for
him, and he shall be clean.
21And if he *be* poor, and cannot get so much; then he shall take
one lamb *for* a trespass offering to be waved, to make an atonement
for him, and one tenth deal of fine flour mingled with oil for a meat
offering, and a log of oil;
22And two turtledoves, or two young pigeons, such as he is able
to get; and the one shall be a sin offering, and the other a burnt
offering.
23And he shall bring them on the eighth day for his cleansing
unto the priest, unto the door of the tabernacle of the congregation, before the LORD.
24And the priest shall take the lamb of the trespass offering, and
the log of oil, and the priest shall wave them *for* a wave offering
before the LORD:
25And he shall kill the lamb of the trespass offering, and the
priest shall take *some* of the blood of the trespass offering, and put
*it* upon the tip of the right ear of him that is to be cleansed, and
upon the thumb of his right hand, and upon the great toe of his
right foot:
26And the priest shall pour of the oil into the palm of his own
left hand:
27And the priest shall sprinkle with his right finger *some* of the
oil that *is* in his left hand seven times before the LORD:
28And the priest shall put of the oil that *is* in his hand upon the
tip of the right ear of him that is to be cleansed, and upon the
thumb of his right hand, and upon the great toe of his right foot,
upon the place of the blood of the trespass offering:
29And the rest of the oil that *is* in the priest's hand he shall put
upon the head of him that is to be cleansed, to make an atonement
for him before the LORD.
30And he shall offer the one of the turtledoves, or of the young
pigeons, such as he can get;
31 *Even* such as he is able to get, the one *for* a sin offering, and
the other *for* a burnt offering, with the meat offering: and the priest
shall make an atonement for him that is to be cleansed before the
LORD.
32This *is* the law *of him* in whom *is* the plague of leprosy, whose
hand is not able to get *that which pertaineth* to his cleansing.
33¶ And the LORD spake unto Moses and unto Aaron, saying,
34When ye be come into the land of Canaan, which I give to you
for a possession, and I put the plague of leprosy in a house of the
land of your possession;
35And he that owneth the house shall come and tell the priest,
saying, It seemeth to me *there is* as it were a plague in the house:
36Then the priest shall command that they empty the house,
before the priest go *into it* to see the plague, that all that *is* in the
house be not made unclean: and afterward the priest shall go in
to see the house:
37And he shall look on the plague, and, behold, *if* the plague
*be* in the walls of the house with hollow strakes, greenish or reddish, which in sight *are* lower than the wall;
38Then the priest shall go out of the house to the door of the
house, and shut up the house seven days:
39And the priest shall come again the seventh day, and shall
look: and, behold, *if* the plague be spread in the walls of the house;
40Then the priest shall command that they take away the stones
in which the plague *is*, and they shall cast them into an unclean
place without the city:
41And he shall cause the house to be scraped within round
about, and they shall pour out the dust that they scrape off without
the city into an unclean place:
42And they shall take other stones, and put *them* in the place
of those stones; and he shall take other mortar, and shall plaster
the house.
43And if the plague come again, and break out in the house,
after that he hath taken away the stones, and after he hath scraped
the house, and after it is plastered;

## Amplified

20And the priest shall offer the burnt offering and the cereal
offering on the altar; and *he* shall make atonement for him, and he
shall be clean.
21If the cleansed leper is poor and cannot afford so much, he
shall take one lamb for a guilt *or* trespass offering to be waved, to
make atonement for him, and one tenth of an ephah of fine flour
mixed with oil for a cereal offering, and a log of oil,
22And two turtledoves or two young pigeons, such as he can
afford, one for a sin offering, the other for a burnt offering.
23He shall bring them on the eighth day for his cleansing to the
priest, at the door of the tent of meeting, before the Lord.
24And the priest shall take the lamb of the guilt *or* trespass
offering, and the log of oil, and shall wave them for a wave offering
before the Lord.
25And he shall kill the lamb of the guilt *or* trespass offering, and
the priest shall take some of the blood of the offering, and put it
on the tip of the right ear of him who is to be cleansed, and on the
thumb of his right hand, and on the great toe of his right foot.
26And the priest shall pour of the oil into the palm of his own
left hand,
27And shall sprinkle with his right finger some of the oil that
is in his left hand seven times before the Lord;
28The priest shall put of the oil in his hand on the tip of the right
ear of the one to be cleansed, and on the thumb of his right hand,
and on the great toe of his right foot, on the places where he has
put the blood of the guilt offering.
29The rest of the oil that is in the priest's hand he shall put on
the head of the one to be cleansed, to make atonement for him
before the Lord.
30And he shall offer one of the turtledoves or of the young
pigeons, such as he is able to get,
31As he can afford, one for a sin offering and the other for a
burnt offering, with the cereal offering; and the priest shall make
atonement for him who is to be cleansed before the Lord.
32This is the law of him in whom is the plague of leprosy, who
is not able to get what is required for his cleansing.
33And the Lord said to Moses and Aaron,
34When you have come into the land of Canaan, which I give
to you for a possession, and I put the disease of leprosy in a house
of the land of your possession,
35Then he who owns the house shall come and tell the priest,
It seems to me there is some sort of disease in my house.
36Then the priest shall command that they empty the house
before [he] goes in to examine the disease, so that all that is in the
house may not be declared unclean; afterward [he] shall go in to
see the house.
37He shall examine the disease, and if it is in the walls of the
house with depressed spots of dark green or dark red appearing
beneath [the surface of] the wall,
38Then the priest shall go out of the door, and shut up the house
seven days.
39The priest shall come again the seventh day, and shall look;
and if the disease has spread in the walls of the house,
40He shall command that they take out the diseased stones and
cast them into an unclean place outside the city.
41He shall cause the house to be scraped within round about,
and the plaster *or* mortar that is scraped off to be emptied out in
an unclean place outside the city.
42And they shall put other stones in the place of those stones,
and he shall plaster the house with fresh mortar.
43If the disease returns, breaking out in the house after he has
removed the stones and has scraped and plastered the house,

## New American Standard

20"And the priest shall offer up the burnt offering and the grain
offering on the altar. Thus the priest shall make atonement for him,
and he shall be clean.
**21**¶ "But if he is poor, and his means are insufficient, then he
is to take one male lamb for a guilt offering as a wave offering to
make atonement for him, and one-tenth *of an ephah* of fine flour
mixed with oil for a grain offering, and a log of oil,
22and two turtledoves or two young pigeons which are within
his means, the one shall be a sin offering and the other a burnt
offering.
23"Then the eighth day he shall bring them for his cleansing to
the priest, at the doorway of the tent of meeting, before the LORD.
24"And the priest shall take the lamb of the guilt offering, and
the log of oil, and the priest shall offer them for a wave offering
before the LORD.
25"Next he shall slaughter the lamb of the guilt offering; and the
priest is to take some of the blood of the guilt offering and put *it*
on the lobe of the right ear of the one to be cleansed and on the
thumb of his right hand, and on the big toe of his right foot.
26"The priest shall also pour some of the oil into his left palm;
27and with his right-hand finger the priest shall sprinkle some
of the oil that is in his left palm seven times before the LORD.
28"The priest shall then put some of the oil that is in his palm
on the lobe of the right ear of the one to be cleansed, and on the
thumb of his right hand, and on the big toe of his right foot, on
the place of the blood of the guilt offering.
29"Moreover, the rest of the oil that is in the priest's palm he
shall put on the head of the one to be cleansed, to make atonement
on his behalf before the LORD.
30"He shall then offer one of the turtledoves or young pigeons,
which are within his means.
31" *He shall offer* what he can afford, the one for a sin offering,
and the other for a burnt offering, together with the grain offering.
So the priest shall make atonement before the LORD on behalf of
the one to be cleansed.
32"This is the law *for him* in whom there is an infection of
leprosy, whose means are limited for his cleansing."

*Cleansing a Leprous House*

**33**¶ The LORD further spoke to Moses and to Aaron, saying,
34"When you enter the land of Canaan, which I give you for a
possession, and I put a mark of leprosy on a house in the land of
your possession,
35then the one who owns the house shall come and tell the
priest, saying, ' *Something* like a mark *of leprosy* has become visible
to me in the house.'
36"The priest shall then order that they empty the house before
the priest goes in to look at the mark, so that everything in the
house need not become unclean; and afterward the priest shall go
in to look at the house.
37"So he shall look at the mark, and if the mark on the walls of
the house has greenish or reddish depressions, and appears deeper than the surface;
38then the priest shall come out of the house, to the doorway,
and quarantine the house for seven days.
39"And the priest shall return on the seventh day and make an
inspection. If the mark has indeed spread in the walls of the house,
40then the priest shall order them to tear out the stones with the
mark in them and throw them away at an unclean place outside
the city.
41"And he shall have the house scraped all around inside, and
they shall dump the plaster that they scrape off at an unclean place
outside the city.
42"Then they shall take other stones and replace *those* stones;
and he shall take other plaster and replaster the house.
**43**¶ "If, however, the mark breaks out again in the house, after
he has torn out the stones and scraped the house, and after it has
been replastered,

## New International

the altar, together with the grain offering, and make atonement for
him, and he will be clean.
21"If, however, he is poor and cannot afford these, he must take
one male lamb as a guilt offering to be waved to make atonement
for him, together with a tenth of an ephah[a] of fine flour mixed with
oil for a grain offering, a log of oil, 22and two doves or two young
pigeons, which he can afford, one for a sin offering and the other
for a burnt offering.
23"On the eighth day he must bring them for his cleansing to
the priest at the entrance to the Tent of Meeting, before the LORD.
24The priest is to take the lamb for the guilt offering, together with
the log of oil, and wave them before the LORD as a wave offering.
25He shall slaughter the lamb for the guilt offering and take some
of its blood and put it on the lobe of the right ear of the one to be
cleansed, on the thumb of his right hand and on the big toe of his
right foot. 26The priest is to pour some of the oil into the palm of
his own left hand, 27and with his right forefinger sprinkle some of
the oil from his palm seven times before the LORD. 28Some of the
oil in his palm he is to put on the same places he put the blood of
the guilt offering—on the lobe of the right ear of the one to be
cleansed, on the thumb of his right hand and on the big toe of his
right foot. 29The rest of the oil in his palm the priest shall put on
the head of the one to be cleansed, to make atonement for him
before the LORD. 30Then he shall sacrifice the doves or the young
pigeons, which the person can afford, 31one[b] as a sin offering and
the other as a burnt offering, together with the grain offering. In
this way the priest will make atonement before the LORD on behalf
of the one to be cleansed."
32These are the regulations for anyone who has an infectious
skin disease and who cannot afford the regular offerings for his
cleansing.

*Cleansing From Mildew*

33The LORD said to Moses and Aaron, 34"When you enter the
land of Canaan, which I am giving you as your possession, and I
put a spreading mildew in a house in that land, 35the owner of the
house must go and tell the priest, 'I have seen something that looks
like mildew in my house.' 36The priest is to order the house to be
emptied before he goes in to examine the mildew, so that nothing
in the house will be pronounced unclean. After this the priest is
to go in and inspect the house. 37He is to examine the mildew on
the walls, and if it has greenish or reddish depressions that appear
to be deeper than the surface of the wall, 38the priest shall go out
the doorway of the house and close it up for seven days. 39On the
seventh day the priest shall return to inspect the house. If the
mildew has spread on the walls, 40he is to order that the contaminated stones be torn out and thrown into an unclean place
outside the town. 41He must have all the inside walls of the house
scraped and the material that is scraped off dumped into an unclean place outside the town. 42Then they are to take other stones
to replace these and take new clay and plaster the house.
43"If the mildew reappears in the house after the stones have
been torn out and the house scraped and plastered, 44the priest is

**NIV** [a] *21* That is, probably about 2 quarts (about 2 liters) [b] *31* Septuagint and Syriac; Hebrew *31such as the person can afford, one*

## King James

44 Then the priest shall come and look, and, behold, *if* the plague be spread in the house, it *is* a fretting leprosy in the house: it *is* unclean.

45 And he shall break down the house, the stones of it, and the timber thereof, and all the mortar of the house; and he shall carry *them* forth out of the city into an unclean place.

46 Moreover he that goeth into the house all the while that it is shut up shall be unclean until the even.

47 And he that lieth in the house shall wash his clothes; and he that eateth in the house shall wash his clothes.

48 And if the priest shall come in, and look *upon it*, and, behold, the plague hath not spread in the house, after the house was plastered: then the priest shall pronounce the house clean, because the plague is healed.

49 And he shall take to cleanse the house two birds, and cedar wood, and scarlet, and hyssop:

50 And he shall kill the one of the birds in an earthen vessel over running water:

51 And he shall take the cedar wood, and the hyssop, and the scarlet, and the living bird, and dip them in the blood of the slain bird, and in the running water, and sprinkle the house seven times:

52 And he shall cleanse the house with the blood of the bird, and with the running water, and with the living bird, and with the cedar wood, and with the hyssop, and with the scarlet:

53 But he shall let go the living bird out of the city into the open fields, and make an atonement for the house: and it shall be clean.

54 This *is* the law for all manner of plague of leprosy, and scall,

55 And for the leprosy of a garment, and of a house,

56 And for a rising, and for a scab, and for a bright spot:

57 To teach when *it is* unclean, and when *it is* clean: this *is* the law of leprosy.

**15** AND THE LORD spake unto Moses and to Aaron, saying,

2 Speak unto the children of Israel, and say unto them, When any man hath a running issue out of his flesh, *because of* his issue he *is* unclean.

3 And this shall be his uncleanness in his issue: whether his flesh run with his issue, or his flesh be stopped from his issue, it *is* his uncleanness.

4 Every bed, whereon he lieth that hath the issue, is unclean: and every thing, whereon he sitteth, shall be unclean.

5 And whosoever toucheth his bed shall wash his clothes, and bathe *himself* in water, and be unclean until the even.

6 And he that sitteth on *any* thing whereon he sat that hath the issue shall wash his clothes, and bathe *himself* in water, and be unclean until the even.

7 And he that toucheth the flesh of him that hath the issue shall wash his clothes, and bathe *himself* in water, and be unclean until the even.

8 And if he that hath the issue spit upon him that is clean; then he shall wash his clothes, and bathe *himself* in water, and be unclean until the even.

9 And what saddle soever he rideth upon that hath the issue shall be unclean.

10 And whosoever toucheth any thing that was under him shall be unclean until the even: and he that beareth *any of* those things shall wash his clothes, and bathe *himself* in water, and be unclean until the even.

11 And whomsoever he toucheth that hath the issue, and hath not rinsed his hands in water, he shall wash his clothes, and bathe *himself* in water, and be unclean until the even.

12 And the vessel of earth, that he toucheth which hath the issue, shall be broken: and every vessel of wood shall be rinsed in water.

## Amplified

44 Then the priest shall come and look, and if the disease is spreading in the house, it is a rotting *or* corroding leprosy in the house; it is unclean.

45 He shall tear down the house, its stones and its timber and all the plaster *or* mortar of the house, and shall carry them forth out of the city to an unclean place.

46 Moreover he who enters the house during the whole time that it is shut up shall be unclean until the evening.

47 And he who lies down or eats in the house shall wash his clothes.

48 But if the priest inspects it, and the disease has not spread after the house was plastered, he shall pronounce the house clean, because the disease is healed.

49 He shall take to cleanse the house two birds, cedar wood, scarlet [stuff], and hyssop;

50 And he shall kill one of the birds in an earthen vessel over running water,

51 And he shall take the cedar wood, and the hyssop and the scarlet [material] and the living bird, and dip them in the blood of the slain bird and in the running water, and sprinkle the house seven times.

52 And he shall cleanse the house with the blood of the bird, the running water, the living bird, the cedar wood, the hyssop and the scarlet [material].

53 But he shall let go the living bird out of the city into the open field; so he shall make atonement for the house, and it shall be clean.

54 This is the law for all kinds of leprous disease, and mange-like condition,

55 Of a garment or of a house,

56 And for a swelling or an eruption *or* a scab or a bright spot,

57 To teach when it is unclean and when it is clean. This is the law of leprosy.

**15** AND THE Lord said to Moses and Aaron,

2 Say to the Israelites, When any man has a running discharge from his body, because of his discharge he is unclean.

3 This shall be [the law concerning] his uncleanness in his discharge: whether his body runs with his discharge, or has stopped [running], it is uncleanness in him.

4 Every bed on which the one who has the discharge lies is unclean, and everything on which he sits shall be unclean.

5 Whoever touches that person's bed shall wash his clothes, and bathe himself in water, and be unclean until the evening.

6 And whoever sits on anything on which he who has the discharge has sat shall wash his clothes, and bathe himself in water, and be unclean until the evening.

7 And he who touches the flesh of him who has the discharge shall wash his clothes, and bathe himself in water, and be unclean until the evening.

8 And if he who has the discharge spits on him who is clean, then he shall wash his clothes, and bathe himself in water, and be unclean until the evening.

9 And any saddle on which he who has the discharge rides shall be unclean.

10 Whoever touches anything that has been under him shall be unclean until evening; and he who carries those things shall wash his clothes, and bathe himself in water, and be unclean until evening.

11 Whomever he who has the discharge touches, without rinsing his hands in water, shall wash his clothes, and bathe himself in water, and be unclean until evening.

12 The earthen vessel that he with the discharge touches shall be broken, and every vessel of wood shall be rinsed in water.

## New American Standard

44then the priest shall come in and make an inspection. If he
sees that the mark has indeed spread in the house, it is a malignant
mark in the house; it is unclean.
45"He shall therefore tear down the house, its stones, and its
timbers, and all the plaster of the house, and he shall take *them*
outside the city to an unclean place.
46"Moreover, whoever goes into the house during the time that
he has quarantined it, becomes unclean until evening.
47"Likewise, whoever lies down in the house shall wash his
clothes, and whoever eats in the house shall wash his clothes.
48¶ "If, on the other hand, the priest comes in and makes an
inspection, and the mark has not indeed spread in the house after
the house has been replastered, then the priest shall pronounce
the house clean because the mark has not reappeared.
49"To cleanse the house then, he shall take two birds and cedar
wood and a scarlet string and hyssop,
50and he shall slaughter the one bird in an earthenware vessel
over running water.
51"Then he shall take the cedar wood and the hyssop and the
scarlet string, with the live bird, and dip them in the blood of the
slain bird, as well as in the running water, and sprinkle the house
seven times.
52"He shall thus cleanse the house with the blood of the bird
and with the running water, along with the live bird and with the
cedar wood and with the hyssop and with the scarlet string.
53"However, he shall let the live bird go free outside the city
into the open field. So he shall make atonement for the house, and
it shall be clean."
54¶ This is the law for any mark of leprosy—even for a scale,
55and for the leprous garment or house,
56and for a swelling, and for a scab, and for a bright spot—
57to teach when they are unclean, and when they are clean. This
is the law of leprosy.

*Cleansing Unhealthiness*

**15** THE LORD also spoke to Moses and to Aaron, saying,
2"Speak to the sons of Israel, and say to them, 'When any
man has a discharge from his body, his discharge is unclean.
3'This, moreover, shall be his uncleanness in his discharge: it
is his uncleanness whether his body allows its discharge to flow,
or whether his body obstructs its discharge.
4'Every bed on which the person with the discharge lies
becomes unclean, and everything on which he sits becomes unclean.
5'Anyone, moreover, who touches his bed shall wash his
clothes and bathe in water and be unclean until evening;
6and whoever sits on the thing on which the man with the
discharge has been sitting, shall wash his clothes and bathe in
water and be unclean until evening.
7'Also whoever touches the person with the discharge shall
wash his clothes and bathe in water and be unclean until evening.
8'Or if the man with the discharge spits on one who is clean,
he too shall wash his clothes and bathe in water and be unclean
until evening.
9'And every saddle on which the person with the discharge
rides becomes unclean.
10'Whoever then touches any of the things which were under
him shall be unclean until evening, and he who carries them shall
wash his clothes and bathe in water and be unclean until evening.
11'Likewise, whomever the one with the discharge touches
without having rinsed his hands in water shall wash his clothes
and bathe in water and be unclean until evening.
12'However, an earthenware vessel which the person with the
discharge touches shall be broken, and every wooden vessel shall
be rinsed in water.

## New International

to go and examine it and, if the mildew has spread in the house,
it is a destructive mildew; the house is unclean. 45It must be torn
down—its stones, timbers and all the plaster—and taken out of the
town to an unclean place.
46"Anyone who goes into the house while it is closed up will
be unclean till evening. 47Anyone who sleeps or eats in the house
must wash his clothes.
48"But if the priest comes to examine it and the mildew has not
spread after the house has been plastered, he shall pronounce the
house clean, because the mildew is gone. 49To purify the house he
is to take two birds and some cedar wood, scarlet yarn and hyssop.
50He shall kill one of the birds over fresh water in a clay pot. 51Then
he is to take the cedar wood, the hyssop, the scarlet yarn and the
live bird, dip them into the blood of the dead bird and the fresh
water, and sprinkle the house seven times. 52He shall purify the
house with the bird's blood, the fresh water, the live bird, the
cedar wood, the hyssop and the scarlet yarn. 53Then he is to
release the live bird in the open fields outside the town. In this way
he will make atonement for the house, and it will be clean."
54These are the regulations for any infectious skin disease, for
an itch, 55for mildew in clothing or in a house, 56and for a swelling,
a rash or a bright spot, 57to determine when something is clean or
unclean.
These are the regulations for infectious skin diseases and mildew.

*Discharges Causing Uncleanness*

**15** THE LORD said to Moses and Aaron, 2"Speak to the
Israelites and say to them: 'When any man has a bodily
discharge, the discharge is unclean. 3Whether it continues flowing
from his body or is blocked, it will make him unclean. This is how
his discharge will bring about uncleanness:
4" 'Any bed the man with a discharge lies on will be unclean,
and anything he sits on will be unclean. 5Anyone who touches his
bed must wash his clothes and bathe with water, and he will be
unclean till evening. 6Whoever sits on anything that the man with
a discharge sat on must wash his clothes and bathe with water, and
he will be unclean till evening.
7" 'Whoever touches the man who has a discharge must wash
his clothes and bathe with water, and he will be unclean till evening.
8" 'If the man with the discharge spits on someone who is clean,
that person must wash his clothes and bathe with water, and he
will be unclean till evening.
9" 'Everything the man sits on when riding will be unclean,
10and whoever touches any of the things that were under him will
be unclean till evening; whoever picks up those things must wash
his clothes and bathe with water, and he will be unclean till evening.
11" 'Anyone the man with a discharge touches without rinsing
his hands with water must wash his clothes and bathe with water,
and he will be unclean till evening.
12" 'A clay pot that the man touches must be broken, and any
wooden article is to be rinsed with water.

## King James

13 And when he that hath an issue is cleansed of his issue; then he shall number to himself seven days for his cleansing, and wash his clothes, and bathe his flesh in running water, and shall be clean.

14 And on the eighth day he shall take to him two turtledoves, or two young pigeons, and come before the LORD unto the door of the tabernacle of the congregation, and give them unto the priest:

15 And the priest shall offer them, the one *for* a sin offering, and the other *for* a burnt offering; and the priest shall make an atonement for him before the LORD for his issue.

16 And if any man's seed of copulation go out from him, then he shall wash all his flesh in water, and be unclean until the even.

17 And every garment, and every skin, whereon is the seed of copulation, shall be washed with water, and be unclean until the even.

18 The woman also with whom man shall lie *with* seed of copulation, they shall *both* bathe *themselves* in water, and be unclean until the even.

19 ¶ And if a woman have an issue, *and* her issue in her flesh be blood, she shall be put apart seven days: and whosoever toucheth her shall be unclean until the even.

20 And every thing that she lieth upon in her separation shall be unclean: every thing also that she sitteth upon shall be unclean.

21 And whosoever toucheth her bed shall wash his clothes, and bathe *himself* in water, and be unclean until the even.

22 And whosoever toucheth any thing that she sat upon shall wash his clothes, and bathe *himself* in water, and be unclean until the even.

23 And if it *be* on *her* bed, or on any thing whereon she sitteth, when he toucheth it, he shall be unclean until the even.

24 And if any man lie with her at all, and her flowers be upon him, he shall be unclean seven days; and all the bed whereon he lieth shall be unclean.

25 And if a woman have an issue of her blood many days out of the time of her separation, or if it run beyond the time of her separation; all the days of the issue of her uncleanness shall be as the days of her separation: she *shall be* unclean.

26 Every bed whereon she lieth all the days of her issue shall be unto her as the bed of her separation: and whatsoever she sitteth upon shall be unclean, as the uncleanness of her separation.

27 And whosoever toucheth those things shall be unclean, and shall wash his clothes, and bathe *himself* in water, and be unclean until the even.

28 But if she be cleansed of her issue, then she shall number to herself seven days, and after that she shall be clean.

29 And on the eighth day she shall take unto her two turtles, or two young pigeons, and bring them unto the priest, to the door of the tabernacle of the congregation.

30 And the priest shall offer the one *for* a sin offering, and the other *for* a burnt offering; and the priest shall make an atonement for her before the LORD for the issue of her uncleanness.

31 Thus shall ye separate the children of Israel from their uncleanness; that they die not in their uncleanness, when they defile my tabernacle that *is* among them.

32 This *is* the law of him that hath an issue, and *of him* whose seed goeth from him, and is defiled therewith;

33 And of her that is sick of her flowers, and of him that hath an issue, of the man, and of the woman, and of him that lieth with her that is unclean.

**16** AND THE LORD spake unto Moses after the death of the two sons of Aaron, when they offered before the LORD, and died;

## Amplified

13 When he who has a discharge is cleansed of it, he shall count seven days for his purification, then wash his clothes, bathe in running water, and be clean.

14 On the eighth day he shall take two turtledoves or two young pigeons, and come before the Lord to the door of the tent of meeting, and give them to the priest;

15 And the priest shall offer them, one for a sin offering and the other for a burnt offering; and [he] shall make atonement for the man before the Lord for his discharge.

16 And if any man has a discharge of semen, he shall wash all his body in water, and be unclean until evening.

17 And every garment and every skin on which the sperm comes shall be washed with water, and be unclean until evening.

18 The woman also with whom a man with emission of semen shall lie, they shall both bathe themselves in water, and be unclean until evening.

19 And if a woman has a discharge, her [regular] discharge of blood of her body, she shall be in her impurity *or* separation for seven days, and whoever touches her shall be unclean until evening.

20 And everything that she lies on in her separation shall be unclean; everything also that she sits on shall be unclean.

21 And whoever touches her bed shall wash his clothes, and bathe himself in water, and be unclean until evening.

22 Whoever touches anything she sat on shall wash his clothes, and bathe himself in water, and be unclean until evening.

23 And if her flow has stained her bed or anything on which she sat, when he touches it, he shall be unclean until evening.

24 And if any man lie with her, and her impurity be upon him, he shall be unclean seven days; and every bed on which he lies shall be unclean.

25 And if a woman has an issue of blood many days not in the time of her separation, or if she has a discharge beyond the time of her [regular] impurity, all the days of the issue of her uncleanness she shall be as in the days of her impurity; she shall be unclean. [Matt. 9:20.]

26 Every bed on which she lies all the days of her discharge shall be as the bed of her impurity, and whatever she sits on shall be unclean, as in her impurity.

27 And whoever touches those things shall be unclean, and shall wash his clothes, and bathe himself in water, and be unclean until evening.

28 But if she is cleansed of her discharge, then she shall wait seven days, and after that she shall be clean.

29 And on the eighth day she shall take two turtledoves or two young pigeons, and bring them to the priest, to the door of the tent of meeting;

30 He shall offer one for a sin offering and the other for a burnt offering; and he shall make atonement for her before the Lord for her unclean discharge.

31 Thus you shall separate the Israelites from their uncleanness, lest they die in their uncleanness by defiling My tabernacle that is in the midst of them.

32 This is the law for him who has a discharge and for him who has emissions of sperm, being made unclean by it;

33 And for her who is sick with her impurity, and for any person who has a discharge, whether man or woman, and for him who lies with her who is unclean.

**16** AFTER THE death of Aaron's two sons, when they drew near before the Lord [offered false fire] and died, [Lev. 10:1, 2.]

## New American Standard

13¶ 'Now when the man with the discharge becomes cleansed
from his discharge, then he shall count off for himself seven days
for his cleansing; he shall then wash his clothes and bathe his body
in running water and shall become clean.
14'Then on the eighth day he shall take for himself two turtledoves or two young pigeons, and come before the LORD to the
doorway of the tent of meeting, and give them to the priest;
15and the priest shall offer them, one for a sin offering, and the
other for a burnt offering. So the priest shall make atonement on
his behalf before the LORD because of his discharge.
16¶ 'Now if a man has a seminal emission, he shall bathe all his
body in water and be unclean until evening.
17'As for any garment or any leather on which there is seminal
emission, it shall be washed with water and be unclean until
evening.
18'If a man lies with a woman *so that* there is a seminal emission,
they shall both bathe in water and be unclean until evening.
19¶ 'When a woman has a discharge, *if* her discharge in her body
is blood, she shall continue in her menstrual impurity for seven
days; and whoever touches her shall be unclean until evening.
20'Everything also on which she lies during her menstrual impurity shall be unclean, and everything on which she sits shall be
unclean.
21'And anyone who touches her bed shall wash his clothes and
bathe in water and be unclean until evening.
22'And whoever touches any thing on which she sits shall wash
his clothes and bathe in water and be unclean until evening.
23'Whether it be on the bed or on the thing on which she is
sitting, when he touches it, he shall be unclean until evening.
24'And if a man actually lies with her, so that her menstrual
impurity is on him, he shall be unclean seven days, and every bed
on which he lies shall be unclean.
25¶ 'Now if a woman has a discharge of her blood many days,
not at the period of her menstrual impurity, or if she has a discharge beyond that period, all the days of her impure discharge
she shall continue as though in her menstrual impurity; she is
unclean.
26'Any bed on which she lies all the days of her discharge shall
be to her like her bed at menstruation; and every thing on which
she sits shall be unclean, like her uncleanness at that time.
27'Likewise, whoever touches them shall be unclean and shall
wash his clothes and bathe in water and be unclean until evening.
28'When she becomes clean from her discharge, she shall count
off for herself seven days; and afterward she shall be clean.
29'Then on the eighth day she shall take for herself two turtledoves or two young pigeons, and bring them in to the priest, to
the doorway of the tent of meeting.
30'And the priest shall offer the one for a sin offering and the
other for a burnt offering. So the priest shall make atonement on
her behalf before the LORD because of her impure discharge.'
31¶ "Thus you shall keep the sons of Israel separated from their
uncleanness, lest they die in their uncleanness by their defiling My
tabernacle that is among them."
32This is the law for the one with a discharge, and for the man
who has a seminal emission so that he is unclean by it,
33and for the woman who is ill because of menstrual impurity,
and for the one who has a discharge, whether a male or a female,
or a man who lies with an unclean woman.

*Law of Atonement*

16 NOW THE LORD spoke to Moses after the death of the two
sons of Aaron, when they had approached the presence
of the LORD and died.

## New International

13" 'When a man is cleansed from his discharge, he is to count
off seven days for his ceremonial cleansing; he must wash his
clothes and bathe himself with fresh water, and he will be clean.
14On the eighth day he must take two doves or two young pigeons
and come before the LORD to the entrance to the Tent of Meeting
and give them to the priest. 15The priest is to sacrifice them, the
one for a sin offering and the other for a burnt offering. In this way
he will make atonement before the LORD for the man because of
his discharge.
16" 'When a man has an emission of semen, he must bathe his
whole body with water, and he will be unclean till evening. 17Any
clothing or leather that has semen on it must be washed with
water, and it will be unclean till evening. 18When a man lies with
a woman and there is an emission of semen, both must bathe with
water, and they will be unclean till evening.
19" 'When a woman has her regular flow of blood, the impurity
of her monthly period will last seven days, and anyone who
touches her will be unclean till evening.
20" 'Anything she lies on during her period will be unclean, and
anything she sits on will be unclean. 21Whoever touches her bed
must wash his clothes and bathe with water, and he will be unclean till evening. 22Whoever touches anything she sits on must
wash his clothes and bathe with water, and he will be unclean till
evening. 23Whether it is the bed or anything she was sitting on,
when anyone touches it, he will be unclean till evening.
24" 'If a man lies with her and her monthly flow touches him,
he will be unclean for seven days; any bed he lies on will be
unclean.
25" 'When a woman has a discharge of blood for many days at
a time other than her monthly period or has a discharge that
continues beyond her period, she will be unclean as long as she
has the discharge, just as in the days of her period. 26Any bed she
lies on while her discharge continues will be unclean, as is her bed
during her monthly period, and anything she sits on will be unclean, as during her period. 27Whoever touches them will be unclean; he must wash his clothes and bathe with water, and he will
be unclean till evening.
28" 'When she is cleansed from her discharge, she must count
off seven days, and after that she will be ceremonially clean. 29On
the eighth day she must take two doves or two young pigeons and
bring them to the priest at the entrance to the Tent of Meeting.
30The priest is to sacrifice one for a sin offering and the other for
a burnt offering. In this way he will make atonement for her before
the LORD for the uncleanness of her discharge.
31" 'You must keep the Israelites separate from things that make
them unclean, so they will not die in their uncleanness for defiling
my dwelling place,[a] which is among them.' "
32These are the regulations for a man with a discharge, for
anyone made unclean by an emission of semen, 33for a woman in
her monthly period, for a man or a woman with a discharge, and
for a man who lies with a woman who is ceremonially unclean.

*The Day of Atonement*

16 THE LORD spoke to Moses after the death of the two sons
of Aaron who died when they approached the LORD. 2The

NIV [a] 31 Or *my tabernacle*

## King James

2And the LORD said unto Moses, Speak unto Aaron thy brother, that he come not at all times into the holy *place* within the veil before the mercy seat, which *is* upon the ark; that he die not: for I will appear in the cloud upon the mercy seat.

3Thus shall Aaron come into the holy *place:* with a young bullock for a sin offering, and a ram for a burnt offering.

4He shall put on the holy linen coat, and he shall have the linen breeches upon his flesh, and shall be girded with a linen girdle, and with the linen mitre shall he be attired: these *are* holy garments; therefore shall he wash his flesh in water, and *so* put them on.

5And he shall take of the congregation of the children of Israel two kids of the goats for a sin offering, and one ram for a burnt offering.

6And Aaron shall offer his bullock of the sin offering, which *is* for himself, and make an atonement for himself, and for his house.

7And he shall take the two goats, and present them before the LORD *at* the door of the tabernacle of the congregation.

8And Aaron shall cast lots upon the two goats; one lot for the LORD, and the other lot for the scapegoat.

9And Aaron shall bring the goat upon which the LORD's lot fell, and offer him *for* a sin offering.

10But the goat, on which the lot fell to be the scapegoat, shall be presented alive before the LORD, to make an atonement with him, *and* to let him go for a scapegoat into the wilderness.

11And Aaron shall bring the bullock of the sin offering, which *is* for himself, and shall make an atonement for himself, and for his house, and shall kill the bullock of the sin offering which *is* for himself:

12And he shall take a censer full of burning coals of fire from off the altar before the LORD, and his hands full of sweet incense beaten small, and bring *it* within the veil:

13And he shall put the incense upon the fire before the LORD, that the cloud of the incense may cover the mercy seat that *is* upon the testimony, that he die not:

14And he shall take of the blood of the bullock, and sprinkle *it* with his finger upon the mercy seat eastward; and before the mercy seat shall he sprinkle of the blood with his finger seven times.

15¶ Then shall he kill the goat of the sin offering, that *is* for the people, and bring his blood within the veil, and do with that blood as he did with the blood of the bullock, and sprinkle it upon the mercy seat, and before the mercy seat:

16And he shall make an atonement for the holy *place,* because of the uncleanness of the children of Israel, and because of their transgressions in all their sins: and so shall he do for the tabernacle of the congregation, that remaineth among them in the midst of their uncleanness.

17And there shall be no man in the tabernacle of the congregation when he goeth in to make an atonement in the holy *place,* until he come out, and have made an atonement for himself, and for his household, and for all the congregation of Israel.

18And he shall go out unto the altar that *is* before the LORD, and make an atonement for it; and shall take of the blood of the bullock, and of the blood of the goat, and put *it* upon the horns of the altar round about.

19And he shall sprinkle of the blood upon it with his finger seven times, and cleanse it, and hallow it from the uncleanness of the children of Israel.

## Amplified

2The Lord said to Moses, Tell Aaron your brother he [a]must not come at all times into the holy of holies within the veil, before the mercy seat upon the ark, lest he die; for I will appear in the cloud on the mercy seat. [Heb. 9:7-15, 25-28.]

3But Aaron shall come into the holy enclosure in this way; with a young bull for a sin offering and a ram for a burnt offering.

4He shall put on the holy linen undergarment, and he shall have the linen breeches upon his body, and be girded with the linen girdle *or* sash, and with the linen miter *or* turban shall he be attired; these are the holy garments; he shall bathe his body in water and then put them on.

5He shall take [at the expense] of the congregation of the Israelites, two male goats for a sin offering, and one ram for a burnt offering.

6And Aaron shall present the bull as the sin offering for himself, and make atonement for himself and for his house [the other priests].

7He shall take the two goats, and present them before the Lord at the door of the tent of meeting.

8Aaron shall cast lots on the two goats; one lot for the Lord, the other lot for Azazel *or* removal.

9And Aaron shall bring the goat on which the Lord's lot fell, and offer him as a sin offering.

10But the goat on which the lot fell for Azazel, *or* removal, shall be presented alive before the Lord to make atonement over him, that he may be let go into the wilderness for Azazel (for dismissal).

11Aaron shall present the bull as the sin offering for his own sins, and shall make atonement for himself and for his house [the other priests]; and shall kill the bull as the sin offering for himself.

12He shall take a censer full of burning coals of fire from off the [bronze] altar before the Lord, and his two hands full of sweet incense beaten small, and bring it within the veil [into the holy of holies],

13And put the incense on the fire [in the censer] before the Lord, that the cloud of the incense may cover the mercy seat that is upon [the ark of] the testimony, lest he die.

14He shall take of the bull's blood, and sprinkle it with his finger on the front [the east side] of the mercy seat, and before the mercy seat he shall sprinkle of the blood with his finger seven times.

15Then shall he kill the goat of the sin offering, that is for [the sins of] the people, and bring its blood within the veil [into the holy of holies], and do with that blood as he did with the blood of the bull, and sprinkle it on the mercy seat and before the mercy seat. [Heb. 2:17.]

16Thus he shall make atonement for the holy place, because of the uncleanness of the Israelites, and because of their transgressions, even all their sins; and so shall he do for the tent of meeting, that remains among them in the midst of their uncleanness. [Heb. 9:22-24.]

17There shall be no man in the tent of meeting when the high priest goes in to make atonement in the holy of holies [within the veil] until he comes out and has made atonement for his own sins and those of his house [the other priests] and of all the congregation of Israel.

18And he shall go out to the altar [of burnt offering in the court] which is before the Lord, and make atonement for it, and shall take some of the blood of the bull and of the goat and put it on the horns of the altar round about.

19And he shall sprinkle some of the blood on it with his fingers seven times, and cleanse it and hallow it from the uncleanness of the Israelites.

**AMP** [a] The priests being warned by the death of Nadab and Abihu to approach to God with reverence and godly fear, directions are here given how the nearest approach might be made . . . Within the veil none must ever come but the high priest only, and he but one day in the year. But see what a blessed change is made by the gospel of Christ; all good Christians have now *boldness to enter into the holiest,* through the veil, every day (Heb. 10:19, 20); and we *come boldly* (not as Aaron must, with fear and trembling) to the *throne of grace,* or mercy seat (Heb. 4:16) . . . Now therefore we are welcome to come at all times into the *holy place not made with hands.* Then Aaron must not come near at all times, *lest he die;* we now must come near at all times that we may live: it is [keeping our] distance only that is our death (Matthew Henry's *Commentary*).

## New American Standard

2And the LORD said to Moses, "Tell your brother Aaron that
he shall not enter at any time into the holy place inside the veil,
before the [b]mercy seat which is on the ark, lest he die; for I will
appear in the cloud over the mercy seat.
3"Aaron shall enter the holy place with this: with a bull for a
sin offering and a ram for a burnt offering.
4"He shall put on the holy linen tunic, and the linen undergarments shall be next to his body, and he shall be girded with the
linen sash, and attired with the linen turban (these are holy garments). Then he shall bathe his body in water and put them on.
5"And he shall take from the congregation of the sons of Israel
two male goats for a sin offering and one ram for a burnt offering.
6"Then Aaron shall offer the bull for the sin offering which is
for himself, that he may make atonement for himself and for his
household.
7"And he shall take the two goats and present them before the
LORD at the doorway of the tent of meeting.
8"And Aaron shall cast lots for the two goats, one lot for the
LORD and the other lot for the [c]scapegoat.
9"Then Aaron shall offer the goat on which the lot for the LORD
fell, and make it a sin offering.
10"But the goat on which the lot for the scapegoat fell, shall be
presented alive before the LORD, to make atonement upon it, to
send it into the wilderness as the scapegoat.
11¶ "Then Aaron shall offer the bull of the sin offering which
is for himself, and make atonement for himself and for his household, and he shall slaughter the bull of the sin offering which is
for himself.
12"And he shall take a firepan full of coals of fire from upon the
altar before the LORD, and two handfuls of finely ground sweet
incense, and bring *it* inside the veil.
13"And he shall put the incense on the fire before the LORD, that
the cloud of incense may cover the mercy seat that is on *the ark of*
the testimony, lest he die.
14"Moreover, he shall take some of the blood of the bull and
sprinkle *it* with his finger on the mercy seat on the east *side*; also
in front of the mercy seat he shall sprinkle some of the blood with
his finger seven times.
15¶ "Then he shall slaughter the goat of the sin offering which
is for the people, and bring its blood inside the veil, and do with
its blood as he did with the blood of the bull, and sprinkle it on
the mercy seat and in front of the mercy seat.
16"And he shall make atonement for the holy place, because of
the impurities of the sons of Israel, and because of their transgressions, in regard to all their sins; and thus he shall do for the tent
of meeting which abides with them in the midst of their impurities.
17"When he goes in to make atonement in the holy place, no
one shall be in the tent of meeting until he comes out, that he may
make atonement for himself and for his household and for all the
assembly of Israel.
18"Then he shall go out to the altar that is before the LORD and
make atonement for it, and shall take some of the blood of the bull
and of the blood of the goat, and put it on the horns of the altar
on all sides.
19"And with his finger he shall sprinkle some of the blood on
it seven times, and cleanse it, and from the impurities of the sons
of Israel consecrate it.

## New International

LORD said to Moses: "Tell your brother Aaron not to come whenever he chooses into the Most Holy Place behind the curtain in
front of the atonement cover on the ark, or else he will die, because
I appear in the cloud over the atonement cover.
3"This is how Aaron is to enter the sanctuary area: with a young
bull for a sin offering and a ram for a burnt offering. 4He is to put
on the sacred linen tunic, with linen undergarments next to his
body; he is to tie the linen sash around him and put on the linen
turban. These are sacred garments; so he must bathe himself with
water before he puts them on. 5From the Israelite community he
is to take two male goats for a sin offering and a ram for a burnt
offering.
6"Aaron is to offer the bull for his own sin offering to make
atonement for himself and his household. 7Then he is to take the
two goats and present them before the LORD at the entrance to the
Tent of Meeting. 8He is to cast lots for the two goats—one lot for
the LORD and the other for the scapegoat.[d] 9Aaron shall bring the
goat whose lot falls to the LORD and sacrifice it for a sin offering.
10But the goat chosen by lot as the scapegoat shall be presented
alive before the LORD to be used for making atonement by sending
it into the desert as a scapegoat.
11"Aaron shall bring the bull for his own sin offering to make
atonement for himself and his household, and he is to slaughter
the bull for his own sin offering. 12He is to take a censer full of
burning coals from the altar before the LORD and two handfuls of
finely ground fragrant incense and take them behind the curtain.
13He is to put the incense on the fire before the LORD, and the
smoke of the incense will conceal the atonement cover above the
Testimony, so that he will not die. 14He is to take some of the bull's
blood and with his finger sprinkle it on the front of the atonement
cover; then he shall sprinkle some of it with his finger seven times
before the atonement cover.
15"He shall then slaughter the goat for the sin offering for the
people and take its blood behind the curtain and do with it as he
did with the bull's blood: He shall sprinkle it on the atonement
cover and in front of it. 16In this way he will make atonement for
the Most Holy Place because of the uncleanness and rebellion of
the Israelites, whatever their sins have been. He is to do the same
for the Tent of Meeting, which is among them in the midst of their
uncleanness. 17No one is to be in the Tent of Meeting from the time
Aaron goes in to make atonement in the Most Holy Place until he
comes out, having made atonement for himself, his household and
the whole community of Israel.
18"Then he shall come out to the altar that is before the LORD
and make atonement for it. He shall take some of the bull's blood
and some of the goat's blood and put it on all the horns of the altar.
19He shall sprinkle some of the blood on it with his finger seven
times to cleanse it and to consecrate it from the uncleanness of the
Israelites.

NAS [b] Lit., *propitiatory* [c] Lit., *goat of removal*, or else a name: *Azazel*

NIV [d] *8* That is, the goat of removal; Hebrew *azazel;* also in verses 10 and 26

## King James

20¶ And when he hath made an end of reconciling the holy *place*,
and the tabernacle of the congregation, and the altar, he shall bring
the live goat:
21And Aaron shall lay both his hands upon the head of the live
goat, and confess over him all the iniquities of the children of
Israel, and all their transgressions in all their sins, putting them
upon the head of the goat, and shall send *him* away by the hand
of a fit man into the wilderness:
22And the goat shall bear upon him all their iniquities unto a
land not inhabited: and he shall let go the goat in the wilderness.
23And Aaron shall come into the tabernacle of the congregation,
and shall put off the linen garments, which he put on when he
went into the holy *place*, and shall leave them there:
24And he shall wash his flesh with water in the holy place, and
put on his garments, and come forth, and offer his burnt offering,
and the burnt offering of the people, and make an atonement for
himself, and for the people.
25And the fat of the sin offering shall he burn upon the altar.
26And he that let go the goat for the scapegoat shall wash his
clothes, and bathe his flesh in water, and afterward come into the
camp.
27And the bullock *for* the sin offering, and the goat *for* the sin
offering, whose blood was brought in to make atonement in the
holy *place*, shall *one* carry forth without the camp; and they shall
burn in the fire their skins, and their flesh, and their dung.
28And he that burneth them shall wash his clothes, and bathe
his flesh in water, and afterward he shall come into the camp.
29¶ And *this* shall be a statute for ever unto you: *that* in the
seventh month, on the tenth *day* of the month, ye shall afflict your
souls, and do no work at all, *whether it be* one of your own country,
or a stranger that sojourneth among you:
30For on that day shall *the priest* make an atonement for you, to
cleanse you, *that* ye may be clean from all your sins before the
LORD.
31It *shall be* a sabbath of rest unto you, and ye shall afflict your
souls, by a statute for ever.
32And the priest, whom he shall anoint, and whom he shall
consecrate to minister in the priest's office in his father's stead,
shall make the atonement, and shall put on the linen clothes, *even*
the holy garments:
33And he shall make an atonement for the holy sanctuary, and
he shall make an atonement for the tabernacle of the congregation,
and for the altar, and he shall make an atonement for the priests,
and for all the people of the congregation.
34And this shall be an everlasting statute unto you, to make an
atonement for the children of Israel for all their sins once a year.
And he did as the LORD commanded Moses.

17 AND THE LORD spake unto Moses, saying,
2Speak unto Aaron, and unto his sons, and unto all the
children of Israel, and say unto them; This *is* the thing which the
LORD hath commanded, saying,
3What man soever *there be* of the house of Israel, that killeth an
ox, or lamb, or goat, in the camp, or that killeth *it* out of the camp,

**AMP** [a] This is suggestive of the part the personal worker has to play in showing the sinner that Christ the great Sin-bearer has made full substitution for him, if he will accept it. Notice the qualifications of this man, sent along to complete the picture of the transaction between the sinner and his only sin-bearer. He is to be a man, says the Hebrew, "timely, ready *and* fit" to do such a task. The expression is not found in the original in any other passage.

## Amplified

20And when he has finished atoning for the holy of holies and
the tent of meeting and the altar [of burnt offering], he shall
present the live goat;
21And Aaron shall lay both his hands upon the head of the live
goat, and confess over him all the iniquities of the Israelites, and
all their transgressions, all their sins; and he shall put them upon
the head of the goat [the sin-bearer], and send him away into the
wilderness by the hand of a man [a]who is timely (ready, fit).
22The goat shall bear upon himself all their iniquities, carrying
them to a land cut off (a land of forgetfulness *and* separation, not
inhabited)! And the man leading it shall let the goat go in the
wilderness. [John 1:29; Isa. 53:11, 12; Ps. 103:12.]
23Aaron shall come into the tent of meeting and put off the linen
garments which he put on when he went into the holy of holies,
and leave them there;
24And he shall bathe his body with water in a sacred place, and
put on his garments, and come forth, and offer his burnt offering
and that of the people, and make atonement for himself and for
them.
25And the fat of the sin offering he shall burn upon the altar.
26The man who led the sin-bearing goat out and let him go for
Azazel *or* removal shall wash his clothes and bathe his body, and
afterward he may come into the camp.
27The bull and the goat for the sin offering, whose blood was
brought in to make atonement in the holy of holies, shall be carried
forth without the camp; their skins, their flesh, and their dung
shall be burned with fire. [Heb. 13:11-13.]
28And he who burns them shall wash his clothes and bathe his
body in water, and afterward he may come into the camp.
29It shall be a statute to you for ever that in the seventh month
[nearly October], on the tenth day of the month, you shall afflict
yourselves [by fasting with penitence and humiliation], and do no
work at all, either the native-born or the stranger who dwells
temporarily among you.
30For on this day atonement shall be made for you, to cleanse
you; from all your sins you shall be clean before the Lord. [Heb.
10:1, 2; I John 1:7, 9.]
31It is a sabbath of (solemn) rest to you, and you shall afflict
yourselves [by fasting with penitence and humiliation]; it is a
statute for ever.
32And the priest who shall be anointed and consecrated to
minister in the priest's office in his father's stead shall make atonement, wearing the holy linen garments;
33He shall make atonement for the holy sanctuary, for the tent
of meeting, and for the altar [of burnt offering in the court], and
shall make atonement for the priests and for all the people of the
assembly.
34This shall be an everlasting statute for you, that atonement
may be made for the Israelites for all their sins, once a year. And
Moses did as the Lord commanded him.

17 AND THE Lord said to Moses,
2Tell Aaron, his sons, and all the Israelites, This is what
the Lord has commanded:
3If any man of the house of Israel kills an ox or lamb or goat in
the camp, or kills it outside the camp,

## New American Standard

20¶ "When he finishes atoning for the holy place, and the tent of meeting and the altar, he shall offer the live goat.

21"Then Aaron shall lay both of his hands on the head of the live goat, and confess over it all the iniquities of the sons of Israel, and all their transgressions in regard to all their sins; and he shall lay them on the head of the goat and send *it* away into the wilderness by the hand of a man who *stands* in readiness.

22"And the goat shall bear on itself all their iniquities to a solitary land; and he shall release the goat in the wilderness.

23¶ "Then Aaron shall come into the tent of meeting, and take off the linen garments which he put on when he went into the holy place, and shall leave them there.

24"And he shall bathe his body with water in a holy place and put on his clothes, and come forth and offer his burnt offering and the burnt offering of the people, and make atonement for himself and for the people.

25"Then he shall offer up in smoke the fat of the sin offering on the altar.

26"And the one who released the goat as the scapegoat shall wash his clothes and bathe his body with water; then afterward he shall come into the camp.

27"But the bull of the sin offering and the goat of the sin offering, whose blood was brought in to make atonement in the holy place, shall be taken outside the camp, and they shall burn their hides, their flesh, and their refuse in the fire.

28"Then the one who burns them shall wash his clothes and bathe his body with water, then afterward he shall come into the camp.

*An Annual Atonement*

29¶ "And *this* shall be a permanent statute for you: in the seventh month, on the tenth day of the month, you shall humble your souls, and not do any work, whether the native, or the alien who sojourns among you;

30for it is on this day that atonement shall be made for you to cleanse you; you shall be clean from all your sins before the LORD.

31"It is to be a sabbath of solemn rest for you, that you may humble your souls; it is a permanent statute.

32"So the priest who is anointed and ordained to serve as priest in his father's place shall make atonement: he shall thus put on the linen garments, the holy garments,

33and make atonement for the holy sanctuary; and he shall make atonement for the tent of meeting and for the altar. He shall also make atonement for the priests and for all the people of the assembly.

34"Now you shall have this as a permanent statute, to make atonement for the sons of Israel for all their sins once every year." And just as the LORD had commanded Moses, *so* he did.

*Blood for Atonement*

**17** THEN THE LORD spoke to Moses, saying,

2"Speak to Aaron and to his sons, and to all the sons of Israel, and say to them, 'This is what the LORD has commanded, saying,

3"Any man from the house of Israel who slaughters an ox, or a lamb, or a goat in the camp, or who slaughters it outside the camp,

## New International

20"When Aaron has finished making atonement for the Most
Holy Place, the Tent of Meeting and the altar, he shall bring
forward the live goat. 21He is to lay both hands on the head of the
live goat and confess over it all the wickedness and rebellion of the
Israelites—all their sins—and put them on the goat's head. He
shall send the goat away into the desert in the care of a man
appointed for the task. 22The goat will carry on itself all their sins
to a solitary place; and the man shall release it in the desert.

23"Then Aaron is to go into the Tent of Meeting and take off the
linen garments he put on before he entered the Most Holy Place,
and he is to leave them there. 24He shall bathe himself with water
in a holy place and put on his regular garments. Then he shall
come out and sacrifice the burnt offering for himself and the burnt
offering for the people, to make atonement for himself and for the
people. 25He shall also burn the fat of the sin offering on the altar.

26"The man who releases the goat as a scapegoat must wash his
clothes and bathe himself with water; afterward he may come into
the camp. 27The bull and the goat for the sin offerings, whose
blood was brought into the Most Holy Place to make atonement,
must be taken outside the camp; their hides, flesh and offal are to
be burned up. 28The man who burns them must wash his clothes
and bathe himself with water; afterward he may come into the
camp.

29"This is to be a lasting ordinance for you: On the tenth day
of the seventh month you must deny yourselves[b] and not do any
work—whether native-born or an alien living among you— 30be-
cause on this day atonement will be made for you, to cleanse you.
Then, before the LORD, you will be clean from all your sins. 31It is
a sabbath of rest, and you must deny yourselves; it is a lasting
ordinance. 32The priest who is anointed and ordained to succeed
his father as high priest is to make atonement. He is to put on the
sacred linen garments 33and make atonement for the Most Holy
Place, for the Tent of Meeting and the altar, and for the priests and
all the people of the community.

34"This is to be a lasting ordinance for you: Atonement is to be
made once a year for all the sins of the Israelites."

And it was done, as the LORD commanded Moses.

*Eating Blood Forbidden*

**17** THE LORD said to Moses, 2"Speak to Aaron and his sons
and to all the Israelites and say to them: 'This is what the
LORD has commanded: 3Any Israelite who sacrifices an ox,[c] a lamb
or a goat in the camp or outside of it 4instead of bringing it to the

NIV [b] 29 Or *must fast;* also in verse 31 [c] 3 The Hebrew word can include both male and female.

## King James

4And bringeth it not unto the door of the tabernacle of the congregation, to offer an offering unto the LORD before the tabernacle of the LORD; blood shall be imputed unto that man; he hath shed blood; and that man shall be cut off from among his people:

5To the end that the children of Israel may bring their sacrifices, which they offer in the open field, even that they may bring them unto the LORD, unto the door of the tabernacle of the congregation, unto the priest, and offer them *for* peace offerings unto the LORD.

6And the priest shall sprinkle the blood upon the altar of the LORD *at* the door of the tabernacle of the congregation, and burn the fat for a sweet savour unto the LORD.

7And they shall no more offer their sacrifices unto devils, after whom they have gone a-whoring. This shall be a statute for ever unto them throughout their generations.

8¶ And thou shalt say unto them, Whatsoever man *there be* of the house of Israel, or of the strangers which sojourn among you, that offereth a burnt offering or sacrifice,

9And bringeth it not unto the door of the tabernacle of the congregation, to offer it unto the LORD; even that man shall be cut off from among his people.

10¶ And whatsoever man *there be* of the house of Israel, or of the strangers that sojourn among you, that eateth any manner of blood; I will even set my face against that soul that eateth blood, and will cut him off from among his people.

11For the life of the flesh *is* in the blood: and I have given it to you upon the altar to make an atonement for your souls: for it *is* the blood *that* maketh an atonement for the soul.

12Therefore I said unto the children of Israel, No soul of you shall eat blood, neither shall any stranger that sojourneth among you eat blood.

13And whatsoever man *there be* of the children of Israel, or of the strangers that sojourn among you, which hunteth and catcheth any beast or fowl that may be eaten; he shall even pour out the blood thereof, and cover it with dust.

14For *it is* the life of all flesh; the blood of it *is* for the life thereof: therefore I said unto the children of Israel, Ye shall eat the blood of no manner of flesh: for the life of all flesh *is* the blood thereof: whosoever eateth it shall be cut off.

15And every soul that eateth that which died *of itself*, or that which was torn *with beasts, whether it be* one of your own country, or a stranger, he shall both wash his clothes, and bathe *himself* in water, and be unclean until the even: then shall he be clean.

16But if he wash *them* not, nor bathe his flesh; then he shall bear his iniquity.

## Amplified

4And does not bring it to the door of the tent of meeting, to offer it as an offering to the Lord before the Lord's tabernacle, [guilt for shedding] [a]blood shall be imputed to that man; he has shed blood and shall be cut off from among his people;

5This is that the Israelites rather than offer their sacrifices [to idols] in the open field [where they slew them] may bring them to the Lord, to the door of the tent of meeting, to the priest, to offer them for peace offerings to the Lord.

6And the priest shall dash the blood on the altar of the Lord at the door of the tent of meeting, and burn the fat for a sweet *and* satisfying fragrance to the Lord.

7So they shall no more offer their sacrifices to goatlike gods *or* demons *or* field spirits, after which they have played the harlot. This shall be a statute for ever to them throughout their generations.

8And you shall say to them, Whoever of the house of Israel or of the strangers who dwell among you temporarily, who offers a burnt offering or sacrifice,

9And does not bring it to the door of the tent of meeting to offer it to the Lord, shall be cut off from among his people.

10Any one of the house of Israel or of the strangers who dwell among them temporarily who eats any kind of blood, against that person I will set My face, and I will cut him off from among his people [that he may not be included in the atonement made for them]. [Cp. Ezek. 33:25.]

11For the life (the animal soul) is in the blood, and I have given it for you upon the altar to make atonement for your souls; for it is the blood that makes atonement, by reason of the life [which it represents]. [Rom. 3:24-26.]

12Therefore I have said to the Israelites, No person among you shall eat blood, neither shall any stranger who dwells temporarily among you eat blood.

13And any of the Israelites, or of the strangers who sojourn among them, who takes in hunting any clean beast or bird, shall pour out its blood and cover it with dust.

14As for the life of all flesh, the blood of it represents the life of it; therefore I said to the Israelites, You shall partake of the blood of no kind of flesh, for the life of all flesh is its blood. Whoever eats of it shall be cut off.

15And every person who eats what dies of itself, or was torn by beasts, whether he is native-born or a temporary resident, shall wash his clothes and bathe himself in water, and be unclean until evening; then shall he be clean. [Acts 15:20.]

16But if he does not wash his clothes or bathe his body, he shall bear his own iniquity [for it shall not be borne by the sacrifice of atonement].

**18** AND THE LORD spake unto Moses, saying,

2Speak unto the children of Israel, and say unto them, I am the LORD your God.

3After the doings of the land of Egypt, wherein ye dwelt, shall ye not do: and after the doings of the land of Canaan, whither I bring you, shall ye not do: neither shall ye walk in their ordinances.

4Ye shall do my judgments, and keep mine ordinances, to walk therein: I *am* the LORD your God.

5Ye shall therefore keep my statutes, and my judgments: which if a man do, he shall live in them: I *am* the LORD.

6¶ None of you shall approach to any that is near of kin to him, to uncover *their* nakedness: I *am* the LORD.

7The nakedness of thy father, or the nakedness of thy mother, shalt thou not uncover: she *is* thy mother; thou shalt not uncover her nakedness.

**18** AND THE Lord said to Moses,

2Say to the Israelites, I am the Lord your God.

3You shall not do as was done in the land of Egypt in which you dwelt, nor shall you do as is done in the land of Canaan to which I am bringing you; neither shall you walk in their statutes.

4You shall do My ordinances and keep My statutes and walk in them. I am the Lord your God.

5You shall therefore keep My statutes and My ordinances, which if a man does, he shall live by them. I am the Lord. [Rom. 10:4, 5; Gal. 3:12; Luke 10:25-28.]

6None of you shall approach any one close of kin to him, to have sexual relations. I am the Lord.

7The nakedness of your father, which is the nakedness of your mother, you shall not uncover; she is your mother; you shall not have intercourse with her.

**AMP** [a] This requirement, that an animal to be killed was to be brought as an offering to the Lord, was no privation for the owner, for after offering it on the altar of burnt offering he received most of it back as a gift from God.

## New American Standard

4and has not brought it to the doorway of the tent of meeting
to present *it* as an offering to the LORD before the tabernacle of the
LORD, bloodguiltiness is to be reckoned to that man. He has shed
blood and that man shall be cut off from among his people.
5"The reason is so that the sons of Israel may bring their
sacrifices which they were sacrificing in the open field, that they
may bring them in to the LORD, at the doorway of the tent of
meeting to the priest, and sacrifice them as sacrifices of peace
offerings to the LORD.
6"And the priest shall sprinkle the blood on the altar of the
LORD at the doorway of the tent of meeting, and offer up the fat
in smoke as a soothing aroma to the LORD.
7"And they shall no longer sacrifice their sacrifices to the goat
demons with which they play the harlot. This shall be a permanent
statute to them throughout their generations." '
8¶ "Then you shall say to them, 'Any man from the house of
Israel, or from the aliens who sojourn among them, who offers a
burnt offering or sacrifice,
9and does not bring it to the doorway of the tent of meeting
to offer it to the LORD, that man also shall be cut off from his
people.
10¶ 'And any man from the house of Israel, or from the aliens
who sojourn among them, who eats any blood, I will set My face
against that person who eats blood, and will cut him off from
among his people.
11'For the life of the flesh is in the blood, and I have given it to
you on the altar to make atonement for your souls; for it is the
blood by reason of the life that makes atonement.'
12"Therefore I said to the sons of Israel, 'No person among you
may eat blood, nor may any alien who sojourns among you eat
blood.'
13"So when any man from the sons of Israel, or from the aliens
who sojourn among them, in hunting catches a beast or a bird
which may be eaten, he shall pour out its blood and cover it with
earth.
14¶ "For *as for the* life of all flesh, its blood is *identified* with its
life. Therefore I said to the sons of Israel, 'You are not to eat the
blood of any flesh, for the life of all flesh is its blood; whoever eats
it shall be cut off.'
15"And when any person eats *an animal* which dies, or is torn
*by beasts*, whether he is a native or an alien, he shall wash his
clothes and bathe in water, and remain unclean until evening; then
he will become clean.
16"But if he does not wash *them* or bathe his body, then he shall
bear his guilt."

*Laws on Immoral Relations*

18 THEN THE LORD spoke to Moses, saying,
2"Speak to the sons of Israel and say to them, 'I am the
LORD your God.
3'You shall not do what is done in the land of Egypt where you
lived, nor are you to do what is done in the land of Canaan where
I am bringing you; you shall not walk in their statutes.
4'You are to perform My judgments and keep My statutes, to
live in accord with them; I am the LORD your God.
5'So you shall keep My statutes and My judgments, by which
a man may live if he does them; I am the LORD.
6¶ 'None of you shall approach any blood relative of his to
uncover nakedness; I am the LORD.
7'You shall not uncover the nakedness of your father, that is,
the nakedness of your mother. She is your mother; you are not to
uncover her nakedness.

## New International

entrance to the Tent of Meeting to present it as an offering to the
LORD in front of the tabernacle of the LORD—that man shall be
considered guilty of bloodshed; he has shed blood and must be cut
off from his people. 5This is so the Israelites will bring to the LORD
the sacrifices they are now making in the open fields. They must
bring them to the priest, that is, to the LORD, at the entrance to the
Tent of Meeting and sacrifice them as fellowship offerings.[b] 6The
priest is to sprinkle the blood against the altar of the LORD at the
entrance to the Tent of Meeting and burn the fat as an aroma
pleasing to the LORD. 7They must no longer offer any of their
sacrifices to the goat idols[c] to whom they prostitute themselves.
This is to be a lasting ordinance for them and for the generations
to come.'
8"Say to them: 'Any Israelite or any alien living among them
who offers a burnt offering or sacrifice 9and does not bring it to the
entrance to the Tent of Meeting to sacrifice it to the LORD—that
man must be cut off from his people.
10" 'Any Israelite or any alien living among them who eats any
blood—I will set my face against that person who eats blood and
will cut him off from his people. 11For the life of a creature is in
the blood, and I have given it to you to make atonement for
yourselves on the altar; it is the blood that makes atonement for
one's life. 12Therefore I say to the Israelites, "None of you may eat
blood, nor may an alien living among you eat blood."
13" 'Any Israelite or any alien living among you who hunts any
animal or bird that may be eaten must drain out the blood and
cover it with earth, 14because the life of every creature is its blood.
That is why I have said to the Israelites, "You must not eat the
blood of any creature, because the life of every creature is its blood;
anyone who eats it must be cut off."
15" 'Anyone, whether native-born or alien, who eats anything
found dead or torn by wild animals must wash his clothes and
bathe with water, and he will be ceremonially unclean till evening;
then he will be clean. 16But if he does not wash his clothes and
bathe himself, he will be held responsible.' "

*Unlawful Sexual Relations*

18 THE LORD said to Moses, 2"Speak to the Israelites and
say to them: 'I am the LORD your God. 3You must not do
as they do in Egypt, where you used to live, and you must not do
as they do in the land of Canaan, where I am bringing you. Do not
follow their practices. 4You must obey my laws and be careful to
follow my decrees. I am the LORD your God. 5Keep my decrees and
laws, for the man who obeys them will live by them. I am the LORD.
6" 'No one is to approach any close relative to have sexual
relations. I am the LORD.
7" 'Do not dishonor your father by having sexual relations with
your mother. She is your mother; do not have relations with her.

NIV [b] 5 Traditionally *peace offerings* [c] 7 Or *demons*

## King James

8The nakedness of thy father's wife shalt thou not uncover: it *is* thy father's nakedness.
9The nakedness of thy sister, the daughter of thy father, or daughter of thy mother, *whether she be* born at home, or born abroad, *even* their nakedness thou shalt not uncover.
10The nakedness of thy son's daughter, or of thy daughter's daughter, *even* their nakedness thou shalt not uncover: for theirs *is* thine own nakedness.
11The nakedness of thy father's wife's daughter, begotten of thy father, she *is* thy sister, thou shalt not uncover her nakedness.
12Thou shalt not uncover the nakedness of thy father's sister: she *is* thy father's near kinswoman.
13Thou shalt not uncover the nakedness of thy mother's sister: for she *is* thy mother's near kinswoman.
14Thou shalt not uncover the nakedness of thy father's brother, thou shalt not approach to his wife: she *is* thine aunt.
15Thou shalt not uncover the nakedness of thy daughter-in-law: she *is* thy son's wife; thou shalt not uncover her nakedness.
16Thou shalt not uncover the nakedness of thy brother's wife: it *is* thy brother's nakedness.
17Thou shalt not uncover the nakedness of a woman and her daughter, neither shalt thou take her son's daughter, or her daughter's daughter, to uncover her nakedness; *for* they *are* her near kinswomen: it *is* wickedness.
18Neither shalt thou take a wife to her sister, to vex *her*, to uncover her nakedness, beside the other in her life *time*.
19Also thou shalt not approach unto a woman to uncover her nakedness, as long as she is put apart for her uncleanness.
20Moreover thou shalt not lie carnally with thy neighbour's wife, to defile thyself with her.
21And thou shalt not let any of thy seed pass through *the fire* to Molech, neither shalt thou profane the name of thy God: I *am* the LORD.
22Thou shalt not lie with mankind, as with womankind: it *is* abomination.
23Neither shalt thou lie with any beast to defile thyself therewith: neither shall any woman stand before a beast to lie down thereto: it *is* confusion.
24Defile not ye yourselves in any of these things: for in all these the nations are defiled which I cast out before you:
25And the land is defiled: therefore I do visit the iniquity thereof upon it, and the land itself vomiteth out her inhabitants.
26Ye shall therefore keep my statutes and my judgments, and shall not commit *any* of these abominations; *neither* any of your own nation, nor any stranger that sojourneth among you:
27(For all these abominations have the men of the land done, which *were* before you, and the land is defiled;)
28That the land spew not you out also, when ye defile it, as it spewed out the nations that *were* before you.
29For whosoever shall commit any of these abominations, even the souls that commit *them* shall be cut off from among their people.
30Therefore shall ye keep mine ordinance, that *ye* commit not *any one* of these abominable customs, which were committed before you, and that ye defile not yourselves therein: I *am* the LORD your God.

**19** AND THE LORD spake unto Moses, saying,
2Speak unto all the congregation of the children of Israel, and say unto them, Ye shall be holy: for I the LORD your God *am* holy.
3¶ Ye shall fear every man his mother, and his father, and keep my sabbaths: I *am* the LORD your God.
4¶ Turn ye not unto idols, nor make to yourselves molten gods: I *am* the LORD your God.

## Amplified

8The nakedness of your father's wife you shall not uncover; it is your father's nakedness.
9You shall not have intercourse with *or* uncover the nakedness of your sister, the daughter of your father or of your mother, whether born at home or born abroad.
10You must not have sexual relations with your son's daughter or your daughter's daughter; their nakedness you shall not uncover, for they are your own flesh.
11You must not have intercourse with your father's wife's daughter; begotten by your father, she is your sister; you shall not uncover her nakedness.
12You shall not have intercourse with your father's sister; she is your father's near kinswoman.
13You shall not have sexual relations with your mother's sister, for she is your mother's near kinswoman.
14You shall not have intercourse with your father's brother's wife; you shall not approach his wife; she is your aunt.
15You shall not uncover the nakedness of your daughter-in-law; she is your son's wife; you shall not have intercourse with her.
16You shall not have intercourse with your brother's wife; she belongs to your brother.
17You shall not marry a woman and her daughter, nor shall you take her son's daughter or her daughter's daughter to have intercourse; they are *her* near kinswomen; it is wickedness *and* an outrageous offense.
18You must not marry a woman in addition to her sister, to be a rival to her, having sexual relations with the second sister when the first one is alive.
19Also you shall not have intercourse with a woman during her [menstrual period or similar] uncleanness.
20Moreover you shall not lie carnally with your neighbor's wife, to defile yourself with her.
21You shall not give any of your children to pass through the fire *and* sacrifice them to Molech [the fire god], nor shall you profane the name of your God [by giving it to false gods]. I am the Lord.
22You shall not lie with a man as with a woman; it is an abomination. [I Cor. 6:9, 10.]
23Neither shall you lie with any beast and defile yourself with it; neither shall any woman yield herself to a beast to lie with it; it is confusion, perversion *and* degradedly carnal.
24Do not defile yourselves in any of these ways, for in all these things the nations are defiled which I am casting out before you.
25And the land is defiled; therefore I visit the iniquity of it upon it, and the land itself vomits out her inhabitants.
26So you shall keep My statutes and My ordinances and shall not commit any of these abominations; neither the native born nor any stranger who sojourns among you;
27For all these abominations have the men of the land done, who were before you, and the land is defiled.
28[Do none of these things] lest the land spew you out when you defile it, as it spewed out of the nation that was before you.
29Whoever commits any of these abominations shall be cut off from among [his] people.
30So keep My charge; do not practice any of these abominable customs which were practiced before you, and defile yourselves by them. I am the Lord your God.

**19** AND THE Lord said to Moses,
2Say to all the assembly of the Israelites, You shall be holy, for I the Lord your God am holy. [I Pet. 1:15.]
3Each of you shall give due respect to his mother and his father, and keep My sabbaths holy. I the Lord am your God.
4Do not turn to idols *and* things of nought or make for yourselves molten gods. I the Lord am your God.

## New American Standard

8'You shall not uncover the nakedness of your father's wife; it
is your father's nakedness.
9'The nakedness of your sister, *either* your father's daughter or
your mother's daughter, whether born at home or born outside,
their nakedness you shall not uncover.
10'The nakedness of your son's daughter or your daughter's
daughter, their nakedness you shall not uncover; for their nakedness is yours.
11'The nakedness of your father's wife's daughter, born to your
father, she is your sister, you shall not uncover her nakedness.
12'You shall not uncover the nakedness of your father's sister;
she is your father's blood relative.
13'You shall not uncover the nakedness of your mother's sister,
for she is your mother's blood relative.
14'You shall not uncover the nakedness of your father's brother;
you shall not approach his wife, she is your aunt.
15'You shall not uncover the nakedness of your daughter-in-
law; she is your son's wife, you shall not uncover her nakedness.
16'You shall not uncover the nakedness of your brother's wife;
it is your brother's nakedness.
17'You shall not uncover the nakedness of a woman and of her
daughter, nor shall you take her son's daughter or her daughter's
daughter, to uncover her nakedness; they are blood relatives. It is
lewdness.
18'And you shall not marry a woman in addition to her sister
as a rival while she is alive, to uncover her nakedness.
19¶ 'Also you shall not approach a woman to uncover her
nakedness during her menstrual impurity.
20'And you shall not have intercourse with your neighbor's
wife, to be defiled with her.
21'Neither shall you give any of your offspring to offer them to
Molech, nor shall you profane the name of your God; I am the
LORD.
22'You shall not lie with a male as one lies with a female; it is
an abomination.
23'Also you shall not have intercourse with any animal to be
defiled with it, nor shall any woman stand before an animal to
mate with it; it is a perversion.
24¶ 'Do not defile yourselves by any of these things; for by all
these the nations which I am casting out before you have become
defiled.
25'For the land has become defiled, therefore I have visited its
punishment upon it, so the land has spewed out its inhabitants.
26'But as for you, you are to keep My statutes and My judgments, and shall not do any of these abominations, *neither* the
native, nor the alien who sojourns among you
27(for the men of the land who have been before you have done
all these abominations, and the land has become defiled);
28so that the land may not spew you out, should you defile it,
as it has spewed out the nation which has been before you.
29'For whoever does any of these abominations, those persons
who do *so* shall be cut off from among their people.
30'Thus you are to keep My charge, that you do not practice any
of the abominable customs which have been practiced before you,
so as not to defile yourselves with them; I am the LORD your
God.' "

*Idolatry Forbidden*

19 THEN THE LORD spoke to Moses, saying,
2"Speak to all the congregation of the sons of Israel and
say to them, 'You shall be holy, for I the LORD your God am holy.
3'Every one of you shall reverence his mother and his father,
and you shall keep My sabbaths; I am the LORD your God.
4'Do not turn to idols or make for yourselves molten gods; I am
the LORD your God.

## New International

8" 'Do not have sexual relations with your father's wife; that
would dishonor your father.
9" 'Do not have sexual relations with your sister, either your
father's daughter or your mother's daughter, whether she was
born in the same home or elsewhere.
10" 'Do not have sexual relations with your son's daughter or
your daughter's daughter; that would dishonor you.
11" 'Do not have sexual relations with the daughter of your
father's wife, born to your father; she is your sister.
12" 'Do not have sexual relations with your father's sister; she
is your father's close relative.
13" 'Do not have sexual relations with your mother's sister,
because she is your mother's close relative.
14" 'Do not dishonor your father's brother by approaching his
wife to have sexual relations; she is your aunt.
15" 'Do not have sexual relations with your daughter-in-law.
She is your son's wife; do not have relations with her.
16" 'Do not have sexual relations with your brother's wife; that
would dishonor your brother.
17" 'Do not have sexual relations with both a woman and her
daughter. Do not have sexual relations with either her son's
daughter or her daughter's daughter; they are her close relatives.
That is wickedness.
18" 'Do not take your wife's sister as a rival wife and have sexual
relations with her while your wife is living.
19" 'Do not approach a woman to have sexual relations during
the uncleanness of her monthly period.
20" 'Do not have sexual relations with your neighbor's wife and
defile yourself with her.
21" 'Do not give any of your children to be sacrificed[a] to Molech, for you must not profane the name of your God. I am the
LORD.
22" 'Do not lie with a man as one lies with a woman; that is
detestable.
23" 'Do not have sexual relations with an animal and defile
yourself with it. A woman must not present herself to an animal
to have sexual relations with it; that is a perversion.
24" 'Do not defile yourselves in any of these ways, because this
is how the nations that I am going to drive out before you became
defiled. 25Even the land was defiled; so I punished it for its sin, and
the land vomited out its inhabitants. 26But you must keep my
decrees and my laws. The native-born and the aliens living among
you must not do any of these detestable things, 27for all these
things were done by the people who lived in the land before you,
and the land became defiled. 28And if you defile the land, it will
vomit you out as it vomited out the nations that were before you.
29" 'Everyone who does any of these detestable things—such
persons must be cut off from their people. 30Keep my requirements
and do not follow any of the detestable customs that were practiced before you came and do not defile yourselves with them. I
am the LORD your God.' "

*Various Laws*

19 THE LORD said to Moses, 2"Speak to the entire assembly
of Israel and say to them: 'Be holy because I, the LORD your
God, am holy.
3" 'Each of you must respect his mother and father, and you
must observe my Sabbaths. I am the LORD your God.
4" 'Do not turn to idols or make gods of cast metal for yourselves. I am the LORD your God.

NIV [a] 21 *Or to be passed through ⌊the fire⌋*

## King James

5¶ And if ye offer a sacrifice of peace offerings unto the LORD, ye shall offer it at your own will.

6It shall be eaten the same day ye offer it, and on the morrow: and if aught remain until the third day, it shall be burnt in the fire.

7And if it be eaten at all on the third day, it *is* abominable; it shall not be accepted.

8Therefore *every one* that eateth it shall bear his iniquity, because he hath profaned the hallowed thing of the LORD: and that soul shall be cut off from among his people.

9¶ And when ye reap the harvest of your land, thou shalt not wholly reap the corners of thy field, neither shalt thou gather the gleanings of thy harvest.

10And thou shalt not glean thy vineyard, neither shalt thou gather *every* grape of thy vineyard; thou shalt leave them for the poor and stranger: I *am* the LORD your God.

11¶ Ye shall not steal, neither deal falsely, neither lie one to another.

12¶ And ye shall not swear by my name falsely, neither shalt thou profane the name of thy God: I *am* the LORD.

13¶ Thou shalt not defraud thy neighbour, neither rob *him:* the wages of him that is hired shall not abide with thee all night until the morning.

14¶ Thou shalt not curse the deaf, nor put a stumblingblock before the blind, but shalt fear thy God: I *am* the LORD.

15¶ Ye shall do no unrighteousness in judgment: thou shalt not respect the person of the poor, nor honour the person of the mighty: *but* in righteousness shalt thou judge thy neighbour.

16¶ Thou shalt not go up and down *as* a talebearer among thy people: neither shalt thou stand against the blood of thy neighbour: I *am* the LORD.

17¶ Thou shalt not hate thy brother in thine heart: thou shalt in any wise rebuke thy neighbour, and not suffer sin upon him.

18¶ Thou shalt not avenge, nor bear any grudge against the children of thy people, but thou shalt love thy neighbour as thyself: I *am* the LORD.

19¶ Ye shall keep my statutes. Thou shalt not let thy cattle gender with a diverse kind: thou shalt not sow thy field with mingled seed: neither shall a garment mingled of linen and woollen come upon thee.

20¶ And whosoever lieth carnally with a woman, that *is* a bondmaid, betrothed to an husband, and not at all redeemed, nor freedom given her; she shall be scourged; they shall not be put to death, because she was not free.

21And he shall bring his trespass offering unto the LORD, unto the door of the tabernacle of the congregation, *even* a ram for a trespass offering.

22And the priest shall make an atonement for him with the ram of the trespass offering before the LORD for his sin which he hath done: and the sin which he hath done shall be forgiven him.

23¶ And when ye shall come into the land, and shall have planted all manner of trees for food, then ye shall count the fruit thereof as uncircumcised: three years shall it be as uncircumcised unto you: it shall not be eaten of.

24But in the fourth year all the fruit thereof shall be holy to praise the LORD *withal.*

25And in the fifth year shall ye eat of the fruit thereof, that it may yield unto you the increase thereof: I *am* the LORD your God.

26¶ Ye shall not eat *any thing* with the blood: neither shall ye use enchantment, nor observe times.

27Ye shall not round the corners of your heads, neither shalt thou mar the corners of thy beard.

28Ye shall not make any cuttings in your flesh for the dead, nor print any marks upon you: I *am* the LORD.

29¶ Do not prostitute thy daughter, to cause her to be a whore; lest the land fall to whoredom, and the land become full of wickedness.

## Amplified

5And when you offer a sacrifice of peace offerings to the Lord, you shall offer it so that you may be accepted.

6It shall be eaten the same day you offer it and on the day following; and if anything remains until the third day, it shall be burned in the fire.

7If it is eaten at all the third day, it is loathsome; it will not be accepted.

8But every one who eats it shall bear his iniquity, for he has profaned a holy thing of the Lord; and that soul shall be cut off from his people [and not be included in the atonement made for them].

9And when you reap the harvest of your land, you shall not reap your field to its very corners, neither shall you gather the fallen ears *or* gleanings of your harvest.

10And you shall not glean your vineyard bare, neither shall you gather its fallen grapes; you shall leave them for the poor and the stranger. I am the Lord your God.

11You shall not steal, or deal falsely, or lie one to another. [Col. 3:9, 10.]

12And you shall not swear by My name falsely, neither shall you profane the name of your God. I am the Lord.

13You shall not defraud *or* oppress your neighbor or rob him; the wages of a hired servant shall not remain with you all night until morning.

14You shall not curse the deaf, or put a stumbling block before the blind, but you shall (reverently) fear your God. I am the Lord.

15You shall do no injustice in judging a case; you shall not be partial to the poor or show a preference for the mighty, but in righteousness *and* according to the merits of the case judge your neighbor.

16You shall not go up and down as a dispenser of gossip *and* scandal among your people, nor shall you [secure yourself by false testimony or by silence and] endanger the life of your neighbor. I am the Lord.

17You shall not hate your brother in your heart; but you shall surely rebuke your neighbor, lest you incur sin because of him. [Gal. 6:1; I John 2:9, 11; 3:15.]

18You shall not take revenge or bear any grudge against the sons of your people, but you shall love your neighbor as yourself. I am the Lord. [Rom. 12:17, 19; Matt. 5:43-46.]

19You shall keep My statutes. You shall not let your domestic animals breed with a different kind [of animal]; you shall not sow your field with mixed seed, neither wear a garment of linen mixed with wool.

20And if a man lies carnally with a woman who is a slave, betrothed to a husband, and not yet ransomed or given her freedom, they shall be punished [after investigation]; they shall not be put to death, because she was not free;

21But he shall bring his guilt *or* trespass offering to the Lord, to the door of the tent of meeting, a ram for a guilt *or* trespass offering.

22The priest shall make atonement for him with the ram of the guilt *or* trespass offering before the Lord for his sin, and he shall be forgiven for committing the sin.

23And when you come into the land, and have planted all kinds of trees for food, then you shall count the fruit of them as inedible *and* forbidden to you for three years; it shall not be eaten.

24In the fourth year all their fruit shall be holy for giving praise to the Lord.

25But in the fifth year you may eat of the fruit [of the trees], that their produce may enrich you; I am the Lord your God.

26You shall not eat anything with the blood; neither shall you use magic, omens *or* witchcraft, [or predict events by horoscope or signs and lucky days].

27You shall not round the corners of the hair of your heads, nor trim the corners of your beard [as some idolaters do].

28You shall not make any cuttings in your flesh for the dead, nor print *or* tattoo any marks upon you; I am the Lord.

29Do not profane your daughter by causing her to be a harlot, lest the land fall into harlotry and become full of wickedness.

## New American Standard

5¶ 'Now when you offer a sacrifice of peace offerings to the
LORD, you shall offer it so that you may be accepted.
6'It shall be eaten the same day you offer *it*, and the next day;
but what remains until the third day shall be burned with fire.
7'So if it is eaten at all on the third day, it is an offense; it will
not be accepted.
8'And everyone who eats it will bear his iniquity, for he has
profaned the holy thing of the LORD; and that person shall be cut
off from his people.

*Sundry Laws*

9¶ 'Now when you reap the harvest of your land, you shall not
reap to the very corners of your field, neither shall you gather the
gleanings of your harvest.
10'Nor shall you glean your vineyard, nor shall you gather the
fallen fruit of your vineyard; you shall leave them for the needy
and for the stranger. I am the LORD your God.
11¶ 'You shall not steal, nor deal falsely, nor lie to one another.
12'And you shall not swear falsely by My name, so as to profane
the name of your God; I am the LORD.
13¶ 'You shall not oppress your neighbor, nor rob *him*. The
wages of a hired man are not to remain with you all night until
morning.
14'You shall not curse a deaf man, nor place a stumbling block
before the blind, but you shall revere your God; I am the LORD.
15¶ 'You shall do no injustice in judgment; you shall not be
partial to the poor nor defer to the great, but you are to judge your
neighbor fairly.
16'You shall not go about as a slanderer among your people, and
you are not to act against the life of your neighbor; I am the LORD.
17¶ 'You shall not hate your fellow countryman in your heart;
you may surely reprove your neighbor, but shall not incur sin
because of him.
18'You shall not take vengeance, nor bear any grudge against
the sons of your people, but you shall love your neighbor as
yourself; I am the LORD.
19¶ 'You are to keep My statutes. You shall not breed together
two kinds of your cattle; you shall not sow your field with two
kinds of seed, nor wear a garment upon you of two kinds of
material mixed together.
20'Now if a man lies carnally with a woman who is a slave
acquired for *another* man, but who has in no way been redeemed,
nor given her freedom, there shall be punishment; they shall not,
*however*, be put to death, because she was not free.
21'And he shall bring his guilt offering to the LORD to the doorway of the tent of meeting, a ram for a guilt offering.
22'The priest shall also make atonement for him with the ram
of the guilt offering before the LORD for his sin which he has
committed, and the sin which he has committed shall be forgiven
him.
23¶ 'And when you enter the land and plant all kinds of trees
for food, then you shall count their fruit as forbidden. Three years
it shall be forbidden to you; *it* shall not be eaten.
24'But in the fourth year all its fruit shall be holy, an offering of
praise to the LORD.
25'And in the fifth year you are to eat of its fruit, that its yield
may increase for you; I am the LORD your God.
26¶ 'You shall not eat *anything* with the blood, nor practice
divination or soothsaying.
27'You shall not round off the side-growth of your heads, nor
harm the edges of your beard.
28'You shall not make any cuts in your body for the dead, nor
make any tattoo marks on yourselves: I am the LORD.
29¶ 'Do not profane your daughter by making her a harlot, so
that the land may not fall to harlotry, and the land become full of
lewdness.

## New International

5" 'When you sacrifice a fellowship offering[a] to the LORD, sacrifice it in such a way that it will be accepted on your behalf. 6It shall
be eaten on the day you sacrifice it or on the next day; anything
left over until the third day must be burned up. 7If any of it is eaten
on the third day, it is impure and will not be accepted. 8Whoever
eats it will be held responsible because he has desecrated what is
holy to the LORD; that person must be cut off from his people.
9" 'When you reap the harvest of your land, do not reap to the
very edges of your field or gather the gleanings of your harvest.
10Do not go over your vineyard a second time or pick up the grapes
that have fallen. Leave them for the poor and the alien. I am the
LORD your God.
11" 'Do not steal.
" 'Do not lie.
" 'Do not deceive one another.
12" 'Do not swear falsely by my name and so profane the name
of your God. I am the LORD.
13" 'Do not defraud your neighbor or rob him.
" 'Do not hold back the wages of a hired man overnight.
14" 'Do not curse the deaf or put a stumbling block in front of
the blind, but fear your God. I am the LORD.
15" 'Do not pervert justice; do not show partiality to the poor
or favoritism to the great, but judge your neighbor fairly.
16" 'Do not go about spreading slander among your people.
" 'Do not do anything that endangers your neighbor's life. I am
the LORD.
17" 'Do not hate your brother in your heart. Rebuke your neighbor frankly so you will not share in his guilt.
18" 'Do not seek revenge or bear a grudge against one of your
people, but love your neighbor as yourself. I am the LORD.
19" 'Keep my decrees.
" 'Do not mate different kinds of animals.
" 'Do not plant your field with two kinds of seed.
" 'Do not wear clothing woven of two kinds of material.
20" 'If a man sleeps with a woman who is a slave girl promised
to another man but who has not been ransomed or given her
freedom, there must be due punishment. Yet they are not to be put
to death, because she had not been freed. 21The man, however,
must bring a ram to the entrance to the Tent of Meeting for a guilt
offering to the LORD. 22With the ram of the guilt offering the priest
is to make atonement for him before the LORD for the sin he has
committed, and his sin will be forgiven.
23" 'When you enter the land and plant any kind of fruit tree,
regard its fruit as forbidden.[b] For three years you are to consider
it forbidden[c]; it must not be eaten. 24In the fourth year all its fruit
will be holy, an offering of praise to the LORD. 25But in the fifth year
you may eat its fruit. In this way your harvest will be increased.
I am the LORD your God.
26" 'Do not eat any meat with the blood still in it.
" 'Do not practice divination or sorcery.
27" 'Do not cut the hair at the sides of your head or clip off the
edges of your beard.
28" 'Do not cut your bodies for the dead or put tattoo marks on
yourselves. I am the LORD.
29" 'Do not degrade your daughter by making her a prostitute,
or the land will turn to prostitution and be filled with wickedness.

NIV [a] 5 Traditionally *peace offering* [b] 23 Hebrew *uncircumcised*
[c] 23 Hebrew *uncircumcised*

## King James

30¶ Ye shall keep my sabbaths, and reverence my sanctuary: I *am* the LORD.

31¶ Regard not them that have familiar spirits, neither seek after wizards, to be defiled by them: I *am* the LORD your God.

32¶ Thou shalt rise up before the hoary head, and honour the face of the old man, and fear thy God: I *am* the LORD.

33¶ And if a stranger sojourn with thee in your land, ye shall not vex him.

34 *But* the stranger that dwelleth with you shall be unto you as one born among you, and thou shalt love him as thyself; for ye were strangers in the land of Egypt: I *am* the LORD your God.

35¶ Ye shall do no unrighteousness in judgment, in meteyard, in weight, or in measure.

36Just balances, just weights, a just ephah, and a just hin, shall ye have: I *am* the LORD your God, which brought you out of the land of Egypt.

37Therefore shall ye observe all my statutes, and all my judgments, and do them: I *am* the LORD.

**20** AND THE LORD spake unto Moses, saying,

2Again, thou shalt say to the children of Israel, Whosoever *he be* of the children of Israel, or of the strangers that sojourn in Israel, that giveth *any* of his seed unto Molech; he shall surely be put to death: the people of the land shall stone him with stones.

3And I will set my face against that man, and will cut him off from among his people; because he hath given of his seed unto Molech, to defile my sanctuary, and to profane my holy name.

4And if the people of the land do any ways hide their eyes from the man, when he giveth of his seed unto Molech, and kill him not:

5Then I will set my face against that man, and against his family, and will cut him off, and all that go a-whoring after him, to commit whoredom with Molech, from among their people.

6¶ And the soul that turneth after such as have familiar spirits, and after wizards, to go a-whoring after them, I will even set my face against that soul, and will cut him off from among his people.

7¶ Sanctify yourselves therefore, and be ye holy: for I *am* the LORD your God.

8And ye shall keep my statutes, and do them: I *am* the LORD which sanctify you.

9¶ For every one that curseth his father or his mother shall be surely put to death: he hath cursed his father or his mother; his blood *shall be* upon him.

10¶ And the man that committeth adultery with *another* man's wife, *even he* that committeth adultery with his neighbour's wife, the adulterer and the adulteress shall surely be put to death.

11And the man that lieth with his father's wife hath uncovered his father's nakedness: both of them shall surely be put to death; their blood *shall be* upon them.

12And if a man lie with his daughter-in-law, both of them shall surely be put to death: they have wrought confusion; their blood *shall be* upon them.

13If a man also lie with mankind, as he lieth with a woman, both of them have committed an abomination: they shall surely be put to death; their blood *shall be* upon them.

## Amplified

30You shall keep My sabbaths, and reverence My sanctuary. I am the Lord.

31Turn not to those [mediums] who have familiar spirits, or to wizards; do not seek them out to be defiled by them. I am the Lord your God.

32You shall rise up before the hoary head, and honor the face of the old man, and (reverently) fear your God. I am the Lord.

33And if a stranger dwells temporarily with you in your land, you shall not suppress *and* mistreat him.

34But the stranger who dwells with you shall be to you as one born among you; and you shall love him as yourself, for you were strangers in the land of Egypt. I am the Lord your God.

35You shall do no unrighteousness in judgment, in measures of length or weight or quantity.

36You shall have accurate *and* just balances, just weights, just ephah and hin measures. I am the Lord your God, Who brought you out of the land of Egypt.

37You shall observe all My statutes and ordinances, and do them. I am the Lord.

**20** AND THE Lord said to Moses,

2Moreover, you shall say to the Israelites, Any one of the Israelites, or of the strangers that sojourn in Israel, who gives any of his children to Molech [the fire god, worshiped with human sacrifices] shall surely be put to death; the people of the land shall stone him with stones.

3I also will set My face against that man [opposing him, withdrawing My protection from him and excluding him from My covenant], and will cut him off from among his people; because he has given of his children to Molech, defiling My sanctuary and profaning My holy name.

4And if the people of the land do at all hide their eyes from the man, when he gives one of his children [as a burnt offering] to Molech [the fire god], *and* they overlook it *or* neglect to take legal action to punish him, winking at his sin, and do not kill him [as this My law requires],

5Then I will set My face against that man and against his family, and will cut him off from among their people, him and all who follow him to [unfaithfulness to Me, and thus] play the harlot after Molech.

6The person who turns to those who have familiar spirits and to wizards, [being unfaithful to Israel's Maker Who is her Husband, and thus] playing the harlot after them, I will set My face against that person and will cut him off from among his people [that he may not be included in the atonement made for them]. [Isa. 54:5.]

7Consecrate yourselves therefore, and be holy; for I am the Lord your God.

8And you shall keep My statutes, and do them. I am the Lord Who sanctifies you.

9Every one who curses his father or mother shall surely be put to death; he has cursed his father or mother; his bloodguilt is upon him.

10The man who commits adultery with another's wife, even his neighbor's wife, the adulterer and the adulteress shall surely be put to death. [John 8:4-11.]

11And the man who lies carnally with his father's wife has uncovered his father's nakedness; both of the guilty ones shall surely be put to death; their blood shall be upon their own heads.

12And if a man lies carnally with his daughter-in-law, both of them shall surely be put to death; they have wrought confusion, perversion *and* defilement; their blood shall be upon their own heads.

13If a man lies with a male as if he were a woman, both men have committed an offense—perverse, unnatural, abhorrent *and* detestable; they shall surely be put to death; their blood shall be upon them.

## New American Standard

30'You shall keep My sabbaths and revere My sanctuary; I am
the LORD.
31¶ 'Do not turn to mediums or spiritists; do not seek them out
to be defiled by them. I am the LORD your God.
32¶ 'You shall rise up before the grayheaded, and honor the
aged, and you shall revere your God; I am the LORD.
33¶ 'When a stranger resides with you in your land, you shall
not do him wrong.
34'The stranger who resides with you shall be to you as the
native among you, and you shall love him as yourself; for you were
aliens in the land of Egypt: I am the LORD your God.
35¶ 'You shall do no wrong in judgment, in measurement of
weight, or capacity.
36'You shall have just balances, just weights, a just [a]ephah, and
a just [b]hin: I am the LORD your God, who brought you out from
the land of Egypt.
37'You shall thus observe all My statutes, and all My ordinances, and do them: I am the LORD.' "

*On Human Sacrifice and Immoralities*

**20** THEN THE LORD spoke to Moses, saying,
2"You shall also say to the sons of Israel, 'Any man from
the sons of Israel or from the aliens sojourning in Israel, who gives
any of his offspring to Molech, shall surely be put to death; the
people of the land shall stone him with stones.
3'I will also set My face against that man and will cut him off
from among his people, because he has given some of his offspring
to Molech, so as to defile My sanctuary and to profane My holy
name.
4'If the people of the land, however, should ever disregard that
man when he gives any of his offspring to Molech, so as not to put
him to death,
5then I Myself will set My face against that man and against
his family; and I will cut off from among their people both him and
all those who play the harlot after him, by playing the harlot after
Molech.
6¶ 'As for the person who turns to mediums and to spiritists,
to play the harlot after them, I will also set My face against that
person and will cut him off from among his people.
7'You shall consecrate yourselves therefore and be holy, for I
am the LORD your God.
8'And you shall keep My statutes and practice them; I am the
LORD who sanctifies you.
9¶ 'If *there is* anyone who curses his father or his mother, he
shall surely be put to death; he has cursed his father or his mother,
his bloodguiltiness is upon him.
10¶ 'If *there is* a man who commits adultery with another man's
wife, one who commits adultery with his friend's wife, the adulterer and the adulteress shall surely be put to death.
11'If *there is* a man who lies with his father's wife, he has uncovered his father's nakedness; both of them shall surely be put to
death, their bloodguiltiness is upon them.
12'If *there is* a man who lies with his daughter-in-law, both of
them shall surely be put to death; they have committed incest,
their bloodguiltiness is upon them.
13'If *there is* a man who lies with a male as those who lie with
a woman, both of them have committed a detestable act; they shall
surely be put to death. Their bloodguiltiness is upon them.

NAS [a] I.e., Approx. one bushel [b] I.e., Approx. one gallon

## New International

30" 'Observe my Sabbaths and have reverence for my sanctuary. I am the LORD.
31" 'Do not turn to mediums or seek out spiritists, for you will
be defiled by them. I am the LORD your God.
32" 'Rise in the presence of the aged, show respect for the
elderly and revere your God. I am the LORD.
33" 'When an alien lives with you in your land, do not mistreat
him. 34The alien living with you must be treated as one of your
native-born. Love him as yourself, for you were aliens in Egypt.
I am the LORD your God.
35" 'Do not use dishonest standards when measuring length,
weight or quantity. 36Use honest scales and honest weights, an
honest ephah[c] and an honest hin.[d] I am the LORD your God, who
brought you out of Egypt.
37" 'Keep all my decrees and all my laws and follow them. I am
the LORD.' "

*Punishments for Sin*

**20** THE LORD said to Moses, 2"Say to the Israelites: 'Any
Israelite or any alien living in Israel who gives[e] any of his
children to Molech must be put to death. The people of the community are to stone him. 3I will set my face against that man and
I will cut him off from his people; for by giving his children to
Molech, he has defiled my sanctuary and profaned my holy name.
4If the people of the community close their eyes when that man
gives one of his children to Molech and they fail to put him to
death, 5I will set my face against that man and his family and will
cut off from their people both him and all who follow him in
prostituting themselves to Molech.
6" 'I will set my face against the person who turns to mediums
and spiritists to prostitute himself by following them, and I will cut
him off from his people.
7" 'Consecrate yourselves and be holy, because I am the LORD
your God. 8Keep my decrees and follow them. I am the LORD, who
makes you holy.[f]
9" 'If anyone curses his father or mother, he must be put to
death. He has cursed his father or his mother, and his blood will
be on his own head.
10" 'If a man commits adultery with another man's wife—with
the wife of his neighbor—both the adulterer and the adulteress
must be put to death.
11" 'If a man sleeps with his father's wife, he has dishonored his
father. Both the man and the woman must be put to death; their
blood will be on their own heads.
12" 'If a man sleeps with his daughter-in-law, both of them must
be put to death. What they have done is a perversion; their blood
will be on their own heads.
13" 'If a man lies with a man as one lies with a woman, both of
them have done what is detestable. They must be put to death;
their blood will be on their own heads.

NIV [c] 36 An ephah was a dry measure. [d] 36 A hin was a liquid measure.
[e] 2 Or *sacrifices;* also in verses 3 and 4 [f] 8 Or *who sanctifies you;* or *who sets you apart as holy*

## King James

14 And if a man take a wife and her mother, it *is* wickedness: they
shall be burnt with fire, both he and they; that there be no wickedness among you.
15 And if a man lie with a beast, he shall surely be put to death:
and ye shall slay the beast.
16 And if a woman approach unto any beast, and lie down
thereto, thou shalt kill the woman, and the beast: they shall surely
be put to death; their blood *shall be* upon them.
17 And if a man shall take his sister, his father's daughter, or his
mother's daughter, and see her nakedness, and she see his nakedness; it *is* a wicked thing; and they shall be cut off in the sight of
their people; he hath uncovered his sister's nakedness; he shall
bear his iniquity.
18 And if a man shall lie with a woman having her sickness, and
shall uncover her nakedness; he hath discovered her fountain, and
she hath uncovered the fountain of her blood: and both of them
shall be cut off from among their people.
19 And thou shalt not uncover the nakedness of thy mother's
sister, nor of thy father's sister: for he uncovereth his near kin: they
shall bear their iniquity.
20 And if a man shall lie with his uncle's wife, he hath uncovered
his uncle's nakedness: they shall bear their sin; they shall die
childless.
21 And if a man shall take his brother's wife, it *is* an unclean
thing: he hath uncovered his brother's nakedness; they shall be
childless.
22 ¶ Ye shall therefore keep all my statutes, and all my judgments, and do them: that the land, whither I bring you to dwell
therein, spew you not out.
23 And ye shall not walk in the manners of the nation, which I
cast out before you: for they committed all these things, and therefore I abhorred them.
24 But I have said unto you, Ye shall inherit their land, and I will
give it unto you to possess it, a land that floweth with milk and
honey: I *am* the LORD your God, which have separated you from
*other* people.
25 Ye shall therefore put difference between clean beasts and
unclean, and between unclean fowls and clean: and ye shall not
make your souls abominable by beast, or by fowl, or by any manner of living thing that creepeth on the ground, which I have
separated from you as unclean.
26 And ye shall be holy unto me: for I the LORD *am* holy, and
have severed you from *other* people, that ye should be mine.
27 ¶ A man also or woman that hath a familiar spirit, or that is
a wizard, shall surely be put to death: they shall stone them with
stones: their blood *shall be* upon them.

**21** AND THE LORD said unto Moses, Speak unto the priests
the sons of Aaron, and say unto them, There shall none
be defiled for the dead among his people:
2 But for his kin, that is near unto him, *that is,* for his mother,
and for his father, and for his son, and for his daughter, and for
his brother,
3 And for his sister a virgin, that is nigh unto him, which hath
had no husband; for her may he be defiled.
4 *But* he shall not defile himself, *being* a chief man among his
people, to profane himself.
5 They shall not make baldness upon their head, neither shall
they shave off the corner of their beard, nor make any cuttings in
their flesh.
6 They shall be holy unto their God, and not profane the name
of their God: for the offerings of the LORD made by fire, *and* the
bread of their God, they do offer: therefore they shall be holy.
7 They shall not take a wife *that is* a whore, or profane; neither
shall they take a woman put away from her husband: for he *is* holy
unto his God.

## Amplified

14 And if a man takes a wife and her mother, it is wickedness
*and* an outrageous offense; they shall all three be burned with fire,
both he and they [after being stoned to death], that there be no
wickedness among you. [Josh. 7:15, 25.]
15 And if a man lies carnally with a beast, he shall surely be
[stoned] to death; and you shall slay the beast.
16 If a woman approaches any beast, and lies carnally with it,
you shall [stone] the woman and the beast; they shall surely be put
to death, their blood is upon them.
17 If a man takes his sister, his father's or his mother's daughter,
and sees her nakedness and she sees his nakedness, it is a wicked
*and* shameful thing; and they shall be cut off in the sight of their
people; he has had sexual relations with his sister; he shall bear his
iniquity.
18 And if a man shall lie with a woman having her menstrual
pains, and shall uncover her nakedness, he has made naked her
fountain, and she has uncovered the fountain of her blood; and
both of them shall be cut off from among their people.
19 You shall not uncover the nakedness of your mother's sister
or of your father's sister; for that is to make naked his close kin;
they shall bear their iniquity.
20 And if a man shall lie carnally with his uncle's wife, he has
uncovered his uncle's nakedness; they shall bear their sin; they
shall die childless [not literally, but in a legal sense].
21 And if a man shall take his brother's wife, it is impurity; he
has uncovered his brother's nakedness; they shall be childless [not
literally, but in a legal sense].
22 You shall therefore keep all My statutes and all My ordinances, and do them; that the land where I am bringing you to
dwell may not vomit you out [as it did those before you]. [Lev.
18:28.]
23 You shall not walk in the customs of the nation which I am
casting out before you; for they did all these things, and therefore
I was wearied *and* grieved by them.
24 But I have said to you, You shall inherit their land, and I will
give it to you to possess, a land flowing with milk and honey. I am
the Lord your God, Who has separated you from the peoples.
25 You shall therefore make a distinction between the clean beast
and the unclean, and between the unclean fowl and the clean; and
you shall not make yourselves detestable with beast or with bird
or with anything with which the ground teems *or* that creeps,
which I have set apart from you as unclean.
26 And you shall be holy to Me; for I the Lord am holy, and have
separated you from the peoples, that you should be Mine.
27 A man or woman who is a medium *and* has a familiar spirit
or is a wizard, shall surely be put to death, be stoned with stones;
their blood shall be upon them.

**21** THE LORD said to Moses, Speak to the priests [exclusive
of the high priest], the sons of Aaron, and say to them that
none of them shall defile himself for the dead among his people
[by touching a corpse or assisting in preparing it for burial],
2 Except for his near [blood] kin, for his mother, father, son,
daughter, brother,
3 And for his sister a virgin, near to him because she has had no
husband; for her he may be defiled.
4 He shall not even defile himself being a [bereaved] husband
[his wife not being his blood kin] *or* being a chief man among his
people, and so profane himself.
5 The priests [like the other Israelite men] shall not shave the
crown of their heads, or clip off the corners of their beard, or make
any cuttings in their flesh.
6 They shall be holy to their God, and not profane the name of
their God; for they offer the offerings made by fire to the Lord, the
bread of their God; therefore they shall be holy.
7 They shall not take a wife who is a harlot or polluted *or* profane
or divorced; for [the priest] is holy to his God.

## New American Standard

14'If *there is* a man who marries a woman and her mother, it is
immorality; both he and they shall be burned with fire, that there
may be no immorality in your midst.
15'If *there is* a man who lies with an animal, he shall surely be
put to death; you shall also kill the animal.
16'If *there is* a woman who approaches any animal to mate with
it, you shall kill the woman and the animal; they shall surely be
put to death. Their bloodguiltiness is upon them.
17¶ 'If *there is* a man who takes his sister, his father's daughter
or his mother's daughter, so that he sees her nakedness and she
sees his nakedness, it is a disgrace; and they shall be cut off in the
sight of the sons of their people. He has uncovered his sister's
nakedness; he bears his guilt.
18'If *there is* a man who lies with a menstruous woman and
uncovers her nakedness, he has laid bare her flow, and she has
exposed the flow of her blood; thus both of them shall be cut off
from among their people.
19'You shall also not uncover the nakedness of your mother's
sister or of your father's sister, for such a one has made naked his
blood relative; they shall bear their guilt.
20'If *there is* a man who lies with his uncle's wife he has uncovered his uncle's nakedness; they shall bear their sin. They shall die
childless.
21'If *there is* a man who takes his brother's wife, it is abhorrent;
he has uncovered his brother's nakedness. They shall be childless.
22¶ 'You are therefore to keep all My statutes and all My ordinances and do them, so that the land to which I am bringing you
to live will not spew you out.
23'Moreover, you shall not follow the customs of the nation
which I shall drive out before you, for they did all these things, and
therefore I have abhorred them.
24'Hence I have said to you, "You are to possess their land, and
I Myself will give it to you to possess it, a land flowing with milk
and honey." I am the LORD your God, who has separated you from
the peoples.
25'You are therefore to make a distinction between the clean
animal and the unclean, and between the unclean bird and the
clean; and you shall not make yourselves detestable by animal or
by bird or by anything that creeps on the ground, which I have
separated for you as unclean.
26'Thus you are to be holy to Me, for I the LORD am holy; and
I have set you apart from the peoples to be Mine.
27¶ 'Now a man or a woman who is a medium or a spiritist shall
surely be put to death. They shall be stoned with stones, their
bloodguiltiness is upon them.' "

*Regulations concerning Priests*

**21** THEN THE LORD said to Moses, "Speak to the priests, the
sons of Aaron, and say to them, 'No one shall defile
himself for a *dead* person among his people,
2except for his relatives who are nearest to him, his mother and
his father and his son and his daughter and his brother,
3also for his virgin sister, who is near to him because she has
had no husband; for her he may defile himself.
4'He shall not defile himself as a relative by marriage among
his people, and so profane himself.
5'They shall not make any baldness on their heads, nor shave
off the edges of their beards, nor make any cuts in their flesh.
6'They shall be holy to their God and not profane the name of
their God, for they present the offerings by fire to the LORD, the
bread of their God; so they shall be holy.
7'They shall not take a woman who is profaned by harlotry, nor
shall they take a woman divorced from her husband; for he is holy
to his God.

## New International

14" 'If a man marries both a woman and her mother, it is
wicked. Both he and they must be burned in the fire, so that no
wickedness will be among you.
15" 'If a man has sexual relations with an animal, he must be put
to death, and you must kill the animal.
16" 'If a woman approaches an animal to have sexual relations
with it, kill both the woman and the animal. They must be put to
death; their blood will be on their own heads.
17" 'If a man marries his sister, the daughter of either his father
or his mother, and they have sexual relations, it is a disgrace. They
must be cut off before the eyes of their people. He has dishonored
his sister and will be held responsible.
18" 'If a man lies with a woman during her monthly period and
has sexual relations with her, he has exposed the source of her
flow, and she has also uncovered it. Both of them must be cut off
from their people.
19" 'Do not have sexual relations with the sister of either your
mother or your father, for that would dishonor a close relative;
both of you would be held responsible.
20" 'If a man sleeps with his aunt, he has dishonored his uncle.
They will be held responsible; they will die childless.
21" 'If a man marries his brother's wife, it is an act of impurity;
he has dishonored his brother. They will be childless.
22" 'Keep all my decrees and laws and follow them, so that the
land where I am bringing you to live may not vomit you out. 23You
must not live according to the customs of the nations I am going
to drive out before you. Because they did all these things, I abhorred them. 24But I said to you, "You will possess their land; I
will give it to you as an inheritance, a land flowing with milk and
honey." I am the LORD your God, who has set you apart from the
nations.
25" 'You must therefore make a distinction between clean and
unclean animals and between unclean and clean birds. Do not
defile yourselves by any animal or bird or anything that moves
along the ground—those which I have set apart as unclean for you.
26You are to be holy to me[a] because I, the LORD, am holy, and I
have set you apart from the nations to be my own.
27" 'A man or woman who is a medium or spiritist among you
must be put to death. You are to stone them; their blood will be
on their own heads.' "

*Rules for Priests*

**21** THE LORD said to Moses, "Speak to the priests, the sons
of Aaron, and say to them: 'A priest must not make himself ceremonially unclean for any of his people who die, 2except
for a close relative, such as his mother or father, his son or daughter, his brother, 3or an unmarried sister who is dependent on him
since she has no husband—for her he may make himself unclean.
4He must not make himself unclean for people related to him by
marriage,[b] and so defile himself.
5" 'Priests must not shave their heads or shave off the edges of
their beards or cut their bodies. 6They must be holy to their God
and must not profane the name of their God. Because they present
the offerings made to the LORD by fire, the food of their God, they
are to be holy.
7" 'They must not marry women defiled by prostitution or divorced from their husbands, because priests are holy to their God.

**NIV** [a] 26 Or *be my holy ones* [b] 4 Or *unclean as a leader among his people*

## King James

8 Thou shalt sanctify him therefore; for he offereth the bread of thy God: he shall be holy unto thee: for I the LORD, which sanctify you, *am* holy.

9 ¶ And the daughter of any priest, if she profane herself by playing the whore, she profaneth her father: she shall be burnt with fire.

10 And *he that is* the high priest among his brethren, upon whose head the anointing oil was poured, and that is consecrated to put on the garments, shall not uncover his head, nor rend his clothes;

11 Neither shall he go in to any dead body, nor defile himself for his father, or for his mother;

12 Neither shall he go out of the sanctuary, nor profane the sanctuary of his God; for the crown of the anointing oil of his God *is* upon him: I *am* the LORD.

13 And he shall take a wife in her virginity.

14 A widow, or a divorced woman, or profane, *or* an harlot, these shall he not take: but he shall take a virgin of his own people to wife.

15 Neither shall he profane his seed among his people: for I the LORD do sanctify him.

16 ¶ And the LORD spake unto Moses, saying,

17 Speak unto Aaron, saying, Whosoever *he be* of thy seed in their generations that hath *any* blemish, let him not approach to offer the bread of his God.

18 For whatsoever man *he be* that hath a blemish, he shall not approach: a blind man, or a lame, or he that hath a flat nose, or any thing superfluous,

19 Or a man that is brokenfooted, or brokenhanded,

20 Or crookbackt, or a dwarf, or that hath a blemish in his eye, or be scurvy, or scabbed, or hath his stones broken;

21 No man that hath a blemish of the seed of Aaron the priest shall come nigh to offer the offerings of the LORD made by fire: he hath a blemish; he shall not come nigh to offer the bread of his God.

22 He shall eat the bread of his God, *both* of the most holy, and of the holy.

23 Only he shall not go in unto the veil, nor come nigh unto the altar, because he hath a blemish; that he profane not my sanctuaries: for I the LORD do sanctify them.

24 And Moses told *it* unto Aaron, and to his sons, and unto all the children of Israel.

**22** AND THE LORD spake unto Moses, saying,

2 Speak unto Aaron and to his sons, that they separate themselves from the holy things of the children of Israel, and that they profane not my holy name *in those things* which they hallow unto me: I *am* the LORD.

3 Say unto them, Whosoever *he be* of all your seed among your generations, that goeth unto the holy things, which the children of Israel hallow unto the LORD, having his uncleanness upon him, that soul shall be cut off from my presence: I *am* the LORD.

4 What man soever of the seed of Aaron *is* a leper, or hath a running issue; he shall not eat of the holy things, until he be clean. And whoso toucheth any thing *that is* unclean *by* the dead, or a man whose seed goeth from him;

5 Or whosoever toucheth any creeping thing, whereby he may be made unclean, or a man of whom he may take uncleanness, whatsoever uncleanness he hath;

6 The soul which hath touched any such shall be unclean until even, and shall not eat of the holy things, unless he wash his flesh with water.

## Amplified

8 You shall consecrate him therefore, for he offers the bread of your God; he shall be holy to you, for I, the Lord Who sanctifies you, am holy.

9 The daughter of any priest who profanes herself by playing the harlot profanes her father; she shall be burned with fire [after being stoned]. [Josh. 7:15, 25.]

10 But he who is the high priest among his brethren, upon whose head the anointing oil was poured, and who is consecrated to put on the [sacred] garments, shall not let the hair of his head hang loose, or rend his clothes [in mourning],

11 Neither shall he go in where any dead body lies, nor defile himself [by doing so, even] for his father or for his mother;

12 Neither shall he go out of the sanctuary, nor desecrate *or* make ceremonially unclean the sanctuary of his God; for the crown *or* consecration of the anointing oil of his God is upon him. I am the Lord.

13 He shall take a wife in her virginity.

14 A widow, or a divorced woman, or a woman who is polluted *or* profane, or a harlot, these he shall not marry; but he shall take as his wife a virgin of his own people, [Cp. I Tim. 3:2-7; Titus 1:7-9.]

15 That he may not profane *or* dishonor his children among his people; for I the Lord do sanctify the high priest.

16 And the Lord said to Moses,

17 Say to Aaron, Any one of your sons in their successive generations who has any blemish, let him not come near to offer the bread of his God.

18 For no man who has a blemish shall approach [God's altar to serve as priest], a man blind or lame, or he who has a disfigured face or a limb too long,

19 Or who has a fractured foot or hand,

20 Or is a hunchback, or a dwarf, or has a defect in his eye, or has scurvy *or* itch, or scabs *or* skin trouble, or has damaged testicles;

21 No man of the offspring of Aaron the priest who has a blemish *and* is disfigured *or* deformed shall come near [the altar] to offer the offerings of the Lord by fire; he has a blemish; he shall not come near to offer the bread of his God.

22 He may eat the bread of his God, both of the most holy and of the holy things,

23 But he shall not come within the veil, or come near the altar [of incense], because he has a blemish; that he may not desecrate *and* make unclean My sanctuaries *and* hallowed things; for I the Lord do sanctify them. [Heb. 7:28.]

24 And Moses told it to Aaron and to his sons and to all the Israelites.

**22** AND THE Lord said to Moses,

2 Say to Aaron and his sons that they shall stay away from the holy things which the Israelites dedicate to Me, that they may not profane My holy name; I am the Lord.

3 Tell them, any one of your offspring throughout your generations who goes to the holy things, which the Israelites dedicate to the Lord, when he is unclean, that [priest] shall be cut off from My presence *and* excluded from the sanctuary; I am the Lord.

4 No man of the offspring of Aaron who is a leper or has a discharge shall eat of the holy things [the offerings and the showbread] until he is clean. And whoever touches any person *or* thing made unclean by contact with a corpse or a man who has had a discharge of semen,

5 Or whoever touches any dead creeping thing by which he may be made unclean or a man from whom he may acquire uncleanness, whatever it may be, [Lev. 11:24-28.]

6 The priest who has touched any such thing shall be unclean until evening and shall not eat of the holy things unless he has bathed with water. [Cp. Heb. 10:22.]

## New American Standard

8'You shall consecrate him, therefore, for he offers the bread of your God; he shall be holy to you; for I the LORD, who sanctifies you, am holy.

9'Also the daughter of any priest, if she profanes herself by harlotry, she profanes her father; she shall be burned with fire.

10¶ 'And the priest who is the highest among his brothers, on whose head the anointing oil has been poured, and who has been consecrated to wear the garments, shall not uncover his head, nor tear his clothes;

11nor shall he approach any dead person, nor defile himself *even* for his father or his mother;

12nor shall he go out of the sanctuary, nor profane the sanctuary of his God; for the consecration of the anointing oil of his God is on him: I am the LORD.

13'And he shall take a wife in her virginity.

14'A widow, or a divorced woman, or one who is profaned by harlotry, these he may not take; but rather he is to marry a virgin of his own people;

15that he may not profane his offspring among his people: for I am the LORD who sanctifies him.' "

16¶ Then the LORD spoke to Moses, saying,

17"Speak to Aaron, saying, 'No man of your offspring throughout their generations who has a defect shall approach to offer the bread of his God.

18'For no one who has a defect shall approach: a blind man, or a lame man, or he who has a disfigured *face*, or any deformed *limb*,

19or a man who has a broken foot or broken hand,

20or a hunchback or a dwarf, or *one who has* a defect in his eye or eczema or scabs or crushed testicles.

21'No man among the descendants of Aaron the priest, who has a defect, is to come near to offer the LORD'S offerings by fire; *since* he has a defect, he shall not come near to offer the bread of his God.

22'He may eat the bread of his God, *both* of the most holy and of the holy,

23only he shall not go in to the veil or come near the altar because he has a defect, that he may not profane My sanctuaries. For I am the LORD who sanctifies them.' "

24So Moses spoke to Aaron and to his sons and to all the sons of Israel.

*Sundry Rules for Priests*

22 THEN THE LORD spoke to Moses, saying,

2"Tell Aaron and his sons to be careful with the holy *gifts* of the sons of Israel, which they dedicate to Me, so as not to profane My holy name; I am the LORD.

3"Say to them, 'If any man among all your descendants throughout your generations approaches the holy *gifts* which the sons of Israel dedicate to the LORD, while he has an uncleanness, that person shall be cut off from before Me. I am the LORD.

4'No man, of the descendants of Aaron, who is a leper or who has a discharge, may eat of the holy *gifts* until he is clean. And if one touches anything made unclean by a corpse or if a man has a seminal emission,

5or if a man touches any teeming things, by which he is made unclean, or any man by whom he is made unclean, whatever his uncleanness;

6a person who touches any such shall be unclean until evening, and shall not eat of the holy *gifts*, unless he has bathed his body in water.

## New International

8Regard them as holy, because they offer up the food of your God.
Consider them holy, because I the LORD am holy—I who make you
holy.[a]
9" 'If a priest's daughter defiles herself by becoming a prostitute, she disgraces her father; she must be burned in the fire.
10" 'The high priest, the one among his brothers who has had
the anointing oil poured on his head and who has been ordained
to wear the priestly garments, must not let his hair become unkempt[b] or tear his clothes. 11He must not enter a place where there
is a dead body. He must not make himself unclean, even for his
father or mother, 12nor leave the sanctuary of his God or desecrate
it, because he has been dedicated by the anointing oil of his God.
I am the LORD.
13" 'The woman he marries must be a virgin. 14He must not
marry a widow, a divorced woman, or a woman defiled by prostitution, but only a virgin from his own people, 15so he will not defile
his offspring among his people. I am the LORD, who makes him
holy.[c] ' "
16The LORD said to Moses, 17"Say to Aaron: 'For the generations
to come none of your descendants who has a defect may come near
to offer the food of his God. 18No man who has any defect may
come near: no man who is blind or lame, disfigured or deformed;
19no man with a crippled foot or hand, 20or who is hunchbacked
or dwarfed, or who has any eye defect, or who has festering or
running sores or damaged testicles. 21No descendant of Aaron the
priest who has any defect is to come near to present the offerings
made to the LORD by fire. He has a defect; he must not come near
to offer the food of his God. 22He may eat the most holy food of
his God, as well as the holy food; 23yet because of his defect, he
must not go near the curtain or approach the altar, and so desecrate my sanctuary. I am the LORD, who makes them holy.[d] ' "
24So Moses told this to Aaron and his sons and to all the Israelites.

22 THE LORD said to Moses, 2"Tell Aaron and his sons to
treat with respect the sacred offerings the Israelites consecrate to me, so they will not profane my holy name. I am the LORD.
3"Say to them: 'For the generations to come, if any of your
descendants is ceremonially unclean and yet comes near the sacred offerings that the Israelites consecrate to the LORD, that person must be cut off from my presence. I am the LORD.
4" 'If a descendant of Aaron has an infectious skin disease[e] or
a bodily discharge, he may not eat the sacred offerings until he is
cleansed. He will also be unclean if he touches something defiled
by a corpse or by anyone who has an emission of semen, 5or if he
touches any crawling thing that makes him unclean, or any person
who makes him unclean, whatever the uncleanness may be. 6The
one who touches any such thing will be unclean till evening. He
must not eat any of the sacred offerings unless he has bathed
himself with water. 7When the sun goes down, he will be clean,

NIV [a] 8 Or *who sanctify you;* or *who set you apart as holy* [b] 10 Or *not uncover his head* [c] 15 Or *who sanctifies him;* or *who sets him apart as holy* [d] 23 Or *who sanctifies them;* or *who sets them apart as holy* [e] 4 Traditionally *leprosy;* the Hebrew word was used for various diseases affecting the skin—not necessarily leprosy.

## King James

7 And when the sun is down, he shall be clean, and shall afterward eat of the holy things; because it *is* his food.

8 That which dieth of itself, or is torn *with beasts,* he shall not eat to defile himself therewith: I *am* the LORD.

9 They shall therefore keep mine ordinance, lest they bear sin for it, and die therefore, if they profane it: I the LORD do sanctify them.

10 There shall no stranger eat *of* the holy thing: a sojourner of the priest, or an hired servant, shall not eat *of* the holy thing.

11 But if the priest buy *any* soul with his money, he shall eat of it, and he that is born in his house: they shall eat of his meat.

12 If the priest's daughter also be *married* unto a stranger, she may not eat of an offering of the holy things.

13 But if the priest's daughter be a widow, or divorced, and have no child, and is returned unto her father's house, as in her youth, she shall eat of her father's meat: but there shall no stranger eat thereof.

14 ¶ And if a man eat *of* the holy thing unwittingly, then he shall put the fifth *part* thereof unto it, and shall give *it* unto the priest with the holy thing.

15 And they shall not profane the holy things of the children of Israel, which they offer unto the LORD;

16 Or suffer them to bear the iniquity of trespass, when they eat their holy things: for I the LORD do sanctify them.

17 ¶ And the LORD spake unto Moses, saying,

18 Speak unto Aaron, and to his sons, and unto all the children of Israel, and say unto them, Whatsoever *he be* of the house of Israel, or of the strangers in Israel, that will offer his oblation for all his vows, and for all his freewill offerings, which they will offer unto the LORD for a burnt offering;

19 *Ye shall offer* at your own will a male without blemish, of the beeves, of the sheep, or of the goats.

20 *But* whatsoever hath a blemish, *that* shall ye not offer: for it shall not be acceptable for you.

21 And whosoever offereth a sacrifice of peace offerings unto the LORD to accomplish *his* vow, or a freewill offering in beeves or sheep, it shall be perfect to be accepted; there shall be no blemish therein.

22 Blind, or broken, or maimed, or having a wen, or scurvy, or scabbed, ye shall not offer these unto the LORD, nor make an offering by fire of them upon the altar unto the LORD.

23 Either a bullock or a lamb that hath any thing superfluous or lacking in his parts, that mayest thou offer *for* a freewill offering; but for a vow it shall not be accepted.

24 Ye shall not offer unto the LORD that which is bruised, or crushed, or broken, or cut; neither shall ye make *any offering thereof* in your land.

25 Neither from a stranger's hand shall ye offer the bread of your God of any of these; because their corruption *is* in them, *and* blemishes *be* in them: they shall not be accepted for you.

26 ¶ And the LORD spake unto Moses, saying,

27 When a bullock, or a sheep, or a goat, is brought forth, then it shall be seven days under the dam; and from the eighth day and thenceforth it shall be accepted for an offering made by fire unto the LORD.

28 And *whether it be* cow or ewe, ye shall not kill it and her young both in one day.

29 And when ye will offer a sacrifice of thanksgiving unto the LORD, offer *it* at your own will.

30 On the same day it shall be eaten up; ye shall leave none of it until the morrow: I *am* the LORD.

31 Therefore shall ye keep my commandments, and do them: I *am* the LORD.

32 Neither shall ye profane my holy name; but I will be hallowed among the children of Israel: I *am* the LORD which hallow you,

33 That brought you out of the land of Egypt, to be your God: I *am* the LORD.

## Amplified

7 When the sun is down, he shall be clean, and afterward may eat of the holy things, for they are his food.

8 That which dies of itself or is torn by beasts he shall not eat, defiling himself with it. I am the Lord.

9 The priests therefore shall observe My ordinance, lest they bear sin for it and die thereby if they profane it. I am the Lord Who sanctifies them.

10 No outsider [not of the family of Aaron] shall eat of the holy thing [which has been offered to God]; a sojourner with the priest, or a hired servant shall not eat of the holy thing.

11 But if a priest buys a slave with his money, the slave may eat of the holy thing, and he also who is born in the priest's house; they may eat of his food.

12 If a priest's daughter is married to an outsider [not of the priestly tribe] she shall not eat of the offering of the holy things.

13 But if a priest's daughter is a widow or divorced, and has no child, and returns to her father's house, as in her youth, she shall eat of her father's food; but no stranger shall eat of it.

14 And if a man eats unknowingly of the holy thing [which has been offered to God] then he shall add one fifth of its value to it, and repay that amount to the priest for the holy thing.

15 The priests shall not profane the holy things the Israelites offer to the Lord,

16 And so cause them [by neglect of any essential observance] to bear the iniquity when they eat their holy things; for I the Lord sanctify them.

17 And the Lord said to Moses,

18 Say to Aaron and his sons and to all the Israelites, Whoever of the house of Israel and of the foreigners in Israel brings his offering, whether to pay a vow or as a freewill offering which is offered to the Lord for a burnt offering,

19 That you may be accepted you shall offer a male without blemish of the young bulls, the sheep, or the goats.

20 But you shall not offer anything which has a blemish, for it will not be acceptable for you. [I Pet. 1:19.]

21 And whoever offers a sacrifice of peace offerings to the Lord to make a special vow to the Lord or for a freewill offering from the herd or from the flock, must bring what is perfect to be accepted; there shall be no blemish in it.

22 Animals blind or made infirm *and* weak or maimed or having sores *or* a wen or an itch or scabs, you shall not offer to the Lord or make an offering of them by fire upon the altar to the Lord.

23 For a freewill offering you may offer either a bull or a lamb which has some part too long or too short, but for [the payment of] a vow it shall not be accepted.

24 You shall not offer to the Lord any animal which has its testicles bruised or crushed or broken or cut, neither sacrifice it in your land.

25 Neither shall you offer as the bread of your God any such animals obtained from a foreigner [who may wish to pay respect to the true God], because their defects render them unfit, there is a blemish in them; they will not be accepted for you.

26 And the Lord said to Moses,

27 When a bull or a sheep or a goat is born, it shall remain seven days with its mother; and from the eighth day on it shall be accepted for an offering made by fire to the Lord.

28 And whether [the mother] is a cow or a ewe, you shall not kill her and her young both in one day.

29 And when you sacrifice an offering of thanksgiving to the Lord, sacrifice it so that you may be accepted.

30 It shall be eaten on the same day; you shall leave none of it until the next day; I am the Lord.

31 So shall you heartily accept My commandments *and* conform your life and conduct to them. I am the Lord.

32 Neither shall you profane My holy name [applying it to an idol, or treating it with irreverence or contempt or as a byword]; but I will be hallowed among the Israelites. I am the Lord Who consecrates *and* makes you holy,

33 Who brought you out of the land of Egypt to be your God. I am the Lord.

## New American Standard

7'But when the sun sets, he shall be clean, and afterward he shall eat of the holy *gifts,* for it is his food.

8'He shall not eat *an animal* which dies or is torn *by beasts,* becoming unclean by it; I am the LORD.

9'They shall therefore keep My charge, so that they may not bear sin because of it, and die thereby because they profane it; I am the LORD who sanctifies them.

10¶ 'No [a]layman, however, is to eat the holy *gift;* a sojourner with the priest or a hired man shall not eat of the holy *gift.*

11'But if a priest buys a slave as *his* property with his money, that one may eat of it, and those who are born in his house may eat of his food.

12'And if a priest's daughter is married to a layman, she shall not eat of the offering of the *gifts.*

13'But if a priest's daughter becomes a widow or divorced, and has no child and returns to her father's house as in her youth, she shall eat of her father's food; but no layman shall eat of it.

14'But if a man eats a holy *gift* unintentionally, then he shall add to it a fifth of it and shall give the holy *gift* to the priest.

15'And they shall not profane the holy *gifts* of the sons of Israel which they offer to the LORD,

16and *so* cause them to bear punishment for guilt by eating their holy *gifts;* for I am the LORD who sanctifies them.' "

*Flawless Animals for Sacrifice*

17¶ Then the LORD spoke to Moses, saying,

18"Speak to Aaron and to his sons and to all the sons of Israel, and say to them, 'Any man of the house of Israel or of the aliens in Israel who presents his offering, whether it is any of their votive or any of their freewill offerings, which they present to the LORD for a burnt offering—

19for you to be accepted— *it must be* a male without defect from the cattle, the sheep, or the goats.

20'Whatever has a defect, you shall not offer, for it will not be accepted for you.

21'And when a man offers a sacrifice of peace offerings to the LORD to fulfill a special vow, or for a freewill offering, of the herd or of the flock, it must be perfect to be accepted; there shall be no defect in it.

22'Those *that are* blind or fractured or maimed or having a running sore or eczema or scabs, you shall not offer to the LORD, nor make of them an offering by fire on the altar to the LORD.

23'In respect to an ox or a lamb which has an overgrown or stunted *member,* you may present it for a freewill offering, but for a vow it shall not be accepted.

24'Also anything *with its testicles* bruised or crushed or torn or cut, you shall not offer to the LORD, or sacrifice in your land,

25nor shall you accept any such from the hand of a foreigner for offering as the food of your God; for their corruption is in them, they have a defect, they shall not be accepted for you.' "

26¶ Then the LORD spoke to Moses, saying,

27"When an ox or a sheep or a goat is born, it shall remain seven days with its mother, and from the eighth day on it shall be accepted as a sacrifice of an offering by fire to the LORD.

28"But, *whether* it is an ox or a sheep, you shall not kill *both* it and its young in one day.

29"And when you sacrifice a sacrifice of thanksgiving to the LORD, you shall sacrifice it so that you may be accepted.

30"It shall be eaten on the same day, you shall leave none of it until morning: I am the LORD.

31"So you shall keep My commandments, and do them: I am the LORD.

32"And you shall not profane My holy name, but I will be sanctified among the sons of Israel: I am the LORD who sanctifies you,

33who brought you out from the land of Egypt, to be your God: I am the LORD."

NAS [a] Lit., *stranger*

## New International

and after that he may eat the sacred offerings, for they are his food.
8He must not eat anything found dead or torn by wild animals, and
so become unclean through it. I am the LORD.
9" 'The priests are to keep my requirements so that they do not
become guilty and die for treating them with contempt. I am the
LORD, who makes them holy.[b]
10" 'No one outside a priest's family may eat the sacred offering,
nor may the guest of a priest or his hired worker eat it. 11But if a
priest buys a slave with money, or if a slave is born in his household, that slave may eat his food. 12If a priest's daughter marries
anyone other than a priest, she may not eat any of the sacred
contributions. 13But if a priest's daughter becomes a widow or is
divorced, yet has no children, and she returns to live in her father's
house as in her youth, she may eat of her father's food. No unauthorized person, however, may eat any of it.
14" 'If anyone eats a sacred offering by mistake, he must make
restitution to the priest for the offering and add a fifth of the value
to it. 15The priests must not desecrate the sacred offerings the
Israelites present to the LORD 16by allowing them to eat the sacred
offerings and so bring upon them guilt requiring payment. I am
the LORD, who makes them holy.' "

*Unacceptable Sacrifices*

17The LORD said to Moses, 18"Speak to Aaron and his sons and
to all the Israelites and say to them: 'If any of you—either an
Israelite or an alien living in Israel—presents a gift for a burnt
offering to the LORD, either to fulfill a vow or as a freewill offering,
19you must present a male without defect from the cattle, sheep
or goats in order that it may be accepted on your behalf. 20Do not
bring anything with a defect, because it will not be accepted on
your behalf. 21When anyone brings from the herd or flock a fellowship offering[c] to the LORD to fulfill a special vow or as a freewill
offering, it must be without defect or blemish to be acceptable.
22Do not offer to the LORD the blind, the injured or the maimed,
or anything with warts or festering or running sores. Do not place
any of these on the altar as an offering made to the LORD by fire.
23You may, however, present as a freewill offering an ox[d] or a
sheep that is deformed or stunted, but it will not be accepted in
fulfillment of a vow. 24You must not offer to the LORD an animal
whose testicles are bruised, crushed, torn or cut. You must not do
this in your own land, 25and you must not accept such animals
from the hand of a foreigner and offer them as the food of your
God. They will not be accepted on your behalf, because they are
deformed and have defects.' "
26The LORD said to Moses, 27"When a calf, a lamb or a goat is
born, it is to remain with its mother for seven days. From the
eighth day on, it will be acceptable as an offering made to the LORD
by fire. 28Do not slaughter a cow or a sheep and its young on the
same day.
29"When you sacrifice a thank offering to the LORD, sacrifice it
in such a way that it will be accepted on your behalf. 30It must be
eaten that same day; leave none of it till morning. I am the LORD.
31"Keep my commands and follow them. I am the LORD. 32Do
not profane my holy name. I must be acknowledged as holy by the
Israelites. I am the LORD, who makes[e] you holy[f] 33and who
brought you out of Egypt to be your God. I am the LORD."

NIV [b] 9 Or *who sanctifies them;* or *who sets them apart as holy;* also in verse 16 [c] *21* Traditionally *peace offering* [d] 23 The Hebrew word can include both male and female. [e] 32 Or *made* [f] 32 Or *who sanctifies you;* or *who sets you apart as holy*

## King James

**23** AND THE LORD spake unto Moses, saying,
2Speak unto the children of Israel, and say unto them, *Concerning* the feasts of the LORD, which ye shall proclaim *to be* holy convocations, *even* these *are* my feasts.

3Six days shall work be done: but the seventh day *is* the sabbath of rest, an holy convocation; ye shall do no work *therein:* it *is* the sabbath of the LORD in all your dwellings.

4¶ These *are* the feasts of the LORD, *even* holy convocations, which ye shall proclaim in their seasons.

5In the fourteenth *day* of the first month at even *is* the LORD's passover.

6And on the fifteenth day of the same month *is* the feast of unleavened bread unto the LORD: seven days ye must eat unleavened bread.

7In the first day ye shall have an holy convocation: ye shall do no servile work therein.

8But ye shall offer an offering made by fire unto the LORD seven days: in the seventh day *is* an holy convocation: ye shall do no servile work *therein.*

9¶ And the LORD spake unto Moses, saying,

10Speak unto the children of Israel, and say unto them, When ye be come into the land which I give unto you, and shall reap the harvest thereof, then ye shall bring a sheaf of the firstfruits of your harvest unto the priest:

11And he shall wave the sheaf before the LORD, to be accepted for you: on the morrow after the sabbath the priest shall wave it.

12And ye shall offer that day when ye wave the sheaf an he lamb without blemish of the first year for a burnt offering unto the LORD.

13And the meat offering thereof *shall be* two tenth deals of fine flour mingled with oil, an offering made by fire unto the LORD *for* a sweet savour: and the drink offering thereof *shall be* of wine, the fourth *part* of an hin.

14And ye shall eat neither bread, nor parched corn, nor green ears, until the selfsame day that ye have brought an offering unto your God: *it shall be* a statute for ever throughout your generations in all your dwellings.

15¶ And ye shall count unto you from the morrow after the sabbath, from the day that ye brought the sheaf of the wave offering; seven sabbaths shall be complete:

16Even unto the morrow after the seventh sabbath shall ye number fifty days; and ye shall offer a new meat offering unto the LORD.

17Ye shall bring out of your habitations two wave loaves of two tenth deals: they shall be of fine flour; they shall be baked with leaven; *they are* the firstfruits unto the LORD.

18And ye shall offer with the bread seven lambs without blemish of the first year, and one young bullock, and two rams: they shall be *for* a burnt offering unto the LORD, with their meat offering, and their drink offerings, *even* an offering made by fire, of sweet savour unto the LORD.

19Then ye shall sacrifice one kid of the goats for a sin offering, and two lambs of the first year for a sacrifice of peace offerings.

20And the priest shall wave them with the bread of the firstfruits *for* a wave offering before the LORD, with the two lambs: they shall be holy to the LORD for the priest.

21And ye shall proclaim on the selfsame day, *that* it may be an holy convocation unto you: ye shall do no servile work *therein: it shall be* a statute for ever in all your dwellings throughout your generations.

22¶ And when ye reap the harvest of your land, thou shalt not make clean riddance of the corners of thy field when thou reapest, neither shalt thou gather any gleaning of thy harvest: thou shalt leave them unto the poor, and to the stranger: I *am* the LORD your God.

23¶ And the LORD spake unto Moses, saying,

24Speak unto the children of Israel, saying, In the seventh month, in the first *day* of the month, shall ye have a sabbath, a memorial of blowing of trumpets, an holy convocation.

## Amplified

**23** THE LORD said to Moses,
2Say to the Israelites, The set feasts *or* appointed seasons of the Lord which you shall proclaim as holy convocations, even My set feasts, are these:

3Six days shall work be done; but the seventh day is the sabbath of rest, a holy convocation *or* assembly by summons; you shall do no work on that day; it is the sabbath of the Lord in all your dwellings.

4These are the set feasts *or* appointed seasons of the Lord, holy convocations you shall proclaim at their stated times.

5On the fourteenth day of the first month between evenings is the Lord's passover.

6On the fifteenth day of the same month is the feast of unleavened bread to the Lord; seven days you shall eat unleavened bread. [I Cor. 5:7, 8.]

7On the first day you shall have a holy calling together; you shall do no servile *or* laborious work on that day.

8But you shall offer an offering made by fire to the Lord seven days; on the seventh day is a holy convocation; you shall do no servile *or* laborious work on that day.

9And the Lord said to Moses,

10Tell the Israelites, When you have come into the land I give you and reap its harvest, you shall bring the sheaf of the first fruits of your harvest to the priest;

11And he shall wave the sheaf before the Lord, that you may be accepted; on the next day after the sabbath the priest shall wave it [before the Lord].

12You shall offer on the day when you wave the sheaf a male lamb a year old without blemish for a burnt offering to the Lord.

13Its cereal offering shall be two tenths of an ephah of fine flour mixed with oil, an offering made by fire to the Lord for a sweet, pleasing *and* satisfying fragrance; and the drink offering of it [to be poured out] shall be of wine, the fourth of a hin.

14And you shall eat neither bread nor parched grain nor green ears, until this same day, when you have brought the offering of your God; it is a statute for ever throughout your generations in all your houses.

15And you shall count from the day after the sabbath, from the day that you brought the sheaf of the wave offering, seven sabbaths; (seven full weeks) shall they be;

16Counting fifty days to the day after the seventh sabbath; then you shall present a cereal offering of new grain to the Lord.

17You shall bring from your dwellings two loaves of bread to be waved, made from two-tenths of an ephah of fine flour; they shall be baked with leaven, for first fruits to the Lord.

18And you shall offer with the bread seven lambs a year old without blemish, and one young bull and two rams; they shall be a burnt offering to the Lord, with their cereal offering and their drink offerings, an offering made by fire of a sweet *and* satisfying fragrance to the Lord.

19Then you shall sacrifice one he-goat for a sin offering, and two he-lambs a year old for a sacrifice of peace offerings.

20The priest shall wave them with the bread of the first fruits for a wave offering before the Lord, with the two lambs; they shall be holy to the Lord for the priest.

21You shall make proclamation the same day, summoning a holy assembly; you shall do no servile work that day; it shall be a statute for ever in all your dwellings throughout your generations.

22And when you reap the harvest of your land, you shall not wholly reap the corners of your field, neither shall you gather the gleanings of your harvest; you shall leave them for the poor and the stranger. I am the Lord your God.

23And the Lord said to Moses,

24Say to the Israelites, On the first day of the seventh month [almost October], you shall observe a day of solemn [sabbatical] rest, a memorial day announced by blowing of trumpets, a holy called assembly.

## New American Standard

*Laws of Religious Festivals*

**23** THE LORD spoke again to Moses, saying,
2"Speak to the sons of Israel, and say to them, 'The LORD's
appointed times which you shall proclaim as holy convocations—
My appointed times are these:
3'For six days work may be done; but on the seventh day there
is a sabbath of complete rest, a holy convocation. You shall not do
any work; it is a sabbath to the LORD in all your dwellings.
4¶ 'These are the appointed times of the LORD, holy convocations which you shall proclaim at the times appointed for them.
5'In the first month, on the fourteenth day of the month at
twilight is the LORD's Passover.
6'Then on the fifteenth day of the same month there is the Feast
of Unleavened Bread to the LORD; for seven days you shall eat
unleavened bread.
7'On the first day you shall have a holy convocation; you shall
not do any laborious work.
8'But for seven days you shall present an offering by fire to the
LORD. On the seventh day is a holy convocation; you shall not do
any laborious work.'"
9¶ Then the LORD spoke to Moses, saying,
10"Speak to the sons of Israel, and say to them, 'When you enter
the land which I am going to give to you and reap its harvest, then
you shall bring in the sheaf of the first fruits of your harvest to the
priest.
11'And he shall wave the sheaf before the LORD for you to be
accepted; on the day after the sabbath the priest shall wave it.
12'Now on the day when you wave the sheaf, you shall offer a
male lamb one year old without defect for a burnt offering to the
LORD.
13'Its grain offering shall then be two-tenths *of an ephah* of fine
flour mixed with oil, an offering by fire to the LORD *for* a soothing
aroma, with its libation, a fourth of a [a]hin of wine.
14'Until this same day, until you have brought in the offering
of your God, you shall eat neither bread nor roasted grain nor new
growth. It is to be a perpetual statute throughout your generations
in all your dwelling places.
15¶ 'You shall also count for yourselves from the day after the
sabbath, from the day when you brought in the sheaf of the wave
offering; there shall be seven complete sabbaths.
16'You shall count fifty days to the day after the seventh sabbath; then you shall present a new grain offering to the LORD.
17'You shall bring in from your dwelling places two *loaves* of
bread for a wave offering, made of two-tenths *of an ephah*; they
shall be of a fine flour, baked with leaven as first fruits to the LORD.
18'Along with the bread, you shall present seven one year old
male lambs without defect, and a bull of the herd, and two rams;
they are to be a burnt offering to the LORD, with their grain offering
and their libations, an offering by fire of a soothing aroma to the
LORD.
19'You shall also offer one male goat for a sin offering and two
male lambs one year old for a sacrifice of peace offerings.
20'The priest shall then wave them with the bread of the first
fruits for a wave offering with two lambs before the LORD; they are
to be holy to the LORD for the priest.
21'On this same day you shall make a proclamation as well; you
are to have a holy convocation. You shall do no laborious work.
It is to be a perpetual statute in all your dwelling places throughout
your generations.
22¶ 'When you reap the harvest of your land, moreover, you
shall not reap to the very corners of your field, nor gather the
gleaning of your harvest; you are to leave them for the needy and
the alien. I am the LORD your God.'"
23¶ Again the LORD spoke to Moses, saying,
24"Speak to the sons of Israel, saying, 'In the seventh month on
the first of the month, you shall have a rest, a reminder by blowing
*of trumpets*, a holy convocation.

NAS [a] I.e., Approx. one gallon

## New International

**23** THE LORD said to Moses, 2"Speak to the Israelites and
say to them: 'These are my appointed feasts, the appointed feasts of the LORD, which you are to proclaim as sacred
assemblies.

*The Sabbath*

3" 'There are six days when you may work, but the seventh day
is a Sabbath of rest, a day of sacred assembly. You are not to do
any work; wherever you live, it is a Sabbath to the LORD.

*The Passover and Unleavened Bread*

4" 'These are the LORD's appointed feasts, the sacred assemblies
you are to proclaim at their appointed times: 5The LORD's Passover
begins at twilight on the fourteenth day of the first month. 6On the
fifteenth day of that month the LORD's Feast of Unleavened Bread
begins; for seven days you must eat bread made without yeast.
7On the first day hold a sacred assembly and do no regular work.
8For seven days present an offering made to the LORD by fire. And
on the seventh day hold a sacred assembly and do no regular
work.'"

*Firstfruits*

9The LORD said to Moses, 10"Speak to the Israelites and say to
them: 'When you enter the land I am going to give you and you
reap its harvest, bring to the priest a sheaf of the first grain you
harvest. 11He is to wave the sheaf before the LORD so it will be
accepted on your behalf; the priest is to wave it on the day after
the Sabbath. 12On the day you wave the sheaf, you must sacrifice
as a burnt offering to the LORD a lamb a year old without defect,
13together with its grain offering of two-tenths of an ephah[b] of fine
flour mixed with oil—an offering made to the LORD by fire, a
pleasing aroma—and its drink offering of a quarter of a hin[c] of
wine. 14You must not eat any bread, or roasted or new grain, until
the very day you bring this offering to your God. This is to be a
lasting ordinance for the generations to come, wherever you live.

*Feast of Weeks*

15" 'From the day after the Sabbath, the day you brought the
sheaf of the wave offering, count off seven full weeks. 16Count off
fifty days up to the day after the seventh Sabbath, and then present
an offering of new grain to the LORD. 17From wherever you live,
bring two loaves made of two-tenths of an ephah of fine flour,
baked with yeast, as a wave offering of firstfruits to the LORD.
18Present with this bread seven male lambs, each a year old and
without defect, one young bull and two rams. They will be a burnt
offering to the LORD, together with their grain offerings and drink
offerings—an offering made by fire, an aroma pleasing to the
LORD. 19Then sacrifice one male goat for a sin offering and two
lambs, each a year old, for a fellowship offering.[d] 20The priest is
to wave the two lambs before the LORD as a wave offering, together
with the bread of the firstfruits. They are a sacred offering to the
LORD for the priest. 21On that same day you are to proclaim a
sacred assembly and do no regular work. This is to be a lasting
ordinance for the generations to come, wherever you live.
22" 'When you reap the harvest of your land, do not reap to the
very edges of your field or gather the gleanings of your harvest.
Leave them for the poor and the alien. I am the LORD your God.'"

*Feast of Trumpets*

23The LORD said to Moses, 24"Say to the Israelites: 'On the first
day of the seventh month you are to have a day of rest, a sacred

NIV [b] *13* That is, probably about 4 quarts (about 4.5 liters); also in verse 17 [c] *13* That is, probably about 1 quart (about 1 liter) [d] *19* Traditionally *peace offering*

## King James

25 Ye shall do no servile work *therein:* but ye shall offer an offering made by fire unto the LORD.

26 ¶ And the LORD spake unto Moses, saying,

27 Also on the tenth *day* of this seventh month *there shall be* a day of atonement: it shall be an holy convocation unto you; and ye shall afflict your souls, and offer an offering made by fire unto the LORD.

28 And ye shall do no work in that same day: for it *is* a day of atonement, to make an atonement for you before the LORD your God.

29 For whatsoever soul *it be* that shall not be afflicted in that same day, he shall be cut off from among his people.

30 And whatsoever soul *it be* that doeth any work in that same day, the same soul will I destroy from among his people.

31 Ye shall do no manner of work: *it shall be* a statute for ever throughout your generations in all your dwellings.

32 It *shall be* unto you a sabbath of rest, and ye shall afflict your souls: in the ninth *day* of the month at even, from even unto even, shall ye celebrate your sabbath.

33 ¶ And the LORD spake unto Moses, saying,

34 Speak unto the children of Israel, saying, The fifteenth day of this seventh month *shall be* the feast of tabernacles *for* seven days unto the LORD.

35 On the first day *shall be* an holy convocation: ye shall do no servile work *therein.*

36 Seven days ye shall offer an offering made by fire unto the LORD: on the eighth day shall be an holy convocation unto you; and ye shall offer an offering made by fire unto the LORD: it *is* a solemn assembly; *and* ye shall do no servile work *therein.*

37 These *are* the feasts of the LORD, which ye shall proclaim *to be* holy convocations, to offer an offering made by fire unto the LORD, a burnt offering, and a meat offering, a sacrifice, and drink offerings, every thing upon his day:

38 Beside the sabbaths of the LORD, and beside your gifts, and beside all your vows, and beside all your freewill offerings, which ye give unto the LORD.

39 Also in the fifteenth day of the seventh month, when ye have gathered in the fruit of the land, ye shall keep a feast unto the LORD seven days: on the first day *shall be* a sabbath, and on the eighth day *shall be* a sabbath.

40 And ye shall take you on the first day the boughs of goodly trees, branches of palm trees, and the boughs of thick trees, and willows of the brook; and ye shall rejoice before the LORD your God seven days.

41 And ye shall keep it a feast unto the LORD seven days in the year. *It shall be* a statute for ever in your generations: ye shall celebrate it in the seventh month.

42 Ye shall dwell in booths seven days; all that are Israelites born shall dwell in booths:

43 That your generations may know that I made the children of Israel to dwell in booths, when I brought them out of the land of Egypt: I *am* the LORD your God.

44 And Moses declared unto the children of Israel the feasts of the LORD.

**24** AND THE LORD spake unto Moses, saying,

2 Command the children of Israel, that they bring unto thee pure oil olive beaten for the light, to cause the lamps to burn continually.

3 Without the veil of the testimony, in the tabernacle of the congregation, shall Aaron order it from the evening unto the morning before the LORD continually: *it shall be* a statute for ever in your generations.

4 He shall order the lamps upon the pure candlestick before the LORD continually.

## Amplified

25 You shall do no servile work on it, but you shall present an offering made by fire to the Lord.

26 And the Lord said to Moses,

27 Also the tenth day of this seventh month is the day of atonement; it shall be a holy called assembly, and you shall afflict yourselves [by fasting in penitence and humility], and present an offering made by fire to the Lord.

28 And you shall do no work on this day, for it is a day of atonement, to make atonement for you before the Lord your God.

29 For whoever is not afflicted [by fasting in penitence and humility] on this day shall be cut off from among his people [that he may not be included in the atonement made for them].

30 And whoever does any work on that same day I will destroy from among his people.

31 You shall do no kind of work [on that day]; it is a statute for ever throughout your generations in all your dwellings.

32 It shall be to you a sabbath of rest, and you shall afflict yourselves [by fasting in penitence and humility]; on the ninth day of the month from evening to evening, you shall keep your sabbath.

33 And the Lord said to Moses,

34 Say to the Israelites, The fifteenth day of this seventh month and for seven days is the feast of tabernacles *or* booths to the Lord.

35 On the first day shall be a holy convocation; you shall do no servile work on that day.

36 Seven days you shall offer an offering made by fire to the Lord; on the eighth day shall be a holy convocation and you shall present an offering made by fire to the Lord; it is a solemn assembly; you shall do no laborious work on that day.

37 These are the set feasts *or* appointed seasons of the Lord, which you shall proclaim to be holy convocations, to present an offering made by fire to the Lord, a burnt offering, and a cereal offering, a sacrifice, and drink offerings, each on its own day.

38 This is in addition to the sabbaths of the Lord, and besides your gifts and all your vowed offerings and all your freewill offerings, which you give to the Lord.

39 Also the fifteenth day of the seventh month [nearly October], when you have gathered in the fruit of the land, you shall keep the feast of the Lord seven days, the first day and the eighth day each a sabbath.

40 And the first day you shall take the fruit of pleasing trees [and make booths of them], branches of palm trees, and boughs of thick (leafy) trees, and willows of the brook; and you shall rejoice before the Lord your God seven days.

41 You shall keep it a feast to the Lord seven days in the year, a statute for ever throughout your generations; you shall keep it in the seventh month.

42 You shall dwell in booths (shelters) seven days; all native Israelites shall dwell in booths,

43 That your generations may know that I made the Israelites dwell in booths when I brought them out of the land of Egypt. I am the Lord your God.

44 Thus Moses declared to the Israelites the set *or* appointed feasts of the Lord.

**24** AND THE Lord said to Moses,

2 Command the Israelites that they bring to you pure oil from beaten olives for the light [of the golden lampstand], to cause a lamp to burn continually.

3 Outside the veil of the testimony [between the holy and the most holy places] in the tent of meeting shall Aaron keep it in order from evening to morning before the Lord continually; it shall be a statute for ever throughout your generations.

4 He shall keep the lamps in order upon the lampstand of pure gold before the Lord continually. [Cp. Rev. 1:12-18.]

## New American Standard

25 'You shall not do any laborious work, but you shall present
an offering by fire to the LORD.' "

*The Day of Atonement*

26¶ And the LORD spoke to Moses, saying,
27 "On exactly the tenth day of this seventh month is the day of
atonement; it shall be a holy convocation for you, and you shall
humble your souls and present an offering by fire to the LORD.
28 "Neither shall you do any work on this same day, for it is a
day of atonement, to make atonement on your behalf before the
LORD your God.
29 "If there is any person who will not humble himself on this
same day, he shall be cut off from his people.
30 "As for any person who does any work on this same day, that
person I will destroy from among his people.
31 "You shall do no work at all. It is to be a perpetual statute
throughout your generations in all your dwelling places.
32 "It is to be a sabbath of complete rest to you, and you shall
humble your souls; on the ninth of the month at evening, from
evening until evening you shall keep your sabbath."
33¶ Again the LORD spoke to Moses, saying,
34 "Speak to the sons of Israel, saying, 'On the fifteenth of this
seventh month is the Feast of Booths for seven days to the LORD.
35 'On the first day is a holy convocation; you shall do no laborious work of any kind.
36 'For seven days you shall present an offering by fire to the
LORD. On the eighth day you shall have a holy convocation and
present an offering by fire to the LORD; it is an assembly. You shall
do no laborious work.
37¶ 'These are the appointed times of the LORD which you shall
proclaim as holy convocations, to present offerings by fire to the
LORD—burnt offerings and grain offerings, sacrifices and libations,
*each* day's matter on its own day—
38 besides *those of* the sabbaths of the LORD, and besides your
gifts, and besides all your votive and freewill offerings, which you
give to the LORD.
39¶ 'On exactly the fifteenth day of the seventh month, when
you have gathered in the crops of the land, you shall celebrate the
feast of the LORD for seven days, with a rest on the first day and
a rest on the eighth day.
40 'Now on the first day you shall take for yourselves the foliage
of beautiful trees, palm branches and boughs of leafy trees and
willows of the brook; and you shall rejoice before the LORD your
God for seven days.
41 'You shall thus celebrate it *as* a feast to the LORD for seven days
in the year. It *shall be* a perpetual statute throughout your generations; you shall celebrate it in the seventh month.
42 'You shall live in booths for seven days; all the native-born in
Israel shall live in booths,
43 so that your generations may know that I had the sons of
Israel live in booths when I brought them out from the land of
Egypt. I am the LORD your God.' "
44 So Moses declared to the sons of Israel the appointed times
of the LORD.

*The Lamp and the Bread of the Sanctuary*

**24** THEN THE LORD spoke to Moses, saying,
2 "Command the sons of Israel that they bring to you clear
oil from beaten olives for the light, to make a lamp burn continually.
3 "Outside the veil of testimony in the tent of meeting, Aaron
shall keep it in order from evening to morning before the LORD
continually; *it shall be* a perpetual statute throughout your generations.
4 "He shall keep the lamps in order on the pure *gold* lampstand
before the LORD continually.

## New International

assembly commemorated with trumpet blasts. 25 Do no regular
work, but present an offering made to the LORD by fire.' "

*Day of Atonement*

26 The LORD said to Moses, 27 "The tenth day of this seventh
month is the Day of Atonement. Hold a sacred assembly and deny
yourselves,[a] and present an offering made to the LORD by fire.
28 Do no work on that day, because it is the Day of Atonement,
when atonement is made for you before the LORD your God.
29 Anyone who does not deny himself on that day must be cut off
from his people. 30 I will destroy from among his people anyone
who does any work on that day. 31 You shall do no work at all. This
is to be a lasting ordinance for the generations to come, wherever
you live. 32 It is a sabbath of rest for you, and you must deny
yourselves. From the evening of the ninth day of the month until
the following evening you are to observe your sabbath."

*Feast of Tabernacles*

33 The LORD said to Moses, 34 "Say to the Israelites: 'On the
fifteenth day of the seventh month the LORD's Feast of Tabernacles
begins, and it lasts for seven days. 35 The first day is a sacred
assembly; do no regular work. 36 For seven days present offerings
made to the LORD by fire, and on the eighth day hold a sacred
assembly and present an offering made to the LORD by fire. It is
the closing assembly; do no regular work.
37 (" 'These are the LORD's appointed feasts, which you are to
proclaim as sacred assemblies for bringing offerings made to the
LORD by fire—the burnt offerings and grain offerings, sacrifices
and drink offerings required for each day. 38 These offerings are in
addition to those for the LORD's Sabbaths and[b] in addition to your
gifts and whatever you have vowed and all the freewill offerings
you give to the LORD.)
39 " 'So beginning with the fifteenth day of the seventh month,
after you have gathered the crops of the land, celebrate the festival
to the LORD for seven days; the first day is a day of rest, and the
eighth day also is a day of rest. 40 On the first day you are to take
choice fruit from the trees, and palm fronds, leafy branches and
poplars, and rejoice before the LORD your God for seven days.
41 Celebrate this as a festival to the LORD for seven days each year.
This is to be a lasting ordinance for the generations to come;
celebrate it in the seventh month. 42 Live in booths for seven days:
All native-born Israelites are to live in booths 43 so your descendants will know that I had the Israelites live in booths when I
brought them out of Egypt. I am the LORD your God.' "
44 So Moses announced to the Israelites the appointed feasts of
the LORD.

*Oil and Bread Set Before the LORD*

**24** THE LORD said to Moses, 2 "Command the Israelites to
bring you clear oil of pressed olives for the light so that the
lamps may be kept burning continually. 3 Outside the curtain of the
Testimony in the Tent of Meeting, Aaron is to tend the lamps
before the LORD from evening till morning, continually. This is to
be a lasting ordinance for the generations to come. 4 The lamps on
the pure gold lampstand before the LORD must be tended continually.

NIV [a] 27 Or *and fast;* also in verses 29 and 32 [b] 38 Or *These feasts are in addition to the LORD's Sabbaths, and these offerings are*

## King James

5¶ And thou shalt take fine flour, and bake twelve cakes thereof:
two tenth deals shall be in one cake.
6And thou shalt set them in two rows, six on a row, upon the
pure table before the LORD.
7And thou shalt put pure frankincense upon *each* row, that it
may be on the bread for a memorial, *even* an offering made by fire
unto the LORD.
8Every sabbath he shall set it in order before the LORD continually, *being taken* from the children of Israel by an everlasting covenant.
9And it shall be Aaron's and his sons'; and they shall eat it in
the holy place: for it *is* most holy unto him of the offerings of the
LORD made by fire by a perpetual statute.
10¶ And the son of an Israelitish woman, whose father *was* an
Egyptian, went out among the children of Israel: and this son of
the Israelitish *woman* and a man of Israel strove together in the
camp;
11And the Israelitish woman's son blasphemed the name *of the
LORD*, and cursed. And they brought him unto Moses: (and his
mother's name *was* Shelomith, the daughter of Dibri, of the tribe
of Dan:)
12And they put him in ward, that the mind of the LORD might
be shown them.
13And the LORD spake unto Moses, saying,
14Bring forth him that hath cursed without the camp; and let all
that heard *him* lay their hands upon his head, and let all the
congregation stone him.
15And thou shalt speak unto the children of Israel, saying,
Whosoever curseth his God shall bear his sin.
16And he that blasphemeth the name of the LORD, he shall
surely be put to death, *and* all the congregation shall certainly stone
him: as well the stranger, as he that is born in the land, when he
blasphemeth the name *of the LORD*, shall be put to death.
17¶ And he that killeth any man shall surely be put to death.
18And he that killeth a beast shall make it good; beast for beast.
19And if a man cause a blemish in his neighbour; as he hath
done, so shall it be done to him;
20Breach for breach, eye for eye, tooth for tooth: as he hath
caused a blemish in a man, so shall it be done to him *again*.
21And he that killeth a beast, he shall restore it: and he that
killeth a man, he shall be put to death.
22Ye shall have one manner of law, as well for the stranger, as
for one of your own country: for I *am* the LORD your God.
23¶ And Moses spake to the children of Israel, that they should
bring forth him that had cursed out of the camp, and stone him
with stones. And the children of Israel did as the LORD commanded Moses.

## Amplified

5And you shall take fine flour, and bake twelve cakes with it;
two tenths of an ephah shall be in each cake [of the showbread *or*
bread of the Presence].
6And you shall set them in two rows, six in a row, upon the
table of pure gold before the Lord.
7You shall put pure frankincense [in a bowl or spoon] beside
each row, that it may be with the bread as a memorial portion, an
offering to be made by fire to the Lord.
8Every sabbath day, Aaron shall set the showbread in order
before the Lord continually; it is on behalf of the Israelites an
everlasting covenant.
9And the bread shall be for Aaron and his sons, and they shall
eat it in a sacred place, for it is for [Aaron] a most holy portion of
the offerings to the Lord made by fire, a perpetual due [to the high
priest].
10Now the son of an Israelite woman, whose father was an
Egyptian, went out among the Israelites; and he and a man of
Israel quarreled *and* strove together in the camp.
11The Israelite woman's son blasphemed the name of the Lord,
and cursed. They brought him to Moses. His mother was Shelomith, daughter of Dibri, of the tribe of Dan.
12And they put him in custody until the will of the Lord might
be declared to them.
13And the Lord said to Moses,
14Bring him who has cursed out of the camp, and let all who
heard him lay their hands upon his head; then let all the congregation stone him.
15And you shall say to the Israelites, Whoever curses his God
shall bear his sin.
16And he who blasphemes the name of the Lord, he shall surely
be put to death, and all the congregation shall certainly stone him;
the stranger as well as he who was born in the land shall be put
to death when he blasphemes the name of the Lord.
17And he who kills any man shall surely be put to death.
18And he who kills a beast shall make it good, beast for beast.
19And if a man causes a blemish *or* disfigurement on his neighbor, it shall be done to him as he had done,
20Fracture for fracture, eye for eye, tooth for tooth; as he has
caused a blemish *or* disfigurement on a man, so shall it be done
to him. [Cp. Matt. 5:38-42; 7:2.]
21He who kills a beast shall replace it; he who kills a man shall
be put to death.
22You shall have the same law for the sojourner among you as
for one of your own nationality; for I am the Lord your God.
23Moses spoke to the Israelites and they brought him who had
cursed out of the camp, and stoned him with stones. Thus the
Israelites did as the Lord commanded Moses.

**25** AND THE LORD spake unto Moses in mount Sinai, saying,
2Speak unto the children of Israel, and say unto them,
When ye come into the land which I give you, then shall the land
keep a sabbath unto the LORD.
3Six years thou shalt sow thy field, and six years thou shalt
prune thy vineyard, and gather in the fruit thereof;
4But in the seventh year shall be a sabbath of rest unto the land,
a sabbath for the LORD: thou shalt neither sow thy field, nor prune
thy vineyard.
5That which groweth of its own accord of thy harvest thou shalt
not reap, neither gather the grapes of thy vine undressed: *for* it is
a year of rest unto the land.
6And the sabbath of the land shall be meat for you; for thee, and
for thy servant, and for thy maid, and for thy hired servant, and
for thy stranger that sojourneth with thee,

**25** THE LORD said to Moses on Mount Sinai,
2Say to the Israelites, When you come into the land which
I give you, then shall the land keep a sabbath to the Lord.
3Six years you shall sow your field, and six years you shall
prune your vineyard, and gather in its fruits;
4But in the seventh year there shall be a sabbath of solemn rest
for the land, a sabbath to the Lord; you shall neither sow your field,
nor prune your vineyard.
5What grows of itself in your harvest you shall not reap, and
the grapes on your uncultivated vine you shall not gather, for it
is a year of rest to the land.
6And the sabbath rest of the [untilled] land shall [in its increase]
furnish food for you, for your male and female slaves, your hired
servant and the temporary resident who lives with you.

## New American Standard

5¶ "Then you shall take fine flour and bake twelve cakes with
it; two-tenths *of an ephah* shall be *in* each cake.
6"And you shall set them *in* two rows, six *to* a row, on the pure
*gold* table before the LORD.
7"And you shall put pure frankincense on each row, that it
may be a memorial portion for the bread, *even* an offering by fire
to the LORD.
8"Every sabbath day he shall set it in order before the LORD
continually; it is an everlasting covenant for the sons of Israel.
9"And it shall be for Aaron and his sons, and they shall eat it
in a holy place; for it is most holy to him from the LORD's offerings
by fire, *his* portion forever."
10¶ Now the son of an Israelite woman, whose father was an
Egyptian, went out among the sons of Israel; and the Israelite
woman's son and a man of Israel struggled with each other in the
camp.
11And the son of the Israelite woman blasphemed the Name
and cursed. So they brought him to Moses. (Now his mother's
name was Shelomith, the daughter of Dibri, of the tribe of Dan.)
12And they put him in custody so that the command of the LORD
might be made clear to them.
13¶ Then the LORD spoke to Moses, saying,
14"Bring the one who has cursed outside the camp, and let all
who heard him lay their hands on his head; then let all the congregation stone him.
15"And you shall speak to the sons of Israel, saying, 'If anyone
curses his God, then he shall bear his sin.
16'Moreover, the one who blasphemes the name of the LORD
shall surely be put to death; all the congregation shall certainly
stone him. The alien as well as the native, when he blasphemes
the Name, shall be put to death.

*"An Eye for an Eye"*

17¶ 'And if a man takes the life of any human being, he shall
surely be put to death.
18'And the one who takes the life of an animal shall make it
good, life for life.
19'And if a man injures his neighbor, just as he has done, so it
shall be done to him:
20fracture for fracture, eye for eye, tooth for tooth; just as he has
injured a man, so it shall be inflicted on him.
21'Thus the one who kills an animal shall make it good, but the
one who kills a man shall be put to death.
22'There shall be one standard for you; it shall be for the stranger
as well as the native, for I am the LORD your God.'"
23Then Moses spoke to the sons of Israel, and they brought the
one who had cursed outside the camp and stoned him with stones.
Thus the sons of Israel did, just as the LORD had commanded
Moses.

*The Sabbatic Year and Year of Jubilee*

**25** THE LORD then spoke to Moses at Mount Sinai, saying,
2"Speak to the sons of Israel, and say to them, 'When you
come into the land which I shall give you, then the land shall have
a sabbath to the LORD.
3'Six years you shall sow your field, and six years you shall
prune your vineyard and gather in its crop,
4but during the seventh year the land shall have a sabbath rest,
a sabbath to the LORD; you shall not sow your field nor prune your
vineyard.
5'Your harvest's [a]aftergrowth you shall not reap, and your
grapes of untrimmed vines you shall not gather; the land shall
have a sabbatical year.
6'And all of you shall have the sabbath *products* of the land for
food; yourself, and your male and female slaves, and your hired
man and your foreign resident, those who live as aliens with you.

NAS [a] Lit., *growth from spilled kernels*

## New International

5"Take fine flour and bake twelve loaves of bread, using two-
tenths of an ephah[b] for each loaf. 6Set them in two rows, six in
each row, on the table of pure gold before the LORD. 7Along each
row put some pure incense as a memorial portion to represent the
bread and to be an offering made to the LORD by fire. 8This bread
is to be set out before the LORD regularly, Sabbath after Sabbath,
on behalf of the Israelites, as a lasting covenant. 9It belongs to
Aaron and his sons, who are to eat it in a holy place, because it
is a most holy part of their regular share of the offerings made to
the LORD by fire."

*A Blasphemer Stoned*

10Now the son of an Israelite mother and an Egyptian father
went out among the Israelites, and a fight broke out in the camp
between him and an Israelite. 11The son of the Israelite woman
blasphemed the Name with a curse; so they brought him to Moses.
(His mother's name was Shelomith, the daughter of Dibri the
Danite.) 12They put him in custody until the will of the LORD
should be made clear to them.
13Then the LORD said to Moses: 14"Take the blasphemer outside
the camp. All those who heard him are to lay their hands on his
head, and the entire assembly is to stone him. 15Say to the Israelites: 'If anyone curses his God, he will be held responsible; 16any-
one who blasphemes the name of the LORD must be put to death.
The entire assembly must stone him. Whether an alien or native-
born, when he blasphemes the Name, he must be put to death.
17" 'If anyone takes the life of a human being, he must be put
to death. 18Anyone who takes the life of someone's animal must
make restitution—life for life. 19If anyone injures his neighbor,
whatever he has done must be done to him: 20fracture for fracture,
eye for eye, tooth for tooth. As he has injured the other, so he is
to be injured. 21Whoever kills an animal must make restitution, but
whoever kills a man must be put to death. 22You are to have the
same law for the alien and the native-born. I am the LORD your
God.' "
23Then Moses spoke to the Israelites, and they took the blasphemer outside the camp and stoned him. The Israelites did as the
LORD commanded Moses.

*The Sabbath Year*

**25** THE LORD said to Moses on Mount Sinai, 2"Speak to the
Israelites and say to them: 'When you enter the land I am
going to give you, the land itself must observe a sabbath to the
LORD. 3For six years sow your fields, and for six years prune your
vineyards and gather their crops. 4But in the seventh year the land
is to have a sabbath of rest, a sabbath to the LORD. Do not sow your
fields or prune your vineyards. 5Do not reap what grows of itself
or harvest the grapes of your untended vines. The land is to have
a year of rest. 6Whatever the land yields during the sabbath year
will be food for you—for yourself, your manservant and maidservant, and the hired worker and temporary resident who live

NIV [b] 5 That is, probably about 4 quarts (about 4.5 liters)

## King James

7And for thy cattle, and for the beast that *are* in thy land, shall all the increase thereof be meat.
8¶ And thou shalt number seven sabbaths of years unto thee, seven times seven years; and the space of the seven sabbaths of years shall be unto thee forty and nine years.
9Then shalt thou cause the trumpet of the jubilee to sound on the tenth *day* of the seventh month, in the day of atonement shall ye make the trumpet sound throughout all your land.
10And ye shall hallow the fiftieth year, and proclaim liberty throughout *all* the land unto all the inhabitants thereof: it shall be a jubilee unto you; and ye shall return every man unto his possession, and ye shall return every man unto his family.
11A jubilee shall that fiftieth year be unto you: ye shall not sow, neither reap that which groweth of itself in it, nor gather *the grapes* in it of thy vine undressed.
12For it *is* the jubilee; it shall be holy unto you: ye shall eat the increase thereof out of the field.
13In the year of this jubilee ye shall return every man unto his possession.
14And if thou sell aught unto thy neighbour, or buyest *aught* of thy neighbour's hand, ye shall not oppress one another:
15According to the number of years after the jubilee thou shalt buy of thy neighbour, *and* according unto the number of years of the fruits he shall sell unto thee:
16According to the multitude of years thou shalt increase the price thereof, and according to the fewness of years thou shalt diminish the price of it: for *according* to the number *of the years* of the fruits doth he sell unto thee.
17Ye shall not therefore oppress one another; but thou shalt fear thy God: for I *am* the LORD your God.
18¶ Wherefore ye shall do my statutes, and keep my judgments, and do them; and ye shall dwell in the land in safety.
19And the land shall yield her fruit, and ye shall eat your fill, and dwell therein in safety.
20And if ye shall say, What shall we eat the seventh year? behold, we shall not sow, nor gather in our increase:
21Then I will command my blessing upon you in the sixth year, and it shall bring forth fruit for three years.
22And ye shall sow the eighth year, and eat *yet* of old fruit until the ninth year; until her fruits come in ye shall eat *of* the old *store*.
23¶ The land shall not be sold for ever: for the land *is* mine; for ye *are* strangers and sojourners with me.
24And in all the land of your possession ye shall grant a redemption for the land.
25¶ If thy brother be waxen poor, and hath sold away *some* of his possession, and if any of his kin come to redeem it, then shall he redeem that which his brother sold.
26And if the man have none to redeem it, and himself be able to redeem it;
27Then let him count the years of the sale thereof, and restore the overplus unto the man to whom he sold it; that he may return unto his possession.
28But if he be not able to restore *it* to him, then that which is sold shall remain in the hand of him that hath bought it until the year of jubilee: and in the jubilee it shall go out, and he shall return unto his possession.
29And if a man sell a dwelling house in a walled city, then he may redeem it within a whole year after it is sold; *within* a full year may he redeem it.
30And if it be not redeemed within the space of a full year, then the house that *is* in the walled city shall be established for ever to him that bought it throughout his generations: it shall not go out in the jubilee.

## Amplified

7For your domestic animals also and for the [wild] beasts in your land; all its yield shall be for food.
8And you shall number seven sabbaths *or* weeks of years for you, seven times seven years, so the total time of the seven weeks of years shall be forty-nine years.
9Then you shall sound abroad the loud trumpet on the tenth day of the seventh month [almost October]; on the day of atonement blow the trumpet in all your land.
10And you shall hallow the fiftieth year, and proclaim liberty throughout all the land to all its inhabitants; it shall be a jubilee to you; and each of you shall return to his ancestral possession [which through poverty he was compelled to sell], and each of you shall return to his family [from whom he was separated in bondservice].
11That fiftieth year shall be a jubilee to you; in it you shall not sow, or reap and store what grows of itself, or gather the grapes of the uncultivated vines.
12For it is a jubilee; it shall be holy to you; you shall eat the [sufficient] increase of it out of the field.
13In this year of jubilee each of you shall return to his ancestral property.
14And if you sell anything to your neighbor or buy from your neighbor, you shall not wrong one another.
15According to the number of years after the jubilee, you shall buy from your neighbor; *and* he shall sell to you according to the number of years [remaining in which you may gather] the crops [before you must restore the property to him].
16If the years [to the next jubilee] are many you may increase the price, and if the years remaining are few you shall diminish the price, for the number of the crops is what he is selling to you.
17You shall not oppress *and* wrong one another, but you shall (reverently) fear your God; for I am the Lord your God.
18Therefore you shall do *and* give effect to My statutes, and keep My ordinances and perform them; and you will dwell in the land in safety.
19The land shall yield its fruit; you shall eat your fill, and dwell there in safety.
20And if you say, What shall we eat the seventh year, if we are not to sow or gather in our increase?
21Then [this is My answer:] I will command My [special] blessings on you in the sixth year, so that it shall bring forth [sufficient] fruit for three years.
22And you shall sow in the eighth year, but eat of the old store of produce; until the crops of the ninth year come in, you shall eat of the old supply.
23The land shall not be sold into perpetual ownership, for the land is Mine; you are [only] strangers and temporary residents with Me. [Cp. Heb. 11:13; I Pet. 2:11-17.]
24And in all the country you possess you shall grant a redemption for the land [in the year of jubilee].
25If your brother has become poor and has sold some of his property, if any of his kin comes to redeem it, he shall [be allowed to] redeem what his brother has sold.
26And if the man has no one to redeem his property, and he himself has become more prosperous *and* has enough to redeem it,
27Then let him count the years since he sold it and restore the over-payment to the man to whom he sold it, and return to his ancestral possession. [I Kings 21:2, 3.]
28But if he is unable to redeem it, it shall remain in the buyer's possession until the year of jubilee, when it shall be set free and he may return to it.
29If a man sells a dwelling house in a fortified city, he may redeem it within a whole year after it is sold; for a full year he may have the right of redemption.
30And if it is not redeemed within a full year, then the house that is in the fortified city shall be made sure, permanently *and* without limitations, for him who bought it, throughout his generations; it shall not go free in the year of jubilee.

## New American Standard

7'Even your cattle and the animals that are in your land shall
have all its crops to eat.
8¶ 'You are also to count off seven sabbaths of years for yourself, seven times seven years, so that you have the time of the
seven sabbaths of years, *namely*, forty-nine years.
9'You shall then sound a ram's horn abroad on the tenth day
of the seventh month; on the day of atonement you shall sound
a horn all through your land.
10'You shall thus consecrate the fiftieth year and proclaim [a]a
release through the land to all its inhabitants. It shall be a jubilee
for you, and each of you shall return to his own property, and each
of you shall return to his family.
11'You shall have the fiftieth year as a jubilee; you shall not sow,
nor reap its aftergrowth, nor gather in *from* its untrimmed vines.
12'For it is a jubilee; it shall be holy to you. You shall eat its crops
out of the field.
13¶ 'On this year of jubilee each of you shall return to his own
property.
14'If you make a sale, moreover, to your friend, or buy from
your friend's hand, you shall not wrong one another.
15'Corresponding to the number of years after the jubilee, you
shall buy from your friend; he is to sell to you according to the
number of years of crops.
16'In proportion to the extent of the years you shall increase its
price, and in proportion to the fewness of the years, you shall
diminish its price; for *it is* a number of crops he is selling to you.
17'So you shall not wrong one another, but you shall fear your
God; for I am the LORD your God.
18¶ 'You shall thus observe My statutes, and keep My judgments, so as to carry them out, that you may live securely on the
land.
19'Then the land will yield its produce, so that you can eat your
fill and live securely on it.
20'But if you say, "What are we going to eat on the seventh year
if we do not sow or gather in our crops?"
21then I will so order My blessing for you in the sixth year that
it will bring forth the crop for three years.
22'When you are sowing the eighth year, you can still eat old
things from the crop, eating *the old* until the ninth year when its
crop comes in.

*The Law of Redemption*

23¶ 'The land, moreover, shall not be sold permanently, for the
land is Mine; for you are *but* aliens and sojourners with Me.
24'Thus for every piece of your property, you are to provide for
the redemption of the land.
25'If a fellow countryman of yours becomes so poor he has to
sell part of his property, then his nearest kinsman is to come and
buy back what his relative has sold.
26'Or in case a man has no kinsman, but so recovers his means
as to find sufficient for its redemption,
27then he shall calculate the years since its sale and refund the
balance to the man to whom he sold it, and so return to his
property.
28'But if he has not found sufficient means to get it back for
himself, then what he has sold shall remain in the hands of its
purchaser until the year of jubilee; but at the jubilee it shall revert,
that he may return to his property.
29¶ 'Likewise, if a man sells a dwelling house in a walled city,
then his redemption right remains valid until a full year from its
sale; his right of redemption lasts a full year.
30'But if it is not bought back for him within the space of a full
year, then the house that is in the walled city passes permanently
to its purchaser throughout his generations; it does not revert in
the jubilee.

NAS [a] Or, *liberty*

## New International

among you, 7as well as for your livestock and the wild animals in
your land. Whatever the land produces may be eaten.

*The Year of Jubilee*

8" 'Count off seven sabbaths of years—seven times seven
years—so that the seven sabbaths of years amount to a period of
forty-nine years. 9Then have the trumpet sounded everywhere on
the tenth day of the seventh month; on the Day of Atonement
sound the trumpet throughout your land. 10Consecrate the fiftieth
year and proclaim liberty throughout the land to all its inhabitants.
It shall be a jubilee for you; each one of you is to return to his family
property and each to his own clan. 11The fiftieth year shall be a
jubilee for you; do not sow and do not reap what grows of itself
or harvest the untended vines. 12For it is a jubilee and is to be holy
for you; eat only what is taken directly from the fields.
13" 'In this Year of Jubilee everyone is to return to his own
property.
14" 'If you sell land to one of your countrymen or buy any from
him, do not take advantage of each other. 15You are to buy from
your countryman on the basis of the number of years since the
Jubilee. And he is to sell to you on the basis of the number of years
left for harvesting crops. 16When the years are many, you are to
increase the price, and when the years are few, you are to decrease
the price, because what he is really selling you is the number of
crops. 17Do not take advantage of each other, but fear your God.
I am the LORD your God.
18" 'Follow my decrees and be careful to obey my laws, and you
will live safely in the land. 19Then the land will yield its fruit, and
you will eat your fill and live there in safety. 20You may ask, "What
will we eat in the seventh year if we do not plant or harvest our
crops?" 21I will send you such a blessing in the sixth year that the
land will yield enough for three years. 22While you plant during
the eighth year, you will eat from the old crop and will continue
to eat from it until the harvest of the ninth year comes in.
23" 'The land must not be sold permanently, because the land
is mine and you are but aliens and my tenants. 24Throughout the
country that you hold as a possession, you must provide for the
redemption of the land.
25" 'If one of your countrymen becomes poor and sells some of
his property, his nearest relative is to come and redeem what his
countryman has sold. 26If, however, a man has no one to redeem
it for him but he himself prospers and acquires sufficient means
to redeem it, 27he is to determine the value for the years since he
sold it and refund the balance to the man to whom he sold it; he
can then go back to his own property. 28But if he does not acquire
the means to repay him, what he sold will remain in the possession
of the buyer until the Year of Jubilee. It will be returned in the
Jubilee, and he can then go back to his property.
29" 'If a man sells a house in a walled city, he retains the right
of redemption a full year after its sale. During that time he may
redeem it. 30If it is not redeemed before a full year has passed, the
house in the walled city shall belong permanently to the buyer and
his descendants. It is not to be returned in the Jubilee. 31But houses

## King James

31 But the houses of the villages which have no wall round about
them shall be counted as the fields of the country: they may be
redeemed, and they shall go out in the jubilee.
32 Notwithstanding the cities of the Levites, *and* the houses of
the cities of their possession, may the Levites redeem at any time.
33 And if a man purchase of the Levites, then the house that was
sold, and the city of his possession, shall go out in *the year of*
jubilee: for the houses of the cities of the Levites *are* their possession among the children of Israel.
34 But the field of the suburbs of their cities may not be sold; for
it *is* their perpetual possession.
35 ¶ And if thy brother be waxen poor, and fallen in decay with
thee; then thou shalt relieve him: *yea, though he be* a stranger, or
a sojourner; that he may live with thee.
36 Take thou no usury of him, or increase: but fear thy God; that
thy brother may live with thee.
37 Thou shalt not give him thy money upon usury, nor lend him
thy victuals for increase.
38 I *am* the LORD your God, which brought you forth out of the
land of Egypt, to give you the land of Canaan, *and* to be your God.
39 ¶ And if thy brother *that dwelleth* by thee be waxen poor, and
be sold unto thee; thou shalt not compel him to serve as a bondservant:
40 *But* as an hired servant, *and* as a sojourner, he shall be with
thee, *and* shall serve thee unto the year of jubilee:
41 And *then* shall he depart from thee, *both* he and his children
with him, and shall return unto his own family, and unto the
possession of his fathers shall he return.
42 For they *are* my servants, which I brought forth out of the land
of Egypt: they shall not be sold as bondmen.
43 Thou shalt not rule over him with rigour; but shalt fear thy
God.
44 Both thy bondmen, and thy bondmaids, which thou shalt
have, *shall be* of the heathen that are round about you; of them shall
ye buy bondmen and bondmaids.
45 Moreover of the children of the strangers that do sojourn
among you, of them shall ye buy, and of their families that *are* with
you, which they begat in your land: and they shall be your possession.
46 And ye shall take them as an inheritance for your children
after you, to inherit *them for* a possession; they shall be your
bondmen for ever: but over your brethren the children of Israel,
ye shall not rule one over another with rigour.
47 ¶ And if a sojourner or stranger wax rich by thee, and thy
brother *that dwelleth* by him wax poor, and sell himself unto the
stranger *or* sojourner by thee, or to the stock of the stranger's
family:
48 After that he is sold he may be redeemed again; one of his
brethren may redeem him:
49 Either his uncle, or his uncle's son, may redeem him, or *any*
that is nigh of kin unto him of his family may redeem him; or if
he be able, he may redeem himself.
50 And he shall reckon with him that bought him from the year
that he was sold to him unto the year of jubilee: and the price of
his sale shall be according unto the number of years, according to
the time of an hired servant shall it be with him.
51 If *there be* yet many years *behind*, according unto them he shall
give again the price of his redemption out of the money that he was
bought for.
52 And if there remain but few years unto the year of jubilee,
then he shall count with him, *and* according unto his years shall
he give him again the price of his redemption.
53 *And* as a yearly hired servant shall he be with him: *and the
other* shall not rule with rigour over him in thy sight.

## Amplified

31 But the houses of the unwalled villages shall be counted with
the fields of the country; they may be redeemed, and they shall go
free in the year of jubilee.
32 Nevertheless the cities of the Levites, the houses in the cities
of their possession, the Levites may redeem at any time.
33 But if a house is not redeemed by a Levite, the sold house in
the city they possess shall go free in the year of jubilee; for the
houses in the Levite cities are their ancestral possession among the
Israelites.
34 But the field of unenclosed *or* pasture lands of their cities may
not be sold; for it is their perpetual possession.
35 And if your [Israelite] brother has become poor, and his hand
wavers [from poverty, sickness or age, and he is unable to support
himself], then you shall uphold (strengthen, relieve) him, [treating
him with the courtesy and consideration that you would] a
stranger or a temporary resident with you [without property], so
that he may live [along] with you. [I John 3:17.]
36 Charge him no interest or [portion of] increase, but fear your
God, so your brother may [continue to] live along with you.
37 You shall not give him your money on interest nor lend him
food at a profit.
38 I am the Lord your God, Who brought you forth out of the
land of Egypt to give you the land of Canaan and to be your God.
39 And if your brother becomes poor beside you, and sells himself to you, you shall not compel him to serve as a bondservant [a
slave, not eligible for redemption],
40 But as a hired servant and as a temporary resident he shall be
with you; he shall serve you till the year of jubilee,
41 And then he shall depart from you, he and his children with
him, and shall go back to his own family, and return to the possession of his fathers.
42 For the Israelites are My servants; I brought them out of the
land of Egypt; they shall not be sold as bondmen. [I Cor. 7:23.]
43 You shall not rule over him with harshness (severity, oppression), but you shall (reverently) fear your God. [Cp. Eph. 6:9; Col.
4:1.]
44 As for your bondmen and your bondmaids whom you may
have, they shall be from the nations round about you, of whom
you may buy bondmen and bondmaids.
45 Moreover of the children of the strangers who sojourn among
you, of them you may buy, and of their families that are with you,
which they have begotten in your land; and they shall be your
possession.
46 And you shall make them an inheritance for your children
after you, to hold for a possession; of them shall you take your
bondmen always; but over your brethren the Israelites you shall
not rule one over another with harshness (severity, oppression).
47 And if a sojourner or stranger with you becomes rich, and
your [Israelite] brother becomes poor beside him and sells himself
to the stranger or sojourner with you, or to a member of the
stranger's family,
48 After he is sold he may be redeemed; one of his brethren may
redeem him,
49 Either his uncle, or his uncle's son may redeem him, or a near
kinsman may redeem him; or if he has enough *and* is able, he may
redeem himself.
50 And *the redeemer* shall reckon with the purchaser of the servant from the year when he sold himself to the purchaser to the
year of jubilee, and the price of his release shall be adjusted according to the number of years. The time he was with his owner shall
be counted as that of a hired servant.
51 If there remain many years *before the year of jubilee* in proportion to them he must refund *to the purchaser* for his release *the
over-payment* for his acquisition.
52 And if little time remains until the year of jubilee he shall
count it over with him and he shall refund the proportionate
amount for his release.
53 And as a servant hired year by year shall he deal with him;
he shall not rule over him with harshness (severity, oppression)
in your sight [make sure of that].

## New American Standard

31'The houses of the villages, however, which have no surrounding wall shall be considered as open fields; they have redemption rights and revert in the jubilee.

32'As for cities of the Levites, the Levites have a permanent right of redemption for the houses of the cities which are their possession.

33'What, therefore, belongs to the Levites may be redeemed and a house sale in the city of this possession reverts in the jubilee, for the houses of the cities of the Levites are their possession among the sons of Israel.

34'But pasture fields of their cities shall not be sold, for that is their perpetual possession.

*Of Poor Countrymen*

35¶ 'Now in case a countryman of yours becomes poor and his means with regard to you falter, then you are to sustain him, like a stranger or a sojourner, that he may live with you.

36'Do not take usurious interest from him, but revere your God, that your countryman may live with you.

37'You shall not give him your silver at interest, nor your food for gain.

38'I am the LORD your God, who brought you out of the land of Egypt to give you the land of Canaan *and* to be your God.

39¶ 'And if a countryman of yours becomes so poor with regard to you that he sells himself to you, you shall not subject him to a slave's service.

40'He shall be with you as a hired man, as if he were a sojourner; he shall serve with you until the year of jubilee.

41'He shall then go out from you, he and his sons with him, and shall go back to his family, that he may return to the property of his forefathers.

42'For they are My servants whom I brought out from the land of Egypt; they are not to be sold *in* a slave sale.

43'You shall not rule over him with severity, but are to revere your God.

44'As for your male and female slaves whom you may have—you may acquire male and female slaves from the pagan nations that are around you.

45'Then, too, *it is* out of the sons of the sojourners who live as aliens among you that you may gain acquisition, and out of their families who are with you, whom they will have produced in your land; they also may become your possession.

46'You may even bequeath them to your sons after you, to receive as a possession; you can use them as permanent slaves. But in respect to your countrymen, the sons of Israel, you shall not rule with severity over one another.

*Of Redeeming a Poor Man*

47¶ 'Now if the means of a stranger or of a sojourner with you becomes sufficient, and a countryman of yours becomes so poor with regard to him as to sell himself to a stranger who is sojourning with you, or to the descendants of a stranger's family,

48then he shall have redemption right after he has been sold. One of his brothers may redeem him,

49or his uncle, or his uncle's son, may redeem him, or one of his blood relatives from his family may redeem him; or if he prospers, he may redeem himself.

50'He then with his purchaser shall calculate from the year when he sold himself to him up to the year of jubilee; and the price of his sale shall correspond to the number of years. *It is* like the days of a hired man *that* he shall be with him.

51'If there are still many years, he shall refund part of his purchase price in proportion to them for his own redemption;

52and if few years remain until the year of jubilee, he shall so calculate with him. In proportion to his years he is to refund *the amount for* his redemption.

53'Like a man hired year by year he shall be with him; he shall not rule over him with severity in your sight.

## New International

in villages without walls around them are to be considered as open
country. They can be redeemed, and they are to be returned in the
Jubilee.
32" 'The Levites always have the right to redeem their houses
in the Levitical towns, which they possess. 33So the property of the
Levites is redeemable—that is, a house sold in any town they
hold—and is to be returned in the Jubilee, because the houses in
the towns of the Levites are their property among the Israelites.
34But the pastureland belonging to their towns must not be sold;
it is their permanent possession.
35" 'If one of your countrymen becomes poor and is unable to
support himself among you, help him as you would an alien or a
temporary resident, so he can continue to live among you. 36Do
not take interest of any kind[a] from him, but fear your God, so that
your countryman may continue to live among you. 37You must not
lend him money at interest or sell him food at a profit. 38I am the
LORD your God, who brought you out of Egypt to give you the land
of Canaan and to be your God.
39" 'If one of your countrymen becomes poor among you and
sells himself to you, do not make him work as a slave. 40He is to
be treated as a hired worker or a temporary resident among you;
he is to work for you until the Year of Jubilee. 41Then he and his
children are to be released, and he will go back to his own clan and
to the property of his forefathers. 42Because the Israelites are my
servants, whom I brought out of Egypt, they must not be sold as
slaves. 43Do not rule over them ruthlessly, but fear your God.
44" 'Your male and female slaves are to come from the nations
around you; from them you may buy slaves. 45You may also buy
some of the temporary residents living among you and members
of their clans born in your country, and they will become your
property. 46You can will them to your children as inherited property and can make them slaves for life, but you must not rule over
your fellow Israelites ruthlessly.
47" 'If an alien or a temporary resident among you becomes rich
and one of your countrymen becomes poor and sells himself to the
alien living among you or to a member of the alien's clan, 48he
retains the right of redemption after he has sold himself. One of
his relatives may redeem him: 49An uncle or a cousin or any blood
relative in his clan may redeem him. Or if he prospers, he may
redeem himself. 50He and his buyer are to count the time from the
year he sold himself up to the Year of Jubilee. The price for his
release is to be based on the rate paid to a hired man for that
number of years. 51If many years remain, he must pay for his
redemption a larger share of the price paid for him. 52If only a few
years remain until the Year of Jubilee, he is to compute that and
pay for his redemption accordingly. 53He is to be treated as a man
hired from year to year; you must see to it that his owner does not
rule over him ruthlessly.

NIV [a] 36 Or *take excessive interest;* similarly in verse 37

## King James

54 And if he be not redeemed in these *years*, then he shall go out in the year of jubilee, *both* he, and his children with him.

55 For unto me the children of Israel *are* servants; they *are* my servants whom I brought forth out of the land of Egypt: I *am* the LORD your God.

**26** YE SHALL make you no idols nor graven image, neither rear you up a standing image, neither shall ye set up *any* image of stone in your land, to bow down unto it: for I *am* the LORD your God.

2 ¶ Ye shall keep my sabbaths, and reverence my sanctuary: I *am* the LORD.

3 ¶ If ye walk in my statutes, and keep my commandments, and do them;

4 Then I will give you rain in due season, and the land shall yield her increase, and the trees of the field shall yield their fruit.

5 And your threshing shall reach unto the vintage, and the vintage shall reach unto the sowing time: and ye shall eat your bread to the full, and dwell in your land safely.

6 And I will give peace in the land, and ye shall lie down, and none shall make *you* afraid: and I will rid evil beasts out of the land, neither shall the sword go through your land.

7 And ye shall chase your enemies, and they shall fall before you by the sword.

8 And five of you shall chase an hundred, and an hundred of you shall put ten thousand to flight: and your enemies shall fall before you by the sword.

9 For I will have respect unto you, and make you fruitful, and multiply you, and establish my covenant with you.

10 And ye shall eat old store, and bring forth the old because of the new.

11 And I will set my tabernacle among you: and my soul shall not abhor you.

12 And I will walk among you, and will be your God, and ye shall be my people.

13 I *am* the LORD your God, which brought you forth out of the land of Egypt, that ye should not be their bondmen; and I have broken the bands of your yoke, and made you go upright.

14 ¶ But if ye will not hearken unto me, and will not do all these commandments;

15 And if ye shall despise my statutes, or if your soul abhor my judgments, so that ye will not do all my commandments, *but* that ye break my covenant:

16 I also will do this unto you; I will even appoint over you terror, consumption, and the burning ague, that shall consume the eyes, and cause sorrow of heart: and ye shall sow your seed in vain, for your enemies shall eat it.

17 And I will set my face against you, and ye shall be slain before your enemies: they that hate you shall reign over you; and ye shall flee when none pursueth you.

18 And if ye will not yet for all this hearken unto me, then I will punish you seven times more for your sins.

19 And I will break the pride of your power; and I will make your heaven as iron, and your earth as brass:

20 And your strength shall be spent in vain: for your land shall not yield her increase, neither shall the trees of the land yield their fruits.

21 ¶ And if ye walk contrary unto me, and will not hearken unto me; I will bring seven times more plagues upon you according to your sins.

**AMP** [a] This chapter abounds in prophecies of what God would do for, or against, His people if they did, or did not, meet His conditions; each of which prophecies were literally fulfilled in the following centuries. The Scripture references indicate where these fulfillments are recorded; there are at least a dozen of them. Yet some people do not seem to have awakened to the fact that God *keeps His word*, whether for us or against us. It all depends on *us*.

## Amplified

54 And if he is not redeemed during these years *and* by these means, then he shall go free in the year of jubilee, he and his children with him.

55 For to Me the Israelites are servants, My servants whom I brought forth out of the land of Egypt. I am the Lord your God.

**26** YOU SHALL make for yourselves no idols, nor shall you erect a graven image, pillar *or* obelisk, nor shall you place any figured stone in your land to which *or* on which to bow down; for I am the Lord your God.

2 You shall keep My sabbaths and reverence My sanctuary. I am the Lord.

3 If you walk in My statutes and keep My commandments and do them,

4 I will give you rain in due season, and the land shall yield her increase, and the trees of the field yield their fruit.

5 And your threshing [time] shall reach to the vintage, and the vintage [time] shall reach to the sowing time; and you shall eat your bread to the full, and dwell in your land securely.

6 I will give peace in the land; you shall lie down, and none shall fill you with dread *or* make you afraid; and I will clear ferocious (wild) beasts out of the land, nor shall the sword go through your land.

7 And you shall chase your enemies, and they shall fall before you by the sword.

8 Five of you shall chase a hundred, and a hundred of you shall put ten thousand to flight; your enemies shall fall before you by the sword.

9 For I will be leaning toward you with favor *and* regard for you, rendering you fruitful, multiplying you, and establishing *and* ratifying My covenant with you. [II Kings 13:23.]

10 And you shall eat the [abundant] old store of produce long kept, and clear out the old [to make room] for the new.

11 I will set My dwelling in *and* among you, and My soul shall not despise *or* reject *or* separate itself from you.

12 And I will walk in *and* with *and* among you, and will be your God, and you shall be My people.

13 I am the Lord your God, Who brought you forth out of the land of Egypt, that you should no more be slaves; and I have broken the bars of your yoke and made you walk erect [as free men].

14 But if you will not hearken to Me, and will not do all these commandments,

15 And if you spurn *and* despise My statutes, and if your soul despises *and* rejects My ordinances, so that you will not do all My commandments, but break My covenant,

16 I will do this: I will appoint over you (sudden) terror (trembling, trouble), even consumption and fever that consume *and* waste the eyes and make the (physical) life pine away; you shall sow your seed in vain, for your enemies shall eat it.

17 I [the Lord] will set My face against you, and [a]you shall be defeated *and* slain before your enemies; they who hate you shall rule over you; you shall flee when no one pursues you. [I Sam. 4:10; 31:1.]

18 And if in spite of all this you still will not listen *and* be obedient to Me, then I will chastise *and* discipline you sevenfold more for your sins.

19 And I will break *and* humble your pride in your power; and I will make your heavens as iron [yielding no answer, no blessing, no rain], and your earth [as sterile] as brass; [I Kings 17:1.]

20 And your strength shall be spent in vain, for your land shall not yield its increase, neither shall the trees of the land yield their fruit.

21 If you walk contrary to Me and will not heed Me, I will bring seven times more plagues upon you according to your sins.

## New American Standard

54'Even if he is not redeemed by these *means,* he shall still go
out in the year of jubilee, he and his sons with him.
55'For the sons of Israel are My servants; they are My servants
whom I brought out from the land of Egypt. I am the LORD your
God.

*Blessings of Obedience*

26 'YOU SHALL not make for yourselves idols, nor shall you
set up for yourselves an image or a *sacred* pillar, nor shall
you place a figured stone in your land to bow down to it; for I am
the LORD your God.
2'You shall keep My sabbaths and reverence My sanctuary; I
am the LORD.
3'If you walk in My statutes and keep My commandments so
as to carry them out,
4then I shall give you rains in their season, so that the land will
yield its produce and the trees of the field will bear their fruit.
5'Indeed, your threshing will last for you until grape gathering,
and grape gathering will last until sowing time. You will thus eat
your food to the full and live securely in your land.
6'I shall also grant peace in the land, so that you may lie down
with no one making *you* tremble. I shall also eliminate harmful
beasts from the land, and no sword will pass through your land.
7'But you will chase your enemies, and they will fall before you
by the sword;
8five of you will chase a hundred, and a hundred of you will
chase ten thousand, and your enemies will fall before you by the
sword.
9'So I will turn toward you and make you fruitful and multiply
you, and I will confirm My covenant with you.
10'And you will eat the old supply and clear out the old because
of the new.
11'Moreover, I will make My dwelling among you, and My soul
will not reject you.
12'I will also walk among you and be your God, and you shall
be My people.
13'I am the LORD your God, who brought you out of the land
of Egypt so that *you* should not be their slaves, and I broke the bars
of your yoke and made you walk erect.

*Penalties of Disobedience*

14¶ 'But if you do not obey Me and do not carry out all these
commandments,
15if, instead, you reject My statutes, and if your soul abhors My
ordinances so as not to carry out all My commandments, *and* so
break My covenant,
16I, in turn, will do this to you: I will appoint over you a sudden
terror, consumption and fever that shall waste away the eyes and
cause the soul to pine away; also, you shall sow your seed uselessly, for your enemies shall eat it up.
17'And I will set My face against you so that you shall be struck
down before your enemies; and those who hate you shall rule over
you, and you shall flee when no one is pursuing you.
18'If also after these things, you do not obey Me, then I will
punish you seven times more for your sins.
19'And I will also break down your pride of power; I will also
make your sky like iron and your earth like bronze.
20'And your strength shall be spent uselessly, for your land
shall not yield its produce and the trees of the land shall not yield
their fruit.
21¶ 'If then, you act with hostility against Me and are unwilling
to obey Me, I will increase the plague on you seven times according
to your sins.

## New International

54" 'Even if he is not redeemed in any of these ways, he and his
children are to be released in the Year of Jubilee, 55for the Israelites
belong to me as servants. They are my servants, whom I brought
out of Egypt. I am the LORD your God.

*Reward for Obedience*

26 " 'DO NOT make idols or set up an image or a sacred
stone for yourselves, and do not place a carved stone in
your land to bow down before it. I am the LORD your God.
2" 'Observe my Sabbaths and have reverence for my sanctuary.
I am the LORD.
3" 'If you follow my decrees and are careful to obey my commands, 4I will send you rain in its season, and the ground will yield
its crops and the trees of the field their fruit. 5Your threshing will
continue until grape harvest and the grape harvest will continue
until planting, and you will eat all the food you want and live in
safety in your land.
6" 'I will grant peace in the land, and you will lie down and no
one will make you afraid. I will remove savage beasts from the
land, and the sword will not pass through your country. 7You will
pursue your enemies, and they will fall by the sword before you.
8Five of you will chase a hundred, and a hundred of you will chase
ten thousand, and your enemies will fall by the sword before you.
9" 'I will look on you with favor and make you fruitful and
increase your numbers, and I will keep my covenant with you.
10You will still be eating last year's harvest when you will have to
move it out to make room for the new. 11I will put my dwelling
place[b] among you, and I will not abhor you. 12I will walk among
you and be your God, and you will be my people. 13I am the LORD
your God, who brought you out of Egypt so that you would no
longer be slaves to the Egyptians; I broke the bars of your yoke and
enabled you to walk with heads held high.

*Punishment for Disobedience*

14" 'But if you will not listen to me and carry out all these
commands, 15and if you reject my decrees and abhor my laws and
fail to carry out all my commands and so violate my covenant,
16then I will do this to you: I will bring upon you sudden terror,
wasting diseases and fever that will destroy your sight and drain
away your life. You will plant seed in vain, because your enemies
will eat it. 17I will set my face against you so that you will be
defeated by your enemies; those who hate you will rule over you,
and you will flee even when no one is pursuing you.
18" 'If after all this you will not listen to me, I will punish you
for your sins seven times over. 19I will break down your stubborn
pride and make the sky above you like iron and the ground
beneath you like bronze. 20Your strength will be spent in vain,
because your soil will not yield its crops, nor will the trees of the
land yield their fruit.
21" 'If you remain hostile toward me and refuse to listen to me,
I will multiply your afflictions seven times over, as your sins deserve. 22I will send wild animals against you, and they will rob you

NIV [b] *11* Or *my tabernacle*

## King James

22I will also send wild beasts among you, which shall rob you of your children, and destroy your cattle, and make you few in number; and your *high* ways shall be desolate.
23And if ye will not be reformed by me by these things, but will walk contrary unto me;
24Then will I also walk contrary unto you, and will punish you yet seven times for your sins.
25And I will bring a sword upon you, that shall avenge the quarrel of *my* covenant: and when ye are gathered together within your cities, I will send the pestilence among you; and ye shall be delivered into the hand of the enemy.
26 *And* when I have broken the staff of your bread, ten women shall bake your bread in one oven, and they shall deliver *you* your bread again by weight: and ye shall eat, and not be satisfied.
27And if ye will not for all this hearken unto me, but walk contrary unto me;
28Then I will walk contrary unto you also in fury; and I, even I, will chastise you seven times for your sins.
29And ye shall eat the flesh of your sons, and the flesh of your daughters shall ye eat.
30And I will destroy your high places, and cut down your images, and cast your carcases upon the carcases of your idols, and my soul shall abhor you.
31And I will make your cities waste, and bring your sanctuaries unto desolation, and I will not smell the savour of your sweet odours.
32And I will bring the land into desolation: and your enemies which dwell therein shall be astonished at it.
33And I will scatter you among the heathen, and will draw out a sword after you: and your land shall be desolate, and your cities waste.
34Then shall the land enjoy her sabbaths, as long as it lieth desolate, and ye *be* in your enemies' land; *even* then shall the land rest, and enjoy her sabbaths.
35As long as it lieth desolate it shall rest; because it did not rest in your sabbaths, when ye dwelt upon it.
36And upon them that are left *alive* of you I will send a faintness into their hearts in the lands of their enemies; and the sound of a shaken leaf shall chase them; and they shall flee, as fleeing from a sword; and they shall fall when none pursueth.
37And they shall fall one upon another, as it were before a sword, when none pursueth: and ye shall have no power to stand before your enemies.
38And ye shall perish among the heathen, and the land of your enemies shall eat you up.
39And they that are left of you shall pine away in their iniquity in your enemies' lands; and also in the iniquities of their fathers shall they pine away with them.
40If they shall confess their iniquity, and the iniquity of their fathers, with their trespass which they trespassed against me, and that also they have walked contrary unto me;
41And *that* I also have walked contrary unto them, and have brought them into the land of their enemies; if then their uncircumcised hearts be humbled, and they then accept of the punishment of their iniquity:
42Then will I remember my covenant with Jacob, and also my covenant with Isaac, and also my covenant with Abraham will I remember; and I will remember the land.
43The land also shall be left of them, and shall enjoy her sabbaths, while she lieth desolate without them: and they shall accept of the punishment of their iniquity: because, even because they despised my judgments, and because their soul abhorred my statutes.

## Amplified

22I will loose the wild beasts of the field among you, which shall rob you of your children, destroy your livestock, and make you few, so that your roads shall be deserted *and* desolate. [II Kings 17:25, 26.]
23If by these means you are not turned to Me, but determine to walk contrary to Me,
24I also will walk contrary to you, and I will smite you sevenfold for your sins.
25And I will bring a sword upon you, that shall execute the vengeance [for the breaking] of My covenant; and you shall be gathered together within your cities, and I will send the pestilence among you; and you shall be delivered into the hand of the enemy. [Num. 16:49; II Sam. 24:15.]
26When I break your staff of bread *and* cut off your supply of food, ten women shall bake your bread in one oven, and they shall ration your bread *and* deliver it again by weight; and you shall eat, and not be satisfied. [Hag. 1:6.]
27And if in spite of all this you will not listen *and* give heed to Me, but walk contrary to Me,
28Then I will walk contrary to you in wrath, and I also will chastise you sevenfold for your sins.
29You shall eat the flesh of your sons *and* of your daughters. [II Kings 6:28, 29.]
30And I will destroy your high places [devoted to idolatrous worship], and cut down your sun images, and throw your dead bodies upon the [wrecked] bodies of your idols, and My soul shall abhor you [with deep and unutterable loathing]. [II Kings 23:8, 20.]
31I will lay your cities waste, bring your sanctuaries to desolation, and I will not smell the fragrance of your sweet *and* soothing odors [of offerings by fire]. [II Kings 25:4-10; II Chron. 36:19.]
32And I will bring the land into desolation; and your enemies who dwell in it shall be astonished at it.
33I will scatter you among the nations, and draw out your enemies' sword after you; and your land shall be desolate and your cities a waste. [Ps. 44:11-14.]
34Then shall the land [of Israel have the opportunity to] enjoy its sabbaths as long as it lies desolate, and you are in your enemies' land; then shall the land rest, to enjoy *and* receive payments for its sabbaths [divinely ordained for it].
35As long as it lies desolate *and* waste it shall have rest, the rest it did not have in your sabbaths when you dwelt upon it. [II Chron. 36:21.]
36As for those who are left of you, I will send dejection (lack of courage, a faintness) into their hearts in the lands of their enemies; the sound of a driven leaf shall put them to hasty *and* tumultuous flight, and they shall flee as if from the sword, and fall when no one pursues them.
37They shall stumble over one another as if to escape a sword, when no one pursues them; and you shall have no power to stand before your enemies.
38You shall perish among the nations; the land of your enemies shall eat you up.
39And those of you who are left shall pine away in their iniquity in your enemies' lands; also in the iniquities of their fathers shall they pine away like them.
40But if they confess their own and their fathers' iniquity in their treachery which they committed against Me, and also that because they walked contrary to Me,
41I also walked contrary to them and brought them into the land of their enemies; if then their uncircumcised heart is humbled, and they then accept the punishment for their iniquity, [II Kings 24:10-14; Dan. 9:11-14.]
42Then will I [earnestly] remember My covenant with Jacob, My covenant with Isaac, and My covenant with Abraham, and [earnestly] remember the land. [Ps. 106:44-46.]
43But the land shall be left behind them, and shall enjoy its sabbaths, while it lies desolate without them; and they shall accept the punishment for their sins *and* make amends, because they despised *and* rejected My ordinances and their soul scorned *and* rejected My statutes.

## New American Standard

22'And I will let loose among you the beasts of the field, which shall bereave you of your children and destroy your cattle and reduce your number so that your roads lie deserted.

**23**¶ 'And if by these things you are not turned to Me, but act with hostility against Me,

24then I will act with hostility against you; and I, even I, will strike you seven times for your sins.

25'I will also bring upon you a sword which will execute vengeance for the covenant; and when you gather together into your cities, I will send pestilence among you, so that you shall be delivered into enemy hands.

26'When I break your staff of bread, ten women will bake your bread in one oven, and they will bring back your bread [a]in rationed amounts, so that you will eat and not be satisfied.

**27**¶ 'Yet if in spite of this, you do not obey Me, but act with hostility against Me,

28then I will act with wrathful hostility against you; and I, even I, will punish you seven times for your sins.

29'Further, you shall eat the flesh of your sons and the flesh of your daughters you shall eat.

30'I then will destroy your high places, and cut down your incense altars, and heap your remains on the remains of your idols; for My soul shall abhor you.

31'I will lay waste your cities as well, and will make your sanctuaries desolate; and I will not smell your soothing aromas.

32'And I will make the land desolate so that your enemies who settle in it shall be appalled over it.

33'You, however, I will scatter among the nations and will draw out a sword after you, as your land becomes desolate and your cities become waste.

**34**¶ 'Then the land will enjoy its sabbaths all the days of the desolation, while you are in your enemies' land; then the land will rest and enjoy its sabbaths.

35'All the days of *its* desolation it will observe the rest which it did not observe on your sabbaths, while you were living on it.

36'As for those of you who may be left, I will also bring weakness into their hearts in the lands of their enemies. And the sound of a driven leaf will chase them and even when no one is pursuing, they will flee as though from the sword, and they will fall.

37'They will therefore stumble over each other as if *running* from the sword, although no one is pursuing; and you will have *no strength* to stand up before your enemies.

38'But you will perish among the nations, and your enemies' land will consume you.

39'So those of you who may be left will rot away because of their iniquity in the lands of your enemies; and also because of the iniquities of their forefathers they will rot away with them.

**40**¶ 'If they confess their iniquity and the iniquity of their forefathers, in their unfaithfulness which they committed against Me, and also in their acting with hostility against Me—

41I also was acting with hostility against them, to bring them into the land of their enemies—or if their uncircumcised heart becomes humbled so that they then make amends for their iniquity,

42then I will remember My covenant with Jacob, and I will remember also My covenant with Isaac, and My covenant with Abraham as well, and I will remember the land.

43'For the land shall be abandoned by them, and shall make up for its sabbaths while it is made desolate without them. They, meanwhile, shall be making amends for their iniquity, because they rejected My ordinances and their soul abhorred My statutes.

## New International

of your children, destroy your cattle and make you so few in
number that your roads will be deserted.

23" 'If in spite of these things you do not accept my correction
but continue to be hostile toward me, 24I myself will be hostile
toward you and will afflict you for your sins seven times over.
25And I will bring the sword upon you to avenge the breaking of
the covenant. When you withdraw into your cities, I will send a
plague among you, and you will be given into enemy hands.
26When I cut off your supply of bread, ten women will be able to
bake your bread in one oven, and they will dole out the bread by
weight. You will eat, but you will not be satisfied.

27" 'If in spite of this you still do not listen to me but continue
to be hostile toward me, 28then in my anger I will be hostile toward
you, and I myself will punish you for your sins seven times over.
29You will eat the flesh of your sons and the flesh of your daughters. 30I will destroy your high places, cut down your incense altars
and pile your dead bodies on the lifeless forms of your idols, and
I will abhor you. 31I will turn your cities into ruins and lay waste
your sanctuaries, and I will take no delight in the pleasing aroma
of your offerings. 32I will lay waste the land, so that your enemies
who live there will be appalled. 33I will scatter you among the
nations and will draw out my sword and pursue you. Your land
will be laid waste, and your cities will lie in ruins. 34Then the land
will enjoy its sabbath years all the time that it lies desolate and you
are in the country of your enemies; then the land will rest and
enjoy its sabbaths. 35All the time that it lies desolate, the land will
have the rest it did not have during the sabbaths you lived in it.

36" 'As for those of you who are left, I will make their hearts so
fearful in the lands of their enemies that the sound of a windblown
leaf will put them to flight. They will run as though fleeing from
the sword, and they will fall, even though no one is pursuing
them. 37They will stumble over one another as though fleeing from
the sword, even though no one is pursuing them. So you will not
be able to stand before your enemies. 38You will perish among the
nations; the land of your enemies will devour you. 39Those of you
who are left will waste away in the lands of their enemies because
of their sins; also because of their fathers' sins they will waste
away.

40" 'But if they will confess their sins and the sins of their
fathers—their treachery against me and their hostility toward me,
41which made me hostile toward them so that I sent them into the
land of their enemies—then when their uncircumcised hearts are
humbled and they pay for their sin, 42I will remember my covenant
with Jacob and my covenant with Isaac and my covenant with
Abraham, and I will remember the land. 43For the land will be
deserted by them and will enjoy its sabbaths while it lies desolate
without them. They will pay for their sins because they rejected
my laws and abhorred my decrees. 44Yet in spite of this, when they

**NAS** [a] Lit., *by weight*

## King James

44And yet for all that, when they be in the land of their enemies, I will not cast them away, neither will I abhor them, to destroy them utterly, and to break my covenant with them: for I *am* the LORD their God.
45But I will for their sakes remember the covenant of their ancestors, whom I brought forth out of the land of Egypt in the sight of the heathen, that I might be their God: I *am* the LORD.
46These *are* the statutes and judgments and laws, which the LORD made between him and the children of Israel in mount Sinai by the hand of Moses.

**27** AND THE LORD spake unto Moses, saying,
2Speak unto the children of Israel, and say unto them, When a man shall make a singular vow, the persons *shall be* for the LORD by thy estimation.
3And thy estimation shall be of the male from twenty years old even unto sixty years old, even thy estimation shall be fifty shekels of silver, after the shekel of the sanctuary.
4And if it *be* a female, then thy estimation shall be thirty shekels.
5And if *it be* from five years old even unto twenty years old, then thy estimation shall be of the male twenty shekels, and for the female ten shekels.
6And if *it be* from a month old even unto five years old, then thy estimation shall be of the male five shekels of silver, and for the female thy estimation *shall be* three shekels of silver.
7And if *it be* from sixty years old and above; if *it be* a male, then thy estimation shall be fifteen shekels, and for the female ten shekels.
8But if he be poorer than thy estimation, then he shall present himself before the priest, and the priest shall value him; according to his ability that vowed shall the priest value him.
9And if *it be* a beast, whereof men bring an offering unto the LORD, all that *any man* giveth of such unto the LORD shall be holy.
10He shall not alter it, nor change it, a good for a bad, or a bad for a good: and if he shall at all change beast for beast, then it and the exchange thereof shall be holy.
11And if *it be* any unclean beast, of which they do not offer a sacrifice unto the LORD, then he shall present the beast before the priest:
12And the priest shall value it, whether it be good or bad: as thou valuest it, *who art* the priest, so shall it be.
13But if he will at all redeem it, then he shall add a fifth *part* thereof unto thy estimation.
14¶ And when a man shall sanctify his house *to be* holy unto the LORD, then the priest shall estimate it, whether it be good or bad: as the priest shall estimate it, so shall it stand.
15And if he that sanctified it will redeem his house, then he shall add the fifth *part* of the money of thy estimation unto it, and it shall be his.
16And if a man shall sanctify unto the LORD *some part* of a field of his possession, then thy estimation shall be according to the seed thereof: an homer of barley seed *shall be valued* at fifty shekels of silver.
17If he sanctify his field from the year of jubilee, according to thy estimation it shall stand.
18But if he sanctify his field after the jubilee, then the priest shall reckon unto him the money according to the years that remain, even unto the year of the jubilee, and it shall be abated from thy estimation.

**AMP** [a] No greater evidence that God keeps His Word is available than the fact of the existence today of the Jews as a nation. Scattered for twenty-five centuries throughout the world with powerful forces determined to wipe them out, yet they are restored to their homeland, because, in spite of all their sins against Him, God refuses to break His covenant with their forefathers and with them. The presence of even a small number of Jews in the world, after all the centuries of diabolical effort to exterminate them, would alone be sufficient assurance that God will keep His promises whether good or bad, to individuals or to nations.

## Amplified

44And [a]yet for all that, when they are in the land of their enemies, I will not spurn *and* cast them away, neither will I despise *and* abhor them, to destroy them utterly and to break My covenant with them, for I am the Lord their God. [Jer. 33:4, 5, 23-26; Deut. 4:31-35; Rom. 11:2-5.]
45But I will for their sake [earnestly] remember the covenant with their forefathers, whom I brought forth out of the land of Egypt in the sight of the nations, that I might be their God. I am the Lord.
46These are the statutes, ordinances, and laws which the Lord made between Him and the Israelites on Mount Sinai by Moses.

**27** AND THE Lord said to Moses,
2Say to the Israelites, When a man shall make a special vow of persons to the Lord at your valuation,
3Then your valuation of a male from twenty years old to sixty years old shall be fifty shekels of silver, according to the shekel of the sanctuary.
4And if the person is a female, your valuation shall be thirty shekels.
5And if the person is from five years old up to twenty years old, then your valuation shall be of the male twenty shekels, and for the female ten shekels.
6And if a child is from a month up to five years old, then your valuation shall be of the male five shekels of silver, and for the female three shekels.
7And if the person is from sixty years old and above, if it be a male, then your valuation shall be fifteen shekels, and for the female ten shekels.
8But if the man is too poor to pay your valuation, then he shall be set before the priest, and the priest shall value him; according to the ability of him who vowed shall the priest value him.
9If it is a beast of which men offer an offering to the Lord, all that any man gives of such to the Lord shall be holy.
10He shall not replace it or exchange it, a good for a bad, or a bad for a good; and if he makes any exchange beast for beast, then both the original offering and that exchanged for it shall be holy.
11If it is an unclean animal, such as is not offered as an offering to the Lord, he shall bring the animal before the priest,
12And the priest shall value it, whether it be good or bad; as you, the priest, value it, so shall it be.
13But if he wishes to redeem it, he shall add a fifth to your valuation.
14If a man dedicates his house to be sacred to the Lord, the priest shall appraise it, whether it be good or bad; as the priest appraises it, so shall it stand.
15If he who dedicates his house wants to redeem it, he shall add the fifth of your valuation to it, and it shall be his.
16And if a man shall dedicate to the Lord some part of a field of his possession, then your valuation shall be according to the seed [required] for it; [a sowing of] a homer of barley shall be valued at fifty shekels of silver.
17If he dedicates his field from the year of jubilee, it shall stand according to your full valuation.
18But if he dedicates his field after the jubilee, then the priest shall count the money value in proportion to the years that remain until the year of jubilee, and it shall be deducted from your valuation.

## New American Standard

44'Yet in spite of this, when they are in the land of their enemies, I will not reject them, nor will I so abhor them as to destroy them, breaking My covenant with them; for I am the LORD their God.

45'But I will remember for them the covenant with their ancestors, whom I brought out of the land of Egypt in the sight of the nations, that I might be their God. I am the LORD.' "

46¶ These are the statutes and ordinances and laws which the LORD established between Himself and the sons of Israel through Moses at Mount Sinai.

*Rules concerning Valuations*

**27** AGAIN, THE LORD spoke to Moses, saying,
2"Speak to the sons of Israel, and say to them, 'When a man makes a difficult vow, he *shall be valued* according to your valuation of persons belonging to the LORD.

3'If your valuation is of the male from twenty years even to sixty years old, then your valuation shall be fifty shekels of silver, after the shekel of the sanctuary.

4'Or if it is a female, then your valuation shall be thirty shekels.

5'And if it be from five years even to twenty years old then your valuation for the male shall be twenty shekels, and for the female ten shekels.

6'But if *they are* from a month even up to five years old, then your valuation shall be five shekels of silver for the male, and for the female your valuation shall be three shekels of silver.

7'And if *they are* from sixty years old and upward, if it is a male, then your valuation shall be fifteen shekels, and for the female ten shekels.

8'But if he is poorer than your valuation, then he shall be placed before the priest, and the priest shall value him; according to the means of the one who vowed, the priest shall value him.

9'Now if it is an animal of the kind which men can present as an offering to the LORD, any such that one gives to the LORD shall be holy.

10'He shall not replace it or exchange it, a good for a bad, or a bad for a good; or if he does exchange animal for animal, then both it and its substitute shall become holy.

11'If, however, it is any unclean animal of the kind which men do not present as an offering to the LORD, then he shall place the animal before the priest.

12'And the priest shall value it as either good or bad; as you, the priest, value it, so it shall be.

13'But if he should ever *wish to* redeem it, then he shall add one-fifth of it to your valuation.

14¶ 'Now if a man consecrates his house as holy to the LORD, then the priest shall value it as either good or bad; as the priest values it, so it shall stand.

15'Yet if the one who consecrates it should *wish to* redeem his house, then he shall add one-fifth of your valuation price to it, so that it may be his.

16¶ 'Again, if a man consecrates to the LORD part of the fields of his own property, then your valuation shall be proportionate to the seed needed for it: a homer of barley seed at fifty shekels of silver.

17'If he consecrates his field as of the year of jubilee, according to your valuation it shall stand.

18'If he consecrates his field after the jubilee, however, then the priest shall calculate the price for him proportionate to the years that are left until the year of jubilee; and it shall be deducted from your valuation.

## New International

are in the land of their enemies, I will not reject them or abhor them
so as to destroy them completely, breaking my covenant with
them. I am the LORD their God. 45But for their sake I will remember
the covenant with their ancestors whom I brought out of Egypt in
the sight of the nations to be their God. I am the LORD.' "

46These are the decrees, the laws and the regulations that the
LORD established on Mount Sinai between himself and the Israelites through Moses.

*Redeeming What Is the LORD's*

**27** THE LORD said to Moses, 2"Speak to the Israelites and
say to them: 'If anyone makes a special vow to dedicate
persons to the LORD by giving equivalent values, 3set the value of
a male between the ages of twenty and sixty at fifty shekels[b] of
silver, according to the sanctuary shekel[c]; 4and if it is a female, set
her value at thirty shekels.[d] 5If it is a person between the ages of
five and twenty, set the value of a male at twenty shekels[e] and of
a female at ten shekels.[f] 6If it is a person between one month and
five years, set the value of a male at five shekels[g] of silver and that
of a female at three shekels[h] of silver. 7If it is a person sixty years
old or more, set the value of a male at fifteen shekels[i] and of a
female at ten shekels. 8If anyone making the vow is too poor to pay
the specified amount, he is to present the person to the priest, who
will set the value for him according to what the man making the
vow can afford.

9" 'If what he vowed is an animal that is acceptable as an offering to the LORD, such an animal given to the LORD becomes holy.
10He must not exchange it or substitute a good one for a bad one,
or a bad one for a good one; if he should substitute one animal for
another, both it and the substitute become holy. 11If what he
vowed is a ceremonially unclean animal—one that is not acceptable as an offering to the LORD—the animal must be presented to
the priest, 12who will judge its quality as good or bad. Whatever
value the priest then sets, that is what it will be. 13If the owner
wishes to redeem the animal, he must add a fifth to its value.

14" 'If a man dedicates his house as something holy to the LORD,
the priest will judge its quality as good or bad. Whatever value the
priest then sets, so it will remain. 15If the man who dedicates his
house redeems it, he must add a fifth to its value, and the house
will again become his.

16" 'If a man dedicates to the LORD part of his family land, its
value is to be set according to the amount of seed required for
it—fifty shekels of silver to a homer[j] of barley seed. 17If he dedicates his field during the Year of Jubilee, the value that has been
set remains. 18But if he dedicates his field after the Jubilee, the
priest will determine the value according to the number of years
that remain until the next Year of Jubilee, and its set value will be
reduced. 19If the man who dedicates the field wishes to redeem it,

NIV [b] *3* That is, about 1 1/4 pounds (about 0.6 kilogram); also in verse 16 [c] *3* That is, about 2/5 ounce (about 11.5 grams); also in verse 25 [d] *4* That is, about 12 ounces (about 0.3 kilogram) [e] *5* That is, about 8 ounces (about 0.2 kilogram) [f] *5* That is, about 4 ounces (about 110 grams); also in verse 7 [g] *6* That is, about 2 ounces (about 55 grams) [h] *6* That is, about 1 1/4 ounces (about 35 grams) [i] *7* That is, about 6 ounces (about 170 grams) [j] *16* That is, probably about 6 bushels (about 220 liters)

## King James

19And if he that sanctified the field will in any wise redeem it,
then he shall add the fifth *part* of the money of thy estimation unto
it, and it shall be assured to him.
20And if he will not redeem the field, or if he have sold the field
to another man, it shall not be redeemed any more.
21But the field, when it goeth out in the jubilee, shall be holy
unto the LORD, as a field devoted; the possession thereof shall be
the priest's.
22And if *a man* sanctify unto the LORD a field which he hath
bought, which *is* not of the fields of his possession;
23Then the priest shall reckon unto him the worth of thy estimation, *even* unto the year of the jubilee: and he shall give thine
estimation in that day, *as* a holy thing unto the LORD.
24In the year of the jubilee the field shall return unto him of
whom it was bought, *even* to him to whom the possession of the
land *did belong*.
25And all thy estimations shall be according to the shekel of the
sanctuary: twenty gerahs shall be the shekel.
26¶ Only the firstling of the beasts, which should be the LORD's
firstling, no man shall sanctify it; whether *it be* ox, or sheep: it *is*
the LORD's.
27And if *it be* of an unclean beast, then he shall redeem *it*
according to thine estimation, and shall add a fifth *part* of it thereto:
or if it be not redeemed, then it shall be sold according to thy
estimation.
28Notwithstanding no devoted thing, that a man shall devote
unto the LORD of all that he hath, *both* of man and beast, and of
the field of his possession, shall be sold or redeemed: every devoted thing *is* most holy unto the LORD.
29None devoted, which shall be devoted of men, shall be redeemed; *but* shall surely be put to death.
30And all the tithe of the land, *whether* of the seed of the land,
*or* of the fruit of the tree, *is* the LORD's: *it is* holy unto the LORD.
31And if a man will at all redeem *aught* of his tithes, he shall add
thereto the fifth *part* thereof.
32And concerning the tithe of the herd, or of the flock, *even* of
whatsoever passeth under the rod, the tenth shall be holy unto the
LORD.
33He shall not search whether it be good or bad, neither shall
he change it: and if he change it at all, then both it and the change
thereof shall be holy; it shall not be redeemed.
34These *are* the commandments, which the LORD commanded
Moses for the children of Israel in mount Sinai.

## Amplified

19If he who dedicates the field wishes to redeem it, then he shall
add the fifth of the money of your appraisal to it, and it shall
remain his.
20But if he does not want to redeem the field, or if he has sold
it to another man, it shall not be redeemed any more.
21But the field, when it is released in the jubilee, shall be holy
to the Lord, as a field devoted [to God or destruction]; the priest
shall have possession of it.
22And if a man dedicates to the Lord a field he has bought,
which is not of the fields of his [ancestral] possession,
23The priest shall compute the amount of your valuation for it
up to the year of jubilee; the man shall give that amount on that
day as a holy thing to the Lord.
24In the year of jubilee the field shall return to him of whom it
was bought, to him to whom the land belonged [as his ancestral
inheritance].
25And all your valuations shall be according to the sanctuary
shekel, twenty gerahs shall make a shekel.
26But the firstling of the animals, since a firstling belongs to the
Lord, no man may dedicate, whether it be ox or sheep. It is the
Lord's [already].
27If it be of an unclean animal, the owner may redeem it according to your valuation, and shall add a fifth to it; or if it is not
redeemed, then it shall be sold according to your valuation.
28But no thing that a man shall devote to the Lord of all that he
has, whether of man or beast or of the field of his possession, shall
be sold or redeemed; every devoted thing is most holy to the Lord.
29No one doomed to death [under the claim of divine justice],
who is to be completely destroyed from among men, shall be
ransomed [from suffering the death penalty]; he shall surely be put
to death.
30And all the tithe of the land, whether of the seed of the land
or of the fruit of the tree, is the Lord's; it is holy to the Lord. [I Cor.
9:11; Gal. 6:6.]
31And if a man wants to redeem any of his tithe, he shall add
a fifth to it.
32And all the tithe of the herd or of the flock, whatever passes
under the herdsman's staff [by means of which each tenth animal
as it passes through a small door is selected and marked], the tenth
shall be holy to the Lord. [Cp. II Cor. 9:7-9.]
33The man shall not examine whether the animal is good or bad,
nor shall he exchange it; if he does exchange it, then both it and
the animal substituted for it shall be holy; it shall not be redeemed.
34These are the commandments, which the Lord commanded
Moses on Mount Sinai for the Israelites. [Rom. 10:4; Heb. 4:2;
12:18-29.]

## New American Standard

19'And if the one who consecrates it should ever wish to redeem the field, then he shall add one-fifth of your valuation price to it, so that it may pass to him.

20'Yet if he will not redeem the field, but has sold the field to another man, it may no longer be redeemed;

21and when it reverts in the jubilee, the field shall be holy to the LORD, like a field set apart; it shall be for the priest as his property.

22'Or if he consecrates to the LORD a field which he has bought, which is not a part of the field of his own property,

23then the priest shall calculate for him the amount of your valuation up to the year of jubilee; and he shall on that day give your valuation as holy to the LORD.

24'In the year of jubilee the field shall return to the one from whom he bought it, to whom the possession of the land belongs.

25'Every valuation of yours, moreover, shall be after the shekel of the sanctuary. The shekel shall be twenty gerahs.

**26**¶ 'However, a first-born among animals, which as a first-born belongs to the LORD, no man may consecrate it; whether ox or sheep, it is the LORD'S.

27'But if *it is* among the unclean animals, then he shall redeem it according to your valuation, and add to it one-fifth of it; and if it is not redeemed, then it shall be sold according to your valuation.

**28**¶ 'Nevertheless, anything which a man [a]sets apart to the LORD out of all that he has, of man or animal or of the fields of his own property, shall not be sold or redeemed. Anything devoted to destruction is most holy to the LORD.

29'No one who may have been set apart among men shall be ransomed; he shall surely be put to death.

**30**¶ 'Thus all the tithe of the land, of the seed of the land or of the fruit of the tree, is the LORD'S; it is holy to the LORD.

31'If, therefore, a man wishes to redeem part of his tithe, he shall add to it one-fifth of it.

32'And for every tenth part of herd or flock, whatever passes under the rod, the tenth one shall be holy to the LORD.

33'He is not to be concerned whether *it is* good or bad, nor shall he exchange it; or if he does exchange it, then both it and its substitute shall become holy. It shall not be redeemed.' "

**34**¶ These are the commandments which the LORD commanded Moses for the sons of Israel at Mount Sinai.

**NAS** [a] Or, *puts under the ban*

## New International

he must add a fifth to its value, and the field will again become his.
20If, however, he does not redeem the field, or if he has sold it to
someone else, it can never be redeemed. 21When the field is
released in the Jubilee, it will become holy, like a field devoted to
the LORD; it will become the property of the priests.[b]
22" 'If a man dedicates to the LORD a field he has bought, which
is not part of his family land, 23the priest will determine its value
up to the Year of Jubilee, and the man must pay its value on that
day as something holy to the LORD. 24In the Year of Jubilee the field
will revert to the person from whom he bought it, the one whose
land it was. 25Every value is to be set according to the sanctuary
shekel, twenty gerahs to the shekel.
26" 'No one, however, may dedicate the firstborn of an animal,
since the firstborn already belongs to the LORD; whether an ox
or a sheep, it is the LORD's. 27If it is one of the unclean animals,
he may buy it back at its set value, adding a fifth of the value to
it. If he does not redeem it, it is to be sold at its set value.
28" 'But nothing that a man owns and devotes[d] to the LORD—
whether man or animal or family land—may be sold or redeemed;
everything so devoted is most holy to the LORD.
29" 'No person devoted to destruction[e] may be ransomed; he
must be put to death.
30" 'A tithe of everything from the land, whether grain from the
soil or fruit from the trees, belongs to the LORD; it is holy to the
LORD. 31If a man redeems any of his tithe, he must add a fifth of
the value to it. 32The entire tithe of the herd and flock—every tenth
animal that passes under the shepherd's rod—will be holy to the
LORD. 33He must not pick out the good from the bad or make any
substitution. If he does make a substitution, both the animal and
its substitute become holy and cannot be redeemed.' "

34These are the commands the LORD gave Moses on Mount
Sinai for the Israelites.

**NIV** [b] *21* Or *priest* [c] *26* The Hebrew word can include both male and female. [d] *28* The Hebrew term refers to the irrevocable giving over of things or persons to the LORD. [e] *29* The Hebrew term refers to the irrevocable giving over of things or persons to the LORD, often by totally destroying them.

## King James

THE FOURTH BOOK OF
MOSES, CALLED

# Numbers

1 AND THE LORD spake unto Moses in the wilderness of Sinai,
in the tabernacle of the congregation, on the first *day* of the
second month, in the second year after they were come out of the
land of Egypt, saying,
2Take ye the sum of all the congregation of the children of Israel,
after their families, by the house of their fathers, with the number
of *their* names, every male by their polls;
3From twenty years old and upward, all that are able to go forth
to war in Israel: thou and Aaron shall number them by their
armies.
4And with you there shall be a man of every tribe; every one
head of the house of his fathers.
5¶ And these *are* the names of the men that shall stand with you:
of *the tribe of* Reuben; Elizur the son of Shedeur.
6Of Simeon; Shelumiel the son of Zurishaddai.
7Of Judah; Nahshon the son of Amminadab.
8Of Issachar; Nethaneel the son of Zuar.
9Of Zebulun; Eliab the son of Helon.
10Of the children of Joseph: of Ephraim; Elishama the son of
Ammihud: of Manasseh; Gamaliel the son of Pedahzur.
11Of Benjamin; Abidan the son of Gideoni.
12Of Dan; Ahiezer the son of Ammishaddai.
13Of Asher; Pagiel the son of Ocran.
14Of Gad; Eliasaph the son of Deuel.
15Of Naphtali; Ahira the son of Enan.
16These *were* the renowned of the congregation, princes of the
tribes of their fathers, heads of thousands in Israel.
17¶ And Moses and Aaron took these men which are expressed
by *their* names:
18And they assembled all the congregation together on the first
*day* of the second month, and they declared their pedigrees after
their families, by the house of their fathers, according to the number of the names, from twenty years old and upward, by their
polls.
19As the LORD commanded Moses, so he numbered them in the
wilderness of Sinai.
20And the children of Reuben, Israel's eldest son, by their generations, after their families, by the house of their fathers, according to the number of the names, by their polls, every male from
twenty years old and upward, all that were able to go forth to war;
21Those that were numbered of them, *even* of the tribe of Reuben, *were* forty and six thousand and five hundred.
22¶ Of the children of Simeon, by their generations, after their
families, by the house of their fathers, those that were numbered
of them, according to the number of the names, by their polls,
every male from twenty years old and upward, all that were able
to go forth to war;
23Those that were numbered of them, *even* of the tribe of Simeon, *were* fifty and nine thousand and three hundred.
24¶ Of the children of Gad, by their generations, after their
families, by the house of their fathers, according to the number of
the names, from twenty years old and upward, all that were able
to go forth to war;

## Amplified

THE FOURTH BOOK OF MOSES,
CALLED

# Numbers

1 THE LORD spoke to Moses in the wilderness of Sinai, in the
tent of meeting on the first day of the second month in the
second year after they came out of the land of Egypt, saying,
2Take a census of all the males of the congregation of the Israelites, by families, by their fathers' houses, according to the number
of names, head by head;
3From twenty years old and upward, all in Israel who are able
to go forth to war you and Aaron shall number, company by
company.
4And with you there shall be a man [to assist you] from each
tribe, each being the head of his father's house.
5And these are the names of the men who shall attend you. Of
Reuben, Elizur son of Shedeur;
6Of Simeon, Shelumiel son of Zurishaddai;
7Of Judah, Nahshon son of Amminadab;
8Of Issachar, Nethanel son of Zuar;
9Of Zebulun, Eliab son of Helon;
10Of the sons of Joseph: of Ephraim, Elishama son of Ammihud;
of Manasseh, Gamaliel son of Pedahzur;
11Of Benjamin, Abidan son of Gideoni;
12Of Dan, Ahiezer son of Ammishaddai;
13Of Asher, Pagiel son of Ochran;
14Of Gad, Eliasaph son of Deuel;
15Of Naphtali, Ahira son of Enan.
16These were those chosen from the congregation, the leaders
of their ancestral tribes, heads of thousands [the highest class of
officers] in Israel.
17And Moses and Aaron took these men who have been named,
18And assembled all the congregation on the first day of the
second month, and they declared their ancestry after their families, by their fathers' houses, according to the number of names
from twenty years old and upward, head by head,
19As the Lord commanded Moses. So he numbered them in the
wilderness of Sinai.
20The sons of Reuben, Israel's first-born, their generations, by
their families, by their fathers' houses, according to the number of
names, head by head, every male from twenty years old and
upward, all who were able to go to war:
21Those of the tribe of Reuben numbered 46,500.
22Of the sons of Simeon, their generations, by their families, by
their fathers' houses, those numbered of them, according to the
number of names, head by head, every male from twenty years old
and upward, all who were able to go to war:
23Those of the tribe of Simeon numbered 59,300.
24Of the sons of Gad, their generations, by their families, by
their fathers' houses, according to the number of names, from
twenty years old and upward, all who were able to go to war:

## New American Standard

# Numbers

### *The Census of Israel's Warriors*

1 THEN THE LORD spoke to Moses in the wilderness of Sinai,
in the tent of meeting, on the first of the second month, in
the second year after they had come out of the land of Egypt,
saying,
2"Take a [a]census of all the congregation of the sons of Israel,
by their families, by their fathers' households, according to the
number of names, every male, head by head
3from twenty years old and upward, whoever *is able to* go out
to war in Israel, you and Aaron shall [b]number them by their
armies.
4"With you, moreover, there shall be a man of each tribe, each
one head of his father's household.
5"These then are the names of the men who shall stand with
you: of Reuben, Elizur the son of Shedeur;
6of Simeon, Shelumiel the son of Zurishaddai;
7of Judah, Nahshon the son of Amminadab;
8of Issachar, Nethanel the son of Zuar;
9of Zebulun, Eliab the son of Helon;
10of the sons of Joseph: of Ephraim, Elishama the son of Ammihud; of Manasseh, Gamaliel the son of Pedahzur;
11of Benjamin, Abidan the son of Gideoni;
12of Dan, Ahiezer the son of Ammishaddai;
13of Asher, Pagiel the son of Ochran;
14of Gad, Eliasaph the son of Deuel;
15of Naphtali, Ahira the son of Enan.
16"These are they who were called of the congregation, the
leaders of their fathers' tribes; they were the heads of [c]divisions
of Israel."
17So Moses and Aaron took these men who had been designated by name,
18and they assembled all the congregation together on the first
of the second month. Then they registered by ancestry in their
families, by their fathers' households, according to the number of
names, from twenty years old and upward, head by head,
19just as the LORD had commanded Moses. So he numbered
them in the wilderness of Sinai.
20¶ Now the sons of Reuben, Israel's first-born, their genealogical registration by their families, by their fathers' households,
according to the number of names, head by head, every male from
twenty years old and upward, whoever *was able to* go out to war,
21their numbered men, of the tribe of Reuben, *were* 46,500.
22¶ Of the sons of Simeon, their genealogical registration by
their families, by their fathers' households, their numbered men,
according to the number of names, head by head, every male from
twenty years old and upward, whoever *was able to* go out to war,
23their numbered men, of the tribe of Simeon, *were* 59,300.
24¶ Of the sons of Gad, their genealogical registration by their
families, by their fathers' households, according to the number of
names, from twenty years old and upward, whoever *was able to* go
out to war,

NAS [a] Lit., *sum* [b] Lit., *muster,* and so throughout this context [c] Lit., *thousands,* or, *clans*

## New International

# Numbers

### *The Census*

1 THE LORD spoke to Moses in the Tent of Meeting in the
Desert of Sinai on the first day of the second month of the
second year after the Israelites came out of Egypt. He said: 2"Take
a census of the whole Israelite community by their clans and
families, listing every man by name, one by one. 3You and Aaron
are to number by their divisions all the men in Israel twenty years
old or more who are able to serve in the army. 4One man from each
tribe, each the head of his family, is to help you. 5These are the
names of the men who are to assist you:

from Reuben, Elizur son of Shedeur;
6from Simeon, Shelumiel son of Zurishaddai;
7from Judah, Nahshon son of Amminadab;
8from Issachar, Nethanel son of Zuar;
9from Zebulun, Eliab son of Helon;
10from the sons of Joseph:
from Ephraim, Elishama son of Ammihud;
from Manasseh, Gamaliel son of Pedahzur;
11from Benjamin, Abidan son of Gideoni;
12from Dan, Ahiezer son of Ammishaddai;
13from Asher, Pagiel son of Ocran;
14from Gad, Eliasaph son of Deuel;
15from Naphtali, Ahira son of Enan."

16These were the men appointed from the community, the
leaders of their ancestral tribes. They were the heads of the clans
of Israel.
17Moses and Aaron took these men whose names had been
given, 18and they called the whole community together on the first
day of the second month. The people indicated their ancestry by
their clans and families, and the men twenty years old or more
were listed by name, one by one, 19as the LORD commanded
Moses. And so he counted them in the Desert of Sinai:

20From the descendants of Reuben the firstborn son of Israel:
All the men twenty years old or more who were able to
serve in the army were listed by name, one by one, according to the records of their clans and families. 21The number from the tribe of Reuben was 46,500.

22From the descendants of Simeon:
All the men twenty years old or more who were able to
serve in the army were counted and listed by name, one
by one, according to the records of their clans and families.
23The number from the tribe of Simeon was 59,300.

24From the descendants of Gad:
All the men twenty years old or more who were able to
serve in the army were listed by name, according to the

## King James

25Those that were numbered of them, *even* of the tribe of Gad, *were* forty and five thousand six hundred and fifty.

26¶ Of the children of Judah, by their generations, after their families, by the house of their fathers, according to the number of the names, from twenty years old and upward, all that were able to go forth to war;

27Those that were numbered of them, *even* of the tribe of Judah, *were* threescore and fourteen thousand and six hundred.

28¶ Of the children of Issachar, by their generations, after their families, by the house of their fathers, according to the number of the names, from twenty years old and upward, all that were able to go forth to war;

29Those that were numbered of them, *even* of the tribe of Issachar, *were* fifty and four thousand and four hundred.

30¶ Of the children of Zebulun, by their generations, after their families, by the house of their fathers, according to the number of the names, from twenty years old and upward, all that were able to go forth to war;

31Those that were numbered of them, *even* of the tribe of Zebulun, *were* fifty and seven thousand and four hundred.

32¶ Of the children of Joseph, *namely,* of the children of Ephraim, by their generations, after their families, by the house of their fathers, according to the number of the names, from twenty years old and upward, all that were able to go forth to war;

33Those that were numbered of them, *even* of the tribe of Ephraim, *were* forty thousand and five hundred.

34¶ Of the children of Manasseh, by their generations, after their families, by the house of their fathers, according to the number of the names, from twenty years old and upward, all that were able to go forth to war;

35Those that were numbered of them, *even* of the tribe of Manasseh, *were* thirty and two thousand and two hundred.

36¶ Of the children of Benjamin, by their generations, after their families, by the house of their fathers, according to the number of the names, from twenty years old and upward, all that were able to go forth to war;

37Those that were numbered of them, *even* of the tribe of Benjamin, *were* thirty and five thousand and four hundred.

38¶ Of the children of Dan, by their generations, after their families, by the house of their fathers, according to the number of the names, from twenty years old and upward, all that were able to go forth to war;

39Those that were numbered of them, *even* of the tribe of Dan, *were* threescore and two thousand and seven hundred.

40¶ Of the children of Asher, by their generations, after their families, by the house of their fathers, according to the number of the names, from twenty years old and upward, all that were able to go forth to war;

41Those that were numbered of them, *even* of the tribe of Asher, *were* forty and one thousand and five hundred.

42¶ Of the children of Naphtali, throughout their generations, after their families, by the house of their fathers, according to the number of the names, from twenty years old and upward, all that were able to go forth to war;

43Those that were numbered of them, *even* of the tribe of Naphtali, *were* fifty and three thousand and four hundred.

44These *are* those that were numbered, which Moses and Aaron numbered, and the princes of Israel, *being* twelve men: each one was for the house of his fathers.

45So were all those that were numbered of the children of Israel, by the house of their fathers, from twenty years old and upward, all that were able to go forth to war in Israel;

46Even all they that were numbered were six hundred thousand and three thousand and five hundred and fifty.

47¶ But the Levites after the tribe of their fathers were not numbered among them.

48For the LORD had spoken unto Moses, saying,

49Only thou shalt not number the tribe of Levi, neither take the sum of them among the children of Israel:

## Amplified

25Those of the tribe of Gad numbered 45,650.

26Of the sons of Judah, their generations, by their families, by their fathers' houses, according to the number of names, from twenty years old and upward, all able to go to war:

27Those of the tribe of Judah numbered 74,600.

28Of the sons of Issachar, their generations, by their families, by their fathers' houses, according to the number of names, from twenty years old and upward, all able to go to war:

29Those of the tribe of Issachar numbered 54,400.

30Of the sons of Zebulun, their generations, by their families, by their fathers' houses, according to the number of names, from twenty years old and upward, all able to go to war:

31Those of the tribe of Zebulun numbered 57,400.

32Of the sons of Joseph: the sons of Ephraim, their generations, by their families, by their fathers' houses, according to the number of names, from twenty years old and upward, all able to go to war:

33Those of the tribe of Ephraim numbered 40,500.

34Of the sons of Manasseh, their generations, by their families, by their fathers' houses, according to the number of names, from twenty years old and upward, all able to go to war:

35Those of the tribe of Manasseh numbered 32,200.

36Of the sons of Benjamin, their generations, by their families, by their fathers' houses, according to the number of names, from twenty years old and upward, all able to go to war:

37Those of the tribe of Benjamin numbered 35,400.

38Of the sons of Dan, their generations, by their families, by their fathers' houses, according to the number of names, from twenty years old and upward, all able to go to war:

39Those of the tribe of Dan numbered 62,700.

40Of the sons of Asher, their generations, by their families, by their fathers' houses, according to the number of names, from twenty years old and upward, all able to go to war:

41Those of the tribe of Asher numbered 41,500.

42Of the sons of Naphtali, their generations, by their families, by their fathers' houses, according to the number of names, from twenty years old and upward, all able to go to war:

43Those of the tribe of Naphtali numbered 53,400.

44These were numbered by Moses and Aaron, and the leaders of Israel, twelve men, each representing his father's house.

45So all those numbered of the Israelites, by their fathers' houses, from twenty years old and upward, able to go to war in Israel,

46All who were numbered were 603,550.

47But the Levites by their fathers' tribe were not numbered with them,

48For the Lord had said to Moses,

49Only the tribe of Levi you shall not number in the census of the Israelites;

## New American Standard

25their numbered men, of the tribe of Gad, *were* 45,650.
**26**¶ Of the sons of Judah, their genealogical registration by their
families, by their fathers' households, according to the number of
names, from twenty years old and upward, whoever *was able to* go
out to war,
27their numbered men, of the tribe of Judah, *were* 74,600.
**28**¶ Of the sons of Issachar, their genealogical registration by
their families, by their fathers' households, according to the number of names, from twenty years old and upward, whoever *was able
to* go out to war,
29their numbered men, of the tribe of Issachar, *were* 54,400.
**30**¶ Of the sons of Zebulun, their genealogical registration by
their families, by their fathers' households, according to the number of names, from twenty years old and upward, whoever *was able
to* go out to war,
31their numbered men, of the tribe of Zebulun, *were* 57,400.
**32**¶ Of the sons of Joseph, *namely,* of the sons of Ephraim, their
genealogical registration by their families, by their fathers'
households, according to the number of names, from twenty years
old and upward, whoever *was able to* go out to war,
33their numbered men, of the tribe of Ephraim, *were* 40,500.
**34**¶ Of the sons of Manasseh, their genealogical registration by
their families, by their fathers' households, according to the number of names, from twenty years old and upward, whoever *was able
to* go out to war,
35their numbered men, of the tribe of Manasseh, *were* 32,200.
**36**¶ Of the sons of Benjamin, their genealogical registration by
their families, by their fathers' households, according to the number of names, from twenty years old and upward, whoever *was able
to* go out to war,
37their numbered men, of the tribe of Benjamin, *were* 35,400.
**38**¶ Of the sons of Dan, their genealogical registration by their
families, by their fathers' households, according to the number of
names, from twenty years old and upward, whoever *was able to* go
out to war,
39their numbered men, of the tribe of Dan, *were* 62,700.
**40**¶ Of the sons of Asher, their genealogical registration by their
families, by their fathers' households, according to the number of
names, from twenty years old and upward, whoever *was able to* go
out to war,
41their numbered men, of the tribe of Asher, *were* 41,500.
**42**¶ Of the sons of Naphtali, their genealogical registration by
their families, by their fathers' households, according to the number of names, from twenty years old and upward, whoever *was able
to* go out to war,
43their numbered men, of the tribe of Naphtali, *were* 53,400.
**44**¶ These are the ones who were numbered, whom Moses and
Aaron numbered, with the leaders of Israel, twelve men, each of
whom was of his father's household.
45So all the numbered men of the sons of Israel by their fathers'
households, from twenty years old and upward, whoever *was able
to* go out to war in Israel,
46even all the numbered men were 603,550.

*Levites Exempted*

**47**¶ The Levites, however, were not numbered among them by
their fathers' tribe.
48For the LORD had spoken to Moses, saying,
49"Only the tribe of Levi you shall not number, nor shall you
take their census among the sons of Israel.

## New International

records of their clans and families. 25The number from the
tribe of Gad was 45,650.

26From the descendants of Judah:
All the men twenty years old or more who were able to
serve in the army were listed by name, according to the
records of their clans and families. 27The number from the
tribe of Judah was 74,600.

28From the descendants of Issachar:
All the men twenty years old or more who were able to
serve in the army were listed by name, according to the
records of their clans and families. 29The number from the
tribe of Issachar was 54,400.

30From the descendants of Zebulun:
All the men twenty years old or more who were able to
serve in the army were listed by name, according to the
records of their clans and families. 31The number from the
tribe of Zebulun was 57,400.

32From the sons of Joseph:
From the descendants of Ephraim:
All the men twenty years old or more who were able to
serve in the army were listed by name, according to the
records of their clans and families. 33The number from the
tribe of Ephraim was 40,500.
34From the descendants of Manasseh:
All the men twenty years old or more who were able to
serve in the army were listed by name, according to the
records of their clans and families. 35The number from the
tribe of Manasseh was 32,200.

36From the descendants of Benjamin:
All the men twenty years old or more who were able to
serve in the army were listed by name, according to the
records of their clans and families. 37The number from the
tribe of Benjamin was 35,400.

38From the descendants of Dan:
All the men twenty years old or more who were able to
serve in the army were listed by name, according to the
records of their clans and families. 39The number from the
tribe of Dan was 62,700.

40From the descendants of Asher:
All the men twenty years old or more who were able to
serve in the army were listed by name, according to the
records of their clans and families. 41The number from the
tribe of Asher was 41,500.

42From the descendants of Naphtali:
All the men twenty years old or more who were able to
serve in the army were listed by name, according to the
records of their clans and families. 43The number from the
tribe of Naphtali was 53,400.

44These were the men counted by Moses and Aaron and the
twelve leaders of Israel, each one representing his family. 45All the
Israelites twenty years old or more who were able to serve in
Israel's army were counted according to their families. 46The total
number was 603,550.
47The families of the tribe of Levi, however, were not counted
along with the others. 48The LORD had said to Moses: 49"You must
not count the tribe of Levi or include them in the census of the
other Israelites. 50Instead, appoint the Levites to be in charge of the

## King James

50But thou shalt appoint the Levites over the tabernacle of testimony, and over all the vessels thereof, and over all things that
*belong* to it: they shall bear the tabernacle, and all the vessels
thereof; and they shall minister unto it, and shall encamp round
about the tabernacle.
51And when the tabernacle setteth forward, the Levites shall
take it down: and when the tabernacle is to be pitched, the Levites
shall set it up: and the stranger that cometh nigh shall be put to
death.
52And the children of Israel shall pitch their tents, every man
by his own camp, and every man by his own standard, throughout
their hosts.
53But the Levites shall pitch round about the tabernacle of testimony, that there be no wrath upon the congregation of the children of Israel: and the Levites shall keep the charge of the tabernacle of testimony.
54And the children of Israel did according to all that the LORD
commanded Moses, so did they.

2 AND THE LORD spake unto Moses and unto Aaron, saying,
2Every man of the children of Israel shall pitch by his own
standard, with the ensign of their father's house: far off about the
tabernacle of the congregation shall they pitch.
3And on the east side toward the rising of the sun shall they of
the standard of the camp of Judah pitch throughout their armies:
and Nahshon the son of Amminadab *shall be* captain of the children
of Judah.
4And his host, and those that were numbered of them, *were*
threescore and fourteen thousand and six hundred.
5And those that do pitch next unto him *shall be* the tribe of
Issachar: and Nethaneel the son of Zuar *shall be* captain of the
children of Issachar.
6And his host, and those that were numbered thereof, *were* fifty
and four thousand and four hundred.
7 *Then* the tribe of Zebulun: and Eliab the son of Helon *shall be*
captain of the children of Zebulun.
8And his host, and those that were numbered thereof, *were* fifty
and seven thousand and four hundred.
9All that were numbered in the camp of Judah *were* an hundred
thousand and fourscore thousand and six thousand and four hundred, throughout their armies. These shall first set forth.
10¶ On the south side *shall be* the standard of the camp of
Reuben according to their armies: and the captain of the children
of Reuben *shall be* Elizur the son of Shedeur.
11And his host, and those that were numbered thereof, *were*
forty and six thousand and five hundred.
12And those which pitch by him *shall be* the tribe of Simeon: and
the captain of the children of Simeon *shall be* Shelumiel the son of
Zurishaddai.
13And his host, and those that were numbered of them, *were*
fifty and nine thousand and three hundred.
14Then the tribe of Gad: and the captain of the sons of Gad *shall
be* Eliasaph the son of Reuel.
15And his host, and those that were numbered of them, *were*
forty and five thousand and six hundred and fifty.
16All that were numbered in the camp of Reuben *were* an hundred thousand and fifty and one thousand and four hundred and
fifty, throughout their armies. And they shall set forth in the
second rank.
17¶ Then the tabernacle of the congregation shall set forward
with the camp of the Levites in the midst of the camp: as they
encamp, so shall they set forward, every man in his place by their
standards.

## Amplified

50But appoint the Levites over the tabernacle of the testimony,
and over all its vessels and furnishings, and all things that belong
to it. They shall carry the tabernacle [when journeying] and all its
furnishings, and they shall minister to it and encamp around it.
51When the tabernacle is to go forward, the Levites shall take
it down; and when the tabernacle is to be pitched, the Levites shall
set it up. And the excluded [any not of the tribe of Levi] who
approach the tabernacle shall be put to death.
52The Israelites shall pitch their tents by their companies, every
man by his own camp, and every man by his own [tribal] standard;
53But the Levites shall encamp around the tabernacle of the
testimony, that there may be no wrath upon the congregation of
the Israelites; and the Levites shall keep charge of the tabernacle
of the testimony.
54Thus did the Israelites; according to all that the Lord commanded Moses, so they did.

2 THE LORD said to Moses and Aaron,
2The Israelites shall encamp each by his own [tribal] standard
*or* banner, with the ensign of their fathers' houses, opposite the
tent of meeting *and* facing it on every side.
3On the east side toward the sunrise shall they of the standard
of the camp of Judah encamp by their companies; Nahshon son of
Amminadab being the leader of the sons of Judah.
4Judah's host as numbered totaled 74,600.
5Next to Judah the tribe of Issachar shall encamp, Nethanel son
of Zuar being the leader of the sons of Issachar.
6Issachar's host as numbered totaled 54,400.
7Then the tribe of Zebulun, Eliab son of Helon being the leader
of the sons of Zebulun.
8Zebulun's host as numbered totaled 57,400.
9All these [three tribes] numbered in the camp of Judah totaled
186,400. They shall set forth first [on the march].
10On the south side shall be the standard of the camp of Reuben
by their companies, the leader of the sons of Reuben being Elizur
son of Shedeur.
11Reuben's host as numbered totaled 46,500.
12Those who encamp next to Reuben shall be the tribe of Simeon, the leader of the sons of Simeon being Shelumiel son of
Zurishaddai.
13Simeon's host as numbered totaled 59,300.
14Then the tribe of Gad, the leader of the sons of Gad being
Eliasaph son of Reuel [Deuel].
15Gad's host as numbered totaled 45,650.
16The whole number in [the three tribes of] the camp of Reuben
was 151,450. They shall take second place [on the march].
17Then the tent of meeting shall set out, with the camp of the
Levites in the midst of the camps; as they encamp, so shall they
set forward, every man in his place, standard after standard.

## New American Standard

50"But you shall appoint the Levites over the [a]tabernacle of the
testimony, and over all its furnishings and over all that belongs to
it. They shall carry the tabernacle and all its furnishings, and they
shall take care of it; they shall also camp around the tabernacle.
51"So when the tabernacle is to set out, the Levites shall take
it down; and when the tabernacle encamps, the Levites shall set
it up. But the [b]layman who comes near shall be put to death.
52"And the sons of Israel shall camp, each man by his own
camp, and each man by his own standard, according to their
armies.
53"But the Levites shall camp around the tabernacle of the
testimony, that there may be no wrath on the congregation of the
sons of Israel. So the Levites shall keep charge of the tabernacle of
the testimony."
54Thus the sons of Israel did; according to all which the LORD
had commanded Moses, so they did.

*Arrangement of the Camps*

**2** NOW THE LORD spoke to Moses and to Aaron, saying,
2"The sons of Israel shall camp, each by his own standard,
with the banners of their fathers' households; they shall camp
around the tent of meeting at a distance.
3"Now those who camp on the east side toward the sunrise
*shall be* of the standard of the camp of Judah, by their armies, and
the leader of the sons of Judah: Nahshon the son of Amminadab,
4and his army, even their numbered men, 74,600.
5"And those who camp next to him *shall be* the tribe of Issachar,
and the leader of the sons of Issachar: Nethanel the son of Zuar,
6and his army, even their numbered men, 54,400.
7"Then *comes* the tribe of Zebulun, and the leader of the sons
of Zebulun: Eliab the son of Helon,
8and his army, even his numbered men, 57,400.
9"The total of the numbered men of the camp of Judah: 186,
400 by their armies. They shall set out first.
10¶ "On the south side *shall be* the standard of the camp of
Reuben by their armies, and the leader of the sons of Reuben:
Elizur the son of Shedeur,
11and his army, even their numbered men, 46,500.
12"And those who camp next to him *shall be* the tribe of Simeon,
and the leader of the sons of Simeon: Shelumiel the son of Zurishaddai,
13and his army, even their numbered men, 59,300.
14"Then *comes* the tribe of Gad, and the leader of the sons of
Gad: Eliasaph the son of Deuel,
15and his army, even their numbered men, 45,650.
16"The total of the numbered men of the camp of Reuben:
151,450 by their armies. And they shall set out second.
17¶ "Then the tent of meeting shall set out *with* the camp of the
Levites in the midst of the camps; just as they camp, so they shall
set out, every man in his place, by their standards.

NAS [a] Lit., *dwelling place,* and so throughout this context [b] Lit., *stranger*

## New International

tabernacle of the Testimony—over all its furnishings and everything belonging to it. They are to carry the tabernacle and all its
furnishings; they are to take care of it and encamp around it.
51Whenever the tabernacle is to move, the Levites are to take it
down, and whenever the tabernacle is to be set up, the Levites
shall do it. Anyone else who goes near it shall be put to death.
52The Israelites are to set up their tents by divisions, each man in
his own camp under his own standard. 53The Levites, however,
are to set up their tents around the tabernacle of the Testimony so
that wrath will not fall on the Israelite community. The Levites are
to be responsible for the care of the tabernacle of the Testimony."
54The Israelites did all this just as the LORD commanded Moses.

*The Arrangement of the Tribal Camps*

**2** THE LORD said to Moses and Aaron: 2"The Israelites are to
camp around the Tent of Meeting some distance from it, each
man under his standard with the banners of his family."

3On the east, toward the sunrise, the divisions of the camp
of Judah are to encamp under their standard. The leader of the
people of Judah is Nahshon son of Amminadab. 4His division
numbers 74,600.
5The tribe of Issachar will camp next to them. The leader
of the people of Issachar is Nethanel son of Zuar. 6His division
numbers 54,400.
7The tribe of Zebulun will be next. The leader of the people
of Zebulun is Eliab son of Helon. 8His division numbers 57,
400.
9All the men assigned to the camp of Judah, according to
their divisions, number 186,400. They will set out first.

10On the south will be the divisions of the camp of Reuben
under their standard. The leader of the people of Reuben is
Elizur son of Shedeur. 11His division numbers 46,500.
12The tribe of Simeon will camp next to them. The leader
of the people of Simeon is Shelumiel son of Zurishaddai. 13His
division numbers 59,300.
14The tribe of Gad will be next. The leader of the people of
Gad is Eliasaph son of Deuel.[c] 15His division numbers 45,650.
16All the men assigned to the camp of Reuben, according
to their divisions, number 151,450. They will set out second.

17Then the Tent of Meeting and the camp of the Levites will
set out in the middle of the camps. They will set out in the
same order as they encamp, each in his own place under his
standard.

NIV [c] *14* Many manuscripts of the Masoretic Text, Samaritan Pentateuch and Vulgate (see also Num. 1:14); most manuscripts of the Masoretic Text *Reuel*

## King James

18¶ On the west side *shall be* the standard of the camp of
Ephraim according to their armies: and the captain of the sons of
Ephraim *shall be* Elishama the son of Ammihud.
19And his host, and those that were numbered of them, *were*
forty thousand and five hundred.
20And by him *shall be* the tribe of Manasseh: and the captain of
the children of Manasseh *shall be* Gamaliel the son of Pedahzur.
21And his host, and those that were numbered of them, *were*
thirty and two thousand and two hundred.
22Then the tribe of Benjamin: and the captain of the sons of
Benjamin *shall be* Abidan the son of Gideoni.
23And his host, and those that were numbered of them, *were*
thirty and five thousand and four hundred.
24All that were numbered of the camp of Ephraim *were* an
hundred thousand and eight thousand and an hundred, throughout their armies. And they shall go forward in the third rank.
25¶ The standard of the camp of Dan *shall be* on the north side
by their armies: and the captain of the children of Dan *shall be*
Ahiezer the son of Ammishaddai.
26And his host, and those that were numbered of them, *were*
threescore and two thousand and seven hundred.
27And those that encamp by him *shall be* the tribe of Asher: and
the captain of the children of Asher *shall be* Pagiel the son of Ocran.
28And his host, and those that were numbered of them, *were*
forty and one thousand and five hundred.
29¶ Then the tribe of Naphtali: and the captain of the children
of Naphtali *shall be* Ahira the son of Enan.
30And his host, and those that were numbered of them, *were*
fifty and three thousand and four hundred.
31All they that were numbered in the camp of Dan *were* an
hundred thousand and fifty and seven thousand and six hundred.
They shall go hindmost with their standards.
32¶ These *are* those which were numbered of the children of
Israel by the house of their fathers: all those that were numbered
of the camps throughout their hosts *were* six hundred thousand
and three thousand and five hundred and fifty.
33But the Levites were not numbered among the children of
Israel; as the LORD commanded Moses.
34And the children of Israel did according to all that the LORD
commanded Moses: so they pitched by their standards, and so
they set forward, every one after their families, according to the
house of their fathers.

3 THESE ALSO *are* the generations of Aaron and Moses in the
day *that* the LORD spake with Moses in mount Sinai.
2And these *are* the names of the sons of Aaron; Nadab the
firstborn, and Abihu, Eleazar, and Ithamar.
3These *are* the names of the sons of Aaron, the priests which
were anointed, whom he consecrated to minister in the priest's
office.
4And Nadab and Abihu died before the LORD, when they offered strange fire before the LORD, in the wilderness of Sinai, and
they had no children: and Eleazar and Ithamar ministered in the
priest's office in the sight of Aaron their father.
5¶ And the LORD spake unto Moses, saying,
6Bring the tribe of Levi near, and present them before Aaron the
priest, that they may minister unto him.
7And they shall keep his charge, and the charge of the whole
congregation before the tabernacle of the congregation, to do the
service of the tabernacle.
8And they shall keep all the instruments of the tabernacle of the
congregation, and the charge of the children of Israel, to do the
service of the tabernacle.
9And thou shalt give the Levites unto Aaron and to his sons:
they *are* wholly given unto him out of the children of Israel.

## Amplified

18On the west side shall be the standard of the camp of Ephraim
by their companies, the leader of the sons of Ephraim being Elishama son of Ammihud.
19Ephraim's host as numbered totaled 40,500.
20Beside Ephraim shall be the tribe of Manasseh, the leader of
the sons of Manasseh being Gamaliel son of Pedahzur.
21Manasseh's host as numbered totaled 32,200.
22Then the tribe of Benjamin, the leader of the sons of Benjamin
being Abidan son of Gideoni.
23Benjamin's host as numbered totaled 35,400.
24The whole number [of the three tribes] in the camp of
Ephraim totaled 108,100. They shall go forward in third place.
25The standard of the camp of Dan shall be on the north side
[of the tabernacle] by their companies, the leader of the sons of
Dan being Ahiezer son of Ammishaddai.
26Dan's host as numbered totaled 62,700.
27Encamped next to Dan shall be the tribe of Asher, the leader
of the sons of Asher being Pagiel son of Ochran.
28Asher's host as numbered totaled 41,500.
29Then the tribe of Naphtali, the leader of the sons of Naphtali
being Ahira son of Enan.
30Naphtali's host as numbered totaled 53,400.
31The whole number [of the three tribes] in the camp of Dan
totaled 157,600. They shall set out last, standard after standard.
32These are the Israelites as numbered by their fathers' houses;
all in the camps who were numbered by their companies were
603,550.
33But the Levites were not numbered with the Israelites, for so
the Lord commanded Moses.
34Thus the Israelites did according to all the Lord commanded
Moses; so they encamped by their standards, and so they set
forward, every one with his [tribal] families, according to their
fathers' houses.

3 NOW THESE are the generations of Aaron and Moses when
the Lord spoke with Moses on Mount Sinai.
2These are the names of the sons of Aaron: Nadab the first-
born, Abihu, Eleazar, and Ithamar.
3These are the names of the sons of Aaron, the priests who were
anointed, whom Aaron consecrated *and* ordained *to* minister in the
priest's office.
4But Nadab and Abihu died before the Lord when they offered
strange fire before the Lord in the wilderness of Sinai; and they had
no children. So Eleazar and Ithamar ministered in the priest's
office in the presence *and* under the supervision of Aaron their
father. [Lev. 10:1-4.]
5And the Lord said to Moses,
6Bring the tribe of Levi near, and set them before Aaron the
priest, that they may minister to him.
7And they shall carry out his instructions and the duties connected with the whole assembly before the tent of meeting, doing
the service of the tabernacle.
8And they shall keep all the instruments *and* furnishings of the
tent of meeting and take charge of [attending] the Israelites, to
serve in the tabernacle.
9And you shall give the Levites [as servants and helpers] to
Aaron and his sons; they are wholly given to him from among the
Israelites.

## New American Standard

18¶ "On the west side *shall be* the standard of the camp of
Ephraim by their armies, and the leader of the sons of Ephraim
*shall be* Elishama the son of Ammihud,
19and his army, even their numbered men, 40,500.
20"And next to him *shall be* the tribe of Manasseh, and the leader
of the sons of Manasseh: Gamaliel the son of Pedahzur,
21and his army, even their numbered men, 32,200.
22"Then *comes* the tribe of Benjamin, and the leader of the sons
of Benjamin: Abidan the son of Gideoni,
23and his army, even their numbered men, 35,400.
24"The total of the numbered men of the camp of Ephraim:
108,100, by their armies. And they shall set out third.
25¶ "On the north side *shall be* the standard of the camp of Dan
by their armies, and the leader of the sons of Dan: Ahiezer the son
of Ammishaddai,
26and his army, even their numbered men, 62,700.
27"And those who camp next to him *shall be* the tribe of Asher,
and the leader of the sons of Asher: Pagiel the son of Ochran,
28and his army, even their numbered men, 41,500.
29"Then *comes* the tribe of Naphtali, and the leader of the sons
of Naphtali: Ahira the son of Enan,
30and his army, even their numbered men, 53,400.
31"The total of the numbered men of the camp of Dan, *was*
157,600. They shall set out last by their standards."
32¶ These are the numbered men of the sons of Israel by their
fathers' households; the total of the numbered men of the camps
by their armies, 603,550.
33The Levites, however, were not numbered among the sons of
Israel, just as the LORD had commanded Moses.
34Thus the sons of Israel did; according to all that the LORD
commanded Moses, so they camped by their standards, and so
they set out, every one by his family, according to his father's
household.

*Levites to Be Priesthood*

3 NOW THESE are *the records of* the generations of Aaron and
Moses at the time when the LORD spoke with Moses on
Mount Sinai.
2These then are the names of the sons of Aaron: Nadab the
first-born, and Abihu, Eleazar and Ithamar.
3These are the names of the sons of Aaron, the anointed
priests, whom he ordained to serve as priests.
4But Nadab and Abihu died before the LORD when they offered
strange fire before the LORD in the wilderness of Sinai; and they
had no children. So Eleazar and Ithamar served as priests in the
lifetime of their father Aaron.
5¶ Then the LORD spoke to Moses, saying,
6"Bring the tribe of Levi near and set them before Aaron the
priest, that they may serve him.
7"And they shall perform the duties for him and for the whole
congregation before the tent of meeting, to do the service of the
tabernacle.
8"They shall also keep all the furnishings of the tent of meeting, along with the duties of the sons of Israel, to do the service
of the tabernacle.
9"You shall thus give the Levites to Aaron and to his sons; they
are wholly given to him from among the sons of Israel.

## New International

18On the west will be the divisions of the camp of Ephraim
under their standard. The leader of the people of Ephraim is
Elishama son of Ammihud. 19His division numbers 40,500.
20The tribe of Manasseh will be next to them. The leader
of the people of Manasseh is Gamaliel son of Pedahzur. 21His
division numbers 32,200.
22The tribe of Benjamin will be next. The leader of the
people of Benjamin is Abidan son of Gideoni. 23His division
numbers 35,400.
24All the men assigned to the camp of Ephraim, according
to their divisions, number 108,100. They will set out third.

25On the north will be the divisions of the camp of Dan,
under their standard. The leader of the people of Dan is
Ahiezer son of Ammishaddai. 26His division numbers 62,700.
27The tribe of Asher will camp next to them. The leader of
the people of Asher is Pagiel son of Ocran. 28His division
numbers 41,500.
29The tribe of Naphtali will be next. The leader of the
people of Naphtali is Ahira son of Enan. 30His division numbers 53,400.
31All men assigned to the camp of Dan number 157,600.
They will set out last, under their standards.

32These are the Israelites, counted according to their families. All those in the camps, by their divisions, number 603,
550. 33The Levites, however, were not counted along with the
other Israelites, as the LORD commanded Moses.

34So the Israelites did everything the LORD commanded Moses;
that is the way they encamped under their standards, and that is
the way they set out, each with his clan and family.

*The Levites*

3 THIS IS the account of the family of Aaron and Moses at the
time the LORD talked with Moses on Mount Sinai.
2The names of the sons of Aaron were Nadab the firstborn and
Abihu, Eleazar and Ithamar. 3Those were the names of Aaron's
sons, the anointed priests, who were ordained to serve as priests.
4Nadab and Abihu, however, fell dead before the LORD when they
made an offering with unauthorized fire before him in the Desert
of Sinai. They had no sons; so only Eleazar and Ithamar served as
priests during the lifetime of their father Aaron.
5The LORD said to Moses, 6"Bring the tribe of Levi and present
them to Aaron the priest to assist him. 7They are to perform duties
for him and for the whole community at the Tent of Meeting by
doing the work of the tabernacle. 8They are to take care of all the
furnishings of the Tent of Meeting, fulfilling the obligations of the
Israelites by doing the work of the tabernacle. 9Give the Levites to
Aaron and his sons; they are the Israelites who are to be given
wholly to him.[a] 10Appoint Aaron and his sons to serve as priests;

NIV [a] 9 Most manuscripts of the Masoretic Text; some manuscripts of the Masoretic Text, Samaritan Pentateuch and Septuagint (see also Num. 8:16) *to me*

## King James

10And thou shalt appoint Aaron and his sons, and they shall wait on their priest's office: and the stranger that cometh nigh shall be put to death.

11And the LORD spake unto Moses, saying,

12And I, behold, I have taken the Levites from among the children of Israel instead of all the firstborn that openeth the matrix among the children of Israel: therefore the Levites shall be mine;

13Because all the firstborn *are* mine; *for* on the day that I smote all the firstborn in the land of Egypt I hallowed unto me all the firstborn in Israel, both man and beast: mine shall they be: I *am* the LORD.

14¶ And the LORD spake unto Moses in the wilderness of Sinai, saying,

15Number the children of Levi after the house of their fathers, by their families: every male from a month old and upward shalt thou number them.

16And Moses numbered them according to the word of the LORD, as he was commanded.

17And these were the sons of Levi by their names; Gershon, and Kohath, and Merari.

18And these *are* the names of the sons of Gershon by their families; Libni, and Shimei.

19And the sons of Kohath by their families; Amram, and Izehar, Hebron, and Uzziel.

20And the sons of Merari by their families; Mahli, and Mushi. These *are* the families of the Levites according to the house of their fathers.

21Of Gershon *was* the family of the Libnites, and the family of the Shimites: these *are* the families of the Gershonites.

22Those that were numbered of them, according to the number of all the males, from a month old and upward, *even* those that were numbered of them *were* seven thousand and five hundred.

23The families of the Gershonites shall pitch behind the tabernacle westward.

24And the chief of the house of the father of the Gershonites *shall be* Eliasaph the son of Lael.

25And the charge of the sons of Gershon in the tabernacle of the congregation *shall be* the tabernacle, and the tent, the covering thereof, and the hanging for the door of the tabernacle of the congregation,

26And the hangings of the court, and the curtain for the door of the court, which *is* by the tabernacle, and by the altar round about, and the cords of it for all the service thereof.

27¶ And of Kohath *was* the family of the Amramites, and the family of the Izeharites, and the family of the Hebronites, and the family of the Uzzielites: these *are* the families of the Kohathites.

28In the number of all the males, from a month old and upward, *were* eight thousand and six hundred, keeping the charge of the sanctuary.

29The families of the sons of Kohath shall pitch on the side of the tabernacle southward.

30And the chief of the house of the father of the families of the Kohathites *shall be* Elizaphan the son of Uzziel.

31And their charge *shall be* the ark, and the table, and the candlestick, and the altars, and the vessels of the sanctuary wherewith they minister, and the hanging, and all the service thereof.

32And Eleazar the son of Aaron the priest *shall be* chief over the chief of the Levites, *and have* the oversight of them that keep the charge of the sanctuary.

33¶ Of Merari *was* the family of the Mahlites, and the family of the Mushites: these *are* the families of Merari.

34And those that were numbered of them, according to the number of all the males, from a month old and upward, *were* six thousand and two hundred.

35And the chief of the house of the father of the families of Merari *was* Zuriel the son of Abihail: *these* shall pitch on the side of the tabernacle northward.

## Amplified

10And you shall appoint Aaron and his sons, and they shall observe *and* attend to their priest's office; but the excluded [any one daring to assume priestly duties or privileges who is not of the house of Aaron and called of God] who comes near [the holy things] shall be put to death.

11And the Lord said to Moses,

12Behold, I have taken the Levites from among the Israelites instead of every first-born who opens the womb among the Israelites, and the Levites shall be Mine;

13For all the first-born are Mine; on the day that I slew all the first-born in the land of Egypt, I consecrated for Myself all the first-born in Israel, both man and beast; Mine they shall be; I am the Lord.

14And the Lord said to Moses in the wilderness of Sinai,

15Number the sons of Levi by their fathers' houses and by families; every male from a month old and upward you shall number.

16So Moses numbered them as he was commanded by the word of the Lord.

17These were the sons of Levi by their names: Gershon, Kohath, and Merari.

18And these are the names of the sons of Gershon by their families: Libni and Shimei.

19The sons of Kohath by their families: Amram, Izhar, Hebron, and Uzziel.

20The sons of Merari by their families: Mahli and Mushi. These are the families of the Levites by their fathers' houses.

21Of Gershon was the family of the Libnites, and of the Shimeites. These are the families of the Gershonites.

22The males who were numbered of them, from a month old and upward, totaled 7,500.

23The families of the Gershonites were to encamp behind the tabernacle on the west,

24The leader of the fathers' house of the Gershonites being Eliasaph son of Lael.

25And the responsibility of the sons of Gershon in the tent of meeting was to be the tabernacle, the tent, its covering, and the hangings for the door of the tent of meeting,

26And the hangings of the court, the curtain for the door of the court which is around the tabernacle and the altar, its cords, and all the service pertaining to them.

27Of Kohath were the families of the Amramites, the Izharites, the Hebronites, and the Uzzielites; these are the families of the Kohathites.

28The number of all the males, from a month old and upward, totaled 8,600 attending to the duties of the sanctuary.

29The families of the sons of Kohath were to encamp on the south side of the tabernacle,

30The chief of the fathers' house of the families of the Kohathites, being Elizaphan son of Uzziel.

31Their charge was to be the ark, the table, the lampstand, the altars, and the utensils of the sanctuary with which the priests minister, and the screen, and all the service having to do with these.

32Eleazar son of Aaron the priest was to be chief over the leaders of the Levites, and have the oversight of those who had charge of the sanctuary.

33Of Merari were the families of the Mahlites and the Mushites; these are the families of Merari.

34Their number, of all the males from a month old and upward, totaled 6,200.

35And the head of the fathers' house of the families of Merari was Zuriel son of Abihail; the Merarites were to encamp on the north side of the tabernacle.

## New American Standard

10"So you shall appoint Aaron and his sons that they may keep their priesthood, but the layman who comes near shall be put to death."

11¶ Again the LORD spoke to Moses, saying,

12"Now, behold, I have taken the Levites from among the sons of Israel instead of every first-born, the first issue of the womb among the sons of Israel. So the Levites shall be Mine.

13"For all the first-born are Mine; on the day that I struck down all the first-born in the land of Egypt, I sanctified to Myself all the first-born in Israel, from man to beast. They shall be Mine; I am the LORD."

14¶ Then the LORD spoke to Moses in the wilderness of Sinai, saying,

15"Number the sons of Levi by their fathers' households, by their families; every male from a month old and upward you shall number."

16So Moses numbered them according to the word of the LORD, just as he had been commanded.

17These then are the sons of Levi by their names: Gershon and Kohath and Merari.

18And these are the names of the sons of Gershon by their families: Libni and Shimei;

19and the sons of Kohath by their families: Amram and Izhar, Hebron and Uzziel;

20and the sons of Merari by their families: Mahli and Mushi. These are the families of the Levites according to their fathers' households.

21¶ Of Gershon *was* the family of the Libnites and the family of the Shimeites; these *were* the families of the Gershonites.

22Their numbered men, in the numbering of every male from a month old and upward, *even* their numbered men *were* 7,500.

23The families of the Gershonites were to camp behind the tabernacle westward,

24and the leader of the fathers' households of the Gershonites *was* Eliasaph the son of Lael.

*Duties of the Priests*

25Now the duties of the sons of Gershon in the tent of meeting *involved* the tabernacle and the tent, its covering, and the screen for the doorway of the tent of meeting,

26and the hangings of the court, and the screen for the doorway of the court, which is around the tabernacle and the altar, and its cords, according to all the service concerning them.

27¶ And of Kohath *was* the family of the Amramites and the family of the Izharites and the family of the Hebronites and the family of the Uzzielites; these were the families of the Kohathites.

28In the numbering of every male from a month old and upward, *there were* 8,600, performing the duties of the sanctuary.

29The families of the sons of Kohath were to camp on the southward side of the tabernacle,

30and the leader of the fathers' households of the Kohathite families was Elizaphan the son of Uzziel.

31Now their duties *involved* the ark, the table, the lampstand, the altars, and the utensils of the sanctuary with which they minister, and the screen, and all the service concerning them;

32and Eleazar the son of Aaron the priest *was* the chief of the leaders of Levi, *and had* the oversight of those who perform the duties of the sanctuary.

33¶ Of Merari *was* the family of the Mahlites and the family of the Mushites; these *were* the families of Merari.

34Their numbered men in the numbering of every male from a month old and upward, *were* 6,200.

35And the leader of the fathers' households of the families of Merari *was* Zuriel the son of Abihail. They *were* to camp on the northward side of the tabernacle.

## New International

anyone else who approaches the sanctuary must be put to death."
11The LORD also said to Moses, 12"I have taken the Levites from
among the Israelites in place of the first male offspring of every
Israelite woman. The Levites are mine, 13for all the firstborn are
mine. When I struck down all the firstborn in Egypt, I set apart for
myself every firstborn in Israel, whether man or animal. They are
to be mine. I am the LORD."
14The LORD said to Moses in the Desert of Sinai, 15"Count the
Levites by their families and clans. Count every male a month old
or more." 16So Moses counted them, as he was commanded by the
word of the LORD.
17These were the names of the sons of Levi:
Gershon, Kohath and Merari.
18These were the names of the Gershonite clans:
Libni and Shimei.
19The Kohathite clans:
Amram, Izhar, Hebron and Uzziel.
20The Merarite clans:
Mahli and Mushi.
These were the Levite clans, according to their families.

21To Gershon belonged the clans of the Libnites and Shimeites;
these were the Gershonite clans. 22The number of all the males a
month old or more who were counted was 7,500. 23The Gershonite
clans were to camp on the west, behind the tabernacle. 24The
leader of the families of the Gershonites was Eliasaph son of Lael.
25At the Tent of Meeting the Gershonites were responsible for the
care of the tabernacle and tent, its coverings, the curtain at the
entrance to the Tent of Meeting, 26the curtains of the courtyard,
the curtain at the entrance to the courtyard surrounding the tabernacle and altar, and the ropes—and everything related to their use.

27To Kohath belonged the clans of the Amramites, Izharites,
Hebronites and Uzzielites; these were the Kohathite clans. 28The
number of all the males a month old or more was 8,600.[a] The
Kohathites were responsible for the care of the sanctuary. 29The
Kohathite clans were to camp on the south side of the tabernacle.
30The leader of the families of the Kohathite clans was Elizaphan
son of Uzziel. 31They were responsible for the care of the ark, the
table, the lampstand, the altars, the articles of the sanctuary used
in ministering, the curtain, and everything related to their use.
32The chief leader of the Levites was Eleazar son of Aaron, the
priest. He was appointed over those who were responsible for the
care of the sanctuary.

33To Merari belonged the clans of the Mahlites and the Mushites; these were the Merarite clans. 34The number of all the males
a month old or more who were counted was 6,200. 35The leader
of the families of the Merarite clans was Zuriel son of Abihail; they
were to camp on the north side of the tabernacle. 36The Merarites

NIV a 28 Hebrew; some Septuagint manuscripts *8,300*

## King James

36And *under* the custody and charge of the sons of Merari *shall be* the boards of the tabernacle, and the bars thereof, and the pillars thereof, and the sockets thereof, and all the vessels thereof, and all that serveth thereto,

37And the pillars of the court round about, and their sockets, and their pins, and their cords.

38¶ But those that encamp before the tabernacle toward the east, *even* before the tabernacle of the congregation eastward, *shall be* Moses, and Aaron and his sons, keeping the charge of the sanctuary for the charge of the children of Israel; and the stranger that cometh nigh shall be put to death.

39All that were numbered of the Levites, which Moses and Aaron numbered at the commandment of the LORD, throughout their families, all the males from a month old and upward, *were* twenty and two thousand.

40¶ And the LORD said unto Moses, Number all the firstborn of the males of the children of Israel from a month old and upward, and take the number of their names.

41And thou shalt take the Levites for me (I *am* the LORD) instead of all the firstborn among the children of Israel; and the cattle of the Levites instead of all the firstlings among the cattle of the children of Israel.

42And Moses numbered, as the LORD commanded him, all the firstborn among the children of Israel.

43And all the firstborn males by the number of names, from a month old and upward, of those that were numbered of them, were twenty and two thousand two hundred and threescore and thirteen.

44¶ And the LORD spake unto Moses, saying,

45Take the Levites instead of all the firstborn among the children of Israel, and the cattle of the Levites instead of their cattle; and the Levites shall be mine: I *am* the LORD.

46And for those that are to be redeemed of the two hundred and threescore and thirteen of the firstborn of the children of Israel, which are more than the Levites;

47Thou shalt even take five shekels apiece by the poll, after the shekel of the sanctuary shalt thou take *them:* (the shekel *is* twenty gerahs:)

48And thou shalt give the money, wherewith the odd number of them is to be redeemed, unto Aaron and to his sons.

49And Moses took the redemption money of them that were over and above them that were redeemed by the Levites:

50Of the firstborn of the children of Israel took he the money; a thousand three hundred and threescore and five *shekels*, after the shekel of the sanctuary:

51And Moses gave the money of them that were redeemed unto Aaron and to his sons, according to the word of the LORD, as the LORD commanded Moses.

**4** AND THE LORD spake unto Moses and unto Aaron, saying,

2Take the sum of the sons of Kohath from among the sons of Levi, after their families, by the house of their fathers,

3From thirty years old and upward even until fifty years old, all that enter into the host, to do the work in the tabernacle of the congregation.

## Amplified

36And the appointed charge of the sons of Merari was the boards *or* frames of the tabernacle, and its bars, pillars, sockets *or* bases, and all the accessories *or* instruments of it, and all the work connected with them,

37And the pillars of the surrounding court and their sockets *or* bases, with their pegs and their cords.

38But those to encamp before the tabernacle toward the east, before the tent of meeting toward the sunrise, were to be Moses and Aaron and his sons, keeping the full charge of the rites of the sanctuary in whatever was required for the Israelites; and the [a]excluded [one not a descendant of Aaron and called of God] who came near [the sanctuary] was to be put to death.

39All the Levites whom Moses and Aaron numbered at the command of the Lord, by their families, all the males from a month old and upward, were 22,000.

40And the Lord said to Moses, Number all the first-born of the males of the Israelites from a month old and upward, and take the number of their names.

41You shall take the Levites for Me instead of all the first-born among the Israelites; I am the Lord; and you shall take the cattle of the Levites for Me instead of all the firstlings among the cattle of the Israelites.

42So Moses numbered, as the Lord commanded him, all the first-born Israelites.

43But all the first-born males from a month old and upward as numbered were 22,273 [273 more than the Levites].

44And the Lord said to Moses,

45Take the Levites [for Me] instead of all the first-born Israelites, and the Levites' cattle instead of their cattle; and the Levites shall be Mine; I am the Lord.

46And for those 273 who are to be redeemed of the first-born of the Israelites who outnumber the Levites,

47You shall take five shekels apiece, reckoning by the sanctuary shekel of twenty gerahs; you shall collect them,

48And you shall give the ransom silver, from the excess number [over the Levites] to be redeemed, to Aaron and his sons.

49So Moses took the redemption money from those who were left over from the number who were redeemed by the Levites.

50Of the first-born of the Israelites, he took the money, 1,365 shekels, after the shekel of the sanctuary.

51And Moses gave the money from those who were ransomed to Aaron and his sons, as the Lord commanded Moses.

**4** AND THE Lord said to Moses and Aaron,

2Take a census of the Kohathite division among the sons of Levi, by their families, by their fathers' house,

3From thirty years old and up to fifty years old, all who can enter the service to do the work in the tent of meeting.

**AMP** [a] This ban against "the excluded" from coming near the sanctuary (the sacred tent, the tabernacle proper) is not to be construed as discrimination against people who were not Israelites. It included every one except the ordained descendants of Levi of the house of Aaron. The tabernacle proper was made up of two small rooms, which no one, except the priest or priests whose assignment it was, was ever to enter. The congregation entered the outside enclosure only. This was true also of the later temples. Neither Jesus nor any of his disciples or Paul ever entered the sanctuary. When Jesus "taught in the temple," or "entered into the temple," the Greek word invariably indicates that He was in the temple enclosure, "hieron," and not in the sanctuary, "naos." (See Trench's *Synonyms of The New Testament.*) For a violation of this ban see II Chron. 26:16-21, which tells of King Uzziah, who attempted to enter the sanctuary to burn incense, and while being forcibly put out by eighty priests became a leper—for the rest of his life.

## New American Standard

36 Now the appointed duties of the sons of Merari *involved* the
frames of the tabernacle, its bars, its pillars, its sockets, all its
equipment, and the service concerning them,
37 and the pillars around the court with their sockets and their
pegs and their cords.
38 ¶ Now those who were to camp before the tabernacle eastward, before the tent of meeting toward the sunrise, are Moses and
Aaron and his sons, performing the duties of the sanctuary for the
obligation of the sons of Israel; but the layman coming near was
to be put to death.
39 All the numbered men of the Levites, whom Moses and
Aaron numbered at the command of the LORD by their families,
every male from a month old and upward, *were* 22,000.

*First-born Redeemed*

40 ¶ Then the LORD said to Moses, "Number every first-born
male of the sons of Israel from a month old and upward, and make
a list of their names.
41 "And you shall take the Levites for Me, I am the LORD, instead
of all the first-born among the sons of Israel, and the cattle of the
Levites instead of all the first-born among the cattle of the sons of
Israel."
42 So Moses numbered all the first-born among the sons of Israel, just as the LORD had commanded him;
43 and all the first-born males by the number of names from a
month old and upward, for their numbered men were 22,273.
44 ¶ Then the LORD spoke to Moses, saying,
45 "Take the Levites instead of all the first-born among the sons
of Israel and the cattle of the Levites. And the Levites shall be
Mine; I am the LORD.
46 "And for the ransom of the 273 of the first-born of the sons
of Israel who are in excess beyond the Levites,
47 you shall take five shekels apiece, per head; you shall take
*them* in terms of the shekel of the sanctuary (the shekel is twenty
[b]gerahs),
48 and give the money, the ransom of those who are in excess
among them, to Aaron and to his sons."
49 So Moses took the ransom money from those who were in
excess, beyond those ransomed by the Levites;
50 from the first-born of the sons of Israel he took the money in
terms of the shekel of the sanctuary, 1,365.
51 Then Moses gave the ransom money to Aaron and to his sons,
at the command of the LORD, just as the LORD had commanded
Moses.

*Duties of the Kohathites*

4 THEN THE LORD spoke to Moses and to Aaron, saying,
2 "Take a census of the descendants of Kohath from among
the sons of Levi, by their families, by their fathers' households,
3 from thirty years and upward, even to fifty years old, all who
enter the service to do the work in the tent of meeting.

NAS [b] I.e., A gerah equals approx. one-fortieth ounce

## New International

were appointed to take care of the frames of the tabernacle, its
crossbars, posts, bases, all its equipment, and everything related
to their use, 37 as well as the posts of the surrounding courtyard
with their bases, tent pegs and ropes.

38 Moses and Aaron and his sons were to camp to the east of the
tabernacle, toward the sunrise, in front of the Tent of Meeting.
They were responsible for the care of the sanctuary on behalf of
the Israelites. Anyone else who approached the sanctuary was to
be put to death.

39 The total number of Levites counted at the LORD's command
by Moses and Aaron according to their clans, including every male
a month old or more, was 22,000.

40 The LORD said to Moses, "Count all the firstborn Israelite
males who are a month old or more and make a list of their names.
41 Take the Levites for me in place of all the firstborn of the Israelites, and the livestock of the Levites in place of all the firstborn of
the livestock of the Israelites. I am the LORD."
42 So Moses counted all the firstborn of the Israelites, as the
LORD commanded him. 43 The total number of firstborn males a
month old or more, listed by name, was 22,273.
44 The LORD also said to Moses, 45 "Take the Levites in place of
all the firstborn of Israel, and the livestock of the Levites in place
of their livestock. The Levites are to be mine. I am the LORD. 46 To
redeem the 273 firstborn Israelites who exceed the number of the
Levites, 47 collect five shekels[c] for each one, according to the sanctuary shekel, which weighs twenty gerahs. 48 Give the money for
the redemption of the additional Israelites to Aaron and his sons."
49 So Moses collected the redemption money from those who
exceeded the number redeemed by the Levites. 50 From the first-
born of the Israelites he collected silver weighing 1,365 shekels,[d]
according to the sanctuary shekel. 51 Moses gave the redemption
money to Aaron and his sons, as he was commanded by the word
of the LORD.

*The Kohathites*

4 THE LORD said to Moses and Aaron: 2 "Take a census of the
Kohathite branch of the Levites by their clans and families.
3 Count all the men from thirty to fifty years of age who come to
serve in the work in the Tent of Meeting.

NIV [c] *47* That is, about 2 ounces (about 55 grams) [d] *50* That is, about 35 pounds (about 15.5 kilograms)

## King James

4 This *shall be* the service of the sons of Kohath in the tabernacle of the congregation, *about* the most holy things:

5 ¶ And when the camp setteth forward, Aaron shall come, and his sons, and they shall take down the covering veil, and cover the ark of testimony with it:

6 And shall put thereon the covering of badgers' skins, and shall spread over *it* a cloth wholly of blue, and shall put in the staves thereof.

7 And upon the table of showbread they shall spread a cloth of blue, and put thereon the dishes, and the spoons, and the bowls, and covers to cover withal: and the continual bread shall be thereon:

8 And they shall spread upon them a cloth of scarlet, and cover the same with a covering of badgers' skins, and shall put in the staves thereof.

9 And they shall take a cloth of blue, and cover the candlestick of the light, and his lamps, and his tongs, and his snuffdishes, and all the oil vessels thereof, wherewith they minister unto it:

10 And they shall put it and all the vessels thereof within a covering of badgers' skins, and shall put *it* upon a bar.

11 And upon the golden altar they shall spread a cloth of blue, and cover it with a covering of badgers' skins, and shall put to the staves thereof:

12 And they shall take all the instruments of ministry, wherewith they minister in the sanctuary, and put *them* in a cloth of blue, and cover them with a covering of badgers' skins, and shall put *them* on a bar:

13 And they shall take away the ashes from the altar, and spread a purple cloth thereon:

14 And they shall put upon it all the vessels thereof, wherewith they minister about it, *even* the censers, the fleshhooks, and the shovels, and the basins, all the vessels of the altar; and they shall spread upon it a covering of badgers' skins, and put to the staves of it.

15 And when Aaron and his sons have made an end of covering the sanctuary, and all the vessels of the sanctuary, as the camp is to set forward; after that the sons of Kohath shall come to bear *it:* but they shall not touch *any* holy thing, lest they die. These *things are* the burden of the sons of Kohath in the tabernacle of the congregation.

16 ¶ And to the office of Eleazar the son of Aaron the priest *pertaineth* the oil for the light, and the sweet incense, and the daily meat offering, and the anointing oil, *and* the oversight of all the tabernacle, and of all that therein *is,* in the sanctuary, and in the vessels thereof.

17 ¶ And the LORD spake unto Moses and unto Aaron, saying,

18 Cut ye not off the tribe of the families of the Kohathites from among the Levites:

19 But thus do unto them, that they may live, and not die, when they approach unto the most holy things: Aaron and his sons shall go in, and appoint them every one to his service and to his burden:

20 But they shall not go in to see when the holy things are covered, lest they die.

21 ¶ And the LORD spake unto Moses, saying,

22 Take also the sum of the sons of Gershon, throughout the houses of their fathers, by their families;

23 From thirty years old and upward until fifty years old shalt thou number them; all that enter in to perform the service, to do the work in the tabernacle of the congregation.

24 This *is* the service of the families of the Gershonites, to serve, and for burdens:

25 And they shall bear the curtains of the tabernacle, and the tabernacle of the congregation, his covering, and the covering of the badgers' skins that *is* above upon it, and the hanging for the door of the tabernacle of the congregation,

## Amplified

4 This shall be the responsibility of the sons of Kohath in the tent of meeting: the most holy things.

5 When the camp prepares to set forward, Aaron and his sons shall take down the veil [screening the holy of holies] and cover the ark of the testimony with it;

6 And shall put on it the covering of dolphin *or* porpoise skin, and shall spread over that a cloth wholly of blue, and shall put in place the poles of the ark.

7 And upon the table of showbread they shall spread a cloth of blue, and put on it the plates, the dishes for incense, the bowls, the flagons for the drink offering, and also the continual showbread.

8 And they shall spread over them a cloth of scarlet, and put over that a covering of dolphin *or* porpoise skin, and put in place the poles [for carrying].

9 And they shall take a cloth of blue, and cover the lampstand for the light, and its lamps, its snuffers, its ashtrays, and all the oil vessels from which it is supplied.

10 And they shall put the lampstand and all its utensils within a covering of dolphin *or* porpoise skin, and shall put it upon the frame [for carrying].

11 And upon the golden [incense] altar they shall spread a cloth of blue, and cover it with a covering of dolphin *or* porpoise skin, and shall put in place its poles [for carrying].

12 And they shall take all the utensils of the service with which they minister in the sanctuary, and put them in a cloth of blue, and cover them with a covering of dolphin *or* porpoise skin, and shall put them on the frame [for carrying].

13 And they shall take away the ashes from the altar [of burnt offering], and spread a purple cloth over it.

14 And they shall put upon it all its vessels *and* utensils with which they minister there, the firepans, the fleshhooks *or* forks, the shovels, the basins, and all the vessels *and* utensils of the altar, and they shall spread over it all a covering of dolphin *or* porpoise skin, and shall put in its poles [for carrying].

15 When Aaron and his sons have finished covering the sanctuary and all its furniture, as the camp sets out, after all that [is done but not before] the sons of Kohath shall come to carry them; but they shall not touch the holy things, lest they die. These are the things of the tent of meeting which the sons of Kohath are to carry.

16 And Eleazar son of Aaron the priest shall have charge of the oil for the light, the fragrant incense, the continual cereal offering, and the anointing oil, with the oversight of all the tabernacle and of all that is in it, of the sanctuary and its utensils.

17 And the Lord said to Moses and Aaron,

18 *Since* the tribe of the families of the Kohathites [are only Levites and not priests], do not [by exposing them to the sin of touching the most holy things] cut them off from among the Levites;

19 But deal thus with them, that they may live and not die when they approach the most holy things: Aaron and his sons shall go in and appoint them each to his work and to his burden [to be carried on the march];

20 But [the Kohathites] shall not go in to see the sanctuary [the holy place and the holy of holies] *or* its holy things even for an instant, lest they die.

21 And the Lord said to Moses,

22 Take a census of the sons of Gershon, by their fathers' house, by their families;

23 From thirty years old and up to fifty years old you shall number them, all who enter for service, to do the work in the tent of meeting.

24 This is the service of the families of the Gershonites, in serving and in bearing burdens [when on the march]:

25 And they shall carry the curtains of the tabernacle, and the tent of meeting, its covering, and the covering of dolphin *or* porpoise skin that is on top of it, and the hanging *or* screen for the door of the tent of meeting,

## New American Standard

4"This is the work of the descendants of Kohath in the tent of meeting, *concerning* the most holy things.

5"When the camp sets out, Aaron and his sons shall go in and they shall take down the veil of the screen and cover the ark of the testimony with it;

6and they shall lay a covering of porpoise skin on it, and shall spread over *it* a cloth of pure blue, and shall insert its poles.

7"Over the table of the bread of the Presence they shall also spread a cloth of blue and put on it the dishes and the pans and the sacrificial bowls and the jars for the libation, and the continual bread shall be on it.

8"And they shall spread over them a cloth of scarlet *material,* and cover the same with a covering of porpoise skin, and they shall insert its poles.

9"Then they shall take a blue cloth and cover the lampstand for the light, along with its lamps and its snuffers, and its trays and all its oil vessels, by which they serve it;

10and they shall put it and all its utensils in a covering of porpoise skin, and shall put it on the carrying bars.

11"And over the golden altar they shall spread a blue cloth and cover it with a covering of porpoise skin, and shall insert its poles;

12and they shall take all the utensils of service, with which they serve in the sanctuary, and put them in a blue cloth and cover them with a covering of porpoise skin, and put them on the carrying bars.

13"Then they shall take away the ashes from the altar, and spread a purple cloth over it.

14"They shall also put on it all its utensils by which they serve in connection with it: the firepans, the forks and shovels and the basins, all the utensils of the altar; and they shall spread a cover of porpoise skin over it and insert its poles.

15"And when Aaron and his sons have finished covering the holy *objects* and all the furnishings of the sanctuary, when the camp is to set out, after that the sons of Kohath shall come to carry *them,* so that they may not touch the holy *objects* and die. These are the things in the tent of meeting which the sons of Kohath are to carry.

16"And the responsibility of Eleazar the son of Aaron the priest is the oil for the light and the fragrant incense and the continual grain offering and the anointing oil—the responsibility of all the tabernacle and of all that is in it, with the sanctuary and its furnishings."

17¶ Then the LORD spoke to Moses and to Aaron, saying,

18"Do not let the tribe of the families of the Kohathites be cut off from among the Levites.

19"But do this to them that they may live and not die when they approach the most holy *objects:* Aaron and his sons shall go in and assign each of them to his work and to his load;

20but they shall not go in to see the holy *objects* even for a moment, lest they die."

*Duties of the Gershonites*

21¶ Then the LORD spoke to Moses, saying,

22"Take a census of the sons of Gershon also, by their fathers' households, by their families;

23from thirty years and upward to fifty years old, you shall number them; all who enter to perform the service to do the work in the tent of meeting.

24"This is the service of the families of the Gershonites, in serving and in carrying:

25they shall carry the curtains of the tabernacle and the tent of meeting *with* its covering and the covering of porpoise skin that is on top of it, and the screen for the doorway of the tent of meeting,

## New International

4"This is the work of the Kohathites in the Tent of Meeting: the
care of the most holy things. 5When the camp is to move, Aaron
and his sons are to go in and take down the shielding curtain and
cover the ark of the Testimony with it. 6Then they are to cover this
with hides of sea cows,[a] spread a cloth of solid blue over that and
put the poles in place.
7"Over the table of the Presence they are to spread a blue cloth
and put on it the plates, dishes and bowls, and the jars for drink
offerings; the bread that is continually there is to remain on it.
8Over these they are to spread a scarlet cloth, cover that with hides
of sea cows and put its poles in place.
9"They are to take a blue cloth and cover the lampstand that is
for light, together with its lamps, its wick trimmers and trays, and
all its jars for the oil used to supply it. 10Then they are to wrap it
and all its accessories in a covering of hides of sea cows and put
it on a carrying frame.
11"Over the gold altar they are to spread a blue cloth and cover
that with hides of sea cows and put its poles in place.
12"They are to take all the articles used for ministering in the
sanctuary, wrap them in a blue cloth, cover that with hides of sea
cows and put them on a carrying frame.
13"They are to remove the ashes from the bronze altar and
spread a purple cloth over it. 14Then they are to place on it all the
utensils used for ministering at the altar, including the firepans,
meat forks, shovels and sprinkling bowls. Over it they are to
spread a covering of hides of sea cows and put its poles in place.
15"After Aaron and his sons have finished covering the holy
furnishings and all the holy articles, and when the camp is ready
to move, the Kohathites are to come to do the carrying. But they
must not touch the holy things or they will die. The Kohathites are
to carry those things that are in the Tent of Meeting.
16"Eleazar son of Aaron, the priest, is to have charge of the oil
for the light, the fragrant incense, the regular grain offering and
the anointing oil. He is to be in charge of the entire tabernacle and
everything in it, including its holy furnishings and articles."
17The LORD said to Moses and Aaron, 18"See that the Kohathite
tribal clans are not cut off from the Levites. 19So that they may live
and not die when they come near the most holy things, do this for
them: Aaron and his sons are to go into the sanctuary and assign
to each man his work and what he is to carry. 20But the Kohathites
must not go in to look at the holy things, even for a moment, or
they will die."

*The Gershonites*

21The LORD said to Moses, 22"Take a census also of the Gershonites by their families and clans. 23Count all the men from
thirty to fifty years of age who come to serve in the work at the Tent
of Meeting.
24"This is the service of the Gershonite clans as they work and
carry burdens: 25They are to carry the curtains of the tabernacle,
the Tent of Meeting, its covering and the outer covering of hides
of sea cows, the curtains for the entrance to the Tent of Meeting,

NIV [a] 6 That is, dugongs; also in verses 8, 10, 11, 12, 14 and 25

## King James

26 And the hangings of the court, and the hanging for the door of the gate of the court, which *is* by the tabernacle and by the altar round about, and their cords, and all the instruments of their service, and all that is made for them: so shall they serve.

27 At the appointment of Aaron and his sons shall be all the service of the sons of the Gershonites, in all their burdens, and in all their service: and ye shall appoint unto them in charge all their burdens.

28 This *is* the service of the families of the sons of Gershon in the tabernacle of the congregation: and their charge *shall be* under the hand of Ithamar the son of Aaron the priest.

29 ¶ As for the sons of Merari, thou shalt number them after their families, by the house of their fathers;

30 From thirty years old and upward even unto fifty years old shalt thou number them, every one that entereth into the service, to do the work of the tabernacle of the congregation.

31 And this *is* the charge of their burden, according to all their service in the tabernacle of the congregation; the boards of the tabernacle, and the bars thereof, and the pillars thereof, and sockets thereof,

32 And the pillars of the court round about, and their sockets, and their pins, and their cords, with all their instruments, and with all their service: and by name ye shall reckon the instruments of the charge of their burden.

33 This *is* the service of the families of the sons of Merari, according to all their service, in the tabernacle of the congregation, under the hand of Ithamar the son of Aaron the priest.

34 ¶ And Moses and Aaron and the chief of the congregation numbered the sons of the Kohathites after their families, and after the house of their fathers,

35 From thirty years old and upward even unto fifty years old, every one that entereth into the service, for the work in the tabernacle of the congregation:

36 And those that were numbered of them by their families were two thousand seven hundred and fifty.

37 These *were* they that were numbered of the families of the Kohathites, all that might do service in the tabernacle of the congregation, which Moses and Aaron did number according to the commandment of the LORD by the hand of Moses.

38 And those that were numbered of the sons of Gershon, throughout their families, and by the house of their fathers,

39 From thirty years old and upward even unto fifty years old, every one that entereth into the service, for the work in the tabernacle of the congregation,

40 Even those that were numbered of them, throughout their families, by the house of their fathers, were two thousand and six hundred and thirty.

41 These *are* they that were numbered of the families of the sons of Gershon, of all that might do service in the tabernacle of the congregation, whom Moses and Aaron did number according to the commandment of the LORD.

42 ¶ And those that were numbered of the families of the sons of Merari, throughout their families, by the house of their fathers,

43 From thirty years old and upward even unto fifty years old, every one that entereth into the service, for the work in the tabernacle of the congregation,

44 Even those that were numbered of them after their families, were three thousand and two hundred.

45 These *be* those that were numbered of the families of the sons of Merari, whom Moses and Aaron numbered according to the word of the LORD by the hand of Moses.

46 All those that were numbered of the Levites, whom Moses and Aaron and the chief of Israel numbered, after their families, and after the house of their fathers,

47 From thirty years old and upward even unto fifty years old, every one that came to do the service of the ministry, and the service of the burden in the tabernacle of the congregation,

48 Even those that were numbered of them, were eight thousand and five hundred and fourscore.

## Amplified

26 And the hangings of the court, and the hanging *or* screen for the entrance of the gate of the court which is around the tabernacle and the altar [of burnt offering], and their cords, and all the equipment for their service; whatever needs to be done with them, that they shall do.

27 Under the direction of Aaron and his sons shall be all the service of the sons of the Gershonites, in all they have to carry and in all they have to do; and you shall assign to their charge all that they are to carry [on the march].

28 This is the service of the families of the sons of Gershon in the tent of meeting; and their work shall be under the direction of Ithamar son of Aaron [high] priest.

29 As for the sons of Merari, you shall number them by their families and their fathers' house;

30 From thirty years old up to fifty years old you shall number them, every one who enters the service, to do the work of the tent of meeting.

31 And this is what they are assigned to carry *and* to guard [on the march], according to all their service in the tent of meeting: the boards *or* frames of the tabernacle and its bars, and its pillars, and its sockets *or* bases,

32 And the pillars of the court round about with their sockets *or* bases, and pegs, and cords, with all their equipment and all their accessories for service; and you shall assign to them by name the articles which they are to carry [on the march].

33 This is the work of the families of the sons of Merari, according to all their tasks in the tent of meeting, under the direction of Ithamar son of Aaron the [high] priest.

34 And Moses and Aaron and the leaders of the congregation numbered the sons of the Kohathites by their families and their fathers' house,

35 From thirty years old up to fifty years old, every one who enters the service to do the work of the tent of meeting;

36 And those who were numbered of them by their families were 2,750.

37 These were numbered of the families of the Kohathites, all who did service in the tent of meeting, whom Moses and Aaron numbered according to the command of the Lord by Moses.

38 And those that were numbered of the sons of Gershon, by their families, and by their fathers' houses,

39 From thirty years old up to fifty years old, every one who entered the service to do the work of the tent of meeting,

40 Those who were enrolled of them, by their families, by their fathers' houses, were 2,630.

41 These were numbered of the families of the sons of Gershon, all who served in the tent of meeting, whom Moses and Aaron numbered as the Lord commanded.

42 And those numbered of the families of the sons of Merari, by their families, by their fathers' house,

43 From thirty years old up to fifty years old, every one who entered into the service for work in the tent of meeting,

44 Even those who were numbered of them by their families, were 3,200.

45 These are those who were numbered of the families of the sons of Merari, whom Moses and Aaron numbered according to the command of the Lord by Moses.

46 All those who were numbered of the Levites, whom Moses and Aaron and the leaders of Israel counted by their families, and by their fathers' houses,

47 From thirty years old up to fifty years old, every one who could enter to do the work of service and of burden bearing in the tent of meeting,

48 Those that were numbered of them were 8,580.

## New American Standard

26and the hangings of the court, and the screen for the doorway
of the gate of the court which is around the tabernacle and the
altar, and their cords and all the equipment for their service; and
all that is to be done, they shall perform.
27"All the service of the sons of the Gershonites, in all their
loads and in all their work, shall be *performed* at the command of
Aaron and his sons; and you shall assign to them as a duty all their
loads.
28"This is the service of the families of the sons of the Gershonites in the tent of meeting, and their duties *shall be* under the
direction of Ithamar the son of Aaron the priest.

*Duties of the Merarites*

29¶ "*As for* the sons of Merari, you shall number them by their
families, by their fathers' households;
30from thirty years and upward even to fifty years old, you shall
number them, everyone who enters the service to do the work of
the tent of meeting.
31"Now this is the duty of their loads, for all their service in the
tent of meeting: the boards of the tabernacle and its bars and its
pillars and its sockets,
32and the pillars around the court and their sockets and their
pegs and their cords, with all their equipment and with all their
service; and you shall assign *each man* by name the items he is to
carry.
33"This is the service of the families of the sons of Merari,
according to all their service in the tent of meeting, under the
direction of Ithamar the son of Aaron the priest."
34¶ So Moses and Aaron and the leaders of the congregation
numbered the sons of the Kohathites by their families, and by their
fathers' households,
35from thirty years and upward even to fifty years old, everyone
who entered the service for work in the tent of meeting.
36And their numbered men by their families were 2,750.
37These are the numbered men of the Kohathite families, everyone who was serving in the tent of meeting, whom Moses and
Aaron numbered according to the commandment of the LORD
through Moses.
38¶ And the numbered men of the sons of Gershon by their
families, and by their fathers' households,
39from thirty years and upward even to fifty years old, everyone
who entered the service for work in the tent of meeting.
40And their numbered men by their families, by their fathers'
households, were 2,630.
41These are the numbered men of the families of the sons of
Gershon, everyone who was serving in the tent of meeting, whom
Moses and Aaron numbered according to the commandment of
the LORD.
42¶ And the numbered men of the families of the sons of Merari
by their families, by their fathers' households,
43from thirty years and upward even to fifty years old, everyone
who entered the service for work in the tent of meeting.
44And their numbered men by their families were 3,200.
45These are the numbered men of the families of the sons of
Merari, whom Moses and Aaron numbered according to the commandment of the LORD through Moses.
46¶ All the numbered men of the Levites, whom Moses and
Aaron and the leaders of Israel numbered, by their families and by
their fathers' households,
47from thirty years and upward even to fifty years old, everyone
who could enter to do the work of service and the work of carrying
in the tent of meeting.
48And their numbered men were 8,580.

## New International

26the curtains of the courtyard surrounding the tabernacle and
altar, the curtain for the entrance, the ropes and all the equipment
used in its service. The Gershonites are to do all that needs to be
done with these things. 27All their service, whether carrying or
doing other work, is to be done under the direction of Aaron and
his sons. You shall assign to them as their responsibility all they
are to carry. 28This is the service of the Gershonite clans at the Tent
of Meeting. Their duties are to be under the direction of Ithamar
son of Aaron, the priest.

*The Merarites*

29"Count the Merarites by their clans and families. 30Count all
the men from thirty to fifty years of age who come to serve in the
work at the Tent of Meeting. 31This is their duty as they perform
service at the Tent of Meeting: to carry the frames of the tabernacle,
its crossbars, posts and bases, 32as well as the posts of the surrounding courtyard with their bases, tent pegs, ropes, all their
equipment and everything related to their use. Assign to each man
the specific things he is to carry. 33This is the service of the Merarite
clans as they work at the Tent of Meeting under the direction of
Ithamar son of Aaron, the priest."

*The Numbering of the Levite Clans*

34Moses, Aaron and the leaders of the community counted the
Kohathites by their clans and families. 35All the men from thirty
to fifty years of age who came to serve in the work in the Tent of
Meeting, 36counted by clans, were 2,750. 37This was the total of all
those in the Kohathite clans who served in the Tent of Meeting.
Moses and Aaron counted them according to the LORD's command
through Moses.
38The Gershonites were counted by their clans and families.
39All the men from thirty to fifty years of age who came to serve
in the work at the Tent of Meeting, 40counted by their clans and
families, were 2,630. 41This was the total of those in the Gershonite
clans who served at the Tent of Meeting. Moses and Aaron counted them according to the LORD's command.
42The Merarites were counted by their clans and families. 43All
the men from thirty to fifty years of age who came to serve in the
work at the Tent of Meeting, 44counted by their clans, were 3,200.
45This was the total of those in the Merarite clans. Moses and
Aaron counted them according to the LORD's command through
Moses.
46So Moses, Aaron and the leaders of Israel counted all the
Levites by their clans and families. 47All the men from thirty to fifty
years of age who came to do the work of serving and carrying the
Tent of Meeting 48numbered 8,580. 49At the LORD's command

## King James

49According to the commandment of the LORD they were numbered by the hand of Moses, every one according to his service, and according to his burden: thus were they numbered of him, as the LORD commanded Moses.

5 AND THE LORD spake unto Moses, saying,
2Command the children of Israel, that they put out of the camp every leper, and every one that hath an issue, and whosoever is defiled by the dead:
3Both male and female shall ye put out, without the camp shall ye put them; that they defile not their camps, in the midst whereof I dwell.
4And the children of Israel did so, and put them out without the camp: as the LORD spake unto Moses, so did the children of Israel.
5¶ And the LORD spake unto Moses, saying,
6Speak unto the children of Israel, When a man or woman shall commit any sin that men commit, to do a trespass against the LORD, and that person be guilty;
7Then they shall confess their sin which they have done: and he shall recompense his trespass with the principal thereof, and add unto it the fifth *part* thereof, and give *it* unto *him* against whom he hath trespassed.
8But if the man have no kinsman to recompense the trespass unto, let the trespass be recompensed unto the LORD, *even* to the priest; beside the ram of the atonement, whereby an atonement shall be made for him.
9And every offering of all the holy things of the children of Israel, which they bring unto the priest, shall be his.
10And every man's hallowed things shall be his: whatsoever any man giveth the priest, it shall be his.
11¶ And the LORD spake unto Moses, saying,
12Speak unto the children of Israel, and say unto them, If any man's wife go aside, and commit a trespass against him,
13And a man lie with her carnally, and it be hid from the eyes of her husband, and be kept close, and she be defiled, and *there be* no witness against her, neither she be taken *with the manner;*
14And the spirit of jealousy come upon him, and he be jealous of his wife, and she be defiled: or if the spirit of jealousy come upon him, and he be jealous of his wife, and she be not defiled:
15Then shall the man bring his wife unto the priest, and he shall bring her offering for her, the tenth *part* of an ephah of barley meal; he shall pour no oil upon it, nor put frankincense thereon; for it *is* an offering of jealousy, an offering of memorial, bringing iniquity to remembrance.
16And the priest shall bring her near, and set her before the LORD:
17And the priest shall take holy water in an earthen vessel; and of the dust that is in the floor of the tabernacle the priest shall take, and put *it* into the water:
18And the priest shall set the woman before the LORD, and uncover the woman's head, and put the offering of memorial in her hands, which *is* the jealousy offering: and the priest shall have in his hand the bitter water that causeth the curse:
19And the priest shall charge her by an oath, and say unto the woman, If no man have lain with thee, and if thou hast not gone aside to uncleanness *with another* instead of thy husband, be thou free from this bitter water that causeth the curse:
20But if thou hast gone aside *to another* instead of thy husband, and if thou be defiled, and some man have lain with thee beside thine husband:

## Amplified

49According to the command of the Lord through Moses they were assigned each to his work of serving and carrying. Thus they were numbered by him, as the Lord had commanded Moses.

5 THE LORD said to Moses,
2Command the Israelites that they put outside the camp every leper, and every one who has a discharge, and whoever is defiled by [coming in contact with] the dead.
3Both male and female you shall put out, without the camp you shall put them, that they may not defile their camp, in the midst of which I dwell.
4The Israelites did so, and put them outside the camp; as the Lord said to Moses, so the Israelites did.
5And the Lord said to Moses,
6Say to the Israelites, When a man or woman commits any sin that men commit by breaking faith with the Lord, and that person is guilty,
7Then he shall confess the sin which he has committed, and he shall make restitution for his wrong in full and add a fifth to it, and give it to him whom he has wronged.
8But if the man [wronged] has no kinsman to whom the restitution may be made, let it be given to the Lord for the priest, besides the ram of atonement with which atonement shall be made for the offender.
9And every offering of all the holy things of the Israelites which they bring to the priest shall be his.
10And every man's hallowed things shall be the priest's; whatever any man gives the priest shall be his.
11And the Lord said to Moses,
12Say to the Israelites, If any man's wife goes astray and commits an offense of guilt against him,
13And a man lies with her carnally, and it is hidden from the eyes of her husband, and it is kept secret though she is defiled, and there is no witness against her, nor was she taken in the act;
14And if the spirit of jealousy comes upon him, and he is jealous *and* suspicious of his wife who has defiled herself; or if the spirit of jealousy comes upon him, and he is jealous *and* suspicious of his wife though she has not defiled herself;
15Then shall the man bring his wife to the priest, and he shall bring the offering required of her, the tenth of an ephah of barley meal; but he shall pour no oil upon it, nor put frankincense on it [symbols of favor and joy], for it is a cereal offering of jealousy *and* suspicion, a memorial offering, bringing iniquity to remembrance.
16And the priest shall bring her near, and set her before the Lord;
17And the priest shall take holy water [probably from the sacred laver] in an earthen vessel, and take some of the dust that is on the floor of the tabernacle and put it in the water.
18And the priest shall set the woman before the Lord, and let the hair of the woman's head hang loose, and put the meal offering of remembrance in her hands, which is the jealousy *and* suspicion offering. And the priest shall have in his hand the water of bitterness that brings the curse.
19Then the priest shall make her take an oath, and say to the woman, If no man has lain with you, and if you have not gone astray to uncleanness with another instead of your husband, then be free from any effect of this water of bitterness which brings the curse.
20But if you have gone astray, and you are defiled, some man having lain with you beside your husband,

## New American Standard

49According to the commandment of the LORD through Moses, they were numbered, everyone by his serving or carrying; thus these were his numbered men, just as the LORD had commanded Moses.

*On Defilement*

5 THEN THE LORD spoke to Moses, saying,

2"Command the sons of Israel that they send away from the camp every leper and everyone having a discharge and everyone who is unclean because of a *dead* person.

3"You shall send away both male and female; you shall send them outside the camp so that they will not defile their camp where I dwell in their midst."

4And the sons of Israel did so and sent them outside the camp; just as the LORD had spoken to Moses, thus the sons of Israel did.

5¶ Then the LORD spoke to Moses, saying,

6"Speak to the sons of Israel, 'When a man or woman commits any of the sins of mankind, acting unfaithfully against the LORD, and that person is guilty,

7then he shall confess his sins which he has committed, and he shall make restitution in full for his wrong, and add to it one-fifth of it, and give *it* to him whom he has wronged.

8'But if the man has no [a]relative to whom restitution may be made for the wrong, the restitution which is made for the wrong *must go* to the LORD for the priest, besides the ram of atonement, by which atonement is made for him.

9'Also every contribution pertaining to all the holy *gifts* of the sons of Israel, which they offer to the priest, shall be his.

10'So every man's holy *gifts* shall be his; whatever any man gives to the priest, it becomes his.'"

*The Adultery Test*

11¶ Then the LORD spoke to Moses, saying,

12"Speak to the sons of Israel, and say to them, 'If any man's wife goes astray and is unfaithful to him,

13and a man has intercourse with her and it is hidden from the eyes of her husband and she is undetected, although she has defiled herself, and there is no witness against her and she has not been caught in the act,

14if a spirit of jealousy comes over him and he is jealous of his wife when she has defiled herself, or if a spirit of jealousy comes over him and he is jealous of his wife when she has not defiled herself,

15the man shall then bring his wife to the priest, and shall bring *as* an offering for her one-tenth of an ephah of barley meal; he shall not pour oil on it, nor put frankincense on it, for it is a grain offering of jealousy, a grain offering of memorial, a reminder of iniquity.

16¶ 'Then the priest shall bring her near and have her stand before the LORD,

17and the priest shall take holy water in an earthenware vessel; and he shall take some of the dust that is on the floor of the tabernacle and put *it* into the water.

18'The priest shall then have the woman stand before the LORD and let *the hair of* the woman's head go loose, and place the grain offering of memorial in her hands, which is the grain offering of jealousy, and in the hand of the priest is to be the water of bitterness that brings a curse.

19'And the priest shall have her take an oath and shall say to the woman, "If no man has lain with you and if you have not gone astray into uncleanness, *being* under *the authority of* your husband, be immune to this water of bitterness that brings a curse;

20if you, however, have gone astray, *being* under *the authority of* your husband, and if you have defiled yourself and a man other than your husband has had intercourse with you"

NAS [a] Lit., *redeemer*

## New International

through Moses, each was assigned his work and told what to
carry.
Thus they were counted, as the LORD commanded Moses.

*The Purity of the Camp*

5 THE LORD said to Moses, 2"Command the Israelites to send
away from the camp anyone who has an infectious skin disease[b] or a discharge of any kind, or who is ceremonially unclean
because of a dead body. 3Send away male and female alike; send
them outside the camp so they will not defile their camp, where
I dwell among them." 4The Israelites did this; they sent them
outside the camp. They did just as the LORD had instructed Moses.

*Restitution for Wrongs*

5The LORD said to Moses, 6"Say to the Israelites: 'When a man
or woman wrongs another in any way[c] and so is unfaithful to the
LORD, that person is guilty 7and must confess the sin he has
committed. He must make full restitution for his wrong, add one
fifth to it and give it all to the person he has wronged. 8But if that
person has no close relative to whom restitution can be made for
the wrong, the restitution belongs to the LORD and must be given
to the priest, along with the ram with which atonement is made
for him. 9All the sacred contributions the Israelites bring to a priest
will belong to him. 10Each man's sacred gifts are his own, but what
he gives to the priest will belong to the priest.'"

*The Test for an Unfaithful Wife*

11Then the LORD said to Moses, 12"Speak to the Israelites and
say to them: 'If a man's wife goes astray and is unfaithful to him
13by sleeping with another man, and this is hidden from her husband and her impurity is undetected (since there is no witness
against her and she has not been caught in the act), 14and if feelings
of jealousy come over her husband and he suspects his wife and
she is impure—or if he is jealous and suspects her even though she
is not impure— 15then he is to take his wife to the priest. He must
also take an offering of a tenth of an ephah[d] of barley flour on her
behalf. He must not pour oil on it or put incense on it, because it
is a grain offering for jealousy, a reminder offering to draw attention to guilt.
16" 'The priest shall bring her and have her stand before the
LORD. 17Then he shall take some holy water in a clay jar and put
some dust from the tabernacle floor into the water. 18After the
priest has had the woman stand before the LORD, he shall loosen
her hair and place in her hands the reminder offering, the grain
offering for jealousy, while he himself holds the bitter water that
brings a curse. 19Then the priest shall put the woman under oath
and say to her, "If no other man has slept with you and you have
not gone astray and become impure while married to your husband, may this bitter water that brings a curse not harm you. 20But
if you have gone astray while married to your husband and you
have defiled yourself by sleeping with a man other than your
husband"— 21here the priest is to put the woman under this curse

NIV [b] 2 Traditionally *leprosy;* the Hebrew word was used for various diseases affecting the skin—not necessarily leprosy. [c] *6* Or *woman commits any wrong common to mankind* [d] *15* That is, probably about 2 quarts (about 2 liters)

## King James

21Then the priest shall charge the woman with an oath of cursing, and the priest shall say unto the woman, The LORD make thee a curse and an oath among thy people, when the LORD doth make thy thigh to rot, and thy belly to swell;

22And this water that causeth the curse shall go into thy bowels, to make *thy* belly to swell, and *thy* thigh to rot: And the woman shall say, Amen, amen.

23And the priest shall write these curses in a book, and he shall blot *them* out with the bitter water:

24And he shall cause the woman to drink the bitter water that causeth the curse: and the water that causeth the curse shall enter into her, *and become* bitter.

25Then the priest shall take the jealousy offering out of the woman's hand, and shall wave the offering before the LORD, and offer it upon the altar:

26And the priest shall take an handful of the offering, *even* the memorial thereof, and burn *it* upon the altar, and afterward shall cause the woman to drink the water.

27And when he hath made her to drink the water, then it shall come to pass, *that*, if she be defiled, and have done trespass against her husband, that the water that causeth the curse shall enter into her, *and become* bitter, and her belly shall swell, and her thigh shall rot: and the woman shall be a curse among her people.

28And if the woman be not defiled, but be clean; then she shall be free, and shall conceive seed.

29This *is* the law of jealousies, when a wife goeth aside *to another* instead of her husband, and is defiled;

30Or when the spirit of jealousy cometh upon him, and he be jealous over his wife, and shall set the woman before the LORD, and the priest shall execute upon her all this law.

31Then shall the man be guiltless from iniquity, and this woman shall bear her iniquity.

6 AND THE LORD spake unto Moses, saying,

2Speak unto the children of Israel, and say unto them, When either man or woman shall separate *themselves* to vow a vow of a Nazarite, to separate *themselves* unto the LORD:

3He shall separate *himself* from wine and strong drink, and shall drink no vinegar of wine, or vinegar of strong drink, neither shall he drink any liquor of grapes, nor eat moist grapes, or dried.

4All the days of his separation shall he eat nothing that is made of the vine tree, from the kernels even to the husk.

5All the days of the vow of his separation there shall no razor come upon his head: until the days be fulfilled, in the which he separateth *himself* unto the LORD, he shall be holy, *and* shall let the locks of the hair of his head grow.

6All the days that he separateth *himself* unto the LORD he shall come at no dead body.

7He shall not make himself unclean for his father, or for his mother, for his brother, or for his sister, when they die: because the consecration of his God *is* upon his head.

8All the days of his separation he *is* holy unto the LORD.

9And if any man die very suddenly by him, and he hath defiled the head of his consecration; then he shall shave his head in the day of his cleansing, on the seventh day shall he shave it.

10And on the eighth day he shall bring two turtles, or two young pigeons, to the priest, to the door of the tabernacle of the congregation:

11And the priest shall offer the one for a sin offering, and the other for a burnt offering, and make an atonement for him, for that he sinned by the dead, and shall hallow his head that same day.

12And he shall consecrate unto the LORD the days of his separation, and shall bring a lamb of the first year for a trespass offering: but the days that were before shall be lost, because his separation was defiled.

## Amplified

21Then the priests shall make the woman take the oath of the curse, and say to the woman, The Lord make you a curse and an oath among your people, when the Lord makes your thigh fall away and your body swell;

22May this water that brings the curse go into your bowels and make your body swell and your thigh fall away. And the woman shall say, So let it be, so let it be.

23The priest shall then write these curses in a book, and shall wash them off into the water of bitterness;

24And he shall cause the woman to drink the water of bitterness that brings the curse, and the water that brings the curse shall enter into her [to try her] bitterly.

25Then the priest shall take the cereal offering of jealousy *and* suspicion out of the woman's hand and shall wave the offering before the Lord and offer it upon the altar.

26And the priest shall take a handful of the cereal offering, as the memorial portion of it, and burn it on the altar and afterward shall cause the woman to drink the water.

27And when he has made her drink the water, then if she is defiled and has committed a trespass against her husband, the curse water which she drank shall be bitterness and cause her body to swell and her thigh to fall away, and the woman shall be a curse among her people.

28But if the woman is not defiled, and is clean, then she shall be free [from the curse] and be able to have children.

29This is the law of jealousy *and* suspicion when a wife goes aside to another instead of her husband and is defiled;

30Or when the spirit of jealousy *and* suspicion comes upon a man and he is jealous *and* suspicious of his wife; then shall he set the woman before the Lord, and the priest shall execute on her all this law.

31The [husband] shall be free from iniquity *and* guilt, and that woman [if guilty] shall bear her iniquity.

6 AND THE Lord said to Moses,

2Say to the Israelites, When either man or woman shall make a special vow, the vow of a Nazirite, that is, one separated *and* consecrated to the Lord,

3He shall separate himself from wine and strong drink, he shall drink no vinegar of wine or of strong drink, and shall drink no grape juice, or eat grapes, fresh or dried. [Luke 1:15.]

4All the days of his separation he shall eat nothing produced from the grapevine, not even the seeds or the skins.

5All the days of the vow of his separation *and* abstinence there shall no razor come upon his head. Until the time is completed for which he separates himself to the Lord, he shall be holy, and shall let the locks of the hair of his head grow long.

6All the days that he separates himself to the Lord he shall not go near a dead body.

7He shall not make himself unclean for his father, mother, brother, or sister, when they die; because his separation *and* abstinence to his God is upon his head.

8All the days of his separation *and* abstinence he is holy to the Lord.

9And if any man die very suddenly beside him and he has defiled his consecrated head, then he shall shave his head on the day of his cleansing; on the seventh day shall he shave it.

10On the eighth day he shall bring two turtledoves or two young pigeons to the priest to the door of the tent of meeting,

11And the priest shall offer the one for a sin offering and the other for a burnt offering, and make atonement for him, because he sinned by reason of the dead body. He shall consecrate his head the same day,

12And he shall consecrate *and* separate himself to the Lord for the days of his separation, and shall bring a male lamb a year old for a trespass *or* guilt offering; but the previous days shall be void *and* lost, because his separation was defiled.

## New American Standard

21(then the priest shall have the woman swear with the oath of
the curse, and the priest shall say to the woman), "the LORD make
you a curse and an oath among your people by the LORD's making
your thigh waste away and your abdomen swell;
22and this water that brings a curse shall go into your stomach,
and make your abdomen swell and your thigh waste away." And
the woman shall say, "Amen. Amen."
**23**¶ 'The priest shall then write these curses on a scroll, and he
shall wash them off into the water of bitterness.
24'Then he shall make the woman drink the water of bitterness
that brings a curse, so that the water which brings a curse will go
into her and *cause* bitterness.
25'And the priest shall take the grain offering of jealousy from
the woman's hand, and he shall wave the grain offering before the
LORD and bring it to the altar;
26and the priest shall take a handful of the grain offering as its
memorial offering and offer *it* up in smoke on the altar, and afterward he shall make the woman drink the water.
27'When he has made her drink the water, then it shall come
about, if she has defiled herself and has been unfaithful to her
husband, that the water which brings a curse shall go into her and
*cause* bitterness, and her abdomen will swell and her thigh will
waste away, and the woman will become a curse among her
people.
28'But if the woman has not defiled herself and is clean, she will
then be free and conceive children.
**29**¶ 'This is the law of jealousy: when a wife, *being* under *the
authority of* her husband, goes astray and defiles herself,
30or when a spirit of jealousy comes over a man and he is jealous
of his wife, he shall then make the woman stand before the LORD,
and the priest shall apply all this law to her.
31'Moreover, the man shall be free from guilt, but that woman
shall bear her guilt.'"

*Law of the Nazirites*

6 AGAIN THE LORD spoke to Moses, saying,
2"Speak to the sons of Israel, and say to them, 'When a man
or woman makes a special vow, the vow of a [a]Nazirite, to dedicate
himself to the LORD,
3he shall abstain from wine and strong drink; he shall drink no
vinegar, whether made from wine or strong drink, neither shall he
drink any grape juice, nor eat fresh or dried grapes.
4'All the days of his [b]separation he shall not eat anything that
is produced by the grape vine, from *the* seeds even to *the* skin.
**5**¶ 'All the days of his vow of separation no razor shall pass over
his head. He shall be holy until the days are fulfilled for which he
separated himself to the LORD; he shall let the locks of hair on his
head grow long.
**6**¶ 'All the days of his separation to the LORD he shall not go
near to a dead person.
7'He shall not make himself unclean for his father or for his
mother, for his brother or for his sister, when they die, because his
separation to God is on his head.
8'All the days of his separation he is holy to the LORD.
**9**¶ 'But if a man dies very suddenly beside him and he defiles
his dedicated head *of hair,* then he shall shave his head on the day
when he becomes clean; he shall shave it on the seventh day.
10'Then on the eighth day he shall bring two turtledoves or two
young pigeons to the priest, to the doorway of the tent of meeting.
11'And the priest shall offer one for a sin offering and *the* other
for a burnt offering, and make atonement for him concerning his
sin because of the *dead* person. And that same day he shall consecrate his head,
12and shall dedicate to the LORD his days as a Nazirite, and shall
bring a male lamb a year old for a guilt offering; but the former days
shall be void because his separation was defiled.

NAS [a] I.e., one separated [b] Or, *living as a Nazirite,* and so through v. 21

## New International

of the oath—"may the LORD cause your people to curse and denounce you when he causes your thigh to waste away and your
abdomen to swell.[c] 22May this water that brings a curse enter your
body so that your abdomen swells and your thigh wastes away.[d]"
" 'Then the woman is to say, "Amen. So be it."
23" 'The priest is to write these curses on a scroll and then wash
them off into the bitter water. 24He shall have the woman drink
the bitter water that brings a curse, and this water will enter her
and cause bitter suffering. 25The priest is to take from her hands
the grain offering for jealousy, wave it before the LORD and bring
it to the altar. 26The priest is then to take a handful of the grain
offering as a memorial offering and burn it on the altar; after that,
he is to have the woman drink the water. 27If she has defiled
herself and been unfaithful to her husband, then when she is made
to drink the water that brings a curse, it will go into her and cause
bitter suffering; her abdomen will swell and her thigh waste
away,[e] and she will become accursed among her people. 28If,
however, the woman has not defiled herself and is free from
impurity, she will be cleared of guilt and will be able to have
children.
29" 'This, then, is the law of jealousy when a woman goes astray
and defiles herself while married to her husband, 30or when feelings of jealousy come over a man because he suspects his wife. The
priest is to have her stand before the LORD and is to apply this
entire law to her. 31The husband will be innocent of any wrongdoing, but the woman will bear the consequences of her sin.' "

*The Nazirite*

6 THE LORD said to Moses, 2"Speak to the Israelites and say
to them: 'If a man or woman wants to make a special vow,
a vow of separation to the LORD as a Nazirite, 3he must abstain
from wine and other fermented drink and must not drink vinegar
made from wine or from other fermented drink. He must not drink
grape juice or eat grapes or raisins. 4As long as he is a Nazirite, he
must not eat anything that comes from the grapevine, not even the
seeds or skins.
5" 'During the entire period of his vow of separation no razor
may be used on his head. He must be holy until the period of his
separation to the LORD is over; he must let the hair of his head grow
long. 6Throughout the period of his separation to the LORD he
must not go near a dead body. 7Even if his own father or mother
or brother or sister dies, he must not make himself ceremonially
unclean on account of them, because the symbol of his separation
to God is on his head. 8Throughout the period of his separation
he is consecrated to the LORD.
9" 'If someone dies suddenly in his presence, thus defiling the
hair he has dedicated, he must shave his head on the day of his
cleansing—the seventh day. 10Then on the eighth day he must
bring two doves or two young pigeons to the priest at the entrance
to the Tent of Meeting. 11The priest is to offer one as a sin offering
and the other as a burnt offering to make atonement for him
because he sinned by being in the presence of the dead body. That
same day he is to consecrate his head. 12He must dedicate himself
to the LORD for the period of his separation and must bring a
year-old male lamb as a guilt offering. The previous days do not
count, because he became defiled during his separation.

NIV [c] 21 Or *causes you to have a miscarrying womb and barrenness* [d] 22 Or *body and cause you to be barren and have a miscarrying womb* [e] 27 Or *suffering; she will have barrenness and a miscarrying womb*

## King James

13¶ And this *is* the law of the Nazarite, when the days of his separation are fulfilled: he shall be brought unto the door of the tabernacle of the congregation:

14And he shall offer his offering unto the LORD, one he lamb of the first year without blemish for a burnt offering, and one ewe lamb of the first year without blemish for a sin offering, and one ram without blemish for peace offerings,

15And a basket of unleavened bread, cakes of fine flour mingled with oil, and wafers of unleavened bread anointed with oil, and their meat offering, and their drink offerings.

16And the priest shall bring *them* before the LORD, and shall offer his sin offering, and his burnt offering:

17And he shall offer the ram *for* a sacrifice of peace offerings unto the LORD, with the basket of unleavened bread: the priest shall offer also his meat offering, and his drink offering.

18And the Nazarite shall shave the head of his separation *at* the door of the tabernacle of the congregation, and shall take the hair of the head of his separation, and put *it* in the fire which *is* under the sacrifice of the peace offerings.

19And the priest shall take the sodden shoulder of the ram, and one unleavened cake out of the basket, and one unleavened wafer, and shall put *them* upon the hands of the Nazarite, after *the hair of* his separation is shaven:

20And the priest shall wave them *for* a wave offering before the LORD: this *is* holy for the priest, with the wave breast and heave shoulder: and after that the Nazarite may drink wine.

21This *is* the law of the Nazarite who hath vowed, *and of* his offering unto the LORD for his separation, beside *that* that his hand shall get: according to the vow which he vowed, so he must do after the law of his separation.

22¶ And the LORD spake unto Moses, saying,

23Speak unto Aaron and unto his sons, saying, On this wise ye shall bless the children of Israel, saying unto them,

24The LORD bless thee, and keep thee:

25The LORD make his face shine upon thee, and be gracious unto thee:

26The LORD lift up his countenance upon thee, and give thee peace.

27And they shall put my name upon the children of Israel; and I will bless them.

**7** AND IT came to pass on the day that Moses had fully set up the tabernacle, and had anointed it, and sanctified it, and all the instruments thereof, both the altar and all the vessels thereof, and had anointed them, and sanctified them;

2That the princes of Israel, heads of the house of their fathers, who *were* the princes of the tribes, and were over them that were numbered, offered:

3And they brought their offering before the LORD, six covered wagons, and twelve oxen; a wagon for two of the princes, and for each one an ox: and they brought them before the tabernacle.

4And the LORD spake unto Moses, saying,

5Take *it* of them, that they may be to do the service of the tabernacle of the congregation; and thou shalt give them unto the Levites, to every man according to his service.

6And Moses took the wagons and the oxen, and gave them unto the Levites.

7Two wagons and four oxen he gave unto the sons of Gershon, according to their service:

8And four wagons and eight oxen he gave unto the sons of Merari, according unto their service, under the hand of Ithamar the son of Aaron the priest.

## Amplified

13And this is the law of the Nazirite, when the days of his separation *and* abstinence are fulfilled: he shall be brought to the door of the tent of meeting,

14And he shall offer his gift to the Lord, one he-lamb a year old without blemish for a burnt offering, and one ewe lamb a year old without blemish for a sin offering, and one ram without blemish for a peace offering,

15And a basket of unleavened bread, cakes of fine flour mingled with oil, and wafers of unleavened bread spread with oil, and their cereal offering, and their drink offerings.

16And the priest shall present them before the Lord, and shall offer the person's sin offering and his burnt offering.

17And he shall offer the ram for a sacrifice of peace offerings to the Lord, with the basket of unleavened bread; the priest shall offer also its cereal offering, and its drink offering.

18And the Nazirite shall shave his consecrated head at the door of the tent of meeting, and shall take the hair and put it on the fire which is under the sacrifice of the peace offerings.

19And the priest shall take the boiled shoulder of the ram, and one unleavened cake out of the basket, and one unleavened wafer, and shall put them upon the hands of the Nazirite, after he has shaven the hair of his separation *and* abstinence.

20And the priest shall wave them for a wave offering before the Lord; they are a holy portion for the priest, with the breast that is waved and the thigh *or* shoulder that is offered; and after that the Nazirite may drink wine.

21This is the law for the Nazirite who has made a vow. His offering to the Lord, besides what else he is able to afford, shall be according to the vow which he has vowed, so shall he do according to the law for his separation *and* abstinence [as a Nazirite]. [Act 21:24, 26.]

22And the Lord said to Moses,

23Say to Aaron and his sons, This is the way you shall bless the Israelites. Say to them,

24The Lord bless you, and watch, guard *and* keep you;

25The Lord make His face to shine upon *and* enlighten you and be gracious (kind, merciful, and giving favor) to you.

26The Lord lift up His [approving] countenance upon you, and give you peace [tranquility of heart *and* life continually].

27And they shall put My name upon the Israelites, and I will bless them.

**7** ON THE day that Moses had fully completed setting up the tabernacle, and had anointed and consecrated it and all its furniture, and the altar and all its utensils, and had anointed and set them apart for holy use,

2The princes *or* leaders of Israel, heads of their fathers' houses, made offerings. These were the leaders of the tribes and were over those who were numbered.

3And they brought their offering before the Lord, six covered wagons and twelve oxen; a wagon for each two of the princes *or* leaders, and an ox for each one; and they brought them before the tabernacle.

4Then the Lord said to Moses,

5Accept the things from them, that they may be used in doing the service of the tent of meeting, and give them to the Levites, to each man according to his service.

6So Moses took the wagons and the oxen, and gave them to the Levites.

7Two wagons and four oxen he gave to the sons of Gershon, according to their service;

8And four wagons and eight oxen he gave to the sons of Merari, according to their service, under the supervision of Ithamar the son of Aaron the [high] priest.

## New American Standard

13¶ 'Now this is the law of the Nazirite when the days of his
separation are fulfilled, he shall bring the offering to the doorway
of the tent of meeting.
14'And he shall present his offering to the LORD: one male lamb
a year old without defect for a burnt offering and one ewe-lamb
a year old without defect for a sin offering and one ram without
defect for a peace offering,
15and a basket of unleavened cakes of fine flour mixed with oil
and unleavened wafers spread with oil, along with their grain
offering and their libations.
16'Then the priest shall present *them* before the LORD and shall
offer his sin offering and his burnt offering.
17'He shall also offer the ram for a sacrifice of peace offerings
to the LORD, together with the basket of unleavened cakes; the
priest shall likewise offer its grain offering and its libation.
18'The Nazirite shall then shave his dedicated head *of hair* at the
doorway of the tent of meeting, and take the dedicated hair of his
head and put *it* on the fire which is under the sacrifice of peace
offerings.
19'And the priest shall take the ram's shoulder *when it has been*
boiled, and one unleavened cake out of the basket, and one unleavened wafer, and shall put *them* on the hands of the Nazirite
after he has shaved his dedicated *hair.*
20'Then the priest shall wave them for a wave offering before
the LORD. It is holy for the priest, together with the breast offered
by waving and the thigh offered by lifting up; and afterward the
Nazirite may drink wine.'
21¶ "This is the law of the Nazirite who vows his offering to the
LORD according to his separation, in addition to what *else* he can
afford; according to his vow which he takes, so he shall do according to the law of his separation."

*Aaron's Benediction*

22¶ Then the LORD spoke to Moses, saying,
23"Speak to Aaron and to his sons, saying, 'Thus you shall bless
the sons of Israel. You shall say to them:

24¶ The LORD bless you, and keep you;
25¶ The LORD make His face shine on you,
And be gracious to you;
26¶ The LORD lift up His countenance on you,
And give you peace.'

27"So they shall invoke My name on the sons of Israel, and I
then will bless them."

*Offerings of the Leaders*

7 NOW IT came about on the day that Moses had finished
setting up the tabernacle, he anointed it and consecrated it
with all its furnishings and the altar and all its utensils; he anointed
them and consecrated them also.
2Then the leaders of Israel, the heads of their fathers'
households, made an offering (they were the leaders of the tribes;
they were the ones who were over the numbered men).
3When they brought their offering before the LORD, six covered
carts and twelve oxen, a cart for *every* two of the leaders and an
ox for each one, then they presented them before the tabernacle.
4Then the LORD spoke to Moses, saying,
5"Accept *these things* from them, that they may be used in the
service of the tent of meeting, and you shall give them to the
Levites, *to* each man according to his service."
6So Moses took the carts and the oxen, and gave them to the
Levites.
7Two carts and four oxen he gave to the sons of Gershon,
according to their service,
8and four carts and eight oxen he gave to the sons of Merari,
according to their service, under the direction of Ithamar the son
of Aaron the priest.

## New International

13" 'Now this is the law for the Nazirite when the period of his
separation is over. He is to be brought to the entrance to the Tent
of Meeting. 14There he is to present his offerings to the LORD: a
year-old male lamb without defect for a burnt offering, a year-old
ewe lamb without defect for a sin offering, a ram without defect
for a fellowship offering,[a] 15together with their grain offerings and
drink offerings, and a basket of bread made without yeast—cakes
made of fine flour mixed with oil, and wafers spread with oil.
16" 'The priest is to present them before the LORD and make the
sin offering and the burnt offering. 17He is to present the basket
of unleavened bread and is to sacrifice the ram as a fellowship
offering to the LORD, together with its grain offering and drink
offering.
18" 'Then at the entrance to the Tent of Meeting, the Nazirite
must shave off the hair that he dedicated. He is to take the hair and
put it in the fire that is under the sacrifice of the fellowship offering.
19" 'After the Nazirite has shaved off the hair of his dedication,
the priest is to place in his hands a boiled shoulder of the ram, and
a cake and a wafer from the basket, both made without yeast.
20The priest shall then wave them before the LORD as a wave
offering; they are holy and belong to the priest, together with the
breast that was waved and the thigh that was presented. After
that, the Nazirite may drink wine.
21" 'This is the law of the Nazirite who vows his offering to the
LORD in accordance with his separation, in addition to whatever
else he can afford. He must fulfill the vow he has made, according
to the law of the Nazirite.' "

*The Priestly Blessing*

22The LORD said to Moses, 23"Tell Aaron and his sons, 'This is
how you are to bless the Israelites. Say to them:

24" ' "The LORD bless you
and keep you;
25the LORD make his face shine upon you
and be gracious to you;
26the LORD turn his face toward you
and give you peace." '

27"So they will put my name on the Israelites, and I will bless
them."

*Offerings at the Dedication of the Tabernacle*

7 WHEN MOSES finished setting up the tabernacle, he anointed it and consecrated it and all its furnishings. He also anointed and consecrated the altar and all its utensils. 2Then the leaders
of Israel, the heads of families who were the tribal leaders in charge
of those who were counted, made offerings. 3They brought as their
gifts before the LORD six covered carts and twelve oxen—an ox
from each leader and a cart from every two. These they presented
before the tabernacle.
4The LORD said to Moses, 5"Accept these from them, that they
may be used in the work at the Tent of Meeting. Give them to the
Levites as each man's work requires."
6So Moses took the carts and oxen and gave them to the Levites.
7He gave two carts and four oxen to the Gershonites, as their work
required, 8and he gave four carts and eight oxen to the Merarites,
as their work required. They were all under the direction of Ithamar son of Aaron, the priest. 9But Moses did not give any to the

NIV [a] 14 Traditionally *peace offering;* also in verses 17 and 18

## King James

9But unto the sons of Kohath he gave none: because the service of the sanctuary belonging unto them *was that* they should bear upon their shoulders.

10¶ And the princes offered for dedicating of the altar in the day that it was anointed, even the princes offered their offering before the altar.

11And the LORD said unto Moses, They shall offer their offering, each prince on his day, for the dedicating of the altar.

12¶ And he that offered his offering the first day was Nahshon the son of Amminadab, of the tribe of Judah:

13And his offering *was* one silver charger, the weight thereof *was* an hundred and thirty *shekels*, one silver bowl of seventy shekels, after the shekel of the sanctuary; both of them *were* full of fine flour mingled with oil for a meat offering:

14One spoon of ten *shekels* of gold, full of incense:

15One young bullock, one ram, one lamb of the first year, for a burnt offering:

16One kid of the goats for a sin offering:

17And for a sacrifice of peace offerings, two oxen, five rams, five he goats, five lambs of the first year: this *was* the offering of Nahshon the son of Amminadab.

18¶ On the second day Nethaneel the son of Zuar, prince of Issachar, did offer:

19He offered *for* his offering one silver charger, the weight whereof *was* an hundred and thirty *shekels*, one silver bowl of seventy shekels, after the shekel of the sanctuary; both of them full of fine flour mingled with oil for a meat offering:

20One spoon of gold of ten *shekels*, full of incense:

21One young bullock, one ram, one lamb of the first year, for a burnt offering:

22One kid of the goats for a sin offering:

23And for a sacrifice of peace offerings, two oxen, five rams, five he goats, five lambs of the first year: this *was* the offering of Nethaneel the son of Zuar.

24¶ On the third day Eliab the son of Helon, prince of the children of Zebulun, *did offer:*

25His offering *was* one silver charger, the weight whereof *was* an hundred and thirty *shekels*, one silver bowl of seventy shekels, after the shekel of the sanctuary; both of them full of fine flour mingled with oil for a meat offering:

26One golden spoon of ten *shekels*, full of incense:

27One young bullock, one ram, one lamb of the first year, for a burnt offering:

28One kid of the goats for a sin offering:

29And for a sacrifice of peace offerings, two oxen, five rams, five he goats, five lambs of the first year: this *was* the offering of Eliab the son of Helon.

30¶ On the fourth day Elizur the son of Shedeur, prince of the children of Reuben, *did offer:*

31His offering *was* one silver charger of the weight of an hundred and thirty *shekels*, one silver bowl of seventy shekels, after the shekel of the sanctuary; both of them full of fine flour mingled with oil for a meat offering:

32One golden spoon of ten *shekels*, full of incense:

## Amplified

9But to the sons of Kohath he gave none; because they were assigned the care of the sanctuary *and* the holy things which had to be carried on their shoulders.

10And the princes *or* leaders offered sacrifices for the dedication of the altar [of burnt offering] on the day that it was anointed; and they offered their sacrifice before the altar.

11And the Lord said to Moses, They shall offer their offerings, each prince *or* leader on his day, for the dedication of the altar.

12He who offered his offering the first day was Nahshon son of Amminadab, of the tribe of Judah.

13And his offering was one silver platter, the weight of which was 130 shekels, one silver basin of seventy shekels, according to the shekel of the sanctuary, both of them full of fine flour mixed with oil for a cereal offering;

14One golden bowl of ten shekels, full of incense;

15One young bull, one ram, one male lamb a year old, for a burnt offering;

16One male goat for a sin offering;

17And [a]for the sacrifice of peace offerings, two oxen, five rams, five male goats, five male lambs a year old. This was the offering of Nahshon son of Amminadab.

18The second day Nethanel son of Zuar, leader [of the tribe] of Issachar, offered.

19He gave for his offering one silver platter, the weight of which was 130 shekels, one silver basin of seventy shekels, after the shekel of the sanctuary, both of them full of fine flour mixed with oil for a cereal offering;

20One golden bowl of ten shekels, full of incense;

21One young bull, one ram, one male lamb a year old, for a burnt offering;

22One male goat for a sin offering;

23And for the sacrifice of peace offerings, two oxen, five rams, five male goats, five male lambs a year old. This was the offering of Nethanel son of Zuar.

24The third day Eliab son of Helon, leader of the sons of Zebulun, offered.

25His offering was one silver platter, the weight of which was 130 shekels, one silver basin of seventy shekels, after the shekel of the sanctuary, both of them full of fine flour mixed with oil for a cereal offering;

26One golden bowl of ten shekels, full of incense;

27One young bull, one ram, one male lamb a year old, for a burnt offering;

28One male goat for a sin offering;

29And for the sacrifice of peace offerings, two oxen, five rams, five male goats, five male lambs a year old. This was the offering of Eliab son of Helon.

30The fourth day Elizur son of Shedeur, leader of the sons of Reuben, offered.

31His offering was one silver platter of the weight of 130 shekels, one silver basin of seventy shekels, after the shekel of the sanctuary, both of them full of fine flour mixed with oil for a cereal offering;

32One golden bowl of ten shekels, full of incense;

**AMP** [a] Verses 12 to 17 give the detailed description of one tribe leader's offering. Then, instead of saying that the gifts of the other tribe leaders were exactly like this one and naming the leaders, the record goes on for *seventy* verses repeating what has already been said, *eleven* more times! Why? These things "were written for our learning" (Rom. 15:4). Let us seek the answer. Other commentators give *Matthew Henry* credit for giving the correct view. He says that, both by appointing that each tribal leader was to have a separate day for his gift, and in giving the reports equal space, regardless of the contrast in the tribe's strength and rank in the camp, God had a definite purpose. It was "that an equal honor might thereby be put on each several tribe . . . Thus it was intimated that all the tribes of Israel had an equal share in the altar, and an equal share in the sacrifices that were offered upon it. Though one tribe was posted more honorably in the camp than another, yet they and their services were all alike acceptable to God . . . Rich and poor meet together before God . . . He was letting us know that what is given is lent to the Lord, and He carefully records it, with every one's name prefixed to his gift, because what is so given (as a labor of love, Heb. 6:10) He will repay. Christ took particular notice of what was cast into the treasury (Mark 12:41)."

## New American Standard

9But he did not give *any* to the sons of Kohath because theirs
*was* the service of the holy *objects, which* they carried on the shoulder.
10And the leaders offered the dedication *offering* for the altar
when it was anointed, so the leaders offered their offering before
the altar.
11Then the LORD said to Moses, "Let them present their offering, one leader each day, for the dedication of the altar."
**12**¶ Now the one who presented his offering on the first day *was*
Nahshon the son of Amminadab, of the tribe of Judah;
13and his offering *was* one silver [b]dish whose weight *was* one
hundred and thirty *shekels*, one silver bowl of seventy shekels,
according to [c]the shekel of the sanctuary, both of them full of fine
flour mixed with oil for a grain offering;
14one gold pan of ten *shekels*, full of incense;
15one bull, one ram, one male lamb one year old, for a burnt
offering;
16one male goat for a sin offering;
17and for the sacrifice of peace offerings, two oxen, five rams,
five male goats, five male lambs one year old. This *was* the offering
of Nahshon the son of Amminadab.
**18**¶ On the second day Nethanel the son of Zuar, leader of
Issachar, presented *an offering;*
19he presented as his offering one silver dish whose weight *was*
one hundred and thirty *shekels*, one silver bowl of seventy shekels,
according to the shekel of the sanctuary, both of them full of fine
flour mixed with oil for a grain offering;
20one gold pan of ten *shekels*, full of incense;
21one bull, one ram, one male lamb one year old, for a burnt
offering;
22one male goat for a sin offering;
23and for the sacrifice of peace offerings, two oxen, five rams,
five male goats, five male lambs one year old. This *was* the offering
of Nethanel the son of Zuar.
**24**¶ On the third day *it was* Eliab the son of Helon, leader of the
sons of Zebulun;
25his offering *was* one silver dish whose weight *was* one hundred and thirty *shekels*, one silver bowl of seventy shekels, according to the shekel of the sanctuary, both of them full of fine flour
mixed with oil for a grain offering;
26one gold pan of ten *shekels*, full of incense;
27one young bull, one ram, one male lamb one year old, for a
burnt offering;
28one male goat for a sin offering;
29and for the sacrifice of peace offerings, two oxen, five rams,
five male goats, five male lambs one year old. This *was* the offering
of Eliab the son of Helon.
**30**¶ On the fourth day *it was* Elizur the son of Shedeur, leader
of the sons of Reuben;
31his offering *was* one silver dish whose weight *was* one hundred and thirty *shekels*, one silver bowl of seventy shekels, according to the shekel of the sanctuary, both of them full of fine flour
mixed with oil for a grain offering;
32one gold pan of ten *shekels*, full of incense;

NAS [b] Or, *platter*, and so through v. 85 [c] I.e., Approx. one-half ounce, and so through v. 86

## New International

Kohathites, because they were to carry on their shoulders the holy
things, for which they were responsible.
10When the altar was anointed, the leaders brought their offerings for its dedication and presented them before the altar. 11For
the LORD had said to Moses, "Each day one leader is to bring his
offering for the dedication of the altar."

12The one who brought his offering on the first day was Nahshon
son of Amminadab of the tribe of Judah.
13His offering was one silver plate weighing a hundred and
thirty shekels,[d] and one silver sprinkling bowl weighing seventy shekels,[e] both according to the sanctuary shekel, each
filled with fine flour mixed with oil as a grain offering; 14one
gold dish weighing ten shekels,[f] filled with incense; 15one
young bull, one ram and one male lamb a year old, for a burnt
offering; 16one male goat for a sin offering; 17and two oxen,
five rams, five male goats and five male lambs a year old, to
be sacrificed as a fellowship offering.[g] This was the offering
of Nahshon son of Amminadab.

18On the second day Nethanel son of Zuar, the leader of Issachar,
brought his offering.
19The offering he brought was one silver plate weighing a
hundred and thirty shekels, and one silver sprinkling bowl
weighing seventy shekels, both according to the sanctuary
shekel, each filled with fine flour mixed with oil as a grain
offering; 20one gold dish weighing ten shekels, filled with
incense; 21one young bull, one ram and one male lamb a year
old, for a burnt offering; 22one male goat for a sin offering;
23and two oxen, five rams, five male goats and five male lambs
a year old, to be sacrificed as a fellowship offering. This was
the offering of Nethanel son of Zuar.

24On the third day, Eliab son of Helon, the leader of the people of
Zebulun, brought his offering.
25His offering was one silver plate weighing a hundred and
thirty shekels, and one silver sprinkling bowl weighing seventy shekels, both according to the sanctuary shekel, each
filled with fine flour mixed with oil as a grain offering; 26one
gold dish weighing ten shekels, filled with incense; 27one
young bull, one ram and one male lamb a year old, for a burnt
offering; 28one male goat for a sin offering; 29and two oxen,
five rams, five male goats and five male lambs a year old, to
be sacrificed as a fellowship offering. This was the offering of
Eliab son of Helon.

30On the fourth day Elizur son of Shedeur, the leader of the people
of Reuben, brought his offering.
31His offering was one silver plate weighing a hundred and
thirty shekels, and one silver sprinkling bowl weighing seventy shekels, both according to the sanctuary shekel, each
filled with fine flour mixed with oil as a grain offering; 32one
gold dish weighing ten shekels, filled with incense; 33one

NIV [d] *13* That is, about 3 1/4 pounds (about 1.5 kilograms); also elsewhere in this chapter [e] *13* That is, about 1 3/4 pounds (about 0.8 kilogram); also elsewhere in this chapter [f] *14* That is, about 4 ounces (about 110 grams); also elsewhere in this chapter [g] *17* Traditionally *peace offering;* also elsewhere in this chapter

## King James

33One young bullock, one ram, one lamb of the first year, for a burnt offering:
34One kid of the goats for a sin offering:
35And for a sacrifice of peace offerings, two oxen, five rams, five he goats, five lambs of the first year: this *was* the offering of Elizur the son of Shedeur.
36¶ On the fifth day Shelumiel the son of Zurishaddai, prince of the children of Simeon, *did offer:*
37His offering *was* one silver charger, the weight whereof *was* an hundred and thirty *shekels,* one silver bowl of seventy shekels, after the shekel of the sanctuary; both of them full of fine flour mingled with oil for a meat offering:
38One golden spoon of ten *shekels,* full of incense:
39One young bullock, one ram, one lamb of the first year, for a burnt offering:
40One kid of the goats for a sin offering:
41And for a sacrifice of peace offerings, two oxen, five rams, five he goats, five lambs of the first year: this *was* the offering of Shelumiel the son of Zurishaddai.
42¶ On the sixth day Eliasaph the son of Deuel, prince of the children of Gad, *offered:*
43His offering *was* one silver charger of the weight of an hundred and thirty *shekels,* a silver bowl of seventy shekels, after the shekel of the sanctuary; both of them full of fine flour mingled with oil for a meat offering:
44One golden spoon of ten *shekels,* full of incense:
45One young bullock, one ram, one lamb of the first year, for a burnt offering:
46One kid of the goats for a sin offering:
47And for a sacrifice of peace offerings, two oxen, five rams, five he goats, five lambs of the first year: this *was* the offering of Eliasaph the son of Deuel.
48¶ On the seventh day Elishama the son of Ammihud, prince of the children of Ephraim, *offered:*
49His offering *was* one silver charger, the weight whereof *was* an hundred and thirty *shekels,* one silver bowl of seventy shekels, after the shekel of the sanctuary; both of them full of fine flour mingled with oil for a meat offering:
50One golden spoon of ten *shekels,* full of incense:
51One young bullock, one ram, one lamb of the first year, for a burnt offering:
52One kid of the goats for a sin offering:
53And for a sacrifice of peace offerings, two oxen, five rams, five he goats, five lambs of the first year: this *was* the offering of Elishama the son of Ammihud.
54¶ On the eighth day *offered* Gamaliel the son of Pedahzur, prince of the children of Manasseh:
55His offering *was* one silver charger of the weight of an hundred and thirty *shekels,* one silver bowl of seventy shekels, after the shekel of the sanctuary; both of them full of fine flour mingled with oil for a meat offering:
56One golden spoon of ten *shekels,* full of incense:
57One young bullock, one ram, one lamb of the first year, for a burnt offering:
58One kid of the goats for a sin offering:
59And for a sacrifice of peace offerings, two oxen, five rams, five he goats, five lambs of the first year: this *was* the offering of Gamaliel the son of Pedahzur.
60¶ On the ninth day Abidan the son of Gideoni, prince of the children of Benjamin, *offered:*
61His offering *was* one silver charger, the weight whereof *was* an hundred and thirty *shekels,* one silver bowl of seventy shekels, after the shekel of the sanctuary; both of them full of fine flour mingled with oil for a meat offering:
62One golden spoon of ten *shekels,* full of incense:
63One young bullock, one ram, one lamb of the first year, for a burnt offering:
64One kid of the goats for a sin offering:

## Amplified

33One young bull, one ram, one male lamb a year old, for a burnt offering;
34One male goat for a sin offering;
35And for the sacrifice of peace offerings, two oxen, five rams, five male goats, five male lambs a year old. This was the offering of Elizur son of Shedeur.
36The fifth day Shelumiel son of Zurishaddai, leader of the sons of Simeon, offered.
37His offering was one silver platter, the weight of which was 130 shekels, one silver basin of seventy shekels, after the shekel of the sanctuary, both of them full of fine flour mixed with oil for a cereal offering;
38One golden bowl of ten shekels, full of incense;
39One young bull, one ram, one male lamb a year old, for a burnt offering;
40One male goat for a sin offering;
41And for the sacrifice of peace offerings, two oxen, five rams, five male goats, five male lambs a year old. This was the offering of Shelumiel son of Zurishaddai.
42The sixth day Eliasaph son of Deuel, leader of the sons of Gad, offered.
43His offering was one silver platter of the weight of 130 shekels, a silver basin of seventy shekels, after the shekel of the sanctuary, both of them full of fine flour mixed with oil for a cereal offering;
44One golden bowl of ten shekels, full of incense;
45One young bull, one ram, one male lamb a year old, for a burnt offering;
46One male goat for a sin offering;
47And for the sacrifice of peace offerings, two oxen, five rams, five male goats *and* five male lambs a year old. This was the offering of Eliasaph son of Deuel.
48The seventh day Elishama son of Ammihud, leader of the sons of Ephraim, offered.
49His offering was one silver platter, the weight of which was 130 shekels, one silver basin of seventy shekels, after the shekel of the sanctuary, both of them full of fine flour mixed with oil for a cereal offering;
50One golden bowl of ten shekels, full of incense;
51One young bull, one ram, one male lamb a year old, for a burnt offering;
52One male goat for a sin offering;
53And for the sacrifice of peace offerings, two oxen, five rams, five male goats *and* five male lambs a year old. This was the offering of Elishama son of Ammihud.
54The eighth day Gamaliel son of Pedahzur, leader of the sons of Manasseh, offered.
55His offering was one silver platter of the weight of 130 shekels, one silver basin of seventy shekels, after the shekel of the sanctuary, both of them full of fine flour mixed with oil for a cereal offering;
56One golden bowl of ten shekels, full of incense;
57One young bull, one ram, one male lamb a year old, for a burnt offering;
58One male goat for a sin offering;
59And for the sacrifice of peace offerings, two oxen, five rams, five male goats, five male lambs a year old. This was the offering of Gamaliel son of Pedahzur.
60The ninth day Abidan the son of Gideoni, prince *or* leader of the sons of Benjamin, offered.
61His offering was one silver platter, the weight of which was 130 shekels, one silver basin of seventy shekels, after the shekel of the sanctuary, both of them full of fine flour mixed with oil for a cereal offering;
62One golden bowl of ten shekels, full of incense;
63One young bull, one ram, one male lamb a year old, for a burnt offering;
64One male goat for a sin offering;

## New American Standard

33one bull, one ram, one male lamb one year old, for a burnt
offering;
34one male goat for a sin offering;
35and for the sacrifice of peace offerings, two oxen, five rams,
five male goats, five male lambs one year old. This *was* the offering
of Elizur the son of Shedeur.
36¶ On the fifth day *it was* Shelumiel the son of Zurishaddai,
leader of the children of Simeon;
37his offering *was* one silver dish whose weight *was* one hundred and thirty *shekels,* one silver bowl of seventy shekels, according to the shekel of the sanctuary, both of them full of fine flour
mixed with oil for a grain offering;
38one gold pan of ten *shekels,* full of incense;
39one bull, one ram, one male lamb one year old, for a burnt
offering;
40one male goat for a sin offering;
41and for the sacrifice of peace offerings, two oxen, five rams,
five male goats, five male lambs one year old. This *was* the offering
of Shelumiel the son of Zurishaddai.
42¶ On the sixth day *it was* Eliasaph the son of Deuel, leader of
the sons of Gad;
43his offering *was* one silver dish whose weight *was* one hundred and thirty *shekels,* one silver bowl of seventy shekels, according to the shekel of the sanctuary, both of them full of fine flour
mixed with oil for a grain offering;
44one gold pan of ten *shekels,* full of incense;
45one bull, one ram, one male lamb one year old, for a burnt
offering;
46one male goat for a sin offering;
47and for the sacrifice of peace offerings, two oxen, five rams,
five male goats, five male lambs one year old. This *was* the offering
of Eliasaph the son of Deuel.
48¶ On the seventh day *it was* Elishama the son of Ammihud,
leader of the sons of Ephraim;
49his offering *was* one silver dish whose weight *was* one hundred and thirty *shekels,* one silver bowl of seventy shekels, according to the shekel of the sanctuary, both of them full of fine flour
mixed with oil for a grain offering;
50one gold pan of ten *shekels,* full of incense;
51one bull, one ram, one male lamb one year old, for a burnt
offering;
52one male goat for a sin offering;
53and for the sacrifice of peace offerings, two oxen, five rams,
five male goats, five male lambs one year old. This *was* the offering
of Elishama the son of Ammihud.
54¶ On the eighth day *it was* Gamaliel the son of Pedahzur,
leader of the sons of Manasseh;
55his offering *was* one silver dish whose weight *was* one hundred and thirty *shekels,* one silver bowl of seventy shekels, according to the shekel of the sanctuary, both of them full of fine flour
mixed with oil for a grain offering;
56one gold pan of ten *shekels,* full of incense;
57one bull, one ram, one male lamb one year old, for a burnt
offering;
58one male goat for a sin offering;
59and for the sacrifice of peace offerings, two oxen, five rams,
five male goats, five male lambs one year old. This *was* the offering
of Gamaliel the son of Pedahzur.
60¶ On the ninth day *it was* Abidan the son of Gideoni, leader
of the sons of Benjamin;
61his offering *was* one silver dish whose weight *was* one hundred and thirty *shekels,* one silver bowl of seventy shekels, according to the shekel of the sanctuary, both of them full of fine flour
mixed with oil for a grain offering;
62one gold pan of ten *shekels,* full of incense;
63one bull, one ram, one male lamb one year old, for a burnt
offering;
64one male goat for a sin offering;

## New International

young bull, one ram and one male lamb a year old, for a burnt
offering; 34one male goat for a sin offering; 35and two oxen,
five rams, five male goats and five male lambs a year old, to
be sacrificed as a fellowship offering. This was the offering of
Elizur son of Shedeur.

36On the fifth day Shelumiel son of Zurishaddai, the leader of the
people of Simeon, brought his offering.
37His offering was one silver plate weighing a hundred and
thirty shekels, and one silver sprinkling bowl weighing seventy shekels, both according to the sanctuary shekel, each
filled with fine flour mixed with oil as a grain offering; 38one
gold dish weighing ten shekels, filled with incense; 39one
young bull, one ram and one male lamb a year old, for a burnt
offering; 40one male goat for a sin offering; 41and two oxen,
five rams, five male goats and five male lambs a year old, to
be sacrificed as a fellowship offering. This was the offering of
Shelumiel son of Zurishaddai.

42On the sixth day Eliasaph son of Deuel, the leader of the people
of Gad, brought his offering.
43His offering was one silver plate weighing a hundred and
thirty shekels, and one silver sprinkling bowl weighing seventy shekels, both according to the sanctuary shekel, each
filled with fine flour mixed with oil as a grain offering; 44one
gold dish weighing ten shekels, filled with incense; 45one
young bull, one ram and one male lamb a year old, for a burnt
offering; 46one male goat for a sin offering; 47and two oxen,
five rams, five male goats and five male lambs a year old, to
be sacrificed as a fellowship offering. This was the offering of
Eliasaph son of Deuel.

48On the seventh day Elishama son of Ammihud, the leader of the
people of Ephraim, brought his offering.
49His offering was one silver plate weighing a hundred and
thirty shekels, and one silver sprinkling bowl weighing seventy shekels, both according to the sanctuary shekel, each
filled with fine flour mixed with oil as a grain offering; 50one
gold dish weighing ten shekels, filled with incense; 51one
young bull, one ram and one male lamb a year old, for a burnt
offering; 52one male goat for a sin offering; 53and two oxen,
five rams, five male goats and five male lambs a year old, to
be sacrificed as a fellowship offering. This was the offering of
Elishama son of Ammihud.

54On the eighth day Gamaliel son of Pedahzur, the leader of the
people of Manasseh, brought his offering.
55His offering was one silver plate weighing a hundred and
thirty shekels, and one silver sprinkling bowl weighing seventy shekels, both according to the sanctuary shekel, each
filled with fine flour mixed with oil as a grain offering; 56one
gold dish weighing ten shekels, filled with incense; 57one
young bull, one ram and one male lamb a year old, for a burnt
offering; 58one male goat for a sin offering; 59and two oxen,
five rams, five male goats and five male lambs a year old, to
be sacrificed as a fellowship offering. This was the offering of
Gamaliel son of Pedahzur.

60On the ninth day Abidan son of Gideoni, the leader of the people
of Benjamin, brought his offering.
61His offering was one silver plate weighing a hundred and
thirty shekels, and one silver sprinkling bowl weighing seventy shekels, both according to the sanctuary shekel, each
filled with fine flour mixed with oil as a grain offering; 62one
gold dish weighing ten shekels, filled with incense; 63one
young bull, one ram and one male lamb a year old, for a burnt
offering; 64one male goat for a sin offering; 65and two oxen,

## King James

65And for a sacrifice of peace offerings, two oxen, five rams, five he goats, five lambs of the first year: this *was* the offering of Abidan the son of Gideoni.

66¶ On the tenth day Ahiezer the son of Ammishaddai, prince of the children of Dan, *offered:*

67His offering *was* one silver charger, the weight whereof *was* an hundred and thirty *shekels,* one silver bowl of seventy shekels, after the shekel of the sanctuary; both of them full of fine flour mingled with oil for a meat offering:

68One golden spoon of ten *shekels,* full of incense:

69One young bullock, one ram, one lamb of the first year, for a burnt offering:

70One kid of the goats for a sin offering:

71And for a sacrifice of peace offerings, two oxen, five rams, five he goats, five lambs of the first year: this *was* the offering of Ahiezer the son of Ammishaddai.

72¶ On the eleventh day Pagiel the son of Ocran, prince of the children of Asher, *offered:*

73His offering *was* one silver charger, the weight whereof *was* an hundred and thirty *shekels,* one silver bowl of seventy shekels, after the shekel of the sanctuary; both of them full of fine flour mingled with oil for a meat offering:

74One golden spoon of ten *shekels,* full of incense:

75One young bullock, one ram, one lamb of the first year, for a burnt offering:

76One kid of the goats for a sin offering:

77And for a sacrifice of peace offerings, two oxen, five rams, five he goats, five lambs of the first year: this *was* the offering of Pagiel the son of Ocran.

78¶ On the twelfth day Ahira the son of Enan, prince of the children of Naphtali, *offered:*

79His offering *was* one silver charger, the weight whereof *was* an hundred and thirty *shekels,* one silver bowl of seventy shekels, after the shekel of the sanctuary; both of them full of fine flour mingled with oil for a meat offering:

80One golden spoon of ten *shekels,* full of incense:

81One young bullock, one ram, one lamb of the first year, for a burnt offering:

82One kid of the goats for a sin offering:

83And for a sacrifice of peace offerings, two oxen, five rams, five he goats, five lambs of the first year: this *was* the offering of Ahira the son of Enan.

84This *was* the dedication of the altar, in the day when it was anointed, by the princes of Israel: twelve chargers of silver, twelve silver bowls, twelve spoons of gold:

85Each charger of silver *weighing* an hundred and thirty *shekels,* each bowl seventy: all the silver vessels *weighed* two thousand and four hundred *shekels,* after the shekel of the sanctuary:

86The golden spoons *were* twelve, full of incense, *weighing* ten *shekels* apiece, after the shekel of the sanctuary: all the gold of the spoons *was* an hundred and twenty *shekels.*

87All the oxen for the burnt offering *were* twelve bullocks, the rams twelve, the lambs of the first year twelve, with their meat offering: and the kids of the goats for sin offering twelve.

88And all the oxen for the sacrifice of the peace offerings *were* twenty and four bullocks, the rams sixty, the he goats sixty, the lambs of the first year sixty. This *was* the dedication of the altar, after that it was anointed.

89And when Moses was gone into the tabernacle of the congregation to speak with him, then he heard the voice of one speaking unto him from off the mercy seat that *was* upon the ark of testimony, from between the two cherubims: and he spake unto him.

## Amplified

65And for the sacrifice of peace offerings, two oxen, five rams, five male goats, five male lambs a year old. This was the offering of Abidan son of Gideoni.

66The tenth day Ahiezer son of Ammishaddai, leader of the sons of Dan, offered.

67His offering was one silver platter, the weight of which was 130 shekels, one silver basin of seventy shekels, after the shekel of the sanctuary, both of them full of fine flour mixed with oil for a cereal offering;

68One golden bowl of ten shekels, full of incense;

69One young bull, one ram, one male lamb a year old, for a burnt offering;

70One male goat for a sin offering;

71And for the sacrifice of peace offerings, two oxen, five rams, five male goats, five male lambs a year old. This was the offering of Ahiezer son of Ammishaddai.

72The eleventh day Pagiel son of Ochran, leader of the sons of Asher, offered.

73His offering was one silver platter, the weight of which was 130 shekels, one silver basin of seventy shekels, after the shekel of the sanctuary, both of them full of fine flour mixed with oil for a cereal offering;

74One golden bowl of ten shekels, full of incense;

75One young bull, one ram, one male lamb a year old, for a burnt offering;

76One male goat for a sin offering;

77And for the sacrifice of peace offerings, two oxen, five rams, five male goats, five male lambs a year old. This was the offering of Pagiel son of Ochran.

78The twelfth day Ahira son of Enan, leader of the sons of Naphtali, offered.

79His offering was one silver platter, the weight of which was 130 shekels, one silver basin of seventy shekels, after the shekel of the sanctuary, both of them full of fine flour mixed with oil for a cereal offering;

80One golden bowl of ten shekels, full of incense;

81One young bull, one ram, one male lamb a year old, for a burnt offering;

82One male goat for a sin offering;

83And for the sacrifice of peace offerings, two oxen, five rams, five male goats, five male lambs a year old. This was the offering of Ahira son of Enan.

84This was the dedication offering for the altar [of burnt offering], on the day when it was anointed, from the leaders of Israel: twelve platters of silver, twelve silver basins, twelve golden bowls;

85Each platter of silver weighing 130 shekels, each basin seventy; all the silver vessels weighed 2,400 shekels after the shekel of the sanctuary,

86The twelve golden bowls full of incense, weighing ten shekels apiece, after the shekel of the sanctuary, all the gold of the bowls being 120 shekels;

87All the oxen for the burnt offering were twelve bulls, the rams twelve, the male lambs a year old twelve, with their cereal offering; and the male goats for a sin offering twelve;

88And all the oxen for the sacrifice of the peace offerings were twenty-four bulls, the rams sixty, the male goats sixty, the male lambs a year old sixty. This was the dedication of the altar [of burnt offering] after it was anointed.

89And when Moses went into the tent of meeting to speak with the Lord, he heard the Voice speaking to him from above the mercy seat that was upon the ark of the testimony, from between the two cherubim; and He spoke to [Moses].

## New American Standard

65and for the sacrifice of peace offerings, two oxen, five rams,
five male goats, five male lambs one year old. This *was* the offering
of Abidan the son of Gideoni.

**66**¶ On the tenth day *it was* Ahiezer the son of Ammishaddai,
leader of the sons of Dan;

67his offering *was* one silver dish whose weight *was* one hundred and thirty *shekels*, one silver bowl of seventy shekels, according to the shekel of the sanctuary, both of them full of fine flour mixed with oil for a grain offering;

68one gold pan of ten *shekels*, full of incense;

69one bull, one ram, one male lamb one year old, for a burnt offering;

70one male goat for a sin offering;

71and for the sacrifice of peace offerings, two oxen, five rams,
five male goats, five male lambs one year old. This *was* the offering
of Ahiezer the son of Ammishaddai.

**72**¶ On the eleventh day *it was* Pagiel the son of Ochran, leader
of the sons of Asher;

73his offering *was* one silver dish whose weight *was* one hundred and thirty *shekels*, one silver bowl of seventy shekels, according to the shekel of the sanctuary, both of them full of fine flour mixed with oil for a grain offering;

74one gold pan of ten *shekels*, full of incense;

75one bull, one ram, one male lamb one year old, for a burnt offering;

76one male goat for a sin offering;

77and for the sacrifice of peace offerings, two oxen, five rams,
five male goats, five male lambs one year old. This *was* the offering
of Pagiel the son of Ochran.

**78**¶ On the twelfth day *it was* Ahira the son of Enan, leader of
the sons of Naphtali;

79his offering *was* one silver dish whose weight *was* one hundred and thirty *shekels*, one silver bowl of seventy shekels, according to the shekel of the sanctuary, both of them full of fine flour mixed with oil for a grain offering;

80one gold pan of ten *shekels*, full of incense;

81one bull, one ram, one male lamb one year old, for a burnt offering;

82one male goat for a sin offering;

83and for the sacrifice of peace offerings, two oxen, five rams,
five male goats, five male lambs one year old. This *was* the offering
of Ahira the son of Enan.

**84**¶ This *was* the dedication *offering* for the altar from the leaders
of Israel when it was anointed: twelve silver dishes, twelve silver
bowls, twelve gold pans,

85each silver dish *weighing* one hundred and thirty *shekels* and
each bowl seventy; all the silver of the utensils *was* 2,400 *shekels*,
according to the shekel of the sanctuary;

86the twelve gold pans, full of incense, *weighing* ten *shekels*
apiece, according to the shekel of the sanctuary, all the gold of the
pans 120 *shekels;*

87all the oxen for the burnt offering twelve bulls, *all* the rams
twelve, the male lambs one year old with their grain offering
twelve, and the male goats for a sin offering twelve;

88and all the oxen for the sacrifice of peace offerings 24 bulls,
*all* the rams 60, the male goats 60, the male lambs one year old 60.
This *was* the dedication *offering* for the altar after it was anointed.

**89**¶ Now when Moses went into the tent of meeting to speak
with Him, he heard the voice speaking to him from above the
mercy seat that was on the ark of the testimony, from between the
two cherubim, so He spoke to him.

## New International

five rams, five male goats and five male lambs a year old, to
be sacrificed as a fellowship offering. This was the offering of
Abidan son of Gideoni.

66On the tenth day Ahiezer son of Ammishaddai, the leader of the
people of Dan, brought his offering.

67His offering was one silver plate weighing a hundred and
thirty shekels, and one silver sprinkling bowl weighing seventy shekels, both according to the sanctuary shekel, each
filled with fine flour mixed with oil as a grain offering; 68one
gold dish weighing ten shekels, filled with incense; 69one
young bull, one ram and one male lamb a year old, for a burnt
offering; 70one male goat for a sin offering; 71and two oxen,
five rams, five male goats and five male lambs a year old, to
be sacrificed as a fellowship offering. This was the offering of
Ahiezer son of Ammishaddai.

72On the eleventh day Pagiel son of Ocran, the leader of the people
of Asher, brought his offering.

73His offering was one silver plate weighing a hundred and
thirty shekels, and one silver sprinkling bowl weighing seventy shekels, both according to the sanctuary shekel, each
filled with fine flour mixed with oil as a grain offering; 74one
gold dish weighing ten shekels, filled with incense; 75one
young bull, one ram and one male lamb a year old, for a burnt
offering; 76one male goat for a sin offering; 77and two oxen,
five rams, five male goats and five male lambs a year old, to
be sacrificed as a fellowship offering. This was the offering of
Pagiel son of Ocran.

78On the twelfth day Ahira son of Enan, the leader of the people
of Naphtali, brought his offering.

79His offering was one silver plate weighing a hundred and
thirty shekels, and one silver sprinkling bowl weighing seventy shekels, both according to the sanctuary shekel, each
filled with fine flour mixed with oil as a grain offering; 80one
gold dish weighing ten shekels, filled with incense; 81one
young bull, one ram and one male lamb a year old, for a burnt
offering; 82one male goat for a sin offering; 83and two oxen,
five rams, five male goats and five male lambs a year old, to
be sacrificed as a fellowship offering. This was the offering of
Ahira son of Enan.

84These were the offerings of the Israelite leaders for the dedication of the altar when it was anointed: twelve silver plates, twelve
silver sprinkling bowls and twelve gold dishes. 85Each silver plate
weighed a hundred and thirty shekels, and each sprinkling bowl
seventy shekels. Altogether, the silver dishes weighed two thousand four hundred shekels,[a] according to the sanctuary shekel.
86The twelve gold dishes filled with incense weighed ten shekels
each, according to the sanctuary shekel. Altogether, the gold
dishes weighed a hundred and twenty shekels.[b] 87The total number of animals for the burnt offering came to twelve young bulls,
twelve rams and twelve male lambs a year old, together with their
grain offering. Twelve male goats were used for the sin offering.
88The total number of animals for the sacrifice of the fellowship
offering came to twenty-four oxen, sixty rams, sixty male goats and
sixty male lambs a year old. These were the offerings for the
dedication of the altar after it was anointed.

89When Moses entered the Tent of Meeting to speak with the
LORD, he heard the voice speaking to him from between the two
cherubim above the atonement cover on the ark of the Testimony.
And he spoke with him.

**NIV** [a] *85* That is, about 60 pounds (about 28 kilograms) [b] *86* That is, about 3 pounds (about 1.4 kilograms)

## King James

8 AND THE LORD spake unto Moses, saying,

2 Speak unto Aaron, and say unto him, When thou lightest the lamps, the seven lamps shall give light over against the candlestick.

3 And Aaron did so; he lighted the lamps thereof over against the candlestick, as the LORD commanded Moses.

4 And this work of the candlestick *was of* beaten gold, unto the shaft thereof, unto the flowers thereof, *was* beaten work: according unto the pattern which the LORD had shown Moses, so he made the candlestick.

5 ¶ And the LORD spake unto Moses, saying,

6 Take the Levites from among the children of Israel, and cleanse them.

7 And thus shalt thou do unto them, to cleanse them: Sprinkle water of purifying upon them, and let them shave all their flesh, and let them wash their clothes, and *so* make themselves clean.

8 Then let them take a young bullock with his meat offering, *even* fine flour mingled with oil, and another young bullock shalt thou take for a sin offering.

9 And thou shalt bring the Levites before the tabernacle of the congregation: and thou shalt gather the whole assembly of the children of Israel together:

10 And thou shalt bring the Levites before the LORD: and the children of Israel shall put their hands upon the Levites:

11 And Aaron shall offer the Levites before the LORD *for* an offering of the children of Israel, that they may execute the service of the LORD.

12 And the Levites shall lay their hands upon the heads of the bullocks: and thou shalt offer the one *for* a sin offering, and the other *for* a burnt offering, unto the LORD, to make an atonement for the Levites.

13 And thou shalt set the Levites before Aaron, and before his sons, and offer them *for* an offering unto the LORD.

14 Thus shalt thou separate the Levites from among the children of Israel: and the Levites shall be mine.

15 And after that shall the Levites go in to do the service of the tabernacle of the congregation: and thou shalt cleanse them, and offer them *for* an offering.

16 For they *are* wholly given unto me from among the children of Israel; instead of such as open every womb, *even instead of* the firstborn of all the children of Israel, have I taken them unto me.

17 For all the firstborn of the children of Israel *are* mine, *both* man and beast: on the day that I smote every firstborn in the land of Egypt I sanctified them for myself.

18 And I have taken the Levites for all the firstborn of the children of Israel.

19 And I have given the Levites *as* a gift to Aaron and to his sons from among the children of Israel, to do the service of the children of Israel in the tabernacle of the congregation, and to make an atonement for the children of Israel: that there be no plague among the children of Israel, when the children of Israel come nigh unto the sanctuary.

20 And Moses, and Aaron, and all the congregation of the children of Israel, did to the Levites according unto all that the LORD commanded Moses concerning the Levites, so did the children of Israel unto them.

21 And the Levites were purified, and they washed their clothes; and Aaron offered them *as* an offering before the LORD; and Aaron made an atonement for them to cleanse them.

## Amplified

8 AND THE Lord said to Moses,

2 Say to Aaron, When you set up *and* light the lamps, the seven lamps shall be made to give light in front of the lampstand.

3 And Aaron did so; he lighted the lamps of the lampstand to give light in front of it, as the Lord commanded Moses.

4 And this was the workmanship of the candlestick, beaten *or* turned gold, being beaten work from its base to its flowers; according to the pattern which the Lord had shown Moses, so he made the lampstand.

5 And the Lord said to Moses,

6 Take the [a]Levites from among the Israelites and cleanse them.

7 And thus you shall do to them to cleanse them: sprinkle the water of purification [water to be used in case of sin] upon them, and let them pass a razor over all their flesh, and wash their clothes and cleanse themselves. [Num. 19:17, 18.]

8 Then let them take a young bull and its cereal offering of fine flour mixed with oil, and another young bull you shall take for a sin offering.

9 You shall present the Levites before the tent of meeting, and you shall assemble the whole Israelite congregation.

10 And you shall present the Levites before the Lord, and the Israelites shall put their hands upon the Levites,

11 And Aaron shall offer the Levites before the Lord as a wave offering from the Israelites *and* on their behalf, that they may do the service of the Lord.

12 Then the Levites shall lay their hands upon the heads of the bulls; and you shall offer the one for a sin offering and the other for a burnt offering to the Lord, to make atonement for the Levites.

13 And you shall present the Levites before Aaron and his sons, and offer them as a wave offering to the Lord.

14 Thus you shall separate the Levites from among the Israelites, and the Levites shall be Mine [in a very special sense].

15 And after that the Levites shall go in to do service at the tent of meeting, when you have cleansed them and offered them as a wave offering.

16 For they are wholly given to Me from among the Israelites; instead of all who open the womb, the first-born of all the Israelites, I have taken the Levites for Myself.

17 For all the first-born of the Israelites are Mine, both of man and beast; on the day that I smote every first-born in the land of Egypt [not of Israel], I consecrated them *and* set them apart for Myself.

18 And I have taken the Levites instead of all the first-born of the Israelites.

19 And I have given the Levites as a gift to Aaron and to his sons from among the Israelites, to do the service of the Israelites at the tent of meeting, and to make atonement for them, that there may be no plague among the Israelites if they should come near the sanctuary.

20 So Moses and Aaron and all the congregation of the Israelites did thus to the Levites; according to all that the Lord commanded Moses concerning [them], so did the Israelites to them.

21 The Levites cleansed *and* purified themselves and they washed their clothes; and Aaron offered them as a wave offering before the Lord, and Aaron made atonement for them to cleanse them.

**AMP** [a] There are many lessons for the Christian in this section (verses 5-22). He sees here the importance of each member of God's family having his own particular task. Cp. I Cor. 12. It is necessary that special men be designated for particular duties in order that the work of God's kingdom shall be done in orderly fashion. Those who do the work of God must be cleansed from all defilement of flesh and spirit. No one is fit in himself to serve God. It is only as we see ourselves as guilty sinners saved through the sacrifice of the Lord Jesus Christ at Calvary that we can do anything that is worth while in God's sight. All our righteousnesses apart from Him are but "filthy rags" (Isa. 64:6). (*The New Bible Commentary*).

## New American Standard

*The Seven Lamps*

8 THEN THE LORD spoke to Moses, saying,
2"Speak to Aaron and say to him, 'When you mount the
lamps, the seven lamps will give light in the front of the lampstand.' "
3Aaron therefore did so; he mounted its lamps at the front of
the lampstand, just as the LORD had commanded Moses.
4Now this was the workmanship of the lampstand, hammered
work of gold; from its base to its flowers, it was hammered work;
according to the pattern which the LORD had showed Moses, so
he made the lampstand.

*Cleansing the Levites*

5¶ Again the LORD spoke to Moses, saying,
6"Take the Levites from among the sons of Israel and cleanse
them.
7"And thus you shall do to them, for their cleansing: *sprinkle*
purifying water on them, and let them use a razor over their whole
body, and wash their clothes, and they shall be clean.
8"Then let them take a bull with its grain offering, fine flour
mixed with oil; and a second bull you shall take for a sin offering.
9"So you shall present the Levites before the tent of meeting.
You shall also assemble the whole congregation of the sons of
Israel,
10and present the Levites before the LORD; and the sons of Israel
shall lay their hands on the Levites.
11"Aaron then shall present the Levites before the LORD as a
wave offering from the sons of Israel, that they may qualify to
perform the service of the LORD.
12"Now the Levites shall lay their hands on the heads of the
bulls; then offer the one for a sin offering and the other for a burnt
offering to the LORD, to make atonement for the Levites.
13"And you shall have the Levites stand before Aaron and
before his sons so as to present them as a wave offering to the
LORD.
14¶ "Thus you shall separate the Levites from among the sons
of Israel, and the Levites shall be Mine.
15"Then after that the Levites may go in to serve the tent of
meeting. But you shall cleanse them and present them as a wave
offering;
16for they are wholly given to Me from among the sons of Israel.
I have taken them for Myself instead of every first issue of the
womb, the first-born of all the sons of Israel.
17"For every first-born among the sons of Israel is Mine, among
the men and among the animals; on the day that I struck down all
the first-born in the land of Egypt I sanctified them for Myself.
18"But I have taken the Levites instead of every first-born
among the sons of Israel.
19"And I have given the Levites as a gift to Aaron and to his
sons from among the sons of Israel, to perform the service of the
sons of Israel at the tent of meeting, and to make atonement on
behalf of the sons of Israel, that there may be no plague among the
sons of Israel by their coming near to the sanctuary."
20¶ Thus did Moses and Aaron and all the congregation of the
sons of Israel to the Levites; according to all that the LORD had
commanded Moses concerning the Levites, so the sons of Israel
did to them.
21The Levites, too, purified themselves from sin and washed
their clothes; and Aaron presented them as a wave offering before
the LORD. Aaron also made atonement for them to cleanse them.

## New International

*Setting Up the Lamps*

8 THE LORD said to Moses, 2"Speak to Aaron and say to him,
'When you set up the seven lamps, they are to light the area
in front of the lampstand.' "
3Aaron did so; he set up the lamps so that they faced forward
on the lampstand, just as the LORD commanded Moses. 4This is
how the lampstand was made: It was made of hammered gold—
from its base to its blossoms. The lampstand was made exactly like
the pattern the LORD had shown Moses.

*The Setting Apart of the Levites*

5The LORD said to Moses: 6"Take the Levites from among the
other Israelites and make them ceremonially clean. 7To purify
them, do this: Sprinkle the water of cleansing on them; then have
them shave their whole bodies and wash their clothes, and so
purify themselves. 8Have them take a young bull with its grain
offering of fine flour mixed with oil; then you are to take a second
young bull for a sin offering. 9Bring the Levites to the front of the
Tent of Meeting and assemble the whole Israelite community.
10You are to bring the Levites before the LORD, and the Israelites
are to lay their hands on them. 11Aaron is to present the Levites
before the LORD as a wave offering from the Israelites, so that they
may be ready to do the work of the LORD.
12"After the Levites lay their hands on the heads of the bulls,
use the one for a sin offering to the LORD and the other for a burnt
offering, to make atonement for the Levites. 13Have the Levites
stand in front of Aaron and his sons and then present them as a
wave offering to the LORD. 14In this way you are to set the Levites
apart from the other Israelites, and the Levites will be mine.
15"After you have purified the Levites and presented them as
a wave offering, they are to come to do their work at the Tent of
Meeting. 16They are the Israelites who are to be given wholly to
me. I have taken them as my own in place of the firstborn, the first
male offspring from every Israelite woman. 17Every firstborn male
in Israel, whether man or animal, is mine. When I struck down all
the firstborn in Egypt, I set them apart for myself. 18And I have
taken the Levites in place of all the firstborn sons in Israel. 19Of all
the Israelites, I have given the Levites as gifts to Aaron and his sons
to do the work at the Tent of Meeting on behalf of the Israelites
and to make atonement for them so that no plague will strike the
Israelites when they go near the sanctuary."
20Moses, Aaron and the whole Israelite community did with the
Levites just as the LORD commanded Moses. 21The Levites purified
themselves and washed their clothes. Then Aaron presented them
as a wave offering before the LORD and made atonement for them
to purify them. 22After that, the Levites came to do their work at

## King James

22And after that went the Levites in to do their service in the
tabernacle of the congregation before Aaron, and before his sons:
as the LORD had commanded Moses concerning the Levites, so did
they unto them.
23¶ And the LORD spake unto Moses, saying,
24This *is it* that *belongeth* unto the Levites: from twenty and five
years old and upward they shall go in to wait upon the service of
the tabernacle of the congregation:
25And from the age of fifty years they shall cease waiting upon
the service *thereof*, and shall serve no more:
26But shall minister with their brethren in the tabernacle of the
congregation, to keep the charge, and shall do no service. Thus
shalt thou do unto the Levites touching their charge.

**9** AND THE LORD spake unto Moses in the wilderness of Sinai,
in the first month of the second year after they were come out
of the land of Egypt, saying,
2Let the children of Israel also keep the passover at his appointed season.
3In the fourteenth day of this month, at even, ye shall keep it
in his appointed season: according to all the rites of it, and according to all the ceremonies thereof, shall ye keep it.
4And Moses spake unto the children of Israel, that they should
keep the passover.
5And they kept the passover on the fourteenth day of the first
month at even in the wilderness of Sinai: according to all that the
LORD commanded Moses, so did the children of Israel.
6¶ And there were certain men, who were defiled by the dead
body of a man, that they could not keep the passover on that day:
and they came before Moses and before Aaron on that day:
7And those men said unto him, We *are* defiled by the dead body
of a man: wherefore are we kept back, that we may not offer an
offering of the LORD in his appointed season among the children
of Israel?
8And Moses said unto them, Stand still, and I will hear what
the LORD will command concerning you.
9¶ And the LORD spake unto Moses, saying,
10Speak unto the children of Israel, saying, If any man of you
or of your posterity shall be unclean by reason of a dead body, or
*be* in a journey afar off, yet he shall keep the passover unto the
LORD.
11The fourteenth day of the second month at even they shall
keep it, *and* eat it with unleavened bread and bitter *herbs*.
12They shall leave none of it unto the morning, nor break any
bone of it: according to all the ordinances of the passover they shall
keep it.
13But the man that *is* clean, and is not in a journey, and forbeareth to keep the passover, even the same soul shall be cut off
from among his people: because he brought not the offering of the
LORD in his appointed season, that man shall bear his sin.
14And if a stranger shall sojourn among you, and will keep the
passover unto the LORD; according to the ordinance of the passover, and according to the manner thereof, so shall he do: ye shall
have one ordinance, both for the stranger, and for him that was
born in the land.
15¶ And on the day that the tabernacle was reared up the cloud
covered the tabernacle, *namely*, the tent of the testimony: and at
even there was upon the tabernacle as it were the appearance of
fire, until the morning.
16So it was always: the cloud covered it *by day*, and the appearance of fire by night.

## Amplified

22And after that the Levites went in to do their service in the
tent of meeting in attendance upon Aaron and his sons; as the Lord
had commanded Moses concerning the Levites, so did they to
them.
23And the Lord said to Moses,
24This is what applies to the Levites: from twenty-five years old
and upward they shall go in to perform the work of the service of
the tent of meeting,
25And from the age of fifty years they shall retire from the
warfare of the service and serve no more,
26But shall help their brethren in the tent of meeting, [to attend
to protecting the sacred things from being profaned], but shall do
no regular *or* heavy service. Thus shall you direct the Levites in
regard to their duties.

**9** THE LORD said to Moses in the wilderness of Sinai, in the
first month of the second year after they had come out of the
land of Egypt,
2Let the Israelites keep the passover at its appointed time.
3On the fourteenth day of this month, in the evening, you shall
keep it at its appointed time; according to all its statutes and
ordinances you shall keep it.
4So Moses told the Israelites they should keep the passover.
5And they kept the passover on the fourteenth day of the first
month in the evening in the wilderness of Sinai; according to all
that the Lord commanded Moses, so the Israelites did.
6And there were certain men who were defiled by touching the
dead body of a man, so they could not keep the passover on that
day; and they came before Moses and Aaron on that day;
7Those men said to [Moses], We are defiled by touching the
dead body. Why are we prevented from offering the Lord's offering at its appointed time among the Israelites?
8And Moses said to them, Stand still, and I will hear what the
Lord will command concerning you.
9And the Lord said to Moses,
10Say to the Israelites, If any man of you or of your posterity
shall be unclean by reason of touching a dead body, or is far off
on a journey, still he shall keep the passover to the Lord.
11The fourteenth day of the second month in the evening they
shall keep it, and eat it with unleavened bread and bitter herbs.
12They shall leave none of it until the morning, nor break any
bone of it; according to all the statute for the passover they shall
keep it. [John 19:36.]
13But the man who is clean, and is not on a journey, yet does
not keep the passover, that person shall be cut off from among his
people; because he did not bring the Lord's offering at its appointed time, that man shall bear [the penalty of] his sin.
14And if a stranger sojourns among you, and will keep the
passover to the Lord, according to [its] statute and its ordinance,
so shall he do; you shall have one statute both for the temporary
resident and for him who was born in the land.
15And on the day that the tabernacle was erected the cloud [of
God's presence] covered the tabernacle, that is, the tent of the
testimony; and at evening it was over the tabernacle, having the
appearance of [a pillar of] fire until the morning. [Exod. 13:21.]
16So it was constantly; the cloud covered it by day, and the
appearance of fire by night.

## New American Standard

22Then after that the Levites went in to perform their service in
the tent of meeting before Aaron and before his sons; just as the
LORD had commanded Moses concerning the Levites, so they did
to them.

*Retirement*

23¶ Now the LORD spoke to Moses, saying,
24"This is what *applies* to the Levites: from twenty-five years old
and upward they shall enter to perform service in the work of the
tent of meeting.
25"But at the age of fifty years they shall retire from service in
the work and not work any more.
26"They may, however, assist their brothers in the tent of meeting, to keep an obligation; but they *themselves* shall do no work.
Thus you shall deal with the Levites concerning their obligations."

*The Passover*

9 THUS THE LORD spoke to Moses in the wilderness of Sinai,
in the first month of the second year after they had come out
of the land of Egypt, saying,
2"Now, let the sons of Israel observe the Passover at its appointed time.
3"On the fourteenth day of this month, at twilight, you shall
observe it at its appointed time; you shall observe it according to
all its statutes and according to all its ordinances."
4So Moses told the sons of Israel to observe the Passover.
5And they observed the Passover in the first *month,* on the
fourteenth day of the month, at twilight, in the wilderness of Sinai;
according to all that the LORD had commanded Moses, so the sons
of Israel did.
6But there were *some* men who were unclean because of *the*
dead person, so that they could not observe Passover on that day;
so they came before Moses and Aaron on that day.
7And those men said to him, "*Though* we are unclean because
of *the* dead person, why are we restrained from presenting the
offering of the LORD at its appointed time among the sons of
Israel?"
8Moses therefore said to them, "Wait, and I will listen to what
the LORD will command concerning you."
9¶ Then the LORD spoke to Moses, saying,
10"Speak to the sons of Israel, saying, 'If any one of you or of
your generations becomes unclean because of a *dead* person, or is
on a distant journey, he may, however, observe the Passover to
the LORD.
11'In the second month on the fourteenth day at twilight, they
shall observe it; they shall eat it with unleavened bread and bitter
herbs.
12'They shall leave none of it until morning, nor break a bone
of it; according to all the statute of the Passover they shall observe
it.
13'But the man who is clean and is not on a journey, and yet
neglects to observe the Passover, that person shall then be cut off
from his people, for he did not present the offering of the LORD
at its appointed time. That man shall bear his sin.
14'And if an alien sojourns among you and observes the Passover to the LORD, according to the statute of the Passover and
according to its ordinance, so he shall do; you shall have one
statute, both for the alien and for the native of the land.' "

*The Cloud on the Tabernacle*

15¶ Now on the day that the tabernacle was erected the cloud
covered the tabernacle, the tent of the testimony, and in the evening it was like the appearance of fire over the tabernacle, until
morning.
16So it was continuously; the cloud would cover it *by day,* and
the appearance of fire by night.

## New International

the Tent of Meeting under the supervision of Aaron and his sons.
They did with the Levites just as the LORD commanded Moses.
23The LORD said to Moses, 24"This applies to the Levites: Men
twenty-five years old or more shall come to take part in the work
at the Tent of Meeting, 25but at the age of fifty, they must retire
from their regular service and work no longer. 26They may assist
their brothers in performing their duties at the Tent of Meeting, but
they themselves must not do the work. This, then, is how you are
to assign the responsibilities of the Levites."

*The Passover*

9 THE LORD spoke to Moses in the Desert of Sinai in the first
month of the second year after they came out of Egypt. He
said, 2"Have the Israelites celebrate the Passover at the appointed
time. 3Celebrate it at the appointed time, at twilight on the fourteenth day of this month, in accordance with all its rules and
regulations."
4So Moses told the Israelites to celebrate the Passover, 5and they
did so in the Desert of Sinai at twilight on the fourteenth day of
the first month. The Israelites did everything just as the LORD
commanded Moses.
6But some of them could not celebrate the Passover on that day
because they were ceremonially unclean on account of a dead
body. So they came to Moses and Aaron that same day 7and said
to Moses, "We have become unclean because of a dead body, but
why should we be kept from presenting the LORD's offering with
the other Israelites at the appointed time?"
8Moses answered them, "Wait until I find out what the LORD
commands concerning you."
9Then the LORD said to Moses, 10"Tell the Israelites: 'When any
of you or your descendants are unclean because of a dead body or
are away on a journey, they may still celebrate the LORD's Passover. 11They are to celebrate it on the fourteenth day of the second
month at twilight. They are to eat the lamb, together with unleavened bread and bitter herbs. 12They must not leave any of it till
morning or break any of its bones. When they celebrate the Passover, they must follow all the regulations. 13But if a man who is
ceremonially clean and not on a journey fails to celebrate the
Passover, that person must be cut off from his people because he
did not present the LORD's offering at the appointed time. That
man will bear the consequences of his sin.
14" 'An alien living among you who wants to celebrate the
LORD's Passover must do so in accordance with its rules and regulations. You must have the same regulations for the alien and the
native-born.' "

*The Cloud Above the Tabernacle*

15On the day the tabernacle, the Tent of the Testimony, was set
up, the cloud covered it. From evening till morning the cloud
above the tabernacle looked like fire. 16That is how it continued to
be; the cloud covered it, and at night it looked like fire. 17Whenever

## King James

17 And when the cloud was taken up from the tabernacle, then after that the children of Israel journeyed: and in the place where the cloud abode, there the children of Israel pitched their tents.

18 At the commandment of the LORD the children of Israel journeyed, and at the commandment of the LORD they pitched: as long as the cloud abode upon the tabernacle they rested in their tents.

19 And when the cloud tarried long upon the tabernacle many days, then the children of Israel kept the charge of the LORD, and journeyed not.

20 And *so* it was, when the cloud was a few days upon the tabernacle; according to the commandment of the LORD they abode in their tents, and according to the commandment of the LORD they journeyed.

21 And *so* it was, when the cloud abode from even unto the morning, and *that* the cloud was taken up in the morning, then they journeyed: whether *it was* by day or by night that the cloud was taken up, they journeyed.

22 Or *whether it were* two days, or a month, or a year, that the cloud tarried upon the tabernacle, remaining thereon, the children of Israel abode in their tents, and journeyed not: but when it was taken up, they journeyed.

23 At the commandment of the LORD they rested in the tents, and at the commandment of the LORD they journeyed: they kept the charge of the LORD, at the commandment of the LORD by the hand of Moses.

**10** AND THE LORD spake unto Moses, saying,

2 Make thee two trumpets of silver; of a whole piece shalt thou make them: that thou mayest use them for the calling of the assembly, and for the journeying of the camps.

3 And when they shall blow with them, all the assembly shall assemble themselves to thee at the door of the tabernacle of the congregation.

4 And if they blow *but* with one *trumpet,* then the princes, *which are* heads of the thousands of Israel, shall gather themselves unto thee.

5 When ye blow an alarm, then the camps that lie on the east parts shall go forward.

6 When ye blow an alarm the second time, then the camps that lie on the south side shall take their journey: they shall blow an alarm for their journeys.

7 But when the congregation is to be gathered together, ye shall blow, but ye shall not sound an alarm.

8 And the sons of Aaron, the priests, shall blow with the trumpets; and they shall be to you for an ordinance for ever throughout your generations.

9 And if ye go to war in your land against the enemy that oppresseth you, then ye shall blow an alarm with the trumpets; and ye shall be remembered before the LORD your God, and ye shall be saved from your enemies.

10 Also in the day of your gladness, and in your solemn days, and in the beginnings of your months, ye shall blow with the trumpets over your burnt offerings, and over the sacrifices of your peace offerings; that they may be to you for a memorial before your God: I *am* the LORD your God.

11 ¶ And it came to pass on the twentieth *day* of the second month, in the second year, that the cloud was taken up from off the tabernacle of the testimony.

12 And the children of Israel took their journeys out of the wilderness of Sinai; and the cloud rested in the wilderness of Paran.

13 And they first took their journey according to the commandment of the LORD by the hand of Moses.

14 ¶ In the first *place* went the standard of the camp of the children of Judah according to their armies: and over his host *was* Nahshon the son of Amminadab.

## Amplified

17 Whenever the cloud was taken up from over the tent, then after that the Israelites journeyed; and in the place where the cloud rested, there the Israelites encamped.

18 At the Lord's command the Israelites journeyed, and at [His] command they encamped; as long as the cloud rested upon the tabernacle they remained encamped.

19 Even when the cloud tarried upon the tabernacle many days, the Israelites kept the Lord's charge, and did not set out.

20 And sometimes the cloud was only a few days upon the tabernacle, but according to the command of the Lord they remained encamped, or they journeyed.

21 And sometimes the cloud remained [over the tabernacle] from evening only until morning, but when the cloud was taken up they journeyed; whether it was taken up by day or by night, they journeyed.

22 Whether it was two days, or a month, or a longer time, that the cloud tarried upon the tabernacle, dwelling on it, the Israelites remained encamped; but when it was taken up, they journeyed.

23 At the command of the Lord they remained encamped, and at [His] command they journeyed; they kept the charge of the Lord, at the command of the Lord by Moses.

**10** AND THE Lord said to Moses,

2 Make two trumpets of silver; of hammered *or* turned work you shall make them, that you may use them to call the congregation, and for breaking camp.

3 When they both are blown, all the congregation shall assemble before you at the door of the tent of meeting.

4 And if one blast on a single trumpet is blown, then the princes *or* leaders, heads of the tribes of Israel, shall gather themselves to you.

5 When you blow an alarm, the camps on the east side [of the tabernacle] shall set out.

6 When you blow an alarm the second time, then the camps on the south side shall set out. An alarm shall be blown whenever they are to set out on their journeys.

7 When the congregation is to be assembled, you shall blow [the trumpets in short, sharp tones], but not blast an alarm.

8 And the sons of Aaron, the priests, shall blow the trumpets, and the trumpets shall be to you for a perpetual statute throughout your generations.

9 When you go to war in your land against the enemy that oppresses you, then blow an alarm with the trumpets, that you may be remembered before the Lord your God, and you shall be saved from your enemies.

10 Also in the day of rejoicing, and in your set feasts and at the beginnings of months, you shall blow the trumpets over your burnt offerings and your peace offerings; thus they may be a remembrance before your God; I am the Lord your God.

11 On the twentieth day of the second month, in the second year [since leaving Egypt], the cloud [of the Lord's presence] was taken up from over the tabernacle of the testimony,

12 And the Israelites took their journey by stages out of the wilderness of Sinai, and the [guiding] cloud rested in the wilderness of Paran.

13 When the journey was to begin, at the command of the Lord by Moses,

14 In the first place went the standard of the camp of the sons of Judah by their companies; and over their host was Nahshon son of Amminadab.

## New American Standard

17And whenever the cloud was lifted from over the tent, afterward the sons of Israel would then set out; and in the place where
the cloud settled down, there the sons of Israel would camp.
18At the command of the LORD the sons of Israel would set out,
and at the command of the LORD they would camp; as long as the
cloud settled over the tabernacle, they remained camped.
19Even when the cloud lingered over the tabernacle for many
days, the sons of Israel would keep the LORD's charge and not set
out.
20If sometimes the cloud remained a few days over the tabernacle, according to the command of the LORD they remained
camped. Then according to the command of the LORD they set out.
21If sometimes the cloud remained from evening until morning,
when the cloud was lifted in the morning, they would move out;
or *if it remained* in the daytime and at night, whenever the cloud
was lifted, they would set out.
22Whether it was two days or a month or a year that the cloud
lingered over the tabernacle, staying above it, the sons of Israel
remained camped and did not set out; but when it was lifted, they
did set out.
23At the command of the LORD they camped, and at the command of the LORD they set out; they kept the LORD's charge,
according to the command of the LORD through Moses.

### *The Silver Trumpets*

**10** THE LORD spoke further to Moses, saying,
2"Make yourself two trumpets of silver, of hammered
work you shall make them; and you shall use them for summoning
the congregation and for having the camps set out.
3"And when both are blown, all the congregation shall gather
themselves to you at the doorway of the tent of meeting.
4"Yet if *only* one is blown, then the leaders, the heads of the
divisions of Israel, shall assemble before you.
5"But when you blow an alarm, the camps that are pitched on
the east side shall set out.
6"And when you blow an alarm the second time, the camps
that are pitched on the south side shall set out; an alarm is to be
blown for them to set out.
7"When convening the assembly, however, you shall blow
without sounding an alarm.
8"The priestly sons of Aaron, moreover, shall blow the trumpets; and this shall be for you a perpetual statute throughout your
generations.
9"And when you go to war in your land against the adversary
who attacks you, then you shall sound an alarm with the trumpets,
that you may be remembered before the LORD your God, and be
saved from your enemies.
10"Also in the day of your gladness and in your appointed
feasts, and on the first *days* of your months, you shall blow the
trumpets over your burnt offerings, and over the sacrifices of your
peace offerings; and they shall be as a reminder of you before your
God. I am the LORD your God."

### *The Tribes Leave Sinai*

11¶ Now it came about in the second year, in the second month,
on the twentieth of the month, that the cloud was lifted from over
the tabernacle of the testimony;
12and the sons of Israel set out on their journeys from the
wilderness of Sinai. Then the cloud settled down in the wilderness
of Paran.
13So they moved out for the first time according to the commandment of the LORD through Moses.
14And the standard of the camp of the sons of Judah, according
to their armies, set out first, with Nahshon the son of Amminadab,
over its army,

## New International

the cloud lifted from above the Tent, the Israelites set out;
wherever the cloud settled, the Israelites encamped. 18At the
LORD's command the Israelites set out, and at his command they
encamped. As long as the cloud stayed over the tabernacle, they
remained in camp. 19When the cloud remained over the tabernacle
a long time, the Israelites obeyed the LORD's order and did not set
out. 20Sometimes the cloud was over the tabernacle only a few
days; at the LORD's command they would encamp, and then at his
command they would set out. 21Sometimes the cloud stayed only
from evening till morning, and when it lifted in the morning, they
set out. Whether by day or by night, whenever the cloud lifted,
they set out. 22Whether the cloud stayed over the tabernacle for
two days or a month or a year, the Israelites would remain in camp
and not set out; but when it lifted, they would set out. 23At the
LORD's command they encamped, and at the LORD's command
they set out. They obeyed the LORD's order, in accordance with his
command through Moses.

### *The Silver Trumpets*

**10** THE LORD said to Moses: 2"Make two trumpets of hammered silver, and use them for calling the community
together and for having the camps set out. 3When both are sounded, the whole community is to assemble before you at the entrance
to the Tent of Meeting. 4If only one is sounded, the leaders—the
heads of the clans of Israel—are to assemble before you. 5When a
trumpet blast is sounded, the tribes camping on the east are to set
out. 6At the sounding of a second blast, the camps on the south
are to set out. The blast will be the signal for setting out. 7To gather
the assembly, blow the trumpets, but not with the same signal.
8"The sons of Aaron, the priests, are to blow the trumpets. This
is to be a lasting ordinance for you and the generations to come.
9When you go into battle in your own land against an enemy who
is oppressing you, sound a blast on the trumpets. Then you will
be remembered by the LORD your God and rescued from your
enemies. 10Also at your times of rejoicing—your appointed feasts
and New Moon festivals—you are to sound the trumpets over your
burnt offerings and fellowship offerings,[a] and they will be a
memorial for you before your God. I am the LORD your God."

### *The Israelites Leave Sinai*

11On the twentieth day of the second month of the second year,
the cloud lifted from above the tabernacle of the Testimony. 12Then
the Israelites set out from the Desert of Sinai and traveled from
place to place until the cloud came to rest in the Desert of Paran.
13They set out, this first time, at the LORD's command through
Moses.
14The divisions of the camp of Judah went first, under their
standard. Nahshon son of Amminadab was in command. 15Ne-

NIV [a] *10* Traditionally *peace offerings*

## King James

15 And over the host of the tribe of the children of Issachar *was* Nethaneel the son of Zuar.

16 And over the host of the tribe of the children of Zebulun *was* Eliab the son of Helon.

17 And the tabernacle was taken down; and the sons of Gershon and the sons of Merari set forward, bearing the tabernacle.

18 ¶ And the standard of the camp of Reuben set forward according to their armies: and over his host *was* Elizur the son of Shedeur.

19 And over the host of the tribe of the children of Simeon *was* Shelumiel the son of Zurishaddai.

20 And over the host of the tribe of the children of Gad *was* Eliasaph the son of Deuel.

21 And the Kohathites set forward, bearing the sanctuary: and *the other* did set up the tabernacle against they came.

22 ¶ And the standard of the camp of the children of Ephraim set forward according to their armies: and over his host *was* Elishama the son of Ammihud.

23 And over the host of the tribe of the children of Manasseh *was* Gamaliel the son of Pedahzur.

24 And over the host of the tribe of the children of Benjamin *was* Abidan the son of Gideoni.

25 ¶ And the standard of the camp of the children of Dan set forward, *which was* the rearward of all the camps throughout their hosts: and over his host *was* Ahiezer the son of Ammishaddai.

26 And over the host of the tribe of the children of Asher *was* Pagiel the son of Ocran.

27 And over the host of the tribe of the children of Naphtali *was* Ahira the son of Enan.

28 Thus *were* the journeyings of the children of Israel according to their armies, when they set forward.

29 ¶ And Moses said unto Hobab, the son of Raguel the Midianite, Moses' father-in-law, We are journeying unto the place of which the LORD said, I will give it you: come thou with us, and we will do thee good: for the LORD hath spoken good concerning Israel.

30 And he said unto him, I will not go; but I will depart to mine own land, and to my kindred.

31 And he said, Leave us not, I pray thee; forasmuch as thou knowest how we are to encamp in the wilderness, and thou mayest be to us instead of eyes.

32 And it shall be, if thou go with us, yea, it shall be, that what goodness the LORD shall do unto us, the same will we do unto thee.

33 ¶ And they departed from the mount of the LORD three days' journey: and the ark of the covenant of the LORD went before them in the three days' journey, to search out a resting place for them.

34 And the cloud of the LORD *was* upon them by day, when they went out of the camp.

35 And it came to pass, when the ark set forward, that Moses said, Rise up, LORD, and let thine enemies be scattered; and let them that hate thee flee before thee.

36 And when it rested, he said, Return, O LORD, unto the many thousands of Israel.

**11** AND *WHEN* the people complained, it displeased the LORD: and the LORD heard *it;* and his anger was kindled; and the fire of the LORD burnt among them, and consumed *them that were* in the uttermost parts of the camp.

2 And the people cried unto Moses; and when Moses prayed unto the LORD, the fire was quenched.

## Amplified

15 And over the host of the tribe of the sons of Issachar was Nethanel son of Zuar.

16 And over the host of the tribe of the sons of Zebulun was Eliab son of Helon.

17 When the tabernacle was taken down, the sons of Gershon and Merari, bearing [it] on their shoulders, set out.

18 The standard of the camp of Reuben set forward by their companies; and over Reuben's host was Elizur son of Shedeur.

19 And over the host of the tribe of the sons of Simeon was Shelumiel son of Zurishaddai.

20 And over the host of the tribe of the sons of Gad was Eliasaph son of Deuel.

21 Then the Kohathites set forward, bearing the holy things, and the tabernacle was set up before they arrived.

22 And the standard of the camp of the sons of Ephraim set forward according to their companies; and over Ephraim's host was Elishama son of Ammihud.

23 Over the host of the tribe of the sons of Manasseh was Gamaliel son of Pedahzur.

24 And over the host of the tribe of the sons of Benjamin was Abidan son of Gideoni.

25 Then the standard of the camp of the sons of Dan, which was the rear guard of all the camps, set forward according to their companies; and over Dan's host was Ahiezer son of Ammishaddai.

26 And over the host of the tribe of the sons of Asher was Pagiel son of Ochran.

27 And over the host of the tribe of the sons of Naphtali was Ahira son of Enan.

28 This was the Israelites' order of march by their hosts, when they set out.

29 And Moses said to Hobab, son of Raguel the Midianite, Moses' father-in-law, We are journeying to the place of which the Lord said, I will give it to you; come with us, and we will do you good; for the Lord has promised good concerning Israel.

30 And Hobab said to him, I will not go; I will depart to my own land and to my family.

31 And Moses said, [a]Do not leave us, I pray you; for you know how we are to encamp in the wilderness and you will serve as eyes for us.

32 And if you will go with us, it shall be that whatever good the Lord does to us, the same we will do to you.

33 They departed from the mountain of the Lord [Mount Sinai] three days' journey; and the ark of the covenant of the Lord went before them in the three days' journey to seek out a resting place for them.

34 The cloud of the Lord was over them by day, when they went forward from the camp.

35 Whenever the ark set out, Moses said, Rise up, Lord; let Your enemies be scattered, and let those who hate You flee before You. [Ps. 68:1, 2.]

36 And when it rested, he said, Return O Lord, to the ten thousand thousands in Israel.

**11** AND THE people grumbled *and* deplored their hardships, which was evil in the ears of the Lord; and when the Lord heard it, His anger was kindled; and the fire of the Lord burned among them, and devoured those in the outlying parts of the camp.

2 The people cried to Moses; and when Moses prayed to the Lord the fire subsided.

**AMP** [a] The record does not say so, but Hobab seems to have remained with the Israelites, for later history shows that his descendants lived in Canaan (Judg. 1:16; I Sam. 15:6).

## New American Standard

15and Nethanel the son of Zuar, over the tribal army of the sons of Issachar;
16and Eliab the son of Helon over the tribal army of the sons of Zebulun.
17¶ Then the tabernacle was taken down; and the sons of Gershon and the sons of Merari, who were carrying the tabernacle, set out.
18Next the standard of the camp of Reuben, according to their armies, set out with Elizur the son of Shedeur, over its army,
19and Shelumiel the son of Zurishaddai over the tribal army of the sons of Simeon,
20and Eliasaph the son of Deuel was over the tribal army of the sons of Gad.
21¶ Then the Kohathites set out, carrying the holy *objects;* and the tabernacle was set up before their arrival.
22Next the standard of the camp of the sons of Ephraim, according to their armies, was set out, with Elishama the son of Ammihud over its army,
23and Gamaliel the son of Pedahzur over the tribal army of the sons of Manasseh;
24and Abidan the son of Gideoni over the tribal army of the sons of Benjamin.
25¶ Then the standard of the camp of the sons of Dan, according to their armies, *which formed* the rear guard for all the camps, set out, with Ahiezer the son of Ammishaddai over its army,
26and Pagiel the son of Ochran over the tribal army of the sons of Asher;
27and Ahira the son of Enan over the tribal army of the sons of Naphtali.
28This was the order of march of the sons of Israel by their armies as they set out.
29¶ Then Moses said to Hobab the son of Reuel the Midianite, Moses' father-in-law, "We are setting out to the place of which the LORD said, 'I will give it to you'; come with us and we will do you good, for the LORD has promised good concerning Israel."
30But he said to him, "I will not come, but rather will go to my *own* land and relatives."
31Then he said, "Please do not leave us, inasmuch as you know where we should camp in the wilderness, and you will be as eyes for us.
32"So it will be, if you go with us, it will come about that whatever good the LORD does for us, we will do for you."
33¶ Thus they set out from the mount of the LORD three days' journey, with the ark of the covenant of the LORD journeying in front of them for the three days, to seek out a resting place for them.
34And the cloud of the LORD was over them by day, when they set out from the camp.
35¶ Then it came about when the ark set out that Moses said,

"Rise up, O LORD!
And let Thine enemies be scattered,
And let those who hate Thee flee [b]before Thee."

36And when it came to rest, he said,

"Return Thou, O LORD,
*To* the myriad thousands of Israel."

### *The People Complain*

**11** NOW THE people became like those who complain of adversity in the hearing of the LORD; and when the LORD heard *it,* His anger was kindled, and the fire of the LORD burned among them and consumed *some* of the outskirts of the camp.
2The people therefore cried out to Moses, and Moses prayed to the LORD, and the fire died out.

## New International

thanel son of Zuar was over the division of the tribe of Issachar,
16and Eliab son of Helon was over the division of the tribe of
Zebulun. 17Then the tabernacle was taken down, and the Gershonites and Merarites, who carried it, set out.
18The divisions of the camp of Reuben went next, under their
standard. Elizur son of Shedeur was in command. 19Shelumiel son
of Zurishaddai was over the division of the tribe of Simeon, 20and
Eliasaph son of Deuel was over the division of the tribe of Gad.
21Then the Kohathites set out, carrying the holy things. The tabernacle was to be set up before they arrived.
22The divisions of the camp of Ephraim went next, under their
standard. Elishama son of Ammihud was in command. 23Gamaliel
son of Pedahzur was over the division of the tribe of Manasseh,
24and Abidan son of Gideoni was over the division of the tribe of
Benjamin.
25Finally, as the rear guard for all the units, the divisions of the
camp of Dan set out, under their standard. Ahiezer son of Ammishaddai was in command. 26Pagiel son of Ocran was over the
division of the tribe of Asher, 27and Ahira son of Enan was over
the division of the tribe of Naphtali. 28This was the order of march
for the Israelite divisions as they set out.
29Now Moses said to Hobab son of Reuel the Midianite, Moses'
father-in-law, "We are setting out for the place about which the
LORD said, 'I will give it to you.' Come with us and we will treat
you well, for the LORD has promised good things to Israel."
30He answered, "No, I will not go; I am going back to my own
land and my own people."
31But Moses said, "Please do not leave us. You know where we
should camp in the desert, and you can be our eyes. 32If you come
with us, we will share with you whatever good things the LORD
gives us."
33So they set out from the mountain of the LORD and traveled
for three days. The ark of the covenant of the LORD went before
them during those three days to find them a place to rest. 34The
cloud of the LORD was over them by day when they set out from
the camp.
35Whenever the ark set out, Moses said,

"Rise up, O LORD!
May your enemies be scattered;
may your foes flee before you."

36Whenever it came to rest, he said,

"Return, O LORD,
to the countless thousands of Israel."

### *Fire From the LORD*

**11** NOW THE people complained about their hardships in
the hearing of the LORD, and when he heard them his
anger was aroused. Then fire from the LORD burned among them
and consumed some of the outskirts of the camp. 2When the
people cried out to Moses, he prayed to the LORD and the fire died

NAS [b] Or, *from Thy presence*

## King James

3 And he called the name of the place Taberah: because the fire of the LORD burnt among them.

4 ¶ And the mixed multitude that *was* among them fell a-lusting: and the children of Israel also wept again, and said, Who shall give us flesh to eat?

5 We remember the fish, which we did eat in Egypt freely; the cucumbers, and the melons, and the leeks, and the onions, and the garlic:

6 But now our soul *is* dried away: *there is* nothing at all, beside this manna, *before* our eyes.

7 And the manna *was* as coriander seed, and the colour thereof as the colour of bdellium.

8 *And* the people went about, and gathered *it*, and ground *it* in mills, or beat *it* in a mortar, and baked *it* in pans, and made cakes of it: and the taste of it was as the taste of fresh oil.

9 And when the dew fell upon the camp in the night, the manna fell upon it.

10 ¶ Then Moses heard the people weep throughout their families, every man in the door of his tent: and the anger of the LORD was kindled greatly; Moses also was displeased.

11 And Moses said unto the LORD, Wherefore hast thou afflicted thy servant? and wherefore have I not found favour in thy sight, that thou layest the burden of all this people upon me?

12 Have I conceived all this people? have I begotten them, that thou shouldest say unto me, Carry them in thy bosom, as a nursing father beareth the sucking child, unto the land which thou swarest unto their fathers?

13 Whence should I have flesh to give unto all this people? for they weep unto me, saying, Give us flesh, that we may eat.

14 I am not able to bear all this people alone, because *it is* too heavy for me.

15 And if thou deal thus with me, kill me, I pray thee, out of hand, if I have found favour in thy sight; and let me not see my wretchedness.

16 ¶ And the LORD said unto Moses, Gather unto me seventy men of the elders of Israel, whom thou knowest to be the elders of the people, and officers over them; and bring them unto the tabernacle of the congregation, that they may stand there with thee.

17 And I will come down and talk with thee there: and I will take of the spirit which *is* upon thee, and will put *it* upon them; and they shall bear the burden of the people with thee, that thou bear *it* not thyself alone.

18 And say thou unto the people, Sanctify yourselves against tomorrow, and ye shall eat flesh: for ye have wept in the ears of the LORD, saying, Who shall give us flesh to eat? for *it was* well with us in Egypt: therefore the LORD will give you flesh, and ye shall eat.

19 Ye shall not eat one day, nor two days, nor five days, neither ten days, nor twenty days;

20 *But* even a whole month, until it come out at your nostrils, and it be loathsome unto you: because that ye have despised the LORD which *is* among you, and have wept before him, saying, Why came we forth out of Egypt?

21 And Moses said, The people, among whom I *am, are* six hundred thousand footmen; and thou hast said, I will give them flesh, that they may eat a whole month.

22 Shall the flocks and the herds be slain for them, to suffice them? or shall all the fish of the sea be gathered together for them, to suffice them?

23 And the LORD said unto Moses, Is the LORD's hand waxed short? thou shalt see now whether my word shall come to pass unto thee or not.

## Amplified

3 He called the name of the place Taberah [burning] because the fire of the Lord burned among them.

4 And the mixed multitude among them [the rabble who followed Israel from Egypt] began to lust greatly [for familiar *and* dainty food]; and the Israelites wept again, and said, Who will give us meat to eat?

5 We remember the fish we ate freely in Egypt *and* without cost, the cucumbers, melons, leeks, onions, and garlic.

6 But now our soul [our strength] is dried up; there is nothing at all [in the way of food] to be seen but this manna.

7 The manna was like coriander seed, and its appearance was like that of bdellium [perhaps a precious stone].

8 The people went about and gathered it, and ground it in mills or beat it in mortars and boiled it in pots, and made cakes of it; and it tasted like cakes baked with fresh oil.

9 And when the dew fell on the camp in the night, the manna fell with it.

10 And Moses heard the people weeping throughout their families, every man at the door of his tent; and the anger of the Lord blazed hotly, and in the eyes of Moses it was evil.

11 And Moses said to the Lord, Why have You dealt ill with Your servants? And why have I not found favor in Your sight, that You lay the burden of all this people on me?

12 Have I conceived all this people? Have I brought them forth, that You should say to me, Carry them in your bosom, as a nursing father carries the sucking child, to the land which You swore to their fathers [to give them]?

13 Where should I get meat to give to all these people? For they weep before me and say, Give us meat, that we may eat.

14 I am not able to carry all these people alone, because the burden is too heavy for me.

15 And if this is the way You deal with me, kill me, I pray You, at once and be granting me a favor, and let me not see my wretchedness [in the failure of all my efforts].

16 And the Lord said to Moses, Gather for Me [a]seventy men of the elders of Israel, whom you know to be the elders of the people and officers over them; and bring them to the tent of meeting, and let them stand there with you.

17 And I will come down and talk with you there; and I will take of the Spirit which is upon you, and will put it upon them; and they shall bear the burden of the people with you, so that you may not have to bear it yourself alone.

18 And say to the people, Consecrate yourselves for tomorrow, and you shall eat meat; for you have wept in the hearing of the Lord, saying, Who will give us meat to eat? For it was well with us in Egypt. Therefore the Lord will give you meat, and you shall eat.

19 You shall not eat one day, or two, or five, or ten, or twenty days;

20 But a whole month, until [you are satiated and vomit it up violently, and it] comes out at your nostrils, and is disgusting to you; because you have rejected *and* despised the Lord Who is among you, and have wept before Him, saying, Why did we come out of Egypt? [Ps. 106:13-15.]

21 But Moses said, The people, among whom I am, are 600,000 footmen [besides all the women and children], and You have said, I will give them meat that they may eat a whole month!

22 Shall flocks and herds be killed to suffice them? Or shall all the fish of the sea be collected to satisfy them?

23 The Lord said to Moses, Has the Lord's hand [His ability and power] become short [thwarted and inadequate]? You shall see now whether My word shall come to pass for you or not. [Isa. 50:2.]

**AMP** [a] A council of seventy elders had existed the year before this (Exod. 24:9), the origin of the Sanhedrin, the highest Jewish assembly for government in the time of our Lord; usually translated "council."

## New American Standard

3So the name of that place was called [b]Taberah, because the fire of the LORD burned among them.

4¶ And the rabble who were among them had greedy desires; and also the sons of Israel wept again and said, "Who will give us meat to eat?

5"We remember the fish which we used to eat free in Egypt, the cucumbers and the melons and the leeks and the onions and the garlic,

6but now our [c]appetite is gone. There is nothing at all to look at except this manna."

7Now the manna was like coriander seed, and its appearance like that of bdellium.

8The people would go about and gather *it* and grind *it* between two millstones or beat *it* in the mortar, and boil *it* in the pot and make cakes with it; and its taste was as the taste of cakes baked with oil.

9And when the dew fell on the camp at night, the manna would fall with it.

*The Complaint of Moses*

10¶ Now Moses heard the people weeping throughout their families, each man at the doorway of his tent; and the anger of the LORD was kindled greatly, and Moses was displeased.

11So Moses said to the LORD, "Why hast Thou [d]been so hard on Thy servant? And why have I not found favor in Thy sight, that Thou hast laid the burden of all this people on me?

12"Was it I who conceived all this people? Was it I who brought them forth, that Thou shouldest say to me, 'Carry them in your bosom as a nurse carries a nursing infant, to the land which Thou didst swear to their fathers'?

13"Where am I to get meat to give to all this people? For they weep before me, saying, 'Give us meat that we may eat!'

14"I alone am not able to carry all this people, because it is too burdensome for me.

15"So if Thou art going to deal thus with me, please kill me at once, if I have found favor in Thy sight, and do not let me see my wretchedness."

*Seventy Elders to Assist*

16¶ The LORD therefore said to Moses, "Gather for Me seventy men from the elders of Israel, whom you know to be the elders of the people and their officers and bring them to the tent of meeting, and let them take their stand there with you.

17"Then I will come down and speak with you there, and I will take of the Spirit who is upon you, and will put *Him* upon them; and they shall bear the burden of the people with you, so that you shall not bear *it* all alone.

18"And say to the people, 'Consecrate yourselves for tomorrow, and you shall eat meat; for you have wept in the ears of the LORD, saying, "Oh that someone would give us meat to eat! For we were well-off in Egypt." Therefore the LORD will give you meat and you shall eat.

19'You shall eat, not one day, nor two days, nor five days, nor ten days, nor twenty days,

20but a whole month, until it comes out of your nostrils and becomes loathsome to you; because you have rejected the LORD who is among you and have wept before Him, saying, "Why did we ever leave Egypt?" ' "

21But Moses said, "The people, among whom I am, are 600,000 on foot; yet Thou hast said, 'I will give them meat in order that they may eat for a whole month.'

22"Should flocks and herds be slaughtered for them, to be sufficient for them? Or should all the fish of the sea be gathered together for them, to be sufficient for them?"

23And the LORD said to Moses, "Is the LORD's power limited? Now you shall see whether My word will come true for you or not."

NAS [b] I.e., burning [c] Lit., *soul is dried up* [d] Lit., *dealt ill with*

## New International

down. 3So that place was called Taberah,[e] because fire from the LORD had burned among them.

*Quail From the LORD*

4The rabble with them began to crave other food, and again the Israelites started wailing and said, "If only we had meat to eat! 5We remember the fish we ate in Egypt at no cost—also the cucumbers, melons, leeks, onions and garlic. 6But now we have lost our appetite; we never see anything but this manna!"

7The manna was like coriander seed and looked like resin. 8The people went around gathering it, and then ground it in a handmill or crushed it in a mortar. They cooked it in a pot or made it into cakes. And it tasted like something made with olive oil. 9When the dew settled on the camp at night, the manna also came down.

10Moses heard the people of every family wailing, each at the entrance to his tent. The LORD became exceedingly angry, and Moses was troubled. 11He asked the LORD, "Why have you brought this trouble on your servant? What have I done to displease you that you put the burden of all these people on me? 12Did I conceive all these people? Did I give them birth? Why do you tell me to carry them in my arms, as a nurse carries an infant, to the land you promised on oath to their forefathers? 13Where can I get meat for all these people? They keep wailing to me, 'Give us meat to eat!' 14I cannot carry all these people by myself; the burden is too heavy for me. 15If this is how you are going to treat me, put me to death right now—if I have found favor in your eyes—and do not let me face my own ruin."

16The LORD said to Moses: "Bring me seventy of Israel's elders who are known to you as leaders and officials among the people. Have them come to the Tent of Meeting, that they may stand there with you. 17I will come down and speak with you there, and I will take of the Spirit that is on you and put the Spirit on them. They will help you carry the burden of the people so that you will not have to carry it alone.

18"Tell the people: 'Consecrate yourselves in preparation for tomorrow, when you will eat meat. The LORD heard you when you wailed, "If only we had meat to eat! We were better off in Egypt!" Now the LORD will give you meat, and you will eat it. 19You will not eat it for just one day, or two days, or five, ten or twenty days, 20but for a whole month—until it comes out of your nostrils and you loathe it—because you have rejected the LORD, who is among you, and have wailed before him, saying, "Why did we ever leave Egypt?" ' "

21But Moses said, "Here I am among six hundred thousand men on foot, and you say, 'I will give them meat to eat for a whole month!' 22Would they have enough if flocks and herds were slaughtered for them? Would they have enough if all the fish in the sea were caught for them?"

23The LORD answered Moses, "Is the LORD's arm too short? You will now see whether or not what I say will come true for you."

NIV [e] 3 *Taberah* means *burning*.

## King James

24¶ And Moses went out, and told the people the words of the
LORD, and gathered the seventy men of the elders of the people,
and set them round about the tabernacle.
25And the LORD came down in a cloud, and spake unto him,
and took of the spirit that *was* upon him, and gave *it* unto the
seventy elders: and it came to pass, *that,* when the spirit rested
upon them, they prophesied, and did not cease.
26But there remained two *of the* men in the camp, the name of
the one *was* Eldad, and the name of the other Medad: and the spirit
rested upon them; and they *were* of them that were written, but
went not out unto the tabernacle: and they prophesied in the
camp.
27And there ran a young man, and told Moses, and said, Eldad
and Medad do prophesy in the camp.
28And Joshua the son of Nun, the servant of Moses, *one* of his
young men, answered and said, My lord Moses, forbid them.
29And Moses said unto him, Enviest thou for my sake? would
God that all the LORD'S people were prophets, *and* that the LORD
would put his spirit upon them!
30And Moses gat him into the camp, he and the elders of Israel.
31¶ And there went forth a wind from the LORD, and brought
quails from the sea, and let *them* fall by the camp, as it were a day's
journey on this side, and as it were a day's journey on the other
side, round about the camp, and as it were two cubits *high* upon
the face of the earth.
32And the people stood up all that day, and all *that* night, and
all the next day, and they gathered the quails: he that gathered
least gathered ten homers: and they spread *them* all abroad for
themselves round about the camp.
33And while the flesh *was* yet between their teeth, ere it was
chewed, the wrath of the LORD was kindled against the people,
and the LORD smote the people with a very great plague.
34And he called the name of that place Kibroth-hattaavah: because there they buried the people that lusted.
35 *And* the people journeyed from Kibroth-hattaavah unto
Hazeroth; and abode at Hazeroth.

**12** AND MIRIAM and Aaron spake against Moses because of
the Ethiopian woman whom he had married: for he had
married an Ethiopian woman.
2And they said, Hath the LORD indeed spoken only by Moses?
hath he not spoken also by us? And the LORD heard *it.*
3(Now the man Moses *was* very meek, above all the men which
*were* upon the face of the earth.)
4And the LORD spake suddenly unto Moses, and unto Aaron,
and unto Miriam, Come out ye three unto the tabernacle of the
congregation. And they three came out.
5And the LORD came down in the pillar of the cloud, and stood
*in* the door of the tabernacle, and called Aaron and Miriam: and
they both came forth.
6And he said, Hear now my words: If there be a prophet among
you, *I* the LORD will make myself known unto him in a vision, *and*
will speak unto him in a dream.
7My servant Moses *is* not so, who *is* faithful in all mine house.

## Amplified

24So Moses went out and told the people the words of the Lord,
and he gathered seventy men of the elders of the people, and set
them round about the tent.
25And the Lord came down in the cloud, and spoke to him, and
took of the Spirit that was upon him, and put it upon the seventy
elders; and when the Spirit rested upon them, they prophesied
[sounding forth the praises of God and declaring His will]. Then
they did so no more. [Cp. v. 29.]
26But there remained two men in the camp, named Eldad and
Medad; the Spirit rested upon them, and they were of those who
were selected *and* listed, yet they did not go out to the tent [as told
to do]; but they prophesied in the camp.
27And a young man ran to Moses and said, Eldad and Medad
are prophesying [sounding forth the praises of God and declaring
His will] in the camp.
28Joshua son of Nun, the minister of Moses, one of his chosen
men, said, My lord Moses, forbid them!
29But Moses said to him, Are you [a]envious *or* jealous for my
sake? Would that all the Lord's people were prophets, and that the
Lord would put His Spirit upon them! [Luke 9:49, 50.]
30And Moses went back into the camp, he and the elders of
Israel.
31And there went forth a wind from the Lord and brought
quails from the sea, and let them fall [so they flew low] beside the
camp, about a day's journey on this side and on the other side,
around the camp, about two cubits above the ground.
32And the people rose all that day, and all night, and all the next
day, and caught *and* gathered the quails; he who gathered least
gathered ten homers; and they spread them out for themselves
round about the camp [to cure them by drying].
33While the meat was yet between their teeth, before it was
consumed, the anger of the Lord was kindled against the people,
and the Lord smote them with a very great plague.
34That place was called Kibroth-hattaavah [the graves of sensuous desire], because there they buried the people who lusted,
whose physical appetite caused them to sin. [I Cor. 10:1-13.]
35The Israelites journeyed from Kibroth-hattaavah to Hazeroth,
where they remained.

**12** NOW MIRIAM and Aaron talked against Moses [their
brother] because of his [b]Cushite wife, for he had married
a Cushite woman.
2And they said, Has the Lord indeed spoken only by Moses?
Has He not spoken also by us? And the Lord heard it.
3Now the man Moses was very meek [gentle, kind and humble]
*or* above all the men on the face of the earth.
4Suddenly the Lord said to Moses, Aaron, and Miriam, Come
out, you three, to the tent of meeting. And they three came out.
5The Lord came down in a pillar of cloud, and stood at the tent
door, and called Aaron and Miriam, and they came forward.
6And He said, Hear now My words: If there is a prophet among
you, I the Lord make Myself known to him in a vision, and speak
to him in a dream.
7But not so with My servant Moses; he is entrusted *and* faithful
in all My house. [Heb. 3:2, 5, 6.]

**AMP** [a] "Moses, the minister of God rebukes our partial love, Who envy at the gifts bestow'd on those we disapprove. We do not our own spirit know, who wish to see suppressed, The men that Jesus' spirit show, the men whom God hath blest." Charles Wesley [b] Zipporah, Moses' wife, seems to have died some time before. Marriage with a Canaanite was forbidden, but not with an Egyptian or Cushite. Joseph's wife was an Egyptian (Gen. 41:45).

## New American Standard

24¶ So Moses went out and told the people the words of the
LORD. Also, he gathered seventy men of the elders of the people,
and stationed them around the tent.
25Then the LORD came down in the cloud and spoke to him; and
He took of the Spirit who was upon him and placed *Him* upon the
seventy elders. And it came about that when the Spirit rested upon
them, they prophesied. But they did not do *it* again.
26¶ But two men had remained in the camp; the name of one
was Eldad and the name of the other Medad. And the Spirit rested
upon them (now they were among those who had been registered,
but had not gone out to the tent), and they prophesied in the camp.
27So a young man ran and told Moses and said, "Eldad and
Medad are prophesying in the camp."
28Then Joshua the son of Nun, the attendant of Moses from his
youth, answered and said, "Moses, my lord, restrain them."
29But Moses said to him, "Are you jealous for my sake? Would
that all the LORD's people were prophets, that the LORD would put
His Spirit upon them!"
30Then Moses returned to the camp, *both* he and the elders of
Israel.

*The Quail and the Plague*

31¶ Now there went forth a wind from the LORD, and it brought
quail from the sea, and let *them* fall beside the camp, about a day's
journey on this side and a day's journey on the other side, all
around the camp, and about two cubits *deep* on the surface of the
ground.
32And the people spent all day and all night and all the next day,
and gathered the quail (he who gathered least gathered ten homers) and they spread *them* out for themselves all around the camp.
33While the meat was still between their teeth, before it was
chewed, the anger of the LORD was kindled against the people, and
the LORD struck the people with a very severe plague.
34So the name of that place was called [c]Kibroth-hattaavah,
because there they buried the people who had been greedy.
35From Kibroth-hattaavah the people set out for Hazeroth, and
they remained at Hazeroth.

*The Murmuring of Miriam and Aaron*

12 THEN MIRIAM and Aaron spoke against Moses because
of the Cushite woman whom he had married (for he had
married a Cushite woman);
2and they said, "Has the LORD indeed spoken only through
Moses? Has He not spoken through us as well?" And the LORD
heard it.
3(Now the man Moses was very humble, more than any man
who was on the face of the earth.)
4And suddenly the LORD said to Moses and Aaron and to
Miriam, "You three come out to the tent of meeting." So the three
of them came out.
5Then the LORD came down in a pillar of cloud and stood at
the doorway of the tent, and He called Aaron and Miriam. When
they had both come forward,
6He said,

"Hear now My words:
If there is a prophet among you,
I, the LORD, shall make Myself known to him in a
vision.
I shall speak with him in a dream.
7 "Not so, with My servant Moses,
He is faithful in all My household;

NAS [c] I.e., the graves of greediness

## New International

24So Moses went out and told the people what the LORD had
said. He brought together seventy of their elders and had them
stand around the Tent. 25Then the LORD came down in the cloud
and spoke with him, and he took of the Spirit that was on him and
put the Spirit on the seventy elders. When the Spirit rested on
them, they prophesied, but they did not do so again.[d]
26However, two men, whose names were Eldad and Medad,
had remained in the camp. They were listed among the elders, but
did not go out to the Tent. Yet the Spirit also rested on them, and
they prophesied in the camp. 27A young man ran and told Moses,
"Eldad and Medad are prophesying in the camp."
28Joshua son of Nun, who had been Moses' aide since youth,
spoke up and said, "Moses, my lord, stop them!"
29But Moses replied, "Are you jealous for my sake? I wish that
all the LORD's people were prophets and that the LORD would put
his Spirit on them!" 30Then Moses and the elders of Israel returned
to the camp.
31Now a wind went out from the LORD and drove quail in from
the sea. It brought them[e] down all around the camp to about three
feet[f] above the ground, as far as a day's walk in any direction.
32All that day and night and all the next day the people went out
and gathered quail. No one gathered less than ten homers.[g] Then
they spread them out all around the camp. 33But while the meat
was still between their teeth and before it could be consumed, the
anger of the LORD burned against the people, and he struck them
with a severe plague. 34Therefore the place was named Kibroth
Hattaavah,[h] because there they buried the people who had craved
other food.
35From Kibroth Hattaavah the people traveled to Hazeroth and
stayed there.

*Miriam and Aaron Oppose Moses*

12 MIRIAM AND Aaron began to talk against Moses because
of his Cushite wife, for he had married a Cushite. 2"Has
the LORD spoken only through Moses?" they asked. "Hasn't he
also spoken through us?" And the LORD heard this.
3(Now Moses was a very humble man, more humble than anyone else on the face of the earth.)
4At once the LORD said to Moses, Aaron and Miriam, "Come
out to the Tent of Meeting, all three of you." So the three of them
came out. 5Then the LORD came down in a pillar of cloud; he stood
at the entrance to the Tent and summoned Aaron and Miriam.
When both of them stepped forward, 6he said, "Listen to my
words:

"When a prophet of the LORD is among you,
I reveal myself to him in visions,
I speak to him in dreams.
7But this is not true of my servant Moses;
he is faithful in all my house.

NIV [d] 25 Or *prophesied and continued to do so* [e] 31 Or *They flew* [f] 31 Hebrew *two cubits* (about 1 meter) [g] 32 That is, probably about 60 bushels (about 2.2 kiloliters) [h] 34 *Kibroth Hattaavah* means *graves of craving.*

## King James

8With him will I speak mouth to mouth, even apparently, and not in dark speeches; and the similitude of the LORD shall he behold: wherefore then were ye not afraid to speak against my servant Moses?
9And the anger of the LORD was kindled against them; and he departed.
10And the cloud departed from off the tabernacle; and, behold, Miriam *became* leprous, *white* as snow: and Aaron looked upon Miriam, and, behold, *she was* leprous.
11And Aaron said unto Moses, Alas, my lord, I beseech thee, lay not the sin upon us, wherein we have done foolishly, and wherein we have sinned.
12Let her not be as one dead, of whom the flesh is half consumed when he cometh out of his mother's womb.
13And Moses cried unto the LORD, saying, Heal her now, O God, I beseech thee.
14¶ And the LORD said unto Moses, If her father had but spit in her face, should she not be ashamed seven days? let her be shut out from the camp seven days, and after that let her be received in *again*.
15And Miriam was shut out from the camp seven days: and the people journeyed not till Miriam was brought in *again*.
16And afterward the people removed from Hazeroth, and pitched in the wilderness of Paran.

13 AND THE LORD spake unto Moses, saying,
2Send thou men, that they may search the land of Canaan, which I give unto the children of Israel: of every tribe of their fathers shall ye send a man, every one a ruler among them.
3And Moses by the commandment of the LORD sent them from the wilderness of Paran: all those men *were* heads of the children of Israel.
4And these *were* their names: of the tribe of Reuben, Shammua the son of Zaccur.
5Of the tribe of Simeon, Shaphat the son of Hori.
6Of the tribe of Judah, Caleb the son of Jephunneh.
7Of the tribe of Issachar, Igal the son of Joseph.
8Of the tribe of Ephraim, Oshea the son of Nun.
9Of the tribe of Benjamin, Palti the son of Raphu.
10Of the tribe of Zebulun, Gaddiel the son of Sodi.
11Of the tribe of Joseph, *namely,* of the tribe of Manasseh, Gaddi the son of Susi.
12Of the tribe of Dan, Ammiel the son of Gemalli.
13Of the tribe of Asher, Sethur the son of Michael.
14Of the tribe of Naphtali, Nahbi the son of Vophsi.
15Of the tribe of Gad, Geuel the son of Machi.
16These *are* the names of the men which Moses sent to spy out the land. And Moses called Oshea the son of Nun Jehoshua.
17¶ And Moses sent them to spy out the land of Canaan, and said unto them, Get you up this *way* southward, and go up into the mountain:
18And see the land, what it *is;* and the people that dwelleth therein, whether they *be* strong or weak, few or many;
19And what the land *is* that they dwell in, whether it *be* good or bad; and what cities *they be* that they dwell in, whether in tents, or in strong holds;
20And what the land *is,* whether it *be* fat or lean, whether there be wood therein, or not. And be ye of good courage, and bring of the fruit of the land. Now the time *was* the time of the firstripe grapes.
21¶ So they went up, and searched the land from the wilderness of Zin unto Rehob, as men come to Hamath.

## Amplified

8With him I speak mouth to mouth [directly] clearly and not in dark speeches; and he beholds the form of the Lord. Why then were you not afraid to speak against My servant Moses?
9And the anger of the Lord was kindled against them, and He departed.
10And when the cloud departed from over the tent, behold Miriam was leprous, as white as snow. And Aaron looked at Miriam, and, behold, she was leprous!
11And Aaron said to Moses, Oh, my lord, I plead with you, lay not the sin upon us, in which we have done foolishly and in which we have sinned.
12Let her not be as one dead, already half decomposed when he comes out of his mother's womb.
13And Moses cried to the Lord, saying, Heal her now, O God, I beseech You!
14And the Lord said to Moses, If her father had but spit in her face, should she not be ashamed seven days? Let her be shut up outside the camp seven days, and after that let her be brought in again.
15So Miriam was shut up without the camp seven days; and the people did not journey on until Miriam was brought in again.
16Afterward [they] removed from Hazeroth, and encamped in the wilderness of Paran.

13 AND THE Lord said to Moses,
2Send men to explore *and* scout out [for yourselves] the land of Canaan, which I give to the Israelites; from each tribe of their fathers you shall send a man, every one a leader *or* head among them.
3So Moses by the command of the Lord sent scouts from the wilderness of Paran, all of them men who were heads of the Israelites.
4These were their names: of the tribe of Reuben, Shammua son of Zaccur.
5Of the tribe of Simeon, Shaphat son of Hori.
6Of the tribe of Judah, Caleb son of Jephunneh.
7Of the tribe of Issachar, Igal son of Joseph.
8Of the tribe of Ephraim, Hoshea [that is, Joshua] son of Nun.
9Of the tribe of Benjamin, Palti son of Raphu.
10Of the tribe of Zebulun, Gaddiel son of Sodi.
11Of the tribe of Joseph, that is, of the tribe of Manasseh, Gaddi son of Susi.
12Of the tribe of Dan, Ammiel son of Gemalli.
13Of the tribe of Asher, Sethur son of Michael.
14Of the tribe of Naphtali, Nahbi son of Vophsi.
15Of the tribe of Gad, Geuel son of Machi.
16These are the names of the men whom Moses sent to explore *and* scout out the land. And Moses called Hoshea son of Nun Joshua.
17Moses sent them to scout out the land of Canaan, and said to them, Get up this way by the Negeb [the South] and go up into the hill country,
18And see what the land is, and whether the people who dwell there are strong or weak, few or many;
19And whether the land they live in is good or bad, and whether the cities they dwell in are camps or strongholds,
20And what the land is, whether it is fat or lean, whether there is timber on it, or not. And be of good courage, and bring some of the fruit of the land. Now the time was the time of the first ripe grapes.
21So they went up, and scouted through the land from the wilderness of Zin to Rehob, to the entrance of Hamath.

## New American Standard

8 With him I speak mouth to mouth,
Even openly, and not in dark sayings,
And he beholds the form of the LORD.
Why then were you not afraid
To speak against My servant, against Moses?"
9¶ So the anger of the LORD burned against them and He
departed.
10But when the cloud had withdrawn from over the tent, behold, Miriam *was* leprous, as *white as* snow. As Aaron turned
toward Miriam, behold, she *was* leprous.
11Then Aaron said to Moses, "Oh, my lord, I beg you, do not
account *this* sin to us, in which we have acted foolishly and in
which we have sinned.
12"Oh, do not let her be like one dead, whose flesh is half eaten
away when he comes from his mother's womb!"
13And Moses cried out to the LORD, saying, "O God, heal her,
I pray!"
14But the LORD said to Moses, "If her father had but spit in her
face, would she not bear her shame for seven days? Let her be shut
up for seven days outside the camp, and afterward she may be
received again."
15So Miriam was shut up outside the camp for seven days, and
the people did not move on until Miriam was received again.
16¶ Afterward, however, the people moved out from Hazeroth
and camped in the wilderness of Paran.

*Spies View the Land*

13 THEN THE LORD spoke to Moses saying,
2"Send out for yourself men so that they may spy out the
land of Canaan, which I am going to give to the sons of Israel; you
shall send a man from each of their fathers' tribes, every one a
leader among them."
3So Moses sent them from the wilderness of Paran at the
command of the LORD, all of them men who were heads of the sons
of Israel.
4These then *were* their names: from the tribe of Reuben, Shammua the son of Zaccur;
5from the tribe of Simeon, Shaphat the son of Hori;
6from the tribe of Judah, Caleb the son of Jephunneh;
7from the tribe of Issachar, Igal the son of Joseph;
8from the tribe of Ephraim, Hoshea the son of Nun;
9from the tribe of Benjamin, Palti the son of Raphu;
10from the tribe of Zebulun, Gaddiel the son of Sodi;
11from the tribe of Joseph, from the tribe of Manasseh, Gaddi
the son of Susi;
12from the tribe of Dan, Ammiel the son of Gemalli;
13from the tribe of Asher, Sethur the son of Michael;
14from the tribe of Naphtali, Nahbi the son of Vophsi;
15from the tribe of Gad, Geuel the son of Machi.
16These are the names of the men whom Moses sent to spy out
the land; but Moses called Hoshea the son of Nun, Joshua.
17¶ When Moses sent them to spy out the land of Canaan, he
said to them, "Go up there into the [a]Negev; then go up into the
hill country.
18"And see what the land is like, and whether the people who
live in it are strong *or* weak, whether they are few or many.
19"And how is the land in which they live, is it good or bad?
And how are the cities in which they live, are *they* like *open* camps
or with fortifications?
20"And how is the land, is it fat or lean? Are there trees in it or
not? Make an effort then to get some of the fruit of the land." Now
the time was the time of the first ripe grapes.
21¶ So they went up and spied out the land from the wilderness
of Zin as far as Rehob, at Lebo-hamath.

NAS [a] I.e., South country, and so throughout this context

## New International

8With him I speak face to face,
clearly and not in riddles;
he sees the form of the LORD.
Why then were you not afraid
to speak against my servant Moses?"
9The anger of the LORD burned against them, and he left them.
10When the cloud lifted from above the Tent, there stood Miriam—leprous,[b] like snow. Aaron turned toward her and saw that
she had leprosy; 11and he said to Moses, "Please, my lord, do not
hold against us the sin we have so foolishly committed. 12Do not
let her be like a stillborn infant coming from its mother's womb
with its flesh half eaten away."
13So Moses cried out to the LORD, "O God, please heal her!"
14The LORD replied to Moses, "If her father had spit in her face,
would she not have been in disgrace for seven days? Confine her
outside the camp for seven days; after that she can be brought
back." 15So Miriam was confined outside the camp for seven days,
and the people did not move on till she was brought back.
16After that, the people left Hazeroth and encamped in the
Desert of Paran.

*Exploring Canaan*

13 THE LORD said to Moses, 2"Send some men to explore
the land of Canaan, which I am giving to the Israelites.
From each ancestral tribe send one of its leaders."
3So at the LORD's command Moses sent them out from the
Desert of Paran. All of them were leaders of the Israelites. 4These
are their names:

from the tribe of Reuben, Shammua son of Zaccur;
5from the tribe of Simeon, Shaphat son of Hori;
6from the tribe of Judah, Caleb son of Jephunneh;
7from the tribe of Issachar, Igal son of Joseph;
8from the tribe of Ephraim, Hoshea son of Nun;
9from the tribe of Benjamin, Palti son of Raphu;
10from the tribe of Zebulun, Gaddiel son of Sodi;
11from the tribe of Manasseh (a tribe of Joseph), Gaddi son of
Susi;
12from the tribe of Dan, Ammiel son of Gemalli;
13from the tribe of Asher, Sethur son of Michael;
14from the tribe of Naphtali, Nahbi son of Vophsi;
15from the tribe of Gad, Geuel son of Maki.

16These are the names of the men Moses sent to explore the land.
(Moses gave Hoshea son of Nun the name Joshua.)
17When Moses sent them to explore Canaan, he said, "Go up
through the Negev and on into the hill country. 18See what the
land is like and whether the people who live there are strong or
weak, few or many. 19What kind of land do they live in? Is it good
or bad? What kind of towns do they live in? Are they unwalled or
fortified? 20How is the soil? Is it fertile or poor? Are there trees on
it or not? Do your best to bring back some of the fruit of the land."
(It was the season for the first ripe grapes.)
21So they went up and explored the land from the Desert of Zin
as far as Rehob, toward Lebo[c] Hamath. 22They went up through

NIV [b] *10* The Hebrew word was used for various diseases affecting the skin—not necessarily leprosy. [c] *21* Or *toward the entrance to*

## King James

22And they ascended by the south, and came unto Hebron;
where Ahiman, Sheshai, and Talmai, the children of Anak, *were*.
(Now Hebron was built seven years before Zoan in Egypt.)
23And they came unto the brook of Eshcol, and cut down from
thence a branch with one cluster of grapes, and they bare it between two upon a staff; and *they brought* of the pomegranates, and
of the figs.
24The place was called the brook Eshcol, because of the cluster
of grapes which the children of Israel cut down from thence.
25And they returned from searching of the land after forty days.
26¶ And they went and came to Moses, and to Aaron, and to
all the congregation of the children of Israel, unto the wilderness
of Paran, to Kadesh; and brought back word unto them, and unto
all the congregation, and showed them the fruit of the land.
27And they told him, and said, We came unto the land whither
thou sentest us, and surely it floweth with milk and honey; and
this *is* the fruit of it.
28Nevertheless the people *be* strong that dwell in the land, and
the cities *are* walled, *and* very great: and moreover we saw the
children of Anak there.
29The Amalekites dwell in the land of the south: and the Hittites, and the Jebusites, and the Amorites, dwell in the mountains:
and the Canaanites dwell by the sea, and by the coast of Jordan.
30And Caleb stilled the people before Moses, and said, Let us
go up at once, and possess it; for we are well able to overcome it.
31But the men that went up with him said, We be not able to
go up against the people; for they *are* stronger than we.
32And they brought up an evil report of the land which they had
searched unto the children of Israel, saying, The land, through
which we have gone to search it, *is* a land that eateth up the
inhabitants thereof; and all the people that we saw in it *are* men
of a great stature.
33And there we saw the giants, the sons of Anak, *which come*
of the giants: and we were in our own sight as grasshoppers, and
so we were in their sight.

**14** AND ALL the congregation lifted up their voice, and
cried; and the people wept that night.
2And all the children of Israel murmured against Moses and
against Aaron: and the whole congregation said unto them, Would
God that we had died in the land of Egypt! or would God we had
died in this wilderness!
3And wherefore hath the LORD brought us unto this land, to fall
by the sword, that our wives and our children should be a prey?
were it not better for us to return into Egypt?
4And they said one to another, Let us make a captain, and let
us return into Egypt.
5Then Moses and Aaron fell on their faces before all the assembly of the congregation of the children of Israel.
6¶ And Joshua the son of Nun, and Caleb the son of Jephunneh,
*which were* of them that searched the land, rent their clothes:
7And they spake unto all the company of the children of Israel,
saying, The land, which we passed through to search it, *is* an
exceeding good land.
8If the LORD delight in us, then he will bring us into this land,
and give it us; a land which floweth with milk and honey.
9Only rebel not ye against the LORD, neither fear ye the people
of the land; for they *are* bread for us: their defence is departed from
them, and the LORD *is* with us: fear them not.

## Amplified

22And then went up into the South [the Negeb], and came to
Hebron; and Ahiman, Sheshai, and Talmai [probably three tribes
of] the sons of Anak were there. (Hebron was built seven years
before Zoan in Egypt.)
23And they came to the Valley of Eshcol, and cut down from
there a branch with one cluster of grapes, and they carried it on
a pole between two [of them]; they brought also some pomegranates and figs.
24That place was called the Valley of Eshcol [cluster], because
of the cluster which the Israelites cut down there.
25And they returned from scouting out the land after forty days.
26They came to Moses and Aaron and to all the Israelite congregation in the wilderness of Paran at Kadesh, and brought them
word, and showed them the land's fruit.
27They told Moses, We came to the land to which you sent us;
surely it flows with milk and honey; this is its fruit.
28But the people who dwell there are strong, and the cities are
[a]fortified *and* very large; moreover there we saw the sons of Anak
[of great stature and courage].
29Amalek dwells in the land of the South [the Negeb]; the
Hittite, the Jebusite, and the Amorite dwell in the hill country; and
the Canaanite dwells by the sea, and along by the side of the
Jordan [River].
30Caleb quieted the people before Moses, and said, Let us go
up at once and possess it; we are well able to conquer it.
31But his fellow scouts said, We are not able to go up against
the people [of Canaan]; for they are stronger than we are.
32So they brought the Israelites an evil report of the land which
they had scouted out, saying, The land, through which we went
to spy it out, is a land that devours its inhabitants; and all the
people that we saw in it are men of great stature.
33There we saw the Nephilim [or giants], the sons of Anak, who
come from the giants; and we were in our own sight as grasshoppers, and so we were in their sight.

**14** AND ALL the congregation cried out with a loud voice,
and [they] wept that night.
2All the Israelites grumbled *and* deplored their situation, accusing Moses and Aaron, to whom the whole congregation said,
Would that we had died in Egypt! Or that we had died in this
wilderness!
3Why does the Lord bring us to this land, to fall by the sword?
Our wives and little ones will be a prey; is it not better for us to
return to Egypt? [Acts 7:37-39.]
4And they said one to another, Let us choose a captain and
return to Egypt.
5Then Moses and Aaron fell on their faces before all the assembly of Israelites.
6And Joshua son of Nun and Caleb son of Jephunneh, who
were among the scouts who had searched the land, rent their
clothes;
7And they said to all the company of Israelites, The land
through which we passed as scouts is an exceedingly good land.
8If the Lord delights in us, then He will bring us into this land
and give it to us, a land flowing with milk and honey.
9Only do not rebel against the Lord, neither fear the people of
the land; for they are bread for us; their defense *and* the shadow
[of protection] is removed from over them, but the Lord is with us;
fear them not.

**AMP** [a] The scouts probably had not seen walled cities before, having lived their childhood in Goshen in Egypt. Those who forgot God's power to help them, naturally found the situation formidable, as happens in the lives of most people. "'But God' makes all the difference between cowards and Calebs."

## New American Standard

22When they had gone up into the Negev, they came to Hebron where Ahiman, Sheshai and Talmai, the descendants of Anak were. (Now Hebron was built seven years before Zoan in Egypt.)

23¶ Then they came to the valley of [b]Eshcol and from there cut down a branch with a single cluster of grapes; and they carried it on a pole between two *men*, with some of the pomegranates and the figs.

24That place was called the valley of Eshcol, because of the cluster which the sons of Israel cut down from there.

*The Spies' Reports*

25¶ When they returned from spying out the land, at the end of forty days,

26they proceeded to come to Moses and Aaron and to all the congregation of the sons of Israel in the wilderness of Paran, at Kadesh; and they brought back word to them and to all the congregation and showed them the fruit of the land.

27Thus they told him, and said, "We went in to the land where you sent us; and it certainly does flow with milk and honey, and this is its fruit.

28"Nevertheless, the people who live in the land are strong, and the cities are fortified *and* very large; and moreover, we saw the descendants of Anak there.

29"Amalek is living in the land of the Negev and the Hittites and the Jebusites and the Amorites are living in the hill country, and the Canaanites are living by the sea and by the side of the Jordan."

30¶ Then Caleb quieted the people before Moses, and said, "We should by all means go up and take possession of it, for we shall surely overcome it."

31But the men who had gone up with him said, "We are not able to go up against the people, for they are too strong for us."

32So they gave out to the sons of Israel a bad report of the land which they had spied out, saying, "The land through which we have gone, in spying it out, is a land that devours its inhabitants; and all the people whom we saw in it are men of *great* size.

33"There also we saw the Nephilim (the sons of Anak are part of the Nephilim); and we became like grasshoppers in our own sight, and so we were in their sight."

*The People Rebel*

14 THEN ALL the congregation lifted up their voices and cried, and the people wept that night.

2And all the sons of Israel grumbled against Moses and Aaron; and the whole congregation said to them, "Would that we had died in the land of Egypt! Or would that we had died in this wilderness!

3"And why is the LORD bringing us into this land, to fall by the sword? Our wives and our little ones will become plunder; would it not be better for us to return to Egypt?"

4So they said to one another, "Let us appoint a leader and return to Egypt."

5¶ Then Moses and Aaron fell on their faces in the presence of all the assembly of the congregation of the sons of Israel.

6And Joshua the son of Nun and Caleb the son of Jephunneh, of those who had spied out the land, tore their clothes;

7and they spoke to all the congregation of the sons of Israel, saying, "The land which we passed through to spy out is an exceedingly good land.

8"If the LORD is pleased with us, then He will bring us into this land, and give it to us—a land which flows with milk and honey.

9"Only do not rebel against the LORD; and do not fear the people of the land, for they shall be our prey. Their protection has been removed from them, and the LORD is with us; do not fear them."

NAS [b] I.e., cluster

## New International

the Negev and came to Hebron, where Ahiman, Sheshai and
Talmai, the descendants of Anak, lived. (Hebron had been built
seven years before Zoan in Egypt.) 23When they reached the Valley
of Eshcol,[c] they cut off a branch bearing a single cluster of grapes.
Two of them carried it on a pole between them, along with some
pomegranates and figs. 24That place was called the Valley of Eshcol
because of the cluster of grapes the Israelites cut off there. 25At the
end of forty days they returned from exploring the land.

*Report on the Exploration*

26They came back to Moses and Aaron and the whole Israelite
community at Kadesh in the Desert of Paran. There they reported
to them and to the whole assembly and showed them the fruit of
the land. 27They gave Moses this account: "We went into the land
to which you sent us, and it does flow with milk and honey! Here
is its fruit. 28But the people who live there are powerful, and the
cities are fortified and very large. We even saw descendants of
Anak there. 29The Amalekites live in the Negev; the Hittites, Jebusites and Amorites live in the hill country; and the Canaanites live
near the sea and along the Jordan."

30Then Caleb silenced the people before Moses and said, "We
should go up and take possession of the land, for we can certainly
do it."

31But the men who had gone up with him said, "We can't attack
those people; they are stronger than we are." 32And they spread
among the Israelites a bad report about the land they had explored.
They said, "The land we explored devours those living in it. All
the people we saw there are of great size. 33We saw the Nephilim
there (the descendants of Anak come from the Nephilim). We
seemed like grasshoppers in our own eyes, and we looked the
same to them."

*The People Rebel*

14 THAT NIGHT all the people of the community raised their
voices and wept aloud. 2All the Israelites grumbled
against Moses and Aaron, and the whole assembly said to them,
"If only we had died in Egypt! Or in this desert! 3Why is the LORD
bringing us to this land only to let us fall by the sword? Our wives
and children will be taken as plunder. Wouldn't it be better for us
to go back to Egypt?" 4And they said to each other, "We should
choose a leader and go back to Egypt."

5Then Moses and Aaron fell facedown in front of the whole
Israelite assembly gathered there. 6Joshua son of Nun and Caleb
son of Jephunneh, who were among those who had explored the
land, tore their clothes 7and said to the entire Israelite assembly,
"The land we passed through and explored is exceedingly good.
8If the LORD is pleased with us, he will lead us into that land, a land
flowing with milk and honey, and will give it to us. 9Only do not
rebel against the LORD. And do not be afraid of the people of the
land, because we will swallow them up. Their protection is gone,
but the LORD is with us. Do not be afraid of them."

NIV [c] 23 *Eshcol* means *cluster;* also in verse 24.

## King James

10But all the congregation bade stone them with stones. And the glory of the LORD appeared in the tabernacle of the congregation before all the children of Israel.

11¶ And the LORD said unto Moses, How long will this people provoke me? and how long will it be ere they believe me, for all the signs which I have shown among them?

12I will smite them with the pestilence, and disinherit them, and will make of thee a greater nation and mightier than they.

13¶ And Moses said unto the LORD, Then the Egyptians shall hear *it*, (for thou broughtest up this people in thy might from among them;)

14And they will tell *it* to the inhabitants of this land: *for* they have heard that thou LORD *art* among this people, that thou LORD art seen face to face, and *that* thy cloud standeth over them, and *that* thou goest before them, by day time in a pillar of a cloud, and in a pillar of fire by night.

15¶ Now *if* thou shalt kill *all* this people as one man, then the nations which have heard the fame of thee will speak, saying,

16Because the LORD was not able to bring this people into the land which he sware unto them, therefore he hath slain them in the wilderness.

17And now, I beseech thee, let the power of my LORD be great, according as thou hast spoken, saying,

18The LORD *is* longsuffering, and of great mercy, forgiving iniquity and transgression, and by no means clearing *the guilty*, visiting the iniquity of the fathers upon the children unto the third and fourth *generation*.

19Pardon, I beseech thee, the iniquity of this people according unto the greatness of thy mercy, and as thou hast forgiven this people, from Egypt even until now.

20And the LORD said, I have pardoned according to thy word:

21But *as* truly *as* I live, all the earth shall be filled with the glory of the LORD.

22Because all those men which have seen my glory, and my miracles, which I did in Egypt and in the wilderness, and have tempted me now these ten times, and have not hearkened to my voice;

23Surely they shall not see the land which I sware unto their fathers, neither shall any of them that provoked me see it:

24But my servant Caleb, because he had another spirit with him, and hath followed me fully, him will I bring into the land whereinto he went; and his seed shall possess it.

25(Now the Amalekites and the Canaanites dwelt in the valley.) Tomorrow turn you, and get you into the wilderness by the way of the Red sea.

26¶ And the LORD spake unto Moses and unto Aaron, saying,

27How long *shall I bear with* this evil congregation, which murmur against me? I have heard the murmurings of the children of Israel, which they murmur against me.

28Say unto them, *As truly as* I live, saith the LORD, as ye have spoken in mine ears, so will I do to you:

29Your carcases shall fall in this wilderness; and all that were numbered of you, according to your whole number, from twenty years old and upward, which have murmured against me,

30Doubtless ye shall not come into the land, *concerning* which I sware to make you dwell therein, save Caleb the son of Jephunneh, and Joshua the son of Nun.

31But your little ones, which ye said should be a prey, them will I bring in, and they shall know the land which ye have despised.

32But *as for* you, your carcases, they shall fall in this wilderness.

33And your children shall wander in the wilderness forty years, and bear your whoredoms, until your carcases be wasted in the wilderness.

## Amplified

10But all the congregation said to stone [Joshua and Caleb] with stones. But the glory of the Lord appeared at the tent of meeting before all the Israelites.

11And the Lord said to Moses, How long will this people provoke (spurn, despise) Me? And how long will it be before they believe Me [trusting in, relying on, clinging to Me], for all the signs which I have performed among them?

12I will smite them with the pestilence, and disinherit them, and will make of you [Moses] a nation greater and mightier than they.

13But Moses said to the Lord, Then the Egyptians will hear of it, for You brought up this people in Your might from among them;

14And they will tell it to the inhabitants of this land. They have heard that You, Lord, are in the midst of this people [of Israel]: that You, Lord, are seen face to face, and that Your cloud stands over them and that You go before them, in a pillar of cloud by day and in a pillar of fire by night.

15Now if You kill all this people as one man, then the nations that have heard Your fame will say,

16Because the Lord was not able to bring this people into the land which He swore to give to them, therefore He has slain them in the wilderness.

17And now, I pray You, let the power of my Lord be great, as You have promised, saying,

18The Lord is longsuffering *and* slow to anger, and abundant in mercy *and* lovingkindness, forgiving iniquity and transgression; but He will by no means clear the guilty, visiting the iniquity of the fathers upon the children, upon the third and fourth generation. [Exod. 34:6, 7.]

19Pardon, I pray You, the iniquity of this people according to the greatness of Your mercy *and* loving-kindness, and as You have forgiven [them] from Egypt until now.

20And the Lord said, I have pardoned according to your word;

21But truly as I live, and as all the earth shall be filled with the glory of the Lord, [Isa. 6:3; 11:9.]

22Because all those men who have seen My glory and My [miraculous] signs, which I performed in Egypt and in the wilderness, yet have tested *and* proved Me these ten times and have not heeded My voice,

23Surely they shall not see the land which I swore to give to their fathers; nor shall any who provoked (spurned, despised) Me see it. [Heb. 6:4-11.]

24But My servant Caleb, because he has a different spirit and has followed Me fully, I will bring into the land into which he went; and his descendants shall possess it.

25Now, because the Amalekites and the Canaanites dwell in the valley, tomorrow turn and go into the wilderness by way of the Red Sea.

26And the Lord said to Moses and Aaron,

27How long will this evil congregation murmur against Me? I have heard the complaints the Israelites murmur against Me.

28Tell them, As I live, says the Lord, what you have said in My hearing I will do to you:

29Your dead bodies shall fall in this wilderness; of all who were numbered of you, from twenty years old and upward, who have murmured against Me, [Heb. 3:17-19.]

30Surely none shall come into the land, in which I swore to make you dwell, except Caleb son of Jephunneh, and Joshua son of Nun.

31But your little ones, whom you said would be a prey, them will I bring in, and they shall know the land which you have despised *and* rejected.

32But as for you, your dead bodies shall fall in this wilderness.

33And your children shall be wanderers *and* shepherds in the wilderness forty years, and shall suffer for your whoredoms [your infidelity to your espoused God], until your corpses are consumed in the wilderness.

## New American Standard

10But all the congregation said to stone them with stones. Then the glory of the LORD appeared in the tent of meeting to all the sons of Israel.

*Moses Pleads for the People*

11¶ And the LORD said to Moses, "How long will this people spurn Me? And how long will they not believe in Me, despite all the signs which I have performed in their midst?

12"I will smite them with pestilence and dispossess them, and I will make you into a nation greater and mightier than they."

13¶ But Moses said to the LORD, "Then the Egyptians will hear of it, for by Thy strength Thou didst bring up this people from their midst,

14and they will tell *it* to the inhabitants of this land. They have heard that Thou, O LORD, art in the midst of this people, for Thou, O LORD, art seen eye to eye, while Thy cloud stands over them; and Thou dost go before them in a pillar of cloud by day and in a pillar of fire by night.

15"Now if Thou dost slay this people as one man, then the nations who have heard of Thy fame will say,

16'Because the LORD could not bring this people into the land which He promised them by oath, therefore He slaughtered them in the wilderness.'

17"But now, I pray, let the power of the Lord be great, just as Thou hast declared,

18'The LORD is slow to anger and abundant in lovingkindness, forgiving iniquity and transgression; but He will by no means clear *the guilty*, visiting the iniquity of the fathers on the children to the third and the fourth *generations*.'

19"Pardon, I pray, the iniquity of this people according to the greatness of Thy lovingkindness, just as Thou also hast forgiven this people, from Egypt even until now."

*The LORD Pardons and Rebukes*

20¶ So the LORD said, "I have pardoned *them* according to your word;

21but indeed, as I live, all the earth will be filled with the glory of the LORD.

22"Surely all the men who have seen My glory and My signs, which I performed in Egypt and in the wilderness, yet have put Me to the test these ten times and have not listened to My voice,

23shall by no means see the land which I swore to their fathers, nor shall any of those who spurned Me see it.

24"But My servant Caleb, because he has had a different spirit and has followed Me fully, I will bring into the land which he entered, and his descendants shall take possession of it.

25"Now the Amalekites and the Canaanites live in the valleys; turn tomorrow and set out to the wilderness by the way of the Red Sea."

26¶ And the LORD spoke to Moses and Aaron, saying,

27"How long *shall I bear* with this evil congregation who are grumbling against Me? I have heard the complaints of the sons of Israel, which they are making against Me.

28"Say to them, 'As I live,' says the LORD, 'just as you have spoken in My hearing, so I will surely do to you;

29your corpses shall fall in this wilderness, even all your numbered men, according to your complete number from twenty years old and upward, who have grumbled against Me.

30'Surely you shall not come into the land in which I swore to settle you, except Caleb the son of Jephunneh and Joshua the son of Nun.

31'Your children, however, whom you said would become a prey—I will bring them in, and they shall know the land which you have rejected.

32'But as for you, your corpses shall fall in this wilderness.

33'And your sons shall be shepherds for forty years in the wilderness, and they shall suffer *for* your unfaithfulness, until your corpses lie in the wilderness.

## New International

10But the whole assembly talked about stoning them. Then the
glory of the LORD appeared at the Tent of Meeting to all the
Israelites. 11The LORD said to Moses, "How long will these people
treat me with contempt? How long will they refuse to believe in
me, in spite of all the miraculous signs I have performed among
them? 12I will strike them down with a plague and destroy them,
but I will make you into a nation greater and stronger than they."
13Moses said to the LORD, "Then the Egyptians will hear about
it! By your power you brought these people up from among them.
14And they will tell the inhabitants of this land about it. They have
already heard that you, O LORD, are with these people and that
you, O LORD, have been seen face to face, that your cloud stays
over them, and that you go before them in a pillar of cloud by day
and a pillar of fire by night. 15If you put these people to death all
at one time, the nations who have heard this report about you will
say, 16'The LORD was not able to bring these people into the land
he promised them on oath; so he slaughtered them in the desert.'
17"Now may the Lord's strength be displayed, just as you have
declared: 18'The LORD is slow to anger, abounding in love and
forgiving sin and rebellion. Yet he does not leave the guilty unpunished; he punishes the children for the sin of the fathers to the third
and fourth generation.' 19In accordance with your great love, forgive the sin of these people, just as you have pardoned them from
the time they left Egypt until now."
20The LORD replied, "I have forgiven them, as you asked.
21Nevertheless, as surely as I live and as surely as the glory of the
LORD fills the whole earth, 22not one of the men who saw my glory
and the miraculous signs I performed in Egypt and in the desert
but who disobeyed me and tested me ten times— 23not one of
them will ever see the land I promised on oath to their forefathers.
No one who has treated me with contempt will ever see it. 24But
because my servant Caleb has a different spirit and follows me
wholeheartedly, I will bring him into the land he went to, and his
descendants will inherit it. 25Since the Amalekites and Canaanites
are living in the valleys, turn back tomorrow and set out toward
the desert along the route to the Red Sea.[a]"
26The LORD said to Moses and Aaron: 27"How long will this
wicked community grumble against me? I have heard the complaints of these grumbling Israelites. 28So tell them, 'As surely as
I live, declares the LORD, I will do to you the very things I heard
you say: 29In this desert your bodies will fall—every one of you
twenty years old or more who was counted in the census and who
has grumbled against me. 30Not one of you will enter the land I
swore with uplifted hand to make your home, except Caleb son of
Jephunneh and Joshua son of Nun. 31As for your children that you
said would be taken as plunder, I will bring them in to enjoy the
land you have rejected. 32But you—your bodies will fall in this
desert. 33Your children will be shepherds here for forty years,
suffering for your unfaithfulness, until the last of your bodies lies
in the desert. 34For forty years—one year for each of the forty days

**NIV** [a] 25 Hebrew *Yam Suph;* that is, Sea of Reeds

## King James

34After the number of the days in which ye searched the land, *even* forty days, each day for a year, shall ye bear your iniquities, *even* forty years, and ye shall know my breach of promise.

35I the LORD have said, I will surely do it unto all this evil congregation, that are gathered together against me: in this wilderness they shall be consumed, and there they shall die.

36And the men, which Moses sent to search the land, who returned, and made all the congregation to murmur against him, by bringing up a slander upon the land,

37Even those men that did bring up the evil report upon the land, died by the plague before the LORD.

38But Joshua the son of Nun, and Caleb the son of Jephunneh, *which were* of the men that went to search the land, lived *still.*

39And Moses told these sayings unto all the children of Israel: and the people mourned greatly.

40¶ And they rose up early in the morning, and gat them up into the top of the mountain, saying, Lo, we *be here,* and will go up unto the place which the LORD hath promised: for we have sinned.

41And Moses said, Wherefore now do ye transgress the commandment of the LORD? but it shall not prosper.

42Go not up, for the LORD *is* not among you; that ye be not smitten before your enemies.

43For the Amalekites and the Canaanites *are* there before you, and ye shall fall by the sword: because ye are turned away from the LORD, therefore the LORD will not be with you.

44But they presumed to go up unto the hill top: nevertheless the ark of the covenant of the LORD, and Moses, departed not out of the camp.

45Then the Amalekites came down, and the Canaanites which dwelt in that hill, and smote them, and discomfited them, *even* unto Hormah.

**15** AND THE LORD spake unto Moses, saying,

2Speak unto the children of Israel, and say unto them, When ye be come into the land of your habitations, which I give unto you,

3And will make an offering by fire unto the LORD, a burnt offering, or a sacrifice in performing a vow, or in a freewill offering, or in your solemn feasts, to make a sweet savour unto the LORD, of the herd, or of the flock:

4Then shall he that offereth his offering unto the LORD bring a meat offering of a tenth deal of flour mingled with the fourth *part* of an hin of oil.

5And the fourth *part* of an hin of wine for a drink offering shalt thou prepare with the burnt offering or sacrifice, for one lamb.

6Or for a ram, thou shalt prepare *for* a meat offering two tenth deals of flour mingled with the third *part* of an hin of oil.

7And for a drink offering thou shalt offer the third *part* of an hin of wine, *for* a sweet savour unto the LORD.

8And when thou preparest a bullock *for* a burnt offering, or *for* a sacrifice in performing a vow, or peace offerings unto the LORD:

9Then shall he bring with a bullock a meat offering of three tenth deals of flour mingled with half an hin of oil.

10And thou shalt bring for a drink offering half an hin of wine, *for* an offering made by fire, of a sweet savour unto the LORD.

11Thus shall it be done for one bullock, or for one ram, or for a lamb, or a kid.

12According to the number that ye shall prepare, so shall ye do to every one according to their number.

## Amplified

34After the number of the days in which you spied out the land [of Canaan], even forty days, for each day a year, shall you bear *and* suffer for your iniquities, even forty years; and you shall know My displeasure [the revoking of My promise *and* My estrangement].

35I the Lord have spoken; surely this will I do to all this evil congregation that are gathered together against Me; in this wilderness they shall be consumed [by war, disease, plagues] and here they shall die. [I Cor. 10:10, 11.]

36And the men whom Moses sent to search the land, who returned and made all the congregation grumble *and* complain against him by bringing back a slanderous report of the land,

37Even those men who brought the evil report of the land, died by a plague before the Lord. [Heb. 3:17-19; Jude 5-7.]

38But Joshua son of Nun and Caleb son of Jephunneh, who were among the men who went to search the land, lived still.

39Moses told [the Lord's] words to all the Israelites, and [they] mourned greatly.

40And they rose early in the morning, and went up to the top of the mountain, saying, Lo, we are here, and we intend to go up to the place which the Lord has promised; for we have sinned.

41But Moses said, Why now do you transgress the command of the Lord [to turn back by way of the Red Sea] since it will not succeed?

42Go not up, for the Lord is not among you, that you be not struck down before your enemies.

43For the Amalekites and the Canaanites are there before you, and you shall fall by the sword; because you have turned away from following after the Lord, therefore the Lord will not be with you.

44But they presumed to go up to the heights of the hill country; however, the ark of the covenant of the Lord, and Moses, did not depart out of the camp.

45Then the Amalekites came down and the Canaanites who dwelt in that hill country, and smote the Israelites and beat them back, even as far as Hormah.

**15** AND THE Lord said to Moses,

2Say to the Israelites, When you come into the land where you are to live, which I am giving you,

3And will make an offering by fire to the Lord from the herd or from the flock, a burnt offering or a sacrifice to fulfill a special vow or as a freewill offering or in your set feasts, to make a pleasant *and* soothing fragrance to the Lord,

4Then shall he who brings his offering to the Lord bring a cereal offering of a tenth of an ephah of fine flour mixed with the fourth of a hin of oil.

5And the fourth of a hin of wine for the drink offering you shall prepare with the burnt offering or for the sacrifice, for each lamb.

6Or for a ram, you shall prepare for a cereal offering two tenths of an ephah of fine flour mixed with the third of a hin of oil.

7And for the drink offering you shall offer the third of a hin of wine, for a sweet *and* pleasing odor to the Lord.

8And when you prepare a bull for a burnt offering, or for a sacrifice in fulfilling a special vow, or peace offerings to the Lord,

9Then shall one offer with the bull a cereal offering of three tenths of an ephah of fine flour mixed with half a hin of oil.

10And you shall bring for the drink offering half a hin of wine, for an offering made by fire, of a pleasant *and* soothing fragrance to the Lord.

11Thus shall it be done for each bull, or for each ram, or for each of the male lambs, or of the kids.

12According to the number that you shall prepare, so shall you do to every one according to their number.

## New American Standard

34'According to the number of days which you spied out the
land, forty days, for every day you shall bear your guilt a year, *even*
forty years, and you shall know My opposition.
35'I, the LORD, have spoken, surely this I will do to all this evil
congregation who are gathered together against Me. In this wilderness they shall be destroyed, and there they shall die.' "
36¶ As for the men whom Moses sent to spy out the land and
who returned and made all the congregation grumble against him
by bringing out a bad report concerning the land,
37even those men who brought out the very bad report of the
land died by a plague before the LORD.
38But Joshua the son of Nun and Caleb the son of Jephunneh
remained alive out of those men who went to spy out the land.

*Israel Repulsed*

39¶ And when Moses spoke these words to all the sons of Israel,
the people mourned greatly.
40In the morning, however, they rose up early and went up to
the ridge of the hill country, saying, "Here we are; we have indeed
sinned, but we will go up to the place which the LORD has promised."
41But Moses said, "Why then are you transgressing the commandment of the LORD, when it will not succeed?
42"Do not go up, lest you be struck down before your enemies,
for the LORD is not among you.
43"For the Amalekites and the Canaanites will be there in front
of you, and you will fall by the sword, inasmuch as you have
turned back from following the LORD. And the LORD will not be
with you."
44But they went up heedlessly to the ridge of the hill country;
neither the ark of the covenant of the LORD nor Moses left the
camp.
45Then the Amalekites and the Canaanites who lived in that hill
country came down, and struck them and beat them down as far
as Hormah.

*Laws for Canaan*

15 NOW THE LORD spoke to Moses, saying,
2"Speak to the sons of Israel, and say to them, 'When you
enter the land where you are to live, which I am giving you,
3then make an offering by fire to the LORD, a burnt offering or
a sacrifice to fulfill a special vow, or as a freewill offering or in your
appointed times, to make a soothing aroma to the LORD, from the
herd or from the flock.
4'And the one who presents his offering shall present to the
LORD a grain offering of one-tenth *of an ephah* of fine flour mixed
with one-fourth of a [a]hin of oil,
5and you shall prepare wine for the libation, one-fourth of a
hin, with the burnt offering or for the sacrifice, for each lamb.
6'Or for a ram you shall prepare as a grain offering two-tenths
*of an ephah* of fine flour mixed with one-third of a hin of oil;
7and for the libation you shall offer one-third of a hin of wine
as a soothing aroma to the LORD.
8'And when you prepare a bull as a burnt offering or a sacrifice,
to fulfill a special vow, or for peace offerings to the LORD,
9then you shall offer with the bull a grain offering of three-
tenths *of an ephah* of fine flour mixed with one-half a hin of oil;
10and you shall offer as the libation one-half a hin of wine as an
offering by fire, as a soothing aroma to the LORD.
11¶ 'Thus it shall be done for each ox, or for each ram, or for each
of the male lambs, or of the goats.
12'According to the number that you prepare, so you shall do
for everyone according to their number.

**NAS** [a] I.e., Approx. one gallon, and so through v. 10

## New International

you explored the land—you will suffer for your sins and know
what it is like to have me against you.' 35I, the LORD, have spoken,
and I will surely do these things to this whole wicked community,
which has banded together against me. They will meet their end
in this desert; here they will die."
36So the men Moses had sent to explore the land, who returned
and made the whole community grumble against him by spreading a bad report about it— 37these men responsible for spreading
the bad report about the land were struck down and died of a
plague before the LORD. 38Of the men who went to explore the
land, only Joshua son of Nun and Caleb son of Jephunneh survived.
39When Moses reported this to all the Israelites, they mourned
bitterly. 40Early the next morning they went up toward the high
hill country. "We have sinned," they said. "We will go up to the
place the LORD promised."
41But Moses said, "Why are you disobeying the LORD's command? This will not succeed! 42Do not go up, because the LORD is
not with you. You will be defeated by your enemies, 43for the
Amalekites and Canaanites will face you there. Because you have
turned away from the LORD, he will not be with you and you will
fall by the sword."
44Nevertheless, in their presumption they went up toward the
high hill country, though neither Moses nor the ark of the LORD's
covenant moved from the camp. 45Then the Amalekites and Canaanites who lived in that hill country came down and attacked
them and beat them down all the way to Hormah.

*Supplementary Offerings*

15 THE LORD said to Moses, 2"Speak to the Israelites and
say to them: 'After you enter the land I am giving you as
a home 3and you present to the LORD offerings made by fire, from
the herd or the flock, as an aroma pleasing to the LORD—whether
burnt offerings or sacrifices, for special vows or freewill offerings
or festival offerings— 4then the one who brings his offering shall
present to the LORD a grain offering of a tenth of an ephah[b] of fine
flour mixed with a quarter of a hin[c] of oil. 5With each lamb for the
burnt offering or the sacrifice, prepare a quarter of a hin of wine
as a drink offering.
6" 'With a ram prepare a grain offering of two-tenths of an
ephah[d] of fine flour mixed with a third of a hin[e] of oil, 7and a third
of a hin of wine as a drink offering. Offer it as an aroma pleasing
to the LORD.
8" 'When you prepare a young bull as a burnt offering or sacrifice, for a special vow or a fellowship offering[f] to the LORD, 9bring
with the bull a grain offering of three-tenths of an ephah[g] of fine
flour mixed with half a hin[h] of oil. 10Also bring half a hin of wine
as a drink offering. It will be an offering made by fire, an aroma
pleasing to the LORD. 11Each bull or ram, each lamb or young goat,
is to be prepared in this manner. 12Do this for each one, for as
many as you prepare.

**NIV** [b] *4* That is, probably about 2 quarts (about 2 liters) [c] *4* That is, probably about 1 quart (about 1 liter); also in verse 5 [d] *6* That is, probably about 4 quarts (about 4.5 liters) [e] *6* That is, probably about 1 1/4 quarts (about 1.2 liters); also in verse 7 [f] *8* Traditionally *peace offering* [g] *9* That is, probably about 6 quarts (about 6.5 liters) [h] *9* That is, probably about 2 quarts (about 2 liters); also in verse 10

## King James

13All that are born of the country shall do these things after this
manner, in offering an offering made by fire, of a sweet savour
unto the LORD.
14And if a stranger sojourn with you, or whosoever *be* among
you in your generations, and will offer an offering made by fire,
of a sweet savour unto the LORD; as ye do, so he shall do.
15One ordinance *shall be both* for you of the congregation, and
also for the stranger that sojourneth *with you,* an ordinance for ever
in your generations: as ye *are,* so shall the stranger be before the
LORD.
16One law and one manner shall be for you, and for the stranger
that sojourneth with you.
17¶ And the LORD spake unto Moses, saying,
18Speak unto the children of Israel, and say unto them, When
ye come into the land whither I bring you,
19Then it shall be, that, when ye eat of the bread of the land,
ye shall offer up an heave offering unto the LORD.
20Ye shall offer up a cake of the first of your dough *for* an heave
offering: as *ye do* the heave offering of the threshingfloor, so shall
ye heave it.
21Of the first of your dough ye shall give unto the LORD an
heave offering in your generations.
22¶ And if ye have erred, and not observed all these commandments, which the LORD hath spoken unto Moses,
23 *Even* all that the LORD hath commanded you by the hand of
Moses, from the day that the LORD commanded *Moses,* and henceforward among your generations;
24Then it shall be, if *aught* be committed by ignorance without
the knowledge of the congregation, that all the congregation shall
offer one young bullock for a burnt offering, for a sweet savour
unto the LORD, with his meat offering, and his drink offering,
according to the manner, and one kid of the goats for a sin offering.
25And the priest shall make an atonement for all the congregation of the children of Israel, and it shall be forgiven them; for it
*is* ignorance: and they shall bring their offering, a sacrifice made
by fire unto the LORD, and their sin offering before the LORD, for
their ignorance:
26And it shall be forgiven all the congregation of the children
of Israel, and the stranger that sojourneth among them; seeing all
the people *were* in ignorance.
27¶ And if any soul sin through ignorance, then he shall bring
a she goat of the first year for a sin offering.
28And the priest shall make an atonement for the soul that
sinneth ignorantly, when he sinneth by ignorance before the
LORD, to make an atonement for him; and it shall be forgiven him.
29Ye shall have one law for him that sinneth through ignorance,
*both for* him that is born among the children of Israel, and for the
stranger that sojourneth among them.
30¶ But the soul that doeth *aught* presumptuously, *whether he be*
born in the land, or a stranger, the same reproacheth the LORD; and
that soul shall be cut off from among his people.
31Because he hath despised the word of the LORD, and hath
broken his commandment, that soul shall utterly be cut off; his
iniquity *shall be* upon him.
32¶ And while the children of Israel were in the wilderness, they
found a man that gathered sticks upon the sabbath day.
33And they that found him gathering sticks brought him unto
Moses and Aaron, and unto all the congregation.
34And they put him in ward, because it was not declared what
should be done to him.
35And the LORD said unto Moses, The man shall be surely put
to death: all the congregation shall stone him with stones without
the camp.
36And all the congregation brought him without the camp, and
stoned him with stones, and he died; as the LORD commanded
Moses.

## Amplified

13All who are native born shall do these things in this way in
bringing an offering made by fire of a sweet *and* pleasant odor to
the Lord.
14And if a stranger sojourns with you, or whoever may be
among you throughout your generations, and will offer an offering
made by fire, of a pleasing *and* soothing fragrance to the Lord, as
you do, so shall he do.
15There shall be one [and the same] statute [both] for you [of
the congregation] and for the stranger who is a temporary resident
with you, a statute for ever throughout your generations: as you
are, so shall the stranger be before the Lord.
16One law and one ordinance shall be for you and for the
stranger who sojourns with you.
17And the Lord said to Moses,
18Say to the Israelites, When you come into the land to which
I am bringing you,
19Then, when you eat of the food of the land, you shall set apart
a portion for a gift to the Lord [called a heave or taken out offering].
20You shall set apart a cake made of the first of your coarse meal
as a gift [to the Lord]; as an offering set apart from the threshing
floor, so shall you lift it out *or* heave it.
21Of the first of your coarse meal you shall give to the Lord a
portion for a gift throughout your generations [your heave or lifted
out offering].
22When you have erred and have not observed all these commandments, which the Lord has spoken to Moses,
23Even all that the Lord has commanded you by Moses, from
the day that the Lord gave commandment, and onward throughout your generations,
24Then it shall be, if it was done unwittingly *or* in error without
the knowledge of the congregation, that all the congregation shall
offer one young bull for a burnt offering, for a pleasant *and* soothing fragrance to the Lord, with its cereal offering, and its drink
offering, according to the ordinance, and one male goat for a sin
offering.
25And the priest shall make atonement for all the congregation
of the Israelites, and they shall be forgiven; for it was an error, and
they have brought their offering, an offering made by fire to the
Lord, and their sin offering before the Lord, for their error.
26And all the congregation of the Israelites shall be forgiven,
and the stranger who lives temporarily among them, because all
the people were involved in the error.
27And if any person sins unknowingly *or* unintentionally he
shall offer a female goat a year old for a sin offering.
28And the priest shall make atonement before the Lord for the
person who commits an error, when he sins unknowingly *or* unintentionally, to make atonement for him; and he shall be forgiven.
29You shall have one law for him who sins unknowingly *or*
unintentionally, whether he is native born among the Israelites or
a stranger who is sojourning among them.
30But the person who does anything [wrong] willfully *and* openly, whether he is native born or a stranger, that one reproaches,
reviles *and* blasphemes the Lord, and that person shall be cut off
from among his people [that the atonement made for them may
not include him].
31Because he has despised and rejected the word of the Lord,
and has broken His commandment, that person shall be utterly cut
off; his iniquity shall be upon him.
32While the Israelites were in the wilderness, they found a man
who was gathering sticks on the sabbath day.
33Those who found him gathering sticks brought him to Moses
and Aaron, and to all the congregation.
34They put him in custody, because it was not certain *or* clear
what should be done to him.
35And the Lord said to Moses, The man shall be surely put to
death; all the congregation shall stone him with stones without the
camp.
36And all the congregation brought him without the camp, and
stoned him to death with stones, as the Lord commanded Moses.

## New American Standard

13'All who are native shall do these things in this manner, in
presenting an offering by fire, as a soothing aroma to the LORD.

*Law of the Sojourner*

14'And if an alien sojourns with you, or one who may be among
you throughout your generations, and he *wishes to* make an offering by fire, as a soothing aroma to the LORD, just as you do, so he
shall do.
15' *As for* the assembly, there shall be one statute for you and
for the alien who sojourns *with you*, a perpetual statute throughout
your generations; as you are, so shall the alien be before the LORD.
16'There is to be one law and one ordinance for you and for the
alien who sojourns with you.' "
17¶ Then the LORD spoke to Moses, saying,
18"Speak to the sons of Israel, and say to them, 'When you enter
the land where I bring you,
19then it shall be, that when you eat of the food of the land, you
shall lift up an offering to the LORD.
20'Of the first of your [a]dough you shall lift up a cake as an
offering; as the offering of the threshing floor, so you shall lift it
up.
21'From the first of your [b]dough you shall give to the LORD an
offering throughout your generations.
22¶ 'But when you unwittingly fail and do not observe all these
commandments, which the LORD has spoken to Moses,
23 *even* all that the LORD has commanded you through Moses,
from the day when the LORD gave commandment and onward
throughout your generations,
24then it shall be, if it is done unintentionally, without the
knowledge of the congregation, that all the congregation shall
offer one bull for a burnt offering, as a soothing aroma to the LORD,
with its grain offering, and its libation, according to the ordinance,
and one male goat for a sin offering.
25'Then the priest shall make atonement for all the congregation
of the sons of Israel, and they shall be forgiven; for it was an error,
and they have brought their offering, an offering by fire to the
LORD, and their sin offering before the LORD, for their error.
26'So all the congregation of the sons of Israel will be forgiven,
with the alien who sojourns among them, for *it happened* to all the
people through error.
27¶ 'Also if one person sins unintentionally, then he shall offer
a one year old female goat for a sin offering.
28'And the priest shall make atonement before the LORD for the
person who goes astray when he sins unintentionally, making
atonement for him that he may be forgiven.
29'You shall have one law for him who does *anything* unintentionally, for him who is native among the sons of Israel and for the
alien who sojourns among them.
30'But the person who does *anything* defiantly, whether he is
native or an alien, that one is blaspheming the LORD; and that
person shall be cut off from among his people.
31'Because he has despised the word of the LORD and has broken His commandment, that person shall be completely cut off; his
guilt *shall be* on him.' "

*Sabbath-breaking Punished*

32¶ Now while the sons of Israel were in the wilderness, they
found a man gathering wood on the sabbath day.
33And those who found him gathering wood brought him to
Moses and Aaron, and to all the congregation;
34and they put him in custody because it had not been declared
what should be done to him.
35Then the LORD said to Moses, "The man shall surely be put
to death; all the congregation shall stone him with stones outside
the camp."
36So all the congregation brought him outside the camp, and
stoned him to death with stones, just as the LORD had commanded
Moses.

NAS [a] Or, *coarse meal* [b] Or, *coarse meal*

## New International

13" 'Everyone who is native-born must do these things in this
way when he brings an offering made by fire as an aroma pleasing
to the LORD. 14For the generations to come, whenever an alien or
anyone else living among you presents an offering made by fire as
an aroma pleasing to the LORD, he must do exactly as you do. 15The
community is to have the same rules for you and for the alien living
among you; this is a lasting ordinance for the generations to come.
You and the alien shall be the same before the LORD: 16The same
laws and regulations will apply both to you and to the alien living
among you.' "
17The LORD said to Moses, 18"Speak to the Israelites and say to
them: 'When you enter the land to which I am taking you 19and
you eat the food of the land, present a portion as an offering to the
LORD. 20Present a cake from the first of your ground meal and
present it as an offering from the threshing floor. 21Throughout the
generations to come you are to give this offering to the LORD from
the first of your ground meal.

*Offerings for Unintentional Sins*

22" 'Now if you unintentionally fail to keep any of these commands the LORD gave Moses— 23any of the LORD's commands to
you through him, from the day the LORD gave them and continuing through the generations to come— 24and if this is done unintentionally without the community being aware of it, then the
whole community is to offer a young bull for a burnt offering as
an aroma pleasing to the LORD, along with its prescribed grain
offering and drink offering, and a male goat for a sin offering.
25The priest is to make atonement for the whole Israelite community, and they will be forgiven, for it was not intentional and they
have brought to the LORD for their wrong an offering made by fire
and a sin offering. 26The whole Israelite community and the aliens
living among them will be forgiven, because all the people were
involved in the unintentional wrong.
27" 'But if just one person sins unintentionally, he must bring
a year-old female goat for a sin offering. 28The priest is to make
atonement before the LORD for the one who erred by sinning
unintentionally, and when atonement has been made for him, he
will be forgiven. 29One and the same law applies to everyone who
sins unintentionally, whether he is a native-born Israelite or an
alien.
30" 'But anyone who sins defiantly, whether native-born or
alien, blasphemes the LORD, and that person must be cut off from
his people. 31Because he has despised the LORD's word and broken
his commands, that person must surely be cut off; his guilt remains
on him.' "

*The Sabbath-Breaker Put to Death*

32While the Israelites were in the desert, a man was found
gathering wood on the Sabbath day. 33Those who found him
gathering wood brought him to Moses and Aaron and the whole
assembly, 34and they kept him in custody, because it was not clear
what should be done to him. 35Then the LORD said to Moses, "The
man must die. The whole assembly must stone him outside the
camp." 36So the assembly took him outside the camp and stoned
him to death, as the LORD commanded Moses.

## King James

37¶ And the LORD spake unto Moses, saying,

38 Speak unto the children of Israel, and bid them that they make them fringes in the borders of their garments throughout their generations, and that they put upon the fringe of the borders a ribband of blue:

39 And it shall be unto you for a fringe, that ye may look upon it, and remember all the commandments of the LORD, and do them; and that ye seek not after your own heart and your own eyes, after which ye use to go a-whoring:

40 That ye may remember, and do all my commandments, and be holy unto your God.

41 I *am* the LORD your God, which brought you out of the land of Egypt, to be your God: I *am* the LORD your God.

16 NOW KORAH, the son of Izhar, the son of Kohath, the son of Levi, and Dathan and Abiram, the sons of Eliab, and On, the son of Peleth, sons of Reuben, took *men:*

2 And they rose up before Moses, with certain of the children of Israel, two hundred and fifty princes of the assembly, famous in the congregation, men of renown:

3 And they gathered themselves together against Moses and against Aaron, and said unto them, *Ye take* too much upon you, seeing all the congregation *are* holy, every one of them, and the LORD *is* among them: wherefore then lift ye up yourselves above the congregation of the LORD?

4 And when Moses heard *it*, he fell upon his face:

5 And he spake unto Korah and unto all his company, saying, Even tomorrow the LORD will show who *are* his, and *who is* holy; and will cause *him* to come near unto him: even *him* whom he hath chosen will he cause to come near unto him.

6 This do; Take you censers, Korah, and all his company;

7 And put fire therein, and put incense in them before the LORD tomorrow: and it shall be *that* the man whom the LORD doth choose, he *shall be* holy: *ye take* too much upon you, ye sons of Levi.

8 And Moses said unto Korah, Hear, I pray you, ye sons of Levi:

9 *Seemeth it but* a small thing unto you, that the God of Israel hath separated you from the congregation of Israel, to bring you near to himself to do the service of the tabernacle of the LORD, and to stand before the congregation to minister unto them?

10 And he hath brought thee near *to him*, and all thy brethren the sons of Levi with thee: and seek ye the priesthood also?

11 For which cause *both* thou and all thy company *are* gathered together against the LORD: and what *is* Aaron, that ye murmur against him?

12¶ And Moses sent to call Dathan and Abiram, the sons of Eliab: which said, We will not come up:

13 *Is it* a small thing that thou hast brought us up out of a land that floweth with milk and honey, to kill us in the wilderness, except thou make thyself altogether a prince over us?

14 Moreover thou hast not brought us into a land that floweth with milk and honey, or given us inheritance of fields and vineyards: wilt thou put out the eyes of these men? we will not come up.

15 And Moses was very wroth, and said unto the LORD, Respect not thou their offering: I have not taken one ass from them, neither have I hurt one of them.

16 And Moses said unto Korah, Be thou and all thy company before the LORD, thou, and they, and Aaron, tomorrow:

17 And take every man his censer, and put incense in them, and bring ye before the LORD every man his censer, two hundred and fifty censers; thou also, and Aaron, each *of you* his censer.

## Amplified

37 And the Lord said to Moses,

38 Speak to the Israelites, and bid them make fringes *or* tassels on the corners in the borders of their garments throughout their generations, and put upon the fringe of the borders *or* upon the tassel of each corner a cord of blue;

39 And it shall be to you a fringe *or* tassel that you may look upon and remember all the commandments of the Lord, and do them, that you may not spy out *and* follow after [the desires of] your own heart and your own eyes, after which you used to follow *and* play the harlot [spiritually, if not physically];

40 That you may remember and do all My commandments, and be holy to your God.

41 I am the Lord your God, Who brought you out of the land of Egypt, to be your God; I am the Lord, your God.

16 NOW KORAH son of Izhar, son of Kohath, son of Levi, with Dathan and Abiram sons of Eliab, and On son of Peleth, sons of Reuben, took men;

2 And they rose up before Moses, with certain of the Israelites, 250 princes *or* leaders of the congregation, called to the assembly, men well-known *and* of distinction;

3 And they gathered together against Moses and Aaron, and said to them, (Enough of you!) You take too much upon yourselves, seeing that all the congregation are holy, every one of them, and the Lord is among them. Why then do you lift yourselves up above the assembly of the Lord?

4 And when Moses heard it, he fell upon his face;

5 And he said to Korah and all his company, In the morning the Lord will show who are His, and who is holy, and will cause him to come near to Him; him whom He has chosen will He cause to come near to Him. [II Tim. 2:19.]

6 Do this: Take censers, Korah and all his company,

7 And put fire in them and put incense upon them before the Lord tomorrow; and the man whom the Lord chooses shall be holy. You take too much upon yourselves, you sons of Levi.

8 And Moses said to Korah, Hear, I pray you, you sons of Levi:

9 Does it seem but a small thing to you that the God of Israel has separated you from the congregation of Israel, to bring you near to Himself to do the service of the tabernacle of the Lord, and to stand before the congregation to minister to them;

10 And that He has brought you near to Him, and all your brethren the sons of Levi with you? Would you seek the priesthood also?

11 Therefore you and all your company are gathered together against the Lord. And Aaron, what is he that you murmur against him?

12 And Moses sent to call Dathan and Abiram sons of Eliab, and they said, We will not come up.

13 Is it a small thing that you have brought us up out of a land flowing with milk and honey, to kill us in the wilderness, but you must also make yourself a prince over us?

14 Moreover you have not brought us into a land that flows with milk and honey, or given us inheritance of fields and vineyards. Will you bore out the eyes of these men? We will not come up!

15 And Moses was very angry, and said to the Lord, Do not respect their offering! I have not taken one donkey from them, nor have I hurt one of them.

16 And Moses said to Korah, You and all your company be before the Lord tomorrow, you and they, and Aaron.

17 And let every man take his censer, and put incense upon it, and bring before the Lord every man his censer, 250 censers; you also, and Aaron, each his censer.

## New American Standard

37¶ The LORD also spoke to Moses, saying,

38"Speak to the sons of Israel, and tell them that they shall make for themselves tassels on the corners of their garments throughout their generations, and that they shall put on the tassel of each corner a cord of blue.

39"And it shall be a tassel for you to look at and remember all the commandments of the LORD, so as to do them and not follow after your own heart and your own eyes, after which you played the harlot,

40in order that you may remember to do all My commandments, and be holy to your God.

41"I am the LORD your God who brought you out from the land of Egypt to be your God; I am the LORD your God."

*Korah's Rebellion*

16 NOW KORAH the son of Izhar, the son of Kohath, the son of Levi, with Dathan and Abiram, the sons of Eliab, and On the son of Peleth, sons of Reuben, took *action,*

2and they rose up before Moses, together with some of the sons of Israel, two hundred and fifty leaders of the congregation, chosen in the assembly, men of renown.

3And they assembled together against Moses and Aaron, and said to them, "You have gone far enough, for all the congregation are holy, every one of them, and the LORD is in their midst; so why do you exalt yourselves above the assembly of the LORD?"

4¶ When Moses heard *this,* he fell on his face;

5and he spoke to Korah and all his company, saying, "Tomorrow morning the LORD will show who is His, and who is holy, and will bring *him* near to Himself; even the one whom He will choose, He will bring near to Himself.

6"Do this: take censers for yourselves, Korah and all your company,

7and put fire in them, and lay incense upon them in the presence of the LORD tomorrow; and the man whom the LORD chooses *shall be* the one who is holy. You have gone far enough, you sons of Levi!"

8¶ Then Moses said to Korah, "Hear now, you sons of Levi,

9is it not enough for you that the God of Israel has separated you from the *rest of* the congregation of Israel, to bring you near to Himself, to do the service of the tabernacle of the LORD, and to stand before the congregation to minister to them;

10and that He has brought you near, *Korah,* and all your brothers, sons of Levi, with you? And are you seeking for the priesthood also?

11"Therefore you and all your company are gathered together against the LORD; but as for Aaron, who is he that you grumble against him?"

12¶ Then Moses sent a summons to Dathan and Abiram, the sons of Eliab; but they said, "We will not come up.

13"Is it not enough that you have brought us up out of a land flowing with milk and honey to have us die in the wilderness, but you would also lord it over us?

14"Indeed, you have not brought us into a land flowing with milk and honey, nor have you given us an inheritance of fields and vineyards. Would you put out the eyes of these men? We will not come up!"

15¶ Then Moses became very angry and said to the LORD, "Do not regard their offering! I have not taken a single donkey from them, nor have I done harm to any of them."

16And Moses said to Korah, "You and all your company be present before the LORD tomorrow, both you and they along with Aaron.

17"And each of you take his firepan and put incense on it, and each of you bring his censer before the LORD, two hundred and fifty firepans; also you and Aaron *shall* each *bring* his firepan."

## New International

*Tassels on Garments*

37The LORD said to Moses, 38"Speak to the Israelites and say to
them: 'Throughout the generations to come you are to make tassels
on the corners of your garments, with a blue cord on each tassel.
39You will have these tassels to look at and so you will remember
all the commands of the LORD, that you may obey them and not
prostitute yourselves by going after the lusts of your own hearts
and eyes. 40Then you will remember to obey all my commands and
will be consecrated to your God. 41I am the LORD your God, who
brought you out of Egypt to be your God. I am the LORD your
God.' "

*Korah, Dathan and Abiram*

16 KORAH SON of Izhar, the son of Kohath, the son of Levi,
and certain Reubenites—Dathan and Abiram, sons of
Eliab, and On son of Peleth—became insolent[a] 2and rose up
against Moses. With them were 250 Israelite men, well-known
community leaders who had been appointed members of the
council. 3They came as a group to oppose Moses and Aaron and
said to them, "You have gone too far! The whole community is
holy, every one of them, and the LORD is with them. Why then do
you set yourselves above the LORD's assembly?"
4When Moses heard this, he fell facedown. 5Then he said to
Korah and all his followers: "In the morning the LORD will show
who belongs to him and who is holy, and he will have that person
come near him. The man he chooses he will cause to come near
him. 6You, Korah, and all your followers are to do this: Take
censers 7and tomorrow put fire and incense in them before the
LORD. The man the LORD chooses will be the one who is holy. You
Levites have gone too far!"
8Moses also said to Korah, "Now listen, you Levites! 9Isn't it
enough for you that the God of Israel has separated you from the
rest of the Israelite community and brought you near himself to do
the work at the LORD's tabernacle and to stand before the community and minister to them? 10He has brought you and all your
fellow Levites near himself, but now you are trying to get the
priesthood too. 11It is against the LORD that you and all your
followers have banded together. Who is Aaron that you should
grumble against him?"
12Then Moses summoned Dathan and Abiram, the sons of
Eliab. But they said, "We will not come! 13Isn't it enough that you
have brought us up out of a land flowing with milk and honey to
kill us in the desert? And now you also want to lord it over us?
14Moreover, you haven't brought us into a land flowing with milk
and honey or given us an inheritance of fields and vineyards. Will
you gouge out the eyes of[b] these men? No, we will not come!"
15Then Moses became very angry and said to the LORD, "Do not
accept their offering. I have not taken so much as a donkey from
them, nor have I wronged any of them."
16Moses said to Korah, "You and all your followers are to appear before the LORD tomorrow—you and they and Aaron. 17Each
man is to take his censer and put incense in it—250 censers in
all—and present it before the LORD. You and Aaron are to present
your censers also." 18So each man took his censer, put fire and

NIV [a] 1 Or *Peleth—took ⌊men⌋* [b] 14 Or *you make slaves of;* or *you deceive*

## King James

18 And they took every man his censer, and put fire in them, and
laid incense thereon, and stood in the door of the tabernacle of the
congregation with Moses and Aaron.
19 And Korah gathered all the congregation against them unto
the door of the tabernacle of the congregation: and the glory of the
LORD appeared unto all the congregation.
20 And the LORD spake unto Moses and unto Aaron, saying,
21 Separate yourselves from among this congregation, that I may
consume them in a moment.
22 And they fell upon their faces, and said, O God, the God of
the spirits of all flesh, shall one man sin, and wilt thou be wroth
with all the congregation?
23 ¶ And the LORD spake unto Moses, saying,
24 Speak unto the congregation, saying, Get you up from about
the tabernacle of Korah, Dathan, and Abiram.
25 And Moses rose up and went unto Dathan and Abiram; and
the elders of Israel followed him.
26 And he spake unto the congregation, saying, Depart, I pray
you, from the tents of these wicked men, and touch nothing of
theirs, lest ye be consumed in all their sins.
27 So they gat up from the tabernacle of Korah, Dathan, and
Abiram, on every side: and Dathan and Abiram came out, and
stood in the door of their tents, and their wives, and their sons,
and their little children.
28 And Moses said, Hereby ye shall know that the LORD hath
sent me to do all these works; for *I have* not *done them* of mine own
mind.
29 If these men die the common death of all men, or if they be
visited after the visitation of all men; *then* the LORD hath not sent
me.
30 But if the LORD make a new thing, and the earth open her
mouth, and swallow them up, with all that *appertain* unto them,
and they go down quick into the pit; then ye shall understand that
these men have provoked the LORD.
31 ¶ And it came to pass, as he had made an end of speaking all
these words, that the ground clave asunder that *was* under them:
32 And the earth opened her mouth, and swallowed them up,
and their houses, and all the men that *appertained* unto Korah, and
all *their* goods.
33 They, and all that *appertained* to them, went down alive into
the pit, and the earth closed upon them: and they perished from
among the congregation.
34 And all Israel that *were* round about them fled at the cry of
them: for they said, Lest the earth swallow us up *also*.
35 And there came out a fire from the LORD, and consumed the
two hundred and fifty men that offered incense.
36 ¶ And the LORD spake unto Moses, saying,
37 Speak unto Eleazar the son of Aaron the priest, that he take
up the censers out of the burning, and scatter thou the fire yonder;
for they are hallowed.
38 The censers of these sinners against their own souls, let them
make them broad plates *for* a covering of the altar: for they offered
them before the LORD, therefore they are hallowed: and they shall
be a sign unto the children of Israel.
39 And Eleazar the priest took the brasen censers, wherewith
they that were burnt had offered; and they were made broad *plates
for* a covering of the altar:
40 *To be* a memorial unto the children of Israel, that no stranger,
which *is* not of the seed of Aaron, come near to offer incense before
the LORD; that he be not as Korah, and as his company: as the LORD
said to him by the hand of Moses.
41 ¶ But on the morrow all the congregation of the children of
Israel murmured against Moses and against Aaron, saying, Ye
have killed the people of the LORD.
42 And it came to pass, when the congregation was gathered
against Moses and against Aaron, that they looked toward the
tabernacle of the congregation: and, behold, the cloud covered it,
and the glory of the LORD appeared.

## Amplified

18 So they took every man his censer, and they put fire in them,
and laid incense upon it, and they stood at the entrance of the tent
of meeting with Moses and Aaron.
19 Then Korah assembled all the congregation against Moses
and Aaron before the entrance of the tent of meeting, and the glory
of the Lord appeared to all the congregation.
20 And the Lord said to Moses and Aaron,
21 Separate yourselves from among this congregation, that I may
consume them in a moment.
22 And they fell upon their faces, and said, O God, the God of
the spirits of all flesh, shall one man sin, and will You be angry
with all the congregation?
23 And the Lord said to Moses,
24 Say to the congregation, Get away from around the tents of
Korah, Dathan, and Abiram.
25 Then Moses rose up and went to Dathan and Abiram, and the
elders of Israel followed him.
26 And he said to the congregation, Depart, I pray you, from the
tents of these wicked men, and touch nothing of theirs, lest you
be consumed in all their sins.
27 So they got away from the tents of Korah, Dathan, and Abiram, on every side; and Dathan and Abiram came out and stood
in the door of their tents, with their wives, and their sons, and their
little ones.
28 And Moses said, By this you shall know that the Lord has sent
me to do all these works; for I do not act of my own accord.
29 If these men die the common death of all men, or if [only]
what happens to everyone happens to them, then the Lord has not
sent me.
30 But if the Lord causes a new thing [to happen], and the earth
opens its mouth, and swallows them up, with all that belongs to
them, and they go down alive into Sheol [the place of the dead],
then you shall understand that these men have provoked
(spurned, despised) the Lord!
31 As soon as he stopped speaking, the ground under the offenders split apart,
32 And the earth opened its mouth, and swallowed them and
their households, and [Korah and] all [his] men, and all their
possessions. [26:10, 11.]
33 They and all that belonged to them, went down alive into
Sheol [the place of the dead], and the earth closed upon them; and
they perished from among the assembly.
34 And all Israel that were round about them fled at their cry, for
they said, Lest the earth swallow us up also.
35 And fire came forth from the Lord, and devoured the 250 men
who offered the incense.
36 And the Lord said to Moses,
37 Speak to Eleazar son of Aaron the priest, that he take up the
censers out of the burning, and scatter the fire at a distance. For
the censers are hallowed,
38 The censers of these men who have sinned against themselves *and* at the cost of their own lives. Let the censers be made
into hammered plates for a covering of the altar [of burnt offering];
for they were used in offering before the Lord, therefore they are
sacred. They shall be a sign [of warning] to the Israelites.
39 Eleazar the priest took the bronze censers with which the
Levites who were burned had offered incense, and they were
hammered into broad sheets for a covering of the [brazen] altar [of
burnt offering];
40 To be a memorial [a warning for ever] to the Israelites, so that
no outsider, that is, no one not of the descendants of Aaron,
should come near to offer incense before the Lord; lest he become
as Korah, and as his company, as the Lord said to Eleazar through
Moses.
41 But on the morrow all the congregation of the Israelites murmured against Moses and Aaron, saying, You have killed the
people of the Lord.
42 When the congregation was gathered against Moses and
Aaron, they looked at the tent of meeting, and lo, the cloud
covered it, and they saw the Lord's glory.

## New American Standard

18So they each took his *own* censer and put fire on it, and laid incense on it; and they stood at the doorway of the tent of meeting, with Moses and Aaron.

19Thus Korah assembled all the congregation against them at the doorway of the tent of meeting. And the glory of the LORD appeared to all the congregation.

**20**¶ Then the LORD spoke to Moses and Aaron, saying,

21"Separate yourselves from among this congregation, that I may consume them instantly."

22But they fell on their faces, and said, "O God, Thou God of the spirits of all flesh, when one man sins, wilt Thou be angry with the entire congregation?"

23Then the LORD spoke to Moses, saying,

24"Speak to the congregation, saying, 'Get back from around the dwellings of Korah, Dathan and Abiram.' "

**25**¶ Then Moses arose and went to Dathan and Abiram, with the elders of Israel following him,

26and he spoke to the congregation, saying, "Depart now from the tents of these wicked men, and touch nothing that belongs to them, lest you be swept away in all their sin."

27So they got back from around the dwellings of Korah, Dathan and Abiram; and Dathan and Abiram came out *and* stood at the doorway of their tents, along with their wives and their sons and their little ones.

28And Moses said, "By this you shall know that the LORD has sent me to do all these deeds; for this is not my doing.

29"If these men die the death of all men, or if they suffer the fate of all men, *then* the LORD has not sent me.

30"But if the LORD brings about an entirely new thing and the ground opens its mouth and swallows them up with all that is theirs, and they descend alive into Sheol, then you will understand that these men have spurned the LORD."

**31**¶ Then it came about as he finished speaking all these words, that the ground that was under them split open;

32and the earth opened its mouth and swallowed them up, and their households, and all the men who belonged to Korah, with *their* possessions.

33So they and all that belonged to them went down alive to Sheol; and the earth closed over them, and they perished from the midst of the assembly.

34And all Israel who *were* around them fled at their outcry, for they said, "The earth may swallow us up!"

35Fire also came forth from the LORD and consumed the two hundred and fifty men who were offering the incense.

**36**¶ Then the LORD spoke to Moses, saying,

37"Say to Eleazar, the son of Aaron the priest, that he shall take up the censers out of the midst of the blaze, for they are holy; and you scatter the burning coals abroad.

38"As for the censers of these men who have sinned at the cost of their lives, let them be made into hammered sheets for a plating of the altar, since they did present them before the LORD and they are holy; and they shall be for a sign to the sons of Israel."

39So Eleazar the priest took the bronze censers which the men who were burned had offered; and they hammered them out as a plating for the altar,

40as a reminder to the sons of Israel that no layman who is not of the descendants of Aaron should come near to burn incense before the LORD; that he might not become like Korah and his company—just as the LORD had spoken to him through Moses.

*Murmuring and Plague*

**41**¶ But on the next day all the congregation of the sons of Israel grumbled against Moses and Aaron, saying, "You are the ones who have caused the death of the LORD's people."

42It came about, however, when the congregation had assembled against Moses and Aaron, that they turned toward the tent of meeting, and behold, the cloud covered it and the glory of the LORD appeared.

## New International

incense in it, and stood with Moses and Aaron at the entrance to
the Tent of Meeting. 19When Korah had gathered all his followers
in opposition to them at the entrance to the Tent of Meeting, the
glory of the LORD appeared to the entire assembly. 20The LORD said
to Moses and Aaron, 21"Separate yourselves from this assembly so
I can put an end to them at once."
22But Moses and Aaron fell facedown and cried out, "O God,
God of the spirits of all mankind, will you be angry with the entire
assembly when only one man sins?"
23Then the LORD said to Moses, 24"Say to the assembly, 'Move
away from the tents of Korah, Dathan and Abiram.' "
25Moses got up and went to Dathan and Abiram, and the elders
of Israel followed him. 26He warned the assembly, "Move back
from the tents of these wicked men! Do not touch anything belonging to them, or you will be swept away because of all their sins."
27So they moved away from the tents of Korah, Dathan and Abiram. Dathan and Abiram had come out and were standing with
their wives, children and little ones at the entrances to their tents.
28Then Moses said, "This is how you will know that the LORD
has sent me to do all these things and that it was not my idea: 29If
these men die a natural death and experience only what usually
happens to men, then the LORD has not sent me. 30But if the LORD
brings about something totally new, and the earth opens its mouth
and swallows them, with everything that belongs to them, and
they go down alive into the grave,[a] then you will know that these
men have treated the LORD with contempt."
31As soon as he finished saying all this, the ground under them
split apart 32and the earth opened its mouth and swallowed them,
with their households and all Korah's men and all their possessions. 33They went down alive into the grave, with everything they
owned; the earth closed over them, and they perished and were
gone from the community. 34At their cries, all the Israelites around
them fled, shouting, "The earth is going to swallow us too!"
35And fire came out from the LORD and consumed the 250 men
who were offering the incense.
36The LORD said to Moses, 37"Tell Eleazar son of Aaron, the
priest, to take the censers out of the smoldering remains and
scatter the coals some distance away, for the censers are holy—
38the censers of the men who sinned at the cost of their lives.
Hammer the censers into sheets to overlay the altar, for they were
presented before the LORD and have become holy. Let them be a
sign to the Israelites."
39So Eleazar the priest collected the bronze censers brought by
those who had been burned up, and he had them hammered out
to overlay the altar, 40as the LORD directed him through Moses.
This was to remind the Israelites that no one except a descendant
of Aaron should come to burn incense before the LORD, or he
would become like Korah and his followers.
41The next day the whole Israelite community grumbled against
Moses and Aaron. "You have killed the LORD's people," they said.
42But when the assembly gathered in opposition to Moses and
Aaron and turned toward the Tent of Meeting, suddenly the cloud
covered it and the glory of the LORD appeared. 43Then Moses and

NIV [a] 30 Hebrew *Sheol;* also in verse 33

## King James

43 And Moses and Aaron came before the tabernacle of the congregation.

44¶ And the LORD spake unto Moses, saying,

45 Get you up from among this congregation, that I may consume them as in a moment. And they fell upon their faces.

46¶ And Moses said unto Aaron, Take a censer, and put fire therein from off the altar, and put on incense, and go quickly unto the congregation, and make an atonement for them: for there is wrath gone out from the LORD; the plague is begun.

47 And Aaron took as Moses commanded, and ran into the midst of the congregation; and, behold, the plague was begun among the people: and he put on incense, and made an atonement for the people.

48 And he stood between the dead and the living; and the plague was stayed.

49 Now they that died in the plague were fourteen thousand and seven hundred, beside them that died about the matter of Korah.

50 And Aaron returned unto Moses unto the door of the tabernacle of the congregation: and the plague was stayed.

**17** AND THE LORD spake unto Moses, saying,

2 Speak unto the children of Israel, and take of every one of them a rod according to the house of *their* fathers, of all their princes according to the house of their fathers twelve rods: write thou every man's name upon his rod.

3 And thou shalt write Aaron's name upon the rod of Levi: for one rod *shall be* for the head of the house of their fathers.

4 And thou shalt lay them up in the tabernacle of the congregation before the testimony, where I will meet with you.

5 And it shall come to pass, *that* the man's rod, whom I shall choose, shall blossom: and I will make to cease from me the murmurings of the children of Israel, whereby they murmur against you.

6¶ And Moses spake unto the children of Israel, and every one of their princes gave him a rod apiece, for each prince one, according to their fathers' houses, *even* twelve rods: and the rod of Aaron *was* among their rods.

7 And Moses laid up the rods before the LORD in the tabernacle of witness.

8 And it came to pass, that on the morrow Moses went into the tabernacle of witness; and, behold, the rod of Aaron for the house of Levi was budded, and brought forth buds, and bloomed blossoms, and yielded almonds.

9 And Moses brought out all the rods from before the LORD unto all the children of Israel: and they looked, and took every man his rod.

10¶ And the LORD said unto Moses, Bring Aaron's rod again before the testimony, to be kept for a token against the rebels; and thou shalt quite take away their murmurings from me, that they die not.

11 And Moses did *so:* as the LORD commanded him, so did he.

12 And the children of Israel spake unto Moses, saying, Behold, we die, we perish, we all perish.

13 Whosoever cometh any thing near unto the tabernacle of the LORD shall die: shall we be consumed with dying?

**18** AND THE LORD said unto Aaron, Thou and thy sons and thy father's house with thee shall bear the iniquity of the sanctuary: and thou and thy sons with thee shall bear the iniquity of your priesthood.

## Amplified

43 And Moses and Aaron came to the front of the tent of meeting.

44 And the Lord said to Moses,

45 Get away from among this congregation, that I may consume them in a moment. And Moses and Aaron fell on their faces.

46 And Moses said to Aaron, Take a censer, and put fire in it from off the altar, and lay incense on it, and carry it quickly to the congregation, and make atonement for them; for there is wrath gone out from the Lord; the plague has begun!

47 So Aaron took the burning censer as Moses commanded, and ran into the midst of the congregation; and behold, the plague was begun among the people; and he put on the incense, and made atonement for the people.

48 And he stood between the dead and the living; and the plague was stayed.

49 Now those who died in the plague were 14,700, besides those who died in the matter of Korah.

50 And Aaron returned to Moses to the door of the tent of meeting, since the plague was stayed.

**17** AND THE Lord said to Moses,

2 Speak to the Israelites and get from them rods *or* staves, one for each father's house, from all their leaders according to their father's houses, twelve rods; write every man's name on his rod.

3 And you shall write Aaron's name on the rod of Levi [his great-grandfather]. For there shall be one rod for the head of each father's house.

4 You shall lay them up in the tent of meeting before [the ark of] the testimony, where I meet with you.

5 And the rod of the man whom I choose shall bud; and I will make to cease from Me the murmurings of the Israelites, which they murmur against you.

6 And Moses spoke to the Israelites, and every one of their leaders gave him a rod *or* staff, one for each leader, according to their fathers' houses, twelve rods; and the rod of Aaron was among their rods.

7 And Moses deposited the rods before the Lord in the tent of the testimony.

8 And the next day Moses went into the tent of the testimony, and behold, the rod of Aaron for the house of Levi had sprouted and brought forth buds, and produced blossoms, and yielded [ripe] almonds.

9 Moses brought out all the rods from before the Lord to all the Israelites; and they looked, and each man took his rod.

10 And the Lord told Moses, Put Aaron's rod back before the testimony [in the ark], to be kept as a [warning] sign for the rebels; and you shall make an end of their murmurings against Me, lest they die.

11 And Moses did so; as the Lord commanded him, so he did.

12 The Israelites said to Moses, Behold, we perish, we are undone, all undone!

13 Every one who comes near, who comes near the tabernacle of the Lord, dies *or* shall die! Are we all to perish?

**18** AND THE Lord said to Aaron, You and your sons and your father's house with you shall bear *and* remove the iniquity of the sanctuary [that is, the guilt for the offenses which the people unknowingly commit when brought into contact with the manifestations of God's presence]. And you and your sons with you shall bear *and* remove the iniquity of your priesthood [your own unintentional offenses].

## New American Standard

43Then Moses and Aaron came to the front of the tent of meeting,
44and the LORD spoke to Moses, saying,
45"Get away from among this congregation, that I may consume them instantly." Then they fell on their faces.
46And Moses said to Aaron, "Take your censer and put in it fire
from the altar, and lay incense *on it;* then bring it quickly to the
congregation and make atonement for them, for wrath has gone
forth from the LORD, the plague has begun!"
47Then Aaron took *it* as Moses had spoken, and ran into the
midst of the assembly, for behold, the plague had begun among
the people. So he put *on* the incense and made atonement for the
people.
48And he took his stand between the dead and the living, so
that the plague was checked.
49But those who died by the plague were 14,700, besides those
who died on account of Korah.
50Then Aaron returned to Moses at the doorway of the tent of
meeting, for the plague had been checked.

*Aaron's Rod Buds*

**17** THEN THE LORD spoke to Moses, saying,
2"Speak to the sons of Israel, and get from them a rod for
each father's household: twelve rods, from all their leaders according to their fathers' households. You shall write each name on his
rod,
3and write Aaron's name on the rod of Levi; for there is one
rod for the head *of each* of their fathers' households.
4"You shall then deposit them in the tent of meeting in front
of the testimony, where I meet with you.
5"And it will come about that the rod of the man whom I
choose will sprout. Thus I shall lessen from upon Myself the
grumblings of the sons of Israel, who are grumbling against you."
6Moses therefore spoke to the sons of Israel, and all their
leaders gave him a rod apiece, for each leader according to their
fathers' households, twelve rods, with the rod of Aaron among
their rods.
7So Moses deposited the rods before the LORD in the tent of the
testimony.
8¶ Now it came about on the next day that Moses went into the
tent of the testimony; and behold, the rod of Aaron for the house
of Levi had sprouted and put forth buds and produced blossoms,
and it bore ripe almonds.
9Moses then brought out all the rods from the presence of the
LORD to all the sons of Israel; and they looked, and each man took
his rod.
10But the LORD said to Moses, "Put back the rod of Aaron before
the testimony to be kept as a sign against the rebels, that you may
put an end to their grumblings against Me, so that they should not
die."
11Thus Moses did; just as the LORD had commanded him, so he
did.
12¶ Then the sons of Israel spoke to Moses, saying, "Behold, we
perish, we are dying, we are all dying!
13"Everyone who comes near, who comes near to the tabernacle
of the LORD, must die. Are we to perish completely?"

*Duties of Levites*

**18** SO THE LORD said to Aaron, "You and your sons and
your father's household with you shall bear the guilt in
connection with the sanctuary; and you and your sons with you
shall bear the guilt in connection with your priesthood.

## New International

Aaron went to the front of the Tent of Meeting, 44and the LORD said
to Moses, 45"Get away from this assembly so I can put an end to
them at once." And they fell facedown.
46Then Moses said to Aaron, "Take your censer and put incense
in it, along with fire from the altar, and hurry to the assembly to
make atonement for them. Wrath has come out from the LORD; the
plague has started." 47So Aaron did as Moses said, and ran into
the midst of the assembly. The plague had already started among
the people, but Aaron offered the incense and made atonement for
them. 48He stood between the living and the dead, and the plague
stopped. 49But 14,700 people died from the plague, in addition to
those who had died because of Korah. 50Then Aaron returned to
Moses at the entrance to the Tent of Meeting, for the plague had
stopped.

*The Budding of Aaron's Staff*

**17** THE LORD said to Moses, 2"Speak to the Israelites and
get twelve staffs from them, one from the leader of each
of their ancestral tribes. Write the name of each man on his staff.
3On the staff of Levi write Aaron's name, for there must be one
staff for the head of each ancestral tribe. 4Place them in the Tent
of Meeting in front of the Testimony, where I meet with you. 5The
staff belonging to the man I choose will sprout, and I will rid myself
of this constant grumbling against you by the Israelites."
6So Moses spoke to the Israelites, and their leaders gave him
twelve staffs, one for the leader of each of their ancestral tribes,
and Aaron's staff was among them. 7Moses placed the staffs before
the LORD in the Tent of the Testimony.
8The next day Moses entered the Tent of the Testimony and saw
that Aaron's staff, which represented the house of Levi, had not
only sprouted but had budded, blossomed and produced almonds. 9Then Moses brought out all the staffs from the LORD's
presence to all the Israelites. They looked at them, and each man
took his own staff.
10The LORD said to Moses, "Put back Aaron's staff in front of
the Testimony, to be kept as a sign to the rebellious. This will put
an end to their grumbling against me, so that they will not die."
11Moses did just as the LORD commanded him.
12The Israelites said to Moses, "We will die! We are lost, we are
all lost! 13Anyone who even comes near the tabernacle of the LORD
will die. Are we all going to die?"

*Duties of Priests and Levites*

**18** THE LORD said to Aaron, "You, your sons and your
father's family are to bear the responsibility for offenses
against the sanctuary, and you and your sons alone are to bear the
responsibility for offenses against the priesthood. 2Bring your fel-

## King James

2 And thy brethren also of the tribe of Levi, the tribe of thy father, bring thou with thee, that they may be joined unto thee, and minister unto thee: but thou and thy sons with thee *shall minister* before the tabernacle of witness.

3 And they shall keep thy charge, and the charge of all the tabernacle: only they shall not come nigh the vessels of the sanctuary and the altar, that neither they, nor ye also, die.

4 And they shall be joined unto thee, and keep the charge of the tabernacle of the congregation, for all the service of the tabernacle: and a stranger shall not come nigh unto you.

5 And ye shall keep the charge of the sanctuary, and the charge of the altar: that there be no wrath any more upon the children of Israel.

6 And I, behold, I have taken your brethren the Levites from among the children of Israel: to you *they are* given *as* a gift for the LORD, to do the service of the tabernacle of the congregation.

7 Therefore thou and thy sons with thee shall keep your priest's office for every thing of the altar, and within the veil; and ye shall serve: I have given your priest's office *unto you as* a service of gift: and the stranger that cometh nigh shall be put to death.

8 ¶ And the LORD spake unto Aaron, Behold, I also have given thee the charge of mine heave offerings of all the hallowed things of the children of Israel; unto thee have I given them by reason of the anointing, and to thy sons, by an ordinance for ever.

9 This shall be thine of the most holy things, *reserved* from the fire: every oblation of theirs, every meat offering of theirs, and every sin offering of theirs, and every trespass offering of theirs, which they shall render unto me, *shall be* most holy for thee and for thy sons.

10 In the most holy *place* shalt thou eat it; every male shall eat it: it shall be holy unto thee.

11 And this *is* thine; the heave offering of their gift, with all the wave offerings of the children of Israel: I have given them unto thee, and to thy sons and to thy daughters with thee, by a statute for ever: every one that is clean in thy house shall eat of it.

12 All the best of the oil, and all the best of the wine, and of the wheat, the firstfruits of them which they shall offer unto the LORD, them have I given thee.

13 *And* whatsoever is first ripe in the land, which they shall bring unto the LORD, shall be thine; every one that is clean in thine house shall eat *of* it.

14 Every thing devoted in Israel shall be thine.

15 Every thing that openeth the matrix in all flesh, which they bring unto the LORD, *whether it be* of men or beasts, shall be thine: nevertheless the firstborn of man shalt thou surely redeem, and the firstling of unclean beasts shalt thou redeem.

16 And those that are to be redeemed from a month old shalt thou redeem, according to thine estimation, for the money of five shekels, after the shekel of the sanctuary, which *is* twenty gerahs.

17 But the firstling of a cow, or the firstling of a sheep, or the firstling of a goat, thou shalt not redeem; they *are* holy: thou shalt sprinkle their blood upon the altar, and shalt burn their fat *for* an offering made by fire, for a sweet savour unto the LORD.

18 And the flesh of them shall be thine, as the wave breast and as the right shoulder are thine.

## Amplified

2 And your brethren also of the tribe of Levi, the tribe of your *fore*father, bring with you, that they may be joined to you and minister to you; but only you and your sons with you shall come before the tent of the testimony [into the holy place where only priests may go and into the most holy place which only the high priest dares enter].

3 And the Levites shall attend you [as servants] and attend to all the duties of the tent; only they shall not come near the sacred vessels of the sanctuary or to the brazen altar, that they, and also you [Aaron], die not.

4 And they shall be joined to you and attend to the duties of the tent of meeting for all the [menial] service of the tent; and no stranger [that is, no layman, any one who is not a Levite] shall come near you [Aaron, and your sons].

5 And you shall attend to the duties of the sanctuary and attend to the altar [of burnt offering and the altar of incense], that there be no wrath any more upon the Israelites [as in the incident of Korah, Dathan and Abiram]. [16:42-50.]

6 And I, behold, I have taken your brethren the Levites from among the Israelites; to you they are a gift, given to the Lord, to do the [menial] service of the tent of meeting,

7 Therefore you and your sons with you shall attend to your priesthood for everything of the altar [of burnt offering and the altar of incense], and [of the holy of holies] within the veil; and you shall serve. I give you your priesthood as a service of gift; and the stranger [any one else than Moses or your sons, Aaron] who comes near shall be put to death. [Exod. 40:18, 20, 26.]

8 And the Lord said to Aaron, And I, behold, I have given you the charge of My heave offerings [that is, whatever is taken out and kept of the offerings made to Me], all the dedicated *and* consecrated things of the Israelites; to you have I given them [as your portion] and to your sons, as a continual allowance for ever, by reason of your anointing as priests. [Lev. 7:35.]

9 This shall be yours of the most holy things, reserved from the fire: every offering of the people, every cereal offering and sin offering and trespass offering of theirs, which they shall render to Me, shall be most holy for you [Aaron] and for your sons.

10 As the most holy thing *and* in a sacred place shall you eat of it; every male [of your house] shall eat of it; it shall be holy to you. [Lev. 22:10-16.]

11 And this also is yours, the heave offering of their gift, with all the wave offerings of the Israelites. I have given them to you and to your sons and to your daughters with you as a continual allowance for ever; everyone in your house who is [ceremonially] clean may eat of it.

12 All the best of the oil, and all the best of the (fresh) wine and of the grain, the first fruits of what they give to the Lord, to you have I given them.

13 Whatever is first ripe in the land, which they bring to the Lord, shall be yours; every one who is [ceremonially] clean in your house may eat of it.

14 [Every thing that has been vowed to the Lord] every devoted thing in Israel shall be yours.

15 Everything that first opens the womb in all flesh, which they bring to the Lord, whether it be of men or beasts, shall be yours. Nevertheless the first-born of man you shall surely redeem, and the firstling of unclean beasts you shall redeem.

16 And those that are to be redeemed of them, from a month old shall you redeem, according to your estimate [of their age], for the fixed price of five shekels in silver, according to the shekel of the sanctuary, which is twenty gerahs.

17 But the firstling of a cow or of a sheep or of a goat, you shall not redeem; they [as the first-born of clean beasts, belong to God and] are holy. You shall sprinkle their blood upon the altar, and shall burn their fat for an offering made by fire, for a sweet *and* soothing odor to the Lord.

18 And the flesh of them shall be yours as the wave breast and as the right shoulder are yours.

## New American Standard

2"But bring with you also your brothers, the tribe of Levi, the tribe of your father, that they may be joined with you and serve you, while you and your sons with you are before the tent of the testimony.

3"And they shall thus attend to your obligation and the obligation of all the tent, but they shall not come near to the furnishings of the sanctuary and the altar, lest both they and you die.

4"And they shall be joined with you and attend to the obligations of the tent of meeting, for all the service of the tent; but an outsider may not come near you.

5"So you shall attend to the obligations of the sanctuary and the obligations of the altar, that there may no longer be wrath on the sons of Israel.

6"And behold, I Myself have taken your fellow Levites from among the sons of Israel; they are a gift to you, dedicated to the LORD, to perform the service for the tent of meeting.

7"But you and your sons with you shall attend to your priesthood for everything concerning the altar and inside the veil, and you are to perform service. I am giving you the priesthood as a bestowed service, but the outsider who comes near shall be put to death."

*The Priests' Portion*

8¶ Then the LORD spoke to Aaron, "Now behold, I Myself have given you charge of My offerings, even all the holy gifts of the sons of Israel, I have given them to you as a portion, and to your sons as a perpetual allotment.

9"This shall be yours from the most holy *gifts, reserved* from the fire; every offering of theirs, even every grain offering and every sin offering and every guilt offering, which they shall render to Me, shall be most holy for you and for your sons.

10"As the most holy *gifts* you shall eat it; every male shall eat it. It shall be holy to you.

11"This also is yours, the offering of their gift, even all the wave offerings of the sons of Israel; I have given them to you and to your sons and daughters with you, as a perpetual allotment. Everyone of your household who is clean may eat it.

12"All the best of the fresh oil and all the best of the fresh wine and of the grain, the first fruits of those which they give to the LORD, I give them to you.

13"The first ripe fruits of all that is in their land, which they bring to the LORD, shall be yours; everyone of your household who is clean may eat it.

14"Every devoted thing in Israel shall be yours.

15"Every first issue of the womb of all flesh, whether man or animal, which they offer to the LORD, shall be yours; nevertheless the first-born of man you shall surely redeem, and the first-born of unclean animals you shall redeem.

16"And as to their redemption price, from a month old you shall redeem them, by your valuation, five [a]shekels in silver, according to the shekel of the sanctuary, which is twenty gerahs.

17"But the first-born of an ox or the first-born of a sheep or the first-born of a goat, you shall not redeem; they are holy. You shall sprinkle their blood on the altar and shall offer up their fat in smoke *as* an offering by fire, for a soothing aroma to the LORD.

18"And their meat shall be yours; it shall be yours like the breast of a wave offering and like the right thigh.

NAS [a] I.e., A shekel equals approx. one-half ounce

## New International

low Levites from your ancestral tribe to join you and assist you when you and your sons minister before the Tent of the Testimony. 3They are to be responsible to you and are to perform all the duties of the Tent, but they must not go near the furnishings of the sanctuary or the altar, or both they and you will die. 4They are to join you and be responsible for the care of the Tent of Meeting—all the work at the Tent—and no one else may come near where you are.

5"You are to be responsible for the care of the sanctuary and the altar, so that wrath will not fall on the Israelites again. 6I myself have selected your fellow Levites from among the Israelites as a gift to you, dedicated to the LORD to do the work at the Tent of Meeting. 7But only you and your sons may serve as priests in connection with everything at the altar and inside the curtain. I am giving you the service of the priesthood as a gift. Anyone else who comes near the sanctuary must be put to death."

*Offerings for Priests and Levites*

8Then the LORD said to Aaron, "I myself have put you in charge of the offerings presented to me; all the holy offerings the Israelites give me I give to you and your sons as your portion and regular share. 9You are to have the part of the most holy offerings that is kept from the fire. From all the gifts they bring me as most holy offerings, whether grain or sin or guilt offerings, that part belongs to you and your sons. 10Eat it as something most holy; every male shall eat it. You must regard it as holy.

11"This also is yours: whatever is set aside from the gifts of all the wave offerings of the Israelites. I give this to you and your sons and daughters as your regular share. Everyone in your household who is ceremonially clean may eat it.

12"I give you all the finest olive oil and all the finest new wine and grain they give the LORD as the firstfruits of their harvest. 13All the land's firstfruits that they bring to the LORD will be yours. Everyone in your household who is ceremonially clean may eat it.

14"Everything in Israel that is devoted[b] to the LORD is yours. 15The first offspring of every womb, both man and animal, that is offered to the LORD is yours. But you must redeem every firstborn son and every firstborn male of unclean animals. 16When they are a month old, you must redeem them at the redemption price set at five shekels[c] of silver, according to the sanctuary shekel, which weighs twenty gerahs.

17"But you must not redeem the firstborn of an ox, a sheep or a goat; they are holy. Sprinkle their blood on the altar and burn their fat as an offering made by fire, an aroma pleasing to the LORD. 18Their meat is to be yours, just as the breast of the wave offering and the right thigh are yours. 19Whatever is set aside from the holy

NIV [b] *14* The Hebrew term refers to the irrevocable giving over of things or persons to the LORD, often by totally destroying them. [c] *16* That is, about 2 ounces (about 55 grams)

## King James

19All the heave offerings of the holy things, which the children of Israel offer unto the LORD, have I given thee, and thy sons and thy daughters with thee, by a statute for ever: it *is* a covenant of salt for ever before the LORD unto thee and to thy seed with thee.

20¶ And the LORD spake unto Aaron, Thou shalt have no inheritance in their land, neither shalt thou have any part among them: I *am* thy part and thine inheritance among the children of Israel.

21And, behold, I have given the children of Levi all the tenth in Israel for an inheritance, for their service which they serve, *even* the service of the tabernacle of the congregation.

22Neither must the children of Israel henceforth come nigh the tabernacle of the congregation, lest they bear sin, and die.

23But the Levites shall do the service of the tabernacle of the congregation, and they shall bear their iniquity: *it shall be* a statute for ever throughout your generations, that among the children of Israel they have no inheritance.

24But the tithes of the children of Israel, which they offer *as* an heave offering unto the LORD, I have given to the Levites to inherit: therefore I have said unto them, Among the children of Israel they shall have no inheritance.

25¶ And the LORD spake unto Moses, saying,

26Thus speak unto the Levites, and say unto them, When ye take of the children of Israel the tithes which I have given you from them for your inheritance, then ye shall offer up an heave offering of it for the LORD, *even* a tenth *part* of the tithe.

27And *this* your heave offering shall be reckoned unto you, as though *it were* the corn of the threshingfloor, and as the fulness of the winepress.

28Thus ye also shall offer an heave offering unto the LORD of all your tithes, which ye receive of the children of Israel; and ye shall give thereof the LORD's heave offering to Aaron the priest.

29Out of all your gifts ye shall offer every heave offering of the LORD, of all the best thereof, *even* the hallowed part thereof out of it.

30Therefore thou shalt say unto them, When ye have heaved the best thereof from it, then it shall be counted unto the Levites as the increase of the threshingfloor, and as the increase of the winepress.

31And ye shall eat it in every place, ye and your households: for it *is* your reward for your service in the tabernacle of the congregation.

32And ye shall bear no sin by reason of it, when ye have heaved from it the best of it: neither shall ye pollute the holy things of the children of Israel, lest ye die.

## Amplified

19All the heave offerings [that is, the lifted out and kept portions] of the holy things which the Israelites give to the Lord, I give to you and to your sons and your daughters with you, as a continual debt for ever. It is a covenant of salt [that cannot be dissolved or violated] for ever before the Lord for you [Aaron] and for your posterity with you.

20And the Lord said to Aaron, You shall have no inheritance in the land [of the Israelites], neither shall you have any part among them. I am your portion and your inheritance among the Israelites.

21And, behold, I have given the Levites all the tithe in Israel for an inheritance, in return for their service which they serve, the [menial] service of the tent of meeting.

22Henceforth the Israelites shall not come near the tent of meeting [the covered sanctuary, the holy place and the holy of holies], lest they incur guilt and die.

23But the Levites shall do the [menial] service of the tent of meeting, and they shall bear and remove the iniquity of the people [that is, be answerable for the legal pollutions of the holy things, and offer the necessary atonements for unintentional offenses in these matters]. It shall be a statute for ever in all your generations, that among the Israelites the Levites have no inheritance [of land].

24But the tithes of the Israelites, which they present as an offering to the Lord, I have given to the Levites to inherit; therefore I have said to them, Among the Israelites they shall have no inheritance. [They have homes and cities and pasturage to use, but not to possess as their personal inheritance.]

25And the Lord said to Moses,

26Moreover you shall say to the Levites, When you take from the Israelites the tithe which I have given you from them for your inheritance, then you shall present an offering from it to the Lord, even a tenth of the tithe [paid by the people].

27And what you lift out and keep [your heave offering] shall be credited to you as though it were the grain of the threshing floor, and as the fully ripe produce of the vine.

28Likewise you shall also present an offering to the Lord of all your tithes which you receive from the Israelites; and therefore you shall give this heave offering [lifted out and kept] for the Lord to Aaron the priest.

29Out of all the gifts to you, you shall present every offering due to the Lord, of all the best of it, even the hallowed part lifted out *and* held back out of it [for the Levites].

30Therefore you shall say to them, When you have lifted out *and* held back the best from it [and presented it to the Lord by giving it to yourselves, the Levites], then it shall be counted to [you] the Levites just as if it were the increase of the threshing floor or of the winepress.

31And you may eat it in every place, you and your households; for it is your reward for your service in the tent of meeting.

32And you shall be guilty of no sin by reason of it when you have lifted out *and* held back the best of it; neither shall you have polluted the holy things of the Israelites, neither shall you die [because of it].

**19** AND THE LORD spake unto Moses and unto Aaron, saying,

2This *is* the ordinance of the law which the LORD hath commanded, saying, Speak unto the children of Israel, that they bring thee a red heifer without spot, wherein *is* no blemish, *and* upon which never came yoke:

3And ye shall give her unto Eleazar the priest, that he may bring her forth without the camp, and *one* shall slay her before his face:

4And Eleazar the priest shall take of her blood with his finger, and sprinkle of her blood directly before the tabernacle of the congregation seven times:

5And *one* shall burn the heifer in his sight; her skin, and her flesh, and her blood, with her dung, shall he burn:

**19** AND THE Lord said to Moses and Aaron,

2This is the ritual of the law which the Lord has commanded: Tell the Israelites to bring you a red heifer without spot, in which is no blemish, upon which a yoke has never come.

3And you shall give her to Eleazer the priest, and he shall bring her outside the camp, and she shall be slaughtered before him.

4Eleazar the priest shall take some of her blood with his finger, and sprinkle it toward the front of the tent of meeting seven times.

5The heifer shall be burned in his sight, her skin, flesh, blood, and dung;

## New American Standard

19"All the offerings of the holy *gifts,* which the sons of Israel offer to the LORD, I have given to you and your sons and your daughters with you, as a perpetual allotment. It is an everlasting covenant of salt before the LORD to you and your descendants with you."

20Then the LORD said to Aaron, "You shall have no inheritance in their land, nor own any portion among them; I am your portion and your inheritance among the sons of Israel.

21¶ "And to the sons of Levi, behold, I have given all the tithe in Israel for an inheritance, in return for their service which they perform, the service of the tent of meeting.

22"And the sons of Israel shall not come near the tent of meeting again, lest they bear sin and die.

23"Only the Levites shall perform the service of the tent of meeting, and they shall bear their iniquity; it shall be a perpetual statute throughout your generations, and among the sons of Israel they shall have no inheritance.

24"For the tithe of the sons of Israel, which they offer as an offering to the LORD, I have given to the Levites for an inheritance; therefore I have said concerning them, 'They shall have no inheritance among the sons of Israel.' "

25¶ Then the LORD spoke to Moses, saying,

26"Moreover, you shall speak to the Levites and say to them, 'When you take from the sons of Israel the tithe which I have given you from them for your inheritance, then you shall present an offering from it to the LORD, a tithe of the tithe.

27'And your offering shall be reckoned to you as the grain from the threshing floor or the full produce from the wine vat.

28'So you shall also present an offering to the LORD from your tithes, which you receive from the sons of Israel; and from it you shall give the LORD's offering to Aaron the priest.

29'Out of all your gifts you shall present every offering due to the LORD, from all the best of them, the sacred part from them.'

30"And you shall say to them, 'When you have offered from it the best of it, then *the rest* shall be reckoned to the Levites as the product of the threshing floor, and as the product of the wine vat.

31'And you may eat it anywhere, you and your households, for it is your compensation in return for your service in the tent of meeting.

32'And you shall bear no sin by reason of it, when you have offered the best of it. But you shall not profane the sacred gifts of the sons of Israel, lest you die.' "

*Ordinance of the Red Heifer*

**19** THEN THE LORD spoke to Moses and Aaron, saying,
2"This is the statute of the law which the LORD has commanded, saying, 'Speak to the sons of Israel that they bring you an unblemished red heifer in which is no defect, *and* on which a yoke has never been placed.

3'And you shall give it to Eleazar the priest, and it shall be brought outside the camp and be slaughtered in his presence.

4'Next Eleazar the priest shall take some of its blood with his finger, and sprinkle some of its blood toward the front of the tent of meeting seven times.

5'Then the heifer shall be burned in his sight; its hide and its flesh and its blood, with its refuse, shall be burned.

## New International

offerings the Israelites present to the LORD I give to you and your
sons and daughters as your regular share. It is an everlasting
covenant of salt before the LORD for both you and your offspring."
20The LORD said to Aaron, "You will have no inheritance in
their land, nor will you have any share among them; I am your
share and your inheritance among the Israelites.
21"I give to the Levites all the tithes in Israel as their inheritance
in return for the work they do while serving at the Tent of Meeting.
22From now on the Israelites must not go near the Tent of Meeting,
or they will bear the consequences of their sin and will die. 23It is
the Levites who are to do the work at the Tent of Meeting and bear
the responsibility for offenses against it. This is a lasting ordinance
for the generations to come. They will receive no inheritance
among the Israelites. 24Instead, I give to the Levites as their inheritance the tithes that the Israelites present as an offering to the
LORD. That is why I said concerning them: 'They will have no
inheritance among the Israelites.' "
25The LORD said to Moses, 26"Speak to the Levites and say to
them: 'When you receive from the Israelites the tithe I give you as
your inheritance, you must present a tenth of that tithe as the
LORD's offering. 27Your offering will be reckoned to you as grain
from the threshing floor or juice from the winepress. 28In this way
you also will present an offering to the LORD from all the tithes you
receive from the Israelites. From these tithes you must give the
LORD's portion to Aaron the priest. 29You must present as the
LORD's portion the best and holiest part of everything given to
you.'
30"Say to the Levites: 'When you present the best part, it will
be reckoned to you as the product of the threshing floor or the
winepress. 31You and your households may eat the rest of it anywhere, for it is your wages for your work at the Tent of Meeting.
32By presenting the best part of it you will not be guilty in this
matter; then you will not defile the holy offerings of the Israelites,
and you will not die.' "

*The Water of Cleansing*

**19** THE LORD said to Moses and Aaron: 2"This is a requirement of the law that the LORD has commanded: Tell
the Israelites to bring you a red heifer without defect or blemish
and that has never been under a yoke. 3Give it to Eleazar the priest;
it is to be taken outside the camp and slaughtered in his presence.
4Then Eleazar the priest is to take some of its blood on his finger
and sprinkle it seven times toward the front of the Tent of Meeting.
5While he watches, the heifer is to be burned—its hide, flesh,
blood and offal. 6The priest is to take some cedar wood, hyssop

## King James

6And the priest shall take cedar wood, and hyssop, and scarlet, and cast *it* into the midst of the burning of the heifer.
7Then the priest shall wash his clothes, and he shall bathe his flesh in water, and afterward he shall come into the camp, and the priest shall be unclean until the even.
8And he that burneth her shall wash his clothes in water, and bathe his flesh in water, and shall be unclean until the even.
9And a man *that is* clean shall gather up the ashes of the heifer, and lay *them* up without the camp in a clean place, and it shall be kept for the congregation of the children of Israel for a water of separation: it *is* a purification for sin.
10And he that gathereth the ashes of the heifer shall wash his clothes, and be unclean until the even: and it shall be unto the children of Israel, and unto the stranger that sojourneth among them, for a statute for ever.
11¶ He that toucheth the dead body of any man shall be unclean seven days.
12He shall purify himself with it on the third day, and on the seventh day he shall be clean: but if he purify not himself the third day, then the seventh day he shall not be clean.
13Whosoever toucheth the dead body of any man that is dead, and purifieth not himself, defileth the tabernacle of the LORD; and that soul shall be cut off from Israel: because the water of separation was not sprinkled upon him, he shall be unclean; his uncleanness *is* yet upon him.
14This *is* the law, when a man dieth in a tent: all that come into the tent, and all that *is* in the tent, shall be unclean seven days.
15And every open vessel, which hath no covering bound upon it, *is* unclean.
16And whosoever toucheth one that is slain with a sword in the open fields, or a dead body, or a bone of a man, or a grave, shall be unclean seven days.
17And for an unclean *person* they shall take of the ashes of the burnt heifer of purification for sin, and running water shall be put thereto in a vessel:
18And a clean person shall take hyssop, and dip *it* in the water, and sprinkle *it* upon the tent, and upon all the vessels, and upon the persons that were there, and upon him that touched a bone, or one slain, or one dead, or a grave:
19And the clean *person* shall sprinkle upon the unclean on the third day, and on the seventh day: and on the seventh day he shall purify himself, and wash his clothes, and bathe himself in water, and shall be clean at even.
20But the man that shall be unclean, and shall not purify himself, that soul shall be cut off from among the congregation, because he hath defiled the sanctuary of the LORD: the water of separation hath not been sprinkled upon him; he *is* unclean.
21And it shall be a perpetual statute unto them, that he that sprinkleth the water of separation shall wash his clothes; and he that toucheth the water of separation shall be unclean until even.
22And whatsoever the unclean *person* toucheth shall be unclean; and the soul that toucheth *it* shall be unclean until even.

**20** THEN CAME the children of Israel, *even* the whole congregation, into the desert of Zin in the first month: and the people abode in Kadesh; and Miriam died there, and was buried there.
2And there was no water for the congregation: and they gathered themselves together against Moses and against Aaron.
3And the people chode with Moses, and spake, saying, Would God that we had died when our brethren died before the LORD!

## Amplified

6And the priest shall take cedar wood, and hyssop and scarlet stuff, and cast them into the midst of the burning of the heifer.
7Then the priest shall wash his clothes and bathe his body in water; afterward he shall come into the camp; but he shall be unclean until evening.
8He who burns the heifer shall wash his clothes and bathe his body in water, and shall be unclean until evening.
9And a man who is clean shall collect the ashes of the heifer and put them outside the camp in a clean place, and they shall be kept for the congregation of the Israelites for the water for impurity; it is a sin offering.
10And he who gathers the ashes of the heifer shall wash his clothes, and be unclean until evening. This shall be to the Israelites, and to the stranger who sojourns among them, a perpetual statute.
11He who touches the dead body of any person shall be unclean seven days.
12He shall purify himself with the water for impurity [made with the ashes of the burned heifer] on the third day, and on the seventh day he shall be clean; but if he does not purify himself the third day, then the seventh day he shall not be clean.
13Whoever touches the corpse of any who has died, and does not purify himself, defiles the tabernacle of the Lord, and that person shall be cut off from Israel; because the water for impurity was not sprinkled upon him, he shall be unclean; his uncleanness is still upon him.
14This is the law when a man dies in a tent: all who come into the tent, and all that is in the tent, shall be unclean seven days.
15And every open vessel, which has no covering fastened upon it, is unclean.
16And whoever in the open fields touches one who is slain with a sword, or a dead body, or a bone of a dead man, or a grave, shall be unclean seven days.
17And for the unclean they shall take of the ashes of the burning of the sin offering, and the running water shall be put with it in a vessel;
18And a clean person shall take hyssop, and dip it in the water, and sprinkle it upon the tent, and upon all the vessels, and upon the persons who were there, and upon him who touched the bone, or the slain, or the naturally dead, or the grave.
19And the clean person shall sprinkle [the water for purification] upon the unclean person on the third day and on the seventh day; and on the seventh day the unclean man shall purify himself, and wash his clothes and bathe himself in water, and shall be clean at evening.
20But the man who is unclean and does not purify himself, that person shall be cut off from among the congregation, because he has defiled the sanctuary of the Lord; the water for purification has not been sprinkled upon him; he is unclean.
21And it shall be a perpetual statute to them. He who sprinkles the water for impurity [upon another] shall wash his clothes; and he who touches the water for impurity shall be unclean until evening.
22And whatever the unclean person touches shall be unclean; and any one who touches it shall be unclean until evening.

**20** AND THE Israelites, the whole congregation, came into the desert of Zin in the first month. And the people dwelt in Kadesh; Miriam died and was buried there.
2Now there was no water for the congregation; and they assembled together against Moses and Aaron.
3And the people contended with Moses, and said, Would that we had died when our brethren died [in the plague] before the Lord! [16:49.]

## New American Standard

6'And the priest shall take cedar wood and hyssop and scarlet *material,* and cast it into the midst of the burning heifer.

7'The priest shall then wash his clothes and bathe his body in water, and afterward come into the camp, but the priest shall be unclean until evening.

8'The one who burns it shall also wash his clothes in water and bathe his body in water, and shall be unclean until evening.

9'Now a man who is clean shall gather up the ashes of the heifer and deposit them outside the camp in a clean place, and the congregation of the sons of Israel shall keep it as water to remove impurity; it is purification from sin.

10'And the one who gathers the ashes of the heifer shall wash his clothes and be unclean until evening; and it shall be a perpetual statute to the sons of Israel and to the alien who sojourns among them.

11¶ 'The one who touches the corpse of any person shall be unclean for seven days.

12'That one shall purify himself from uncleanness with the water on the third day and on the seventh day, *and then* he shall be clean; but if he does not purify himself on the third day and on the seventh day, he shall not be clean.

13'Anyone who touches a corpse, the body of a man who has died, and does not purify himself, defiles the tabernacle of the LORD; and that person shall be cut off from Israel. Because the water for impurity was not sprinkled on him, he shall be unclean; his uncleanness is still on him.

14¶ 'This is the law when a man dies in a tent: everyone who comes into the tent and everyone who is in the tent shall be unclean for seven days.

15'And every open vessel, which has no covering tied down on it, shall be unclean.

16'Also, anyone who in the open field touches one who has been slain with a sword or who has died *naturally,* or a human bone or a grave, shall be unclean for seven days.

17'Then for the unclean *person* they shall take some of the ashes of the burnt purification from sin and flowing water shall be added to them in a vessel.

18'And a clean person shall take hyssop and dip *it* in the water, and sprinkle *it* on the tent and on all the furnishings and on the persons who were there, and on the one who touched the bone or the one slain or the one dying *naturally* or the grave.

19'Then the clean *person* shall sprinkle on the unclean on the third day and on the seventh day; and on the seventh day he shall purify him from uncleanness, and he shall wash his clothes and bathe *himself* in water and shall be clean by evening.

20¶ 'But the man who is unclean and does not purify himself from uncleanness, that person shall be cut off from the midst of the assembly, because he has defiled the sanctuary of the LORD; the water for impurity has not been sprinkled on him, he is unclean.

21'So it shall be a perpetual statute for them. And he who sprinkles the water for impurity shall wash his clothes, and he who touches the water for impurity shall be unclean until evening.

22'Furthermore, anything that the unclean *person* touches shall be unclean; and the person who touches *it* shall be unclean until evening.' "

## New International

and scarlet wool and throw them onto the burning heifer. 7After
that, the priest must wash his clothes and bathe himself with
water. He may then come into the camp, but he will be ceremonially unclean till evening. 8The man who burns it must also wash
his clothes and bathe with water, and he too will be unclean till
evening.
9"A man who is clean shall gather up the ashes of the heifer and
put them in a ceremonially clean place outside the camp. They
shall be kept by the Israelite community for use in the water of
cleansing; it is for purification from sin. 10The man who gathers up
the ashes of the heifer must also wash his clothes, and he too will
be unclean till evening. This will be a lasting ordinance both for the
Israelites and for the aliens living among them.
11"Whoever touches the dead body of anyone will be unclean
for seven days. 12He must purify himself with the water on the
third day and on the seventh day; then he will be clean. But if he
does not purify himself on the third and seventh days, he will not
be clean. 13Whoever touches the dead body of anyone and fails to
purify himself defiles the LORD's tabernacle. That person must be
cut off from Israel. Because the water of cleansing has not been
sprinkled on him, he is unclean; his uncleanness remains on him.
14"This is the law that applies when a person dies in a tent:
Anyone who enters the tent and anyone who is in it will be unclean
for seven days, 15and every open container without a lid fastened
on it will be unclean.
16"Anyone out in the open who touches someone who has been
killed with a sword or someone who has died a natural death, or
anyone who touches a human bone or a grave, will be unclean for
seven days.
17"For the unclean person, put some ashes from the burned
purification offering into a jar and pour fresh water over them.
18Then a man who is ceremonially clean is to take some hyssop,
dip it in the water and sprinkle the tent and all the furnishings and
the people who were there. He must also sprinkle anyone who has
touched a human bone or a grave or someone who has been killed
or someone who has died a natural death. 19The man who is clean
is to sprinkle the unclean person on the third and seventh days,
and on the seventh day he is to purify him. The person being
cleansed must wash his clothes and bathe with water, and that
evening he will be clean. 20But if a person who is unclean does not
purify himself, he must be cut off from the community, because
he has defiled the sanctuary of the LORD. The water of cleansing
has not been sprinkled on him, and he is unclean. 21This is a lasting
ordinance for them.
"The man who sprinkles the water of cleansing must also wash
his clothes, and anyone who touches the water of cleansing will
be unclean till evening. 22Anything that an unclean person touches
becomes unclean, and anyone who touches it becomes unclean till
evening."

*Death of Miriam*

20 THEN THE sons of Israel, the whole congregation, came to the wilderness of Zin in the first month; and the people stayed at Kadesh. Now Miriam died there and was buried there.

2¶ And there was no water for the congregation; and they assembled themselves against Moses and Aaron.

3The people thus contended with Moses and spoke, saying, "If only we had perished when our brothers perished before the LORD!

*Water From the Rock*

20 IN THE first month the whole Israelite community arrived
at the Desert of Zin, and they stayed at Kadesh. There
Miriam died and was buried.
2Now there was no water for the community, and the people
gathered in opposition to Moses and Aaron. 3They quarreled with
Moses and said, "If only we had died when our brothers fell dead
before the LORD! 4Why did you bring the LORD's community into

## King James

4 And why have ye brought up the congregation of the LORD into this wilderness, that we and our cattle should die there?

5 And wherefore have ye made us to come up out of Egypt, to bring us in unto this evil place? it *is* no place of seed, or of figs, or of vines, or of pomegranates; neither *is* there any water to drink.

6 And Moses and Aaron went from the presence of the assembly unto the door of the tabernacle of the congregation, and they fell upon their faces: and the glory of the LORD appeared unto them.

7 ¶ And the LORD spake unto Moses, saying,

8 Take the rod, and gather thou the assembly together, thou, and Aaron thy brother, and speak ye unto the rock before their eyes; and it shall give forth his water, and thou shalt bring forth to them water out of the rock: so thou shalt give the congregation and their beasts drink.

9 And Moses took the rod from before the LORD, as he commanded him.

10 And Moses and Aaron gathered the congregation together before the rock, and he said unto them, Hear now, ye rebels; must we fetch you water out of this rock?

11 And Moses lifted up his hand, and with his rod he smote the rock twice: and the water came out abundantly, and the congregation drank, and their beasts *also*.

12 ¶ And the LORD spake unto Moses and Aaron, Because ye believed me not, to sanctify me in the eyes of the children of Israel, therefore ye shall not bring this congregation into the land which I have given them.

13 This *is* the water of Meribah; because the children of Israel strove with the LORD, and he was sanctified in them.

14 ¶ And Moses sent messengers from Kadesh unto the king of Edom, Thus saith thy brother Israel, Thou knowest all the travail that hath befallen us:

15 How our fathers went down into Egypt, and we have dwelt in Egypt a long time; and the Egyptians vexed us, and our fathers:

16 And when we cried unto the LORD, he heard our voice, and sent an angel, and hath brought us forth out of Egypt: and, behold, we *are* in Kadesh, a city in the uttermost of thy border:

17 Let us pass, I pray thee, through thy country: we will not pass through the fields, or through the vineyards, neither will we drink *of* the water of the wells: we will go by the king's *high* way, we will not turn to the right hand nor to the left, until we have passed thy borders.

18 And Edom said unto him, Thou shalt not pass by me, lest I come out against thee with the sword.

19 And the children of Israel said unto him, We will go by the high way: and if I and my cattle drink of thy water, then I will pay for it: I will only, without *doing* any thing *else*, go through on my feet.

20 And he said, Thou shalt not go through. And Edom came out against him with much people, and with a strong hand.

21 Thus Edom refused to give Israel passage through his border: wherefore Israel turned away from him.

22 ¶ And the children of Israel, *even* the whole congregation, journeyed from Kadesh, and came unto mount Hor.

23 And the LORD spake unto Moses and Aaron in mount Hor, by the coast of the land of Edom, saying,

## Amplified

4 And why have you brought up the congregation of the Lord into this wilderness, that we should die here, we and our livestock?

5 And why have you made us come up out of Egypt, to bring us into this evil place? It is no place of grain, or of figs, or of vines, or of pomegranates; and there is no water to drink.

6 Then Moses and Aaron went from the presence of the assembly to the door of the tent of meeting, and fell on their faces. Then the glory of the Lord appeared to them.

7 And the Lord said to Moses,

8 Take the rod, and assemble the congregation, you and Aaron your brother, and tell the rock before their eyes to give forth its water, and you shall bring forth to them water out of the rock; so you shall give the congregation and their livestock drink.

9 So Moses took the rod from before the Lord, as He commanded him.

10 And Moses and Aaron assembled the congregation before the rock, and Moses said to them, Hear now, you rebels; must we bring you water out of this rock?

11 And Moses lifted up his hand, and with his rod he smote the rock [a]twice: and the water came out abundantly, and the congregation drank, and their livestock.

12 And the Lord said to Moses and Aaron, Because you did not believe in (rely on, cling to) Me, to sanctify Me in the eyes of the Israelites, you therefore [b]shall not bring this congregation into the land which I have given them. [Ps. 106:32, 33.]

13 These are the waters of Meribah [meaning, strife], where the Israelites contended with the Lord, and He showed Himself holy among them.

14 And Moses sent messengers from Kadesh to the king of Edom, saying, Thus says your kinsman Israel, You know all the adversity *and* birth pangs that have come upon us [as a nation]:

15 How our fathers went down to Egypt; we dwelt there a long time, and the Egyptians dealt evilly with us and our fathers.

16 But when we cried to the Lord, He heard us, and sent an angel, and brought us forth out of Egypt. Now behold, we are in Kadesh, a city on your country's edge.

17 Let us pass, I pray you, through your country. We will not pass through field or vineyard, or drink of the water of the wells. We will go along the King's Highway; we will not turn aside to the right hand or to the left, until we have passed your borders.

18 But Edom said to him, You shall not go through, lest I come out against you with the sword.

19 And the Israelites said to him, We will go by the highway; and if I and my livestock drink of your water, I will pay for it. Only let me pass through on foot, nothing else.

20 But Edom said, You shall not go through. And Edom came out against Israel with many people and a strong hand.

21 Thus Edom refused to give Israel passage through his territory, [c]so Israel turned away from him.

22 They journeyed from Kadesh, and the Israelites, even the whole congregation, came to Mount Hor.

23 And the Lord said to Moses and Aaron at Mount Hor, on the border of the land of Edom,

**AMP** [a] "And the Rock was Christ," as I Cor. 10:4 explains. Once smitten, at Rephidim (Exod. 17:6), He did not need to be smitten, crucified, again. To smite the rock twice was to imply that Christ's death on the cross was not effectual or sufficient for time and eternity. [b] Possibly Moses was not aware of the significance of what he had been ordered to do, but God held him responsible for not obeying Him exactly, nevertheless. Obedience to His will is vitally important, whether we understand His purpose or not. "God's will; nothing more; nothing less; nothing else; at any cost," would have been priceless to Moses and Aaron that day, if they had only followed it. [c] Israel (Jacob's offspring) did not fight Edom, the offspring of Jacob's brother Esau, because of the Lord's warning, later conveyed in definite instructions (Deut. 23:7). But what had begun as only a quarrel between twin brothers (Gen. 27:41) had now been passed on for generations and was to cost countless lives, extending throughout the Old Testament and into the New, where Herod, remotely related to Esau, tried to take the life of the Babe of Bethlehem, a descendant of Jacob. "See how much wood *or* how great a forest a tiny spark can set ablaze!" (James 3:5, Amp.).

## New American Standard

4"Why then have you brought the LORD's assembly into this
wilderness, for us and our beasts to die here?
5"And why have you made us come up from Egypt, to bring
us in to this wretched place? It is not a place of grain or figs or vines
or pomegranates, nor is there water to drink."
6Then Moses and Aaron came in from the presence of the
assembly to the doorway of the tent of meeting, and fell on their
faces. Then the glory of the LORD appeared to them;
7and the LORD spoke to Moses, saying,

*The Water of Meribah*

8"Take the rod; and you and your brother Aaron assemble the
congregation and speak to the rock before their eyes, that it may
yield its water. You shall thus bring forth water for them out of the
rock and let the congregation and their beasts drink."
9So Moses took the rod from before the LORD, just as He had
commanded him;
10and Moses and Aaron gathered the assembly before the rock.
And he said to them, "Listen now, you rebels; shall we bring forth
water for you out of this rock?"
11Then Moses lifted up his hand and struck the rock twice with
his rod; and water came forth abundantly, and the congregation
and their beasts drank.
12But the LORD said to Moses and Aaron, "Because you have
not believed Me, to treat Me as holy in the sight of the sons of
Israel, therefore you shall not bring this assembly into the land
which I have given them."
13Those *were* the waters of [d]Meribah, because the sons of Israel
contended with the LORD, and He proved Himself holy among
them.
**14**¶ From Kadesh Moses then sent messengers to the king of
Edom: "Thus your brother Israel has said, 'You know all the hardship that has befallen us;
15that our fathers went down to Egypt, and we stayed in Egypt
a long time, and the Egyptians treated us and our fathers badly.
16'But when we cried out to the LORD, He heard our voice and
sent an angel and brought us out from Egypt; now behold, we are
at Kadesh, a town on the edge of your territory.
17'Please let us pass through your land. We shall not pass
through field or through vineyard; we shall not even drink water
from a well. We shall go along the king's highway, not turning to
the right or left, until we pass through your territory.'"
18Edom, however, said to him, "You shall not pass through us,
lest I come out with the sword against you."
19Again, the sons of Israel said to him, "We shall go up by the
highway, and if I and my livestock do drink any of your water,
then I will pay its price. Let me only pass through on my feet,
nothing *else*."
20But he said, "You shall not pass through." And Edom came
out against him with a heavy force, and with a strong hand.
21Thus Edom refused to allow Israel to pass through his territory; so Israel turned away from him.
**22**¶ Now when they set out from Kadesh, the sons of Israel, the
whole congregation, came to Mount Hor.

*Death of Aaron*

23Then the LORD spoke to Moses and Aaron at Mount Hor by
the border of the land of Edom, saying,

NAS [d] I.e., contention

## New International

this desert, that we and our livestock should die here? 5Why did
you bring us up out of Egypt to this terrible place? It has no grain
or figs, grapevines or pomegranates. And there is no water to
drink!"
6Moses and Aaron went from the assembly to the entrance to
the Tent of Meeting and fell facedown, and the glory of the LORD
appeared to them. 7The LORD said to Moses, 8"Take the staff, and
you and your brother Aaron gather the assembly together. Speak
to that rock before their eyes and it will pour out its water. You will
bring water out of the rock for the community so they and their
livestock can drink."
9So Moses took the staff from the LORD's presence, just as he
commanded him. 10He and Aaron gathered the assembly together
in front of the rock and Moses said to them, "Listen, you rebels,
must we bring you water out of this rock?" 11Then Moses raised
his arm and struck the rock twice with his staff. Water gushed out,
and the community and their livestock drank.
12But the LORD said to Moses and Aaron, "Because you did not
trust in me enough to honor me as holy in the sight of the Israelites,
you will not bring this community into the land I give them."
13These were the waters of Meribah,[e] where the Israelites quarreled with the LORD and where he showed himself holy among
them.

*Edom Denies Israel Passage*

14Moses sent messengers from Kadesh to the king of Edom,
saying:

"This is what your brother Israel says: You know about all
the hardships that have come upon us. 15Our forefathers
went down into Egypt, and we lived there many years. The
Egyptians mistreated us and our fathers, 16but when we cried
out to the LORD, he heard our cry and sent an angel and
brought us out of Egypt.
"Now we are here at Kadesh, a town on the edge of your
territory. 17Please let us pass through your country. We will
not go through any field or vineyard, or drink water from any
well. We will travel along the king's highway and not turn to
the right or to the left until we have passed through your
territory."

18But Edom answered:

"You may not pass through here; if you try, we will march
out and attack you with the sword."

19The Israelites replied:

"We will go along the main road, and if we or our livestock
drink any of your water, we will pay for it. We only want to
pass through on foot—nothing else."

20Again they answered:

"You may not pass through."

Then Edom came out against them with a large and powerful
army. 21Since Edom refused to let them go through their territory,
Israel turned away from them.

*The Death of Aaron*

22The whole Israelite community set out from Kadesh and came
to Mount Hor. 23At Mount Hor, near the border of Edom, the LORD
said to Moses and Aaron, 24"Aaron will be gathered to his people.

NIV [e] *13 Meribah* means *quarreling.*

## King James

24 Aaron shall be gathered unto his people: for he shall not enter into the land which I have given unto the children of Israel, because ye rebelled against my word at the water of Meribah.

25 Take Aaron and Eleazar his son, and bring them up unto mount Hor:

26 And strip Aaron of his garments, and put them upon Eleazar his son: and Aaron shall be gathered *unto his people,* and shall die there.

27 And Moses did as the LORD commanded: and they went up into mount Hor in the sight of all the congregation.

28 And Moses stripped Aaron of his garments, and put them upon Eleazar his son; and Aaron died there in the top of the mount: and Moses and Eleazar came down from the mount.

29 And when all the congregation saw that Aaron was dead, they mourned for Aaron thirty days, *even* all the house of Israel.

**21** AND *WHEN* king Arad the Canaanite, which dwelt in the south, heard tell that Israel came by the way of the spies; then he fought against Israel, and took *some* of them prisoners.

2 And Israel vowed a vow unto the LORD, and said, If thou wilt indeed deliver this people into my hand, then I will utterly destroy their cities.

3 And the LORD hearkened to the voice of Israel, and delivered up the Canaanites; and they utterly destroyed them and their cities: and he called the name of the place Hormah.

4 ¶ And they journeyed from mount Hor by the way of the Red sea, to compass the land of Edom: and the soul of the people was much discouraged because of the way.

5 And the people spake against God, and against Moses, Wherefore have ye brought us up out of Egypt to die in the wilderness? for *there is* no bread, neither *is there any* water; and our soul loatheth this light bread.

6 And the LORD sent fiery serpents among the people, and they bit the people; and much people of Israel died.

7 ¶ Therefore the people came to Moses, and said, We have sinned, for we have spoken against the LORD, and against thee; pray unto the LORD, that he take away the serpents from us. And Moses prayed for the people.

8 And the LORD said unto Moses, Make thee a fiery serpent, and set it upon a pole: and it shall come to pass, that every one that is bitten, when he looketh upon it, shall live.

9 And Moses made a serpent of brass, and put it upon a pole, and it came to pass, that if a serpent had bitten any man, when he beheld the serpent of brass, he lived.

10 ¶ And the children of Israel set forward, and pitched in Oboth.

11 And they journeyed from Oboth, and pitched at Ije-abarim, in the wilderness which *is* before Moab, toward the sunrising.

12 ¶ From thence they removed, and pitched in the valley of Zared.

13 From thence they removed, and pitched on the other side of Arnon, which *is* in the wilderness that cometh out of the coasts of the Amorites: for Arnon *is* the border of Moab, between Moab and the Amorites.

14 Wherefore it is said in the book of the wars of the LORD, What he did in the Red sea, and in the brooks of Arnon,

## Amplified

24 Aaron shall be gathered to his people; for he shall not enter the land which I have given to the Israelites, because you both rebelled against My instructions at the waters of Meribah.

25 Take Aaron and Eleazar his son, and bring them up to Mount Hor;

26 Strip Aaron of his vestments, and put them on Eleazar his son; and Aaron shall be gathered to his people, and shall die there.

27 And Moses did as the Lord commanded; and they went up Mount Hor in the sight of all the congregation.

28 And Moses stripped Aaron of his [priestly] garments, and put them on Eleazar his son; and Aaron died there on the mountain top; and Moses and Eleazar came down from the mountain.

29 When all the congregation saw that Aaron was dead, they wept *and* mourned for him thirty days, all the house of Israel.

**21** WHEN THE Canaanite king of Arad, who dwelt in the South (the Negeb), heard that Israel was coming by the way of Atharim [the route traveled by the spies sent out by Moses] he fought against Israel, and took some of them captive.

2 And Israel vowed a vow to the Lord, and said, If You will indeed deliver this people into my hand, then I will utterly destroy their cities.

3 And the Lord hearkened to Israel, and gave over the Canaanites; and they utterly destroyed them and their cities; and the name of the place was called Hormah [a banned or devoted thing].

4 And they journeyed from Mount Hor by the way to the Red Sea, to go around the land of Edom, and the people became impatient (depressed, much discouraged), because [of the trials] of the way.

5 And the people said against God and against Moses, Why have you brought us out of Egypt to die in the wilderness? For there is no bread, neither is there any water, and we loathe this light (contemptible, unsubstantial) manna.

6 Then the Lord sent fiery (burning) serpents among the people, and they bit the people; and many Israelites died.

7 And the people came to Moses, and said, We have sinned, for we have spoken against the Lord and against you; pray to the Lord, that He may take away the serpents from us. So Moses prayed for the people.

8 And the Lord said to Moses, Make a fiery serpent [of bronze], and set it on a pole; and every one who is bitten, when he looks at it, shall live.

9 And Moses made a serpent of bronze and put it on a pole, and if a serpent had bitten any man, when he looked to the serpent of bronze [ [a]attentively, expectantly, with a steady and absorbing gaze], he lived.

10 And the Israelites journeyed on, and encamped at Oboth.

11 They journeyed from Oboth, and encamped at Iye-abarim, in the wilderness opposite Moab, toward the sunrising.

12 From there they journeyed, and encamped in the Valley of Zared.

13 From there they journeyed and encamped on the other side of [the river] Arnon, which is in the desert *or* wilderness that extends from the frontier of the Amorites; for [the river] Arnon is the boundary of Moab, between Moab and the Amorites.

14 That is why it is said in the Book of the Wars of the Lord, Waheb in Suphah, and the valleys of [the branches of] the Arnon [River],

**AMP** [a] Jesus said that as Moses lifted up the serpent in the wilderness, so must the Son of man be lifted up, "that every one who believes in Him—who cleaves to Him, trusts and relies on Him—may not perish, but have eternal life and [actually] live for ever!" (John 3:14, 15). Obviously this implies that the look that caused the victim of a fiery serpent to be healed was something far more than a casual glance. A "look" would save, but what kind of a look? The Hebrew text here means "look attentively, expectantly, with a steady and absorbing gaze." Or, as Jesus said in the last verse of the chapter quoted above, "He who believes on—has faith in, clings to, relies on—the Son has (now possesses) eternal life." But whoever does not so believe in, cling to, and rely on the Son, "will never see . . . life." The look that saves is not just a fleeting glance; it is a God-honoring, God-answered, fixed and absorbing gaze!

## New American Standard

24"Aaron shall be gathered to his people; for he shall not enter
the land which I have given to the sons of Israel, because you
rebelled against My command at the waters of Meribah.
25"Take Aaron and his son Eleazar, and bring them up to
Mount Hor;
26and strip Aaron of his garments and put them on his son
Eleazar. So Aaron will be gathered *to his people*, and will die there."
27So Moses did just as the LORD had commanded, and they
went up to Mount Hor in the sight of all the congregation.
28And after Moses had stripped Aaron of his garments and put
them on his son Eleazar, Aaron died there on the mountain top.
Then Moses and Eleazar came down from the mountain.
29And when all the congregation saw that Aaron had died, all
the house of Israel wept for Aaron thirty days.

*Arad Conquered*

**21** WHEN THE Canaanite, the king of Arad, who lived in the
[b]Negev, heard that Israel was coming by the way of
[c]Atharim, then he fought against Israel, and took some of them
captive.
2So Israel made a vow to the LORD, and said, "If Thou wilt
indeed deliver this people into my hand, then I will utterly destroy
their cities."
3And the LORD heard the voice of Israel, and delivered up the
Canaanites; then they utterly destroyed them and their cities. Thus
the name of the place was called [d]Hormah.
4¶ Then they set out from Mount Hor by the way of the Red
Sea, to go around the land of Edom; and the people became impatient because of the journey.
5And the people spoke against God and Moses, "Why have
you brought us up out of Egypt to die in the wilderness? For there
is no food and no water, and we loathe this miserable food."

*The Bronze Serpent*

6And the LORD sent fiery serpents among the people and they
bit the people, so that many people of Israel died.
7So the people came to Moses and said, "We have sinned,
because we have spoken against the LORD and you; intercede with
the LORD, that He may remove the serpents from us." And Moses
interceded for the people.
8Then the LORD said to Moses, "Make a fiery *serpent*, and set
it on a standard; and it shall come about, that everyone who is
bitten, when he looks at it, he shall live."
9And Moses made a bronze serpent and set it on the standard;
and it came about, that if a serpent bit any man, when he looked
to the bronze serpent, he lived.
10¶ Now the sons of Israel moved out and camped in Oboth.
11And they journeyed from Oboth, and camped at Iyeabarim,
in the wilderness which is opposite Moab, to the east.
12From there they set out and camped in [e]Wadi Zered.
13From there they journeyed and camped on the other side of
the Arnon, which is in the wilderness that comes out of the border
of the Amorites, for the Arnon is the border of Moab, between
Moab and the Amorites.
14Therefore it is said in the Book of the Wars of the LORD,
"Waheb in Suphah,
And the wadis of the Arnon,

NAS [b] I.e., South country [c] Or, *the spies* [d] I.e., a devoted thing; or, Destruction [e] I.e., a dry ravine except during rainy season

## New International

He will not enter the land I give the Israelites, because both of you
rebelled against my command at the waters of Meribah. 25Get
Aaron and his son Eleazar and take them up Mount Hor. 26Re-
move Aaron's garments and put them on his son Eleazar, for
Aaron will be gathered to his people; he will die there."
27Moses did as the LORD commanded: They went up Mount
Hor in the sight of the whole community. 28Moses removed
Aaron's garments and put them on his son Eleazar. And Aaron
died there on top of the mountain. Then Moses and Eleazar came
down from the mountain, 29and when the whole community
learned that Aaron had died, the entire house of Israel mourned
for him thirty days.

*Arad Destroyed*

**21** WHEN THE Canaanite king of Arad, who lived in the
Negev, heard that Israel was coming along the road to
Atharim, he attacked the Israelites and captured some of them.
2Then Israel made this vow to the LORD: "If you will deliver these
people into our hands, we will totally destroy[f] their cities." 3The
LORD listened to Israel's plea and gave the Canaanites over to
them. They completely destroyed them and their towns; so the
place was named Hormah.[g]

*The Bronze Snake*

4They traveled from Mount Hor along the route to the Red
Sea,[h] to go around Edom. But the people grew impatient on the
way; 5they spoke against God and against Moses, and said, "Why
have you brought us up out of Egypt to die in the desert? There
is no bread! There is no water! And we detest this miserable food!"
6Then the LORD sent venomous snakes among them; they bit
the people and many Israelites died. 7The people came to Moses
and said, "We sinned when we spoke against the LORD and against
you. Pray that the LORD will take the snakes away from us." So
Moses prayed for the people.
8The LORD said to Moses, "Make a snake and put it up on a pole;
anyone who is bitten can look at it and live." 9So Moses made a
bronze snake and put it up on a pole. Then when anyone was
bitten by a snake and looked at the bronze snake, he lived.

*The Journey to Moab*

10The Israelites moved on and camped at Oboth. 11Then they
set out from Oboth and camped in Iye Abarim, in the desert that
faces Moab toward the sunrise. 12From there they moved on and
camped in the Zered Valley. 13They set out from there and camped
alongside the Arnon, which is in the desert extending into Amorite
territory. The Arnon is the border of Moab, between Moab and the
Amorites. 14That is why the Book of the Wars of the LORD says:
"... Waheb in Suphah[i] and the ravines,
the Arnon 15and[j] the slopes of the ravines

NIV [f] 2 The Hebrew term refers to the irrevocable giving over of things or persons to the LORD, often by totally destroying them; also in verse 3. [g] 3 *Hormah* means *destruction*. [h] 4 Hebrew *Yam Suph*; that is, Sea of Reeds [i] 14 The meaning of the Hebrew for this phrase is uncertain. [j] 14,15 Or *"I have been given from Suphah and the ravines / of the Arnon* [15]*to*

## King James

15And at the stream of the brooks that goeth down to the
dwelling of Ar, and lieth upon the border of Moab.
16And from thence *they went* to Beer: that *is* the well whereof
the LORD spake unto Moses, Gather the people together, and I will
give them water.
17¶ Then Israel sang this song, Spring up, O well; sing ye unto
it:
18The princes digged the well, the nobles of the people digged
it, by *the direction of* the lawgiver, with their staves. And from the
wilderness *they went* to Mattanah:
19And from Mattanah to Nahaliel: and from Nahaliel to Bamoth:
20And from Bamoth *in* the valley, that *is* in the country of Moab,
to the top of Pisgah, which looketh toward Jeshimon.
21¶ And Israel sent messengers unto Sihon king of the Amorites, saying,
22Let me pass through thy land: we will not turn into the fields,
or into the vineyards; we will not drink *of* the waters of the well:
*but* we will go along by the king's *high* way, until we be past thy
borders.
23And Sihon would not suffer Israel to pass through his border:
but Sihon gathered all his people together, and went out against
Israel into the wilderness: and he came to Jahaz, and fought
against Israel.
24And Israel smote him with the edge of the sword, and possessed his land from Arnon unto Jabbok, even unto the children
of Ammon: for the border of the children of Ammon *was* strong.
25And Israel took all these cities: and Israel dwelt in all the cities
of the Amorites, in Heshbon, and in all the villages thereof.
26For Heshbon *was* the city of Sihon the king of the Amorites,
who had fought against the former king of Moab, and taken all his
land out of his hand, even unto Arnon.
27Wherefore they that speak in proverbs say, Come into Heshbon, let the city of Sihon be built and prepared:
28For there is a fire gone out of Heshbon, a flame from the city
of Sihon: it hath consumed Ar of Moab, *and* the lords of the high
places of Arnon.
29Woe to thee, Moab! thou art undone, O people of Chemosh:
he hath given his sons that escaped, and his daughters, into captivity unto Sihon king of the Amorites.
30We have shot at them; Heshbon is perished even unto Dibon,
and we have laid them waste even unto Nophah, which *reacheth*
unto Medeba.
31¶ Thus Israel dwelt in the land of the Amorites.
32And Moses sent to spy out Jaazer, and they took the villages
thereof, and drove out the Amorites that *were* there.
33¶ And they turned and went up by the way of Bashan: and
Og the king of Bashan went out against them, he, and all his
people, to the battle at Edrei.
34And the LORD said unto Moses, Fear him not: for I have
delivered him into thy hand, and all his people, and his land; and
thou shalt do to him as thou didst unto Sihon king of the Amorites,
which dwelt at Heshbon.
35So they smote him, and his sons, and all his people, until
there was none left him alive: and they possessed his land.

## Amplified

15And the slope of the valleys that stretch toward the site of Ar,
and find support on the border of Moab.
16From there the Israelites went on to Beer [meaning, a well];
that is the well of which the Lord had said to Moses, Assemble the
people together, and I will give them water. [Cp. John 7:37-39.]
17Then Israel sang this song, Spring up, O well! Let all sing to
it! [Rom. 14:17.]
18The fountain the princes opened, which the nobles of the
people hollowed out from their staves. And from the wilderness
*or* desert [Israel] *journeyed* to Mattanah;
19And from Mattanah to Nahaliel; and from Nahaliel to Bamoth;
20And from Bamoth to the valley that is in the field of Moab,
to the top of Pisgah, which looks down upon Jeshimon *and* the
desert.
21And Israel sent messengers to Sihon king of the Amorites,
saying,
22Let me pass through your land. We will not turn aside into
field or vineyard; we will not drink the water of the wells. We will
go by the King's Highway until we have passed your border.
23But Sihon would not allow Israel to pass through his border.
Instead Sihon gathered all his people together and went out
against Israel into the wilderness, and came to Jahaz, and he
fought against Israel.
24And Israel smote the king of the Amorites with the edge of
the sword, and possessed his land from the river Arnon to the river
Jabbok, as far as to the Ammonites, for the boundary of the Ammonites was strong.
25And Israel took all these cities, and dwelt in all the cities of
the Amorites, in Heshbon, and in all its towns.
26For Heshbon was the city of Sihon the king of the Amorites,
who had fought against the former king of Moab and taken all his
land out of his hand, as far as [the river] Arnon.
27That is why those who sing ballads say, Come to Heshbon,
let the city of Sihon be built and established;
28For fire has gone out of Heshbon, a flame from the city of
Sihon; it has devoured Ar of Moab and the lords of the heights of
the Arnon.
29Woe to you, Moab! You are undone, O people of [the god]
Chemosh! Moab has given his sons as fugitives, and his daughters
into captivity, to Sihon king of the Amorites.
30We have shot them down; Heshbon has perished as far as
Dibon, and we have laid them waste as far as Nophah, which
reaches to Medeba.
31Thus Israel dwelt in the land of the Amorites.
32And Moses sent to spy out Jazer, and they took its villages,
and dispossessed the Amorites who were there.
33Then they turned and went up by the way of Bashan; and Og
the king of Bashan went out against them, he and all his people,
to battle at Edrei.
34But the Lord said to Moses, Do not fear him, for I have
delivered him and all his people and his land into your hand; and
you shall do to him as you did to Sihon king of the Amorites, who
dwelt at Heshbon.
35So the Israelites slew Og, and his sons, and all his people,
until there was not one left alive; and they possessed his land.

# New American Standard

15 And the slope of the wadis
That extends to the site of Ar,
And leans to the border of Moab."
16And from there *they continued* to Beer, that is the well where
the LORD said to Moses, "Assemble the people, that I may give
them water."
17¶ Then Israel sang this song:
"Spring up, O well! Sing to it!
18 "The well, which the leaders sank,
Which the nobles of the people dug,
With the scepter *and* with their staffs."
And from the wilderness *they continued* to Mattanah,
19and from Mattanah to Nahaliel, and from Nahaliel to Bamoth,
20and from Bamoth to the valley that is in the land of Moab, at
the top of Pisgah which overlooks the wasteland.

*Two Victories*

21¶ Then Israel sent messengers to Sihon, king of the Amorites,
saying,
22"Let me pass through your land. We will not turn off into field
or vineyard; we will not drink water from wells. We will go by the
king's highway until we have passed through your border."
23But Sihon would not permit Israel to pass through his border.
So Sihon gathered all his people and went out against Israel in the
wilderness, and came to Jahaz and fought against Israel.
24Then Israel struck him with the edge of the sword, and took
possession of his land from the Arnon to the Jabbok, as far as the
sons of Ammon; for the border of the sons of Ammon *was* Jazer.
25And Israel took all these cities and Israel lived in all the cities
of the Amorites, in Heshbon, and in all her villages.
26For Heshbon was the city of Sihon, king of the Amorites, who
had fought against the former king of Moab and had taken all his
land out of his hand, as far as the Arnon.
27Therefore those who use proverbs say,
"Come to Heshbon! Let it be built!
So let the city of Sihon be established.
28 "For a fire went forth from Heshbon,
A flame from the town of Sihon;
It devoured Ar of Moab,
The dominant heights of the Arnon.
29 "Woe to you, O Moab!
You are ruined, O people of Chemosh!
He has given his sons as fugitives,
And his daughters into captivity,
To an Amorite king, Sihon.
30 "But we have cast them down,
Heshbon is ruined as far as Dibon,
Then we have laid waste even to Nophah,
Which *reaches* to Medeba."
31Thus Israel lived in the land of the Amorites.
32And Moses sent to spy out Jazer, and they captured its vil-
lages and dispossessed the Amorites who *were* there.
33¶ Then they turned and went up by the way of Bashan, and
Og the king of Bashan went out with all his people, for battle at
Edrei.
34But the LORD said to Moses, "Do not fear him, for I have given
him into your hand, and all his people and his land; and you shall
do to him as you did to Sihon, king of the Amorites, who lived at
Heshbon."
35So they killed him and his sons and all his people, until there
was no remnant left him; and they possessed his land.

# New International

that lead to the site of Ar
and lie along the border of Moab."
16From there they continued on to Beer, the well where the LORD
said to Moses, "Gather the people together and I will give them
water."
17Then Israel sang this song:
"Spring up, O well!
Sing about it,
18about the well that the princes dug,
that the nobles of the people sank—
the nobles with scepters and staffs."
Then they went from the desert to Mattanah, 19from Mattanah to
Nahaliel, from Nahaliel to Bamoth, 20and from Bamoth to the
valley in Moab where the top of Pisgah overlooks the wasteland.

*Defeat of Sihon and Og*

21Israel sent messengers to say to Sihon king of the Amorites:
22"Let us pass through your country. We will not turn
aside into any field or vineyard, or drink water from any well.
We will travel along the king's highway until we have passed
through your territory."
23But Sihon would not let Israel pass through his territory. He
mustered his entire army and marched out into the desert against
Israel. When he reached Jahaz, he fought with Israel. 24Israel,
however, put him to the sword and took over his land from the
Arnon to the Jabbok, but only as far as the Ammonites, because
their border was fortified. 25Israel captured all the cities of the
Amorites and occupied them, including Heshbon and all its surrounding settlements. 26Heshbon was the city of Sihon king of the
Amorites, who had fought against the former king of Moab and
had taken from him all his land as far as the Arnon.
27That is why the poets say:
"Come to Heshbon and let it be rebuilt;
let Sihon's city be restored.
28"Fire went out from Heshbon,
a blaze from the city of Sihon.
It consumed Ar of Moab,
the citizens of Arnon's heights.
29Woe to you, O Moab!
You are destroyed, O people of Chemosh!
He has given up his sons as fugitives
and his daughters as captives
to Sihon king of the Amorites.
30"But we have overthrown them;
Heshbon is destroyed all the way to Dibon.
We have demolished them as far as Nophah,
which extends to Medeba."
31So Israel settled in the land of the Amorites.
32After Moses had sent spies to Jazer, the Israelites captured its
surrounding settlements and drove out the Amorites who were
there. 33Then they turned and went up along the road toward
Bashan, and Og king of Bashan and his whole army marched out
to meet them in battle at Edrei.
34The LORD said to Moses, "Do not be afraid of him, for I have
handed him over to you, with his whole army and his land. Do
to him what you did to Sihon king of the Amorites, who reigned
in Heshbon."
35So they struck him down, together with his sons and his
whole army, leaving them no survivors. And they took possession
of his land.

## King James

**22** AND THE children of Israel set forward, and pitched in the plains of Moab on this side Jordan *by* Jericho.

2¶ And Balak the son of Zippor saw all that Israel had done to the Amorites.

3 And Moab was sore afraid of the people, because they *were* many: and Moab was distressed because of the children of Israel.

4 And Moab said unto the elders of Midian, Now shall this company lick up all *that are* round about us, as the ox licketh up the grass of the field. And Balak the son of Zippor *was* king of the Moabites at that time.

5 He sent messengers therefore unto Balaam the son of Beor to Pethor, which *is* by the river of the land of the children of his people, to call him, saying, Behold, there is a people come out from Egypt: behold, they cover the face of the earth, and they abide over against me:

6 Come now therefore, I pray thee, curse me this people; for they *are* too mighty for me: peradventure I shall prevail, *that* we may smite them, and *that* I may drive them out of the land: for I wot that he whom thou blessest *is* blessed, and he whom thou cursest is cursed.

7 And the elders of Moab and the elders of Midian departed with the rewards of divination in their hand; and they came unto Balaam, and spake unto him the words of Balak.

8 And he said unto them, Lodge here this night, and I will bring you word again, as the LORD shall speak unto me: and the princes of Moab abode with Balaam.

9 And God came unto Balaam, and said, What men *are* these with thee?

10 And Balaam said unto God, Balak the son of Zippor, king of Moab, hath sent unto me, *saying*,

11 Behold, *there is* a people come out of Egypt, which covereth the face of the earth: come now, curse me them; peradventure I shall be able to overcome them, and drive them out.

12 And God said unto Balaam, Thou shalt not go with them; thou shalt not curse the people: for they *are* blessed.

13 And Balaam rose up in the morning, and said unto the princes of Balak, Get you into your land: for the LORD refuseth to give me leave to go with you.

14 And the princes of Moab rose up, and they went unto Balak, and said, Balaam refuseth to come with us.

15¶ And Balak sent yet again princes, more, and more honourable than they.

16 And they came to Balaam, and said to him, Thus saith Balak the son of Zippor, Let nothing, I pray thee, hinder thee from coming unto me:

17 For I will promote thee unto very great honour, and I will do whatsoever thou sayest unto me: come therefore, I pray thee, curse me this people.

18 And Balaam answered and said unto the servants of Balak, If Balak would give me his house full of silver and gold, I cannot go beyond the word of the LORD my God, to do less or more.

19 Now therefore, I pray you, tarry ye also here this night, that I may know what the LORD will say unto me more.

20 And God came unto Balaam at night, and said unto him, If the men come to call thee, rise up, *and* go with them; but yet the word which I shall say unto thee, that shalt thou do.

21 And Balaam rose up in the morning, and saddled his ass, and went with the princes of Moab.

22¶ And God's anger was kindled because he went: and the angel of the LORD stood in the way for an adversary against him. Now he was riding upon his ass, and his two servants *were* with him.

## Amplified

**22** THE ISRAELITES journeyed and encamped in the plains of Moab, on the east side of the Jordan [River] at Jericho.

2 And [the king of Moab] Balak son of Zippor saw all that Israel had done to the Amorites.

3 And Moab was terrified at the people *and* full of dread, because they were many; Moab was distressed *and* overcome with fear because of the Israelites.

4 And Moab said to the elders of Midian, Now will this multitude lick up all that is round about us, as the ox licks up the grass of the field. So Balak son of Zippor the king of the Moabites at that time,

5 Sent messengers to Balaam [a foreteller of events] son of Beor at Pethor, which is by the [Euphrates] River, even to the land of the children of his people, to say to him, There is a people come out from Egypt; behold, they cover the face of the earth, and they have settled down *and* dwell opposite me.

6 Now come, I beg of you, curse this people for me, for they are too powerful for me; perhaps I may be able to defeat them and drive them out of the land, for I know that he whom you bless is blessed, and he whom you curse is cursed.

7 And the elders of Moab and of Midian departed with the rewards of foretelling in their hand; and they came to Balaam, and told him the words of Balak.

8 And he said to them, Lodge here tonight, and I will bring you word, as the Lord may speak to me. And the princes of Moab abode with Balaam [that night].

9 And God came to Balaam, and said, What men are these with you?

10 And Balaam said to God, Balak the son of Zippor, king of Moab, has sent to me, saying,

11 Behold, the people who came out of Egypt cover the face of the earth; come now, curse them for me; perhaps I shall be able to fight against them and drive them out.

12 And God said to Balaam, You shall not go with them; you shall not curse the people, for they are blessed.

13 And Balaam rose up in the morning, and said to the princes of Balak, Go back to your own land, for the Lord refuses to permit me to go with you.

14 So the princes of Moab rose up and went to Balak, and said, Balaam refuses to come with us.

15 Then Balak again sent princes, more of them and more honorable than the first ones.

16 And they came to Balaam, and said to him, Thus says Balak son of Zippor, I beg of you, let nothing hinder you from coming to me.

17 For I will promote you to very great honor, and I will do whatever you tell me; so come, I beg of you, curse this people for me.

18 And Balaam answered the servants of Balak, If Balak would give me his house full of silver and gold, I cannot go beyond the word of the Lord my God, to do less or more.

19 Now therefore, I pray you, tarry here again tonight that I may know what more the Lord will say to me.

20 And God came to Balaam at night, and said to him, If the men come to call you, rise up and go with them; but still only what I tell you may you do.

21 And Balaam rose up in the morning, and saddled his donkey and went with the princes of Moab.

22 And God's anger was kindled because he went; and the [a]Angel of the Lord stood in the way as an adversary against him. Now he was riding upon his donkey, and his two servants were with him.

**AMP** [a] In the report of Moses and the burning bush, "the Angel of the Lord" is identified as the Lord Himself: "the Angel of the Lord appeared to him . . . out of the midst of a bush . . . God called to him out of the midst of the bush . . . Moreover He said, I am . . . God" (Exod. 3:2, 4, 6).

# New American Standard

*Balak Sends for Balaam*

**22** THEN THE sons of Israel journeyed, and camped in the
plains of Moab beyond the Jordan *opposite* Jericho.
2¶ Now Balak the son of Zippor saw all that Israel had done
to the Amorites.
3So Moab was in great fear because of the people, for they were
numerous; and Moab was in dread of the sons of Israel.
4And Moab said to the elders of Midian, "Now this horde will
lick up all that is around us, as the ox licks up the grass of the
field." And Balak the son of Zippor was king of Moab at that time.
5So he sent messengers to Balaam the son of Beor, at Pethor,
which is near the [b]River, *in* the land of the sons of his people, to
call him, saying, "Behold, a people came out of Egypt; behold,
they cover the surface of the land, and they are living opposite me.
6"Now, therefore, please come, curse this people for me since
they are too mighty for me; perhaps I may be able to defeat them
and drive them out of the land. For I know that he whom you bless
is blessed, and he whom you curse is cursed."
7¶ So the elders of Moab and the elders of Midian departed
with the *fees for* divination in their hand; and they came to Balaam
and repeated Balak's words to him.
8And he said to them, "Spend the night here, and I will bring
word back to you as the LORD may speak to me." And the leaders
of Moab stayed with Balaam.
9Then God came to Balaam and said, "Who are these men with
you?"
10And Balaam said to God, "Balak the son of Zippor, king of
Moab, has sent *word* to me,
11'Behold, there is a people who came out of Egypt and they
cover the surface of the land; now come, curse them for me;
perhaps I may be able to fight against them, and drive them out.' "
12And God said to Balaam, "Do not go with them; you shall not
curse the people; for they are blessed."
13So Balaam arose in the morning and said to Balak's leaders,
"Go back to your land, for the LORD has refused to let me go with
you."
14And the leaders of Moab arose and went to Balak, and said,
"Balaam refused to come with us."
15¶ Then Balak again sent leaders, more numerous and more
distinguished than the former.
16And they came to Balaam and said to him, "Thus says Balak
the son of Zippor, 'Let nothing, I beg you, hinder you from coming
to me;
17for I will indeed honor you richly, and I will do whatever you
say to me. Please come then, curse this people for me.' "
18And Balaam answered and said to the servants of Balak,
"Though Balak were to give me his house full of silver and gold,
I could not do anything, either small or great, contrary to the
command of the LORD my God.
19"And now please, you also stay here tonight, and I will find
out what else the LORD will speak to me."
20And God came to Balaam at night and said to him, "If the men
have come to call you, rise up *and* go with them; but only the word
which I speak to you shall you do."
21¶ So Balaam arose in the morning, and saddled his donkey,
and went with the leaders of Moab.

*The Angel and Balaam*

22But God was angry because he was going, and the angel of
the LORD took his stand in the way as an adversary against him.
Now he was riding on his donkey and his two servants were with
him.

NAS [b] I.e., Euphrates

# New International

*Balak Summons Balaam*

**22** THEN THE Israelites traveled to the plains of Moab and
camped along the Jordan across from Jericho.[c]
2Now Balak son of Zippor saw all that Israel had done to the
Amorites, 3and Moab was terrified because there were so many
people. Indeed, Moab was filled with dread because of the Israelites.
4The Moabites said to the elders of Midian, "This horde is going
to lick up everything around us, as an ox licks up the grass of the
field."
So Balak son of Zippor, who was king of Moab at that time,
5sent messengers to summon Balaam son of Beor, who was at
Pethor, near the River,[d] in his native land. Balak said:

"A people has come out of Egypt; they cover the face of the
land and have settled next to me. 6Now come and put a curse
on these people, because they are too powerful for me. Perhaps then I will be able to defeat them and drive them out of
the country. For I know that those you bless are blessed, and
those you curse are cursed."

7The elders of Moab and Midian left, taking with them the fee
for divination. When they came to Balaam, they told him what
Balak had said.
8"Spend the night here," Balaam said to them, "and I will bring
you back the answer the LORD gives me." So the Moabite princes
stayed with him.
9God came to Balaam and asked, "Who are these men with
you?"
10Balaam said to God, "Balak son of Zippor, king of Moab, sent
me this message: 11'A people that has come out of Egypt covers
the face of the land. Now come and put a curse on them for me.
Perhaps then I will be able to fight them and drive them away.' "
12But God said to Balaam, "Do not go with them. You must not
put a curse on those people, because they are blessed."
13The next morning Balaam got up and said to Balak's princes,
"Go back to your own country, for the LORD has refused to let me
go with you."
14So the Moabite princes returned to Balak and said, "Balaam
refused to come with us."
15Then Balak sent other princes, more numerous and more
distinguished than the first. 16They came to Balaam and said:

"This is what Balak son of Zippor says: Do not let anything
keep you from coming to me, 17because I will reward you
handsomely and do whatever you say. Come and put a curse
on these people for me."

18But Balaam answered them, "Even if Balak gave me his palace
filled with silver and gold, I could not do anything great or small
to go beyond the command of the LORD my God. 19Now stay here
tonight as the others did, and I will find out what else the LORD
will tell me."
20That night God came to Balaam and said, "Since these men
have come to summon you, go with them, but do only what I tell
you."

*Balaam's Donkey*

21Balaam got up in the morning, saddled his donkey and went
with the princes of Moab. 22But God was very angry when he
went, and the angel of the LORD stood in the road to oppose him.
Balaam was riding on his donkey, and his two servants were with
him. 23When the donkey saw the angel of the LORD standing in the

NIV [c] *1* Hebrew *Jordan of Jericho;* possibly an ancient name for the Jordan
River [d] *5* That is, the Euphrates

## King James

23 And the ass saw the angel of the LORD standing in the way,
and his sword drawn in his hand: and the ass turned aside out of
the way, and went into the field: and Balaam smote the ass, to turn
her into the way.
24 But the angel of the LORD stood in a path of the vineyards, a
wall *being* on this side, and a wall on that side.
25 And when the ass saw the angel of the LORD, she thrust
herself unto the wall, and crushed Balaam's foot against the wall:
and he smote her again.
26 And the angel of the LORD went further, and stood in a
narrow place, where *was* no way to turn either to the right hand
or to the left.
27 And when the ass saw the angel of the LORD, she fell down
under Balaam: and Balaam's anger was kindled, and he smote the
ass with a staff.
28 And the LORD opened the mouth of the ass, and she said unto
Balaam, What have I done unto thee, that thou hast smitten me
these three times?
29 And Balaam said unto the ass, Because thou hast mocked me:
I would there were a sword in mine hand, for now would I kill
thee.
30 And the ass said unto Balaam, *Am* not I thine ass, upon which
thou hast ridden ever since *I was* thine unto this day? was I ever
wont to do so unto thee? And he said, Nay.
31 Then the LORD opened the eyes of Balaam, and he saw the
angel of the LORD standing in the way, and his sword drawn in
his hand: and he bowed down his head, and fell flat on his face.
32 And the angel of the LORD said unto him, Wherefore hast
thou smitten thine ass these three times? behold, I went out to
withstand thee, because *thy* way is perverse before me:
33 And the ass saw me, and turned from me these three times:
unless she had turned from me, surely now also I had slain thee,
and saved her alive.
34 And Balaam said unto the angel of the LORD, I have sinned;
for I knew not that thou stoodest in the way against me: now
therefore, if it displease thee, I will get me back again.
35 And the angel of the LORD said unto Balaam, Go with the
men: but only the word that I shall speak unto thee, that thou shalt
speak. So Balaam went with the princes of Balak.
36 ¶ And when Balak heard that Balaam was come, he went out
to meet him unto a city of Moab, which *is* in the border of Arnon,
which *is* in the utmost coast.
37 And Balak said unto Balaam, Did I not earnestly send unto
thee to call thee? wherefore camest thou not unto me? am I not able
indeed to promote thee to honour?
38 And Balaam said unto Balak, Lo, I am come unto thee: have
I now any power at all to say any thing? the word that God putteth
in my mouth, that shall I speak.
39 And Balaam went with Balak, and they came unto Kirjath-
huzoth.
40 And Balak offered oxen and sheep, and sent to Balaam, and
to the princes that *were* with him.
41 And it came to pass on the morrow, that Balak took Balaam,
and brought him up into the high places of Baal, that thence he
might see the utmost *part* of the people.

**23** AND BALAAM said unto Balak, Build me here seven
altars, and prepare me here seven oxen and seven rams.
2 And Balak did as Balaam had spoken; and Balak and Balaam
offered on *every* altar a bullock and a ram.
3 And Balaam said unto Balak, Stand by thy burnt offering, and
I will go: peradventure the LORD will come to meet me: and whatsoever he showeth me I will tell thee. And he went to an high
place.

## Amplified

23 And the donkey saw the Angel of the Lord standing in the
way and His sword drawn in His hand, and the donkey turned
aside out of the way, and went into the field; and Balaam struck
the donkey to turn her into the way.
24 But the Angel of the Lord stood in a path of the vineyards,
a wall on this side and a wall on that side.
25 And when the donkey saw the Angel of the Lord, she thrust
herself against the wall, and crushed Balaam's foot against it, and
he struck her again.
26 And the Angel of the Lord went further, and stood in a
narrow place, where there was no room to turn either to the right
hand or to the left.
27 And when the donkey saw the Angel of the Lord, she fell
down under Balaam; and Balaam's anger was kindled, and he
struck the donkey with his staff.
28 And the Lord opened the mouth of the donkey, and she said
to Balaam, What have I done to you that you should strike me
these three times?
29 And Balaam said to the donkey, Because you have ridiculed
*and* provoked me; I wish there were a sword in my hand, for now
I would kill you!
30 And the donkey said to Balaam, Am not I your donkey, upon
which you have ridden all your life long until this day? Was I ever
accustomed to do so to you? And he said, No.
31 Then the Lord opened Balaam's eyes, and he saw the Angel
of the Lord standing in the way with His sword drawn in His hand;
and he bowed his head, and fell on his face.
32 And the Angel of the Lord said to him, Why have you struck
your donkey these three times? See, I came out to stand against
*and* resist you, for your behavior is willfully obstinate *and* contrary
before Me.
33 And the ass saw Me, and turned from Me these three times.
If she had not turned from Me, surely I would have slain you, and
saved her alive.
34 Balaam said to the Angel of the Lord, I have sinned; for I did
not know You stood in the way against me. But now, if my going
displeases You, I will return.
35 The Angel of the Lord said to Balaam, Go with the men; but
you shall speak only what I tell you. So Balaam went with the
princes of Balak.
36 When Balak heard that Balaam had come, he went out to meet
him at the city of Moab, on the border formed by the Arnon
[River], at the farthest end of the boundary.
37 Balak said to Balaam, Did I not [earnestly] send to you to ask
you *to come* to me? Why did you not come? Am not I able to
promote you to honor?
38 And Balaam said to Balak, Indeed, I have come to you, but
do I now have any power at all to say anything? The word that God
puts in my mouth, that shall I speak.
39 And Balaam went with Balak, and they came to Kiriath-
huzoth.
40 And Balak offered oxen and sheep, and sent [portions] to
Balaam and to the princes who were with him.
41 And on the following day Balak took Balaam and brought him
up into the high places of Bamoth-baal; from there he saw the
nearest of the Israelites.

**23** AND BALAAM said to Balak, Build me here seven altars,
and prepare me here seven oxen and seven rams.
2 And Balak did as Balaam had spoken; and Balak and Balaam
offered on every altar a bull and a ram.
3 And Balaam said to Balak, Stand by your burnt offering, and
I will go; perhaps the Lord will come to meet me; and whatever
He shows me I will tell you. And he went to a bare height.

## New American Standard

23When the donkey saw the angel of the LORD standing in the way with his drawn sword in his hand, the donkey turned off from the way and went into the field; but Balaam struck the donkey to turn her back into the way.

24Then the angel of the LORD stood in a narrow path of the vineyards, *with* a wall on this side and a wall on that side.

25When the donkey saw the angel of the LORD, she pressed herself to the wall and pressed Balaam's foot against the wall, so he struck her again.

26And the angel of the LORD went further, and stood in a narrow place where there was no way to turn to the right hand or the left.

27When the donkey saw the angel of the LORD, she lay down under Balaam; so Balaam was angry and struck the donkey with his stick.

28And the LORD opened the mouth of the donkey, and she said to Balaam, "What have I done to you, that you have struck me these three times?"

29Then Balaam said to the donkey, "Because you have made a mockery of me! If there had been a sword in my hand, I would have killed you by now."

30And the donkey said to Balaam, "Am I not your donkey on which you have ridden all your life to this day? Have I ever been accustomed to do so to you?" And he said, "No."

31¶ Then the LORD opened the eyes of Balaam, and he saw the angel of the LORD standing in the way with his drawn sword in his hand; and he bowed all the way to the ground.

32And the angel of the LORD said to him, "Why have you struck your donkey these three times? Behold, I have come out as an adversary, because your way was contrary to me.

33"But the donkey saw me and turned aside from me these three times. If she had not turned aside from me, I would surely have killed you just now, and let her live."

34And Balaam said to the angel of the LORD, "I have sinned, for I did not know that you were standing in the way against me. Now then, if it is displeasing to you, I will turn back."

35But the angel of the LORD said to Balaam, "Go with the men, but you shall speak only the word which I shall tell you." So Balaam went along with the leaders of Balak.

36¶ When Balak heard that Balaam was coming, he went out to meet him at the city of Moab, which is on the Arnon border, at the extreme end of the border.

37Then Balak said to Balaam, "Did I not urgently send to you to call you? Why did you not come to me? Am I really unable to honor you?"

38So Balaam said to Balak, "Behold, I have come now to you! Am I able to speak anything at all? The word that God puts in my mouth, that I shall speak."

39And Balaam went with Balak, and they came to Kiriath-huzoth.

40And Balak sacrificed oxen and sheep, and sent *some* to Balaam and the leaders who were with him.

41¶ Then it came about in the morning that Balak took Balaam, and brought him up to the high places of Baal; and he saw from there a portion of the people.

*The Prophecies of Balaam*

**23** THEN BALAAM said to Balak, "Build seven altars for me here, and prepare seven bulls and seven rams for me here."

2And Balak did just as Balaam had spoken, and Balak and Balaam offered up a bull and a ram on each altar.

3Then Balaam said to Balak, "Stand beside your burnt offering, and I will go; perhaps the LORD will come to meet me, and whatever He shows me I will tell you." So he went to a bare hill.

## New International

road with a drawn sword in his hand, she turned off the road into a field. Balaam beat her to get her back on the road.

24Then the angel of the LORD stood in a narrow path between two vineyards, with walls on both sides. 25When the donkey saw the angel of the LORD, she pressed close to the wall, crushing Balaam's foot against it. So he beat her again.

26Then the angel of the LORD moved on ahead and stood in a narrow place where there was no room to turn, either to the right or to the left. 27When the donkey saw the angel of the LORD, she lay down under Balaam, and he was angry and beat her with his staff. 28Then the LORD opened the donkey's mouth, and she said to Balaam, "What have I done to you to make you beat me these three times?"

29Balaam answered the donkey, "You have made a fool of me! If I had a sword in my hand, I would kill you right now."

30The donkey said to Balaam, "Am I not your own donkey, which you have always ridden, to this day? Have I been in the habit of doing this to you?"

"No," he said.

31Then the LORD opened Balaam's eyes, and he saw the angel of the LORD standing in the road with his sword drawn. So he bowed low and fell facedown.

32The angel of the LORD asked him, "Why have you beaten your donkey these three times? I have come here to oppose you because your path is a reckless one before me.[a] 33The donkey saw me and turned away from me these three times. If she had not turned away, I would certainly have killed you by now, but I would have spared her."

34Balaam said to the angel of the LORD, "I have sinned. I did not realize you were standing in the road to oppose me. Now if you are displeased, I will go back."

35The angel of the LORD said to Balaam, "Go with the men, but speak only what I tell you." So Balaam went with the princes of Balak.

36When Balak heard that Balaam was coming, he went out to meet him at the Moabite town on the Arnon border, at the edge of his territory. 37Balak said to Balaam, "Did I not send you an urgent summons? Why didn't you come to me? Am I really not able to reward you?"

38"Well, I have come to you now," Balaam replied. "But can I say just anything? I must speak only what God puts in my mouth."

39Then Balaam went with Balak to Kiriath Huzoth. 40Balak sacrificed cattle and sheep, and gave some to Balaam and the princes who were with him. 41The next morning Balak took Balaam up to Bamoth Baal, and from there he saw part of the people.

*Balaam's First Oracle*

**23** BALAAM SAID, "Build me seven altars here, and prepare seven bulls and seven rams for me." 2Balak did as Balaam said, and the two of them offered a bull and a ram on each altar.

3Then Balaam said to Balak, "Stay here beside your offering while I go aside. Perhaps the LORD will come to meet with me. Whatever he reveals to me I will tell you." Then he went off to a barren height.

NIV [a] 32 The meaning of the Hebrew for this clause is uncertain.

## King James

4 And God met Balaam: and he said unto him, I have prepared seven altars, and I have offered upon *every* altar a bullock and a ram.

5 And the LORD put a word in Balaam's mouth, and said, Return unto Balak, and thus thou shalt speak.

6 And he returned unto him, and, lo, he stood by his burnt sacrifice, he, and all the princes of Moab.

7 And he took up his parable, and said, Balak the king of Moab hath brought me from Aram, out of the mountains of the east, *saying*, Come, curse me Jacob, and come, defy Israel.

8 How shall I curse, whom God hath not cursed? or how shall I defy, *whom* the LORD hath not defied?

9 For from the top of the rocks I see him, and from the hills I behold him: lo, the people shall dwell alone, and shall not be reckoned among the nations.

10 Who can count the dust of Jacob, and the number of the fourth *part* of Israel? Let me die the death of the righteous, and let my last end be like his!

11 And Balak said unto Balaam, What hast thou done unto me? I took thee to curse mine enemies, and, behold, thou hast blessed *them* altogether.

12 And he answered and said, Must I not take heed to speak that which the LORD hath put in my mouth?

13 And Balak said unto him, Come, I pray thee, with me unto another place, from whence thou mayest see them: thou shalt see but the utmost part of them, and shalt not see them all: and curse me them from thence.

14 ¶ And he brought him into the field of Zophim, to the top of Pisgah, and built seven altars, and offered a bullock and a ram on *every* altar.

15 And he said unto Balak, Stand here by thy burnt offering, while I meet *the LORD* yonder.

16 And the LORD met Balaam, and put a word in his mouth, and said, Go again unto Balak, and say thus.

17 And when he came to him, behold, he stood by his burnt offering, and the princes of Moab with him. And Balak said unto him, What hath the LORD spoken?

18 And he took up his parable, and said, Rise up, Balak, and hear; hearken unto me, thou son of Zippor:

19 God *is* not a man, that he should lie; neither the son of man, that he should repent: hath he said, and shall he not do *it?* or hath he spoken, and shall he not make it good?

20 Behold, I have received *commandment* to bless: and he hath blessed: and I cannot reverse it.

21 He hath not beheld iniquity in Jacob, neither hath he seen perverseness in Israel; the LORD his God *is* with him, and the shout of a king *is* among them.

22 God brought them out of Egypt; he hath as it were the strength of an unicorn.

23 Surely *there is* no enchantment against Jacob, neither *is there* any divination against Israel: according to this time it shall be said of Jacob and of Israel, What hath God wrought!

24 Behold, the people shall rise up as a great lion, and lift up himself as a young lion: he shall not lie down until he eat *of* the prey, and drink the blood of the slain.

## Amplified

4 God met Balaam, who said to Him, I have prepared seven altars, and I have offered on each altar a bull and a ram.

5 And the Lord put a speech in Balaam's mouth, and said, Return to Balak, and thus shall you speak.

6 Balaam returned to Balak, who was standing by his burnt sacrifice, he and all the princes of Moab.

7 Balaam took up his [figurative] speech and said, Balak the king of Moab has brought me from Aram, out of the mountains of the east, saying, Come, curse Jacob for me, and come, violently denounce Israel.

8 How can I curse those God has not cursed? Or how can I [violently] denounce those the Lord has not denounced?

9 For from the top of the rocks I see Israel, and from the hills I behold him. Lo, the people [of Israel] shall [a]dwell alone, and shall not be reckoned *and* esteemed among the nations.

10 Who can count the dust [the descendants] of Jacob, and the number of the fourth part of Israel? Let me die the death of the righteous [those who are upright and in right standing with God], and let my last end be like his! [Ps. 37:37; Rev. 14:13.]

11 And Balak said to Balaam, What have you done to me? I brought you to curse my enemies, and here you have (thoroughly) blessed them instead!

12 And Balaam answered, Must I not be obedient *and* speak what the Lord has put in my mouth?

13 Balak said to him, Come with me, I implore you, to another place from which you can see them, though you will see only the nearest and not all of them; and curse them for me from there.

14 So he took Balaam into the field of Zophim, to the top of [Mount] Pisgah, and built seven altars, and offered a bull and a ram on each altar.

15 Balaam said to Balak, Stand here by your burnt offering, while I go to meet the Lord yonder.

16 And the Lord met Balaam, and put a speech in his mouth, and said, Go again to Balak, and speak thus.

17 And when he returned to Balak he was standing beside his burnt offering, and the princes of Moab with him. And Balak said to him, What has the Lord said?

18 Balaam took up his [figurative] discourse and said, Rise up, Balak, and hear; listen [closely] to me, son of Zippor:

19 God is not a man, that He should tell *or* act a lie, neither the son of man, that He should feel repentance *or* compunction [for what He has promised]. Has He said, and shall He not do it? Or has He spoken and shall He not make it good?

20 You see, I have received His command to bless Israel. He has blessed, and I cannot reverse *or* qualify it.

21 [God] has not beheld iniquity in Jacob [for he is forgiven], neither has He seen mischief *or* perverseness in Israel [for the same reason]. The Lord his God is with Israel, and the shout of praise to their King is among the people. [Rom. 4:7, 8; I John 3:1, 2.]

22 God brought them forth out of Egypt; they have as it were the strength of a wild ox.

23 Surely there is no enchantment with *or* against Jacob, neither is there any divination with *or* against Israel. [In due season and even] now it shall be said of Jacob and of Israel, What has God wrought!

24 Behold, a people! He rises up as a lioness, and lifts himself up as a lion; he shall not lie down until he devours the prey, and drinks the blood of the slain.

**AMP** [a] The literal fulfillment of this prophecy has been obvious during the whole more than thirty-four centuries since it was spoken. The Jews have always been separate as a nation from other peoples. Though conquered many times, they have never been absorbed by their conquerors or lost their identity. The prophecy had to become true, "for the Lord put [it] . . . in Balaam's mouth" (v. 5).

## New American Standard

4Now God met Balaam, and he said to Him, "I have set up the seven altars, and I have offered up a bull and a ram on each altar."
5Then the LORD put a word in Balaam's mouth and said, "Return to Balak, and you shall speak thus."
6So he returned to him, and behold, he was standing beside his burnt offering, he and all the leaders of Moab.
7And he took up his [b]discourse and said,

"From Aram Balak has brought me,
Moab's king from the mountains of the East,
'Come curse Jacob for me,
And come, denounce Israel!'
8 "How shall I curse, whom God has not cursed?
And how can I denounce, whom the LORD has not denounced?
9 "As I see him from the top of the rocks,
And I look at him from the hills;
Behold, a people *who* dwells apart,
And shall not be reckoned among the nations.
10 "Who can count the dust of Jacob,
Or number the fourth part of Israel?
Let me die the death of the upright,
And let my end be like his!"

11¶ Then Balak said to Balaam, "What have you done to me? I took you to curse my enemies, but behold, you have actually blessed them!"
12And he answered and said, "Must I not be careful to speak what the LORD puts in my mouth?"
13¶ Then Balak said to him, "Please come with me to another place from where you may see them, although you will only see the extreme end of them, and will not see all of them; and curse them for me from there."
14So he took him to the field of Zophim, to the top of Pisgah, and built seven altars and offered a bull and a ram on *each* altar.
15And he said to Balak, "Stand here beside your burnt offering, while I myself meet *the LORD* yonder."
16Then the LORD met Balaam and put a word in his mouth and said, "Return to Balak, and thus you shall speak."
17And he came to him, and behold, he was standing beside his burnt offering, and the leaders of Moab with him. And Balak said to him, "What has the LORD spoken?"
18Then he took up his [c]discourse and said,

"Arise, O Balak, and hear;
Give ear to me, O son of Zippor!
19 "God is not a man, that He should lie,
Nor a son of man, that He should repent;
Has He said, and will He not do it?
Or has He spoken, and will He not make it good?
20 "Behold, I have received *a command* to bless;
When He has blessed, then I cannot revoke it.
21 "He has not observed misfortune in Jacob;
Nor has He seen trouble in Israel;
The LORD his God is with him,
And the shout of a king is among them.
22 "God brings them out of Egypt,
He is for them like the horns of the wild ox.
23 "For there is no omen against Jacob,
Nor is there any divination against Israel;
At the proper time it shall be said to Jacob
And to Israel, what God has done.
24 "Behold, a people rises like a lioness,
And as a lion it lifts itself;
It shall not lie down until it devours the prey,
And drinks the blood of the slain."

NAS [b] Lit., *parable,* and so throughout this context [c] Lit., *parable,* and so throughout this context

## New International

4God met with him, and Balaam said, "I have prepared seven altars, and on each altar I have offered a bull and a ram."
5The LORD put a message in Balaam's mouth and said, "Go back to Balak and give him this message."
6So he went back to him and found him standing beside his offering, with all the princes of Moab. 7Then Balaam uttered his oracle:

"Balak brought me from Aram,
the king of Moab from the eastern mountains.
'Come,' he said, 'curse Jacob for me;
come, denounce Israel.'
8How can I curse
those whom God has not cursed?
How can I denounce
those whom the LORD has not denounced?
9From the rocky peaks I see them,
from the heights I view them.
I see a people who live apart
and do not consider themselves one of the nations.
10Who can count the dust of Jacob
or number the fourth part of Israel?
Let me die the death of the righteous,
and may my end be like theirs!"

11Balak said to Balaam, "What have you done to me? I brought you to curse my enemies, but you have done nothing but bless them!"
12He answered, "Must I not speak what the LORD puts in my mouth?"

*Balaam's Second Oracle*

13Then Balak said to him, "Come with me to another place where you can see them; you will see only a part but not all of them. And from there, curse them for me." 14So he took him to the field of Zophim on the top of Pisgah, and there he built seven altars and offered a bull and a ram on each altar.
15Balaam said to Balak, "Stay here beside your offering while I meet with him over there."
16The LORD met with Balaam and put a message in his mouth and said, "Go back to Balak and give him this message."
17So he went to him and found him standing beside his offering, with the princes of Moab. Balak asked him, "What did the LORD say?"
18Then he uttered his oracle:

"Arise, Balak, and listen;
hear me, son of Zippor.
19God is not a man, that he should lie,
nor a son of man, that he should change his mind.
Does he speak and then not act?
Does he promise and not fulfill?
20I have received a command to bless;
he has blessed, and I cannot change it.
21"No misfortune is seen in Jacob,
no misery observed in Israel.[d]
The LORD their God is with them;
the shout of the King is among them.
22God brought them out of Egypt;
they have the strength of a wild ox.
23There is no sorcery against Jacob,
no divination against Israel.
It will now be said of Jacob
and of Israel, 'See what God has done!'
24The people rise like a lioness;
they rouse themselves like a lion
that does not rest till he devours his prey
and drinks the blood of his victims."

NIV [d] 21 *Or He has not looked on Jacob's offenses / or on the wrongs found in Israel.*

## King James

25 ¶ And Balak said unto Balaam, Neither curse them at all, nor bless them at all.

26 But Balaam answered and said unto Balak, Told not I thee, saying, All that the LORD speaketh, that I must do?

27 ¶ And Balak said unto Balaam, Come, I pray thee, I will bring thee unto another place; peradventure it will please God that thou mayest curse me them from thence.

28 And Balak brought Balaam unto the top of Peor, that looketh toward Jeshimon.

29 And Balaam said unto Balak, Build me here seven altars, and prepare me here seven bullocks and seven rams.

30 And Balak did as Balaam had said, and offered a bullock and a ram on *every* altar.

**24** AND WHEN Balaam saw that it pleased the LORD to bless Israel, he went not, as at other times, to seek for enchantments, but he set his face toward the wilderness.

2 And Balaam lifted up his eyes, and he saw Israel abiding *in his tents* according to their tribes; and the spirit of God came upon him.

3 And he took up his parable, and said, Balaam the son of Beor hath said, and the man whose eyes are open hath said:

4 He hath said, which heard the words of God, which saw the vision of the Almighty, falling *into a trance,* but having his eyes open:

5 How goodly are thy tents, O Jacob, *and* thy tabernacles, O Israel!

6 As the valleys are they spread forth, as gardens by the river's side, as the trees of lign aloes which the LORD hath planted, *and* as cedar trees beside the waters.

7 He shall pour the water out of his buckets, and his seed *shall be* in many waters, and his king shall be higher than Agag, and his kingdom shall be exalted.

8 God brought him forth out of Egypt; he hath as it were the strength of an unicorn: he shall eat up the nations his enemies, and shall break their bones, and pierce *them* through with his arrows.

9 He couched, he lay down as a lion, and as a great lion: who shall stir him up? Blessed *is* he that blesseth thee, and cursed *is* he that curseth thee.

10 ¶ And Balak's anger was kindled against Balaam, and he smote his hands together: and Balak said unto Balaam, I called thee to curse mine enemies, and, behold, thou hast altogether blessed *them* these three times.

11 Therefore now flee thou to thy place: I thought to promote thee unto great honour; but, lo, the LORD hath kept thee back from honour.

12 And Balaam said unto Balak, Spake I not also to thy messengers which thou sentest unto me, saying,

13 If Balak would give me his house full of silver and gold, I cannot go beyond the commandment of the LORD, to do *either* good or bad of mine own mind; *but* what the LORD saith, that will I speak?

14 And now, behold, I go unto my people: come *therefore, and* I will advertise thee what this people shall do to thy people in the latter days.

15 ¶ And he took up his parable, and said, Balaam the son of Beor hath said, and the man whose eyes are open hath said:

## Amplified

25 And Balak said to Balaam, Neither curse them at all, nor bless them at all.

26 But Balaam answered Balak, Did I not say to you, All the Lord speaks, that I must do?

27 And Balak said to Balaam, Come, I implore you; I will take you to another place; perhaps it will please God to let you curse them for me from there.

28 So Balak brought Balaam to the top of [Mount] Peor, that overlooks [the wilderness or desert] Jeshimon.

29 And Balaam said to Balak, Build me here seven altars, and prepare me here seven bulls and seven rams.

30 And Balak did as Balaam had said, and offered a bull and a ram on each altar.

**24** WHEN BALAAM saw that it pleased the Lord to bless Israel, he did not go as he had done each time before [superstitiously] to meet with omens *and* signs in the natural world, but he set his face toward the wilderness *or* desert.

2 And Balaam lifted up his eyes, and he saw Israel abiding in their tents according to their tribes. And the Spirit of God came upon him,

3 And he took up his [figurative] discourse and said, Balaam son of Beor, the man whose eye is opened [at last, to see clearly the purposes and will of God],

4 He [Balaam] who hears the words of God, who sees the vision of the Almighty; falling down, but having his eyes open *and* uncovered, he says:

5 How attractive *and* considerable are your tents, O Jacob, *and* your tabernacles, O Israel!

6 As valleys are they spread forth, as gardens by the riverside, as [rare spice] of lign aloes which the Lord has planted, and as cedar trees beside the waters. [Ps. 1:3.]

7 [Israel] shall pour water out of his own buckets [have his own sources of rich blessing *and* plenty], and his offspring shall dwell by many waters, and his king shall be higher than [a]Agag, and his kingdom shall be exalted.

8 God brought [Israel] forth out of Egypt; [Israel] has strength like the wild ox; he shall eat up the nations his enemies, crushing their bones and piercing them through with his arrows.

9 He couched, he lay down as a lion; and as a lioness, who shall rouse him? Blessed [of God] is he who blesses you [who prays for *and* contributes to your welfare] and cursed [of God] is he who curses you [who in word, thought, or deed would bring harm upon you]. [Matt. 25:40.]

10 Then Balak's anger was kindled against Balaam, and he smote his hands together; and Balak said to Balaam, I called you to curse my enemies, and, behold, you have done nothing but bless them these three times.

11 Therefore now go back where you belong *and* do it in a hurry! I had intended to promote you to great honor; but lo, the Lord has held you back from honor.

12 Balaam said to Balak, Did I not say to your messengers whom you sent to me,

13 If Balak would give me his house full of silver and gold, I cannot go beyond the command of the Lord, to do either good or bad of my own will, but what the Lord says, that will I speak?

14 And now, behold, I am going to my people; come, I will tell you what this people [Israel] will do to your people [Moab] in the latter days.

15 And he took up his [figurative] discourse, and said, Balaam son of Beor speaks; the man whose eye is opened speaks;

**AMP** [a] "Agag" was the title of Amalekite kings, and it represents here the kingdom of the Gentiles. The Amalekites at that time were the most powerful of all the desert tribes (v. 20).

## New American Standard

25Then Balak said to Balaam, "Do not curse them at all nor bless
them at all!"
26But Balaam answered and said to Balak, "Did I not tell you,
'Whatever the LORD speaks, that I must do'?"
27¶ Then Balak said to Balaam, "Please come, I will take you to
another place; perhaps it will be agreeable with God that you curse
them for me from there."
28So Balak took Balaam to the top of Peor which overlooks the
wasteland.
29And Balaam said to Balak, "Build seven altars for me here and
prepare seven bulls and seven rams for me here."
30And Balak did just as Balaam had said, and offered up a bull
and a ram on *each* altar.

*The Prophecy from Peor*

**24** WHEN BALAAM saw that it pleased the LORD to bless
Israel, he did not go as at other times to seek omens but
he set his face toward the wilderness.
2And Balaam lifted up his eyes and saw Israel camping tribe
by tribe; and the Spirit of God came upon him.
3And he took up his discourse and said,
"The oracle of Balaam the son of Beor,
And the oracle of the man whose eye is opened;
4 The oracle of him who hears the words of God,
Who sees the vision of the Almighty,
Falling down, yet having his eyes uncovered,
5 How fair are your tents, O Jacob,
Your dwellings, O Israel!
6 "Like valleys that stretch out,
Like gardens beside the river,
Like aloes planted by the LORD,
Like cedars beside the waters.
7 "Water shall flow from his buckets,
And his seed *shall be* by many waters,
And his king shall be higher than Agag,
And his kingdom shall be exalted.
8 "God brings him out of Egypt,
He is for him like the horns of the wild ox.
He shall devour the nations *who are* his adversaries,
And shall crush their bones in pieces,
And shatter *them* with his arrows.
9 "He couches, he lies down as a lion,
And as a lion, who dares rouse him?
Blessed is everyone who blesses you,
And cursed is everyone who curses you."
10¶ Then Balak's anger burned against Balaam, and he struck his
hands together; and Balak said to Balaam, "I called you to curse
my enemies, but behold, you have persisted in blessing them these
three times!
11"Therefore, flee to your place now. I said I would honor you
greatly, but behold, the LORD has held you back from honor."
12And Balaam said to Balak, "Did I not tell your messengers
whom you had sent to me, saying,
13'Though Balak were to give me his house full of silver and
gold, I could not do anything contrary to the command of the
LORD, either good or bad, of my own accord. What the LORD
speaks, that I will speak'?
14"And now behold, I am going to my people; come, *and* I will
advise you what this people will do to your people in the days to
come."
15And he took up his discourse and said,
"The oracle of Balaam the son of Beor,
And the oracle of the man whose eye is opened,

## New International

25Then Balak said to Balaam, "Neither curse them at all nor
bless them at all!"
26Balaam answered, "Did I not tell you I must do whatever the
LORD says?"

*Balaam's Third Oracle*

27Then Balak said to Balaam, "Come, let me take you to another
place. Perhaps it will please God to let you curse them for me from
there." 28And Balak took Balaam to the top of Peor, overlooking
the wasteland.
29Balaam said, "Build me seven altars here, and prepare seven
bulls and seven rams for me." 30Balak did as Balaam had said, and
offered a bull and a ram on each altar.

**24** NOW WHEN Balaam saw that it pleased the LORD to bless
Israel, he did not resort to sorcery as at other times, but
turned his face toward the desert. 2When Balaam looked out and
saw Israel encamped tribe by tribe, the Spirit of God came upon
him 3and he uttered his oracle:

"The oracle of Balaam son of Beor,
the oracle of one whose eye sees clearly,
4the oracle of one who hears the words of God,
who sees a vision from the Almighty,[b]
who falls prostrate, and whose eyes are opened:

5"How beautiful are your tents, O Jacob,
your dwelling places, O Israel!

6"Like valleys they spread out,
like gardens beside a river,
like aloes planted by the LORD,
like cedars beside the waters.
7Water will flow from their buckets;
their seed will have abundant water.

"Their king will be greater than Agag;
their kingdom will be exalted.

8"God brought them out of Egypt;
they have the strength of a wild ox.
They devour hostile nations
and break their bones in pieces;
with their arrows they pierce them.
9Like a lion they crouch and lie down,
like a lioness—who dares to rouse them?

"May those who bless you be blessed
and those who curse you be cursed!"

10Then Balak's anger burned against Balaam. He struck his
hands together and said to him, "I summoned you to curse my
enemies, but you have blessed them these three times. 11Now
leave at once and go home! I said I would reward you handsomely,
but the LORD has kept you from being rewarded."
12Balaam answered Balak, "Did I not tell the messengers you
sent me, 13'Even if Balak gave me his palace filled with silver and
gold, I could not do anything of my own accord, good or bad, to
go beyond the command of the LORD—and I must say only what
the LORD says'? 14Now I am going back to my people, but come,
let me warn you of what this people will do to your people in days
to come."

*Balaam's Fourth Oracle*

15Then he uttered his oracle:

"The oracle of Balaam son of Beor,
the oracle of one whose eye sees clearly,

NIV [b] 4 Hebrew *Shaddai;* also in verse 16

## King James

16 He hath said, which heard the words of God, and knew the knowledge of the most High, *which* saw the vision of the Almighty, falling *into a trance,* but having his eyes open:

17 I shall see him, but not now: I shall behold him, but not nigh: there shall come a Star out of Jacob, and a Sceptre shall rise out of Israel, and shall smite the corners of Moab, and destroy all the children of Sheth.

18 And Edom shall be a possession, Seir also shall be a possession for his enemies; and Israel shall do valiantly.

19 Out of Jacob shall come he that shall have dominion, and shall destroy him that remaineth of the city.

20 ¶ And when he looked on Amalek, he took up his parable, and said, Amalek *was* the first of the nations; but his latter end *shall be* that he perish for ever.

21 And he looked on the Kenites, and took up his parable, and said, Strong is thy dwellingplace, and thou puttest thy nest in a rock.

22 Nevertheless the Kenite shall be wasted, until Asshur shall carry thee away captive.

23 And he took up his parable, and said, Alas, who shall live when God doeth this!

24 And ships *shall come* from the coast of Chittim, and shall afflict Asshur, and shall afflict Eber, and he also shall perish for ever.

25 And Balaam rose up, and went and returned to his place: and Balak also went his way.

## Amplified

16 He speaks, who heard the words of God, and knew the knowledge of the Most High, who saw the vision of the Almighty, falling down, but having his eyes open *and* uncovered:

17 I see Him but He is not now; I behold Him, but He is not near; a [a]star shall come forth out of Jacob, and a scepter shall rise out of Israel and shall crush all the corners of Moab, and break down all the sons of Sheth [Moab's sons of tumult]. [Matt. 2:2; Rom. 15:12.]

18 And Edom shall be [taken as] a possession, [Mount] Seir also shall be dispossessed, who were Israel's enemies; while Israel does valiantly.

19 Out of Jacob shall one come having dominion, and shall destroy the remnant from the city.

20 *Balaam* looked on Amalek and took up his [prophetic] utterance, and said, Amalek is the foremost of the [neighboring] nations, but in his latter end he shall [b]come to destruction.

21 And he looked on the Kenite, and took up his [prophetic] utterance, and said, Strong is your dwelling place, and you set your nest in the rock.

22 Nevertheless the Kenites shall be wasted. How long shall Asshur [Assyria] take you away captive?

23 And he took up his [prophetic] speech, and said, Alas, who shall live when God does this *and* establishes [Assyria]?

24 But ships shall come from Kittim [Cyprus, and the greater part of the Mediterranean's east coast], and shall afflict Assyria and Eber [the Hebrews, certain Arabs, and descendants of Nahor]; and he [the victor], also shall come to destruction.

25 And Balaam rose up, returned to his place, and Balak also went his way.

## King James

**25** AND ISRAEL abode in Shittim, and the people began to commit whoredom with the daughters of Moab.

2 And they called the people unto the sacrifices of their gods: and the people did eat, and bowed down to their gods.

3 And Israel joined himself unto Baal-peor: and the anger of the LORD was kindled against Israel.

4 And the LORD said unto Moses, Take all the heads of the people, and hang them up before the LORD against the sun, that the fierce anger of the LORD may be turned away from Israel.

5 And Moses said unto the judges of Israel, Slay ye every one his men that were joined unto Baal-peor.

6 ¶ And, behold, one of the children of Israel came and brought unto his brethren a Midianitish woman in the sight of Moses, and in the sight of all the congregation of the children of Israel, who *were* weeping *before* the door of the tabernacle of the congregation.

## Amplified

**25** ISRAEL SETTLED down *and* remained in Shittim, and the people began to play the harlot with the daughters of Moab,

2 Who invited the [Israelites] to the sacrifices of their gods, and [they] ate and bowed down to Moab's gods.

3 So Israel joined himself to [the god] Baal of Peor. And the anger of the Lord was kindled against Israel.

4 And the Lord said to Moses, Take all the leaders *or* chiefs of the people, and hang them before the Lord in the sun [after killing them], that the fierce anger of the Lord may turn away from Israel.

5 And Moses said to the judges of Israel, Every one of you slay his men who joined themselves to Baal of Peor.

6 And, behold, one of the Israelites came and brought to his brethren a Midianitish woman in the sight of Moses and of all the congregation of Israel, while they were weeping at the door of the tent of meeting [over the divine judgment and the punishment].

**AMP** [a] "This imagery in the hieroglyphic language of the East denotes some eminent ruler—primarily David; but secondarily and pre-eminently, the Messiah" (*Jamieson, Fausett and Brown's Commentary*). Notice that the principal time for these events is set in the prophecy for "the latter days," verse 14. "The prophecy [concerning Moab] was partially, or typically, fulfilled in the time of David (II Sam. 8:2). Moab and Edom represented symbolically the enemies of Christ and His church, and as such will eventually be subdued by the King of kings (Cp. Ps. 60:8)." (*Ellicott's Commentary*). "The star which the wise men from the East saw, and which led them in the way to the newborn 'King of the Jews,' refers clearly to the prophecy of Balaam (Matt. 2:1,2)." (*Lange's Commentary*).
[b] After the time of David (who was forced to rescue two of his wives from Amalekite bandits, I Sam. 30:18), and once later in Hezekiah's time when the Amalekites are mentioned, "they disappear from the field of history . . . So that the word of God here also stood fast; and the first of the surrounding tribes who impiously sought to measure their strength with the cause and people of God were likewise the first to lose their national existence" (*Fairbairn's Bible Encyclopedia*).

## New American Standard

16 The oracle of him who hears the words of God,
And knows the knowledge of the Most High,
Who sees the vision of the Almighty,
Falling down, yet having his eyes uncovered.
17 "I see him, but not now;
I behold him, but not near;
A star shall come forth from Jacob,
And a scepter shall rise from Israel,
And shall crush through the forehead of Moab,
And tear down all the sons of [c]Sheth.
18 "And Edom shall be a possession,
Seir, its enemies, also shall be a possession,
While Israel performs valiantly.
19 "One from Jacob shall have dominion,
And shall destroy the remnant from the city."
20 And he looked at Amalek and took up his discourse and said,
"Amalek was the first of the nations,
But his end *shall be* destruction."
21 And he looked at the Kenite, and took up his discourse and
said,
"Your dwelling place is enduring,
And your nest is set in the cliff.
22 "Nevertheless Kain shall be consumed;
How long shall Asshur keep you captive?"
23 And he took up his discourse and said,
"Alas, who can live except God has ordained it?
24 "But ships *shall come* from the coast of Kittim,
And they shall afflict Asshur and shall afflict Eber;
So they also *shall come* to destruction."
25 Then Balaam arose and departed and returned to his place,
and Balak also went his way.

*The Sin of Peor*

25 WHILE ISRAEL remained at Shittim, the people began to
play the harlot with the daughters of Moab.
2 For they invited the people to the sacrifices of their gods, and
the people ate and bowed down to their gods.
3 So Israel joined themselves to Baal of Peor, and the LORD was
angry against Israel.
4 And the LORD said to Moses, "Take all the leaders of the
people and execute them in broad daylight before the LORD, so that
the fierce anger of the LORD may turn away from Israel."
5 So Moses said to the judges of Israel, "Each of you slay his
men who have joined themselves to Baal of Peor."
6 ¶ Then behold, one of the sons of Israel came and brought to
his relatives a Midianite woman, in the sight of Moses and in the
sight of all the congregation of the sons of Israel, while they were
weeping at the doorway of the tent of meeting.

NAS [c] I.e., tumult

## New International

16 the oracle of one who hears the words of God,
who has knowledge from the Most High,
who sees a vision from the Almighty,
who falls prostrate, and whose eyes are opened:
17 "I see him, but not now;
I behold him, but not near.
A star will come out of Jacob;
a scepter will rise out of Israel.
He will crush the foreheads of Moab,
the skulls[d] of[e] all the sons of Sheth.[f]
18 Edom will be conquered;
Seir, his enemy, will be conquered,
but Israel will grow strong.
19 A ruler will come out of Jacob
and destroy the survivors of the city."

*Balaam's Final Oracles*

20 Then Balaam saw Amalek and uttered his oracle:
"Amalek was first among the nations,
but he will come to ruin at last."
21 Then he saw the Kenites and uttered his oracle:
"Your dwelling place is secure,
your nest is set in a rock;
22 yet you Kenites will be destroyed
when Asshur takes you captive."
23 Then he uttered his oracle:
"Ah, who can live when God does this?[g]
24 Ships will come from the shores of Kittim;
they will subdue Asshur and Eber,
but they too will come to ruin."
25 Then Balaam got up and returned home and Balak went his
own way.

*Moab Seduces Israel*

25 WHILE ISRAEL was staying in Shittim, the men began to
indulge in sexual immorality with Moabite women, 2 who
invited them to the sacrifices to their gods. The people ate and
bowed down before these gods. 3 So Israel joined in worshiping the
Baal of Peor. And the LORD's anger burned against them.
4 The LORD said to Moses, "Take all the leaders of these people,
kill them and expose them in broad daylight before the LORD, so
that the LORD's fierce anger may turn away from Israel."
5 So Moses said to Israel's judges, "Each of you must put to
death those of your men who have joined in worshiping the Baal
of Peor."
6 Then an Israelite man brought to his family a Midianite woman
right before the eyes of Moses and the whole assembly of Israel
while they were weeping at the entrance to the Tent of Meeting.

NIV [d] 17 Samaritan Pentateuch (see also Jer. 48:45); the meaning of the word in the Masoretic Text is uncertain. [e] 17 Or possibly *Moab, / batter* [f] 17 Or *all the noisy boasters* [g] 23 Masoretic Text; with a different word division of the Hebrew *A people will gather from the north.*

## King James

7 And when Phinehas, the son of Eleazar, the son of Aaron the priest, saw *it*, he rose up from among the congregation, and took a javelin in his hand;

8 And he went after the man of Israel into the tent, and thrust both of them through, the man of Israel, and the woman through her belly. So the plague was stayed from the children of Israel.

9 And those that died in the plague were twenty and four thousand.

10 ¶ And the LORD spake unto Moses, saying,

11 Phinehas, the son of Eleazar, the son of Aaron the priest, hath turned my wrath away from the children of Israel, while he was zealous for my sake among them, that I consumed not the children of Israel in my jealousy.

12 Wherefore say, Behold, I give unto him my covenant of peace:

13 And he shall have it, and his seed after him, *even* the covenant of an everlasting priesthood; because he was zealous for his God, and made an atonement for the children of Israel.

14 Now the name of the Israelite that was slain, *even* that was slain with the Midianitish woman, *was* Zimri, the son of Salu, a prince of a chief house among the Simeonites.

15 And the name of the Midianitish woman that was slain *was* Cozbi, the daughter of Zur; he *was* head over a people, *and* of a chief house in Midian.

16 ¶ And the LORD spake unto Moses, saying,

17 Vex the Midianites, and smite them:

18 For they vex you with their wiles, wherewith they have beguiled you in the matter of Peor, and in the matter of Cozbi, the daughter of a prince of Midian, their sister, which was slain in the day of the plague for Peor's sake.

**26** AND IT came to pass after the plague, that the LORD spake unto Moses and unto Eleazar the son of Aaron the priest, saying,

2 Take the sum of all the congregation of the children of Israel, from twenty years old and upward, throughout their fathers' house, all that are able to go to war in Israel.

3 And Moses and Eleazar the priest spake with them in the plains of Moab by Jordan *near* Jericho, saying,

4 *Take the sum of the people*, from twenty years old and upward; as the LORD commanded Moses and the children of Israel, which went forth out of the land of Egypt.

5 ¶ Reuben, the eldest son of Israel: the children of Reuben; Hanoch, *of whom cometh* the family of the Hanochites: of Pallu, the family of the Palluites:

6 Of Hezron, the family of the Hezronites: of Carmi, the family of the Carmites.

7 These *are* the families of the Reubenites: and they that were numbered of them were forty and three thousand and seven hundred and thirty.

8 And the sons of Pallu; Eliab.

9 And the sons of Eliab; Nemuel, and Dathan, and Abiram. This *is that* Dathan and Abiram, *which were* famous in the congregation, who strove against Moses and against Aaron in the company of Korah, when they strove against the LORD:

10 And the earth opened her mouth, and swallowed them up together with Korah, when that company died, what time the fire devoured two hundred and fifty men: and they became a sign.

11 Notwithstanding the children of Korah died not.

12 ¶ The sons of Simeon after their families: of Nemuel, the family of the Nemuelites: of Jamin, the family of the Jaminites: of Jachin, the family of the Jachinites:

13 Of Zerah, the family of the Zarhites: of Shaul, the family of the Shaulites.

14 These *are* the families of the Simeonites, twenty and two thousand and two hundred.

## Amplified

7 And when Phinehas son of Eleazar, son of Aaron the priest, saw it, he rose up from the midst of the congregation, and took a spear in his hand

8 And went after the man of Israel into the inner room, and thrust both of them through, the man of Israel, and the woman, through her body. Then the (smiting) plague was stayed from the Israelites.

9 Nevertheless those who died in the (smiting) plague were 24,000.

10 And the Lord said to Moses,

11 Phinehas son of Eleazar, son of Aaron the priest, has turned my wrath away from the Israelites, in that he was jealous with My jealousy among them, so that I did not consume the Israelites in My jealousy.

12 Therefore say, Behold, I give to Phinehas the priest My covenant of peace;

13 And he shall have it, and his descendants after him, the covenant of an everlasting priesthood; because he was jealous for his God, and made atonement for the Israelites. [Ps. 106:28-31.]

14 Now the man of Israel who was slain with the Midianitish woman was Zimri son of Salu, a head of a father's house among the Simeonites.

15 And the Midianitish woman who was slain was Cozbi daughter of Zur; he was head of a father's house in Midian.

16 And the Lord said to Moses,

17 Provoke hostilities with the Midianites and attack them;

18 For they harass you with their wiles, with which they have beguiled you in the matter of Peor, and of Cozbi the daughter of the prince of Midian, their sister, who was slain on the day of the plague in the matter of Peor.

**26** AFTER THE plague the Lord said to Moses and Eleazar son of Aaron the priest,

2 Take a census of all the [male] congregation of the Israelites from twenty years old and upward, by their fathers' houses, all in Israel able to go to war.

3 And Moses and Eleazar the priest told [the people] in the plains of Moab by Jordan at Jericho,

4 A census of the people shall be taken, from twenty years old and upward, as the Lord commanded Moses. And the Israelites who came forth out of the land of Egypt were:

5 Reuben, the first-born of Israel; the sons of Reuben: of Hanoch, the family of the Hanochites; of Pallu, the family of the Palluites;

6 Of Hezron, the family of the Hezronites; of Carmi, the family of the Carmites.

7 These are the families of the Reubenites; and their number was 43,730.

8 And the sons of Pallu: Eliab.

9 The sons of Eliab: Nemuel, Dathan, and Abiram. These are the Dathan and Abiram, chosen from the congregation, who contended against Moses and Aaron in the company of Korah, when they contended against the Lord.

10 And the earth opened its mouth and swallowed them up together with Korah, when that company died, and the fire devoured 250 men; and they became a [warning] sign.

11 But Korah's sons did not die.

12 The sons of Simeon according to their families: of Nemuel, the family of the Nemuelites; of Jamin, the family of the Jaminites; of Jachin, the family of the Jachinites;

13 Of Zerah, the family of the Zerahites; of Shaul, the family of the Shaulites.

14 These are the families of the Simeonites, 22,200.

## New American Standard

7When Phinehas the son of Eleazar, the son of Aaron the priest, saw it, he arose from the midst of the congregation, and took a spear in his hand;

8and he went after the man of Israel into the tent, and pierced both of them through, the man of Israel and the woman, through the body. So the plague on the sons of Israel was checked.

9And those who died by the plague were 24,000.

*The Zeal of Phinehas*

**10**¶ Then the LORD spoke to Moses, saying,

11"Phinehas the son of Eleazar, the son of Aaron the priest, has turned away My wrath from the sons of Israel, in that he was jealous with My jealousy among them, so that I did not destroy the sons of Israel in My jealousy.

12"Therefore say, 'Behold, I give him My covenant of peace;

13and it shall be for him and his descendants after him, a covenant of a perpetual priesthood, because he was jealous for his God, and made atonement for the sons of Israel.' "

**14**¶ Now the name of the slain man of Israel who was slain with the Midianite woman, was Zimri the son of Salu, a leader of a father's household among the Simeonites.

15And the name of the Midianite woman who was slain was Cozbi the daughter of Zur, who was head of the people of a father's household in Midian.

**16**¶ Then the LORD spoke to Moses, saying,

17"Be hostile to the Midianites and strike them;

18for they have been hostile to you with their tricks, with which they have deceived you in the affair of Peor, and in the affair of Cozbi, the daughter of the leader of Midian, their sister who was slain on the day of the plague because of Peor."

*Census of a New Generation*

**26** THEN IT came about after the plague, that the LORD spoke to Moses and to Eleazar the son of Aaron the priest, saying,

2"Take a census of all the congregation of the sons of Israel from twenty years old and upward, by their fathers' households, whoever is able to go out to war in Israel."

3So Moses and Eleazar the priest spoke with them in the plains of Moab by the Jordan at Jericho, saying,

4" *Take a census of the people* from twenty years old and upward, as the LORD has commanded Moses."

¶ Now the sons of Israel who came out of the land of Egypt *were:*

5Reuben, Israel's first-born, the sons of Reuben: *of* Hanoch, the family of the Hanochites; of Pallu, the family of the Palluites;

6of Hezron, the family of the Hezronites; of Carmi, the family of the Carmites.

7These are the families of the Reubenites, and those who were numbered of them were 43,730.

8And the son of Pallu: Eliab.

9And the sons of Eliab: Nemuel and Dathan and Abiram. These are the Dathan and Abiram who were called by the congregation, who contended against Moses and against Aaron in the company of Korah, when they contended against the LORD,

10and the earth opened its mouth and swallowed them up along with Korah, when that company died, when the fire devoured 250 men, so that they became a warning.

11The sons of Korah, however, did not die.

**12**¶ The sons of Simeon according to their families: of Nemuel, the family of the Nemuelites; of Jamin, the family of the Jaminites; of Jachin, the family of the Jachinites;

13of Zerah, the family of the Zerahites; of Shaul, the family of the Shaulites.

14These are the families of the Simeonites, 22,200.

## New International

7When Phinehas son of Eleazar, the son of Aaron, the priest, saw
this, he left the assembly, took a spear in his hand 8and followed
the Israelite into the tent. He drove the spear through both of
them—through the Israelite and into the woman's body. Then the
plague against the Israelites was stopped; 9but those who died in
the plague numbered 24,000.
10The LORD said to Moses, 11"Phinehas son of Eleazar, the son
of Aaron, the priest, has turned my anger away from the Israelites;
for he was as zealous as I am for my honor among them, so that
in my zeal I did not put an end to them. 12Therefore tell him I am
making my covenant of peace with him. 13He and his descendants
will have a covenant of a lasting priesthood, because he was zealous for the honor of his God and made atonement for the Israelites."

14The name of the Israelite who was killed with the Midianite
woman was Zimri son of Salu, the leader of a Simeonite family.
15And the name of the Midianite woman who was put to death was
Cozbi daughter of Zur, a tribal chief of a Midianite family.
16The LORD said to Moses, 17"Treat the Midianites as enemies
and kill them, 18because they treated you as enemies when they
deceived you in the affair of Peor and their sister Cozbi, the daughter of a Midianite leader, the woman who was killed when the
plague came as a result of Peor."

*The Second Census*

**26** AFTER THE plague the LORD said to Moses and Eleazar
son of Aaron, the priest, 2"Take a census of the whole
Israelite community by families—all those twenty years old or
more who are able to serve in the army of Israel." 3So on the plains
of Moab by the Jordan across from Jericho,[a] Moses and Eleazar the
priest spoke with them and said, 4"Take a census of the men
twenty years old or more, as the LORD commanded Moses."

These were the Israelites who came out of Egypt:

5The descendants of Reuben, the firstborn son of Israel, were:
through Hanoch, the Hanochite clan;
through Pallu, the Palluite clan;
6through Hezron, the Hezronite clan;
through Carmi, the Carmite clan.
7These were the clans of Reuben; those numbered were 43,730.
8The son of Pallu was Eliab, 9and the sons of Eliab were Nemuel, Dathan and Abiram. The same Dathan and Abiram were the
community officials who rebelled against Moses and Aaron and
were among Korah's followers when they rebelled against the
LORD. 10The earth opened its mouth and swallowed them along
with Korah, whose followers died when the fire devoured the 250
men. And they served as a warning sign. 11The line of Korah,
however, did not die out.

12The descendants of Simeon by their clans were:
through Nemuel, the Nemuelite clan;
through Jamin, the Jaminite clan;
through Jakin, the Jakinite clan;
13through Zerah, the Zerahite clan;
through Shaul, the Shaulite clan.
14These were the clans of Simeon; there were 22,200 men.

**NIV** [a] 3 Hebrew *Jordan of Jericho;* possibly an ancient name for the Jordan River; also in verse 63

## King James

15¶ The children of Gad after their families: of Zephon, the
family of the Zephonites: of Haggi, the family of the Haggites: of
Shuni, the family of the Shunites:
16Of Ozni, the family of the Oznites: of Eri, the family of the
Erites:
17Of Arod, the family of the Arodites: of Areli, the family of the
Arelites.
18These *are* the families of the children of Gad according to those
that were numbered of them, forty thousand and five hundred.
19¶ The sons of Judah *were* Er and Onan: and Er and Onan died
in the land of Canaan.
20And the sons of Judah after their families were; of Shelah, the
family of the Shelanites: of Pharez, the family of the Pharzites: of
Zerah, the family of the Zarhites.
21And the sons of Pharez were; of Hezron, the family of the
Hezronites: of Hamul, the family of the Hamulites.
22These *are* the families of Judah according to those that were
numbered of them, threescore and sixteen thousand and five hundred.
23¶ *Of* the sons of Issachar after their families: *of* Tola, the family
of the Tolaites: of Pua, the family of the Punites:
24Of Jashub, the family of the Jashubites: of Shimron, the family
of the Shimronites.
25These *are* the families of Issachar according to those that were
numbered of them, threescore and four thousand and three hundred.
26¶ *Of* the sons of Zebulun after their families: of Sered, the
family of the Sardites: of Elon, the family of the Elonites: of Jahleel,
the family of the Jahleelites.
27These *are* the families of the Zebulunites according to those
that were numbered of them, threescore thousand and five hundred.
28¶ The sons of Joseph after their families *were* Manasseh and
Ephraim.
29Of the sons of Manasseh: of Machir, the family of the Machirites: and Machir begat Gilead: of Gilead *come* the family of the
Gileadites.
30These *are* the sons of Gilead: *of* Jeezer, the family of the Jeezer-
ites: of Helek, the family of the Helekites:
31And *of* Asriel, the family of the Asrielites: and *of* Shechem, the
family of the Shechemites:
32And *of* Shemida, the family of the Shemidaites: and *of* Hepher,
the family of the Hepherites.
33¶ And Zelophehad the son of Hepher had no sons, but daughters: and the names of the daughters of Zelophehad *were* Mahlah,
and Noah, Hoglah, Milcah, and Tirzah.
34These *are* the families of Manasseh, and those that were numbered of them, fifty and two thousand and seven hundred.
35¶ These *are* the sons of Ephraim after their families: of Shuthelah, the family of the Shuthalhites: of Becher, the family of the
Bachrites: of Tahan, the family of the Tahanites.
36And these *are* the sons of Shuthelah: of Eran, the family of the
Eranites.
37These *are* the families of the sons of Ephraim according to
those that were numbered of them, thirty and two thousand and
five hundred. These *are* the sons of Joseph after their families.
38¶ The sons of Benjamin after their families: of Bela, the family
of the Belaites: of Ashbel, the family of the Ashbelites: of Ahiram,
the family of the Ahiramites:
39Of Shupham, the family of the Shuphamites: of Hupham, the
family of the Huphamites.

## Amplified

15The sons of Gad after their families: of Zephon, the family of
the Zephonites; of Haggi, the family of the Haggites; of Shuni, the
family of the Shunites;
16Of Ozni, the family of the Oznites; of Eri, the family of the
Erites;
17Of Arod, the family of the Arodites; of Areli, the family of the
Arelites.
18These, the families of the sons of Gad according to their
numbering, totaled 40,500.
19The sons of Judah were Er and Onan; and Er and Onan died
in the land of Canaan.
20And the sons of Judah according to their families were: of
Shelah, the family of the Shelanites; of Perez, the family of the
Perezites; of Zerah, the family of the Zerahites.
21And the sons of Perez were: of Hezron, the family of the
Hezronites; of Hamul, the family of the Hamulites.
22These, the families of Judah according to their numbering,
totaled 76,500.
23The sons of Issachar after their families: of Tola, the family of
the Tolaites; of Puvah, the family of the Punites;
24Of Jashub, the family of the Jashubites; of Shimron, the family
of the Shimronites.
25These, the families of Issachar according to their numbering,
totaled 64,300.
26The sons of Zebulun after their families: of Sered, the family
of the Seredites; of Elon, the family of the Elonites; of Jahleel, the
family of the Jahleelites.
27These, the families of the Zebulunites according to their numbering, totaled 60,500.
28The sons of Joseph after their families were Manasseh and
Ephraim.
29The sons of Manasseh: of Machir, the family of the Machirites;
and Machir was the father of Gilead; of Gilead, the family of the
Gileadites.
30These are the sons of Gilead: of Iezer, the family of the Iezer-
ites; of Helek, the family of the Helekites;
31Of Asriel, the family of the Asrielites; of Shechem, the family
of the Shechemites;
32Of Shemida, the family of the Shemidaites; and of Hepher,
the family of the Hepherites.
33Zelophehad son of Hepher had no sons, but daughters: and
their names were Mahlah, Noah, Hoglah, Milcah, and Tirzah.
34These are the families of Manasseh, and their number was
52,700.
35These are the sons of Ephraim according to their families: of
Shuthelah, the family of the Shuthelahites; of Becher, the family
of the Becherites; of Tahan, the family of the Tahanites.
36And these are the sons of Shuthelah: of Eran, the family of the
Eranites.
37These, the families of the sons of Ephraim according to their
number, totaled 32,500. These are the sons of Joseph after their
families.
38The sons of Benjamin according to their families: of Bela, the
family of the Belaites; of Ashbel, the family of the Ashbelites; of
Ahiram, the family of the Ahiramites;
39Of Shephupham, the family of the Shuphamites; of Hupham,
the family of the Huphamites.

## New American Standard

15¶ The sons of Gad according to their families: of Zephon, the
family of the Zephonites; of Haggi, the family of the Haggites; of
Shuni, the family of the Shunites;
16of Ozni, the family of the Oznites; of Eri, the family of the
Erites;
17of Arod, the family of the Arodites; of Areli, the family of the
Arelites.
18These are the families of the sons of Gad according to those
who were numbered of them, 40,500.
19¶ The sons of Judah *were* Er and Onan, but Er and Onan died
in the land of Canaan.
20And the sons of Judah according to their families were: of
Shelah, the family of the Shelanites; of Perez, the family of the
Perezites; of Zerah, the family of the Zerahites.
21And the sons of Perez were: of Hezron, the family of the
Hezronites; of Hamul, the family of the Hamulites.
22These are the families of Judah according to those who were
numbered of them, 76,500.
23¶ The sons of Issachar according to their families: *of* Tola, the
family of the Tolaites; of Puvah, the family of the Punites;
24of Jashub, the family of the Jashubites; of Shimron, the family
of the Shimronites.
25These are the families of Issachar according to those who were
numbered of them, 64,300.
26¶ The sons of Zebulun according to their families: of Sered, the
family of the Seredites; of Elon, the family of the Elonites; of
Jahleel, the family of the Jahleelites.
27These are the families of the Zebulunites according to those
who were numbered of them, 60,500.
28¶ The sons of Joseph according to their families: Manasseh
and Ephraim.
29The sons of Manasseh: of Machir, the family of the Machirites;
and Machir became the father of Gilead: of Gilead, the family of
the Gileadites.
30These are the sons of Gilead: *of* Iezer, the family of the Iezer-
ites; of Helek, the family of the Helekites;
31and *of* Asriel, the family of the Asrielites; and *of* Shechem, the
family of the Shechemites;
32and *of* Shemida, the family of the Shemidaites; and *of* Hepher,
the family of the Hepherites.
33Now Zelophehad the son of Hepher had no sons, but only
daughters; and the names of the daughters of Zelophehad were
Mahlah, Noah, Hoglah, Milcah and Tirzah.
34These are the families of Manasseh; and those who were
numbered of them were 52,700.
35¶ These are the sons of Ephraim according to their families:
of Shuthelah, the family of the Shuthelahites; of Becher, the family
of the Becherites; of Tahan, the family of the Tahanites.
36And these are the sons of Shuthelah: of Eran, the family of the
Eranites.
37These are the families of the sons of Ephraim according to
those who were numbered of them, 32,500. These are the sons of
Joseph according to their families.
38¶ The sons of Benjamin according to their families: of Bela, the
family of the Belaites; of Ashbel, the family of the Ashbelites; of
Ahiram, the family of the Ahiramites;
39of Shephupham, the family of the Shuphamites; of Hupham,
the family of the Huphamites.

## New International

15The descendants of Gad by their clans were:
through Zephon, the Zephonite clan;
through Haggi, the Haggite clan;
through Shuni, the Shunite clan;
16through Ozni, the Oznite clan;
through Eri, the Erite clan;
17through Arodi,[a] the Arodite clan;
through Areli, the Arelite clan.
18These were the clans of Gad; those numbered were 40,500.

19Er and Onan were sons of Judah, but they died in Canaan.
20The descendants of Judah by their clans were:
through Shelah, the Shelanite clan;
through Perez, the Perezite clan;
through Zerah, the Zerahite clan.
21The descendants of Perez were:
through Hezron, the Hezronite clan;
through Hamul, the Hamulite clan.
22These were the clans of Judah; those numbered were 76,500.

23The descendants of Issachar by their clans were:
through Tola, the Tolaite clan;
through Puah, the Puite[b] clan;
24through Jashub, the Jashubite clan;
through Shimron, the Shimronite clan.
25These were the clans of Issachar; those numbered were 64,300.

26The descendants of Zebulun by their clans were:
through Sered, the Seredite clan;
through Elon, the Elonite clan;
through Jahleel, the Jahleelite clan.
27These were the clans of Zebulun; those numbered were 60,500.

28The descendants of Joseph by their clans through Manasseh and
Ephraim were:
29The descendants of Manasseh:
through Makir, the Makirite clan (Makir was the father of
Gilead);
through Gilead, the Gileadite clan.
30These were the descendants of Gilead:
through Iezer, the Iezerite clan;
through Helek, the Helekite clan;
31through Asriel, the Asrielite clan;
through Shechem, the Shechemite clan;
32through Shemida, the Shemidaite clan;
through Hepher, the Hepherite clan.
33(Zelophehad son of Hepher had no sons; he had only
daughters, whose names were Mahlah, Noah, Hoglah,
Milcah and Tirzah.)
34These were the clans of Manasseh; those numbered were 52,700.
35These were the descendants of Ephraim by their clans:
through Shuthelah, the Shuthelahite clan;
through Beker, the Bekerite clan;
through Tahan, the Tahanite clan.
36These were the descendants of Shuthelah:
through Eran, the Eranite clan.
37These were the clans of Ephraim; those numbered were 32,500.

These were the descendants of Joseph by their clans.

38The descendants of Benjamin by their clans were:
through Bela, the Belaite clan;
through Ashbel, the Ashbelite clan;
through Ahiram, the Ahiramite clan;
39through Shupham,[c] the Shuphamite clan;
through Hupham, the Huphamite clan.

**NIV** [a] *17* Samaritan Pentateuch and Syriac (see also Gen. 46:16); Masoretic Text *Arod* [b] *23* Samaritan Pentateuch, Septuagint, Vulgate and Syriac (see also 1 Chron. 7:1); Masoretic Text *through Puvah, the Punite* [c] *39* A few manuscripts of the Masoretic Text, Samaritan Pentateuch, Vulgate and Syriac (see also Septuagint); most manuscripts of the Masoretic Text *Shephupham*

## King James

40And the sons of Bela were Ard and Naaman: *of Ard,* the family of the Ardites: *and* of Naaman, the family of the Naamites.

41These *are* the sons of Benjamin after their families: and they that were numbered of them *were* forty and five thousand and six hundred.

42¶ These *are* the sons of Dan after their families: of Shuham, the family of the Shuhamites. These *are* the families of Dan after their families.

43All the families of the Shuhamites, according to those that were numbered of them, *were* threescore and four thousand and four hundred.

44¶ *Of* the children of Asher after their families: of Jimna, the family of the Jimnites: of Jesui, the family of the Jesuites: of Beriah, the family of the Beriites.

45Of the sons of Beriah: of Heber, the family of the Heberites: of Malchiel, the family of the Malchielites.

46And the name of the daughter of Asher *was* Sarah.

47These *are* the families of the sons of Asher according to those that were numbered of them; *who were* fifty and three thousand and four hundred.

48¶ *Of* the sons of Naphtali after their families: of Jahzeel, the family of the Jahzeelites: of Guni, the family of the Gunites:

49Of Jezer, the family of the Jezerites: of Shillem, the family of the Shillemites.

50These *are* the families of Naphtali according to their families: and they that were numbered of them *were* forty and five thousand and four hundred.

51These *were* the numbered of the children of Israel, six hundred thousand and a thousand seven hundred and thirty.

52¶ And the LORD spake unto Moses, saying,

53Unto these the land shall be divided for an inheritance according to the number of names.

54To many thou shalt give the more inheritance, and to few thou shalt give the less inheritance: to every one shall his inheritance be given according to those that were numbered of him.

55Notwithstanding the land shall be divided by lot: according to the names of the tribes of their fathers they shall inherit.

56According to the lot shall the possession thereof be divided between many and few.

57¶ And these *are* they that were numbered of the Levites after their families: of Gershon, the family of the Gershonites: of Kohath, the family of the Kohathites: of Merari, the family of the Merarites.

58These *are* the families of the Levites: the family of the Libnites, the family of the Hebronites, the family of the Mahlites, the family of the Mushites, the family of the Korathites. And Kohath begat Amram.

59And the name of Amram's wife *was* Jochebed, the daughter of Levi, whom *her mother* bare to Levi in Egypt: and she bare unto Amram Aaron and Moses, and Miriam their sister.

60And unto Aaron was born Nadab, and Abihu, Eleazar, and Ithamar.

61And Nadab and Abihu died, when they offered strange fire before the LORD.

62And those that were numbered of them were twenty and three thousand, all males from a month old and upward: for they were not numbered among the children of Israel, because there was no inheritance given them among the children of Israel.

63¶ These *are* they that were numbered by Moses and Eleazar the priest, who numbered the children of Israel in the plains of Moab by Jordan *near* Jericho.

64But among these there was not a man of them whom Moses and Aaron the priest numbered, when they numbered the children of Israel in the wilderness of Sinai.

65For the LORD had said of them, They shall surely die in the wilderness. And there was not left a man of them, save Caleb the son of Jephunneh, and Joshua the son of Nun.

## Amplified

40And the sons of Bela were Ard and Naaman; of Ard, the family of the Ardites; of Naaman, the family of the Naamites.

41These are the sons of Benjamin according to their families; and their number was 45,600.

42These are the sons of Dan according to their families: of Shuham, the family of the Shuhamites. These are the families of Dan according to their families.

43All the families of the Shuhamites, according to their number were 64,400.

44Of the sons of Asher according to their families: of Imnah, the family of the Imnites; of Ishvi, the family of the Ishvites; of Beriah, the family of the Beriites.

45Of the sons of Beriah: of Heber, the family of the Heberites; of Malchiel, the family of the Malchielites.

46And the name of the daughter of Asher was Serah.

47These, the families of the sons of Asher according to their number, totaled 53,400.

48Of the sons of Naphtali after their families: of Jahzeel, the family of the Jahzeelites; of Guni, the family of the Gunites;

49Of Jezer, the family of the Jezerites; of Shillem, the family of the Shillemites.

50These, the families of Naphtali according to their families; and their number totaled 45,400.

51This was the number of the Israelites, 601,730.

52And the Lord said to Moses,

53To these the land shall be divided for inheritance according to the number of names.

54To a larger tribe you shall give the greater inheritance, and to a small tribe the less inheritance; to each tribe shall its inheritance be given according to its numbers.

55But the land shall be divided by lot; according to the names of the tribes of their fathers they shall inherit.

56According to the lot shall their inheritance be divided between the larger and the smaller.

57And these were numbered of the Levites according to their families: of Gershon, the family of the Gershonites; of Kohath, the family of the Kohathites; of Merari, the family of the Merarites.

58These are the families of Levi: the family of the Libnites, the family of the Hebronites, the family of the Mahlites, the family of the Mushites, the family of the Korahites. And Kohath was the father of Amram.

59Amram's wife was Jochebed daughter of Levi, who was born to Levi in Egypt; and she bore to Amram Aaron, Moses, and Miriam their sister.

60And to Aaron were born Nadab, Abihu, Eleazar, and Ithamar.

61But Nadab and Abihu died when they offered strange *and* unholy fire before the Lord.

62And those numbered of them were 23,000, every male from a month old and upward; for they were not numbered among the Israelites, because there was no inheritance given them among the Israelites.

63These were those numbered by Moses and Eleazar the priest, who numbered the Israelites in the plains of Moab by Jordan at Jericho.

64But among these there was not a man of those numbered by Moses and Aaron the priest, when they numbered the Israelites in the wilderness of Sinai.

65For the Lord had said of them, They shall surely die in the wilderness. There was not left a man of them, except Caleb son of Jephunneh and Joshua son of Nun.

## New American Standard

40And the sons of Bela were Ard and Naaman: *of Ard,* the family of the Ardites; of Naaman, the family of the Naamites.
41These are the sons of Benjamin according to their families; and those who were numbered of them were 45,600.
**42**¶ These are the sons of Dan according to their families: of Shuham, the family of the Shuhamites. These are the families of Dan according to their families.
43All the families of the Shuhamites, according to those who were numbered of them, were 64,400.
**44**¶ The sons of Asher according to their families: of Imnah, the family of the Imnites; of Ishvi, the family of the Ishvites; of Beriah, the family of the Beriites.
45Of the sons of Beriah: of Heber, the family of the Heberites; of Malchiel, the family of the Malchielites.
46And the name of the daughter of Asher *was* Serah.
47These are the families of the sons of Asher according to those who were numbered of them, 53,400.
**48**¶ The sons of Naphtali according to their families: of Jahzeel, the family of the Jahzeelites; of Guni, the family of the Gunites;
49of Jezer, the family of the Jezerites; of Shillem, the family of the Shillemites.
50These are the families of Naphtali according to their families; and those who were numbered of them were 45,400.
**51**¶ These are those who were numbered of the sons of Israel, 601,730.
**52**¶ Then the LORD spoke to Moses, saying,
53"Among these the land shall be divided for an inheritance according to the number of names.
54"To the larger *group* you shall increase their inheritance, and to the smaller *group* you shall diminish their inheritance; each shall be given their inheritance according to those who were numbered of them.
55"But the land shall be divided by lot. They shall receive their inheritance according to the names of the tribes of their fathers.
56"According to the selection by lot, their inheritance shall be divided between the larger and the smaller *groups.*"
**57**¶ And these are those who were numbered of the Levites according to their families: of Gershon, the family of the Gershonites; of Kohath, the family of the Kohathites; of Merari, the family of the Merarites.
58These are the families of Levi: the family of the Libnites, the family of the Hebronites, the family of the Mahlites, the family of the Mushites, the family of the Korahites. And Kohath became the father of Amram.
59And the name of Amram's wife was Jochebed, the daughter of Levi, who was born to Levi in Egypt; and she bore to Amram: Aaron and Moses and their sister Miriam.
60And to Aaron were born Nadab and Abihu, Eleazar and Ithamar.
61But Nadab and Abihu died when they offered strange fire before the LORD.
62And those who were numbered of them were 23,000, every male from a month old and upward, for they were not numbered among the sons of Israel since no inheritance was given to them among the sons of Israel.
**63**¶ These are those who were numbered by Moses and Eleazar the priest, who numbered the sons of Israel in the plains of Moab by the Jordan at Jericho.
64But among these there was not a man of those who were numbered by Moses and Aaron the priest, who numbered the sons of Israel in the wilderness of Sinai.
65For the LORD had said of them, "They shall surely die in the wilderness." And not a man was left of them, except Caleb the son of Jephunneh, and Joshua the son of Nun.

## New International

40The descendants of Bela through Ard and Naaman were:
through Ard,[a] the Ardite clan;
through Naaman, the Naamite clan.
41These were the clans of Benjamin; those numbered were 45,600.

42These were the descendants of Dan by their clans:
through Shuham, the Shuhamite clan.
These were the clans of Dan: 43All of them were Shuhamite clans; and those numbered were 64,400.

44The descendants of Asher by their clans were:
through Imnah, the Imnite clan;
through Ishvi, the Ishvite clan;
through Beriah, the Beriite clan;
45and through the descendants of Beriah:
through Heber, the Heberite clan;
through Malkiel, the Malkielite clan.
46(Asher had a daughter named Serah.)
47These were the clans of Asher; those numbered were 53,400.

48The descendants of Naphtali by their clans were:
through Jahzeel, the Jahzeelite clan;
through Guni, the Gunite clan;
49through Jezer, the Jezerite clan;
through Shillem, the Shillemite clan.
50These were the clans of Naphtali; those numbered were 45,400.

51The total number of the men of Israel was 601,730.

52The LORD said to Moses, 53"The land is to be allotted to them
as an inheritance based on the number of names. 54To a larger
group give a larger inheritance, and to a smaller group a smaller
one; each is to receive its inheritance according to the number of
those listed. 55Be sure that the land is distributed by lot. What each
group inherits will be according to the names for its ancestral tribe.
56Each inheritance is to be distributed by lot among the larger and
smaller groups."

57These were the Levites who were counted by their clans:
through Gershon, the Gershonite clan;
through Kohath, the Kohathite clan;
through Merari, the Merarite clan.
58These also were Levite clans:
the Libnite clan,
the Hebronite clan,
the Mahlite clan,
the Mushite clan,
the Korahite clan.
(Kohath was the forefather of Amram; 59the name of Amram's
wife was Jochebed, a descendant of Levi, who was born to the
Levites[b] in Egypt. To Amram she bore Aaron, Moses and
their sister Miriam. 60Aaron was the father of Nadab and
Abihu, Eleazar and Ithamar. 61But Nadab and Abihu died
when they made an offering before the LORD with unauthorized fire.)

62All the male Levites a month old or more numbered 23,000. They were not counted along with the other Israelites because they received no inheritance among them.

63These are the ones counted by Moses and Eleazar the priest
when they counted the Israelites on the plains of Moab by the
Jordan across from Jericho. 64Not one of them was among those
counted by Moses and Aaron the priest when they counted the
Israelites in the Desert of Sinai. 65For the LORD had told those
Israelites they would surely die in the desert, and not one of them
was left except Caleb son of Jephunneh and Joshua son of Nun.

**NIV** [a] *40* Samaritan Pentateuch and Vulgate (see also Septuagint); Masoretic Text does not have *through Ard.* [b] *59* Or *Jochebed, a daughter of Levi, who was born to Levi*

## King James

**27** THEN CAME the daughters of Zelophehad, the son of Hepher, the son of Gilead, the son of Machir, the son of Manasseh, of the families of Manasseh the son of Joseph: and these *are* the names of his daughters; Mahlah, Noah, and Hoglah, and Milcah, and Tirzah.

2And they stood before Moses, and before Eleazar the priest, and before the princes and all the congregation, *by* the door of the tabernacle of the congregation, saying,

3Our father died in the wilderness, and he was not in the company of them that gathered themselves together against the LORD in the company of Korah; but died in his own sin, and had no sons.

4Why should the name of our father be done away from among his family, because he hath no son? Give unto us *therefore* a possession among the brethren of our father.

5And Moses brought their cause before the LORD.

6¶ And the LORD spake unto Moses, saying,

7The daughters of Zelophehad speak right: thou shalt surely give them a possession of an inheritance among their father's brethren; and thou shalt cause the inheritance of their father to pass unto them.

8And thou shalt speak unto the children of Israel, saying, If a man die, and have no son, then ye shall cause his inheritance to pass unto his daughter.

9And if he have no daughter, then ye shall give his inheritance unto his brethren.

10And if he have no brethren, then ye shall give his inheritance unto his father's brethren.

11And if his father have no brethren, then ye shall give his inheritance unto his kinsman that is next to him of his family, and he shall possess it: and it shall be unto the children of Israel a statute of judgment, as the LORD commanded Moses.

12¶ And the LORD said unto Moses, Get thee up into this mount Abarim, and see the land which I have given unto the children of Israel.

13And when thou hast seen it, thou also shalt be gathered unto thy people, as Aaron thy brother was gathered.

14For ye rebelled against my commandment in the desert of Zin, in the strife of the congregation, to sanctify me at the water before their eyes: that *is* the water of Meribah in Kadesh in the wilderness of Zin.

15¶ And Moses spake unto the LORD, saying,

16Let the LORD, the God of the spirits of all flesh, set a man over the congregation,

17Which may go out before them, and which may go in before them, and which may lead them out, and which may bring them in; that the congregation of the LORD be not as sheep which have no shepherd.

18¶ And the LORD said unto Moses, Take thee Joshua the son of Nun, a man in whom *is* the spirit, and lay thine hand upon him;

19And set him before Eleazar the priest, and before all the congregation; and give him a charge in their sight.

20And thou shalt put *some* of thine honour upon him, that all the congregation of the children of Israel may be obedient.

21And he shall stand before Eleazar the priest, who shall ask *counsel* for him after the judgment of Urim before the LORD: at his word shall they go out, and at his word they shall come in, *both* he, and all the children of Israel with him, even all the congregation.

22And Moses did as the LORD commanded him: and he took Joshua, and set him before Eleazar the priest, and before all the congregation:

23And he laid his hands upon him, and gave him a charge, as the LORD commanded by the hand of Moses.

## Amplified

**27** THEN CAME the daughters of Zelophehad son of Hepher, son of Gilead, son of Machir, son of Manasseh, from the families of Manasseh son of Joseph. The names of his daughters: Mahlah, Noah, Hoglah, Milcah, and Tirzah.

2They stood before Moses, Eleazar the priest, and the leaders and all the congregation, at the door of the tent of meeting, saying,

3Our father died in the wilderness; he was not among those who assembled together against the Lord in the company of Korah, but died for his own sin [as did all those who rebelled at Kadesh]; and he had no sons. [Num. 14:26-35.]

4Why should the name of our father be removed from his family, because he had no son? Give to us a possession among our father's brethren.

5Moses brought their case before the Lord.

6And the Lord said to Moses,

7The daughters of Zelophehad are justified *and* speak correctly; you shall surely give them an inheritance among their father's brethren, and you shall cause their father's inheritance to pass to them.

8And say to the Israelites, If a man dies, and has no son, you shall cause his inheritance to pass to his daughter.

9If he has no daughter, you shall give his inheritance to his brethren.

10If he has no brethren, give his inheritance to his father's brethren.

11And if his father has no brethren, then give his inheritance to his next of kin, and he shall possess it. It shall be to the Israelites a statute and ordinance, as the Lord commanded Moses.

12And the Lord said to Moses, Go up into this mountain of Abarim, and behold the land I have given to the Israelites.

13And when you have seen it, you also shall be gathered to your [departed] people as Aaron your brother was gathered,

14For you disobeyed My order in the wilderness of Zin during the strife of the congregation, to uphold My sanctity [by strict obedience to My authority] at the waters before their eyes. [These are the waters of Meribah in Kadesh in the wilderness of Zin.] [Num. 20:10-12.]

15And Moses said to the Lord,

16Let the Lord, the God of the spirits of all flesh, set a man over the congregation,

17Who shall go out and come in before them, leading them out and bringing them in; that the congregation of the Lord may not be as sheep which have no shepherd.

18The Lord said to Moses, Take Joshua son of Nun, a man in whom is the Spirit, and lay your hand upon him;

19And set him before Eleazar the priest and all the congregation, and give him a charge in their sight;

20And put some of your honor *and* authority upon him, that all the congregation of the Israelites may obey him.

21He shall stand before Eleazar the priest, who shall inquire for him before the Lord by the judgment of the Urim [one of two articles in the priest's breastplate worn when asking counsel of the Lord for the people]. At Joshua's word the people shall go out and come in, both he and all the Israelite congregation with him.

22And Moses did as the Lord commanded him; he took Joshua, and set him before Eleazar the priest and all the congregation,

23And he laid his hands upon him, and commissioned him, as the Lord commanded through Moses.

## New American Standard

*A Law of Inheritance*

**27** THEN THE daughters of Zelophehad, the son of Hepher,
the son of Gilead, the son of Machir, the son of Manasseh,
of the families of Manasseh the son of Joseph, came near; and these
are the names of his daughters: Mahlah, Noah and Hoglah and
Milcah and Tirzah.
2And they stood before Moses and before Eleazar the priest
and before the leaders and all the congregation, at the doorway of
the tent of meeting, saying,
3"Our father died in the wilderness, yet he was not among the
company of those who gathered themselves together against the
LORD in the company of Korah; but he died in his own sin, and
he had no sons.
4"Why should the name of our father be withdrawn from
among his family because he had no son? Give us a possession
among our father's brothers."
5And Moses brought their case before the LORD.
6¶ Then the LORD spoke to Moses, saying,
7"The daughters of Zelophehad are right in *their* statements.
You shall surely give them a hereditary possession among their
father's brothers, and you shall transfer the inheritance of their
father to them.
8"Further, you shall speak to the sons of Israel, saying, 'If a
man dies and has no son, then you shall transfer his inheritance
to his daughter.
9'And if he has no daughter, then you shall give his inheritance
to his brothers.
10'And if he has no brothers, then you shall give his inheritance
to his father's brothers.
11'And if his father has no brothers, then you shall give his
inheritance to his nearest relative in his own family, and he shall
possess it; and it shall be a statutory ordinance to the sons of Israel,
just as the LORD commanded Moses.'"
12¶ Then the LORD said to Moses, "Go up to this mountain of
Abarim, and see the land which I have given to the sons of Israel.
13"And when you have seen it, you too shall be gathered to
your people, as Aaron your brother was;
14for in the wilderness of Zin, during the strife of the congregation, you rebelled against My command to treat Me as holy before
their eyes at the water." (These are the waters of Meribah of
Kadesh in the wilderness of Zin.)

*Joshua to Succeed Moses*

15¶ Then Moses spoke to the LORD, saying,
16"May the LORD, the God of the spirits of all flesh, appoint a
man over the congregation,
17who will go out and come in before them, and who will lead
them out and bring them in, that the congregation of the LORD may
not be like sheep which have no shepherd."
18So the LORD said to Moses, "Take Joshua the son of Nun, a
man in whom is the Spirit, and lay your hand on him;
19and have him stand before Eleazar the priest and before all the
congregation; and commission him in their sight.
20"And you shall put some of your authority on him, in order
that all the congregation of the sons of Israel may obey *him*.
21"Moreover, he shall stand before Eleazar the priest, who shall
inquire for him by the judgment of the Urim before the LORD. At
his command they shall go out and at his command they shall
come in, *both* he and the sons of Israel with him, even all the
congregation."
22And Moses did just as the LORD commanded him; and he took
Joshua and set him before Eleazar the priest, and before all the
congregation.
23Then he laid his hands on him and commissioned him, just
as the LORD had spoken through Moses.

## New International

*Zelophehad's Daughters*

**27** THE DAUGHTERS of Zelophehad son of Hepher, the son
of Gilead, the son of Makir, the son of Manasseh, belonged to the clans of Manasseh son of Joseph. The names of the
daughters were Mahlah, Noah, Hoglah, Milcah and Tirzah. They
approached 2the entrance to the Tent of Meeting and stood before
Moses, Eleazar the priest, the leaders and the whole assembly, and
said, 3"Our father died in the desert. He was not among Korah's
followers, who banded together against the LORD, but he died for
his own sin and left no sons. 4Why should our father's name
disappear from his clan because he had no son? Give us property
among our father's relatives."
5So Moses brought their case before the LORD 6and the LORD
said to him, 7"What Zelophehad's daughters are saying is right.
You must certainly give them property as an inheritance among
their father's relatives and turn their father's inheritance over to
them.
8"Say to the Israelites, 'If a man dies and leaves no son, turn
his inheritance over to his daughter. 9If he has no daughter, give
his inheritance to his brothers. 10If he has no brothers, give his
inheritance to his father's brothers. 11If his father had no brothers,
give his inheritance to the nearest relative in his clan, that he may
possess it. This is to be a legal requirement for the Israelites, as the
LORD commanded Moses.'"

*Joshua to Succeed Moses*

12Then the LORD said to Moses, "Go up this mountain in the
Abarim range and see the land I have given the Israelites. 13After
you have seen it, you too will be gathered to your people, as your
brother Aaron was, 14for when the community rebelled at the
waters in the Desert of Zin, both of you disobeyed my command
to honor me as holy before their eyes." (These were the waters of
Meribah Kadesh, in the Desert of Zin.)
15Moses said to the LORD, 16"May the LORD, the God of the
spirits of all mankind, appoint a man over this community 17to go
out and come in before them, one who will lead them out and bring
them in, so the LORD's people will not be like sheep without a
shepherd."
18So the LORD said to Moses, "Take Joshua son of Nun, a man
in whom is the spirit,[a] and lay your hand on him. 19Have him
stand before Eleazar the priest and the entire assembly and commission him in their presence. 20Give him some of your authority
so the whole Israelite community will obey him. 21He is to stand
before Eleazar the priest, who will obtain decisions for him by
inquiring of the Urim before the LORD. At his command he and the
entire community of the Israelites will go out, and at his command
they will come in."
22Moses did as the LORD commanded him. He took Joshua and
had him stand before Eleazar the priest and the whole assembly.
23Then he laid his hands on him and commissioned him, as the
LORD instructed through Moses.

NIV [a] *18* Or *Spirit*

## King James

28 AND THE LORD spake unto Moses, saying,

2 Command the children of Israel, and say unto them, My offering, *and* my bread for my sacrifices made by fire, *for* a sweet savour unto me, shall ye observe to offer unto me in their due season.

3 And thou shalt say unto them, This *is* the offering made by fire which ye shall offer unto the LORD; two lambs of the first year without spot day by day, *for* a continual burnt offering.

4 The one lamb shalt thou offer in the morning, and the other lamb shalt thou offer at even;

5 And a tenth *part* of an ephah of flour for a meat offering, mingled with the fourth *part* of an hin of beaten oil.

6 *It is* a continual burnt offering, which was ordained in mount Sinai for a sweet savour, a sacrifice made by fire unto the LORD.

7 And the drink offering thereof *shall be* the fourth *part* of an hin for the one lamb: in the holy *place* shalt thou cause the strong wine to be poured unto the LORD *for* a drink offering.

8 And the other lamb shalt thou offer at even: as the meat offering of the morning, and as the drink offering thereof, thou shalt offer *it*, a sacrifice made by fire, of a sweet savour unto the LORD.

9 ¶ And on the sabbath day two lambs of the first year without spot, and two tenth deals of flour *for* a meat offering, mingled with oil, and the drink offering thereof:

10 *This is* the burnt offering of every sabbath, beside the continual burnt offering, and his drink offering.

11 ¶ And in the beginnings of your months ye shall offer a burnt offering unto the LORD; two young bullocks, and one ram, seven lambs of the first year without spot;

12 And three tenth deals of flour *for* a meat offering, mingled with oil, for one bullock; and two tenth deals of flour *for* a meat offering, mingled with oil, for one ram;

13 And a several tenth deal of flour mingled with oil *for* a meat offering unto one lamb; *for* a burnt offering of a sweet savour, a sacrifice made by fire unto the LORD.

14 And their drink offerings shall be half an hin of wine unto a bullock, and the third *part* of an hin unto a ram, and a fourth *part* of an hin unto a lamb: this *is* the burnt offering of every month throughout the months of the year.

15 And one kid of the goats for a sin offering unto the LORD shall be offered, beside the continual burnt offering, and his drink offering.

16 And in the fourteenth day of the first month *is* the passover of the LORD.

17 And in the fifteenth day of this month *is* the feast: seven days shall unleavened bread be eaten.

18 In the first day *shall be* an holy convocation; ye shall do no manner of servile work *therein*:

19 But ye shall offer a sacrifice made by fire *for* a burnt offering unto the LORD; two young bullocks, and one ram, and seven lambs of the first year: they shall be unto you without blemish:

20 And their meat offering *shall be of* flour mingled with oil: three tenth deals shall ye offer for a bullock, and two tenth deals for a ram;

21 A several tenth deal shalt thou offer for every lamb, throughout the seven lambs:

22 And one goat *for* a sin offering, to make an atonement for you.

23 Ye shall offer these beside the burnt offering in the morning, which *is* for a continual burnt offering.

24 After this manner ye shall offer daily, throughout the seven days, the meat of the sacrifice made by fire, of a sweet savour unto the LORD: it shall be offered beside the continual burnt offering, and his drink offering.

25 And on the seventh day ye shall have an holy convocation; ye shall do no servile work.

26 ¶ Also in the day of the firstfruits, when ye bring a new meat offering unto the LORD, after your weeks *be out*, ye shall have an holy convocation; ye shall do no servile work:

## Amplified

28 AND THE Lord said to Moses,

2 Command the Israelites, saying, My offering, My food for My offerings by fire, My sweet *and* soothing odor, you shall be careful to offer to Me at its proper time.

3 And you shall say to the people, This is the offering by fire which you shall offer to the Lord: two male lambs a year old without spot *or* blemish, two day by day, for a continual burnt offering.

4 One lamb you shall offer in the morning, and the other in the evening;

5 Also a tenth of an ephah of flour for a cereal offering, mixed with the fourth of a hin of beaten oil.

6 It is a continual burnt offering, which was ordained in Mount Sinai for a sweet *and* soothing odor, an offering made by fire to the Lord.

7 Its drink offering shall be the fourth of a hin for each lamb; in the holy place you shall pour out a fermented drink offering to the Lord.

8 And the other lamb you shall offer in the evening; like the cereal offering of the morning, and like its drink offering, you shall offer it, an offering made by fire, a sweet *and* soothing odor to the Lord.

9 And on the sabbath day two male lambs a year old without spot *or* blemish, and two tenths of an ephah of flour for a cereal offering, mixed with oil, and its drink offering;

10 This is the burnt offering of every sabbath, besides the continual burnt offering and its drink offering.

11 And at the beginnings of your months you shall offer a burnt offering to the Lord: two young bulls, one ram, seven male lambs a year old without spot *or* blemish;

12 And three tenths of an ephah of fine flour for a cereal offering, mixed with oil for each bull; and two tenths of an ephah of fine flour for a cereal offering, mixed with oil, for the one ram.

13 And a tenth part of fine flour mixed with oil as a cereal offering for each lamb; for a burnt offering of a sweet *and* pleasant fragrance, an offering made by fire to the Lord.

14 And their drink offerings shall be half a hin of wine for a bull, and the third of a hin for a ram, and a fourth of a hin for a lamb; this is the burnt offering of each month throughout the months of the year.

15 And one male goat for a sin offering to the Lord; it shall be offered in addition to the continual burnt offering and its drink offering.

16 On the fourteenth day of the first month is the Lord's passover.

17 On the fifteenth day of this month is a feast; seven days shall unleavened bread be eaten.

18 On the first day there shall be a holy [summoned] assembly; you shall do no servile work that day.

19 But you shall offer an offering by fire, a burnt offering to the Lord: two young bulls, one ram, and seven male lambs a year old; they shall be without blemish to your knowledge.

20 And their cereal offering shall be of fine flour mixed with oil; three tenths of an ephah shall you offer for a bull, and two tenths for a ram;

21 A tenth shall you offer for each of the seven male lambs,

22 Also one male goat for a sin offering, to make atonement for you.

23 You shall offer these in addition to the burnt offering of the morning, which is for a continual burnt offering.

24 In this way you shall offer daily, for seven days, the food of an offering by fire, a sweet *and* soothing odor to the Lord; it shall be offered in addition to the continual burnt offering and its drink offering.

25 And on the seventh day you shall have a holy [summoned] assembly; you shall do no work befitting a slave *or* a servant.

26 Also in the day of the first fruits, when you offer a cereal offering of new grain to the Lord, at your feast of weeks, you shall have a holy [summoned] assembly; you shall do no servile work.

## New American Standard

*Laws for Offerings*

28 THEN THE LORD spoke to Moses, saying,
2"Command the sons of Israel and say to them, 'You shall
be careful to present My offering, My food for My offerings by fire,
of a soothing aroma to Me, at their appointed time.'
3"And you shall say to them, 'This is the offering by fire which
you shall offer to the LORD; two male lambs one year old without
defect *as* a continual burnt offering every day.
4'You shall offer the one lamb in the morning, and the other
lamb you shall offer at twilight;
5also a tenth of an ephah of fine flour for a grain offering, mixed
with a fourth of a hin of beaten oil.
6'It is a continual burnt offering which was ordained in Mount
Sinai as a soothing aroma, an offering by fire to the LORD.
7'Then the libation with it *shall be* a fourth of a hin for each
lamb, in the holy place you shall pour out a libation of strong drink
to the LORD.
8'And the other lamb you shall offer at twilight; as the grain
offering of the morning and as its libation, you shall offer it, an
offering by fire, a soothing aroma to the LORD.
9¶ 'Then on the sabbath day two male lambs one year old
without defect, and two-tenths *of an ephah* of fine flour mixed with
oil as a grain offering, and its libation:
10 '*This is* the burnt offering of every sabbath in addition to the
continual burnt offering and its libation.
11¶ 'Then at the beginning of each of your months you shall
present a burnt offering to the LORD; two bulls and one ram, seven
male lambs one year old without defect,
12and three-tenths *of an ephah* of fine flour for a grain offering,
mixed with oil, for each bull; and two-tenths of fine flour for a grain
offering, mixed with oil, for the one ram;
13and a tenth *of an ephah* of fine flour mixed with oil for a grain
offering for each lamb, for a burnt offering of a soothing aroma,
an offering by fire to the LORD.
14'And their libations shall be half a hin of wine for a bull and
a third of a hin for the ram and a fourth of a hin for a lamb; this
is the burnt offering of each month throughout the months of the
year.
15'And one male goat for a sin offering to the LORD; it shall be
offered with its libation in addition to the continual burnt offering.
16¶ 'Then on the fourteenth day of the first month shall be the
LORD's Passover.
17'And on the fifteenth day of this month *shall be* a feast, unleavened bread *shall be* eaten for seven days.
18'On the first day *shall be* a holy convocation; you shall do no
laborious work.
19'And you shall present an offering by fire, a burnt offering to
the LORD: two bulls and one ram and seven male lambs one year
old, having them without defect.
20'And for their grain offering, you shall offer fine flour mixed
with oil: three-tenths *of an ephah* for a bull and two-tenths for the
ram.
21'A tenth *of an ephah* you shall offer for each of the seven lambs,
22and one male goat for a sin offering, to make atonement for
you.
23'You shall present these besides the burnt offering of the
morning, which is for a continual burnt offering.
24'After this manner you shall present daily, for seven days, the
food of the offering by fire, of a soothing aroma to the LORD; it shall
be presented with its libation in addition to the continual burnt
offering.
25'And on the seventh day you shall have a holy convocation;
you shall do no laborious work.
26¶ 'Also on the day of the first fruits, when you present a new
grain offering to the LORD in your *Feast of* Weeks, you shall have
a holy convocation; you shall do no laborious work.

## New International

*Daily Offerings*

28 THE LORD said to Moses, 2"Give this command to the
Israelites and say to them: 'See that you present to me at
the appointed time the food for my offerings made by fire, as an
aroma pleasing to me.' 3Say to them: 'This is the offering made by
fire that you are to present to the LORD: two lambs a year old
without defect, as a regular burnt offering each day. 4Prepare one
lamb in the morning and the other at twilight, 5together with a
grain offering of a tenth of an ephah[a] of fine flour mixed with a
quarter of a hin[b] of oil from pressed olives. 6This is the regular
burnt offering instituted at Mount Sinai as a pleasing aroma, an
offering made to the LORD by fire. 7The accompanying drink offering is to be a quarter of a hin of fermented drink with each lamb.
Pour out the drink offering to the LORD at the sanctuary. 8Prepare
the second lamb at twilight, along with the same kind of grain
offering and drink offering that you prepare in the morning. This
is an offering made by fire, an aroma pleasing to the LORD.

*Sabbath Offerings*

9" 'On the Sabbath day, make an offering of two lambs a year
old without defect, together with its drink offering and a grain
offering of two-tenths of an ephah[c] of fine flour mixed with oil.
10This is the burnt offering for every Sabbath, in addition to the
regular burnt offering and its drink offering.

*Monthly Offerings*

11" 'On the first of every month, present to the LORD a burnt
offering of two young bulls, one ram and seven male lambs a year
old, all without defect. 12With each bull there is to be a grain
offering of three-tenths of an ephah[d] of fine flour mixed with oil;
with the ram, a grain offering of two-tenths of an ephah of fine
flour mixed with oil; 13and with each lamb, a grain offering of a
tenth of an ephah of fine flour mixed with oil. This is for a burnt
offering, a pleasing aroma, an offering made to the LORD by fire.
14With each bull there is to be a drink offering of half a hin[e] of
wine; with the ram, a third of a hin[f]; and with each lamb, a quarter
of a hin. This is the monthly burnt offering to be made at each new
moon during the year. 15Besides the regular burnt offering with its
drink offering, one male goat is to be presented to the LORD as a
sin offering.

*The Passover*

16" 'On the fourteenth day of the first month the LORD's Passover is to be held. 17On the fifteenth day of this month there is to
be a festival; for seven days eat bread made without yeast. 18On
the first day hold a sacred assembly and do no regular work.
19Present to the LORD an offering made by fire, a burnt offering of
two young bulls, one ram and seven male lambs a year old, all
without defect. 20With each bull prepare a grain offering of three-
tenths of an ephah of fine flour mixed with oil; with the ram,
two-tenths; 21and with each of the seven lambs, one-tenth. 22In-
clude one male goat as a sin offering to make atonement for you.
23Prepare these in addition to the regular morning burnt offering.
24In this way prepare the food for the offering made by fire every
day for seven days as an aroma pleasing to the LORD; it is to be
prepared in addition to the regular burnt offering and its drink
offering. 25On the seventh day hold a sacred assembly and do no
regular work.

*Feast of Weeks*

26" 'On the day of firstfruits, when you present to the LORD an
offering of new grain during the Feast of Weeks, hold a sacred
assembly and do no regular work. 27Present a burnt offering of two

NIV [a] *5* That is, probably about 2 quarts (about 2 liters); also in verses 13, 21 and 29 [b] *5* That is, probably about 1 quart (about 1 liter); also in verses 7 and 14 [c] *9* That is, probably about 4 quarts (about 4.5 liters); also in verses 12, 20 and 28 [d] *12* That is, probably about 6 quarts (about 6.5 liters); also in verses 20 and 28 [e] *14* That is, probably about 2 quarts (about 2 liters) [f] *14* That is, probably about 1 1/4 quarts (about 1.2 liters)

## King James

27 But ye shall offer the burnt offering for a sweet savour unto the LORD; two young bullocks, one ram, seven lambs of the first year;

28 And their meat offering of flour mingled with oil, three tenth deals unto one bullock, two tenth deals unto one ram,

29 A several tenth deal unto one lamb, throughout the seven lambs;

30 *And* one kid of the goats, to make an atonement for you.

31 Ye shall offer *them* beside the continual burnt offering, and his meat offering, (they shall be unto you without blemish) and their drink offerings.

**29** AND IN the seventh month, on the first *day* of the month, ye shall have an holy convocation; ye shall do no servile work: it is a day of blowing the trumpets unto you.

2 And ye shall offer a burnt offering for a sweet savour unto the LORD; one young bullock, one ram, *and* seven lambs of the first year without blemish:

3 And their meat offering *shall be of* flour mingled with oil, three tenth deals for a bullock, *and* two tenth deals for a ram,

4 And one tenth deal for one lamb, throughout the seven lambs:

5 And one kid of the goats *for* a sin offering, to make an atonement for you:

6 Beside the burnt offering of the month, and his meat offering, and the daily burnt offering, and his meat offering, and their drink offerings, according unto their manner, for a sweet savour, a sacrifice made by fire unto the LORD.

7 ¶ And ye shall have on the tenth *day* of this seventh month an holy convocation; and ye shall afflict your souls: ye shall not do any work *therein:*

8 But ye shall offer a burnt offering unto the LORD *for* a sweet savour; one young bullock, one ram, *and* seven lambs of the first year; they shall be unto you without blemish:

9 And their meat offering *shall be of* flour mingled with oil, three tenth deals to a bullock, *and* two tenth deals to one ram,

10 A several tenth deal for one lamb, throughout the seven lambs:

11 One kid of the goats *for* a sin offering; beside the sin offering of atonement, and the continual burnt offering, and the meat offering of it, and their drink offerings.

12 ¶ And on the fifteenth day of the seventh month ye shall have an holy convocation; ye shall do no servile work, and ye shall keep a feast unto the LORD seven days:

13 And ye shall offer a burnt offering, a sacrifice made by fire, of a sweet savour unto the LORD; thirteen young bullocks, two rams, *and* fourteen lambs of the first year; they shall be without blemish:

14 And their meat offering *shall be of* flour mingled with oil, three tenth deals unto every bullock of the thirteen bullocks, two tenth deals to each ram of the two rams,

15 And a several tenth deal to each lamb of the fourteen lambs:

16 And one kid of the goats *for* a sin offering; beside the continual burnt offering, his meat offering, and his drink offering.

17 ¶ And on the second day *ye shall offer* twelve young bullocks, two rams, fourteen lambs of the first year without spot:

18 And their meat offering and their drink offerings for the bullocks, for the rams, and for the lambs, *shall be* according to their number, after the manner:

19 And one kid of the goats *for* a sin offering; beside the continual burnt offering, and the meat offering thereof, and their drink offerings.

20 ¶ And on the third day eleven bullocks, two rams, fourteen lambs of the first year without blemish;

21 And their meat offering and their drink offerings for the bullocks, for the rams, and for the lambs, *shall be* according to their number, after the manner:

## Amplified

27 But you shall offer the burnt offering for a sweet, pleasing *and* soothing fragrance to the Lord; two young bulls, one ram, seven male lambs a year old;

28 And their cereal offering of fine flour mixed with oil, three tenths of an ephah for each bull, two tenths for one ram,

29 A tenth for each of the seven male lambs;

30 And one male goat to make atonement for you.

31 You shall offer them in addition to the continual burnt offering and its cereal offering and their drink offerings. See that they are without blemish.

**29** ON THE first day of the seventh month [that is, on New Year's day of the civil year], you shall have a holy [summoned] assembly; you shall do no servile work; it is a day of blowing of trumpets for you [every one blowing who will, proclaiming that the glad New Year has come and that the great day of atonement and the feast of tabernacles are now approaching].

2 And you shall offer a burnt offering for a sweet *and* pleasing odor to the Lord: one young bull, one ram, and seven male lambs a year old without blemish.

3 Their cereal offering shall be of fine flour mixed with oil, three tenths of an ephah for a bull, two tenths for a ram,

4 And one tenth of an ephah for each of the seven lambs.

5 And one male goat for a sin offering, to make atonement for you.

6 These in addition to the burnt offering of the new moon, and its cereal offering, and the daily burnt offering and its cereal offering, and their drink offerings, according to the ordinance for them, for a pleasant *and* soothing fragrance, an offering by fire to the Lord.

7 And you shall have on the tenth day of this seventh month a holy [summoned] assembly; [it is the great day of atonement, a day of humiliation] and you shall humble *and* abase yourselves; you shall not do any work in it.

8 But you shall offer a burnt offering to the Lord for a sweet *and* soothing fragrance; one young bull, one ram, and seven male lambs a year old; see that they are without blemish.

9 And their cereal offering shall be of fine flour mixed with oil, three tenths of an ephah for the bull, two tenths for the one ram,

10 A tenth for each of the seven male lambs;

11 One male goat for a sin offering, in addition to the sin offering of atonement, and the continual burnt offering and its cereal offering, and their drink offerings.

12 And on the fifteenth day of the seventh month you shall have a holy [summoned] assembly; you shall do no servile work, and you shall keep a feast to the Lord seven days.

13 And you shall offer a burnt offering, an offering by fire, of a sweet *and* pleasing fragrance to the Lord; thirteen young bulls, two rams, and fourteen male lambs a year old; they shall be without blemish.

14 And their cereal offering shall be of fine flour mixed with oil, three tenths of an ephah for each of the thirteen bulls, two tenths for each of the two rams,

15 And a tenth part for each of the fourteen male lambs;

16 Also one male goat for a sin offering, in addition to the continual burnt offering, its cereal offering and its drink offering.

17 And on the second day you shall offer twelve young bulls, two rams, fourteen male lambs a year old without spot *or* blemish,

18 With the cereal offering and the drink offerings for the bulls, the rams, and the lambs, by number according to the ordinance;

19 Also one male goat for a sin offering, besides the continual burnt offering, its cereal offering, and their drink offerings.

20 And on the third day eleven bulls, two rams, fourteen male lambs a year old without blemish,

21 With their cereal and drink offerings for the bulls, the rams, and the lambs, by number, according to the ordinance.

## New American Standard

27'And you shall offer a burnt offering for a soothing aroma to the LORD, two young bulls, one ram, seven male lambs one year old,
28and their grain offering, fine flour mixed with oil, three-tenths *of an ephah* for each bull, two-tenths for the one ram,
29a tenth for each of the seven lambs,
30one male goat to make atonement for you.
31'Besides the continual burnt offering and its grain offering, you shall present *them* with their libations. They shall be without defect.

*Offerings of the Seventh Month*

**29** 'NOW IN the seventh month, on the first day of the month, you shall also have a holy convocation; you shall do no laborious work. It will be to you a day for blowing trumpets.
2'And you shall offer a burnt offering as a soothing aroma to the LORD: one bull, one ram, *and* seven male lambs one year old without defect;
3also their grain offering, fine flour mixed with oil, three-tenths *of an ephah* for the bull, two-tenths for the ram,
4and one-tenth for each of the seven lambs.
5'And *offer* one male goat for a sin offering, to make atonement for you,
6besides the burnt offering of the new moon, and its grain offering, and the continual burnt offering and its grain offering, and their libations, according to their ordinance, for a soothing aroma, an offering by fire to the LORD.
7¶ 'Then on the tenth day of this seventh month you shall have a holy convocation, and you shall humble yourselves; you shall not do any work.
8'And you shall present a burnt offering to the LORD *as* a soothing aroma: one bull, one ram, seven male lambs one year old, having them without defect;
9and their grain offering, fine flour mixed with oil, three-tenths *of an ephah* for the bull, two-tenths for the one ram,
10a tenth for each of the seven lambs;
11one male goat for a sin offering, besides the sin offering of atonement and the continual burnt offering and its grain offering, and their libations.
12¶ 'Then on the fifteenth day of the seventh month you shall have a holy convocation; you shall do no laborious work, and you shall observe a feast to the LORD for seven days.
13'And you shall present a burnt offering, an offering by fire as a soothing aroma to the LORD: thirteen bulls, two rams, fourteen male lambs one year old, which are without defect,
14and their grain offering, fine flour mixed with oil, three-tenths *of an ephah* for each of the thirteen bulls, two-tenths for each of the two rams,
15and a tenth for each of the fourteen lambs;
16and one male goat for a sin offering, besides the continual burnt offering, its grain offering and its libation.
17¶ 'Then on the second day: twelve bulls, two rams, fourteen male lambs one year old without defect;
18and their grain offering and their libations for the bulls, for the rams and for the lambs, by their number according to the ordinance;
19and one male goat for a sin offering, besides the continual burnt offering and its grain offering, and their libations.
20¶ 'Then on the third day: eleven bulls, two rams, fourteen male lambs one year old without defect;
21and their grain offering and their libations for the bulls, for the rams and for the lambs, by their number according to the ordinance;

## New International

young bulls, one ram and seven male lambs a year old as an aroma
pleasing to the LORD. 28With each bull there is to be a grain offering
of three-tenths of an ephah of fine flour mixed with oil; with the
ram, two-tenths; 29and with each of the seven lambs, one-tenth.
30Include one male goat to make atonement for you. 31Prepare
these together with their drink offerings, in addition to the regular
burnt offering and its grain offering. Be sure the animals are without defect.

*Feast of Trumpets*

**29** " 'ON THE first day of the seventh month hold a sacred
assembly and do no regular work. It is a day for you to
sound the trumpets. 2As an aroma pleasing to the LORD, prepare
a burnt offering of one young bull, one ram and seven male lambs
a year old, all without defect. 3With the bull prepare a grain offering of three-tenths of an ephah[a] of fine flour mixed with oil; with
the ram, two-tenths[b]; 4and with each of the seven lambs, one-
tenth.[c] 5Include one male goat as a sin offering to make atonement
for you. 6These are in addition to the monthly and daily burnt
offerings with their grain offerings and drink offerings as specified. They are offerings made to the LORD by fire—a pleasing
aroma.

*Day of Atonement*

7" 'On the tenth day of this seventh month hold a sacred assembly. You must deny yourselves[d] and do no work. 8Present as an
aroma pleasing to the LORD a burnt offering of one young bull, one
ram and seven male lambs a year old, all without defect. 9With the
bull prepare a grain offering of three-tenths of an ephah of fine
flour mixed with oil; with the ram, two-tenths; 10and with each of
the seven lambs, one-tenth. 11Include one male goat as a sin offering, in addition to the sin offering for atonement and the regular
burnt offering with its grain offering, and their drink offerings.

*Feast of Tabernacles*

12" 'On the fifteenth day of the seventh month, hold a sacred
assembly and do no regular work. Celebrate a festival to the LORD
for seven days. 13Present an offering made by fire as an aroma
pleasing to the LORD, a burnt offering of thirteen young bulls, two
rams and fourteen male lambs a year old, all without defect. 14With
each of the thirteen bulls prepare a grain offering of three-tenths
of an ephah of fine flour mixed with oil; with each of the two rams,
two-tenths; 15and with each of the fourteen lambs, one-tenth.
16Include one male goat as a sin offering, in addition to the regular
burnt offering with its grain offering and drink offering.
17" 'On the second day prepare twelve young bulls, two rams
and fourteen male lambs a year old, all without defect. 18With the
bulls, rams and lambs, prepare their grain offerings and drink
offerings according to the number specified. 19Include one male
goat as a sin offering, in addition to the regular burnt offering with
its grain offering, and their drink offerings.
20" 'On the third day prepare eleven bulls, two rams and fourteen male lambs a year old, all without defect. 21With the bulls,
rams and lambs, prepare their grain offerings and drink offerings
according to the number specified. 22Include one male goat as a sin

NIV [a] 3 That is, probably about 6 quarts (about 6.5 liters); also in verses 9 and 14 [b] 3 That is, probably about 4 quarts (about 4.5 liters); also in verses 9 and 14 [c] 4 That is, probably about 2 quarts (about 2 liters); also in verses 10 and 15 [d] 7 Or *must fast*

## King James

22And one goat *for* a sin offering; beside the continual burnt offering, and his meat offering, and his drink offering.
23¶ And on the fourth day ten bullocks, two rams, *and* fourteen lambs of the first year without blemish:
24Their meat offering and their drink offerings for the bullocks, for the rams, and for the lambs, *shall be* according to their number, after the manner:
25And one kid of the goats *for* a sin offering; beside the continual burnt offering, his meat offering, and his drink offering.
26¶ And on the fifth day nine bullocks, two rams, *and* fourteen lambs of the first year without spot:
27And their meat offering and their drink offerings for the bullocks, for the rams, and for the lambs, *shall be* according to their number, after the manner:
28And one goat *for* a sin offering; beside the continual burnt offering, and his meat offering, and his drink offering.
29¶ And on the sixth day eight bullocks, two rams, *and* fourteen lambs of the first year without blemish:
30And their meat offering and their drink offerings for the bullocks, for the rams, and for the lambs, *shall be* according to their number, after the manner:
31And one goat *for* a sin offering; beside the continual burnt offering, his meat offering, and his drink offering.
32¶ And on the seventh day seven bullocks, two rams, *and* fourteen lambs of the first year without blemish:
33And their meat offering and their drink offerings for the bullocks, for the rams, and for the lambs, *shall be* according to their number, after the manner:
34And one goat *for* a sin offering; beside the continual burnt offering, his meat offering, and his drink offering.
35¶ On the eighth day ye shall have a solemn assembly: ye shall do no servile work *therein:*
36But ye shall offer a burnt offering, a sacrifice made by fire, of a sweet savour unto the LORD: one bullock, one ram, seven lambs of the first year without blemish:
37Their meat offering and their drink offerings for the bullock, for the ram, and for the lambs, *shall be* according to their number, after the manner:
38And one goat *for* a sin offering; beside the continual burnt offering, and his meat offering, and his drink offering.
39These *things* ye shall do unto the LORD in your set feasts, beside your vows, and your freewill offerings, for your burnt offerings, and for your meat offerings, and for your drink offerings, and for your peace offerings.
40And Moses told the children of Israel according to all that the LORD commanded Moses.

**30** AND MOSES spake unto the heads of the tribes concerning the children of Israel, saying, This *is* the thing which the LORD hath commanded.
2If a man vow a vow unto the LORD, or swear an oath to bind his soul with a bond; he shall not break his word, he shall do according to all that proceedeth out of his mouth.
3If a woman also vow a vow unto the LORD, and bind *herself* by a bond, *being* in her father's house in her youth;
4And her father hear her vow, and her bond wherewith she hath bound her soul, and her father shall hold his peace at her: then all her vows shall stand, and every bond wherewith she hath bound her soul shall stand.
5But if her father disallow her in the day that he heareth; not any of her vows, or of her bonds wherewith she hath bound her soul, shall stand: and the LORD shall forgive her, because her father disallowed her.
6And if she had at all an husband, when she vowed, or uttered aught out of her lips, wherewith she bound her soul;

## Amplified

22And one male goat for a sin offering, besides the continual burnt offering, its cereal and drink offerings.
23On the fourth day ten bulls, two rams, and fourteen male lambs a year old without blemish,
24Their cereal offering and their drink offerings for the bulls, the rams, and the lambs, shall be by number, according to the ordinance.
25And one male goat for a sin offering, besides the continual burnt offering, its cereal and its drink offerings.
26And on the fifth day nine bulls, two rams, and fourteen male lambs a year old without spot *or* blemish.
27And their cereal and drink offerings for the bulls, the rams, and the lambs, by number, according to the ordinance.
28And one goat for a sin offering, besides the continual burnt offering, and its cereal and drink offerings.
29And on the sixth day eight bulls, two rams, and fourteen male lambs a year old without blemish.
30And their cereal offering and their drink offerings for the bulls, the rams, and the lambs, by number, according to the ordinance.
31And one goat for a sin offering; besides the continual burnt offering, its cereal and its drink offerings.
32And on the seventh day seven bulls, two rams, and fourteen male lambs a year old without blemish.
33And their cereal and drink offerings for the bulls, the rams, and the lambs, by number, according to the ordinance.
34And one male goat for a sin offering; besides the continual burnt offering, and its cereal and drink offerings.
35On the eighth day you shall have a solemn assembly; you shall do no servile work.
36You shall offer a burnt offering, an offering by fire, of a sweet *and* pleasing fragrance to the Lord: one bull, one ram, seven male lambs a year old without blemish.
37Their cereal and drink offerings for the bull, the ram, and the lambs, shall be by number, according to the ordinance.
38And one male goat for a sin offering, besides the continual burnt offering and its cereal and drink offerings.
39These you shall offer to the Lord at your appointed feasts, besides the offerings you have vowed and your freewill offerings, for your burnt offerings, cereal offerings, drink offerings, and peace offerings.
40And Moses told the Israelites all that the Lord commanded him.

**30** AND MOSES said to the heads *or* leaders of the tribes of Israel, This is the thing which the Lord has commanded:
2If a man vows a vow to the Lord, or swears an oath to bind himself by a pledge, he shall not break *and* profane his word; he shall do according to all that proceeds out of his mouth.
3Also when a woman vows a vow to the Lord, and binds herself by a pledge, being in her father's house in her youth,
4And her father hears her vow and her pledge with which she has bound herself, and he offers no objection; then all her vows shall stand, and every pledge with which she has bound herself shall stand.
5But if her father refuses to allow her [to carry out her vow] on the day that he hears about it, not any of her vows, or of her pledges with which she has bound herself, shall stand. And the Lord will forgive her, because her father refused to let her [carry out her purpose].
6And if she is married to a husband while her vows are upon her, or, she has bound herself by a rash utterance,

## New American Standard

22and one male goat for a sin offering, besides the continual
burnt offering and its grain offering and its libation.
23¶ 'Then on the fourth day: ten bulls, two rams, fourteen male
lambs one year old without defect;
24their grain offering and their libations for the bulls, for the
rams and for the lambs, by their number according to the ordinance;
25and one male goat for a sin offering, besides the continual
burnt offering, its grain offering and its libation.
26¶ 'Then on the fifth day: nine bulls, two rams, fourteen male
lambs one year old without defect;
27and their grain offering and their libations for the bulls, for the
rams and for the lambs, by their number according to the ordinance;
28and one male goat for a sin offering, besides the continual
burnt offering and its grain offering and its libation.
29¶ 'Then on the sixth day: eight bulls, two rams, fourteen male
lambs one year old without defect;
30and their grain offering and their libations for the bulls, for the
rams and for the lambs, by their number according to the ordinance;
31and one male goat for a sin offering, besides the continual
burnt offering, its grain offering and its libations.
32¶ 'Then on the seventh day: seven bulls, two rams, fourteen
male lambs one year old without defect;
33and their grain offering and their libations for the bulls, for the
rams and for the lambs, by their number according to the ordinance;
34and one male goat for a sin offering, besides the continual
burnt offering, its grain offering and its libation.
35¶ 'On the eighth day you shall have a solemn assembly; you
shall do no laborious work.
36'But you shall present a burnt offering, an offering by fire, as
a soothing aroma to the LORD: one bull, one ram, seven male lambs
one year old without defect;
37their grain offering and their libations for the bull, for the ram
and for the lambs, by their number according to the ordinance;
38and one male goat for a sin offering, besides the continual
burnt offering and its grain offering and its libation.
39¶ 'You shall present these to the LORD at your appointed
times, besides your votive offerings and your freewill offerings, for
your burnt offerings and for your grain offerings and for your
libations and for your peace offerings.' "
40And Moses spoke to the sons of Israel in accordance with all
that the LORD had commanded Moses.

*The Law of Vows*

**30** THEN MOSES spoke to the heads of the tribes of the sons
of Israel, saying, "This is the word which the LORD has
commanded.
2"If a man makes a vow to the LORD, or takes an oath to bind
himself with a binding obligation, he shall not violate his word; he
shall do according to all that proceeds out of his mouth.
3"Also if a woman makes a vow to the LORD, and binds herself
by an obligation in her father's house in her youth,
4and her father hears her vow and her obligation by which she
has bound herself, and her father says nothing to her, then all her
vows shall stand, and every obligation by which she has bound
herself shall stand.
5"But if her father should forbid her on the day he hears *of it*,
none of her vows or her obligations by which she has bound
herself shall stand; and the LORD will forgive her because her father
had forbidden her.
6¶ "However, if she should marry while under her vows or the
rash statement of her lips by which she has bound herself,

## New International

offering, in addition to the regular burnt offering with its grain
offering and drink offering.
23" 'On the fourth day prepare ten bulls, two rams and fourteen
male lambs a year old, all without defect. 24With the bulls, rams
and lambs, prepare their grain offerings and drink offerings according to the number specified. 25Include one male goat as a sin
offering, in addition to the regular burnt offering with its grain
offering and drink offering.
26" 'On the fifth day prepare nine bulls, two rams and fourteen
male lambs a year old, all without defect. 27With the bulls, rams
and lambs, prepare their grain offerings and drink offerings according to the number specified. 28Include one male goat as a sin
offering, in addition to the regular burnt offering with its grain
offering and drink offering.
29" 'On the sixth day prepare eight bulls, two rams and fourteen
male lambs a year old, all without defect. 30With the bulls, rams
and lambs, prepare their grain offerings and drink offerings according to the number specified. 31Include one male goat as a sin
offering, in addition to the regular burnt offering with its grain
offering and drink offering.
32" 'On the seventh day prepare seven bulls, two rams and
fourteen male lambs a year old, all without defect. 33With the bulls,
rams and lambs, prepare their grain offerings and drink offerings
according to the number specified. 34Include one male goat as a sin
offering, in addition to the regular burnt offering with its grain
offering and drink offering.
35" 'On the eighth day hold an assembly and do no regular
work. 36Present an offering made by fire as an aroma pleasing to
the LORD, a burnt offering of one bull, one ram and seven male
lambs a year old, all without defect. 37With the bull, the ram and
the lambs, prepare their grain offerings and drink offerings according to the number specified. 38Include one male goat as a sin
offering, in addition to the regular burnt offering with its grain
offering and drink offering.
39" 'In addition to what you vow and your freewill offerings,
prepare these for the LORD at your appointed feasts: your burnt
offerings, grain offerings, drink offerings and fellowship offerings.[a] ' "
40Moses told the Israelites all that the LORD commanded him.

*Vows*

**30** MOSES SAID to the heads of the tribes of Israel: "This is
what the LORD commands: 2When a man makes a vow to
the LORD or takes an oath to obligate himself by a pledge, he must
not break his word but must do everything he said.
3"When a young woman still living in her father's house makes
a vow to the LORD or obligates herself by a pledge 4and her father
hears about her vow or pledge but says nothing to her, then all her
vows and every pledge by which she obligated herself will stand.
5But if her father forbids her when he hears about it, none of her
vows or the pledges by which she obligated herself will stand; the
LORD will release her because her father has forbidden her.
6"If she marries after she makes a vow or after her lips utter a
rash promise by which she obligates herself 7and her husband

NIV [a] 39 Traditionally *peace offerings*

## King James

7And her husband heard *it*, and held his peace at her in the day that he heard *it:* then her vows shall stand, and her bonds wherewith she bound her soul shall stand.

8But if her husband disallowed her on the day that he heard *it;* then he shall make her vow which she vowed, and that which she uttered with her lips, wherewith she bound her soul, of none effect: and the LORD shall forgive her.

9But every vow of a widow, and of her that is divorced, wherewith they have bound their souls, shall stand against her.

10And if she vowed in her husband's house, or bound her soul by a bond with an oath;

11And her husband heard *it*, and held his peace at her, *and* disallowed her not: then all her vows shall stand, and every bond wherewith she bound her soul shall stand.

12But if her husband hath utterly made them void on the day he heard *them; then* whatsoever proceeded out of her lips concerning her vows, or concerning the bond of her soul, shall not stand: her husband hath made them void; and the LORD shall forgive her.

13Every vow, and every binding oath to afflict the soul, her husband may establish it, or her husband may make it void.

14But if her husband altogether hold his peace at her from day to day; then he establisheth all her vows, or all her bonds, which *are* upon her: he confirmeth them, because he held his peace at her in the day that he heard *them.*

15But if he shall any ways make them void after that he hath heard *them;* then he shall bear her iniquity.

16These *are* the statutes, which the LORD commanded Moses, between a man and his wife, between the father and his daughter, *being yet* in her youth in her father's house.

31 AND THE LORD spake unto Moses, saying,

2Avenge the children of Israel of the Midianites: afterward shalt thou be gathered unto thy people.

3And Moses spake unto the people, saying, Arm some of yourselves unto the war, and let them go against the Midianites, and avenge the LORD of Midian.

4Of every tribe a thousand, throughout all the tribes of Israel, shall ye send to the war.

5So there were delivered out of the thousands of Israel, a thousand of *every* tribe, twelve thousand armed for war.

6And Moses sent them to the war, a thousand of *every* tribe, them and Phinehas the son of Eleazar the priest, to the war, with the holy instruments, and the trumpets to blow in his hand.

7And they warred against the Midianites, as the LORD commanded Moses; and they slew all the males.

8And they slew the kings of Midian, beside the rest of them that were slain; *namely,* Evi, and Rekem, and Zur, and Hur, and Reba, five kings of Midian: Balaam also the son of Beor they slew with the sword.

9And the children of Israel took *all* the women of Midian captives, and their little ones, and took the spoil of all their cattle, and all their flocks, and all their goods.

10And they burnt all their cities wherein they dwelt, and all their goodly castles, with fire.

11And they took all the spoil, and all the prey, *both* of men and of beasts.

12And they brought the captives, and the prey, and the spoil, unto Moses, and Eleazar the priest, and unto the congregation of the children of Israel, unto the camp at the plains of Moab, which *are* by Jordan *near* Jericho.

13¶ And Moses, and Eleazar the priest, and all the princes of the congregation, went forth to meet them without the camp.

14And Moses was wroth with the officers of the host, *with* the captains over thousands, and captains over hundreds, which came from the battle.

## Amplified

7And her husband hears of it, and holds his peace concerning it on the day that he hears it, then her vows shall stand, and her pledge with which she bound herself shall stand.

8But if her husband refuses to allow her [to keep her vow or pledge] on the day that he hears of it, then he shall make void *and* annul her vow which is upon her, and the rash utterance of her lips by which she bound herself; and the Lord will forgive her.

9But the vow of a widow, or of a divorced woman, with which she has bound herself, shall stand against her.

10And if she vowed in her husband's house, or bound herself by a pledge with an oath,

11And her husband heard it, and did not oppose or prohibit her, then all her vows and every pledge with which she bound herself shall stand.

12But if her husband positively made them void on the day he heard them, then whatever proceeded out of her lips concerning her vows, or concerning her pledge of herself, shall not stand; her husband has annulled them, and the Lord will forgive her.

13Every vow, and every binding oath to humble *or* afflict herself, her husband may establish it, or her husband may annul it.

14But if her husband altogether holds his peace [concerning the matter] with her from day to day, then he establishes *and* confirms all her vows or all her pledges which are upon her; he establishes them because he said nothing to [restrain] her on the day he heard of them.

15But if he shall nullify them after he hears of them, then he shall be responsible for *and* bear her iniquity.

16These are the statutes which the Lord commanded Moses, between a man and his wife, and between a father and his daughter, while in her youth in her father's house.

31 THE LORD said to Moses,

2Avenge the Israelites on the Midianites; afterward you shall be gathered to your [departed] people.

3And Moses said to the people, Arm men from among you for the war, that they may go against Midian, and execute the Lord's vengeance on Midian [for seducing Israel]. [Num. 25:16-18.]

4From each of the tribes of Israel, you shall send 1,000 to the war.

5So there were provided out of the thousands of Israel, 1,000 from each tribe, 12,000 armed for war.

6And Moses sent them to the war, 1,000 from each tribe, together with Phinehas son of Eleazar the priest, with the [sacred] vessels of the sanctuary and the trumpets to blow the alarm in his hand.

7They fought with Midian, as the Lord commanded Moses, and slew every male,

8Including the five kings of Midian: Evi, Rekem, Zur, Hur, and Reba; also Balaam son of Beor they slew with the sword. [22:31-35; Neh. 13:1, 2.]

9And the Israelites took captive the women of Midian and their little ones, and all their cattle, their flocks, and their goods as booty.

10They burned all the cities in which they dwelt, and all their encampments.

11And they took all the spoil and all the prey, both of man and of beast.

12Then they brought the captives, the prey, and the spoil to Moses and Eleazar the priest, and to the congregation of the Israelites, at the camp on the plains of Moab by Jordan at Jericho.

13Moses and Eleazar the priest, and all the princes *or* leaders of the congregation went to meet them outside the camp.

14But Moses was angry with the officers of the army, the commanders of thousands and of hundreds, who served in the war.

## New American Standard

7and her husband hears of it and says nothing to her on the
day he hears *it*, then her vows shall stand and her obligations by
which she has bound herself shall stand.
8"But if on the day her husband hears *of it*, he forbids her, then
he shall annul her vow which she is under and the rash statement
of her lips by which she has bound herself; and the LORD will
forgive her.
9¶ "But the vow of a widow or of a divorced woman, everything by which she has bound herself, shall stand against her.
10"However, if she vowed in her husband's house, or bound
herself by an obligation with an oath,
11and her husband heard *it*, but said nothing to her *and* did not
forbid her, then all her vows shall stand, and every obligation by
which she bound herself shall stand.
12"But if her husband indeed annuls them on the day he hears
*them*, then whatever proceeds out of her lips concerning her vows
or concerning the obligation of herself, shall not stand; her husband has annulled them, and the LORD will forgive her.
13¶ "Every vow and every binding oath to humble herself, her
husband may confirm it or her husband may annul it.
14"But if her husband indeed says nothing to her from day to
day, then he confirms all her vows or all her obligations which are
on her; he has confirmed them, because he said nothing to her on
the day he heard them.
15"But if he indeed annuls them after he has heard them, then
he shall bear her guilt."
16¶ These are the statutes which the LORD commanded Moses,
*as* between a man and his wife, *and as* between a father and his
daughter, *while she is* in her youth in her father's house.

*The Slaughter of Midian*

**31** THEN THE LORD spoke to Moses, saying,
2"Take full vengeance for the sons of Israel on the Midianites; afterward you will be gathered to your people."
3And Moses spoke to the people, saying, "Arm men from
among you for the war, that they may go against Midian, to
execute the LORD's vengeance on Midian.
4"A thousand from each tribe of all the tribes of Israel you shall
send to the war."
5So there were furnished from the thousands of Israel, a thousand from each tribe, twelve thousand armed for war.
6And Moses sent them, a thousand from each tribe, to the war,
and Phinehas the son of Eleazar the priest, to the war with them,
and the holy vessels and the trumpets for the alarm in his hand.
7So they made war against Midian, just as the LORD had commanded Moses, and they killed every male.
8And they killed the kings of Midian along with the *rest of* their
slain: Evi and Rekem and Zur and Hur and Reba, the five kings
of Midian; they also killed Balaam the son of Beor with the sword.
9And the sons of Israel captured the women of Midian and
their little ones; and all their cattle and all their flocks and all their
goods, they plundered.
10Then they burned all their cities where they lived and all their
camps with fire.
11And they took all the spoil and all the prey, both of man and
of beast.
12And they brought the captives and the prey and the spoil to
Moses, and to Eleazar the priest and to the congregation of the
sons of Israel, to the camp at the plains of Moab, which are by the
Jordan opposite Jericho.
13¶ And Moses and Eleazar the priest and all the leaders of the
congregation went out to meet them outside the camp.
14And Moses was angry with the officers of the army, the
captains of thousands and the captains of hundreds, who had
come from service in the war.

## New International

hears about it but says nothing to her, then her vows or the pledges
by which she obligated herself will stand. 8But if her husband
forbids her when he hears about it, he nullifies the vow that
obligates her or the rash promise by which she obligates herself,
and the LORD will release her.
9"Any vow or obligation taken by a widow or divorced woman
will be binding on her.
10"If a woman living with her husband makes a vow or obligates herself by a pledge under oath 11and her husband hears
about it but says nothing to her and does not forbid her, then all
her vows or the pledges by which she obligated herself will stand.
12But if her husband nullifies them when he hears about them,
then none of the vows or pledges that came from her lips will
stand. Her husband has nullified them, and the LORD will release
her. 13Her husband may confirm or nullify any vow she makes or
any sworn pledge to deny herself. 14But if her husband says nothing to her about it from day to day, then he confirms all her vows
or the pledges binding on her. He confirms them by saying nothing to her when he hears about them. 15If, however, he nullifies
them some time after he hears about them, then he is responsible
for her guilt."
16These are the regulations the LORD gave Moses concerning
relationships between a man and his wife, and between a father
and his young daughter still living in his house.

*Vengeance on the Midianites*

**31** THE LORD said to Moses, 2"Take vengeance on the Midianites for the Israelites. After that, you will be gathered
to your people."
3So Moses said to the people, "Arm some of your men to go to
war against the Midianites and to carry out the LORD's vengeance
on them. 4Send into battle a thousand men from each of the tribes
of Israel." 5So twelve thousand men armed for battle, a thousand
from each tribe, were supplied from the clans of Israel. 6Moses sent
them into battle, a thousand from each tribe, along with Phinehas
son of Eleazar, the priest, who took with him articles from the
sanctuary and the trumpets for signaling.
7They fought against Midian, as the LORD commanded Moses,
and killed every man. 8Among their victims were Evi, Rekem, Zur,
Hur and Reba—the five kings of Midian. They also killed Balaam
son of Beor with the sword. 9The Israelites captured the Midianite
women and children and took all the Midianite herds, flocks and
goods as plunder. 10They burned all the towns where the Midianites had settled, as well as all their camps. 11They took all the
plunder and spoils, including the people and animals, 12and
brought the captives, spoils and plunder to Moses and Eleazar the
priest and the Israelite assembly at their camp on the plains of
Moab, by the Jordan across from Jericho.[a]
13Moses, Eleazar the priest and all the leaders of the community
went to meet them outside the camp. 14Moses was angry with the
officers of the army—the commanders of thousands and commanders of hundreds—who returned from the battle.

**NIV** [a] *12* Hebrew *Jordan of Jericho;* possibly an ancient name for the Jordan River

## King James

15 And Moses said unto them, Have ye saved all the women alive?

16 Behold, these caused the children of Israel, through the counsel of Balaam, to commit trespass against the LORD in the matter of Peor, and there was a plague among the congregation of the LORD.

17 Now therefore kill every male among the little ones, and kill every woman that hath known man by lying with him.

18 But all the women children, that have not known a man by lying with him, keep alive for yourselves.

19 And do ye abide without the camp seven days: whosoever hath killed any person, and whosoever hath touched any slain, purify *both* yourselves and your captives on the third day, and on the seventh day.

20 And purify all *your* raiment, and all that is made of skins, and all work of goats' *hair*, and all things made of wood.

21 ¶ And Eleazar the priest said unto the men of war which went to the battle, This *is* the ordinance of the law which the LORD commanded Moses;

22 Only the gold, and the silver, the brass, the iron, the tin, and the lead,

23 Every thing that may abide the fire, ye shall make *it* go through the fire, and it shall be clean: nevertheless it shall be purified with the water of separation: and all that abideth not the fire ye shall make go through the water.

24 And ye shall wash your clothes on the seventh day, and ye shall be clean, and afterward ye shall come into the camp.

25 ¶ And the LORD spake unto Moses, saying,

26 Take the sum of the prey that was taken, *both* of man and of beast, thou, and Eleazar the priest, and the chief fathers of the congregation:

27 And divide the prey into two parts; between them that took the war upon them, who went out to battle, and between all the congregation:

28 And levy a tribute unto the LORD of the men of war which went out to battle: one soul of five hundred, *both* of the persons, and of the beeves, and of the asses, and of the sheep:

29 Take *it* of their half, and give *it* unto Eleazar the priest, *for* an heave offering of the LORD.

30 And of the children of Israel's half, thou shalt take one portion of fifty, of the persons, of the beeves, of the asses, and of the flocks, of all manner of beasts, and give them unto the Levites, which keep the charge of the tabernacle of the LORD.

31 And Moses and Eleazar the priest did as the LORD commanded Moses.

32 And the booty, *being* the rest of the prey which the men of war had caught, was six hundred thousand and seventy thousand and five thousand sheep,

33 And threescore and twelve thousand beeves,

34 And threescore and one thousand asses,

35 And thirty and two thousand persons in all, of women that had not known man by lying with him.

36 And the half, *which was* the portion of them that went out to war, was in number three hundred thousand and seven and thirty thousand and five hundred sheep:

37 And the LORD's tribute of the sheep was six hundred and threescore and fifteen.

38 And the beeves *were* thirty and six thousand; of which the LORD's tribute *was* threescore and twelve.

39 And the asses *were* thirty thousand and five hundred; of which the LORD's tribute *was* threescore and one.

40 And the persons *were* sixteen thousand; of which the LORD's tribute *was* thirty and two persons.

41 And Moses gave the tribute, *which was* the LORD's heave offering, unto Eleazar the priest, as the LORD commanded Moses.

42 And of the children of Israel's half, which Moses divided from the men that warred,

## Amplified

15 And Moses said to them, Have you let all the women live?

16 Behold, these caused the Israelites, by the counsel of Balaam, to trespass *and* act treacherously against the Lord in the matter of Peor, and so a (smiting) plague came among the congregation of the Lord. [v. 8; 25:1-9.]

17 Now therefore, kill every male among the little ones, and kill every woman who is not a virgin.

18 But all the young girls who have not known man by lying with him, keep alive for yourselves.

19 Encamp outside the camp seven days; whoever has killed any person, and whoever has touched any slain, purify yourselves and your captives on the third day and on the seventh day.

20 You shall purify every garment, all that is made of skins, all work of goats' hair, and every article of wood.

21 And Eleazar the priest said to the men of war who had gone to battle, This is the statute of the law which the Lord has commanded Moses:

22 Only the gold, the silver, the bronze, the iron, the tin, and the lead,

23 Everything that can stand fire, you shall make go through fire, and it shall be clean. Nevertheless it shall also be purified with the water of impurity; and all that cannot stand fire [such as fabrics] you shall pass through water.

24 And you shall wash your clothes on the seventh day, and you shall be clean, then you shall come into the camp.

25 And the Lord said to Moses,

26 Take the count of the prey that was taken, both of man and of beast, you and Eleazar the priest and the heads of the fathers' houses of the congregation;

27 Divide the booty into two [equal] parts, between the warriors who went out to battle, and all the congregation.

28 And levy a tribute to the Lord from the warriors who went to battle, one out of 500 of the persons, the oxen, the donkeys, and the flocks.

29 Take [this tribute] from the warrior's half and give it to Eleazar the priest as an offering to the Lord.

30 And from the Israelites' half [of the booty] you shall take one out of every fifty of the persons, the oxen, the donkeys, the flocks, and of all livestock, and give them to the Levites who have charge of the tabernacle of the Lord.

31 And Moses and Eleazar the priest did as the Lord commanded Moses.

32 The prey, besides the booty which the men of war took, was: 675,000 sheep,

33 And 72,000 cattle,

34 And 61,000 donkeys,

35 And 32,000 persons in all, of women who were virgins.

36 And the half, the portion of those who went to war, was 337,500 sheep.

37 And the Lord's tribute of the sheep was 675.

38 The cattle were 36,000, of which the Lord's tribute was 72.

39 The donkeys were 30,500, of which the Lord's tribute was 61.

40 The persons were 16,000, of whom the Lord's tribute was 32 persons.

41 And Moses gave the tribute, which was the Lord's offering, to Eleazar the priest, as the Lord commanded Moses.

42 And the Israelites' half, Moses separated from that of the warriors;

## New American Standard

15And Moses said to them, "Have you spared all the women?
16"Behold, these caused the sons of Israel, through the counsel
of Balaam, to trespass against the LORD in the matter of Peor, so
the plague was among the congregation of the LORD.
17"Now therefore, kill every male among the little ones, and kill
every woman who has known man intimately.
18"But all the girls who have not known man intimately, spare
for yourselves.
19"And you, camp outside the camp seven days; whoever has
killed any person, and whoever has touched any slain, purify
yourselves, you and your captives, on the third day and on the
seventh day.
20"And you shall purify for yourselves every garment and every
article of leather and all the work of goats' *hair*, and all articles of
wood."
**21¶** Then Eleazar the priest said to the men of war who had gone
to battle, "This is the statute of the law which the LORD has commanded Moses:
22only the gold and the silver, the bronze, the iron, the tin and
the lead,
23everything that can stand the fire, you shall pass through the
fire, and it shall be clean, but it shall be purified with water for
impurity. But whatever cannot stand the fire you shall pass
through the water.
24"And you shall wash your clothes on the seventh day and be
clean, and afterward you may enter the camp."

*Division of the Booty*

**25¶** Then the LORD spoke to Moses, saying,
26"You and Eleazar the priest and the heads of the fathers'
*households* of the congregation, take a count of the booty that was
captured, both of man and of animal;
27and divide the booty between the warriors who went out to
battle and all the congregation.
28"And levy a tax for the LORD from the men of war who went
out to battle, one in five hundred of the persons and of the cattle
and of the donkeys and of the sheep;
29take it from their half and give it to Eleazar the priest, as an
offering to the LORD.
30"And from the sons of Israel's half, you shall take one drawn
out of every fifty of the persons, of the cattle, of the donkeys and
of the sheep, from all the animals, and give them to the Levites
who keep charge of the tabernacle of the LORD."
31And Moses and Eleazar the priest did just as the LORD had
commanded Moses.
**32¶** Now the booty that remained from the spoil which the men
of war had plundered was 675,000 sheep,
33and 72,000 cattle,
34and 61,000 donkeys,
35and of human beings, of the women who had not known man
intimately, all the persons were 32,000.
36And the half, the portion of those who went out to war, was
*as follows:* the number of sheep was 337,500,
37and the LORD's levy of the sheep was 675,
38and the cattle were 36,000, from which the LORD's levy was
72.
39And the donkeys were 30,500, from which the LORD's levy
was 61.
40And the human beings were 16,000, from whom the LORD's
levy was 32 persons.
41And Moses gave the levy *which was* the LORD's offering to
Eleazar the priest, just as the LORD had commanded Moses.
**42¶** As for the sons of Israel's half, which Moses separated from
the men who had gone to war—

## New International

15"Have you allowed all the women to live?" he asked them.
16"They were the ones who followed Balaam's advice and were the
means of turning the Israelites away from the LORD in what happened at Peor, so that a plague struck the LORD's people. 17Now
kill all the boys. And kill every woman who has slept with a man,
18but save for yourselves every girl who has never slept with a
man.
19"All of you who have killed anyone or touched anyone who
was killed must stay outside the camp seven days. On the third
and seventh days you must purify yourselves and your captives.
20Purify every garment as well as everything made of leather, goat
hair or wood."
21Then Eleazar the priest said to the soldiers who had gone into
battle, "This is the requirement of the law that the LORD gave
Moses: 22Gold, silver, bronze, iron, tin, lead 23and anything else
that can withstand fire must be put through the fire, and then it
will be clean. But it must also be purified with the water of cleansing. And whatever cannot withstand fire must be put through that
water. 24On the seventh day wash your clothes and you will be
clean. Then you may come into the camp."

*Dividing the Spoils*

25The LORD said to Moses, 26"You and Eleazar the priest and
the family heads of the community are to count all the people and
animals that were captured. 27Divide the spoils between the soldiers who took part in the battle and the rest of the community.
28From the soldiers who fought in the battle, set apart as tribute
for the LORD one out of every five hundred, whether persons,
cattle, donkeys, sheep or goats. 29Take this tribute from their half
share and give it to Eleazar the priest as the LORD's part. 30From
the Israelites' half, select one out of every fifty, whether persons,
cattle, donkeys, sheep, goats or other animals. Give them to the
Levites, who are responsible for the care of the LORD's tabernacle."
31So Moses and Eleazar the priest did as the LORD commanded
Moses.
32The plunder remaining from the spoils that the soldiers took
was 675,000 sheep, 3372,000 cattle, 3461,000 donkeys 35and 32,000
women who had never slept with a man.
36The half share of those who fought in the battle was:

337,500 sheep, 37of which the tribute for the LORD was 675;
3836,000 cattle, of which the tribute for the LORD was 72;
3930,500 donkeys, of which the tribute for the LORD was 61;
4016,000 people, of which the tribute for the LORD was 32.

41Moses gave the tribute to Eleazar the priest as the LORD's part,
as the LORD commanded Moses.
42The half belonging to the Israelites, which Moses set apart
from that of the fighting men— 43the community's half—was

## King James

43(Now the half *that pertained unto* the congregation was three hundred thousand and thirty thousand *and* seven thousand and five hundred sheep,

44And thirty and six thousand beeves,

45And thirty thousand asses and five hundred,

46And sixteen thousand persons;)

47Even of the children of Israel's half, Moses took one portion of fifty, *both* of man and of beast, and gave them unto the Levites, which kept the charge of the tabernacle of the LORD; as the LORD commanded Moses.

48¶ And the officers which *were* over thousands of the host, the captains of thousands, and captains of hundreds, came near unto Moses:

49And they said unto Moses, Thy servants have taken the sum of the men of war which *are* under our charge, and there lacketh not one man of us.

50We have therefore brought an oblation for the LORD, what every man hath gotten, of jewels of gold, chains, and bracelets, rings, earrings, and tablets, to make an atonement for our souls before the LORD.

51And Moses and Eleazar the priest took the gold of them, *even* all wrought jewels.

52And all the gold of the offering that they offered up to the LORD, of the captains of thousands, and of the captains of hundreds, was sixteen thousand seven hundred and fifty shekels.

53( *For* the men of war had taken spoil, every man for himself.)

54And Moses and Eleazar the priest took the gold of the captains of thousands and of hundreds, and brought it into the tabernacle of the congregation, *for* a memorial for the children of Israel before the LORD.

**32** NOW THE children of Reuben and the children of Gad had a very great multitude of cattle: and when they saw the land of Jazer, and the land of Gilead, that, behold, the place *was* a place for cattle;

2The children of Gad and the children of Reuben came and spake unto Moses, and to Eleazar the priest, and unto the princes of the congregation, saying,

3Ataroth, and Dibon, and Jazer, and Nimrah, and Heshbon, and Elealeh, and Shebam, and Nebo, and Beon,

4 *Even* the country which the LORD smote before the congregation of Israel, *is* a land for cattle, and thy servants have cattle:

5Wherefore, said they, if we have found grace in thy sight, let this land be given unto thy servants for a possession, *and* bring us not over Jordan.

6¶ And Moses said unto the children of Gad and to the children of Reuben, Shall your brethren go to war, and shall ye sit here?

7And wherefore discourage ye the heart of the children of Israel from going over into the land which the LORD hath given them?

8Thus did your fathers, when I sent them from Kadesh-barnea to see the land.

9For when they went up unto the valley of Eshcol, and saw the land, they discouraged the heart of the children of Israel, that they should not go into the land which the LORD had given them.

10And the LORD's anger was kindled the same time, and he sware, saying,

11Surely none of the men that came up out of Egypt, from twenty years old and upward, shall see the land which I sware unto Abraham, unto Isaac, and unto Jacob; because they have not wholly followed me:

12Save Caleb the son of Jephunneh the Kenezite, and Joshua the son of Nun: for they have wholly followed the LORD.

13And the LORD's anger was kindled against Israel, and he made them wander in the wilderness forty years, until all the generation, that had done evil in the sight of the LORD, was consumed.

## Amplified

43(Now the congregation's half was 337,500 sheep,

44And 36,000 cattle,

45And 30,500 donkeys,

46And 16,000 persons),

47Even of the Israelites' half, Moses took one of every 50, both of persons and of beasts, and gave them to the Levites, who had charge of the tabernacle of the Lord, as the Lord commanded Moses.

48And the officers who were over the thousands of the army, the commanders of thousands and hundreds, came to Moses.

49They told [him], Your servants have counted the warriors under our command, and not one man of us is missing.

50We have brought the Lord's offering, what each man obtained, articles of gold, armlets, bracelets, signet rings, earrings, neck ornaments, to make atonement for ourselves before the Lord.

51Moses and Eleazar the priest took the gold from them, all wrought articles.

52And all the gold of the offering that they offered to the Lord, from the commanders of thousands and of hundreds, was 16,750 shekels—

53For the men of war had taken booty, every man for himself.

54And Moses and Eleazar the priest received the gold from the commanders of thousands and of hundreds and brought it into the tent of meeting, as a memorial for the Israelites before the Lord.

**32** NOW THE sons of Reuben and of Gad had a very great multitude of cattle; and they saw the land of Jazer and the land of Gilead [on the east side of the Jordan], and behold, the place was one for cattle.

2So the sons of Gad and of Reuben came and said to Moses, Eleazar the priest, and the leaders of the congregation:

3[The country around] Ataroth, Dibon, Jazer, Nimrah, Heshbon, Elealeh, Sebam, Nebo, and Beon,

4The land the Lord smote before the congregation of Israel, is a land for cattle; and your servants have cattle.

5And they said, If we have found favor in your sight, let this land be given to your servants for a possession; do not take us over the Jordan.

6And Moses said to the sons of Gad and of Reuben, Shall your brethren go to war while you sit here?

7Why do you discourage the heart of the Israelites from going over into the land which the Lord has given them?

8Thus your fathers did when I sent them from Kadesh-barnea to see the land!

9For when they went up to the Valley of Eshcol, and saw the land, they discouraged the heart of the Israelites from going into the land the Lord had given them;

10And the Lord's anger was kindled on that day, and He swore, saying,

11Surely none of the men who came up out of Egypt, from twenty years old and upward, shall see the land which I swore to Abraham, to Isaac, and to Jacob, because they have not wholly followed Me,

12Except Caleb son of Jephunneh the Kenizzite, and Joshua son of Nun, for they have wholly followed the Lord.

13And the Lord's anger was kindled against Israel, and He made them wander in the wilderness for forty years, until all the generation that had done evil in the sight of the Lord was consumed.

## New American Standard

43now the congregation's half was 337,500 sheep,
44and 36,000 cattle,
45and 30,500 donkeys,
46and the human beings were 16,000—
47and from the sons of Israel's half, Moses took one drawn out
of every fifty, both of man and of animals, and gave them to the
Levites, who kept charge of the tabernacle of the LORD, just as the
LORD had commanded Moses.
48¶ Then the officers who were over the thousands of the army,
the captains of thousands and the captains of hundreds, approached Moses;
49and they said to Moses, "Your servants have taken a census
of men of war who are in our charge, and no man of us is missing.
50"So we have brought as an offering to the LORD what each
man found, articles of gold, armlets and bracelets, signet rings,
earrings and necklaces, to make atonement for ourselves before
the LORD."
51And Moses and Eleazar the priest took the gold from them,
all kinds of wrought articles.
52And all the gold of the offering which they offered up to the
LORD, from the captains of thousands and the captains of hundreds, was 16,750 shekels.
53The men of war had taken booty, every man for himself.
54So Moses and Eleazar the priest took the gold from the captains of thousands and of hundreds, and brought it to the tent of
meeting as a memorial for the sons of Israel before the LORD.

*Reuben and Gad Settle in Gilead*

32 NOW THE sons of Reuben and the sons of Gad had an
exceedingly large number of livestock. So when they saw
the land of Jazer and the land of Gilead, that it was indeed a place
suitable for livestock,
2the sons of Gad and the sons of Reuben came and spoke to
Moses and to Eleazar the priest and to the leaders of the congregation, saying,
3"Ataroth, Dibon, Jazer, Nimrah, Heshbon, Elealeh, Sebam,
Nebo and Beon,
4the land which the LORD conquered before the congregation
of Israel, is a land for livestock; and your servants have livestock."
5And they said, "If we have found favor in your sight, let this
land be given to your servants as a possession; do not take us
across the Jordan."
6¶ But Moses said to the sons of Gad and to the sons of Reuben,
"Shall your brothers go to war while you yourselves sit here?
7"Now why are you discouraging the sons of Israel from crossing over into the land which the LORD has given them?
8"This is what your fathers did when I sent them from Kadesh-
barnea to see the land.
9"For when they went up to the valley of Eshcol and saw the
land, they discouraged the sons of Israel so that they did not go
into the land which the LORD had given them.
10"So the LORD's anger burned in that day, and He swore,
saying,
11'None of the men who came up from Egypt, from twenty
years old and upward, shall see the land which I swore to Abraham, to Isaac and to Jacob; for they did not follow Me fully,
12except Caleb the son of Jephunneh the Kenizzite and Joshua
the son of Nun, for they have followed the LORD fully.'
13"So the LORD's anger burned against Israel, and He made
them wander in the wilderness forty years, until the entire generation of those who had done evil in the sight of the LORD was
destroyed.

## New International

337,500 sheep, 4436,000 cattle, 4530,500 donkeys 46and 16,000
people. 47From the Israelites' half, Moses selected one out of every
fifty persons and animals, as the LORD commanded him, and gave
them to the Levites, who were responsible for the care of the
LORD's tabernacle.
48Then the officers who were over the units of the army—the
commanders of thousands and commanders of hundreds—went
to Moses 49and said to him, "Your servants have counted the
soldiers under our command, and not one is missing. 50So we have
brought as an offering to the LORD the gold articles each of us
acquired—armlets, bracelets, signet rings, earrings and necklaces—to make atonement for ourselves before the LORD."
51Moses and Eleazar the priest accepted from them the gold—
all the crafted articles. 52All the gold from the commanders of
thousands and commanders of hundreds that Moses and Eleazar
presented as a gift to the LORD weighed 16,750 shekels.[a] 53Each
soldier had taken plunder for himself. 54Moses and Eleazar the
priest accepted the gold from the commanders of thousands and
commanders of hundreds and brought it into the Tent of Meeting
as a memorial for the Israelites before the LORD.

*The Transjordan Tribes*

32 THE REUBENITES and Gadites, who had very large herds
and flocks, saw that the lands of Jazer and Gilead were
suitable for livestock. 2So they came to Moses and Eleazar the
priest and to the leaders of the community, and said, 3"Ataroth,
Dibon, Jazer, Nimrah, Heshbon, Elealeh, Sebam, Nebo and Beon— 4the land the LORD subdued before the people of Israel—are
suitable for livestock, and your servants have livestock. 5If we have
found favor in your eyes," they said, "let this land be given to your
servants as our possession. Do not make us cross the Jordan."
6Moses said to the Gadites and Reubenites, "Shall your countrymen go to war while you sit here? 7Why do you discourage the
Israelites from going over into the land the LORD has given them?
8This is what your fathers did when I sent them from Kadesh
Barnea to look over the land. 9After they went up to the Valley of
Eshcol and viewed the land, they discouraged the Israelites from
entering the land the LORD had given them. 10The LORD's anger
was aroused that day and he swore this oath: 11'Because they have
not followed me wholeheartedly, not one of the men twenty years
old or more who came up out of Egypt will see the land I promised
on oath to Abraham, Isaac and Jacob— 12not one except Caleb son
of Jephunneh the Kenizzite and Joshua son of Nun, for they followed the LORD wholeheartedly.' 13The LORD's anger burned
against Israel and he made them wander in the desert forty years,
until the whole generation of those who had done evil in his sight
was gone.

NIV [a] 52 That is, about 420 pounds (about 190 kilograms)

## King James

14And, behold, ye are risen up in your fathers' stead, an increase of sinful men, to augment yet the fierce anger of the LORD toward Israel.

15For if ye turn away from after him, he will yet again leave them in the wilderness; and ye shall destroy all this people.

16¶ And they came near unto him, and said, We will build sheepfolds here for our cattle, and cities for our little ones:

17But we ourselves will go ready armed before the children of Israel, until we have brought them unto their place: and our little ones shall dwell in the fenced cities because of the inhabitants of the land.

18We will not return unto our houses, until the children of Israel have inherited every man his inheritance.

19For we will not inherit with them on yonder side Jordan, or forward; because our inheritance is fallen to us on this side Jordan eastward.

20¶ And Moses said unto them, If ye will do this thing, if ye will go armed before the LORD to war,

21And will go all of you armed over Jordan before the LORD, until he hath driven out his enemies from before him,

22And the land be subdued before the LORD: then afterward ye shall return, and be guiltless before the LORD, and before Israel; and this land shall be your possession before the LORD.

23But if ye will not do so, behold, ye have sinned against the LORD: and be sure your sin will find you out.

24Build you cities for your little ones, and folds for your sheep; and do that which hath proceeded out of your mouth.

25And the children of Gad and the children of Reuben spake unto Moses, saying, Thy servants will do as my lord commandeth.

26Our little ones, our wives, our flocks, and all our cattle, shall be there in the cities of Gilead:

27But thy servants will pass over, every man armed for war, before the LORD to battle, as my lord saith.

28So concerning them Moses commanded Eleazar the priest, and Joshua the son of Nun, and the chief fathers of the tribes of the children of Israel:

29And Moses said unto them, If the children of Gad and the children of Reuben will pass with you over Jordan, every man armed to battle, before the LORD, and the land shall be subdued before you; then ye shall give them the land of Gilead for a possession:

30But if they will not pass over with you armed, they shall have possessions among you in the land of Canaan.

31And the children of Gad and the children of Reuben answered, saying, As the LORD hath said unto thy servants, so will we do.

32We will pass over armed before the LORD into the land of Canaan, that the possession of our inheritance on this side Jordan *may be* ours.

33And Moses gave unto them, *even* to the children of Gad, and to the children of Reuben, and unto half the tribe of Manasseh the son of Joseph, the kingdom of Sihon king of the Amorites, and the kingdom of Og king of Bashan, the land, with the cities thereof in the coasts, *even* the cities of the country round about.

34¶ And the children of Gad built Dibon, and Ataroth, and Aroer,

35And Atroth, Shophan, and Jaazer, and Jogbehah,

36And Beth-nimrah, and Beth-haran, fenced cities: and folds for sheep.

37And the children of Reuben built Heshbon, and Elealeh, and Kirjathaim,

38And Nebo and Baal-meon, (their names being changed,) and Shibmah: and gave other names unto the cities which they builded.

39And the children of Machir the son of Manasseh went to Gilead, and took it, and dispossessed the Amorite which *was* in it.

40And Moses gave Gilead unto Machir the son of Manasseh; and he dwelt therein.

41And Jair the son of Manasseh went and took the small towns thereof, and called them Havoth-jair.

## Amplified

14And behold, you are risen up in your fathers' stead, a brood of sinful men, to increase still more the fierce anger of the Lord against Israel.

15For if you turn from following Him, He will again abandon them in the wilderness, and you will destroy all this people.

16But they came near to him, and said, We will build sheepfolds here for our flocks, and walled settlements for our little ones,

17But we will be ready armed to go before the Israelites, until we have brought them to their place. Our little ones shall dwell in the fortified settlements because of the people of the land.

18We will not return to our homes until the Israelites have inherited every man his inheritance.

19For we will not inherit with them on the [west] side of Jordan and beyond, because our inheritance is fallen to us on this side of Jordan eastward.

20Moses replied, If you will do as you say, going armed before the Lord to war,

21And every armed man of you will pass over Jordan before the Lord, until He has driven out His enemies before Him,

22And the land is subdued before the Lord; then afterward you shall return and be guiltless [in this matter] before the Lord and before Israel, and this land shall be your possession before the Lord.

23But if you will not do so, behold, you have sinned against the Lord; and be sure your sin will find you out.

24Build settlements for your little ones, and folds for your sheep; and do that of which you have spoken.

25And the sons of Gad and of Reuben said to Moses, Your servants will do as my lord commands.

26Our little ones, our wives, our flocks, and all our cattle, shall be there in the cities of Gilead;

27But your servants will pass over, every man armed for war, before the Lord to battle, as my lord says.

28So Moses gave command concerning them to Eleazar the priest and Joshua son of Nun and the heads of the fathers' houses of the tribes of Israel;

29And Moses said to them, If the sons of Gad and Reuben will pass with you over Jordan, every man armed to battle before the Lord, and the land shall be subdued before you, then you shall give them the land of Gilead for a possession;

30But if they will not pass over with you armed, they shall have possessions among you in the land of Canaan.

31The sons of Gad and Reuben answered, As the Lord has said to your servants, so will we do.

32We will pass over armed before the Lord into the land of Canaan, that the possession of our inheritance on this side Jordan may be ours.

33Moses gave to them, to the sons of Gad and of Reuben and to half the tribe of Manasseh son of Joseph, the kingdom of Sihon king of the Amorites and the kingdom of Og king of Bashan, the land with its cities and their territories, even the cities round about the country.

34And the sons of Gad built Dibon, Ataroth, Aroer,

35Atroth-shophan, Jazer, Jogbehah,

36Beth-nimrah, and Beth-haran, fortified cities, and folds for sheep.

37And the sons of Reuben built Heshbon, Elealeh, Kiriathaim,

38Nebo, and Baal-meon (their names to be changed), and Shibmah; and they gave other names to the cities they built.

39And the sons of Machir son of Manasseh went to Gilead, and took it, and dispossessed the Amorites who were in it.

40And Moses gave Gilead to Machir son of Manasseh, and he settled in it.

41Jair son of Manasseh took their villages, and called them Havvoth-jair.

## New American Standard

14"Now behold, you have risen up in your fathers' place, a brood of sinful men, to add still more to the burning anger of the LORD against Israel.

15"For if you turn away from following Him, He will once more abandon them in the wilderness; and you will destroy all these people."

16¶ Then they came near to him and said, "We will build here sheepfolds for our livestock and cities for our little ones;

17but we ourselves will be armed ready *to go* before the sons of Israel, until we have brought them to their place, while our little ones live in the fortified cities because of the inhabitants of the land.

18"We will not return to our homes until every one of the sons of Israel has possessed his inheritance.

19"For we will not have an inheritance with them on the other side of the Jordan and beyond, because our inheritance has fallen to us on this side of the Jordan toward the east."

20¶ So Moses said to them, "If you will do this, if you will arm yourselves before the LORD for the war,

21and all of you armed men cross over the Jordan before the LORD until He has driven His enemies out from before Him,

22and the land is subdued before the LORD, then afterward you shall return and be free of obligation toward the LORD and toward Israel, and this land shall be yours for a possession before the LORD.

23"But if you will not do so, behold, you have sinned against the LORD, and be sure your sin will find you out.

24"Build yourselves cities for your little ones, and sheepfolds for your sheep; and do what you have promised."

25And the sons of Gad and the sons of Reuben spoke to Moses, saying, "Your servants will do just as my lord commands.

26"Our little ones, our wives, our livestock and all our cattle shall remain there in the cities of Gilead;

27while your servants, everyone who is armed for war, will cross over in the presence of the LORD to battle, just as my lord says."

28¶ So Moses gave command concerning them to Eleazar the priest, and to Joshua the son of Nun, and to the heads of the fathers' *households* of the tribes of the sons of Israel.

29And Moses said to them, "If the sons of Gad and the sons of Reuben, everyone who is armed for battle, will cross with you over the Jordan in the presence of the LORD, and the land will be subdued before you, then you shall give them the land of Gilead for a possession;

30but if they will not cross over with you armed, they shall have possessions among you in the land of Canaan."

31And the sons of Gad and the sons of Reuben answered, saying, "As the LORD has said to your servants, so we will do.

32"We ourselves will cross over armed in the presence of the LORD into the land of Canaan, and the possession of our inheritance *shall remain* with us across the Jordan."

33¶ So Moses gave to them, to the sons of Gad and to the sons of Reuben and to the half-tribe of Joseph's son Manasseh, the kingdom of Sihon, king of the Amorites and the kingdom of Og, the king of Bashan, the land with its cities with *their* territories, the cities of the surrounding land.

34And the sons of Gad built Dibon and Ataroth and Aroer,

35and Atroth-shophan and Jazer and Jogbehah,

36and Beth-nimrah and Beth-haran as fortified cities, and sheepfolds for sheep.

37And the sons of Reuben built Heshbon and Elealeh and Kiriathaim,

38and Nebo and Baal-meon— *their* names being changed—and Sibmah, and they gave *other* names to the cities which they built.

39And the sons of Machir the son of Manasseh went to Gilead and took it, and dispossessed the Amorites who were in it.

40So Moses gave Gilead to Machir the son of Manasseh, and he lived in it.

41And Jair the son of Manasseh went and took its towns, and called them Havvoth-jair.

## New International

14"And here you are, a brood of sinners, standing in the place
of your fathers and making the LORD even more angry with Israel.
15If you turn away from following him, he will again leave all this
people in the desert, and you will be the cause of their destruction."

16Then they came up to him and said, "We would like to build
pens here for our livestock and cities for our women and children.
17But we are ready to arm ourselves and go ahead of the Israelites
until we have brought them to their place. Meanwhile our women
and children will live in fortified cities, for protection from the
inhabitants of the land. 18We will not return to our homes until
every Israelite has received his inheritance. 19We will not receive
any inheritance with them on the other side of the Jordan, because
our inheritance has come to us on the east side of the Jordan."

20Then Moses said to them, "If you will do this—if you will arm
yourselves before the LORD for battle, 21and if all of you will go
armed over the Jordan before the LORD until he has driven his
enemies out before him— 22then when the land is subdued before
the LORD, you may return and be free from your obligation to the
LORD and to Israel. And this land will be your possession before
the LORD.

23"But if you fail to do this, you will be sinning against the LORD;
and you may be sure that your sin will find you out. 24Build cities
for your women and children, and pens for your flocks, but do
what you have promised."

25The Gadites and Reubenites said to Moses, "We your servants
will do as our lord commands. 26Our children and wives, our
flocks and herds will remain here in the cities of Gilead. 27But your
servants, every man armed for battle, will cross over to fight before
the LORD, just as our lord says."

28Then Moses gave orders about them to Eleazar the priest and
Joshua son of Nun and to the family heads of the Israelite tribes.
29He said to them, "If the Gadites and Reubenites, every man
armed for battle, cross over the Jordan with you before the LORD,
then when the land is subdued before you, give them the land of
Gilead as their possession. 30But if they do not cross over with you
armed, they must accept their possession with you in Canaan."

31The Gadites and Reubenites answered, "Your servants will
do what the LORD has said. 32We will cross over before the LORD
into Canaan armed, but the property we inherit will be on this side
of the Jordan."

33Then Moses gave to the Gadites, the Reubenites and the
half-tribe of Manasseh son of Joseph the kingdom of Sihon king
of the Amorites and the kingdom of Og king of Bashan—the whole
land with its cities and the territory around them.

34The Gadites built up Dibon, Ataroth, Aroer, 35Atroth Shophan, Jazer, Jogbehah, 36Beth Nimrah and Beth Haran as fortified
cities, and built pens for their flocks. 37And the Reubenites rebuilt
Heshbon, Elealeh and Kiriathaim, 38as well as Nebo and Baal
Meon (these names were changed) and Sibmah. They gave names
to the cities they rebuilt.

39The descendants of Makir son of Manasseh went to Gilead,
captured it and drove out the Amorites who were there. 40So
Moses gave Gilead to the Makirites, the descendants of Manasseh,
and they settled there. 41Jair, a descendant of Manasseh, captured
their settlements and called them Havvoth Jair.[a] 42And Nobah

**NIV** [a] 41 Or *them the settlements of Jair*

## King James

42 And Nobah went and took Kenath, and the villages thereof, and called it Nobah, after his own name.

# 33

THESE *ARE* the journeys of the children of Israel, which went forth out of the land of Egypt with their armies under the hand of Moses and Aaron.

2 And Moses wrote their goings out according to their journeys by the commandment of the LORD: and these *are* their journeys according to their goings out.

3 And they departed from Rameses in the first month, on the fifteenth day of the first month; on the morrow after the passover the children of Israel went out with an high hand in the sight of all the Egyptians.

4 For the Egyptians buried all *their* firstborn, which the LORD had smitten among them: upon their gods also the LORD executed judgments.

5 And the children of Israel removed from Rameses, and pitched in Succoth.

6 And they departed from Succoth, and pitched in Etham, which *is* in the edge of the wilderness.

7 And they removed from Etham, and turned again unto Pi-hahiroth, which *is* before Baal-zephon: and they pitched before Migdol.

8 And they departed from before Pi-hahiroth, and passed through the midst of the sea into the wilderness, and went three days' journey in the wilderness of Etham, and pitched in Marah.

9 And they removed from Marah, and came unto Elim: and in Elim *were* twelve fountains of water, and threescore and ten palm trees; and they pitched there.

10 And they removed from Elim, and encamped by the Red sea.

11 And they removed from the Red sea, and encamped in the wilderness of Sin.

12 And they took their journey out of the wilderness of Sin, and encamped in Dophkah.

13 And they departed from Dophkah, and encamped in Alush.

14 And they removed from Alush, and encamped at Rephidim, where was no water for the people to drink.

15 And they departed from Rephidim, and pitched in the wilderness of Sinai.

16 And they removed from the desert of Sinai, and pitched at Kibroth-hattaavah.

17 And they departed from Kibroth-hattaavah, and encamped at Hazeroth.

18 And they departed from Hazeroth, and pitched in Rithmah.

19 And they departed from Rithmah, and pitched at Rimmon-parez.

20 And they departed from Rimmon-parez, and pitched in Libnah.

21 And they removed from Libnah, and pitched at Rissah.

22 And they journeyed from Rissah, and pitched in Kehelathah.

23 And they went from Kehelathah, and pitched in mount Shapher.

24 And they removed from mount Shapher, and encamped in Haradah.

25 And they removed from Haradah, and pitched in Makheloth.

26 And they removed from Makheloth, and encamped at Tahath.

27 And they departed from Tahath, and pitched at Tarah.

28 And they removed from Tarah, and pitched in Mithcah.

29 And they went from Mithcah, and pitched in Hashmonah.

30 And they departed from Hashmonah, and encamped at Moseroth.

31 And they departed from Moseroth, and pitched in Bene-jaakan.

## Amplified

42 And Nobah took Kenath and its villages, and called it Nobah, after his own name.

# 33

THESE ARE the stages of the journeys of the Israelites, by which they went out of the land of Egypt by their hosts under the leadership of Moses and Aaron.

2 Moses recorded their starting places, as the Lord commanded, stage by stage; and these are their journeying stages from their starting places.

3 They set out from Rameses, the fifteenth day of the first month; on the day after the passover the Israelites went out [of Egypt] with a high hand *and* triumphantly in the sight of all the Egyptians,

4 While the Egyptians were burying all their firstborn whom the Lord had struck down among them; upon their gods also the Lord executed judgments.

5 The Israelites set out from Rameses, and encamped in Succoth.

6 And they departed from Succoth, and encamped in Etham, which is at the edge of the wilderness.

7 They set out from Etham, and turned back to Pi-hahiroth, east of Baal-zephon; and they encamped before Migdol.

8 And they journeyed from before Pi-hahiroth, and passed through the midst of the [Red] sea into the wilderness; and they went a three days' journey in the wilderness of Etham, and encamped at Marah.

9 They journeyed from Marah, and came to Elim; at Elim were twelve springs of water, and seventy palm trees; and they encamped there.

10 They set out from Elim, and encamped by the Red Sea.

11 They journeyed from the Red Sea, and encamped in the wilderness of Sin.

12 And they traveled on from the wilderness of Sin, and encamped at Dophkah.

13 And they departed from Dophkah, and encamped at Alush.

14 And they set out from Alush, and encamped at Rephidim, where there was no water for the people to drink.

15 And they departed from Rephidim, and encamped in the wilderness of Sinai.

16 And they journeyed from the desert of Sinai, and encamped at Kibroth-hattaavah.

17 And they traveled on from Kibroth-hattaavah, and encamped at Hazeroth.

18 And they journeyed from Hazeroth, and encamped at Rithmah.

19 And they departed from Rithmah, and encamped at Rimmon-perez.

20 And they departed from Rimmon-perez, and encamped at Libnah.

21 And they removed from Libnah, and encamped at Rissah.

22 And they journeyed from Rissah, and encamped at Kehelathah.

23 And they went from Kehelathah, and encamped at Mount Shepher.

24 And they removed from Mount Shepher, and encamped at Haradah.

25 And they set out from Haradah, and encamped at Makheloth.

26 And they removed from Makheloth, and encamped at Tahath.

27 And they departed from Tahath, and encamped at Terah.

28 And they removed from Terah, and encamped at Mithkah.

29 And they set out from Mithkah, and encamped at Hashmonah.

30 And they traveled on from Hashmonah, and encamped at Moseroth.

31 And they journeyed from Moseroth, and pitched in Bene-jaakan.

## New American Standard

42 And Nobah went and took Kenath and its villages, and called
it Nobah after his own name.

*Review of the Journey from Egypt to Jordan*

**33** THESE ARE the journeys of the sons of Israel, by which
they came out from the land of Egypt by their armies,
under the leadership of Moses and Aaron.
2 And Moses recorded their starting places according to their
journeys by the command of the LORD, and these are their journeys according to their starting places.
3 And they journeyed from Rameses in the first month, on the
fifteenth day of the first month; on the next day after the Passover
the sons of Israel started out boldly in the sight of all the Egyptians,
4 while the Egyptians were burying all their first-born whom
the LORD had struck down among them. The LORD had also executed judgments on their gods.
5 ¶ Then the sons of Israel journeyed from Rameses, and
camped in Succoth.
6 And they journeyed from Succoth, and camped in Etham,
which is on the edge of the wilderness.
7 And they journeyed from Etham, and turned back to Pi-
hahiroth, which faces Baal-zephon; and they camped before Migdol.
8 And they journeyed from before Hahiroth, and passed
through the midst of the sea into the wilderness; and they went
three days' journey in the wilderness of Etham, and camped at
Marah.
9 And they journeyed from Marah, and came to Elim; and in
Elim there were twelve springs of water and seventy palm trees;
and they camped there.
10 And they journeyed from Elim, and camped by the Red Sea.
11 And they journeyed from the Red Sea, and camped in the
wilderness of Sin.
12 And they journeyed from the wilderness of Sin, and camped
at Dophkah.
13 And they journeyed from Dophkah, and camped at Alush.
14 And they journeyed from Alush, and camped at Rephidim;
now it was there that the people had no water to drink.
15 And they journeyed from Rephidim, and camped in the wilderness of Sinai.
16 And they journeyed from the wilderness of Sinai, and
camped at Kibroth-hattaavah.
17 ¶ And they journeyed from Kibroth-hattaavah, and camped
at Hazeroth.
18 And they journeyed from Hazeroth, and camped at Rithmah.
19 And they journeyed from Rithmah, and camped at Rimmon-
perez.
20 And they journeyed from Rimmon-perez, and camped at Libnah.
21 And they journeyed from Libnah, and camped at Rissah.
22 And they journeyed from Rissah, and camped in Kehelathah.
23 And they journeyed from Kehelathah, and camped at Mount
Shepher.
24 And they journeyed from Mount Shepher, and camped at
Haradah.
25 And they journeyed from Haradah, and camped at Makheloth.
26 And they journeyed from Makheloth, and camped at Tahath.
27 And they journeyed from Tahath, and camped at Terah.
28 And they journeyed from Terah, and camped at Mithkah.
29 And they journeyed from Mithkah, and camped at Hashmonah.
30 And they journeyed from Hashmonah, and camped at Moseroth.
31 And they journeyed from Moseroth, and camped at Bene-jaakan.

## New International

captured Kenath and its surrounding settlements and called it
Nobah after himself.

*Stages in Israel's Journey*

**33** HERE ARE the stages in the journey of the Israelites when
they came out of Egypt by divisions under the leadership
of Moses and Aaron. 2 At the LORD's command Moses recorded the
stages in their journey. This is their journey by stages:

3 The Israelites set out from Rameses on the fifteenth day
of the first month, the day after the Passover. They marched
out boldly in full view of all the Egyptians, 4 who were burying
all their firstborn, whom the LORD had struck down among
them; for the LORD had brought judgment on their gods.
5 The Israelites left Rameses and camped at Succoth.
6 They left Succoth and camped at Etham, on the edge of
the desert.
7 They left Etham, turned back to Pi Hahiroth, to the east
of Baal Zephon, and camped near Migdol.
8 They left Pi Hahiroth[a] and passed through the sea into
the desert, and when they had traveled for three days in the
Desert of Etham, they camped at Marah.
9 They left Marah and went to Elim, where there were
twelve springs and seventy palm trees, and they camped
there.
10 They left Elim and camped by the Red Sea.[b]
11 They left the Red Sea and camped in the Desert of Sin.
12 They left the Desert of Sin and camped at Dophkah.
13 They left Dophkah and camped at Alush.
14 They left Alush and camped at Rephidim, where there
was no water for the people to drink.
15 They left Rephidim and camped in the Desert of Sinai.
16 They left the Desert of Sinai and camped at Kibroth Hattaavah.
17 They left Kibroth Hattaavah and camped at Hazeroth.
18 They left Hazeroth and camped at Rithmah.
19 They left Rithmah and camped at Rimmon Perez.
20 They left Rimmon Perez and camped at Libnah.
21 They left Libnah and camped at Rissah.
22 They left Rissah and camped at Kehelathah.
23 They left Kehelathah and camped at Mount Shepher.
24 They left Mount Shepher and camped at Haradah.
25 They left Haradah and camped at Makheloth.
26 They left Makheloth and camped at Tahath.
27 They left Tahath and camped at Terah.
28 They left Terah and camped at Mithcah.
29 They left Mithcah and camped at Hashmonah.
30 They left Hashmonah and camped at Moseroth.
31 They left Moseroth and camped at Bene Jaakan.

**NIV** [a] *8* Many manuscripts of the Masoretic Text, Samaritan Pentateuch and Vulgate; most manuscripts of the Masoretic Text *left from before Hahiroth*
[b] *10* Hebrew *Yam Suph;* that is, Sea of Reeds; also in verse 11

## King James

32And they removed from Bene-jaakan, and encamped at Hor-hagidgad.

33And they went from Hor-hagidgad, and pitched in Jotbathah.

34And they removed from Jotbathah, and encamped at Ebronah.

35And they departed from Ebronah, and encamped at Ezion-geber.

36And they removed from Ezion-geber, and pitched in the wilderness of Zin, which *is* Kadesh.

37And they removed from Kadesh, and pitched in mount Hor, in the edge of the land of Edom.

38And Aaron the priest went up into mount Hor at the commandment of the LORD, and died there, in the fortieth year after the children of Israel were come out of the land of Egypt, in the first *day* of the fifth month.

39And Aaron *was* an hundred and twenty and three years old when he died in mount Hor.

40And king Arad the Canaanite, which dwelt in the south in the land of Canaan, heard of the coming of the children of Israel.

41And they departed from mount Hor, and pitched in Zalmonah.

42And they departed from Zalmonah, and pitched in Punon.

43And they departed from Punon, and pitched in Oboth.

44And they departed from Oboth, and pitched in Ije-abarim, in the border of Moab.

45And they departed from Iim, and pitched in Dibon-gad.

46And they removed from Dibon-gad, and encamped in Almon-diblathaim.

47And they removed from Almon-diblathaim, and pitched in the mountains of Abarim, before Nebo.

48And they departed from the mountains of Abarim, and pitched in the plains of Moab by Jordan *near* Jericho.

49And they pitched by Jordan, from Beth-jeshimoth *even* unto Abel-shittim in the plains of Moab.

50¶ And the LORD spake unto Moses in the plains of Moab by Jordan *near* Jericho, saying,

51Speak unto the children of Israel, and say unto them, When ye are passed over Jordan into the land of Canaan;

52Then ye shall drive out all the inhabitants of the land from before you, and destroy all their pictures, and destroy all their molten images, and quite pluck down all their high places:

53And ye shall dispossess *the inhabitants of* the land, and dwell therein: for I have given you the land to possess it.

54And ye shall divide the land by lot for an inheritance among your families: *and* to the more ye shall give the more inheritance, and to the fewer ye shall give the less inheritance: every man's *inheritance* shall be in the place where his lot falleth; according to the tribes of your fathers ye shall inherit.

55But if ye will not drive out the inhabitants of the land from before you; then it shall come to pass, that those which ye let remain of them *shall be* pricks in your eyes, and thorns in your sides, and shall vex you in the land wherein ye dwell.

56Moreover it shall come to pass, *that* I shall do unto you, as I thought to do unto them.

**34** AND THE LORD spake unto Moses, saying,

2Command the children of Israel, and say unto them, When ye come into the land of Canaan; (this *is* the land that shall fall unto you for an inheritance, *even* the land of Canaan with the coasts thereof:)

3Then your south quarter shall be from the wilderness of Zin along by the coast of Edom, and your south border shall be the outmost coast of the salt sea eastward:

## Amplified

32And they set out from Bene-jaakan, and encamped at Hor-haggidgad.

33And they set out from Hor-haggidgad, and encamped at Jotbathah.

34And they journeyed from Jotbathah, and encamped at Abronah.

35And they traveled on from Abronah, and encamped at Ezion-geber.

36And they removed from Ezion-geber, and encamped in the wilderness of Zin, which is Kadesh.

37And they removed from Kadesh, and encamped at Mount Hor, on the edge of Edom.

38Aaron the priest went up on Mount Hor at the command of the Lord, and died there, in the fortieth year after the Israelites came out of Egypt, the first day of the fifth month. [20:23-29.]

39Aaron was 123 years old when he died on Mount Hor.

40The Canaanite king of Arad, who lived in the South (the Negeb) in the land of Canaan, heard of the coming of the Israelites.

41They set out from Mount Hor, and encamped at Zalmonah.

42And they set out from Zalmonah, and encamped at Punon.

43And they set out from Punon, and encamped at Oboth.

44And they traveled on from Oboth, and encamped at Iye-abarim, in the border of Moab.

45And they departed from Iyim, and encamped at Dibon-gad.

46And they set out from Dibon-gad, and encamped in Almon-diblathaim.

47And they traveled on from Almon-diblathaim, and encamped in the mountains of Abarim, before Nebo.

48And they departed from the mountains of Abarim, and encamped in the plains of Moab by the Jordan at Jericho.

49And they encamped by the Jordan, from Beth-jeshimoth as far as Abel-shittim in the plains of Moab.

50And the Lord said to Moses in the plains of Moab by the Jordan at Jericho,

51Tell the Israelites, When you have passed over Jordan into the land of Canaan,

52Then you shall drive out all the inhabitants of the land before you, and destroy all their figured stones, and all their molten images, and completely demolish all their [idolatrous] high places,

53And you shall take possession of the land and dwell in it, for to you I have given the land to possess it.

54You shall inherit the land by lot according to your families; to the large tribe you shall give a larger inheritance, and to the small tribe you shall give a smaller inheritance; wherever the lot falls to any man, that shall be his; according to the tribes of your fathers you shall inherit.

55But if you will not drive out the inhabitants of the land from before you, then those you let remain of them shall be as pricks in your eyes, and as thorns in your sides, and they shall vex you in the land in which you dwell.

56And as I thought to do to them, so will I do to you.

**34** AND THE Lord said to Moses,

2Command the Israelites, When you come into the land of Canaan (which is the land that shall be yours for an inheritance, the land of Canaan according to its boundaries),

3Your south side shall be from the wilderness of Zin along the side of Edom, and your southern boundary from the end of the Salt [Dead] Sea eastward;

## New American Standard

32And they journeyed from Bene-jaakan, and camped at Hor-
haggidgad.
33And they journeyed from Hor-haggidgad, and camped at
Jotbathah.
34And they journeyed from Jotbathah, and camped at Abronah.
35And they journeyed from Abronah, and camped at Ezion-
geber.
36And they journeyed from Ezion-geber, and camped in the
wilderness of Zin, that is, Kadesh.
37And they journeyed from Kadesh, and camped at Mount Hor,
at the edge of the land of Edom.
38¶ Then Aaron the priest went up to Mount Hor at the command of the LORD, and died there, in the fortieth year after the
sons of Israel had come from the land of Egypt on the first *day* in
the fifth month.
39And Aaron was one hundred twenty-three years old when he
died on Mount Hor.
40¶ Now the Canaanite, the king of Arad who lived in the Negev
in the land of Canaan, heard of the coming of the sons of Israel.
41¶ Then they journeyed from Mount Hor, and camped at Zalmonah.
42And they journeyed from Zalmonah, and camped at Punon.
43And they journeyed from Punon, and camped at Oboth.
44And they journeyed from Oboth, and camped at Iye-abarim,
at the border of Moab.
45And they journeyed from Iyim, and camped at Dibon-gad.
46And they journeyed from Dibon-gad, and camped at Almon-
diblathaim.
47And they journeyed from Almon-diblathaim, and camped in
the mountains of Abarim, before Nebo.
48And they journeyed from the mountains of Abarim, and
camped in the plains of Moab by the Jordan *opposite* Jericho.
49And they camped by the Jordan, from Beth-jeshimoth as far
as Abel-shittim in the plains of Moab.

*Law of Possessing the Land*

50¶ Then the LORD spoke to Moses in the plains of Moab by the
Jordan *opposite* Jericho, saying,
51"Speak to the sons of Israel and say to them, 'When you cross
over the Jordan into the land of Canaan,
52then you shall drive out all the inhabitants of the land from
before you, and destroy all their figured stones, and destroy all
their molten images and demolish all their high places;
53and you shall take possession of the land and live in it, for I
have given the land to you to possess it.
54'And you shall inherit the land by lot according to your families; to the larger you shall give more inheritance, and to the
smaller you shall give less inheritance. Wherever the lot falls to
anyone, that shall be his. You shall inherit according to the tribes
of your fathers.
55'But if you do not drive out the inhabitants of the land from
before you, then it shall come about that those whom you let
remain of them *will become* as pricks in your eyes and as thorns in
your sides, and they shall trouble you in the land in which you live.
56'And it shall come about that as I plan to do to them, so I will
do to you.' "

*Instruction for Apportioning Canaan*

34 THEN THE LORD spoke to Moses, saying,
2"Command the sons of Israel and say to them, 'When
you enter the land of Canaan, this is the land that shall fall to you
as an inheritance, *even the* land of Canaan according to its borders.
3'Your southern sector shall extend from the wilderness of Zin
along the side of Edom, and your southern border shall extend
from the end of the Salt Sea eastward.

## New International

32They left Bene Jaakan and camped at Hor Haggidgad.
33They left Hor Haggidgad and camped at Jotbathah.
34They left Jotbathah and camped at Abronah.
35They left Abronah and camped at Ezion Geber.
36They left Ezion Geber and camped at Kadesh, in the
Desert of Zin.
37They left Kadesh and camped at Mount Hor, on the
border of Edom. 38At the LORD's command Aaron the priest
went up Mount Hor, where he died on the first day of the fifth
month of the fortieth year after the Israelites came out of
Egypt. 39Aaron was a hundred and twenty-three years old
when he died on Mount Hor.
40The Canaanite king of Arad, who lived in the Negev of
Canaan, heard that the Israelites were coming.
41They left Mount Hor and camped at Zalmonah.
42They left Zalmonah and camped at Punon.
43They left Punon and camped at Oboth.
44They left Oboth and camped at Iye Abarim, on the border
of Moab.
45They left Iyim[a] and camped at Dibon Gad.
46They left Dibon Gad and camped at Almon Diblathaim.
47They left Almon Diblathaim and camped in the mountains of Abarim, near Nebo.
48They left the mountains of Abarim and camped on the
plains of Moab by the Jordan across from Jericho.[b] 49There on
the plains of Moab they camped along the Jordan from Beth
Jeshimoth to Abel Shittim.
50On the plains of Moab by the Jordan across from Jericho the
LORD said to Moses, 51"Speak to the Israelites and say to them:
'When you cross the Jordan into Canaan, 52drive out all the inhabitants of the land before you. Destroy all their carved images and
their cast idols, and demolish all their high places. 53Take possession of the land and settle in it, for I have given you the land to
possess. 54Distribute the land by lot, according to your clans. To
a larger group give a larger inheritance, and to a smaller group a
smaller one. Whatever falls to them by lot will be theirs. Distribute
it according to your ancestral tribes.
55" 'But if you do not drive out the inhabitants of the land, those
you allow to remain will become barbs in your eyes and thorns in
your sides. They will give you trouble in the land where you will
live. 56And then I will do to you what I plan to do to them.' "

*Boundaries of Canaan*

34 THE LORD said to Moses, 2"Command the Israelites and
say to them: 'When you enter Canaan, the land that will
be allotted to you as an inheritance will have these boundaries:
3" 'Your southern side will include some of the Desert of Zin
along the border of Edom. On the east, your southern boundary
will start from the end of the Salt Sea,[c] 4cross south of Scorpion[d]

NIV [a] 45 That is, Iye Abarim [b] 48 Hebrew *Jordan of Jericho*; possibly an ancient name for the Jordan River; also in verse 50 [c] 3 That is, the Dead Sea; also in verse 12 [d] 4 Hebrew *Akrabbim*

## King James

4And your border shall turn from the south to the ascent of Akrabbim, and pass on to Zin: and the going forth thereof shall be from the south to Kadesh-barnea, and shall go on to Hazar-addar, and pass on to Azmon:
5And the border shall fetch a compass from Azmon unto the river of Egypt, and the goings out of it shall be at the sea.
6And *as for* the western border, ye shall even have the great sea for a border: this shall be your west border.
7And this shall be your north border: from the great sea ye shall point out for you mount Hor:
8From mount Hor ye shall point out *your border* unto the entrance of Hamath; and the goings forth of the border shall be to Zedad:
9¶ And the border shall go on to Ziphron, and the goings out of it shall be at Hazar-enan: this shall be your north border.
10And ye shall point out your east border from Hazar-enan to Shepham:
11And the coast shall go down from Shepham to Riblah, on the east side of Ain; and the border shall descend, and shall reach unto the side of the sea of Chinnereth eastward:
12And the border shall go down to Jordan, and the goings out of it shall be at the salt sea: this shall be your land with the coasts thereof round about.
13And Moses commanded the children of Israel, saying, This *is* the land which ye shall inherit by lot, which the LORD commanded to give unto the nine tribes, and to the half tribe:
14For the tribe of the children of Reuben according to the house of their fathers, and the tribe of the children of Gad according to the house of their fathers, have received *their inheritance;* and half the tribe of Manasseh have received their inheritance:
15The two tribes and the half tribe have received their inheritance on this side Jordan *near* Jericho eastward, toward the sunrising.
16And the LORD spake unto Moses, saying,
17These *are* the names of the men which shall divide the land unto you: Eleazar the priest, and Joshua the son of Nun.
18And ye shall take one prince of every tribe, to divide the land by inheritance.
19And the names of the men *are* these: Of the tribe of Judah, Caleb the son of Jephunneh.
20And of the tribe of the children of Simeon, Shemuel the son of Ammihud.
21Of the tribe of Benjamin, Elidad the son of Chislon.
22And the prince of the tribe of the children of Dan, Bukki the son of Jogli.
23The prince of the children of Joseph, for the tribe of the children of Manasseh, Hanniel the son of Ephod.
24And the prince of the tribe of the children of Ephraim, Kemuel the son of Shiphtan.
25And the prince of the tribe of the children of Zebulun, Elizaphan the son of Parnach.
26And the prince of the tribe of the children of Issachar, Paltiel the son of Azzan.
27And the prince of the tribe of the children of Asher, Ahihud the son of Shelomi.
28And the prince of the tribe of the children of Naphtali, Pedahel the son of Ammihud.
29These *are they* whom the LORD commanded to divide the inheritance unto the children of Israel in the land of Canaan.

**35** AND THE LORD spake unto Moses in the plains of Moab by Jordan *near* Jericho, saying,

## Amplified

4Your boundary shall turn south of the ascent of Akrabbim, and pass on to Zin; and its end shall be south of Kadesh-barnea, then it shall go on to Hazar-addar, and pass to Azmon;
5Then the boundary shall turn from Azmon to the Brook of Egypt, and it shall terminate at the [Mediterranean] Sea.
6For the western boundary, you shall have the Great Sea and its coast.
7And this shall be your north border: from the Great Sea mark out your boundary line to Mount Hor;
8From Mount Hor you shall mark out your boundary to the entrance of Hamath, and its end shall be at Zedad;
9Then the northern boundary shall go on to Ziphron, and the end of it shall be at Hazar-enan.
10You shall mark out your eastern boundary from Hazar-enan to Shepham;
11The boundary shall go down from Shepham to Riblah on the east side of Ain, and shall descend and reach to the shoulder of the Sea of Chinnereth [that is, the Sea of Galilee] on the east;
12And the boundary shall do down to the Jordan, and the end shall be at the Salt Sea. This shall be your land with its boundaries all around.
13Moses commanded the Israelites, This is the land you shall inherit by lot, which the Lord has commanded to give to the nine tribes and the half tribe [of Manasseh];
14For the tribes of the sons of Reuben and of Gad by their fathers' houses, have received their inheritance, and also the half-tribe of Manasseh.
15The two and one-half tribes have received their inheritance east of the Jordan at Jericho, toward the sunrise.
16And the Lord said to Moses,
17These are the men who shall divide the land to you for inheritance: Eleazar the priest and Joshua son of Nun.
18And [with them] you shall take one head *or* prince of each tribe, to divide the land for inheritance.
19The names of the men are: Of the tribe of Judah, Caleb son of Jephunneh.
20Of the tribe of the sons of Simeon, Shemuel son of Ammihud.
21Of the tribe of Benjamin, Elidad son of Chislon.
22Of the tribe of the sons of Dan, a leader, Bukki son of Jogli.
23Of the sons of Joseph: for the tribe of the sons of Manasseh a leader, Hanniel son of Ephod.
24And of the tribe of the sons of Ephraim a leader, Kemuel son of Shiphtan.
25And of the tribe of the sons of Zebulun a leader, Elizaphan son of Parnach.
26And of the tribe of the sons of Issachar a leader, Paltiel son of Azzan.
27And of the tribe of the sons of Asher a leader, Ahihud son of Shelomi.
28And of the tribe of the sons of Naphtali a leader, Pedahel son of Ammihud.
29These are the men whom the Lord commanded to divide the inheritance to the Israelites in the land of Canaan.

**35** AND THE Lord said to Moses in the plains of Moab by the Jordan at Jericho,

## New American Standard

4'Then your border shall turn *direction* from the south to the
ascent of Akrabbim, and continue to Zin, and its [a]termination
shall be to the south of Kadesh-barnea; and it shall reach Hazarad-
dar, and continue to Azmon.
5'And the border shall turn *direction* from Azmon to the brook
of Egypt, and its termination shall be at the sea.
6¶ 'As for the western border, you shall have the Great Sea,
that is, *its* coastline; this shall be your west border.
7¶ 'And this shall be your north border: you shall draw your
*border* line from the Great Sea to Mount Hor.
8'You shall draw a line from Mount Hor to the Lebo-hamath,
and the termination of the border shall be at Zedad;
9and the border shall proceed to Ziphron, and its termination
shall be at Hazar-enan. This shall be your north border.
10¶ 'For your eastern border you shall also draw a line from
Hazar-enan to Shepham,
11and the border shall go down from Shepham to Riblah on the
east side of Ain; and the border shall go down and reach to the
[b]slope on the east side of the Sea of Chinnereth.
12'And the border shall go down to the Jordan and its termination shall be at the Salt Sea. This shall be your land according to
its borders all around.' "
13¶ So Moses commanded the sons of Israel, saying, "This is the
land that you are to apportion by lot among you as a possession,
which the LORD has commanded to give to the nine and a half
tribes.
14"For the tribe of the sons of Reuben have received *theirs*
according to their fathers' households, and the tribe of the sons of
Gad according to their fathers' households, and the half-tribe of
Manasseh have received their possession.
15"The two and a half tribes have received their possession
across the Jordan opposite Jericho, eastward toward the sunrising."
16¶ Then the LORD spoke to Moses, saying,
17"These are the names of the men who shall apportion the land
to you for inheritance: Eleazar the priest and Joshua the son of
Nun.
18"And you shall take one leader of every tribe to apportion the
land for inheritance.
19"And these are the names of the men: of the tribe of Judah,
Caleb the son of Jephunneh.
20"And of the tribe of the sons of Simeon, Samuel the son of
Ammihud.
21"Of the tribe of Benjamin, Elidad the son of Chislon.
22"And of the tribe of the sons of Dan a leader, Bukki the son
of Jogli.
23"Of the sons of Joseph: of the tribe of the sons of Manasseh
a leader, Hanniel the son of Ephod.
24"And of the tribe of the sons of Ephraim a leader, Kemuel the
son of Shiphtan.
25"And of the tribe of the sons of Zebulun a leader, Elizaphan
the son of Parnach.
26"And of the tribe of the sons of Issachar a leader, Paltiel the
son of Azzan.
27"And of the tribe of the sons of Asher a leader, Ahihud the
son of Shelomi.
28"And of the tribe of the sons of Naphtali a leader, Pedahel the
son of Ammihud."
29These are those whom the LORD commanded to apportion the
inheritance to the sons of Israel in the land of Canaan.

*Cities for the Levites*

**35** NOW THE LORD spoke to Moses in the plains of Moab by
the Jordan opposite Jericho, saying,

NAS [a] Lit., *goings out,* and so throughout this context [b] Lit., *shoulder*

## New International

Pass, continue on to Zin and go south of Kadesh Barnea. Then it
will go to Hazar Addar and over to Azmon, 5where it will turn, join
the Wadi of Egypt and end at the Sea.[c]
6" 'Your western boundary will be the coast of the Great Sea.
This will be your boundary on the west.
7" 'For your northern boundary, run a line from the Great Sea
to Mount Hor 8and from Mount Hor to Lebo[d] Hamath. Then the
boundary will go to Zedad, 9continue to Ziphron and end at Hazar
Enan. This will be your boundary on the north.
10" 'For your eastern boundary, run a line from Hazar Enan to
Shepham. 11The boundary will go down from Shepham to Riblah
on the east side of Ain and continue along the slopes east of the
Sea of Kinnereth.[e] 12Then the boundary will go down along the
Jordan and end at the Salt Sea.
" 'This will be your land, with its boundaries on every side.' "
13Moses commanded the Israelites: "Assign this land by lot as
an inheritance. The LORD has ordered that it be given to the nine
and a half tribes, 14because the families of the tribe of Reuben, the
tribe of Gad and the half-tribe of Manasseh have received their
inheritance. 15These two and a half tribes have received their inheritance on the east side of the Jordan of Jericho,[f] toward the
sunrise."
16The LORD said to Moses, 17"These are the names of the men
who are to assign the land for you as an inheritance: Eleazar the
priest and Joshua son of Nun. 18And appoint one leader from each
tribe to help assign the land. 19These are their names:

Caleb son of Jephunneh,
from the tribe of Judah;
20Shemuel son of Ammihud,
from the tribe of Simeon;
21Elidad son of Kislon,
from the tribe of Benjamin;
22Bukki son of Jogli,
the leader from the tribe of Dan;
23Hanniel son of Ephod,
the leader from the tribe of Manasseh son of Joseph;
24Kemuel son of Shiphtan,
the leader from the tribe of Ephraim son of Joseph;
25Elizaphan son of Parnach,
the leader from the tribe of Zebulun;
26Paltiel son of Azzan,
the leader from the tribe of Issachar;
27Ahihud son of Shelomi,
the leader from the tribe of Asher;
28Pedahel son of Ammihud,
the leader from the tribe of Naphtali."
29These are the men the LORD commanded to assign the inheritance to the Israelites in the land of Canaan.

*Towns for the Levites*

**35** ON THE plains of Moab by the Jordan across from Jericho,[g] the LORD said to Moses, 2"Command the Israelites

NIV [c] 5 That is, the Mediterranean; also in verses 6 and 7 [d] 8 Or *to the entrance to* [e] 11 That is, Galilee [f] 15 *Jordan of Jericho* was possibly an ancient name for the Jordan River. [g] 1 Hebrew *Jordan of Jericho;* possibly an ancient name for the Jordan River

## King James

2 Command the children of Israel, that they give unto the Levites of the inheritance of their possession cities to dwell in; and ye shall give *also* unto the Levites suburbs for the cities round about them.

3 And the cities shall they have to dwell in; and the suburbs of them shall be for their cattle, and for their goods, and for all their beasts.

4 And the suburbs of the cities, which ye shall give unto the Levites, *shall reach* from the wall of the city and outward a thousand cubits round about.

5 And ye shall measure from without the city on the east side two thousand cubits, and on the south side two thousand cubits, and on the west side two thousand cubits, and on the north side two thousand cubits; and the city *shall be* in the midst: this shall be to them the suburbs of the cities.

6 And among the cities which ye shall give unto the Levites *there shall be* six cities for refuge, which ye shall appoint for the manslayer, that he may flee thither: and to them ye shall add forty and two cities.

7 *So* all the cities which ye shall give to the Levites *shall be* forty and eight cities: them *shall ye give* with their suburbs.

8 And the cities which ye shall give *shall be* of the possession of the children of Israel: from *them that have* many ye shall give many; but from *them that have* few ye shall give few: every one shall give of his cities unto the Levites according to his inheritance which he inheriteth.

9 ¶ And the LORD spake unto Moses, saying,

10 Speak unto the children of Israel, and say unto them, When ye be come over Jordan into the land of Canaan;

11 Then ye shall appoint you cities to be cities of refuge for you; that the slayer may flee thither, which killeth any person at unawares.

12 And they shall be unto you cities for refuge from the avenger; that the manslayer die not, until he stand before the congregation in judgment.

13 And of these cities which ye shall give six cities shall ye have for refuge.

14 Ye shall give three cities on this side Jordan, and three cities shall ye give in the land of Canaan, *which* shall be cities of refuge.

15 These six cities shall be a refuge, *both* for the children of Israel, and for the stranger, and for the sojourner among them: that every one that killeth any person unawares may flee thither.

16 And if he smite him with an instrument of iron, so that he die, he *is* a murderer: the murderer shall surely be put to death.

17 And if he smite him with throwing a stone, wherewith he may die, and he die, he *is* a murderer: the murderer shall surely be put to death.

18 Or *if* he smite him with an handweapon of wood, wherewith he may die, and he die, he *is* a murderer: the murderer shall surely be put to death.

19 The revenger of blood himself shall slay the murderer: when he meeteth him, he shall slay him.

20 But if he thrust him of hatred, or hurl at him by laying of wait, that he die;

21 Or in enmity smite him with his hand, that he die: he that smote *him* shall surely be put to death; *for* he *is* a murderer: the revenger of blood shall slay the murderer, when he meeteth him.

22 But if he thrust him suddenly without enmity, or have cast upon him any thing without laying of wait,

23 Or with any stone, wherewith a man may die, seeing *him* not, and cast *it* upon him, that he die, and *was* not his enemy, neither sought his harm:

24 Then the congregation shall judge between the slayer and the revenger of blood according to these judgments:

25 And the congregation shall deliver the slayer out of the hand of the revenger of blood, and the congregation shall restore him to the city of his refuge, whither he was fled: and he shall abide in it unto the death of the high priest, which was anointed with the holy oil.

## Amplified

2 Command the Israelites, that they give to the Levites, from the inheritance of their possession, cities to dwell in; and [suburb] pasture lands round about the cities' walls you shall give to the Levites also.

3 They shall have the cities to dwell in, and their [suburb] pasture lands shall be for their cattle, for their wealth [in flocks], and for all their beasts.

4 And the pasture lands of the cities, which you shall give to the Levites, shall reach from the wall of the city and outward 1,000 cubits round about.

5 You shall measure from the wall of the city outward on the east, south, west, and north sides 2,000 cubits, the city being in the center. This shall belong to [the Levites] as [suburb] pasture lands for their cities.

6 Of the cities which you shall give to the Levites there shall be the six cities of refuge, which you shall give for the manslayer to flee into; and in addition to them you shall give forty-two cities.

7 So all the cities which you shall give to the Levites shall be forty-eight; you shall give them with their adjacent [suburb] pasture lands.

8 As for the cities you shall give from the possession of the Israelites, from the larger tribes you shall take many, and from the smaller tribes few; each tribe shall give of its cities to the Levites in proportion to its inheritance.

9 And the Lord said to Moses,

10 Say to the Israelites, When you cross the Jordan into the land of Canaan,

11 Then you shall select cities to be cities of refuge for you, that the slayer who kills any person unintentionally *and* unawares may flee there.

12 And the cities shall be to you for refuge from the avenger, that the manslayer may not die until he has had a fair trial before the congregation.

13 And of the cities which you give there shall be your six cities for refuge.

14 You shall give three cities on this [east] side of Jordan and three cities in the land of Canaan, to be cities of refuge.

15 These six cities shall be a refuge for the Israelites and for the stranger and the temporary resident among them; that any one who kills any person unintentionally *and* unawares may flee there.

16 But if he struck him down with an instrument of iron, so that he died, he is a murderer; the murderer shall surely be put to death.

17 And if he struck him down by throwing a stone, by which a person may die, and he died, he is a murderer; the murderer shall surely be put to death.

18 Or if he struck him down with a weapon of wood in his hand, by which one may die, and he died, the offender is a murderer; he shall surely be put to death.

19 The avenger of blood shall himself slay the murderer; when he meets him, he shall slay him.

20 But if he stabbed him through hatred, or hurled at him by lying in wait, so that he died,

21 Or in enmity struck him down with his hand, so that he died, he that smote him shall surely be put to death; he is a murderer; the avenger of blood shall slay the murderer, when he meets him.

22 But if he stabbed him suddenly without enmity, or threw anything at *or* upon him without lying in wait,

23 Or with any stone, with which a man may be killed, not seeing him, and threw it at him, so that he died, and was not his enemy, nor sought to harm him,

24 Then the congregation shall judge between the slayer and the avenger of blood according to these ordinances.

25 And the congregation shall rescue the manslayer from the hand of the avenger of blood and restore him to his city of refuge to which he had fled; and he shall live in it until the high priest dies who was anointed with the sacred oil.

## New American Standard

2"Command the sons of Israel that they give to the Levites from the inheritance of their possession, cities to live in; and you shall give to the Levites pasture lands around the cities.

3"And the cities shall be theirs to live in; and their pasture lands shall be for their cattle and for their herds and for all their beasts.

4¶ "And the pasture lands of the cities which you shall give to the Levites *shall extend* from the wall of the city outward a thousand cubits around.

5"You shall also measure outside the city on the east side two thousand cubits, and on the south side two thousand cubits, and on the west side two thousand cubits, and on the north side two thousand cubits, with the city in the center. This shall become theirs as pasture lands for the cities.

*Cities of Refuge*

6"And the cities which you shall give to the Levites *shall be* the six cities of refuge, which you shall give for the manslayer to flee to; and in addition to them you shall give forty-two cities.

7"All the cities which you shall give to the Levites *shall be* forty-eight cities, together with their pasture lands.

8"As for the cities which you shall give from the possession of the sons of Israel, you shall take more from the larger and you shall take less from the smaller; each shall give some of his cities to the Levites in proportion to his possession which he inherits."

9¶ Then the LORD spoke to Moses, saying,

10"Speak to the sons of Israel and say to them, 'When you cross the Jordan into the land of Canaan,

11then you shall select for yourselves cities to be your cities of refuge, that the manslayer who has killed any person unintentionally may flee there.

12'And the cities shall be to you as a refuge from the avenger, so that the manslayer may not die until he stands before the congregation for trial.

13'And the cities which you are to give shall be your six cities of refuge.

14'You shall give three cities across the Jordan and three cities in the land of Canaan; they are to be cities of refuge.

15'These six cities shall be for refuge for the sons of Israel, and for the alien and for the sojourner among them; that anyone who kills a person unintentionally may flee there.

16¶ 'But if he struck him down with an iron object, so that he died, he is a murderer; the murderer shall surely be put to death.

17'And if he struck him down with a stone in the hand, by which he may die, and *as a result* he died, he is a murderer; the murderer shall surely be put to death.

18'Or if he struck him with a wooden object in the hand, by which he may die, and *as a result* he died, he is a murderer; the murderer shall surely be put to death.

19'The blood avenger himself shall put the murderer to death; he shall put him to death when he meets him.

20'And if he pushed him of hatred, or threw something at him lying in wait and *as a result* he died,

21or if he struck him down with his hand in enmity, and *as a result* he died, the one who struck him shall surely be put to death, he is a murderer; the blood avenger shall put the murderer to death when he meets him.

22¶ 'But if he pushed him suddenly without enmity, or threw something at him without lying in wait,

23or with any deadly object of stone, and without seeing it dropped on him so that he died, while he was not his enemy nor seeking his injury,

24then the congregation shall judge between the slayer and the blood avenger according to these ordinances.

25'And the congregation shall deliver the manslayer from the hand of the blood avenger, and the congregation shall restore him to his city of refuge to which he fled; and he shall live in it until the death of the high priest who was anointed with the holy oil.

## New International

to give the Levites towns to live in from the inheritance the Israelites will possess. And give them pasturelands around the towns.
3Then they will have towns to live in and pasturelands for their
cattle, flocks and all their other livestock.
4"The pasturelands around the towns that you give the Levites
will extend out fifteen hundred feet[a] from the town wall. 5Outside
the town, measure three thousand feet[b] on the east side, three
thousand on the south side, three thousand on the west and three
thousand on the north, with the town in the center. They will have
this area as pastureland for the towns.

*Cities of Refuge*

6"Six of the towns you give the Levites will be cities of refuge,
to which a person who has killed someone may flee. In addition,
give them forty-two other towns. 7In all you must give the Levites
forty-eight towns, together with their pasturelands. 8The towns
you give the Levites from the land the Israelites possess are to be
given in proportion to the inheritance of each tribe: Take many
towns from a tribe that has many, but few from one that has few."
9Then the LORD said to Moses: 10"Speak to the Israelites and say
to them: 'When you cross the Jordan into Canaan, 11select some
towns to be your cities of refuge, to which a person who has killed
someone accidentally may flee. 12They will be places of refuge
from the avenger, so that a person accused of murder may not die
before he stands trial before the assembly. 13These six towns you
give will be your cities of refuge. 14Give three on this side of the
Jordan and three in Canaan as cities of refuge. 15These six towns
will be a place of refuge for Israelites, aliens and any other people
living among them, so that anyone who has killed another accidentally can flee there.
16" 'If a man strikes someone with an iron object so that he dies,
he is a murderer; the murderer shall be put to death. 17Or if anyone
has a stone in his hand that could kill, and he strikes someone so
that he dies, he is a murderer; the murderer shall be put to death.
18Or if anyone has a wooden object in his hand that could kill, and
he hits someone so that he dies, he is a murderer; the murderer
shall be put to death. 19The avenger of blood shall put the murderer to death; when he meets him, he shall put him to death. 20If
anyone with malice aforethought shoves another or throws something at him intentionally so that he dies 21or if in hostility he hits
him with his fist so that he dies, that person shall be put to death;
he is a murderer. The avenger of blood shall put the murderer to
death when he meets him.
22" 'But if without hostility someone suddenly shoves another
or throws something at him unintentionally 23or, without seeing
him, drops a stone on him that could kill him, and he dies, then
since he was not his enemy and he did not intend to harm him,
24the assembly must judge between him and the avenger of blood
according to these regulations. 25The assembly must protect the
one accused of murder from the avenger of blood and send him
back to the city of refuge to which he fled. He must stay there until
the death of the high priest, who was anointed with the holy oil.

NIV [a] 4 Hebrew *a thousand cubits* (about 450 meters) [b] 5 Hebrew *two thousand cubits* (about 900 meters)

## King James

26But if the slayer shall at any time come without the border of the city of his refuge, whither he was fled;

27And the revenger of blood find him without the borders of the city of his refuge, and the revenger of blood kill the slayer; he shall not be guilty of blood:

28Because he should have remained in the city of his refuge until the death of the high priest: but after the death of the high priest the slayer shall return into the land of his possession.

29So these *things* shall be for a statute of judgment unto you throughout your generations in all your dwellings.

30Whoso killeth any person, the murderer shall be put to death by the mouth of witnesses: but one witness shall not testify against any person *to cause him* to die.

31Moreover ye shall take no satisfaction for the life of a murderer, which *is* guilty of death: but he shall be surely put to death.

32And ye shall take no satisfaction for him that is fled to the city of his refuge, that he should come again to dwell in the land, until the death of the priest.

33So ye shall not pollute the land wherein ye *are:* for blood it defileth the land: and the land cannot be cleansed of the blood that is shed therein, but by the blood of him that shed it.

34Defile not therefore the land which ye shall inhabit, wherein I dwell: for I the LORD dwell among the children of Israel.

36 AND THE chief fathers of the families of the children of Gilead, the son of Machir, the son of Manasseh, of the families of the sons of Joseph, came near, and spake before Moses, and before the princes, the chief fathers of the children of Israel:

2And they said, The LORD commanded my lord to give the land for an inheritance by lot to the children of Israel: and my lord was commanded by the LORD to give the inheritance of Zelophehad our brother unto his daughters.

3And if they be married to any of the sons of the *other* tribes of the children of Israel, then shall their inheritance be taken from the inheritance of our fathers, and shall be put to the inheritance of the tribe whereunto they are received: so shall it be taken from the lot of our inheritance.

4And when the jubilee of the children of Israel shall be, then shall their inheritance be put unto the inheritance of the tribe whereunto they are received: so shall their inheritance be taken away from the inheritance of the tribe of our fathers.

5And Moses commanded the children of Israel according to the word of the LORD, saying, The tribe of the sons of Joseph hath said well.

6This *is* the thing which the LORD doth command concerning the daughters of Zelophehad, saying, Let them marry to whom they think best; only to the family of the tribe of their father shall they marry.

7So shall not the inheritance of the children of Israel remove from tribe to tribe: for every one of the children of Israel shall keep himself to the inheritance of the tribe of his fathers.

8And every daughter, that possesseth an inheritance in any tribe of the children of Israel, shall be wife unto one of the family of the tribe of her father, that the children of Israel may enjoy every man the inheritance of his fathers.

9Neither shall the inheritance remove from *one* tribe to another tribe; but every one of the tribes of the children of Israel shall keep himself to his own inheritance.

10Even as the LORD commanded Moses, so did the daughters of Zelophehad:

11For Mahlah, Tirzah, and Hoglah, and Milcah, and Noah, the daughters of Zelophehad, were married unto their father's brothers' sons:

## Amplified

26But if the slayer shall at any time come outside the limits of his city of refuge to which he had fled,

27And the avenger of blood finds him outside the limits of his city of refuge and kills the manslayer, he shall not be guilty of blood.

28Because the manslayer should have remained in his city of refuge until the death of the high priest; but after the high priest's death the manslayer shall return to the land of his possession.

29And these things shall be for a statute *and* ordinance to you throughout your generations in all your dwellings.

30Whoever kills any person [intentionally], the murderer shall be put to death on the testimony of witnesses; but no one shall be put to death on the testimony of one witness.

31Moreover you shall take no ransom for the life of a murderer guilty of death; but he shall surely be put to death.

32And you shall accept no ransom for him who has fled to his city of refuge, so that he may return to dwell in the land before the death of the high priest.

33So you shall not thus pollute the land in which you live; for blood pollutes the land, and no atonement can be made for the land, for the blood shed in it, but by the blood of him who shed it.

34And you shall not defile the land in which you live, in the midst of which I dwell; for I the Lord dwell in the midst of the people of Israel.

36 THE HEADS of the fathers' houses of the families of the sons of Gilead son of Machir, son of Manasseh, of the fathers' houses of the sons of Joseph, came near and spoke before Moses and the leaders, the heads of the fathers' houses of the Israelites.

2They said, The Lord commanded [you] my lord to give the land for inheritance by lot to the Israelites; and my lord was commanded by the Lord to give the inheritance of Zelophehad our brother to his daughters.

3But if they are married to any of the sons of the other tribes of the Israelites, then their inheritance will be taken from that of our fathers, and added to the inheritance of the tribe to which they are received *and* belong; so it will be taken out of the lot of our inheritance.

4And when the jubilee of the Israelites comes, then their inheritance will be added to that of the tribe to which they are received *and* belong; so will their inheritance be taken away from that of the tribe of our fathers.

5And Moses commanded the Israelites according to the word of the Lord, saying, The tribe of the sons of Joseph is right.

6This is what the Lord commands concerning the daughters of Zelophehad, Let them marry whom they think best; only they shall marry within the family of the tribe of their father.

7So shall no inheritance of the Israelites be transferred from tribe to tribe; for every one of the Israelites shall cling to the inheritance of the tribe of his fathers.

8And every daughter who possesses an inheritance in any tribe of the Israelites shall be wife to one of the family of the tribe of her father, so that the Israelites may each one possess the inheritance of his fathers.

9So shall no inheritance be transferred from one tribe to another; but each of the tribes of the Israelites shall cling to its own inheritance.

10The daughters of Zelophehad did as the Lord commanded Moses;

11For Mahlah, Tirzah, Hoglah, Milcah, and Noah, the daughters of Zelophehad, were married to sons of their father's brothers.

## New American Standard

26'But if the manslayer shall at any time go beyond the border
of his city of refuge to which he may flee,
27and the blood avenger finds him outside the border of his city
of refuge, and the blood avenger kills the manslayer, he shall not
be guilty of blood
28because he should have remained in his city of refuge until the
death of the high priest. But after the death of the high priest the
manslayer shall return to the land of his possession.
29¶ 'And these things shall be for a statutory ordinance to you
throughout your generations in all your dwellings.
30'If anyone kills a person, the murderer shall be put to death
at the evidence of witnesses, but no person shall be put to death
on the testimony of one witness.
31'Moreover, you shall not take ransom for the life of a murderer
who is guilty of death, but he shall surely be put to death.
32'And you shall not take ransom for him who has fled to his
city of refuge, that he may return to live in the land before the
death of the priest.
33'So you shall not pollute the land in which you are; for blood
pollutes the land and no expiation can be made for the land for the
blood that is shed on it, except by the blood of him who shed it.
34'And you shall not defile the land in which you live, in the
midst of which I dwell; for I the LORD am dwelling in the midst of
the sons of Israel.' "

*Inheritance by Marriage*

36 AND THE heads of the fathers' *households* of the family of
the sons of Gilead, the son of Machir, the son of Manasseh, of the families of the sons of Joseph, came near and spoke
before Moses and before the leaders, the heads of the fathers'
*households* of the sons of Israel,
2and they said, "The LORD commanded my lord to give the
land by lot to the sons of Israel as an inheritance, and my lord was
commanded by the LORD to give the inheritance of Zelophehad our
brother to his daughters.
3"But if they marry one of the sons of the *other* tribes of the sons
of Israel, their inheritance will be withdrawn from the inheritance
of our fathers and will be added to the inheritance of the tribe to
which they belong; thus it will be withdrawn from our allotted
inheritance.
4"And when the jubilee of the sons of Israel comes, then their
inheritance will be added to the inheritance of the tribe to which
they belong; so their inheritance will be withdrawn from the inheritance of the tribe of our fathers."
5¶ Then Moses commanded the sons of Israel according to the
word of the LORD, saying, "The tribe of the sons of Joseph are right
in *their* statements.
6"This is what the LORD has commanded concerning the
daughters of Zelophehad, saying, 'Let them marry whom they
wish; only they must marry within the family of the tribe of their
father.'
7"Thus no inheritance of the sons of Israel shall be transferred
from tribe to tribe, for the sons of Israel shall each hold to the
inheritance of the tribe of his fathers.
8"And every daughter who comes into possession of an inheritance of any tribe of the sons of Israel, shall be wife to one of the
family of the tribe of her father, so that the sons of Israel each may
possess the inheritance of his fathers.
9"Thus no inheritance shall be transferred from one tribe to
another tribe, for the tribes of the sons of Israel shall each hold to
his own inheritance."
10¶ Just as the LORD had commanded Moses, so the daughters
of Zelophehad did:
11Mahlah, Tirzah, Hoglah, Milcah and Noah, the daughters of
Zelophehad married their uncles' sons.

## New International

26" 'But if the accused ever goes outside the limits of the city of
refuge to which he has fled 27and the avenger of blood finds him
outside the city, the avenger of blood may kill the accused without
being guilty of murder. 28The accused must stay in his city of
refuge until the death of the high priest; only after the death of the
high priest may he return to his own property.
29" 'These are to be legal requirements for you throughout the
generations to come, wherever you live.
30" 'Anyone who kills a person is to be put to death as a murderer only on the testimony of witnesses. But no one is to be put
to death on the testimony of only one witness.
31" 'Do not accept a ransom for the life of a murderer, who
deserves to die. He must surely be put to death.
32" 'Do not accept a ransom for anyone who has fled to a city
of refuge and so allow him to go back and live on his own land
before the death of the high priest.
33" 'Do not pollute the land where you are. Bloodshed pollutes
the land, and atonement cannot be made for the land on which
blood has been shed, except by the blood of the one who shed it.
34Do not defile the land where you live and where I dwell, for I,
the LORD, dwell among the Israelites.' "

*Inheritance of Zelophehad's Daughters*

36 THE FAMILY heads of the clan of Gilead son of Makir, the
son of Manasseh, who were from the clans of the descendants of Joseph, came and spoke before Moses and the leaders, the
heads of the Israelite families. 2They said, "When the LORD commanded my lord to give the land as an inheritance to the Israelites
by lot, he ordered you to give the inheritance of our brother Zelophehad to his daughters. 3Now suppose they marry men from
other Israelite tribes; then their inheritance will be taken from our
ancestral inheritance and added to that of the tribe they marry into.
And so part of the inheritance allotted to us will be taken away.
4When the Year of Jubilee for the Israelites comes, their inheritance
will be added to that of the tribe into which they marry, and their
property will be taken from the tribal inheritance of our forefathers."
5Then at the LORD's command Moses gave this order to the
Israelites: "What the tribe of the descendants of Joseph is saying
is right. 6This is what the LORD commands for Zelophehad's
daughters: They may marry anyone they please as long as they
marry within the tribal clan of their father. 7No inheritance in Israel
is to pass from tribe to tribe, for every Israelite shall keep the tribal
land inherited from his forefathers. 8Every daughter who inherits
land in any Israelite tribe must marry someone in her father's tribal
clan, so that every Israelite will possess the inheritance of his
fathers. 9No inheritance may pass from tribe to tribe, for each
Israelite tribe is to keep the land it inherits."
10So Zelophehad's daughters did as the LORD commanded
Moses. 11Zelophehad's daughters—Mahlah, Tirzah, Hoglah, Milcah and Noah—married their cousins on their father's side. 12They

## King James

12 *And* they were married into the families of the sons of Manasseh the son of Joseph, and their inheritance remained in the
tribe of the family of their father.
13These *are* the commandments and the judgments, which the
LORD commanded by the hand of Moses unto the children of Israel
in the plains of Moab by Jordan *near* Jericho.

## Amplified

12They married into the families of the sons of Manasseh son
of Joseph, and their inheritance remained in the tribe of the family
of their father.
13These are the commandments and ordinances which the Lord
commanded the Israelites by Moses in the plains of Moab by the
Jordan [River] at Jericho.

## New American Standard

12They married *those* from the families of the sons of Manasseh the son of Joseph, and their inheritance remained with the tribe of the family of their father.

13¶ These are the commandments and the ordinances which the LORD commanded to the sons of Israel through Moses in the plains of Moab by the Jordan *opposite* Jericho.

## New International

married within the clans of the descendants of Manasseh son of Joseph, and their inheritance remained in their father's clan and tribe.

13These are the commands and regulations the LORD gave through Moses to the Israelites on the plains of Moab by the Jordan across from Jericho.[a]

NIV [a] *13* Hebrew *Jordan of Jericho;* possibly an ancient name for the Jordan River

## King James

THE FIFTH BOOK OF

MOSES, CALLED

# Deuteronomy

1 THESE *BE* the words which Moses spake unto all Israel on this side Jordan in the wilderness, in the plain over against the Red *sea,* between Paran, and Tophel, and Laban, and Hazeroth, and Dizahab.

2( *There are* eleven days' *journey* from Horeb by the way of mount Seir unto Kadesh-barnea.)

3And it came to pass in the fortieth year, in the eleventh month, on the first *day* of the month, *that* Moses spake unto the children of Israel, according unto all that the LORD had given him in commandment unto them;

4After he had slain Sihon the king of the Amorites, which dwelt in Heshbon, and Og the king of Bashan, which dwelt at Astaroth in Edrei:

5On this side Jordan, in the land of Moab, began Moses to declare this law, saying,

6The LORD our God spake unto us in Horeb, saying, Ye have dwelt long enough in this mount:

7Turn you, and take your journey, and go to the mount of the Amorites, and unto all *the places* nigh thereunto, in the plain, in the hills, and in the vale, and in the south, and by the sea side, to the land of the Canaanites, and unto Lebanon, unto the great river, the river Euphrates.

8Behold, I have set the land before you: go in and possess the land which the LORD sware unto your fathers, Abraham, Isaac, and Jacob, to give unto them and to their seed after them.

9¶ And I spake unto you at that time, saying, I am not able to bear you myself alone:

10The LORD your God hath multiplied you, and, behold, ye *are* this day as the stars of heaven for multitude.

11(The LORD God of your fathers make you a thousand times so many more as ye *are,* and bless you, as he hath promised you!)

12How can I myself alone bear your cumbrance, and your burden, and your strife?

13Take you wise men, and understanding, and known among your tribes, and I will make them rulers over you.

14And ye answered me, and said, The thing which thou hast spoken *is* good *for us* to do.

15So I took the chief of your tribes, wise men, and known, and made them heads over you, captains over thousands, and captains over hundreds, and captains over fifties, and captains over tens, and officers among your tribes.

16And I charged your judges at that time, saying, Hear *the causes* between your brethren, and judge righteously between *every* man and his brother, and the stranger *that is* with him.

17Ye shall not respect persons in judgment; *but* ye shall hear the small as well as the great; ye shall not be afraid of the face of man; for the judgment *is* God's: and the cause that is too hard for you, bring *it* unto me, and I will hear it.

18And I commanded you at that time all the things which ye should do.

## Amplified

THE FIFTH BOOK OF MOSES,

CALLED

# Deuteronomy

1 THESE ARE the words which Moses spoke to all Israel, [still] on the [east] side of the Jordan [River] in the wilderness, in the Arabah [that is, the deep valley running north and south from the eastern arm of the Red Sea to beyond the Dead Sea] over near Suph, between Paran and Tophel, Laban, Hazeroth, and Dizahab.

2It is [only] eleven days' journey from Horeb by the way of Mount Seir to Kadesh-barnea [on Canaan's border; yet Israel took forty years to get beyond it].

3And in the fortieth year, on the first day of the eleventh month, Moses spoke to the Israelites according to all that the Lord had given him in commandment to them,

4After he had defeated Sihon king of the Amorites, who lived in Heshbon, and Og the king of Bashan, who lived in Ashtaroth *and* Edrei.

5Beyond [east of] the Jordan, in the land of Moab, Moses began to explain this law, saying,

6The Lord our God said to us in Horeb, You have dwelt long enough on this mountain;

7Turn and take up your journey, and go to the hill country of the Amorites, and to all their neighbors in the Arabah, in the hill country, in the lowland, in the South [the Negeb], and on the coast, the land of the Canaanites, and Lebanon, as far as the great river, the river Euphrates.

8Behold, I have set the land before you; go in and take possession of the land which the Lord swore to your fathers, to Abraham, to Isaac, and to Jacob, to give to them and to their descendants after them.

9I said to you at that time, I am not able to bear you alone;

10The Lord your God has multiplied you, and behold, you are this day as the stars of the heavens for multitude.

11May the Lord, the God of your fathers make you 1,000 times as many as you are, and bless you, as He has promised you!

12How can I bear alone the weariness *and* pressure and burden of you and your strife?

13Choose wise, understanding, experienced *and* respected men, according to your tribes, and I will make them heads over you.

14And you answered me, The thing which you have spoken is good for us to do.

15So I took the heads of your tribes, wise, experienced *and* respected men, and made them heads over you, commanders of thousands, and hundreds, and fifties, and tens, and officers according to your tribes.

16And I charged your judges at that time, Hear the cases between your brethren, and judge righteously between a man and his brother or the stranger *or* sojourner who is with him.

17You shall not be partial in judgment; but you shall hear the small as well as the great; you shall not be afraid of the face of man, for the judgment is God's; and the case that is too hard for you, you shall bring to me, and I will hear it.

18And I commanded you at that time all the things that you should do.

## New American Standard

# Deuteronomy

*Israel's History after the Exodus*

1 THESE ARE the words which Moses spoke to all Israel across
the Jordan in the wilderness, in the Arabah opposite Suph,
between Paran and Tophel and Laban and Hazeroth and Dizahab.
2It is eleven days' *journey* from Horeb by the way of Mount Seir
to Kadesh-barnea.
3And it came about in the fortieth year, on the first day of the
eleventh month, that Moses spoke to the children of Israel, according to all that the LORD had commanded him *to give* to them,
4after he had defeated Sihon the king of the Amorites, who
lived in Heshbon, and Og the king of Bashan, who lived in Ashtaroth and Edrei.
5Across the Jordan in the land of Moab, Moses undertook to
expound this law, saying,
6"The LORD our God spoke to us at Horeb, saying, 'You have
stayed long enough at this mountain.
7'Turn and set your journey, and go to the hill country of the
Amorites, and to all their neighbors in the Arabah, in the hill
country and in the lowland and in the [a]Negev and by the seacoast,
the land of the Canaanites, and Lebanon, as far as the great river,
the river Euphrates.
8'See, I have placed the land before you; go in and possess the
land which the LORD swore to give to your fathers, to Abraham,
to Isaac, and to Jacob, to them and their descendants after them.'
9¶ "And I spoke to you at that time, saying, 'I am not able to
bear *the burden* of you alone.
10'The LORD your God has multiplied you, and behold, you are
this day as the stars of heaven for multitude.
11'May the LORD, the God of your fathers, increase you a thou-
sand-fold more than you are, and bless you, just as He has promised you!
12'How can I alone bear the load and burden of you and your
strife?
13'Choose wise and discerning and experienced men from your
tribes, and I will appoint them as your heads.'
14"And you answered me and said, 'The thing which you have
said to do is good.'
15"So I took the heads of your tribes, wise and experienced
men, and appointed them heads over you, leaders of thousands,
and of hundreds, of fifties and of tens, and officers for your tribes.
16¶ "Then I charged your judges at that time, saying, 'Hear *the
cases* between your fellow countrymen, and judge righteously between a man and his fellow countryman, or the alien who is with
him.
17'You shall not show partiality in judgment; you shall hear the
small and the great alike. You shall not fear man, for the judgment
is God's. And the case that is too hard for you, you shall bring to
me, and I will hear it.'
18"And I commanded you at that time all the things that you
should do.

NAS [a] I.e., South country

## New International

# Deuteronomy

*The Command to Leave Horeb*

1 THESE ARE the words Moses spoke to all Israel in the desert
east of the Jordan—that is, in the Arabah—opposite Suph,
between Paran and Tophel, Laban, Hazeroth and Dizahab. 2(It
takes eleven days to go from Horeb to Kadesh Barnea by the
Mount Seir road.)
3In the fortieth year, on the first day of the eleventh month,
Moses proclaimed to the Israelites all that the LORD had commanded him concerning them. 4This was after he had defeated
Sihon king of the Amorites, who reigned in Heshbon, and at Edrei
had defeated Og king of Bashan, who reigned in Ashtaroth.
5East of the Jordan in the territory of Moab, Moses began to
expound this law, saying:
6The LORD our God said to us at Horeb, "You have stayed long
enough at this mountain. 7Break camp and advance into the hill
country of the Amorites; go to all the neighboring peoples in the
Arabah, in the mountains, in the western foothills, in the Negev
and along the coast, to the land of the Canaanites and to Lebanon,
as far as the great river, the Euphrates. 8See, I have given you this
land. Go in and take possession of the land that the LORD swore
he would give to your fathers—to Abraham, Isaac and Jacob—and
to their descendants after them."

*The Appointment of Leaders*

9At that time I said to you, "You are too heavy a burden for me
to carry alone. 10The LORD your God has increased your numbers
so that today you are as many as the stars in the sky. 11May the
LORD, the God of your fathers, increase you a thousand times and
bless you as he has promised! 12But how can I bear your problems
and your burdens and your disputes all by myself? 13Choose some
wise, understanding and respected men from each of your tribes,
and I will set them over you."
14You answered me, "What you propose to do is good."
15So I took the leading men of your tribes, wise and respected
men, and appointed them to have authority over you—as commanders of thousands, of hundreds, of fifties and of tens and as
tribal officials. 16And I charged your judges at that time: Hear the
disputes between your brothers and judge fairly, whether the case
is between brother Israelites or between one of them and an alien.
17Do not show partiality in judging; hear both small and great
alike. Do not be afraid of any man, for judgment belongs to God.
Bring me any case too hard for you, and I will hear it. 18And at that
time I told you everything you were to do.

## King James

19¶ And when we departed from Horeb, we went through all that great and terrible wilderness, which ye saw by the way of the mountain of the Amorites, as the LORD our God commanded us; and we came to Kadesh-barnea.

20And I said unto you, Ye are come unto the mountain of the Amorites, which the LORD our God doth give unto us.

21Behold, the LORD thy God hath set the land before thee: go up *and* possess *it*, as the LORD God of thy fathers hath said unto thee; fear not, neither be discouraged.

22¶ And ye came near unto me every one of you, and said, We will send men before us, and they shall search us out the land, and bring us word again by what way we must go up, and into what cities we shall come.

23And the saying pleased me well: and I took twelve men of you, one of a tribe:

24And they turned and went up into the mountain, and came unto the valley of Eshcol, and searched it out.

25And they took of the fruit of the land in their hands, and brought *it* down unto us, and brought us word again, and said, *It is* a good land which the LORD our God doth give us.

26Notwithstanding ye would not go up, but rebelled against the commandment of the LORD your God:

27And ye murmured in your tents, and said, Because the LORD hated us, he hath brought us forth out of the land of Egypt, to deliver us into the hand of the Amorites, to destroy us.

28Whither shall we go up? our brethren have discouraged our heart, saying, The people *is* greater and taller than we; the cities *are* great and walled up to heaven; and moreover we have seen the sons of the Anakims there.

29Then I said unto you, Dread not, neither be afraid of them.

30The LORD your God which goeth before you, he shall fight for you, according to all that he did for you in Egypt before your eyes;

31And in the wilderness, where thou hast seen how that the LORD thy God bare thee, as a man doth bear his son, in all the way that ye went, until ye came into this place.

32Yet in this thing ye did not believe the LORD your God,

33Who went in the way before you, to search you out a place to pitch your tents *in*, in fire by night, to show you by what way ye should go, and in a cloud by day.

34And the LORD heard the voice of your words, and was wroth, and sware, saying,

35Surely there shall not one of these men of this evil generation see that good land, which I sware to give unto your fathers,

36Save Caleb the son of Jephunneh; he shall see it, and to him will I give the land that he hath trodden upon, and to his children, because he hath wholly followed the LORD.

37Also the LORD was angry with me for your sakes, saying, Thou also shalt not go in thither.

38 *But* Joshua the son of Nun, which standeth before thee, he shall go in thither: encourage him: for he shall cause Israel to inherit it.

39Moreover your little ones, which ye said should be a prey, and your children, which in that day had no knowledge between good and evil, they shall go in thither, and unto them will I give it, and they shall possess it.

40But *as for* you, turn you, and take your journey into the wilderness by the way of the Red sea.

41Then ye answered and said unto me, We have sinned against the LORD, we will go up and fight, according to all that the LORD our God commanded us. And when ye had girded on every man his weapons of war, ye were ready to go up into the hill.

42And the LORD said unto me, Say unto them, Go not up, neither fight; for I *am* not among you; lest ye be smitten before your enemies.

43So I spake unto you; and ye would not hear, but rebelled against the commandment of the LORD, and went presumptuously up into the hill.

## Amplified

19And when we departed from Horeb, we went through all tha great and terrible wilderness, which you saw on the way to the hil country of the Amorites, as the Lord our God commanded us; anc we came to Kadesh-barnea.

20And I said to you, You have come to the hill country of the Amorites, which the Lord our God gives us.

21Behold, the Lord your God has set the land before you; go up and possess it, as the Lord God of your fathers has said to you; fea not, neither be dismayed.

22Then you all came near to me and said, Let us send mer before us, that they may search us out the land, and bring us word again by what way we should go up, and the cities into which we shall come.

23The thing pleased me well, and I took twelve men of you, one for each tribe.

24And they turned and went up into the hill country, and came to the Valley of Eshcol and spied it out.

25And they took of the fruit of the land in their hands, and brought it down to us, and brought us word again, and said, It is a good land which the Lord our God gives us.

26Yet you would not go up, but rebelled against the commandment of the Lord your God;

27You were peevish *and* discontented in your tents, and said, Because the Lord hated us He brought us forth out of the land of Egypt, to deliver us into the hand of the Amorites, to destroy us.

28To what are we going up? Our brethren have made our hearts melt, saying, The people are bigger and taller than we are; the cities are great and fortified to the heavens; and moreover we have seen the [giant-like] sons of the Anakim there.

29Then I said to you, Dread not, neither be afraid of them.

30The Lord your God Who goes before you, He will fight for you just as He did for you in Egypt before your eyes,

31And in the wilderness, where you have seen how the Lord your God bore you, as a man carries his son, in all the way that you went until you came to this place.

32Yet in spite of this word you did not believe [trust, rely on and remain steadfast to] the Lord your God;

33Who went in the way before you to search out a place to pitch your tents, in fire by night, to show you by what way you should go, and in the cloud by day.

34And the Lord heard your words, and was angered, and He swore,

35Not one of these men of this evil generation shall see that good land which I swore to give to your fathers,

36Except [Joshua, of course; and] Caleb son of Jephunneh, he shall see it, and to him and to his children I will give the land upon which he has walked, because he has wholly followed the Lord.

37The Lord was angry with me also for your sakes, and said, You also shall not enter Canaan.

38But Joshua the son of Nun, who stands before you, he shall enter there; encourage him, for he shall cause Israel to inherit it.

39Moreover your little ones, whom you said would become a prey, and your children, who at this time cannot discern between good and evil, they shall enter Canaan, and to them I will give it, and they shall possess it.

40But as for you, turn and journey into the wilderness by way of the Red Sea.

41Then you said to me, We have sinned against the Lord; we will go up and fight, as the Lord our God commanded us. And you girded on every man his battle weapons and thought it a simple matter to go up into the hill country.

42And the Lord said to me, Say to them, Do not go up or fight, for I am not among you; lest you be dangerously hurt by your enemies.

43So I spoke to you; and you would not hear, but rebelled against the commandment of the Lord, and were presumptuous and went up into the hill country.

## New American Standard

19¶ "Then we set out from Horeb, and went through all that
great and terrible wilderness which you saw, on the way to the hill
country of the Amorites, just as the LORD our God had commanded us; and we came to Kadesh-barnea.
20"And I said to you, 'You have come to the hill country of the
Amorites which the LORD our God is about to give us.
21'See, the LORD your God has placed the land before you; go
up, take possession, as the LORD, the God of your fathers, has
spoken to you. Do not fear or be dismayed.'
22"Then all of you approached me and said, 'Let us send men
before us, that they may search out the land for us, and bring back
to us word of the way by which we should go up, and the cities
which we shall enter.'
23"And the thing pleased me and I took twelve of your men,
one man for each tribe.
24"And they turned and went up into the hill country, and came
to the valley of Eshcol, and spied it out.
25"Then they took *some* of the fruit of the land in their hands
and brought it down to us; and they brought us back a report and
said, 'It is a good land which the LORD our God is about to give
us.'
26¶ "Yet you were not willing to go up, but rebelled against the
command of the LORD your God;
27and you grumbled in your tents and said, 'Because the LORD
hates us, He has brought us out of the land of Egypt to deliver us
into the hand of the Amorites to destroy us.
28'Where can we go up? Our brethren have made our hearts
melt, saying, "The people are bigger and taller than we; the cities
are large and fortified to heaven. And besides, we saw the sons of
the Anakim there." '
29"Then I said to you, 'Do not be shocked, nor fear them.
30'The LORD your God who goes before you will Himself fight
on your behalf, just as He did for you in Egypt before your eyes,
31and in the wilderness where you saw how the LORD your God
carried you, just as a man carries his son, in all the way which you
have walked, until you came to this place.'
32"But for all this, you did not trust the LORD your God,
33who goes before you on *your* way, to seek out a place for you
to encamp, in fire by night and cloud by day, to show you the way
in which you should go.
34¶ "Then the LORD heard the sound of your words, and He was
angry and took an oath, saying,
35'Not one of these men, this evil generation, shall see the good
land which I swore to give your fathers,
36except Caleb the son of Jephunneh; he shall see it, and to him
and to his sons I will give the land on which he has set foot,
because he has followed the LORD fully.'
37"The LORD was angry with me also on your account, saying,
'Not even you shall enter there.
38'Joshua the son of Nun, who stands before you, he shall enter
there; encourage him, for he shall cause Israel to inherit it.
39'Moreover, your little ones who you said would become a
prey, and your sons, who this day have no knowledge of good or
evil, shall enter there, and I will give it to them, and they shall
possess it.
40'But as for you, turn around and set out for the wilderness by
the way to the Red Sea.'
41¶ "Then you answered and said to me, 'We have sinned
against the LORD; we will indeed go up and fight, just as the LORD
our God commanded us.' And every man of you girded on his
weapons of war, and regarded it as easy to go up into the hill
country.
42"And the LORD said to me, 'Say to them, "Do not go up, nor
fight, for I am not among you; lest you be defeated before your
enemies." '
43"So I spoke to you, but you would not listen. Instead you
rebelled against the command of the LORD, and acted presumptuously and went up into the hill country.

## New International

*Spies Sent Out*

19Then, as the LORD our God commanded us, we set out from
Horeb and went toward the hill country of the Amorites through
all that vast and dreadful desert that you have seen, and so we
reached Kadesh Barnea. 20Then I said to you, "You have reached
the hill country of the Amorites, which the LORD our God is giving
us. 21See, the LORD your God has given you the land. Go up and
take possession of it as the LORD, the God of your fathers, told you.
Do not be afraid; do not be discouraged."
22Then all of you came to me and said, "Let us send men ahead
to spy out the land for us and bring back a report about the route
we are to take and the towns we will come to."
23The idea seemed good to me; so I selected twelve of you, one
man from each tribe. 24They left and went up into the hill country,
and came to the Valley of Eshcol and explored it. 25Taking with
them some of the fruit of the land, they brought it down to us and
reported, "It is a good land that the LORD our God is giving us."

*Rebellion Against the LORD*

26But you were unwilling to go up; you rebelled against the
command of the LORD your God. 27You grumbled in your tents
and said, "The LORD hates us; so he brought us out of Egypt to
deliver us into the hands of the Amorites to destroy us. 28Where
can we go? Our brothers have made us lose heart. They say, 'The
people are stronger and taller than we are; the cities are large, with
walls up to the sky. We even saw the Anakites there.' "
29Then I said to you, "Do not be terrified; do not be afraid of
them. 30The LORD your God, who is going before you, will fight
for you, as he did for you in Egypt, before your very eyes, 31and
in the desert. There you saw how the LORD your God carried you,
as a father carries his son, all the way you went until you reached
this place."
32In spite of this, you did not trust in the LORD your God, 33who
went ahead of you on your journey, in fire by night and in a cloud
by day, to search out places for you to camp and to show you the
way you should go.
34When the LORD heard what you said, he was angry and
solemnly swore: 35"Not a man of this evil generation shall see the
good land I swore to give your forefathers, 36except Caleb son of
Jephunneh. He will see it, and I will give him and his descendants
the land he set his feet on, because he followed the LORD wholeheartedly."
37Because of you the LORD became angry with me also and said,
"You shall not enter it, either. 38But your assistant, Joshua son of
Nun, will enter it. Encourage him, because he will lead Israel to
inherit it. 39And the little ones that you said would be taken captive, your children who do not yet know good from bad—they will
enter the land. I will give it to them and they will take possession
of it. 40But as for you, turn around and set out toward the desert
along the route to the Red Sea.[a] "
41Then you replied, "We have sinned against the LORD. We will
go up and fight, as the LORD our God commanded us." So every
one of you put on his weapons, thinking it easy to go up into the
hill country.
42But the LORD said to me, "Tell them, 'Do not go up and fight,
because I will not be with you. You will be defeated by your
enemies.' "
43So I told you, but you would not listen. You rebelled against
the LORD's command and in your arrogance you marched up into
the hill country. 44The Amorites who lived in those hills came out

**NIV** [a] 40 Hebrew *Yam Suph;* that is, Sea of Reeds

## King James

44 And the Amorites, which dwelt in that mountain, came out against you, and chased you, as bees do, and destroyed you in Seir, *even* unto Hormah.

45 And ye returned and wept before the LORD; but the LORD would not hearken to your voice, nor give ear unto you.

46 So ye abode in Kadesh many days, according unto the days that ye abode *there*.

**2** THEN WE turned, and took our journey into the wilderness by the way of the Red sea, as the LORD spake unto me: and we compassed mount Seir many days.

2 And the LORD spake unto me, saying,

3 Ye have compassed this mountain long enough: turn you northward.

4 And command thou the people, saying, Ye *are* to pass through the coast of your brethren the children of Esau, which dwell in Seir; and they shall be afraid of you: take ye good heed unto yourselves therefore:

5 Meddle not with them; for I will not give you of their land, no, not so much as a footbreadth; because I have given mount Seir unto Esau *for* a possession.

6 Ye shall buy meat of them for money, that ye may eat; and ye shall also buy water of them for money, that ye may drink.

7 For the LORD thy God hath blessed thee in all the works of thy hand: he knoweth thy walking through this great wilderness: these forty years the LORD thy God *hath been* with thee; thou hast lacked nothing.

8 And when we passed by from our brethren the children of Esau, which dwelt in Seir, through the way of the plain from Elath, and from Ezion-geber, we turned and passed by the way of the wilderness of Moab.

9 And the LORD said unto me, Distress not the Moabites, neither contend with them in battle: for I will not give thee of their land *for* a possession; because I have given Ar unto the children of Lot *for* a possession.

10 The Emims dwelt therein in times past, a people great, and many, and tall, as the Anakims;

11 Which also were accounted giants, as the Anakims; but the Moabites call them Emims.

12 The Horims also dwelt in Seir beforetime; but the children of Esau succeeded them, when they had destroyed them from before them, and dwelt in their stead; as Israel did unto the land of his possession, which the LORD gave unto them.

13 Now rise up, *said I*, and get you over the brook Zered. And we went over the brook Zered.

14 And the space in which we came from Kadesh-barnea, until we were come over the brook Zered, *was* thirty and eight years; until all the generation of the men of war were wasted out from among the host, as the LORD sware unto them.

15 For indeed the hand of the LORD was against them, to destroy them from among the host, until they were consumed.

16 ¶ So it came to pass, when all the men of war were consumed and dead from among the people,

17 That the LORD spake unto me, saying,

18 Thou art to pass over through Ar, the coast of Moab, this day:

19 And *when* thou comest nigh over against the children of Ammon, distress them not, nor meddle with them: for I will not give thee of the land of the children of Ammon *any* possession; because I have given it unto the children of Lot *for* a possession.

20 (That also was accounted a land of giants: giants dwelt therein in old time; and the Ammonites call them Zamzummims;

21 A people great, and many, and tall, as the Anakims; but the LORD destroyed them before them; and they succeeded them, and dwelt in their stead:

22 As he did to the children of Esau, which dwelt in Seir, when he destroyed the Horims from before them; and they succeeded them, and dwelt in their stead even unto this day:

## Amplified

44 Then the Amorites who lived in that hill country came out against you and chased you as bees do and struck you down in Seir as far as Hormah.

45 And you returned and wept before the Lord; but the Lord would not heed your voice or listen to you.

46 So you remained in Kadesh; many days you remained there.

**2** THEN WE turned, and took our journey into the wilderness by the way of the Red Sea, as the Lord directed me; and for many days we journeyed around Mount Seir.

2 And the Lord spoke to me [Moses], saying,

3 You have roamed around this mountain country long enough; turn northward.

4 And command the Israelites, You are to pass through the territory of your kinsmen the sons of Esau, who live in Seir; and they will be afraid of you. So watch yourselves carefully;

5 Do not provoke *or* stir them up; for I will not give you of their land, no, not enough for the sole of your foot to tread on, for I have given Mount Seir to Esau for a possession.

6 You shall buy food of them for money, that you may eat, and you shall also buy water of them for money, that you may drink.

7 For the Lord your God has blessed you in all the work of your hand; He knows your walking through this great wilderness; these forty years the Lord your God has been with you; you have lacked nothing.

8 So we passed on from our brethren the sons of Esau, who dwelt in Seir, away from the Arabah (wilderness) and from Elath, and from Ezion-geber. We turned and went by the way of the wilderness of Moab.

9 And the Lord said to me, Do not trouble *or* assault Moab or contend with them in battle, for I will not give you any of their land for a possession, because I have given Ar to the sons of Lot for a possession.

10 (The Emim dwelt there in times past, a people great and many, and tall as the Anakim;

11 These also are known as Rephaim [of giant stature], as are the Anakim, but the Moabites call them Emim.

12 The Horites also formerly lived in Seir, but the sons of Esau dispossessed them and destroyed them from before them, and dwelt in their stead; as Israel did to the land of their possession, which the Lord gave to them.)

13 Now rise up, and go over the brook Zered. So we went over the brook Zered.

14 And the time from our leaving Kadesh-barnea until we had come over the brook Zered was thirty-eight years, until the whole generation of the men of war had perished from the camp, as the Lord had sworn to them.

15 Moreover the hand of the Lord was against them, to exterminate them from the midst of the camp, until they were all gone.

16 So when all the men of war had died from among the people,

17 The Lord spoke to me [Moses], saying,

18 You are this day to pass through Ar, the border of Moab.

19 But when you come near the territory of the sons of Ammon, do not trouble *or* assault them, or provoke *or* stir them up, for I will not give you any of the land of the Ammonites for a possession, because I have given it to the sons of Lot for a possession.

20 (That also is known as a land of Rephaim [of giant stature]; Rephaim dwelt there formerly, but the Ammonites call them Zamzummim,

21 A people great and many, and tall as the Anakim; but the Lord destroyed them before [Ammon]; and they dispossessed them and settled in their stead;

22 As He did for the sons of Esau, who dwell in Seir, when He destroyed the Horites from before them, and they dispossessed them, and settled in their stead even to this day.

## New American Standard

44"And the Amorites who lived in that hill country came out
gainst you, and chased you as bees do, and crushed you from Seir
o Hormah.
45"Then you returned and wept before the LORD; but the LORD
lid not listen to your voice, nor give ear to you.
46"So you remained in Kadesh many days, the days that you
pent *there*.

*Vanderings in the Wilderness*

2 "THEN WE turned and set out for the wilderness by the way
to the Red Sea, as the LORD spoke to me, and circled Mount
Seir for many days.
2"And the LORD spoke to me, saying,
3'You have circled this mountain long enough. *Now* turn north,
4and command the people, saying, "You will pass through the
erritory of your brothers the sons of Esau who live in Seir; and
hey will be afraid of you. So be very careful;
5do not provoke them, for I will not give you any of their land,
even *as little as* a footstep because I have given Mount Seir to Esau
as a possession.
6"You shall buy food from them with money so that you may
eat, and you shall also purchase water from them with money so
that you may drink.
7"For the LORD your God has blessed you in all that you have
done; He has known your wanderings through this great wilderness. These forty years the LORD your God has been with you; you
have not lacked a thing." '
8¶ "So we passed beyond our brothers the sons of Esau, who
live in Seir, away from the Arabah road, away from Elath and from
Ezion-geber. And we turned and passed through by the way of the
wilderness of Moab.
9"Then the LORD said to me, 'Do not harass Moab, nor provoke
them to war, for I will not give you any of their land as a possession, because I have given Ar to the sons of Lot as a possession.
10(The Emim lived there formerly, a people as great, numerous,
and tall as the Anakim.
11Like the Anakim, they are also regarded as Rephaim, but the
Moabites call them Emim.
12The Horites formerly lived in Seir, but the sons of Esau dispossessed them and destroyed them from before them and settled
in their place, just as Israel did to the land of their possession
which the LORD gave to them.)
13'Now arise and cross over the brook Zered yourselves.' So we
crossed over the brook Zered.
14"Now the time that it took for us to come from Kadesh-barnea, until we crossed over the brook Zered, was thirty-eight years;
until all the generation of the men of war perished from within the
camp, as the LORD had sworn to them.
15"Moreover the hand of the LORD was against them, to destroy
them from within the camp, until they all perished.
16¶ "So it came about when all the men of war had finally
perished from among the people,
17that the LORD spoke to me, saying,
18'You shall cross over Ar, the border of Moab, today.
19'And when you come opposite the sons of Ammon, do not
harass them nor provoke them, for I will not give you any of the
land of the sons of Ammon as a possession, because I have given
it to the sons of Lot as a possession.'
20(It is also regarded as the land of the Rephaim, *for* Rephaim
formerly lived in it, but the Ammonites call them Zamzummin,
21a people as great, numerous, and tall as the Anakim, but the
LORD destroyed them before them. And they dispossessed them
and settled in their place,
22just as He did for the sons of Esau, who live in Seir, when He
destroyed the Horites from before them; and they dispossessed
them, and settled in their place even to this day.

## New International

against you; they chased you like a swarm of bees and beat you
down from Seir all the way to Hormah. 45You came back and wept
before the LORD, but he paid no attention to your weeping and
turned a deaf ear to you. 46And so you stayed in Kadesh many
days—all the time you spent there.

*Wanderings in the Desert*

2 THEN WE turned back and set out toward the desert along
the route to the Red Sea,[a] as the LORD had directed me. For
a long time we made our way around the hill country of Seir.
2Then the LORD said to me, 3"You have made your way around
this hill country long enough; now turn north. 4Give the people
these orders: 'You are about to pass through the territory of your
brothers the descendants of Esau, who live in Seir. They will be
afraid of you, but be very careful. 5Do not provoke them to war,
for I will not give you any of their land, not even enough to put
your foot on. I have given Esau the hill country of Seir as his own.
6You are to pay them in silver for the food you eat and the water
you drink.' "
7The LORD your God has blessed you in all the work of your
hands. He has watched over your journey through this vast desert.
These forty years the LORD your God has been with you, and you
have not lacked anything.
8So we went on past our brothers the descendants of Esau, who
live in Seir. We turned from the Arabah road, which comes up
from Elath and Ezion Geber, and traveled along the desert road of
Moab.
9Then the LORD said to me, "Do not harass the Moabites or
provoke them to war, for I will not give you any part of their land.
I have given Ar to the descendants of Lot as a possession."
10(The Emites used to live there—a people strong and numerous, and as tall as the Anakites. 11Like the Anakites, they too were
considered Rephaites, but the Moabites called them Emites. 12Hor-
ites used to live in Seir, but the descendants of Esau drove them
out. They destroyed the Horites from before them and settled in
their place, just as Israel did in the land the LORD gave them as their
possession.)
13And the LORD said, "Now get up and cross the Zered Valley."
So we crossed the valley.
14Thirty-eight years passed from the time we left Kadesh Barnea
until we crossed the Zered Valley. By then, that entire generation
of fighting men had perished from the camp, as the LORD had
sworn to them. 15The LORD's hand was against them until he had
completely eliminated them from the camp.
16Now when the last of these fighting men among the people
had died, 17the LORD said to me, 18"Today you are to pass by the
region of Moab at Ar. 19When you come to the Ammonites, do not
harass them or provoke them to war, for I will not give you possession of any land belonging to the Ammonites. I have given it as
a possession to the descendants of Lot."
20(That too was considered a land of the Rephaites, who used
to live there; but the Ammonites called them Zamzummites.
21They were a people strong and numerous, and as tall as the
Anakites. The LORD destroyed them from before the Ammonites,
who drove them out and settled in their place. 22The LORD had
done the same for the descendants of Esau, who lived in Seir,
when he destroyed the Horites from before them. They drove
them out and have lived in their place to this day. 23And as for the

NIV [a] 1 Hebrew *Yam Suph;* that is, Sea of Reeds

## King James

23And the Avims which dwelt in Hazerim, *even* unto Azzah, the
Caphtorims, which came forth out of Caphtor, destroyed them,
and dwelt in their stead.)
24¶ Rise ye up, take your journey, and pass over the river
Arnon: behold, I have given into thine hand Sihon the Amorite,
king of Heshbon, and his land: begin to possess *it*, and contend
with him in battle.
25This day will I begin to put the dread of thee and the fear of
thee upon the nations *that are* under the whole heaven, who shall
hear report of thee, and shall tremble, and be in anguish because
of thee.
26¶ And I sent messengers out of the wilderness of Kedemoth
unto Sihon king of Heshbon with words of peace, saying,
27Let me pass through thy land: I will go along by the high way,
I will neither turn unto the right hand nor to the left.
28Thou shalt sell me meat for money, that I may eat; and give
me water for money, that I may drink: only I will pass through on
my feet;
29(As the children of Esau which dwell in Seir, and the Moabites
which dwell in Ar, did unto me;) until I shall pass over Jordan into
the land which the LORD our God giveth us.
30But Sihon king of Heshbon would not let us pass by him: for
the LORD thy God hardened his spirit, and made his heart obstinate, that he might deliver him into thy hand, as *appeareth* this day.
31And the LORD said unto me, Behold, I have begun to give
Sihon and his land before thee: begin to possess, that thou mayest
inherit his land.
32Then Sihon came out against us, he and all his people, to fight
at Jahaz.
33And the LORD our God delivered him before us; and we smote
him, and his sons, and all his people.
34And we took all his cities at that time, and utterly destroyed
the men, and the women, and the little ones, of every city, we left
none to remain:
35Only the cattle we took for a prey unto ourselves, and the
spoil of the cities which we took.
36From Aroer, which *is* by the brink of the river of Arnon, and
*from* the city that *is* by the river, even unto Gilead, there was not
one city too strong for us: the LORD our God delivered all unto us:
37Only unto the land of the children of Ammon thou camest
not, *nor* unto any place of the river Jabbok, nor unto the cities in
the mountains, nor unto whatsoever the LORD our God forbad us.

3 THEN WE turned, and went up the way to Bashan: and Og
the king of Bashan came out against us, he and all his people,
to battle at Edrei.
2And the LORD said unto me, Fear him not: for I will deliver
him, and all his people, and his land, into thy hand; and thou shalt
do unto him as thou didst unto Sihon king of the Amorites, which
dwelt at Heshbon.
3So the LORD our God delivered into our hands Og also, the
king of Bashan, and all his people: and we smote him until none
was left to him remaining.
4And we took all his cities at that time, there was not a city
which we took not from them, threescore cities, all the region of
Argob, the kingdom of Og in Bashan.
5All these cities *were* fenced with high walls, gates, and bars;
beside unwalled towns a great many.
6And we utterly destroyed them, as we did unto Sihon king of
Heshbon, utterly destroying the men, women, and children, of
every city.

## Amplified

23As for the Avvim, who dwelt in villages as far as Gaza, the
Caphtorim, who came from Caphtor, destroyed them, and dwelt
in their stead.)
24Rise up, take your journey, and pass over the valley of the
Arnon; behold, I have given into your hand Sihon the Amorite,
king of Heshbon, and his land; begin to possess it, and contend
with him in battle.
25This day will I begin to put the dread and fear of you upon
the peoples that are under the whole heavens, who shall hear the
report of you, and shall tremble and be in anguish because of you.
26So I sent messengers from the wilderness of Kedemoth to
Sihon king of Heshbon with words of peace, saying,
27Let me pass through your land; I will go only by the road,
turning aside neither to the right nor to the left.
28You shall sell me food to eat, and sell me water to drink; only
let me walk through,
29As the sons of Esau who dwell in Seir and the Moabites who
dwell in Ar [a]did for me, until I go over the Jordan into the land
which the Lord our God gives us.
30But Sihon king of Heshbon would not let us pass by him; for
the Lord your God hardened his spirit, and made his heart obstinate, that He might give him into your hand, as at this day.
31And the Lord said to me [Moses], Behold, I have begun to give
Sihon and his land over to you; begin to take possession, that you
may succeed him *and* occupy his land.
32Then Sihon came out against us, he and all his people, to fight
at Jahaz.
33And the Lord our God gave him over to us; and we defeated
him and his sons and all his people.
34At the same time we took all his cities, and utterly destroyed
every city, men, women, and children; we left none to remain.
35Only the cattle we took as booty for ourselves, and the spoil
of the cities which we had captured.
36From Aroer, which is on the edge of the Arnon valley, and
from the city that is in the valley, as far as Gilead, there was no
city too high *and* strong for us; the Lord our God delivered all to
us.
37Only you did not go near the land of the Ammonites, that is,
to any bank of the river Jabbok and the cities of the hill country,
and wherever the Lord our God had forbidden us.

3 THEN WE turned, and went up the road to Bashan; and Og
the king of Bashan came out against us, he and all his people,
to battle at Edrei.
2And the Lord said to me, Do not fear him; for I have given him
and all his people and his land into your hand; and you shall do
to him as you did to Sihon king of the Amorites, who lived at
Heshbon.
3So the Lord our God gave into our hands Og also, the king of
Bashan, and all his people; and we smote him until not one was
left to him.
4And we took all his cities at that time; there was not a city
which we did not take from them, sixty cities, the whole region of
Argob, the kingdom of Og in Bashan.
5All these cities were fortified with high *and* haughty walls,
gates, and bars; besides a great many unwalled villages.
6And we utterly destroyed them, as we did to Sihon king of
Heshbon, utterly destroying every city, men, women, and children.

**AMP** [a] All that is said here is that the Edomites and Moabites sold Israel bread and water. There is no denial, expressed or implied, of their hostility to Israel, and their desire for his destruction. The passage is in entire harmony with Num. 20:17, 21, and Deut. 23:3, 4. (*Lange's Commentary.*)

## New American Standard

23And the Avvim, who lived in villages as far as Gaza, the [b]Caphtorim who came from [c]Caphtor, destroyed them and lived in their place.)

24'Arise, set out, and pass through the valley of Arnon. Look! I have given Sihon the Amorite, king of Heshbon, and his land into your hand; begin to take possession and contend with him in battle.

25'This day I will begin to put the dread and fear of you upon the peoples everywhere under the heavens, who, when they hear the report of you, shall tremble and be in anguish because of you.'

**26**¶ "So I sent messengers from the wilderness of Kedemoth to Sihon king of Heshbon with words of peace, saying,

27'Let me pass through your land, I will travel only on the highway; I will not turn aside to the right or to the left.

28'You will sell me food for money so that I may eat, and give me water for money so that I may drink, only let me pass through on foot,

29just as the sons of Esau who live in Seir and the Moabites who live in Ar did for me, until I cross over the Jordan into the land which the LORD our God is giving to us.'

30"But Sihon king of Heshbon was not willing for us to pass through his land; for the LORD your God hardened his spirit and made his heart obstinate, in order to deliver him into your hand, as *he is* today.

31"And the LORD said to me, 'See, I have begun to deliver Sihon and his land over to you. Begin to occupy, that you may possess his land.'

**32**¶ "Then Sihon with all his people came out to meet us in battle at Jahaz.

33"And the LORD our God delivered him over to us; and we defeated him with his sons and all his people.

34"So we captured all his cities at that time, and utterly destroyed the men, women and children of every city. We left no survivor.

35"We took only the animals as our booty and the spoil of the cities which we had captured.

36"From Aroer which is on the edge of the valley of Arnon and *from* the city which is in the valley, even to Gilead, there was no city that was too high for us; the LORD our God delivered all over to us.

37"Only you did not go near to the land of the sons of Ammon, all along the river Jabbok and the cities of the hill country, and wherever the LORD our God had commanded us.

*Conquests Recounted*

**3** "THEN WE turned and went up the road to Bashan, and Og, king of Bashan, with all his people came out to meet us in battle at Edrei.

2"But the LORD said to me, 'Do not fear him, for I have delivered him and all his people and his land into your hand; and you shall do to him just as you did to Sihon king of the Amorites, who lived at Heshbon.'

3"So the LORD our God delivered Og also, king of Bashan, with all his people into our hand, and we smote them until no survivor was left.

4"And we captured all his cities at that time; there was not a city which we did not take from them: sixty cities, all the region of Argob, the kingdom of Og in Bashan.

5"All these were cities fortified with high walls, gates and bars, besides a great many unwalled towns.

6"And we utterly destroyed them, as we did to Sihon king of Heshbon, utterly destroying the men, women and children of every city.

NAS [b] I.e., Philistines [c] I.e., Crete

## New International

Avvites who lived in villages as far as Gaza, the Caphtorites coming out from Caphtor[d] destroyed them and settled in their place.)

*Defeat of Sihon King of Heshbon*

24"Set out now and cross the Arnon Gorge. See, I have given
into your hand Sihon the Amorite, king of Heshbon, and his
country. Begin to take possession of it and engage him in battle.
25This very day I will begin to put the terror and fear of you on all
the nations under heaven. They will hear reports of you and will
tremble and be in anguish because of you."

26From the desert of Kedemoth I sent messengers to Sihon king
of Heshbon offering peace and saying, 27"Let us pass through your
country. We will stay on the main road; we will not turn aside to
the right or to the left. 28Sell us food to eat and water to drink for
their price in silver. Only let us pass through on foot— 29as the
descendants of Esau, who live in Seir, and the Moabites, who live
in Ar, did for us—until we cross the Jordan into the land the LORD
our God is giving us." 30But Sihon king of Heshbon refused to let
us pass through. For the LORD your God had made his spirit
stubborn and his heart obstinate in order to give him into your
hands, as he has now done.

31The LORD said to me, "See, I have begun to deliver Sihon and
his country over to you. Now begin to conquer and possess his
land."

32When Sihon and all his army came out to meet us in battle at
Jahaz, 33the LORD our God delivered him over to us and we struck
him down, together with his sons and his whole army. 34At that
time we took all his towns and completely destroyed[e] them—men,
women and children. We left no survivors. 35But the livestock and
the plunder from the towns we had captured we carried off for
ourselves. 36From Aroer on the rim of the Arnon Gorge, and from
the town in the gorge, even as far as Gilead, not one town was too
strong for us. The LORD our God gave us all of them. 37But in
accordance with the command of the LORD our God, you did not
encroach on any of the land of the Ammonites, neither the land
along the course of the Jabbok nor that around the towns in the
hills.

*Defeat of Og King of Bashan*

**3** NEXT WE turned and went up along the road toward Bashan,
and Og king of Bashan with his whole army marched out to
meet us in battle at Edrei. 2The LORD said to me, "Do not be afraid
of him, for I have handed him over to you with his whole army
and his land. Do to him what you did to Sihon king of the Amorites, who reigned in Heshbon."

3So the LORD our God also gave into our hands Og king of
Bashan and all his army. We struck them down, leaving no survivors. 4At that time we took all his cities. There was not one of the
sixty cities that we did not take from them—the whole region of
Argob, Og's kingdom in Bashan. 5All these cities were fortified
with high walls and with gates and bars, and there were also a
great many unwalled villages. 6We completely destroyed[f] them,
as we had done with Sihon king of Heshbon, destroying[g] every

NIV [d] *23* That is, Crete [e] *34* The Hebrew term refers to the irrevocable giving over of things or persons to the LORD, often by totally destroying them. [f] *6* The Hebrew term refers to the irrevocable giving over of things or persons to the LORD, often by totally destroying them. [g] *6* The Hebrew term refers to the irrevocable giving over of things or persons to the LORD, often by totally destroying them.

## King James

7But all the cattle, and the spoil of the cities, we took for a prey
to ourselves.
8And we took at that time out of the hand of the two kings of
the Amorites the land that *was* on this side Jordan, from the river
of Arnon unto mount Hermon;
9(*Which* Hermon the Sidonians call Sirion; and the Amorites call
it Shenir;)
10All the cities of the plain, and all Gilead, and all Bashan, unto
Salchah and Edrei, cities of the kingdom of Og in Bashan.
11For only Og king of Bashan remained of the remnant of giants;
behold, his bedstead *was* a bedstead of iron; *is* it not in Rabbath of
the children of Ammon? nine cubits *was* the length thereof, and
four cubits the breadth of it, after the cubit of a man.
12And this land, *which* we possessed at that time, from Aroer,
which *is* by the river Arnon, and half mount Gilead, and the cities
thereof, gave I unto the Reubenites and to the Gadites.
13And the rest of Gilead, and all Bashan, *being* the kingdom of
Og, gave I unto the half tribe of Manasseh; all the region of Argob,
with all Bashan, which was called the land of giants.
14Jair the son of Manasseh took all the country of Argob unto
the coasts of Geshuri and Maachathi; and called them after his own
name, Bashan-havoth-jair, unto this day.
15And I gave Gilead unto Machir.
16And unto the Reubenites and unto the Gadites I gave from
Gilead even unto the river Arnon half the valley, and the border
even unto the river Jabbok, *which is* the border of the children of
Ammon;
17The plain also, and Jordan, and the coast *thereof*, from Chinnereth even unto the sea of the plain, *even* the salt sea, under
Ashdoth-pisgah eastward.
18¶ And I commanded you at that time, saying, The LORD your
God hath given you this land to possess it: ye shall pass over armed
before your brethren the children of Israel, all *that are* meet for the
war.
19But your wives, and your little ones, and your cattle, (*for* I
know that ye have much cattle,) shall abide in your cities which
I have given you;
20Until the LORD have given rest unto your brethren, as well as
unto you, and *until* they also possess the land which the LORD your
God hath given them beyond Jordan: and *then* shall ye return every
man unto his possession, which I have given you.
21¶ And I commanded Joshua at that time, saying, Thine eyes
have seen all that the LORD your God hath done unto these two
kings: so shall the LORD do unto all the kingdoms whither thou
passest.
22Ye shall not fear them: for the LORD your God he shall fight
for you.
23And I besought the LORD at that time, saying,
24O Lord GOD, thou hast begun to show thy servant thy greatness, and thy mighty hand: for what God *is there* in heaven or in
earth, that can do according to thy works, and according to thy
might?
25I pray thee, let me go over, and see the good land that *is*
beyond Jordan, that goodly mountain, and Lebanon.
26But the LORD was wroth with me for your sakes, and would
not hear me: and the LORD said unto me, Let it suffice thee; speak
no more unto me of this matter.
27Get thee up into the top of Pisgah, and lift up thine eyes
westward, and northward, and southward, and eastward, and
behold *it* with thine eyes: for thou shalt not go over this Jordan.
28But charge Joshua, and encourage him, and strengthen him:
for he shall go over before this people, and he shall cause them to
inherit the land which thou shalt see.
29So we abode in the valley over against Beth-peor.

## Amplified

7But all the cattle, and the spoil of the cities, we took for booty
for ourselves.
8So we took the land at that time out of the hand of the two
kings of the Amorites who were beyond the Jordan, from the
valley of the Arnon to Mount Hermon
9(The Sidonians call Hermon, Sirion, and the Amorites call it
Senir),
10All the cities of the plain and all Gilead and all Bashan, as far
as Salecah and Edrei, cities of the kingdom of Og in Bashan.
11For only Og king of Bashan remained of the remnant of the
[gigantic] Rephaim; behold, his bedstead was of iron; is it not in
Rabbah of the Ammonites? Nine cubits was its length, and four
cubits its breadth, using the cubit of a man [the forearm to the end
of the middle finger].
12When we took possession of this land, I gave to the Reubenites and the Gadites the territory from Aroer, which is on the edge
of the valley of Arnon, and half the hill country of Gilead and its
cities;
13The rest of Gilead, and all Bashan, the kingdom of Og, that
is, all the region of Argob, with all Bashan, I gave to the half-tribe
of Manasseh. It is called the land of Rephaim [of giant stature].
14Jair son of Manasseh took all the region of Argob, that is,
Bashan, as far as the border of the Geshurites and the Ma-acathites, and called the villages after his own name, Havvoth-jair, so
called to this day.
15And I gave Gilead to Machir [son of Manasseh].
16And to the Reubenites and Gadites I gave from Gilead even
to the valley of the Arnon, with the middle of the valley as the
boundary of it, as far over as the river Jabbok, the boundary of the
Ammonites.
17The Arabah also, with the Jordan as its boundary, from Chinnereth as far as the sea of the Arabah, the Salt [Dead] Sea, under
the cliffs [of the headlands] of Pisgah on the east.
18And I commanded you at that time, saying, The Lord your
God has given you this land to possess it; you [Reuben, Gad, and
the half-tribe of Manasseh] shall go over [the Jordan] armed before
your brethren the other Israelites, all that are able for war.
19But your wives, and your little ones, and your cattle (I know
that you have many cattle) shall remain in your cities which I have
given you,
20Until the Lord has given rest to your brethren, as to you, and
until they also possess the land which the Lord your God has given
them beyond Jordan; then shall you return every man to his
possession, which I have given you.
21And I commanded Joshua at that time, saying, Your *own* eyes
have seen all that the Lord your God has done to these two kings
[Sihon and Og]; so shall the Lord do to all the kingdoms into which
you are going over [the Jordan].
22You shall not fear them, for the Lord your God shall fight for
you.
23And I besought the Lord at that time, saying,
24O Lord God, You have only begun to show Your servant Your
greatness and Your mighty hand; for what god is there in Heaven
or on earth, that can do according to Your works, and according
to Your might?
25I pray You, [will You not just] let me go over and see the good
land that is beyond Jordan, that goodly mountain country [with
Hermon], and Lebanon?
26But the Lord was angry with me on your account, and would
not listen to me; and the Lord said to me, That is enough; say no
more to Me about it.
27Get up to the top of Pisgah, and lift up your eyes westward,
and northward, and southward, and eastward, and behold it with
your eyes; for you shall not go over this Jordan.
28But charge Joshua, and encourage and strengthen him; for he
shall go over before this people, and he shall cause them to possess
the land which you shall see.
29So we remained in the valley opposite Beth-peor.

## New American Standard

7"But all the animals and the spoil of the cities we took as our booty.

8"Thus we took the land at that time from the hand of the two kings of the Amorites who were beyond the Jordan, from the valley of Arnon to Mount Hermon

9(Sidonians call Hermon Sirion, and the Amorites call it Senir):

10all the cities of the tableland and all Gilead and all Bashan, as far as Salecah and Edrei, cities of the kingdom of Og in Bashan.

11(For only Og king of Bashan was left of the remnant of the Rephaim. Behold, his bedstead was an iron bedstead; it is in Rabbah of the sons of Ammon. Its length was nine cubits and its width four cubits by ordinary cubit.)

12¶ "So we took possession of this land at that time. From Aroer, which is by the valley of Arnon, and half the hill country of Gilead and its cities, I gave to the Reubenites and to the Gadites.

13"And the rest of Gilead, and all Bashan, the kingdom of Og, I gave to the half-tribe of Manasseh, all the region of Argob (concerning all Bashan, it is called the land of Rephaim.

14Jair the son of Manasseh took all the region of Argob as far as the border of the Geshurites and the Maacathites, and called it, *that is*, Bashan, after his own name, Havvoth-jair, *as it is* to this day.)

15"And to Machir I gave Gilead.

16"And to the Reubenites and to the Gadites, I gave from Gilead even as far as the valley of Arnon, the middle of the valley as a border and as far as the river Jabbok, the border of the sons of Ammon;

17the Arabah also, with the Jordan as *a* border, from [a]Chinnereth even as far as the sea of the Arabah, the Salt Sea, at the foot of the slopes of Pisgah on the east.

18¶ "Then I commanded you at that time, saying, 'The LORD your God has given you this land to possess it; all you valiant men shall cross over armed before your brothers, the sons of Israel.

19'But your wives and your little ones and your livestock (I know that you have much livestock), shall remain in your cities which I have given you,

20until the LORD gives rest to your fellow countrymen as to you, and they also possess the land which the LORD your God will give them beyond the Jordan. Then you may return every man to his possession, which I have given you.'

21"And I commanded Joshua at that time, saying, 'Your eyes have seen all that the LORD your God has done to these two kings; so the LORD shall do to all the kingdoms into which you are about to cross.

22'Do not fear them, for the LORD your God is the one fighting for you.'

23¶ "I also pleaded with the LORD at that time, saying,

24'O Lord GOD, Thou hast begun to show Thy servant Thy greatness and Thy strong hand; for what god is there in heaven or on earth who can do such works and mighty acts as Thine?

25'Let me, I pray, cross over and see the fair land that is beyond the Jordan, that good hill country and Lebanon.'

26"But the LORD was angry with me on your account, and would not listen to me; and the LORD said to me, 'Enough! Speak to Me no more of this matter.

27'Go up to the top of Pisgah and lift up your eyes to the west and north and south and east, and see *it* with your eyes, for you shall not cross over this Jordan.

28'But charge Joshua and encourage him and strengthen him; for he shall go across at the head of this people, and he shall give them as an inheritance the land which you will see.'

29"So we remained in the valley opposite Beth-peor.

NAS [a] I.e., the Sea of Galilee

## New International

city—men, women and children. 7But all the livestock and the
plunder from their cities we carried off for ourselves.
8So at that time we took from these two kings of the Amorites
the territory east of the Jordan, from the Arnon Gorge as far as
Mount Hermon. 9(Hermon is called Sirion by the Sidonians; the
Amorites call it Senir.) 10We took all the towns on the plateau, and
all Gilead, and all Bashan as far as Salecah and Edrei, towns of Og's
kingdom in Bashan. 11(Only Og king of Bashan was left of the
remnant of the Rephaites. His bed[b] was made of iron and was
more than thirteen feet long and six feet wide.[c] It is still in Rabbah
of the Ammonites.)

### *Division of the Land*

12Of the land that we took over at that time, I gave the Reubenites and the Gadites the territory north of Aroer by the Arnon
Gorge, including half the hill country of Gilead, together with its
towns. 13The rest of Gilead and also all of Bashan, the kingdom of
Og, I gave to the half tribe of Manasseh. (The whole region of
Argob in Bashan used to be known as a land of the Rephaites.
14Jair, a descendant of Manasseh, took the whole region of Argob
as far as the border of the Geshurites and the Maacathites; it was
named after him, so that to this day Bashan is called Havvoth
Jair.[d]) 15And I gave Gilead to Makir. 16But to the Reubenites and
the Gadites I gave the territory extending from Gilead down to the
Arnon Gorge (the middle of the gorge being the border) and out
to the Jabbok River, which is the border of the Ammonites. 17Its
western border was the Jordan in the Arabah, from Kinnereth to
the Sea of the Arabah (the Salt Sea[e]), below the slopes of Pisgah.
18I commanded you at that time: "The LORD your God has given
you this land to take possession of it. But all your able-bodied men,
armed for battle, must cross over ahead of your brother Israelites.
19However, your wives, your children and your livestock (I know
you have much livestock) may stay in the towns I have given you,
20until the LORD gives rest to your brothers as he has to you, and
they too have taken over the land that the LORD your God is giving
them, across the Jordan. After that, each of you may go back to the
possession I have given you."

### *Moses Forbidden to Cross the Jordan*

21At that time I commanded Joshua: "You have seen with your
own eyes all that the LORD your God has done to these two kings.
The LORD will do the same to all the kingdoms over there where
you are going. 22Do not be afraid of them; the LORD your God
himself will fight for you."
23At that time I pleaded with the LORD: 24"O Sovereign LORD,
you have begun to show to your servant your greatness and your
strong hand. For what god is there in heaven or on earth who can
do the deeds and mighty works you do? 25Let me go over and see
the good land beyond the Jordan—that fine hill country and Lebanon."
26But because of you the LORD was angry with me and would
not listen to me. "That is enough," the LORD said. "Do not speak
to me anymore about this matter. 27Go up to the top of Pisgah and
look west and north and south and east. Look at the land with your
own eyes, since you are not going to cross this Jordan. 28But
commission Joshua, and encourage and strengthen him, for he
will lead this people across and will cause them to inherit the land
that you will see." 29So we stayed in the valley near Beth Peor.

NIV [b] *11* Or *sarcophagus* [c] *11* Hebrew *nine cubits long and four cubits wide* (about 4 meters long and 1.8 meters wide) [d] *14* Or *called the settlements of Jair* [e] *17* That is, the Dead Sea

## King James

**4** NOW THEREFORE hearken, O Israel, unto the statutes and unto the judgments, which I teach you, for to do *them,* that ye may live, and go in and possess the land which the LORD God of your fathers giveth you.

2 Ye shall not add unto the word which I command you, neither shall ye diminish *aught* from it, that ye may keep the commandments of the LORD your God which I command you.

3 Your eyes have seen what the LORD did because of Baal-peor: for all the men that followed Baal-peor, the LORD thy God hath destroyed them from among you.

4 But ye that did cleave unto the LORD your God *are* alive every one of you this day.

5 Behold, I have taught you statutes and judgments, even as the LORD my God commanded me, that ye should do so in the land whither ye go to possess it.

6 Keep therefore and do *them;* for this *is* your wisdom and your understanding in the sight of the nations, which shall hear all these statutes, and say, Surely this great nation *is* a wise and understanding people.

7 For what nation *is there so* great, who *hath* God *so* nigh unto them, as the LORD our God *is* in all *things that* we call upon him *for?*

8 And what nation *is there so* great, that hath statutes and judgments *so* righteous as all this law, which I set before you this day?

9 Only take heed to thyself, and keep thy soul diligently, lest thou forget the things which thine eyes have seen, and lest they depart from thy heart all the days of thy life: but teach them thy sons, and thy sons' sons;

10 *Specially* the day that thou stoodest before the LORD thy God in Horeb, when the LORD said unto me, Gather me the people together, and I will make them hear my words, that they may learn to fear me all the days that they shall live upon the earth, and *that* they may teach their children.

11 And ye came near and stood under the mountain; and the mountain burned with fire unto the midst of heaven, with darkness, clouds, and thick darkness.

12 And the LORD spake unto you out of the midst of the fire: ye heard the voice of the words, but saw no similitude; only *ye heard* a voice.

13 And he declared unto you his covenant, which he commanded you to perform, *even* ten commandments; and he wrote them upon two tables of stone.

14 ¶ And the LORD commanded me at that time to teach you statutes and judgments, that ye might do them in the land whither ye go over to possess it.

15 Take ye therefore good heed unto yourselves; for ye saw no manner of similitude on the day *that* the LORD spake unto you in Horeb out of the midst of the fire:

16 Lest ye corrupt *yourselves,* and make you a graven image, the similitude of any figure, the likeness of male or female,

17 The likeness of any beast that *is* on the earth, the likeness of any winged fowl that flieth in the air,

18 The likeness of any thing that creepeth on the ground, the likeness of any fish that *is* in the waters beneath the earth:

19 And lest thou lift up thine eyes unto heaven, and when thou seest the sun, and the moon, and the stars, *even* all the host of heaven, shouldest be driven to worship them, and serve them, which the LORD thy God hath divided unto all nations under the whole heaven.

20 But the LORD hath taken you, and brought you forth out of the iron furnace, *even* out of Egypt, to be unto him a people of inheritance, as *ye are* this day.

21 Furthermore the LORD was angry with me for your sakes, and sware that I should not go over Jordan, and that I should not go in unto that good land, which the LORD thy God giveth thee *for* an inheritance:

## Amplified

**4** NOW LISTEN *and* give heed, O Israel, to the statutes and ordinances which I teach you, and do them, that you may live, and go in and possess the land which the Lord, the God of your fathers, gives you.

2 You shall not add to the word which I command you, neither shall you diminish it, that you may keep the commandments of the Lord your God which I command you.

3 Your eyes still see what the Lord did because of Baal-peor; for all the men who followed the Baal of Peor the Lord your God has destroyed from among you; [Num. 25:1-9.]

4 But you who clung fast to the Lord your God are alive, every one of you, this day.

5 Behold, I have taught you statutes and ordinances as the Lord my God commanded me, that you should do them in the land which you are entering to possess.

6 So keep them and do them; for that is your wisdom and your understanding in the sight of the peoples, who, when they hear all these statutes, will say, Surely this great nation is a wise and understanding people.

7 For what great nation is there who has a god so near to them as the Lord our God is to us in all things for which we call upon Him?

8 And what large *and* important nation has statutes and ordinances so upright *and* just as all this law which I set before you today?

9 Only take heed, and guard your life diligently, lest you forget the things which your eyes have seen, and lest they depart from your [mind and] heart all the days of your life; teach them to your children, and your children's children;

10 Especially how on the day that you stood before the Lord your God in Horeb, the Lord said to me, Gather the people together to Me, and I will make them hear My words, that they may learn (reverently) to fear Me all the days they live upon the earth, and that they may teach their children.

11 And you came near and stood at the foot of the mountain; and the mountain burned with fire to the heart of Heaven, with darkness, cloud, and thick gloom.

12 And the Lord spoke to you out of the midst of the fire; you heard the voice of the words, but saw no form; there was only a voice.

13 And He declared to you His covenant, which He commanded you to perform, the ten commandments; and He wrote them on two tables of stone.

14 And the Lord commanded me at that time to teach you statutes and precepts, that you might do them in the land which you are going over to possess.

15 Therefore take good heed to yourselves; since you saw no form of Him on the day the Lord spoke to you on Horeb out of the midst of the fire,

16 Beware lest you become corrupt by making for yourself [to worship] a graven image in the form of any figure, the likeness of male or female,

17 The likeness of any beast that is on the earth, or of any winged fowl that flies in the air,

18 The likeness of anything that creeps on the ground, or of any fish that is in the waters beneath the earth.

19 And beware lest you lift up your eyes to the heavens, and when you see the sun, moon, and stars, even all the host of the heavens, you be drawn away and worship them and serve them, things which the Lord your God has allotted to all nations under the whole heavens.

20 But the Lord has taken you, and brought you forth out of the iron furnace, out of Egypt, to be to Him a people of His own possession, as this day.

21 Furthermore the Lord was angry with me because of you, and He swore that I should not go over the Jordan, and that I should not enter the good land, which the Lord your God gives you for an inheritance.

## New American Standard

*Israel Urged to Obey God's Law*

**4** "AND NOW, O Israel, listen to the statutes and the judgments which I am teaching you to perform, in order that you may live and go in and take possession of the land which the LORD, the God of your fathers, is giving you.

2"You shall not add to the word which I am commanding you, nor take away from it, that you may keep the commandments of the LORD your God which I command you.

3"Your eyes have seen what the LORD has done in the case of Baal-peor, for all the men who followed Baal-peor, the LORD your God has destroyed them from among you.

4"But you who held fast to the LORD your God are alive today, every one of you.

5"See, I have taught you statutes and judgments just as the LORD my God commanded me, that you should do thus in the land where you are entering to possess it.

6"So keep and do *them*, for that is your wisdom and your understanding in the sight of the peoples who will hear all these statutes and say, 'Surely this great nation is a wise and understanding people.'

7"For what great nation is there that has a god so near to it as is the LORD our God whenever we call on Him?

8"Or what great nation is there that has statutes and judgments as righteous as this whole law which I am setting before you today?

9¶ "Only give heed to yourself and keep your soul diligently, lest you forget the things which your eyes have seen, and lest they depart from your heart all the days of your life; but make them known to your sons and your grandsons.

10" *Remember* the day you stood before the LORD your God at Horeb, when the LORD said to me, 'Assemble the people to Me, that I may let them hear My words so they may learn to [a]fear Me all the days they live on the earth, and that they may teach their children.'

11"And you came near and stood at the foot of the mountain, and the mountain burned with fire to the *very* heart of the heavens: darkness, cloud and thick gloom.

12"Then the LORD spoke to you from the midst of the fire; you heard the sound of words, but you saw no form—only a voice.

13"So He declared to you His covenant which He commanded you to perform, *that is,* the ten commandments; and He wrote them on two tablets of stone.

14"And the LORD commanded me at that time to teach you statutes and judgments, that you might perform them in the land where you are going over to possess it.

15¶ "So watch yourselves carefully, since you did not see any form on the day the LORD spoke to you at Horeb from the midst of the fire,

16lest you act corruptly and make a graven image for yourselves in the form of any figure, the likeness of male or female,

17the likeness of any animal that is on the earth, the likeness of any winged bird that flies in the sky,

18the likeness of anything that creeps on the ground, the likeness of any fish that is in the water below the earth.

19"And *beware,* lest you lift up your eyes to heaven and see the sun and the moon and the stars, all the host of heaven, and be drawn away and worship them and serve them, those which the LORD your God has allotted to all the peoples under the whole heaven.

20"But the LORD has taken you and brought you out of the iron furnace, from Egypt, to be a people for His own possession, as today.

21"Now the LORD was angry with me on your account, and swore that I should not cross the Jordan, and that I should not enter the good land which the LORD your God is giving you as an inheritance.

NAS [a] Or, *reverence*

## New International

*Obedience Commanded*

**4** HEAR NOW, O Israel, the decrees and laws I am about to teach you. Follow them so that you may live and may go in and take possession of the land that the LORD, the God of your fathers, is giving you. 2Do not add to what I command you and do not subtract from it, but keep the commands of the LORD your God that I give you.

3You saw with your own eyes what the LORD did at Baal Peor. The LORD your God destroyed from among you everyone who followed the Baal of Peor, 4but all of you who held fast to the LORD your God are still alive today.

5See, I have taught you decrees and laws as the LORD my God commanded me, so that you may follow them in the land you are entering to take possession of it. 6Observe them carefully, for this will show your wisdom and understanding to the nations, who will hear about all these decrees and say, "Surely this great nation is a wise and understanding people." 7What other nation is so great as to have their gods near them the way the LORD our God is near us whenever we pray to him? 8And what other nation is so great as to have such righteous decrees and laws as this body of laws I am setting before you today?

9Only be careful, and watch yourselves closely so that you do not forget the things your eyes have seen or let them slip from your heart as long as you live. Teach them to your children and to their children after them. 10Remember the day you stood before the LORD your God at Horeb, when he said to me, "Assemble the people before me to hear my words so that they may learn to revere me as long as they live in the land and may teach them to their children." 11You came near and stood at the foot of the mountain while it blazed with fire to the very heavens, with black clouds and deep darkness. 12Then the LORD spoke to you out of the fire. You heard the sound of words but saw no form; there was only a voice. 13He declared to you his covenant, the Ten Commandments, which he commanded you to follow and then wrote them on two stone tablets. 14And the LORD directed me at that time to teach you the decrees and laws you are to follow in the land that you are crossing the Jordan to possess.

*Idolatry Forbidden*

15You saw no form of any kind the day the LORD spoke to you at Horeb out of the fire. Therefore watch yourselves very carefully, 16so that you do not become corrupt and make for yourselves an idol, an image of any shape, whether formed like a man or a woman, 17or like any animal on earth or any bird that flies in the air, 18or like any creature that moves along the ground or any fish in the waters below. 19And when you look up to the sky and see the sun, the moon and the stars—all the heavenly array—do not be enticed into bowing down to them and worshiping things the LORD your God has apportioned to all the nations under heaven. 20But as for you, the LORD took you and brought you out of the iron-smelting furnace, out of Egypt, to be the people of his inheritance, as you now are.

21The LORD was angry with me because of you, and he solemnly swore that I would not cross the Jordan and enter the good land the LORD your God is giving you as your inheritance. 22I will die

## King James

22 But I must die in this land, I must not go over Jordan: but ye shall go over, and possess that good land.

23 Take heed unto yourselves, lest ye forget the covenant of the LORD your God, which he made with you, and make you a graven image, *or* the likeness of any *thing*, which the LORD thy God hath forbidden thee.

24 For the LORD thy God *is* a consuming fire, *even* a jealous God.

25 ¶ When thou shalt beget children, and children's children, and ye shall have remained long in the land, and shall corrupt *yourselves*, and make a graven image, *or* the likeness of any *thing*, and shall do evil in the sight of the LORD thy God, to provoke him to anger:

26 I call heaven and earth to witness against you this day, that ye shall soon utterly perish from off the land whereunto ye go over Jordan to possess it; ye shall not prolong *your* days upon it, but shall utterly be destroyed.

27 And the LORD shall scatter you among the nations, and ye shall be left few in number among the heathen, whither the LORD shall lead you.

28 And there ye shall serve gods, the work of men's hands, wood and stone, which neither see, nor hear, nor eat, nor smell.

29 But if from thence thou shalt seek the LORD thy God, thou shalt find *him*, if thou seek him with all thy heart and with all thy soul.

30 When thou art in tribulation, and all these things are come upon thee, *even* in the latter days, if thou turn to the LORD thy God, and shalt be obedient unto his voice;

31 (For the LORD thy God *is* a merciful God;) he will not forsake thee, neither destroy thee, nor forget the covenant of thy fathers which he sware unto them.

32 For ask now of the days that are past, which were before thee, since the day that God created man upon the earth, and *ask* from the one side of heaven unto the other, whether there hath been *any such thing* as this great thing *is*, or hath been heard like it?

33 Did *ever* people hear the voice of God speaking out of the midst of the fire, as thou hast heard, and live?

34 Or hath God assayed to go *and* take him a nation from the midst of *another* nation, by temptations, by signs, and by wonders, and by war, and by a mighty hand, and by a stretched out arm, and by great terrors, according to all that the LORD your God did for you in Egypt before your eyes?

35 Unto thee it was shown, that thou mightest know that the LORD he *is* God; *there is* none else beside him.

36 Out of heaven he made thee to hear his voice, that he might instruct thee: and upon earth he showed thee his great fire; and thou heardest his words out of the midst of the fire.

37 And because he loved thy fathers, therefore he chose their seed after them, and brought thee out in his sight with his mighty power out of Egypt;

38 To drive out nations from before thee greater and mightier than thou *art*, to bring thee in, to give thee their land *for* an inheritance, as *it is* this day.

39 Know therefore this day, and consider *it* in thine heart, that the LORD he *is* God in heaven above, and upon the earth beneath: *there is* none else.

40 Thou shalt keep therefore his statutes, and his commandments, which I command thee this day, that it may go well with thee, and with thy children after thee, and that thou mayest prolong *thy* days upon the earth, which the LORD thy God giveth thee, for ever.

41 ¶ Then Moses severed three cities on this side Jordan toward the sunrising;

42 That the slayer might flee thither, which should kill his neighbour unawares, and hated him not in times past; and that fleeing unto one of these cities he might live:

43 *Namely*, Bezer in the wilderness, in the plain country, of the Reubenites; and Ramoth in Gilead, of the Gadites; and Golan in Bashan, of the Manassites.

44 ¶ And this *is* the law which Moses set before the children of Israel:

## Amplified

22 But I must die in this land, I must not cross the Jordan; but you shall go over and possess that good land.

23 Take heed to yourselves, lest you forget the covenant of the Lord your God, which He made with you, and make you a graven image in the form of anything, which the Lord your God has forbidden you.

24 For the Lord your God is a consuming fire, a jealous God.

25 When children shall be born to you, and children's children, and you have grown old in the land, if you corrupt yourselves by making a graven image in the form of anything, and do evil in the sight of the Lord your God, provoking Him to anger,

26 I call Heaven and earth to witness against you this day, that you shall soon utterly perish from off the land which you are going over the Jordan to possess; you will not live long upon it, but will be utterly destroyed.

27 And the Lord will scatter you among the peoples, and you will be left few in number among the nations to which the Lord will drive you.

28 There you will serve gods, the work of men's hands, wood and stone, which neither see, nor hear, nor eat, nor smell.

29 But if from there you will seek [inquire of and require as necessity] the Lord your God, you will find Him, if you [truly] seek Him with all your heart (and mind) and soul and life.

30 When you are in tribulation, and all these things come upon you in the latter days, if you turn to the Lord your God, and are obedient to His voice,

31 For the Lord your God is a merciful God, He will not fail you, or destroy you, or forget the covenant of your fathers which He swore to them.

32 For ask now of the days that are past, which were before you, since the day that God created man upon the earth, and ask from one end of the heavens to the other, whether any such a great thing as this has ever occurred or been heard of anywhere?

33 Did ever people hear the voice of God speaking out of the midst of the fire, as you heard, and live?

34 Or has God ever tried to go and take for Himself a nation from the midst of another nation, by trials, by signs, by wonders, by war, by a mighty hand, by an outstretched arm, and by great terrors, as the Lord your God did for you in Egypt before your eyes?

35 To you it was shown, that you might realize *and* have personal knowledge that the Lord is God; there is no other besides Him.

36 Out of Heaven He made you hear His voice, that He might correct, discipline *and* admonish you; and on earth He made you see His great fire, and you heard His words out of the midst of the fire.

37 And because He loved your fathers, He chose their descendants after them, and brought you out with His own presence, by His mighty power from Egypt,

38 Driving out nations from before you, greater and mightier than yourselves, to bring you in, to give you their land for an inheritance, as this day;

39 Know, recognize *and* understand therefore this day, and turn your [mind and] heart to it, that the Lord is God in the heavens above, and upon the earth beneath; there is no other.

40 Therefore you shall keep His statutes and His commandments, which I command you this day, that it may go well with you and your children after you, and that you may prolong your days in the land which the Lord your God gives you for ever.

41 Then Moses set apart three cities [of refuge] beyond the Jordan to the east,

42 That the manslayer might flee there, who slew his neighbor unintentionally, and had not previously been at enmity with him, that fleeing to one of these cities he might save his life:

43 Bezer in the wilderness on the tableland for the Reubenites, and Ramoth in Gilead for the Gadites, and Golan in Bashan for the Manassites.

44 This is the law which Moses set before the Israelites;

## New American Standard

22"For I shall die in this land, I shall not cross the Jordan, but
you shall cross and take possession of this good land.
23"So watch yourselves, lest you forget the covenant of the
LORD your God, which He made with you, and make for yourselves a graven image in the form of anything *against* which the
LORD your God has commanded you.
24"For the LORD your God is a consuming fire, a jealous God.
**25**¶ "When you become the father of children and children's
children and have remained long in the land, and act corruptly,
and make an idol in the form of anything, and do that which is evil
in the sight of the LORD your God *so as* to provoke Him to anger,
26I call heaven and earth to witness against you today, that you
shall surely perish quickly from the land where you are going over
the Jordan to possess it. You shall not live long on it, but shall be
utterly destroyed.
27"And the LORD will scatter you among the peoples, and you
shall be left few in number among the nations, where the LORD
shall drive you.
28"And there you will serve gods, the work of man's hands,
wood and stone, which neither see nor hear nor eat nor smell.
29"But from there you will seek the LORD your God, and you
will find *Him* if you search for Him with all your heart and all your
soul.
30"When you are in distress and all these things have come
upon you, in the latter days, you will return to the LORD your God
and listen to His voice.
31"For the LORD your God is a compassionate God; He will not
fail you nor destroy you nor forget the covenant with your fathers
which He swore to them.
**32**¶ "Indeed, ask now concerning the former days which were
before you, since the day that God created man on the earth, and
*inquire* from one end of the heavens to the other. Has *anything* been
done like this great thing, or has *anything* been heard like it?
33"Has *any* people heard the voice of God speaking from the
midst of the fire, as you have heard *it*, and survived?
34"Or has a god tried to go to take for himself a nation from
within *another* nation by trials, by signs and wonders and by war
and by a mighty hand and by an outstretched arm and by great
terrors, as the LORD your God did for you in Egypt before your
eyes?
35"To you it was shown that you might know that the LORD, He
is God; there is no other besides Him.
36"Out of the heavens He let you hear His voice to discipline
you; and on earth He let you see His great fire, and you heard His
words from the midst of the fire.
37"Because He loved your fathers, therefore He chose their
descendants after them. And He personally brought you from
Egypt by His great power,
38driving out from before you nations greater and mightier than
you, to bring you in *and* to give you their land for an inheritance,
as it is today.
39"Know therefore today, and take it to your heart, that the
LORD, He is God in heaven above and on the earth below; there
is no other.
40"So you shall keep His statutes and His commandments
which I am giving you today, that it may go well with you and with
your children after you, and that you may live long on the land
which the LORD your God is giving you for all time."
**41**¶ Then Moses set apart three cities across the Jordan to the
east,
42that a manslayer might flee there, who unintentionally slew
his neighbor without having enmity toward him in time past; and
by fleeing to one of these cities he might live:
43Bezer in the wilderness on the plateau for the Reubenites, and
Ramoth in Gilead for the Gadites, and Golan in Bashan for the
Manassites.
**44**¶ Now this is the law which Moses set before the sons of Israel;

## New International

in this land; I will not cross the Jordan; but you are about to cross
over and take possession of that good land. 23Be careful not to
forget the covenant of the LORD your God that he made with you;
do not make for yourselves an idol in the form of anything the
LORD your God has forbidden. 24For the LORD your God is a
consuming fire, a jealous God.
25After you have had children and grandchildren and have
lived in the land a long time—if you then become corrupt and
make any kind of idol, doing evil in the eyes of the LORD your God
and provoking him to anger, 26I call heaven and earth as witnesses
against you this day that you will quickly perish from the land that
you are crossing the Jordan to possess. You will not live there long
but will certainly be destroyed. 27The LORD will scatter you among
the peoples, and only a few of you will survive among the nations
to which the LORD will drive you. 28There you will worship man-
made gods of wood and stone, which cannot see or hear or eat or
smell. 29But if from there you seek the LORD your God, you will
find him if you look for him with all your heart and with all your
soul. 30When you are in distress and all these things have happened to you, then in later days you will return to the LORD your
God and obey him. 31For the LORD your God is a merciful God; he
will not abandon or destroy you or forget the covenant with your
forefathers, which he confirmed to them by oath.

*The LORD Is God*

32Ask now about the former days, long before your time, from
the day God created man on the earth; ask from one end of the
heavens to the other. Has anything so great as this ever happened,
or has anything like it ever been heard of? 33Has any other people
heard the voice of God[a] speaking out of fire, as you have, and
lived? 34Has any god ever tried to take for himself one nation out
of another nation, by testings, by miraculous signs and wonders,
by war, by a mighty hand and an outstretched arm, or by great and
awesome deeds, like all the things the LORD your God did for you
in Egypt before your very eyes?
35You were shown these things so that you might know that the
LORD is God; besides him there is no other. 36From heaven he
made you hear his voice to discipline you. On earth he showed you
his great fire, and you heard his words from out of the fire. 37Be-
cause he loved your forefathers and chose their descendants after
them, he brought you out of Egypt by his Presence and his great
strength, 38to drive out before you nations greater and stronger
than you and to bring you into their land to give it to you for your
inheritance, as it is today.
39Acknowledge and take to heart this day that the LORD is God
in heaven above and on the earth below. There is no other. 40Keep
his decrees and commands, which I am giving you today, so that
it may go well with you and your children after you and that you
may live long in the land the LORD your God gives you for all time.

*Cities of Refuge*

41Then Moses set aside three cities east of the Jordan, 42to which
anyone who had killed a person could flee if he had unintentionally killed his neighbor without malice aforethought. He could flee
into one of these cities and save his life. 43The cities were these:
Bezer in the desert plateau, for the Reubenites; Ramoth in Gilead,
for the Gadites; and Golan in Bashan, for the Manassites.

*Introduction to the Law*

44This is the law Moses set before the Israelites. 45These are the

NIV [a] 33 Or *of a god*

## King James

45These *are* the testimonies, and the statutes, and the judgments, which Moses spake unto the children of Israel, after they
came forth out of Egypt,
46On this side Jordan, in the valley over against Beth-peor, in
the land of Sihon king of the Amorites, who dwelt at Heshbon,
whom Moses and the children of Israel smote, after they were
come forth out of Egypt:
47And they possessed his land, and the land of Og king of
Bashan, two kings of the Amorites, which *were* on this side Jordan
toward the sunrising;
48From Aroer, which *is* by the bank of the river Arnon, even
unto mount Sion, which *is* Hermon,
49And all the plain on this side Jordan eastward, even unto the
sea of the plain, under the springs of Pisgah.

**5** AND MOSES called all Israel, and said unto them, Hear, O
Israel, the statutes and judgments which I speak in your ears
this day, that ye may learn them, and keep, and do them.
2The LORD our God made a covenant with us in Horeb.
3The LORD made not this covenant with our fathers, but with
us, *even* us, who *are* all of us here alive this day.
4The LORD talked with you face to face in the mount out of the
midst of the fire,
5(I stood between the LORD and you at that time, to show you
the word of the LORD: for ye were afraid by reason of the fire, and
went not up into the mount;) saying,
6¶ I *am* the LORD thy God, which brought thee out of the land
of Egypt, from the house of bondage.
7Thou shalt have none other gods before me.
8Thou shalt not make thee *any* graven image, *or* any likeness *of*
*any thing* that *is* in heaven above, or that *is* in the earth beneath,
or that *is* in the waters beneath the earth:
9Thou shalt not bow down thyself unto them, nor serve them:
for I the LORD thy God *am* a jealous God, visiting the iniquity of
the fathers upon the children unto the third and fourth *generation*
of them that hate me,
10And showing mercy unto thousands of them that love me and
keep my commandments.
11Thou shalt not take the name of the LORD thy God in vain: for
the LORD will not hold *him* guiltless that taketh his name in vain.
12Keep the sabbath day to sanctify it, as the LORD thy God hath
commanded thee.
13Six days thou shalt labour, and do all thy work:
14But the seventh day *is* the sabbath of the LORD thy God: *in it*
thou shalt not do any work, thou, nor thy son, nor thy daughter,
nor thy manservant, nor thy maidservant, nor thine ox, nor thine
ass, nor any of thy cattle, nor thy stranger that *is* within thy gates;
that thy manservant and thy maidservant may rest as well as thou.
15And remember that thou wast a servant in the land of Egypt,
and *that* the LORD thy God brought thee out thence through a
mighty hand and by a stretched out arm: therefore the LORD thy
God commanded thee to keep the sabbath day.
16¶ Honour thy father and thy mother, as the LORD thy God
hath commanded thee; that thy days may be prolonged, and that
it may go well with thee, in the land which the LORD thy God
giveth thee.
17Thou shalt not kill.
18Neither shalt thou commit adultery.
19Neither shalt thou steal.
20Neither shalt thou bear false witness against thy neighbour.

## Amplified

45These are the testimonies, and the laws, and the precepts,
which Moses spoke to the Israelites when they came out of Egypt,
46Beyond the Jordan in the valley opposite Bethpeor, in the land
of Sihon king of the Amorites, who dwelt at Heshbon, whom
Moses and the Israelites smote when they came out of Egypt.
47And they took possession of his land and the land of Og king
of Bashan, the two kings of the Amorites, who lived beyond the
Jordan to the east;
48From Aroer, which is on the edge of the valley of the Arnon,
as far as Mount Sirion (that is, Hermon),
49And all the Arabah (lowlands) beyond the Jordan eastward,
as far as the Sea of the Arabah [the Dead Sea], under the slopes
*and* springs of Pisgah.

**5** AND MOSES called all Israel, and said to them, Hear, O
Israel, the statutes and ordinances which I speak in your
hearing this day, that you may learn them, and take heed and do
them.
2The Lord our God made a covenant with us in Horeb.
3The Lord made this covenant not with our fathers, but with us,
who are all of us here alive this day.
4The Lord spoke with you face to face in the mount out of the
midst of the fire.
5I stood between the Lord and you at that time, to show you
the word of the Lord; for you were afraid because of the fire, and
went not up into the mount. He said,
6I am the Lord your God, Who brought you out of the land of
Egypt, from the house of bondage.
7You shall have no other gods before Me *or* besides Me.
8You shall not make for yourself [to worship] a graven image,
or any likeness of anything that is in the heavens above, or that
is in the earth beneath, or that is in the water under the earth;
9You shall not bow down yourself to them or serve them; for
I the Lord your God am a jealous God, visiting the iniquity of the
fathers upon the children to the third and fourth generations of
those who hate Me,
10And showing mercy *and* steadfast love to thousands *and* to a
thousand generations of those who love Me and keep My commandments.
11You shall not take the name of the Lord your God in vain; for
the Lord will not hold him guiltless who takes His name in falsehood *or* without purpose.
12Observe the sabbath day to keep it holy, as the Lord your God
commanded you.
13Six days you shall labor and do all your work;
14But the seventh day is a sabbath to the Lord your God; in it
you shall not do any work, you or your son, or your daughter, or
your manservant, or your maidservant, or your ox, or your donkey, or any of your livestock, or the stranger *or* sojourner who is
within your gates, that your manservant and your maidservant
may rest as well as you.
15And (earnestly) remember that you were a servant in the land
of Egypt, and that the Lord your God brought you out from there
with a mighty hand and an outstretched arm; therefore the Lord
your God commanded you to observe *and* take heed to the sabbath
day.
16Honor your father and your mother, as the Lord your God
commanded you, that your days may be prolonged, and that it
may go well with you in the land which the Lord your God gives
you.
17You shall not murder.
18Neither shall you commit adultery.
19Neither shall you act slyly *or* steal.
20Neither shall you witness falsely against your neighbor.

## New American Standard

45these are the testimonies and the statutes and the ordinances
which Moses spoke to the sons of Israel, when they came out from
Egypt,
46across the Jordan, in the valley opposite Beth-peor, in the land
of Sihon king of the Amorites who lived at Heshbon, whom Moses
and the sons of Israel defeated when they came out from Egypt.
47And they took possession of his land and the land of Og king
of Bashan, the two kings of the Amorites, *who were* across the
Jordan to the east,
48from Aroer, which is on the edge of the valley of Arnon, even
as far as Mount Sion (that is, Hermon),
49with all the Arabah across the Jordan to the east, even as far
as the sea of the Arabah, at the foot of the slopes of Pisgah.

*The Ten Commandments Repeated*

5 THEN MOSES summoned all Israel, and said to them, "Hear,
O Israel, the statutes and the ordinances which I am speaking
today in your hearing, that you may learn them and observe them
carefully.
2"The LORD our God made a covenant with us at Horeb.
3"The LORD did not make this covenant with our fathers, but
with us, *with* all those of us alive here today.
4"The LORD spoke to you face to face at the mountain from the
midst of the fire,
5 *while* I was standing between the LORD and you at that time,
to declare to you the word of the LORD; for you were afraid because
of the fire and did not go up the mountain. He said,
6¶ 'I am the LORD your God, who brought you out of the land
of Egypt, out of the house of slavery.
7¶ 'You shall have no other gods before Me.
8¶ 'You shall not make for yourself an idol, *or* any likeness *of*
what is in heaven above or on the earth beneath or in the water
under the earth.
9'You shall not worship them or serve them; for I, the LORD
your God, am a jealous God, visiting the iniquity of the fathers on
the children, and on the third and the fourth *generations* of those
who hate Me,
10but showing lovingkindness to thousands, to those who love
Me and keep My commandments.
11¶ 'You shall not take the name of the LORD your God in vain,
for the LORD will not leave him unpunished who takes His name
in vain.
12¶ 'Observe the sabbath day to keep it holy, as the LORD your
God commanded you.
13'Six days you shall labor and do all your work,
14but the seventh day is a sabbath of the LORD your God; *in it*
you shall not do any work, you or your son or your daughter or
your male servant or your female servant or your ox or your
donkey or any of your cattle or your sojourner who stays with you,
so that your male servant and your female servant may rest as well
as you.
15'And you shall remember that you were a slave in the land of
Egypt, and the LORD your God brought you out of there by a
mighty hand and by an outstretched arm; therefore the LORD your
God commanded you to observe the sabbath day.
16¶ 'Honor your father and your mother, as the LORD your God
has commanded you, that your days may be prolonged, and that
it may go well with you on the land which the LORD your God gives
you.
17¶ 'You shall not murder.
18¶ 'You shall not commit adultery.
19¶ 'You shall not steal.
20¶ 'You shall not bear false witness against your neighbor.

## New International

stipulations, decrees and laws Moses gave them when they came
out of Egypt 46and were in the valley near Beth Peor east of the
Jordan, in the land of Sihon king of the Amorites, who reigned in
Heshbon and was defeated by Moses and the Israelites as they
came out of Egypt. 47They took possession of his land and the land
of Og king of Bashan, the two Amorite kings east of the Jordan.
48This land extended from Aroer on the rim of the Arnon Gorge
to Mount Siyon[a] (that is, Hermon), 49and included all the Arabah
east of the Jordan, as far as the Sea of the Arabah,[b] below the
slopes of Pisgah.

*The Ten Commandments*

5 MOSES SUMMONED all Israel and said:
Hear, O Israel, the decrees and laws I declare in your hearing
today. Learn them and be sure to follow them. 2The LORD our God
made a covenant with us at Horeb. 3It was not with our fathers that
the LORD made this covenant, but with us, with all of us who are
alive here today. 4The LORD spoke to you face to face out of the
fire on the mountain. 5(At that time I stood between the LORD and
you to declare to you the word of the LORD, because you were
afraid of the fire and did not go up the mountain.) And he said:

6"I am the LORD your God, who brought you out of Egypt, out
of the land of slavery.
7"You shall have no other gods before[c] me.
8"You shall not make for yourself an idol in the form of anything in heaven above or on the earth beneath or in the
waters below. 9You shall not bow down to them or
worship them; for I, the LORD your God, am a jealous
God, punishing the children for the sin of the fathers to
the third and fourth generation of those who hate me,
10but showing love to a thousand generations of those
who love me and keep my commandments.
11"You shall not misuse the name of the LORD your God, for
the LORD will not hold anyone guiltless who misuses his
name.
12"Observe the Sabbath day by keeping it holy, as the LORD
your God has commanded you. 13Six days you shall
labor and do all your work, 14but the seventh day is a
Sabbath to the LORD your God. On it you shall not do
any work, neither you, nor your son or daughter, nor
your manservant or maidservant, nor your ox, your
donkey or any of your animals, nor the alien within
your gates, so that your manservant and maidservant
may rest, as you do. 15Remember that you were slaves
in Egypt and that the LORD your God brought you out
of there with a mighty hand and an outstretched arm.
Therefore the LORD your God has commanded you to
observe the Sabbath day.
16"Honor your father and your mother, as the LORD your God
has commanded you, so that you may live long and that
it may go well with you in the land the LORD your God
is giving you.
17"You shall not murder.
18"You shall not commit adultery.
19"You shall not steal.
20"You shall not give false testimony against your neighbor.

NIV [a] 48 Hebrew; Syriac (see also Deut. 3:9) *Sirion* [b] 49 That is, the Dead Sea [c] 7 Or *besides*

## King James

21 Neither shalt thou desire thy neighbour's wife, neither shalt thou covet thy neighbour's house, his field, or his manservant, or his maidservant, his ox, or his ass, or any *thing* that *is* thy neighbour's.

22 ¶ These words the LORD spake unto all your assembly in the mount out of the midst of the fire, of the cloud, and of the thick darkness, with a great voice: and he added no more. And he wrote them in two tables of stone, and delivered them unto me.

23 And it came to pass, when ye heard the voice out of the midst of the darkness, (for the mountain did burn with fire,) that ye came near unto me, *even* all the heads of your tribes, and your elders;

24 And ye said, Behold, the LORD our God hath shown us his glory and his greatness, and we have heard his voice out of the midst of the fire: we have seen this day that God doth talk with man, and he liveth.

25 Now therefore why should we die? for this great fire will consume us: if we hear the voice of the LORD our God any more, then we shall die.

26 For who *is there of* all flesh, that hath heard the voice of the living God speaking out of the midst of the fire, as we *have,* and lived?

27 Go thou near, and hear all that the LORD our God shall say: and speak thou unto us all that the LORD our God shall speak unto thee; and we will hear *it,* and do *it.*

28 And the LORD heard the voice of your words, when ye spake unto me; and the LORD said unto me, I have heard the voice of the words of this people, which they have spoken unto thee: they have well said all that they have spoken.

29 O that there were such an heart in them, that they would fear me, and keep all my commandments always, that it might be well with them, and with their children for ever!

30 Go say to them, Get you into your tents again.

31 But as for thee, stand thou here by me, and I will speak unto thee all the commandments, and the statutes, and the judgments, which thou shalt teach them, that they may do *them* in the land which I give them to possess it.

32 Ye shall observe to do therefore as the LORD your God hath commanded you: ye shall not turn aside to the right hand or to the left.

33 Ye shall walk in all the ways which the LORD your God hath commanded you, that ye may live, and *that it may be* well with you, and *that* ye may prolong *your* days in the land which ye shall possess.

**6** NOW THESE *are* the commandments, the statutes, and the judgments, which the LORD your God commanded to teach you, that ye might do *them* in the land whither ye go to possess it:

2 That thou mightest fear the LORD thy God, to keep all his statutes and his commandments, which I command thee, thou, and thy son, and thy son's son, all the days of thy life; and that thy days may be prolonged.

3 ¶ Hear therefore, O Israel, and observe to do *it;* that it may be well with thee, and that ye may increase mightily, as the LORD God of thy fathers hath promised thee, in the land that floweth with milk and honey.

4 Hear, O Israel: The LORD our God *is* one LORD:

5 And thou shalt love the LORD thy God with all thine heart, and with all thy soul, and with all thy might.

6 And these words, which I command thee this day, shall be in thine heart:

7 And thou shalt teach them diligently unto thy children, and shalt talk of them when thou sittest in thine house, and when thou walkest by the way, and when thou liest down, and when thou risest up.

## Amplified

21 Neither shall you covet your neighbor's wife, nor desire your neighbor's house, his field, his manservant, or his maidservant, his ox or his donkey, or anything that is your neighbor's.

22 These words the Lord spoke to all your assembly at the mountain out of the midst of the fire, the cloud, and the thick darkness, with a loud voice; and He spoke not again—added no more. He wrote them on two tables of stone, and gave them to me [Moses].

23 And when you heard the voice out of the midst of the darkness, while the mountain was burning with fire, you came near me, all the heads of your tribes, and your elders;

24 And you said, Behold, the Lord our God has shown us His glory and His greatness, and we have heard His voice out of the midst of the fire; we have this day seen that God speaks with man and man still lives.

25 Now therefore why should we die? For this great fire will consume us; if we hear the voice of the Lord our God any more, we shall die.

26 For who is there of all flesh, who has heard the voice of the living God speaking out of the midst of fire, as we have, and lived?

27 Go near [Moses], and hear all that the Lord our God will say; and speak to us all that the Lord our God will speak to you; and we will hear and do it.

28 And the Lord heard your words, when you spoke to me; and the Lord said to me, I have heard the words of this people, which they have spoken to you; they have well said all that they have spoken.

29 O that they had such a [mind and] heart in them always, (reverently) to fear Me, and keep all My commandments, that it might go well with them, and with their children for ever!

30 Go and say to them, Return to your tents.

31 But you [Moses], stand here by Me, and I will tell you all the commandments and the statutes and the precepts which you shall teach them, that they may do them in the land which I give them to possess.

32 Therefore you people shall be watchful to do as the Lord your God has commanded you; you shall not turn aside to the right hand or to the left.

33 You shall walk in all the way which the Lord your God has commanded you, that you may live, and that it may go well with you, and that you may live long in the land which you shall possess.

**6** NOW THIS is the instruction, the laws, and the precepts, which the Lord your God commanded me to teach you, that you might do them in the land to which you go to possess it;

2 That you may (reverently) fear the Lord your God, you and your son and your son's son, and keep all His statutes and His commandments, which I command you, all the days of your life; and that your days may be prolonged.

3 Hear therefore, O Israel, and be watchful to do them; that it may be well with you, and that you may increase exceedingly as the Lord God of your fathers has promised you, in a land flowing with milk and honey.

4 Hear, O Israel: the Lord our God is one Lord—the only Lord.

5 And you shall love the Lord your God with all your [mind and] heart, and with your entire being, and with all your might.

6 And these words, which I am commanding you this day, shall be [first] in your *own* mind *and* heart; [then]

7 You shall whet *and* sharpen them, so as to make them penetrate, *and* teach *and* impress them diligently upon the [minds and] hearts of your children, and shall talk of them when you sit in your house, and when you walk by the way, and when you lie down and when you rise up.

## New American Standard

21¶ 'You shall not covet your neighbor's wife, and you shall not desire your neighbor's house, his field or his male servant or his female servant, his ox or his donkey or anything that belongs to your neighbor.'

*Moses Interceded*

22¶ "These words the LORD spoke to all your assembly at the mountain from the midst of the fire, *of* the cloud and *of* the thick gloom, with a great voice, and He added no more. And He wrote them on two tablets of stone and gave them to me.

23"And it came about, when you heard the voice from the midst of the darkness, while the mountain was burning with fire, that you came near to me, all the heads of your tribes and your elders.

24"And you said, 'Behold, the LORD our God has shown us His glory and His greatness, and we have heard His voice from the midst of the fire; we have seen today that God speaks with man, yet he lives.

25'Now then why should we die? For this great fire will consume us; if we hear the voice of the LORD our God any longer, then we shall die.

26'For who is there of all flesh, who has heard the voice of the living God speaking from the midst of the fire, as we *have*, and lived?

27'Go near and hear all that the LORD our God says; then speak to us all that the LORD our God will speak to you, and we will hear and do *it*.'

28¶ "And the LORD heard the voice of your words when you spoke to me, and the LORD said to me, 'I have heard the voice of the words of this people which they have spoken to you. They have done well in all that they have spoken.

29'Oh that they had such a heart in them, that they would fear Me, and keep all My commandments always, that it may be well with them and with their sons forever!

30'Go, say to them, "Return to your tents."

31'But as for you, stand here by Me, that I may speak to you all the commandments and the statutes and the judgments which you shall teach them, that they may observe *them* in the land which I give them to possess.'

32"So you shall observe to do just as the LORD your God has commanded you; you shall not turn aside to the right or to the left.

33"You shall walk in all the way which the LORD your God has commanded you, that you may live, and that it may be well with you, and that you may prolong *your* days in the land which you shall possess.

*Obey God and Prosper*

6 "NOW THIS is the commandment, the statutes and the judgments which the LORD your God has commanded *me* to teach you, that you might do *them* in the land where you are going over to possess it,

2so that you and your son and your grandson might fear the LORD your God, to keep all His statutes and His commandments, which I command you, all the days of your life, and that your days may be prolonged.

3"O Israel, you should listen and be careful to do *it*, that it may be well with you and that you may multiply greatly, just as the LORD, the God of your fathers, has promised you, *in* a land flowing with milk and honey.

4¶ "Hear, O Israel! The LORD is our God, the LORD is one!

5"And you shall love the LORD your God with all your heart and with all your soul and with all your might.

6"And these words, which I am commanding you today, shall be on your heart;

7and you shall teach them diligently to your sons and shall talk of them when you sit in your house and when you walk by the way and when you lie down and when you rise up.

## New International

21"You shall not covet your neighbor's wife. You shall not set
your desire on your neighbor's house or land, his manservant or maidservant, his ox or donkey, or anything
that belongs to your neighbor."

22These are the commandments the LORD proclaimed in a loud
voice to your whole assembly there on the mountain from out of
the fire, the cloud and the deep darkness; and he added nothing
more. Then he wrote them on two stone tablets and gave them to
me.
23When you heard the voice out of the darkness, while the
mountain was ablaze with fire, all the leading men of your tribes
and your elders came to me. 24And you said, "The LORD our God
has shown us his glory and his majesty, and we have heard his
voice from the fire. Today we have seen that a man can live even
if God speaks with him. 25But now, why should we die? This great
fire will consume us, and we will die if we hear the voice of the
LORD our God any longer. 26For what mortal man has ever heard
the voice of the living God speaking out of fire, as we have, and
survived? 27Go near and listen to all that the LORD our God says.
Then tell us whatever the LORD our God tells you. We will listen
and obey."
28The LORD heard you when you spoke to me and the LORD said
to me, "I have heard what this people said to you. Everything they
said was good. 29Oh, that their hearts would be inclined to fear me
and keep all my commands always, so that it might go well with
them and their children forever!
30"Go, tell them to return to their tents. 31But you stay here with
me so that I may give you all the commands, decrees and laws you
are to teach them to follow in the land I am giving them to possess."
32So be careful to do what the LORD your God has commanded
you; do not turn aside to the right or to the left. 33Walk in all the
way that the LORD your God has commanded you, so that you may
live and prosper and prolong your days in the land that you will
possess.

*Love the LORD Your God*

6 THESE ARE the commands, decrees and laws the LORD your
God directed me to teach you to observe in the land that you
are crossing the Jordan to possess, 2so that you, your children and
their children after them may fear the LORD your God as long as
you live by keeping all his decrees and commands that I give you,
and so that you may enjoy long life. 3Hear, O Israel, and be careful
to obey so that it may go well with you and that you may increase
greatly in a land flowing with milk and honey, just as the LORD,
the God of your fathers, promised you.
4Hear, O Israel: The LORD our God, the LORD is one.[a] 5Love the
LORD your God with all your heart and with all your soul and with
all your strength. 6These commandments that I give you today are
to be upon your hearts. 7Impress them on your children. Talk
about them when you sit at home and when you walk along the
road, when you lie down and when you get up. 8Tie them as

NIV [a] 4 Or *The LORD our God is one LORD;* or *The LORD is our God, the LORD is one;* or *The LORD is our God, the LORD alone*

## King James

8 And thou shalt bind them for a sign upon thine hand, and they shall be as frontlets between thine eyes.

9 And thou shalt write them upon the posts of thy house, and on thy gates.

10 And it shall be, when the LORD thy God shall have brought thee into the land which he sware unto thy fathers, to Abraham, to Isaac, and to Jacob, to give thee great and goodly cities, which thou buildest not,

11 And houses full of all good *things,* which thou filledst not, and wells digged, which thou diggedst not, vineyards and olive trees, which thou plantedst not; when thou shalt have eaten and be full;

12 *Then* beware lest thou forget the LORD, which brought thee forth out of the land of Egypt, from the house of bondage.

13 Thou shalt fear the LORD thy God, and serve him, and shalt swear by his name.

14 Ye shall not go after other gods, of the gods of the people which *are* round about you;

15 (For the LORD thy God *is* a jealous God among you) lest the anger of the LORD thy God be kindled against thee, and destroy thee from off the face of the earth.

16 ¶ Ye shall not tempt the LORD your God, as ye tempted *him* in Massah.

17 Ye shall diligently keep the commandments of the LORD your God, and his testimonies, and his statutes, which he hath commanded thee.

18 And thou shalt do *that which is* right and good in the sight of the LORD: that it may be well with thee, and that thou mayest go in and possess the good land which the LORD sware unto thy fathers,

19 To cast out all thine enemies from before thee, as the LORD hath spoken.

20 *And* when thy son asketh thee in time to come, saying, What *mean* the testimonies, and the statutes, and the judgments, which the LORD our God hath commanded you?

21 Then thou shalt say unto thy son, We were Pharaoh's bondmen in Egypt; and the LORD brought us out of Egypt with a mighty hand:

22 And the LORD showed signs and wonders, great and sore, upon Egypt, upon Pharaoh, and upon all his household, before our eyes:

23 And he brought us out from thence, that he might bring us in, to give us the land which he sware unto our fathers.

24 And the LORD commanded us to do all these statutes, to fear the LORD our God, for our good always, that he might preserve us alive, as *it is* at this day.

25 And it shall be our righteousness, if we observe to do all these commandments before the LORD our God, as he hath commanded us.

**7** WHEN THE LORD thy God shall bring thee into the land whither thou goest to possess it, and hath cast out many nations before thee, the Hittites, and the Girgashites, and the Amorites, and the Canaanites, and the Perizzites, and the Hivites, and the Jebusites, seven nations greater and mightier than thou;

2 And when the LORD thy God shall deliver them before thee; thou shalt smite them, *and* utterly destroy them; thou shalt make no covenant with them, nor show mercy unto them:

3 Neither shalt thou make marriages with them; thy daughter thou shalt not give unto his son, nor his daughter shalt thou take unto thy son.

4 For they will turn away thy son from following me, that they may serve other gods: so will the anger of the LORD be kindled against you, and destroy thee suddenly.

## Amplified

8 And you shall bind them as a sign upon your hand, and they shall be as frontlets (forehead bands) between your eyes.

9 And you shall write them upon the doorposts of your house and on your gates.

10 And when the Lord your God brings you into the land which He swore to your fathers, to Abraham, Isaac, and Jacob, to give you, with great and goodly cities, which you did not build,

11 And houses full of all good things, which you did not fill, and cisterns hewn out, which you did not hew, and vineyards and olive trees, which you did not plant, and when you eat and are full,

12 Then beware lest you forget the Lord, Who brought you out of the land of Egypt, out of the house of bondage.

13 You shall (reverently) fear the Lord your God, and serve Him, and swear by His name [and presence].

14 You shall not go after other gods, of the gods of the peoples who are round about you;

15 For the Lord your God in the midst of you is a jealous God; lest the anger of the Lord your God be kindled against you, and He destroy you from off the face of the earth.

16 You shall not tempt *and* try the Lord your God, as you tempted *and* tried Him in Massah. [Exod. 17:7.]

17 You shall diligently keep the commandments of the Lord your God, and His exhortations, and His statutes, which He commanded you.

18 And you shall do what is right and good in the sight of the Lord, that it may go well with you, and that you may go in and possess the good land which the Lord swore to give to your fathers,

19 To cast out all your enemies from before you, as the Lord has promised.

20 When your son asks you in time to come, What is the meaning of the testimonies and statutes and precepts, which the Lord our God has commanded you?

21 Then you shall say to your son, We were Pharaoh's bondmen in Egypt, and the Lord brought us out of Egypt with a mighty hand;

22 And the Lord showed signs and wonders, great and evil, against Egypt, against Pharaoh and all his household, before our eyes;

23 And He brought us out from there, that He might bring us in, to give us the land which He swore to give our fathers.

24 And the Lord commanded us to do all these statutes, to (reverently) fear the Lord our God, for our good always, that He might preserve us alive, as at this day.

25 And it will be accounted as righteousness [conformity to God's will in word, thought, and action] for us, if we are watchful to do all this commandment before the Lord our God, as He has commanded us.

**7** WHEN THE Lord your God brings you into the land which you are entering to possess, and has plucked away many nations before you, the Hittites, the Girgashites, the Amorites, the Canaanites, the Perizzites, the Hivites, and the Jebusites, seven nations greater and mightier than yourselves,

2 And when the Lord your God gives them over to you, and you smite them; then you must utterly destroy them; you shall make no covenant with them, or show mercy to them.

3 You shall not make marriages with them; your daughter you shall not give to his son, nor shall you take his daughter for your son.

4 For they will turn away your sons from following Me, that they may serve other gods; so will the anger of the Lord be kindled against you, and He will destroy you quickly.

## New American Standard

8"And you shall bind them as a sign on your hand and they shall be as frontals on your forehead.

9"And you shall write them on the doorposts of your house and on your gates.

10¶ "Then it shall come about when the LORD your God brings you into the land which He swore to your fathers, Abraham, Isaac and Jacob, to give you, great and splendid cities which you did not build,

11and houses full of all good things which you did not fill, and hewn cisterns which you did not dig, vineyards and olive trees which you did not plant, and you shall eat and be satisfied,

12then watch yourself, lest you forget the LORD who brought you from the land of Egypt, out of the house of slavery.

13"You shall [a]fear *only* the LORD your God; and you shall worship Him, and swear by His name.

14"You shall not follow other gods, any of the gods of the peoples who surround you,

15for the LORD your God in the midst of you is a jealous God; otherwise the anger of the LORD your God will be kindled against you, and He will wipe you off the face of the earth.

16¶ "You shall not put the LORD your God to the test, as you tested *Him* at Massah.

17"You should diligently keep the commandments of the LORD your God, and His testimonies and His statutes which He has commanded you.

18"And you shall do what is right and good in the sight of the LORD, that it may be well with you and that you may go in and possess the good land which the LORD swore to *give* your fathers,

19by driving out all your enemies from before you, as the LORD has spoken.

20¶ "When your son asks you in time to come, saying, 'What *do* the testimonies and the statutes and the judgments *mean* which the LORD our God commanded you?'

21then you shall say to your son, 'We were slaves to Pharaoh in Egypt; and the LORD brought us from Egypt with a mighty hand.

22'Moreover, the LORD showed great and distressing signs and wonders before our eyes against Egypt, Pharaoh and all his household;

23and He brought us out from there in order to bring us in, to give us the land which He had sworn to our fathers.'

24"So the LORD commanded us to observe all these statutes, to fear the LORD our God for our good always and for our survival, as *it is* today.

25"And it will be righteousness for us if we are careful to observe all this commandment before the LORD our God, just as He commanded us.

*Warnings*

**7** "WHEN THE LORD your God shall bring you into the land where you are entering to possess it, and shall clear away many nations before you, the Hittites and the Girgashites and the Amorites and the Canaanites and the Perizzites and the Hivites and the Jebusites, seven nations greater and stronger than you,

2and when the LORD your God shall deliver them before you, and you shall defeat them, then you shall utterly destroy them. You shall make no covenant with them and show no favor to them.

3"Furthermore, you shall not intermarry with them; you shall not give your daughters to their sons, nor shall you take their daughters for your sons.

4"For they will turn your sons away from following Me to serve other gods; then the anger of the LORD will be kindled against you, and He will quickly destroy you.

NAS [a] Or, *reverence*

## New International

symbols on your hands and bind them on your foreheads. 9Write
them on the doorframes of your houses and on your gates.
10When the LORD your God brings you into the land he swore
to your fathers, to Abraham, Isaac and Jacob, to give you—a land
with large, flourishing cities you did not build, 11houses filled with
all kinds of good things you did not provide, wells you did not dig,
and vineyards and olive groves you did not plant—then when you
eat and are satisfied, 12be careful that you do not forget the LORD,
who brought you out of Egypt, out of the land of slavery.
13Fear the LORD your God, serve him only and take your oaths
in his name. 14Do not follow other gods, the gods of the peoples
around you; 15for the LORD your God, who is among you, is a
jealous God and his anger will burn against you, and he will
destroy you from the face of the land. 16Do not test the LORD your
God as you did at Massah. 17Be sure to keep the commands of the
LORD your God and the stipulations and decrees he has given you.
18Do what is right and good in the LORD's sight, so that it may go
well with you and you may go in and take over the good land that
the LORD promised on oath to your forefathers, 19thrusting out all
your enemies before you, as the LORD said.
20In the future, when your son asks you, "What is the meaning
of the stipulations, decrees and laws the LORD our God has commanded you?" 21tell him: "We were slaves of Pharaoh in Egypt,
but the LORD brought us out of Egypt with a mighty hand. 22Before
our eyes the LORD sent miraculous signs and wonders—great and
terrible—upon Egypt and Pharaoh and his whole household. 23But
he brought us out from there to bring us in and give us the land
that he promised on oath to our forefathers. 24The LORD commanded us to obey all these decrees and to fear the LORD our God,
so that we might always prosper and be kept alive, as is the case
today. 25And if we are careful to obey all this law before the LORD
our God, as he has commanded us, that will be our righteousness."

*Driving Out the Nations*

**7** WHEN THE LORD your God brings you into the land you are
entering to possess and drives out before you many nations—
the Hittites, Girgashites, Amorites, Canaanites, Perizzites, Hivites
and Jebusites, seven nations larger and stronger than you— 2and
when the LORD your God has delivered them over to you and you
have defeated them, then you must destroy them totally.[b] Make
no treaty with them, and show them no mercy. 3Do not intermarry
with them. Do not give your daughters to their sons or take their
daughters for your sons, 4for they will turn your sons away from
following me to serve other gods, and the LORD's anger will burn
against you and will quickly destroy you. 5This is what you are to

NIV [b] 2 The Hebrew term refers to the irrevocable giving over of things or persons to the LORD, often by totally destroying them; also in verse 26.

## King James

5But thus shall ye deal with them; ye shall destroy their altars, and break down their images, and cut down their groves, and burn their graven images with fire.

6For thou *art* an holy people unto the LORD thy God: the LORD thy God hath chosen thee to be a special people unto himself, above all people that *are* upon the face of the earth.

7The LORD did not set his love upon you, nor choose you, because ye were more in number than any people; for ye *were* the fewest of all people:

8But because the LORD loved you, and because he would keep the oath which he had sworn unto your fathers, hath the LORD brought you out with a mighty hand, and redeemed you out of the house of bondmen, from the hand of Pharaoh king of Egypt.

9Know therefore that the LORD thy God, he *is* God, the faithful God, which keepeth covenant and mercy with them that love him and keep his commandments to a thousand generations;

10And repayeth them that hate him to their face, to destroy them: he will not be slack to him that hateth him, he will repay him to his face.

11Thou shalt therefore keep the commandments, and the statutes, and the judgments, which I command thee this day, to do them.

12¶ Wherefore it shall come to pass, if ye hearken to these judgments, and keep, and do them, that the LORD thy God shall keep unto thee the covenant and the mercy which he sware unto thy fathers:

13And he will love thee, and bless thee, and multiply thee: he will also bless the fruit of thy womb, and the fruit of thy land, thy corn, and thy wine, and thine oil, the increase of thy kine, and the flocks of thy sheep, in the land which he sware unto thy fathers to give thee.

14Thou shalt be blessed above all people: there shall not be male or female barren among you, or among your cattle.

15And the LORD will take away from thee all sickness, and will put none of the evil diseases of Egypt, which thou knowest, upon thee; but will lay them upon all *them* that hate thee.

16And thou shalt consume all the people which the LORD thy God shall deliver thee; thine eye shall have no pity upon them: neither shalt thou serve their gods; for that *will be* a snare unto thee.

17If thou shalt say in thine heart, These nations *are* more than I; how can I dispossess them?

18Thou shalt not be afraid of them: *but* shalt well remember what the LORD thy God did unto Pharaoh, and unto all Egypt;

19The great temptations which thine eyes saw, and the signs, and the wonders, and the mighty hand, and the stretched out arm, whereby the LORD thy God brought thee out: so shall the LORD thy God do unto all the people of whom thou art afraid.

20Moreover the LORD thy God will send the hornet among them, until they that are left, and hide themselves from thee, be destroyed.

21Thou shalt not be affrighted at them: for the LORD thy God *is* among you, a mighty God and terrible.

22And the LORD thy God will put out those nations before thee by little and little: thou mayest not consume them at once, lest the beasts of the field increase upon thee.

23But the LORD thy God shall deliver them unto thee, and shall destroy them with a mighty destruction, until they be destroyed.

24And he shall deliver their kings into thine hand, and thou shalt destroy their name from under heaven: there shall no man be able to stand before thee, until thou have destroyed them.

25The graven images of their gods shall ye burn with fire: thou shalt not desire the silver or gold *that is* on them, nor take *it* unto thee, lest thou be snared therein: for it *is* an abomination to the LORD thy God.

## Amplified

5But thus shall you deal with them: you shall break down their altars, and dash in pieces their pillars, and hew down their Asherim, and burn their graven images with fire.

6For you are a holy *and* set apart people to the Lord your God; the Lord your God has chosen you to be a special people to Himself, out of all the peoples on the face of the earth.

7The Lord did not set His love upon you and choose you, because you were more in number than any other people, for you were the fewest of all people;

8But because the Lord loves you, and because He would keep the oath which He had sworn to your fathers, the Lord has brought you out with a mighty hand, and redeemed you out of the house of bondage, from the hand of Pharaoh king of Egypt.

9Know, recognize *and* understand therefore that the Lord your God, He is God, the faithful God, Who keeps covenant and steadfast love *and* mercy with those who love Him and keep His commandments, to a thousand generations;

10And repays those who hate Him to their face, by destroying them; He will not be slack to him who hates Him, but will requite him to his face.

11You shall therefore keep and do the instruction, laws, and precepts which I command you this day.

12And if you hearken to these precepts and keep and do them, the Lord your God will keep with you the covenant and the steadfast love which He swore to your fathers;

13And He will love you, bless you, and multiply you; He will also bless the fruit of your body and the fruit of your land, your grain, your new wine, and your oil, the increase of your cattle and the young of your flock, in the land which He swore to your fathers to give you.

14You shall be blessed above all peoples; there shall not be male or female barren among you, or among your cattle.

15And the Lord will take away from you all sickness, and none of the evil diseases of Egypt, which you knew, will He put upon you, but will lay them upon all who hate you.

16And you shall consume all the peoples whom the Lord your God will give over to you; your eye shall not pity them; neither shall you serve their gods, for that would be a snare to you.

17If you say in your [mind and] heart, These nations are more than I; how can I dispossess them?

18You shall not be afraid of them, but remember (earnestly) what the Lord your God did to Pharaoh, and to all Egypt,

19The great trials which your eyes saw, the signs, the wonders, the mighty hand, and the outstretched arm by which the Lord your God brought you out; so shall the Lord your God do to all the people of whom you are afraid.

20Moreover the Lord your God will send the [a]hornet among them, until those who are left and hide themselves from you are destroyed.

21You shall not dread them; for the Lord your God is among you, a mighty and terrible God.

22And the Lord your God will clear out those nations before you little by little; you may not consume them quickly, lest the beasts of the field increase among you.

23But the Lord your God will give them over to you, and will confuse them with a mighty panic until they are destroyed.

24And He will give their kings into your hand, and you shall make their name perish from under the heavens; there shall no man be able to stand before you, until you have destroyed them.

25The graven images of their gods you shall burn with fire; you shall not desire the silver or gold that is on them, nor take it for yourself, lest you be ensnared by it; for it is an abomination to the Lord your God.

**AMP** [a] " . . . the hornet" with the article, meaning collective as a species or kind, is thus evidently to be understood, as 2:25, of the terrors of God which should go before Israel, with which also Josh. 24:12 and Ps. 44:2 fully agree. (*Lange's Commentary*, adapted.)

## New American Standard

5"But thus you shall do to them: you shall tear down their altars, and smash their *sacred* pillars, and hew down their [b]Asherim, and burn their graven images with fire.

6¶ "For you are a holy people to the LORD your God; the LORD your God has chosen you to be a people for His own possession out of all the peoples who are on the face of the earth.

7"The LORD did not set His love on you nor choose you because you were more in number than any of the peoples, for you were the fewest of all peoples,

8but because the LORD loved you and kept the oath which He swore to your forefathers, the LORD brought you out by a mighty hand, and redeemed you from the house of slavery, from the hand of Pharaoh king of Egypt.

9"Know therefore that the LORD your God, He is God, the faithful God, who keeps His covenant and His lovingkindness to a thousandth generation with those who love Him and keep His commandments;

10but repays those who hate Him to their faces, to destroy them; He will not delay with him who hates Him, He will repay him to his face.

11"Therefore, you shall keep the commandment and the statutes and the judgments which I am commanding you today, to do them.

*Promises of God*

12¶ "Then it shall come about, because you listen to these judgments and keep and do them, that the LORD your God will keep with you His covenant and His lovingkindness which He swore to your forefathers.

13"And He will love you and bless you and multiply you; He will also bless the fruit of your womb and the fruit of your ground, your grain and your new wine and your oil, the increase of your herd and the young of your flock, in the land which He swore to your forefathers to give you.

14"You shall be blessed above all peoples; there shall be no male or female barren among you or among your cattle.

15"And the LORD will remove from you all sickness; and He will not put on you any of the harmful diseases of Egypt which you have known, but He will lay them on all who hate you.

16"And you shall consume all the peoples whom the LORD your God will deliver to you; your eye shall not pity them, neither shall you serve their gods, for that *would be* a snare to you.

17¶ "If you should say in your heart, 'These nations are greater than I; how can I dispossess them?'

18you shall not be afraid of them; you shall well remember what the LORD your God did to Pharaoh and to all Egypt:

19the great trials which your eyes saw and the signs and the wonders and the mighty hand and the outstretched arm by which the LORD your God brought you out. So shall the LORD your God do to all the peoples of whom you are afraid.

20"Moreover, the LORD your God will send the hornet against them, until those who are left and hide themselves from you perish.

21"You shall not dread them, for the LORD your God is in your midst, a great and awesome God.

22"And the LORD your God will clear away these nations before you little by little; you will not be able to put an end to them quickly, lest the wild beasts grow too numerous for you.

23"But the LORD your God shall deliver them before you, and will throw them into great confusion until they are destroyed.

24"And He will deliver their kings into your hand so that you shall make their name perish from under heaven; no man will be able to stand before you until you have destroyed them.

25"The graven images of their gods you are to burn with fire; you shall not covet the silver or the gold that is on them, nor take it for yourselves, lest you be snared by it, for it is an abomination to the LORD your God.

NAS [b] I.e., wooden symbols of a female deity

## New International

do to them: Break down their altars, smash their sacred stones, cut
down their Asherah poles[c] and burn their idols in the fire. 6For
you are a people holy to the LORD your God. The LORD your God
has chosen you out of all the peoples on the face of the earth to
be his people, his treasured possession.
7The LORD did not set his affection on you and choose you
because you were more numerous than other peoples, for you
were the fewest of all peoples. 8But it was because the LORD loved
you and kept the oath he swore to your forefathers that he brought
you out with a mighty hand and redeemed you from the land of
slavery, from the power of Pharaoh king of Egypt. 9Know therefore that the LORD your God is God; he is the faithful God, keeping
his covenant of love to a thousand generations of those who love
him and keep his commands. 10But

those who hate him he will repay to their face by
destruction;
he will not be slow to repay to their face those who
hate him.

11Therefore, take care to follow the commands, decrees and laws
I give you today.
12If you pay attention to these laws and are careful to follow
them, then the LORD your God will keep his covenant of love with
you, as he swore to your forefathers. 13He will love you and bless
you and increase your numbers. He will bless the fruit of your
womb, the crops of your land—your grain, new wine and oil—the
calves of your herds and the lambs of your flocks in the land that
he swore to your forefathers to give you. 14You will be blessed
more than any other people; none of your men or women will be
childless, nor any of your livestock without young. 15The LORD will
keep you free from every disease. He will not inflict on you the
horrible diseases you knew in Egypt, but he will inflict them on all
who hate you. 16You must destroy all the peoples the LORD your
God gives over to you. Do not look on them with pity and do not
serve their gods, for that will be a snare to you.
17You may say to yourselves, "These nations are stronger than
we are. How can we drive them out?" 18But do not be afraid of
them; remember well what the LORD your God did to Pharaoh and
to all Egypt. 19You saw with your own eyes the great trials, the
miraculous signs and wonders, the mighty hand and outstretched
arm, with which the LORD your God brought you out. The LORD
your God will do the same to all the peoples you now fear. 20More-
over, the LORD your God will send the hornet among them until
even the survivors who hide from you have perished. 21Do not be
terrified by them, for the LORD your God, who is among you, is
a great and awesome God. 22The LORD your God will drive out
those nations before you, little by little. You will not be allowed to
eliminate them all at once, or the wild animals will multiply around
you. 23But the LORD your God will deliver them over to you,
throwing them into great confusion until they are destroyed. 24He
will give their kings into your hand, and you will wipe out their
names from under heaven. No one will be able to stand up against
you; you will destroy them. 25The images of their gods you are to
burn in the fire. Do not covet the silver and gold on them, and do
not take it for yourselves, or you will be ensnared by it, for it is

NIV [c] 5 That is, symbols of the goddess Asherah; here and elsewhere in Deuteronomy

## King James

26 Neither shalt thou bring an abomination into thine house, lest thou be a cursed thing like it: *but* thou shalt utterly detest it, and thou shalt utterly abhor it; for it *is* a cursed thing.

**8** ALL THE commandments which I command thee this day shall ye observe to do, that ye may live, and multiply, and go in and possess the land which the LORD sware unto your fathers.

2 And thou shalt remember all the way which the LORD thy God led thee these forty years in the wilderness, to humble thee, *and* to prove thee, to know what *was* in thine heart, whether thou wouldest keep his commandments, or no.

3 And he humbled thee, and suffered thee to hunger, and fed thee with manna, which thou knewest not, neither did thy fathers know; that he might make thee know that man doth not live by bread only, but by every *word* that proceedeth out of the mouth of the LORD doth man live.

4 Thy raiment waxed not old upon thee, neither did thy foot swell, these forty years.

5 Thou shalt also consider in thine heart, that, as a man chasteneth his son, *so* the LORD thy God chasteneth thee.

6 Therefore thou shalt keep the commandments of the LORD thy God, to walk in his ways, and to fear him.

7 For the LORD thy God bringeth thee into a good land, a land of brooks of water, of fountains and depths that spring out of valleys and hills;

8 A land of wheat, and barley, and vines, and fig trees, and pomegranates; a land of oil olive, and honey;

9 A land wherein thou shalt eat bread without scarceness, thou shalt not lack any *thing* in it; a land whose stones *are* iron, and out of whose hills thou mayest dig brass.

10 When thou hast eaten and art full, then thou shalt bless the LORD thy God for the good land which he hath given thee.

11 Beware that thou forget not the LORD thy God, in not keeping his commandments, and his judgments, and his statutes, which I command thee this day:

12 Lest *when* thou hast eaten and art full, and hast built goodly houses, and dwelt *therein;*

13 And *when* thy herds and thy flocks multiply, and thy silver and thy gold is multiplied, and all that thou hast is multiplied;

14 Then thine heart be lifted up, and thou forget the LORD thy God, which brought thee forth out of the land of Egypt, from the house of bondage;

15 Who led thee through that great and terrible wilderness, *wherein were* fiery serpents, and scorpions, and drought, where *there was* no water; who brought thee forth water out of the rock of flint;

16 Who fed thee in the wilderness with manna, which thy fathers knew not, that he might humble thee, and that he might prove thee, to do thee good at thy latter end;

17 And thou say in thine heart, My power and the might of *mine* hand hath gotten me this wealth.

18 But thou shalt remember the LORD thy God: for *it is* he that giveth thee power to get wealth, that he may establish his covenant which he sware unto thy fathers, as *it is* this day.

19 And it shall be, if thou do at all forget the LORD thy God, and walk after other gods, and serve them, and worship them, I testify against you this day that ye shall surely perish.

20 As the nations which the LORD destroyeth before your face, so shall ye perish; because ye would not be obedient unto the voice of the LORD your God.

## Amplified

26 Neither shall you bring an abomination (an idol) into your house, lest you become an accursed thing like it; but you shall utterly detest and abhor it, for it is an accursed thing.

**8** ALL THE commandments which I command you this day you shall be watchful to do, that you may live, and multiply, and go in and possess the land which the Lord swore to give to your fathers.

2 And you shall (earnestly) remember all the way which the Lord your God led you these forty years in the wilderness, to humble you, and to prove you, to know what was in your [mind and] heart, whether you would keep His commandments or not.

3 And He humbled you and allowed you to hunger, and fed you with manna, which you did not know, nor did your fathers know; that He might make you recognize *and* personally know that man does not live by bread only, but man lives by every word that proceeds out of the mouth of the Lord.

4 Your clothing did not become old upon you, nor did your foot swell, these forty years.

5 Know also in your [mind and] heart that, as a man disciplines *and* instructs his son, so the Lord your God disciplines *and* instructs you.

6 So you shall keep the commandments of the Lord your God, to walk in His ways and (reverently) fear Him. [Prov. 8:13.]

7 For the Lord your God is bringing you into a good land, a land of brooks of water, of fountains and springs, flowing forth in valleys and hills;

8 A land of wheat and barley, and vines and fig trees and pomegranates, a land of olive trees and honey,

9 A land in which you shall eat food without shortage, and lack nothing in it, a land whose stones are iron, and out of whose hills you can dig copper.

10 When you have eaten and are full, then you shall bless the Lord your God for all the good land which He has given you.

11 Beware that you do not forget the Lord your God, by not keeping His commandments, His precepts, and His statutes, which I command you today,

12 Lest when you have eaten and are full, and have built goodly houses, and live in them,

13 And when your herds and flocks multiply, and your silver and gold is multiplied, and all you have is multiplied;

14 Then your [mind and] heart be lifted up, and you forget the Lord your God Who brought you out of the land of Egypt, out of the house of bondage,

15 Who led you through the great and terrible wilderness, with its fiery serpents and scorpions and thirsty ground where there was no water, but Who brought you forth water out of the flinty rock;

16 Who fed you in the wilderness with manna which your fathers did not know, that He might humble you and test you, to do you good in the end.

17 And beware lest you say in your [mind and] heart, My power and the might of my hand have gotten me this wealth.

18 But you shall (earnestly) remember the Lord your God; for it is He Who gives you power to get wealth, that He may establish His covenant which He swore to your fathers, as at this day.

19 And if you forget the Lord your God, and walk after other gods, and serve them, and worship them, I testify against you this day that you shall surely perish.

20 Like the nations which the Lord makes perish before you, so shall you perish, because you would not obey the voice of the Lord your God.

## New American Standard

26"And you shall not bring an abomination into your house, and like it come under the ban; you shall utterly detest it and you shall utterly abhor it, for it is something banned.

*God's Gracious Dealings*

8 "ALL THE commandments that I am commanding you today you shall be careful to do, that you may live and multiply, and go in and possess the land which the LORD swore *to give* to your forefathers.

2"And you shall remember all the way which the LORD your God has led you in the wilderness these forty years, that He might humble you, testing you, to know what was in your heart, whether you would keep His commandments or not.

3"And He humbled you and let you be hungry, and fed you with manna which you did not know, nor did your fathers know, that He might make you understand that man does not live by bread alone, but man lives by everything that proceeds out of the mouth of the LORD.

4"Your clothing did not wear out on you, nor did your foot swell these forty years.

5"Thus you are to know in your heart that the LORD your God was disciplining you just as a man disciplines his son.

6"Therefore, you shall keep the commandments of the LORD your God, to walk in His ways and to fear Him.

7"For the LORD your God is bringing you into a good land, a land of brooks of water, of fountains and springs, flowing forth in valleys and hills;

8a land of wheat and barley, of vines and fig trees and pomegranates, a land of olive oil and honey;

9a land where you shall eat food without scarcity, in which you shall not lack anything; a land whose stones are iron, and out of whose hills you can dig copper.

10"When you have eaten and are satisfied, you shall bless the LORD your God for the good land which He has given you.

11¶ "Beware lest you forget the LORD your God by not keeping His commandments and His ordinances and His statutes which I am commanding you today;

12lest, when you have eaten and are satisfied, and have built good houses and lived *in them,*

13and when your herds and your flocks multiply, and your silver and gold multiply, and all that you have multiplies,

14then your heart becomes proud, and you forget the LORD your God who brought you out from the land of Egypt, out of the house of slavery.

15"He led you through the great and terrible wilderness, *with its* fiery serpents and scorpions and thirsty ground where there was no water; He brought water for you out of the rock of flint.

16"In the wilderness He fed you manna which your fathers did not know, that He might humble you and that He might test you, to do good for you in the end.

17"Otherwise, you may say in your heart, 'My power and the strength of my hand made me this wealth.'

18"But you shall remember the LORD your God, for it is He who is giving you power to make wealth, that He may confirm His covenant which He swore to your fathers, as *it is* this day.

19"And it shall come about if you ever forget the LORD your God, and go after other gods and serve them and worship them, I testify against you today that you shall surely perish.

20"Like the nations that the LORD makes to perish before you, so you shall perish; because you would not listen to the voice of the LORD your God.

## New International

detestable to the LORD your God. 26Do not bring a detestable thing
into your house or you, like it, will be set apart for destruction.
Utterly abhor and detest it, for it is set apart for destruction.

*Do Not Forget the LORD*

8 BE CAREFUL to follow every command I am giving you today, so that you may live and increase and may enter and possess the land that the LORD promised on oath to your forefathers. 2Remember how the LORD your God led you all the way
in the desert these forty years, to humble you and to test you in
order to know what was in your heart, whether or not you would
keep his commands. 3He humbled you, causing you to hunger and
then feeding you with manna, which neither you nor your fathers
had known, to teach you that man does not live on bread alone
but on every word that comes from the mouth of the LORD. 4Your
clothes did not wear out and your feet did not swell during these
forty years. 5Know then in your heart that as a man disciplines his
son, so the LORD your God disciplines you.

6Observe the commands of the LORD your God, walking in his
ways and revering him. 7For the LORD your God is bringing you
into a good land—a land with streams and pools of water, with
springs flowing in the valleys and hills; 8a land with wheat and
barley, vines and fig trees, pomegranates, olive oil and honey; 9a
land where bread will not be scarce and you will lack nothing; a
land where the rocks are iron and you can dig copper out of the
hills.

10When you have eaten and are satisfied, praise the LORD your
God for the good land he has given you. 11Be careful that you do
not forget the LORD your God, failing to observe his commands,
his laws and his decrees that I am giving you this day. 12Other-
wise, when you eat and are satisfied, when you build fine houses
and settle down, 13and when your herds and flocks grow large and
your silver and gold increase and all you have is multiplied, 14then
your heart will become proud and you will forget the LORD your
God, who brought you out of Egypt, out of the land of slavery.
15He led you through the vast and dreadful desert, that thirsty and
waterless land, with its venomous snakes and scorpions. He
brought you water out of hard rock. 16He gave you manna to eat
in the desert, something your fathers had never known, to humble
and to test you so that in the end it might go well with you. 17You
may say to yourself, "My power and the strength of my hands
have produced this wealth for me." 18But remember the LORD your
God, for it is he who gives you the ability to produce wealth, and
so confirms his covenant, which he swore to your forefathers, as
it is today.

19If you ever forget the LORD your God and follow other gods
and worship and bow down to them, I testify against you today
that you will surely be destroyed. 20Like the nations the LORD
destroyed before you, so you will be destroyed for not obeying the
LORD your God.

## King James

9 HEAR, O Israel: Thou *art* to pass over Jordan this day, to go in to possess nations greater and mightier than thyself, cities great and fenced up to heaven,

2A people great and tall, the children of the Anakims, whom thou knowest, and *of whom* thou hast heard *say*, Who can stand before the children of Anak!

3Understand therefore this day, that the LORD thy God *is* he which goeth over before thee; *as* a consuming fire he shall destroy them, and he shall bring them down before thy face: so shalt thou drive them out, and destroy them quickly, as the LORD hath said unto thee.

4Speak not thou in thine heart, after that the LORD thy God hath cast them out from before thee, saying, For my righteousness the LORD hath brought me in to possess this land: but for the wickedness of these nations the LORD doth drive them out from before thee.

5Not for thy righteousness, or for the uprightness of thine heart, dost thou go to possess their land: but for the wickedness of these nations the LORD thy God doth drive them out from before thee, and that he may perform the word which the LORD sware unto thy fathers, Abraham, Isaac, and Jacob.

6Understand therefore, that the LORD thy God giveth thee not this good land to possess it for thy righteousness; for thou *art* a stiffnecked people.

7¶ Remember, *and* forget not, how thou provokedst the LORD thy God to wrath in the wilderness: from the day that thou didst depart out of the land of Egypt, until ye came unto this place, ye have been rebellious against the LORD.

8Also in Horeb ye provoked the LORD to wrath, so that the LORD was angry with you to have destroyed you.

9When I was gone up into the mount to receive the tables of stone, *even* the tables of the covenant which the LORD made with you, then I abode in the mount forty days and forty nights, I neither did eat bread nor drink water:

10And the LORD delivered unto me two tables of stone written with the finger of God; and on them *was written* according to all the words, which the LORD spake with you in the mount out of the midst of the fire in the day of the assembly.

11And it came to pass at the end of forty days and forty nights, *that* the LORD gave me the two tables of stone, *even* the tables of the covenant.

12And the LORD said unto me, Arise, get thee down quickly from hence; for thy people which thou hast brought forth out of Egypt have corrupted *themselves;* they are quickly turned aside out of the way which I commanded them; they have made them a molten image.

13Furthermore the LORD spake unto me, saying, I have seen this people, and, behold, it *is* a stiffnecked people:

14Let me alone, that I may destroy them, and blot out their name from under heaven: and I will make of thee a nation mightier and greater than they.

15So I turned and came down from the mount, and the mount burned with fire: and the two tables of the covenant *were* in my two hands.

16And I looked, and, behold, ye had sinned against the LORD your God, *and* had made you a molten calf: ye had turned aside quickly out of the way which the LORD had commanded you.

17And I took the two tables, and cast them out of my two hands, and brake them before your eyes.

18And I fell down before the LORD, as at the first, forty days and forty nights: I did neither eat bread, nor drink water, because of all your sins which ye sinned, in doing wickedly in the sight of the LORD, to provoke him to anger.

19For I was afraid of the anger and hot displeasure, wherewith the LORD was wroth against you to destroy you. But the LORD hearkened unto me at that time also.

20And the LORD was very angry with Aaron to have destroyed him: and I prayed for Aaron also the same time.

## Amplified

9 HEAR, O Israel; you are to cross the Jordan today, to go in to dispossess nations greater and mightier than you are, cities great and fortified up to the heavens,

2A people great and tall, the sons of the Anakim, whom you know, and of whom you have heard it said, Who can stand before the sons of Anak?

3Know therefore this day, that the Lord your God is He Who goes over before you as a devouring fire; He will destroy them and bring them down before you; so you shall dispossess them and make them perish quickly, as the Lord has promised you.

4Do not say in your [mind and] heart, after the Lord your God has thrust them out from before you, It is because of my righteousness that the Lord has brought me in to possess this land; whereas it is because of the wickedness of these nations that the Lord is dispossessing them before you.

5Not for your righteousness, or for the uprightness of your [mind and] heart, do you go to possess their land; but because of the wickedness of these nations the Lord your God is driving them out before you, and that He may fulfill the promise which the Lord swore to your fathers, Abraham, Isaac, and Jacob.

6Know therefore, that the Lord your God does not give you this good land to possess because of your righteousness, for you are a hard *and* stubborn people.

7(Earnestly) remember, and forget not, how you provoked the Lord your God to wrath in the wilderness; from the day you left the land of Egypt until you came to this place, you have been rebellious against the Lord.

8Even in Horeb you provoked the Lord to wrath, and the Lord was so angry with you that He would have destroyed you.

9When I went up the mountain to receive the tables of stone, the tables of the covenant which the Lord made with you, I remained on the mountain forty days and forty nights; I neither ate food nor drank water.

10And the Lord delivered to me the two tables of stone written with the finger of God; and on them were all the words which the Lord spoke with you on the mountain out of the midst of the fire in the day of the assembly.

11And at the end of forty days and forty nights the Lord gave me the two tables of stone, the tables of the covenant.

12And the Lord said to me, Arise, go down from here quickly; for your people whom you brought out of Egypt have corrupted themselves; they have quickly turned aside out of the way which I commanded them; they have made themselves a molten image.

13Furthermore the Lord said to me, I have seen this people, and behold, it is stubborn *and* hard;

14Let me alone, that I may destroy them, and blot out their name from under the heavens; and I will make of you a nation mightier and greater than they.

15So I turned and came down from the mountain, and the mountain was burning with fire; and the two tables of the covenant were in my two hands.

16And I looked, and behold, you had sinned against the Lord your God; you had made you a molten calf; you had turned aside quickly from the way which the Lord had commanded you.

17I took the two tables, cast them out of my two hands, and broke them before your eyes.

18Then I fell down before the Lord, as before, forty days and forty nights; I neither ate food, nor drank water, because of all the sin you had committed in doing wickedly in the sight of the Lord, to provoke Him to anger.

19For I was afraid of the anger and hot displeasure which the Lord held against you, enough to destroy you. But the Lord listened to me that time also.

20And the Lord was very angry with Aaron, enough to have destroyed him; and I prayed for Aaron also at the same time.

# New American Standard

*Israel Provoked God*

**9** "HEAR, O Israel! You are crossing over the Jordan today to go in to dispossess nations greater and mightier than you, great cities fortified to heaven,

2 a people great and tall, the sons of the Anakim, whom you know and of whom you have heard *it said*, 'Who can stand before the sons of Anak?'

3 "Know therefore today that it is the LORD your God who is crossing over before you as a consuming fire. He will destroy them and He will subdue them before you, so that you may drive them out and destroy them quickly, just as the LORD has spoken to you.

4 "Do not say in your heart when the LORD your God has driven them out before you, 'Because of my righteousness the LORD has brought me in to possess this land,' but *it is* because of the wickedness of these nations *that* the LORD is dispossessing them before you.

5 "It is not for your righteousness or for the uprightness of your heart that you are going to possess their land, but *it is* because of the wickedness of these nations *that* the LORD your God is driving them out before you, in order to confirm the oath which the LORD swore to your fathers, to Abraham, Isaac and Jacob.

6 "Know, then, *it is* not because of your righteousness *that* the LORD your God is giving you this good land to possess, for you are a stubborn people.

7 ¶ "Remember, do not forget how you provoked the LORD your God to wrath in the wilderness; from the day that you left the land of Egypt until you arrived at this place, you have been rebellious against the LORD.

8 "Even at Horeb you provoked the LORD to wrath, and the LORD was so angry with you that He would have destroyed you.

9 "When I went up to the mountain to receive the tablets of stone, the tablets of the covenant which the LORD had made with you, then I remained on the mountain forty days and nights; I neither ate bread nor drank water.

10 "And the LORD gave me the two tablets of stone written by the finger of God; and on them *were* all the words which the LORD had spoken with you at the mountain from the midst of the fire on the day of the assembly.

11 "And it came about at the end of forty days and nights that the LORD gave me the two tablets of stone, the tablets of the covenant.

12 "Then the LORD said to me, 'Arise, go down from here quickly, for your people whom you brought out of Egypt have acted corruptly. They have quickly turned aside from the way which I commanded them; they have made a molten image for themselves.'

13 "The LORD spoke further to me, saying, 'I have seen this people, and indeed, it is a stubborn people.

14 'Let Me alone, that I may destroy them and blot out their name from under heaven; and I will make of you a nation mightier and greater than they.'

15 "So I turned and came down from the mountain while the mountain was burning with fire, and the two tablets of the covenant were in my two hands.

16 "And I saw that you had indeed sinned against the LORD your God. You had made for yourselves a molten calf; you had turned aside quickly from the way which the LORD had commanded you.

17 "And I took hold of the two tablets and threw them from my hands, and smashed them before your eyes.

18 "And I fell down before the LORD, as at the first, forty days and nights; I neither ate bread nor drank water, because of all your sin which you had committed in doing what was evil in the sight of the LORD to provoke Him to anger.

19 "For I was afraid of the anger and hot displeasure with which the LORD was wrathful against you in order to destroy you, but the LORD listened to me that time also.

20 "And the LORD was angry enough with Aaron to destroy him; so I also prayed for Aaron at the same time.

# New International

*Not Because of Israel's Righteousness*

**9** HEAR, O Israel. You are now about to cross the Jordan to go
in and dispossess nations greater and stronger than you, with
large cities that have walls up to the sky. 2 The people are strong
and tall—Anakites! You know about them and have heard it said:
"Who can stand up against the Anakites?" 3 But be assured today
that the LORD your God is the one who goes across ahead of you
like a devouring fire. He will destroy them; he will subdue them
before you. And you will drive them out and annihilate them
quickly, as the LORD has promised you.
4 After the LORD your God has driven them out before you, do
not say to yourself, "The LORD has brought me here to take possession of this land because of my righteousness." No, it is on account
of the wickedness of these nations that the LORD is going to drive
them out before you. 5 It is not because of your righteousness or
your integrity that you are going in to take possession of their land;
but on account of the wickedness of these nations, the LORD your
God will drive them out before you, to accomplish what he swore
to your fathers, to Abraham, Isaac and Jacob. 6 Understand, then,
that it is not because of your righteousness that the LORD your God
is giving you this good land to possess, for you are a stiff-necked
people.

*The Golden Calf*

7 Remember this and never forget how you provoked the LORD
your God to anger in the desert. From the day you left Egypt until
you arrived here, you have been rebellious against the LORD. 8 At
Horeb you aroused the LORD's wrath so that he was angry enough
to destroy you. 9 When I went up on the mountain to receive the
tablets of stone, the tablets of the covenant that the LORD had made
with you, I stayed on the mountain forty days and forty nights; I
ate no bread and drank no water. 10 The LORD gave me two stone
tablets inscribed by the finger of God. On them were all the commandments the LORD proclaimed to you on the mountain out of
the fire, on the day of the assembly.
11 At the end of the forty days and forty nights, the LORD gave
me the two stone tablets, the tablets of the covenant. 12 Then the
LORD told me, "Go down from here at once, because your people
whom you brought out of Egypt have become corrupt. They have
turned away quickly from what I commanded them and have
made a cast idol for themselves."
13 And the LORD said to me, "I have seen this people, and they
are a stiff-necked people indeed! 14 Let me alone, so that I may
destroy them and blot out their name from under heaven. And I
will make you into a nation stronger and more numerous than
they."
15 So I turned and went down from the mountain while it was
ablaze with fire. And the two tablets of the covenant were in my
hands.[a] 16 When I looked, I saw that you had sinned against the
LORD your God; you had made for yourselves an idol cast in the
shape of a calf. You had turned aside quickly from the way that
the LORD had commanded you. 17 So I took the two tablets and
threw them out of my hands, breaking them to pieces before your
eyes.
18 Then once again I fell prostrate before the LORD for forty days
and forty nights; I ate no bread and drank no water, because of all
the sin you had committed, doing what was evil in the LORD's sight
and so provoking him to anger. 19 I feared the anger and wrath of
the LORD, for he was angry enough with you to destroy you. But
again the LORD listened to me. 20 And the LORD was angry enough
with Aaron to destroy him, but at that time I prayed for Aaron too.

NIV [a] 15 Or *And I had the two tablets of the covenant with me, one in each hand*

## King James

21And I took your sin, the calf which ye had made, and burnt
it with fire, and stamped it, *and* ground *it* very small, *even* until it
was as small as dust: and I cast the dust thereof into the brook that
descended out of the mount.
22And at Taberah, and at Massah, and at Kibroth-hattaavah, ye
provoked the LORD to wrath.
23Likewise when the LORD sent you from Kadesh-barnea, saying, Go up and possess the land which I have given you; then ye
rebelled against the commandment of the LORD your God, and ye
believed him not, nor hearkened to his voice.
24Ye have been rebellious against the LORD from the day that
I knew you.
25Thus I fell down before the LORD forty days and forty nights,
as I fell down *at the first;* because the LORD had said he would
destroy you.
26I prayed therefore unto the LORD, and said, O Lord GOD,
destroy not thy people and thine inheritance, which thou hast
redeemed through thy greatness, which thou hast brought forth
out of Egypt with a mighty hand.
27Remember thy servants, Abraham, Isaac, and Jacob; look not
unto the stubbornness of this people, nor to their wickedness, nor
to their sin:
28Lest the land whence thou broughtest us out say, Because the
LORD was not able to bring them into the land which he promised
them, and because he hated them, he hath brought them out to
slay them in the wilderness.
29Yet they *are* thy people and thine inheritance, which thou
broughtest out by thy mighty power and by thy stretched out arm.

**10** AT THAT time the LORD said unto me, Hew thee two
tables of stone like unto the first, and come up unto me
into the mount, and make thee an ark of wood.
2And I will write on the tables the words that were in the first
tables which thou brakest, and thou shalt put them in the ark.
3And I made an ark of shittim wood, and hewed two tables of
stone like unto the first, and went up into the mount, having the
two tables in mine hand.
4And he wrote on the tables, according to the first writing, the
ten commandments, which the LORD spake unto you in the mount
out of the midst of the fire in the day of the assembly: and the LORD
gave them unto me.
5And I turned myself and came down from the mount, and put
the tables in the ark which I had made; and there they be, as the
LORD commanded me.
6¶ And the children of Israel took their journey from Beeroth of
the children of Jaakan to Mosera: there Aaron died, and there he
was buried; and Eleazar his son ministered in the priest's office in
his stead.
7From thence they journeyed unto Gudgodah; and from Gudgodah to Jotbath, a land of rivers of waters.
8¶ At that time the LORD separated the tribe of Levi, to bear the
ark of the covenant of the LORD, to stand before the LORD to
minister unto him, and to bless in his name, unto this day.
9Wherefore Levi hath no part nor inheritance with his brethren;
the LORD *is* his inheritance, according as the LORD thy God promised him.
10And I stayed in the mount, according to the first time, forty
days and forty nights; and the LORD hearkened unto me at that
time also, *and* the LORD would not destroy thee.

## Amplified

21And I took your sin, the calf which you had made, and burned
it with fire and crushed it, grinding it very small, until it was as
fine as dust; and I cast the dust of it into the brook that came down
out of the mountain.
22At Taberah also, and at Massah, and at Kibroth-hattaavah,
you provoked the Lord to wrath.
23Likewise when the Lord sent you from Kadesh-barnea, saying, Go up and possess the land which I have given you; then you
rebelled against the commandment of the Lord your God, and you
did not believe Him *or* trust *and* rely on Him or obey His voice.
24You have been rebellious against the Lord from the day that
I knew you.
25So I fell down *and* lay prostrate before the Lord forty days and
nights, for the Lord had said He would destroy you.
26And I prayed to the Lord, O Lord God, do not destroy Your
people and Your heritage, whom You have redeemed through
Your greatness, whom You have brought out of Egypt with a
mighty hand.
27Remember [earnestly] Your servants, Abraham, Isaac, and
Jacob; look not at the stubbornness of this people, or at their
wickedness, or at their sin,
28Lest the land from which You brought us out say, Because the
Lord was not able to bring them into the land which He promised
them, and because He hated them, He has brought them out to
slay them in the wilderness.
29Yet they are Your people and Your inheritance, whom You
brought out by Your mighty power and by Your outstretched arm.

**10** AT THAT time the Lord said to me, Hew two tables of
stone like the first, and come up to Me on the mountain,
and make an ark of wood.
2And I will write on the tables the words that were on the first
tables which you broke, and you shall put them in the ark.
3So I [Moses] made an ark of acacia wood, and hewed two tables
of stone like the first, and went up the mountain [a]with the two
tables of stone in my [one] hand.
4And the Lord wrote on the tables, as at the first writing, the
ten commandments, which the Lord had spoken to you on the
mountain out of the midst of the fire on the day of the assembly;
and the Lord gave them to me.
5And I turned and came down from the mountain, and put the
tables in the ark which I had made; and there they are, as the Lord
commanded me.
6(The Israelites journeyed from the wells of the sons of Jaakan
to Moserah. There Aaron died, and there he was buried, and
Eleazar his son ministered in the priest's office in his stead.
7From there they journeyed to Gudgodah; then to Jotbathah, a
land of brooks [dividing the valley].
8At that time the Lord set apart the tribe of Levi, to bear the ark
of the covenant of the Lord, to stand before the Lord to minister
to Him, and to bless in His name, unto this day.
9Therefore Levi has no part or inheritance with his brethren; the
Lord is his inheritance, as the Lord your God promised him.)
10And I [Moses] stayed on the mountain, as the first time, forty
days and nights; and the Lord listened to me at that time also; the
Lord would not destroy you.

**AMP** [a] One of the many misconceptions of articles and events mentioned in the Bible, which have been innocently perpetuated by artists without adequate knowledge, is that of the size of the two tables of stone on which the ten commandments were written. They were not great tombstone-sized slabs, but probably small rectangular plates, two of which could easily be carried in one hand. Dr. George L. Robinson brought from the Sinai area a pair of "tables of stone" believed comparable to those mentioned here, which he put in his coat pocket. Moses says here, "I went up the mountain with the two tables of stone in my [one] hand;" and he confirms it in Exod. 34:4.

## New American Standard

21"And I took your sinful *thing*, the calf which you had made, and burned it with fire and crushed it, grinding it very small until it was as fine as dust; and I threw its dust into the brook that came down from the mountain.

22¶ "Again at Taberah and at Massah and at Kibroth-hattaavah you provoked the LORD to wrath.

23"And when the LORD sent you from Kadesh-barnea, saying, 'Go up and possess the land which I have given you,' then you rebelled against the command of the LORD your God; you neither believed Him nor listened to His voice.

24"You have been rebellious against the LORD from the day I knew you.

25¶ "So I fell down before the LORD the forty days and nights, which I did because the LORD had said He would destroy you.

26"And I prayed to the LORD, and said, 'O Lord GOD, do not destroy Thy people, even Thine inheritance, whom Thou hast redeemed through Thy greatness, whom Thou hast brought out of Egypt with a mighty hand.

27'Remember Thy servants, Abraham, Isaac, and Jacob; do not look at the stubbornness of this people or at their wickedness or their sin.

28'Otherwise the land from which Thou didst bring us may say, "Because the LORD was not able to bring them into the land which He had promised them and because He hated them He has brought them out to slay them in the wilderness."

29'Yet they are Thy people, even Thine inheritance, whom Thou hast brought out by Thy great power and Thine outstretched arm.'

*The Tablets Rewritten*

**10** "AT THAT time the LORD said to me, 'Cut out for yourself two tablets of stone like the former ones, and come up to Me on the mountain, and make an ark of wood for yourself.

2'And I will write on the tablets the words that were on the former tablets which you shattered, and you shall put them in the ark.'

3"So I made an ark of acacia wood and cut out two tablets of stone like the former ones, and went up on the mountain with the two tablets in my hand.

4"And He wrote on the tablets, like the former writing, the Ten Commandments which the LORD had spoken to you on the mountain from the midst of the fire on the day of the assembly; and the LORD gave them to me.

5"Then I turned and came down from the mountain, and put the tablets in the ark which I had made; and there they are, as the LORD commanded me."

6¶ (Now the sons of Israel set out from Beeroth Bene-jaakan to Moserah. There Aaron died and there he was buried and Eleazar his son ministered as priest in his place.

7From there they set out to Gudgodah; and from Gudgodah to Jotbathah, a land of brooks of water.

8At that time the LORD set apart the tribe of Levi to carry the ark of the covenant of the LORD, to stand before the LORD to serve Him and to bless in His name until this day.

9Therefore, Levi does not have a portion or inheritance with his brothers; the LORD is his inheritance, just as the LORD your God spoke to him.)

10¶ "I, moreover, stayed on the mountain forty days and forty nights like the first time, and the LORD listened to me that time also; the LORD was not willing to destroy you.

## New International

21Also I took that sinful thing of yours, the calf you had made, and
burned it in the fire. Then I crushed it and ground it to powder as
fine as dust and threw the dust into a stream that flowed down the
mountain.
22You also made the LORD angry at Taberah, at Massah and at
Kibroth Hattaavah.
23And when the LORD sent you out from Kadesh Barnea, he
said, "Go up and take possession of the land I have given you."
But you rebelled against the command of the LORD your God. You
did not trust him or obey him. 24You have been rebellious against
the LORD ever since I have known you.
25I lay prostrate before the LORD those forty days and forty
nights because the LORD had said he would destroy you. 26I prayed
to the LORD and said, "O Sovereign LORD, do not destroy your
people, your own inheritance that you redeemed by your great
power and brought out of Egypt with a mighty hand. 27Remember
your servants Abraham, Isaac and Jacob. Overlook the stubbornness of this people, their wickedness and their sin. 28Otherwise,
the country from which you brought us will say, 'Because the LORD
was not able to take them into the land he had promised them, and
because he hated them, he brought them out to put them to death
in the desert.' 29But they are your people, your inheritance that
you brought out by your great power and your outstretched arm."

*Tablets Like the First Ones*

**10** AT THAT time the LORD said to me, "Chisel out two stone
tablets like the first ones and come up to me on the mountain. Also make a wooden chest.[b] 2I will write on the tablets the
words that were on the first tablets, which you broke. Then you
are to put them in the chest."
3So I made the ark out of acacia wood and chiseled out two
stone tablets like the first ones, and I went up on the mountain
with the two tablets in my hands. 4The LORD wrote on these tablets
what he had written before, the Ten Commandments he had
proclaimed to you on the mountain, out of the fire, on the day of
the assembly. And the LORD gave them to me. 5Then I came back
down the mountain and put the tablets in the ark I had made, as
the LORD commanded me, and they are there now.
6(The Israelites traveled from the wells of the Jaakanites to
Moserah. There Aaron died and was buried, and Eleazar his son
succeeded him as priest. 7From there they traveled to Gudgodah
and on to Jotbathah, a land with streams of water. 8At that time
the LORD set apart the tribe of Levi to carry the ark of the covenant
of the LORD, to stand before the LORD to minister and to pronounce
blessings in his name, as they still do today. 9That is why the
Levites have no share or inheritance among their brothers; the
LORD is their inheritance, as the LORD your God told them.)
10Now I had stayed on the mountain forty days and nights, as
I did the first time, and the LORD listened to me at this time also.
It was not his will to destroy you. 11"Go," the LORD said to me,

NIV [b] *1* That is, an ark

## King James

11 And the LORD said unto me, Arise, take *thy* journey before the people, that they may go in and possess the land, which I sware unto their fathers to give unto them.

12¶ And now, Israel, what doth the LORD thy God require of thee, but to fear the LORD thy God, to walk in all his ways, and to love him, and to serve the LORD thy God with all thy heart and with all thy soul,

13 To keep the commandments of the LORD, and his statutes, which I command thee this day for thy good?

14 Behold, the heaven and the heaven of heavens *is* the LORD's thy God, the earth *also*, with all that therein *is*.

15 Only the LORD had a delight in thy fathers to love them, and he chose their seed after them, *even* you above all people, as *it is* this day.

16 Circumcise therefore the foreskin of your heart, and be no more stiffnecked.

17 For the LORD your God *is* God of gods, and Lord of lords, a great God, a mighty, and a terrible, which regardeth not persons, nor taketh reward:

18 He doth execute the judgment of the fatherless and widow, and loveth the stranger, in giving him food and raiment.

19 Love ye therefore the stranger: for ye were strangers in the land of Egypt.

20 Thou shalt fear the LORD thy God; him shalt thou serve, and to him shalt thou cleave, and swear by his name.

21 He *is* thy praise, and he *is* thy God, that hath done for thee these great and terrible things, which thine eyes have seen.

22 Thy fathers went down into Egypt with threescore and ten persons; and now the LORD thy God hath made thee as the stars of heaven for multitude.

**11** THEREFORE THOU shalt love the LORD thy God, and keep his charge, and his statutes, and his judgments, and his commandments, always.

2 And know ye this day: for *I speak* not with your children which have not known, and which have not seen the chastisement of the LORD your God, his greatness, his mighty hand, and his stretched out arm,

3 And his miracles, and his acts, which he did in the midst of Egypt unto Pharaoh the king of Egypt, and unto all his land;

4 And what he did unto the army of Egypt, unto their horses, and to their chariots; how he made the water of the Red sea to overflow them as they pursued after you, and *how* the LORD hath destroyed them unto this day;

5 And what he did unto you in the wilderness, until ye came into this place;

6 And what he did unto Dathan and Abiram, the sons of Eliab, the son of Reuben: how the earth opened her mouth, and swallowed them up, and their households, and their tents, and all the substance that *was* in their possession, in the midst of all Israel:

7 But your eyes have seen all the great acts of the LORD which he did.

8 Therefore shall ye keep all the commandments which I command you this day, that ye may be strong, and go in and possess the land, whither ye go to possess it;

9 And that ye may prolong *your* days in the land, which the LORD sware unto your fathers to give unto them and to their seed, a land that floweth with milk and honey.

10¶ For the land, whither thou goest in to possess it, *is* not as the land of Egypt, from whence ye came out, where thou sowedst thy seed, and wateredst *it* with thy foot, as a garden of herbs:

11 But the land, whither ye go to possess it, *is* a land of hills and valleys, *and* drinketh water of the rain of heaven:

## Amplified

11 And the Lord said to me, Arise, journey on before the people, that they may go in and possess the land, which I swore to their fathers to give to them.

12 And now, Israel, what does the Lord your God require of you, but (reverently) to fear the Lord your God: [that is,] to walk in all His ways, and to love Him, and to serve the Lord your God with all your [mind and] heart and with your entire being,

13 To keep the commandments of the Lord, and His statutes, which I command you today for your good?

14 Behold, the heavens and the Heaven of heavens belong to the Lord your God, the earth also, with all that is in it *and* on it;

15 Yet the Lord had a delight in loving your fathers, and He chose their descendants after them, you above all people, as this day.

16 So circumcise the foreskin of your [mind and] heart; be no longer stubborn *and* hardened.

17 For the Lord your God is God of gods and Lord of lords, the great, the mighty, the terrible God, Who is not partial and takes no bribe.

18 He executes justice for the fatherless and widow, and loves the stranger *or* temporary resident and gives him food and clothing.

19 Therefore love the stranger *and* sojourner, for you were strangers *and* sojourners in the land of Egypt.

20 You shall (reverently) fear the Lord your God; you shall serve Him and cling to Him, and by His name *and* presence you shall swear.

21 He is your praise; He is your God, Who has done for you these great and terrible things which your eyes have seen.

22 Your fathers went down to Egypt seventy persons; and now the Lord your God has made you as the stars of the heavens for multitude.

**11** THEREFORE YOU shall love the Lord your God, and keep His charge, His statutes, His precepts, and His commandments always.

2 And know this day (for I am not speaking to your children who have not [personally] known and seen it), the instruction *and* discipline of the Lord your God, His greatness, His mighty hand, and His outstretched arm,

3 His signs and His deeds which He did in Egypt to Pharaoh the king of Egypt and to all his land;

4 And what He did to the army of Egypt, to their horses and chariots; how He made the water of the Red Sea overflow them as they pursued after you, and how the Lord has destroyed them to this day;

5 And what He did to you in the wilderness, until you came to this place;

6 And what He did to Dathan and Abiram sons of Eliab, son of Reuben; how the earth opened its mouth and swallowed up them, their households, their tents, and every living thing that followed them, in the midst of all Israel; [Num. 26:9, 10.]

7 For your eyes have seen all the great work of the Lord which He did.

8 Therefore you shall keep all the commandments which I command you today, that you may be strong, and go in and possess the land which you go across [Jordan] to possess;

9 And that you may live long in the land, which the Lord swore to your fathers to give them and to their descendants, a land flowing with milk and honey.

10 For the land which you go in to possess is not like the land of Egypt, from which you came out, where you sowed your seed and watered it with your foot laboriously, as a garden of vegetables;

11 But the land, which you enter to possess, is a land of hills and valleys, and drinks water of the rain of the heavens;

## New American Standard

11 "Then the LORD said to me, 'Arise, proceed on your journey
ahead of the people, that they may go in and possess the land
which I swore to their fathers to give them.'
12¶ "And now, Israel, what does the LORD your God require
from you, but to fear the LORD your God, to walk in all His ways
and love Him, and to serve the LORD your God with all your heart
and with all your soul,
13 *and* to keep the LORD's commandments and His statutes
which I am commanding you today for your good?
14 "Behold, to the LORD your God belong heaven and the highest heavens, the earth and all that is in it.
15 "Yet on your fathers did the LORD set His affection to love
them, and He chose their descendants after them, *even* you above
all peoples, as *it is* this day.
16 "Circumcise then your heart, and stiffen your neck no more.
17 "For the LORD your God is the God of gods and the Lord of
lords, the great, the mighty, and the awesome God who does not
show partiality, nor take a bribe.
18 "He executes justice for the orphan and the widow, and
shows His love for the alien by giving him food and clothing.
19 "So show your love for the alien, for you were aliens in the
land of Egypt.
20 "You shall fear the LORD your God; you shall serve Him and
cling to Him, and you shall swear by His name.
21 "He is your praise and He is your God, who has done these
great and awesome things for you which your eyes have seen.
22 "Your fathers went down to Egypt seventy persons *in all*, and
now the LORD your God has made you as numerous as the stars
of heaven.

## New International

"and lead the people on their way, so that they may enter and
possess the land that I swore to their fathers to give them."

*Fear the LORD*

12 And now, O Israel, what does the LORD your God ask of you
but to fear the LORD your God, to walk in all his ways, to love him,
to serve the LORD your God with all your heart and with all your
soul, 13 and to observe the LORD's commands and decrees that I am
giving you today for your own good?
14 To the LORD your God belong the heavens, even the highest
heavens, the earth and everything in it. 15 Yet the LORD set his
affection on your forefathers and loved them, and he chose you,
their descendants, above all the nations, as it is today. 16 Circumcise your hearts, therefore, and do not be stiff-necked any longer.
17 For the LORD your God is God of gods and Lord of lords, the
great God, mighty and awesome, who shows no partiality and
accepts no bribes. 18 He defends the cause of the fatherless and the
widow, and loves the alien, giving him food and clothing. 19 And
you are to love those who are aliens, for you yourselves were aliens
in Egypt. 20 Fear the LORD your God and serve him. Hold fast to
him and take your oaths in his name. 21 He is your praise; he is your
God, who performed for you those great and awesome wonders
you saw with your own eyes. 22 Your forefathers who went down
into Egypt were seventy in all, and now the LORD your God has
made you as numerous as the stars in the sky.

### New American Standard

*Rewards of Obedience*

11 "YOU SHALL therefore love the LORD your God, and
always keep His charge, His statutes, His ordinances, and
His commandments.
2 "And know this day that I *am* not *speaking* with your sons who
have not known and who have not seen the [a]discipline of the LORD
your God—His greatness, His mighty hand, and His outstretched
arm,
3 and His signs and His works which He did in the midst of
Egypt to Pharaoh the king of Egypt and to all his land;
4 and what He did to Egypt's army, to its horses and its chariots, when He made the water of the Red Sea to engulf them while
they were pursuing you, and the LORD completely destroyed
them;
5 and what He did to you in the wilderness until you came to
this place;
6 and what He did to Dathan and Abiram, the sons of Eliab, the
son of Reuben, when the earth opened its mouth and swallowed
them, their households, their tents, and every living thing that
followed them, among all Israel—
7 but your own eyes have seen all the great work of the LORD
which He did.
8¶ "You shall therefore keep every commandment which I am
commanding you today, so that you may be strong and go in and
possess the land into which you are about to cross to possess it;
9 so that you may prolong *your* days on the land which the LORD
swore to your fathers to give to them and to their descendants, a
land flowing with milk and honey.
10 "For the land, into which you are entering to possess it, is not
like the land of Egypt from which you came, where you used to
sow your seed and water it with your [b]foot like a vegetable garden.
11 "But the land into which you are about to cross to possess it,
a land of hills and valleys, drinks water from the rain of heaven,

### New International

*Love and Obey the LORD*

11 LOVE THE LORD your God and keep his requirements, his
decrees, his laws and his commands always. 2 Remember
today that your children were not the ones who saw and experienced the discipline of the LORD your God: his majesty, his mighty
hand, his outstretched arm; 3 the signs he performed and the
things he did in the heart of Egypt, both to Pharaoh king of Egypt
and to his whole country; 4 what he did to the Egyptian army, to
its horses and chariots, how he overwhelmed them with the waters of the Red Sea[c] as they were pursuing you, and how the LORD
brought lasting ruin on them. 5 It was not your children who saw
what he did for you in the desert until you arrived at this place,
6 and what he did to Dathan and Abiram, sons of Eliab the Reubenite, when the earth opened its mouth right in the middle of all
Israel and swallowed them up with their households, their tents
and every living thing that belonged to them. 7 But it was your own
eyes that saw all these great things the LORD has done.
8 Observe therefore all the commands I am giving you today, so
that you may have the strength to go in and take over the land that
you are crossing the Jordan to possess, 9 and so that you may live
long in the land that the LORD swore to your forefathers to give to
them and their descendants, a land flowing with milk and honey.
10 The land you are entering to take over is not like the land of
Egypt, from which you have come, where you planted your seed
and irrigated it by foot as in a vegetable garden. 11 But the land you
are crossing the Jordan to take possession of is a land of mountains
and valleys that drinks rain from heaven. 12 It is a land the LORD

NAS [a] Or, *instruction* [b] I.e., probably a treadmill

NIV [c] 4 Hebrew *Yam Suph;* that is, Sea of Reeds

## King James

12A land which the LORD thy God careth for: the eyes of the LORD thy God *are* always upon it, from the beginning of the year even unto the end of the year.

13¶ And it shall come to pass, if ye shall hearken diligently unto my commandments which I command you this day, to love the LORD your God, and to serve him with all your heart and with all your soul,

14That I will give *you* the rain of your land in his due season, the first rain and the latter rain, that thou mayest gather in thy corn, and thy wine, and thine oil.

15And I will send grass in thy fields for thy cattle, that thou mayest eat and be full.

16Take heed to yourselves, that your heart be not deceived, and ye turn aside, and serve other gods, and worship them;

17And *then* the LORD's wrath be kindled against you, and he shut up the heaven, that there be no rain, and that the land yield not her fruit; and *lest* ye perish quickly from off the good land which the LORD giveth you.

18¶ Therefore shall ye lay up these my words in your heart and in your soul, and bind them for a sign upon your hand, that they may be as frontlets between your eyes.

19And ye shall teach them your children, speaking of them when thou sittest in thine house, and when thou walkest by the way, when thou liest down, and when thou risest up.

20And thou shalt write them upon the door posts of thine house, and upon thy gates:

21That your days may be multiplied, and the days of your children, in the land which the LORD sware unto your fathers to give them, as the days of heaven upon the earth.

22¶ For if ye shall diligently keep all these commandments which I command you, to do them, to love the LORD your God, to walk in all his ways, and to cleave unto him;

23Then will the LORD drive out all these nations from before you, and ye shall possess greater nations and mightier than yourselves.

24Every place whereon the soles of your feet shall tread shall be yours: from the wilderness and Lebanon, from the river, the river Euphrates, even unto the uttermost sea shall your coast be.

25There shall no man be able to stand before you: *for* the LORD your God shall lay the fear of you and the dread of you upon all the land that ye shall tread upon, as he hath said unto you.

26¶ Behold, I set before you this day a blessing and a curse;

27A blessing, if ye obey the commandments of the LORD your God, which I command you this day:

28And a curse, if ye will not obey the commandments of the LORD your God, but turn aside out of the way which I command you this day, to go after other gods, which ye have not known.

29And it shall come to pass, when the LORD thy God hath brought thee in unto the land whither thou goest to possess it, that thou shalt put the blessing upon mount Gerizim, and the curse upon mount Ebal.

30 *Are* they not on the other side Jordan, by the way where the sun goeth down, in the land of the Canaanites, which dwell in the champaign over against Gilgal, beside the plains of Moreh?

31For ye shall pass over Jordan to go in to possess the land which the LORD your God giveth you, and ye shall possess it, and dwell therein.

32And ye shall observe to do all the statutes and judgments which I set before you this day.

**12** THESE *ARE* the statutes and judgments, which ye shall observe to do in the land, which the LORD God of thy fathers giveth thee to possess it, all the days that ye live upon the earth.

## Amplified

12A land for which the Lord your God cares; the eyes of the Lord your God are always upon it, from the beginning of the year to the end of the year.

13And if you will diligently heed My commandments which I command you this day, to love the Lord your God, and to serve Him with all your [mind and] heart and with your entire being,

14I will give the rain for your land in its season, the early rain and the latter rain, that you may gather in your grain, your new wine, and your oil.

15And I will give grass in your fields for your cattle, that you may eat and be full.

16Take heed to yourselves, lest your [mind and] heart be deceived, and you turn aside and serve other gods and worship them,

17And the Lord's anger be kindled against you, and He shut up the heavens, so that there will be no rain, and the land yield not its fruit, and you perish quickly off the good land which the Lord gives you.

18Therefore you shall lay up these My words in your [mind and] heart and in your [entire] being, and bind them for a sign upon your hand, and as forehead bands between your eyes.

19And you shall teach them to your children, speaking of them when you sit in your house, and when you walk along the road, when you lie down and when you rise up.

20And you shall write them upon the doorposts of your house, and on your gates,

21That your days and the days of your children may be multiplied in the land which the Lord swore to your fathers to give them, as long as the heavens are above the earth.

22For if you diligently keep all this commandment which I command you to do, to love the Lord your God, to walk in all His ways, and to cleave to Him,

23Then the Lord will drive out all these nations before you, and you shall dispossess nations greater and mightier than yourselves.

24Every place upon which the sole of your foot shall tread shall be yours; from the wilderness to Lebanon, and from the River, the river Euphrates, to the western [Mediterranean] sea your territory shall be.

25There shall no man be able to stand before you; the Lord your God shall lay the fear and the dread of you upon all the land that you shall tread, as He has said to you.

26Behold, I set before you this day a blessing and a curse;

27The blessing, if you obey the commandments of the Lord your God, which I command you this day;

28And the curse, if you will not obey the commandments of the Lord your God, but turn aside from the way which I command you this day, to go after other gods which you have not known.

29And when the Lord your God has brought you into the land which you go to possess, you shall set the blessing on Mount Gerizim and the curse on Mount Ebal. [Josh. 8:33.]

30Are they not beyond the Jordan, west of the road where the sun goes down, in the land of the Canaanites, living in the Arabah opposite Gilgal, beside the oaks *or* terebinths of Moreh?

31For you are to cross over the Jordan to go in to possess the land which the Lord your God gives you, and you shall possess it, and live in it.

32And you shall be watchful to do all the statutes and ordinances which I set before you this day.

**12** THESE ARE the statutes and ordinances which you shall be watchful to do in the land, which the Lord, God of your fathers, gives you to possess all the days you live on the earth.

## New American Standard

12a land for which the LORD your God cares; the eyes of the LORD your God are always on it, from the beginning even to the end of the year.

13¶ "And it shall come about, if you listen obediently to my commandments which I am commanding you today, to love the LORD your God and to serve Him with all your heart and all your soul,

14that He will give the rain for your land in its season, the [a]early and late rain, that you may gather in your grain and your new wine and your oil.

15"And He will give grass in your fields for your cattle, and you shall eat and be satisfied.

16"Beware, lest your hearts be deceived and you turn away and serve other gods and worship them.

17"Or the anger of the LORD will be kindled against you, and He will shut up the heavens so that there will be no rain and the ground will not yield its fruit; and you will perish quickly from the good land which the LORD is giving you.

18¶ "You shall therefore impress these words of mine on your heart and on your soul; and you shall bind them as a sign on your hand, and they shall be as frontals on your forehead.

19"And you shall teach them to your sons, talking of them when you sit in your house and when you walk along the road and when you lie down and when you rise up.

20"And you shall write them on the doorposts of your house and on your gates,

21so that your days and the days of your sons may be multiplied on the land which the LORD swore to your fathers to give them, as long as the heavens *remain* above the earth.

22"For if you are careful to keep all this commandment which I am commanding you, to do it, to love the LORD your God, to walk in all His ways and hold fast to Him;

23then the LORD will drive out all these nations from before you, and you will dispossess nations greater and mightier than you.

24"Every place on which the sole of your foot shall tread shall be yours; your border shall be from the wilderness to Lebanon, *and* from the river, the river Euphrates, as far as [b]the western sea.

25"There shall no man be able to stand before you; the LORD your God shall lay the dread of you and the fear of you on all the land on which you set foot, as He has spoken to you.

26¶ "See, I am setting before you today a blessing and a curse:

27the blessing, if you listen to the commandments of the LORD your God, which I am commanding you today;

28and the curse, if you do not listen to the commandments of the LORD your God, but turn aside from the way which I am commanding you today, by following other gods which you have not known.

29"And it shall come about, when the LORD your God brings you into the land where you are entering to possess it, that you shall place the blessing on Mount Gerizim and the curse on Mount Ebal.

30"Are they not across the Jordan, west of the way toward the sunset, in the land of the Canaanites who live in the Arabah, opposite Gilgal, beside the oaks of Moreh?

31"For you are about to cross the Jordan to go in to possess the land which the LORD your God is giving you, and you shall possess it and live in it,

32and you shall be careful to do all the statutes and the judgments which I am setting before you today.

*Laws of the Sanctuary*

**12** "THESE ARE the statutes and the judgments which you shall carefully observe in the land which the LORD, the God of your fathers, has given you to possess as long as you live on the earth.

NAS [a] I.e., autumn and spring rain [b] I.e., the Mediterranean

## New International

your God cares for; the eyes of the LORD your God are continually
on it from the beginning of the year to its end.
13So if you faithfully obey the commands I am giving you today—to love the LORD your God and to serve him with all your
heart and with all your soul— 14then I will send rain on your land
in its season, both autumn and spring rains, so that you may
gather in your grain, new wine and oil. 15I will provide grass in
the fields for your cattle, and you will eat and be satisfied.
16Be careful, or you will be enticed to turn away and worship
other gods and bow down to them. 17Then the LORD's anger will
burn against you, and he will shut the heavens so that it will not
rain and the ground will yield no produce, and you will soon
perish from the good land the LORD is giving you. 18Fix these
words of mine in your hearts and minds; tie them as symbols on
your hands and bind them on your foreheads. 19Teach them to
your children, talking about them when you sit at home and when
you walk along the road, when you lie down and when you get
up. 20Write them on the doorframes of your houses and on your
gates, 21so that your days and the days of your children may be
many in the land that the LORD swore to give your forefathers, as
many as the days that the heavens are above the earth.
22If you carefully observe all these commands I am giving you
to follow—to love the LORD your God, to walk in all his ways and
to hold fast to him— 23then the LORD will drive out all these nations
before you, and you will dispossess nations larger and stronger
than you. 24Every place where you set your foot will be yours: Your
territory will extend from the desert to Lebanon, and from the
Euphrates River to the western sea.[c] 25No man will be able to
stand against you. The LORD your God, as he promised you, will
put the terror and fear of you on the whole land, wherever you go.
26See, I am setting before you today a blessing and a curse—
27the blessing if you obey the commands of the LORD your God that
I am giving you today; 28the curse if you disobey the commands
of the LORD your God and turn from the way that I command you
today by following other gods, which you have not known.
29When the LORD your God has brought you into the land you are
entering to possess, you are to proclaim on Mount Gerizim the
blessings, and on Mount Ebal the curses. 30As you know, these
mountains are across the Jordan, west of the road,[d] toward the
setting sun, near the great trees of Moreh, in the territory of those
Canaanites living in the Arabah in the vicinity of Gilgal. 31You are
about to cross the Jordan to enter and take possession of the land
the LORD your God is giving you. When you have taken it over and
are living there, 32be sure that you obey all the decrees and laws
I am setting before you today.

*The One Place of Worship*

**12** THESE ARE the decrees and laws you must be careful to
follow in the land that the LORD, the God of your fathers,
has given you to possess—as long as you live in the land. 2Destroy

NIV [c] *24* That is, the Mediterranean [d] *30* Or *Jordan, westward*

## King James

2Ye shall utterly destroy all the places, wherein the nations
which ye shall possess served their gods, upon the high mountains, and upon the hills, and under every green tree:
3And ye shall overthrow their altars, and break their pillars, and
burn their groves with fire; and ye shall hew down the graven
images of their gods, and destroy the names of them out of that
place.
4Ye shall not do so unto the LORD your God.
5But unto the place which the LORD your God shall choose out
of all your tribes to put his name there, *even* unto his habitation
shall ye seek, and thither thou shalt come:
6And thither ye shall bring your burnt offerings, and your
sacrifices, and your tithes, and heave offerings of your hand, and
your vows, and your freewill offerings, and the firstlings of your
herds and of your flocks:
7And there ye shall eat before the LORD your God, and ye shall
rejoice in all that ye put your hand unto, ye and your households,
wherein the LORD thy God hath blessed thee.
8Ye shall not do after all *the things* that we do here this day,
every man whatsoever *is* right in his own eyes.
9For ye are not as yet come to the rest and to the inheritance,
which the LORD your God giveth you.
10But *when* ye go over Jordan, and dwell in the land which the
LORD your God giveth you to inherit, and *when* he giveth you rest
from all your enemies round about, so that ye dwell in safety;
11Then there shall be a place which the LORD your God shall
choose to cause his name to dwell there; thither shall ye bring all
that I command you; your burnt offerings, and your sacrifices,
your tithes, and the heave offering of your hand, and all your
choice vows which ye vow unto the LORD:
12And ye shall rejoice before the LORD your God, ye, and your
sons, and your daughters, and your menservants, and your maidservants, and the Levite that *is* within your gates; forasmuch as he
hath no part nor inheritance with you.
13Take heed to thyself that thou offer not thy burnt offerings in
every place that thou seest:
14But in the place which the LORD shall choose in one of thy
tribes, there thou shalt offer thy burnt offerings, and there thou
shalt do all that I command thee.
15Notwithstanding thou mayest kill and eat flesh in all thy
gates, whatsoever thy soul lusteth after, according to the blessing
of the LORD thy God which he hath given thee: the unclean and
the clean may eat thereof, as of the roebuck, and as of the hart.
16Only ye shall not eat the blood; ye shall pour it upon the earth
as water.
17¶ Thou mayest not eat within thy gates the tithe of thy corn,
or of thy wine, or of thy oil, or the firstlings of thy herds or of thy
flock, nor any of thy vows which thou vowest, nor thy freewill
offerings, or heave offering of thine hand:
18But thou must eat them before the LORD thy God in the place
which the LORD thy God shall choose, thou, and thy son, and thy
daughter, and thy manservant, and thy maidservant, and the
Levite that *is* within thy gates: and thou shalt rejoice before the
LORD thy God in all that thou puttest thine hands unto.
19Take heed to thyself that thou forsake not the Levite as long
as thou livest upon the earth.
20¶ When the LORD thy God shall enlarge thy border, as he hath
promised thee, and thou shalt say, I will eat flesh, because thy soul
longeth to eat flesh; thou mayest eat flesh, whatsoever thy soul
lusteth after.

## Amplified

2You shall surely destroy all the places where the nations you
dispossess served their gods, upon the high mountains and the
hills and under every green tree;
3You shall break down their altars, and dash in pieces their
pillars, and burn their Asherim with fire; you shall hew down the
graven images of their gods, and destroy their name out of that
place.
4You shall not behave so toward the Lord your God.
5But you shall seek the place which the Lord your God shall
choose out of all your tribes to put His name and make His dwellingplace, and there shall you come;
6And there you shall bring your burnt offerings, and your sacrifices, your tithes, and the offering of your hands and your vows,
and your freewill offerings, and the firstlings of your herd and of
your flock;
7And there you shall eat before the Lord your God, and you
shall rejoice in all to which you put your hand, you and your
households, in which the Lord your God has blessed you.
8You [a]shall not do according to all we do here [in the camp] this
day, every man doing whatever looks right in his own eyes.
9For you have not yet come to the rest and to the inheritance
which the Lord your God gives you.
10But when you go over the Jordan and dwell in the land which
the Lord your God causes you to inherit, and He gives you rest
from all your enemies round about, so that you dwell in safety,
11Then there shall be a place which the Lord your God shall
choose to cause His name [and His presence] to dwell there; to it
you shall bring all that I command you; your burnt offerings, your
sacrifices, your tithes, and what the hand presents [as a first gift
from the fruits of the ground], and all your choicest offerings
which you vow to the Lord.
12And you shall rejoice before the Lord your God, you and your
sons and your daughters, and your menservants and your maidservants, and the Levite that is within your towns; since he has no
part or inheritance with you.
13Be watchful not to offer your burnt offerings in every place
you see;
14But in the place which the Lord shall choose in one of your
tribes, there you shall offer your burnt offerings, and there you
shall do all I command you.
15However, you may kill and eat flesh in any of your towns,
whenever you desire, according to the provision for the support
of life with which the Lord your God has blessed you; those
[ceremonially] unclean and the clean may eat of it, as of the gazelle
and the hart.
16Only you shall not eat the blood; you shall pour it upon the
ground as water.
17You may not eat within your towns the tithe of your grain or
of your new wine or of your oil or the firstlings of your herd or
flock, or anything you have vowed, or your freewill offerings, or
the offerings from your hand [of garden products].
18But you shall eat them before the Lord your God in the place
which the Lord your God shall choose, you and your son and your
daughter, your manservant and your maidservant, and the Levite
that is within your towns; and you shall rejoice before the Lord
your God in all that you undertake.
19Take heed not to forsake *or* neglect the Levite [God's minister]
as long as you live in your land.
20When the Lord your God enlarges your territory, as He promised you, and you say, I will eat flesh, because you crave flesh, you
may eat flesh, whenever you desire.

**AMP** [a] "It has been too much overlooked that the Law of Moses had a prophetic side. It was given to him and to Israel when they were not in a position to keep it [fully]. It was *the law of the land* which God would give them. In many ways its observance depended on the completion of the conquest of the land, and upon the quietness of the times in which they lived. This prophetic aspect was certainly not unrecognized by the Jews, or they would not (for example) have neglected to dwell in booths at the Feast of Tabernacles from the time of Joshua to Nehemiah. See Neh. 8:17." *(Ellicott's Commentary.)*

## New American Standard

2"You shall utterly destroy all the places where the nations whom you shall dispossess serve their gods, on the high mountains and on the hills and under every green tree.

3"And you shall tear down their altars and smash their *sacred* pillars and burn their [b]Asherim with fire, and you shall cut down the engraved images of their gods, and you shall obliterate their name from that place.

4"You shall not act like this toward the LORD your God.

5"But you shall seek *the LORD* at the place which the LORD your God shall choose from all your tribes, to establish His name there for His dwelling, and there you shall come.

6"And there you shall bring your burnt offerings, your sacrifices, your tithes, the contribution of your hand, your votive offerings, your freewill offerings, and the first-born of your herd and of your flock.

7"There also you and your households shall eat before the LORD your God, and rejoice in all your undertakings in which the LORD your God has blessed you.

8"You shall not do at all what we are doing here today, every man *doing* whatever is right in his own eyes;

9for you have not as yet come to the resting place and the inheritance which the LORD your God is giving you.

10"When you cross the Jordan and live in the land which the LORD your God is giving you to inherit, and He gives you rest from all your enemies around *you* so that you live in security,

11then it shall come about that the place in which the LORD your God shall choose for His name to dwell, there you shall bring all that I command you: your burnt offerings and your sacrifices, your tithes and the contribution of your hand, and all your choice votive offerings which you will vow to the LORD.

12"And you shall rejoice before the LORD your God, you and your sons and daughters, your male and female servants, and the Levite who is within your gates, since he has no portion or inheritance with you.

13"Be careful that you do not offer your burnt offerings in every *cultic* place you see,

14but in the place which the LORD chooses in one of your tribes, there you shall offer your burnt offerings, and there you shall do all that I command you.

**15**¶ "However, you may slaughter and eat meat within any of your gates, whatever you desire, according to the blessing of the LORD your God which He has given you; the unclean and the clean may eat of it, as of the gazelle and the deer.

16"Only you shall not eat the blood; you are to pour it out on the ground like water.

17"You are not allowed to eat within your gates the tithe of your grain, or new wine, or oil, or the first-born of your herd or flock, or any of your votive offerings which you vow, or your freewill offerings, or the contribution of your hand.

18"But you shall eat them before the LORD your God in the place which the LORD your God will choose, you and your son and daughter, and your male and female servants, and the Levite who is within your gates; and you shall rejoice before the LORD your God in all your undertakings.

19"Be careful that you do not forsake the Levite as long as you live in your land.

**20**¶ "When the LORD your God extends your border as He has promised you, and you say, 'I will eat meat,' because you desire to eat meat, *then* you may eat meat, whatever you desire.

NAS [b] I.e., wooden symbols of a female deity

## New International

completely all the places on the high mountains and on the hills
and under every spreading tree where the nations you are dispossessing worship their gods. 3Break down their altars, smash their
sacred stones and burn their Asherah poles in the fire; cut down
the idols of their gods and wipe out their names from those places.
4You must not worship the LORD your God in their way. 5But
you are to seek the place the LORD your God will choose from
among all your tribes to put his Name there for his dwelling. To
that place you must go; 6there bring your burnt offerings and
sacrifices, your tithes and special gifts, what you have vowed to
give and your freewill offerings, and the firstborn of your herds
and flocks. 7There, in the presence of the LORD your God, you and
your families shall eat and shall rejoice in everything you have put
your hand to, because the LORD your God has blessed you.
8You are not to do as we do here today, everyone as he sees fit,
9since you have not yet reached the resting place and the inheritance the LORD your God is giving you. 10But you will cross the
Jordan and settle in the land the LORD your God is giving you as
an inheritance, and he will give you rest from all your enemies
around you so that you will live in safety. 11Then to the place the
LORD your God will choose as a dwelling for his Name—there you
are to bring everything I command you: your burnt offerings and
sacrifices, your tithes and special gifts, and all the choice possessions you have vowed to the LORD. 12And there rejoice before the
LORD your God, you, your sons and daughters, your menservants
and maidservants, and the Levites from your towns, who have no
allotment or inheritance of their own. 13Be careful not to sacrifice
your burnt offerings anywhere you please. 14Offer them only at
the place the LORD will choose in one of your tribes, and there
observe everything I command you.
15Nevertheless, you may slaughter your animals in any of your
towns and eat as much of the meat as you want, as if it were gazelle
or deer, according to the blessing the LORD your God gives you.
Both the ceremonially unclean and the clean may eat it. 16But you
must not eat the blood; pour it out on the ground like water. 17You
must not eat in your own towns the tithe of your grain and new
wine and oil, or the firstborn of your herds and flocks, or whatever
you have vowed to give, or your freewill offerings or special gifts.
18Instead, you are to eat them in the presence of the LORD your
God at the place the LORD your God will choose—you, your sons
and daughters, your menservants and maidservants, and the Levites from your towns—and you are to rejoice before the LORD
your God in everything you put your hand to. 19Be careful not to
neglect the Levites as long as you live in your land.
20When the LORD your God has enlarged your territory as he
promised you, and you crave meat and say, "I would like some
meat," then you may eat as much of it as you want. 21If the place

## King James

21If the place which the LORD thy God hath chosen to put his name there be too far from thee, then thou shalt kill of thy herd and of thy flock, which the LORD hath given thee, as I have commanded thee, and thou shalt eat in thy gates whatsoever thy soul lusteth after.

22Even as the roebuck and the hart is eaten, so thou shalt eat them: the unclean and the clean shall eat *of* them alike.

23Only be sure that thou eat not the blood: for the blood *is* the life; and thou mayest not eat the life with the flesh.

24Thou shalt not eat it; thou shalt pour it upon the earth as water.

25Thou shalt not eat it; that it may go well with thee, and with thy children after thee, when thou shalt do *that which is* right in the sight of the LORD.

26Only thy holy things which thou hast, and thy vows, thou shalt take, and go unto the place which the LORD shall choose:

27And thou shalt offer thy burnt offerings, the flesh and the blood, upon the altar of the LORD thy God: and the blood of thy sacrifices shall be poured out upon the altar of the LORD thy God, and thou shalt eat the flesh.

28Observe and hear all these words which I command thee, that it may go well with thee, and with thy children after thee for ever, when thou doest *that which is* good and right in the sight of the LORD thy God.

29¶ When the LORD thy God shall cut off the nations from before thee, whither thou goest to possess them, and thou succeedest them, and dwellest in their land;

30Take heed to thyself that thou be not snared by following them, after that they be destroyed from before thee; and that thou inquire not after their gods, saying, How did these nations serve their gods? even so will I do likewise.

31Thou shalt not do so unto the LORD thy God: for every abomination to the LORD, which he hateth, have they done unto their gods; for even their sons and their daughters they have burnt in the fire to their gods.

32What thing soever I command you, observe to do it: thou shalt not add thereto, nor diminish from it.

**13** IF THERE arise among you a prophet, or a dreamer of dreams, and giveth thee a sign or a wonder,

2And the sign or the wonder come to pass, whereof he spake unto thee, saying, Let us go after other gods, which thou hast not known, and let us serve them;

3Thou shalt not hearken unto the words of that prophet, or that dreamer of dreams: for the LORD your God proveth you, to know whether ye love the LORD your God with all your heart and with all your soul.

4Ye shall walk after the LORD your God, and fear him, and keep his commandments, and obey his voice, and ye shall serve him, and cleave unto him.

5And that prophet, or that dreamer of dreams, shall be put to death; because he hath spoken to turn *you* away from the LORD your God, which brought you out of the land of Egypt, and redeemed you out of the house of bondage, to thrust thee out of the way which the LORD thy God commanded thee to walk in. So shalt thou put the evil away from the midst of thee.

6¶ If thy brother, the son of thy mother, or thy son, or thy daughter, or the wife of thy bosom, or thy friend, which *is* as thine own soul, entice thee secretly, saying, Let us go and serve other gods, which thou hast not known, thou, nor thy fathers;

7 *Namely*, of the gods of the people which *are* round about you, nigh unto thee, or far off from thee, from the *one* end of the earth even unto the *other* end of the earth;

8Thou shalt not consent unto him, nor hearken unto him; neither shall thine eye pity him, neither shalt thou spare, neither shalt thou conceal him:

## Amplified

21If the place where the Lord your God has chosen to put His name [and presence] is too far from you, then you shall kill from your herd or flock which the Lord has given you, as I [Moses] have commanded you; eat in your towns as much as you desire.

22Just as the roebuck and the hart is eaten, so you may eat of it [but not offer it]; the unclean and the clean alike may eat of it.

23Only be sure that you do not eat the blood; for the blood is the life; and you may not eat the life with the flesh.

24You shall not eat it; you shall pour it out on the earth like water.

25You shall not eat it; that all may go well with you and with your children after you, when you do what is right in the sight of the Lord.

26Only your holy things which you have [to offer], and what you have vowed, you shall take, and go to the place [before the sanctuary] which the Lord shall choose,

27And offer your burnt offerings, the flesh and the blood, upon the altar of the Lord your God; and the blood of your sacrifices shall be poured out on the altar of the Lord your God, and you may eat the flesh.

28Be watchful and obey all these words which I command you, that it may go well with you and with your children after you for ever, when you do what is good and right in the sight of the Lord your God.

29When the Lord your God cuts off before you the nations whom you go to dispossess, and you dispossess them and live in their land,

30Be watchful that you are not ensnared into following them after they have been destroyed before you, and that you do not inquire after their gods, saying, How did these nations serve their gods? I will do likewise.

31You shall not do so to the Lord your God; for every abominable thing which the Lord hates they have done for their gods; for even their sons and their daughters they have burned in the fire to their gods.

32Whatever I command you, be watchful to do it; you shall not add to it or diminish it.

**13** IF A prophet arises among you, or a dreamer of dreams, and gives you a sign or a wonder,

2And the sign or the wonder he foretells to you comes to pass, and if he says, Let us go after other gods, which you have not known, and let us serve them,

3You shall not listen to the words of that prophet or to that dreamer of dreams; for the Lord your God is testing you, to know whether you love the Lord your God with all your [mind and] heart and with your entire being.

4You shall walk after the Lord your God and (reverently) fear Him, and keep His commandments and obey His voice, and you shall serve Him, and cling to Him.

5But that prophet or that dreamer of dreams shall be put to death, because he has talked rebellion *and* turning away from the Lord your God, Who brought you out of the land of Egypt, and redeemed you out of the house of bondage; that man has tried to draw you aside from the way in which the Lord your God commanded you to walk. So shall you put the evil away from your midst.

6If your brother, the son of your mother, or your son or daughter, or the wife of your bosom, or your friend, who is as your own life, entice you secretly, saying, Let us go and serve other gods, which you have not known, you nor your fathers;

7Of the gods of the peoples who are round about you, near you or far away from you, from one end of the earth to the other,

8You shall not consent to him, or listen to him; nor shall your eye pity him, nor shall you spare him or conceal him;

## New American Standard

21"If the place which the LORD your God chooses to put His name is too far from you, then you may slaughter of your herd and flock which the LORD has given you, as I have commanded you; and you may eat within your gates whatever you desire.

22"Just as a gazelle or a deer is eaten, so you shall eat it; the unclean and the clean alike may eat of it.

23"Only be sure not to eat the blood, for the blood is the life, and you shall not eat the life with the flesh.

24"You shall not eat it; you shall pour it out on the ground like water.

25"You shall not eat it, in order that it may be well with you and your sons after you, for you will be doing what is right in the sight of the LORD.

26"Only your holy things which you may have and your votive offerings, you shall take and go to the place which the LORD chooses.

27"And you shall offer your burnt offerings, the flesh and the blood, on the altar of the LORD your God; and the blood of your sacrifices shall be poured out on the altar of the LORD your God, and you shall eat the flesh.

28"Be careful to listen to all these words which I command you, in order that it may be well with you and your sons after you forever, for you will be doing what is good and right in the sight of the LORD your God.

**29**¶ "When the LORD your God cuts off before you the nations which you are going in to dispossess, and you dispossess them and dwell in their land,

30beware that you are not ensnared to follow them, after they are destroyed before you, and that you do not inquire after their gods, saying, 'How do these nations serve their gods, that I also may do likewise?'

31"You shall not behave thus toward the LORD your God, for every abominable act which the LORD hates they have done for their gods; for they even burn their sons and daughters in the fire to their gods.

**32**¶ "Whatever I command you, you shall be careful to do; you shall not add to nor take away from it.

*Shun Idolatry*

**13** "IF A prophet or a dreamer of dreams arises among you and gives you a sign or a wonder,

2and the sign or the wonder comes true, concerning which he spoke to you, saying, 'Let us go after other gods (whom you have not known) and let us serve them,'

3you shall not listen to the words of that prophet or that dreamer of dreams; for the LORD your God is testing you to find out if you love the LORD your God with all your heart and with all your soul.

4"You shall follow the LORD your God and fear Him; and you shall keep His commandments, listen to His voice, serve Him, and cling to Him.

5"But that prophet or that dreamer of dreams shall be put to death, because he has counseled rebellion against the LORD your God who brought you from the land of Egypt and redeemed you from the house of slavery, to seduce you from the way in which the LORD your God commanded you to walk. So you shall purge the evil from among you.

**6**¶ "If your brother, your mother's son, or your son or daughter, or the wife you cherish, or your friend who is as your own soul, entice you secretly, saying, 'Let us go and serve other gods' (whom neither you nor your fathers have known,

7of the gods of the peoples who are around you, near you or far from you, from one end of the earth to the other end),

8you shall not yield to him or listen to him; and your eye shall not pity him, nor shall you spare or conceal him.

## New International

where the LORD your God chooses to put his Name is too far away
from you, you may slaughter animals from the herds and flocks
the LORD has given you, as I have commanded you, and in your
own towns you may eat as much of them as you want. 22Eat them
as you would gazelle or deer. Both the ceremonially unclean and
the clean may eat. 23But be sure you do not eat the blood, because
the blood is the life, and you must not eat the life with the meat.
24You must not eat the blood; pour it out on the ground like water.
25Do not eat it, so that it may go well with you and your children
after you, because you will be doing what is right in the eyes of
the LORD.

26But take your consecrated things and whatever you have
vowed to give, and go to the place the LORD will choose. 27Present
your burnt offerings on the altar of the LORD your God, both the
meat and the blood. The blood of your sacrifices must be poured
beside the altar of the LORD your God, but you may eat the meat.
28Be careful to obey all these regulations I am giving you, so that
it may always go well with you and your children after you,
because you will be doing what is good and right in the eyes of the
LORD your God.

29The LORD your God will cut off before you the nations you are
about to invade and dispossess. But when you have driven them
out and settled in their land, 30and after they have been destroyed
before you, be careful not to be ensnared by inquiring about their
gods, saying, "How do these nations serve their gods? We will do
the same." 31You must not worship the LORD your God in their
way, because in worshiping their gods, they do all kinds of detestable things the LORD hates. They even burn their sons and daughters in the fire as sacrifices to their gods.

32See that you do all I command you; do not add to it or take
away from it.

*Worshiping Other Gods*

**13** IF A prophet, or one who foretells by dreams, appears
among you and announces to you a miraculous sign or
wonder, 2and if the sign or wonder of which he has spoken takes
place, and he says, "Let us follow other gods" (gods you have not
known) "and let us worship them," 3you must not listen to the
words of that prophet or dreamer. The LORD your God is testing
you to find out whether you love him with all your heart and with
all your soul. 4It is the LORD your God you must follow, and him
you must revere. Keep his commands and obey him; serve him
and hold fast to him. 5That prophet or dreamer must be put to
death, because he preached rebellion against the LORD your God,
who brought you out of Egypt and redeemed you from the land
of slavery; he has tried to turn you from the way the LORD your
God commanded you to follow. You must purge the evil from
among you.

6If your very own brother, or your son or daughter, or the wife
you love, or your closest friend secretly entices you, saying, "Let
us go and worship other gods" (gods that neither you nor your
fathers have known, 7gods of the peoples around you, whether
near or far, from one end of the land to the other), 8do not yield
to him or listen to him. Show him no pity. Do not spare him or
shield him. 9You must certainly put him to death. Your hand must

## King James

9But thou shalt surely kill him; thine hand shall be first upon him to put him to death, and afterwards the hand of all the people.

10And thou shalt stone him with stones, that he die; because he hath sought to thrust thee away from the LORD thy God, which brought thee out of the land of Egypt, from the house of bondage.

11And all Israel shall hear, and fear, and shall do no more any such wickedness as this is among you.

12¶ If thou shalt hear *say* in one of thy cities, which the LORD thy God hath given thee to dwell there, saying,

13 *Certain* men, the children of Belial, are gone out from among you, and have withdrawn the inhabitants of their city, saying, Let us go and serve other gods, which ye have not known;

14Then shalt thou inquire, and make search, and ask diligently; and, behold, *if it be* truth, *and* the thing certain, *that* such abomination is wrought among you;

15Thou shalt surely smite the inhabitants of that city with the edge of the sword, destroying it utterly, and all that *is* therein, and the cattle thereof, with the edge of the sword.

16And thou shalt gather all the spoil of it into the midst of the street thereof, and shalt burn with fire the city, and all the spoil thereof every whit, for the LORD thy God: and it shall be an heap for ever; it shall not be built again.

17And there shall cleave nought of the cursed thing to thine hand: that the LORD may turn from the fierceness of his anger, and show thee mercy, and have compassion upon thee, and multiply thee, as he hath sworn unto thy fathers;

18When thou shalt hearken to the voice of the LORD thy God, to keep all his commandments which I command thee this day, to do *that which is* right in the eyes of the LORD thy God.

**14** YE *ARE* the children of the LORD your God: ye shall not cut yourselves, nor make any baldness between your eyes for the dead.

2For thou *art* an holy people unto the LORD thy God, and the LORD hath chosen thee to be a peculiar people unto himself, above all the nations that *are* upon the earth.

3¶ Thou shalt not eat any abominable thing.

4These *are* the beasts which ye shall eat: the ox, the sheep, and the goat,

5The hart, and the roebuck, and the fallow deer, and the wild goat, and the pygarg, and the wild ox, and the chamois.

6And every beast that parteth the hoof, and cleaveth the cleft into two claws, *and* cheweth the cud among the beasts, that ye shall eat.

7Nevertheless these ye shall not eat of them that chew the cud, or of them that divide the cloven hoof; *as* the camel, and the hare, and the coney: for they chew the cud, but divide not the hoof; *therefore* they *are* unclean unto you.

8And the swine, because it divideth the hoof, yet cheweth not the cud, it *is* unclean unto you: ye shall not eat of their flesh, nor touch their dead carcase.

9¶ These ye shall eat of all that *are* in the waters: all that have fins and scales shall ye eat:

10And whatsoever hath not fins and scales ye may not eat; it *is* unclean unto you.

11¶ *Of* all clean birds ye shall eat.

12But these *are they* of which ye shall not eat: the eagle, and the ossifrage, and the ospray,

13And the glede, and the kite, and the vulture after his kind,

14And every raven after his kind,

15And the owl, and the night hawk, and the cuckoo, and the hawk after his kind,

16The little owl, and the great owl, and the swan,

17And the pelican, and the gier eagle, and the cormorant,

18And the stork, and the heron after her kind, and the lapwing, and the bat.

## Amplified

9But you shall surely kill him; your hand shall be first upon him to put him to death, and afterwards the hand of all the people.

10And you shall stone him to death with stones, because he has tried to draw you away from the Lord your God, Who brought you out of the land of Egypt, from the house of bondage.

11And all Israel shall hear, and (reverently) fear, and shall do no more any such wickedness as this among you.

12If you hear it said in one of your cities, which the Lord your God has given you in which to dwell,

13That certain base fellows have gone out from your midst, and have enticed away the inhabitants of their city, saying, Let us go and serve other gods, which you have not known;

14Then you shall inquire and make search and ask diligently and, behold, if it be true and certain that such an abominable thing has been done among you,

15You shall surely smite the inhabitants of that city with the edge of the sword, destroying it utterly, and all who are in it, and its beasts, with the edge of the sword.

16And you shall collect all its spoil into the midst of its open square, and shall burn the city with fire, with every bit of its spoil [as a whole burnt offering] to the Lord your God; it shall be a heap [of ruins] for ever; it shall not be built again.

17And nothing of the accursed thing shall cling to your hand that the Lord may turn from the fierceness of His anger, and show you mercy, and have compassion on you, and multiply you, as He swore to your fathers,

18If you obey the voice of the Lord your God, to keep all His commandments which I command you this day, to do what is right in the eyes of the Lord your God.

**14** YOU ARE the sons of the Lord your God; you shall not cut yourselves, or make any baldness on your foreheads for the dead.

2For you are a holy people (set apart) to the Lord your God, and the Lord has chosen you to be a peculiar people to Himself, above all the nations on the earth.

3You shall not eat anything that is abominable [to the Lord and so forbidden by Him].

4These are the beasts which you may eat: the ox, the sheep, and the goat,

5The hart, the gazelle, the roebuck, the wild goat, the ibex, the antelope, and the mountain sheep.

6And every beast that parts the hoof and has it divided into two, and brings up *and* chews the cud, among the beasts, you may eat.

7Yet these you shall not eat of those that chew the cud or have the hoof split in two: the camel, the hare, and the coney, because they chew the cud but divide not the hoof; they are unclean to you.

8And the swine, because it parts the hoof but does not chew the cud; it is unclean to you; you shall not eat of their flesh, or touch their dead bodies.

9These you may eat of all that are in the waters: whatever has fins and scales you may eat;

10And whatsoever has not fins and scales you may not eat; it is unclean to you.

11Of all clean birds you may eat.

12But these are they of which you shall not eat: the eagle, the vulture, the ospray,

13The buzzard, the kite in its several species,

14The raven in all its species,

15The ostrich, the night-hawk, the sea gull, the hawk of any variety,

16The little owl, the great owl, the horned owl,

17The pelican, the carrion vulture, the cormorant,

18The stork, the heron of any variety, the hoopoe, and the bat

## New American Standard

9 "But you shall surely kill him; your hand shall be first against him to put him to death, and afterwards the hand of all the people.

10 "So you shall stone him to death because he has sought to seduce you from the LORD your God who brought you out from the land of Egypt, out of the house of slavery.

11 "Then all Israel will hear and be afraid, and will never again do such a wicked thing among you.

12 ¶ "If you hear in one of your cities, which the LORD your God is giving you to live in, *anyone* saying *that*

13 some worthless men have gone out from among you and have seduced the inhabitants of their city, saying, 'Let us go and serve other gods' (whom you have not known),

14 then you shall investigate and search out and inquire thoroughly. And if it is true *and* the matter established that this abomination has been done among you,

15 you shall surely strike the inhabitants of that city with the edge of the sword, utterly destroying it and all that is in it and its cattle with the edge of the sword.

16 "Then you shall gather all its booty into the middle of its open square and burn the city and all its booty with fire as a whole burnt offering to the LORD your God; and it shall be a ruin forever. It shall never be rebuilt.

17 "And nothing from that which is put under the ban shall cling to your hand, in order that the LORD may turn from His burning anger and show mercy to you, and have compassion on you and make you increase, just as He has sworn to your fathers,

18 if you will listen to the voice of the LORD your God, keeping all His commandments which I am commanding you today, and doing what is right in the sight of the LORD your God.

*Clean and Unclean Animals*

**14** "YOU ARE the sons of the LORD your God; you shall not cut yourselves nor shave your forehead for the sake of the dead.

2 "For you are a holy people to the LORD your God; and the LORD has chosen you to be a people for His own possession out of all the peoples who are on the face of the earth.

3 ¶ "You shall not eat any detestable thing.

4 "These are the animals which you may eat: the ox, the sheep, the goat,

5 the deer, the gazelle, the roebuck, the wild goat, the ibex, the antelope and the mountain sheep.

6 "And any animal that divides the hoof and has the hoof split in two *and* chews the cud, among the animals, that you may eat.

7 "Nevertheless, you are not to eat of these among those which chew the cud, or among those that divide the hoof in two: the camel and the rabbit and the rock-badger, for though they chew the cud, they do not divide the hoof; they are unclean for you.

8 "And the pig, because it divides the hoof but *does* not *chew* the cud, it is unclean for you. You shall not eat any of their flesh nor touch their carcasses.

9 ¶ "These you may eat of all that are in water: anything that has fins and scales you may eat,

10 but anything that does not have fins and scales you shall not eat; it is unclean for you.

11 ¶ "You may eat any clean bird.

12 "But these are the ones which you shall not eat: the eagle and the vulture and the buzzard,

13 and the red kite, the falcon, and the kite in their kinds,

14 and every raven in its kind,

15 and the ostrich, the owl, the sea gull, and the hawk in their kinds,

16 the little owl, the great owl, the white owl,

17 the pelican, the carrion vulture, the cormorant,

18 the stork, and the heron in their kinds, and the hoopoe and the bat.

## New International

be the first in putting him to death, and then the hands of all the
people. 10 Stone him to death, because he tried to turn you away
from the LORD your God, who brought you out of Egypt, out of
the land of slavery. 11 Then all Israel will hear and be afraid, and
no one among you will do such an evil thing again.
12 If you hear it said about one of the towns the LORD your God
is giving you to live in 13 that wicked men have arisen among you
and have led the people of their town astray, saying, "Let us go
and worship other gods" (gods you have not known), 14 then you
must inquire, probe and investigate it thoroughly. And if it is true
and it has been proved that this detestable thing has been done
among you, 15 you must certainly put to the sword all who live in
that town. Destroy it completely,[a] both its people and its livestock.
16 Gather all the plunder of the town into the middle of the public
square and completely burn the town and all its plunder as a whole
burnt offering to the LORD your God. It is to remain a ruin forever,
never to be rebuilt. 17 None of those condemned things[b] shall be
found in your hands, so that the LORD will turn from his fierce
anger; he will show you mercy, have compassion on you, and
increase your numbers, as he promised on oath to your forefathers, 18 because you obey the LORD your God, keeping all his
commands that I am giving you today and doing what is right in
his eyes.

*Clean and Unclean Food*

**14** YOU ARE the children of the LORD your God. Do not cut
yourselves or shave the front of your heads for the dead,
2 for you are a people holy to the LORD your God. Out of all the
peoples on the face of the earth, the LORD has chosen you to be
his treasured possession.
3 Do not eat any detestable thing. 4 These are the animals you
may eat: the ox, the sheep, the goat, 5 the deer, the gazelle, the roe
deer, the wild goat, the ibex, the antelope and the mountain
sheep.[c] 6 You may eat any animal that has a split hoof divided in
two and that chews the cud. 7 However, of those that chew the cud
or that have a split hoof completely divided you may not eat the
camel, the rabbit or the coney.[d] Although they chew the cud, they
do not have a split hoof; they are ceremonially unclean for you.
8 The pig is also unclean; although it has a split hoof, it does not
chew the cud. You are not to eat their meat or touch their carcasses.
9 Of all the creatures living in the water, you may eat any that
has fins and scales. 10 But anything that does not have fins and
scales you may not eat; for you it is unclean.
11 You may eat any clean bird. 12 But these you may not eat: the
eagle, the vulture, the black vulture, 13 the red kite, the black kite,
any kind of falcon, 14 any kind of raven, 15 the horned owl, the
screech owl, the gull, any kind of hawk, 16 the little owl, the great
owl, the white owl, 17 the desert owl, the osprey, the cormorant,
18 the stork, any kind of heron, the hoopoe and the bat.

NIV [a] *15,17* The Hebrew term refers to the irrevocable giving over of things or persons to the LORD, often by totally destroying them. [b] *15,17* The Hebrew term refers to the irrevocable giving over of things or persons to the LORD, often by totally destroying them. [c] *5* The precise identification of some of the birds and animals in this chapter is uncertain. [d] *7* That is, the hyrax or rock badger

## King James

19And every creeping thing that flieth *is* unclean unto you: they shall not be eaten.

20 *But of* all clean fowls ye may eat.

21¶ Ye shall not eat *of* any thing that dieth of itself: thou shalt give it unto the stranger that *is* in thy gates, that he may eat it; or thou mayest sell it unto an alien: for thou *art* an holy people unto the LORD thy God. Thou shalt not seethe a kid in his mother's milk.

22Thou shalt truly tithe all the increase of thy seed, that the field bringeth forth year by year.

23And thou shalt eat before the LORD thy God, in the place which he shall choose to place his name there, the tithe of thy corn, of thy wine, and of thine oil, and the firstlings of thy herds and of thy flocks; that thou mayest learn to fear the LORD thy God always.

24And if the way be too long for thee, so that thou art not able to carry it; *or* if the place be too far from thee, which the LORD thy God shall choose to set his name there, when the LORD thy God hath blessed thee:

25Then shalt thou turn *it* into money, and bind up the money in thine hand, and shalt go unto the place which the LORD thy God shall choose:

26And thou shalt bestow that money for whatsoever thy soul lusteth after, for oxen, or for sheep, or for wine, or for strong drink, or for whatsoever thy soul desireth: and thou shalt eat there before the LORD thy God, and thou shalt rejoice, thou, and thine household,

27And the Levite that *is* within thy gates; thou shalt not forsake him; for he hath no part nor inheritance with thee.

28¶ At the end of three years thou shalt bring forth all the tithe of thine increase the same year, and shalt lay *it* up within thy gates:

29And the Levite, (because he hath no part nor inheritance with thee,) and the stranger, and the fatherless, and the widow, which *are* within thy gates, shall come, and shall eat and be satisfied; that the LORD thy God may bless thee in all the work of thine hand which thou doest.

**15** AT THE end of *every* seven years thou shalt make a release.

2And this *is* the manner of the release: Every creditor that lendeth *aught* unto his neighbour shall release *it;* he shall not exact *it* of his neighbour, or of his brother; because it is called the LORD's release.

3Of a foreigner thou mayest exact *it again:* but *that* which is thine with thy brother thine hand shall release;

4Save when there shall be no poor among you; for the LORD shall greatly bless thee in the land which the LORD thy God giveth thee *for* an inheritance to possess it:

5Only if thou carefully hearken unto the voice of the LORD thy God, to observe to do all these commandments which I command thee this day.

6For the LORD thy God blesseth thee, as he promised thee: and thou shalt lend unto many nations, but thou shalt not borrow; and thou shalt reign over many nations, but they shall not reign over thee.

7¶ If there be among you a poor man of one of thy brethren within any of thy gates in thy land which the LORD thy God giveth thee, thou shalt not harden thine heart, nor shut thine hand from thy poor brother:

8But thou shalt open thine hand wide unto him, and shalt surely lend him sufficient for his need, *in that* which he wanteth.

## Amplified

19And all flying insects are unclean for you; they shall not be eaten.

20But of all clean winged things you may eat.

21You shall not eat of anything that dies of itself; you may give it to the stranger *or* the foreigner who is within your towns, that he may eat it, or you may sell it to an alien; [they are not under God's law in this matter] but you are a people holy to the Lord your God. You shall not [even] boil a kid in its mother's milk.

22You shall surely tithe all the yield of your seed, produced by your field each year.

23And you shall eat before the Lord your God, in the place in which He will cause His name [and presence] to dwell, the tithe (tenth) of your grain, your new wine, your oil, and the firstlings of your herd and your flock, that you may learn (reverently) to fear the Lord your God always.

24And if the distance is too long for you to carry your tithe, or the place where the Lord your God chooses to set His name [and presence] is too far away for you, when the Lord your God has blessed you,

25Then you shall turn it into money, and bind up the money in your hand, and shall go to the place [of worship] which the Lord your God has chosen;

26And you may spend that money for whatever your appetite craves, for oxen, or sheep, or new wine or strong *er* drink, or whatever you desire; and you shall eat there before the Lord your God and you shall rejoice, you and your household.

27And you shall not forsake *or* neglect the Levite [God's minister] in your towns, for he has been given no share or inheritance with you.

28At the end of every three years you shall bring forth all the tithe of your increase the same year, and lay it up within your towns;

29And the Levite [because he has no part or inheritance with you], and the stranger *or* temporary resident, and the fatherless, and the widow, who are in your towns, shall come and eat and be satisfied; that the Lord your God may bless you in all the work of your hands that you do.

**15** AT THE end of every seven years you shall grant a release.

2And this is the manner of the release: every creditor shall release that which he has lent to his neighbor; he shall not exact it of his neighbor, his brother; for the Lord's release is proclaimed.

3Of a foreigner you may exact it; but whatever of yours is with your brother [Israelite] your hand shall release.

4But there will be no poor among you, for the Lord will surely bless you in the land which the Lord your God gives you for an inheritance to possess,

5If only you carefully listen to the voice of the Lord your God, to do watchfully all these commandments which I command you this day.

6When the Lord your God blesses you as He promised you, then you shall lend to many nations, but you shall not borrow; and you shall rule over many nations, but they shall not rule over you.

7If there is among you a poor man, one of your kinsmen in any of the towns of your land which the Lord your God gives you, you shall not harden your [mind and] heart, or close your hand to your poor brother;

8But you shall open your hand wide to him, and shall surely lend him sufficient for his need, which he lacks.

## New American Standard

19"And all the teeming life with wings are unclean to you; they
shall not be eaten.
20"You may eat any clean bird.
21¶ "You shall not eat anything which dies *of itself*. You may give
it to the alien who is in your town, so that he may eat it, or you
may sell it to a foreigner, for you are a holy people to the LORD your
God. You shall not boil a kid in its mother's milk.
22¶ "You shall surely tithe all the produce from what you sow,
which comes out of the field every year.
23"And you shall eat in the presence of the LORD your God, at
the place where He chooses to establish His name, the tithe of your
grain, your new wine, your oil, and the first-born of your herd and
your flock, in order that you may learn to fear the LORD your God
always.
24"And if the distance is so great for you that you are not able
to bring *the tithe*, since the place where the LORD your God chooses
to set His name is too far away from you when the LORD your God
blesses you,
25then you shall exchange *it* for money, and bind the money in
your hand and go to the place which the LORD your God chooses.
26"And you may spend the money for whatever your heart
desires, for oxen, or sheep, or wine, or strong drink, or whatever
your heart desires; and there you shall eat in the presence of the
LORD your God and rejoice, you and your household.
27"Also you shall not neglect the Levite who is in your town,
for he has no portion or inheritance among you.
28¶ "At the end of every third year you shall bring out all the
tithe of your produce in that year, and shall deposit *it* in your town.
29"And the Levite, because he has no portion or inheritance
among you, and the alien, the orphan and the widow who are in
your town, shall come and eat and be satisfied, in order that the
LORD your God may bless you in all the work of your hand which
you do.

*The Sabbatic Year*

**15** "AT THE end of *every* seven years you shall [a]grant a
remission *of debts*.
2"And this is the manner of remission: every creditor shall
release what he has loaned to his neighbor; he shall not exact it of
his neighbor and his brother, because the LORD's remission has
been proclaimed.
3"From a foreigner you may exact *it*, but your hand shall
release whatever of yours is with your brother.
4"However, there shall be no poor among you, since the LORD
will surely bless you in the land which the LORD your God is giving
you as an inheritance to possess,
5if only you listen obediently to the voice of the LORD your
God, to observe carefully all this commandment which I am commanding you today.
6"For the LORD your God shall bless you as He has promised
you, and you will lend to many nations, but you will not borrow;
and you will rule over many nations, but they will not rule over
you.
7¶ "If there is a poor man with you, one of your brothers, in
any of your towns in your land which the LORD your God is giving
you, you shall not harden your heart, nor close your hand from
your poor brother;
8but you shall freely open your hand to him, and shall generously lend him sufficient for his need *in* whatever he lacks.

NAS [a] Lit., *make a release*

## New International

19All flying insects that swarm are unclean to you; do not eat
them. 20But any winged creature that is clean you may eat.
21Do not eat anything you find already dead. You may give it
to an alien living in any of your towns, and he may eat it, or you
may sell it to a foreigner. But you are a people holy to the LORD
your God.
Do not cook a young goat in its mother's milk.

*Tithes*

22Be sure to set aside a tenth of all that your fields produce each
year. 23Eat the tithe of your grain, new wine and oil, and the
firstborn of your herds and flocks in the presence of the LORD your
God at the place he will choose as a dwelling for his Name, so that
you may learn to revere the LORD your God always. 24But if that
place is too distant and you have been blessed by the LORD your
God and cannot carry your tithe (because the place where the LORD
will choose to put his Name is so far away), 25then exchange your
tithe for silver, and take the silver with you and go to the place the
LORD your God will choose. 26Use the silver to buy whatever you
like: cattle, sheep, wine or other fermented drink, or anything you
wish. Then you and your household shall eat there in the presence
of the LORD your God and rejoice. 27And do not neglect the Levites
living in your towns, for they have no allotment or inheritance of
their own.
28At the end of every three years, bring all the tithes of that
year's produce and store it in your towns, 29so that the Levites
(who have no allotment or inheritance of their own) and the aliens,
the fatherless and the widows who live in your towns may come
and eat and be satisfied, and so that the LORD your God may bless
you in all the work of your hands.

*The Year for Canceling Debts*

**15** AT THE end of every seven years you must cancel debts.
2This is how it is to be done: Every creditor shall cancel the
loan he has made to his fellow Israelite. He shall not require
payment from his fellow Israelite or brother, because the LORD's
time for canceling debts has been proclaimed. 3You may require
payment from a foreigner, but you must cancel any debt your
brother owes you. 4However, there should be no poor among you,
for in the land the LORD your God is giving you to possess as your
inheritance, he will richly bless you, 5if only you fully obey the
LORD your God and are careful to follow all these commands I am
giving you today. 6For the LORD your God will bless you as he has
promised, and you will lend to many nations but will borrow from
none. You will rule over many nations but none will rule over you.
7If there is a poor man among your brothers in any of the towns
of the land that the LORD your God is giving you, do not be
hardhearted or tightfisted toward your poor brother. 8Rather be
openhanded and freely lend him whatever he needs. 9Be careful

## King James

9 Beware that there be not a thought in thy wicked heart, saying, The seventh year, the year of release, is at hand; and thine eye be evil against thy poor brother, and thou givest him nought; and he cry unto the LORD against thee, and it be sin unto thee.

10 Thou shalt surely give him, and thine heart shall not be grieved when thou givest unto him: because that for this thing the LORD thy God shall bless thee in all thy works, and in all that thou puttest thine hand unto.

11 For the poor shall never cease out of the land: therefore I command thee, saying, Thou shalt open thine hand wide unto thy brother, to thy poor, and to thy needy, in thy land.

12 ¶ *And* if thy brother, an Hebrew man, or an Hebrew woman, be sold unto thee, and serve thee six years; then in the seventh year thou shalt let him go free from thee.

13 And when thou sendest him out free from thee, thou shalt not let him go away empty:

14 Thou shalt furnish him liberally out of thy flock, and out of thy floor, and out of thy winepress: *of that* wherewith the LORD thy God hath blessed thee thou shalt give unto him.

15 And thou shalt remember that thou wast a bondman in the land of Egypt, and the LORD thy God redeemed thee: therefore I command thee this thing today.

16 And it shall be, if he say unto thee, I will not go away from thee; because he loveth thee and thine house, because he is well with thee;

17 Then thou shalt take an awl, and thrust *it* through his ear unto the door, and he shall be thy servant for ever. And also unto thy maidservant thou shalt do likewise.

18 It shall not seem hard unto thee, when thou sendest him away free from thee; for he hath been worth a double hired servant *to thee,* in serving thee six years: and the LORD thy God shall bless thee in all that thou doest.

19 ¶ All the firstling males that come of thy herd and of thy flock thou shalt sanctify unto the LORD thy God: thou shalt do no work with the firstling of thy bullock, nor shear the firstling of thy sheep.

20 Thou shalt eat *it* before the LORD thy God year by year in the place which the LORD shall choose, thou and thy household.

21 And if there be *any* blemish therein, *as if it be* lame, or blind, *or have* any ill blemish, thou shalt not sacrifice it unto the LORD thy God.

22 Thou shalt eat it within thy gates: the unclean and the clean *person shall eat it* alike, as the roebuck, and as the hart.

23 Only thou shalt not eat the blood thereof; thou shalt pour it upon the ground as water.

**16** OBSERVE THE month of Abib, and keep the passover unto the LORD thy God: for in the month of Abib the LORD thy God brought thee forth out of Egypt by night.

2 Thou shalt therefore sacrifice the passover unto the LORD thy God, of the flock and the herd, in the place which the LORD shall choose to place his name there.

3 Thou shalt eat no leavened bread with it; seven days shalt thou eat unleavened bread therewith, *even* the bread of affliction; for thou camest forth out of the land of Egypt in haste: that thou mayest remember the day when thou camest forth out of the land of Egypt all the days of thy life.

4 And there shall be no leavened bread seen with thee in all thy coast seven days; neither shall there *any thing* of the flesh, which thou sacrificedst the first day at even, remain all night until the morning.

5 Thou mayest not sacrifice the passover within any of thy gates, which the LORD thy God giveth thee:

6 But at the place which the LORD thy God shall choose to place his name in, there thou shalt sacrifice the passover at even, at the going down of the sun, at the season that thou camest forth out of Egypt.

## Amplified

9 Beware lest there be a base thought in your [mind and] heart, and you say, The seventh year, the year of release, is at hand; and your eye be evil against your poor brother, and you give him nothing, and he cry to the Lord against you, and it be sin in you.

10 You shall give to him freely without begrudging it; because for this the Lord will bless you in all your work and in all you undertake.

11 For the poor will never cease out of the land; therefore I command you, You shall open wide your hand to your brother, to your needy, and to your poor in your land.

12 And if your brother, a Hebrew man, or a Hebrew woman, be sold to you and serve you six years, then in the seventh year you shall let him go free from you.

13 And when you send him out free from you, you shall not let him go away empty-handed;

14 You shall furnish him liberally out of your flock, your threshing floor, and your winepress; of what the Lord your God has blessed you, you shall give to him.

15 And you shall [earnestly] remember that you were a bondman in the land of Egypt, and the Lord your God redeemed you; therefore I give you this command today.

16 But if the servant says to you, I will not go away from you, because he loves you and your household, since he does well with you,

17 Then take an awl and pierce his ear through to the door, and he shall be your servant always. And also to your bondwoman you shall do likewise.

18 It shall not seem hard to you when you let him go free from you; for at half the cost of a hired servant he has served you six years, and the Lord your God will bless you in all you do.

19 All the firstling males that are born of your herd and flock you shall set apart for the Lord your God; you shall do no work with the firstling of your herd, nor shear the firstling of your flock.

20 You shall eat it before the Lord your God annually in the place [for worship] which the Lord shall choose, you and your household.

21 But if it has any blemish, if it is lame, blind, or has any bad blemish whatever, you shall not sacrifice it to the Lord your God.

22 You shall eat it within your towns; the [ceremonially] unclean and the clean alike may eat it, as if it were a gazelle or a hart.

23 Only you shall not eat its blood; you shall pour it on the ground like water.

**16** OBSERVE THE month of Abib, and keep the passover to the Lord your God; for in the month of Abib the Lord your God brought you out of Egypt by night.

2 You shall offer the passover sacrifice to the Lord your God from the flock or the herd, in the place where the Lord will choose to make His name [and His presence] dwell.

3 You shall eat no leavened bread with it; seven days you shall eat it with unleavened bread, the bread of affliction—for you fled from the land of Egypt in haste—that all the days of your life you may [earnestly] remember the day when you came out of Egypt.

4 No leaven shall be seen with you in all your territory for seven days; nor shall any of the flesh which you sacrificed the first day at evening be left all night until the morning.

5 You may not offer the passover sacrifices within any of your towns which the Lord your God gives you;

6 But at the place which the Lord your God will choose in which to make His name [and His presence] dwell, there you shall offer the passover sacrifice in the evening at sunset, at the season that you came out of Egypt.

## New American Standard

9"Beware, lest there is a base thought in your heart, saying,
'The seventh year, the year of remission, is near,' and your eye is
hostile toward your poor brother, and you give him nothing; then
he may cry to the LORD against you, and it will be a sin in you.
10"You shall generously give to him, and your heart shall not
be grieved when you give to him, because for this thing the LORD
your God will bless you in all your work and in all your undertakings.
11"For the poor will never cease *to be* in the land; therefore I
command you, saying, 'You shall freely open your hand to your
brother, to your needy and poor in your land.'
12¶ "If your kinsman, a Hebrew man or woman, is sold to you,
then he shall serve you six years, but in the seventh year you shall
set him free.
13"And when you set him free, you shall not send him away
empty-handed.
14"You shall furnish him liberally from your flock and from your
threshing floor and from your wine vat; you shall give to him as
the LORD your God has blessed you.
15"And you shall remember that you were a slave in the land
of Egypt, and the LORD your God redeemed you; therefore I command you this today.
16"And it shall come about if he says to you, 'I will not go out
from you,' because he loves you and your household, since he
fares well with you;
17then you shall take an awl and pierce it through his ear into
the door, and he shall be your servant forever. And also you shall
do likewise to your maidservant.
18"It shall not seem hard to you when you set him free, for he
has given you six years *with* double the service of a hired man; so
the LORD your God will bless you in whatever you do.
19¶ "You shall consecrate to the LORD your God all the first-born
males that are born of your herd and of your flock; you shall not
work with the first-born of your herd, nor shear the first-born of
your flock.
20"You and your household shall eat it every year before the
LORD your God in the place which the LORD chooses.
21"But if it has any defect, *such as* lameness or blindness, *or* any
serious defect, you shall not sacrifice it to the LORD your God.
22"You shall eat it within your gates; the unclean and the clean
alike *may eat it,* as a gazelle or a deer.
23"Only you shall not eat its blood; you are to pour it out on the
ground like water.

*The Feasts of Passover, of Weeks, and of Booths*

16 "OBSERVE THE month of Abib and celebrate the Passover to the LORD your God, for in the month of Abib the
LORD your God brought you out of Egypt by night.
2"And you shall sacrifice the Passover to the LORD your God
from the flock and the herd, in the place where the LORD chooses
to establish His name.
3"You shall not eat leavened bread with it; seven days you
shall eat with it unleavened bread, the bread of affliction (for you
came out of the land of Egypt in haste), in order that you may
remember all the days of your life the day when you came out of
the land of Egypt.
4"For seven days no leaven shall be seen with you in all your
territory, and none of the flesh which you sacrifice on the evening
of the first day shall remain overnight until morning.
5"You are not allowed to sacrifice the Passover in any of your
towns which the LORD your God is giving you;
6but at the place where the LORD your God chooses to establish
His name, you shall sacrifice the Passover in the evening at sunset,
at the time that you came out of Egypt.

## New International

not to harbor this wicked thought: "The seventh year, the year for
canceling debts, is near," so that you do not show ill will toward
your needy brother and give him nothing. He may then appeal to
the LORD against you, and you will be found guilty of sin. 10Give
generously to him and do so without a grudging heart; then because of this the LORD your God will bless you in all your work and
in everything you put your hand to. 11There will always be poor
people in the land. Therefore I command you to be openhanded
toward your brothers and toward the poor and needy in your land.

*Freeing Servants*

12If a fellow Hebrew, a man or a woman, sells himself to you
and serves you six years, in the seventh year you must let him go
free. 13And when you release him, do not send him away empty-
handed. 14Supply him liberally from your flock, your threshing
floor and your winepress. Give to him as the LORD your God has
blessed you. 15Remember that you were slaves in Egypt and the
LORD your God redeemed you. That is why I give you this command today.
16But if your servant says to you, "I do not want to leave you,"
because he loves you and your family and is well off with you,
17then take an awl and push it through his ear lobe into the door,
and he will become your servant for life. Do the same for your
maidservant.
18Do not consider it a hardship to set your servant free, because
his service to you these six years has been worth twice as much
as that of a hired hand. And the LORD your God will bless you in
everything you do.

*The Firstborn Animals*

19Set apart for the LORD your God every firstborn male of your
herds and flocks. Do not put the firstborn of your oxen to work,
and do not shear the firstborn of your sheep. 20Each year you and
your family are to eat them in the presence of the LORD your God
at the place he will choose. 21If an animal has a defect, is lame or
blind, or has any serious flaw, you must not sacrifice it to the LORD
your God. 22You are to eat it in your own towns. Both the ceremonially unclean and the clean may eat it, as if it were gazelle or deer.
23But you must not eat the blood; pour it out on the ground like
water.

*Passover*

16 OBSERVE THE month of Abib and celebrate the Passover
of the LORD your God, because in the month of Abib he
brought you out of Egypt by night. 2Sacrifice as the Passover to the
LORD your God an animal from your flock or herd at the place the
LORD will choose as a dwelling for his Name. 3Do not eat it with
bread made with yeast, but for seven days eat unleavened bread,
the bread of affliction, because you left Egypt in haste—so that all
the days of your life you may remember the time of your departure
from Egypt. 4Let no yeast be found in your possession in all your
land for seven days. Do not let any of the meat you sacrifice on the
evening of the first day remain until morning.
5You must not sacrifice the Passover in any town the LORD your
God gives you 6except in the place he will choose as a dwelling for
his Name. There you must sacrifice the Passover in the evening,
when the sun goes down, on the anniversary[a] of your departure
from Egypt. 7Roast it and eat it at the place the LORD your God will

NIV [a] 6 Or *down, at the time of day*

## King James

7And thou shalt roast and eat *it* in the place which the LORD thy God shall choose: and thou shalt turn in the morning, and go unto thy tents.

8Six days thou shalt eat unleavened bread: and on the seventh day *shall be* a solemn assembly to the LORD thy God: thou shalt do no work *therein*.

9¶ Seven weeks shalt thou number unto thee: begin to number the seven weeks from *such time as* thou beginnest *to put* the sickle to the corn.

10And thou shalt keep the feast of weeks unto the LORD thy God with a tribute of a freewill offering of thine hand, which thou shalt give *unto the LORD thy God*, according as the LORD thy God hath blessed thee:

11And thou shalt rejoice before the LORD thy God, thou, and thy son, and thy daughter, and thy manservant, and thy maidservant, and the Levite that *is* within thy gates, and the stranger, and the fatherless, and the widow, that *are* among you, in the place which the LORD thy God hath chosen to place his name there.

12And thou shalt remember that thou wast a bondman in Egypt: and thou shalt observe and do these statutes.

13¶ Thou shalt observe the feast of tabernacles seven days, after that thou hast gathered in thy corn and thy wine:

14And thou shalt rejoice in thy feast, thou, and thy son, and thy daughter, and thy manservant, and thy maidservant, and the Levite, the stranger, and the fatherless, and the widow, that *are* within thy gates.

15Seven days shalt thou keep a solemn feast unto the LORD thy God in the place which the LORD shall choose: because the LORD thy God shall bless thee in all thine increase, and in all the works of thine hands, therefore thou shalt surely rejoice.

16¶ Three times in a year shall all thy males appear before the LORD thy God in the place which he shall choose; in the feast of unleavened bread, and in the feast of weeks, and in the feast of tabernacles: and they shall not appear before the LORD empty:

17Every man *shall give* as he is able, according to the blessing of the LORD thy God which he hath given thee.

18¶ Judges and officers shalt thou make thee in all thy gates, which the LORD thy God giveth thee, throughout thy tribes: and they shall judge the people with just judgment.

19Thou shalt not wrest judgment; thou shalt not respect persons, neither take a gift: for a gift doth blind the eyes of the wise, and pervert the words of the righteous.

20That which is altogether just shalt thou follow, that thou mayest live, and inherit the land which the LORD thy God giveth thee.

21¶ Thou shalt not plant thee a grove of any trees near unto the altar of the LORD thy God, which thou shalt make thee.

22Neither shalt thou set thee up *any* image; which the LORD thy God hateth.

**17** THOU SHALT not sacrifice unto the LORD thy God *any* bullock, or sheep, wherein is blemish, *or* any evilfavouredness: for that *is* an abomination unto the LORD thy God.

2¶ If there be found among you, within any of thy gates which the LORD thy God giveth thee, man or woman, that hath wrought wickedness in the sight of the LORD thy God, in transgressing his covenant,

3And hath gone and served other gods, and worshipped them, either the sun, or moon, or any of the host of heaven, which I have not commanded;

4And it be told thee, and thou hast heard *of it*, and inquired diligently, and, behold, *it be* true, *and* the thing certain, *that* such abomination is wrought in Israel:

5Then shalt thou bring forth that man or that woman, which have committed that wicked thing, unto thy gates, *even* that man or that woman, and shalt stone them with stones, till they die.

## Amplified

7And you shall roast *or* boil and eat it in the place which the Lord your God will choose; and in the morning you shall turn and go to your tents.

8Six days you shall eat unleavened bread; and on the seventh day there shall be a solemn assembly to the Lord your God; you shall do no work on it.

9You shall count seven weeks; begin to number the seven weeks from the time you begin to put the sickle to the standing grain.

10Then you shall keep the feast of weeks to the Lord your God with a tribute of a freewill offering from your hand, which you shall give to the Lord your God, as the Lord your God blesses you.

11And you shall rejoice before the Lord your God, you and your son and daughter, your manservant and maidservant, and the Levite who is within your towns, the stranger *or* temporary resident, the fatherless, and the widow who are among you, at the place in which the Lord your God chooses to make His name [and His presence] dwell.

12And you shall (earnestly) remember that you were a slave in Egypt; and you shall be watchful and obey these statutes.

13You shall observe the feast of tabernacles *or* booths seven days, after you have gathered in from your threshing floor and wine vat.

14You shall rejoice in your feast, you, your son and daughter, your manservant and maidservant, the Levite, the transient *and* the stranger, the fatherless, and the widow, that are within your towns.

15Seven days you shall keep a solemn feast to the Lord your God in the place which the Lord chooses; because the Lord your God will bless you in all your produce, and in all the works of your hands, so that you will be altogether joyful.

16Three times a year shall all your males appear before the Lord your God in the place which He chooses, in the feast of unleavened bread, in the feast of weeks, and in the feast of tabernacles *or* booths. They shall not appear before the Lord empty-handed;

17Every man shall give as he is able, according to the blessing of the Lord your God which He has given you.

18You shall appoint judges and officers in all your towns which the Lord your God gives you, according to your tribes; and they shall judge the people with righteous judgment.

19You shall not misinterpret *or* misapply judgment; you shall not be partial, or take a bribe; for a bribe blinds the eyes of the wise, and perverts the words of the righteous.

20Follow what is altogether just [that is, uncompromisingly righteous], that you may live and inherit the land which your God gives you.

21You shall not plant you any kind of tree as an Asherah beside the altar of the Lord your God which you shall make.

22Neither shall you set up an idolatrous stone *or* image, which the Lord your God hates.

**17** YOU SHALL not sacrifice to the Lord your God an ox or sheep with a blemish or any defect whatever; for that is an abomination to the Lord your God.

2If there is found among you, within any of your towns which the Lord your God gives you, a man or woman who does what is wicked in the sight of the Lord your God, by transgressing His covenant,

3Who has gone and served other gods and worshiped them, or the sun or moon or any of the host of the heavens, which I have forbidden,

4And it is told and you hear of it; then inquire diligently, and if it is certainly true that such an abomination has been committed in Israel,

5Then you shall bring forth to your town's gates that man or woman who has done that wicked thing, and you shall stone that man or woman to death.

## New American Standard

7"And you shall cook and eat *it* in the place which the LORD
your God chooses. And in the morning you are to return to your
tents.
8"Six days you shall eat unleavened bread, and on the seventh
day there shall be a solemn assembly to the LORD your God; you
shall do no work *on it.*
9¶ "You shall count seven weeks for yourself; you shall begin
to count seven weeks from the time you begin to put the sickle to
the standing grain.
10"Then you shall celebrate the Feast of Weeks to the LORD your
God with a tribute of a freewill offering of your hand, which you
shall give just as the LORD your God blesses you;
11and you shall rejoice before the LORD your God, you and your
son and your daughter and your male and female servants and the
Levite who is in your town, and the stranger and the orphan and
the widow who are in your midst, in the place where the LORD
your God chooses to establish His name.
12"And you shall remember that you were a slave in Egypt, and
you shall be careful to observe these statutes.
13¶ "You shall celebrate the Feast of Booths seven days after you
have gathered in from your threshing floor and your wine vat;
14and you shall rejoice in your feast, you and your son and your
daughter and your male and female servants and the Levite and
the stranger and the orphan and the widow who are in your
towns.
15"Seven days you shall celebrate a feast to the LORD your God
in the place which the LORD chooses, because the LORD your God
will bless you in all your produce and in all the work of your hands,
so that you shall be altogether joyful.
16"Three times in a year all your males shall appear before the
LORD your God in the place which He chooses, at the Feast of
Unleavened Bread and at the Feast of Weeks and at the Feast of
Booths, and they shall not appear before the LORD empty-handed.
17"Every man shall give as he is able, according to the blessing
of the LORD your God which He has given you.
18¶ "You shall appoint for yourself judges and officers in all
your towns which the LORD your God is giving you, according to
your tribes, and they shall judge the people with righteous judgment.
19"You shall not distort justice; you shall not be partial, and you
shall not take a bribe, for a bribe blinds the eyes of the wise and
perverts the words of the righteous.
20"Justice, *and only* justice, you shall pursue, that you may live
and possess the land which the LORD your God is giving you.
21¶ "You shall not plant for yourself an Asherah of any kind of
tree beside the altar of the LORD your God, which you shall make
for yourself.
22"Neither shall you set up for yourself a *sacred* pillar which the
LORD your God hates.

## New International

choose. Then in the morning return to your tents. 8For six days eat
unleavened bread and on the seventh day hold an assembly to the
LORD your God and do no work.

*Feast of Weeks*

9Count off seven weeks from the time you begin to put the
sickle to the standing grain. 10Then celebrate the Feast of Weeks
to the LORD your God by giving a freewill offering in proportion
to the blessings the LORD your God has given you. 11And rejoice
before the LORD your God at the place he will choose as a dwelling
for his Name—you, your sons and daughters, your menservants
and maidservants, the Levites in your towns, and the aliens, the
fatherless and the widows living among you. 12Remember that
you were slaves in Egypt, and follow carefully these decrees.

*Feast of Tabernacles*

13Celebrate the Feast of Tabernacles for seven days after you
have gathered the produce of your threshing floor and your winepress. 14Be joyful at your Feast—you, your sons and daughters,
your menservants and maidservants, and the Levites, the aliens,
the fatherless and the widows who live in your towns. 15For seven
days celebrate the Feast to the LORD your God at the place the LORD
will choose. For the LORD your God will bless you in all your
harvest and in all the work of your hands, and your joy will be
complete.
16Three times a year all your men must appear before the LORD
your God at the place he will choose: at the Feast of Unleavened
Bread, the Feast of Weeks and the Feast of Tabernacles. No man
should appear before the LORD empty-handed: 17Each of you must
bring a gift in proportion to the way the LORD your God has blessed
you.

*Judges*

18Appoint judges and officials for each of your tribes in every
town the LORD your God is giving you, and they shall judge the
people fairly. 19Do not pervert justice or show partiality. Do not
accept a bribe, for a bribe blinds the eyes of the wise and twists the
words of the righteous. 20Follow justice and justice alone, so that
you may live and possess the land the LORD your God is giving
you.

*Worshiping Other Gods*

21Do not set up any wooden Asherah pole[a] beside the altar you
build to the LORD your God, 22and do not erect a sacred stone, for
these the LORD your God hates.

*Administration of Justice*

17 "YOU SHALL not sacrifice to the LORD your God an ox or
a sheep which has a blemish or any defect, for that is a
detestable thing to the LORD your God.
2¶ "If there is found in your midst, in any of your towns, which
the LORD your God is giving you, a man or a woman who does
what is evil in the sight of the LORD your God, by transgressing
His covenant,
3and has gone and served other gods and worshiped them, or
the sun or the moon or any of the heavenly host, which I have not
commanded,
4and if it is told you and you have heard of it, then you shall
inquire thoroughly. And behold, if it is true and the thing certain
that this detestable thing has been done in Israel,
5then you shall bring out that man or that woman who has
done this evil deed, to your gates, *that is,* the man or the woman,
and you shall stone them to death.

17 DO NOT sacrifice to the LORD your God an ox or a sheep
that has any defect or flaw in it, for that would be detestable to him.
2If a man or woman living among you in one of the towns the
LORD gives you is found doing evil in the eyes of the LORD your
God in violation of his covenant, 3and contrary to my command
has worshiped other gods, bowing down to them or to the sun or
the moon or the stars of the sky, 4and this has been brought to your
attention, then you must investigate it thoroughly. If it is true and
it has been proved that this detestable thing has been done in
Israel, 5take the man or woman who has done this evil deed to your
city gate and stone that person to death. 6On the testimony of two

NIV [a] 21 Or *Do not plant any tree dedicated to Asherah*

## King James

6At the mouth of two witnesses, or three witnesses, shall he that is worthy of death be put to death; *but* at the mouth of one witness he shall not be put to death.

7The hands of the witnesses shall be first upon him to put him to death, and afterward the hands of all the people. So thou shalt put the evil away from among you.

8¶ If there arise a matter too hard for thee in judgment, between blood and blood, between plea and plea, and between stroke and stroke, *being* matters of controversy within thy gates: then shalt thou arise, and get thee up into the place which the LORD thy God shall choose;

9And thou shalt come unto the priests the Levites, and unto the judge that shall be in those days, and inquire; and they shall show thee the sentence of judgment:

10And thou shalt do according to the sentence, which they of that place which the LORD shall choose shall show thee; and thou shalt observe to do according to all that they inform thee:

11According to the sentence of the law which they shall teach thee, and according to the judgment which they shall tell thee, thou shalt do: thou shalt not decline from the sentence which they shall show thee, *to* the right hand, nor *to* the left.

12And the man that will do presumptuously, and will not hearken unto the priest that standeth to minister there before the LORD thy God, or unto the judge, even that man shall die: and thou shalt put away the evil from Israel.

13And all the people shall hear, and fear, and do no more presumptuously.

14¶ When thou art come unto the land which the LORD thy God giveth thee, and shalt possess it, and shalt dwell therein, and shalt say, I will set a king over me, like as all the nations that *are* about me;

15Thou shalt in any wise set *him* king over thee, whom the LORD thy God shall choose: *one* from among thy brethren shalt thou set king over thee: thou mayest not set a stranger over thee, which *is* not thy brother.

16But he shall not multiply horses to himself, nor cause the people to return to Egypt, to the end that he should multiply horses: forasmuch as the LORD hath said unto you, Ye shall henceforth return no more that way.

17Neither shall he multiply wives to himself, that his heart turn not away: neither shall he greatly multiply to himself silver and gold.

18And it shall be, when he sitteth upon the throne of his kingdom, that he shall write him a copy of this law in a book out of *that which is* before the priests the Levites:

19And it shall be with him, and he shall read therein all the days of his life: that he may learn to fear the LORD his God, to keep all the words of this law and these statutes, to do them:

20That his heart be not lifted up above his brethren, and that he turn not aside from the commandment, *to* the right hand, or *to* the left: to the end that he may prolong *his* days in his kingdom, he, and his children, in the midst of Israel.

## Amplified

6On the evidence of two or three witnesses, he who is worthy of death shall be put to death; he shall not be put to death on the evidence of one witness.

7The hands of the witnesses shall be the first against him to put him to death, and afterward the hands of all the people. So you shall purge the evil from among you.

8If there arise a matter too hard for you in judgment, between one kind of bloodshed and another, between one legality and another, between one kind of assault and another, matters of controversy within your towns, then arise and go to the place which the Lord your God chooses,

9And you shall come to the Levitical priests, and to the judge who is in office in those days, and you shall consult them, and they shall make clear to you the decision.

10And you shall do according to the decision which they declare to you from that place which the Lord chooses, and you shall be watchful to do according to all that they tell you;

11According to the decision of the law which they shall teach you, and the judgment which they shall announce to you, you shall do; you shall not turn aside from the verdict they give you, either to the right hand or the left. [a]

12The man who does presumptuously, and will not listen to the priest who stands to minister there before the Lord your God, or to the judge, that man shall die; so you shall purge the evil from Israel.

13And all the people shall hear, and (reverently) fear, and not act presumptuously again.

14When you come to the land which the Lord your God gives you, and you possess it and live there, and then say, I will set a king over me, like all the nations that are about me;

15You shall surely set as king over you him whom the Lord your God will choose; one from among your brethren you shall set as king over you; you may not set a foreigner, who is not your brother, over you.

16But he shall not multiply horses to himself, or cause the people to return to Egypt in order to multiply horses, since the Lord said to you, You shall never return that way.

17And he shall not multiply wives to himself, that his [mind and] heart turn not away; neither shall he greatly multiply to himself silver and gold.

18And when he sits on his royal throne, he shall write him a copy of this law in a book out of what is before the Levitical priests;

19And he shall keep it with him, and he shall read in it all the days of his life, that he may learn (reverently) to fear the Lord his God, by keeping all the words of this law and these statutes, and doing them;

20That his [mind and] heart may not be lifted up above his brethren, and that he may not turn aside from the commandment, to the right hand or to the left; so that he may continue long, he and his sons, in his kingdom in Israel.

## King James

**18** THE PRIESTS the Levites, *and* all the tribe of Levi, shall have no part nor inheritance with Israel: they shall eat the offerings of the LORD made by fire, and his inheritance.

2Therefore shall they have no inheritance among their brethren: the LORD *is* their inheritance, as he hath said unto them.

3¶ And this shall be the priest's due from the people, from them that offer a sacrifice, whether *it be* ox or sheep; and they shall give unto the priest the shoulder, and the two cheeks, and the maw.

4The firstfruit *also* of thy corn, of thy wine, and of thine oil, and the first of the fleece of thy sheep, shalt thou give him.

## Amplified

**18** THE LEVITICAL priests and all the tribe of Levi shall have no part or inheritance with Israel; they shall eat the offerings made by fire to the Lord, and His rightful dues.

2They shall have no inheritance among their brethren; the Lord is their inheritance, as He promised them.

3And this shall be the priest's due from the people, from those who offer a sacrifice, whether it be ox or sheep: they shall give to the priest the shoulder and the two cheeks and the stomach.

4The first fruits of your grain, of your new wine, and of your oil, and the first *or* best of the fleece of your sheep, you shall give the priest.

AMP [a] Hebrew is obscure.

## New American Standard

6"On the evidence of two witnesses or three witnesses, he who
is to die shall be put to death; he shall not be put to death on the
evidence of one witness.
7"The hand of the witnesses shall be first against him to put
him to death, and afterward the hand of all the people. So you shall
purge the evil from your midst.
8¶ "If any case is too difficult for you to decide, between one
kind of homicide or another, between one kind of lawsuit or another, and between one kind of assault or another, being cases of
dispute in your courts, then you shall arise and go up to the place
which the LORD your God chooses.
9"So you shall come to the Levitical priest or the judge who is
*in office* in those days, and you shall inquire *of them*, and they will
declare to you the verdict in the case.
10"And you shall do according to the terms of the verdict which
they declare to you from that place which the LORD chooses; and
you shall be careful to observe according to all that they teach you.
11"According to the terms of the law which they teach you, and
according to the verdict which they tell you, you shall do; you shall
not turn aside from the word which they declare to you, to the
right or the left.
12"And the man who acts presumptuously by not listening to
the priest who stands there to serve the LORD your God, nor to the
judge, that man shall die; thus you shall purge the evil from Israel.
13"Then all the people will hear and be afraid, and will not act
presumptuously again.
14¶ "When you enter the land which the LORD your God gives
you, and you possess it and live in it, and you say, 'I will set a king
over me like all the nations who are around me,'
15you shall surely set a king over you whom the LORD your God
chooses, *one* from among your countrymen you shall set as king
over yourselves; you may not put a foreigner over yourselves who
is not your countryman.
16"Moreover, he shall not multiply horses for himself, nor shall
he cause the people to return to Egypt to multiply horses, since the
LORD has said to you, 'You shall never again return that way.'
17"Neither shall he multiply wives for himself, lest his heart
turn away; nor shall he greatly increase silver and gold for himself.
18¶ "Now it shall come about when he sits on the throne of his
kingdom, he shall write for himself a copy of this law on a scroll
in the presence of the Levitical priests.
19"And it shall be with him, and he shall read it all the days of
his life, that he may learn to fear the LORD his God, by carefully
observing all the words of this law and these statutes,
20that his heart may not be lifted up above his countrymen and
that he may not turn aside from the commandment, to the right
or the left; in order that he and his sons may continue long in his
kingdom in the midst of Israel.

*Portion of the Levites*

18 "THE LEVITICAL priests, the whole tribe of Levi, shall
have no portion or inheritance with Israel; they shall eat
the LORD's offerings by fire and His portion.
2"And they shall have no inheritance among their countrymen; the LORD is their inheritance, as He promised them.
3¶ "Now this shall be the priests' due from the people, from
those who offer a sacrifice, either an ox or a sheep, of which they
shall give to the priest the shoulder and the two cheeks and the
stomach.
4"You shall give him the first fruits of your grain, your new
wine, and your oil, and the first shearing of your sheep.

## New International

or three witnesses a man shall be put to death, but no one shall
be put to death on the testimony of only one witness. 7The hands
of the witnesses must be the first in putting him to death, and then
the hands of all the people. You must purge the evil from among
you.

*Law Courts*

8If cases come before your courts that are too difficult for you
to judge—whether bloodshed, lawsuits or assaults—take them to
the place the LORD your God will choose. 9Go to the priests, who
are Levites, and to the judge who is in office at that time. Inquire
of them and they will give you the verdict. 10You must act according to the decisions they give you at the place the LORD will choose.
Be careful to do everything they direct you to do. 11Act according
to the law they teach you and the decisions they give you. Do not
turn aside from what they tell you, to the right or to the left. 12The
man who shows contempt for the judge or for the priest who
stands ministering there to the LORD your God must be put to
death. You must purge the evil from Israel. 13All the people will
hear and be afraid, and will not be contemptuous again.

*The King*

14When you enter the land the LORD your God is giving you and
have taken possession of it and settled in it, and you say, "Let us
set a king over us like all the nations around us," 15be sure to
appoint over you the king the LORD your God chooses. He must
be from among your own brothers. Do not place a foreigner over
you, one who is not a brother Israelite. 16The king, moreover, must
not acquire great numbers of horses for himself or make the people
return to Egypt to get more of them, for the LORD has told you,
"You are not to go back that way again." 17He must not take many
wives, or his heart will be led astray. He must not accumulate large
amounts of silver and gold.
18When he takes the throne of his kingdom, he is to write for
himself on a scroll a copy of this law, taken from that of the priests,
who are Levites. 19It is to be with him, and he is to read it all the
days of his life so that he may learn to revere the LORD his God and
follow carefully all the words of this law and these decrees 20and
not consider himself better than his brothers and turn from the law
to the right or to the left. Then he and his descendants will reign
a long time over his kingdom in Israel.

*Offerings for Priests and Levites*

18 THE PRIESTS, who are Levites—indeed the whole tribe of
Levi—are to have no allotment or inheritance with Israel.
They shall live on the offerings made to the LORD by fire, for that
is their inheritance. 2They shall have no inheritance among their
brothers; the LORD is their inheritance, as he promised them.
3This is the share due the priests from the people who sacrifice
a bull or a sheep: the shoulder, the jowls and the inner parts. 4You
are to give them the firstfruits of your grain, new wine and oil, and
the first wool from the shearing of your sheep, 5for the LORD your

## King James

5For the LORD thy God hath chosen him out of all thy tribes, to stand to minister in the name of the LORD, him and his sons for ever.

6¶ And if a Levite come from any of thy gates out of all Israel, where he sojourned, and come with all the desire of his mind unto the place which the LORD shall choose;

7Then he shall minister in the name of the LORD his God, as all his brethren the Levites *do*, which stand there before the LORD.

8They shall have like portions to eat, beside that which cometh of the sale of his patrimony.

9¶ When thou art come into the land which the LORD thy God giveth thee, thou shalt not learn to do after the abominations of those nations.

10There shall not be found among you *any one* that maketh his son or his daughter to pass through the fire, *or* that useth divination, *or* an observer of times, or an enchanter, or a witch,

11Or a charmer, or a consulter with familiar spirits, or a wizard, or a necromancer.

12For all that do these things *are* an abomination unto the LORD: and because of these abominations the LORD thy God doth drive them out from before thee.

13Thou shalt be perfect with the LORD thy God.

14For these nations, which thou shalt possess, hearkened unto observers of times, and unto diviners: but as for thee, the LORD thy God hath not suffered thee so *to do*.

15¶ The LORD thy God will raise up unto thee a Prophet from the midst of thee, of thy brethren, like unto me; unto him ye shall hearken;

16According to all that thou desiredst of the LORD thy God in Horeb in the day of the assembly, saying, Let me not hear again the voice of the LORD my God, neither let me see this great fire any more, that I die not.

17And the LORD said unto me, They have well *spoken that* which they have spoken.

18I will raise them up a Prophet from among their brethren, like unto thee, and will put my words in his mouth; and he shall speak unto them all that I shall command him.

19And it shall come to pass, *that* whosoever will not hearken unto my words which he shall speak in my name, I will require *it* of him.

20But the prophet, which shall presume to speak a word in my name, which I have not commanded him to speak, or that shall speak in the name of other gods, even that prophet shall die.

21And if thou say in thine heart, How shall we know the word which the LORD hath not spoken?

22When a prophet speaketh in the name of the LORD, if the thing follow not, nor come to pass, that *is* the thing which the LORD hath not spoken, *but* the prophet hath spoken it presumptuously: thou shalt not be afraid of him.

## Amplified

5For the Lord your God has chosen him out of all your tribes, to stand to minister in the name [and presence] of the Lord, him and his sons for ever.

6And if a Levite comes from any of your towns out of all Israel, where he is a temporary resident, he may come whenever he desires to [the sanctuary] the place the Lord will choose,

7Then he may minister in the name [and presence of] the Lord his God, like all his brethren the Levites, who stand to minister there before the Lord.

8They shall have equal portions to eat, besides what may come of the sale of his patrimony. [Jer. 32:6-15.]

9When you come into the land which the Lord your God gives you, you shall not learn to follow the abominable practices of these nations.

10There shall not be found among you any one who makes his son or daughter pass through the fire, or who uses divination, or is a soothsayer, or an augur, or a sorcerer,

11Or a charmer, or a medium, or a wizard, or a necromancer.

12For all who do these things are an abomination to the Lord; and it is because of these abominable practices that the Lord your God is driving them out from before you.

13You shall be blameless (and absolutely true) to the Lord your God.

14For these nations, whom you shall dispossess, listen to soothsayers and diviners, but as for you, the Lord your God has not allowed you to do so.

15The Lord your God will raise up for you [a]a prophet from the midst of your brethren, like me [Moses]; to him you shall listen.

16This is what you desired (and asked) of the Lord your God at Horeb on the day of the assembly, when you said, Let me not hear again the voice of the Lord my God, or see this great fire any more, lest I die.

17And the Lord said to me, They have well said all that they have spoken.

18I will raise up for them a prophet from among their brethren, like you, and will put My words in his mouth; and he shall speak to them all that I command him.

19And whoever will not hearken to My words which he shall speak in My name, I Myself will require it of him.

20But the prophet who presumes to speak a word in My name which I have not commanded him to speak, or who speaks in the name of other gods, that same prophet shall die.

21And if you say in your [mind and] heart, How shall we know which words the Lord has not spoken?

22When a prophet speaks in the name of the Lord, if the word does not come to pass or prove true, that is a word which the Lord has not spoken; the prophet has spoken it presumptuously; you shall not be afraid of him.

### King James

**19** WHEN THE LORD thy God hath cut off the nations, whose land the LORD thy God giveth thee, and thou succeedest them, and dwellest in their cities, and in their houses;

2Thou shalt separate three cities for thee in the midst of thy land, which the LORD thy God giveth thee to possess it.

### Amplified

**19** WHEN THE Lord your God has cut off the nations whose land the Lord your God gives you, and you dispossess them and dwell in their cities and in their houses;

2You shall set apart three cities for you in the land which the Lord your God gives you to possess.

**AMP** [a] The insertion of this promise in connection with the preceding prohibition, might warrant the application which some make of it, to that order of true prophets whom God commissioned in unbroken succession to instruct, to direct, and warn His people; and in this view the gist of it is, "there is no need to consult with diviners and soothsayers, for I shall afford you the benefit of divinely appointed prophets, for judging of whose identity a sure clue is given" (vs. 20, 22). But the prophet here promised was pre-eminently the Messiah, for He alone was "like unto Moses in His mediatorial character; in the peculiar excellence of His ministry; in the number, variety and magnitude of His miracles; in His close and familiar communion with God; and in His being the author of a new dispensation of religion." This prediction was fulfulled 1500 years afterwards, and was expressly applied to Christ by Peter (Acts 3:22, 23), and by Stephen (Acts 7:37)—*Jamieson, Fausset and Brown Commentary.*

## New American Standard

5"For the LORD your God has chosen him and his sons from
all your tribes, to stand and serve in the name of the LORD forever.
6¶ "Now if a Levite comes from any of your towns throughout
Israel where he resides, and comes whenever he desires to the
place which the LORD chooses,
7then he shall serve in the name of the LORD his God, like all
his fellow Levites who stand there before the LORD.
8"They shall eat equal portions, except *what they receive* from
the sale of their fathers' *estates*.

*Spiritism Forbidden*

9¶ "When you enter the land which the LORD your God gives
you, you shall not learn to imitate the detestable things of those
nations.
10"There shall not be found among you anyone who makes his
son or his daughter pass through the fire, one who uses divination,
one who practices witchcraft, or one who interprets omens, or a
sorcerer,
11or one who casts a spell, or a medium, or a spiritist, or one
who calls up the dead.
12"For whoever does these things is detestable to the LORD; and
because of these detestable things the LORD your God will drive
them out before you.
13"You shall be blameless before the LORD your God.
14¶ "For those nations, which you shall dispossess, listen to
those who practice witchcraft and to diviners, but as for you, the
LORD your God has not allowed you *to do* so.
15"The LORD your God will raise up for you a prophet like me
from among you, from your countrymen, you shall listen to him.
16"This is according to all that you asked of the LORD your God
in Horeb on the day of the assembly, saying, 'Let me not hear again
the voice of the LORD my God, let me not see this great fire
anymore, lest I die.'
17"And the LORD said to me, 'They have spoken well.
18'I will raise up a prophet from among their countrymen like
you, and I will put My words in his mouth, and he shall speak to
them all that I command him.
19'And it shall come about that whoever will not listen to My
words which he shall speak in My name, I Myself will require *it*
of him.
20'But the prophet who shall speak a word presumptuously in
My name which I have not commanded him to speak, or which he
shall speak in the name of other gods, that prophet shall die.'
21"And you may say in your heart, 'How shall we know the
word which the LORD has not spoken?'
22"When a prophet speaks in the name of the LORD, if the thing
does not come about or come true, that is the thing which the LORD
has not spoken. The prophet has spoken it presumptuously; you
shall not be afraid of him.

*Cities of Refuge*

**19** "WHEN THE LORD your God cuts off the nations, whose
land the LORD your God gives you, and you dispossess
them and settle in their cities and in their houses,
2you shall set aside three cities for yourself in the midst of your
land, which the LORD your God gives you to possess.

## New International

God has chosen them and their descendants out of all your tribes
to stand and minister in the LORD's name always.
6If a Levite moves from one of your towns anywhere in Israel
where he is living, and comes in all earnestness to the place the
LORD will choose, 7he may minister in the name of the LORD his
God like all his fellow Levites who serve there in the presence of
the LORD. 8He is to share equally in their benefits, even though he
has received money from the sale of family possessions.

*Detestable Practices*

9When you enter the land the LORD your God is giving you, do
not learn to imitate the detestable ways of the nations there. 10Let
no one be found among you who sacrifices his son or daughter in[b]
the fire, who practices divination or sorcery, interprets omens,
engages in witchcraft, 11or casts spells, or who is a medium or
spiritist or who consults the dead. 12Anyone who does these
things is detestable to the LORD, and because of these detestable
practices the LORD your God will drive out those nations before
you. 13You must be blameless before the LORD your God.

*The Prophet*

14The nations you will dispossess listen to those who practice
sorcery or divination. But as for you, the LORD your God has not
permitted you to do so. 15The LORD your God will raise up for you
a prophet like me from among your own brothers. You must listen
to him. 16For this is what you asked of the LORD your God at Horeb
on the day of the assembly when you said, "Let us not hear the
voice of the LORD our God nor see this great fire anymore, or we
will die."
17The LORD said to me: "What they say is good. 18I will raise up
for them a prophet like you from among their brothers; I will put
my words in his mouth, and he will tell them everything I command him. 19If anyone does not listen to my words that the
prophet speaks in my name, I myself will call him to account. 20But
a prophet who presumes to speak in my name anything I have not
commanded him to say, or a prophet who speaks in the name of
other gods, must be put to death."
21You may say to yourselves, "How can we know when a
message has not been spoken by the LORD?" 22If what a prophet
proclaims in the name of the LORD does not take place or come
true, that is a message the LORD has not spoken. That prophet has
spoken presumptuously. Do not be afraid of him.

*Cities of Refuge*

**19** WHEN THE LORD your God has destroyed the nations
whose land he is giving you, and when you have driven
them out and settled in their towns and houses, 2then set aside for
yourselves three cities centrally located in the land the LORD your
God is giving you to possess. 3Build roads to them and divide into

NIV [b] 10 Or *who makes his son or daughter pass through*

## King James

3Thou shalt prepare thee a way, and divide the coasts of thy land, which the LORD thy God giveth thee to inherit, into three parts, that every slayer may flee thither.
4¶ And this *is* the case of the slayer, which shall flee thither, that he may live: Whoso killeth his neighbour ignorantly, whom he hated not in time past;
5As when a man goeth into the wood with his neighbour to hew wood, and his hand fetcheth a stroke with the axe to cut down the tree, and the head slippeth from the helve, and lighteth upon his neighbour, that he die; he shall flee unto one of those cities, and live:
6Lest the avenger of the blood pursue the slayer, while his heart is hot, and overtake him, because the way is long, and slay him; whereas he *was* not worthy of death, inasmuch as he hated him not in time past.
7Wherefore I command thee, saying, Thou shalt separate three cities for thee.
8And if the LORD thy God enlarge thy coast, as he hath sworn unto thy fathers, and give thee all the land which he promised to give unto thy fathers;
9If thou shalt keep all these commandments to do them, which I command thee this day, to love the LORD thy God, and to walk ever in his ways; then shalt thou add three cities more for thee, beside these three:
10That innocent blood be not shed in thy land, which the LORD thy God giveth thee *for* an inheritance, and *so* blood be upon thee.
11¶ But if any man hate his neighbour, and lie in wait for him, and rise up against him, and smite him mortally that he die, and fleeth into one of these cities:
12Then the elders of his city shall send and fetch him thence, and deliver him into the hand of the avenger of blood, that he may die.
13Thine eye shall not pity him, but thou shalt put away *the guilt of* innocent blood from Israel, that it may go well with thee.
14¶ Thou shalt not remove thy neighbour's landmark, which they of old time have set in thine inheritance, which thou shalt inherit in the land that the LORD thy God giveth thee to possess it.
15¶ One witness shall not rise up against a man for any iniquity, or for any sin, in any sin that he sinneth: at the mouth of two witnesses, or at the mouth of three witnesses, shall the matter be established.
16¶ If a false witness rise up against any man to testify against him *that which is* wrong;
17Then both the men, between whom the controversy *is,* shall stand before the LORD, before the priests and the judges, which shall be in those days;
18And the judges shall make diligent inquisition: and, behold, *if* the witness *be* a false witness, *and* hath testified falsely against his brother;
19Then shall ye do unto him, as he had thought to have done unto his brother: so shalt thou put the evil away from among you.
20And those which remain shall hear, and fear, and shall henceforth commit no more any such evil among you.
21And thine eye shall not pity; *but* life *shall go* for life, eye for eye, tooth for tooth, hand for hand, foot for foot.

**20** WHEN THOU goest out to battle against thine enemies, and seest horses, and chariots, *and* a people more than thou, be not afraid of them: for the LORD thy God *is* with thee, which brought thee up out of the land of Egypt.
2And it shall be, when ye are come nigh unto the battle, that the priest shall approach and speak unto the people,
3And shall say unto them, Hear, O Israel, ye approach this day unto battle against your enemies: let not your hearts faint, fear not, and do not tremble, neither be ye terrified because of them;

## Amplified

3You shall prepare the road, and divide the territory of your land, which the Lord your God gives you to possess, into three parts, so that any manslayer can flee to them.
4And this is the case of the slayer who shall flee there that he may live. Whoever kills his neighbor unintentionally, for whom he had no enmity in time past;
5As when a man goes into the wood with his neighbor to hew wood, and his hand strikes with the axe to cut down the tree, and the head slips off the handle and lights on his neighbor, and kills him; he may flee to one of those cities and live;
6Lest the avenger of the blood pursue the slayer, while his [mind and] heart are hot with anger, and overtake him, because the way is long, and slay him; although the slayer was not worthy of death, since he had not been at enmity with him previously.
7Therefore I command you, You shall set apart three [refuge] cities.
8And if the Lord your God enlarges your territory, as He has sworn to your fathers to do, and gives you all the land which He promised to your fathers to give,
9If you keep all these commandments to do them, which I command you this day, to love the Lord your God, and to walk always in His ways; then you shall add three other cities to these three,
10Lest innocent blood be shed in your land, which the Lord your God gives you for an inheritance, and so blood guilt be upon you.
11But if any man hates his neighbor, and lies in wait for him, and attacks him and wounds him mortally so that he dies, and the assailant flees into one of these cities,
12Then the elders of his own city shall send and fetch him there, and give him over to the avenger of blood, so that he may die.
13Your eye shall not pity him, but you shall clear Israel of the guilt of innocent blood, that it may be well with you.
14You shall not remove your neighbor's landmark, in the land which the Lord your God gives you to possess, which the men of old [the first dividers of the land] set.
15One witness shall not prevail against a man for any crime or any wrong in connection with any sin he commits; only on the testimony of two or three witnesses shall a charge be established.
16If a false witness rises up against any man to accuse him of wrongdoing,
17Then both parties to the controversy shall stand before the Lord, before the priests and the judges who are in office in those days;
18The judges shall inquire diligently, and if the witness is a false witness and has accused his brother falsely,
19Then you shall do to him as he had intended to do to his brother; so you shall put away the evil from among you.
20And those who remain shall hear, and (reverently) fear, and shall henceforth commit no such evil among you.
21Your eye shall not pity; it shall be life for life, eye for eye, tooth for tooth, hand for hand, foot for foot.

**20** WHEN YOU go forth to battle against your enemies, and see horses and chariots and an army greater than your own, do not be afraid of them; for the Lord your God, Who brought you out of the land of Egypt, is with you.
2And when you come near to the battle, the priest shall approach and speak to the men,
3And shall say to them, Hear, O Israel, you draw near this day to battle against your enemies; let not your [minds and] hearts faint; fear not, and do not tremble, or be terrified (and in dread) because of them.

## New American Standard

3"You shall prepare the roads for yourself, and divide into three parts the territory of your land, which the LORD your God will give you as a possession, so that any manslayer may flee there.

4¶ "Now this is the case of the manslayer who may flee there and live: when he kills his friend unintentionally, not hating him previously—

5as when *a man* goes into the forest with his friend to cut wood, and his hand swings the axe to cut down the tree, and the iron *head* slips off the handle and strikes his friend so that he dies—he may flee to one of these cities and live;

6lest the avenger of blood pursue the manslayer in the heat of his anger, and overtake him, because the way is long, and take his life, though he was not deserving of death, since he had not hated him previously.

7"Therefore, I command you, saying, 'You shall set aside three cities for yourself.'

8"And if the LORD your God enlarges your territory, just as He has sworn to your fathers, and gives you all the land which He promised to give your fathers—

9if you carefully observe all this commandment, which I command you today, to love the LORD your God, and to walk in His ways always—then you shall add three more cities for yourself, besides these three.

10"So innocent blood will not be shed in the midst of your land which the LORD your God gives you as an inheritance, and bloodguiltiness be on you.

11¶ "But if there is a man who hates his neighbor and lies in wait for him and rises up against him and strikes him so that he dies, and he flees to one of these cities,

12then the elders of his city shall send and take him from there and deliver him into the hand of the avenger of blood, that he may die.

13"You shall not pity him, but you shall purge the blood of the innocent from Israel, that it may go well with you.

*Laws of Landmark and Testimony*

14¶ "You shall not move your neighbor's boundary mark, which the ancestors have set, in your inheritance which you shall inherit in the land that the LORD your God gives you to possess.

15¶ "A single witness shall not rise up against a man on account of any iniquity or any sin which he has committed; on the evidence of two or three witnesses a matter shall be confirmed.

16"If a malicious witness rises up against a man to accuse him of wrongdoing,

17then both the men who have the dispute shall stand before the LORD, before the priests and the judges who will be *in office* in those days.

18"And the judges shall investigate thoroughly; and if the witness is a false witness *and* he has accused his brother falsely,

19then you shall do to him just as he had intended to do to his brother. Thus you shall purge the evil from among you.

20"And the rest will hear and be afraid, and will never again do such an evil thing among you.

21"Thus you shall not show pity: life for life, eye for eye, tooth for tooth, hand for hand, foot for foot.

*Laws of Warfare*

**20** "WHEN YOU go out to battle against your enemies and see horses and chariots *and* people more numerous than you, do not be afraid of them; for the LORD your God, who brought you up from the land of Egypt, is with you.

2"Now it shall come about that when you are approaching the battle, the priest shall come near and speak to the people.

3"And he shall say to them, 'Hear, O Israel, you are approaching the battle against your enemies today. Do not be fainthearted. Do not be afraid, or panic, or tremble before them,

## New International

three parts the land the LORD your God is giving you as an inheritance, so that anyone who kills a man may flee there.
4This is the rule concerning the man who kills another and flees
there to save his life—one who kills his neighbor unintentionally,
without malice aforethought. 5For instance, a man may go into the
forest with his neighbor to cut wood, and as he swings his ax to
fell a tree, the head may fly off and hit his neighbor and kill him.
That man may flee to one of these cities and save his life. 6Other-
wise, the avenger of blood might pursue him in a rage, overtake
him if the distance is too great, and kill him even though he is not
deserving of death, since he did it to his neighbor without malice
aforethought. 7This is why I command you to set aside for yourselves three cities.
8If the LORD your God enlarges your territory, as he promised
on oath to your forefathers, and gives you the whole land he
promised them, 9because you carefully follow all these laws I
command you today—to love the LORD your God and to walk
always in his ways—then you are to set aside three more cities.
10Do this so that innocent blood will not be shed in your land,
which the LORD your God is giving you as your inheritance, and
so that you will not be guilty of bloodshed.
11But if a man hates his neighbor and lies in wait for him,
assaults and kills him, and then flees to one of these cities, 12the
elders of his town shall send for him, bring him back from the city,
and hand him over to the avenger of blood to die. 13Show him no
pity. You must purge from Israel the guilt of shedding innocent
blood, so that it may go well with you.
14Do not move your neighbor's boundary stone set up by your
predecessors in the inheritance you receive in the land the LORD
your God is giving you to possess.

*Witnesses*

15One witness is not enough to convict a man accused of any
crime or offense he may have committed. A matter must be established by the testimony of two or three witnesses.
16If a malicious witness takes the stand to accuse a man of a
crime, 17the two men involved in the dispute must stand in the
presence of the LORD before the priests and the judges who are in
office at the time. 18The judges must make a thorough investigation, and if the witness proves to be a liar, giving false testimony
against his brother, 19then do to him as he intended to do to his
brother. You must purge the evil from among you. 20The rest of
the people will hear of this and be afraid, and never again will such
an evil thing be done among you. 21Show no pity: life for life, eye
for eye, tooth for tooth, hand for hand, foot for foot.

*Going to War*

**20** WHEN YOU go to war against your enemies and see
horses and chariots and an army greater than yours, do
not be afraid of them, because the LORD your God, who brought
you up out of Egypt, will be with you. 2When you are about to go
into battle, the priest shall come forward and address the army.
3He shall say: "Hear, O Israel, today you are going into battle
against your enemies. Do not be fainthearted or afraid; do not be
terrified or give way to panic before them. 4For the LORD your God

## King James

4For the LORD your God *is* he that goeth with you, to fight for you against your enemies, to save you.

5¶ And the officers shall speak unto the people, saying, What man *is there* that hath built a new house, and hath not dedicated it? let him go and return to his house, lest he die in the battle, and another man dedicate it.

6And what man *is he* that hath planted a vineyard, and hath not *yet* eaten of it? let him *also* go and return unto his house, lest he die in the battle, and another man eat of it.

7And what man *is there* that hath betrothed a wife, and hath not taken her? let him go and return unto his house, lest he die in the battle, and another man take her.

8And the officers shall speak further unto the people, and they shall say, What man *is there that is* fearful and fainthearted? let him go and return unto his house, lest his brethren's heart faint as well as his heart.

9And it shall be, when the officers have made an end of speaking unto the people, that they shall make captains of the armies to lead the people.

10¶ When thou comest nigh unto a city to fight against it, then proclaim peace unto it.

11And it shall be, if it make thee answer of peace, and open unto thee, then it shall be, *that* all the people *that is* found therein shall be tributaries unto thee, and they shall serve thee.

12And if it will make no peace with thee, but will make war against thee, then thou shalt besiege it:

13And when the LORD thy God hath delivered it into thine hands, thou shalt smite every male thereof with the edge of the sword:

14But the women, and the little ones, and the cattle, and all that is in the city, *even* all the spoil thereof, shalt thou take unto thyself; and thou shalt eat the spoil of thine enemies, which the LORD thy God hath given thee.

15Thus shalt thou do unto all the cities *which are* very far off from thee, which *are* not of the cities of these nations.

16But of the cities of these people, which the LORD thy God doth give thee *for* an inheritance, thou shalt save alive nothing that breatheth:

17But thou shalt utterly destroy them; *namely,* the Hittites, and the Amorites, the Canaanites, and the Perizzites, the Hivites, and the Jebusites; as the LORD thy God hath commanded thee:

18That they teach you not to do after all their abominations, which they have done unto their gods; so should ye sin against the LORD your God.

19¶ When thou shalt besiege a city a long time, in making war against it to take it, thou shalt not destroy the trees thereof by forcing an axe against them: for thou mayest eat of them, and thou shalt not cut them down (for the tree of the field *is* man's *life*) to employ *them* in the siege:

20Only the trees which thou knowest that they *be* not trees for meat, thou shalt destroy and cut them down; and thou shalt build bulwarks against the city that maketh war with thee, until it be subdued.

**21** IF *ONE* be found slain in the land which the LORD thy God giveth thee to possess it, lying in the field, *and* it be not known who hath slain him:

2Then thy elders and thy judges shall come forth, and they shall measure unto the cities which *are* round about him that is slain:

3And it shall be, *that* the city *which is* next unto the slain man, even the elders of that city shall take an heifer, which hath not been wrought with, *and* which hath not drawn in the yoke;

4And the elders of that city shall bring down the heifer unto a rough valley, which is neither eared nor sown, and shall strike off the heifer's neck there in the valley:

## Amplified

4For the Lord your God is He Who goes with you, to fight for you against your enemies, to save you. [I Sam. 17:45.]

5And the officers shall speak to the people, saying, What man is there who has built a new house and has not dedicated it? Let him return to his house, lest he die in the battle and another man dedicate it.

6And what man has planted a vineyard and has not used the fruit of it? Let him also return to his house, lest he die in the battle, and another man use the fruit of it.

7And what man has betrothed a wife, and has not taken her? Let him return to his house, lest he die in the battle and another man take her.

8And the officers shall speak further to the people, and say, What man is fearful and fainthearted? Let him return to his house, lest [because of him] his brethren's [mind and] heart faint as does his own.

9And when the officers finish speaking to the people, they shall appoint commanders at the head of the people.

10When you draw near to a city to fight against it, then proclaim peace to it.

11And if that city makes an answer of peace to you and opens to you, then all the people found in it shall be tributary to you and they shall serve you.

12But if it refuses to make peace with you and fights against you, then you shall besiege it;

13And when the Lord your God has given it into your hands, you shall smite every male there with the edge of the sword.

14But the women, the little ones, the beasts, and all that is in the city, all the spoil in it, you shall take for yourselves, and you shall use the spoil of your enemies which the Lord your God has given you.

15So shall you treat all the cities which are very far off from you, that do not belong to the cities of these nations.

16But of the cities of these people, which the Lord your God gives you for an inheritance, you shall save alive nothing that breathes.

17But you shall utterly exterminate them, the Hittites, the Amorites, the Canaanites, the Perizzites, the Hivites, and the Jebusites; as the Lord your God has commanded you;

18So they may not teach you all the abominable practices they have carried on for their gods, and so cause you to sin against the Lord your God.

19When you besiege a city for a long time, making war against it to take it, you shall not destroy its trees by using an ax on them, for you can eat their fruit; you must not cut them down, for is the tree of the field a man, that it should be besieged by you?

20Only the trees which you know are not trees for food you may destroy and cut down, that you may build siegeworks against the city that makes war with you, until it falls.

**21** IF ONE be found slain in the land which the Lord your God gives you to possess, lying in the field, and it is not known who has killed him,

2Then your elders and judges shall come forth and measure the distance to the cities around him who is slain;

3And the city which is nearest to the slain man, the elders of that city shall take a heifer, which has never been worked, never pulled in the yoke;

4And the elders of that city shall bring the heifer down to a valley with running water, which is neither plowed nor sown, and shall break the heifer's neck there in the valley.

## New American Standard

4for the LORD your God is the one who goes with you, to fight
for you against your enemies, to save you.'
5"The officers also shall speak to the people, saying, 'Who is
the man that has built a new house and has not dedicated it? Let
him depart and return to his house, lest he die in the battle and
another man dedicate it.
6'And who is the man that has planted a vineyard and has not
begun to use its fruit? Let him depart and return to his house, lest
he die in the battle and another man begin to use its fruit.
7'And who is the man that is engaged to a woman and has not
married her? Let him depart and return to his house, lest he die
in the battle and another man marry her.'
8"Then the officers shall speak further to the people, and they
shall say, 'Who is the man that is afraid and fainthearted? Let him
depart and return to his house, so that he might not make his
brothers' hearts melt like his heart.'
9"And it shall come about that when the officers have finished
speaking to the people, they shall appoint commanders of armies
at the head of the people.
10¶ "When you approach a city to fight against it, you shall offer
it terms of peace.
11"And it shall come about, if it agrees to make peace with you
and opens to you, then it shall be that all the people who are found
in it shall become your forced labor and shall serve you.
12"However, if it does not make peace with you, but makes war
against you, then you shall besiege it.
13"When the LORD your God gives it into your hand, you shall
strike all the men in it with the edge of the sword.
14"Only the women and the children and the animals and all
that is in the city, all its spoil, you shall take as booty for yourself;
and you shall use the spoil of your enemies which the LORD your
God has given you.
15"Thus you shall do to all the cities that are very far from you,
which are not of the cities of these nations nearby.
16"Only in the cities of these peoples that the LORD your God
is giving you as an inheritance, you shall not leave alive anything
that breathes.
17"But you shall utterly destroy them, the Hittite and the Amorite, the Canaanite and the Perizzite, the Hivite and the Jebusite,
as the LORD your God has commanded you,
18in order that they may not teach you to do according to all
their detestable things which they have done for their gods, so that
you would sin against the LORD your God.
19¶ "When you besiege a city a long time, to make war against
it in order to capture it, you shall not destroy its trees by swinging
an axe against them; for you may eat from them, and you shall not
cut them down. For is the tree of the field a man, that it should
be besieged by you?
20"Only the trees which you know are not fruit trees you shall
destroy and cut down, that you may construct siegeworks against
the city that is making war with you until it falls.

*Expiation of a Crime*

**21** "IF A slain person is found lying in the open country in
the land which the LORD your God gives you to possess,
*and* it is not known who has struck him,
2then your elders and your judges shall go out and measure
*the distance* to the cities which are around the slain one.
3"And it shall be that the city which is nearest to the slain man,
that is, the elders of that city, shall take a heifer of the herd, which
has not been worked and which has not pulled in a yoke;
4and the elders of that city shall bring the heifer down to a
valley with running water, which has not been plowed or sown,
and shall break the heifer's neck there in the valley.

## New International

is the one who goes with you to fight for you against your enemies
to give you victory."
5The officers shall say to the army: "Has anyone built a new
house and not dedicated it? Let him go home, or he may die in
battle and someone else may dedicate it. 6Has anyone planted a
vineyard and not begun to enjoy it? Let him go home, or he may
die in battle and someone else enjoy it. 7Has anyone become
pledged to a woman and not married her? Let him go home, or he
may die in battle and someone else marry her." 8Then the officers
shall add, "Is any man afraid or fainthearted? Let him go home so
that his brothers will not become disheartened too." 9When the
officers have finished speaking to the army, they shall appoint
commanders over it.
10When you march up to attack a city, make its people an offer
of peace. 11If they accept and open their gates, all the people in it
shall be subject to forced labor and shall work for you. 12If they
refuse to make peace and they engage you in battle, lay siege to
that city. 13When the LORD your God delivers it into your hand,
put to the sword all the men in it. 14As for the women, the children, the livestock and everything else in the city, you may take
these as plunder for yourselves. And you may use the plunder the
LORD your God gives you from your enemies. 15This is how you
are to treat all the cities that are at a distance from you and do not
belong to the nations nearby.
16However, in the cities of the nations the LORD your God is
giving you as an inheritance, do not leave alive anything that
breathes. 17Completely destroy[a] them—the Hittites, Amorites,
Canaanites, Perizzites, Hivites and Jebusites—as the LORD your
God has commanded you. 18Otherwise, they will teach you to
follow all the detestable things they do in worshiping their gods,
and you will sin against the LORD your God.
19When you lay siege to a city for a long time, fighting against
it to capture it, do not destroy its trees by putting an ax to them,
because you can eat their fruit. Do not cut them down. Are the
trees of the field people, that you should besiege them?[b] 20How-
ever, you may cut down trees that you know are not fruit trees and
use them to build siege works until the city at war with you falls.

*Atonement for an Unsolved Murder*

**21** IF A man is found slain, lying in a field in the land the
LORD your God is giving you to possess, and it is not
known who killed him, 2your elders and judges shall go out and
measure the distance from the body to the neighboring towns.
3Then the elders of the town nearest the body shall take a heifer
that has never been worked and has never worn a yoke 4and lead
her down to a valley that has not been plowed or planted and
where there is a flowing stream. There in the valley they are to
break the heifer's neck. 5The priests, the sons of Levi, shall step

**NIV** [a] *17* The Hebrew term refers to the irrevocable giving over of things or persons to the LORD, often by totally destroying them. [b] *19* Or *down to use in the siege, for the fruit trees are for the benefit of man.*

## King James

5And the priests the sons of Levi shall come near; for them the LORD thy God hath chosen to minister unto him, and to bless in the name of the LORD; and by their word shall every controversy and every stroke be *tried:*

6And all the elders of that city, *that are* next unto the slain *man,* shall wash their hands over the heifer that is beheaded in the valley:

7And they shall answer and say, Our hands have not shed this blood, neither have our eyes seen *it.*

8Be merciful, O LORD, unto thy people Israel, whom thou hast redeemed, and lay not innocent blood unto thy people of Israel's charge. And the blood shall be forgiven them.

9So shalt thou put away the *guilt of* innocent blood from among you, when thou shalt do *that which is* right in the sight of the LORD.

10¶ When thou goest forth to war against thine enemies, and the LORD thy God hath delivered them into thine hands, and thou hast taken them captive,

11And seest among the captives a beautiful woman, and hast a desire unto her, that thou wouldest have her to thy wife;

12Then thou shalt bring her home to thine house; and she shall shave her head, and pare her nails;

13And she shall put the raiment of her captivity from off her, and shall remain in thine house, and bewail her father and her mother a full month: and after that thou shalt go in unto her, and be her husband, and she shall be thy wife.

14And it shall be, if thou have no delight in her, then thou shalt let her go whither she will; but thou shalt not sell her at all for money, thou shalt not make merchandise of her, because thou hast humbled her.

15¶ If a man have two wives, one beloved, and another hated, and they have born him children, *both* the beloved and the hated; and *if* the firstborn son be hers that was hated:

16Then it shall be, when he maketh his sons to inherit *that* which he hath, *that* he may not make the son of the beloved firstborn before the son of the hated, *which is indeed* the firstborn:

17But he shall acknowledge the son of the hated *for* the firstborn, by giving him a double portion of all that he hath: for he *is* the beginning of his strength; the right of the firstborn *is* his.

18¶ If a man have a stubborn and rebellious son, which will not obey the voice of his father, or the voice of his mother, and *that,* when they have chastened him, will not hearken unto them:

19Then shall his father and his mother lay hold on him, and bring him out unto the elders of his city, and unto the gate of his place;

20And they shall say unto the elders of his city, This our son *is* stubborn and rebellious, he will not obey our voice; *he is* a glutton, and a drunkard.

21And all the men of his city shall stone him with stones, that he die: so shalt thou put evil away from among you; and all Israel shall hear, and fear.

22¶ And if a man have committed a sin worthy of death, and he be to be put to death, and thou hang him on a tree:

23His body shall not remain all night upon the tree, but thou shalt in any wise bury him that day; (for he that is hanged *is* accursed of God;) that thy land be not defiled, which the LORD thy God giveth thee *for* an inheritance.

**22** THOU SHALT not see thy brother's ox or his sheep go astray, and hide thyself from them: thou shalt in any case bring them again unto thy brother.

## Amplified

5And the priests the sons of Levi shall come near, for the Lord your God has chosen them to minister to Him and to bless in the name [and presence] of the Lord, and by their word shall every controversy and every assault be settled.

6And all the elders of that city nearest to the slain man shall wash their hands over the heifer whose neck was broken in the valley;

7And they shall testify, Our hands have not shed this blood, neither have our eyes seen it.

8Forgive, O Lord, Your people Israel whom You have redeemed, and do not allow the shedding of innocent blood to be charged to Your people Israel. And the guilt of blood shall be forgiven them.

9So shall you purge the guilt of innocent blood from among you, when you do what is right in the sight of the Lord.

10When you go forth to battle against your enemies, and the Lord your God has given them into your hands, and you carry them away captive,

11And you see among the captives a beautiful woman, and desire her, that you may have her as your wife,

12Then you shall bring her home to your house; and she shall shave her head and pare her nails [in purification from heathenism],

13And put off her prisoner's garb and shall remain in your house, and bewail her father and her mother a full month. After that you may go in to her and be her husband, and she shall be your wife.

14And if you have no delight in her, then you shall let her go absolutely free; you shall not sell her at all for money, you shall not deal with her as a slave *or* a servant, because you have humbled her.

15If a man has two wives, one loved and the other disliked, and they both have borne him children, and if the first-born son is hers who is disliked,

16Then on the day when he wills his possessions to his sons, he shall not put the first-born of his loved wife in place of the first-born of the disliked, who is older.

17But he shall acknowledge the son of the disliked as the first-born, by giving him a double portion of all that he has, for he was the first issue of his strength; the right of the first-born is his.

18If a man has a stubborn and rebellious son, who will not obey the voice of his father or his mother, and though they chasten him, will not listen to them;

19Then his father and mother shall take hold of him, and bring him out to the elders of his city at the gate of the place where he lives,

20And they shall say to the elders of his city, This our son is stubborn and rebellious, he will not obey our voice; he is a glutton and a drunkard. [Prov. 23:20-22.]

21Then all the men of his city shall stone him to death; so you shall cleanse out the evil from your midst, and all Israel shall hear, and (reverently) fear.

22And if a man has committed a sin worthy of death, and he is put to death, and [afterward] you hang him on a tree, [Josh. 10:26, 27.]

23His body shall not remain all night upon the tree, but you shall surely bury him the same day, for a hanged man is accursed by God; thus you shall not defile your land which the Lord your God gives you for an inheritance. [Gal. 3:13.]

**22** YOU SHALL not see your brother's ox or his sheep being driven away *or* stolen, and hide yourself from [your duty to help] them; you shall surely take them back to your brother. [Cp. Prov. 24:12.]

## New American Standard

5"Then the priests, the sons of Levi, shall come near, for the
LORD your God has chosen them to serve Him and to bless in the
name of the LORD; and every dispute and every assault shall be
settled by them.

6"And all the elders of that city which is nearest to the slain
man shall wash their hands over the heifer whose neck was broken
in the valley;

7and they shall answer and say, 'Our hands have not shed this
blood, nor did our eyes see *it*.

8 [a]Forgive Thy people Israel whom Thou hast redeemed, O
LORD, and do not place the guilt of innocent blood in the midst of
Thy people Israel.' And the bloodguiltiness shall be forgiven them.

9"So you shall remove the guilt of innocent blood from your
midst, when you do what is right in the eyes of the LORD.

*Domestic Relations*

10¶ "When you go out to battle against your enemies, and the
LORD your God delivers them into your hands, and you take them
away captive,

11and see among the captives a beautiful woman, and have a
desire for her and would take her as a wife for yourself,

12then you shall bring her home to your house, and she shall
shave her head and trim her nails.

13"She shall also remove the clothes of her captivity and shall
remain in your house, and mourn her father and mother a full
month; and after that you may go in to her and be her husband
and she shall be your wife.

14"And it shall be, if you are not pleased with her, then you
shall let her go wherever she wishes; but you shall certainly not
sell her for money, you shall not mistreat her, because you have
humbled her.

15¶ "If a man has two wives, the one loved and the other
unloved, and *both* the loved and the unloved have borne him sons,
if the first-born son belongs to the unloved,

16then it shall be in the day he wills what he has to his sons,
he cannot make the son of the loved the first-born before the son
of the unloved, who is the first-born.

17"But he shall acknowledge the first-born, the son of the unloved, by giving him a double portion of all that he has, for he is
the beginning of his strength; to him belongs the right of the
first-born.

18¶ "If any man has a stubborn and rebellious son who will not
obey his father or his mother, and when they chastise him, he will
not even listen to them,

19then his father and mother shall seize him, and bring him out
to the elders of his city at the gateway of his home town.

20"And they shall say to the elders of his city, 'This son of ours
is stubborn and rebellious, he will not obey us, he is a glutton and
a drunkard.'

21"Then all the men of his city shall stone him to death; so you
shall remove the evil from your midst, and all Israel shall hear *of*
*it* and fear.

22¶ "And if a man has committed a sin worthy of death, and he
is put to death, and you hang him on a tree,

23his corpse shall not hang all night on the tree, but you shall
surely bury him on the same day (for he who is hanged is accursed
of God), so that you do not defile your land which the LORD your
God gives you as an inheritance.

*Sundry Laws*

**22** "YOU SHALL not see your countryman's ox or his sheep
straying away, and pay no attention to them; you shall
certainly bring them back to your countryman.

NAS [a] Lit., *Cover over, atone for*

## New International

forward, for the LORD your God has chosen them to minister and
to pronounce blessings in the name of the LORD and to decide all
cases of dispute and assault. 6Then all the elders of the town
nearest the body shall wash their hands over the heifer whose neck
was broken in the valley, 7and they shall declare: "Our hands did
not shed this blood, nor did our eyes see it done. 8Accept this
atonement for your people Israel, whom you have redeemed, O
LORD, and do not hold your people guilty of the blood of an
innocent man." And the bloodshed will be atoned for. 9So you will
purge from yourselves the guilt of shedding innocent blood, since
you have done what is right in the eyes of the LORD.

*Marrying a Captive Woman*

10When you go to war against your enemies and the LORD your
God delivers them into your hands and you take captives, 11if you
notice among the captives a beautiful woman and are attracted to
her, you may take her as your wife. 12Bring her into your home
and have her shave her head, trim her nails 13and put aside the
clothes she was wearing when captured. After she has lived in
your house and mourned her father and mother for a full month,
then you may go to her and be her husband and she shall be your
wife. 14If you are not pleased with her, let her go wherever she
wishes. You must not sell her or treat her as a slave, since you have
dishonored her.

*The Right of the Firstborn*

15If a man has two wives, and he loves one but not the other,
and both bear him sons but the firstborn is the son of the wife he
does not love, 16when he wills his property to his sons, he must
not give the rights of the firstborn to the son of the wife he loves
in preference to his actual firstborn, the son of the wife he does not
love. 17He must acknowledge the son of his unloved wife as the
firstborn by giving him a double share of all he has. That son is the
first sign of his father's strength. The right of the firstborn belongs
to him.

*A Rebellious Son*

18If a man has a stubborn and rebellious son who does not obey
his father and mother and will not listen to them when they
discipline him, 19his father and mother shall take hold of him and
bring him to the elders at the gate of his town. 20They shall say to
the elders, "This son of ours is stubborn and rebellious. He will not
obey us. He is a profligate and a drunkard." 21Then all the men
of his town shall stone him to death. You must purge the evil from
among you. All Israel will hear of it and be afraid.

*Various Laws*

22If a man guilty of a capital offense is put to death and his body
is hung on a tree, 23you must not leave his body on the tree
overnight. Be sure to bury him that same day, because anyone who
is hung on a tree is under God's curse. You must not desecrate the
land the LORD your God is giving you as an inheritance.

**22** IF YOU see your brother's ox or sheep straying, do not
ignore it but be sure to take it back to him. 2If the brother

## King James

2And if thy brother *be* not nigh unto thee, or if thou know him not, then thou shalt bring it unto thine own house, and it shall be with thee until thy brother seek after it, and thou shalt restore it to him again.

3In like manner shalt thou do with his ass; and so shalt thou do with his raiment; and with all lost thing of thy brother's, which he hath lost, and thou hast found, shalt thou do likewise: thou mayest not hide thyself.

4¶ Thou shalt not see thy brother's ass or his ox fall down by the way, and hide thyself from them: thou shalt surely help him to lift *them* up again.

5¶ The woman shall not wear that which pertaineth unto a man, neither shall a man put on a woman's garment: for all that do so *are* abomination unto the LORD thy God.

6¶ If a bird's nest chance to be before thee in the way in any tree, or on the ground, *whether they be* young ones, or eggs, and the dam sitting upon the young, or upon the eggs, thou shalt not take the dam with the young:

7 *But* thou shalt in any wise let the dam go, and take the young to thee; that it may be well with thee, and *that* thou mayest prolong *thy* days.

8¶ When thou buildest a new house, then thou shalt make a battlement for thy roof, that thou bring not blood upon thine house, if any man fall from thence.

9¶ Thou shalt not sow thy vineyard with divers seeds: lest the fruit of thy seed which thou hast sown, and the fruit of thy vineyard, be defiled.

10¶ Thou shalt not plow with an ox and an ass together.

11¶ Thou shalt not wear a garment of divers sorts, *as* of woollen and linen together.

12¶ Thou shalt make thee fringes upon the four quarters of thy vesture, wherewith thou coverest *thyself*.

13¶ If any man take a wife, and go in unto her, and hate her,

14And give occasions of speech against her, and bring up an evil name upon her, and say, I took this woman, and when I came to her, I found her not a maid:

15Then shall the father of the damsel, and her mother, take and bring forth *the tokens of* the damsel's virginity unto the elders of the city in the gate:

16And the damsel's father shall say unto the elders, I gave my daughter unto this man to wife, and he hateth her;

17And, lo, he hath given occasions of speech *against her*, saying, I found not thy daughter a maid; and yet these *are the tokens of* my daughter's virginity. And they shall spread the cloth before the elders of the city.

18And the elders of that city shall take that man and chastise him;

19And they shall amerce him in an hundred *shekels* of silver, and give *them* unto the father of the damsel, because he hath brought up an evil name upon a virgin of Israel: and she shall be his wife; he may not put her away all his days.

20But if this thing be true, *and the tokens of* virginity be not found for the damsel:

21Then they shall bring out the damsel to the door of her father's house, and the men of her city shall stone her with stones that she die: because she hath wrought folly in Israel, to play the whore in her father's house: so shalt thou put evil away from among you.

22¶ If a man be found lying with a woman married to an husband, then they shall both of them die, *both* the man that lay with the woman, and the woman: so shalt thou put away evil from Israel.

23¶ If a damsel *that is* a virgin be betrothed unto an husband, and a man find her in the city, and lie with her;

24Then ye shall bring them both out unto the gate of that city, and ye shall stone them with stones that they die; the damsel, because she cried not, *being* in the city; and the man, because he hath humbled his neighbour's wife: so thou shalt put away evil from among you.

## Amplified

2And if your brother [the owner] is not near you, or if you do not know who he is, you shall bring the animal to your house, and it shall be with you until your brother comes looking for it; then you shall restore it to him.

3And so shall you do with his donkey, or his garment, or with anything which your brother has lost and you have found; you shall not hide yourself from [your duty concerning] them.

4You shall not see your brother's donkey or his ox fall down by the way, and hide from [your duty concerning] them; you shall surely help him to lift them up again.

5The woman shall not wear that which pertains to a man, neither shall a man put on a woman's garment; for all that do so are an abomination to the Lord your God.

6If a bird's nest chance to be before you in the way in any tree or on the ground, with young ones or eggs, and the mother bird is sitting on the young or on the eggs, you shall not take the mother bird with the young.

7You shall surely let the mother bird go, and take only the young, that it may be well with you, and that you may prolong your days.

8When you build a new house, then you shall put a railing around your [flat] roof, so that no one may fall from there, and bring guilt of blood upon your house.

9You shall not plant your vineyard with two kinds of seed, lest the whole crop be forfeited [under this ban], the seed which you have sown and the yield of the vineyard forfeited to the sanctuary.

10You shall not plow with an ox [a clean animal] and a donkey [unclean] together. [II Cor. 6:14-16.]

11You shall not wear a garment of mingled stuff, wool and linen together. [Ezek. 44:18; Rev. 19:8.]

12You shall make yourself tassels on the four corners of your cloak with which you cover yourself. [Num. 15:37-40.]

13If any man takes a wife, and goes in to her, and then scorns her,

14And charges her with shameful things and gives her an evil reputation, and says, I took this woman, and when I came to her, I did not find in her the tokens of a virgin,

15Then the father of the young woman, and her mother, shall get and bring out the tokens of her virginity to the elders of the city in the gate;

16And her father shall say to the elders, I gave my daughter to this man as wife, and he hates *and* spurns her,

17And, lo, he has made shameful charges against her, saying, I found not in your daughter the evidences of her virginity; and yet these are the tokens of my daughter's virginity. And they shall spread the garment before the elders of the city.

18And the elders of that city shall take the man and rebuke *and* whip him;

19And they shall fine him 100 shekels of silver, and give them to the father of the young woman, because he has brought an evil name upon a virgin of Israel; and she shall be his wife; he may not divorce her all his days.

20But if it is true that the evidences of virginity were not found in the young woman,

21Then they shall bring her to the door of her father's house, and the men of her city shall stone her to death; because she has wrought [criminal] folly in Israel, by playing the harlot in her father's house. So you shall put away the evil from among you.

22If a man is found lying with another man's wife, they shall both die, the man who lay with the woman and the woman. So you shall purge the evil from Israel.

23If a maiden who is a virgin is engaged to be married, and a man find her in the city, and lie with her;

24Then you shall bring them both out to the gate of that city and shall stone them to death, the young woman because she did not cry for help though she was in the city, and the man because he has violated his neighbor's [promised] wife. So shall you put away evil from among you.

## New American Standard

2"And if your countryman is not near you, or if you do not know him, then you shall bring it home to your house, and it shall remain with you until your countryman looks for it; then you shall restore it to him.

3"And thus you shall do with his donkey, and you shall do the same with his garment, and you shall do likewise with anything lost by your countryman, which he has lost and you have found. You are not allowed to neglect *them.*

4"You shall not see your countryman's donkey or his ox fallen down on the way, and pay no attention to them; you shall certainly help him to raise *them* up.

5¶ "A woman shall not wear man's clothing, nor shall a man put on a woman's clothing; for whoever does these things is an abomination to the LORD your God.

6¶ "If you happen to come upon a bird's nest along the way, in any tree or on the ground, with young ones or eggs, and the mother sitting on the young or on the eggs, you shall not take the mother with the young;

7you shall certainly let the mother go, but the young you may take for yourself, in order that it may be well with you, and that you may prolong your days.

8¶ "When you build a new house, you shall make a parapet for your roof, that you may not bring bloodguilt on your house if anyone falls from it.

9¶ "You shall not sow your vineyard with two kinds of seed, lest all the produce of the seed which you have sown, and the increase of the vineyard become defiled.

10"You shall not plow with an ox and a donkey together.

11"You shall not wear a material mixed of wool and linen together.

12¶ "You shall make yourself tassels on the four corners of your garment with which you cover yourself.

*Laws on Morality*

13¶ "If any man takes a wife and goes in to her and *then* turns against her,

14and charges her with shameful deeds and publicly defames her, and says, 'I took this woman, *but* when I came near her, I did not find her a virgin,'

15then the girl's father and her mother shall take and bring out the *evidence* of the girl's virginity to the elders of the city at the gate.

16"And the girl's father shall say to the elders, 'I gave my daughter to this man for a wife, but he turned against her;

17and behold, he has charged her with shameful deeds, saying, "I did not find your daughter a virgin." But this is the *evidence* of my daughter's virginity.' And they shall spread the garment before the elders of the city.

18"So the elders of that city shall take the man and chastise him,

19and they shall fine him a hundred *shekels* of silver and give it to the girl's father, because he publicly defamed a virgin of Israel. And she shall remain his wife; he cannot divorce her all his days.

20"But if this charge is true, that the girl was not found a virgin,

21then they shall bring out the girl to the doorway of her father's house, and the men of her city shall stone her to death because she has committed an act of folly in Israel, by playing the harlot in her father's house; thus you shall purge the evil from among you.

22¶ "If a man is found lying with a married woman, then both of them shall die, the man who lay with the woman, and the woman; thus you shall purge the evil from Israel.

23¶ "If there is a girl who is a virgin engaged to a man, and *another* man finds her in the city and lies with her,

24then you shall bring them both out to the gate of that city and you shall stone them to death; the girl, because she did not cry out in the city, and the man, because he has violated his neighbor's wife. Thus you shall purge the evil from among you.

## New International

does not live near you or if you do not know who he is, take it
home with you and keep it until he comes looking for it. Then give
it back to him. 3Do the same if you find your brother's donkey or
his cloak or anything he loses. Do not ignore it.
4If you see your brother's donkey or his ox fallen on the road,
do not ignore it. Help him get it to its feet.
5A woman must not wear men's clothing, nor a man wear
women's clothing, for the LORD your God detests anyone who
does this.
6If you come across a bird's nest beside the road, either in a tree
or on the ground, and the mother is sitting on the young or on the
eggs, do not take the mother with the young. 7You may take the
young, but be sure to let the mother go, so that it may go well with
you and you may have a long life.
8When you build a new house, make a parapet around your
roof so that you may not bring the guilt of bloodshed on your
house if someone falls from the roof.
9Do not plant two kinds of seed in your vineyard; if you do, not
only the crops you plant but also the fruit of the vineyard will be
defiled.[a]
10Do not plow with an ox and a donkey yoked together.
11Do not wear clothes of wool and linen woven together.
12Make tassels on the four corners of the cloak you wear.

*Marriage Violations*

13If a man takes a wife and, after lying with her, dislikes her
14and slanders her and gives her a bad name, saying, "I married
this woman, but when I approached her, I did not find proof of
her virginity," 15then the girl's father and mother shall bring proof
that she was a virgin to the town elders at the gate. 16The girl's
father will say to the elders, "I gave my daughter in marriage to
this man, but he dislikes her. 17Now he has slandered her and said,
'I did not find your daughter to be a virgin.' But here is the proof
of my daughter's virginity." Then her parents shall display the
cloth before the elders of the town, 18and the elders shall take the
man and punish him. 19They shall fine him a hundred shekels of
silver[b] and give them to the girl's father, because this man has
given an Israelite virgin a bad name. She shall continue to be his
wife; he must not divorce her as long as he lives.
20If, however, the charge is true and no proof of the girl's
virginity can be found, 21she shall be brought to the door of her
father's house and there the men of her town shall stone her to
death. She has done a disgraceful thing in Israel by being promiscuous while still in her father's house. You must purge the evil
from among you.
22If a man is found sleeping with another man's wife, both the
man who slept with her and the woman must die. You must purge
the evil from Israel.
23If a man happens to meet in a town a virgin pledged to be
married and he sleeps with her, 24you shall take both of them to
the gate of that town and stone them to death—the girl because
she was in a town and did not scream for help, and the man
because he violated another man's wife. You must purge the evil
from among you.

**NIV** [a] *9* Or *be forfeited to the sanctuary* [b] *19* That is, about 2 1/2 pounds (about 1 kilogram)

## King James

25¶ But if a man find a betrothed damsel in the field, and the man force her, and lie with her: then the man only that lay with her shall die:
26But unto the damsel thou shalt do nothing; *there is* in the damsel no sin *worthy* of death: for as when a man riseth against his neighbour, and slayeth him, even so *is* this matter:
27For he found her in the field, *and* the betrothed damsel cried, and *there was* none to save her.
28¶ If a man find a damsel *that is* a virgin, which is not betrothed, and lay hold on her, and lie with her, and they be found;
29Then the man that lay with her shall give unto the damsel's father fifty *shekels* of silver, and she shall be his wife; because he hath humbled her, he may not put her away all his days.
30¶ A man shall not take his father's wife, nor discover his father's skirt.

23 HE THAT is wounded in the stones, or hath his privy member cut off, shall not enter into the congregation of the LORD.
2A bastard shall not enter into the congregation of the LORD; even to his tenth generation shall he not enter into the congregation of the LORD.
3An Ammonite or Moabite shall not enter into the congregation of the LORD; even to their tenth generation shall they not enter into the congregation of the LORD for ever:
4Because they met you not with bread and with water in the way, when ye came forth out of Egypt; and because they hired against thee Balaam the son of Beor of Pethor of Mesopotamia, to curse thee.
5Nevertheless the LORD thy God would not hearken unto Balaam; but the LORD thy God turned the curse into a blessing unto thee, because the LORD thy God loved thee.
6Thou shalt not seek their peace nor their prosperity all thy days for ever.
7¶ Thou shalt not abhor an Edomite; for he *is* thy brother: thou shalt not abhor an Egyptian; because thou wast a stranger in his land.
8The children that are begotten of them shall enter into the congregation of the LORD in their third generation.
9¶ When the host goeth forth against thine enemies, then keep thee from every wicked thing.
10¶ If there be among you any man, that is not clean by reason of uncleanness that chanceth him by night, then shall he go abroad out of the camp, he shall not come within the camp:
11But it shall be, when evening cometh on, he shall wash *himself* with water: and when the sun is down, he shall come into the camp *again*.
12¶ Thou shalt have a place also without the camp, whither thou shalt go forth abroad:
13And thou shalt have a paddle upon thy weapon; and it shall be, when thou wilt ease thyself abroad, thou shalt dig therewith, and shalt turn back and cover that which cometh from thee:
14For the LORD thy God walketh in the midst of thy camp, to deliver thee, and to give up thine enemies before thee; therefore shall thy camp be holy: that he see no unclean thing in thee, and turn away from thee.
15¶ Thou shalt not deliver unto his master the servant which is escaped from his master unto thee:
16He shall dwell with thee, *even* among you, in that place which he shall choose in one of thy gates, where it liketh him best: thou shalt not oppress him.

## Amplified

25But if a man finds the betrothed maiden in the open country, and the man seizes her and lies with her, then only the man who lay with her shall die.
26But you shall do nothing to the young woman; she has committed no sin punishable by death, for this is as when a man attacks and slays his neighbor;
27For he came upon her in the open country, and the betrothed girl cried out, but there was no one to save her.
28If a man find a girl who is a virgin, who is not betrothed, and he seizes her and lies with her, and they are found,
29Then the man who lay with her shall give to the girl's father fifty shekels of silver, and she shall be his wife, because he has violated her; he may not divorce her all his days.
30A man shall not take his father's former wife, nor shall he uncover her who belongs to his father.

23 HE WHO is wounded in the testicles, or has been made a eunuch, shall not enter into the congregation of the Lord.
2A person begotten out of wedlock shall not enter into the assembly of the Lord; even to his tenth generation shall his descendants not enter into the congregation of the Lord.
3An Ammonite or [a]Moabite shall not enter into the congregation of the Lord; even to their tenth generation their descendants shall not enter into the assembly of the Lord for ever;
4Because they did not meet you with food and water on the way when you came forth out of Egypt, and because they hired Balaam son of Beor of Pethor of Mesopotamia, against you to curse you.
5Nevertheless the Lord your God would not listen to Balaam; but the Lord your God turned the curse into a blessing to you, because the Lord your God loved you.
6You shall not seek their peace or their prosperity all your days for ever.
7You shall not abhor an Edomite, for he is your brother [Esau's descendant]. You shall not abhor an Egyptian, because you were a stranger *and* temporary resident in his land.
8Their children may enter into the congregation of the Lord in their third generation.
9When you go forth against your enemies and are in camp, you shall keep yourself from every evil thing.
10If there is among you any man who is not clean by reason of what happens to him at night, then he shall go outside the camp, he shall not come within the camp;
11But when evening comes he shall bathe himself in water, and when the sun is down, he may return to the camp.
12You shall have a place also outside the camp to which you shall go [as a comfort station];
13And you shall have a paddle *or* shovel among your weapons, and when you sit down outside [to relieve yourself], you shall dig a hole with it, and turn back and cover up what has come from you.
14For the Lord your God walks in the midst of your camp to deliver you and to give up your enemies before you; therefore shall your camp be holy, that He may see nothing indecent among you, and turn away from you.
15You shall not give up to his master a servant who has escaped from his master to you;
16He shall dwell with you in your midst, where he chooses in one of your towns, where it pleases him best. You shall not defraud *or* oppress him.

**AMP** [a] It must be remembered that the children, according to the Jewish law, followed the father, not the mother. [That is, the family of Boaz, for example, although his wife Ruth was a Moabitess, was considered Israelite, including his wife.] The case of Ruth would not, therefore, be touched by this precept *(Ellicott's Commentary)*.

## New American Standard

25"But if in the field the man finds the girl who is engaged, and
the man forces her and lies with her, then only the man who lies
with her shall die.
26"But you shall do nothing to the girl; there is no sin in the girl
worthy of death, for just as a man rises against his neighbor and
murders him, so is this case.
27"When he found her in the field, the engaged girl cried out,
but there was no one to save her.
28¶ "If a man finds a girl who is a virgin, who is not engaged,
and seizes her and lies with her and they are discovered,
29then the man who lay with her shall give to the girl's father
fifty *shekels* of silver, and she shall become his wife because he has
violated her; he cannot divorce her all his days.
30¶ "A man shall not take his father's wife so that he shall not
uncover his father's skirt.

*Persons Excluded from the Assembly*

23 "NO ONE who is emasculated, or has his male organ cut
off, shall enter the assembly of the LORD.
2"No one of illegitimate birth shall enter the assembly of the
LORD; none of his *descendants*, even to the tenth generation, shall
enter the assembly of the LORD.
3"No Ammonite or Moabite shall enter the assembly of the
LORD; none of their *descendants*, even to the tenth generation, shall
ever enter the assembly of the LORD,
4because they did not meet you with food and water on the
way when you came out of Egypt, and because they hired against
you Balaam the son of Beor from Pethor of Mesopotamia, to curse
you.
5"Nevertheless, the LORD your God was not willing to listen
to Balaam, but the LORD your God turned the curse into a blessing
for you because the LORD your God loves you.
6"You shall never seek their peace or their prosperity all your
days.
7¶ "You shall not detest an Edomite, for he is your brother; you
shall not detest an Egyptian, because you were an alien in his land.
8"The sons of the third generation who are born to them may
enter the assembly of the LORD.
9¶ "When you go out as an army against your enemies, then
you shall keep yourself from every evil thing.
10"If there is among you any man who is unclean because of a
nocturnal emission, then he must go outside the camp; he may not
reenter the camp.
11"But it shall be when evening approaches, he shall bathe
himself with water, and at sundown he may reenter the camp.
12"You shall also have a place outside the camp and go out
there,
13and you shall have a spade among your tools, and it shall be
when you sit down outside, you shall dig with it and shall turn to
cover up your excrement.
14"Since the LORD your God walks in the midst of your camp
to deliver you and to defeat your enemies before you, therefore
your camp must be holy; and He must not see anything indecent
among you lest He turn away from you.
15¶ "You shall not hand over to his master a slave who has
escaped from his master to you.
16"He shall live with you in your midst, in the place which he
shall choose in one of your towns where it pleases him; you shall
not mistreat him.

## New International

25But if out in the country a man happens to meet a girl pledged
to be married and rapes her, only the man who has done this shall
die. 26Do nothing to the girl; she has committed no sin deserving
death. This case is like that of someone who attacks and murders
his neighbor, 27for the man found the girl out in the country, and
though the betrothed girl screamed, there was no one to rescue
her.
28If a man happens to meet a virgin who is not pledged to be
married and rapes her and they are discovered, 29he shall pay the
girl's father fifty shekels of silver.[b] He must marry the girl, for he
has violated her. He can never divorce her as long as he lives.
30A man is not to marry his father's wife; he must not dishonor
his father's bed.

*Exclusion From the Assembly*

23 NO ONE who has been emasculated by crushing or cutting may enter the assembly of the LORD.
2No one born of a forbidden marriage[c] nor any of his descendants may enter the assembly of the LORD, even down to the tenth
generation.
3No Ammonite or Moabite or any of his descendants may enter
the assembly of the LORD, even down to the tenth generation. 4For
they did not come to meet you with bread and water on your way
when you came out of Egypt, and they hired Balaam son of Beor
from Pethor in Aram Naharaim[d] to pronounce a curse on you.
5However, the LORD your God would not listen to Balaam but
turned the curse into a blessing for you, because the LORD your
God loves you. 6Do not seek a treaty of friendship with them as
long as you live.
7Do not abhor an Edomite, for he is your brother. Do not abhor
an Egyptian, because you lived as an alien in his country. 8The
third generation of children born to them may enter the assembly
of the LORD.

*Uncleanness in the Camp*

9When you are encamped against your enemies, keep away
from everything impure. 10If one of your men is unclean because
of a nocturnal emission, he is to go outside the camp and stay
there. 11But as evening approaches he is to wash himself, and at
sunset he may return to the camp.
12Designate a place outside the camp where you can go to
relieve yourself. 13As part of your equipment have something to
dig with, and when you relieve yourself, dig a hole and cover up
your excrement. 14For the LORD your God moves about in your
camp to protect you and to deliver your enemies to you. Your
camp must be holy, so that he will not see among you anything
indecent and turn away from you.

*Miscellaneous Laws*

15If a slave has taken refuge with you, do not hand him over
to his master. 16Let him live among you wherever he likes and in
whatever town he chooses. Do not oppress him.

NIV [b] 29 That is, about 1 1/4 pounds (about 0.6 kilogram) [c] 2 Or *one of illegitimate birth* [d] 4 That is, Northwest Mesopotamia

## King James

17¶ There shall be no whore of the daughters of Israel, nor a sodomite of the sons of Israel.

18Thou shalt not bring the hire of a whore, or the price of a dog, into the house of the LORD thy God for any vow: for even both these *are* abomination unto the LORD thy God.

19¶ Thou shalt not lend upon usury to thy brother; usury of money, usury of victuals, usury of any thing that is lent upon usury:

20Unto a stranger thou mayest lend upon usury; but unto thy brother thou shalt not lend upon usury: that the LORD thy God may bless thee in all that thou settest thine hand to in the land whither thou goest to possess it.

21¶ When thou shalt vow a vow unto the LORD thy God, thou shalt not slack to pay it: for the LORD thy God will surely require it of thee; and it would be sin in thee.

22But if thou shalt forbear to vow, it shall be no sin in thee.

23That which is gone out of thy lips thou shalt keep and perform; *even* a freewill offering, according as thou hast vowed unto the LORD thy God, which thou hast promised with thy mouth.

24¶ When thou comest into thy neighbour's vineyard, then thou mayest eat grapes thy fill at thine own pleasure; but thou shalt not put *any* in thy vessel.

25When thou comest into the standing corn of thy neighbour, then thou mayest pluck the ears with thine hand; but thou shalt not move a sickle unto thy neighbour's standing corn.

**24** WHEN A man hath taken a wife, and married her, and it come to pass that she find no favour in his eyes, because he hath found some uncleanness in her: then let him write her a bill of divorcement, and give *it* in her hand, and send her out of his house.

2And when she is departed out of his house, she may go and be another man's *wife.*

3And *if* the latter husband hate her, and write her a bill of divorcement, and giveth *it* in her hand, and sendeth her out of his house; or if the latter husband die, which took her *to be* his wife;

4Her former husband, which sent her away, may not take her again to be his wife, after that she is defiled; for that *is* abomination before the LORD: and thou shalt not cause the land to sin, which the LORD thy God giveth thee *for* an inheritance.

5¶ When a man hath taken a new wife, he shall not go out to war, neither shall he be charged with any business: *but* he shall be free at home one year, and shall cheer up his wife which he hath taken.

6¶ No man shall take the nether or the upper millstone to pledge: for he taketh *a man's* life to pledge.

7¶ If a man be found stealing any of his brethren of the children of Israel, and maketh merchandise of him, or selleth him; then that thief shall die; and thou shalt put evil away from among you.

8¶ Take heed in the plague of leprosy, that thou observe diligently, and do according to all that the priests the Levites shall teach you: as I commanded them, *so* ye shall observe to do.

9Remember what the LORD thy God did unto Miriam by the way, after that ye were come forth out of Egypt.

10¶ When thou dost lend thy brother any thing, thou shalt not go into his house to fetch his pledge.

11Thou shalt stand abroad, and the man to whom thou dost lend shall bring out the pledge abroad unto thee.

12And if the man *be* poor, thou shalt not sleep with his pledge:

13In any case thou shalt deliver him the pledge again when the sun goeth down, that he may sleep in his own raiment, and bless thee: and it shall be righteousness unto thee before the LORD thy God.

## Amplified

17There shall be no cult prostitute of the daughters of Israel, neither shall there be a cult prostitute (a sodomite) of the sons of Israel.

18You shall not bring the hire of a harlot or the price of a dog [a sodomite] into the house of the Lord your God, in payment for a vow; for both of these—the gift and the giver—are an abomination to the Lord your God.

19You shall not lend on interest to your brother, interest on money, on victuals, on anything that is lent for interest.

20You may lend on interest to a foreigner; but to your brother you shall not lend on interest, that the Lord your God may bless you in all that you undertake in the land to which you go to possess it.

21When you make a vow to the Lord your God, you shall not be slack in paying it; for the Lord your God will surely require it of you, and slackness would be sin in you.

22But if you refrain from vowing, it will not be sin in you.

23The vow which has passed your lips you shall be watchful to perform, a voluntary offering which you have made to the Lord your God, which you have promised with your mouth.

24When you come into your neighbor's vineyard, you may eat your fill of grapes as many as you please; but you shall not put any in your vessel.

25When you come into the standing grain of your neighbor, you may pluck the ears with your hand; but you shall not put a sickle to your neighbor's standing grain.

**24** WHEN A man takes a wife and marries her, if then she finds no favor in his eyes because he has found some indecency in her, and he writes her a bill of divorce, puts it in her hand and sends her out of his house,

2And when she departs out of his house, she goes and marries another man,

3And if the latter husband dislikes her and writes her a bill of divorce and puts it in her hand and sends her out of his house; or if the last husband dies, who took her as his wife,

4Then her former husband, who sent her away, may not take her again to be his wife, after she is defiled; for that is an abomination before the Lord; and you shall not bring guilt upon the land which the Lord your God gives you for an inheritance.

5When a man is newly married, he shall not go out with the army or be charged with any business; he shall be free at home one year, and shall cheer his wife whom he has taken.

6No man shall take a mill or an upper millstone in pledge, for he would be taking a life in pledge.

7If a man be found kidnapping any of his brethren of the Israelites, and treats him as a slave *or* a servant, or sells him, then that thief shall die. So you shall put evil from among you.

8Take heed in the plague of leprosy, that you watch diligently, and do according to all that the Levitical priests shall teach you. As I commanded them, so you shall be watchful and do. [Lev. 13:14, 15.]

9Remember [earnestly] what the Lord your God did to Miriam by the way, after you had come out of Egypt. [Num. 12:10.]

10When you lend your brother anything, you shall not go into his house to get his pledge.

11You shall stand outside, and the man to whom you lend shall bring the pledge out to you.

12And if the man is poor, you shall not keep his pledge over night.

13You shall surely restore to him the pledge at sunset that he may sleep in his garment and bless you; and it shall be credited to you as righteousness (rightness and justice) before the Lord your God.

## New American Standard

17¶ "None of the daughters of Israel shall be a cult prostitute,
nor shall any of the sons of Israel be a cult prostitute.
18"You shall not bring the hire of a harlot or the wages of a [a]dog
into the house of the LORD your God for any votive offering, for
both of these are an abomination to the LORD your God.
19"You shall not charge interest to your countrymen: interest on
money, food, *or* anything that may be loaned at interest.
20"You may charge interest to a foreigner, but to your countryman you shall not charge interest, so that the LORD your God may
bless you in all that you undertake in the land which you are about
to enter to possess.
21¶ "When you make a vow to the LORD your God, you shall
not delay to pay it, for it would be sin in you, and the LORD your
God will surely require it of you.
22"However, if you refrain from vowing, it would not be sin in
you.
23"You shall be careful to perform what goes out from your lips,
just as you have voluntarily vowed to the LORD your God, what
you have promised.
24¶ "When you enter your neighbor's vineyard, then you may
eat grapes until you are fully satisfied, but you shall not put any
in your basket.
25"When you enter your neighbor's standing grain, then you
may pluck the heads with your hand, but you shall not wield a
sickle in your neighbor's standing grain.

## New International

17No Israelite man or woman is to become a shrine prostitute.
18You must not bring the earnings of a female prostitute or of a
male prostitute[b] into the house of the LORD your God to pay any
vow, because the LORD your God detests them both.
19Do not charge your brother interest, whether on money or
food or anything else that may earn interest. 20You may charge a
foreigner interest, but not a brother Israelite, so that the LORD your
God may bless you in everything you put your hand to in the land
you are entering to possess.
21If you make a vow to the LORD your God, do not be slow to
pay it, for the LORD your God will certainly demand it of you and
you will be guilty of sin. 22But if you refrain from making a vow,
you will not be guilty. 23Whatever your lips utter you must be sure
to do, because you made your vow freely to the LORD your God
with your own mouth.
24If you enter your neighbor's vineyard, you may eat all the
grapes you want, but do not put any in your basket. 25If you enter
your neighbor's grainfield, you may pick kernels with your hands,
but you must not put a sickle to his standing grain.

*Law of Divorce*

24 "WHEN A man takes a wife and marries her, and it happens that she finds no favor in his eyes because he has
found some indecency in her, and he writes her a certificate of
divorce and puts *it* in her hand and sends her out from his house,
2and she leaves his house and goes and becomes another
man's *wife,*
3and if the latter husband turns against her and writes her a
certificate of divorce and puts *it* in her hand and sends her out of
his house, or if the latter husband dies who took her to be his wife,
4 *then* her former husband who sent her away is not allowed
to take her again to be his wife, since she has been defiled; for that
is an abomination before the LORD, and you shall not bring sin on
the land which the LORD your God gives you as an inheritance.
5¶ "When a man takes a new wife, he shall not go out with the
army, nor be charged with any duty; he shall be free at home one
year and shall give happiness to his wife whom he has taken.

*Sundry Laws*

6¶ "No one shall take a handmill or an upper millstone in
pledge, for he would be taking a life in pledge.
7¶ "If a man is caught kidnapping any of his countrymen of the
sons of Israel, and he deals with him violently, or sells him, then
that thief shall die; so you shall purge the evil from among you.
8¶ "Be careful against an infection of leprosy, that you diligently observe and do according to all that the Levitical priests shall
teach you; as I have commanded them, so you shall be careful to
do.
9"Remember what the LORD your God did to Miriam on the
way as you came out of Egypt.
10¶ "When you make your neighbor a loan of any sort, you shall
not enter his house to take his pledge.
11"You shall remain outside, and the man to whom you make
the loan shall bring the pledge out to you.
12"And if he is a poor man, you shall not sleep with his pledge.
13"When the sun goes down you shall surely return the pledge
to him, that he may sleep in his cloak and bless you; and it will be
righteousness for you before the LORD your God.

24 IF A man marries a woman who becomes displeasing to
him because he finds something indecent about her, and
he writes her a certificate of divorce, gives it to her and sends her
from his house, 2and if after she leaves his house she becomes the
wife of another man, 3and her second husband dislikes her and
writes her a certificate of divorce, gives it to her and sends her from
his house, or if he dies, 4then her first husband, who divorced her,
is not allowed to marry her again after she has been defiled. That
would be detestable in the eyes of the LORD. Do not bring sin upon
the land the LORD your God is giving you as an inheritance.
5If a man has recently married, he must not be sent to war or
have any other duty laid on him. For one year he is to be free to
stay at home and bring happiness to the wife he has married.
6Do not take a pair of millstones—not even the upper one—as
security for a debt, because that would be taking a man's livelihood
as security.
7If a man is caught kidnapping one of his brother Israelites and
treats him as a slave or sells him, the kidnapper must die. You
must purge the evil from among you.
8In cases of leprous[c] diseases be very careful to do exactly as
the priests, who are Levites, instruct you. You must follow carefully what I have commanded them. 9Remember what the LORD
your God did to Miriam along the way after you came out of Egypt.
10When you make a loan of any kind to your neighbor, do not
go into his house to get what he is offering as a pledge. 11Stay
outside and let the man to whom you are making the loan bring
the pledge out to you. 12If the man is poor, do not go to sleep with
his pledge in your possession. 13Return his cloak to him by sunset
so that he may sleep in it. Then he will thank you, and it will be
regarded as a righteous act in the sight of the LORD your God.

NAS [a] I.e., male prostitute, sodomite

NIV [b] *18* Hebrew *of a dog* [c] *8* The Hebrew word was used for various diseases affecting the skin—not necessarily leprosy.

## King James

14¶ Thou shalt not oppress an hired servant *that is* poor and needy, *whether he be* of thy brethren, or of thy strangers that *are* in thy land within thy gates:

15At his day thou shalt give *him* his hire, neither shall the sun go down upon it; for he *is* poor, and setteth his heart upon it: lest he cry against thee unto the LORD, and it be sin unto thee.

16The fathers shall not be put to death for the children, neither shall the children be put to death for the fathers: every man shall be put to death for his own sin.

17¶ Thou shalt not pervert the judgment of the stranger, *nor* of the fatherless; nor take a widow's raiment to pledge:

18But thou shalt remember that thou wast a bondman in Egypt, and the LORD thy God redeemed thee thence: therefore I command thee to do this thing.

19¶ When thou cuttest down thine harvest in thy field, and hast forgot a sheaf in the field, thou shalt not go again to fetch it: it shall be for the stranger, for the fatherless, and for the widow: that the LORD thy God may bless thee in all the work of thine hands.

20When thou beatest thine olive tree, thou shalt not go over the boughs again: it shall be for the stranger, for the fatherless, and for the widow.

21When thou gatherest the grapes of thy vineyard, thou shalt not glean *it* afterward: it shall be for the stranger, for the fatherless, and for the widow.

22And thou shalt remember that thou wast a bondman in the land of Egypt: therefore I command thee to do this thing.

**25** IF THERE be a controversy between men, and they come unto judgment, that *the judges* may judge them; then they shall justify the righteous, and condemn the wicked.

2And it shall be, if the wicked man *be* worthy to be beaten, that the judge shall cause him to lie down, and to be beaten before his face, according to his fault, by a certain number.

3Forty stripes he may give him, *and* not exceed: lest, *if* he should exceed, and beat him above these with many stripes, then thy brother should seem vile unto thee.

4¶ Thou shalt not muzzle the ox when he treadeth out *the corn.*

5¶ If brethren dwell together, and one of them die, and have no child, the wife of the dead shall not marry without unto a stranger: her husband's brother shall go in unto her, and take her to him to wife, and perform the duty of an husband's brother unto her.

6And it shall be, *that* the firstborn which she beareth shall succeed in the name of his brother *which is* dead, that his name be not put out of Israel.

7And if the man like not to take his brother's wife, then let his brother's wife go up to the gate unto the elders, and say, My husband's brother refuseth to raise up unto his brother a name in Israel, he will not perform the duty of my husband's brother.

8Then the elders of his city shall call him, and speak unto him: and *if* he stand *to it*, and say, I like not to take her;

9Then shall his brother's wife come unto him in the presence of the elders, and loose his shoe from off his foot, and spit in his face, and shall answer and say, So shall it be done unto that man that will not build up his brother's house.

10And his name shall be called in Israel, The house of him that hath his shoe loosed.

11¶ When men strive together one with another, and the wife of the one draweth near for to deliver her husband out of the hand of him that smiteth him, and putteth forth her hand, and taketh him by the secrets:

12Then thou shalt cut off her hand, thine eye shall not pity *her.*

13¶ Thou shalt not have in thy bag divers weights, a great and a small.

## Amplified

14You shall not oppress *or* extort from a hired servant who is poor and needy, whether he is of your brethren, or of your strangers *and* sojourners who are in your land inside your towns.

15You shall give him his hire on the day he earns it, before the sun goes down; for he is poor, and sets his heart upon it; lest he cry against you to the Lord, and it be sin to you.

16The fathers shall not be put to death for the children, neither shall the children be put to death for the fathers; only for his own sin shall any one be put to death.

17You shall not pervert justice due the stranger *or* the sojourner or the fatherless, or take a widow's garment in pledge;

18But you shall [earnestly] remember that you were a slave in Egypt and the Lord your God redeemed you from there; therefore I command you to do this:

19When you reap your harvest in your field and have forgotten a sheaf in the field, you shall not go back to get it; it shall be for the stranger *and* the sojourner, the fatherless, and the widow; that the Lord your God may bless you in all the work of your hands.

20When you beat your olive tree, do not go over the boughs again; the leavings shall be for the stranger *and* the sojourner, the fatherless, and the widow.

21When you gather the grapes of your vineyard, you shall not glean it afterward; it shall be for the stranger *and* the sojourner, the fatherless, and the widow.

22You shall [earnestly] remember that you were a slave in the land of Egypt; therefore I command you to do this.

**25** IF THERE is a controversy between men, and they come into court, and the judges decide between them, justifying the innocent and condemning the guilty,

2Then if the guilty man deserves to be beaten, the judge shall cause him to lie down and be beaten in his presence with a certain number of stripes, according to his offense.

3Forty stripes may be given him, but not more; lest, if he should be beaten with many stripes your brother should [be treated like a beast and] seem low and worthless to you.

4You shall not muzzle the ox when he treads out the grain. [I Cor. 9:9, 10; I Tim. 5:17, 18.]

5If brothers live together, and one of them dies and has no son, his wife shall not marry outside the family to a stranger [an exluded man]; her husband's brother shall go in to her, and take her as his wife, and perform the duty of a husband's brother to her.

6And the first-born son shall succeed to the name of the dead brother, that his name be not blotted out of Israel.

7And if the man does not want to take his brother's wife, then let his brother's wife go up to the gate to the elders, and say, My husband's brother refuses to continue his brother's name in Israel; he will not perform the duty of my husband's brother.

8Then the elders of his city shall call him, and speak to him; and if he stands firm and says, I do not want to take her,

9Then shall his brother's wife come to him in the presence of the elders, and pull his shoe off his foot, and spit in his face, and shall answer, So shall it be done to that man who does not build up his brother's house.

10And his family shall be called in Israel, The house of him whose shoe was loosed.

11When men strive together one with another, and the wife of the one draws near to rescue her husband out of the hand of him who is beating him, and puts out her hand, and seizes the other man by the private parts;

12Then you shall cut off her hand; your eye shall not pity her.

13You shall not have in your bag true and false weights, a large and a small.

## New American Standard

14¶ "You shall not oppress a hired servant *who is* poor and
needy, whether *he is* one of your countrymen or one of your aliens
who is in your land in your towns.
15"You shall give him his wages on his day before the sun sets,
for he is poor and sets his heart on it; so that he may not cry against
you to the LORD and it become sin in you.
16¶ "Fathers shall not be put to death for *their* sons, nor shall
sons be put to death for *their* fathers; everyone shall be put to death
for his own sin.
17¶ "You shall not pervert the justice due an alien *or* [a]an orphan, nor take a widow's garment in pledge.
18"But you shall remember that you were a slave in Egypt, and
that the LORD your God redeemed you from there; therefore I am
commanding you to do this thing.
19¶ "When you reap your harvest in your field and have forgotten a sheaf in the field, you shall not go back to get it; it shall be
for the alien, for the orphan, and for the widow, in order that the
LORD your God may bless you in all the work of your hands.
20"When you beat your olive tree, you shall not go over the
boughs again; it shall be for the alien, for the orphan, and for the
widow.
21"When you gather the grapes of your vineyard, you shall not
go over it again; it shall be for the alien, for the orphan, and for
the widow.
22"And you shall remember that you were a slave in the land
of Egypt; therefore I am commanding you to do this thing.

*Sundry Laws*

25 "IF THERE is a dispute between men and they go to court,
and the judges decide their case, and they justify the
righteous and condemn the wicked,
2then it shall be if the wicked man deserves to be beaten, the
judge shall then make him lie down and be beaten in his presence
with the number of stripes according to his guilt.
3"He may beat him forty times *but* no more, lest he beat him
with many more stripes than these, and your brother be degraded
in your eyes.
4¶ "You shall not muzzle the ox while he is threshing.
5¶ "When brothers live together and one of them dies and has
no son, the wife of the deceased shall not be *married* outside *the
family* to a strange man. Her husband's brother shall go in to her
and take her to himself as wife and perform the duty of a husband's brother to her.
6"And it shall be that the first-born whom she bears shall
assume the name of his dead brother, that his name may not be
blotted out from Israel.
7"But if the man does not desire to take his brother's wife, then
his brother's wife shall go up to the gate to the elders and say, 'My
husband's brother refuses to establish a name for his brother in
Israel; he is not willing to perform the duty of a husband's brother
to me.'
8"Then the elders of his city shall summon him and speak to
him. And *if* he persists and says, 'I do not desire to take her,'
9then his brother's wife shall come to him in the sight of the
elders, and pull his sandal off his foot and spit in his face; and she
shall declare, 'Thus it is done to the man who does not build up
his brother's house.'
10"And in Israel his name shall be called, 'The house of him
whose sandal is removed.'
11¶ "If *two* men, a man and his countryman, are struggling
together, and the wife of one comes near to deliver her husband
from the hand of the one who is striking him, and puts out her
hand and seizes his genitals,
12then you shall cut off her hand; you shall not show pity.
13¶ "You shall not have in your bag differing weights, a large
and a small.

NAS [a] Or, *the fatherless*, and so throughout this context

## New International

14Do not take advantage of a hired man who is poor and needy,
whether he is a brother Israelite or an alien living in one of your
towns. 15Pay him his wages each day before sunset, because he is
poor and is counting on it. Otherwise he may cry to the LORD
against you, and you will be guilty of sin.
16Fathers shall not be put to death for their children, nor children put to death for their fathers; each is to die for his own sin.
17Do not deprive the alien or the fatherless of justice, or take the
cloak of the widow as a pledge. 18Remember that you were slaves
in Egypt and the LORD your God redeemed you from there. That
is why I command you to do this.
19When you are harvesting in your field and you overlook a
sheaf, do not go back to get it. Leave it for the alien, the fatherless
and the widow, so that the LORD your God may bless you in all
the work of your hands. 20When you beat the olives from your
trees, do not go over the branches a second time. Leave what
remains for the alien, the fatherless and the widow. 21When you
harvest the grapes in your vineyard, do not go over the vines
again. Leave what remains for the alien, the fatherless and the
widow. 22Remember that you were slaves in Egypt. That is why
I command you to do this.

25 WHEN MEN have a dispute, they are to take it to court
and the judges will decide the case, acquitting the innocent and condemning the guilty. 2If the guilty man deserves to be
beaten, the judge shall make him lie down and have him flogged
in his presence with the number of lashes his crime deserves, 3but
he must not give him more than forty lashes. If he is flogged more
than that, your brother will be degraded in your eyes.
4Do not muzzle an ox while it is treading out the grain.
5If brothers are living together and one of them dies without a
son, his widow must not marry outside the family. Her husband's
brother shall take her and marry her and fulfill the duty of a
brother-in-law to her. 6The first son she bears shall carry on the
name of the dead brother so that his name will not be blotted out
from Israel.
7However, if a man does not want to marry his brother's wife,
she shall go to the elders at the town gate and say, "My husband's
brother refuses to carry on his brother's name in Israel. He will not
fulfill the duty of a brother-in-law to me." 8Then the elders of his
town shall summon him and talk to him. If he persists in saying,
"I do not want to marry her," 9his brother's widow shall go up to
him in the presence of the elders, take off one of his sandals, spit
in his face and say, "This is what is done to the man who will not
build up his brother's family line." 10That man's line shall be
known in Israel as The Family of the Unsandaled.
11If two men are fighting and the wife of one of them comes to
rescue her husband from his assailant, and she reaches out and
seizes him by his private parts, 12you shall cut off her hand. Show
her no pity.
13Do not have two differing weights in your bag—one heavy,
one light. 14Do not have two differing measures in your house—

## King James

14Thou shalt not have in thine house divers measures, a great and a small.

15 *But* thou shalt have a perfect and just weight, a perfect and just measure shalt thou have: that thy days may be lengthened in the land which the LORD thy God giveth thee.

16For all that do such things, *and* all that do unrighteously, *are* an abomination unto the LORD thy God.

17¶ Remember what Amalek did unto thee by the way, when ye were come forth out of Egypt;

18How he met thee by the way, and smote the hindmost of thee, *even* all *that were* feeble behind thee, when thou *wast* faint and weary; and he feared not God.

19Therefore it shall be, when the LORD thy God hath given thee rest from all thine enemies round about, in the land which the LORD thy God giveth thee *for* an inheritance to possess it, *that* thou shalt blot out the remembrance of Amalek from under heaven; thou shalt not forget *it*.

**26** AND IT shall be, when thou *art* come in unto the land which the LORD thy God giveth thee *for* an inheritance, and possessest it, and dwellest therein;

2That thou shalt take of the first of all the fruit of the earth, which thou shalt bring of thy land that the LORD thy God giveth thee, and shalt put *it* in a basket, and shalt go unto the place which the LORD thy God shall choose to place his name there.

3And thou shalt go unto the priest that shall be in those days, and say unto him, I profess this day unto the LORD thy God, that I am come unto the country which the LORD sware unto our fathers for to give us.

4And the priest shall take the basket out of thine hand, and set it down before the altar of the LORD thy God.

5And thou shalt speak and say before the LORD thy God, A Syrian ready to perish *was* my father, and he went down into Egypt, and sojourned there with a few, and became there a nation, great, mighty, and populous:

6And the Egyptians evil entreated us, and afflicted us, and laid upon us hard bondage:

7And when we cried unto the LORD God of our fathers, the LORD heard our voice, and looked on our affliction, and our labour, and our oppression:

8And the LORD brought us forth out of Egypt with a mighty hand, and with an outstretched arm, and with great terribleness, and with signs, and with wonders:

9And he hath brought us into this place, and hath given us this land, *even* a land that floweth with milk and honey.

10And now, behold, I have brought the firstfruits of the land, which thou, O LORD, hast given me. And thou shalt set it before the LORD thy God, and worship before the LORD thy God:

11And thou shalt rejoice in every good *thing* which the LORD thy God hath given unto thee, and unto thine house, thou, and the Levite, and the stranger that *is* among you.

12¶ When thou hast made an end of tithing all the tithes of thine increase the third year, *which is* the year of tithing, and hast given *it* unto the Levite, the stranger, the fatherless, and the widow, that they may eat within thy gates, and be filled;

13Then thou shalt say before the LORD thy God, I have brought away the hallowed things out of *mine* house, and also have given them unto the Levite, and unto the stranger, to the fatherless, and to the widow, according to all thy commandments which thou hast commanded me: I have not transgressed thy commandments, neither have I forgotten *them*:

## Amplified

14You shall not have in your house true and false measures, a large and a small.

15But you shall have a perfect and just weight, and a perfect and just measure; that your days may be prolonged in the land which the Lord your God gives you.

16For all who do such things, and all who do unrighteously, are an abomination to the Lord your God.

17Remember what Amalek did to you on the way, when you had come forth from Egypt;

18How he did not fear God, but when you were faint and weary he attacked you along the way and cut off all the stragglers in your rear. [Exod. 17:14.]

19Therefore when the Lord your God has given you rest from all your enemies round about, in the land which the Lord your God gives you to possess for an inheritance, you shall blot out the remembrance of Amalek from under the heavens; you must not forget it.

**26** WHEN YOU have come into the land which the Lord your God gives you for an inheritance, and possess it, and live in it,

2You shall take some of all the produce of the soil which you harvest from the land that the Lord your God gives you, and put it in a basket, and go to the place [the sanctuary] which the Lord your God has chosen as the abiding place of His name [and His presence].

3And you shall go to the priest who is in office in those days, and say to him, I give thanks this day to the Lord your God that I have come to the land which the Lord swore to our fathers to give us;

4And the priest shall take the basket from your hand, and set it down before the altar of the Lord your God.

5And you shall say before the Lord your God, A wandering *and* lost Aramean ready to perish was my father [Jacob], and he went down into Egypt, and sojourned there, few in number, and he became there a nation, great, mighty, and numerous.

6And the Egyptians treated us very badly, and afflicted us, and laid upon us hard bondage.

7And when we cried to the Lord, the God of our fathers, the Lord heard our voice, and looked on our affliction, and our labor, and our (cruel) oppression;

8And the Lord brought us forth out of Egypt with a mighty hand, and with an outstretched arm, and with great (awesome) power, and with signs, and with wonders;

9And He brought us into this place, and gave us this land, a land flowing with milk and honey.

10And now, behold, I bring the first fruits of the ground, which You, O Lord, have given me. And you shall set it down before the Lord your God, and worship before the Lord your God;

11And you shall rejoice in all the good which the Lord your God has given you and your household, you and the Levite, and the stranger *and* the sojourner among you.

12When you have finished paying all the tithe of your produce the third year, which is the year of tithing, and have given it to the Levite, the stranger *and* the sojourner, the fatherless, and to the widow, that they may eat within your towns and be filled,

13Then you shall say before the Lord your God, I have brought the hallowed things [the tithe] out of my house, and moreover have given them to the Levite, to the stranger *and* the sojourner, to the fatherless, and to the widow, according to all your commandments which you have commanded me; I have not transgressed any of your commandments, neither have I forgotten them.

## New American Standard

14"You shall not have in your house differing measures, a large and a small.

15"You shall have a full and just weight; you shall have a full and just measure, that your days may be prolonged in the land which the LORD your God gives you.

16"For everyone who does these things, everyone who acts unjustly is an abomination to the LORD your God.

17¶ "Remember what Amalek did to you along the way when you came out from Egypt,

18how he met you along the way and attacked among you all the stragglers at your rear when you were faint and weary; and he did not [a]fear God.

19"Therefore it shall come about when the LORD your God has given you rest from all your surrounding enemies, in the land which the LORD your God gives you as an inheritance to possess, you shall blot out the memory of Amalek from under heaven; you must not forget.

*Offering First Fruits*

**26** "THEN IT shall be, when you enter the land which the LORD your God gives you as an inheritance, and you possess it and live in it,

2that you shall take some of the first of all the produce of the ground which you shall bring in from your land that the LORD your God gives you, and you shall put *it* in a basket and go to the place where the LORD your God chooses to establish His name.

3"And you shall go to the priest who is in office at that time, and say to him, 'I declare this day to the LORD my God that I have entered the land which the LORD swore to our fathers to give us.'

4"Then the priest shall take the basket from your hand and set it down before the altar of the LORD your God.

5"And you shall answer and say before the LORD your God, 'My father was a wandering Aramean, and he went down to Egypt and sojourned there, few in number; but there he became a great, mighty and populous nation.

6'And the Egyptians treated us harshly and afflicted us, and imposed hard labor on us.

7'Then we cried to the LORD, the God of our fathers, and the LORD heard our voice and saw our affliction and our toil and our oppression;

8and the LORD brought us out of Egypt with a mighty hand and an outstretched arm and with great terror and with signs and wonders;

9and He has brought us to this place, and has given us this land, a land flowing with milk and honey.

10'And now behold, I have brought the first of the produce of the ground which Thou, O LORD hast given me.' And you shall set it down before the LORD your God, and worship before the LORD your God;

11and you and the Levite and the alien who is among you shall rejoice in all the good which the LORD your God has given you and your household.

12¶ "When you have finished paying all the tithe of your increase in the third year, the year of tithing, then you shall give it to the Levite, to the stranger, to the orphan and to the widow, that they may eat in your towns, and be satisfied.

13"And you shall say before the LORD your God, 'I have removed the sacred *portion* from *my* house, and also have given it to the Levite and the alien, the orphan and the widow, according to all Thy commandments which Thou hast commanded me; I have not transgressed or forgotten any of Thy commandments.

NAS [a] Or, *reverence*

## New International

one large, one small. 15You must have accurate and honest weights
and measures, so that you may live long in the land the LORD your
God is giving you. 16For the LORD your God detests anyone who
does these things, anyone who deals dishonestly.
17Remember what the Amalekites did to you along the way
when you came out of Egypt. 18When you were weary and worn
out, they met you on your journey and cut off all who were lagging
behind; they had no fear of God. 19When the LORD your God gives
you rest from all the enemies around you in the land he is giving
you to possess as an inheritance, you shall blot out the memory
of Amalek from under heaven. Do not forget!

*Firstfruits and Tithes*

**26** WHEN YOU have entered the land the LORD your God is
giving you as an inheritance and have taken possession of
it and settled in it, 2take some of the firstfruits of all that you
produce from the soil of the land the LORD your God is giving you
and put them in a basket. Then go to the place the LORD your God
will choose as a dwelling for his Name 3and say to the priest in
office at the time, "I declare today to the LORD your God that I have
come to the land the LORD swore to our forefathers to give us."
4The priest shall take the basket from your hands and set it down
in front of the altar of the LORD your God. 5Then you shall declare
before the LORD your God: "My father was a wandering Aramean,
and he went down into Egypt with a few people and lived there
and became a great nation, powerful and numerous. 6But the
Egyptians mistreated us and made us suffer, putting us to hard
labor. 7Then we cried out to the LORD, the God of our fathers, and
the LORD heard our voice and saw our misery, toil and oppression.
8So the LORD brought us out of Egypt with a mighty hand and an
outstretched arm, with great terror and with miraculous signs and
wonders. 9He brought us to this place and gave us this land, a land
flowing with milk and honey; 10and now I bring the firstfruits of
the soil that you, O LORD, have given me." Place the basket before
the LORD your God and bow down before him. 11And you and the
Levites and the aliens among you shall rejoice in all the good
things the LORD your God has given to you and your household.
12When you have finished setting aside a tenth of all your
produce in the third year, the year of the tithe, you shall give it to
the Levite, the alien, the fatherless and the widow, so that they
may eat in your towns and be satisfied. 13Then say to the LORD
your God: "I have removed from my house the sacred portion and
have given it to the Levite, the alien, the fatherless and the widow,
according to all you commanded. I have not turned aside from
your commands nor have I forgotten any of them. 14I have not

## King James

14I have not eaten thereof in my mourning, neither have I taken
away *aught* thereof for *any* unclean *use*, nor given *aught* thereof for
the dead: *but* I have hearkened to the voice of the LORD my God,
*and* have done according to all that thou hast commanded me.
15Look down from thy holy habitation, from heaven, and bless
thy people Israel, and the land which thou hast given us, as thou
swarest unto our fathers, a land that floweth with milk and honey.
16¶ This day the LORD thy God hath commanded thee to do
these statutes and judgments: thou shalt therefore keep and do
them with all thine heart, and with all thy soul.
17Thou hast avouched the LORD this day to be thy God, and to
walk in his ways, and to keep his statutes, and his commandments, and his judgments, and to hearken unto his voice:
18And the LORD hath avouched thee this day to be his peculiar
people, as he hath promised thee, and that *thou* shouldest keep all
his commandments;
19And to make thee high above all nations which he hath made,
in praise, and in name, and in honour; and that thou mayest be
an holy people unto the LORD thy God, as he hath spoken.

**27** AND MOSES with the elders of Israel commanded the
people, saying, Keep all the commandments which I command you this day.
2And it shall be on the day when ye shall pass over Jordan unto
the land which the LORD thy God giveth thee, that thou shalt set
thee up great stones, and plaster them with plaster:
3And thou shalt write upon them all the words of this law,
when thou art passed over, that thou mayest go in unto the land
which the LORD thy God giveth thee, a land that floweth with milk
and honey; as the LORD God of thy fathers hath promised thee.
4Therefore it shall be when ye be gone over Jordan, *that* ye shall
set up these stones, which I command you this day, in mount Ebal,
and thou shalt plaster them with plaster.
5And there shalt thou build an altar unto the LORD thy God, an
altar of stones: thou shalt not lift up *any* iron *tool* upon them.
6Thou shalt build the altar of the LORD thy God of whole stones:
and thou shalt offer burnt offerings thereon unto the LORD thy
God:
7And thou shalt offer peace offerings, and shalt eat there, and
rejoice before the LORD thy God.
8And thou shalt write upon the stones all the words of this law
very plainly.
9¶ And Moses and the priests the Levites spake unto all Israel,
saying, Take heed, and hearken, O Israel; this day thou art become
the people of the LORD thy God.
10Thou shalt therefore obey the voice of the LORD thy God, and
do his commandments and his statutes, which I command thee
this day.
11¶ And Moses charged the people the same day, saying,
12These shall stand upon mount Gerizim to bless the people,
when ye are come over Jordan; Simeon, and Levi, and Judah, and
Issachar, and Joseph, and Benjamin:
13And these shall stand upon mount Ebal to curse; Reuben,
Gad, and Asher, and Zebulun, Dan, and Naphtali.
14¶ And the Levites shall speak, and say unto all the men of
Israel with a loud voice,
15Cursed *be* the man that maketh *any* graven or molten image,
an abomination unto the LORD, the work of the hands of the
craftsman, and putteth *it* in *a* secret *place*. And all the people shall
answer and say, Amen.
16Cursed *be* he that setteth light by his father or his mother. And
all the people shall say, Amen.
17Cursed *be* he that removeth his neighbour's landmark. And
all the people shall say, Amen.
18Cursed *be* he that maketh the blind to wander out of the way.
And all the people shall say, Amen.

## Amplified

14I have not eaten of the tithe in my mourning [making the tithe
unclean], nor have I handled any of it when I was unclean, or given
any of it to the dead; I have hearkened to the voice of the Lord my
God, and have done according to all that You have commanded
me.
15Look down from Your holy habitation, from Heaven, and
bless Your people Israel, and the land which You have given us,
as You swore to our fathers, a land flowing with milk and honey.
16This day the Lord your God has commanded you to do these
statutes and ordinances; therefore you shall keep and do them
with all your [mind and] heart and with all your being.
17You have (openly) declared the Lord this day to be your God,
[pledging] to walk in His ways, to keep His statutes, and His
commandments, and His precepts, and to hearken to His voice.
18And the Lord has declared this day that you are His peculiar
people, as He promised you, and you are to keep all His commandments;
19And He will make you high above all nations which He has
made, in praise and in fame and in honor, and that you shall be
a holy people to the Lord your God, as He has spoken.

**27** AND MOSES with the elders of Israel commanded the
people, Keep all the commandments with which I charge
you today.
2And on the day when you pass over the Jordan to the land
which the Lord your God gives you, you shall set you up great
stones, and cover them with plaster.
3And you shall write on them all the words of this law, when
you have passed over, that you may go into the land which the
Lord your God is giving you, a land flowing with milk and honey,
as the Lord, the God of your fathers, has promised you.
4And when you have gone over the Jordan, you shall set up
these stones, which I command you this day, on Mount Ebal, and
coat them with plaster.
5And there you shall build an altar to the Lord your God, an
altar of stones; you shall not lift up any iron tool upon them.
6You shall build the altar of the Lord your God of whole stones,
and offer burnt offerings on it to Him;
7And you shall offer peace offerings, and eat there, and rejoice
before the Lord your God.
8And you shall write upon the stones all the words of this law
very plainly.
9And Moses and the Levitical priests said to all Israel, Keep
silence, and hear, O Israel; this day you have become the people
of the Lord your God.
10So you shall obey the voice of the Lord your God, and do His
commandments and statutes, which I command you today.
11And Moses charged the people the same day, saying,
12These [tribes] shall stand on Mount Gerizim to bless the
people, when you have passed over the Jordan: Simeon, Levi,
Judah, Issachar, Joseph's [sons], and Benjamin.
13And these [tribes] shall stand upon Mount Ebal to pronounce
the curse [for disobedience]: Reuben, Gad, Asher, Zebulun, Dan,
and Naphtali.
14And the Levites shall declare with a loud voice to all the men
of Israel:
15Cursed be the man who makes a graven or molten image, an
abomination to the Lord, the work of the hands of the craftsman,
and sets it up in secret. All the people shall answer, Amen.
16Cursed be he who dishonors his father or his mother. All the
people shall say, Amen.
17Cursed be he who moves (back) his neighbor's landmark. All
the people shall say, Amen.
18Cursed be he who misleads a blind man from his way. All the
people shall say, Amen.

## New American Standard

14'I have not eaten of it while mourning, nor have I removed any of it while I was unclean, nor offered any of it to the dead. I have listened to the voice of the LORD my God; I have done according to all that Thou hast commanded me.

15'Look down from Thy holy habitation, from heaven, and bless Thy people Israel, and the ground which Thou hast given us, a land flowing with milk and honey, as Thou didst swear to our fathers.'

16¶ "This day the LORD your God commands you to do these statutes and ordinances. You shall therefore be careful to do them with all your heart and with all your soul.

17"You have today declared the LORD to be your God, and that you would walk in His ways and keep His statutes, His commandments and His ordinances, and listen to His voice.

18"And the LORD has today declared you to be His people, a treasured possession, as He promised you, and that you should keep all His commandments;

19and that He shall set you high above all nations which He has made, for praise, fame, and honor; and that you shall be a consecrated people to the LORD your God, as He has spoken."

## New International

eaten any of the sacred portion while I was in mourning, nor have
I removed any of it while I was unclean, nor have I offered any of
it to the dead. I have obeyed the LORD my God; I have done
everything you commanded me. 15Look down from heaven, your
holy dwelling place, and bless your people Israel and the land you
have given us as you promised on oath to our forefathers, a land
flowing with milk and honey."

*Follow the LORD's Commands*

16The LORD your God commands you this day to follow these
decrees and laws; carefully observe them with all your heart and
with all your soul. 17You have declared this day that the LORD is
your God and that you will walk in his ways, that you will keep
his decrees, commands and laws, and that you will obey him.
18And the LORD has declared this day that you are his people, his
treasured possession as he promised, and that you are to keep all
his commands. 19He has declared that he will set you in praise,
fame and honor high above all the nations he has made and that
you will be a people holy to the LORD your God, as he promised.

*The Curses of Mount Ebal*

27 THEN MOSES and the elders of Israel charged the people, saying, "Keep all the commandments which I command you today.

2"So it shall be on the day when you shall cross the Jordan to the land which the LORD your God gives you, that you shall set up for yourself large stones, and coat them with lime

3and write on them all the words of this law, when you cross over, in order that you may enter the land which the LORD your God gives you, a land flowing with milk and honey, as the LORD, the God of your fathers, promised you.

4"So it shall be when you cross the Jordan, you shall set up on Mount Ebal, these stones, as I am commanding you today, and you shall coat them with lime.

5"Moreover, you shall build there an altar to the LORD your God, an altar of stones; you shall not wield an iron *tool* on them.

6"You shall build the altar of the LORD your God of uncut stones; and you shall offer on it burnt offerings to the LORD your God;

7and you shall sacrifice peace offerings and eat there, and you shall rejoice before the LORD your God.

8"And you shall write on the stones all the words of this law very distinctly."

9¶ Then Moses and the Levitical priests spoke to all Israel, saying, "Be silent and listen, O Israel! This day you have become a people for the LORD your God.

10"You shall therefore obey the LORD your God, and do His commandments and His statutes which I command you today."

11¶ Moses also charged the people on that day, saying,

12"When you cross the Jordan, these shall stand on Mount Gerizim to bless the people: Simeon, Levi, Judah, Issachar, Joseph, and Benjamin.

13"And for the curse, these shall stand on Mount Ebal: Reuben, Gad, Asher, Zebulun, Dan, and Naphtali.

14"The Levites shall then answer and say to all the men of Israel with a loud voice,

15¶ 'Cursed is the man who makes an idol or a molten image, an abomination to the LORD, the work of the hands of the craftsman, and sets *it* up in secret.' And all the people shall answer and say, 'Amen.'

16¶ 'Cursed is he who dishonors his father or mother.' And all the people shall say, 'Amen.'

17¶ 'Cursed is he who moves his neighbor's boundary mark.' And all the people shall say, 'Amen.'

18¶ 'Cursed is he who misleads a blind *person* on the road.' And all the people shall say, 'Amen.'

*The Altar on Mount Ebal*

27 MOSES AND the elders of Israel commanded the people:
"Keep all these commands that I give you today. 2When
you have crossed the Jordan into the land the LORD your God is
giving you, set up some large stones and coat them with plaster.
3Write on them all the words of this law when you have crossed
over to enter the land the LORD your God is giving you, a land
flowing with milk and honey, just as the LORD, the God of your
fathers, promised you. 4And when you have crossed the Jordan,
set up these stones on Mount Ebal, as I command you today, and
coat them with plaster. 5Build there an altar to the LORD your God,
an altar of stones. Do not use any iron tool upon them. 6Build the
altar of the LORD your God with fieldstones and offer burnt offerings on it to the LORD your God. 7Sacrifice fellowship offerings[a]
there, eating them and rejoicing in the presence of the LORD your
God. 8And you shall write very clearly all the words of this law on
these stones you have set up."

*Curses From Mount Ebal*

9Then Moses and the priests, who are Levites, said to all Israel,
"Be silent, O Israel, and listen! You have now become the people
of the LORD your God. 10Obey the LORD your God and follow his
commands and decrees that I give you today."
11On the same day Moses commanded the people:
12When you have crossed the Jordan, these tribes shall stand on
Mount Gerizim to bless the people: Simeon, Levi, Judah, Issachar,
Joseph and Benjamin. 13And these tribes shall stand on Mount
Ebal to pronounce curses: Reuben, Gad, Asher, Zebulun, Dan and
Naphtali.
14The Levites shall recite to all the people of Israel in a loud
voice:

15"Cursed is the man who carves an image or casts an idol—a thing detestable to the LORD, the work of the craftsman's hands—and sets it up in secret."

Then all the people shall say, "Amen!"

16"Cursed is the man who dishonors his father or his mother."

Then all the people shall say, "Amen!"

17"Cursed is the man who moves his neighbor's boundary stone."

Then all the people shall say, "Amen!"

18"Cursed is the man who leads the blind astray on the road."

Then all the people shall say, "Amen!"

NIV [a] 7 Traditionally *peace offerings*

## King James

19Cursed *be* he that perverteth the judgment of the stranger, fatherless, and widow. And all the people shall say, Amen.
20Cursed *be* he that lieth with his father's wife; because he uncovereth his father's skirt. And all the people shall say, Amen.
21Cursed *be* he that lieth with any manner of beast. And all the people shall say, Amen.
22Cursed *be* he that lieth with his sister, the daughter of his father, or the daughter of his mother. And all the people shall say, Amen.
23Cursed *be* he that lieth with his mother-in-law. And all the people shall say, Amen.
24Cursed *be* he that smiteth his neighbour secretly. And all the people shall say, Amen.
25Cursed *be* he that taketh reward to slay an innocent person. And all the people shall say, Amen.
26Cursed *be* he that confirmeth not *all* the words of this law to do them. And all the people shall say, Amen.

**28** AND IT shall come to pass, if thou shalt hearken diligently unto the voice of the LORD thy God, to observe *and* to do all his commandments which I command thee this day, that the LORD thy God will set thee on high above all nations of the earth:
2And all these blessings shall come on thee, and overtake thee, if thou shalt hearken unto the voice of the LORD thy God.
3Blessed *shalt* thou *be* in the city, and blessed *shalt* thou *be* in the field.
4Blessed *shall be* the fruit of thy body, and the fruit of thy ground, and the fruit of thy cattle, the increase of thy kine, and the flocks of thy sheep.
5Blessed *shall be* thy basket and thy store.
6Blessed *shalt* thou *be* when thou comest in, and blessed *shalt* thou *be* when thou goest out.
7The LORD shall cause thine enemies that rise up against thee to be smitten before thy face: they shall come out against thee one way, and flee before thee seven ways.
8The LORD shall command the blessing upon thee in thy storehouses, and in all that thou settest thine hand unto; and he shall bless thee in the land which the LORD thy God giveth thee.
9The LORD shall establish thee an holy people unto himself, as he hath sworn unto thee, if thou shalt keep the commandments of the LORD thy God, and walk in his ways.
10And all people of the earth shall see that thou art called by the name of the LORD; and they shall be afraid of thee.
11And the LORD shall make thee plenteous in goods, in the fruit of thy body, and in the fruit of thy cattle, and in the fruit of thy ground, in the land which the LORD sware unto thy fathers to give thee.
12The LORD shall open unto thee his good treasure, the heaven to give the rain unto thy land in his season, and to bless all the work of thine hand: and thou shalt lend unto many nations, and thou shalt not borrow.
13And the LORD shall make thee the head, and not the tail; and thou shalt be above only, and thou shalt not be beneath; if that thou hearken unto the commandments of the LORD thy God, which I command thee this day, to observe and to do *them:*
14And thou shalt not go aside from any of the words which I command thee this day, *to* the right hand, or *to* the left, to go after other gods to serve them.

## Amplified

19Cursed be he who perverts the justice due to the sojourner *or* the stranger, the fatherless, and the widow. All the people shall say, Amen.
20Cursed be he who lies with his father's wife, because he uncovers what belongs to his father. All the people shall say, Amen.
21Cursed be he who lies with any beast. All the people shall say, Amen.
22Cursed be he who lies with his half-sister, whether his father's or his mother's daughter. All the people shall say, Amen.
23Cursed be he who lies with his mother-in-law. All the people shall say, Amen.
24Cursed be he who slays his neighbor secretly. All the people shall say, Amen.
25Cursed be he who takes a bribe to slay an innocent person. All the people shall say, Amen.
26Cursed be he who does not support *and* give assent to the words of this law to do them [as the rule of his life]. All the people shall say, Amen.

**28** IF YOU will listen diligently to the voice of the Lord your God, being watchful to do all His commandments which I command you this day, the Lord your God will set you high above all the nations of the earth,
2And all these blessings shall come upon you and overtake you, if you heed the voice of the Lord your God.
3Blessed shall you be in the city, and blessed shall you be in the field.
4Blessed shall be the fruit of your body, and the fruit of your ground, and the fruit of your beasts, the increase of your cattle, and the young of your flock.
5Blessed shall be your basket and your kneading trough.
6Blessed shall you be when you come in, and blessed shall you be when you go out.
7The Lord shall cause your enemies who rise up against you to be defeated before your face; they shall come out against you one way, and flee before you seven ways.
8The Lord shall command the blessing upon you in your storehouse, and in all that you undertake; and He will bless you in the land which the Lord your God gives you.
9The Lord will establish you as a people holy to Himself, as He has sworn to you, if you keep the commandments of the Lord your God, and walk in His ways.
10And all people of the earth shall see that you are called by the name [and in the presence of] the Lord; and they shall be afraid of you.
11And the Lord shall make you have a surplus of prosperity, through the fruit of your body, of your livestock, and of your ground, in the land which the Lord swore to your fathers to give you.
12The Lord shall open to you His good treasury, the heavens to give the rain of your land in its season, and to bless all the work of your hand; and you shall lend to many nations, but you shall not borrow.
13And the Lord shall make you the head, and not the tail; and you shall be above only, and you shall not be beneath, if you heed the commandments of the Lord your God, which I command you this day, and are watchful to do them.
14And you shall not go aside from any of the words which I command you this day, to the right hand or to the left, to go after other gods to serve them.

## New American Standard

19¶ 'Cursed is he who distorts the justice due an alien, orphan,
and widow.' And all the people shall say, 'Amen.'
20¶ 'Cursed is he who lies with his father's wife, because he has
uncovered his father's skirt.' And all the people shall say, 'Amen.'
21¶ 'Cursed is he who lies with any animal.' And all the people
shall say, 'Amen.'
22¶ 'Cursed is he who lies with his sister, the daughter of his
father or of his mother.' And all the people shall say, 'Amen.'
23¶ 'Cursed is he who lies with his mother-in-law.' And all the
people shall say, 'Amen.'
24¶ 'Cursed is he who strikes his neighbor in secret.' And all the
people shall say, 'Amen.'
25¶ 'Cursed is he who accepts a bribe to strike down an innocent
person.' And all the people shall say, 'Amen.'
26¶ 'Cursed is he who does not confirm the words of this law
by doing them.' And all the people shall say, 'Amen.'

*Blessings at Gerizim*

**28** "NOW IT shall be, if you will diligently obey the LORD
your God, being careful to do all His commandments
which I command you today, the LORD your God will set you high
above all the nations of the earth.
2"And all these blessings shall come upon you and overtake
you, if you will obey the LORD your God.
3"Blessed *shall* you *be* in the city, and blessed *shall* you *be* in the
country.
4"Blessed *shall be* the offspring of your body and the produce
of your ground and the offspring of your beasts, the increase of
your herd and the young of your flock.
5"Blessed *shall be* your basket and your kneading bowl.
6"Blessed *shall* you *be* when you come in, and blessed *shall* you
*be* when you go out.
7¶ "The LORD will cause your enemies who rise up against you
to be defeated before you; they shall come out against you one way
and shall flee before you seven ways.
8"The LORD will command the blessing upon you in your barns
and in all that you put your hand to, and He will bless you in the
land which the LORD your God gives you.
9"The LORD will establish you as a holy people to Himself, as
He swore to you, if you will keep the commandments of the LORD
your God, and walk in His ways.
10"So all the peoples of the earth shall see that you are called
by the name of the LORD; and they shall be afraid of you.
11"And the LORD will make you abound in prosperity, in the
offspring of your body and in the offspring of your beast and in
the produce of your ground, in the land which the LORD swore to
your fathers to give you.
12"The LORD will open for you His good storehouse, the heavens, to give rain to your land in its season and to bless all the work
of your hand; and you shall lend to many nations, but you shall
not borrow.
13"And the LORD shall make you the head and not the tail, and
you only shall be above, and you shall not be underneath, if you
will listen to the commandments of the LORD your God, which I
charge you today, to observe *them* carefully,
14and do not turn aside from any of the words which I command you today, to the right or to the left, to go after other gods
to serve them.

## New International

19"Cursed is the man who withholds justice from the alien,
the fatherless or the widow."
Then all the people shall say, "Amen!"
20"Cursed is the man who sleeps with his father's wife, for
he dishonors his father's bed."
Then all the people shall say, "Amen!"
21"Cursed is the man who has sexual relations with any
animal."
Then all the people shall say, "Amen!"
22"Cursed is the man who sleeps with his sister, the
daughter of his father or the daughter of his mother."
Then all the people shall say, "Amen!"
23"Cursed is the man who sleeps with his mother-in-law."
Then all the people shall say, "Amen!"
24"Cursed is the man who kills his neighbor secretly."
Then all the people shall say, "Amen!"
25"Cursed is the man who accepts a bribe to kill an innocent person."
Then all the people shall say, "Amen!"
26"Cursed is the man who does not uphold the words of
this law by carrying them out."
Then all the people shall say, "Amen!"

*Blessings for Obedience*

**28** IF YOU fully obey the LORD your God and carefully follow
all his commands I give you today, the LORD your God will
set you high above all the nations on earth. 2All these blessings will
come upon you and accompany you if you obey the LORD your
God:

3You will be blessed in the city and blessed in the country.
4The fruit of your womb will be blessed, and the crops of
your land and the young of your livestock—the calves of your
herds and the lambs of your flocks.
5Your basket and your kneading trough will be blessed.
6You will be blessed when you come in and blessed when
you go out.
7The LORD will grant that the enemies who rise up against you
will be defeated before you. They will come at you from one
direction but flee from you in seven.
8The LORD will send a blessing on your barns and on everything
you put your hand to. The LORD your God will bless you in the
land he is giving you.
9The LORD will establish you as his holy people, as he promised
you on oath, if you keep the commands of the LORD your God and
walk in his ways. 10Then all the peoples on earth will see that you
are called by the name of the LORD, and they will fear you. 11The
LORD will grant you abundant prosperity—in the fruit of your
womb, the young of your livestock and the crops of your ground—
in the land he swore to your forefathers to give you.
12The LORD will open the heavens, the storehouse of his bounty, to send rain on your land in season and to bless all the work
of your hands. You will lend to many nations but will borrow from
none. 13The LORD will make you the head, not the tail. If you pay
attention to the commands of the LORD your God that I give you
this day and carefully follow them, you will always be at the top,
never at the bottom. 14Do not turn aside from any of the commands I give you today, to the right or to the left, following other
gods and serving them.

## King James

15¶ But it shall come to pass, if thou wilt not hearken unto the voice of the LORD thy God, to observe to do all his commandments and his statutes which I command thee this day; that all these curses shall come upon thee, and overtake thee:

16Cursed *shalt* thou *be* in the city, and cursed *shalt* thou *be* in the field.

17Cursed *shall be* thy basket and thy store.

18Cursed *shall be* the fruit of thy body, and the fruit of thy land, the increase of thy kine, and the flocks of thy sheep.

19Cursed *shalt* thou *be* when thou comest in, and cursed *shalt* thou *be* when thou goest out.

20The LORD shall send upon thee cursing, vexation, and rebuke, in all that thou settest thine hand unto for to do, until thou be destroyed, and until thou perish quickly; because of the wickedness of thy doings, whereby thou hast forsaken me.

21The LORD shall make the pestilence cleave unto thee, until he have consumed thee from off the land, whither thou goest to possess it.

22The LORD shall smite thee with a consumption, and with a fever, and with an inflammation, and with an extreme burning, and with the sword, and with blasting, and with mildew; and they shall pursue thee until thou perish.

23And thy heaven that *is* over thy head shall be brass, and the earth that *is* under thee *shall be* iron.

24The LORD shall make the rain of thy land powder and dust: from heaven shall it come down upon thee, until thou be destroyed.

25The LORD shall cause thee to be smitten before thine enemies: thou shalt go out one way against them, and flee seven ways before them: and shalt be removed into all the kingdoms of the earth.

26And thy carcase shall be meat unto all fowls of the air, and unto the beasts of the earth, and no man shall fray *them* away.

27The LORD will smite thee with the botch of Egypt, and with the emerods, and with the scab, and with the itch, whereof thou canst not be healed.

28The LORD shall smite thee with madness, and blindness, and astonishment of heart:

29And thou shalt grope at noonday, as the blind gropeth in darkness, and thou shalt not prosper in thy ways: and thou shalt be only oppressed and spoiled evermore, and no man shall save *thee*.

30Thou shalt betroth a wife, and another man shall lie with her: thou shalt build an house, and thou shalt not dwell therein: thou shalt plant a vineyard, and shalt not gather the grapes thereof.

31Thine ox *shall be* slain before thine eyes, and thou shalt not eat thereof: thine ass *shall be* violently taken away from before thy face, and shall not be restored to thee: thy sheep *shall be* given unto thine enemies, and thou shalt have none to rescue *them*.

32Thy sons and thy daughters *shall be* given unto another people, and thine eyes shall look, and fail *with longing* for them all the day long: and *there shall be* no might in thine hand.

33The fruit of thy land, and all thy labours, shall a nation which thou knowest not eat up; and thou shalt be only oppressed and crushed always:

34So that thou shalt be mad for the sight of thine eyes which thou shalt see.

35The LORD shall smite thee in the knees, and in the legs, with a sore botch that cannot be healed, from the sole of thy foot unto the top of thy head.

36The LORD shall bring thee, and thy king which thou shalt set over thee, unto a nation which neither thou nor thy fathers have known; and there shalt thou serve other gods, wood and stone.

37And thou shalt become an astonishment, a proverb, and a byword, among all nations whither the LORD shall lead thee.

38Thou shalt carry much seed out into the field, and shalt gather *but* little in; for the locust shall consume it.

## Amplified

15But if you will not obey the voice of the Lord your God, being watchful to do all His commandments and His statutes which I command you this day, then all these curses shall come upon you and overtake you:

16Cursed shall you be in the city, and cursed shall you be in the field.

17Cursed shall be your basket and your kneading trough.

18Cursed shall be the fruit of your body, of your land, of the increase of your cattle and the young of your sheep.

19Cursed shall you be when you come in, and cursed shall you be when you go out.

20The Lord shall send you curses, confusion, and rebuke in every enterprise to which you set your hand, until you are destroyed, perishing quickly, because of the evil of your doings, by which you have forsaken me [Moses and God as one].

21The Lord will make the pestilence cling to you until He has consumed you from off the land, which you go to possess.

22The Lord will smite you with consumption, with fever, and inflammation, fiery heat, sword *and* drought, blasting, and mildew; they shall pursue you until you perish.

23The heavens over your head shall be brass, and the earth under you shall be iron.

24The Lord shall make the rain of your land powdered soil and dust; from the heavens it shall come down upon you until you are destroyed.

25The Lord shall cause you to be struck down before your enemies; you shall go out one way against them, and flee seven ways before them, and you shall be tossed to and fro *and* be a terror among all the kingdoms of the earth. [Fulfilled, II Chron. 29:8.]

26And your dead body shall be food for all birds of the air and beasts of the earth, and there shall be no one to frighten them away.

27The Lord will smite you with the boils of Egypt and the tumors, the scurvy and the itch, of which you cannot be healed.

28The Lord will smite you with madness and blindness and dismay of [mind and] heart.

29And you shall grope at noonday, as the blind grope in darkness, and you shall not prosper in your ways; and you shall be only oppressed and robbed continually, and there shall be no one to save you.

30You shall betroth a wife, and another man shall lie with her; you shall build a house, and not live in it; you shall plant a vineyard and not gather its grapes.

31Your ox shall be slain before your eyes, and you shall not eat of it; your donkey shall be violently taken away before your face, and not be restored to you; your sheep shall be given to your enemies, and you shall have no one to help you.

32Your sons and daughters shall be given to another people, and your eyes shall look and fail with longing for them all the day; and there shall be no power in your hands to prevent it. [Fulfilled, II Chron. 29:9.]

33A nation which you have not known shall eat up the fruit of your land and of all your labors; and you shall be only oppressed and crushed continually, [Fulfilled, Judg. 6:1-6; 13:1.]

34So that you shall be driven mad by the sight which your eyes shall see.

35The Lord will smite you on the knees and on the legs with a sore boil that cannot be healed, from the sole of your foot to the top of your head.

36The Lord shall bring you and your king whom you have set over you, to a nation which neither you nor your fathers have known, and there you shall [be forced to] serve other gods, of wood and stone. [Fulfilled, II Kings 17:4, 6; 24:12, 14; 25:7, 11; Dan. 6:11, 12.]

37And you shall become an amazement, a proverb, and a byword, among all peoples to which the Lord will lead you.

38You shall carry much seed out into the field, and shall gather little in; for the locust shall consume it. [Fulfilled, Hag. 1:6.]

# New American Standard

*Consequences of Disobedience*

15¶ "But it shall come about, if you will not obey the LORD your God, to observe to do all His commandments and His statutes with which I charge you today, that all these curses shall come upon you and overtake you.

16"Cursed *shall* you *be* in the city, and cursed *shall* you *be* in the country.

17"Cursed *shall be* your basket and your kneading bowl.

18"Cursed *shall be* the offspring of your body and the produce of your ground, the increase of your herd and the young of your flock.

19"Cursed *shall* you *be* when you come in, and cursed *shall* you *be* when you go out.

20¶ "The LORD will send upon you curses, confusion, and rebuke, in all you undertake to do, until you are destroyed and until you perish quickly, on account of the evil of your deeds, because you have forsaken Me.

21"The LORD will make the pestilence cling to you until He has consumed you from the land, where you are entering to possess it.

22"The LORD will smite you with consumption and with fever and with inflammation and with fiery heat and with [a]the sword and with blight and with mildew, and they shall pursue you until you perish.

23"And the heaven which is over your head shall be bronze, and the earth which is under you, iron.

24"The LORD will make the rain of your land powder and dust; from heaven it shall come down on you until you are destroyed.

25"The LORD will cause you to be defeated before your enemies; you shall go out one way against them, but you shall flee seven ways before them, and you shall be *an example of* terror to all the kingdoms of the earth.

26"And your carcasses shall be food to all birds of the sky and to the beasts of the earth, and there shall be no one to frighten *them* away.

27¶ "The LORD will smite you with the boils of Egypt and with tumors and with the scab and with the itch, from which you cannot be healed.

28"The LORD will smite you with madness and with blindness and with bewilderment of heart;

29and you shall grope at noon, as the blind man gropes in darkness, and you shall not prosper in your ways; but you shall only be oppressed and robbed continually, with none to save you.

30"You shall betroth a wife, but another man shall violate her; you shall build a house, but you shall not live in it; you shall plant a vineyard, but you shall not use its fruit.

31"Your ox shall be slaughtered before your eyes, but you shall not eat of it; your donkey shall be torn away from you, and shall not be restored to you; your sheep shall be given to your enemies, and you shall have none to save you.

32"Your sons and your daughters shall be given to another people, while your eyes shall look on and yearn for them continually; but there shall be nothing you can do.

33"A people whom you do not know shall eat up the produce of your ground and all your labors, and you shall never be anything but oppressed and crushed continually.

34"And you shall be driven mad by the sight of what you see.

35"The LORD will strike you on the knees and legs with sore boils, from which you cannot be healed, from the sole of your foot to the crown of your head.

36"The LORD will bring you and your king, whom you shall set over you, to a nation which neither you nor your fathers have known, and there you shall serve other gods, wood and stone.

37"And you shall become a horror, a proverb, and a taunt among all the people where the LORD will drive you.

38¶ "You shall bring out much seed to the field but you shall gather in little, for the locust shall consume it.

NAS [a] Another reading is *drought*

# New International

*Curses for Disobedience*

15However, if you do not obey the LORD your God and do not carefully follow all his commands and decrees I am giving you today, all these curses will come upon you and overtake you:

16You will be cursed in the city and cursed in the country.
17Your basket and your kneading trough will be cursed.
18The fruit of your womb will be cursed, and the crops of your land, and the calves of your herds and the lambs of your flocks.
19You will be cursed when you come in and cursed when you go out.

20The LORD will send on you curses, confusion and rebuke in
everything you put your hand to, until you are destroyed and
come to sudden ruin because of the evil you have done in forsaking
him.[b] 21The LORD will plague you with diseases until he has
destroyed you from the land you are entering to possess. 22The
LORD will strike you with wasting disease, with fever and inflammation, with scorching heat and drought, with blight and mildew,
which will plague you until you perish. 23The sky over your head
will be bronze, the ground beneath you iron. 24The LORD will turn
the rain of your country into dust and powder; it will come down
from the skies until you are destroyed.
25The LORD will cause you to be defeated before your enemies.
You will come at them from one direction but flee from them in
seven, and you will become a thing of horror to all the kingdoms
on earth. 26Your carcasses will be food for all the birds of the air
and the beasts of the earth, and there will be no one to frighten
them away. 27The LORD will afflict you with the boils of Egypt and
with tumors, festering sores and the itch, from which you cannot
be cured. 28The LORD will afflict you with madness, blindness and
confusion of mind. 29At midday you will grope about like a blind
man in the dark. You will be unsuccessful in everything you do;
day after day you will be oppressed and robbed, with no one to
rescue you.
30You will be pledged to be married to a woman, but another
will take her and ravish her. You will build a house, but you will
not live in it. You will plant a vineyard, but you will not even begin
to enjoy its fruit. 31Your ox will be slaughtered before your eyes,
but you will eat none of it. Your donkey will be forcibly taken from
you and will not be returned. Your sheep will be given to your
enemies, and no one will rescue them. 32Your sons and daughters
will be given to another nation, and you will wear out your eyes
watching for them day after day, powerless to lift a hand. 33A
people that you do not know will eat what your land and labor
produce, and you will have nothing but cruel oppression all your
days. 34The sights you see will drive you mad. 35The LORD will
afflict your knees and legs with painful boils that cannot be cured,
spreading from the soles of your feet to the top of your head.
36The LORD will drive you and the king you set over you to a
nation unknown to you or your fathers. There you will worship
other gods, gods of wood and stone. 37You will become a thing of
horror and an object of scorn and ridicule to all the nations where
the LORD will drive you.
38You will sow much seed in the field but you will harvest little,
because locusts will devour it. 39You will plant vineyards and

NIV [b] 20 Hebrew *me*

# King James

39Thou shalt plant vineyards, and dress *them*, but shalt neither drink *of* the wine, nor gather *the grapes;* for the worms shall eat them.

40Thou shalt have olive trees throughout all thy coasts, but thou shalt not anoint *thyself* with the oil; for thine olive shall cast *his fruit*.

41Thou shalt beget sons and daughters, but thou shalt not enjoy them; for they shall go into captivity.

42All thy trees and fruit of thy land shall the locust consume.

43The stranger that *is* within thee shall get up above thee very high; and thou shalt come down very low.

44He shall lend to thee, and thou shalt not lend to him: he shall be the head, and thou shalt be the tail.

45Moreover all these curses shall come upon thee, and shall pursue thee, and overtake thee, till thou be destroyed; because thou hearkenedst not unto the voice of the LORD thy God, to keep his commandments and his statutes which he commanded thee:

46And they shall be upon thee for a sign and for a wonder, and upon thy seed for ever.

47Because thou servedst not the LORD thy God with joyfulness, and with gladness of heart, for the abundance of all *things;*

48Therefore shalt thou serve thine enemies which the LORD shall send against thee, in hunger, and in thirst, and in nakedness, and in want of all *things:* and he shall put a yoke of iron upon thy neck, until he have destroyed thee.

49The LORD shall bring a nation against thee from far, from the end of the earth, *as swift* as the eagle flieth; a nation whose tongue thou shalt not understand;

50A nation of fierce countenance, which shall not regard the person of the old, nor show favour to the young:

51And he shall eat the fruit of thy cattle, and the fruit of thy land, until thou be destroyed: which *also* shall not leave thee *either* corn, wine, or oil, *or* the increase of thy kine, or flocks of thy sheep, until he have destroyed thee.

52And he shall besiege thee in all thy gates, until thy high and fenced walls come down, wherein thou trustedst, throughout all thy land: and he shall besiege thee in all thy gates throughout all thy land, which the LORD thy God hath given thee.

53And thou shalt eat the fruit of thine own body, the flesh of thy sons and of thy daughters, which the LORD thy God hath given thee, in the siege, and in the straitness, wherewith thine enemies shall distress thee:

54 *So that* the man *that is* tender among you, and very delicate, his eye shall be evil toward his brother, and toward the wife of his bosom, and toward the remnant of his children which he shall leave:

55So that he will not give to any of them of the flesh of his children whom he shall eat: because he hath nothing left him in the siege, and in the straitness, wherewith thine enemies shall distress thee in all thy gates.

56The tender and delicate woman among you, which would not adventure to set the sole of her foot upon the ground for delicateness and tenderness, her eye shall be evil toward the husband of her bosom, and toward her son, and toward her daughter,

57And toward her young one that cometh out from between her feet, and toward her children which she shall bear: for she shall eat them for want of all *things* secretly in the siege and straitness, wherewith thine enemy shall distress thee in thy gates.

58If thou wilt not observe to do all the words of this law that are written in this book, that thou mayest fear this glorious and fearful name, THE LORD THY GOD;

59Then the LORD will make thy plagues wonderful, and the plagues of thy seed, *even* great plagues, and of long continuance, and sore sicknesses, and of long continuance.

60Moreover he will bring upon thee all the diseases of Egypt, which thou wast afraid of; and they shall cleave unto thee.

# Amplified

39You shall plant vineyards and dress them, but shall neither drink of the wine nor gather the grapes; for the worm shall eat them.

40You shall have olive trees throughout all your territory, but you shall not anoint yourself with the oil; for your olive trees shall drop their fruit.

41You shall beget sons and daughters, but shall not enjoy them; for they shall go into captivity. [Fulfilled, Lam. 1:5.]

42All your trees and the fruit of your ground shall the locust possess. [Fulfilled, Joel 1:4.]

43The transient (stranger) among you shall mount up higher and higher above you, and you shall come down lower and lower.

44He shall lend to you, and you shall not lend to him; he shall be the head, and you shall be the tail.

45All these curses shall come upon you and shall pursue you and overtake you, till you are destroyed, because you do not obey the voice of the Lord your God, to keep His commandments and His statutes which He commanded you;

46They shall be upon you for a sign [of warning to other nations] and for a wonder, and upon your descendants for ever.

47Because you did not serve the Lord your God with joyfulness of [mind and] heart [in gratitude] for the abundance of all [with which He had blessed you],

48Therefore you shall serve your enemies whom the Lord shall send against you, in hunger and thirst, in nakedness, and in want of all things; and He will put a yoke of iron upon your neck, until He has destroyed you.

49The Lord will bring a nation against you from afar, from the end of the earth, as swift as the eagle flies, a nation whose language you shall not understand;

50A nation of unyielding countenance, who will not regard the person of the old, or show favor to the young,

51And shall eat the fruit of your cattle and the fruit of your ground, until you are destroyed; who also shall not leave you grain, new wine, oil, the increase of your cattle or the young of your sheep until they have caused you to perish.

52They shall besiege you in all your towns, until your high and fortified walls, in which you trusted, come down throughout all your land; and they shall besiege you in all your towns throughout all your land, which the Lord your God has given you.

53And you shall eat the fruit of your own body, the flesh of your sons and daughters, whom the Lord your God has given you, in the siege and in the (pressing) misery with which your enemies shall distress you. [Fulfilled, II Kings 6:24-29.]

54The man who is most tender among you, and extremely particular *and* well-bred, his eye shall be cruel *and* grudging of food toward his brother, and toward the wife of his bosom, and toward those of his children still remaining;

55So that he will not give to any of them any of the flesh of his children which he is eating, because he has nothing left him in the siege and in the distress with which your enemies shall distress you in all your towns.

56The most tender and daintily bred woman among you, who would not venture to set the sole of her foot upon the ground because she is so dainty and kind, will grudge to the husband of her bosom, to her son and to her daughter,

57Her afterbirth that comes out from her body and the children whom she shall bear; for she will eat them secretly for want of all else in the siege and distress with which your enemies shall distress you in your towns.

58If you will not be watchful to do all the words of this law that are written in this book, that you may (reverently) fear this glorious and fearful name [and presence], THE LORD YOUR GOD;

59Then the Lord will bring upon you and your descendants extraordinary strokes and blows, great plagues of long continuance, and grievous sicknesses of long duration.

60Moreover He will bring upon you all the diseases of Egypt, of which you were afraid, and they shall cling to you.

## New American Standard

39 "You shall plant and cultivate vineyards, but you shall neither drink of the wine nor gather *the grapes,* for the worm shall devour them.

40 "You shall have olive trees throughout your territory but you shall not anoint yourself with the oil, for your olives shall drop off.

41 "You shall have sons and daughters but they shall not be yours, for they shall go into captivity.

42 "The cricket shall possess all your trees and the produce of your ground.

43 "The alien who is among you shall rise above you higher and higher, but you shall go down lower and lower.

44 "He shall lend to you, but you shall not lend to him; he shall be the head, and you shall be the tail.

45 "So all these curses shall come on you and pursue you and overtake you until you are destroyed, because you would not obey the LORD your God by keeping His commandments and His statutes which He commanded you.

46 "And they shall become a sign and a wonder on you and your descendants forever.

47 "Because you did not serve the LORD your God with joy and a glad heart, for the abundance of all things;

48 therefore you shall serve your enemies whom the LORD shall send against you, in hunger, in thirst, in nakedness, and in the lack of all things; and He will put an iron yoke on your neck until He has destroyed you.

**49**¶ "The LORD will bring a nation against you from afar, from the end of the earth, as the eagle swoops down, a nation whose language you shall not understand,

50 a nation of fierce countenance who shall have no respect for the old, nor show favor to the young.

51 "Moreover, it shall eat the offspring of your herd and the produce of your ground until you are destroyed, who also leaves you no grain, new wine, or oil, nor the increase of your herd or the young of your flock until they have caused you to perish.

52 "And it shall besiege you in all your towns until your high and fortified walls in which you trusted come down throughout your land, and it shall besiege you in all your towns throughout your land which the LORD your God has given you.

53 "Then you shall eat the offspring of your own body, the flesh of your sons and of your daughters whom the LORD your God has given you, during the siege and the distress by which your enemy shall oppress you.

54 "The man who is refined and very delicate among you shall be hostile toward his brother and toward the wife he cherishes and toward the rest of his children who remain,

55 so that he will not give *even* one of them any of the flesh of his children which he shall eat, since he has nothing *else* left, during the siege and the distress by which your enemy shall oppress you in all your towns.

56 "The refined and delicate woman among you, who would not venture to set the sole of her foot on the ground for delicateness and refinement, shall be hostile toward the husband she cherishes and toward her son and daughter,

57 and toward her afterbirth which issues from between her legs and toward her children whom she bears; for she shall eat them secretly for lack of anything *else,* during the siege and the distress by which your enemy shall oppress you in your towns.

**58**¶ "If you are not careful to observe all the words of this law which are written in this book, to fear this honored and awesome name, the LORD your God,

59 then the LORD will bring extraordinary plagues on you and your descendants, even severe and lasting plagues, and miserable and chronic sicknesses.

60 "And He will bring back on you all the diseases of Egypt of which you were afraid, and they shall cling to you.

## New International

cultivate them but you will not drink the wine or gather the grapes,
because worms will eat them. 40 You will have olive trees throughout your country but you will not use the oil, because the olives
will drop off. 41 You will have sons and daughters but you will not
keep them, because they will go into captivity. 42 Swarms of locusts
will take over all your trees and the crops of your land.
43 The alien who lives among you will rise above you higher and
higher, but you will sink lower and lower. 44 He will lend to you,
but you will not lend to him. He will be the head, but you will be
the tail.
45 All these curses will come upon you. They will pursue you
and overtake you until you are destroyed, because you did not
obey the LORD your God and observe the commands and decrees
he gave you. 46 They will be a sign and a wonder to you and your
descendants forever. 47 Because you did not serve the LORD your
God joyfully and gladly in the time of prosperity, 48 therefore in
hunger and thirst, in nakedness and dire poverty, you will serve
the enemies the LORD sends against you. He will put an iron yoke
on your neck until he has destroyed you.
49 The LORD will bring a nation against you from far away, from
the ends of the earth, like an eagle swooping down, a nation
whose language you will not understand, 50 a fierce-looking nation
without respect for the old or pity for the young. 51 They will
devour the young of your livestock and the crops of your land until
you are destroyed. They will leave you no grain, new wine or oil,
nor any calves of your herds or lambs of your flocks until you are
ruined. 52 They will lay siege to all the cities throughout your land
until the high fortified walls in which you trust fall down. They will
besiege all the cities throughout the land the LORD your God is
giving you.
53 Because of the suffering that your enemy will inflict on you
during the siege, you will eat the fruit of the womb, the flesh of
the sons and daughters the LORD your God has given you. 54 Even
the most gentle and sensitive man among you will have no compassion on his own brother or the wife he loves or his surviving
children, 55 and he will not give to one of them any of the flesh of
his children that he is eating. It will be all he has left because of
the suffering your enemy will inflict on you during the siege of all
your cities. 56 The most gentle and sensitive woman among you—
so sensitive and gentle that she would not venture to touch the
ground with the sole of her foot—will begrudge the husband she
loves and her own son or daughter 57 the afterbirth from her womb
and the children she bears. For she intends to eat them secretly
during the siege and in the distress that your enemy will inflict on
you in your cities.
58 If you do not carefully follow all the words of this law, which
are written in this book, and do not revere this glorious and awesome name—the LORD your God— 59 the LORD will send fearful
plagues on you and your descendants, harsh and prolonged disasters, and severe and lingering illnesses. 60 He will bring upon you
all the diseases of Egypt that you dreaded, and they will cling to
you. 61 The LORD will also bring on you every kind of sickness and

## King James

61 Also every sickness, and every plague, which *is* not written
in the book of this law, them will the LORD bring upon thee, until
thou be destroyed.
62 And ye shall be left few in number, whereas ye were as the
stars of heaven for multitude; because thou wouldest not obey the
voice of the LORD thy God.
63 And it shall come to pass, *that* as the LORD rejoiced over you
to do you good, and to multiply you; so the LORD will rejoice over
you to destroy you, and to bring you to nought; and ye shall be
plucked from off the land whither thou goest to possess it.
64 And the LORD shall scatter thee among all people, from the
one end of the earth even unto the other; and there thou shalt serve
other gods, which neither thou nor thy fathers have known, *even*
wood and stone.
65 And among these nations shalt thou find no ease, neither
shall the sole of thy foot have rest: but the LORD shall give thee
there a trembling heart, and failing of eyes, and sorrow of mind:
66 And thy life shall hang in doubt before thee; and thou shalt
fear day and night, and shalt have none assurance of thy life:
67 In the morning thou shalt say, Would God it were even! and
at even thou shalt say, Would God it were morning! for the fear
of thine heart wherewith thou shalt fear, and for the sight of thine
eyes which thou shalt see.
68 And the LORD shall bring thee into Egypt again with ships, by
the way whereof I spake unto thee, Thou shalt see it no more
again: and there ye shall be sold unto your enemies for bondmen
and bondwomen, and no man shall buy *you*.

**29** THESE *ARE* the words of the covenant, which the LORD
commanded Moses to make with the children of Israel in
the land of Moab, beside the covenant which he made with them
in Horeb.
2 ¶ And Moses called unto all Israel, and said unto them, Ye have
seen all that the LORD did before your eyes in the land of Egypt
unto Pharaoh, and unto all his servants, and unto all his land;
3 The great temptations which thine eyes have seen, the signs,
and those great miracles:
4 Yet the LORD hath not given you an heart to perceive, and eyes
to see, and ears to hear, unto this day.
5 And I have led you forty years in the wilderness: your clothes
are not waxen old upon you, and thy shoe is not waxen old upon
thy foot.
6 Ye have not eaten bread, neither have ye drunk wine or strong
drink: that ye might know that I *am* the LORD your God.
7 And when ye came unto this place, Sihon the king of Heshbon,
and Og the king of Bashan, came out against us unto battle, and
we smote them:
8 And we took their land, and gave it for an inheritance unto the
Reubenites, and to the Gadites, and to the half tribe of Manasseh.

## Amplified

61 Also every sickness and every affliction which is not written
in the book of this law, the Lord will bring upon you, until you are
destroyed.
62 And you shall be [a]left few in number, whereas you had been
as the stars of the heavens for multitude; because you would not
obey the voice of the Lord your God.
63 And as the Lord rejoiced over you to do you good, and to
multiply you, so the Lord will rejoice to bring ruin upon you and
to destroy you; and you shall be [b]plucked from off the land which
you go to possess.
64 And the Lord shall scatter you among all peoples from one
end of the earth to the other; and there you shall [be forced to]
serve other gods, of wood and stone, which neither you nor your
fathers have known. [Fulfilled, Dan. 3:6.]
65 And among these nations you shall find no ease and there
shall be no rest for the sole of your foot; but the Lord will give you
there a trembling heart, failing of eyes [from disappointment of
hope], fainting of mind *and* languishing of spirit.
66 Your life shall hang in doubt before you; day and night you
shall be worried, and have no assurance of your life.
67 In the morning you shall say, Would it were evening! and at
evening you shall say, Would it were morning! because of the
anxiety *and* dread of your [mind and] heart, and the sights which
you shall see with your [own] eyes.
68 And the Lord shall [c]bring you into Egypt again with ships,
by the way about which I said to you, You shall never see it again;
and there you shall be sold to your enemies for bondmen and
bondwomen, and no man shall buy you. [Hos. 8:13.]

**29** THESE ARE the words of the covenant, which the Lord
commanded Moses to make with the Israelites in the land
of Moab, besides the covenant which he made with them in Horeb.
2 Moses called to all Israel, and said to them, You have seen all
that the Lord did before your eyes in the land of Egypt to Pharaoh,
to all his servants, and to all his land;
3 The great trials which your eyes saw, the signs, and those great
wonders;
4 Yet the Lord has not given you a [mind and] heart to understand, and eyes to see, and ears to hear, to this day.
5 I have led you forty years in the wilderness; your clothes have
not worn out upon you, and your sandals have not worn off your
feet.
6 You have not eaten [grain] bread, nor have you drunk wine or
strong drink, that you might recognize *and* know [your dependence on Him Who is saying], I am the Lord your God.
7 And when you came to this place, Sihon the king of Heshbon
and Og the king of Bashan came out against us to battle, but we
defeated them;
8 We took their land, and gave it for an inheritance to the Reubenites, the Gadites, and the half-tribe of the Manassites.

**AMP** [a] The informed reader scarcely needs to be reminded of how literally fulfilled have been many of these predictions of evil made against the chosen people because of their idolatry and rebellion against God. Such verses as 25, 32, 33, 36, 38, 41, 42, and 53, foretell historical facts now recorded in Jewish history both sacred and secular. Here verse 62 foretells how the Jewish race "has been thinned, and kept down, again and again." [b] [The Roman emperor] Hadrian issued a proclamation forbidding any Jews to reside in Judea, or even to approach its confines *(Gray and Adams' Commentary)*. [c] "Observe the contrast, you came out from bondage by God's high hand, monuments of His grace and power; you shall be carried back into bondage in men's slave-ships. This was literally fulfilled under [the Roman emperor] Titus, and also under Hadrian" *(Gray and Adams' Commentary)*. The curses . . . were also fulfilled in a terrible manner during the middle ages, and are still in a course of fulfillment, though frequently less sensibly felt *(Lange's Commentary)*. "Here, then, are prophecies delivered above 3,000 years ago, and yet being fulfilled in the world at this very time . . . I must acknowledge, they not only convince, but amaze and astonish me beyond expression; they are truly as Moses foretold (vs. 45, 46) they would be, 'a sign and a wonder for ever' " (Bishop Newton, quoted in *Jamieson, Fausset and Brown Commentary*).

## New American Standard

61"Also every sickness and every plague which, not written in
the book of this law, the LORD will bring on you until you are
destroyed.
62"Then you shall be left few in number, whereas you were as
the stars of heaven for multitude, because you did not obey the
LORD your God.
63"And it shall come about that as the LORD delighted over you
to prosper you, and multiply you, so the LORD will delight over
you to make you perish and destroy you; and you shall be torn
from the land where you are entering to possess it.
64"Moreover, the LORD will scatter you among all peoples, from
one end of the earth to the other end of the earth; and there you
shall serve other gods, wood and stone, which you or your fathers
have not known.
65"And among those nations you shall find no rest, and there
shall be no resting place for the sole of your foot; but there the LORD
will give you a trembling heart, failing of eyes, and despair of soul.
66"So your life shall hang in doubt before you; and you shall be
in dread night and day, and shall have no assurance of your life.
67"In the morning you shall say, 'Would that it were evening!'
And at evening you shall say, 'Would that it were morning!' because of the dread of your heart which you dread, and for the sight
of your eyes which you shall see.
68"And the LORD will bring you back to Egypt in ships, by the
way about which I spoke to you, 'You will never see it again!' And
there you shall offer yourselves for sale to your enemies as male
and female slaves, but there will be no buyer."

*The Covenant in Moab*

29 THESE ARE the words of the covenant which the LORD
commanded Moses to make with the sons of Israel in the
land of Moab, besides the covenant which He had made with them
at Horeb.
2¶ And Moses summoned all Israel and said to them, "You
have seen all that the LORD did before your eyes in the land of
Egypt to Pharaoh and all his servants and all his land;
3the great trials which your eyes have seen, those great signs
and wonders.
4"Yet to this day the LORD has not given you a heart to know,
nor eyes to see, nor ears to hear.
5"And I have led you forty years in the wilderness; your
clothes have not worn out on you, and your sandal has not worn
out on your foot.
6"You have not eaten bread, nor have you drunk wine or
strong drink, in order that you might know that I am the LORD your
God.
7"When you reached this place, Sihon the king of Heshbon
and Og the king of Bashan came out to meet us for battle, but we
defeated them;
8and we took their land and gave it as an inheritance to the
Reubenites, the Gadites, and the half-tribe of the Manassites.

## New International

disaster not recorded in this Book of the Law, until you are destroyed. 62You who were as numerous as the stars in the sky will
be left but few in number, because you did not obey the LORD your
God. 63Just as it pleased the LORD to make you prosper and increase in number, so it will please him to ruin and destroy you.
You will be uprooted from the land you are entering to possess.
64Then the LORD will scatter you among all nations, from one
end of the earth to the other. There you will worship other gods—
gods of wood and stone, which neither you nor your fathers have
known. 65Among those nations you will find no repose, no resting
place for the sole of your foot. There the LORD will give you an
anxious mind, eyes weary with longing, and a despairing heart.
66You will live in constant suspense, filled with dread both night
and day, never sure of your life. 67In the morning you will say, "If
only it were evening!" and in the evening, "If only it were morning!"—because of the terror that will fill your hearts and the sights
that your eyes will see. 68The LORD will send you back in ships to
Egypt on a journey I said you should never make again. There you
will offer yourselves for sale to your enemies as male and female
slaves, but no one will buy you.

*Renewal of the Covenant*

29 THESE ARE the terms of the covenant the LORD commanded Moses to make with the Israelites in Moab, in
addition to the covenant he had made with them at Horeb.
2Moses summoned all the Israelites and said to them:

Your eyes have seen all that the LORD did in Egypt to Pharaoh,
to all his officials and to all his land. 3With your own eyes you saw
those great trials, those miraculous signs and great wonders. 4But
to this day the LORD has not given you a mind that understands
or eyes that see or ears that hear. 5During the forty years that I led
you through the desert, your clothes did not wear out, nor did the
sandals on your feet. 6You ate no bread and drank no wine or other
fermented drink. I did this so that you might know that I am the
LORD your God.
7When you reached this place, Sihon king of Heshbon and Og
king of Bashan came out to fight against us, but we defeated them.
8We took their land and gave it as an inheritance to the Reubenites,
the Gadites and the half-tribe of Manasseh.

## King James

9Keep therefore the words of this covenant, and do them, that
ye may prosper in all that ye do.
10¶ Ye stand this day all of you before the LORD your God; your
captains of your tribes, your elders, and your officers, *with* all the
men of Israel,
11Your little ones, your wives, and thy stranger that *is* in thy
camp, from the hewer of thy wood unto the drawer of thy water:
12That thou shouldest enter into covenant with the LORD thy
God, and into his oath, which the LORD thy God maketh with thee
this day:
13That he may establish thee today for a people unto himself,
and *that* he may be unto thee a God, as he hath said unto thee, and
as he hath sworn unto thy fathers, to Abraham, to Isaac, and to
Jacob.
14Neither with you only do I make this covenant and this oath;
15But with *him* that standeth here with us this day before the
LORD our God, and also with *him* that *is* not here with us this day:
16(For ye know how we have dwelt in the land of Egypt; and
how we came through the nations which ye passed by;
17And ye have seen their abominations, and their idols, wood
and stone, silver and gold, which *were* among them:)
18Lest there should be among you man, or woman, or family,
or tribe, whose heart turneth away this day from the LORD our
God, to go *and* serve the gods of these nations; lest there should
be among you a root that beareth gall and wormwood;
19And it come to pass, when he heareth the words of this curse,
that he bless himself in his heart, saying, I shall have peace,
though I walk in the imagination of mine heart, to add drunkenness to thirst:
20The LORD will not spare him, but then the anger of the LORD
and his jealousy shall smoke against that man, and all the curses
that are written in this book shall lie upon him, and the LORD shall
blot out his name from under heaven.
21And the LORD shall separate him unto evil out of all the tribes
of Israel, according to all the curses of the covenant that are written
in this book of the law:
22So that the generation to come of your children that shall rise
up after you, and the stranger that shall come from a far land, shall
say, when they see the plagues of that land, and the sicknesses
which the LORD hath laid upon it;
23 *And that* the whole land thereof *is* brimstone, and salt, *and*
burning, *that* it is not sown, nor beareth, nor any grass groweth
therein, like the overthrow of Sodom, and Gomorrah, Admah, and
Zeboim, which the LORD overthrew in his anger, and in his wrath:
24Even all nations shall say, Wherefore hath the LORD done thus
unto this land? what *meaneth* the heat of this great anger?
25Then men shall say, Because they have forsaken the covenant
of the LORD God of their fathers, which he made with them when
he brought them forth out of the land of Egypt:
26For they went and served other gods, and worshipped them,
gods whom they knew not, and *whom* he had not given unto them:
27And the anger of the LORD was kindled against this land, to
bring upon it all the curses that are written in this book:
28And the LORD rooted them out of their land in anger, and in
wrath, and in great indignation, and cast them into another land,
as *it is* this day.
29The secret *things belong* unto the LORD our God: but those
*things which are* revealed *belong* unto us and to our children for
ever, that *we* may do all the words of this law.

## Amplified

9Therefore keep the words of this covenant, and do them, that
you may deal wisely *and* prosper in all that you do.
10All of you stand today before the Lord your God; your heads,
your tribes, your elders, and your officers, even all the men of
Israel,
11Your little ones, your wives, and the stranger *and* sojourner
in your camp, from the hewer of your wood to the drawer of your
water;
12That you may enter into the covenant of the Lord your God,
and into His oath, which He makes with you today;
13That He may establish you this day as a people for Himself,
and that He may be to you a God, as He said to you and as He
swore to your fathers, Abraham, Isaac, and Jacob.
14It is not with you only that I make this sworn covenant,
15But with future Israelites who do not stand here with us today
before the Lord our God, as well as with those who are here with
us this day.
16You know how we lived in the land of Egypt, and how we
came through the midst of the nations you crossed;
17And you have seen their abominations, and their idols, wood
and stone, silver and gold, which were among them.
18Beware lest there should be among you a man or woman or
family or tribe, whose [mind and] heart turns away this day from
the Lord our God to go and serve the gods of these nations; lest
there should be among you a [poisonous] root that bears gall and
wormwood;
19And lest, when he hears the words of this curse *and* oath, he
flatter *and* congratulate himself in his [mind and] heart, saying, I
shall have peace *and* safety, [a]though I walk in the stubbornness
of my [mind and] heart [bringing down a hurricane of destruction]
and sweep away the watered land with the dry.
20The Lord will not pardon him, but then the anger of the Lord
and His jealousy will smoke against that man, and all the curse that
is written in this book shall settle on him; the Lord will blot out his
very name from under the heavens;
21And the Lord will single him out for ruin *and* destruction from
all the tribes of Israel, according to all the curses of the covenant
that are written in this book of the law,
22So that the next generation, your children who rise up after
you, and the foreigner who shall come from a distant land, shall
say, when they see the plagues of this land, and the diseases with
which the Lord has made it sick—
23The whole land is brimstone and salt, and a burned waste, not
sown or bearing anything, where no grass can take root, like the
overthrow of Sodom and Gomorrah with Admah and Zeboiim,
which the Lord overthrew in His anger and wrath—
24Even all the nations shall say, Why has the Lord done thus
to this land? What does the heat of this great anger mean?
25Then men shall say, Because they forsook the covenant of the
Lord, the God of their fathers, which He made with them when
He brought them forth out of the land of Egypt,
26For they went and served other gods, and worshiped them,
gods they knew not, and that He had not given to them;
27So the anger of the Lord was kindled against this land, bringing upon it all the curses that are written in this book;
28And the Lord rooted them out of their land in anger and in
wrath and in great indignation, and cast them into another land,
as this day.
29The secret things belong unto the Lord our God; but the
things which are revealed belong to us and to our children for ever,
that we may do all of the words of this law.

**AMP** [a] It is on the strength of the Lord's oath to be Israel's God and so to protect them, that this Israelite flatters himself he is secure, no matter how he may behave. In the history of religion such a delusion has been lamentably frequent, and persons depending upon the unlimited protection of election have presumed on this and recklessly indulged in evil (*Cambridge Bible*, condensed). The Bible emphasizes the "security of the saints," but it is equally emphatic concerning the insecurity of those in conscious and continued indifference to God. [Ezek. 3:20; 18:24, 26; Rev. 22:14; James 1:21; Gal. 6:8; II Pet. 1:10, 11.]

## New American Standard

9"So keep the words of this covenant to do them, that you may prosper in all that you do.
10¶ "You stand today, all of you, before the LORD your God: your chiefs, your tribes, your elders and your officers, *even* all the men of Israel,
11your little ones, your wives, and the alien who is within your camps, from the one who chops your wood to the one who draws your water,
12that you may enter into the covenant with the LORD your God, and into His oath which the LORD your God is making with you today,
13in order that He may establish you today as His people and that He may be your God, just as He spoke to you and as He swore to your fathers, to Abraham, Isaac, and Jacob.
14¶ "Now not with you alone am I making this covenant and this oath,
15but both with those who stand here with us today in the presence of the LORD our God and with those who are not with us here today
16(for you know how we lived in the land of Egypt, and how we came through the midst of the nations through which you passed.
17"Moreover, you have seen their abominations and their idols *of* wood, stone, silver, and gold, which *they had* with them);
18lest there shall be among you a man or woman, or family or tribe, whose heart turns away today from the LORD our God, to go and serve the gods of those nations; lest there shall be among you a root bearing poisonous fruit and wormwood.
19"And it shall be when he hears the words of this curse, that he will boast, saying, 'I have peace though I walk in the stubbornness of my heart in order to destroy the watered *land* with the dry.'
20"The LORD shall never be willing to forgive him, but rather the anger of the LORD and His jealousy will burn against that man, and every curse which is written in this book will rest on him, and the LORD will blot out his name from under heaven.
21"Then the LORD will single him out for adversity from all the tribes of Israel, according to all the curses of the covenant which are written in this book of the law.
22¶ "Now the generation to come, your sons who rise up after you and the foreigner who comes from a distant land, when they see the plagues of the land and the diseases with which the LORD has afflicted it, will say,
23'All its land is brimstone and salt, a burning waste, unsown and unproductive, and no grass grows in it, like the overthrow of Sodom and Gomorrah, Admah and Zeboiim, which the LORD overthrew in His anger and in His wrath.'
24"And all the nations shall say, 'Why has the LORD done thus to this land? Why this great outburst of anger?'
25"Then *men* shall say, 'Because they forsook the covenant of the LORD, the God of their fathers, which He made with them when He brought them out of the land of Egypt.
26'And they went and served other gods and worshiped them, gods whom they have not known and whom He had not allotted to them.
27'Therefore, the anger of the LORD burned against that land, to bring upon it every curse which is written in this book;
28and the LORD uprooted them from their land in anger and in fury and in great wrath, and cast them into another land, as *it is* this day.'
29¶ "The secret things belong to the LORD our God, but the things revealed belong to us and to our sons forever, that we may observe all the words of this law.

## New International

9Carefully follow the terms of this covenant, so that you may
prosper in everything you do. 10All of you are standing today in
the presence of the LORD your God—your leaders and chief men,
your elders and officials, and all the other men of Israel, 11together
with your children and your wives, and the aliens living in your
camps who chop your wood and carry your water. 12You are
standing here in order to enter into a covenant with the LORD your
God, a covenant the LORD is making with you this day and sealing
with an oath, 13to confirm you this day as his people, that he may
be your God as he promised you and as he swore to your fathers,
Abraham, Isaac and Jacob. 14I am making this covenant, with its
oath, not only with you 15who are standing here with us today in
the presence of the LORD our God but also with those who are not
here today.
16You yourselves know how we lived in Egypt and how we
passed through the countries on the way here. 17You saw among
them their detestable images and idols of wood and stone, of silver
and gold. 18Make sure there is no man or woman, clan or tribe
among you today whose heart turns away from the LORD our God
to go and worship the gods of those nations; make sure there is
no root among you that produces such bitter poison.
19When such a person hears the words of this oath, he invokes
a blessing on himself and therefore thinks, "I will be safe, even
though I persist in going my own way." This will bring disaster
on the watered land as well as the dry.[b] 20The LORD will never be
willing to forgive him; his wrath and zeal will burn against that
man. All the curses written in this book will fall upon him, and the
LORD will blot out his name from under heaven. 21The LORD will
single him out from all the tribes of Israel for disaster, according
to all the curses of the covenant written in this Book of the Law.
22Your children who follow you in later generations and foreigners who come from distant lands will see the calamities that
have fallen on the land and the diseases with which the LORD has
afflicted it. 23The whole land will be a burning waste of salt and
sulfur—nothing planted, nothing sprouting, no vegetation growing on it. It will be like the destruction of Sodom and Gomorrah,
Admah and Zeboiim, which the LORD overthrew in fierce anger.
24All the nations will ask: "Why has the LORD done this to this
land? Why this fierce, burning anger?"
25And the answer will be: "It is because this people abandoned
the covenant of the LORD, the God of their fathers, the covenant
he made with them when he brought them out of Egypt. 26They
went off and worshiped other gods and bowed down to them,
gods they did not know, gods he had not given them. 27Therefore
the LORD's anger burned against this land, so that he brought on
it all the curses written in this book. 28In furious anger and in great
wrath the LORD uprooted them from their land and thrust them
into another land, as it is now."
29The secret things belong to the LORD our God, but the things
revealed belong to us and to our children forever, that we may
follow all the words of this law.

NIV [b] 19 Or *way, in order to add drunkenness to thirst."*

## King James

30 AND IT shall come to pass, when all these things are come
upon thee, the blessing and the curse, which I have set
before thee, and thou shalt call *them* to mind among all the nations,
whither the LORD thy God hath driven thee,
2And shalt return unto the LORD thy God, and shalt obey his
voice according to all that I command thee this day, thou and thy
children, with all thine heart, and with all thy soul;
3That then the LORD thy God will turn thy captivity, and have
compassion upon thee, and will return and gather thee from all the
nations, whither the LORD thy God hath scattered thee.
4If *any* of thine be driven out unto the outmost *parts* of heaven,
from thence will the LORD thy God gather thee, and from thence
will he fetch thee:
5And the LORD thy God will bring thee into the land which thy
fathers possessed, and thou shalt possess it; and he will do thee
good, and multiply thee above thy fathers.
6And the LORD thy God will circumcise thine heart, and the
heart of thy seed, to love the LORD thy God with all thine heart,
and with all thy soul, that thou mayest live.
7And the LORD thy God will put all these curses upon thine
enemies, and on them that hate thee, which persecuted thee.
8And thou shalt return and obey the voice of the LORD, and do
all his commandments which I command thee this day.
9And the LORD thy God will make thee plenteous in every work
of thine hand, in the fruit of thy body, and in the fruit of thy cattle,
and in the fruit of thy land, for good: for the LORD will again rejoice
over thee for good, as he rejoiced over thy fathers:
10If thou shalt hearken unto the voice of the LORD thy God, to
keep his commandments and his statutes which are written in this
book of the law, *and* if thou turn unto the LORD thy God with all
thine heart, and with all thy soul.
11¶ For this commandment which I command thee this day, it
*is* not hidden from thee, neither *is* it far off.
12It *is* not in heaven, that thou shouldest say, Who shall go up
for us to heaven, and bring it unto us, that we may hear it, and
do it?
13Neither *is* it beyond the sea, that thou shouldest say, Who
shall go over the sea for us, and bring it unto us, that we may hear
it, and do it?
14But the word *is* very nigh unto thee, in thy mouth, and in thy
heart, that thou mayest do it.
15¶ See, I have set before thee this day life and good, and death
and evil;
16In that I command thee this day to love the LORD thy God, to
walk in his ways, and to keep his commandments and his statutes
and his judgments, that thou mayest live and multiply: and the
LORD thy God shall bless thee in the land whither thou goest to
possess it.
17But if thine heart turn away, so that thou wilt not hear, but
shalt be drawn away, and worship other gods, and serve them;
18I denounce unto you this day, that ye shall surely perish, *and
that* ye shall not prolong *your* days upon the land, whither thou
passest over Jordan to go to possess it.
19I call heaven and earth to record this day against you, *that* I
have set before you life and death, blessing and cursing: therefore
choose life, that both thou and thy seed may live:
20That thou mayest love the LORD thy God, *and* that thou mayest obey his voice, and that thou mayest cleave unto him: for he
*is* thy life, and the length of thy days: that thou mayest dwell in
the land which the LORD sware unto thy fathers, to Abraham, to
Isaac, and to Jacob, to give them.

## Amplified

30 AND WHEN all these things have come upon you, the
blessing and the curse, which I have set before you, and
you shall call them to mind among all the nations, where the Lord
your God has driven you,
2And shall return to the Lord your God and obey His voice
according to all that I command you today, you and your children,
with all your [mind and] heart, and with all your being;
3Then the Lord your God will restore your fortunes, and have
compassion upon you, and will gather you again from all the
nations, where He has scattered you.
4Even if any of your dispersed are in the uttermost parts of the
heavens, from there the Lord your God will gather you, and from
there will He bring you.
5And the Lord your God will bring you into the land which your
fathers possessed, and you shall possess it; and He will do you
good, and multiply you above your fathers.
6And the Lord your God will circumcise your heart, and the
heart of your descendants, to love the Lord your God with all your
[mind and] heart, and with all your being, that you may live.
7And the Lord your God will put all these curses upon your
enemies, and on those who hate you, who persecute you.
8And you shall return and obey the voice of the Lord, and do
all His commandments which I command you today.
9And the Lord your God will make you abundantly prosperous
in every work of your hand, in the fruit of your body, of your cattle,
of your land, for good; for the Lord will again delight in prospering
you, as He took delight in your fathers,
10If you obey the voice of the Lord your God, to keep His
commandments and His statutes which are written in this book of
the law, and if you turn to the Lord your God with all your [mind
and] heart, and with all your being.
11For this commandment which I command you this day, is not
too difficult for you, nor is it far off.
12It is not [a secret laid up] in Heaven, that you should say, Who
shall go up for us to Heaven, and bring it to us, that we may hear
and do it?
13Neither is it beyond the sea, that you should say, Who shall
go over the sea for us, and bring it to us, that we may hear and
do it?
14But the word is very near you, in your mouth, and in your
mind *and* in your heart, so that you can do it.
15See, I have set before you this day life and good, and death
and evil.
16[If you obey the commandments of the Lord your God which]
I command you today, to love the Lord your God, to walk in His
ways, and to keep His commandments and His statutes and His
ordinances, then you shall live and multiply, and the Lord your
God will bless you in the land which you go to possess.
17But if your [mind and] heart turn away, and you will not hear,
but are drawn away to worship other gods and serve them,
18I declare to you today, that you shall surely perish, and you
shall not live long in the land which you pass over the Jordan to
enter and possess.
19I call Heaven and earth to witness this day against you, that
I have set before you life and death, the blessing and the curse;
therefore choose life, that you and your descendants may live;
20To love the Lord your God, to obey His voice, and to cling to
Him; for He is your life, and the length of your days, that you may
dwell in the land which the Lord swore to give to your fathers, to
Abraham, Isaac, and Jacob.

## New American Standard

*Restoration Promised*

**30** "SO IT shall be when all of these things have come upon
you, the blessing and the curse which I have set before
you, and you call *them* to mind in all nations where the LORD your
God has banished you,
2and you return to the LORD your God and obey Him with all
your heart and soul according to all that I command you today, you
and your sons,
3then the LORD your God will restore you from captivity, and
have compassion on you, and will gather you again from all the
peoples where the LORD your God has scattered you.
4"If your outcasts are at the ends of the earth, from there the
LORD your God will gather you, and from there He will bring you
back.
5"And the LORD your God will bring you into the land which
your fathers possessed, and you shall possess it; and He will
prosper you and multiply you more than your fathers.
6"Moreover the LORD your God will circumcise your heart and
the heart of your descendants, to love the LORD your God with all
your heart and with all your soul, in order that you may live.
7"And the LORD your God will inflict all these curses on your
enemies and on those who hate you, who persecuted you.
8"And you shall again obey the LORD, and observe all His
commandments which I command you today.
9"Then the LORD your God will prosper you abundantly in all
the work of your hand, in the offspring of your body and in the
offspring of your cattle and in the produce of your ground, for the
LORD will again rejoice over you for good, just as He rejoiced over
your fathers;
10if you obey the LORD your God to keep His commandments
and His statutes which are written in this book of the law, if you
turn to the LORD your God with all your heart and soul.
11¶ "For this commandment which I command you today is not
too difficult for you, nor is it out of reach.
12"It is not in heaven, that you should say, 'Who will go up to
heaven for us to get it for us and make us hear it, that we may
observe it?'
13"Nor is it beyond the sea, that you should say, 'Who will cross
the sea for us to get it for us and make us hear it, that we may
observe it?'
14"But the word is very near you, in your mouth and in your
heart, that you may observe it.

*Choose Life*

15¶ "See, I have set before you today life and prosperity, and
death and adversity;
16in that I command you today to love the LORD your God, to
walk in His ways and to keep His commandments and His statutes
and His judgments, that you may live and multiply, and that the
LORD your God may bless you in the land where you are entering
to possess it.
17"But if your heart turns away and you will not obey, but are
drawn away and worship other gods and serve them,
18I declare to you today that you shall surely perish. You shall
not prolong *your* days in the land where you are crossing the
Jordan to enter and possess it.
19"I call heaven and earth to witness against you today, that I
have set before you life and death, the blessing and the curse. So
choose life in order that you may live, you and your descendants,
20by loving the LORD your God, by obeying His voice, and by
holding fast to Him; for this is your life and the length of your days,
that you may live in the land which the LORD swore to your fathers,
to Abraham, Isaac, and Jacob, to give them."

## New International

*Prosperity After Turning to the LORD*

**30** WHEN ALL these blessings and curses I have set before
you come upon you and you take them to heart wherever
the LORD your God disperses you among the nations, 2and when
you and your children return to the LORD your God and obey him
with all your heart and with all your soul according to everything
I command you today, 3then the LORD your God will restore your
fortunes[a] and have compassion on you and gather you again from
all the nations where he scattered you. 4Even if you have been
banished to the most distant land under the heavens, from there
the LORD your God will gather you and bring you back. 5He will
bring you to the land that belonged to your fathers, and you will
take possession of it. He will make you more prosperous and
numerous than your fathers. 6The LORD your God will circumcise
your hearts and the hearts of your descendants, so that you may
love him with all your heart and with all your soul, and live. 7The
LORD your God will put all these curses on your enemies who hate
and persecute you. 8You will again obey the LORD and follow all
his commands I am giving you today. 9Then the LORD your God
will make you most prosperous in all the work of your hands and
in the fruit of your womb, the young of your livestock and the
crops of your land. The LORD will again delight in you and make
you prosperous, just as he delighted in your fathers, 10if you obey
the LORD your God and keep his commands and decrees that are
written in this Book of the Law and turn to the LORD your God with
all your heart and with all your soul.

*The Offer of Life or Death*

11Now what I am commanding you today is not too difficult for
you or beyond your reach. 12It is not up in heaven, so that you
have to ask, "Who will ascend into heaven to get it and proclaim
it to us so we may obey it?" 13Nor is it beyond the sea, so that you
have to ask, "Who will cross the sea to get it and proclaim it to us
so we may obey it?" 14No, the word is very near you; it is in your
mouth and in your heart so you may obey it.
15See, I set before you today life and prosperity, death and
destruction. 16For I command you today to love the LORD your
God, to walk in his ways, and to keep his commands, decrees and
laws; then you will live and increase, and the LORD your God will
bless you in the land you are entering to possess.
17But if your heart turns away and you are not obedient, and
if you are drawn away to bow down to other gods and worship
them, 18I declare to you this day that you will certainly be destroyed. You will not live long in the land you are crossing the
Jordan to enter and possess.
19This day I call heaven and earth as witnesses against you that
I have set before you life and death, blessings and curses. Now
choose life, so that you and your children may live 20and that you
may love the LORD your God, listen to his voice, and hold fast to
him. For the LORD is your life, and he will give you many years
in the land he swore to give to your fathers, Abraham, Isaac and
Jacob.

**NIV** [a] 3 Or *will bring you back from captivity*

## King James

**31** AND MOSES went and spake these words unto all Israel.

2And he said unto them, I *am* an hundred and twenty years old this day; I can no more go out and come in: also the LORD hath said unto me, Thou shalt not go over this Jordan.

3The LORD thy God, he will go over before thee, *and* he will destroy these nations from before thee, and thou shalt possess them: *and* Joshua, he shall go over before thee, as the LORD hath said.

4And the LORD shall do unto them as he did to Sihon and to Og, kings of the Amorites, and unto the land of them, whom he destroyed.

5And the LORD shall give them up before your face, that ye may do unto them according unto all the commandments which I have commanded you.

6Be strong and of a good courage, fear not, nor be afraid of them: for the LORD thy God, he *it is* that doth go with thee; he will not fail thee, nor forsake thee.

7¶ And Moses called unto Joshua, and said unto him in the sight of all Israel, Be strong and of a good courage: for thou must go with this people unto the land which the LORD hath sworn unto their fathers to give them; and thou shalt cause them to inherit it.

8And the LORD, he *it is* that doth go before thee; he will be with thee, he will not fail thee, neither forsake thee: fear not, neither be dismayed.

9¶ And Moses wrote this law, and delivered it unto the priests the sons of Levi, which bare the ark of the covenant of the LORD, and unto all the elders of Israel.

10And Moses commanded them, saying, At the end of *every* seven years, in the solemnity of the year of release, in the feast of tabernacles,

11When all Israel is come to appear before the LORD thy God in the place which he shall choose, thou shalt read this law before all Israel in their hearing.

12Gather the people together, men, and women, and children, and thy stranger that *is* within thy gates, that they may hear, and that they may learn, and fear the LORD your God, and observe to do all the words of this law:

13And *that* their children, which have not known *any thing*, may hear, and learn to fear the LORD your God, as long as ye live in the land whither ye go over Jordan to possess it.

14¶ And the LORD said unto Moses, Behold, thy days approach that thou must die: call Joshua, and present yourselves in the tabernacle of the congregation, that I may give him a charge. And Moses and Joshua went, and presented themselves in the tabernacle of the congregation.

15And the LORD appeared in the tabernacle in a pillar of a cloud: and the pillar of the cloud stood over the door of the tabernacle.

16¶ And the LORD said unto Moses, Behold, thou shalt sleep with thy fathers; and this people will rise up, and go a-whoring after the gods of the strangers of the land, whither they go *to be* among them, and will forsake me, and break my covenant which I have made with them.

17Then my anger shall be kindled against them in that day, and I will forsake them, and I will hide my face from them, and they shall be devoured, and many evils and troubles shall befall them; so that they will say in that day, Are not these evils come upon us, because our God *is* not among us?

18And I will surely hide my face in that day for all the evils which they shall have wrought, in that they are turned unto other gods.

19Now therefore write ye this song for you, and teach it the children of Israel: put it in their mouths, that this song may be a witness for me against the children of Israel.

20For when I shall have brought them into the land which I sware unto their fathers, that floweth with milk and honey; and they shall have eaten and filled themselves, and waxen fat; then will they turn unto other gods, and serve them, and provoke me, and break my covenant.

## Amplified

**31** AND MOSES went on speaking these words to all Israel.

2And he said to them, I am 120 years old this day; I can no more go out and come in; and the Lord has said to me, You shall not go over this Jordan.

3The Lord your God will Himself go over before you, and He will destroy these nations from before you, and you shall dispossess them; and Joshua shall go over before you, as the Lord has said.

4And the Lord will do to them as He did to Sihon and Og, the kings of the Amorites, and to their land, when He destroyed them.

5And the Lord will give them over to you, and you shall do to them according to all the commandments which I have commanded you.

6Be strong, courageous *and* firm, fear not, nor be in terror before them; for it is the Lord your God Who goes with you; He will not fail you or forsake you.

7And Moses called to Joshua, and said to him in the sight of all Israel, Be strong, courageous *and* firm; for you shall go with this people into the land which the Lord has sworn to their fathers to give them; and you shall cause them to possess it.

8It is the Lord Who goes before you; He will [march] with you; He will not fail you *or* let you go, or forsake you; [let there be no cowardice or flinching, but] fear not, neither become broken [in spirit] (depressed, dismayed and unnerved with alarm).

9And Moses wrote this law, and delivered it to the Levitical priests, who carried the ark of the covenant of the Lord, and to all the elders of Israel.

10And Moses commanded them, At the end of every seven years, at the set time of the year of release [of debtors from their debts], at the feast of booths,

11When all Israel comes to appear before the Lord your God in the place which He chooses [for His sanctuary], you shall read this law before all Israel in their hearing.

12Assemble the people, men, women, and children, and the stranger *and* the sojourner within your towns, that they may hear and learn (reverently) to fear the Lord your God, and be watchful to do all the words of this law,

13And that their children, who have not known it, may hear, and learn (reverently) to fear the Lord your God, as long as you live in the land which you go over Jordan to possess.

14And the Lord said to Moses, Behold, your days are nearing when you must die. Call Joshua, and present yourselves in the tent of meeting, that I may give him his charge. And Moses and Joshua went, and presented themselves in the tent of meeting.

15And the Lord appeared in the tent in a pillar of cloud; and the pillar of cloud stood over the door of the tent.

16And the Lord said to Moses, Behold, you shall sleep with your fathers; and this people will rise up, and play the harlot after the strange gods of the land where they go to be among them, and they will forsake Me, and break My covenant which I have made with them.

17Then My anger will be kindled against them in that day, and I will forsake them and hide My face from them, and they shall be devoured, and many evils and troubles shall befall them; so that they will say in that day, Have not these evils come upon us because our God is not among us?

18And I will surely hide My face in that day because of all the evil which they have done in turning to other gods.

19And now write this song for you, and teach it to the Israelites; put it in their mouths, that this song may be a witness for Me against the Israelites.

20For when I have brought them into the land which I swore to their fathers, that flows with milk and honey, and they have eaten and filled themselves, and become fat; then they will turn to other gods, and serve them, and despise *and* scorn Me, and break My covenant.

## New American Standard

*Moses' Last Counsel*

**31** SO MOSES went and spoke these words to all Israel.
2And he said to them, "I am a hundred and twenty years
old today; I am no longer able to come and go, and the LORD has
said to me, 'You shall not cross this Jordan.'

3"It is the LORD your God who will cross ahead of you; He will
destroy these nations before you, and you shall dispossess them.
Joshua is the one who will cross ahead of you, just as the LORD has
spoken.

4"And the LORD will do to them just as He did to Sihon and
Og, the kings of the Amorites, and to their land, when He destroyed them.

5"And the LORD will deliver them up before you, and you shall
do to them according to all the commandments which I have
commanded you.

6"Be strong and courageous, do not be afraid or tremble at
them, for the LORD your God is the one who goes with you. He
will not fail you or forsake you."

7Then Moses called to Joshua and said to him in the sight of
all Israel, "Be strong and courageous, for you shall go with this
people into the land which the LORD has sworn to their fathers to
give them, and you shall give it to them as an inheritance.

8"And the LORD is the one who goes ahead of you; He will be
with you. He will not fail you or forsake you. Do not fear, or be
dismayed."

9¶ So Moses wrote this law and gave it to the priests, the sons
of Levi who carried the ark of the covenant of the LORD, and to all
the elders of Israel.

10Then Moses commanded them, saying, "At the end of *every*
seven years, at the time of the year of remission of debts, at the
Feast of Booths,

11when all Israel comes to appear before the LORD your God at
the place which He will choose, you shall read this law in front of
all Israel in their hearing.

12"Assemble the people, the men and the women and children
and the alien who is in your town, in order that they may hear and
learn and fear the LORD your God, and be careful to observe all the
words of this law.

13"And their children, who have not known, will hear and learn
to fear the LORD your God, as long as you live on the land which
you are about to cross the Jordan to possess."

*Israel Will Fall Away*

14¶ Then the LORD said to Moses, "Behold, the time for you to
die is near; call Joshua, and present yourselves at the tent of
meeting, that I may commission him." So Moses and Joshua went
and presented themselves at the tent of meeting.

15And the LORD appeared in the tent in a pillar of cloud, and
the pillar of cloud stood at the doorway of the tent.

16And the LORD said to Moses, "Behold, you are about to lie
down with your fathers; and this people will arise and play the
harlot with the strange gods of the land, into the midst of which
they are going, and will forsake Me and break My covenant which
I have made with them.

17"Then My anger will be kindled against them in that day, and
I will forsake them and hide My face from them, and they shall be
consumed, and many evils and troubles shall come upon them; so
that they will say in that day, 'Is it not because our God is not
among us that these evils have come upon us?'

18"But I will surely hide My face in that day because of all the
evil which they will do, for they will turn to other gods.

19"Now therefore, write this song for yourselves, and teach it
to the sons of Israel; put it on their lips, in order that this song may
be a witness for Me against the sons of Israel.

20"For when I bring them into the land flowing with milk and
honey, which I swore to their fathers, and they have eaten and are
satisfied and become prosperous, then they will turn to other gods
and serve them, and spurn Me and break My covenant.

## New International

*Joshua to Succeed Moses*

**31** THEN MOSES went out and spoke these words to all
Israel: 2"I am now a hundred and twenty years old and I
am no longer able to lead you. The LORD has said to me, 'You shall
not cross the Jordan.' 3The LORD your God himself will cross over
ahead of you. He will destroy these nations before you, and you
will take possession of their land. Joshua also will cross over ahead
of you, as the LORD said. 4And the LORD will do to them what he
did to Sihon and Og, the kings of the Amorites, whom he destroyed along with their land. 5The LORD will deliver them to you,
and you must do to them all that I have commanded you. 6Be
strong and courageous. Do not be afraid or terrified because of
them, for the LORD your God goes with you; he will never leave
you nor forsake you."

7Then Moses summoned Joshua and said to him in the presence
of all Israel, "Be strong and courageous, for you must go with this
people into the land that the LORD swore to their forefathers to give
them, and you must divide it among them as their inheritance.
8The LORD himself goes before you and will be with you; he will
never leave you nor forsake you. Do not be afraid; do not be
discouraged."

*The Reading of the Law*

9So Moses wrote down this law and gave it to the priests, the
sons of Levi, who carried the ark of the covenant of the LORD, and
to all the elders of Israel. 10Then Moses commanded them: "At the
end of every seven years, in the year for canceling debts, during
the Feast of Tabernacles, 11when all Israel comes to appear before
the LORD your God at the place he will choose, you shall read this
law before them in their hearing. 12Assemble the people—men,
women and children, and the aliens living in your towns—so they
can listen and learn to fear the LORD your God and follow carefully
all the words of this law. 13Their children, who do not know this
law, must hear it and learn to fear the LORD your God as long as
you live in the land you are crossing the Jordan to possess."

*Israel's Rebellion Predicted*

14The LORD said to Moses, "Now the day of your death is near.
Call Joshua and present yourselves at the Tent of Meeting, where
I will commission him." So Moses and Joshua came and presented
themselves at the Tent of Meeting.

15Then the LORD appeared at the Tent in a pillar of cloud, and
the cloud stood over the entrance to the Tent. 16And the LORD said
to Moses: "You are going to rest with your fathers, and these
people will soon prostitute themselves to the foreign gods of the
land they are entering. They will forsake me and break the covenant I made with them. 17On that day I will become angry with
them and forsake them; I will hide my face from them, and they
will be destroyed. Many disasters and difficulties will come upon
them, and on that day they will ask, 'Have not these disasters
come upon us because our God is not with us?' 18And I will
certainly hide my face on that day because of all their wickedness
in turning to other gods.

19"Now write down for yourselves this song and teach it to the
Israelites and have them sing it, so that it may be a witness for me
against them. 20When I have brought them into the land flowing
with milk and honey, the land I promised on oath to their forefathers, and when they eat their fill and thrive, they will turn to
other gods and worship them, rejecting me and breaking my covenant. 21And when many disasters and difficulties come upon

## King James

21And it shall come to pass, when many evils and troubles are befallen them, that this song shall testify against them as a witness; for it shall not be forgotten out of the mouths of their seed: for I know their imagination which they go about, even now, before I have brought them into the land which I sware.
22¶ Moses therefore wrote this song the same day, and taught it the children of Israel.
23And he gave Joshua the son of Nun a charge, and said, Be strong and of a good courage: for thou shalt bring the children of Israel into the land which I sware unto them: and I will be with thee.
24¶ And it came to pass, when Moses had made an end of writing the words of this law in a book, until they were finished,
25That Moses commanded the Levites, which bare the ark of the covenant of the LORD, saying,
26Take this book of the law, and put it in the side of the ark of the covenant of the LORD your God, that it may be there for a witness against thee.
27For I know thy rebellion, and thy stiff neck: behold, while I am yet alive with you this day, ye have been rebellious against the LORD; and how much more after my death?
28¶ Gather unto me all the elders of your tribes, and your officers, that I may speak these words in their ears, and call heaven and earth to record against them.
29For I know that after my death ye will utterly corrupt *yourselves*, and turn aside from the way which I have commanded you; and evil will befall you in the latter days; because ye will do evil in the sight of the LORD, to provoke him to anger through the work of your hands.
30And Moses spake in the ears of all the congregation of Israel the words of this song, until they were ended.

**32** GIVE EAR, O ye heavens, and I will speak; and hear, O earth, the words of my mouth.
2My doctrine shall drop as the rain, my speech shall distil as the dew, as the small rain upon the tender herb, and as the showers upon the grass:
3Because I will publish the name of the LORD: ascribe ye greatness unto our God.
4 *He is* the Rock, his work *is* perfect: for all his ways *are* judgment: a God of truth and without iniquity, just and right *is* he.
5They have corrupted themselves, their spot *is* not *the spot* of his children: *they are* a perverse and crooked generation.
6Do ye thus requite the LORD, O foolish people and unwise? *is* not he thy father *that* hath bought thee? hath he not made thee, and established thee?
7¶ Remember the days of old, consider the years of many generations: ask thy father, and he will show thee; thy elders, and they will tell thee.
8When the Most High divided to the nations their inheritance, when he separated the sons of Adam, he set the bounds of the people according to the number of the children of Israel.
9For the LORD's portion *is* his people; Jacob *is* the lot of his inheritance.

## Amplified

21And when many evils and troubles have befallen them, this [sacred] song will confront them as a witness, for it will never be forgotten from the mouths of their descendants; for I know their strong desire *and* the purposes which they are forming even now, before I have brought them into the land which I swore to give them.
22Moses wrote this song the same day, and taught it to the Israelites. [See 32:1-43.]
23And [the Lord] charged Joshua son of Nun, Be strong and courageous *and* firm; for you shall bring the Israelites into the land which I swore to give them; and I will be with you.
24And when Moses had finished writing the words of this law in a book to the very end,
25He commanded the Levites who carried the ark of the covenant of the Lord,
26Take this book of the law, and put it by the side of the ark of the covenant of the Lord your God, that it may be there for a witness against you.
27For I know your rebellion and stubbornness; behold, while I am yet alive with you, today you have been rebellious against the Lord; and how much more after my death!
28Gather to me all the elders of your tribes, and your officers, that I may speak these words in their ears and call Heaven and earth to witness against them.
29For I know that after my death you will utterly corrupt yourselves, and turn aside from the way which I have commanded you; and evil will befall you in the latter days; because you will do what is evil in the sight of the Lord, to provoke Him to anger through the work of your hands.
30And Moses spoke in the hearing of all the congregation of Israel the words of this song, until they were ended.

**32** GIVE EAR, O heavens, and I [Moses] will speak; and let the earth hear the words of my mouth.
2My message shall drop as the rain, my speech shall distil as the dew, as the light rain upon the tender grass, and as the showers upon the herb.
3For I will proclaim the name [and presence] of the Lord. Concede *and* ascribe greatness to our God.
4He is the Rock, His work is perfect; for all His ways are law *and* justice, a God of faithfulness, without breach *or* deviation, just and right is He.
5They [Israel] have spoiled themselves. They are not sons to Him, that is their blemish. A perverse and crooked generation!
6Do you thus repay the Lord, you foolish and senseless people? Is not He your Father Who acquired you for His own? Who made and established you [as a nation]?
7Remember the days of old, consider the years of many generations; ask your father, and he will show you, your elders, and they will tell you.
8When the Most High gave to the nations their inheritance, when He separated the children of men, He set the bounds of the peoples according to the number of the Israelites.
9For the Lord's portion is His people; Jacob (Israel) is the lot of His inheritance.

## New American Standard

21"Then it shall come about, when many evils and troubles have come upon them, that this song will testify before them as a witness (for it shall not be forgotten from the lips of their descendants); for I know their intent which they are developing today, before I have brought them into the land which I swore."

22So Moses wrote this song the same day, and taught it to the sons of Israel.

*Joshua Is Commissioned*

23¶ Then He commissioned Joshua the son of Nun, and said, "Be strong and courageous, for you shall bring the sons of Israel into the land which I swore to them, and I will be with you."

24¶ And it came about, when Moses finished writing the words of this law in a book until they were complete,

25that Moses commanded the Levites who carried the ark of the covenant of the LORD, saying,

26"Take this book of the law and place it beside the ark of the covenant of the LORD your God, that it may remain there as a witness against you.

27"For I know your rebellion and your stubbornness; behold, while I am still alive with you today, you have been rebellious against the LORD; how much more, then, after my death?

28"Assemble to me all the elders of your tribes and your officers, that I may speak these words in their hearing and call the heavens and the earth to witness against them.

29"For I know that after my death you will act corruptly and turn from the way which I have commanded you; and evil will befall you in the latter days, for you will do that which is evil in the sight of the LORD, provoking Him to anger with the work of your hands."

30¶ Then Moses spoke in the hearing of all the assembly of Israel the words of this song, until they were complete:

*The Song of Moses*

**32** "GIVE EAR, O heavens, and let me speak;
And let the earth hear the words of my mouth.
2 "Let my teaching drop as the rain,
My speech distill as the dew,
As the droplets on the fresh grass
And as the showers on the herb.
3 "For I proclaim the name of the LORD;
Ascribe greatness to our God!
4 "The Rock! His work is perfect,
For all His ways are just;
A God of faithfulness and without injustice,
Righteous and upright is He.
5 "They have acted corruptly toward Him,
*They are* not His children, because of their defect;
*But are* a perverse and crooked generation.
6 "Do you thus repay the LORD,
O foolish and unwise people?
Is not He your Father who has bought you?
He has made you and established you.
7 "Remember the days of old,
Consider the years of all generations.
Ask your father, and he will inform you,
Your elders, and they will tell you.
8 "When the Most High gave the nations their inheritance,
When He separated the sons of man,
He set the boundaries of the peoples
According to the number of the sons of Israel.
9 "For the LORD's portion is His people;
Jacob is the allotment of His inheritance.

## New International

them, this song will testify against them, because it will not be
forgotten by their descendants. I know what they are disposed to
do, even before I bring them into the land I promised them on
oath." 22So Moses wrote down this song that day and taught it to
the Israelites.

23The LORD gave this command to Joshua son of Nun: "Be
strong and courageous, for you will bring the Israelites into the
land I promised them on oath, and I myself will be with you."

24After Moses finished writing in a book the words of this law
from beginning to end, 25he gave this command to the Levites who
carried the ark of the covenant of the LORD: 26"Take this Book of
the Law and place it beside the ark of the covenant of the LORD
your God. There it will remain as a witness against you. 27For I
know how rebellious and stiff-necked you are. If you have been
rebellious against the LORD while I am still alive and with you, how
much more will you rebel after I die! 28Assemble before me all the
elders of your tribes and all your officials, so that I can speak these
words in their hearing and call heaven and earth to testify against
them. 29For I know that after my death you are sure to become
utterly corrupt and to turn from the way I have commanded you.
In days to come, disaster will fall upon you because you will do
evil in the sight of the LORD and provoke him to anger by what
your hands have made."

*The Song of Moses*

30And Moses recited the words of this song from beginning to
end in the hearing of the whole assembly of Israel:

**32** LISTEN, O heavens, and I will speak;
hear, O earth, the words of my mouth.
2Let my teaching fall like rain
and my words descend like dew,
like showers on new grass,
like abundant rain on tender plants.

3I will proclaim the name of the LORD.
Oh, praise the greatness of our God!
4He is the Rock, his works are perfect,
and all his ways are just.
A faithful God who does no wrong,
upright and just is he.
5They have acted corruptly toward him;
to their shame they are no longer his children,
but a warped and crooked generation.[a]
6Is this the way you repay the LORD,
O foolish and unwise people?
Is he not your Father, your Creator,[b]
who made you and formed you?

7Remember the days of old;
consider the generations long past.
Ask your father and he will tell you,
your elders, and they will explain to you.
8When the Most High gave the nations their inheritance,
when he divided all mankind,
he set up boundaries for the peoples
according to the number of the sons of Israel.[c]
9For the LORD's portion is his people,
Jacob his allotted inheritance.

**NIV** [a] 5 Or *Corrupt are they and not his children, / a generation warped and twisted to their shame* [b] 6 Or *Father, who bought you* [c] 8 Masoretic Text; Dead Sea Scrolls (see also Septuagint) *sons of God*

## King James

10He found him in a desert land, and in the waste howling wilderness; he led him about, he instructed him, he kept him as the apple of his eye.

11As an eagle stirreth up her nest, fluttereth over her young, spreadeth abroad her wings, taketh them, beareth them on her wings:

12 *So* the LORD alone did lead him, and *there was* no strange god with him.

13He made him ride on the high places of the earth, that he might eat the increase of the fields; and he made him to suck honey out of the rock, and oil out of the flinty rock;

14Butter of kine, and milk of sheep, with fat of lambs, and rams of the breed of Bashan, and goats, with the fat of kidneys of wheat; and thou didst drink the pure blood of the grape.

15¶ But Jeshurun waxed fat, and kicked: thou art waxen fat, thou art grown thick, thou art covered *with fatness;* then he forsook God *which* made him, and lightly esteemed the Rock of his salvation.

16They provoked him to jealousy with strange *gods,* with abominations provoked they him to anger.

17They sacrificed unto devils, not to God; to gods whom they knew not, to new *gods that* came newly up, whom your fathers feared not.

18Of the Rock *that* begat thee thou art unmindful, and hast forgotten God that formed thee.

19And when the LORD saw *it,* he abhorred *them,* because of the provoking of his sons, and of his daughters.

20And he said, I will hide my face from them, I will see what their end *shall be:* for they *are* a very froward generation, children in whom *is* no faith.

21They have moved me to jealousy with *that which is* not God; they have provoked me to anger with their vanities: and I will move them to jealousy with *those which are* not a people; I will provoke them to anger with a foolish nation.

22For a fire is kindled in mine anger, and shall burn unto the lowest hell, and shall consume the earth with her increase, and set on fire the foundations of the mountains.

23I will heap mischiefs upon them; I will spend mine arrows upon them.

24 *They shall be* burnt with hunger, and devoured with burning heat, and with bitter destruction: I will also send the teeth of beasts upon them, with the poison of serpents of the dust.

25The sword without, and terror within, shall destroy both the young man and the virgin, the suckling *also* with the man of gray hairs.

26I said, I would scatter them into corners, I would make the remembrance of them to cease from among men:

27Were it not that I feared the wrath of the enemy, lest their adversaries should behave themselves strangely, *and* lest they should say, Our hand *is* high, and the LORD hath not done all this.

28For they *are* a nation void of counsel, neither *is there any* understanding in them.

## Amplified

10He found him in a desert land, in the howling void of the wilderness; He kept circling around him, He scanned him (penetratingly), He kept him as the pupil of His eye.

11As an eagle that stirs up her nest, that flutters over her young, He spread abroad His wings; He took them, He bore them on His pinions. [Luke 13:34.]

12So the Lord alone led him; there was no foreign god with Him.

13He made Israel ride on the high places of the earth, and he ate the increase of the field; and He made him to suck honey out of the rock and oil out of the flinty rock;

14Butter *and* curds of the herd and milk of the flock, with fat of lambs, and rams of the breed of Bashan and he-goats, with the finest of the wheat; and you drank wine of the blood of the grape.

15But Jeshurun (Israel) grew fat and kicked. You became fat, you grew thick, you were gorged *and* sleek! Then he forsook God Who made him, and forsook *and* despised the Rock of his salvation.

16They provoked Him to jealousy with strange gods, with abominations they provoked Him to anger.

17They sacrificed to demons, not to God; to gods whom they knew not, to new gods lately come up, whom your fathers never knew or feared.

18Of the Rock that bore you you were unmindful; you forgot the God Who travailed in your birth.

19And the Lord saw it, He spurned *and* rejected them, from indignation with His sons and His daughters.

20And He said, I will hide My face from them, I will see what their end will be. For they are a perverse generation, children in whom is no faithfulness.

21They have moved Me to jealousy with what is not God; they have angered Me with their idols; so I will move them to jealousy with those not a people; I will anger them with a foolish nation.

22For a fire is kindled by My anger, and it burns to the depths of Sheol, devours the earth with its increase, and sets on fire the foundations of the mountains.

23And I will heap evils upon them; I will spend My arrows upon them.

24They shall be wasted with hunger, and devoured with burning heat and poisonous pestilence; and the teeth of beasts will I send against them, with the poison of crawling things of the dust.

25From without the sword shall bereave, and in the chambers shall be terror, destroying both young man and virgin, the sucking child with the man of gray hairs.

26I said, I would scatter them afar, and I would have made the remembrance of them to cease from among men,

27Had I not feared the provocation of the foe, lest their enemies misconstrue it, and lest they should say, Our own hand has prevailed; all this was not the work of the Lord.

28For they are a nation void of counsel, and there is no understanding in them.

## New American Standard

10 "He found him in a desert land,
And in the howling waste of a wilderness;
He encircled him, He cared for him,
He guarded him as the pupil of His eye.
11 "Like an eagle that stirs up its nest,
That hovers over its young,
He spread His wings and caught them,
He carried them on His pinions.
12 "The LORD alone guided him,
And there was no foreign god with him.
13 "He made him ride on the high places of the earth,
And he ate the produce of the field;
And He made him suck honey from the rock,
And oil from the flinty rock,
14 Curds of cows, and milk of the flock,
With fat of lambs,
And rams, the breed of Bashan, and goats,
With the finest of the wheat—
And of the blood of grapes you drank wine.
15¶ "But [a]Jeshurun grew fat and kicked—
You are grown fat, thick, and sleek—
Then he forsook God who made him,
And scorned the Rock of his salvation.
16 "They made Him jealous with strange *gods;*
With abominations they provoked Him to anger.
17 "They sacrificed to demons who were not God,
To gods whom they have not known,
New *gods* who came lately,
Whom your fathers did not dread.
18 "You neglected the Rock who begot you,
And forgot the God who gave you birth.
19¶ "And the LORD saw *this,* and spurned *them*
Because of the provocation of His sons and daughters.
20 "Then He said, 'I will hide My face from them,
I will see what their end *shall be;*
For they are a perverse generation,
Sons in whom is no faithfulness.
21 'They have made Me jealous with *what* is not God;
They have provoked Me to anger with their idols.
So I will make them jealous with *those who* are not a people;
I will provoke them to anger with a foolish nation,
22 For a fire is kindled in My anger,
And burns to the lowest part of Sheol,
And consumes the earth with its yield,
And sets on fire the foundations of the mountains.

23¶ 'I will heap misfortunes on them;
I will use My arrows on them.
24 '*They shall be* wasted by famine, and consumed by plague
And bitter destruction;
And the teeth of beasts I will send upon them,
With the venom of crawling things of the dust.
25 'Outside the sword shall bereave,
And inside terror—
Both young man and virgin,
The nursling with the man of gray hair.
26 'I would have said, "I will cut them to pieces,
I will remove the memory of them from men,"
27 Had I not feared the provocation by the enemy,
Lest their adversaries should misjudge,
Lest they should say, "Our hand is triumphant,
And the LORD has not done all this." '

28¶ "For they are a nation lacking in counsel,
And there is no understanding in them.

NAS [a] I.e., Israel

## New International

10In a desert land he found him,
in a barren and howling waste.
He shielded him and cared for him;
he guarded him as the apple of his eye,
11like an eagle that stirs up its nest
and hovers over its young,
that spreads its wings to catch them
and carries them on its pinions.
12The LORD alone led him;
no foreign god was with him.

13He made him ride on the heights of the land
and fed him with the fruit of the fields.
He nourished him with honey from the rock,
and with oil from the flinty crag,
14with curds and milk from herd and flock
and with fattened lambs and goats,
with choice rams of Bashan
and the finest kernels of wheat.
You drank the foaming blood of the grape.
15Jeshurun[b] grew fat and kicked;
filled with food, he became heavy and sleek.
He abandoned the God who made him
and rejected the Rock his Savior.
16They made him jealous with their foreign gods
and angered him with their detestable idols.
17They sacrificed to demons, which are not God—
gods they had not known,
gods that recently appeared,
gods your fathers did not fear.
18You deserted the Rock, who fathered you;
you forgot the God who gave you birth.

19The LORD saw this and rejected them
because he was angered by his sons and daughters.
20"I will hide my face from them," he said,
"and see what their end will be;
for they are a perverse generation,
children who are unfaithful.
21They made me jealous by what is no god
and angered me with their worthless idols.
I will make them envious by those who are not a people;
I will make them angry by a nation that has no understanding.
22For a fire has been kindled by my wrath,
one that burns to the realm of death[c] below.
It will devour the earth and its harvests
and set afire the foundations of the mountains.

23"I will heap calamities upon them
and spend my arrows against them.
24I will send wasting famine against them,
consuming pestilence and deadly plague;
I will send against them the fangs of wild beasts,
the venom of vipers that glide in the dust.
25In the street the sword will make them childless;
in their homes terror will reign.
Young men and young women will perish,
infants and gray-haired men.
26I said I would scatter them
and blot out their memory from mankind,
27but I dreaded the taunt of the enemy,
lest the adversary misunderstand
and say, 'Our hand has triumphed;
the LORD has not done all this.' "

28They are a nation without sense,
there is no discernment in them.

NIV [b] *15 Jeshurun* means *the upright one,* that is, Israel. [c] *22* Hebrew *to Sheol*

## King James

29O that they were wise, *that* they understood this, *that* they would consider their latter end!

30How should one chase a thousand, and two put ten thousand to flight, except their Rock had sold them, and the LORD had shut them up?

31For their rock *is* not as our Rock, even our enemies themselves *being* judges.

32For their vine *is* of the vine of Sodom, and of the fields of Gomorrah: their grapes *are* grapes of gall, their clusters *are* bitter:

33Their wine *is* the poison of dragons, and the cruel venom of asps.

34 *Is* not this laid up in store with me, *and* sealed up among my treasures?

35To me *belongeth* vengeance, and recompence; their foot shall slide in *due* time: for the day of their calamity *is* at hand, and the things that shall come upon them make haste.

36For the LORD shall judge his people, and repent himself for his servants, when he seeth that *their* power is gone, and *there is* none shut up, or left.

37And he shall say, Where *are* their gods, *their* rock in whom they trusted,

38Which did eat the fat of their sacrifices, *and* drank the wine of their drink offerings? let them rise up and help you, *and* be your protection.

39See now that I, *even* I, *am* he, and *there is* no god with me: I kill, and I make alive; I wound, and I heal: neither *is there any* that can deliver out of my hand.

40For I lift up my hand to heaven, and say, I live for ever.

41If I whet my glittering sword, and mine hand take hold on judgment; I will render vengeance to mine enemies, and will reward them that hate me.

42I will make mine arrows drunk with blood, and my sword shall devour flesh; *and that* with the blood of the slain and of the captives, from the beginning of revengers upon the enemy.

43Rejoice, O ye nations, *with* his people: for he will avenge the blood of his servants, and will render vengeance to his adversaries, and will be merciful unto his land, *and* to his people.

44¶ And Moses came and spake all the words of this song in the ears of the people, he, and Hoshea the son of Nun.

45And Moses made an end of speaking all these words to all Israel:

46And he said unto them, Set your hearts unto all the words which I testify among you this day, which ye shall command your children to observe to do, all the words of this law.

47For it *is* not a vain thing for you; because it *is* your life: and through this thing ye shall prolong *your* days in the land, whither ye go over Jordan to possess it.

48And the LORD spake unto Moses that selfsame day, saying,

49Get thee up into this mountain Abarim, *unto* mount Nebo, which *is* in the land of Moab, that *is* over against Jericho; and behold the land of Canaan, which I give unto the children of Israel for a possession:

## Amplified

29O that they were wise, and would see through this [present triumph] to their ultimate fate!

30How could one have chased 1,000 and two put 10,000 to flight, except their rock had sold them, and the Lord had delivered them up?

31For their rock is not as our Rock, even our enemies themselves being judges.

32For their vine comes from the vine of Sodom, and from the fields of Gomorrah; their grapes are grapes of (poisonous) gall, their clusters are bitter;

33Their wine is the (furious) venom of serpents, and the pitiless poison of vipers;

34Is not this laid up in store with Me, sealed up in My treasuries?

35Vengeance is Mine, and recompense, for the time when their foot shall slide; for the day of their disaster is at hand, and their doom comes speedily.

36For the Lord will pass sentence for His people, and relent for His servants' sake, when He sees that their power is gone, and none remain, whether bond or free.

37And He will say, Where are their gods, the rock in which they took refuge,

38Who ate the fat of their sacrifices, and drank the wine of their drink offering? Let them rise up and help you, let them be your protection.

39See now that I, I am He, and there is no god beside Me; I kill, and I make alive; I wound, and I heal; and there is none who can deliver out of My hand.

40For I lift up My hand to Heaven, and swear, As I live for ever,

41If I whet My lightning sword, and My hand takes hold on judgment, I will wreak vengeance on My foes, and recompense those who hate Me.

42I will make My arrows drunk with blood, and My sword shall devour flesh with the blood of the slain and the captives, from the long-haired heads of the foe.

43Rejoice *with* His people, O you nations, for He avenges the blood of His servants, and vengeance He inflicts on His foes, and clears guilt from the land of His people.

44And Moses came and spoke all the words of this song in the ears of the people, he and Hoshea (Joshua) son of Nun.

45And when Moses had finished speaking all these words to all Israel,

46He said to them, Set your [minds and] hearts on all the words which I command you this day, that you may command them to your children, that they may be watchful to do all the words of this law.

47For it is not an empty *and* worthless trifle for you; it is your *very* life; by it you shall live long in the land which you are going over the Jordan to possess.

48And the Lord said to Moses that same day,

49Get up into this mountain of the Abarim, Mount Nebo, which is in the land of Moab, opposite Jericho; and look at the land of Canaan, which I give to the Israelites for a possession;

## New American Standard

29 "Would that they were wise, that they understood this,
That they would discern their future!
30 "How could one chase a thousand,
And two put ten thousand to flight,
Unless their Rock had sold them,
And the LORD had given them up?
31 "Indeed their rock is not like our Rock,
Even our enemies themselves judge this.
32 "For their vine is from the vine of Sodom,
And from the fields of Gomorrah;
Their grapes are grapes of poison,
Their clusters, bitter.
33 "Their wine is the venom of serpents,
And the deadly poison of cobras.
**34**¶ 'Is it not laid up in store with Me,
Sealed up in My treasuries?
35 'Vengeance is Mine, and retribution,
In due time their foot will slip;
For the day of their calamity is near,
And the impending things are hastening upon them.'
36 "For the LORD will vindicate His people,
And will have compassion on His servants;
When He sees that *their* strength is gone,
And there is none *remaining,* bond or free.
37 "And He will say, 'Where are their gods,
The rock in which they sought refuge?
38 'Who ate the fat of their sacrifices,
*And* drank the wine of their libation?
Let them rise up and help you,
Let them be your hiding place!
39 'See now that I, I am He,
And there is no god besides Me;
It is I who put to death and give life.
I have wounded, and it is I who heal;
And there is no one who can deliver from My hand.
40 'Indeed, I lift up My hand to heaven,
And say, as I live forever,
41 If I sharpen My flashing sword,
And My hand takes hold on justice,
I will render vengeance on My adversaries,
And I will repay those who hate Me.
42 'I will make My arrows drunk with blood,
And My sword shall devour flesh,
With the blood of the slain and the captives,
From the long-haired leaders of the enemy.'
43 "Rejoice, O nations, *with* His people;
For He will avenge the blood of His servants,
And will render vengeance on His adversaries,
And will atone for His land *and* His people."

**44**¶ Then Moses came and spoke all the words of this song in the hearing of the people, he, with Joshua the son of Nun.

45When Moses had finished speaking all these words to all Israel,

46he said to them, "Take to your heart all the words with which I am warning you today, which you shall command your sons to observe carefully, *even* all the words of this law.

47"For it is not an idle word for you; indeed it is your life. And by this word you shall prolong your days in the land, which you are about to cross the Jordan to possess."

**48**¶ And the LORD spoke to Moses that very same day, saying,

49"Go up to this mountain of the Abarim, Mount Nebo, which is in the land of Moab opposite Jericho, and look at the land of Canaan, which I am giving to the sons of Israel for a possession.

## New International

29If only they were wise and would understand this
and discern what their end will be!
30How could one man chase a thousand,
or two put ten thousand to flight,
unless their Rock had sold them,
unless the LORD had given them up?
31For their rock is not like our Rock,
as even our enemies concede.
32Their vine comes from the vine of Sodom
and from the fields of Gomorrah.
Their grapes are filled with poison,
and their clusters with bitterness.
33Their wine is the venom of serpents,
the deadly poison of cobras.

34"Have I not kept this in reserve
and sealed it in my vaults?
35It is mine to avenge; I will repay.
In due time their foot will slip;
their day of disaster is near
and their doom rushes upon them."
36The LORD will judge his people
and have compassion on his servants
when he sees their strength is gone
and no one is left, slave or free.
37He will say: "Now where are their gods,
the rock they took refuge in,
38the gods who ate the fat of their sacrifices
and drank the wine of their drink offerings?
Let them rise up to help you!
Let them give you shelter!

39"See now that I myself am He!
There is no god besides me.
I put to death and I bring to life,
I have wounded and I will heal,
and no one can deliver out of my hand.
40I lift my hand to heaven and declare:
As surely as I live forever,
41when I sharpen my flashing sword
and my hand grasps it in judgment,
I will take vengeance on my adversaries
and repay those who hate me.
42I will make my arrows drunk with blood,
while my sword devours flesh:
the blood of the slain and the captives,
the heads of the enemy leaders."

43Rejoice, O nations, with his people,[a,b]
for he will avenge the blood of his servants;
he will take vengeance on his enemies
and make atonement for his land and people.

44Moses came with Joshua[c] son of Nun and spoke all the words of this song in the hearing of the people. 45When Moses finished reciting all these words to all Israel, 46he said to them, "Take to heart all the words I have solemnly declared to you this day, so that you may command your children to obey carefully all the words of this law. 47They are not just idle words for you—they are your life. By them you will live long in the land you are crossing the Jordan to possess."

*Moses to Die on Mount Nebo*

48On that same day the LORD told Moses, 49"Go up into the Abarim Range to Mount Nebo in Moab, across from Jericho, and view Canaan, the land I am giving the Israelites as their own possession. 50There on the mountain that you have climbed you

**NIV** [a] 43 Or *Make his people rejoice, O nations* [b] 43 Masoretic Text; Dead Sea Scrolls (see also Septuagint) *people, / and let all the angels worship him /* [c] 44 Hebrew *Hoshea,* a variant of *Joshua*

## King James

50And die in the mount whither thou goest up, and be gathered
unto thy people; as Aaron thy brother died in mount Hor, and was
gathered unto his people:
51Because ye trespassed against me among the children of Israel
at the waters of Meribah-Kadesh, in the wilderness of Zin; because
ye sanctified me not in the midst of the children of Israel.
52Yet thou shalt see the land before *thee;* but thou shalt not go
thither unto the land which I give the children of Israel.

**33** AND THIS *is* the blessing, wherewith Moses the man of
God blessed the children of Israel before his death.
2And he said, The LORD came from Sinai, and rose up from Seir
unto them; he shined forth from mount Paran, and he came with
ten thousands of saints: from his right hand *went* a fiery law for
them.
3Yea, he loved the people; all his saints *are* in thy hand: and they
sat down at thy feet; *every one* shall receive of thy words.
4Moses commanded us a law, *even* the inheritance of the congregation of Jacob.
5And he was king in Jeshurun, when the heads of the people
*and* the tribes of Israel were gathered together.
6¶ Let Reuben live, and not die; and let *not* his men be few.
7¶ And this *is the blessing* of Judah: and he said, Hear, LORD, the
voice of Judah, and bring him unto his people: let his hands be
sufficient for him; and be thou an help *to him* from his enemies.
8¶ And of Levi he said, *Let* thy Thummim and thy Urim *be* with
thy holy one, whom thou didst prove at Massah, *and with* whom
thou didst strive at the waters of Meribah;
9Who said unto his father and to his mother, I have not seen
him; neither did he acknowledge his brethren, nor knew his own
children: for they have observed thy word, and kept thy covenant.
10They shall teach Jacob thy judgments, and Israel thy law: they
shall put incense before thee, and whole burnt sacrifice upon thine
altar.
11Bless, LORD, his substance, and accept the work of his hands:
smite through the loins of them that rise against him, and of them
that hate him, that they rise not again.
12¶ *And* of Benjamin he said, The beloved of the LORD shall
dwell in safety by him; *and the LORD* shall cover him all the day long,
and he shall dwell between his shoulders.

## Amplified

50And die on the mountain which you ascend, and be gathered
to your people, as Aaron your brother died on Mount Hor and was
gathered to his people;
51Because you broke faith with Me in the midst of the Israelites
at the waters of Meribah of Kadesh, in the wilderness of Zin;
because you did not set Me apart as holy in the midst of the
Israelites.
52For you shall see the land over opposite you, but you shall not
go there, into the land which I give the Israelites.

**33** THIS IS the blessing with which Moses the man of God
blessed the Israelites before his death.
2He said, The Lord came from Sinai and beamed upon us from
Seir; He flashed forth from Mount Paran, from among ten thousands of holy ones, a flaming fire, a law, at His right hand.
3Yes, He loves [the tribes] His people; all those consecrated to
Him are in Your hand. They followed in Your steps; they [accepted
Your word and] received direction from You,
4When Moses commanded us a law, as a possession for the
assembly of Jacob.
5[The Lord] was King in Jeshurun (Israel), when the heads of
the people were gathered, all the tribes of Israel together.
6Let [the tribe of] Reuben live, and not die out, but [a]let his men
be few.
7And this [Moses] said to Judah: Hear, O Lord, the voice of
Judah, and bring him to his people! With his hands he contended
for himself, but You be a help to him against his enemies.
8And of Levi he said, Your Thummim and Your Urim [by which
the priest sought God's will for the nation] are for your pious one
[Aaron for the tribe], whom You tried *and* proved at Massah, with
whom You contended at the waters of Meribah; [Num. 20:1-13.]
9[Aaron], who [b]said of his father and mother, I do not regard
them, nor did he acknowledge his brothers, or openly recognize
his own children. For the priests observed Your word and kept
Your covenant [as to their limitations].
10[The priests] shall teach Jacob Your ordinances, and Israel
Your law; they shall put incense before You, and whole burnt
offering upon Your altar.
11Bless, O Lord, [Levi's] substance, and accept the work of his
hands; crush the loins of his adversaries, and of those who hate
him, that they arise no more.
12Of Benjamin he said, The beloved of the Lord shall [c]dwell in
safety by Him; He covers him all the day long, and makes His
dwelling between his shoulders.

**AMP** [a] The earlier Bible translators could not believe that Moses meant to say of Reuben, "let his men be few," so they put "not" in it in italics: "let *not* his men be few." But Reuben had committed a grave offense (Gen. 49:3, 4), which canceled his birthright, and God meant exactly what He directed Moses to say, as continuous fulfillment of the prophecy proves. "In Judg. 5:16 the tribe [of Reuben] is scorned for its failure to join the others against the Canaanites, and except for I Chron. 5:3-20 it does not again appear in Israel's history. Nor does Misha of Moab, ninth century, B.C. name it" *(Cambridge Bible).* Furthermore, by 1951 A.D. no Jew was permitted to enter the territory once allotted to the tribe of Reuben. "The whole territory, which is . . . quite capable of cultivation, is now deserted by its settled inhabitants" *(Davis' Bible Dictionary).* It was then being restored, not by Israelites, but by Arabs. [b] The law required that the high priest act as impartially when one of his immediate family died as if the departed were no kin to him (Lev. 21:10-12). This throws light on Christ's attitude toward His mother and brethren in Matt. 12:46-50. Cp. Heb. 8:1-6; 3:1-3. [c] The temple in Jerusalem was located almost between the ridges of the territory of Benjamin, suggesting "between his shoulders" (cp. Josh. 15:8). Moses sees it as a symbol of the Lord's presence covering Benjamin continually.

## New American Standard

50"Then die on the mountain where you ascend, and be gathered to your people, as Aaron your brother died on Mount Hor and was gathered to his people,
51because you broke faith with Me in the midst of the sons of Israel at the waters of Meribah-kadesh, in the wilderness of Zin, because you did not treat Me as holy in the midst of the sons of Israel.
52"For you shall see the land at a distance, but you shall not go there, into the land which I am giving the sons of Israel."

*The Blessing of Moses*

**33** NOW THIS is the blessing with which Moses the man of God blessed the sons of Israel before his death.
2And he said,
"The LORD came from Sinai,
And dawned on them from Seir;
He shone forth from Mount Paran,
And He came from the midst of ten thousand holy ones;
At His right hand there was flashing lightning for them.
3 "Indeed, He loves the people;
All Thy holy ones are in Thy hand,
And they followed in Thy steps;
*Everyone* receives of Thy words.
4 "Moses charged us with a law,
A possession for the assembly of Jacob.
5 "And He was king in Jeshurun,
When the heads of the people were gathered,
The tribes of Israel together.

6¶ "May Reuben live and not die,
Nor his men be few."

7¶ And this regarding Judah; so he said,
"Hear, O LORD, the voice of Judah,
And bring him to his people.
With his hands he contended for them;
And mayest Thou be a help against his adversaries."

8¶ And of Levi he said,
"*Let* Thy Thummim and Thy Urim *belong* to Thy godly man,
Whom Thou didst prove at Massah,
With whom Thou didst contend at the waters of Meribah;
9 Who said of his father and his mother,
'I did not consider them';
And he did not acknowledge his brothers,
Nor did he regard his own sons,
For they observed Thy word,
And kept Thy covenant.
10 "They shall teach Thine ordinances to Jacob,
And Thy law to Israel.
They shall put incense before Thee,
And whole burnt offerings on Thine altar.
11 "O LORD, bless his substance,
And accept the work of his hands;
Shatter the loins of those who rise up against him,
And those who hate him, so that they may not rise *again*."

12¶ Of Benjamin he said,
"May the beloved of the LORD dwell in security by Him,
Who shields him all the day,
And he dwells between His shoulders."

## New International

will die and be gathered to your people, just as your brother Aaron died on Mount Hor and was gathered to his people. 51This is because both of you broke faith with me in the presence of the Israelites at the waters of Meribah Kadesh in the Desert of Zin and because you did not uphold my holiness among the Israelites. 52Therefore, you will see the land only from a distance; you will not enter the land I am giving to the people of Israel."

*Moses Blesses the Tribes*

**33** THIS IS the blessing that Moses the man of God pronounced on the Israelites before his death. 2He said:

"The LORD came from Sinai
and dawned over them from Seir;
he shone forth from Mount Paran.
He came with[d] myriads of holy ones
from the south, from his mountain slopes.[e]
3Surely it is you who love the people;
all the holy ones are in your hand.
At your feet they all bow down,
and from you receive instruction,
4the law that Moses gave us,
the possession of the assembly of Jacob.
5He was king over Jeshurun[f]
when the leaders of the people assembled,
along with the tribes of Israel.
6"Let Reuben live and not die,
nor[g] his men be few."

7And this he said about Judah:

"Hear, O LORD, the cry of Judah;
bring him to his people.
With his own hands he defends his cause.
Oh, be his help against his foes!"

8About Levi he said:

"Your Thummim and Urim belong
to the man you favored.
You tested him at Massah;
you contended with him at the waters of Meribah.
9He said of his father and mother,
'I have no regard for them.'
He did not recognize his brothers
or acknowledge his own children,
but he watched over your word
and guarded your covenant.
10He teaches your precepts to Jacob
and your law to Israel.
He offers incense before you
and whole burnt offerings on your altar.
11Bless all his skills, O LORD,
and be pleased with the work of his hands.
Smite the loins of those who rise up against him;
strike his foes till they rise no more."

12About Benjamin he said:

"Let the beloved of the LORD rest secure in him,
for he shields him all day long,
and the one the LORD loves rests between his shoulders."

**NIV** d 2 Or *from* e 2 The meaning of the Hebrew for this phrase is uncertain. f 5 *Jeshurun* means *the upright one,* that is, Israel; also in verse 26. g 6 Or *but let*

## King James

13¶ And of Joseph he said, Blessed of the LORD *be* his land, for the precious things of heaven, for the dew, and for the deep that coucheth beneath,

14 And for the precious fruits *brought forth* by the sun, and for the precious things put forth by the moon,

15 And for the chief things of the ancient mountains, and for the precious things of the lasting hills,

16 And for the precious things of the earth and fulness thereof, and *for* the good will of him that dwelt in the bush: let *the blessing* come upon the head of Joseph, and upon the top of the head of him *that was* separated from his brethren.

17 His glory *is like* the firstling of his bullock, and his horns *are like* the horns of unicorns: with them he shall push the people together to the ends of the earth: and they *are* the ten thousands of Ephraim, and they *are* the thousands of Manasseh.

18¶ And of Zebulun he said, Rejoice, Zebulun, in thy going out; and, Issachar, in thy tents.

19 They shall call the people unto the mountain; there they shall offer sacrifices of righteousness: for they shall suck *of* the abundance of the seas, and *of* treasures hid in the sand.

20¶ And of Gad he said, Blessed *be* he that enlargeth Gad: he dwelleth as a lion, and teareth the arm with the crown of the head.

21 And he provided the first part for himself, because there, *in* a portion of the lawgiver, *was he* seated; and he came with the heads of the people, he executed the justice of the LORD, and his judgments with Israel.

22¶ And of Dan he said, Dan *is* a lion's whelp: he shall leap from Bashan.

23¶ And of Naphtali he said, O Naphtali, satisfied with favour, and full with the blessing of the LORD: possess thou the west and the south.

24¶ And of Asher he said, *Let* Asher *be* blessed with children; let him be acceptable to his brethren, and let him dip his foot in oil.

25 Thy shoes *shall be* iron and brass; and as thy days, *so shall* thy strength *be*.

26¶ *There is* none like unto the God of Jeshurun, *who* rideth upon the heaven in thy help, and in his excellency on the sky.

27 The eternal God *is thy* refuge, and underneath *are* the everlasting arms: and he shall thrust out the enemy from before thee; and shall say, Destroy *them*.

28 Israel then shall dwell in safety alone: the fountain of Jacob *shall be* upon a land of corn and wine; also his heavens shall drop down dew.

## Amplified

13 And of Joseph he said, Blessed by the Lord be his land, with the precious gifts of Heaven, from the dew, and from the deep that couches beneath,

14 From the precious things of the fruits of the sun, and from the precious yield of the months,

15 From the chief products of the ancient mountains, and from the precious things of the everlasting hills,

16 With the precious things of the earth and its fullness, and the favor *and* good will of Him Who dwelt in the bush. Let these blessings come upon the head of Joseph, upon the crown of the head of him who was separate *and* prince among his brothers. [Exod. 3:4.]

17 Like a firstling young bull his majesty is, and his horns like the horns of the wild ox; with them he shall push the peoples, all of them, to the ends of the earth; and they are the ten thousands of Ephraim, and they are the thousands of Manasseh.

18 And of Zebulun he said, [a]Rejoice, Zebulun, in your interests abroad; and you, Issachar, in your tents [at home].

19 They shall call the people unto Mount [Carmel]; there they shall offer sacrifices of righteousness, for [b]they shall suck the abundance of the seas, and the treasures hid in the sand.

20 And of Gad he said, Blessed be He Who enlarges Gad! Gad lurks like a lioness, and tears the arm, yes, the crown of the head.

21 He selected the best land for himself, for there was the leader's portion reserved; yet he came with the chiefs of the nation, and the righteous will of the Lord he performed, and His ordinances with Israel. [Num. 32:29-33.]

22 Of Dan he said, Dan is a lion's whelp that leaps forth from Bashan.

23 Of Naphtali he said, O Naphtali, [c]satisfied with favor, and full of the blessing of the Lord, possess the sea [of Galilee] and [its warm, sunny climate like] the south.

24 Of Asher he said, Blessed above sons be Asher; let him be acceptable to his brothers, and [d]let him dip his foot in oil.

25 Your castles and strongholds shall have bars of iron and bronze; and as your day so shall your strength, your rest *and* security, be.

26 There is none like God, O Jeshurun [Israel], Who rides through the heavens to your help, and in His majestic glory through the sky.

27 The eternal God is your refuge *and* dwelling place, and underneath are the everlasting arms; He drove the enemy before you *and* thrust them out, saying, Destroy!

28 And Israel dwells in safety, the fountain of Jacob alone in a land of grain and new wine; yes, His heavens drop dew.

**AMP** [a] Not until 1934 was this prophecy notably in process of fulfillment, when Haifa's bay became one of the great harbors of the Mediterranean, with commerce affecting the whole world. [b] The great oil pipeline path across Palestine was first opened in 1935. Until then this prophecy fell far short of fulfillment. But 3400 years before, Moses sent out the inspired headlines, "Zebulun . . . Issachar . . . shall suck of the abundance of the seas, and of the treasures hid in the sand." Our omnipotent God was "declaring the end *and* the result from the beginning, and from ancient times the things that are not yet done, saying, My counsel shall stand" (Isa. 46:10). [c] For many centuries much of the territory of upper Naphtali was little more than a miasmic swamp, unfit for man or beast. But when the Jews last returned to Palestine they drained and redeemed the area, and by 1940 it was dotted over with thriving colonies, as Moses had foretold, "satisfied with favor, and full of the blessing of the Lord." [d] The maps of the territory of Asher suggest sometimes the sole of a foot, sometimes the shape of a leg and foot; but in either case the Great International Iraq-Petroleum Enterprise, opened in 1935, crossed the area just at the toe of Asher's "foot." Oil brought nearly 1,000 miles across the sands from Mesopotamia began pouring through pipes into the Haifa harbor a million gallons of oil a day. Jacob had said, "In the latter days . . . Asher, his bread shall be fat" (Gen. 49:1, 20), and here Moses says of Asher, "Let him dip his foot in oil"!

## New American Standard

13¶ And of Joseph he said,
"Blessed of the LORD *be* his land,
With the choice things of heaven, with the dew,
And from the deep lying beneath,
14 And with the choice yield of the sun,
And with the choice produce of the months.
15 "And with the best things of the ancient mountains,
And with the choice things of the everlasting hills,
16 And with the choice things of the earth and its fulness,
And the favor of Him who dwelt in the bush.
Let it come to the head of Joseph,
And to the crown of the head of the one distinguished among his brothers.
17 "As the first-born of his ox, majesty is his,
And his horns are the horns of the wild ox;
With them he shall push the peoples,
All at once, *to* the ends of the earth.
And those are the ten thousands of Ephraim,
And those are the thousands of Manasseh."

18¶ And of Zebulun he said,
"Rejoice, Zebulun, in your going forth,
And, Issachar, in your tents.
19 "They shall call peoples *to* the mountain;
There they shall offer righteous sacrifices;
For they shall draw out the abundance of the seas,
And the hidden treasures of the sand."

20¶ And of Gad he said,
"Blessed is the one who enlarges Gad;
He lies down as a lion,
And tears the arm, also the crown of the head.
21 "Then he provided the first *part* for himself,
For there the ruler's portion was reserved;
And he came *with* the leaders of the people;
He executed the justice of the LORD,
And His ordinances with Israel."

22¶ And of Dan he said,
"Dan is a lion's whelp,
That leaps forth from Bashan."

23¶ And of Naphtali he said,
"O Naphtali, satisfied with favor,
And full of the blessing of the LORD,
Take possession of the sea and the south."

24¶ And of Asher he said,
"More blessed than sons is Asher;
May he be favored by his brothers,
And may he dip his foot in oil.
25 "Your locks shall be iron and bronze,
And according to your days, so shall your leisurely walk be.

26¶ "There is none like the God of [e]Jeshurun,
Who rides the heavens to your help,
And through the skies in His majesty.
27 "The eternal God is a dwelling place,
And underneath are the everlasting arms;
And He drove out the enemy from before you,
And said, 'Destroy!'
28 "So Israel dwells in security,
The fountain of Jacob secluded,
In a land of grain and new wine;
His heavens also drop down dew.

NAS [e] I.e., Israel

## New International

13 About Joseph he said:

"May the LORD bless his land
with the precious dew from heaven above
and with the deep waters that lie below;
14 with the best the sun brings forth
and the finest the moon can yield;
15 with the choicest gifts of the ancient mountains
and the fruitfulness of the everlasting hills;
16 with the best gifts of the earth and its fullness
and the favor of him who dwelt in the burning bush.
Let all these rest on the head of Joseph,
on the brow of the prince among[f] his brothers.
17 In majesty he is like a firstborn bull;
his horns are the horns of a wild ox.
With them he will gore the nations,
even those at the ends of the earth.
Such are the ten thousands of Ephraim;
such are the thousands of Manasseh."

18 About Zebulun he said:

"Rejoice, Zebulun, in your going out,
and you, Issachar, in your tents.
19 They will summon peoples to the mountain
and there offer sacrifices of righteousness;
they will feast on the abundance of the seas,
on the treasures hidden in the sand."

20 About Gad he said:

"Blessed is he who enlarges Gad's domain!
Gad lives there like a lion,
tearing at arm or head.
21 He chose the best land for himself;
the leader's portion was kept for him.
When the heads of the people assembled,
he carried out the LORD's righteous will,
and his judgments concerning Israel."

22 About Dan he said:

"Dan is a lion's cub,
springing out of Bashan."

23 About Naphtali he said:

"Naphtali is abounding with the favor of the LORD
and is full of his blessing;
he will inherit southward to the lake."

24 About Asher he said:

"Most blessed of sons is Asher;
let him be favored by his brothers,
and let him bathe his feet in oil.
25 The bolts of your gates will be iron and bronze,
and your strength will equal your days.

26 "There is no one like the God of Jeshurun,
who rides on the heavens to help you
and on the clouds in his majesty.
27 The eternal God is your refuge,
and underneath are the everlasting arms.
He will drive out your enemy before you,
saying, 'Destroy him!'
28 So Israel will live in safety alone;
Jacob's spring is secure
in a land of grain and new wine,
where the heavens drop dew.

NIV [f] 16 Or *of the one separated from*

## King James

29Happy *art* thou, O Israel: who *is* like unto thee, O people saved by the LORD, the shield of thy help, and who *is* the sword of thy excellency! and thine enemies shall be found liars unto thee; and thou shalt tread upon their high places.

**34** AND MOSES went up from the plains of Moab unto the mountain of Nebo, to the top of Pisgah, that *is* over against Jericho. And the LORD showed him all the land of Gilead, unto Dan,

2And all Naphtali, and the land of Ephraim, and Manasseh, and all the land of Judah, unto the utmost sea,

3And the south, and the plain of the valley of Jericho, the city of palm trees, unto Zoar.

4And the LORD said unto him, This *is* the land which I sware unto Abraham, unto Isaac, and unto Jacob, saying, I will give it unto thy seed: I have caused thee to see *it* with thine eyes, but thou shalt not go over thither.

5¶ So Moses the servant of the LORD died there in the land of Moab, according to the word of the LORD.

6And he buried him in a valley in the land of Moab, over against Beth-peor: but no man knoweth of his sepulchre unto this day.

7¶ And Moses *was* an hundred and twenty years old when he died: his eye was not dim, nor his natural force abated.

8¶ And the children of Israel wept for Moses in the plains of Moab thirty days: so the days of weeping *and* mourning for Moses were ended.

9¶ And Joshua the son of Nun was full of the spirit of wisdom; for Moses had laid his hands upon him: and the children of Israel hearkened unto him, and did as the LORD commanded Moses.

10¶ And there arose not a prophet since in Israel like unto Moses, whom the LORD knew face to face,

11In all the signs and the wonders, which the LORD sent him to do in the land of Egypt to Pharaoh, and to all his servants, and to all his land,

12And in all that mighty hand, and in all the great terror which Moses showed in the sight of all Israel.

## Amplified

29Happy are you, O Israel, *and* blessing is yours! Who is like you, a people saved by the Lord, the shield of your help, the sword that exalts you! Your enemies shall come fawning *and* cringing, *and* submit feigned obedience to you, and you shall march on their high places.

**34** AND MOSES went up from the plains of Moab to Mount Nebo, to the top of Pisgah, that is opposite Jericho. And the Lord showed him all the land, Gilead to Dan,

2And all Naphtali, and the land of Ephraim and Manasseh, and all the land of Judah, to the western [Mediterranean] sea.

3And the South (the Negeb) and the Plain, that is, the valley of Jericho the city of palm trees, as far as Zoar.

4And the Lord said to him, This is the land which I swore to Abraham, Isaac, and Jacob, saying, I will give it to your descendants. I have let you see it with your eyes, but you shall not go over there.

5So Moses the servant of the Lord died there in the land of Moab, according to the word of the Lord,

6And He buried him in the valley of the land of Moab, opposite Beth-peor; but no man knows where his tomb is to this day.

7Moses was 120 years old when he died; his eye was not dim, nor his natural force abated. [But cp. 31:2.]

8And the Israelites wept for Moses in the plains of Moab thirty days; then the days of weeping and mourning for Moses were ended.

9And Joshua son of Nun was full of the spirit of wisdom, for Moses had laid his hands upon him; so the Israelites listened to him, and did as the Lord commanded Moses.

10And there arose not a prophet since in Israel like Moses, whom the Lord knew face to face,

11[None equal to him] in all the signs and wonders, which the Lord sent him to do in the land of Egypt, to Pharaoh and to all his servants and to all his land,

12And in all the mighty power and all the great and terrible deeds which Moses wrought in the sight of all Israel.

## New American Standard

29 "Blessed are you, O Israel;
Who is like you, a people saved by the LORD,
Who is the shield of your help,
And the sword of your majesty!
So your enemies shall cringe before you,
And you shall tread upon their high places."

*The Death of Moses*

**34** NOW MOSES went up from the plains of Moab to Mount Nebo, to the top of Pisgah, which is opposite Jericho. And the LORD showed him all the land, Gilead as far as Dan,

2and all Naphtali and the land of Ephraim and Manasseh, and all the land of Judah as far as the [a]western sea,

3and the Negev and the plain in the valley of Jericho, the city of palm trees, as far as Zoar.

4Then the LORD said to him, "This is the land which I swore to Abraham, Isaac, and Jacob, saying, 'I will give it to your descendants'; I have let you see *it* with your eyes, but you shall not go over there."

5So Moses the servant of the LORD died there in the land of Moab, according to the word of the LORD.

6And He buried him in the valley in the land of Moab, opposite Beth-peor; but no man knows his burial place to this day.

7Although Moses was one hundred and twenty years old when he died, his eye was not dim, nor his vigor abated.

8So the sons of Israel wept for Moses in the plains of Moab thirty days; then the days of weeping *and* mourning for Moses came to an end.

9¶ Now Joshua the son of Nun was filled with the spirit of wisdom, for Moses had laid his hands on him; and the sons of Israel listened to him and did as the LORD had commanded Moses.

10Since then no prophet has risen in Israel like Moses, whom the LORD knew face to face,

11for all the signs and wonders which the LORD sent him to perform in the land of Egypt against Pharaoh, all his servants, and all his land,

12and for all the mighty power and for all the great terror which Moses performed in the sight of all Israel.

NAS [a] I.e., Mediterranean Sea

## New International

29Blessed are you, O Israel!
Who is like you,
a people saved by the LORD?
He is your shield and helper
and your glorious sword.
Your enemies will cower before you,
and you will trample down their high places.[b]"

*The Death of Moses*

**34** THEN MOSES climbed Mount Nebo from the plains of
Moab to the top of Pisgah, across from Jericho. There the
LORD showed him the whole land—from Gilead to Dan, 2all of
Naphtali, the territory of Ephraim and Manasseh, all the land of
Judah as far as the western sea,[c] 3the Negev and the whole region
from the Valley of Jericho, the City of Palms, as far as Zoar. 4Then
the LORD said to him, "This is the land I promised on oath to
Abraham, Isaac and Jacob when I said, 'I will give it to your
descendants.' I have let you see it with your eyes, but you will not
cross over into it."
5And Moses the servant of the LORD died there in Moab, as the
LORD had said. 6He buried him[d] in Moab, in the valley opposite
Beth Peor, but to this day no one knows where his grave is. 7Moses
was a hundred and twenty years old when he died, yet his eyes
were not weak nor his strength gone. 8The Israelites grieved for
Moses in the plains of Moab thirty days, until the time of weeping
and mourning was over.
9Now Joshua son of Nun was filled with the spirit[e] of wisdom
because Moses had laid his hands on him. So the Israelites listened
to him and did what the LORD had commanded Moses.
10Since then, no prophet has risen in Israel like Moses, whom
the LORD knew face to face, 11who did all those miraculous signs
and wonders the LORD sent him to do in Egypt—to Pharaoh and
to all his officials and to his whole land. 12For no one has ever
shown the mighty power or performed the awesome deeds that
Moses did in the sight of all Israel.

NIV [b] 29 Or *will tread upon their bodies* [c] 2 That is, the Mediterranean [d] 6 Or *He was buried* [e] 9 Or *Spirit*

## King James

THE BOOK OF

# Joshua

1 NOW AFTER the death of Moses the servant of the LORD it
came to pass, that the LORD spake unto Joshua the son of
Nun, Moses' minister, saying,
2Moses my servant is dead; now therefore arise, go over this
Jordan, thou, and all this people, unto the land which I do give to
them, *even* to the children of Israel.
3Every place that the sole of your foot shall tread upon, that
have I given unto you, as I said unto Moses.
4From the wilderness and this Lebanon even unto the great
river, the river Euphrates, all the land of the Hittites, and unto the
great sea toward the going down of the sun, shall be your coast.
5There shall not any man be able to stand before thee all the
days of thy life: as I was with Moses, *so* I will be with thee: I will
not fail thee, nor forsake thee.
6Be strong and of a good courage: for unto this people shalt thou
divide for an inheritance the land, which I sware unto their fathers
to give them.
7Only be thou strong and very courageous, that thou mayest
observe to do according to all the law, which Moses my servant
commanded thee: turn not from it *to* the right hand or *to* the left,
that thou mayest prosper whithersoever thou goest.
8This book of the law shall not depart out of thy mouth; but thou
shalt meditate therein day and night, that thou mayest observe to
do according to all that is written therein: for then thou shalt make
thy way prosperous, and then thou shalt have good success.
9Have not I commanded thee? Be strong and of a good courage;
be not afraid, neither be thou dismayed: for the LORD thy God *is*
with thee whithersoever thou goest.
10¶ Then Joshua commanded the officers of the people, saying,
11Pass through the host, and command the people, saying,
Prepare you victuals; for within three days ye shall pass over this
Jordan, to go in to possess the land, which the LORD your God
giveth you to possess it.
12¶ And to the Reubenites, and to the Gadites, and to half the
tribe of Manasseh, spake Joshua, saying,
13Remember the word which Moses the servant of the LORD
commanded you, saying, The LORD your God hath given you rest,
and hath given you this land.
14Your wives, your little ones, and your cattle, shall remain in
the land which Moses gave you on this side Jordan; but ye shall
pass before your brethren armed, all the mighty men of valour,
and help them;

## Amplified

THE BOOK OF

# Joshua

1 AFTER THE death of Moses the servant of the Lord, the Lord
said to Joshua, son of Nun, Moses' minister, [Deut. 34:4-8.]
2Moses My servant is dead; so now arise [take his place], go
over this Jordan, you and all this people, into the land which I am
giving to them, the Israelites.
3Every place upon which the sole of your foot shall tread, that
I have given to you, as I promised Moses.
4From the wilderness and this Lebanon to the great river Euphrates, all the land of the [a]Hittites [meaning Canaan], and to the
Great [Mediterranean] Sea on the west shall be your territory.
5No man shall be able to stand before you all the days of your
life. As I was with Moses, so I will be with you; I will not fail you
or forsake you.
6Be strong [confident], and of good courage, for you shall cause
this people to inherit the land, which I swore to their fathers to give
them.
7Only you be strong, and very courageous, that you may do
according to all the law, which Moses My servant commanded
you. Turn not from it to the right hand or to the left, that you may
prosper wherever you go.
8This book of the law shall not depart out of your mouth, but
you shall meditate on it day and night, that you may observe *and*
do according to all that is written in it; for then you shall make your
way prosperous, and then you shall deal wisely *and* have good
[b]success.
9Have not I commanded you? Be strong, vigorous and very
courageous; be not afraid, neither be dismayed; for the Lord your
God is with you wherever you go.
10Then Joshua commanded the officers of the people, saying,
11Pass through the camp, and command the people, Prepare
your provisions; for within three days you shall pass over this
Jordan, to go in to take possession of the land, which the Lord your
God is giving you to possess.
12And to the Reubenites, the Gadites, and the half-tribe of
Manasseh Joshua said,
13Remember what Moses the servant of the Lord commanded
you, saying, The Lord your God is giving you [of these two and
a half tribes a place of] rest, and will give you this land [east of the
Jordan].
14Your wives, your little ones, and your cattle shall dwell in the
land which Moses gave you on this side Jordan; but all your mighty
men of valor shall pass on before your brethren [of the other tribes]
armed, and help them [possess their land].

**AMP** [a] Although the Hittites are mentioned forty-eight times in the Bible, some critics long refused to accept the possibility or at least the probability of the importance of such an ancient people. But archaeological discoveries of the twentieth century have confirmed the importance of the Hittites beyond all question. For instance, G. A. Barton in *Archaeology and the Bible* records the existence of an archive of clay tablets containing among other things a military treaty made by the Egyptians and the Hittites nearly thirteen centuries before the birth of Christ. [b] This is the only place in the early English versions where the word "success" is found. The secret of success is given in verses 5 to 9. Joshua accepted Moses' place of leadership without misgivings. God's will for him was his will, and he did not hesitate. To be all-out for God was already habitual with him; it is the unfailing prerequisite of eternal success. (Deut. 6:3-5; Luke 10:25-28; Ps. 1:1-3).

## New American Standard

# Joshua

*God's Charge to Joshua*

**1** NOW IT came about after the death of Moses the servant of the LORD that the LORD spoke to Joshua the son of Nun, Moses' [c]servant, saying,

2"Moses My servant is dead; now therefore arise, cross this Jordan, you and all this people, to the land which I am giving to them, to the sons of Israel.

3"Every place on which the sole of your foot treads, I have given it to you, just as I spoke to Moses.

4"From the wilderness and this Lebanon, even as far as the great river, the river Euphrates, all the land of the Hittites, and as far as the Great Sea toward the setting of the sun, will be your territory.

5"No man will *be able to* stand before you all the days of your life. Just as I have been with Moses, I will be with you; I will not fail you or forsake you.

6"Be strong and courageous, for you shall give this people possession of the land which I swore to their fathers to give them.

7"Only be strong and very courageous; be careful to do according to all the law which Moses My servant commanded you; do not turn from it to the right or to the left, so that you may have success wherever you go.

8"This book of the law shall not depart from your mouth, but you shall meditate on it day and night, so that you may be careful to do according to all that is written in it; for then you will make your way prosperous, and then you will have success.

9"Have I not commanded you? Be strong and courageous! Do not tremble or be dismayed, for the LORD your God is with you wherever you go."

*Joshua Assumes Command*

10¶ Then Joshua commanded the officers of the people, saying,

11"Pass through the midst of the camp and command the people, saying, 'Prepare provisions for yourselves, for within three days you are to cross this Jordan, to go in to possess the land which the LORD your God is giving you, to possess it.' "

12¶ And to the Reubenites and to the Gadites and to the half-tribe of Manasseh, Joshua said,

13"Remember the word which Moses the servant of the LORD commanded you, saying, 'The LORD your God gives you rest, and will give you this land.'

14"Your wives, your little ones, and your cattle shall remain in the land which Moses gave you beyond the Jordan, but you shall cross before your brothers in battle array, all your valiant warriors, and shall help them,

NAS [c] Or, *minister*

## New International

# Joshua

*The LORD Commands Joshua*

**1** AFTER THE death of Moses the servant of the LORD, the LORD
said to Joshua son of Nun, Moses' aide: 2"Moses my servant
is dead. Now then, you and all these people, get ready to cross the
Jordan River into the land I am about to give to them—to the
Israelites. 3I will give you every place where you set your foot, as
I promised Moses. 4Your territory will extend from the desert to
Lebanon, and from the great river, the Euphrates—all the Hittite
country—to the Great Sea[d] on the west. 5No one will be able to
stand up against you all the days of your life. As I was with Moses,
so I will be with you; I will never leave you nor forsake you.
6"Be strong and courageous, because you will lead these people
to inherit the land I swore to their forefathers to give them. 7Be
strong and very courageous. Be careful to obey all the law my
servant Moses gave you; do not turn from it to the right or to the
left, that you may be successful wherever you go. 8Do not let this
Book of the Law depart from your mouth; meditate on it day and
night, so that you may be careful to do everything written in it.
Then you will be prosperous and successful. 9Have I not commanded you? Be strong and courageous. Do not be terrified; do not
be discouraged, for the LORD your God will be with you wherever
you go."
10So Joshua ordered the officers of the people: 11"Go through
the camp and tell the people, 'Get your supplies ready. Three days
from now you will cross the Jordan here to go in and take possession of the land the LORD your God is giving you for your own.' "
12But to the Reubenites, the Gadites and the half-tribe of Manasseh, Joshua said, 13"Remember the command that Moses the
servant of the LORD gave you: 'The LORD your God is giving you
rest and has granted you this land.' 14Your wives, your children
and your livestock may stay in the land that Moses gave you east
of the Jordan, but all your fighting men, fully armed, must cross
over ahead of your brothers. You are to help your brothers 15until

NIV [d] 4 That is, the Mediterranean

## King James

15 Until the LORD have given your brethren rest, as *he hath given* you, and they also have possessed the land which the LORD your God giveth them: then ye shall return unto the land of your possession, and enjoy it, which Moses the LORD's servant gave you on this side Jordan toward the sunrising.

16 ¶ And they answered Joshua, saying, All that thou commandest us we will do, and whithersoever thou sendest us, we will go.

17 According as we hearkened unto Moses in all things, so will we hearken unto thee: only the LORD thy God be with thee, as he was with Moses.

18 Whosoever *he be* that doth rebel against thy commandment, and will not hearken unto thy words in all that thou commandest him, he shall be put to death: only be strong and of a good courage.

## Amplified

15 Until the Lord gives your brethren rest, as He has given you, and they also possess the land the Lord your God is giving them. Then you shall return to the land of your possession, and possess it, the land Moses the Lord's servant gave you on the sunrise side of the Jordan.

16 They answered Joshua, All you command us we will do, and wherever you send us, we will go.

17 As we hearkened to Moses in all things, so will we hearken to you; only the Lord your God be with you, as He was with Moses.

18 Whoever rebels against your commandment, and will not hearken to all you command him, shall be put to death. Only be strong, vigorous *and* of good courage.

## King James

2 AND JOSHUA the son of Nun sent out of Shittim two men to spy secretly, saying, Go view the land, even Jericho. And they went, and came into an harlot's house, named Rahab, and lodged there.

2 And it was told the king of Jericho, saying, Behold, there came men in hither tonight of the children of Israel to search out the country.

3 And the king of Jericho sent unto Rahab, saying, Bring forth the men that are come to thee, which are entered into thine house: for they be come to search out all the country.

4 And the woman took the two men, and hid them, and said thus, There came men unto me, but I wist not whence they *were:*

5 And it came to pass *about the time* of shutting of the gate, when it was dark, that the men went out: whither the men went I wot not: pursue after them quickly; for ye shall overtake them.

6 But she had brought them up to the roof of the house, and hid them with the stalks of flax, which she had laid in order upon the roof.

7 And the men pursued after them the way to Jordan unto the fords: and as soon as they which pursued after them were gone out, they shut the gate.

8 ¶ And before they were laid down, she came up unto them upon the roof;

9 And she said unto the men, I know that the LORD hath given you the land, and that your terror is fallen upon us, and that all the inhabitants of the land faint because of you.

10 For we have heard how the LORD dried up the water of the Red sea for you, when ye came out of Egypt; and what ye did unto the two kings of the Amorites, that *were* on the other side Jordan, Sihon and Og, whom ye utterly destroyed.

11 And as soon as we had heard *these things*, our hearts did melt, neither did there remain any more courage in any man, because of you: for the LORD your God, he *is* God in heaven above, and in earth beneath.

12 Now therefore, I pray you, swear unto me by the LORD, since I have shown you kindness, that ye will also show kindness unto my father's house, and give me a true token:

13 And *that* ye will save alive my father, and my mother, and my brethren, and my sisters, and all that they have, and deliver our lives from death.

14 And the men answered her, Our life for yours, if ye utter not this our business. And it shall be, when the LORD hath given us the land, that we will deal kindly and truly with thee.

15 Then she let them down by a cord through the window: for her house *was* upon the town wall, and she dwelt upon the wall.

16 And she said unto them, Get you to the mountain, lest the pursuers meet you; and hide yourselves there three days, until the pursuers be returned: and afterward may ye go your way.

17 And the men said unto her, We *will be* blameless of this thine oath which thou hast made us swear.

## Amplified

2 JOSHUA SON of Nun sent two men secretly from Shittim as scouts, saying, Go, view the land, and Jericho. And they went, and came to the house of a harlot named Rahab, and lodged there.

2 It was told the king of Jericho, Behold, there came men in here tonight of the Israelites to search out the country.

3 And the king of Jericho sent to Rahab, saying, Bring forth the men who have come to you, who entered your house, for they have come to search out the land.

4 But the woman had taken the two men and hidden them. So she said, Yes, two men came to me, but I did not know from where they came;

5 And at gate-closing time, after dark, the men went out. Where they went I do not know. Pursue them quickly, for you will overtake them.

6 But she had brought them up to the roof, and hid them under the stalks of flax, which she had laid in order there.

7 So the men pursued them to Jordan as far as the fords. As soon as the pursuers had gone, the city's gate was shut.

8 Before the two men had lain down, Rahab came up to them on the roof;

9 And she said to the men, I know that the Lord has given you the land, and that your terror is fallen upon us, and that all the inhabitants of the land faint because of you.

10 For we have heard how the Lord dried up the water of the Red Sea for you, when you came out of Egypt, and what you did to the two kings of the Amorites who were on the [east] side Jordan, Sihon and Og, whom you utterly destroyed.

11 When we heard it, our hearts melted, neither did spirit *or* courage remain any more in any man, because of you; for the Lord your God, He is God in Heaven above, and on earth beneath. [Heb. 11:31.]

12 Now then, I pray you, swear to me by the Lord, since I have shown you kindness, that you also will show kindness to my father's house, and give me a sure sign,

13 And save alive my father and mother, my brothers and sisters, and all they have, and deliver us from death.

14 And the men said to her, Our life for yours! If you do not tell this business of ours, then when the Lord gives us the land we will deal kindly and faithfully with you.

15 Then she let them down by a rope through the window; for her house was built into the [town] wall, so she dwelt in the wall.

16 And she said to them, Get you to the mountain, lest the pursuers meet you; hide yourselves there three days, until the pursuers have returned; and afterward you may go your way.

17 The men said to her, We will be blameless of this oath you have made us swear. [The responsibility is now yours.]

## New American Standard

15until the LORD gives your brothers rest, as *He gives* you, and
they also possess the land which the LORD your God is giving
them. Then you shall return to your own land, and possess that
which Moses the servant of the LORD gave you beyond the Jordan
toward the sunrise."
16And they answered Joshua, saying, "All that you have commanded us we will do, and wherever you send us we will go.
17"Just as we obeyed Moses in all things, so we will obey you;
only may the LORD your God be with you, as He was with Moses.
18"Anyone who rebels against your command and does not
obey your words in all that you command him, shall be put to
death; only be strong and courageous."

*Rahab Shelters Spies*

2 THEN JOSHUA the son of Nun sent two men as spies secretly
from Shittim, saying, "Go, view the land, especially Jericho."
So they went and came into the house of a harlot whose name was
Rahab, and lodged there.
2And it was told the king of Jericho, saying, "Behold, men
from the sons of Israel have come here tonight to search out the
land."
3And the king of Jericho sent *word* to Rahab, saying, "Bring out
the men who have come to you, who have entered your house, for
they have come to search out all the land."
4But the woman had taken the two men and hidden them, and
she said, "Yes, the men came to me, but I did not know where they
were from.
5"And it came about when *it was time* to shut the gate, at dark,
that the men went out; I do not know where the men went. Pursue
them quickly, for you will overtake them."
6But she had brought them up to the roof and hidden them in
the stalks of flax which she had laid in order on the roof.
7So the men pursued them on the road to the Jordan to the
fords; and as soon as those who were pursuing them had gone out,
they shut the gate.
8¶ Now before they lay down, she came up to them on the roof,
9and said to the men, "I know that the LORD has given you the
land, and that the terror of you has fallen on us, and that all the
inhabitants of the land have melted away before you.
10"For we have heard how the LORD dried up the water of the
Red Sea before you when you came out of Egypt, and what you
did to the two kings of the Amorites who were beyond the Jordan,
to Sihon and Og, whom you utterly destroyed.
11"And when we heard *it,* our hearts melted and no courage
remained in any man any longer because of you; for the LORD your
God, He is God in heaven above and on earth beneath.
12"Now therefore, please swear to me by the LORD, since I have
dealt kindly with you, that you also will deal kindly with my
father's household, and give me a pledge of truth,
13and spare my father and my mother and my brothers and my
sisters, with all who belong to them, and deliver our [a]lives from
death."
14So the men said to her, "Our life for yours if you do not tell
this business of ours; and it shall come about when the LORD gives
us the land that we will deal kindly and faithfully with you."

*The Promise to Rahab*

15¶ Then she let them down by a rope through the window, for
her house was on the city wall, so that she was living on the wall.
16And she said to them, "Go to the hill country, lest the pursuers happen upon you, and hide yourselves there for three days,
until the pursuers return. Then afterward you may go on your
way."
17And the men said to her, "We *shall be* free from this oath to
you which you have made us swear,

NAS [a] Lit., *souls*

## New International

the LORD gives them rest, as he has done for you, and until they
too have taken possession of the land that the LORD your God is
giving them. After that, you may go back and occupy your own
land, which Moses the servant of the LORD gave you east of the
Jordan toward the sunrise."
16Then they answered Joshua, "Whatever you have commanded us we will do, and wherever you send us we will go. 17Just
as we fully obeyed Moses, so we will obey you. Only may the LORD
your God be with you as he was with Moses. 18Whoever rebels
against your word and does not obey your words, whatever you
may command them, will be put to death. Only be strong and
courageous!"

*Rahab and the Spies*

2 THEN JOSHUA son of Nun secretly sent two spies from
Shittim. "Go, look over the land," he said, "especially Jericho." So they went and entered the house of a prostitute[b] named
Rahab and stayed there.
2The king of Jericho was told, "Look! Some of the Israelites have
come here tonight to spy out the land." 3So the king of Jericho sent
this message to Rahab: "Bring out the men who came to you and
entered your house, because they have come to spy out the whole
land."
4But the woman had taken the two men and hidden them. She
said, "Yes, the men came to me, but I did not know where they
had come from. 5At dusk, when it was time to close the city gate,
the men left. I don't know which way they went. Go after them
quickly. You may catch up with them." 6(But she had taken them
up to the roof and hidden them under the stalks of flax she had
laid out on the roof.) 7So the men set out in pursuit of the spies
on the road that leads to the fords of the Jordan, and as soon as
the pursuers had gone out, the gate was shut.
8Before the spies lay down for the night, she went up on the
roof 9and said to them, "I know that the LORD has given this land
to you and that a great fear of you has fallen on us, so that all who
live in this country are melting in fear because of you. 10We have
heard how the LORD dried up the water of the Red Sea[c] for you
when you came out of Egypt, and what you did to Sihon and Og,
the two kings of the Amorites east of the Jordan, whom you
completely destroyed.[d] 11When we heard of it, our hearts melted
and everyone's courage failed because of you, for the LORD your
God is God in heaven above and on the earth below. 12Now then,
please swear to me by the LORD that you will show kindness to my
family, because I have shown kindness to you. Give me a sure sign
13that you will spare the lives of my father and mother, my brothers and sisters, and all who belong to them, and that you will save
us from death."
14"Our lives for your lives!" the men assured her. "If you don't
tell what we are doing, we will treat you kindly and faithfully
when the LORD gives us the land."
15So she let them down by a rope through the window, for the
house she lived in was part of the city wall. 16Now she had said
to them, "Go to the hills so the pursuers will not find you. Hide
yourselves there three days until they return, and then go on your
way."
17The men said to her, "This oath you made us swear will not
be binding on us 18unless, when we enter the land, you have tied

NIV [b] *1* Or possibly *an innkeeper* [c] *10* Hebrew *Yam Suph;* that is, Sea of Reeds [d] *10* The Hebrew term refers to the irrevocable giving over of things or persons to the LORD, often by totally destroying them.

## King James

18 Behold, *when* we come into the land, thou shalt bind this line of scarlet thread in the window which thou didst let us down by: and thou shalt bring thy father, and thy mother, and thy brethren, and all thy father's household, home unto thee.

19 And it shall be, *that* whosoever shall go out of the doors of thy house into the street, his blood *shall be* upon his head, and we *will be* guiltless: and whosoever shall be with thee in the house, his blood *shall be* on our head, if *any* hand be upon him.

20 And if thou utter this our business, then we will be quit of thine oath which thou hast made us to swear.

21 And she said, According unto your words, so *be* it. And she sent them away, and they departed: and she bound the scarlet line in the window.

22 And they went, and came unto the mountain, and abode there three days, until the pursuers were returned: and the pursuers sought *them* throughout all the way, but found *them* not.

23 ¶ So the two men returned, and descended from the mountain, and passed over, and came to Joshua the son of Nun, and told him all *things* that befell them:

24 And they said unto Joshua, Truly the LORD hath delivered into our hands all the land; for even all the inhabitants of the country do faint because of us.

**3** AND JOSHUA rose early in the morning; and they removed from Shittim, and came to Jordan, he and all the children of Israel, and lodged there before they passed over.

2 And it came to pass after three days, that the officers went through the host;

3 And they commanded the people, saying, When ye see the ark of the covenant of the LORD your God, and the priests the Levites bearing it, then ye shall remove from your place, and go after it.

4 Yet there shall be a space between you and it, about two thousand cubits by measure: come not near unto it, that ye may know the way by which ye must go: for ye have not passed *this* way heretofore.

5 And Joshua said unto the people, Sanctify yourselves: for to-morrow the LORD will do wonders among you.

6 And Joshua spake unto the priests, saying, Take up the ark of the covenant, and pass over before the people. And they took up the ark of the covenant, and went before the people.

7 ¶ And the LORD said unto Joshua, This day will I begin to magnify thee in the sight of all Israel, that they may know that, as I was with Moses, *so* I will be with thee.

8 And thou shalt command the priests that bear the ark of the covenant, saying, When ye are come to the brink of the water of Jordan, ye shall stand still in Jordan.

9 ¶ And Joshua said unto the children of Israel, Come hither, and hear the words of the LORD your God.

10 And Joshua said, Hereby ye shall know that the living God *is* among you, and *that* he will without fail drive out from before you the Canaanites, and the Hittites, and the Hivites, and the Perizzites, and the Girgashites, and the Amorites, and the Jebusites.

11 Behold, the ark of the covenant of the Lord of all the earth passeth over before you into Jordan.

12 Now therefore take you twelve men out of the tribes of Israel, out of every tribe a man.

## Amplified

18 Behold, when we come into the land, you shall bind this scarlet cord in the window through which you let us down, and you shall bring your father and mother, your brothers, and all your father's household, into your house.

19 And if any one goes out of the doors of your house into the street, his blood shall be upon his head, and we will be guiltless; but if a hand is laid upon any one who is with you in the house, his blood shall be on our head.

20 But if you tell this business of ours we shall be guiltless of your oath which you made us swear.

21 And she said, According to your words, so it is. Then she sent them away, and they departed; and she bound the [a]scarlet cord in the window.

22 They left and went to the mountain, and stayed there three days, until the pursuers returned, who had searched all along the way without finding them.

23 So the two men descended from the mountain, passed over [Jordan] and came to Joshua son of Nun, and told him all that had befallen them.

24 They said to Joshua, Truly the Lord has given all the land into our hands; for all the inhabitants of the country are faint because of us.

**3** JOSHUA ROSE early in the morning, and they removed from Shittim, and came to the Jordan, he and all the Israelites, and lodged there before passing over.

2 After three days, the officers went through the camp,

3 Commanding the people, When you see the ark of the covenant of the Lord your God being borne by the Levitical priests, set out from where you are and follow it.

4 Yet a space must be kept between you and it, about 2,000 cubits by measure; come not near it, that you may [be able to see the ark and] know the way you must go, for you have not passed this way before.

5 And Joshua said to the people, Sanctify yourselves [that is, separate yourselves for special holy purpose], for tomorrow the Lord will do wonders among you.

6 Joshua said to the priests, Take up the ark of the covenant, and pass over before the people. And they took it up and went on before the people.

7 The Lord said to Joshua, This day I will begin to magnify you in the sight of all Israel, so they may know that, as I was with Moses, so I will be with you.

8 You shall command the priests who bear the ark of the covenant, When you come to the brink of the waters of the Jordan, you shall stand still in the Jordan.

9 Joshua said to the Israelites, Come near; hear the words of the Lord your God.

10 Joshua said, Hereby you shall know that the living God is among you, and that He will surely drive out from before you the Canaanites, Hittites, Hivites, Perizzites, Girgashites, Amorites, and Jebusites.

11 Behold, the ark of the covenant; the Lord of all the earth is passing over before you into Jordan!

12 So now take twelve men from the tribes of Israel, one from each tribe.

**AMP** [a] What the blood on the doorposts, on the first passover night in Egypt, was to the houses of Israel (Exod. 12:13), that the scarlet cord in the window was to the house of Rahab. Her sinful years of ignorance God ignored (Acts 17:30, 31); she became an ancestress, as did Ruth, of David and of Jesus Christ (Matt. 1:1, 5, 6).

## New American Standard

18unless, when we come into the land, you tie this cord of scarlet thread in the window through which you let us down, and gather to yourself into the house your father and your mother and your brothers and all your father's household.

19"And it shall come about that anyone who goes out of the doors of your house into the street, his blood *shall be* on his own head, and we *shall be* free; but anyone who is with you in the house, his blood *shall be* on our head, if a hand is *laid* on him.

20"But if you tell this business of ours, then we shall be free from the oath which you have made us swear."

21And she said, "According to your words, so be it." So she sent them away, and they departed; and she tied the scarlet cord in the window.

22¶ And they departed and came to the hill country, and remained there for three days until the pursuers returned. Now the pursuers had sought *them* all along the road, but had not found *them*.

23Then the two men returned and came down from the hill country and crossed over and came to Joshua the son of Nun, and they related to him all that had happened to them.

24And they said to Joshua, "Surely the LORD has given all the land into our hands, and all the inhabitants of the land, moreover, have melted away before us."

*Israel Crosses the Jordan*

**3** THEN JOSHUA rose early in the morning; and he and all the sons of Israel set out from Shittim and came to the Jordan, and they lodged there before they crossed.

2And it came about at the end of three days that the officers went through the midst of the camp;

3and they commanded the people, saying, "When you see the ark of the covenant of the LORD your God with the Levitical priests carrying it, then you shall set out from your place and go after it.

4"However, there shall be between you and it a distance of about 2,000 cubits by measure. Do not come near it, that you may know the way by which you shall go, for you have not passed this way before."

5¶ Then Joshua said to the people, "Consecrate yourselves, for tomorrow the LORD will do wonders among you."

6And Joshua spoke to the priests, saying, "Take up the ark of the covenant and cross over ahead of the people." So they took up the ark of the covenant and went ahead of the people.

7¶ Now the LORD said to Joshua, "This day I will begin to exalt you in the sight of all Israel, that they may know that just as I have been with Moses, I will be with you.

8"You shall, moreover, command the priests who are carrying the ark of the covenant, saying, 'When you come to the edge of the waters of the Jordan, you shall stand *still* in the Jordan.'"

9Then Joshua said to the sons of Israel, "Come here, and hear the words of the LORD your God."

10And Joshua said, "By this you shall know that the living God is among you, and that He will assuredly dispossess from before you the Canaanite, the Hittite, the Hivite, the Perizzite, the Girgashite, the Amorite, and the Jebusite.

11"Behold, the ark of the covenant of the Lord of all the earth is crossing over ahead of you into the Jordan.

12"Now then, take for yourselves twelve men from the tribes of Israel, one man for each tribe.

## New International

this scarlet cord in the window through which you let us down,
and unless you have brought your father and mother, your brothers and all your family into your house. 19If anyone goes outside
your house into the street, his blood will be on his own head; we
will not be responsible. As for anyone who is in the house with
you, his blood will be on our head if a hand is laid on him. 20But
if you tell what we are doing, we will be released from the oath
you made us swear."
21"Agreed," she replied. "Let it be as you say." So she sent
them away and they departed. And she tied the scarlet cord in the
window.
22When they left, they went into the hills and stayed there three
days, until the pursuers had searched all along the road and returned without finding them. 23Then the two men started back.
They went down out of the hills, forded the river and came to
Joshua son of Nun and told him everything that had happened to
them. 24They said to Joshua, "The LORD has surely given the
whole land into our hands; all the people are melting in fear
because of us."

*Crossing the Jordan*

**3** EARLY IN the morning Joshua and all the Israelites set out
from Shittim and went to the Jordan, where they camped
before crossing over. 2After three days the officers went throughout the camp, 3giving orders to the people: "When you see the ark
of the covenant of the LORD your God, and the priests, who are
Levites, carrying it, you are to move out from your positions and
follow it. 4Then you will know which way to go, since you have
never been this way before. But keep a distance of about a thousand yards[b] between you and the ark; do not go near it."
5Joshua told the people, "Consecrate yourselves, for tomorrow
the LORD will do amazing things among you."
6Joshua said to the priests, "Take up the ark of the covenant and
pass on ahead of the people." So they took it up and went ahead
of them.
7And the LORD said to Joshua, "Today I will begin to exalt you
in the eyes of all Israel, so they may know that I am with you as
I was with Moses. 8Tell the priests who carry the ark of the covenant: 'When you reach the edge of the Jordan's waters, go and
stand in the river.'"
9Joshua said to the Israelites, "Come here and listen to the
words of the LORD your God. 10This is how you will know that the
living God is among you and that he will certainly drive out before
you the Canaanites, Hittites, Hivites, Perizzites, Girgashites, Amorites and Jebusites. 11See, the ark of the covenant of the Lord of
all the earth will go into the Jordan ahead of you. 12Now then,
choose twelve men from the tribes of Israel, one from each tribe.

NIV [b] 4 Hebrew *about two thousand cubits* (about 900 meters)

## King James

13 And it shall come to pass, as soon as the soles of the feet of the priests that bear the ark of the LORD, the Lord of all the earth, shall rest in the waters of Jordan, *that* the waters of Jordan shall be cut off *from* the waters that come down from above; and they shall stand upon an heap.

14 ¶ And it came to pass, when the people removed from their tents, to pass over Jordan, and the priests bearing the ark of the covenant before the people;

15 And as they that bare the ark were come unto Jordan, and the feet of the priests that bare the ark were dipped in the brim of the water, (for Jordan overfloweth all his banks all the time of harvest,)

16 That the waters which came down from above stood *and* rose up upon an heap very far from the city Adam, that *is* beside Zaretan: and those that came down toward the sea of the plain, *even* the salt sea, failed, *and* were cut off: and the people passed over right against Jericho.

17 And the priests that bare the ark of the covenant of the LORD stood firm on dry ground in the midst of Jordan, and all the Israelites passed over on dry ground, until all the people were passed clean over Jordan.

## Amplified

13 When the soles of the feet of the priests who bear the ark of the Lord of all the earth shall rest in the Jordan, the waters of the Jordan coming down from above shall be cut off, and they shall stand in one heap.

14 So, when the people set out from their tents to pass over the Jordan with the priests bearing the ark of the covenant before the people,

15 And when those who bore the ark had come to the Jordan, and the feet of the priests bearing the ark were in the brink of the water (for the Jordan overflows all its banks through the time of harvest),

16 Then the [a]waters which came down from above stood and rose up in a heap far off, at Adam, the city that is beside Zarethan; and those flowing down toward the sea of the Arabah, the Salt [Dead] Sea, were wholly cut off, and the people passed over opposite Jericho. [Ps. 114.]

17 And while all Israel were passing over on dry ground, the priests who bore the ark of the covenant of the Lord stood firm on dry ground in the midst of the Jordan, until all the nation finished passing over the Jordan.

## King James

4 AND IT came to pass, when all the people were clean passed over Jordan, that the LORD spake unto Joshua, saying,

2 Take you twelve men out of the people, out of every tribe a man,

3 And command ye them, saying, Take you hence out of the midst of Jordan, out of the place where the priests' feet stood firm, twelve stones, and ye shall carry them over with you, and leave them in the lodging place, where ye shall lodge this night.

4 Then Joshua called the twelve men, whom he had prepared of the children of Israel, out of every tribe a man:

5 And Joshua said unto them, Pass over before the ark of the LORD your God into the midst of Jordan, and take you up every man of you a stone upon his shoulder, according unto the number of the tribes of the children of Israel:

6 That this may be a sign among you, *that* when your children ask *their fathers* in time to come, saying, What *mean* ye by these stones?

7 Then ye shall answer them, That the waters of Jordan were cut off before the ark of the covenant of the LORD; when it passed over Jordan, the waters of Jordan were cut off: and these stones shall be for a memorial unto the children of Israel for ever.

8 And the children of Israel did so as Joshua commanded, and took up twelve stones out of the midst of Jordan, as the LORD spake unto Joshua, according to the number of the tribes of the children of Israel, and carried them over with them unto the place where they lodged, and laid them down there.

9 And Joshua set up twelve stones in the midst of Jordan, in the place where the feet of the priests which bare the ark of the covenant stood: and they are there unto this day.

10 ¶ For the priests which bare the ark stood in the midst of Jordan, until every thing was finished that the LORD commanded Joshua to speak unto the people, according to all that Moses commanded Joshua: and the people hasted and passed over.

## Amplified

4 WHEN ALL the nation had fully passed over the Jordan, the Lord said to Joshua,

2 Take twelve men from among the people, out of every tribe a man.

3 And command them, Take twelve stones out of the midst of the Jordan from the place where the priests' feet stood firm; carry them over with you, and leave them at the place where you lodge tonight.

4 Then Joshua called the twelve men of the Israelites, whom he had appointed, a man from each tribe.

5 And Joshua said to them, Pass over before the ark of the Lord your God in the midst of the Jordan, and take up every man of you a stone on his shoulder, as is the number of the tribes of the Israelites;

6 That this may be a sign among you, when your children ask in time to come, What do these stones mean to you?

7 Then you shall tell them that the waters of the Jordan were cut off before the ark of the covenant of the Lord; when it passed over the Jordan, the waters of Jordan were cut off. So these stones shall be to the Israelites a memorial for ever.

8 And the Israelites did as Joshua commanded, and took up twelve stones out of the midst of the Jordan, according to the number of the tribes of the Israelites, as the Lord told Joshua, and carried them over with them to the place where they lodged, and laid them down there.

9 And Joshua set up twelve stones in the midst of the Jordan, in the place where the feet of the priests bearing the ark of the covenant had stood; and they are there to this day.

10 For the priests who bore the ark stood in the midst of the Jordan, until everything was finished that the Lord commanded Joshua to tell the people, according to all that Moses had commanded Joshua. The people passed over in haste.

**AMP** [a] The city of Adam has been placed 16 miles up the river from Jericho, and it seems probable that a stretch of 20 or 30 miles of the river bed was left dry. An interesting parallel of the event here recorded has been found in the pages of an Arabic historian telling how in 1266 A.D. near a place many experts have identified with Adam, the bed of the [Jordan] river was left dry for ten hours as the result of a landslip. Garstang cites other parallels in 1906 and 1927; but to accept this "natural" explanation of what happened centuries earlier does not detract in any way from the supernatural intervention which opened the way to Israel just at the moment when they needed to cross. The priests standing in the dry bed of the river as the whole nation passed over were the sign [3:10] that this was the doing of the Lord. (Condensed from *The New Bible Commentary*.)

## New American Standard

13"And it shall come about when the soles of the feet of the
priests who carry the ark of the LORD, the Lord of all the earth, shall
rest in the waters of the Jordan, the waters of the Jordan shall be
cut off, *and* the waters which are flowing down from above shall
stand in one heap."
14¶ So it came about when the people set out from their tents
to cross the Jordan with the priests carrying the ark of the covenant
before the people,
15and when those who carried the ark came into the Jordan, and
the feet of the priests carrying the ark were dipped in the edge of
the water (for the Jordan overflows all its banks all the days of
harvest),
16that the waters which were flowing down from above stood
*and* rose up in one heap, a great distance away at Adam, the city
that is beside Zarethan; and those which were flowing down
toward the sea of the Arabah, the Salt Sea, were completely cut off.
So the people crossed opposite Jericho.
17And the priests who carried the ark of the covenant of the
LORD stood firm on dry ground in the middle of the Jordan while
all Israel crossed on dry ground, until all the nation had finished
crossing the Jordan.

*Memorial Stones from Jordan*

4 NOW IT came about when all the nation had finished crossing the Jordan, that the LORD spoke to Joshua, saying,
2"Take for yourselves twelve men from the people, one man
from each tribe,
3and command them, saying, 'Take up for yourselves twelve
stones from here out of the middle of the Jordan, from the place
where the priests' feet are standing firm, and carry them over with
you, and lay them down in the lodging place where you will lodge
tonight.' "
4So Joshua called the twelve men whom he had appointed
from the sons of Israel, one man from each tribe;
5and Joshua said to them, "Cross again to the ark of the LORD
your God into the middle of the Jordan, and each of you take up
a stone on his shoulder, according to the number of the tribes of
the sons of Israel.
6"Let this be a sign among you, so that when your children ask
later, saying, 'What do these stones mean to you?'
7then you shall say to them, 'Because the waters of the Jordan
were cut off before the ark of the covenant of the LORD; when it
crossed the Jordan, the waters of the Jordan were cut off.' So these
stones shall become a memorial to the sons of Israel forever."
8¶ And thus the sons of Israel did, as Joshua commanded, and
took up twelve stones from the middle of the Jordan, just as the
LORD spoke to Joshua, according to the number of the tribes of the
sons of Israel; and they carried them over with them to the lodging
place, and put them down there.
9Then Joshua set up twelve stones in the middle of the Jordan
at the place where the feet of the priests who carried the ark of the
covenant were standing, and they are there to this day.
10For the priests who carried the ark were standing in the middle of the Jordan until everything was completed that the LORD had
commanded Joshua to speak to the people, according to all that
Moses had commanded Joshua. And the people hurried and
crossed;

## New International

13And as soon as the priests who carry the ark of the LORD—the
Lord of all the earth—set foot in the Jordan, its waters flowing
downstream will be cut off and stand up in a heap."
14So when the people broke camp to cross the Jordan, the
priests carrying the ark of the covenant went ahead of them.
15Now the Jordan is at flood stage all during harvest. Yet as soon
as the priests who carried the ark reached the Jordan and their feet
touched the water's edge, 16the water from upstream stopped
flowing. It piled up in a heap a great distance away, at a town
called Adam in the vicinity of Zarethan, while the water flowing
down to the Sea of the Arabah (the Salt Sea[b]) was completely cut
off. So the people crossed over opposite Jericho. 17The priests who
carried the ark of the covenant of the LORD stood firm on dry
ground in the middle of the Jordan, while all Israel passed by until
the whole nation had completed the crossing on dry ground.

4 WHEN THE whole nation had finished crossing the Jordan,
the LORD said to Joshua, 2"Choose twelve men from among
the people, one from each tribe, 3and tell them to take up twelve
stones from the middle of the Jordan from right where the priests
stood and to carry them over with you and put them down at the
place where you stay tonight."
4So Joshua called together the twelve men he had appointed
from the Israelites, one from each tribe, 5and said to them, "Go
over before the ark of the LORD your God into the middle of the
Jordan. Each of you is to take up a stone on his shoulder, according
to the number of the tribes of the Israelites, 6to serve as a sign
among you. In the future, when your children ask you, 'What do
these stones mean?' 7tell them that the flow of the Jordan was cut
off before the ark of the covenant of the LORD. When it crossed the
Jordan, the waters of the Jordan were cut off. These stones are to
be a memorial to the people of Israel forever."
8So the Israelites did as Joshua commanded them. They took
twelve stones from the middle of the Jordan, according to the
number of the tribes of the Israelites, as the LORD had told Joshua;
and they carried them over with them to their camp, where they
put them down. 9Joshua set up the twelve stones that had been[c]
in the middle of the Jordan at the spot where the priests who
carried the ark of the covenant had stood. And they are there to
this day.
10Now the priests who carried the ark remained standing in the
middle of the Jordan until everything the LORD had commanded
Joshua was done by the people, just as Moses had directed Joshua.
The people hurried over, 11and as soon as all of them had crossed,

NIV [b] 16 That is, the Dead Sea [c] 9 Or *Joshua also set up twelve stones*

## King James

11And it came to pass, when all the people were clean passed
over, that the ark of the LORD passed over, and the priests, in the
presence of the people.
12And the children of Reuben, and the children of Gad, and half
the tribe of Manasseh, passed over armed before the children of
Israel, as Moses spake unto them:
13About forty thousand prepared for war passed over before the
LORD unto battle, to the plains of Jericho.
14¶ On that day the LORD magnified Joshua in the sight of all
Israel; and they feared him, as they feared Moses, all the days of
his life.
15And the LORD spake unto Joshua, saying,
16Command the priests that bear the ark of the testimony, that
they come up out of Jordan.
17Joshua therefore commanded the priests, saying, Come ye up
out of Jordan.
18And it came to pass, when the priests that bare the ark of the
covenant of the LORD were come up out of the midst of Jordan, *and*
the soles of the priests' feet were lifted up unto the dry land, that
the waters of Jordan returned unto their place, and flowed over all
his banks, as *they did* before.
19¶ And the people came up out of Jordan on the tenth *day* of
the first month, and encamped in Gilgal, in the east border of
Jericho.
20And those twelve stones, which they took out of Jordan, did
Joshua pitch in Gilgal.
21And he spake unto the children of Israel, saying, When your
children shall ask their fathers in time to come, saying, What *mean*
these stones?
22Then ye shall let your children know, saying, Israel came over
this Jordan on dry land.
23For the LORD your God dried up the waters of Jordan from
before you, until ye were passed over, as the LORD your God did
to the Red sea, which he dried up from before us, until we were
gone over:
24That all the people of the earth might know the hand of the
LORD, that it *is* mighty: that ye might fear the LORD your God for
ever.

5 AND IT came to pass, when all the kings of the Amorites,
which *were* on the side of Jordan westward, and all the kings
of the Canaanites, which *were* by the sea, heard that the LORD had
dried up the waters of the Jordan from before the children of Israel,
until we were passed over, that their heart melted, neither was
there spirit in them any more, because of the children of Israel.
2¶ At that time the LORD said unto Joshua, Make thee sharp
knives, and circumcise again the children of Israel the second time.
3And Joshua made him sharp knives, and circumcised the children of Israel at the hill of the foreskins.
4And this *is* the cause why Joshua did circumcise: All the people
that came out of Egypt, *that were* males, *even* all the men of war,
died in the wilderness by the way, after they came out of Egypt.
5Now all the people that came out were circumcised: but all the
people *that were* born in the wilderness by the way as they came
forth out of Egypt, *them* they had not circumcised.
6For the children of Israel walked forty years in the wilderness,
till all the people *that were* men of war, which came out of Egypt,
were consumed, because they obeyed not the voice of the LORD:
unto whom the LORD sware that he would not show them the land,
which the LORD sware unto their fathers that he would give us, a
land that floweth with milk and honey.
7And their children, *whom* he raised up in their stead, them
Joshua circumcised: for they were uncircumcised, because they
had not circumcised them by the way.

## Amplified

11When all the people had passed over, the ark of the Lord and
the priests went over, in the presence of the people.
12And the sons of Reuben, Gad, and half the tribe of Manasseh,
passed over armed before the [other] Israelites, as Moses had
bidden them;
13About 40,000 [of these] prepared for war passed over before
the Lord for battle, to the plains of Jericho.
14On that day the Lord magnified Joshua in the sight of all
Israel; and they stood in awe of him, as they stood in awe of Moses,
all the days of his life.
15And the Lord said to Joshua,
16Order the priests bearing the ark of the testimony to come up
out of the Jordan.
17So Joshua commanded the priests, Come up out of the Jordan.
18And when the priests who bore the ark of the covenant of the
Lord had come up out of the midst of the Jordan, and the soles of
their feet were lifted up to the dry land, the waters of the Jordan
returned to their place, and flowed over all its banks, as they had
before.
19And the people came up out of the Jordan on the tenth day
of the first month and encamped in Gilgal on the east border of
Jericho.
20And those twelve stones, which they took out of the Jordan,
Joshua set up in Gilgal.
21And he said to the Israelites, When your children ask their
fathers in time to come, What do these stones mean?
22You shall let your children know, Israel came over this Jordan
on dry land.
23For the Lord your God dried up the waters of the Jordan for
you until you passed over, as the Lord your God did to the Red
Sea, which He dried up for us, until we passed over,
24That all the peoples of the earth may know that the hand of
the Lord is mighty; that you may reverence *and* fear the Lord your
God for ever.

5 WHEN ALL the kings of the Amorites who were beyond the
Jordan to the west, and all the kings of the Canaanites who
were by the sea, heard that the Lord had dried up the waters of
the Jordan before the Israelites until we had crossed over, their
hearts melted, and there was no spirit in them any more, because
of the Israelites.
2At that time the Lord said to Joshua, Make knives of flint and
circumcise the [new generation of] Israelites as before.
3So Joshua made knives of flint and circumcised the sons of
Israel at Gibeath-haaraloth.
4And this is the reason Joshua circumcised them: all the males
of the people who came out of Egypt, all the men of war, had died
on the way in the wilderness, after they came out of Egypt.
5Though all the people who came out were circumcised, yet all
the people who were born in the wilderness on the way after Israel
came out of Egypt had not been circumcised.
6For the Israelites walked forty years in the wilderness, till all
who were men of war who came out of Egypt perished, because
they did not hearken to the voice of the Lord; to them the Lord
swore that He would not let them see the land, which the Lord
swore to their fathers to give us, a land flowing with milk and
honey.
7So it was their uncircumcised children, whom He raised up in
their stead, whom Joshua circumcised; because the rite had not
been performed on the way.

## New American Standard

11and it came about when all the people had finished crossing, that the ark of the LORD and the priests crossed before the people.

12And the sons of Reuben and the sons of Gad and the half-tribe of Manasseh crossed over in battle array before the sons of Israel, just as Moses had spoken to them;

13about 40,000, equipped for war, crossed for battle before the LORD to the desert plains of Jericho.

14On that day the LORD exalted Joshua in the sight of all Israel; so that they [a]revered him, just as they had revered Moses all the days of his life.

15¶ Now the LORD said to Joshua,

16"Command the priests who carry the ark of the testimony that they come up from the Jordan."

17So Joshua commanded the priests, saying, "Come up from the Jordan."

18And it came about when the priests who carried the ark of the covenant of the LORD had come up from the middle of the Jordan, and the soles of the priests' feet were lifted up to the dry ground, that the waters of the Jordan returned to their place, and went over all its banks as before.

19¶ Now the people came up from the Jordan on the tenth of the first month and camped at Gilgal on the eastern edge of Jericho.

20And those twelve stones which they had taken from the Jordan, Joshua set up at Gilgal.

21And he said to the sons of Israel, "When your children ask their fathers in time to come, saying, 'What are these stones?'

22then you shall inform your children, saying, 'Israel crossed this Jordan on dry ground.'

23"For the LORD your God dried up the waters of the Jordan before you until you had crossed, just as the LORD your God had done to the Red Sea, which He dried up before us until we had crossed;

24that all the peoples of the earth may know that the hand of the LORD is mighty, so that you may fear the LORD your God forever."

*Israel Is Circumcised*

**5** NOW IT came about when all the kings of the Amorites who *were* beyond the Jordan to the west, and all the kings of the Canaanites who *were* by the sea, heard how the LORD had dried up the waters of the Jordan before the sons of Israel until they had crossed, that their hearts melted, and there was no spirit in them any longer, because of the sons of Israel.

2¶ At that time the LORD said to Joshua, "Make for yourself flint knives and circumcise again the sons of Israel the second time."

3So Joshua made himself flint knives and circumcised the sons of Israel at [b]Gibeath-haaraloth.

4And this is the reason why Joshua circumcised them: all the people who came out of Egypt who were males, all the men of war, died in the wilderness along the way, after they came out of Egypt.

5For all the people who came out were circumcised, but all the people who were born in the wilderness along the way as they came out of Egypt had not been circumcised.

6For the sons of Israel walked forty years in the wilderness, until all the nation, *that is,* the men of war who came out of Egypt, perished because they did not listen to the voice of the LORD, to whom the LORD had sworn that He would not let them see the land which the LORD had sworn to their fathers to give us, a land flowing with milk and honey.

7And their children whom He raised up in their place, Joshua circumcised; for they were uncircumcised, because they had not circumcised them along the way.

**NAS** [a] Or, *feared* [b] I.e., the hill of the foreskins

## New International

the ark of the LORD and the priests came to the other side while
the people watched. 12The men of Reuben, Gad and the half-tribe
of Manasseh crossed over, armed, in front of the Israelites, as
Moses had directed them. 13About forty thousand armed for battle
crossed over before the LORD to the plains of Jericho for war.
14That day the LORD exalted Joshua in the sight of all Israel; and
they revered him all the days of his life, just as they had revered
Moses.
15Then the LORD said to Joshua, 16"Command the priests carrying the ark of the Testimony to come up out of the Jordan."
17So Joshua commanded the priests, "Come up out of the Jordan."
18And the priests came up out of the river carrying the ark of
the covenant of the LORD. No sooner had they set their feet on the
dry ground than the waters of the Jordan returned to their place
and ran at flood stage as before.
19On the tenth day of the first month the people went up from
the Jordan and camped at Gilgal on the eastern border of Jericho.
20And Joshua set up at Gilgal the twelve stones they had taken out
of the Jordan. 21He said to the Israelites, "In the future when your
descendants ask their fathers, 'What do these stones mean?' 22tell
them, 'Israel crossed the Jordan on dry ground.' 23For the LORD
your God dried up the Jordan before you until you had crossed
over. The LORD your God did to the Jordan just what he had done
to the Red Sea[c] when he dried it up before us until we had crossed
over. 24He did this so that all the peoples of the earth might know
that the hand of the LORD is powerful and so that you might always
fear the LORD your God."

*Circumcision at Gilgal*

**5** NOW WHEN all the Amorite kings west of the Jordan and all
the Canaanite kings along the coast heard how the LORD had
dried up the Jordan before the Israelites until we had crossed over,
their hearts melted and they no longer had the courage to face the
Israelites.
2At that time the LORD said to Joshua, "Make flint knives and
circumcise the Israelites again." 3So Joshua made flint knives and
circumcised the Israelites at Gibeath Haaraloth.[d]
4Now this is why he did so: All those who came out of Egypt—
all the men of military age—died in the desert on the way after
leaving Egypt. 5All the people that came out had been circumcised,
but all the people born in the desert during the journey from Egypt
had not. 6The Israelites had moved about in the desert forty years
until all the men who were of military age when they left Egypt
had died, since they had not obeyed the LORD. For the LORD had
sworn to them that they would not see the land that he had
solemnly promised their fathers to give us, a land flowing with
milk and honey. 7So he raised up their sons in their place, and
these were the ones Joshua circumcised. They were still uncircumcised because they had not been circumcised on the way. 8And

**NIV** [c] 23 Hebrew *Yam Suph;* that is, Sea of Reeds [d] 3 *Gibeath Haaraloth* means *hill of foreskins.*

## King James

8And it came to pass, when they had done circumcising all the people, that they abode in their places in the camp, till they were whole.

9And the LORD said unto Joshua, This day have I rolled away the reproach of Egypt from off you. Wherefore the name of the place is called Gilgal unto this day.

10¶ And the children of Israel encamped in Gilgal, and kept the passover on the fourteenth day of the month at even in the plains of Jericho.

11And they did eat of the old corn of the land on the morrow after the passover, unleavened cakes, and parched *corn* in the selfsame day.

12¶ And the manna ceased on the morrow after they had eaten of the old corn of the land; neither had the children of Israel manna any more; but they did eat of the fruit of the land of Canaan that year.

13¶ And it came to pass, when Joshua was by Jericho, that he lifted up his eyes and looked, and, behold, there stood a man over against him with his sword drawn in his hand: and Joshua went unto him, and said unto him, *Art* thou for us, or for our adversaries?

14And he said, Nay; but *as* captain of the host of the LORD am I now come. And Joshua fell on his face to the earth, and did worship, and said unto him, What saith my lord unto his servant?

15And the captain of the LORD's host said unto Joshua, Loose thy shoe from off thy foot; for the place whereon thou standest *is* holy. And Joshua did so.

**6** NOW JERICHO was straitly shut up because of the children of Israel: none went out, and none came in.

2And the LORD said unto Joshua, See, I have given into thine hand Jericho, and the king thereof, *and* the mighty men of valour.

3And ye shall compass the city, all *ye* men of war, *and* go round about the city once. Thus shalt thou do six days.

4And seven priests shall bear before the ark seven trumpets of rams' horns: and the seventh day ye shall compass the city seven times, and the priests shall blow with the trumpets.

5And it shall come to pass, that when they make a long *blast* with the ram's horn, *and* when ye hear the sound of the trumpet, all the people shall shout with a great shout; and the wall of the city shall fall down flat, and the people shall ascend up every man straight before him.

6¶ And Joshua the son of Nun called the priests, and said unto them, Take up the ark of the covenant, and let seven priests bear seven trumpets of rams' horns before the ark of the LORD.

7And he said unto the people, Pass on, and compass the city, and let him that is armed pass on before the ark of the LORD.

8¶ And it came to pass, when Joshua had spoken unto the people, that the seven priests bearing the seven trumpets of rams' horns passed on before the LORD, and blew with the trumpets: and the ark of the covenant of the LORD followed them.

9¶ And the armed men went before the priests that blew with the trumpets, and the rearward came after the ark, *the priests* going on, and blowing with the trumpets.

10And Joshua had commanded the people, saying, Ye shall not shout, nor make any noise with your voice, neither shall *any* word proceed out of your mouth, until the day I bid you shout; then shall ye shout.

11So the ark of the LORD compassed the city, going about *it* once: and they came into the camp, and lodged in the camp.

## Amplified

8When they finished circumcising all the males of the nation, they remained in their places in the camp till they were healed.

9And the Lord said to Joshua, This day have I rolled away the reproach of Egypt from you. So the name of the place is called Gilgal [rolling] to this day.

10And the Israelites encamped in Gilgal; and they kept the passover on the fourteenth day of the month at evening in the plains of Jericho.

11And on that same day, they ate the produce of the land, unleavened cakes and parched grain.

12And the manna ceased on the day after they ate of the produce of the land; and the Israelites had manna no more, but they ate of the fruit of the land of Canaan that year.

13When Joshua was by Jericho, he looked up, and behold, a Man stood near him with His drawn sword in His hand. And Joshua went to Him, and said to Him, Are you for us, or for our adversaries?

14And He said, No [neither]; but as Prince of the Lord's host am I now come. And Joshua fell on his face to the earth, and worshiped, and said to Him, What says my Lord to His servant?

15And the Prince of the Lord's host said to Joshua, [a]Loose your shoes from off your feet; for the place where you stand is holy. And Joshua did so. [Exod. 3:5.]

**6** NOW JERICHO [a fenced town with high walls] was tightly closed because of the Israelites; no one went out or came in.

2And the Lord said to Joshua, See, I have given Jericho, its king and mighty men of valor, into your hand.

3You shall march around the enclosure, all the men of war going around the city once. This you shall do six days.

4And seven priests shall bear before the ark seven trumpets of rams' horns; and the seventh day you shall march around the enclosure seven times, and the priests shall blow the trumpets.

5When they make a long blast with the ram's horn, and you hear the sound of the trumpet, all the people shall shout with a great shout; and the wall of the enclosure shall fall down in its place, and the people shall go up [over it] every man straight before him.

6So Joshua son of Nun called the priests, and said to them, Take up the ark of the covenant, and let seven priests bear seven trumpets of rams' horns before the ark of the Lord.

7He said to the people, Go on; march around the enclosure, and let the armed men pass on before the ark of the Lord.

8When Joshua had spoken to the people, the seven priests bearing the seven trumpets of rams' horns passed on before the Lord, and blew the trumpets, and the ark of the covenant of the Lord followed them.

9The armed men went before the priests who blew the trumpets, and the rear guard came after the ark, the priests blowing the trumpets as they went.

10But Joshua commanded the people, You shall not shout or let your voice be heard, nor shall any word proceed out of your mouth until the day I tell you to shout; then you shall shout.

11So he caused the ark of the Lord to go around the city once; and they came into the camp, and lodged in the camp.

**AMP** [a] "The real character of this personage was disclosed by His accepting the homage of worship (cp. Acts 10:25, 26; Rev. 19:10), and still further in the command, 'Loose thy shoe from off thy foot'" (Jamieson, Fausset & Brown's *Commentary*). The *New Bible Commentary* supports this position, as do Lange, *The Cambridge Bible,* Ellicott, and many others, when it says, "We believe that this was the Son of God Himself."

## New American Standard

8 Now it came about when they had finished circumcising all the nation, that they remained in their places in the camp until they were healed.

9 Then the LORD said to Joshua, "Today I have rolled away the reproach of Egypt from you." So the name of that place is called [b]Gilgal to this day.

10 While the sons of Israel camped at Gilgal, they observed the Passover on the evening of the fourteenth day of the month on the desert plains of Jericho.

11 And on the day after the Passover, on that very day, they ate some of the produce of the land, unleavened cakes and parched *grain.*

12 And the manna ceased on the day after they had eaten some of the produce of the land, so that the sons of Israel no longer had manna, but they ate some of the yield of the land of Canaan during that year.

13¶ Now it came about when Joshua was by Jericho, that he lifted up his eyes and looked, and behold, a man was standing opposite him with his sword drawn in his hand, and Joshua went to him and said to him, "Are you for us or for our adversaries?"

14 And he said, "No, rather I indeed come now *as* captain of the host of the LORD." And Joshua fell on his face to the earth, and bowed down, and said to him, "What has my lord to say to his servant?"

15 And the captain of the LORD's host said to Joshua, "Remove your sandals from your feet, for the place where you are standing is holy." And Joshua did so.

*The Conquest of Jericho*

**6** NOW JERICHO was tightly shut because of the sons of Israel; no one went out and no one came in.

2 And the LORD said to Joshua, "See, I have given Jericho into your hand, with its king *and* the valiant warriors.

3 "And you shall march around the city, all the men of war circling the city once. You shall do so for six days.

4 "Also seven priests shall carry seven trumpets of rams' horns before the ark; then on the seventh day you shall march around the city seven times, and the priests shall blow the trumpets.

5 "And it shall be that when they make a long blast with the ram's horn, and when you hear the sound of the trumpet, all the people shall shout with a great shout; and the wall of the city will fall down flat, and the people will go up every man straight ahead."

6¶ So Joshua the son of Nun called the priests and said to them, "Take up the ark of the covenant, and let seven priests carry seven trumpets of rams' horns before the ark of the LORD."

7 Then he said to the people, "Go forward, and march around the city, and let the armed men go on before the ark of the LORD."

8 And it was *so,* that when Joshua had spoken to the people, the seven priests carrying the seven trumpets of rams' horns before the LORD went forward and blew the trumpets; and the ark of the covenant of the LORD followed them.

9 And the armed men went before the priests who blew the trumpets, and the rear guard came after the ark, while they continued to blow the trumpets.

10 But Joshua commanded the people, saying, "You shall not shout nor let your voice be heard, nor let a word proceed out of your mouth, until the day I tell you, 'Shout!' Then you shall shout!"

11 So he had the ark of the LORD taken around the city, circling *it* once; then they came into the camp and spent the night in the camp.

NAS [b] I.e., rolling

## New International

after the whole nation had been circumcised, they remained where they were in camp until they were healed.

9 Then the LORD said to Joshua, "Today I have rolled away the reproach of Egypt from you." So the place has been called Gilgal[c] to this day.

10 On the evening of the fourteenth day of the month, while camped at Gilgal on the plains of Jericho, the Israelites celebrated the Passover. 11 The day after the Passover, that very day, they ate some of the produce of the land: unleavened bread and roasted grain. 12 The manna stopped the day after[d] they ate this food from the land; there was no longer any manna for the Israelites, but that year they ate of the produce of Canaan.

*The Fall of Jericho*

13 Now when Joshua was near Jericho, he looked up and saw a man standing in front of him with a drawn sword in his hand. Joshua went up to him and asked, "Are you for us or for our enemies?"

14 "Neither," he replied, "but as commander of the army of the LORD I have now come." Then Joshua fell facedown to the ground in reverence, and asked him, "What message does my Lord[e] have for his servant?"

15 The commander of the LORD's army replied, "Take off your sandals, for the place where you are standing is holy." And Joshua did so.

**6** NOW JERICHO was tightly shut up because of the Israelites. No one went out and no one came in.

2 Then the LORD said to Joshua, "See, I have delivered Jericho into your hands, along with its king and its fighting men. 3 March around the city once with all the armed men. Do this for six days. 4 Have seven priests carry trumpets of rams' horns in front of the ark. On the seventh day, march around the city seven times, with the priests blowing the trumpets. 5 When you hear them sound a long blast on the trumpets, have all the people give a loud shout; then the wall of the city will collapse and the people will go up, every man straight in."

6 So Joshua son of Nun called the priests and said to them, "Take up the ark of the covenant of the LORD and have seven priests carry trumpets in front of it." 7 And he ordered the people, "Advance! March around the city, with the armed guard going ahead of the ark of the LORD."

8 When Joshua had spoken to the people, the seven priests carrying the seven trumpets before the LORD went forward, blowing their trumpets, and the ark of the LORD's covenant followed them. 9 The armed guard marched ahead of the priests who blew the trumpets, and the rear guard followed the ark. All this time the trumpets were sounding. 10 But Joshua had commanded the people, "Do not give a war cry, do not raise your voices, do not say a word until the day I tell you to shout. Then shout!" 11 So he had the ark of the LORD carried around the city, circling it once. Then the people returned to camp and spent the night there.

NIV [c] 9 *Gilgal* sounds like the Hebrew for *roll.* [d] 12 Or *the day* [e] 14 Or *lord*

## King James

12¶ And Joshua rose early in the morning, and the priests took up the ark of the LORD.

13And seven priests bearing seven trumpets of rams' horns before the ark of the LORD went on continually, and blew with the trumpets: and the armed men went before them; but the rearward came after the ark of the LORD, *the priests* going on, and blowing with the trumpets.

14And the second day they compassed the city once, and returned into the camp: so they did six days.

15And it came to pass on the seventh day, that they rose early about the dawning of the day, and compassed the city after the same manner seven times: only on that day they compassed the city seven times.

16And it came to pass at the seventh time, when the priests blew with the trumpets, Joshua said unto the people, Shout; for the LORD hath given you the city.

17¶ And the city shall be accursed, *even* it, and all that *are* therein, to the LORD: only Rahab the harlot shall live, she and all that *are* with her in the house, because she hid the messengers that we sent.

18And ye, in any wise keep *yourselves* from the accursed thing, lest ye make *yourselves* accursed, when ye take of the accursed thing, and make the camp of Israel a curse, and trouble it.

19But all the silver, and gold, and vessels of brass and iron, *are* consecrated unto the LORD: they shall come into the treasury of the LORD.

20So the people shouted when *the priests* blew with the trumpets: and it came to pass, when the people heard the sound of the trumpet, and the people shouted with a great shout, that the wall fell down flat, so that the people went up into the city, every man straight before him, and they took the city.

21And they utterly destroyed all that *was* in the city, both man and woman, young and old, and ox, and sheep, and ass, with the edge of the sword.

22But Joshua had said unto the two men that had spied out the country, Go into the harlot's house, and bring out thence the woman, and all that she hath, as ye sware unto her.

23And the young men that were spies went in, and brought out Rahab, and her father, and her mother, and her brethren, and all that she had; and they brought out all her kindred, and left them without the camp of Israel.

24And they burnt the city with fire, and all that *was* therein: only the silver, and the gold, and the vessels of brass and of iron, they put into the treasury of the house of the LORD.

25And Joshua saved Rahab the harlot alive, and her father's household, and all that she had; and she dwelleth in Israel *even* unto this day; because she hid the messengers, which Joshua sent to spy out Jericho.

## Amplified

12Joshua rose early in the morning, and the priests took up the ark of the Lord.

13And the seven priests bearing the seven trumpets of rams' horns before the ark of the Lord passed on, blowing the trumpets continually; and the armed men went before them, and the rear guard came after the ark of the Lord, the priests blowing the trumpets as they went.

14The second day they compassed the city enclosure once, and returned to the camp. So they did six days.

15On the seventh day, they rose early at daybreak and marched around the city as usual, only that one day they compassed the city [a]seven times.

16And the seventh time, when the priests had blown the trumpets, Joshua said to the people, Shout; for the Lord has given you the city.

17And the city and all that is in it shall be devoted to the Lord [for destruction]; only Rahab the harlot and all who are with her in her house shall live, because she hid the messengers whom we sent.

18But you, keep yourselves from the accursed *and* devoted thing, lest when you have devoted it [to destruction], you take of the accursed thing, and so make the camp of Israel accursed, and trouble it.

19But all the silver, and gold, and vessels of bronze and iron, are consecrated to the Lord; they shall come into the treasury of the Lord.

20So the people shouted, and the trumpets were blown. When the people heard the sound of the trumpet, they raised a great shout, and [Jericho's] wall fell down in its place, so that the [Israelites] went up into the city every man straight before him, and they took the city.

21Then they utterly destroyed all that was in the city, both man and woman, young and old, ox, sheep, and donkey, with the edge of the sword.

22But Joshua said to the two men who had spied out the land, Go into the harlot's house, and bring out the woman, and all that she has, as you swore to her.

23So the young men, the spies, went in and brought out Rahab, her father and mother, her brethren, and all that she had; and they brought out all her kindred, and set them outside the camp of Israel.

24And they [b]burned the city with fire, and all that was in it; only the silver, the gold, and the vessels of bronze and of iron, they put into the treasury of the house of the Lord.

25So Joshua saved Rahab the harlot alive, and her father's household, and all that she had; and she lives in Israel even to this day, because she hid the messengers whom Joshua sent to spy out Jericho.

**AMP** [a] Any walled town was called a "city" and its head man was called "a king" in ancient times, but the fact that Joshua's army could march around the whole of Jericho seven times in one day shows that it was a very small place. Sir Charles Marston in *New Bible Evidence* echoes the reports of other archaeologists when he says that the excavations of ancient Jericho do not confirm the conceptions of our youth. Though the walls were so formidable, the area they enclosed only measures seven acres. The whole circumference of the city was about 650 yards. Our disappointment is somewhat modified by the fact that Jebusite Jerusalem which David captured was about the same size. Schliemann experienced a like disillusionment in 1873 when he excavated the city of Troy which Homer tells us so long withstood the Grecian hosts. Indeed it would almost seem that these ancient cities were more in the nature of places of refuge resorted to on the approach of an enemy. Under peaceful conditions a large proportion of the inhabitants would dwell outside the city's walls (Marston, condensed). [b] Important details of this story are fully substantiated by the findings of Dr. J. B. Garstang in his several excavations of Jericho. 1. The city was thoroughly burned by fire. 2. It had not been thoroughly plundered. Stored grain, for example, was found burned, but undisturbed. 3. But "the silver, the gold, and the vessels of bronze and of iron" were missing. 4. The walls had fallen, but the one gate had a tower left standing. 5. Well supported houses had been built on the walls. 6. The gate tower was "an imposing edifice," 54 ft. by 24 ft., remarkably well built of gray brick. Its ruins still stand 16 ft. high. 7. Only on one side of Jericho is there a mountain, and that is a mountain ridge, beginning a mile west of the city. (Adapted from various sources including *The Story of Jericho* by Garstang and *Archaeology and Bible History*, by Joseph P. Free.)

## New American Standard

12¶ Now Joshua rose early in the morning, and the priests took up the ark of the LORD.

13And the seven priests carrying the seven trumpets of rams' horns before the ark of the LORD went on continually, and blew the trumpets; and the armed men went before them, and the rear guard came after the ark of the LORD, while they continued to blow the trumpets.

14Thus the second day they marched around the city once and returned to the camp; they did so for six days.

15¶ Then it came about on the seventh day that they rose early at the dawning of the day and marched around the city in the same manner seven times; only on that day they marched around the city seven times.

16And it came about at the seventh time, when the priests blew the trumpets, Joshua said to the people, "Shout! For the LORD has given you the city.

17"And the city shall be under the ban, it and all that is in it belongs to the LORD; only Rahab the harlot and all who are with her in the house shall live, because she hid the messengers whom we sent.

18"But as for you, only keep yourselves from the things under the ban, lest you covet *them* and take some of the things under the ban, so you would make the camp of Israel accursed and bring trouble on it.

19"But all the silver and gold and articles of bronze and iron are holy to the LORD; they shall go into the treasury of the LORD."

20So the people shouted, and *priests* blew the trumpets; and it came about, when the people heard the sound of the trumpet, that the people shouted with a great shout and the wall fell down flat, so that the people went up into the city, every man straight ahead, and they took the city.

21And they utterly destroyed everything in the city, both man and woman, young and old, and ox and sheep and donkey, with the edge of the sword.

22¶ And Joshua said to the two men who had spied out the land, "Go into the harlot's house and bring the woman and all she has out of there, as you have sworn to her."

23So the young men who were spies went in and brought out Rahab and her father and her mother and her brothers and all she had; they also brought out all her relatives, and placed them outside the camp of Israel.

24And they burned the city with fire, and all that was in it. Only the silver and gold and articles of bronze and iron, they put into the treasury of the [c]house of the LORD.

25However, Rahab the harlot and her father's household and all she had, Joshua spared; and she has lived in the midst of Israel to this day, for she hid the messengers whom Joshua sent to spy out Jericho.

NAS [c] I.e., tabernacle

## New International

12Joshua got up early the next morning and the priests took up
the ark of the LORD. 13The seven priests carrying the seven trumpets went forward, marching before the ark of the LORD and blowing the trumpets. The armed men went ahead of them and the rear
guard followed the ark of the LORD, while the trumpets kept
sounding. 14So on the second day they marched around the city
once and returned to the camp. They did this for six days.
15On the seventh day, they got up at daybreak and marched
around the city seven times in the same manner, except that on
that day they circled the city seven times. 16The seventh time
around, when the priests sounded the trumpet blast, Joshua commanded the people, "Shout! For the LORD has given you the city!
17The city and all that is in it are to be devoted[d] to the LORD. Only
Rahab the prostitute[e] and all who are with her in her house shall
be spared, because she hid the spies we sent. 18But keep away
from the devoted things, so that you will not bring about your own
destruction by taking any of them. Otherwise you will make the
camp of Israel liable to destruction and bring trouble on it. 19All
the silver and gold and the articles of bronze and iron are sacred
to the LORD and must go into his treasury."
20When the trumpets sounded, the people shouted, and at the
sound of the trumpet, when the people gave a loud shout, the wall
collapsed; so every man charged straight in, and they took the city.
21They devoted the city to the LORD and destroyed with the sword
every living thing in it—men and women, young and old, cattle,
sheep and donkeys.
22Joshua said to the two men who had spied out the land, "Go
into the prostitute's house and bring her out and all who belong
to her, in accordance with your oath to her." 23So the young men
who had done the spying went in and brought out Rahab, her
father and mother and brothers and all who belonged to her. They
brought out her entire family and put them in a place outside the
camp of Israel.
24Then they burned the whole city and everything in it, but they
put the silver and gold and the articles of bronze and iron into the
treasury of the LORD's house. 25But Joshua spared Rahab the prostitute, with her family and all who belonged to her, because she
hid the men Joshua had sent as spies to Jericho—and she lives
among the Israelites to this day.

NIV [d] *17* The Hebrew term refers to the irrevocable giving over of things or persons to the LORD, often by totally destroying them; also in verses 18 and 21.
[e] *17* Or possibly *innkeeper;* also in verses 22 and 25

## King James

26¶ And Joshua adjured *them* at that time, saying, Cursed *be* the man before the LORD, that riseth up and buildeth this city Jericho: he shall lay the foundation thereof in his firstborn, and in his youngest *son* shall he set up the gates of it.
27So the LORD was with Joshua; and his fame was *noised* throughout all the country.

**7** BUT THE children of Israel committed a trespass in the accursed thing: for Achan, the son of Carmi, the son of Zabdi, the son of Zerah, of the tribe of Judah, took of the accursed thing: and the anger of the LORD was kindled against the children of Israel.
2And Joshua sent men from Jericho to Ai, which *is* beside Beth-aven, on the east side of Beth-el, and spake unto them, saying, Go up and view the country. And the men went up and viewed Ai.
3And they returned to Joshua, and said unto him, Let not all the people go up; but let about two or three thousand man go up and smite Ai; *and* make not all the people to labour thither; for they *are but* few.
4So there went up thither of the people about three thousand men: and they fled before the men of Ai.
5And the men of Ai smote of them about thirty and six men: for they chased them *from* before the gate *even* unto Shebarim, and smote them in the going down: wherefore the hearts of the people melted, and became as water.
6¶ And Joshua rent his clothes, and fell to the earth upon his face before the ark of the LORD until the eventide, he and the elders of Israel, and put dust upon their heads.
7And Joshua said, Alas, O Lord GOD, wherefore hast thou at all brought this people over Jordan, to deliver us into the hand of the Amorites, to destroy us? would to God we had been content, and dwelt on the other side Jordan!
8O Lord, what shall I say, when Israel turneth their backs before their enemies!
9For the Canaanites and all the inhabitants of the land shall hear *of it,* and shall environ us round, and cut off our name from the earth: and what wilt thou do unto thy great name?
10¶ And the LORD said unto Joshua, Get thee up; wherefore liest thou thus upon thy face?
11Israel hath sinned, and they have also transgressed my covenant which I commanded them: for they have even taken of the accursed thing, and have also stolen, and dissembled also, and they have put *it* even among their own stuff.
12Therefore the children of Israel could not stand before their enemies, *but* turned *their* backs before their enemies, because they were accursed: neither will I be with you any more, except ye destroy the accursed from among you.
13Up, sanctify the people, and say, Sanctify yourselves against tomorrow: for thus saith the LORD God of Israel, *There is* an accursed thing in the midst of thee, O Israel: thou canst not stand before thine enemies, until ye take away the accursed thing from among you.
14In the morning therefore ye shall be brought according to your tribes: and it shall be, *that* the tribe which the LORD taketh shall come according to the families *thereof;* and the family which the LORD shall take shall come by households; and the household which the LORD shall take shall come man by man.
15And it shall be, *that* he that is taken with the accursed thing shall be burnt with fire, he and all that he hath: because he hath transgressed the covenant of the LORD, and because he hath wrought folly in Israel.

## Amplified

26Then Joshua laid this oath on them, Cursed be the man before the Lord, who rises up and rebuilds this city, Jericho. With the loss of his first-born shall he lay its foundation, and with the loss of his youngest son shall he set up its gates. [See I Kings 16:34.]
27So the Lord was with Joshua; and his fame was in all the land.

**7** BUT THE Israelites committed a trespass in the devoted thing; for Achan son of Carmi, son of Zabdi, son of Zerah, of the tribe of Judah, took some of the things devoted [for destruction]; and the anger of the Lord burned against Israel.
2Joshua sent men from Jericho to Ai, which is near Beth-aven, east of Bethel, and said to them, Go up and spy out the land. So the men went up and spied out Ai.
3And they returned to Joshua, and said to him, Let not all the men go up; but let about two thousand or three thousand go up and attack Ai; do not make the whole army toil up there, for they of Ai are few.
4So about three thousand Israelites went up there, and they fled before the men of Ai,
5And the men of Ai killed about thirty-six men of them, for they chased them from before the gate as far as Shebarim, and slew them at the descent. And the hearts of the people melted, and became as water.
6Then Joshua rent his clothes, and lay on the earth upon his face before the ark of the Lord until evening, he and the elders of Israel; and they put dust on their heads.
7Joshua said, Alas, O Lord God, Why have You brought this people over the Jordan at all, only to give us into the hand of the Amorites to destroy us? Would that we had been content to dwell beyond Jordan!
8O Lord, what can I say, when Israel has turned to flee before their enemies!
9For the Canaanites and all the inhabitants of the land will hear of it, and will surround us, and cut off our name from the earth; and what will You do for Your great name?
10The Lord said to Joshua, Get up! Why do you lie thus upon your face?
11Israel has sinned; they have transgressed My covenant which I commanded them; they have taken of the things devoted [for destruction]; they have stolen, and lied, and put them among their own baggage.
12That is why the Israelites could not stand before their enemies, but fled before them; they are accursed *and* have become devoted [for destruction], I will cease to be with you, unless you destroy the accursed [devoted] things among you.
13Up, sanctify [set apart for holy purpose] the people, and say, Sanctify yourselves for tomorrow; for thus says the Lord, the God of Israel, There is an accursed thing in the midst of you, O Israel; you can not stand before your enemies until you take away from among you the thing devoted [to destruction].
14In the morning therefore you shall present your tribes; and the tribe which the Lord takes shall come by families; and the family which the Lord takes shall come by households; and the household which the Lord takes shall come by persons.
15And he who is taken with the devoted thing shall be [killed and his body] burned with fire, he and all he has, because he has transgressed the covenant of the Lord, and because he has done a shameful *and* wicked thing in Israel. [Verse 25.]

## New American Standard

26¶ Then Joshua made them take an oath at that time, saying,
"Cursed before the LORD is the man who rises up and builds this
city Jericho; with *the loss of* his first-born he shall lay its foundation,
and with *the loss of* his youngest son he shall set up its gates."
27So the LORD was with Joshua, and his fame was in all the land.

*Israel Is Defeated at Ai*

7 BUT THE sons of Israel acted unfaithfully in regard to the
things under the ban, for Achan, the son of Carmi, the son
of Zabdi, the son of Zerah, from the tribe of Judah, took some of
the things under the ban, therefore the anger of the LORD burned
against the sons of Israel.
2¶ Now Joshua sent men from Jericho to Ai, which is near
Beth-aven, east of Bethel, and said to them, "Go up and spy out
the land." So the men went up and spied out Ai.
3And they returned to Joshua and said to him, "Do not let all
the people go up; *only* about two or three thousand men need go
up to Ai; do not make all the people toil up there, for they are few."
4So about three thousand men from the people went up there,
but they fled from the men of Ai.
5And the men of Ai struck down about thirty-six of their men,
and pursued them from the gate as far as Shebarim, and struck
them down on the descent, so the hearts of the people melted and
became as water.
6¶ Then Joshua tore his clothes and fell to the earth on his face
before the ark of the LORD until the evening, *both* he and the elders
of Israel; and they put dust on their heads.
7And Joshua said, "Alas, O Lord GOD, why didst Thou ever
bring this people over the Jordan, *only* to deliver us into the hand
of the Amorites, to destroy us? If only we had been willing to dwell
beyond the Jordan!
8"O Lord, what can I say since Israel has turned *their* back
before their enemies?
9"For the Canaanites and all the inhabitants of the land will
hear of it, and they will surround us and cut off our name from
the earth. And what wilt Thou do for Thy great name?"
10¶ So the LORD said to Joshua, "Rise up! Why is it that you have
fallen on your face?
11"Israel has sinned, and they have also transgressed My covenant which I commanded them. And they have even taken some
of the things under the ban and have both stolen and deceived.
Moreover, they have also put *them* among their own things.
12"Therefore the sons of Israel cannot stand before their enemies; they turn *their* backs before their enemies, for they have
become accursed. I will not be with you anymore unless you
destroy the things under the ban from your midst.
13"Rise up! Consecrate the people and say, 'Consecrate yourselves for tomorrow, for thus the LORD, the God of Israel, has said,
"There are things under the ban in your midst, O Israel. You
cannot stand before your enemies until you have removed the
things under the ban from your midst."
14'In the morning then you shall come near by your tribes. And
it shall be that the tribe which the LORD takes *by lot* shall come near
by families, and the family which the LORD takes shall come near
by households, and the household which the LORD takes shall
come near man by man.
15'And it shall be that the one who is taken with the things
under the ban shall be burned with fire, he and all that belongs to
him, because he has transgressed the covenant of the LORD, and
because he has committed a disgraceful thing in Israel.' "

## New International

26At that time Joshua pronounced this solemn oath: "Cursed
before the LORD is the man who undertakes to rebuild this city,
Jericho:

"At the cost of his firstborn son
 will he lay its foundations;
at the cost of his youngest
 will he set up its gates."

27So the LORD was with Joshua, and his fame spread throughout the land.

*Achan's Sin*

7 BUT THE Israelites acted unfaithfully in regard to the devoted
things[a]; Achan son of Carmi, the son of Zimri,[b] the son of
Zerah, of the tribe of Judah, took some of them. So the LORD's
anger burned against Israel.
2Now Joshua sent men from Jericho to Ai, which is near Beth
Aven to the east of Bethel, and told them, "Go up and spy out the
region." So the men went up and spied out Ai.
3When they returned to Joshua, they said, "Not all the people
will have to go up against Ai. Send two or three thousand men to
take it and do not weary all the people, for only a few men are
there." 4So about three thousand men went up; but they were
routed by the men of Ai, 5who killed about thirty-six of them. They
chased the Israelites from the city gate as far as the stone quarries[c]
and struck them down on the slopes. At this the hearts of the
people melted and became like water.
6Then Joshua tore his clothes and fell facedown to the ground
before the ark of the LORD, remaining there till evening. The elders
of Israel did the same, and sprinkled dust on their heads. 7And
Joshua said, "Ah, Sovereign LORD, why did you ever bring this
people across the Jordan to deliver us into the hands of the Amorites to destroy us? If only we had been content to stay on the other
side of the Jordan! 8O Lord, what can I say, now that Israel has
been routed by its enemies? 9The Canaanites and the other people
of the country will hear about this and they will surround us and
wipe out our name from the earth. What then will you do for your
own great name?"
10The LORD said to Joshua, "Stand up! What are you doing
down on your face? 11Israel has sinned; they have violated my
covenant, which I commanded them to keep. They have taken
some of the devoted things; they have stolen, they have lied, they
have put them with their own possessions. 12That is why the
Israelites cannot stand against their enemies; they turn their backs
and run because they have been made liable to destruction. I will
not be with you anymore unless you destroy whatever among you
is devoted to destruction.
13"Go, consecrate the people. Tell them, 'Consecrate yourselves in preparation for tomorrow; for this is what the LORD, the
God of Israel, says: That which is devoted is among you, O Israel.
You cannot stand against your enemies until you remove it.
14" 'In the morning, present yourselves tribe by tribe. The tribe
that the LORD takes shall come forward clan by clan; the clan that
the LORD takes shall come forward family by family; and the family
that the LORD takes shall come forward man by man. 15He who is
caught with the devoted things shall be destroyed by fire, along
with all that belongs to him. He has violated the covenant of the
LORD and has done a disgraceful thing in Israel!' "

**NIV** [a] *1* The Hebrew term refers to the irrevocable giving over of things or persons to the LORD, often by totally destroying them; also in verses 11, 12, 13 and 15. [b] *1* See Septuagint and 1 Chron. 2:6; Hebrew *Zabdi;* also in verses 17 and 18. [c] *5* Or *as far as Shebarim*

## King James

16¶ So Joshua rose up early in the morning, and brought Israel by their tribes; and the tribe of Judah was taken:

17And he brought the family of Judah; and he took the family of the Zarhites: and he brought the family of the Zarhites man by man; and Zabdi was taken:

18And he brought his household man by man; and Achan, the son of Carmi, the son of Zabdi, the son of Zerah, of the tribe of Judah, was taken.

19And Joshua said unto Achan, My son, give, I pray thee, glory to the LORD God of Israel, and make confession unto him; and tell me now what thou hast done; hide *it* not from me.

20And Achan answered Joshua, and said, Indeed I have sinned against the LORD God of Israel, and thus and thus have I done:

21When I saw among the spoils a goodly Babylonish garment, and two hundred shekels of silver, and a wedge of gold of fifty shekels weight, then I coveted them, and took them; and, behold, they *are* hid in the earth in the midst of my tent, and the silver under it.

22¶ So Joshua sent messengers, and they ran unto the tent; and, behold, *it was* hid in his tent, and the silver under it.

23And they took them out of the midst of the tent, and brought them unto Joshua, and unto all the children of Israel, and laid them out before the LORD.

24And Joshua, and all Israel with him, took Achan the son of Zerah, and the silver, and the garment, and the wedge of gold, and his sons, and his daughters, and his oxen, and his asses, and his sheep, and his tent, and all that he had: and they brought them unto the valley of Achor.

25And Joshua said, Why hast thou troubled us? the LORD shall trouble thee this day. And all Israel stoned him with stones, and burned them with fire, after they had stoned them with stones.

26And they raised over him a great heap of stones unto this day. So the LORD turned from the fierceness of his anger. Wherefore the name of that place was called, The valley of Achor, unto this day.

8 AND THE LORD said unto Joshua, Fear not, neither be thou dismayed: take all the people of war with thee, and arise, go up to Ai: see, I have given into thy hand the king of Ai, and his people, and his city, and his land:

2And thou shalt do to Ai and her king as thou didst unto Jericho and her king: only the spoil thereof, and the cattle thereof, shall ye take for a prey unto yourselves: lay thee an ambush for the city behind it.

3¶ So Joshua arose, and all the people of war, to go up against Ai: and Joshua chose out thirty thousand mighty men of valour, and sent them away by night.

4And he commanded them, saying, Behold, ye shall lie in wait against the city, *even* behind the city: go not very far from the city, but be ye all ready:

5And I, and all the people that *are* with me, will approach unto the city: and it shall come to pass, when they come out against us, as at the first, that we will flee before them,

6(For they will come out after us) till we have drawn them from the city; for they will say, They flee before us, as at the first: therefore we will flee before them.

7Then ye shall rise up from the ambush, and seize upon the city: for the LORD your God will deliver it into your hand.

8And it shall be, when ye have taken the city, *that* ye shall set the city on fire: according to the commandment of the LORD shall ye do. See, I have commanded you.

9¶ Joshua therefore sent them forth: and they went to lie in ambush, and abode between Beth-el and Ai, on the west side of Ai: but Joshua lodged that night among the people.

## Amplified

16So Joshua rose up early in the morning and brought Israel near by their tribes; and the tribe of Judah was taken;

17He brought near the family of Judah, and the family of the Zarhites was taken; and he brought near the family of the Zarhites man by man, and Zabdi was taken;

18He brought near his household man by man, and Achan son of Carmi, son of Zabdi, son of Zerah of the tribe of Judah, was taken.

19And Joshua said to Achan, My son, give glory to the Lord God of Israel, make confession to Him; and tell me now what you have done; do not hide it from me.

20And Achan answered Joshua, In truth I have sinned against the Lord, the God of Israel, and this have I done:

21When I saw among the spoils an attractive mantle from Shinar, and two hundred shekels of silver, and a bar of gold weighing fifty shekels, I coveted them and took them. Behold, they are hidden in the earth inside my tent, with the silver underneath.

22So Joshua sent messengers, who ran to the tent; and lo, the spoil was hidden in his tent with the silver underneath.

23And they took them from the tent and brought them to Joshua and all the Israelites, and laid them out before the Lord.

24And Joshua and all Israel with him took Achan son of Zerah, and the silver, the garment, the wedge of gold, his sons, his daughters, his oxen, his donkeys, his sheep, his tent, and all that he had; and they brought them to the valley of Achor.

25And Joshua said, Why have you brought trouble on us? The Lord will trouble you this day. And all Israel stoned him and those with him with stones, and afterward burned their bodies with fire.

26And they raised over him a great heap of stones that remains to this day; then the Lord turned from the fierceness of His anger. Therefore the name of that place was called the Valley of Achor *or* Troubling, to this day.

8 AND THE Lord said to Joshua, Fear not nor be dismayed; take all the men of war with you, and arise, go up to Ai; see, I have given into your hand the king of Ai, his people, his city, and his land;

2And you shall do to Ai and her king as you did to Jericho and her king; only its spoil and its cattle [this time] you shall take as booty for yourselves. Lay an ambush against the city behind it.

3So Joshua arose, and all the people of war, to go up against Ai; [he] chose thirty thousand mighty men of strength and sent them forth by night.

4And he commanded them, Behold, you shall lie in wait against the city behind it. Do not go very far from the city, but be all ready.

5And I, and all the people who are with me, will approach the city. And when they come out against us, as the first time, we will flee before them,

6Till we have drawn them from the city; for they will say, They are fleeing from us as before. So we will flee before them.

7Then you shall rise up from the ambush, and seize the city; for the Lord your God will deliver it into your hand.

8When you have taken the city, you shall set it afire; as the Lord commanded you shall do. See, I have commanded you.

9So Joshua sent them forth; and they went to the place of ambush, and remained between Bethel and Ai, on the west side of Ai; but Joshua lodged that night among the people.

## New American Standard

*The Sin of Achan*

16¶ So Joshua arose early in the morning and brought Israel near by tribes, and the tribe of Judah was taken.

17And he brought the family of Judah near, and he took the family of the Zerahites; and he brought the family of the Zerahites near man by man, and Zabdi was taken.

18And he brought his household near man by man; and Achan, son of Carmi, son of Zabdi, son of Zerah, from the tribe of Judah, was taken.

19Then Joshua said to Achan, "My son, I implore you, give glory to the LORD, the God of Israel, and give praise to Him; and tell me now what you have done. Do not hide it from me."

20So Achan answered Joshua and said, "Truly, I have sinned against the LORD, the God of Israel, and this is what I did:

21when I saw among the spoil a beautiful mantle from Shinar and two hundred shekels of silver and a bar of gold fifty shekels in weight, then I coveted them and took them; and behold, they are concealed in the earth inside my tent with the silver underneath it."

22¶ So Joshua sent messengers, and they ran to the tent; and behold, it was concealed in his tent with the silver underneath it.

23And they took them from inside the tent and brought them to Joshua and to all the sons of Israel, and they poured them out before the LORD.

24Then Joshua and all Israel with him, took Achan the son of Zerah, the silver, the mantle, the bar of gold, his sons, his daughters, his oxen, his donkeys, his sheep, his tent and all that belonged to him; and they brought them up to the valley of [a]Achor.

25And Joshua said, "Why have you troubled us? The LORD will trouble you this day." And all Israel stoned them with stones; and they burned them with fire after they had stoned them with stones.

26And they raised over him a great heap of stones that stands to this day, and the LORD turned from the fierceness of His anger. Therefore the name of that place has been called the valley of [b]Achor to this day.

*The Conquest of Ai*

8 NOW THE LORD said to Joshua, "Do not fear or be dismayed. Take all the people of war with you and arise, go up to Ai; see, I have given into your hand the king of Ai, his people, his city, and his land.

2"And you shall do to Ai and its king just as you did to Jericho and its king; you shall take only its spoil and its cattle as plunder for yourselves. Set an ambush for the city behind it."

3¶ So Joshua rose with all the people of war to go up to Ai; and Joshua chose 30,000 men, valiant warriors, and sent them out at night.

4And he commanded them, saying, "See, you are going to ambush the city from behind it. Do not go very far from the city, but all of you be ready.

5"Then I and all the people who are with me will approach the city. And it will come about when they come out to meet us as at the first, that we will flee before them.

6"And they will come out after us until we have drawn them away from the city, for they will say, '*They* are fleeing before us as at the first.' So we will flee before them.

7"And you shall rise from *your* ambush and take possession of the city, for the LORD your God will deliver it into your hand.

8"Then it will be when you have seized the city, that you shall set the city on fire. You shall do *it* according to the word of the LORD. See, I have commanded you."

9So Joshua sent them away, and they went to the place of ambush and remained between Bethel and Ai, on the west side of Ai; but Joshua spent that night among the people.

NAS [a] I.e., trouble [b] I.e., trouble

## New International

16Early the next morning Joshua had Israel come forward by
tribes, and Judah was taken. 17The clans of Judah came forward,
and he took the Zerahites. He had the clan of the Zerahites come
forward by families, and Zimri was taken. 18Joshua had his family
come forward man by man, and Achan son of Carmi, the son of
Zimri, the son of Zerah, of the tribe of Judah, was taken.
19Then Joshua said to Achan, "My son, give glory to the LORD,[c]
the God of Israel, and give him the praise.[d] Tell me what you have
done; do not hide it from me."
20Achan replied, "It is true! I have sinned against the LORD, the
God of Israel. This is what I have done: 21When I saw in the
plunder a beautiful robe from Babylonia,[e] two hundred shekels[f]
of silver and a wedge of gold weighing fifty shekels,[g] I coveted
them and took them. They are hidden in the ground inside my
tent, with the silver underneath."
22So Joshua sent messengers, and they ran to the tent, and there
it was, hidden in his tent, with the silver underneath. 23They took
the things from the tent, brought them to Joshua and all the
Israelites and spread them out before the LORD.
24Then Joshua, together with all Israel, took Achan son of
Zerah, the silver, the robe, the gold wedge, his sons and daughters, his cattle, donkeys and sheep, his tent and all that he had,
to the Valley of Achor. 25Joshua said, "Why have you brought this
trouble on us? The LORD will bring trouble on you today."
Then all Israel stoned him, and after they had stoned the rest,
they burned them. 26Over Achan they heaped up a large pile of
rocks, which remains to this day. Then the LORD turned from his
fierce anger. Therefore that place has been called the Valley of
Achor[h] ever since.

*Ai Destroyed*

8 THEN THE LORD said to Joshua, "Do not be afraid; do not be discouraged. Take the whole army with you, and go up and
attack Ai. For I have delivered into your hands the king of Ai, his
people, his city and his land. 2You shall do to Ai and its king as
you did to Jericho and its king, except that you may carry off their
plunder and livestock for yourselves. Set an ambush behind the
city."
3So Joshua and the whole army moved out to attack Ai. He
chose thirty thousand of his best fighting men and sent them out
at night 4with these orders: "Listen carefully. You are to set an
ambush behind the city. Don't go very far from it. All of you be
on the alert. 5I and all those with me will advance on the city, and
when the men come out against us, as they did before, we will flee
from them. 6They will pursue us until we have lured them away
from the city, for they will say, 'They are running away from us
as they did before.' So when we flee from them, 7you are to rise
up from ambush and take the city. The LORD your God will give
it into your hand. 8When you have taken the city, set it on fire. Do
what the LORD has commanded. See to it; you have my orders."
9Then Joshua sent them off, and they went to the place of
ambush and lay in wait between Bethel and Ai, to the west of
Ai—but Joshua spent that night with the people.

NIV [c] 19 A solemn charge to tell the truth [d] 19 Or *and confess to him* [e] 21 Hebrew *Shinar* [f] 21 That is, about 5 pounds (about 2.3 kilograms) [g] 21 That is, about 1 1/4 pounds (about 0.6 kilogram) [h] 26 *Achor* means *trouble.*

## King James

10And Joshua rose up early in the morning, and numbered the people, and went up, he and the elders of Israel, before the people to Ai.

11And all the people, *even the people* of war that *were* with him, went up, and drew nigh, and came before the city, and pitched on the north side of Ai: now *there was* a valley between them and Ai.

12And he took about five thousand men, and set them to lie in ambush between Beth-el and Ai, on the west side of the city.

13And when they had set the people, *even* all the host that *was* on the north of the city, and their liers in wait on the west of the city, Joshua went that night into the midst of the valley.

14¶ And it came to pass, when the king of Ai saw *it*, that they hasted and rose up early, and the men of the city went out against Israel to battle, he and all his people, at a time appointed, before the plain; but he wist not that *there were* liers in ambush against him behind the city.

15And Joshua and all Israel made as if they were beaten before them, and fled by the way of the wilderness.

16And all the people that *were* in Ai were called together to pursue after them: and they pursued after Joshua, and were drawn away from the city.

17And there was not a man left in Ai or Beth-el, that went not out after Israel: and they left the city open, and pursued after Israel.

18And the LORD said unto Joshua, Stretch out the spear that *is* in thy hand toward Ai; for I will give it into thine hand. And Joshua stretched out the spear that *he had* in his hand toward the city.

19And the ambush arose quickly out of their place, and they ran as soon as he had stretched out his hand: and they entered into the city, and took it, and hasted and set the city on fire.

20And when the men of Ai looked behind them, they saw, and, behold, the smoke of the city ascended up to heaven, and they had no power to flee this way or that way: and the people that fled to the wilderness turned back upon the pursuers.

21And when Joshua and all Israel saw that the ambush had taken the city, and that the smoke of the city ascended, then they turned again, and slew the men of Ai.

22And the other issued out of the city against them; so they were in the midst of Israel, some on this side, and some on that side: and they smote them, so that they let none of them remain or escape.

23And the king of Ai they took alive, and brought him to Joshua.

24And it came to pass, when Israel had made an end of slaying all the inhabitants of Ai in the field, in the wilderness wherein they chased them, and when they were all fallen on the edge of the sword, until they were consumed, that all the Israelites returned unto Ai, and smote it with the edge of the sword.

25And *so* it was, *that* all that fell that day, both of men and women, *were* twelve thousand, *even* all the men of Ai.

26For Joshua drew not his hand back, wherewith he stretched out the spear, until he had utterly destroyed all the inhabitants of Ai.

27Only the cattle and the spoil of that city Israel took for a prey unto themselves, according unto the word of the LORD which he commanded Joshua.

28And Joshua burnt Ai, and made it an heap for ever, *even* a desolation unto this day.

29And the king of Ai he hanged on a tree until eventide: and as soon as the sun was down, Joshua commanded that they should take his carcase down from the tree, and cast it at the entering of the gate of the city, and raise thereon a great heap of stones, *that remaineth* unto this day.

30¶ Then Joshua built an altar unto the LORD God of Israel in mount Ebal,

31As Moses the servant of the LORD commanded the children of Israel, as it is written in the book of the law of Moses, an altar of whole stones, over which no man hath lift up *any* iron: and they offered thereon burnt offerings unto the LORD, and sacrificed peace offerings.

## Amplified

10Joshua rose up early in the morning, and mustered the men, and went up with the elders of Israel, before the warriors to Ai.

11And all the fighting men who were with him, went up, and drew near before the city, and encamped on the north side of [it], with a ravine between them and Ai.

12And he took about five thousand men, and set them in ambush between Bethel and Ai, west of the city.

13So they stationed all the army, the main encampment that was north of the city, and their men in ambush behind *and* on the west of the city, and Joshua went that night into the midst of the ravine.

14When the king *and people* of Ai saw it, they hastily rose early, and the men of the city went out against Israel to battle, [at a time *and* place appointed,] before the Arabah [plain]; but he did not know of the ambush against him behind the city.

15And Joshua and all Israel pretended to be beaten by them, and fled toward the wilderness.

16So all the people in Ai were called together to pursue them; and they pursued Joshua, and were drawn away from the city.

17Not a man was left in Ai or Bethel, who did not go out after Israel. Leaving the city open, they pursued Israel.

18Then the Lord said to Joshua, Stretch out the javelin that is in your hand toward Ai; for I will give it into your hand. So Joshua stretched out the javelin in his hand toward the city.

19The ambush arose quickly out of their place and ran when he stretched out his hand; and they entered the city and took it, then hastened and set it afire.

20When the men of Ai looked back, behold, the smoke of the city went up to the heavens, and they had no power to flee this way or that way. Then the Israelites who fled to the wilderness turned back upon the pursuers.

21When Joshua and all Israel saw that the ambush had taken the city, and that the smoke of the city went up, they turned again and slew the men of Ai.

22And the others came forth out of the city against them of Ai; so they were in the midst of Israel, some on this side, and some on that side. And [the Israelites] smote them, so that they let none of them remain or escape.

23But they took the king of Ai alive, and brought him to Joshua.

24When Israel had finished slaying all the inhabitants of Ai in the field, and in the wilderness into which they pursued them, and they were all fallen by the sword until they were consumed, then all the Israelites returned to Ai and smote it with the sword.

25And all that fell that day, both of men and women, were twelve thousand, including all the men of Ai.

26For Joshua drew not back his hand with which he stretched out the javelin, until he had utterly destroyed all the inhabitants of Ai.

27Only the livestock and the spoil of that city Israel took as booty for themselves, according to the word of the Lord which He commanded Joshua.

28So Joshua burned Ai, and made it a heap of ruins for ever, even a desolation to this day.

29And he hanged the king of Ai on a tree until evening; and at sunset Joshua commanded, and they took the body down from the tree, and cast it at the entrance of the city's gate, and raised a great heap of stones over it, there to this day.

30Then Joshua built an altar to the Lord, the God of Israel, on Mount Ebal,

31As Moses the servant of the Lord commanded the Israelites, as it is written in the book of the law of Moses, an altar of unhewn stones, upon which no man has lifted up an iron tool; and they offered on it burnt offerings to the Lord, and sacrificed peace offerings.

## New American Standard

10¶ Now Joshua rose early in the morning and mustered the
people, and he went up with the elders of Israel before the people
to Ai.
11Then all the people of war who *were* with him went up and
drew near and arrived in front of the city, and camped on the north
side of Ai. Now *there was* a valley between him and Ai.
12And he took about 5,000 men and set them in ambush between Bethel and Ai, on the west side of the city.
13So they stationed the people, all the army that was on the
north side of the city, and its rear guard on the west side of the
city, and Joshua spent that night in the midst of the valley.
14And it came about when the king of Ai saw *it,* that the men
of the city hurried and rose up early and went out to meet Israel
in battle, he and all his people at the appointed place before the
desert plain. But he did not know that *there was* an ambush against
him behind the city.
15And Joshua and all Israel pretended to be beaten before them,
and fled by the way of the wilderness.
16And all the people who were in the city were called together
to pursue them, and they pursued Joshua, and were drawn away
from the city.
17So not a man was left in Ai or Bethel who had not gone out
after Israel, and they left the city unguarded and pursued Israel.
18¶ Then the LORD said to Joshua, "Stretch out the javelin that
is in your hand toward Ai, for I will give it into your hand." So
Joshua stretched out the javelin that was in his hand toward the
city.
19And the *men in* ambush rose quickly from their place, and
when he had stretched out his hand, they ran and entered the city
and captured it; and they quickly set the city on fire.
20When the men of Ai turned back and looked, behold, the
smoke of the city ascended to the sky, and they had no place to
flee this way or that, for the people who had been fleeing to the
wilderness turned against the pursuers.
21When Joshua and all Israel saw that the *men in* ambush had
captured the city and that the smoke of the city ascended, they
turned back and slew the men of Ai.
22And the others came out from the city to encounter them, so
that they were *trapped* in the midst of Israel, some on this side and
some on that side; and they slew them until no one was left of
those who survived or escaped.
23But they took alive the king of Ai and brought him to Joshua.
24¶ Now it came about when Israel had finished killing all the
inhabitants of Ai in the field in the wilderness where they pursued
them, and all of them were fallen by the edge of the sword until
they were destroyed, then all Israel returned to Ai and struck it
with the edge of the sword.
25And all who fell that day, both men and women, were
12,000—all the people of Ai.
26For Joshua did not withdraw his hand with which he
stretched out the javelin until he had utterly destroyed all the
inhabitants of Ai.
27Israel took only the cattle and the spoil of that city as plunder
for themselves, according to the word of the LORD which He had
commanded Joshua.
28So Joshua burned Ai and made it a heap forever, a desolation
until this day.
29And he hanged the king of Ai on a tree until evening; and at
sunset Joshua gave command and they took his body down from
the tree, and threw it at the entrance of the city gate, and raised
over it a great heap of stones *that stands* to this day.
30¶ Then Joshua built an altar to the LORD, the God of Israel, in
Mount Ebal,
31just as Moses the servant of the LORD had commanded the
sons of Israel, as it is written in the book of the law of Moses, an
altar of uncut stones, on which no man had wielded an iron *tool;*
and they offered burnt offerings on it to the LORD, and sacrificed
peace offerings.

## New International

10Early the next morning Joshua mustered his men, and he and
the leaders of Israel marched before them to Ai. 11The entire force
that was with him marched up and approached the city and arrived in front of it. They set up camp north of Ai, with the valley
between them and the city. 12Joshua had taken about five thousand men and set them in ambush between Bethel and Ai, to the
west of the city. 13They had the soldiers take up their positions—all
those in the camp to the north of the city and the ambush to the
west of it. That night Joshua went into the valley.
14When the king of Ai saw this, he and all the men of the city
hurried out early in the morning to meet Israel in battle at a certain
place overlooking the Arabah. But he did not know that an ambush
had been set against him behind the city. 15Joshua and all Israel
let themselves be driven back before them, and they fled toward
the desert. 16All the men of Ai were called to pursue them, and
they pursued Joshua and were lured away from the city. 17Not a
man remained in Ai or Bethel who did not go after Israel. They left
the city open and went in pursuit of Israel.
18Then the LORD said to Joshua, "Hold out toward Ai the javelin
that is in your hand, for into your hand I will deliver the city." So
Joshua held out his javelin toward Ai. 19As soon as he did this, the
men in the ambush rose quickly from their position and rushed
forward. They entered the city and captured it and quickly set it
on fire.
20The men of Ai looked back and saw the smoke of the city
rising against the sky, but they had no chance to escape in any
direction, for the Israelites who had been fleeing toward the desert
had turned back against their pursuers. 21For when Joshua and all
Israel saw that the ambush had taken the city and that smoke was
going up from the city, they turned around and attacked the men
of Ai. 22The men of the ambush also came out of the city against
them, so that they were caught in the middle, with Israelites on
both sides. Israel cut them down, leaving them neither survivors
nor fugitives. 23But they took the king of Ai alive and brought him
to Joshua.
24When Israel had finished killing all the men of Ai in the fields
and in the desert where they had chased them, and when every
one of them had been put to the sword, all the Israelites returned
to Ai and killed those who were in it. 25Twelve thousand men and
women fell that day—all the people of Ai. 26For Joshua did not
draw back the hand that held out his javelin until he had destroyed[a] all who lived in Ai. 27But Israel did carry off for themselves the livestock and plunder of this city, as the LORD had
instructed Joshua.
28So Joshua burned Ai and made it a permanent heap of ruins,
a desolate place to this day. 29He hung the king of Ai on a tree and
left him there until evening. At sunset, Joshua ordered them to
take his body from the tree and throw it down at the entrance of
the city gate. And they raised a large pile of rocks over it, which
remains to this day.

### *The Covenant Renewed at Mount Ebal*

30Then Joshua built on Mount Ebal an altar to the LORD, the God
of Israel, 31as Moses the servant of the LORD had commanded the
Israelites. He built it according to what is written in the Book of
the Law of Moses—an altar of uncut stones, on which no iron tool
had been used. On it they offered to the LORD burnt offerings and
sacrificed fellowship offerings.[b] 32There, in the presence of the

**NIV** [a] *26* The Hebrew term refers to the irrevocable giving over of things or persons to the LORD, often by totally destroying them. [b] *31* Traditionally *peace offerings*

## King James

32¶ And he wrote there upon the stones a copy of the law of Moses, which he wrote in the presence of the children of Israel.
33And all Israel, and their elders, and officers, and their judges, stood on this side the ark and on that side before the priests the Levites, which bare the ark of the covenant of the LORD, as well the stranger, as he that was born among them; half of them over against mount Gerizim, and half of them over against mount Ebal; as Moses the servant of the LORD had commanded before, that they should bless the people of Israel.
34And afterward he read all the words of the law, the blessings and cursings, according to all that is written in the book of the law.
35There was not a word of all that Moses commanded, which Joshua read not before all the congregation of Israel, with the women, and the little ones, and the strangers that were conversant among them.

9 AND IT came to pass, when all the kings which *were* on this side Jordan, in the hills, and in the valleys, and in all the coasts of the great sea over against Lebanon, the Hittite, and the Amorite, the Canaanite, the Perizzite, the Hivite, and the Jebusite, heard *thereof;*
2That they gathered themselves together, to fight with Joshua and with Israel, with one accord.
3¶ And when the inhabitants of Gibeon heard what Joshua had done unto Jericho and to Ai,
4They did work wilily, and went and made as if they had been ambassadors, and took old sacks upon their asses, and wine bottles, old, and rent, and bound up;
5And old shoes and clouted upon their feet, and old garments upon them; and all the bread of their provision was dry *and* mouldy.
6And they went to Joshua unto the camp at Gilgal, and said unto him, and to the men of Israel, We be come from a far country: now therefore make ye a league with us.
7And the men of Israel said unto the Hivites, Peradventure ye dwell among us; and how shall we make a league with you?
8And they said unto Joshua, We *are* thy servants. And Joshua said unto them, Who *are* ye? and from whence come ye?
9And they said unto him, From a very far country thy servants are come because of the name of the LORD thy God: for we have heard the fame of him, and all that he did in Egypt,
10And all that he did to the two kings of the Amorites, that *were* beyond Jordan, to Sihon king of Heshbon, and to Og king of Bashan, which *was* at Ashtaroth.
11Wherefore our elders and all the inhabitants of our country spake to us, saying, Take victuals with you for the journey, and go to meet them, and say unto them, We *are* your servants: therefore now make ye a league with us.
12This our bread we took hot *for* our provision out of our houses on the day we came forth to go unto you; but now, behold, it is dry, and it is mouldy:
13And these bottles of wine, which we filled, *were* new; and, behold, they be rent: and these our garments and our shoes are become old by reason of the very long journey.
14And the men took of their victuals, and asked not *counsel* at the mouth of the LORD.
15And Joshua made peace with them, and made a league with them, to let them live: and the princes of the congregation sware unto them.
16¶ And it came to pass at the end of three days after they had made a league with them, that they heard that they *were* their neighbours, and *that* they dwelt among them.
17And the children of Israel journeyed, and came unto their cities on the third day. Now their cities *were* Gibeon, and Chephirah, and Beeroth, and Kirjath-jearim.

## Amplified

32And there in the presence of the Israelites, [Joshua] wrote on the stones a copy of the law of Moses.
33And all Israel, sojourner as well as he who was born among them, with their elders, officers, and judges, stood on either side of the ark before the Levitical priests who carried the ark of the covenant of the Lord, half of them in front of Mount Gerizim, and half of them in front of Mount Ebal, as Moses the servant of the Lord had commanded before, that they should bless the Israelites.
34Afterward Joshua read all the words of the law, the blessing and cursing, all that is written in the book of the law.
35There was not a word of all that Moses commanded which Joshua did not read before all the assembly of Israel, and the women, and little ones, and the foreigners who were living among them.

9 WHEN ALL the kings beyond the Jordan in the hill country and in the lowland and all along the coast of the Great [Mediterranean] Sea toward Lebanon, the Hittites, Amorites, Canaanites, Perizzites, Hivites, and Jebusites heard this,
2They gathered together with one accord to fight Joshua and Israel.
3But when the people of Gibeon heard what Joshua had done to Jericho and Ai,
4They worked cunningly, and went pretending to be ambassadors, and took [provisions and] old sacks on their donkeys, and wineskins, old, torn, and mended;
5And old and patched shoes on their feet, and wearing old garments; and all their supply of food was dry and moldy.
6And they went to Joshua in the camp at Gilgal, and said to him and the men of Israel, We have come from a far country; so now make a covenant with us.
7But the men of Israel said to the Hivites, Perhaps you live among us; then how can we make a covenant with you?
8They said to Joshua, We are your servants. And Joshua said to them, Who are you? From where have you come?
9They said to him, From a very far country your servants have come because of the name of the Lord your God; for we have heard the fame of Him, and all that He did in Egypt,
10And all that He did to the two kings of the Amorites, who were beyond the Jordan, to Sihon king of Heshbon, and to Og king of Bashan, who lived in Ashtaroth.
11So our elders and all the residents of our country said to us, Take provisions for the journey, and go to meet [the Israelites], and say to them, We are your servants; and now make a covenant with us.
12This our bread we took hot for our provision out of our houses on the day we set out to go to you; but now, behold, it is dry, and has become moldy.
13These wineskin [bottles], which we filled, were new; and behold, they are torn; and our garments and our shoes have become old because of the very long journey.
14So the [Israelite] men partook of their food, and did not consult the Lord.
15Joshua made peace with them, covenanting with them to let them live; and the assembly's leaders swore to them.
16Then three days after they had made a covenant with [the strangers, the Israelites] heard that they were their neighbors, and that they dwelt among them.
17And the Israelites set out and came to their cities on the third day. Now their cities were Gibeon, Chephirah, Beeroth, and Kiriath-jearim.

## New American Standard

32And he wrote there on the stones a copy of the law of Moses,
which he had written, in the presence of the sons of Israel.
33And all Israel with their elders and officers and their judges
were standing on both sides of the ark before the Levitical priests
who carried the ark of the covenant of the LORD, the stranger as
well as the native. Half of them *stood* in front of Mount Gerizim and
half of them in front of Mount Ebal, just as Moses the servant of
the LORD had given command at first to bless the people of Israel.
34Then afterward he read all the words of the law, the blessing
and the curse, according to all that is written in the book of the law.
35There was not a word of all that Moses had commanded
which Joshua did not read before all the assembly of Israel with the
women and the little ones and the strangers who were living
among them.

*Guile of the Gibeonites*

9 NOW IT came about when all the kings who were beyond the
Jordan, in the hill country and in the lowland and on all the
coast of the Great Sea toward Lebanon, the Hittite and the Amorite, the Canaanite, the Perizzite, the Hivite and the Jebusite, heard
of it,
2that they gathered themselves together with one accord to
fight with Joshua and with Israel.
3¶ When the inhabitants of Gibeon heard what Joshua had
done to Jericho and to Ai,
4they also acted craftily and set out as envoys, and took worn-
out sacks on their donkeys, and wineskins, worn-out and torn and
mended,
5and worn-out and patched sandals on their feet, and worn-
out clothes on themselves; and all the bread of their provision was
dry *and* had become crumbled.
6And they went to Joshua to the camp at Gilgal, and said to
him and to the men of Israel, "We have come from a far country;
now therefore, make a covenant with us."
7And the men of Israel said to the Hivites, "Perhaps you are
living within our land; how then shall we make a covenant with
you?"
8But they said to Joshua, "We are your servants." Then Joshua
said to them, "Who are you, and where do you come from?"
9And they said to him, "Your servants have come from a very
far country because of the fame of the LORD your God; for we have
heard the report of Him and all that He did in Egypt,
10and all that He did to the two kings of the Amorites who were
beyond the Jordan, to Sihon king of Heshbon and to Og king of
Bashan who was at Ashtaroth.
11"So our elders and all the inhabitants of our country spoke to
us, saying, 'Take provisions in your hand for the journey, and go
to meet them and say to them, "We are your servants; now then,
make a covenant with us."'
12"This our bread *was* warm *when* we took it for our provisions
out of our houses on the day that we left to come to you; but now
behold, it is dry and has become crumbled.
13"And these wineskins which we filled were new, and behold,
they are torn; and these our clothes and our sandals are worn out
because of the very long journey."
14So the men *of Israel* took some of their provisions, and did not
ask for the counsel of the LORD.
15And Joshua made peace with them and made a covenant with
them, to let them live; and the leaders of the congregation swore
*an oath* to them.
16¶ And it came about at the end of three days after they had
made a covenant with them, that they heard that they were neighbors and that they were living within their land.
17Then the sons of Israel set out and came to their cities on the
third day. Now their cities *were* Gibeon and Chephirah and
Beeroth and Kiriath-jearim.

## New International

Israelites, Joshua copied on stones the law of Moses, which he had
written. 33All Israel, aliens and citizens alike, with their elders,
officials and judges, were standing on both sides of the ark of the
covenant of the LORD, facing those who carried it—the priests,
who were Levites. Half of the people stood in front of Mount
Gerizim and half of them in front of Mount Ebal, as Moses the
servant of the LORD had formerly commanded when he gave instructions to bless the people of Israel.
34Afterward, Joshua read all the words of the law—the blessings and the curses—just as it is written in the Book of the Law.
35There was not a word of all that Moses had commanded that
Joshua did not read to the whole assembly of Israel, including the
women and children, and the aliens who lived among them.

*The Gibeonite Deception*

9 NOW WHEN all the kings west of the Jordan heard about
these things—those in the hill country, in the western foothills, and along the entire coast of the Great Sea[a] as far as Lebanon
(the kings of the Hittites, Amorites, Canaanites, Perizzites, Hivites
and Jebusites)— 2they came together to make war against Joshua
and Israel.
3However, when the people of Gibeon heard what Joshua had
done to Jericho and Ai, 4they resorted to a ruse: They went as a
delegation whose donkeys were loaded[b] with worn-out sacks and
old wineskins, cracked and mended. 5The men put worn and
patched sandals on their feet and wore old clothes. All the bread
of their food supply was dry and moldy. 6Then they went to
Joshua in the camp at Gilgal and said to him and the men of Israel,
"We have come from a distant country; make a treaty with us."
7The men of Israel said to the Hivites, "But perhaps you live
near us. How then can we make a treaty with you?"
8"We are your servants," they said to Joshua.
But Joshua asked, "Who are you and where do you come
from?"
9They answered: "Your servants have come from a very distant
country because of the fame of the LORD your God. For we have
heard reports of him: all that he did in Egypt, 10and all that he did
to the two kings of the Amorites east of the Jordan—Sihon king of
Heshbon, and Og king of Bashan, who reigned in Ashtaroth.
11And our elders and all those living in our country said to us,
'Take provisions for your journey; go and meet them and say to
them, "We are your servants; make a treaty with us."' 12This
bread of ours was warm when we packed it at home on the day
we left to come to you. But now see how dry and moldy it is. 13And
these wineskins that we filled were new, but see how cracked they
are. And our clothes and sandals are worn out by the very long
journey."
14The men of Israel sampled their provisions but did not inquire
of the LORD. 15Then Joshua made a treaty of peace with them to
let them live, and the leaders of the assembly ratified it by oath.
16Three days after they made the treaty with the Gibeonites, the
Israelites heard that they were neighbors, living near them. 17So
the Israelites set out and on the third day came to their cities:
Gibeon, Kephirah, Beeroth and Kiriath Jearim. 18But the Israelites

**NIV** [a] *1* That is, the Mediterranean [b] *4* Most Hebrew manuscripts; some Hebrew manuscripts, Vulgate and Syriac (see also Septuagint) *They prepared provisions and loaded their donkeys*

## King James

18 And the children of Israel smote them not, because the
princes of the congregation had sworn unto them by the LORD God
of Israel. And all the congregation murmured against the princes.
19 But all the princes said unto all the congregation, We have
sworn unto them by the LORD God of Israel: now therefore we may
not touch them.
20 This we will do to them; we will even let them live, lest wrath
be upon us, because of the oath which we sware unto them.
21 And the princes said unto them, Let them live; but let them
be hewers of wood and drawers of water unto all the congregation;
as the princes had promised them.
22 ¶ And Joshua called for them, and he spake unto them, saying, Wherefore have ye beguiled us, saying, We *are* very far from
you; when ye dwell among us?
23 Now therefore ye *are* cursed, and there shall none of you be
freed from being bondmen, and hewers of wood and drawers of
water for the house of my God.
24 And they answered Joshua, and said, Because it was certainly
told thy servants, how that the LORD thy God commanded his
servant Moses to give you all the land, and to destroy all the
inhabitants of the land from before you, therefore we were sore
afraid of our lives because of you, and have done this thing.
25 And now, behold, we *are* in thine hand: as it seemeth good
and right unto thee to do unto us, do.
26 And so did he unto them, and delivered them out of the hand
of the children of Israel, that they slew them not.
27 And Joshua made them that day hewers of wood and drawers
of water for the congregation, and for the altar of the LORD, even
unto this day, in the place which he should choose.

**10** NOW IT came to pass, when Adoni-zedec king of Jerusalem had heard how Joshua had taken Ai, and had utterly
destroyed it; as he had done to Jericho and her king, so he had
done to Ai and her king; and how the inhabitants of Gibeon had
made peace with Israel, and were among them;
2 That they feared greatly, because Gibeon *was* a great city, as
one of the royal cities, and because it *was* greater than Ai, and all
the men thereof *were* mighty.
3 Wherefore Adoni-zedec king of Jerusalem sent unto Hoham
king of Hebron, and unto Piram king of Jarmuth, and unto Japhia
king of Lachish, and unto Debir king of Eglon, saying,
4 Come up unto me, and help me, that we may smite Gibeon:
for it hath made peace with Joshua and with the children of Israel.
5 Therefore the five kings of the Amorites, the king of Jerusalem,
the king of Hebron, the king of Jarmuth, the king of Lachish, the
king of Eglon, gathered themselves together, and went up, they
and all their hosts, and encamped before Gibeon, and made war
against it.
6 ¶ And the men of Gibeon sent unto Joshua to the camp to
Gilgal, saying, Slack not thy hand from thy servants; come up to
us quickly, and save us, and help us: for all the kings of the
Amorites that dwell in the mountains are gathered together
against us.
7 So Joshua ascended from Gilgal, he, and all the people of war
with him, and all the mighty men of valour.
8 ¶ And the LORD said unto Joshua, Fear them not: for I have
delivered them into thine hand; there shall not a man of them
stand before thee.
9 Joshua therefore came unto them suddenly, *and* went up from
Gilgal all night.
10 And the LORD discomfited them before Israel, and slew them
with a great slaughter at Gibeon, and chased them along the way
that goeth up to Beth-horon, and smote them to Azekah, and unto
Makkedah.

## Amplified

18 But the Israelites did not slay them, because the leaders of the
assembly had sworn to them by the Lord the God of Israel [to spare
them]. And all the assembly murmured against the leaders.
19 But all the leaders said to all the assembly, We have sworn to
them by the Lord the God of Israel; so now we may not touch
them.
20 This we will do to them; we will let them live, lest wrath be
upon us, because of the oath which we swore to them.
21 And the leaders said to them, Let them live [and be our
slaves]. So they became hewers of wood and drawers of water for
all the assembly; as the leaders had said of them.
22 Joshua called the men, and said, Why did you deceive us,
saying, We live very far from you, when you dwell among us?
23 Now therefore you are cursed, and of you there shall always
be slaves, hewers of wood and drawers of water for the house of
my God.
24 They answered Joshua, Because it was surely told your servants that the Lord your God commanded His servant Moses to
give you all the land, and to destroy all the land's inhabitants from
before you. So we feared greatly for our lives because of you, and
have done this thing.
25 And now, behold, we are in your hand; do as it seems good
and right in your sight to do to us.
26 So he did to them, and delivered them out of the hand of the
Israelites, so that they did not kill them.
27 But Joshua then made them hewers of wood and drawers of
water for the congregation and for the altar of the Lord, to this day,
in the place which He should choose.

**10** WHEN ADONIZEDEK king of Jerusalem heard how
Joshua had taken Ai, and had utterly destroyed it, doing
to Jericho and its king as he had done to Ai and its king, and how
the residents of Gibeon had made peace with Israel, and were
among them,
2 He feared greatly, because Gibeon was a great city, like one of
the royal cities, and because it was greater than Ai, and all its men
were mighty.
3 So Adonizedek king of Jerusalem sent to Hoham king of Hebron, to Piram king of Jarmuth, to Japhia king of Lachish, and to
Debir king of Eglon, saying,
4 Come up to me, and help me, and let us smite Gibeon; for it
has made peace with Joshua and with the Israelites.
5 Then the five kings of the Amorites, the kings of Jerusalem,
Hebron, Jarmuth, Lachish and Eglon, gathered their forces and
went up with all their armies and encamped before Gibeon, to fight
against it.
6 And the men of Gibeon sent to Joshua at the camp in Gilgal,
saying, Do not relax your hand from your servants; come up to us
quickly, and save us, and help us; for all the kings of the Amorites
who dwell in the hill country are gathered against us.
7 So Joshua went up from Gilgal, he and all the warriors with
him, and all the mighty men of valor.
8 And the Lord said to Joshua, Do not fear them, for I have given
them into your hand; there shall not a man of them stand before
you.
9 So Joshua came upon them suddenly, having gone up from
Gilgal all night.
10 And the Lord caused [the enemies] to panic before Israel, who
slew them with a great slaughter at Gibeon, and chased them along
the way that goes up to Beth-horon, and smote them as far as
Azekah and Makkedah.

## New American Standard

18And the sons of Israel did not strike them because the leaders of the congregation had sworn to them by the LORD the God of Israel. And the whole congregation grumbled against the leaders.

19But all the leaders said to the whole congregation, "We have sworn to them by the LORD, the God of Israel, and now we cannot touch them.

20"This we will do to them, even let them live, lest wrath be upon us for the oath which we swore to them."

21And the leaders said to them, "Let them live." So they became hewers of wood and drawers of water for the whole congregation, just as the leaders had spoken to them.

22¶ Then Joshua called for them and spoke to them, saying, "Why have you deceived us, saying, 'We are very far from you,' when you are living within our land?

23"Now therefore, you are cursed, and you shall never cease being slaves, both hewers of wood and drawers of water for the house of my God."

24So they answered Joshua and said, "Because it was certainly told your servants that the LORD your God had commanded His servant Moses to give you all the land, and to destroy all the inhabitants of the land before you; therefore we feared greatly for our lives because of you, and have done this thing.

25"And now behold, we are in your hands; do as it seems good and right in your sight to do to us."

26Thus he did to them, and delivered them from the hands of the sons of Israel, and they did not kill them.

27But Joshua made them that day hewers of wood and drawers of water for the congregation and for the altar of the LORD, to this day, in the place which He would choose.

*Five Kings Attack Gibeon*

**10** NOW IT came about when Adoni-zedek king of Jerusalem heard that Joshua had captured Ai, and had utterly destroyed it (just as he had done to Jericho and its king, so he had done to Ai and its king), and that the inhabitants of Gibeon had made peace with Israel and were within their land,

2that he feared greatly, because Gibeon *was* a great city, like one of the royal cities, and because it was greater than Ai, and all its men *were* mighty.

3Therefore Adoni-zedek king of Jerusalem sent *word* to Hoham king of Hebron and to Piram king of Jarmuth and to Japhia king of Lachish and to Debir king of Eglon, saying,

4"Come up to me and help me, and let us attack Gibeon, for it has made peace with Joshua and with the sons of Israel."

5So the five kings of the Amorites, the king of Jerusalem, the king of Hebron, the king of Jarmuth, the king of Lachish, *and* the king of Eglon, gathered together and went up, they with all their armies, and camped by Gibeon and fought against it.

6¶ Then the men of Gibeon sent *word* to Joshua to the camp at Gilgal, saying, "Do not abandon your servants; come up to us quickly and save us and help us, for all the kings of the Amorites that live in the hill country have assembled against us."

7So Joshua went up from Gilgal, he and all the people of war with him and all the valiant warriors.

8And the LORD said to Joshua, "Do not fear them, for I have given them into your hands; not one of them shall stand before you."

9So Joshua came upon them suddenly by marching all night from Gilgal.

10And the LORD confounded them before Israel, and He slew them with a great slaughter at Gibeon, and pursued them by the way of the ascent of Beth-horon, and struck them as far as Azekah and Makkedah.

## New International

did not attack them, because the leaders of the assembly had sworn an oath to them by the LORD, the God of Israel.
The whole assembly grumbled against the leaders, 19but all the
leaders answered, "We have given them our oath by the LORD, the
God of Israel, and we cannot touch them now. 20This is what we
will do to them: We will let them live, so that wrath will not fall
on us for breaking the oath we swore to them." 21They continued,
"Let them live, but let them be woodcutters and water carriers for the entire community." So the leaders' promise to them was kept.

22Then Joshua summoned the Gibeonites and said, "Why did you deceive us by saying, 'We live a long way from you,' while actually you live near us? 23You are now under a curse: You will never cease to serve as woodcutters and water carriers for the house of my God."

24They answered Joshua, "Your servants were clearly told how the LORD your God had commanded his servant Moses to give you the whole land and to wipe out all its inhabitants from before you. So we feared for our lives because of you, and that is why we did
this. 25We are now in your hands. Do to us whatever seems good and right to you."

26So Joshua saved them from the Israelites, and they did not kill
them. 27That day he made the Gibeonites woodcutters and water carriers for the community and for the altar of the LORD at the place the LORD would choose. And that is what they are to this day.

*The Sun Stands Still*

**10** NOW ADONI-ZEDEK king of Jerusalem heard that Joshua had taken Ai and totally destroyed[a] it, doing to Ai and its king as he had done to Jericho and its king, and that the people of Gibeon had made a treaty of peace with Israel and were
living near them. 2He and his people were very much alarmed at this, because Gibeon was an important city, like one of the royal cities; it was larger than Ai, and all its men were good fighters. 3So
Adoni-Zedek king of Jerusalem appealed to Hoham king of Hebron, Piram king of Jarmuth, Japhia king of Lachish and Debir king of Eglon. 4"Come up and help me attack Gibeon," he said, "because it has made peace with Joshua and the Israelites."

5Then the five kings of the Amorites—the kings of Jerusalem, Hebron, Jarmuth, Lachish and Eglon—joined forces. They moved up with all their troops and took up positions against Gibeon and attacked it.

6The Gibeonites then sent word to Joshua in the camp at Gilgal: "Do not abandon your servants. Come up to us quickly and save us! Help us, because all the Amorite kings from the hill country have joined forces against us."

7So Joshua marched up from Gilgal with his entire army, including all the best fighting men. 8The LORD said to Joshua, "Do not be afraid of them; I have given them into your hand. Not one of them will be able to withstand you."

9After an all-night march from Gilgal, Joshua took them by
surprise. 10The LORD threw them into confusion before Israel, who defeated them in a great victory at Gibeon. Israel pursued them along the road going up to Beth Horon and cut them down all the way to Azekah and Makkedah. 11As they fled before Israel on the

NIV [a] *1* The Hebrew term refers to the irrevocable giving over of things or persons to the LORD, often by totally destroying them; also in verses 28, 35, 37, 39 and 40.

## King James

11And it came to pass, as they fled from before Israel, *and* were
in the going down to Beth-horon, that the LORD cast down great
stones from heaven upon them unto Azekah, and they died: *they*
*were* more which died with hailstones than *they* whom the children
of Israel slew with the sword.
12¶ Then spake Joshua to the LORD in the day when the LORD
delivered up the Amorites before the children of Israel, and he said
in the sight of Israel, Sun, stand thou still upon Gibeon; and thou,
Moon, in the valley of Ajalon.
13And the sun stood still, and the moon stayed, until the people
had avenged themselves upon their enemies. *Is* not this written in
the book of Jasher? So the sun stood still in the midst of heaven,
and hasted not to go down about a whole day.
14And there was no day like that before it or after it, that the
LORD hearkened unto the voice of a man: for the LORD fought for
Israel.
15¶ And Joshua returned, and all Israel with him, unto the camp
to Gilgal.
16But these five kings fled, and hid themselves in a cave at
Makkedah.
17And it was told Joshua, saying, The five kings are found hid
in a cave at Makkedah.
18And Joshua said, Roll great stones upon the mouth of the
cave, and set men by it for to keep them:
19And stay ye not, *but* pursue after your enemies, and smite the
hindmost of them; suffer them not to enter into their cities: for the
LORD your God hath delivered them into your hand.
20And it came to pass, when Joshua and the children of Israel
had made an end of slaying them with a very great slaughter, till
they were consumed, that the rest *which* remained of them entered
into fenced cities.
21And all the people returned to the camp to Joshua at Makkedah in peace: none moved his tongue against any of the children
of Israel.
22Then said Joshua, Open the mouth of the cave, and bring out
those five kings unto me out of the cave.
23And they did so, and brought forth those five kings unto him
out of the cave, the king of Jerusalem, the king of Hebron, the king
of Jarmuth, the king of Lachish, *and* the king of Eglon.
24And it came to pass, when they brought out those kings unto
Joshua, that Joshua called for all the men of Israel, and said unto
the captains of the men of war which went with him, Come near,
put your feet upon the necks of these kings. And they came near,
and put their feet upon the necks of them.
25And Joshua said unto them, Fear not, nor be dismayed, be
strong and of good courage: for thus shall the LORD do to all your
enemies against whom ye fight.
26And afterward Joshua smote them, and slew them, and
hanged them on five trees: and they were hanging upon the trees
until the evening.
27And it came to pass at the time of the going down of the sun,
*that* Joshua commanded, and they took them down off the trees,
and cast them into the cave wherein they had been hid, and laid
great stones in the cave's mouth, *which remain* until this very day.
28¶ And that day Joshua took Makkedah, and smote it with the
edge of the sword, and the king thereof he utterly destroyed,
them, and all the souls that *were* therein; he let none remain: and
he did to the king of Makkedah as he did unto the king of Jericho.
29Then Joshua passed from Makkedah, and all Israel with him,
unto Libnah, and fought against Libnah:

## Amplified

11As they fled before Israel, while they were descending [the
pass] to Beth-horon, the Lord cast great stones from the heavens
on them as far as Azekah, killing them. More died because of the
hailstones than the Israelites slew with the sword.
12Then Joshua spoke to the Lord the day when the Lord gave
the Amorites over to the Israelites; and he said in the sight of Israel,
Sun, be silent *and* stand still at Gibeon; and you, Moon, in the
valley of Ajalon!
13And the sun stood still, and the moon stayed, until the nation
took vengeance upon their enemies. Is not this written in the book
of Jasher? So the sun stood still in the midst of the heavens, and
did not hasten to go down for about a whole day.
14There was no day like it before or since, when the Lord
heeded the voice of a man; for the Lord fought for Israel.
15Then Joshua returned, and all Israel with him, to the camp at
Gilgal.
16Those five kings fled, and hid themselves in the cave of Makkedah.
17And it was told Joshua, The five kings are hidden in the cave
at Makkedah.
18Joshua said, Roll great stones to the cave's mouth, and set
men to guard them;
19But do not stay; pursue your enemies, and fall upon their rear;
do not allow them to enter their cities, for the Lord your God has
given them into your hand.
20When Joshua and the Israelites had ended slaying them until
they were wiped out, and the remnant remaining of them had
entered into fortified cities,
21All the people returned to the camp to Joshua at Makkedah
in peace; none moved his tongue against any of the Israelites.
22Then said Joshua, Open the mouth of the cave, and bring out
those five kings to me from the cave.
23They brought the five kings out of the cave to him, the kings
of Jerusalem, Hebron, Jarmuth, Lachish and Eglon.
24When they brought out those kings to Joshua, [he] called for
all the Israelites and told the commanders of the men of war who
went with him, Come, put your feet on the necks of these kings.
And they came and put their feet on the [kings'] necks.
25Joshua said to them, Fear not nor be dismayed; be strong and
of good courage; for thus shall the Lord do to all your enemies
against whom you fight.
26Afterward Joshua smote and slew them, and hanged their
bodies on five trees; and they hung on the trees until evening.
27At sunset Joshua ordered and they took the bodies down from
the trees, and cast them into the cave where the kings had hidden,
and laid great stones on the cave's mouth, which remain to this
very day.
28Joshua took Makkedah that day and smote it and its king with
the sword, and utterly destroyed every one in it, he left none
remaining; and he did to the king of Makkedah as he had done to
the king of Jericho. [Josh. 6:21.]
29Then Joshua and all Israel went from Makkedah to Libnah,
and attacked Libnah;

## New American Standard

11And it came about as they fled from before Israel, *while* they
were at the descent of Beth-horon, that the LORD threw large
stones from heaven on them as far as Azekah, and they died; *there
were* more who died from the hailstones than those whom the sons
of Israel killed with the sword.
12¶ Then Joshua spoke to the LORD in the day when the LORD
delivered up the Amorites before the sons of Israel, and he said in
the sight of Israel,

"O sun, stand still at Gibeon,
And O moon in the valley of Aijalon."
13 So the sun stood still, and the moon stopped,
Until the nation avenged themselves of their enemies.

Is it not written in the book of Jashar? And the sun stopped in the
middle of the sky, and did not hasten to go *down* for about a whole
day.
14And there was no day like that before it or after it, when the
LORD listened to the voice of a man; for the LORD fought for Israel.
15Then Joshua and all Israel with him returned to the camp to
Gilgal.

*Victory at Makkedah*

16¶ Now these five kings had fled and hidden themselves in the
cave at Makkedah.
17And it was told Joshua, saying, "The five kings have been
found hidden in the cave at Makkedah."
18And Joshua said, "Roll large stones against the mouth of the
cave, and assign men by it to guard them,
19but do not stay *there* yourselves; pursue your enemies and
attack them in the rear. Do not allow them to enter their cities, for
the LORD your God has delivered them into your hand."
20And it came about when Joshua and the sons of Israel had
finished slaying them with a very great slaughter, until they were
destroyed, and the survivors *who* remained of them had entered
the fortified cities,
21that all the people returned to the camp to Joshua at Makkedah in peace. No one uttered a word against any of the sons of
Israel.
22¶ Then Joshua said, "Open the mouth of the cave and bring
these five kings out to me from the cave."
23And they did so, and brought these five kings out to him from
the cave: the king of Jerusalem, the king of Hebron, the king of
Jarmuth, the king of Lachish, *and* the king of Eglon.
24And it came about when they brought these kings out to
Joshua, that Joshua called for all the men of Israel, and said to the
chiefs of the men of war who had gone with him, "Come near, put
your feet on the necks of these kings." So they came near and put
their feet on their necks.
25Joshua then said to them, "Do not fear or be dismayed! Be
strong and courageous, for thus the LORD will do to all your
enemies with whom you fight."
26So afterward Joshua struck them and put them to death, and
he hanged them on five trees; and they hung on the trees until
evening.
27And it came about at sunset that Joshua commanded, and
they took them down from the trees and threw them into the cave
where they had hidden themselves, and put large stones over the
mouth of the cave, to this very day.
28¶ Now Joshua captured Makkedah on that day, and struck it
and its king with the edge of the sword; he utterly destroyed it and
every [a]person who was in it. He left no survivor. Thus he did to
the king of Makkedah just as he had done to the king of Jericho.

*Joshua's Conquest of Southern Palestine*

29¶ Then Joshua and all Israel with him passed on from Makkedah to Libnah, and fought against Libnah.

NAS [a] Lit., *soul*, and so throughout this context

## New International

road down from Beth Horon to Azekah, the LORD hurled large
hailstones down on them from the sky, and more of them died
from the hailstones than were killed by the swords of the Israelites.
12On the day the LORD gave the Amorites over to Israel, Joshua
said to the LORD in the presence of Israel:

"O sun, stand still over Gibeon,
O moon, over the Valley of Aijalon."
13So the sun stood still,
and the moon stopped,
till the nation avenged itself on[b] its enemies,

as it is written in the Book of Jashar.
The sun stopped in the middle of the sky and delayed going
down about a full day. 14There has never been a day like it before
or since, a day when the LORD listened to a man. Surely the LORD
was fighting for Israel!
15Then Joshua returned with all Israel to the camp at Gilgal.

*Five Amorite Kings Killed*

16Now the five kings had fled and hidden in the cave at Makkedah. 17When Joshua was told that the five kings had been found
hiding in the cave at Makkedah, 18he said, "Roll large rocks up to
the mouth of the cave, and post some men there to guard it. 19But
don't stop! Pursue your enemies, attack them from the rear and
don't let them reach their cities, for the LORD your God has given
them into your hand."
20So Joshua and the Israelites destroyed them completely—
almost to a man—but the few who were left reached their fortified
cities. 21The whole army then returned safely to Joshua in the
camp at Makkedah, and no one uttered a word against the Israelites.
22Joshua said, "Open the mouth of the cave and bring those five
kings out to me." 23So they brought the five kings out of the
cave—the kings of Jerusalem, Hebron, Jarmuth, Lachish and
Eglon. 24When they had brought these kings to Joshua, he summoned all the men of Israel and said to the army commanders who
had come with him, "Come here and put your feet on the necks
of these kings." So they came forward and placed their feet on
their necks.
25Joshua said to them, "Do not be afraid; do not be discouraged.
Be strong and courageous. This is what the LORD will do to all the
enemies you are going to fight." 26Then Joshua struck and killed
the kings and hung them on five trees, and they were left hanging
on the trees until evening.
27At sunset Joshua gave the order and they took them down
from the trees and threw them into the cave where they had been
hiding. At the mouth of the cave they placed large rocks, which
are there to this day.
28That day Joshua took Makkedah. He put the city and its king
to the sword and totally destroyed everyone in it. He left no
survivors. And he did to the king of Makkedah as he had done to
the king of Jericho.

*Southern Cities Conquered*

29Then Joshua and all Israel with him moved on from Makkedah to Libnah and attacked it. 30The LORD also gave that city and

NIV [b] 13 Or *nation triumphed over*

## King James

30 And the LORD delivered it also, and the king thereof, into the hand of Israel; and he smote it with the edge of the sword, and all the souls that *were* therein; he let none remain in it; but did unto the king thereof as he did unto the king of Jericho.

31 ¶ And Joshua passed from Libnah, and all Israel with him, unto Lachish, and encamped against it, and fought against it:

32 And the LORD delivered Lachish into the hand of Israel, which took it on the second day, and smote it with the edge of the sword, and all the souls that *were* therein, according to all that he had done to Libnah.

33 ¶ Then Horam king of Gezer came up to help Lachish; and Joshua smote him and his people, until he had left him none remaining.

34 ¶ And from Lachish Joshua passed unto Eglon, and all Israel with him; and they encamped against it, and fought against it:

35 And they took it on that day, and smote it with the edge of the sword, and all the souls that *were* therein he utterly destroyed that day, according to all that he had done to Lachish.

36 And Joshua went up from Eglon, and all Israel with him, unto Hebron; and they fought against it:

37 And they took it, and smote it with the edge of the sword, and the king thereof, and all the cities thereof, and all the souls that *were* therein; he left none remaining, according to all that he had done to Eglon; but destroyed it utterly, and all the souls that *were* therein.

38 ¶ And Joshua returned, and all Israel with him, to Debir; and fought against it:

39 And he took it, and the king thereof, and all the cities thereof; and they smote them with the edge of the sword, and utterly destroyed all the souls that *were* therein; he left none remaining: as he had done to Hebron, so he did to Debir, and to the king thereof; as he had done also to Libnah, and to her king.

40 ¶ So Joshua smote all the country of the hills, and of the south, and of the vale, and of the springs, and all their kings: he left none remaining, but utterly destroyed all that breathed, as the LORD God of Israel commanded.

41 And Joshua smote them from Kadesh-barnea even unto Gaza, and all the country of Goshen, even unto Gibeon.

42 And all these kings and their land did Joshua take at one time, because the LORD God of Israel fought for Israel.

43 And Joshua returned, and all Israel with him, unto the camp to Gilgal.

11 AND IT came to pass, when Jabin king of Hazor had heard *those things,* that he sent to Jobab king of Madon, and to the king of Shimron, and to the king of Achshaph,

2 And to the kings that *were* on the north of the mountains, and of the plains south of Chinneroth, and in the valley, and in the borders of Dor on the west,

3 *And to* the Canaanite on the east and on the west, and *to* the Amorite, and the Hittite, and the Perizzite, and the Jebusite in the mountains, and *to* the Hivite under Hermon in the land of Mizpeh.

4 And they went out, they and all their hosts with them, much people, even as the sand that *is* upon the sea shore in multitude, with horses and chariots very many.

5 And when all these kings were met together, they came and pitched together at the waters of Merom, to fight against Israel.

## Amplified

30 And the Lord gave it also, and its king, into Israel's hand, and Joshua smote it with the sword, and all the people in it; he left none remaining in it; and he did to its king as he did to the king of Jericho.

31 And Joshua passed from Libnah, and all Israel with him, to Lachish, and encamped against it, and attacked it.

32 And the Lord delivered Lachish into the hand of Israel, and Joshua took it on the second day, and smote it with the sword, and all the people in it, as he had done to Libnah.

33 Then Horam king of Gezer came up to help Lachish; and Joshua smote him and his people, until he had left none remaining.

34 From Lachish Joshua and all Israel went on to Eglon, laid siege to it, and attacked it.

35 And they took it that day, and smote it with the sword, and utterly destroyed all who were in it that day, as he had done to Lachish.

36 Then Joshua with all Israel went up from Eglon to Hebron; and they attacked it,

37 And took it, and smote it with the sword, and its king and all its towns, and every one in it; he left none remaining, as he had done to Eglon, and utterly destroyed it and all its people.

38 And Joshua and all Israel with him, returned to Debir, and attacked it.

39 And he took it, with its king and all its towns; and they smote them with the sword, and utterly destroyed everyone in it; he left none remaining; as he had done to Hebron and to Libnah and its king, so he did to Debir and its king.

40 So Joshua smote all the land, the hill country, the South, the lowland, and the slopes, and all their kings; he left none remaining, but utterly destroyed all that breathed, as the [a]Lord the God of Israel commanded. [Deut. 20:16.]

41 And Joshua smote them from Kadesh-barnea even to Gaza, and all the country of Goshen, even to Gibeon.

42 Joshua took all these kings and their land at one time, because the Lord the God of Israel fought for Israel.

43 And Joshua returned, and all Israel with him, to the camp at Gilgal.

11 WHEN JABIN king of Hazor had heard of this he sent to Jobab king of Madon, and to the kings of Shimron and Achshaph,

2 And to the kings who were in the north, in the hill country, and in the Arabah south of Chinneroth, and in the lowland, and in the heights of Dor on the west,

3 To the Canaanites in the east and west, the Amorites, the Hittites, the Perizzites, the Jebusites in the hill country, and the Hivites below [Mount] Hermon in the land of Mizpah.

4 And they went out, with all their hosts, much people, like the sand on the seashore in number, with very many horses and chariots.

5 And all these kings met and came and encamped together at the waters of Merom, to fight with Israel.

**AMP** [a] As the presence of "the Prince of the Lord's host" (Josh. 5:13, 14) indicates, Jehovah will take part in this conflict, not as an ally or an adversary, but as commander-in-chief. It is not Israel's quarrel, in which they are to ask the Divine assistance. It is the Lord's own quarrel, and Israel and Joshua are but a division in His host. The wars of Israel in Canaan are always presented by the Old Testament as "the wars of the Lord." The conquest of Canaan is too often treated as an enterprise of the Israelites, carried out with great cruelties, for which they claimed the Divine sanction. The Old Testament presents the matter in an entirely different light . . . Jehovah fights for His own right hand, and Israel is but a fragment of His army. "The sun stood still," the stars in their courses fought against His foes (Ellicott's *Commentary*).

## New American Standard

30And the LORD gave it also with its king into the hands of
Israel, and he struck it and every person who *was* in it with the
edge of the sword. He left no survivor in it. Thus he did to its king
just as he had done to the king of Jericho.
31¶ And Joshua and all Israel with him passed on from Libnah
to Lachish, and they camped by it and fought against it.
32And the LORD gave Lachish into the hands of Israel; and he
captured it on the second day, and struck it and every person who
*was* in it with the edge of the sword, according to all that he had
done to Libnah.
33¶ Then Horam king of Gezer came up to help Lachish, and
Joshua defeated him and his people until he had left him no
survivor.
34¶ And Joshua and all Israel with him passed on from Lachish
to Eglon, and they camped by it and fought against it.
35And they captured it on that day and struck it with the edge
of the sword; and he utterly destroyed that day every person who
*was* in it, according to all that he had done to Lachish.
36¶ Then Joshua and all Israel with him went up from Eglon to
Hebron, and they fought against it.
37And they captured it and struck it and its king and all its cities
and all the persons who *were* in it with the edge of the sword. He
left no survivor, according to all that he had done to Eglon. And
he utterly destroyed it and every person who *was* in it.
38¶ Then Joshua and all Israel with him returned to Debir, and
they fought against it.
39And he captured it and its king and all its cities, and they
struck them with the edge of the sword, and utterly destroyed
every person *who was* in it. He left no survivor. Just as he had done
to Hebron, so he did to Debir and its king, as he had also done to
Libnah and its king.
40¶ Thus Joshua struck all the land, the hill country and the
[b]Negev and the lowland and the slopes and all their kings. He left
no survivor, but he utterly destroyed all who breathed, just as the
LORD, the God of Israel, had commanded.
41And Joshua struck them from Kadesh-barnea even as far as
Gaza, and all the country of Goshen even as far as Gibeon.
42And Joshua captured all these kings and their lands at one
time, because the LORD, the God of Israel, fought for Israel.
43So Joshua and all Israel with him returned to the camp at
Gilgal.

*Northern Palestine Taken*

11 THEN IT came about, when Jabin king of Hazor heard *of
it*, that he sent to Jobab king of Madon and to the king of
Shimron and to the king of Achshaph,
2and to the kings who were of the north in the hill country, and
in the Arabah—south of [c]Chinneroth and in the lowland and on
the heights of Dor on the west—
3to the Canaanite on the east and on the west, and the Amorite
and the Hittite and the Perizzite and the Jebusite in the hill country,
and the Hivite at the foot of Hermon in the land of Mizpeh.
4And they came out, they and all their armies with them, *as*
many people *as* the sand that is on the seashore, with very many
horses and chariots.
5So all of these kings having agreed to meet, came and encamped
together at the waters of Merom, to fight against Israel.

NAS [b] I.e., South country [c] I.e., Sea of Galilee

## New International

its king into Israel's hand. The city and everyone in it Joshua put
to the sword. He left no survivors there. And he did to its king as
he had done to the king of Jericho.
31Then Joshua and all Israel with him moved on from Libnah
to Lachish; he took up positions against it and attacked it. 32The
LORD handed Lachish over to Israel, and Joshua took it on the
second day. The city and everyone in it he put to the sword, just
as he had done to Libnah. 33Meanwhile, Horam king of Gezer had
come up to help Lachish, but Joshua defeated him and his army—
until no survivors were left.
34Then Joshua and all Israel with him moved on from Lachish
to Eglon; they took up positions against it and attacked it. 35They
captured it that same day and put it to the sword and totally
destroyed everyone in it, just as they had done to Lachish.
36Then Joshua and all Israel with him went up from Eglon to
Hebron and attacked it. 37They took the city and put it to the
sword, together with its king, its villages and everyone in it. They
left no survivors. Just as at Eglon, they totally destroyed it and
everyone in it.
38Then Joshua and all Israel with him turned around and attacked
Debir. 39They took the city, its king and its villages, and put
them to the sword. Everyone in it they totally destroyed. They left
no survivors. They did to Debir and its king as they had done to
Libnah and its king and to Hebron.
40So Joshua subdued the whole region, including the hill country,
the Negev, the western foothills and the mountain slopes,
together with all their kings. He left no survivors. He totally destroyed
all who breathed, just as the LORD, the God of Israel, had
commanded. 41Joshua subdued them from Kadesh Barnea to Gaza
and from the whole region of Goshen to Gibeon. 42All these kings
and their lands Joshua conquered in one campaign, because the
LORD, the God of Israel, fought for Israel.
43Then Joshua returned with all Israel to the camp at Gilgal.

*Northern Kings Defeated*

11 WHEN JABIN king of Hazor heard of this, he sent word
to Jobab king of Madon, to the kings of Shimron and
Acshaph, 2and to the northern kings who were in the mountains,
in the Arabah south of Kinnereth, in the western foothills and in
Naphoth Dor[d] on the west; 3to the Canaanites in the east and west;
to the Amorites, Hittites, Perizzites and Jebusites in the hill country;
and to the Hivites below Hermon in the region of Mizpah.
4They came out with all their troops and a large number of horses
and chariots—a huge army, as numerous as the sand on the seashore.
5All these kings joined forces and made camp together at
the Waters of Merom, to fight against Israel.

NIV [d] 2 Or *in the heights of Dor*

## King James

6¶ And the LORD said unto Joshua, Be not afraid because of them: for tomorrow about this time will I deliver them up all slain before Israel: thou shalt hough their horses, and burn their chariots with fire.

7So Joshua came, and all the people of war with him, against them by the waters of Merom suddenly; and they fell upon them.

8And the LORD delivered them into the hand of Israel, who smote them, and chased them unto great Zidon, and unto Misrephoth-maim, and unto the valley of Mizpeh eastward; and they smote them, until they left them none remaining.

9And Joshua did unto them as the LORD bade him: he houghed their horses, and burnt their chariots with fire.

10¶ And Joshua at that time turned back, and took Hazor, and smote the king thereof with the sword: for Hazor beforetime was the head of all those kingdoms.

11And they smote all the souls that *were* therein with the edge of the sword, utterly destroying *them:* there was not any left to breathe: and he burnt Hazor with fire.

12And all the cities of those kings, and all the kings of them, did Joshua take, and smote them with the edge of the sword, *and* he utterly destroyed them, as Moses the servant of the LORD commanded.

13But *as for* the cities that stood still in their strength, Israel burned none of them, save Hazor only; *that* did Joshua burn.

14And all the spoil of these cities, and the cattle, the children of Israel took for a prey unto themselves; but every man they smote with the edge of the sword, until they had destroyed them, neither left they any to breathe.

15¶ As the LORD commanded Moses his servant, so did Moses command Joshua, and so did Joshua; he left nothing undone of all that the LORD commanded Moses.

16So Joshua took all that land, the hills, and all the south country, and all the land of Goshen, and the valley, and the plain, and the mountain of Israel, and the valley of the same;

17 *Even* from the mount Halak, that goeth up to Seir, even unto Baal-gad in the valley of Lebanon under mount Hermon: and all their kings he took, and smote them, and slew them.

18Joshua made war a long time with all those kings.

19There was not a city that made peace with the children of Israel, save the Hivites the inhabitants of Gibeon: all *other* they took in battle.

20For it was of the LORD to harden their hearts, that they should come against Israel in battle, that he might destroy them utterly, *and* that they might have no favour, but that he might destroy them, as the LORD commanded Moses.

21¶ And at that time came Joshua, and cut off the Anakims from the mountains, from Hebron, from Debir, from Anab, and from all the mountains of Judah, and from all the mountains of Israel: Joshua destroyed them utterly with their cities.

22There was none of the Anakims left in the land of the children of Israel: only in Gaza, in Gath, and in Ashdod, there remained.

23So Joshua took the whole land, according to all that the LORD said unto Moses; and Joshua gave it for an inheritance unto Israel according to their divisions by their tribes. And the land rested from war.

## Amplified

6But the Lord said to Joshua, Do not be afraid because of them; for tomorrow by this time I will give them up all slain to Israel; you shall hock their horses, and burn their chariots with fire.

7So Joshua and all the people of war with him, came against them suddenly by the waters of Merom, and fell upon them.

8And the Lord gave them into the hand of Israel, who smote them and chased them [toward] populous Sidon and Misrephoth-maim, and eastward as far as the valley of Mizpah; they smote them, until none remained.

9And Joshua did to them as the Lord had commanded him; he hamstrung their horses, and burned their chariots with fire.

10And Joshua at that time turned back, and took Hazor, and smote its king with the sword; for Hazor previously was the head of all those kingdoms.

11They smote all the people in it with the sword, utterly destroying them; none were left alive, and he burned Hazor with fire.

12And Joshua took all the cities of those kings, and all the kings, and smote them with the sword, utterly destroying them, as Moses the servant of the Lord commanded. [Deut. 20:16.]

13But Israel burned none of the cities that stood [fortified] on mounds, except Hazor only; that Joshua burned.

14And all the spoil of these cities, and the livestock, the Israelites took for their booty; but every man they smote with the sword, until they had destroyed them, and they left none who breathed.

15As the Lord had commanded Moses His servant, so Moses commanded Joshua, and so Joshua did; he left nothing undone of all that the Lord commanded Moses.

16So Joshua took all that land, the hill country, all the South, all the land of Goshen, the lowland, the Arabah [plain], the hill country of Israel, and its lowland;

17From Mount Halak, that rises toward Seir, as far as Baal-gad in the valley of Lebanon, below Mount Hermon. He captured all their kings, and slew them.

18Joshua had waged war a long time [at least five years] with all those kings.

19Not a city made peace with the Israelites, except the Hivites, the people of Gibeon; all the others they took in battle.

20For it was of the Lord to harden their hearts, that they should come against Israel in battle, that [Israel] might [a]destroy them utterly, and that without favor, as the Lord commanded Moses.

21Joshua came at that time and cut off the Anakim [large in stature] from the hill country, from Hebron, from Debir, from Anab, and from all the hill country of Judah and of Israel; Joshua destroyed them utterly with their cities.

22None of the Anakim were left in the land of the Israelites; only in Gaza, Gath, and Ashdod [of Philistia], some remained.

23So Joshua took the whole land, according to all that the Lord had spoken to Moses; and Joshua gave it for an inheritance to Israel according to their allotments by tribes. And the land had rest from war.

**AMP** [a] Infidels say that it seems wholly inconsistent with what we should suppose to be the merciful character of God, that He should thus command whole nations to be destroyed by the sword . . . (But) when we see juries in our own country bringing in a verdict of guilty, the judge pronouncing sentence of death, and that sentence executed, we do not complain that there is anything unjust in the act. These Canaanites are proved to have polluted and stained the land with [intolerable] crimes; it was merely the holy judge pronouncing sentence on flagrant criminals and [Joshua] the righteous governor executing that sentence to the letter. It was not an act of arbitrary or private revenge, but the execution of the sentence of retributive justice, and such as had perhaps as great mercy to the innocent as justice to the guilty (Cumming, quoted in *Gray and Adams Commentary*, condensed).

## New American Standard

6¶ Then the LORD said to Joshua, "Do not be afraid because of them, for tomorrow at this time I will deliver all of them slain before Israel; you shall hamstring their horses and burn their chariots with fire."

7So Joshua and all the people of war with him came upon them suddenly by the waters of Merom, and attacked them.

8And the LORD delivered them into the hand of Israel, so that they defeated them, and pursued them as far as Great Sidon and Misrephoth-maim and the valley of Mizpeh to the east; and they struck them until no survivor was left to them.

9And Joshua did to them as the LORD had told him; he hamstrung their horses, and burned their chariots with fire.

10¶ Then Joshua turned back at that time, and captured Hazor and struck its king with the sword; for Hazor formerly was the head of all these kingdoms.

11And they struck every person who was in it with the edge of the sword, utterly destroying *them;* there was no one left who breathed. And he burned Hazor with fire.

12And Joshua captured all the cities of these kings, and all their kings, and he struck them with the edge of the sword, *and* utterly destroyed them; just as Moses the servant of the LORD had commanded.

13However, Israel did not burn any cities that stood on their mounds, except Hazor alone, *which* Joshua burned.

14And all the spoil of these cities and the cattle, the sons of Israel took as their plunder; but they struck every man with the edge of the sword, until they had destroyed them. They left no one who breathed.

15Just as the LORD had commanded Moses his servant, so Moses commanded Joshua, and so Joshua did; he left nothing undone of all that the LORD had commanded Moses.

16¶ Thus Joshua took all that land: the hill country and all the Negev, all that land of Goshen, the lowland, the Arabah, the hill country of Israel and its lowland

17from Mount Halak, that rises toward Seir, even as far as Baal-gad in the valley of Lebanon at the foot of Mount Hermon. And he captured all their kings and struck them down and put them to death.

18Joshua waged war a long time with all these kings.

19There was not a city which made peace with the sons of Israel except the Hivites living in Gibeon; they took them all in battle.

20For it was of the LORD to harden their hearts, to meet Israel in battle in order that he might utterly destroy them, that they might receive no mercy, but that he might destroy them, just as the LORD had commanded Moses.

21¶ Then Joshua came at that time and cut off the Anakim from the hill country, from Hebron, from Debir, from Anab and from all the hill country of Judah and from all the hill country of Israel. Joshua utterly destroyed them with their cities.

22There were no Anakim left in the land of the sons of Israel; only in Gaza, in Gath, and in Ashdod some remained.

23So Joshua took the whole land, according to all that the LORD had spoken to Moses, and Joshua gave it for an inheritance to Israel according to their divisions by their tribes. Thus the land had rest from war.

## New International

6The LORD said to Joshua, "Do not be afraid of them, because
by this time tomorrow I will hand all of them over to Israel, slain.
You are to hamstring their horses and burn their chariots."
7So Joshua and his whole army came against them suddenly at
the Waters of Merom and attacked them, 8and the LORD gave them
into the hand of Israel. They defeated them and pursued them all
the way to Greater Sidon, to Misrephoth Maim, and to the Valley
of Mizpah on the east, until no survivors were left. 9Joshua did to
them as the LORD had directed: He hamstrung their horses and
burned their chariots.
10At that time Joshua turned back and captured Hazor and put
its king to the sword. (Hazor had been the head of all these kingdoms.)
11Everyone in it they put to the sword. They totally destroyed[b] them, not sparing anything that breathed, and he burned
up Hazor itself.
12Joshua took all these royal cities and their kings and put them
to the sword. He totally destroyed them, as Moses the servant of
the LORD had commanded. 13Yet Israel did not burn any of the
cities built on their mounds—except Hazor, which Joshua burned.
14The Israelites carried off for themselves all the plunder and livestock of these cities, but all the people they put to the sword until
they completely destroyed them, not sparing anyone that
breathed. 15As the LORD commanded his servant Moses, so Moses
commanded Joshua, and Joshua did it; he left nothing undone of
all that the LORD commanded Moses.
16So Joshua took this entire land: the hill country, all the Negev,
the whole region of Goshen, the western foothills, the Arabah and
the mountains of Israel with their foothills, 17from Mount Halak,
which rises toward Seir, to Baal Gad in the Valley of Lebanon
below Mount Hermon. He captured all their kings and struck them
down, putting them to death. 18Joshua waged war against all these
kings for a long time. 19Except for the Hivites living in Gibeon, not
one city made a treaty of peace with the Israelites, who took them
all in battle. 20For it was the LORD himself who hardened their
hearts to wage war against Israel, so that he might destroy them
totally, exterminating them without mercy, as the LORD had commanded Moses.
21At that time Joshua went and destroyed the Anakites from the
hill country: from Hebron, Debir and Anab, from all the hill country of Judah, and from all the hill country of Israel. Joshua totally
destroyed them and their towns. 22No Anakites were left in Israelite territory; only in Gaza, Gath and Ashdod did any survive. 23So
Joshua took the entire land, just as the LORD had directed Moses,
and he gave it as an inheritance to Israel according to their tribal
divisions.

Then the land had rest from war.

NIV [b] *11* The Hebrew term refers to the irrevocable giving over of things or persons to the LORD, often by totally destroying them; also in verses 12, 20 and 21.

## King James

12 NOW THESE *are* the kings of the land, which the children
of Israel smote, and possessed their land on the other side
Jordan toward the rising of the sun, from the river Arnon unto
mount Hermon, and all the plain on the east:
2Sihon king of the Amorites, who dwelt in Heshbon, *and* ruled
from Aroer, which *is* upon the bank of the river Arnon, and from
the middle of the river, and from half Gilead, even unto the river
Jabbok, *which is* the border of the children of Ammon;
3And from the plain to the sea of Chinneroth on the east, and
unto the sea of the plain, *even* the salt sea on the east, the way to
Beth-jeshimoth; and from the south, under Ashdoth-pisgah:
4¶ And the coast of Og king of Bashan, *which was* of the remnant
of the giants, that dwelt at Ashtaroth and at Edrei,
5And reigned in mount Hermon, and in Salcah, and in all
Bashan, unto the border of the Geshurites and the Maachathites,
and half Gilead, the border of Sihon king of Heshbon.
6Them did Moses the servant of the LORD and the children of
Israel smite: and Moses the servant of the LORD gave it *for* a
possession unto the Reubenites, and the Gadites, and the half tribe
of Manasseh.
7¶ And these *are* the kings of the country which Joshua and the
children of Israel smote on this side Jordan on the west, from
Baal-gad in the valley of Lebanon even unto the mount Halak, that
goeth up to Seir; which Joshua gave unto the tribes of Israel *for* a
possession according to their divisions;
8In the mountains, and in the valleys, and in the plains, and in
the springs, and in the wilderness, and in the south country; the
Hittites, the Amorites, and the Canaanites, the Perizzites, the
Hivites, and the Jebusites:
9¶ The king of Jericho, one; the king of Ai, which *is* beside
Beth-el, one;
10The king of Jerusalem, one; the king of Hebron, one;
11The king of Jarmuth, one; the king of Lachish, one;
12The king of Eglon, one; the king of Gezer, one;
13The king of Debir, one; the king of Geder, one;
14The king of Hormah, one; the king of Arad, one;
15The king of Libnah, one; the king of Adullam, one;
16The king of Makkedah, one; the king of Beth-el, one;
17The king of Tappuah, one; the king of Hepher, one;
18The king of Aphek, one; the king of Lasharon, one;
19The king of Madon, one; the king of Hazor, one;
20The king of Shimron-meron, one; the king of Achshaph, one;
21The king of Taanach, one; the king of Megiddo, one;
22The king of Kedesh, one; the king of Jokneam of Carmel, one;
23The king of Dor in the coast of Dor, one; the king of the
nations of Gilgal, one;
24The king of Tirzah, one: all the kings thirty and one.

## Amplified

12 NOW THESE are the kings of the land, whom the Israelites defeated, and took possession of their land east of the
Jordan from the river Arnon to Mount Hermon, and all the Arabah
eastward:
2Sihon king of the Amorites, who dwelt in Heshbon, and ruled
from Aroer, on the edge of the valley of the river Arnon, and from
the middle of the valley as far as the river Jabbok, the boundary
of the Ammonites, that is, the half of Gilead,
3And the Arabah to the Sea of Chinneroth eastward, and in the
direction of Beth-jeshimoth, to the sea of the Arabah, the Salt [or
Dead] Sea, southward to the foot of the slopes of Pisgah;
4And Og king of Bashan, one of the remnant of the Rephaim
who lived at Ashtaroth and at Edrei,
5And ruled over Mount Hermon and Salecah and all Bashan to
the boundary of the Geshurites and the Ma-acathites, and over half
of Gilead to the boundary of Sihon king of Heshbon.
6These Moses, the servant of the Lord, and the Israelites defeated; and Moses the servant of the Lord gave their land for a
possession to the Reubenites, the Gadites, and the half-tribe of
Manasseh.
7These are the kings of the land whom Joshua and the Israelites
defeated on the west side of the Jordan, from Baal-gad in the valley
of Lebanon to Mount Halak, that rises toward Seir. Joshua gave
their land to the tribes of Israel for a possession according to their
allotments,
8In the hill country, in the lowland, in the Arabah, on the
slopes, in the wilderness, and in the Negeb, the land of the Hittites, Amorites, Canaanites, Perizzites, Hivites, and Jebusites.
9The king of Jericho, one; the king of Ai, which is beside Bethel,
one;
10The king of Jerusalem, one; the king of Hebron, one;
11The king of Jarmuth, one; the king of Lachish, one;
12The king of Eglon, one; the king of Gezer, one;
13The king of Debir, one; the king of Geder, one;
14The king of Hormah, one; the king of Arad, one;
15The king of Libnah, one; the king of Adullam, one;
16The king of Makkedah, one; the king of Bethel, one;
17The king of Tappuah, one; the king of Hepher, one;
18The king of Aphek, one; the king of Lasharon, one;
19The king of Madon, one; the king of Hazor, one;
20The king of Shimron-meron, one; the king of Achshaph, one;
21The king of Taanach, one; the king of Megiddo, one;
22The king of Kedesh, one; the king of Jokneam in Carmel, one;
23The king of Dor in the height of Dor, one; the king of Goiim
in Galilee, one;
24The king of Tirzah, one. In all, thirty-one kings.

## New American Standard

*Kings Defeated by Israel*

**12** NOW THESE are the kings of the land whom the sons of Israel defeated, and whose land they possessed beyond the Jordan toward the sunrise, from the valley of the Arnon as far as Mount Hermon, and all the Arabah to the east:

2 Sihon king of the Amorites, who lived in Heshbon, *and* ruled from Aroer, which is on the edge of the valley of the Arnon, both the middle of the valley and half of Gilead, even as far as the brook Jabbok, the border of the sons of Ammon;

3 and the Arabah as far as the Sea of [a]Chinneroth toward the east, and as far as the sea of the Arabah, *even* the Salt Sea, eastward toward Beth-jeshimoth, and on the south, at the foot of the slopes of Pisgah;

4 and the territory of Og king of Bashan, one of the remnant of Rephaim, who lived at Ashtaroth and at Edrei,

5 and ruled over Mount Hermon and Salecah and all Bashan, as far as the border of the Geshurites and the Maacathites, and half of Gilead, *as far as* the border of Sihon king of Heshbon.

6 Moses the servant of the LORD and the sons of Israel defeated them; and Moses the servant of the LORD gave it to the Reubenites and the Gadites, and the half-tribe of Manasseh as a possession.

7 ¶ Now these are the kings of the land whom Joshua and the sons of Israel defeated beyond the Jordan toward the west, from Baal-gad in the valley of Lebanon even as far as Mount Halak, which rises toward Seir; and Joshua gave it to the tribes of Israel as a possession according to their divisions,

8 in the hill country, in the lowland, in the Arabah, on the slopes, and in the wilderness, and in the Negev; the Hittite, the Amorite and the Canaanite, the Perizzite, the Hivite and the Jebusite:

9 the king of Jericho, one; the king of Ai, which is beside Bethel, one;

10 the king of Jerusalem, one; the king of Hebron, one;

11 the king of Jarmuth, one; the king of Lachish, one;

12 the king of Eglon, one; the king of Gezer, one;

13 the king of Debir, one; the king of Geder, one;

14 the king of Hormah, one; the king of Arad, one;

15 the king of Libnah, one; the king of Adullam, one;

16 the king of Makkedah, one; the king of Bethel, one;

17 the king of Tappuah, one; the king of Hepher, one;

18 the king of Aphek, one; the king of Lasharon, one;

19 the king of Madon, one; the king of Hazor, one;

20 the king of Shimron-meron, one; the king of Achshaph, one;

21 the king of Taanach, one; the king of Megiddo, one;

22 the king of Kedesh, one; the king of Jokneam in Carmel, one;

23 the king of Dor in the heights of Dor, one; the king of Goiim in Gilgal, one;

24 the king of Tirzah, one: in all, thirty-one kings.

NAS [a] I.e., Galilee

## New International

*List of Defeated Kings*

**12** THESE ARE the kings of the land whom the Israelites had defeated and whose territory they took over east of the Jordan, from the Arnon Gorge to Mount Hermon, including all the eastern side of the Arabah:

2 Sihon king of the Amorites,
who reigned in Heshbon. He ruled from Aroer on the rim of
the Arnon Gorge—from the middle of the gorge—to the Jabbok River, which is the border of the Ammonites. This included half of Gilead.
3 He also ruled over the eastern Arabah
from the Sea of Kinnereth[b] to the Sea of the Arabah (the Salt
Sea[c]), to Beth Jeshimoth, and then southward below the
slopes of Pisgah.

4 And the territory of Og king of Bashan,
one of the last of the Rephaites, who reigned in Ashtaroth and
Edrei.
5 He ruled over Mount Hermon, Salecah, all of Bashan
to the border of the people of Geshur and Maacah, and half
of Gilead to the border of Sihon king of Heshbon.

6 Moses, the servant of the LORD, and the Israelites conquered them. And Moses the servant of the LORD gave their land to the Reubenites, the Gadites and the half-tribe of Manasseh to be their possession.

7 These are the kings of the land that Joshua and the Israelites
conquered on the west side of the Jordan, from Baal Gad in the
Valley of Lebanon to Mount Halak, which rises toward Seir (their
lands Joshua gave as an inheritance to the tribes of Israel according
to their tribal divisions—
8 the hill country, the western foothills,
the Arabah, the mountain slopes, the desert and the Negev—the
lands of the Hittites, Amorites, Canaanites, Perizzites, Hivites and
Jebusites):

| | |
|---|---|
| 9 the king of Jericho | one |
| the king of Ai (near Bethel) | one |
| 10 the king of Jerusalem | one |
| the king of Hebron | one |
| 11 the king of Jarmuth | one |
| the king of Lachish | one |
| 12 the king of Eglon | one |
| the king of Gezer | one |
| 13 the king of Debir | one |
| the king of Geder | one |
| 14 the king of Hormah | one |
| the king of Arad | one |
| 15 the king of Libnah | one |
| the king of Adullam | one |
| 16 the king of Makkedah | one |
| the king of Bethel | one |
| 17 the king of Tappuah | one |
| the king of Hepher | one |
| 18 the king of Aphek | one |
| the king of Lasharon | one |
| 19 the king of Madon | one |
| the king of Hazor | one |
| 20 the king of Shimron Meron | one |
| the king of Acshaph | one |
| 21 the king of Taanach | one |
| the king of Megiddo | one |
| 22 the king of Kedesh | one |
| the king of Jokneam in Carmel | one |
| 23 the king of Dor (in Naphoth Dor[d]) | one |
| the king of Goyim in Gilgal | one |
| 24 the king of Tirzah | one |

thirty-one kings in all.

NIV [b] 3 That is, Galilee [c] 3 That is, the Dead Sea [d] 23 Or *in the heights of Dor*

# King James

**13** NOW JOSHUA was old *and* stricken in years; and the LORD said unto him, Thou art old *and* stricken in years, and there remaineth yet very much land to be possessed.

2This *is* the land that yet remaineth: all the borders of the Philistines, and all Geshuri,

3From Sihor, which *is* before Egypt, even unto the borders of Ekron northward, *which* is counted to the Canaanite: five lords of the Philistines; the Gazathites, and the Ashdothites, the Eshkalonites, the Gittites, and the Ekronites; also the Avites:

4From the south, all the land of the Canaanites, and Mearah that *is* beside the Sidonians, unto Aphek, to the borders of the Amorites:

5And the land of the Giblites, and all Lebanon, toward the sunrising, from Baal-gad under mount Hermon unto the entering into Hamath.

6All the inhabitants of the hill country from Lebanon unto Misrephoth-maim, *and* all the Sidonians, them will I drive out from before the children of Israel: only divide thou it by lot unto the Israelites for an inheritance, as I have commanded thee.

7Now therefore divide this land for an inheritance unto the nine tribes, and the half tribe of Manasseh,

8With whom the Reubenites and the Gadites have received their inheritance, which Moses gave them, beyond Jordan eastward, *even* as Moses the servant of the LORD gave them;

9From Aroer, that *is* upon the bank of the river Arnon, and the city that *is* in the midst of the river, and all the plain of Medeba unto Dibon;

10And all the cities of Sihon king of the Amorites, which reigned in Heshbon, unto the border of the children of Ammon;

11And Gilead, and the border of the Geshurites and Maachathites, and all mount Hermon, and all Bashan unto Salcah;

12All the kingdom of Og in Bashan, which reigned in Ashtaroth and in Edrei, who remained of the remnant of the giants: for these did Moses smite, and cast them out.

13Nevertheless the children of Israel expelled not the Geshurites, nor the Maachathites: but the Geshurites and the Maachathites dwell among the Israelites until this day.

14Only unto the tribe of Levi he gave none inheritance; the sacrifices of the LORD God of Israel made by fire *are* their inheritance, as he said unto them.

15¶ And Moses gave unto the tribe of the children of Reuben *inheritance* according to their families.

16And their coast was from Aroer, that *is* on the bank of the river Arnon, and the city that *is* in the midst of the river, and all the plain by Medeba;

17Heshbon, and all her cities that *are* in the plain; Dibon, and Bamoth-baal, and Beth-baal-meon,

18And Jahaza, and Kedemoth, and Mephaath,

19And Kirjathaim, and Sibmah, and Zareth-shahar in the mount of the valley,

20And Beth-peor, and Ashdoth-pisgah, and Beth-jeshimoth,

21And all the cities of the plain, and all the kingdom of Sihon king of the Amorites, which reigned in Heshbon, whom Moses smote with the princes of Midian, Evi, and Rekem, and Zur, and Hur, and Reba, *which were* dukes of Sihon, dwelling in the country.

22¶ Balaam also the son of Beor, the soothsayer, did the children of Israel slay with the sword among them that were slain by them.

23And the border of the children of Reuben was Jordan, and the border *thereof*. This *was* the inheritance of the children of Reuben after their families, the cities and the villages thereof.

24And Moses gave *inheritance* unto the tribe of Gad, *even* unto the children of Gad according to their families.

25And their coast was Jazer, and all the cities of Gilead, and half the land of the children of Ammon, unto Aroer that *is* before Rabbah;

26And from Heshbon unto Ramath-mizpeh, and Betonim; and from Mahanaim unto the border of Debir;

# Amplified

**13** NOW JOSHUA was old and gone far in years [over 100]; and the Lord said to him, You have grown old and are gone far in years, and very much land still remains to be possessed.

2This is the land that yet remains: all the regions of the Philistines, and all those of the Geshurites,

3From the Shihor, which is east of Egypt, northward to the boundary of Ekron, it is counted as Canaanite; there are five rulers of the Philistines, those of Gaza, Ashdod, Ashkelon, Gath, and Ekron, and those of the Avvim,

4In the south, all the land of the Canaanites, and Mearah which belongs to the Sidonians, to Aphek, to the boundary of the Amorites,

5And the land of the Gebalites, and all Lebanon, toward the east, from Baal-gad below Mount Hermon to the gate of Hamath;

6All the inhabitants of the hill country from Lebanon to Misrephoth-maim, even all the Sidonians. I will Myself drive them out from before the Israelites; only allot the land to Israel for an inheritance, as I have commanded you.

7So now divide this land for an inheritance to the nine tribes, and the half-tribe of Manasseh.

8With the other half-tribe of Manasseh the Reubenites and the Gadites received their inheritance, beyond Jordan eastward, as Moses the servant of the Lord gave them:

9From Aroer, on the edge of the valley of the river Arnon, and the city in the midst of the valley, and all the tableland of Medeba as far as Dibon;

10And all the cities of Sihon king of the Amorites, who ruled in Heshbon, as far as the boundary of the Ammonites;

11And Gilead, and the region of the Geshurites and Ma-acathites, and all Mount Hermon, and all Bashan to Salecah;

12All the kingdom of Og in Bashan, who reigned in Ashtaroth and Edrei, and alone was left of the Rephaim [giants]; for these Moses had defeated and driven out.

13Yet the Israelites did not drive out the Geshurites or the Ma-acathites; but Geshur and Ma-acath dwell among [them] still.

14Only to the tribe of Levi Moses gave no inheritance; the sacrifices to the Lord God of Israel made by fire are their inheritance, as He said to him.

15And Moses gave an inheritance to the tribe of the Reubenites according to their families.

16Their territory was from Aroer, on the edge of the valley of the river Arnon, and the city in the midst of the valley, and all the tableland by Medeba;

17With Heshbon, and all its cities that are on the plain; Dibon, Bamoth-baal, and Beth-baal-meon,

18Jahaz, Kedemoth, Mephaath,

19Kiriathaim, Sibmah, and Zereth-shahar on the hill of the valley,

20Bethpeor, Pisgah's slopes, and Beth-jeshimoth,

21All the cities of the plain, and all the kingdom of Sihon king of the Amorites, who ruled in Heshbon, whom Moses defeated with the leaders of Midian, Evi, Rekem, Zur, Hur, and Reba, the princes of Sihon, who lived in the land.

22Balaam also, the son of Beor, the soothsayer, the Israelites killed with the sword among the rest of their slain. [Num. 31:16.]

23And the border of the Reubenites was the Jordan. This was the inheritance of the Reubenites according to their families with their cities and villages.

24Moses gave an inheritance also to the tribe of the Gadites according to their families.

25Their territory was Jazer, and all the cities of Gilead, and half the land of the Ammonites, to Aroer east of Rabbah,

26And from Heshbon to Ramath-mizpeh and Betonim, and from Mahanaim to the territory of Debir,

## New American Standard

*Canaan Divided among the Tribes*

**13** NOW JOSHUA was old *and* advanced in years when the LORD said to him, "You are old *and* advanced in years, and very much of the land remains to be possessed.

2 "This is the land that remains: all the regions *of* the Philistines and all *those of* the Geshurites;

3 from the Shihor which is east of Egypt, even as far as the border of Ekron to the north (it is counted as Canaanite); the five lords of the Philistines: the Gazite, the Ashdodite, the Ashkelonite, the Gittite, the Ekronite; and the Avvite

4 to the south, all the land of the Canaanite, and Mearah that belongs to the Sidonians, as far as Aphek, to the border of the Amorite;

5 and the land of the Gebalite, and all of Lebanon, toward the east, from Baal-gad below Mount Hermon as far as Lebo-hamath.

6 "All the inhabitants of the hill country from Lebanon as far as Misrephoth-maim, all the Sidonians, I will drive them out from before the sons of Israel; only allot it to Israel for an inheritance as I have commanded you.

7 "Now therefore, apportion this land for an inheritance to the nine tribes, and the half-tribe of Manasseh."

8 ¶ With the other half-tribe, the Reubenites and the Gadites received their inheritance which Moses gave them beyond the Jordan to the east, just as Moses the servant of the LORD gave to them;

9 from Aroer, which is on the edge of the valley of the Arnon, with the city which is in the middle of the valley, and all the plain of Medeba, as far as Dibon;

10 and all the cities of Sihon king of the Amorites, who reigned in Heshbon, as far as the border of the sons of Ammon;

11 and Gilead, and the territory of the Geshurites and Maacathites, and all Mount Hermon, and all Bashan as far as Salecah;

12 all the kingdom of Og in Bashan, who reigned in Ashtaroth and in Edrei (he alone was left of the remnant of the Rephaim); for Moses struck them and dispossessed them.

13 But the sons of Israel did not dispossess the Geshurites or the Maacathites; for Geshur and Maacath live among Israel until this day.

14 Only to the tribe of Levi he did not give an inheritance; the offerings by fire to the LORD, the God of Israel, are their inheritance, as He spoke to him.

15 ¶ So Moses gave *an inheritance* to the tribe of the sons of Reuben according to their families.

16 And their territory was from Aroer, which is on the edge of the valley of the Arnon, with the city which is in the middle of the valley and all the plain by Medeba;

17 Heshbon, and all its cities which are on the plain: Dibon and Bamoth-baal and Beth-baal-meon,

18 and Jahaz and Kedemoth and Mephaath,

19 and Kiriathaim and Sibmah and Zereth-shahar on the hill of the valley,

20 and Beth-peor and the slopes of Pisgah and Beth-jeshimoth,

21 even all the cities of the plain and all the kingdom of Sihon king of the Amorites who reigned in Heshbon, whom Moses struck with the chiefs of Midian, Evi and Rekem and Zur and Hur and Reba, the princes of Sihon, who lived in the land.

22 The sons of Israel also killed Balaam the son of Beor, the diviner, with the sword among *the rest of* their slain.

23 And the border of the sons of Reuben was the Jordan. This was the inheritance of the sons of Reuben according to their families, the cities and their villages.

24 ¶ Moses also gave *an inheritance* to the tribe of Gad, to the sons of Gad, according to their families.

25 And their territory was Jazer, and all the cities of Gilead, and half the land of the sons of Ammon, as far as Aroer which is before Rabbah;

26 and from Heshbon as far as Ramath-mizpeh and Betonim, and from Mahanaim as far as the border of Debir;

## New International

*Land Still to Be Taken*

**13** WHEN JOSHUA was old and well advanced in years, the LORD said to him, "You are very old, and there are still very large areas of land to be taken over.

2 "This is the land that remains: all the regions of the Philistines and Geshurites: 3 from the Shihor River on the east of
Egypt to the territory of Ekron on the north, all of it counted
as Canaanite (the territory of the five Philistine rulers in Gaza,
Ashdod, Ashkelon, Gath and Ekron—that of the Avvites);
4 from the south, all the land of the Canaanites, from Arah of
the Sidonians as far as Aphek, the region of the Amorites, 5 the
area of the Gebalites[a]; and all Lebanon to the east, from Baal
Gad below Mount Hermon to Lebo[b] Hamath.

6 "As for all the inhabitants of the mountain regions from Lebanon to Misrephoth Maim, that is, all the Sidonians, I myself will
drive them out before the Israelites. Be sure to allocate this land
to Israel for an inheritance, as I have instructed you, 7 and divide
it as an inheritance among the nine tribes and half of the tribe of
Manasseh."

*Division of the Land East of the Jordan*

8 The other half of Manasseh,[c] the Reubenites and the Gadites had
received the inheritance that Moses had given them east of the
Jordan, as he, the servant of the LORD, had assigned it to them.

9 It extended from Aroer on the rim of the Arnon Gorge, and
from the town in the middle of the gorge, and included the
whole plateau of Medeba as far as Dibon, 10 and all the towns
of Sihon king of the Amorites, who ruled in Heshbon, out to
the border of the Ammonites. 11 It also included Gilead, the
territory of the people of Geshur and Maacah, all of Mount
Hermon and all Bashan as far as Salecah— 12 that is, the whole
kingdom of Og in Bashan, who had reigned in Ashtaroth and
Edrei and had survived as one of the last of the Rephaites.
Moses had defeated them and taken over their land. 13 But the
Israelites did not drive out the people of Geshur and Maacah,
so they continue to live among the Israelites to this day.

14 But to the tribe of Levi he gave no inheritance, since the
offerings made by fire to the LORD, the God of Israel, are their
inheritance, as he promised them.

15 This is what Moses had given to the tribe of Reuben, clan by clan:

16 The territory from Aroer on the rim of the Arnon Gorge, and
from the town in the middle of the gorge, and the whole
plateau past Medeba 17 to Heshbon and all its towns on the
plateau, including Dibon, Bamoth Baal, Beth Baal Meon,
18 Jahaz, Kedemoth, Mephaath, 19 Kiriathaim, Sibmah, Zereth
Shahar on the hill in the valley, 20 Beth Peor, the slopes of
Pisgah, and Beth Jeshimoth 21—all the towns on the plateau
and the entire realm of Sihon king of the Amorites, who ruled
at Heshbon. Moses had defeated him and the Midianite
chiefs, Evi, Rekem, Zur, Hur and Reba—princes allied with
Sihon—who lived in that country. 22 In addition to those slain
in battle, the Israelites had put to the sword Balaam son of
Beor, who practiced divination. 23 The boundary of the Reubenites was the bank of the Jordan. These towns and their
villages were the inheritance of the Reubenites, clan by clan.

24 This is what Moses had given to the tribe of Gad, clan by clan:

25 The territory of Jazer, all the towns of Gilead and half the
Ammonite country as far as Aroer, near Rabbah; 26 and from
Heshbon to Ramath Mizpah and Betonim, and from Maha-
naim to the territory of Debir; 27 and in the valley, Beth Haram,

**NIV** [a] 5 That is, the area of Byblos [b] 5 Or *to the entrance to* [c] 8 Hebrew *With it* (that is, with the other half of Manasseh)

## King James

27 And in the valley, Beth-aram, and Beth-nimrah, and Succoth, and Zaphon, the rest of the kingdom of Sihon king of Heshbon, Jordan and *his* border, *even* unto the edge of the sea of Chinnereth on the other side Jordan eastward.

28 This *is* the inheritance of the children of Gad after their families, the cities, and their villages.

29 ¶ And Moses gave *inheritance* unto the half tribe of Manasseh: and *this* was *the possession* of the half tribe of the children of Manasseh by their families.

30 And their coast was from Mahanaim, all Bashan, all the kingdom of Og king of Bashan, and all the towns of Jair, which *are* in Bashan, threescore cities:

31 And half Gilead, and Ashtaroth, and Edrei, cities of the kingdom of Og in Bashan, *were pertaining* unto the children of Machir the son of Manasseh, *even* to the one half of the children of Machir by their families.

32 These *are the countries* which Moses did distribute for inheritance in the plains of Moab, on the other side Jordan, by Jericho, eastward.

33 But unto the tribe of Levi Moses gave not *any* inheritance: the LORD God of Israel *was* their inheritance, as he said unto them.

**14** AND THESE *are the countries* which the children of Israel inherited in the land of Canaan, which Eleazar the priest, and Joshua the son of Nun, and the heads of the fathers of the tribes of the children of Israel, distributed for inheritance to them.

2 By lot *was* their inheritance, as the LORD commanded by the hand of Moses, for the nine tribes, and *for* the half tribe.

3 For Moses had given the inheritance of two tribes and an half tribe on the other side Jordan: but unto the Levites he gave none inheritance among them.

4 For the children of Joseph were two tribes, Manasseh and Ephraim: therefore they gave no part unto the Levites in the land, save cities to dwell *in,* with their suburbs for their cattle and for their substance.

5 As the LORD commanded Moses, so the children of Israel did, and they divided the land.

6 ¶ Then the children of Judah came unto Joshua in Gilgal: and Caleb the son of Jephunneh the Kenezite said unto him, Thou knowest the thing that the LORD said unto Moses the man of God concerning me and thee in Kadesh-barnea.

7 Forty years old *was* I when Moses the servant of the LORD sent me from Kadesh-barnea to espy out the land; and I brought him word again as *it was* in mine heart.

8 Nevertheless my brethren that went up with me made the heart of the people melt: but I wholly followed the LORD my God.

9 And Moses sware on that day, saying, Surely the land whereon thy feet have trodden shall be thine inheritance, and thy children's for ever, because thou hast wholly followed the LORD my God.

10 And now, behold, the LORD hath kept me alive, as he said, these forty and five years, even since the LORD spake this word unto Moses, while *the children of* Israel wandered in the wilderness: and now, lo, I *am* this day fourscore and five years old.

11 As yet I *am as* strong this day as *I was* in the day that Moses sent me: as my strength *was* then, even so *is* my strength now, for war, both to go out, and to come in.

12 Now therefore give me this mountain, whereof the LORD spake in that day; for thou heardest in that day how the Anakims *were* there, and *that* the cities *were* great *and* fenced: if so be the LORD *will be* with me, then I shall be able to drive them out, as the LORD said.

13 And Joshua blessed him, and gave unto Caleb the son of Jephunneh Hebron for an inheritance.

## Amplified

27 And in the valley of Beth-haram, Beth-nimrah, Succoth, and Zaphon, the rest of the realm of Sihon king of Heshbon, with the Jordan as a boundary, to the lower end of the Sea of Chinnereth east of the Jordan.

28 This is the inheritance of the Gadites according to their families, with their cities and villages.

29 And Moses gave an inheritance to the half-tribe of Manasseh; it was allotted to them according to their families.

30 Their region extended from Mahanaim, through all Bashan, the entire kingdom of Og king of Bashan, and all the towns of Jair, which are in Bashan; sixty cities,

31 And half Gilead, and Ashtaroth, and Edrei, cities of the kingdom of Og in Bashan; these were allotted to the people of Machir son of Manasseh for the half of the Machirites according to their families.

32 These are the inheritances which Moses distributed in the plains of Moab, beyond the Jordan east of Jericho.

33 But to the tribe of Levi Moses gave no inheritance; the Lord the God of Israel was their inheritance, as He told them.

**14** THESE ARE the inheritances in the land of Canaan, distributed to the Israelites by Eleazar the priest, Joshua the son of Nun, and the heads of the fathers' houses of their tribes.

2 Their inheritance was by lot, as the Lord commanded Moses, for the nine and one-half tribes.

3 For Moses had given an inheritance to the two and one-half tribes beyond the Jordan; but to the Levites he gave no inheritance among them.

4 For the people of Joseph were two tribes, Manasseh and Ephraim; and no part was given in the land to the Levites, except cities in which to live, with their pasture lands for their livestock and for their possession.

5 As the Lord commanded Moses, so the Israelites did, and they divided the land.

6 Then the people of Judah came to Joshua in Gilgal, and Caleb son of Jephunneh the Kenizzite said to him, You know what the Lord said to Moses the man of God concerning me and you in Kadesh-barnea.

7 Forty years old was I when Moses the servant of the Lord sent me from Kadesh-barnea to scout out the land; and I brought him report as it was in my heart.

8 But my brethren who went up with me made the heart of the people melt; yet I wholly followed the Lord my God.

9 And Moses swore on that day, Surely the land on which your feet have walked shall be an inheritance to you and your children always, because you have wholly followed the Lord my God. [Deut. 1:35, 36.]

10 And now, behold, the Lord has kept me alive, as He said, these forty-five years since the Lord spoke this word to Moses, while the Israelites wandered in the wilderness; and now, lo, I am this day eighty-five years old.

11 Yet I am as strong today as I was the day Moses sent me; as my strength was then, so is my strength now, for war, and to go out, and to come in.

12 So now give me this hill country, of which the Lord spoke that day; for you heard then how the [giant-like] Anakim were there, and that the cities were great and fortified; if the Lord will be with me, I shall drive them out, as the Lord said.

13 Then Joshua blessed him, and gave Hebron to Caleb son of Jephunneh for an inheritance.

## New American Standard

27and in the valley, Beth-haram and Beth-nimrah and Succoth and Zaphon, the rest of the kingdom of Sihon king of Heshbon, with the Jordan as a border, as far as the *lower* end of the Sea of Chinnereth beyond the Jordan to the east.

28This is the inheritance of the sons of Gad according to their families, the cities and their villages.

29¶ Moses also gave *an inheritance* to the half-tribe of Manasseh; and it was for the half-tribe of the sons of Manasseh according to their families.

30And their territory was from Mahanaim, all Bashan, all the kingdom of Og king of Bashan, and all the towns of Jair, which are in Bashan, sixty cities;

31also half of Gilead, with Ashtaroth and Edrei, the cities of the kingdom of Og in Bashan, *were* for the sons of Machir the son of Manasseh, for half of the sons of Machir according to their families.

32¶ These are *the territories* which Moses apportioned for an inheritance in the plains of Moab, beyond the Jordan at Jericho to the east.

33But to the tribe of Levi, Moses did not give an inheritance; the LORD, the God of Israel, is their inheritance, as He had promised to them.

*Caleb's Request*

14 NOW THESE are *the territories* which the sons of Israel inherited in the land of Canaan, which Eleazar the priest, and Joshua the son of Nun, and the heads of the households of the tribes of the sons of Israel apportioned to them for an inheritance,

2by the lot of their inheritance, as the LORD commanded through Moses, for the nine tribes and the half-tribe.

3For Moses had given the inheritance of the two tribes and the half-tribe beyond the Jordan; but he did not give an inheritance to the Levites among them.

4For the sons of Joseph were two tribes, Manasseh and Ephraim, and they did not give a portion to the Levites in the land, except cities to live in, with their pasture lands for their livestock and for their property.

5Thus the sons of Israel did just as the LORD had commanded Moses, and they divided the land.

6¶ Then the sons of Judah drew near to Joshua in Gilgal, and Caleb the son of Jephunneh the Kenizzite said to him, "You know the word which the LORD spoke to Moses the man of God concerning you and me in Kadesh-barnea.

7"I was forty years old when Moses the servant of the LORD sent me from Kadesh-barnea to spy out the land, and I brought word back to him as *it was* in my heart.

8"Nevertheless my brethren who went up with me made the heart of the people melt with fear; but I followed the LORD my God fully.

9"So Moses swore on that day, saying, 'Surely the land on which your foot has trodden shall be an inheritance to you and to your children forever, because you have followed the LORD my God fully.'

10"And now behold, the LORD has let me live, just as He spoke, these forty-five years, from the time that the LORD spoke this word to Moses, when Israel walked in the wilderness; and now behold, I am eighty-five years old today.

11"I am still as strong today as I was in the day Moses sent me; as my strength was then, so my strength is now, for war and for going out and coming in.

12"Now then, give me this hill country about which the LORD spoke on that day, for you heard on that day that Anakim *were* there, with great fortified cities; perhaps the LORD will be with me, and I shall drive them out as the LORD has spoken."

13¶ So Joshua blessed him, and gave Hebron to Caleb the son of Jephunneh for an inheritance.

## New International

Beth Nimrah, Succoth and Zaphon with the rest of the realm
of Sihon king of Heshbon (the east side of the Jordan, the
territory up to the end of the Sea of Kinnereth[a]). 28These
towns and their villages were the inheritance of the Gadites,
clan by clan.

29This is what Moses had given to the half-tribe of Manasseh, that is, to half the family of the descendants of Manasseh, clan by clan:

30The territory extending from Mahanaim and including all of
Bashan, the entire realm of Og king of Bashan—all the settlements of Jair in Bashan, sixty towns, 31half of Gilead, and
Ashtaroth and Edrei (the royal cities of Og in Bashan). This
was for the descendants of Makir son of Manasseh—for half
of the sons of Makir, clan by clan.

32This is the inheritance Moses had given when he was in the
plains of Moab across the Jordan east of Jericho. 33But to the tribe
of Levi, Moses had given no inheritance; the LORD, the God of
Israel, is their inheritance, as he promised them.

*Division of the Land West of the Jordan*

14 NOW THESE are the areas the Israelites received as an
inheritance in the land of Canaan, which Eleazar the
priest, Joshua son of Nun and the heads of the tribal clans of Israel
allotted to them. 2Their inheritances were assigned by lot to the
nine-and-a-half tribes, as the LORD had commanded through
Moses. 3Moses had granted the two-and-a-half tribes their inheritance east of the Jordan but had not granted the Levites an inheritance among the rest, 4for the sons of Joseph had become two
tribes—Manasseh and Ephraim. The Levites received no share of
the land but only towns to live in, with pasturelands for their flocks
and herds. 5So the Israelites divided the land, just as the LORD had
commanded Moses.

*Hebron Given to Caleb*

6Now the men of Judah approached Joshua at Gilgal, and Caleb
son of Jephunneh the Kenizzite said to him, "You know what the
LORD said to Moses the man of God at Kadesh Barnea about you
and me. 7I was forty years old when Moses the servant of the LORD
sent me from Kadesh Barnea to explore the land. And I brought
him back a report according to my convictions, 8but my brothers
who went up with me made the hearts of the people melt with fear.
I, however, followed the LORD my God wholeheartedly. 9So on
that day Moses swore to me, 'The land on which your feet have
walked will be your inheritance and that of your children forever,
because you have followed the LORD my God wholeheartedly.'[b]

10"Now then, just as the LORD promised, he has kept me alive
for forty-five years since the time he said this to Moses, while Israel
moved about in the desert. So here I am today, eighty-five years
old! 11I am still as strong today as the day Moses sent me out; I'm
just as vigorous to go out to battle now as I was then. 12Now give
me this hill country that the LORD promised me that day. You
yourself heard then that the Anakites were there and their cities
were large and fortified, but, the LORD helping me, I will drive
them out just as he said."

13Then Joshua blessed Caleb son of Jephunneh and gave him
Hebron as his inheritance. 14So Hebron has belonged to Caleb son

NIV [a] 27 That is, Galilee [b] 9 Deut. 1:36

## King James

14Hebron therefore became the inheritance of Caleb the son of Jephunneh the Kenezite unto this day, because that he wholly followed the LORD God of Israel.

15And the name of Hebron before *was* Kirjath-arba; *which Arba was* a great man among the Anakims. And the land had rest from war.

**15** *THIS* THEN was the lot of the tribe of the children of Judah by their families; *even* to the border of Edom the wilderness of Zin southward *was* the uttermost part of the south coast.

2And their south border was from the shore of the salt sea, from the bay that looketh southward:

3And it went out to the south side to Maaleh-acrabbim, and passed along to Zin, and ascended up on the south side unto Kadesh-barnea, and passed along to Hezron, and went up to Adar, and fetched a compass to Karkaa:

4 *From thence* it passed toward Azmon, and went out unto the river of Egypt; and the goings out of that coast were at the sea: this shall be your south coast.

5And the east border *was* the salt sea, *even* unto the end of Jordan. And *their* border in the north quarter *was* from the bay of the sea at the uttermost part of Jordan:

6And the border went up to Beth-hoglah, and passed along by the north by Beth-arabah; and the border went up to the stone of Bohan the son of Reuben:

7And the border went up toward Debir from the valley of Achor, and so northward, looking toward Gilgal, that *is* before the going up to Adummim, which *is* on the south side of the river: and the border passed toward the waters of En-shemesh, and the goings out thereof were at En-rogel:

8And the border went up by the valley of the son of Hinnom unto the south side of the Jebusite; the same *is* Jerusalem: and the border went up to the top of the mountain that *lieth* before the valley of Hinnom westward, which *is* at the end of the valley of the giants northward:

9And the border was drawn from the top of the hill unto the fountain of the water of Nephtoah, and went out to the cities of mount Ephron; and the border was drawn to Baalah, which *is* Kirjath-jearim:

10And the border compassed from Baalah westward unto mount Seir, and passed along unto the side of mount Jearim, which *is* Chesalon, on the north side, and went down to Beth-shemesh, and passed on to Timnah:

11And the border went out unto the side of Ekron northward: and the border was drawn to Shicron, and passed along to mount Baalah, and went out unto Jabneel; and the goings out of the border were at the sea.

12And the west border *was* to the great sea, and the coast *thereof*. This *is* the coast of the children of Judah round about according to their families.

13¶ And unto Caleb the son of Jephunneh he gave a part among the children of Judah, according to the commandment of the LORD to Joshua, *even* the city of Arba the father of Anak, which *city is* Hebron.

14And Caleb drove thence the three sons of Anak, Sheshai, and Ahiman, and Talmai, the children of Anak.

15And he went up thence to the inhabitants of Debir: and the name of Debir before *was* Kirjath-sepher.

16¶ And Caleb said, He that smiteth Kirjath-sepher, and taketh it, to him will I give Achsah my daughter to wife.

17And Othniel the son of Kenaz, the brother of Caleb, took it: and he gave him Achsah his daughter to wife.

18And it came to pass, as she came *unto him*, that she moved him to ask of her father a field: and she lighted off *her* ass; and Caleb said unto her, What wouldest thou?

## Amplified

14So Hebron became the inheritance of Caleb son of Jephunneh the Kenizzite to this day, because he wholly followed the Lord, the God of Israel.

15The name of Hebron before was Kiriath-arba [meaning, city of Arba]. This Arba was the greatest of the Anakim. And the land had rest from war.

**15** THE LOT for the tribe of Judah according to *its* families reached southward to the boundary of Edom, to the wilderness of Zin at its most southern part.

2And their south boundary was from the end of the Salt [Dead] Sea, from the bay that faces southward;

3It went out south of the ascent of Akrabbim, passed along to Zin, and went up south of Kadesh-barnea, along by Hezron, up to Addar, and turned about to Karka,

4Passed along to Azmon, went out by the brook of Egypt, and ended at the sea. This was their southern frontier.

5The eastern boundary was the Salt [Dead] Sea, as far as the mouth of the Jordan. The northern boundary was from the bay of the sea at the mouth of the Jordan;

6And the boundary went up to Beth-hogla, and passed along north of Beth-arabah, and [it] went up to the [landmark] stone of Bohan son of Reuben.

7And the boundary went up to Debir from the Valley of Achor, and so northward, turning toward Gilgal, which is opposite the ascent to Adummim, on the south side of the valley; and *it* passed on to the waters of En-shemesh, and ended at En-rogel;

8Then the boundary went up by the valley of the son of Hinnom at the southern shoulder of the Jebusite (that is, Jerusalem); and the boundary went up to the top of the mountain that lies before the valley of Hinnom on the west, at the northern end of the valley of Rephaim.

9Then the boundary extended from the top of the mountain to the spring of the Waters of Nephtoah, and went on to the cities of Mount Ephron; then *it* bent round to Baalah, that is, Kiriath-jearim.

10And the boundary went around west of Baalah to Mount Seir, passed along to the northern side of Mount Jearim, which is Chesalon, and went down to Beth-shemesh, then passed on by Timnah;

11And the boundary went out to the shoulder of the hill north of Ekron, then it bent round to Shikkeron, and passed along to Mount Baalah, and went out to Jabneel; then the boundary ended at the sea.

12And the west boundary was the Great Sea with its coastline. This is the boundary round about the people of Judah according to their families.

13And to Caleb son of Jephunneh [Joshua] gave a part among the people of Judah, as the Lord commanded [him]; it was Kiriath-arba, which is Hebron, [named for] Arba the father of Anak.

14And Caleb drove from there the three sons of Anak, Sheshai, and Ahiman, and Talmai, the descendants of Anak.

15He went up from there against the people of Debir. Debir was formerly named Kiriath-sepher.

16Caleb said, He who smites Kiriath-sepher, and takes it, to him will I give Achsah my daughter as wife.

17And Othniel the son of Kenaz, Caleb's brother, took it; and he gave him Achsah his daughter as wife.

18When Achsah came to Othniel, she got his consent to ask her father for a field. Then she returned to Caleb and when she lighted off her donkey, Caleb said, What do you wish?

## New American Standard

14Therefore, Hebron became the inheritance of Caleb the son of Jephunneh the Kenizzite until this day, because he followed the LORD God of Israel fully.

15Now the name of Hebron was formerly Kiriath-arba; *for Arba* was the greatest man among the Anakim. Then the land had rest from war.

*Territory of Judah*

**15** NOW THE lot for the tribe of the sons of Judah according to their families reached the border of Edom, southward to the wilderness of Zin at the extreme south.

2And their south border was from the lower end of the Salt Sea, from the bay that turns to the south.

3Then it proceeded southward to the ascent of Akrabbim and continued to Zin, then went up by the south of Kadesh-barnea and continued to Hezron, and went up to Addar and turned about to Karka.

4And it continued to Azmon and proceeded to the brook of Egypt; and the border ended at the sea. This shall be your south border.

5And the east border *was* the Salt Sea, as far as the mouth of the Jordan. And the border of the north side was from the bay of the sea at the mouth of the Jordan.

6Then the border went up to Beth-hoglah, and continued on the north of Beth-arabah, and the border went up to the stone of Bohan the son of Reuben.

7And the border went up to Debir from the valley of Achor, and turned northward toward Gilgal which is opposite the ascent of Adummim, which is on the south of the valley; and the border continued to the waters of En-shemesh, and it ended at En-rogel.

8Then the border went up the valley of Ben-hinnom to the slope of the Jebusite on the south (that is, Jerusalem); and the border went up to the top of the mountain which is before the valley of Hinnom to the west, which is at the end of the valley of Rephaim toward the north.

9And from the top of the mountain the border curved to the spring of the waters of Nephtoah and proceeded to the cities of Mount Ephron, then the border curved to Baalah (that is, Kiriath-jearim).

10And the border turned about from Baalah westward to Mount Seir, and continued to the slope of Mount Jearim on the north (that is, Chesalon), and went down to Beth-shemesh and continued through Timnah.

11And the border proceeded to the side of Ekron northward. Then the border curved to Shikkeron and continued to Mount Baalah and proceeded to Jabneel, and the border ended at the sea.

12And the west border *was* at the Great Sea, even *its* coastline. This is the border around the sons of Judah according to their families.

13¶ Now he gave to Caleb the son of Jephunneh a portion among the sons of Judah, according to the command of the LORD to Joshua, *namely,* Kiriath-arba, *Arba being* the father of Anak (that is, Hebron).

14And Caleb drove out from there the three sons of Anak: Sheshai and Ahiman and Talmai, the children of Anak.

15Then he went up from there against the inhabitants of Debir; now the name of Debir formerly was Kiriath-sepher.

16And Caleb said, "The one who attacks Kiriath-sepher and captures it, I will give him Achsah my daughter as a wife."

17And Othniel the son of Kenaz, the brother of Caleb, captured it; so he gave him Achsah his daughter as a wife.

18And it came about that when she came *to him,* she persuaded him to ask her father for a field. So she alighted from the donkey, and Caleb said to her, "What do you want?"

## New International

of Jephunneh the Kenizzite ever since, because he followed the
LORD, the God of Israel, wholeheartedly. 15(Hebron used to be
called Kiriath Arba after Arba, who was the greatest man among
the Anakites.)
Then the land had rest from war.

*Allotment for Judah*

**15** THE ALLOTMENT for the tribe of Judah, clan by clan,
extended down to the territory of Edom, to the Desert of
Zin in the extreme south.
2Their southern boundary started from the bay at the
southern end of the Salt Sea,[a] 3crossed south of Scorpion[b]
Pass, continued on to Zin and went over to the south of
Kadesh Barnea. Then it ran past Hezron up to Addar and
curved around to Karka. 4It then passed along to Azmon and
joined the Wadi of Egypt, ending at the sea. This is their[c]
southern boundary.
5The eastern boundary is the Salt Sea as far as the mouth
of the Jordan.
The northern boundary started from the bay of the sea at
the mouth of the Jordan, 6went up to Beth Hoglah and continued north of Beth Arabah to the Stone of Bohan son of
Reuben. 7The boundary then went up to Debir from the Valley of Achor and turned north to Gilgal, which faces the Pass
of Adummim south of the gorge. It continued along to the
waters of En Shemesh and came out at En Rogel. 8Then it ran
up the Valley of Ben Hinnom along the southern slope of the
Jebusite city (that is, Jerusalem). From there it climbed to the
top of the hill west of the Hinnom Valley at the northern end
of the Valley of Rephaim. 9From the hilltop the boundary
headed toward the spring of the waters of Nephtoah, came
out at the towns of Mount Ephron and went down toward
Baalah (that is, Kiriath Jearim). 10Then it curved westward
from Baalah to Mount Seir, ran along the northern slope of
Mount Jearim (that is, Kesalon), continued down to Beth
Shemesh and crossed to Timnah. 11It went to the northern
slope of Ekron, turned toward Shikkeron, passed along to
Mount Baalah and reached Jabneel. The boundary ended at
the sea.
12The western boundary is the coastline of the Great Sea.[d]
These are the boundaries around the people of Judah by their
clans.

13In accordance with the LORD's command to him, Joshua gave
to Caleb son of Jephunneh a portion in Judah—Kiriath Arba, that
is, Hebron. (Arba was the forefather of Anak.) 14From Hebron
Caleb drove out the three Anakites—Sheshai, Ahiman and Talmai—descendants of Anak. 15From there he marched against the
people living in Debir (formerly called Kiriath Sepher). 16And
Caleb said, "I will give my daughter Acsah in marriage to the man
who attacks and captures Kiriath Sepher." 17Othniel son of Kenaz,
Caleb's brother, took it; so Caleb gave his daughter Acsah to him
in marriage.
18One day when she came to Othniel, she urged him[e] to ask
her father for a field. When she got off her donkey, Caleb asked
her, "What can I do for you?"

**NIV** [a] 2 That is, the Dead Sea; also in verse 5 [b] 3 Hebrew *Akrabbim*
[c] 4 Hebrew *your* [d] 12 That is, the Mediterranean; also in verse 47
[e] 18 Hebrew and some Septuagint manuscripts; other Septuagint manuscripts (see also note at Judges 1:14) *Othniel, he urged her*

## King James

19Who answered, Give me a blessing; for thou hast given me
a south land; give me also springs of water. And he gave her the
upper springs, and the nether springs.
20This *is* the inheritance of the tribe of the children of Judah
according to their families.
21And the uttermost cities of the tribe of the children of Judah
toward the coast of Edom southward were Kabzeel, and Eder, and
Jagur,
22And Kinah, and Dimonah, and Adadah,
23And Kedesh, and Hazor, and Ithnan,
24Ziph, and Telem, and Bealoth,
25And Hazor, Hadattah, and Kerioth, *and* Hezron, which *is*
Hazor,
26Amam, and Shema, and Moladah,
27And Hazar-gaddah, and Heshmon, and Beth-palet,
28And Hazar-shual, and Beer-sheba, and Bizjothjah,
29Baalah, and Iim, and Azem,
30And Eltolad, and Chesil, and Hormah,
31And Ziklag, and Madmannah, and Sansannah,
32And Lebaoth, and Shilhim, and Ain, and Rimmon: all the
cities *are* twenty and nine, with their villages:
33 *And* in the valley, Eshtaol, and Zoreah, and Ashnah,
34And Zanoah, and En-gannim, Tappuah, and Enam,
35Jarmuth, and Adullam, Socoh, and Azekah,
36And Sharaim, and Adithaim, and Gederah, and Gederothaim; fourteen cities with their villages:
37Zenan, and Hadashah, and Migdal-gad,
38And Dilean, and Mizpeh, and Joktheel,
39Lachish, and Bozkath, and Eglon,
40And Cabbon, and Lahmam, and Kithlish,
41And Gederoth, Beth-dagon, and Naamah, and Makkedah;
sixteen cities with their villages:
42Libnah, and Ether, and Ashan,
43And Jiphtah, and Ashnah, and Nezib,
44And Keilah, and Achzib, and Mareshah; nine cities with their
villages:
45Ekron, with her towns and her villages:
46From Ekron even unto the sea, all that *lay* near Ashdod, with
their villages:
47Ashdod with her towns and her villages, Gaza with her towns
and her villages, unto the river of Egypt, and the great sea, and
the border *thereof*:
48¶ And in the mountains, Shamir, and Jattir, and Socoh,
49And Dannah, and Kirjath-sannah, which *is* Debir,
50And Anab, and Eshtemoh, and Anim,
51And Goshen, and Holon, and Giloh; eleven cities with their
villages:
52Arab, and Dumah, and Eshean,
53And Janum, and Beth-tappuah, and Aphekah,
54And Humtah, and Kirjath-arba, which *is* Hebron, and Zior;
nine cities with their villages:
55Maon, Carmel, and Ziph, and Juttah,
56And Jezreel, and Jokdeam, and Zanoah,
57Cain, Gibeah, and Timnah; ten cities with their villages:
58Halhul, Beth-zur, and Gedor,
59And Maarath, and Beth-anoth, and Eltekon; six cities with
their villages:
60Kirjath-baal, which *is* Kirjath-jearim, and Rabbah; two cities
with their villages:
61In the wilderness, Beth-arabah, Middin, and Secacah,
62And Nibshan, and the city of Salt, and En-gedi; six cities with
their villages.
63¶ As for the Jebusites the inhabitants of Jerusalem, the children of Judah could not drive them out: but the Jebusites dwell
with the children of Judah at Jerusalem unto this day.

## Amplified

19Achsah answered, Give me a present; since you have set me
in the [dry] Negeb, give me also springs of water. And he gave her
the [sloping field with] upper and lower springs.
20This is the inheritance of the tribe of Judahites according to
their families.
21The cities of the tribe of Judah in the extreme south, toward
the boundary of Edom, were Kabzeel, Eder, Jagur,
22Kinah, Dimonah, Adadah,
23Kedesh, Hazor, Ithnan,
24Ziph, Telem, Bealoth,
25Hazor-hadattah, Kerioth-hezron (Hazor),
26Amam, Shema, Moladah,
27Hazar-gaddah, Heshmon, Beth-pelet,
28Hazar-shual, Beer-sheba, Biziothiah,
29Baalah, Iim, Ezem,
30Eltolad, Chesil, Hormah,
31Ziklag, Madmannah, Sansannah,
32Lebaoth, Shilhim, Ain, and Rimmon. All the cities were
twenty-nine [later thirty-six], with their villages.
33In the lowland, Eshtaol, Zorah, Ashnah,
34Zanoah, Engannim, Tappuah, Enam,
35Jarmuth, Adullam, Soco, Azekah,
36Shaaraim, Adithaim, and Gederah and Gederothaim, fourteen cities with their villages.
37Zenan, Hadashah, Migdalgad,
38Dilean, Mizpah, Joktheel,
39Lachish, Bozkath, Eglon,
40Cabbon, Lahmam, Chitlish,
41Gederoth, Beth-dagon, Naamah, and Makkedah; sixteen cities with their villages.
42Libnah, Ether, Ashan,
43Iphtah, Ashnah, Nezib,
44Keilah, Achzib, and Mareshah; nine cities with their villages.
45Ekron, with its towns and villages.
46From Ekron to the sea, all that lay beside Ashdod, with their
villages.
47Ashdod with its towns and its villages, Gaza with its towns
and its villages, to the brook of Egypt, and the great [Mediter-
ranean] Sea with its coastline.
48In the hill country, Shamir, Jattir, Soco,
49Dannah, Kiriath-sannah (that is, Debir),
50Anab, Eshtemoh, Anim,
51Goshen, Holon, and Giloh; eleven cities with their villages.
52Arab, Dumah, Eshan,
53Janim, Beth-tappuah, Aphekah,
54Humtah, Kiriath-arba (that is, Hebron), and Zior; nine cities
with their villages.
55Maon, Carmel, Ziph, Juttah,
56Jezreel, Jokdeam, Zanoah,
57Kain, Gibeah, and Timnah; ten cities with their villages.
58Halhul, Bethzur, Gedor,
59Maarath, Bethanoth, and Eltekon; six cities with their villages.
60Kiriath-baal (that is, Kiriath-jearim), and Rabbah; two cities
with their villages.
61In the wilderness, Beth-arabah, Middin, Secacah,
62Nibshan, the City of Salt, and Engedi; six cities with their
villages.
63But the Jebusites, the inhabitants of Jerusalem, the people of
Judah could not drive out; so the Jebusites dwell with the people
of Judah at Jerusalem to this day.

## New American Standard

19Then she said, "Give me a blessing; since you have given me
the land of the Negev, give me also springs of water." So he gave
her the upper springs and the lower springs.
20¶ This is the inheritance of the tribe of the sons of Judah
according to their families.
21¶ Now the cities at the extremity of the tribe of the sons of
Judah toward the border of Edom in the south were Kabzeel and
Eder and Jagur,
22and Kinah and Dimonah and Adadah,
23and Kedesh and Hazor and Ithnan,
24Ziph and Telem and Bealoth,
25and Hazor-hadattah and Kerioth-hezron (that is, Hazor),
26Amam and Shema and Moladah,
27and Hazar-gaddah and Heshmon and Beth-pelet,
28and Hazar-shual and Beersheba and Biziothiah,
29Baalah and Iim and Ezem,
30and Eltolad and Chesil and Hormah,
31and Ziklag and Madmannah and Sansannah,
32and Lebaoth and Shilhim and Ain and Rimmon; in all,
twenty-nine cities with their villages.
33¶ In the lowland: Eshtaol and Zorah and Ashnah,
34and Zanoah and En-gannim, Tappuah and Enam,
35Jarmuth and Adullam, Socoh and Azekah,
36and Shaaraim and Adithaim and Gederah and Gederothaim;
fourteen cities with their villages.
37¶ Zenan and Hadashah and Migdal-gad,
38and Dilean and Mizpeh and Joktheel,
39Lachish and Bozkath and Eglon,
40and Cabbon and Lahmas and Chitlish,
41and Gederoth, Beth-dagon and Naamah and Makkedah; sixteen cities with their villages.
42¶ Libnah and Ether and Ashan,
43and Iphtah and Ashnah and Nezib,
44and Keilah and Achzib and Mareshah; nine cities with their
villages.
45¶ Ekron, with its towns and its villages;
46from Ekron even to the sea, all that were by the side of
Ashdod, with their villages.
47¶ Ashdod, its towns and its villages; Gaza, its towns and its
villages; as far as the brook of Egypt and the Great Sea, even *its*
coastline.
48¶ And in the hill country: Shamir and Jattir and Socoh,
49and Dannah and Kiriath-sannah (that is, Debir),
50and Anab and Eshtemoh and Anim,
51and Goshen and Holon and Giloh; eleven cities with their
villages.
52¶ Arab and Dumah and Eshan,
53and Janum and Beth-tappuah and Aphekah,
54and Humtah and Kiriath-arba (that is, Hebron), and Zior; nine
cities with their villages.
55¶ Maon, Carmel and Ziph and Juttah,
56and Jezreel and Jokdeam and Zanoah,
57Kain, Gibeah and Timnah; ten cities with their villages.
58¶ Halhul, Beth-zur and Gedor,
59and Maarath and Beth-anoth and Eltekon; six cities with their
villages.
60¶ Kiriath-baal (that is, Kiriath-jearim), and Rabbah; two cities
with their villages.
61¶ In the wilderness: Beth-arabah, Middin and Secacah,
62and Nibshan and the City of Salt and Engedi; six cities with
their villages.
63¶ Now as for the Jebusites, the inhabitants of Jerusalem, the
sons of Judah could not drive them out; so the Jebusites live with
the sons of Judah at Jerusalem until this day.

## New International

19She replied, "Do me a special favor. Since you have given me
land in the Negev, give me also springs of water." So Caleb gave
her the upper and lower springs.

20This is the inheritance of the tribe of Judah, clan by clan:
21The southernmost towns of the tribe of Judah in the Negev
toward the boundary of Edom were:
Kabzeel, Eder, Jagur, 22Kinah, Dimonah, Adadah, 23Ke-
desh, Hazor, Ithnan, 24Ziph, Telem, Bealoth, 25Hazor Hadattah, Kerioth Hezron (that is, Hazor), 26Amam, Shema, Moladah, 27Hazar Gaddah, Heshmon, Beth Pelet, 28Hazar Shual,
Beersheba, Biziothiah, 29Baalah, Iim, Ezem, 30Eltolad, Kesil,
Hormah, 31Ziklag, Madmannah, Sansannah, 32Lebaoth, Shilhim, Ain and Rimmon—a total of twenty-nine towns and
their villages.

33In the western foothills:
Eshtaol, Zorah, Ashnah, 34Zanoah, En Gannim, Tappuah,
Enam, 35Jarmuth, Adullam, Socoh, Azekah, 36Shaaraim, Adithaim and Gederah (or Gederothaim)[a] —fourteen towns and
their villages.
37Zenan, Hadashah, Migdal Gad, 38Dilean, Mizpah, Joktheel, 39Lachish, Bozkath, Eglon, 40Cabbon, Lahmas, Kitlish,
41Gederoth, Beth Dagon, Naamah and Makkedah—sixteen
towns and their villages.
42Libnah, Ether, Ashan, 43Iphtah, Ashnah, Nezib, 44Kei-
lah, Aczib and Mareshah—nine towns and their villages.
45Ekron, with its surrounding settlements and villages;
46west of Ekron, all that were in the vicinity of Ashdod, together with their villages; 47Ashdod, its surrounding settlements and villages; and Gaza, its settlements and villages, as
far as the Wadi of Egypt and the coastline of the Great Sea.

48In the hill country:
Shamir, Jattir, Socoh, 49Dannah, Kiriath Sannah (that is,
Debir), 50Anab, Eshtemoh, Anim, 51Goshen, Holon and
Giloh—eleven towns and their villages.
52Arab, Dumah, Eshan, 53Janim, Beth Tappuah, Aphekah,
54Humtah, Kiriath Arba (that is, Hebron) and Zior—nine
towns and their villages.
55Maon, Carmel, Ziph, Juttah, 56Jezreel, Jokdeam, Zanoah, 57Kain, Gibeah and Timnah—ten towns and their villages.
58Halhul, Beth Zur, Gedor, 59Maarath, Beth Anoth and
Eltekon—six towns and their villages.
60Kiriath Baal (that is, Kiriath Jearim) and Rabbah—two
towns and their villages.

61In the desert:
Beth Arabah, Middin, Secacah, 62Nibshan, the City of Salt
and En Gedi—six towns and their villages.
63Judah could not dislodge the Jebusites, who were living in
Jerusalem; to this day the Jebusites live there with the people of
Judah.

NIV [a] 36 Or *Gederah and Gederothaim*

## King James

**16** AND THE lot of the children of Joseph fell from Jordan by
Jericho, unto the water of Jericho on the east, to the wilderness that goeth up from Jericho throughout mount Beth-el,
2And goeth out from Beth-el to Luz, and passeth along unto the
borders of Archi to Ataroth,
3And goeth down westward to the coast of Japhleti, unto the
coast of Beth-horon the nether, and to Gezer: and the goings out
thereof are at the sea.
4So the children of Joseph, Manasseh and Ephraim, took their
inheritance.
5¶ And the border of the children of Ephraim according to their
families was *thus:* even the border of their inheritance on the east
side was Ataroth-addar, unto Beth-horon the upper;
6And the border went out toward the sea to Michmethah on the
north side; and the border went about eastward unto Taanath-
shiloh, and passed by it on the east to Janohah;
7And it went down from Janohah to Ataroth, and to Naarath,
and came to Jericho, and went out at Jordan.
8The border went out from Tappuah westward unto the river
Kanah; and the goings out thereof were at the sea. This *is* the
inheritance of the tribe of the children of Ephraim by their families.
9And the separate cities for the children of Ephraim *were* among
the inheritance of the children of Manasseh, all the cities with their
villages.
10And they drave not out the Canaanites that dwelt in Gezer:
but the Canaanites dwell among the Ephraimites unto this day,
and serve under tribute.

**17** THERE WAS also a lot for the tribe of Manasseh; for he
*was* the firstborn of Joseph; *to wit,* for Machir the firstborn
of Manasseh, the father of Gilead: because he was a man of war,
therefore he had Gilead and Bashan.
2There was also *a lot* for the rest of the children of Manasseh by
their families; for the children of Abiezer, and for the children of
Helek, and for the children of Asriel, and for the children of
Shechem, and for the children of Hepher, and for the children of
Shemida: these *were* the male children of Manasseh the son of
Joseph by their families.
3¶ But Zelophehad, the son of Hepher, the son of Gilead, the
son of Machir, the son of Manasseh, had no sons, but daughters:
and these *are* the names of his daughters, Mahlah, and Noah,
Hoglah, Milcah, and Tirzah.
4And they came near before Eleazar the priest, and before
Joshua the son of Nun, and before the princes, saying, The LORD
commanded Moses to give us an inheritance among our brethren.
Therefore according to the commandment of the LORD he gave
them an inheritance among the brethren of their father.
5And there fell ten portions to Manasseh, beside the land of
Gilead and Bashan, which *were* on the other side Jordan;
6Because the daughters of Manasseh had an inheritance among
his sons: and the rest of Manasseh's sons had the land of Gilead.
7¶ And the coast of Manasseh was from Asher to Michmethah,
that *lieth* before Shechem; and the border went along on the right
hand unto the inhabitants of En-tappuah.
8 *Now* Manasseh had the land of Tappuah: but Tappuah on the
border of Manasseh *belonged* to the children of Ephraim;
9And the coast descended unto the river Kanah, southward of
the river: these cities of Ephraim *are* among the cities of Manasseh:
the coast of Manasseh also *was* on the north side of the river, and
the outgoings of it were at the sea:
10Southward *it was* Ephraim's, and northward *it was* Manasseh's, and the sea is his border; and they met together in Asher
on the north, and in Issachar on the east.

## Amplified

**16** THE ALLOTMENT of the people of Joseph went from the
Jordan by Jericho, east of the waters of Jericho, into the
wilderness, going up from Jericho into the hill country to Bethel;
2Then went from Bethel to Luz, and passed on to Ataroth, the
border of the Archites,
3And it went down westward to the territory of the Japhletites,
to the outskirts of Lower Beth-horon, then to Gezer, and ended at
the sea.
4The descendants of Joseph, Manasseh and Ephraim, received
their inheritance.
5The boundary of the Ephraimites according to their families
was thus: on the east side their border was Ataroth-adder as far
as Upper Beth-horon.
6Then the boundary went from there to the sea; on the north
was Michmethath; then on the east the boundary went out to
Taanath-shiloh, and eastward to Janoah,
7Then it went down from Janoah to Ataroth, and to Naarah,
touched Jericho, and ended at the Jordan [River].
8The border went out from Tappuah westward to the brook
Kanah, and ended at the [Mediterranean] Sea. This is the inheritance of the Ephraimites by their families,
9With the towns set apart for the Ephraimites within the inheritance of the Manassites, all those towns with their villages.
10But they did not drive out the Canaanites who dwelt in Gezer;
but the Canaanites dwell among the Ephraimites to this day, and
they became slaves to do forced labor.

**17** ALLOTMENT WAS made to the tribe of Manasseh, for he
was the first-born of Joseph. To Machir the first-born of
Manasseh, the father of Gilead, were allotted Gilead and Bashan,
because he was a man of war.
2Allotment was also made to the other Manassites by their
families, for the sons of Abiezer, of Helek, Asriel, Shechem, Hepher, and Shemida, the male offspring of Manasseh son of Joseph
by their families.
3But Zelophehad son of Hepher, son of Gilead, son of Machir,
son of Manasseh, had no sons, but daughters; their names were
Mahlah, Noah, Hoglah, Milcah, and Tirzah.
4They came before Eleazar the priest and Joshua son of Nun and
the leaders, and said, The Lord commanded Moses to give us an
inheritance with our brethren. So according to the Lord's command Joshua gave them an inheritance among their father's brethren.
5So there fell ten portions to Manasseh, besides the land of
Gilead and Bashan, which is on the other side of the Jordan;
6Because the [five] daughters of Manasseh received an inheritance among his [five] sons. The land of Gilead belonged to the
other [half] of the Manassites.
7The territory of Manasseh reached from Asher to Michmethah,
east of Shechem; and the border went along southward to the
inhabitants of En-tappuah.
8The land of Tappuah belonged to Manasseh, but the town of
Tappuah on the border of Manasseh belonged to the Ephraimites.
9Then the boundary went down to the brook Kanah. The cities
south of the brook, among the cities of Manasseh, belonged to
Ephraim. Then Manasseh's boundary went on north of the brook
and ended at the sea;
10The land to the south was Ephraim's, and that to the north
was Manasseh's, and the sea was the boundary; on the north
Asher was reached, and on the east Issachar.

## New American Standard

*Territory of Ephraim*

**16** THEN THE lot for the sons of Joseph went from the Jordan
at Jericho to the waters of Jericho on the east into the
wilderness, going up from Jericho through the hill country to
Bethel.
2And it went from Bethel to Luz, and continued to the border
of the Archites at Ataroth.
3And it went down westward to the territory of the Japhletites,
as far as the territory of lower Beth-horon even to Gezer, and it
ended at the sea.
4¶ And the sons of Joseph, Manasseh and Ephraim, received
their inheritance.
5Now *this* was the territory of the sons of Ephraim according
to their families: the border of their inheritance eastward was
Ataroth-addar, as far as upper Beth-horon.
6Then the border went westward at Michmethath on the
north, and the border turned about eastward to Taanath-shiloh,
and continued *beyond* it to the east of Janoah.
7And it went down from Janoah to Ataroth and to Naarah,
then reached Jericho and came out at the Jordan.
8From Tappuah the border continued westward to the brook
of Kanah, and it ended at the sea. This is the inheritance of the tribe
of the sons of Ephraim according to their families,
9 *together* with the cities which were set apart for the sons of
Ephraim in the midst of the inheritance of the sons of Manasseh,
all the cities with their villages.
10But they did not drive out the Canaanites who lived in Gezer,
so the Canaanites live in the midst of Ephraim to this day, and they
became forced laborers.

*Territory of Manasseh*

**17** NOW *THIS* was the lot for the tribe of Manasseh, for he
was the first-born of Joseph. To Machir the first-born of
Manasseh, the father of Gilead, was allotted Gilead and Bashan,
because he was a man of war.
2So *the lot* was *made* for the rest of the sons of Manasseh
according to their families: for the sons of Abiezer and for the sons
of Helek and for the sons of Asriel and for the sons of Shechem
and for the sons of Hepher and for the sons of Shemida; these *were*
the male *descendants* of Manasseh the son of Joseph according to
their families.
3However, Zelophehad, the son of Hepher, the son of Gilead,
the son of Machir, the son of Manasseh, had no sons, only daughters; and these are the names of his daughters: Mahlah and Noah,
Hoglah, Milcah and Tirzah.
4And they came near before Eleazar the priest and before
Joshua the son of Nun and before the leaders, saying, "The LORD
commanded Moses to give us an inheritance among our brothers."
So according to the command of the LORD he gave them an inheritance among their father's brothers.
5Thus there fell ten portions to Manasseh, besides the land of
Gilead and Bashan, which is beyond the Jordan,
6because the daughters of Manasseh received an inheritance
among his sons. And the land of Gilead belonged to the rest of the
sons of Manasseh.
7¶ And the border of Manasseh ran from Asher to Michmethath which was east of Shechem; then the border went southward
to the inhabitants of En-tappuah.
8The land of Tappuah belonged to Manasseh, but Tappuah on
the border of Manasseh *belonged* to the sons of Ephraim.
9And the border went down to the brook of Kanah, southward
of the brook (these cities *belonged* to Ephraim among the cities of
Manasseh), and the border of Manasseh *was* on the north side of
the brook, and it ended at the sea.
10The south side *belonged* to Ephraim and the north side to
Manasseh, and the sea was their border; and they reached to Asher
on the north and to Issachar on the east.

## New International

*Allotment for Ephraim and Manasseh*

**16** THE ALLOTMENT for Joseph began at the Jordan of
Jericho,[a] east of the waters of Jericho, and went up
from there through the desert into the hill country of Bethel.
2It went on from Bethel (that is, Luz),[b] crossed over to the
territory of the Arkites in Ataroth, 3descended westward to
the territory of the Japhletites as far as the region of Lower
Beth Horon and on to Gezer, ending at the sea.
4So Manasseh and Ephraim, the descendants of Joseph, received
their inheritance.
5This was the territory of Ephraim, clan by clan:
The boundary of their inheritance went from Ataroth Addar in the east to Upper Beth Horon 6and continued to the sea.
From Micmethath on the north it curved eastward to Taanath
Shiloh, passing by it to Janoah on the east. 7Then it went
down from Janoah to Ataroth and Naarah, touched Jericho
and came out at the Jordan. 8From Tappuah the border went
west to the Kanah Ravine and ended at the sea. This was the
inheritance of the tribe of the Ephraimites, clan by clan. 9It
also included all the towns and their villages that were set
aside for the Ephraimites within the inheritance of the Manassites.
10They did not dislodge the Canaanites living in Gezer; to this day
the Canaanites live among the people of Ephraim but are required
to do forced labor.

**17** THIS WAS the allotment for the tribe of Manasseh as
Joseph's firstborn, that is, for Makir, Manasseh's first-
born. Makir was the ancestor of the Gileadites, who had received
Gilead and Bashan because the Makirites were great soldiers. 2So
this allotment was for the rest of the people of Manasseh—the
clans of Abiezer, Helek, Asriel, Shechem, Hepher and Shemida.
These are the other male descendants of Manasseh son of Joseph
by their clans.
3Now Zelophehad son of Hepher, the son of Gilead, the son of
Makir, the son of Manasseh, had no sons but only daughters,
whose names were Mahlah, Noah, Hoglah, Milcah and Tirzah.
4They went to Eleazar the priest, Joshua son of Nun, and the
leaders and said, "The LORD commanded Moses to give us an
inheritance among our brothers." So Joshua gave them an inheritance along with the brothers of their father, according to the
LORD's command. 5Manasseh's share consisted of ten tracts of
land besides Gilead and Bashan east of the Jordan, 6because the
daughters of the tribe of Manasseh received an inheritance among
the sons. The land of Gilead belonged to the rest of the descendants of Manasseh.
7The territory of Manasseh extended from Asher to Micmethath east of Shechem. The boundary ran southward from
there to include the people living at En Tappuah. 8(Manasseh
had the land of Tappuah, but Tappuah itself, on the boundary
of Manasseh, belonged to the Ephraimites.) 9Then the boundary continued south to the Kanah Ravine. There were towns
belonging to Ephraim lying among the towns of Manasseh,
but the boundary of Manasseh was the northern side of the
ravine and ended at the sea. 10On the south the land belonged
to Ephraim, on the north to Manasseh. The territory of Manasseh reached the sea and bordered Asher on the north and
Issachar on the east.

**NIV** [a] 1 *Jordan of Jericho* was possibly an ancient name for the Jordan River.
[b] 2 Septuagint; Hebrew *Bethel to Luz*

# King James

11And Manasseh had in Issachar and in Asher Beth-shean and her towns, and Ibleam and her towns, and the inhabitants of Dor and her towns, and the inhabitants of En-dor and her towns, and the inhabitants of Taanach and her towns, and the inhabitants of Megiddo and her towns, *even* three countries.

12Yet the children of Manasseh could not drive out *the inhabitants of* those cities; but the Canaanites would dwell in that land.

13Yet it came to pass, when the children of Israel were waxen strong, that they put the Canaanites to tribute; but did not utterly drive them out.

14And the children of Joseph spake unto Joshua, saying, Why hast thou given me *but* one lot and one portion to inherit, seeing I *am* a great people, forasmuch as the LORD hath blessed me hitherto?

15And Joshua answered them, If thou *be* a great people, *then* get thee up to the wood *country*, and cut down for thyself there in the land of the Perizzites, and of the giants, if mount Ephraim be too narrow for thee.

16And the children of Joseph said, The hill is not enough for us: and all the Canaanites that dwell in the land of the valley have chariots of iron, *both they* who *are* of Beth-shean and her towns, and *they* who *are* of the valley of Jezreel.

17And Joshua spake unto the house of Joseph, *even* to Ephraim and to Manasseh, saying, Thou *art* a great people, and hast great power: thou shalt not have one lot *only:*

18But the mountain shall be thine; for it *is* a wood, and thou shalt cut it down: and the outgoings of it shall be thine: for thou shalt drive out the Canaanites, though they have iron chariots, *and* though they *be* strong.

**18** AND THE whole congregation of the children of Israel assembled together at Shiloh, and set up the tabernacle of the congregation there. And the land was subdued before them.

2And there remained among the children of Israel seven tribes, which had not yet received their inheritance.

3And Joshua said unto the children of Israel, How long *are* ye slack to go to possess the land, which the LORD God of your fathers hath given you?

4Give out from among you three men for *each* tribe: and I will send them, and they shall rise, and go through the land, and describe it according to the inheritance of them; and they shall come *again* to me.

5And they shall divide it into seven parts: Judah shall abide in their coast on the south, and the house of Joseph shall abide in their coasts on the north.

6Ye shall therefore describe the land *into* seven parts, and bring *the description* hither to me, that I may cast lots for you here before the LORD our God.

7But the Levites have no part among you; for the priesthood of the LORD *is* their inheritance: and Gad, and Reuben, and half the tribe of Manasseh, have received their inheritance beyond Jordan on the east, which Moses the servant of the LORD gave them.

8¶ And the men arose, and went away: and Joshua charged them that went to describe the land, saying, Go and walk through the land, and describe it, and come again to me, that I may here cast lots for you before the LORD in Shiloh.

9And the men went and passed through the land, and described it by cities into seven parts in a book, and came *again* to Joshua to the host at Shiloh.

10¶ And Joshua cast lots for them in Shiloh before the LORD: and there Joshua divided the land unto the children of Israel according to their divisions.

# Amplified

11Also Manasseh had in Issachar and in Asher [these six towns], their inhabitants and their villages, Beth-shean, Ibleam, Dor, En-dor, Taanach, and Megiddo.

12Yet the sons of Manasseh could not drive out the inhabitants of those cities; but the Canaanites persisted in dwelling in that land.

13When the Israelites became strong they put the Canaanites to forced labor, but did not utterly drive them out.

14The tribe of Joseph spoke to Joshua, saying, Why have you given [us] but one lot and one portion as an inheritance, when [we] are a great [abundant] people, for until now the Lord has blessed [us]?

15Joshua replied, If you are a great people, get up to the forest, and clear ground for yourselves in the land of the Perizzites and the Rephaim, since the Ephraim hill country is too narrow for you.

16The Josephites said, The hill country is not enough for us: and all the Canaanites who dwell in the valley have iron chariots, both those in Beth-shean and its villages, and in the Valley of Jezreel.

17And Joshua said to the house of Joseph, to Ephraim and to Manasseh, You are a great *and* numerous people, and have great power; you shall not have only one lot,

18But the hill country shall be yours; though it is a forest, you shall clear and possess it to its farthest borders; for you shall drive out the Canaanites, though they have iron chariots and are strong.

**18** AND THE whole congregation of the Israelites assembled at Shiloh, and set up the tent of meeting there; and the land was subdued before them.

2And there remained among the Israelites seven tribes, to whom their inheritance had not yet been divided.

3Joshua asked the Israelites, How long will you be slack to go in and possess the land, which the Lord God of your fathers has given you?

4Provide three men from each tribe, and I will send them to go through the land, and write a description of it according to their [tribal] inheritances, then return to me.

5And they shall divide it into seven parts: Judah shall remain in his territory on the south, and the house of Joseph shall remain in their territory on the north.

6You shall describe the land in seven divisions, and bring the description here to me, that I may cast lots for you here before the Lord our God.

7But the Levites have no portion among you; for the priesthood of the Lord is their inheritance. Gad and Reuben and half the tribe of Manasseh have received their inheritance east of the Jordan, which Moses the servant of the Lord gave them.

8So the men arose and went; and Joshua charged them saying, Go and walk through the land, and describe it, and come again to me, and I will cast lots for you here before the Lord in Shiloh.

9And the men went and passed through the land, and described it by cities in seven portions in a book; and they came again to Joshua to the camp at Shiloh.

10Joshua cast lots for them in Shiloh before the Lord; and there [he] divided the land to the Israelites, to each [tribe] his portion.

## New American Standard

11And in Issachar and in Asher, Manasseh had Beth-shean and
its towns and Ibleam and its towns, and the inhabitants of Dor and
its towns, and the inhabitants of En-dor and its towns, and the
inhabitants of Taanach and its towns, and the inhabitants of
Megiddo and its towns, the third is Napheth.
12But the sons of Manasseh could not take possession of these
cities, because the Canaanites persisted in living in that land.
13And it came about when the sons of Israel became strong,
they put the Canaanites to forced labor, but they did not drive
them out completely.
14¶ Then the sons of Joseph spoke to Joshua, saying, "Why have
you given me only one lot and one portion for an inheritance, since
I am a numerous people whom the LORD has thus far blessed?"
15And Joshua said to them, "If you are a numerous people, go
up to the forest and clear a place for yourself there in the land of
the Perizzites and of the Rephaim, since the hill country of
Ephraim is too narrow for you."
16And the sons of Joseph said, "The hill country is not enough
for us, and all the Canaanites who live in the valley land have
chariots of iron, both those who are in Beth-shean and its towns,
and those who are in the valley of Jezreel."
17And Joshua spoke to the house of Joseph, to Ephraim and
Manasseh, saying, "You are a numerous people and have great
power; you shall not have one lot *only*,
18but the hill country shall be yours. For though it is a forest,
you shall clear it, and to its farthest borders it shall be yours; for
you shall drive out the Canaanites, even though they have chariots
of iron *and* though they are strong."

*Rest of the Land Divided*

18 THEN THE whole congregation of the sons of Israel assembled themselves at Shiloh, and set up the tent of meeting there; and the land was subdued before them.
2And there remained among the sons of Israel seven tribes
who had not divided their inheritance.
3So Joshua said to the sons of Israel, "How long will you put
off entering to take possession of the land which the LORD, the God
of your fathers, has given you?
4"Provide for yourselves three men from each tribe that I may
send them, and that they may arise and walk through the land and
write a description of it according to their inheritance; then they
shall return to me.
5"And they shall divide it into seven portions; Judah shall stay
in its territory on the south, and the house of Joseph shall stay in
their territory on the north.
6"And you shall describe the land in seven divisions, and bring
*the description* here to me. And I will cast lots for you here before
the LORD our God.
7"For the Levites have no portion among you, because the
priesthood of the LORD is their inheritance. Gad and Reuben and
the half-tribe of Manasseh also have received their inheritance
eastward beyond the Jordan, which Moses the servant of the LORD
gave them."
8¶ Then the men arose and went, and Joshua commanded
those who went to describe the land, saying, "Go and walk
through the land and describe it, and return to me; then I will cast
lots for you here before the LORD in Shiloh."
9So the men went and passed through the land, and described
it by cities in seven divisions in a book; and they came to Joshua
to the camp at Shiloh.
10And Joshua cast lots for them in Shiloh before the LORD, and
there Joshua divided the land to the sons of Israel according to
their divisions.

## New International

11Within Issachar and Asher, Manasseh also had Beth
Shan, Ibleam and the people of Dor, Endor, Taanach and
Megiddo, together with their surrounding settlements (the
third in the list is Naphoth[a]).
12Yet the Manassites were not able to occupy these towns, for the
Canaanites were determined to live in that region. 13However,
when the Israelites grew stronger, they subjected the Canaanites
to forced labor but did not drive them out completely.
14The people of Joseph said to Joshua, "Why have you given us
only one allotment and one portion for an inheritance? We are a
numerous people and the LORD has blessed us abundantly."
15"If you are so numerous," Joshua answered, "and if the hill
country of Ephraim is too small for you, go up into the forest and
clear land for yourselves there in the land of the Perizzites and
Rephaites."
16The people of Joseph replied, "The hill country is not enough
for us, and all the Canaanites who live in the plain have iron
chariots, both those in Beth Shan and its settlements and those in
the Valley of Jezreel."
17But Joshua said to the house of Joseph—to Ephraim and
Manasseh—"You are numerous and very powerful. You will have
not only one allotment 18but the forested hill country as well. Clear
it, and its farthest limits will be yours; though the Canaanites have
iron chariots and though they are strong, you can drive them out."

*Division of the Rest of the Land*

18 THE WHOLE assembly of the Israelites gathered at Shiloh
and set up the Tent of Meeting there. The country was
brought under their control, 2but there were still seven Israelite
tribes who had not yet received their inheritance.
3So Joshua said to the Israelites: "How long will you wait before
you begin to take possession of the land that the LORD, the God
of your fathers, has given you? 4Appoint three men from each
tribe. I will send them out to make a survey of the land and to write
a description of it, according to the inheritance of each. Then they
will return to me. 5You are to divide the land into seven parts.
Judah is to remain in its territory on the south and the house of
Joseph in its territory on the north. 6After you have written descriptions of the seven parts of the land, bring them here to me and
I will cast lots for you in the presence of the LORD our God. 7The
Levites, however, do not get a portion among you, because the
priestly service of the LORD is their inheritance. And Gad, Reuben
and the half-tribe of Manasseh have already received their inheritance on the east side of the Jordan. Moses the servant of the LORD
gave it to them."
8As the men started on their way to map out the land, Joshua
instructed them, "Go and make a survey of the land and write a
description of it. Then return to me, and I will cast lots for you here
at Shiloh in the presence of the LORD." 9So the men left and went
through the land. They wrote its description on a scroll, town by
town, in seven parts, and returned to Joshua in the camp at Shiloh.
10Joshua then cast lots for them in Shiloh in the presence of the
LORD, and there he distributed the land to the Israelites according
to their tribal divisions.

NIV [a] *11* That is, Naphoth Dor

## King James

11¶ And the lot of the tribe of the children of Benjamin came up
according to their families: and the coast of their lot came forth
between the children of Judah and the children of Joseph.
12And their border on the north side was from Jordan; and the
border went up to the side of Jericho on the north side, and went
up through the mountains westward; and the goings out thereof
were at the wilderness of Beth-aven.
13And the border went over from thence toward Luz, to the side
of Luz, which *is* Beth-el, southward; and the border descended to
Ataroth-adar, near the hill that *lieth* on the south side of the nether
Beth-horon.
14And the border was drawn *thence*, and compassed the corner
of the sea southward, from the hill that *lieth* before Beth-horon
southward; and the goings out thereof were at Kirjath-baal, which
*is* Kirjath-jearim, a city of the children of Judah: this *was* the west
quarter.
15And the south quarter *was* from the end of Kirjath-jearim, and
the border went out on the west, and went out to the well of waters
of Nephtoah:
16And the border came down to the end of the mountain that
*lieth* before the valley of the son of Hinnom, *and* which *is* in the
valley of the giants on the north, and descended to the valley of
Hinnom, to the side of Jebusi on the south, and descended to
En-rogel,
17And was drawn from the north, and went forth to En-
shemesh, and went forth toward Geliloth, which *is* over against
the going up of Adummim, and descended to the stone of Bohan
the son of Reuben,
18And passed along toward the side over against Arabah northward, and went down unto Arabah:
19And the border passed along to the side of Beth-hoglah northward: and the outgoings of the border were at the north bay of the
salt sea at the south end of Jordan: this *was* the south coast.
20And Jordan was the border of it on the east side. This *was* the
inheritance of the children of Benjamin, by the coasts thereof
round about, according to their families.
21Now the cities of the tribe of the children of Benjamin according to their families were Jericho, and Beth-hoglah, and the valley
of Keziz,
22And Beth-arabah, and Zemaraim, and Beth-el,
23And Avim, and Parah, and Ophrah,
24And Chephar-haammonai, and Ophni, and Gaba; twelve cities with their villages:
25Gibeon, and Ramah, and Beeroth,
26And Mizpeh, and Chephirah, and Mozah,
27And Rekem, and Irpeel, and Taralah,
28And Zelah, Eleph, and Jebusi, which *is* Jerusalem, Gibeath,
*and* Kirjath; fourteen cities with their villages. This *is* the inheritance of the children of Benjamin according to their families.

**19** AND THE second lot came forth to Simeon, *even* for the
tribe of the children of Simeon according to their families:
and their inheritance was within the inheritance of the children of
Judah.
2And they had in their inheritance Beer-sheba, or Sheba, and
Moladah,
3And Hazar-shual, and Balah, and Azem,
4And Eltolad, and Bethul, and Hormah,
5And Ziklag, and Beth-marcaboth, and Hazar-susah,
6And Beth-lebaoth, and Sharuhen; thirteen cities and their villages:
7Ain, Remmon, and Ether, and Ashan; four cities and their
villages:

## Amplified

11And the lot of the Benjamites came up according to their
families; and the territory of their lot fell between the tribes of
Judah and Joseph.
12On the north side their boundary began at the Jordan; then
it went up to the shoulder of Jericho on the north, and up through
the hill country westward, and ended at the Beth-aven wilderness.
13Then the boundary passed over southward toward Luz, to the
shoulder of Luz (that is, Bethel); then it went down to Ataroth-
addar, by the mountain that lies south of Lower Beth-horon.
14The boundary extended from there, and turning about on the
western side southward from the mountain that lies to the south,
opposite Beth-horon, it ended at Kiriath-baal (that is, Kiriath-
jearim), a city of the tribe of Judah. This formed the western side
[of Benjamin's territory].
15The southern side began at the edge of Kiriath-jearim, and the
boundary went on westward to the spring of the Waters of Nephtoah;
16Then the boundary went down to the edge of the mountain
overlooking the valley of the son of Hinnom, which is at the north
end of the valley of Rephaim; and descended to the valley of
Hinnom, south of the shoulder of the Jebusites, and went on down
to En-rogel;
17Then it bent toward the north and went on to En-shemesh,
and on to Geliloth, which was opposite the ascent of Adummim,
and went down to the stone of Bohan son of Reuben,
18And went on to the north of the shoulder [of Beth] Arabah
and down to the Arabah;
19Then the boundary passed along to the north of the shoulder
of Beth-hoglah, and ended at the northern bay of the Salt [Dead]
Sea, at the south end of the Jordan; this is the southern border.
20And the Jordan was its boundary on the east side. This was
the inheritance of the sons of Benjamin, by its boundaries round
about, according to their families.
21Now the cities of the tribe of Benjamin according to [its]
families were Jericho, Beth-hoglah, Emek-keziz,
22Beth-arabah, Zemaraim, Bethel,
23Avvim, Parah, Ophrah,
24Chephar-ammoni, Ophni, and Geba; twelve cities with their
villages;
25Gibeon, Ramah, Beeroth,
26Mizpah, Chephirah, Mozah,
27Rekem, Irpeel, Taralah,
28Zela, Ha-eleph, *Jebus* (that is, Jerusalem), Gibeath, and
Kiriath-[jearim]; fourteen cities with their villages. This is the inheritance of the tribe of Benjamin according to its families.

**19** THE SECOND lot fell to Simeon, for the tribe of the Simeonites, according to their families; and their inheritance
lay within that of the people of Judah.
2And they had for their inheritance Beer-sheba or Sheba, Moladah,
3Hazarshual, Balah, Ezem,
4Eltolad, Bethul, Hormah,
5Ziklag, Beth-marcaboth, Hazar-susah,
6Beth-lebaoth, and Sharuhen, [making] thirteen cities and their
villages;
7Ain [with] Rimmon, Ether, and Ashan, [making] four cities
and their villages;

## New American Standard

*The Territory of Benjamin*

11¶ Now the lot of the tribe of the sons of Benjamin came up
according to their families, and the territory of their lot lay between
the sons of Judah and the sons of Joseph.
12And their border on the north side was from the Jordan, then
the border went up to the side of Jericho on the north, and went
up through the hill country westward; and [a]it ended at the wilderness of Beth-aven.
13And from there the border continued to Luz, to the side of Luz
(that is, Bethel) southward; and the border went down to Ataroth-
addar, near the hill which *lies* on the south of lower Beth-horon.
14And the border extended *from there,* and turned round on the
west side southward, from the hill which *lies* before Beth-horon
southward; and [b]it ended at Kiriath-baal (that is, Kiriath-jearim),
a city of the sons of Judah. This *was* the west side.
15Then the south side *was* from the edge of Kiriath-jearim, and
the border went westward and went to the fountain of the waters
of Nephtoah.
16And the border went down to the edge of the hill which is in
the valley of Ben-hinnom, which is in the valley of Rephaim northward; and it went down to the valley of Hinnom, to the slope of
the Jebusite southward, and went down to En-rogel.
17And it extended northward and went to En-shemesh and
went to Geliloth, which is opposite the ascent of Adummim, and
it went down to the stone of Bohan the son of Reuben.
18And it continued to the side in front of the Arabah northward,
and went down to the Arabah.
19And the border continued to the side of Beth-hoglah northward; and the [c]border ended at the north bay of the Salt Sea, at
the south end of the Jordan. This *was* the south border.
20Moreover, the Jordan was its border on the east side. This *was*
the inheritance of the sons of Benjamin, according to their families
*and* according to its borders all around.
21¶ Now the cities of the tribe of the sons of Benjamin according
to their families were Jericho and Beth-hoglah and Emek-keziz,
22and Beth-arabah and Zemaraim and Bethel,
23and Avvim and Parah and Ophrah,
24and Chephar-ammoni and Ophni and Geba; twelve cities
with their villages.
25Gibeon and Ramah and Beeroth,
26and Mizpeh and Chephirah and Mozah,
27and Rekem and Irpeel and Taralah,
28and Zelah, Haeleph and the Jebusite (that is, Jerusalem), Gibeah, Kiriath; fourteen cities with their villages. This is the inheritance of the sons of Benjamin according to their families.

*Territory of Simeon*

**19** THEN THE second lot fell to Simeon, to the tribe of the
sons of Simeon according to their families, and their inheritance was in the midst of the inheritance of the sons of Judah.
2So they had as their inheritance Beersheba or Sheba and Moladah,
3and Hazar-shual and Balah and Ezem,
4and Eltolad and Bethul and Hormah,
5and Ziklag and Beth-marcaboth and Hazar-susah,
6and Beth-lebaoth and Sharuhen, thirteen cities with their villages;
7Ain, Rimmon and Ether and Ashan, four cities with their
villages;

NAS [a] Lit., *goings out of it were* [b] Lit., *goings out of it were* [c] Lit., *goings out of it were*

## New International

*Allotment for Benjamin*

11The lot came up for the tribe of Benjamin, clan by clan. Their
allotted territory lay between the tribes of Judah and Joseph:
12On the north side their boundary began at the Jordan,
passed the northern slope of Jericho and headed west into the
hill country, coming out at the desert of Beth Aven. 13From
there it crossed to the south slope of Luz (that is, Bethel) and
went down to Ataroth Addar on the hill south of Lower Beth
Horon.
14From the hill facing Beth Horon on the south the boundary turned south along the western side and came out at
Kiriath Baal (that is, Kiriath Jearim), a town of the people of
Judah. This was the western side.
15The southern side began at the outskirts of Kiriath Jearim
on the west, and the boundary came out at the spring of the
waters of Nephtoah. 16The boundary went down to the foot
of the hill facing the Valley of Ben Hinnom, north of the Valley
of Rephaim. It continued down the Hinnom Valley along the
southern slope of the Jebusite city and so to En Rogel. 17It then
curved north, went to En Shemesh, continued to Geliloth,
which faces the Pass of Adummim, and ran down to the Stone
of Bohan son of Reuben. 18It continued to the northern slope
of Beth Arabah[d] and on down into the Arabah. 19It then went
to the northern slope of Beth Hoglah and came out at the
northern bay of the Salt Sea,[e] at the mouth of the Jordan in
the south. This was the southern boundary.
20The Jordan formed the boundary on the eastern side.
These were the boundaries that marked out the inheritance of the
clans of Benjamin on all sides.

21The tribe of Benjamin, clan by clan, had the following cities:
Jericho, Beth Hoglah, Emek Keziz, 22Beth Arabah, Zemaraim, Bethel, 23Avvim, Parah, Ophrah, 24Kephar Ammoni,
Ophni and Geba—twelve towns and their villages.
25Gibeon, Ramah, Beeroth, 26Mizpah, Kephirah, Mozah,
27Rekem, Irpeel, Taralah, 28Zelah, Haeleph, the Jebusite city
(that is, Jerusalem), Gibeah and Kiriath—fourteen towns and
their villages.
This was the inheritance of Benjamin for its clans.

*Allotment for Simeon*

**19** THE SECOND lot came out for the tribe of Simeon, clan
by clan. Their inheritance lay within the territory of Judah.
2It included:
Beersheba (or Sheba),[f] Moladah, 3Hazar Shual, Balah,
Ezem, 4Eltolad, Bethul, Hormah, 5Ziklag, Beth Marcaboth,
Hazar Susah, 6Beth Lebaoth and Sharuhen—thirteen towns
and their villages;
7Ain, Rimmon, Ether and Ashan—four towns and their

NIV [d] *18* Septuagint; Hebrew *slope facing the Arabah* [e] *19* That is, the Dead Sea [f] *2* Or *Beersheba, Sheba;* 1 Chron. 4:28 does not have *Sheba.*

## King James

8And all the villages that *were* round about these cities to
Baalath-beer, Ramath of the south. This *is* the inheritance of the
tribe of the children of Simeon according to their families.
9Out of the portion of the children of Judah *was* the inheritance
of the children of Simeon: for the part of the children of Judah was
too much for them: therefore the children of Simeon had their
inheritance within the inheritance of them.
10¶ And the third lot came up for the children of Zebulun
according to their families: and the border of their inheritance was
unto Sarid:
11And their border went up toward the sea, and Maralah, and
reached to Dabbasheth, and reached to the river that *is* before
Jokneam;
12And turned from Sarid eastward toward the sunrising unto
the border of Chisloth-tabor, and then goeth out to Daberath, and
goeth up to Japhia,
13And from thence passeth on along on the east to Gittah-
hepher, to Ittah-kazin, and goeth out to Remmon-methoar to
Neah;
14And the border compasseth it on the north side to Hannathon: and the outgoings thereof are in the valley of Jiphthah-el:
15And Kattath, and Nahallal, and Shimron, and Idalah, and
Bethlehem: twelve cities with their villages.
16This *is* the inheritance of the children of Zebulun according to
their families, these cities with their villages.
17¶ *And* the fourth lot came out to Issachar, for the children of
Issachar according to their families.
18And their border was toward Jezreel, and Chesulloth, and
Shunem,
19And Haphraim, and Shion, and Anaharath,
20And Rabbith, and Kishion, and Abez,
21And Remeth, and En-gannim, and En-haddah, and Beth-
pazzez;
22And the coast reacheth to Tabor, and Shahazimah, and Beth-
shemesh; and the outgoings of their border were at Jordan: sixteen
cities with their villages.
23This *is* the inheritance of the tribe of the children of Issachar
according to their families, the cities and their villages.
24¶ And the fifth lot came out for the tribe of the children of
Asher according to their families.
25And their border was Helkath, and Hali, and Beten, and
Achshaph,
26And Alammelech, and Amad, and Misheal; and reacheth to
Carmel westward, and to Shihor-libnath;
27And turneth toward the sunrising to Beth-dagon, and
reacheth to Zebulun, and to the valley of Jiphthah-el toward the
north side of Beth-emek, and Neiel, and goeth out to Cabul on the
left hand,
28And Hebron, and Rehob, and Hammon, and Kanah, *even*
unto great Zidon;
29And *then* the coast turneth to Ramah, and to the strong city
Tyre; and the coast turneth to Hosah; and the outgoings thereof
are at the sea from the coast to Achzib:
30Ummah also, and Aphek, and Rehob: twenty and two cities
with their villages.
31This *is* the inheritance of the tribe of the children of Asher
according to their families, these cities with their villages.
32¶ The sixth lot came out to the children of Naphtali, *even* for
the children of Naphtali according to their families.
33And their coast was from Heleph, from Allon to Zaanannim,
and Adami, Nekeb, and Jabneel, unto Lakum; and the outgoings
thereof were at Jordan:

## Amplified

8And all the villages around these cities as far as Baalath-beer,
or Ramah of the Negeb. This was the possession of the Simeonites
according to their families.
9Out of the part assigned to the Judahites was the inheritance
of the tribe of Simeon; for the portion of the tribe of Judah was too
large for them, therefore the tribe of Simeon had its inheritance in
the midst of Judah's inheritance.
10The third lot came up for the tribe of Zebulun according to its
families. The border of its inheritance extended to Sarid;
11Then its boundary went up westward and on to Mareal, and
reached to Dabbesheth, and to the brook east of Jokneam;
12And it turned from Sarid eastward to the border of Chisloth-
tabor, and it went out to Daberath, and on up to Japhia;
13Then passed eastward to Gath-hepher [Jonah's birthplace],
and to Eth-kazin; and went on to Rimmon bending toward Neah.
14The boundary circled on the north to Hannathon, ending at
the valley of Iphtahel;
15And Kattath, Nahalal, Shimron, Idalah, and Bethlehem;
twelve cities with their villages.
16This is the inheritance of the people of Zebulun according to
their families, these cities with their villages.
17The fourth lot fell to Issachar, for its people according to their
families.
18Their territory included Jezreel, Chesulloth, Shunem,
19Hapharaim, Shion, Anaharath,
20Rabbith, Kishion, Ebez,
21Remeth, Engannim, Enhaddah, and Beth-pazzez;
22The boundary reached to Tabor, Shahazumah, and Beth-
shemesh, and ended at the Jordan; sixteen cities with their villages.
23This is the inheritance of the tribe of Issachar according to its
families, the cities and their villages.
24The fifth lot fell to the tribe of Asher according to its families.
25Its territory included Helkath, Hali, Beten, Achshaph,
26Allammelech, Amad, and Mishal; and on the west it touched
Carmel and Shihor-libnath,
27Then it turned eastward to Beth-dagon, touching Zebulun
and the valley of Iphtahel northward to Beth-emek, and Neiel, and
continued in the north to Cabul,
28Ebron, Rehob, Hammon, and Kanah, even to populous Sidon;
29Then the boundary turned to Ramah, reaching to the fortified
city of Tyre; and *it* turned to Hosah, and ended at the sea—
Mahalab, Achzib,
30Ummah, Aphek, and Rehob; twenty-two cities with their villages.
31This is the inheritance of the tribe of Asher according to its
families, these cities with their villages.
32The sixth lot fell to the tribe of Naphtali, according to its
families.
33Its boundary ran from Heleph, from the oak in Za-anannim,
and Adami-nekeb, and Jabneel, as far as Lakkum; and it ended at
the Jordan.

## New American Standard

8and all the villages which *were* around these cities as far as Baalath-beer, Ramah of the Negev. This *was* the inheritance of the tribe of the sons of Simeon according to their families.
9The inheritance of the sons of Simeon *was taken* from the portion of the sons of Judah, for the share of the sons of Judah was too large for them; so the sons of Simeon received *an* inheritance in the midst of Judah's inheritance.

*Territory of Zebulun*

**10**¶ Now the third lot came up for the sons of Zebulun according to their families. And the territory of their inheritance was as far as Sarid.
11Then their border went up to the west and to Maralah, it then touched Dabbesheth, and reached to the brook that is before Jokneam.
12Then it turned from Sarid to the east toward the sunrise as far as the border of Chisloth-tabor, and it proceeded to Daberath and up to Japhia.
13And from there it continued eastward toward the sunrise to Gath-hepher, to Eth-kazin, and it proceeded to Rimmon which stretches to Neah.
14And the border circled around it on the north to Hannathon, and it ended at the valley of Iphtahel.
15 *Included* also *were* Kattah and Nahalal and Shimron and Idalah and Bethlehem; twelve cities with their villages.
16This *was* the inheritance of the sons of Zebulun according to their families, these cities with their villages.

*Territory of Issachar*

**17**¶ The fourth lot fell to Issachar, to the sons of Issachar according to their families.
18And their territory was to Jezreel and *included* Chesulloth and Shunem,
19and Hapharaim and Shion and Anaharath,
20and Rabbith and Kishion and Ebez,
21and Remeth and En-gannim and En-haddah and Beth-pazzez.
22And the border reached to Tabor and Shahazumah and Beth-shemesh, and their border ended at the Jordan; sixteen cities with their villages.
23This *was* the inheritance of the tribe of the sons of Issachar according to their families, the cities with their villages.

*Territory of Asher*

**24**¶ Now the fifth lot fell to the tribe of the sons of Asher according to their families.
25And their territory was Helkath and Hali and Beten and Achshaph,
26and Allammelech and Amad and Mishal; and it reached to Carmel on the west and to Shihor-libnath.
27And it turned toward the east to Beth-dagon, and reached to Zebulun, and to the valley of Iphtahel northward to Beth-emek and Neiel; then it proceeded on north to Cabul,
28and Ebron and Rehob and Hammon and Kanah, as far as Great Sidon.
29And the border turned to Ramah, and to the fortified city of Tyre; then the border turned to Hosah, and it ended at the sea by the region of Achzib.
30 *Included* also *were* Ummah, and Aphek and Rehob; twenty-two cities with their villages.
31This *was* the inheritance of the tribe of the sons of Asher according to their families, these cities with their villages.

*Territory of Naphtali*

**32**¶ The sixth lot fell to the sons of Naphtali; to the sons of Naphtali according to their families.
33And their border was from Heleph, from the oak in Zaanannim and Adami-nekeb and Jabneel, as far as Lakkum; and it ended at the Jordan.

## New International

villages— 8and all the villages around these towns as far as
Baalath Beer (Ramah in the Negev).
This was the inheritance of the tribe of the Simeonites, clan by clan.
9The inheritance of the Simeonites was taken from the share of
Judah, because Judah's portion was more than they needed. So the
Simeonites received their inheritance within the territory of Judah.

*Allotment for Zebulun*

10The third lot came up for Zebulun, clan by clan:
The boundary of their inheritance went as far as Sarid.
11Going west it ran to Maralah, touched Dabbesheth, and
extended to the ravine near Jokneam. 12It turned east from
Sarid toward the sunrise to the territory of Kisloth Tabor and
went on to Daberath and up to Japhia. 13Then it continued
eastward to Gath Hepher and Eth Kazin; it came out at Rimmon and turned toward Neah. 14There the boundary went
around on the north to Hannathon and ended at the Valley
of Iphtah El. 15Included were Kattath, Nahalal, Shimron, Idalah and Bethlehem. There were twelve towns and their villages.
16These towns and their villages were the inheritance of Zebulun,
clan by clan.

*Allotment for Issachar*

17The fourth lot came out for Issachar, clan by clan. 18Their territory included:
Jezreel, Kesulloth, Shunem, 19Hapharaim, Shion, Anaharath, 20Rabbith, Kishion, Ebez, 21Remeth, En Gannim, En
Haddah and Beth Pazzez. 22The boundary touched Tabor,
Shahazumah and Beth Shemesh, and ended at the Jordan.
There were sixteen towns and their villages.
23These towns and their villages were the inheritance of the tribe
of Issachar, clan by clan.

*Allotment for Asher*

24The fifth lot came out for the tribe of Asher, clan by clan. 25Their
territory included:
Helkath, Hali, Beten, Acshaph, 26Allammelech, Amad and
Mishal. On the west the boundary touched Carmel and Shihor Libnath. 27It then turned east toward Beth Dagon,
touched Zebulun and the Valley of Iphtah El, and went north
to Beth Emek and Neiel, passing Cabul on the left. 28It went
to Abdon,[a] Rehob, Hammon and Kanah, as far as Greater
Sidon. 29The boundary then turned back toward Ramah and
went to the fortified city of Tyre, turned toward Hosah and
came out at the sea in the region of Aczib, 30Ummah, Aphek
and Rehob. There were twenty-two towns and their villages.
31These towns and their villages were the inheritance of the tribe
of Asher, clan by clan.

*Allotment for Naphtali*

32The sixth lot came out for Naphtali, clan by clan:
33Their boundary went from Heleph and the large tree in
Zaanannim, passing Adami Nekeb and Jabneel to Lakkum
and ending at the Jordan. 34The boundary ran west through

**NIV** [a] *28* Some Hebrew manuscripts (see also Joshua 21:30); most Hebrew manuscripts *Ebron*

## King James

34And *then* the coast turneth westward to Aznoth-tabor, and goeth out from thence to Hukkok, and reacheth to Zebulun on the south side, and reacheth to Asher on the west side, and to Judah upon Jordan toward the sunrising.

35And the fenced cities *are* Ziddim, Zer, and Hammath, Rakkath, and Chinnereth,

36And Adamah, and Ramah, and Hazor,

37And Kedesh, and Edrei, and En-hazor,

38And Iron, and Migdal-el, Horem, and Beth-anath, and Beth-shemesh; nineteen cities with their villages.

39This *is* the inheritance of the tribe of the children of Naphtali according to their families, the cities and their villages.

40¶ *And* the seventh lot came out for the tribe of the children of Dan according to their families.

41And the coast of their inheritance was Zorah, and Eshtaol, and Ir-shemesh,

42And Shaalabbin, and Ajalon, and Jethlah,

43And Elon, and Thimnathah, and Ekron,

44And Eltekeh, and Gibbethon, and Baalath,

45And Jehud, and Bene-berak, and Gath-rimmon,

46And Me-jarkon, and Rakkon, with the border before Japho.

47And the coast of the children of Dan went out *too little* for them: therefore the children of Dan went up to fight against Leshem, and took it, and smote it with the edge of the sword, and possessed it, and dwelt therein, and called Leshem, Dan, after the name of Dan their father.

48This *is* the inheritance of the tribe of the children of Dan according to their families, these cities with their villages.

49¶ When they had made an end of dividing the land for inheritance by their coasts, the children of Israel gave an inheritance to Joshua the son of Nun among them:

50According to the word of the LORD they gave him the city which he asked, *even* Timnath-serah in mount Ephraim: and he built the city, and dwelt therein.

51These *are* the inheritances, which Eleazar the priest, and Joshua the son of Nun, and the heads of the fathers of the tribes of the children of Israel, divided for an inheritance by lot in Shiloh before the LORD, at the door of the tabernacle of the congregation. So they made an end of dividing the country.

**20** THE LORD also spake unto Joshua, saying,

2Speak to the children of Israel, saying, Appoint out for you cities of refuge, whereof I spake unto you by the hand of Moses:

3That the slayer that killeth *any* person unawares *and* unwittingly may flee thither: and they shall be your refuge from the avenger of blood.

4And when he that doth flee unto one of those cities shall stand at the entering of the gate of the city, and shall declare his cause in the ears of the elders of that city, they shall take him into the city unto them, and give him a place, that he may dwell among them.

5And if the avenger of blood pursue after him, then they shall not deliver the slayer up into his hand; because he smote his neighbour unwittingly, and hated him not beforetime.

6And he shall dwell in that city, until he stand before the congregation for judgment, *and* until the death of the high priest that shall be in those days: then shall the slayer return, and come unto his own city, and unto his own house, unto the city from whence he fled.

7¶ And they appointed Kedesh in Galilee in mount Naphtali, and Shechem in mount Ephraim, and Kirjath-arba, which *is* Hebron, in the mountain of Judah.

## Amplified

34Then the boundary turned westward to Aznoth-tabor, and went from there to Hukkok, touching Zebulun on the south, Asher on the west, and Judah on the east at the Jordan.

35The fortified cities included Ziddim, Zer, and Hammath, Rakkath, Chinnereth,

36Adamah, Ramah, Hazor,

37Kedesh, Edrei, En-hazor,

38Yiron, Migdalel, Horem, Beth-anath, and Beth-shemesh; nineteen cities and their villages.

39This is the inheritance of the tribe of Naphtali according to its families, the cities and their villages.

40And the seventh lot fell to the tribe of Dan according to its families.

41The territory of its inheritance included Zorah, Esthtaol, Ir-shemesh,

42Sha-alabbin, Aijalon, Ithlah,

43Elon, Timnah, Ekron,

44Eltekeh, Gibbethon, Baalath,

45Jehud, Bene-berak, Gath-rimmon,

46Mejarkon, and Rakkon, with the territory before Joppa.

47The territory of the tribe of Dan had to be extended [because of the crowding in of the Amorites and Philistines]; so the sons of Dan went up to fight against Leshem [Laish], and took it, and smote it with the sword, and possessed it, and dwelt there, and called Leshem [Laish], Dan, after Dan their [forefather]. [Judg. 1:34; 18:7-10, 27.]

48This is the inheritance of the tribe of Dan according to *its* families, these cities with their villages.

49When they had finished dividing the land for inheritance by their boundaries, the Israelites gave an inheritance among them to Joshua the son of Nun.

50According to the word of the Lord they gave him the city which he asked. Timnath-serah in the hills of Ephraim; and he built the city, and dwelt in it.

51These are the inheritances, which Eleazar the priest, Joshua son of Nun, and the heads of the fathers' houses of the tribes of Israel distributed by lot in Shiloh before the Lord, at the door of the tent of meeting. So they finished dividing the land.

**20** THE LORD said also to Joshua,

2Say to the Israelites, Appoint among you cities of refuge, of which I spoke to you through Moses,

3That the slayer who kills any one accidentally and unintentionally may flee there; and they shall be your refuge from the avenger of blood. [Num. 35:10ff.]

4He who flees to one of those cities shall stand at the entrance of the gate of the city and explain his case to the elders of that city; they shall receive him to [the protection of] that city, and give him a place to dwell among them.

5If the avenger of blood pursues him, they shall not deliver the slayer up into his hand; because he killed his neighbor unintentionally, having had no hatred for him previously.

6And he shall dwell in that city, until he has been tried before the congregation and until the death of him who is the high priest in those days. Then the slayer shall return to his own city from which he fled, and to his own house.

7And they set apart *and* consecrated Kedesh in Galilee in the hill country of Naphtali, and Shechem in the hill country of Ephraim, and Kiriath-arba (that is, Hebron), in the hill country of Judah.

## New American Standard

34Then the border turned westward to Aznoth-tabor, and proceeded from there to Hukkok; and it reached to Zebulun on the
south and touched Asher on the west, and to Judah at the Jordan
toward the east.
35And the fortified cities *were* Ziddim, Zer and Hammath, Rakkath and Chinnereth,
36and Adamah and Ramah and Hazor,
37and Kedesh and Edrei and En-hazor,
38and Yiron and Migdal-el, Horem and Beth-anath and Beth-
shemesh; nineteen cities with their villages.
39This *was* the inheritance of the tribe of the sons of Naphtali
according to their families, the cities with their villages.

*Territory of Dan*

40¶ The seventh lot fell to the tribe of the sons of Dan according
to their families.
41And the territory of their inheritance was Zorah and Eshtaol
and Ir-shemesh,
42and Shaalabbin and Aijalon and Ithlah,
43and Elon and Timnah and Ekron,
44and Eltekeh and Gibbethon and Baalath,
45and Jehud and Bene-berak and Gath-rimmon,
46and Me-jarkon and Rakkon, with the territory over against
Joppa.
47And the territory of the sons of Dan proceeded beyond them;
for the sons of Dan went up and fought with Leshem and captured
it. Then they struck it with the edge of the sword and possessed
it and settled in it; and they called Leshem Dan after the name of
Dan their father.
48This *was* the inheritance of the tribe of the sons of Dan according to their families, these cities with their villages.
49¶ When they finished apportioning the land for inheritance by
its borders, the sons of Israel gave an inheritance in their midst to
Joshua the son of Nun.
50In accordance with the command of the LORD they gave him
the city for which he asked, Timnath-serah in the hill country of
Ephraim. So he built the city and settled in it.
51¶ These are the inheritances which Eleazar the priest and
Joshua the son of Nun and the heads of the households of the
tribes of the sons of Israel distributed by lot in Shiloh before the
LORD, at the doorway of the tent of meeting. So they finished
dividing the land.

*Six Cities of Refuge*

20 THEN THE LORD spoke to Joshua, saying,
2"Speak to the sons of Israel, saying, 'Designate the cities
of refuge, of which I spoke to you through Moses,
3that the manslayer who kills any person unintentionally,
without premeditation, may flee there, and they shall become your
refuge from the avenger of blood.
4'And he shall flee to one of these cities, and shall stand at the
entrance of the gate of the city and state his case in the hearing of
the elders of that city; and they shall take him into the city to them
and give him a place, so that he may dwell among them.
5'Now if the avenger of blood pursues him, then they shall not
deliver the manslayer into his hand, because he struck his neighbor without premeditation and did not hate him beforehand.
6'And he shall dwell in that city until he stands before the
congregation for judgment, until the death of the one who is high
priest in those days. Then the manslayer shall return to his own
city and to his own house, to the city from which he fled.' "
7¶ So they set apart Kedesh in Galilee in the hill country of
Naphtali and Shechem in the hill country of Ephraim, and Kiriath-
arba (that is, Hebron) in the hill country of Judah.

## New International

Aznoth Tabor and came out at Hukkok. It touched Zebulun
on the south, Asher on the west and the Jordan[a] on the east.
35The fortified cities were Ziddim, Zer, Hammath, Rakkath,
Kinnereth, 36Adamah, Ramah, Hazor, 37Kedesh, Edrei, En
Hazor, 38Iron, Migdal El, Horem, Beth Anath and Beth Shemesh. There were nineteen towns and their villages.
39These towns and their villages were the inheritance of the tribe
of Naphtali, clan by clan.

*Allotment for Dan*

40The seventh lot came out for the tribe of Dan, clan by clan. 41The
territory of their inheritance included:
Zorah, Eshtaol, Ir Shemesh, 42Shaalabbin, Aijalon, Ithlah,
43Elon, Timnah, Ekron, 44Eltekeh, Gibbethon, Baalath,
45Jehud, Bene Berak, Gath Rimmon, 46Me Jarkon and Rakkon, with the area facing Joppa.
47(But the Danites had difficulty taking possession of their territory, so they went up and attacked Leshem, took it, put it to the
sword and occupied it. They settled in Leshem and named it Dan
after their forefather.)
48These towns and their villages were the inheritance of the tribe
of Dan, clan by clan.

*Allotment for Joshua*

49When they had finished dividing the land into its allotted
portions, the Israelites gave Joshua son of Nun an inheritance
among them, 50as the LORD had commanded. They gave him the
town he asked for—Timnath Serah[b] in the hill country of Ephraim.
And he built up the town and settled there.
51These are the territories that Eleazar the priest, Joshua son of
Nun and the heads of the tribal clans of Israel assigned by lot at
Shiloh in the presence of the LORD at the entrance to the Tent of
Meeting. And so they finished dividing the land.

*Cities of Refuge*

20 THEN THE LORD said to Joshua: 2"Tell the Israelites to
designate the cities of refuge, as I instructed you through
Moses, 3so that anyone who kills a person accidentally and unintentionally may flee there and find protection from the avenger of
blood.
4"When he flees to one of these cities, he is to stand in the
entrance of the city gate and state his case before the elders of that
city. Then they are to admit him into their city and give him a place
to live with them. 5If the avenger of blood pursues him, they must
not surrender the one accused, because he killed his neighbor
unintentionally and without malice aforethought. 6He is to stay in
that city until he has stood trial before the assembly and until the
death of the high priest who is serving at that time. Then he may
go back to his own home in the town from which he fled."
7So they set apart Kedesh in Galilee in the hill country of Naphtali, Shechem in the hill country of Ephraim, and Kiriath Arba (that
is, Hebron) in the hill country of Judah. 8On the east side of the

NIV [a] 34 Septuagint; Hebrew *west, and Judah, the Jordan,* [b] 50 Also known as *Timnath Heres* (see Judges 2:9)

## King James

8 And on the other side Jordan by Jericho eastward, they assigned Bezer in the wilderness upon the plain out of the tribe of Reuben, and Ramoth in Gilead out of the tribe of Gad, and Golan in Bashan out of the tribe of Manasseh.

9 These were the cities appointed for all the children of Israel, and for the stranger that sojourneth among them, that whosoever killeth *any* person at unawares might flee thither, and not die by the hand of the avenger of blood, until he stood before the congregation.

**21** THEN CAME near the heads of the fathers of the Levites unto Eleazar the priest, and unto Joshua the son of Nun, and unto the heads of the fathers of the tribes of the children of Israel;

2 And they spake unto them at Shiloh in the land of Canaan, saying, The LORD commanded by the hand of Moses to give us cities to dwell in, with the suburbs thereof for our cattle.

3 And the children of Israel gave unto the Levites out of their inheritance, at the commandment of the LORD, these cities and their suburbs.

4 And the lot came out for the families of the Kohathites: and the children of Aaron the priest, *which were* of the Levites, had by lot out of the tribe of Judah, and out of the tribe of Simeon, and out of the tribe of Benjamin, thirteen cities.

5 And the rest of the children of Kohath *had* by lot out of the families of the tribe of Ephraim, and out of the tribe of Dan, and out of the half tribe of Manasseh, ten cities.

6 And the children of Gershon *had* by lot out of the families of the tribe of Issachar, and out of the tribe of Asher, and out of the tribe of Naphtali, and out of the half tribe of Manasseh in Bashan, thirteen cities.

7 The children of Merari by their families *had* out of the tribe of Reuben, and out of the tribe of Gad, and out of the tribe of Zebulun, twelve cities.

8 And the children of Israel gave by lot unto the Levites these cities with their suburbs, as the LORD commanded by the hand of Moses.

9 ¶ And they gave out of the tribe of the children of Judah, and out of the tribe of the children of Simeon, these cities which are *here* mentioned by name,

10 Which the children of Aaron, *being* of the families of the Kohathites, *who were* of the children of Levi, had: for their's was the first lot.

11 And they gave them the city of Arba the father of Anak, which *city is* Hebron, in the hill *country* of Judah, with the suburbs thereof round about it.

12 But the fields of the city, and the villages thereof, gave they to Caleb the son of Jephunneh for his possession.

13 ¶ Thus they gave to the children of Aaron the priest Hebron with her suburbs, *to be* a city of refuge for the slayer; and Libnah with her suburbs,

14 And Jattir with her suburbs, and Eshtemoa with her suburbs,

15 And Holon with her suburbs, and Debir with her suburbs,

16 And Ain with her suburbs, and Juttah with her suburbs, *and* Beth-shemesh with her suburbs; nine cities out of those two tribes.

17 And out of the tribe of Benjamin, Gibeon with her suburbs, Geba with her suburbs,

18 Anathoth with her suburbs, and Almon with her suburbs; four cities.

## Amplified

8 Beyond the Jordan east of Jericho, they appointed Bezer in the wilderness tableland, from the tribe of Reuben, and Ramoth in Gilead, from the tribe of Gad, and Golan in Bashan, from the tribe of Manasseh.

9 These cities were for all the Israelites and the stranger sojourning among them, that whoever killed a person unintentionally might flee there, and not be slain by the avenger of blood, until he had been tried before the congregation.

**21** THEN THE heads of the fathers' houses of the Levites came to Eleazar the priest and Joshua son of Nun, and the heads of the fathers' houses of the Israelite tribes;

2 They said to them at Shiloh in Canaan, The Lord commanded by Moses that we should be given cities to dwell in, with their pasture lands [suburbs] for our cattle.

3 So the Israelites gave to the Levites out of their inheritance, at the command of the Lord, these cities and their suburbs.

4 The [first] lot came out for the families of the Kohathites. So those [a]Levites who were descendants of Aaron the priest, received by lot from the tribes of Judah, Simeon and Benjamin, thirteen cities.

5 And the rest of the Kohathites received by lot from the families of the tribes of Ephraim, Dan, and the half tribe of Manasseh, ten cities.

6 The Gershonites received by lot from the families of the tribes of Issachar, Asher, Naphtali, and the half tribe of Manasseh in Bashan, thirteen cities.

7 The Merarites received according to their families from the tribes of Reuben, Gad, and Zebulun, twelve cities.

8 The Israelites gave by lot to the Levites these cities with their pasture lands [suburbs], as the Lord commanded by Moses.

9 They gave from the tribes of Judah and Simeon the cities here mentioned by name,

10 Which went to the families of the descendants of Aaron, of the Kohathite branch of the Levites; for the lot fell to them first.

11 They gave them [the city of] Kiriath-arba, Arba being the father of Anak, which city is Hebron, in the hill country of Judah, with its pasture lands round about it.

12 But the city's fields and villages they gave to Caleb son of Jephunneh as his own.

13 Thus to the descendants of Aaron the priest they gave Hebron with its pasture lands [suburbs] the city of refuge for the slayer, and with *their* suburbs, Libnah,

14 Jattir, Eshtemoa,

15 Holon, Debir,

16 Ain, Juttah, and Beth-shemesh; nine cities, each with its suburbs, out of those two tribes.

17 Out of the tribe of Benjamin, Gibeon, Geba,

18 Anathoth and Almon; four cities, each with its suburbs.

**AMP** [a] The Levites were divided into three groups, the descendants of Levi's three sons, Gershon, Kohath, and Merari. But only those Israelites could be priests who were descendants of Levi through Kohath's grandson Aaron. The priesthood was made hereditary in the family of Aaron and restricted to it; however, even some of these were debarred by legal disabilities (Lev. 21:16ff). The other families of Levi's descendants, the Gershonites and Merarites and those Kohathites who were not descended from Aaron were charged with the care of the sanctuary. The priests ministered at the altar.

## New American Standard

8And beyond the Jordan east of Jericho, they designated Bezer
in the wilderness on the plain from the tribe of Reuben, and
Ramoth in Gilead from the tribe of Gad, and Golan in Bashan from
the tribe of Manasseh.
9These were the appointed cities for all the sons of Israel and
for the stranger who sojourns among them, that whoever kills any
person unintentionally may flee there, and not die by the hand of
the avenger of blood until he stands before the congregation.

*Forty-eight Cities of the Levites*

**21** THEN THE heads of households of the Levites approached Eleazar the priest and Joshua the son of Nun
and the heads of households of the tribes of the sons of Israel.
2And they spoke to them at Shiloh in the land of Canaan,
saying, "The LORD commanded through Moses to give us cities to
live in, with their pasture lands for our cattle."
3So the sons of Israel gave the Levites from their inheritance
these cities with their pasture lands, according to the command of
the LORD.
4Then the lot came out for the families of the Kohathites. And
the sons of Aaron the priest, who were of the Levites, received
thirteen cities by lot from the tribe of Judah and from the tribe of
the Simeonites and from the tribe of Benjamin.
5And the rest of the sons of Kohath received ten cities by lot
from the families of the tribe of Ephraim and from the tribe of Dan
and from the half-tribe of Manasseh.
6And the sons of Gershon received thirteen cities by lot from
the families of the tribe of Issachar and from the tribe of Asher and
from the tribe of Naphtali and from the half-tribe of Manasseh in
Bashan.
7The sons of Merari according to their families received twelve
cities from the tribe of Reuben and from the tribe of Gad and from
the tribe of Zebulun.
8Now the sons of Israel gave by lot to the Levites these cities
with their pasture lands, as the LORD had commanded through
Moses.
9¶ And they gave these cities which are *here* mentioned by
name from the tribe of the sons of Judah and from the tribe of the
sons of Simeon;
10and they were for the sons of Aaron, one of the families of the
Kohathites, of the sons of Levi, for the lot was theirs first.
11Thus they gave them Kiriath-arba, *Arba being* the father of
Anak (that is, Hebron), in the hill country of Judah, with its surrounding pasture lands.
12But the fields of the city and its villages, they gave to Caleb
the son of Jephunneh as his possession.
13¶ So to the sons of Aaron the priest they gave Hebron, the city
of refuge for the manslayer, with its pasture lands, and Libnah
with its pasture lands,
14and Jattir with its pasture lands and Eshtemoa with its pasture
lands,
15and Holon with its pasture lands and Debir with its pasture
lands,
16and Ain with its pasture lands and Juttah with its pasture
lands *and* Beth-shemesh with its pasture lands; nine cities from
these two tribes.
17And from the tribe of Benjamin, Gibeon with its pasture
lands, Geba with its pasture lands,
18Anathoth with its pasture lands and Almon with its pasture
lands; four cities.

## New International

Jordan of Jericho[b] they designated Bezer in the desert on the
plateau in the tribe of Reuben, Ramoth in Gilead in the tribe of
Gad, and Golan in Bashan in the tribe of Manasseh. 9Any of the
Israelites or any alien living among them who killed someone
accidentally could flee to these designated cities and not be killed
by the avenger of blood prior to standing trial before the assembly.

*Towns for the Levites*

**21** NOW THE family heads of the Levites approached Eleazar the priest, Joshua son of Nun, and the heads of the
other tribal families of Israel 2at Shiloh in Canaan and said to them,
"The LORD commanded through Moses that you give us towns to
live in, with pasturelands for our livestock." 3So, as the LORD had
commanded, the Israelites gave the Levites the following towns
and pasturelands out of their own inheritance:
4The first lot came out for the Kohathites, clan by clan. The
Levites who were descendants of Aaron the priest were allotted
thirteen towns from the tribes of Judah, Simeon and Benjamin.
5The rest of Kohath's descendants were allotted ten towns from
the clans of the tribes of Ephraim, Dan and half of Manasseh.
6The descendants of Gershon were allotted thirteen towns from
the clans of the tribes of Issachar, Asher, Naphtali and the half-
tribe of Manasseh in Bashan.
7The descendants of Merari, clan by clan, received twelve
towns from the tribes of Reuben, Gad and Zebulun.
8So the Israelites allotted to the Levites these towns and their
pasturelands, as the LORD had commanded through Moses.

9From the tribes of Judah and Simeon they allotted the following
towns by name 10(these towns were assigned to the descendants
of Aaron who were from the Kohathite clans of the Levites, because the first lot fell to them):
11They gave them Kiriath Arba (that is, Hebron), with its
surrounding pastureland, in the hill country of Judah. (Arba
was the forefather of Anak.) 12But the fields and villages
around the city they had given to Caleb son of Jephunneh as
his possession.
13So to the descendants of Aaron the priest they gave
Hebron (a city of refuge for one accused of murder), Libnah,
14Jattir, Eshtemoa, 15Holon, Debir, 16Ain, Juttah and Beth
Shemesh, together with their pasturelands—nine towns from
these two tribes.
17And from the tribe of Benjamin they gave them Gibeon,
Geba, 18Anathoth and Almon, together with their pasturelands—four towns.

NIV [b] 8 *Jordan of Jericho* was possibly an ancient name for the Jordan River.

## King James

19 All the cities of the children of Aaron, the priests, *were* thirteen cities with their suburbs.

20 ¶ And the families of the children of Kohath, the Levites which remained of the children of Kohath, even they had the cities of their lot out of the tribe of Ephraim.

21 For they gave them Shechem with her suburbs in mount Ephraim, *to be* a city of refuge for the slayer; and Gezer with her suburbs,

22 And Kibzaim with her suburbs, and Beth-horon with her suburbs; four cities.

23 And out of the tribe of Dan, Eltekeh with her suburbs, Gibbethon with her suburbs,

24 Aijalon with her suburbs, Gathrimmon with her suburbs; four cities.

25 And out of the half tribe of Manasseh, Tanach with her suburbs, and Gath-rimmon with her suburbs; two cities.

26 All the cities *were* ten with their suburbs for the families of the children of Kohath that remained.

27 ¶ And unto the children of Gershon, of the families of the Levites, out of the *other* half tribe of Manasseh *they gave* Golan in Bashan with her suburbs, *to be* a city of refuge for the slayer; and Beesh-terah with her suburbs; two cities.

28 And out of the tribe of Issachar, Kishon with her suburbs, Dabareh with her suburbs,

29 Jarmuth with her suburbs, En-gannim with her suburbs; four cities.

30 And out of the tribe of Asher, Mishal with her suburbs, Abdon with her suburbs,

31 Helkath with her suburbs, and Rehob with her suburbs; four cities.

32 And out of the tribe of Naphtali, Kedesh in Galilee with her suburbs, *to be* a city of refuge for the slayer; and Hammoth-dor with her suburbs, and Kartan with her suburbs; three cities.

33 All the cities of the Gershonites according to their families *were* thirteen cities with their suburbs.

34 ¶ And unto the families of the children of Merari, the rest of the Levites, out of the tribe of Zebulun, Jokneam with her suburbs, and Kartah with her suburbs,

35 Dimnah with her suburbs, Nahalal with her suburbs; four cities.

36 And out of the tribe of Reuben, Bezer with her suburbs, and Jahazah with her suburbs,

37 Kedemoth with her suburbs, and Mephaath with her suburbs; four cities.

38 And out of the tribe of Gad, Ramoth in Gilead with her suburbs, *to be* a city of refuge for the slayer; and Mahanaim with her suburbs,

39 Heshbon with her suburbs, Jazer with her suburbs; four cities in all.

40 So all the cities for the children of Merari by their families, which were remaining of the families of the Levites, were *by* their lot twelve cities.

41 All the cities of the Levites within the possession of the children of Israel *were* forty and eight cities with their suburbs.

42 These cities were every one with their suburbs round about them: thus *were* all these cities.

43 ¶ And the LORD gave unto Israel all the land which he sware to give unto their fathers; and they possessed it, and dwelt therein.

44 And the LORD gave them rest round about, according to all that he sware unto their fathers: and there stood not a man of all their enemies before them; the LORD delivered all their enemies into their hand.

45 There failed not aught of any good thing which the LORD had spoken unto the house of Israel; all came to pass.

## Amplified

19 The cities of the sons of Aaron, the priests, were thirteen, with their suburbs.

20 The rest of the Kohathites belonging to the Levitical families were allotted cities out of the tribe of Ephraim.

21 To them were given, each with its pasture lands [suburbs], Shechem in the hill country of Ephraim, as the city of refuge for the slayer, and Gezer,

22 And Kibzaim, and Beth-horon; four cities, each with its pasture lands [suburbs].

23 And out of the tribe of Dan, each with its pasture lands [suburbs], Elteke, Gibbethon,

24 Aijalon, and Gath-rimmon; four cities, each with its pasture lands [suburbs].

25 And out of the half tribe of Manasseh, Taanach, and [another] Gath-rimmon; two cities, each with its pasture lands [suburbs].

26 All the cities for the families of the remaining Kohathites were ten, with their pasture lands [suburbs].

27 And to the Gershonites, of the families of the Levites, they gave out of the other half tribe of Manasseh the city of Golan in Bashan, as the city of refuge for the slayer, and Be-eshterah; two cities, each with its pasture lands.

28 Out of the tribe of Issachar, Kishion, Daberath,

29 Jarmuth, and En-gannim; four cities, each with its suburbs.

30 Out of the tribe of Asher, Mishal, Abdon,

31 Helkath, and Rehob; four cities, each with its pasture lands.

32 And out of the tribe of Naphtali, Kedesh in Galilee, city of refuge for the slayer; and Hammoth-dor, and Kartan; three cities, each with its suburbs.

33 All the cities of the Gershonite families were thirteen with their pasture lands [suburbs].

34 And to the families of the Merarites, the rest of the Levites, out of the tribe of Zebulun were given Jokneam, Kartah,

35 Dimnah, and Nahalal; four cities, each with its pasture lands [suburbs].

36 And out of the tribe of Reuben, Bezer, Jahaz,

37 Kedemoth, and Mephaath; four cities, each with its pasture lands [suburbs].

38 And out of the tribe of Gad, Ramoth in Gilead as the city of refuge for the slayer; and Mahanaim,

39 Heshbon, and Jazer; four cities in all, each with its pasture lands [suburbs].

40 So all the cities allotted to the Merarite families, that is, the remainder of the Levite families, were twelve cities.

41 The cities of the Levites in the midst of the possession of the Israelites were in all forty-eight cities with their pasture lands [suburbs].

42 These cities all had their pasture lands [suburbs] around them.

43 And the Lord gave to Israel all the land which He swore to give to their fathers; and they possessed it, and dwelt in it.

44 The Lord gave them rest round about just as He swore to their fathers; not one of all their enemies withstood them; the Lord delivered all their enemies into their hand.

45 There failed no part of any good thing which the Lord had promised to the house of Israel; all came to pass.

## New American Standard

19All the cities of the sons of Aaron, the priests, were thirteen
cities with their pasture lands.
20¶ Then the cities from the tribe of Ephraim were allotted to the
families of the sons of Kohath, the Levites, *even to* the rest of the
sons of Kohath.
21And they gave them Shechem, the city of refuge for the manslayer, with its pasture lands, in the hill country of Ephraim, and
Gezer with its pasture lands,
22and Kibzaim with its pasture lands and Beth-horon with its
pasture lands; four cities.
23And from the tribe of Dan, Elteke with its pasture lands,
Gibbethon with its pasture lands,
24Aijalon with its pasture lands, Gath-rimmon with its pasture
lands; four cities.
25And from the half-tribe of Manasseh, *they allotted* Taanach
with its pasture lands and Gath-rimmon with its pasture lands;
two cities.
26All the cities with their pasture lands for the families of the
rest of the sons of Kohath were ten.
27¶ And to the sons of Gershon, one of the families of the
Levites, from the half-tribe of Manasseh, *they gave* Golan in Bashan, the city of refuge for the manslayer, with its pasture lands,
and Be-eshterah with its pasture lands; two cities.
28And from the tribe of Issachar, *they gave* Kishion with its
pasture lands, Daberath with its pasture lands,
29Jarmuth with its pasture lands, En-gannim with its pasture
lands; four cities.
30And from the tribe of Asher, *they gave* Mishal with its pasture
lands, Abdon with its pasture lands,
31Helkath with its pasture lands and Rehob with its pasture
lands; four cities.
32And from the tribe of Naphtali, *they gave* Kedesh in Galilee,
the city of refuge for the manslayer, with its pasture lands and
Hammoth-dor with its pasture lands and Kartan with its pasture
lands; three cities.
33All the cities of the Gershonites according to their families
were thirteen cities with their pasture lands.
34¶ And to the families of the sons of Merari, the rest of the
Levites, *they gave* from the tribe of Zebulun, Jokneam with its
pasture lands and Kartah with its pasture lands.
35Dimnah with its pasture lands, Nahalal with its pasture lands;
four cities.
36And from the tribe of Reuben, *they gave* Bezer with its pasture
lands and Jahaz with its pasture lands,
37Kedemoth with its pasture lands and Mephaath with its pasture lands; four cities.
38And from the tribe of Gad, *they gave* Ramoth in Gilead, the city
of refuge for the manslayer, with its pasture lands and Mahanaim
with its pasture lands,
39Heshbon with its pasture lands, Jazer with its pasture lands;
four cities in all.
40All *these were* the cities of the sons of Merari according to their
families, the rest of the families of the Levites; and their lot was
twelve cities.
41¶ All the cities of the Levites in the midst of the possession of
the sons of Israel were forty-eight cities with their pasture lands.
42These cities each had its surrounding pasture lands; thus *it
was* with all these cities.
43¶ So the LORD gave Israel all the land which He had sworn to
give to their fathers, and they possessed it and lived in it.
44And the LORD gave them rest on every side, according to all
that He had sworn to their fathers, and no one of all their enemies
stood before them; the LORD gave all their enemies into their hand.
45Not one of the good promises which the LORD had made to
the house of Israel failed; all came to pass.

## New International

19All the towns for the priests, the descendants of Aaron, were
thirteen, together with their pasturelands.

20The rest of the Kohathite clans of the Levites were allotted towns
from the tribe of Ephraim:
21In the hill country of Ephraim they were given Shechem
(a city of refuge for one accused of murder) and Gezer, 22Kib-
zaim and Beth Horon, together with their pasturelands—four
towns.
23Also from the tribe of Dan they received Eltekeh, Gibbethon, 24Aijalon and Gath Rimmon, together with their pasturelands—four towns.
25From half the tribe of Manasseh they received Taanach
and Gath Rimmon, together with their pasturelands—two
towns.
26All these ten towns and their pasturelands were given to the rest
of the Kohathite clans.
27The Levite clans of the Gershonites were given:
from the half-tribe of Manasseh,
Golan in Bashan (a city of refuge for one accused of murder)
and Be Eshtarah, together with their pasturelands—two
towns;
28from the tribe of Issachar,
Kishion, Daberath, 29Jarmuth and En Gannim, together with
their pasturelands—four towns;
30from the tribe of Asher,
Mishal, Abdon, 31Helkath and Rehob, together with their
pasturelands—four towns;
32from the tribe of Naphtali,
Kedesh in Galilee (a city of refuge for one accused of murder),
Hammoth Dor and Kartan, together with their pasturelands—three towns.
33All the towns of the Gershonite clans were thirteen, together
with their pasturelands.
34The Merarite clans (the rest of the Levites) were given:
from the tribe of Zebulun,
Jokneam, Kartah, 35Dimnah and Nahalal, together with their
pasturelands—four towns;
36from the tribe of Reuben,
Bezer, Jahaz, 37Kedemoth and Mephaath, together with their
pasturelands—four towns;
38from the tribe of Gad,
Ramoth in Gilead (a city of refuge for one accused of murder),
Mahanaim, 39Heshbon and Jazer, together with their pasturelands—four towns in all.
40All the towns allotted to the Merarite clans, who were the rest
of the Levites, were twelve.
41The towns of the Levites in the territory held by the Israelites
were forty-eight in all, together with their pasturelands. 42Each of
these towns had pasturelands surrounding it; this was true for all
these towns.
43So the LORD gave Israel all the land he had sworn to give their
forefathers, and they took possession of it and settled there. 44The
LORD gave them rest on every side, just as he had sworn to their
forefathers. Not one of their enemies withstood them; the LORD
handed all their enemies over to them. 45Not one of all the LORD's
good promises to the house of Israel failed; every one was fulfilled.

## King James

22 THEN JOSHUA called the Reubenites, and the Gadites,
and the half tribe of Manasseh,
2And said unto them, Ye have kept all that Moses the servant
of the LORD commanded you, and have obeyed my voice in all that
I commanded you:
3Ye have not left your brethren these many days unto this day,
but have kept the charge of the commandment of the LORD your
God.
4And now the LORD your God hath given rest unto your brethren, as he promised them: therefore now return ye, and get you
unto your tents, *and* unto the land of your possession, which
Moses the servant of the LORD gave you on the other side Jordan.
5But take diligent heed to do the commandment and the law,
which Moses the servant of the LORD charged you, to love the
LORD your God, and to walk in all his ways, and to keep his
commandments, and to cleave unto him, and to serve him with all
your heart and with all your soul.
6So Joshua blessed them, and sent them away: and they went
unto their tents.
7¶ Now to the *one* half of the tribe of Manasseh Moses had given
*possession* in Bashan: but unto the *other* half thereof gave Joshua
among their brethren on this side Jordan westward. And when
Joshua sent them away also unto their tents, then he blessed them,
8And he spake unto them, saying, Return with much riches
unto your tents, and with very much cattle, with silver, and with
gold, and with brass, and with iron, and with very much raiment:
divide the spoil of your enemies with your brethren.
9¶ And the children of Reuben and the children of Gad and the
half tribe of Manasseh returned, and departed from the children
of Israel out of Shiloh, which *is* in the land of Canaan, to go unto
the country of Gilead, to the land of their possession, whereof they
were possessed, according to the word of the LORD by the hand
of Moses.
10¶ And when they came unto the borders of Jordan, that *are*
in the land of Canaan, the children of Reuben and the children of
Gad and the half tribe of Manasseh built there an altar by Jordan,
a great altar to see to.
11¶ And the children of Israel heard say, Behold, the children
of Reuben and the children of Gad and the half tribe of Manasseh
have built an altar over against the land of Canaan, in the borders
of Jordan, at the passage of the children of Israel.
12And when the children of Israel heard *of it*, the whole congregation of the children of Israel gathered themselves together at
Shiloh, to go up to war against them.
13And the children of Israel sent unto the children of Reuben,
and to the children of Gad, and to the half tribe of Manasseh, into
the land of Gilead, Phinehas the son of Eleazar the priest,
14And with him ten princes, of each chief house a prince
throughout all the tribes of Israel; and each one *was* an head of the
house of their fathers among the thousands of Israel.
15¶ And they came unto the children of Reuben, and to the
children of Gad, and to the half tribe of Manasseh, unto the land
of Gilead, and they spake with them, saying,
16Thus saith the whole congregation of the LORD, What trespass
*is* this that ye have committed against the God of Israel, to turn
away this day from following the LORD, in that ye have builded
you an altar, that ye might rebel this day against the LORD?
17 *Is* the iniquity of Peor too little for us, from which we are not
cleansed until this day, although there was a plague in the congregation of the LORD,
18But that ye must turn away this day from following the LORD?
and it will be, *seeing* ye rebel today against the LORD, that tomorrow he will be wroth with the whole congregation of Israel.
19Notwithstanding, if the land of your possession *be* unclean,
*then* pass ye over unto the land of the possession of the LORD,
wherein the LORD's tabernacle dwelleth, and take possession
among us: but rebel not against the LORD, nor rebel against us, in
building you an altar beside the altar of the LORD our God.

## Amplified

22 THEN JOSHUA called the Reubenites, the Gadites, and
the half tribe of Manasseh,
2And said to them, You have kept all that Moses the servant of
the Lord commanded you, and have obeyed my voice in all that
I commanded you;
3You have not deserted your brethren [the other tribes] these
many days until now, but have carefully kept the charge of the
Lord your God.
4But now the Lord your God has given rest to your brethren,
as He promised them; so now go, return to your homes in the land
of your possession, which Moses the servant of the Lord gave you
on the *east* side of the Jordan.
5But take diligent heed to do the commandment and the law,
which Moses the servant of the Lord charged you, to love the Lord
your God, and to walk in all His ways, and to keep His commandments, and to cling to *and* unite with Him, and to serve Him with
all your heart and soul [your very life].
6So Joshua blessed them, and sent them away; and they went
to their homes.
7Now to one-half of the tribe of Manasseh Moses had given a
possession in Bashan; but to the other half Joshua gave a possession on this the west side of the Jordan among their brethren. Also
when Joshua sent them away to their homes, he blessed them,
8And he said to them, Return with much riches to your tents,
and with very much livestock, with silver, gold, bronze, iron, and
very much clothing. Divide the spoil of your enemies with your
brethren.
9So the Reubenites, Gadites, and the half-tribe of Manasseh
returned home, parting from the [other] Israelites at Shiloh in the
land of Canaan, to go to the land of Gilead, their own land of which
they had been given possession by the command of the Lord
through Moses.
10And when they came to the region of the Jordan, in the land
of Canaan, the Reubenites, Gadites, and the half-tribe of Manasseh built there an altar by the Jordan, an altar great to behold.
11And the [other] Israelites heard it said, Behold, the Reubenites, Gadites, and the half-tribe of Manasseh have built an altar at
the edge of the land of Canaan, in the region [west] of Jordan, in
the passage [belonging to us], the Israelites.
12When the Israelites heard of it, the whole congregation of the
sons of Israel gathered at Shiloh, to make war on them.
13And the [other] Israelites sent to the Reubenites, Gadites, and
the half-tribe of Manasseh, in the land of Gilead, Phinehas son of
Eleazar the priest,
14And with him ten chiefs, one from each of the tribal families
of Israel; and each one was a head of a fathers' house among the
clans of Israel.
15And they came to the Reubenites, Gadites, and the half-tribe
of Manasseh, in the land of Gilead, and they said to them,
16The whole congregation of the Lord says, What trespass is
this that you have committed against the God of Israel, to turn
away this day from following the Lord, in that you have built you
an altar, to rebel this day against the Lord?
17Is the iniquity of Peor too little for us, from which we are not
cleansed even now, although there came a plague [in which 24,000
died] in the congregation of the Lord, [Num. 25:1-9.]
18That you must turn away this day from following the Lord?
The result will be, since you rebel today against the Lord, that
tomorrow He will be angry with the whole congregation of Israel.
19But now, if your land is unclean, pass over into the Lord's
land, where the Lord's tabernacle resides, and take for yourselves
a possession among us. But do not rebel against the Lord, or rebel
against us, by building you an altar other than the altar of the Lord
our God.

## New American Standard

*Tribes beyond Jordan Return*

**22** THEN JOSHUA summoned the Reubenites and the Gadites and the half-tribe of Manasseh,

2and said to them, "You have kept all that Moses the servant of the LORD commanded you, and have listened to my voice in all that I commanded you.

3"You have not forsaken your brothers these many days to this day, but have kept the charge of the commandment of the LORD your God.

4"And now the LORD your God has given rest to your brothers, as He spoke to them; therefore turn now and go to your tents, to the land of your possession, which Moses the servant of the LORD gave you beyond the Jordan.

5"Only be very careful to observe the commandment and the law which Moses the servant of the LORD commanded you, to love the LORD your God and walk in all His ways and keep His commandments and hold fast to Him and serve Him with all your heart and with all your soul."

6So Joshua blessed them and sent them away, and they went to their tents.

7¶ Now to the one half-tribe of Manasseh Moses had given *a possession* in Bashan, but to the other half Joshua gave *a possession* among their brothers westward beyond the Jordan. So when Joshua sent them away to their tents, he blessed them,

8and said to them, "Return to your tents with great riches and with very much livestock, with silver, gold, bronze, iron, and with very many clothes; divide the spoil of your enemies with your brothers."

9And the sons of Reuben and the sons of Gad and the half-tribe of Manasseh returned *home* and departed from the sons of Israel at Shiloh which is in the land of Canaan, to go to the land of Gilead, to the land of their possession which they had possessed, according to the command of the LORD through Moses.

*The Offensive Altar*

10¶ And when they came to the region of the Jordan which is in the land of Canaan, the sons of Reuben and the sons of Gad and the half-tribe of Manasseh built an altar there by the Jordan, a large altar in appearance.

11And the sons of Israel heard *it* said, "Behold, the sons of Reuben and the sons of Gad and the half-tribe of Manasseh have built an altar at the frontier of the land of Canaan, in the region of the Jordan, on the side *belonging to* the sons of Israel."

12And when the sons of Israel heard *of it*, the whole congregation of the sons of Israel gathered themselves at Shiloh, to go up against them in war.

13¶ Then the sons of Israel sent to the sons of Reuben and to the sons of Gad and to the half-tribe of Manasseh, into the land of Gilead, Phinehas the son of Eleazar the priest,

14and with him ten chiefs, one chief for each father's household from each of the tribes of Israel; and each one of them *was* the head of his father's household among the thousands of Israel.

15And they came to the sons of Reuben and to the sons of Gad and to the half-tribe of Manasseh, to the land of Gilead, and they spoke with them saying,

16"Thus says the whole congregation of the LORD, 'What is this unfaithful act which you have committed against the God of Israel, turning away from following the LORD this day, by building yourselves an altar, to rebel against the LORD this day?

17'Is not the iniquity of Peor enough for us, from which we have not cleansed ourselves to this day, although a plague came on the congregation of the LORD,

18that you must turn away this day from following the LORD? And it will come about if you rebel against the LORD today, that He will be angry with the whole congregation of Israel tomorrow.

19'If, however, the land of your possession is unclean, then cross into the land of the possession of the LORD, where the LORD's tabernacle stands, and take possession among us. Only do not rebel against the LORD, or rebel against us by building an altar for yourselves, besides the altar of the LORD our God.

## New International

*Eastern Tribes Return Home*

**22** THEN JOSHUA summoned the Reubenites, the Gadites
and the half-tribe of Manasseh 2and said to them, "You
have done all that Moses the servant of the LORD commanded, and
you have obeyed me in everything I commanded. 3For a long time
now—to this very day—you have not deserted your brothers but
have carried out the mission the LORD your God gave you. 4Now
that the LORD your God has given your brothers rest as he promised, return to your homes in the land that Moses the servant of
the LORD gave you on the other side of the Jordan. 5But be very
careful to keep the commandment and the law that Moses the
servant of the LORD gave you: to love the LORD your God, to walk
in all his ways, to obey his commands, to hold fast to him and to
serve him with all your heart and all your soul."

6Then Joshua blessed them and sent them away, and they went
to their homes. 7(To the half-tribe of Manasseh Moses had given
land in Bashan, and to the other half of the tribe Joshua gave land
on the west side of the Jordan with their brothers.) When Joshua
sent them home, he blessed them, 8saying, "Return to your homes
with your great wealth—with large herds of livestock, with silver,
gold, bronze and iron, and a great quantity of clothing—and divide
with your brothers the plunder from your enemies."

9So the Reubenites, the Gadites and the half-tribe of Manasseh
left the Israelites at Shiloh in Canaan to return to Gilead, their own
land, which they had acquired in accordance with the command
of the LORD through Moses.

10When they came to Geliloth near the Jordan in the land of
Canaan, the Reubenites, the Gadites and the half-tribe of Manasseh built an imposing altar there by the Jordan. 11And when the
Israelites heard that they had built the altar on the border of
Canaan at Geliloth near the Jordan on the Israelite side, 12the
whole assembly of Israel gathered at Shiloh to go to war against
them.

13So the Israelites sent Phinehas son of Eleazar, the priest, to the
land of Gilead—to Reuben, Gad and the half-tribe of Manasseh.
14With him they sent ten of the chief men, one for each of the tribes
of Israel, each the head of a family division among the Israelite
clans.

15When they went to Gilead—to Reuben, Gad and the half-tribe
of Manasseh—they said to them: 16"The whole assembly of the
LORD says: 'How could you break faith with the God of Israel like
this? How could you turn away from the LORD and build yourselves an altar in rebellion against him now? 17Was not the sin of
Peor enough for us? Up to this very day we have not cleansed
ourselves from that sin, even though a plague fell on the community of the LORD! 18And are you now turning away from the LORD?

"'If you rebel against the LORD today, tomorrow he will be
angry with the whole community of Israel. 19If the land you possess is defiled, come over to the LORD's land, where the LORD's
tabernacle stands, and share the land with us. But do not rebel
against the LORD or against us by building an altar for yourselves,
other than the altar of the LORD our God. 20When Achan son of

## King James

20Did not Achan the son of Zerah commit a trespass in the accursed thing, and wrath fell on all the congregation of Israel? and that man perished not alone in his iniquity.

21¶ Then the children of Reuben and the children of Gad and the half tribe of Manasseh answered, and said unto the heads of the thousands of Israel,

22The LORD God of gods, the LORD God of gods, he knoweth, and Israel he shall know; if *it be* in rebellion, or if in transgression against the LORD, (save us not this day,)

23That we have built us an altar to turn from following the LORD, or if to offer thereon burnt offering or meat offering, or if to offer peace offerings thereon, let the LORD himself require *it;*

24And if we have not *rather* done it for fear of *this* thing, saying, In time to come your children might speak unto our children, saying, What have ye to do with the LORD God of Israel?

25For the LORD hath made Jordan a border between us and you, ye children of Reuben and children of Gad; ye have no part in the LORD: so shall your children make our children cease from fearing the LORD.

26Therefore we said, Let us now prepare to build us an altar, not for burnt offering, nor for sacrifice:

27But *that* it *may be* a witness between us, and you, and our generations after us, that we might do the service of the LORD before him with our burnt offerings, and with our sacrifices, and with our peace offerings; that your children may not say to our children in time to come, Ye have no part in the LORD.

28Therefore said we, that it shall be, when they should *so* say to us or to our generations in time to come, that we may say *again,* Behold the pattern of the altar of the LORD, which our fathers made, not for burnt offerings, nor for sacrifices; but it *is* a witness between us and you.

29God forbid that we should rebel against the LORD, and turn this day from following the LORD, to build an altar for burnt offerings, for meat offerings, or for sacrifices, beside the altar of the LORD our God that *is* before his tabernacle.

30¶ And when Phinehas the priest, and the princes of the congregation and heads of the thousands of Israel which *were* with him, heard the words that the children of Reuben and the children of Gad and the children of Manasseh spake, it pleased them.

31And Phinehas the son of Eleazar the priest said unto the children of Reuben, and to the children of Gad, and to the children of Manasseh, This day we perceive that the LORD *is* among us, because ye have not committed this trespass against the LORD: now ye have delivered the children of Israel out of the hand of the LORD.

32¶ And Phinehas the son of Eleazar the priest, and the princes, returned from the children of Reuben, and from the children of Gad, out of the land of Gilead, unto the land of Canaan, to the children of Israel, and brought them word again.

33And the thing pleased the children of Israel; and the children of Israel blessed God, and did not intend to go up against them in battle, to destroy the land wherein the children of Reuben and Gad dwelt.

34And the children of Reuben and the children of Gad called the altar *Ed:* for it *shall be* a witness between us that the LORD *is* God.

## Amplified

20Did not Achan, son of Zerah, commit a trespass in the matter of taking accursed things [devoted to destruction], and wrath fell on all the congregation of Israel? And he did not perish alone in his perversity *and* iniquity. [Josh. 7.]

21Then the Reubenites, Gadites, and the half-tribe of Manasseh said to the heads of the clans of Israel,

22The Mighty One, God, the Lord! The Mighty One, God, the Lord! He knows, and let Israel itself know! If it was in rebellion, or in transgression against the Lord, spare us not today;

23If we have built us an altar to turn away from following the Lord, or if we did so to offer on it burnt offerings or cereal offerings or peace offerings, may the Lord Himself take vengeance.

24No! But we did it from fear that in time to come your children might say to our children, What have you to do with the Lord God of Israel?

25For the Lord has made the Jordan a boundary between us and you, you Reubenites and Gadites; you have no part in the Lord. So your children might make our children cease from fearing the Lord.

26So we said, Let us now prepare to build us an altar, not for burnt offering, nor for sacrifice,

27But to be a witness between us and you, and between the generations after us, that we do perform the service of the Lord before Him with our burnt offerings and sacrifices and peace offerings; lest your children say to our children in time to come, You have no portion in the Lord.

28So we thought, if that should be said to us or to our descendants in time to come, we can reply, Behold the copy of the altar of the Lord, which our fathers made, not for burnt offerings, nor for sacrifices; but to be a witness between us and you.

29Far be it from us that we should rebel against the Lord, and turn this day from following the Lord, to build an altar for burnt offerings, for cereal offerings, or for sacrifices, besides the altar of the Lord our God that is before His tabernacle.

30And when Phinehas the priest, and the chiefs of the congregation, and heads of the clans of Israel who were with him, heard the words that the Reubenites, Gadites, and Manassites spoke, it pleased them.

31Phinehas son of Eleazar the priest said to the Reubenites, Gadites, and Manassites, Today we know the Lord is among us, because you have not committed this trespass *and* treachery against the Lord; now you have saved the Israelites from the Lord's hand.

32Then Phinehas son of Eleazar the priest, and the chiefs, returned from the Reubenites and Gadites in the land of Gilead to the land of Canaan, to the [other] Israelites, and brought back word to them.

33The report pleased the Israelites; they blessed God, and spoke no more of going to war against them, to destroy the land in which the Reubenites and Gadites dwelt.

34The Reubenites and Gadites called the altar Ed [witness], saying, It shall be a witness between us that the Lord is God.

**23** AND IT came to pass a long time after that the LORD had given rest unto Israel from all their enemies round about, that Joshua waxed old *and* stricken in age.

2And Joshua called for all Israel, *and* for their elders, and for their heads, and for their judges, and for their officers, and said unto them, I am old *and* stricken in age:

**23** A LONG time after that, when the Lord had given Israel rest from all their enemies round about, and Joshua had grown old and advanced in years,

2Joshua summoned all Israel, their elders, heads, judges, and officers, and said to them, I am old and advanced in years;

## New American Standard

20'Did not Achan the son of Zerah act unfaithfully in the things under the ban, and wrath fall on all the congregation of Israel? And that man did not perish alone in his iniquity.' "

21¶ Then the sons of Reuben and the sons of Gad and the half-tribe of Manasseh answered, and spoke to the heads of the families of Israel.

22"The Mighty One, God, the LORD, the Mighty One, God, the LORD! He knows, and may Israel itself know. If *it was* in rebellion, or if in an unfaithful act against the LORD do not Thou save us this day!

23"If we have built us an altar to turn away from following the LORD, or if to offer a burnt offering or grain offering on it, or if to offer sacrifices of peace offerings on it, may the LORD Himself require it.

24"But truly we have done this out of concern, for a reason, saying, 'In time to come your sons may say to our sons, "What have you to do with the LORD, the God of Israel?

25"For the LORD has made the Jordan a border between us and you, *you* sons of Reuben and sons of Gad; you have no portion in the LORD." So your sons may make our sons stop fearing the LORD.'

26¶ "Therefore we said, 'Let us build an altar, not for burnt offering or for sacrifice;

27rather it shall be a witness between us and you and between our generations after us, that we are to perform the service of the LORD before Him with our burnt offerings, and with our sacrifices and with our peace offerings, that your sons may not say to our sons in time to come, "You have no portion in the LORD." '

28"Therefore we said, 'It shall also come about if they say *this* to us or to our generations in time to come, then we shall say, "See the copy of the altar of the LORD which our fathers made, not for burnt offering or for sacrifice; rather it is a witness between us and you." '

29"Far be it from us that we should rebel against the LORD and turn away from following the LORD this day, by building an altar for burnt offering, for grain offering or for sacrifice, besides the altar of the LORD our God which is before His [a]tabernacle."

30¶ So when Phinehas the priest and the leaders of the congregation, even the heads of the families of Israel who *were* with him, heard the words which the sons of Reuben and the sons of Gad and the sons of Manasseh spoke, it pleased them.

31And Phinehas the son of Eleazar the priest said to the sons of Reuben and to the sons of Gad and to the sons of Manasseh, "Today we know that the LORD is in our midst, because you have not committed this unfaithful act against the LORD; now you have delivered the sons of Israel from the hand of the LORD."

32Then Phinehas the son of Eleazar the priest and the leaders returned from the sons of Reuben and from the sons of Gad, from the land of Gilead, to the land of Canaan, to the sons of Israel, and brought back word to them.

33And the word pleased the sons of Israel, and the sons of Israel blessed God; and they did not speak of going up against them in war, to destroy the land in which the sons of Reuben and the sons of Gad were living.

34And the sons of Reuben and the sons of Gad called the altar *Witness;* "For," *they said,* "it is a witness between us that the LORD is God."

*Joshua's Farewell Address*

**23** NOW IT came about after many days, when the LORD had given rest to Israel from all their enemies on every side, and Joshua was old, advanced in years,

2that Joshua called for all Israel, for their elders and their heads and their judges and their officers, and said to them, "I am old, advanced in years.

NAS [a] Lit., *dwelling place*

## New International

Zerah acted unfaithfully regarding the devoted things,[b] did not
wrath come upon the whole community of Israel? He was not the
only one who died for his sin.' "
21Then Reuben, Gad and the half-tribe of Manasseh replied to
the heads of the clans of Israel: 22"The Mighty One, God, the LORD!
The Mighty One, God, the LORD! He knows! And let Israel know!
If this has been in rebellion or disobedience to the LORD, do not
spare us this day. 23If we have built our own altar to turn away
from the LORD and to offer burnt offerings and grain offerings, or
to sacrifice fellowship offerings[c] on it, may the LORD himself call
us to account.
24"No! We did it for fear that some day your descendants might
say to ours, 'What do you have to do with the LORD, the God of
Israel? 25The LORD has made the Jordan a boundary between us
and you—you Reubenites and Gadites! You have no share in the
LORD.' So your descendants might cause ours to stop fearing the
LORD.
26"That is why we said, 'Let us get ready and build an altar—but
not for burnt offerings or sacrifices.' 27On the contrary, it is to be
a witness between us and you and the generations that follow, that
we will worship the LORD at his sanctuary with our burnt offerings,
sacrifices and fellowship offerings. Then in the future your descendants will not be able to say to ours, 'You have no share in the
LORD.'
28"And we said, 'If they ever say this to us, or to our descendants, we will answer: Look at the replica of the LORD's altar, which
our fathers built, not for burnt offerings and sacrifices, but as a
witness between us and you.'
29"Far be it from us to rebel against the LORD and turn away
from him today by building an altar for burnt offerings, grain
offerings and sacrifices, other than the altar of the LORD our God
that stands before his tabernacle."
30When Phinehas the priest and the leaders of the community—
the heads of the clans of the Israelites—heard what Reuben, Gad
and Manasseh had to say, they were pleased. 31And Phinehas son
of Eleazar, the priest, said to Reuben, Gad and Manasseh, "Today
we know that the LORD is with us, because you have not acted
unfaithfully toward the LORD in this matter. Now you have rescued the Israelites from the LORD's hand."
32Then Phinehas son of Eleazar, the priest, and the leaders
returned to Canaan from their meeting with the Reubenites and
Gadites in Gilead and reported to the Israelites. 33They were glad
to hear the report and praised God. And they talked no more about
going to war against them to devastate the country where the
Reubenites and the Gadites lived.
34And the Reubenites and the Gadites gave the altar this name:
A Witness Between Us that the LORD is God.

*Joshua's Farewell to the Leaders*

**23** AFTER A long time had passed and the LORD had given
Israel rest from all their enemies around them, Joshua, by
then old and well advanced in years, 2summoned all Israel—their
elders, leaders, judges and officials—and said to them: "I am old
and well advanced in years. 3You yourselves have seen everything

NIV [b] 20 The Hebrew term refers to the irrevocable giving over of things or persons to the LORD, often by totally destroying them. [c] 23 Traditionally *peace offerings;* also in verse 27

## King James

3And ye have seen all that the LORD your God hath done unto all these nations because of you; for the LORD your God *is* he that hath fought for you.

4Behold, I have divided unto you by lot these nations that remain, to be an inheritance for your tribes, from Jordan, with all the nations that I have cut off, even unto the great sea westward.

5And the LORD your God, he shall expel them from before you, and drive them from out of your sight; and ye shall possess their land, as the LORD your God hath promised unto you.

6Be ye therefore very courageous to keep and to do all that is written in the book of the law of Moses, that ye turn not aside therefrom *to* the right hand or *to* the left;

7That ye come not among these nations, these that remain among you; neither make mention of the name of their gods, nor cause to swear *by them,* neither serve them, nor bow yourselves unto them:

8But cleave unto the LORD your God, as ye have done unto this day.

9For the LORD hath driven out from before you great nations and strong: but *as for* you, no man hath been able to stand before you unto this day.

10One man of you shall chase a thousand: for the LORD your God, he *it is* that fighteth for you, as he hath promised you.

11Take good heed therefore unto yourselves, that ye love the LORD your God.

12Else if ye do in any wise go back, and cleave unto the remnant of these nations, *even* these that remain among you, and shall make marriages with them, and go in unto them, and they to you:

13Know for a certainty that the LORD your God will no more drive out *any of* these nations from before you; but they shall be snares and traps unto you, and scourges in your sides, and thorns in your eyes, until ye perish from off this good land which the LORD your God hath given you.

14And, behold, this day I *am* going the way of all the earth: and ye know in all your hearts and in all your souls, that not one thing hath failed of all the good things which the LORD your God spake concerning you; all are come to pass unto you, *and* not one thing hath failed thereof.

15Therefore it shall come to pass, *that* as all good things are come upon you, which the LORD your God promised you; so shall the LORD bring upon you all evil things, until he have destroyed you from off this good land which the LORD your God hath given you.

16When ye have transgressed the covenant of the LORD your God, which he commanded you, and have gone and served other gods, and bowed yourselves to them; then shall the anger of the LORD be kindled against you, and ye shall perish quickly from off the good land which he hath given unto you.

**24** AND JOSHUA gathered all the tribes of Israel to Shechem, and called for the elders of Israel, and for their heads, and for their judges, and for their officers; and they presented themselves before God.

2And Joshua said unto all the people, Thus saith the LORD God of Israel, Your fathers dwelt on the other side of the flood in old time, *even* Terah, the father of Abraham, and the father of Nachor: and they served other gods.

## Amplified

3And you have seen all that the Lord your God has done to all these nations for your sake, for it is the Lord your God Who has fought for you. [Exod. 14:14.]

4Behold, I have allotted to you, as an inheritance for your tribes those nations that remain, with all the nations I have cut off, from the Jordan to the Great Sea on the west.

5The Lord your God will thrust them out from before you, and drive them out of your sight; and you shall possess their land, as the Lord your God [a]promised you.

6So be very courageous *and* steadfast to keep and do all that is written in the book of the law of Moses, turning not aside from it to the right hand or the left,

7That you may not mix with these nations that remain among you, or make mention of the names of their gods, or swear by them, or serve them, or bow down to them;

8But cling to the Lord your God as you have done to this day.

9For the Lord has driven out from before you great and strong nations; and as for you, no man has been able to withstand you to this day.

10One man of you shall put to flight a thousand; for it is the Lord your God Who fights for you, as He promised you.

11Be very watchful of yourselves, therefore, to [b]love the Lord your God.

12For if you turn back and adhere to the remnant of these nations left among you, and make marriages with them, you marrying their women and they yours,

13Know for a certainty that the Lord your God will not continue to drive these nations from before you, but they shall be a snare and trap to you, and a scourge in your sides, and thorns in your eyes, until you perish from off this good land which the Lord your God has given you.

14And behold, this day I am going the way of all the earth; know in all your hearts and in all your souls, that not one thing has failed of all the good things which the Lord your God promised concerning you; all have come to pass for you, not one thing of them has failed.

15But just as all good things which the Lord has promised you have come to you, so will the Lord carry out [His] every [warning of] evil upon you, until He has destroyed you from off this good land which the Lord your God has given you.

16If you transgress the covenant of the Lord your God, which He commanded you, if you serve other gods, and bow down to them, then the anger of the Lord will be kindled against you, and you shall perish quickly from off the good land He has given you.

**24** THEN JOSHUA gathered all the tribes of Israel to Shechem, and summoned the elders of Israel, and their heads, their judges, and their officers; they presented themselves before God.

2Joshua said to all the people, Thus says the Lord, the God of Israel, Your fathers dwelt in olden times beyond the Euphrates River, Terah, the father of Abraham and Nahor; and they served other gods.

**AMP** [a] All through the time of Joshua's leadership he kept giving as his warrant of faith the fact that the Lord had said, had promised. The word of God is the guaranty of faith. Genuine faith always advances on the authority expressed in Heb. 13:5, 6, "HE (God) Himself has said . . . So WE take comfort *and* are encouraged *and* confidently *and* boldly SAY . . ." [b] All depended on whether or not Israel would continue faithful to the covenant. Joshua's words do not conceal his apprehension. Seven times he refers to the idolatrous nations still left in Canaan. He knew the snare they would be to Israel, and he therefore prescribed three safeguards. First, there must be brave *adherence to God's word* (v. 6). Second, there must be a vigilantly continued *separation* from the Canaanite nations (v. 7). And, there must be a cleaving to the Lord with real and fervent *love* (vv. 8-11). (J. Sidlow Baxter in *Explore the Book.*)

## New American Standard

3"And you have seen all that the LORD your God has done to
all these nations because of you, for the LORD your God is He who
has been fighting for you.
4"See, I have apportioned to you these nations which remain
as an inheritance for your tribes, with all the nations which I have
cut off, from the Jordan even to the Great Sea toward the setting
of the sun.
5"And the LORD your God, He shall thrust them out from
before you and drive them from before you; and you shall possess
their land, just as the LORD your God promised you.
6"Be very firm, then, to keep and do all that is written in the
book of the law of Moses, so that you may not turn aside from it
to the right hand or to the left,
7in order that you may not associate with these nations, these
which remain among you, or mention the name of their gods, or
make *anyone* swear *by them,* or serve them, or bow down to them.
8"But you are to cling to the LORD your God, as you have done
to this day.
9"For the LORD has driven out great and strong nations from
before you; and as for you, no man has stood before you to this
day.
10"One of your men puts to flight a thousand, for the LORD your
God is He who fights for you, just as He promised you.
11"So take diligent heed to yourselves to love the LORD your
God.
12"For if you ever go back and cling to the rest of these nations,
these which remain among you, and intermarry with them, so that
you associate with them and they with you,
13know with certainty that the LORD your God will not continue
to drive these nations out from before you; but they shall be a snare
and a trap to you, and a whip on your sides and thorns in your
eyes, until you perish from off this good land which the LORD your
God has given you.
14¶ "Now behold, today I am going the way of all the earth, and
you know in all your hearts and in all your souls that not one word
of all the good words which the LORD your God spoke concerning
you has failed; all have been fulfilled for you, not one of them has
failed.
15"And it shall come about that just as all the good words which
the LORD your God spoke to you have come upon you, so the LORD
will bring upon you all the threats, until He has destroyed you
from off this good land which the LORD your God has given you.
16"When you transgress the covenant of the LORD your God,
which He commanded you, and go and serve other gods, and bow
down to them, then the anger of the LORD will burn against you,
and you shall perish quickly from off the good land which He has
given you."

*Joshua Reviews Israel's History*

24 THEN JOSHUA gathered all the tribes of Israel to Shechem, and called for the elders of Israel and for their heads
and their judges and their officers; and they presented themselves
before God.
2And Joshua said to all the people, "Thus says the LORD, the
God of Israel, 'From ancient times your fathers lived beyond the
[c]River, *namely,* Terah, the father of Abraham and the father of
Nahor, and they served other gods.

NAS [c] I.e., Euphrates

## New International

the LORD your God has done to all these nations for your sake; it
was the LORD your God who fought for you. 4Remember how I
have allotted as an inheritance for your tribes all the land of the
nations that remain—the nations I conquered—between the Jordan and the Great Sea[d] in the west. 5The LORD your God himself
will drive them out of your way. He will push them out before you,
and you will take possession of their land, as the LORD your God
promised you.
6"Be very strong; be careful to obey all that is written in the Book
of the Law of Moses, without turning aside to the right or to the
left. 7Do not associate with these nations that remain among you;
do not invoke the names of their gods or swear by them. You must
not serve them or bow down to them. 8But you are to hold fast to
the LORD your God, as you have until now.
9"The LORD has driven out before you great and powerful nations; to this day no one has been able to withstand you. 10One of
you routs a thousand, because the LORD your God fights for you,
just as he promised. 11So be very careful to love the LORD your
God.
12"But if you turn away and ally yourselves with the survivors
of these nations that remain among you and if you intermarry with
them and associate with them, 13then you may be sure that the
LORD your God will no longer drive out these nations before you.
Instead, they will become snares and traps for you, whips on your
backs and thorns in your eyes, until you perish from this good
land, which the LORD your God has given you.
14"Now I am about to go the way of all the earth. You know
with all your heart and soul that not one of all the good promises
the LORD your God gave you has failed. Every promise has been
fulfilled; not one has failed. 15But just as every good promise of the
LORD your God has come true, so the LORD will bring on you all
the evil he has threatened, until he has destroyed you from this
good land he has given you. 16If you violate the covenant of the
LORD your God, which he commanded you, and go and serve
other gods and bow down to them, the LORD's anger will burn
against you, and you will quickly perish from the good land he has
given you."

*The Covenant Renewed at Shechem*

24 THEN JOSHUA assembled all the tribes of Israel at Shechem. He summoned the elders, leaders, judges and officials of Israel, and they presented themselves before God.
2Joshua said to all the people, "This is what the LORD, the God
of Israel, says: 'Long ago your forefathers, including Terah the
father of Abraham and Nahor, lived beyond the River[e] and worshiped other gods. 3But I took your father Abraham from the land

NIV [d] 4 That is, the Mediterranean [e] 2 That is, the Euphrates; also in verses 3, 14 and 15

## King James

3And I took your father Abraham from the other side of the flood, and led him throughout all the land of Canaan, and multiplied his seed, and gave him Isaac.

4And I gave unto Isaac Jacob and Esau: and I gave unto Esau mount Seir, to possess it; but Jacob and his children went down into Egypt.

5I sent Moses also and Aaron, and I plagued Egypt, according to that which I did among them: and afterward I brought you out.

6And I brought your fathers out of Egypt: and ye came unto the sea; and the Egyptians pursued after your fathers with chariots and horsemen unto the Red sea.

7And when they cried unto the LORD, he put darkness between you and the Egyptians, and brought the sea upon them, and covered them; and your eyes have seen what I have done in Egypt: and ye dwelt in the wilderness a long season.

8And I brought you into the land of the Amorites, which dwelt on the other side Jordan; and they fought with you: and I gave them into your hand, that ye might possess their land; and I destroyed them from before you.

9Then Balak the son of Zippor, king of Moab, arose and warred against Israel, and sent and called Balaam the son of Beor to curse you:

10But I would not hearken unto Balaam; therefore he blessed you still: so I delivered you out of his hand.

11And ye went over Jordan, and came unto Jericho: and the men of Jericho fought against you, the Amorites, and the Perizzites, and the Canaanites, and the Hittites, and the Girgashites, the Hivites, and the Jebusites; and I delivered them into your hand.

12And I sent the hornet before you, which drave them out from before you, *even* the two kings of the Amorites; *but* not with thy sword, nor with thy bow.

13And I have given you a land for which ye did not labour, and cities which ye built not, and ye dwell in them; of the vineyards and oliveyards which ye planted not do ye eat.

14¶ Now therefore fear the LORD, and serve him in sincerity and in truth: and put away the gods which your fathers served on the other side of the flood, and in Egypt; and serve ye the LORD.

15And if it seem evil unto you to serve the LORD, choose you this day whom ye will serve; whether the gods which your fathers served that *were* on the other side of the flood, or the gods of the Amorites, in whose land ye dwell: but as for me and my house, we will serve the LORD.

16And the people answered and said, God forbid that we should forsake the LORD, to serve other gods;

17For the LORD our God, he *it is* that brought us up and our fathers out of the land of Egypt, from the house of bondage, and which did those great signs in our sight, and preserved us in all the way wherein we went, and among all the people through whom we passed:

18And the LORD drave out from before us all the people, even the Amorites which dwelt in the land: *therefore* will we also serve the LORD; for he *is* our God.

19And Joshua said unto the people, Ye cannot serve the LORD: for he *is* an holy God; he *is* a jealous God; he will not forgive your transgressions nor your sins.

20If ye forsake the LORD, and serve strange gods, then he will turn and do you hurt, and consume you, after that he hath done you good.

21And the people said unto Joshua, Nay; but we will serve the LORD.

22And Joshua said unto the people, Ye *are* witnesses against yourselves that ye have chosen you the LORD, to serve him. And they said, *We are* witnesses.

## Amplified

3And I took your father Abraham from beyond the Euphrates River and led him through all the land of Canaan, and multiplied his offspring. I gave him Isaac;

4And I gave to Isaac Jacob and Esau. And I gave to Esau the hill country of Seir to possess, and Jacob and his children went down to Egypt.

5I sent Moses and Aaron, and I plagued Egypt with what I did in the midst of it; and afterward I brought you out.

6I brought your fathers out of Egypt, and came to the sea; and the Egyptians pursued your fathers with chariots and horsemen to the Red Sea.

7When they cried to the Lord, He put darkness between you and the Egyptians, and brought the sea upon them and covered them; and your eyes saw what I did in Egypt, and you lived in the wilderness a long time [forty years]. [Josh. 5:6.]

8I brought you into the land of the Amorites, who lived on the other side of the Jordan; they fought with you, and I gave them into your hand, and you possessed their land, and I destroyed them before you.

9Then Balak son of Zippor, king of Moab, arose and warred against Israel, and sent and called Balaam son of Beor to curse you.

10But I would not listen to Balaam; therefore he blessed you; so I delivered you out of Balak's hand. [Deut: 23:5.]

11You went over Jordan, and came to Jericho, and the men of Jericho fought against you, as did the Amorites, Perizzites, Canaanites, Hittites, Girgashites, Hivites, and Jebusites; and I gave them into your hand.

12I sent the hornet [that is, terror of you] before you, which drove the two kings of the Amorites out before you; but it was not by your sword or by your bow. [Exod. 23:27, 28; Deut. 2:25; 7:20, footnote.]

13I have given you a land for which you did not labor, and cities you did not build, and you dwell in them; you eat from vineyards and oliveyards you did not plant.

14Now therefore [reverently] fear the Lord, and serve Him in sincerity and in truth; put away the gods which your fathers served on the other side of the [Euphrates] River and in Egypt, and serve the Lord.

15And if it seems evil to you to serve the Lord, choose you this day whom you will serve, whether the gods which your fathers served on the other side of the River, or the gods of the Amorites in whose land you dwell; but as for me and my house, we will serve the Lord.

16The people answered, Far be it from us to forsake the Lord, to serve other gods;

17For it is the Lord our God Who brought us and our fathers up out of the land of Egypt, from the house of bondage, Who did those great signs in our sight, and preserved us in all the way that we went, and among all the peoples through whom we passed;

18And the Lord drove out before us all the people, the Amorites which dwelt in the land; therefore we also will serve the Lord, for He is our God.

19And Joshua said to the people, You cannot serve the Lord; for He is a holy God; He is a jealous God; He will not forgive your transgressions or your sins,

20If you forsake the Lord and [a]serve strange gods; then He will turn and do you harm, and consume you, after having done you good.

21And the people said to Joshua, No; but we will serve the Lord.

22Then Joshua said to the people, You are witnesses against yourselves that you have chosen the Lord, to serve Him. And they said, We are witnesses.

**AMP** [a] Anything which we keep in our hearts in the place which God ought to have is an idol, whether it be an image of wood or stone or gold, or whether it be money, or desire for fame, or love of pleasure, or some secret sin which we will not give up. If God does not really occupy the highest place in our hearts, controlling all, something else does, and that something else is an idol (J. R. Miller, in *Devotional Hours with the Bible*).

## New American Standard

3'Then I took your father Abraham from beyond the [b]River,
and led him through all the land of Canaan, and multiplied his
descendants and gave him Isaac.
4'And to Isaac I gave Jacob and Esau, and to Esau I gave Mount
Seir, to possess it; but Jacob and his sons went down to Egypt.
5'Then I sent Moses and Aaron, and I plagued Egypt by what
I did in its midst; and afterward I brought you out.
6'And I brought your fathers out of Egypt, and you came to the
sea; and Egypt pursued your fathers with chariots and horsemen
to the Red Sea.
7'But when they cried out to the LORD, He put darkness between you and the Egyptians, and brought the sea upon them and
covered them; and your own eyes saw what I did in Egypt. And
you lived in the wilderness for a long time.
8'Then I brought you into the land of the Amorites who lived
beyond the Jordan, and they fought with you; and I gave them into
your hand, and you took possession of their land when I destroyed
them before you.
9'Then Balak the son of Zippor, king of Moab, arose and fought
against Israel, and he sent and summoned Balaam the son of Beor
to curse you.
10'But I was not willing to listen to Balaam. So he had to bless
you, and I delivered you from his hand.
11'And you crossed the Jordan and came to Jericho; and the
citizens of Jericho fought against you, *and* the Amorite and
the Perizzite and the Canaanite and the Hittite and the Girgashite,
the Hivite and the Jebusite. Thus I gave them into your hand.
12'Then I sent the hornet before you and it drove out the two
kings of the Amorites from before you, *but* not by your sword or
your bow.
13'And I gave you a land on which you had not labored, and
cities which you had not built, and you have lived in them; you
are eating of vineyards and olive groves which you did not plant.'

### *"We Will Serve the LORD"*

**14**¶ "Now, therefore, fear the LORD and serve Him in sincerity
and truth; and put away the gods which your fathers served
beyond the River and in Egypt, and serve the LORD.
15"And if it is disagreeable in your sight to serve the LORD,
choose for yourselves today whom you will serve: whether the
gods which your fathers served which were beyond the River, or
the gods of the Amorites in whose land you are living; but as for
me and my house, we will serve the LORD."
**16**¶ And the people answered and said, "Far be it from us that
we should forsake the LORD to serve other gods;
17for the LORD our God is He who brought us and our fathers
up out of the land of Egypt, from the house of bondage, and who
did these great signs in our sight and preserved us through all the
way in which we went and among all the peoples through whose
midst we passed.
18"And the LORD drove out from before us all the peoples, even
the Amorites who lived in the land. We also will serve the LORD,
for He is our God."
**19**¶ Then Joshua said to the people, "You will not be able to
serve the LORD, for He is a holy God. He is a jealous God; He will
not forgive your transgression or your sins.
20"If you forsake the LORD and serve foreign gods, then He will
turn and do you harm and consume you after He has done good
to you."
21And the people said to Joshua, "No, but we will serve the
LORD."
22And Joshua said to the people, "You are witnesses against
yourselves that you have chosen for yourselves the LORD, to serve
Him." And they said, "We are witnesses."

**NAS** [b] I.e., Euphrates

## New International

beyond the River and led him throughout Canaan and gave him
many descendants. I gave him Isaac, 4and to Isaac I gave Jacob and
Esau. I assigned the hill country of Seir to Esau, but Jacob and his
sons went down to Egypt.
5" 'Then I sent Moses and Aaron, and I afflicted the Egyptians
by what I did there, and I brought you out. 6When I brought your
fathers out of Egypt, you came to the sea, and the Egyptians
pursued them with chariots and horsemen[c] as far as the Red Sea.[d]
7But they cried to the LORD for help, and he put darkness between
you and the Egyptians; he brought the sea over them and covered
them. You saw with your own eyes what I did to the Egyptians.
Then you lived in the desert for a long time.
8" 'I brought you to the land of the Amorites who lived east of
the Jordan. They fought against you, but I gave them into your
hands. I destroyed them from before you, and you took possession
of their land. 9When Balak son of Zippor, the king of Moab, prepared to fight against Israel, he sent for Balaam son of Beor to put
a curse on you. 10But I would not listen to Balaam, so he blessed
you again and again, and I delivered you out of his hand.
11" 'Then you crossed the Jordan and came to Jericho. The
citizens of Jericho fought against you, as did also the Amorites,
Perizzites, Canaanites, Hittites, Girgashites, Hivites and Jebusites,
but I gave them into your hands. 12I sent the hornet ahead of you,
which drove them out before you—also the two Amorite kings.
You did not do it with your own sword and bow. 13So I gave you
a land on which you did not toil and cities you did not build; and
you live in them and eat from vineyards and olive groves that you
did not plant.'
14"Now fear the LORD and serve him with all faithfulness.
Throw away the gods your forefathers worshiped beyond the
River and in Egypt, and serve the LORD. 15But if serving the LORD
seems undesirable to you, then choose for yourselves this day
whom you will serve, whether the gods your forefathers served
beyond the River, or the gods of the Amorites, in whose land you
are living. But as for me and my household, we will serve the
LORD."
16Then the people answered, "Far be it from us to forsake the
LORD to serve other gods! 17It was the LORD our God himself who
brought us and our fathers up out of Egypt, from that land of
slavery, and performed those great signs before our eyes. He
protected us on our entire journey and among all the nations
through which we traveled. 18And the LORD drove out before us
all the nations, including the Amorites, who lived in the land. We
too will serve the LORD, because he is our God."
19Joshua said to the people, "You are not able to serve the LORD.
He is a holy God; he is a jealous God. He will not forgive your
rebellion and your sins. 20If you forsake the LORD and serve foreign
gods, he will turn and bring disaster on you and make an end of
you, after he has been good to you."
21But the people said to Joshua, "No! We will serve the LORD."
22Then Joshua said, "You are witnesses against yourselves that
you have chosen to serve the LORD."
"Yes, we are witnesses," they replied.

**NIV** [c] 6 Or *charioteers* [d] 6 Hebrew *Yam Suph;* that is, Sea of Reeds

# King James

23Now therefore put away, *said he*, the strange gods which *are* among you, and incline your heart unto the LORD God of Israel.

24And the people said unto Joshua, The LORD our God will we serve, and his voice will we obey.

25So Joshua made a covenant with the people that day, and set them a statute and an ordinance in Shechem.

26¶ And Joshua wrote these words in the book of the law of God, and took a great stone, and set it up there under an oak, that *was* by the sanctuary of the LORD.

27And Joshua said unto all the people, Behold, this stone shall be a witness unto us; for it hath heard all the words of the LORD which he spake unto us: it shall be therefore a witness unto you, lest ye deny your God.

28So Joshua let the people depart, every man unto his inheritance.

29¶ And it came to pass after these things, that Joshua the son of Nun, the servant of the LORD, died, *being* an hundred and ten years old.

30And they buried him in the border of his inheritance in Timnath-serah, which *is* in mount Ephraim, on the north side of the hill of Gaash.

31And Israel served the LORD all the days of Joshua, and all the days of the elders that overlived Joshua, and which had known all the works of the LORD, that he had done for Israel.

32¶ And the bones of Joseph, which the children of Israel brought up out of Egypt, buried they in Shechem, in a parcel of ground which Jacob bought of the sons of Hamor the father of Shechem for an hundred pieces of silver: and it became the inheritance of the children of Joseph.

33And Eleazar the son of Aaron died; and they buried him in a hill *that pertained to* Phinehas his son, which was given him in mount Ephraim.

# Amplified

23Then put away, said he, the foreign gods that are among you, and incline your heart to the Lord, the God of Israel.

24The people said to Joshua, The Lord our God we will serve; His voice we will obey.

25So Joshua made a covenant with the people that day, and made statutes and ordinances for them at Shechem.

26And Joshua wrote these words in the book of the law of God; and he took a great stone, and set it up there under an oak that was in [the court of] the sanctuary of the Lord.

27And Joshua said to all the people, See, this stone shall be a witness against us; for it has heard all the words the Lord spoke to us; so it shall be a witness against you, lest [afterward] you lie [pretend] *and* deny your God.

28So Joshua sent the people away, every man to his inheritance.

29After this, Joshua, son of Nun, the servant of the Lord, died, being 110 years old.

30They buried him at the edge of his inheritance in Timnath-serah, in the hill country of Ephraim, on the north side of the hill of Gaash.

31Israel served the Lord all the days of Joshua, and of the elders who outlived Joshua and had known all the works the Lord had done for Israel.

32And the bones of Joseph, which the Israelites brought up out of Egypt, they buried in Shechem, in the portion of ground Jacob bought from the sons of Hamor father of Shechem for 100 pieces of money; and it became the inheritance of the Josephites.

33And Eleazar son of Aaron died; and they buried him at Gibeah [on the hill] of Phinehas his son, which was given him in the hill country of Ephraim.

## New American Standard

23"Now therefore, put away the foreign gods which are in your
midst, and incline your hearts to the LORD, the God of Israel."
24And the people said to Joshua, "We will serve the LORD our
God and we will obey His voice."
25So Joshua made a covenant with the people that day, and
made for them a statute and an ordinance in Shechem.
26And Joshua wrote these words in the book of the law of God;
and he took a large stone and set it up there under the oak that
was by the sanctuary of the LORD.
27And Joshua said to all the people, "Behold, this stone shall be
for a witness against us, for it has heard all the words of the LORD
which He spoke to us; thus it shall be for a witness against you,
lest you deny your God."
28Then Joshua dismissed the people, each to his inheritance.

*Joshua's Death and Burial*

**29**¶ And it came about after these things that Joshua the son of
Nun, the servant of the LORD, died, being one hundred and ten
years old.
30And they buried him in the territory of his inheritance in
Timnath-serah, which is in the hill country of Ephraim, on the
north of Mount Gaash.
31And Israel served the LORD all the days of Joshua and all the
days of the elders who survived Joshua, and had known all the
deeds of the LORD which He had done for Israel.
**32**¶ Now they buried the bones of Joseph, which the sons of
Israel brought up from Egypt, at Shechem, in the piece of ground
which Jacob had bought from the sons of Hamor the father of
Shechem for one hundred pieces of money; and they became the
inheritance of Joseph's sons.
33And Eleazar the son of Aaron died; and they buried him at
Gibeah of Phinehas his son, which was given him in the hill
country of Ephraim.

## New International

23"Now then," said Joshua, "throw away the foreign gods that
are among you and yield your hearts to the LORD, the God of
Israel."
24And the people said to Joshua, "We will serve the LORD our
God and obey him."
25On that day Joshua made a covenant for the people, and there
at Shechem he drew up for them decrees and laws. 26And Joshua
recorded these things in the Book of the Law of God. Then he took
a large stone and set it up there under the oak near the holy place
of the LORD.
27"See!" he said to all the people. "This stone will be a witness
against us. It has heard all the words the LORD has said to us. It
will be a witness against you if you are untrue to your God."

*Buried in the Promised Land*

28Then Joshua sent the people away, each to his own inheritance.
29After these things, Joshua son of Nun, the servant of the
LORD, died at the age of a hundred and ten. 30And they buried him
in the land of his inheritance, at Timnath Serah[a] in the hill country
of Ephraim, north of Mount Gaash.
31Israel served the LORD throughout the lifetime of Joshua and
of the elders who outlived him and who had experienced everything the LORD had done for Israel.
32And Joseph's bones, which the Israelites had brought up from
Egypt, were buried at Shechem in the tract of land that Jacob
bought for a hundred pieces of silver[b] from the sons of Hamor, the
father of Shechem. This became the inheritance of Joseph's descendants.
33And Eleazar son of Aaron died and was buried at Gibeah,
which had been allotted to his son Phinehas in the hill country of
Ephraim.

**NIV** [a] 30 Also known as *Timnath Heres* (see Judges 2:9) [b] 32 Hebrew *hundred kesitahs;* a kesitah was a unit of money of unknown weight and value.

## King James

THE BOOK OF

# Judges

1 NOW AFTER the death of Joshua it came to pass, that the
children of Israel asked the LORD, saying, Who shall go up for
us against the Canaanites first, to fight against them?
2And the LORD said, Judah shall go up: behold, I have delivered
the land into his hand.
3And Judah said unto Simeon his brother, Come up with me
into my lot, that we may fight against the Canaanites; and I likewise will go with thee into thy lot. So Simeon went with him.
4And Judah went up; and the LORD delivered the Canaanites
and the Perizzites into their hand: and they slew of them in Bezek
ten thousand men.
5And they found Adoni-bezek in Bezek: and they fought
against him, and they slew the Canaanites and the Perizzites.
6But Adoni-bezek fled; and they pursued after him, and caught
him, and cut off his thumbs and his great toes.
7And Adoni-bezek said, Threescore and ten kings, having their
thumbs and their great toes cut off, gathered *their meat* under my
table: as I have done, so God hath requited me. And they brought
him to Jerusalem, and there he died.
8Now the children of Judah had fought against Jerusalem, and
had taken it, and smitten it with the edge of the sword, and set
the city on fire.
9¶ And afterward the children of Judah went down to fight
against the Canaanites, that dwelt in the mountain, and in the
south, and in the valley.
10And Judah went against the Canaanites that dwelt in Hebron:
(now the name of Hebron before *was* Kirjath-arba:) and they slew
Sheshai, and Ahiman, and Talmai.
11And from thence he went against the inhabitants of Debir:
and the name of Debir before *was* Kirjath-sepher:
12And Caleb said, He that smiteth Kirjath-sepher, and taketh it,
to him will I give Achsah my daughter to wife.
13And Othniel the son of Kenaz, Caleb's younger brother, took
it: and he gave him Achsah his daughter to wife.
14And it came to pass, when she came *to him*, that she moved
him to ask of her father a field: and she lighted from off *her* ass;
and Caleb said unto her, What wilt thou?
15And she said unto him, Give me a blessing: for thou hast
given me a south land; give me also springs of water. And Caleb
gave her the upper springs and the nether springs.
16¶ And the children of the Kenite, Moses' father-in-law, went
up out of the city of palm trees with the children of Judah into the
wilderness of Judah, which *lieth* in the south of Arad; and they
went and dwelt among the people.
17And Judah went with Simeon his brother, and they slew the
Canaanites that inhabited Zephath, and utterly destroyed it. And
the name of the city was called Hormah.

## Amplified

THE BOOK OF

# Judges

1 AFTER THE death of Joshua the Israelites asked the Lord,
Who shall go up first for us against the Canaanites, to fight
against them?
2And the Lord said, Judah shall go up; behold, I have delivered
the land into his hand.
3And Judah [the tribe] said to [the tribe of] Simeon his brother,
Come up with me into my allotment, that we may fight against the
Canaanites; and I likewise will go with you into your territory. So
Simeon went with him.
4Then Judah went up, and the Lord delivered the Canaanites
and the Perizzites into their hand; and they smote 10,000 of them
in Bezek.
5And they found Adoni-bezek in Bezek, and fought against
him, and they smote the Canaanites and the Perizzites.
6Adoni-bezek fled; but they pursued him, and caught him, and
cut off his thumbs and his big toes.
7Adoni-bezek said, Seventy kings with their thumbs and big
toes cut off had to gather their food under my table. As I have
done, so God has repaid me. And they brought him to Jerusalem,
and there he died.
8And the men of Judah fought against [Jebusite] Jerusalem, and
took it, and smote it with the edge of the sword, and set the city
on fire.
9Afterward the men of Judah went down to fight against the
Canaanites who dwelt in the hill country, in the Negeb (South),
and in the lowland.
10And Judah went against the Canaanites who dwelt in Hebron. The name of Hebron before was Kiriath-arba. And they
defeated Sheshai and Ahiman and Talmai.
11From there [Judah] went against the inhabitants of Debir. The
name of Debir before was Kiriath-sepher [city of books and
scribes].
12And Caleb said, Whoever attacks Kiriath-sepher and takes it,
to him will I give Achsah my daughter as wife.
13And Othniel son of Kenaz, Caleb's younger brother, took it;
and he gave him Achsah his daughter as wife.
14And when she came to [Othniel], she got his consent to ask
her father for a [sloping] field. And she alighted off her donkey,
and Caleb said to her, What do you want?
15And she said to him, Give me a present; since you have set
me in the land of the Negeb, give me also springs of water. And
Caleb gave her the upper and lower springs.
16And the descendants of the Kenite, Moses' father-in-law,
went up with the Judahites from the city of palms [Jericho] into the
wilderness of Judah, which lies in the Negeb near Arad; and they
went and dwelt with the people.
17And [the tribe of] Judah went with Simeon his brother, and
they slew the Canaanites who inhabited Zephath, and utterly
destroyed it. So the city was called Hormah [destruction].

## New American Standard

# Judges

*Jerusalem Is Captured*

1 NOW IT came about after the death of Joshua that the sons
of Israel inquired of the LORD, saying, "Who shall go up first
for us against the Canaanites, to fight against them?"
2And the LORD said, "Judah shall go up; behold, I have given
the land into his hand."
3Then Judah said to Simeon his brother, "Come up with me
into the territory allotted me, that we may fight against the Canaanites; and I in turn will go with you into the territory allotted
you." So Simeon went with him.
4And Judah went up, and the LORD gave the Canaanites and
the Perizzites into their hands; and they defeated ten thousand
men at Bezek.
5And they found Adoni-bezek in Bezek and fought against him
and they defeated the Canaanites and the Perizzites.
6But Adoni-bezek fled; and they pursued him and caught him
and cut off his thumbs and big toes.
7And Adoni-bezek said, "Seventy kings with their thumbs and
their big toes cut off used to gather up *scraps* under my table; as
I have done, so God has repaid me." So they brought him to
Jerusalem and he died there.
8¶ Then the sons of Judah fought against Jerusalem and captured it and struck it with the edge of the sword and set the city
on fire.
9And afterward the sons of Judah went down to fight against
the Canaanites living in the hill country and in the [a]Negev and in
the lowland.
10So Judah went against the Canaanites who lived in Hebron
(now the name of Hebron formerly *was* Kiriath-arba); and they
struck Sheshai and Ahiman and Talmai.

*Capture of Other Cities*

11¶ Then from there he went against the inhabitants of Debir
(now the name of Debir formerly *was* Kiriath-sepher).
12And Caleb said, "The one who attacks Kiriath-sepher and
captures it, I will even give him my daughter Achsah for a wife."
13And Othniel the son of Kenaz, Caleb's younger brother, captured it; so he gave him his daughter Achsah for a wife.
14Then it came about when she came *to him*, that she persuaded
him to ask her father for a field. Then she alighted from her
donkey, and Caleb said to her, "What do you want?"
15And she said to him, "Give me a blessing, since you have
given me the land of the [b]Negev, give me also springs of water."
So Caleb gave her the upper springs and the lower springs.
16¶ And the descendants of the Kenite, Moses' father-in-law,
went up from the city of palms with the sons of Judah, to the
wilderness of Judah which is in the south of Arad; and they went
and lived with the people.
17Then Judah went with Simeon his brother, and they struck
the Canaanites living in Zephath, and utterly destroyed it. So the
name of the city was called Hormah.

NAS [a] I.e., South country [b] I.e., South country

## New International

# Judges

*Israel Fights the Remaining Canaanites*

1 AFTER THE death of Joshua, the Israelites asked the LORD,
"Who will be the first to go up and fight for us against the
Canaanites?"
2The LORD answered, "Judah is to go; I have given the land into
their hands."
3Then the men of Judah said to the Simeonites their brothers,
"Come up with us into the territory allotted to us, to fight against
the Canaanites. We in turn will go with you into yours." So the
Simeonites went with them.
4When Judah attacked, the LORD gave the Canaanites and Perizzites into their hands and they struck down ten thousand men
at Bezek. 5It was there that they found Adoni-Bezek and fought
against him, putting to rout the Canaanites and Perizzites. 6Adoni-
Bezek fled, but they chased him and caught him, and cut off his
thumbs and big toes.
7Then Adoni-Bezek said, "Seventy kings with their thumbs and
big toes cut off have picked up scraps under my table. Now God
has paid me back for what I did to them." They brought him to
Jerusalem, and he died there.
8The men of Judah attacked Jerusalem also and took it. They put
the city to the sword and set it on fire.
9After that, the men of Judah went down to fight against the
Canaanites living in the hill country, the Negev and the western
foothills. 10They advanced against the Canaanites living in Hebron
(formerly called Kiriath Arba) and defeated Sheshai, Ahiman and
Talmai.
11From there they advanced against the people living in Debir
(formerly called Kiriath Sepher). 12And Caleb said, "I will give my
daughter Acsah in marriage to the man who attacks and captures
Kiriath Sepher." 13Othniel son of Kenaz, Caleb's younger brother,
took it; so Caleb gave his daughter Acsah to him in marriage.
14One day when she came to Othniel, she urged him[c] to ask
her father for a field. When she got off her donkey, Caleb asked
her, "What can I do for you?"
15She replied, "Do me a special favor. Since you have given me
land in the Negev, give me also springs of water." Then Caleb gave
her the upper and lower springs.
16The descendants of Moses' father-in-law, the Kenite, went up
from the City of Palms[d] with the men of Judah to live among the
people of the Desert of Judah in the Negev near Arad.
17Then the men of Judah went with the Simeonites their brothers and attacked the Canaanites living in Zephath, and they totally
destroyed[e] the city. Therefore it was called Hormah.[f] 18The men

NIV [c] 14 Hebrew; Septuagint and Vulgate *Othniel, he urged her* [d] 16 That is, Jericho [e] 17 The Hebrew term refers to the irrevocable giving over of things or persons to the LORD, often by totally destroying them. [f] 17 *Hormah* means *destruction.*

## King James

18 Also Judah took Gaza with the coast thereof, and Askelon with the coast thereof, and Ekron with the coast thereof.

19 And the LORD was with Judah; and he drave out *the inhabitants of* the mountain; but could not drive out the inhabitants of the valley, because they had chariots of iron.

20 And they gave Hebron unto Caleb, as Moses said: and he expelled thence the three sons of Anak.

21 And the children of Benjamin did not drive out the Jebusites that inhabited Jerusalem; but the Jebusites dwell with the children of Benjamin in Jerusalem unto this day.

22 ¶ And the house of Joseph, they also went up against Beth-el: and the LORD *was* with them.

23 And the house of Joseph sent to descry Beth-el. (Now the name of the city before *was* Luz.)

24 And the spies saw a man come forth out of the city, and they said unto him, Show us, we pray thee, the entrance into the city, and we will show thee mercy.

25 And when he showed them the entrance into the city, they smote the city with the edge of the sword; but they let go the man and all his family.

26 And the man went into the land of the Hittites, and built a city, and called the name thereof Luz: which *is* the name thereof unto this day.

27 ¶ Neither did Manasseh drive out *the inhabitants of* Beth-shean and her towns, nor Taanach and her towns, nor the inhabitants of Dor and her towns, nor the inhabitants of Ibleam and her towns, nor the inhabitants of Megiddo and her towns: but the Canaanites would dwell in that land.

28 And it came to pass, when Israel was strong, that they put the Canaanites to tribute, and did not utterly drive them out.

29 ¶ Neither did Ephraim drive out the Canaanites that dwelt in Gezer; but the Canaanites dwelt in Gezer among them.

30 ¶ Neither did Zebulun drive out the inhabitants of Kitron, nor the inhabitants of Nahalol; but the Canaanites dwelt among them, and became tributaries.

31 ¶ Neither did Asher drive out the inhabitants of Accho, nor the inhabitants of Zidon, nor of Ahlab, nor of Achzib, nor of Helbah, nor of Aphik, nor of Rehob:

32 But the Asherites dwelt among the Canaanites, the inhabitants of the land: for they did not drive them out.

33 ¶ Neither did Naphtali drive out the inhabitants of Beth-shemesh, nor the inhabitants of Beth-anath; but he dwelt among the Canaanites, the inhabitants of the land: nevertheless the inhabitants of Beth-shemesh and of Beth-anath became tributaries unto them.

34 And the Amorites forced the children of Dan into the mountain: for they would not suffer them to come down to the valley:

35 But the Amorites would dwell in mount Heres in Aijalon, and in Shaalbim: yet the hand of the house of Joseph prevailed, so that they became tributaries.

36 And the coast of the Amorites *was* from the going up to Akrabbim, from the rock, and upward.

**2** AND AN angel of the LORD came up from Gilgal to Bochim, and said, I made you to go up out of Egypt, and have brought you unto the land which I sware unto your fathers; and I said, I will never break my covenant with you.

2 And ye shall make no league with the inhabitants of this land; ye shall throw down their altars: but ye have not obeyed my voice: why have ye done this?

3 Wherefore I also said, I will not drive them out from before you; but they shall be *as thorns* in your sides, and their gods shall be a snare unto you.

## Amplified

18 Also Judah took Gaza, Askelon, and Ekron, each with its territory.

19 The Lord was with Judah, and [Judah] drove out the inhabitants of the hill-country; but he could not drive out those inhabiting the [difficult] valley-basin, because they had chariots of iron.

20 Hebron was given to Caleb, as Moses said; and he expelled from there the three sons of Anak. [Josh. 14:6, 9.]

21 But the Benjamites did not drive out the Jebusites who inhabited Jerusalem; the Jebusites dwell with the Benjamites at Jerusalem to this day.

22 The house of Joseph also went up against Bethel; and the Lord was with them.

23 And the house of Joseph sent to spy out Bethel. The name of the city formerly had been Luz.

24 And the spies saw a man coming out of the city, and they said to him, Show us, we pray, the way into the city, and we will show you mercy.

25 When he showed them the entrance to the city, they smote the city with the sword; but they let the man and all his family go.

26 And the man went into the land of the Hittites, and built a city, and called it Luz, which is its name to this day.

27 Neither did Manasseh drive out the inhabitants of Beth-shean and its villages, or of Taanach or Dor or Ibleam or Megiddo and their villages, but the Canaanites remained in that land.

28 When Israel became strong, they put the Canaanites to forced labor, but did not utterly drive them out.

29 Neither did Ephraim drive out the Canaanites who dwelt in Gezer; but the Canaanites dwelt in Gezer among them.

30 Neither did Zebulun drive out the inhabitants of Kitron, or of Nahalol; but the Canaanites dwelt among them, and were put to forced labor.

31 Neither did Asher drive out the inhabitants of Acco, or of Sidon, or of Ahlab, or of Achzib, or of Helbah, or of Aphik, or of Rehob;

32 But the Asherites dwelt among the Canaanites, the inhabitants of the land; for they did not drive them out.

33 Neither did Naphtali drive out the inhabitants of Beth-shemesh, or of Beth-anath, but dwelt among the Canaanites, the inhabitants of the land; but the inhabitants of Beth-shemesh and of Beth-anath became subject to forced labor for them.

34 The Amorites forced the Danites back into the hill country, for they would not allow them to come down to the plain;

35 The Amorites remained fixed in Mount Heres [Sun-mountain] in Aijalon, and in Sha-albim; yet the hand of the house of Joseph prevailed, so that they became subject to forced labor.

36 And the border of the Amorites was from the ascent of Akrabbim, from the rock Sela and onward.

**2** NOW THE Angel of the Lord went up from Gilgal to Bochim. And He said, I brought you up from Egypt, and have brought you to the land which I swore to give to your fathers; and I said, I will never break My covenant with you; [Exod. 20:2.]

2 And you shall make no covenant with the inhabitants of this land; you shall break down their altars. But you have not obeyed My voice. Why have you done this?

3 So now I say, I will not drive them out from before you; but they shall be as thorns in your sides, and their gods shall be a snare to you.

## New American Standard

18 And Judah took Gaza with its territory and Ashkelon with its territory and Ekron with its territory.
19 Now the LORD was with Judah, and they took possession of the hill country; but they could not drive out the inhabitants of the valley because they had iron chariots.
20 Then they gave Hebron to Caleb, as Moses had promised; and he drove out from there the three sons of Anak.
21 But the sons of Benjamin did not drive out the Jebusites who lived in Jerusalem; so the Jebusites have lived with the sons of Benjamin in Jerusalem to this day.
22 ¶ Likewise the house of Joseph went up against Bethel, and the LORD was with them.
23 And the house of Joseph spied out Bethel (now the name of the city was formerly Luz).
24 And the spies saw a man coming out of the city, and they said to him, "Please show us the entrance to the city and we will treat you kindly."
25 So he showed them the entrance to the city, and they struck the city with the edge of the sword, but they let the man and all his family go free.
26 And the man went into the land of the Hittites and built a city and named it Luz which is its name to this day.

*Places Not Conquered*

27 ¶ But Manasseh did not take possession of Beth-shean and its villages, or Taanach and its villages, or the inhabitants of Dor and its villages, or the inhabitants of Ibleam and its villages, or the inhabitants of Megiddo and its villages; so the Canaanites persisted in living in that land.
28 And it came about when Israel became strong, that they put the Canaanites to forced labor, but they did not drive them out completely.
29 ¶ Neither did Ephraim drive out the Canaanites who were living in Gezer; so the Canaanites lived in Gezer among them.
30 ¶ Zebulun did not drive out the inhabitants of Kitron, or the inhabitants of Nahalol; so the Canaanites lived among them and became subject to forced labor.
31 ¶ Asher did not drive out the inhabitants of Acco, or the inhabitants of Sidon, or of Ahlab, or of Achzib, or of Helbah, or of Aphik, or of Rehob.
32 So the Asherites lived among the Canaanites, the inhabitants of the land; for they did not drive them out.
33 ¶ Naphtali did not drive out the inhabitants of Beth-shemesh, or the inhabitants of Beth-anath, but lived among the Canaanites, the inhabitants of the land; and the inhabitants of Beth-shemesh and Beth-anath became forced labor for them.
34 ¶ Then the Amorites forced the sons of Dan into the hill country, for they did not allow them to come down to the valley;
35 yet the Amorites persisted in living in Mount Heres, in Aijalon and in Shaalbim; but when the power of the house of Joseph grew strong, they became forced labor.
36 And the border of the Amorites ran from the ascent of Akrabbim, from Sela and upward.

*Israel Rebuked*

**2** NOW THE angel of the LORD came up from Gilgal to Bochim. And he said, "I brought you up out of Egypt and led you into the land which I have sworn to your fathers; and I said, 'I will never break My covenant with you,
2 and as for you, you shall make no covenant with the inhabitants of this land; you shall tear down their altars.' But you have not obeyed Me; what is this you have done?
3 "Therefore I also said, 'I will not drive them out before you; but they shall [a]become *as thorns* in your sides, and their gods shall be a snare to you.'"

NAS [a] Some ancient mss. read *be adversaries, and*

## New International

of Judah also took[b] Gaza, Ashkelon and Ekron—each city with its territory.
19 The LORD was with the men of Judah. They took possession
of the hill country, but they were unable to drive the people from
the plains, because they had iron chariots. 20 As Moses had promised, Hebron was given to Caleb, who drove from it the three sons
of Anak. 21 The Benjamites, however, failed to dislodge the Jebusites, who were living in Jerusalem; to this day the Jebusites live
there with the Benjamites.
22 Now the house of Joseph attacked Bethel, and the LORD was
with them. 23 When they sent men to spy out Bethel (formerly
called Luz), 24 the spies saw a man coming out of the city and they
said to him, "Show us how to get into the city and we will see that
you are treated well." 25 So he showed them, and they put the city
to the sword but spared the man and his whole family. 26 He then
went to the land of the Hittites, where he built a city and called
it Luz, which is its name to this day.
27 But Manasseh did not drive out the people of Beth Shan or
Taanach or Dor or Ibleam or Megiddo and their surrounding settlements, for the Canaanites were determined to live in that land.
28 When Israel became strong, they pressed the Canaanites into
forced labor but never drove them out completely. 29 Nor did
Ephraim drive out the Canaanites living in Gezer, but the Canaanites continued to live there among them. 30 Neither did Zebulun
drive out the Canaanites living in Kitron or Nahalol, who remained
among them; but they did subject them to forced labor. 31 Nor did
Asher drive out those living in Acco or Sidon or Ahlab or Aczib
or Helbah or Aphek or Rehob, 32 and because of this the people of
Asher lived among the Canaanite inhabitants of the land.
33 Neither did Naphtali drive out those living in Beth Shemesh or
Beth Anath; but the Naphtalites too lived among the Canaanite
inhabitants of the land, and those living in Beth Shemesh and Beth
Anath became forced laborers for them. 34 The Amorites confined
the Danites to the hill country, not allowing them to come down
into the plain. 35 And the Amorites were determined also to hold
out in Mount Heres, Aijalon and Shaalbim, but when the power
of the house of Joseph increased, they too were pressed into forced
labor. 36 The boundary of the Amorites was from Scorpion[c] Pass
to Sela and beyond.

*The Angel of the LORD at Bokim*

**2** THE ANGEL of the LORD went up from Gilgal to Bokim and said, "I brought you up out of Egypt and led you into the land
that I swore to give to your forefathers. I said, 'I will never break
my covenant with you, 2 and you shall not make a covenant with
the people of this land, but you shall break down their altars.' Yet
you have disobeyed me. Why have you done this? 3 Now therefore
I tell you that I will not drive them out before you; they will be
⌊thorns⌋ in your sides and their gods will be a snare to you."

NIV [b] *18* Hebrew; Septuagint *Judah did not take* [c] *36* Hebrew *Akrabbim*

## King James

4 And it came to pass, when the angel of the LORD spake these words unto all the children of Israel, that the people lifted up their voice, and wept.

5 And they called the name of that place Bochim: and they sacrificed there unto the LORD.

6 ¶ And when Joshua had let the people go, the children of Israel went every man unto his inheritance to possess the land.

7 And the people served the LORD all the days of Joshua, and all the days of the elders that outlived Joshua, who had seen all the great works of the LORD, that he did for Israel.

8 And Joshua the son of Nun, the servant of the LORD, died, *being* an hundred and ten years old.

9 And they buried him in the border of his inheritance in Timnath-heres, in the mount of Ephraim, on the north side of the hill Gaash.

10 And also all that generation were gathered unto their fathers: and there arose another generation after them, which knew not the LORD, nor yet the works which he had done for Israel.

11 ¶ And the children of Israel did evil in the sight of the LORD, and served Baalim:

12 And they forsook the LORD God of their fathers, which brought them out of the land of Egypt, and followed other gods, of the gods of the people that *were* round about them, and bowed themselves unto them, and provoked the LORD to anger.

13 And they forsook the LORD, and served Baal and Ashtaroth.

14 ¶ And the anger of the LORD was hot against Israel, and he delivered them into the hands of spoilers that spoiled them, and he sold them into the hands of their enemies round about, so that they could not any longer stand before their enemies.

15 Whithersoever they went out, the hand of the LORD was against them for evil, as the LORD had said, and as the LORD had sworn unto them: and they were greatly distressed.

16 ¶ Nevertheless the LORD raised up judges, which delivered them out of the hand of those that spoiled them.

17 And yet they would not hearken unto their judges, but they went a-whoring after other gods, and bowed themselves unto them: they turned quickly out of the way which their fathers walked in, obeying the commandments of the LORD; *but* they did not so.

18 And when the LORD raised them up judges, then The LORD was with the judge, and delivered them out of the hand of their enemies all the days of the judge: for it repented the LORD because of their groanings by reason of them that oppressed them and vexed them.

19 And it came to pass, when the judge was dead, *that* they returned, and corrupted *themselves* more than their fathers, in following other gods to serve them, and to bow down unto them; they ceased not from their own doings, nor from their stubborn way.

20 ¶ And the anger of the LORD was hot against Israel; and he said, Because that this people hath transgressed my covenant which I commanded their fathers, and have not hearkened unto my voice;

21 I also will not henceforth drive out any from before them of the nations which Joshua left when he died:

22 That through them I may prove Israel, whether they will keep the way of the LORD to walk therein, as their fathers did keep *it*, or not.

23 Therefore the LORD left those nations, without driving them out hastily; neither delivered he them into the hand of Joshua.

## Amplified

4 When the Angel of the Lord spoke these words to all the Israelites, the people lifted up their voice and wept.

5 They named that place Bochim [weepers], and they sacrificed there to the Lord.

6 And when Joshua had let the people go, the Israelites went every man to his inheritance to possess the land.

7 And the people served the Lord all the days of Joshua, and all the days of the elders who outlived Joshua, who had seen all the great works of the Lord, which He did for Israel.

8 And Joshua son of Nun, the servant of the Lord, died, being 110 years old.

9 And they buried him within the boundary of his inheritance in Timnath-heres, in the hill country of Ephraim, north of Mount Gaash.

10 And also all that generation were gathered to their fathers; and there arose another generation after them, who did not know (recognize, understand) the Lord or even the work which He had done for Israel.

11 And the people of Israel did evil in the sight of the Lord, and served the Baals;

12 And they forsook the Lord, the God of their fathers, Who brought them out of the land of Egypt; they went after other gods of the peoples round about them, and bowed down to them, and provoked the Lord to anger.

13 And they forsook the Lord, and served the Baals [masculine] and the Ashtaroth [feminine plural].

14 So the anger of the Lord was kindled against Israel, and He gave them into the power of plunderers who robbed them, and He sold them into the hands of their enemies round about, so that they could no longer stand before their foes.

15 Whenever they went out, the hand of the Lord was against them for evil, as the Lord had said, and as the Lord had sworn to them; and they were bitterly distressed. [Lev. 26:14-46.]

16 But the Lord raised up judges, who delivered them out of the hand of those who robbed them.

17 And yet they did not listen to their judges; for they played the harlot after other gods and bowed down to them; they turned quickly out of the way in which their fathers had walked, who had obeyed the commandments of the Lord, and they did not so.

18 When the Lord raised them up judges, then He was with the judge, and delivered them out of the hand of their enemies all the days of the judge; for the Lord was moved to relent because of their groanings by reason of those who oppressed and vexed them.

19 But when the judge was dead, they turned back and corrupted themselves more than their fathers, following and serving other gods, and bowing down to them; they did not cease from their practices or their stubborn way.

20 So the anger of the Lord was kindled against Israel; and He said, Because this people have transgressed My covenant which I commanded their fathers, and have not listened to My voice,

21 I from now on will also not drive out from before them any of the nations which Joshua left when he died,

22 That through them I may prove Israel, whether they will keep the way of the Lord to walk in it, as their fathers kept it, or not.

23 So the Lord left those nations, without driving them out at once, nor had He delivered them into Joshua's power.

## New American Standard

4And it came about when the angel of the LORD spoke these
words to all the sons of Israel, that the people lifted up their voices
and wept.
5So they named that place [a]Bochim; and there they sacrificed
to the LORD.

*Joshua Dies*

6¶ When Joshua had dismissed the people, the sons of Israel
went each to his inheritance to possess the land.
7And the people served the LORD all the days of Joshua, and
all the days of the elders who survived Joshua, who had seen all
the great work of the LORD which He had done for Israel.
8Then Joshua the son of Nun, the servant of the LORD, died at
the age of one hundred and ten.
9And they buried him in the territory of his inheritance in
Timnath-heres, in the hill country of Ephraim, north of Mount
Gaash.
10And all that generation also were gathered to their fathers;
and there arose another generation after them who did not know
the LORD, nor yet the work which He had done for Israel.

*Israel Serves Baals*

11¶ Then the sons of Israel did evil in the sight of the LORD, and
[b]served the Baals,
12and they forsook the LORD, the God of their fathers, who had
brought them out of the land of Egypt, and followed other gods
from *among* the gods of the peoples who were around them, and
bowed themselves down to them; thus they provoked the LORD to
anger.
13So they forsook the LORD and served Baal and the Ashtaroth.
14And the anger of the LORD burned against Israel, and He gave
them into the hands of plunderers who plundered them; and He
sold them into the hands of their enemies around *them,* so that
they could no longer stand before their enemies.
15Wherever they went, the hand of the LORD was against them
for evil, as the LORD had spoken and as the LORD had sworn to
them, so that they were severely distressed.
16Then the LORD raised up judges who delivered them from the
hands of those who plundered them.
17And yet they did not listen to their judges, for they played the
harlot after other gods and bowed themselves down to them. They
turned aside quickly from the way in which their fathers had
walked in obeying the commandments of the LORD; they did not
do as *their fathers.*
18And when the LORD raised up judges for them, the LORD was
with the judge and delivered them from the hand of their enemies
all the days of the judge; for the LORD was moved to pity by their
groaning because of those who oppressed and afflicted them.
19But it came about when the judge died, that they would turn
back and act more corruptly than their fathers, in following other
gods to serve them and bow down to them; they did not abandon
their practices or their stubborn ways.
20So the anger of the LORD burned against Israel, and He said,
"Because this nation has transgressed My covenant which I commanded their fathers, and has not listened to My voice,
21I also will no longer drive out before them any of the nations
which Joshua left when he died,
22in order to test Israel by them, whether they will keep the way
of the LORD to walk in it as their fathers did, or not."
23So the LORD allowed those nations to remain, not driving
them out quickly; and He did not give them into the hand of
Joshua.

NAS [a] I.e., weepers [b] Or, *worshiped*

## New International

4When the angel of the LORD had spoken these things to all the
Israelites, the people wept aloud, 5and they called that place
Bokim.[c] There they offered sacrifices to the LORD.

*Disobedience and Defeat*

6After Joshua had dismissed the Israelites, they went to take
possession of the land, each to his own inheritance. 7The people
served the LORD throughout the lifetime of Joshua and of the elders
who outlived him and who had seen all the great things the LORD
had done for Israel.
8Joshua son of Nun, the servant of the LORD, died at the age of
a hundred and ten. 9And they buried him in the land of his
inheritance, at Timnath Heres[d] in the hill country of Ephraim,
north of Mount Gaash.
10After that whole generation had been gathered to their fathers, another generation grew up, who knew neither the LORD
nor what he had done for Israel. 11Then the Israelites did evil in
the eyes of the LORD and served the Baals. 12They forsook the
LORD, the God of their fathers, who had brought them out of
Egypt. They followed and worshiped various gods of the peoples
around them. They provoked the LORD to anger 13because they
forsook him and served Baal and the Ashtoreths. 14In his anger
against Israel the LORD handed them over to raiders who plundered them. He sold them to their enemies all around, whom they
were no longer able to resist. 15Whenever Israel went out to fight,
the hand of the LORD was against them to defeat them, just as he
had sworn to them. They were in great distress.
16Then the LORD raised up judges,[e] who saved them out of the
hands of these raiders. 17Yet they would not listen to their judges
but prostituted themselves to other gods and worshiped them.
Unlike their fathers, they quickly turned from the way in which
their fathers had walked, the way of obedience to the LORD's
commands. 18Whenever the LORD raised up a judge for them, he
was with the judge and saved them out of the hands of their
enemies as long as the judge lived; for the LORD had compassion
on them as they groaned under those who oppressed and afflicted
them. 19But when the judge died, the people returned to ways
even more corrupt than those of their fathers, following other gods
and serving and worshiping them. They refused to give up their
evil practices and stubborn ways.
20Therefore the LORD was very angry with Israel and said,
"Because this nation has violated the covenant that I laid down for
their forefathers and has not listened to me, 21I will no longer drive
out before them any of the nations Joshua left when he died. 22I
will use them to test Israel and see whether they will keep the way
of the LORD and walk in it as their forefathers did." 23The LORD had
allowed those nations to remain; he did not drive them out at once
by giving them into the hands of Joshua.

NIV [c] 5 *Bokim* means *weepers.* [d] 9 Also known as *Timnath Serah* (see Joshua 19:50 and 24:30) [e] 16 Or *leaders;* similarly in verses 17-19

## King James

3 NOW THESE *are* the nations which the LORD left, to prove Israel by them, *even* as many *of Israel* as had not known all the wars of Canaan;
2Only that the generations of the children of Israel might know, to teach them war, at the least such as before knew nothing thereof;
3 *Namely*, five lords of the Philistines, and all the Canaanites, and the Sidonians, and the Hivites that dwelt in mount Lebanon, from mount Baal-hermon unto the entering in of Hamath.
4And they were to prove Israel by them, to know whether they would hearken unto the commandments of the LORD, which he commanded their fathers by the hand of Moses.
5¶ And the children of Israel dwelt among the Canaanites, Hittites, and Amorites, and Perizzites, and Hivites, and Jebusites:
6And they took their daughters to be their wives, and gave their daughters to their sons, and served their gods.
7And the children of Israel did evil in the sight of the LORD, and forgat the LORD their God, and served Baalim and the groves.
8¶ Therefore the anger of the LORD was hot against Israel, and he sold them into the hand of Chushan-rishathaim king of Mesopotamia: and the children of Israel served Chushan-rishathaim eight years.
9And when the children of Israel cried unto the LORD, the LORD raised up a deliverer to the children of Israel, who delivered them, *even* Othniel the son of Kenaz, Caleb's younger brother.
10And the spirit of the LORD came upon him, and he judged Israel, and went out to war: and the LORD delivered Chushan-rishathaim king of Mesopotamia into his hand; and his hand prevailed against Chushan-rishathaim.
11And the land had rest forty years. And Othniel the son of Kenaz died.
12¶ And the children of Israel did evil again in the sight of the LORD: and the LORD strengthened Eglon the king of Moab against Israel, because they had done evil in the sight of the LORD.
13And he gathered unto him the children of Ammon and Amalek, and went and smote Israel, and possessed the city of palm trees.
14So the children of Israel served Eglon the king of Moab eighteen years.
15But when the children of Israel cried unto the LORD, the LORD raised them up a deliverer, Ehud the son of Gera, a Benjamite, a man lefthanded: and by him the children of Israel sent a present unto Eglon the king of Moab.
16But Ehud made him a dagger which had two edges, of a cubit length; and he did gird it under his raiment upon his right thigh.
17And he brought the present unto Eglon king of Moab: and Eglon *was* a very fat man.
18And when he had made an end to offer the present, he sent away the people that bare the present.
19But he himself turned again from the quarries that *were* by Gilgal, and said, I have a secret errand unto thee, O king: who said, Keep silence. And all that stood by him went out from him.
20And Ehud came unto him; and he was sitting in a summer parlour, which he had for himself alone. And Ehud said, I have a message from God unto thee. And he arose out of *his* seat.
21And Ehud put forth his left hand, and took the dagger from his right thigh, and thrust it into his belly:
22And the haft also went in after the blade; and the fat closed upon the blade, so that he could not draw the dagger out of his belly; and the dirt came out.
23Then Ehud went forth through the porch, and shut the doors of the parlour upon him, and locked them.

## Amplified

3 NOW THESE are the nations which the Lord left, to prove Israel by them, that is, all in Israel who had not previously experienced war in Canaan;
2It was only that the generations of the Israelites might know and be taught war, at least those who previously knew nothing of it.
3The remaining nations are: the five lords of the Philistines, all the Canaanites, the Sidonians, and the Hivites who dwelt on Mount Lebanon, from Mount Baal-hermon to the entrance of Hamath.
4They were for the testing *and* proving of Israel, to know whether Israel would listen *and* obey the commandments of the Lord, which He commanded their fathers by Moses.
5And the Israelites dwelt among the Canaanites, Hittites, Amorites, Perizzites, Hivites, and Jebusites;
6And they married their daughters, and gave their own daughters to their sons, and served their gods. [Exod. 34:12-16.]
7And the Israelites did evil in the sight of the Lord, and forgot the Lord their God, and served the Baals [masculine] and the Ashtaroth [feminine plural].
8So the anger of the Lord was kindled against Israel, and He sold them into the hand of Chushan-rishathaim king of Mesopotamia; and the Israelites served Chushan-rishathaim eight years.
9But when the Israelites cried to the Lord, the Lord raised up a deliverer for the people of Israel, who delivered them, Othniel son of Kenaz, Caleb's younger brother.
10The Spirit of the Lord came upon him, and he judged Israel; he went out to war, and the Lord delivered Chushan-rishathaim king of Mesopotamia into his hand; and his hand prevailed over Chushan-rishathaim.
11And the land had rest forty years. Then Othniel son of Kenaz died.
12And the Israelites again did evil in the sight of the Lord; and the Lord strengthened Eglon king of Moab against Israel, because they had done what was evil in the sight of the Lord.
13And [Eglon] gathered to him the men of Ammon and Amalek, and went and smote Israel, and they possessed the city of palm trees [Jericho].
14And the Israelites served Eglon the king of Moab eighteen years.
15But when the Israelites cried to the Lord, the Lord raised them up a deliverer, Ehud son of Gera, a Benjamite, a left-handed man; and by him the Israelites sent tribute to Eglon the king of Moab.
16Ehud made for himself a sword, a cubit long, which had two edges; and he girded it on his right thigh under his clothing.
17And he brought the tribute to Eglon king of Moab. Now Eglon was a very fat man.
18And when Ehud had finished presenting the tribute, he sent away the people who had carried it.
19He himself went [with them] as far as the sculptured [boundary] stones near Gilgal, and then turned back and came to Eglon, and said, I have a secret errand to you, O king. Eglon commanded silence, and all who stood by him went out from him.
20When Ehud had come [near] to him as he was sitting alone in his cool upper apartment, Ehud said, I have a commission from God to execute to you. And the king arose from his seat.
21Then Ehud put forth his left hand, and took the sword from his right thigh, and thrust it into Eglon's belly;
22And the hilt also went in after the blade; and the fat closed upon the blade, for [Ehud] did not draw the sword out of his belly, and the dirt came out.
23Then Ehud went out into the vestibule, and shut the doors of the upper room upon [Eglon], and locked them.

## New American Standard

*Idolatry Leads to Servitude*

3 NOW THESE are the nations which the LORD left, to test Israel by them ( *that is,* all who had not experienced any of the wars of Canaan;

2only in order that the generations of the sons of Israel might be taught war, those who had not experienced it formerly).

3 *These nations are:* the five lords of the Philistines and all the Canaanites and the Sidonians and the Hivites who lived in Mount Lebanon, from Mount Baal-hermon as far as Lebo-hamath.

4And they were for testing Israel, to find out if they would obey the commandments of the LORD, which He had commanded their fathers through Moses.

5And the sons of Israel lived among the Canaanites, the Hittites, the Amorites, the Perizzites, the Hivites, and the Jebusites;

6and they took their daughters for themselves as wives, and gave their own daughters to their sons, and served their gods.

7And the sons of Israel did what was evil in the sight of the LORD, and forgot the LORD their God, and served the Baals and the [a]Asheroth.

8Then the anger of the LORD was kindled against Israel, so that He sold them into the hands of Cushan-rishathaim king of Mesopotamia; and the sons of Israel served Cushan-rishathaim eight years.

*The First Judge Delivers Israel*

9And when the sons of Israel cried to the LORD, the LORD raised up a deliverer for the sons of Israel to deliver them, Othniel the son of Kenaz, Caleb's younger brother.

10And the Spirit of the LORD came upon him, and he judged Israel. When he went out to war, the LORD gave Cushan-rishathaim king of Mesopotamia into his hand, so that he prevailed over Cushan-rishathaim.

11Then the land had rest forty years. And Othniel the son of Kenaz died.

12¶ Now the sons of Israel again did evil in the sight of the LORD. So the LORD strengthened Eglon the king of Moab against Israel, because they had done evil in the sight of the LORD.

13And he gathered to himself the sons of Ammon and Amalek; and he went and defeated Israel, and they possessed the city of the palm trees.

14And the sons of Israel served Eglon the king of Moab eighteen years.

*Ehud Delivers from Moab*

15¶ But when the sons of Israel cried to the LORD, the LORD raised up a deliverer for them, Ehud the son of Gera, the Benjamite, a left-handed man. And the sons of Israel sent tribute by him to Eglon the king of Moab.

16And Ehud made himself a sword which had two edges, a cubit in length; and he bound it on his right thigh under his cloak.

17And he presented the tribute to Eglon king of Moab. Now Eglon was a very fat man.

18And it came about when he had finished presenting the tribute, that he sent away the people who had carried the tribute.

19But he himself turned back from the idols which were at Gilgal, and said, "I have a secret message for you, O king." And he said, "Keep silence." And all who attended him left him.

20And Ehud came to him while he was sitting alone in his cool roof chamber. And Ehud said, "I have a message from God for you." And he arose from his seat.

21And Ehud stretched out his left hand, took the sword from his right thigh and thrust it into his belly.

22The handle also went in after the blade, and the fat closed over the blade, for he did not draw the sword out of his belly; and the refuse came out.

23Then Ehud went out into the vestibule and shut the doors of the roof chamber behind him, and locked *them.*

NAS [a] I.e., wooden symbol of a female deity

## New International

3 THESE ARE the nations the LORD left to test all those Isarel-
ites who had not experienced any of the wars in Canaan 2(he
did this only to teach warfare to the descendants of the Israelites
who had not had previous battle experience): 3the five rulers of the
Philistines, all the Canaanites, the Sidonians, and the Hivites living in the Lebanon mountains from Mount Baal Hermon to Lebo[b]
Hamath. 4They were left to test the Israelites to see whether they
would obey the LORD's commands, which he had given their
forefathers through Moses.
5The Israelites lived among the Canaanites, Hittites, Amorites,
Perizzites, Hivites and Jebusites. 6They took their daughters in
marriage and gave their own daughters to their sons, and served
their gods.

*Othniel*

7The Israelites did evil in the eyes of the LORD; they forgot the
LORD their God and served the Baals and the Asherahs. 8The anger
of the LORD burned against Israel so that he sold them into the
hands of Cushan-Rishathaim king of Aram Naharaim,[c] to whom
the Israelites were subject for eight years. 9But when they cried out
to the LORD, he raised up for them a deliverer, Othniel son of
Kenaz, Caleb's younger brother, who saved them. 10The Spirit of
the LORD came upon him, so that he became Israel's judge[d] and
went to war. The LORD gave Cushan-Rishathaim king of Aram into
the hands of Othniel, who overpowered him. 11So the land had
peace for forty years, until Othniel son of Kenaz died.

*Ehud*

12Once again the Israelites did evil in the eyes of the LORD, and
because they did this evil the LORD gave Eglon king of Moab power
over Israel. 13Getting the Ammonites and Amalekites to join him,
Eglon came and attacked Israel, and they took possession of the
City of Palms.[e] 14The Israelites were subject to Eglon king of Moab
for eighteen years.
15Again the Israelites cried out to the LORD, and he gave them
a deliverer—Ehud, a left-handed man, the son of Gera the Benjamite. The Israelites sent him with tribute to Eglon king of Moab.
16Now Ehud had made a double-edged sword about a foot and a
half[f] long, which he strapped to his right thigh under his clothing.
17He presented the tribute to Eglon king of Moab, who was a very
fat man. 18After Ehud had presented the tribute, he sent on their
way the men who had carried it. 19At the idols[g] near Gilgal he
himself turned back and said, "I have a secret message for you, O
king."
The king said, "Quiet!" And all his attendants left him.
20Ehud then approached him while he was sitting alone in the
upper room of his summer palace[h] and said, "I have a message
from God for you." As the king rose from his seat, 21Ehud reached
with his left hand, drew the sword from his right thigh and
plunged it into the king's belly. 22Even the handle sank in after the
blade, which came out his back. Ehud did not pull the sword out,
and the fat closed in over it. 23Then Ehud went out to the porch[i];
he shut the doors of the upper room behind him and locked them.

NIV [b] 3 Or *to the entrance to* [c] *8* That is, Northwest Mesopotamia [d] *10* Or *leader* [e] *13* That is, Jericho [f] *16* Hebrew *a cubit* (about 0.5 meter) [g] *19* Or *the stone quarries;* also in verse 26 [h] *20* The meaning of the Hebrew for this phrase is uncertain. [i] *23* The meaning of the Hebrew for this word is uncertain.

## King James

24When he was gone out, his servants came; and when they saw that, behold, the doors of the parlour *were* locked, they said, Surely he covereth his feet in his summer chamber.

25And they tarried till they were ashamed: and, behold, he opened not the doors of the parlour; therefore they took a key, and opened *them:* and, behold, their lord *was* fallen down dead on the earth.

26And Ehud escaped while they tarried, and passed beyond the quarries, and escaped unto Seirath.

27And it came to pass, when he was come, that he blew a trumpet in the mountain of Ephraim, and the children of Israel went down with him from the mount, and he before them.

28And he said unto them, Follow after me: for the LORD hath delivered your enemies the Moabites into your hand. And they went down after him, and took the fords of Jordan toward Moab, and suffered not a man to pass over.

29And they slew of Moab at that time about ten thousand men, all lusty, and all men of valour; and there escaped not a man.

30So Moab was subdued that day under the hand of Israel. And the land had rest fourscore years.

31¶ And after him was Shamgar the son of Anath, which slew of the Philistines six hundred men with an ox goad: and he also delivered Israel.

**4** AND THE children of Israel again did evil in the sight of the LORD, when Ehud was dead.

2And the LORD sold them into the hand of Jabin king of Canaan, that reigned in Hazor; the captain of whose host *was* Sisera, which dwelt in Harosheth of the Gentiles.

3And the children of Israel cried unto the LORD: for he had nine hundred chariots of iron; and twenty years he mightily oppressed the children of Israel.

4¶ And Deborah, a prophetess, the wife of Lapidoth, she judged Israel at that time.

5And she dwelt under the palm tree of Deborah between Ramah and Beth-el in mount Ephraim: and the children of Israel came up to her for judgment.

6And she sent and called Barak the son of Abinoam out of Kedesh-naphtali, and said unto him, Hath not the LORD God of Israel commanded, *saying,* Go and draw toward mount Tabor, and take with thee ten thousand men of the children of Naphtali and of the children of Zebulun?

7And I will draw unto thee to the river Kishon Sisera, the captain of Jabin's army, with his chariots and his multitude; and I will deliver him into thine hand.

8And Barak said unto her, If thou wilt go with me, then I will go: but if thou wilt not go with me, *then* I will not go.

9And she said, I will surely go with thee: notwithstanding the journey that thou takest shall not be for thine honour; for the LORD shall sell Sisera into the hand of a woman. And Deborah arose, and went with Barak to Kedesh.

## Amplified

24When [Ehud] had gone out, [Eglon's] servants came; and when they saw the doors of the upper room were locked, they thought, Surely he [is seeking privacy while he] relieves himself in the closet of the cool chamber.

25They waited long, until they became embarrassed *and* uneasy; but when he still did not open the doors of the upper room, they took the key, and opened them; and there lay their master fallen to the floor, dead!

26Ehud escaped while they delayed, and passed beyond the sculptured [boundary] stones [images] and escaped to Se-irah.

27When he arrived, he blew a trumpet in the hill country of Ephraim, and the Israelites went down from the hill country, with him at their head.

28And he said to them, Follow me; for the Lord has delivered your enemies the Moabites into your hand. So they went down after him, and seized the fords of the Jordan against the Moabites, and permitted not a man to pass over.

29They slew at that time about 10,000 Moabites, all strong, courageous men; not a man escaped.

30So Moab was subdued that day under the hand of Israel, and the land had peace *and* rest for eighty years.

31After *Ehud* was Shamgar son of Anath, who slew 600 Philistine men with an oxgoad; he also delivered Israel.

**4** BUT AFTER Ehud died the Israelites again did evil in the sight of the Lord.

2So the Lord sold them into the hand of Jabin king of Canaan, who reigned in Hazor; the commander of his army was Sisera, who dwelt in Harosheth-ha-goiim [fortress or city of the nations].

3Then the Israelites cried to the Lord; for [Jabin] had 900 chariots of iron, and had severely oppressed the Israelites for twenty years.

4Now Deborah, a [a]prophetess, the wife of Lappidoth, judged Israel at that time.

5She sat under the palm tree of Deborah between Ramah and Bethel in the hill country of Ephraim; and the Israelites came up to her for judgment.

6And she sent and called Barak son of Abinoam from Kedesh in Naphtali, and said to him, Has not the Lord, the God of Israel commanded *you,* Go, gather your men at Mount Tabor, taking 10,000 men from the tribes of Naphtali and Zebulun?

7And I will draw out Sisera, the general of Jabin's army, to meet you at the river Kishon, with his chariots and his multitude; and I will deliver him into your hand?

8And Barak said to her, If you will go with me, then I will go; but if you will not go with me, I will not go.

9And she said, I will surely go with you; nevertheless, the trip you take will not be for your glory; for the Lord will sell Sisera into the hand of a woman. And Deborah arose and went with Barak to Kedesh. [See verse 22 for fulfillment.]

**AMP** [a] According to Num. 11:25, the prophetic gift has its source in the "Spirit of the Lord." The prophet is a spokesman of God and for Him. Miriam was the first prophetess who praised God before all the people (Exod. 15:20). Deborah was not like Miriam, the sister of such men as Moses and Aaron. The objective spirit of her God alone elevates her above her people, above heroes before and after her. Not only the ecstasy of enthusiasm, but the calm wisdom of that Spirit who informs the law, dwells in her. Of no Judge until Samuel [the last of the Judges] is it expressly said that he was a "prophet." Of none until him can it be said that he was possessed of the popular authority needful for the office of Judge. The position of Deborah in Israel is therefore a twofold testimony: it proves the relaxation of spiritual and manly energy, but also the undying might of divine truth, as delivered by Moses, comes brilliantly to view. History shows many instances where in times of distress, when men despaired, women arose and saved their nation; but in all such cases there must be an unextinguished spark of the old fire in the people themselves. Israel, formerly encouraged by the great exploit of a left-handed man, is now quickened by the glowing word of a noble woman (condensed from *Lange's Commentary*).

## New American Standard

24¶ When he had gone out, his servants came and looked, and
behold, the doors of the roof chamber were locked; and they said,
"He is only relieving himself in the cool room."
25And they waited until they became anxious; but behold, he
did not open the doors of the roof chamber. Therefore they took
the key and opened them, and behold, their master had fallen to
the floor dead.
26¶ Now Ehud escaped while they were delaying, and he
passed by the idols and escaped to Seirah.
27And it came about when he had arrived, that he blew the
trumpet in the hill country of Ephraim; and the sons of Israel went
down with him from the hill country, and he *was* in front of them.
28And he said to them, "Pursue *them,* for the LORD has given
your enemies the Moabites into your hands." So they went down
after him and seized the fords of the Jordan opposite Moab, and
did not allow anyone to cross.
29And they struck down at that time about ten thousand Moabites, all robust and valiant men; and no one escaped.
30So Moab was subdued that day under the hand of Israel. And
the land was undisturbed for eighty years.

*Shamgar Delivers from Philistines*

31¶ And after him came Shamgar the son of Anath, who struck
down six hundred Philistines with an oxgoad; and he also saved
Israel.

*Deborah and Barak Deliver from Canaanites*

4 THEN THE sons of Israel again did evil in the sight of the
LORD, after Ehud died.
2And the LORD sold them into the hand of Jabin king of Canaan, who reigned in Hazor; and the commander of his army was
Sisera, who lived in Harosheth-hagoyim.
3And the sons of Israel cried to the LORD; for he had nine
hundred iron chariots, and he oppressed the sons of Israel severely
for twenty years.
4¶ Now Deborah, a prophetess, the wife of Lappidoth, was
judging Israel at that time.
5And she used to sit under the palm tree of Deborah between
Ramah and Bethel in the hill country of Ephraim; and the sons of
Israel came up to her for judgment.
6Now she sent and summoned Barak the son of Abinoam from
Kedesh-naphtali, and said to him, "Behold, the LORD, the God of
Israel, has commanded, 'Go and march to Mount Tabor, and take
with you ten thousand men from the sons of Naphtali and from
the sons of Zebulun.
7'And I will draw out to you Sisera, the commander of Jabin's
army, with his chariots and his many *troops* to the river Kishon;
and I will give him into your hand.' "
8Then Barak said to her, "If you will go with me, then I will
go; but if you will not go with me, I will not go."
9And she said, "I will surely go with you; nevertheless, the
honor shall not be yours on the journey that you are about to take,
for the LORD will sell Sisera into the hands of a woman." Then
Deborah arose and went with Barak to Kedesh.

## New International

24After he had gone, the servants came and found the doors of
the upper room locked. They said, "He must be relieving himself
in the inner room of the house." 25They waited to the point of
embarrassment, but when he did not open the doors of the room,
they took a key and unlocked them. There they saw their lord
fallen to the floor, dead.
26While they waited, Ehud got away. He passed by the idols
and escaped to Seirah. 27When he arrived there, he blew a trumpet
in the hill country of Ephraim, and the Israelites went down with
him from the hills, with him leading them.
28"Follow me," he ordered, "for the LORD has given Moab, your
enemy, into your hands." So they followed him down and, taking
possession of the fords of the Jordan that led to Moab, they allowed no one to cross over. 29At that time they struck down about
ten thousand Moabites, all vigorous and strong; not a man escaped. 30That day Moab was made subject to Israel, and the land
had peace for eighty years.

*Shamgar*

31After Ehud came Shamgar son of Anath, who struck down six
hundred Philistines with an oxgoad. He too saved Israel.

*Deborah*

4 AFTER EHUD died, the Israelites once again did evil in the
eyes of the LORD. 2So the LORD sold them into the hands of
Jabin, a king of Canaan, who reigned in Hazor. The commander
of his army was Sisera, who lived in Harosheth Haggoyim. 3Be-
cause he had nine hundred iron chariots and had cruelly oppressed the Israelites for twenty years, they cried to the LORD for
help.
4Deborah, a prophetess, the wife of Lappidoth, was leading[b]
Israel at that time. 5She held court under the Palm of Deborah
between Ramah and Bethel in the hill country of Ephraim, and the
Israelites came to her to have their disputes decided. 6She sent for
Barak son of Abinoam from Kedesh in Naphtali and said to him,
"The LORD, the God of Israel, commands you: 'Go, take with you
ten thousand men of Naphtali and Zebulun and lead the way to
Mount Tabor. 7I will lure Sisera, the commander of Jabin's army,
with his chariots and his troops to the Kishon River and give him
into your hands.' "
8Barak said to her, "If you go with me, I will go; but if you don't
go with me, I won't go."
9"Very well," Deborah said, "I will go with you. But because
of the way you are going about this,[c] the honor will not be yours,
for the LORD will hand Sisera over to a woman." So Deborah went
with Barak to Kedesh, 10where he summoned Zebulun and Naph-

NIV [b] 4 Traditionally *judging* [c] 9 Or *But on the expedition you are undertaking*

# King James

10¶ And Barak called Zebulun and Naphtali to Kedesh; and he went up with ten thousand men at his feet: and Deborah went up with him.

11Now Heber the Kenite, *which was* of the children of Hobab the father-in-law of Moses, had severed himself from the Kenites, and pitched his tent unto the plain of Zaanaim, which *is* by Kedesh.

12And they showed Sisera that Barak the son of Abinoam was gone up to mount Tabor.

13And Sisera gathered together all his chariots, *even* nine hundred chariots of iron, and all the people that *were* with him, from Harosheth of the Gentiles unto the river of Kishon.

14And Deborah said unto Barak, Up; for this *is* the day in which the LORD hath delivered Sisera into thine hand: is not the LORD gone out before thee? So Barak went down from mount Tabor, and ten thousand men after him.

15And the LORD discomfited Sisera, and all *his* chariots, and all *his* host, with the edge of the sword before Barak; so that Sisera lighted down off *his* chariot, and fled away on his feet.

16But Barak pursued after the chariots, and after the host, unto Harosheth of the Gentiles: and all the host of Sisera fell upon the edge of the sword; *and* there was not a man left.

17Howbeit Sisera fled away on his feet to the tent of Jael the wife of Heber the Kenite: for *there was* peace between Jabin the king of Hazor and the house of Heber the Kenite.

18¶ And Jael went out to meet Sisera, and said unto him, Turn in, my lord, turn in to me; fear not. And when he had turned in unto her into the tent, she covered him with a mantle.

19And he said unto her, Give me, I pray thee, a little water to drink; for I am thirsty. And she opened a bottle of milk, and gave him drink, and covered him.

20Again he said unto her, Stand in the door of the tent, and it shall be, when any man doth come and inquire of thee, and say, Is there any man here? that thou shalt say, No.

21Then Jael Heber's wife took a nail of the tent, and took an hammer in her hand, and went softly unto him, and smote the nail into his temples, and fastened it into the ground: for he was fast asleep and weary. So he died.

22And, behold, as Barak pursued Sisera, Jael came out to meet him, and said unto him, Come, and I will show thee the man whom thou seekest. And when he came into her *tent*, behold, Sisera lay dead, and the nail *was* in his temples.

23So God subdued on that day Jabin the king of Canaan before the children of Israel.

24And the hand of the children of Israel prospered, and prevailed against Jabin the king of Canaan, until they had destroyed Jabin king of Canaan.

5 THEN SANG Deborah and Barak the son of Abinoam on that day, saying,

2Praise ye the LORD for the avenging of Israel, when the people willingly offered themselves.

3Hear, O ye kings; give ear, O ye princes; I, *even* I, will sing unto the LORD; I will sing *praise* to the LORD God of Israel.

4LORD, when thou wentest out of Seir, when thou marchedst out of the field of Edom, the earth trembled, and the heavens dropped, the clouds also dropped water.

5The mountains melted from before the LORD, *even* that Sinai from before the LORD God of Israel.

# Amplified

10And Barak called Zebulun and Naphtali to Kedesh; and he went up with 10,000 men at his heels; and Deborah went up with him.

11Now Heber the Kenite, of the descendants of Hobab, father-in-law of Moses, had separated from the Kenites, and encamped as far away as the oak in Zaanannim, which is near Kedesh.

12When it was told Sisera that Barak son of Abinoam had gone up to Mount Tabor,

13Sisera gathered together all his chariots, even 900 chariots of iron, and all the men who were with him, from Harosheth-ha-goiim to the river Kishon.

14And Deborah said to Barak, Up! For this is the day when the Lord has given Sisera into your hand. Is not the Lord gone out before you? So Barak went down from Mount Tabor with 10,000 men following him.

15And the Lord confused *and* terrified Sisera and all his chariot drivers and all his army before Barak with the sword. And Sisera alighted from his chariot and fled on foot.

16But Barak pursued after the chariots and the army to Harosheth-ha-goiim; and all the army of Sisera fell by the sword; not a man was left.

17But Sisera fled on foot to the tent of Jael, the wife of Heber the Kenite; for there was peace between Jabin the king of Hazor and the house of Heber the Kenite.

18And Jael went out to meet Sisera, and said to him, Turn aside, my lord, turn aside to me; have no fear. So he turned aside to her into the tent, and she covered him with a rug.

19And he said to her, Give me, I pray you, a little water to drink, for I am thirsty. And she opened a skin of milk and gave him a drink and covered him.

20And he said to her, Stand at the door of the tent, and if any man comes and asks you, Is there any man here? Tell him, No.

21But Jael, Heber's wife, took a tent pin and a hammer in her hand, and went softly to him and drove the pin through his temples and into the ground; for he was in a deep sleep from weariness. So he died.

22And behold, as Barak pursued Sisera, Jael came out to meet him, and said to him, Come, and I will show you the man you seek. And when he came into her tent, behold, Sisera lay dead, and the tent pin was in his temples.

23So God subdued on that day Jabin the king of Canaan before the Israelites.

24And the hand of the Israelites bore more and more upon Jabin the king of Canaan, until they had destroyed [him].

5 THEN SANG Deborah and Barak the son of Abinoam on that day, saying,

2For the leaders who took the lead in Israel, for the people who offered themselves willingly, bless the Lord!

3Hear, O kings; give ear, O princes; I will sing to the Lord; I will sing praise to the Lord, the God of Israel.

4Lord, when You went forth out of Seir, when You marched out of the field of Edom, the earth trembled, and the heavens also dropped, yes, the clouds dropped water.

5The mountains quaked at the presence of the Lord, yes, yonder Sinai at the presence of the Lord, the God of Israel.

## New American Standard

10And Barak called Zebulun and Naphtali together to Kedesh,
and ten thousand men went up with him; Deborah also went up
with him.
11¶ Now Heber the Kenite had separated himself from the Kenites, from the sons of Hobab the father-in-law of Moses, and had
pitched his tent as far away as the oak in Zaanannim, which is near
Kedesh.
12¶ Then they told Sisera that Barak the son of Abinoam had
gone up to Mount Tabor.
13And Sisera called together all his chariots, nine hundred iron
chariots, and all the people who *were* with him, from Harosheth-
hagoyim to the river Kishon.
14And Deborah said to Barak, "Arise! For this is the day in
which the LORD has given Sisera into your hands; [a]behold, the
LORD has gone out before you." So Barak went down from Mount
Tabor with ten thousand men following him.
15And the LORD routed Sisera and all *his* chariots and all *his*
army, with the edge of the sword before Barak; and Sisera alighted
from *his* chariot and fled away on foot.
16But Barak pursued the chariots and the army as far as
Harosheth-hagoyim, and all the army of Sisera fell by the edge of
the sword; not even one was left.
17¶ Now Sisera fled away on foot to the tent of Jael the wife of
Heber the Kenite, for *there was* peace between Jabin the king of
Hazor and the house of Heber the Kenite.
18And Jael went out to meet Sisera, and said to him, "Turn
aside, my master, turn aside to me! Do not be afraid." And he
turned aside to her into the tent, and she covered him with a rug.
19And he said to her, "Please give me a little water to drink, for
I am thirsty." So she opened a [b]bottle of milk and gave him a drink;
then she covered him.
20And he said to her, "Stand in the doorway of the tent, and
it shall be if anyone comes and inquires of you, and says, 'Is there
anyone here?' that you shall say, 'No.' "
21But Jael, Heber's wife, took a tent peg and seized a hammer
in her hand, and went secretly to him and drove the peg into his
temple, and it went through into the ground; for he was sound
asleep and exhausted. So he died.
22And behold, as Barak pursued Sisera, Jael came out to meet
him and said to him, "Come, and I will show you the man whom
you are seeking." And he entered with her, and behold Sisera was
lying dead with the tent peg in his temple.
23¶ So God subdued on that day Jabin the king of Canaan before
the sons of Israel.
24And the hand of the sons of Israel pressed heavier and heavier
upon Jabin the king of Canaan, until they had destroyed Jabin the
king of Canaan.

*The Song of Deborah and Barak*

**5** THEN DEBORAH and Barak the son of Abinoam sang on that
day, saying,

2 "That the leaders led in Israel,
That the people volunteered,
Bless the LORD!
3 "Hear, O kings; give ear, O rulers!
I—to the LORD, I will sing,
I will sing praise to the LORD, the God of Israel.
4 "LORD, when Thou didst go out from Seir,
When Thou didst march from the field of Edom,
The earth quaked, the heavens also dripped,
Even the clouds dripped water.
5 "The mountains quaked at the presence of the LORD,
This Sinai, at the presence of the LORD, the God of
Israel.

NAS [a] Or, *has not the LORD gone . . . ?* [b] I.e., skin container

## New International

tali. Ten thousand men followed him, and Deborah also went with
him.
11Now Heber the Kenite had left the other Kenites, the descendants of Hobab, Moses' brother-in-law,[c] and pitched his tent by the
great tree in Zaanannim near Kedesh.
12When they told Sisera that Barak son of Abinoam had gone
up to Mount Tabor, 13Sisera gathered together his nine hundred
iron chariots and all the men with him, from Harosheth Haggoyim
to the Kishon River.
14Then Deborah said to Barak, "Go! This is the day the LORD
has given Sisera into your hands. Has not the LORD gone ahead
of you?" So Barak went down Mount Tabor, followed by ten
thousand men. 15At Barak's advance, the LORD routed Sisera and
all his chariots and army by the sword, and Sisera abandoned his
chariot and fled on foot. 16But Barak pursued the chariots and
army as far as Harosheth Haggoyim. All the troops of Sisera fell
by the sword; not a man was left.
17Sisera, however, fled on foot to the tent of Jael, the wife of
Heber the Kenite, because there were friendly relations between
Jabin king of Hazor and the clan of Heber the Kenite.
18Jael went out to meet Sisera and said to him, "Come, my lord,
come right in. Don't be afraid." So he entered her tent, and she
put a covering over him.
19"I'm thirsty," he said. "Please give me some water." She
opened a skin of milk, gave him a drink, and covered him up.
20"Stand in the doorway of the tent," he told her. "If someone
comes by and asks you, 'Is anyone here?' say 'No.' "
21But Jael, Heber's wife, picked up a tent peg and a hammer and
went quietly to him while he lay fast asleep, exhausted. She drove
the peg through his temple into the ground, and he died.
22Barak came by in pursuit of Sisera, and Jael went out to meet
him. "Come," she said, "I will show you the man you're looking
for." So he went in with her, and there lay Sisera with the tent peg
through his temple—dead.
23On that day God subdued Jabin, the Canaanite king, before
the Israelites. 24And the hand of the Israelites grew stronger and
stronger against Jabin, the Canaanite king, until they destroyed
him.

*The Song of Deborah*

**5** ON THAT day Deborah and Barak son of Abinoam sang this
song:

2"When the princes in Israel take the lead,
when the people willingly offer themselves—
praise the LORD!

3"Hear this, you kings! Listen, you rulers!
I will sing to[d] the LORD, I will sing;
I will make music to[e] the LORD, the God of Israel.

4"O LORD, when you went out from Seir,
when you marched from the land of Edom,
the earth shook, the heavens poured,
the clouds poured down water.
5The mountains quaked before the LORD, the One of Sinai,
before the LORD, the God of Israel.

NIV [c] 11 Or *father-in-law* [d] 3 Or *of* [e] 3 Or / *with song I will praise*

## King James

6 In the days of Shamgar the son of Anath, in the days of Jael, the highways were unoccupied, and the travellers walked through byways.

7 *The inhabitants of* the villages ceased, they ceased in Israel, until that I Deborah arose, that I arose a mother in Israel.

8 They chose new gods; then *was* war in the gates: was there a shield or spear seen among forty thousand in Israel?

9 My heart *is* toward the governors of Israel, that offered themselves willingly among the people. Bless ye the LORD.

10 Speak, ye that ride on white asses, ye that sit in judgment, and walk by the way.

11 *They that are delivered* from the noise of archers in the places of drawing water, there shall they rehearse the righteous acts of the LORD, *even* the righteous acts *toward the inhabitants* of his villages in Israel: then shall the people of the LORD go down to the gates.

12 Awake, awake, Deborah: awake, awake, utter a song: arise, Barak, and lead thy captivity captive, thou son of Abinoam.

13 Then he made him that remaineth have dominion over the nobles among the people: the LORD made me have dominion over the mighty.

14 Out of Ephraim *was there* a root of them against Amalek; after thee, Benjamin, among thy people; out of Machir came down governors, and out of Zebulun they that handle the pen of the writer.

15 And the princes of Issachar *were* with Deborah; even Issachar, and also Barak: he was sent on foot into the valley. For the divisions of Reuben *there were* great thoughts of heart.

16 Why abodest thou among the sheepfolds, to hear the bleatings of the flocks? For the divisions of Reuben *there were* great searchings of heart.

17 Gilead abode beyond Jordan: and why did Dan remain in ships? Asher continued on the sea shore, and abode in his breaches.

18 Zebulun and Naphtali *were* a people *that* jeoparded their lives unto the death in the high places of the field.

19 The kings came *and* fought, then fought the kings of Canaan in Taanach by the waters of Megiddo; they took no gain of money.

20 They fought from heaven; the stars in their courses fought against Sisera.

21 The river of Kishon swept them away, that ancient river, the river Kishon. O my soul, thou hast trodden down strength.

22 Then were the horsehoofs broken by the means of the pransings, the pransings of their mighty ones.

23 Curse ye Meroz, said the angel of the LORD, curse ye bitterly the inhabitants thereof; because they came not to the help of the LORD, to the help of the LORD against the mighty.

## Amplified

6 After the days of Shamgar son of Anath, after the days of Jael [meaning here Ehud] the caravans ceased, travelers walked through byways.

7 The villages were unoccupied, *and* rulers ceased in Israel, until [a]you arose, you, Deborah, arose, a mother in Israel.

8 [Formerly] they chose new gods; then was war in the gates. Was there a shield or spear seen among 40,000 in Israel?

9 My heart goes out to the commanders of Israel, who offered themselves willingly among the people. Bless the Lord!

10 Tell of it, you who ride on white donkeys, you who sit on rich carpets, and you who walk by the way.

11 Far from the noise of archers, in the places of drawing water, there shall they rehearse the righteous acts of the Lord, even the righteous acts toward His villagers in Israel. Then the people of the Lord went down to the gates.

12 Awake, awake, Deborah! Awake, awake, utter a song! Arise, Barak, and lead away your captives, you son of Abinoam.

13 Then down marched the remnant of the nobles; the people of the Lord marched down for *Me* against the mighty.

14 Out of Ephraim they came down whose root is in Amalek; after you, Benjamin, with your kinsmen; out of Machir came down commanders *and* lawgivers, and out of Zebulun those who [b]handle the pen *or* stylus of the writer.

15 And the princes of Issachar came with Deborah, and Issachar faithful to Barak; into the valley they rushed forth at his heels. *But* among the clans of Reuben were great searchings of heart.

16 Why, *Reuben*, did you linger among the sheepfolds, listening to the piping for the flocks? Among the clans of Reuben there were great searchings of heart.

17 Gilead remained beyond Jordan; and why did Dan stay with the ships? Asher sat still on the sea coast, and remained by his creeks. [These came not forth to battle for God's people.]

18 But Zebulun was a people who endangered their lives to the death; Naphtali did also, on the heights of the field.

19 The kings came and fought; then fought the kings of Canaan, at Taanach by the waters of Megiddo; gain of booty they did not obtain.

20 From the heavens the stars fought, from their courses they fought against Sisera.

21 The torrent Kishon swept [the foe] away, the onrushing torrent, the torrent Kishon. O my soul, march on with strength!

22 Then the horses' hoofs beat loudly, because of the galloping of [fleeing] valiant riders.

23 Curse Meroz, said the messenger of the Lord, curse bitterly its inhabitants; because they came not to the help of the Lord, to the help of the Lord against the mighty!

**AMP** [a] F. F. Bruce in *The New Bible Dictionary* calls attention to the fact that the repeated Hebrew verb here "may be understood not as the normal first person singular ('I arose') but as an archaic second person singular ('thou didst arise')." [b] Reference at this date (c. 1150 B.C.) to a writer is no more surprising than the mention of "the city of books" in 1:11. Writing, and alphabetical writing at that, had been practiced for some centuries along the Syrian Coast . . . Quantities of papyrus [the pith of papyrus was used for writing] were exported from Egypt to Phoenicia c. 1100 B.C. Cp. Judg. 8:14 (condensed from *The New Bible Commentary*). "Zebulun, formerly known only for his experts with the ciphering-pencil, had now become a people courageous unto death" *(Lange's Commentary)*.

## New American Standard

6¶ "In the days of Shamgar the son of Anath,
In the days of Jael, the highways were deserted,
And travelers went by roundabout ways.
7 "The peasantry ceased, they ceased in Israel,
Until I, Deborah, arose,
Until I arose, a mother in Israel.
8 "New gods were chosen;
Then war *was* in the gates.
Not a shield or a spear was seen
Among forty thousand in Israel.
9 "My heart *goes out* to the commanders of Israel,
The volunteers among the people;
Bless the LORD!
10 "You who ride on white donkeys,
You who sit on *rich* carpets,
And you who travel on the road—sing!
11 "At the sound of those who divide *flocks* among the watering places,
There they shall recount the righteous deeds of the LORD,
The righteous deeds for His peasantry in Israel.
Then the people of the LORD went down to the gates.

12¶ "Awake, awake, Deborah;
Awake, awake, sing a song!
Arise, Barak, and take away your captives, O son of Abinoam.
13 "Then survivors came down to the nobles;
The people of the LORD came down to me as warriors.
14 "From Ephraim those whose root is in Amalek *came down,*
Following you, Benjamin, with your peoples;
From Machir commanders came down,
And from Zebulun those who wield the staff of office.
15 "And the princes of Issachar *were* with Deborah;
As *was* Issachar, so *was* Barak;
Into the valley they rushed at his heels;
Among the divisions of Reuben
*There were* great resolves of heart.
16 "Why did you sit among the [c]sheepfolds,
To hear the piping for the flocks?
Among the divisions of Reuben
*There were* great searchings of heart.
17 "Gilead remained across the Jordan;
And why did Dan stay in ships?
Asher sat at the seashore,
And remained by its landings.
18 "Zebulun *was* a people who despised their lives *even* to death,
And Naphtali also, on the high places of the field.

19¶ "The kings came *and* fought;
Then fought the kings of Canaan
At Taanach near the waters of Megiddo;
They took no plunder in silver.
20 "The stars fought from heaven,
From their courses they fought against Sisera.
21 "The torrent of Kishon swept them away,
The ancient torrent, the torrent Kishon.
O my soul, march on with strength.
22 "Then the horses' hoofs beat
From the dashing, the dashing of his valiant steeds.
23 'Curse Meroz,' said the angel of the LORD,
'Utterly curse its inhabitants;
Because they did not come to the help of the LORD,
To the help of the LORD against the warriors.'

NAS [c] Or, *saddlebags*

## New International

6"In the days of Shamgar son of Anath,
in the days of Jael, the roads were abandoned;
travelers took to winding paths.
7Village life[d] in Israel ceased,
ceased until I,[e] Deborah, arose,
arose a mother in Israel.
8When they chose new gods,
war came to the city gates,
and not a shield or spear was seen
among forty thousand in Israel.
9My heart is with Israel's princes,
with the willing volunteers among the people.
Praise the LORD!

10"You who ride on white donkeys,
sitting on your saddle blankets,
and you who walk along the road,
consider 11the voice of the singers[f] at the watering places.
They recite the righteous acts of the LORD,
the righteous acts of his warriors[g] in Israel.
"Then the people of the LORD
went down to the city gates.
12'Wake up, wake up, Deborah!
Wake up, wake up, break out in song!
Arise, O Barak!
Take captive your captives, O son of Abinoam.'

13"Then the men who were left
came down to the nobles;
the people of the LORD
came to me with the mighty.
14Some came from Ephraim, whose roots were in Amalek;
Benjamin was with the people who followed you.
From Makir captains came down,
from Zebulun those who bear a commander's staff.
15The princes of Issachar were with Deborah;
yes, Issachar was with Barak,
rushing after him into the valley.
In the districts of Reuben
there was much searching of heart.
16Why did you stay among the campfires[h]
to hear the whistling for the flocks?
In the districts of Reuben
there was much searching of heart.
17Gilead stayed beyond the Jordan.
And Dan, why did he linger by the ships?
Asher remained on the coast
and stayed in his coves.
18The people of Zebulun risked their very lives;
so did Naphtali on the heights of the field.

19"Kings came, they fought;
the kings of Canaan fought
at Taanach by the waters of Megiddo,
but they carried off no silver, no plunder.
20From the heavens the stars fought,
from their courses they fought against Sisera.
21The river Kishon swept them away,
the age-old river, the river Kishon.
March on, my soul; be strong!
22Then thundered the horses' hoofs—
galloping, galloping go his mighty steeds.
23'Curse Meroz,' said the angel of the LORD.
'Curse its people bitterly,
because they did not come to help the LORD,
to help the LORD against the mighty.'

NIV [d] *7* Or *Warriors* [e] *7* Or *you* [f] *11* Or *archers;* the meaning of the Hebrew for this word is uncertain. [g] *11* Or *villagers* [h] *16* Or *saddlebags*

## King James

24Blessed above women shall Jael the wife of Heber the Kenite
be, blessed shall she be above women in the tent.
25He asked water, *and* she gave *him* milk; she brought forth
butter in a lordly dish.
26She put her hand to the nail, and her right hand to the workmen's hammer; and with the hammer she smote Sisera, she smote
off his head, when she had pierced and stricken through his temples.
27At her feet he bowed, he fell, he lay down: at her feet he
bowed, he fell: where he bowed, there he fell down dead.
28The mother of Sisera looked out at a window, and cried
through the lattice, Why is his chariot *so* long in coming? why tarry
the wheels of his chariot?
29Her wise ladies answered her, yea, she returned answer to
herself,
30Have they not sped? have they *not* divided the prey; to every
man a damsel *or* two; to Sisera a prey of divers colours, a prey of
divers colours of needlework, of divers colours of needlework on
both sides, *meet* for the necks of *them that take* the spoil?
31So let all thine enemies perish, O LORD: but *let* them that love
him *be* as the sun when he goeth forth in his might. And the land
had rest forty years.

6 AND THE children of Israel did evil in the sight of the LORD:
and the LORD delivered them into the hand of Midian seven
years.
2And the hand of Midian prevailed against Israel: *and* because
of the Midianites the children of Israel made them the dens which
*are* in the mountains, and caves, and strong holds.
3And *so* it was, when Israel had sown, that the Midianites came
up, and the Amalekites, and the children of the east, even they
came up against them;
4And they encamped against them, and destroyed the increase
of the earth, till thou come unto Gaza, and left no sustenance for
Israel, neither sheep, nor ox, nor ass.
5For they came up with their cattle and their tents, and they
came as grasshoppers for multitude; *for* both they and their camels
were without number: and they entered into the land to destroy
it.
6And Israel was greatly impoverished because of the Midianites; and the children of Israel cried unto the LORD.
7¶ And it came to pass, when the children of Israel cried unto
the LORD because of the Midianites,
8That the LORD sent a prophet unto the children of Israel, which
said unto them, Thus saith the LORD God of Israel, I brought you
up from Egypt, and brought you forth out of the house of bondage;
9And I delivered you out of the hand of the Egyptians, and out
of the hand of all that oppressed you, and drave them out from
before you, and gave you their land;
10And I said unto you, I *am* the LORD your God; fear not the
gods of the Amorites, in whose land ye dwell: but ye have not
obeyed my voice.

## Amplified

24Blessed above women shall Jael the wife of Heber the Kenite
be, blessed shall she be above women in the tent.
25[Sisera] asked water, *and she* gave *him* milk; she brought him
curds in a lordly dish.
26She put her [left] hand to the tent-pin, and her right hand to
the workmen's hammer; and with the wooden hammer she smote
Sisera, she smote through his head, yes, she pierced and struck
through his temples.
27He sank, he fell, he lay still at her feet; at her feet he sank, he
fell; where he sank, there he fell dead!
28The [a]mother of Sisera looked out at a window, and wailed
through the lattice, Why is his chariot so long in coming? Why do
the hoof-beats of his chariots tarry?
29Her wise ladies answered her, yet she repeated her words to
herself,
30Have they not found and been dividing the spoil? A maiden
or two for every man, spoil of dyed garments for Sisera, spoil of
dyed stuffs embroidered, two pieces of dyed work embroidered
for my neck as spoil?
31So let all Your enemies perish, O Lord! But let those who love
Him be like the sun when he rises in his might. And the land had
peace *and* rest for forty years.

6 BUT THE Israelites did evil in the sight of the Lord; and the
Lord gave them into the hand of Midian for seven years.
2And the hand of Midian prevailed against Israel; because of
Midian the Israelites made themselves the dens which are in the
mountains, and the caves and strongholds.
3For whenever Israel had sown their seed, the Midianites and
the Amalekites and the people of the East came up against them;
4And they would encamp against them and destroy the crops,
as far as Gaza, and leave no nourishment for Israel, and no ox or
sheep or donkey,
5For they came up with their cattle and their tents, and they
came like locusts for multitude; both they and their camels could
not be counted; so they wasted the land as they entered it.
6And Israel was greatly impoverished because of the Midianites, and the Israelites cried to the Lord.
7And when they cried to the Lord because of Midian,
8The Lord sent a prophet to the Israelites, who said to them,
Thus says the Lord, the God of Israel, I brought you up from
Egypt, and brought you forth out of the house of bondage;
9And I delivered you out of the hand of the Egyptians, and out
of the hand of all who oppressed you, and drove them out from
before you, and gave you their land;
10And I said to you, I am the Lord your God; fear not the gods
of the Amorites, in whose land you dwell. But you have not
obeyed My voice.

**AMP** [a] Who should first suffer anxiety [in the palace of the women], if not the mother? Of a wife, nothing is said; such love thrives not in the harem of a prince. He is his mother's pride, the great hero, who had hitherto been invincible. What she has in him, and what she loses, concerns no other woman *(Lange's Commentary)*.

## New American Standard

24¶ "Most blessed of women is Jael,
The wife of Heber the Kenite;
Most blessed is she of women in the tent.
25 "He asked for water *and* she gave him milk;
In a magnificent bowl she brought him curds.
26 "She reached out her hand for the tent peg,
And her right hand for the workmen's hammer.
Then she struck Sisera, she smashed his head;
And she shattered and pierced his temple.
27 "Between her feet he bowed, he fell, he lay;
Between her feet he bowed, he fell;
Where he bowed, there he fell dead.

28¶ "Out of the window she looked and lamented,
The mother of Sisera through the lattice,
'Why does his chariot delay in coming?
Why do the hoofbeats of his chariots tarry?'
29 "Her wise princesses would answer her,
Indeed she repeats her words to herself,
30 'Are they not finding, are they not dividing the spoil?
A maiden, two maidens for every warrior;
To Sisera a spoil of dyed work,
A spoil of dyed work embroidered,
Dyed work of double embroidery on the neck of the spoiler?'
31 "Thus let all Thine enemies perish, O LORD;
But let those who love Him be like the rising of the sun in its might."
And the land was undisturbed for forty years.

*Israel Oppressed by Midian*

6 THEN THE sons of Israel did what was evil in the sight of the
LORD; and the LORD gave them into the hands of Midian
seven years.
2And the power of Midian prevailed against Israel. Because of
Midian the sons of Israel made for themselves the dens which were
in the mountains and the caves and the strongholds.
3For it was when Israel had sown, that the Midianites would
come up with the Amalekites and the sons of the east and go
against them.
4So they would camp against them and destroy the produce of
the earth as far as Gaza, and leave no sustenance in Israel as well
as no sheep, ox, or donkey.
5For they would come up with their livestock and their tents,
they would come in like locusts for number, both they and their
camels were innumerable; and they came into the land to devastate
it.
6So Israel was brought very low because of Midian, and the
sons of Israel cried to the LORD.
7¶ Now it came about when the sons of Israel cried to the LORD
on account of Midian,
8that the LORD sent a prophet to the sons of Israel, and he said
to them, "Thus says the LORD, the God of Israel, 'It was I who
brought you up from Egypt, and brought you out from the house
of slavery.
9'And I delivered you from the hands of the Egyptians and
from the hands of all your oppressors, and dispossessed them
before you and gave you their land,
10and I said to you, "I am the LORD your God; you shall not fear
the gods of the Amorites in whose land you live. But you have not
obeyed Me." ' "

## New International

24"Most blessed of women be Jael,
the wife of Heber the Kenite,
most blessed of tent-dwelling women.
25He asked for water, and she gave him milk;
in a bowl fit for nobles she brought him curdled milk.
26Her hand reached for the tent peg,
her right hand for the workman's hammer.
She struck Sisera, she crushed his head,
she shattered and pierced his temple.
27At her feet he sank,
he fell; there he lay.
At her feet he sank, he fell;
where he sank, there he fell—dead.

28"Through the window peered Sisera's mother;
behind the lattice she cried out,
'Why is his chariot so long in coming?
Why is the clatter of his chariots delayed?'
29The wisest of her ladies answer her;
indeed, she keeps saying to herself,
30'Are they not finding and dividing the spoils:
a girl or two for each man,
colorful garments as plunder for Sisera,
colorful garments embroidered,
highly embroidered garments for my neck—
all this as plunder?'

31"So may all your enemies perish, O LORD!
But may they who love you be like the sun
when it rises in its strength."

Then the land had peace forty years.

*Gideon*

6 AGAIN THE Israelites did evil in the eyes of the LORD, and
for seven years he gave them into the hands of the Midianites.
2Because the power of Midian was so oppressive, the Israelites
prepared shelters for themselves in mountain clefts, caves and
strongholds. 3Whenever the Israelites planted their crops, the
Midianites, Amalekites and other eastern peoples invaded the
country. 4They camped on the land and ruined the crops all the
way to Gaza and did not spare a living thing for Israel, neither
sheep nor cattle nor donkeys. 5They came up with their livestock
and their tents like swarms of locusts. It was impossible to count
the men and their camels; they invaded the land to ravage it.
6Midian so impoverished the Israelites that they cried out to the
LORD for help.
7When the Israelites cried to the LORD because of Midian, 8he
sent them a prophet, who said, "This is what the LORD, the God
of Israel, says: I brought you up out of Egypt, out of the land of
slavery. 9I snatched you from the power of Egypt and from the
hand of all your oppressors. I drove them from before you and
gave you their land. 10I said to you, 'I am the LORD your God; do
not worship the gods of the Amorites, in whose land you live.' But
you have not listened to me."

## King James

11¶ And there came an angel of the LORD, and sat under an oak which *was* in Ophrah, that *pertained* unto Joash the Abi-ezrite: and his son Gideon threshed wheat by the winepress, to hide *it* from the Midianites.

12And the angel of the LORD appeared unto him, and said unto him, The LORD *is* with thee, thou mighty man of valour.

13And Gideon said unto him, Oh my Lord, if the LORD be with us, why then is all this befallen us? and where *be* all his miracles which our fathers told us of, saying, Did not the LORD bring us up from Egypt? but now the LORD hath forsaken us, and delivered us into the hands of the Midianites.

14And the LORD looked upon him, and said, Go in this thy might, and thou shalt save Israel from the hand of the Midianites: have not I sent thee?

15And he said unto him, Oh my Lord, wherewith shall I save Israel? behold, my family *is* poor in Manasseh, and I *am* the least in my father's house.

16And the LORD said unto him, Surely I will be with thee, and thou shalt smite the Midianites as one man.

17And he said unto him, If now I have found grace in thy sight, then shew me a sign that thou talkest with me.

18Depart not hence, I pray thee, until I come unto thee, and bring forth my present, and set *it* before thee. And he said, I will tarry until thou come again.

19¶ And Gideon went in, and made ready a kid, and unleavened cakes of an ephah of flour: the flesh he put in a basket, and he put the broth in a pot, and brought *it* out unto him under the oak, and presented *it*.

20And the angel of God said unto him, Take the flesh and the unleavened cakes, and lay *them* upon this rock, and pour out the broth. And he did so.

21¶ Then the angel of the LORD put forth the end of the staff that *was* in his hand, and touched the flesh and the unleavened cakes; and there rose up fire out of the rock, and consumed the flesh and the unleavened cakes. Then the angel of the LORD departed out of his sight.

22And when Gideon perceived that he *was* an angel of the LORD, Gideon said, Alas, O Lord GOD! for because I have seen an angel of the LORD face to face.

23And the LORD said unto him, Peace *be* unto thee; fear not: thou shalt not die.

24Then Gideon built an altar there unto the LORD, and called it Jehovah-shalom: unto this day it *is* yet in Ophrah of the Abi-ezrites.

25¶ And it came to pass the same night, that the LORD said unto him, Take thy father's young bullock, even the second bullock of seven years old, and throw down the altar of Baal that thy father hath, and cut down the grove that *is* by it:

26And build an altar unto the LORD thy God upon the top of this rock, in the ordered place, and take the second bullock, and offer a burnt sacrifice with the wood of the grove which thou shalt cut down.

27Then Gideon took ten men of his servants, and did as the LORD had said unto him: and *so* it was, because he feared his father's household, and the men of the city, that he could not do *it* by day, that he did *it* by night.

28¶ And when the men of the city arose early in the morning, behold, the altar of Baal was cast down, and the grove was cut down that *was* by it, and the second bullock was offered upon the altar *that was* built.

29And they said one to another, Who hath done this thing? And when they inquired and asked, they said, Gideon the son of Joash hath done this thing.

30Then the men of the city said unto Joash, Bring out thy son, that he may die: because he hath cast down the altar of Baal, and because he hath cut down the grove that *was* by it.

## Amplified

11Now the Angel of the Lord came and sat under the oak [terebinth] at Ophrah, which belonged to Joash the Abiezrite, and his son Gideon was beating wheat in the winepress, to hide it from the Midianites.

12And the Angel of the Lord appeared to him and said to him, The Lord is with you, you mighty man of [fearless] courage.

13And Gideon said to him, O sir, if the Lord is with us, why is all this befallen us? And where are all His wondrous works of which our fathers told us, saying, Did not the Lord bring us up from Egypt? But now the Lord has forsaken us, and given us into the hand of Midian.

14The Lord turned to him, and said, Go in this your might, and you shall save Israel from the hand of Midian. Have I not sent you?

15Gideon said to Him, Oh, Lord, how can I deliver Israel? Behold, my clan is the poorest in Manasseh, and I am the least in my father's house.

16The Lord said to him, Surely I will be with you, and you shall smite the Midianites as one man.

17Gideon said to Him, If now I have found favor in Your sight, then show me a sign that it is You Who talks with me.

18Do not leave here, I pray You, until I return to You, and bring my offering, and set it before You. And He said, I will wait until you return.

19The Gideon went in and prepared a kid and unleavened cakes of an ephah of flour. The meat he put in a basket and the broth in a pot, and brought them to Him under the oak and presented them.

20And the Angel of God said to him, Take the meat and unleavened cakes and lay them on this rock, and pour the broth over them. And he did so.

21Then the Angel of the Lord reached out the tip of the staff that was in His hand, and touched the meat and the unleavened cakes; and there flared up fire from the rock and consumed the meat and the unleavened cakes. Then the Angel of the Lord vanished from his sight.

22And when Gideon perceived that He was the Angel of the Lord, Gideon said, Alas, O Lord God! For now I have seen the Angel of the Lord face to face!

23The Lord said to him, Peace be to you; do not fear, you shall not die.

24Then Gideon built an altar there to the Lord, and called it, The Lord is peace. To this day it still stands in Ophrah, which belongs to the Abiezrites.

25That night the Lord said to Gideon, Take your father's bull, the second bull seven years old, and pull down the altar of Baal that your father has, and cut down the Asherah that is beside it;

26And build an altar to the Lord your God on top of this stronghold, with stones laid in proper order; then take the second bull, and offer a burnt sacrifice with the wood of the Asherah which you shall cut down.

27Then Gideon took ten men of his servants, and did as the Lord had told him; but because he was too afraid of his father's household and the men of the city to do it by day, he did it by night.

28And when the men of the city arose early in the morning, behold, the altar of Baal was cast down, and the Asherah was cut down that was beside it, and the second bull was offered on the altar which had been built.

29And they said to one another, Who has done this thing? And when they searched and asked, they were told, Gideon son of Joash has done this thing.

30Then the men of the city commanded Joash, Bring out your son, that he may die; for he has pulled down the altar of Baal and cut down the Asherah beside it.

## New American Standard

*Gideon Is Visited*

11¶ Then the angel of the LORD came and sat under the oak that
was in Ophrah, which belonged to Joash the Abiezrite as his son
Gideon was beating out wheat in the wine press in order to save
*it* from the Midianites.
12And the angel of the LORD appeared to him and said to him,
"The LORD is with you, O valiant warrior."
13Then Gideon said to him, "O my lord, if the LORD is with us,
why then has all this happened to us? And where are all His
miracles which our fathers told us about, saying, 'Did not the LORD
bring us up from Egypt?' But now the LORD has abandoned us and
given us into the hand of Midian."
14And the LORD looked at him and said, "Go in this your
strength and deliver Israel from the hand of Midian. Have I not
sent you?"
15And he said to Him, "O Lord, how shall I deliver Israel?
Behold, my family is the least in Manasseh, and I am the youngest
in my father's house."
16But the LORD said to him, "Surely I will be with you, and you
shall defeat Midian as one man."
17So Gideon said to Him, "If now I have found favor in Thy
sight, then show me a sign that it is Thou who speakest with me.
18"Please do not depart from here, until I come *back* to Thee, and
bring out my offering and lay it before Thee." And He said, "I will
remain until you return."
19¶ Then Gideon went in and prepared a kid and unleavened
bread from an [a]ephah of flour; he put the meat in a basket and the
broth in a pot, and brought *them* out to him under the oak, and
presented *them*.
20And the angel of God said to him, "Take the meat and the
unleavened bread and lay them on this rock, and pour out the
broth." And he did so.
21Then the angel of the LORD put out the end of the staff that
was in his hand and touched the meat and the unleavened bread;
and fire sprang up from the rock and consumed the meat and the
unleavened bread. Then the angel of the LORD vanished from his
sight.
22When Gideon saw that he was the angel of the LORD, he said,
"Alas, O Lord GOD! For now I have seen the angel of the LORD face
to face."
23And the LORD said to him, "Peace to you, do not fear; you
shall not die."
24Then Gideon built an altar there to the LORD and named it The
LORD is Peace. To this day it is still in Ophrah of the Abiezrites.
25¶ Now the same night it came about that the LORD said to him,
"Take your father's bull and a second bull seven years old, and pull
down the altar of Baal which belongs to your father, and cut down
the [b]Asherah that is beside it;
26and build an altar to the LORD your God on the top of this
stronghold in an orderly manner, and take a second bull and offer
a burnt offering with the wood of the Asherah which you shall cut
down."
27Then Gideon took ten men of his servants and did as the LORD
had spoken to him; and it came about, because he was too afraid
of his father's household and the men of the city to do it by day,
that he did it by night.

*The Altar of Baal Destroyed*

28¶ When the men of the city arose early in the morning, behold,
the altar of Baal was torn down, and the Asherah which was beside
it was cut down, and the second bull was offered on the altar which
had been built.
29And they said to one another, "Who did this thing?" And
when they searched about and inquired, they said, "Gideon the
son of Joash did this thing."
30Then the men of the city said to Joash, "Bring out your son,
that he may die, for he has torn down the altar of Baal, and indeed,
he has cut down the Asherah which was beside it."

NAS [a] I.e., Approx. one bushel [b] I.e., wooden symbol of a female deity

## New International

11The angel of the LORD came and sat down under the oak in
Ophrah that belonged to Joash the Abiezrite, where his son Gideon was threshing wheat in a winepress to keep it from the Midianites. 12When the angel of the LORD appeared to Gideon, he said,
"The LORD is with you, mighty warrior."
13"But sir," Gideon replied, "if the LORD is with us, why has
all this happened to us? Where are all his wonders that our fathers
told us about when they said, 'Did not the LORD bring us up out
of Egypt?' But now the LORD has abandoned us and put us into
the hand of Midian."
14The LORD turned to him and said, "Go in the strength you
have and save Israel out of Midian's hand. Am I not sending you?"
15"But Lord,[c]" Gideon asked, "how can I save Israel? My clan
is the weakest in Manasseh, and I am the least in my family."
16The LORD answered, "I will be with you, and you will strike
down all the Midianites together."
17Gideon replied, "If now I have found favor in your eyes, give
me a sign that it is really you talking to me. 18Please do not go away
until I come back and bring my offering and set it before you."
And the LORD said, "I will wait until you return."
19Gideon went in, prepared a young goat, and from an ephah[d]
of flour he made bread without yeast. Putting the meat in a basket
and its broth in a pot, he brought them out and offered them to
him under the oak.
20The angel of God said to him, "Take the meat and the unleavened bread, place them on this rock, and pour out the broth." And
Gideon did so. 21With the tip of the staff that was in his hand, the
angel of the LORD touched the meat and the unleavened bread. Fire
flared from the rock, consuming the meat and the bread. And the
angel of the LORD disappeared. 22When Gideon realized that it was
the angel of the LORD, he exclaimed, "Ah, Sovereign LORD! I have
seen the angel of the LORD face to face!"
23But the LORD said to him, "Peace! Do not be afraid. You are
not going to die."
24So Gideon built an altar to the LORD there and called it The
LORD is Peace. To this day it stands in Ophrah of the Abiezrites.
25That same night the LORD said to him, "Take the second bull
from your father's herd, the one seven years old.[e] Tear down your
father's altar to Baal and cut down the Asherah pole[f] beside it.
26Then build a proper kind of[g] altar to the LORD your God on the
top of this height. Using the wood of the Asherah pole that you
cut down, offer the second[h] bull as a burnt offering."
27So Gideon took ten of his servants and did as the LORD told
him. But because he was afraid of his family and the men of the
town, he did it at night rather than in the daytime.
28In the morning when the men of the town got up, there was
Baal's altar, demolished, with the Asherah pole beside it cut down
and the second bull sacrificed on the newly built altar!
29They asked each other, "Who did this?"
When they carefully investigated, they were told, "Gideon son
of Joash did it."
30The men of the town demanded of Joash, "Bring out your
son. He must die, because he has broken down Baal's altar and cut
down the Asherah pole beside it."

NIV [c] *15 Or sir* [d] *19* That is, probably about 3/5 bushel (about 22 liters) [e] *25 Or Take a full-grown, mature bull from your father's herd* [f] *25* That is, a symbol of the goddess Asherah; here and elsewhere in Judges [g] *26 Or build with layers of stone an* [h] *26 Or full-grown;* also in verse 28

## King James

31And Joash said unto all that stood against him, Will ye plead for Baal? will ye save him? he that will plead for him, let him be put to death whilst *it is yet* morning: if he *be* a god, let him plead for himself, because *one* hath cast down his altar.

32Therefore on that day he called him Jerubbaal, saying, Let Baal plead against him, because he hath thrown down his altar.

33¶ Then all the Midianites and the Amalekites and the children of the east were gathered together, and went over, and pitched in the valley of Jezreel.

34But the spirit of the LORD came upon Gideon, and he blew a trumpet; and Abiezer was gathered after him.

35And he sent messengers throughout all Manasseh; who also was gathered after him: and he sent messengers unto Asher, and unto Zebulun, and unto Naphtali; and they came up to meet them.

36¶ And Gideon said unto God, If thou wilt save Israel by mine hand, as thou hast said,

37Behold, I will put a fleece of wool in the floor; *and* if the dew be on the fleece only, and *it be* dry upon all the earth *beside*, then shall I know that thou wilt save Israel by mine hand, as thou hast said.

38And it was so: for he rose up early on the morrow, and thrust the fleece together, and wringed the dew out of the fleece, a bowl full of water.

39And Gideon said unto God, Let not thine anger be hot against me, and I will speak but this once: let me prove, I pray thee, but this once with the fleece; let it now be dry only upon the fleece, and upon all the ground let there be dew.

40And God did so that night: for it was dry upon the fleece only, and there was dew on all the ground.

7 THEN JERUBBAAL, who *is* Gideon, and all the people that *were* with him, rose up early, and pitched beside the well of Harod: so that the host of the Midianites were on the north side of them, by the hill of Moreh, in the valley.

2And the LORD said unto Gideon, The people that *are* with thee *are* too many for me to give the Midianites into their hands, lest Israel vaunt themselves against me, saying, Mine own hand hath saved me.

3Now therefore go to, proclaim in the ears of the people, saying, Whosoever *is* fearful and afraid, let him return and depart early from mount Gilead. And there returned of the people twenty and two thousand; and there remained ten thousand.

4And the LORD said unto Gideon, The people *are* yet *too* many; bring them down unto the water, and I will try them for thee there: and it shall be, *that* of whom I say unto thee, This shall go with thee, the same shall go with thee; and of whomsoever I say unto thee, This shall not go with thee, the same shall not go.

5So he brought down the people unto the water: and the LORD said unto Gideon, Every one that lappeth of the water with his tongue, as a dog lappeth, him shalt thou set by himself; likewise every one that boweth down upon his knees to drink.

6And the number of them that lapped, *putting* their hand to their mouth, were three hundred men: but all the rest of the people bowed down upon their knees to drink water.

7And the LORD said unto Gideon, By the three hundred men that lapped will I save you, and deliver the Midianites into thine hand: and let all the *other* people go every man unto his place.

8So the people took victuals in their hand, and their trumpets: and he sent all *the rest of* Israel every man unto his tent, and retained those three hundred men: and the host of Midian was beneath him in the valley.

9¶ And it came to pass the same night, that the LORD said unto him, Arise, get thee down unto the host; for I have delivered it into thine hand.

## Amplified

31But Joash said to all who stood against him, Will you contend for Baal? Or will you save him? He who will contend for Baal, let him be put to death while it is still morning. If Baal is a god, let him contend for himself, because one has pulled down his altar.

32Therefore on that day he called Gideon Jerubbaal, meaning, Let Baal contend against him, because he had pulled down his altar.

33Then all the Midianites and the Amalekites and the people of the East came together, and crossing the Jordan encamped in the Valley of Jezreel.

34But the Spirit of the Lord clothed Gideon with Himself *and* took possession of him; and he blew a trumpet, and [the clan of] Abiezer was gathered after him.

35And he sent messengers throughout all Manasseh, and the Manassites were called to follow him; and he sent messengers to Asher, to Zebulun, and to Naphtali, and they came up to meet them.

36And Gideon said to God, If You will deliver Israel by my hand as You have said,

37Behold, I will put a fleece of wool on the threshing floor; if there is dew on the fleece only, and it is dry on all the ground, then I shall know that You will deliver Israel by my hand, as You have said.

38And it was so. When he rose early next morning and squeezed the dew out of the fleece, he wrung from it a bowlful of water.

39And Gideon said to God, Let not your anger be kindled against me, and I will speak but this once; let me make trial only this once with the fleece, I pray; let it now be dry only upon the fleece, and upon all the ground let there be dew.

40And God did so that night; for it was dry on the fleece only, and there was dew on all the ground.

7 THEN JERUBBAAL, that is Gideon, and all the people who were with him rose early and encamped beside the spring of Harod; and the camp of Midian was north of them, by the hill of Moreh, in the valley.

2The Lord said to Gideon, The people who are with you are too many for Me to give the Midianites into their hand, lest Israel boast about themselves against Me, saying, My own hand has delivered me.

3So now proclaim in the ears of the men, saying, Whoever is fearful and trembling, let him turn back and depart from Mount Gilead. And 22,000 of the men returned, but 10,000 remained.

4And the Lord said to Gideon, The men are still too many; bring them down to the water, and I will test them for you there; and he of whom I say to you, This man shall go with you, shall go with you; and he of whom I say to you, This man shall not go with you, shall not go.

5So he brought the men down to the water; and the Lord said to Gideon, Every one who laps up the water with his tongue, as a dog laps it, you shall set by himself; likewise every one who bows down on his knees to drink.

6And the number of those who lapped, putting their hand to their mouth, were 300 men; but all the rest of the people bowed down upon their knees to drink water.

7And the Lord said to Gideon, By the 300 men who lapped I will deliver you, and give the Midianites into your hand. Let all the others return every man to his home.

8So the people took provisions in their hand, and their trumpets; and he sent all the rest of Israel every man to his home, and retained those 300 men; and the host of Midian was below him in the valley.

9That same night the Lord said to Gideon, Arise, go down against their camp, for I have given it into your hand.

## New American Standard

31But Joash said to all who stood against him, "Will you contend
for Baal, or will you deliver him? Whoever will plead for him shall
be put to death by morning. If he is a god, let him contend for
himself, because someone has torn down his altar."
32Therefore on that day he named him Jerubbaal, that is to say,
"Let Baal contend against him," because he had torn down his
altar.
33¶ Then all the Midianites and the Amalekites and the sons of
the east assembled themselves; and they crossed over and camped
in the valley of Jezreel.
34So the Spirit of the LORD came upon Gideon; and he blew a
trumpet, and the Abiezrites were called together to follow him.
35And he sent messengers throughout Manasseh, and they also
were called together to follow him; and he sent messengers to
Asher, Zebulun, and Naphtali, and they came up to meet them.

*Sign of the Fleece*

36¶ Then Gideon said to God, "If Thou wilt deliver Israel
through me, as Thou hast spoken,
37behold, I will put a fleece of wool on the threshing floor. If
there is dew on the fleece only, and it is dry on all the ground, then
I will know that Thou wilt deliver Israel through me, as Thou hast
spoken."
38And it was so. When he arose early the next morning and
squeezed the fleece, he drained the dew from the fleece, a bowl
full of water.
39Then Gideon said to God, "Do not let Thine anger burn
against me that I may speak once more; please let me make a test
once more with the fleece, let it now be dry only on the fleece, and
let there be dew on all the ground."
40And God did so that night; for it was dry only on the fleece,
and dew was on all the ground.

*Gideon's 300 Chosen Men*

7 THEN JERUBBAAL (that is, Gideon) and all the people who
were with him, rose early and camped beside the spring of
Harod; and the camp of Midian was on the north side of them by
the hill of Moreh in the valley.
2¶ And the LORD said to Gideon, "The people who are with you
are too many for Me to give Midian into their hands, lest Israel
become boastful, saying, 'My own power has delivered me.'
3"Now therefore come, proclaim in the hearing of the people,
saying, 'Whoever is afraid and trembling, let him return and depart from Mount Gilead.' " So 22,000 people returned, but 10,000
remained.
4¶ Then the LORD said to Gideon, "The people are still too
many; bring them down to the water and I will test them for you
there. Therefore it shall be that he of whom I say to you, 'This one
shall go with you,' he shall go with you; but everyone of whom
I say to you, 'This one shall not go with you,' he shall not go."
5So he brought the people down to the water. And the LORD
said to Gideon, "You shall separate everyone who laps the water
with his tongue, as a dog laps, as well as everyone who kneels to
drink."
6Now the number of those who lapped, putting their hand to
their mouth, was 300 men; but all the rest of the people kneeled
to drink water.
7And the LORD said to Gideon, "I will deliver you with the 300
men who lapped and will give the Midianites into your hands; so
let all the *other* people go, each man to his home."
8So the 300 men took the people's provisions and their trumpets into their hands. And Gideon sent all the *other* men of Israel,
each to his tent, but retained the 300 men; and the camp of Midian
was below him in the valley.
9¶ Now the same night it came about that the LORD said to him,
"Arise, go down against the camp, for I have given it into your
hands.

## New International

31But Joash replied to the hostile crowd around him, "Are you
going to plead Baal's cause? Are you trying to save him? Whoever
fights for him shall be put to death by morning! If Baal really is a
god, he can defend himself when someone breaks down his altar."
32So that day they called Gideon "Jerub-Baal,[a]" saying, "Let Baal
contend with him," because he broke down Baal's altar.
33Now all the Midianites, Amalekites and other eastern peoples
joined forces and crossed over the Jordan and camped in the Valley
of Jezreel. 34Then the Spirit of the LORD came upon Gideon, and
he blew a trumpet, summoning the Abiezrites to follow him. 35He
sent messengers throughout Manasseh, calling them to arms, and
also into Asher, Zebulun and Naphtali, so that they too went up
to meet them.
36Gideon said to God, "If you will save Israel by my hand as you
have promised— 37look, I will place a wool fleece on the threshing
floor. If there is dew only on the fleece and all the ground is dry,
then I will know that you will save Israel by my hand, as you said."
38And that is what happened. Gideon rose early the next day; he
squeezed the fleece and wrung out the dew—a bowlful of water.
39Then Gideon said to God, "Do not be angry with me. Let me
make just one more request. Allow me one more test with the
fleece. This time make the fleece dry and the ground covered with
dew." 40That night God did so. Only the fleece was dry; all the
ground was covered with dew.

*Gideon Defeats the Midianites*

7 EARLY IN the morning, Jerub-Baal (that is, Gideon) and all
his men camped at the spring of Harod. The camp of Midian
was north of them in the valley near the hill of Moreh. 2The LORD
said to Gideon, "You have too many men for me to deliver Midian
into their hands. In order that Israel may not boast against me that
her own strength has saved her, 3announce now to the people,
'Anyone who trembles with fear may turn back and leave Mount
Gilead.' " So twenty-two thousand men left, while ten thousand
remained.
4But the LORD said to Gideon, "There are still too many men.
Take them down to the water, and I will sift them for you there.
If I say, 'This one shall go with you,' he shall go; but if I say, 'This
one shall not go with you,' he shall not go."
5So Gideon took the men down to the water. There the LORD
told him, "Separate those who lap the water with their tongues like
a dog from those who kneel down to drink." 6Three hundred men
lapped with their hands to their mouths. All the rest got down on
their knees to drink.
7The LORD said to Gideon, "With the three hundred men that
lapped I will save you and give the Midianites into your hands. Let
all the other men go, each to his own place." 8So Gideon sent the
rest of the Israelites to their tents but kept the three hundred, who
took over the provisions and trumpets of the others.
Now the camp of Midian lay below him in the valley. 9During
that night the LORD said to Gideon, "Get up, go down against the
camp, because I am going to give it into your hands. 10If you are

**NIV** [a] 32 *Jerub-Baal* means *let Baal contend.*

## King James

10 But if thou fear to go down, go thou with Phurah thy servant down to the host:

11 And thou shalt hear what they say; and afterward shall thine hands be strengthened to go down unto the host. Then went he down with Phurah his servant unto the outside of the armed men that *were* in the host.

12 And the Midianites and the Amalekites and all the children of the east lay along in the valley like grasshoppers for multitude; and their camels *were* without number, as the sand by the sea side for multitude.

13 And when Gideon was come, behold, *there was* a man that told a dream unto his fellow, and said, Behold, I dreamed a dream, and, lo, a cake of barley bread tumbled into the host of Midian, and came unto a tent, and smote it that it fell, and overturned it, that the tent lay along.

14 And his fellow answered and said, This *is* nothing else save the sword of Gideon the son of Joash, a man of Israel: *for* into his hand hath God delivered Midian, and all the host.

15 ¶ And it was *so,* when Gideon heard the telling of the dream, and the interpretation thereof, that he worshipped, and returned into the host of Israel, and said, Arise; for the LORD hath delivered into your hand the host of Midian.

16 And he divided the three hundred men *into* three companies, and he put a trumpet in every man's hand, with empty pitchers, and lamps within the pitchers.

17 And he said unto them, Look on me, and do likewise: and, behold, when I come to the outside of the camp, it shall be *that,* as I do, so shall ye do.

18 When I blow with a trumpet, I and all that *are* with me, then blow ye the trumpets also on every side of all the camp, and say, *The sword* of the LORD, and of Gideon.

19 ¶ So Gideon, and the hundred men that *were* with him, came unto the outside of the camp in the beginning of the middle watch; and they had but newly set the watch: and they blew the trumpets, and brake the pitchers that *were* in their hands.

20 And the three companies blew the trumpets, and brake the pitchers, and held the lamps in their left hands, and the trumpets in their right hands to blow *withal:* and they cried, The sword of the LORD, and of Gideon.

21 And they stood every man in his place round about the camp: and all the host ran, and cried, and fled.

22 And the three hundred blew the trumpets, and the LORD set every man's sword against his fellow, even throughout all the host: and the host fled to Beth-shittah in Zererath, *and* to the border of Abel-meholah, unto Tabbath.

23 And the men of Israel gathered themselves together out of Naphtali, and out of Asher, and out of all Manasseh, and pursued after the Midianites.

24 ¶ And Gideon sent messengers throughout all mount Ephraim, saying, Come down against the Midianites, and take before them the waters unto Beth-barah and Jordan. Then all the men of Ephraim gathered themselves together, and took the waters unto Beth-barah and Jordan.

25 And they took two princes of the Midianites, Oreb and Zeeb; and they slew Oreb upon the rock Oreb, and Zeeb they slew at the winepress of Zeeb, and pursued Midian, and brought the heads of Oreb and Zeeb to Gideon on the other side Jordan.

**8** AND THE men of Ephraim said unto him, Why hast thou served us thus, that thou calledst us not, when thou wentest to fight with the Midianites? And they did chide with him sharply.

## Amplified

10 But if you fear to go down, go with Purah your servant down to the camp;

11 And you shall hear what they say, and afterward your hands shall be strengthened to go down against the camp. Then he went down with Purah his servant to the outposts of the camp of the armed men.

12 And the Midianites and the Amalekites and all the sons of the East lay along the valley like locusts for multitude; and their camels were without number, as the sand on the seashore for multitude.

13 When Gideon arrived, behold, a man was telling a dream to his comrade; and he said, Behold, I dreamed a dream; and, lo, a cake of [a]barley bread tumbled into the camp of Midian, and came to the tent, and struck it so that it fell, and turned it upside down, so that the tent lay flat.

14 And his comrade replied, This is nothing else but the sword of Gideon son of Joash, a man of Israel. Into his hand God has given Midian and all the host.

15 When Gideon heard the telling of the dream and its interpretation, he worshiped, and returned to the camp of Israel, and said, Arise; for the Lord has given into your hand the host of Midian.

16 And he divided the 300 men into three companies, and he put into the hands of all of them trumpets and empty pitchers, with torches inside the pitchers.

17 And he said to them, Look at me, then do likewise; when I come to the edge of their camp, do as I do.

18 When I blow the trumpet, I and all who are with me, then you blow the trumpets also on every side of all the camp, and shout, For the Lord and for Gideon!

19 So Gideon and the 100 men who were with him came to the outskirts of the camp at the beginning of the middle watch, when the guards had just been changed; and they blew the trumpets and smashed the pitchers that were in their hands.

20 And the three companies blew the trumpets, and shattered the pitchers, holding the torches in their left hands, and in their right hands the trumpets to blow [leaving no chance to use swords]; and they cried, The sword for the Lord and Gideon!

21 They stood every man in his place round about the camp, and all the [Midianite] army ran; they cried out and fled.

22 When [Gideon's men] blew the 300 trumpets, the Lord set every [Midianite's] sword against his comrade and against all the army; and the army fled as far as Bethshittah toward Zererah, as far as the border of Abel-meholah, by Tabbath.

23 And the men of Israel were called together out of Naphtali and Asher, and all Manasseh, and they pursued after Midian.

24 And Gideon sent messengers throughout all the hill country of Ephraim, saying, Come down against the Midianites, and take all the intervening fords as far as Beth-barah, and also the Jordan. So all the men of Ephraim were gathered together, and took all the fords as far as Beth-barah, and also the Jordan.

25 And [the men of Ephraim] took the two princes of Midian, Oreb and Zeeb; and they slew Oreb at the rock of Oreb, and Zeeb they slew at the winepress of Zeeb, and pursued Midian, and they brought the heads of Oreb and Zeeb to Gideon beyond the Jordan.

**8** AND THE men of Ephraim said to Gideon, Why have you treated us like this, not calling us when you went to fight with Midian? And they quarreled with him furiously.

**AMP** [a] Alluding to the insignificance of Gideon and his family, or perhaps of his whole troop. Barley then, as it is still, was distinguished from "fine flour." "To heare himselfe but a Barly-cake, troubled him not. It matters not how base wee be thought, so wee be victorious" (Bishop Hall, quoted in *Cambridge Bible*).

## New American Standard

10"But if you are afraid to go down, go with Purah your servant
down to the camp,
11and you will hear what they say; and afterward your hands
will be strengthened that you may go down against the camp." So
he went with Purah his servant down to the outposts of the army
that was in the camp.
12Now the Midianites and the Amalekites and all the sons of the
east were lying in the valley as numerous as locusts; and their
camels were without number, as numerous as the sand on the
seashore.
13When Gideon came, behold, a man was relating a dream to
his friend. And he said, "Behold, I had a dream; a loaf of barley
bread was tumbling into the camp of Midian, and it came to the
tent and struck it so that it fell, and turned it upside down so that
the tent lay flat."
14And his friend answered and said, "This is nothing less than
the sword of Gideon the son of Joash, a man of Israel; God has
given Midian and all the camp into his hand."
15¶ And it came about when Gideon heard the account of the
dream and its interpretation, that he bowed in worship. He returned to the camp of Israel and said, "Arise, for the LORD has
given the camp of Midian into your hands."
16And he divided the 300 men into three companies, and he put
trumpets and empty pitchers into the hands of all of them, with
torches inside the pitchers.
17And he said to them, "Look at me, and do likewise. And
behold, when I come to the outskirts of the camp, do as I do.
18"When I and all who are with me blow the trumpet, then you
also blow the trumpets all around the camp, and say, 'For the LORD
and for Gideon.' "

*Confusion of the Enemy*

19¶ So Gideon and the hundred men who were with him came
to the outskirts of the camp at the beginning of the middle watch,
when they had just posted the watch; and they blew the trumpets
and smashed the pitchers that were in their hands.
20When the three companies blew the trumpets and broke the
pitchers, they held the torches in their left hands and the trumpets
in their right hands for blowing, and cried, "A sword for the LORD
and for Gideon!"
21And each stood in his place around the camp; and all the
[b]army ran, crying out as they fled.
22And when they blew 300 trumpets, the LORD set the sword
of one against another even throughout the whole army; and the
army fled as far as Beth-shittah toward Zererah, as far as the edge
of Abel-meholah, by Tabbath.
23And the men of Israel were summoned from Naphtali and
Asher and all Manasseh, and they pursued Midian.
24¶ And Gideon sent messengers throughout all the hill country
of Ephraim, saying, "Come down against Midian and take the
waters before them, as far as Beth-barah and the Jordan." So all
the men of Ephraim were summoned, and they took the waters as
far as Beth-barah and the Jordan.
25And they captured the two leaders of Midian, Oreb and Zeeb,
and they killed Oreb at the rock of Oreb, and they killed Zeeb at
the wine press of Zeeb, while they pursued Midian; and they
brought the heads of Oreb and Zeeb to Gideon from across the
Jordan.

*Zeba and Zalmunna Routed*

8 THEN THE men of Ephraim said to him, "What is this thing
you have done to us, not calling us when you went to fight
against Midian?" And they contended with him vigorously.

NAS [b] Or, *camp*

## New International

afraid to attack, go down to the camp with your servant Purah
11and listen to what they are saying. Afterward, you will be encouraged to attack the camp." So he and Purah his servant went
down to the outposts of the camp. 12The Midianites, the Amalekites and all the other eastern peoples had settled in the valley, thick
as locusts. Their camels could no more be counted than the sand
on the seashore.
13Gideon arrived just as a man was telling a friend his dream.
"I had a dream," he was saying. "A round loaf of barley bread
came tumbling into the Midianite camp. It struck the tent with
such force that the tent overturned and collapsed."
14His friend responded, "This can be nothing other than the
sword of Gideon son of Joash, the Israelite. God has given the
Midianites and the whole camp into his hands."
15When Gideon heard the dream and its interpretation, he worshiped God. He returned to the camp of Israel and called out, "Get
up! The LORD has given the Midianite camp into your hands."
16Dividing the three hundred men into three companies, he placed
trumpets and empty jars in the hands of all of them, with torches
inside.
17"Watch me," he told them. "Follow my lead. When I get to
the edge of the camp, do exactly as I do. 18When I and all who are
with me blow our trumpets, then from all around the camp blow
yours and shout, 'For the LORD and for Gideon.' "
19Gideon and the hundred men with him reached the edge of
the camp at the beginning of the middle watch, just after they had
changed the guard. They blew their trumpets and broke the jars
that were in their hands. 20The three companies blew the trumpets
and smashed the jars. Grasping the torches in their left hands and
holding in their right hands the trumpets they were to blow, they
shouted, "A sword for the LORD and for Gideon!" 21While each
man held his position around the camp, all the Midianites ran,
crying out as they fled.
22When the three hundred trumpets sounded, the LORD caused
the men throughout the camp to turn on each other with their
swords. The army fled to Beth Shittah toward Zererah as far as the
border of Abel Meholah near Tabbath. 23Israelites from Naphtali,
Asher and all Manasseh were called out, and they pursued the
Midianites. 24Gideon sent messengers throughout the hill country
of Ephraim, saying, "Come down against the Midianites and seize
the waters of the Jordan ahead of them as far as Beth Barah."
So all the men of Ephraim were called out and they took the
waters of the Jordan as far as Beth Barah. 25They also captured two
of the Midianite leaders, Oreb and Zeeb. They killed Oreb at the
rock of Oreb, and Zeeb at the winepress of Zeeb. They pursued
the Midianites and brought the heads of Oreb and Zeeb to Gideon,
who was by the Jordan.

*Zebah and Zalmunna*

8 NOW THE Ephraimites asked Gideon, "Why have you treated us like this? Why didn't you call us when you went to fight
Midian?" And they criticized him sharply.

# King James

2And he said unto them, What have I done now in comparison of you? *Is* not the gleaning of the grapes of Ephraim better than the vintage of Abiezer?

3God hath delivered into your hands the princes of Midian, Oreb and Zeeb: and what was I able to do in comparison of you? Then their anger was abated toward him, when he had said that.

4¶ And Gideon came to Jordan, *and* passed over, he, and the three hundred men that *were* with him, faint, yet pursuing *them.*

5And he said unto the men of Succoth, Give, I pray you, loaves of bread unto the people that follow me; for they *be* faint, and I am pursuing after Zebah and Zalmunna, kings of Midian.

6¶ And the princes of Succoth said, *Are* the hands of Zebah and Zalmunna now in thine hand, that we should give bread unto thine army?

7And Gideon said, Therefore when the LORD hath delivered Zebah and Zalmunna into mine hand, then I will tear your flesh with the thorns of the wilderness and with briers.

8¶ And he went up thence to Penuel, and spake unto them likewise: and the men of Penuel answered him as the men of Succoth had answered *him.*

9And he spake also unto the men of Penuel, saying, When I come again in peace, I will break down this tower.

10¶ Now Zebah and Zalmunna *were* in Karkor, and their hosts with them, about fifteen thousand *men,* all that were left of all the hosts of the children of the east: for there fell an hundred and twenty thousand men that drew sword.

11¶ And Gideon went up by the way of them that dwelt in tents on the east of Nobah and Jogbehah, and smote the host: for the host was secure.

12And when Zebah and Zalmunna fled, he pursued after them, and took the two kings of Midian, Zebah and Zalmunna, and discomfited all the host.

13¶ And Gideon the son of Joash returned from battle before the sun *was up,*

14And caught a young man of the men of Succoth, and inquired of him: and he described unto him the princes of Succoth, and the elders thereof, *even* threescore and seventeen men.

15And he came unto the men of Succoth, and said, Behold Zebah and Zalmunna, with whom ye did upbraid me, saying, *Are* the hands of Zebah and Zalmunna now in thine hand, that we should give bread unto thy men *that are* weary?

16And he took the elders of the city, and thorns of the wilderness and briers, and with them he taught the men of Succoth.

17And he beat down the tower of Penuel, and slew the men of the city.

18¶ Then said he unto Zebah and Zalmunna, What manner of men *were they* whom ye slew at Tabor? And they answered, As thou *art,* so *were* they; each one resembled the children of a king.

19And he said, they *were* my brethren, *even* the sons of my mother: *as* the LORD liveth, if ye had saved them alive, I would not slay you.

20And he said unto Jether his firstborn, Up, *and* slay them. But the youth drew not his sword: for he feared, because he *was* yet a youth.

21Then Zebah and Zalmunna said, Rise thou, and fall upon us: for as the man *is, so is* his strength. And Gideon arose, and slew Zebah and Zalmunna, and took away the ornaments that *were* on their camels' necks.

22¶ Then the men of Israel said unto Gideon, Rule thou over us, both thou, and thy son, and thy son's son also: for thou hast delivered us from the hand of Midian.

23And Gideon said unto them, I will not rule over you, neither shall my son rule over you: the LORD shall rule over you.

# Amplified

2And he said to them, What have I done now in comparison with you? Is not the gleaning of the grapes of [your big tribe of] Ephraim better than the vintage of [my little clan of] Abiezer?

3 [a]God has given into your hands the princes of Midian, Oreb and Zeeb; and what was I able to do in comparison with you? Then their anger toward him was abated, when he had said that.

4And Gideon came to the Jordan, and passed over, he and the 300 men with him, faint, yet pursuing.

5And he said to the men of Succoth, Give, I pray you, loaves of bread to the people who follow me; for they are faint, and I am pursuing after Zebah and Zalmunna, kings of Midian.

6And the princes of Succoth said, Are Zebah and Zalmunna already in your hand, that we should give bread to your army?

7And Gideon said, For that, when the Lord has delivered Zebah and Zalmunna into my hand, I will thresh your flesh with the thorns and briers of the wilderness!

8And he went from there up to Penuel, and made the same request; and the men of Penuel answered him as the men of Succoth had done.

9And [Gideon] said to the men of Penuel, When I come again in peace, I will break down this tower.

10Now Zebah and Zalmunna were in Karkor with their army, about 15,000 men, all who were left of all the army of the sons of the East; for there had fallen 120,000 men who drew the sword.

11And Gideon went up by the route of those who dwelt in tents east of Nobah and Jogbehah, and smote their camp [unexpectedly]; for the army thought itself secure.

12And Zebah and Zalmunna fled, and he pursued them and took the two kings of Midian, Zebah and Zalmunna, and terrified all the army.

13Then Gideon son of Joash returned from the battle by the ascent of Heres.

14And he caught a young man of Succoth, and inquired of him; and [the youth] wrote down for him *the names of* the officials of Succoth and its elders, seventy-seven men.

15And he came to the men of Succoth, and said, Behold Zebah and Zalmunna, about whom you scoffed at me, saying, Are Zebah and Zalmunna now in your hand, that we should give bread to your men who are faint?

16And he took the elders of the city and thorns of the wilderness and briers, and with them he taught the men of Succoth.

17And he broke down the tower of Penuel, and slew the men of the city.

18Then [Gideon] said to Zebah and Zalmunna, What kind of men were they whom you slew at Tabor? And they replied, They were like you, each of them; they resembled the sons of a king.

19And he said, They were my brothers, the sons of my mother. As the Lord lives, if you had saved them alive, I would not slay you.

20And [Gideon] said to Jether his first-born [to embarrass them], Up, and slay them. But the youth drew not his sword, for he feared, because he was yet a lad.

21Then Zebah and Zalmunna said, Rise yourself, and fall on us; for as the man is, so is his strength. And Gideon arose and slew Zebah and Zalmunna, and took the [crescent-shaped] ornaments that were on their camels' necks.

22Then the men of Israel said to Gideon, Rule over us, you and your son and your son's son also; for you have delivered us from the hand of Midian.

23And Gideon said to them, I will not rule over you, and my son will not rule over you; the Lord will rule over you.

**AMP** [a] "Gideon's good words were as victorious as his sword" (Bishop Hall, quoted in *Ellicott's Commentary*). "He might have said that he could place but little dependence upon his brethren when, through faintheartedness, 22,000 left him at one time [Judg. 7:3], but he passed this by and took a more excellent way" *(Clarke's Commentary).* "The improving of a victory is often more honorable, and of greater consequence, than the winning of it . . . Humility of deportment is the . . . surest method of ending strife" *(Matthew Henry's Commentary).*

# New American Standard

2But he said to them, "What have I done now in comparison
with you? Is not the gleaning *of the grapes* of Ephraim better than
the vintage of Abiezer?
3"God has given the leaders of Midian, Oreb and Zeeb into
your hands; and what was I able to do in comparison with you?"
Then their anger toward him subsided when he said that.
4¶ Then Gideon and the 300 men who were with him came to
the Jordan *and* crossed over, weary yet pursuing.
5And he said to the men of Succoth, "Please give loaves of
bread to the people who are following me, for they are weary, and
I am pursuing Zebah and Zalmunna, the kings of Midian."
6And the leaders of Succoth said, "Are the hands of Zebah and
Zalmunna already in your hands, that we should give bread to
your army?"
7And Gideon said, "All right, when the LORD has given Zebah
and Zalmunna into my hand, then I will thrash your bodies with
the thorns of the wilderness and with briers."
8And he went up from there to Penuel, and spoke similarly to
them; and the men of Penuel answered him just as the men of
Succoth had answered.
9So he spoke also to the men of Penuel, saying, "When I return
safely, I will tear down this tower."
10Now Zebah and Zalmunna were in Karkor, and their armies
with them, about 15,000 men, all who were left of the entire army
of the sons of the east; for the fallen were 120,000 swordsmen.
11And Gideon went up by the way of those who lived in tents
on the east of Nobah and Jogbehah, and attacked the camp, when
the camp was unsuspecting.
12When Zebah and Zalmunna fled, he pursued them and captured the two kings of Midian, Zebah and Zalmunna, and routed
the whole army.
13¶ Then Gideon the son of Joash returned from the battle by
the ascent of Heres.
14And he captured a youth from Succoth and questioned him.
Then *the youth* wrote down for him the princes of Succoth and its
elders, seventy-seven men.
15And he came to the men of Succoth and said, "Behold Zebah
and Zalmunna, concerning whom you taunted me, saying, 'Are
the hands of Zebah and Zalmunna already in your hand, that we
should give bread to your men who are weary?'"
16And he took the elders of the city, and thorns of the wilderness and briers, and he disciplined the men of Succoth with them.
17And he tore down the tower of Penuel and killed the men of
the city.
18¶ Then he said to Zebah and Zalmunna, "What kind of men
*were* they whom you killed at Tabor?" And they said, "They were
like you, each one resembling the son of a king."
19And he said, "They *were* my brothers, the sons of my mother.
*As* the LORD lives, if only you had let them live, I would not kill
you."
20So he said to Jether his first-born, "Rise, kill them." But the
youth did not draw his sword, for he was afraid, because he was
still a youth.
21Then Zebah and Zalmunna said, "Rise up yourself, and fall
on us; for as the man, so is his strength." So Gideon arose and
killed Zebah and Zalmunna, and took the crescent ornaments
which were on their camels' necks.
22¶ Then the men of Israel said to Gideon, "Rule over us, both
you and your son, also your son's son, for you have delivered us
from the hand of Midian."
23But Gideon said to them, "I will not rule over you, nor shall
my son rule over you; the LORD shall rule over you."

# New International

2But he answered them, "What have I accomplished compared
to you? Aren't the gleanings of Ephraim's grapes better than the
full grape harvest of Abiezer? 3God gave Oreb and Zeeb, the
Midianite leaders, into your hands. What was I able to do compared to you?" At this, their resentment against him subsided.
4Gideon and his three hundred men, exhausted yet keeping up
the pursuit, came to the Jordan and crossed it. 5He said to the men
of Succoth, "Give my troops some bread; they are worn out, and
I am still pursuing Zebah and Zalmunna, the kings of Midian."
6But the officials of Succoth said, "Do you already have the
hands of Zebah and Zalmunna in your possession? Why should
we give bread to your troops?"
7Then Gideon replied, "Just for that, when the LORD has given
Zebah and Zalmunna into my hand, I will tear your flesh with
desert thorns and briers."
8From there he went up to Peniel[b] and made the same request
of them, but they answered as the men of Succoth had. 9So he said
to the men of Peniel, "When I return in triumph, I will tear down
this tower."
10Now Zebah and Zalmunna were in Karkor with a force of
about fifteen thousand men, all that were left of the armies of the
eastern peoples; a hundred and twenty thousand swordsmen had
fallen. 11Gideon went up by the route of the nomads east of Nobah
and Jogbehah and fell upon the unsuspecting army. 12Zebah and
Zalmunna, the two kings of Midian, fled, but he pursued them and
captured them, routing their entire army.
13Gideon son of Joash then returned from the battle by the Pass
of Heres. 14He caught a young man of Succoth and questioned
him, and the young man wrote down for him the names of the
seventy-seven officials of Succoth, the elders of the town. 15Then
Gideon came and said to the men of Succoth, "Here are Zebah and
Zalmunna, about whom you taunted me by saying, 'Do you already have the hands of Zebah and Zalmunna in your possession?
Why should we give bread to your exhausted men?' " 16He took
the elders of the town and taught the men of Succoth a lesson by
punishing them with desert thorns and briers. 17He also pulled
down the tower of Peniel and killed the men of the town.
18Then he asked Zebah and Zalmunna, "What kind of men did
you kill at Tabor?"
"Men like you," they answered, "each one with the bearing of
a prince."
19Gideon replied, "Those were my brothers, the sons of my
own mother. As surely as the LORD lives, if you had spared their
lives, I would not kill you." 20Turning to Jether, his oldest son, he
said, "Kill them!" But Jether did not draw his sword, because he
was only a boy and was afraid.
21Zebah and Zalmunna said, "Come, do it yourself. 'As is the
man, so is his strength.' " So Gideon stepped forward and killed
them, and took the ornaments off their camels' necks.

*Gideon's Ephod*

22The Israelites said to Gideon, "Rule over us—you, your son
and your grandson—because you have saved us out of the hand
of Midian."
23But Gideon told them, "I will not rule over you, nor will my
son rule over you. The LORD will rule over you." 24And he said,

**NIV** [b] *8* Hebrew *Penuel,* a variant of *Peniel;* also in verses 9 and 17

## King James

24¶ And Gideon said unto them, I would desire a request of you,
that ye would give me every man the earrings of his prey. (For they
had golden earrings, because they *were* Ishmaelites.)
25And they answered, We will willingly give *them*. And they
spread a garment, and did cast therein every man the earrings of
his prey.
26And the weight of the golden earrings that he requested was
a thousand and seven hundred *shekels* of gold; beside ornaments,
and collars, and purple raiment that *was* on the kings of Midian,
and beside the chains that *were* about their camels' necks.
27And Gideon made an ephod thereof, and put it in his city,
*even* in Ophrah: and all Israel went thither a-whoring after it: which
thing became a snare unto Gideon, and to his house.
28¶ Thus was Midian subdued before the children of Israel, so
that they lifted up their heads no more. And the country was in
quietness forty years in the days of Gideon.
29¶ And Jerubbaal the son of Joash went and dwelt in his own
house.
30And Gideon had threescore and ten sons of his body begotten: for he had many wives.
31And his concubine that *was* in Shechem, she also bare him a
son, whose name he called Abimelech.
32¶ And Gideon the son of Joash died in a good old age, and
was buried in the sepulchre of Joash his father, in Ophrah of the
Abi-ezrites.
33And it came to pass, as soon as Gideon was dead, that the
children of Israel turned again, and went a-whoring after Baalim,
and made Baal-berith their god.
34And the children of Israel remembered not the LORD their
God, who had delivered them out of the hands of all their enemies
on every side:
35Neither showed they kindness to the house of Jerubbaal,
*namely*, Gideon, according to all the goodness which he had shown
unto Israel.

9 AND ABIMELECH the son of Jerubbaal went to Shechem
unto his mother's brethren, and communed with them, and
with all the family of the house of his mother's father, saying,
2Speak, I pray you, in the ears of all the men of Shechem,
Whether *is* better for you, either that all the sons of Jerubbaal,
*which are* threescore and ten persons, reign over you, or that one
reign over you? remember also that I *am* your bone and your flesh.
3And his mother's brethren spake of him in the ears of all the
men of Shechem all these words: and their hearts inclined to follow
Abimelech; for they said, He *is* our brother.
4And they gave him threescore and ten *pieces* of silver out of the
house of Baal-berith, wherewith Abimelech hired vain and light
persons, which followed him.
5And he went unto his father's house at Ophrah, and slew his
brethren the sons of Jerubbaal, *being* threescore and ten persons,
upon one stone: notwithstanding yet Jotham the youngest son of
Jerubbaal was left; for he hid himself.
6And all the men of Shechem gathered together, and all the
house of Millo, and went, and made Abimelech king, by the plain
of the pillar that *was* in Shechem.
7¶ And when they told *it* to Jotham, he went and stood in the
top of mount Gerizim, and lifted up his voice, and cried, and said
unto them, Hearken unto me, ye men of Shechem, that God may
hearken unto you.

## Amplified

24And Gideon said to them, Let me make a request of you; every
man of you give me the earrings of his spoil. For [the Midianites]
had gold earrings because they were Ishmaelites [general term for
all descendants of Keturah].
25And they answered, We will willingly give them. And they
spread a garment, and every man cast on it the earrings of his
spoil.
26And the weight of the golden earrings that he requested was
1,700 shekels of gold; besides the crescents and pendants and the
purple garments worn by the kings of Midian, and the chains that
were about their camels' necks.
27And Gideon made an ephod [a sacred, high priest's garment]
of it, and put it in his city of Ophrah; and all Israel paid homage
to it there, and [a]it became a snare to Gideon and to his family.
28Thus was Midian subdued before the Israelites, so that they
lifted up their heads no more. And the land had peace *and* rest for
forty years in the days of Gideon.
29Jerubbaal [Gideon] son of Joash went and dwelt in his own
house.
30Now Gideon had seventy sons born to him, for he had many
wives.
31And his concubine who was in Shechem, also bore him a son,
whom he named Abimelech.
32Gideon son of Joash died in a good old age, and was buried
in the tomb of Joash his father, in Ophrah of the Abiezrites.
33As soon as Gideon was dead, the Israelites turned again and
played the harlot after the Baals, and made Baal-berith their god.
34And the Israelites did not remember the Lord their God, Who
had delivered them out of the hand of all their enemies on every
side;
35Neither did they show kindness to the family of Jerubbaal,
that is, Gideon, in return for all the good which he had done to
Israel.

9 NOW ABIMELECH son of Jerubbaal [Gideon] went to Shechem to his mother's kinsmen, and said to them and to the
whole clan of his mother's family,
2Say, I pray you, in the hearing of all the men of Shechem,
Which is better for you, that all seventy of the sons of Jerubbaal
reign over you, or that one rule over you? Remember also that I
am your bone and your flesh.
3And his mother's kinsmen spoke all these words concerning
him in the hearing of all the men of Shechem; and their hearts
inclined to follow Abimelech, for they said, He is our brother.
4And they gave him seventy pieces of silver out of the house
of Baal-berith, with which Abimelech hired worthless and foolhardy men who followed him.
5And he went to his father's house at Ophrah, and slew his
brothers the sons of Jerubbaal, seventy men upon one stone; but
Jotham the youngest son of Jerubbaal was left, for he hid himself.
6And all the men of Shechem gathered together, and all of
Beth-millo, and went and made Abimelech king, by the oak [tere-
binth] of the pillar at Shechem.
7When it was told to Jotham, he went and stood at the top of
Mount Gerizim, and shouted to them, Hear me, men of Shechem,
that God may hear you.

**AMP** [a] The gold and purple of the spoil enabled Gideon to make an ephod, presumably on the pattern of that described in Exodus 28. It was not exactly an idol but a kind of fetish, and it diverted the thoughts of the people from Shiloh and the spiritual worship of the unseen and eternal God. So apt is the human heart to cling to some outward emblem—it may be a crucifix, a wafer, or a church—and miss that worship in spirit and in truth for which the Father seeks [John 4:24]. (F. B. Meyer in *Devotional Commentary*).

## New American Standard

24 Yet Gideon said to them, "I would request of you, that each
of you give me an earring from his spoil." (For they had gold
earrings, because they were Ishmaelites.)
25 And they said, "We will surely give *them*." So they spread out
a garment, and every one of them threw an earring there from his
spoil.
26 And the weight of the gold earrings that he requested was
1,700 *shekels* of gold, besides the crescent ornaments and the pendants and the purple robes which *were* on the kings of Midian, and
besides the neck bands that *were* on their camels' necks.
27 And Gideon made it into an ephod, and placed it in his city,
Ophrah, and all Israel played the harlot with it there, so that it
became a snare to Gideon and his household.

*Forty Years of Peace*

28 So Midian was subdued before the sons of Israel, and they did
not lift up their heads anymore. And the land was undisturbed for
forty years in the days of Gideon.
29¶ Then Jerubbaal the son of Joash went and lived in his own
house.
30 Now Gideon had seventy sons who were his direct descendants, for he had many wives.
31 And his concubine who was in Shechem also bore him a son,
and he named him Abimelech.
32 And Gideon the son of Joash died at a ripe old age and was
buried in the tomb of his father Joash, in Ophrah of the Abiezrites.
33¶ Then it came about, as soon as Gideon was dead, that the
sons of Israel again played the harlot with the Baals, and made
Baal-berith their god.
34 Thus the sons of Israel did not remember the LORD their God,
who had delivered them from the hands of all their enemies on
every side;
35 nor did they show kindness to the household of Jerubbaal
(*that is,* Gideon), in accord with all the good that he had done to
Israel.

*Abimelech's Conspiracy*

9 AND ABIMELECH the son of Jerubbaal went to Shechem to
his mother's relatives, and spoke to them and to the whole
clan of the household of his mother's father, saying,
2 "Speak, now, in the hearing of all the leaders of Shechem,
'Which is better for you, that seventy men, all the sons of Jerubbaal, rule over you, or that one man rule over you?' Also, remember that I am your bone and your flesh."
3 And his mother's relatives spoke all these words on his behalf
in the hearing of all the leaders of Shechem; and they were inclined
to follow Abimelech, for they said, "He is our relative."
4 And they gave him seventy *pieces* of silver from the house of
Baal-berith with which Abimelech hired worthless and reckless
fellows, and they followed him.
5 Then he went to his father's house at Ophrah, and killed his
brothers the sons of Jerubbaal, seventy men, on one stone. But
Jotham the youngest son of Jerubbaal was left, for he hid himself.
6 And all the men of Shechem and all [b]Beth-millo assembled
together, and they went and made Abimelech king, by the oak of
the pillar which was in Shechem.
7¶ Now when they told Jotham, he went and stood on the top
of Mount Gerizim, and lifted his voice and called out. Thus he said
to them, "Listen to me, O men of Shechem, that God may listen
to you.

NAS [b] Or, *the house of Millo*

## New International

"I do have one request, that each of you give me an earring from
your share of the plunder." (It was the custom of the Ishmaelites
to wear gold earrings.)
25 They answered, "We'll be glad to give them." So they spread
out a garment, and each man threw a ring from his plunder onto
it. 26 The weight of the gold rings he asked for came to seventeen
hundred shekels,[c] not counting the ornaments, the pendants and
the purple garments worn by the kings of Midian or the chains that
were on their camels' necks. 27 Gideon made the gold into an
ephod, which he placed in Ophrah, his town. All Israel prostituted
themselves by worshiping it there, and it became a snare to Gideon
and his family.

*Gideon's Death*

28 Thus Midian was subdued before the Israelites and did not
raise its head again. During Gideon's lifetime, the land enjoyed
peace forty years.
29 Jerub-Baal son of Joash went back home to live. 30 He had
seventy sons of his own, for he had many wives. 31 His concubine,
who lived in Shechem, also bore him a son, whom he named
Abimelech. 32 Gideon son of Joash died at a good old age and was
buried in the tomb of his father Joash in Ophrah of the Abiezrites.
33 No sooner had Gideon died than the Israelites again prostituted themselves to the Baals. They set up Baal-Berith as their god
and 34 did not remember the LORD their God, who had rescued
them from the hands of all their enemies on every side. 35 They also
failed to show kindness to the family of Jerub-Baal (that is, Gideon)
for all the good things he had done for them.

*Abimelech*

9 ABIMELECH SON of Jerub-Baal went to his mother's brothers in Shechem and said to them and to all his mother's clan,
2 "Ask all the citizens of Shechem, 'Which is better for you: to have
all seventy of Jerub-Baal's sons rule over you, or just one man?'
Remember, I am your flesh and blood."
3 When the brothers repeated all this to the citizens of Shechem,
they were inclined to follow Abimelech, for they said, "He is our
brother." 4 They gave him seventy shekels[d] of silver from the
temple of Baal-Berith, and Abimelech used it to hire reckless adventurers, who became his followers. 5 He went to his father's
home in Ophrah and on one stone murdered his seventy brothers,
the sons of Jerub-Baal. But Jotham, the youngest son of Jerub-Baal,
escaped by hiding. 6 Then all the citizens of Shechem and Beth
Millo gathered beside the great tree at the pillar in Shechem to
crown Abimelech king.
7 When Jotham was told about this, he climbed up on the top
of Mount Gerizim and shouted to them, "Listen to me, citizens of
Shechem, so that God may listen to you. 8 One day the trees went

NIV [c] 26 That is, about 43 pounds (about 19.5 kilograms) [d] 4 That is, about 1 3/4 pounds (about 0.8 kilogram)

## King James

8 The trees went forth *on a time* to anoint a king over them; and they said unto the olive tree, Reign thou over us.

9 But the olive tree said unto them, Should I leave my fatness, wherewith by me they honour God and man, and go to be promoted over the trees?

10 And the trees said to the fig tree, Come thou, *and* reign over us.

11 But the fig tree said unto them, Should I forsake my sweetness, and my good fruit, and go to be promoted over the trees?

12 Then said the trees unto the vine, Come thou, *and* reign over us.

13 And the vine said unto them, Should I leave my wine, which cheereth God and man, and go to be promoted over the trees?

14 Then said all the trees unto the bramble, Come thou, *and* reign over us.

15 And the bramble said unto the trees, If in truth ye anoint me king over you, *then* come *and* put your trust in my shadow: and if not, let fire come out of the bramble, and devour the cedars of Lebanon.

16 Now therefore, if ye have done truly and sincerely, in that ye have made Abimelech king, and if ye have dealt well with Jerubbaal and his house, and have done unto him according to the deserving of his hands;

17 (For my father fought for you, and adventured his life far, and delivered you out of the hand of Midian:

18 And ye are risen up against my father's house this day, and have slain his sons, threescore and ten persons, upon one stone, and have made Abimelech, the son of his maidservant, king over the men of Shechem, because he *is* your brother;)

19 If ye then have dealt truly and sincerely with Jerubbaal and with his house this day, *then* rejoice ye in Abimelech, and let him also rejoice in you:

20 But if not, let fire come out from Abimelech, and devour the men of Shechem, and the house of Millo; and let fire come out from the men of Shechem, and from the house of Millo, and devour Abimelech.

21 And Jotham ran away, and fled, and went to Beer, and dwelt there, for fear of Abimelech his brother.

22 ¶ When Abimelech had reigned three years over Israel,

23 Then God sent an evil spirit between Abimelech and the men of Shechem; and the men of Shechem dealt treacherously with Abimelech:

24 That the cruelty *done* to the threescore and ten sons of Jerubbaal might come, and their blood be laid upon Abimelech their brother, which slew them; and upon the men of Shechem, which aided him in the killing of his brethren.

25 And the men of Shechem set liers in wait for him in the top of the mountains, and they robbed all that came along that way by them: and it was told Abimelech.

26 And Gaal the son of Ebed came with his brethren, and went over to Shechem: and the men of Shechem put their confidence in him.

27 And they went out into the fields, and gathered their vineyards, and trode *the grapes*, and made merry, and went into the house of their god, and did eat and drink, and cursed Abimelech.

28 And Gaal the son of Ebed said, Who *is* Abimelech, and who *is* Shechem, that we should serve him? *is* not *he* the son of Jerubbaal? and Zebul his officer? serve the men of Hamor the father of Shechem: for why should we serve him?

29 And would to God this people were under my hand! then would I remove Abimelech. And he said to Abimelech, Increase thine army, and come out.

30 ¶ And when Zebul the ruler of the city heard the words of Gaal the son of Ebed, his anger was kindled.

31 And he sent messengers unto Abimelech privily, saying, Behold, Gaal the son of Ebed and his brethren be come to Shechem; and, behold, they fortify the city against thee.

32 Now therefore up by night, thou and the people that *is* with thee, and lie in wait in the field:

## Amplified

8 One time the trees went forth to anoint a king over them, and they said to the olive tree, Reign over us.

9 But the olive tree said to them, Should I leave my fatness, by which God and man are honored, and go to wave over the trees?

10 Then the trees said to the fig tree, You come, and reign over us.

11 But the fig tree said to them, Should I leave my sweetness and my good fruit and go to wave over the trees?

12 Then the trees said to the vine [grapevine], You come, and reign over us.

13 And the vine [grapevine] replied, Should I leave my new wine, which rejoices God and man, and go to wave over the trees?

14 Then all the trees said to the bramble, You come, and reign over us.

15 And the bramble said to the trees, If in good faith you are anointing me king over you, then come and take refuge in my shade; but if not, let fire come out of the bramble and devour the cedars of Lebanon.

16 Now therefore, if you acted sincerely and honorably when you made Abimelech king, and if you have dealt well with Jerubbaal and his house, and have done to him as his deeds deserved—

17 For my father fought for you, and jeopardized his life, and rescued you from the hand of Midian;

18 And you have risen up against my father's house this day, and have slain his sons, seventy men on one stone, and have made Abimelech, son of his maidservant, king over the people of Shechem, because he is your kinsman—

19 If you then have acted sincerely and honorably with Jerubbaal and his house this day, then rejoice in Abimelech, and let him also rejoice in you;

20 But if not, let fire come out from Abimelech, and devour the people of Shechem and Beth-millo; and let fire come out from the people of Shechem and Beth-millo, and devour Abimelech.

21 And Jotham ran away and fled, and went to Beer and dwelt there, for fear of Abimelech his brother.

22 Abimelech reigned three years over Israel.

23 And God sent an evil spirit between Abimelech and the men of Shechem; and the men of Shechem dealt treacherously with Abimelech;

24 That the violence done to the seventy sons of Jerubbaal might come and that their blood might be laid upon Abimelech their brother, who slew them, and upon the men of Shechem, who strengthened his hands to slay his brothers.

25 And the men of Shechem set men in ambush against [Abimelech] on the mountain tops, and they robbed all who passed by them along that way; and it was told Abimelech.

26 And Gaal son of Ebed came with his kinsmen and moved into Shechem; and the men of Shechem put confidence in him.

27 And they went out into the field, gathered their vineyard fruits and trod them, and held festival; and going into the house of their god, they ate and drank and cursed Abimelech.

28 Gaal son of Ebed said, Who is Abimelech, and who are we of Shechem, that we should serve him? Were not the son of Jerubbaal and Zebul his officer servants of the men of Hamor the father *and* founder of Shechem? Then why should we serve him?

29 Would that this people were under my hand! Then would I remove Abimelech, and say to him, Increase your army, and come out.

30 When Zebul the city's mayor heard the words of Gaal son of Ebed, his anger was kindled.

31 And he sent messengers to Abimelech slyly, saying, Behold, Gaal son of Ebed and his kinsmen have come to Shechem; and behold, they stir up the city to rise against you.

32 Now therefore rise up by night, you and the men with you, and lie in wait in the field.

## New American Standard

8"Once the trees went forth to anoint a king over them, and they said to the olive tree, 'Reign over us!'

9"But the olive tree said to them, 'Shall I leave my fatness with which God and men are honored, and go to wave over the trees?'

10"Then the trees said to the fig tree, 'You come, reign over us!'

11"But the fig tree said to them, 'Shall I leave my sweetness and my good fruit, and go to wave over the trees?'

12"Then the trees said to the vine, 'You come, reign over us!'

13"But the vine said to them, 'Shall I leave my new wine, which cheers God and men, and go to wave over the trees?'

14"Finally all the trees said to the bramble, 'You come, reign over us!'

15"And the bramble said to the trees, 'If in truth you are anointing me as king over you, come and take refuge in my shade; but if not, may fire come out from the bramble and consume the cedars of Lebanon.'

16¶ "Now therefore, if you have dealt in truth and integrity in making Abimelech king, and if you have dealt well with Jerubbaal and his house, and have dealt with him as he deserved—

17for my father fought for you and risked his life and delivered you from the hand of Midian;

18but you have risen against my father's house today and have killed his sons, seventy men, on one stone, and have made Abimelech, the son of his maidservant, king over the men of Shechem, because he is your relative—

19if then you have dealt in truth and integrity with Jerubbaal and his house this day, rejoice in Abimelech, and let him also rejoice in you.

20"But if not, let fire come out from Abimelech and consume the men of Shechem and Beth-millo; and let fire come out from the men of Shechem and from Beth-millo, and consume Abimelech."

21Then Jotham escaped and fled, and went to Beer and remained there because of Abimelech his brother.

*Shechem and Abimelech Fall*

22¶ Now Abimelech ruled over Israel three years.

23Then God sent an evil spirit between Abimelech and the men of Shechem; and the men of Shechem dealt treacherously with Abimelech,

24in order that the violence done to the seventy sons of Jerubbaal might come, and their blood might be laid on Abimelech their brother, who killed them, and on the men of Shechem, who strengthened his hands to kill his brothers.

25And the men of Shechem set men in ambush against him on the tops of the mountains, and they robbed all who might pass by them along the road; and it was told to Abimelech.

26¶ Now Gaal the son of Ebed came with his relatives, and crossed over into Shechem; and the men of Shechem put their trust in him.

27And they went out into the field and gathered *the grapes of* their vineyards and trod *them*, and held a festival; and they went into the house of their god, and ate and drank and cursed Abimelech.

28Then Gaal the son of Ebed said, "Who is Abimelech, and who is Shechem, that we should serve him? Is he not the son of Jerubbaal, and *is* Zebul *not* his lieutenant? Serve the men of Hamor the father of Shechem; but why should we serve him?

29"Would, therefore, that this people were under my authority! Then I would remove Abimelech." And he said to Abimelech, "Increase your army, and come out."

30¶ And when Zebul the ruler of the city heard the words of Gaal the son of Ebed, his anger burned.

31And he sent messengers to Abimelech deceitfully, saying, "Behold, Gaal the son of Ebed and his relatives have come to Shechem; and behold, they are stirring up the city against you.

32"Now therefore, arise by night, you and the people who are with you, and lie in wait in the field.

## New International

out to anoint a king for themselves. They said to the olive tree, 'Be our king.'

9"But the olive tree answered, 'Should I give up my oil, by which both gods and men are honored, to hold sway over the trees?'

10"Next, the trees said to the fig tree, 'Come and be our king.'

11"But the fig tree replied, 'Should I give up my fruit, so good and sweet, to hold sway over the trees?'

12"Then the trees said to the vine, 'Come and be our king.'

13"But the vine answered, 'Should I give up my wine, which cheers both gods and men, to hold sway over the trees?'

14"Finally all the trees said to the thornbush, 'Come and be our king.'

15"The thornbush said to the trees, 'If you really want to anoint me king over you, come and take refuge in my shade; but if not, then let fire come out of the thornbush and consume the cedars of Lebanon!'

16"Now if you have acted honorably and in good faith when
you made Abimelech king, and if you have been fair to Jerub-Baal
and his family, and if you have treated him as he deserves— 17and
to think that my father fought for you, risked his life to rescue you
from the hand of Midian 18(but today you have revolted against my
father's family, murdered his seventy sons on a single stone, and
made Abimelech, the son of his slave girl, king over the citizens
of Shechem because he is your brother)— 19if then you have acted
honorably and in good faith toward Jerub-Baal and his family
today, may Abimelech be your joy, and may you be his, too! 20But
if you have not, let fire come out from Abimelech and consume
you, citizens of Shechem and Beth Millo, and let fire come out from
you, citizens of Shechem and Beth Millo, and consume Abimelech!"

21Then Jotham fled, escaping to Beer, and he lived there because he was afraid of his brother Abimelech.

22After Abimelech had governed Israel three years, 23God sent
an evil spirit between Abimelech and the citizens of Shechem, who
acted treacherously against Abimelech. 24God did this in order that
the crime against Jerub-Baal's seventy sons, the shedding of their
blood, might be avenged on their brother Abimelech and on the
citizens of Shechem, who had helped him murder his brothers.
25In opposition to him these citizens of Shechem set men on the
hilltops to ambush and rob everyone who passed by, and this was
reported to Abimelech.

26Now Gaal son of Ebed moved with his brothers into Shechem,
and its citizens put their confidence in him. 27After they had gone
out into the fields and gathered the grapes and trodden them, they
held a festival in the temple of their god. While they were eating
and drinking, they cursed Abimelech. 28Then Gaal son of Ebed
said, "Who is Abimelech, and who is Shechem, that we should be
subject to him? Isn't he Jerub-Baal's son, and isn't Zebul his deputy? Serve the men of Hamor, Shechem's father! Why should we
serve Abimelech? 29If only this people were under my command!
Then I would get rid of him. I would say to Abimelech, 'Call out
your whole army!' "[a]

30When Zebul the governor of the city heard what Gaal son of
Ebed said, he was very angry. 31Under cover he sent messengers
to Abimelech, saying, "Gaal son of Ebed and his brothers have
come to Shechem and are stirring up the city against you. 32Now
then, during the night you and your men should come and lie in
wait in the fields. 33In the morning at sunrise, advance against the

**NIV** [a] 29 Septuagint; Hebrew *him." Then he said to Abimelech, "Call out your whole army!"*

## King James

33 And it shall be, *that* in the morning, as soon as the sun is up, thou shalt rise early, and set upon the city: and, behold, *when* he and the people that *is* with him come out against thee, then mayest thou do to them as thou shalt find occasion.

34 ¶ And Abimelech rose up, and all the people that *were* with him, by night, and they laid wait against Shechem in four companies.

35 And Gaal the son of Ebed went out, and stood in the entering of the gate of the city: and Abimelech rose up, and the people that *were* with him, from lying in wait.

36 And when Gaal saw the people, he said to Zebul, Behold, there come people down from the top of the mountains. And Zebul said unto him, Thou seest the shadow of the mountains as *if they were* men.

37 And Gaal spake again and said, See there come people down by the middle of the land, and another company come along by the plain of Meonenim.

38 Then said Zebul unto him, Where *is* now thy mouth, wherewith thou saidst, Who *is* Abimelech, that we should serve him? *is* not this the people that thou hast despised? go out, I pray now, and fight with them.

39 And Gaal went out before the men of Shechem, and fought with Abimelech.

40 And Abimelech chased him, and he fled before him, and many were overthrown *and* wounded, *even* unto the entering of the gate.

41 And Abimelech dwelt at Arumah: and Zebul thrust out Gaal and his brethren, that they should not dwell in Shechem.

42 And it came to pass on the morrow, that the people went out into the field; and they told Abimelech.

43 And he took the people, and divided them into three companies, and laid wait in the field, and looked, and, behold, the people *were* come forth out of the city; and he rose up against them, and smote them.

44 And Abimelech, and the company that *was* with him, rushed forward, and stood in the entering of the gate of the city: and the two *other* companies ran upon all *the people* that *were* in the fields, and slew them.

45 And Abimelech fought against the city all that day; and he took the city, and slew the people that *was* therein, and beat down the city, and sowed it with salt.

46 ¶ And when all the men of the tower of Shechem heard *that*, they entered into an hold of the house of the god Berith.

47 And it was told Abimelech, that all the men of the tower of Shechem were gathered together.

48 And Abimelech gat him up to mount Zalmon, he and all the people that *were* with him; and Abimelech took an axe in his hand, and cut down a bough from the trees, and took it, and laid *it* on his shoulder, and said unto the people that *were* with him, What ye have seen me do, make haste, *and* do as I *have done*.

49 And all the people likewise cut down every man his bough, and followed Abimelech, and put *them* to the hold, and set the hold on fire upon them; so that all the men of the tower of Shechem died also, about a thousand men and women.

50 ¶ Then went Abimelech to Thebez, and encamped against Thebez, and took it.

51 But there was a strong tower within the city, and thither fled all the men and women, and all they of the city, and shut *it* to them, and gat them up to the top of the tower.

## Amplified

33 Then in the morning, as soon as the sun is up, rise early, and set upon the city; and when Gaal and the men with him come out against you, do to them as opportunity permits.

34 And Abimelech rose up by night, and all the men with him, and they laid wait against Shechem in four companies.

35 And Gaal son of Ebed came out and stood in the entrance of the city's gate. Then Abimelech and the men with him rose up from ambush.

36 When Gaal saw the men, he said to Zebul, Look, men are coming down from the mountain tops! Zebul said to him, The shadow of the mountains looks to you like men.

37 And Gaal spoke again and said, See, men are coming down from the center of the land, and one company is coming from the direction of the Oak of Meonenim [the sorcerers].

38 Then said Zebul to Gaal, Where is your [big] mouth now, you who said, Who is Abimelech, that we should serve him? Are not these the men whom you have despised? Go out now and fight with them.

39 And Gaal went out ahead of the men of Shechem, and fought with Abimelech.

40 And Abimelech chased him, and he fled before him, and many fell wounded, even to the entrance of the gate.

41 And Abimelech lodged at Arumah; and Zebul thrust out Gaal and his kinsmen, so they could not live in Shechem.

42 The next day the men went out into the fields; and Abimelech was told.

43 He took his men and divided them into three companies, and laid wait in the field; and he looked, and behold, the people were coming out of the city; and he rose up against them and smote them.

44 And Abimelech and the company with him rushed forward and stood in the entrance of the city's gate, while the two other companies rushed upon all who were in the field and slew them.

45 And Abimelech fought against the city all that day; he took the city, and slew the people who were in it; he demolished the city and [a]sowed it with salt.

46 And when all the men of the Tower of Shechem heard of it, they entered the stronghold of the house of El-berith [the god of Berith].

47 Abimelech was told that all the people of the Tower of Shechem were gathered together.

48 And Abimelech went up to Mount Zalmon, he and all the men with him; and Abimelech took an ax in his hand, and cut down a bundle of brush, picked it up and laid it on his shoulder. And he said to the men with him, What you have seen me do, make haste to do also.

49 So each of the men cut down his bundle and following Abimelech put it against the stronghold, and set [the stronghold] on fire over the people in it, so that all the people of the Tower of Shechem also died, about 1,000 men and women.

50 Then Abimelech went to Thebez, and encamped against Thebez, and took it.

51 But there was a strong tower in the city, and all the people of the city, men and women, fled to it, and shut themselves in, and went to the roof of the tower.

**AMP** [a] This strewing of salt over Shechem was not intended (even if Abimelech had been able to supply enough salt) actually to make the ground unfruitful; but it was a symbol of perpetual desolation, and that Shechem never would be rebuilt. However, such a forecast of a city's fate made by a true prophet of God, or by the Lord Himself, was one thing; but this forecast, symbolized by the wicked usurper Abimelech, was quite another thing. For Shechem was later rebuilt (I Kings 12:25), and so was denounced Jericho (I Kings 16:34). But this is not true of Samaria (Mic. 1:6), or Nineveh (Nah. 1:9-12), or Ashkelon (Zeph. 2:4), or the cities of Edom (Ezek. 35:9), or Tyre (Ezek. 26:3, 14), or Chorazin, or Bethsaida, or Capernaum (Matt. 11:20, 21, 23). For that these cities, as such, would never be rebuilt permanently was foretold on the authority and by order of God Himself. "Sky and earth shall pass away, but My words shall not pass away" (Matt. 24:35).

## New American Standard

33"And it shall come about in the morning, as soon as the sun
is up, that you shall rise early and rush upon the city; and behold,
when he and the people who are with him come out against you,
you shall do to them whatever you can."
34¶ So Abimelech and all the people who *were* with him arose
by night and lay in wait against Shechem in four companies.
35Now Gaal the son of Ebed went out and stood in the entrance
of the city gate; and Abimelech and the people who *were* with him
arose from the ambush.
36And when Gaal saw the people, he said to Zebul, "Look,
people are coming down from the tops of the mountains." But
Zebul said to him, "You are seeing the shadow of the mountains
as *if they were* men."
37And Gaal spoke again and said, "Behold, people are coming
down from the highest part of the land, and one company comes
by the way of the diviners' oak."
38Then Zebul said to him, "Where is your boasting now with
which you said, 'Who is Abimelech that we should serve him?' Is
this not the people whom you despised? Go out now and fight
with them!"
39So Gaal went out before the leaders of Shechem and fought
with Abimelech.
40And Abimelech chased him, and he fled before him; and
many fell wounded up to the entrance of the gate.
41Then Abimelech remained at Arumah, but Zebul drove out
Gaal and his relatives so that they could not remain in Shechem.
42¶ Now it came about the next day, that the people went out
to the field, and it was told to Abimelech.
43So he took his people and divided them into three companies,
and lay in wait in the field; when he looked and saw the people
coming out from the city, he arose against them and slew them.
44Then Abimelech and the company who was with him dashed
forward and stood in the entrance of the city gate; the other two
companies then dashed against all who *were* in the field and slew
them.
45And Abimelech fought against the city all that day, and he
captured the city and killed the people who *were* in it; then he razed
the city and sowed it with salt.
46¶ When all the leaders of the tower of Shechem heard of *it*,
they entered the inner chamber of the temple of El-berith.
47And it was told Abimelech that all the leaders of the tower of
Shechem were gathered together.
48So Abimelech went up to Mount Zalmon, he and all the
people who *were* with him; and Abimelech took an axe in his hand
and cut down a branch from the trees, and lifted it and laid *it* on
his shoulder. Then he said to the people who *were* with him,
"What you have seen me do, hurry *and* do likewise."
49And all the people also cut down each one his branch and
followed Abimelech, and put *them* on the inner chamber and set
the inner chamber on fire over those *inside*, so that all the men of
the tower of Shechem also died, about a thousand men and
women.
50¶ Then Abimelech went to Thebez, and he camped against
Thebez and captured it.
51But there was a strong tower in the center of the city, and all
the men and women with all the leaders of the city fled there and
shut themselves in; and they went up on the roof of the tower.

## New International

city. When Gaal and his men come out against you, do whatever
your hand finds to do."
34So Abimelech and all his troops set out by night and took up
concealed positions near Shechem in four companies. 35Now Gaal
son of Ebed had gone out and was standing at the entrance to the
city gate just as Abimelech and his soldiers came out from their
hiding place.
36When Gaal saw them, he said to Zebul, "Look, people are
coming down from the tops of the mountains!"
Zebul replied, "You mistake the shadows of the mountains for
men."
37But Gaal spoke up again: "Look, people are coming down
from the center of the land, and a company is coming from the
direction of the soothsayers' tree."
38Then Zebul said to him, "Where is your big talk now, you
who said, 'Who is Abimelech that we should be subject to him?'
Aren't these the men you ridiculed? Go out and fight them!"
39So Gaal led out[b] the citizens of Shechem and fought Abimelech. 40Abimelech chased him, and many fell wounded in the
flight—all the way to the entrance to the gate. 41Abimelech stayed
in Arumah, and Zebul drove Gaal and his brothers out of Shechem.
42The next day the people of Shechem went out to the fields,
and this was reported to Abimelech. 43So he took his men, divided
them into three companies and set an ambush in the fields. When
he saw the people coming out of the city, he rose to attack them.
44Abimelech and the companies with him rushed forward to a
position at the entrance to the city gate. Then two companies
rushed upon those in the fields and struck them down. 45All that
day Abimelech pressed his attack against the city until he had
captured it and killed its people. Then he destroyed the city and
scattered salt over it.
46On hearing this, the citizens in the tower of Shechem went
into the stronghold of the temple of El-Berith. 47When Abimelech
heard that they had assembled there, 48he and all his men went
up Mount Zalmon. He took an ax and cut off some branches,
which he lifted to his shoulders. He ordered the men with him,
"Quick! Do what you have seen me do!" 49So all the men cut
branches and followed Abimelech. They piled them against the
stronghold and set it on fire over the people inside. So all the
people in the tower of Shechem, about a thousand men and
women, also died.
50Next Abimelech went to Thebez and besieged it and captured
it. 51Inside the city, however, was a strong tower, to which all the
men and women—all the people of the city—fled. They locked
themselves in and climbed up on the tower roof. 52Abimelech went

NIV [b] 39 Or *Gaal went out in the sight of*

## King James

52And Abimelech came unto the tower, and fought against it, and went hard unto the door of the tower to burn it with fire.

53And a certain woman cast a piece of a millstone upon Abimelech's head, and all to brake his skull.

54Then he called hastily unto the young man his armourbearer, and said unto him, Draw thy sword, and slay me, that men say not of me, A woman slew him. And his young man thrust him through, and he died.

55And when the men of Israel saw that Abimelech was dead, they departed every man unto his place.

56¶ Thus God rendered the wickedness of Abimelech, which he did unto his father, in slaying his seventy brethren:

57And all the evil of the men of Shechem did God render upon their heads: and upon them came the curse of Jotham the son of Jerubbaal.

**10** AND AFTER Abimelech there arose to defend Israel Tola the son of Puah, the son of Dodo, a man of Issachar; and he dwelt in Shamir in mount Ephraim.

2And he judged Israel twenty and three years, and died, and was buried in Shamir.

3¶ And after him arose Jair, a Gileadite, and judged Israel twenty and two years.

4And he had thirty sons that rode on thirty ass colts, and they had thirty cities, which are called Havoth-jair unto this day, which *are* in the land of Gilead.

5And Jair died, and was buried in Camon.

6¶ And the children of Israel did evil again in the sight of the LORD, and served Baalim, and Ashtaroth, and the gods of Syria, and the gods of Zidon, and the gods of Moab, and the gods of the children of Ammon, and the gods of the Philistines, and forsook the LORD, and served not him.

7And the anger of the LORD was hot against Israel, and he sold them into the hands of the Philistines, and into the hands of the children of Ammon.

8And that year they vexed and oppressed the children of Israel: eighteen years, all the children of Israel that *were* on the other side Jordan in the land of the Amorites, which *is* in Gilead.

9Moreover the children of Ammon passed over Jordan to fight also against Judah, and against Benjamin, and against the house of Ephraim; so that Israel was sore distressed.

10¶ And the children of Israel cried unto the LORD, saying, We have sinned against thee, both because we have forsaken our God, and also served Baalim.

11And the LORD said unto the children of Israel, *Did* not *I deliver you* from the Egyptians, and from the Amorites, from the children of Ammon, and from the Philistines?

12The Zidonians also, and the Amalekites, and the Maonites, did oppress you; and ye cried to me, and I delivered you out of their hand.

13Yet ye have forsaken me, and served other gods: wherefore I will deliver you no more.

14Go and cry unto the gods which ye have chosen; let them deliver you in the time of your tribulation.

15¶ And the children of Israel said unto the LORD, We have sinned: do thou unto us whatsoever seemeth good unto thee; deliver us only, we pray thee, this day.

16And they put away the strange gods from among them, and served the LORD: and his soul was grieved for the misery of Israel.

17Then the children of Ammon were gathered together, and encamped in Gilead. And the children of Israel assembled themselves together, and encamped in Mizpeh.

18And the people *and* princes of Gilead said one to another, What man *is he* that will begin to fight against the children of Ammon? he shall be head over all the inhabitants of Gilead.

## Amplified

52And Abimelech came to the tower, and fought against it, and drew near the door of the tower to burn it with fire.

53But a certain woman cast an upper millstone *down* upon Abimelech's head, and broke his skull.

54Then he called hastily to the young man his armor-bearer, and said to him, Draw your sword and slay me, that men may not say of me, A woman slew him. And his young man thrust him through, and he died.

55And when the men of Israel saw that Abimelech was dead, they departed each man to his home.

56Thus God repaid the wickedness of Abimelech, which he did to his father [Gideon] in slaying his seventy brothers;

57And all the wickedness of the men of Shechem God repaid upon their heads, and caused to come upon them the curse of Jotham son of Jerubaal. [Vss. 19, 20.]

**10** AFTER ABIMELECH there arose to rescue Israel, Tola son of Puah, son of Dodo, a man of Issachar; and he lived at Shamir in the hill country of Ephraim.

2He judged Israel twenty-three years; then died, and was buried in Shamir.

3After him arose Jair, the Gileadite; and he judged Israel twenty-two years.

4And he had thirty sons who rode on thirty donkey colts, and they had thirty towns called Havoth [towns of]-jair to this day, which are in the land of Gilead.

5And Jair died, and was buried in Kamon.

6And the Israelites again did what was evil in the sight of the Lord, and served the Baals, the Ashtaroth [plu.], and the gods of Syria, of Sidon, of Moab, of the Ammonites, and of the Philistines; they forsook the Lord and did not serve Him.

7And the anger of the Lord was kindled against Israel, and He sold them into the hand of the Philistines and of the Ammonites,

8And they oppressed and crushed *and* broke the Israelites that year. For eighteen years they oppressed all the Israelites beyond the Jordan in the land of the Amorites, which is in Gilead.

9And the Ammonites passed over the Jordan to fight also against Judah and Benjamin and the house of Ephraim; so that Israel was sorely distressed.

10And the Israelites cried to the Lord, saying, We have sinned against You, because we have forsaken our God and have served the Baals.

11And the Lord said to the Israelites, Did I not deliver you from the Egyptians, and the Amorites, the Ammonites, and the Philistines?

12The Sidonians also, and the Amalekites, and the Maonites, oppressed *and* crushed you; and you cried to Me, and I delivered you out of their hand.

13Yet you have forsaken Me and served other gods; therefore I will deliver you no more.

14Go, cry to the gods you have chosen; let them deliver you in your time of distress.

15And the Israelites said to the Lord, We have sinned; do to us whatever seems good to You; only deliver us, we pray You, this day.

16So they put away the foreign gods from among them and served the Lord; and His heart became impatient over the misery of Israel.

17Then the Ammonites were gathered together, and they encamped in Gilead. And the Israelites assembled and encamped at Mizpah.

18And the [Israelites], the leaders of Gilead, said one to another, Who is the man who will begin to fight against the Ammonites? He shall be head over all the inhabitants of Gilead.

## New American Standard

52So Abimelech came to the tower and fought against it, and
approached the entrance of the tower to burn it with fire.
53But a certain woman threw an upper millstone on Abimelech's head, crushing his skull.
54Then he called quickly to the young man, his armor bearer,
and said to him, "Draw your sword and kill me, lest it be said of
me, 'A woman slew him.'" So the young man pierced him
through, and he died.
55And when the men of Israel saw that Abimelech was dead,
each departed to his home.
56Thus God repaid the wickedness of Abimelech, which he had
done to his father, in killing his seventy brothers.
57Also God returned all the wickedness of the men of Shechem
on their heads, and the curse of Jotham the son of Jerubbaal came
upon them.

*Oppression of Philistines and Ammonites*

**10** NOW AFTER Abimelech died, Tola the son of Puah, the
son of Dodo, a man of Issachar, arose to save Israel; and
he lived in Shamir in the hill country of Ephraim.
2And he judged Israel twenty-three years. Then he died and
was buried in Shamir.
3¶ And after him, Jair the Gileadite arose, and judged Israel
twenty-two years.
4And he had thirty sons who rode on thirty donkeys, and they
had thirty cities in the land of Gilead that are called Havvoth-jair
to this day.
5And Jair died and was buried in Kamon.
6¶ Then the sons of Israel again did evil in the sight of the LORD,
served the Baals and the Ashtaroth, the gods of Aram, the gods
of Sidon, the gods of Moab, the gods of the sons of Ammon, and
the gods of the Philistines; thus they forsook the LORD and did not
serve Him.
7And the anger of the LORD burned against Israel, and He sold
them into the hands of the Philistines, and into the hands of the
sons of Ammon.
8And they afflicted and crushed the sons of Israel that year; for
eighteen years they *afflicted* all the sons of Israel who were beyond
the Jordan in Gilead in the land of the Amorites.
9And the sons of Ammon crossed the Jordan to fight also
against Judah, Benjamin, and the house of Ephraim, so that Israel
was greatly distressed.
10¶ Then the sons of Israel cried out to the LORD, saying, "We
have sinned against Thee, for indeed, we have forsaken our God
and served the Baals."
11And the LORD said to the sons of Israel, "*Did I* not *deliver you*
from the Egyptians, the Amorites, the sons of Ammon, and the
Philistines?
12"Also when the Sidonians, the Amalekites and the Maonites
oppressed you, you cried out to Me, and I delivered you from their
hands.
13"Yet you have forsaken Me and served other gods; therefore
I will deliver you no more.
14"Go and cry out to the gods which you have chosen; let them
deliver you in the time of your distress."
15And the sons of Israel said to the LORD, "We have sinned, do
to us whatever seems good to Thee; only please deliver us this
day."
16So they put away the foreign gods from among them, and
served the LORD; and He could bear the misery of Israel no longer.
17¶ Then the sons of Ammon were summoned, and they
camped in Gilead. And the sons of Israel gathered together, and
camped in Mizpah.
18And the people, the leaders of Gilead, said to one another,
"Who is the man who will begin to fight against the sons of
Ammon? He shall become head over all the inhabitants of Gilead."

## New International

to the tower and stormed it. But as he approached the entrance to
the tower to set it on fire, 53a woman dropped an upper millstone
on his head and cracked his skull.
54Hurriedly he called to his armor-bearer, "Draw your sword
and kill me, so that they can't say, 'A woman killed him.'" So his
servant ran him through, and he died. 55When the Israelites saw
that Abimelech was dead, they went home.
56Thus God repaid the wickedness that Abimelech had done to
his father by murdering his seventy brothers. 57God also made the
men of Shechem pay for all their wickedness. The curse of Jotham
son of Jerub-Baal came on them.

*Tola*

**10** AFTER THE time of Abimelech a man of Issachar, Tola son
of Puah, the son of Dodo, rose to save Israel. He lived in
Shamir, in the hill country of Ephraim. 2He led[a] Israel twenty-
three years; then he died, and was buried in Shamir.

*Jair*

3He was followed by Jair of Gilead, who led Israel twenty-two
years. 4He had thirty sons, who rode thirty donkeys. They controlled thirty towns in Gilead, which to this day are called Havvoth
Jair.[b] 5When Jair died, he was buried in Kamon.

*Jephthah*

6Again the Israelites did evil in the eyes of the LORD. They
served the Baals and the Ashtoreths, and the gods of Aram, the
gods of Sidon, the gods of Moab, the gods of the Ammonites and
the gods of the Philistines. And because the Israelites forsook the
LORD and no longer served him, 7he became angry with them. He
sold them into the hands of the Philistines and the Ammonites,
8who that year shattered and crushed them. For eighteen years
they oppressed all the Israelites on the east side of the Jordan in
Gilead, the land of the Amorites. 9The Ammonites also crossed the
Jordan to fight against Judah, Benjamin and the house of Ephraim;
and Israel was in great distress. 10Then the Israelites cried out to
the LORD, "We have sinned against you, forsaking our God and
serving the Baals."
11The LORD replied, "When the Egyptians, the Amorites, the
Ammonites, the Philistines, 12the Sidonians, the Amalekites and
the Maonites[c] oppressed you and you cried to me for help, did I
not save you from their hands? 13But you have forsaken me and
served other gods, so I will no longer save you. 14Go and cry out
to the gods you have chosen. Let them save you when you are in
trouble!"
15But the Israelites said to the LORD, "We have sinned. Do with
us whatever you think best, but please rescue us now." 16Then
they got rid of the foreign gods among them and served the LORD.
And he could bear Israel's misery no longer.
17When the Ammonites were called to arms and camped in
Gilead, the Israelites assembled and camped at Mizpah. 18The
leaders of the people of Gilead said to each other, "Whoever will
launch the attack against the Ammonites will be the head of all
those living in Gilead."

**NIV** [a] 2 Traditionally *judged;* also in verse 3 [b] 4 Or *called the settlements of Jair*
[c] 12 Hebrew; some Septuagint manuscripts *Midianites*

## King James

**11** NOW JEPHTHAH the Gileadite was a mighty man of valour, and he *was* the son of an harlot: and Gilead begat Jephthah.

2 And Gilead's wife bare him sons; and his wife's sons grew up, and they thrust out Jephthah, and said unto him, Thou shalt not inherit in our father's house; for thou *art* the son of a strange woman.

3 Then Jephthah fled from his brethren, and dwelt in the land of Tob: and there were gathered vain men to Jephthah, and went out with him.

4 ¶ And it came to pass in process of time, that the children of Ammon made war against Israel.

5 And it was so, that when the children of Ammon made war against Israel, the elders of Gilead went to fetch Jephthah out of the land of Tob:

6 And they said unto Jephthah, Come, and be our captain, that we may fight with the children of Ammon.

7 And Jephthah said unto the elders of Gilead, Did not ye hate me, and expel me out of my father's house? and why are ye come unto me now when ye are in distress?

8 And the elders of Gilead said unto Jephthah, Therefore we turn again to thee now, that thou mayest go with us, and fight against the children of Ammon, and be our head over all the inhabitants of Gilead.

9 And Jephthah said unto the elders of Gilead, If ye bring me home again to fight against the children of Ammon, and the LORD deliver them before me, shall I be your head?

10 And the elders of Gilead said unto Jephthah, The LORD be witness between us, if we do not so according to thy words.

11 Then Jephthah went with the elders of Gilead, and the people made him head and captain over them: and Jephthah uttered all his words before the LORD in Mizpeh.

12 ¶ And Jephthah sent messengers unto the king of the children of Ammon, saying, What hast thou to do with me, that thou art come against me to fight in my land?

13 And the king of the children of Ammon answered unto the messengers of Jephthah, Because Israel took away my land, when they came up out of Egypt, from Arnon even unto Jabbok, and unto Jordan: now therefore restore those *lands* again peaceably.

14 And Jephthah sent messengers again unto the king of the children of Ammon:

15 And said unto him, Thus saith Jephthah, Israel took not away the land of Moab, nor the land of the children of Ammon:

16 But when Israel came up from Egypt, and walked through the wilderness unto the Red sea, and came to Kadesh;

17 Then Israel sent messengers unto the king of Edom, saying, Let me, I pray thee, pass through thy land: but the king of Edom would not hearken *thereto.* And in like manner they sent unto the king of Moab: but he would not *consent:* and Israel abode in Kadesh.

18 Then they went along through the wilderness, and compassed the land of Edom, and the land of Moab, and came by the east side of the land of Moab, and pitched on the other side of Arnon, but came not within the border of Moab: for Arnon *was* the border of Moab.

19 And Israel sent messengers unto Sihon king of the Amorites, the king of Heshbon; and Israel said unto him, Let us pass, we pray thee, through thy land into my place.

20 But Sihon trusted not Israel to pass through his coast: but Sihon gathered all his people together, and pitched in Jahaz, and fought against Israel.

21 And the LORD God of Israel delivered Sihon and all his people into the hand of Israel, and they smote them: so Israel possessed all the land of the Amorites, the inhabitants of that country.

22 And they possessed all the coasts of the Amorites, from Arnon even unto Jabbok, and from the wilderness even unto Jordan.

23 So now the LORD God of Israel hath dispossessed the Amorites from before his people Israel, and shouldest thou possess it?

## Amplified

**11** NOW JEPHTHAH the Gileadite was a mighty warrior, but he was the son of a harlot. Gilead was Jephthah's father.

2 And Gilead's wife also bore him sons; and when his wife's sons grew up, they thrust Jephthah out, and said to him, You shall not inherit in our father's house; for you are the son of another woman.

3 Then Jephthah fled from his brothers, and dwelt in the land of Tob; and worthless men gathered around Jephthah, and went on raids with him.

4 And after a time, the Ammonites made war against Israel.

5 And when the Ammonites made war against Israel, the elders of Gilead went to bring Jephthah out of the land of Tob;

6 And they said to Jephthah, Come and be our leader, that we may fight with the Ammonites.

7 But Jephthah said to the elders of Gilead, Did you not hate me, and drive me out of my father's house? Why have you come to me now when you are in trouble?

8 And the elders of Gilead said to Jephthah, That is why we have turned to you now, that you may go with us and fight the Ammonites and be our head over all the citizens of Gilead.

9 Jephthah said to the elders of Gilead, If you bring me home again to fight against the Ammonites, and the Lord gives them over to me, [understand that] I will be your head.

10 And the elders of Gilead said to Jephthah, The Lord be witness between us, if we do not what you say.

11 So Jephthah went with the elders of Gilead, and the people made him head and leader over them; and Jephthah repeated all he had promised before the Lord at Mizpah.

12 And Jephthah sent messengers to the king of the Ammonites, saying, What have you to do with me, that you have come against me to fight in my land?

13 The Ammonites' king replied to the messengers of Jephthah, Because Israel took away my land [which was not true], when they came up out of Egypt [300 years before] from the Arnon even to Jabbok and to the Jordan; now therefore restore those lands peaceably.

14 And Jephthah sent messengers again to the king of the Ammonites:

15 And said to him, Thus says Jephthah, Israel did not take the land of Moab or the land of the Ammonites;

16 But when [Israel] came up from Egypt, [they] walked through the wilderness to the Red Sea and came to Kadesh.

17 Then Israel sent messengers to the king of Edom, saying, Let us, we pray, pass through your land; but the king of Edom would not listen. Also they sent to the king of Moab, but he would not consent. So Israel remained at Kadesh.

18 Then they went through the wilderness, and went around the land of Edom, and the land of Moab, and came by the east side of the land of Moab, and camped on the other side of the Arnon, but came not within the territory of Moab; for the Arnon was the boundary of Moab.

19 Then Israel sent messengers to Sihon king of the Amorites, king of Heshbon; and Israel said to him, Let us pass, we pray you, through your land to our country.

20 But Sihon did not trust Israel to pass through his territory; so Sihon gathered all his people together, and encamped at Jahaz, and fought with Israel.

21 And the Lord, the God of Israel, gave Sihon and all his people into the hand of Israel, and they defeated them; so Israel took possession of all the land of the Amorites, the inhabitants of that country.

22 They possessed all the territory of the Amorites, from the Arnon even to the Jabbok, and from the wilderness even to the Jordan.

23 So now the Lord God of Israel has dispossessed the Amorites from before His people Israel, and should you possess them?

## New American Standard

*Jephthah the Ninth Judge*

**11** NOW JEPHTHAH the Gileadite was a valiant warrior, but
he was the son of a harlot. And Gilead was the father of
Jephthah.
2And Gilead's wife bore him sons; and when his wife's sons
grew up, they drove Jephthah out and said to him, "You shall not
have an inheritance in our father's house, for you are the son of
another woman."
3So Jephthah fled from his brothers and lived in the land of
Tob; and worthless fellows gathered themselves about Jephthah,
and they went out with him.
4¶ And it came about after a while that the sons of Ammon
fought against Israel.
5And it happened when the sons of Ammon fought against
Israel that the elders of Gilead went to get Jephthah from the land
of Tob;
6and they said to Jephthah, "Come and be our chief that we
may fight against the sons of Ammon."
7Then Jephthah said to the elders of Gilead, "Did you not hate
me and drive me from my father's house? So why have you come
to me now when you are in trouble?"
8And the elders of Gilead said to Jephthah, "For this reason we
have now returned to you, that you may go with us and fight with
the sons of Ammon and become head over all the inhabitants of
Gilead."
9So Jephthah said to the elders of Gilead, "If you take me back
to fight against the sons of Ammon and the LORD gives them up
to me, will I become your head?"
10And the elders of Gilead said to Jephthah, "The LORD is
witness between us; surely we will do as you have said."
11Then Jephthah went with the elders of Gilead, and the people
made him head and chief over them; and Jephthah spoke all his
words before the LORD at Mizpah.
12¶ Now Jephthah sent messengers to the king of the sons of
Ammon, saying, "What is between you and me, that you have
come to me to fight against my land?"
13And the king of the sons of Ammon said to the messengers
of Jephthah, "Because Israel took away my land when they came
up from Egypt, from the Arnon as far as the Jabbok and the Jordan;
therefore, return them peaceably now."
14But Jephthah sent messengers again to the king of the sons
of Ammon,
15and they said to him, "Thus says Jephthah, 'Israel did not take
away the land of Moab, nor the land of the sons of Ammon.
16'For when they came up from Egypt, and Israel went through
the wilderness to the Red Sea and came to Kadesh,
17then Israel sent messengers to the king of Edom, saying,
"Please let us pass through your land," but the king of Edom
would not listen. And they also sent to the king of Moab, but he
would not consent. So Israel remained at Kadesh.
18'Then they went through the wilderness and around the land
of Edom and the land of Moab, and came to the east side of the
land of Moab, and they camped beyond the Arnon; but they did
not enter the territory of Moab, for the Arnon *was* the border of
Moab.
19'And Israel sent messengers to Sihon king of the Amorites,
the king of Heshbon, and Israel said to him, "Please let us pass
through your land to our place."
20'But Sihon did not trust Israel to pass through his territory; so
Sihon gathered all his people and camped in Jahaz, and fought
with Israel.
21'And the LORD, the God of Israel, gave Sihon and all his
people into the hand of Israel, and they defeated them; so Israel
possessed all the land of the Amorites, the inhabitants of that
country.
22'So they possessed all the territory of the Amorites, from the
Arnon as far as the Jabbok, and from the wilderness as far as the
Jordan.
23'Since now the LORD, the God of Israel, drove out the Amorites from before His people Israel, are you then to possess it?

## New International

**11** JEPHTHAH THE Gileadite was a mighty warrior. His father was Gilead; his mother was a prostitute. 2Gilead's
wife also bore him sons, and when they were grown up, they
drove Jephthah away. "You are not going to get any inheritance
in our family," they said, "because you are the son of another
woman." 3So Jephthah fled from his brothers and settled in the
land of Tob, where a group of adventurers gathered around him
and followed him.
4Some time later, when the Ammonites made war on Israel,
5the elders of Gilead went to get Jephthah from the land of Tob.
6"Come," they said, "be our commander, so we can fight the
Ammonites."
7Jephthah said to them, "Didn't you hate me and drive me from
my father's house? Why do you come to me now, when you're in
trouble?"
8The elders of Gilead said to him, "Nevertheless, we are turning
to you now; come with us to fight the Ammonites, and you will
be our head over all who live in Gilead."
9Jephthah answered, "Suppose you take me back to fight the
Ammonites and the LORD gives them to me—will I really be your
head?"
10The elders of Gilead replied, "The LORD is our witness; we
will certainly do as you say." 11So Jephthah went with the elders
of Gilead, and the people made him head and commander over
them. And he repeated all his words before the LORD in Mizpah.
12Then Jephthah sent messengers to the Ammonite king with
the question: "What do you have against us that you have attacked
our country?"
13The king of the Ammonites answered Jephthah's messengers,
"When Israel came up out of Egypt, they took away my land from
the Arnon to the Jabbok, all the way to the Jordan. Now give it back
peaceably."
14Jephthah sent back messengers to the Ammonite king, 15say-
ing:

"This is what Jephthah says: Israel did not take the land of
Moab or the land of the Ammonites. 16But when they came
up out of Egypt, Israel went through the desert to the Red
Sea[a] and on to Kadesh. 17Then Israel sent messengers to the
king of Edom, saying, 'Give us permission to go through your
country,' but the king of Edom would not listen. They sent
also to the king of Moab, and he refused. So Israel stayed at
Kadesh.
18"Next they traveled through the desert, skirted the lands
of Edom and Moab, passed along the eastern side of the
country of Moab, and camped on the other side of the Arnon.
They did not enter the territory of Moab, for the Arnon was
its border.
19"Then Israel sent messengers to Sihon king of the Amorites, who ruled in Heshbon, and said to him, 'Let us pass
through your country to our own place.' 20Sihon, however,
did not trust Israel[b] to pass through his territory. He mustered all his men and encamped at Jahaz and fought with
Israel.
21"Then the LORD, the God of Israel, gave Sihon and all his
men into Israel's hands, and they defeated them. Israel took
over all the land of the Amorites who lived in that country,
22capturing all of it from the Arnon to the Jabbok and from the
desert to the Jordan.
23"Now since the LORD, the God of Israel, has driven the
Amorites out before his people Israel, what right have you to
take it over? 24Will you not take what your god Chemosh

**NIV** [a] 16 Hebrew *Yam Suph;* that is, Sea of Reeds [b] 20 Or *however, would not make an agreement for Israel*

## King James

24Wilt not thou possess that which Chemosh thy god giveth thee to possess? So whomsoever the LORD our God shall drive out from before us, them will we possess.

25And now *art* thou any thing better than Balak the son of Zippor, king of Moab? did he ever strive against Israel, or did he ever fight against them,

26While Israel dwelt in Heshbon and her towns, and in Aroer and her towns, and in all the cities that *be* along by the coasts of Arnon, three hundred years? why therefore did ye not recover *them* within that time?

27Wherefore I have not sinned against thee, but thou doest me wrong to war against me: the LORD the Judge be judge this day between the children of Israel and the children of Ammon.

28Howbeit the king of the children of Ammon hearkened not unto the words of Jephthah which he sent him.

29¶ Then the spirit of the LORD came upon Jephthah, and he passed over Gilead, and Manasseh, and passed over Mizpeh of Gilead, and from Mizpeh of Gilead he passed over *unto* the children of Ammon.

30And Jephthah vowed a vow unto the LORD, and said, If thou shalt without fail deliver the children of Ammon into mine hands,

31Then it shall be, that whatsoever cometh forth of the doors of my house to meet me, when I return in peace from the children of Ammon, shall surely be the LORD'S, and I will offer it up for a burnt offering.

32¶ So Jephthah passed over unto the children of Ammon to fight against them; and the LORD delivered them into his hands.

33And he smote them from Aroer, even till thou come to Minnith, *even* twenty cities, and unto the plain of the vineyards, with a very great slaughter. Thus the children of Ammon were subdued before the children of Israel.

34¶ And Jephthah came to Mizpeh unto his house, and, behold, his daughter came out to meet him with timbrels and with dances: and she *was his* only child; beside her he had neither son nor daughter.

35And it came to pass, when he saw her, that he rent his clothes, and said, Alas, my daughter! thou hast brought me very low, and thou art one of them that trouble me: for I have opened my mouth unto the LORD, and I cannot go back.

36And she said unto him, My father, *if* thou hast opened thy mouth unto the LORD, do to me according to that which hath proceeded out of thy mouth; forasmuch as the LORD hath taken vengeance for thee of thine enemies, *even* of the children of Ammon.

37And she said unto her father, Let this thing be done for me: let me alone two months, that I may go up and down upon the mountains, and bewail my virginity, I and my fellows.

38And he said, Go. And he sent her away *for* two months: and she went with her companions, and bewailed her virginity upon the mountains.

39And it came to pass at the end of two months, that she returned unto her father, who did with her *according* to his vow which he had vowed: and she knew no man. And it was a custom in Israel,

## Amplified

24Will you not possess what Chemosh your god gives you to possess? And all the Lord our God dispossessed before us, we will possess.

25Now are you any better than Balak son of Zippor, king of Moab? Did he ever strive against Israel, or did he ever go to war with them?

26While Israel dwelt in Heshbon and its villages, and in Aroer and its villages, and in all the cities along the banks of the Arnon for 300 years, why did you not recover [your lost lands] during that time?

27So I have not sinned against you, but you are doing me wrong to war against me. The Lord, the [righteous] Judge, be judge this day between the Israelites and the Ammonites.

28But the king of the Ammonites did not listen to the message Jephthah sent him.

29Then the Spirit of the Lord came upon Jephthah, and he passed through Gilead and Manasseh and Mizpah of Gilead, and from Mizpah of Gilead he passed on to the Ammonites.

30And Jephthah made a vow to the Lord, and said, If You will indeed give the Ammonites into my hand,

31Then whatever *or* whoever comes forth from the doors of my house to meet me, when I return in peace from the Ammonites, it shall be the Lord's, and I will offer it *or* him up for a burnt offering.

32Then Jephthah crossed over to the Ammonites to fight with them; and the Lord gave them into his hand.

33And from Aroer to Minnith he smote them, twenty cities, and as far as Abel-cheramim [the meadow of vineyards], with a very great slaughter. So the Ammonites were subdued before the Israelites.

34Then Jephthah came to Mizpah to his home, and behold, his daughter came out to meet him with timbrels and with dances! And she was his only child; beside her he had neither son nor daughter.

35And when he saw her, he rent his clothes, and said, Alas, my daughter! You have brought me very low, and are the cause of great trouble to me; for I have opened my mouth [in a vow] to the Lord, and I cannot take it back.

36And she said to him, My father, if you have opened your mouth to the Lord, do to me according to what you have vowed, since the Lord has taken vengeance for you on your enemies, the Ammonites.

37And she said to her father, Let this thing be done for me; let me alone two months, that I may go and wander upon the mountains, and bewail my virginity, I and my companions.

38And he said, Go. And he sent her away for two months; and she went with her companions, and bewailed her virginity upon the mountains.

39At the end of two months she returned to her father, who [a]did with her according to his vow which he had vowed. She never mated with a man. And it became a custom in Israel

**AMP** [a] Scholars fail to agree as to what Jephthah really did. For example, "This plain and restrained statement that *he did with her according to his vow* is best taken as implying her actual sacrifice. Although human sacrifice was strictly forbidden to Israelites, we need not be surprised at a man of Jephthah's half-Canaanite antecedents following Canaanite usage in this matter" *(New Bible Commentary)*. And, "Although the lapse of two months might be supposed to have afforded time for reflection, and a better sense of his duty, there is but too much reason to conclude that he was impelled to the fulfillment by the dictates of a pious but unenlightened conscience" *(Jamieson, Fausset and Brown's Bible Commentary)*. And, "The religious system of Israel had fallen into suspension. From the days of Phinehas [Judg. 20:27, 28] to the time of Samuel, we hear nothing of the high priest, the ark or the tabernacle" *(Cambridge Bible)*. On the other hand, *Lange* sums up the position of many scholars when he calls attention to stories in Greek mythology in which the *virginity* of a goddess was celebrated by Greek maidens with song and dance. "At all events, it does not 'stand there in the text,' as Luther wrote, that she was offered in sacrifice" *(Lange's Commentary)*. And the fact that the maidens mourned her virginity and not her death seems to prove that she did not die.

## New American Standard

24'Do you not possess what Chemosh your god gives you to possess? So whatever the LORD our God has driven out before us, we will possess it.

25'And now are you any better than Balak the son of Zippor, king of Moab? Did he ever strive with Israel, or did he ever fight against them?

26'While Israel lived in Heshbon and its villages, and in Aroer and its villages, and in all the cities that are on the banks of the Arnon, three hundred years, why did you not recover them within that time?

27'I therefore have not sinned against you, but you are doing me wrong by making war against me; may the LORD, the Judge, judge today between the sons of Israel and the sons of Ammon.'"

28But the king of the sons of Ammon disregarded the message which Jephthah sent him.

*Jephthah's Tragic Vow*

**29**¶ Now the Spirit of the LORD came upon Jephthah, so that he passed through Gilead and Manasseh; then he passed through Mizpah of Gilead, and from Mizpah of Gilead he went on to the sons of Ammon.

30And Jephthah made a vow to the LORD and said, "If Thou wilt indeed give the sons of Ammon into my hand,

31then it shall be that whatever comes out of the doors of my house to meet me when I return in peace from the sons of Ammon, it shall be the LORD's, and I will offer it up as a burnt offering."

32So Jephthah crossed over to the sons of Ammon to fight against them; and the LORD gave them into his hand.

33And he struck them with a very great slaughter from Aroer to the entrance of Minnith, twenty cities, and as far as Abel-keramim. So the sons of Ammon were subdued before the sons of Israel.

**34**¶ When Jephthah came to his house at Mizpah, behold, his daughter was coming out to meet him with tambourines and with dancing. Now she was his one *and* only child; besides her he had neither son nor daughter.

35And it came about when he saw her, that he tore his clothes and said, "Alas, my daughter! You have brought me very low, and you are among those who trouble me; for I have given my word to the LORD, and I cannot take *it* back."

36So she said to him, "My father, you have given your word to the LORD; do to me as you have said, since the LORD has avenged you of your enemies, the sons of Ammon."

37And she said to her father, "Let this thing be done for me; let me alone two months, that I may go to the mountains and weep because of my virginity, I and my companions."

38Then he said, "Go." So he sent her away for two months; and she left with her companions, and wept on the mountains because of her virginity.

39And it came about at the end of two months that she returned to her father, who did to her according to the vow which he had made; and she had no relations with a man. Thus it became a custom in Israel,

## New International

gives you? Likewise, whatever the LORD our God has given us, we will possess. 25Are you better than Balak son of Zippor, king of Moab? Did he ever quarrel with Israel or fight with them? 26For three hundred years Israel occupied Heshbon, Aroer, the surrounding settlements and all the towns along the Arnon. Why didn't you retake them during that time? 27I have not wronged you, but you are doing me wrong by waging war against me. Let the LORD, the Judge,[b] decide the dispute this day between the Israelites and the Ammonites."

28The king of Ammon, however, paid no attention to the message Jephthah sent him.

29Then the Spirit of the LORD came upon Jephthah. He crossed Gilead and Manasseh, passed through Mizpah of Gilead, and from there he advanced against the Ammonites. 30And Jephthah made a vow to the LORD: "If you give the Ammonites into my hands, 31whatever comes out of the door of my house to meet me when I return in triumph from the Ammonites will be the LORD's, and I will sacrifice it as a burnt offering."

32Then Jephthah went over to fight the Ammonites, and the LORD gave them into his hands. 33He devastated twenty towns from Aroer to the vicinity of Minnith, as far as Abel Keramim. Thus Israel subdued Ammon.

34When Jephthah returned to his home in Mizpah, who should come out to meet him but his daughter, dancing to the sound of tambourines! She was an only child. Except for her he had neither son nor daughter. 35When he saw her, he tore his clothes and cried, "Oh! My daughter! You have made me miserable and wretched, because I have made a vow to the LORD that I cannot break."

36"My father," she replied, "you have given your word to the LORD. Do to me just as you promised, now that the LORD has avenged you of your enemies, the Ammonites. 37But grant me this one request," she said. "Give me two months to roam the hills and weep with my friends, because I will never marry."

38"You may go," he said. And he let her go for two months. She and the girls went into the hills and wept because she would never marry. 39After the two months, she returned to her father and he did to her as he had vowed. And she was a virgin.

From this comes the Israelite custom 40that each year the young

NIV [b] 27 Or *Ruler*

## King James

40 *That* the daughters of Israel went yearly to lament the daughter of Jephthah the Gileadite four days in a year.

12 AND THE men of Ephraim gathered themselves together,
and went northward, and said unto Jephthah, Wherefore
passedst thou over to fight against the children of Ammon, and
didst not call us to go with thee? we will burn thine house upon
thee with fire.
2 And Jephthah said unto them, I and my people were at great
strife with the children of Ammon; and when I called you, ye
delivered me not out of their hands.
3 And when I saw that ye delivered *me* not, I put my life in my
hands, and passed over against the children of Ammon, and the
LORD delivered them into my hand: wherefore then are ye come
up unto me this day, to fight against me?
4 Then Jephthah gathered together all the men of Gilead, and
fought with Ephraim: and the men of Gilead smote Ephraim,
because they said, Ye Gileadites *are* fugitives of Ephraim among
the Ephraimites, *and* among the Manassites.
5 And the Gileadites took the passages of Jordan before the
Ephraimites: and it was *so,* that when those Ephraimites which
were escaped said, Let me go over; that the men of Gilead said
unto him, *Art* thou an Ephraimite? If he said, Nay;
6 Then said they unto him, Say now Shibboleth: and he said
Sibboleth: for he could not frame to pronounce *it* right. Then they
took him, and slew him at the passages of Jordan: and there fell
at that time of the Ephraimites forty and two thousand.
7 And Jephthah judged Israel six years. Then died Jephthah the
Gileadite, and was buried in *one of* the cities of Gilead.
8 ¶ And after him Ibzan of Bethlehem judged Israel.
9 And he had thirty sons, and thirty daughters, *whom* he sent
abroad, and took in thirty daughters from abroad for his sons. And
he judged Israel seven years.
10 Then died Ibzan, and was buried at Bethlehem.
11 ¶ And after him Elon, a Zebulonite, judged Israel; and he
judged Israel ten years.
12 And Elon the Zebulonite died, and was buried in Aijalon in
the country of Zebulun.
13 ¶ And after him Abdon the son of Hillel, a Pirathonite, judged
Israel.
14 And he had forty sons and thirty nephews, that rode on
threescore and ten ass colts: and he judged Israel eight years.
15 And Abdon the son of Hillel the Pirathonite died, and was
buried in Pirathon in the land of Ephraim, in the mount of the
Amalekites.

13 AND THE children of Israel did evil again in the sight of
the LORD; and the LORD delivered them into the hand of
the Philistines forty years.
2 ¶ And there was a certain man of Zorah, of the family of the
Danites, whose name *was* Manoah; and his wife *was* barren, and
bare not.
3 And the angel of the LORD appeared unto the woman, and said
unto her, Behold now, thou *art* barren, and bearest not: but thou
shalt conceive, and bear a son.
4 Now therefore beware, I pray thee, and drink not wine nor
strong drink, and eat not any unclean *thing:*
5 For, lo, thou shalt conceive, and bear a son; and no razor shall
come on his head: for the child shall be a Nazarite unto God from
the womb: and he shall begin to deliver Israel out of the hand of
the Philistines.

## Amplified

40 That the daughters of Israel went yearly to mourn the daughter of Jephthah the Gileadite four days in a year.

12 THE MEN of Ephraim were summoned together, and
crossed to Zaphon, and said to Jephthah, Why did you
cross over to fight with the Ammonites and did not summon us
to go with you? We will burn your house over you with fire.
2 And Jephthah said to them, I and my people were in a severe
conflict with the Ammonites, and I did call you and you did not
rescue me from their hands.
3 And when I saw that you would not rescue me, I put my life
in my hands, and crossed over against the Ammonites, and the
Lord delivered them into my hand. Why then have you come up
to me this day, to fight against me?
4 Then Jephthah gathered all the men of Gilead and fought with
Ephraim; and the men of Gilead smote Ephraim, because they had
said, You Gileadites are fugitives of Ephraim in the midst of
Ephraim and Manasseh.
5 And the Gileadites took the fords of the Jordan before the
Ephraimites; and when any of those Ephraimites who had escaped
said, Let me go over, the men of Gilead said to him, Are you an
Ephraimite? If he said, No,
6 They said to him, Then say Shibboleth, and He said Sibboleth,
for he could not pronounce it right. Then they seized him and slew
him at the fords of the Jordan. And there fell at that time 42,000
of the Ephraimites.
7 Jephthah judged Israel six years. Then Jephthah the Gileadite
died, and was buried in one of the cities of Gilead.
8 And after him Ibzan of Bethlehem judged Israel.
9 And he had thirty sons; and thirty daughters he gave [to
husbands] outside his tribe, and thirty daughters [daughters-in-
law] he brought in from outside his tribe for his sons. And he
judged Israel seven years.
10 Then Ibzan died, and was buried at Bethlehem.
11 After him Elon, a Zebulunite, judged Israel; and he judged
Israel ten years.
12 Then Elon the Zebulunite died, and was buried at Aijalon in
the land of Zebulun.
13 And after him Abdon son of Hillel the Pirathonite judged
Israel.
14 And he had forty sons and thirty grandsons who rode on
seventy donkey colts; and he judged Israel eight years.
15 Then Abdon son of Hillel the Pirathonite died, and was buried
at Pirathon in the land of Ephraim, in the hill country of the
Amalekites.

13 AND THE Israelites did what was evil again in the sight
of the Lord; and the Lord gave them into the hand of the
Philistines for forty years.
2 And there was a certain man of Zorah, of the tribe of the
Danites, whose name was Manoah; and his wife was barren and
had no children.
3 And the Angel of the Lord appeared to the woman, and said
to her, Behold, you are barren and have no children; but you shall
become pregnant and bear a son.
4 Therefore beware, and drink no wine or strong drink, and eat
nothing unclean,
5 For lo, you shall become pregnant and bear a son. No razor
shall come upon his head, for the child shall be a Nazirite to God
from birth; and he shall begin to deliver Israel out of the hand of
the Philistines.

## New American Standard

40that the daughters of Israel went yearly to commemorate the
daughter of Jephthah the Gileadite four days in the year.

*Jephthah and His Successors*

**12** THEN THE men of Ephraim were summoned, and they
crossed to Zaphon and said to Jephthah, "Why did you
cross over to fight against the sons of Ammon without calling us
to go with you? We will burn your house down on you."
2And Jephthah said to them, "I and my people were at great
strife with the sons of Ammon; when I called you, you did not
deliver me from their hand.
3"And when I saw that you would not deliver *me*, I took my
life in my hands and crossed over against the sons of Ammon, and
the LORD gave them into my hand. Why then have you come up
to me this day, to fight against me?"
4Then Jephthah gathered all the men of Gilead and fought
Ephraim; and the men of Gilead defeated Ephraim, because they
said, "You are fugitives of Ephraim, O Gileadites, in the midst of
Ephraim *and* in the midst of Manasseh."
5And the Gileadites captured the fords of the Jordan opposite
Ephraim. And it happened when *any of* the fugitives of Ephraim
said, "Let me cross over," the men of Gilead would say to him,
"Are you an Ephraimite?" If he said, "No,"
6then they would say to him, "Say now, 'Shibboleth.' " But he
said, "Sibboleth," for he could not pronounce it correctly. Then
they seized him and slew him at the fords of the Jordan. Thus there
fell at that time 42,000 of Ephraim.
7And Jephthah judged Israel six years. Then Jephthah the
Gileadite died and was buried in *one of* the cities of Gilead.
8¶ Now Ibzan of Bethlehem judged Israel after him.
9And he had thirty sons, and thirty daughters *whom* he gave
in marriage outside *the family*, and he brought in thirty daughters
from outside for his sons. And he judged Israel seven years.
10Then Ibzan died and was buried in Bethlehem.
11¶ Now Elon the Zebulunite judged Israel after him; and he
judged Israel ten years.
12Then Elon the Zebulunite died and was buried at Aijalon in
the land of Zebulun.
13¶ Now Abdon the son of Hillel the Pirathonite judged Israel
after him.
14And he had forty sons and thirty grandsons who rode on
seventy donkeys; and he judged Israel eight years.
15Then Abdon the son of Hillel the Pirathonite died and was
buried at Pirathon in the land of Ephraim, in the hill country of the
Amalekites.

*Philistines Oppress Again*

**13** NOW THE sons of Israel again did evil in the sight of the
LORD, so that the LORD gave them into the hands of the
Philistines forty years.
2¶ And there was a certain man of Zorah, of the family of the
Danites, whose name was Manoah; and his wife was barren and
had borne no *children.*
3Then the angel of the LORD appeared to the woman, and said
to her, "Behold now, you are barren and have borne no *children,*
but you shall conceive and give birth to a son.
4"Now therefore, be careful not to drink wine or strong drink,
nor eat any unclean thing.
5"For behold, you shall conceive and give birth to a son, and
no razor shall come upon his head, for the boy shall be a Nazirite
to God from the womb; and he shall begin to deliver Israel from
the hands of the Philistines."

## New International

women of Israel go out for four days to commemorate the daughter
of Jephthah the Gileadite.

*Jephthah and Ephraim*

**12** THE MEN of Ephraim called out their forces, crossed over
to Zaphon and said to Jephthah, "Why did you go to fight
the Ammonites without calling us to go with you? We're going to
burn down your house over your head."
2Jephthah answered, "I and my people were engaged in a great
struggle with the Ammonites, and although I called, you didn't
save me out of their hands. 3When I saw that you wouldn't help,
I took my life in my hands and crossed over to fight the Ammonites, and the LORD gave me the victory over them. Now why have
you come up today to fight me?"
4Jephthah then called together the men of Gilead and fought
against Ephraim. The Gileadites struck them down because the
Ephraimites had said, "You Gileadites are renegades from
Ephraim and Manasseh." 5The Gileadites captured the fords of the
Jordan leading to Ephraim, and whenever a survivor of Ephraim
said, "Let me cross over," the men of Gilead asked him, "Are you
an Ephraimite?" If he replied, "No," 6they said, "All right, say
'Shibboleth.' " If he said, "Sibboleth," because he could not pronounce the word correctly, they seized him and killed him at the
fords of the Jordan. Forty-two thousand Ephraimites were killed
at that time.
7Jephthah led[a] Israel six years. Then Jephthah the Gileadite
died, and was buried in a town in Gilead.

*Ibzan, Elon and Abdon*

8After him, Ibzan of Bethlehem led Israel. 9He had thirty sons
and thirty daughters. He gave his daughters away in marriage to
those outside his clan, and for his sons he brought in thirty young
women as wives from outside his clan. Ibzan led Israel seven
years. 10Then Ibzan died, and was buried in Bethlehem.
11After him, Elon the Zebulunite led Israel ten years. 12Then
Elon died, and was buried in Aijalon in the land of Zebulun.
13After him, Abdon son of Hillel, from Pirathon, led Israel. 14He
had forty sons and thirty grandsons, who rode on seventy donkeys. He led Israel eight years. 15Then Abdon son of Hillel died,
and was buried at Pirathon in Ephraim, in the hill country of the
Amalekites.

*The Birth of Samson*

**13** AGAIN THE Israelites did evil in the eyes of the LORD, so
the LORD delivered them into the hands of the Philistines
for forty years.
2A certain man of Zorah, named Manoah, from the clan of the
Danites, had a wife who was sterile and remained childless. 3The
angel of the LORD appeared to her and said, "You are sterile and
childless, but you are going to conceive and have a son. 4Now see
to it that you drink no wine or other fermented drink and that you
do not eat anything unclean, 5because you will conceive and give
birth to a son. No razor may be used on his head, because the boy
is to be a Nazirite, set apart to God from birth, and he will begin
the deliverance of Israel from the hands of the Philistines."

NIV [a] 7 Traditionally *judged;* also in verses 8-14

## King James

6¶ Then the woman came and told her husband, saying, A man
of God came unto me, and his countenance *was* like the countenance of an angel of God, very terrible: but I asked him not whence
he *was*, neither told he me his name:
7But he said unto me, Behold, thou shalt conceive, and bear a
son; and now drink no wine nor strong drink, neither eat any
unclean *thing:* for the child shall be a Nazarite to God from the
womb to the day of his death.
8¶ Then Manoah entreated the LORD, and said, O my Lord, let
the man of God which thou didst send come again unto us, and
teach us what we shall do unto the child that shall be born.
9And God hearkened to the voice of Manoah; and the angel of
God came again unto the woman as she sat in the field: but Manoah her husband *was* not with her.
10And the woman made haste, and ran, and showed her husband, and said unto him, Behold, the man hath appeared unto me,
that came unto me the *other* day.
11And Manoah arose, and went after his wife, and came to the
man, and said unto him, *Art* thou the man that spakest unto the
woman? And he said, I *am.*
12And Manoah said, Now let thy words come to pass. How
shall we order the child, and *how* shall we do unto him?
13And the angel of the LORD said unto Manoah, Of all that I said
unto the woman let her beware.
14She may not eat of any *thing* that cometh of the vine, neither
let her drink wine or strong drink, nor eat any unclean *thing:* all
that I commanded her let her observe.
15¶ And Manoah said unto the angel of the LORD, I pray thee,
let us detain thee, until we shall have made ready a kid for thee.
16And the angel of the LORD said unto Manoah, Though thou
detain me, I will not eat of thy bread: and if thou wilt offer a burnt
offering, thou must offer it unto the LORD. For Manoah knew not
that he *was* an angel of the LORD.
17And Manoah said unto the angel of the LORD, What *is* thy
name, that when thy sayings come to pass we may do thee honour?
18And the angel of the LORD said unto him, Why askest thou
thus after my name, seeing it *is* secret?
19So Manoah took a kid with a meat offering, and offered *it*
upon a rock unto the LORD: and *the angel* did wondrously; and
Manoah and his wife looked on.
20For it came to pass, when the flame went up toward heaven
from off the altar, that the angel of the LORD ascended in the flame
of the altar. And Manoah and his wife looked on *it*, and fell on their
faces to the ground.
21But the angel of the LORD did no more appear to Manoah and
to his wife. Then Manoah knew that he *was* an angel of the LORD.
22And Manoah said unto his wife, We shall surely die, because
we have seen God.
23But his wife said unto him, If the LORD were pleased to kill
us, he would not have received a burnt offering and a meat offering at our hands, neither would he have shown us all these *things*,
nor would as at this time have told us *such things* as these.
24¶ And the woman bare a son, and called his name Samson:
and the child grew, and the LORD blessed him.
25And the spirit of the LORD began to move him at times in the
camp of Dan between Zorah and Eshtaol.

**14** AND SAMSON went down to Timnath, and saw a
woman in Timnath of the daughters of the Philistines.
2And he came up, and told his father and his mother, and said,
I have seen a woman in Timnath of the daughters of the Philistines:
now therefore get her for me to wife.

## Amplified

6Then the woman went and told her husband, saying, A man
of God came to me, and his face was like the face of the Angel of
God, to be greatly and reverently feared; I did not ask him from
where he came, and he did not tell me his name.
7But he said to me, Behold, you shall become pregnant and bear
a son; and now drink no wine or strong drink, and eat nothing
unclean, for the child shall be a Nazirite to God from birth to the
day of his death.
8Then Manoah entreated the Lord, and said, O Lord, let the
man of God whom You sent come again to us, and teach us what
we shall do with the child that shall be born.
9And God listened to the voice of Manoah, and the Angel of
God came again to the woman as she sat in the field; but Manoah
her husband was not with her.
10And the woman ran in haste and told her husband, and said
to him, Behold, the man who came to me the other day has
appeared to me.
11And Manoah arose, and went after his wife, and came to the
Man and said to Him, Are you the Man who spoke to this woman?
And He said, I am.
12And Manoah said, Now when your words come true, how
shall we manage the child, and what is he to do?
13And the Angel of the Lord said to Manoah, Let the mother
beware of all that I told her.
14She may not eat of anything that comes from the grapevine,
or drink wine or strong drink, or eat any unclean thing; all that I
commanded her let her observe.
15And Manoah said to the Angel of the Lord, Pray, let us detain
you that we may prepare a kid for you.
16And the Angel of the Lord said to Manoah, Though you
detain me, I will not eat of your food; but if you make ready a burnt
offering, offer it to the Lord. For Manoah did not know He was the
Angel of the Lord.
17And Manoah said to the Angel of the Lord, What is your
name, so that when your words come true, we may do you honor?
18And the Angel of the Lord said to him, Why do you ask My
name, seeing it is wonderful? [Isa. 9:6.]
19So Manoah took the kid with the cereal offering, and offered
it upon a rock to the Lord, the Angel working wonders, while
Manoah and his wife looked on.
20For when the flame went up toward the heavens from off the
altar, the Angel of the Lord ascended in the altar flame. And
Manoah and his wife looked on; and they fell on their faces to the
ground.
21The Angel of the Lord did not appear again to Manoah or to
his wife. Then Manoah knew that He was the Angel of the Lord.
22And Manoah said to his wife, We shall surely die, because we
have seen God.
23But his [sensible] wife said to him, If the Lord were pleased
to kill us, He would not have received a burnt offering and a cereal
offering at our hands, or have shown us all these things, or now
have announced such things as these.
24And the woman [in due time] bore a son, and called his name
Samson; and the child grew, and the Lord blessed him.
25And the Spirit of the Lord began to move him at times in
Mahaneh-dan [the camp of Dan] between Zorah and Eshtaol.

**14** SAMSON WENT down to Timnah, and at Timnah he saw
one of the daughters of the Philistines.
2And he came up, and told his father and mother, I saw one of
the daughters of the Philistines at Timnah; now get her for me as
my wife.

## New American Standard

6Then the woman came and told her husband, saying, "A man
of God came to me and his appearance was like the appearance of
the angel of God, very awesome. And I did not ask him where he
*came* from, nor did he tell me his name.
7"But he said to me, 'Behold, you shall conceive and give birth
to a son, and now you shall not drink wine or strong drink nor eat
any unclean thing, for the boy shall be a Nazirite to God from the
womb to the day of his death.' "
8¶ Then Manoah entreated the LORD and said, "O Lord, please
let the man of God whom Thou hast sent come to us again that he
may teach us what to do for the boy who is to be born."
9And God listened to the voice of Manoah; and the angel of
God came again to the woman as she was sitting in the field, but
Manoah her husband was not with her.
10So the woman ran quickly and told her husband, "Behold, the
man who came the *other* day has appeared to me."
11Then Manoah arose and followed his wife, and when he came
to the man he said to him, "Are you the man who spoke to the
woman?" And he said, "I am."
12And Manoah said, "Now when your words come *to pass*,
what shall be the boy's mode of life and his vocation?"
13So the angel of the LORD said to Manoah, "Let the woman pay
attention to all that I said.
14"She should not eat anything that comes from the vine nor
drink wine or strong drink, nor eat any unclean thing; let her
observe all that I commanded."
15¶ Then Manoah said to the angel of the LORD, "Please let us
detain you so that we may prepare a kid for you."
16And the angel of the LORD said to Manoah, "Though you
detain me, I will not eat your food, but if you prepare a burnt
offering, *then* offer it to the LORD." For Manoah did not know that
he was the angel of the LORD.
17And Manoah said to the angel of the LORD, "What is your
name, so that when your words come *to pass*, we may honor you?"
18But the angel of the LORD said to him, "Why do you ask my
name, seeing it is [a]wonderful?"
19So Manoah took the kid with the grain offering and offered
it on the rock to the LORD, and He performed wonders while
Manoah and his wife looked on.
20For it came about when the flame went up from the altar
toward heaven, that the angel of the LORD ascended in the flame
of the altar. When Manoah and his wife saw *this*, they fell on their
faces to the ground.
21Now the angel of the LORD appeared no more to Manoah or
his wife. Then Manoah knew that he was the angel of the LORD.
22So Manoah said to his wife, "We shall surely die, for we have
seen God."
23But his wife said to him, "If the LORD had desired to kill us,
He would not have accepted a burnt offering and a grain offering
from our hands, nor would He have shown us all these things, nor
would He have let us hear *things* like this at this time."
24¶ Then the woman gave birth to a son and named him Samson; and the child grew up and the LORD blessed him.
25And the Spirit of the LORD began to stir him in
[b]Mahaneh-dan, between Zorah and Eshtaol.

*Samson's Marriage*

**14** THEN SAMSON went down to Timnah and saw a woman
in Timnah, *one* of the daughters of the Philistines.
2So he came back and told his father and mother, "I saw a
woman in Timnah, *one* of the daughters of the Philistines; now
therefore, get her for me as a wife."

NAS [a] I.e., incomprehensible [b] I.e., the camp of Dan

## New International

6Then the woman went to her husband and told him, "A man
of God came to me. He looked like an angel of God, very awesome.
I didn't ask him where he came from, and he didn't tell me his
name. 7But he said to me, 'You will conceive and give birth to a
son. Now then, drink no wine or other fermented drink and do not
eat anything unclean, because the boy will be a Nazirite of God
from birth until the day of his death.' "
8Then Manoah prayed to the LORD: "O Lord, I beg you, let the
man of God you sent to us come again to teach us how to bring
up the boy who is to be born."
9God heard Manoah, and the angel of God came again to the
woman while she was out in the field; but her husband Manoah
was not with her. 10The woman hurried to tell her husband, "He's
here! The man who appeared to me the other day!"
11Manoah got up and followed his wife. When he came to the
man, he said, "Are you the one who talked to my wife?"
"I am," he said.
12So Manoah asked him, "When your words are fulfilled, what
is to be the rule for the boy's life and work?"
13The angel of the LORD answered, "Your wife must do all that
I have told her. 14She must not eat anything that comes from the
grapevine, nor drink any wine or other fermented drink nor eat
anything unclean. She must do everything I have commanded
her."
15Manoah said to the angel of the LORD, "We would like you
to stay until we prepare a young goat for you."
16The angel of the LORD replied, "Even though you detain me,
I will not eat any of your food. But if you prepare a burnt offering,
offer it to the LORD." (Manoah did not realize that it was the angel
of the LORD.)
17Then Manoah inquired of the angel of the LORD, "What is
your name, so that we may honor you when your word comes
true?"
18He replied, "Why do you ask my name? It is beyond understanding.[c] " 19Then Manoah took a young goat, together with the
grain offering, and sacrificed it on a rock to the LORD. And the
LORD did an amazing thing while Manoah and his wife watched:
20As the flame blazed up from the altar toward heaven, the angel
of the LORD ascended in the flame. Seeing this, Manoah and his
wife fell with their faces to the ground. 21When the angel of the
LORD did not show himself again to Manoah and his wife, Manoah
realized that it was the angel of the LORD.
22"We are doomed to die!" he said to his wife. "We have seen
God!"
23But his wife answered, "If the LORD had meant to kill us, he
would not have accepted a burnt offering and grain offering from
our hands, nor shown us all these things or now told us this."
24The woman gave birth to a boy and named him Samson. He
grew and the LORD blessed him, 25and the Spirit of the LORD began
to stir him while he was in Mahaneh Dan, between Zorah and
Eshtaol.

*Samson's Marriage*

**14** SAMSON WENT down to Timnah and saw there a young
Philistine woman. 2When he returned, he said to his father and mother, "I have seen a Philistine woman in Timnah; now
get her for me as my wife."

NIV [c] *18* Or *is wonderful*

## King James

3Then his father and his mother said unto him, *Is there* never
a woman among the daughters of thy brethren, or among all my
people, that thou goest to take a wife of the uncircumcised Philistines? And Samson said unto his father, Get her for me; for she
pleaseth me well.
4But his father and his mother knew not that it *was* of the LORD,
that he sought an occasion against the Philistines: for at that time
the Philistines had dominion over Israel.
5¶ Then went Samson down, and his father and his mother, to
Timnath, and came to the vineyards of Timnath: and, behold, a
young lion roared against him.
6And the spirit of the LORD came mightily upon him, and he
rent him as he would have rent a kid, and *he had* nothing in his
hand: but he told not his father or his mother what he had done.
7And he went down, and talked with the woman; and she
pleased Samson well.
8¶ And after a time he returned to take her, and he turned aside
to see the carcase of the lion: and, behold, *there was* a swarm of bees
and honey in the carcase of the lion.
9And he took thereof in his hands, and went on eating, and
came to his father and mother, and he gave them, and they did
eat: but he told not them that he had taken the honey out of the
carcase of the lion.
10¶ So his father went down unto the woman: and Samson
made there a feast; for so used the young men to do.
11And it came to pass, when they saw him, that they brought
thirty companions to be with him.
12¶ And Samson said unto them, I will now put forth a riddle
unto you: if ye can certainly declare it me within the seven days
of the feast, and find *it* out, then I will give you thirty sheets and
thirty change of garments:
13But if ye cannot declare *it* me, then shall ye give me thirty
sheets and thirty change of garments. And they said unto him, Put
forth thy riddle, that we may hear it.
14And he said unto them, Out of the eater came forth meat, and
out of the strong came forth sweetness. And they could not in
three days expound the riddle.
15And it came to pass on the seventh day, that they said unto
Samson's wife, Entice thy husband, that he may declare unto us
the riddle, lest we burn thee and thy father's house with fire: have
ye called us to take that we have? *is it* not *so?*
16And Samson's wife wept before him, and said, Thou dost but
hate me, and lovest me not: thou hast put forth a riddle unto the
children of my people, and hast not told *it* me. And he said unto
her, Behold, I have not told *it* my father nor my mother, and shall
I tell *it* thee?
17And she wept before him the seven days, while their feast
lasted: and it came to pass on the seventh day, that he told her,
because she lay sore upon him: and she told the riddle to the
children of her people.
18And the men of the city said unto him on the seventh day
before the sun went down, What *is* sweeter than honey? and what
*is* stronger than a lion? And he said unto them, If ye had not
plowed with my heifer, ye had not found out my riddle.
19¶ And the spirit of the LORD came upon him, and he went
down to Ashkelon, and slew thirty men of them, and took their
spoil, and gave change of garments unto them which expounded
the riddle. And his anger was kindled, and he went up to his
father's house.
20But Samson's wife was *given* to his companion, whom he had
used as his friend.

## Amplified

3But his father and mother said to him, Is there not a woman
among the daughters of your kinsmen, or among all our people,
that you must go to take a wife from the uncircumcised Philistines?
And Samson said to his father, Get her for me; for she is all right
in my eyes.
4His father and mother did not know that it was of the Lord,
and that He sought an occasion for assailing the Philistines. At that
time the Philistines had dominion over Israel.
5Then Samson and his father and mother went down to Timnah, and came to the vineyards of Timnah. And behold, a young
lion roared against him;
6And the Spirit of the Lord came mightily upon him, and he tore
the lion as he would have torn a kid, and he had nothing in his
hand; but he did not tell his father or mother what he had done.
7And he went down, and talked with the woman; and she
pleased Samson well.
8And after a while he returned to take her; and he turned aside
to see the body of the lion, and behold, there was a swarm of bees
in the body of the lion, and honey.
9And he scraped some of the honey out into his hands and went
along eating, and he came to his father and mother and gave them
some, and they ate it; but he did not tell them he had taken the
honey from the body of the lion.
10His father went down to the woman; and Samson made a
feast there; for that was the customary thing for young men to do.
11And when the people saw him, they brought thirty companions to be with him.
12And Samson said to them, I will now put forth a riddle to you;
if you can tell me what it is, within the seven days of the feast, and
find it out, then I will give you thirty linen undergarments and
thirty changes of raiment.
13But if you cannot declare it me, then shall you give me thirty
linen undergarments and thirty changes of festive [costly] raiment.
And they said to him, Put forth your riddle, that we may hear it.
14And he said to them, Out of the eater came forth food, and
out of the strong came forth sweetness. And they could not in
three days solve the riddle.
15And on the seventh day they said to Samson's wife, Entice
your husband to declare to us the riddle, lest we burn you and your
father's household with fire. Have you invited us to make us poor?
Is it not true?
16And Samson's wife wept before him, and said, You only hate
me, you do not love me; you have put forth a riddle to my countrymen and have not told the answer to me. And he said to her,
Behold, I have not told my father or my mother, and shall I tell
you?
17And Samson's wife wept before him the seven days their feast
lasted, and on the seventh day he told her, because she pressed
him with entreaties. Then she told the riddle to her countrymen.
18And the men of the city said to [Samson] on the seventh day
before sundown, What is sweeter than honey? What is stronger
than a lion? And he said to them, If you had not plowed with my
heifer, you would not have solved my riddle.
19And the Spirit of the Lord came upon [Samson], and he went
down to Ashkelon, and slew thirty men of them, and took their
apparel [as spoil], and gave the changes of garments to those who
explained the riddle. And his anger was kindled, and he went up
to his father's house.
20But Samson's wife was *given* to his companion, who was his
[best] friend.

## New American Standard

3Then his father and his mother said to him, "Is there no
woman among the daughters of your relatives, or among all our
people, that you go to take a wife from the uncircumcised Philistines?" But Samson said to his father, "Get her for me, for she
looks good to me."
4However, his father and mother did not know that it was of
the LORD, for He was seeking an occasion against the Philistines.
Now at that time the Philistines were ruling over Israel.
5¶ Then Samson went down to Timnah with his father and
mother, and came as far as the vineyards of Timnah; and behold,
a young lion *came* roaring toward him.
6And the Spirit of the LORD came upon him mightily, so that
he tore him as one tears a kid though he had nothing in his hand;
but he did not tell his father or mother what he had done.
7So he went down and talked to the woman; and she looked
good to Samson.
8When he returned later to take her, he turned aside to look
at the carcass of the lion; and behold, a swarm of bees and honey
were in the body of the lion.
9So he scraped the honey into his hands and went on, eating
as he went. When he came to his father and mother, he gave *some*
to them and they ate *it;* but he did not tell them that he had scraped
the honey out of the body of the lion.
10¶ Then his father went down to the woman; and Samson
made a feast there, for the young men customarily did this.
11And it came about when they saw him that they brought
thirty companions to be with him.

*Samson's Riddle*

12Then Samson said to them, "Let me now propound a riddle
to you; if you will indeed tell it to me within the seven days of the
feast, and find it out, then I will give you thirty linen wraps and
thirty changes of clothes.
13"But if you are unable to tell me, then you shall give me thirty
linen wraps and thirty changes of clothes." And they said to him,
"Propound your riddle, that we may hear it."
14So he said to them,
"Out of the eater came something to eat,
And out of the strong came something sweet."
But they could not tell the riddle in three days.
15¶ Then it came about on the fourth day that they said to
Samson's wife, "Entice your husband, that he may tell us the
riddle, lest we burn you and your father's house with fire. Have
you invited us to impoverish us? Is this not *so?*"
16And Samson's wife wept before him and said, "You only hate
me, and you do not love me; you have propounded a riddle to the
sons of my people, and have not told *it* to me." And he said to her,
"Behold, I have not told *it* to my father or mother; so should I tell
you?"
17However she wept before him seven days while their feast
lasted. And it came about on the seventh day that he told her
because she pressed him so hard. She then told the riddle to the
sons of her people.
18So the men of the city said to him on the seventh day before
the sun went down,
"What is sweeter than honey?
And what is stronger than a lion?"
And he said to them,
"If you had not plowed with my heifer,
You would not have found out my riddle."
19Then the Spirit of the LORD came upon him mightily, and he
went down to Ashkelon and killed thirty of them and took their
spoil, and gave the changes *of clothes* to those who told the riddle.
And his anger burned, and he went up to his father's house.
20But Samson's wife was *given* to his companion who had been
his friend.

## New International

3His father and mother replied, "Isn't there an acceptable
woman among your relatives or among all our people? Must you
go to the uncircumcised Philistines to get a wife?"
But Samson said to his father, "Get her for me. She's the right
one for me." 4(His parents did not know that this was from the
LORD, who was seeking an occasion to confront the Philistines; for
at that time they were ruling over Israel.) 5Samson went down to
Timnah together with his father and mother. As they approached
the vineyards of Timnah, suddenly a young lion came roaring
toward him. 6The Spirit of the LORD came upon him in power so
that he tore the lion apart with his bare hands as he might have
torn a young goat. But he told neither his father nor his mother
what he had done. 7Then he went down and talked with the
woman, and he liked her.
8Some time later, when he went back to marry her, he turned
aside to look at the lion's carcass. In it was a swarm of bees and
some honey, 9which he scooped out with his hands and ate as he
went along. When he rejoined his parents, he gave them some,
and they too ate it. But he did not tell them that he had taken the
honey from the lion's carcass.
10Now his father went down to see the woman. And Samson
made a feast there, as was customary for bridegrooms. 11When he
appeared, he was given thirty companions.
12"Let me tell you a riddle," Samson said to them. "If you can
give me the answer within the seven days of the feast, I will give
you thirty linen garments and thirty sets of clothes. 13If you can't
tell me the answer, you must give me thirty linen garments and
thirty sets of clothes."
"Tell us your riddle," they said. "Let's hear it."
14He replied,
"Out of the eater, something to eat;
out of the strong, something sweet."
For three days they could not give the answer.
15On the fourth[a] day, they said to Samson's wife, "Coax your
husband into explaining the riddle for us, or we will burn you and
your father's household to death. Did you invite us here to rob
us?"
16Then Samson's wife threw herself on him, sobbing, "You hate
me! You don't really love me. You've given my people a riddle, but
you haven't told me the answer."
"I haven't even explained it to my father or mother," he replied,
"so why should I explain it to you?" 17She cried the whole seven
days of the feast. So on the seventh day he finally told her, because
she continued to press him. She in turn explained the riddle to her
people.
18Before sunset on the seventh day the men of the town said
to him,
"What is sweeter than honey?
What is stronger than a lion?"
Samson said to them,
"If you had not plowed with my heifer,
you would not have solved my riddle."
19Then the Spirit of the LORD came upon him in power. He went
down to Ashkelon, struck down thirty of their men, stripped them
of their belongings and gave their clothes to those who had explained the riddle. Burning with anger, he went up to his father's
house. 20And Samson's wife was given to the friend who had
attended him at his wedding.

NIV [a] *15* Some Septuagint manuscripts and Syriac; Hebrew *seventh*

## King James

**15** BUT IT came to pass within a while after, in the time of wheat harvest, that Samson visited his wife with a kid; and he said, I will go in to my wife into the chamber. But her father would not suffer him to go in.

2 And her father said, I verily thought that thou hadst utterly hated her; therefore I gave her to thy companion: *is* not her younger sister fairer than she? take her, I pray thee, instead of her.

3 ¶ And Samson said concerning them, Now shall I be more blameless than the Philistines, though I do them a displeasure.

4 And Samson went and caught three hundred foxes, and took firebrands, and turned tail to tail, and put a firebrand in the midst between two tails.

5 And when he had set the brands on fire, he let *them* go into the standing corn of the Philistines, and burnt up both the shocks, and also the standing corn, with the vineyards *and* olives.

6 ¶ Then the Philistines said, Who hath done this? And they answered, Samson, the son-in-law of the Timnite, because he had taken his wife, and given her to his companion. And the Philistines came up, and burnt her and her father with fire.

7 ¶ And Samson said unto them, Though ye have done this, yet will I be avenged of you, and after that I will cease.

8 And he smote them hip and thigh with a great slaughter: and he went down and dwelt in the top of the rock Etam.

9 ¶ Then the Philistines went up, and pitched in Judah, and spread themselves in Lehi.

10 And the men of Judah said, Why are ye come up against us? And they answered, To bind Samson are we come up, to do to him as he hath done to us.

11 Then three thousand men of Judah went to the top of the rock Etam, and said to Samson, Knowest thou not that the Philistines *are* rulers over us? what *is* this *that* thou hast done unto us? And he said unto them, As they did unto me, so have I done unto them.

12 And they said unto him, We are come down to bind thee, that we may deliver thee into the hand of the Philistines. And Samson said unto them, Swear unto me, that ye will not fall upon me yourselves.

13 And they spake unto him, saying, No; but we will bind thee fast, and deliver thee into their hand: but surely we will not kill thee. And they bound him with two new cords, and brought him up from the rock.

14 ¶ *And* when he came unto Lehi, the Philistines shouted against him: and the spirit of the LORD came mightily upon him, and the cords that *were* upon his arms became as flax that was burnt with fire, and his bands loosed from off his hands.

15 And he found a new jawbone of an ass, and put forth his hand, and took it, and slew a thousand men therewith.

16 And Samson said, With the jawbone of an ass, heaps upon heaps, with the jaw of an ass have I slain a thousand men.

17 And it came to pass, when he had made an end of speaking, that he cast away the jawbone out of his hand, and called that place Ramath-lehi.

18 ¶ And he was sore athirst, and called on the LORD, and said, Thou hast given this great deliverance into the hand of thy servant: and now shall I die for thirst, and fall into the hand of the uncircumcised?

19 But God clave an hollow place that *was* in the jaw, and there came water thereout; and when he had drunk, his spirit came again, and he revived: wherefore he called the name thereof En-hakkore, which *is* in Lehi unto this day.

20 And he judged Israel in the days of the Philistines twenty years.

## Amplified

**15** BUT SOME days later, in the time of wheat harvest, Samson went to visit his wife, taking along a kid [as a token of reconciliation]; and he said, I will go unto my wife in the inner chamber. But her father would not allow him to go in.

2 And her father said, I truly thought you utterly hated her, so I gave her to your companion. Is her younger sister not fairer than she? Take her, I pray you, instead of her.

3 And Samson said of them, This time shall I be blameless as regards the Philistines, though I do them evil.

4 So Samson went and caught 300 foxes *or* jackals, and took torches, and turning the foxes tail to tail, he put a torch between each two tails.

5 And when he had set the torches ablaze, he let the foxes go into the standing grain of the Philistines, and burned up the shocks and the standing grain, and also the olive orchards.

6 Then the Philistines said, Who has done this? And they were told, Samson, the son-in-law of the Timnite, because he has taken his wife, and given her to his companion. And the Philistines came up, and burned her and her father with fire.

7 And Samson said to them, If this is the way you do, surely I will take revenge on you, and after that I will quit.

8 And he smote them hip and thigh, a great slaughter; and he went down and dwelt in the cleft of the rock of Etam.

9 Then the Philistines came up and encamped in Judah, and spread themselves in Lehi.

10 And the men of Judah said, Why have you come up against us? And they answered, We have come up to bind Samson, to do to him as he has done to us.

11 Then 3,000 men of Judah went down to the cleft of the rock Etam, and said to Samson, Have you not known that the Philistines are rulers over us? What is this that you have done to us? He said to them, As they did to me, so have I done to them.

12 And they said to him, We have come down to bind you, that we may deliver you into the hand of the Philistines. And Samson said to them, Swear to me, that you will not fall upon me yourselves.

13 And they said to him, No; we will bind you fast and give you into their hand; but surely we will not kill you. So they bound him with two new ropes, and brought him up from the rock.

14 And when he came to Lehi, the Philistines came shouting to meet him; and the Spirit of the Lord came mightily upon [Samson], and the ropes on his arms became as flax that had caught fire, and his bonds melted off his hands.

15 And he found a still moist jawbone of a donkey, and reached out and took it, and slew 1,000 men with it.

16 And Samson said, With the jawbone of a donkey, heaps upon heaps, with the jawbone of a donkey I have slain 1,000 men!

17 And when he stopped speaking, he cast the jawbone from his hand; and that place was called Ramath-lehi [the hill of the jawbone].

18 Samson was very thirsty, and prayed to the Lord and said, You have given this great deliverance by the hand of Your servant; and now shall I die of thirst, and fall into the hand of the uncircumcised?

19 And God split open the hollow place that was at Lehi, and water came out of it. And when [Samson] drank, his spirit returned, and he revived. Therefore the name of it was called En-hakkore [the spring of him who prayed], which is at Lehi to this day.

20 And [Samson] judged [defended] Israel in the days of the Philistines twenty years. [17:6.]

## New American Standard

*Samson Burns Philistine Crops*

**15** BUT AFTER a while, in the time of wheat harvest, it came
about that Samson visited his wife with a young goat, and
said, "I will go in to my wife in *her* room." But her father did not
let him enter.
2And her father said, "I really thought that you hated her
intensely; so I gave her to your companion. Is not her younger
sister more beautiful than she? Please let her be yours instead."
3Samson then said to them, "This time I shall be blameless in
regard to the Philistines when I do them harm."
4And Samson went and caught three hundred foxes, and took
torches, and turned *the foxes* tail to tail, and put one torch in the
middle between two tails.
5When he had set fire to the torches, he released the foxes into
the standing grain of the Philistines, thus burning up both the
shocks and the standing grain, along with the vineyards *and*
groves.
6Then the Philistines said, "Who did this?" And they said,
"Samson, the son-in-law of the Timnite, because he took his wife
and gave her to his companion." So the Philistines came up and
burned her and her father with fire.
7And Samson said to them, "Since you act like this, I will
surely take revenge on you, but after that I will quit."
8And he struck them ruthlessly with a great slaughter; and he
went down and lived in the cleft of the rock of Etam.
9¶ Then the Philistines went up and camped in Judah, and
spread out in Lehi.
10And the men of Judah said, "Why have you come up against
us?" And they said, "We have come up to bind Samson in order
to do to him as he did to us."
11Then 3,000 men of Judah went down to the cleft of the rock
of Etam and said to Samson, "Do you not know that the Philistines
are rulers over us? What then is this that you have done to us?"
And he said to them, "As they did to me, so I have done to them."
12And they said to him, "We have come down to bind you so
that we may give you into the hands of the Philistines." And
Samson said to them, "Swear to me that you will not kill me."
13So they said to him, "No, but we will bind you fast and give
you into their hands; yet surely we will not kill you." Then they
bound him with two new ropes and brought him up from the rock.
14¶ When he came to Lehi, the Philistines shouted as they met
him. And the Spirit of the LORD came upon him mightily so that
the ropes that were on his arms were as flax that is burned with
fire, and his bonds dropped from his hands.
15And he found a fresh jawbone of a donkey, so he reached out
and took it and killed a thousand men with it.
16Then Samson said,
"With the jawbone of a donkey,
Heaps upon heaps,
With the jawbone of a donkey
I have killed a thousand men."
17And it came about when he had finished speaking, that he
threw the jawbone from his hand; and he named that place
[a]Ramath-lehi.
18Then he became very thirsty, and he called to the LORD and
said, "Thou hast given this great deliverance by the hand of Thy
servant, and now shall I die of thirst and fall into the hands of the
uncircumcised?"
19But God split the hollow place that is in Lehi so that water
came out of it. When he drank, his strength returned and he
revived. Therefore, he named it En-hakkore, which is in Lehi to
this day.
20So he judged Israel twenty years in the days of the Philistines.

NAS [a] I.e., the high place of the jawbone

## New International

*Samson's Vengeance on the Philistines*

**15** LATER ON, at the time of wheat harvest, Samson took a
young goat and went to visit his wife. He said, "I'm going
to my wife's room." But her father would not let him go in.
2"I was so sure you thoroughly hated her," he said, "that I gave
her to your friend. Isn't her younger sister more attractive? Take
her instead."
3Samson said to them, "This time I have a right to get even with
the Philistines; I will really harm them." 4So he went out and
caught three hundred foxes and tied them tail to tail in pairs. He
then fastened a torch to every pair of tails, 5lit the torches and let
the foxes loose in the standing grain of the Philistines. He burned
up the shocks and standing grain, together with the vineyards and
olive groves.
6When the Philistines asked, "Who did this?" they were told,
"Samson, the Timnite's son-in-law, because his wife was given to
his friend."
So the Philistines went up and burned her and her father to
death. 7Samson said to them, "Since you've acted like this, I won't
stop until I get my revenge on you." 8He attacked them viciously
and slaughtered many of them. Then he went down and stayed
in a cave in the rock of Etam.
9The Philistines went up and camped in Judah, spreading out
near Lehi. 10The men of Judah asked, "Why have you come to fight
us?"
"We have come to take Samson prisoner," they answered, "to
do to him as he did to us."
11Then three thousand men from Judah went down to the cave
in the rock of Etam and said to Samson, "Don't you realize that
the Philistines are rulers over us? What have you done to us?"
He answered, "I merely did to them what they did to me."
12They said to him, "We've come to tie you up and hand you
over to the Philistines."
Samson said, "Swear to me that you won't kill me yourselves."
13"Agreed," they answered. "We will only tie you up and hand
you over to them. We will not kill you." So they bound him with
two new ropes and led him up from the rock. 14As he approached
Lehi, the Philistines came toward him shouting. The Spirit of the
LORD came upon him in power. The ropes on his arms became like
charred flax, and the bindings dropped from his hands. 15Finding
a fresh jawbone of a donkey, he grabbed it and struck down a
thousand men.
16Then Samson said,
"With a donkey's jawbone
I have made donkeys of them.[b]
With a donkey's jawbone
I have killed a thousand men."
17When he finished speaking, he threw away the jawbone; and the
place was called Ramath Lehi.[c]
18Because he was very thirsty, he cried out to the LORD, "You
have given your servant this great victory. Must I now die of thirst
and fall into the hands of the uncircumcised?" 19Then God opened
up the hollow place in Lehi, and water came out of it. When
Samson drank, his strength returned and he revived. So the spring
was called En Hakkore,[d] and it is still there in Lehi.
20Samson led[e] Israel for twenty years in the days of the Philistines.

**NIV** [b] *16* Or *made a heap or two;* the Hebrew for *donkey* sounds like the Hebrew for *heap.* [c] *17 Ramath Lehi* means *jawbone hill.* [d] *19 En Hakkore* means *caller's spring.* [e] *20* Traditionally *judged*

## King James

16 THEN WENT Samson to Gaza, and saw there an harlot, and went in unto her.

2 *And it was told* the Gazites, saying, Samson is come hither. And they compassed *him* in, and laid wait for him all night in the gate of the city, and were quiet all the night, saying, In the morning, when it is day, we shall kill him.

3 And Samson lay till midnight, and arose at midnight, and took the doors of the gate of the city, and the two posts, and went away with them, bar and all, and put *them* upon his shoulders, and carried them up to the top of an hill that *is* before Hebron.

4 ¶ And it came to pass afterward, that he loved a woman in the valley of Sorek, whose name *was* Delilah.

5 And the lords of the Philistines came up unto her, and said unto her, Entice him, and see wherein his great strength *lieth*, and by what *means* we may prevail against him, that we may bind him to afflict him: and we will give thee every one of us eleven hundred *pieces* of silver.

6 ¶ And Delilah said to Samson, Tell me, I pray thee, wherein thy great strength *lieth*, and wherewith thou mightest be bound to afflict thee.

7 And Samson said unto her, If they bind me with seven green withs that were never dried, then shall I be weak, and be as another man.

8 Then the lords of the Philistines brought up to her seven green withs which had not been dried, and she bound him with them.

9 Now *there were* men lying in wait, abiding with her in the chamber. And she said unto him, The Philistines *be* upon thee, Samson. And he brake the withs, as a thread of tow is broken when it toucheth the fire. So his strength was not known.

10 And Delilah said unto Samson, Behold, thou hast mocked me, and told me lies: now tell me, I pray thee, wherewith thou mightest be bound.

11 And he said unto her, If they bind me fast with new ropes that never were occupied, then shall I be weak, and be as another man.

12 Delilah therefore took new ropes, and bound him therewith, and said unto him, The Philistines *be* upon thee, Samson. And *there were* liers in wait abiding in the chamber. And he brake them from off his arms like a thread.

13 And Delilah said unto Samson, Hitherto thou hast mocked me, and told me lies: tell me wherewith thou mightest be bound. And he said unto her, If thou weavest the seven locks of my head with the web.

14 And she fastened *it* with the pin, and said unto him, The Philistines *be* upon thee, Samson. And he awaked out of his sleep, and went away with the pin of the beam, and with the web.

15 ¶ And she said unto him, How canst thou say, I love thee, when thine heart *is* not with me? thou hast mocked me these three times, and hast not told me wherein thy great strength *lieth*.

16 And it came to pass, when she pressed him daily with her words, and urged him, *so* that his soul was vexed unto death;

17 That he told her all his heart, and said unto her, There hath not come a razor upon mine head; for I *have been* a Nazarite unto God from my mother's womb: if I be shaven, then my strength will go from me, and I shall become weak, and be like any *other* man.

18 And when Delilah saw that he had told her all his heart, she sent and called for the lords of the Philistines, saying, Come up this once, for he hath shown me all his heart. Then the lords of the Philistines came up unto her, and brought money in their hand.

19 And she made him sleep upon her knees; and she called for a man, and she caused him to shave off the seven locks of his head; and she began to afflict him, and his strength went from him.

## Amplified

16 THEN SAMSON went to Gaza, and saw there a harlot, and went in to her.

2 The Gazites were told, Samson has come here. And they surrounded the place and lay in wait for him all night at the gate of the city. They were quiet all night, saying, In the morning, when it is light, we will kill him.

3 But Samson lay till midnight, and [then] he arose and took hold of the doors of the city's gate and the two posts, and pulling them up, bar and all, he put them on his shoulders and carried them to the top of the hill that is before Hebron.

4 After this he loved a woman in the valley of Sorek, whose name was Delilah.

5 And the lords of the Philistines came to her and said to her, Entice him, and see in what his great strength lies, and by what means we may overpower him, that we may bind him to subdue him, and we will each give you 1,100 pieces of silver.

6 And Delilah said to Samson, Tell me, I pray, wherein your great strength lies, and with what you might be bound to subdue you.

7 And Samson said to her, If they bind me with seven fresh strong gutstrings, still moist, then shall I be weak, and be as another man.

8 Then the Philistine lords brought to her seven fresh, strong bowstrings, still moist, and she bound him with them.

9 Now she had men lying in wait in an inner room. And she said to him, The Philistines are upon you, Samson! And he broke the bowstrings as a string of tow breaks when it touches the fire. So the secret of his strength was not known.

10 And Delilah said to Samson, Behold, you have mocked me, and told me lies; now tell me, I pray you, how you might be bound.

11 And he said to her, If they bind me fast with new ropes that have not been used, then I shall become weak, and be like any other man.

12 So Delilah took new ropes, and bound him with them, and said to him, The Philistines are upon you, Samson! And the men lying in wait were in the inner room. But he snapped the ropes off his arms like [sewing] thread.

13 And Delilah said to Samson, Until now you have mocked me, and told me lies; tell me with what you might be bound. And he said to her, If you weave the seven braids of [the hair of] my head with the web.

14 And she did so and fastened it with the pin, and said to him, The Philistines are upon you, Samson! And he awoke out of his sleep, and went away with the pin of the [weaver's] beam, and with the web.

15 And she said to him, How can you say, I love you, when your heart is not with me? You have mocked me these three times, and have not told me in what your great strength lies.

16 And when she pressed him day after day with her words, and urged him, he was vexed to death.

17 Then he told her all his mind, and said to her, A razor has never come upon my head, for I have been a Nazirite to God from my birth. If I am shaved, then my strength will go from me, and I shall become weak, and be like any other man.

18 And when Delilah saw that he had told her all his mind, she went and called for the Philistine lords, saying, Come up this once, for he has told me all he knows. Then the Philistine lords came up to her, and brought the money in their hand.

19 And she made Samson sleep upon her knees; and she called a man, and caused him to shave off the seven braids of his head. Then she began to torment [Samson], and his strength went from him.

## New American Standard

*Samson's Weakness*

**16** NOW SAMSON went to Gaza and saw a harlot there, and
went in to her.
2 *When it was told* to the Gazites, saying, "Samson has come
here," they surrounded *the place* and lay in wait for him all night
at the gate of the city. And they kept silent all night, saying, "*Let
us wait* until the morning light, then we will kill him."
3Now Samson lay until midnight, and at midnight he arose
and took hold of the doors of the city gate and the two posts and
pulled them up along with the bars; then he put them on his
shoulders and carried them up to the top of the mountain which
is opposite Hebron.
4¶ After this it came about that he loved a woman in the valley
of Sorek, whose name was Delilah.
5And the lords of the Philistines came up to her, and said to
her, "Entice him, and see where his great strength *lies* and how we
may overpower him that we may bind him to afflict him. Then we
will each give you eleven hundred *pieces* of silver."
6So Delilah said to Samson, "Please tell me where your great
strength is and how you may be bound to afflict you."
7And Samson said to her, "If they bind me with seven fresh
cords that have not been dried, then I shall become weak and be
like any *other* man."
8Then the lords of the Philistines brought up to her seven fresh
cords that had not been dried, and she bound him with them.
9Now she had *men* lying in wait in an inner room. And she said
to him, "The Philistines are upon you, Samson!" But he snapped
the cords as a string of tow snaps when it touches fire. So his
strength was not discovered.
10¶ Then Delilah said to Samson, "Behold, you have deceived
me and told me lies; now please tell me, how you may be bound."
11And he said to her, "If they bind me tightly with new ropes
which have not been used, then I shall become weak and be like
any *other* man."
12So Delilah took new ropes and bound him with them and said
to him, "The Philistines are upon you, Samson!" For the *men* were
lying in wait in the inner room. But he snapped the ropes from his
arms like a thread.
13¶ Then Delilah said to Samson, "Up to now you have deceived
me and told me lies; tell me how you may be bound." And he said
to her, "If you weave the seven locks of my hair with the web
[a][and fasten it with a pin, then I shall become weak and be like
any other man."
14So while he slept, Delilah took the seven locks of his hair and
wove them into the web]. And she fastened *it* with the pin, and
said to him, "The Philistines are upon you, Samson!" But he
awoke from his sleep and pulled out the pin of the loom and the
web.

*Delilah Extracts His Secret*

15¶ Then she said to him, "How can you say, 'I love you,' when
your heart is not with me? You have deceived me these three times
and have not told me where your great strength is."
16And it came about when she pressed him daily with her
words and urged him, that his soul was annoyed to death.
17So he told her all *that was* in his heart and said to her, "A razor
has never come on my head, for I have been a Nazirite to God from
my mother's womb. If I am shaved, then my strength will leave
me and I shall become weak and be like any *other* man."
18¶ When Delilah saw that he had told her all *that was* in his
heart, she sent and called the lords of the Philistines, saying,
"Come up once more, for he has told me all *that is* in his heart."
Then the lords of the Philistines came up to her, and brought the
money in their hands.
19And she made him sleep on her knees, and called for a man
and had him shave off the seven locks of his hair. Then she began
to afflict him, and his strength left him.

**NAS** [a] The passage in brackets is found in Gr. but not in any Heb. mss.

## New International

*Samson and Delilah*

**16** ONE DAY Samson went to Gaza, where he saw a prostitute. He went in to spend the night with her. 2The people
of Gaza were told, "Samson is here!" So they surrounded the place
and lay in wait for him all night at the city gate. They made no
move during the night, saying, "At dawn we'll kill him."
3But Samson lay there only until the middle of the night. Then
he got up and took hold of the doors of the city gate, together with
the two posts, and tore them loose, bar and all. He lifted them to
his shoulders and carried them to the top of the hill that faces
Hebron.
4Some time later, he fell in love with a woman in the Valley of
Sorek whose name was Delilah. 5The rulers of the Philistines went
to her and said, "See if you can lure him into showing you the
secret of his great strength and how we can overpower him so we
may tie him up and subdue him. Each one of us will give you
eleven hundred shekels[b] of silver."
6So Delilah said to Samson, "Tell me the secret of your great
strength and how you can be tied up and subdued."
7Samson answered her, "If anyone ties me with seven fresh
thongs[c] that have not been dried, I'll become as weak as any other
man."
8Then the rulers of the Philistines brought her seven fresh
thongs that had not been dried, and she tied him with them. 9With
men hidden in the room, she called to him, "Samson, the Philistines are upon you!" But he snapped the thongs as easily as a piece
of string snaps when it comes close to a flame. So the secret of his
strength was not discovered.
10Then Delilah said to Samson, "You have made a fool of me;
you lied to me. Come now, tell me how you can be tied."
11He said, "If anyone ties me securely with new ropes that have
never been used, I'll become as weak as any other man."
12So Delilah took new ropes and tied him with them. Then,
with men hidden in the room, she called to him, "Samson, the
Philistines are upon you!" But he snapped the ropes off his arms
as if they were threads.
13Delilah then said to Samson, "Until now, you have been
making a fool of me and lying to me. Tell me how you can be tied."
He replied, "If you weave the seven braids of my head into the
fabric ⌞on the loom⌟ and tighten it with the pin, I'll become as weak
as any other man." So while he was sleeping, Delilah took the
seven braids of his head, wove them into the fabric 14and[d] tightened it with the pin.
Again she called to him, "Samson, the Philistines are upon
you!" He awoke from his sleep and pulled up the pin and the
loom, with the fabric.
15Then she said to him, "How can you say, 'I love you,' when
you won't confide in me? This is the third time you have made a
fool of me and haven't told me the secret of your great strength."
16With such nagging she prodded him day after day until he was
tired to death.
17So he told her everything. "No razor has ever been used on
my head," he said, "because I have been a Nazirite set apart to God
since birth. If my head were shaved, my strength would leave me,
and I would become as weak as any other man."
18When Delilah saw that he had told her everything, she sent
word to the rulers of the Philistines, "Come back once more; he
has told me everything." So the rulers of the Philistines returned
with the silver in their hands. 19Having put him to sleep on her
lap, she called a man to shave off the seven braids of his hair, and
so began to subdue him.[e] And his strength left him.

**NIV** [b] *5* That is, about 28 pounds (about 13 kilograms) [c] *7* Or *bowstrings;* also in verses 8 and 9 [d] *13,14* Some Septuagint manuscripts; Hebrew *"I can⌟ if you weave the seven braids of my head into the fabric ⌞on the loom⌟." 14So she* [e] *19* Hebrew; some Septuagint manuscripts *and he began to weaken*

## King James

20 And she said, The Philistines *be* upon thee, Samson. And he awoke out of his sleep, and said, I will go out as at other times before, and shake myself. And he wist not that the LORD was departed from him.

21 ¶ But the Philistines took him, and put out his eyes, and brought him down to Gaza, and bound him with fetters of brass; and he did grind in the prison house.

22 Howbeit the hair of his head began to grow again after he was shaven.

23 Then the lords of the Philistines gathered them together for to offer a great sacrifice unto Dagon their god, and to rejoice: for they said, Our god hath delivered Samson our enemy into our hand.

24 And when the people saw him, they praised their god: for they said, Our god hath delivered into our hands our enemy, and the destroyer of our country, which slew many of us.

25 And it came to pass, when their hearts were merry, that they said, Call for Samson, that he may make us sport. And they called for Samson out of the prison house; and he made them sport: and they set him between the pillars.

26 And Samson said unto the lad that held him by the hand, Suffer me that I may feel the pillars whereupon the house standeth, that I may lean upon them.

27 Now the house was full of men and women; and all the lords of the Philistines *were* there; and *there were* upon the roof about three thousand men and women, that beheld while Samson made sport.

28 And Samson called unto the LORD, and said, O Lord GOD, remember me, I pray thee, and strengthen me, I pray thee, only this once, O God, that I may be at once avenged of the Philistines for my two eyes.

29 And Samson took hold of the two middle pillars upon which the house stood, and on which it was borne up, of the one with his right hand, and of the other with his left.

30 And Samson said, Let me die with the Philistines. And he bowed himself with *all his* might; and the house fell upon the lords, and upon all the people that *were* therein. So the dead which he slew at his death were more than *they* which he slew in his life.

31 Then his brethren and all the house of his father came down, and took him, and brought *him* up, and buried him between Zorah and Eshtaol in the buryingplace of Manoah his father. And he judged Israel twenty years.

**17** AND THERE was a man of mount Ephraim, whose name *was* Micah.

2 And he said unto his mother, The eleven hundred *shekels* of silver that were taken from thee, about which thou cursedst, and spakest of also in mine ears, behold, the silver *is* with me; I took it. And his mother said, Blessed *be thou* of the LORD, my son.

3 And when he had restored the eleven hundred *shekels* of silver to his mother, his mother said, I had wholly dedicated the silver unto the LORD from my hand for my son, to make a graven image and a molten image: now therefore I will restore it unto thee.

4 Yet he restored the money unto his mother; and his mother took two hundred *shekels* of silver, and gave them to the founder, who made thereof a graven image and a molten image: and they were in the house of Micah.

5 And the man Micah had an house of gods, and made an ephod, and teraphim, and consecrated one of his sons, who became his priest.

6 In those days *there was* no king in Israel, *but* every man did *that which was* right in his own eyes.

## Amplified

20 She said, The Philistines are upon you, Samson! And he awoke out of his sleep, and said, I will go out as I have time after time, and shake myself free. For Samson did not know that the Lord had departed from him.

21 But the Philistines laid hold of him, and bored out his eyes, and brought him down to Gaza, and bound him with [two] bronze fetters; and he ground at the mill in the prison.

22 But the hair of his head began to grow again after it had been shaved.

23 Then the Philistine lords gathered together to offer a great sacrifice to Dagon their god, and to rejoice; for they said, Our god has given Samson our enemy into our hand.

24 And when the people saw Samson, they praised their god; for they said, Our god has delivered into our hand our enemy, the ravager of our country, who has slain many of us.

25 And when their hearts were merry, they said, Call for Samson, that he may make sport for us. So they called [blind] Samson out of the prison, and he made sport before them; they made him stand between the pillars.

26 And Samson said to the lad who held him by the hand, Allow me to feel the pillars upon which the house rests that I may lean against them.

27 Now the house was full of men and women; all the Philistine princes were there, and on the roof were about 3,000 men and women, who looked on while Samson made sport.

28 Then Samson called to the Lord and said, O Lord God [earnestly] remember me, I pray You, and strengthen me, I pray You, only this once, O God, and let me have one vengeance upon the Philistines for both my eyes.

29 And Samson laid hold of the two middle pillars by which the house was borne up, of one with his right hand, and of the other with his left.

30 And Samson cried, Let me die with the Philistines! And he bowed himself mightily; and the house fell upon the princes, and upon all the people that were in it. So the dead whom he slew at his death were more than they whom he slew in his life.

31 Then his kinsmen and all the tribal family of his father came down, and took his body, and brought it up, and they buried him between Zorah and Eshtaol in the burial place of Manoah his father. He had judged Israel [that is, had defended the Israelites] for twenty years. [17:6; Heb. 11:32.]

**17** THERE WAS a man of the hill country of Ephraim, whose name was Micah.

2 And he said to his mother, The 1,100 shekels of silver that were taken from you, about which you cursed, and also spoke in my hearing, behold, I have the silver with me; I took it. And his mother said, Blessed be you by the Lord, my son!

3 He restored the 1,100 shekels of silver to his mother, and she said, I had truly dedicated the silver to the Lord from my hand for my son, to make a graven image and a molten image; now therefore I will restore it to you.

4 So when he restored the money to his mother, she took 200 pieces of silver, and gave them to the silversmith, who made of it a graven image and a molten image; and they were in the house of Micah.

5 And the man Micah had a house of gods, and he made an ephod, and teraphim, and dedicated one of his sons, who became his priest.

6 In those days there was no king in Israel; every man did what was right in his own eyes.

## New American Standard

20And she said, "The Philistines are upon you, Samson!" And
he awoke from his sleep and said, "I will go out as at other times
and shake myself free." But he did not know that the LORD had
departed from him.
21Then the Philistines seized him and gouged out his eyes; and
they brought him down to Gaza and bound him with bronze
chains, and he was a grinder in the prison.
22However, the hair of his head began to grow again after it was
shaved off.
23¶ Now the lords of the Philistines assembled to offer a great
sacrifice to Dagon their god, and to rejoice, for they said,
"Our god has given Samson our enemy into our hands."
24When the people saw him, they praised their god, for they
said,

"Our god has given our enemy into our hands,
Even the destroyer of our country,
Who has slain many of us."

25It so happened when they were in high spirits, that they said,
"Call for Samson, that he may amuse us." So they called for
Samson from the prison, and he entertained them. And they made
him stand between the pillars.
26Then Samson said to the boy who was holding his hand, "Let
me feel the pillars on which the house rests, that I may lean against
them."
27Now the house was full of men and women, and all the lords
of the Philistines were there. And about 3,000 men and women
were on the roof looking on while Samson was amusing *them*.

*Samson Is Avenged*

28¶ Then Samson called to the LORD and said, "O Lord GOD,
please remember me and please strengthen me just this time, O
God, that I may at once be avenged of the Philistines for my two
eyes."
29And Samson grasped the two middle pillars on which the
house rested, and braced himself against them, the one with his
right hand and the other with his left.
30And Samson said, "Let me die with the Philistines!" And he
bent with all his might so that the house fell on the lords and all
the people who were in it. So the dead whom he killed at his death
were more than those whom he killed in his life.
31Then his brothers and all his father's household came down,
took him, brought him up, and buried him between Zorah and
Eshtaol in the tomb of Manoah his father. Thus he had judged
Israel twenty years.

*Micah's Idolatry*

**17** NOW THERE was a man of the hill country of Ephraim
whose name was Micah.
2And he said to his mother, "The eleven hundred *pieces* of
silver which were taken from you, about which you uttered a curse
in my hearing, behold, the silver is with me; I took it." And his
mother said, "Blessed be my son by the LORD."
3He then returned the eleven hundred *pieces* of silver to his
mother, and his mother said, "I wholly dedicate the silver from my
hand to the LORD for my son to make a graven image and a molten
image; now therefore, I will return them to you."
4So when he returned the silver to his mother, his mother took
two hundred *pieces* of silver and gave them to the silversmith who
made them into a graven image and a molten image, and they were
in the house of Micah.
5And the man Micah had a [a]shrine and he made an ephod and
household idols and consecrated one of his sons, that he might
become his priest.
6In those days there was no king in Israel; every man did what
was right in his own eyes.

NAS [a] Lit., *house of gods*

## New International

20Then she called, "Samson, the Philistines are upon you!"
He awoke from his sleep and thought, "I'll go out as before and
shake myself free." But he did not know that the LORD had left
him.
21Then the Philistines seized him, gouged out his eyes and took
him down to Gaza. Binding him with bronze shackles, they set him
to grinding in the prison. 22But the hair on his head began to grow
again after it had been shaved.

*The Death of Samson*

23Now the rulers of the Philistines assembled to offer a great
sacrifice to Dagon their god and to celebrate, saying, "Our god has
delivered Samson, our enemy, into our hands."
24When the people saw him, they praised their god, saying,

"Our god has delivered our enemy
into our hands,
the one who laid waste our land
and multiplied our slain."

25While they were in high spirits, they shouted, "Bring out
Samson to entertain us." So they called Samson out of the prison,
and he performed for them.
When they stood him among the pillars, 26Samson said to the
servant who held his hand, "Put me where I can feel the pillars
that support the temple, so that I may lean against them." 27Now
the temple was crowded with men and women; all the rulers of the
Philistines were there, and on the roof were about three thousand
men and women watching Samson perform. 28Then Samson
prayed to the LORD, "O Sovereign LORD, remember me. O God,
please strengthen me just once more, and let me with one blow get
revenge on the Philistines for my two eyes." 29Then Samson
reached toward the two central pillars on which the temple stood.
Bracing himself against them, his right hand on the one and his
left hand on the other, 30Samson said, "Let me die with the Philistines!" Then he pushed with all his might, and down came the
temple on the rulers and all the people in it. Thus he killed many
more when he died than while he lived.
31Then his brothers and his father's whole family went down
to get him. They brought him back and buried him between Zorah
and Eshtaol in the tomb of Manoah his father. He had led[b] Israel
twenty years.

*Micah's Idols*

**17** NOW A man named Micah from the hill country of
Ephraim 2said to his mother, "The eleven hundred
shekels[c] of silver that were taken from you and about which I
heard you utter a curse—I have that silver with me; I took it."
Then his mother said, "The LORD bless you, my son!"
3When he returned the eleven hundred shekels of silver to his
mother, she said, "I solemnly consecrate my silver to the LORD for
my son to make a carved image and a cast idol. I will give it back
to you."
4So he returned the silver to his mother, and she took two
hundred shekels[d] of silver and gave them to a silversmith, who
made them into the image and the idol. And they were put in
Micah's house.
5Now this man Micah had a shrine, and he made an ephod and
some idols and installed one of his sons as his priest. 6In those days
Israel had no king; everyone did as he saw fit.

NIV [b] *31* Traditionally *judged* [c] *2* That is, about 28 pounds (about 13 kilograms) [d] *4* That is, about 5 pounds (about 2.3 kilograms)

## King James

7¶ And there was a young man out of Bethlehem-judah of the family of Judah, who *was* a Levite, and he sojourned there.

8And the man departed out of the city from Bethlehem-judah to sojourn where he could find *a place:* and he came to mount Ephraim to the house of Micah, as he journeyed.

9And Micah said unto him, Whence comest thou? And he said unto him, I *am* a Levite of Bethlehem-judah, and I go to sojourn where I may find *a place.*

10And Micah said unto him, Dwell with me, and be unto me a father and a priest, and I will give thee ten *shekels* of silver by the year, and a suit of apparel, and thy victuals. So the Levite went in.

11And the Levite was content to dwell with the man; and the young man was unto him as one of his sons.

12And Micah consecrated the Levite; and the young man became his priest, and was in the house of Micah.

13Then said Micah, Now know I that the LORD will do me good, seeing I have a Levite to *my* priest.

18 IN THOSE days *there was* no king in Israel: and in those days the tribe of the Danites sought them an inheritance to dwell in; for unto that day *all their* inheritance had not fallen unto them among the tribes of Israel.

2And the children of Dan sent of their family five men from their coasts, men of valour, from Zorah, and from Eshtaol, to spy out the land, and to search it; and they said unto them, Go, search the land: who when they came to mount Ephraim, to the house of Micah, they lodged there.

3When they *were* by the house of Micah, they knew the voice of the young man the Levite: and they turned in thither, and said unto him, Who brought thee hither? and what makest thou in this *place?* and what hast thou here?

4And he said unto them, Thus and thus dealeth Micah with me, and hath hired me, and I am his priest.

5And they said unto him, Ask counsel, we pray thee, of God, that we may know whether our way which we go shall be prosperous.

6And the priest said unto them, Go in peace: before the LORD *is* your way wherein ye go.

7¶ Then the five men departed, and came to Laish, and saw the people that *were* therein, how they dwelt careless, after the manner of the Zidonians, quiet and secure; and *there was* no magistrate in the land, that might put *them* to shame in *any* thing; and they *were* far from the Zidonians, and had no business with *any* man.

8And they came unto their brethren to Zorah and Eshtaol: and their brethren said unto them, What *say* ye?

9And they said, Arise, that we may go up against them: for we have seen the land, and, behold, it *is* very good: and *are* ye still? be not slothful to go, *and* to enter to possess the land.

10When ye go, ye shall come unto a people secure, and to a large land: for God hath given it into your hands; a place where *there is* no want of any thing that *is* in the earth.

11¶ And there went from thence of the family of the Danites, out of Zorah and out of Eshtaol, six hundred men appointed with weapons of war.

12And they went up, and pitched in Kirjath-jearim, in Judah: wherefore they called that place Mahaneh-dan unto this day: behold, *it is* behind Kirjath-jearim.

13And they passed thence unto mount Ephraim, and came unto the house of Micah.

## Amplified

7And there was a young man in Bethlehem of Judah, of the family of Judah, who was a Levite, and he sojourned there.

8And the man departed from the town of Bethlehem in Judah to sojourn where he could find a place; and as he journeyed he came to the hill country of Ephraim to the house of Micah.

9And Micah said to him, From where do you come? And he said to him, I am a Levite of Bethlehem in Judah, and I go to sojourn where I may find a place.

10And Micah said to him, Dwell with me, and be to me a father and a priest, and I will give you ten pieces of silver each year, and a suit of clothes, and your living. So the Levite went in.

11And the Levite was content to dwell with the man; and the young man was to Micah as one of his sons.

12And Micah consecrated the Levite; and the young man became his priest, and was in the house of Micah.

13Then said Micah, Now I know that the Lord will favor me, since I have a Levite to be my priest.

18 IN THOSE days there was no king in Israel. And in those days the tribe of the Danites sought for itself an inheritance to dwell in; for until then no [sufficient] inheritance had been acquired by them among the tribes of Israel.

2So the Danites sent from the whole number of their tribe five brave men, from Zorah and Eshtaol, to spy out the land and to explore it; and they said to them, Go, explore the land. They came to the hill country of Ephraim, to the house of Micah, and lodged there.

3When they went by the house of Micah, they recognized the voice of the young Levite; and they turned aside there and said to him, Who brought you here? And what do you do in this place? And what have you here?

4And he said to them, Thus and thus Micah deals with me, and has hired me, and I am his priest.

5And they said to him, Ask counsel, we pray you, of God, that we may know whether our journey will be successful.

6And the priest said to them, Go in peace. The way in which you go is [before, under the eye of] the Lord.

7Then the five men departed, and came to Laish, and saw the people who were there, how they dwelt securely after the manner of the Sidonians, quiet and feeling safe; and there was no magistrate in the land, who might put them to shame in anything *or* injure them; and they were far from the Sidonians and had no dealings with any one.

8The five men came to their brethren at Zorah and Eshtaol, and their brethren said to them, What do you say?

9They said, Arise, let us go up against them; for we have seen the land, and behold, it is very fertile. And will you do nothing? Do not be slow to go and enter in and possess the land.

10When you go, you will come to people [feeling] safe and secure. The land is broad—widely extended on all sides; and God has given it into your hands; a place where there is no want of anything that is in the earth.

11And there went from there of the tribe of the Danites, out of Zorah and Eshtaol, 600 men armed with weapons of war.

12And they went up and encamped at Kiriath-jearim, in Judah. Therefore they called that place Mahaneh-dan [camp of Dan] to this day. It is west of Kiriath-jearim.

13And they passed from there to the hill country of Ephraim, and came to Micah's house.

## New American Standard

7¶ Now there was a young man from Bethlehem in Judah, of the family of Judah, who was a Levite; and he was staying there. 8Then the man departed from the city, from Bethlehem in Judah, to stay wherever he might find *a place;* and as he made his journey, he came to the hill country of Ephraim to the house of Micah.

9And Micah said to him, "Where do you come from?" And he said to him, "I am a Levite from Bethlehem in Judah, and I am going to stay wherever I may find *a place.*"

10Micah then said to him, "Dwell with me and be a father and a priest to me, and I will give you ten *pieces* of silver a year, a suit of clothes, and your maintenance." So the Levite went *in.*

11And the Levite agreed to live with the man; and the young man became to him like one of his sons.

12So Micah consecrated the Levite, and the young man became his priest and lived in the house of Micah.

13Then Micah said, "Now I know that the LORD will prosper me, seeing I have a Levite as priest."

*Danites Seek Territory*

**18** IN THOSE days there was no king of Israel; and in those days the tribe of the Danites was seeking an inheritance for themselves to live in, for until that day an inheritance had not been allotted to them as a possession among the tribes of Israel.

2So the sons of Dan sent from their family five men out of their whole number, valiant men from Zorah and Eshtaol, to spy out the land and to search it; and they said to them, "Go, search the land." And they came to the hill country of Ephraim, to the house of Micah, and lodged there.

3When they were near the house of Micah, they recognized the voice of the young man, the Levite; and they turned aside there, and said to him, "Who brought you here? And what are you doing in this *place?* And what do you have here?"

4And he said to them, "Thus and so has Micah done to me, and he has hired me, and I have become his priest."

5And they said to him, "Inquire of God, please, that we may know whether our way on which we are going will be prosperous."

6And the priest said to them, "Go in peace; your way in which you are going has the LORD's approval."

7¶ Then the five men departed and came to Laish and saw the people who were in it living in security, after the manner of the Sidonians, quiet and secure; for there was no ruler humiliating *them* for anything in the land, and they were far from the Sidonians and had no dealings with anyone.

8When they came back to their brothers at Zorah and Eshtaol, their brothers said to them, "What *do* you *report?*"

9And they said, "Arise, and let us go up against them; for we have seen the land, and behold, it is very good. And will you sit still? Do not delay to go, to enter, to possess the land.

10"When you enter, you shall come to a secure people with a spacious land; for God has given it into your hand, a place where there is no lack of anything that is on the earth."

11¶ Then from the family of the Danites, from Zorah and from Eshtaol, six hundred men armed with weapons of war set out.

12And they went up and camped at Kiriath-jearim in Judah. Therefore they called that place [a]Mahaneh-dan to this day; behold, it is west of Kiriath-jearim.

13And they passed from there to the hill country of Ephraim and came to the house of Micah.

**NAS** [a] I.e., the camp of Dan

## New International

7A young Levite from Bethlehem in Judah, who had been living within the clan of Judah, 8left that town in search of some other place to stay. On his way[b] he came to Micah's house in the hill country of Ephraim.

9Micah asked him, "Where are you from?"

"I'm a Levite from Bethlehem in Judah," he said, "and I'm looking for a place to stay."

10Then Micah said to him, "Live with me and be my father and priest, and I'll give you ten shekels[c] of silver a year, your clothes and your food." 11So the Levite agreed to live with him, and the young man was to him like one of his sons. 12Then Micah installed the Levite, and the young man became his priest and lived in his house. 13And Micah said, "Now I know that the LORD will be good to me, since this Levite has become my priest."

*Danites Settle in Laish*

**18** IN THOSE days Israel had no king.

And in those days the tribe of the Danites was seeking a place of their own where they might settle, because they had not yet come into an inheritance among the tribes of Israel. 2So the Danites sent five warriors from Zorah and Eshtaol to spy out the land and explore it. These men represented all their clans. They told them, "Go, explore the land."

The men entered the hill country of Ephraim and came to the house of Micah, where they spent the night. 3When they were near Micah's house, they recognized the voice of the young Levite; so they turned in there and asked him, "Who brought you here? What are you doing in this place? Why are you here?"

4He told them what Micah had done for him, and said, "He has hired me and I am his priest."

5Then they said to him, "Please inquire of God to learn whether our journey will be successful."

6The priest answered them, "Go in peace. Your journey has the LORD's approval."

7So the five men left and came to Laish, where they saw that the people were living in safety, like the Sidonians, unsuspecting and secure. And since their land lacked nothing, they were prosperous.[d] Also, they lived a long way from the Sidonians and had no relationship with anyone else.[e]

8When they returned to Zorah and Eshtaol, their brothers asked them, "How did you find things?"

9They answered, "Come on, let's attack them! We have seen that the land is very good. Aren't you going to do something? Don't hesitate to go there and take it over. 10When you get there, you will find an unsuspecting people and a spacious land that God has put into your hands, a land that lacks nothing whatever."

11Then six hundred men from the clan of the Danites, armed for battle, set out from Zorah and Eshtaol. 12On their way they set up camp near Kiriath Jearim in Judah. This is why the place west of Kiriath Jearim is called Mahaneh Dan[f] to this day. 13From there they went on to the hill country of Ephraim and came to Micah's house.

**NIV** [b] *8* Or *To carry on his profession* [c] *10* That is, about 4 ounces (about 110 grams) [d] *7* The meaning of the Hebrew for this clause is uncertain. [e] *7* Hebrew; some Septuagint manuscripts *with the Arameans* [f] *12 Mahaneh Dan* means *Dan's camp.*

## King James

14¶ Then answered the five men that went to spy out the country of Laish, and said unto their brethren, Do ye know that there is in these houses an ephod, and teraphim, and a graven image, and a molten image? now therefore consider what ye have to do.

15And they turned thitherward, and came to the house of the young man the Levite, *even* unto the house of Micah, and saluted him.

16And the six hundred men appointed with their weapons of war, which *were* of the children of Dan, stood by the entering of the gate.

17And the five men that went to spy out the land went up, *and* came in thither, *and* took the graven image, and the ephod, and the teraphim, and the molten image: and the priest stood in the entering of the gate with the six hundred men *that were* appointed with weapons of war.

18And these went into Micah's house, and fetched the carved image, the ephod, and the teraphim, and the molten image. Then said the priest unto them, What do ye?

19And they said unto him, Hold thy peace, lay thine hand upon thy mouth, and go with us, and be to us a father and a priest: *is it* better for thee to be a priest unto the house of one man, or that thou be a priest unto a tribe and a family in Israel?

20And the priest's heart was glad, and he took the ephod, and the teraphim, and the graven image, and went in the midst of the people.

21So they turned and departed, and put the little ones and the cattle and the carriage before them.

22¶ *And* when they were a good way from the house of Micah, the men that *were* in the houses near to Micah's house were gathered together, and overtook the children of Dan.

23And they cried unto the children of Dan. And they turned their faces, and said unto Micah, What aileth thee, that thou comest with such a company?

24And he said, Ye have taken away my gods which I made, and the priest, and ye are gone away: and what have I more? and what *is* this *that* ye say unto me, What aileth thee?

25And the children of Dan said unto him, Let not thy voice be heard among us, lest angry fellows run upon thee, and thou lose thy life, with the lives of thy household.

26And the children of Dan went their way: and when Micah saw that they *were* too strong for him, he turned and went back unto his house.

27And they took *the things* which Micah had made, and the priest which he had, and came unto Laish, unto a people *that were* at quiet and secure: and they smote them with the edge of the sword, and burnt the city with fire.

28And *there was* no deliverer, because it *was* far from Zidon, and they had no business with *any* man; and it was in the valley that *lieth* by Beth-rehob. And they built a city, and dwelt therein.

29And they called the name of the city Dan, after the name of Dan their father, who was born unto Israel: howbeit the name of the city *was* Laish at the first.

30¶ And the children of Dan set up the graven image: and Jonathan, the son of Gershom, the son of Manasseh, he and his sons were priests to the tribe of Dan until the day of the captivity of the land.

31And they set them up Micah's graven image, which he made, all the time that the house of God was in Shiloh.

## Amplified

14Then the five men who had gone to spy out the country of Laish said to their brethren, Do you know that there are in these houses an ephod, and teraphim, and a graven image, and a molten image? Now therefore consider what you have to do.

15And they turned in that direction, and came to the house of the young Levite, at the home of Micah, and saluted him.

16Now the 600 Danites with their weapons of war stood at Micah's gate.

17And the five men who had gone to spy out the land went up, and entered the house and took the graven image, the ephod, the teraphim, and the molten image, while the priest stood by the entrance of the gate with the 600 men armed with weapons of war.

18And when these went into Micah's house, and took the carved image, the ephod, the teraphim, and the molten image, the priest said to them, What are you doing?

19And they said to him, Be still, put your hand over your mouth and come with us, and be to us a father and a priest. Is it better for you to be a priest to the house of one man, or that you be a priest to a tribe and family in Israel?

20And the priest's heart was glad; he took the ephod, the teraphim, and the graven image, and went in the midst of the people.

21So they turned and departed, and put the little ones, the cattle and the baggage in front of them.

22When they were a good way from the house of Micah, the men who were Micah's near neighbors were called out and overtook the Danites.

23They shouted to the Danites, who turned and said to Micah, What ails you, that you come with such a company?

24And he said, You take away my gods, which I made, and the priest, and go away; and what have I left? How can you say to me, What ails you?

25And the men of Dan said to him, Let not your voice be heard among us, lest angry fellows fall upon you, and you lose your life with the lives of your household.

26And the Danites went their way; and when Micah saw that they were too strong for him, he turned and went back to his house.

27And they took the things which Micah had made, and his priest, and came to Laish, to a people quiet and feeling secure; and they smote them with the sword, and burned the city.

28And there was no deliverer because it was far from Sidon, and they had no business with any one. It was in the valley which belongs to Beth-rehob. And they rebuilt the city, and dwelt in it.

29They named the city Dan, after Dan their forefather, who was born to Israel; however the name of the city was Laish at first.

30And the Danites set up the graven image for themselves; and Jonathan son of Gershom, son of Moses, and his sons were priests to the tribe of Dan until the day of the captivity of the land.

31So they set them up Micah's graven image which he made, as long as the house of God was at Shiloh.

## New American Standard

*Danites Take Micah's Idols*

14¶ Then the five men who went to spy out the country of Laish
answered and said to their kinsmen, "Do you know that there are
in these houses an ephod and [a]household idols and a graven
image and a molten image? Now therefore, consider what you
should do."
15And they turned aside there and came to the house of the
young man, the Levite, to the house of Micah, and asked him of
his welfare.
16And the six hundred men armed with their weapons of war,
who were of the sons of Dan, stood by the entrance of the gate.
17Now the five men who went to spy out the land went up *and*
entered there, *and* took the graven image and the ephod and
household idols and the molten image, while the priest stood by
the entrance of the gate with the six hundred men armed with
weapons of war.
18And when these went into Micah's house and took the graven
image, the ephod and household idols and the molten image, the
priest said to them, "What are you doing?"
19And they said to him, "Be silent, put your hand over your
mouth and come with us, and be to us a father and a priest. Is it
better for you to be a priest to the house of one man, or to be priest
to a tribe and a family in Israel?"
20And the priest's heart was glad, and he took the ephod and
household idols and the graven image, and went among the
people.
21¶ Then they turned and departed, and put the little ones and
the livestock and the valuables in front of them.
22When they had gone some distance from the house of Micah,
the men who *were* in the houses near Micah's house assembled and
overtook the sons of Dan.
23And they cried to the sons of Dan, who turned around and
said to Micah, "What is *the matter* with you, that you have assembled together?"
24And he said, "You have taken away my gods which I made,
and the priest, and have gone away, and what do I have besides?
So how can you say to me, 'What is *the matter* with you?' "
25And the sons of Dan said to him, "Do not let your voice be
heard among us, lest fierce men fall upon you and you lose your
life, with the lives of your household."
26So the sons of Dan went on their way; and when Micah saw
that they were too strong for him, he turned and went back to his
house.
27¶ Then they took what Micah had made and the priest who
had belonged to him, and came to Laish, to a people quiet and
secure, and struck them with the edge of the sword; and they
burned the city with fire.
28And there was no one to deliver *them*, because it was far from
Sidon and they had no dealings with anyone, and it was in the
valley which is near Beth-rehob. And they rebuilt the city and lived
in it.
29And they called the name of the city Dan, after the name of
Dan their father who was born in Israel; however, the name of the
city formerly was Laish.
30And the sons of Dan set up for themselves the graven image;
and Jonathan, the son of Gershom, the son of [b]Manasseh, he and
his sons were priests to the tribe of the Danites until the day of the
captivity of the land.
31So they set up for themselves Micah's graven image which he
had made, all the time that the house of God was at Shiloh.

NAS [a] Heb., *teraphim*, and so throughout this context [b] Some ancient versions read *Moses*

## New International

14Then the five men who had spied out the land of Laish said
to their brothers, "Do you know that one of these houses has an
ephod, other household gods, a carved image and a cast idol? Now
you know what to do." 15So they turned in there and went to the
house of the young Levite at Micah's place and greeted him. 16The
six hundred Danites, armed for battle, stood at the entrance to the
gate. 17The five men who had spied out the land went inside and
took the carved image, the ephod, the other household gods and
the cast idol while the priest and the six hundred armed men stood
at the entrance to the gate.
18When these men went into Micah's house and took the carved
image, the ephod, the other household gods and the cast idol, the
priest said to them, "What are you doing?"
19They answered him, "Be quiet! Don't say a word. Come with
us, and be our father and priest. Isn't it better that you serve a tribe
and clan in Israel as priest rather than just one man's household?"
20Then the priest was glad. He took the ephod, the other household gods and the carved image and went along with the people.
21Putting their little children, their livestock and their possessions
in front of them, they turned away and left.
22When they had gone some distance from Micah's house, the
men who lived near Micah were called together and overtook the
Danites. 23As they shouted after them, the Danites turned and said
to Micah, "What's the matter with you that you called out your
men to fight?"
24He replied, "You took the gods I made, and my priest, and
went away. What else do I have? How can you ask, 'What's the
matter with you?' "
25The Danites answered, "Don't argue with us, or some hot-
tempered men will attack you, and you and your family will lose
your lives." 26So the Danites went their way, and Micah, seeing
that they were too strong for him, turned around and went back
home.
27Then they took what Micah had made, and his priest, and
went on to Laish, against a peaceful and unsuspecting people.
They attacked them with the sword and burned down their city.
28There was no one to rescue them because they lived a long way
from Sidon and had no relationship with anyone else. The city was
in a valley near Beth Rehob.
The Danites rebuilt the city and settled there. 29They named it
Dan after their forefather Dan, who was born to Israel—though the
city used to be called Laish. 30There the Danites set up for themselves the idols, and Jonathan son of Gershom, the son of Moses,[c]
and his sons were priests for the tribe of Dan until the time of the
captivity of the land. 31They continued to use the idols Micah had
made, all the time the house of God was in Shiloh.

NIV [c] *30* An ancient Hebrew scribal tradition, some Septuagint manuscripts and Vulgate; Masoretic Text *Manasseh*

## King James

**19** AND IT came to pass in those days, when *there was* no king in Israel, that there was a certain Levite sojourning on the side of mount Ephraim, who took to him a concubine out of Bethlehem-judah.

2And his concubine played the whore against him, and went away from him unto her father's house to Bethlehem-judah, and was there four whole months.

3And her husband arose, and went after her, to speak friendly unto her, *and* to bring her again, having his servant with him, and a couple of asses: and she brought him into her father's house: and when the father of the damsel saw him, he rejoiced to meet him.

4And his father-in-law, the damsel's father, retained him; and he abode with him three days: so they did eat and drink, and lodged there.

5¶ And it came to pass on the fourth day, when they arose early in the morning, that he rose up to depart: and the damsel's father said unto his son-in-law, Comfort thine heart with a morsel of bread, and afterward go your way.

6And they sat down, and did eat and drink both of them together: for the damsel's father had said unto the man, Be content, I pray thee, and tarry all night, and let thine heart be merry.

7And when the man rose up to depart, his father-in-law urged him: therefore he lodged there again.

8And he arose early in the morning on the fifth day to depart: and the damsel's father said, Comfort thine heart, I pray thee. And they tarried until afternoon, and they did eat both of them.

9And when the man rose up to depart, he, and his concubine, and his servant, his father-in-law, the damsel's father, said unto him, Behold, now the day draweth toward evening, I pray you tarry all night: behold, the day groweth to an end, lodge here, that thine heart may be merry; and tomorrow get you early on your way, that thou mayest go home.

10But the man would not tarry that night, but he rose up and departed, and came over against Jebus, which *is* Jerusalem; and *there were* with him two asses saddled, his concubine also *was* with him.

11 *And* when they *were* by Jebus, the day was far spent; and the servant said unto his master, Come, I pray thee, and let us turn in into this city of the Jebusites, and lodge in it.

12And his master said unto him, We will not turn aside hither into the city of a stranger, that *is* not of the children of Israel; we will pass over to Gibeah.

13And he said unto his servant, Come, and let us draw near to one of these places to lodge all night, in Gibeah, or in Ramah.

14And they passed on and went their way; and the sun went down upon them *when they were* by Gibeah, which *belongeth* to Benjamin.

15And they turned aside thither, to go in *and* to lodge in Gibeah: and when he went in, he sat him down in a street of the city: for *there was* no man that took them into his house to lodging.

16¶ And, behold, there came an old man from his work out of the field at even, which *was* also of mount Ephraim; and he sojourned in Gibeah: but the men of the place *were* Benjamites.

17And when he had lifted up his eyes, he saw a wayfaring man in the street of the city: and the old man said, Whither goest thou? and whence comest thou?

18And he said unto him, We *are* passing from Bethlehem-judah toward the side of mount Ephraim; from thence *am* I: and I went to Bethlehem-judah, but I *am now* going to the house of the LORD; and there *is* no man that receiveth me to house.

19Yet there is both straw and provender for our asses; and there is bread and wine also for me, and for thy handmaid, and for the young man *which is* with thy servants: *there is* no want of any thing.

20And the old man said, Peace *be* with thee; howsoever *let* all thy wants *lie* upon me; only lodge not in the street.

21So he brought him into his house, and gave provender unto the asses: and they washed their feet, and did eat and drink.

## Amplified

**19** IN THOSE days, when there was no king in Israel, a certain Levite was living temporarily in the most remote part of the hill district of Ephraim, who took to himself a wife of inferior station from Bethlehem in Judah.

2And his [a]concubine was untrue to him, and went away from him to her father's house at Bethlehem of Judah and stayed the space of four months.

3Then her husband arose, and went after her, to speak kindly to her [to her heart] and to bring her back, having with him his servant and a couple of donkeys. And she brought him into her father's house, and when her father saw him, he rejoiced to meet him.

4And his father-in-law, the girl's father, [insistently] detained him, and he remained with him three days. So they ate and drank, and he lodged there.

5On the fourth day they arose early in the morning, and the [Levite] prepared to leave; but the girl's father said to his son-in-law, Strengthen your heart with a morsel of bread, and afterward go your way.

6So both men sat down and ate and drank together, and the girl's father said to the man, Consent to stay all night, and let your heart be merry.

7And when the man rose up to depart, his father-in-law urged him, so he lodged there again.

8And he arose early in the morning on the fifth day to depart, but the girl's father said, Strengthen your heart, and tarry until toward evening. So they ate, both of them.

9And when the man and his concubine and his servant rose up to leave, his father-in-law the girl's father, said to him, Behold, now the day draws toward evening, I pray you stay all night. Behold, now the day grows to an end, lodge here and let your heart be merry; and tomorrow get early on your way, and go home.

10But the man would not stay that night; he rose up and departed, and came opposite to Jebus, which is Jerusalem. With him were two saddled donkeys [and his servant], and his concubine.

11When they were near Jebus, it was late, and the servant said to his master, Come I pray, and let us turn into this Jebusite city and lodge in it.

12His master said to him, We will not turn aside into the city of foreigners, where there are no Israelites. We will go on to Gibeah.

13And he said to his servant, Come, and let us go to one of these places and spend the night in Gibeah or in Ramah.

14So they passed on and went their way; and the sun went down on them near Gibeah, which belongs to Benjamin,

15And they turned aside there, to go in and lodge at Gibeah. And the Levite went in and sat down in the open square of the city, for no man took them into his house to spend the night.

16And behold, an old man was coming from his work in the field at evening; he was from the hill country of Ephraim but was living temporarily in Gibeah; the men of the place were Benjamites.

17And when he looked up, he saw the wayfarer in the city square; and the old man said, Where are you going? And from where did you come?

18The Levite replied, We are passing from Bethlehem of Judah to the rear side of the hill country of Ephraim; I am from there. I went to Bethlehem of Judah, but I am [now] going [home] to the house of the Lord [where I serve]; and there is no man who receives me into his house.

19Yet we have both straw and provender for our donkeys, and bread and wine also for me and your handmaid and the young man who is with your servants; there is no lack of anything.

20And the old man said, Peace be to you; but leave all your wants to me; only do not lodge in the street.

21So he brought him into his house, and gave provender to the donkeys. And the guests washed their feet, and ate and drank.

AMP [a] Josephus gives her name as Drumah.

## New American Standard

*A Levite's Concubine Degraded*

19 NOW IT came about in those days, when there was no king in Israel, that there was a certain Levite staying in the remote part of the hill country of Ephraim, who took a concubine for himself from Bethlehem in Judah.

2 But his concubine played the harlot against him, and she went away from him to her father's house in Bethlehem in Judah, and was there for a period of four months.

3 Then her husband arose and went after her to speak tenderly to her in order to bring her back, taking with him his servant and a pair of donkeys. So she brought him into her father's house, and when the girl's father saw him, he was glad to meet him.

4 And his father-in-law, the girl's father, detained him; and he remained with him three days. So they ate and drank and lodged there.

5 Now it came about on the fourth day that they got up early in the morning, and he prepared to go; and the girl's father said to his son-in-law, "Sustain yourself with a piece of bread, and afterward you may go."

6 So both of them sat down and ate and drank together; and the girl's father said to the man, "Please be willing to spend the night, and let your heart be merry."

7 Then the man arose to go, but his father-in-law urged him so that he spent the night there again.

8 And on the fifth day he arose to go early in the morning, and the girl's father said, "Please sustain yourself, and wait until afternoon"; so both of them ate.

9 When the man arose to go along with his concubine and servant, his father-in-law, the girl's father, said to him, "Behold now, the day has drawn to a close; please spend the night. Lo, the day is coming to an end; spend the night here that your heart may be merry. Then tomorrow you may arise early for your journey so that you may go home."

10 ¶ But the man was not willing to spend the night, so he arose and departed and came to *a place* opposite Jebus (that is, Jerusalem). And there were with him a pair of saddled donkeys; his concubine also was with him.

11 When they *were* near Jebus, the day was almost gone; and the servant said to his master, "Please come, and let us turn aside into this city of the Jebusites and spend the night in it."

12 However, his master said to him, "We will not turn aside into the city of foreigners who are not of the sons of Israel; but we will go on as far as Gibeah."

13 And he said to his servant, "Come and let us approach one of these places; and we will spend the night in Gibeah or Ramah."

14 So they passed along and went their way, and the sun set on them near Gibeah which belongs to Benjamin.

15 And they turned aside there in order to enter *and* lodge in Gibeah. When they entered, they sat down in the open square of the city, for no one took them into *his* house to spend the night.

16 ¶ Then behold, an old man was coming out of the field from his work at evening. Now the man was from the hill country of Ephraim, and he was staying in Gibeah, but the men of the place were Benjamites.

17 And he lifted up his eyes and saw the traveler in the open square of the city; and the old man said, "Where are you going, and where do you come from?"

18 And he said to him, "We are passing from Bethlehem in Judah to the remote part of the hill country of Ephraim, *for* I am from there, and I went to Bethlehem in Judah. But I am *now* going to my house, and no man will take me into his house.

19 "Yet there is both straw and fodder for our donkeys, and also bread and wine for me, your maidservant, and the young man who is with your servants; there is no lack of anything."

20 And the old man said, "Peace to you. Only let me *take care of* all your needs; however, do not spend the night in the open square."

21 So he took him into his house and gave the donkeys fodder, and they washed their feet and ate and drank.

## New International

*A Levite and His Concubine*

19 IN THOSE days Israel had no king.
Now a Levite who lived in a remote area in the hill country
of Ephraim took a concubine from Bethlehem in Judah. 2 But she
was unfaithful to him. She left him and went back to her father's
house in Bethlehem, Judah. After she had been there four months,
3 her husband went to her to persuade her to return. He had with
him his servant and two donkeys. She took him into her father's
house, and when her father saw him, he gladly welcomed him.
4 His father-in-law, the girl's father, prevailed upon him to stay; so
he remained with him three days, eating and drinking, and sleeping there.
5 On the fourth day they got up early and he prepared to leave,
but the girl's father said to his son-in-law, "Refresh yourself with
something to eat; then you can go." 6 So the two of them sat down
to eat and drink together. Afterward the girl's father said, "Please
stay tonight and enjoy yourself." 7 And when the man got up to
go, his father-in-law persuaded him, so he stayed there that night.
8 On the morning of the fifth day, when he rose to go, the girl's
father said, "Refresh yourself. Wait till afternoon!" So the two of
them ate together.
9 Then when the man, with his concubine and his servant, got
up to leave, his father-in-law, the girl's father, said, "Now look,
it's almost evening. Spend the night here; the day is nearly over.
Stay and enjoy yourself. Early tomorrow morning you can get up
and be on your way home." 10 But, unwilling to stay another night,
the man left and went toward Jebus (that is, Jerusalem), with his
two saddled donkeys and his concubine.
11 When they were near Jebus and the day was almost gone, the
servant said to his master, "Come, let's stop at this city of the
Jebusites and spend the night."
12 His master replied, "No. We won't go into an alien city,
whose people are not Israelites. We will go on to Gibeah." 13 He
added, "Come, let's try to reach Gibeah or Ramah and spend the
night in one of those places." 14 So they went on, and the sun set
as they neared Gibeah in Benjamin. 15 There they stopped to spend
the night. They went and sat in the city square, but no one took
them into his home for the night.
16 That evening an old man from the hill country of Ephraim,
who was living in Gibeah (the men of the place were Benjamites),
came in from his work in the fields. 17 When he looked and saw the
traveler in the city square, the old man asked, "Where are you
going? Where did you come from?"
18 He answered, "We are on our way from Bethlehem in Judah
to a remote area in the hill country of Ephraim where I live. I have
been to Bethlehem in Judah and now I am going to the house of
the LORD. No one has taken me into his house. 19 We have both
straw and fodder for our donkeys and bread and wine for ourselves your servants—me, your maidservant, and the young man
with us. We don't need anything."
20 "You are welcome at my house," the old man said. "Let me
supply whatever you need. Only don't spend the night in the
square." 21 So he took him into his house and fed his donkeys.
After they had washed their feet, they had something to eat and
drink.

## King James

22¶ *Now* as they were making their hearts merry, behold, the men of the city, certain sons of Belial, beset the house round about, *and* beat at the door, and spake to the master of the house, the old man, saying, Bring forth the man that came into thine house, that we may know him.

23And the man, the master of the house, went out unto them, and said unto them, Nay, my brethren, *nay*, I pray you, do not *so* wickedly; seeing that this man is come into mine house, do not this folly.

24Behold, *here is* my daughter a maiden, and his concubine; them I will bring out now, and humble ye them, and do with them what seemeth good unto you: but unto this man do not so vile a thing.

25But the men would not hearken to him: so the man took his concubine, and brought her forth unto them; and they knew her, and abused her all the night until the morning: and when the day began to spring, they let her go.

26Then came the woman in the dawning of the day, and fell down at the door of the man's house where her lord *was*, till it was light.

27And her lord rose up in the morning, and opened the doors of the house, and went out to go his way: and, behold, the woman his concubine was fallen down *at* the door of the house, and her hands *were* upon the threshold.

28And he said unto her, Up, and let us be going. But none answered. Then the man took her *up* upon an ass, and the man rose up, and gat him unto his place.

29¶ And when he was come into his house, he took a knife, and laid hold on his concubine, and divided her, *together* with her bones, into twelve pieces, and sent her into all the coasts of Israel.

30And it was so, that all that saw it said, There was no such deed done nor seen from the day that the children of Israel came up out of the land of Egypt unto this day: consider of it, take advice, and speak *your minds*.

**20** THEN ALL the children of Israel went out, and the congregation was gathered together as one man, from Dan even to Beer-sheba, with the land of Gilead, unto the LORD in Mizpeh.

2And the chief of all the people, *even* of all the tribes of Israel, presented themselves in the assembly of the people of God, four hundred thousand footmen that drew sword.

3(Now the children of Benjamin heard that the children of Israel were gone up to Mizpeh.) Then said the children of Israel, Tell *us*, how was this wickedness?

4And the Levite, the husband of the woman that was slain, answered and said, I came into Gibeah that *belongeth* to Benjamin, I and my concubine, to lodge.

5And the men of Gibeah rose against me, and beset the house round about upon me by night, *and* thought to have slain me: and my concubine have they forced, that she is dead.

6And I took my concubine, and cut her in pieces, and sent her throughout all the country of the inheritance of Israel: for they have committed lewdness and folly in Israel.

7Behold, ye *are* all children of Israel; give here your advice and counsel.

8¶ And all the people arose as one man, saying, We will not any *of us* go to his tent, neither will we any *of us* turn into his house.

9But now this *shall be* the thing which we will do to Gibeah; *we will go up* by lot against it;

10And we will take ten men of an hundred throughout all the tribes of Israel, and an hundred of a thousand, and a thousand out of ten thousand, to fetch victual for the people, that they may do, when they come to Gibeah of Benjamin, according to all the folly that they have wrought in Israel.

11So all the men of Israel were gathered against the city, knit together as one man.

## Amplified

22Now as they were making their hearts merry, behold, the men of the city, certain worthless fellows, beset the house round about, and beat on the door, and said to the master of the house, the old man, Bring forth the man who came to your house, that we may have intercourse with him.

23And the man, the master of the house, went out and said to them, No, my kinsmen, I pray you, do not so wickedly; seeing that this man is my guest, do not this [wicked] folly.

24Behold, here are my virgin daughter and this man's concubine; them I will bring out now; debase them and do with them what seems good to you, but to this man do not so vile a thing.

25But the men would not listen to him. So the man took his concubine, and forced her forth to them and they had intercourse with her, and abused her all the night until morning. And when the dawn began to break they let her go.

26At daybreak the woman came and fell down and lay at the door of the man's house where her master was, till it was light.

27And her master rose up in the morning and opened the doors of the house, and went out to go his way; and behold, his concubine had fallen down at the door of the house, and her hands were upon the threshold.

28And he said to her, Up, and let us be going. But there was no answer. Then he put her [dead body] upon the donkey; and the man rose up, and went home.

29And when he came into his house, he took a knife, and took hold of his dead concubine, and divided her [body] limb by limb into twelve pieces, and sent her [body] throughout all the territory of Israel.

30And all who saw it said, There was no such deed done or seen from the day that the Israelites came up out of the land of Egypt to this day; consider it, take counsel, and speak [your minds].

**20** THEN ALL the Israelites came out, and the congregation assembled as one man to the Lord at Mizpah, from Dan even to Beersheba, including the land of Gilead.

2And the chiefs of all the people, of all the tribes of Israel, presented themselves in the assembly of the people of God, 400,000 men on foot who drew the sword.

3(Now the Benjamites [among whom the vile tragedy occurred] heard that the [other] Israelites had gone up to Mizpah.) There the Israelites asked, How did this wickedness happen?

4And the Levite, the husband of the woman who was murdered, replied, I came to Gibeah which belongs to Benjamin, I and my concubine, to spend the night.

5And the men of Gibeah rose against me, and beset the house round about me by night; they meant to kill me, and they raped my concubine, and she is dead.

6And I took my concubine, and cut her in pieces, and sent her throughout all the country of the inheritance of Israel; for they have committed abomination and [wicked] folly in Israel.

7Behold, you Israelites, all of you, give here your advice and counsel.

8And all the people arose as one man, saying, We will not any of us go to his tent, and none of us will return to his home.

9But now this we will do to Gibeah: we will go up by lot against it,

10And we will take ten men of 100 throughout all the tribes of Israel, and 100 of 1,000, and 1,000 out of 10,000, to bring provisions for the men, that when they come to Gibeah of Benjamin they may do to it according to all the [wicked] folly which they have committed in Israel.

11So all the men of Israel gathered against the city, united as one man.

## New American Standard

22¶ While they were making merry, behold, the men of the city,
certain worthless fellows, surrounded the house, pounding the
door; and they spoke to the owner of the house, the old man,
saying, "Bring out the man who came into your house that we may
have relations with him."
23Then the man, the owner of the house, went out to them and
said to them, "No, my fellows, please do not act so wickedly; since
this man has come into my house, do not commit this act of folly.
24"Here is my virgin daughter and his concubine. Please let me
bring them out that you may ravish them and do to them whatever
you wish. But do not commit such an act of folly against this man."
25But the men would not listen to him, so the man seized his
concubine and brought *her* out to them. And they raped her and
abused her all night until morning, then let her go at the approach
of dawn.
26As the day began to dawn, the woman came and fell down
at the doorway of the man's house where her master was, until *full*
daylight.
27¶ When her master arose in the morning and opened the
doors of the house and went out to go on his way, then behold,
his concubine was lying at the doorway of the house, with her
hands on the threshold.
28And he said to her, "Get up and let us go," but there was no
answer. Then he placed her on the donkey; and the man arose and
went to his home.
29When he entered his house, he took a knife and laid hold of
his concubine and cut her in twelve pieces, limb by limb, and sent
her throughout the territory of Israel.
30And it came about that all who saw *it* said, "Nothing like this
has *ever* happened or been seen from the day when the sons of
Israel came up from the land of Egypt to this day. Consider it, take
counsel and speak up!"

*Resolve to Punish the Guilty*

20 THEN ALL the sons of Israel from Dan to Beersheba,
including the land of Gilead, came out, and the congregation assembled as one man to the LORD at Mizpah.
2And the chiefs of all the people, *even* of all the tribes of Israel,
took their stand in the assembly of the people of God, 400,000 foot
soldiers who drew the sword.
3(Now the sons of Benjamin heard that the sons of Israel had
gone up to Mizpah.) And the sons of Israel said, "Tell *us*, how did
this wickedness take place?"
4So the Levite, the husband of the woman who was murdered,
answered and said, "I came with my concubine to spend the night
at Gibeah which belongs to Benjamin.
5"But the men of Gibeah rose up against me and surrounded
the house at night because of me. They intended to kill me; instead, they ravished my concubine so that she died.
6"And I took hold of my concubine and cut her in pieces and
sent her throughout the land of Israel's inheritance; for they have
committed a lewd and disgraceful act in Israel.
7"Behold, all you sons of Israel, give your advice and counsel
here."
8¶ Then all the people arose as one man, saying, "Not one of
us will go to his tent, nor will any of us return to his house.
9"But now this is the thing which we will do to Gibeah; *we will*
*go up* against it by lot.
10"And we will take 10 men out of 100 throughout the tribes of
Israel, and 100 out of 1,000, and 1,000 out of 10,000 to supply food
for the people, that when they come to Gibeah of Benjamin, they
may punish *them* for all the disgraceful acts that they have committed in Israel."
11Thus all the men of Israel were gathered against the city,
united as one man.

## New International

22While they were enjoying themselves, some of the wicked
men of the city surrounded the house. Pounding on the door, they
shouted to the old man who owned the house, "Bring out the man
who came to your house so we can have sex with him."
23The owner of the house went outside and said to them, "No,
my friends, don't be so vile. Since this man is my guest, don't do
this disgraceful thing. 24Look, here is my virgin daughter, and his
concubine. I will bring them out to you now, and you can use them
and do to them whatever you wish. But to this man, don't do such
a disgraceful thing."
25But the men would not listen to him. So the man took his
concubine and sent her outside to them, and they raped her and
abused her throughout the night, and at dawn they let her go. 26At
daybreak the woman went back to the house where her master was
staying, fell down at the door and lay there until daylight.
27When her master got up in the morning and opened the door
of the house and stepped out to continue on his way, there lay his
concubine, fallen in the doorway of the house, with her hands on
the threshold. 28He said to her, "Get up; let's go." But there was
no answer. Then the man put her on his donkey and set out for
home.
29When he reached home, he took a knife and cut up his concubine, limb by limb, into twelve parts and sent them into all the
areas of Israel. 30Everyone who saw it said, "Such a thing has
never been seen or done, not since the day the Israelites came up
out of Egypt. Think about it! Consider it! Tell us what to do!"

*Israelites Fight the Benjamites*

20 THEN ALL the Israelites from Dan to Beersheba and from
the land of Gilead came out as one man and assembled
before the LORD in Mizpah. 2The leaders of all the people of the
tribes of Israel took their places in the assembly of the people of
God, four hundred thousand soldiers armed with swords. 3(The
Benjamites heard that the Israelites had gone up to Mizpah.) Then
the Israelites said, "Tell us how this awful thing happened."
4So the Levite, the husband of the murdered woman, said, "I
and my concubine came to Gibeah in Benjamin to spend the night.
5During the night the men of Gibeah came after me and surrounded the house, intending to kill me. They raped my concubine, and
she died. 6I took my concubine, cut her into pieces and sent one
piece to each region of Israel's inheritance, because they committed this lewd and disgraceful act in Israel. 7Now, all you Israelites,
speak up and give your verdict."
8All the people rose as one man, saying, "None of us will go
home. No, not one of us will return to his house. 9But now this
is what we'll do to Gibeah: We'll go up against it as the lot directs.
10We'll take ten men out of every hundred from all the tribes of
Israel, and a hundred from a thousand, and a thousand from ten
thousand, to get provisions for the army. Then, when the army
arrives at Gibeah[a] in Benjamin, it can give them what they deserve
for all this vileness done in Israel." 11So all the men of Israel got
together and united as one man against the city.

**NIV** [a] *10* One Hebrew manuscript; most Hebrew manuscripts *Geba,* a variant of *Gibeah*

## King James

12¶ And the tribes of Israel sent men through all the tribe of Benjamin, saying, What wickedness *is* this that is done among you?

13Now therefore deliver *us* the men, the children of Belial, which *are* in Gibeah, that we may put them to death, and put away evil from Israel. But the children of Benjamin would not hearken to the voice of their brethren the children of Israel:

14But the children of Benjamin gathered themselves together out of the cities unto Gibeah, to go out to battle against the children of Israel.

15And the children of Benjamin were numbered at that time out of the cities twenty and six thousand men that drew sword, beside the inhabitants of Gibeah, which were numbered seven hundred chosen men.

16Among all this people *there were* seven hundred chosen men lefthanded; every one could sling stones at an hair *breadth*, and not miss.

17And the men of Israel, beside Benjamin, were numbered four hundred thousand men that drew sword: all these *were* men of war.

18¶ And the children of Israel arose, and went up to the house of God, and asked counsel of God, and said, Which of us shall go up first to the battle against the children of Benjamin? And the LORD said, Judah *shall go up* first.

19And the children of Israel rose up in the morning, and encamped against Gibeah.

20And the men of Israel went out to battle against Benjamin; and the men of Israel put themselves in array to fight against them at Gibeah.

21And the children of Benjamin came forth out of Gibeah, and destroyed down to the ground of the Israelites that day twenty and two thousand men.

22And the people the men of Israel encouraged themselves, and set their battle again in array in the place where they put themselves in array the first day.

23(And the children of Israel went up and wept before the LORD until even, and asked counsel of the LORD, saying, Shall I go up again to battle against the children of Benjamin my brother? And the LORD said, Go up against him.)

24And the children of Israel came near against the children of Benjamin the second day.

25And Benjamin went forth against them out of Gibeah the second day, and destroyed down to the ground of the children of Israel again eighteen thousand men; all these drew the sword.

26¶ Then all the children of Israel, and all the people, went up, and came unto the house of God, and wept, and sat there before the LORD, and fasted that day until even, and offered burnt offerings and peace offerings before the LORD.

27And the children of Israel inquired of the LORD, (for the ark of the covenant of God *was* there in those days,

28And Phinehas, the son of Eleazar, the son of Aaron, stood before it in those days,) saying, Shall I yet again go out to battle against the children of Benjamin my brother, or shall I cease? And the LORD said, Go up; for tomorrow I will deliver them into thine hand.

29And Israel set liers in wait round about Gibeah.

30And the children of Israel went up against the children of Benjamin on the third day, and put themselves in array against Gibeah, as at other times.

31And the children of Benjamin went out against the people, *and* were drawn away from the city; and they began to smite of the people, *and* kill, as at other times, in the highways, of which one goeth up to the house of God, and the other to Gibeah in the field, about thirty men of Israel.

32And the children of Benjamin said, They *are* smitten down before us, as at the first. But the children of Israel said, Let us flee, and draw them from the city unto the highways.

33And all the men of Israel rose up out of their place, and put themselves in array at Baal-tamar: and the liers in wait of Israel came forth out of their places, *even* out of the meadows of Gibeah.

## Amplified

12And the tribes of Israel sent men through all the tribe of Benjamin, saying, What wickedness is this that has been done among you?

13Now therefore, give up the men [involved], the base fellows in Gibeah, that we may put them to death, and put away evil from Israel. But the Benjamites would not listen to the voice of their kinsmen the Israelites.

14But the Benjamites out of the cities assembled at Gibeah to go out to battle against the other Israelites.

15And the Benjamites mustered out of their cities at that time 26,000 men who drew the sword, besides the inhabitants of Gibeah, who mustered 700 chosen men.

16Among all these were 700 chosen left-handed men; every one could sling stones at a hair, and not miss.

17And the men of Israel, other than Benjamin, mustered 400,000 men who drew the sword; all these were men of war.

18The Israelites arose, and went up to the house of God [Bethel], and asked counsel of God, and said, Which of us shall take the lead to battle against the Benjamites? And the Lord said, Judah shall go up first.

19Then the Israelites rose in the morning, and encamped against Gibeah.

20And the men of Israel went out to battle against Benjamin, and set the battle in array against them at Gibeah.

21The Benjamites came forth out of Gibeah, and felled to the ground that day 22,000 men of the Israelites.

22But the people, the men of Israel, took courage *and* strengthened themselves and again set their battle line in the same place where they formed it the first day.

23And the Israelites went up and wept before the Lord until evening; and asked of the Lord, Shall we go up again to battle against our brethren the Benjamites? And the Lord said, Go up against them.

24So the Israelites came near against the Benjamites the second day.

25And Benjamin went forth out of Gibeah against them the second day and felled to the ground the Israelites again, 18,000 men; all of whom were swordsmen.

26Then all the Israelites, the whole army, went up, and came to the house of God [Bethel], and wept, and sat there before the Lord, and fasted that day until evening, and offered burnt offerings, and peace offerings before the Lord.

27And the Israelites inquired of the Lord (for the ark of the covenant of God was there [at Bethel] in those days,

28And Phinehas son of Eleazar, son of Aaron, ministered before it in those days), saying, Shall we yet again go out to battle against our brethren the Benjamites, or shall we quit? And the Lord said, Go up; for tomorrow I will deliver them into your hand.

29So Israel set men in ambush round about Gibeah.

30And the Israelites went up against the Benjamites on the third day, and set themselves in array against Gibeah, as at other times.

31And the Benjamites went out against their army, and were drawn away from the city; and they began to smite and kill some of the people, as at other times, in the highways, one of which goes up to Bethel and the other to Gibeah, in the open country, about thirty men of Israel.

32And the Benjamites said, They are routed before us, as at first. But the Israelites said, Let us flee, and draw them from the city to the highways.

33And all the men of Israel rose out of their place, and set themselves in array at Baal-tamar; and the men of Israel in ambush rushed out of their place in the meadow of Geba.

## New American Standard

12¶ Then the tribes of Israel sent men through the entire tribe
of Benjamin, saying, "What is this wickedness that has taken place
among you?
13"Now then, deliver up the men, the [a]worthless fellows in
Gibeah, that we may put them to death and remove *this* wickedness from Israel." But the sons of Benjamin would not listen to the
voice of their brothers, the sons of Israel.
14And the sons of Benjamin gathered from the cities to Gibeah,
to go out to battle against the sons of Israel.
15And from the cities on that day the sons of Benjamin were
numbered, 26,000 men who draw the sword, besides the inhabitants of Gibeah who were numbered, 700 choice men.
16Out of all these people 700 choice men were left-handed; each
one could sling a stone at a hair and not miss.
17¶ Then the men of Israel besides Benjamin were numbered,
400,000 men who draw the sword; all these were men of war.

*Civil War, Benjamin Defeated*

18Now the sons of Israel arose, went up to Bethel, and inquired
of God, and said, "Who shall go up first for us to battle against the
sons of Benjamin?" Then the LORD said, "Judah *shall go up* first."
19¶ So the sons of Israel arose in the morning and camped
against Gibeah.
20And the men of Israel went out to battle against Benjamin,
and the men of Israel arrayed for battle against them at Gibeah.
21Then the sons of Benjamin came out of Gibeah and felled to
the ground on that day 22,000 men of Israel.
22But the people, the men of Israel, encouraged themselves and
arrayed for battle again in the place where they had arrayed themselves the first day.
23And the sons of Israel went up and wept before the LORD until
evening, and inquired of the LORD, saying, "Shall we again draw
near for battle against the sons of my brother Benjamin?" And the
LORD said, "Go up against him."
24¶ Then the sons of Israel came against the sons of Benjamin
the second day.
25And Benjamin went out against them from Gibeah the second
day and felled to the ground again 18,000 men of the sons of Israel;
all these drew the sword.
26Then all the sons of Israel and all the people went up and came
to Bethel and wept; thus they remained there before the LORD and
fasted that day until evening. And they offered burnt offerings and
peace offerings before the LORD.
27And the sons of Israel inquired of the LORD (for the ark of the
covenant of God *was* there in those days,
28and Phinehas the son of Eleazar, Aaron's son, stood before it
to *minister* in those days), saying, "Shall I yet again go out to battle
against the sons of my brother Benjamin, or shall I cease?" And
the LORD said, "Go up, for tomorrow I will deliver them into your
hand."
29¶ So Israel set men in ambush around Gibeah.
30And the sons of Israel went up against the sons of Benjamin
on the third day and arrayed themselves against Gibeah, as at
other times.
31And the sons of Benjamin went out against the people and
were drawn away from the city, and they began to strike and kill
some of the people, as at other times, on the highways, one of
which goes up to Bethel and the other to Gibeah, *and* in the field,
about thirty men of Israel.
32And the sons of Benjamin said, "They are struck down before
us, as at the first." But the sons of Israel said, "Let us flee that we
may draw them away from the city to the highways."
33Then all the men of Israel arose from their place and arrayed
themselves at Baal-tamar; and the men of Israel in ambush broke
out of their place, even out of Maareh-geba.

NAS [a] Lit., *sons of Belial*

## New International

12The tribes of Israel sent men throughout the tribe of Benjamin,
saying, "What about this awful crime that was committed among
you? 13Now surrender those wicked men of Gibeah so that we may
put them to death and purge the evil from Israel."
But the Benjamites would not listen to their fellow Israelites.
14From their towns they came together at Gibeah to fight against
the Israelites. 15At once the Benjamites mobilized twenty-six thousand swordsmen from their towns, in addition to seven hundred
chosen men from those living in Gibeah. 16Among all these soldiers there were seven hundred chosen men who were left-handed, each of whom could sling a stone at a hair and not miss.
17Israel, apart from Benjamin, mustered four hundred thousand swordsmen, all of them fighting men.
18The Israelites went up to Bethel[b] and inquired of God. They
said, "Who of us shall go first to fight against the Benjamites?"
The LORD replied, "Judah shall go first."
19The next morning the Israelites got up and pitched camp near
Gibeah. 20The men of Israel went out to fight the Benjamites and
took up battle positions against them at Gibeah. 21The Benjamites
came out of Gibeah and cut down twenty-two thousand Israelites
on the battlefield that day. 22But the men of Israel encouraged one
another and again took up their positions where they had stationed themselves the first day. 23The Israelites went up and wept
before the LORD until evening, and they inquired of the LORD.
They said, "Shall we go up again to battle against the Benjamites,
our brothers?"
The LORD answered, "Go up against them."
24Then the Israelites drew near to Benjamin the second day.
25This time, when the Benjamites came out from Gibeah to oppose
them, they cut down another eighteen thousand Israelites, all of
them armed with swords.
26Then the Israelites, all the people, went up to Bethel, and
there they sat weeping before the LORD. They fasted that day until
evening and presented burnt offerings and fellowship offerings[c]
to the LORD. 27And the Israelites inquired of the LORD. (In those
days the ark of the covenant of God was there, 28with Phinehas
son of Eleazar, the son of Aaron, ministering before it.) They
asked, "Shall we go up again to battle with Benjamin our brother,
or not?"
The LORD responded, "Go, for tomorrow I will give them into
your hands."
29Then Israel set an ambush around Gibeah. 30They went up
against the Benjamites on the third day and took up positions
against Gibeah as they had done before. 31The Benjamites came
out to meet them and were drawn away from the city. They began
to inflict casualties on the Israelites as before, so that about thirty
men fell in the open field and on the roads—the one leading to
Bethel and the other to Gibeah.
32While the Benjamites were saying, "We are defeating them as
before," the Israelites were saying, "Let's retreat and draw them
away from the city to the roads."
33All the men of Israel moved from their places and took up
positions at Baal Tamar, and the Israelite ambush charged out of
its place on the west[d] of Gibeah.[e] 34Then ten thousand of Israel's

NIV [b] *18* Or *to the house of God;* also in verse 26 [c] *26* Traditionally *peace offerings* [d] *33* Some Septuagint manuscripts and Vulgate; the meaning of the Hebrew for this word is uncertain. [e] *33* Hebrew *Geba,* a variant of *Gibeah*

## King James

34And there came against Gibeah ten thousand chosen men out of all Israel, and the battle was sore: but they knew not that evil *was* near them.

35And the LORD smote Benjamin before Israel: and the children of Israel destroyed of the Benjamites that day twenty and five thousand and an hundred men: all these drew the sword.

36So the children of Benjamin saw that they were smitten: for the men of Israel gave place to the Benjamites, because they trusted unto the liers in wait which they had set beside Gibeah.

37And the liers in wait hasted, and rushed upon Gibeah; and the liers in wait drew *themselves* along, and smote all the city with the edge of the sword.

38Now there was an appointed sign between the men of Israel and the liers in wait, that they should make a great flame with smoke rise up out of the city.

39And when the men of Israel retired in the battle, Benjamin began to smite *and* kill of the men of Israel about thirty persons: for they said, Surely they are smitten down before us, as *in* the first battle.

40But when the flame began to arise up out of the city with a pillar of smoke, the Benjamites looked behind them, and, behold, the flame of the city ascended up to heaven.

41And when the men of Israel turned again, the men of Benjamin were amazed: for they saw that evil was come upon them.

42Therefore they turned *their backs* before the men of Israel unto the way of the wilderness; but the battle overtook them; and them which *came* out of the cities they destroyed in the midst of them.

43 *Thus* they inclosed the Benjamites round about, *and* chased them, *and* trode them down with ease over against Gibeah toward the sunrising.

44And there fell of Benjamin eighteen thousand men; all these *were* men of valour.

45And they turned and fled toward the wilderness unto the rock of Rimmon: and they gleaned of them in the highways five thousand men; and pursued hard after them unto Gidom, and slew two thousand men of them.

46So that all which fell that day of Benjamin were twenty and five thousand men that drew the sword; all these *were* men of valour.

47But six hundred men turned and fled to the wilderness unto the rock Rimmon, and abode in the rock Rimmon four months.

48And the men of Israel turned again upon the children of Benjamin, and smote them with the edge of the sword, as well the men of *every* city, as the beast, and all that came to hand: also they set on fire all the cities that they came to.

**21** NOW THE men of Israel had sworn in Mizpeh, saying, There shall not any of us give his daughter unto Benjamin to wife.

2And the people came to the house of God, and abode there till even before God, and lifted up their voices, and wept sore;

3And said, O LORD God of Israel, why is this come to pass in Israel, that there should be today one tribe lacking in Israel?

4And it came to pass on the morrow, that the people rose early, and built there an altar, and offered burnt offerings and peace offerings.

5And the children of Israel said, Who *is there* among all the tribes of Israel that came not up with the congregation unto the LORD? For they had made a great oath concerning him that came not up to the LORD to Mizpeh, saying, He shall surely be put to death.

6And the children of Israel repented them for Benjamin their brother, and said, There is one tribe cut off from Israel this day.

7How shall we do for wives for them that remain, seeing we have sworn by the LORD that we will not give them of our daughters to wives?

## Amplified

34And there came against Gibeah 10,000 chosen men out of all Israel, and the battle was hard; but the Benjamites did not know disaster was close upon them.

35And the Lord overcame Benjamin before Israel; and the Israelites destroyed of the Benjamites that day 25,100 men, all of whom were swordsmen.

36So the Benjamites saw that they were defeated. The men of Israel gave ground to the Benjamites, because they trusted to the men in ambush whom they had set against Gibeah.

37And the men in ambush quickly rushed upon Gibeah; and the liers-in-wait moved out and smote all the city with the sword.

38Now the appointed signal between the men of Israel and the men in ambush was that when they made a great cloud of smoke arise from the city,

39The men of Israel should all turn back in battle. Now Benjamin had begun to smite and kill some of the men of Israel, about thirty persons. They said, Surely they are falling before us, as in the first battle.

40But when the [signal] cloud began to rise out of the city in a pillar of smoke, the Benjamites looked behind them, and behold, the whole of the city went up in smoke to the heavens.

41When the men of Israel turned back again, the men of Benjamin were dismayed, for they saw that disaster had come upon them.

42Therefore they turned their backs before the men of Israel and fled toward the wilderness; but the battle followed close after *and* overtook them; and the inhabitants of the cities destroyed those [Benjamites] who came through them, in their midst.

43They surrounded the Benjamites, pursued them, and overtook *and* trod them down at their resting place as far as opposite Gibeah toward the east.

44And there fell 18,000 men of Benjamin, all of them men of valor.

45And [the Benjamites] turned and fled toward the wilderness to the rock of Rimmon; and Israel picked off on the highways 5,000 men of them; they pursued hard after them to Gidom, and slew 2,000 more of them.

46So that all of Benjamin who fell that day were 25,000 men who drew the sword, all of them men of valor.

47But 600 men turned and fled to the wilderness to the rock Rimmon, and remained at the rock Rimmon four months.

48And the men of Israel turned back against the Benjamites, and smote them with the sword, men and beasts and all that they found. Also they set on fire all the towns to which they came.

**21** NOW THE men of Israel had sworn at Mizpah, None of us shall give his daughter in marriage to Benjamin.

2And the Israelites came to the house of God [Bethel] and sat there until evening before God, and lifted up their voices, and wept bitterly. [20:27.]

3And said, O Lord, the God of Israel, why has this come to pass in Israel, that there should be today one tribe lacking in Israel?

4And next morning the people rose early, and built there an altar, and offered burnt offerings and peace offerings.

5And the Israelites said, Which among all the tribes of Israel did not come up with the assembly to the Lord? For they had taken a great oath concerning him who did not come up to the Lord to Mizpah, saying, He shall surely die.

6And the Israelites changed their purpose [and had compassion] for the Benjamites their kinsmen, and said, There is one tribe cut off from Israel today.

7What shall we do for wives for those who are left, seeing we have sworn by the Lord that we will not give them our daughters as wives?

## New American Standard

34When ten thousand choice men from all Israel came against
Gibeah, the battle became fierce; but Benjamin did not know that
disaster was close to them.
35And the LORD struck Benjamin before Israel, so that the sons
of Israel destroyed 25,100 men of Benjamin that day, all who draw
the sword.
36¶ So the sons of Benjamin saw that they were defeated. When
the men of Israel gave ground to Benjamin because they relied on
the men in ambush whom they had set against Gibeah,
37the men in ambush hurried and rushed against Gibeah; the
men in ambush also deployed and struck all the city with the edge
of the sword.
38Now the appointed sign between the men of Israel and the
men in ambush was that they should make a great cloud of smoke
rise from the city.
39Then the men of Israel turned in the battle, and Benjamin
began to strike and kill about thirty men of Israel, for they said,
"Surely they are defeated before us, as in the first battle."
40But when the cloud began to rise from the city in a column
of smoke, Benjamin looked behind them; and behold, the whole
city was going up *in smoke* to heaven.
41Then the men of Israel turned, and the men of Benjamin were
terrified; for they saw that disaster was close to them.
42Therefore, they turned their backs before the men of Israel
toward the direction of the wilderness, but the battle overtook
them while those who came out of the cities destroyed them in the
midst of them.
43They surrounded Benjamin, pursued them without rest *and*
trod them down opposite Gibeah toward the east.
44Thus 18,000 men of Benjamin fell; all these were valiant warriors.
45The rest turned and fled toward the wilderness to the rock of
Rimmon, but they caught 5,000 of them on the highways and
overtook them at Gidom and killed 2,000 of them.
46So all of Benjamin who fell that day were 25,000 men who
draw the sword; all these were valiant warriors.
47But 600 men turned and fled toward the wilderness to the rock
of Rimmon, and they remained at the rock of Rimmon four
months.
48The men of Israel then turned back against the sons of Benjamin and struck them with the edge of the sword, both the entire
city with the cattle and all that they found; they also set on fire all
the cities which they found.

*Mourning Lost Tribe*

21 NOW THE men of Israel had sworn in Mizpah, saying,
"None of us shall give his daughter to Benjamin in marriage."
2So the people came to Bethel and sat there before God until
evening, and lifted up their voices and wept bitterly.
3And they said, "Why, O LORD, God of Israel, has this come
about in Israel, so that one tribe should be *missing* today in Israel?"
4And it came about the next day that the people arose early and
built an altar there, and offered burnt offerings and peace offerings.
5¶ Then the sons of Israel said, "Who is there among all the
tribes of Israel who did not come up in the assembly to the LORD?"
For they had taken a great oath concerning him who did not come
up to the LORD at Mizpah, saying, "He shall surely be put to
death."
6And the sons of Israel were sorry for their brother Benjamin
and said, "One tribe is cut off from Israel today.
7"What shall we do for wives for those who are left, since we
have sworn by the LORD not to give them any of our daughters in
marriage?"

## New International

finest men made a frontal attack on Gibeah. The fighting was so
heavy that the Benjamites did not realize how near disaster was.
35The LORD defeated Benjamin before Israel, and on that day the
Israelites struck down 25,100 Benjamites, all armed with swords.
36Then the Benjamites saw that they were beaten.
Now the men of Israel had given way before Benjamin, because
they relied on the ambush they had set near Gibeah. 37The men
who had been in ambush made a sudden dash into Gibeah, spread
out and put the whole city to the sword. 38The men of Israel had
arranged with the ambush that they should send up a great cloud
of smoke from the city, 39and then the men of Israel would turn
in the battle.
The Benjamites had begun to inflict casualties on the men of
Israel (about thirty), and they said, "We are defeating them as in
the first battle." 40But when the column of smoke began to rise
from the city, the Benjamites turned and saw the smoke of the
whole city going up into the sky. 41Then the men of Israel turned
on them, and the men of Benjamin were terrified, because they
realized that disaster had come upon them. 42So they fled before
the Israelites in the direction of the desert, but they could not
escape the battle. And the men of Israel who came out of the towns
cut them down there. 43They surrounded the Benjamites, chased
them and easily[a] overran them in the vicinity of Gibeah on the
east. 44Eighteen thousand Benjamites fell, all of them valiant fighters. 45As they turned and fled toward the desert to the rock of
Rimmon, the Israelites cut down five thousand men along the
roads. They kept pressing after the Benjamites as far as Gidom and
struck down two thousand more.
46On that day twenty-five thousand Benjamite swordsmen fell,
all of them valiant fighters. 47But six hundred men turned and fled
into the desert to the rock of Rimmon, where they stayed four
months. 48The men of Israel went back to Benjamin and put all the
towns to the sword, including the animals and everything else
they found. All the towns they came across they set on fire.

*Wives for the Benjamites*

21 THE MEN of Israel had taken an oath at Mizpah: "Not one
of us will give his daughter in marriage to a Benjamite."
2The people went to Bethel,[b] where they sat before God until
evening, raising their voices and weeping bitterly. 3"O LORD, the
God of Israel," they cried, "why has this happened to Israel? Why
should one tribe be missing from Israel today?"
4Early the next day the people built an altar and presented burnt
offerings and fellowship offerings.[c]
5Then the Israelites asked, "Who from all the tribes of Israel has
failed to assemble before the LORD?" For they had taken a solemn
oath that anyone who failed to assemble before the LORD at Mizpah
should certainly be put to death.
6Now the Israelites grieved for their brothers, the Benjamites.
"Today one tribe is cut off from Israel," they said. 7"How can we
provide wives for those who are left, since we have taken an oath
by the LORD not to give them any of our daughters in marriage?"

NIV [a] 43 The meaning of the Hebrew for this word is uncertain. [b] 2 Or *to the house of God* [c] 4 Traditionally *peace offerings*

## King James

8¶ And they said, What one *is there* of the tribes of Israel that came not up to Mizpeh to the LORD? And, behold, there came none to the camp from Jabesh-gilead to the assembly.

9For the people were numbered, and, behold, *there were* none of the inhabitants of Jabesh-gilead there.

10And the congregation sent thither twelve thousand men of the valiantest, and commanded them, saying, Go and smite the inhabitants of Jabesh-gilead with the edge of the sword, with the women and the children.

11And this *is* the thing that ye shall do, Ye shall utterly destroy every male, and every woman that hath lain by man.

12And they found among the inhabitants of Jabesh-gilead four hundred young virgins, that had known no man by lying with any male: and they brought them unto the camp to Shiloh, which *is* in the land of Canaan.

13And the whole congregation sent *some* to speak to the children of Benjamin that *were* in the rock Rimmon, and to call peaceably unto them.

14And Benjamin came again at that time; and they gave them wives which they had saved alive of the women of Jabesh-gilead: and yet so they sufficed them not.

15And the people repented them for Benjamin, because that the LORD had made a breach in the tribes of Israel.

16¶ Then the elders of the congregation said, How shall we do for wives for them that remain, seeing the women are destroyed out of Benjamin?

17And they said, *There must be* an inheritance for them that be escaped of Benjamin, that a tribe be not destroyed out of Israel.

18Howbeit we may not give them wives of our daughters: for the children of Israel have sworn, saying, Cursed *be* he that giveth a wife to Benjamin.

19Then they said, Behold, *there is* a feast of the LORD in Shiloh yearly *in a place* which *is* on the north side of Beth-el, on the east side of the highway that goeth up from Beth-el to Shechem, and on the south of Lebonah.

20Therefore they commanded the children of Benjamin, saying, Go and lie in wait in the vineyards;

21And see, and, behold, if the daughters of Shiloh come out to dance in dances, then come ye out of the vineyards, and catch you every man his wife of the daughters of Shiloh, and go to the land of Benjamin.

22And it shall be, when their fathers or their brethren come unto us to complain, that we will say unto them, Be favourable unto them for our sakes: because we reserved not to each man his wife in the war: for ye did not give unto them at this time, *that* ye should be guilty.

23And the children of Benjamin did so, and took *them* wives, according to their number, of them that danced, whom they caught: and they went and returned unto their inheritance, and repaired the cities, and dwelt in them.

24And the children of Israel departed thence at that time, every man to his tribe and to his family, and they went out from thence every man to his inheritance.

25In those days *there was* no king in Israel: every man did *that which was* right in his own eyes.

## Amplified

8And they said, What one is there of the tribes of Israel that did not come up to Mizpah to the Lord? And behold, no one had come to the camp from Jabesh-gilead, to the assembly.

9For when the people were mustered, behold, not one of the citizens of Jabesh-gilead was there.

10And the congregation sent there 12,000 of the bravest men, saying, Go and smite the inhabitants of Jabesh-gilead with the sword, also the women and the little ones.

11And this is what you shall do; utterly destroy every male, and every woman who is not a virgin.

12And they found among the inhabitants of Jabesh-gilead 400 young virgins, who had known no man by lying with him; and they brought them to the camp at Shiloh, which is in the land of Canaan.

13And the whole congregation sent word to the Benjamites who were at the rock of Rimmon, and invited them to be friendly with them.

14And Benjamin returned at that time; and they gave them the women whom they had saved alive of the women of Jabesh-gilead; and yet there were not enough for them.

15And the people had compassion on Benjamin, because the Lord had made a breach in the tribes of Israel.

16Then the elders of the congregation said, What shall we do for wives for those who are left, since the women of Benjamin are destroyed?

17And they said, There must be an inheritance for the survivors of Benjamin, so a tribe shall not be wiped out of Israel.

18But we cannot give them wives of our daughters, for the Israelites have sworn, Cursed be he who gives a wife to Benjamin.

19So they said, Behold, there is the yearly feast of the Lord at Shiloh, which is north of Bethel, on the east of the highway that goes up from Bethel to Shechem, and south of Lebonah.

20So they commanded the Benjamites, Go and lie in wait in the vineyards,

21And watch; if the daughters of Shiloh come out to dance in the dances, then come out of the vineyards, and catch every man his wife from the daughters of Shiloh, and go to the land of Benjamin.

22And when their fathers or their brothers come to us to complain, we will say to them, Grant them graciously unto us, because we did not reserve a wife for each of them in battle, neither did you give wives to them, for that would have made you guilty [of breaking your oath].

23And the Benjamites did so, and took wives, according to their number, from the dancers whom they carried off; then they went and returned to their inheritance, and repaired the towns, and dwelt in them.

24And the Israelites left there then, every man to his tribe and family, and they went out from there every man to his inheritance.

25In those days [a]there was no king in Israel; every man did what was right in his own eyes.

**AMP** [a] This statement is made three times in these latter chapters. All was well while Joshua and those who assisted him lived, then gradually came disorder. "What is the meaning of this? . . . There was no king [or counselor] in Israel because in Israel there was no God. The Lord is King. You cannot have a [true] king if you have not a God. There was no nominal renunciation of God, no public and blatant atheism, no boastful impiety; there was a deadlier heresy—namely, keeping God as a sign, but paying no tribute to Him as a King, worshiping Him possibly in outward form, but knowing nothing of the subduing and directing power of godliness. That is more to be dreaded than any intellectual difficulty of a theological kind . . . Dead consciences, prayerless prayers, mechanical formalities—these are the impediments which overturn . . . the chariots of progress. This was the case in Israel. Where God is, the king is not [merely] a man with a crown on, but a king in the sense of kingliness, sovereignty, authority, rule—the spirit of obligation and responsibility . . . You find the right monarch where you find the right God" (Joseph Parker, quoted in *Gray and Adams' Commentary,* condensed).

## New American Standard

*Provision for Their Survival*

8¶ And they said, "What one is there of the tribes of Israel who
did not come up to the LORD at Mizpah?" And behold, no one had
come to the camp from Jabesh-gilead to the assembly.
9For when the people were numbered, behold, not one of the
inhabitants of Jabesh-gilead was there.
10And the congregation sent 12,000 of the valiant warriors
there, and commanded them, saying, "Go and strike the inhabitants of Jabesh-gilead with the edge of the sword, with the women
and the little ones.
11"And this is the thing that you shall do: you shall utterly
destroy every man and every woman who has lain with a man."
12And they found among the inhabitants of Jabesh-gilead 400
young virgins who had not known a man by lying with him; and
they brought them to the camp at Shiloh, which is in the land of
Canaan.
13¶ Then the whole congregation sent *word* and spoke to the
sons of Benjamin who were at the rock of Rimmon, and proclaimed
peace to them.
14And Benjamin returned at that time, and they gave them the
women whom they had kept alive from the women of Jabesh-
gilead; yet they were not enough for them.
15And the people were sorry for Benjamin because the LORD
had made a breach in the tribes of Israel.
16¶ Then the elders of the congregation said, "What shall we do
for wives for those who are left, since the women are destroyed
out of Benjamin?"
17And they said, "*There must be* an inheritance for the survivors
of Benjamin, that a tribe may not be blotted out from Israel.
18"But we cannot give them wives of our daughters." For the
sons of Israel had sworn, saying, "Cursed is he who gives a wife
to Benjamin."
19¶ So they said, "Behold, there is a feast of the LORD from year
to year in Shiloh, which is on the north side of Bethel, on the east
side of the highway that goes up from Bethel to Shechem, and on
the south side of Lebonah."
20And they commanded the sons of Benjamin, saying, "Go and
lie in wait in the vineyards,
21and watch; and behold, if the daughters of Shiloh come out
to take part in the dances, then you shall come out of the vineyards
and each of you shall catch his wife from the daughters of Shiloh,
and go to the land of Benjamin.
22"And it shall come about, when their fathers or their brothers
come to complain to us, that we shall say to them, 'Give them to
us voluntarily, because we did not take for each man *of Benjamin*
a wife in battle, nor did you give *them* to them, *else* you would now
be guilty.'"
23And the sons of Benjamin did so, and took wives according
to their number from those who danced, whom they carried away.
And they went and returned to their inheritance, and rebuilt the
cities and lived in them.
24And the sons of Israel departed from there at that time, every
man to his tribe and family, and each one of them went out from
there to his inheritance.
25¶ In those days there was no king in Israel; everyone did what
was right in his own eyes.

## New International

8Then they asked, "Which one of the tribes of Israel failed to
assemble before the LORD at Mizpah?" They discovered that no
one from Jabesh Gilead had come to the camp for the assembly.
9For when they counted the people, they found that none of the
people of Jabesh Gilead were there.
10So the assembly sent twelve thousand fighting men with
instructions to go to Jabesh Gilead and put to the sword those
living there, including the women and children. 11"This is what
you are to do," they said. "Kill every male and every woman who
is not a virgin." 12They found among the people living in Jabesh
Gilead four hundred young women who had never slept with a
man, and they took them to the camp at Shiloh in Canaan.
13Then the whole assembly sent an offer of peace to the Benjamites at the rock of Rimmon. 14So the Benjamites returned at that
time and were given the women of Jabesh Gilead who had been
spared. But there were not enough for all of them.
15The people grieved for Benjamin, because the LORD had made
a gap in the tribes of Israel. 16And the elders of the assembly said,
"With the women of Benjamin destroyed, how shall we provide
wives for the men who are left? 17The Benjamite survivors must
have heirs," they said, "so that a tribe of Israel will not be wiped
out. 18We can't give them our daughters as wives, since we Israelites have taken this oath: 'Cursed be anyone who gives a wife to
a Benjamite.' 19But look, there is the annual festival of the LORD
in Shiloh, to the north of Bethel, and east of the road that goes from
Bethel to Shechem, and to the south of Lebonah."
20So they instructed the Benjamites, saying, "Go and hide in the
vineyards 21and watch. When the girls of Shiloh come out to join
in the dancing, then rush from the vineyards and each of you seize
a wife from the girls of Shiloh and go to the land of Benjamin.
22When their fathers or brothers complain to us, we will say to
them, 'Do us a kindness by helping them, because we did not get
wives for them during the war, and you are innocent, since you
did not give your daughters to them.'"
23So that is what the Benjamites did. While the girls were dancing, each man caught one and carried her off to be his wife. Then
they returned to their inheritance and rebuilt the towns and settled
in them.
24At that time the Israelites left that place and went home to
their tribes and clans, each to his own inheritance.
25In those days Israel had no king; everyone did as he saw fit.

## King James

THE BOOK OF

# Ruth

**1** NOW IT came to pass in the days when the judges ruled, that there was a famine in the land. And a certain man of Bethlehem-judah went to sojourn in the country of Moab, he, and his wife, and his two sons.

2And the name of the man *was* Elimelech, and the name of his wife Naomi, and the name of his two sons Mahlon and Chilion, Ephrathites of Bethlehem-judah. And they came into the country of Moab, and continued there.

3And Elimelech Naomi's husband died; and she was left, and her two sons.

4And they took them wives of the women of Moab; the name of the one *was* Orpah, and the name of the other Ruth: and they dwelled there about ten years.

5And Mahlon and Chilion died also both of them; and the woman was left of her two sons and her husband.

6¶ Then she arose with her daughters-in-law, that she might return from the country of Moab: for she had heard in the country of Moab how that the LORD had visited his people in giving them bread.

7Wherefore she went forth out of the place where she was, and her two daughters-in-law with her; and they went on the way to return unto the land of Judah.

8And Naomi said unto her two daughters-in-law, Go, return each to her mother's house: the LORD deal kindly with you, as ye have dealt with the dead, and with me.

9The LORD grant you that ye may find rest, each *of you* in the house of her husband. Then she kissed them; and they lifted up their voice, and wept.

10And they said unto her, Surely we will return with thee unto thy people.

11And Naomi said, Turn again, my daughters: why will ye go with me? *are* there yet *any more* sons in my womb, that they may be your husbands?

12Turn again, my daughters, go *your way;* for I am too old to have an husband. If I should say, I have hope, *if* I should have an husband also tonight, and should also bear sons;

13Would ye tarry for them till they were grown? would ye stay for them from having husbands? nay, my daughters; for it grieveth me much for your sakes that the hand of the LORD is gone out against me.

14And they lifted up their voice, and wept again: and Orpah kissed her mother-in-law; but Ruth clave unto her.

15And she said, Behold, thy sister-in-law is gone back unto her people, and unto her gods: return thou after thy sister-in-law.

## Amplified

THE BOOK OF

# Ruth

**1** IN THE days when the judges ruled there was a famine in the land. And a certain man of Bethlehem of Judah went to sojourn in the country of Moab, he, his wife, and his two sons.

2The man's name was Elimelech, and his wife's name was Naomi, and his two sons were named Mahlon (invalid) and Chilion (pining); they were Ephrathites from Bethlehem of Judah. They went to the country of Moab, and continued there.

3But Elimelech, Naomi's husband, died, and she was left, and her two sons.

4And they took wives of the women of Moab; the name of one was Orpah and the name of the other Ruth. They dwelt there about ten years;

5And Mahlon and Chilion died *also,* both of them, so the woman was bereft of her two sons and her husband.

6Then she arose with her daughters-in-law, to return from the country of Moab; for she had heard in Moab how the Lord had visited His people in giving them food.

7So she left the place where she was, her two daughters-in-law with her, and they started on the way back to Judah.

8But Naomi said to her two daughters-in-law, Go, return each of you to her mother's house. May the Lord deal kindly with you, as you have dealt with the dead and with me.

9The Lord grant that you may find a home *and* rest, each in the house of her husband! Then she kissed them, and they wept aloud.

10And they said to her, No, we will return with you to your people.

11But Naomi said, Turn back, my daughters, why will you go with me? Have I yet sons in my womb that may become your husbands?

12Turn back, my daughters, go; for I am too old to have a husband. If I should say I have hope, even if I should have a husband tonight and should bear sons,

13Would you therefore wait till they were grown? Would you therefore refrain from marrying? No, my daughters; it is far more bitter for me than for you that the hand of the Lord is gone out against me.

14Then they wept aloud again; and Orpah [a]kissed her mother-in-law [goodbye], but Ruth clung to her.

15And Naomi said, See, your sister-in-law has gone back to her people and to her god; return after your sister-in-law.

**AMP** [a] "How many part with Christ at this cross-way! Like Orpah they go a furlong or two with Christ, till He goes to take them off from their worldly hopes, and bids them prepare for hardship, and then they fairly kiss and leave Him" (Gurnall, quoted in *Gray and Adams' Commentary*).

## New American Standard

# Ruth

*Naomi Widowed*

1 NOW IT came about in the days when the judges governed, that there was a famine in the land. And a certain man of Bethlehem in Judah went to sojourn in the land of Moab with his wife and his two sons.

2 And the name of the man *was* Elimelech, and the name of his wife, Naomi; and the names of his two sons *were* Mahlon and Chilion, Ephrathites of Bethlehem in Judah. Now they entered the land of Moab and remained there.

3 Then Elimelech, Naomi's husband, died; and she was left with her two sons.

4 And they took for themselves Moabite women *as* wives; the name of the one was Orpah and the name of the other Ruth. And they lived there about ten years.

5 Then both Mahlon and Chilion also died; and the woman was bereft of her two children and her husband.

6¶ Then she arose with her daughters-in-law that she might return from the land of Moab, for she had heard in the land of Moab that the LORD had visited His people in giving them food.

7 So she departed from the place where she was, and her two daughters-in-law with her; and they went on the way to return to the land of Judah.

8 And Naomi said to her two daughters-in-law, "Go, return each of you to her mother's house. May the LORD deal kindly with you as you have dealt with the dead and with me.

9 "May the LORD grant that you may find rest, each in the house of her husband." Then she kissed them, and they lifted up their voices and wept.

10 And they said to her, "*No,* but we will surely return with you to your people."

11 But Naomi said, "Return, my daughters. Why should you go with me? Have I yet sons in my womb, that they may be your husbands?

12 "Return, my daughters! Go, for I am too old to have a husband. If I said I have hope, if I should even have a husband tonight and also bear sons,

13 would you therefore wait until they were grown? Would you therefore refrain from marrying? No, my daughters; for it is harder for me than for you, for the hand of the LORD has gone forth against me."

*Ruth's Loyalty*

14 And they lifted up their voices and wept again; and Orpah kissed her mother-in-law, but Ruth clung to her.

15¶ Then she said, "Behold, your sister-in-law has gone back to her people and her gods; return after your sister-in-law."

## New International

# Ruth

*Naomi and Ruth*

1 IN THE days when the judges ruled,[b] there was a famine in
the land, and a man from Bethlehem in Judah, together with
his wife and two sons, went to live for a while in the country of
Moab. 2 The man's name was Elimelech, his wife's name Naomi,
and the names of his two sons were Mahlon and Kilion. They were
Ephrathites from Bethlehem, Judah. And they went to Moab and
lived there.
3 Now Elimelech, Naomi's husband, died, and she was left with
her two sons. 4 They married Moabite women, one named Orpah
and the other Ruth. After they had lived there about ten years,
5 both Mahlon and Kilion also died, and Naomi was left without
her two sons and her husband.
6 When she heard in Moab that the LORD had come to the aid
of his people by providing food for them, Naomi and her
daughters-in-law prepared to return home from there. 7 With her
two daughters-in-law she left the place where she had been living
and set out on the road that would take them back to the land of
Judah.
8 Then Naomi said to her two daughters-in-law, "Go back, each
of you, to your mother's home. May the LORD show kindness to
you, as you have shown to your dead and to me. 9 May the LORD
grant that each of you will find rest in the home of another husband."
Then she kissed them and they wept aloud 10 and said to her,
"We will go back with you to your people."
11 But Naomi said, "Return home, my daughters. Why would
you come with me? Am I going to have any more sons, who could
become your husbands? 12 Return home, my daughters; I am too
old to have another husband. Even if I thought there was still hope
for me—even if I had a husband tonight and then gave birth to
sons— 13 would you wait until they grew up? Would you remain
unmarried for them? No, my daughters. It is more bitter for me
than for you, because the LORD's hand has gone out against me!"
14 At this they wept again. Then Orpah kissed her mother-in-law good-by, but Ruth clung to her.
15 "Look," said Naomi, "your sister-in-law is going back to her
people and her gods. Go back with her."

NIV [b] *1* Traditionally *judged*

## King James

16And Ruth said, Entreat me not to leave thee, *or* to return from
following after thee: for whither thou goest, I will go; and where
thou lodgest, I will lodge: thy people *shall be* my people, and thy
God my God:
17Where thou diest, will I die, and there will I be buried: the
LORD do so to me, and more also, *if aught* but death part thee and
me.
18When she saw that she was stedfastly minded to go with her,
then she left speaking unto her.
19¶ So they two went until they came to Bethlehem. And it came
to pass, when they were come to Bethlehem, that all the city was
moved about them, and they said, *Is* this Naomi?
20And she said unto them, Call me not Naomi, call me Mara:
for the Almighty hath dealt very bitterly with me.
21I went out full, and the LORD hath brought me home again
empty: why *then* call ye me Naomi, seeing the LORD hath testified
against me, and the Almighty hath afflicted me?
22So Naomi returned, and Ruth the Moabitess, her daughter-in-
law, with her, which returned out of the country of Moab: and they
came to Bethlehem in the beginning of barley harvest.

2 AND NAOMI had a kinsman of her husband's, a mighty man
of wealth, of the family of Elimelech; and his name *was* Boaz.
2And Ruth the Moabitess said unto Naomi, Let me now go to
the field, and glean ears of corn after *him* in whose sight I shall find
grace. And she said unto her, Go, my daughter.
3And she went, and came, and gleaned in the field after the
reapers: and her hap was to light on a part of the field *belonging*
unto Boaz, who *was* of the kindred of Elimelech.
4¶ And, behold, Boaz came from Bethlehem, and said unto the
reapers, The LORD *be* with you. And they answered him, The LORD
bless thee.
5Then said Boaz unto his servant that was set over the reapers,
Whose damsel *is* this?
6And the servant that was set over the reapers answered and
said, It *is* the Moabitish damsel that came back with Naomi out of
the country of Moab:
7And she said, I pray you, let me glean and gather after the
reapers among the sheaves: so she came, and hath continued even
from the morning until now, that she tarried a little in the house.
8Then said Boaz unto Ruth, Hearest thou not, my daughter? Go
not to glean in another field, neither go from hence, but abide here
fast by my maidens:
9 *Let* thine eyes *be* on the field that they do reap, and go thou
after them: have I not charged the young men that they shall not
touch thee? and when thou art athirst, go unto the vessels, and
drink of *that* which the young men have drawn.
10Then she fell on her face, and bowed herself to the ground,
and said unto him, Why have I found grace in thine eyes, that thou
shouldest take knowledge of me, seeing I *am* a stranger?
11And Boaz answered and said unto her, It hath fully been
shown me, all that thou hast done unto thy mother-in-law since
the death of thine husband: and *how* thou hast left thy father and
thy mother, and the land of thy nativity, and art come unto a
people which thou knewest not heretofore.

## Amplified

16And Ruth said, Urge me not to leave you, or to return from
following you; for where you go, I will go; and where you lodge,
I will lodge; [a]your people shall be my people, and your God my
God;
17Where you die, I will die, and there will I be buried. The Lord
do so to me, and more also, if anything but death parts me from
you.
18When Naomi saw that Ruth was determined to go with her,
she said no more.
19So they two went on until they came to Bethlehem. And when
they arrived in Bethlehem, the whole town was stirred about
them, and said, Is this Naomi?
20And she said to them, Call me not Naomi [pleasant], call me
Mara [bitter]; for the Almighty has dealt very bitterly with me.
21I went out full, and the Lord has brought me home again
empty; why call me Naomi, since the Lord has testified against me,
and the Almighty has afflicted me?
22So Naomi returned, and Ruth the Moabitess her daughter-in-
law with her, returned from the country of Moab; and they came
to Bethlehem in the beginning of barley harvest.

2 NOW NAOMI had a kinsman of her husband's, a man of
wealth, of the family of Elimelech, whose name was Boaz.
2And Ruth the Moabitess said to Naomi, Let me go to the field,
and glean among the ears of grain after him in whose sight I shall
find favor. Naomi said to her, Go, my daughter.
3And [Ruth] went and gleaned in a field after the reapers; and
she happened to stop at the part of the field belonging to Boaz,
who was of the family of Elimelech.
4And behold, Boaz came from Bethlehem, and said to the reapers, The Lord be with you! And they answered him, The Lord bless
you!
5Then Boaz said to his servant who was set over the reapers,
Whose maiden is this?
6And the servant set over the reapers answered, It is the Moabitish girl who came back with Naomi from the country of Moab;
7And she said, I pray you, let me glean and gather after the
reapers among the sheaves. So she came, and has continued from
early morning until now, except when she rested a little in the
house.
8Then Boaz said to Ruth, Listen, my daughter, do not go to
glean in another field, or leave this one, but stay here close by my
maidens.
9Watch which field they reap, and follow them. Have I not
charged the young men not to molest you? And when you are
thirsty, go to the vessels and drink what the young men have
drawn.
10Then she fell on her face, bowing to the ground, and said to
him, Why have I found favor in your eyes, that you should notice
me, when I am a foreigner?
11And Boaz said to her, I have been made fully aware of all you
have done for your mother-in-law since the death of your husband; and how you have left your father and mother, and the land
of your birth and have come to a people unknown to you before.

**AMP** [a] "Ruth is a prophecy, than which none could be more beautiful and engaging, of the entrance of the heathen world into the kingdom of God. She comes forth out of Moab, an idolatrous people full of wantonness and sin, and is herself so tender and pure. In a land where dissolute sensuality formed one of the elements of idol worship, a woman appears, as wife and daughter, chaste as the rose of spring and unsurpassed in these relations by any other [human] character in Holy Writ. . . . Ruth's confession of God and His people originated in the home of her married life. It sprang from the love with which she was permitted to embrace Israelites . . . The conduct of one Israelitish woman [Naomi] in a foreign land, was able to call forth a love and a confession of God like that of Ruth . . . Ruth loves a woman, and is thereby led to the God whom that woman confesses" *(Lange's Commentary).*

## New American Standard

16 But Ruth said, "Do not urge me to leave you *or* turn back from
following you; for where you go, I will go, and where you lodge,
I will lodge. Your people *shall be* my people, and your God, my
God.
17 "Where you die, I will die, and there I will be buried. Thus
may the LORD do to me, and worse, if *anything but* death parts you
and me."
18 When she saw that she was determined to go with her, she
said no more to her.
19 ¶ So they both went until they came to Bethlehem. And it
came about when they had come to Bethlehem, that all the city was
stirred because of them, and the women said, "Is this Naomi?"
20 And she said to them, "Do not call me [b]Naomi; call me
[c]Mara, for the Almighty has dealt very bitterly with me.
21 "I went out full, but the LORD has brought me back empty.
Why do you call me Naomi, since the LORD has witnessed against
me and the Almighty has afflicted me?"
22 ¶ So Naomi returned, and with her Ruth the Moabitess, her
daughter-in-law, who returned from the land of Moab. And they
came to Bethlehem at the beginning of barley harvest.

*Ruth Gleans in Boaz' Field*

**2** NOW NAOMI had a kinsman of her husband, a man of great
wealth, of the family of Elimelech, whose name was Boaz.
2 And Ruth the Moabitess said to Naomi, "Please let me go to
the field and glean among the ears of grain after one in whose sight
I may find favor." And she said to her, "Go, my daughter."
3 So she departed and went and gleaned in the field after the
reapers; and she happened to come to the portion of the field
belonging to Boaz, who was of the family of Elimelech.
4 Now behold, Boaz came from Bethlehem and said to the
reapers, "May the LORD be with you." And they said to him, "May
the LORD bless you."
5 Then Boaz said to his servant who was in charge of the reapers, "Whose young woman is this?"
6 And the servant in charge of the reapers answered and said,
"She is the young Moabite woman who returned with Naomi from
the land of Moab.
7 "And she said, 'Please let me glean and gather after the reapers among the sheaves.' Thus she came and has remained from the
morning until now; she has been sitting in the house for a little
while."
8 ¶ Then Boaz said to Ruth, "Listen carefully, my daughter. Do
not go to glean in another field; furthermore, do not go on from
this one, but stay here with my maids.
9 "Let your eyes be on the field which they reap, and go after
them. Indeed, I have commanded the servants not to touch you.
When you are thirsty, go to the water jars and drink from what the
servants draw."
10 Then she fell on her face, bowing to the ground and said to
him, "Why have I found favor in your sight that you should take
notice of me, since I am a foreigner?"
11 And Boaz answered and said to her, "All that you have done
for your mother-in-law after the death of your husband has been
fully reported to me, and how you left your father and your mother
and the land of your birth, and came to a people that you did not
previously know.

NAS [b] I.e., pleasant [c] I.e., bitter

## New International

16 But Ruth replied, "Don't urge me to leave you or to turn back
from you. Where you go I will go, and where you stay I will stay.
Your people will be my people and your God my God. 17 Where
you die I will die, and there I will be buried. May the LORD deal
with me, be it ever so severely, if anything but death separates you
and me." 18 When Naomi realized that Ruth was determined to go
with her, she stopped urging her.
19 So the two women went on until they came to Bethlehem.
When they arrived in Bethlehem, the whole town was stirred
because of them, and the women exclaimed, "Can this be Naomi?"
20 "Don't call me Naomi,[d]" she told them. "Call me Mara,[e]
because the Almighty[f] has made my life very bitter. 21 I went away
full, but the LORD has brought me back empty. Why call me
Naomi? The LORD has afflicted[g] me; the Almighty has brought
misfortune upon me."
22 So Naomi returned from Moab accompanied by Ruth the
Moabitess, her daughter-in-law, arriving in Bethlehem as the barley harvest was beginning.

*Ruth Meets Boaz*

**2** NOW NAOMI had a relative on her husband's side, from the
clan of Elimelech, a man of standing, whose name was Boaz.
2 And Ruth the Moabitess said to Naomi, "Let me go to the fields
and pick up the leftover grain behind anyone in whose eyes I find
favor."
Naomi said to her, "Go ahead, my daughter." 3 So she went out
and began to glean in the fields behind the harvesters. As it turned
out, she found herself working in a field belonging to Boaz, who
was from the clan of Elimelech.
4 Just then Boaz arrived from Bethlehem and greeted the harvesters, "The LORD be with you!"
"The LORD bless you!" they called back.
5 Boaz asked the foreman of his harvesters, "Whose young
woman is that?"
6 The foreman replied, "She is the Moabitess who came back
from Moab with Naomi. 7 She said, 'Please let me glean and gather
among the sheaves behind the harvesters.' She went into the field
and has worked steadily from morning till now, except for a short
rest in the shelter."
8 So Boaz said to Ruth, "My daughter, listen to me. Don't go and
glean in another field and don't go away from here. Stay here with
my servant girls. 9 Watch the field where the men are harvesting,
and follow along after the girls. I have told the men not to touch
you. And whenever you are thirsty, go and get a drink from the
water jars the men have filled."
10 At this, she bowed down with her face to the ground. She
exclaimed, "Why have I found such favor in your eyes that you
notice me—a foreigner?"
11 Boaz replied, "I've been told all about what you have done for
your mother-in-law since the death of your husband—how you
left your father and mother and your homeland and came to live
with a people you did not know before. 12 May the LORD repay you

NIV [d] 20 *Naomi* means *pleasant;* also in verse 21. [e] 20 *Mara* means *bitter.*
[f] 20 Hebrew *Shaddai;* also in verse 21 [g] 21 Or *has testified against*

## King James

12The LORD recompense thy work, and a full reward be given thee of the LORD God of Israel, under whose wings thou art come to trust.

13Then she said, Let me find favour in thy sight, my lord; for that thou hast comforted me, and for that thou hast spoken friendly unto thine handmaid, though I be not like unto one of thine handmaidens.

14And Boaz said unto her, At mealtime come thou hither, and eat of the bread, and dip thy morsel in the vinegar. And she sat beside the reapers: and he reached her parched *corn*, and she did eat, and was sufficed, and left.

15And when she was risen up to glean, Boaz commanded his young men, saying, Let her glean even among the sheaves, and reproach her not:

16And let fall also *some* of the handfuls of purpose for her, and leave *them*, that she may glean *them*, and rebuke her not.

17So she gleaned in the field until even, and beat out that she had gleaned: and it was about an ephah of barley.

18¶ And she took *it* up, and went into the city: and her mother-in-law saw what she had gleaned: and she brought forth, and gave to her that she had reserved after she was sufficed.

19And her mother-in-law said unto her, Where hast thou gleaned today? and where wroughtest thou? blessed be he that did take knowledge of thee. And she showed her mother-in-law with whom she had wrought, and said, The man's name with whom I wrought today *is* Boaz.

20And Naomi said unto her daughter-in-law, Blessed *be* he of the LORD, who hath not left off his kindness to the living and to the dead. And Naomi said unto her, The man *is* near of kin unto us, one of our next kinsmen.

21And Ruth the Moabitess said, He said unto me also, Thou shalt keep fast by my young men, until they have ended all my harvest.

22And Naomi said unto Ruth her daughter-in-law, *It is* good, my daughter, that thou go out with his maidens, that they meet thee not in any other field.

23So she kept fast by the maidens of Boaz to glean unto the end of barley harvest and of wheat harvest; and dwelt with her mother-in-law.

**3** THEN NAOMI her mother-in-law said unto her, My daughter, shall I not seek rest for thee, that it may be well with thee?

2And now *is* not Boaz of our kindred, with whose maidens thou wast? Behold, he winnoweth barley tonight in the threshingfloor.

3Wash thyself therefore, and anoint thee, and put thy raiment upon thee, and get thee down to the floor: *but* make not thyself known unto the man, until he shall have done eating and drinking.

4And it shall be, when he lieth down, that thou shalt mark the place where he shall lie, and thou shalt go in, and uncover his feet, and lay thee down; and he will tell thee what thou shalt do.

5And she said unto her, All that thou sayest unto me I will do.

6¶ And she went down unto the floor, and did according to all that her mother-in-law bade her.

7And when Boaz had eaten and drunk, and his heart was merry, he went to lie down at the end of the heap of corn: and she came softly, and uncovered his feet, and laid her down.

8¶ And it came to pass at midnight, that the man was afraid, and turned himself: and, behold, a woman lay at his feet.

9And he said, Who *art* thou? And she answered, I *am* Ruth thine handmaid: spread therefore thy skirt over thine handmaid; for thou *art* a near kinsman.

## Amplified

12The Lord recompense you for what you have done, and a full reward be given you by the Lord, the God of Israel, under Whose wings you have come to take refuge!

13Then she said, Let me find favor in your sight, my lord; for you have comforted me and have spoken to the heart of your maidservant, though I am not as one of your maidservants.

14And at mealtime Boaz said to her, Come here and eat of the bread, and dip your morsel in the sour wine [mixed with oil]. And she sat beside the reapers; and he passed her parched grain, and she ate until she was satisfied, and she had some left [for Naomi].

15And when she got up to glean, Boaz ordered his young men, Let her glean even among the sheaves, and do not reproach her;

16And let fall some handfuls for her on purpose, and let them lie there for her to glean, and do not rebuke her.

17So she gleaned in the field until evening; then she beat out what she had gleaned. It was about an ephah of barley.

18And she took it up, and went into the town; she showed her mother-in-law what she had gleaned, and brought forth and gave her the food she had reserved after she was satisfied.

19And her mother-in-law said to her, Where have you gleaned today? Where did you work? Blessed be the man who noticed you. So [Ruth] told [her], The name of him with whom I worked today is Boaz.

20And Naomi said to her daughter-in-law, Blessed be he of the Lord, who has not ceased his kindness to the living and to the dead. And Naomi said to her, The man is a near relative of ours, one who has the right to redeem us. [Lev. 25:25.]

21And Ruth the Moabitess said, He said to me also, Stay close to my young men until they have harvested my entire crop.

22And Naomi said to Ruth, It is good, my daughter, for you to go out with his maidens, lest in any other field you be molested.

23So she kept close to the maidens of Boaz, gleaning until the end of the barley and wheat harvests; and she lived with her mother-in-law.

**3** THEN NAOMI her mother-in-law said to Ruth, My daughter, shall I not seek rest *or* a home for you, that you may prosper?

2And now is not Boaz, with whose maidens you were, our relative? See, he is winnowing barley tonight at the threshing floor.

3Wash and anoint yourself therefore, and put on your best clothes and go down to the threshing floor; but do not make yourself known to the man until he has finished eating and drinking.

4But when he lies down, notice the place where he lies; then go and uncover his feet and lie down; and he will tell you what to do.

5And Ruth said to her, All that you say to me I will do.

6So she went down to the floor, and did just as her mother-in-law had told her.

7And when Boaz had eaten and drunk, and his heart was merry, he went to lie down at the end of the heap of grain. Then [Ruth] came softly and uncovered his feet and lay down.

8At midnight, the man was startled, and turned over, and behold, a woman lay at his feet!

9And he said, Who are you? And she answered, I am Ruth your maidservant. Spread your wing (of protection) over your maidservant, for you are next of kin.

## New American Standard

12"May the LORD reward your work, and your wages be full
from the LORD, the God of Israel, under whose wings you have
come to seek refuge."
13Then she said, "I have found favor in your sight, my lord, for
you have comforted me and indeed have spoken kindly to your
maidservant, though I am not like one of your maidservants."
14¶ And at mealtime Boaz said to her, "Come here, that you may
eat of the bread and dip your piece of bread in the vinegar." So
she sat beside the reapers; and he served her roasted grain, and
she ate and was satisfied and had some left.
15When she rose to glean, Boaz commanded his servants, saying, "Let her glean even among the sheaves, and do not insult her.
16"And also you shall purposely pull out for her *some grain* from
the bundles and leave *it* that she may glean, and do not rebuke
her."
17¶ So she gleaned in the field until evening. Then she beat out
what she had gleaned, and it was about an ephah of barley.
18And she took *it* up and went into the city, and her mother-in-
law saw what she had gleaned. She also took *it* out and gave
Naomi what she had left after she was satisfied.
19Her mother-in-law then said to her, "Where did you glean
today and where did you work? May he who took notice of you
be blessed." So she told her mother-in-law with whom she had
worked and said, "The name of the man with whom I worked
today is Boaz."
20And Naomi said to her daughter-in-law, "May he be blessed
of the LORD who has not withdrawn his kindness to the living and
to the dead." Again Naomi said to her, "The man is our relative,
he is one of our closest relatives."
21Then Ruth the Moabitess said, "Furthermore, he said to me,
'You should stay close to my servants until they have finished all
my harvest.' "
22And Naomi said to Ruth her daughter-in-law, "It is good, my
daughter, that you go out with his maids, lest *others* fall upon you
in another field."
23So she stayed close by the maids of Boaz in order to glean until
the end of the barley harvest and the wheat harvest. And she lived
with her mother-in-law.

*Boaz Will Redeem Ruth*

3 THEN NAOMI her mother-in-law said to her, "My daughter,
shall I not seek security for you, that it may be well with you?
2"And now is not Boaz our kinsman, with whose maids you
were? Behold, he winnows barley at the threshing floor tonight.
3"Wash yourself therefore, and anoint yourself and put on
your *best* clothes, and go down to the threshing floor; *but* do not
make yourself known to the man until he has finished eating and
drinking.
4"And it shall be when he lies down, that you shall notice the
place where he lies, and you shall go and uncover his feet and lie
down; then he will tell you what you shall do."
5And she said to her, "All that you say I will do."
6¶ So she went down to the threshing floor and did according
to all that her mother-in-law had commanded her.
7When Boaz had eaten and drunk and his heart was merry, he
went to lie down at the end of the heap of grain; and she came
secretly, and uncovered his feet and lay down.
8And it happened in the middle of the night that the man was
startled and bent forward; and behold, a woman was lying at his
feet.
9And he said, "Who are you?" And she answered, "I am Ruth
your maid. So spread your covering over your maid, for you are
a [a]close relative."

NAS [a] Or, *redeemer*, and so throughout this context

## New International

for what you have done. May you be richly rewarded by the LORD,
the God of Israel, under whose wings you have come to take
refuge."
13"May I continue to find favor in your eyes, my lord," she said.
"You have given me comfort and have spoken kindly to your
servant—though I do not have the standing of one of your servant
girls."
14At mealtime Boaz said to her, "Come over here. Have some
bread and dip it in the wine vinegar."
When she sat down with the harvesters, he offered her some
roasted grain. She ate all she wanted and had some left over. 15As
she got up to glean, Boaz gave orders to his men, "Even if she
gathers among the sheaves, don't embarrass her. 16Rather, pull
out some stalks for her from the bundles and leave them for her
to pick up, and don't rebuke her."
17So Ruth gleaned in the field until evening. Then she threshed
the barley she had gathered, and it amounted to about an ephah.[b]
18She carried it back to town, and her mother-in-law saw how
much she had gathered. Ruth also brought out and gave her what
she had left over after she had eaten enough.
19Her mother-in-law asked her, "Where did you glean today?
Where did you work? Blessed be the man who took notice of you!"
Then Ruth told her mother-in-law about the one at whose place
she had been working. "The name of the man I worked with today
is Boaz," she said.
20"The LORD bless him!" Naomi said to her daughter-in-law.
"He has not stopped showing his kindness to the living and the
dead." She added, "That man is our close relative; he is one of our
kinsman-redeemers."
21Then Ruth the Moabitess said, "He even said to me, 'Stay
with my workers until they finish harvesting all my grain.' "
22Naomi said to Ruth her daughter-in-law, "It will be good for
you, my daughter, to go with his girls, because in someone else's
field you might be harmed."
23So Ruth stayed close to the servant girls of Boaz to glean until
the barley and wheat harvests were finished. And she lived with
her mother-in-law.

*Ruth and Boaz at the Threshing Floor*

3 ONE DAY Naomi her mother-in-law said to her, "My daughter, should I not try to find a home[c] for you, where you will
be well provided for? 2Is not Boaz, with whose servant girls you
have been, a kinsman of ours? Tonight he will be winnowing
barley on the threshing floor. 3Wash and perfume yourself, and
put on your best clothes. Then go down to the threshing floor, but
don't let him know you are there until he has finished eating and
drinking. 4When he lies down, note the place where he is lying.
Then go and uncover his feet and lie down. He will tell you what
to do."
5"I will do whatever you say," Ruth answered. 6So she went
down to the threshing floor and did everything her mother-in-law
told her to do.
7When Boaz had finished eating and drinking and was in good
spirits, he went over to lie down at the far end of the grain pile.
Ruth approached quietly, uncovered his feet and lay down. 8In the
middle of the night something startled the man, and he turned and
discovered a woman lying at his feet.
9"Who are you?" he asked.
"I am your servant Ruth," she said. "Spread the corner of your
garment over me, since you are a kinsman-redeemer."

NIV [b] *17* That is, probably about 3/5 bushel (about 22 liters) [c] *1* Hebrew *find rest* (see Ruth 1:9)

## King James

10And he said, Blessed *be* thou of the LORD, my daughter: *for*
thou hast shown more kindness in the latter end than at the
beginning, inasmuch as thou followedst not young men, whether
poor or rich.
11And now, my daughter, fear not; I will do to thee all that thou
requirest: for all the city of my people doth know that thou *art* a
virtuous woman.
12And now it is true that I *am thy* near kinsman: howbeit there
is a kinsman nearer than I.
13Tarry this night, and it shall be in the morning, *that* if he will
perform unto thee the part of a kinsman, well; let him do the
kinsman's part: but if he will not do the part of a kinsman to thee,
then will I do the part of a kinsman to thee, *as* the LORD liveth: lie
down until the morning.
14¶ And she lay at his feet until the morning: and she rose up
before one could know another. And he said, Let it not be known
that a woman came into the floor.
15Also he said, Bring the veil that *thou hast* upon thee, and hold
it. And when she held it, he measured six *measures* of barley, and
laid *it* on her: and she went into the city.
16And when she came to her mother-in-law, she said, Who *art*
thou, my daughter? And she told her all that the man had done
to her.
17And she said, These six *measures* of barley gave he me; for he
said to me, Go not empty unto thy mother-in-law.
18Then said she, Sit still, my daughter, until thou know how the
matter will fall: for the man will not be in rest, until he have
finished the thing this day.

**4** THEN WENT Boaz up to the gate, and sat him down there:
and, behold, the kinsman of whom Boaz spake came by; unto
whom he said, Ho, such a one! turn aside, sit down here. And he
turned aside, and sat down.
2And he took ten men of the elders of the city, and said, Sit ye
down here. And they sat down.
3And he said unto the kinsman, Naomi, that is come again out
of the country of Moab, selleth a parcel of land, which *was* our
brother Elimelech's:
4And I thought to advertise thee, saying, Buy *it* before the
inhabitants, and before the elders of my people. If thou wilt redeem *it*, redeem *it*: but if thou wilt not redeem *it*, *then* tell me, that
I may know: for *there is* none to redeem *it* beside thee; and I *am* after
thee. And he said, I will redeem *it*.
5Then said Boaz, What day thou buyest the field of the hand
of Naomi, thou must buy *it* also of Ruth the Moabitess, the wife
of the dead, to raise up the name of the dead upon his inheritance.
6¶ And the kinsman said, I cannot redeem *it* for myself, lest I
mar mine own inheritance: redeem thou my right to thyself; for I
cannot redeem *it*.
7Now this *was the manner* in former time in Israel concerning
redeeming and concerning changing, for to confirm all things; a
man plucked off his shoe, and gave *it* to his neighbour: and this
*was* a testimony in Israel.
8Therefore the kinsman said unto Boaz, Buy *it* for thee. So he
drew off his shoe.
9¶ And Boaz said unto the elders, and *unto* all the people, Ye
*are* witnesses this day, that I have bought all that *was* Elimelech's,
and all that *was* Chilion's and Mahlon's, of the hand of Naomi.
10Moreover Ruth the Moabitess, the wife of Mahlon, have I
purchased to be my wife, to raise up the name of the dead upon
his inheritance, that the name of the dead be not cut off from
among his brethren, and from the gate of his place: ye *are* witnesses this day.

## Amplified

10And he said, Blessed be you of the Lord, my daughter; for you
have made this last loving-kindness greater than the former, for
you have not gone after young men, whether poor or rich.
11And now, my daughter, fear not; I will do for you all you
require; for all the city of my people know that you are a woman
of strength—worth, bravery, capability.
12It is true that I am your near kinsman; however there is a
kinsman nearer than I.
13Remain tonight, and in the morning, if he will perform for you
the part of a kinsman, well; let him do it; but if he will not do the
part of a kinsman for you, then, as the Lord lives, I will do the part
of a kinsman for you; lie down until the morning.
14And she lay at his feet until the morning, but arose before one
could recognize another. For he said, Let it not be known that the
woman came to the floor.
15Also he said, Bring the mantle you are wearing and hold it.
So [Ruth] held it, and he measured out six measures of barley, and
laid it on her; and she went into the town.
16And when she came home her mother-in-law said, How have
you fared, my daughter? And Ruth told her all that the man had
done for her.
17And she said, He gave me these six measures of barley, for
he said to me, Do not go empty-handed to your mother-in-law.
18Then said she, Sit still, my daughter, until you learn how the
matter turns out; for the man will not rest until he finishes the
matter today.

**4** THEN BOAZ went up to the city's gate and sat down there;
and behold, the kinsman of whom Boaz had spoken came by.
He said to him, Ho! Turn aside and sit down here. So he turned
aside and sat down.
2And Boaz took ten men of the elders of the city, and said, Sit
down here. And they sat down.
3And he said to the kinsman, Naomi, who has returned from
the country of Moab, has sold the parcel of land which belonged
to our brother Elimelech.
4And I thought to let you hear of it, and say, Buy it in the
presence of those sitting here, and before the elders of my people.
If you will redeem it, redeem it; but if you will not redeem it, then
say so, that I may know; for there is no one besides you to redeem
it; and I am [next of kin] after you. And he said, I will redeem it.
5Then Boaz said, The day you buy the field of Naomi, you must
buy it also of Ruth the Moabitess, the widow of the dead, to restore
the name of the dead to his inheritance.
6And the kinsman said, I cannot redeem it for myself, lest [by
marrying a Moabitess] I endanger my own inheritance; take my
right of redemption yourself, for I cannot redeem it. [Deut. 23:3,
4.]
7Now formerly in Israel this was the custom concerning redeeming and exchanging. To confirm a transaction, a man pulled
off his sandal and gave it to the other. This was the way of attesting
in Israel.
8Therefore, when the kinsman said to Boaz, Buy it for yourself,
he pulled off his sandal.
9And Boaz said to the elders, and to all the people, You are
witnesses this day, that I have bought all that was Elimelech's, and
all that was Chilion's and Mahlon's, from the hand of Naomi.
10Also Ruth the Moabitess, the widow of Mahlon, I have bought
to be my wife, to restore the name of the dead to his inheritance,
that the name of the dead may not be cut off from among his
brethren, and from the gate of his birthplace. You are witnesses
this day.

## New American Standard

10Then he said, "May you be blessed of the LORD, my daughter. You have shown your last kindness to be better than the first by not going after young men, whether poor or rich.

11"And now, my daughter, do not fear. I will do for you whatever you ask, for all my people in the city know that you are a woman of excellence.

12"And now it is true I am a close relative; however, there is a relative closer than I.

13"Remain this night, and when morning comes, if he will redeem you, good; let him redeem you. But if he does not wish to redeem you, then I will redeem you, as the LORD lives. Lie down until morning."

14¶ So she lay at his feet until morning and rose before one could recognize another; and he said, "Let it not be known that the woman came to the threshing floor."

15Again he said, "Give me the cloak that is on you and hold it." So she held it, and he measured six *measures* of barley and laid *it* on her. Then she went into the city.

16And when she came to her mother-in-law, she said, "How did it go, my daughter?" And she told her all that the man had done for her.

17And she said, "These six *measures* of barley he gave to me, for he said, 'Do not go to your mother-in-law empty-handed.' "

18Then she said, "Wait, my daughter, until you know how the matter turns out; for the man will not rest until he has settled it today."

*The Marriage of Ruth*

**4** NOW BOAZ went up to the gate and sat down there, and behold, the close relative of whom Boaz spoke was passing by, so he said, "Turn aside, friend, sit down here." And he turned aside and sat down.

2And he took ten men of the elders of the city and said, "Sit down here." So they sat down.

3Then he said to the closest relative, "Naomi, who has come back from the land of Moab, has to sell the piece of land which belonged to our brother Elimelech.

4"So I thought to inform you, saying, 'Buy *it* before those who are sitting *here,* and before the elders of my people. If you will redeem *it*, redeem *it;* but if not, tell me that I may know; for there is no one but you to redeem *it*, and I am after you.' " And he said, "I will redeem *it*."

5Then Boaz said, "On the day you buy the field from the hand of Naomi, you must also acquire Ruth the Moabitess, the widow of the deceased, in order to raise up the name of the deceased on his inheritance."

6And the closest relative said, "I cannot redeem *it* for myself, lest I jeopardize my own inheritance. Redeem *it* for yourself; you *may have* my right of redemption, for I cannot redeem *it*."

7¶ Now this was *the custom* in former times in Israel concerning the redemption and the exchange *of land* to confirm any matter: a man removed his sandal and gave it to another; and this was the *manner of* attestation in Israel.

8So the closest relative said to Boaz, "Buy *it* for yourself." And he removed his sandal.

9Then Boaz said to the elders and all the people, "You are witnesses today that I have bought from the hand of Naomi all that belonged to Elimelech and all that belonged to Chilion and Mahlon.

10"Moreover, I have acquired Ruth the Moabitess, the widow of Mahlon, to be my wife in order to raise up the name of the deceased on his inheritance, so that the name of the deceased may not be cut off from his brothers or from the court of his *birth* place; you are witnesses today."

## New International

10"The LORD bless you, my daughter," he replied. "This kindness is greater than that which you showed earlier: You have not run after the younger men, whether rich or poor. 11And now, my daughter, don't be afraid. I will do for you all you ask. All my fellow townsmen know that you are a woman of noble character. 12Although it is true that I am near of kin, there is a kinsman-redeemer nearer than I. 13Stay here for the night, and in the morning if he wants to redeem, good; let him redeem. But if he is not willing, as surely as the LORD lives I will do it. Lie here until morning."

14So she lay at his feet until morning, but got up before anyone could be recognized; and he said, "Don't let it be known that a woman came to the threshing floor."

15He also said, "Bring me the shawl you are wearing and hold it out." When she did so, he poured into it six measures of barley and put it on her. Then he[a] went back to town.

16When Ruth came to her mother-in-law, Naomi asked, "How did it go, my daughter?"

Then she told her everything Boaz had done for her 17and added, "He gave me these six measures of barley, saying, 'Don't go back to your mother-in-law empty-handed.' "

18Then Naomi said, "Wait, my daughter, until you find out what happens. For the man will not rest until the matter is settled today."

*Boaz Marries Ruth*

**4** MEANWHILE BOAZ went up to the town gate and sat there. When the kinsman-redeemer he had mentioned came along, Boaz said, "Come over here, my friend, and sit down." So he went over and sat down.

2Boaz took ten of the elders of the town and said, "Sit here," and they did so. 3Then he said to the kinsman-redeemer, "Naomi, who has come back from Moab, is selling the piece of land that belonged to our brother Elimelech. 4I thought I should bring the matter to your attention and suggest that you buy it in the presence of these seated here and in the presence of the elders of my people. If you will redeem it, do so. But if you[b] will not, tell me, so I will know. For no one has the right to do it except you, and I am next in line."

"I will redeem it," he said.

5Then Boaz said, "On the day you buy the land from Naomi and from Ruth the Moabitess, you acquire[c] the dead man's widow, in order to maintain the name of the dead with his property."

6At this, the kinsman-redeemer said, "Then I cannot redeem it because I might endanger my own estate. You redeem it yourself. I cannot do it."

7(Now in earlier times in Israel, for the redemption and transfer of property to become final, one party took off his sandal and gave it to the other. This was the method of legalizing transactions in Israel.)

8So the kinsman-redeemer said to Boaz, "Buy it yourself." And he removed his sandal.

9Then Boaz announced to the elders and all the people, "Today you are witnesses that I have bought from Naomi all the property of Elimelech, Kilion and Mahlon. 10I have also acquired Ruth the Moabitess, Mahlon's widow, as my wife, in order to maintain the name of the dead with his property, so that his name will not disappear from among his family or from the town records. Today you are witnesses!"

**NIV** [a] *15* Most Hebrew manuscripts; many Hebrew manuscripts, Vulgate and Syriac *she* [b] *4* Many Hebrew manuscripts, Septuagint, Vulgate and Syriac; most Hebrew manuscripts *he* [c] *5* Hebrew; Vulgate and Syriac *Naomi, you acquire Ruth the Moabitess,*

## King James

11And all the people that *were* in the gate, and the elders, said, *We are* witnesses. The LORD make the woman that is come into thine house like Rachel and like Leah, which two did build the house of Israel: and do thou worthily in Ephratah, and be famous in Bethlehem:

12And let thy house be like the house of Pharez, whom Tamar bare unto Judah, of the seed which the LORD shall give thee of this young woman.

13¶ So Boaz took Ruth, and she was his wife: and when he went in unto her, the LORD gave her conception, and she bare a son.

14And the women said unto Naomi, Blessed *be* the LORD, which hath not left thee this day without a kinsman, that his name may be famous in Israel.

15And he shall be unto thee a restorer of *thy* life, and a nourisher of thine old age: for thy daughter-in-law, which loveth thee, which is better to thee than seven sons, hath borne him.

16And Naomi took the child, and laid it in her bosom, and became nurse unto it.

17And the women her neighbours gave it a name, saying, There is a son born to Naomi; and they called his name Obed: he *is* the father of Jesse, the father of David.

18¶ Now these *are* the generations of Pharez: Pharez begat Hezron,

19And Hezron begat Ram, and Ram begat Amminadab,

20And Amminadab begat Nahshon, and Nahshon begat Salmon,

21And Salmon begat Boaz, and Boaz begat Obed,

22And Obed begat Jesse, and Jesse begat David.

## Amplified

11And all the people at the gate, and the elders, said, We are witnesses. The Lord make the woman who is coming into your house like Rachel and Leah, the two who built the household of Israel. May you do worthily *and* get wealth (power) in Ephratah, and be famous in Bethlehem.

12And let your house be like the house of Perez, whom Tamar bore to Judah, because of the offspring which the Lord will give you by this young woman.

13So Boaz took Ruth, and she became his wife; and he went in to her, and the Lord caused her to conceive and she bore a son.

14And the women said to Naomi, Blessed be the Lord, Who has not left you this day without a close kinsman, and may his name be famous in Israel.

15And may he be to you a restorer of life, and a nourisher *and* support of your old age, for your daughter-in-law who loves you, who is better to you than seven sons, has borne him.

16Then Naomi took the child, and laid him in her bosom, and became his nurse.

17And her neighbor women gave him a name, saying, A son is born to Naomi. They named him Obed; he was the father of Jesse, father of David [the ancestor of Jesus Christ].

18Now these are the descendants of Perez: Perez was father of Hezron,

19Hezron of Ram, Ram of Amminadab,

20Amminadab of Nahshon, Nahshon of Salmon,

21Salmon of Boaz, Boaz of Obed,

22Obed of Jesse, and Jesse of David [the ancestor of Jesus Christ].

## New American Standard

11And all the people who were in the court, and the elders, said,
"*We are* witnesses. May the LORD make the woman who is coming
into your home like Rachel and Leah, both of whom built the
house of Israel; and may you achieve wealth in Ephrathah and
become famous in Bethlehem.
12"Moreover, may your house be like the house of Perez whom
Tamar bore to Judah, through the offspring which the LORD shall
give you by this young woman."
13¶ So Boaz took Ruth, and she became his wife, and he went
in to her. And the LORD enabled her to conceive, and she gave birth
to a son.
14Then the women said to Naomi, "Blessed is the LORD who has
not left you without a redeemer today, and may his name become
famous in Israel.
15"May he also be to you a restorer of life and a sustainer of your
old age; for your daughter-in-law, who loves you and is better to
you than seven sons, has given birth to him."

*The Line of David Began Here*

16Then Naomi took the child and laid him in her lap, and
became his nurse.
17And the neighbor women gave him a name, saying, "A son
has been born to Naomi!" So they named him Obed. He is the
father of Jesse, the father of David.
18¶ Now these are the generations of Perez: to Perez was born
Hezron,
19and to Hezron was born Ram, and to Ram, Amminadab,
20and to Amminadab was born Nahshon, and to Nahshon,
Salmon,
21and to Salmon was born Boaz, and to Boaz, Obed,
22and to Obed was born Jesse, and to Jesse, David.

## New International

11Then the elders and all those at the gate said, "We are witnesses. May the LORD make the woman who is coming into your
home like Rachel and Leah, who together built up the house of
Israel. May you have standing in Ephrathah and be famous in
Bethlehem. 12Through the offspring the LORD gives you by this
young woman, may your family be like that of Perez, whom Tamar
bore to Judah."

*The Genealogy of David*

13So Boaz took Ruth and she became his wife. Then he went to
her, and the LORD enabled her to conceive, and she gave birth to
a son. 14The women said to Naomi: "Praise be to the LORD, who
this day has not left you without a kinsman-redeemer. May he
become famous throughout Israel! 15He will renew your life and
sustain you in your old age. For your daughter-in-law, who loves
you and who is better to you than seven sons, has given him
birth."
16Then Naomi took the child, laid him in her lap and cared for
him. 17The women living there said, "Naomi has a son." And they
named him Obed. He was the father of Jesse, the father of David.
18This, then, is the family line of Perez:

Perez was the father of Hezron,
19Hezron the father of Ram,
Ram the father of Amminadab,
20Amminadab the father of Nahshon,
Nahshon the father of Salmon,[a]
21Salmon the father of Boaz,
Boaz the father of Obed,
22Obed the father of Jesse,
and Jesse the father of David.

**NIV** [a] *20* A few Hebrew manuscripts, some Septuagint manuscripts and Vulgate (see also verse 21 and Septuagint of 1 Chron. 2:11); most Hebrew manuscripts *Salma*

## King James

THE FIRST BOOK OF

# Samuel

OTHERWISE CALLED

THE FIRST BOOK OF THE KINGS

**1** NOW THERE was a certain man of Ramathaim-zophim, of
mount Ephraim, and his name *was* Elkanah, the son of Jeroham, the son of Elihu, the son of Tohu, the son of Zuph, an
Ephrathite:
2And he had two wives; the name of the one *was* Hannah, and
the name of the other Peninnah: and Peninnah had children, but
Hannah had no children.
3And this man went up out of his city yearly to worship and to
sacrifice unto the LORD of hosts in Shiloh. And the two sons of Eli,
Hophni and Phinehas, the priests of the LORD, *were* there.
4¶ And when the time was that Elkanah offered, he gave to
Peninnah his wife, and to all her sons and her daughters, portions:
5But unto Hannah he gave a worthy portion; for he loved Hannah: but the LORD had shut up her womb.
6And her adversary also provoked her sore, for to make her fret,
because the LORD had shut up her womb.
7And *as* he did so year by year, when she went up to the house
of the LORD, so she provoked her; therefore she wept, and did not
eat.
8Then said Elkanah her husband to her, Hannah, why weepest
thou? and why eatest thou not? and why is thy heart grieved? *am*
not I better to thee than ten sons?
9¶ So Hannah rose up after they had eaten in Shiloh, and after
they had drunk. Now Eli the priest sat upon a seat by a post of the
temple of the LORD.
10And she *was* in bitterness of soul, and prayed unto the LORD,
and wept sore.
11And she vowed a vow, and said, O LORD of hosts, if thou wilt
indeed look on the affliction of thine handmaid, and remember
me, and not forget thine handmaid, but wilt give unto thine handmaid a man child, then I will give him unto the LORD all the days
of his life, and there shall no razor come upon his head.
12And it came to pass, as she continued praying before the
LORD, that Eli marked her mouth.
13Now Hannah, she spake in her heart; only her lips moved,
but her voice was not heard: therefore Eli thought she had been
drunken.
14And Eli said unto her, How long wilt thou be drunken? put
away thy wine from thee.
15And Hannah answered and said, No, my lord, I *am* a woman
of a sorrowful spirit: I have drunk neither wine nor strong drink,
but have poured out my soul before the LORD.
16Count not thine handmaid for a daughter of Belial: for out of
the abundance of my complaint and grief have I spoken hitherto.
17Then Eli answered and said, Go in peace: and the God of
Israel grant *thee* thy petition that thou hast asked of him.
18And she said, Let thine handmaid find grace in thy sight. So
the woman went her way, and did eat, and her countenance was
no more *sad*.

## Amplified

THE FIRST BOOK OF

# Samuel

**1** THERE WAS a certain man of Ramathaim-zophim, of the hill
country of Ephraim, named Elkanah son of Jeroham, son of
Elihu, son of Tohu, son of Zuph, an Ephraimite.
2He had two wives, one named Hannah, and the other named
Peninnah. Peninnah had children, but Hannah had none.
3This man went from his city year by year to worship and
sacrifice to the Lord of hosts at Shiloh, where Hophni and Phinehas, sons of Eli, were the Lord's priests.
4When the day came that Elkanah sacrificed, he would give to
Peninnah his wife, and all her sons and daughters, portions [of the
sacrificial meat];
5But to Hannah he gave a double portion; for he loved Hannah,
but the Lord had given her no children.
6[This embarrassed and grieved Hannah] and her rival provoked her greatly, to vex her, because the Lord had left her childless.
7So it was year after year, when Hannah went up to the Lord's
house Peninnah provoked her; so she wept and did not eat.
8Then Elkanah her husband said to her, Hannah, why do you
cry? And why do you not eat? And why are you grieving? Am I
not more to you than ten sons?
9So Hannah rose, after they had eaten and drunk in Shiloh.
Now Eli the priest was sitting on his seat beside a post of the [tent]
temple of the Lord.
10And [Hannah] was in distress of soul praying to the Lord, and
weeping bitterly.
11She vowed, saying, O Lord of hosts, if You will indeed look
on the affliction of Your handmaid, and [earnestly] remember and
not forget Your handmaid, but will give me a son, I will give him
to the Lord all his life; no razor shall touch his head.
12And as she continued praying before the Lord, Eli noticed her
mouth.
13Hannah was speaking in her heart; only her lips moved, and
her voice was not heard; so Eli thought she was drunk.
14Eli said to her, How long will you be intoxicated? Put wine
away from you.
15But Hannah answered, No, my lord, I am a woman of a
sorrowful spirit. I have drunk neither wine nor [a]strong drink, but
I was pouring out my soul before the Lord.
16Regard not your handmaid as a wicked woman; for out of my
great complaint and bitter provocation I have been speaking.
17Then Eli said, Go in peace; and the God of Israel grant your
petition which you have asked of Him.
18Hannah said, Let your handmaid find grace in your sight. So
[she] went her way, and ate, her countenance no longer sad.

**AMP** [a] Genesis 19:34.

## New American Standard

# 1 Samuel

*Elkanah and His Wives*

**1** NOW THERE was a certain man from Ramathaim-zophim
from the hill country of Ephraim, and his name was Elkanah
the son of Jeroham, the son of Elihu, the son of Tohu, the son of
Zuph, an Ephraimite.

2And he had two wives: the name of one was Hannah and the
name of the other Peninnah; and Peninnah had children, but
Hannah had no children.

3Now this man would go up from his city yearly to worship
and to sacrifice to the LORD of hosts in Shiloh. And the two sons
of Eli, Hophni and Phinehas were priests to the LORD there.

4And when the day came that Elkanah sacrificed, he would
give portions to Peninnah his wife and to all her sons and her
daughters;

5but to Hannah he would give a double portion, for he loved
Hannah, but the LORD had closed her womb.

6Her rival, however, would provoke her bitterly to irritate her,
because the LORD had closed her womb.

7And it happened year after year, as often as she went up to
the house of the LORD, she would provoke her, so she wept and
would not eat.

8Then Elkanah her husband said to her, "Hannah, why do you
weep and why do you not eat and why is your heart sad? Am I
not better to you than ten sons?"

**9**¶ Then Hannah rose after eating and drinking in Shiloh. Now
Eli the priest was sitting on the seat by the doorpost of the temple
of the LORD.

10And she, greatly distressed, prayed to the LORD and wept
bitterly.

11And she made a vow and said, "O LORD of hosts, if Thou wilt
indeed look on the affliction of Thy maidservant and remember
me, and not forget Thy maidservant, but wilt give Thy maidservant a son, then I will give him to the LORD all the days of his
life, and a razor shall never come on his head."

**12**¶ Now it came about, as she continued praying before the
LORD, that Eli was watching her mouth.

13As for Hannah, she was speaking in her heart, only her lips
were moving, but her voice was not heard. So Eli thought she was
drunk.

14Then Eli said to her, "How long will you make yourself
drunk? Put away your wine from you."

15But Hannah answered and said, "No, my lord, I am a woman
oppressed in spirit; I have drunk neither wine nor strong drink,
but I have poured out my soul before the LORD.

16"Do not consider your maidservant as a worthless woman; for
I have spoken until now out of my great concern and provocation."

17Then Eli answered and said, "Go in peace; and may the God
of Israel grant your petition that you have asked of Him."

18And she said, "Let your maidservant find favor in your
sight." So the woman went her way and ate, and her face was no
longer *sad*.

## New International

# 1 Samuel

*The Birth of Samuel*

**1** THERE WAS a certain man from Ramathaim, a Zuphite[b]
from the hill country of Ephraim, whose name was Elkanah
son of Jeroham, the son of Elihu, the son of Tohu, the son of Zuph,
an Ephraimite. 2He had two wives; one was called Hannah and the
other Peninnah. Peninnah had children, but Hannah had none.

3Year after year this man went up from his town to worship and
sacrifice to the LORD Almighty at Shiloh, where Hophni and Phinehas, the two sons of Eli, were priests of the LORD. 4Whenever the
day came for Elkanah to sacrifice, he would give portions of the
meat to his wife Peninnah and to all her sons and daughters. 5But
to Hannah he gave a double portion because he loved her, and the
LORD had closed her womb. 6And because the LORD had closed her
womb, her rival kept provoking her in order to irritate her. 7This
went on year after year. Whenever Hannah went up to the house
of the LORD, her rival provoked her till she wept and would not
eat. 8Elkanah her husband would say to her, "Hannah, why are
you weeping? Why don't you eat? Why are you downhearted?
Don't I mean more to you than ten sons?"

9Once when they had finished eating and drinking in Shiloh,
Hannah stood up. Now Eli the priest was sitting on a chair by the
doorpost of the LORD's temple.[c] 10In bitterness of soul Hannah
wept much and prayed to the LORD. 11And she made a vow,
saying, "O LORD Almighty, if you will only look upon your servant's misery and remember me, and not forget your servant but
give her a son, then I will give him to the LORD for all the days of
his life, and no razor will ever be used on his head."

12As she kept on praying to the LORD, Eli observed her mouth.
13Hannah was praying in her heart, and her lips were moving but
her voice was not heard. Eli thought she was drunk 14and said to
her, "How long will you keep on getting drunk? Get rid of your
wine."

15"Not so, my lord," Hannah replied, "I am a woman who is
deeply troubled. I have not been drinking wine or beer; I was
pouring out my soul to the LORD. 16Do not take your servant for
a wicked woman; I have been praying here out of my great anguish
and grief."

17Eli answered, "Go in peace, and may the God of Israel grant
you what you have asked of him."

18She said, "May your servant find favor in your eyes." Then
she went her way and ate something, and her face was no longer
downcast.

NIV [b] *1* Or *from Ramathaim Zuphim* [c] *9* That is, tabernacle

## King James

19¶ And they rose up in the morning early, and worshipped before the LORD, and returned, and came to their house to Ramah: and Elkanah knew Hannah his wife; and the LORD remembered her.

20 Wherefore it came to pass, when the time was come about after Hannah had conceived, that she bare a son, and called his name Samuel, *saying,* Because I have asked him of the LORD.

21 And the man Elkanah, and all his house, went up to offer unto the LORD the yearly sacrifice, and his vow.

22 But Hannah went not up; for she said unto her husband, *I will not go up* until the child be weaned, and *then* I will bring him, that he may appear before the LORD, and there abide for ever.

23 And Elkanah her husband said unto her, Do what seemeth thee good; tarry until thou have weaned him; only the LORD establish his word. So the woman abode, and gave her son suck until she weaned him.

24¶ And when she had weaned him, she took him up with her, with three bullocks, and one ephah of flour, and a bottle of wine, and brought him unto the house of the LORD in Shiloh: and the child *was* young.

25 And they slew a bullock, and brought the child to Eli.

26 And she said, Oh my lord, *as* thy soul liveth, my lord, I *am* the woman that stood by thee here, praying unto the LORD.

27 For this child I prayed; and the LORD hath given me my petition which I asked of him:

28 Therefore also I have lent him to the LORD; as long as he liveth he shall be lent to the LORD. And he worshipped the LORD there.

**2** AND HANNAH prayed, and said, My heart rejoiceth in the LORD, mine horn is exalted in the LORD: my mouth is enlarged over mine enemies; because I rejoice in thy salvation.

2 *There is* none holy as the LORD: for *there is* none beside thee: neither *is there* any rock like our God.

3 Talk no more so exceeding proudly; let *not* arrogancy come out of your mouth: for the LORD *is* a God of knowledge, and by him actions are weighed.

4 The bows of the mighty men *are* broken, and they that stumbled are girded with strength.

5 *They that were* full have hired out themselves for bread; and *they that were* hungry ceased: so that the barren hath born seven; and she that hath many children is waxed feeble.

6 The LORD killeth, and maketh alive: he bringeth down to the grave, and bringeth up.

7 The LORD maketh poor, and maketh rich: he bringeth low, and lifteth up.

8 He raiseth up the poor out of the dust, *and* lifteth up the beggar from the dunghill, to set *them* among princes, and to make them inherit the throne of glory: for the pillars of the earth *are* the LORD'S, and he hath set the world upon them.

**AMP** [a] He would then be two or three years old . . . There were women engaged in the tabernacle service to whose care he might have been committed. It was important that he should be dedicated as soon as possible. The earliest impressions of his boyhood were to be those of the house of God *(Cambridge Bible).*

## Amplified

19 The family rose early next morning, worshiped before the Lord, and returned to their home in Ramah. Elkanah knew Hannah his wife, and the Lord remembered her.

20 Hannah became pregnant, and in due time bore a son, and named him Samuel [heard of God], Because she said, I have asked him of the Lord.

21 And Elkanah, and all his house, went up to offer to the Lord the yearly sacrifice, and his vow.

22 But Hannah did not go, for she said to her husband, I will not go until the child is weaned, and then I will bring him, that he may appear before the Lord, and remain there as long as he lives.

23 Elkanah her husband said to her, Do what seems best to you, wait until you have weaned him; only, may the Lord establish His word. So Hannah remained and nursed her son until she weaned him.

24 When she had [a]weaned him, she took him with her, with a three-year-old bull, an ephah of flour, and a skin-bottle of wine [to pour over the burnt offering for a sweet odor], and brought Samuel to the Lord's house in Shiloh. The child was growing.

25 Then they slew the bull, and brought the child to Eli.

26 Hannah said, Oh, my lord! As your soul lives, my lord, I am the woman who stood by you here, praying to the Lord.

27 For this child I prayed, and the Lord has granted my petition made to Him.

28 Therefore I have given him to the Lord; as long as he lives he is given to the Lord. And they worshiped the Lord there.

**2** HANNAH PRAYED, and said, My heart exults *and* triumphs in the Lord; my horn (my strength) is lifted up in the Lord. My mouth is no longer silent, for it is opened wide over my enemies, because I rejoice in Your salvation.

2 There is none holy like the Lord, there is none besides You; there is no rock like our God.

3 Talk no more so very proudly; let not arrogance go forth from your mouth; for the Lord is a God of knowledge, and by Him actions are weighed.

4 The bows of the mighty are broken, and those who stumbled are girded with strength.

5 Those who were full have hired themselves out for bread; but those who were hungry have ceased to hunger. The barren has borne seven, but she who has many children languishes *and* is forlorn.

6 The Lord slays and makes alive; He brings down to Sheol and raises up.

7 The Lord makes poor and makes rich; He brings low and He lifts up.

8 He raises up the poor out of the dust, and lifts up the needy from the ash heap, to make them sit with the noble, and inherit the throne of glory. For the pillars of the earth are the Lord's, and He has set the world upon them.

## New American Standard

*Samuel Is Born to Hannah*

19¶ Then they arose early in the morning and worshiped before
the LORD, and returned again to their house in Ramah. And Elkanah had relations with Hannah his wife, and the LORD remembered her.
20And it came about in due time, after Hannah had conceived,
that she gave birth to a son; and she named him Samuel, *saying,*
"Because I have asked him of the LORD."
21¶ Then the man Elkanah went up with all his household to
offer to the LORD the yearly sacrifice and *pay* his vow.
22But Hannah did not go up, for she said to her husband, "*I
will not go up* until the child is weaned; then I will bring him, that
he may appear before the LORD and stay there forever."
23And Elkanah her husband said to her, "Do what seems best
to you. Remain until you have weaned him; only may the LORD
confirm His word." So the woman remained and nursed her son
until she weaned him.
24Now when she had weaned him, she took him up with her,
with a three-year-old bull and one ephah of flour and a jug of wine,
and brought him to the house of the LORD in Shiloh, although the
child was young.
25Then they slaughtered the bull, and brought the boy to Eli.
26And she said, "Oh, my lord! As your soul lives, my lord, I am
the woman who stood here beside you, praying to the LORD.
27"For this boy I prayed, and the LORD has given me my petition
which I asked of Him.
28"So I have also [b]dedicated him to the LORD; as long as he lives
he is [c]dedicated to the LORD." And he worshiped the LORD there.

*Hannah's Song of Thanksgiving*

**2** THEN HANNAH prayed and said,
"My heart exults in the LORD;
My horn is exalted in the LORD,
My mouth speaks boldly against my enemies,
Because I rejoice in Thy salvation.
2 "There is no one holy like the LORD,
Indeed, there is no one besides Thee,
Nor is there any rock like our God.
3 "Boast no more so very proudly,
Do not let arrogance come out of your mouth;
For the LORD is a God of knowledge,
And with Him actions are weighed.
4 "The bows of the mighty are shattered,
But the feeble gird on strength.
5 "Those who were full hire themselves out for bread,
But those who were hungry cease *to hunger.*
Even the barren gives birth to seven,
But she who has many children languishes.
6 "The LORD kills and makes alive;
He brings down to Sheol and raises up.
7 "The LORD makes poor and rich;
He brings low, He also exalts.
8 "He raises the poor from the dust,
He lifts the needy from the ash heap
To make them sit with nobles,
And inherit a seat of honor;
For the pillars of the earth are the LORD'S,
And He set the world on them.

NAS [b] Lit., *lent* [c] Lit., *lent*

## New International

19Early the next morning they arose and worshiped before the
LORD and then went back to their home at Ramah. Elkanah lay
with Hannah his wife, and the LORD remembered her. 20So in the
course of time Hannah conceived and gave birth to a son. She
named him Samuel,[d] saying, "Because I asked the LORD for him."

*Hannah Dedicates Samuel*

21When the man Elkanah went up with all his family to offer
the annual sacrifice to the LORD and to fulfill his vow, 22Hannah
did not go. She said to her husband, "After the boy is weaned, I
will take him and present him before the LORD, and he will live
there always."
23"Do what seems best to you," Elkanah her husband told her.
"Stay here until you have weaned him; only may the LORD make
good his[e] word." So the woman stayed at home and nursed her
son until she had weaned him.
24After he was weaned, she took the boy with her, young as he
was, along with a three-year-old bull,[f] an ephah[g] of flour and a
skin of wine, and brought him to the house of the LORD at Shiloh.
25When they had slaughtered the bull, they brought the boy to Eli,
26and she said to him, "As surely as you live, my lord, I am the
woman who stood here beside you praying to the LORD. 27I prayed
for this child, and the LORD has granted me what I asked of him.
28So now I give him to the LORD. For his whole life he will be given
over to the LORD." And he worshiped the LORD there.

*Hannah's Prayer*

**2** THEN HANNAH prayed and said:
"My heart rejoices in the LORD;
in the LORD my horn[h] is lifted high.
My mouth boasts over my enemies,
for I delight in your deliverance.

2"There is no one holy[i] like the LORD;
there is no one besides you;
there is no Rock like our God.

3"Do not keep talking so proudly
or let your mouth speak such arrogance,
for the LORD is a God who knows,
and by him deeds are weighed.

4"The bows of the warriors are broken,
but those who stumbled are armed with strength.
5Those who were full hire themselves out for food,
but those who were hungry hunger no more.
She who was barren has borne seven children,
but she who has had many sons pines away.

6"The LORD brings death and makes alive;
he brings down to the grave[j] and raises up.
7The LORD sends poverty and wealth;
he humbles and he exalts.
8He raises the poor from the dust
and lifts the needy from the ash heap;
he seats them with princes
and has them inherit a throne of honor.

"For the foundations of the earth are the LORD's;
upon them he has set the world.

NIV [d] 20 *Samuel* sounds like the Hebrew for *heard of God.* [e] 23 Masoretic Text; Dead Sea Scrolls, Septuagint and Syriac *your* [f] 24 Dead Sea Scrolls, Septuagint and Syriac; Masoretic Text *with three bulls* [g] 24 That is, probably about 3/5 bushel (about 22 liters) [h] 1 *Horn* here symbolizes strength; also in verse 10. [i] 2 Or *no Holy One* [j] 6 Hebrew *Sheol*

## King James

9He will keep the feet of his saints, and the wicked shall be silent
in darkness; for by strength shall no man prevail.
10The adversaries of the LORD shall be broken to pieces; out of
heaven shall he thunder upon them: the LORD shall judge the ends
of the earth; and he shall give strength unto his king, and exalt the
horn of his anointed.
11And Elkanah went to Ramah to his house. And the child did
minister unto the LORD before Eli the priest.
12¶ Now the sons of Eli *were* sons of Belial; they knew not the
LORD.
13And the priests' custom with the people *was, that,* when any
man offered sacrifice, the priest's servant came, while the flesh
was in seething, with a fleshhook of three teeth in his hand;
14And he struck *it* into the pan, or kettle, or caldron, or pot; all
that the fleshhook brought up the priest took for himself. So they
did in Shiloh unto all the Israelites that came thither.
15Also before they burnt the fat, the priest's servant came, and
said to the man that sacrificed, Give flesh to roast for the priest;
for he will not have sodden flesh of thee, but raw.
16And *if* any man said unto him, Let them not fail to burn the
fat presently, and *then* take *as much* as thy soul desireth; then he
would answer him, *Nay;* but thou shalt give *it me* now: and if not,
I will take *it* by force.
17Wherefore the sin of the young men was very great before the
LORD: for men abhorred the offering of the LORD.
18¶ But Samuel ministered before the LORD, *being* a child, girded
with a linen ephod.
19Moreover his mother made him a little coat, and brought *it* to
him from year to year, when she came up with her husband to
offer the yearly sacrifice.
20¶ And Eli blessed Elkanah and his wife, and said, The LORD
give thee seed of this woman for the loan which is lent to the LORD.
And they went unto their own home.
21And the LORD visited Hannah, so that she conceived, and
bare three sons and two daughters. And the child Samuel grew
before the LORD.
22¶ Now Eli was very old, and heard all that his sons did unto
all Israel; and how they lay with the women that assembled *at* the
door of the tabernacle of the congregation.
23And he said unto them, Why do ye such things? for I hear of
your evil dealings by all this people.
24Nay, my sons; for *it is* no good report that I hear: ye make the
LORD'S people to transgress.
25If one man sin against another, the judge shall judge him: but
if a man sin against the LORD, who shall entreat for him? Notwithstanding they hearkened not unto the voice of their father, because
the LORD would slay them.
26And the child Samuel grew on, and was in favour both with
the LORD, and also with men.
27¶ And there came a man of God unto Eli, and said unto him,
Thus saith the LORD, Did I plainly appear unto the house of thy
father, when they were in Egypt in Pharaoh's house?
28And did I choose him out of all the tribes of Israel *to be* my
priest, to offer upon mine altar, to burn incense, to wear an ephod
before me? and did I give unto the house of thy father all the
offerings made by fire of the children of Israel?

## Amplified

9He will guard the feet of His godly ones, and the wicked shall
be silenced *and* perish in darkness; for by strength shall no man
prevail.
10The adversaries of the Lord shall be broken to pieces; against
them will He thunder in Heaven. The Lord will judge [all peoples]
to the ends of the earth; and He will give strength to [a]His king,
and exalt the power of His Anointed—[b]His Christ. [Luke 1:46.]
11Elkanah and his wife Hannah returned to Ramah to his house.
But the child ministered to the Lord before Eli the priest.
12The sons of Eli were base *and* worthless; they did not know
*or* regard the Lord.
13And the custom of the priests with the people was this: when
any man offered sacrifice, the priest's servant came, while the flesh
was boiling, with a fleshhook of three prongs in his hand;
14And he thrust it into the pan, or kettle, or caldron, or pot; all
that the fleshhook brought up the priest took for himself. So they
did in Shiloh with all the Israelites who came there.
15Also before they burned the fat, the priest's servant came and
said to the man who sacrificed, Give meat to roast for the priest;
for he will not accept boiled meat from you, but raw.
16And if the man said to him, Let them burn the fat first, and
then you may take as much as you want, the priest's servant would
say, No! Give it to me now, or I will take it by force.
17So the sin of the *two* young men was very great before the
Lord; for they despised the offering of the Lord.
18But Samuel ministered before the Lord, a child, girded with
a linen ephod.
19Moreover his mother made him a little robe, and brought it
to him from year to year, when she came up with her husband to
offer the yearly sacrifice.
20And Eli would bless Elkanah and his wife, and say, The Lord
give you children of this woman for the gift she asked *and* gave to
the Lord. Then they would go to their own home.
21And the Lord visited Hannah, so that she bore three sons and
two daughters. And the child Samuel grew before the Lord.
22Now Eli was very old, and heard all that his sons did to all
Israel, and how they lay with the women who served at the door
of the tent of meeting.
23And he said to them, Why do you do such things? For I hear
of your evil dealings from all the people.
24No, my sons; it is no good report which I hear the Lord's
people spreading abroad.
25If one man wrongs another, God will mediate for him; but if
a man wrongs the Lord, who shall intercede for him? Yet they did
not listen to their father, for it was the Lord's will to slay them.
26Now the boy Samuel grew and was in favor both with the
Lord and with men.
27A man of God came to Eli, and said to him, Thus has the Lord
said, I plainly revealed Myself to the house of your father [fore-
father Aaron] when they were in Egypt in bondage to Pharaoh's
house.
28Moreover, I selected him out of all the tribes of Israel to be My
priest, to offer on My altar, to burn incense, to wear an ephod
before Me. And I gave [from then on] to the house of your father
[forefather] all the offerings of the Israelites made by fire.

**AMP** [a] Hannah's prophetic prayer was but partially fulfilled in the king soon to be anointed by her son as the deliverer of Israel; it reaches forward to . . . the King Messiah, in Whom alone the lofty anticipations of the prophetess are to be completely realized *(Cambridge Bible).* [b] Both the Septuagint (Greek) and the Vulgate (Latin) read "His Christ" (cp. Luke 2:26).

## New American Standard

9 "He keeps the feet of His godly ones,
But the wicked ones are silenced in darkness;
For not by might shall a man prevail.
10 "Those who contend with the LORD will be shattered;
Against them He will thunder in the heavens,
The LORD will judge the ends of the earth;
And He will give strength to His king,
And will exalt the horn of His anointed."

11¶ Then Elkanah went to his home at Ramah. But the boy
ministered to the LORD before Eli the priest.

*The Sin of Eli's Sons*

12¶ Now the sons of Eli were [c]worthless men; they did not
know the LORD
13and the custom of the priests with the people. When any man
was offering a sacrifice, the priest's servant would come while the
meat was boiling, with a three-pronged fork in his hand.
14Then he would thrust it into the pan, or kettle, or caldron, or
pot; all that the fork brought up the priest would take for himself.
Thus they did in Shiloh to all the Israelites who came there.
15Also, before they burned the fat, the priest's servant would
come and say to the man who was sacrificing, "Give the priest
meat for roasting, as he will not take boiled meat from you, only
raw."
16And if the man said to him, "They must surely burn the fat
first, and then take as much as you desire," then he would say,
"No, but you shall give *it to me* now; and if not, I will take it by
force."
17Thus the sin of the young men was very great before the
LORD, for the men despised the offering of the LORD.

*Samuel before the LORD as a Boy*

18¶ Now Samuel was ministering before the LORD, *as* a boy
wearing a linen ephod.
19And his mother would make him a little robe and bring it to
him from year to year when she would come up with her husband
to offer the yearly sacrifice.
20Then Eli would bless Elkanah and his wife and say, "May the
LORD give you children from this woman in place of the one she
dedicated to the LORD." And they went to their own home.
21And the LORD visited Hannah; and she conceived and gave
birth to three sons and two daughters. And the boy Samuel grew
before the LORD.

*Eli Rebukes His Sons*

22¶ Now Eli was very old; and he heard all that his sons were
doing to all Israel, and how they lay with the women who served
at the doorway of the tent of meeting.
23And he said to them, "Why do you do such things, the evil
things that I hear from all these people?
24"No, my sons; for the report is not good which I hear the
LORD's people circulating.
25"If one man sins against another, God will mediate for him;
but if a man sins against the LORD, who can intercede for him?"
But they would not listen to the voice of their father, for the LORD
desired to put them to death.
26Now the boy Samuel was growing in stature and in favor both
with the LORD and with men.
27¶ Then a man of God came to Eli and said to him, "Thus says
the LORD, 'Did I *not* indeed reveal Myself to the house of your
father when they were in Egypt *in bondage* to Pharaoh's house?
28'And did I *not* choose them from all the tribes of Israel to be
My priests, to go up to My altar, to burn incense, to carry an ephod
before Me; and did I *not* give to the house of your father all the fire
*offerings* of the sons of Israel?

NAS [c] Lit., *sons of Belial*

## New International

9He will guard the feet of his saints,
but the wicked will be silenced in darkness.
"It is not by strength that one prevails;
10 those who oppose the LORD will be shattered.
He will thunder against them from heaven;
the LORD will judge the ends of the earth.
"He will give strength to his king
and exalt the horn of his anointed."

11Then Elkanah went home to Ramah, but the boy ministered
before the LORD under Eli the priest.

*Eli's Wicked Sons*

12Eli's sons were wicked men; they had no regard for the LORD.
13Now it was the practice of the priests with the people that whenever anyone offered a sacrifice and while the meat was being
boiled, the servant of the priest would come with a three-pronged
fork in his hand. 14He would plunge it into the pan or kettle or
caldron or pot, and the priest would take for himself whatever the
fork brought up. This is how they treated all the Israelites who
came to Shiloh. 15But even before the fat was burned, the servant
of the priest would come and say to the man who was sacrificing,
"Give the priest some meat to roast; he won't accept boiled meat
from you, but only raw."
16If the man said to him, "Let the fat be burned up first, and
then take whatever you want," the servant would then answer,
"No, hand it over now; if you don't, I'll take it by force."
17This sin of the young men was very great in the LORD's sight,
for they[d] were treating the LORD's offering with contempt.
18But Samuel was ministering before the LORD—a boy wearing
a linen ephod. 19Each year his mother made him a little robe and
took it to him when she went up with her husband to offer the
annual sacrifice. 20Eli would bless Elkanah and his wife, saying,
"May the LORD give you children by this woman to take the place
of the one she prayed for and gave to the LORD." Then they would
go home. 21And the LORD was gracious to Hannah; she conceived
and gave birth to three sons and two daughters. Meanwhile, the
boy Samuel grew up in the presence of the LORD.
22Now Eli, who was very old, heard about everything his sons
were doing to all Israel and how they slept with the women who
served at the entrance to the Tent of Meeting. 23So he said to them,
"Why do you do such things? I hear from all the people about these
wicked deeds of yours. 24No, my sons; it is not a good report that
I hear spreading among the LORD's people. 25If a man sins against
another man, God[e] may mediate for him; but if a man sins against
the LORD, who will intercede for him?" His sons, however, did not
listen to their father's rebuke, for it was the LORD's will to put them
to death.
26And the boy Samuel continued to grow in stature and in favor
with the LORD and with men.

*Prophecy Against the House of Eli*

27Now a man of God came to Eli and said to him, "This is what
the LORD says: 'Did I not clearly reveal myself to your father's
house when they were in Egypt under Pharaoh? 28I chose your
father out of all the tribes of Israel to be my priest, to go up to my
altar, to burn incense, and to wear an ephod in my presence. I also
gave your father's house all the offerings made with fire by the
Israelites. 29Why do you[f] scorn my sacrifice and offering that I

NIV [d] 17 Or *men* [e] 25 Or *the judges* [f] 29 The Hebrew is plural.

## King James

29 Wherefore kick ye at my sacrifice and at mine offering, which I have commanded *in my* habitation; and honourest thy sons above me, to make yourselves fat with the chiefest of all the offerings of Israel my people?

30 Wherefore the LORD God of Israel saith, I said indeed *that* thy house, and the house of thy father, should walk before me for ever: but now the LORD saith, Be it far from me; for them that honour me I will honour, and they that despise me shall be lightly esteemed.

31 Behold, the days come, that I will cut off thine arm, and the arm of thy father's house, that there shall not be an old man in thine house.

32 And thou shalt see an enemy *in my* habitation, in all *the wealth* which *God* shall give Israel: and there shall not be an old man in thine house for ever.

33 And the man of thine, *whom* I shall not cut off from mine altar, *shall be* to consume thine eyes, and to grieve thine heart: and all the increase of thine house shall die in the flower of their age.

34 And this *shall be* a sign unto thee, that shall come upon thy two sons, on Hophni and Phinehas; in one day they shall die both of them.

35 And I will raise me up a faithful priest, *that* shall do according to *that* which *is* in mine heart and in my mind: and I will build him a sure house; and he shall walk before mine anointed for ever.

36 And it shall come to pass, *that* every one that is left in thine house shall come *and* crouch to him for a piece of silver and a morsel of bread, and shall say, Put me, I pray thee, into one of the priests' offices, that I may eat a piece of bread.

**3** AND THE child Samuel ministered unto the LORD before Eli. And the word of the LORD was precious in those days; *there was* no open vision.

2 And it came to pass at that time, when Eli *was* laid down in his place, and his eyes began to wax dim, *that* he could not see;

3 And ere the lamp of God went out in the temple of the LORD, where the ark of God *was,* and Samuel was laid down *to sleep;*

4 That the LORD called Samuel: and he answered, Here *am* I.

5 And he ran unto Eli, and said, Here *am* I; for thou calledst me. And he said, I called not; lie down again. And he went and lay down.

6 And the LORD called yet again, Samuel. And Samuel arose and went to Eli, and said, Here *am* I; for thou didst call me. And he answered, I called not, my son; lie down again.

7 Now Samuel did not yet know the LORD, neither was the word of the LORD yet revealed unto him.

8 And the LORD called Samuel again the third time. And he arose and went to Eli, and said, Here *am* I; for thou didst call me. And Eli perceived that the LORD had called the child.

9 Therefore Eli said unto Samuel, Go, lie down: and it shall be, if he call thee, that thou shalt say, Speak, LORD; for thy servant heareth. So Samuel went and lay down in his place.

10 And the LORD came, and stood, and called as at other times, Samuel, Samuel. Then Samuel answered, Speak; for thy servant heareth.

11 ¶ And the LORD said to Samuel, Behold, I will do a thing in Israel, at which both the ears of every one that heareth it shall tingle.

12 In that day I will perform against Eli all *things* which I have spoken concerning his house: when I begin, I will also make an end.

## Amplified

29 Why then do you kick [trample upon, treat with contempt] My sacrifice and My offering, which I commanded; and honor your sons above Me by fattening yourselves upon the choicest part of every offering of My people Israel?

30 Therefore the Lord the God of Israel says, I did promise that your house and that of your father [forefather Aaron] should go in and out before Me for ever. But now the Lord says, Be it far from Me; for those who honor Me I will honor, and those who despise Me shall be lightly esteemed.

31 Behold, the time is coming when I will cut off your strength and the strength of your own father's house, that there shall not be an old man in your house.

32 And you shall behold the distress of My house, even in all the prosperity which God will give Israel, and there shall not be an old man in your house for ever.

33 Yet I will not cut off from My altar every man of yours; some shall survive to weep and mourn [over the family's ruin]; but all the increase of your house shall die in their best years. [I Sam. 22:17-20.]

34 And what befalls your two sons, Hophni and Phinehas, shall be a sign to you; in one day they both shall die. [Fulfilled, I Sam. 4:17, 18.]

35 And I will raise Me up a [a]faithful priest, who shall do according to what is in My heart and mind. And I will build him a sure house; and he shall walk before My Anointed for ever. [Verse 10.]

36 Every one who is left in your house shall come crouching to him for a piece of silver and a bit of bread, and say, Put me, I pray you, into a priest's office, so I may have a piece of bread.

**3** NOW THE boy Samuel ministered to the Lord before Eli. The word of the Lord was rare *and* precious in those days; there was no frequent *or* widely spread vision.

2 At that time Eli, whose eyesight had dimmed so that he could not see, was lying down in his own place;

3 The lamp of God had not yet gone out in the temple of the Lord, where the ark of God was, and Samuel was lying down,

4 When the Lord called, Samuel! And he answered, Here I am.

5 He ran to Eli and said, Here I am, for you called me. Eli said, I did not call you; lie down again. So he went and lay down.

6 And the Lord called again, Samuel! And Samuel arose and went to Eli, and said, Here am I, you did call me. Eli answered, I did not call, my son; lie down again.

7 Now Samuel did not yet know the Lord, and the word of the Lord was not yet revealed to him.

8 And the Lord called Samuel the third time. And he went to Eli, and said, Here I am, for you did call me. Then Eli perceived that the Lord was calling the boy.

9 So Eli said to Samuel, Go, lie down. And if He calls you, you shall say, Speak, Lord, for Your servant is listening. So Samuel went and lay down in his place.

10 And the Lord came, and stood, and called as at other times, Samuel! Samuel! Then Samuel answered, Speak, Lord, for Your servant is listening.

11 The Lord told Samuel, Behold, I am about to do a thing in Israel, at which both ears of all who hear it shall tingle.

12 On that day I will perform against Eli all that I have spoken concerning his house, from beginning to end.

**AMP** [a] This person is not identified, but (as Lange's *Commentary* points out) this prophecy found its fulfillment from the standpoint of historical exposition in Samuel. Christian writers usually adopt also the Messianic interpretation. The text does not allow an exclusive reference to Christ, looking plainly as it does to the then existing order of things, but rather it points to Christ as the consummation of the blessedness which it promises.

## New American Standard

29'Why do you kick at My sacrifice and at My offering which I
have commanded *in My* dwelling, and honor your sons above Me,
by making yourselves fat with the choicest of every offering of My
people Israel?'
30"Therefore the LORD God of Israel declares, 'I did indeed say
that your house and the house of your father should walk before
Me forever'; but now the LORD declares, 'Far be it from Me—for
those who honor Me I will honor, and those who despise Me will
be lightly esteemed.
31'Behold, the days are coming when I will break your strength
and the strength of your father's house so that there will not be
an old man in your house.
32'And you will see the distress of *My* dwelling, in *spite of* all that
I do good for Israel; and an old man will not be in your house
forever.
33'Yet I will not cut off every man of yours from My altar that
your eyes may fail *from weeping* and your soul grieve, and all the
increase of your house will die in the prime of life.
34'And this will be the sign to you which shall come concerning
your two sons, Hophni and Phinehas: on the same day both of
them shall die.
35'But I will raise up for Myself a faithful priest who will do
according to what is in My heart and in My soul; and I will build
him an enduring house, and he will walk before My anointed
always.
36'And it shall come about that everyone who is left in your
house shall come and bow down to him for a piece of silver or a
loaf of bread, and say, "Please assign me to one of the priest's
offices so that I may eat a piece of bread." ' "

*The Prophetic Call to Samuel*

3 NOW THE boy Samuel was ministering to the LORD before
Eli. And word from the LORD was rare in those days, visions
were infrequent.
2And it happened at that time as Eli was lying down in his
place (now his eyesight had begun to grow dim *and* he could not
see well),
3and the lamp of God had not yet gone out, and Samuel was
lying down in the temple of the LORD where the ark of God *was*,
4that the LORD called Samuel; and he said, "Here I am."
5Then he ran to Eli and said, "Here I am, for you called me."
But he said, "I did not call, lie down again." So he went and lay
down.
6And the LORD called yet again, "Samuel!" So Samuel arose
and went to Eli, and said, "Here I am, for you called me." But he
answered, "I did not call, my son, lie down again."
7Now Samuel did not yet know the LORD, nor had the word
of the LORD yet been revealed to him.
8So the LORD called Samuel again for the third time. And he
arose and went to Eli, and said, "Here I am, for you called me."
Then Eli discerned that the LORD was calling the boy.
9And Eli said to Samuel, "Go lie down, and it shall be if He calls
you, that you shall say, 'Speak, LORD, for Thy servant is listening.' " So Samuel went and lay down in his place.
10¶ Then the LORD came and stood and called as at other times,
"Samuel! Samuel!" And Samuel said, "Speak, for Thy servant is
listening."
11And the LORD said to Samuel, "Behold, I am about to do a
thing in Israel at which both ears of everyone who hears it will
tingle.
12"In that day I will carry out against Eli all that I have spoken
concerning his house, from beginning to end.

## New International

prescribed for my dwelling? Why do you honor your sons more
than me by fattening yourselves on the choice parts of every offering made by my people Israel?'
30"Therefore the LORD, the God of Israel, declares: 'I promised
that your house and your father's house would minister before me
forever.' But now the LORD declares: 'Far be it from me! Those who
honor me I will honor, but those who despise me will be disdained. 31The time is coming when I will cut short your strength
and the strength of your father's house, so that there will not be
an old man in your family line 32and you will see distress in my
dwelling. Although good will be done to Israel, in your family line
there will never be an old man. 33Every one of you that I do not
cut off from my altar will be spared only to blind your eyes with
tears and to grieve your heart, and all your descendants will die
in the prime of life.
34" 'And what happens to your two sons, Hophni and Phinehas, will be a sign to you—they will both die on the same day. 35I
will raise up for myself a faithful priest, who will do according to
what is in my heart and mind. I will firmly establish his house, and
he will minister before my anointed one always. 36Then everyone
left in your family line will come and bow down before him for a
piece of silver and a crust of bread and plead, "Appoint me to some
priestly office so I can have food to eat." ' "

*The LORD Calls Samuel*

3 THE BOY Samuel ministered before the LORD under Eli. In
those days the word of the LORD was rare; there were not
many visions.
2One night Eli, whose eyes were becoming so weak that he
could barely see, was lying down in his usual place. 3The lamp of
God had not yet gone out, and Samuel was lying down in the
temple[b] of the LORD, where the ark of God was. 4Then the LORD
called Samuel.
Samuel answered, "Here I am." 5And he ran to Eli and said,
"Here I am; you called me."
But Eli said, "I did not call; go back and lie down." So he went
and lay down.
6Again the LORD called, "Samuel!" And Samuel got up and
went to Eli and said, "Here I am; you called me."
"My son," Eli said, "I did not call; go back and lie down."
7Now Samuel did not yet know the LORD: The word of the LORD
had not yet been revealed to him.
8The LORD called Samuel a third time, and Samuel got up and
went to Eli and said, "Here I am; you called me."
Then Eli realized that the LORD was calling the boy. 9So Eli told
Samuel, "Go and lie down, and if he calls you, say, 'Speak, LORD,
for your servant is listening.' " So Samuel went and lay down in
his place.
10The LORD came and stood there, calling as at the other times,
"Samuel! Samuel!"
Then Samuel said, "Speak, for your servant is listening."
11And the LORD said to Samuel: "See, I am about to do something in Israel that will make the ears of everyone who hears of it
tingle. 12At that time I will carry out against Eli everything I spoke
against his family—from beginning to end. 13For I told him that I

NIV [b]3 That is, tabernacle

## King James

13For I have told him that I will judge his house for ever for the iniquity which he knoweth; because his sons made themselves vile, and he restrained them not.
14And therefore I have sworn unto the house of Eli, that the iniquity of Eli's house shall not be purged with sacrifice nor offering for ever.
15¶ And Samuel lay until the morning, and opened the doors of the house of the LORD. And Samuel feared to show Eli the vision.
16Then Eli called Samuel, and said, Samuel, my son. And he answered, Here *am* I.
17And he said, What *is* the thing that *the* LORD hath said unto thee? I pray thee hide *it* not from me: God do so to thee, and more also, if thou hide *any* thing from me of all the things that he said unto thee.
18And Samuel told him every whit, and hid nothing from him. And he said, It *is* the LORD: let him do what seemeth him good.
19¶ And Samuel grew, and the LORD was with him, and did let none of his words fall to the ground.
20And all Israel from Dan even to Beer-sheba knew that Samuel *was* established *to be* a prophet of the LORD.
21And the LORD appeared again in Shiloh: for the LORD revealed himself to Samuel in Shiloh by the word of the LORD.

4 AND THE word of Samuel came to all Israel. Now Israel went out against the Philistines to battle, and pitched beside Eben-ezer: and the Philistines pitched in Aphek.
2And the Philistines put themselves in array against Israel: and when they joined battle, Israel was smitten before the Philistines: and they slew of the army in the field about four thousand men.
3¶ And when the people were come into the camp, the elders of Israel said, Wherefore hath the LORD smitten us today before the Philistines? Let us fetch the ark of the covenant of the LORD out of Shiloh unto us, that, when it cometh among us, it may save us out of the hand of our enemies.
4So the people sent to Shiloh, that they might bring from thence the ark of the covenant of the LORD of hosts, which dwelleth *between* the cherubims: and the two sons of Eli, Hophni and Phinehas, *were* there with the ark of the covenant of God.
5And when the ark of the covenant of the LORD came into the camp, all Israel shouted with a great shout, so that the earth rang again.
6And when the Philistines heard the noise of the shout, they said, What *meaneth* the noise of this great shout in the camp of the Hebrews? And they understood that the ark of the LORD was come into the camp.
7And the Philistines were afraid, for they said, God is come into the camp. And they said, Woe unto us! for there hath not been such a thing heretofore.
8Woe unto us! who shall deliver us out of the hand of these mighty Gods? these *are* the Gods that smote the Egyptians with all the plagues in the wilderness.
9Be strong, and quit yourselves like men, O ye Philistines, that ye be not servants unto the Hebrews, as they have been to you: quit yourselves like men, and fight.
10¶ And the Philistines fought, and Israel was smitten, and they fled every man into his tent: and there was a very great slaughter; for there fell of Israel thirty thousand footmen.
11And the ark of God was taken; and the two sons of Eli, Hophni and Phinehas, were slain.
12¶ And there ran a man of Benjamin out of the army, and came to Shiloh the same day with his clothes rent, and with earth upon his head.
13And when he came, lo, Eli sat upon a seat by the wayside watching: for his heart trembled for the ark of God. And when the man came into the city, and told *it*, all the city cried out.

## Amplified

13And I [now] announce to him that I will judge *and* punish his house for ever for the iniquity of which he knew, for his sons were [blaspheming God] bringing curse upon themselves, and he did not restrain them.
14Therefore I have sworn to the house of Eli, that the iniquity of Eli's house shall not be atoned for *or* purged with sacrifice or offering for ever.
15Samuel lay until morning; then he opened the doors of the Lord's house. And [he] was afraid to tell the vision to Eli.
16But Eli called Samuel, and said, Samuel, my son. And he answered, Here I am.
17Eli said, What is it He told you? Pray do not hide it from me. God do so to you and more also, if you hide anything from me of all that He said to you.
18And Samuel told him everything, hiding nothing. And Eli said, It is the Lord; let Him do what seems good to Him.
19Samuel grew; the Lord was with him and let none of his words fall to the ground. [Cp. Josh. 23:14.]
20And all Israel from Dan to Beersheba knew that Samuel was established to be a prophet of the Lord.
21And the Lord continued to appear in Shiloh, for the Lord revealed Himself to Samuel in Shiloh in the word of the Lord.

4 AND THE word of [the Lord through] Samuel came to all Israel. Now Israel went out to battle against the Philistines, and encamped beside Ebenezer; the Philistines encamped at Aphek.
2The Philistines drew up against Israel, and when the battle spread, Israel was smitten by the Philistines, who slew about 4,000 men on the *battle* field.
3When the troops had come into the camp, the elders of Israel said, Why has the Lord smitten us today before the Philistines? Let us bring the ark of the covenant of the Lord here from Shiloh, that He may come among us and save us from the power of our enemies.
4So the people sent to Shiloh and brought from there the ark of the covenant of the Lord of hosts, Who dwells above the cherubim; and the two sons of Eli, Hophni and Phinehas, were with the ark of the covenant of God.
5And when the ark of the covenant of the Lord came into the camp, all Israel shouted with a great shout, so that the earth resounded.
6And when the Philistines heard the noise of the shout, they said, What does this great shout in the camp of the Hebrews mean? When they understood that the ark of the Lord had come into the camp,
7The Philistines were afraid, for they said, God is come into the camp. And they said, Woe to us! For such a thing has not happened before.
8Woe to us! Who shall deliver us out of the hand of these mighty gods? These are the gods that smote the Egyptians with every kind of plague in the wilderness.
9Be strong, and acquit yourselves like men, O you Philistines, that you may not become servants to the Hebrews, as they have been to you; behave yourselves like men, and fight!
10And the Philistines fought; Israel was smitten, and they fled every man to his own home. There was a very great slaughter, for 30,000 foot soldiers of Israel fell.
11And the ark of God was taken; and the two sons of Eli, Hophni and Phinehas, were slain. [Foretold, I Sam. 2:34.]
12Now a man of Benjamin ran from the battle line and came to Shiloh that day, with his clothes torn and earth on his head.
13When he arrived, Eli was sitting by the road watching, for his heart trembled for the ark of God. When the man told the news in the city, all the city [people] cried out.

## New American Standard

13"For I have told him that I am about to judge his house forever for the iniquity which he knew, because his sons brought a curse on themselves and he did not rebuke them.

14"And therefore I have sworn to the house of Eli that the iniquity of Eli's house shall not be atoned for by sacrifice or offering forever."

15¶ So Samuel lay down until morning. Then he opened the doors of the house of the LORD. But Samuel was afraid to tell the vision to Eli.

16Then Eli called Samuel and said, "Samuel, my son." And he said, "Here I am."

17And he said, "What is the word that He spoke to you? Please do not hide it from me. May God do so to you, and more also, if you hide anything from me of all the words that He spoke to you."

18So Samuel told him everything and hid nothing from him. And he said, "It is the LORD; let Him do what seems good to Him."

19¶ Thus Samuel grew and the LORD was with him and let none of his words fail.

20And all Israel from Dan even to Beersheba knew that Samuel was confirmed as a prophet of the LORD.

21And the LORD appeared again at Shiloh, because the LORD revealed Himself to Samuel at Shiloh by the word of the LORD.

*Philistines Take the Ark in Victory*

**4** THUS THE word of Samuel came to all Israel. Now Israel went out to meet the Philistines in battle and camped beside Ebenezer while the Philistines camped in Aphek.

2And the Philistines drew up in battle array to meet Israel. When the battle spread, Israel was defeated before the Philistines who killed about four thousand men on the battlefield.

3When the people came into the camp, the elders of Israel said, "Why has the LORD defeated us today before the Philistines? Let us take to ourselves from Shiloh the ark of the covenant of the LORD, that it may come among us and deliver us from the power of our enemies."

4So the people sent to Shiloh, and from there they carried the ark of the covenant of the LORD of hosts who sits *above* the cherubim; and the two sons of Eli, Hophni and Phinehas, *were* there with the ark of the covenant of God.

5¶ And it happened as the ark of the covenant of the LORD came into the camp, that all Israel shouted with a great shout, so that the earth resounded.

6And when the Philistines heard the noise of the shout, they said, "What *does* the noise of this great shout in the camp of the Hebrews *mean?*" Then they understood that the ark of the LORD had come into the camp.

7And the Philistines were afraid, for they said, "God has come into the camp." And they said, "Woe to us! For nothing like this has happened before.

8"Woe to us! Who shall deliver us from the hand of these mighty gods? These are the gods who smote the Egyptians with all *kinds of* plagues in the wilderness.

9"Take courage and be men, O Philistines, lest you become slaves to the Hebrews, as they have been slaves to you; therefore, be men and fight."

10So the Philistines fought and Israel was defeated, and every man fled to his tent, and the slaughter was very great; for there fell of Israel thirty thousand foot soldiers.

11And the ark of God was taken; and the two sons of Eli, Hophni and Phinehas, died.

12¶ Now a man of Benjamin ran from the battle line and came to Shiloh the same day with his clothes torn and dust on his head.

13When he came, behold, Eli was sitting on *his* seat by the road eagerly watching, because his heart was trembling for the ark of God. So the man came to tell *it* in the city, and all the city cried out.

## New International

would judge his family forever because of the sin he knew about; his sons made themselves contemptible,[a] and he failed to restrain them. 14Therefore, I swore to the house of Eli, 'The guilt of Eli's house will never be atoned for by sacrifice or offering.'"

15Samuel lay down until morning and then opened the doors of the house of the LORD. He was afraid to tell Eli the vision, 16but Eli called him and said, "Samuel, my son."

Samuel answered, "Here I am."

17"What was it he said to you?" Eli asked. "Do not hide it from me. May God deal with you, be it ever so severely, if you hide from me anything he told you." 18So Samuel told him everything, hiding nothing from him. Then Eli said, "He is the LORD; let him do what is good in his eyes."

19The LORD was with Samuel as he grew up, and he let none of his words fall to the ground. 20And all Israel from Dan to Beersheba recognized that Samuel was attested as a prophet of the LORD. 21The LORD continued to appear at Shiloh, and there he revealed himself to Samuel through his word.

**4** AND SAMUEL'S word came to all Israel.

*The Philistines Capture the Ark*

Now the Israelites went out to fight against the Philistines. The Israelites camped at Ebenezer, and the Philistines at Aphek. 2The Philistines deployed their forces to meet Israel, and as the battle spread, Israel was defeated by the Philistines, who killed about four thousand of them on the battlefield. 3When the soldiers returned to camp, the elders of Israel asked, "Why did the LORD bring defeat upon us today before the Philistines? Let us bring the ark of the LORD's covenant from Shiloh, so that it[b] may go with us and save us from the hand of our enemies."

4So the people sent men to Shiloh, and they brought back the ark of the covenant of the LORD Almighty, who is enthroned between the cherubim. And Eli's two sons, Hophni and Phinehas, were there with the ark of the covenant of God.

5When the ark of the LORD's covenant came into the camp, all Israel raised such a great shout that the ground shook. 6Hearing the uproar, the Philistines asked, "What's all this shouting in the Hebrew camp?"

When they learned that the ark of the LORD had come into the camp, 7the Philistines were afraid. "A god has come into the camp," they said. "We're in trouble! Nothing like this has happened before. 8Woe to us! Who will deliver us from the hand of these mighty gods? They are the gods who struck the Egyptians with all kinds of plagues in the desert. 9Be strong, Philistines! Be men, or you will be subject to the Hebrews, as they have been to you. Be men, and fight!"

10So the Philistines fought, and the Israelites were defeated and every man fled to his tent. The slaughter was very great; Israel lost thirty thousand foot soldiers. 11The ark of God was captured, and Eli's two sons, Hophni and Phinehas, died.

*Death of Eli*

12That same day a Benjamite ran from the battle line and went to Shiloh, his clothes torn and dust on his head. 13When he arrived, there was Eli sitting on his chair by the side of the road, watching, because his heart feared for the ark of God. When the man entered the town and told what had happened, the whole town sent up a cry.

**NIV** [a] *13* Masoretic Text; an ancient Hebrew scribal tradition and Septuagint *sons blasphemed God* [b] *3* Or *he*

## King James

14 And when Eli heard the noise of the crying, he said, What *meaneth* the noise of this tumult? And the man came in hastily, and told Eli.

15 Now Eli was ninety and eight years old; and his eyes were dim, that he could not see.

16 And the man said unto Eli, I *am* he that came out of the army, and I fled today out of the army. And he said, What is there done, my son?

17 And the messenger answered and said, Israel is fled before the Philistines, and there hath been also a great slaughter among the people, and thy two sons also, Hophni and Phinehas, are dead, and the ark of God is taken.

18 And it came to pass, when he made mention of the ark of God, that he fell from off the seat backward by the side of the gate, and his neck brake, and he died: for he was an old man, and heavy. And he had judged Israel forty years.

19 ¶ And his daughter-in-law, Phinehas' wife, was with child, *near* to be delivered: and when she heard the tidings that the ark of God was taken, and that her father-in-law and her husband were dead, she bowed herself and travailed; for her pains came upon her.

20 And about the time of her death the women that stood by her said unto her, Fear not; for thou hast borne a son. But she answered not, neither did she regard *it*.

21 And she named the child I-chabod, saying, The glory is departed from Israel: because the ark of God was taken, and because of her father-in-law and her husband.

22 And she said, The glory is departed from Israel: for the ark of God is taken.

**5** AND THE Philistines took the ark of God, and brought it from Eben-ezer unto Ashdod.

2 When the Philistines took the ark of God, they brought it into the house of Dagon, and set it by Dagon.

3 ¶ And when they of Ashdod arose early on the morrow, behold, Dagon *was* fallen upon his face to the earth before the ark of the LORD. And they took Dagon, and set him in his place again.

4 And when they arose early on the morrow morning, behold, Dagon *was* fallen upon his face to the ground before the ark of the LORD; and the head of Dagon and both the palms of his hands *were* cut off upon the threshold; only *the stump of* Dagon was left to him.

5 Therefore neither the priests of Dagon, nor any that come into Dagon's house, tread on the threshold of Dagon in Ashdod unto this day.

6 But the hand of the LORD was heavy upon them of Ashdod, and he destroyed them, and smote them with emerods, *even* Ashdod and the coasts thereof.

7 And when the men of Ashdod saw that *it was* so, they said, The ark of the God of Israel shall not abide with us: for his hand is sore upon us, and upon Dagon our god.

8 They sent therefore and gathered all the lords of the Philistines unto them, and said, What shall we do with the ark of the God of Israel? And they answered, Let the ark of the God of Israel be carried about unto Gath. And they carried the ark of the God of Israel about *thither*.

9 And it was *so*, that, after they had carried it about, the hand of the LORD was against the city with a very great destruction: and he smote the men of the city, both small and great, and they had emerods in their secret parts.

10 ¶ Therefore they sent the ark of God to Ekron. And it came to pass, as the ark of God came to Ekron, that the Ekronites cried out, saying, They have brought about the ark of the God of Israel to us, to slay us and our people.

## Amplified

14 When Eli heard the noise of the crying, he said, What is this uproar? And the man came hastily and told Eli.

15 Now Eli was 98 years old; his eyes were dim, so he could not see.

16 The man said to Eli, I have come from the battle; I fled from the battle today. Eli said, How did it go, my son?

17 The messenger replied, Israel fled before the Philistines, and there has been a great slaughter among the people; also your two sons, Hophni and Phinehas, are dead, and the ark of God is captured.

18 And when he mentioned the ark of God, Eli fell off the seat backward by the side of the gate; his neck was broken and he died, for he was an old man, and heavy. He had judged Israel forty years.

19 Now his daughter-in-law, Phinehas' wife, was with child about to be delivered. And when she heard that the ark of God was captured, and that her father-in-law and her husband were dead, she bowed herself and gave birth; for her pains came upon her.

20 And about the time of her death the women attending her said to her, Fear not, for you have borne a son. But she did not answer or notice.

21 And she named the child Ichabod, saying, The glory is departed from Israel! Because the ark of God had been captured and because of her father-in-law and her husband.

22 She said, The glory is gone from Israel, for the ark of God has been taken.

**5** THE PHILISTINES brought the ark of God from Ebenezer to Ashdod.

2 They took the ark of God into the house of Dagon and set it beside Dagon [their idol].

3 When they of Ashdod arose early on the morrow, behold, Dagon had fallen upon his face on the ground before the ark of the Lord. So they took Dagon and set him in his place again.

4 But when they arose early the next morning, behold, Dagon had again fallen on his face on the ground before the ark of the Lord, and [his] head and both the palms of his hands were lying cut off on the threshold; only the trunk of Dagon was left him.

5 This is the reason neither the priests of Dagon, nor any who come into Dagon's house, tread on the threshold of Dagon in Ashdod to this day.

6 But the hand of the Lord was heavy upon the people of Ashdod, and He caused [mice to spring up and there was] very deadly destruction, and He smote the people with [very painful] tumors *or* boils, both Ashdod and its territory.

7 When the men of Ashdod saw that it was so, they said, The ark of the God of Israel must not remain with us; for His hand is heavy on us and on Dagon our god.

8 So they sent and gathered all the lords of the Philistines to them, and said, What shall we do with the ark of the God of Israel? They answered, Let [it] be carried around to Gath. So they carried the ark of the God of Israel there.

9 But after they had carried it to Gath, the hand of the Lord was against the city, causing an exceedingly great panic [at the deaths from the plague], for He afflicted the people of the city, both small and great, and tumors *or* boils broke out on them.

10 So they sent the ark of God to Ekron. And as [it] came the people of Ekron cried out, They have brought the ark of the God of Israel to us, to slay us and our people!

## New American Standard

14When Eli heard the noise of the outcry, he said, "What *does*
the noise of this commotion *mean?*" Then the man came hurriedly
and told Eli.
15Now Eli was ninety-eight years old, and his eyes were set so
that he could not see.
16And the man said to Eli, "I am the one who came from the
battle line. Indeed, I escaped from the battle line today." And he
said, "How did things go, my son?"
17Then the one who brought the news answered and said,
"Israel has fled before the Philistines and there has also been a
great slaughter among the people, and your two sons also, Hophni
and Phinehas, are dead, and the ark of God has been taken."
18And it came about when he mentioned the ark of God that Eli
fell off the seat backward beside the gate, and his neck was broken
and he died, for he was old and heavy. Thus he judged Israel forty
years.
19¶ Now his daughter-in-law, Phinehas' wife, was pregnant
and about to give birth; and when she heard the news that the ark
of God was taken and that her father-in-law and her husband had
died, she kneeled down and gave birth, for her pains came upon
her.
20And about the time of her death the women who stood by her
said to her, "Do not be afraid, for you have given birth to a son."
But she did not answer or pay attention.
21And she called the boy [a]Ichabod, saying, "The glory has
departed from Israel," because the ark of God was taken and
because of her father-in-law and her husband.
22And she said, "The glory has departed from Israel, for the ark
of God was taken."

*Capture of the Ark Provokes God*

5 NOW THE Philistines took the ark of God and brought it from
Ebenezer to Ashdod.
2Then the Philistines took the ark of God and brought it to the
house of Dagon, and set it by Dagon.
3When the Ashdodites arose early the next morning, behold,
Dagon had fallen on his face to the ground before the ark of the
LORD. So they took Dagon and set him in his place again.
4But when they arose early the next morning, behold, Dagon
had fallen on his face to the ground before the ark of the LORD. And
the head of Dagon and both the palms of his hands *were* cut off on
the threshold; only the trunk of Dagon was left to him.
5Therefore neither the priests of Dagon nor all who enter Dagon's house tread on the threshold of Dagon in Ashdod to this
day.
6¶ Now the hand of the LORD was heavy on the Ashdodites,
and He ravaged them and smote them with tumors, both Ashdod
and its territories.
7When the men of Ashdod saw that it was so, they said, "The
ark of the God of Israel must not remain with us, for His hand is
severe on us and on Dagon our god."
8So they sent and gathered all the lords of the Philistines to
them and said, "What shall we do with the ark of the God of
Israel?" And they said, "Let the ark of the God of Israel be brought
around to Gath." And they brought the ark of the God of Israel
*around.*
9And it came about that after they had brought it around, the
hand of the LORD was against the city with very great confusion;
and He smote the men of the city, both young and old, so that
tumors broke out on them.
10So they sent the ark of God to Ekron. And it happened as the
ark of God came to Ekron that the Ekronites cried out, saying,
"They have brought the ark of the God of Israel around to us, to
kill us and our people."

NAS [a] I.e., no glory

## New International

14Eli heard the outcry and asked, "What is the meaning of this
uproar?"
The man hurried over to Eli, 15who was ninety-eight years old
and whose eyes were set so that he could not see. 16He told Eli,
"I have just come from the battle line; I fled from it this very day."
Eli asked, "What happened, my son?"
17The man who brought the news replied, "Israel fled before
the Philistines, and the army has suffered heavy losses. Also your
two sons, Hophni and Phinehas, are dead, and the ark of God has
been captured."
18When he mentioned the ark of God, Eli fell backward off his
chair by the side of the gate. His neck was broken and he died, for
he was an old man and heavy. He had led[b] Israel forty years.
19His daughter-in-law, the wife of Phinehas, was pregnant and
near the time of delivery. When she heard the news that the ark
of God had been captured and that her father-in-law and her
husband were dead, she went into labor and gave birth, but was
overcome by her labor pains. 20As she was dying, the women
attending her said, "Don't despair; you have given birth to a son."
But she did not respond or pay any attention.
21She named the boy Ichabod,[c] saying, "The glory has departed from Israel"—because of the capture of the ark of God and
the deaths of her father-in-law and her husband. 22She said, "The
glory has departed from Israel, for the ark of God has been captured."

*The Ark in Ashdod and Ekron*

5 AFTER THE Philistines had captured the ark of God, they
took it from Ebenezer to Ashdod. 2Then they carried the ark
into Dagon's temple and set it beside Dagon. 3When the people of
Ashdod rose early the next day, there was Dagon, fallen on his face
on the ground before the ark of the LORD! They took Dagon and
put him back in his place. 4But the following morning when they
rose, there was Dagon, fallen on his face on the ground before the
ark of the LORD! His head and hands had been broken off and were
lying on the threshold; only his body remained. 5That is why to
this day neither the priests of Dagon nor any others who enter
Dagon's temple at Ashdod step on the threshold.
6The LORD's hand was heavy upon the people of Ashdod and
its vicinity; he brought devastation upon them and afflicted them
with tumors.[d] 7When the men of Ashdod saw what was happening, they said, "The ark of the god of Israel must not stay here with
us, because his hand is heavy upon us and upon Dagon our god."
8So they called together all the rulers of the Philistines and asked
them, "What shall we do with the ark of the god of Israel?"
They answered, "Have the ark of the god of Israel moved to
Gath." So they moved the ark of the God of Israel.
9But after they had moved it, the LORD's hand was against that
city, throwing it into a great panic. He afflicted the people of the
city, both young and old, with an outbreak of tumors.[e] 10So they
sent the ark of God to Ekron.
As the ark of God was entering Ekron, the people of Ekron cried
out, "They have brought the ark of the god of Israel around to us
to kill us and our people." 11So they called together all the rulers

NIV [b] 18 Traditionally *judged* [c] 21 *Ichabod* means *no glory.* [d] 6 Hebrew; Septuagint and Vulgate *tumors. And rats appeared in their land, and death and destruction were throughout the city* [e] 9 Or *with tumors in the groin* (see Septuagint)

## King James

11So they sent and gathered together all the lords of the Philistines, and said, Send away the ark of the God of Israel, and let it go again to his own place, that it slay us not, and our people: for there was a deadly destruction throughout all the city; the hand of God was very heavy there.
12And the men that died not were smitten with the emerods: and the cry of the city went up to heaven.

**6** AND THE ark of the LORD was in the country of the Philistines seven months.
2And the Philistines called for the priests and the diviners, saying, What shall we do to the ark of the LORD? tell us wherewith we shall send it to his place.
3And they said, If ye send away the ark of the God of Israel, send it not empty; but in any wise return him a trespass offering: then ye shall be healed, and it shall be known to you why his hand is not removed from you.
4Then said they, What *shall be* the trespass offering which we shall return to him? They answered, Five golden emerods, and five golden mice, *according to* the number of the lords of the Philistines: for one plague *was* on you all, and on your lords.
5Wherefore ye shall make images of your emerods, and images of your mice that mar the land; and ye shall give glory unto the God of Israel: peradventure he will lighten his hand from off you, and from off your gods, and from off your land.
6Wherefore then do ye harden your hearts, as the Egyptians and Pharaoh hardened their hearts? when he had wrought wonderfully among them, did they not let the people go, and they departed?
7Now therefore make a new cart, and take two milch kine, on which there hath come no yoke, and tie the kine to the cart, and bring their calves home from them:
8And take the ark of the LORD, and lay it upon the cart; and put the jewels of gold, which ye return him *for* a trespass offering, in a coffer by the side thereof; and send it away, that it may go.
9And see, if it goeth up by the way of his own coast to Beth-shemesh, *then* he hath done us this great evil: but if not, then we shall know that *it is* not his hand *that* smote us; it *was* a chance *that* happened to us.
10¶ And the men did so; and took two milch kine, and tied them to the cart, and shut up their calves at home:
11And they laid the ark of the LORD upon the cart, and the coffer with the mice of gold and the images of their emerods.
12And the kine took the straight way to the way of Beth-shemesh, *and* went along the highway, lowing as they went, and turned not aside *to* the right hand or *to* the left; and the lords of the Philistines went after them unto the border of Beth-shemesh.
13And *they of* Beth-shemesh *were* reaping their wheat harvest in the valley: and they lifted up their eyes, and saw the ark, and rejoiced to see *it*.
14And the cart came into the field of Joshua, a Beth-shemite, and stood there, where *there was* a great stone: and they clave the wood of the cart, and offered the kine a burnt offering unto the LORD.
15And the Levites took down the ark of the LORD, and the coffer that *was* with it, wherein the jewels of gold *were*, and put *them* on the great stone: and the men of Beth-shemesh offered burnt offerings and sacrificed sacrifices the same day unto the LORD.
16And when the five lords of the Philistines had seen *it*, they returned to Ekron the same day.
17And these *are* the golden emerods which the Philistines returned *for* a trespass offering unto the LORD; for Ashdod one, for Gaza one, for Askelon one, for Gath one, for Ekron one;

## Amplified

11So they sent and assembled all the lords of the Philistines, and said, Send away the ark of the God of Israel; let it return to its own place, that it may not slay us and our people. For there was a deadly panic throughout all the city; the hand of God was very heavy there.
12The men who had not died were stricken with the very painful tumors *or* boils, and the cry of the city went up to Heaven.

**6** THE ARK of the Lord was in the country of the Philistines seven months.
2And the Philistines called for the priests and the diviners, saying, What shall we do to the ark of the Lord? Tell us with what we shall send it to its place.
3And they said, If you send away the ark of the God of Israel, do not send it empty, but at least return Him a guilt offering; then you will be healed, and it will be known to you why His hand is not removed [and healing granted you].
4Then they said, What shall be the guilt offering which we shall return to Him? They answered, Five golden tumors, and five golden mice, according to the number of the Philistine lords; for one plague was on you all, even on your lords.
5Therefore you must make images of your tumors and of your mice that destroy the land, and give glory to the God of Israel. Perhaps He will lighten His hand from off you and your gods and your land.
6Why then do you harden your hearts, as the Egyptians and Pharaoh hardened their hearts? When He had done wonders *and* made a mock of them, did they not let the people go, and they departed?
7Now then make and prepare a new cart, and two milch cows on which no yoke has ever come, and yoke the cows to the cart, but take their calves home, away from them.
8And take the ark of the Lord and place it upon the cart, and put in a box at its side the figures of gold, which you are returning to Him as a guilt offering. Then send it away, and let it be gone.
9And watch; if it goes up by the way of its own land to Beth-shemesh, then He has done us this great evil; but if not, then we shall know that it is not His hand that struck us, it happened to us by chance.
10And the men did so, and took two milch cows and yoked them to the cart, and shut up their calves at home.
11And they put the ark of the Lord on the cart, and the box with the mice of gold, and the images of their tumors.
12And the cows went straight toward Beth-shemesh along the highway, lowing as they went, and turned not aside to the right or the left, and the Philistine lords followed them as far as the border of Beth-shemesh.
13Now the men of Beth-shemesh were reaping their wheat harvest in the valley; and they lifted up their eyes and saw the ark, and rejoiced to see it.
14The cart came into the field of Joshua of Beth-shemesh and stopped there. A great stone was there, and the men split up the wood of the cart and offered the cows as a burnt offering to the Lord.
15The Levites took down the ark of the Lord, and the box beside it in which were the figures of gold and put them upon the great stone. And the men of Beth-shemesh offered burnt offerings and sacrifices that day to the Lord.
16When the five lords of the Philistines saw it, they returned that day to Ekron.
17And these are the tumors of gold which the Philistines returned for a guilt offering to the Lord: one each for Ashdod, Gaza, Ashkelon, Gath and Ekron;

## New American Standard

11They sent therefore and gathered all the lords of the Philistines and said, "Send away the ark of the God of Israel, and let it
return to its own place, that it may not kill us and our people." For
there was a deadly confusion throughout the city; the hand of God
was very heavy there.
12And the men who did not die were smitten with tumors and
the cry of the city went up to heaven.

*The Ark Returned to Israel*

6 NOW THE ark of the LORD had been in the country of the
Philistines seven months.
2And the Philistines called for the priests and the diviners,
saying, "What shall we do with the ark of the LORD? Tell us how
we shall send it to its place."
3And they said, "If you send away the ark of the God of Israel,
do not send it empty; but you shall surely return to Him a guilt
offering. Then you shall be healed and it shall be known to you
why His hand is not removed from you."
4Then they said, "What shall be the guilt offering which we
shall return to Him?" And they said, "Five golden tumors and five
golden mice *according to* the number of the lords of the Philistines,
for one plague was on all of you and on your lords.
5"So you shall make likenesses of your tumors and likenesses
of your mice that ravage the land, and you shall give glory to the
God of Israel; perhaps He will ease His hand from you, your gods,
and your land.
6"Why then do you harden your hearts as the Egyptians and
Pharaoh hardened their hearts? When He had severely dealt with
them, did they not allow the people to go, and they departed?
7"Now therefore take and prepare a new cart and two milch
cows on which there has never been a yoke; and hitch the cows
to the cart and take their calves home, away from them.
8"And take the ark of the LORD and place it on the cart; and
put the articles of gold which you return to Him as a guilt offering
in a box by its side. Then send it away that it may go.
9"And watch, if it goes up by the way of its own territory to
Beth-shemesh, then He has done us this great evil. But if not, then
we shall know that it was not His hand that struck us; it happened
to us by chance."
10¶ Then the men did so, and took two milch cows and hitched
them to the cart, and shut up their calves at home.
11And they put the ark of the LORD on the cart, and the box with
the golden mice and the likenesses of their tumors.
12And the cows took the straight way in the direction of Beth-
shemesh; they went along the highway, lowing as they went, and
did not turn aside to the right or to the left. And the lords of the
Philistines followed them to the border of Beth-shemesh.
13Now *the people of* Beth-shemesh were reaping their wheat
harvest in the valley, and they raised their eyes and saw the ark
and were glad to see *it*.
14And the cart came into the field of Joshua the Beth-shemite
and stood there where there *was* a large stone; and they split the
wood of the cart and offered the cows as a burnt offering to the
LORD.
15And the Levites took down the ark of the LORD and the box
that was with it, in which were the articles of gold, and put them
on the large stone; and the men of Beth-shemesh offered burnt
offerings and sacrificed sacrifices that day to the LORD.
16And when the five lords of the Philistines saw it, they returned to Ekron that day.
17¶ And these are the golden tumors which the Philistines returned for a guilt offering to the LORD: one for Ashdod, one for
Gaza, one for Ashkelon, one for Gath, one for Ekron;

## New International

of the Philistines and said, "Send the ark of the god of Israel away;
let it go back to its own place, or it[a] will kill us and our people."
For death had filled the city with panic; God's hand was very
heavy upon it. 12Those who did not die were afflicted with tumors,
and the outcry of the city went up to heaven.

*The Ark Returned to Israel*

6 WHEN THE ark of the LORD had been in Philistine territory
seven months, 2the Philistines called for the priests and the
diviners and said, "What shall we do with the ark of the LORD? Tell
us how we should send it back to its place."
3They answered, "If you return the ark of the god of Israel, do
not send it away empty, but by all means send a guilt offering to
him. Then you will be healed, and you will know why his hand
has not been lifted from you."
4The Philistines asked, "What guilt offering should we send to
him?"
They replied, "Five gold tumors and five gold rats, according
to the number of the Philistine rulers, because the same plague has
struck both you and your rulers. 5Make models of the tumors and
of the rats that are destroying the country, and pay honor to
Israel's god. Perhaps he will lift his hand from you and your gods
and your land. 6Why do you harden your hearts as the Egyptians
and Pharaoh did? When he[b] treated them harshly, did they not
send the Israelites out so they could go on their way?
7"Now then, get a new cart ready, with two cows that have
calved and have never been yoked. Hitch the cows to the cart, but
take their calves away and pen them up. 8Take the ark of the LORD
and put it on the cart, and in a chest beside it put the gold objects
you are sending back to him as a guilt offering. Send it on its way,
9but keep watching it. If it goes up to its own territory, toward Beth
Shemesh, then the LORD has brought this great disaster on us. But
if it does not, then we will know that it was not his hand that struck
us and that it happened to us by chance."
10So they did this. They took two such cows and hitched them
to the cart and penned up their calves. 11They placed the ark of the
LORD on the cart and along with it the chest containing the gold
rats and the models of the tumors. 12Then the cows went straight
up toward Beth Shemesh, keeping on the road and lowing all the
way; they did not turn to the right or to the left. The rulers of the
Philistines followed them as far as the border of Beth Shemesh.
13Now the people of Beth Shemesh were harvesting their wheat
in the valley, and when they looked up and saw the ark, they
rejoiced at the sight. 14The cart came to the field of Joshua of Beth
Shemesh, and there it stopped beside a large rock. The people
chopped up the wood of the cart and sacrificed the cows as a burnt
offering to the LORD. 15The Levites took down the ark of the LORD,
together with the chest containing the gold objects, and placed
them on the large rock. On that day the people of Beth Shemesh
offered burnt offerings and made sacrifices to the LORD. 16The five
rulers of the Philistines saw all this and then returned that same
day to Ekron.
17These are the gold tumors the Philistines sent as a guilt offering to the LORD—one each for Ashdod, Gaza, Ashkelon, Gath and
Ekron. 18And the number of the gold rats was according to the

NIV [a] *11* Or *he* [b] *6* That is, God

## King James

18 And the golden mice, *according to* the number of all the cities of the Philistines *belonging* to the five lords, *both* of fenced cities, and of country villages, even unto the great *stone of* Abel, whereon they set down the ark of the LORD: *which stone remaineth* unto this day in the field of Joshua, the Beth-shemite.

19 ¶ And he smote the men of Beth-shemesh, because they had looked into the ark of the LORD, even he smote of the people fifty thousand and threescore and ten men: and the people lamented, because the LORD had smitten *many* of the people with a great slaughter.

20 And the men of Beth-shemesh said, Who is able to stand before this holy LORD God? and to whom shall he go up from us?

21 ¶ And they sent messengers to the inhabitants of Kirjath-jearim, saying, The Philistines have brought again the ark of the LORD; come ye down, *and* fetch it up to you.

**7** AND THE men of Kirjath-jearim came, and fetched up the ark of the LORD, and brought it into the house of Abinadab in the hill, and sanctified Eleazar his son to keep the ark of the LORD.

2 And it came to pass, while the ark abode in Kirjath-jearim, that the time was long; for it was twenty years: and all the house of Israel lamented after the LORD.

3 ¶ And Samuel spake unto all the house of Israel, saying, If ye do return unto the LORD with all your hearts, *then* put away the strange gods and Ashtaroth from among you, and prepare your hearts unto the LORD, and serve him only: and he will deliver you out of the hand of the Philistines.

4 Then the children of Israel did put away Baalim and Ashtaroth, and served the LORD only.

5 And Samuel said, Gather all Israel to Mizpeh, and I will pray for you unto the LORD.

6 And they gathered together to Mizpeh, and drew water, and poured *it* out before the LORD, and fasted on that day, and said there, We have sinned against the LORD. And Samuel judged the children of Israel in Mizpeh.

7 And when the Philistines heard that the children of Israel were gathered together to Mizpeh, the lords of the Philistines went up against Israel. And when the children of Israel heard *it*, they were afraid of the Philistines.

8 And the children of Israel said to Samuel, Cease not to cry unto the LORD our God for us, that he will save us out of the hand of the Philistines.

9 ¶ And Samuel took a sucking lamb, and offered *it for* a burnt offering wholly unto the LORD: and Samuel cried unto the LORD for Israel; and the LORD heard him.

10 And as Samuel was offering up the burnt offering, the Philistines drew near to battle against Israel: but the LORD thundered with a great thunder on that day upon the Philistines, and discomfited them; and they were smitten before Israel.

11 And the men of Israel went out of Mizpeh, and pursued the Philistines, and smote them, until *they came* under Beth-car.

12 Then Samuel took a stone, and set *it* between Mizpeh and Shen, and called the name of it Eben-ezer, saying, Hitherto hath the LORD helped us.

13 ¶ So the Philistines were subdued, and they came no more into the coast of Israel: and the hand of the LORD was against the Philistines all the days of Samuel.

14 And the cities which the Philistines had taken from Israel were restored to Israel, from Ekron even unto Gath; and the coasts thereof did Israel deliver out of the hands of the Philistines. And there was peace between Israel and the Amorites.

15 And Samuel judged Israel all the days of his life.

## Amplified

18 Also the mice of gold according to the number of all the cities of the Philistines belonging to the five lords, both fortified cities and country villages. The great stone, on which they set the ark of the Lord, remains as a witness to this day in the field of Joshua of Beth-shemesh.

19 And the Lord slew some of the men of Beth-shemesh, because they had looked into the ark of the Lord; He slew seventy men of them [fifty thousand men], and the people mourned, because the Lord had made a great slaughter among them.

20 And the men of Beth-shemesh said, Who is able to stand before the Lord, this holy God? And to whom shall He go away from us?

21 And they sent messengers to the inhabitants of Kiriath-jearim, saying, The Philistines have returned the ark of the Lord. Come down and take it up to you.

**7** SO THE men of Kiriath-jearim came, and took the ark of the Lord, and brought it into the house of Abinadab on the hill, and consecrated Eleazar his son to have charge of the ark of the Lord.

2 And the ark remained in Kiriath-jearim a very long time [nearly 100 years, through Samuel's entire judgeship, Saul's reign, and well into David's, when it was brought to Jerusalem]. For it was twenty years before all the house of Israel lamented after the Lord. [I Chron. 13:5-7.]

3 Then Samuel said to all the house of Israel, If you are returning to the Lord with all your heart, then put away the foreign gods and the Ashtaroth from among you, and direct your hearts to the Lord, and serve Him only, and He will deliver you out of the hand of the Philistines.

4 So the Israelites put away the Baals and the Ashtaroth [fem. plu.], and served the Lord only.

5 Samuel said, Gather all Israel to Mizpah, and I will pray to the Lord for you.

6 So they gathered at Mizpah, and drew water and poured it out before the Lord, and fasted on that day, and said there, We have sinned against the Lord. And Samuel judged the Israelites at Mizpah.

7 Now when the Philistines heard that the Israelites had gathered at Mizpah, the lords of the Philistines went up against Israel. And when the Israelites heard of it they were afraid of the Philistines.

8 And the Israelites said to Samuel, Do not cease to cry to the Lord our God for us, that He will save us from the hand of the Philistines.

9 So Samuel took a sucking lamb, and offered it as a whole burnt offering to the Lord; and Samuel cried to the Lord for Israel, and the Lord answered him.

10 As Samuel was offering up the burnt offering, the Philistines drew near to attack Israel; but the Lord thundered with a great voice that day against the Philistines, and threw them into confusion; and they were defeated before Israel.

11 And the men of Israel went out of Mizpah, and pursued the Philistines, and smote them, as far as below Beth-car.

12 Then Samuel took a stone, and set it between Mizpah and Jeshanah, and called the name of it Ebenezer [stone of help], saying, Heretofore the Lord has helped us.

13 So the Philistines were subdued, and came no more into Israelite territory. And the hand of the Lord was against the Philistines all the days of Samuel.

14 The cities the Philistines had taken from Israel were restored to Israel, from Ekron to Gath; and Israel rescued [the cities'] territory from the Philistines. There was peace also between Israel and the Amorites.

15 And Samuel judged Israel all his days.

## New American Standard

18and the golden mice, *according* to the number of all the cities
of the Philistines belonging to the five lords, both of fortified cities
and of country villages. The large stone on which they set the ark
of the LORD *is a witness* to this day in the field of Joshua the
Beth-shemite.
19¶ And He struck down some of the men of Beth-shemesh
because they had looked into the ark of the LORD. He struck down
of all the people, 50,070 men, and the people mourned because the
LORD had struck the people with a great slaughter.
20And the men of Beth-shemesh said, "Who is able to stand
before the LORD, this holy God? And to whom shall He go up from
us?"
21So they sent messengers to the inhabitants of Kiriath-jearim,
saying, "The Philistines have brought back the ark of the LORD;
come down and take it up to you."

*Deliverance from the Philistines*

7 AND THE men of Kiriath-jearim came and took the ark of the
LORD and brought it into the house of Abinadab on the hill,
and consecrated Eleazar his son to keep the ark of the LORD.
2And it came about from the day that the ark remained at
Kiriath-jearim that the time was long, for it was twenty years; and
all the house of Israel lamented after the LORD.
3¶ Then Samuel spoke to all the house of Israel, saying, "If you
return to the LORD with all your heart, remove the foreign gods
and the Ashtaroth from among you and direct your hearts to the
LORD and serve Him alone; and He will deliver you from the hand
of the Philistines."
4So the sons of Israel removed the Baals and the Ashtaroth and
served the LORD alone.
5¶ Then Samuel said, "Gather all Israel to Mizpah, and I will
pray to the LORD for you."
6And they gathered to Mizpah, and drew water and poured it
out before the LORD, and fasted on that day, and said there, "We
have sinned against the LORD." And Samuel judged the sons of
Israel at Mizpah.
7Now when the Philistines heard that the sons of Israel had
gathered to Mizpah, the lords of the Philistines went up against
Israel. And when the sons of Israel heard it, they were afraid of
the Philistines.
8Then the sons of Israel said to Samuel, "Do not cease to cry
to the LORD our God for us, that He may save us from the hand
of the Philistines."
9And Samuel took a suckling lamb and offered it for a whole
burnt offering to the LORD; and Samuel cried to the LORD for Israel
and the LORD answered him.
10Now Samuel was offering up the burnt offering, and the
Philistines drew near to battle against Israel. But the LORD thundered with a great thunder on that day against the Philistines and
confused them, so that they were routed before Israel.
11And the men of Israel went out of Mizpah and pursued the
Philistines, and struck them down as far as below Beth-car.
12¶ Then Samuel took a stone and set it between Mizpah and
Shen, and named it [a]Ebenezer, saying, "Thus far the LORD has
helped us."
13So the Philistines were subdued and they did not come anymore within the border of Israel. And the hand of the LORD was
against the Philistines all the days of Samuel.
14And the cities which the Philistines had taken from Israel
were restored to Israel, from Ekron even to Gath; and Israel delivered their territory from the hand of the Philistines. So there was
peace between Israel and the Amorites.

*Samuel's Ministry*

15¶ Now Samuel judged Israel all the days of his life.

NAS [a] I.e., the stone of help

## New International

number of Philistine towns belonging to the five rulers—the fortified towns with their country villages. The large rock, on which[b]
they set the ark of the LORD, is a witness to this day in the field
of Joshua of Beth Shemesh.
19But God struck down some of the men of Beth Shemesh,
putting seventy[c] of them to death because they had looked into
the ark of the LORD. The people mourned because of the heavy
blow the LORD had dealt them, 20and the men of Beth Shemesh
asked, "Who can stand in the presence of the LORD, this holy God?
To whom will the ark go up from here?"
21Then they sent messengers to the people of Kiriath Jearim,
saying, "The Philistines have returned the ark of the LORD. Come
down and take it up to your place."

7 SO THE men of Kiriath Jearim came and took up the ark of
the LORD. They took it to Abinadab's house on the hill and
consecrated Eleazar his son to guard the ark of the LORD.

*Samuel Subdues the Philistines at Mizpah*

2It was a long time, twenty years in all, that the ark remained
at Kiriath Jearim, and all the people of Israel mourned and sought
after the LORD. 3And Samuel said to the whole house of Israel, "If
you are returning to the LORD with all your hearts, then rid yourselves of the foreign gods and the Ashtoreths and commit yourselves to the LORD and serve him only, and he will deliver you out
of the hand of the Philistines." 4So the Israelites put away their
Baals and Ashtoreths, and served the LORD only.
5Then Samuel said, "Assemble all Israel at Mizpah and I will
intercede with the LORD for you." 6When they had assembled at
Mizpah, they drew water and poured it out before the LORD. On
that day they fasted and there they confessed, "We have sinned
against the LORD." And Samuel was leader[d] of Israel at Mizpah.
7When the Philistines heard that Israel had assembled at Mizpah, the rulers of the Philistines came up to attack them. And
when the Israelites heard of it, they were afraid because of the
Philistines. 8They said to Samuel, "Do not stop crying out to the
LORD our God for us, that he may rescue us from the hand of the
Philistines." 9Then Samuel took a suckling lamb and offered it up
as a whole burnt offering to the LORD. He cried out to the LORD
on Israel's behalf, and the LORD answered him.
10While Samuel was sacrificing the burnt offering, the Philistines drew near to engage Israel in battle. But that day the LORD
thundered with loud thunder against the Philistines and threw
them into such a panic that they were routed before the Israelites.
11The men of Israel rushed out of Mizpah and pursued the Philistines, slaughtering them along the way to a point below Beth Car.
12Then Samuel took a stone and set it up between Mizpah and
Shen. He named it Ebenezer,[e] saying, "Thus far has the LORD
helped us." 13So the Philistines were subdued and did not invade
Israelite territory again.
Throughout Samuel's lifetime, the hand of the LORD was
against the Philistines. 14The towns from Ekron to Gath that the
Philistines had captured from Israel were restored to her, and
Israel delivered the neighboring territory from the power of the
Philistines. And there was peace between Israel and the Amorites.
15Samuel continued as judge over Israel all the days of his life.

NIV [b] *18* A few Hebrew manuscripts (see also Septuagint); most Hebrew manuscripts *villages as far as Greater Abel, where* [c] *19* A few Hebrew manuscripts; most Hebrew manuscripts and Septuagint *50,070* [d] *6* Traditionally *judge* [e] *12 Ebenezer* means *stone of help.*

## King James

16And he went from year to year in circuit to Beth-el, and Gilgal, and Mizpeh, and judged Israel in all those places.

17And his return *was* to Ramah; for there *was* his house; and there he judged Israel; and there he built an altar unto the LORD.

8 AND IT came to pass, when Samuel was old, that he made his sons judges over Israel.

2Now the name of his firstborn was Joel; and the name of his second, Abiah: *they were* judges in Beer-sheba.

3And his sons walked not in his ways, but turned aside after lucre, and took bribes, and perverted judgment.

4Then all the elders of Israel gathered themselves together, and came to Samuel unto Ramah,

5And said unto him, Behold, thou art old, and thy sons walk not in thy ways: now make us a king to judge us like all the nations.

6¶ But the thing displeased Samuel, when they said, Give us a king to judge us. And Samuel prayed unto the LORD.

7And the LORD said unto Samuel, Hearken unto the voice of the people in all that they say unto thee: for they have not rejected thee, but they have rejected me, that I should not reign over them.

8According to all the works which they have done since the day that I brought them up out of Egypt even unto this day, wherewith they have forsaken me, and served other gods, so do they also unto thee.

9Now therefore hearken unto their voice: howbeit yet protest solemnly unto them, and show them the manner of the king that shall reign over them.

10¶ And Samuel told all the words of the LORD unto the people that asked of him a king.

11And he said, This will be the manner of the king that shall reign over you: He will take your sons, and appoint *them* for himself, for his chariots, and *to be* his horsemen; and *some* shall run before his chariots.

12And he will appoint him captains over thousands, and captains over fifties; and *will set them* to ear his ground, and to reap his harvest, and to make his instruments of war, and instruments of his chariots.

13And he will take your daughters *to be* confectionaries, and *to be* cooks, and *to be* bakers.

14And he will take your fields, and your vineyards, and your oliveyards, *even* the best *of them*, and give *them* to his servants.

15And he will take the tenth of your seed, and of your vineyards, and give to his officers, and to his servants.

16And he will take your menservants, and your maidservants, and your goodliest young men, and your asses, and put *them* to his work.

17He will take the tenth of your sheep: and ye shall be his servants.

18And ye shall cry out in that day because of your king which ye shall have chosen you; and the LORD will not hear you in that day.

19¶ Nevertheless the people refused to obey the voice of Samuel; and they said, Nay; but we will have a king over us;

20That we also may be like all the nations; and that our king may judge us, and go out before us, and fight our battles.

21And Samuel heard all the words of the people, and he rehearsed them in the ears of the LORD.

22And the LORD said to Samuel, Hearken unto their voice, and make them a king. And Samuel said unto the men of Israel, Go ye every man unto his city.

## Amplified

16And he went from year to year in circuit to Bethel, Gilgal, and Mizpah, and was judge for Israel in all those places.

17Then he would return to Ramah, for his home was there; there he judged Israel, and there he built an altar to the Lord.

8 WHEN SAMUEL was old, he made his sons judges over Israel.

2Now the name of his first-born was Joel, and the name of his second, Abiah. They were judges in Beersheba.

3His sons did not walk in his ways, but turned aside after gain, took bribes, and perverted justice.

4All the elders of Israel assembled and came to Samuel at Ramah,

5And said to him, Behold, you are old, and your sons do not walk in your ways; now appoint us a king to rule over us like all the other nations.

6But it displeased Samuel when they said, Give us a king to govern us. And Samuel prayed to the Lord.

7And the Lord said to Samuel, Hearken to the voice of the people in all they say to you; for they have not rejected you, but they have rejected Me, that I should not be king over them.

8According to all the works which they have done since I brought them up out of Egypt even to this day, forsaking Me and serving other gods, so they also do to you.

9So listen now to their voice, only solemnly warn them, and show them the ways of the king who shall reign over them.

10So Samuel told all the words of the Lord to the people who asked of him a king.

11And he said, These will be the ways of the king who shall reign over you: he will take your sons and appoint them to his chariots, and to be his horsemen, and to run before his chariots.

12He will appoint them for himself for commanders over thousands, and over fifties, and to plow his ground, and to reap his harvest, and to make his implements of war, and equipment for his chariots.

13He will take your daughters to be perfumers, cooks, and bakers.

14He will take your fields, your vineyards, and your olive orchards, even the best of them, and give them to his servants.

15He will take the tenth of your grain and of your vineyards, and give to his officers and to his servants.

16He will take your men and women servants, and the best of your cattle and your donkeys, and put them to his work.

17He will take the tenth of your flocks, and you shall be his slaves.

18In that day you will cry out because of your king you have chosen for yourselves; but the Lord will not hear you then.

19Nevertheless the people refused to listen to the voice of Samuel; and they said, No! We will have a king over us,

20That we also may be like all the nations, and that our king may govern us, and go out before us and fight our battles.

21Samuel heard all the people's words, and repeated them in the Lord's ears.

22And the Lord said to Samuel, Hearken to their voice, and appoint them a king. And Samuel said to the men of Israel, Go every man to his city.

## New American Standard

16And he used to go annually on circuit to Bethel and Gilgal and
Mizpah, and he judged Israel in all these places.
17Then his return *was* to Ramah, for his house *was* there, and
there he judged Israel; and he built there an altar to the LORD.

*Israel Demands a King*

**8** AND IT came about when Samuel was old that he appointed
his sons judges over Israel.
2Now the name of his first-born was Joel, and the name of his
second, Abijah; *they* were judging in Beersheba.
3His sons, however, did not walk in his ways, but turned aside
after dishonest gain and took bribes and perverted justice.
4¶ Then all the elders of Israel gathered together and came to
Samuel at Ramah;
5and they said to him, "Behold, you have grown old, and your
sons do not walk in your ways. Now appoint a king for us to judge
us like all the nations."
6But the thing was displeasing in the sight of Samuel when
they said, "Give us a king to judge us." And Samuel prayed to the
LORD.
7And the LORD said to Samuel, "Listen to the voice of the
people in regard to all that they say to you, for they have not
rejected you, but they have rejected Me from being king over
them.
8"Like all the deeds which they have done since the day that
I brought them up from Egypt even to this day—in that they have
forsaken Me and served other gods—so they are doing to you also.
9"Now then, listen to their voice; however, you shall solemnly
warn them and tell them of the [a]procedure of the king who will
reign over them."

*Warning concerning a King*

10¶ So Samuel spoke all the words of the LORD to the people who
had asked of him a king.
11And he said, "This will be the procedure of the king who will
reign over you: he will take your sons and place *them* for himself
in his chariots and among his horsemen and they will run before
his chariots.
12"And he will appoint for himself commanders of thousands
and of fifties, and *some* to do his plowing and to reap his harvest
and to make his weapons of war and equipment for his chariots.
13"He will also take your daughters for perfumers and cooks
and bakers.
14"And he will take the best of your fields and your vineyards
and your olive groves, and give *them* to his servants.
15"And he will take a tenth of your seed and of your vineyards,
and give to his officers and to his servants.
16"He will also take your male servants and your female servants and your best young men and your donkeys, and use *them*
for his work.
17"He will take a tenth of your flocks, and you yourselves will
become his servants.
18"Then you will cry out in that day because of your king whom
you have chosen for yourselves, but the LORD will not answer you
in that day."
19¶ Nevertheless, the people refused to listen to the voice of
Samuel, and they said, "No, but there shall be a king over us,
20that we also may be like all the nations, that our king may
judge us and go out before us and fight our battles."
21Now after Samuel had heard all the words of the people, he
repeated them in the LORD's hearing.
22And the LORD said to Samuel, "Listen to their voice, and
appoint them a king." So Samuel said to the men of Israel, "Go
every man to his city."

NAS [a] Lit., *custom*

## New International

16From year to year he went on a circuit from Bethel to Gilgal to
Mizpah, judging Israel in all those places. 17But he always went
back to Ramah, where his home was, and there he also judged
Israel. And he built an altar there to the LORD.

*Israel Asks for a King*

**8** WHEN SAMUEL grew old, he appointed his sons as judges
for Israel. 2The name of his firstborn was Joel and the name
of his second was Abijah, and they served at Beersheba. 3But his
sons did not walk in his ways. They turned aside after dishonest
gain and accepted bribes and perverted justice.
4So all the elders of Israel gathered together and came to Samuel
at Ramah. 5They said to him, "You are old, and your sons do not
walk in your ways; now appoint a king to lead[b] us, such as all the
other nations have."
6But when they said, "Give us a king to lead us," this displeased Samuel; so he prayed to the LORD. 7And the LORD told
him: "Listen to all that the people are saying to you; it is not you
they have rejected, but they have rejected me as their king. 8As
they have done from the day I brought them up out of Egypt until
this day, forsaking me and serving other gods, so they are doing
to you. 9Now listen to them; but warn them solemnly and let them
know what the king who will reign over them will do."
10Samuel told all the words of the LORD to the people who were
asking him for a king. 11He said, "This is what the king who will
reign over you will do: He will take your sons and make them serve
with his chariots and horses, and they will run in front of his
chariots. 12Some he will assign to be commanders of thousands
and commanders of fifties, and others to plow his ground and reap
his harvest, and still others to make weapons of war and equipment for his chariots. 13He will take your daughters to be perfumers and cooks and bakers. 14He will take the best of your fields and
vineyards and olive groves and give them to his attendants. 15He
will take a tenth of your grain and of your vintage and give it to
his officials and attendants. 16Your menservants and maidservants
and the best of your cattle[c] and donkeys he will take for his own
use. 17He will take a tenth of your flocks, and you yourselves will
become his slaves. 18When that day comes, you will cry out for
relief from the king you have chosen, and the LORD will not answer
you in that day."
19But the people refused to listen to Samuel. "No!" they said.
"We want a king over us. 20Then we will be like all the other
nations, with a king to lead us and to go out before us and fight
our battles."
21When Samuel heard all that the people said, he repeated it
before the LORD. 22The LORD answered, "Listen to them and give
them a king."
Then Samuel said to the men of Israel, "Everyone go back to his
town."

NIV [b] 5 Traditionally *judge;* also in verses 6 and 20 [c] *16* Septuagint; Hebrew *young men*

## King James

9 NOW THERE was a man of Benjamin, whose name *was* Kish,
the son of Abiel, the son of Zeror, the son of Bechorath, the
son of Aphiah, a Benjamite, a mighty man of power.
2 And he had a son, whose name *was* Saul, a choice young man,
and a goodly: and *there was* not among the children of Israel a
goodlier person than he: from his shoulders and upward *he was*
higher than any of the people.
3 And the asses of Kish Saul's father were lost. And Kish said
to Saul his son, Take now one of the servants with thee, and arise,
go seek the asses.
4 And he passed through mount Ephraim, and passed through
the land of Shalisha, but they found *them* not: then they passed
through the land of Shalim, and *there they were* not: and he passed
through the land of the Benjamites, but they found *them* not.
5 *And* when they were come to the land of Zuph, Saul said to
his servant that *was* with him, Come, and let us return; lest my
father leave *caring* for the asses, and take thought for us.
6 And he said unto him, Behold now, *there is* in this city a man
of God, and *he is* an honourable man; all that he saith cometh
surely to pass: now let us go thither; peradventure he can show
us our way that we should go.
7 Then said Saul to his servant, But, behold, *if* we go, what shall
we bring the man? for the bread is spent in our vessels, and *there
is* not a present to bring to the man of God: what have we?
8 And the servant answered Saul again, and said, Behold, I have
here at hand the fourth part of a shekel of silver: *that* will I give
to the man of God, to tell us our way.
9 (Beforetime in Israel, when a man went to inquire of God, thus
he spake, Come, and let us go to the seer: for *he that is* now *called*
a Prophet was beforetime called a Seer.)
10 Then said Saul to his servant, Well said; come, let us go. So
they went unto the city where the man of God *was*.
11 ¶ *And* as they went up the hill to the city, they found young
maidens going out to draw water, and said unto them, Is the seer
here?
12 And they answered them, and said, He is; behold, *he is* before
you: make haste now, for he came today to the city; for *there is* a
sacrifice of the people today in the high place:
13 As soon as ye be come into the city, ye shall straightway find
him, before he go up to the high place to eat: for the people will
not eat until he come, because he doth bless the sacrifice; *and*
afterwards they eat that be bidden. Now therefore get you up; for
about this time ye shall find him.
14 And they went up into the city: *and* when they were come into
the city, behold, Samuel came out against them, for to go up to the
high place.
15 ¶ Now the LORD had told Samuel in his ear a day before Saul
came, saying,
16 Tomorrow about this time I will send thee a man out of the
land of Benjamin, and thou shalt anoint him *to be* captain over my
people Israel, that he may save my people out of the hand of the
Philistines: for I have looked upon my people, because their cry is
come unto me.
17 And when Samuel saw Saul, the LORD said unto him, Behold
the man whom I spake to thee of! this same shall reign over my
people.
18 Then Saul drew near to Samuel in the gate, and said, Tell me,
I pray thee, where the seer's house *is*.
19 And Samuel answered Saul, and said, I *am* the seer: go up
before me unto the high place; for ye shall eat with me today, and
tomorrow I will let thee go, and will tell thee all that *is* in thine
heart.
20 And as for thine asses that were lost three days ago, set not
thy mind on them; for they are found. And on whom *is* all the
desire of Israel? *Is it* not on thee, and on all thy father's house?

## Amplified

9 THERE WAS a man of Benjamin whose name was Kish, son
of Abiel, son of Zeror, son of Becorath, son of Aphiah, a
Benjamite, a mighty man of wealth *and* valor.
2 Kish had a son named Saul, a choice young man and handsome; among all the Israelites there was not a man more handsome
than he. He was a head taller than any of the people.
3 The donkeys of Kish, Saul's father, were lost. Kish said to Saul,
Take a servant with you, and go, look for the donkeys.
4 And they passed through the hill country of Ephraim, and the
land of Shalishah, but did not find them. Then they went through
the land of Shaalim, and the land of Benjamin, but did not find
them.
5 And when they came to the land of Zuph, Saul said to his
servant, Come, let us return, lest my father stop worrying about
the donkeys and become concerned about us.
6 The servant said to him, Behold now, there is in this city a man
of God, a man held in honor; all that he says surely comes true.
Now let us go there. Perhaps he can show us where we should go.
7 Then Saul said to his servant, But if we go, what shall we bring
the man? The bread in our sacks is gone, and there is no gift for
the man of God. What have we?
8 The servant replied, I have here a quarter of a shekel of silver.
I will give that to the man of God to tell us our way.
9 (Formerly in Israel, when a man went to inquire of God, he
said, Come, let us go to the seer; for he that is now called a prophet
was formerly called a seer.)
10 Saul said to his servant, Well said; come, let us go. So they
went to the city where the man of God was.
11 As they went up the hill to the city, they met young maidens
going out to draw water, and said to them, Is the seer here?
12 They answered, He is; behold, he is just beyond you. Hurry,
for he came today to the city because the people have a sacrifice
today on the high place.
13 As you enter the city you will find him before he goes up to
the high place to eat. The people will not eat until he comes to ask
the blessing on the sacrifice. Afterward those who are invited eat.
So go on up, for about now you will find him.
14 So they went up to the city, and as they were entering, behold
Samuel came toward them, going up to the high place.
15 Now a day before Saul came, the Lord had revealed to Samuel
in his ear,
16 Tomorrow about this time I will send you a man from the land
of Benjamin, and you shall anoint him to be leader over My people
Israel, and he shall save them out of the hand of the Philistines;
for I have looked upon the distress of My people, because their cry
has come to Me.
17 When Samuel saw Saul, the Lord told him, There is the man
of whom I told you. He shall have authority over My people.
18 Then Saul came near to Samuel in the gate, and said, Tell me,
where is the seer's house?
19 Samuel answered Saul, I am the seer; go up before me to the
high place, for you shall eat with me today, and tomorrow I will
let you go, and will tell you all that is on your mind.
20 As for your donkeys that were lost three days ago, do not be
thinking about them, for they are found. And for whom are all the
desirable things of Israel? Are they not for you and for all your
father's house?

## New American Standard

*Saul's Search*

9 NOW THERE was a man of Benjamin whose name was Kish
the son of Abiel, the son of Zeror, the son of Becorath, the
son of Aphiah, the son of a Benjamite, a mighty man of valor.
2And he had a son whose name was Saul, a choice and handsome *man,* and there was not a more handsome person than he
among the sons of Israel; from his shoulders and up he was taller
than any of the people.
3Now the donkeys of Kish, Saul's father, were lost. So Kish
said to his son Saul, "Take now with you one of the servants, and
arise, go search for the donkeys."
4And he passed through the hill country of Ephraim and
passed through the land of Shalishah, but they did not find *them.*
Then they passed through the land of Shaalim, but *they were* not
*there.* Then he passed through the land of the Benjamites, but they
did not find *them.*
5¶ When they came to the land of Zuph, Saul said to his servant
who was with him, "Come, and let us return, lest my father cease
*to be concerned* about the donkeys and become anxious for us."
6And he said to him, "Behold now, there is a man of God in
this city, and the man is held in honor; all that he says surely comes
true. Now let us go there, perhaps he can tell us about our journey
on which we have set out."
7Then Saul said to his servant, "But behold, if we go, what
shall we bring the man? For the bread is gone from our sack and
there is no present to bring to the man of God. What do we have?"
8And the servant answered Saul again and said, "Behold, I
have in my hand a fourth of a shekel of silver; I will give *it* to the
man of God and he will tell us our way."
9(Formerly in Israel, when a man went to inquire of God, he
used to say, "Come, and let us go to the seer"; for *he who is called*
a prophet now was formerly called a seer.)
10Then Saul said to his servant, "Well said; come, let us go."
So they went to the city where the man of God was.
11¶ As they went up the slope to the city, they found young
women going out to draw water, and said to them, "Is the seer
here?"
12And they answered them and said, "He is; see, *he is* ahead
of you. Hurry now, for he has come into the city today, for the
people have a sacrifice on the high place today.
13"As soon as you enter the city you will find him before he goes
up to the high place to eat, for the people will not eat until he
comes, because he must bless the sacrifice; afterward those who
are invited will eat. Now therefore, go up for you will find him at
once."
14So they went up to the city. As they came into the city, behold,
Samuel was coming out toward them to go up to the high place.

*God's Choice for King*

15¶ Now a day before Saul's coming, the LORD had revealed *this*
to Samuel saying,
16"About this time tomorrow I will send you a man from the
land of Benjamin, and you shall anoint him to be prince over My
people Israel; and he shall deliver My people from the hand of the
Philistines. For I have regarded My people, because their cry has
come to Me."
17When Samuel saw Saul, the LORD said to him, "Behold, the
man of whom I spoke to you! This one shall rule over My people."
18Then Saul approached Samuel in the gate, and said, "Please
tell me where the seer's house is."
19And Samuel answered Saul and said, "I am the seer. Go up
before me to the high place, for you shall eat with me today; and
in the morning I will let you go, and will tell you all that is on your
mind.
20"And as for your donkeys which were lost three days ago, do
not set your mind on them, for they have been found. And for
whom is all that is desirable in Israel? Is it not for you and for all
your father's household?"

## New International

*Samuel Anoints Saul*

9 THERE WAS a Benjamite, a man of standing, whose name
was Kish son of Abiel, the son of Zeror, the son of Becorath,
the son of Aphiah of Benjamin. 2He had a son named Saul, an
impressive young man without equal among the Israelites—a head
taller than any of the others.
3Now the donkeys belonging to Saul's father Kish were lost,
and Kish said to his son Saul, "Take one of the servants with you
and go and look for the donkeys." 4So he passed through the hill
country of Ephraim and through the area around Shalisha, but
they did not find them. They went on into the district of Shaalim,
but the donkeys were not there. Then he passed through the
territory of Benjamin, but they did not find them.
5When they reached the district of Zuph, Saul said to the servant who was with him, "Come, let's go back, or my father will
stop thinking about the donkeys and start worrying about us."
6But the servant replied, "Look, in this town there is a man of
God; he is highly respected, and everything he says comes true.
Let's go there now. Perhaps he will tell us what way to take."
7Saul said to his servant, "If we go, what can we give the man?
The food in our sacks is gone. We have no gift to take to the man
of God. What do we have?"
8The servant answered him again. "Look," he said, "I have a
quarter of a shekel[a] of silver. I will give it to the man of God so
that he will tell us what way to take." 9(Formerly in Israel, if a man
went to inquire of God, he would say, "Come, let us go to the
seer," because the prophet of today used to be called a seer.)
10"Good," Saul said to his servant. "Come, let's go." So they
set out for the town where the man of God was.
11As they were going up the hill to the town, they met some
girls coming out to draw water, and they asked them, "Is the seer
here?"
12"He is," they answered. "He's ahead of you. Hurry now; he
has just come to our town today, for the people have a sacrifice at
the high place. 13As soon as you enter the town, you will find him
before he goes up to the high place to eat. The people will not begin
eating until he comes, because he must bless the sacrifice; afterward, those who are invited will eat. Go up now; you should find
him about this time."
14They went up to the town, and as they were entering it, there
was Samuel, coming toward them on his way up to the high place.
15Now the day before Saul came, the LORD had revealed this to
Samuel: 16"About this time tomorrow I will send you a man from
the land of Benjamin. Anoint him leader over my people Israel; he
will deliver my people from the hand of the Philistines. I have
looked upon my people, for their cry has reached me."
17When Samuel caught sight of Saul, the LORD said to him,
"This is the man I spoke to you about; he will govern my people."
18Saul approached Samuel in the gateway and asked, "Would
you please tell me where the seer's house is?"
19"I am the seer," Samuel replied. "Go up ahead of me to the
high place, for today you are to eat with me, and in the morning
I will let you go and will tell you all that is in your heart. 20As for
the donkeys you lost three days ago, do not worry about them;
they have been found. And to whom is all the desire of Israel
turned, if not to you and all your father's family?"

NIV [a] *8* That is, about 1/10 ounce (about 3 grams)

## King James

21And Saul answered and said, *Am* not I a Benjamite, of the
smallest of the tribes of Israel? and my family the least of all the
families of the tribe of Benjamin? wherefore then speakest thou so
to me?
22And Samuel took Saul and his servant, and brought them into
the parlour, and made them sit in the chiefest place among them
that were bidden, which *were* about thirty persons.
23And Samuel said unto the cook, Bring the portion which I
gave thee, of which I said unto thee, Set it by thee.
24And the cook took up the shoulder, and *that* which *was* upon
it, and set *it* before Saul. And *Samuel* said, Behold that which is left!
set *it* before thee, *and* eat: for unto this time hath it been kept for
thee since I said, I have invited the people. So Saul did eat with
Samuel that day.
25¶ And when they were come down from the high place into
the city, *Samuel* communed with Saul upon the top of the house.
26And they arose early: and it came to pass about the spring of
the day, that Samuel called Saul to the top of the house, saying,
Up, that I may send thee away. And Saul arose, and they went out
both of them, he and Samuel, abroad.
27 *And* as they were going down to the end of the city, Samuel
said to Saul, Bid the servant pass on before us, (and he passed on,)
but stand thou still a while, that I may show thee the word of God.

**10** THEN SAMUEL took a vial of oil, and poured *it* upon his
head, and kissed him, and said, *Is it* not because the LORD
hath anointed thee *to be* captain over his inheritance?
2When thou art departed from me today, then thou shalt find
two men by Rachel's sepulchre in the border of Benjamin at Zelzah; and they will say unto thee, The asses which thou wentest to
seek are found: and, lo, thy father hath left the care of the asses,
and sorroweth for you, saying, What shall I do for my son?
3Then shalt thou go on forward from thence, and thou shalt
come to the plain of Tabor, and there shall meet thee three men
going up to God to Beth-el, one carrying three kids, and another
carrying three loaves of bread, and another carrying a bottle of
wine:
4And they will salute thee, and give thee two *loaves* of bread;
which thou shalt receive of their hands.
5After that thou shalt come to the hill of God, where *is* the
garrison of the Philistines: and it shall come to pass, when thou art
come thither to the city, that thou shalt meet a company of prophets coming down from the high place with a psaltery, and a tabret,
and a pipe, and a harp, before them; and they shall prophesy:
6And the spirit of the LORD will come upon thee, and thou shalt
prophesy with them, and shalt be turned into another man.
7And let it be, when these signs are come unto thee, *that* thou
do as occasion serve thee; for God *is* with thee.
8And thou shalt go down before me to Gilgal; and, behold, I will
come down unto thee, to offer burnt offerings, *and* to sacrifice
sacrifices of peace offerings: seven days shalt thou tarry, till I come
to thee, and show thee what thou shalt do.
9¶ And it was *so,* that when he had turned his back to go from
Samuel, God gave him another heart: and all those signs came to
pass that day.
10And when they came thither to the hill, behold, a company
of prophets met him; and the spirit of God came upon him, and
he prophesied among them.
11And it came to pass, when all that knew him beforetime saw
that, behold, he prophesied among the prophets, then the people
said one to another, What *is* this *that* is come unto the son of Kish?
*Is* Saul also among the prophets?

## Amplified

21And Saul said, Am I not a Benjamite, of the smallest of the
tribes of Israel? And is not my family the least of all the families
of the clans of Benjamin? Why then do you speak this way to me?
22Then Samuel took Saul and his servant, and brought them
into the guest room [at the high place], and had them sit in the
chief place among the about thirty persons who were invited. [The
other people feasted outside.]
23And Samuel said to the cook, Bring the portion which I gave
you, of which I said to you, Set it aside.
24And the cook lifted high the shoulder and what was on it
[indicating that it was the priest's honored portion] and set it
before Saul. [Samuel] said, See what was reserved for you. Eat; for
until the hour appointed it was kept for you ever since I invited
the people. So Saul ate that day with Samuel.
25When they had come down from the high place into the city,
Samuel conversed with Saul on the top of the house.
26They arose early, and about dawn Samuel called Saul [who
was sleeping] on the top of the house, saying, Up, that I may send
you on your way. Saul arose, and both he and Samuel went out
on the street.
27And as they were going down to the outskirts of the city,
Samuel said to Saul, Bid the servant pass on before us; and he
passed on. But you stand still, first, that I may cause you to hear
the Word of God.

**10** THEN SAMUEL took the vial of oil, and poured it on
Saul's head, and kissed him, and said, Has not the Lord
anointed you to be prince over His heritage Israel?
2When you have left me today, you will meet two men by
Rachel's tomb in the territory of Benjamin at Zelzah, and they will
say to you, The donkeys you sought are found, and your father
has quit caring about them, and is anxious for you, asking, What
shall I do about my son?
3Then you will go on from there and you will come to the oak
of Tabor, and three men going up to God at Bethel will meet you
there, one carrying three kids, another carrying three loaves of
bread, and another carrying a skin-bottle of wine.
4They will greet you and give you two loaves of bread, which
you shall accept from their hand.
5After that you will come to the hill of God, where the garrison
of the Philistines is; and when you come to the city you will meet
a company of prophets coming down from the high place with
harp, tambourine, flute, and lyre, before them, prophesying.
6Then the Spirit of the Lord will come upon you mightily and
you will show yourself a prophet with them; and you will be
turned into another man.
7When these signs meet you, do whatever you find to be done,
for God is with you.
8You shall go down before me to Gilgal; and behold, I will come
down to you to offer burnt offerings and to sacrifice peace offerings. You shall wait seven days, until I come to you and show you
what you shall do.
9And when [Saul] had turned his back to leave Samuel, God
gave him another heart; and all these signs came to pass that day.
10When they came to the hill [Gibeah], behold, a band of prophets met him; and the Spirit of God came mightily upon him, and
he spoke under divine inspiration among them.
11And when all who knew Saul before saw that he spoke by
inspiration among the [schooled] prophets, the people said one to
another, What has come over [him, who is nobody but] the son of
Kish? Is Saul also among the prophets?

## New American Standard

21And Saul answered and said, "Am I not a Benjamite, of the
smallest of the tribes of Israel, and my family the least of all the
families of the tribe of Benjamin? Why then do you speak to me
in this way?"
22¶ Then Samuel took Saul and his servant and brought them
into the hall, and gave them a place at the head of those who were
invited, who were about thirty men.
23And Samuel said to the cook, "Bring the portion that I gave
you, concerning which I said to you, 'Set it aside.' "
24Then the cook took up the leg with what was on it and set *it*
before Saul. And *Samuel* said, "Here is what has been reserved! Set
*it* before you *and* eat, because it has been kept for you until the
appointed time, since I said I have invited the people." So Saul ate
with Samuel that day.
25¶ When they came down from the high place into the city,
*Samuel* spoke with Saul on the roof. [a]
26And they arose early; and it came about at daybreak that
Samuel called to Saul on the roof, saying, "Get up, that I may send
you away." So Saul arose, and both he and Samuel went out into
the street.
27As they were going down to the edge of the city, Samuel said
to Saul, "Say to the servant that he might go ahead of us and pass
on, but you remain standing now, that I may proclaim the word
of God to you."

*Saul among Prophets*

**10** THEN SAMUEL took the flask of oil, poured it on his
head, kissed him and said, "Has not the LORD anointed
you a ruler over His inheritance?
2"When you go from me today, then you will find two men
close to Rachel's tomb in the territory of Benjamin at Zelzah; and
they will say to you, 'The donkeys which you went to look for have
been found. Now behold, your father has ceased to be concerned
about the donkeys and is anxious for you, saying, "What shall I
do about my son?" '
3"Then you will go on further from there, and you will come
as far as the oak of Tabor, and there three men going up to God
at Bethel will meet you, one carrying three kids, another carrying
three loaves of bread, and another carrying a jug of wine;
4and they will greet you and give you two *loaves* of bread,
which you will accept from their hand.
5"Afterward you will come to the hill of God where the Philistine garrison is; and it shall be as soon as you have come there to
the city, that you will meet a group of prophets coming down from
the high place with harp, tambourine, flute, and a lyre before
them, and they will be prophesying.
6"Then the Spirit of the LORD will come upon you mightily,
and you shall prophesy with them and be changed into another
man.
7"And it shall be when these signs come to you, do for yourself
what the occasion requires; for God is with you.
8"And you shall go down before me to Gilgal; and behold, I
will come down to you to offer burnt offerings and sacrifice peace
offerings. You shall wait seven days until I come to you and show
you what you should do."
9¶ Then it happened when he turned his back to leave Samuel,
God changed his heart; and all those signs came about on that day.
10When they came to the hill there, behold, a group of prophets
met him; and the Spirit of God came upon him mightily, so that
he prophesied among them.
11And it came about, when all who knew him previously saw
that he prophesied now with the prophets, that the people said to
one another, "What has happened to the son of Kish? Is Saul also
among the prophets?"

NAS [a] Gr. adds *and they spread a bed for Saul on the roof and he slept.*

## New International

21Saul answered, "But am I not a Benjamite, from the smallest
tribe of Israel, and is not my clan the least of all the clans of the
tribe of Benjamin? Why do you say such a thing to me?"
22Then Samuel brought Saul and his servant into the hall and
seated them at the head of those who were invited—about thirty
in number. 23Samuel said to the cook, "Bring the piece of meat I
gave you, the one I told you to lay aside."
24So the cook took up the leg with what was on it and set it in
front of Saul. Samuel said, "Here is what has been kept for you.
Eat, because it was set aside for you for this occasion, from the time
I said, 'I have invited guests.' " And Saul dined with Samuel that
day.
25After they came down from the high place to the town, Samuel talked with Saul on the roof of his house. 26They rose about
daybreak and Samuel called to Saul on the roof, "Get ready, and
I will send you on your way." When Saul got ready, he and Samuel
went outside together. 27As they were going down to the edge of
the town, Samuel said to Saul, "Tell the servant to go on ahead of
us"—and the servant did so—"but you stay here awhile, so that
I may give you a message from God."

**10** THEN SAMUEL took a flask of oil and poured it on Saul's
head and kissed him, saying, "Has not the LORD anointed
you leader over his inheritance?[b] 2When you leave me today, you
will meet two men near Rachel's tomb, at Zelzah on the border of
Benjamin. They will say to you, 'The donkeys you set out to look
for have been found. And now your father has stopped thinking
about them and is worried about you. He is asking, "What shall
I do about my son?" '
3"Then you will go on from there until you reach the great tree
of Tabor. Three men going up to God at Bethel will meet you there.
One will be carrying three young goats, another three loaves of
bread, and another a skin of wine. 4They will greet you and offer
you two loaves of bread, which you will accept from them.
5"After that you will go to Gibeah of God, where there is a
Philistine outpost. As you approach the town, you will meet a
procession of prophets coming down from the high place with
lyres, tambourines, flutes and harps being played before them,
and they will be prophesying. 6The Spirit of the LORD will come
upon you in power, and you will prophesy with them; and you
will be changed into a different person. 7Once these signs are
fulfilled, do whatever your hand finds to do, for God is with you.
8"Go down ahead of me to Gilgal. I will surely come down to
you to sacrifice burnt offerings and fellowship offerings,[c] but you
must wait seven days until I come to you and tell you what you
are to do."

*Saul Made King*

9As Saul turned to leave Samuel, God changed Saul's heart, and
all these signs were fulfilled that day. 10When they arrived at
Gibeah, a procession of prophets met him; the Spirit of God came
upon him in power, and he joined in their prophesying. 11When
all those who had formerly known him saw him prophesying with
the prophets, they asked each other, "What is this that has happened to the son of Kish? Is Saul also among the prophets?"

NIV [b] *1* Hebrew; Septuagint and Vulgate *over his people Israel? You will reign over the LORD's people and save them from the power of their enemies round about. And this will be a sign to you that the LORD has anointed you leader over his inheritance:*
[c] *8* Traditionally *peace offerings*

## King James

12 And one of the same place answered and said, But who *is*
their father? Therefore it became a proverb, *Is* Saul also among the
prophets?
13 And when he had made an end of prophesying, he came to
the high place.
14 ¶ And Saul's uncle said unto him and to his servant, Whither
went ye? And he said, To seek the asses: and when we saw that
*they were* no where, we came to Samuel.
15 And Saul's uncle said, Tell me, I pray thee, what Samuel said
unto you.
16 And Saul said unto his uncle, He told us plainly that the asses
were found. But of the matter of the kingdom, whereof Samuel
spake, he told him not.
17 ¶ And Samuel called the people together unto the LORD to
Mizpeh;
18 And said unto the children of Israel, Thus saith the LORD God
of Israel, I brought up Israel out of Egypt, and delivered you out
of the hand of the Egyptians, and out of the hand of all kingdoms,
*and* of them that oppressed you:
19 And ye have this day rejected your God, who himself saved
you out of all your adversities and your tribulations; and ye have
said unto him, *Nay,* but set a king over us. Now therefore present
yourselves before the LORD by your tribes, and by your thousands.
20 And when Samuel had caused all the tribes of Israel to come
near, the tribe of Benjamin was taken.
21 When he had caused the tribe of Benjamin to come near by
their families, the family of Matri was taken, and Saul the son of
Kish was taken: and when they sought him, he could not be found.
22 Therefore they inquired of the LORD further, if the man should
yet come thither. And the LORD answered, Behold, he hath hid
himself among the stuff.
23 And they ran and fetched him thence: and when he stood
among the people, he was higher than any of the people from his
shoulders and upward.
24 And Samuel said to all the people, See ye him whom the LORD
hath chosen, that *there is* none like him among all the people? And
all the people shouted, and said, God save the king.
25 Then Samuel told the people the manner of the kingdom, and
wrote *it* in a book, and laid *it* up before the LORD. And Samuel sent
all the people away, every man to his house.
26 ¶ And Saul also went home to Gibeah; and there went with
him a band of men, whose hearts God had touched.
27 But the children of Belial said, How shall this man save us?
And they despised him, and brought him no presents. But he held
his peace.

**11** THEN NAHASH the Ammonite came up, and encamped
against Jabesh-gilead: and all the men of Jabesh said unto
Nahash, Make a covenant with us, and we will serve thee.
2 And Nahash the Ammonite answered them, On this *condition*
will I make *a covenant* with you, that I may thrust out all your right
eyes, and lay it *for* a reproach upon all Israel.
3 And the elders of Jabesh said unto him, Give us seven days'
respite, that we may send messengers unto all the coasts of Israel:
and then, if *there be* no man to save us, we will come out to thee.
4 ¶ Then came the messengers to Gibeah of Saul, and told the
tidings in the ears of the people: and all the people lifted up their
voices, and wept.
5 And, behold, Saul came after the herd out of the field; and Saul
said, What *aileth* the people that they weep? And they told him the
tidings of the men of Jabesh.
6 And the spirit of God came upon Saul when he heard those
tidings, and his anger was kindled greatly.

## Amplified

12 One of the same place answered, But who is the father of the
others? So it became a proverb, Is Saul also among the prophets?
13 When [Saul] had ended his inspired speaking, he went to the
high place.
14 Saul's uncle said to him and to his servant, Where did you go?
And Saul said, To look for the donkeys, and when we found them
nowhere, we went to Samuel.
15 Saul's uncle said, Tell me, what did Samuel say to you?
16 And Saul said to his uncle, He told us plainly that the donkeys
were found. But of the matter of the kingdom, of which Samuel
spoke, he told him nothing.
17 And Samuel called the people together to the Lord at Mizpah,
18 And said to the Israelites, Thus says the Lord God of Israel,
It was I Who brought up Israel out of Egypt, and delivered you out
of the hand of the Egyptians and of all kingdoms that oppressed
you.
19 But you have this day rejected your God, Who Himself saves
you from all your calamities and distresses; and you have said to
Him, No! Set a king over us. So now present yourselves before the
Lord by your tribes, and by your thousands.
20 And when Samuel had caused all the tribes of Israel to come
near, the tribe of Benjamin was taken [probably by lot].
21 When he had caused the tribe of Benjamin to come near by
their families, the family of Matri was taken, and Saul the son of
Kish was taken. But when they looked for him, he could not be
found.
22 Therefore they inquired of the Lord further, if the man would
yet come back. And the Lord answered, Behold, he has hidden
himself among the baggage. [Exod. 28:30.]
23 They ran and brought him from there. And when he stood
among the people, he was a head taller than any of them.
24 And Samuel said to all the people, Do you see him whom the
Lord has chosen, that none like him is among all the people? And
all the people shouted, and said, Long live the king!
25 Then Samuel told the people the manner of the kingdom
[defining the position of the king in relation to God and to the
people], and wrote it in a book, and laid it up before the Lord. And
Samuel sent all the people away, each one to his home.
26 Saul also went home to Gibeah; and there went with him a
band of valiant men, whose hearts God had touched.
27 But some worthless fellows said, How can this man save us?
And they despised him, and brought him no gift. But he held his
peace *and* was as if deaf.

**11** AND NAHASH the Ammonite went up and besieged
Jabesh-gilead; and all the men of Jabesh said to Nahash,
Make a treaty with us, and we will serve you.
2 But Nahash the Ammonite told them, On this condition I will
make a treaty with you, that I thrust out all your right eyes, and
thus lay disgrace on all Israel.
3 The elders of Jabesh said to Nahash, Give us seven days' time,
that we may send messengers through all the territory of Israel.
Then, if there is no man to save us, we will come out to you.
4 Then messengers came to Gibeah of Saul, and told the news
in the ears of the people; and all the people wept aloud.
5 Now Saul came after the oxen out of the field; and [he] said,
What ails the people that they are weeping? And they told him the
words of the men of Jabesh.
6 The Spirit of God came mightily upon Saul when he heard
those tidings, and his anger was greatly kindled.

## New American Standard

12And a man there answered and said, "Now, who is their
father?" Therefore it became a proverb: "Is Saul also among the
prophets?"
13When he had finished prophesying, he came to the high
place.
14¶ Now Saul's uncle said to him and his servant, "Where did
you go?" And he said, "To look for the donkeys. When we saw
that they could not be found, we went to Samuel."
15And Saul's uncle said, "Please tell me what Samuel said to
you."
16So Saul said to his uncle, "He told us plainly that the donkeys
had been found." But he did not tell him about the matter of the
kingdom which Samuel had mentioned.

*Saul Publicly Chosen King*

17¶ Thereafter Samuel called the people together to the LORD at
Mizpah;
18and he said to the sons of Israel, "Thus says the LORD, the God
of Israel, 'I brought Israel up from Egypt, and I delivered you from
the hand of the Egyptians, and from the power of all the kingdoms
that were oppressing you.'
19"But you today rejected your God, who delivers you from all
your calamities and your distresses; yet you have said, 'No, but set
a king over us!' Now therefore, present yourselves before the LORD
by your tribes and by your clans."
20Thus Samuel brought all the tribes of Israel near, and the tribe
of Benjamin was taken by lot.
21Then he brought the tribe of Benjamin near by its families,
and the Matrite family was taken. And Saul the son of Kish was
taken; but when they looked for him, he could not be found.
22Therefore they inquired further of the LORD, "Has the man
come here yet?" So the LORD said, "Behold, he is hiding himself
by the baggage."
23So they ran and took him from there, and when he stood
among the people, he was taller than any of the people from his
shoulders upward.
24And Samuel said to all the people, "Do you see him whom
the LORD has chosen? Surely there is no one like him among all the
people." So all the people shouted and said, "*Long* live the king!"
25Then Samuel told the people the ordinances of the kingdom,
and wrote *them* in the book and placed *it* before the LORD. And
Samuel sent all the people away, each one to his house.
26And Saul also went to his house at Gibeah; and the valiant *men*
whose hearts God had touched went with him.
27But certain worthless men said, "How can this one deliver
us?" And they despised him and did not bring him any present.
But he kept silent.

*Saul Defeats the Ammonites*

**11** NOW NAHASH the Ammonite came up and besieged
Jabesh-gilead; and all the men of Jabesh said to Nahash,
"Make a covenant with us and we will serve you."
2But Nahash the Ammonite said to them, "I will make *it* with
you on this condition, that I will gouge out the right eye of every
one of you, thus I will make it a reproach on all Israel."
3And the elders of Jabesh said to him, "Let us alone for seven
days, that we may send messengers throughout the territory of
Israel. Then, if there is no one to deliver us, we will come out to
you."
4Then the messengers came to Gibeah of Saul and spoke these
words in the hearing of the people, and all the people lifted up
their voices and wept.
5Now behold, Saul was coming from the field behind the oxen;
and he said, "What is *the matter* with the people that they weep?"
So they related to him the words of the men of Jabesh.
6¶ Then the Spirit of God came upon Saul mightily when he
heard these words, and he became very angry.

## New International

12A man who lived there answered, "And who is their father?"
So it became a saying: "Is Saul also among the prophets?" 13After
Saul stopped prophesying, he went to the high place.
14Now Saul's uncle asked him and his servant, "Where have
you been?"
"Looking for the donkeys," he said. "But when we saw they
were not to be found, we went to Samuel."
15Saul's uncle said, "Tell me what Samuel said to you."
16Saul replied, "He assured us that the donkeys had been
found." But he did not tell his uncle what Samuel had said about
the kingship.
17Samuel summoned the people of Israel to the LORD at Mizpah
18and said to them, "This is what the LORD, the God of Israel, says:
'I brought Israel up out of Egypt, and I delivered you from the
power of Egypt and all the kingdoms that oppressed you.' 19But
you have now rejected your God, who saves you out of all your
calamities and distresses. And you have said, 'No, set a king over
us.' So now present yourselves before the LORD by your tribes and
clans."
20When Samuel brought all the tribes of Israel near, the tribe of
Benjamin was chosen. 21Then he brought forward the tribe of
Benjamin, clan by clan, and Matri's clan was chosen. Finally Saul
son of Kish was chosen. But when they looked for him, he was not
to be found. 22So they inquired further of the LORD, "Has the man
come here yet?"
And the LORD said, "Yes, he has hidden himself among the
baggage."
23They ran and brought him out, and as he stood among the
people he was a head taller than any of the others. 24Samuel said
to all the people, "Do you see the man the LORD has chosen? There
is no one like him among all the people."
Then the people shouted, "Long live the king!"
25Samuel explained to the people the regulations of the kingship. He wrote them down on a scroll and deposited it before the
LORD. Then Samuel dismissed the people, each to his own home.
26Saul also went to his home in Gibeah, accompanied by valiant
men whose hearts God had touched. 27But some troublemakers
said, "How can this fellow save us?" They despised him and
brought him no gifts. But Saul kept silent.

*Saul Rescues the City of Jabesh*

**11** NAHASH THE Ammonite went up and besieged Jabesh
Gilead. And all the men of Jabesh said to him, "Make a
treaty with us, and we will be subject to you."
2But Nahash the Ammonite replied, "I will make a treaty with
you only on the condition that I gouge out the right eye of every
one of you and so bring disgrace on all Israel."
3The elders of Jabesh said to him, "Give us seven days so we
can send messengers throughout Israel; if no one comes to rescue
us, we will surrender to you."
4When the messengers came to Gibeah of Saul and reported
these terms to the people, they all wept aloud. 5Just then Saul was
returning from the fields, behind his oxen, and he asked, "What
is wrong with the people? Why are they weeping?" Then they
repeated to him what the men of Jabesh had said.
6When Saul heard their words, the Spirit of God came upon him
in power, and he burned with anger. 7He took a pair of oxen, cut

# King James

7And he took a yoke of oxen, and hewed them in pieces, and sent *them* throughout all the coasts of Israel by the hands of messengers, saying, Whosoever cometh not forth after Saul and after Samuel, so shall it be done unto his oxen. And the fear of the Lord fell on the people, and they came out with one consent.

8And when he numbered them in Bezek, the children of Israel were three hundred thousand, and the men of Judah thirty thousand.

9And they said unto the messengers that came, Thus shall ye say unto the men of Jabesh-gilead, Tomorrow, by *that time* the sun be hot, ye shall have help. And the messengers came and showed *it* to the men of Jabesh; and they were glad.

10Therefore the men of Jabesh said, Tomorrow we will come out unto you, and ye shall do with us all that seemeth good unto you.

11And it was *so* on the morrow, that Saul put the people in three companies; and they came into the midst of the host in the morning watch, and slew the Ammonites until the heat of the day: and it came to pass, that they which remained were scattered, so that two of them were not left together.

12¶ And the people said unto Samuel, Who *is* he that said, Shall Saul reign over us? bring the men, that we may put them to death.

13And Saul said, There shall not a man be put to death this day: for today the Lord hath wrought salvation in Israel.

14Then said Samuel to the people, Come, and let us go to Gilgal, and renew the kingdom there.

15And all the people went to Gilgal; and there they made Saul king before the Lord in Gilgal; and there they sacrificed sacrifices of peace offerings before the Lord; and there Saul and all the men of Israel rejoiced greatly.

**12** AND SAMUEL said unto all Israel, Behold, I have hearkened unto your voice in all that ye said unto me, and have made a king over you.

2And now, behold, the king walketh before you: and I am old and grayheaded; and, behold, my sons *are* with you: and I have walked before you from my childhood unto this day.

3Behold, here I *am*: witness against me before the Lord, and before his anointed: whose ox have I taken? or whose ass have I taken? or whom have I defrauded? whom have I oppressed? or of whose hand have I received *any* bribe to blind mine eyes therewith? and I will restore it you.

4And they said, Thou hast not defrauded us, nor oppressed us, neither hast thou taken aught of any man's hand.

5And he said unto them, The Lord *is* witness against you, and his anointed *is* witness this day, that ye have not found aught in my hand. And they answered, *He is* witness.

6¶ And Samuel said unto the people, *It is* the Lord that advanced Moses and Aaron, and that brought your fathers up out of the land of Egypt.

7Now therefore stand still, that I may reason with you before the Lord of all the righteous acts of the Lord, which he did to you and to your fathers.

8When Jacob was come into Egypt, and your fathers cried unto the Lord, then the Lord sent Moses and Aaron, which brought forth your fathers out of Egypt, and made them dwell in this place.

9And when they forgat the Lord their God, he sold them into the hand of Sisera, captain of the host of Hazor, and into the hand of the Philistines, and into the hand of the king of Moab, and they fought against them.

10And they cried unto the Lord, and said, We have sinned, because we have forsaken the Lord, and have served Baalim and Ashtaroth: but now deliver us out of the hand of our enemies, and we will serve thee.

# Amplified

7And he took a yoke of oxen and cut them in pieces and sent them throughout all the territory of Israel by the hands of messengers, saying, Whoever does not come forth after Saul and Samuel, so shall it be done to his oxen! And terror from the Lord fell on the people, and they came out with one consent.

8And he numbered them at Bezek, and the Israelites were 300,000, and the men of Judah 30,000.

9The messengers who came were told, Say to the men of Jabesh-gilead, Tomorrow by the time the sun is hot, you shall have help. The messengers came and reported to the men of Jabesh, and they were glad.

10So the men of Jabesh said to Nahash, Tomorrow we will come out to you, and you may do with us all that seems good to you.

11Next day Saul put the men in three companies; and they came into the midst of the enemy's camp in the [darkness of the] morning watch, and slew the Ammonites until midday, and the survivors were scattered, so that no two of them remained together.

12The people said to Samuel, Who is he who said, Shall Saul reign over us? Bring the men, that we may put them to death.

13But Saul said, There shall not a man be put to death this day; for today the Lord has brought deliverance to Israel.

14Samuel said to the people, Come, let us go to Gilgal, and there renew the kingdom.

15All the people went to Gilgal, and there they made Saul king before the Lord; and there they sacrificed peace offerings before the Lord, and there Saul and all the men of Israel rejoiced greatly.

**12** AND SAMUEL said to all Israel, I have listened to you in all that you have said to me, and have made a king over you.

2And now, behold, the king walks before you; and I am old and gray, and behold, my sons are with you; and I have walked before you from my childhood to this day.

3Here I am; testify against me before the Lord and Saul his anointed. Whose ox or donkey have I taken? Or whom have I defrauded or oppressed? Or of whose hand have I received any bribe to blind my eyes? Tell me and I will restore it to you.

4And they said, You have not defrauded us, or oppressed us, or taken anything from any man's hand.

5And Samuel said to them, The Lord is witness against you, and His anointed is witness this day, that you have not found anything in my hand. And they answered, He is witness.

6And Samuel said to the people, It is the Lord Who appointed Moses and Aaron and brought your fathers up out of Egypt.

7Now present yourselves, that I may plead with you before the Lord concerning all the righteous acts of the Lord, which He did to you and to your fathers.

8When Jacob and his sons had come into Egypt [and the Egyptians oppressed them], and your fathers cried to the Lord, then the Lord sent Moses and Aaron, who brought forth your fathers out of Egypt, and made them dwell in this place.

9But when they forgot the Lord their God, He sold them into the hand of Sisera, commander of Hazor's army, and into the hand of the Philistines, and of the king of Moab; and they fought those foes.

10And they cried to the Lord, saying, We have sinned, because we have forsaken the Lord, and have served the Baals and Ashtaroth; but now deliver us from the hand of our enemies, and we will serve You.

## New American Standard

7And he took a yoke of oxen and cut them in pieces, and sent
*them* throughout the territory of Israel by the hand of messengers,
saying, "Whoever does not come out after Saul and after Samuel,
so shall it be done to his oxen." Then the dread of the LORD fell
on the people, and they came out as one man.
8And he numbered them in Bezek; and the sons of Israel were
300,000, and the men of Judah 30,000.
9And they said to the messengers who had come, "Thus you
shall say to the men of Jabesh-gilead, 'Tomorrow, by the time the
sun is hot, you shall have deliverance.' " So the messengers went
and told the men of Jabesh; and they were glad.
10Then the men of Jabesh said, "Tomorrow we will come out
to you, and you may do to us whatever seems good to you."
11And it happened the next morning that Saul put the people
in three companies; and they came into the midst of the camp at
the morning watch, and struck down the Ammonites until the heat
of the day. And it came about that those who survived were
scattered, so that no two of them were left together.
12¶ Then the people said to Samuel, "Who is he that said, 'Shall
Saul reign over us?' Bring the men, that we may put them to
death."
13But Saul said, "Not a man shall be put to death this day, for
today the LORD has accomplished deliverance in Israel."
14¶ Then Samuel said to the people, "Come and let us go to
Gilgal and renew the kingdom there."
15So all the people went to Gilgal, and there they made Saul
king before the LORD in Gilgal. There they also offered sacrifices
of peace offerings before the LORD; and there Saul and all the men
of Israel rejoiced greatly.

*Samuel Addresses Israel*

12 THEN SAMUEL said to all Israel, "Behold, I have listened
to your voice in all that you said to me, and I have appointed a king over you.
2"And now, here is the king walking before you, but I am old
and gray, and behold my sons are with you. And I have walked
before you from my youth even to this day.
3"Here I am; bear witness against me before the LORD and His
anointed. Whose ox have I taken, or whose donkey have I taken,
or whom have I defrauded? Whom have I oppressed, or from
whose hand have I taken a bribe to blind my eyes with it? I will
restore *it* to you."
4And they said, "You have not defrauded us, or oppressed us,
or taken anything from any man's hand."
5And he said to them, "The LORD is witness against you, and
His anointed is witness this day that you have found nothing in
my hand." And they said, " *He is* witness."
6¶ Then Samuel said to the people, "It is the LORD who appointed Moses and Aaron and who brought your fathers up from
the land of Egypt.
7"So now, take your stand, that I may plead with you before
the LORD concerning all the righteous acts of the LORD which He
did for you and your fathers.
8"When Jacob went into Egypt and your fathers cried out to the
LORD, then the LORD sent Moses and Aaron who brought your
fathers out of Egypt and settled them in this place.
9"But they forgot the LORD their God, so He sold them into the
hand of Sisera, captain of the army of Hazor, and into the hand
of the Philistines and into the hand of the king of Moab, and they
fought against them.
10"And they cried out to the LORD and said, 'We have sinned
because we have forsaken the LORD and have served the Baals and
the Ashtaroth; but now deliver us from the hands of our enemies,
and we will serve Thee.'

## New International

them into pieces, and sent the pieces by messengers throughout
Israel, proclaiming, "This is what will be done to the oxen of
anyone who does not follow Saul and Samuel." Then the terror of
the LORD fell on the people, and they turned out as one man.
8When Saul mustered them at Bezek, the men of Israel numbered
three hundred thousand and the men of Judah thirty thousand.
9They told the messengers who had come, "Say to the men of
Jabesh Gilead, 'By the time the sun is hot tomorrow, you will be
delivered.' " When the messengers went and reported this to the
men of Jabesh, they were elated. 10They said to the Ammonites,
"Tomorrow we will surrender to you, and you can do to us whatever seems good to you."
11The next day Saul separated his men into three divisions;
during the last watch of the night they broke into the camp of the
Ammonites and slaughtered them until the heat of the day. Those
who survived were scattered, so that no two of them were left
together.

*Saul Confirmed as King*

12The people then said to Samuel, "Who was it that asked,
'Shall Saul reign over us?' Bring these men to us and we will put
them to death."
13But Saul said, "No one shall be put to death today, for this
day the LORD has rescued Israel."
14Then Samuel said to the people, "Come, let us go to Gilgal
and there reaffirm the kingship." 15So all the people went to Gilgal
and confirmed Saul as king in the presence of the LORD. There they
sacrificed fellowship offerings[a] before the LORD, and Saul and all
the Israelites held a great celebration.

*Samuel's Farewell Speech*

12 SAMUEL SAID to all Israel, "I have listened to everything
you said to me and have set a king over you. 2Now you
have a king as your leader. As for me, I am old and gray, and my
sons are here with you. I have been your leader from my youth
until this day. 3Here I stand. Testify against me in the presence of
the LORD and his anointed. Whose ox have I taken? Whose donkey
have I taken? Whom have I cheated? Whom have I oppressed?
From whose hand have I accepted a bribe to make me shut my
eyes? If I have done any of these, I will make it right."
4"You have not cheated or oppressed us," they replied. "You
have not taken anything from anyone's hand."
5Samuel said to them, "The LORD is witness against you, and
also his anointed is witness this day, that you have not found
anything in my hand."
"He is witness," they said.
6Then Samuel said to the people, "It is the LORD who appointed
Moses and Aaron and brought your forefathers up out of Egypt.
7Now then, stand here, because I am going to confront you with
evidence before the LORD as to all the righteous acts performed by
the LORD for you and your fathers.
8"After Jacob entered Egypt, they cried to the LORD for help,
and the LORD sent Moses and Aaron, who brought your forefathers out of Egypt and settled them in this place.
9"But they forgot the LORD their God; so he sold them into the
hand of Sisera, the commander of the army of Hazor, and into the
hands of the Philistines and the king of Moab, who fought against
them. 10They cried out to the LORD and said, 'We have sinned; we
have forsaken the LORD and served the Baals and the Ashtoreths.
But now deliver us from the hands of our enemies, and we will
serve you.' 11Then the LORD sent Jerub-Baal,[b] Barak,[c] Jephthah

**NIV** [a] *15* Traditionally *peace offerings* [b] *11* Also called *Gideon* [c] *11* Some Septuagint manuscripts and Syriac; Hebrew *Bedan*

## King James

11 And the LORD sent Jerubbaal, and Bedan, and Jephthah, and Samuel, and delivered you out of the hand of your enemies on every side, and ye dwelled safe.

12 And when ye saw that Nahash the king of the children of Ammon came against you, ye said unto me, Nay; but a king shall reign over us: when the LORD your God *was* your king.

13 Now therefore behold the king whom ye have chosen, *and* whom ye have desired! and, behold, the LORD hath set a king over you.

14 If ye will fear the LORD, and serve him, and obey his voice, and not rebel against the commandment of the LORD, then shall both ye and also the king that reigneth over you continue following the LORD your God:

15 But if ye will not obey the voice of the LORD, but rebel against the commandment of the LORD, then shall the hand of the LORD be against you, as *it was* against your fathers.

16 ¶ Now therefore stand and see this great thing, which the LORD will do before your eyes.

17 *Is it* not wheat harvest today? I will call unto the LORD, and he shall send thunder and rain; that ye may perceive and see that your wickedness *is* great, which ye have done in the sight of the LORD, in asking you a king.

18 So Samuel called unto the LORD; and the LORD sent thunder and rain that day: and all the people greatly feared the LORD and Samuel.

19 And all the people said unto Samuel, Pray for thy servants unto the LORD thy God, that we die not: for we have added unto all our sins *this* evil, to ask us a king.

20 ¶ And Samuel said unto the people, Fear not: ye have done all this wickedness: yet turn not aside from following the LORD, but serve the LORD with all your heart;

21 And turn ye not aside: for *then should ye go* after vain *things*, which cannot profit nor deliver; for they *are* vain.

22 For the LORD will not forsake his people for his great name's sake: because it hath pleased the LORD to make you his people.

23 Moreover as for me, God forbid that I should sin against the LORD in ceasing to pray for you: but I will teach you the good and the right way:

24 Only fear the LORD, and serve him in truth with all your heart: for consider how great *things* he hath done for you.

25 But if ye shall still do wickedly, ye shall be consumed, both ye and your king.

**13** SAUL REIGNED one year; and when he had reigned two years over Israel,

2 Saul chose him three thousand *men* of Israel; *whereof* two thousand were with Saul in Michmash and in mount Beth-el, and a thousand were with Jonathan in Gibeah of Benjamin: and the rest of the people he sent every man to his tent.

3 And Jonathan smote the garrison of the Philistines that *was* in Geba, and the Philistines heard *of it*. And Saul blew the trumpet throughout all the land, saying, Let the Hebrews hear.

4 And all Israel heard say *that* Saul had smitten a garrison of the Philistines, and *that* Israel also was had in abomination with the Philistines. And the people were called together after Saul to Gilgal.

5 ¶ And the Philistines gathered themselves together to fight with Israel, thirty thousand chariots, and six thousand horsemen, and people as the sand which *is* on the sea shore in multitude: and they came up, and pitched in Michmash, eastward from Beth-aven.

## Amplified

11 And the Lord sent Jerubbaal, and Barak, and Jephthah, and Samuel, and delivered you out of the hand of your enemies on every side, and you dwelt safely.

12 But when you saw that Nahash king of the Ammonites came against you, you said to me, No! A king shall reign over us, when the Lord your God was your King!

13 Now see the king whom you have chosen, and for whom you have asked; behold, the Lord has set a king over you.

14 If you will revere *and* fear the Lord and serve Him and hearken to His voice and not rebel against His commandment, and if both you and your king will follow the Lord your God, it will be well.

15 But if you will not hearken to the Lord's voice, but rebel against His commandment, then the hand of the Lord will be against you, as it was against your fathers.

16 So stand still and see this great thing the Lord will do before your eyes now.

17 Is it not wheat harvest today? I will call to the Lord, and He will send thunder and rain; that you shall know and see that your wickedness is great, which you have done in the sight of the Lord, in asking a king for yourselves.

18 So Samuel called to the Lord, and He sent thunder and rain that day; and all the people greatly feared the Lord and Samuel.

19 And [they] all said to Samuel, Pray for your servants to the Lord your God, that we may not die; for we have added to all our sins this evil, to ask for us a king.

20 And Samuel said to the people, Fear not; you have indeed done all this evil; yet turn not aside from following the Lord, but serve Him with all your heart;

21 And turn not aside after vain *and* worthless things which cannot profit or deliver you, for they are empty *and* futile.

22 The Lord will not forsake His people, for His great name's sake, for it has pleased Him to make you a people for Himself.

23 Moreover as for me, far be it from me that I should sin against the Lord by ceasing to pray for you; but I will instruct you in the good and right way.

24 Only fear the Lord, and serve Him faithfully with all your heart; for consider how great are the things He has done for you.

25 But if you still do wickedly, both you and your king shall be swept away.

**13** SAUL WAS [ [a] *forty*] years old when he began to reign; and when he had reigned two years over Israel,

2 Saul chose 3,000 men of Israel; 2,000 were with [him] in Michmash and the hill country of Bethel, and 1,000 with Jonathan in Gibeah of Benjamin; the rest of the men he sent away, each one to his home.

3 Jonathan smote the Philistine garrison at Geba, and the Philistines heard of it. And Saul blew the trumpet throughout all the land, saying, Let the Hebrews hear!

4 All Israel heard that Saul had defeated the Philistine garrison, and also that Israel had become an abomination to the Philistines. And the people were called out to join Saul at Gilgal.

5 And the Philistines gathered to fight with Israel, 30,000 chariots and 6,000 horsemen, and troops like sand on the seashore in multitude. They came up and encamped at Michmash, east of Beth-aven.

**AMP** [a] The complete numbers in this verse are missing in the Hebrew. The word "forty" is supplied by the best available estimate.

## New American Standard

11"Then the LORD sent Jerubbaal and [b]Bedan and Jephthah and
Samuel, and delivered you from the hands of your enemies all
around, so that you lived in security.

*The King Confirmed*

12"When you saw that Nahash the king of the sons of Ammon
came against you, you said to me, 'No, but a king shall reign over
us,' although the LORD your God *was* your king.

13"Now therefore, here is the king whom you have chosen,
whom you have asked for, and behold, the LORD has set a king
over you.

14"If you will fear the LORD and serve Him, and listen to His
voice and not rebel against the command of the LORD, then both
you and also the king who reigns over you will follow the LORD
your God.

15"And if you will not listen to the voice of the LORD, but rebel
against the command of the LORD, then the hand of the LORD will
be against you, *as it was* against your fathers.

16"Even now, take your stand and see this great thing which the
LORD will do before your eyes.

17"Is it not the wheat harvest today? I will call to the LORD, that
He may send thunder and rain. Then you will know and see that
your wickedness is great which you have done in the sight of the
LORD by asking for yourselves a king."

18So Samuel called to the LORD, and the LORD sent thunder and
rain that day; and all the people greatly feared the LORD and
Samuel.

19¶ Then all the people said to Samuel, "Pray for your servants
to the LORD your God, so that we may not die, for we have added
to all our sins *this* evil by asking for ourselves a king."

20And Samuel said to the people, "Do not fear. You have committed all this evil, yet do not turn aside from following the LORD,
but serve the LORD with all your heart.

21"And you must not turn aside, for *then you would go* after futile
things which can not profit or deliver, because they are futile.

22"For the LORD will not abandon His people on account of His
great name, because the LORD has been pleased to make you a
people for Himself.

23"Moreover, as for me, far be it from me that I should sin
against the LORD by ceasing to pray for you; but I will instruct you
in the good and right way.

24"Only [c]fear the LORD and serve Him in truth with all your
heart; for consider what great things He has done for you.

25"But if you still do wickedly, both you and your king shall be
swept away."

*War with the Philistines*

**13** SAUL WAS *forty* years old when he began to reign, and
he reigned *thirty*-two years over Israel.

2Now Saul chose for himself 3,000 men of Israel, of which 2,000
were with Saul in Michmash and in the hill country of Bethel,
while 1,000 were with Jonathan at Gibeah of Benjamin. But he sent
away the rest of the people, each to his tent.

3And Jonathan smote the garrison of the Philistines that was
in Geba, and the Philistines heard of *it*. Then Saul blew the trumpet throughout the land, saying, "Let the Hebrews hear."

4And all Israel heard the news that Saul had smitten the garrison of the Philistines, and also that Israel had become odious to
the Philistines. The people were then summoned to Saul at Gilgal.

5¶ Now the Philistines assembled to fight with Israel, 30,000
chariots and 6,000 horsemen, and people like the sand which is on
the seashore in abundance; and they came up and camped in
Michmash, east of Beth-aven.

NAS [b] Gr. and Syr. read *Barak* [c] Or, *reverence*

## New International

and Samuel,[d] and he delivered you from the hands of your enemies on every side, so that you lived securely.

12"But when you saw that Nahash king of the Ammonites was
moving against you, you said to me, 'No, we want a king to rule
over us'—even though the LORD your God was your king.
13Now
here is the king you have chosen, the one you asked for; see, the
LORD has set a king over you.
14If you fear the LORD and serve and
obey him and do not rebel against his commands, and if both you
and the king who reigns over you follow the LORD your God—
good!
15But if you do not obey the LORD, and if you rebel against
his commands, his hand will be against you, as it was against your
fathers.

16"Now then, stand still and see this great thing the LORD is
about to do before your eyes!
17Is it not wheat harvest now? I will
call upon the LORD to send thunder and rain. And you will realize
what an evil thing you did in the eyes of the LORD when you asked
for a king."

18Then Samuel called upon the LORD, and that same day the
LORD sent thunder and rain. So all the people stood in awe of the
LORD and of Samuel.

19The people all said to Samuel, "Pray to the LORD your God
for your servants so that we will not die, for we have added to all
our other sins the evil of asking for a king."

20"Do not be afraid," Samuel replied. "You have done all this
evil; yet do not turn away from the LORD, but serve the LORD with
all your heart.
21Do not turn away after useless idols. They can do
you no good, nor can they rescue you, because they are useless.
22For the sake of his great name the LORD will not reject his people,
because the LORD was pleased to make you his own.
23As for me,
far be it from me that I should sin against the LORD by failing to
pray for you. And I will teach you the way that is good and right.
24But be sure to fear the LORD and serve him faithfully with all your
heart; consider what great things he has done for you.
25Yet if you
persist in doing evil, both you and your king will be swept away."

*Samuel Rebukes Saul*

**13** SAUL WAS ⌞thirty⌟[e] years old when he became king, and
he reigned over Israel ⌞forty-⌟[f] two years.

2Saul[g] chose three thousand men from Israel; two thousand
were with him at Micmash and in the hill country of Bethel, and
a thousand were with Jonathan at Gibeah in Benjamin. The rest of
the men he sent back to their homes.

3Jonathan attacked the Philistine outpost at Geba, and the Philistines heard about it. Then Saul had the trumpet blown throughout the land and said, "Let the Hebrews hear!"
4So all Israel heard
the news: "Saul has attacked the Philistine outpost, and now Israel
has become a stench to the Philistines." And the people were
summoned to join Saul at Gilgal.

5The Philistines assembled to fight Israel, with three thousand[h]
chariots, six thousand charioteers, and soldiers as numerous as the
sand on the seashore. They went up and camped at Micmash, east
of Beth Aven.
6When the men of Israel saw that their situation was

NIV [d] *11* Hebrew; some Septuagint manuscripts and Syriac *Samson* [e] *1* A few late manuscripts of the Septuagint; Hebrew does not have *thirty*. [f] *1* See the round number in Acts 13:21; Hebrew does not have *forty-*. [g] *1,2* Or *and when he had reigned over Israel two years, 2he* [h] *5* Some Septuagint manuscripts and Syriac; Hebrew *thirty thousand*

## King James

6 When the men of Israel saw that they were in a strait, (for the people were distressed,) then the people did hide themselves in caves, and in thickets, and in rocks, and in high places, and in pits.

7 And *some of* the Hebrews went over Jordan to the land of Gad and Gilead. As for Saul, he *was* yet in Gilgal, and all the people followed him trembling.

8 ¶ And he tarried seven days, according to the set time that Samuel *had appointed:* but Samuel came not to Gilgal; and the people were scattered from him.

9 And Saul said, Bring hither a burnt offering to me, and peace offerings. And he offered the burnt offering.

10 And it came to pass, that as soon as he had made an end of offering the burnt offering, behold, Samuel came; and Saul went out to meet him, that he might salute him.

11 ¶ And Samuel said, What hast thou done? And Saul said, Because I saw that the people were scattered from me, and *that* thou camest not within the days appointed, and *that* the Philistines gathered themselves together at Michmash;

12 Therefore said I, The Philistines will come down now upon me to Gilgal, and I have not made supplication unto the LORD: I forced myself therefore, and offered a burnt offering.

13 And Samuel said to Saul, Thou hast done foolishly: thou hast not kept the commandment of the LORD thy God, which he commanded thee: for now would the LORD have established thy kingdom upon Israel for ever.

14 But now thy kingdom shall not continue: the LORD hath sought him a man after his own heart, and the LORD hath commanded him *to be* captain over his people, because thou hast not kept *that* which the LORD commanded thee.

15 And Samuel arose, and gat him up from Gilgal unto Gibeah of Benjamin. And Saul numbered the people *that were* present with him, about six hundred men.

16 And Saul, and Jonathan his son, and the people *that were* present with them, abode in Gibeah of Benjamin: but the Philistines encamped in Michmash.

17 ¶ And the spoilers came out of the camp of the Philistines in three companies: one company turned unto the way *that leadeth to* Ophrah, unto the land of Shual:

18 And another company turned the way *to* Beth-horon: and another company turned *to* the way of the border that looketh to the valley of Zeboim toward the wilderness.

19 ¶ Now there was no smith found throughout all the land of Israel: for the Philistines said, Lest the Hebrews make *them* swords or spears:

20 But all the Israelites went down to the Philistines, to sharpen every man his share, and his coulter, and his axe, and his mattock.

21 Yet they had a file for the mattocks, and for the coulters, and for the forks, and for the axes, and to sharpen the goads.

22 So it came to pass in the day of battle, that there was neither sword nor spear found in the hand of any of the people that *were* with Saul and Jonathan: but with Saul and with Jonathan his son was there found.

23 And the garrison of the Philistines went out to the passage of Michmash.

**14** NOW IT came to pass upon a day, that Jonathan the son of Saul said unto the young man that bare his armour, Come, and let us go over to the Philistines' garrison, that *is* on the other side. But he told not his father.

## Amplified

6 When the men of Israel saw that they were in a tight situation (for their troops were hard pressed), they hid in caves, holes, rocks, tombs, and pits *or* cisterns.

7 Some Hebrews had gone over Jordan to the land of Gad and Gilead. As for Saul, he was still in Gilgal, and all the people followed him trembling.

8 Saul waited seven days, according to the set time Samuel had appointed. But Samuel had not come to Gilgal, and the people were scattering from Saul.

9 So Saul said, Bring me a burnt offering and peace offerings. And he offered the burnt offering [which he was forbidden to do].

10 And just as he finished sacrificing the burnt offering, behold, Samuel came! Saul went out to meet and greet him.

11 Samuel said, What have you done? Saul said, Because I saw that the people were scattering from me, and that you did not come within the days appointed, and that the Philistines were assembled at Michmash,

12 I thought, The Philistines will come down now upon me to Gilgal, and I have not made supplication to the Lord; so I forced myself to offer a burnt offering.

13 And Samuel said to Saul, You have done foolishly! You have not kept the commandment of the Lord your God, which He commanded you; for the Lord would have established your kingdom over Israel for ever;

14 But now your kingdom shall not continue. The Lord has sought out [David] a man after His own [a]heart, and the Lord has commanded him to be prince *and* ruler over His people, because you have not kept what the Lord commanded you.

15 And Samuel went up from Gilgal to Gibeah of Benjamin. And Saul numbered the people that were left with him, *only* about 600.

16 Saul and Jonathan his son, and the people with them, remained in Gibeah of Benjamin; but the Philistines encamped at Michmash.

17 And raiders came out of the Philistine camp in three companies; one company turned toward Ophrah, to the land of Shual;

18 Another turned toward Beth-horon, and another toward the border overlooking the valley of Zeboim toward the wilderness.

19 Now there was no metal worker to be found throughout all the land of Israel; for the Philistines said, Lest the Hebrews make them swords or spears;

20 But each of the Israelites had to go down to the Philistines to get his plowshare, mattock, axe, or sickle sharpened;

21 And the price for plowshares and mattocks was a pim, and a third of a shekel for axes and for setting goads. [So that blunt edges resulted for the sickles, mattocks, forks, axes, and goads.]

22 So on the day of battle neither sword nor spear was found in the hand of any of the men who were with Saul and Jonathan; but Saul and Jonathan his son had them.

23 And the garrison of the Philistines went out to the pass of Michmash.

**14** ONE DAY Jonathan son of Saul said to his armor-bearer, Come, let us go over to the Philistine garrison, on the other side. But he did not tell his father.

AMP [a] See footnote on I Sam. 27:10.

## New American Standard

6When the men of Israel saw that they were in a strait (for the
people were hard-pressed), then the people hid themselves in
caves, in thickets, in cliffs, in cellars, and in pits.
7Also *some of* the Hebrews crossed the Jordan into the land of
Gad and Gilead. But as for Saul, he *was* still in Gilgal, and all the
people followed him trembling.
8¶ Now he waited seven days, according to the appointed time
set by Samuel, but Samuel did not come to Gilgal; and the people
were scattering from him.
9So Saul said, "Bring to me the burnt offering and the peace
offerings." And he offered the burnt offering.
10And it came about as soon as he finished offering the burnt
offering, that behold, Samuel came; and Saul went out to meet him
*and* to greet him.

*Saul Assumes Priestly Office*

11But Samuel said, "What have you done?" And Saul said,
"Because I saw that the people were scattering from me, and that
you did not come within the appointed days, and that the Philistines were assembling at Michmash,
12therefore I said, 'Now the Philistines will come down against
me at Gilgal, and I have not asked the favor of the LORD.' So I
forced myself and offered the burnt offering."
13And Samuel said to Saul, "You have acted foolishly; you have
not kept the commandment of the LORD your God, which He
commanded you, for now the LORD would have established your
kingdom over Israel forever.
14"But now your kingdom shall not endure. The LORD has
sought out for Himself a man after His own heart, and the LORD
has appointed him as ruler over His people, because you have not
kept what the LORD commanded you."
15¶ Then Samuel arose and went up from Gilgal to Gibeah of
Benjamin. And Saul numbered the people who were present with
him, about six hundred men.
16Now Saul and his son Jonathan and the people who were
present with them were staying in Geba of Benjamin while the
Philistines camped at Michmash.
17And the raiders came from the camp of the Philistines in three
companies: one company turned toward Ophrah, to the land of
Shual,
18and another company turned toward Beth-horon, and another company turned toward the border which overlooks the
valley of Zeboim toward the wilderness.
19¶ Now no blacksmith could be found in all the land of Israel,
for the Philistines said, "Lest the Hebrews make swords or
spears."
20So all Israel went down to the Philistines, each to sharpen his
plowshare, his mattock, his axe, and his hoe.
21And the charge was two-thirds of a shekel for the plowshares,
the mattocks, the forks, and the axes, and to fix the hoes.
22So it came about on the day of battle that neither sword nor
spear was found in the hands of any of the people who *were* with
Saul and Jonathan, but they were found with Saul and his son
Jonathan.
23And the garrison of the Philistines went out to the pass of
Michmash.

*Jonathan's Victory*

14 NOW THE day came that Jonathan, the son of Saul, said
to the young man who was carrying his armor, "Come
and let us cross over to the Philistines' garrison that is on yonder
side." But he did not tell his father.

## New International

critical and that their army was hard pressed, they hid in caves and
thickets, among the rocks, and in pits and cisterns. 7Some Hebrews even crossed the Jordan to the land of Gad and Gilead.
Saul remained at Gilgal, and all the troops with him were quaking with fear. 8He waited seven days, the time set by Samuel; but
Samuel did not come to Gilgal, and Saul's men began to scatter.
9So he said, "Bring me the burnt offering and the fellowship offerings.[b]" And Saul offered up the burnt offering. 10Just as he finished making the offering, Samuel arrived, and Saul went out to
greet him.
11"What have you done?" asked Samuel.
Saul replied, "When I saw that the men were scattering, and
that you did not come at the set time, and that the Philistines were
assembling at Micmash, 12I thought, 'Now the Philistines will
come down against me at Gilgal, and I have not sought the LORD's
favor.' So I felt compelled to offer the burnt offering."
13"You acted foolishly," Samuel said. "You have not kept the
command the LORD your God gave you; if you had, he would have
established your kingdom over Israel for all time. 14But now your
kingdom will not endure; the LORD has sought out a man after his
own heart and appointed him leader of his people, because you
have not kept the LORD's command."
15Then Samuel left Gilgal[c] and went up to Gibeah in Benjamin,
and Saul counted the men who were with him. They numbered
about six hundred.

*Israel Without Weapons*

16Saul and his son Jonathan and the men with them were staying in Gibeah[d] in Benjamin, while the Philistines camped at Micmash. 17Raiding parties went out from the Philistine camp in three
detachments. One turned toward Ophrah in the vicinity of Shual,
18another toward Beth Horon, and the third toward the borderland
overlooking the Valley of Zeboim facing the desert.
19Not a blacksmith could be found in the whole land of Israel,
because the Philistines had said, "Otherwise the Hebrews will
make swords or spears!" 20So all Israel went down to the Philistines to have their plowshares, mattocks, axes and sickles[e]
sharpened. 21The price was two thirds of a shekel[f] for sharpening
plowshares and mattocks, and a third of a shekel[g] for sharpening
forks and axes and for repointing goads.
22So on the day of the battle not a soldier with Saul and Jonathan
had a sword or spear in his hand; only Saul and his son Jonathan
had them.

*Jonathan Attacks the Philistines*

23Now a detachment of Philistines had gone out to the pass at
Micmash.

14 ONE DAY Jonathan son of Saul said to the young man
bearing his armor, "Come, let's go over to the Philistine
outpost on the other side." But he did not tell his father.

**NIV** [b] 9 Traditionally *peace offerings* [c] 15 Hebrew; Septuagint *Gilgal and went his way; the rest of the people went after Saul to meet the army, and they went out of Gilgal* [d] 16 Two Hebrew manuscripts; most Hebrew manuscripts *Geba*, a variant of *Gibeah* [e] 20 Septuagint; Hebrew *plowshares* [f] 21 Hebrew *pim*; that is, about 1/4 ounce (about 8 grams) [g] 21 That is, about 1/8 ounce (about 4 grams)

## King James

2And Saul tarried in the uttermost part of Gibeah under a pomegranate tree which *is* in Migron: and the people that *were* with him *were* about six hundred men;

3And Ahiah, the son of Ahitub, Ichabod's brother, the son of Phinehas, the son of Eli, the LORD's priest in Shiloh, wearing an ephod. And the people knew not that Jonathan was gone.

4¶ And between the passages, by which Jonathan sought to go over unto the Philistines' garrison, *there was* a sharp rock on the one side, and a sharp rock on the other side: and the name of the one *was* Bozez, and the name of the other Seneh.

5The forefront of the one *was* situate northward over against Michmash, and the other southward over against Gibeah.

6And Jonathan said to the young man that bare his armour, Come, and let us go over unto the garrison of these uncircumcised: it may be that the LORD will work for us: for *there is* no restraint to the LORD to save by many or by few.

7And his armourbearer said unto him, Do all that *is* in thine heart: turn thee; behold, I *am* with thee according to thy heart.

8Then said Jonathan, Behold, we will pass over unto *these* men, and we will discover ourselves unto them.

9If they say thus unto us, Tarry until we come to you; then we will stand still in our place, and will not go up unto them.

10But if they say thus, Come up unto us; then we will go up: for the LORD hath delivered them into our hand: and this *shall be* a sign unto us.

11And both of them discovered themselves unto the garrison of the Philistines: and the Philistines said, Behold, the Hebrews come forth out of the holes where they had hid themselves.

12And the men of the garrison answered Jonathan and his armourbearer, and said, Come up to us, and we will show you a thing. And Jonathan said unto his armourbearer, Come up after me: for the LORD hath delivered them into the hand of Israel.

13And Jonathan climbed up upon his hands and upon his feet, and his armourbearer after him: and they fell before Jonathan; and his armourbearer slew after him.

14And that first slaughter, which Jonathan and his armourbearer made, was about twenty men, within as it were an half acre of land, *which* a yoke *of oxen might plow*.

15And there was trembling in the host, in the field, and among all the people: the garrison, and the spoilers, they also trembled, and the earth quaked: so it was a very great trembling.

16And the watchmen of Saul in Gibeah of Benjamin looked; and, behold, the multitude melted away, and they went on beating down *one another*.

17Then said Saul unto the people that *were* with him, Number now, and see who is gone from us. And when they had numbered, behold, Jonathan and his armourbearer *were* not *there*.

18And Saul said unto Ahiah, Bring hither the ark of God. For the ark of God was at that time with the children of Israel.

19¶ And it came to pass, while Saul talked unto the priest, that the noise that *was* in the host of the Philistines went on and increased: and Saul said unto the priest, Withdraw thine hand.

20And Saul and all the people that *were* with him assembled themselves, and they came to the battle: and, behold, every man's sword was against his fellow, *and there was* a very great discomfiture.

21Moreover the Hebrews *that* were with the Philistines before that time, which went up with them into the camp *from the country* round about, even they also *turned* to be with the Israelites that *were* with Saul and Jonathan.

22Likewise all the men of Israel which had hid themselves in mount Ephraim, *when* they heard that the Philistines fled, even they also followed hard after them in the battle.

23So the LORD saved Israel that day: and the battle passed over unto Beth-aven.

## Amplified

2Saul was remaining in the outskirts of Gibeah under a pomegranate tree in Migron; and with him were about 600 men,

3And Ahiah son of Ahitub, Ichabod's brother, son of Phinehas, son of Eli, the Lord's priest in Shiloh, wearing the ephod. And the people did not know Jonathan was gone.

4Between the passes by which Jonathan sought to go over to the Philistine garrison, there was a rocky crag on the one side and a rocky crag on the other side; one was named Bozez, and the other Seneh.

5The one crag rose on the north in front of Michmash, and the other on the south in front of Geba.

6And Jonathan said to his young armor-bearer, Come, and let us go over to the garrison of these uncircumcised; it may be that the Lord will work for us; for there is nothing to prevent the Lord from saving by many or by few.

7And his armor-bearer said to him, Do all that is in your mind; I am with you in whatever you think [best].

8Jonathan said, We will pass over to these men, and we will let them see us.

9If they say to us, Wait until we come to you, then we will stand still in our place, and will not go up to them.

10But if they say, Come up to us, we will go up; for the Lord has delivered them into our hand, and this will be our sign.

11So they both let the Philistine garrison see them. And the Philistines said, Behold, the Hebrews are coming out of the holes where they have hid themselves.

12The garrison men said to Jonathan and his armor-bearer, Come up to us, and we will show you a thing. Jonathan said to his armor-bearer, Come up after me, for the Lord has given them into Israel's hand.

13Then Jonathan climbed up on his hands and feet, his armor-bearer after him; and the enemy fell before Jonathan, and his armor-bearer killed them after him.

14And that first slaughter, which Jonathan and his armor-bearer made, was about twenty men, within about a half acre of land, which a yoke of oxen might plow.

15And there was trembling *and* panic in the [Philistine] camp, in the field, and among all the men; the garrison, and even the raiders trembled; the earth quaked, and it became a terror from God.

16Saul's watchmen in Gibeah of Benjamin looked, and behold, the multitude melted away, and went hither and thither.

17Then Saul said to the men with him, Number, and see who is gone from us. When they numbered, behold, Jonathan and his armor-bearer were missing.

18Saul said to Ahijah, Bring here the ark of God, for at that time the ark of God was with the children of Israel.

19While Saul talked to the priest, the tumult in the Philistine camp kept increasing. Then Saul said to the priest, Withdraw your hand.

20Then Saul and all the people with him rallied and went into the battle, and behold, every [Philistine's] sword was against his fellow in wild confusion.

21Moreover the Hebrews who were with the Philistines before that time, who went up with them into the camp from the country round about, even they also turned to be with the Israelites who were with Saul and Jonathan.

22Likewise all the men of Israel who had hid themselves in the hill country of Ephraim, when they heard that the Philistines fled, they also went after them in hot pursuit in the battle.

23So the Lord delivered Israel that day, and the battle passed beyond Beth-aven.

## New American Standard

2And Saul was staying in the outskirts of Gibeah under the pomegranate tree which is in Migron. And the people who *were* with him *were* about six hundred men,

3and Ahijah, the son of Ahitub, Ichabod's brother, the son of Phinehas, the son of Eli, the priest of the LORD at Shiloh, was wearing an ephod. And the people did not know that Jonathan had gone.

4And between the passes by which Jonathan sought to cross over to the Philistines' garrison, there was a sharp crag on the one side, and a sharp crag on the other side, and the name of the one was Bozez, and the name of the other Seneh.

5The one crag rose on the north opposite Michmash, and the other on the south opposite Geba.

6¶ Then Jonathan said to the young man who was carrying his armor, "Come and let us cross over to the garrison of these uncircumcised; perhaps the LORD will work for us, for the LORD is not restrained to save by many or by few."

7And his armor bearer said to him, "Do all that is in your heart; turn yourself, *and* here I am with you according to your desire."

8Then Jonathan said, "Behold, we will cross over to the men and reveal ourselves to them.

9"If they say to us, 'Wait until we come to you'; then we will stand in our place and not go up to them.

10"But if they say, 'Come up to us,' then we will go up, for the LORD has given them into our hands; and this shall be the sign to us."

11And when both of them revealed themselves to the garrison of the Philistines, the Philistines said, "Behold, Hebrews are coming out of the holes where they have hidden themselves."

12So the men of the garrison hailed Jonathan and his armor bearer and said, "Come up to us and we will tell you something." And Jonathan said to his armor bearer, "Come up after me, for the LORD has given them into the hands of Israel."

13Then Jonathan climbed up on his hands and feet, with his armor bearer behind him; and they fell before Jonathan, and his armor bearer put some to death after him.

14And that first slaughter which Jonathan and his armor bearer made was about twenty men within about half a furrow in an acre of land.

15And there was a trembling in the camp, in the field, and among all the people. Even the garrison and the raiders trembled, and the earth quaked so that it became a [a]great trembling.

16¶ Now Saul's watchmen in Gibeah of Benjamin looked, and behold, the multitude melted away; and they went here and *there.*

17And Saul said to the people who *were* with him, "Number now and see who has gone from us." And when they had numbered, behold, Jonathan and his armor bearer were not *there.*

18Then Saul said to Ahijah, "Bring the ark of God here." For the ark of God was at that time with the sons of Israel.

19And it happened while Saul talked to the priest, that the commotion in the camp of the Philistines continued and increased; so Saul said to the priest, "Withdraw your hand."

20Then Saul and all the people who *were* with him rallied and came to the battle; and behold, every man's sword was against his fellow, *and there was* very great confusion.

21Now the Hebrews *who* were with the Philistines previously, who went up with them all around in the camp, even they also *turned* to be with the Israelites who *were* with Saul and Jonathan.

22When all the men of Israel who had hidden themselves in the hill country of Ephraim heard that the Philistines had fled, even they also pursued them closely in the battle.

23So the LORD delivered Israel that day, and the battle spread beyond Beth-aven.

NAS [a] Lit., *trembling of God*

## New International

2Saul was staying on the outskirts of Gibeah under a pomegranate tree in Migron. With him were about six hundred men, 3among whom was Ahijah, who was wearing an ephod. He was a son of Ichabod's brother Ahitub son of Phinehas, the son of Eli, the LORD's priest in Shiloh. No one was aware that Jonathan had left.

4On each side of the pass that Jonathan intended to cross to reach the Philistine outpost was a cliff; one was called Bozez, and the other Seneh. 5One cliff stood to the north toward Micmash, the other to the south toward Geba.

6Jonathan said to his young armor-bearer, "Come, let's go over to the outpost of those uncircumcised fellows. Perhaps the LORD will act in our behalf. Nothing can hinder the LORD from saving, whether by many or by few."

7"Do all that you have in mind," his armor-bearer said. "Go ahead; I am with you heart and soul."

8Jonathan said, "Come, then; we will cross over toward the men and let them see us. 9If they say to us, 'Wait there until we come to you,' we will stay where we are and not go up to them. 10But if they say, 'Come up to us,' we will climb up, because that will be our sign that the LORD has given them into our hands."

11So both of them showed themselves to the Philistine outpost. "Look!" said the Philistines. "The Hebrews are crawling out of the holes they were hiding in." 12The men of the outpost shouted to Jonathan and his armor-bearer, "Come up to us and we'll teach you a lesson."

So Jonathan said to his armor-bearer, "Climb up after me; the LORD has given them into the hand of Israel."

13Jonathan climbed up, using his hands and feet, with his armor-bearer right behind him. The Philistines fell before Jonathan, and his armor-bearer followed and killed behind him. 14In that first attack Jonathan and his armor-bearer killed some twenty men in an area of about half an acre.[b]

*Israel Routs the Philistines*

15Then panic struck the whole army—those in the camp and field, and those in the outposts and raiding parties—and the ground shook. It was a panic sent by God.[c]

16Saul's lookouts at Gibeah of Benjamin saw the army melting away in all directions. 17Then Saul said to the men who were with him, "Muster the forces and see who has left us." When they did, it was Jonathan and his armor-bearer who were not there.

18Saul said to Ahijah, "Bring the ark of God." (At that time it was with the Israelites.)[d] 19While Saul was talking to the priest, the tumult in the Philistine camp increased more and more. So Saul said to the priest, "Withdraw your hand."

20Then Saul and all his men assembled and went to the battle. They found the Philistines in total confusion, striking each other with their swords. 21Those Hebrews who had previously been with the Philistines and had gone up with them to their camp went over to the Israelites who were with Saul and Jonathan. 22When all the Israelites who had hidden in the hill country of Ephraim heard that the Philistines were on the run, they joined the battle in hot pursuit. 23So the LORD rescued Israel that day, and the battle moved on beyond Beth Aven.

NIV [b] *14* Hebrew *half a yoke;* a "yoke" was the land plowed by a yoke of oxen in one day. [c] *15* Or *a terrible panic* [d] *18* Hebrew; Septuagint *"Bring the ephod." (At that time he wore the ephod before the Israelites.)*

## King James

24¶ And the men of Israel were distressed that day: for Saul had adjured the people, saying, Cursed *be* the man that eateth *any* food until evening, that I may be avenged on mine enemies. So none of the people tasted *any* food.

25And all *they of* the land came to a wood; and there was honey upon the ground.

26And when the people were come into the wood, behold, the honey dropped; but no man put his hand to his mouth: for the people feared the oath.

27But Jonathan heard not when his father charged the people with the oath: wherefore he put forth the end of the rod that *was* in his hand, and dipped it in an honeycomb, and put his hand to his mouth; and his eyes were enlightened.

28Then answered one of the people, and said, Thy father straitly charged the people with an oath, saying, Cursed *be* the man that eateth *any* food this day. And the people were faint.

29Then said Jonathan, My father hath troubled the land: see, I pray you, how mine eyes have been enlightened, because I tasted a little of this honey.

30How much more, if haply the people had eaten freely today of the spoil of their enemies which they found? for had there not been now a much greater slaughter among the Philistines?

31And they smote the Philistines that day from Michmash to Aijalon: and the people were very faint.

32And the people flew upon the spoil, and took sheep, and oxen, and calves, and slew *them* on the ground: and the people did eat *them* with the blood.

33¶ Then they told Saul, saying, Behold, the people sin against the LORD, in that they eat with the blood. And he said, Ye have transgressed: roll a great stone unto me this day.

34And Saul said, Disperse yourselves among the people, and say unto them, Bring me hither every man his ox, and every man his sheep, and slay *them* here, and eat; and sin not against the LORD in eating with the blood. And all the people brought every man his ox with him that night, and slew *them* there.

35And Saul built an altar unto the LORD: the same was the first altar that he built unto the LORD.

36¶ And Saul said, Let us go down after the Philistines by night, and spoil them until the morning light, and let us not leave a man of them. And they said, Do whatsoever seemeth good unto thee. Then said the priest, Let us draw near hither unto God.

37And Saul asked counsel of God, Shall I go down after the Philistines? wilt thou deliver them into the hand of Israel? But he answered him not that day.

38And Saul said, Draw ye near hither, all the chief of the people: and know and see wherein this sin hath been this day.

39For, *as* the LORD liveth, which saveth Israel, though it be in Jonathan my son, he shall surely die. But *there was* not a man among all the people *that* answered him.

40Then said he unto all Israel, Be ye on one side, and I and Jonathan my son will be on the other side. And the people said unto Saul, Do what seemeth good unto thee.

41Therefore Saul said unto the LORD God of Israel, Give a perfect *lot*. And Saul and Jonathan were taken: but the people escaped.

42And Saul said, Cast *lots* between me and Jonathan my son. And Jonathan was taken.

43Then Saul said to Jonathan, Tell me what thou hast done. And Jonathan told him, and said, I did but taste a little honey with the end of the rod that *was* in mine hand, *and*, lo, I must die.

44And Saul answered, God do so and more also: for thou shalt surely die, Jonathan.

45And the people said unto Saul, Shall Jonathan die, who hath wrought this great salvation in Israel? God forbid: *as* the LORD liveth, there shall not one hair of his head fall to the ground; for he hath wrought with God this day. So the people rescued Jonathan, that he died not.

46Then Saul went up from following the Philistines: and the Philistines went to their own place.

## Amplified

24But the men of Israel were distressed that day; for Saul had caused them to take an oath, saying, Cursed be the man who eats any food until evening and I have taken vengeance on my enemies. So none of the men tasted any food.

25And all they of the land came to a wood; and there was honey on the ground.

26When the men entered the wood, behold, the honey was dripping; but no man tasted it, for the men feared the oath.

27But Jonathan had not heard when his father charged the people with the oath. So he dipped the end of the rod in his hand into a honeycomb, and put it to his mouth; and his [weary] eyes brightened.

28Then one of the men told him, Your father strictly charged the men with an oath, saying, Cursed be the man who eats any food today. And the people were exhausted *and* faint.

29Then Jonathan said, My father has troubled the land; see how my eyes have brightened, because I tasted a little of this honey.

30How much better if the men had eaten freely today of the spoil of their enemies which they found; for the slaughter of the Philistines has not been great.

31They smote the Philistines that day from Michmash to Aijalon. And the people were very faint.

32[When night came and the oath expired] the men flew upon the spoil. They took sheep, oxen, and calves, slew them on the ground, and ate them [raw] with the blood.

33Then Saul was told, Behold, the men are sinning against the Lord by eating with the blood. And he said, You have transgressed; roll a great stone to me here.

34Saul said, Disperse yourselves among the people, and tell them, Bring me every man his ox, or his sheep, and butcher them here, and eat; and sin not against the Lord by eating the blood. So all the men brought each one his ox that night, and butchered them there.

35And Saul built an altar to the Lord; it was the first altar he built to the Lord.

36Then Saul said, Let us go down after the Philistines by night, and seize and plunder them until daylight, and let us not leave a man of them. They said, Do whatever seems good to you. Then the priest said, Let us draw near here to God.

37And Saul asked counsel of God, Shall I go down after the Philistines? Will You deliver them into the hand of Israel? But He did not answer him that day.

38Then Saul said, Draw near, all the chief of the people; and let us see how this sin [causing God's silence] arose today.

39For, as the Lord lives, Who delivers Israel, though it be in Jonathan my son, he shall surely die. But not a man among all the people answered him.

40Then he said to all Israel, You be on one side, and I and Jonathan my son will be on the other side. The people said to Saul, Do what seems good to you.

41Therefore Saul said to the Lord, the God of Israel, Give a perfect lot *and* show the right. And Saul and Jonathan were taken [by lot], but the other men went free.

42Saul said, Cast lots between me and Jonathan my son. And Jonathan was taken.

43Saul said to Jonathan, Tell me what you have done. And Jonathan said, I tasted a little honey with the end of the rod that was in my hand. And lo, I must die.

44Saul answered, God do so and more also; for you shall surely die, Jonathan.

45But the people said to Saul, Shall Jonathan, who has wrought this great deliverance to Israel, die? God forbid! As the Lord lives, there shall not one hair of his head perish, for he has wrought this great deliverance with God this day. So the people rescued Jonathan, and he did not die.

46Then Saul ceased pursuing the Philistines, and they went to their own place.

## New American Standard

*Saul's Foolish Order*

**24**¶ Now the men of Israel were hard-pressed on that day, for
Saul had put the people under oath, saying, "Cursed be the man
who eats food before evening, and until I have avenged myself on
my enemies." So none of the people tasted food.
25And all *the people of* the land entered the forest, and there was
honey on the ground.
26When the people entered the forest, behold, *there was* a flow
of honey; but no man put his hand to his mouth, for the people
feared the oath.
27But Jonathan had not heard when his father put the people
under oath; therefore, he put out the end of the staff that *was* in
his hand and dipped it in the honeycomb, and put his hand to his
mouth, and his eyes brightened.
28Then one of the people answered and said, "Your father
strictly put the people under oath, saying, 'Cursed be the man who
eats food today.' " And the people were weary.
29Then Jonathan said, "My father has troubled the land. See
now, how my eyes have brightened because I tasted a little of this
honey.
30"How much more, if only the people had eaten freely today
of the spoil of their enemies which they found! For now the slaughter among the Philistines has not been great."
**31**¶ And they struck among the Philistines that day from Michmash to Aijalon. And the people were very weary.
32And the people rushed greedily upon the spoil, and took
sheep and oxen and calves, and slew *them* on the ground; and the
people ate *them* with the blood.
33Then they told Saul, saying, "Behold, the people are sinning
against the LORD by eating with the blood." And he said, "You
have acted treacherously; roll a great stone to me today."
34And Saul said, "Disperse yourselves among the people and
say to them, 'Each one of you bring me his ox or his sheep, and
slaughter *it* here and eat; and do not sin against the LORD by eating
with the blood.' " So all the people that night brought each one his
ox with him, and slaughtered *it* there.
35And Saul built an altar to the LORD; it was the first altar that
he built to the LORD.
**36**¶ Then Saul said, "Let us go down after the Philistines by
night and take spoil among them until the morning light, and let
us not leave a man of them." And they said, "Do whatever seems
good to you." So the priest said, "Let us draw near to God here."
37And Saul inquired of God, "Shall I go down after the Philistines? Wilt Thou give them into the hand of Israel?" But He did
not answer him on that day.
38And Saul said, "Draw near here, all you chiefs of the people,
and investigate and see how this sin has happened today.
39"For as the LORD lives, who delivers Israel, though it is in
Jonathan my son, he shall surely die." But not one of all the people
answered him.
40Then he said to all Israel, "You shall be on one side and I and
Jonathan my son will be on the other side." And the people said
to Saul, "Do what seems good to you."
41Therefore, Saul said to the LORD, the God of Israel, "Give a
perfect *lot*." And Jonathan and Saul were taken, but the people
escaped.
42And Saul said, "Cast *lots* between me and Jonathan my son."
And Jonathan was taken.
**43**¶ Then Saul said to Jonathan, "Tell me what you have done."
So Jonathan told him and said, "I indeed tasted a little honey with
the end of the staff that was in my hand. Here I am, I must die!"
44And Saul said, "May God do this *to me* and more also, for you
shall surely die, Jonathan."
45But the people said to Saul, "Must Jonathan die, who has
brought about this great deliverance in Israel? Far from it! As the
LORD lives, there shall not one hair of his head fall to the ground,
for he has worked with God this day." So the people rescued
Jonathan and he did not die.
46Then Saul went up from pursuing the Philistines, and the
Philistines went to their own place.

## New International

*Jonathan Eats Honey*

24Now the men of Israel were in distress that day, because Saul
had bound the people under an oath, saying, "Cursed be any man
who eats food before evening comes, before I have avenged myself
on my enemies!" So none of the troops tasted food.
25The entire army[a] entered the woods, and there was honey on
the ground. 26When they went into the woods, they saw the honey
oozing out, yet no one put his hand to his mouth, because they
feared the oath. 27But Jonathan had not heard that his father had
bound the people with the oath, so he reached out the end of the
staff that was in his hand and dipped it into the honeycomb. He
raised his hand to his mouth, and his eyes brightened.[b] 28Then
one of the soldiers told him, "Your father bound the army under
a strict oath, saying, 'Cursed be any man who eats food today!'
That is why the men are faint."
29Jonathan said, "My father has made trouble for the country.
See how my eyes brightened[c] when I tasted a little of this honey.
30How much better it would have been if the men had eaten today
some of the plunder they took from their enemies. Would not the
slaughter of the Philistines have been even greater?"
31That day, after the Israelites had struck down the Philistines
from Micmash to Aijalon, they were exhausted. 32They pounced
on the plunder and, taking sheep, cattle and calves, they butchered them on the ground and ate them, together with the blood.
33Then someone said to Saul, "Look, the men are sinning against
the LORD by eating meat that has blood in it."
"You have broken faith," he said. "Roll a large stone over here
at once." 34Then he said, "Go out among the men and tell them,
'Each of you bring me your cattle and sheep, and slaughter them
here and eat them. Do not sin against the LORD by eating meat with
blood still in it.' "
So everyone brought his ox that night and slaughtered it there.
35Then Saul built an altar to the LORD; it was the first time he had
done this.
36Saul said, "Let us go down after the Philistines by night and
plunder them till dawn, and let us not leave one of them alive."
"Do whatever seems best to you," they replied.
But the priest said, "Let us inquire of God here."
37So Saul asked God, "Shall I go down after the Philistines? Will
you give them into Israel's hand?" But God did not answer him
that day.
38Saul therefore said, "Come here, all you who are leaders of
the army, and let us find out what sin has been committed today.
39As surely as the LORD who rescues Israel lives, even if it lies with
my son Jonathan, he must die." But not one of the men said a
word.
40Saul then said to all the Israelites, "You stand over there; I and
Jonathan my son will stand over here."
"Do what seems best to you," the men replied.
41Then Saul prayed to the LORD, the God of Israel, "Give me
the right answer."[d] And Jonathan and Saul were taken by lot, and
the men were cleared. 42Saul said, "Cast the lot between me and
Jonathan my son." And Jonathan was taken.
43Then Saul said to Jonathan, "Tell me what you have done."
So Jonathan told him, "I merely tasted a little honey with the
end of my staff. And now must I die?"
44Saul said, "May God deal with me, be it ever so severely, if
you do not die, Jonathan."
45But the men said to Saul, "Should Jonathan die—he who has
brought about this great deliverance in Israel? Never! As surely as
the LORD lives, not a hair of his head will fall to the ground, for
he did this today with God's help." So the men rescued Jonathan,
and he was not put to death.
46Then Saul stopped pursuing the Philistines, and they withdrew to their own land.

**NIV** [a] 25 Or *Now all the people of the land* [b] 27 Or *his strength was renewed* [c] 29 Or *my strength was renewed* [d] 41 Hebrew; Septuagint *"Why have you not answered your servant today? If the fault is in me or my son Jonathan, respond with Urim, but if the men of Israel are at fault, respond with Thummim."*

## King James

47¶ So Saul took the kingdom over Israel, and fought against all his enemies on every side, against Moab, and against the children of Ammon, and against Edom, and against the kings of Zobah, and against the Philistines: and whithersoever he turned himself, he vexed *them*.

48And he gathered an host, and smote the Amalekites, and delivered Israel out of the hands of them that spoiled them.

49Now the sons of Saul were Jonathan, and Ishui, and Melchi-shua: and the names of his two daughters *were these;* the name of the firstborn Merab, and the name of the younger Michal:

50And the name of Saul's wife *was* Ahinoam, the daughter of Ahimaaz: and the name of the captain of his host *was* Abner, the son of Ner, Saul's uncle.

51And Kish *was* the father of Saul; and Ner the father of Abner *was* the son of Abiel.

52And there was sore war against the Philistines all the days of Saul: and when Saul saw any strong man, or any valiant man, he took him unto him.

**15** SAMUEL ALSO said unto Saul, The LORD sent me to anoint thee *to be* king over his people, over Israel: now therefore hearken thou unto the voice of the words of the LORD.

2Thus saith the LORD of hosts, I remember *that* which Amalek did to Israel, how he laid *wait* for him in the way, when he came up from Egypt.

3Now go and smite Amalek, and utterly destroy all that they have, and spare them not; but slay both man and woman, infant and suckling, ox and sheep, camel and ass.

4And Saul gathered the people together, and numbered them in Telaim, two hundred thousand footmen, and ten thousand men of Judah.

5And Saul came to a city of Amalek, and laid wait in the valley.

6¶ And Saul said unto the Kenites, Go, depart, get you down from among the Amalekites, lest I destroy you with them: for ye showed kindness to all the children of Israel, when they came up out of Egypt. So the Kenites departed from among the Amalekites.

7And Saul smote the Amalekites from Havilah *until* thou comest to Shur, that *is* over against Egypt.

8And he took Agag the king of the Amalekites alive, and utterly destroyed all the people with the edge of the sword.

9But Saul and the people spared Agag, and the best of the sheep, and of the oxen, and of the fatlings, and the lambs, and all *that was* good, and would not utterly destroy them: but every thing *that was* vile and refuse, that they destroyed utterly.

10¶ Then came the word of the LORD unto Samuel, saying,

11It repenteth me that I have set up Saul *to be* king: for he is turned back from following me, and hath not performed my commandments. And it grieved Samuel; and he cried unto the LORD all night.

12And when Samuel rose early to meet Saul in the morning, it was told Samuel, saying, Saul came to Carmel, and, behold, he set him up a place, and is gone about, and passed on, and gone down to Gilgal.

13And Samuel came to Saul: and Saul said unto him, Blessed *be* thou of the LORD: I have performed the commandment of the LORD.

14And Samuel said, What *meaneth* then this bleating of the sheep in mine ears, and the lowing of the oxen which I hear?

15And Saul said, They have brought them from the Amalekites: for the people spared the best of the sheep and of the oxen, to sacrifice unto the LORD thy God; and the rest we have utterly destroyed.

16Then Samuel said unto Saul, Stay, and I will tell thee what the LORD hath said to me this night. And he said unto him, Say on.

17And Samuel said, When thou *wast* little in thine own sight, *wast* thou not *made* the head of the tribes of Israel, and the LORD anointed thee king over Israel?

## Amplified

47When Saul took over the kingdom of Israel, he fought against all his enemies on every side: Moab, the Ammonites, Edom; the kings of Zobah, and the Philistines. Wherever he turned he made it worse for them.

48He did valiantly, and smote the Amalekites, and delivered Israel out of the hands of those who plundered them.

49Now Saul's sons were Jonathan, Ishvi, and Malchi-shua; and the names of his two daughters were, of the first-born, Merab; and of the younger, Michal.

50The name of Saul's wife was Ahinoam daughter of Ahimaaz. The commander of his army was Abner son of Ner, Saul's uncle.

51Kish the father of Saul and Ner the father of Abner were sons of Abiel.

52There was severe war against the Philistines all the days of Saul, and whenever Saul saw any mighty or [outstandingly] courageous man, he attached him to himself.

**15** SAMUEL TOLD Saul, The Lord sent me to anoint you king over His people Israel. Now listen and heed the words of the Lord.

2Thus says the Lord of hosts, I have considered *and* will punish what Amalek did to Israel, how he set himself against him in the way, when [Israel] came out of Egypt.

3Now go and smite Amalek, and utterly destroy all they have; do not spare them, but kill both man and woman, infant and suckling, ox and sheep, camel and donkey.

4So Saul assembled the men and numbered them at Telaim, 200,000 men on foot, and 10,000 men of Judah.

5And Saul came to the city of Amalek, and laid wait in the valley.

6Saul warned the Kenites, Go, depart, get down from among the Amalekites, lest I destroy you with them; for you showed kindness to all the Israelites when they came up out of Egypt. So the Kenites departed from among the Amalekites.

7Saul smote the Amalekites from Havilah as far as Shur, that is east of Egypt.

8And he took Agag the king of the Amalekites alive, though he utterly destroyed all the rest of the people with the sword.

9Saul and the people spared Agag, and the best of the sheep, oxen, fatlings, lambs, and all that was good, and would not utterly destroy them; but all that was undesirable or worthless they destroyed utterly.

10Then the word of the Lord came to Samuel, saying,

11I regret making Saul king, for he has turned back from following Me, and has not performed My commands. And Samuel was grieved *and* angry [with Saul], and he cried to the Lord all night.

12When Samuel rose early to meet Saul in the morning, he was told, Saul came to Carmel, and behold, he set up for himself a monument or trophy [of his victory], and passed on, and went down to Gilgal.

13And Samuel came to Saul, and Saul said to him, Blessed be you of the Lord. I have performed what the Lord ordered.

14And Samuel said, What then means this bleating of the sheep in my ears, and the lowing of the oxen which I hear?

15Saul said, They have brought them from the Amalekites; for the people spared the best of the sheep and oxen, to sacrifice to the Lord your God; but the rest we have utterly destroyed.

16Then Samuel said to Saul, Stop! I will tell you what the Lord said to me tonight. Saul said to him, Say on.

17Samuel said, When you were small in your own sight, were you not made the head of the tribes of Israel, and the Lord anointed you king over Israel?

## New American Standard

*Constant Warfare*

47¶ Now when Saul had taken the kingdom over Israel, he
fought against all his enemies on every side, against Moab, the
sons of Ammon, Edom, the kings of Zobah, and the Philistines;
and wherever he turned, he inflicted punishment.
48And he acted valiantly and defeated the Amalekites, and
delivered Israel from the hands of those who plundered them.
49¶ Now the sons of Saul were Jonathan and Ishvi and Malchi-
shua; and the names of his two daughters *were these:* the name of
the first-born Merab and the name of the younger Michal.
50And the name of Saul's wife was Ahinoam the daughter of
Ahimaaz. And the name of the captain of his army was Abner the
son of Ner, Saul's uncle.
51And Kish *was* the father of Saul, and Ner the father of Abner
*was* the son of Abiel.
52¶ Now the war against the Philistines was severe all the days
of Saul; and when Saul saw any mighty man or any valiant man,
he attached him to his staff.

*Saul's Disobedience*

15 THEN SAMUEL said to Saul, "The LORD sent me to anoint
you as king over His people, over Israel; now therefore,
listen to the words of the LORD.
2"Thus says the LORD of hosts, 'I will punish Amalek *for* what
he did to Israel, how he set himself against him on the way while
he was coming up from Egypt.
3'Now go and strike Amalek and utterly destroy all that he has,
and do not spare him; but put to death both man and woman, child
and infant, ox and sheep, camel and donkey.' "
4¶ Then Saul summoned the people and numbered them in
Telaim, 200,000 foot soldiers and 10,000 men of Judah.
5And Saul came to the city of Amalek, and set an ambush in
the valley.
6And Saul said to the Kenites, "Go, depart, go down from
among the Amalekites, lest I destroy you with them; for you
showed kindness to all the sons of Israel when they came up from
Egypt." So the Kenites departed from among the Amalekites.
7So Saul defeated the Amalekites, from Havilah as you go to
Shur, which is east of Egypt.
8And he captured Agag the king of the Amalekites alive, and
utterly destroyed all the people with the edge of the sword.
9But Saul and the people spared Agag and the best of the
sheep, the oxen, the fatlings, the lambs, and all that was good, and
were not willing to destroy them utterly; but everything despised
and worthless, that they utterly destroyed.

*Samuel Rebukes Saul*

10¶ Then the word of the LORD came to Samuel, saying,
11"I regret that I have made Saul king, for he has turned back
from following Me, and has not carried out My commands." And
Samuel was distressed and cried out to the LORD all night.
12And Samuel rose early in the morning to meet Saul; and it was
told Samuel, saying, "Saul came to Carmel, and behold, he set up
a monument for himself, then turned and proceeded on down to
Gilgal."
13And Samuel came to Saul, and Saul said to him, "Blessed are
you of the LORD! I have carried out the command of the LORD."
14But Samuel said, "What then is this bleating of the sheep in
my ears, and the lowing of the oxen which I hear?"
15And Saul said, "They have brought them from the Amalekites, for the people spared the best of the sheep and oxen, to
sacrifice to the LORD your God; but the rest we have utterly destroyed."
16Then Samuel said to Saul, "Wait, and let me tell you what the
LORD said to me last night." And he said to him, "Speak!"
17¶ And Samuel said, "Is it not true, though you were little in
your own eyes, you were *made* the head of the tribes of Israel? And
the LORD anointed you king over Israel,

## New International

47After Saul had assumed rule over Israel, he fought against
their enemies on every side: Moab, the Ammonites, Edom, the
kings[a] of Zobah, and the Philistines. Wherever he turned, he
inflicted punishment on them.[b] 48He fought valiantly and defeated the Amalekites, delivering Israel from the hands of those
who had plundered them.

*Saul's Family*

49Saul's sons were Jonathan, Ishvi and Malki-Shua. The name
of his older daughter was Merab, and that of the younger was
Michal. 50His wife's name was Ahinoam daughter of Ahimaaz.
The name of the commander of Saul's army was Abner son of Ner,
and Ner was Saul's uncle. 51Saul's father Kish and Abner's father
Ner were sons of Abiel.
52All the days of Saul there was bitter war with the Philistines,
and whenever Saul saw a mighty or brave man, he took him into
his service.

*The LORD Rejects Saul as King*

15 SAMUEL SAID to Saul, "I am the one the LORD sent to
anoint you king over his people Israel; so listen now to the
message from the LORD. 2This is what the LORD Almighty says: 'I
will punish the Amalekites for what they did to Israel when they
waylaid them as they came up from Egypt. 3Now go, attack the
Amalekites and totally destroy[c] everything that belongs to them.
Do not spare them; put to death men and women, children and
infants, cattle and sheep, camels and donkeys.' "
4So Saul summoned the men and mustered them at Telaim—
two hundred thousand foot soldiers and ten thousand men from
Judah. 5Saul went to the city of Amalek and set an ambush in the
ravine. 6Then he said to the Kenites, "Go away, leave the Amalekites so that I do not destroy you along with them; for you showed
kindness to all the Israelites when they came up out of Egypt." So
the Kenites moved away from the Amalekites.
7Then Saul attacked the Amalekites all the way from Havilah to
Shur, to the east of Egypt. 8He took Agag king of the Amalekites
alive, and all his people he totally destroyed with the sword. 9But
Saul and the army spared Agag and the best of the sheep and
cattle, the fat calves[d] and lambs—everything that was good. These
they were unwilling to destroy completely, but everything that
was despised and weak they totally destroyed.
10Then the word of the LORD came to Samuel: 11"I am grieved
that I have made Saul king, because he has turned away from me
and has not carried out my instructions." Samuel was troubled,
and he cried out to the LORD all that night.
12Early in the morning Samuel got up and went to meet Saul,
but he was told, "Saul has gone to Carmel. There he has set up
a monument in his own honor and has turned and gone on down
to Gilgal."
13When Samuel reached him, Saul said, "The LORD bless you!
I have carried out the LORD's instructions."
14But Samuel said, "What then is this bleating of sheep in my
ears? What is this lowing of cattle that I hear?"
15Saul answered, "The soldiers brought them from the Amalekites; they spared the best of the sheep and cattle to sacrifice to the
LORD your God, but we totally destroyed the rest."
16"Stop!" Samuel said to Saul. "Let me tell you what the LORD
said to me last night."
"Tell me," Saul replied.
17Samuel said, "Although you were once small in your own
eyes, did you not become the head of the tribes of Israel? The LORD
anointed you king over Israel. 18And he sent you on a mission,

**NIV** [a] 47 Masoretic Text; Dead Sea Scrolls and Septuagint *king* [b] 47 Hebrew; Septuagint *he was victorious* [c] 3 The Hebrew term refers to the irrevocable giving over of things or persons to the LORD, often by totally destroying them; also in verses 8, 9, 15, 18, 20 and 21. [d] 9 Or *the grown bulls;* the meaning of the Hebrew for this phrase is uncertain.

## King James

18 And the LORD sent thee on a journey, and said, Go and utterly destroy the sinners the Amalekites, and fight against them until they be consumed.

19 Wherefore then didst thou not obey the voice of the LORD, but didst fly upon the spoil, and didst evil in the sight of the LORD?

20 And Saul said unto Samuel, Yea, I have obeyed the voice of the LORD, and have gone the way which the LORD sent me, and have brought Agag the king of Amalek, and have utterly destroyed the Amalekites.

21 But the people took of the spoil, sheep and oxen, the chief of the things which should have been utterly destroyed, to sacrifice unto the LORD thy God in Gilgal.

22 And Samuel said, Hath the LORD *as great* delight in burnt offerings and sacrifices, as in obeying the voice of the LORD? Behold, to obey *is* better than sacrifice, *and* to hearken than the fat of rams.

23 For rebellion *is as* the sin of witchcraft, and stubbornness *is as* iniquity and idolatry. Because thou hast rejected the word of the LORD, he hath also rejected thee from *being* king.

24 ¶ And Saul said unto Samuel, I have sinned: for I have transgressed the commandment of the LORD, and thy words: because I feared the people, and obeyed their voice.

25 Now therefore, I pray thee, pardon my sin, and turn again with me, that I may worship the LORD.

26 And Samuel said unto Saul, I will not return with thee: for thou hast rejected the word of the LORD, and the LORD hath rejected thee from being king over Israel.

27 And as Samuel turned about to go away, he laid hold upon the skirt of his mantle, and it rent.

28 And Samuel said unto him, The LORD hath rent the kingdom of Israel from thee this day, and hath given it to a neighbour of thine, *that is* better than thou.

29 And also the Strength of Israel will not lie nor repent: for he *is* not a man, that he should repent.

30 Then he said, I have sinned: *yet* honour me now, I pray thee, before the elders of my people, and before Israel, and turn again with me, that I may worship the LORD thy God.

31 So Samuel turned again after Saul; and Saul worshipped the LORD.

32 ¶ Then said Samuel, Bring ye hither to me Agag the king of the Amalekites. And Agag came unto him delicately. And Agag said, Surely the bitterness of death is past.

33 And Samuel said, As thy sword hath made women childless, so shall thy mother be childless among women. And Samuel hewed Agag in pieces before the LORD in Gilgal.

34 ¶ Then Samuel went to Ramah; and Saul went up to his house to Gibeah of Saul.

35 And Samuel came no more to see Saul until the day of his death: nevertheless Samuel mourned for Saul: and the LORD repented that he had made Saul king over Israel.

**16** AND THE LORD said unto Samuel, How long wilt thou mourn for Saul, seeing I have rejected him from reigning over Israel? fill thine horn with oil, and go, I will send thee to Jesse the Bethlehemite: for I have provided me a king among his sons.

2 And Samuel said, How can I go? if Saul hear *it,* he will kill me. And the LORD said, Take an heifer with thee, and say, I am come to sacrifice to the LORD.

3 And call Jesse to the sacrifice, and I will show thee what thou shalt do: and thou shalt anoint unto me *him* whom I name unto thee.

## Amplified

18 And the Lord sent you on a mission, and said, Go, utterly destroy the sinners, the Amalekites, and fight against them until they are consumed.

19 Why then did you not obey the voice of the Lord, but swooped down upon the plunder and did evil in the Lord's sight?

20 Saul said to Samuel, Yes, I have obeyed the voice of the Lord, and have gone the way which the Lord sent me, and have brought Agag the king of Amalek, and have utterly destroyed the Amalekites.

21 But the people took of the spoil, sheep and oxen, the chief of the things to be utterly destroyed, to sacrifice to the Lord your God in Gilgal.

22 Samuel said, Has the Lord as great delight in burnt offerings and sacrifices, as in obeying the voice of the Lord? Behold, to obey is better than sacrifice, and to hearken than the fat of rams.

23 For rebellion is as the sin of witchcraft, and stubbornness is as idolatry and teraphim (good luck images). Because you have rejected the word of the Lord, He also has rejected you from being king.

24 And Saul said to Samuel, I have sinned; for I have transgressed the commandment of the Lord and your words, because I feared the people and obeyed their voice.

25 Now, I pray you, pardon my sin, and go back with me, that I may worship the Lord.

26 And Samuel said to Saul, I will not return with you, for you have rejected the word of the Lord, and the Lord has rejected you from being king over Israel.

27 And as Samuel turned to go away, Saul seized the skirt of Samuel's mantle, and it tore.

28 And Samuel said to him, The Lord has torn the kingdom of Israel from you this day, and has given it to a neighbor of yours, who is better than you.

29 And also the Strength of Israel will not lie or repent; for He is not a man, that He should repent.

30 Saul said, I have sinned; yet honor me now, I pray you, before the elders of my people and before Israel, and return with me, that I may worship the Lord your God.

31 So Samuel turned back after Saul; and Saul worshiped the Lord.

32 Then Samuel said, Bring here to me Agag, king of the Amalekites. And Agag came to him cheerfully. And Agag said, Surely the bitterness of death is past.

33 Samuel said, As your sword has made women childless, so shall your mother be childless among women. And Samuel hewed Agag in pieces before the Lord in Gilgal.

34 Then Samuel went to Ramah, and Saul went up to his house in Gibeah of Saul.

35 And Samuel came no more to see Saul to the day of his death, but Samuel grieved over Saul; and the Lord repented that he had made Saul king over Israel.

**16** THE LORD said to Samuel, How long will you mourn for Saul, seeing I have rejected him from reigning over Israel? Fill your horn with oil; I will send you to Jesse the Bethlehemite; for I have provided for Myself a king among his sons.

2 Samuel said, How can I go? If Saul hears it, he will kill me. And the Lord said, Take a heifer with you, and say, I have come to sacrifice to the Lord.

3 And invite Jesse to the sacrifice, and I will show you what you shall do; and you shall anoint for Me him I name to you.

## New American Standard

18and the LORD sent you on a mission, and said, 'Go and utterly
destroy the sinners, the Amalekites, and fight against them until
they are exterminated.'
19"Why then did you not obey the voice of the LORD, but rushed
upon the spoil and did what was evil in the sight of the LORD?"
20¶ Then Saul said to Samuel, "I did obey the voice of the LORD,
and went on the mission on which the LORD sent me, and have
brought back Agag the king of Amalek, and have utterly destroyed
the Amalekites.
21"But the people took *some* of the spoil, sheep and oxen, the
choicest of the things devoted to destruction, to sacrifice to the
LORD your God at Gilgal."
22And Samuel said,

"Has the LORD as much delight in burnt offerings and
sacrifices
As in obeying the voice of the LORD?
Behold, to obey is better than sacrifice,
*And* to heed than the fat of rams.

23 "For rebellion is as the sin of divination,
And insubordination is as iniquity and idolatry.
Because you have rejected the word of the LORD,
He has also rejected you from *being* king."

24¶ Then Saul said to Samuel, "I have sinned; I have indeed
transgressed the command of the LORD and your words, because
I feared the people and listened to their voice.
25"Now therefore, please pardon my sin and return with me,
that I may worship the LORD."
26But Samuel said to Saul, "I will not return with you; for you
have rejected the word of the LORD, and the LORD has rejected you
from being king over Israel."
27And as Samuel turned to go, *Saul* seized the edge of his robe,
and it tore.
28So Samuel said to him, "The LORD has torn the kingdom of
Israel from you today, and has given it to your neighbor who is
better than you.
29"And also the Glory of Israel will not lie or change His mind;
for He is not a man that He should change His mind."
30Then he said, "I have sinned; *but* please honor me now before
the elders of my people and before Israel, and go back with me,
that I may worship the LORD your God."
31So Samuel went back following Saul, and Saul worshiped the
LORD.
32¶ Then Samuel said, "Bring me Agag, the king of the Amalekites." And Agag came to him cheerfully. And Agag said, "Surely
the bitterness of death is past."
33But Samuel said, "As your sword has made women childless,
so shall your mother be childless among women." And Samuel
hewed Agag to pieces before the LORD at Gilgal.
34¶ Then Samuel went to Ramah, but Saul went up to his house
at Gibeah of Saul.
35And Samuel did not see Saul again until the day of his death;
for Samuel grieved over Saul. And the LORD regretted that He had
made Saul king over Israel.

*Samuel Goes to Bethlehem*

16 NOW THE LORD said to Samuel, "How long will you
grieve over Saul, since I have rejected him from being king
over Israel? Fill your horn with oil, and go; I will send you to Jesse
the Bethlehemite, for I have selected a king for Myself among his
sons."
2But Samuel said, "How can I go? When Saul hears *of it*, he will
kill me." And the LORD said, "Take a heifer with you, and say, 'I
have come to sacrifice to the LORD.'
3"And you shall invite Jesse to the sacrifice, and I will show
you what you shall do; and you shall anoint for Me the one whom
I designate to you."

## New International

saying, 'Go and completely destroy those wicked people, the
Amalekites; make war on them until you have wiped them out.'
19Why did you not obey the LORD? Why did you pounce on the
plunder and do evil in the eyes of the LORD?"
20"But I did obey the LORD," Saul said. "I went on the mission
the LORD assigned me. I completely destroyed the Amalekites and
brought back Agag their king. 21The soldiers took sheep and cattle
from the plunder, the best of what was devoted to God, in order
to sacrifice them to the LORD your God at Gilgal."
22But Samuel replied:

"Does the LORD delight in burnt offerings and sacrifices
as much as in obeying the voice of the LORD?
To obey is better than sacrifice,
and to heed is better than the fat of rams.
23For rebellion is like the sin of divination,
and arrogance like the evil of idolatry.
Because you have rejected the word of the LORD,
he has rejected you as king."

24Then Saul said to Samuel, "I have sinned. I violated the
LORD's command and your instructions. I was afraid of the people
and so I gave in to them. 25Now I beg you, forgive my sin and come
back with me, so that I may worship the LORD."
26But Samuel said to him, "I will not go back with you. You have
rejected the word of the LORD, and the LORD has rejected you as
king over Israel!"
27As Samuel turned to leave, Saul caught hold of the hem of his
robe, and it tore. 28Samuel said to him, "The LORD has torn the
kingdom of Israel from you today and has given it to one of your
neighbors—to one better than you. 29He who is the Glory of Israel
does not lie or change his mind; for he is not a man, that he should
change his mind."
30Saul replied, "I have sinned. But please honor me before the
elders of my people and before Israel; come back with me, so that
I may worship the LORD your God." 31So Samuel went back with
Saul, and Saul worshiped the LORD.
32Then Samuel said, "Bring me Agag king of the Amalekites."
Agag came to him confidently,[a] thinking, "Surely the bitterness of death is past."
33But Samuel said,

"As your sword has made women childless,
so will your mother be childless among women."

And Samuel put Agag to death before the LORD at Gilgal.
34Then Samuel left for Ramah, but Saul went up to his home
in Gibeah of Saul. 35Until the day Samuel died, he did not go to
see Saul again, though Samuel mourned for him. And the LORD
was grieved that he had made Saul king over Israel.

*Samuel Anoints David*

16 THE LORD said to Samuel, "How long will you mourn for
Saul, since I have rejected him as king over Israel? Fill your
horn with oil and be on your way; I am sending you to Jesse of
Bethlehem. I have chosen one of his sons to be king."
2But Samuel said, "How can I go? Saul will hear about it and
kill me."
The LORD said, "Take a heifer with you and say, 'I have come
to sacrifice to the LORD.' 3Invite Jesse to the sacrifice, and I will
show you what to do. You are to anoint for me the one I indicate."

NIV [a] 32 Or *him trembling, yet*

## King James

4 And Samuel did that which the LORD spake, and came to Bethlehem. And the elders of the town trembled at his coming, and said, Comest thou peaceably?

5 And he said, Peaceably: I am come to sacrifice unto the LORD: sanctify yourselves, and come with me to the sacrifice. And he sanctified Jesse and his sons, and called them to the sacrifice.

6 ¶ And it came to pass, when they were come, that he looked on Eliab, and said, Surely the LORD's anointed *is* before him.

7 But the LORD said unto Samuel, Look not on his countenance, or on the height of his stature; because I have refused him: for *the* LORD *seeth* not as man seeth; for man looketh on the outward appearance, but the LORD looketh on the heart.

8 Then Jesse called Abinadab, and made him pass before Samuel. And he said, Neither hath the LORD chosen this.

9 Then Jesse made Shammah to pass by. And he said, Neither hath the LORD chosen this.

10 Again, Jesse made seven of his sons to pass before Samuel. And Samuel said unto Jesse, The LORD hath not chosen these.

11 And Samuel said unto Jesse, Are here all *thy* children? And he said, There remaineth yet the youngest, and, behold, he keepeth the sheep. And Samuel said unto Jesse, Send and fetch him: for we will not sit down till he come hither.

12 And he sent, and brought him in. Now he *was* ruddy, *and* withal of a beautiful countenance, and goodly to look to. And the LORD said, Arise, anoint him: for this *is* he.

13 Then Samuel took the horn of oil, and anointed him in the midst of his brethren: and the spirit of the LORD came upon David from that day forward. So Samuel rose up, and went to Ramah.

14 ¶ But the spirit of the LORD departed from Saul, and an evil spirit from the LORD troubled him.

15 And Saul's servants said unto him, Behold now, an evil spirit from God troubleth thee.

16 Let our lord now command thy servants, *which are* before thee, to seek out a man, *who is* a cunning player on an harp: and it shall come to pass, when the evil spirit from God is upon thee, that he shall play with his hand, and thou shalt be well.

17 And Saul said unto his servants, Provide me now a man that can play well, and bring *him* to me.

18 Then answered one of the servants, and said, Behold, I have seen a son of Jesse the Bethlehemite, *that is* cunning in playing, and a mighty valiant man, and a man of war, and prudent in matters, and a comely person, and the LORD *is* with him.

19 ¶ Wherefore Saul sent messengers unto Jesse, and said, Send me David thy son, which *is* with the sheep.

20 And Jesse took an ass *laden* with bread, and a bottle of wine, and a kid, and sent *them* by David his son unto Saul.

21 And David came to Saul, and stood before him: and he loved him greatly; and he became his armourbearer.

22 And Saul sent to Jesse, saying, Let David, I pray thee, stand before me; for he hath found favour in my sight.

23 And it came to pass, when the *evil* spirit from God was upon Saul, that David took an harp, and played with his hand: so Saul was refreshed, and was well, and the evil spirit departed from him.

**17** NOW THE Philistines gathered together their armies to battle, and were gathered together at Shochoh, which *belongeth* to Judah, and pitched between Shochoh and Azekah, in Ephes-dammim.

2 And Saul and the men of Israel were gathered together, and pitched by the valley of Elah, and set the battle in array against the Philistines.

## Amplified

4 And Samuel did what the Lord said, and came to Bethlehem. And the elders of the town trembled at his coming, and said, Have you come peaceably?

5 And he said, Peaceably. I have come to sacrifice to the Lord; consecrate yourselves, and come with me to the sacrifice. And he consecrated Jesse and his sons, and called them to the sacrifice.

6 When they had come, he looked on Eliab [the eldest son], and said, Surely the Lord's anointed is before Him.

7 But the Lord said to Samuel, Look not on his appearance or at the height of his stature, for I have rejected him; for the Lord sees not as man sees; for man looks on the outward appearance, but the Lord looks on the heart.

8 Then Jesse called Abinadab, and made him pass before Samuel. But Samuel said, Neither has the Lord chosen this one.

9 Then Jesse made Shammah pass by. Samuel said, Nor has the Lord chosen him.

10 Jesse made seven of his sons pass before Samuel. And Samuel said to Jesse, The Lord has not chosen any of these.

11 Then [he] said to Jesse, Are all your sons here? [Jesse] said, There is yet the youngest; he is tending the sheep. Samuel said to Jesse, Send for him, for we will not sit down to eat until he is here.

12 Jesse sent and brought him. David had reddish hair *and* fair skin, beautiful eyes, and was fine looking. The Lord said [to Samuel], Arise, anoint him; this is he.

13 Then Samuel took the horn of oil, and anointed David in the midst of his brothers; and the Spirit of the Lord came mightily upon David from that day forward. And Samuel arose and went to Ramah.

14 But the Spirit of the Lord departed from Saul, and an evil spirit from the Lord tormented *and* troubled him.

15 Saul's servants said to him, Behold, an evil spirit from God torments you.

16 Let our lord now command your servants here before you to find a man who plays skillfully on the lyre, and when the evil spirit from God is upon you, he will play it, and you will be well.

17 Saul told his servants, Find me a man who plays well, and bring him to me.

18 One of the young men said, I have seen a son of Jesse the Bethlehemite, who plays skillfully, a valiant man, a man of war, prudent in speech *and* eloquent, an attractive person, and the Lord is with him.

19 So Saul sent messengers to Jesse, and said, Send me David your son, who is with the sheep.

20 And Jesse took a donkey loaded with bread, a skin of wine, and a kid, and sent them by David his son to Saul.

21 And David came to Saul, and served him. Saul became very fond of him, and he became his armor-bearer.

22 Saul sent to Jesse, saying, Let David remain in my service, for he pleases me.

23 And when the evil spirit from God was upon Saul, David took a lyre and played it; so Saul was refreshed and became well, and the evil spirit left him.

**17** NOW THE Philistines gathered their armies for battle, and were assembled at Soco, which belongs to Judah, and encamped between Soco and Azekah in Ephes-dammim.

2 Saul and the men of Israel were encamped in the valley of Elah, and drew up in battle array against the Philistines.

## New American Standard

4So Samuel did what the LORD said, and came to Bethlehem.
And the elders of the city came trembling to meet him and said,
"Do you come in peace?"
5And he said, "In peace; I have come to sacrifice to the LORD.
Consecrate yourselves and come with me to the sacrifice." He also
consecrated Jesse and his sons, and invited them to the sacrifice.
6¶ Then it came about when they entered, that he looked at
Eliab and thought, "Surely the LORD's anointed is before Him."
7But the LORD said to Samuel, "Do not look at his appearance
or at the height of his stature, because I have rejected him; for God
*sees* not as man sees, for man looks at the outward appearance, but
the LORD looks at the heart."
8Then Jesse called Abinadab, and made him pass before Samuel. And he said, "Neither has the LORD chosen this one."
9Next Jesse made Shammah pass by. And he said, "Neither
has the LORD chosen this one."
10Thus Jesse made seven of his sons pass before Samuel. But
Samuel said to Jesse, "The LORD has not chosen these."
11And Samuel said to Jesse, "Are these all the children?" And
he said, "There remains yet the youngest, and behold, he is tending the sheep." Then Samuel said to Jesse, "Send and bring him;
for we will not sit down until he comes here."

*David Anointed*

12So he sent and brought him in. Now he was ruddy, with
beautiful eyes and a handsome appearance. And the LORD said,
"Arise, anoint him; for this is he."
13Then Samuel took the horn of oil and anointed him in the
midst of his brothers; and the Spirit of the LORD came mightily
upon David from that day forward. And Samuel arose and went
to Ramah.
14¶ Now the Spirit of the LORD departed from Saul, and an evil
spirit from the LORD terrorized him.
15Saul's servants then said to him, "Behold now, an evil spirit
from God is terrorizing you.
16"Let our lord now command your servants who are before
you. Let them seek a man who is a skillful player on the harp; and
it shall come about when the evil spirit from God is on you, that
he shall play *the harp* with his hand, and you will be well."
17So Saul said to his servants, "Provide for me now a man who
can play well, and bring *him* to me."
18Then one of the young men answered and said, "Behold, I
have seen a son of Jesse the Bethlehemite who is a skillful musician, a mighty man of valor, a warrior, one prudent in speech, and
a handsome man; and the LORD is with him."
19So Saul sent messengers to Jesse, and said, "Send me your
son David who is with the flock."
20And Jesse took a donkey *loaded with* bread and a jug of wine
and a young goat, and sent *them* to Saul by David his son.
21Then David came to Saul and attended him, and Saul loved
him greatly; and he became his armor bearer.
22And Saul sent to Jesse, saying, "Let David now stand before
me; for he has found favor in my sight."
23So it came about whenever the *evil* spirit from God came to
Saul, David would take the harp and play *it* with his hand; and
Saul would be refreshed and be well, and the evil spirit would
depart from him.

*Goliath's Challenge*

17 NOW THE Philistines gathered their armies for battle; and
they were gathered at Socoh which belongs to Judah, and
they camped between Socoh and Azekah, in Ephes-dammim.
2And Saul and the men of Israel were gathered, and camped
in the valley of Elah, and drew up in battle array to encounter the
Philistines.

## New International

4Samuel did what the LORD said. When he arrived at Bethlehem, the elders of the town trembled when they met him. They
asked, "Do you come in peace?"
5Samuel replied, "Yes, in peace; I have come to sacrifice to the
LORD. Consecrate yourselves and come to the sacrifice with me."
Then he consecrated Jesse and his sons and invited them to the
sacrifice.
6When they arrived, Samuel saw Eliab and thought, "Surely the
LORD's anointed stands here before the LORD."
7But the LORD said to Samuel, "Do not consider his appearance
or his height, for I have rejected him. The LORD does not look at
the things man looks at. Man looks at the outward appearance, but
the LORD looks at the heart."
8Then Jesse called Abinadab and had him pass in front of Samuel. But Samuel said, "The LORD has not chosen this one either."
9Jesse then had Shammah pass by, but Samuel said, "Nor has the
LORD chosen this one." 10Jesse had seven of his sons pass before
Samuel, but Samuel said to him, "The LORD has not chosen these."
11So he asked Jesse, "Are these all the sons you have?"
"There is still the youngest," Jesse answered, "but he is tending
the sheep."
Samuel said, "Send for him; we will not sit down[a] until he
arrives."
12So he sent and had him brought in. He was ruddy, with a fine
appearance and handsome features.
Then the LORD said, "Rise and anoint him; he is the one."
13So Samuel took the horn of oil and anointed him in the presence of his brothers, and from that day on the Spirit of the LORD
came upon David in power. Samuel then went to Ramah.

*David in Saul's Service*

14Now the Spirit of the LORD had departed from Saul, and an
evil[b] spirit from the LORD tormented him.
15Saul's attendants said to him, "See, an evil spirit from God is
tormenting you. 16Let our lord command his servants here to
search for someone who can play the harp. He will play when the
evil spirit from God comes upon you, and you will feel better."
17So Saul said to his attendants, "Find someone who plays well
and bring him to me."
18One of the servants answered, "I have seen a son of Jesse of
Bethlehem who knows how to play the harp. He is a brave man
and a warrior. He speaks well and is a fine-looking man. And the
LORD is with him."
19Then Saul sent messengers to Jesse and said, "Send me your
son David, who is with the sheep." 20So Jesse took a donkey
loaded with bread, a skin of wine and a young goat and sent them
with his son David to Saul.
21David came to Saul and entered his service. Saul liked him
very much, and David became one of his armor-bearers. 22Then
Saul sent word to Jesse, saying, "Allow David to remain in my
service, for I am pleased with him."
23Whenever the spirit from God came upon Saul, David would
take his harp and play. Then relief would come to Saul; he would
feel better, and the evil spirit would leave him.

*David and Goliath*

17 NOW THE Philistines gathered their forces for war and
assembled at Socoh in Judah. They pitched camp at Ephes
Dammim, between Socoh and Azekah. 2Saul and the Israelites
assembled and camped in the Valley of Elah and drew up their

NIV [a] *11* Some Septuagint manuscripts; Hebrew *not gather around* [b] *14* Or *injurious;* also in verses 15, 16 and 23

## King James

3 And the Philistines stood on a mountain on the one side, and Israel stood on a mountain on the other side: and *there was* a valley between them.

4 ¶ And there went out a champion out of the camp of the Philistines, named Goliath, of Gath, whose height *was* six cubits and a span.

5 And *he had* an helmet of brass upon his head, and he *was* armed with a coat of mail; and the weight of the coat *was* five thousand shekels of brass.

6 And *he had* greaves of brass upon his legs, and a target of brass between his shoulders.

7 And the staff of his spear *was* like a weaver's beam; and his spear's head *weighed* six hundred shekels of iron: and one bearing a shield went before him.

8 And he stood and cried unto the armies of Israel, and said unto them, Why are ye come out to set *your* battle in array? *am* not I a Philistine, and ye servants to Saul? choose you a man for you, and let him come down to me.

9 If he be able to fight with me, and to kill me, then will we be your servants: but if I prevail against him, and kill him, then shall ye be our servants, and serve us.

10 And the Philistine said, I defy the armies of Israel this day; give me a man, that we may fight together.

11 When Saul and all Israel heard those words of the Philistine, they were dismayed, and greatly afraid.

12 ¶ Now David *was* the son of that Ephrathite of Bethlehem-judah, whose name *was* Jesse; and he had eight sons: and the man went among men *for* an old man in the days of Saul.

13 And the three eldest sons of Jesse went *and* followed Saul to the battle: and the names of his three sons that went to the battle *were* Eliab the firstborn, and next unto him Abinadab, and the third Shammah.

14 And David *was* the youngest: and the three eldest followed Saul.

15 But David went and returned from Saul to feed his father's sheep at Bethlehem.

16 And the Philistine drew near morning and evening, and presented himself forty days.

17 And Jesse said unto David his son, Take now for thy brethren an ephah of this parched *corn*, and these ten loaves, and run to the camp to thy brethren;

18 And carry these ten cheeses unto the captain of *their* thousand, and look how thy brethren fare, and take their pledge.

19 Now Saul, and they, and all the men of Israel, *were* in the valley of Elah, fighting with the Philistines.

20 ¶ And David rose up early in the morning, and left the sheep with a keeper, and took, and went, as Jesse had commanded him; and he came to the trench, as the host was going forth to the fight, and shouted for the battle.

21 For Israel and the Philistines had put the battle in array, army against army.

22 And David left his carriage in the hand of the keeper of the carriage, and ran into the army, and came and saluted his brethren.

23 And as he talked with them, behold, there came up the champion, the Philistine of Gath, Goliath by name, out of the armies of the Philistines, and spake according to the same words: and David heard *them*.

24 And all the men of Israel, when they saw the man, fled from him, and were sore afraid.

25 And the men of Israel said, Have ye seen this man that is come up? surely to defy Israel is he come up: and it shall be, *that* the man who killeth him, the king will enrich him with great riches, and will give him his daughter, and make his father's house free in Israel.

## Amplified

3 And the Philistines stood on a mountain on one side, and Israel stood on a mountain on the other side, with a valley between them.

4 And a champion went out of the camp of the Philistines, named Goliath of Gath, whose height was six cubits and a span [almost ten feet].

5 And he had a bronze helmet on his head, and wore a coat of mail; and the coat weighed 5,000 shekels of bronze.

6 He had bronze shin-armor on his legs, and a bronze javelin across his shoulders.

7 And the shaft of his spear was like a weaver's beam; his spear's head weighed 600 shekels of iron; and a shield-bearer went before him.

8 Goliath stood and shouted to the ranks of Israel, Why have you come out to draw up for battle? Am I not a Philistine and you servants of Saul? Choose a man for you, and let him come down to me.

9 If he is able to fight with me and kill me, then we will be your servants; but if I prevail against him and kill him, then you shall be our servants and serve us.

10 And the Philistine said, I defy the ranks of Israel this day; give me a man, that we may fight together.

11 When Saul and all Israel heard those words of the Philistine, they were dismayed and greatly afraid.

12 David was the son of an Ephrathite of Bethlehem in Judah, named Jesse, who had eight sons. [Jesse] in the days of Saul was old, advanced in years.

13 [His] three eldest sons had followed Saul into battle. Their names were Eliab the first-born, next Abinadab, and third Shammah.

14 David was the youngest; the three eldest followed Saul,

15 But David went back and forth from Saul to feed his father's sheep at Bethlehem.

16 The Philistine came out morning and evening, presenting himself forty days.

17 And Jesse said to David his son, Take for your brothers an ephah of this parched grain, and these ten loaves, and carry them quickly to your brothers at the camp.

18 Also take these ten cheeses to the commander of their thousand. See how your brothers fare and bring some token from them.

19 Now Saul, and the brothers, and all the men of Israel, were in the valley of Elah, fighting with the Philistines.

20 So David rose up early next morning, left the sheep with a keeper, took the provisions, and went, as Jesse had commanded him; and he came to the encampment as the host going forth to the battle ground shouted the battle cry.

21 And Israel and the Philistines put the battle in array, army against army.

22 David left his packages in the care of the baggage keeper, and ran into the ranks, and came and greeted his brothers.

23 As they talked, behold, Goliath the champion, the Philistine of Gath, came forth from the Philistine ranks and spoke the same words as before, and David heard him.

24 And all the men of Israel, when they saw the man, fled from him, terrified.

25 And the Israelites said, Have you seen this man who has come out? Surely he has come out to defy Israel, and the man who kills him the king will enrich with great riches, and will give him his daughter, and make his father's house free [from taxes and service] in Israel.

## New American Standard

3And the Philistines stood on the mountain on one side while Israel stood on the mountain on the other side, with the valley between them.

4Then a champion came out from the armies of the Philistines named Goliath, from Gath, whose height was six [a]cubits and a span.

5And *he had* a bronze helmet on his head, and he was clothed with scale-armor which weighed five thousand shekels of bronze.

6 *He* also *had* bronze [b]greaves on his legs and a bronze javelin *slung* between his shoulders.

7And the shaft of his spear was like a weaver's beam, and the head of his spear *weighed* six hundred shekels of iron; his shield-carrier also walked before him.

8And he stood and shouted to the ranks of Israel, and said to them, "Why do you come out to draw up in battle array? Am I not the Philistine and you servants of Saul? Choose a man for yourselves and let him come down to me.

9"If he is able to fight with me and kill me, then we will become your servants; but if I prevail against him and kill him, then you shall become our servants and serve us."

10Again the Philistine said, "I defy the ranks of Israel this day; give me a man that we may fight together."

11When Saul and all Israel heard these words of the Philistine, they were dismayed and greatly afraid.

12¶ Now David was the son of the Ephrathite of Bethlehem in Judah, whose name was Jesse, and he had eight sons. And Jesse was old in the days of Saul, advanced *in years* among men.

13And the three older sons of Jesse had gone after Saul to the battle. And the names of his three sons who went to the battle were Eliab the first-born, and the second to him Abinadab, and the third Shammah.

14And David was the youngest. Now the three oldest followed Saul,

15but David went back and forth from Saul to tend his father's flock at Bethlehem.

16And the Philistine came forward morning and evening for forty days, and took his stand.

17¶ Then Jesse said to David his son, "Take now for your brothers an ephah of this roasted grain and these ten loaves, and run to the camp to your brothers.

18"Bring also these ten cuts of cheese to the commander of *their* thousand, and look into the welfare of your brothers, and bring back news of them.

19"For Saul and they and all the men of Israel are in the valley of Elah, fighting with the Philistines."

*David Accepts the Challenge*

20¶ So David arose early in the morning and left the flock with a keeper and took *the supplies* and went as Jesse had commanded him. And he came to the circle of the camp while the army was going out in battle array shouting the war cry.

21And Israel and the Philistines drew up in battle array, army against army.

22Then David left his baggage in the care of the baggage keeper, and ran to the battle line and entered in order to greet his brothers.

23As he was talking with them, behold, the champion, the Philistine from Gath named Goliath, was coming up from the army of the Philistines, and he spoke these same words; and David heard *them*.

24When all the men of Israel saw the man, they fled from him and were greatly afraid.

25And the men of Israel said, "Have you seen this man who is coming up? Surely he is coming up to defy Israel. And it will be that the king will enrich the man who kills him with great riches and will give him his daughter and make his father's house [c]free in Israel."

NAS [a] I.e., One cubit equals approx. 18 in. [b] Or, *shin guards* [c] I.e., free from taxes and public service

## New International

battle line to meet the Philistines. 3The Philistines occupied one hill
and the Israelites another, with the valley between them.
4A champion named Goliath, who was from Gath, came out of
the Philistine camp. He was over nine feet[d] tall. 5He had a bronze
helmet on his head and wore a coat of scale armor of bronze
weighing five thousand shekels[e]; 6on his legs he wore bronze
greaves, and a bronze javelin was slung on his back. 7His spear
shaft was like a weaver's rod, and its iron point weighed six
hundred shekels.[f] His shield bearer went ahead of him.
8Goliath stood and shouted to the ranks of Israel, "Why do you
come out and line up for battle? Am I not a Philistine, and are you
not the servants of Saul? Choose a man and have him come down
to me. 9If he is able to fight and kill me, we will become your
subjects; but if I overcome him and kill him, you will become our
subjects and serve us." 10Then the Philistine said, "This day I defy
the ranks of Israel! Give me a man and let us fight each other."
11On hearing the Philistine's words, Saul and all the Israelites were
dismayed and terrified.
12Now David was the son of an Ephrathite named Jesse, who
was from Bethlehem in Judah. Jesse had eight sons, and in Saul's
time he was old and well advanced in years. 13Jesse's three oldest
sons had followed Saul to the war: The firstborn was Eliab; the
second, Abinadab; and the third, Shammah. 14David was the
youngest. The three oldest followed Saul, 15but David went back
and forth from Saul to tend his father's sheep at Bethlehem.
16For forty days the Philistine came forward every morning and
evening and took his stand.
17Now Jesse said to his son David, "Take this ephah[g] of roasted
grain and these ten loaves of bread for your brothers and hurry to
their camp. 18Take along these ten cheeses to the commander of
their unit.[h] See how your brothers are and bring back some assurance[i] from them. 19They are with Saul and all the men of Israel
in the Valley of Elah, fighting against the Philistines."
20Early in the morning David left the flock with a shepherd,
loaded up and set out, as Jesse had directed. He reached the camp
as the army was going out to its battle positions, shouting the war
cry. 21Israel and the Philistines were drawing up their lines facing
each other. 22David left his things with the keeper of supplies, ran
to the battle lines and greeted his brothers. 23As he was talking
with them, Goliath, the Philistine champion from Gath, stepped
out from his lines and shouted his usual defiance, and David heard
it. 24When the Israelites saw the man, they all ran from him in great
fear.
25Now the Israelites had been saying, "Do you see how this
man keeps coming out? He comes out to defy Israel. The king will
give great wealth to the man who kills him. He will also give him
his daughter in marriage and will exempt his father's family from
taxes in Israel."

NIV [d] *4* Hebrew *was six cubits and a span* (about 3 meters) [e] *5* That is, about 125 pounds (about 57 kilograms) [f] *7* That is, about 15 pounds (about 7 kilograms) [g] *17* That is, probably about 3/5 bushel (about 22 liters) [h] *18* Hebrew *thousand* [i] *18* Or *some token;* or *some pledge of spoils*

## King James

26 And David spake to the men that stood by him, saying, What shall be done to the man that killeth this Philistine, and taketh away the reproach from Israel? for who *is* this uncircumcised Philistine, that he should defy the armies of the living God?

27 And the people answered him after this manner, saying, So shall it be done to the man that killeth him.

28 ¶ And Eliab his eldest brother heard when he spake unto the men; and Eliab's anger was kindled against David, and he said, Why camest thou down hither? and with whom hast thou left those few sheep in the wilderness? I know thy pride, and the naughtiness of thine heart; for thou art come down that thou mightest see the battle.

29 And David said, What have I now done? *Is there* not a cause?

30 ¶ And he turned from him toward another, and spake after the same manner: and the people answered him again after the former manner.

31 And when the words were heard which David spake, they rehearsed *them* before Saul: and he sent for him.

32 ¶ And David said to Saul, Let no man's heart fail because of him; thy servant will go and fight with this Philistine.

33 And Saul said to David, Thou art not able to go against this Philistine to fight with him: for thou *art but* a youth, and he a man of war from his youth.

34 And David said unto Saul, Thy servant kept his father's sheep, and there came a lion, and a bear, and took a lamb out of the flock:

35 And I went out after him, and smote him, and delivered *it* out of his mouth: and when he arose against me, I caught *him* by his beard, and smote him, and slew him.

36 Thy servant slew both the lion and the bear: and this uncircumcised Philistine shall be as one of them, seeing he hath defied the armies of the living God.

37 David said moreover, The LORD that delivered me out of the paw of the lion, and out of the paw of the bear, he will deliver me out of the hand of this Philistine. And Saul said unto David, Go, and the LORD be with thee.

38 ¶ And Saul armed David with his armour, and he put an helmet of brass upon his head; also he armed him with a coat of mail.

39 And David girded his sword upon his armour, and he assayed to go; for he had not proved *it*. And David said unto Saul, I cannot go with these; for I have not proved *them*. And David put them off him.

40 And he took his staff in his hand, and chose him five smooth stones out of the brook, and put them in a shepherd's bag which he had, even in a scrip; and his sling *was* in his hand: and he drew near to the Philistine.

41 And the Philistine came on and drew near unto David; and the man that bare the shield *went* before him.

42 And when the Philistine looked about, and saw David, he disdained him: for he was *but* a youth, and ruddy, and of a fair countenance.

43 And the Philistine said unto David, *Am* I a dog, that thou comest to me with staves? And the Philistine cursed David by his gods.

44 And the Philistine said to David, Come to me, and I will give thy flesh unto the fowls of the air, and to the beasts of the field.

45 Then said David to the Philistine, Thou comest to me with a sword, and with a spear, and with a shield: but I come to thee in the name of the LORD of hosts, the God of the armies of Israel, whom thou hast defied.

46 This day will the LORD deliver thee into mine hand; and I will smite thee, and take thine head from thee; and I will give the carcases of the host of the Philistines this day unto the fowls of the air, and to the wild beasts of the earth; that all the earth may know that there is a God in Israel.

47 And all this assembly shall know that the LORD saveth not with sword and spear: for the battle *is* the LORD's, and he will give you into our hands.

## Amplified

26 And David said to the men standing by him, What shall be done for the man who kills this Philistine, and takes away the reproach from Israel? For who is this uncircumcised Philistine, that he should defy the armies of the living God?

27 And the [men] told him, Thus shall it be done for the man who kills him.

28 Now Eliab his eldest brother heard what he said to the men; and Eliab's anger was kindled against David, and he said, Why did you come here? With whom have you left those few sheep in the wilderness? I know your presumption and evilness of heart for you came down that you might see the battle.

29 And David said, What have I done now? Was it not a harmless question?

30 And David turned away from Eliab to another, whom he asked the same question, and again the men gave him the same answer.

31 When David's words were heard, they were repeated to Saul, and he sent for him.

32 David said to Saul, Let no man's heart fail because of this Philistine; your servant will go out and fight with him.

33 And Saul said to David, You are not able to go to fight against this Philistine. You are only an adolescent, and he has been a warrior from his youth.

34 And David said to Saul, Your servant kept his father's sheep, and when there came a lion, and again a bear, and took a lamb out of the flock,

35 I went out after him, and smote him and delivered it out of his mouth; and when he arose against me, I caught him by his beard, and smote him, and killed him.

36 Your servant killed both the lion and the bear; and this uncircumcised Philistine shall be as one of them, for he has defied the armies of the living God!

37 David said, The Lord, Who delivered me out of the paw of the lion and out of the paw of the bear, He will deliver me out of the hand of this Philistine. And Saul said to David, Go, and the Lord be with you!

38 Then Saul clothed David with his armor; he put a bronze helmet on his head, and clothed him with a coat of mail.

39 And David girded his sword over his armor. Then he tried to go, but could not, for he was not used to it. And David said to Saul, I cannot go with these, for I am not used to them. And David took them off.

40 Then he took his staff in his hand, and chose five smooth stones out of the brook, and put them in his shepherd's [lunch] bag [a whole kid's skin, slung from his shoulder], in his scrip; and his sling was in his hand, and he drew near the Philistine.

41 The Philistine came on and drew near to David, the man who bore the shield going before him.

42 And when the Philistine looked around and saw David, he scorned *and* despised him; for he was but an adolescent, with a healthy reddish color, and a fair face.

43 And the Philistine said to David, Am I a dog, that you should come to me with sticks? And the Philistine cursed David by his gods.

44 The Philistine said to David, Come to me and I will give your flesh to the birds of the air and the beasts of the field.

45 Then said David to the Philistine, You come to me with a sword, a spear, and a javelin; but I come to you in the name of the Lord of hosts, the God of the ranks of Israel, Whom you have defied.

46 This day the Lord will deliver you into my hand; and I will smite you, and cut off your head; and I will give the corpses of the army of the Philistines this day to the birds of the air and the wild beasts of the earth; that all the earth may know that there is a God in Israel.

47 And all this assembly shall know that the Lord saves not with sword and spear; for the battle is the Lord's, and He will give you into our hand.

## New American Standard

26¶ Then David spoke to the men who were standing by him,
saying, "What will be done for the man who kills this Philistine,
and takes away the reproach from Israel? For who is this uncircumcised Philistine, that he should taunt the armies of the living God?"
27And the people answered him in accord with this word, saying, "Thus it will be done for the man who kills him."
28¶ Now Eliab his oldest brother heard when he spoke to the
men; and Eliab's anger burned against David and he said, "Why
have you come down? And with whom have you left those few
sheep in the wilderness? I know your insolence and the wickedness of your heart; for you have come down in order to see the
battle."
29But David said, "What have I done now? Was it not just a
question?"
30Then he turned away from him to another and said the same
thing; and the people answered the same thing as before.

*David Kills Goliath*

31¶ When the words which David spoke were heard, they told
*them* to Saul, and he sent for him.
32And David said to Saul, "Let no man's heart fail on account
of him; your servant will go and fight with this Philistine."
33Then Saul said to David, "You are not able to go against this
Philistine to fight with him; for you are *but* a youth while he has
been a warrior from his youth."
34But David said to Saul, "Your servant was tending his father's
sheep. When a lion or a bear came and took a lamb from the flock,
35I went out after him and attacked him, and rescued *it* from his
mouth; and when he rose up against me, I seized *him* by his beard
and struck him and killed him.
36"Your servant has killed both the lion and the bear; and this
uncircumcised Philistine will be like one of them, since he has
taunted the armies of the living God."
37And David said, "The LORD who delivered me from the paw
of the lion and from the paw of the bear, He will deliver me from
the hand of this Philistine." And Saul said to David, "Go, and may
the LORD be with you."
38Then Saul clothed David with his garments and put a bronze
helmet on his head, and he clothed him with armor.
39And David girded his sword over his armor and tried to walk,
for he had not tested *them*. So David said to Saul, "I cannot go with
these, for I have not tested *them*." And David took them off.
40And he took his stick in his hand and chose for himself five
smooth stones from the brook, and put them in the shepherd's bag
which he had, even in *his* pouch, and his sling was in his hand;
and he approached the Philistine.
41¶ Then the Philistine came on and approached David, with the
shield-bearer in front of him.
42When the Philistine looked and saw David, he disdained him;
for he was *but* a youth, and ruddy, with a handsome appearance.
43And the Philistine said to David, "Am I a dog, that you come
to me with sticks?" And the Philistine cursed David by his gods.
44The Philistine also said to David, "Come to me, and I will give
your flesh to the birds of the sky and the beasts of the field."
45Then David said to the Philistine, "You come to me with a
sword, a spear, and a javelin, but I come to you in the name of the
LORD of hosts, the God of the armies of Israel, whom you have
taunted.
46"This day the LORD will deliver you up into my hands, and
I will strike you down and remove your head from you. And I will
give the dead bodies of the army of the Philistines this day to the
birds of the sky and the wild beasts of the earth, that all the earth
may know that there is a God in Israel,
47and that all this assembly may know that the LORD does not
deliver by sword or by spear; for the battle is the LORD's and He
will give you into our hands."

## New International

26David asked the men standing near him, "What will be done
for the man who kills this Philistine and removes this disgrace from
Israel? Who is this uncircumcised Philistine that he should defy the
armies of the living God?"
27They repeated to him what they had been saying and told
him, "This is what will be done for the man who kills him."
28When Eliab, David's oldest brother, heard him speaking with
the men, he burned with anger at him and asked, "Why have you
come down here? And with whom did you leave those few sheep
in the desert? I know how conceited you are and how wicked your
heart is; you came down only to watch the battle."
29"Now what have I done?" said David. "Can't I even speak?"
30He then turned away to someone else and brought up the same
matter, and the men answered him as before. 31What David said
was overheard and reported to Saul, and Saul sent for him.
32David said to Saul, "Let no one lose heart on account of this
Philistine; your servant will go and fight him."
33Saul replied, "You are not able to go out against this Philistine
and fight him; you are only a boy, and he has been a fighting man
from his youth."
34But David said to Saul, "Your servant has been keeping his
father's sheep. When a lion or a bear came and carried off a sheep
from the flock, 35I went after it, struck it and rescued the sheep
from its mouth. When it turned on me, I seized it by its hair, struck
it and killed it. 36Your servant has killed both the lion and the bear;
this uncircumcised Philistine will be like one of them, because he
has defied the armies of the living God. 37The LORD who delivered
me from the paw of the lion and the paw of the bear will deliver
me from the hand of this Philistine."
Saul said to David, "Go, and the LORD be with you."
38Then Saul dressed David in his own tunic. He put a coat of
armor on him and a bronze helmet on his head. 39David fastened
on his sword over the tunic and tried walking around, because he
was not used to them.
"I cannot go in these," he said to Saul, "because I am not used
to them." So he took them off. 40Then he took his staff in his hand,
chose five smooth stones from the stream, put them in the pouch
of his shepherd's bag and, with his sling in his hand, approached
the Philistine.
41Meanwhile, the Philistine, with his shield bearer in front of
him, kept coming closer to David. 42He looked David over and saw
that he was only a boy, ruddy and handsome, and he despised
him. 43He said to David, "Am I a dog, that you come at me with
sticks?" And the Philistine cursed David by his gods. 44"Come
here," he said, "and I'll give your flesh to the birds of the air and
the beasts of the field!"
45David said to the Philistine, "You come against me with
sword and spear and javelin, but I come against you in the name
of the LORD Almighty, the God of the armies of Israel, whom you
have defied. 46This day the LORD will hand you over to me, and
I'll strike you down and cut off your head. Today I will give the
carcasses of the Philistine army to the birds of the air and the beasts
of the earth, and the whole world will know that there is a God
in Israel. 47All those gathered here will know that it is not by sword
or spear that the LORD saves; for the battle is the LORD's, and he
will give all of you into our hands."

## King James

48And it came to pass, when the Philistine arose, and came and
drew nigh to meet David, that David hasted, and ran toward the
army to meet the Philistine.
49And David put his hand in his bag, and took thence a stone,
and slang *it*, and smote the Philistine in his forehead, that the
stone sunk into his forehead; and he fell upon his face to the earth.
50So David prevailed over the Philistine with a sling and with
a stone, and smote the Philistine, and slew him; but *there was* no
sword in the hand of David.
51Therefore David ran, and stood upon the Philistine, and took
his sword, and drew it out of the sheath thereof, and slew him,
and cut off his head therewith. And when the Philistines saw their
champion was dead, they fled.
52And the men of Israel and of Judah arose, and shouted, and
pursued the Philistines, until thou come to the valley, and to the
gates of Ekron. And the wounded of the Philistines fell down by
the way to Shaaraim, even unto Gath, and unto Ekron.
53And the children of Israel returned from chasing after the
Philistines, and they spoiled their tents.
54And David took the head of the Philistine, and brought it to
Jerusalem; but he put his armour in his tent.
55¶ And when Saul saw David go forth against the Philistine,
he said unto Abner, the captain of the host, Abner, whose son *is*
this youth? And Abner said, *As* thy soul liveth, O king, I cannot
tell.
56And the king said, Inquire thou whose son the stripling *is*.
57And as David returned from the slaughter of the Philistine,
Abner took him, and brought him before Saul with the head of the
Philistine in his hand.
58And Saul said to him, Whose son *art* thou, *thou* young man?
And David answered, *I am* the son of thy servant Jesse the
Bethlehemite.

**18** AND IT came to pass, when he had made an end of
speaking unto Saul, that the soul of Jonathan was knit
with the soul of David, and Jonathan loved him as his own soul.
2And Saul took him that day, and would let him go no more
home to his father's house.
3Then Jonathan and David made a covenant, because he loved
him as his own soul.
4And Jonathan stripped himself of the robe that *was* upon him,
and gave it to David, and his garments, even to his sword, and to
his bow, and to his girdle.
5¶ And David went out whithersoever Saul sent him, *and*
behaved himself wisely: and Saul set him over the men of war, and
he was accepted in the sight of all the people, and also in the sight
of Saul's servants.
6And it came to pass as they came, when David was returned
from the slaughter of the Philistine, that the women came out of
all cities of Israel, singing and dancing, to meet king Saul, with
tabrets, with joy, and with instruments of music.
7And the women answered *one another* as they played, and said,
Saul hath slain his thousands, and David his ten thousands.
8And Saul was very wroth, and the saying displeased him; and
he said, They have ascribed unto David ten thousands, and to me
they have ascribed *but* thousands: and *what* can he have more but
the kingdom?
9And Saul eyed David from that day and forward.
10¶ And it came to pass on the morrow, that the evil spirit from
God came upon Saul, and he prophesied in the midst of the house:
and David played with his hand, as at other times: and *there was*
a javelin in Saul's hand.

## Amplified

48When the Philistine came forward to meet David, David ran
quickly toward the battle line to meet the Philistine.
49David put his hand in his bag, and took out a stone and slung
it, and it struck the Philistine, sinking into his forehead, and he fell
on his face to the earth.
50So David prevailed over the Philistine with a sling and with
a stone, and struck down the Philistine, and slew him. But no
sword was in David's hand,
51So he ran and stood over the Philistine, took his sword and
drew it out of its sheath, and killed him, and cut off his head with
it. When the Philistines saw their mighty champion was dead, they
fled.
52And the men of Israel and Judah rose with a shout and pursued the Philistines as far as Gath and the gates of Ekron, so the
wounded Philistines fell along the way from Sha-araim as far as
Gath and Ekron.
53The Israelites returned from pursuit of the Philistines and
plundered their tents.
54David took the head of the Philistine and brought it to Jerusalem, but he put his armor in his tent.
55When Saul saw David go out against the Philistine, he said to
Abner, the captain of the host, Abner, whose son is this youth?
And Abner said, As your soul lives, O king, I cannot tell.
56And the king said, Inquire whose son the stripling is.
57When David returned from killing Goliath the Philistine, Abner brought him before Saul with the head of the Philistine in his
hand.
58And Saul said to him, Whose son are you, young man? And
David answered, I am the son of your servant Jesse of Bethlehem.

**18** WHEN DAVID had finished speaking to Saul, the soul of
Jonathan was knit with the soul of David, and Jonathan
loved him as his own life.
2Saul took David that day, and would not let him return to his
father's house.
3Then Jonathan made a covenant with David, because he loved
him as his own life.
4And Jonathan stripped himself of the robe that was on him,
and gave it to David, and his armor, even to his sword, his bow,
and his girdle.
5And David went out wherever Saul sent him, and he prospered *and* behaved himself wisely; and Saul set him over the men
of war, and it was satisfactory both to the people and to Saul's
servants.
6As they were coming home, when David returned from killing
the Philistine, the women came out of all the Israelite towns,
singing and dancing, to meet King Saul, with timbrels, songs of
joy, and instruments of music.
7And the women responded, as they laughed *and* frolicked,
saying, Saul has slain his thousands, and David his ten thousands.
8And Saul was very angry, for the saying displeased him; and
he said, They have ascribed to David ten thousands, and to me
they have ascribed but thousands. What more can he have but the
kingdom?
9And Saul [jealously] eyed David from that day forward.
10Next day an evil spirit from God came mightily upon Saul,
and he raved [madly] in his house, while David played with his
hand, as at other times; and there was a javelin in Saul's hand.

## New American Standard

48 Then it happened when the Philistine rose and came and drew near to meet David, that David ran quickly toward the battle line to meet the Philistine.

49 And David put his hand into his bag and took from it a stone and slung *it*, and struck the Philistine on his forehead. And the stone sank into his forehead, so that he fell on his face to the ground.

50 ¶ Thus David prevailed over the Philistine with a sling and a stone, and he struck the Philistine and killed him; but there was no sword in David's hand.

51 Then David ran and stood over the Philistine and took his sword and drew it out of its sheath and killed him, and cut off his head with it. When the Philistines saw that their champion was dead, they fled.

52 And the men of Israel and Judah arose and shouted and pursued the Philistines as far as the valley, and to the gates of Ekron. And the slain Philistines lay along the way to Shaaraim, even to Gath and Ekron.

53 And the sons of Israel returned from chasing the Philistines and plundered their camps.

54 Then David took the Philistine's head and brought it to Jerusalem, but he put his weapons in his tent.

55 ¶ Now when Saul saw David going out against the Philistine, he said to Abner the commander of the army, "Abner, whose son is this young man?" And Abner said, "By your life, O king, I do not know."

56 And the king said, "You inquire whose son the youth is."

57 So when David returned from killing the Philistine, Abner took him and brought him before Saul with the Philistine's head in his hand.

58 And Saul said to him, "Whose son are you, young man?" And David answered, "*I am* the son of your servant Jesse the Bethlehemite."

*Jonathan and David*

**18** NOW IT came about when he had finished speaking to Saul, that the soul of Jonathan was knit to the soul of David, and Jonathan loved him as himself.

2 And Saul took him that day and did not let him return to his father's house.

3 Then Jonathan made a covenant with David because he loved him as himself.

4 And Jonathan stripped himself of the robe that was on him and gave it to David, with his armor, including his sword and his bow and his belt.

5 So David went out wherever Saul sent him, *and* prospered; and Saul set him over the men of war. And it was pleasing in the sight of all the people and also in the sight of Saul's servants.

6 ¶ And it happened as they were coming, when David returned from killing the Philistine, that the women came out of all the cities of Israel, singing and dancing, to meet King Saul, with tambourines, with joy and with [a]musical instruments.

7 And the women sang as they played, and said,

"Saul has slain his thousands,
And David his ten thousands."

8 Then Saul became very angry, for this saying displeased him; and he said, "They have ascribed to David ten thousands, but to me they have ascribed thousands. Now what more can he have but the kingdom?"

9 And Saul looked at David with suspicion from that day on.

*Saul Turns against David*

10 ¶ Now it came about on the next day that an evil spirit from God came mightily upon Saul, and he raved in the midst of the house, while David was playing *the harp* with his hand, as usual; and a spear *was* in Saul's hand.

**NAS** [a] I.e., triangles, or three-stringed instruments

## New International

48 As the Philistine moved closer to attack him, David ran
quickly toward the battle line to meet him. 49 Reaching into his bag
and taking out a stone, he slung it and struck the Philistine on the
forehead. The stone sank into his forehead, and he fell facedown
on the ground.
50 So David triumphed over the Philistine with a sling and a
stone; without a sword in his hand he struck down the Philistine
and killed him.
51 David ran and stood over him. He took hold of the Philistine's
sword and drew it from the scabbard. After he killed him, he cut
off his head with the sword.
When the Philistines saw that their hero was dead, they turned
and ran. 52 Then the men of Israel and Judah surged forward with
a shout and pursued the Philistines to the entrance of Gath[b] and
to the gates of Ekron. Their dead were strewn along the Shaaraim
road to Gath and Ekron. 53 When the Israelites returned from chasing the Philistines, they plundered their camp. 54 David took the
Philistine's head and brought it to Jerusalem, and he put the
Philistine's weapons in his own tent.
55 As Saul watched David going out to meet the Philistine, he
said to Abner, commander of the army, "Abner, whose son is that
young man?"
Abner replied, "As surely as you live, O king, I don't know."
56 The king said, "Find out whose son this young man is."
57 As soon as David returned from killing the Philistine, Abner
took him and brought him before Saul, with David still holding the
Philistine's head.
58 "Whose son are you, young man?" Saul asked him.
David said, "I am the son of your servant Jesse of Bethlehem."

*Saul's Jealousy of David*

**18** AFTER DAVID had finished talking with Saul, Jonathan
became one in spirit with David, and he loved him as
himself. 2 From that day Saul kept David with him and did not let
him return to his father's house. 3 And Jonathan made a covenant
with David because he loved him as himself. 4 Jonathan took off the
robe he was wearing and gave it to David, along with his tunic,
and even his sword, his bow and his belt.
5 Whatever Saul sent him to do, David did it so successfully[c]
that Saul gave him a high rank in the army. This pleased all the
people, and Saul's officers as well.
6 When the men were returning home after David had killed the
Philistine, the women came out from all the towns of Israel to meet
King Saul with singing and dancing, with joyful songs and with
tambourines and lutes. 7 As they danced, they sang:

"Saul has slain his thousands,
and David his tens of thousands."

8 Saul was very angry; this refrain galled him. "They have credited David with tens of thousands," he thought, "but me with only
thousands. What more can he get but the kingdom?" 9 And from
that time on Saul kept a jealous eye on David.
10 The next day an evil[d] spirit from God came forcefully upon
Saul. He was prophesying in his house, while David was playing
the harp, as he usually did. Saul had a spear in his hand 11 and he

**NIV** [b] 52 Some Septuagint manuscripts; Hebrew *a valley* [c] 5 Or *wisely* [d] *10* Or *injurious*

## King James

11 And Saul cast the javelin; for he said, I will smite David even
to the wall *with it*. And David avoided out of his presence twice.
12 ¶ And Saul was afraid of David, because the LORD was with
him, and was departed from Saul.
13 Therefore Saul removed him from him, and made him his
captain over a thousand; and he went out and came in before the
people.
14 And David behaved himself wisely in all his ways; and the
LORD *was* with him.
15 Wherefore when Saul saw that he behaved himself very wisely, he was afraid of him.
16 But all Israel and Judah loved David, because he went out and
came in before them.
17 ¶ And Saul said to David, Behold my elder daughter Merab,
her will I give thee to wife: only be thou valiant for me, and fight
the LORD's battles. For Saul said, Let not mine hand be upon him,
but let the hand of the Philistines be upon him.
18 And David said unto Saul, Who *am* I? and what *is* my life, *or*
my father's family in Israel, that I should be son-in-law to the king?
19 But it came to pass at the time when Merab Saul's daughter
should have been given to David, that she was given unto Adriel
the Meholathite to wife.
20 And Michal Saul's daughter loved David: and they told Saul,
and the thing pleased him.
21 And Saul said, I will give him her, that she may be a snare to
him, and that the hand of the Philistines may be against him.
Wherefore Saul said to David, Thou shalt this day be my son-in-
law in *the one of* the twain.
22 ¶ And Saul commanded his servants, *saying*, Commune with
David secretly, and say, Behold, the king hath delight in thee, and
all his servants love thee: now therefore be the king's son-in-law.
23 And Saul's servants spake those words in the ears of David.
And David said, Seemeth it to you *a* light *thing* to be a king's
son-in-law, seeing that I *am* a poor man, and lightly esteemed?
24 And the servants of Saul told him, saying, On this manner
spake David.
25 And Saul said, Thus shall ye say to David, The king desireth
not any dowry, but an hundred foreskins of the Philistines, to be
avenged of the king's enemies. But Saul thought to make David
fall by the hand of the Philistines.
26 And when his servants told David these words, it pleased
David well to be the king's son-in-law: and the days were not
expired.
27 Wherefore David arose and went, he and his men, and slew
of the Philistines two hundred men; and David brought their
foreskins, and they gave them in full tale to the king, that he might
be the king's son-in-law. And Saul gave him Michal his daughter
to wife.
28 ¶ And Saul saw and knew that the LORD *was* with David, and
*that* Michal Saul's daughter loved him.
29 And Saul was yet the more afraid of David; and Saul became
David's enemy continually.
30 Then the princes of the Philistines went forth: and it came to
pass, after they went forth, *that* David behaved himself more
wisely than all the servants of Saul; so that his name was much set
by.

## Amplified

11 And Saul cast the javelin; for he thought, I will pin David to
the wall. And David evaded him twice.
12 Saul was afraid of David, because the Lord was with him, but
had departed from Saul.
13 So Saul removed David from him, and made him his commander over a thousand; and he went and came before the people.
14 David acted wisely in all his ways *and* succeeded, and the
Lord was with him.
15 When Saul saw how capable *and* successful David was, he
stood in awe of him.
16 But all Israel and Judah loved David, for he went and came
before them.
17 Saul said to David, My elder daughter Merab I will give you
as wife; only serve me courageously and fight the Lord's battles.
For Saul thought, Let not my hand, but the Philistines' hand, be
upon him.
18 David said to Saul, Who am I, and what is my life or my
father's family in Israel, that I should be the king's son-in-law?
19 But at the time when Merab Saul's daughter should have been
given to David, she was given to Adriel the Meholathite as wife.
20 Now Michal Saul's daughter loved David; and they told Saul,
and it pleased him.
21 Saul thought, I will give her to him that she may be a snare
to him, and that the hand of the Philistines may be against him.
So Saul said to David a second time, You shall now be my son-in-
law.
22 And Saul commanded his servants to speak to David privately
and say, The king delights in you, and all his servants love you;
now then become [his] son-in-law.
23 Saul's servants told those words to David. David said, Does
it seem to you a light thing to be a king's son-in-law, seeing I am
a poor man, and lightly esteemed?
24 And the servants of Saul told him what David said.
25 Saul said, Say this to David, The king wants no dowry, but
a hundred foreskins of the Philistines, to avenge him of the king's
enemies. But Saul thought to make David fall by the Philistines'
hand.
26 When his servants told David these words, it pleased [him]
well to be the king's son-in-law. Before the days expired,
27 David went, he and his men, and slew two hundred Philistine
men; and brought their foreskins, and gave them in full number
to the king, that he might be the king's son-in-law. And Saul gave
him Michal his daughter as wife.
28 When Saul saw and knew that the Lord was with David, and
that Michal [his] daughter loved him,
29 Saul was still more afraid of David; and Saul became David's
constant enemy.
30 Then the Philistine princes came out to battle; and when they
did so, David had more success *and* behaved himself more wisely
than all Saul's servants; so that his name was very dear *and* highly
esteemed.

**19** AND SAUL spake to Jonathan his son, and to all his
servants, that they should kill David.
2 But Jonathan Saul's son delighted much in David: and Jonathan told David, saying, Saul my father seeketh to kill thee: now
therefore, I pray thee, take heed to thyself until the morning, and
abide in a secret *place*, and hide thyself:
3 And I will go out and stand beside my father in the field where
thou *art*, and I will commune with my father of thee; and what I
see, that I will tell thee.

**19** NOW SAUL told Jonathan his son and all his servants,
that they must kill David.
2 But Jonathan Saul's son delighted much in David, and he told
David, Saul my father is seeking to kill you. Now therefore, take
heed to yourself in the morning, and stay in a secret place and hide
yourself.
3 And I will go out and stand beside my father in the field where
you are, and I will converse with my father about you; and if I learn
anything I will tell you.

## New American Standard

11And Saul hurled the spear for he thought, "I will pin David
to the wall." But David escaped from his presence twice.
12Now Saul was afraid of David, for the LORD was with him but
had departed from Saul.
13Therefore Saul removed him from his presence, and appointed him as his commander of a thousand; and he went out and
came in before the people.
14And David was prospering in all his ways for the LORD *was*
with him.
15When Saul saw that he was prospering greatly, he dreaded
him.
16But all Israel and Judah loved David, and he went out and
came in before them.
17¶ Then Saul said to David, "Here is my older daughter Merab;
I will give her to you as a wife, only be a valiant man for me and
fight the LORD's battles." For Saul thought, "My hand shall not be
against him, but let the hand of the Philistines be against him."
18But David said to Saul, "Who am I, and what is my life *or* my
father's family in Israel, that I should be the king's son-in-law?"
19So it came about at the time when Merab, Saul's daughter,
should have been given to David, that she was given to Adriel the
Meholathite for a wife.

*David Marries Saul's Daughter*

20¶ Now Michal, Saul's daughter, loved David. When they told
Saul, the thing was agreeable to him.
21And Saul thought, "I will give her to him that she may become
a snare to him, and that the hand of the Philistines may be against
him." Therefore Saul said to David, "For a second time you may
be my son-in-law today."
22Then Saul commanded his servants, "Speak to David secretly, saying, 'Behold, the king delights in you, and all his servants
love you; now therefore, become the king's son-in-law.' "
23So Saul's servants spoke these words to David. But David
said, "Is it trivial in your sight to become the king's son-in-law,
since I am a poor man and lightly esteemed?"
24And the servants of Saul reported to him according to these
words *which* David spoke.
25Saul then said, "Thus you shall say to David, 'The king does
not desire any dowry except a hundred foreskins of the Philistines,
to take vengeance on the king's enemies.' " Now Saul planned to
make David fall by the hand of the Philistines.
26When his servants told David these words, it pleased David
to become the king's son-in-law. Before the days had expired
27David rose up and went, he and his men, and struck down
two hundred men among the Philistines. Then David brought
their foreskins, and they gave them in full number to the king, that
he might become the king's son-in-law. So Saul gave him Michal
his daughter for a wife.
28When Saul saw and knew that the LORD was with David, and
*that* Michal, Saul's daughter, loved him,
29then Saul was even more afraid of David. Thus Saul was
David's enemy continually.
30¶ Then the commanders of the Philistines went out *to battle*,
and it happened as often as they went out, that David behaved
himself more wisely than all the servants of Saul. So his name was
highly esteemed.

*David Protected from Saul*

**19** NOW SAUL told Jonathan his son and all his servants to
put David to death. But Jonathan, Saul's son, greatly delighted in David.
2So Jonathan told David saying, "Saul my father is seeking to
put you to death. Now therefore, please be on guard in the morning, and stay in a secret place and hide yourself.
3"And I will go out and stand beside my father in the field
where you are, and I will speak with my father about you; if I find
out anything, then I shall tell you."

## New International

hurled it, saying to himself, "I'll pin David to the wall." But David
eluded him twice.
12Saul was afraid of David, because the LORD was with David
but had left Saul. 13So he sent David away from him and gave him
command over a thousand men, and David led the troops in their
campaigns. 14In everything he did he had great success,[a] because
the LORD was with him. 15When Saul saw how successful[b] he was,
he was afraid of him. 16But all Israel and Judah loved David,
because he led them in their campaigns.
17Saul said to David, "Here is my older daughter Merab. I will
give her to you in marriage; only serve me bravely and fight the
battles of the LORD." For Saul said to himself, "I will not raise a
hand against him. Let the Philistines do that!"
18But David said to Saul, "Who am I, and what is my family or
my father's clan in Israel, that I should become the king's son-in-
law?" 19So[c] when the time came for Merab, Saul's daughter, to be
given to David, she was given in marriage to Adriel of Meholah.
20Now Saul's daughter Michal was in love with David, and
when they told Saul about it, he was pleased. 21"I will give her to
him," he thought, "so that she may be a snare to him and so that
the hand of the Philistines may be against him." So Saul said to
David, "Now you have a second opportunity to become my son-
in-law."
22Then Saul ordered his attendants: "Speak to David privately
and say, 'Look, the king is pleased with you, and his attendants
all like you; now become his son-in-law.' "
23They repeated these words to David. But David said, "Do you
think it is a small matter to become the king's son-in-law? I'm only
a poor man and little known."
24When Saul's servants told him what David had said, 25Saul
replied, "Say to David, 'The king wants no other price for the bride
than a hundred Philistine foreskins, to take revenge on his enemies.' " Saul's plan was to have David fall by the hands of the
Philistines.
26When the attendants told David these things, he was pleased
to become the king's son-in-law. So before the allotted time
elapsed, 27David and his men went out and killed two hundred
Philistines. He brought their foreskins and presented the full number to the king so that he might become the king's son-in-law.
Then Saul gave him his daughter Michal in marriage.
28When Saul realized that the LORD was with David and that his
daughter Michal loved David, 29Saul became still more afraid of
him, and he remained his enemy the rest of his days.
30The Philistine commanders continued to go out to battle, and
as often as they did, David met with more success[d] than the rest
of Saul's officers, and his name became well known.

*Saul Tries to Kill David*

**19** SAUL TOLD his son Jonathan and all the attendants to kill
David. But Jonathan was very fond of David 2and warned
him, "My father Saul is looking for a chance to kill you. Be on your
guard tomorrow morning; go into hiding and stay there. 3I will go
out and stand with my father in the field where you are. I'll speak
to him about you and will tell you what I find out."

**NIV** [a] 14 Or *he was very wise* [b] 15 Or *wise* [c] 19 Or *However,* [d] 30 Or
*David acted more wisely*

## King James

4¶ And Jonathan spake good of David unto Saul his father, and said unto him, Let not the king sin against his servant, against David; because he hath not sinned against thee, and because his works *have been* to thee-ward very good:

5For he did put his life in his hand, and slew the Philistine, and the LORD wrought a great salvation for all Israel: thou sawest *it*, and didst rejoice: wherefore then wilt thou sin against innocent blood, to slay David without a cause?

6And Saul hearkened unto the voice of Jonathan: and Saul sware, *As* the LORD liveth, he shall not be slain.

7And Jonathan called David, and Jonathan showed him all those things. And Jonathan brought David to Saul, and he was in his presence, as in times past.

8¶ And there was war again: and David went out, and fought with the Philistines, and slew them with a great slaughter; and they fled from him.

9And the evil spirit from the LORD was upon Saul, as he sat in his house with his javelin in his hand: and David played with *his* hand.

10And Saul sought to smite David even to the wall with the javelin; but he slipped away out of Saul's presence, and he smote the javelin into the wall: and David fled, and escaped that night.

11Saul also sent messengers unto David's house, to watch him, and to slay him in the morning: and Michal David's wife told him, saying, If thou save not thy life tonight, tomorrow thou shalt be slain.

12¶ So Michal let David down through a window: and he went, and fled, and escaped.

13And Michal took an image, and laid *it* in the bed, and put a pillow of goats' *hair* for his bolster, and covered *it* with a cloth.

14And when Saul sent messengers to take David, she said, He *is* sick.

15And Saul sent the messengers *again* to see David, saying, Bring him up to me in the bed, that I may slay him.

16And when the messengers were come in, behold, *there was* an image in the bed, with a pillow of goats' *hair* for his bolster.

17And Saul said unto Michal, Why hast thou deceived me so, and sent away mine enemy, that he is escaped? And Michal answered Saul, He said unto me, Let me go; why should I kill thee?

18¶ So David fled, and escaped, and came to Samuel to Ramah, and told him all that Saul had done to him. And he and Samuel went and dwelt in Naioth.

19And it was told Saul, saying, Behold, David *is* at Naioth in Ramah.

20And Saul sent messengers to take David: and when they saw the company of the prophets prophesying, and Samuel standing *as* appointed over them, the spirit of God was upon the messengers of Saul, and they also prophesied.

21And when it was told Saul, he sent other messengers, and they prophesied likewise. And Saul sent messengers again the third time, and they prophesied also.

22Then went he also to Ramah, and came to a great well that *is* in Sechu: and he asked and said, Where *are* Samuel and David? And *one* said, Behold, *they be* at Naioth in Ramah.

23And he went thither to Naioth in Ramah: and the spirit of God was upon him also, and he went on, and prophesied, until he came to Naioth in Ramah.

24And he stripped off his clothes also, and prophesied before Samuel in like manner, and lay down naked all that day and all that night. Wherefore they say, *Is* Saul also among the prophets?

## Amplified

4And Jonathan spoke good of David to Saul his father, and said to him, Let not the king sin against his servant David, for he has not sinned against you, and his deeds have been of good service to you.

5For he took his life in his hand and slew the Philistine, and the Lord wrought a great deliverance for all Israel; you saw it and rejoiced; why then will you sin against innocent blood and kill David without a cause?

6Saul heeded Jonathan and swore, As the Lord lives, David shall not be slain.

7So Jonathan called David, and told him all these things. And Jonathan brought David to Saul, and he was in his presence, as in times past.

8Then there was war again; and David went out and fought with the Philistines, and made a great slaughter among them, and they fled before him.

9Then an evil spirit from the Lord came upon Saul, as he sat in his house with his spear in his hand; and David was playing [the lyre] with his hand.

10Saul sought to pin David to the wall with the spear, but he slipped away, so that Saul struck the spear into the wall. Then David fled, and escaped that night.

11Saul sent messengers that night to David's house to watch him that he might kill him in the morning. But Michal, David's wife, told him, If you do not save your life tonight, tomorrow you will be killed.

12So Michal let David down through the window; and he fled and escaped.

13And Michal took the teraphim [household good-luck image] and laid it in the bed, put a pillow of goats' hair at its head, and covered it with a bedspread.

14And when Saul sent messengers to take David, she said, He is sick.

15Then Saul sent the messengers again to see David, saying, Bring him up to me in the bed, that I may slay him.

16And when the messengers came in, behold, there was an image in the bed, with a pillow of goats' hair at its head.

17Saul said to Michal, Why have you deceived me so, and sent away my enemy, so that he has escaped? Michal answered Saul, He said to me, Let me go; why should I kill you?

18So David fled, and escaped, and came to Samuel at Ramah, and told him all that Saul had done to him. And he and Samuel went and dwelt in Naioth.

19And it was told Saul, Behold, David is at Naioth in Ramah.

20And Saul sent messengers to take David; and when they saw the company of the prophets prophesying, and Samuel standing as appointed head over them, the Spirit of God came upon the messengers of Saul, and they also prophesied.

21When it was told Saul, he sent other messengers, and they also prophesied. And Saul sent messengers again the third time, and they also prophesied.

22Then Saul himself went to Ramah, and came to a great well that is in Secu; and he asked, Where are Samuel and David? And was told, They are at Naioth in Ramah.

23So he went on to Naioth in Ramah; and the Spirit of God came upon him also, and as he went on he prophesied, until he came to Naioth in Ramah.

24He took off his royal robes, and prophesied before Samuel and lay down stripped thus all that day and night. So they say, Is Saul also among the prophets? [I Sam. 10:10.]

## New American Standard

4Then Jonathan spoke well of David to Saul his father, and said
to him, "Do not let the king sin against his servant David, since
he has not sinned against you, and since his deeds *have been* very
beneficial to you.
5"For he took his life in his hand and struck the Philistine, and
the LORD brought about a great deliverance for all Israel; you saw
*it* and rejoiced. Why then will you sin against innocent blood, by
putting David to death without a cause?"
6And Saul listened to the voice of Jonathan, and Saul vowed,
"As the LORD lives, he shall not be put to death."
7Then Jonathan called David, and Jonathan told him all these
words. And Jonathan brought David to Saul, and he was in his
presence as formerly.
**8**¶ When there was war again, David went out and fought with
the Philistines, and defeated them with great slaughter, so that
they fled before him.
9Now there was an evil spirit from the LORD on Saul as he was
sitting in his house with his spear in his hand, and David was
playing *the harp* with *his* hand.
10And Saul tried to pin David to the wall with the spear, but he
slipped away out of Saul's presence, so that he stuck the spear into
the wall. And David fled and escaped that night.
**11**¶ Then Saul sent messengers to David's house to watch him,
in order to put him to death in the morning. But Michal, David's
wife, told him, saying, "If you do not save your life tonight,
tomorrow you will be put to death."
12So Michal let David down through a window, and he went
out and fled and escaped.
13And Michal took the household idol and laid *it* on the bed,
and put a quilt of goats' *hair* at its head, and covered *it* with clothes.
14When Saul sent messengers to take David, she said, "He is
sick."
15Then Saul sent messengers to see David, saying, "Bring him
up to me on his bed, that I may put him to death."
16When the messengers entered, behold, the household idol
*was* on the bed with the quilt of goats' *hair* at its head.
17So Saul said to Michal, "Why have you deceived me like this
and let my enemy go, so that he has escaped?" And Michal said
to Saul, "He said to me, 'Let me go! Why should I put you to
death?' "
**18**¶ Now David fled and escaped and came to Samuel at Ramah,
and told him all that Saul had done to him. And he and Samuel
went and stayed in Naioth.
19And it was told Saul, saying, "Behold, David is at Naioth in
Ramah."
20Then Saul sent messengers to take David, but when they saw
the company of the prophets prophesying, with Samuel standing
*and* presiding over them, the Spirit of God came upon the messengers of Saul; and they also prophesied.
21And when it was told Saul, he sent other messengers, and
they also prophesied. So Saul sent messengers again the third
time, and they also prophesied.
22Then he himself went to Ramah, and came as far as the large
well that is in Secu; and he asked and said, "Where are Samuel and
David?" And *someone* said, "Behold, they are at Naioth in Ramah."
23And he proceeded there to Naioth in Ramah; and the Spirit
of God came upon him also, so that he went along prophesying
continually until he came to Naioth in Ramah.
24And he also stripped off his clothes, and he too prophesied
before Samuel and lay down naked all that day and all that night.
Therefore they say, "Is Saul also among the prophets?"

## New International

4Jonathan spoke well of David to Saul his father and said to him,
"Let not the king do wrong to his servant David; he has not
wronged you, and what he has done has benefited you greatly.
5He took his life in his hands when he killed the Philistine. The
LORD won a great victory for all Israel, and you saw it and were
glad. Why then would you do wrong to an innocent man like
David by killing him for no reason?"
6Saul listened to Jonathan and took this oath: "As surely as the
LORD lives, David will not be put to death."
7So Jonathan called David and told him the whole conversation.
He brought him to Saul, and David was with Saul as before.
8Once more war broke out, and David went out and fought the
Philistines. He struck them with such force that they fled before
him.
9But an evil[a] spirit from the LORD came upon Saul as he was
sitting in his house with his spear in his hand. While David was
playing the harp, 10Saul tried to pin him to the wall with his spear,
but David eluded him as Saul drove the spear into the wall. That
night David made good his escape.
11Saul sent men to David's house to watch it and to kill him in
the morning. But Michal, David's wife, warned him, "If you don't
run for your life tonight, tomorrow you'll be killed." 12So Michal
let David down through a window, and he fled and escaped.
13Then Michal took an idol[b] and laid it on the bed, covering it with
a garment and putting some goats' hair at the head.
14When Saul sent the men to capture David, Michal said, "He
is ill."
15Then Saul sent the men back to see David and told them,
"Bring him up to me in his bed so that I may kill him." 16But when
the men entered, there was the idol in the bed, and at the head
was some goats' hair.
17Saul said to Michal, "Why did you deceive me like this and
send my enemy away so that he escaped?"
Michal told him, "He said to me, 'Let me get away. Why should
I kill you?' "
18When David had fled and made his escape, he went to Samuel
at Ramah and told him all that Saul had done to him. Then he and
Samuel went to Naioth and stayed there. 19Word came to Saul:
"David is in Naioth at Ramah"; 20so he sent men to capture him.
But when they saw a group of prophets prophesying, with Samuel
standing there as their leader, the Spirit of God came upon Saul's
men and they also prophesied. 21Saul was told about it, and he
sent more men, and they prophesied too. Saul sent men a third
time, and they also prophesied. 22Finally, he himself left for
Ramah and went to the great cistern at Secu. And he asked,
"Where are Samuel and David?"
"Over in Naioth at Ramah," they said.
23So Saul went to Naioth at Ramah. But the Spirit of God came
even upon him, and he walked along prophesying until he came
to Naioth. 24He stripped off his robes and also prophesied in
Samuel's presence. He lay that way all that day and night. This is
why people say, "Is Saul also among the prophets?"

NIV [a] 9 Or *injurious* [b] 13 Hebrew *teraphim;* also in verse 16

## King James

**20** AND DAVID fled from Naioth in Ramah, and came and
said before Jonathan, What have I done? what *is* mine
iniquity? and what *is* my sin before thy father, that he seeketh my
life?
2 And he said unto him, God forbid; thou shalt not die: behold,
my father will do nothing either great or small, but that he will
show it me: and why should my father hide this thing from me?
it *is* not *so*.
3 And David sware moreover, and said, Thy father certainly
knoweth that I have found grace in thine eyes; and he saith, Let
not Jonathan know this, lest he be grieved: but truly *as* the LORD
liveth, and *as* thy soul liveth, *there is* but a step between me and
death.
4 Then said Jonathan unto David, Whatsoever thy soul desireth,
I will even do *it* for thee.
5 And David said unto Jonathan, Behold, tomorrow *is* the new
moon, and I should not fail to sit with the king at meat: but let me
go, that I may hide myself in the field unto the third *day* at even.
6 If thy father at all miss me, then say, David earnestly asked
*leave* of me that he might run to Bethlehem his city: for *there is* a
yearly sacrifice there for all the family.
7 If he say thus, *It is* well; thy servant shall have peace: but if he
be very wroth, *then* be sure that evil is determined by him.
8 Therefore thou shalt deal kindly with thy servant; for thou hast
brought thy servant into a covenant of the LORD with thee: notwithstanding, if there be in me iniquity, slay me thyself; for why
shouldest thou bring me to thy father?
9 And Jonathan said, Far be it from thee: for if I knew certainly
that evil were determined by my father to come upon thee, then
would not I tell it thee?
10 Then said David to Jonathan, Who shall tell me? or what *if* thy
father answer thee roughly?
11 ¶ And Jonathan said unto David, Come, and let us go out into
the field. And they went out both of them into the field.
12 And Jonathan said unto David, O LORD God of Israel, when
I have sounded my father about tomorrow any time, *or* the third
*day*, and, behold, *if there be* good toward David, and I then send
not unto thee, and show it thee;
13 The LORD do so and much more to Jonathan: but if it please
my father *to do* thee evil, then I will show it thee, and send thee
away, that thou mayest go in peace: and the LORD be with thee,
as he hath been with my father.
14 And thou shalt not only while yet I live show me the kindness
of the LORD, that I die not:
15 But *also* thou shalt not cut off thy kindness from my house for
ever: no, not when the LORD hath cut off the enemies of David
every one from the face of the earth.
16 So Jonathan made *a covenant* with the house of David, *saying*,
Let the LORD even require *it* at the hand of David's enemies.
17 And Jonathan caused David to swear again, because he loved
him: for he loved him as he loved his own soul.
18 Then Jonathan said to David, Tomorrow *is* the new moon: and
thou shalt be missed, because thy seat will be empty.
19 And *when* thou hast stayed three days, *then* thou shalt go
down quickly, and come to the place where thou didst hide thyself
when the business was *in hand*, and shalt remain by the stone Ezel.
20 And I will shoot three arrows on the side *thereof*, as though
I shot at a mark.
21 And, behold, I will send a lad, *saying*, Go, find out the arrows.
If I expressly say unto the lad, Behold, the arrows *are* on this side
of thee, take them; then come thou: for *there is* peace to thee, and
no hurt; *as* the LORD liveth.
22 But if I say thus unto the young man, Behold, the arrows *are*
beyond thee; go thy way: for the LORD hath sent thee away.
23 And *as touching* the matter which thou and I have spoken of,
behold, the LORD *be* between thee and me for ever.
24 ¶ So David hid himself in the field: and when the new moon
was come, the king sat him down to eat meat.

## Amplified

**20** DAVID FLED from Naioth in Ramah, and came and said
to Jonathan, What have I done? Of what am I guilty? What
is my sin before your father, that he seeks my life?
2 Jonathan said, God forbid! You shall not die. My father does
nothing great or small but what he tells me; and why should [he]
hide this thing from me? It is not so.
3 But David replied, Your father certainly knows that I have
found favor in your eyes; and he thinks, Let not Jonathan know
this, lest he be grieved. But truly as the Lord lives, and as your soul
lives, there is but a step between me and death.
4 Then Jonathan said to David, Whatever you desire, I will do
for you.
5 David said to Jonathan, Tomorrow is the new moon, and I
should not fail to sit at the table with the king; but let me go, that
I may hide myself in the field till the third day at evening.
6 If your father misses me at all, then say, David earnestly asked
leave of me that he might run to Bethlehem his city; for there is
a yearly sacrifice there for all the family.
7 If he says, All right, then it will be well with your servant; but
if he is angry, then be sure that evil is determined by him.
8 Therefore deal kindly with your servant, for you have brought
[me] into a covenant of the Lord with you. But if there is guilt in
me, kill me yourself; for why should you bring me to your father?
9 And Jonathan said, Far be it from you! If I knew that evil was
determined for you by my father, would I not tell you?
10 Then said David to Jonathan, Who will tell me if your father
answers you roughly?
11 Jonathan said, Come, let us go into the field. So they went into
the field.
12 Jonathan said to David, The Lord, the God of Israel be witness. When I have sounded my father about this time tomorrow,
or the third day, behold, if he is well inclined toward David, and
I do not send and let you know it,
13 The Lord do so and much more to Jonathan. But if it please
my father to do you harm, then I will disclose it to you, and send
you away, that you may go in safety. And the Lord be with you,
as He has been with my father.
14 While I am still alive you shall not only show me the loving-
kindness of the Lord that I die not,
15 But also you shall not cut off your kindness from my house
for ever; no, not when the Lord has cut off every enemy of David
from the face of the earth.
16 So Jonathan made a covenant with the house of David, saying, And the Lord will require that this covenant be kept at the
hand of David's enemies.
17 And Jonathan caused David to swear again, by his love for
him, for Jonathan loved him as he loved his own life.
18 Then Jonathan said to David, Tomorrow is the new moon;
and you will be missed, for your seat will be empty.
19 On the third day you will go quickly, and come to the place
where you hid yourself when the matter was in hand, and remain
by the stone Ezel.
20 And I will shoot three arrows on the side of it, as though I shot
at a mark.
21 And I will send a lad, saying, Go, find the arrows. If I expressly say to the lad, Look, the arrows are on this side of you, take
them; then you are to come, for it is safe for you and there is no
danger, as the Lord lives.
22 But if I say to the youth, Look, the arrows are beyond you,
then go; for the Lord has sent you away.
23 And as touching the matter of which you and I have spoken,
behold, the Lord is between you and me for ever.
24 So David hid himself in the field; and when the new moon
came, the king sat down to eat food.

## New American Standard

*David and Jonathan Covenant*

**20** THEN DAVID fled from Naioth in Ramah, and came and said to Jonathan, "What have I done? What is my iniquity? And what is my sin before your father, that he is seeking my life?"

2And he said to him, "Far from it, you shall not die. Behold, my father does nothing either great or small without disclosing it to me. So why should my father hide this thing from me? It is not so!"

3Yet David vowed again, saying, "Your father knows well that I have found favor in your sight, and he has said, 'Do not let Jonathan know this, lest he be grieved.' But truly as the LORD lives and as your soul lives, there is hardly a step between me and death."

4Then Jonathan said to David, "Whatever you say, I will do for you."

5So David said to Jonathan, "Behold, tomorrow is the new moon, and I ought to sit down to eat with the king. But let me go, that I may hide myself in the field until the third evening.

6"If your father misses me at all, then say, 'David earnestly asked *leave* of me to run to Bethlehem his city, because it is the yearly sacrifice there for the whole family.'

7"If he says, 'It is good,' your servant *shall be* safe; but if he is very angry, know that he has decided on evil.

8"Therefore deal kindly with your servant, for you have brought your servant into a covenant of the LORD with you. But if there is iniquity in me, put me to death yourself; for why then should you bring me to your father?"

9And Jonathan said, "Far be it from you! For if I should indeed learn that evil has been decided by my father to come upon you, then would I not tell you about it?"

10Then David said to Jonathan, "Who will tell me if your father answers you harshly?"

11And Jonathan said to David, "Come, and let us go out into the field." So both of them went out to the field.

12¶ Then Jonathan said to David, "The LORD, the God of Israel, *be witness*! When I have sounded out my father about this time tomorrow, *or* the third day, behold, if there is good *feeling* toward David, shall I not then send to you and make it known to you?

13"If it please my father *to do* you harm, may the LORD do so to Jonathan and more also, if I do not make it known to you and send you away, that you may go in safety. And may the LORD be with you as He has been with my father.

14"And if I am still alive, will you not show me the lovingkindness of the LORD, that I may not die?

15"And you shall not cut off your lovingkindness from my house forever, not even when the LORD cuts off every one of the enemies of David from the face of the earth."

16So Jonathan made a *covenant* with the house of David, *saying*, "May the LORD require *it* at the hands of David's enemies."

17And Jonathan made David vow again because of his love for him, because he loved him as he loved his own life.

18¶ Then Jonathan said to him, "Tomorrow is the new moon, and you will be missed because your seat will be empty.

19"When you have stayed for three days, you shall go down quickly and come to the place where you hid yourself on that eventful day, and you shall remain by the stone Ezel.

20"And I will shoot three arrows to the side, as though I shot at a target.

21"And behold, I will send the lad, *saying*, 'Go, find the arrows.' If I specifically say to the lad, 'Behold, the arrows are on this side of you, get them,' then come; for there is safety for you and no harm, as the LORD lives.

22"But if I say to the youth, 'Behold, the arrows are beyond you,' go, for the LORD has sent you away.

23"As for the agreement of which you and I have spoken, behold, the LORD is between you and me forever."

24¶ So David hid in the field; and when the new moon came, the king sat down to eat food.

## New International

*David and Jonathan*

**20** THEN DAVID fled from Naioth at Ramah and went to
Jonathan and asked, "What have I done? What is my
crime? How have I wronged your father, that he is trying to take
my life?"
2"Never!" Jonathan replied. "You are not going to die! Look,
my father doesn't do anything, great or small, without confiding
in me. Why would he hide this from me? It's not so!"
3But David took an oath and said, "Your father knows very well
that I have found favor in your eyes, and he has said to himself,
'Jonathan must not know this or he will be grieved.' Yet as surely
as the LORD lives and as you live, there is only a step between me
and death."
4Jonathan said to David, "Whatever you want me to do, I'll do
for you."
5So David said, "Look, tomorrow is the New Moon festival, and
I am supposed to dine with the king; but let me go and hide in the
field until the evening of the day after tomorrow. 6If your father
misses me at all, tell him, 'David earnestly asked my permission
to hurry to Bethlehem, his hometown, because an annual sacrifice
is being made there for his whole clan.' 7If he says, 'Very well,'
then your servant is safe. But if he loses his temper, you can be
sure that he is determined to harm me. 8As for you, show kindness
to your servant, for you have brought him into a covenant with
you before the LORD. If I am guilty, then kill me yourself! Why
hand me over to your father?"
9"Never!" Jonathan said. "If I had the least inkling that my
father was determined to harm you, wouldn't I tell you?"
10David asked, "Who will tell me if your father answers you
harshly?"
11"Come," Jonathan said, "let's go out into the field." So they
went there together.
12Then Jonathan said to David: "By the LORD, the God of Israel,
I will surely sound out my father by this time the day after tomorrow! If he is favorably disposed toward you, will I not send you
word and let you know? 13But if my father is inclined to harm you,
may the LORD deal with me, be it ever so severely, if I do not let
you know and send you away safely. May the LORD be with you
as he has been with my father. 14But show me unfailing kindness
like that of the LORD as long as I live, so that I may not be killed,
15and do not ever cut off your kindness from my family—not even
when the LORD has cut off every one of David's enemies from the
face of the earth."
16So Jonathan made a covenant with the house of David, saying, "May the LORD call David's enemies to account." 17And Jonathan had David reaffirm his oath out of love for him, because he
loved him as he loved himself.
18Then Jonathan said to David: "Tomorrow is the New Moon
festival. You will be missed, because your seat will be empty. 19The
day after tomorrow, toward evening, go to the place where you hid
when this trouble began, and wait by the stone Ezel. 20I will shoot
three arrows to the side of it, as though I were shooting at a target.
21Then I will send a boy and say, 'Go, find the arrows.' If I say to
him, 'Look, the arrows are on this side of you; bring them here,'
then come, because, as surely as the LORD lives, you are safe; there
is no danger. 22But if I say to the boy, 'Look, the arrows are beyond
you,' then you must go, because the LORD has sent you away.
23And about the matter you and I discussed—remember, the LORD
is witness between you and me forever."
24So David hid in the field, and when the New Moon festival
came, the king sat down to eat. 25He sat in his customary place by

## King James

25And the king sat upon his seat, as at other times, *even* upon
a seat by the wall: and Jonathan arose, and Abner sat by Saul's
side, and David's place was empty.
26Nevertheless Saul spake not any thing that day: for he
thought, Something hath befallen him, he *is* not clean; surely he
*is* not clean.
27And it came to pass on the morrow, *which was* the second *day*
of the month, that David's place was empty: and Saul said unto
Jonathan his son, Wherefore cometh not the son of Jesse to meat,
neither yesterday, nor today?
28And Jonathan answered Saul, David earnestly asked *leave* of
me *to go* to Bethlehem:
29And he said, Let me go, I pray thee; for our family hath a
sacrifice in the city; and my brother, he hath commanded me *to be
there:* and now, if I have found favour in thine eyes, let me get
away, I pray thee, and see my brethren. Therefore he cometh not
unto the king's table.
30Then Saul's anger was kindled against Jonathan, and he said
unto him, Thou son of the perverse rebellious *woman,* do not I
know that thou hast chosen the son of Jesse to thine own confusion, and unto the confusion of thy mother's nakedness?
31For as long as the son of Jesse liveth upon the ground, thou
shalt not be established, nor thy kingdom. Wherefore now send
and fetch him unto me, for he shall surely die.
32And Jonathan answered Saul his father, and said unto him,
Wherefore shall he be slain? what hath he done?
33And Saul cast a javelin at him to smite him: whereby Jonathan
knew that it was determined of his father to slay David.
34So Jonathan arose from the table in fierce anger, and did eat
no meat the second day of the month: for he was grieved for David,
because his father had done him shame.
35¶ And it came to pass in the morning, that Jonathan went out
into the field at the time appointed with David, and a little lad with
him.
36And he said unto his lad, Run, find out now the arrows which
I shoot. *And* as the lad ran, he shot an arrow beyond him.
37And when the lad was come to the place of the arrow which
Jonathan had shot, Jonathan cried after the lad, and said, *Is* not the
arrow beyond thee?
38And Jonathan cried after the lad, Make speed, haste, stay not.
And Jonathan's lad gathered up the arrows, and came to his master.
39But the lad knew not any thing: only Jonathan and David
knew the matter.
40And Jonathan gave his artillery unto his lad, and said unto
him, Go, carry *them* to the city.
41¶ *And* as soon as the lad was gone, David arose out of *a place*
toward the south, and fell on his face to the ground, and bowed
himself three times: and they kissed one another, and wept one
with another, until David exceeded.
42And Jonathan said to David, Go in peace, forasmuch as we
have sworn both of us in the name of the LORD, saying, The LORD
be between me and thee, and between my seed and thy seed for
ever. And he arose and departed: and Jonathan went into the city.

**21** THEN CAME David to Nob to Ahimelech the priest: and
Ahimelech was afraid at the meeting of David, and said
unto him, Why *art* thou alone, and no man with thee?
2And David said unto Ahimelech the priest, The king hath
commanded me a business, and hath said unto me, Let no man
know any thing of the business whereabout I send thee, and what
I have commanded thee: and I have appointed *my* servants to such
and such a place.

## Amplified

25The king sat, as at other times, on his seat by the wall; and
Jonathan sat opposite, and Abner sat by Saul's side, but David's
place was empty.
26Yet Saul said nothing that day; for he thought, Something has
befallen him, he is not clean; surely he is not clean.
27But on the morrow, the second day after the new moon,
David's place was empty; and Saul said to Jonathan his son, Why
has not the son of Jesse come to the meal, either yesterday or
today?
28And Jonathan answered, David earnestly asked leave of me
to go to Bethlehem.
29He said, Let me go, I pray, for our family holds a sacrifice in
the city; and my brother commanded me to be there. Now, if I have
found favor in your eyes, let me get away and see my brothers.
That is why he has not come to the king's table.
30Then Saul's anger was kindled against Jonathan, and he said
to him, You son of a perverse, rebellious woman, do not I know
that you have chosen the son of Jesse to your own shame, and to
the shame of your mother who bore you?
31For as long as the son of Jesse lives upon the earth you shall
not be established nor your kingdom. So now send and bring him
to me, for he shall surely die.
32Jonathan answered Saul his father, Why should he be killed?
What has he done?
33But Saul cast his spear at him to smite him, by which Jonathan
knew that his father had determined to kill David.
34So Jonathan arose from the table in fierce anger and ate no
food that second day of the month, for he grieved for David,
because his father had disgraced him.
35In the morning Jonathan went out into the field at the time
appointed with David, and a little lad with him.
36And he said to his lad, Run, find the arrows which I shoot.
And as the lad ran, he shot an arrow beyond him.
37When the lad came to the place where Jonathan had shot the
arrow, Jonathan called to [him], Is not the arrow beyond you?
38And Jonathan cried after the lad, Make speed, haste, stay not!
The lad gathered up the arrows, and came to his master.
39But the lad knew nothing; only Jonathan and David knew the
matter.
40Jonathan gave his weapons to his lad, and told him, Go, carry
them to the city.
41And as soon as the lad was gone, David arose from beside the
heap of stones, and fell on his face to the ground, and bowed
himself three times. And they kissed one another, and wept with
one another, until David got control of himself.
42And Jonathan told David, Go in peace, forasmuch as we have
sworn both of us in the name of the Lord, saying, The Lord shall
be between me and you, and between my descendants and yours
for ever. And Jonathan arose and departed into the city.

**21** THEN DAVID went to Nob, to Ahimelech the priest; and
Ahimelech was afraid at meeting David, and said to him,
Why are you alone, and no man with you?
2David said to Ahimelech the priest, The king has charged me
with a matter and has told me, Let no man know anything of the
mission on which I send you, and with what I have charged you.
I have appointed the young men to a certain place.

## New American Standard

25And the king sat on his seat as usual, the seat by the wall; then Jonathan rose up and Abner sat down by Saul's side, but David's place was empty.

26Nevertheless Saul did not speak anything that day, for he thought, "It is an accident, he is not clean, surely *he is* not clean."

27And it came about the next day, the second *day* of the new moon, that David's place was empty; so Saul said to Jonathan his son, "Why has the son of Jesse not come to the meal, either yesterday or today?"

28Jonathan then answered Saul, "David earnestly asked leave of me *to go* to Bethlehem,

29for he said, 'Please let me go, since our family has a sacrifice in the city, and my brother has commanded me to attend. And now, if I have found favor in your sight, please let me get away that I may see my brothers.' For this reason he has not come to the king's table."

*Saul Is Angry with Jonathan*

30¶ Then Saul's anger burned against Jonathan and he said to him, "You son of a perverse, rebellious woman! Do I not know that you are choosing the son of Jesse to your own shame and to the shame of your mother's nakedness?

31"For as long as the son of Jesse lives on the earth, neither you nor your kingdom will be established. Therefore now, send and bring him to me, for he must surely die."

32But Jonathan answered Saul his father and said to him, "Why should he be put to death? What has he done?"

33Then Saul hurled his spear at him to strike him down; so Jonathan knew that his father had decided to put David to death.

34Then Jonathan arose from the table in fierce anger, and did not eat food on the second day of the new moon, for he was grieved over David because his father had dishonored him.

35¶ Now it came about in the morning that Jonathan went out into the field for the appointment with David, and a little lad *was* with him.

36And he said to his lad, "Run, find now the arrows which I am about to shoot." As the lad was running, he shot an arrow past him.

37When the lad reached the place of the arrow which Jonathan had shot, Jonathan called after the lad, and said, "Is not the arrow beyond you?"

38And Jonathan called after the lad, "Hurry, be quick, do not stay!" And Jonathan's lad picked up the arrow and came to his master.

39But the lad was not aware of anything; only Jonathan and David knew about the matter.

40Then Jonathan gave his weapons to his lad and said to him, "Go, bring *them* to the city."

41When the lad was gone, David rose from the south side and fell on his face to the ground, and bowed three times. And they kissed each other and wept together, but David more.

42And Jonathan said to David, "Go in safety, inasmuch as we have sworn to each other in the name of the LORD, saying, 'The LORD will be between me and you, and between my descendants and your descendants forever.' " Then he rose and departed, while Jonathan went into the city.

*David Takes Consecrated Bread*

**21** THEN DAVID came to Nob to Ahimelech the priest; and Ahimelech came trembling to meet David, and said to him, "Why are you alone and no one with you?"

2And David said to Ahimelech the priest, "The king has commissioned me with a matter, and has said to me, 'Let no one know anything about the matter on which I am sending you and with which I have commissioned you; and I have directed the young men to a certain place.'

## New International

the wall, opposite Jonathan,[a] and Abner sat next to Saul, but
David's place was empty. 26Saul said nothing that day, for he
thought, "Something must have happened to David to make him
ceremonially unclean—surely he is unclean." 27But the next day,
the second day of the month, David's place was empty again. Then
Saul said to his son Jonathan, "Why hasn't the son of Jesse come
to the meal, either yesterday or today?"
28Jonathan answered, "David earnestly asked me for permission to go to Bethlehem. 29He said, 'Let me go, because our family
is observing a sacrifice in the town and my brother has ordered me
to be there. If I have found favor in your eyes, let me get away to
see my brothers.' That is why he has not come to the king's table."
30Saul's anger flared up at Jonathan and he said to him, "You
son of a perverse and rebellious woman! Don't I know that you
have sided with the son of Jesse to your own shame and to the
shame of the mother who bore you? 31As long as the son of Jesse
lives on this earth, neither you nor your kingdom will be established. Now send and bring him to me, for he must die!"
32"Why should he be put to death? What has he done?" Jonathan asked his father. 33But Saul hurled his spear at him to kill him.
Then Jonathan knew that his father intended to kill David.
34Jonathan got up from the table in fierce anger; on that second
day of the month he did not eat, because he was grieved at his
father's shameful treatment of David.
35In the morning Jonathan went out to the field for his meeting
with David. He had a small boy with him, 36and he said to the boy,
"Run and find the arrows I shoot." As the boy ran, he shot an
arrow beyond him. 37When the boy came to the place where
Jonathan's arrow had fallen, Jonathan called out after him, "Isn't
the arrow beyond you?" 38Then he shouted, "Hurry! Go quickly!
Don't stop!" The boy picked up the arrow and returned to his
master. 39(The boy knew nothing of all this; only Jonathan and
David knew.) 40Then Jonathan gave his weapons to the boy and
said, "Go, carry them back to town."
41After the boy had gone, David got up from the south side ⌊of
the stone⌋ and bowed down before Jonathan three times, with his
face to the ground. Then they kissed each other and wept together—but David wept the most.
42Jonathan said to David, "Go in peace, for we have sworn
friendship with each other in the name of the LORD, saying, 'The
LORD is witness between you and me, and between your descendants and my descendants forever.' " Then David left, and Jonathan
went back to the town.

*David at Nob*

**21** DAVID WENT to Nob, to Ahimelech the priest. Ahimelech trembled when he met him, and asked, "Why are you
alone? Why is no one with you?"
2David answered Ahimelech the priest, "The king charged me
with a certain matter and said to me, 'No one is to know anything
about your mission and your instructions.' As for my men, I have
told them to meet me at a certain place. 3Now then, what do you

NIV [a] 25 Septuagint; Hebrew *wall. Jonathan arose*

## King James

3Now therefore what is under thine hand? give *me* five *loaves of* bread in mine hand, or what there is present.

4And the priest answered David, and said, *There is* no common bread under mine hand, but there is hallowed bread; if the young men have kept themselves at least from women.

5And David answered the priest, and said unto him, Of a truth women *have been* kept from us about these three days, since I came out, and the vessels of the young men are holy, and *the bread is* in a manner common, yea, though it were sanctified this day in the vessel.

6So the priest gave him hallowed *bread:* for there was no bread there but the showbread, that was taken from before the LORD, to put hot bread in the day when it was taken away.

7Now a certain man of the servants of Saul *was* there that day, detained before the LORD; and his name *was* Doeg, an Edomite, the chiefest of the herdmen that *belonged* to Saul.

8¶ And David said unto Ahimelech, And is there not here under thine hand spear or sword? for I have neither brought my sword nor my weapons with me, because the king's business required haste.

9And the priest said, The sword of Goliath the Philistine, whom thou slewest in the valley of Elah, behold, it *is here* wrapped in a cloth behind the ephod: if thou wilt take that, take *it:* for *there is* no other save that here. And David said, *There is* none like that; give it me.

10¶ And David arose, and fled that day for fear of Saul, and went to Achish the king of Gath.

11And the servants of Achish said unto him, *Is* not this David the king of the land? did they not sing one to another of him in dances, saying, Saul hath slain his thousands, and David his ten thousands?

12And David laid up these words in his heart, and was sore afraid of Achish the king of Gath.

13And he changed his behaviour before them, and feigned himself mad in their hands, and scrabbled on the doors of the gate, and let his spittle fall down upon his beard.

14Then said Achish unto his servants, Lo, ye see the man is mad: wherefore *then* have ye brought him to me?

15Have I need of mad men, that ye have brought this *fellow* to play the mad man in my presence? shall this *fellow* come into my house?

**22** DAVID THEREFORE departed thence, and escaped to the cave Adullam: and when his brethren and all his father's house heard *it,* they went down thither to him.

2And every one *that was* in distress, and every one that *was* in debt, and every one *that was* discontented, gathered themselves unto him; and he became a captain over them: and there were with him about four hundred men.

3¶ And David went thence to Mizpeh of Moab: and he said unto the king of Moab, Let my father and my mother, I pray thee, come forth, *and be* with you, till I know what God will do for me.

4And he brought them before the king of Moab: and they dwelt with him all the while that David was in the hold.

5¶ And the prophet Gad said unto David, Abide not in the hold; depart, and get thee into the land of Judah. Then David departed, and came into the forest of Hareth.

6¶ When Saul heard that David was discovered, and the men that *were* with him, (now Saul abode in Gibeah under a tree in Ramah, having his spear in his hand, and all his servants *were* standing about him;)

7Then Saul said unto his servants that stood about him, Hear now, ye Benjamites; will the son of Jesse give every one of you fields and vineyards, *and* make you all captains of thousands, and captains of hundreds;

## Amplified

3Now what do you have on hand? Give me five loaves of bread, or what you may have.

4And the priest answered David, There is no common bread on hand, but there is hallowed bread; if the young men have kept themselves at least from women.

5And David told the priest, Truly women have been kept from us about these three days, since I came out, and the food bags *and* utensils of the young men are clean, and although the bread will be used in a secular way, it will be set apart in the clean bags.

6So the priest gave him holy bread; for there was no bread there but the showbread, which was taken from before the Lord, to put hot bread in its place the day when it was taken away.

7Now a certain man of Saul's servants was there that day, detained before the Lord; his name was Doeg, an Edomite, the chief of Saul's herdsmen.

8David said to Ahimelech, Do you have at hand a sword or spear? The king's business required haste, and I brought neither my sword nor my weapons with me.

9The priest said, The sword of Goliath the Philistine, whom you slew in the valley of Elah, see, it is here wrapped in a cloth behind the ephod; if you will take that, do so, for there is no other here. And David said, There is none like that; give it to me.

10David arose, and fled that day from Saul, and went to Achish king of Gath.

11The servants of Achish said to him, Is not this David the king of the land? Did they not sing one to another of him in dances, Saul has slain his thousands, and David his ten thousands?

12David took these words to heart and was much afraid of Achish king of Gath.

13And he changed his behavior before them, and pretended to be insane in their [Philistine] hands, and scribbled on the gate doors, and drooled on his beard.

14Then said Achish to his servants, You see the man is mad; why then have you brought him to me?

15Have I need of mad men, that you bring this fellow to play the mad man in my presence? Shall this fellow come into my house?

**22** SO DAVID departed, and escaped to the cave Adullam: and when his brothers and all his father's house heard it, they went down there to him.

2And every one in distress, or in debt, or discontented, gathered to him; and he became a commander over them; and there were with him about 400 men.

3And David went from there to Mizpah of Moab; and he said to the king of Moab, Let my father [of Moabite descent] and my mother, I pray, come out [of Judah] and be with you, till I know what God will do for me. [Cp. Ruth 4:13, 17.]

4And he brought them before the king of Moab, and they dwelt with him all the while that David was in the mountain-fastness [in Moab].

5Then the prophet Gad said to David, Do not remain in the stronghold; leave, and get into the land of Judah. So David left and went into the forest of Hareth.

6Saul heard that David was discovered, and the men that were with him. Saul was sitting in Gibeah under the tamarisk tree on the height, his spear in his hand, and all his servants standing about him.

7Saul said to his servants who stood about him, Hear now, you Benjamites; will the son of Jesse give every one of you fields and vineyards, and make you all commanders of thousands and hundreds,

## New American Standard

3"Now therefore, what do you have on hand? Give me five
loaves of bread, or whatever can be found."
4And the priest answered David and said, "There is no ordinary bread on hand, but there is consecrated bread; if only the
young men have kept themselves from women."
5And David answered the priest and said to him, "Surely
women have been kept from us as previously when I set out and
the vessels of the young men were holy, though it was an ordinary
journey; how much more then today will their vessels *be holy*?"
6So the priest gave him consecrated *bread*; for there was no
bread there but the bread of the Presence which was removed from
before the LORD, in order to put hot bread *in its place* when it was
taken away.
7¶ Now one of the servants of Saul was there that day, detained
before the LORD; and his name was Doeg the Edomite, the chief
of Saul's shepherds.
8¶ And David said to Ahimelech, "Now is there not a spear or
a sword on hand? For I brought neither my sword nor my weapons
with me, because the king's matter was urgent."
9Then the priest said, "The sword of Goliath the Philistine,
whom you killed in the valley of Elah, behold, it is wrapped in a
cloth behind the ephod; if you would take it for yourself, take *it*.
For there is no other except it here." And David said, "There is
none like it; give it to me."
10¶ Then David arose and fled that day from Saul, and went to
Achish king of Gath.
11But the servants of Achish said to him, "Is this not David the
king of the land? Did they not sing of this one as they danced,
saying,

'Saul has slain his thousands,
And David his ten thousands'?"

12And David took these words to heart, and greatly feared
Achish king of Gath.
13So he disguised his sanity before them, and acted insanely in
their hands, and scribbled on the doors of the gate, and let his
saliva run down into his beard.
14Then Achish said to his servants, "Behold, you see the man
behaving as a madman. Why do you bring him to me?
15"Do I lack madmen, that you have brought this one to act the
madman in my presence? Shall this one come into my house?"

*The Priests Slain at Nob*

22 SO DAVID departed from there and escaped to the cave
of Adullam; and when his brothers and all his father's
household heard *of it*, they went down there to him.
2And everyone who was in distress, and everyone who was in
debt, and everyone who was discontented, gathered to him; and
he became captain over them. Now there were about four hundred
men with him.
3¶ And David went from there to Mizpah of Moab; and he said
to the king of Moab, "Please let my father and my mother come
*and stay* with you until I know what God will do for me."
4Then he left them with the king of Moab; and they stayed with
him all the time that David was in the stronghold.
5And the prophet Gad said to David, "Do not stay in the
stronghold; depart, and go into the land of Judah." So David
departed and went into the forest of Hereth.
6¶ Then Saul heard that David and the men who were with him
had been discovered. Now Saul was sitting in Gibeah, under the
tamarisk tree on the height with his spear in his hand, and all his
servants were standing around him.
7And Saul said to his servants who stood around him, "Hear
now, O Benjamites! Will the son of Jesse also give to all of you
fields and vineyards? Will he make you all commanders of thousands and commanders of hundreds?

## New International

have on hand? Give me five loaves of bread, or whatever you can
find."
4But the priest answered David, "I don't have any ordinary
bread on hand; however, there is some consecrated bread here—
provided the men have kept themselves from women."
5David replied, "Indeed women have been kept from us, as
usual whenever[a] I set out. The men's things[b] are holy even on
missions that are not holy. How much more so today!" 6So the
priest gave him the consecrated bread, since there was no bread
there except the bread of the Presence that had been removed from
before the LORD and replaced by hot bread on the day it was taken
away.
7Now one of Saul's servants was there that day, detained before
the LORD; he was Doeg the Edomite, Saul's head shepherd.
8David asked Ahimelech, "Don't you have a spear or a sword
here? I haven't brought my sword or any other weapon, because
the king's business was urgent."
9The priest replied, "The sword of Goliath the Philistine, whom
you killed in the Valley of Elah, is here; it is wrapped in a cloth
behind the ephod. If you want it, take it; there is no sword here
but that one."
David said, "There is none like it; give it to me."

*David at Gath*

10That day David fled from Saul and went to Achish king of
Gath. 11But the servants of Achish said to him, "Isn't this David,
the king of the land? Isn't he the one they sing about in their
dances:

"'Saul has slain his thousands,
and David his tens of thousands'?"

12David took these words to heart and was very much afraid of
Achish king of Gath. 13So he pretended to be insane in their
presence; and while he was in their hands he acted like a madman,
making marks on the doors of the gate and letting saliva run down
his beard.
14Achish said to his servants, "Look at the man! He is insane!
Why bring him to me? 15Am I so short of madmen that you have
to bring this fellow here to carry on like this in front of me? Must
this man come into my house?"

*David at Adullam and Mizpah*

22 DAVID LEFT Gath and escaped to the cave of Adullam.
When his brothers and his father's household heard about
it, they went down to him there. 2All those who were in distress
or in debt or discontented gathered around him, and he became
their leader. About four hundred men were with him.
3From there David went to Mizpah in Moab and said to the king
of Moab, "Would you let my father and mother come and stay with
you until I learn what God will do for me?" 4So he left them with
the king of Moab, and they stayed with him as long as David was
in the stronghold.
5But the prophet Gad said to David, "Do not stay in the stronghold. Go into the land of Judah." So David left and went to the
forest of Hereth.

*Saul Kills the Priests of Nob*

6Now Saul heard that David and his men had been discovered.
And Saul, spear in hand, was seated under the tamarisk tree on
the hill at Gibeah, with all his officials standing around him. 7Saul
said to them, "Listen, men of Benjamin! Will the son of Jesse give
all of you fields and vineyards? Will he make all of you commanders of thousands and commanders of hundreds? 8Is that why you

NIV [a] 5 Or *from us in the past few days since* [b] 5 Or *bodies*

## King James

8That all of you have conspired against me, and *there is* none that showeth me that my son hath made a league with the son of Jesse, and *there is* none of you that is sorry for me, or showeth unto me that my son hath stirred up my servant against me, to lie in wait, as at this day?

9¶ Then answered Doeg the Edomite, which was set over the servants of Saul, and said, I saw the son of Jesse coming to Nob, to Ahimelech the son of Ahitub.

10And he inquired of the LORD for him, and gave him victuals, and gave him the sword of Goliath the Philistine.

11Then the king sent to call Ahimelech the priest, the son of Ahitub, and all his father's house, the priests that *were* in Nob: and they came all of them to the king.

12And Saul said, Hear now, thou son of Ahitub. And he answered, Here I *am*, my lord.

13And Saul said unto him, Why have ye conspired against me, thou and the son of Jesse, in that thou hast given him bread, and a sword, and hast inquired of God for him, that he should rise against me, to lie in wait, as at this day?

14Then Ahimelech answered the king, and said, And who *is so* faithful among all thy servants as David, which is the king's son-in-law, and goeth at thy bidding, and is honourable in thine house?

15Did I then begin to inquire of God for him? be it far from me: let not the king impute *any* thing unto his servant, *nor* to all the house of my father: for thy servant knew nothing of all this, less or more.

16And the king said, Thou shalt surely die, Ahimelech, thou, and all thy father's house.

17¶ And the king said unto the footmen that stood about him, Turn, and slay the priests of the LORD; because their hand also *is* with David, and because they knew when he fled, and did not show it to me. But the servants of the king would not put forth their hand to fall upon the priests of the LORD.

18And the king said to Doeg, Turn thou, and fall upon the priests. And Doeg the Edomite turned, and he fell upon the priests, and slew on that day fourscore and five persons that did wear a linen ephod.

19And Nob, the city of the priests, smote he with the edge of the sword, both men and women, children and sucklings, and oxen, and asses, and sheep, with the edge of the sword.

20¶ And one of the sons of Ahimelech the son of Ahitub, named Abiathar, escaped, and fled after David.

21And Abiathar showed David that Saul had slain the LORD's priests.

22And David said unto Abiathar, I knew *it* that day, when Doeg the Edomite *was* there, that he would surely tell Saul: I have occasioned *the death* of all the persons of thy father's house.

23Abide thou with me, fear not: for he that seeketh my life seeketh thy life: but with me thou *shalt be* in safeguard.

**23** THEN THEY told David, saying, Behold, the Philistines fight against Keilah, and they rob the threshingfloors.

2Therefore David inquired of the LORD, saying, Shall I go and smite these Philistines? And the LORD said unto David, Go, and smite the Philistines, and save Keilah.

3And David's men said unto him, Behold, we be afraid here in Judah: how much more then if we come to Keilah against the armies of the Philistines?

4Then David inquired of the LORD yet again. And the LORD answered him and said, Arise, go down to Keilah; for I will deliver the Philistines into thine hand.

5So David and his men went to Keilah, and fought with the Philistines, and brought away their cattle, and smote them with a great slaughter. So David saved the inhabitants of Keilah.

## Amplified

8That all of you have conspired against me? No one discloses to me when my son makes a league with the son of Jesse; none of you is sorry for me or discloses that my son has stirred up my servant against me, to lie in wait, as this day?

9Then Doeg the Edomite, who stood with Saul's servants, said, I saw the son of Jesse come to Nob, to Ahimelech, son of Ahitub.

10And [Ahimelech] inquired of the Lord for him, and gave him provisions and the sword of Goliath the Philistine.

11Then the king sent to call Ahimelech the priest, the son of Ahitub, and all his father's house, the priests who were at Nob; and they all came to the king.

12Saul said, Hear now, you son of Ahitub. He replied, Here I am, my lord.

13Saul said to him, Why have you conspired against me, you and the son of Jesse, giving him bread, and a sword, and inquiring of God for him, so he could rise against me, to lie in wait, as this day?

14Then Ahimelech answered the king, And who is so faithful among all your servants as David, who is the king's son-in-law, and is taken into your council, and honored in your house?

15Have I only today begun inquiring of God for him? No! Let not the king impute any wrong to his servant, nor to all the house of my father; for your servant has known nothing of all this, little or much.

16[Saul] said, You shall surely die, Ahimelech, you and all your father's house.

17And the king said to the guard that stood about him, Turn, and slay the Lord's priests; because their hand also is with David, and because they knew that he fled, and did not disclose it to me. But the servants of the king would not put forth their hand against the Lord's priests.

18The king said to Doeg, You turn and fall upon the priests. And Doeg the Edomite turned, and attacked the priests, and slew that day eighty-five persons who wore the priest's linen ephod.

19And Nob, the city of the priests, he smote with the sword; both men and women, children and sucklings, oxen and donkeys and sheep, he put to the sword.

20And one of the sons of Ahimelech the son of Ahitub, named Abiathar, escaped, and fled after David.

21And Abiathar told David that Saul had slain the Lord's priests.

22David said to Abiathar, I knew that day when Doeg the Edomite was there, that he would surely tell Saul. I have occasioned the death of all your father's house.

23Stay with me, fear not; for he who seeks my life seeks your life; but with me you shall be safeguarded.

**23** THEN THEY told David, Behold, the Philistines are fighting against Keilah, and are robbing the threshing floors.

2So David inquired of the Lord, Shall I go and attack these Philistines? And the Lord said to David, Go, smite the Philistines, and save Keilah.

3David's men said to him, Behold, we are afraid here in Judah. How much more then if we come to Keilah against the armies of the Philistines?

4Then David inquired of the Lord again. And the Lord answered him, Arise, go down to Keilah, for I will deliver the Philistines into your hand.

5So David and his men went to Keilah, and fought the Philistines with a great slaughter, and brought away their cattle. So David delivered the people of Keilah.

## New American Standard

8"For all of you have conspired against me so that there is no
one who discloses to me when my son makes *a covenant* with the
son of Jesse, and there is none of you who is sorry for me or
discloses to me that my son has stirred up my servant against me
to lie in ambush, as *it is* this day."
9Then Doeg the Edomite, who was standing by the servants
of Saul, answered and said, "I saw the son of Jesse coming to Nob,
to Ahimelech the son of Ahitub.
10"And he inquired of the LORD for him, gave him provisions,
and gave him the sword of Goliath the Philistine."
**11**¶ Then the king sent someone to summon Ahimelech the
priest, the son of Ahitub, and all his father's household, the priests
who were in Nob; and all of them came to the king.
12And Saul said, "Listen now, son of Ahitub." And he answered, "Here I am, my lord."
13Saul then said to him, "Why have you and the son of Jesse
conspired against me, in that you have given him bread and a
sword and have inquired of God for him, that he should rise up
against me by lying in ambush as *it is* this day?"
14Then Ahimelech answered the king and said, "And who
among all your servants is as faithful as David, even the king's
son-in-law, who is captain over your guard, and is honored in your
house?
15"Did I *just* begin to inquire of God for him today? Far be it
from me! Do not let the king impute anything to his servant *or* to
any of the household of my father, for your servant knows nothing
at all of this whole affair."
16But the king said, "You shall surely die, Ahimelech, you and
all your father's household!"
17And the king said to the guards who were attending him,
"Turn around and put the priests of the LORD to death, because
their hand also is with David and because they knew that he was
fleeing and did not reveal it to me." But the servants of the king
were not willing to put forth their hands to attack the priests of the
LORD.
18Then the king said to Doeg, "You turn around and attack the
priests." And Doeg the Edomite turned around and attacked the
priests, and he killed that day eighty-five men who wore the linen
ephod.
19And he struck Nob the city of the priests with the edge of the
sword, both men and women, children and infants; also oxen,
donkeys, and sheep, *he struck* with the edge of the sword.
**20**¶ But one son of Ahimelech the son of Ahitub, named Abiathar, escaped and fled after David.
21And Abiathar told David that Saul had killed the priests of the
LORD.
22Then David said to Abiathar, "I knew on that day, when Doeg
the Edomite was there, that he would surely tell Saul. I have
brought about *the death* of every person in your father's household.
23"Stay with me, do not be afraid, for he who seeks my life seeks
your life; for you are safe with me."

*David Delivers Keilah*

**23** THEN THEY told David, saying, "Behold, the Philistines
are fighting against Keilah, and are plundering the threshing floors."
2So David inquired of the LORD, saying, "Shall I go and attack
these Philistines?" And the LORD said to David, "Go and attack the
Philistines, and deliver Keilah."
3But David's men said to him, "Behold, we are afraid here in
Judah. How much more then if we go to Keilah against the ranks
of the Philistines?"
4Then David inquired of the LORD once more. And the LORD
answered him and said, "Arise, go down to Keilah, for I will give
the Philistines into your hand."
5So David and his men went to Keilah and fought with the
Philistines; and he led away their livestock and struck them with
a great slaughter. Thus David delivered the inhabitants of Keilah.

## New International

have all conspired against me? No one tells me when my son
makes a covenant with the son of Jesse. None of you is concerned
about me or tells me that my son has incited my servant to lie in
wait for me, as he does today."
9But Doeg the Edomite, who was standing with Saul's officials,
said, "I saw the son of Jesse come to Ahimelech son of Ahitub at
Nob. 10Ahimelech inquired of the LORD for him; he also gave him
provisions and the sword of Goliath the Philistine."
11Then the king sent for the priest Ahimelech son of Ahitub and
his father's whole family, who were the priests at Nob, and they
all came to the king. 12Saul said, "Listen now, son of Ahitub."
"Yes, my lord," he answered.
13Saul said to him, "Why have you conspired against me, you
and the son of Jesse, giving him bread and a sword and inquiring
of God for him, so that he has rebelled against me and lies in wait
for me, as he does today?"
14Ahimelech answered the king, "Who of all your servants is
as loyal as David, the king's son-in-law, captain of your bodyguard
and highly respected in your household? 15Was that day the first
time I inquired of God for him? Of course not! Let not the king
accuse your servant or any of his father's family, for your servant
knows nothing at all about this whole affair."
16But the king said, "You will surely die, Ahimelech, you and
your father's whole family."
17Then the king ordered the guards at his side: "Turn and kill
the priests of the LORD, because they too have sided with David.
They knew he was fleeing, yet they did not tell me."
But the king's officials were not willing to raise a hand to strike
the priests of the LORD.
18The king then ordered Doeg, "You turn and strike down the
priests." So Doeg the Edomite turned and struck them down. That
day he killed eighty-five men who wore the linen ephod. 19He also
put to the sword Nob, the town of the priests, with its men and
women, its children and infants, and its cattle, donkeys and sheep.
20But Abiathar, a son of Ahimelech son of Ahitub, escaped and
fled to join David. 21He told David that Saul had killed the priests
of the LORD. 22Then David said to Abiathar: "That day, when Doeg
the Edomite was there, I knew he would be sure to tell Saul. I am
responsible for the death of your father's whole family. 23Stay with
me; don't be afraid; the man who is seeking your life is seeking
mine also. You will be safe with me."

*David Saves Keilah*

**23** WHEN DAVID was told, "Look, the Philistines are fighting against Keilah and are looting the threshing floors,"
2he inquired of the LORD, saying, "Shall I go and attack these
Philistines?"
The LORD answered him, "Go, attack the Philistines and save
Keilah."
3But David's men said to him, "Here in Judah we are afraid.
How much more, then, if we go to Keilah against the Philistine
forces!"
4Once again David inquired of the LORD, and the LORD answered him, "Go down to Keilah, for I am going to give the
Philistines into your hand." 5So David and his men went to Keilah,
fought the Philistines and carried off their livestock. He inflicted
heavy losses on the Philistines and saved the people of Keilah.

## King James

6And it came to pass, when Abiathar the son of Ahimelech fled
to David to Keilah, *that* he came down *with* an ephod in his hand.
7¶ And it was told Saul that David was come to Keilah. And Saul
said, God hath delivered him into mine hand; for he is shut in, by
entering into a town that hath gates and bars.
8And Saul called all the people together to war, to go down to
Keilah, to besiege David and his men.
9¶ And David knew that Saul secretly practised mischief against
him; and he said to Abiathar the priest, Bring hither the ephod.
10Then said David, O LORD God of Israel, thy servant hath
certainly heard that Saul seeketh to come to Keilah, to destroy the
city for my sake.
11Will the men of Keilah deliver me up into his hand? will Saul
come down, as thy servant hath heard? O LORD God of Israel, I
beseech thee, tell thy servant. And the LORD said, He will come
down.
12Then said David, Will the men of Keilah deliver me and my
men into the hand of Saul? And the LORD said, They will deliver
*thee* up.
13¶ Then David and his men, *which were* about six hundred,
arose and departed out of Keilah, and went whithersoever they
could go. And it was told Saul that David was escaped from Keilah;
and he forbare to go forth.
14And David abode in the wilderness in strong holds, and
remained in a mountain in the wilderness of Ziph. And Saul
sought him every day, but God delivered him not into his hand.
15And David saw that Saul was come out to seek his life: and
David *was* in the wilderness of Ziph in a wood.
16¶ And Jonathan Saul's son arose, and went to David into the
wood, and strengthened his hand in God.
17And he said unto him, Fear not: for the hand of Saul my father
shall not find thee; and thou shalt be king over Israel, and I shall
be next unto thee; and that also Saul my father knoweth.
18And they two made a covenant before the LORD: and David
abode in the wood, and Jonathan went to his house.
19¶ Then came up the Ziphites to Saul to Gibeah, saying, Doth
not David hide himself with us in strong holds in the wood, in the
hill of Hachilah, which *is* on the south of Jeshimon?
20Now therefore, O king, come down according to all the desire
of thy soul to come down; and our part *shall be* to deliver him into
the king's hand.
21And Saul said, Blessed *be* ye of the LORD; for ye have compassion on me.
22Go, I pray you, prepare yet, and know and see his place
where his haunt is, *and* who hath seen him there: for it is told me
*that* he dealeth very subtly.
23See therefore, and take knowledge of all the lurking places
where he hideth himself, and come ye again to me with the certainty, and I will go with you: and it shall come to pass, if he be in the
land, that I will search him out throughout all the thousands of
Judah.
24And they arose, and went to Ziph before Saul: but David and
his men *were* in the wilderness of Maon, in the plain on the south
of Jeshimon.
25Saul also and his men went to seek *him*. And they told David:
wherefore he came down into a rock, and abode in the wilderness
of Maon. And when Saul heard *that*, he pursued after David in the
wilderness of Maon.
26And Saul went on this side of the mountain, and David and
his men on that side of the mountain: and David made haste to get
away for fear of Saul; for Saul and his men compassed David and
his men round about to take them.
27¶ But there came a messenger unto Saul, saying, Haste thee,
and come; for the Philistines have invaded the land.
28Wherefore Saul returned from pursuing after David, and
went against the Philistines: therefore they called that place Sela-
hammahlekoth.

## Amplified

6When Abiathar son of Ahimelech fled to David at Keilah, he
came with an ephod in his hand.
7Now it was told Saul that David had come to Keilah. Saul said,
God has delivered him into my hand; for he is shut in by going into
a town that has gates and bars.
8Saul summoned all the men for war, to go to Keilah to besiege
David and his men.
9David knew that Saul was plotting evil against him; and he
said to Abiathar the priest, Bring the ephod here.
10Then David said, O Lord, the God of Israel, Your servant has
surely heard that Saul intends to come and destroy the city of
Keilah on my account.
11Will the men of Keilah deliver me into his hand? Will Saul
come down, as Your servant has heard? O Lord God of Israel, I
beseech You, tell Your servant. And the Lord said, He will come
down.
12Then David asked, Will the men of Keilah deliver me and my
men into Saul's hand? The Lord said, They will deliver you up.
13Then David and his men, about 600, arose and left Keilah,
going wherever they could go. When Saul was told David had
escaped from Keilah, he gave up going there.
14David remained in the wilderness strongholds, in the hill
country of the Wilderness of Ziph. Saul sought him every day, but
God did not give him into his hand.
15David saw that Saul had come out to seek his life. David was
in the Wilderness of Ziph in the wood [at Horesh].
16And Jonathan Saul's son rose, and went into the wood, to
David [at Horesh], and strengthened his hand in God.
17He said to him, Fear not; the hand of Saul my father shall not
find you. You shall be king over Israel, and I shall be next to you;
Saul my father knows that too.
18And they two made a covenant before the Lord. And David
remained in the wood [at Horesh], and Jonathan went to his
house.
19Then the Ziphites came to Saul at Gibeah, saying, Does not
David hide himself with us in strongholds in the wood [at Horesh],
on the hill of Hachilah, which is south of Jeshimon?
20Now come down, O king, according to all your heart's desire
to come down, and our part shall be to deliver him into the king's
hand.
21And Saul said, The Lord bless you, for you have compassion
on me.
22Go, make yet more sure, and know and see where his haunt
is, and who has seen him there; for I am told he deals very craftily.
23See and take note of all his hiding places, and come back to
me with the certain facts, and I will go with you. If he is in the land,
I will search him out among all the thousands of Judah.
24So they arose, and went to Ziph ahead of Saul. Now David
and his men were in the wilderness of Maon, in the Arabah south
of Jeshimon.
25Saul and his men went to seek him. And David was told; so
he went down to the rock in the wilderness of Maon and stayed.
When Saul heard that, he pursued David in the wilderness of
Maon.
26And Saul went on one side of the mountain, and David and
his men on the other side of the mountain. And David made haste
to get away for fear of Saul; for Saul and his men were surrounding
[him] and his men to capture them.
27But a messenger came to Saul, saying, Make haste and come,
for the Philistines have made a raid on the land.
28So Saul returned from pursuing David, and went against the
Philistines. So they called that place the Rock of Escape.

## New American Standard

6¶ Now it came about, when Abiathar the son of Ahimelech
fled to David at Keilah, *that* he came down *with* an ephod in his
hand.
7When it was told Saul that David had come to Keilah, Saul
said, "God has delivered him into my hand, for he shut himself
in by entering a city with double gates and bars."
8So Saul summoned all the people for war, to go down to
Keilah to besiege David and his men.
9Now David knew that Saul was plotting evil against him; so
he said to Abiathar the priest, "Bring the ephod here."
10Then David said, "O LORD God of Israel, Thy servant has
heard for certain that Saul is seeking to come to Keilah to destroy
the city on my account.
11"Will the men of Keilah surrender me into his hand? Will Saul
come down just as Thy servant has heard? O LORD God of Israel,
I pray, tell Thy servant." And the LORD said, "He will come
down."
12Then David said, "Will the men of Keilah surrender me and
my men into the hand of Saul?" And the LORD said, "They will
surrender you."
13Then David and his men, about six hundred, arose and departed from Keilah, and they went wherever they could go. When
it was told Saul that David had escaped from Keilah, he gave up
the pursuit.
14And David stayed in the wilderness in the strongholds, and
remained in the hill country in the wilderness of Ziph. And Saul
sought him every day, but God did not deliver him into his hand.

*Saul Pursues David*

15¶ Now David became aware that Saul had come out to seek
his life while David was in the wilderness of Ziph at Horesh.
16And Jonathan, Saul's son, arose and went to David at Horesh,
and [a]encouraged him in God.
17Thus he said to him, "Do not be afraid, because the hand of
Saul my father shall not find you, and you will be king over Israel
and I will be next to you; and Saul my father knows that also."
18So the two of them made a covenant before the LORD; and
David stayed at Horesh while Jonathan went to his house.
19¶ Then Ziphites came up to Saul at Gibeah, saying, "Is David
not hiding with us in the strongholds at Horesh, on the hill of
Hachilah, which is on the south of [b]Jeshimon?
20"Now then, O king, come down according to all the desire of
your soul to do so; and our part *shall be* to surrender him into the
king's hand."
21And Saul said, "May you be blessed of the LORD; for you have
had compassion on me.
22"Go now, make more sure, and investigate and see his place
where his haunt is, *and* who has seen him there; for I am told that
he is very cunning.
23"So look, and learn about all the hiding places where he hides
himself, and return to me with certainty, and I will go with you;
and it shall come about if he is in the land that I will search him
out among all the thousands of Judah."
24¶ Then they arose and went to Ziph before Saul. Now David
and his men were in the wilderness of Maon, in the Arabah to the
south of Jeshimon.
25When Saul and his men went to seek *him*, they told David,
and he came down to the rock and stayed in the wilderness of
Maon. And when Saul heard *it*, he pursued David in the wilderness of Maon.
26And Saul went on one side of the mountain, and David and
his men on the other side of the mountain; and David was hurrying to get away from Saul, for Saul and his men were surrounding
David and his men to seize them.
27But a messenger came to Saul, saying, "Hurry and come, for
the Philistines have made a raid on the land."
28So Saul returned from pursuing David, and went to meet the
Philistines; therefore they called that place the Rock of Escape.

NAS [a] Lit., *strengthened his hand* [b] Or, *the desert*

## New International

6(Now Abiathar son of Ahimelech had brought the ephod down
with him when he fled to David at Keilah.)

*Saul Pursues David*

7Saul was told that David had gone to Keilah, and he said, "God
has handed him over to me, for David has imprisoned himself by
entering a town with gates and bars." 8And Saul called up all his
forces for battle, to go down to Keilah to besiege David and his
men.
9When David learned that Saul was plotting against him, he
said to Abiathar the priest, "Bring the ephod." 10David said, "O
LORD, God of Israel, your servant has heard definitely that Saul
plans to come to Keilah and destroy the town on account of me.
11Will the citizens of Keilah surrender me to him? Will Saul come
down, as your servant has heard? O LORD, God of Israel, tell your
servant."
And the LORD said, "He will."
12Again David asked, "Will the citizens of Keilah surrender me
and my men to Saul?"
And the LORD said, "They will."
13So David and his men, about six hundred in number, left
Keilah and kept moving from place to place. When Saul was told
that David had escaped from Keilah, he did not go there.
14David stayed in the desert strongholds and in the hills of the
Desert of Ziph. Day after day Saul searched for him, but God did
not give David into his hands.
15While David was at Horesh in the Desert of Ziph, he learned
that Saul had come out to take his life. 16And Saul's son Jonathan
went to David at Horesh and helped him find strength in God.
17"Don't be afraid," he said. "My father Saul will not lay a hand
on you. You will be king over Israel, and I will be second to you.
Even my father Saul knows this." 18The two of them made a
covenant before the LORD. Then Jonathan went home, but David
remained at Horesh.
19The Ziphites went up to Saul at Gibeah and said, "Is not
David hiding among us in the strongholds at Horesh, on the hill
of Hakilah, south of Jeshimon? 20Now, O king, come down whenever it pleases you to do so, and we will be responsible for handing
him over to the king."
21Saul replied, "The LORD bless you for your concern for me.
22Go and make further preparation. Find out where David usually
goes and who has seen him there. They tell me he is very crafty.
23Find out about all the hiding places he uses and come back to me
with definite information.[c] Then I will go with you; if he is in the
area, I will track him down among all the clans of Judah."
24So they set out and went to Ziph ahead of Saul. Now David
and his men were in the Desert of Maon, in the Arabah south of
Jeshimon. 25Saul and his men began the search, and when David
was told about it, he went down to the rock and stayed in the
Desert of Maon. When Saul heard this, he went into the Desert of
Maon in pursuit of David.
26Saul was going along one side of the mountain, and David
and his men were on the other side, hurrying to get away from
Saul. As Saul and his forces were closing in on David and his men
to capture them, 27a messenger came to Saul, saying, "Come
quickly! The Philistines are raiding the land." 28Then Saul broke
off his pursuit of David and went to meet the Philistines. That is

NIV [c] 23 Or *me at Nacon*

## King James

29¶ And David went up from thence, and dwelt in strong holds at En-gedi.

**24** AND IT came to pass, when Saul was returned from following the Philistines, that it was told him, saying, Behold, David *is* in the wilderness of En-gedi.

2Then Saul took three thousand chosen men out of all Israel, and went to seek David and his men upon the rocks of the wild goats.

3And he came to the sheepcotes by the way, where *was* a cave; and Saul went in to cover his feet: and David and his men remained in the sides of the cave.

4And the men of David said unto him, Behold the day of which the LORD said unto thee, Behold, I will deliver thine enemy into thine hand, that thou mayest do to him as it shall seem good unto thee. Then David arose, and cut off the skirt of Saul's robe privily.

5And it came to pass afterward, that David's heart smote him, because he had cut off Saul's skirt.

6And he said unto his men, The LORD forbid that I should do this thing unto my master, the LORD's anointed, to stretch forth mine hand against him, seeing he *is* the anointed of the LORD.

7So David stayed his servants with these words, and suffered them not to rise against Saul. But Saul rose up out of the cave, and went on *his* way.

8David also arose afterward, and went out of the cave, and cried after Saul, saying, My lord the king. And when Saul looked behind him, David stooped with his face to the earth, and bowed himself.

9¶ And David said to Saul, Wherefore hearest thou men's words, saying, Behold, David seeketh thy hurt?

10Behold, this day thine eyes have seen how that the LORD had delivered thee today into mine hand in the cave: and *some* bade *me* kill thee: but *mine eye* spared thee; and I said, I will not put forth mine hand against my lord; for he *is* the LORD's anointed.

11Moreover, my father, see, yea, see the skirt of thy robe in my hand: for in that I cut off the skirt of thy robe, and killed thee not, know thou and see that *there is* neither evil nor transgression in mine hand, and I have not sinned against thee; yet thou huntest my soul to take it.

12The LORD judge between me and thee, and the LORD avenge me of thee: but mine hand shall not be upon thee.

13As saith the proverb of the ancients, Wickedness proceedeth from the wicked: but mine hand shall not be upon thee.

14After whom is the king of Israel come out? after whom dost thou pursue? after a dead dog, after a flea.

15The LORD therefore be judge, and judge between me and thee, and see, and plead my cause, and deliver me out of thine hand.

16¶ And it came to pass, when David had made an end of speaking these words unto Saul, that Saul said, *Is* this thy voice, my son David? And Saul lifted up his voice, and wept.

17And he said to David, Thou *art* more righteous than I: for thou hast rewarded me good, whereas I have rewarded thee evil.

18And thou hast shown this day how that thou hast dealt well with me: forasmuch as when the LORD had delivered me into thine hand, thou killedst me not.

19For if a man find his enemy, will he let him go well away? wherefore the LORD reward thee good for that thou hast done unto me this day.

20And now, behold, I know well that thou shalt surely be king, and that the kingdom of Israel shall be established in thine hand.

21Swear now therefore unto me by the LORD, that thou wilt not cut off my seed after me, and that thou wilt not destroy my name out of my father's house.

22And David sware unto Saul. And Saul went home; but David and his men gat them up unto the hold.

## Amplified

29David went up from there, and dwelt in the strongholds of Engedi.

**24** WHEN SAUL returned from following the Philistines, he was told, Behold, David is in the wilderness of Engedi.

2Then Saul took 3,000 chosen men out of all Israel, and went to seek David and his men among the Rocks of the Wild Goats.

3He came to the sheepfolds on the way, where there was a cave; and Saul went in to relieve himself. Now David and his men were sitting in the cave's innermost recesses.

4David's men said to him, Behold the day of which the Lord said to you, Lo, I will deliver your enemy into your hand, and you shall do to him as seems good to you. Then David arose [in the darkness] and stealthily cut off the skirt of Saul's robe.

5Afterward, David's heart smote him, because he had cut off Saul's skirt.

6He said to his men, The Lord forbid that I should do this to my master, the Lord's anointed, to put my hand out against him, when he is the anointed of the Lord.

7So David checked his men with these words, and did not let them rise against Saul. But Saul rose up and left the cave, and went on his way.

8David also arose afterward, and went out of the cave, and called after Saul, saying, My lord the king! And when Saul looked behind him, David bowed with his face to the earth, and did obeisance.

9And David said to Saul, Why do you listen to the words of men who say, David seeks to do you harm?

10Lo, your eyes have seen how the Lord gave you today into my hand in the cave. Some told me to kill you, but I spared you. I said, I will not put forth my hand against my lord; for he is the Lord's anointed.

11See, my father, see the skirt of your robe in my hand. Since I cut off the skirt of your robe and did not kill you, you know and see that there is no evil or treason in my hands. I have not sinned against you, yet you hunt my life to take it.

12The Lord judge between me and you, and the Lord avenge me upon you; but my hand shall not be upon you.

13As the proverb of the ancients says, Out of the wicked comes forth wickedness; but my hand shall not be against you.

14After whom is the king of Israel come out? After whom do you pursue? After a dead dog! After a flea!

15May the Lord be judge, and judge between me and you, and see, plead my cause, and deliver me out of your hand. [Ps. 142.]

16When David had said this to Saul, Saul said, Is this your voice, my son David? And Saul lifted up his voice and wept.

17He said to David, You are more upright in God's eyes than I, for you have repaid me good, and I have rewarded you evil.

18You have declared today how you have dealt well with me, for when the Lord gave me into your hand you did not kill me.

19For if a man finds his enemy, will he let him go away unharmed? Therefore may the Lord reward you with good for what you have done for me this day.

20And now, lo, I well know that you shall surely be king, and that the kingdom of Israel shall be established in your hand.

21Swear now therefore to me by the Lord, that you will not cut off my descendants after me, and that you will not destroy my name out of my father's house.

22David gave Saul his oath, and Saul went home; but David and his men got up to the stronghold.

## New American Standard

29And David went up from there and stayed in the strongholds of Engedi.

*David Spares Saul's Life*

**24** NOW IT came about when Saul returned from pursuing the Philistines, he was told, saying, "Behold, David is in the wilderness of Engedi."

2Then Saul took three thousand chosen men from all Israel, and went to seek David and his men in front of the Rocks of the Wild Goats.

3And he came to the sheepfolds on the way, where there *was* a cave; and Saul went in to relieve himself. Now David and his men were sitting in the inner recesses of the cave.

4And the men of David said to him, "Behold, *this is* the day of which the LORD said to you, 'Behold; I am about to give your enemy into your hand, and you shall do to him as it seems good to you.'" Then David arose and cut off the edge of Saul's robe secretly.

5And it came about afterward that David's conscience bothered him because he had cut off the edge of Saul's *robe*.

6So he said to his men, "Far be it from me because of the LORD that I should do this thing to my lord, the LORD's anointed, to stretch out my hand against him, since he is the LORD's anointed."

7And David persuaded his men with *these* words and did not allow them to rise up against Saul. And Saul arose, left the cave, and went on *his* way.

8¶ Now afterward David arose and went out of the cave and called after Saul, saying, "My lord the king!" And when Saul looked behind him, David bowed with his face to the ground and prostrated himself.

9And David said to Saul, "Why do you listen to the words of men, saying, 'Behold, David seeks to harm you'?

10"Behold, this day your eyes have seen that the LORD had given you today into my hand in the cave, and some said to kill you, but *my eye* had pity on you; and I said, 'I will not stretch out my hand against my lord, for he is the LORD's anointed.'

11"Now, my father, see! Indeed, see the edge of your robe in my hand! For in that I cut off the edge of your robe and did not kill you, know and perceive that there is no evil or rebellion in my hands, and I have not sinned against you, though you are lying in wait for my life to take it.

12"May the LORD judge between you and me, and may the LORD avenge me on you; but my hand shall not be against you.

13"As the proverb of the ancients says, 'Out of the wicked comes forth wickedness'; but my hand shall not be against you.

14"After whom has the king of Israel come out? Whom are you pursuing? A dead dog, a single flea?

15"The LORD therefore be judge and decide between you and me; and may He see and plead my cause, and deliver me from your hand."

16¶ Now it came about when David had finished speaking these words to Saul, that Saul said, "Is this your voice, my son David?" Then Saul lifted up his voice and wept.

17And he said to David, "You are more righteous than I; for you have dealt well with me, while I have dealt wickedly with you.

18"And you have declared today that you have done good to me, that the LORD delivered me into your hand and *yet* you did not kill me.

19"For if a man finds his enemy, will he let him go away safely? May the LORD therefore reward you with good in return for what you have done to me this day.

20"And now, behold, I know that you shall surely be king, and that the kingdom of Israel shall be established in your hand.

21"So now swear to me by the LORD that you will not cut off my descendants after me, and that you will not destroy my name from my father's household."

22And David swore to Saul. And Saul went to his home, but David and his men went up to the stronghold.

## New International

why they call this place Sela Hammahlekoth.[a] 29And David went
up from there and lived in the strongholds of En Gedi.

*David Spares Saul's Life*

**24** AFTER SAUL returned from pursuing the Philistines, he
was told, "David is in the Desert of En Gedi." 2So Saul
took three thousand chosen men from all Israel and set out to look
for David and his men near the Crags of the Wild Goats.
3He came to the sheep pens along the way; a cave was there,
and Saul went in to relieve himself. David and his men were far
back in the cave. 4The men said, "This is the day the LORD spoke
of when he said[b] to you, 'I will give your enemy into your hands
for you to deal with as you wish.'" Then David crept up unnoticed
and cut off a corner of Saul's robe.
5Afterward, David was conscience-stricken for having cut off a
corner of his robe. 6He said to his men, "The LORD forbid that I
should do such a thing to my master, the LORD's anointed, or lift
my hand against him; for he is the anointed of the LORD." 7With
these words David rebuked his men and did not allow them to
attack Saul. And Saul left the cave and went his way.
8Then David went out of the cave and called out to Saul, "My
lord the king!" When Saul looked behind him, David bowed down
and prostrated himself with his face to the ground. 9He said to
Saul, "Why do you listen when men say, 'David is bent on harming you'? 10This day you have seen with your own eyes how the
LORD delivered you into my hands in the cave. Some urged me to
kill you, but I spared you; I said, 'I will not lift my hand against
my master, because he is the LORD's anointed.' 11See, my father,
look at this piece of your robe in my hand! I cut off the corner of
your robe but did not kill you. Now understand and recognize that
I am not guilty of wrongdoing or rebellion. I have not wronged
you, but you are hunting me down to take my life. 12May the LORD
judge between you and me. And may the LORD avenge the wrongs
you have done to me, but my hand will not touch you. 13As the
old saying goes, 'From evildoers come evil deeds,' so my hand will
not touch you.
14"Against whom has the king of Israel come out? Whom are
you pursuing? A dead dog? A flea? 15May the LORD be our judge
and decide between us. May he consider my cause and uphold it;
may he vindicate me by delivering me from your hand."
16When David finished saying this, Saul asked, "Is that your
voice, David my son?" And he wept aloud. 17"You are more
righteous than I," he said. "You have treated me well, but I have
treated you badly. 18You have just now told me of the good you
did to me; the LORD delivered me into your hands, but you did not
kill me. 19When a man finds his enemy, does he let him get away
unharmed? May the LORD reward you well for the way you treated
me today. 20I know that you will surely be king and that the
kingdom of Israel will be established in your hands. 21Now swear
to me by the LORD that you will not cut off my descendants or wipe
out my name from my father's family."
22So David gave his oath to Saul. Then Saul returned home, but
David and his men went up to the stronghold.

NIV [a] *28 Sela Hammahlekoth* means *rock of parting.* [b] *4* Or *"Today the LORD is saying*

## King James

**25** AND SAMUEL died; and all the Israelites were gathered together, and lamented him, and buried him in his house at Ramah. And David arose, and went down to the wilderness of Paran.

2And *there was* a man in Maon, whose possessions *were* in Carmel; and the man *was* very great, and he had three thousand sheep, and a thousand goats: and he was shearing his sheep in Carmel.

3Now the name of the man *was* Nabal; and the name of his wife Abigail: and *she was* a woman of good understanding, and of a beautiful countenance: but the man *was* churlish and evil in his doings; and he *was* of the house of Caleb.

4¶ And David heard in the wilderness that Nabal did shear his sheep.

5And David sent out ten young men, and David said unto the young men, Get you up to Carmel, and go to Nabal, and greet him in my name:

6And thus shall ye say to him that liveth *in prosperity,* Peace *be* both to thee, and peace *be* to thine house, and peace *be* unto all that thou hast.

7And now I have heard that thou hast shearers: now thy shepherds which were with us, we hurt them not, neither was there aught missing unto them, all the while they were in Carmel.

8Ask thy young men, and they will show thee. Wherefore let the young men find favour in thine eyes: for we come in a good day: give, I pray thee, whatsoever cometh to thine hand unto thy servants, and to thy son David.

9And when David's young men came, they spake to Nabal according to all those words in the name of David, and ceased.

10¶ And Nabal answered David's servants, and said, Who *is* David? and who *is* the son of Jesse? there be many servants now a days that break away every man from his master.

11Shall I then take my bread, and my water, and my flesh that I have killed for my shearers, and give *it* unto men, whom I know not whence they *be?*

12So David's young men turned their way, and went again, and came and told him all those sayings.

13And David said unto his men, Gird ye on every man his sword. And they girded on every man his sword; and David also girded on his sword: and there went up after David about four hundred men; and two hundred abode by the stuff.

14¶ But one of the young men told Abigail, Nabal's wife, saying, Behold, David sent messengers out of the wilderness to salute our master; and he railed on them.

15But the men *were* very good unto us, and we were not hurt, neither missed we any thing, as long as we were conversant with them, when we were in the fields:

16They were a wall unto us both by night and day, all the while we were with them keeping the sheep.

17Now therefore know and consider what thou wilt do; for evil is determined against our master, and against all his household: for he *is such* a son of Belial, that *a man* cannot speak to him.

18¶ Then Abigail made haste, and took two hundred loaves, and two bottles of wine, and five sheep ready dressed, and five measures of parched *corn,* and an hundred clusters of raisins, and two hundred cakes of figs, and laid *them* on asses.

19And she said unto her servants, Go on before me; behold, I come after you. But she told not her husband Nabal.

20And it was *so, as* she rode on the ass, that she came down by the covert of the hill, and, behold, David and his men came down against her; and she met them.

21Now David had said, Surely in vain have I kept all that this *fellow* hath in the wilderness, so that nothing was missed of all that *pertained* unto him: and he hath requited me evil for good.

## Amplified

**25** NOW SAMUEL died; and all the Israelites assembled and mourned for him, and buried him at his house in Ramah. David arose, and went to the wilderness of Paran.

2A very rich man was in Maon, whose possessions *and* business were in Carmel. He had 3,000 sheep and 1,000 goats, and he was shearing his sheep in Carmel.

3The man's name was Nabal, and his wife's name was Abigail; she was a woman of good understanding, and beautiful. But the man was rough and evil in his doings; he was a Calebite.

4David heard in the wilderness that Nabal was shearing his sheep.

5And David sent out ten young men, and said to [them], Go up to Carmel to Nabal, and greet him in my name;

6And salute him thus: Peace be to you and to your house and to all that you have.

7I have heard that you have shearers. Now your shepherds have been with us, and we did them no harm, and they missed nothing, all the time they were in Carmel.

8Ask your young men, and they will tell you. Therefore let my young men find favor in your sight, for we come at an opportune time. Pray, give whatever you have at hand to your servants and to your son David.

9And when David's young men came, they said all this to Nabal in the name of David, and then paused.

10And Nabal answered David's servants, and said, Who is David? Who is the son of Jesse? There are many servants nowadays each breaking away from his master.

11Shall I then take my bread, and my water, and my meat that I have killed for my shearers, and give it to men, when I do not know where they belong?

12So David's young men turned away, and came and told him all that was said.

13And David said to his men, Every man gird on his sword. And they did so, and David also girded on his sword; and there went up after David about 400 men, and 200 remained with the baggage.

14But one of Nabal's young men told Abigail, Nabal's wife, Behold, David sent messengers out of the wilderness to salute our master; and he railed at them.

15But David's men were very good to us, and we were not harmed, nor did we miss anything as long as we went with them, when we were in the fields;

16They were a wall to us night and day, all the time we were with them keeping the sheep.

17So know this and consider what you will do; for evil is determined against our master and all his house; for he is such a wicked man one cannot speak to him.

18Then Abigail made haste, and took 200 loaves, two skins of wine, five sheep ready dressed, five measures of parched grain, 100 clusters of raisins, and 200 cakes of figs, and laid them on donkeys.

19And she said to her servants, Go on before me; behold, I come after you. But she did not tell her husband Nabal.

20As she rode on her donkey she came down hidden by the mountain, and behold, David and his men came down opposite her, and she met them.

21Now David had said, Surely in vain have I protected all that this fellow has in the wilderness, so that nothing was missed of all that belonged to him; and he has repaid me evil for good.

## New American Standard

*Samuel's Death*

**25** THEN SAMUEL died; and all Israel gathered together and mourned for him, and buried him at his house in Ramah. And David arose and went down to the wilderness of Paran.

*Nabal and Abigail*

2¶ Now *there was* a man in Maon whose business was in Carmel; and the man was very rich, and he had three thousand sheep and a thousand goats. And it came about while he was shearing his sheep in Carmel

3(now the man's name was Nabal, and his wife's name was Abigail. And the woman was intelligent and beautiful in appearance, but the man was harsh and evil in *his* dealings, and he was a Calebite),

4that David heard in the wilderness that Nabal was shearing his sheep.

5So David sent ten young men, and David said to the young men, "Go up to Carmel, visit Nabal and greet him in my name;

6and thus you shall say, 'Have a long life, peace be to you, and peace be to your house, and peace be to all that you have.

7'And now I have heard that you have shearers; now your shepherds have been with us and we have not insulted them, nor have they missed anything all the days they were in Carmel.

8'Ask your young men and they will tell you. Therefore let *my* young men find favor in your eyes, for we have come on a festive day. Please give whatever you find at hand to your servants and to your son David.' "

9¶ When David's young men came, they spoke to Nabal according to all these words in David's name; then they waited.

10But Nabal answered David's servants, and said, "Who is David? And who is the son of Jesse? There are many servants today who are each breaking away from his master.

11"Shall I then take my bread and my water and my meat that I have slaughtered for my shearers, and give it to men whose origin I do not know?"

12So David's young men retraced their way and went back; and they came and told him according to all these words.

13And David said to his men, "Each *of you* gird on his sword." So each man girded on his sword. And David also girded on his sword, and about four hundred men went up behind David while two hundred stayed with the baggage.

14¶ But one of the young men told Abigail, Nabal's wife, saying, "Behold, David sent messengers from the wilderness to greet our master, and he scorned them.

15"Yet the men were very good to us, and we were not insulted, nor did we miss anything as long as we went about with them, while we were in the fields.

16"They were a wall to us both by night and by day, all the time we were with them tending the sheep.

17"Now therefore, know and consider what you should do, for evil is plotted against our master and against all his household; and he is such a worthless man that no one can speak to him."

*Abigail Intercedes*

18¶ Then Abigail hurried and took two hundred *loaves* of bread and two jugs of wine and five sheep already prepared and five measures of roasted grain and a hundred clusters of raisins and two hundred cakes of figs, and loaded *them* on donkeys.

19And she said to her young men, "Go on before me; behold, I am coming after you." But she did not tell her husband Nabal.

20And it came about as she was riding on her donkey and coming down by the hidden part of the mountain, that behold, David and his men were coming down toward her; so she met them.

21Now David had said, "Surely in vain I have guarded all that this *man* has in the wilderness, so that nothing was missed of all that belonged to him; and he has returned me evil for good.

## New International

*David, Nabal and Abigail*

**25** NOW SAMUEL died, and all Israel assembled and
mourned for him; and they buried him at his home in
Ramah.

Then David moved down into the Desert of Maon.[a] 2A certain
man in Maon, who had property there at Carmel, was very
wealthy. He had a thousand goats and three thousand sheep,
which he was shearing in Carmel. 3His name was Nabal and his
wife's name was Abigail. She was an intelligent and beautiful
woman, but her husband, a Calebite, was surly and mean in his
dealings.

4While David was in the desert, he heard that Nabal was shearing sheep. 5So he sent ten young men and said to them, "Go up
to Nabal at Carmel and greet him in my name. 6Say to him: 'Long
life to you! Good health to you and your household! And good
health to all that is yours!

7" 'Now I hear that it is sheep-shearing time. When your shepherds were with us, we did not mistreat them, and the whole time
they were at Carmel nothing of theirs was missing. 8Ask your own
servants and they will tell you. Therefore be favorable toward my
young men, since we come at a festive time. Please give your
servants and your son David whatever you can find for them.' "

9When David's men arrived, they gave Nabal this message in
David's name. Then they waited.

10Nabal answered David's servants, "Who is this David? Who
is this son of Jesse? Many servants are breaking away from their
masters these days. 11Why should I take my bread and water, and
the meat I have slaughtered for my shearers, and give it to men
coming from who knows where?"

12David's men turned around and went back. When they arrived, they reported every word. 13David said to his men, "Put on
your swords!" So they put on their swords, and David put on his.
About four hundred men went up with David, while two hundred
stayed with the supplies.

14One of the servants told Nabal's wife Abigail: "David sent
messengers from the desert to give our master his greetings, but
he hurled insults at them. 15Yet these men were very good to us.
They did not mistreat us, and the whole time we were out in the
fields near them nothing was missing. 16Night and day they were
a wall around us all the time we were herding our sheep near
them. 17Now think it over and see what you can do, because
disaster is hanging over our master and his whole household. He
is such a wicked man that no one can talk to him."

18Abigail lost no time. She took two hundred loaves of bread,
two skins of wine, five dressed sheep, five seahs[b] of roasted grain,
a hundred cakes of raisins and two hundred cakes of pressed figs,
and loaded them on donkeys. 19Then she told her servants, "Go
on ahead; I'll follow you." But she did not tell her husband Nabal.

20As she came riding her donkey into a mountain ravine, there
were David and his men descending toward her, and she met
them. 21David had just said, "It's been useless—all my watching
over this fellow's property in the desert so that nothing of his was
missing. He has paid me back evil for good. 22May God deal with

**NIV** [a] *1* Some Septuagint manuscripts; Hebrew *Paran* [b] *18* That is, probably about a bushel (about 37 liters)

## King James

22 So and more also do God unto the enemies of David, if I leave
of all that *pertain* to him by the morning light any that pisseth
against the wall.
23 And when Abigail saw David, she hasted, and lighted off the
ass, and fell before David on her face, and bowed herself to the
ground,
24 And fell at his feet, and said, Upon me, my lord, *upon* me *let*
*this* iniquity *be:* and let thine handmaid, I pray thee, speak in thine
audience, and hear the words of thine handmaid.
25 Let not my lord, I pray thee, regard this man of Belial, *even*
Nabal: for as his name *is,* so *is* he; Nabal *is* his name, and folly *is*
with him: but I thine handmaid saw not the young men of my lord,
whom thou didst send.
26 Now therefore, my lord, *as* the LORD liveth, and *as* thy soul
liveth, seeing the LORD hath withholden thee from coming to *shed*
blood, and from avenging thyself with thine own hand, now let
thine enemies, and they that seek evil to my lord, be as Nabal.
27 And now this blessing which thine handmaid hath brought
unto my lord, let it even be given unto the young men that follow
my lord.
28 I pray thee, forgive the trespass of thine handmaid: for the
LORD will certainly make my lord a sure house; because my lord
fighteth the battles of the LORD, and evil hath not been found in
thee *all* thy days.
29 Yet a man is risen to pursue thee, and to seek thy soul: but
the soul of my lord shall be bound in the bundle of life with the
LORD thy God; and the souls of thine enemies, them shall he sling
out, *as out* of the middle of a sling.
30 And it shall come to pass, when the LORD shall have done to
my lord according to all the good that he hath spoken concerning
thee, and shall have appointed thee ruler over Israel;
31 That this shall be no grief unto thee, nor offence of heart unto
my lord, either that thou hast shed blood causeless, or that my lord
hath avenged himself: but when the LORD shall have dealt well
with my lord, then remember thine handmaid.
32 ¶ And David said to Abigail, Blessed *be* the LORD God of Israel,
which sent thee this day to meet me:
33 And blessed *be* thy advice, and blessed *be* thou, which hast
kept me this day from coming to *shed* blood, and from avenging
myself with mine own hand.
34 For in very deed, *as* the LORD God of Israel liveth, which hath
kept me back from hurting thee, except thou hadst hasted and
come to meet me, surely there had not been left unto Nabal by the
morning light any that pisseth against the wall.
35 So David received of her hand *that* which she had brought
him, and said unto her, Go up in peace to thine house; see, I have
hearkened to thy voice, and have accepted thy person.
36 ¶ And Abigail came to Nabal; and, behold, he held a feast in
his house, like the feast of a king; and Nabal's heart *was* merry
within him, for he *was* very drunken: wherefore she told him
nothing, less or more, until the morning light.
37 But it came to pass in the morning, when the wine was gone
out of Nabal, and his wife had told him these things, that his heart
died within him, and he became *as* a stone.
38 And it came to pass about ten days *after,* that the LORD smote
Nabal, that he died.

## Amplified

22 God do so and more also to David, [a]if I leave of all who belong
to him one male alive by morning.
23 When Abigail saw David, she hasted and lighted off the donkey, and fell before David on her face, and did obeisance.
24 Kneeling at his feet she said, Upon me alone let this guilt be,
my lord; and let your handmaid, I pray, speak in your presence,
and hear the words of your handmaid.
25 Let not my lord, I pray, regard this foolish *and* wicked fellow
Nabal, for as his name is, so is he; Nabal [foolish, wicked] is his
name, and folly is with him. But I your handmaid did not see my
lord's young men whom you sent.
26 So now, my lord, as the Lord lives, and as your soul lives,
seeing that the Lord has prevented you from blood guiltiness, and
from avenging yourself with your own hand, now let your enemies and those who seek to do evil to my lord be as Nabal.
27 And now this gift which your handmaid has brought my lord,
let it be given to the young men who follow my lord.
28 Forgive, I pray you, the trespass of your handmaid; for the
Lord will certainly make my lord a sure house; because my lord is
fighting the Lord's battles, and evil has not been found in you all
your days.
29 Though man be risen up to pursue you and to seek your life,
yet the life of my lord shall be bound in the living bundle with the
Lord your God. And the lives of your enemies, them shall He sling
out, as out of the center of a sling.
30 And when the Lord has done to my lord according to all the
good that He has promised concerning you, and has made you
ruler over Israel,
31 This shall be no staggering grief to you, or cause for pangs of
conscience to my lord, either that you have shed blood without
cause, or that my lord has avenged himself. And when the Lord
has dealt well with my lord, then [ [b]earnestly] remember your
handmaid.
32 And David said to Abigail, Blessed be the Lord God of Israel,
Who sent you this day to meet me.
33 And blessed be your discretion *and* advice, and blessed be
you, who have kept me today from blood guiltiness and from
avenging myself with my own hand.
34 For as the Lord God of Israel lives, Who has prevented me
from hurting you, if you had not hurried and come to meet me,
surely by morning there would not have been left so much as one
male to Nabal.
35 So David accepted what she had brought him, and said to her,
Go up in peace to your house; see, I have hearkened to your voice
and have granted your petition.
36 And Abigail came to Nabal; and behold, he was holding a
feast in his house, like the feast of a king; and *his* heart was merry,
for he was very drunk; so she told him nothing at all until the
morning light.
37 But in the morning, when the wine was gone out of Nabal,
and his wife told him these things, his heart died within him, and
he became [paralyzed, helpless as] a stone.
38 And about ten days after that, the Lord smote Nabal and he
died.

**AMP** [a] The Septuagint (Greek) Version so reads. The Hebrew reads *David's enemies.* [b] Whenever God's inspired Word says "(earnestly) remember," one is certain to miss something if he does not stop, look, and really listen to what the Holy Spirit is wanting to tell him—or her. "(Earnestly) remember" Abigail, the woman whom God has specifically held up as a pattern of right behavior in an unfortunate marriage. Here are a dozen vital questions answered through Abigail's example. She could not have known that thousands of years later people in similar circumstances would become "more than conquerors" because of her, but God knew. Study her until you know her God-given secrets of success; then pass them on to the people who are letting an unfortunate marriage wreck them, rather than sanctify them for service. In *Through the Bible Day by Day,* F. B. Meyer said, "Never let the evil disposition of one mate hinder the devotion and grace of the other. Never let the difficulties of your home lead you to abdicate your throne. Do not step down to the level of your circumstances, but lift them to your own high calling in Christ. (Be not conformed . . . be transformed. Rom. 12:1, 2)."

## New American Standard

22"May God do so to the enemies of David, and more also, if
by morning I leave *as much as* one male of any who belong to him."
**23**¶ When Abigail saw David, she hurried and dismounted from
her donkey, and fell on her face before David, and bowed herself
to the ground.
24And she fell at his feet and said, "On me alone, my lord, be
the blame. And please let your maidservant speak to you, and
listen to the words of your maidservant.
25"Please do not let my lord pay attention to this worthless
man, Nabal, for as his name is, so is he. Nabal is his name and folly
is with him; but I your maidservant did not see the young men of
my lord whom you sent.
26"Now therefore, my lord, as the LORD lives, and as your soul
lives, since the LORD has restrained you from shedding blood, and
from avenging yourself by your own hand, now then let your
enemies, and those who seek evil against my lord, be as Nabal.
27"And now let this gift which your maidservant has brought
to my lord be given to the young men who accompany my lord.
28"Please forgive the transgression of your maidservant; for the
LORD will certainly make for my lord an enduring house, because
my lord is fighting the battles of the LORD, and evil shall not be
found in you all your days.
29"And should anyone rise up to pursue you and to seek your
life, then the life of my lord shall be bound in the bundle of the
living with the LORD your God; but the lives of your enemies He
will sling out as from the hollow of a sling.
30"And it shall come about when the LORD shall do for my lord
according to all the good that He has spoken concerning you, and
shall appoint you ruler over Israel,
31that this will not cause grief or a troubled heart to my lord,
both by having shed blood without cause and by my lord having
avenged himself. When the LORD shall deal well with my lord,
then remember your maidservant."
**32**¶ Then David said to Abigail, "Blessed be the LORD God of
Israel, who sent you this day to meet me,
33and blessed be your discernment, and blessed be you, who
have kept me this day from bloodshed, and from avenging myself
by my own hand.
34"Nevertheless, as the LORD God of Israel lives, who has restrained me from harming you, unless you had come quickly to
meet me, surely there would not have been left to Nabal until the
morning light *as much as* one male."
35So David received from her hand what she had brought him,
and he said to her, "Go up to your house in peace. See, I have
listened to you and granted your request."
**36**¶ Then Abigail came to Nabal, and behold, he was holding a
feast in his house, like the feast of a king. And Nabal's heart was
merry within him, for he was very drunk; so she did not tell him
anything at all until the morning light.
37But it came about in the morning, when the wine had gone
out of Nabal, that his wife told him these things, and his heart died
within him so that he became *as* a stone.
38And about ten days later, it happened that the LORD struck
Nabal, and he died.

## New International

David,[c] be it ever so severely, if by morning I leave alive one male
of all who belong to him!"
23When Abigail saw David, she quickly got off her donkey and
bowed down before David with her face to the ground. 24She fell
at his feet and said: "My lord, let the blame be on me alone. Please
let your servant speak to you; hear what your servant has to say.
25May my lord pay no attention to that wicked man Nabal. He is
just like his name—his name is Fool, and folly goes with him. But
as for me, your servant, I did not see the men my master sent.
26"Now since the LORD has kept you, my master, from bloodshed and from avenging yourself with your own hands, as surely
as the LORD lives and as you live, may your enemies and all who
intend to harm my master be like Nabal. 27And let this gift, which
your servant has brought to my master, be given to the men who
follow you. 28Please forgive your servant's offense, for the LORD
will certainly make a lasting dynasty for my master, because he
fights the LORD's battles. Let no wrongdoing be found in you as
long as you live. 29Even though someone is pursuing you to take
your life, the life of my master will be bound securely in the bundle
of the living by the LORD your God. But the lives of your enemies
he will hurl away as from the pocket of a sling. 30When the LORD
has done for my master every good thing he promised concerning
him and has appointed him leader over Israel, 31my master will not
have on his conscience the staggering burden of needless bloodshed or of having avenged himself. And when the LORD has
brought my master success, remember your servant."
32David said to Abigail, "Praise be to the LORD, the God of
Israel, who has sent you today to meet me. 33May you be blessed
for your good judgment and for keeping me from bloodshed this
day and from avenging myself with my own hands. 34Otherwise,
as surely as the LORD, the God of Israel, lives, who has kept me
from harming you, if you had not come quickly to meet me, not
one male belonging to Nabal would have been left alive by daybreak."
35Then David accepted from her hand what she had brought
him and said, "Go home in peace. I have heard your words and
granted your request."
36When Abigail went to Nabal, he was in the house holding a
banquet like that of a king. He was in high spirits and very drunk.
So she told him nothing until daybreak. 37Then in the morning,
when Nabal was sober, his wife told him all these things, and his
heart failed him and he became like a stone. 38About ten days later,
the LORD struck Nabal and he died.

**NIV** [c] 22 Some Septuagint manuscripts; Hebrew *with David's enemies*

## King James

39¶ And when David heard that Nabal was dead, he said, Blessed *be* the LORD, that hath pleaded the cause of my reproach from the hand of Nabal, and hath kept his servant from evil: for the LORD hath returned the wickedness of Nabal upon his own head. And David sent and communed with Abigail, to take her to him to wife.

40And when the servants of David were come to Abigail to Carmel, they spake unto her, saying, David sent us unto thee, to take thee to him to wife.

41And she arose, and bowed herself on *her* face to the earth, and said, Behold, *let* thine handmaid *be* a servant to wash the feet of the servants of my lord.

42And Abigail hasted, and arose, and rode upon an ass, with five damsels of hers that went after her; and she went after the messengers of David, and became his wife.

43David also took Ahinoam of Jezreel; and they were also both of them his wives.

44¶ But Saul had given Michal his daughter, David's wife, to Phalti the son of Laish, which *was* of Gallim.

**26** AND THE Ziphites came unto Saul to Gibeah, saying, Doth not David hide himself in the hill of Hachilah, *which is* before Jeshimon?

2Then Saul arose, and went down to the wilderness of Ziph, having three thousand chosen men of Israel with him, to seek David in the wilderness of Ziph.

3And Saul pitched in the hill of Hachilah, which *is* before Jeshimon, by the way. But David abode in the wilderness, and he saw that Saul came after him into the wilderness.

4David therefore sent out spies, and understood that Saul was come in very deed.

5¶ And David arose, and came to the place where Saul had pitched: and David beheld the place where Saul lay, and Abner the son of Ner, the captain of his host: and Saul lay in the trench, and the people pitched round about him.

6Then answered David and said to Ahimelech the Hittite, and to Abishai the son of Zeruiah, brother to Joab, saying, Who will go down with me to Saul to the camp? And Abishai said, I will go down with thee.

7So David and Abishai came to the people by night: and, behold, Saul lay sleeping within the trench, and his spear stuck in the ground at his bolster: but Abner and the people lay round about him.

8Then said Abishai to David, God hath delivered thine enemy into thine hand this day: now therefore let me smite him, I pray thee, with the spear even to the earth at once, and I will not *smite* him the second time.

9And David said to Abishai, Destroy him not: for who can stretch forth his hand against the LORD's anointed, and be guiltless?

10David said furthermore, *As* the LORD liveth, the LORD shall smite him; or his day shall come to die; or he shall descend into battle, and perish.

11The LORD forbid that I should stretch forth mine hand against the LORD's anointed: but, I pray thee, take thou now the spear that *is* at his bolster, and the cruse of water, and let us go.

12So David took the spear and the cruse of water from Saul's bolster; and they gat them away, and no man saw *it*, nor knew *it*, neither awaked: for they *were* all asleep; because a deep sleep from the LORD was fallen upon them.

13¶ Then David went over to the other side, and stood on the top of an hill afar off; a great space *being* between them:

14And David cried to the people, and to Abner the son of Ner, saying, Answerest thou not, Abner? Then Abner answered and said, Who *art* thou *that* criest to the king?

## Amplified

39When David heard that Nabal was dead, he said, Blessed be the Lord, Who has pleaded the cause of my reproach at the hand of Nabal, and kept His servant from evil. For the Lord has returned the wickedness of Nabal upon his own head. And David sent and communed with Abigail, to take her to him as his wife.

40And when the servants of David had come to Abigail at Carmel, they said to her, David sent us to you, to take you to him to be his wife.

41And she arose, and bowed herself to the earth, and said, Behold, let your handmaid be a servant to wash the feet of the servants of my lord.

42And Abigail hastened and arose, and rode on a donkey, with five of her maids who followed her, and she went after the messengers of David, and became his wife.

43David also took Ahinoam of Jezreel; and they both became his wives.

44Saul had given Michal his daughter, David's wife, to Phalti son of Laish, who was of Gallim.

**26** THE ZIPHITES came to Saul at Gibeah, saying, Does not David hide himself on the hill of Hachilah, east of Jeshimon?

2So Saul arose and went down to the wilderness of Ziph, with 3,000 chosen men of Israel, to seek David [there].

3Saul encamped on the hill of Hachilah, which is beside the road east of Jeshimon. But David remained in the wilderness; and when he saw that Saul came after him into the wilderness,

4David sent out spies, and learned that Saul had actually come.

5David arose, and came to the place where Saul had encamped, and saw where Saul lay with Abner son of Ner, commander of his army; and Saul was lying in the encampment, with the army encamped around him.

6Then David said to Ahimelech the Hittite, and to Abishai son of Zeruiah, brother of Joab, Who will go down with me into the camp of Saul? And Abishai said, I will go down with you.

7So David and Abishai went to the army by night; and there Saul lay sleeping within the encampment, with his spear stuck in the ground at his head, and Abner and the army lay round about him.

8Then said Abishai to David, God has given your enemy into your hand this day. Now therefore let me smite him to the earth at once with one stroke of the spear, and I will not strike him twice.

9David said to Abishai, Do not destroy him; for who can raise his hand against the Lord's anointed, and be guiltless?

10David said, As the Lord lives, [He] will smite him; or his day will come to die; or he will go down in battle and perish.

11The Lord forbid that I should raise my hand against the Lord's anointed; but take now the spear that is at his head, and the bottle of water, and let us go.

12So David took the spear and the bottle of water from Saul's head, and they got away; and no man saw, or knew, or wakened, for they were all asleep because a deep sleep from the Lord had fallen upon them.

13Then David went over to the other side, and stood on the top of the mountain afar off, a great space being between them;

14David called to the army and Abner son of Ner, Will you answer, Abner? Abner replied, Who are you, calling [and disturbing] the king?

## New American Standard

*David Marries Abigail*

39¶ When David heard that Nabal was dead, he said, "Blessed
be the LORD, who has pleaded the cause of my reproach from the
hand of Nabal, and has kept back His servant from evil. The LORD
has also returned the evildoing of Nabal on his own head." Then
David sent a proposal to Abigail, to take her as his wife.
40When the servants of David came to Abigail at Carmel, they
spoke to her, saying, "David has sent us to you, to take you as his
wife."
41And she arose and bowed with her face to the ground and
said, "Behold, your maidservant is a maid to wash the feet of my
lord's servants."
42Then Abigail quickly arose, and rode on a donkey, with her
five maidens who attended her; and she followed the messengers
of David, and became his wife.
43¶ David had also taken Ahinoam of Jezreel, and they both
became his wives.
44¶ Now Saul had given Michal his daughter, David's wife, to
Palti the son of Laish, who was from Gallim.

*David Again Spares Saul*

26 THEN THE Ziphites came to Saul at Gibeah, saying, "Is
not David hiding on the hill of Hachilah, *which is* before
[a]Jeshimon?"
2So Saul arose and went down to the wilderness of Ziph,
having with him three thousand chosen men of Israel, to search
for David in the wilderness of Ziph.
3And Saul camped in the hill of Hachilah, which is before
[b]Jeshimon, beside the road, and David was staying in the wilderness. When he saw that Saul came after him into the wilderness,
4David sent out spies, and he knew that Saul was definitely
coming.
5David then arose and came to the place where Saul had
camped. And David saw the place where Saul lay, and Abner the
son of Ner, the commander of his army; and Saul was lying in the
circle of the camp, and the people were camped around him.
6¶ Then David answered and said to Ahimelech the Hittite and
to Abishai the son of Zeruiah, Joab's brother, saying, "Who will
go down with me to Saul in the camp?" And Abishai said, "I will
go down with you."
7So David and Abishai came to the people by night, and behold, Saul lay sleeping inside the circle of the camp, with his spear
stuck in the ground at his head; and Abner and the people were
lying around him.
8Then Abishai said to David, "Today God has delivered your
enemy into your hand; now therefore, please let me strike him
with the spear to the ground with one stroke, and I will not strike
him the second time."
9But David said to Abishai, "Do not destroy him, for who can
stretch out his hand against the LORD's anointed and be without
guilt?"
10David also said, "As the LORD lives, surely the LORD will
strike him, or his day will come that he dies, or he will go down
into battle and perish.
11"The LORD forbid that I should stretch out my hand against
the LORD's anointed; but now please take the spear that is at his
head and the jug of water, and let us go."
12So David took the spear and the jug of water from *beside* Saul's
head, and they went away, but no one saw or knew *it*, nor did any
awake, for they were all asleep, because a sound sleep from the
LORD had fallen on them.
13¶ Then David crossed over to the other side, and stood on top
of the mountain at a distance *with* a large area between them.
14And David called to the people and to Abner the son of Ner,
saying, "Will you not answer, Abner?" Then Abner answered and
said, "Who are you who calls to the king?"

NAS [a] Or, *the desert* [b] Or, *the desert*

## New International

39When David heard that Nabal was dead, he said, "Praise be
to the LORD, who has upheld my cause against Nabal for treating
me with contempt. He has kept his servant from doing wrong and
has brought Nabal's wrongdoing down on his own head."
Then David sent word to Abigail, asking her to become his wife.
40His servants went to Carmel and said to Abigail, "David has sent
us to you to take you to become his wife."
41She bowed down with her face to the ground and said, "Here
is your maidservant, ready to serve you and wash the feet of my
master's servants." 42Abigail quickly got on a donkey and, attended by her five maids, went with David's messengers and became
his wife. 43David had also married Ahinoam of Jezreel, and they
both were his wives. 44But Saul had given his daughter Michal,
David's wife, to Paltiel[c] son of Laish, who was from Gallim.

*David Again Spares Saul's Life*

26 THE ZIPHITES went to Saul at Gibeah and said, "Is not
David hiding on the hill of Hakilah, which faces Jeshimon?"
2So Saul went down to the Desert of Ziph, with his three thousand chosen men of Israel, to search there for David. 3Saul made
his camp beside the road on the hill of Hakilah facing Jeshimon,
but David stayed in the desert. When he saw that Saul had followed him there, 4he sent out scouts and learned that Saul had
definitely arrived.[d]
5Then David set out and went to the place where Saul had
camped. He saw where Saul and Abner son of Ner, the commander of the army, had lain down. Saul was lying inside the
camp, with the army encamped around him.
6David then asked Ahimelech the Hittite and Abishai son of
Zeruiah, Joab's brother, "Who will go down into the camp with me
to Saul?"
"I'll go with you," said Abishai.
7So David and Abishai went to the army by night, and there was
Saul, lying asleep inside the camp with his spear stuck in the
ground near his head. Abner and the soldiers were lying around
him.
8Abishai said to David, "Today God has delivered your enemy
into your hands. Now let me pin him to the ground with one thrust
of my spear; I won't strike him twice."
9But David said to Abishai, "Don't destroy him! Who can lay
a hand on the LORD's anointed and be guiltless? 10As surely as the
LORD lives," he said, "the LORD himself will strike him; either his
time will come and he will die, or he will go into battle and perish.
11But the LORD forbid that I should lay a hand on the LORD's
anointed. Now get the spear and water jug that are near his head,
and let's go."
12So David took the spear and water jug near Saul's head, and
they left. No one saw or knew about it, nor did anyone wake up.
They were all sleeping, because the LORD had put them into a deep
sleep.
13Then David crossed over to the other side and stood on top
of the hill some distance away; there was a wide space between
them. 14He called out to the army and to Abner son of Ner, "Aren't
you going to answer me, Abner?"
Abner replied, "Who are you who calls to the king?"

NIV [c] 44 Hebrew *Palti*, a variant of *Paltiel* [d] 4 Or *had come to Nacon*

## King James

15And David said to Abner, *Art* not thou a *valiant* man? and who *is* like to thee in Israel? wherefore then hast thou not kept thy lord the king? for there came one of the people in to destroy the king thy lord.

16This thing *is* not good that thou hast done. *As* the LORD liveth, ye *are* worthy to die, because ye have not kept your master, the LORD's anointed. And now see where the king's spear *is*, and the cruse of water that *was* at his bolster.

17And Saul knew David's voice, and said, *Is* this thy voice, my son David? And David said, *It is* my voice, my lord, O king.

18And he said, Wherefore doth my lord thus pursue after his servant? for what have I done? or what evil *is* in mine hand?

19Now therefore, I pray thee, let my lord the king hear the words of his servant. If the LORD have stirred thee up against me, let him accept an offering: but if *they be* the children of men, cursed *be* they before the LORD; for they have driven me out this day from abiding in the inheritance of the LORD, saying, Go, serve other gods.

20Now therefore, let not my blood fall to the earth before the face of the LORD: for the king of Israel is come out to seek a flea, as when one doth hunt a partridge in the mountains.

21¶ Then said Saul, I have sinned: return, my son David: for I will no more do thee harm, because my soul was precious in thine eyes this day: behold, I have played the fool, and have erred exceedingly.

22And David answered and said, Behold the king's spear! and let one of the young men come over and fetch it.

23The LORD render to every man his righteousness and his faithfulness: for the LORD delivered thee into *my* hand today, but I would not stretch forth mine hand against the LORD's anointed.

24And, behold, as thy life was much set by this day in mine eyes, so let my life be much set by in the eyes of the LORD, and let him deliver me out of all tribulation.

25Then Saul said to David, Blessed *be* thou, my son David: thou shalt both do great *things*, and also shalt still prevail. So David went on his way, and Saul returned to his place.

**27** AND DAVID said in his heart, I shall now perish one day by the hand of Saul: *there is* nothing better for me than that I should speedily escape into the land of the Philistines; and Saul shall despair of me, to seek me any more in any coast of Israel: so shall I escape out of his hand.

2And David arose, and he passed over with the six hundred men that *were* with him unto Achish, the son of Maoch, king of Gath.

3And David dwelt with Achish at Gath, he and his men, every man with his household, *even* David with his two wives, Ahinoam the Jezreelitess, and Abigail the Carmelitess, Nabal's wife.

4And it was told Saul that David was fled to Gath: and he sought no more again for him.

5¶ And David said unto Achish, If I have now found grace in thine eyes, let them give me a place in some town in the country, that I may dwell there: for why should thy servant dwell in the royal city with thee?

## Amplified

15David said to Abner, Are you not a valiant man? Who is like you in Israel? Why then have you not guarded your lord the king? For one of the people came in [to your camp] to destroy the king your lord.

16This thing is not good that you have done. As the Lord lives, you deserve to die, because you have not guarded your master, the Lord's anointed. And now see where the king's spear is, and the bottle of water that was at his head.

17And Saul knew David's voice, and said, Is this your voice, my son David? And David said, My voice, my lord, O king!

18And David said, Why does my lord thus pursue his servant? What have I done? Or what evil is in my hand [tonight]?

19Now therefore, I pray, let my lord the king hear the words of his servant. If the Lord has stirred you up against me, let Him accept an offering; but if it is men, cursed be they before the Lord; for they have driven me out this day that I should have no share in the inheritance of the Lord, saying, Go, serve other gods.

20Now therefore, let not my blood fall to the earth away from the presence of the Lord; for the king of Israel is come out to seek one flea, as when one hunts a partridge in the mountains.

21Then said Saul, I have sinned; return, my son David; for I will no more do you harm, because my life was precious in your eyes this day. Behold, I have [a]played the fool, and have erred exceedingly.

22David answered, See, the king's spear! Let one of the young men come and get it.

23The Lord rewards every man for his righteousness and his faithfulness; for the Lord delivered you into my hand today, but I would not stretch forth my hand against the Lord's anointed.

24And, behold, as your life was precious today in my sight, so let my life be precious in the sight of the Lord, and let Him deliver me out of all tribulation.

25Then Saul said to David, May you be blessed, my son David; you will both do mightily and surely prevail. So David went on his way, and Saul returned to his place.

**27** BUT DAVID said in his heart, I shall now perish one day by the hand of Saul; there is nothing better for me than that I should escape into the land of the Philistines; then Saul will despair of seeking me any more within the borders of Israel, and I shall escape out of his hand.

2So David arose, and went over with the 600 men who were with him, to Achish son of Maoch, king of Gath.

3And David dwelt with Achish at Gath, he and his men, every man with his household, and David with his two wives, Ahinoam the Jezreelitess, and Abigail the Carmelitess, Nabal's widow.

4When it was told Saul that David had fled to Gath, he sought for him no more.

5And David said to Achish, If I have now found favor in your eyes, let me be given a place to dwell in some country town; for why should your servant live in the royal city with you?

**AMP** [a] "When for a moment a man is off guard, in all probability you will know more truth about him than in all his attempts either to reveal himself or to hide himself. The ever-present consciousness, habitually hidden, flashes forth. Later, he may apologize, and say he did not mean what he said. The fact is that he was surprised into saying what he was constantly thinking. In all probability Saul had never said that before, and would never say it again; but he had been thinking it for a long time—'I played the fool.' There is no escape for any man, as long as reason continues, from the naked truth about himself. He may practice deceit so skilfully as not only to hide himself from his fellow men, but in his unutterable folly to imagine he has hidden himself from God; but he can never hide himself from *himself*. In some moment of stress and strain, he says what he has been thinking all the time . . . Ere Saul knew it, he had said, 'Behold, I have played the fool.' That is the whole story of the man" (*G. Campbell Morgan*, quoted by J. Sidlow Baxter in *Explore the Book*).

## New American Standard

15So David said to Abner, "Are you not a man? And who is like
you in Israel? Why then have you not guarded your lord the king?
For one of the people came to destroy the king your lord.
16"This thing that you have done is not good. As the LORD lives,
*all* of you must surely die, because you did not guard your lord,
the LORD'S anointed. And now, see where the king's spear is, and
the jug of water that was at his head."
17¶ Then Saul recognized David's voice and said, "Is this your
voice, my son David?" And David said, "It is my voice, my lord
the king."
18He also said, "Why then is my lord pursuing his servant? For
what have I done? Or what evil is in my hand?
19"Now therefore, please let my lord the king listen to the
words of his servant. If the LORD has stirred you up against me,
let Him accept an offering; but if it is men, cursed are they before
the LORD, for they have driven me out today that I should have
no attachment with the inheritance of the LORD, saying, 'Go, serve
other gods.'
20"Now then, do not let my blood fall to the ground away from
the presence of the LORD; for the king of Israel has come out to
search for a single flea, just as one hunts a partridge in the mountains."
21¶ Then Saul said, "I have sinned. Return, my son David, for
I will not harm you again because my life was precious in your
sight this day. Behold, I have played the fool and have committed
a serious error."
22And David answered and said, "Behold the spear of the king!
Now let one of the young men come over and take it.
23"And the LORD will repay each man *for* his righteousness and
his faithfulness; for the LORD delivered you into *my* hand today,
but I refused to stretch out my hand against the LORD's anointed.
24"Now behold, as your life was highly valued in my sight this
day, so may my life be highly valued in the sight of the LORD, and
may He deliver me from all distress."
25Then Saul said to David, "Blessed are you, my son David; you
will both accomplish much and surely prevail." So David went on
his way, and Saul returned to his place.

### *David Flees to the Philistines*

27 THEN DAVID said to himself, "Now I will perish one day
by the hand of Saul. There is nothing better for me than
to escape into the land of the Philistines. Saul then will despair of
searching for me anymore in all the territory of Israel, and I will
escape from his hand."
2So David arose and crossed over, he and the six hundred men
who were with him, to Achish the son of Maoch, king of Gath.
3And David lived with Achish at Gath, he and his men, each
with his household, *even* David with his two wives, Ahinoam the
Jezreelitess, and Abigail the Carmelitess, Nabal's widow.
4Now it was told Saul that David had fled to Gath, so he no
longer searched for him.
5¶ Then David said to Achish, "If now I have found favor in
your sight, let them give me a place in one of the cities in the
country, that I may live there; for why should your servant live in
the royal city with you?"

## New International

15David said, "You're a man, aren't you? And who is like you
in Israel? Why didn't you guard your lord the king? Someone came
to destroy your lord the king. 16What you have done is not good.
As surely as the LORD lives, you and your men deserve to die,
because you did not guard your master, the LORD'S anointed. Look
around you. Where are the king's spear and water jug that were
near his head?"
17Saul recognized David's voice and said, "Is that your voice,
David my son?"
David replied, "Yes it is, my lord the king." 18And he added,
"Why is my lord pursuing his servant? What have I done, and
what wrong am I guilty of? 19Now let my lord the king listen to
his servant's words. If the LORD has incited you against me, then
may he accept an offering. If, however, men have done it, may
they be cursed before the LORD! They have now driven me from
my share in the LORD'S inheritance and have said, 'Go, serve other
gods.' 20Now do not let my blood fall to the ground far from the
presence of the LORD. The king of Israel has come out to look for
a flea—as one hunts a partridge in the mountains."
21Then Saul said, "I have sinned. Come back, David my son.
Because you considered my life precious today, I will not try to
harm you again. Surely I have acted like a fool and have erred
greatly."
22"Here is the king's spear," David answered. "Let one of your
young men come over and get it. 23The LORD rewards every man
for his righteousness and faithfulness. The LORD delivered you
into my hands today, but I would not lay a hand on the LORD'S
anointed. 24As surely as I valued your life today, so may the LORD
value my life and deliver me from all trouble."
25Then Saul said to David, "May you be blessed, my son David;
you will do great things and surely triumph."
So David went on his way, and Saul returned home.

### *David Among the Philistines*

27 BUT DAVID thought to himself, "One of these days I will
be destroyed by the hand of Saul. The best thing I can do
is to escape to the land of the Philistines. Then Saul will give up
searching for me anywhere in Israel, and I will slip out of his
hand."
2So David and the six hundred men with him left and went over
to Achish son of Maoch king of Gath. 3David and his men settled
in Gath with Achish. Each man had his family with him, and David
had his two wives: Ahinoam of Jezreel and Abigail of Carmel, the
widow of Nabal. 4When Saul was told that David had fled to Gath,
he no longer searched for him.
5Then David said to Achish, "If I have found favor in your eyes,
let a place be assigned to me in one of the country towns, that I
may live there. Why should your servant live in the royal city with
you?"

## King James

6Then Achish gave him Ziklag that day: wherefore Ziklag pertaineth unto the kings of Judah unto this day.
7And the time that David dwelt in the country of the Philistines
was a full year and four months.
8¶ And David and his men went up, and invaded the Geshurites, and the Gezrites, and the Amalekites: for those *nations were*
of old the inhabitants of the land, as thou goest to Shur, even unto
the land of Egypt.
9And David smote the land, and left neither man nor woman
alive, and took away the sheep, and the oxen, and the asses, and
the camels, and the apparel, and returned, and came to Achish.
10And Achish said, Whither have ye made a road today? And
David said, Against the south of Judah, and against the south of
the Jerahmeelites, and against the south of the Kenites.
11And David saved neither man nor woman alive, to bring
*tidings* to Gath, saying, Lest they should tell on us, saying, So did
David, and so *will be* his manner all the while he dwelleth in the
country of the Philistines.
12And Achish believed David, saying, He hath made his people
Israel utterly to abhor him; therefore he shall be my servant for
ever.

**28** AND IT came to pass in those days, that the Philistines
gathered their armies together for warfare, to fight with
Israel. And Achish said unto David, Know thou assuredly, that
thou shalt go out with me to battle, thou and thy men.
2And David said to Achish, Surely thou shalt know what thy
servant can do. And Achish said to David, Therefore will I make
thee keeper of mine head for ever.
3¶ Now Samuel was dead, and all Israel had lamented him, and
buried him in Ramah, even in his own city. And Saul had put away
those that had familiar spirits, and the wizards, out of the land.
4And the Philistines gathered themselves together, and came
and pitched in Shunem: and Saul gathered all Israel together, and
they pitched in Giboa.
5And when Saul saw the host of the Philistines, he was afraid,
and his heart greatly trembled.
6And when Saul inquired of the LORD, the LORD answered him
not, neither by dreams, nor by Urim, nor by prophets.
7¶ Then said Saul unto his servants, Seek me a woman that hath
a familiar spirit, that I may go to her, and inquire of her. And his
servants said to him, Behold, *there is* a woman that hath a familiar
spirit at En-dor.
8And Saul disguised himself, and put on other raiment, and he
went, and two men with him, and they came to the woman by
night: and he said, I pray thee, divine unto me by the familiar
spirit, and bring me *him* up, whom I shall name unto thee.
9And the woman said unto him, Behold, thou knowest what
Saul hath done, how he hath cut off those that have familiar spirits,
and the wizards, out of the land: wherefore then layest thou a
snare for my life, to cause me to die?
10And Saul sware to her by the LORD, saying, *As* the LORD
liveth, there shall no punishment happen to thee for this thing.

## Amplified

6Then Achish gave David the town of Ziklag that day. Therefore
Ziklag belongs to the kings of Judah to this day.
7The time David dwelt in the Philistines' country was a year and
four months.
8Now David and his men went up and made attacks on the
Geshurites, Girzites, and Amalekites [enemies of Israel Joshua had
failed to exterminate]. For from of old those nations inhabited the
land, as one goes to Shur, even to the land of Egypt. [Deut. 25:19;
Josh. 13:1, 2, 13.]
9And David smote the land, and left neither man nor woman
alive, and took away the sheep, oxen, donkeys, camels, and the
apparel, and returned to Achish.
10Achish would ask, Against whom have you made a raid today? And David would reply, [a]Against the South of Judah, or of
the Jerahmeelites, or of the Kenites.
11And David saved neither man nor woman alive, to bring
tidings to Gath, thinking, Lest they should say about us, So did
David, and so will he do as long as he dwells in the Philistines'
country.
12And Achish believed David, saying, He has made his people
Israel utterly abhor him; so he shall be my servant always.

**28** IN THOSE days the Philistines gathered their forces for
war against Israel. Achish said to David, Understand that
you and your men shall go with me to battle.
2David said to Achish, All right, you shall know what your
servant can do. Achish said to David, Therefore I will make you
my bodyguard always.
3Now Samuel was dead, and all Israel had mourned for him and
buried him in Ramah, his own city. And Saul had put the mediums
and the wizards out of the land.
4And the Philistines assembled, and came and encamped at
Shunem; and Saul gathered all Israel, and they encamped at Gilboa.
5When Saul saw the Philistine host, he was afraid; his heart
trembled greatly.
6When Saul inquired of the Lord, He refused to answer him,
either by dreams, or by Urim [a symbol worn by the priest, when
seeking the will of God for Israel], or by the prophets. [Prov.
1:24-30.]
7Then Saul said to his servants, Find me a woman who is a
medium [between the living and the dead], that I may go and
inquire of her. His servants said, Behold, there is a woman who
is a medium at Endor.
8So Saul disguised himself, put on other raiment, and he and
two men with him went and came to the woman at night. He said
to her, Perceive for me by the familiar spirit, and bring up for me
the dead person whom I shall name to you.
9The woman said, See here, you know what Saul has done,
how he has cut off those who are mediums and the wizards, out
of the land. Why then do you lay a trap for my life to cause my
death?
10And Saul swore to her by the Lord, saying, As the Lord lives,
there shall no punishment come to you for this.

**AMP** [a] How could David be "a man after God's own heart" (13:14) and lie and deceive like that? God hates lying (Prov. 12:22), and those who deal in falsehood and deception are to be excluded from Heaven (Rev. 22:15). The truth is that David had gone through such a long period of persecution and threatening circumstances that he had fallen into a bit of mistrust of God Himself. God had sworn to make him king, to rid him of his enemies, to give him a sure house; yet here he was in a panic, concluding God had forsaken him and that if he was to remain alive he must manage it himself. It was very dishonoring to God. But God was standing by His stricken child, waiting for the moment when he would realize his own utter helplessness and turn in blessed surrender to the almighty arms of Him who had been watching over him all along. That time came at Ziklag, when in the bitterest hour of his life, we are told, "But David encouraged *and* strengthened himself in the Lord" (30:6), truly "a man after God's own heart."

## New American Standard

6So Achish gave him Ziklag that day; therefore Ziklag has
belonged to the kings of Judah to this day.
7And the number of days that David lived in the country of the
Philistines was a year and four months.
8¶ Now David and his men went up and raided the Geshurites
and the Girzites and the Amalekites; for they were the inhabitants
of the land from ancient times, as you come to Shur even as far as
the land of Egypt.
9And David attacked the land and did not leave a man or a
woman alive, and he took away the sheep, the cattle, the donkeys,
the camels, and the clothing. Then he returned and came to
Achish.
10Now Achish said, "Where have you made a raid today?" And
David said, "Against the [b]Negev of Judah and against the Negev
of the Jerahmeelites and against the Negev of the Kenites."
11And David did not leave a man or a woman alive, to bring to
Gath, saying, "Lest they should tell about us, saying, 'So has
David done and so *has been* his practice all the time he has lived
in the country of the Philistines.' "
12So Achish believed David, saying, "He has surely made himself odious among his people Israel; therefore he will become my
servant forever."

*Saul and the Spirit Medium*

**28** NOW IT came about in those days that the Philistines
gathered their armed camps for war, to fight against Israel. And Achish said to David, "Know assuredly that you will go
out with me in the camp, you and your men."
2And David said to Achish, "Very well, you shall know what
your servant can do." So Achish said to David, "Very well, I will
make you my bodyguard for life."
3¶ Now Samuel was dead, and all Israel had lamented him and
buried him in Ramah his own city. And Saul had removed from
the land those who were mediums and spiritists.
4So the Philistines gathered together and came and camped in
Shunem; and Saul gathered all Israel together and they camped in
Gilboa.
5When Saul saw the camp of the Philistines, he was afraid and
his heart trembled greatly.
6When Saul inquired of the LORD, the LORD did not answer
him, either by dreams or by Urim or by prophets.
7Then Saul said to his servants, "Seek for me a woman who
is a medium, that I may go to her and inquire of her." And his
servants said to him, "Behold, there is a woman who is a medium
at En-dor."
8¶ Then Saul disguised himself by putting on other clothes,
and went, he and two men with him, and they came to the woman
by night; and he said, "Conjure up for me, please, and bring up
for me whom I shall name to you."
9But the woman said to him, "Behold, you know what Saul has
done, how he has cut off those who are mediums and spiritists
from the land. Why are you then laying a snare for my life to bring
about my death?"
10And Saul vowed to her by the LORD, saying, "As the LORD
lives, there shall no punishment come upon you for this thing."

NAS [b] I.e., South country

## New International

6So on that day Achish gave him Ziklag, and it has belonged
to the kings of Judah ever since. 7David lived in Philistine territory
a year and four months.
8Now David and his men went up and raided the Geshurites,
the Girzites and the Amalekites. (From ancient times these peoples
had lived in the land extending to Shur and Egypt.) 9Whenever
David attacked an area, he did not leave a man or woman alive,
but took sheep and cattle, donkeys and camels, and clothes. Then
he returned to Achish.
10When Achish asked, "Where did you go raiding today?"
David would say, "Against the Negev of Judah" or "Against the
Negev of Jerahmeel" or "Against the Negev of the Kenites." 11He
did not leave a man or woman alive to be brought to Gath, for he
thought, "They might inform on us and say, 'This is what David
did.' " And such was his practice as long as he lived in Philistine
territory. 12Achish trusted David and said to himself, "He has
become so odious to his people, the Israelites, that he will be my
servant forever."

*Saul and the Witch of Endor*

**28** IN THOSE days the Philistines gathered their forces to
fight against Israel. Achish said to David, "You must understand that you and your men will accompany me in the army."
2David said, "Then you will see for yourself what your servant
can do."
Achish replied, "Very well, I will make you my bodyguard for
life."
3Now Samuel was dead, and all Israel had mourned for him and
buried him in his own town of Ramah. Saul had expelled the
mediums and spiritists from the land.
4The Philistines assembled and came and set up camp at Shunem, while Saul gathered all the Israelites and set up camp at
Gilboa. 5When Saul saw the Philistine army, he was afraid; terror
filled his heart. 6He inquired of the LORD, but the LORD did not
answer him by dreams or Urim or prophets. 7Saul then said to his
attendants, "Find me a woman who is a medium, so I may go and
inquire of her."
"There is one in Endor," they said.
8So Saul disguised himself, putting on other clothes, and at
night he and two men went to the woman. "Consult a spirit for
me," he said, "and bring up for me the one I name."
9But the woman said to him, "Surely you know what Saul has
done. He has cut off the mediums and spiritists from the land.
Why have you set a trap for my life to bring about my death?"
10Saul swore to her by the LORD, "As surely as the LORD lives,
you will not be punished for this."

## King James

11Then said the woman, Whom shall I bring up unto thee? And he said, Bring me up Samuel.

12And when the woman saw Samuel, she cried with a loud voice: and the woman spake to Saul, saying, Why hast thou deceived me? for thou *art* Saul.

13And the king said unto her, Be not afraid: for what sawest thou? And the woman said unto Saul, I saw gods ascending out of the earth.

14And he said unto her, What form *is* he of? And she said, An old man cometh up; and he *is* covered with a mantle. And Saul perceived that it *was* Samuel, and he stooped with *his* face to the ground, and bowed himself.

15¶ And Samuel said to Saul, Why hast thou disquieted me, to bring me up? And Saul answered, I am sore distressed; for the Philistines make war against me, and God is departed from me, and answereth me no more, neither by prophets, nor by dreams: therefore I have called thee, that thou mayest make known unto me what I shall do.

16Then said Samuel, Wherefore then dost thou ask of me, seeing the LORD is departed from thee, and is become thine enemy?

17And the LORD hath done to him, as he spake by me: for the LORD hath rent the kingdom out of thine hand, and given it to thy neighbour, *even* to David:

18Because thou obeyedst not the voice of the LORD, nor executedst his fierce wrath upon Amalek, therefore hath the LORD done this thing unto thee this day.

19Moreover the LORD will also deliver Israel with thee into the hand of the Philistines: and tomorrow *shalt* thou and thy sons *be* with me: the LORD also shall deliver the host of Israel into the hand of the Philistines.

20Then Saul fell straightway all along on the earth, and was sore afraid, because of the words of Samuel: and there was no strength in him; for he had eaten no bread all the day, nor all the night.

21¶ And the woman came unto Saul, and saw that he was sore troubled, and said unto him, Behold, thine handmaid hath obeyed thy voice, and I have put my life in my hand, and have hearkened unto thy words which thou spakest unto me.

22Now therefore, I pray thee, hearken thou also unto the voice of thine handmaid, and let me set a morsel of bread before thee; and eat, that thou mayest have strength, when thou goest on thy way.

23But he refused, and said, I will not eat. But his servants, together with the woman, compelled him; and he hearkened unto their voice. So he arose from the earth, and sat upon the bed.

24And the woman had a fat calf in the house; and she hasted, and killed it, and took flour, and kneaded *it*, and did bake unleavened bread thereof:

25And she brought *it* before Saul, and before his servants; and they did eat. Then they rose up, and went away that night.

**29** NOW THE Philistines gathered together all their armies to Aphek: and the Israelites pitched by a fountain which *is* in Jezreel.

2And the lords of the Philistines passed on by hundreds, and by thousands: but David and his men passed on in the rearward with Achish.

3Then said the princes of the Philistines, What *do* these Hebrews *here?* And Achish said unto the princes of the Philistines, *Is* not this David, the servant of Saul the king of Israel, which hath been with me these days, or these years, and I have found no fault in him since he fell *unto me* unto this day?

## Amplified

11The woman said, Whom shall I bring up for you? He said, Bring up Samuel for me.

12And when the woman saw Samuel she screamed, and she said to Saul, Why have you deceived me? For you are Saul!

13The king said to her, Be not afraid; what do you see? The woman said to Saul, I see a god [terrorizing superhuman being] coming up out of the earth!

14He said to her, In what form is he? And she said, An old man comes up, covered with a mantle. And Saul perceived that it was Samuel, and he stooped with his face to the ground, and made obeisance.

15And Samuel said to Saul, Why have you disturbed me, to bring me up? Saul answered, I am bitterly distressed; for the Philistines make war against me, and God has departed from me, and answers me no more, either by prophets, or by dreams. Therefore I have called you, that you may make known to me what I shall do.

16Samuel said, Why then do you ask of me, seeing the Lord has turned from you and has become your enemy?

17The Lord has done to you as He said through me He would do; for [He] has torn the kingdom out of your hand and given it to your neighbor, David. [I Sam. 15:22-28.]

18Because you did not obey the voice of the Lord, or execute His fierce wrath upon Amalek, therefore the Lord has done this thing to you this day.

19Moreover the Lord will also give Israel with you into the hand of the Philistines; and tomorrow you and your sons shall be with me [among the dead]. The Lord also will give the army of Israel into the hand of the Philistines.

20Then immediately Saul fell full length upon the earth floor [of the medium's house], and was exceedingly afraid because of Samuel's words. There was no strength in him, for he had eaten nothing all day and all night.

21The woman came to Saul, and seeing that he was greatly troubled, she said to him, Behold, your handmaid has obeyed you, and I have put my life in my hand, and have listened to what you said to me.

22So now, I pray you, listen also to the voice of your handmaid, and let me set a morsel of food before you, and eat, so you may have strength when you go your way.

23But he said, I will not eat. But his servants, together with the woman, urged him, and he heeded their words. So he arose from the ground, and sat upon the bed.

24The woman had a fat calf in the house; she hurried and killed it, and took flour, kneaded it, and baked unleavened bread.

25Then she brought it before Saul and his servants, and they ate. Then they rose up, and went away that night.

**29** NOW THE Philistines gathered all their forces at Aphek; and the Israelites encamped by the fountain in Jezreel.

2As the Philistine lords were passing on by hundreds and by thousands, and David and his men were in the rear with Achish,

3The Philistine princes said, What are these Hebrews doing here? Achish said to the Philistine princes, Is not this David, servant of Saul king of Israel, who has been with me these days and years, and I have found no fault in him since he deserted to me unto this day?

## New American Standard

11Then the woman said, "Whom shall I bring up for you?" And he said, "Bring up Samuel for me."

12When the woman saw Samuel, she cried out with a loud voice; and the woman spoke to Saul, saying, "Why have you deceived me? For you are Saul."

13And the king said to her, "Do not be afraid; but what do you see?" And the woman said to Saul, "I see a divine being coming up out of the earth."

14And he said to her, "What is his form?" And she said, "An old man is coming up, and he is wrapped with a robe." And Saul knew that it was Samuel, and he bowed with his face to the ground and did homage.

15¶ Then Samuel said to Saul, "Why have you disturbed me by bringing me up?" And Saul answered, "I am greatly distressed; for the Philistines are waging war against me, and God has departed from me and answers me no more, either through prophets or by dreams; therefore I have called you, that you may make known to me what I should do."

16And Samuel said, "Why then do you ask me, since the LORD has departed from you and has become your adversary?

17"And the LORD has done accordingly as He spoke through me; for the LORD has torn the kingdom out of your hand and given it to your neighbor, to David.

18"As you did not obey the LORD and did not execute His fierce wrath on Amalek, so the LORD has done this thing to you this day.

19"Moreover the LORD will also give over Israel along with you into the hands of the Philistines, therefore tomorrow you and your sons will be with me. Indeed the LORD will give over the army of Israel into the hands of the Philistines!"

20¶ Then Saul immediately fell full length upon the ground and was very afraid because of the words of Samuel; also there was no strength in him, for he had eaten no food all day and all night.

21And the woman came to Saul and saw that he was terrified, and said to him, "Behold, your maidservant has obeyed you, and I have taken my life in my hand, and have listened to your words which you spoke to me.

22"So now also, please listen to the voice of your maidservant, and let me set a piece of bread before you that *you may* eat and have strength when you go on *your* way."

23But he refused and said, "I will not eat." However, his servants together with the woman urged him, and he listened to them. So he arose from the ground and sat on the bed.

24And the woman had a fattened calf in the house, and she quickly slaughtered it; and she took flour, kneaded it, and baked unleavened bread from it.

25And she brought *it* before Saul and his servants, and they ate. Then they arose and went away that night.

*The Philistines Mistrust David*

**29** NOW THE Philistines gathered together all their armies to Aphek, while the Israelites were camping by the spring which is in Jezreel.

2And the lords of the Philistines were proceeding on by hundreds and by thousands, and David and his men were proceeding on in the rear with Achish.

3Then the commanders of the Philistines said, "What *are* these Hebrews *doing here*?" And Achish said to the commanders of the Philistines, "Is this not David, the servant of Saul the king of Israel, who has been with me these days, or *rather* these years, and I have found no fault in him from the day he deserted *to me* to this day?"

## New International

11Then the woman asked, "Whom shall I bring up for you?"

"Bring up Samuel," he said.

12When the woman saw Samuel, she cried out at the top of her voice and said to Saul, "Why have you deceived me? You are Saul!"

13The king said to her, "Don't be afraid. What do you see?"

The woman said, "I see a spirit[a] coming up out of the ground."

14"What does he look like?" he asked.

"An old man wearing a robe is coming up," she said.

Then Saul knew it was Samuel, and he bowed down and prostrated himself with his face to the ground.

15Samuel said to Saul, "Why have you disturbed me by bringing me up?"

"I am in great distress," Saul said. "The Philistines are fighting against me, and God has turned away from me. He no longer answers me, either by prophets or by dreams. So I have called on you to tell me what to do."

16Samuel said, "Why do you consult me, now that the LORD has turned away from you and become your enemy? 17The LORD has done what he predicted through me. The LORD has torn the kingdom out of your hands and given it to one of your neighbors—to David. 18Because you did not obey the LORD or carry out his fierce wrath against the Amalekites, the LORD has done this to you today. 19The LORD will hand over both Israel and you to the Philistines, and tomorrow you and your sons will be with me. The LORD will also hand over the army of Israel to the Philistines."

20Immediately Saul fell full length on the ground, filled with fear because of Samuel's words. His strength was gone, for he had eaten nothing all that day and night.

21When the woman came to Saul and saw that he was greatly shaken, she said, "Look, your maidservant has obeyed you. I took my life in my hands and did what you told me to do. 22Now please listen to your servant and let me give you some food so you may eat and have the strength to go on your way."

23He refused and said, "I will not eat."

But his men joined the woman in urging him, and he listened to them. He got up from the ground and sat on the couch.

24The woman had a fattened calf at the house, which she butchered at once. She took some flour, kneaded it and baked bread without yeast. 25Then she set it before Saul and his men, and they ate. That same night they got up and left.

*Achish Sends David Back to Ziklag*

**29** THE PHILISTINES gathered all their forces at Aphek, and Israel camped by the spring in Jezreel. 2As the Philistine rulers marched with their units of hundreds and thousands, David and his men were marching at the rear with Achish. 3The commanders of the Philistines asked, "What about these Hebrews?"

Achish replied, "Is this not David, who was an officer of Saul king of Israel? He has already been with me for over a year, and from the day he left Saul until now, I have found no fault in him."

NIV [a] 13 Or *see spirits;* or *see gods*

## King James

4And the princes of the Philistines were wroth with him; and the princes of the Philistines said unto him, Make this fellow return, that he may go again to his place which thou hast appointed him, and let him not go down with us to battle, lest in the battle he be an adversary to us: for wherewith should he reconcile himself unto his master? *should it* not *be* with the heads of these men?

5 *Is* not this David, of whom they sang one to another in dances, saying, Saul slew his thousands, and David his ten thousands?

6¶ Then Achish called David, and said unto him, Surely, *as* the LORD liveth, thou hast been upright, and thy going out and thy coming in with me in the host *is* good in my sight: for I have not found evil in thee since the day of thy coming unto me unto this day: nevertheless the lords favour thee not.

7Wherefore now return, and go in peace, that thou displease not the lords of the Philistines.

8¶ And David said unto Achish, But what have I done? and what hast thou found in thy servant so long as I have been with thee unto this day, that I may not go fight against the enemies of my lord the king?

9And Achish answered and said to David, I know that thou *art* good in my sight, as an angel of God: notwithstanding the princes of the Philistines have said, He shall not go up with us to the battle.

10Wherefore now rise up early in the morning with thy master's servants that are come with thee: and as soon as ye be up early in the morning, and have light, depart.

11So David and his men rose up early to depart in the morning, to return into the land of the Philistines. And the Philistines went up to Jezreel.

**30** AND IT came to pass, when David and his men were come to Ziklag on the third day, that the Amalekites had invaded the south, and Ziklag, and smitten Ziklag, and burned it with fire;

2And had taken the women captives, that *were* therein: they slew not any, either great or small, but carried *them* away, and went on their way.

3¶ So David and his men came to the city, and, behold, *it was* burned with fire; and their wives, and their sons, and their daughters, were taken captives.

4Then David and the people that *were* with him lifted up their voice and wept, until they had no more power to weep.

5And David's two wives were taken captives, Ahinoam the Jezreelitess, and Abigail the wife of Nabal the Carmelite.

6And David was greatly distressed; for the people spake of stoning him, because the soul of all the people was grieved, every man for his sons and for his daughters: but David encouraged himself in the LORD his God.

7And David said to Abiathar the priest, Ahimelech's son, I pray thee, bring me hither the ephod. And Abiathar brought thither the ephod to David.

8And David inquired at the LORD, saying, Shall I pursue after this troop? shall I overtake them? And he answered him, Pursue: for thou shalt surely overtake *them,* and without fail recover *all.*

9So David went, he and the six hundred men that *were* with him, and came to the brook Besor, where those that were left behind stayed.

10But David pursued, he and four hundred men: for two hundred abode behind, which were so faint that they could not go over the brook Besor.

11¶ And they found an Egyptian in the field, and brought him to David, and gave him bread, and he did eat; and they made him drink water;

## Amplified

4And the Philistine princes were angry with Achish, and they said to him, Make this fellow return, that he may go again to his place which you have assigned him, and let him not go down with us to battle, lest in the battle he become an adversary to us. For how could David reconcile himself to his master? Would it not be with the heads of the men here?

5Is not this David, of whom they sang to one another in dances, Saul slew his thousands, and David his ten thousands?

6Then Achish called David, and said to him, Surely, as the Lord lives, you have been honest *and* upright, and for you to go out and come in with me in the army is good in my sight, for I have found no evil in you from the day of your coming to me to this day. Yet the lords do not approve of you.

7So return now, and go peaceably, so as not to displease the Philistine lords.

8David said to Achish, But what have I done? And what have you found in your servant as long as I have been with you to this day, that I may not go fight against the enemies of my lord the king?

9And Achish said to David, I know that you are as blameless in my sight as an angel of God; nevertheless the princes of the Philistines have said, He shall not go up with us to the battle.

10So now rise up early in the morning with your master's servants who have come with you, and as soon as you are up and have light, depart.

11So David and his men rose up early in the morning, to return to the land of the Philistines. But the Philistines went up to Jezreel [to fight against Israel].

**30** NOW WHEN David and his men came home to Ziklag on the third day, they found that the Amalekites had made a raid on the South and on Ziklag, and had struck Ziklag, and burned it with fire,

2And had taken the women and all who were there, both great and small, captive. They killed no one, but carried them off, and went on their way.

3So David and his men came to the town, and behold, it was burned; and their wives and sons and daughters were taken captive.

4Then David and the men with him lifted up their voices and wept, until they had no more strength to weep.

5David's two wives also had been taken captive, Ahinoam the Jezreelitess, and Abigail the widow of Nabal the Carmelite.

6David was greatly distressed; for the men spoke of stoning him, because the soul of them all was bitterly grieved, each man for his sons and daughters; but David encouraged *and* strengthened himself in the Lord his God.

7David said to Abiathar the priest, Ahimelech's son, I pray you, bring me the ephod. And Abiathar brought him the ephod.

8And David inquired of the Lord, saying, Shall I pursue this troop? Shall I overtake them? The Lord answered him, Pursue; for you shall surely overtake them, and without fail recover all.

9So David went, he and the 600 men with him, and came to the brook Besor; there those remained who were left behind.

10But David pursued, he and 400 men, for 200 stayed behind who were too exhausted *and* faint to cross the brook Besor.

11They found an Egyptian in the field, and brought him to David, and gave him bread and he ate, and water to drink,

## New American Standard

4But the commanders of the Philistines were angry with him,
and the commanders of the Philistines said to him, "Make the man
go back, that he may return to his place where you have assigned
him, and do not let him go down to battle with us, lest in the battle
he become an adversary to us. For with what could this *man* make
himself acceptable to his lord? *Would it* not *be* with the heads of
these men?
5"Is this not David, of whom they sing in the dances, saying,
'Saul has slain his thousands,
And David his ten thousands'?"
6¶ Then Achish called David and said to him, " *As* the LORD
lives, you *have been* upright, and your going out and your coming
in with me in the army are pleasing in my sight; for I have not
found evil in you from the day of your coming to me to this day.
Nevertheless, you are not pleasing in the sight of the lords.
7"Now therefore return, and go in peace, that you may not
displease the lords of the Philistines."
8And David said to Achish, "But what have I done? And what
have you found in your servant from the day when I came before
you to this day, that I may not go and fight against the enemies
of my lord the king?"
9But Achish answered and said to David, "I know that you are
pleasing in my sight, like an angel of God; nevertheless the commanders
of the Philistines have said, 'He must not go up with us
to the battle.'
10"Now then arise early in the morning with the servants of
your lord who have come with you, and as soon as you have arisen
early in the morning and have light, depart."
11So David arose early, he and his men, to depart in the morning,
to return to the land of the Philistines. And the Philistines
went up to Jezreel.

*David's Victory over the Amalekites*

**30** THEN IT happened when David and his men came to
Ziklag on the third day, that the Amalekites had made a
raid on the Negev and on Ziklag, and had overthrown Ziklag and
burned it with fire;
2and they took captive the women *and all* who were in it, both
small and great, without killing anyone, and carried *them* off and
went their way.
3And when David and his men came to the city, behold, it was
burned with fire, and their wives and their sons and their daughters
had been taken captive.
4Then David and the people who were with him lifted their
voices and wept until there was no strength in them to weep.
5Now David's two wives had been taken captive, Ahinoam the
Jezreelitess and Abigail the widow of Nabal the Carmelite.
6Moreover David was greatly distressed because the people
spoke of stoning him, for all the people were embittered, each one
because of his sons and his daughters. But David strengthened
himself in the LORD his God.
7¶ Then David said to Abiathar the priest, the son of Ahimelech,
"Please bring me the ephod." So Abiathar brought the ephod
to David.
8And David inquired of the LORD, saying, "Shall I pursue this
band? Shall I overtake them?" And He said to him, "Pursue, for
you shall surely overtake them, and you shall surely rescue *all*."
9So David went, he and the six hundred men who were with
him, and came to the brook Besor, *where* those left behind remained.
10But David pursued, he and four hundred men, for two hundred
who were too exhausted to cross the brook Besor, remained
*behind*.
11¶ Now they found an Egyptian in the field and brought him
to David, and gave him bread and he ate, and they provided him
water to drink.

## New International

4But the Philistine commanders were angry with him and said,
"Send the man back, that he may return to the place you assigned
him. He must not go with us into battle, or he will turn against us
during the fighting. How better could he regain his master's favor
than by taking the heads of our own men? 5Isn't this the David
they sang about in their dances:
" 'Saul has slain his thousands,
and David his tens of thousands'?"
6So Achish called David and said to him, "As surely as the LORD
lives, you have been reliable, and I would be pleased to have you
serve with me in the army. From the day you came to me until
now, I have found no fault in you, but the rulers don't approve
of you. 7Turn back and go in peace; do nothing to displease the
Philistine rulers."
8"But what have I done?" asked David. "What have you found
against your servant from the day I came to you until now? Why
can't I go and fight against the enemies of my lord the king?"
9Achish answered, "I know that you have been as pleasing in
my eyes as an angel of God; nevertheless, the Philistine commanders
have said, 'He must not go up with us into battle.' 10Now get
up early, along with your master's servants who have come with
you, and leave in the morning as soon as it is light."
11So David and his men got up early in the morning to go back
to the land of the Philistines, and the Philistines went up to Jezreel.

*David Destroys the Amalekites*

**30** DAVID AND his men reached Ziklag on the third day.
Now the Amalekites had raided the Negev and Ziklag.
They had attacked Ziklag and burned it, 2and had taken captive
the women and all who were in it, both young and old. They killed
none of them, but carried them off as they went on their way.
3When David and his men came to Ziklag, they found it destroyed
by fire and their wives and sons and daughters taken
captive. 4So David and his men wept aloud until they had no
strength left to weep. 5David's two wives had been captured—
Ahinoam of Jezreel and Abigail, the widow of Nabal of Carmel.
6David was greatly distressed because the men were talking of
stoning him; each one was bitter in spirit because of his sons and
daughters. But David found strength in the LORD his God.
7Then David said to Abiathar the priest, the son of Ahimelech,
"Bring me the ephod." Abiathar brought it to him, 8and David
inquired of the LORD, "Shall I pursue this raiding party? Will I
overtake them?"
"Pursue them," he answered. "You will certainly overtake
them and succeed in the rescue."
9David and the six hundred men with him came to the Besor
Ravine, where some stayed behind, 10for two hundred men were
too exhausted to cross the ravine. But David and four hundred
men continued the pursuit.
11They found an Egyptian in a field and brought him to David.
They gave him water to drink and food to eat— 12part of a cake

## King James

12And they gave him a piece of a cake of figs, and two clusters of raisins: and when he had eaten, his spirit came again to him: for he had eaten no bread, nor drunk *any* water, three days and three nights.

13And David said unto him, To whom *belongest* thou? and whence *art* thou? And he said, I *am* a young man of Egypt, servant to an Amalekite; and my master left me, because three days agone I fell sick.

14We made an invasion *upon* the south of the Cherethites, and upon *the coast* which *belongeth* to Judah, and upon the south of Caleb; and we burned Ziklag with fire.

15And David said to him, Canst thou bring me down to this company? And he said, Swear unto me by God, that thou wilt neither kill me, nor deliver me into the hands of my master, and I will bring thee down to this company.

16¶ And when he had brought him down, behold, *they were* spread abroad upon all the earth, eating and drinking, and dancing, because of all the great spoil that they had taken out of the land of the Philistines, and out of the land of Judah.

17And David smote them from the twilight even unto the evening of the next day: and there escaped not a man of them, save four hundred young men, which rode upon camels, and fled.

18And David recovered all that the Amalekites had carried away: and David rescued his two wives.

19And there was nothing lacking to them, neither small nor great, neither sons nor daughters, neither spoil, nor any *thing* that they had taken to them: David recovered all.

20And David took all the flocks and the herds, *which* they drave before those *other* cattle, and said, This *is* David's spoil.

21¶ And David came to the two hundred men, which were so faint that they could not follow David, whom they had made also to abide at the brook Besor: and they went forth to meet David, and to meet the people that *were* with him: and when David came near to the people, he saluted them.

22Then answered all the wicked men and *men* of Belial, of those that went with David, and said, Because they went not with us, we will not give them *aught* of the spoil that we have recovered, save to every man his wife and his children, that they may lead *them* away, and depart.

23Then said David, Ye shall not do so, my brethren, with that which the LORD hath given us, who hath preserved us, and delivered the company that came against us into our hand.

24For who will hearken unto you in this matter? but as his part *is* that goeth down to the battle, so *shall* his part *be* that tarrieth by the stuff: they shall part alike.

25And it was *so* from that day forward, that he made it a statute and an ordinance for Israel unto this day.

26¶ And when David came to Ziklag, he sent of the spoil unto the elders of Judah, *even* to his friends, saying, Behold a present for you of the spoil of the enemies of the LORD;

27To *them* which *were* in Beth-el, and to *them* which *were* in south Ramoth, and to *them* which *were* in Jattir,

28And to *them* which *were* in Aroer, and to *them* which *were* in Siphmoth, and to *them* which *were* in Eshtemoa,

29And to *them* which *were* in Rachal, and to *them* which *were* in the cities of the Jerahmeelites, and to *them* which *were* in the cities of the Kenites,

30And to *them* which which *were* in Hormah, and to *them* which *were* in Chor-ashan, and to *them* which *were* in Athach,

31And to *them* which *were* in Hebron, and to all the places where David himself and his men were wont to haunt.

**31** NOW THE Philistines fought against Israel: and the men of Israel fled from before the Philistines, and fell down slain in mount Gilboa.

## Amplified

12And a piece of a cake of figs, and two clusters of raisins; and when he had eaten, his spirit returned to him; for he had eaten no food, or drunk any water, three days and three nights.

13And David said to him, To whom do you belong? And from where have you come? He said, I am a young man of Egypt, servant to an Amalekite; and my master left me, because three days ago I fell sick.

14We had made a raid on the South of the Cherethites, and upon that which belongs to Judah, and upon the South of Caleb; and we burned Ziklag with fire.

15And David said to him, Can you take me down to this band? And he said, Swear to me by God that you will neither kill me nor deliver me into the hands of my master, and I will bring you down to this band.

16And when he had brought David down, behold, the raiders were spread abroad over all the land, eating and drinking and dancing, because of all the great spoil they had taken from the land of the Philistines, and from the land of Judah.

17And David smote them from twilight even to the evening of the next day, and not a man of them escaped, except 400 youths who rode camels and fled.

18David recovered all that the Amalekites had taken, and rescued his two wives.

19Nothing was missing, small or great, sons or daughters, spoil, or anything that had been taken; David recovered all.

20Also David captured all the flocks and herds [which the enemy had]; and the people drove those animals before him, and said, This is David's spoil.

21And David came to the 200 men, who were so exhausted *and* faint that they could not follow [him] and had been left at the brook Besor [with the baggage]. They came to meet David and those with him, and when he came near to the men, he saluted them.

22Then all the wicked and base men who went with David, said, Because they did not go with us, we will give them nothing of the spoil we have recovered, except that every man may lead away his wife and children and depart.

23David said, You shall not do so, my brethren, with what the Lord has given us; He has preserved us, and has delivered into our hand the troop that came against us.

24Who would listen to you in this matter? For as is the share of him who goes into the battle, so shall his share be who stays by the baggage. They shall share alike.

25And from that day to this he made it a statute and ordinance for Israel.

26When David came to Ziklag, he sent part of the spoil to the elders of Judah, his friends, saying, Here is a gift for you of the spoil of the enemies of the Lord:

27For those in Bethel, Ramoth of the Negeb, Jattir,

28Aroer, Siphmoth, Eshtemoa,

29Racal, the cities of the Jerahmeelites, the city of the Kenites,

30Hormah, Borashan, Athach,

31Hebron, and all the places David and his men had habitually haunted.

**31** NOW THE Philistines fought against Israel; and the men of Israel fled before [them] and fell slain on Mount Gilboa.

## New American Standard

12 And they gave him a piece of fig cake and two clusters of raisins, and he ate; then his spirit revived. For he had not eaten bread or drunk water for three days and three nights.

13 And David said to him, "To whom do you belong? And where are you from?" And he said, "I am a young man of Egypt, a servant of an Amalekite; and my master left me behind when I fell sick three days ago.

14 "We made a raid on the Negev of the Cherethites, and on that which belongs to Judah, and on the Negev of Caleb, and we burned Ziklag with fire."

15 Then David said to him, "Will you bring me down to this band?" And he said, "Swear to me by God that you will not kill me or deliver me into the hands of my master, and I will bring you down to this band."

**16**¶ And when he had brought him down, behold, they were spread over all the land, eating and drinking and dancing because of all the great spoil that they had taken from the land of the Philistines and from the land of Judah.

17 And David slaughtered them from the twilight until the evening of the next day; and not a man of them escaped, except four hundred young men who rode on camels and fled.

18 So David recovered all that the Amalekites had taken, and rescued his two wives.

19 But nothing of theirs was missing, whether small or great, sons or daughters, spoil or anything that they had taken for themselves; David brought *it* all back.

20 So David had captured all the sheep and the cattle *which the people* drove ahead of the *other* livestock, and they said, "This is David's spoil."

*The Spoils Are Divided*

**21**¶ When David came to the two hundred men who were too exhausted to follow David, who had also been left at the brook Besor, and they went out to meet David and to meet the people who were with him, then David approached the people and greeted them.

22 Then all the wicked and worthless men among those who went with David answered and said, "Because they did not go with us, we will not give them any of the spoil that we have recovered, except to every man his wife and his children, that they may lead *them* away and depart."

23 Then David said, "You must not do so, my brothers, with what the LORD has given us, who has kept us and delivered into our hand the band that came against us.

24 "And who will listen to you in this matter? For as his share is who goes down to the battle, so shall his share be who stays by the baggage; they shall share alike."

25 And so it has been from that day forward, that he made it a statute and an ordinance for Israel to this day.

**26**¶ Now when David came to Ziklag, he sent *some* of the spoil to the elders of Judah, to his friends, saying, "Behold, a gift for you from the spoil of the enemies of the LORD:

27 to those who were in Bethel, and to those who were in Ramoth of the Negev, and to those who were in Jattir,

28 and to those who were in Aroer, and to those who were in Siphmoth, and to those who were in Eshtemoa,

29 and to those who were in Racal, and to those who were in the cities of the Jerahmeelites, and to those who were in the cities of the Kenites,

30 and to those who were in Hormah, and to those who were in Bor-ashan, and to those who were in Athach,

31 and to those who were in Hebron, and to all the places where David himself and his men were accustomed to go."

*Saul and His Sons Slain*

**31** NOW THE Philistines were fighting against Israel, and the men of Israel fled from before the Philistines and fell slain on Mount Gilboa.

## New International

of pressed figs and two cakes of raisins. He ate and was revived,
for he had not eaten any food or drunk any water for three days
and three nights.
13 David asked him, "To whom do you belong, and where do
you come from?"
He said, "I am an Egyptian, the slave of an Amalekite. My
master abandoned me when I became ill three days ago. 14 We
raided the Negev of the Kerethites and the territory belonging to
Judah and the Negev of Caleb. And we burned Ziklag."
15 David asked him, "Can you lead me down to this raiding
party?"
He answered, "Swear to me before God that you will not kill
me or hand me over to my master, and I will take you down to
them."
16 He led David down, and there they were, scattered over the
countryside, eating, drinking and reveling because of the great
amount of plunder they had taken from the land of the Philistines
and from Judah. 17 David fought them from dusk until the evening
of the next day, and none of them got away, except four hundred
young men who rode off on camels and fled. 18 David recovered
everything the Amalekites had taken, including his two wives.
19 Nothing was missing: young or old, boy or girl, plunder or
anything else they had taken. David brought everything back.
20 He took all the flocks and herds, and his men drove them ahead
of the other livestock, saying, "This is David's plunder."
21 Then David came to the two hundred men who had been too
exhausted to follow him and who were left behind at the Besor
Ravine. They came out to meet David and the people with him.
As David and his men approached, he greeted them. 22 But all the
evil men and troublemakers among David's followers said, "Because they did not go out with us, we will not share with them the
plunder we recovered. However, each man may take his wife and
children and go."
23 David replied, "No, my brothers, you must not do that with
what the LORD has given us. He has protected us and handed over
to us the forces that came against us. 24 Who will listen to what you
say? The share of the man who stayed with the supplies is to be
the same as that of him who went down to the battle. All will share
alike." 25 David made this a statute and ordinance for Israel from
that day to this.
26 When David arrived in Ziklag, he sent some of the plunder
to the elders of Judah, who were his friends, saying, "Here is a
present for you from the plunder of the LORD's enemies."
27 He sent it to those who were in Bethel, Ramoth Negev and
Jattir; 28 to those in Aroer, Siphmoth, Eshtemoa 29 and Racal; to
those in the towns of the Jerahmeelites and the Kenites; 30 to those
in Hormah, Bor Ashan, Athach 31 and Hebron; and to those in all
the other places where David and his men had roamed.

*Saul Takes His Life*

**31** NOW THE Philistines fought against Israel; the Israelites fled before them, and many fell slain on Mount Gilboa.

## King James

2And the Philistines followed hard upon Saul and upon his sons; and the Philistines slew Jonathan, and Abinadab, and Melchi-shua, Saul's sons.
3And the battle went sore against Saul, and the archers hit him; and he was sore wounded of the archers.
4Then said Saul unto his armourbearer, Draw thy sword, and thrust me through therewith; lest these uncircumcised come and thrust me through, and abuse me. But his armourbearer would not; for he was sore afraid. Therefore Saul took a sword, and fell upon it.
5And when his armourbearer saw that Saul was dead, he fell likewise upon his sword, and died with him.
6So Saul died, and his three sons, and his armourbearer, and all his men, that same day together.
7¶ And when the men of Israel that *were* on the other side of the valley, and *they* that *were* on the other side Jordan, saw that the men of Israel fled, and that Saul and his sons were dead, they forsook the cities, and fled; and the Philistines came and dwelt in them.
8And it came to pass on the morrow, when the Philistines came to strip the slain, that they found Saul and his three sons fallen in mount Gilboa.
9And they cut off his head, and stripped off his armour, and sent into the land of the Philistines round about, to publish *it in* the house of their idols, and among the people.
10And they put his armour in the house of Ashtaroth: and they fastened his body to the wall of Beth-shan.
11¶ And when the inhabitants of Jabesh-gilead heard of that which the Philistines had done to Saul;
12All the valiant men arose, and went all night, and took the body of Saul and the bodies of his sons from the wall of Beth-shan, and came to Jabesh, and burnt them there.
13And they took their bones, and buried *them* under a tree at Jabesh, and fasted seven days.

## Amplified

2And the Philistines pursued Saul and his sons, and slew Jonathan and Abinadab and Malchishua, Saul's sons.
3The battle went heavily against Saul, and the archers severely wounded him.
4Saul said to his armor-bearer, Draw your sword and thrust me through, lest these uncircumcised come and thrust me through, and abuse *and* mock me. But his armor-bearer would not, for he was terrified. So [a]Saul took a sword and fell upon it.
5When his armor-bearer saw that Saul was dead, he likewise fell upon his sword, and died with him.
6So Saul, his three sons, his armor-bearer, and all his men, died that day together.
7And when the men of Israel on the other side of the valley and beyond the Jordan saw that the Israelites fled, and that Saul and his sons were dead, they forsook the cities, and fled; and the Philistines came and dwelt in them.
8Next day, when the Philistines came to strip the slain, they found Saul and his three sons fallen on Mount Gilboa.
9They cut off Saul's head, and stripped off his armor, and sent them round about the land of the Philistines, to publish it in the house of their idols, and among the people.
10And they put Saul's armor in the house of [the idols] Ashtaroth; and they fastened his body to the wall of Beth-shan.
11When the people of Jabesh-gilead heard what the Philistines had done to Saul,
12All the valiant men arose, and went all night, and took the bodies of Saul and his sons from the wall of Beth-shan, and came to Jabesh, and cremated them there.
13And they took their bones, and buried them under a tree at Jabesh, and fasted seven days.

**AMP** [a] This account of Saul's death obviously contradicts that given by the Amalekite who came to David with Saul's spear and crown, claiming to have killed him (II Sam. 1:9ff). His story was [probably] a fabrication. He found the king's body on the battlefield, stripped it, and brought the spoil to David hoping for a reward, as *The Cambridge Bible* comments. However, it is possible that Saul was not entirely dead when the Amalekite found him, though his armor-bearer had thought him dead and had killed himself, in which case the Amalekite's story may have been true.

## New American Standard

2And the Philistines overtook Saul and his sons; and the Philistines killed Jonathan and Abinadab and Malchi-shua the sons of Saul.

3And the battle went heavily against Saul, and the archers hit him; and he was badly wounded by the archers.

4Then Saul said to his armor bearer, "Draw your sword and pierce me through with it, lest these uncircumcised come and pierce me through and make sport of me." But his armor bearer would not, for he was greatly afraid. So Saul took his sword and fell on it.

5And when his armor bearer saw that Saul was dead, he also fell on his sword and died with him.

6Thus Saul died with his three sons, his armor bearer, and all his men on that day together.

7¶ And when the men of Israel who were on the other side of the valley, with those who were beyond the Jordan, saw that the men of Israel had fled and that Saul and his sons were dead, they abandoned the cities and fled; then the Philistines came and lived in them.

8And it came about on the next day when the Philistines came to strip the slain, that they found Saul and his three sons fallen on Mount Gilboa.

9And they cut off his head, and stripped off his weapons, and sent *them* throughout the land of the Philistines, to carry the good news to the house of their idols and to the people.

10And they put his weapons in the temple of Ashtaroth, and they fastened his body to the wall of Beth-shan.

11Now when the inhabitants of Jabesh-gilead heard what the Philistines had done to Saul,

12all the valiant men rose and walked all night, and took the body of Saul and the bodies of his sons from the wall of Beth-shan, and they came to Jabesh, and burned them there.

13And they took their bones and buried them under the tamarisk tree at Jabesh, and fasted seven days.

## New International

2The Philistines pressed hard after Saul and his sons, and they
killed his sons Jonathan, Abinadab and Malki-Shua. 3The fighting
grew fierce around Saul, and when the archers overtook him, they
wounded him critically.

4Saul said to his armor-bearer, "Draw your sword and run me through, or these uncircumcised fellows will come and run me through and abuse me."

But his armor-bearer was terrified and would not do it; so Saul
took his own sword and fell on it. 5When the armor-bearer saw
that Saul was dead, he too fell on his sword and died with him.
6So Saul and his three sons and his armor-bearer and all his men
died together that same day.

7When the Israelites along the valley and those across the Jordan saw that the Israelite army had fled and that Saul and his sons had died, they abandoned their towns and fled. And the Philistines came and occupied them.

8The next day, when the Philistines came to strip the dead, they
found Saul and his three sons fallen on Mount Gilboa. 9They cut
off his head and stripped off his armor, and they sent messengers
throughout the land of the Philistines to proclaim the news in the
temple of their idols and among their people. 10They put his armor
in the temple of the Ashtoreths and fastened his body to the wall
of Beth Shan.

11When the people of Jabesh Gilead heard of what the Philistines had done to Saul, 12all their valiant men journeyed through
the night to Beth Shan. They took down the bodies of Saul and his
sons from the wall of Beth Shan and went to Jabesh, where they
burned them. 13Then they took their bones and buried them under
a tamarisk tree at Jabesh, and they fasted seven days.

## King James

THE SECOND BOOK OF

# Samuel

OTHERWISE CALLED

THE SECOND BOOK OF THE KINGS

1 NOW IT came to pass after the death of Saul, when David
was returned from the slaughter of the Amalekites, and David had abode two days in Ziklag;
2It came even to pass on the third day, that, behold, a man came
out of the camp from Saul with his clothes rent, and earth upon
his head: and *so* it was, when he came to David, that he fell to the
earth, and did obeisance.
3And David said unto him, From whence comest thou? And he
said unto him, Out of the camp of Israel am I escaped.
4And David said unto him, How went the matter? I pray thee,
tell me. And he answered, That the people are fled from the battle,
and many of the people also are fallen and dead; and Saul and
Jonathan his son are dead also.
5And David said unto the young man that told him, How
knowest thou that Saul and Jonathan his son be dead?
6And the young man that told him said, As I happened by
chance upon mount Gilboa, behold, Saul leaned upon his spear;
and, lo, the chariots and horsemen followed hard after him.
7And when he looked behind him, he saw me, and called unto
me. And I answered, Here *am* I.
8And he said unto me, Who *art* thou? And I answered him, I
*am* an Amalekite.
9He said unto me again, Stand, I pray thee, upon me, and slay
me: for anguish is come upon me, because my life *is* yet whole in
me.
10So I stood upon him, and slew him, because I was sure that
he could not live after that he was fallen: and I took the crown that
*was* upon his head, and the bracelet that *was* on his arm, and have
brought them hither unto my lord.
11Then David took hold on his clothes, and rent them; and
likewise all the men that *were* with him:
12And they mourned, and wept, and fasted until even, for Saul,
and for Jonathan his son, and for the people of the LORD, and for
the house of Israel; because they were fallen by the sword.
13¶ And David said unto the young man that told him, Whence
*art* thou? And he answered, I *am* the son of a stranger, an Amalekite.
14And David said unto him, How wast thou not afraid to stretch
forth thine hand to destroy the LORD's anointed?
15And David called one of the young men, and said, Go near,
*and* fall upon him. And he smote him that he died.
16And David said unto him, Thy blood *be* upon thy head; for
thy mouth hath testified against thee, saying, I have slain the
LORD's anointed.
17¶ And David lamented with this lamentation over Saul and
over Jonathan his son:
18(Also he bade them teach the children of Judah *the use of* the
bow: behold, *it is* written in the book of Jasher.)
19The beauty of Israel is slain upon thy high places: how are the
mighty fallen!

## Amplified

THE SECOND BOOK OF

# Samuel

1 NOW AFTER the death of Saul, when David returned from
the slaughter of the Amalekites, he had stayed two days in
Ziklag,
2When on the third day a man came from Saul's camp with his
clothes torn and dust on his head. When he came to David, he fell
to the ground and did obeisance.
3David said to him, Where have you come from? He said, I have
escaped from the camp of Israel.
4David said to him, How did it go? Tell me. He answered, The
men have fled from the battle; many have fallen and are dead; Saul
and Jonathan his son are dead also.
5David said to the young man, How do you know Saul and
Jonathan his son are dead?
6The young man said, By chance I happened to be on Mount
Gilboa and I saw Saul leaning on his spear, and lo, the chariots and
horsemen were close after him.
7When he looked behind him, he saw me, and called to me. I
answered, Here I am.
8He asked me, Who are you? I answered, An Amalekite.
9He said to me, Rise up against me, and slay me; for terrible
dizziness has come upon me, yet my life is still in me [and I will
be taken alive].
10So I stood up against him, and slew him, because I was sure
he could not live after he had fallen. So I took the crown on his
head, and the bracelet on his arm, and have brought them here to
my lord.
11Then David grasped his own clothes and tore them; so did all
the men with him.
12They mourned and wept for Saul and Jonathan his son, and
fasted until evening for the Lord's people and the house of Israel,
because of their defeat in battle.
13David said to the young man who told him, Where are you
from? He answered, I am the son of a foreigner, an Amalekite.
14David said to him, Why were you not afraid to stretch forth
your hand to destroy the Lord's anointed?
15David called one of the young men, and said, Go near, and
fall upon him. And he smote him so that he died.
16David said to [the fallen man], Your blood be upon your own
head; for you have testified against yourself, saying, I have slain
the Lord's anointed.
17David lamented with this lamentation over Saul and Jonathan
his son,
18And he commanded to teach it, The Bow, to the Israelites.
Behold, it is written in the book of Jashar.
19Your glory, O Israel, is slain upon your high places. How are
the mighty fallen!

## New American Standard

# 2 Samuel

*David Learns of Saul's Death*

1 NOW IT came about after the death of Saul, when David had
returned from the slaughter of the Amalekites, that David
remained two days in Ziklag.
2And it happened on the third day, that behold, a man came
out of the camp from Saul, with his clothes torn and dust on his
head. And it came about when he came to David that he fell to the
ground and prostrated himself.
3Then David said to him, "From where do you come?" And he
said to him, "I have escaped from the camp of Israel."
4And David said to him, "How did things go? Please tell me."
And he said, "The people have fled from the battle, and also many
of the people have fallen and are dead; and Saul and Jonathan his
son are dead also."
5So David said to the young man who told him, "How do you
know that Saul and his son Jonathan are dead?"
6And the young man who told him said, "By chance I happened to be on Mount Gilboa, and behold, Saul was leaning on his
spear. And behold, the chariots and the horsemen pursued him
closely.
7"And when he looked behind him, he saw me and called to
me. And I said, 'Here I am.'
8"And he said to me, 'Who are you?' And I answered him, 'I
am an Amalekite.'
9"Then he said to me, 'Please stand beside me and kill me; for
agony has seized me because my life still lingers in me.'
10"So I stood beside him and killed him, because I knew that
he could not live after he had fallen. And I took the crown which
*was* on his head and the bracelet which *was* on his arm, and I have
brought them here to my lord."
11¶ Then David took hold of his clothes and tore them, and *so*
also *did* all the men who *were* with him.
12And they mourned and wept and fasted until evening for Saul
and his son Jonathan and for the people of the LORD and the house
of Israel, because they had fallen by the sword.
13And David said to the young man who told him, "Where are
you from?" And he answered, "I am the son of an alien, an
Amalekite."
14Then David said to him, "How is it you were not afraid to
stretch out your hand to destroy the LORD's anointed?"
15And David called one of the young men and said, "Go, cut
him down." So he struck him and he died.
16And David said to him, "Your blood is on your head, for your
mouth has testified against you, saying, 'I have killed the LORD's
anointed.' "

*David's Dirge for Saul and Jonathan*

17¶ Then David chanted with this lament over Saul and Jonathan his son,
18and he told *them* to teach the sons of Judah *the song of* the bow;
behold, it is written in the book of Jashar.
19 "Your beauty, O Israel, is slain on your high places!
How have the mighty fallen!

## New International

# 2 Samuel

*David Hears of Saul's Death*

1 AFTER THE death of Saul, David returned from defeating the
Amalekites and stayed in Ziklag two days. 2On the third day
a man arrived from Saul's camp, with his clothes torn and with
dust on his head. When he came to David, he fell to the ground
to pay him honor.
3"Where have you come from?" David asked him.
He answered, "I have escaped from the Israelite camp."
4"What happened?" David asked. "Tell me."
He said, "The men fled from the battle. Many of them fell and
died. And Saul and his son Jonathan are dead."
5Then David said to the young man who brought him the
report, "How do you know that Saul and his son Jonathan are
dead?"
6"I happened to be on Mount Gilboa," the young man said,
"and there was Saul, leaning on his spear, with the chariots and
riders almost upon him. 7When he turned around and saw me, he
called out to me, and I said, 'What can I do?'
8"He asked me, 'Who are you?'
" 'An Amalekite,' I answered.
9"Then he said to me, 'Stand over me and kill me! I am in the
throes of death, but I'm still alive.'
10"So I stood over him and killed him, because I knew that after
he had fallen he could not survive. And I took the crown that was
on his head and the band on his arm and have brought them here
to my lord."
11Then David and all the men with him took hold of their
clothes and tore them. 12They mourned and wept and fasted till
evening for Saul and his son Jonathan, and for the army of the
LORD and the house of Israel, because they had fallen by the
sword.
13David said to the young man who brought him the report,
"Where are you from?"
"I am the son of an alien, an Amalekite," he answered.
14David asked him, "Why were you not afraid to lift your hand
to destroy the LORD's anointed?"
15Then David called one of his men and said, "Go, strike him
down!" So he struck him down, and he died. 16For David had said
to him, "Your blood be on your own head. Your own mouth
testified against you when you said, 'I killed the LORD's anointed.' "

*David's Lament for Saul and Jonathan*

17David took up this lament concerning Saul anu his son Jonathan, 18and ordered that the men of Judah be taught this lament
of the bow (it is written in the Book of Jashar):
19"Your glory, O Israel, lies slain on your heights.
How the mighty have fallen!

## King James

20 Tell *it* not in Gath, publish *it* not in the streets of Askelon; lest the daughters of the Philistines rejoice, lest the daughters of the uncircumcised triumph.

21 Ye mountains of Gilboa, *let there be* no dew, neither *let there be* rain, upon you, nor fields of offerings: for there the shield of the mighty is vilely cast away, the shield of Saul, *as though he had* not *been* anointed with oil.

22 From the blood of the slain, from the fat of the mighty, the bow of Jonathan turned not back, and the sword of Saul returned not empty.

23 Saul and Jonathan *were* lovely and pleasant in their lives, and in their death they were not divided: they were swifter than eagles, they were stronger than lions.

24 Ye daughters of Israel, weep over Saul, who clothed you in scarlet, with *other* delights, who put on ornaments of gold upon your apparel.

25 How are the mighty fallen in the midst of the battle! O Jonathan, *thou wast* slain in thine high places.

26 I am distressed for thee, my brother Jonathan: very pleasant hast thou been unto me: thy love to me was wonderful, passing the love of women.

27 How are the mighty fallen, and the weapons of war perished!

**2** AND IT came to pass after this, that David inquired of the LORD, saying, Shall I go up into any of the cities of Judah? And the LORD said unto him, Go up. And David said, Whither shall I go up? And he said, Unto Hebron.

2 So David went up thither, and his two wives also, Ahinoam the Jezreelitess, and Abigail Nabal's wife the Carmelite.

3 And his men that *were* with him did David bring up, every man with his household: and they dwelt in the cities of Hebron.

4 And the men of Judah came, and there they anointed David king over the house of Judah. And they told David, saying, *That* the men of Jabesh-gilead *were they* that buried Saul.

5 ¶ And David sent messengers unto the men of Jabesh-gilead, and said unto them, Blessed *be* ye of the LORD, that ye have shown this kindness unto your lord, *even* unto Saul, and have buried him.

6 And now the LORD show kindness and truth unto you: and I also will requite you this kindness, because ye have done this thing.

7 Therefore now let your hands be strengthened, and be ye valiant: for your master Saul is dead, and also the house of Judah have anointed me king over them.

8 ¶ But Abner the son of Ner, captain of Saul's host, took Ish-bosheth the son of Saul, and brought him over to Mahanaim;

9 And made him king over Gilead, and over the Ashurites, and over Jezreel, and over Ephraim, and over Benjamin, and over all Israel.

10 Ish-bosheth Saul's son *was* forty years old when he began to reign over Israel, and reigned two years. But the house of Judah followed David.

## Amplified

20 Tell it not in Gath, announce it not in the streets of Askelon; lest the daughters of the Philistines rejoice, lest the daughters of the uncircumcised exult.

21 O mountains of Gilboa, let there be no dew or rain upon you, or fields with offerings. For there the shield of the mighty was defiled, the shield of Saul, as though he were not anointed with oil.

22 From the blood of the slain, from the fat of the mighty, the bow of Jonathan turned not back, and the sword of Saul returned not empty.

23 Saul, and Jonathan beloved and lovely! In their lives and in their death they were not divided; they were swifter than eagles, they were stronger than lions.

24 You daughters of Israel, weep over Saul, who clothed you in scarlet, with [other] delights, who put ornaments of gold upon your apparel.

25 How are the mighty fallen in the midst of the battle! Jonathan lies slain upon your high places.

26 I am distressed for you, my brother Jonathan; very pleasant have you been to me; your love to me was wonderful, passing the love of women.

27 How are the mighty fallen, and the weapons of war perished!

**2** AFTER THIS, David inquired of the Lord, saying, Shall I go up into any of the cities of Judah? And the Lord said to him, Go up. David said, To which shall I go up? And He said, To Hebron.

2 So David went up there, with his two wives, Ahinoam the Jezreelitess, and Abigail widow of Nabal of Carmel.

3 And David brought up his men who were with him, each one with his household; and they dwelt in the towns of Hebron.

4 And the men of Judah came, and there they anointed David king over the house of Judah. They told David, The men of Jabesh-gilead buried Saul. [I Sam. 31:11-13.]

5 And David sent messengers to the men of Jabesh-gilead, saying, May the Lord bless you, because you showed kindness *and* loyalty to Saul your king and buried him.

6 And now the Lord show loving-kindness and faithfulness to you. I also will do well by you because you have done this.

7 So now let your hands be strengthened, and be valiant; for your master Saul is dead, and the house of Judah has anointed me king over them.

8 Now Abner son of Ner, commander of Saul's army, took Ish-bosheth son of Saul, and brought him over to Mahanaim;

9 And he made him king over Gilead, the Ashurites, Jezreel, Ephraim, Benjamin, and all Israel.

10 Ishbosheth, Saul's son, was forty years old when he began his two years' reign over Israel. But the house of Judah followed David.

## New American Standard

20 "Tell *it* not in Gath,
Proclaim it not in the streets of Ashkelon;
Lest the daughters of the Philistines rejoice,
Lest the daughters of the uncircumcised exult.
21 "O mountains of Gilboa,
Let not dew or rain be on you, nor fields of offerings;
For there the shield of the mighty was defiled,
The shield of Saul, not anointed with oil.
22 "From the blood of the slain, from the fat of the mighty,
The bow of Jonathan did not turn back,
And the sword of Saul did not return empty.
23 "Saul and Jonathan, beloved and pleasant in their life,
And in their death they were not parted;
They were swifter than eagles,
They were stronger than lions.
24 "O daughters of Israel, weep over Saul,
Who clothed you luxuriously in scarlet,
Who put ornaments of gold on your apparel.
25 "How have the mighty fallen in the midst of the battle!
Jonathan is slain on your high places.
26 "I am distressed for you, my brother Jonathan;
You have been very pleasant to me.
Your love to me was more wonderful
Than the love of women.
27 "How have the mighty fallen,
And the weapons of war perished!"

*David Made King over Judah*

2 THEN IT came about afterwards that David inquired of the
LORD, saying, "Shall I go up to one of the cities of Judah?"
And the LORD said to him, "Go up." So David said, "Where shall
I go up?" And He said, "To Hebron."
2So David went up there, and his two wives also, Ahinoam the
Jezreelitess and Abigail the widow of Nabal the Carmelite.
3And David brought up his men who *were* with him, each with
his household; and they lived in the cities of Hebron.
4Then the men of Judah came and there anointed David king
over the house of Judah.
¶And they told David, saying, "It was the men of Jabesh-
gilead who buried Saul."
5And David sent messengers to the men of Jabesh-gilead, and
said to them, "May you be blessed of the LORD because you have
shown this kindness to Saul your lord, and have buried him.
6"And now may the LORD show lovingkindness and truth to
you; and I also will show this goodness to you, because you have
done this thing.
7"Now therefore, let your hands be strong, and be valiant; for
Saul your lord is dead, and also the house of Judah has anointed
me king over them."

*Ish-bosheth Made King over Israel*

8¶ But Abner the son of Ner, commander of Saul's army, had
taken [a]Ish-bosheth the son of Saul, and brought him over to
Mahanaim.
9And he made him king over Gilead, over the Ashurites, over
Jezreel, over Ephraim, and over Benjamin, even over all Israel.
10Ish-bosheth, Saul's son, was forty years old when he became
king over Israel, and he was king for two years. The house of
Judah, however, followed David.

NAS [a] I.e., man of shame

## New International

20"Tell it not in Gath,
proclaim it not in the streets of Ashkelon,
lest the daughters of the Philistines be glad,
lest the daughters of the uncircumcised rejoice.

21"O mountains of Gilboa,
may you have neither dew nor rain,
nor fields that yield offerings of grain.
For there the shield of the mighty was defiled,
the shield of Saul—no longer rubbed with oil.
22From the blood of the slain,
from the flesh of the mighty,
the bow of Jonathan did not turn back,
the sword of Saul did not return unsatisfied.

23"Saul and Jonathan—
in life they were loved and gracious,
and in death they were not parted.
They were swifter than eagles,
they were stronger than lions.

24"O daughters of Israel,
weep for Saul,
who clothed you in scarlet and finery,
who adorned your garments with ornaments of gold.

25"How the mighty have fallen in battle!
Jonathan lies slain on your heights.
26I grieve for you, Jonathan my brother;
you were very dear to me.
Your love for me was wonderful,
more wonderful than that of women.

27"How the mighty have fallen!
The weapons of war have perished!"

*David Anointed King Over Judah*

2 IN THE course of time, David inquired of the LORD. "Shall I
go up to one of the towns of Judah?" he asked.
The LORD said, "Go up."
David asked, "Where shall I go?"
"To Hebron," the LORD answered.
2So David went up there with his two wives, Ahinoam of Jezreel and Abigail, the widow of Nabal of Carmel. 3David also took
the men who were with him, each with his family, and they settled
in Hebron and its towns. 4Then the men of Judah came to Hebron
and there they anointed David king over the house of Judah.
When David was told that it was the men of Jabesh Gilead who
had buried Saul, 5he sent messengers to the men of Jabesh Gilead
to say to them, "The LORD bless you for showing this kindness to
Saul your master by burying him. 6May the LORD now show you
kindness and faithfulness, and I too will show you the same favor
because you have done this. 7Now then, be strong and brave, for
Saul your master is dead, and the house of Judah has anointed me
king over them."

*War Between the Houses of David and Saul*

8Meanwhile, Abner son of Ner, the commander of Saul's army,
had taken Ish-Bosheth son of Saul and brought him over to Mahanaim. 9He made him king over Gilead, Ashuri[b] and Jezreel, and
also over Ephraim, Benjamin and all Israel.
10Ish-Bosheth son of Saul was forty years old when he became
king over Israel, and he reigned two years. The house of Judah,
however, followed David. 11The length of time David was king in

NIV [b] 9 Or *Asher*

## King James

11And the time that David was king in Hebron over the house of Judah was seven years and six months.

12¶ And Abner the son of Ner, and the servants of Ish-bosheth the son of Saul, went out from Mahanaim to Gibeon.

13And Joab the son of Zeruiah, and the servants of David, went out, and met together by the pool of Gibeon: and they sat down, the one on the one side of the pool, and the other on the other side of the pool.

14And Abner said to Joab, Let the young men now arise, and play before us. And Joab said, Let them arise.

15Then there arose and went over by number twelve of Benjamin, which *pertained* to Ish-bosheth the son of Saul, and twelve of the servants of David.

16And they caught every one his fellow by the head, and *thrust* his sword in his fellow's side; so they fell down together: wherefore that place was called Helkath-hazzurim, which *is* in Gibeon.

17And there was a very sore battle that day; and Abner was beaten, and the men of Israel, before the servants of David.

18¶ And there were three sons of Zeruiah there, Joab, and Abishai, and Asahel: and Asahel *was as* light of foot as a wild roe.

19And Asahel pursued after Abner; and in going he turned not to the right hand nor to the left from following Abner.

20Then Abner looked behind him, and said, *Art* thou Asahel? And he answered, I *am*.

21And Abner said to him, Turn thee aside to thy right hand or to thy left, and lay thee hold on one of the young men, and take thee his armour. But Asahel would not turn aside from following of him.

22And Abner said again to Asahel, Turn thee aside from following me: wherefore should I smite thee to the ground? how then should I hold up my face to Joab thy brother?

23Howbeit he refused to turn aside: wherefore Abner with the hinder end of the spear smote him under the fifth *rib*, that the spear came out behind him; and he fell down there, and died in the same place: and it came to pass, *that* as many as came to the place where Asahel fell down and died stood still.

24Joab also and Abishai pursued after Abner: and the sun went down when they were come to the hill of Ammah, that *lieth* before Giah by the way of the wilderness of Gibeon.

25¶ And the children of Benjamin gathered themselves together after Abner, and became one troop, and stood on the top of an hill.

26Then Abner called to Joab, and said, Shall the sword devour for ever? knowest thou not that it will be bitterness in the latter end? how long shall it be then, ere thou bid the people return from following their brethren?

27And Joab said, *As* God liveth, unless thou hadst spoken, surely then in the morning the people had gone up every one from following his brother.

28So Joab blew a trumpet, and all the people stood still, and pursued after Israel no more, neither fought they any more.

29And Abner and his men walked all that night through the plain, and passed over Jordan, and went through all Bithron, and they came to Mahanaim.

30And Joab returned from following Abner: and when he had gathered all the people together, there lacked of David's servants nineteen men and Asahel.

31But the servants of David had smitten of Benjamin, and of Abner's men, *so that* three hundred and threescore men died.

32¶ And they took up Asahel, and buried him in the sepulchre of his father, which *was in* Bethlehem. And Joab and his men went all night, and they came to Hebron at break of day.

## Amplified

11And David was king in Hebron over the house of Judah seven years and six months.

12And Abner son of Ner, and the servants of Ishbosheth son of Saul, went out from Mahanaim to Gibeon.

13Joab son of Zeruiah, and the servants of David, went out also, and the two groups met by the pool of Gibeon, seating themselves, one group on either side of the pool.

14And Abner said to Joab, Let the young men now arise, and have a contest before us. And Joab said, Let them arise.

15Then there arose and went over by number, twelve of Benjamin, who were with Ishbosheth son of Saul, and twelve of the servants of David.

16And each caught his opponent by the head and thrust his sword into his side; so they all fell together. Therefore that place was called the field of sharp knives, which is at Gibeon.

17A very fierce battle followed, and Abner with the men of Israel was beaten before the servants of David.

18Three sons of Zeruiah [the half sister of David] were there, Joab, Abishai, and Asahel. Now Asahel was as light of foot as a wild roe *or* antelope.

19Asahel pursued Abner; and as he ran he turned not to the right hand or to the left from following Abner.

20Then Abner looked behind him, and said, Are you Asahel? He answered, I am.

21Abner said to him, Turn aside to your right or left, and seize one of the young men, and take his armor. But Asahel would not turn aside from following him.

22And Abner said again to Asahel, Turn aside from following me. Why should I strike you to the ground? How then should I be able to face Joab your brother?

23Asahel refused to turn aside; so Abner with the rear end of his spear smote him through the abdomen, and he fell, and died where he fell. And all who came to the place where Asahel fell and died, stood still.

24But Joab and Abishai [his brothers] pursued Abner; the sun was going down as they came to the hill of Ammah, before Giah on the way to the wilderness of Gibeon.

25And the Benjamites gathered together behind Abner, and became one troop, and took their stand on the top of a hill.

26Then Abner called to Joab, Shall the sword devour for ever? Do you not know that bitterness will be the result? How long will it be then before you bid the people stop pursuing their brethren?

27Joab said, As God lives, if you had not spoken, surely the men would have stopped pursuing their brethren in the morning.

28So Joab blew a trumpet, and all the people stood still, and pursued Israel no more, nor did they fight any more.

29Abner and his men went all night through the Arabah [plain], crossed the Jordan, and went through all the Bithron [district of ravines] and came to Mahanaim.

30Joab returned from pursuing Abner; and when he had gathered all the people together, there were missing of David's servants nineteen men besides Asahel.

31But the servants of David had slain of Benjamin, 360 of Abner's men.

32And they took up Asahel, and buried him in the tomb of his father, at Bethlehem. And Joab and his men walked all night, and came to Hebron at daybreak.

## New American Standard

11And the time that David was king in Hebron over the house
of Judah was seven years and six months.

*Civil War*

**12**¶ Now Abner the son of Ner, went out from Mahanaim to
Gibeon with the servants of Ish-bosheth the son of Saul.
13And Joab the son of Zeruiah and the servants of David went
out and met them by the pool of Gibeon; and they sat down, one
on the one side of the pool and the other on the other side of the
pool.
14Then Abner said to Joab, "Now let the young men arise and
[a]hold a contest before us." And Joab said, "Let them arise."
15So they arose and went over by count, twelve for Benjamin
and Ish-bosheth the son of Saul, and twelve of the servants of
David.
16And each one of them seized his opponent by the head, and
*thrust* his sword in his opponent's side; so they fell down together.
Therefore that place was called [b]Helkath-hazzurim, which is in
Gibeon.
17And that day the battle was very severe, and Abner and the
men of Israel were beaten before the servants of David.
**18**¶ Now the three sons of Zeruiah were there, Joab and Abishai
and Asahel; and Asahel *was as* swift-footed as one of the gazelles
which is in the field.
19And Asahel pursued Abner and did not turn to the right or
to the left from following Abner.
20Then Abner looked behind him and said, "Is that you, Asahel?" And he answered, "It is I."
21So Abner said to him, "Turn to your right or to your left, and
take hold of one of the young men for yourself, and take for
yourself his spoil." But Asahel was not willing to turn aside from
following him.
22And Abner repeated again to Asahel, "Turn aside from following me. Why should I strike you to the ground? How then
could I lift up my face to your brother Joab?"
23However, he refused to turn aside; therefore Abner struck
him in the belly with the butt end of the spear, so that the spear
came out at his back. And he fell there and died on the spot. And
it came about that all who came to the place where Asahel had
fallen and died, stood still.
**24**¶ But Joab and Abishai pursued Abner, and when the sun was
going down, they came to the hill of Ammah, which is in front of
Giah by the way of the wilderness of Gibeon.
25And the sons of Benjamin gathered together behind Abner
and became one band, and they stood on the top of a certain hill.
26Then Abner called to Joab and said, "Shall the sword devour
forever? Do you not know that it will be bitter in the end? How long
will you refrain from telling the people to turn back from following
their brothers?"
27And Joab said, "As God lives, if you had not spoken, surely
then the people would have gone away in the morning, each from
following his brother."
28So Joab blew the trumpet; and all the people halted and pursued Israel no longer, nor did they continue to fight anymore.
29Abner and his men then went through the Arabah all that
night; so they crossed the Jordan, walked all morning, and came
to Mahanaim.
**30**¶ Then Joab returned from following Abner; when he had
gathered all the people together, nineteen of David's servants
besides Asahel were missing.
31But the servants of David had struck down many of Benjamin
and Abner's men, *so that* three hundred and sixty men died.
32And they took up Asahel and buried him in his father's tomb
which was in Bethlehem. Then Joab and his men went all night
until the day dawned at Hebron.

**NAS** [a] Lit., *make sport* [b] I.e., the field of sword-edges

## New International

Hebron over the house of Judah was seven years and six months.
12Abner son of Ner, together with the men of Ish-Bosheth son
of Saul, left Mahanaim and went to Gibeon. 13Joab son of Zeruiah
and David's men went out and met them at the pool of Gibeon.
One group sat down on one side of the pool and one group on the
other side.
14Then Abner said to Joab, "Let's have some of the young men
get up and fight hand to hand in front of us."
"All right, let them do it," Joab said.
15So they stood up and were counted off—twelve men for Benjamin and Ish-Bosheth son of Saul, and twelve for David. 16Then
each man grabbed his opponent by the head and thrust his dagger
into his opponent's side, and they fell down together. So that place
in Gibeon was called Helkath Hazzurim.[c]
17The battle that day was very fierce, and Abner and the men
of Israel were defeated by David's men.
18The three sons of Zeruiah were there: Joab, Abishai and Asahel. Now Asahel was as fleet-footed as a wild gazelle. 19He chased
Abner, turning neither to the right nor to the left as he pursued
him. 20Abner looked behind him and asked, "Is that you, Asahel?"
"It is," he answered.
21Then Abner said to him, "Turn aside to the right or to the left;
take on one of the young men and strip him of his weapons." But
Asahel would not stop chasing him.
22Again Abner warned Asahel, "Stop chasing me! Why should
I strike you down? How could I look your brother Joab in the face?"
23But Asahel refused to give up the pursuit; so Abner thrust the
butt of his spear into Asahel's stomach, and the spear came out
through his back. He fell there and died on the spot. And every
man stopped when he came to the place where Asahel had fallen
and died.
24But Joab and Abishai pursued Abner, and as the sun was
setting, they came to the hill of Ammah, near Giah on the way to
the wasteland of Gibeon. 25Then the men of Benjamin rallied
behind Abner. They formed themselves into a group and took
their stand on top of a hill.
26Abner called out to Joab, "Must the sword devour forever?
Don't you realize that this will end in bitterness? How long before
you order your men to stop pursuing their brothers?"
27Joab answered, "As surely as God lives, if you had not
spoken, the men would have continued the pursuit of their brothers until morning.[d]"
28So Joab blew the trumpet, and all the men came to a halt; they
no longer pursued Israel, nor did they fight anymore.
29All that night Abner and his men marched through the Arabah. They crossed the Jordan, continued through the whole Bithron[e] and came to Mahanaim.
30Then Joab returned from pursuing Abner and assembled all
his men. Besides Asahel, nineteen of David's men were found
missing. 31But David's men had killed three hundred and sixty
Benjamites who were with Abner. 32They took Asahel and buried
him in his father's tomb at Bethlehem. Then Joab and his men
marched all night and arrived at Hebron by daybreak.

**NIV** [c] 16 *Helkath Hazzurim* means *field of daggers* or *field of hostilities.* [d] 27 Or *spoken this morning, the men would not have taken up the pursuit of their brothers;* or *spoken, the men would have given up the pursuit of their brothers by morning* [e] 29 Or *morning;* or *ravine;* the meaning of the Hebrew for this word is uncertain.

## King James

3 NOW THERE was long war between the house of Saul and
the house of David: but David waxed stronger and stronger,
and the house of Saul waxed weaker and weaker.
2¶ And unto David were sons born in Hebron: and his firstborn
was Amnon, of Ahinoam the Jezreelitess;
3And his second, Chileab, of Abigail the wife of Nabal the
Carmelite; and the third, Absalom the son of Maacah the daughter
of Talmai king of Geshur;
4And the fourth, Adonijah the son of Haggith; and the fifth,
Shephatiah the son of Abital;
5And the sixth, Ithream, by Eglah David's wife. These were
born to David in Hebron.
6¶ And it came to pass, while there was war between the house
of Saul and the house of David, that Abner made himself strong
for the house of Saul.
7And Saul had a concubine, whose name *was* Rizpah, the
daughter of Aiah: and *Ish-bosheth* said to Abner, Wherefore hast
thou gone in unto my father's concubine?
8Then was Abner very wroth for the words of Ish-bosheth, and
said, *Am* I a dog's head, which against Judah do show kindness
this day unto the house of Saul thy father, to his brethren, and to
his friends, and have not delivered thee into the hand of David,
that thou chargest me today with a fault concerning this woman?
9So do God to Abner, and more also, except, as the LORD hath
sworn to David, even so I do to him;
10To translate the kingdom from the house of Saul, and to set
up the throne of David over Israel and over Judah, from Dan even
to Beer-sheba.
11And he could not answer Abner a word again, because he
feared him.
12¶ And Abner sent messengers to David on his behalf, saying,
Whose *is* the land? saying *also,* Make thy league with me, and,
behold, my hand *shall be* with thee, to bring about all Israel unto
thee.
13¶ And he said, Well; I will make a league with thee: but one
thing I require of thee, that is, Thou shalt not see my face, except
thou first bring Michal Saul's daughter, when thou comest to see
my face.
14And David sent messengers to Ish-bosheth Saul's son, saying, Deliver *me* my wife Michal, which I espoused to me for an
hundred foreskins of the Philistines.
15And Ish-bosheth sent, and took her from *her* husband, *even*
from Phaltiel the son of Laish.
16And her husband went with her along weeping behind her
to Bahurim. Then said Abner unto him, Go, return. And he returned.
17¶ And Abner had communication with the elders of Israel,
saying, Ye sought for David in times past *to be* king over you:
18Now then do *it:* for the LORD hath spoken of David, saying,
By the hand of my servant David I will save my people Israel out
of the hand of the Philistines, and out of the hand of all their
enemies.
19And Abner also spake in the ears of Benjamin: and Abner
went also to speak in the ears of David in Hebron all that seemed
good to Israel, and that seemed good to the whole house of Benjamin.
20So Abner came to David to Hebron, and twenty men with
him. And David made Abner and the men that *were* with him a
feast.
21And Abner said unto David, I will arise and go, and will
gather all Israel unto my lord the king, that they may make a league
with thee, and that thou mayest reign over all that thine heart
desireth. And David sent Abner away; and he went in peace.
22¶ And, behold, the servants of David and Joab came from
*pursuing* a troop, and brought in a great spoil with them: but Abner
*was* not with David in Hebron; for he had sent him away, and he
was gone in peace.

## Amplified

3 THERE WAS a long war between the house of Saul and the
house of David; but David grew stronger and stronger, and
the house of Saul grew weaker and weaker.
2Sons were born to David in Hebron: his first-born was Amnon,
of Ahinoam the Jezreelitess;
3His second, Chileab, of Abigail widow of Nabal of Carmel; the
third, Absalom son of Maacah daughter of Talmai king of Geshur;
4The fourth, Adonijah son of Haggith; the fifth, Shephatiah son
of Abital;
5And the sixth, Ithream of Eglah, David's wife. These were born
to David in Hebron.
6While there was war between the houses of Saul and David,
Abner was making himself strong in the house of Saul.
7Now Saul had a concubine, whose name was Rizpah daughter
of Aiah; and Ishbosheth said to Abner, Why have you gone in to
my father's concubine?
8Then Abner was very angry at the words of Ishbosheth, and
said, Am I a dog's head [despicable and hostile] against Judah?
This day I keep showing kindness *and* loyalty to the house of Saul
your father, to his brothers, and his friends; and have not delivered
you into the hand of David; and yet you charge me today with a
fault concerning this woman?
9God do so to Abner, and more also, if I do not do for David
what the Lord has sworn to him;
10To transfer the kingdom from the house of Saul, and set the
throne of David over Israel and Judah, from Dan to Beer-sheba.
11And Ishbosheth could not answer Abner a word, because he
feared him.
12And Abner sent messengers to David where he was [at He-
bron], saying, Whose is the land? Make your league with me, and
my hand shall be with you, to bring all Israel over to you.
13And David said, Good. I will make a league with you. But I
require one thing of you; that is, you shall not see my face unless
you first bring Michal, Saul's daughter, when you come to see me.
14And David sent messengers to Ishbosheth Saul's son, saying,
Give me my wife Michal, whom I betrothed for a hundred foreskins of the Philistines.
15And Ishbosheth sent, and took her from her [second] husband, from Paltiel son of Laish [to whom Saul had given her].
16But her husband went with her, weeping behind her all the
way to Bahurim. Then Abner said to him, Go back. And he did so.
17Abner talked with the seniors of Israel, saying, In times past
you sought to make David king over you.
18Now then do it; for the Lord has spoken of David, saying, By
the hand of My servant David I will save My people Israel from
the hand of the Philistines and of all their enemies. [I Sam. 9:16
with 15:27, 28.]
19Abner also spoke to [the men of] Benjamin. Then [he] went
to Hebron to tell David all that seemed good to Israel and the whole
house of Benjamin to do.
20So Abner came to David at Hebron, and twenty men with
him. And David made Abner and the men with him a feast.
21Abner said to David, I will go and gather all Israel to my lord
the king, that they may make a league with you, and that you may
reign over all that your heart desires. So David sent Abner away
in peace.
22Then the servants of David came with Joab from pursuing a
troop, and brought much spoil with them. But Abner was not with
David in Hebron, for he had sent him away, and he had gone in
peace.

## New American Standard

*The House of David Strengthened*

3 NOW THERE was a long war between the house of Saul and
the house of David; and David grew steadily stronger, but the
house of Saul grew weaker continually.
2¶ Sons were born to David at Hebron: his first-born was
Amnon, by Ahinoam the Jezreelitess;
3and his second, Chileab, by Abigail the widow of Nabal the
Carmelite; and the third, Absalom the son of Maacah, the daughter
of Talmai, king of Geshur;
4and the fourth, Adonijah the son of Haggith; and the fifth,
Shephatiah the son of Abital;
5and the sixth, Ithream, by David's wife Eglah. These were
born to David at Hebron.

*Abner Joins David*

6¶ And it came about while there was war between the house
of Saul and the house of David that Abner was making himself
strong in the house of Saul.
7Now Saul had a concubine whose name was Rizpah, the
daughter of Aiah; and Ish-bosheth said to Abner, "Why have you
gone in to my father's concubine?"
8Then Abner was very angry over the words of Ish-bosheth
and said, "Am I a dog's head that belongs to Judah? Today I show
kindness to the house of Saul your father, to his brothers and to
his friends, and have not delivered you into the hands of David;
and yet today you charge me with a guilt concerning the woman.
9"May God do so to Abner, and more also, if as the LORD has
sworn to David, I do not accomplish this for him,
10to transfer the kingdom from the house of Saul, and to establish the throne of David over Israel and over Judah, from Dan even
to Beersheba."
11And he could no longer answer Abner a word, because he
was afraid of him.
12¶ Then Abner sent messengers to David in his place, saying,
"Whose is the land? Make your covenant with me, and behold, my
hand shall be with you to bring all Israel over to you."
13And he said, "Good! I will make a covenant with you, but I
demand one thing of you, namely, you shall not see my face unless
you first bring Michal, Saul's daughter, when you come to see
me."
14So David sent messengers to Ish-bosheth, Saul's son, saying,
"Give me my wife Michal, to whom I was betrothed for a hundred
foreskins of the Philistines."
15And Ish-bosheth sent and took her from *her* husband, from
Paltiel the son of Laish.
16But her husband went with her, weeping as he went, and
followed her as far as Bahurim. Then Abner said to him, "Go,
return." So he returned.
17¶ Now Abner had consultation with the elders of Israel, saying, "In times past you were seeking for David to be king over you.
18"Now then, do *it*! For the LORD has spoken of David, saying,
'By the hand of My servant David I will save My people Israel from
the hand of the Philistines and from the hand of all their enemies.' "
19And Abner also spoke in the hearing of Benjamin; and in
addition Abner went to speak in the hearing of David in Hebron
all that seemed good to Israel and to the whole house of Benjamin.
20¶ Then Abner and twenty men with him came to David at
Hebron. And David made a feast for Abner and the men who were
with him.
21And Abner said to David, "Let me arise and go, and gather
all Israel to my lord the king that they may make a covenant with
you, and that you may be king over all that your soul desires." So
David sent Abner away, and he went in peace.
22¶ And behold, the servants of David and Joab came from a raid
and brought much spoil with them; but Abner was not with David
in Hebron, for he had sent him away, and he had gone in peace.

## New International

3 THE WAR between the house of Saul and the house of David
lasted a long time. David grew stronger and stronger, while
the house of Saul grew weaker and weaker.
2Sons were born to David in Hebron:
His firstborn was Amnon the son of Ahinoam of Jezreel;
3his second, Kileab the son of Abigail the widow of Nabal
of Carmel;
the third, Absalom the son of Maacah daughter of Talmai
king of Geshur;
4the fourth, Adonijah the son of Haggith;
the fifth, Shephatiah the son of Abital;
5and the sixth, Ithream the son of David's wife Eglah.
These were born to David in Hebron.

*Abner Goes Over to David*

6During the war between the house of Saul and the house of
David, Abner had been strengthening his own position in the
house of Saul. 7Now Saul had had a concubine named Rizpah
daughter of Aiah. And Ish-Bosheth said to Abner, "Why did you
sleep with my father's concubine?"
8Abner was very angry because of what Ish-Bosheth said and
he answered, "Am I a dog's head—on Judah's side? This very day
I am loyal to the house of your father Saul and to his family and
friends. I haven't handed you over to David. Yet now you accuse
me of an offense involving this woman! 9May God deal with Abner, be it ever so severely, if I do not do for David what the LORD
promised him on oath 10and transfer the kingdom from the house
of Saul and establish David's throne over Israel and Judah from
Dan to Beersheba." 11Ish-Bosheth did not dare to say another word
to Abner, because he was afraid of him.
12Then Abner sent messengers on his behalf to say to David,
"Whose land is it? Make an agreement with me, and I will help you
bring all Israel over to you."
13"Good," said David. "I will make an agreement with you. But
I demand one thing of you: Do not come into my presence unless
you bring Michal daughter of Saul when you come to see me."
14Then David sent messengers to Ish-Bosheth son of Saul, demanding, "Give me my wife Michal, whom I betrothed to myself
for the price of a hundred Philistine foreskins."
15So Ish-Bosheth gave orders and had her taken away from her
husband Paltiel son of Laish. 16Her husband, however, went with
her, weeping behind her all the way to Bahurim. Then Abner said
to him, "Go back home!" So he went back.
17Abner conferred with the elders of Israel and said, "For some
time you have wanted to make David your king. 18Now do it! For
the LORD promised David, 'By my servant David I will rescue my
people Israel from the hand of the Philistines and from the hand
of all their enemies.' "
19Abner also spoke to the Benjamites in person. Then he went
to Hebron to tell David everything that Israel and the whole house
of Benjamin wanted to do. 20When Abner, who had twenty men
with him, came to David at Hebron, David prepared a feast for him
and his men. 21Then Abner said to David, "Let me go at once and
assemble all Israel for my lord the king, so that they may make a
compact with you, and that you may rule over all that your heart
desires." So David sent Abner away, and he went in peace.

*Joab Murders Abner*

22Just then David's men and Joab returned from a raid and
brought with them a great deal of plunder. But Abner was no
longer with David in Hebron, because David had sent him away,
and he had gone in peace. 23When Joab and all the soldiers with

## King James

23 When Joab and all the host that *was* with him were come, they told Joab, saying, Abner the son of Ner came to the king, and he hath sent him away, and he is gone in peace.

24 Then Joab came to the king, and said, What hast thou done? behold, Abner came unto thee; why *is* it *that* thou hast sent him away, and he is quite gone?

25 Thou knowest Abner the son of Ner, that he came to deceive thee, and to know thy going out and thy coming in, and to know all that thou doest.

26 And when Joab was come out from David, he sent messengers after Abner, which brought him again from the well of Sirah: but David knew *it* not.

27 And when Abner was returned to Hebron, Joab took him aside in the gate to speak with him quietly, and smote him there under the fifth *rib*, that he died, for the blood of Asahel his brother.

28 ¶ And afterward when David heard *it*, he said, I and my kingdom *are* guiltless before the LORD for ever from the blood of Abner the son of Ner:

29 Let it rest on the head of Joab, and on all his father's house; and let there not fail from the house of Joab one that hath an issue, or that is a leper, or that leaneth on a staff, or that falleth on the sword, or that lacketh bread.

30 So Joab and Abishai his brother slew Abner, because he had slain their brother Asahel at Gibeon in the battle.

31 ¶ And David said to Joab, and to all the people that *were* with him, Rend your clothes, and gird you with sackcloth, and mourn before Abner. And king David *himself* followed the bier.

32 And they buried Abner in Hebron: and the king lifted up his voice, and wept at the grave of Abner; and all the people wept.

33 And the king lamented over Abner, and said, Died Abner as a fool dieth?

34 Thy hands *were* not bound, nor thy feet put into fetters: as a man falleth before wicked men, *so* fellest thou. And all the people wept again over him.

35 And when all the people came to cause David to eat meat while it was yet day, David sware, saying, So do God to me, and more also, if I taste bread, or aught else, till the sun be down.

36 And all the people took notice *of it*, and it pleased them: as whatsoever the king did pleased all the people.

37 For all the people and all Israel understood that day that it was not of the king to slay Abner the son of Ner.

38 And the king said unto his servants, Know ye not that there is a prince and a great man fallen this day in Israel?

39 And I *am* this day weak, though anointed king; and these men the sons of Zeruiah *be* too hard for me: the LORD shall reward the doer of evil according to his wickedness.

4 AND WHEN Saul's son heard that Abner was dead in Hebron, his hands were feeble, and all the Israelites were troubled.

2 And Saul's son had two men *that were* captains of bands: the name of the one *was* Baanah, and the name of the other Rechab, the sons of Rimmon a Beerothite, of the children of Benjamin: (for Beeroth also was reckoned to Benjamin:

3 And the Beerothites fled to Gittaim, and were sojourners there until this day.)

## Amplified

23 When Joab and all the army with him had come, it was told Joab, Abner son of Ner came to the king, and he has sent him away, and he is gone in peace.

24 Then Joab came to the king, and said, What have you done? Behold, Abner came to you. Why is it you have sent him away, and he is quite gone?

25 You know that Abner son of Ner came to deceive you, and to know your going out and coming in and all you are doing.

26 When Joab came from seeing David, he sent messengers after Abner, who brought him back from the well of Sirah; but David did not know it.

27 And when Abner returned to Hebron, Joab took him aside to the center of the gate to speak to him privately, and there he smote Abner in the abdomen, so he died, to avenge the blood of Asahel Joab's brother.

28 When David heard of it, he said, I and my kingdom are guiltless before the Lord for ever of the blood of Abner son of Ner.

29 Let it fall on the head of Joab, and on all his father's house; and let the house of Joab never be without one who has a discharge, or is a leper, or walks with a crutch *or* is a distaff holder [unfit for war], or who falls by the sword, or lacks food!

30 So Joab and Abishai his brother slew Abner, because he had slain their brother Asahel at Gibeon in the battle.

31 And David said to Joab and to all the people with him, Rend your clothes, gird yourselves with sackcloth, and mourn before Abner. And King David followed the bier.

32 They buried Abner in Hebron. And the king lifted up his voice and wept at the grave of Abner; and all the people wept.

33 And the king lamented over Abner, and said, Should Abner die as a fool dies?

34 Your hands were not bound, or your feet put into fetters; as a man falls before wicked men, so you fell. And all the people wept again over him.

35 All the people came to urge David to eat food while it was yet day; but David took an oath, saying, May God do so to me and more also if I taste bread or anything else, till the sun is down.

36 And all the people took notice of it, and it pleased them, as whatever the king did pleased all the people.

37 For all the people and all Israel understood that day that it was not the king's will to slay Abner son of Ner.

38 King David said to his servants, Do you not know that a prince and a great man has fallen this day in Israel?

39 And I am this day weak, though anointed [but not crowned] king; these sons of Zeruiah are too hard for me. The Lord repay the evildoer according to his wickedness!

4 WHEN ISHBOSHETH, Saul's son [king over Israel], heard that Abner was dead in Hebron, his courage failed, and all the Israelites were troubled *and* dismayed.

2 Saul's son had two men who were captains of raiding bands; one was named Baanah, and the other Rechab, sons of Rimmon the Beerothite of Benjamin (for Beeroth also was reckoned to Benjamin.

3 And the Beerothites fled to Gittaim, and have been sojourners there to this day).

## New American Standard

23When Joab and all the army that was with him arrived, they
told Joab, saying, "Abner the son of Ner came to the king, and he
has sent him away, and he has gone in peace."
24Then Joab came to the king and said, "What have you done?
Behold, Abner came to you; why then have you sent him away and
he is already gone?
25"You know Abner the son of Ner, that he came to deceive you
and to learn of your going out and coming in, and to find out all
that you are doing."

*Joab Murders Abner*

26¶ When Joab came out from David, he sent messengers after
Abner, and they brought him back from the well of Sirah; but
David did not know *it*.
27So when Abner returned to Hebron, Joab took him aside into
the middle of the gate to speak with him privately, and there he
struck him in the belly so that he died on account of the blood of
Asahel his brother.
28And afterward when David heard it, he said, "I and my
kingdom are innocent before the LORD forever of the blood of
Abner the son of Ner.
29"May it fall on the head of Joab and on all his father's house;
and may there not fail from the house of Joab one who has a
discharge, or who is a leper, or who takes hold of a distaff, or who
falls by the sword, or who lacks bread."
30So Joab and Abishai his brother killed Abner because he had
put their brother Asahel to death in the battle at Gibeon.

*David Mourns Abner*

31¶ Then David said to Joab and to all the people who were with
him, "Tear your clothes and gird on sackcloth and lament before
Abner." And King David walked behind the bier.
32Thus they buried Abner in Hebron; and the king lifted up his
voice and wept at the grave of Abner, and all the people wept.
33And the king chanted a *lament* for Abner and said,
"Should Abner die as a fool dies?
34 "Your hands were not bound, nor your feet put in
fetters;
As one falls before the wicked, you have fallen."
And all the people wept again over him.
35Then all the people came to persuade David to eat bread while
it was still day; but David vowed, saying, "May God do so to me,
and more also, if I taste bread or anything else before the sun goes
down."
36Now all the people took note *of it*, and it pleased them, just
as everything the king did pleased all the people.
37So all the people and all Israel understood that day that it had
not been *the will* of the king to put Abner the son of Ner to death.
38Then the king said to his servants, "Do you not know that a
prince and a great man has fallen this day in Israel?
39"And I am weak today, though anointed king; and these men
the sons of Zeruiah are too difficult for me. May the LORD repay
the evildoer according to his evil."

*Ish-bosheth Murdered*

4 NOW WHEN Ish-bosheth, Saul's son, heard that Abner had
died in Hebron, he lost courage, and all Israel was disturbed.
2And Saul's son *had* two men who were commanders of bands:
the name of the one was Baanah and the name of the other Rechab,
sons of Rimmon the Beerothite, of the sons of Benjamin (for
Beeroth is also considered *part* of Benjamin,
3and the Beerothites fled to Gittaim, and have been aliens there
until this day).

## New International

him arrived, he was told that Abner son of Ner had come to the
king and that the king had sent him away and that he had gone
in peace.
24So Joab went to the king and said, "What have you done?
Look, Abner came to you. Why did you let him go? Now he is
gone! 25You know Abner son of Ner; he came to deceive you and
observe your movements and find out everything you are doing."
26Joab then left David and sent messengers after Abner, and
they brought him back from the well of Sirah. But David did not
know it. 27Now when Abner returned to Hebron, Joab took him
aside into the gateway, as though to speak with him privately. And
there, to avenge the blood of his brother Asahel, Joab stabbed him
in the stomach, and he died.
28Later, when David heard about this, he said, "I and my kingdom are forever innocent before the LORD concerning the blood of
Abner son of Ner. 29May his blood fall upon the head of Joab and
upon all his father's house! May Joab's house never be without
someone who has a running sore or leprosy[a] or who leans on a
crutch or who falls by the sword or who lacks food."
30(Joab and his brother Abishai murdered Abner because he
had killed their brother Asahel in the battle at Gibeon.)
31Then David said to Joab and all the people with him, "Tear
your clothes and put on sackcloth and walk in mourning in front
of Abner." King David himself walked behind the bier. 32They
buried Abner in Hebron, and the king wept aloud at Abner's tomb.
All the people wept also.
33The king sang this lament for Abner:
"Should Abner have died as the lawless die?
34 Your hands were not bound,
your feet were not fettered.
You fell as one falls before wicked men."
And all the people wept over him again.
35Then they all came and urged David to eat something while
it was still day; but David took an oath, saying, "May God deal
with me, be it ever so severely, if I taste bread or anything else
before the sun sets!"
36All the people took note and were pleased; indeed, everything the king did pleased them. 37So on that day all the people
and all Israel knew that the king had no part in the murder of
Abner son of Ner.
38Then the king said to his men, "Do you not realize that a
prince and a great man has fallen in Israel this day? 39And today,
though I am the anointed king, I am weak, and these sons of
Zeruiah are too strong for me. May the LORD repay the evildoer
according to his evil deeds!"

*Ish-Bosheth Murdered*

4 WHEN ISH-BOSHETH son of Saul heard that Abner had died
in Hebron, he lost courage, and all Israel became alarmed.
2Now Saul's son had two men who were leaders of raiding bands.
One was named Baanah and the other Recab; they were sons of
Rimmon the Beerothite from the tribe of Benjamin—Beeroth is
considered part of Benjamin, 3because the people of Beeroth fled
to Gittaim and have lived there as aliens to this day.

**NIV** [a] 29 The Hebrew word was used for various diseases affecting the skin—not necessarily leprosy.

## King James

4And Jonathan, Saul's son, had a son *that was* lame of *his* feet. He was five years old when the tidings came of Saul and Jonathan out of Jezreel, and his nurse took him up, and fled: and it came to pass, as she made haste to flee, that he fell, and became lame. And his name *was* Mephibosheth.

5And the sons of Rimmon the Beerothite, Rechab and Baanah, went, and came about the heat of the day to the house of Ish-bosheth, who lay on a bed at noon.

6And they came thither into the midst of the house, *as though* they would have fetched wheat; and they smote him under the fifth *rib:* and Rechab and Baanah his brother escaped.

7For when they came into the house, he lay on his bed in his bedchamber, and they smote him, and slew him, and beheaded him, and took his head, and gat them away through the plain all night.

8And they brought the head of Ish-bosheth unto David to Hebron, and said to the king, Behold the head of Ish-bosheth the son of Saul thine enemy, which sought thy life; and the LORD hath avenged my lord the king this day of Saul, and of his seed.

9¶ And David answered Rechab and Baanah his brother, the sons of Rimmon the Beerothite, and said unto them, *As* the LORD liveth, who hath redeemed my soul out of all adversity,

10When one told me, saying, Behold, Saul is dead, thinking to have brought good tidings, I took hold of him, and slew him in Ziklag, who *thought* that I would have given him a reward for his tidings:

11How much more, when wicked men have slain a righteous person in his own house upon his bed? shall I not therefore now require his blood of your hand, and take you away from the earth?

12And David commanded his young men, and they slew them, and cut off their hands and their feet, and hanged *them* up over the pool in Hebron. But they took the head of Ish-bosheth, and buried *it* in the sepulchre of Abner in Hebron.

**5** THEN CAME all the tribes of Israel to David unto Hebron, and spake, saying, Behold, we *are* thy bone and thy flesh.

2Also in time past, when Saul was king over us, thou wast he that leddest out and broughtest in Israel: and the LORD said to thee, Thou shalt feed my people Israel, and thou shalt be a captain over Israel.

3So all the elders of Israel came to the king to Hebron; and king David made a league with them in Hebron before the LORD: and they anointed David king over Israel.

4¶ David *was* thirty years old when he began to reign, *and* he reigned forty years.

5In Hebron he reigned over Judah seven years and six months: and in Jerusalem he reigned thirty and three years over all Israel and Judah.

6¶ And the king and his men went to Jerusalem unto the Jebusites, the inhabitants of the land: which spake unto David, saying, Except thou take away the blind and the lame, thou shalt not come in hither: thinking, David cannot come in hither.

7Nevertheless David took the strong hold of Zion: the same *is* the city of David.

8And David said on that day, Whosoever getteth up to the gutter, and smiteth the Jebusites, and the lame and the blind, *that are* hated of David's soul, *he shall be chief and captain.* Wherefore they said, The blind and the lame shall not come into the house.

9So David dwelt in the fort, and called it the city of David. And David built round about from Millo and inward.

10And David went on, and grew great, and the LORD God of hosts *was* with him.

11¶ And Hiram king of Tyre sent messengers to David, and cedar trees, and carpenters, and masons: and they built David an house.

## Amplified

4Jonathan, Saul's son, had a son who was a cripple in his feet. He was five years old when the news came out of Jezreel [of the death] of Saul and Jonathan; and the boy's nurse took him up and fled; and in her haste he fell and became lame. His name was Mephibosheth.

5Now the sons of Rimmon the Beerothite, Rechab and Baanah, went about the heat of the day to the house of Ishbosheth, who lay resting on his bed at noon.

6And they came into the interior of the house as though they were delivering wheat; and they smote him in the body; and Rechab and Baanah his brother escaped.

7Now when they had come into the house, and he lay on his bed in his bedroom, they [not only] smote and slew him, [but] beheaded him, and took his head and went by the way of the plain all night;

8And brought the head of Ishbosheth to David at Hebron, and said to the king, Behold the head of Ishbosheth son of Saul, your enemy, who sought your life; and the Lord has avenged my lord the king this day on Saul and on his offspring.

9And David answered Rechab and Baanah his brother, sons of Rimmon the Beerothite, As the Lord lives Who redeemed my life out of all adversity,

10When one told me, Behold, Saul is dead, thinking he was bringing good news, I seized and slew him in Ziklag, who expected me to give him a reward for his news.

11How much more, when wicked men have slain a just man in his own house on his bed, shall I not now require his blood of your hand, and remove you from the earth?

12David commanded his young men, and they slew them, and cut off their hands and feet, and hanged them over the pool in Hebron. But they took Ishbosheth's head and buried it in Hebron in the tomb of Abner [his relative and once chief supporter].

**5** THEN ALL the tribes of Israel came to David at Hebron, and said, Behold, we are your bone and your flesh.

2In times past, when Saul was king over us, it was you who led out and brought in Israel, and the Lord told you, You shall feed My people Israel and be prince over [them]. [Cp. I Sam. 16:1 with 15:27-29.]

3So all the elders of Israel came to the king at Hebron; and King David made a covenant with them [there] before the Lord, and they anointed [him] king over Israel.

4David was thirty years old when he began his forty years' reign.

5In Hebron he reigned over Judah seven years and six months; and in Jerusalem he reigned thirty-three years over all Israel and Judah.

6And the king and his men went to Jerusalem against the Jebusites, the inhabitants of the land, who said to David, You shall not enter here, for the blind and the lame will prevent you; thinking, David cannot come in here.

7Nevertheless David took the stronghold of Zion, that is, the city of David.

8David said on that day, Whoever smites the Jebusites, let him get up the water shaft and smite the lame and the blind, who are detested by David's soul. So they say, The blind and the lame shall not come into the house.

9So David dwelt in the stronghold, and called it the city of David. And he built round about from Millo and inward.

10David became greater and greater, for the Lord, the God of hosts, was with him.

11Hiram king of Tyre sent messengers to David, and cedar trees, carpenters, and masons; and they built David a house.

## New American Standard

4¶ Now Jonathan, Saul's son, had a son crippled in his feet. He
was five years old when the report of Saul and Jonathan came from
Jezreel, and his nurse took him up and fled. And it happened that
in her hurry to flee, he fell and became lame. And his name was
Mephibosheth.
5¶ So the sons of Rimmon the Beerothite, Rechab and Baanah,
departed and came to the house of Ish-bosheth in the heat of the
day while he was taking his midday rest.
6And they came to the middle of the house as if to get wheat,
and they struck him in the belly; and Rechab and Baanah his
brother escaped.
7Now when they came into the house, as he was lying on his
bed in his bedroom, they struck him and killed him and beheaded
him. And they took his head and traveled by way of the Arabah
all night.
8Then they brought the head of Ish-bosheth to David at Hebron, and said to the king, "Behold, the head of Ish-bosheth, the
son of Saul, your enemy, who sought your life; thus the LORD has
given my lord the king vengeance this day on Saul and his descendants."
9¶ And David answered Rechab and Baanah his brother, sons
of Rimmon the Beerothite, and said to them, "As the LORD lives,
who has redeemed my life from all distress,
10when one told me, saying, 'Behold, Saul is dead,' and thought
he was bringing good news, I seized him and killed him in Ziklag,
which was the reward I gave him for *his* news.
11"How much more, when wicked men have killed a righteous
man in his own house on his bed, shall I not now require his blood
from your hand, and destroy you from the earth?"
12Then David commanded the young men, and they killed
them and cut off their hands and feet, and hung them up beside
the pool in Hebron. But they took the head of Ish-bosheth and
buried it in the grave of Abner in Hebron.

*David King over All Israel*

5 THEN ALL the tribes of Israel came to David at Hebron and
said, "Behold, we are your bone and your flesh.
2"Previously, when Saul was king over us, you were the one
who led Israel out and in. And the LORD said to you, 'You will
shepherd My people Israel, and you will be a ruler over Israel.'"
3So all the elders of Israel came to the king at Hebron, and King
David made a covenant with them before the LORD at Hebron; then
they anointed David king over Israel.
4David was thirty years old when he became king, *and* he
reigned forty years.
5At Hebron he reigned over Judah seven years and six months,
and in Jerusalem he reigned thirty-three years over all Israel and
Judah.
6¶ Now the king and his men went to Jerusalem against the
Jebusites, the inhabitants of the land, and they said to David, "You
shall not come in here, but the blind and lame shall turn you
away"; thinking, "David cannot enter here."
7Nevertheless, David captured the stronghold of Zion, that is
the city of David.
8And David said on that day, "Whoever would strike the
Jebusites, let him reach the lame and the blind, who are hated by
David's soul, through the water tunnel." Therefore they say, "The
blind or the lame shall not come into the house."
9So David lived in the stronghold, and called it the city of
David. And David built all around from the [a]Millo and inward.
10And David became greater and greater, for the LORD God of
hosts was with him.
11¶ Then Hiram king of Tyre sent messengers to David with
cedar trees and carpenters and stonemasons; and they built a
house for David.

NAS [a] I.e., citadel

## New International

4(Jonathan son of Saul had a son who was lame in both feet. He
was five years old when the news about Saul and Jonathan came
from Jezreel. His nurse picked him up and fled, but as she hurried
to leave, he fell and became crippled. His name was Mephibosheth.)
5Now Recab and Baanah, the sons of Rimmon the Beerothite,
set out for the house of Ish-Bosheth, and they arrived there in the
heat of the day while he was taking his noonday rest. 6They went
into the inner part of the house as if to get some wheat, and they
stabbed him in the stomach. Then Recab and his brother Baanah
slipped away.
7They had gone into the house while he was lying on the bed
in his bedroom. After they stabbed and killed him, they cut off his
head. Taking it with them, they traveled all night by way of the
Arabah. 8They brought the head of Ish-Bosheth to David at Hebron and said to the king, "Here is the head of Ish-Bosheth son
of Saul, your enemy, who tried to take your life. This day the LORD
has avenged my lord the king against Saul and his offspring."
9David answered Recab and his brother Baanah, the sons of
Rimmon the Beerothite, "As surely as the LORD lives, who has
delivered me out of all trouble, 10when a man told me, 'Saul is
dead,' and thought he was bringing good news, I seized him and
put him to death in Ziklag. That was the reward I gave him for his
news! 11How much more—when wicked men have killed an innocent man in his own house and on his own bed—should I not now
demand his blood from your hand and rid the earth of you!"
12So David gave an order to his men, and they killed them. They
cut off their hands and feet and hung the bodies by the pool in
Hebron. But they took the head of Ish-Bosheth and buried it in
Abner's tomb at Hebron.

*David Becomes King Over Israel*

5 ALL THE tribes of Israel came to David at Hebron and said,
"We are your own flesh and blood. 2In the past, while Saul
was king over us, you were the one who led Israel on their military
campaigns. And the LORD said to you, 'You will shepherd my
people Israel, and you will become their ruler.'"
3When all the elders of Israel had come to King David at Hebron, the king made a compact with them at Hebron before the
LORD, and they anointed David king over Israel.
4David was thirty years old when he became king, and he
reigned forty years. 5In Hebron he reigned over Judah seven years
and six months, and in Jerusalem he reigned over all Israel and
Judah thirty-three years.

*David Conquers Jerusalem*

6The king and his men marched to Jerusalem to attack the
Jebusites, who lived there. The Jebusites said to David, "You will
not get in here; even the blind and the lame can ward you off."
They thought, "David cannot get in here." 7Nevertheless, David
captured the fortress of Zion, the City of David.
8On that day, David said, "Anyone who conquers the Jebusites
will have to use the water shaft[b] to reach those 'lame and blind'
who are David's enemies.[c]" That is why they say, "The 'blind and
lame' will not enter the palace."
9David then took up residence in the fortress and called it the
City of David. He built up the area around it, from the supporting
terraces[d] inward. 10And he became more and more powerful,
because the LORD God Almighty was with him.
11Now Hiram king of Tyre sent messengers to David, along
with cedar logs and carpenters and stonemasons, and they built
a palace for David. 12And David knew that the LORD had estab-

NIV [b] 8 Or *use scaling hooks* [c] 8 Or *are hated by David* [d] 9 Or *the Millo*

## King James

12And David perceived that the LORD had established him king over Israel, and that he had exalted his kingdom for his people Israel's sake.

13¶ And David took *him* more concubines and wives out of Jerusalem, after he was come from Hebron: and there were yet sons and daughters born to David.

14And these *be* the names of those that were born unto him in Jerusalem; Shammuah, and Shobab, and Nathan, and Solomon,

15Ibhar also, and Elishua, and Nepheg, and Japhia,

16And Elishama, and Eliada, and Eliphalet.

17¶ But when the Philistines heard that they had anointed David king over Israel, all the Philistines came up to seek David; and David heard *of it*, and went down to the hold.

18The Philistines also came and spread themselves in the valley of Rephaim.

19And David inquired of the LORD, saying, Shall I go up to the Philistines? wilt thou deliver them into mine hand? And the LORD said unto David, Go up: for I will doubtless deliver the Philistines into thine hand.

20And David came to Baal-perazim, and David smote them there, and said, The LORD hath broken forth upon mine enemies before me, as the breach of waters. Therefore he called the name of that place Baal-perazim.

21And there they left their images, and David and his men burned them.

22¶ And the Philistines came up yet again, and spread themselves in the valley of Rephaim.

23And when David inquired of the LORD, he said, Thou shalt not go up; *but* fetch a compass behind them, and come upon them over against the mulberry trees.

24And let it be, when thou hearest the sound of a going in the tops of the mulberry trees, that then thou shalt bestir thyself: for then shall the LORD go out before thee, to smite the host of the Philistines.

25And David did so, as the LORD had commanded him; and smote the Philistines from Geba until thou come to Gazer.

**6** AGAIN, DAVID gathered together all *the* chosen *men* of Israel, thirty thousand.

2And David arose, and went with all the people that *were* with him from Baale of Judah, to bring up from thence the ark of God, whose name is called by the name of the LORD of hosts that dwelleth *between* the cherubims.

3And they set the ark of God upon a new cart, and brought it out of the house of Abinadab that *was* in Gibeah: and Uzzah and Ahio, the sons of Abinadab, drave the new cart.

4And they brought it out of the house of Abinadab which *was* at Gibeah, accompanying the ark of God: and Ahio went before the ark.

5And David and all the house of Israel played before the LORD on all manner of *instruments made of* fir wood, even on harps, and on psalteries, and on timbrels, and on cornets, and on cymbals.

6¶ And when they came to Nachon's threshingfloor, Uzzah put forth *his hand* to the ark of God, and took hold of it; for the oxen shook *it*.

7And the anger of the LORD was kindled against Uzzah; and God smote him there for *his* error; and there he died by the ark of God.

## Amplified

12And David perceived that the Lord had established him king over Israel, and that He had exalted his kingdom for His people Israel's sake.

13And David took him more concubines and wives out of Jerusalem, after he came from Hebron; and other sons and daughters were born to [him].

14And these are the names of those who were born to him in Jerusalem: Shammua, Shobab, Nathan, Solomon,

15Ibhar, Elishua, Nepheg, Japhia,

16Elishama, Eliada, and Eliphelet.

17When the Philistines heard that David had been anointed king over Israel, they all went up to find [him]; but [he] heard of it and went down to the stronghold.

18The Philistines also came and spread themselves in the valley of Rephaim.

19David inquired of the Lord, saying, Shall I go up against the Philistines? Will You deliver them into my hand? And the Lord said to David, Go up; for I will surely deliver [them] into your hand.

20And David came to Baal-perazim, and he smote them there, and said, The Lord has broken through my enemies before me, like the bursting out of great waters. So he called the name of that place Baal-perazim [Lord of breaking through].

21There the Philistines left their [a]images, and David and his men took them away.

22The Philistines came up again, and spread themselves in the valley of Rephaim.

23When David inquired of the Lord, He said, You shall not go up; but go around behind them, and come upon them over opposite the mulberry (or balsam) trees.

24And when you hear the sound of marching in the tops of the mulberry trees, then bestir yourself; for then has the Lord gone out before you, to smite the army of the Philistines.

25And David did as the Lord had commanded him, and smote the Philistines from Geba to Gezer.

**6** AGAIN, DAVID gathered together all the chosen men of Israel, 30,000.

2And [he] arose, and went with all the people who were with him to Baale-judah [Kiriath-jearim] to bring up from there the ark of God, which is called by the name of the Lord of hosts Who sits enthroned above the cherubim.

3And they set the ark of God upon a new cart, and brought it [b]out of the house of Abinadab that was on the hill; and Uzzah and Ahio, sons of Abinadab, drove the new cart.

4And they brought it out of the house of Abinadab, which was in the hill, with the ark of God; and Ahio went before the ark.

5And David and all the house of Israel played before the Lord with all their might, with songs, lyres, harps, tambourines, castanets, and cymbals.

6And when they came to Nacon's threshing floor, Uzzah put out his hand to the ark of God, and took hold of it, for the oxen stumbled *and* shook it.

7And the anger of the Lord was kindled against Uzzah; and God smote him there for touching the ark; and he died there by the ark of God.

**AMP** [a] The Israelites took as spoil the images of the Philistines; perhaps to display in triumphal procession, though they were afterward burned (I Chron. 14:12) in compliance with the law of Deut. 7:5, 25. Thus the old disgrace of the capture of the Ark by the Philistines was avenged (I Sam. 4:4, 10, 11)—*Cambridge Bible.* [b] How long had the ark been in the house of Abinadab? See I Sam. 7:2, *Amp.*

## New American Standard

12And David realized that the LORD had established him as king
over Israel, and that He had exalted his kingdom for the sake of
His people Israel.
13¶ Meanwhile David took more concubines and wives from
Jerusalem, after he came from Hebron; and more sons and daughters were born to David.
14Now these are the names of those who were born to him in
Jerusalem: Shammua, Shobab, Nathan, Solomon,
15Ibhar, Elishua, Nepheg, Japhia,
16Elishama, Eliada and Eliphelet.

*War with the Philistines*

17¶ When the Philistines heard that they had anointed David
king over Israel, all the Philistines went up to seek out David; and
when David heard *of it*, he went down to the stronghold.
18Now the Philistines came and spread themselves out in the
valley of Rephaim.
19Then David inquired of the LORD, saying, "Shall I go up
against the Philistines? Wilt Thou give them into my hand?" And
the LORD said to David, "Go up, for I will certainly give the Philistines into your hand."
20So David came to Baal-perazim, and defeated them there; and
he said, "The LORD has broken through my enemies before me like
the breakthrough of waters." Therefore he named that place
[c]Baal-perazim.
21And they abandoned their idols there, so David and his men
carried them away.
22¶ Now the Philistines came up once again and spread themselves out in the valley of Rephaim.
23And when David inquired of the LORD, He said, "You shall
not go *directly* up; circle around behind them and come at them in
front of the [d]balsam trees.
24"And it shall be, when you hear the sound of marching in the
tops of the [e]balsam trees, then you shall act promptly, for then
the LORD will have gone out before you to strike the army of the
Philistines."
25Then David did so, just as the LORD had commanded him,
and struck down the Philistines from Geba as far as Gezer.

*Peril in Moving the Ark*

6 NOW DAVID again gathered all the chosen men of Israel,
thirty thousand.
2And David arose and went with all the people who were with
him to Baale-judah, to bring up from there the ark of God which
is called by the Name, the very name of the LORD of hosts who is
enthroned *above* the cherubim.
3And they placed the ark of God on a new cart that they might
bring it from the house of Abinadab which was on the hill; and
Uzzah and Ahio, the sons of Abinadab, were leading the new cart.
4So they brought it with the ark of God from the house of
Abinadab, which was on the hill; and Ahio was walking ahead of
the ark.
5Meanwhile, David and all the house of Israel were celebrating
before the LORD with all kinds of *instruments made of* fir wood, and
with lyres, harps, tambourines, castanets and cymbals.
6¶ But when they came to the threshing floor of Nacon, Uzzah
reached out toward the ark of God and took hold of it, for the oxen
nearly upset *it*.
7And the anger of the LORD burned against Uzzah, and God
struck him down there for his irreverence; and he died there by the
ark of God.

NAS [c] I.e., the master of breakthrough [d] Or, *baka-shrubs* [e] Or, *baka-shrubs*

## New International

lished him as king over Israel and had exalted his kingdom for the
sake of his people Israel.
13After he left Hebron, David took more concubines and wives
in Jerusalem, and more sons and daughters were born to him.
14These are the names of the children born to him there: Shammua, Shobab, Nathan, Solomon, 15Ibhar, Elishua, Nepheg,
Japhia, 16Elishama, Eliada and Eliphelet.

*David Defeats the Philistines*

17When the Philistines heard that David had been anointed
king over Israel, they went up in full force to search for him, but
David heard about it and went down to the stronghold. 18Now the
Philistines had come and spread out in the Valley of Rephaim; 19so
David inquired of the LORD, "Shall I go and attack the Philistines?
Will you hand them over to me?"
The LORD answered him, "Go, for I will surely hand the Philistines over to you."
20So David went to Baal Perazim, and there he defeated them.
He said, "As waters break out, the LORD has broken out against
my enemies before me." So that place was called Baal Perazim.[f]
21The Philistines abandoned their idols there, and David and his
men carried them off.
22Once more the Philistines came up and spread out in the
Valley of Rephaim; 23so David inquired of the LORD, and he answered, "Do not go straight up, but circle around behind them and
attack them in front of the balsam trees. 24As soon as you hear the
sound of marching in the tops of the balsam trees, move quickly,
because that will mean the LORD has gone out in front of you to
strike the Philistine army." 25So David did as the LORD commanded him, and he struck down the Philistines all the way from
Gibeon[g] to Gezer.

*The Ark Brought to Jerusalem*

6 DAVID AGAIN brought together out of Israel chosen men,
thirty thousand in all. 2He and all his men set out from Baalah
of Judah[h] to bring up from there the ark of God, which is called
by the Name,[i] the name of the LORD Almighty, who is enthroned
between the cherubim that are on the ark. 3They set the ark of God
on a new cart and brought it from the house of Abinadab, which
was on the hill. Uzzah and Ahio, sons of Abinadab, were guiding
the new cart 4with the ark of God on it,[j] and Ahio was walking
in front of it. 5David and the whole house of Israel were celebrating
with all their might before the LORD, with songs[k] and with harps,
lyres, tambourines, sistrums and cymbals.
6When they came to the threshing floor of Nacon, Uzzah
reached out and took hold of the ark of God, because the oxen
stumbled. 7The LORD's anger burned against Uzzah because of his
irreverent act; therefore God struck him down and he died there
beside the ark of God.

NIV [f] 20 *Baal Perazim* means *the lord who breaks out.* [g] 25 Septuagint (see also 1 Chronicles 14:16); Hebrew *Geba* [h] 2 That is, Kiriath Jearim; Hebrew *Baale Judah*, a variant of *Baalah of Judah* [i] 2 Hebrew; Septuagint and Vulgate do not have *the Name.* [j] 3,4 Dead Sea Scrolls and some Septuagint manuscripts; Masoretic Text *cart* [4] *and they brought it with the ark of God from the house of Abinadab, which was on the hill* [k] 5 See Dead Sea Scrolls, Septuagint and 1 Chronicles 13:8; Masoretic Text *celebrating before the LORD with all kinds of instruments made of pine.*

## King James

8And David was displeased, because the LORD had made a
breach upon Uzzah: and he called the name of the place Perez-
uzzah to this day.
9And David was afraid of the LORD that day, and said, How
shall the ark of the LORD come to me?
10So David would not remove the ark of the LORD unto him into
the city of David: but David carried it aside into the house of
Obed-edom the Gittite.
11And the ark of the LORD continued in the house of Obed-
edom the Gittite three months: and the LORD blessed Obed-edom,
and all his household.
12¶ And it was told king David, saying, The LORD hath blessed
the house of Obed-edom, and all that *pertaineth* unto him, because
of the ark of God. So David went and brought up the ark of God
from the house of Obed-edom into the city of David with gladness.
13And it was *so*, that when they that bare the ark of the LORD
had gone six paces, he sacrificed oxen and fatlings.
14And David danced before the LORD with all *his* might; and
David *was* girded with a linen ephod.
15So David and all the house of Israel brought up the ark of the
LORD with shouting, and with the sound of the trumpet.
16And as the ark of the LORD came into the city of David, Michal
Saul's daughter looked through a window, and saw king David
leaping and dancing before the LORD; and she despised him in her
heart.
17¶ And they brought in the ark of the LORD, and set it in his
place, in the midst of the tabernacle that David had pitched for it:
and David offered burnt offerings and peace offerings before the
LORD.
18And as soon as David had made an end of offering burnt
offerings and peace offerings, he blessed the people in the name
of the LORD of hosts.
19And he dealt among all the people, *even* among the whole
multitude of Israel, as well to the women as men, to every one a
cake of bread, and a good piece *of flesh,* and a flagon *of wine.* So
all the people departed every one to his house.
20¶ Then David returned to bless his household. And Michal the
daughter of Saul came out to meet David, and said, How glorious
was the king of Israel today, who uncovered himself today in the
eyes of the handmaids of his servants, as one of the vain fellows
shamelessly uncovereth himself!
21And David said unto Michal, *It was* before the LORD, which
chose me before thy father, and before all his house, to appoint me
ruler over the people of the LORD, over Israel: therefore will I play
before the LORD.
22And I will yet be more vile than thus, and will be base in mine
own sight: and of the maidservants which thou hast spoken of, of
them shall I be had in honour.
23Therefore Michal the daughter of Saul had no child unto the
day of her death.

7 AND IT came to pass, when the king sat in his house, and
the LORD had given him rest round about from all his enemies;
2That the king said unto Nathan the prophet, See now, I dwell
in an house of cedar, but the ark of God dwelleth within curtains.
3And Nathan said to the king, Go, do all that *is* in thine heart;
for the LORD *is* with thee.
4¶ And it came to pass that night, that the word of the LORD
came unto Nathan, saying,
5Go and tell my servant David, Thus saith the LORD, Shalt thou
build me an house for me to dwell in?
6Whereas I have not dwelt in *any* house since the time that I
brought up the children of Israel out of Egypt, even to this day,
but have walked in a tent and in a tabernacle.

## Amplified

8David was grieved *and* offended because the Lord had broken
forth upon Uzzah; and that place is called Perez-uzzah [the breaking forth upon Uzzah] to this day.
9David was afraid of the Lord that day, and said, How can the
ark of the Lord come to me?
10So David was not willing to take the ark of the Lord to him
into the city of David; but he took it aside into the house of
Obed-edom the Gittite.
11And the ark of the Lord remained in the house of Obed-edom
the Gittite three months; and the Lord blessed Obed-edom and all
his household.
12And it was told king David, The Lord has blessed the house
of Obed-edom, and all that belongs to him, because of the ark of
God. So David went and brought up the ark of God from the house
of Obed-edom into the city of David with rejoicing;
13And when those who bore the ark of the Lord had gone six
paces, he sacrificed an ox and a fatling.
14And David danced before the Lord with all his might, clad in
a linen ephod [a priest's upper garment].
15So David and all the house of Israel brought up the ark of the
Lord with shouting, and with the sound of the trumpet.
16As the ark of the Lord came into the city of David, Michal,
Saul's daughter [David's wife], looked out of the window, and saw
King David leaping and dancing before the Lord, and she despised
him in her heart.
17They brought in the ark of the Lord, and set it in its place
inside the tent which David had pitched for it; and David offered
burnt offerings and peace offerings before the Lord.
18When David had finished offering the burnt offering and
peace offerings, he blessed the people in the name [and presence]
of the Lord of hosts,
19And distributed among all the people, the whole multitude of
Israel, both to men and women, to each a cake of bread, a portion
of meat, and a cake of raisins. So all the people departed, each to
his house.
20Then David returned to bless his household. And [his wife]
Michal daughter of Saul came out to meet David, and said, How
glorious was the king of Israel today, who stripped himself of his
kingly robes *and* uncovered himself in the eyes of his servants'
maids, as one of the worthless fellows shamelessly uncovers himself!
21David said to Michal, It was before the Lord, who chose me
above your father and all his house, to appoint me as prince over
Israel, the people of the Lord. Therefore will I make merry (in pure
enjoyment) before the Lord.
22I will be still more lightly esteemed than this, and will humble
*and* lower myself in my own sight [and yours]; but by the maids
you mentioned I will be held in honor.
23And Michal the daughter of Saul had no child to the day of
her death.

7 WHEN KING David dwelt in his house, and the Lord had
given him rest from all his surrounding enemies,
2The king said to Nathan the prophet, See now, I dwell in a
house of cedar, but the ark of God dwells within curtains.
3And Nathan said to the king, Go, do all that is in your heart;
for the Lord is with you.
4That night, the word of the Lord came to Nathan, saying,
5Go and tell My servant David, Thus says the Lord: Shall you
build Me a house in which to dwell?
6For I have not dwelt in a house since I brought the Israelites
out of Egypt to this day, but have moved about with a tent for My
dwelling.

## New American Standard

8And David became angry because of the LORD's outburst
against Uzzah, and that place is called [a]Perez-uzzah to this day.
9So David was afraid of the LORD that day; and he said, "How
can the ark of the LORD come to me?"
10And David was unwilling to move the ark of the LORD into
the city of David with him; but David took it aside to the house of
Obed-edom the Gittite.
11Thus the ark of the LORD remained in the house of Obed-
edom the Gittite three months, and the LORD blessed Obed-edom
and all his household.

*The Ark Is Brought to Jerusalem*

12¶ Now it was told King David, saying, "The LORD has blessed
the house of Obed-edom and all that belongs to him, on account
of the ark of God." And David went and brought up the ark of God
from the house of Obed-edom into the city of David with gladness.
13And so it was, that when the bearers of the ark of the LORD
had gone six paces, he sacrificed an ox and a fatling.
14And David was dancing before the LORD with all *his* might,
and David was wearing a linen ephod.
15So David and all the house of Israel were bringing up the ark
of the LORD with shouting and the sound of the trumpet.
16Then it happened *as* the ark of the LORD came into the city of
David that Michal the daughter of Saul looked out of the window
and saw King David leaping and dancing before the LORD; and she
despised him in her heart.
17So they brought in the ark of the LORD and set it in its place
inside the tent which David had pitched for it; and David offered
burnt offerings and peace offerings before the LORD.
18And when David had finished offering the burnt offering and
the peace offering, he blessed the people in the name of the LORD
of hosts.
19Further, he distributed to all the people, to all the multitude
of Israel, both to men and women, a cake of bread and one of dates
and one of raisins to each one. Then all the people departed each
to his house.
20¶ But when David returned to bless his household, Michal the
daughter of Saul came out to meet David and said, "How the king
of Israel distinguished himself today! He uncovered himself today
in the eyes of his servants' maids as one of the foolish ones shamelessly uncovers himself!"
21So David said to Michal, "*It was* before the LORD, who chose
me above your father and above all his house, to appoint me ruler
over the people of the LORD, over Israel; therefore I will celebrate
before the LORD.
22"And I will be more lightly esteemed than this and will be
humble in my own eyes, but with the maids of whom you have
spoken, with them I will be distinguished."
23And Michal the daughter of Saul had no child to the day of
her death.

*David Plans to Build a Temple*

7 NOW IT came about when the king lived in his house, and
the LORD had given him rest on every side from all his enemies,
2that the king said to Nathan the prophet, "See now, I dwell
in a house of cedar, but the ark of God dwells within tent curtains."
3And Nathan said to the king, "Go, do all that is in your mind,
for the LORD is with you."
4But it came about in the same night that the word of the LORD
came to Nathan, saying,
5"Go and say to My servant David, 'Thus says the LORD, "Are
you the one who should build Me a house to dwell in?
6"For I have not dwelt in a house since the day I brought up
the sons of Israel from Egypt, even to this day; but I have been
moving about in a tent, even in a tabernacle.

NAS [a] I.e., the breakthrough of Uzzah

## New International

8Then David was angry because the LORD's wrath had broken
out against Uzzah, and to this day that place is called Perez Uzzah.[b]
9David was afraid of the LORD that day and said, "How can the
ark of the LORD ever come to me?" 10He was not willing to take
the ark of the LORD to be with him in the City of David. Instead,
he took it aside to the house of Obed-Edom the Gittite. 11The ark
of the LORD remained in the house of Obed-Edom the Gittite for
three months, and the LORD blessed him and his entire household.
12Now King David was told, "The LORD has blessed the household of Obed-Edom and everything he has, because of the ark of
God." So David went down and brought up the ark of God from
the house of Obed-Edom to the City of David with rejoicing.
13When those who were carrying the ark of the LORD had taken
six steps, he sacrificed a bull and a fattened calf. 14David, wearing
a linen ephod, danced before the LORD with all his might, 15while
he and the entire house of Israel brought up the ark of the LORD
with shouts and the sound of trumpets.
16As the ark of the LORD was entering the City of David, Michal
daughter of Saul watched from a window. And when she saw King
David leaping and dancing before the LORD, she despised him in
her heart.
17They brought the ark of the LORD and set it in its place inside
the tent that David had pitched for it, and David sacrificed burnt
offerings and fellowship offerings[c] before the LORD. 18After he
had finished sacrificing the burnt offerings and fellowship offerings, he blessed the people in the name of the LORD Almighty.
19Then he gave a loaf of bread, a cake of dates and a cake of raisins
to each person in the whole crowd of Israelites, both men and
women. And all the people went to their homes.
20When David returned home to bless his household, Michal
daughter of Saul came out to meet him and said, "How the king
of Israel has distinguished himself today, disrobing in the sight of
the slave girls of his servants as any vulgar fellow would!"
21David said to Michal, "It was before the LORD, who chose me
rather than your father or anyone from his house when he appointed me ruler over the LORD's people Israel—I will celebrate
before the LORD. 22I will become even more undignified than this,
and I will be humiliated in my own eyes. But by these slave girls
you spoke of, I will be held in honor."
23And Michal daughter of Saul had no children to the day of her
death.

*God's Promise to David*

7 AFTER THE king was settled in his palace and the LORD had
given him rest from all his enemies around him, 2he said to
Nathan the prophet, "Here I am, living in a palace of cedar, while
the ark of God remains in a tent."
3Nathan replied to the king, "Whatever you have in mind, go
ahead and do it, for the LORD is with you."
4That night the word of the LORD came to Nathan, saying:
5"Go and tell my servant David, 'This is what the LORD
says: Are you the one to build me a house to dwell in? 6I have
not dwelt in a house from the day I brought the Israelites up
out of Egypt to this day. I have been moving from place to
place with a tent as my dwelling. 7Wherever I have moved

NIV [b] *8 Perez Uzzah* means *outbreak against Uzzah.* [c] *17* Traditionally *peace offerings;* also in verse 18

## King James

[7]In all *the places* wherein I have walked with all the children of Israel spake I a word with any of the tribes of Israel, whom I commanded to feed my people Israel, saying, Why build ye not me an house of cedar?
[8]Now therefore so shalt thou say unto my servant David, Thus saith the LORD of hosts, I took thee from the sheepcote, from following the sheep, to be ruler over my people, over Israel:
[9]And I was with thee whithersoever thou wentest, and have cut off all thine enemies out of thy sight, and have made thee a great name, like unto the name of the great *men* that *are* in the earth.
[10]Moreover I will appoint a place for my people Israel, and will plant them, that they may dwell in a place of their own, and move no more; neither shall the children of wickedness afflict them any more, as beforetime,
[11]And as since the time that I commanded judges *to be* over my people Israel, and have caused thee to rest from all thine enemies. Also the LORD telleth thee that he will make thee an house.
[12]¶ And when thy days be fulfilled, and thou shalt sleep with thy fathers, I will set up thy seed after thee, which shall proceed out of thy bowels, and I will establish his kingdom.
[13]He shall build an house for my name, and I will stablish the throne of his kingdom for ever.
[14]I will be his father, and he shall be my son. If he commit iniquity, I will chasten him with the rod of men, and with the stripes of the children of men:
[15]But my mercy shall not depart away from him, as I took *it* from Saul, whom I put away before thee.
[16]And thine house and thy kingdom shall be established for ever before thee: thy throne shall be established for ever.
[17]According to all these words, and according to all this vision, so did Nathan speak unto David.
[18]¶ Then went king David in, and sat before the LORD, and he said, Who *am* I, O Lord GOD? and what *is* my house, that thou hast brought me hitherto?
[19]And this was yet a small thing in thy sight, O Lord GOD; but thou hast spoken also of thy servant's house for a great while to come. And *is* this the manner of man, O Lord GOD?
[20]And what can David say more unto thee? for thou, Lord GOD, knowest thy servant.
[21]For thy word's sake, and according to thine own heart, hast thou done all these great things, to make thy servant know *them*.
[22]Wherefore thou art great, O LORD God: for *there is* none like thee, neither *is there any* God beside thee, according to all that we have heard with our ears.
[23]And what one nation in the earth *is* like thy people, *even* like Israel, whom God went to redeem for a people to himself, and to make him a name, and to do for you great things and terrible, for thy land, before thy people, which thou redeemedst to thee from Egypt, *from* the nations and their gods?
[24]For thou hast confirmed to thyself thy people Israel *to be* a people unto thee for ever: and thou, LORD, art become their God.
[25]And now, O LORD God, the word that thou hast spoken concerning thy servant, and concerning his house, establish *it* for ever, and do as thou hast said.
[26]And let thy name be magnified for ever, saying, The LORD of hosts *is* the God over Israel: and let the house of thy servant David be established before thee.
[27]For thou, O LORD of hosts, God of Israel, hast revealed to thy servant, saying, I will build thee an house: therefore hath thy servant found in his heart to pray this prayer unto thee.
[28]And now, O Lord GOD, thou *art* that God, and thy words be true, and thou hast promised this goodness unto thy servant:

## Amplified

[7]In all places where I have moved with all the Israelites, did I speak a word to any from the tribes of Israel whom I commanded to be shepherd of My people Israel, asking, Why do you not build Me a house of cedar?
[8]So now say this to My servant David, Thus says the Lord of hosts, I took you from the pasture, from following the sheep, to be prince over My people Israel;
[9]And I was with you wherever you went, and have cut off all your enemies from before you, and I will make you a great name, like [that] of the great of the earth.
[10]And I will appoint a place for My people Israel, and will plant them, that they may dwell in a place of their own, and be moved no more; and wicked men shall afflict them no more, as formerly,
[11]And as from the time that I appointed judges over My people Israel; and I will cause you to rest from all your enemies. Also the Lord declares to you that He will make you a house.
[12]And when your days are fulfilled, and you sleep with your fathers, I will set up after you your offspring who shall be born to you, and I will establish his kingdom.
[13]He shall build a house for My name [and My presence] and I will establish the throne of his kingdom for ever.
[14]I will be his Father, and he shall be My son. When he commits iniquity, I will chasten him with the rod of men, and with the stripes of the sons of men;
[15]But My mercy *and* loving-kindness shall not depart from him, as I took [them] from Saul, whom I took away before you.
[16]And your house and your kingdom shall be made sure for ever before you; your throne shall be established for ever.
[17]In accordance with all these words and all this vision, Nathan spoke to David.
[18]Then King David went in and sat before the Lord, and said, Who am I, O Lord God, and what is my house, that You have brought me this far?
[19]Then as if this were a little thing in Your eyes, O Lord God, You have spoken also of Your servant's house in the far distant future. And this is the law for man, O Lord God!
[20]What more can David say to You? For You know Your servant, Lord God.
[21]Because of Your promise, and as Your own heart dictates, You have done all these astounding things, to make Your servant know *and* understand.
[22]Therefore You are great, O Lord God; for none is like You, nor is there any God besides You, according to all [You have made] our ears to hear.
[23]What (other) one nation on earth is like Your people Israel, whom God went to redeem to be a people for Himself and to make for Him a name? You have done great and terrible things for You *and* for Your land, before Your people, whom You redeemed *and* delivered for Yourself from Egypt, from the nations and their gods.
[24]And You have established for Yourself Your people Israel to be Your people for ever; and You, Lord, became their God.
[25]Now, O Lord God, confirm for ever the word You have given as to Your servant and his house, and do as You have said;
[26]And Your name [and presence] shall be magnified for ever, saying, The Lord of hosts is God over Israel; and the house of Your servant David will be made firm before You.
[27]For You, O Lord of hosts, God of Israel, have revealed this to Your servant: I will build You a house; so Your servant has found courage to pray this prayer to You.
[28]And now, O Lord God, You are God and Your words are truth, and You have promised this good thing to Your servant.

## New American Standard

7"Wherever I have gone with all the sons of Israel, did I speak a word with one of the tribes of Israel, which I commanded to shepherd My people Israel, saying, 'Why have you not built Me a house of cedar?'"'

*God's Covenant with David*

8"Now therefore, thus you shall say to My servant David, 'Thus says the LORD of hosts, "I took you from the pasture, from following the sheep, that you should be ruler over My people Israel.

9"And I have been with you wherever you have gone and have cut off all your enemies from before you; and I will make you a great name, like the names of the great men who are on the earth.

10"I will also appoint a place for My people Israel and will plant them, that they may live in their own place and not be disturbed again, nor will the wicked afflict them any more as formerly,

11even from the day that I commanded judges to be over My people Israel; and I will give you rest from all your enemies. The LORD also declares to you that the LORD will make a house for you.

12"When your days are complete and you lie down with your fathers, I will raise up your descendant after you, who will come forth from you, and I will establish his kingdom.

13"He shall build a house for My name, and I will establish the throne of his kingdom forever.

14"I will be a father to him and he will be a son to Me; when he commits iniquity, I will correct him with the rod of men and the strokes of the sons of men,

15but My lovingkindness shall not depart from him, as I took *it* away from Saul, whom I removed from before you.

16"And your house and your kingdom shall endure before Me forever; your throne shall be established forever."'"

17In accordance with all these words and all this vision, so Nathan spoke to David.

*David's Prayer*

18¶ Then David the king went in and sat before the LORD, and he said, "Who am I, O Lord GOD, and what is my house, that Thou hast brought me this far?

19"And yet this was insignificant in Thine eyes, O Lord GOD, for Thou hast spoken also of the house of Thy servant concerning the distant future. And this is the custom of man, O Lord GOD.

20"And again what more can David say to Thee? For Thou knowest Thy servant, O Lord GOD!

21"For the sake of Thy word, and according to Thine own heart, Thou hast done all this greatness to let Thy servant know.

22"For this reason Thou art great, O Lord GOD; for there is none like Thee, and there is no God besides Thee, according to all that we have heard with our ears.

23"And what one nation on the earth is like Thy people Israel, whom God went to redeem for Himself as a people and to make a name for Himself, and to do a great thing for Thee and awesome things for Thy land, before Thy people whom Thou hast redeemed for Thyself from Egypt, *from* nations and their gods?

24"For Thou hast established for Thyself Thy people Israel as Thine own people forever, and Thou, O LORD, hast become their God.

25"Now therefore, O LORD God, the word that Thou hast spoken concerning Thy servant and his house, confirm *it* forever, and do as Thou hast spoken,

26that Thy name may be magnified forever, by saying, 'The LORD of hosts is God over Israel'; and may the house of Thy servant David be established before Thee.

27"For Thou, O LORD of hosts, the God of Israel, hast made a revelation to Thy servant, saying, 'I will build you a house'; therefore Thy servant has found courage to pray this prayer to Thee.

28"And now, O Lord GOD, Thou art God, and Thy words are truth, and Thou hast promised this good thing to Thy servant.

## New International

with all the Israelites, did I ever say to any of their rulers
whom I commanded to shepherd my people Israel, "Why
have you not built me a house of cedar?"'

8"Now then, tell my servant David, 'This is what the LORD
Almighty says: I took you from the pasture and from following the flock to be ruler over my people Israel. 9I have been
with you wherever you have gone, and I have cut off all your
enemies from before you. Now I will make your name great,
like the names of the greatest men of the earth. 10And I will
provide a place for my people Israel and will plant them so
that they can have a home of their own and no longer be
disturbed. Wicked people will not oppress them anymore, as
they did at the beginning 11and have done ever since the time
I appointed leaders[a] over my people Israel. I will also give
you rest from all your enemies.
"'The LORD declares to you that the LORD himself will
establish a house for you: 12When your days are over and you
rest with your fathers, I will raise up your offspring to succeed
you, who will come from your own body, and I will establish
his kingdom. 13He is the one who will build a house for my
Name, and I will establish the throne of his kingdom forever.
14I will be his father, and he will be my son. When he does
wrong, I will punish him with the rod of men, with floggings
inflicted by men. 15But my love will never be taken away from
him, as I took it away from Saul, whom I removed from before
you. 16Your house and your kingdom will endure forever
before me[b]; your throne will be established forever.'"

17Nathan reported to David all the words of this entire revelation.

*David's Prayer*

18Then King David went in and sat before the LORD, and he
said:

"Who am I, O Sovereign LORD, and what is my family, that
you have brought me this far? 19And as if this were not
enough in your sight, O Sovereign LORD, you have also
spoken about the future of the house of your servant. Is this
your usual way of dealing with man, O Sovereign LORD?

20"What more can David say to you? For you know your
servant, O Sovereign LORD. 21For the sake of your word and
according to your will, you have done this great thing and
made it known to your servant.

22"How great you are, O Sovereign LORD! There is no one
like you, and there is no God but you, as we have heard with
our own ears. 23And who is like your people Israel—the one
nation on earth that God went out to redeem as a people for
himself, and to make a name for himself, and to perform great
and awesome wonders by driving out nations and their gods
from before your people, whom you redeemed from Egypt?[c]
24You have established your people Israel as your very own
forever, and you, O LORD, have become their God.

25"And now, LORD God, keep forever the promise you
have made concerning your servant and his house. Do as you
promised, 26so that your name will be great forever. Then
men will say, 'The LORD Almighty is God over Israel!' And the
house of your servant David will be established before you.

27"O LORD Almighty, God of Israel, you have revealed this
to your servant, saying, 'I will build a house for you.' So your
servant has found courage to offer you this prayer. 28O Sovereign LORD, you are God! Your words are trustworthy, and you
have promised these good things to your servant. 29Now be

NIV [a] *11* Traditionally *judges* [b] *16* Some Hebrew manuscripts and Septuagint; most Hebrew manuscripts *you* [c] *23* See Septuagint and 1 Chronicles 17:21; Hebrew *wonders for your land and before your people, whom you redeemed from Egypt, from the nations and their gods.*

## King James

29 Therefore now let it please thee to bless the house of thy
servant, that it may continue for ever before thee: for thou, O Lord
GOD, hast spoken *it:* and with thy blessing let the house of thy
servant be blessed for ever.

**8** AND AFTER this it came to pass, that David smote the Philistines, and subdued them: and David took Metheg-ammah
out of the hand of the Philistines.
2 And he smote Moab, and measured them with a line, casting
them down to the ground; even with two lines measured he to put
to death, and with one full line to keep alive. And *so* the Moabites
became David's servants, *and* brought gifts.
3 ¶ David smote also Hadadezer, the son of Rehob, king of
Zobah, as he went to recover his border at the river Euphrates.
4 And David took from him a thousand *chariots*, and seven hundred horsemen, and twenty thousand footmen: and David
houghed all the chariot *horses*, but reserved of them *for* an hundred
chariots.
5 And when the Syrians of Damascus came to succour Hadadezer king of Zobah, David slew of the Syrians two and twenty
thousand men.
6 Then David put garrisons in Syria of Damascus: and the Syrians became servants to David, *and* brought gifts. And the LORD
preserved David whithersoever he went.
7 And David took the shields of gold that were on the servants
of Hadadezer, and brought them to Jerusalem.
8 And from Betah, and from Berothai, cities of Hadadezer, king
David took exceeding much brass.
9 ¶ When Toi king of Hamath heard that David had smitten all
the host of Hadadezer,
10 Then Toi sent Joram his son unto king David, to salute him,
and to bless him, because he had fought against Hadadezer, and
smitten him: for Hadadezer had wars with Toi. And *Joram* brought
with him vessels of silver, and vessels of gold, and vessels of brass:
11 Which also king David did dedicate unto the LORD, with the
silver and gold that he had dedicated of all nations which he
subdued;
12 Of Syria, and of Moab, and of the children of Ammon, and
of the Philistines, and of Amalek, and of the spoil of Hadadezer,
son of Rehob, king of Zobah.
13 And David gat *him* a name when he returned from smiting of
the Syrians in the valley of salt, *being* eighteen thousand *men.*
14 ¶ And he put garrisons in Edom; throughout all Edom put he
garrisons, and all they of Edom became David's servants. And the
LORD preserved David whithersoever he went.
15 And David reigned over all Israel; and David executed judgment and justice unto all his people.
16 And Joab the son of Zeruiah *was* over the host; and Jehoshaphat the son of Ahilud *was* recorder;
17 And Zadok the son of Ahitub, and Ahimelech the son of
Abiathar, *were* the priests; and Seraiah *was* the scribe;
18 And Benaiah the son of Jehoiada *was over* both the Cherethites
and the Pelethites; and David's sons were chief rulers.

**9** AND DAVID said, Is there yet any that is left of the house
of Saul, that I may show him kindness for Jonathan's sake?

## Amplified

29 Therefore now let it please You to bless the house of Your
servant, that it may continue for ever before You; for You, O Lord
God, have spoken it, and with Your blessing let [his] house be
blessed for ever.

**8** AFTER THIS David smote the Philistines and subdued them,
and he took Metheg-ammah out of the hand of the Philistines.
2 He defeated Moab, and measured them with a line, making
them lie down on the ground; two lines he measured to be put to
death, and one full line to keep alive. And the Moabites became
servants to David, bringing tribute.
3 David also defeated Hadadezer son of Rehob, king of Zobah,
as he went to restore his power at the river [Euphrates].
4 David took from him 1700 horsemen, and 20,000 foot soldiers;
and David hamstrung all the chariot horses, except he reserved
enough of them for 100 chariots.
5 And when the Syrians of Damascus came to help Hadadezer
king of Zobah, David slew 22,000 of them.
6 David put garrisons in Syrian Damascus; and the Syrians
became [his] servants, and brought tribute. The Lord preserved
*and* gave victory to David wherever he went.
7 And David took the shields of gold that were on the servants
of Hadadezer, and brought them to Jerusalem.
8 And from Betah and Berothai, cities of Hadadezer, King David
exacted an immense amount of bronze.
9 When Toi king of Hamath heard of David's defeat of all the
forces of Hadadezer,
10 [He] sent Joram his son to King David to salute *and* congratulate him about his battle and defeat of Hadadezer. For Hadadezer
had had wars with Toi. Joram brought vessels of silver, gold, and
bronze.
11 These King David dedicated to the Lord, with the silver and
gold that he had dedicated from all the nations he subdued:
12 From Syria, Moab, the Ammonites, Philistines, Amalek, and
from the spoil of Hadadezer son of Rehob, king of Zobah.
13 David won renown. When he returned he slew 18,000 Edomites in the Valley of Salt.
14 He put garrisons throughout all Edom and all the Edomites
became his servants. And the Lord preserved *and* gave victory to
[him] wherever he went.
15 So David reigned over all Israel, and executed justice and
righteousness to all his people.
16 Joab son of Zeruiah was over the army; Jehoshaphat son of
Ahilud was recorder;
17 Zadok son of Ahitub, and Ahimelech son of Abiathar were the
[chief] priests, and Seraiah was the scribe;
18 Benaiah son of Jehoiada was over both the Cherethites and
Pelethites [the king's bodyguard]; and David's sons were chief
[confidential] assistants to the king.

**9** AND DAVID said, Is there still any one left of the house of
Saul, to whom I may show kindness for Jonathan's sake?

## New American Standard

29"Now therefore, may it please Thee to bless the house of Thy
servant, that it may continue forever before Thee. For Thou, O
Lord GOD, hast spoken; and with Thy blessing may the house of
Thy servant be blessed forever."

*David's Triumphs*

**8** NOW AFTER this it came about that David defeated the
Philistines and subdued them; and David took control of the
chief city from the hand of the Philistines.
2And he defeated Moab, and measured them with the line,
making them lie down on the ground; and he measured two lines
to put to death and one full line to keep alive. And the Moabites
became servants to David, bringing tribute.
3¶ Then David defeated Hadadezer, the son of Rehob king of
Zobah, as he went to restore his rule at the [a]River.
4And David captured from him 1,700 horsemen and 20,000
foot soldiers; and David hamstrung the chariot horses, but reserved *enough* of them for 100 chariots.
5And when the Arameans of Damascus came to help Hadadezer, king of Zobah, David killed 22,000 Arameans.
6Then David put garrisons among the Arameans of Damascus,
and the Arameans became servants to David, bringing tribute.
And the LORD helped David wherever he went.
7And David took the shields of gold which were carried by the
servants of Hadadezer, and brought them to Jerusalem.
8And from Betah and from Berothai, cities of Hadadezer, King
David took a very large amount of bronze.
9¶ Now when Toi king of Hamath heard that David had defeated all the army of Hadadezer,
10Toi sent Joram his son to King David to greet him and bless
him, because he had fought against Hadadezer and defeated him;
for Hadadezer had been at war with Toi. And *Joram* brought with
him articles of silver, of gold and of bronze.
11King David also dedicated these to the LORD, with the silver
and gold that he had dedicated from all the nations which he had
subdued:
12from [b]Aram and Moab and the sons of Ammon and the
Philistines and Amalek, and from the spoil of Hadadezer, son of
Rehob, king of Zobah.
13¶ So David made a name *for himself* when he returned from
killing 18,000 [c]Arameans in the Valley of Salt.
14And he put garrisons in Edom. In all Edom he put garrisons,
and all the Edomites became servants to David. And the LORD
helped David wherever he went.
15¶ So David reigned over all Israel; and David administered
justice and righteousness for all his people.
16And Joab the son of Zeruiah *was* over the army, and Jehoshaphat the son of Ahilud *was* recorder.
17And Zadok the son of Ahitub and Ahimelech the son of
Abiathar *were* priests, and Seraiah *was* secretary.
18And Benaiah the son of Jehoiada was over the Cherethites and
the Pelethites; and David's sons were chief ministers.

*David's Kindness to Mephibosheth*

**9** THEN DAVID said, "Is there yet anyone left of the house of
Saul, that I may show him kindness for Jonathan's sake?"

**NAS** [a] I.e., Euphrates [b] Some mss. read *Edom(ites)* [c] Some mss. read *Edom(ites)*

## New International

pleased to bless the house of your servant, that it may continue forever in your sight; for you, O Sovereign LORD, have
spoken, and with your blessing the house of your servant will
be blessed forever."

*David's Victories*

**8** IN THE course of time, David defeated the Philistines and
subdued them, and he took Metheg Ammah from the control
of the Philistines.
2David also defeated the Moabites. He made them lie down on
the ground and measured them off with a length of cord. Every
two lengths of them were put to death, and the third length was
allowed to live. So the Moabites became subject to David and
brought tribute.
3Moreover, David fought Hadadezer son of Rehob, king of
Zobah, when he went to restore his control along the Euphrates
River. 4David captured a thousand of his chariots, seven thousand
charioteers[d] and twenty thousand foot soldiers. He hamstrung all
but a hundred of the chariot horses.
5When the Arameans of Damascus came to help Hadadezer
king of Zobah, David struck down twenty-two thousand of them.
6He put garrisons in the Aramean kingdom of Damascus, and the
Arameans became subject to him and brought tribute. The LORD
gave David victory wherever he went.
7David took the gold shields that belonged to the officers of
Hadadezer and brought them to Jerusalem. 8From Tebah[e] and
Berothai, towns that belonged to Hadadezer, King David took a
great quantity of bronze.
9When Tou[f] king of Hamath heard that David had defeated the
entire army of Hadadezer, 10he sent his son Joram[g] to King David
to greet him and congratulate him on his victory in battle over
Hadadezer, who had been at war with Tou. Joram brought with
him articles of silver and gold and bronze.
11King David dedicated these articles to the LORD, as he had
done with the silver and gold from all the nations he had subdued:
12Edom[h] and Moab, the Ammonites and the Philistines, and Amalek. He also dedicated the plunder taken from Hadadezer son of
Rehob, king of Zobah.
13And David became famous after he returned from striking
down eighteen thousand Edomites[i] in the Valley of Salt.
14He put garrisons throughout Edom, and all the Edomites
became subject to David. The LORD gave David victory wherever
he went.

*David's Officials*

15David reigned over all Israel, doing what was just and right
for all his people. 16Joab son of Zeruiah was over the army; Jehoshaphat son of Ahilud was recorder; 17Zadok son of Ahitub and
Ahimelech son of Abiathar were priests; Seraiah was secretary;
18Benaiah son of Jehoiada was over the Kerethites and Pelethites;
and David's sons were royal advisers.[j]

*David and Mephibosheth*

**9** DAVID ASKED, "Is there anyone still left of the house of Saul
to whom I can show kindness for Jonathan's sake?"

**NIV** [d] *4* Septuagint (see also Dead Sea Scrolls and 1 Chron. 18:4); Masoretic Text *captured seventeen hundred of his charioteers* [e] *8* See some Septuagint manuscripts (see also 1 Chron. 18:8); Hebrew *Betah.* [f] *9* Hebrew *Toi,* a variant of *Tou;* also in verse 10 [g] *10* A variant of *Hadoram* [h] *12* Some Hebrew manuscripts, Septuagint and Syriac (see also 1 Chron. 18:11); most Hebrew manuscripts *Aram* [i] *13* A few Hebrew manuscripts, Septuagint and Syriac (see also 1 Chron. 18:12); most Hebrew manuscripts *Aram* (that is, Arameans) [j] *18* Or *were priests*

## King James

2 And *there was* of the house of Saul a servant whose name *was* Ziba. And when they had called him unto David, the king said unto him, *Art* thou Ziba? And he said, Thy servant *is he.*

3 And the king said, *Is* there not yet any of the house of Saul, that I may show the kindness of God unto him? And Ziba said unto the king, Jonathan hath yet a son, *which is* lame on *his* feet.

4 And the king said unto him, Where *is* he? And Ziba said unto the king, Behold, he *is* in the house of Machir, the son of Ammiel, in Lo-debar.

5 ¶ Then king David sent, and fetched him out of the house of Machir, the son of Ammiel, from Lo-debar.

6 Now when Mephibosheth, the son of Jonathan, the son of Saul, was come unto David, he fell on his face, and did reverence. And David said, Mephibosheth. And he answered, Behold thy servant!

7 ¶ And David said unto him, Fear not: for I will surely show thee kindness for Jonathan thy father's sake, and will restore thee all the land of Saul thy father; and thou shalt eat bread at my table continually.

8 And he bowed himself, and said, What *is* thy servant, that thou shouldest look upon such a dead dog as I *am?*

9 ¶ Then the king called to Ziba, Saul's servant, and said unto him, I have given unto thy master's son all that pertained to Saul and to all his house.

10 Thou therefore, and thy sons, and thy servants, shall till the land for him, and thou shalt bring in *the fruits,* that thy master's son may have food to eat: but Mephibosheth thy master's son shall eat bread always at my table. Now Ziba had fifteen sons and twenty servants.

11 Then said Ziba unto the king, According to all that my lord the king hath commanded his servant, so shall thy servant do. As for Mephibosheth, *said the king,* he shall eat at my table, as one of the king's sons.

12 And Mephibosheth had a young son, whose name *was* Micha. And all that dwelt in the house of Ziba *were* servants unto Mephibosheth.

13 So Mephibosheth dwelt in Jerusalem: for he did eat continually at the king's table; and was lame on both his feet.

**10** AND IT came to pass after this, that the king of the children of Ammon died, and Hanun his son reigned in his stead.

2 Then said David, I will show kindness unto Hanun the son of Nahash, as his father showed kindness unto me. And David sent to comfort him by the hand of his servants for his father. And David's servants came into the land of the children of Ammon.

3 And the princes of the children of Ammon said unto Hanun their lord, Thinkest thou that David doth honour thy father, that he hath sent comforters unto thee? hath not David *rather* sent his servants unto thee, to search the city, and to spy it out, and to overthrow it?

4 Wherefore Hanun took David's servants, and shaved off the one half of their beards, and cut off their garments in the middle, *even* to their buttocks, and sent them away.

5 When they told *it* unto David, he sent to meet them, because the men were greatly ashamed: and the king said, Tarry at Jericho until your beards be grown, and *then* return.

6 ¶ And when the children of Ammon saw that they stank before David, the children of Ammon sent and hired the Syrians of Beth-rehob, and the Syrians of Zoba, twenty thousand footmen, and of king Maacah a thousand men, and of Ish-tob twelve thousand men.

7 And when David heard of *it,* he sent Joab, and all the host of the mighty men.

## Amplified

2 And of the house of Saul there was a servant whose name was Ziba. When they had called him to David, he said to him, Are you Ziba? He said, I, your servant, am he.

3 The king said, Is there not still some one of the house of Saul to whom I may show the [unfailing, unsought, unlimited] mercy *and* kindness of God? Ziba replied, Jonathan has yet a son, who is lame in his feet. [I Sam. 20:14-17.]

4 And the king said, Where is he? Ziba replied, He is in the house of Machir son of Ammiel, in Lodebar.

5 Then King David sent and brought him from the house of Machir son of Ammiel, at Lodebar.

6 And Mephibosheth son of Jonathan, son of Saul, came to David and fell on his face and did obeisance. David said, Mephibosheth! And he answered, Behold your servant!

7 David said to him, Fear not; for I will surely show you kindness for Jonathan your father's sake, and will restore to you all the land of Saul your father [grandfather] and you shall eat at my table always.

8 And [the cripple] bowed himself, and said, What is your servant, that you should look upon such a dead dog as I am?

9 Then the king called to Ziba, Saul's servant, and said to him, I have given your master's son [grandson] all that belonged to Saul and to all his house.

10 And you shall till the land for him, you, your sons, and your servants, and you shall bring in the produce that your master's heir may have food to eat; but Mephibosheth your master's son [grandson] shall eat always at my table. Now Ziba had fifteen sons and twenty servants.

11 Then Ziba said to the king, Your servant will do according to all my lord the king commands. So Mephibosheth ate at David's table, as one of the king's sons.

12 Mephibosheth had a young son, whose name was Micha. And all who dwelt in Ziba's house were servants to Mephibosheth.

13 So Mephibosheth dwelt in Jerusalem, for he ate continually at the king's table, [even though] he was lame in both feet.

**10** LATER, THE king of the Ammonites died, and Hanun his son reigned in his stead.

2 David said, I will show kindness to Hanun son of Nahash, as his father did to me. So David sent by his servants to console him for his father's death, and they came into the land of the Ammonites,

3 But the princes of the Ammonites said to Hanun their lord, Do you think that it is because David honors your father that he has sent comforters to you? Has he not rather sent his servants to you to search the city, spy it out, and overthrow it?

4 So Hanun took David's servants, and shaved off half their beards, and cut off their garments in the middle at their hips, and sent them away.

5 When it was told David, he sent to meet them, for the men were greatly ashamed. And the king said, Tarry at Jericho until your beards are grown, and then return.

6 And when the Ammonites saw that they had made themselves obnoxious *and* disgusting to David, they sent and hired the Syrians of Beth-rehob and of Zobah, 20,000 foot soldiers, and of the king of Maacah 1,000 men, and of Tob 12,000 men.

7 When David heard of it, he sent Joab and all the army of the mighty men.

## New American Standard

2Now there was a servant of the house of Saul whose name
was Ziba, and they called him to David; and the king said to him,
"Are you Ziba?" And he said, "*I am* your servant."
3And the king said, "Is there not yet anyone of the house of
Saul to whom I may show the kindness of God?" And Ziba said
to the king, "There is still a son of Jonathan who is crippled in both
feet."
4So the king said to him, "Where is he?" And Ziba said to the
king, "Behold, he is in the house of Machir the son of Ammiel in
Lo-debar."
5Then King David sent and brought him from the house of
Machir the son of Ammiel, from Lo-debar.
6And Mephibosheth, the son of Jonathan the son of Saul, came
to David and fell on his face and prostrated himself. And David
said, "Mephibosheth." And he said, "Here is your servant!"
7And David said to him, "Do not fear, for I will surely show
kindness to you for the sake of your father Jonathan, and will
restore to you all the land of your grandfather Saul; and you shall
eat at my table regularly."
8Again he prostrated himself and said, "What is your servant,
that you should regard a dead dog like me?"
9¶ Then the king called Saul's servant Ziba, and said to him,
"All that belonged to Saul and to all his house I have given to your
master's grandson.
10"And you and your sons and your servants shall cultivate the
land for him, and you shall bring in *the produce* so that your master's grandson may have food; nevertheless Mephibosheth your
master's grandson shall eat at my table regularly." Now Ziba had
fifteen sons and twenty servants.
11Then Ziba said to the king, "According to all that my lord the
king commands his servant so your servant will do." So Mephibosheth ate at David's table as one of the king's sons.
12And Mephibosheth had a young son whose name was Mica.
And all who lived in the house of Ziba were servants to Mephibosheth.
13So Mephibosheth lived in Jerusalem, for he ate at the king's
table regularly. Now he was lame in both feet.

### *Ammon and Aram Defeated*

**10** NOW IT happened afterwards that the king of the Ammonites died, and Hanun his son became king in his
place.
2Then David said, "I will show kindness to Hanun the son of
Nahash, just as his father showed kindness to me." So David sent
some of his servants to console him concerning his father. But
when David's servants came to the land of the Ammonites,
3the princes of the Ammonites said to Hanun their lord, "Do
you think that David is honoring your father because he has sent
consolers to you? Has David not sent his servants to you in order
to search the city, to spy it out and overthrow it?"
4So Hanun took David's servants and shaved off half of their
beards, and cut off their garments in the middle as far as their hips,
and sent them away.
5When they told *it* to David, he sent to meet them, for the men
were greatly humiliated. And the king said, "Stay at Jericho until
your beards grow, and *then* return."
6¶ Now when the sons of Ammon saw that they had become
odious to David, the sons of Ammon sent and hired the Arameans
of Beth-rehob and the Arameans of Zobah, 20,000 foot soldiers,
and the king of Maacah with 1,000 men, and the men of Tob with
12,000 men.
7When David heard *of it*, he sent Joab and all the army, the
mighty men.

## New International

2Now there was a servant of Saul's household named Ziba.
They called him to appear before David, and the king said to him,
"Are you Ziba?"
"Your servant," he replied.
3The king asked, "Is there no one still left of the house of Saul
to whom I can show God's kindness?"
Ziba answered the king, "There is still a son of Jonathan; he is
crippled in both feet."
4"Where is he?" the king asked.
Ziba answered, "He is at the house of Makir son of Ammiel in
Lo Debar."
5So King David had him brought from Lo Debar, from the
house of Makir son of Ammiel.
6When Mephibosheth son of Jonathan, the son of Saul, came
to David, he bowed down to pay him honor.
David said, "Mephibosheth!"
"Your servant," he replied.
7"Don't be afraid," David said to him, "for I will surely show
you kindness for the sake of your father Jonathan. I will restore to
you all the land that belonged to your grandfather Saul, and you
will always eat at my table."
8Mephibosheth bowed down and said, "What is your servant,
that you should notice a dead dog like me?"
9Then the king summoned Ziba, Saul's servant, and said to
him, "I have given your master's grandson everything that belonged to Saul and his family. 10You and your sons and your
servants are to farm the land for him and bring in the crops, so that
your master's grandson may be provided for. And Mephibosheth,
grandson of your master, will always eat at my table." (Now Ziba
had fifteen sons and twenty servants.)
11Then Ziba said to the king, "Your servant will do whatever
my lord the king commands his servant to do." So Mephibosheth
ate at David's[a] table like one of the king's sons.
12Mephibosheth had a young son named Mica, and all the
members of Ziba's household were servants of Mephibosheth.
13And Mephibosheth lived in Jerusalem, because he always ate at
the king's table, and he was crippled in both feet.

### *David Defeats the Ammonites*

**10** IN THE course of time, the king of the Ammonites died,
and his son Hanun succeeded him as king. 2David
thought, "I will show kindness to Hanun son of Nahash, just as
his father showed kindness to me." So David sent a delegation to
express his sympathy to Hanun concerning his father.
When David's men came to the land of the Ammonites, 3the
Ammonite nobles said to Hanun their lord, "Do you think David
is honoring your father by sending men to you to express sympathy? Hasn't David sent them to you to explore the city and spy it
out and overthrow it?" 4So Hanun seized David's men, shaved off
half of each man's beard, cut off their garments in the middle at
the buttocks, and sent them away.
5When David was told about this, he sent messengers to meet
the men, for they were greatly humiliated. The king said, "Stay at
Jericho till your beards have grown, and then come back."
6When the Ammonites realized that they had become a stench
in David's nostrils, they hired twenty thousand Aramean foot
soldiers from Beth Rehob and Zobah, as well as the king of Maacah
with a thousand men, and also twelve thousand men from Tob.
7On hearing this, David sent Joab out with the entire army of
fighting men. 8The Ammonites came out and drew up in battle

NIV [a] *11* Septuagint; Hebrew *my*

# King James

8And the children of Ammon came out, and put the battle in array at the entering in of the gate: and the Syrians of Zoba, and of Rehob, and Ish-tob, and Maacah, *were* by themselves in the field.

9When Joab saw that the front of the battle was against him before and behind, he chose of all the choice *men* of Israel, and put *them* in array against the Syrians:

10And the rest of the people he delivered into the hand of Abishai his brother, that he might put *them* in array against the children of Ammon.

11And he said, If the Syrians be too strong for me, then thou shalt help me: but if the children of Ammon be too strong for thee, then I will come and help thee.

12Be of good courage, and let us play the men for our people, and for the cities of our God: and the LORD do that which seemeth him good.

13And Joab drew nigh, and the people that *were* with him, unto the battle against the Syrians: and they fled before him.

14And when the children of Ammon saw that the Syrians were fled, then fled they also before Abishai, and entered into the city. So Joab returned from the children of Ammon, and came to Jerusalem.

15¶ And when the Syrians saw that they were smitten before Israel, they gathered themselves together.

16And Hadarezer sent, and brought out the Syrians that *were* beyond the river: and they came to Helam; and Shobach the captain of the host of Hadarezer *went* before them.

17And when it was told David, he gathered all Israel together, and passed over Jordan, and came to Helam. And the Syrians set themselves in array against David, and fought with him.

18And the Syrians fled before Israel; and David slew *the men of* seven hundred chariots of the Syrians, and forty thousand horsemen, and smote Shobach the captain of their host, who died there.

19And when all the kings *that were* servants to Hadarezer saw that they were smitten before Israel, they made peace with Israel, and served them. So the Syrians feared to help the children of Ammon any more.

**11** AND IT came to pass, after the year was expired, at the time when kings go forth *to battle*, that David sent Joab, and his servants with him, and all Israel; and they destroyed the children of Ammon, and besieged Rabbah. But David tarried still at Jerusalem.

2¶ And it came to pass in an eveningtide, that David arose from off his bed, and walked upon the roof of the king's house: and from the roof he saw a woman washing herself; and the woman *was* very beautiful to look upon.

3And David sent and inquired after the woman. And *one* said, *Is* not this Bath-sheba, the daughter of Eliam, the wife of Uriah the Hittite?

4And David sent messengers, and took her; and she came in unto him, and he lay with her; for she was purified from her uncleanness: and she returned unto her house.

5And the woman conceived, and sent and told David, and said, I *am* with child.

6¶ And David sent to Joab, *saying*, Send me Uriah the Hittite. And Joab sent Uriah to David.

7And when Uriah was come unto him, David demanded *of him* how Joab did, and how the people did, and how the war prospered.

8And David said to Uriah, Go down to thy house, and wash thy feet. And Uriah departed out of the king's house, and there followed him a mess *of meat* from the king.

9But Uriah slept at the door of the king's house with all the servants of his lord, and went not down to his house.

# Amplified

8And the Ammonites came out and put the battle in array at the entrance of the gate; but the Syrians of Zobah and of Rehob, and the men of Tob and Maacah, were stationed by themselves in the open country.

9When Joab saw that the battle front was against him before and behind, he picked some of all the choice men of Israel, and put them in array against the Syrians;

10The rest of the men Joab gave over to Abishai his brother, that he might put them in array against the Ammonites.

11Joab said, If the Syrians are too strong for me, then you shall help me; but if the Ammonites are too strong for you, I will come and help you.

12Be of good courage; let us play the man for our people and the cities of our God; and the Lord do what seems good to Him.

13And Joab and the people who were with him drew near to battle against the Syrians; and they fled before him.

14And when the Ammonites saw that the Syrians had fled, they also fled before Abishai, and entered the city. So Joab returned from battling against the Ammonites and came to Jerusalem.

15When the Syrians saw that they were defeated by Israel, they gathered together.

16Hadadezer sent, and brought the Syrians who were beyond the river [Euphrates], and they came to Helam, with Shobach commander of the army of Hadadezer leading them.

17When David was told, he gathered all Israel, crossed the Jordan, and came to Helam. Then the Syrians set themselves in array against David, and fought with him.

18The Syrians fled before Israel; and David slew of [them] the men of 700 chariots, and 40,000 horsemen, and smote Shobach captain of their army, who died there.

19And when all the kings serving Hadadezer saw that they were defeated by Israel, they made peace with Israel, and served them. So the Syrians were afraid to help the Ammonites any more.

**11** IN THE spring, when kings go forth to battle, David sent Joab with his servants, and all Israel, and they ravaged the Ammonites [country] and besieged Rabbah. But David remained in Jerusalem.

2One evening David arose from his couch and was walking on the roof of the king's house, when from there he saw a woman bathing, and she was very lovely to behold.

3David sent and inquired about the woman. One said, Is not this Bathsheba daughter of Eliam, wife of Uriah the Hittite?

4And David sent messengers, and took her; and she came in to him, and he lay with her (for she was purified from her uncleanness); then she returned to her house.

5And the woman became pregnant, and sent and told David, I am with child.

6David sent to Joab, saying, Send me Uriah the Hittite. So Joab sent [him] Uriah.

7When Uriah had come to him, David asked him how Joab was, how the people fared, and how the war progressed.

8David said to Uriah, Go down to your house, and wash your feet. Uriah went out of the king's house, and there followed him a mess of food [a gift] from the king;

9But Uriah slept at the door of the king's house with all the servants of his lord, and did not go down to his house.

## New American Standard

8And the sons of Ammon came out and drew up in battle array
at the entrance of the city, while the Arameans of Zobah and of
Rehob and the men of Tob and Maacah *were* by themselves in the
field.
9¶ Now when Joab saw that the battle was set against him in
front and in the rear, he selected from all the choice men of Israel,
and arrayed *them* against the Arameans.
10But the remainder of the people he placed in the hand of
Abishai his brother, and he arrayed *them* against the sons of Ammon.
11And he said, "If the Arameans are too strong for me, then you
shall help me, but if the sons of Ammon are too strong for you,
then I will come to help you.
12"Be strong, and let us show ourselves courageous for the sake
of our people and for the cities of our God; and may the LORD do
what is good in His sight."
13So Joab and the people who were with him drew near to the
battle against the Arameans, and they fled before him.
14When the sons of Ammon saw that the Arameans fled, they
*also* fled before Abishai and entered the city. Then Joab returned
from *fighting* against the sons of Ammon and came to Jerusalem.
15¶ When the Arameans saw that they had been defeated by
Israel, they gathered themselves together.
16And Hadadezer sent and brought out the Arameans who
were beyond the [a]River, and they came to Helam; and Shobach
the commander of the army of Hadadezer led them.
17Now when it was told David, he gathered all Israel together
and crossed the Jordan, and came to Helam. And the Arameans
arrayed themselves to meet David and fought against him.
18But the Arameans fled before Israel, and David killed 700
charioteers of the Arameans and 40,000 horsemen and struck
down Shobach the commander of their army, and he died there.
19When all the kings, servants of Hadadezer, saw that they
were defeated by Israel, they made peace with Israel and served
them. So the Arameans feared to help the sons of Ammon anymore.

*Bathsheba, David's Great Sin*

**11** THEN IT happened in the spring, at the time when kings
go out *to battle,* that David sent Joab and his servants with
him and all Israel, and they destroyed the sons of Ammon and
besieged Rabbah. But David stayed at Jerusalem.
2¶ Now when evening came David arose from his bed and
walked around on the roof of the king's house, and from the roof
he saw a woman bathing; and the woman was very beautiful in
appearance.
3So David sent and inquired about the woman. And one said,
"Is this not Bathsheba, the daughter of Eliam, the wife of Uriah the
Hittite?"
4And David sent messengers and took her, and when she came
to him, he lay with her; and when she had purified herself from
her uncleanness, she returned to her house.
5And the woman conceived; and she sent and told David, and
said, "I am pregnant."
6¶ Then David sent to Joab, *saying,* "Send me Uriah the Hittite." So Joab sent Uriah to David.
7When Uriah came to him, David asked concerning the welfare
of Joab and the people and the state of the war.
8Then David said to Uriah, "Go down to your house, and wash
your feet." And Uriah went out of the king's house, and a present
from the king was sent out after him.
9But Uriah slept at the door of the king's house with all the
servants of his lord, and did not go down to his house.

NAS [a] I.e., Euphrates

## New International

formation at the entrance to their city gate, while the Arameans of
Zobah and Rehob and the men of Tob and Maacah were by themselves in the open country.
9Joab saw that there were battle lines in front of him and behind
him; so he selected some of the best troops in Israel and deployed
them against the Arameans. 10He put the rest of the men under
the command of Abishai his brother and deployed them against
the Ammonites. 11Joab said, "If the Arameans are too strong for
me, then you are to come to my rescue; but if the Ammonites are
too strong for you, then I will come to rescue you. 12Be strong and
let us fight bravely for our people and the cities of our God. The
LORD will do what is good in his sight."
13Then Joab and the troops with him advanced to fight the
Arameans, and they fled before him. 14When the Ammonites saw
that the Arameans were fleeing, they fled before Abishai and went
inside the city. So Joab returned from fighting the Ammonites and
came to Jerusalem.
15After the Arameans saw that they had been routed by Israel,
they regrouped. 16Hadadezer had Arameans brought from beyond
the River[b]; they went to Helam, with Shobach the commander of
Hadadezer's army leading them.
17When David was told of this, he gathered all Israel, crossed
the Jordan and went to Helam. The Arameans formed their battle
lines to meet David and fought against him. 18But they fled before
Israel, and David killed seven hundred of their charioteers and
forty thousand of their foot soldiers.[c] He also struck down Shobach the commander of their army, and he died there. 19When all
the kings who were vassals of Hadadezer saw that they had been
defeated by Israel, they made peace with the Israelites and became
subject to them.
So the Arameans were afraid to help the Ammonites anymore.

*David and Bathsheba*

**11** IN THE spring, at the time when kings go off to war,
David sent Joab out with the king's men and the whole
Israelite army. They destroyed the Ammonites and besieged Rabbah. But David remained in Jerusalem.
2One evening David got up from his bed and walked around
on the roof of the palace. From the roof he saw a woman bathing.
The woman was very beautiful, 3and David sent someone to find
out about her. The man said, "Isn't this Bathsheba, the daughter
of Eliam and the wife of Uriah the Hittite?" 4Then David sent
messengers to get her. She came to him, and he slept with her.
(She had purified herself from her uncleanness.) Then[d] she went
back home. 5The woman conceived and sent word to David, saying, "I am pregnant."
6So David sent this word to Joab: "Send me Uriah the Hittite."
And Joab sent him to David. 7When Uriah came to him, David
asked him how Joab was, how the soldiers were and how the war
was going. 8Then David said to Uriah, "Go down to your house
and wash your feet." So Uriah left the palace, and a gift from the
king was sent after him. 9But Uriah slept at the entrance to the
palace with all his master's servants and did not go down to his
house.

NIV [b] *16* That is, the Euphrates [c] *18* Some Septuagint manuscripts (see also 1 Chron. 19:18); Hebrew *horsemen* [d] *4* Or *with her. When she purified herself from her uncleanness,*

## King James

10And when they had told David, saying, Uriah went not down unto his house, David said unto Uriah, Camest thou not from *thy* journey? why *then* didst thou not go down unto thine house?

11And Uriah said unto David, The ark, and Israel, and Judah, abide in tents; and my lord Joab, and the servants of my lord, are encamped in the open fields; shall I then go into mine house, to eat and to drink, and to lie with my wife? *as* thou livest, and *as* thy soul liveth, I will not do this thing.

12And David said to Uriah, Tarry here today also, and tomorrow I will let thee depart. So Uriah abode in Jerusalem that day, and the morrow.

13And when David had called him, he did eat and drink before him; and he made him drunk: and at even he went out to lie on his bed with the servants of his lord, but went not down to his house.

14¶ And it came to pass in the morning, that David wrote a letter to Joab, and sent *it* by the hand of Uriah.

15And he wrote in the letter, saying, Set ye Uriah in the forefront of the hottest battle, and retire ye from him, that he may be smitten, and die.

16And it came to pass, when Joab observed the city, that he assigned Uriah unto a place where he knew that valiant men *were*.

17And the men of the city went out, and fought with Joab: and there fell *some* of the people of the servants of David; and Uriah the Hittite died also.

18¶ Then Joab sent and told David all the things concerning the war;

19And charged the messenger, saying, When thou hast made an end of telling the matters of the war unto the king,

20And if so be that the king's wrath arise, and he say unto thee, Wherefore approached ye so nigh unto the city when ye did fight? knew ye not that they would shoot from the wall?

21Who smote Abimelech the son of Jerubbesheth? did not a woman cast a piece of a millstone upon him from the wall, that he died in Thebez? why went ye nigh the wall? then say thou, Thy servant Uriah the Hittite is dead also.

22¶ So the messenger went, and came and showed David all that Joab had sent him for.

23And the messenger said unto David, Surely the men prevailed against us, and came out unto us into the field, and we were upon them even unto the entering of the gate.

24And the shooters shot from off the wall upon thy servants; and *some* of the king's servants be dead, and thy servant Uriah the Hittite is dead also.

25Then David said unto the messenger, Thus shalt thou say unto Joab, Let not this thing displease thee, for the sword devoureth one as well as another: make thy battle more strong against the city, and overthrow it: and encourage thou him.

26¶ And when the wife of Uriah heard that Uriah her husband was dead, she mourned for her husband.

27And when the mourning was past, David sent and fetched her to his house, and she became his wife, and bare him a son. But the thing that David had done displeased the LORD.

**12** AND THE LORD sent Nathan unto David. And he came unto him, and said unto him, There were two men in one city; the one rich, and the other poor.

2The rich *man* had exceeding many flocks and herds:

3But the poor *man* had nothing, save one little ewe lamb, which he had bought and nourished up: and it grew up together with him, and with his children; it did eat of his own meat, and drank of his own cup, and lay in his bosom, and was unto him as a daughter.

## Amplified

10When they told David, Uriah did not go down to his house, David said to Uriah, Have you not come from a journey? Why did you not go down to your house?

11Uriah said to David, The ark and Israel and Judah live in tents; and my lord Joab, and the servants of my lord are camping in the open field; shall I then go to my house, to eat and drink, and lie with my wife? As you live and as my soul lives, I will not do this thing.

12And David said to Uriah, Remain here today also, and tomorrow I will let you depart. So Uriah remained in Jerusalem that day and the next.

13David invited him and he ate with him and drank so that he made him drunk; but that night he went out to lie on his bed with the servants of his lord, and did not go down to his house.

14In the morning David wrote a letter to Joab, and sent it by Uriah.

15And he wrote in the letter, Put Uriah in the front line of the heaviest fighting and withdraw from him, that he may be struck down and die.

16So when Joab was besieging the city, he assigned Uriah opposite where he knew the enemy's most valiant men were.

17And the men of the city came out and fought with Joab; and some of the servants of David fell. Uriah the Hittite died also.

18Then Joab sent and told David all the things concerning the war;

19And charged the messenger, When you have finished reporting matters of the war to the king,

20Then if the king's anger rises, and he says to you, Why did you go so near to the city to fight? Did you not know they would shoot from the wall?

21Who killed Abimelech son of Jerubbesheth [Gideon]? Did not a woman cast an upper millstone upon him from the wall, so that he died in Thebez? Why did you go near the wall? Then say, Your servant Uriah the Hittite is dead also. [Judg. 9:35, 53.]

22So the messenger went and told David all for which Joab had sent him.

23The messenger said to David, Surely the men prevailed against us, and came out to us in to the field, and we were upon them even to the entrance of the gate.

24Then the archers shot at your servants from the wall. Some of the king's servants are dead, and your servant Uriah the Hittite is dead also.

25Then David said to the messenger, Say to Joab, Let not this thing disturb you, for the sword devours one as well as another; strengthen your attack upon the city, and overthrow it. And encourage Joab.

26When Uriah's wife heard that her husband was dead, she mourned for Uriah.

27And when the mourning was past, David sent and brought her to his house, and she became his wife, and bore him a son. But the thing that David had done was evil in the sight of the Lord.

**12** AND THE Lord sent Nathan to David. He came and said to him, There were two men in a city, one rich and the other poor.

2The rich man had very many flocks and herds;

3But the poor man had nothing but one little ewe lamb, which he had bought and brought up, and it grew up with him and his children. It ate of his own morsel, drank from his own cup, lay in his bosom, and was like a daughter to him.

## New American Standard

10 Now when they told David, saying, "Uriah did not go down
to his house," David said to Uriah, "Have you not come from a
journey? Why did you not go down to your house?"
11 And Uriah said to David, "The ark and Israel and Judah are
staying in temporary shelters, and my lord Joab and the servants
of my lord are camping in the open field. Shall I then go to my
house to eat and to drink and to lie with my wife? By your life and
the life of your soul, I will not do this thing."
12 Then David said to Uriah, "Stay here today also, and tomorrow I will let you go." So Uriah remained in Jerusalem that day and
the next.
13 Now David called him, and he ate and drank before him, and
he made him drunk; and in the evening he went out to lie on his
bed with his lord's servants, but he did not go down to his house.
**14**¶ Now it came about in the morning that David wrote a letter
to Joab, and sent *it* by the hand of Uriah.
15 And he had written in the letter, saying, "Place Uriah in the
front line of the fiercest battle and withdraw from him, so that he
may be struck down and die."
16 So it was as Joab kept watch on the city, that he put Uriah at
the place where he knew there *were* valiant men.
17 And the men of the city went out and fought against Joab, and
some of the people among David's servants fell; and Uriah the
Hittite also died.
18 Then Joab sent and reported to David all the events of the war.
19 And he charged the messenger, saying, "When you have
finished telling all the events of the war to the king,
20 and if it happens that the king's wrath rises and he says to
you, 'Why did you go so near to the city to fight? Did you not know
that they would shoot from the wall?
21 'Who struck down Abimelech the son of Jerubbesheth? Did
not a woman throw an upper millstone on him from the wall so
that he died at Thebez? Why did you go so near the wall?'—then
you shall say, 'Your servant Uriah the Hittite is dead also.'"
**22**¶ So the messenger departed and came and reported to David
all that Joab had sent him *to tell*.
23 And the messenger said to David, "The men prevailed against
us and came out against us in the field, but we pressed them as
far as the entrance of the gate.
24 "Moreover, the archers shot at your servants from the wall;
so some of the king's servants are dead, and your servant Uriah
the Hittite is also dead."
25 Then David said to the messenger, "Thus you shall say to
Joab, 'Do not let this thing displease you, for the sword devours
one as well as another; make your battle against the city stronger
and overthrow it'; and *so* encourage him."
**26**¶ Now when the wife of Uriah heard that Uriah her husband
was dead, she mourned for her husband.
27 When the *time of* mourning was over, David sent and brought
her to his house and she became his wife; then she bore him a son.
But the thing that David had done was evil in the sight of the LORD.

*Nathan Rebukes David*

**12** THEN THE LORD sent Nathan to David. And he came to
him, and said,
"There were two men in one city, the one rich and the
other poor.
2 "The rich man had a great many flocks and herds.
3 "But the poor man had nothing except one little ewe
lamb
Which he bought and nourished;
And it grew up together with him and his children.
It would eat of his bread and drink of his cup and lie in
his bosom,
And was like a daughter to him.

## New International

10 When David was told, "Uriah did not go home," he asked
him, "Haven't you just come from a distance? Why didn't you go
home?"
11 Uriah said to David, "The ark and Israel and Judah are staying
in tents, and my master Joab and my lord's men are camped in the
open fields. How could I go to my house to eat and drink and lie
with my wife? As surely as you live, I will not do such a thing!"
12 Then David said to him, "Stay here one more day, and tomorrow I will send you back." So Uriah remained in Jerusalem that day
and the next. 13 At David's invitation, he ate and drank with him,
and David made him drunk. But in the evening Uriah went out to
sleep on his mat among his master's servants; he did not go home.
14 In the morning David wrote a letter to Joab and sent it with
Uriah. 15 In it he wrote, "Put Uriah in the front line where the
fighting is fiercest. Then withdraw from him so he will be struck
down and die."
16 So while Joab had the city under siege, he put Uriah at a place
where he knew the strongest defenders were. 17 When the men of
the city came out and fought against Joab, some of the men in
David's army fell; moreover, Uriah the Hittite was dead.
18 Joab sent David a full account of the battle. 19 He instructed the
messenger: "When you have finished giving the king this account
of the battle, 20 the king's anger may flare up, and he may ask you,
'Why did you get so close to the city to fight? Didn't you know they
would shoot arrows from the wall? 21 Who killed Abimelech son of
Jerub-Besheth[a] ? Didn't a woman throw an upper millstone on him
from the wall, so that he died in Thebez? Why did you get so close
to the wall?' If he asks you this, then say to him, 'Also, your
servant Uriah the Hittite is dead.'"
22 The messenger set out, and when he arrived he told David
everything Joab had sent him to say. 23 The messenger said to
David, "The men overpowered us and came out against us in the
open, but we drove them back to the entrance to the city gate.
24 Then the archers shot arrows at your servants from the wall, and
some of the king's men died. Moreover, your servant Uriah the
Hittite is dead."
25 David told the messenger, "Say this to Joab: 'Don't let this
upset you; the sword devours one as well as another. Press the
attack against the city and destroy it.' Say this to encourage Joab."
26 When Uriah's wife heard that her husband was dead, she
mourned for him. 27 After the time of mourning was over, David
had her brought to his house, and she became his wife and bore
him a son. But the thing David had done displeased the LORD.

*Nathan Rebukes David*

**12** THE LORD sent Nathan to David. When he came to him,
he said, "There were two men in a certain town, one rich
and the other poor. 2 The rich man had a very large number of
sheep and cattle, 3 but the poor man had nothing except one little
ewe lamb he had bought. He raised it, and it grew up with him
and his children. It shared his food, drank from his cup and even
slept in his arms. It was like a daughter to him.

NIV [a] *21* Also known as *Jerub-Baal* (that is, Gideon)

## King James

4And there came a traveller unto the rich man, and he spared to take of his own flock and of his own herd, to dress for the wayfaring man that was come unto him; but took the poor man's lamb, and dressed it for the man that was come to him.

5And David's anger was greatly kindled against the man; and he said to Nathan, *As* the LORD liveth, the man that hath done this *thing* shall surely die:

6And he shall restore the lamb fourfold, because he did this thing, and because he had no pity.

7¶ And Nathan said to David, Thou *art* the man. Thus saith the LORD God of Israel, I anointed thee king over Israel, and I delivered thee out of the hand of Saul;

8And I gave thee thy master's house, and thy master's wives into thy bosom, and gave thee the house of Israel and of Judah; and if *that had been* too little, I would moreover have given unto thee such and such things.

9Wherefore hast thou despised the commandment of the LORD, to do evil in his sight? thou hast killed Uriah the Hittite with the sword, and hast taken his wife *to be* thy wife, and hast slain him with the sword of the children of Ammon.

10Now therefore the sword shall never depart from thine house; because thou hast despised me, and hast taken the wife of Uriah the Hittite to be thy wife.

11Thus saith the LORD, Behold, I will raise up evil against thee out of thine own house, and I will take thy wives before thine eyes, and give *them* unto thy neighbour, and he shall lie with thy wives in the sight of this sun.

12For thou didst *it* secretly: but I will do this thing before all Israel, and before the sun.

13And David said unto Nathan, I have sinned against the LORD. And Nathan said unto David, The LORD also hath put away thy sin; thou shalt not die.

14Howbeit, because by this deed thou hast given great occasion to the enemies of the LORD to blaspheme, the child also *that is* born unto thee shall surely die.

15¶ And Nathan departed unto his house. And the LORD struck the child that Uriah's wife bare unto David, and it was very sick.

16David therefore besought God for the child; and David fasted, and went in, and lay all night upon the earth.

17And the elders of his house arose, *and went* to him, to raise him up from the earth: but he would not, neither did he eat bread with them.

18And it came to pass on the seventh day, that the child died. And the servants of David feared to tell him that the child was dead: for they said, Behold, while the child was yet alive, we spake unto him, and he would not hearken unto our voice: how will he then vex himself, if we tell him that the child is dead?

19But when David saw that his servants whispered, David perceived that the child was dead: therefore David said unto his servants, Is the child dead? And they said, He is dead.

20Then David arose from the earth, and washed, and anointed *himself,* and changed his apparel, and came into the house of the LORD, and worshipped: then he came to his own house; and when he required, they set bread before him, and he did eat.

21Then said his servants unto him, What thing *is* this that thou hast done? thou didst fast and weep for the child, *while it was* alive; but when the child was dead, thou didst rise and eat bread.

22And he said, While the child was yet alive, I fasted and wept: for I said, Who can tell *whether* GOD will be gracious to me, that the child may live?

**AMP** [a] This sentence was fulfilled in the agony brought on David by his lawless children: Amnon's scandalous behavior with his half sister Tamar, and his consequent murder by his brother Absalom; Absalom's escape to a foreign land, and his return after three years, without recognition by David for two more years; his deliberate, rebellious attempt to win the hearts of the people and supplant his father; David's flight from Jerusalem, with the mass of the people against him; followed by a terrible battle in the wood of Ephraim, won by David's forces, but Absalom was killed in flight. David's agony of heart is echoed repeatedly in the history of these tragedies [II Sam. 13:1, to 19:8] and in some of his Psalms. Even when the great king was dying his son Adonijah was attempting to usurp the throne, and was later executed as a traitor.

## Amplified

4Now a traveler came to the rich man, and to avoid taking one of his own flock or herd to prepare for the wayfaring man who had come to him, he took the poor man's lamb, and prepared it for his guest.

5Then David's anger was greatly kindled against the man, and he said to Nathan, As the Lord lives, the man who has done this is a son [worthy] of death.

6He shall restore the lamb fourfold, because he did this thing and had no pity.

7Then Nathan said to David, You are the man! Thus says the Lord, the God of Israel: I anointed you king of Israel and I delivered you out of the hand of Saul;

8And I gave you your master's house, and your master's wives into your bosom, and gave you the house of Israel and of Judah; and if that had been too little, I would have added that much again.

9Why have you despised the commandment of the Lord, doing evil in His sight? You have slain Uriah the Hittite with the sword, and have taken his wife to be your wife; you have murdered him with the sword of the Ammonites. [Lev. 20:10; 24:17.]

10Now therefore the sword shall never depart from your house; because [you have not only despised My command, but] you have despised Me, and have taken the wife of Uriah the Hittite to be your wife.

11Thus says the Lord, Behold, I will raise up evil against you out of your [a]own house; and I will take your wives before your eyes and give them to your neighbor, and he shall lie with your wives in the sight of this sun.

12For you did it secretly; but I will do this thing before all Israel, and before the sun. [Fulfilled, II Sam. 16:21, 22.]

13And David said to Nathan, I have sinned against the Lord. And Nathan said to David, The Lord also has put away your sin; you shall not die. [Ps. 51.]

14Nevertheless, because by this deed you have utterly scorned the Lord, *and* given great occasion to the enemies of the Lord to blaspheme, the child that is born to you shall surely die.

15Then Nathan departed to his house. And the Lord struck the child that Uriah's widow bore to David, and it was very sick.

16David therefore besought God for the child; and David fasted, and went in, and lay all night [repeatedly] on the floor.

17His older house servants arose [in the night] and went to him, to raise him up from the floor; but he would not, nor did he eat food with them.

18And on the seventh day the child died. David's servants feared to tell him the child was dead, for they said, While the child was yet alive, we spoke to him, and he would not listen to our voice; will he then harm himself, if we tell him the child is dead?

19But when David saw that his servants whispered, he perceived that the child was dead. So he said to them, Is the child dead? And they said, He is.

20Then David arose from the floor, washed, anointed himself, changed his apparel, and went into the house of the Lord and worshiped. Then he came to his own house; and when he asked, they set food before him, and he ate.

21Then his servants said to him, What is this that you have done? You fasted and wept while the child was alive; but when the child was dead, you arose and ate food.

22David said, While the child was still alive, I fasted and wept; for I said, Who knows whether the Lord will be gracious to me and let the child live?

## New American Standard

4 "Now a traveler came to the rich man,
And he was unwilling to take from his own flock or his own herd,
To prepare for the wayfarer who had come to him;
Rather he took the poor man's ewe lamb and prepared it for the man who had come to him."

5 Then David's anger burned greatly against the man, and he said to Nathan, "As the LORD lives, surely the man who has done this deserves to die.

6 "And he must make restitution for the lamb fourfold, because he did this thing and had no compassion."

7 ¶ Nathan then said to David, "You are the man! Thus says the LORD God of Israel, 'It is I who anointed you king over Israel and it is I who delivered you from the hand of Saul.

8 'I also gave you your master's house and your master's wives into your care, and I gave you the house of Israel and Judah; and if *that had been* too little, I would have added to you many more things like these!

9 'Why have you despised the word of the LORD by doing evil in His sight? You have struck down Uriah the Hittite with the sword, have taken his wife to be your wife, and have killed him with the sword of the sons of Ammon.

10 'Now therefore, the sword shall never depart from your house, because you have despised Me and have taken the wife of Uriah the Hittite to be your wife.'

11 "Thus says the LORD, 'Behold, I will raise up evil against you from your own household; I will even take your wives before your eyes, and give *them* to your companion, and he shall lie with your wives in broad daylight.

12 'Indeed you did it secretly, but I will do this thing before all Israel, and under the sun.' "

13 Then David said to Nathan, "I have sinned against the LORD." And Nathan said to David, "The LORD also has taken away your sin; you shall not die.

14 "However, because by this deed you have given occasion to the enemies of the LORD to blaspheme, the child also that is born to you shall surely die."

15 So Nathan went to his house.

*Loss of a Child*

¶ Then the LORD struck the child that Uriah's widow bore to David, so that he was *very* sick.

16 David therefore inquired of God for the child; and David fasted and went and lay all night on the ground.

17 And the elders of his household stood beside him in order to raise him up from the ground, but he was unwilling and would not eat food with them.

18 Then it happened on the seventh day that the child died. And the servants of David were afraid to tell him that the child was dead, for they said, "Behold, while the child was *still* alive, we spoke to him and he did not listen to our voice. How then can we tell him that the child is dead, since he might do *himself* harm!"

19 But when David saw that his servants were whispering together, David perceived that the child was dead; so David said to his servants, "Is the child dead?" And they said, "He is dead."

20 So David arose from the ground, washed, anointed *himself*, and changed his clothes; and he came into the house of the LORD and worshiped. Then he came to his own house, and when he requested, they set food before him and he ate.

21 Then his servants said to him, "What is this thing that you have done? While the child was alive, you fasted and wept; but when the child died, you arose and ate food."

22 And he said, "While the child was *still* alive, I fasted and wept; for I said, 'Who knows, the LORD may be gracious to me, that the child may live.'

## New International

4 "Now a traveler came to the rich man, but the rich man refrained from taking one of his own sheep or cattle to prepare a meal
for the traveler who had come to him. Instead, he took the ewe
lamb that belonged to the poor man and prepared it for the one
who had come to him."

5 David burned with anger against the man and said to Nathan,
"As surely as the LORD lives, the man who did this deserves to die!
6 He must pay for that lamb four times over, because he did such
a thing and had no pity."

7 Then Nathan said to David, "You are the man! This is what the
LORD, the God of Israel, says: 'I anointed you king over Israel, and
I delivered you from the hand of Saul. 8 I gave your master's house
to you, and your master's wives into your arms. I gave you the
house of Israel and Judah. And if all this had been too little, I would
have given you even more. 9 Why did you despise the word of the
LORD by doing what is evil in his eyes? You struck down Uriah the
Hittite with the sword and took his wife to be your own. You killed
him with the sword of the Ammonites. 10 Now, therefore, the
sword will never depart from your house, because you despised
me and took the wife of Uriah the Hittite to be your own.'

11 "This is what the LORD says: 'Out of your own household I
am going to bring calamity upon you. Before your very eyes I will
take your wives and give them to one who is close to you, and he
will lie with your wives in broad daylight. 12 You did it in secret,
but I will do this thing in broad daylight before all Israel.' "

13 Then David said to Nathan, "I have sinned against the LORD."
Nathan replied, "The LORD has taken away your sin. You are
not going to die. 14 But because by doing this you have made the
enemies of the LORD show utter contempt,[b] the son born to you
will die."

15 After Nathan had gone home, the LORD struck the child that
Uriah's wife had borne to David, and he became ill. 16 David pleaded with God for the child. He fasted and went into his house and
spent the nights lying on the ground. 17 The elders of his household stood beside him to get him up from the ground, but he
refused, and he would not eat any food with them.

18 On the seventh day the child died. David's servants were
afraid to tell him that the child was dead, for they thought, "While
the child was still living, we spoke to David but he would not listen
to us. How can we tell him the child is dead? He may do something
desperate."

19 David noticed that his servants were whispering among
themselves and he realized the child was dead. "Is the child
dead?" he asked.

"Yes," they replied, "he is dead."

20 Then David got up from the ground. After he had washed,
put on lotions and changed his clothes, he went into the house of
the LORD and worshiped. Then he went to his own house, and at
his request they served him food, and he ate.

21 His servants asked him, "Why are you acting this way? While
the child was alive, you fasted and wept, but now that the child
is dead, you get up and eat!"

22 He answered, "While the child was still alive, I fasted and
wept. I thought, 'Who knows? The LORD may be gracious to me
and let the child live.' 23 But now that he is dead, why should I fast?

**NIV** [b] *14* Masoretic Text; an ancient Hebrew scribal tradition *this you have shown utter contempt for the LORD*

# King James

23But now he is dead, wherefore should I fast? can I bring him
back again? I shall go to him, but he shall not return to me.
24¶ And David comforted Bath-sheba his wife, and went in unto
her, and lay with her: and she bare a son, and he called his name
Solomon: and the LORD loved him.
25And he sent by the hand of Nathan the prophet; and he called
his name Jedidiah, because of the LORD.
26¶ And Joab fought against Rabbah of the children of Ammon,
and took the royal city.
27And Joab sent messengers to David, and said, I have fought
against Rabbah, and have taken the city of waters.
28Now therefore gather the rest of the people together, and
encamp against the city, and take it: lest I take the city, and it be
called after my name.
29And David gathered all the people together, and went to
Rabbah, and fought against it, and took it.
30And he took their king's crown from off his head, the weight
whereof *was* a talent of gold with the precious stones: and it was
*set* on David's head. And he brought forth the spoil of the city in
great abundance.
31And he brought forth the people that *were* therein, and put
*them* under saws, and under harrows of iron, and under axes of
iron, and made them pass through the brickkiln: and thus did he
unto all the cities of the children of Ammon. So David and all the
people returned unto Jerusalem.

**13** AND IT came to pass after this, that Absalom the son of
David had a fair sister, whose name *was* Tamar; and Amnon the son of David loved her.
2And Amnon was so vexed, that he fell sick for his sister Tamar;
for she *was* a virgin; and Amnon thought it hard for him to do any
thing to her.
3But Amnon had a friend, whose name *was* Jonadab, the son of
Shimeah David's brother: and Jonadab *was* a very subtle man.
4And he said unto him, Why *art* thou, *being* the king's son, lean
from day to day? wilt thou not tell me? And Amnon said unto him,
I love Tamar, my brother Absalom's sister.
5And Jonadab said unto him, Lay thee down on thy bed, and
make thyself sick: and when thy father cometh to see thee, say
unto him, I pray thee, let my sister Tamar come, and give me meat,
and dress the meat in my sight, that I may see *it*, and eat *it* at her
hand.
6¶ So Amnon lay down, and made himself sick: and when the
king was come to see him, Amnon said unto the king, I pray thee,
let Tamar my sister come, and make me a couple of cakes in my
sight, that I may eat at her hand.
7Then David sent home to Tamar, saying, Go now to thy brother Amnon's house, and dress him meat.
8So Tamar went to her brother Amnon's house; and he was laid
down. And she took flour, and kneaded *it*, and made cakes in his
sight, and did bake the cakes.
9And she took a pan, and poured *them* out before him; but he
refused to eat. And Amnon said, Have out all men from me. And
they went out every man from him.
10And Amnon said unto Tamar, Bring the meat into the chamber, that I may eat of thine hand. And Tamar took the cakes which
she had made, and brought *them* into the chamber to Amnon her
brother.
11And when she had brought *them* unto him to eat, he took hold
of her, and said unto her, Come lie with me, my sister.

# Amplified

23But now he is dead, why should I fast? Can I bring him back
again? I shall go to him, but he will not return to me.
24David comforted Bathsheba his wife, and went to her, and lay
with her; and she bore a son, and she called his name Solomon.
And the Lord loved [the child];
25He sent [a message] by the hand of Nathan the prophet; and
[Nathan] called the boy's [special] name Jedidiah [beloved of the
Lord], because the Lord [loved the child].
26Now Joab fought against Rabbah of the Ammonites, and took
the royal city.
27And Joab sent messengers to David, and said, I have fought
against Rabbah, and have taken the city of waters.
28Now therefore assemble the rest of the men, encamp against
the city, and take it; lest I take the city, and it be called after my
name.
29So David gathered all the men, went to Rabbah, fought
against it, and took it.
30And he took the crown of their king [of Malcham] from off his
head; the weight of it was a talent of gold and in it were precious
stones; and it was set on David's head. And he brought forth
exceedingly much spoil from the city.
31And he brought forth the people who were there, and put
them to [work with] saws and iron threshing-sledges and axes,
and made them labor at the brickkiln. And he did this to all the
Ammonite cities. Then [he] and all the men returned to Jerusalem.

**13** ABSALOM SON of David had a fair sister, whose name
was Tamar; and Amnon [her half brother] son of David
loved her.
2And Amnon was so troubled that he fell sick for his [half] sister
Tamar, for she was a virgin; and Amnon thought it impossible for
him to do anything to her.
3But Amnon had a friend, whose name was Jonadab son of
Shimeah, David's brother, and Jonadab was a very crafty man.
4He said to Amnon, Why are you, the king's son, so lean and
weak-looking from day to day? Will you not tell me? And Amnon
said to him, I love Tamar, my [half] brother Absalom's sister.
5Jonadab said to him, Go to bed and pretend you are sick; and
when your father David comes to see you, say to him, Let my sister
Tamar come and give me food, and prepare it in my sight, that I
may see it and eat it from her hand.
6So Amnon lay down and pretended to be sick; and when the
king came to see him, Amnon said to the king, Pray let my sister
Tamar come and make me a couple of cakes in my sight, that I may
eat from her hand.
7Then David sent home and told Tamar, Go now to your brother Amnon's house, and prepare food for him.
8So Tamar went to her brother Amnon's house, and he was in
bed. And she took dough, and kneaded it, and made cakes in his
sight and baked them.
9She took the pan and emptied it out before him, but he refused
to eat. And Amnon said, Send every one out from me. So every
one went out from him.
10Then Amnon said to Tamar, Bring the food here into the
bedroom, so I may eat from your hand. So Tamar took the cakes
she had made, and brought them into the room to Amnon her
brother.
11And when she brought them to him, he took hold of her, and
said, Come lie with me, my sister.

## New American Standard

23"But now he has died; why should I fast? Can I bring him back
again? I shall go to him, but he will not return to me."

*Solomon Born*

24¶ Then David comforted his wife Bathsheba, and went in to
her and lay with her; and she gave birth to a son, and he named
him Solomon. Now the LORD loved him
25and sent *word* through Nathan the prophet, and he named
him [a]Jedidiah for the LORD'S sake.

*War Again*

26¶ Now Joab fought against Rabbah of the sons of Ammon, and
captured the royal city.
27And Joab sent messengers to David and said, "I have fought
against Rabbah, I have even captured the city of waters.
28"Now therefore, gather the rest of the people together and
camp against the city and capture it, lest I capture the city myself
and it be named after me."
29So David gathered all the people and went to Rabbah, fought
against it, and captured it.
30Then he took the crown of their king from his head; and its
weight *was* a talent of gold, and *in it was* a precious stone; and it
was *placed* on David's head. And he brought out the spoil of the
city in great amounts.
31He also brought out the people who were in it, and set *them*
under saws, sharp iron instruments, and iron axes, and made
them pass through the brickkiln. And thus he did to all the cities
of the sons of Ammon. Then David and all the people returned *to*
Jerusalem.

*Amnon and Tamar*

**13** NOW IT was after this that Absalom the son of David had
a beautiful sister whose name was Tamar, and Amnon the
son of David loved her.
2And Amnon was so frustrated because of his sister Tamar that
he made himself ill, for she was a virgin, and it seemed hard to
Amnon to do anything to her.
3But Amnon had a friend whose name was Jonadab, the son
of Shimeah, David's brother; and Jonadab was a very shrewd man.
4And he said to him, "O son of the king, why are you so
depressed morning after morning? Will you not tell me?" Then
Amnon said to him, "I am in love with Tamar, the sister of my
brother Absalom."
5Jonadab then said to him, "Lie down on your bed and pretend
to be ill; when your father comes to see you, say to him, 'Please
let my sister Tamar come and give me *some* food to eat, and let her
prepare the food in my sight, that I may see *it* and eat from her
hand.' "
6So Amnon lay down and pretended to be ill; when the king
came to see him, Amnon said to the king, "Please let my sister
Tamar come and make me a couple of cakes in my sight, that I may
eat from her hand."
7¶ Then David sent to the house for Tamar, saying, "Go now
to your brother Amnon's house, and prepare food for him."
8So Tamar went to her brother Amnon's house, and he was
lying down. And she took dough, kneaded *it*, made cakes in his
sight, and baked the cakes.
9And she took the pan and dished *them* out before him, but he
refused to eat. And Amnon said, "Have everyone go out from
me." So everyone went out from him.
10Then Amnon said to Tamar, "Bring the food into the bedroom, that I may eat from your hand." So Tamar took the cakes
which she had made and brought them into the bedroom to her
brother Amnon.
11When she brought *them* to him to eat, he took hold of her and
said to her, "Come, lie with me, my sister."

NAS [a] I.e., beloved of the LORD

## New International

Can I bring him back again? I will go to him, but he will not return
to me."
24Then David comforted his wife Bathsheba, and he went to her
and lay with her. She gave birth to a son, and they named him
Solomon. The LORD loved him; 25and because the LORD loved him,
he sent word through Nathan the prophet to name him Jedidiah.[b]
26Meanwhile Joab fought against Rabbah of the Ammonites and
captured the royal citadel. 27Joab then sent messengers to David,
saying, "I have fought against Rabbah and taken its water supply.
28Now muster the rest of the troops and besiege the city and
capture it. Otherwise I will take the city, and it will be named after
me."
29So David mustered the entire army and went to Rabbah, and
attacked and captured it. 30He took the crown from the head of
their king[c]—its weight was a talent[d] of gold, and it was set with
precious stones—and it was placed on David's head. He took a
great quantity of plunder from the city 31and brought out the
people who were there, consigning them to labor with saws and
with iron picks and axes, and he made them work at brickmak-
ing.[e] He did this to all the Ammonite towns. Then David and his
entire army returned to Jerusalem.

*Amnon and Tamar*

**13** IN THE course of time, Amnon son of David fell in love
with Tamar, the beautiful sister of Absalom son of David.
2Amnon became frustrated to the point of illness on account of
his sister Tamar, for she was a virgin, and it seemed impossible for
him to do anything to her.
3Now Amnon had a friend named Jonadab son of Shimeah,
David's brother. Jonadab was a very shrewd man. 4He asked
Amnon, "Why do you, the king's son, look so haggard morning
after morning? Won't you tell me?"
Amnon said to him, "I'm in love with Tamar, my brother Absalom's sister."
5"Go to bed and pretend to be ill," Jonadab said. "When your
father comes to see you, say to him, 'I would like my sister Tamar
to come and give me something to eat. Let her prepare the food
in my sight so I may watch her and then eat it from her hand.' "
6So Amnon lay down and pretended to be ill. When the king
came to see him, Amnon said to him, "I would like my sister Tamar
to come and make some special bread in my sight, so I may eat
from her hand."
7David sent word to Tamar at the palace: "Go to the house of
your brother Amnon and prepare some food for him." 8So Tamar
went to the house of her brother Amnon, who was lying down.
She took some dough, kneaded it, made the bread in his sight and
baked it. 9Then she took the pan and served him the bread, but
he refused to eat.
"Send everyone out of here," Amnon said. So everyone left
him. 10Then Amnon said to Tamar, "Bring the food here into my
bedroom so I may eat from your hand." And Tamar took the bread
she had prepared and brought it to her brother Amnon in his
bedroom. 11But when she took it to him to eat, he grabbed her and
said, "Come to bed with me, my sister."

NIV [b] 25 *Jedidiah* means *loved by the LORD.* [c] 30 Or *of Milcom* (that is, Molech) [d] 30 That is, about 75 pounds (about 34 kilograms) [e] 31 The meaning of the Hebrew for this clause is uncertain.

## King James

12And she answered him, Nay, my brother, do not force me; for no such thing ought to be done in Israel: do not thou this folly.

13And I, whither shall I cause my shame to go? and as for thee, thou shalt be as one of the fools in Israel. Now therefore, I pray thee, speak unto the king; for he will not withhold me from thee.

14Howbeit he would not hearken unto her voice: but, being stronger than she, forced her, and lay with her.

15¶ Then Amnon hated her exceedingly; so that the hatred wherewith he hated her *was* greater than the love wherewith he had loved her. And Amnon said unto her, Arise, be gone.

16And she said unto him, *There is* no cause: this evil in sending me away *is* greater than the other that thou didst unto me. But he would not hearken unto her.

17Then he called his servant that ministered unto him, and said, Put now this *woman* out from me, and bolt the door after her.

18And *she had* a garment of divers colours upon her: for with such robes were the king's daughters *that were* virgins apparelled. Then his servant brought her out, and bolted the door after her.

19¶ And Tamar put ashes on her head, and rent her garment of divers colours that *was* on her, and laid her hand on her head, and went on crying.

20And Absalom her brother said unto her, Hath Amnon thy brother been with thee? but hold now thy peace, my sister: he *is* thy brother; regard not this thing. So Tamar remained desolate in her brother Absalom's house.

21¶ But when king David heard of all these things, he was very wroth.

22And Absalom spake unto his brother Amnon neither good nor bad: for Absalom hated Amnon, because he had forced his sister Tamar.

23¶ And it came to pass after two full years, that Absalom had sheepshearers in Baal-hazor, which *is* beside Ephraim: and Absalom invited all the king's sons.

24And Absalom came to the king, and said, Behold now, thy servant hath sheepshearers; let the king, I beseech thee, and his servants go with thy servant.

25And the king said to Absalom, Nay, my son, let us not all now go, lest we be chargeable unto thee. And he pressed him: howbeit he would not go, but blessed him.

26Then said Absalom, If not, I pray thee, let my brother Amnon go with us. And the king said unto him, Why should he go with thee?

27But Absalom pressed him, that he let Amnon and all the king's sons go with him.

28¶ Now Absalom had commanded his servants, saying, Mark ye now when Amnon's heart is merry with wine, and when I say unto you, Smite Amnon; then kill him, fear not: have not I commanded you? be courageous, and be valiant.

29And the servants of Absalom did unto Amnon as Absalom had commanded. Then all the king's sons arose, and every man gat him up upon his mule, and fled.

30¶ And it came to pass, while they were in the way, that tidings came to David, saying, Absalom hath slain all the king's sons, and there is not one of them left.

31Then the king arose, and tare his garments, and lay on the earth; and all his servants stood by with their clothes rent.

32And Jonadab, the son of Shimeah David's brother, answered and said, Let not my lord suppose *that* they have slain all the young men the king's sons; for Amnon only is dead: for by the appointment of Absalom this hath been determined from the day that he forced his sister Tamar.

33Now therefore let not my lord the king take the thing to his heart, to think that all the king's sons are dead: for Amnon only is dead.

## Amplified

12She replied, No! My brother, do not force *and* humble me, for no such thing should be done in Israel! Do not do this foolhardy, scandalous thing! [Gen. 34:7.]

13And I, how could I rid myself of my shame? And you, you will be [considered] one of the stupid fools in Israel. Now therefore, I pray you, speak to the king; for he will not withold me from you.

14But he would not listen to her, and, being stronger than she, he forced her, and lay with her.

15Then Amnon hated her exceedingly; so that his hatred for her was greater than the love with which he had loved her. And Amnon said to her, Get up, and get out!

16But she said, No! This great evil of sending me away is worse than what you did to me. But he would not listen to her.

17He called the servant who served him, and said, Put this woman out of my presence, now, and bolt the door after her!

18Now [Tamar] was wearing a long robe with sleeves *and* of various colors, for in such robes were the king's virgin daughters clad of old. Then Amnon's servant brought her out, and bolted the door after her.

19And [she] put ashes on her head, and tore the long, sleeved robe which she wore, and she laid her hand on her head, and went away shrieking *and* wailing.

20And Absalom her brother said to her, Has your brother Amnon been with you? Be quiet now, my sister. He is your brother; take not this matter to heart. So Tamar dwelt in her brother Absalom's house, a desolate woman.

21But when King David heard of all these things, he was very angry.

22And Absalom spoke to Amnon neither good nor bad; for Absalom hated Amnon, because he had humbled his sister Tamar.

23After two full years Absalom had sheepshearers at Baal-hazor, near Ephraim; and Absalom invited all the king's sons.

24Absalom came to the king, and said, Behold your servant has sheepshearers; pray let the king and his servants go with your servant.

25And the king said to Absalom, No, my son, let us not all go, lest we be burdensome to you. Absalom urged David; still he would not go, but he blessed him.

26Then said Absalom, If not, pray let my brother Amnon go with us. And the king said to him, Why should he go with you?

27But Absalom urged him, and he let Amnon and all the king's sons go with him.

28Now Absalom commanded his servants, Notice now when Amnon's heart is merry with wine, and when I say to you, Strike Amnon, then kill him. Fear not; have I not commanded you? Be courageous and brave.

29And the servants of Absalom did to Amnon as Absalom had commanded. Then all the king's sons arose, and every man mounted his mule and fled.

30While they were on the way, the word came to David, Absalom has killed all the king's sons, and not one of them is left.

31Then the king arose, and tore his garments, and lay on the floor and all his servants standing by tore their clothes.

32But Jonadab son of Shimeah David's brother, said, Let not my lord suppose they have killed all the king's sons, for Amnon only is dead; this purpose has shown itself on Absalom's determined mouth ever since the day Amnon humiliated his sister Tamar.

33So let not my lord the king take the thing to heart, and think all the king's sons are dead; for Amnon only is dead.

## New American Standard

12But she answered him, "No, my brother, do not violate me,
for such a thing is not done in Israel; do not do this disgraceful
thing!
13"As for me, where could I get rid of my reproach? And as for
you, you will be like one of the fools in Israel. Now therefore,
please speak to the king, for he will not withhold me from you."
14However, he would not listen to her; since he was stronger
than she, he violated her and lay with her.
15¶ Then Amnon hated her with a very great hatred; for the
hatred with which he hated her was greater than the love with
which he had loved her. And Amnon said to her, "Get up, go
away!"
16But she said to him, "No, because this wrong in sending me
away is greater than the other that you have done to me!" Yet he
would not listen to her.
17Then he called his young man who attended him and said,
"Now throw this woman out of my *presence*, and lock the door
behind her."
18Now she had on a long-sleeved garment; for in this manner
the virgin daughters of the king dressed themselves in robes. Then
his attendant took her out and locked the door behind her.
19And Tamar put ashes on her head, and tore her long-sleeved
garment which *was* on her; and she put her hand on her head and
went away, crying aloud as she went.
20¶ Then Absalom her brother said to her, "Has Amnon your
brother been with you? But now keep silent, my sister, he is your
brother; do not take this matter to heart." So Tamar remained and
was desolate in her brother Absalom's house.
21Now when King David heard of all these matters, he was very
angry.
22But Absalom did not speak to Amnon either good or bad; for
Absalom hated Amnon because he had violated his sister Tamar.
23¶ Now it came about after two full years that Absalom had
sheepshearers in Baal-hazor, which is near Ephraim, and Absalom
invited all the king's sons.

*Absalom Avenges Tamar*

24And Absalom came to the king and said, "Behold now, your
servant has sheepshearers; please let the king and his servants go
with your servant."
25But the king said to Absalom, "No, my son, we should not
all go, lest we be burdensome to you." Although he urged him,
he would not go, but blessed him.
26Then Absalom said, "If not, please let my brother Amnon go
with us." And the king said to him, "Why should he go with you?"
27But when Absalom urged him, he let Amnon and all the
king's sons go with him.
28¶ And Absalom commanded his servants, saying, "See now,
when Amnon's heart is merry with wine, and when I say to you,
'Strike Amnon,' then put him to death. Do not fear; have not I
myself commanded you? Be courageous and be valiant."
29And the servants of Absalom did to Amnon just as Absalom
had commanded. Then all the king's sons arose and each mounted
his mule and fled.
30¶ Now it was while they were on the way that the report came
to David, saying, "Absalom has struck down all the king's sons,
and not one of them is left."
31Then the king arose, tore his clothes and lay on the ground;
and all his servants were standing by with clothes torn.
32And Jonadab, the son of Shimeah, David's brother, responded, "Do not let my lord suppose they have put to death all the
young men, the king's sons, for Amnon alone is dead; because by
the intent of Absalom this has been determined since the day that
he violated his sister Tamar.
33"Now therefore, do not let my lord the king take the report
to heart, namely, 'all the king's sons are dead,' for only Amnon is
dead."

## New International

12"Don't, my brother!" she said to him. "Don't force me. Such
a thing should not be done in Israel! Don't do this wicked thing.
13What about me? Where could I get rid of my disgrace? And what
about you? You would be like one of the wicked fools in Israel.
Please speak to the king; he will not keep me from being married
to you." 14But he refused to listen to her, and since he was stronger
than she, he raped her.
15Then Amnon hated her with intense hatred. In fact, he hated
her more than he had loved her. Amnon said to her, "Get up and
get out!"
16"No!" she said to him. "Sending me away would be a greater
wrong than what you have already done to me."
But he refused to listen to her. 17He called his personal servant
and said, "Get this woman out of here and bolt the door after her."
18So his servant put her out and bolted the door after her. She was
wearing a richly ornamented[a] robe, for this was the kind of garment the virgin daughters of the king wore. 19Tamar put ashes on
her head and tore the ornamented[b] robe she was wearing. She put
her hand on her head and went away, weeping aloud as she went.
20Her brother Absalom said to her, "Has that Amnon, your
brother, been with you? Be quiet now, my sister; he is your brother. Don't take this thing to heart." And Tamar lived in her brother
Absalom's house, a desolate woman.
21When King David heard all this, he was furious. 22Absalom
never said a word to Amnon, either good or bad; he hated Amnon
because he had disgraced his sister Tamar.

*Absalom Kills Amnon*

23Two years later, when Absalom's sheepshearers were at Baal
Hazor near the border of Ephraim, he invited all the king's sons
to come there. 24Absalom went to the king and said, "Your servant
has had shearers come. Will the king and his officials please join
me?"
25"No, my son," the king replied. "All of us should not go; we
would only be a burden to you." Although Absalom urged him,
he still refused to go, but gave him his blessing.
26Then Absalom said, "If not, please let my brother Amnon
come with us."
The king asked him, "Why should he go with you?" 27But
Absalom urged him, so he sent with him Amnon and the rest of
the king's sons.
28Absalom ordered his men, "Listen! When Amnon is in high
spirits from drinking wine and I say to you, 'Strike Amnon down,'
then kill him. Don't be afraid. Have not I given you this order? Be
strong and brave." 29So Absalom's men did to Amnon what Absalom had ordered. Then all the king's sons got up, mounted their
mules and fled.
30While they were on their way, the report came to David:
"Absalom has struck down all the king's sons; not one of them is
left." 31The king stood up, tore his clothes and lay down on the
ground; and all his servants stood by with their clothes torn.
32But Jonadab son of Shimeah, David's brother, said, "My lord
should not think that they killed all the princes; only Amnon is
dead. This has been Absalom's expressed intention ever since the
day Amnon raped his sister Tamar. 33My lord the king should not
be concerned about the report that all the king's sons are dead.
Only Amnon is dead."

**NIV** [a] *18* The meaning of the Hebrew for this phrase is uncertain. [b] *19* The meaning of the Hebrew for this word is uncertain.

## King James

34 But Absalom fled. And the young man that kept the watch lifted up his eyes, and looked, and, behold, there came much people by the way of the hill side behind him.

35 And Jonadab said unto the king, Behold, the king's sons come: as thy servant said, so it is.

36 And it came to pass, as soon as he had made an end of speaking, that, behold, the king's sons came, and lifted up their voice and wept: and the king also and all his servants wept very sore.

37 ¶ But Absalom fled, and went to Talmai, the son of Ammihud, king of Geshur. And *David* mourned for his son every day.

38 So Absalom fled, and went to Geshur, and was there three years.

39 And *the soul of* king David longed to go forth unto Absalom: for he was comforted concerning Amnon, seeing he was dead.

**14** NOW JOAB the son of Zeruiah perceived that the king's heart *was* toward Absalom.

2 And Joab sent to Tekoah, and fetched thence a wise woman, and said unto her, I pray thee, feign thyself to be a mourner, and put on now mourning apparel, and anoint not thyself with oil, but be as a woman that had a long time mourned for the dead:

3 And come to the king, and speak on this manner unto him. So Joab put the words in her mouth.

4 ¶ And when the woman of Tekoah spake to the king, she fell on her face to the ground, and did obeisance, and said, Help, O king.

5 And the king said unto her, What aileth thee? And she answered, I *am* indeed a widow woman, and mine husband is dead.

6 And thy handmaid had two sons, and they two strove together in the field, and *there was* none to part them, but the one smote the other, and slew him.

7 And, behold, the whole family is risen against thine handmaid, and they said, Deliver him that smote his brother, that we may kill him, for the life of his brother whom he slew; and we will destroy the heir also: and so they shall quench my coal which is left, and shall not leave to my husband *neither* name nor remainder upon the earth.

8 And the king said unto the woman, Go to thine house, and I will give charge concerning thee.

9 And the woman of Tekoah said unto the king, My lord, O king, the iniquity *be* on me, and on my father's house: and the king and his throne *be* guiltless.

10 And the king said, Whosoever saith *aught* unto thee, bring him to me, and he shall not touch thee any more.

11 Then said she, I pray thee, let the king remember the LORD thy God, that thou wouldest not suffer the revengers of blood to destroy any more, lest they destroy my son. And he said, *As* the LORD liveth, there shall not one hair of thy son fall to the earth.

12 Then the woman said, Let thine handmaid, I pray thee, speak *one* word unto my lord the king. And he said, Say on.

13 And the woman said, Wherefore then hast thou thought such a thing against the people of God? for the king doth speak this thing as one which is faulty, in that the king doth not fetch home again his banished.

14 For we must needs die, and *are* as water spilt on the ground, which cannot be gathered up again; neither doth God respect *any* person: yet doth he devise means, that his banished be not expelled from him.

15 Now therefore that I am come to speak of this thing unto my lord the king, *it is* because the people have made me afraid: and thy handmaid said, I will now speak unto the king; it may be that the king will perform the request of his handmaid.

## Amplified

34 But Absalom fled. And the young man who kept the watch looked up, and behold, many people were coming by the way of the hillside behind him.

35 And Jonadab said to the king, See, the king's sons are coming. It is as your servant said.

36 And as he finished speaking the king's sons came, and lifted up their voices and wept; and the king also and all his servants wept very bitterly.

37 But Absalom fled, and went to [his mother's father] Talmai son of Ammihud, king of Geshur. And David mourned for his son [Amnon] every day.

38 So Absalom fled to Geshur, and was there three years;

39 And the spirit of King David longed to go forth to Absalom, for he was comforted about Amnon, seeing he was dead.

**14** NOW JOAB son of Zeruiah knew that the king's heart was toward Absalom.

2 And Joab sent to Tekoah, and brought from there a wise woman, and said to her, Pretend to be a mourner; put on mourning apparel; do not anoint yourself with oil, but act like a woman who has long been mourning for the dead;

3 And go to the king and speak thus to him. And Joab told her what to say.

4 When the woman of Tekoah spoke to the king, she fell on her face to the ground and did obeisance, and said, Help, O king!

5 The king asked her, What troubles you? She said, I am a widow; my husband is dead.

6 And your handmaid had two sons, and they quarreled with one another in the field. There was no one to separate them, and one struck the other and killed him.

7 And, behold, our whole family is risen against your handmaid, and they say, Deliver him who slew his brother, that we may kill him, for the life of his brother whom he slew; and so they would destroy the heir also. And so quenching my coal which is left, they would leave to my husband neither name nor remnant upon the earth.

8 David said to the woman, Go home, and I will give orders concerning you.

9 And the woman of Tekoah said to the king, My lord, O king, the guilt be on me, and on my father's house; let the king and his throne be guiltless.

10 The king said, If any one says anything to you, bring him to me, and he shall not touch you again.

11 Then she said, I pray you, let the king remember the Lord your God, that the avenger of blood destroy not any more, lest they destroy my son. And David said, As the Lord lives, there shall not one hair of your son fall to the earth.

12 Then the woman said, Let your handmaid, I pray you, speak one word to my lord the king. He said, Say on.

13 [She] said, Why then have you planned such a thing against God's people? For in speaking this word the king is as one who is guilty, in that [he] does not bring home his banished one.

14 We must all die, we are like water spilled on the ground, which cannot be gathered up again; and God does not take away life, but devises means that he who is banished may not be an utter outcast from Him.

15 And now I have come to speak of this thing to my lord the king because the people have made me afraid; and I thought, I will speak to the king; it may be that he will perform the request of his servant.

## New American Standard

34¶ Now Absalom had fled. And the young man who was the
watchman raised his eyes and looked, and behold, many people
were coming from the road behind him by the side of the mountain.
35And Jonadab said to the king, "Behold, the king's sons have
come; according to your servant's word, so it happened."
36And it came about as soon as he had finished speaking, that
behold, the king's sons came and lifted their voices and wept; and
also the king and all his servants wept very bitterly.
37¶ Now Absalom fled and went to Talmai the son of Ammihud,
the king of Geshur. And *David* mourned for his son every day.
38So Absalom had fled and gone to Geshur, and was there three
years.
39And *the heart of* King David longed to go out to Absalom; for
he was comforted concerning Amnon, since he was dead.

*The Woman of Tekoa*

14 NOW JOAB the son of Zeruiah perceived that the king's
heart *was inclined* toward Absalom.
2So Joab sent to Tekoa and brought a wise woman from there
and said to her, "Please pretend to be a mourner, and put on
mourning garments now, and do not anoint yourself with oil, but
be like a woman who has been mourning for the dead many days;
3then go to the king and speak to him in this manner." So Joab
put the words in her mouth.
4¶ Now when the woman of Tekoa [a]spoke to the king, she fell
on her face to the ground and prostrated herself and said, "Help,
O king."
5And the king said to her, "What is your trouble?" And she
answered, "Truly I am a widow, for my husband is dead.
6"And your maidservant had two sons, but the two of them
struggled together in the field, and there was no [b]one to separate
them, so one struck the other and killed him.
7"Now behold, the whole family has risen against your maidservant, and they say, 'Hand over the one who struck his brother,
that we may put him to death for the life of his brother whom he
killed, and destroy the heir also.' Thus they will extinguish my coal
which is left, so as to leave my husband neither name nor remnant
on the face of the earth."
8¶ Then the king said to the woman, "Go to your house, and
I will give orders concerning you."
9And the woman of Tekoa said to the king, "O my lord, the
king, the iniquity is on me and my father's house, but the king and
his throne are guiltless."
10So the king said, "Whoever speaks to you, bring him to me,
and he will not touch you anymore."
11Then she said, "Please let the king remember the LORD your
God, *so that* the avenger of blood may not continue to destroy, lest
they destroy my son." And he said, "As the LORD lives, not one
hair of your son shall fall to the ground."
12¶ Then the woman said, "Please let your maidservant speak
a word to my lord the king." And he said, "Speak."
13And the woman said, "Why then have you planned such a
thing against the people of God? For in speaking this word the king
is as one who is guilty, *in that* the king does not bring back his
banished one.
14"For we shall surely die and are like water spilled on the
ground which cannot be gathered up again. Yet God does not take
away life, but plans ways so that the banished one may not be cast
out from him.
15"Now the reason I have come to speak this word to my lord
the king is because the people have made me afraid; so your
maidservant said, 'Let me now speak to the king, perhaps the king
will perform the request of his maidservant.

NAS [a] Many mss. and ancient versions read *came* [b] Lit., *deliverer between*

## New International

34Meanwhile, Absalom had fled.
Now the man standing watch looked up and saw many people
on the road west of him, coming down the side of the hill. The
watchman went and told the king, "I see men in the direction of
Horonaim, on the side of the hill."[c]
35Jonadab said to the king, "See, the king's sons are here; it has
happened just as your servant said."
36As he finished speaking, the king's sons came in, wailing
loudly. The king, too, and all his servants wept very bitterly.
37Absalom fled and went to Talmai son of Ammihud, the king
of Geshur. But King David mourned for his son every day.
38After Absalom fled and went to Geshur, he stayed there three
years. 39And the spirit of the king[d] longed to go to Absalom, for
he was consoled concerning Amnon's death.

*Absalom Returns to Jerusalem*

14 JOAB SON of Zeruiah knew that the king's heart longed
for Absalom. 2So Joab sent someone to Tekoa and had a
wise woman brought from there. He said to her, "Pretend you are
in mourning. Dress in mourning clothes, and don't use any cos-
metic lotions. Act like a woman who has spent many days grieving
for the dead. 3Then go to the king and speak these words to him."
And Joab put the words in her mouth.
4When the woman from Tekoa went[e] to the king, she fell with
her face to the ground to pay him honor, and she said, "Help me,
O king!"
5The king asked her, "What is troubling you?"
She said, "I am indeed a widow; my husband is dead. 6I your
servant had two sons. They got into a fight with each other in the
field, and no one was there to separate them. One struck the other
and killed him. 7Now the whole clan has risen up against your
servant; they say, 'Hand over the one who struck his brother
down, so that we may put him to death for the life of his brother
whom he killed; then we will get rid of the heir as well.' They
would put out the only burning coal I have left, leaving my husband neither name nor descendant on the face of the earth."
8The king said to the woman, "Go home, and I will issue an
order in your behalf."
9But the woman from Tekoa said to him, "My lord the king, let
the blame rest on me and on my father's family, and let the king
and his throne be without guilt."
10The king replied, "If anyone says anything to you, bring him
to me, and he will not bother you again."
11She said, "Then let the king invoke the LORD his God to
prevent the avenger of blood from adding to the destruction, so
that my son will not be destroyed."
"As surely as the LORD lives," he said, "not one hair of your
son's head will fall to the ground."
12Then the woman said, "Let your servant speak a word to my
lord the king."
"Speak," he replied.
13The woman said, "Why then have you devised a thing like
this against the people of God? When the king says this, does he
not convict himself, for the king has not brought back his banished
son? 14Like water spilled on the ground, which cannot be recovered, so we must die. But God does not take away life; instead, he
devises ways so that a banished person may not remain estranged
from him.
15"And now I have come to say this to my lord the king because
the people have made me afraid. Your servant thought, 'I will
speak to the king; perhaps he will do what his servant asks. 16Per-

NIV [c] 34 Septuagint; Hebrew does not have this sentence. [d] 39 Dead Sea Scrolls and some Septuagint manuscripts; Masoretic Text *But the spirit of David the king* [e] 4 Many Hebrew manuscripts, Septuagint, Vulgate and Syriac; most Hebrew manuscripts *spoke*

## King James

16For the king will hear, to deliver his handmaid out of the hand of the man *that would* destroy me and my son together out of the inheritance of God.
17Then thine handmaid said, The word of my lord the king shall now be comfortable: for as an angel of God, so *is* my lord the king to discern good and bad: therefore the LORD thy God will be with thee.
18Then the king answered and said unto the woman, Hide not from me, I pray thee, the thing that I shall ask thee. And the woman said, Let my lord the king now speak.
19And the king said, *Is not* the hand of Joab with thee in all this? And the woman answered and said, *As* thy soul liveth, my lord the king, none can turn to the right hand or to the left from aught that my lord the king hath spoken: for thy servant Joab, he bade me, and he put all these words in the mouth of thine handmaid:
20To fetch about this form of speech hath thy servant Joab done this thing: and my lord *is* wise, according to the wisdom of an angel of God, to know all *things* that *are* in the earth.
21¶ And the king said unto Joab, Behold now, I have done this thing: go therefore, bring the young man Absalom again.
22And Joab fell to the ground on his face, and bowed himself, and thanked the king: and Joab said, Today thy servant knoweth that I have found grace in thy sight, my lord, O king, in that the king hath fulfilled the request of his servant.
23So Joab arose and went to Geshur, and brought Absalom to Jerusalem.
24And the king said, Let him turn to his own house, and let him not see my face. So Absalom returned to his own house, and saw not the king's face.
25¶ But in all Israel there was none to be so much praised as Absalom for his beauty: from the sole of his foot even to the crown of his head there was no blemish in him.
26And when he polled his head, (for it was at every year's end that he polled *it:* because *the hair* was heavy on him, therefore he polled it:) he weighed the hair of his head at two hundred shekels after the king's weight.
27And unto Absalom there were born three sons, and one daughter, whose name *was* Tamar: she was a woman of a fair countenance.
28¶ So Absalom dwelt two full years in Jerusalem, and saw not the king's face.
29Therefore Absalom sent for Joab, to have sent him to the king; but he would not come to him: and when he sent again the second time, he would not come.
30Therefore he said unto his servants, See, Joab's field is near mine, and he hath barley there; go and set it on fire. And Absalom's servants set the field on fire.
31Then Joab arose, and came to Absalom unto *his* house, and said unto him, Wherefore have thy servants set my field on fire?
32And Absalom answered Joab, Behold, I sent unto thee, saying, Come hither, that I may send thee to the king, to say, Wherefore am I come from Geshur? *it had been* good for me *to have been* there still: now therefore let me see the king's face; and if there be *any* iniquity in me, let him kill me.
33So Joab came to the king, and told him: and when he had called for Absalom, he came to the king, and bowed himself on his face to the ground before the king: and the king kissed Absalom.

**15** AND IT came to pass after this, that Absalom prepared him chariots and horses, and fifty men to run before him.

## Amplified

16For the king will hear, to deliver his handmaid from the hand of the man who would destroy me and my son together from [Israel] the inheritance of God.
17And the woman said, The word of my lord the king will now give me rest *and* security, for as an angel of God is my lord the king to hear *and* discern good and evil. The Lord your God be with you!
18Then the king said to the woman, Hide not from me anything I ask you. And the woman said, Let my lord the king speak.
19The king said, Is the hand of Joab with you in all this? And the woman answered, As your soul lives, my lord the king, none can turn to the right hand or to the left from anything my lord the king has said; it was your servant Joab who directed me; he put all these words in my mouth.
20In order to change the course of matters [between Absalom and his father] your servant Joab did this. But my lord has wisdom like the wisdom of the Angel of God, to know all things that are on the earth.
21Then the king said to Joab, Behold now, I grant this; go, bring back the young man Absalom.
22And Joab fell to the ground on his face, and did obeisance, and thanked the king. And Joab said, Today your servant knows that I have found favor in your sight, my lord, O king, in that the king has performed the request of his servant.
23So Joab arose, went to Geshur, and brought Absalom to Jerusalem.
24And the king said, Let him go to his own house, and let him not see my face. So Absalom went to his own house, and did not see the king's face.
25But in all Israel there was none so much to be praised for his beauty as Absalom; from the sole of his foot to the crown of his head there was no blemish in him.
26And when he cut the hair of his head he weighed it (for at each year's end he cut it, because its weight was a burden to him) and it weighed 200 shekels by the king's weight.
27There were born to Absalom three sons, and one daughter whose name was Tamar; she was a beautiful woman.
28Absalom dwelt two full years in Jerusalem, and did not see the king's face.
29So Absalom sent for Joab, to send him to the king; but he would not come to him; even when he sent again the second time, he would not come.
30Therefore Absalom said to his servants, See, Joab's field is near mine, and he has barley there; go and set it on fire. So Absalom's servants set the field afire.
31Then Joab arose and went to Absalom at his house, and said to him, Why have your servants set my field on fire?
32Absalom answered Joab, I sent to you, saying, Come here, that I may send you to the king, to ask, Why have I come from Geshur? It would be better for me to be there still. Now therefore [Joab], let me see the king; and if there be iniquity *and* guilt in me, let him kill me.
33So Joab came to the king, and told him; and when David had called for Absalom, he came to him, and bowed himself on his face to the ground before the king; and [David] kissed Absalom.

**15** AFTER THIS, Absalom got a chariot and horses, and fifty men to run before him.

## New American Standard

16'For the king will hear and deliver his maidservant from the
hand of the man who would destroy both me and my son from the
inheritance of God.'
17"Then your maidservant said, 'Please let the word of my lord
the king be comforting, for as the angel of God, so is my lord the
king to discern good and evil. And may the LORD your God be with
you.' "
18¶ Then the king answered and said to the woman, "Please do
not hide anything from me that I am about to ask you." And the
woman said, "Let my lord the king please speak."
19So the king said, "Is the hand of Joab with you in all this?"
And the woman answered and said, "As your soul lives, my lord
the king, no one can turn to the right or to the left from anything
that my lord the king has spoken. Indeed, it was your servant Joab
who commanded me, and it was he who put all these words in the
mouth of your maidservant;
20in order to change the appearance of things your servant Joab
has done this thing. But my lord is wise, like the wisdom of the
angel of God, to know all that is in the earth."

*Absalom Is Recalled*

21¶ Then the king said to Joab, "Behold now, I will surely do
this thing; go therefore, bring back the young man Absalom."
22And Joab fell on his face to the ground, prostrated himself and
blessed the king; then Joab said, "Today your servant knows that
I have found favor in your sight, O my lord, the king, in that the
king has performed the request of his servant."
23So Joab arose and went to Geshur, and brought Absalom to
Jerusalem.
24However the king said, "Let him turn to his own house, and
let him not see my face." So Absalom turned to his own house and
did not see the king's face.
25¶ Now in all Israel was no one as handsome as Absalom, so
highly praised; from the sole of his foot to the crown of his head
there was no defect in him.
26And when he cut the hair of his head (and it was at the end
of every year that he cut *it*, for it was heavy on him so he cut it),
he weighed the hair of his head at 200 shekels by the king's weight.
27And to Absalom there were born three sons, and one daughter whose name was Tamar; she was a woman of beautiful appearance.
28¶ Now Absalom lived two full years in Jerusalem, and did not
see the king's face.
29Then Absalom sent for Joab, to send him to the king, but he
would not come to him. So he sent again a second time, but he
would not come.
30Therefore he said to his servants, "See, Joab's [a]field is next
to mine, and he has barley there; go and set it on fire." So Absalom's servants set the field on fire.
31Then Joab arose, came to Absalom at his house and said to
him, "Why have your servants set my [b]field on fire?"
32And Absalom answered Joab, "Behold, I sent for you, saying,
'Come here, that I may send you to the king, to say, "Why have
I come from Geshur? It would be better for me still to be there." '
Now therefore, let me see the king's face; and if there is iniquity
in me, let him put me to death."
33So when Joab came to the king and told him, he called for
Absalom. Thus he came to the king and prostrated himself on his
face to the ground before the king, and the king kissed Absalom.

*Absalom's Conspiracy*

**15** NOW IT came about after this that Absalom provided for
himself a chariot and horses, and fifty men as runners
before him.

NAS [a] Lit., *portion* [b] Lit., *portion*

## New International

haps the king will agree to deliver his servant from the hand of the
man who is trying to cut off both me and my son from the inheritance God gave us.'
17"And now your servant says, 'May the word of my lord the
king bring me rest, for my lord the king is like an angel of God in
discerning good and evil. May the LORD your God be with you.' "
18Then the king said to the woman, "Do not keep from me the
answer to what I am going to ask you."
"Let my lord the king speak," the woman said.
19The king asked, "Isn't the hand of Joab with you in all this?"
The woman answered, "As surely as you live, my lord the king,
no one can turn to the right or to the left from anything my lord
the king says. Yes, it was your servant Joab who instructed me to
do this and who put all these words into the mouth of your
servant. 20Your servant Joab did this to change the present situation. My lord has wisdom like that of an angel of God—he knows
everything that happens in the land."
21The king said to Joab, "Very well, I will do it. Go, bring back
the young man Absalom."
22Joab fell with his face to the ground to pay him honor, and
he blessed the king. Joab said, "Today your servant knows that he
has found favor in your eyes, my lord the king, because the king
has granted his servant's request."
23Then Joab went to Geshur and brought Absalom back to
Jerusalem. 24But the king said, "He must go to his own house; he
must not see my face." So Absalom went to his own house and
did not see the face of the king.
25In all Israel there was not a man so highly praised for his
handsome appearance as Absalom. From the top of his head to the
sole of his foot there was no blemish in him. 26Whenever he cut
the hair of his head—he used to cut his hair from time to time when
it became too heavy for him—he would weigh it, and its weight
was two hundred shekels[c] by the royal standard.
27Three sons and a daughter were born to Absalom. The daughter's name was Tamar, and she became a beautiful woman.
28Absalom lived two years in Jerusalem without seeing the
king's face. 29Then Absalom sent for Joab in order to send him to
the king, but Joab refused to come to him. So he sent a second time,
but he refused to come. 30Then he said to his servants, "Look,
Joab's field is next to mine, and he has barley there. Go and set it
on fire." So Absalom's servants set the field on fire.
31Then Joab did go to Absalom's house and he said to him,
"Why have your servants set my field on fire?"
32Absalom said to Joab, "Look, I sent word to you and said,
'Come here so I can send you to the king to ask, "Why have I come
from Geshur? It would be better for me if I were still there!" ' Now
then, I want to see the king's face, and if I am guilty of anything,
let him put me to death."
33So Joab went to the king and told him this. Then the king
summoned Absalom, and he came in and bowed down with his
face to the ground before the king. And the king kissed Absalom.

*Absalom's Conspiracy*

**15** IN THE course of time, Absalom provided himself with a
chariot and horses and with fifty men to run ahead of him.

NIV [c] 26 That is, about 5 pounds (about 2.3 kilograms)

## King James

2And Absalom rose up early, and stood beside the way of the gate: and it was *so*, that when any man that had a controversy came to the king for judgment, then Absalom called unto him, and said, Of what city *art* thou? And he said, Thy servant *is* of one of the tribes of Israel.

3And Absalom said unto him, See, thy matters *are* good and right; but *there is* no man *deputed* of the king to hear thee.

4Absalom said moreover, Oh that I were made judge in the land, that every man which hath any suit or cause might come unto me, and I would do him justice!

5And it was *so*, that when any man came nigh *to him* to do him obeisance, he put forth his hand, and took him, and kissed him.

6And on this manner did Absalom to all Israel that came to the king for judgment: so Absalom stole the hearts of the men of Israel.

7¶ And it came to pass after forty years, that Absalom said unto the king, I pray thee, let me go and pay my vow, which I have vowed unto the LORD, in Hebron.

8For thy servant vowed a vow while I abode at Geshur in Syria, saying, If the LORD shall bring me again indeed to Jerusalem, then I will serve the LORD.

9And the king said unto him, Go in peace. So he arose, and went to Hebron.

10¶ But Absalom sent spies throughout all the tribes of Israel, saying, As soon as ye hear the sound of the trumpet, then ye shall say, Absalom reigneth in Hebron.

11And with Absalom went two hundred men out of Jerusalem, *that were* called; and they went in their simplicity, and they knew not any thing.

12And Absalom sent for Ahithophel the Gilonite, David's counsellor, from his city, *even* from Giloh, while he offered sacrifices. And the conspiracy was strong; for the people increased continually with Absalom.

13¶ And there came a messenger to David, saying, The hearts of the men of Israel are after Absalom.

14And David said unto all his servants that *were* with him at Jerusalem, Arise, and let us flee; for we shall not *else* escape from Absalom: make speed to depart, lest he overtake us suddenly, and bring evil upon us, and smite the city with the edge of the sword.

15And the king's servants said unto the king, Behold, thy servants *are ready to do* whatsoever my lord the king shall appoint.

16And the king went forth, and all his household after him. And the king left ten women, *which were* concubines, to keep the house.

17And the king went forth, and all the people after him, and tarried in a place that was far off.

18And all his servants passed on beside him; and all the Cherethites, and all the Pelethites, and all the Gittites, six hundred men which came after him from Gath, passed on before the king.

19¶ Then said the king to Ittai the Gittite, Wherefore goest thou also with us? return to thy place, and abide with the king: for thou *art* a stranger, and also an exile.

20Whereas thou camest *but* yesterday, should I this day make thee go up and down with us? seeing I go whither I may, return thou, and take back thy brethren: mercy and truth *be* with thee.

21And Ittai answered the king, and said, *As* the LORD liveth, and *as* my lord the king liveth, surely in what place my lord the king shall be, whether in death or life, even there also will thy servant be.

22And David said to Ittai, Go and pass over. And Ittai the Gittite passed over, and all his men, and all the little ones that *were* with him.

23And all the country wept with a loud voice, and all the people passed over: the king also himself passed over the brook Kidron, and all the people passed over, toward the way of the wilderness.

## Amplified

2And [he] rose up early, and stood beside the gate way; and when any man who had a controversy came to the king for judgment, Absalom called to him, Of what city are you? And he would say, Your servant is of such and such a tribe of Israel.

3Absalom would say to him, Your claims are good and right; but there is no man appointed as the king's agent to hear you.

4Absalom added, Oh, that I were judge in the land! Then every man with any suit or cause might come to me, and I would do him justice!

5And whenever a man came near to do obeisance to him, he would put out his hand, take hold of him, and kiss him.

6Thus Absalom did to all Israel that came to the king for judgment. So Absalom stole the hearts of the men of Israel.

7And after [four] years Absalom said to the king, Pray let me go to Hebron [his birthplace] and pay my vow to the Lord.

8For your servant vowed while I dwelt at Geshur in Syria, If the Lord will bring me again to Jerusalem, then I will serve the Lord [by offering a sacrifice].

9And the king said to him, Go in peace. So he arose, and went to Hebron.

10But Absalom sent secret messengers throughout all the tribes of Israel, saying, As soon as you hear the sound of the trumpet, then say, Absalom is king at Hebron.

11With Absalom went 200 men from Jerusalem, who were invited [as guests to his sacrificial feast]; and they went in their simplicity, and they knew not a thing.

12And while Absalom was offering the sacrifices, he sent for Ahithophel the Gilonite, David's counselor, from his city Giloh. And the conspiracy was strong; the people with Absalom increased continually.

13And there came a messenger to David, saying, The hearts of the men of Israel have gone after Absalom.

14David said to all his servants that were with him at Jerusalem, Arise, and let us flee; or else none of us will escape from Absalom. Make haste to depart, lest he overtake us suddenly, and bring evil upon us and smite the city with the sword.

15And the king's servants said to the king, Behold, your servants are ready to do whatever my lord the king says.

16So the king and all his household after him went forth. But he left ten women, who were concubines, to keep the house.

17The king went forth with all the people after him, and halted at the last house.

18All David's servants passed on beside him; and [his bodyguard] all the Cherethites, Pelethites, also all the Gittites, 600 men who came after him from Gath, passed on before the king.

19The king said to Ittai the Gittite, Why do you go with us also? Return to your place and remain with the king [Absalom], for you are a foreigner and an exile.

20Since you came only yesterday, should I make you go up and down with us? Since I must go where I may, you return, and take back your brethren with you. Loving-kindness and faithfulness be with you.

21But Ittai answered the king, As the Lord lives, and as my lord the king lives, wherever my lord the king shall be, whether for death or life, even there also will your servant be.

22So David said to Ittai, Go on and pass over [Kidron]. And Ittai the Gittite passed over, and all his men and all the little ones who were with him.

23All the country wept with a loud voice as all the people passed over. The king crossed the brook Kidron, and all the people went on toward the wilderness.

## New American Standard

2And Absalom used to rise early and stand beside the way to
the gate; and it happened that when any man had a suit to come
to the king for judgment, Absalom would call to him and say,
"From what city are you?" And he would say, "Your servant is
from one of the tribes of Israel."
3Then Absalom would say to him, "See, your claims are good
and right, but no man listens to you on the part of the king."
4Moreover, Absalom would say, "Oh that one would appoint
me judge in the land, then every man who has any suit or cause
could come to me, and I would give him justice."
5And it happened that when a man came near to prostrate
himself before him, he would put out his hand and take hold of
him and kiss him.
6And in this manner Absalom dealt with all Israel who came
to the king for judgment; so Absalom stole away the hearts of the
men of Israel.
7¶ Now it came about at the end of [a]forty years that Absalom
said to the king, "Please let me go and pay my vow which I have
vowed to the LORD, in Hebron.
8"For your servant vowed a vow while I was living at Geshur
in Aram, saying, 'If the LORD shall indeed bring me back to Jerusalem, then I will serve the LORD.' "
9And the king said to him, "Go in peace." So he arose and
went to Hebron.
10But Absalom sent spies throughout all the tribes of Israel,
saying, "As soon as you hear the sound of the trumpet, then you
shall say, 'Absalom is king in Hebron.' "
11Then two hundred men went with Absalom from Jerusalem,
who were invited and went innocently, and they did not know
anything.
12And Absalom sent for Ahithophel the Gilonite, David's counselor, from his city Giloh, while he was offering the sacrifices. And
the conspiracy was strong, for the people increased continually
with Absalom.

*David Flees Jerusalem*

**13**¶ Then a messenger came to David, saying, "The hearts of the
men of Israel are with Absalom."
14And David said to all his servants who were with him at
Jerusalem, "Arise and let us flee, for *otherwise* none of us shall
escape from Absalom. Go in haste, lest he overtake us quickly and
bring down calamity on us and strike the city with the edge of the
sword."
15Then the king's servants said to the king, "Behold, your servants *are ready to do* whatever my lord the king chooses."
16So the king went out and all his household with him. But the
king left ten concubines to keep the house.
17And the king went out and all the people with him, and they
stopped at the last house.
18Now all his servants passed on beside him, all the Cherethites, all the Pelethites, and all the Gittites, six hundred men who
had come with him from Gath, passed on before the king.
**19**¶ Then the king said to Ittai the Gittite, "Why will you also
go with us? Return and remain with the king, for you are a foreigner and also an exile; *return* to your own place.
20"You came *only* yesterday, and shall I today make you wander
with us, while I go where I will? Return and take back your brothers; mercy and truth be with you."
21But Ittai answered the king and said, "As the LORD lives, and
as my lord the king lives, surely wherever my lord the king may
be, whether for death or for life, there also your servant will be."
22Therefore David said to Ittai, "Go and pass over." So Ittai the
Gittite passed over with all his men and all the little ones who *were*
with him.
23While all the country was weeping with a loud voice, all the
people passed over. The king also passed over the brook Kidron,
and all the people passed over toward the way of the wilderness.

**NAS** [a] Some ancient versions render *four*

## New International

2He would get up early and stand by the side of the road leading
to the city gate. Whenever anyone came with a complaint to be
placed before the king for a decision, Absalom would call out to
him, "What town are you from?" He would answer, "Your servant
is from one of the tribes of Israel." 3Then Absalom would say to
him, "Look, your claims are valid and proper, but there is no
representative of the king to hear you." 4And Absalom would add,
"If only I were appointed judge in the land! Then everyone who
has a complaint or case could come to me and I would see that he
gets justice."
5Also, whenever anyone approached him to bow down before
him, Absalom would reach out his hand, take hold of him and kiss
him. 6Absalom behaved in this way toward all the Israelites who
came to the king asking for justice, and so he stole the hearts of
the men of Israel.
7At the end of four[b] years, Absalom said to the king, "Let me
go to Hebron and fulfill a vow I made to the LORD. 8While your
servant was living at Geshur in Aram, I made this vow: 'If the LORD
takes me back to Jerusalem, I will worship the LORD in Hebron.[c] ' "
9The king said to him, "Go in peace." So he went to Hebron.
10Then Absalom sent secret messengers throughout the tribes
of Israel to say, "As soon as you hear the sound of the trumpets,
then say, 'Absalom is king in Hebron.' " 11Two hundred men from
Jerusalem had accompanied Absalom. They had been invited as
guests and went quite innocently, knowing nothing about the
matter. 12While Absalom was offering sacrifices, he also sent for
Ahithophel the Gilonite, David's counselor, to come from Giloh,
his hometown. And so the conspiracy gained strength, and Absalom's following kept on increasing.

*David Flees*

13A messenger came and told David, "The hearts of the men of
Israel are with Absalom."
14Then David said to all his officials who were with him in
Jerusalem, "Come! We must flee, or none of us will escape from
Absalom. We must leave immediately, or he will move quickly to
overtake us and bring ruin upon us and put the city to the sword."
15The king's officials answered him, "Your servants are ready
to do whatever our lord the king chooses."
16The king set out, with his entire household following him; but
he left ten concubines to take care of the palace. 17So the king set
out, with all the people following him, and they halted at a place
some distance away. 18All his men marched past him, along with
all the Kerethites and Pelethites; and all the six hundred Gittites
who had accompanied him from Gath marched before the king.
19The king said to Ittai the Gittite, "Why should you come along
with us? Go back and stay with King Absalom. You are a foreigner,
an exile from your homeland. 20You came only yesterday. And
today shall I make you wander about with us, when I do not know
where I am going? Go back, and take your countrymen. May
kindness and faithfulness be with you."
21But Ittai replied to the king, "As surely as the LORD lives, and
as my lord the king lives, wherever my lord the king may be,
whether it means life or death, there will your servant be."
22David said to Ittai, "Go ahead, march on." So Ittai the Gittite
marched on with all his men and the families that were with him.
23The whole countryside wept aloud as all the people passed
by. The king also crossed the Kidron Valley, and all the people
moved on toward the desert.

**NIV** [b] *7* Some Septuagint manuscripts, Syriac and Josephus; Hebrew *forty*
[c] *8* Some Septuagint manuscripts; Hebrew does not have *in Hebron.*

## King James

24¶ And lo Zadok also, and all the Levites *were* with him, bearing
the ark of the covenant of God: and they set down the ark of God;
and Abiathar went up, until all the people had done passing out
of the city.
25And the king said unto Zadok, Carry back the ark of God into
the city: if I shall find favour in the eyes of the LORD, he will bring
me again, and show me *both* it, and his habitation:
26But if he thus say, I have no delight in thee; behold, *here am*
I, let him do to me as seemeth good unto him.
27The king said also unto Zadok the priest, *Art not* thou a seer?
return into the city in peace, and your two sons with you, Ahimaaz
thy son, and Jonathan the son of Abiathar.
28See, I will tarry in the plain of the wilderness, until there come
word from you to certify me.
29Zadok therefore and Abiathar carried the ark of God again to
Jerusalem: and they tarried there.
30¶ And David went up by the ascent of *mount* Olivet, and wept
as he went up, and had his head covered, and he went barefoot:
and all the people that *was* with him covered every man his head,
and they went up, weeping as they went up.
31¶ And *one* told David, saying, Ahithophel *is* among the conspirators with Absalom. And David said, O LORD, I pray thee, turn
the counsel of Ahithophel into foolishness.
32¶ And it came to pass, that *when* David was come to the top
*of the mount*, where he worshipped God, behold, Hushai the Archite came to meet him with his coat rent, and earth upon his head:
33Unto whom David said, If thou passest on with me, then thou
shalt be a burden unto me:
34But if thou return to the city, and say unto Absalom, I will be
thy servant, O king; *as* I *have been* thy father's servant hitherto, so
*will* I now also *be* thy servant: then mayest thou for me defeat the
counsel of Ahithophel.
35And *hast thou* not there with thee Zadok and Abiathar the
priests? therefore it shall be, *that* what thing soever thou shalt hear
out of the king's house, thou shalt tell *it* to Zadok and Abiathar the
priests.
36Behold, *they have* there with them their two sons, Ahimaaz
Zadok's *son*, and Jonathan Abiathar's *son*; and by them ye shall
send unto me every thing that ye can hear.
37So Hushai David's friend came into the city, and Absalom
came into Jerusalem.

16 AND WHEN David was a little past the top *of the hill*,
behold, Ziba the servant of Mephibosheth met him, with
a couple of asses saddled, and upon them two hundred *loaves* of
bread, and an hundred bunches of raisins, and an hundred of
summer fruits, and a bottle of wine.
2And the king said unto Ziba, What meanest thou by these?
And Ziba said, The asses *be* for the king's household to ride on;
and the bread and summer fruit for the young men to eat; and the
wine, that such as be faint in the wilderness may drink.
3And the king said, And where *is* thy master's son? And Ziba
said unto the king, Behold, he abideth at Jerusalem: for he said,
Today shall the house of Israel restore me the kingdom of my
father.
4Then said the king to Ziba, Behold, thine *are* all that *pertained*
unto Mephibosheth. And Ziba said, I humbly beseech thee *that* I
may find grace in thy sight, my lord, O king.
5¶ And when king David came to Bahurim, behold, thence came
out a man of the family of the house of Saul, whose name *was*
Shimei, the son of Gera: he came forth, and cursed still as he came.

## Amplified

24Abiathar [the priest], and lo, Zadok came also, and all the
Levites with him, bearing the ark of the covenant of God; and they
set down the ark of God, until all the people had gone from the
city.
25Then the king told Zadok, Take back the ark of God to the city.
If I find favor in the Lord's eyes, He will bring me back and let me
see both it and His house.
26But if He says, I have no delight in you, then, here I am; let
Him do to me what seems good to Him.
27The king also said to Zadok the priest, Are you not a seer?
[You and Abiathar] return to the city in peace, and your two sons
with you, Ahimaaz your son, and Jonathan son of Abiathar.
28See, I will wait at the fords [at the Jordan] of the wilderness,
until word comes from you to inform me.
29Zadok therefore and Abiathar carried the ark of God back to
Jerusalem; and they stayed there.
30And David went up over the Mount of Olives, and wept as
he went, barefoot and his head covered. And all the people who
were with him covered their heads, weeping as they went.
31David was told, Ahithophel [your counselor] is among the
conspirators with Absalom. David said, O Lord, I pray You, turn
Ahithophel's counsel into foolishness.
32When David came to the summit [of Olivet], where he worshiped God, behold, Hushai the Archite came to meet him with
his coat rent, and earth upon his head.
33David said to him, If you go with me, you will be a burden
to me;
34But if you return to the city, and say to Absalom, I will be your
servant, O king; as I have been your father's servant in the past,
so will I be your servant now; then you may defeat for me the
counsel of Ahithophel.
35Will not Zadok and Abiathar the priests be with you? So
whatever you hear from the king's house, just tell it to [them].
36Behold, their two sons are there with them, Ahimaaz Zadok's
son, and Jonathan Abiathar's son; and by them send to me everything you hear.
37So Hushai, David's friend, returned, and Absalom also came
into Jerusalem.

16 WHEN DAVID was a little past the top [of Olivet] behold,
Ziba the servant of Mephibosheth met him, with a couple
of donkeys saddled, and upon them 200 loaves of bread, 100
bunches of raisins, 100 of summer fruits, and a skin of wine.
2The king said to Ziba, What do you mean by these? Ziba said,
The donkeys are for the king's household to ride on; the bread and
summer fruit for the young men to eat; and the wine is for those
to drink who become faint in the wilderness.
3The king said, And where is your master's son [grandson
Mephibosheth]? Ziba said to the king, Behold, he remains in
Jerusalem; for he said, Today the house of Israel will give me back
the kingdom of my father [grandfather Saul].
4Then the king said to Ziba, Lo, all that belonged to Mephibosheth is now yours. Ziba said, I do obeisance; let me ever find favor
in your sight, my lord, O king.
5When King David came to Bahurim, a man of the family of the
house of Saul, Shimei son of Gera, came out and cursed continually as he came.

## New American Standard

24¶ Now behold, Zadok also *came,* and all the Levites with him
carrying the ark of the covenant of God. And they set down the
ark of God, and Abiathar came up until all the people had finished
passing from the city.
25And the king said to Zadok, "Return the ark of God to the city.
If I find favor in the sight of the LORD, then He will bring me back
again, and show me both it and His habitation.
26"But if He should say thus, 'I have no delight in you,' behold,
here I am, let Him do to me as seems good to Him."
27The king said also to Zadok the priest, "Are you *not* a seer?
Return to the city in peace and your two sons with you, your son
Ahimaaz and Jonathan the son of Abiathar.
28"See, I am going to wait at the fords of the wilderness until
word comes from you to inform me."
29Therefore Zadok and Abiathar returned the ark of God to
Jerusalem and remained there.
30¶ And David went up the ascent of the *Mount of* Olives, and
wept as he went, and his head was covered and he walked barefoot. Then all the people who were with him each covered his head
and went up weeping as they went.
31Now someone told David, saying, "Ahithophel is among the
conspirators with Absalom." And David said, "O LORD, I pray,
make the counsel of Ahithophel foolishness."
32It happened as David was coming to the summit, where God
was worshiped, that behold, Hushai the Archite met him with his
coat torn, and dust on his head.
33And David said to him, "If you pass over with me, then you
will be a burden to me.
34"But if you return to the city, and say to Absalom, 'I will be
your servant, O king; as I have been your father's servant in time
past, so I will now be your servant,' then you can thwart the
counsel of Ahithophel for me.
35"And are not Zadok and Abiathar the priests with you there?
So it shall be that whatever you hear from the king's house, you
shall report to Zadok and Abiathar the priests.
36"Behold their two sons are with them there, Ahimaaz,
Zadok's son and Jonathan, Abiathar's son; and by them you shall
send me everything that you hear."
37So Hushai, David's friend, came into the city, and Absalom
came into Jerusalem.

*Ziba, a False Servant*

16 NOW WHEN David had passed a little beyond the summit, behold, Ziba the servant of Mephibosheth met him
with a couple of saddled donkeys, and on them *were* two hundred
loaves of bread, a hundred clusters of raisins, a hundred summer
fruits, and a jug of wine.
2And the king said to Ziba, "Why do you have these?" And
Ziba said, "The donkeys are for the king's household to ride, and
the bread and summer fruit for the young men to eat, and the
wine, for whoever is faint in the wilderness to drink."
3Then the king said, "And where is your master's son?" And
Ziba said to the king, "Behold, he is staying in Jerusalem, for he
said, 'Today the house of Israel will restore the kingdom of my
father to me.'"
4So the king said to Ziba, "Behold, all that belongs to Mephibosheth is yours." And Ziba said, "I prostrate myself; let me find
favor in your sight, O my lord, the king!"

*David Is Cursed*

5¶ When King David came to Bahurim, behold, there came out
from there a man of the family of the house of Saul whose name
was Shimei, the son of Gera; he came out cursing continually as
he came.

## New International

24Zadok was there, too, and all the Levites who were with him
were carrying the ark of the covenant of God. They set down the
ark of God, and Abiathar offered sacrifices[a] until all the people had
finished leaving the city.
25Then the king said to Zadok, "Take the ark of God back into
the city. If I find favor in the LORD's eyes, he will bring me back
and let me see it and his dwelling place again. 26But if he says, 'I
am not pleased with you,' then I am ready; let him do to me
whatever seems good to him."
27The king also said to Zadok the priest, "Aren't you a seer? Go
back to the city in peace, with your son Ahimaaz and Jonathan son
of Abiathar. You and Abiathar take your two sons with you. 28I will
wait at the fords in the desert until word comes from you to inform
me." 29So Zadok and Abiathar took the ark of God back to Jerusalem and stayed there.
30But David continued up the Mount of Olives, weeping as he
went; his head was covered and he was barefoot. All the people
with him covered their heads too and were weeping as they went
up. 31Now David had been told, "Ahithophel is among the conspirators with Absalom." So David prayed, "O LORD, turn Ahithophel's counsel into foolishness."
32When David arrived at the summit, where people used to
worship God, Hushai the Arkite was there to meet him, his robe
torn and dust on his head. 33David said to him, "If you go with
me, you will be a burden to me. 34But if you return to the city and
say to Absalom, 'I will be your servant, O king; I was your father's
servant in the past, but now I will be your servant,' then you can
help me by frustrating Ahithophel's advice. 35Won't the priests
Zadok and Abiathar be there with you? Tell them anything you
hear in the king's palace. 36Their two sons, Ahimaaz son of Zadok
and Jonathan son of Abiathar, are there with them. Send them to
me with anything you hear."
37So David's friend Hushai arrived at Jerusalem as Absalom was
entering the city.

*David and Ziba*

16 WHEN DAVID had gone a short distance beyond the
summit, there was Ziba, the steward of Mephibosheth,
waiting to meet him. He had a string of donkeys saddled and
loaded with two hundred loaves of bread, a hundred cakes of
raisins, a hundred cakes of figs and a skin of wine.
2The king asked Ziba, "Why have you brought these?"
Ziba answered, "The donkeys are for the king's household to
ride on, the bread and fruit are for the men to eat, and the wine
is to refresh those who become exhausted in the desert."
3The king then asked, "Where is your master's grandson?"
Ziba said to him, "He is staying in Jerusalem, because he thinks,
'Today the house of Israel will give me back my grandfather's
kingdom.'"
4Then the king said to Ziba, "All that belonged to Mephibosheth is now yours."
"I humbly bow," Ziba said. "May I find favor in your eyes, my
lord the king."

*Shimei Curses David*

5As King David approached Bahurim, a man from the same clan
as Saul's family came out from there. His name was Shimei son of
Gera, and he cursed as he came out. 6He pelted David and all the

NIV [a] 24 Or *Abiathar went up*

## King James

6And he cast stones at David, and at all the servants of king David: and all the people and all the mighty men *were* on his right hand and on his left.

7And thus said Shimei when he cursed, Come out, come out, thou bloody man, and thou man of Belial:

8The LORD hath returned upon thee all the blood of the house of Saul, in whose stead thou hast reigned; and the LORD hath delivered the kingdom into the hand of Absalom thy son: and, behold, thou *art taken* in thy mischief, because thou *art* a bloody man.

9¶ Then said Abishai the son of Zeruiah unto the king, Why should this dead dog curse my lord the king? let me go over, I pray thee, and take off his head.

10And the king said, What have I to do with you, ye sons of Zeruiah? so let him curse, because the LORD hath said unto him, Curse David. Who shall then say, Wherefore hast thou done so?

11And David said to Abishai, and to all his servants, Behold, my son, which came forth of my bowels, seeketh my life: how much more now *may this* Benjamite *do it?* let him alone, and let him curse; for the LORD hath bidden him.

12It may be that the LORD will look on mine affliction, and that the LORD will requite me good for his cursing this day.

13And as David and his men went by the way, Shimei went along on the hill's side over against him, and cursed as he went, and threw stones at him, and cast dust.

14And the king, and all the people that *were* with him, came weary, and refreshed themselves there.

15¶ And Absalom, and all the people the men of Israel, came to Jerusalem, and Ahithophel with him.

16And it came to pass, when Hushai the Archite, David's friend, was come unto Absalom, that Hushai said unto Absalom, God save the king, God save the king.

17And Absalom said to Hushai, *Is* this thy kindness to thy friend? why wentest thou not with thy friend?

18And Hushai said unto Absalom, Nay; but whom the LORD, and this people, and all the men of Israel, choose, his will I be, and with him will I abide.

19And again, whom should I serve? *should I* not *serve* in the presence of his son? as I have served in thy father's presence, so will I be in thy presence.

20¶ Then said Absalom to Ahithophel, Give counsel among you what we shall do.

21And Ahithophel said unto Absalom, Go in unto thy father's concubines, which he hath left to keep the house; and all Israel shall hear that thou art abhorred of thy father: then shall the hands of all that *are* with thee be strong.

22So they spread Absalom a tent upon the top of the house; and Absalom went in unto his father's concubines in the sight of all Israel.

23And the counsel of Ahithophel, which he counselled in those days, *was* as if a man had inquired at the oracle of God: so *was* all the counsel of Ahithophel both with David and with Absalom.

**17** MOREOVER AHITHOPHEL said unto Absalom, Let me now choose out twelve thousand men, and I will arise and pursue after David this night:

2And I will come upon him while he *is* weary and weak handed, and will make him afraid: and all the people that *are* with him shall flee; and I will smite the king only:

3And I will bring back all the people unto thee: the man whom thou seekest *is* as if all returned: *so* all the people shall be in peace.

4And the saying pleased Absalom well, and all the elders of Israel.

5Then said Absalom, Call now Hushai the Archite also, and let us hear likewise what he saith.

## Amplified

6And he cast stones at David, and at all the servants of King David; and all the people and all the mighty men were on his right hand and on his left.

7Shimei said as he cursed, Get out, get out, you man of blood, you base fellow!

8The Lord has avenged upon you all the blood of the house of Saul, in whose stead you have reigned; and the Lord has delivered the kingdom into the hand of Absalom your son. Behold, the calamity is upon you, because you are a bloody man!

9Then said [David's nephew] Abishai son of Zeruiah to the king, Why should this dead dog curse my lord the king? Let me go over and take off his head.

10The king said, What have I to do with you, you sons of Zeruiah? If he is cursing because the Lord said to him, Curse David, who then shall ask, Why have you done so?

11And David said to Abishai, and to all his servants, Behold, my son, who was born to me, seeks my life. With how much more reason now may this Benjamite do it? Let him alone, and let him curse; for the Lord has bidden him do it.

12It may be that the Lord will look on the iniquity done me, and will recompense me good for his cursing this day.

13So David and his men went by the road, and Shimei went along on the hillside opposite David, and cursed as he went, and threw stones and dust at him.

14And the king, and all the people who were with him, came [to the Jordan] weary, and he refreshed himself there.

15And Absalom, and all the people, the men of Israel, came to Jerusalem, and Ahithophel with him.

16And when Hushai the Archite, David's friend, came to Absalom, Hushai said to [him], Long live the king! Long live the king!

17Absalom said to Hushai, Is this your kindness *and* loyalty to your friend? Why did you not go with your friend?

18Hushai said to Absalom, No, for whom the Lord and this people and all the men of Israel choose, his will I be, and with him I will remain.

19And again, whom should I serve? Should it not be his son? As I have served your father, so will I serve you.

20Then Absalom said to Ahithophel, Give your counsel; what shall we do?

21And Ahithophel said to Absalom, Go in to your father's concubines, whom he has left to keep the house; and all Israel will hear that you are abhorred by your father; then the hands of all who are with you will be made strong.

22So they spread Absalom a tent on the top of the [king's] house; and Absalom went in to his father's harem in the sight of all Israel.

23And the counsel of Ahithophel in those days, was as if a man had consulted the word of God; so was all Ahithophel's counsel considered both by David and by Absalom.

**17** MOREOVER AHITHOPHEL said to Absalom, Let me choose 12,000 men, and I will set out and pursue David this night.

2I will come upon him while he is exhausted and weak, and cause him to panic; all the people with him will flee; then I will strike down the king alone.

3I will bring back all the people to you. [The removal of] the man whom you seek is the assurance that all will return, and all the people will be at peace.

4And what he said pleased Absalom well, and all the elders of Israel.

5Absalom said, Now call Hushai the Archite also, and let us hear what he says.

## New American Standard

6And he threw stones at David and at all the servants of King
David; and all the people and all the mighty men were at his right
hand and at his left.
7And thus Shimei said when he cursed, "Get out, get out, you
man of bloodshed, and worthless fellow!
8"The LORD has returned upon you all the bloodshed of the
house of Saul, in whose place you have reigned; and the LORD has
given the kingdom into the hand of your son Absalom. And behold, you are *taken* in your own evil, for you are a man of bloodshed!"
9¶ Then Abishai the son of Zeruiah said to the king, "Why
should this dead dog curse my lord the king? Let me go over now,
and cut off his head."
10But the king said, "What have I to do with you, O sons of
Zeruiah? If he curses, and if the LORD has told him, 'Curse David,'
then who shall say, 'Why have you done so?' "
11Then David said to Abishai and to all his servants, "Behold,
my son who came out from me seeks my life; how much more now
this Benjamite? Let him alone and let him curse, for the LORD has
told him.
12"Perhaps the LORD will look on my affliction and return good
to me instead of his cursing this day."
13So David and his men went on the way; and Shimei went
along on the hillside parallel with him and as he went he cursed,
and cast stones and threw dust at him.
14And the king and all the people who were with him arrived
weary and he refreshed himself there.

*Absalom Enters Jerusalem*

15¶ Then Absalom and all the people, the men of Israel, entered
Jerusalem, and Ahithophel with him.
16Now it came about when Hushai the Archite, David's friend,
came to Absalom, that Hushai said to Absalom, " *Long* live the
king! *Long* live the king!"
17And Absalom said to Hushai, "Is this your loyalty to your
friend? Why did you not go with your friend?"
18Then Hushai said to Absalom, "No! For whom the LORD, this
people, and all the men of Israel have chosen, his will I be, and
with him I will remain.
19"And besides, whom should I serve? *Should I* not *serve* in the
presence of his son? As I have served in your father's presence, so
I will be in your presence."
20¶ Then Absalom said to Ahithophel, "Give your advice. What
shall we do?"
21And Ahithophel said to Absalom, "Go in to your father's
concubines, whom he has left to keep the house; then all Israel will
hear that you have made yourself odious to your father. The hands
of all who are with you will also be strengthened."
22So they pitched a tent for Absalom on the roof, and Absalom
went in to his father's concubines in the sight of all Israel.
23And the advice of Ahithophel, which he gave in those days,
*was* as if one inquired of the word of God; so was all the advice of
Ahithophel *regarded* by both David and Absalom.

*Hushai's Counsel*

17 FURTHERMORE, AHITHOPHEL said to Absalom,
"Please let me choose 12,000 men that I may arise and
pursue David tonight.
2"And I will come upon him while he is weary and exhausted
and will terrify him so that all the people who are with him will
flee. Then I will strike down the king alone,
3and I will bring back all the people to you. The return of
everyone depends on the man you seek; *then* all the people shall
be at peace."
4So the plan pleased Absalom and all the elders of Israel.
5¶ Then Absalom said, "Now call Hushai the Archite also, and
let us hear what he has to say."

## New International

king's officials with stones, though all the troops and the special
guard were on David's right and left. 7As he cursed, Shimei said,
"Get out, get out, you man of blood, you scoundrel! 8The LORD has
repaid you for all the blood you shed in the household of Saul, in
whose place you have reigned. The LORD has handed the kingdom
over to your son Absalom. You have come to ruin because you are
a man of blood!"
9Then Abishai son of Zeruiah said to the king, "Why should
this dead dog curse my lord the king? Let me go over and cut off
his head."
10But the king said, "What do you and I have in common, you
sons of Zeruiah? If he is cursing because the LORD said to him,
'Curse David,' who can ask, 'Why do you do this?' "
11David then said to Abishai and all his officials, "My son, who
is of my own flesh, is trying to take my life. How much more, then,
this Benjamite! Leave him alone; let him curse, for the LORD has
told him to. 12It may be that the LORD will see my distress and
repay me with good for the cursing I am receiving today."
13So David and his men continued along the road while Shimei
was going along the hillside opposite him, cursing as he went and
throwing stones at him and showering him with dirt. 14The king
and all the people with him arrived at their destination exhausted.
And there he refreshed himself.

*The Advice of Hushai and Ahithophel*

15Meanwhile, Absalom and all the men of Israel came to Jerusalem, and Ahithophel was with him. 16Then Hushai the Arkite,
David's friend, went to Absalom and said to him, "Long live the
king! Long live the king!"
17Absalom asked Hushai, "Is this the love you show your
friend? Why didn't you go with your friend?"
18Hushai said to Absalom, "No, the one chosen by the LORD,
by these people, and by all the men of Israel—his I will be, and I
will remain with him. 19Furthermore, whom should I serve?
Should I not serve the son? Just as I served your father, so I will
serve you."
20Absalom said to Ahithophel, "Give us your advice. What
should we do?"
21Ahithophel answered, "Lie with your father's concubines
whom he left to take care of the palace. Then all Israel will hear
that you have made yourself a stench in your father's nostrils, and
the hands of everyone with you will be strengthened." 22So they
pitched a tent for Absalom on the roof, and he lay with his father's
concubines in the sight of all Israel.
23Now in those days the advice Ahithophel gave was like that
of one who inquires of God. That was how both David and Absalom regarded all of Ahithophel's advice.

17 AHITHOPHEL SAID to Absalom, "I would[a] choose
twelve thousand men and set out tonight in pursuit of
David. 2I would[b] attack him while he is weary and weak. I would[c]
strike him with terror, and then all the people with him will flee.
I would[d] strike down only the king 3and bring all the people back
to you. The death of the man you seek will mean the return of all;
all the people will be unharmed." 4This plan seemed good to
Absalom and to all the elders of Israel.
5But Absalom said, "Summon also Hushai the Arkite, so we can
hear what he has to say." 6When Hushai came to him, Absalom

NIV [a] *1* Or *Let me* [b] 2 Or *will* [c] 2 Or *will* [d] 2 Or *will*

## King James

6And when Hushai was come to Absalom, Absalom spake unto him, saying, Ahithophel hath spoken after this manner: shall we do *after* his saying? if not; speak thou.

7And Hushai said unto Absalom, The counsel that Ahithophel hath given *is* not good at this time.

8For, said Hushai, thou knowest thy father and his men, that they *be* mighty men, and they *be* chafed in their minds, as a bear robbed of her whelps in the field: and thy father *is* a man of war, and will not lodge with the people.

9Behold, he is hid now in some pit, or in some *other* place: and it will come to pass, when some of them be overthrown at the first, that whosoever heareth it will say, There is a slaughter among the people that follow Absalom.

10And he also *that is* valiant, whose heart *is* as the heart of a lion, shall utterly melt: for all Israel knoweth that thy father *is* a mighty man, and *they* which *be* with him *are* valiant men.

11Therefore I counsel that all Israel be generally gathered unto thee, from Dan even to Beer-sheba, as the sand that *is* by the sea for multitude; and that thou go to battle in thine own person.

12So shall we come upon him in some place where he shall be found, and we will light upon him as the dew falleth on the ground: and of him and of all the men that *are* with him there shall not be left so much as one.

13Moreover, if he be gotten into a city, then shall all Israel bring ropes to that city, and we will draw it into the river, until there be not one small stone found there.

14And Absalom and all the men of Israel said, The counsel of Hushai the Archite *is* better than the counsel of Ahithophel. For the LORD had appointed to defeat the good counsel of Ahithophel, to the intent that the LORD might bring evil upon Absalom.

15¶ Then said Hushai unto Zadok and to Abiathar the priests, Thus and thus did Ahithophel counsel Absalom and the elders of Israel; and thus and thus have I counselled.

16Now therefore send quickly, and tell David, saying, Lodge not this night in the plains of the wilderness, but speedily pass over; lest the king be swallowed up, and all the people that *are* with him.

17Now Jonathan and Ahimaaz stayed by En-rogel; for they might not be seen to come into the city: and a wench went and told them; and they went and told king David.

18Nevertheless a lad saw them, and told Absalom: but they went both of them away quickly, and came to a man's house in Bahurim, which had a well in his court; whither they went down.

19And the woman took and spread a covering over the well's mouth, and spread ground corn thereon; and the thing was not known.

20And when Absalom's servants came to the woman to the house, they said, Where *is* Ahimaaz and Jonathan? And the woman said unto them, They be gone over the brook of water. And when they had sought and could not find *them,* they returned to Jerusalem.

21And it came to pass, after they were departed, that they came up out of the well, and went and told king David, and said unto David, Arise, and pass quickly over the water: for thus hath Ahithophel counselled against you.

22Then David arose, and all the people that *were* with him, and they passed over Jordan: by the morning light there lacked not one of them that was not gone over Jordan.

23¶ And when Ahithophel saw that his counsel was not followed, he saddled *his* ass, and arose, and gat him home to his house, to his city, and put his household in order, and hanged himself, and died, and was buried in the sepulchre of his father.

24Then David came to Mahanaim. And Absalom passed over Jordan, he and all the men of Israel with him.

25¶ And Absalom made Amasa captain of the host instead of Joab: which Amasa *was* a man's son, whose name *was* Ithra an Israelite, that went in to Abigail the daughter of Nahash, sister to Zeruiah Joab's mother.

26So Israel and Absalom pitched in the land of Gilead.

## Amplified

6When Hushai came, Absalom said to him, Ahithophel has counseled thus. Shall we do what he says? If not, speak up.

7And Hushai said to Absalom, The counsel that Ahithophel has given is not good at this time.

8For, said Hushai, you know your father and his men, that they are mighty men, and they are embittered *and* enraged like a bear robbed of her whelps in the field; and your father is a man of war, and will not lodge with the people.

9Behold, he is hid even now in some pit, or other place; and when some of them are overthrown at the first, whoever hears it will say, There is a slaughter among the followers of Absalom.

10And even he who is brave, whose heart is as the heart of a lion, will utterly melt; for all Israel knows that your father is a mighty man, and they who are with him are brave men.

11Therefore I counsel that all [the men of] Israel be gathered to you, from Dan even to Beer-sheba, as the sand that is by the sea for multitude; and that you go to battle in your own person.

12So shall we come upon [David] some place where he shall be found, and we will light upon him as the dew settles [unseen and unheard] on the ground; and of him and of all the men with him there shall not be left so much as one.

13If he withdraws into a city, then shall all Israel bring ropes to that city, and we will drag it into the ravine, until not one pebble is left there.

14Absalom and all the men of Israel said, The counsel of Hushai the Archite is better than that of Ahithophel. For the Lord had ordained to defeat the good counsel of Ahithophel, so that the Lord might bring evil upon Absalom.

15Then said Hushai to Zadok and Abiathar the priests, Thus and thus did Ahithophel counsel Absalom and the elders of Israel; and thus and thus have I counseled.

16Now send quickly, and tell David, Lodge not this night at the fords of the [Jordan] wilderness, but by all means pass over, lest the king be swallowed up, and all the people with him.

17Now [the youths] Jonathan and Ahimaaz stayed by En-rogel, for they must not be seen to come into the city. But a maidservant went and told them, and they went and told King David.

18But a lad saw them, and told Absalom; but they left quickly, and came to the house of a man in Bahurim, who had a well in his court, and they went down into it.

19And the woman spread a covering over the well's mouth, and spread ground corn on it; and the thing was not discovered.

20For when Absalom's servants came to the woman at the house, they said, Where are Ahimaaz and Jonathan? And the woman said to them, They went over the brook of water. When they had sought and could not find them, they returned to Jerusalem.

21After they had departed, the boys came up out of the well, and went and told King David, and said, Arise, and pass quickly over the river Jordan, for thus and so Ahithophel counseled against you.

22David arose, and all the people with him, and passed over Jordan. By daybreak not one was left who had not crossed.

23But when Ahithophel saw that his counsel was not followed, he saddled his donkey, went home to his city, put his household in order, and hanged himself and died, and was buried in the tomb of his father.

24Then David came to Mahanaim. And Absalom passed over Jordan, he and all the men of Israel with him.

25Absalom made Amasa captain of the army instead of Joab; Amasa was the son of an [Ishmaelite] named Ithra, who married Abigail daughter of Nahash, [half sister of David and] sister of Zeruiah Joab's mother.

26So Israel and Absalom encamped in the land of Gilead.

## New American Standard

6When Hushai had come to Absalom, Absalom said to him,
"Ahithophel has spoken thus. Shall we carry out his plan? If not,
you speak."
7So Hushai said to Absalom, "This time the advice that Ahithophel has given is not good."
8Moreover, Hushai said, "You know your father and his men,
that they are mighty men and they are fierce, like a bear robbed
of her cubs in the field. And your father is an expert in warfare,
and will not spend the night with the people.
9"Behold, he has now hidden himself in one of the caves or in
another place; and it will be when he falls on them at the first
attack, that whoever hears *it* will say, 'There has been a slaughter
among the people who follow Absalom.'
10"And even the one who is valiant, whose heart is like the
heart of a lion, will completely lose heart; for all Israel knows that
your father is a mighty man and those who are with him are valiant
men.
11"But I counsel that all Israel be surely gathered to you, from
Dan even to Beersheba, as the sand that is by the sea in abundance,
and that you personally go into battle.
12"So we shall come to him in one of the places where he can
be found, and we will fall on him as the dew falls on the ground;
and of him and of all the men who are with him, not even one will
be left.
13"And if he withdraws into a city, then all Israel shall bring
ropes to that city, and we will drag it into the valley until not even
a small stone is found there."
14Then Absalom and all the men of Israel said, "The counsel of
Hushai the Archite is better than the counsel of Ahithophel." For
the LORD had ordained to thwart the good counsel of Ahithophel,
in order that the LORD might bring calamity on Absalom.

*Hushai's Warning Saves David*

**15**¶ Then Hushai said to Zadok and to Abiathar the priests,
"This is what Ahithophel counseled Absalom and the elders of
Israel, and this is what I have counseled.
16"Now therefore, send quickly and tell David, saying, 'Do not
spend the night at the fords of the wilderness, but by all means
cross over, lest the king and all the people who are with him be
destroyed.' "
17Now Jonathan and Ahimaaz were staying at En-rogel, and a
maidservant would go and tell them, and they would go and tell
King David, for they could not be seen entering the city.
18But a lad did see them, and told Absalom; so the two of them
departed quickly and came to the house of a man in Bahurim, who
had a well in his courtyard, and they went down into it.
19And the woman took a covering and spread it over the well's
mouth and scattered grain on it, so that nothing was known.
20Then Absalom's servants came to the woman at the house and
said, "Where are Ahimaaz and Jonathan?" And the woman said
to them, "They have crossed the brook of water." And when they
searched and could not find *them*, they returned to Jerusalem.
**21**¶ And it came about after they had departed that they came
up out of the well and went and told King David; and they said
to David, "Arise and cross over the water quickly for thus Ahithophel has counseled against you."
22Then David and all the people who *were* with him arose and
crossed the Jordan; and by dawn not even one remained who had
not crossed the Jordan.
23Now when Ahithophel saw that his counsel was not followed, he saddled *his* donkey and arose and went to his home, to
his city, and set his house in order, and strangled himself; thus he
died and was buried in the grave of his father.
**24**¶ Then David came to Mahanaim. And Absalom crossed the
Jordan, he and all the men of Israel with him.
25And Absalom set Amasa over the army in place of Joab. Now
Amasa was the son of a man whose name was Ithra the Israelite,
who went in to Abigail the daughter of Nahash, sister of Zeruiah,
Joab's mother.
26And Israel and Absalom camped in the land of Gilead.

## New International

said, "Ahithophel has given this advice. Should we do what he
says? If not, give us your opinion."
7Hushai replied to Absalom, "The advice Ahithophel has given
is not good this time. 8You know your father and his men; they
are fighters, and as fierce as a wild bear robbed of her cubs.
Besides, your father is an experienced fighter; he will not spend
the night with the troops. 9Even now, he is hidden in a cave or
some other place. If he should attack your troops first,[a] whoever
hears about it will say, 'There has been a slaughter among the
troops who follow Absalom.' 10Then even the bravest soldier,
whose heart is like the heart of a lion, will melt with fear, for all
Israel knows that your father is a fighter and that those with him
are brave.
11"So I advise you: Let all Israel, from Dan to Beersheba—as
numerous as the sand on the seashore—be gathered to you, with
you yourself leading them into battle. 12Then we will attack him
wherever he may be found, and we will fall on him as dew settles
on the ground. Neither he nor any of his men will be left alive. 13If
he withdraws into a city, then all Israel will bring ropes to that city,
and we will drag it down to the valley until not even a piece of it
can be found."
14Absalom and all the men of Israel said, "The advice of Hushai
the Arkite is better than that of Ahithophel." For the LORD had
determined to frustrate the good advice of Ahithophel in order to
bring disaster on Absalom.
15Hushai told Zadok and Abiathar, the priests, "Ahithophel
has advised Absalom and the elders of Israel to do such and such,
but I have advised them to do so and so. 16Now send a message
immediately and tell David, 'Do not spend the night at the fords
in the desert; cross over without fail, or the king and all the people
with him will be swallowed up.' "
17Jonathan and Ahimaaz were staying at En Rogel. A servant
girl was to go and inform them, and they were to go and tell King
David, for they could not risk being seen entering the city. 18But
a young man saw them and told Absalom. So the two of them left
quickly and went to the house of a man in Bahurim. He had a well
in his courtyard, and they climbed down into it. 19His wife took
a covering and spread it out over the opening of the well and
scattered grain over it. No one knew anything about it.
20When Absalom's men came to the woman at the house, they
asked, "Where are Ahimaaz and Jonathan?"
The woman answered them, "They crossed over the brook."[b]
The men searched but found no one, so they returned to Jerusalem.
21After the men had gone, the two climbed out of the well and
went to inform King David. They said to him, "Set out and cross
the river at once; Ahithophel has advised such and such against
you." 22So David and all the people with him set out and crossed
the Jordan. By daybreak, no one was left who had not crossed the
Jordan.
23When Ahithophel saw that his advice had not been followed,
he saddled his donkey and set out for his house in his hometown.
He put his house in order and then hanged himself. So he died and
was buried in his father's tomb.
24David went to Mahanaim, and Absalom crossed the Jordan
with all the men of Israel. 25Absalom had appointed Amasa over
the army in place of Joab. Amasa was the son of a man named
Jether,[c] an Israelite[d] who had married Abigail,[e] the daughter of
Nahash and sister of Zeruiah the mother of Joab. 26The Israelites
and Absalom camped in the land of Gilead.

**NIV** [a] 9 Or *When some of the men fall at the first attack* [b] 20 Or *"They passed by the sheep pen toward the water."* [c] 25 Hebrew *Ithra*, a variant of *Jether* [d] 25 Hebrew and some Septuagint manuscripts; other Septuagint manuscripts (see also 1 Chron. 2:17) *Ishmaelite* or *Jezreelite* [e] 25 Hebrew *Abigal*, a variant of *Abigail*

## King James

27¶ And it came to pass, when David was come to Mahanaim,
that Shobi the son of Nahash of Rabbah of the children of Ammon,
and Machir the son of Ammiel of Lo-debar, and Barzillai the Gileadite of Rogelim,
28Brought beds, and basins, and earthen vessels, and wheat,
and barley, and flour, and parched *corn*, and beans, and lentiles,
and parched *pulse*,
29And honey, and butter, and sheep, and cheese of kine, for
David, and for the people that *were* with him, to eat: for they said,
The people *is* hungry, and weary, and thirsty, in the wilderness.

18 AND DAVID numbered the people that *were* with him,
and set captains of thousands and captains of hundreds
over them.
2And David sent forth a third part of the people under the hand
of Joab, and a third part under the hand of Abishai the son of
Zeruiah, Joab's brother, and a third part under the hand of Ittai the
Gittite. And the king said unto the people, I will surely go forth
with you myself also.
3But the people answered, Thou shalt not go forth: for if we flee
away, they will not care for us; neither if half of us die, will they
care for us: but now *thou art* worth ten thousand of us: therefore
now *it is* better that thou succour us out of the city.
4And the king said unto them, What seemeth you best I will do.
And the king stood by the gate side, and all the people came out
by hundreds and by thousands.
5And the king commanded Joab and Abishai and Ittai, saying,
*Deal* gently for my sake with the young man, *even* with Absalom.
And all the people heard when the king gave all the captains
charge concerning Absalom.
6¶ So the people went out into the field against Israel: and the
battle was in the wood of Ephraim;
7Where the people of Israel were slain before the servants of
David, and there was there a great slaughter that day of twenty
thousand *men*.
8For the battle was there scattered over the face of all the country: and the wood devoured more people that day than the sword
devoured.
9¶ And Absalom met the servants of David. And Absalom rode
upon a mule, and the mule went under the thick boughs of a great
oak, and his head caught hold of the oak, and he was taken up
between the heaven and the earth; and the mule that *was* under
him went away.
10And a certain man saw *it*, and told Joab, and said, Behold, I
saw Absalom hanged in an oak.
11And Joab said unto the man that told him, And, behold, thou
sawest *him*, and why didst thou not smite him there to the ground?
and I would have given thee ten *shekels* of silver, and a girdle.
12And the man said unto Joab, Though I should receive a thousand *shekels* of silver in mine hand, *yet* would I not put forth mine
hand against the king's son: for in our hearing the king charged
thee and Abishai and Ittai, saying, Beware that none *touch* the
young man Absalom.
13Otherwise I should have wrought falsehood against mine
own life: for there is no matter hid from the king, and thou thyself
wouldest have set thyself against *me*.
14Then said Joab, I may not tarry thus with thee. And he took
three darts in his hand, and thrust them through the heart of
Absalom, while he *was* yet alive in the midst of the oak.
15And ten young men that bare Joab's armour compassed about
and smote Absalom, and slew him.
16And Joab blew the trumpet, and the people returned from
pursuing after Israel: for Joab held back the people.
17And they took Absalom, and cast him into a great pit in the
wood, and laid a very great heap of stones upon him: and all Israel
fled every one to his tent.

## Amplified

27When David came to Mahanaim, Shobi son of Nahash of
Rabbah of the Ammonites, and Machir son of Ammiel of Lodebar,
and Barzillai the Gileadite of Rogelim,
28Brought beds, basins, earthen vessels, wheat, barley, meal,
parched grain, beans, lentils, parched [pulse, peas and beans],
29Honey, curds, sheep, and cheese of cows, for David and the
people with him to eat; for they said, The people are hungry,
weary, and thirsty in the wilderness.

18 DAVID NUMBERED the men who were with him, and set
over them commanders of thousands and of hundreds.
2David sent forth the army, a third under command of Joab, a
third under Abishai son of Zeruiah, Joab's brother, and a third
under Ittai the Gittite. [He] told the men, I myself will go out with
you also.
3But the men said, You shall not go out. For if we flee, they will
not care about us; if half of us die, they will not care about us. But
you are worth 10,000 such as we are. So now it is better that you
be able to help us from the city.
4The king said to them, What seems best to you I will do. So
he stood beside the gate and all the army came out, by hundreds
and by thousands.
5The king commanded Joab, Abishai, and Ittai, saying, Deal
gently for my sake with the young man Absalom. And all the
people heard when the king gave orders to all the commanders
about Absalom.
6So the army went out into the field against Israel; and the battle
was fought in the forest of Ephraim.
7[Absalom's] men of Israel were defeated by the servants of
David, and there was a great slaughter that day of 20,000 men.
8For the battle spread over the face of all the country; and the
forest devoured more men that day than did the sword.
9Then Absalom [unavoidably] met the servants of David. Absalom rode on a mule, and the mule went under the thick boughs
of a great oak, and Absalom's head caught fast [in a fork] of the
oak; and the mule under him ran away, leaving him hanging
between the heavens and the earth.
10A certain man saw it, and told Joab, Behold, I saw Absalom
hanging in an oak.
11Joab said to the man, You saw him, why did you not strike
him down to the ground? I would have given you ten shekels of
silver and a girdle.
12The man told Joab, Though I should recieve 1,000 pieces of
silver, yet I would not put forth my hand against the king's son;
for in our hearing the king charged you, Abishai, and Ittai, Have
a care whoever you be, of the young man Absalom.
13Otherwise if I had dealt falsely against his life (for nothing is
hidden from the king) you yourself would have taken sides against
me.
14Joab said, I will not tarry thus with you. He took three darts
in his hand, and thrust them into the body of Absalom, while he
was yet alive in the midst of the oak.
15And ten young men, Joab's armor bearers, surrounded and
struck Absalom, and killed him.
16Then Joab blew the trumpet, and the troops returned from
pursuing Israel; for Joab restrained *and* spared them.
17They took Absalom, and cast him into a great pit in the forest,
and raised a very great heap of stones upon him; and all Israel fled
every one to his own home.

## New American Standard

27¶ Now when David had come to Mahanaim, Shobi the son of
Nahash from Rabbah of the sons of Ammon, Machir the son of
Ammiel from Lo-debar, and Barzillai the Gileadite from Rogelim,
28brought beds, basins, pottery, wheat, barley, flour, parched
*grain*, beans, lentils, parched *seeds*,
29honey, curds, sheep, and cheese of the herd, for David and
for the people who *were* with him, to eat; for they said, "The people
are hungry and weary and thirsty in the wilderness."

*Absalom Slain*

**18** THEN DAVID numbered the people who were with him
and set over them commanders of thousands and commanders of hundreds.
2And David sent the people out, one third under the command
of Joab, one third under the command of Abishai the son of Zeruiah, Joab's brother, and one third under the command of Ittai the
Gittite. And the king said to the people, "I myself will surely go
out with you also."
3But the people said, "You should not go out; for if we indeed
flee, they will not care about us, even if half of us die, they will
not care about us. But you are worth ten thousand of us; therefore
now it is better that you *be ready* to help us from the city."
4Then the king said to them, "Whatever seems best to you I
will do." So the king stood beside the gate, and all the people went
out by hundreds and thousands.
5And the king charged Joab and Abishai and Ittai, saying, "
*Deal* gently for my sake with the young man Absalom." And all
the people heard when the king charged all the commanders concerning Absalom.
6¶ Then the people went out into the field against Israel, and
the battle took place in the forest of Ephraim.
7And the people of Israel were defeated there before the servants of David, and the slaughter there that day was great, 20,000
men.
8For the battle there was spread over the whole countryside,
and the forest devoured more people that day than the sword
devoured.
9¶ Now Absalom happened to meet the servants of David. For
Absalom was riding on *his* mule, and the mule went under the
thick branches of a great oak. And his head caught fast in the oak,
so he was left hanging between heaven and earth, while the mule
that was under him kept going.
10When a certain man saw *it*, he told Joab and said, "Behold,
I saw Absalom hanging in an oak."
11Then Joab said to the man who had told him, "Now behold,
you saw *him!* Why then did you not strike him there to the ground?
And I would have given you ten *pieces* of silver and a belt."
12And the man said to Joab, "Even if I should receive a thousand *pieces of* silver in my hand, I would not put out my hand
against the king's son; for in our hearing the king charged you and
Abishai and Ittai, saying, 'Protect for me the young man Absalom!'
13"Otherwise, if I had dealt treacherously against his life (and
there is nothing hidden from the king), then you yourself would
have stood aloof."
14Then Joab said, "I will not waste time here with you." So he
took three spears in his hand and thrust them through the heart
of Absalom while he was yet alive in the midst of the oak.
15And ten young men who carried Joab's armor gathered
around and struck Absalom and killed him.
16¶ Then Joab blew the trumpet, and the people returned from
pursuing Israel, for Joab restrained the people.
17And they took Absalom and cast him into a deep pit in the
forest and erected over him a very great heap of stones. And all
Israel fled, each to his tent.

## New International

27When David came to Mahanaim, Shobi son of Nahash from
Rabbah of the Ammonites, and Makir son of Ammiel from Lo
Debar, and Barzillai the Gileadite from Rogelim 28brought bedding
and bowls and articles of pottery. They also brought wheat and
barley, flour and roasted grain, beans and lentils,[a] 29honey and
curds, sheep, and cheese from cows' milk for David and his people
to eat. For they said, "The people have become hungry and tired
and thirsty in the desert."

*Absalom's Death*

**18** DAVID MUSTERED the men who were with him and
appointed over them commanders of thousands and commanders of hundreds. 2David sent the troops out—a third under
the command of Joab, a third under Joab's brother Abishai son of
Zeruiah, and a third under Ittai the Gittite. The king told the
troops, "I myself will surely march out with you."
3But the men said, "You must not go out; if we are forced to flee,
they won't care about us. Even if half of us die, they won't care;
but you are worth ten thousand of us.[b] It would be better now for
you to give us support from the city."
4The king answered, "I will do whatever seems best to you."
So the king stood beside the gate while all the men marched out
in units of hundreds and of thousands. 5The king commanded
Joab, Abishai and Ittai, "Be gentle with the young man Absalom
for my sake." And all the troops heard the king giving orders
concerning Absalom to each of the commanders.
6The army marched into the field to fight Israel, and the battle
took place in the forest of Ephraim. 7There the army of Israel was
defeated by David's men, and the casualties that day were great—
twenty thousand men. 8The battle spread out over the whole
countryside, and the forest claimed more lives that day than the
sword.
9Now Absalom happened to meet David's men. He was riding
his mule, and as the mule went under the thick branches of a large
oak, Absalom's head got caught in the tree. He was left hanging
in midair, while the mule he was riding kept on going.
10When one of the men saw this, he told Joab, "I just saw
Absalom hanging in an oak tree."
11Joab said to the man who had told him this, "What! You saw
him? Why didn't you strike him to the ground right there? Then
I would have had to give you ten shekels[c] of silver and a warrior's
belt."
12But the man replied, "Even if a thousand shekels[d] were
weighed out into my hands, I would not lift my hand against the
king's son. In our hearing the king commanded you and Abishai
and Ittai, 'Protect the young man Absalom for my sake.[e]' 13And
if I had put my life in jeopardy[f] —and nothing is hidden from the
king—you would have kept your distance from me."
14Joab said, "I'm not going to wait like this for you." So he took
three javelins in his hand and plunged them into Absalom's heart
while Absalom was still alive in the oak tree. 15And ten of Joab's
armor-bearers surrounded Absalom, struck him and killed him.
16Then Joab sounded the trumpet, and the troops stopped pursuing Israel, for Joab halted them. 17They took Absalom, threw
him into a big pit in the forest and piled up a large heap of rocks
over him. Meanwhile, all the Israelites fled to their homes.

**NIV** [a] *28* Most Septuagint manuscripts and Syriac; Hebrew *lentils, and roasted grain* [b] *3* Two Hebrew manuscripts, some Septuagint manuscripts and Vulgate; most Hebrew manuscripts *care; for now there are ten thousand like us* [c] *11* That is, about 4 ounces (about 115 grams) [d] *12* That is, about 25 pounds (about 11 kilograms) [e] *12* A few Hebrew manuscripts, Septuagint, Vulgate and Syriac; most Hebrew manuscripts may be translated *Absalom, whoever you may be.* [f] *13* Or *Otherwise, if I had acted treacherously toward him*

## King James

18¶ Now Absalom in his lifetime had taken and reared up for himself a pillar, which *is* in the king's dale: for he said, I have no son to keep my name in remembrance: and he called the pillar after his own name: and it is called unto this day, Absalom's place.

19¶ Then said Ahimaaz the son of Zadok, Let me now run, and bear the king tidings, how that the LORD hath avenged him of his enemies.

20And Joab said unto him, Thou shalt not bear tidings this day, but thou shalt bear tidings another day: but this day thou shalt bear no tidings, because the king's son is dead.

21Then said Joab to Cushi, Go tell the king what thou hast seen. And Cushi bowed himself unto Joab, and ran.

22Then said Ahimaaz the son of Zadok yet again to Joab, But howsoever, let me, I pray thee, also run after Cushi. And Joab said, Wherefore wilt thou run, my son, seeing that thou hast no tidings ready?

23But howsoever, *said he,* let me run. And he said unto him, Run. Then Ahimaaz ran by the way of the plain, and overran Cushi.

24And David sat between the two gates: and the watchman went up to the roof over the gate unto the wall, and lifted up his eyes, and looked, and behold a man running alone.

25And the watchman cried, and told the king. And the king said, If he *be* alone, *there is* tidings in his mouth. And he came apace, and drew near.

26And the watchman saw another man running: and the watchman called unto the porter, and said, Behold *another* man running alone. And the king said, He also bringeth tidings.

27And the watchman said, Me thinketh the running of the foremost is like the running of Ahimaaz the son of Zadok. And the king said, He *is* a good man, and cometh with good tidings.

28And Ahimaaz called, and said unto the king, All is well. And he fell down to the earth upon his face before the king, and said, Blessed *be* the LORD thy God, which hath delivered up the men that lifted up their hand against my lord the king.

29And the king said, Is the young man Absalom safe? And Ahimaaz answered, When Joab sent the king's servant, and *me* thy servant, I saw a great tumult, but I knew not what *it was.*

30And the king said *unto him,* Turn aside, *and* stand here. And he turned aside, and stood still.

31And, behold, Cushi came; and Cushi said, Tidings, my lord the king: for the LORD hath avenged thee this day of all them that rose up against thee.

32And the king said unto Cushi, *Is* the young man Absalom safe? And Cushi answered, The enemies of my lord the king, and all that rise against thee to do *thee* hurt, be as *that* young man *is.*

33¶ And the king was much moved, and went up to the chamber over the gate, and wept: and as he went, thus he said, O my son Absalom, my son, my son Absalom! would God I had died for thee, O Absalom, my son, my son!

**19** AND IT was told Joab, Behold, the king weepeth and mourneth for Absalom.

2And the victory that day was *turned* into mourning unto all the people: for the people heard say that day how the king was grieved for his son.

3And the people gat them by stealth that day into the city, as people being ashamed steal away when they flee in battle.

4But the king covered his face, and the king cried with a loud voice, O my son Absalom, O Absalom, my son, my son!

## Amplified

18Now Absalom in his lifetime had reared up for himself a pillar, which is in the King's Valley, for he said, I have no son to keep my name in remembrance. He called the pillar after his own name; and to this day it is called Absalom's monument.

19Then said Ahimaaz son of Zadok, Let me now run, and bear the king tidings, how the Lord has avenged David of his enemies.

20Joab told him, You shall not carry news today, but another time. Today you shall bear no news for the king's son is dead.

21Then said Joab to Cushi [an Ethiopian], Go tell the king what you have seen. And the Cushite bowed to Joab, and ran.

22Then said Ahimaaz son of Zadok again to Joab, But anyhow, let me, I pray, also run after the Cushite. Joab said, Why should you run, my son, seeing you will have no reward, for you have not sufficient tidings?

23But he said, Let me run anyhow. So Joab said to him, Run. Then Ahimaaz ran by the way of the plain, and outran Cushi.

24Now David was sitting between two gates; and the watchman went up to the roof over the gate by the wall, and when he looked, he saw a man running alone.

25The watchman called out and told the king. The king said, If he is alone, he has news to tell. And he came on and drew near.

26Then the watchman saw another man running; and the watchman called to the gatekeeper, Behold another man running alone. The king said, He also brings news.

27The watchman said, I think the man in front runs like Ahimaaz son of Zadok. The king said, He is a good man, and comes with good tidings.

28And Ahimaaz called, and said to the king, All is well! And he fell down to the ground on his face before the king, and said, Blessed be the Lord your God, Who has shut up the men who lifted up their hand against my lord the king.

29The king said, Is the young man Absalom safe? Ahimaaz answered, When Joab the king's servant sent me, your servant, I saw a great tumult, but I do not know what it was.

30The king told him, Turn aside; stand here. And he turned aside, and stood still.

31And behold, the Cushite [Ethiopian] came; and he said, News, my lord the king! For the Lord has delivered you this day from all who rose up against you.

32The king said to the Cushite, Is the young man Absalom safe? The Cushite replied, May the enemies of my lord the king, and all that rise against you to do evil, be like that young man is.

33And the king was deeply moved, and went up to the chamber over the gate, and wept; and as he went, he said, O my son Absalom, my son, my son Absalom! Would God I had died for you, O Absalom, my son, my son!

**19** IT WAS told Joab, Behold, the king is weeping and mourning for Absalom.

2So the victory that day was turned into mourning for all the people; for they heard it said, The king grieves for his son.

3The people slipped into the city stealthily that day, as humiliated people steal away when they flee in battle.

4But the king covered his face, and cried with a loud voice, O my son Absalom, O Absalom, my son, my son!

## New American Standard

18Now Absalom in his lifetime had taken and set up for himself
a pillar which is in the King's Valley, for he said, "I have no son
to preserve my name." So he named the pillar after his own name,
and it is called Absalom's monument to this day.

*David Is Grief-stricken*

19¶ Then Ahimaaz the son of Zadok said, "Please let me run and
bring the king news that the LORD has freed him from the hand
of his enemies."
20But Joab said to him, "You are not the man to carry news this
day, but you shall carry news another day; however, you shall
carry no news today because the king's son is dead."
21Then Joab said to the Cushite, "Go, tell the king what you
have seen." So the Cushite bowed to Joab and ran.
22Now Ahimaaz the son of Zadok said once more to Joab, "But
whatever happens, please let me also run after the Cushite." And
Joab said, "Why would you run, my son, since you will have no
reward for going?"
23"But whatever happens," *he said,* "I will run." So he said to
him, "Run." Then Ahimaaz ran by way of the plain and passed
up the Cushite.
24¶ Now David was sitting between the two gates; and the
watchman went up to the roof of the gate by the wall, and raised
his eyes and looked, and behold, a man running by himself.
25And the watchman called and told the king. And the king
said, "If he is by himself there is good news in his mouth." And
he came nearer and nearer.
26Then the watchman saw another man running; and the
watchman called to the gatekeeper and said, "Behold, *another* man
running by himself." And the king said, "This one also is bringing
good news."
27And the watchman said, "I think the running of the first one
is like the running of Ahimaaz the son of Zadok." And the king
said, "This is a good man and comes with good news."
28¶ And Ahimaaz called and said to the king, "[a]All is well."
And he prostrated himself before the king with his face to the
ground. And he said, "Blessed is the LORD your God, who has
delivered up the men who lifted their hands against my lord the
king."
29And the king said, "Is it well with the young man Absalom?"
And Ahimaaz answered, "When Joab sent the king's servant, and
your servant, I saw a great tumult, but I did not know what *it was.*"
30Then the king said, "Turn aside and stand here." So he
turned aside and stood still.
31¶ And behold, the Cushite arrived, and the Cushite said, "Let
my lord the king receive good news, for the LORD has freed you
this day from the hand of all those who rose up against you."
32Then the king said to the Cushite, "Is it well with the young
man Absalom?" And the Cushite answered, "Let the enemies of
my lord the king, and all who rise up against you for evil, be as
that young man!"
33And the king was deeply moved and went up to the chamber
over the gate and wept. And thus he said as he walked, "O my
son Absalom, my son, my son Absalom! Would I had died instead
of you, O Absalom, my son, my son!"

*Joab Reproves David's Lament*

19 THEN IT was told Joab, "Behold, the king is weeping and
mourns for Absalom."
2And the victory that day was turned to mourning for all the
people, for the people heard *it* said that day, "The king is grieved
for his son."
3So the people went by stealth into the city that day, as people
who are humiliated steal away when they flee in battle.
4And the king covered his face and cried out with a loud voice,
"O my son Absalom, O Absalom, my son, my son!"

NAS [a] Lit., *Peace.*

## New International

18During his lifetime Absalom had taken a pillar and erected it
in the King's Valley as a monument to himself, for he thought, "I
have no son to carry on the memory of my name." He named the
pillar after himself, and it is called Absalom's Monument to this
day.

*David Mourns*

19Now Ahimaaz son of Zadok said, "Let me run and take the
news to the king that the LORD has delivered him from the hand
of his enemies."
20"You are not the one to take the news today," Joab told him.
"You may take the news another time, but you must not do so
today, because the king's son is dead."
21Then Joab said to a Cushite, "Go, tell the king what you have
seen." The Cushite bowed down before Joab and ran off.
22Ahimaaz son of Zadok again said to Joab, "Come what may,
please let me run behind the Cushite."
But Joab replied, "My son, why do you want to go? You don't
have any news that will bring you a reward."
23He said, "Come what may, I want to run."
So Joab said, "Run!" Then Ahimaaz ran by way of the plain[b]
and outran the Cushite.
24While David was sitting between the inner and outer gates,
the watchman went up to the roof of the gateway by the wall. As
he looked out, he saw a man running alone. 25The watchman
called out to the king and reported it.
The king said, "If he is alone, he must have good news." And
the man came closer and closer.
26Then the watchman saw another man running, and he called
down to the gatekeeper, "Look, another man running alone!"
The king said, "He must be bringing good news, too."
27The watchman said, "It seems to me that the first one runs
like Ahimaaz son of Zadok."
"He's a good man," the king said. "He comes with good news."
28Then Ahimaaz called out to the king, "All is well!" He bowed
down before the king with his face to the ground and said, "Praise
be to the LORD your God! He has delivered up the men who lifted
their hands against my lord the king."
29The king asked, "Is the young man Absalom safe?"
Ahimaaz answered, "I saw great confusion just as Joab was
about to send the king's servant and me, your servant, but I don't
know what it was."
30The king said, "Stand aside and wait here." So he stepped
aside and stood there.
31Then the Cushite arrived and said, "My lord the king, hear
the good news! The LORD has delivered you today from all who
rose up against you."
32The king asked the Cushite, "Is the young man Absalom
safe?"
The Cushite replied, "May the enemies of my lord the king and
all who rise up to harm you be like that young man."
33The king was shaken. He went up to the room over the
gateway and wept. As he went, he said: "O my son Absalom! My
son, my son Absalom! If only I had died instead of you—O Absalom, my son, my son!"

19 JOAB WAS told, "The king is weeping and mourning for
Absalom." 2And for the whole army the victory that day
was turned into mourning, because on that day the troops heard
it said, "The king is grieving for his son." 3The men stole into the
city that day as men steal in who are ashamed when they flee from
battle. 4The king covered his face and cried aloud, "O my son
Absalom! O Absalom, my son, my son!"

NIV [b] 23 That is, the plain of the Jordan

## King James

5 And Joab came into the house to the king, and said, Thou hast shamed this day the faces of all thy servants, which this day have saved thy life, and the lives of thy sons and of thy daughters, and the lives of thy wives, and the lives of thy concubines;

6 In that thou lovest thine enemies, and hatest thy friends. For thou hast declared this day, that thou regardest neither princes nor servants: for this day I perceive, that if Absalom had lived, and all we had died this day, then it had pleased thee well.

7 Now therefore arise, go forth, and speak comfortably unto thy servants: for I swear by the LORD, if thou go not forth, there will not tarry one with thee this night: and that will be worse unto thee than all the evil that befell thee from thy youth until now.

8 Then the king arose, and sat in the gate. And they told unto all the people, saying, Behold, the king doth sit in the gate. And all the people came before the king: for Israel had fled every man to his tent.

9 ¶ And all the people were at strife throughout all the tribes of Israel, saying, The king saved us out of the hand of our enemies, and he delivered us out of the hand of the Philistines; and now he is fled out of the land for Absalom.

10 And Absalom, whom we anointed over us, is dead in battle. Now therefore why speak ye not a word of bringing the king back?

11 ¶ And king David sent to Zadok and to Abiathar the priests, saying, Speak unto the elders of Judah, saying, Why are ye the last to bring the king back to his house? seeing the speech of all Israel is come to the king, *even* to his house.

12 Ye *are* my brethren, ye *are* my bones and my flesh: wherefore then are ye the last to bring back the king?

13 And say ye to Amasa, *Art* thou not of my bone, and of my flesh? God do so to me, and more also, if thou be not captain of the host before me continually in the room of Joab.

14 And he bowed the heart of all the men of Judah, even as *the heart of* one man; so that they sent *this word* unto the king, Return thou, and all thy servants.

15 So the king returned, and came to Jordan. And Judah came to Gilgal, to go to meet the king, to conduct the king over Jordan.

16 ¶ And Shimei the son of Gera, a Benjamite, which *was* of Bahurim, hasted and came down with the men of Judah to meet king David.

17 And *there were* a thousand men of Benjamin with him, and Ziba the servant of the house of Saul, and his fifteen sons and his twenty servants with him; and they went over Jordan before the king.

18 And there went over a ferry boat to carry over the king's household, and to do what he thought good. And Shimei the son of Gera fell down before the king, as he was come over Jordan;

19 And said unto the king, Let not my lord impute iniquity unto me, neither do thou remember that which thy servant did perversely the day that my lord the king went out of Jerusalem, that the king should take it to his heart.

20 For thy servant doth know that I have sinned: therefore, behold, I am come the first this day of all the house of Joseph to go down to meet my lord the king.

21 But Abishai the son of Zeruiah answered and said, Shall not Shimei be put to death for this, because he cursed the LORD's anointed?

22 And David said, What have I to do with you, ye sons of Zeruiah, that ye should this day be adversaries unto me? shall there any man be put to death this day in Israel? for do not I know that I *am* this day king over Israel?

23 Therefore the king said unto Shimei, Thou shalt not die. And the king sware unto him.

## Amplified

5 And Joab came into the house to the king, and said, You have today covered the faces of all your servants with shame, who this day have saved your life and the lives of your sons and your daughters, and the lives of your wives and concubines;

6 For you love those who hate you, and hate those who love you. You have declared today that princes and servants are nothing to you; for today I see that if Absalom had lived and all the rest of us had died, you would be well pleased.

7 So now arise, go out and speak kindly and encouragingly to your servants; for I swear by the Lord, if you do not go, not a man will remain with you this night; and this will be worse for you than all the evil that has befallen you from your youth until now.

8 Then the king arose and sat in the gate. And all [his followers] were told, The king is sitting in the gate; and *they* all came before the king. Now Israel [Absalom's troops] had fled every man to his home.

9 And all the people were at strife throughout all the tribes of Israel, saying, The king delivered us from the hand of our enemies, and he saved us from the hand of the Philistines; and now he has fled out of the land from Absalom.

10 And Absalom, whom we anointed over us, is dead in battle. So now, why do you say nothing about bringing back the king?

11 And King David sent to Zadok and to Abiathar the priests, saying, Say to the elders of Judah, Why are you the last to bring the king back to his house, when the word of all Israel has come to the king, to bring him to his house?

12 You are my kinsmen, you are my bone and my flesh. Why then are you the last to bring back the king?

13 And say to Amasa, Are you not of my bone and of my flesh? God do so to me and more also, if you are not commander of my army hereafter in place of Joab.

14 He inclined the heart of all the men of Judah as one man, so they sent word to [him], Return, you and all your servants.

15 So [David] returned, and came to Jordan. And Judah came to Gilgal, to meet the king, to conduct him over Jordan.

16 And Shimei son of Gera, a Benjamite of Bahurim, hastily came down with the men of Judah to meet King David,

17 And 1,000 men of Benjamin with him. And Ziba servant of the house of Saul, and his fifteen sons and twenty servants with him, rushed to the Jordan *and* pressed quickly into the king's presence.

18 And there went over a ferry boat to bring over the king's household, and to do what he thought good. And Shimei son of Gera fell down before the king, as David came to the Jordan,

19 And said to the king, Let not my lord impute iniquity to me *and* hold me guilty, or remember what your servant did the day my lord went out of Jerusalem [when Shimei grossly insulted David]; may the king not take it to heart.

20 For your servant knows that I have sinned; therefore, behold, I am today first of all the house of Joseph to come down to meet my lord the king.

21 But Abishai son of Zeruiah said, Shall not Shimei be put to death for this, because he cursed the Lord's anointed?

22 David said, What have I to do with you, you sons of Zeruiah, that you should be an adversary to me today? Shall any one be put to death today in Israel? For do not I know I am this day king over Israel?

23 Therefore the king said to Shimei, You shall not die [at my hand]. And the king gave him his oath. [I Kings 2:44-46.]

## New American Standard

5Then Joab came into the house to the king and said, "Today
you have covered with shame the faces of all your servants, who
today have saved your life and the lives of your sons and daughters, the lives of your wives, and the lives of your concubines,
6by loving those who hate you, and by hating those who love
you. For you have shown today that princes and servants are
nothing to you; for I know this day that if Absalom were alive and
all of us were dead today, then you would be pleased.
7"Now therefore arise, go out and speak kindly to your servants, for I swear by the LORD, if you do not go out, surely not a
man will pass the night with you, and this will be worse for you
than all the evil that has come upon you from your youth until
now."

*David Restored as King*

8So the king arose and sat in the gate. When they told all the
people, saying, "Behold, the king is sitting in the gate," then all
the people came before the king.
¶Now Israel had fled, each to his tent.
9And all the people were quarreling throughout all the tribes
of Israel, saying, "The king delivered us from the hand of our
enemies and saved us from the hand of the Philistines, but now
he has fled out of the land from Absalom.
10"However, Absalom, whom we anointed over us, has died in
battle. Now then, why are you silent about bringing the king
back?"
**11**¶ Then King David sent to Zadok and Abiathar the priests,
saying, "Speak to the elders of Judah, saying, 'Why are you the
last to bring the king back to his house, since the word of all Israel
has come to the king, *even* to his house?
12'You are my brothers; you are my bone and my flesh. Why
then should you be the last to bring back the king?'
13"And say to Amasa, 'Are you not my bone and my flesh? May
God do so to me, and more also, if you will not be commander of
the army before me continually in place of Joab.' "
14Thus he turned the hearts of all the men of Judah as one man,
so that they sent *word* to the king, *saying*, "Return, you and all your
servants."
15The king then returned and came as far as the Jordan. And
Judah came to Gilgal in order to go to meet the king, to bring the
king across the Jordan.
**16**¶ Then Shimei the son of Gera, the Benjamite who was from
Bahurim, hurried and came down with the men of Judah to meet
King David.
17And there were a thousand men of Benjamin with him, with
Ziba the servant of the house of Saul, and his fifteen sons and his
twenty servants with him; and they rushed to the Jordan before
the king.
18Then they kept crossing the ford to bring over the king's
household, and to do what was good in his sight. And Shimei the
son of Gera fell down before the king as he was about to cross the
Jordan.
19So he said to the king, "Let not my lord consider me guilty,
nor remember what your servant did wrong on the day when my
lord the king came out from Jerusalem, so that the king should take
*it* to heart.
20"For your servant knows that I have sinned; therefore behold,
I have come today, the first of all the house of Joseph to go down
to meet my lord the king."
21But Abishai the son of Zeruiah answered and said, "Should
not Shimei be put to death for this, because he cursed the LORD's
anointed?"
22David then said, "What have I to do with you, O sons of
Zeruiah, that you should this day be an adversary to me? Should
any man be put to death in Israel today? For do I not know that
I am king over Israel today?"
23And the king said to Shimei, "You shall not die." Thus the
king swore to him.

## New International

5Then Joab went into the house to the king and said, "Today
you have humiliated all your men, who have just saved your life
and the lives of your sons and daughters and the lives of your
wives and concubines. 6You love those who hate you and hate
those who love you. You have made it clear today that the commanders and their men mean nothing to you. I see that you would
be pleased if Absalom were alive today and all of us were dead.
7Now go out and encourage your men. I swear by the LORD that
if you don't go out, not a man will be left with you by nightfall.
This will be worse for you than all the calamities that have come
upon you from your youth till now."
8So the king got up and took his seat in the gateway. When the
men were told, "The king is sitting in the gateway," they all came
before him.

*David Returns to Jerusalem*

Meanwhile, the Israelites had fled to their homes. 9Throughout
the tribes of Israel, the people were all arguing with each other,
saying, "The king delivered us from the hand of our enemies; he
is the one who rescued us from the hand of the Philistines. But
now he has fled the country because of Absalom; 10and Absalom,
whom we anointed to rule over us, has died in battle. So why do
you say nothing about bringing the king back?"
11King David sent this message to Zadok and Abiathar, the
priests: "Ask the elders of Judah, 'Why should you be the last to
bring the king back to his palace, since what is being said throughout Israel has reached the king at his quarters? 12You are my
brothers, my own flesh and blood. So why should you be the last
to bring back the king?' 13And say to Amasa, 'Are you not my own
flesh and blood? May God deal with me, be it ever so severely, if
from now on you are not the commander of my army in place of
Joab.' "
14He won over the hearts of all the men of Judah as though they
were one man. They sent word to the king, "Return, you and all
your men." 15Then the king returned and went as far as the Jordan.
Now the men of Judah had come to Gilgal to go out and meet
the king and bring him across the Jordan. 16Shimei son of Gera,
the Benjamite from Bahurim, hurried down with the men of Judah
to meet King David. 17With him were a thousand Benjamites,
along with Ziba, the steward of Saul's household, and his fifteen
sons and twenty servants. They rushed to the Jordan, where the
king was. 18They crossed at the ford to take the king's household
over and to do whatever he wished.
When Shimei son of Gera crossed the Jordan, he fell prostrate
before the king 19and said to him, "May my lord not hold me
guilty. Do not remember how your servant did wrong on the day
my lord the king left Jerusalem. May the king put it out of his mind.
20For I your servant know that I have sinned, but today I have
come here as the first of the whole house of Joseph to come down
and meet my lord the king."
21Then Abishai son of Zeruiah said, "Shouldn't Shimei be put
to death for this? He cursed the LORD's anointed."
22David replied, "What do you and I have in common, you sons
of Zeruiah? This day you have become my adversaries! Should
anyone be put to death in Israel today? Do I not know that today
I am king over Israel?" 23So the king said to Shimei, "You shall not
die." And the king promised him on oath.

## King James

24¶ And Mephibosheth the son of Saul came down to meet the king, and had neither dressed his feet, nor trimmed his beard, nor washed his clothes, from the day the king departed until the day he came *again* in peace.

25And it came to pass, when he was come to Jerusalem to meet the king, that the king said unto him, Wherefore wentest not thou with me, Mephibosheth?

26And he answered, My lord, O king, my servant deceived me: for thy servant said, I will saddle me an ass, that I may ride thereon, and go to the king; because thy servant *is* lame.

27And he hath slandered thy servant unto my lord the king; but my lord the king *is* as an angel of God: do therefore *what is* good in thine eyes.

28For all *of* my father's house were but dead men before my lord the king: yet didst thou set thy servant among them that did eat at thine own table. What right therefore have I yet to cry any more unto the king?

29And the king said unto him, Why speakest thou any more of thy matters? I have said, Thou and Ziba divide the land.

30And Mephibosheth said unto the king, Yea, let him take all, forasmuch as my lord the king is come again in peace unto his own house.

31¶ And Barzillai the Gileadite came down from Rogelim, and went over Jordan with the king, to conduct him over Jordan.

32Now Barzillai was a very aged man, *even* fourscore years old: and he had provided the king of sustenance while he lay at Mahanaim; for he *was* a very great man.

33And the king said unto Barzillai, Come thou over with me, and I will feed thee with me in Jerusalem.

34And Barzillai said unto the king, How long have I to live, that I should go up with the king unto Jerusalem?

35I *am* this day fourscore years old: *and* can I discern between good and evil? can thy servant taste what I eat or what I drink? can I hear any more the voice of singing men and singing women? wherefore then should thy servant be yet a burden unto my lord the king?

36Thy servant will go a little way over Jordan with the king: and why should the king recompense it me with such a reward?

37Let thy servant, I pray thee, turn back again, that I may die in mine own city, *and be buried* by the grave of my father and of my mother. But behold thy servant Chimham; let him go over with my lord the king; and do to him what shall seem good unto thee.

38And the king answered, Chimham shall go over with me, and I will do to him that which shall seem good unto thee: and whatsoever thou shalt require of me, *that* will I do for thee.

39And all the people went over Jordan. And when the king was come over, the king kissed Barzillai, and blessed him; and he returned unto his own place.

40Then the king went on to Gilgal, and Chimham went on with him: and all the people of Judah conducted the king, and also half the people of Israel.

41¶ And, behold, all the men of Israel came to the king, and said unto the king, Why have our brethren the men of Judah stolen thee away, and have brought the king, and his household, and all David's men with him, over Jordan?

42And all the men of Judah answered the men of Israel, Because the king *is* near of kin to us: wherefore then be ye angry for this matter? have we eaten at all of the king's *cost?* or hath he given us any gift?

43And the men of Israel answered the men of Judah, and said, We have ten parts in the king, and we have also more *right* in David than ye: why then did ye despise us, that our advice should not be first had in bringing back our king? And the words of the men of Judah were fiercer than the words of the men of Israel.

## Amplified

24Mephibosheth the son [grandson] of Saul came down to meet the king, and had not dressed his feet, trimmed his beard, or washed his clothes, from the day the king left until he returned in peace *and* safety.

25And when he came to Jerusalem to meet the king, David said to him, Why did you not go with me, Mephibosheth?

26He said, My lord, O king, my servant [Ziba] deceived me; for I said, Saddle me the donkey that I may ride on it and go to the king, for your servant is lame [but he took the donkey and left without me].

27He has slandered your servant to my lord the king; but the king is as an angel of God; so do what is good in your eyes.

28For all of my father's house were but doomed to death before my lord the king; yet you set your servant among those who ate at your own table. What right therefore have I to cry any more to the king?

29The king said to him, Why speak any more of your affairs? I say, You and Ziba divide the land.

30Mephibosheth said to the king, Oh, let him take it all, since my lord the king has returned home in safety *and* peace.

31Now Barzillai the Gileadite came down from Rogelim, and went on to the Jordan with the king to conduct him over Jordan.

32Now Barzillai was a very aged man, even eighty years old; and he had provided the king with food while he remained at Mahanaim; for he was a very great man.

33And the king said to Barzillai, Come over with me, and I will provide for you with me Jerusalem.

34And Barzillai said to the king, How much longer have I to live, that it would be worthwhile for me to go up with the king to Jerusalem?

35I am this day eighty years old; could I now [be useful as a counselor to] discern between good and evil? Can your servant appreciate what I eat or drink? Can I longer enjoy the voice of singing men and women? Why then should your servant be still a burden to my lord the king?

36Your servant will only go over the Jordan with the king. Why should the king repay me with such a reward?

37Let your servant turn back again, that I may die in my own city, and be buried by the grave of my father and mother. But here is your servant Chimham; let him go over with my lord the king; and do to him what shall seem good to you.

38The king answered, Chimham shall go over with me, and I will do to him what seems good to you; and whatever you ask of me I will do for you.

39So all the people went over Jordan. When the king had crossed over, he kissed Barzillai, and blessed him; and [the great man] returned to his own place.

40Then the king went on to Gilgal, and Chimham went with him; and all the people of Judah and also half the people of Israel escorted the king.

41And all the men of Israel came to the king, and said to him, Why have our kinsmen the men of Judah stolen you away, and have brought the king and his household over Jordan, and all David's men with him?

42But all the men of Judah answered the men of Israel, Because the king is near of kin to us. Why then be angry about it? Have we eaten at all at the king's expense? Or has he given us any gift?

43Then the men of Israel answered the men of Judah, We have ten [tribes'] shares in the king, and we have more right in David than you have; why then did you despise *and* ignore us? Were we not the first to speak of our bringing back our king? But the words of the men of Judah were more violent than the charges of the men of Israel.

## New American Standard

24¶ Then Mephibosheth the [a]son of Saul came down to meet the
king; and he had neither cared for his feet, nor trimmed his mustache, nor washed his clothes, from the day the king departed until
the day he came *home* in peace.
25And it was when he came from Jerusalem to meet the king,
that the king said to him, "Why did you not go with me, Mephibosheth?"
26So he answered, "O my lord, the king, my servant deceived
me; for your servant said, 'I will saddle a donkey for myself that
I may ride on it and go with the king,' because your servant is lame.
27"Moreover, he has slandered your servant to my lord the
king; but my lord the king is like the angel of God, therefore do
what is good in your sight.
28"For all my father's household was nothing but dead men
before my lord the king; yet you set your servant among those who
ate at your own table. What right do I have yet that I should
complain anymore to the king?"
29So the king said to him, "Why do you still speak of your
affairs? I have decided, 'You and Ziba shall divide the land.'"
30And Mephibosheth said to the king, "Let him even take it all,
since my lord the king has come safely to his own house."
31¶ Now Barzillai the Gileadite had come down from Rogelim;
and he went on to the Jordan with the king to escort him over the
Jordan.
32Now Barzillai was very old, being eighty years old; and he had
sustained the king while he stayed at Mahanaim, for he was a very
great man.
33And the king said to Barzillai, "You cross over with me and
I will sustain you in Jerusalem with me."
34But Barzillai said to the king, "How long have I yet to live, that
I should go up with the king to Jerusalem?
35"I am now eighty years old. Can I distinguish between good
and bad? Or can your servant taste what I eat or what I drink? Or
can I hear anymore the voice of singing men and women? Why
then should your servant be an added burden to my lord the king?
36"Your servant would merely cross over the Jordan with the
king. Why should the king compensate me *with* this reward?
37"Please let your servant return, that I may die in my own city
near the grave of my father and my mother. However, here is your
servant Chimham, let him cross over with my lord the king, and
do for him what is good in your sight."
38And the king answered, "Chimham shall cross over with me,
and I will do for him what is good in your sight; and whatever you
require of me, I will do for you."
39All the people crossed over the Jordan and the king crossed
too. The king then kissed Barzillai and blessed him, and he returned to his place.
40¶ Now the king went on to Gilgal, and Chimham went on with
him; and all the people of Judah and also half the people of Israel
accompanied the king.
41And behold, all the men of Israel came to the king and said
to the king, "Why had our brothers the men of Judah stolen you
away, and brought the king and his household and all David's men
with him over the Jordan?"
42Then all the men of Judah answered the men of Israel, "Because the king is a close relative to us. Why then are you angry
about this matter? Have we eaten at all at the king's *expense*, or has
anything been taken for us?"
43But the men of Israel answered the men of Judah and said,
"We have ten parts in the king, therefore we also have more *claim*
on David than you. Why then did you treat us with contempt? Was
it not our advice first to bring back our king?" Yet the words of the
men of Judah were harsher than the words of the men of Israel.

## New International

24Mephibosheth, Saul's grandson, also went down to meet the
king. He had not taken care of his feet or trimmed his mustache
or washed his clothes from the day the king left until the day he
returned safely. 25When he came from Jerusalem to meet the king,
the king asked him, "Why didn't you go with me, Mephibosheth?"
26He said, "My lord the king, since I your servant am lame, I
said, 'I will have my donkey saddled and will ride on it, so I can
go with the king.' But Ziba my servant betrayed me. 27And he has
slandered your servant to my lord the king. My lord the king is like
an angel of God; so do whatever pleases you. 28All my grandfather's descendants deserved nothing but death from my lord the
king, but you gave your servant a place among those who sat at
your table. So what right do I have to make any more appeals to
the king?"
29The king said to him, "Why say more? I order you and Ziba
to divide the fields."
30Mephibosheth said to the king, "Let him take everything,
now that my lord the king has arrived home safely."
31Barzillai the Gileadite also came down from Rogelim to cross
the Jordan with the king and to send him on his way from there.
32Now Barzillai was a very old man, eighty years of age. He had
provided for the king during his stay in Mahanaim, for he was a
very wealthy man. 33The king said to Barzillai, "Cross over with
me and stay with me in Jerusalem, and I will provide for you."
34But Barzillai answered the king, "How many more years will
I live, that I should go up to Jerusalem with the king? 35I am now
eighty years old. Can I tell the difference between what is good and
what is not? Can your servant taste what he eats and drinks? Can
I still hear the voices of men and women singers? Why should your
servant be an added burden to my lord the king? 36Your servant
will cross over the Jordan with the king for a short distance, but
why should the king reward me in this way? 37Let your servant
return, that I may die in my own town near the tomb of my father
and mother. But here is your servant Kimham. Let him cross over
with my lord the king. Do for him whatever pleases you."
38The king said, "Kimham shall cross over with me, and I will
do for him whatever pleases you. And anything you desire from
me I will do for you."
39So all the people crossed the Jordan, and then the king
crossed over. The king kissed Barzillai and gave him his blessing,
and Barzillai returned to his home.
40When the king crossed over to Gilgal, Kimham crossed with
him. All the troops of Judah and half the troops of Israel had taken
the king over.
41Soon all the men of Israel were coming to the king and saying
to him, "Why did our brothers, the men of Judah, steal the king
away and bring him and his household across the Jordan, together
with all his men?"
42All the men of Judah answered the men of Israel, "We did this
because the king is closely related to us. Why are you angry about
it? Have we eaten any of the king's provisions? Have we taken
anything for ourselves?"
43Then the men of Israel answered the men of Judah, "We have
ten shares in the king; and besides, we have a greater claim on
David than you have. So why do you treat us with contempt? Were
we not the first to speak of bringing back our king?"
But the men of Judah responded even more harshly than the
men of Israel.

NAS [a] I.e., grandson

## King James

20 AND THERE happened to be there a man of Belial, whose
name *was* Sheba, the son of Bichri, a Benjamite: and he
blew a trumpet, and said, We have no part in David, neither have
we inheritance in the son of Jesse: every man to his tents, O Israel.
2So every man of Israel went up from after David, *and* followed
Sheba the son of Bichri: but the men of Judah clave unto their king,
from Jordan even to Jerusalem.
3¶ And David came to his house at Jerusalem; and the king took
the ten women *his* concubines, whom he had left to keep the
house, and put them in ward, and fed them, but went not in unto
them. So they were shut up unto the day of their death, living in
widowhood.
4¶ Then said the king to Amasa, Assemble me the men of Judah
within three days, and be thou here present.
5So Amasa went to assemble *the men of* Judah: but he tarried
longer than the set time which he had appointed him.
6And David said to Abishai, Now shall Sheba the son of Bichri
do us more harm than *did* Absalom: take thou thy lord's servants,
and pursue after him, lest he get him fenced cities, and escape us.
7And there went out after him Joab's men, and the Cherethites,
and the Pelethites, and all the mighty men: and they went out of
Jerusalem, to pursue after Sheba the son of Bichri.
8When they *were* at the great stone which *is* in Gibeon, Amasa
went before them. And Joab's garment that he had put on was
girded unto him, and upon it a girdle *with* a sword fastened upon
his loins in the sheath thereof; and as he went forth it fell out.
9And Joab said to Amasa, *Art* thou in health, my brother? And
Joab took Amasa by the beard with the right hand to kiss him.
10But Amasa took no heed to the sword that *was* in Joab's hand:
so he smote him therewith in the fifth *rib,* and shed out his bowels
to the ground, and struck him not again; and he died. So Joab and
Abishai his brother pursued after Sheba the son of Bichri.
11And one of Joab's men stood by him, and said, He that favour-
eth Joab, and he that *is* for David, *let him go* after Joab.
12And Amasa wallowed in blood in the midst of the highway.
And when the man saw that all the people stood still, he removed
Amasa out of the highway into the field, and cast a cloth upon him,
when he saw that every one that came by him stood still.
13When he was removed out of the highway, all the people
went on after Joab, to pursue after Sheba the son of Bichri.
14¶ And he went through all the tribes of Israel unto Abel, and
to Beth-maachah, and all the Berites: and they were gathered
together, and went also after him.
15And they came and besieged him in Abel of Beth-maachah,
and they cast up a bank against the city, and it stood in the trench:
and all the people that *were* with Joab battered the wall, to throw
it down.
16¶ Then cried a wise woman out of the city, Hear, hear; say,
I pray you, unto Joab, Come near hither, that I may speak with
thee.
17And when he was come near unto her, the woman said, *Art*
thou Joab? And he answered, I *am he.* Then she said unto him,
Hear the words of thine handmaid. And he answered, I do hear.
18Then she spake, saying, They were wont to speak in old time,
saying, They shall surely ask *counsel* at Abel: and so they ended *the
matter*.
19I *am one of them that are* peaceable *and* faithful in Israel: thou
seekest to destroy a city and a mother in Israel: why wilt thou
swallow up the inheritance of the LORD?
20And Joab answered and said, Far be it, far be it from me, that
I should swallow up or destroy.

## Amplified

20 THERE HAPPENED to be there a base *and* contemptible
fellow, named Sheba son of Bichri, a Benjamite. He blew
a trumpet, and said, We have no portion in David and no inheritance in the son of Jesse! Every man to his tents, O Israel!
2So all the men of Israel withdrew from David, and followed
Sheba son of Bichri; but the men of Judah stayed faithfully with
their king, from Jordan to Jerusalem.
3So David came to his house at Jerusalem. And the king took
the ten women his concubines, whom he had left to keep the
house, and put them away under guard, and provided for them,
but did not go in to them. So they were shut up to the day of their
death, living in widowhood.
4Then said the king to Amasa, Assemble the men of Judah to
me within three days, and you be present here.
5So Amasa went to assemble the men of Judah; but he tarried
longer than the set time which had been appointed him.
6And David said to Abishai, Now will Sheba son of Bichri do
us more harm than Absalom did. Take your lord's servants and
pursue him, lest he get him fenced cities, and snatch away our very
eyes.
7And there went after him Joab's men and [David's bodyguard]
the Cherethites and Pelethites, and all the mighty men, from
Jerusalem to pursue Sheba son of Bichri.
8When they were at the great stone in Gibeon, Amasa came to
meet them. Joab was wearing a soldier's garment, and over it was
a sheathed sword fastened around his hips, and as he went forward it fell out.
9Joab said to Amasa, Are you well, my brother? And Joab took
Amasa by the beard with the right hand [as if] to kiss him.
10But Amasa did not notice the sword in Joab's hand. So [Joab]
struck him [who was to have been his successor] with it in the
body, shedding his bowels to the ground without another blow,
and [soon] he died. So Joab and Abishai his brother pursued Sheba
the son of Bichri.
11And one of Joab's men stood by him, and said, Who favors
Joab and is for David, follow Joab.
12And Amasa wallowed in blood in the highway. And when the
man saw that all the people who came by stood still, he removed
Amasa out of the highway into the field and spread a cloth over
him.
13When Amasa was removed from the highway, all the people
went on after Joab, to pursue Sheba son of Bichri.
14Joab went through all the tribes of Israel to Abel of Beth-
maacah, and all the Berites assembled and also went after [Sheba]
ardently.
15And they came and besieged Sheba in Abel of Beth-maacah,
and they cast up a siege-mound against the city, and it stood
against the rampart; and all the men with Joab battered *and* under-
mined the wall to make it fall.
16Then a wise woman of the city cried, Hear, hear! Say to Joab,
Come here, so I can speak to you.
17And when he came near her, the woman said, Are you Joab?
He answered, I am. Then she said to him, Hear the words of your
handmaid. He answered, I am listening.
18Then she said, People used to say, Let them but ask counsel
at Abel; and so they settled the matter.
19I am one of the peaceable and faithful in Israel. You seek to
destroy a city which is a mother in Israel. Why will you swallow
up the inheritance of the Lord?
20Joab answered, Far be it, far be it from me, that I should
swallow up or destroy!

## New American Standard

*Sheba's Revolt*

20 NOW A worthless fellow happened to be there whose
name was Sheba, the son of Bichri, a Benjamite; and he
blew the trumpet and said,

"We have no portion in David,
Nor do we have inheritance in the son of Jesse;
Every man to his tents, O Israel!"

2So all the men of Israel withdrew from following David, *and*
followed Sheba the son of Bichri; but the men of Judah remained
steadfast to their king, from the Jordan even to Jerusalem.
3¶ Then David came to his house at Jerusalem, and the king
took the ten women, the concubines whom he had left to keep the
house, and placed them under guard and provided them with
sustenance, but did not go in to them. So they were shut up until
the day of their death, living as widows.
4¶ Then the king said to Amasa, "Call out the men of Judah
for me within three days, and be present here yourself."
5So Amasa went to call out *the men of* Judah, but he delayed
longer than the set time which he had appointed him.
6And David said to Abishai, "Now Sheba the son of Bichri will
do us more harm than Absalom; take your lord's servants and
pursue him, lest he find for himself fortified cities and escape from
our sight."
7So Joab's men went out after him, along with the Cherethites
and the Pelethites and all the mighty men; and they went out from
Jerusalem to pursue Sheba the son of Bichri.
8When they were at the large stone which is in Gibeon, Amasa
came to meet them. Now Joab was dressed in his military attire,
and over it was a belt with a sword in its sheath fastened at his
waist; and as he went forward, it fell out.
9And Joab said to Amasa, "Is it well with you, my brother?"
And Joab took Amasa by the beard with his right hand to kiss him.

*Amasa Murdered*

10But Amasa was not on guard against the sword which was in
Joab's hand so he struck him in the belly with it and poured out
his inward parts on the ground, and did not *strike* him again; and
he died. Then Joab and Abishai his brother pursued Sheba the son
of Bichri.
11Now there stood by him one of Joab's young men, and said,
"Whoever favors Joab and whoever is for David, *let him* follow
Joab."
12But Amasa lay wallowing in *his* blood in the middle of the
highway. And when the man saw that all the people stood still,
he removed Amasa from the highway into the field and threw a
garment over him when he saw that everyone who came by him
stood still.

*Revolt Put Down*

13As soon as he was removed from the highway, all the men
passed on after Joab to pursue Sheba the son of Bichri.
14Now he went through all the tribes of Israel to Abel even to
Beth-maacah and all the Berites; and they were gathered together
and also went after him.
15And they came and besieged him in Abel Beth-maacah, and
they cast up a mound against the city, and it stood by the rampart;
and all the people who were with Joab were wreaking destruction
in order to topple the wall.
16Then a wise woman called from the city, "Hear, hear! Please
tell Joab, 'Come here that I may speak with you.'"
17So he approached her, and the woman said, "Are you Joab?"
And he answered, "I am." Then she said to him, "Listen to the
words of your maidservant." And he answered, "I am listening."
18Then she spoke, saying, "Formerly they used to say, 'They
will surely ask *advice* at Abel,' and thus they ended *the dispute*.
19"I am of those who are peaceable *and* faithful in Israel. You
are seeking to destroy a city even a mother in Israel. Why would
you swallow up the inheritance of the LORD?"
20And Joab answered and said, "Far be it, far be it from me that
I should swallow up or destroy!

## New International

*Sheba Rebels Against David*

20 NOW A troublemaker named Sheba son of Bicri, a Benjamite, happened to be there. He sounded the trumpet and
shouted,

"We have no share in David,
no part in Jesse's son!
Every man to his tent, O Israel!"

2So all the men of Israel deserted David to follow Sheba son of
Bicri. But the men of Judah stayed by their king all the way from
the Jordan to Jerusalem.
3When David returned to his palace in Jerusalem, he took the
ten concubines he had left to take care of the palace and put them
in a house under guard. He provided for them, but did not lie with
them. They were kept in confinement till the day of their death,
living as widows.
4Then the king said to Amasa, "Summon the men of Judah to
come to me within three days, and be here yourself." 5But when
Amasa went to summon Judah, he took longer than the time the
king had set for him.
6David said to Abishai, "Now Sheba son of Bicri will do us more
harm than Absalom did. Take your master's men and pursue him,
or he will find fortified cities and escape from us." 7So Joab's men
and the Kerethites and Pelethites and all the mighty warriors went
out under the command of Abishai. They marched out from
Jerusalem to pursue Sheba son of Bicri.
8While they were at the great rock in Gibeon, Amasa came to
meet them. Joab was wearing his military tunic, and strapped over
it at his waist was a belt with a dagger in its sheath. As he stepped
forward, it dropped out of its sheath.
9Joab said to Amasa, "How are you, my brother?" Then Joab
took Amasa by the beard with his right hand to kiss him. 10Amasa
was not on his guard against the dagger in Joab's hand, and Joab
plunged it into his belly, and his intestines spilled out on the
ground. Without being stabbed again, Amasa died. Then Joab and
his brother Abishai pursued Sheba son of Bicri.
11One of Joab's men stood beside Amasa and said, "Whoever
favors Joab, and whoever is for David, let him follow Joab!"
12Amasa lay wallowing in his blood in the middle of the road, and
the man saw that all the troops came to a halt there. When he
realized that everyone who came up to Amasa stopped, he
dragged him from the road into a field and threw a garment over
him. 13After Amasa had been removed from the road, all the men
went on with Joab to pursue Sheba son of Bicri.
14Sheba passed through all the tribes of Israel to Abel Beth
Maacah[a] and through the entire region of the Berites, who gathered together and followed him. 15All the troops with Joab came
and besieged Sheba in Abel Beth Maacah. They built a siege ramp
up to the city, and it stood against the outer fortifications. While
they were battering the wall to bring it down, 16a wise woman
called from the city, "Listen! Listen! Tell Joab to come here so I can
speak to him." 17He went toward her, and she asked, "Are you
Joab?"

"I am," he answered.

She said, "Listen to what your servant has to say."

"I'm listening," he said.

18She continued, "Long ago they used to say, 'Get your answer
at Abel,' and that settled it. 19We are the peaceful and faithful in
Israel. You are trying to destroy a city that is a mother in Israel.
Why do you want to swallow up the LORD's inheritance?"
20"Far be it from me!" Joab replied, "Far be it from me to
swallow up or destroy! 21That is not the case. A man named Sheba

NIV [a] 14 Or *Abel, even Beth Maacah*; also in verse 15

## King James

21The matter *is* not so: but a man of mount Ephraim, Sheba the
son of Bichri by name, hath lifted up his hand against the king, *even*
against David: deliver him only, and I will depart from the city.
And the woman said unto Joab, Behold, his head shall be thrown
to thee over the wall.
22Then the woman went unto all the people in her wisdom.
And they cut off the head of Sheba the son of Bichri, and cast *it*
out to Joab. And he blew a trumpet, and they retired from the city,
every man to his tent. And Joab returned to Jerusalem unto the
king.
23¶ Now Joab *was* over all the host of Israel: and Benaiah the son
of Jehoiada *was* over the Cherethites and over the Pelethites:
24And Adoram *was* over the tribute: and Jehoshaphat the son
of Ahilud *was* recorder:
25And Sheva *was* scribe: and Zadok and Abiathar *were* the
priests:
26And Ira also the Jairite was a chief ruler about David.

**21** THEN THERE was a famine in the days of David three
years, year after year; and David inquired of the LORD.
And the LORD answered, *It is* for Saul, and for *his* bloody house,
because he slew the Gibeonites.
2And the king called the Gibeonites, and said unto them; (now
the Gibeonites *were* not of the children of Israel, but of the remnant
of the Amorites; and the children of Israel had sworn unto them:
and Saul sought to slay them in his zeal to the children of Israel
and Judah.)
3Wherefore David said unto the Gibeonites, What shall I do for
you? and wherewith shall I make the atonement, that ye may bless
the inheritance of the LORD?
4And the Gibeonites said unto him, We will have no silver nor
gold of Saul, nor of his house; neither for us shalt thou kill any man
in Israel. And he said, What ye shall say, *that* will I do for you.
5And they answered the king, The man that consumed us, and
that devised against us *that* we should be destroyed from remaining in any of the coasts of Israel,
6Let seven men of his sons be delivered unto us, and we will
hang them up unto the LORD in Gibeah of Saul, *whom* the LORD
did choose. And the king said, I will give *them*.
7But the king spared Mephibosheth, the son of Jonathan the son
of Saul, because of the LORD's oath that *was* between them, between David and Jonathan the son of Saul.
8But the king took the two sons of Rizpah the daughter of Aiah,
whom she bare unto Saul, Armoni and Mephibosheth; and the five
sons of Michal the daughter of Saul, whom she brought up for
Adriel the son of Barzillai the Meholathite:
9And he delivered them into the hands of the Gibeonites, and
they hanged them in the hill before the LORD: and they fell *all* seven
together, and were put to death in the days of harvest, in the first
*days*, in the beginning of barley harvest.
10¶ And Rizpah the daughter of Aiah took sackcloth, and spread
it for her upon the rock, from the beginning of harvest until water
dropped upon them out of heaven, and suffered neither the birds
of the air to rest on them by day, nor the beasts of the field by night.
11And it was told David what Rizpah the daughter of Aiah, the
concubine of Saul, had done.
12¶ And David went and took the bones of Saul and the bones
of Jonathan his son from the men of Jabesh-gilead, which had
stolen them from the street of Beth-shan, where the Philistines had
hanged them, when the Philistines had slain Saul in Gilboa:
13And he brought up from thence the bones of Saul and the
bones of Jonathan his son; and they gathered the bones of them
that were hanged.

## Amplified

21That is not true. But a man of the hill country of Ephraim,
Sheba son of Bichri, has lifted up his hand against King David.
Deliver him only, and I will depart from the city. And the woman
said, Behold, his head shall be thrown to you over the wall.
22Then the woman in her wisdom went to all the people. And
they cut off the head of Sheba son of Bichri, and cast it down to
Joab. So he blew the trumpet, and they retired from the city, every
man to his own home. And Joab returned to Jerusalem to the king.
[Eccl. 9:13-16.]
23Joab was over the host of Israel; Benaiah son of Jehoiada was
over [the king's bodyguard] the Cherethites and Pelethites;
24Adoram was over the tribute; Jehoshaphat son of Ahilud was
recorder;
25Sheva was scribe, and Zadok and Abiathar were the priests;
26Also Ira the Jairite was chief minister to David.

**21** THERE WAS a three years' famine in the days of David,
year after year; and David inquired of the Lord. The Lord
replied, It is on account of Saul and his bloody house, for he put
to death the Gibeonites.
2So the king called the Gibeonites. (Now the Gibeonites were
not Israelites, but of the remnant of the Amorites. The Israelites
had sworn to spare them, but Saul in his zeal for the people of
Israel and Judah had sought to slay the Gibeonites.)
3So David said to the Gibeonites, What shall I do for you? How
can I make atonement that you may bless the Lord's inheritance?
4The Gibeonites said to him, We will accept no silver or gold of
Saul, or of his house; neither for us shall you kill any man in Israel.
David said, I will do for you what you say.
5They said to the king, The man who consumed us and planned
to prevent us from remaining in any territory of Israel,
6Let seven men of his sons be delivered to us and we will hang
them up before the Lord at Gibeah of Saul, [on the mountain] of
the Lord. And the king said, I will give them.
7But the king spared Mephibosheth son of Jonathan, son of
Saul, because of the Lord's oath that was between David and
Jonathan son of Saul.
8But the king took the two sons of Rizpah daughter of Aiah,
whom she bore to Saul, Armoni and Mephibosheth, and the five
sons of [Merab] daughter of Saul, whom she bore to Adriel son of
Barzillai the Meholathite.
9He delivered them into the hands of the Gibeonites, and they
hung them up on the hill before the Lord, and all seven perished
together. They were put to death in the first days of barley harvest.
10Rizpah daughter of Aiah took sackcloth, and spread it for
herself on the rock, from the beginning of harvest until rain fell on
them, and she did not allow either the birds of the air to come upon
them by day, or the beasts of the field by night.
11It was told David what Rizpah daughter of Aiah, the concubine of Saul, had done.
12And David went and took the bones of Saul and Jonathan his
son from the men of Jabesh-gilead, who had stolen them from the
street of Beth-shan, where the Philistines had hung them up when
the Philistines had slain Saul in Gilboa;
13He brought from there the bones of Saul and of Jonathan his
son, and they gathered the bones of those who were hung up.

## New American Standard

21 "Such is not the case. But a man from the hill country of
Ephraim, Sheba the son of Bichri by name, has lifted up his hand
against King David. Only hand him over, and I will depart from
the city." And the woman said to Joab, "Behold, his head will be
thrown to you over the wall."
22 Then the woman wisely came to all the people. And they cut
off the head of Sheba the son of Bichri and threw it to Joab. So he
blew the trumpet, and they were dispersed from the city, each to
his tent. Joab also returned to the king at Jerusalem.
23 ¶ Now Joab was over the whole army of Israel, and Benaiah
the son of Jehoiada was over the Cherethites and the Pelethites;
24 and Adoram was over the forced labor, and Jehoshaphat the
son of Ahilud was the recorder;
25 and Sheva was scribe, and Zadok and Abiathar were priests;
26 and Ira the Jairite was also a priest to David.

*Gibeonite Revenge*

**21** NOW THERE was a famine in the days of David for three
years, year after year; and David sought the presence of
the LORD. And the LORD said, "It is for Saul and his bloody house,
because he put the Gibeonites to death."
2 So the king called the Gibeonites and spoke to them (now the
Gibeonites were not of the sons of Israel but of the remnant of the
Amorites, and the sons of Israel made a covenant with them, but
Saul had sought to kill them in his zeal for the sons of Israel and
Judah).
3 Thus David said to the Gibeonites, "What should I do for you?
And how can I make atonement that you may bless the inheritance
of the LORD?"
4 Then the Gibeonites said to him, "We have no *concern* of silver
or gold with Saul or his house, nor is it for us to put any man to
death in Israel." And he said, "I will do for you whatever you say."
5 So they said to the king, "The man who consumed us, and
who planned to exterminate us from remaining within any border
of Israel,
6 let seven men from his sons be given to us, and we will hang
them before the LORD in Gibeah of Saul, the chosen of the LORD."
And the king said, "I will give *them*."
7 ¶ But the king spared Mephibosheth, the son of Jonathan the
son of Saul, because of the oath of the LORD which was between
them, between David and Saul's son Jonathan.
8 So the king took the two sons of Rizpah the daughter of Aiah,
Armoni and Mephibosheth whom she had born to Saul, and the
five sons of Merab the daughter of Saul, whom she had born to
Adriel the son of Barzillai the Meholathite.
9 Then he gave them into the hands of the Gibeonites, and they
hanged them in the mountain before the LORD, so that the seven
of them fell together; and they were put to death in the first days
of harvest at the beginning of barley harvest.
10 ¶ And Rizpah the daughter of Aiah took sackcloth and spread
it for herself on the rock, from the beginning of harvest until it
rained on them from the sky; and she allowed neither the birds of
the sky to rest on them by day nor the beasts of the field by night.
11 When it was told David what Rizpah the daughter of Aiah,
the concubine of Saul, had done,
12 then David went and took the bones of Saul and the bones of
Jonathan his son from the men of Jabesh-gilead, who had stolen
them from the open square of Bethshan, where the Philistines had
hanged them on the day the Philistines struck down Saul in Gilboa.
13 And he brought up the bones of Saul and the bones of Jonathan his son from there, and they gathered the bones of those who
had been hanged.

## New International

son of Bicri, from the hill country of Ephraim, has lifted up his
hand against the king, against David. Hand over this one man, and
I'll withdraw from the city."
The woman said to Joab, "His head will be thrown to you from
the wall."
22 Then the woman went to all the people with her wise advice,
and they cut off the head of Sheba son of Bicri and threw it to Joab.
So he sounded the trumpet, and his men dispersed from the city,
each returning to his home. And Joab went back to the king in
Jerusalem.
23 Joab was over Israel's entire army; Benaiah son of Jehoiada
was over the Kerethites and Pelethites; 24 Adoniram[a] was in charge
of forced labor; Jehoshaphat son of Ahilud was recorder; 25 Sheva
was secretary; Zadok and Abiathar were priests; 26 and Ira the
Jairite was David's priest.

*The Gibeonites Avenged*

**21** DURING THE reign of David, there was a famine for three
successive years; so David sought the face of the LORD.
The LORD said, "It is on account of Saul and his blood-stained
house; it is because he put the Gibeonites to death."
2 The king summoned the Gibeonites and spoke to them. (Now
the Gibeonites were not a part of Israel but were survivors of the
Amorites; the Israelites had sworn to ⌊spare⌋ them, but Saul in his
zeal for Israel and Judah had tried to annihilate them.) 3 David
asked the Gibeonites, "What shall I do for you? How shall I make
amends so that you will bless the LORD's inheritance?"
4 The Gibeonites answered him, "We have no right to demand
silver or gold from Saul or his family, nor do we have the right to
put anyone in Israel to death."
"What do you want me to do for you?" David asked.
5 They answered the king, "As for the man who destroyed us
and plotted against us so that we have been decimated and have
no place anywhere in Israel, 6 let seven of his male descendants be
given to us to be killed and exposed before the LORD at Gibeah of
Saul—the Lord's chosen one."
So the king said, "I will give them to you."
7 The king spared Mephibosheth son of Jonathan, the son of
Saul, because of the oath before the LORD between David and
Jonathan son of Saul. 8 But the king took Armoni and Mephibosheth, the two sons of Aiah's daughter Rizpah, whom she had
borne to Saul, together with the five sons of Saul's daughter
Merab,[b] whom she had borne to Adriel son of Barzillai the Meholathite. 9 He handed them over to the Gibeonites, who killed and
exposed them on a hill before the LORD. All seven of them fell
together; they were put to death during the first days of the harvest, just as the barley harvest was beginning.
10 Rizpah daughter of Aiah took sackcloth and spread it out for
herself on a rock. From the beginning of the harvest till the rain
poured down from the heavens on the bodies, she did not let the
birds of the air touch them by day or the wild animals by night.
11 When David was told what Aiah's daughter Rizpah, Saul's concubine, had done, 12 he went and took the bones of Saul and his
son Jonathan from the citizens of Jabesh Gilead. (They had taken
them secretly from the public square at Beth Shan, where the
Philistines had hung them after they struck Saul down on Gilboa.)
13 David brought the bones of Saul and his son Jonathan from
there, and the bones of those who had been killed and exposed
were gathered up.

**NIV** [a] *24* Some Septuagint manuscripts (see also 1 Kings 4:6 and 5:14); Hebrew *Adoram* [b] *8* Two Hebrew manuscripts, some Septuagint manuscripts and Syriac (see also 1 Samuel 18:19); most Hebrew and Septuagint manuscripts *Michal*

## King James

14 And the bones of Saul and Jonathan his son buried they in the country of Benjamin in Zelah, in the sepulchre of Kish his father: and they performed all that the king commanded. And after that God was entreated for the land.

15¶ Moreover the Philistines had yet war again with Israel; and David went down, and his servants with him, and fought against the Philistines: and David waxed faint.

16 And Ishbi-benob, which *was* of the sons of the giant, the weight of whose spear *weighed* three hundred *shekels* of brass in weight, he being girded with a new *sword*, thought to have slain David.

17 But Abishai the son of Zeruiah succoured him, and smote the Philistine, and killed him. Then the men of David sware unto him, saying, Thou shalt go no more out with us to battle, that thou quench not the light of Israel.

18 And it came to pass after this, that there was again a battle with the Philistines at Gob: then Sibbechai the Hushathite slew Saph, which *was* of the sons of the giant.

19 And there was again a battle in Gob with the Philistines, where Elhanan the son of Jaare-oregim, a Bethlehemite, slew *the brother of* Goliath the Gittite, the staff of whose spear *was* like a weaver's beam.

20 And there was yet a battle in Gath, where was a man of *great* stature, that had on every hand six fingers, and on every foot six toes, four and twenty in number; and he also was born to the giant.

21 And when he defied Israel, Jonathan the son of Shimeah the brother of David slew him.

22 These four were born to the giant in Gath, and fell by the hand of David, and by the hand of his servants.

**22** AND DAVID spake unto the LORD the words of this song in the day *that* the LORD had delivered him out of the hand of all his enemies, and out of the hand of Saul:

2 And he said, The LORD *is* my rock, and my fortress, and my deliverer;

3 The God of my rock; in him will I trust: *he is* my shield, and the horn of my salvation, my high tower, and my refuge, my saviour; thou savest me from violence.

4 I will call on the LORD, *who is* worthy to be praised: so shall I be saved from mine enemies.

5 When the waves of death compassed me, the floods of ungodly men made me afraid;

6 The sorrows of hell compassed me about; the snares of death prevented me;

7 In my distress I called upon the LORD, and cried to my God: and he did hear my voice out of his temple, and my cry *did enter* into his ears.

8 Then the earth shook and trembled; the foundations of heaven moved and shook, because he was wroth.

9 There went up a smoke out of his nostrils, and fire out of his mouth devoured: coals were kindled by it.

10 He bowed the heavens also, and came down; and darkness *was* under his feet.

11 And he rode upon a cherub, and did fly: and he was seen upon the wings of the wind.

## Amplified

14 And the bones of Saul and Jonathan his son they buried in the country of Benjamin in Zelah, in the tomb of Kish [Saul's] father, and they did all that the king commanded. And after that God heard *and* answered when His people prayed for the land.

15 The Philistines had war again with Israel; and David went down, and his servants with him, and fought against the Philistines; and David became faint.

16 Ishbi-benob, who was of the sons of the giants, the weight of whose spear was 300 shekels of bronze, was girded with a new sword and thought to kill David.

17 But Abishai son of Zeruiah came to David's aid, and smote and killed the Philistine. Then David's men charged him, You shall no more go out with us to battle, lest you quench the lamp of Israel.

18 After this, there was again war with the Philistines of Gob [Gezer]. Then Sibbecai the Hushathite slew Saph [Sippai], who was a descendant of the giant.

19 There was again war at Gob with the Philistines; and Elhanan son of Jaare-oregim, a Bethlehemite, slew Goliath the Gittite, whose spear shaft was like a weaver's beam.

20 And there was again war at Gath, where there was a man of great stature, who had six fingers on each hand and six toes on each foot, twenty-four in number; he also was a descendant of the giants.

21 And when he defied Israel, Jonathan son of Shimei, brother of David, slew him.

22 These four were descended from the giant in Gath, and they fell by the hand of David and his servants.

**22** DAVID SPOKE to the Lord the words of this song on the day when the Lord delivered him from the hand of all his enemies, and from the hand of Saul:

2 He said, The Lord is my rock [of escape from Saul] and my fortress [in the wilderness] and my deliverer; [I Sam. 23:25, 28, 14.]

3 My God, my rock; in Him will I take refuge; my shield, and the horn of my salvation, my stronghold, and my refuge, my savior; You save me from violence. [Gen. 15:1.]

4 I call on the Lord, Who is worthy to be praised, and I am saved from my enemies.

5 For the waves of death enveloped me, the torrents of destruction made me afraid;

6 The cords of Sheol were entangling me; I encountered the snares of death.

7 In my distress I called upon the Lord; I cried to my God, and He heard my voice from His temple; my cry came into His ears.

8 Then the earth reeled and quaked; the foundations of the heavens trembled and shook, because He was angry.

9 Smoke went up from His nostrils, and devouring fire from His mouth; coals were kindled by it.

10 He bowed the heavens, and came down; thick darkness was under His feet.

11 He rode on a cherub, and flew; He was seen upon the wings of the wind.

## New American Standard

14And they buried the bones of Saul and Jonathan his son in the
country of Benjamin in Zela, in the grave of Kish his father; thus
they did all that the king commanded, and after that God was
moved by entreaty for the land.
15¶ Now when the Philistines were at war again with Israel,
David went down and his servants with him; and as they fought
against the Philistines, David became weary.
16Then Ishbi-benob, who was among the descendants of the
giant, the weight of whose spear was three hundred *shekels* of
bronze in weight, was girded with a new *sword*, and he intended
to kill David.
17But Abishai the son of Zeruiah helped him, and struck the
Philistine and killed him. Then the men of David swore to him,
saying, "You shall not go out again with us to battle, that you may
not extinguish the lamp of Israel."
18¶ Now it came about after this that there was war again with
the Philistines at Gob; then Sibbecai the Hushathite struck down
Saph, who was among the descendants of the giant.
19And there was war with the Philistines again at Gob, and
Elhanan the son of Jaare-oregim the Bethlehemite killed Goliath
the Gittite, the shaft of whose spear was like a weaver's beam.
20And there was war at Gath again, where there was a man of
*great* stature who had six fingers on each hand and six toes on each
foot, twenty-four in number; and he also had been born to the
giant.
21And when he defied Israel, Jonathan the son of Shimei, David's brother, struck him down.
22These four were born to the giant in Gath, and they fell by the
hand of David and by the hand of his servants.

*David's Psalm of Deliverance*

**22** AND DAVID spoke the words of this song to the LORD in the day that the LORD delivered him from the hand of all his enemies and from the hand of Saul.
2And he said,

"The LORD is my rock and my fortress and my deliverer;
3 My God, my rock, in whom I take refuge;
My shield and the horn of my salvation, my stronghold
and my refuge;
My savior, Thou dost save me from violence.
4 "I call upon the LORD, who is worthy to be praised;
And I am saved from my enemies.
5 "For the waves of death encompassed me;
The torrents of destruction overwhelmed me;
6 The cords of Sheol surrounded me;
The snares of death confronted me.
7 "In my distress I called upon the LORD,
Yes, I cried to my God;
And from His temple He heard my voice,
And my cry for help *came* into His ears.
8 "Then the earth shook and quaked,
The foundations of heaven were trembling
And were shaken, because He was angry.
9 "Smoke went up out of His nostrils,
And fire from His mouth devoured;
Coals were kindled by it.
10 "He bowed the heavens also, and came down
With thick darkness under His feet.
11 "And He rode on a cherub and flew;
And He appeared on the wings of the wind.

## New International

14They buried the bones of Saul and his son Jonathan in the
tomb of Saul's father Kish, at Zela in Benjamin, and did everything
the king commanded. After that, God answered prayer in behalf
of the land.

*Wars Against the Philistines*

15Once again there was a battle between the Philistines and
Israel. David went down with his men to fight against the Philistines, and he became exhausted. 16And Ishbi-Benob, one of the
descendants of Rapha, whose bronze spearhead weighed three
hundred shekels[a] and who was armed with a new ⌞sword⌟, said he
would kill David. 17But Abishai son of Zeruiah came to David's
rescue; he struck the Philistine down and killed him. Then David's
men swore to him, saying, "Never again will you go out with us
to battle, so that the lamp of Israel will not be extinguished."
18In the course of time, there was another battle with the Philistines, at Gob. At that time Sibbecai the Hushathite killed Saph, one
of the descendants of Rapha.
19In another battle with the Philistines at Gob, Elhanan son of
Jaare-Oregim[b] the Bethlehemite killed Goliath[c] the Gittite, who
had a spear with a shaft like a weaver's rod.
20In still another battle, which took place at Gath, there was a
huge man with six fingers on each hand and six toes on each
foot—twenty-four in all. He also was descended from Rapha.
21When he taunted Israel, Jonathan son of Shimeah, David's
brother, killed him.
22These four were descendants of Rapha in Gath, and they fell
at the hands of David and his men.

*David's Song of Praise*

**22** DAVID SANG to the LORD the words of this song when the LORD delivered him from the hand of all his enemies
and from the hand of Saul. 2He said:

"The LORD is my rock, my fortress and my deliverer;
3 my God is my rock, in whom I take refuge,
my shield and the horn[d] of my salvation.
He is my stronghold, my refuge and my savior—
from violent men you save me.
4I call to the LORD, who is worthy of praise,
and I am saved from my enemies.
5"The waves of death swirled about me;
the torrents of destruction overwhelmed me.
6The cords of the grave[e] coiled around me;
the snares of death confronted me.
7In my distress I called to the LORD;
I called out to my God.
From his temple he heard my voice;
my cry came to his ears.
8"The earth trembled and quaked,
the foundations of the heavens[f] shook;
they trembled because he was angry.
9Smoke rose from his nostrils;
consuming fire came from his mouth,
burning coals blazed out of it.
10He parted the heavens and came down;
dark clouds were under his feet.
11He mounted the cherubim and flew;
he soared[g] on the wings of the wind.

**NIV** [a] *16* That is, about 7 1/2 pounds (about 3.5 kilograms) [b] *19* Or *son of Jair the weaver* [c] *19* Hebrew and Septuagint; 1 Chron. 20:5 *son of Jair killed Lahmi the brother of Goliath* [d] *3 Horn* here symbolizes strength. [e] *6* Hebrew *Sheol* [f] *8* Hebrew; Vulgate and Syriac (see also Psalm 18:7) *mountains* [g] *11* Many Hebrew manuscripts (see also Psalm 18:10); most Hebrew manuscripts *appeared*

## King James

12And he made darkness pavilions round about him, dark waters, *and* thick clouds of the skies.

13Through the brightness before him were coals of fire kindled.

14The LORD thundered from heaven, and the most High uttered his voice.

15And he sent out arrows, and scattered them; lightning, and discomfited them.

16And the channels of the sea appeared, the foundations of the world were discovered, at the rebuking of the LORD, at the blast of the breath of his nostrils.

17He sent from above, he took me; he drew me out of many waters;

18He delivered me from my strong enemy, *and* from them that hated me: for they were too strong for me.

19They prevented me in the day of my calamity: but the LORD was my stay.

20He brought me forth also into a large place: he delivered me, because he delighted in me.

21The LORD rewarded me according to my righteousness: according to the cleanness of my hands hath he recompensed me.

22For I have kept the ways of the LORD, and have not wickedly departed from my God.

23For all his judgments *were* before me: and *as for* his statutes, I did not depart from them.

24I was also upright before him, and have kept myself from mine iniquity.

25Therefore the LORD hath recompensed me according to my righteousness; according to my cleanness in his eyesight.

26With the merciful thou wilt show thyself merciful, *and* with the upright man thou wilt show thyself upright.

27With the pure thou wilt show thyself pure; and with the froward thou wilt show thyself unsavoury.

28And the afflicted people thou wilt save: but thine eyes *are* upon the haughty, *that* thou mayest bring *them* down.

29For thou *art* my lamp, O LORD: and the LORD will lighten my darkness.

30For by thee I have run through a troop: by my God have I leaped over a wall.

31 *As for* God, his way *is* perfect; the word of the LORD *is* tried: he *is* a buckler to all them that trust in him.

32For who *is* God, save the LORD? and who *is* a rock, save our God?

33God *is* my strength *and* power: and he maketh my way perfect.

34He maketh my feet like hinds' *feet:* and setteth me upon my high places.

35He teacheth my hands to war; so that a bow of steel is broken by mine arms.

36Thou hast also given me the shield of thy salvation: and thy gentleness hath made me great.

37Thou hast enlarged my steps under me; so that my feet did not slip.

38I have pursued mine enemies, and destroyed them; and turned not again until I had consumed them.

## Amplified

12He made darkness around about Him His canopy, gathering of waters, thick clouds of the skies.

13Out of the brightness before Him coals of fire flamed forth.

14The Lord thundered from Heaven, and the Most High uttered His voice.

15He sent out arrows, and scattered them; lightning confused *and* troubled them.

16The channels of the sea were visible, the foundations of the world were uncovered, at the rebuke of the Lord, at the blast of the breath of His nostrils.

17He sent from above, He took me, He drew me out of great waters,

18He delivered me from my strong enemy, from those who hated me; for they were too mighty for me.

19They came upon me in the day of my calamity, but the Lord was my stay.

20He brought me forth into a large place; He delivered me, because He delighted in me.

21The Lord rewarded me according to my uprightness with Him; He compensated *and* benefited me according to the cleanness of my hands.

22For I have kept the ways of the Lord, and have not wickedly departed from my God.

23For all His ordinances were before me, and from His statutes I did not turn aside.

24I was also blameless before Him, and kept myself from guilt *and* iniquity.

25Therefore the Lord has recompensed me according to my righteousness, according to my cleanness in His [holy] sight.

26Toward the loving *and* loyal You will show Yourself loving *and* loyal, and with the upright *and* blameless You will show Yourself upright *and* blameless.

27To the pure You will show Yourself pure, and to the willful You will show Yourself willful.

28And the afflicted people You will deliver, but Your eyes are upon the haughty, whom You will bring down.

29For You, O Lord, are my lamp; the Lord lightens my darkness.

30For by You I run through a troop; by my God I leap over a wall.

31As for God, His way is perfect; the word of the Lord is tried; He is a shield to all those who trust *and* take refuge in Him.

32For who is God, but the Lord? And who is a rock, except our God?

33God is my strong fortress; He guides the blameless in His way *and* sets him free.

34He makes my feet like the hinds' [firm and able]; He sets me secure *and* confident upon the heights.

35He trains my hands for war, so that my arms can bend a bow of bronze.

36You have also given me the shield of Your salvation; and Your condescension *and* gentleness have made me great.

37You have enlarged my steps under me, so that my feet have not slipped.

38I have pursued my enemies, and destroyed them, and did not turn back until they were consumed.

## New American Standard

12 "And He made darkness canopies around Him,
A mass of waters, thick clouds of the sky.
13 "From the brightness before Him
Coals of fire were kindled.
14 "The LORD thundered from heaven,
And the Most High uttered His voice.
15 "And He sent out arrows, and scattered them,
Lightning, and routed them.
16 "Then the channels of the sea appeared,
The foundations of the world were laid bare,
By the rebuke of the LORD,
At the blast of the breath of His nostrils.
17 "He sent from on high, He took me;
He drew me out of many waters.
18 "He delivered me from my strong enemy,
From those who hated me, for they were too strong for me.
19 "They confronted me in the day of my calamity,
But the LORD was my support.
20 "He also brought me forth into a broad place;
He rescued me, because He delighted in me.
21 "The LORD has rewarded me according to my righteousness;
According to the cleanness of my hands He has recompensed me.
22 "For I have kept the ways of the LORD,
And have not acted wickedly against my God.
23 "For all His ordinances *were* before me;
And *as for* His statutes, I did not depart from them.
24 "I was also blameless toward Him,
And I kept myself from my iniquity.
25 "Therefore the LORD has recompensed me according to my righteousness,
According to my cleanness before His eyes.
26 "With the kind Thou dost show Thyself kind,
With the blameless Thou dost show Thyself blameless;
27 With the pure Thou dost show Thyself pure,
And with the perverted Thou dost show Thyself astute.
28 "And Thou dost save an afflicted people;
But Thine eyes are on the haughty *whom* Thou dost abase.
29 "For Thou art my lamp, O LORD;
And the LORD illumines my darkness.
30 "For by Thee I can [a]run upon a troop;
By my God I can leap over a wall.
31 "As for God, His way is blameless;
The word of the LORD is tested;
He is a shield to all who take refuge in Him.
32 "For who is God, besides the LORD?
And who is a rock, besides our God?
33 "God is my strong fortress;
And He sets the blameless in His way.
34 "He makes my feet like hinds' *feet*,
And sets me on my high places.
35 "He trains my hands for battle,
So that my arms can bend a bow of bronze.
36 "Thou hast also given me the shield of Thy salvation,
And Thy help makes me great.
37 "Thou dost enlarge my steps under me,
And my feet have not slipped.
38 "I pursued my enemies and destroyed them,
And I did not turn back until they were consumed.

NAS [a] Or, *crush a troop*

## New International

12He made darkness his canopy around him—
the dark[b] rain clouds of the sky.
13Out of the brightness of his presence
bolts of lightning blazed forth.
14The LORD thundered from heaven;
the voice of the Most High resounded.
15He shot arrows and scattered ⌊the enemies⌋,
bolts of lightning and routed them.
16The valleys of the sea were exposed
and the foundations of the earth laid bare
at the rebuke of the LORD,
at the blast of breath from his nostrils.

17"He reached down from on high and took hold of me;
he drew me out of deep waters.
18He rescued me from my powerful enemy,
from my foes, who were too strong for me.
19They confronted me in the day of my disaster,
but the LORD was my support.
20He brought me out into a spacious place;
he rescued me because he delighted in me.

21"The LORD has dealt with me according to my righteousness;
according to the cleanness of my hands he has rewarded me.
22For I have kept the ways of the LORD;
I have not done evil by turning from my God.
23All his laws are before me;
I have not turned away from his decrees.
24I have been blameless before him
and have kept myself from sin.
25The LORD has rewarded me according to my righteousness,
according to my cleanness[c] in his sight.

26"To the faithful you show yourself faithful,
to the blameless you show yourself blameless,
27to the pure you show yourself pure,
but to the crooked you show yourself shrewd.
28You save the humble,
but your eyes are on the haughty to bring them low.
29You are my lamp, O LORD;
the LORD turns my darkness into light.
30With your help I can advance against a troop[d];
with my God I can scale a wall.

31"As for God, his way is perfect;
the word of the LORD is flawless.
He is a shield
for all who take refuge in him.
32For who is God besides the LORD?
And who is the Rock except our God?
33It is God who arms me with strength[e]
and makes my way perfect.
34He makes my feet like the feet of a deer;
he enables me to stand on the heights.
35He trains my hands for battle;
my arms can bend a bow of bronze.
36You give me your shield of victory;
you stoop down to make me great.
37You broaden the path beneath me,
so that my ankles do not turn.

38"I pursued my enemies and crushed them;
I did not turn back till they were destroyed.

NIV [b] *12* Septuagint and Vulgate (see also Psalm 18:11); Hebrew *massed* [c] *25* Hebrew; Septuagint and Vulgate (see also Psalm 18:24) *to the cleanness of my hands* [d] *30* Or *can run through a barricade* [e] *33* Dead Sea Scrolls, some Septuagint manuscripts, Vulgate and Syriac (see also Psalm 18:32); Masoretic Text *who is my strong refuge*

# King James

39And I have consumed them, and wounded them, that they could not arise: yea, they are fallen under my feet.

40For thou hast girded me with strength to battle: them that rose up against me hast thou subdued under me.

41Thou hast also given me the necks of mine enemies, that I might destroy them that hate me.

42They looked, but *there was* none to save; *even* unto the LORD, but he answered them not.

43Then did I beat them as small as the dust of the earth, I did stamp them as the mire of the street, *and* did spread them abroad.

44Thou also hast delivered me from the strivings of my people, thou hast kept me *to be* head of the heathen: a people *which* I knew not shall serve me.

45Strangers shall submit themselves unto me: as soon as they hear, they shall be obedient unto me.

46Strangers shall fade away, and they shall be afraid out of their close places.

47The LORD liveth; and blessed *be* my rock; and exalted be the God of the rock of my salvation.

48It *is* God that avengeth me, and that bringeth down the people under me,

49And that bringeth me forth from mine enemies: thou also hast lifted me up on high above them that rose up against me: thou hast delivered me from the violent man.

50Therefore I will give thanks unto thee, O LORD, among the heathen, and I will sing praises unto thy name.

51 *He is* the tower of salvation for his king: and showeth mercy to his anointed, unto David, and to his seed for evermore.

**23** NOW THESE *be* the last words of David. David the son of Jesse said, and the man *who was* raised up on high, the anointed of the God of Jacob, and the sweet psalmist of Israel, said,

2The spirit of the LORD spake by me, and his word *was* in my tongue.

3The God of Israel said, the Rock of Israel spake to me, He that ruleth over men *must be* just, ruling in the fear of God.

4And *he shall be* as the light of the morning, *when* the son riseth, *even* a morning without clouds; *as* the tender grass *springing* out of the earth by clear shining after rain.

5Although my house *be* not so with God; yet he hath made with me an everlasting covenant, ordered in all *things,* and sure: for *this is* all my salvation, and all *my* desire, although he make *it* not to grow.

6¶ But *the sons* of Belial *shall be* all of them as thorns thrust away, because they cannot be taken with hands:

7But the man *that* shall touch them must be fenced with iron and the staff of a spear; and they shall be utterly burned with fire in the *same* place.

# Amplified

39I consumed them, and thrust them through, so that they did not arise; they fell at my feet.

40For You girded me with strength for the battle; those who rose up against me You subdued under me.

41You have made my enemies turn their backs to me, that I might cut off those who hate me.

42They looked, but there was none to save; even to the Lord, but He did not answer them.

43Then I beat them small as the dust of the earth, I crushed them as the mire of the street, and scattered them abroad.

44You also have delivered me from strife with my people; You kept me as the head of the nations; people whom I had not known served me.

45Foreigners yielded feigned obedience to me; as soon as they heard of me, they became obedient to me.

46Foreigners faded away; they came limping *and* trembling from their hiding fastnesses.

47The Lord lives; blessed be my rock, and exalted be God, the rock of my salvation.

48It is God who executes vengeance for me, and Who brought down [and disciplined] the peoples under me,

49Who brought me out from my enemies; You also lifted me up above those who rose up against me; You delivered me from the violent man.

50For this I will give thanks *and* extol You, O Lord, among the nations; I will sing praises to Your name.

51He is a tower of salvation *and* great deliverance to His king, and shows loving-kindness to His anointed, to David and his offspring for ever.

**23** NOW THESE are the last words of David: David son of Jesse says, and the man who was raised on high, the anointed of the God of Jacob, and the sweet psalmist of Israel, says,

2The Spirit of the Lord spoke in *and* by me, and His word was upon my tongue.

3The God of Israel spoke, the Rock of Israel said to me, When one rules over men righteously, ruling in the fear of God,

4He dawns on them like the morning light, when the sun rises on a cloudless morning, when the tender grass springs out of the earth, through clear shining after rain.

5Truly, does not my house stand so with God? For He has made with me an everlasting covenant, ordered in all things, and sure. For will He not cause to prosper all my help and my desire?

6But wicked, godless, *and* worthless lives are all like thorns to be thrust away; because they cannot be taken with the hand;

7But the man who touches them arms himself with iron and the shaft of a spear, and they are utterly consumed with fire on the spot.

## New American Standard

39 "And I have devoured them and shattered them, so that
they did not rise;
And they fell under my feet.
40 "For Thou hast girded me with strength for battle;
Thou hast subdued under me those who rose up
against me.
41 "Thou hast also made my enemies turn *their* backs to
me,
And I destroyed those who hated me.
42 "They looked, but there was none to save;
*Even* to the LORD, but He did not answer them.
43 "Then I pulverized them as the dust of the earth,
I crushed *and* stamped them as the mire of the streets.
44 "Thou hast also delivered me from the contentions of my
people;
Thou hast kept me as head of the nations;
A people whom I have not known serve me.
45 "Foreigners pretend obedience to me;
As soon as they hear, they obey me.
46 "Foreigners lose heart,
And come trembling out of their fortresses.
47 "The LORD lives, and blessed be my rock;
And exalted be God, the rock of my salvation,
48 The God who executes vengeance for me,
And brings down peoples under me,
49 Who also brings me out from my enemies;
Thou dost even lift me above those who rise up against
me;
Thou dost rescue me from the violent man.
50 "Therefore I will give thanks to Thee, O LORD, among
the nations,
And I will sing praises to Thy name.
51 "*He* is a tower of [a]deliverance to His king,
And shows lovingkindness to His anointed,
To David and his descendants forever."

*David's Last Song*

23 NOW THESE are the last words of David.
David the son of Jesse declares,
And the man who was raised on high declares,
The anointed of the God of Jacob,
And the sweet psalmist of Israel,
2 "The Spirit of the LORD spoke by me,
And His word was on my tongue.
3 "The God of Israel said,
The Rock of Israel spoke to me,
'He who rules over men righteously,
Who rules in the fear of God,
4 Is as the light of the morning *when* the sun rises,
A morning without clouds,
*When* the tender grass *springs* out of the earth,
Through sunshine after rain.'
5 "Truly is not my house so with God?
For He has made an everlasting covenant with me,
Ordered in all things, and secured;
For all my salvation and all *my* desire,
Will He not indeed make *it* grow?
6 "But the worthless, every one of them will be thrust
away like thorns,
Because they cannot be taken in hand;
7 But the man who touches them
Must be armed with iron and the shaft of a spear,
And they will be completely burned with fire in *their*
place."

NAS [a] I.e., victories

## New International

39 I crushed them completely, and they could not rise;
they fell beneath my feet.
40 You armed me with strength for battle;
you made my adversaries bow at my feet.
41 You made my enemies turn their backs in flight,
and I destroyed my foes.
42 They cried for help, but there was no one to save them—
to the LORD, but he did not answer.
43 I beat them as fine as the dust of the earth;
I pounded and trampled them like mud in the streets.

44 "You have delivered me from the attacks of my people;
you have preserved me as the head of nations.
People I did not know are subject to me,
45 and foreigners come cringing to me;
as soon as they hear me, they obey me.
46 They all lose heart;
they come trembling[b] from their strongholds.
47 "The LORD lives! Praise be to my Rock!
Exalted be God, the Rock, my Savior!
48 He is the God who avenges me,
who puts the nations under me,
49 who sets me free from my enemies.
You exalted me above my foes;
from violent men you rescued me.
50 Therefore I will praise you, O LORD, among the nations;
I will sing praises to your name.
51 He gives his king great victories;
he shows unfailing kindness to his anointed,
to David and his descendants forever."

*The Last Words of David*

23 THESE ARE the last words of David:

"The oracle of David son of Jesse,
the oracle of the man exalted by the Most High,
the man anointed by the God of Jacob,
Israel's singer of songs[c]:

2 "The Spirit of the LORD spoke through me;
his word was on my tongue.
3 The God of Israel spoke,
the Rock of Israel said to me:
'When one rules over men in righteousness,
when he rules in the fear of God,
4 he is like the light of morning at sunrise
on a cloudless morning,
like the brightness after rain
that brings the grass from the earth.'
5 "Is not my house right with God?
Has he not made with me an everlasting covenant,
arranged and secured in every part?
Will he not bring to fruition my salvation
and grant me my every desire?
6 But evil men are all to be cast aside like thorns,
which are not gathered with the hand.
7 Whoever touches thorns
uses a tool of iron or the shaft of a spear;
they are burned up where they lie."

NIV [b] *46* Some Septuagint manuscripts and Vulgate (see also Psalm 18:45); Masoretic Text *they arm themselves.* [c] *1* Or *Israel's beloved singer*

## King James

8 ¶ These *be* the names of the mighty men whom David had: The Tachmonite that sat in the seat, chief among the captains; the same *was* Adino the Eznite: *he lift up his spear* against eight hundred, whom he slew at one time.

9 And after him *was* Eleazar the son of Dodo the Ahohite, *one* of the three mighty men with David, when they defied the Philistines *that* were there gathered together to battle, and the men of Israel were gone away:

10 He arose, and smote the Philistines until his hand was weary, and his hand clave unto the sword: and the LORD wrought a great victory that day; and the people returned after him only to spoil.

11 And after him *was* Shammah the son of Agee the Hararite. And the Philistines were gathered together into a troop, where was a piece of ground full of lentiles: and the people fled from the Philistines.

12 But he stood in the midst of the ground, and defended it, and slew the Philistines: and the LORD wrought a great victory.

13 And three of the thirty chief went down, and came to David in the harvest time unto the cave of Adullam: and the troop of the Philistines pitched in the valley of Rephaim.

14 And David *was* then in an hold, and the garrison of the Philistines *was* then *in* Bethlehem.

15 And David longed, and said, Oh that one would give me drink of the water of the well of Bethlehem, which *is* by the gate!

16 And the three mighty men brake through the host of the Philistines, and drew water out of the well of Bethlehem, that *was* by the gate, and took *it*, and brought *it* to David: nevertheless he would not drink thereof, but poured it out unto the LORD.

17 And he said, Be it far from me, O LORD, that I should do this: *is not this* the blood of the men that went in jeopardy of their lives? therefore he would not drink it. These things did these three mighty men.

18 And Abishai, the brother of Joab, the son of Zeruiah, was chief among three. And he lifted up his spear against three hundred, *and* slew *them*, and had the name among three.

19 Was he not most honourable of three? therefore he was their captain: howbeit he attained not unto the *first* three.

20 And Benaiah the son of Jehoiada, the son of a valiant man, of Kabzeel, who had done many acts, he slew two lionlike men of Moab: he went down also and slew a lion in the midst of a pit in time of snow:

21 And he slew an Egyptian, a goodly man: and the Egyptian had a spear in his hand; but he went down to him with a staff, and plucked the spear out of the Egyptian's hand, and slew him with his own spear.

22 These *things* did Benaiah the son of Jehoiada, and had the name among three mighty men.

23 He was more honourable than the thirty, but he attained not to the *first* three. And David set him over his guard.

24 Asahel the brother of Joab *was* one of the thirty; Elhanan the son of Dodo of Bethlehem,

25 Shammah the Harodite, Elika the Harodite,

26 Helez the Paltite, Ira the son of Ikkesh the Tekoite,

27 Abiezer the Anethothite, Mebunnai the Hushathite,

28 Zalmon the Ahohite, Maharai the Netophathite,

29 Heleb the son of Baanah, a Netophathite, Ittai the son of Ribai out of Gibeah of the children of Benjamin,

## Amplified

8 These are the names of the mighty men whom David had: Josheb-basshebeth a Tah-chemonite, chief of the three [heroes], known also as Adino the Eznite; he wielded his spear and went against 800 men, who were slain at one time. [I Chron. 11:11.]

9 Next to him among the three mighty men was Eleazar son of Dodo, son of Ahohi. He was with David when they defied the Philistines assembled there for battle, and the men of Israel had departed.

10 [Eleazar] arose and struck down the Philistines until his hand was weary and clung to the sword. The Lord wrought a great deliverance *and* victory that day; the men returned after him only to take the spoil.

11 Next to [Eleazar] was Shammah son of Agee the Hararite. The Philistines were gathered at Lehi, on a piece of ground full of lentils; and the [Israelites] fled from the Philistines.

12 But he stood in the midst of the ground and defended it, and slew the Philistines; and the Lord wrought a great victory.

13 And three of the thirty chief men went down in harvest time to David in the cave of Adullam; and a troop of Philistines was encamped in the valley of Rephaim.

14 And David was then in the stronghold, and the garrison of the Philistines was then in Bethlehem.

15 And David said longingly, O that someone would give me a drink of water from the well of Bethlehem, by the gate!

16 And the three mighty men broke through the army of the Philistines, and drew water out of the well of Bethlehem, by the gate, and brought it to David; but he would not drink it, but poured it out to the Lord.

17 And he said, Be it far from me, O Lord, to drink this. Is it not [the same as] the blood of the men who went at the risk of their lives? So he would not drink it. These things did the three mighty men.

18 Now Abishai brother of Joab, son of Zeruiah, was chief of the three. He wielded his spear against 300 men and slew them, and won a name beside the three.

19 Was he not most renowned of the three? So he was their captain; however, he did not attain to the three.

20 And Benaiah son of Jehoiada, a valiant man of Kabzeel, who had done many notable acts, slew two lionlike men of Moab. He went down also and slew a lion in a pit on a snowy day.

21 And he slew an Egyptian, a handsome man. The Egyptian had a spear in his hand; but Benaiah went down to him with a staff, snatched the spear out of the Egyptian's hand, and slew the man with his own spear.

22 These things Benaiah son of Jehoiada did, and won a name beside the three mighty men.

23 He was more renowned than the thirty, but he attained not to the first three. David set him over his guard *or* council.

24 Asahel brother of Joab was one of the thirty; then Elhanan son of Dodo of Bethlehem,

25 Shammah of Harod, Elika of Harod,

26 Helez the Paltite, Ira son of Ikkesh of Tekoa,

27 Abiezer of Anathoth, Mebunnai the Hushathite,

28 Zalmon the Ahohite, Maharai of Netophah,

29 Heleb son of Baanah, of Netophah, Ittai son of Ribai of Gibeah of the Benjamites.

# New American Standard

*His Mighty Men*

8¶ These are the names of the mighty men whom David had: Josheb-basshebeth a Tahchemonite, chief of the captains, he was *called* Adino the Eznite, because of eight hundred slain *by him* at one time;

9and after him was Eleazar the son of Dodo the Ahohite, one of the three mighty men with David when they defied the Philistines who were gathered there to battle and the men of Israel had withdrawn.

10He arose and struck the Philistines until his hand was weary and clung to the sword, and the LORD brought about a great victory that day; and the people returned after him only to strip *the slain.*

11¶ Now after him was Shammah the son of Agee a Hararite. And the Philistines were gathered into a troop, where there was a plot of ground full of lentils, and the people fled from the Philistines.

12But he took his stand in the midst of the plot, defended it and struck the Philistines; and the LORD brought about a great victory.

13¶ Then three of the thirty chief men went down and came to David in the harvest time to the cave of Adullam, while the troop of the Philistines was camping in the valley of Rephaim.

14And David was then in the stronghold, while the garrison of the Philistines was then in Bethlehem.

15And David had a craving and said, "Oh that someone would give me water to drink from the well of Bethlehem which is by the gate!"

16So the three mighty men broke through the camp of the Philistines, and drew water from the well of Bethlehem which was by the gate, and took *it* and brought *it* to David. Nevertheless he would not drink it, but poured it out to the LORD;

17and he said, "Be it far from me, O LORD, that I should do this. *Shall I drink* the blood of the men who went in *jeopardy* of their lives?" Therefore he would not drink it. These things the three mighty men did.

18¶ And Abishai, the brother of Joab, the son of Zeruiah, was chief of the thirty. And he swung his spear against three hundred and killed *them,* and had a name as well as the three.

19He was most honored of the thirty, therefore he became their commander; however, he did not attain to the three.

20¶ Then Benaiah the son of Jehoiada, the son of a valiant man of Kabzeel, who had done mighty deeds, killed the two *sons of* Ariel of Moab. He also went down and killed a lion in the middle of a pit on a snowy day.

21And he killed an Egyptian, an impressive man. Now the Egyptian *had* a spear in his hand, but he went down to him with a club and snatched the spear from the Egyptian's hand, and killed him with his own spear.

22These *things* Benaiah the son of Jehoiada did, and had a name as well as the three mighty men.

23He was honored among the thirty, but he did not attain to the three. And David appointed him over his guard.

24¶ Asahel the brother of Joab was among the thirty; Elhanan the son of Dodo of Bethlehem,

25Shammah the Harodite, Elika the Harodite,

26Helez the Paltite, Ira the son of Ikkesh the Tekoite,

27Abiezer the Anathothite, Mebunnai the Hushathite,

28Zalmon the Ahohite, Maharai the Netophathite,

29Heleb the son of Baanah the Netophathite, Ittai the son of Ribai of Gibeah of the sons of Benjamin,

# New International

*David's Mighty Men*

8These are the names of David's mighty men:

Josheb-Basshebeth,[a] a Tahkemonite,[b] was chief of the Three;
he raised his spear against eight hundred men, whom he killed[c]
in one encounter.

9Next to him was Eleazar son of Dodai the Ahohite. As one of
the three mighty men, he was with David when they taunted the
Philistines gathered [at Pas Dammim,][d] for battle. Then the men of
Israel retreated, 10but he stood his ground and struck down the
Philistines till his hand grew tired and froze to the sword. The
LORD brought about a great victory that day. The troops returned
to Eleazar, but only to strip the dead.

11Next to him was Shammah son of Agee the Hararite. When
the Philistines banded together at a place where there was a field
full of lentils, Israel's troops fled from them. 12But Shammah took
his stand in the middle of the field. He defended it and struck the
Philistines down, and the LORD brought about a great victory.

13During harvest time, three of the thirty chief men came down
to David at the cave of Adullam, while a band of Philistines was
encamped in the Valley of Rephaim. 14At that time David was in
the stronghold, and the Philistine garrison was at Bethlehem.
15David longed for water and said, "Oh, that someone would get
me a drink of water from the well near the gate of Bethlehem!" 16So
the three mighty men broke through the Philistine lines, drew
water from the well near the gate of Bethlehem and carried it back
to David. But he refused to drink it; instead, he poured it out before
the LORD. 17"Far be it from me, O LORD, to do this!" he said. "Is
it not the blood of men who went at the risk of their lives?" And
David would not drink it.

Such were the exploits of the three mighty men.

18Abishai the brother of Joab son of Zeruiah was chief of the
Three.[e] He raised his spear against three hundred men, whom he
killed, and so he became as famous as the Three. 19Was he not held
in greater honor than the Three? He became their commander,
even though he was not included among them.

20Benaiah son of Jehoiada was a valiant fighter from Kabzeel,
who performed great exploits. He struck down two of Moab's best
men. He also went down into a pit on a snowy day and killed a
lion. 21And he struck down a huge Egyptian. Although the Egyptian had a spear in his hand, Benaiah went against him with a club.
He snatched the spear from the Egyptian's hand and killed him
with his own spear. 22Such were the exploits of Benaiah son of
Jehoiada; he too was as famous as the three mighty men. 23He was
held in greater honor than any of the Thirty, but he was not
included among the Three. And David put him in charge of his
bodyguard.

24Among the Thirty were:

Asahel the brother of Joab,
Elhanan son of Dodo from Bethlehem,
25Shammah the Harodite,
Elika the Harodite,
26Helez the Paltite,
Ira son of Ikkesh from Tekoa,
27Abiezer from Anathoth,
Mebunnai[f] the Hushathite,
28Zalmon the Ahohite,
Maharai the Netophathite,
29Heled[g] son of Baanah the Netophathite,
Ithai son of Ribai from Gibeah in Benjamin,

NIV [a] *8* Hebrew; some Septuagint manuscripts suggest *Ish-Bosheth,* that is, *Esh-Baal* (see also 1 Chron. 11:11 *Jashobeam*). [b] *8* Probably a variant of *Hacmonite* (see 1 Chron. 11:11) [c] *8* Some Septuagint manuscripts (see also 1 Chron. 11:11); Hebrew and other Septuagint manuscripts *Three; it was Adino the Eznite who killed eight hundred men* [d] *9* See 1 Chron. 11:13; Hebrew *gathered there.* [e] *18* Most Hebrew manuscripts (see also 1 Chron. 11:20); two Hebrew manuscripts and Syriac *Thirty* [f] *27* Hebrew; some Septuagint manuscripts (see also 1 Chron. 11:29) *Sibbecai* [g] *29* Some Hebrew manuscripts and Vulgate (see also 1 Chron. 11:30); most Hebrew manuscripts *Heleb*

## King James

30 Benaiah the Pirathonite, Hiddai of the brooks of Gaash,
31 Abi-albon the Arbathite, Azmaveth the Barhumite,
32 Eliahba the Shaalbonite, of the sons of Jashen, Jonathan,
33 Shammah the Hararite, Ahiam the son of Sharar the Hararite,
34 Eliphelet the son of Ahasbai, the son of the Maachathite, Eliam the son of Ahithophel the Gilonite,
35 Hezrai the Carmelite, Paarai the Arbite,
36 Igal the son of Nathan of Zobah, Bani the Gadite,
37 Zelek the Ammonite, Nahari the Beerothite, armourbearer to Joab the son of Zeruiah,
38 Ira an Ithrite, Gareb an Ithrite,
39 Uriah the Hittite: thirty and seven in all.

**24** AND AGAIN the anger of the LORD was kindled against Israel, and he moved David against them to say, Go, number Israel and Judah.

2 For the king said to Joab the captain of the host, which *was* with him, Go now through all the tribes of Israel, from Dan even to Beer-sheba, and number ye the people, that I may know the number of the people.

3 And Joab said unto the king, Now the LORD thy God add unto the people, how many soever they be, an hundredfold, and that the eyes of my lord the king may see *it:* but why doth my lord the king delight in this thing?

4 Notwithstanding the king's word prevailed against Joab, and against the captains of the host. And Joab and the captains of the host went out from the presence of the king, to number the people of Israel.

5 ¶ And they passed over Jordan, and pitched in Aroer, on the right side of the city that *lieth* in the midst of the river of Gad, and toward Jazer:

6 Then they came to Gilead, and to the land of Tahtim-hodshi; and they came to Dan-jaan, and about to Zidon,

7 And came to the strong hold of Tyre, and to all the cities of the Hivites, and of the Canaanites: and they went out to the south of Judah, *even* to Beer-sheba.

8 So when they had gone through all the land, they came to Jerusalem at the end of nine months and twenty days.

9 And Joab gave up the sum of the number of the people unto the king: and there were in Israel eight hundred thousand valiant men that drew the sword; and the men of Judah *were* five hundred thousand men.

10 ¶ And David's heart smote him after that he had numbered the people. And David said unto the LORD, I have sinned greatly in that I have done: and now, I beseech thee, O LORD, take away the iniquity of thy servant; for I have done very foolishly.

11 For when David was up in the morning, the word of the LORD came unto the prophet Gad, David's seer, saying,

12 Go and say unto David, Thus saith the LORD, I offer thee three *things;* choose thee one of them, that I may *do it* unto thee.

13 So Gad came to David, and told him, and said unto him, Shall seven years of famine come unto thee in thy land? or wilt thou flee three months before thine enemies, while they pursue thee? or that there be three days' pestilence in thy land? now advise, and see what answer I shall return to him that sent me.

## Amplified

30 Benaiah of Pirathon, Hiddai of the brooks of Gaash,
31 Abi-albon the Arbathite, Azmaveth of Bahurim,
32 Eliahba of Sha-albon, the sons of Jashen, Jonathan,
33 Shammah the Hararite, Ahiam son of Sharar the Hararite,
34 Eliphelet son of Ahasbai, son of Maacah, Eliam son of Ahithophel of Gilo,
35 Hezro (Hezrai) of Carmel, Paarai the Arbite,
36 Igal son of Nathan of Zobah, Bani the Gadite,
37 Zelek the Ammonite, Naharai of Beeroth, armor-bearer of Joab son of Zeruiah,
38 Ira the Ithrite, Gareb the Ithrite,
39 Uriah the Hittite; thirty-seven in all.

**24** AGAIN THE anger of the Lord was kindled against Israel, and He moved David against them saying, Go, number Israel and Judah.

2 For the king said to Joab the captain of the host, who was with him, Go now through all the tribes of Israel, from Dan even to Beer-sheba, and count the people, that I may know their number.

3 And Joab said to the king, May the Lord your God add a hundred times as many people as there are, and let the eyes of my lord the king see it; but why does my lord the king delight in this thing?

4 But the king's word prevailed against Joab and the commanders of the army. So they went from the king's presence to number the Israelites.

5 They passed over Jordan and encamped in Aroer, on the south side of the city lying in the midst of the ravine [of the Arnon] toward Gad, and on to Jazer.

6 Then they came to Gilead, and to the land of Tahtimhodshi; and they came to Dan-jaan [Dan in the forest] and around to Sidon,

7 And came to the stronghold of Tyre, and to all the cities of the Hivites, and Canaanites; and they went out to the Negeb [the South] of Judah at Beer-sheba.

8 So when they had gone through all the land [taking the census], they came to Jerusalem at the end of nine months and twenty days.

9 And Joab gave the sum of the numbering of the people to the king. There were in Israel 800,000 valiant men who drew the sword; and the men of Judah were 500,000.

10 But David's heart smote him after he had numbered the people. David said to the Lord, I have sinned greatly in what I have done. I beseech You, O Lord, take away the iniquity of Your servant, for I have done very foolishly.

11 When David arose in the morning, the word of the Lord came to the prophet Gad, David's seer, saying,

12 Go and say to David, Thus says the Lord, I hold over you three choices; select one of them, so I may bring it upon you.

13 So Gad came to David, and told him, and said, Shall seven years of famine come to your land? Or will you flee three months before your pursuing enemies? Or do you prefer three days of pestilence in your land? Consider, and see what answer I shall return to Him Who sent me.

## New American Standard

30Benaiah a Pirathonite, Hiddai of the brooks of Gaash,
31Abi-albon the Arbathite, Azmaveth the Barhumite,
32Eliahba the Shaalbonite, the sons of Jashen, Jonathan,
33Shammah the Hararite, Ahiam the son of Sharar the Ararite,
34Eliphelet the son of Ahasbai, the son of the Maacathite, Eliam
the son of Ahithophel the Gilonite,
35Hezro the Carmelite, Paarai the Arbite,
36Igal the son of Nathan of Zobah, Bani the Gadite,
37Zelek the Ammonite, Naharai the Beerothite, armor bearers
of Joab the son of Zeruiah,
38Ira the Ithrite, Gareb the Ithrite,
39Uriah the Hittite; thirty-seven in all.

*The Census Taken*

**24** NOW AGAIN the anger of the LORD burned against Israel,
and it incited David against them to say, "Go, number
Israel and Judah."
2And the king said to Joab the commander of the army who
was with him, "Go about now through all the tribes of Israel, from
Dan to Beersheba, and register the people, that I may know the
number of the people."
3But Joab said to the king, "Now may the LORD your God add
to the people a hundred times as many as they are, while the eyes
of my lord the king *still* see; but why does my lord the king delight
in this thing?"
4Nevertheless, the king's word prevailed against Joab and
against the commanders of the army. So Joab and the commanders
of the army went out from the presence of the king, to register the
people of Israel.
5And they crossed the Jordan and camped in Aroer, on the
right side of the city that is in the middle of the valley of Gad, and
toward Jazer.
6Then they came to Gilead and to [a]the land of Tahtim-hodshi,
and they came to Dan-jaan and around to Sidon,
7and came to the fortress of Tyre and to all the cities of the
Hivites and of the Canaanites, and they went out to the south of
Judah, *to* Beersheba.
8So when they had gone about through the whole land, they
came to Jerusalem at the end of nine months and twenty days.
9And Joab gave the number of the registration of the people to
the king; and there were in Israel eight hundred thousand valiant
men who drew the sword, and the men of Judah were five hundred thousand men.
10¶ Now David's heart troubled him after he had numbered the
people. So David said to the LORD, "I have sinned greatly in what
I have done. But now, O LORD, please take away the iniquity of
Thy servant, for I have acted very foolishly."
11When David arose in the morning, the word of the LORD came
to the prophet Gad, David's seer, saying,
12"Go and speak to David, 'Thus the LORD says, "I am offering
you three things; choose for yourself one of them, which I may do
to you." ' "
13So Gad came to David and told him, and said to him, "Shall
seven years of famine come to you in your land? Or will you flee
three months before your foes while they pursue you? Or shall
there be three days' pestilence in your land? Now consider and see
what answer I shall return to Him who sent me."

NAS [a] Or, *Kadesh in the land of the Hittite*

## New International

30Benaiah the Pirathonite,
Hiddai[b] from the ravines of Gaash,
31Abi-Albon the Arbathite,
Azmaveth the Barhumite,
32Eliahba the Shaalbonite,
the sons of Jashen,
Jonathan 33son of[c] Shammah the Hararite,
Ahiam son of Sharar[d] the Hararite,
34Eliphelet son of Ahasbai the Maacathite,
Eliam son of Ahithophel the Gilonite,
35Hezro the Carmelite,
Paarai the Arbite,
36Igal son of Nathan from Zobah,
the son of Hagri,[e]
37Zelek the Ammonite,
Naharai the Beerothite, the armor-bearer of Joab son of
Zeruiah,
38Ira the Ithrite,
Gareb the Ithrite
39and Uriah the Hittite.
There were thirty-seven in all.

*David Counts the Fighting Men*

**24** AGAIN THE anger of the LORD burned against Israel, and
he incited David against them, saying, "Go and take a
census of Israel and Judah."
2So the king said to Joab and the army commanders[f] with him,
"Go throughout the tribes of Israel from Dan to Beersheba and
enroll the fighting men, so that I may know how many there are."
3But Joab replied to the king, "May the LORD your God multiply
the troops a hundred times over, and may the eyes of my lord the
king see it. But why does my lord the king want to do such a
thing?"
4The king's word, however, overruled Joab and the army commanders; so they left the presence of the king to enroll the fighting
men of Israel.
5After crossing the Jordan, they camped near Aroer, south of
the town in the gorge, and then went through Gad and on to Jazer.
6They went to Gilead and the region of Tahtim Hodshi, and on to
Dan Jaan and around toward Sidon. 7Then they went toward the
fortress of Tyre and all the towns of the Hivites and Canaanites.
Finally, they went on to Beersheba in the Negev of Judah.
8After they had gone through the entire land, they came back
to Jerusalem at the end of nine months and twenty days.
9Joab reported the number of the fighting men to the king: In
Israel there were eight hundred thousand able-bodied men who
could handle a sword, and in Judah five hundred thousand.
10David was conscience-stricken after he had counted the fighting men, and he said to the LORD, "I have sinned greatly in what
I have done. Now, O LORD, I beg you, take away the guilt of your
servant. I have done a very foolish thing."
11Before David got up the next morning, the word of the LORD
had come to Gad the prophet, David's seer: 12"Go and tell David,
'This is what the LORD says: I am giving you three options. Choose
one of them for me to carry out against you.' "
13So Gad went to David and said to him, "Shall there come
upon you three[g] years of famine in your land? Or three months
of fleeing from your enemies while they pursue you? Or three days
of plague in your land? Now then, think it over and decide how
I should answer the one who sent me."

NIV [b] *30* Hebrew; some Septuagint manuscripts (see also 1 Chron. 11:32) *Hurai* [c] *33* Some Septuagint manuscripts (see also 1 Chron. 11:34); Hebrew does not have *son of.* [d] *33* Hebrew; some Septuagint manuscripts (see also 1 Chron. 11:35) *Sacar* [e] *36* Some Septuagint manuscripts (see also 1 Chron. 11:38); Hebrew *Haggadi* [f] *2* Septuagint (see also verse 4 and 1 Chron. 21:2); Hebrew *Joab the army commander* [g] *13* Septuagint (see also 1 Chron. 21:12); Hebrew *seven*

## King James

14And David said unto Gad, I am in a great strait: let us fall now
into the hand of the LORD; for his mercies *are* great: and let me not
fall into the hand of man.
15¶ So the LORD sent a pestilence upon Israel from the morning
even to the time appointed: and there died of the people from Dan
even to Beer-sheba seventy thousand men.
16And when the angel stretched out his hand upon Jerusalem
to destroy it, the LORD repented him of the evil, and said to the
angel that destroyed the people, It is enough: stay now thine hand.
And the angel of the LORD was by the threshingplace of Araunah
the Jebusite.
17And David spake unto the LORD when he saw the angel that
smote the people, and said, Lo, I have sinned, and I have done
wickedly: but these sheep, what have they done? let thine hand,
I pray thee, be against me, and against my father's house.
18¶ And Gad came that day to David, and said unto him, Go up,
rear an altar unto the LORD in the threshingfloor of Araunah the
Jebusite.
19And David, according to the saying of Gad, went up as the
LORD commanded.
20And Araunah looked, and saw the king and his servants
coming on toward him: and Araunah went out, and bowed himself
before the king on his face upon the ground.
21And Araunah said, Wherefore is my lord the king come to his
servant? And David said, To buy the threshingfloor of thee, to
build an altar unto the LORD, that the plague may be stayed from
the people.
22And Araunah said unto David, Let my lord the king take and
offer up what *seemeth* good unto him: behold, *here be* oxen for burnt
sacrifice, and threshing instruments and *other* instruments of the
oxen for wood.
23All these *things* did Araunah, *as* a king, give unto the king.
And Araunah said unto the king, The LORD thy God accept thee.
24And the king said unto Araunah, Nay; but I will surely buy
*it* of thee at a price: neither will I offer burnt offerings unto the
LORD my God of that which doth cost me nothing. So David
bought the threshingfloor and the oxen for fifty shekels of silver.
25And David built there an altar unto the LORD, and offered
burnt offerings and peace offerings. So the LORD was entreated for
the land, and the plague was stayed from Israel.

## Amplified

14And David said to Gad, I am in great distress; let us fall into
the hand of the Lord, for His mercies are many *and* great; but let
me not fall into the hand of man.
15So the Lord sent a pestilence upon Israel from the morning
even to the time appointed; and there died of the people from Dan
even to Beer-sheba 70,000 men.
16And when the angel stretched out his hand upon Jerusalem
to destroy it, the Lord relented of the evil *and* reversed His judgment, and said to the destroying angel, It is enough; now stay your
hand. And the Angel of the Lord was by the threshing floor of
Araunah the Jebusite.
17When David saw the angel who was smiting the people, he
spoke to the Lord and said, Lo, I have sinned, and I have done
wickedly; but these sheep, what have they done? Let Your hand,
I pray You, be [only] against me and against my father's house.
18Then Gad came to David, and said, Go up, rear an altar to the
Lord on the threshing floor of Araunah the Jebusite.
19So David went up according to Gad's word, as the Lord
commanded.
20Araunah looked, and saw the king and his servants coming
toward him; and [he] went out, and bowed himself before the king
with his face to the ground.
21Araunah said, Why has my lord the king come to his servant?
And David said, To buy the threshing floor from you, to build
there an altar to the Lord, that the plague may be stayed from the
people.
22And Araunah said to David, Let my lord the king take and
offer up what seems good to him; behold, here are oxen for burnt
sacrifice, and threshing instruments and the yokes of the oxen for
wood.
23All this, O king, Araunah gives to the king. And Araunah said
to the king, The Lord your God accept you.
24But King David said to Araunah, No, but I will buy it of you
for a price; I will not offer burnt offerings to the Lord my God of
that which costs me nothing. So David bought the threshing floor
and the oxen for fifty shekels of silver.
25David built there an altar to the Lord, and offered burnt and
peace offerings. So the Lord heeded the prayers for the land, and
Israel's plague was stayed.

## New American Standard

14Then David said to Gad, "I am in great distress. Let us now
fall into the hand of the LORD for His mercies are great, but do not
let me fall into the hand of man."

*Pestilence Sent*

15¶ So the LORD sent a pestilence upon Israel from the morning
until the appointed time; and seventy thousand men of the people
from Dan to Beersheba died.
16When the angel stretched out his hand toward Jerusalem to
destroy it, the LORD relented from the calamity, and said to the
angel who destroyed the people, "It is enough! Now relax your
hand!" And the angel of the LORD was by the threshing floor of
Araunah the Jebusite.
17Then David spoke to the LORD when he saw the angel who
was striking down the people, and said, "Behold, it is I who have
sinned, and it is I who have done wrong; but these sheep, what
have they done? Please let Thy hand be against me and against my
father's house."

*David Builds an Altar*

18¶ So Gad came to David that day and said to him, "Go up,
erect an altar to the LORD on the threshing floor of Araunah the
Jebusite."
19And David went up according to the word of Gad, just as the
LORD had commanded.
20And Araunah looked down and saw the king and his servants
crossing over toward him; and Araunah went out and bowed his
face to the ground before the king.
21Then Araunah said, "Why has my lord the king come to his
servant?" And David said, "To buy the threshing floor from you,
in order to build an altar to the LORD, that the plague may be held
back from the people."
22And Araunah said to David, "Let my lord the king take and
offer up what is good in his sight. Look, the oxen for the burnt
offering, the threshing sledges and the yokes of the oxen for the
wood.
23"Everything, O king, Araunah gives to the king." And Araunah said to the king, "May the LORD your God accept you."
24However, the king said to Araunah, "No, but I will surely buy
*it* from you for a price, for I will not offer burnt offerings to the
LORD my God which cost me nothing." So David bought the
threshing floor and the oxen for fifty shekels of silver.
25And David built there an altar to the LORD, and offered burnt
offerings and peace offerings. Thus the LORD was moved by entreaty for the land, and the plague was held back from Israel.

## New International

14David said to Gad, "I am in deep distress. Let us fall into the
hands of the LORD, for his mercy is great; but do not let me fall into
the hands of men."
15So the LORD sent a plague on Israel from that morning until
the end of the time designated, and seventy thousand of the
people from Dan to Beersheba died. 16When the angel stretched
out his hand to destroy Jerusalem, the LORD was grieved because
of the calamity and said to the angel who was afflicting the people,
"Enough! Withdraw your hand." The angel of the LORD was then
at the threshing floor of Araunah the Jebusite.
17When David saw the angel who was striking down the
people, he said to the LORD, "I am the one who has sinned and
done wrong. These are but sheep. What have they done? Let your
hand fall upon me and my family."

*David Builds an Altar*

18On that day Gad went to David and said to him, "Go up and
build an altar to the LORD on the threshing floor of Araunah the
Jebusite." 19So David went up, as the LORD had commanded
through Gad. 20When Araunah looked and saw the king and his
men coming toward him, he went out and bowed down before the
king with his face to the ground.
21Araunah said, "Why has my lord the king come to his servant?"
"To buy your threshing floor," David answered, "so I can build
an altar to the LORD, that the plague on the people may be
stopped."
22Araunah said to David, "Let my lord the king take whatever
pleases him and offer it up. Here are oxen for the burnt offering,
and here are threshing sledges and ox yokes for the wood. 23O
king, Araunah gives all this to the king." Araunah also said to him,
"May the LORD your God accept you."
24But the king replied to Araunah, "No, I insist on paying you
for it. I will not sacrifice to the LORD my God burnt offerings that
cost me nothing."
So David bought the threshing floor and the oxen and paid fifty
shekels[a] of silver for them. 25David built an altar to the LORD there
and sacrificed burnt offerings and fellowship offerings.[b] Then the
LORD answered prayer in behalf of the land, and the plague on
Israel was stopped.

**NIV** [a] *24* That is, about 1 1/4 pounds (about 0.6 kilogram) [b] *25* Traditionally *peace offerings*

## King James

THE FIRST BOOK OF THE

# Kings

COMMONLY CALLED

THE THIRD BOOK OF THE KINGS

1 NOW KING David was old *and* stricken in years; and they
covered him with clothes, but he gat no heat.
2Wherefore his servants said unto him, Let there be sought for
my lord the king a young virgin: and let her stand before the king,
and let her cherish him, and let her lie in thy bosom, that my lord
the king may get heat.
3So they sought for a fair damsel throughout all the coasts of
Israel, and found Abishag a Shunammite, and brought her to the
king.
4And the damsel *was* very fair, and cherished the king, and
ministered to him: but the king knew her not.
5¶ Then Adonijah the son of Haggith exalted himself, saying,
I will be king: and he prepared him chariots and horsemen, and
fifty men to run before him.
6And his father had not displeased him at any time in saying,
Why hast thou done so? and he also *was a* very goodly *man;* and
*his mother* bare him after Absalom.
7And he conferred with Joab the son of Zeruiah, and with
Abiathar the priest: and they following Adonijah helped *him*.
8But Zadok the priest, and Benaiah the son of Jehoiada, and
Nathan the prophet, and Shimei, and Rei, and the mighty men
which *belonged* to David, were not with Adonijah.
9And Adonijah slew sheep and oxen and fat cattle by the stone
of Zoheleth, which *is* by En-rogel, and called all his brethren the
king's sons, and all the men of Judah the king's servants:
10But Nathan the prophet, and Benaiah, and the mighty men,
and Solomon his brother, he called not.
11¶ Wherefore Nathan spake unto Bath-sheba the mother of
Solomon, saying, Hast thou not heard that Adonijah the son of
Haggith doth reign, and David our lord knoweth *it* not?
12Now therefore come, let me, I pray thee, give thee counsel,
that thou mayest save thine own life, and the life of thy son
Solomon.
13Go and get thee in unto king David, and say unto him, Didst
not thou, my lord, O king, swear unto thine handmaid, saying,
Assuredly Solomon thy son shall reign after me, and he shall sit
upon my throne? why then doth Adonijah reign?
14Behold, while thou yet talkest there with the king, I also will
come in after thee, and confirm thy words.
15¶ And Bath-sheba went in unto the king into the chamber: and
the king was very old; and Abishag the Shunammite ministered
unto the king.
16And Bath-sheba bowed, and did obeisance unto the king.
And the king said, What wouldest thou?
17And she said unto him, My lord, thou swarest by the LORD
thy God unto thine handmaid, *saying,* Assuredly Solomon thy son
shall reign after me, and he shall sit upon my throne.
18And now, behold, Adonijah reigneth; and now, my lord the
king, thou knowest *it* not:

## Amplified

THE FIRST BOOK OF THE

# Kings

1 AND KING David was old and advanced in years; they
covered him with [bed] clothes, but he could not get warm.
2So his servants [the [a]physicians] said to him, Let there be
sought for my lord the king a young virgin, and let her wait on and
be useful to the king; let her lie in your bosom, that my lord the
king may get warmth.
3So they sought for a fair maiden through all the territory of
Israel, and found Abishag the Shunammite, and brought her to the
king.
4The maiden was beautiful, and she waited on and nursed him.
But the king had no intercourse with her.
5Then Adonijah son of [David's wife] Haggith exalted himself,
saying, I [the eldest living son] will be king; and he prepared him
chariots and horsemen, and fifty men to run before him.
6David his father had never in his life displeased him by asking,
Why have you done so? He was also a very attractive man, and
was born after Absalom.
7He conferred with [b]Joab son of Zeruiah [David's half sister]
and with Abiathar the priest; and they followed Adonijah and
helped him.
8But Zadok the priest, Benaiah son of Jehoiada, Nathan the
prophet, Shimei, Rei, and David's mighty men did not side with
Adonijah.
9Adonijah sacrificed sheep, oxen, and fatlings by the stone of
Zoheleth, which is beside [the well] En-rogel, and he invited all his
brothers, the king's sons, and all the royal officials of Judah.
10But Nathan the prophet, Benaiah, the mighty men, and Solomon his brother, he did not invite.
11Then Nathan said to Bathsheba the mother of Solomon, Have
you not heard that Adonijah son of Haggith reigns, and David our
lord does not know it?
12Come now, let me advise you how to save your own life and
your son Solomon's.
13Go to King David, and say, Did you not, my lord, O king,
swear to your handmaid saying, Assuredly Solomon your son
shall reign after me, and he shall sit upon my throne? Why then
does Adonijah reign?
14Behold, while you are still talking there with the king, I also
will come in after you and confirm your words.
15So Bathsheba went to the king into his chamber. Now the king
was very old *and* feeble, and Abishag the Shunammite was ministering to [him].
16Bathsheba bowed, and did obeisance to the king. The king
said, What do you wish?
17And she said to him, My lord, you swore by the Lord your
God to your handmaid, saying, Assuredly Solomon your son shall
reign after me and sit upon my throne.
18And now, behold, Adonijah is reigning, and, my lord the
king, you do not know it.

**AMP** [a] Josephus, *Ant.* 14, 3. [b] Commander of Israel's army.

## New American Standard

# 1 Kings

*David in Old Age*

1 NOW KING David was old, advanced in age; and they
covered him with clothes, but he could not keep warm.
2So his servants said to him, "Let them seek a young virgin for
my lord the king, and let her attend the king and become his nurse;
and let her lie in your bosom, that my lord the king may keep
warm."
3So they searched for a beautiful girl throughout all the territory of Israel, and found Abishag the Shunammite, and brought
her to the king.
4And the girl was very beautiful; and she became the king's
nurse and served him, but the king did not cohabit with her.
5¶ Now Adonijah the son of Haggith exalted himself, saying,
"I will be king." So he prepared for himself chariots and horsemen
with fifty men to run before him.
6And his father had never crossed him at any time by asking,
"Why have you done so?" And he was also a very handsome man;
and he was born after Absalom.
7And he had conferred with Joab the son of Zeruiah and with
Abiathar the priest; and following Adonijah they helped him.
8But Zadok the priest, Benaiah the son of Jehoiada, Nathan the
prophet, Shimei, Rei, and the mighty men who belonged to David,
were not with Adonijah.
9And Adonijah sacrificed sheep and oxen and fatlings by the
[c]stone of Zoheleth, which is beside En-rogel; and he invited all his
brothers, the king's sons, and all the men of Judah, the king's
servants.
10But he did not invite Nathan the prophet, Benaiah, the mighty
men, and Solomon his brother.

*Nathan and Bathsheba*

11¶ Then Nathan spoke to Bathsheba the mother of Solomon,
saying, "Have you not heard that Adonijah the son of Haggith has
become king, and David our lord does not know *it?*
12"So now come, please let me give you counsel and save your
life and the life of your son Solomon.
13"Go at once to King David and say to him, 'Have you not, my
lord, O king, sworn to your maidservant, saying, "Surely Solomon
your son shall be king after me, and he shall sit on my throne"?
Why then has Adonijah become king?'
14"Behold, while you are still there speaking with the king, I
will come in after you and confirm your words."
15¶ So Bathsheba went in to the king in the bedroom. Now the
king was very old, and Abishag the Shunammite was ministering
to the king.
16Then Bathsheba bowed and prostrated herself before the
king. And the king said, "What do you wish?"
17And she said to him, "My lord, you swore to your maidservant by the LORD your God, *saying,* 'Surely your son Solomon
shall be king after me and he shall sit on my throne.'
18"And now, behold, Adonijah is king; and now, my lord the
king, you do not know *it.*

NAS [c] Or, *Gliding* or *Serpent Stone*

## New International

# 1 Kings

*Adonijah Sets Himself Up as King*

1 WHEN KING David was old and well advanced in years, he
could not keep warm even when they put covers over him.
2So his servants said to him, "Let us look for a young virgin to
attend the king and take care of him. She can lie beside him so that
our lord the king may keep warm."
3Then they searched throughout Israel for a beautiful girl and
found Abishag, a Shunammite, and brought her to the king. 4The
girl was very beautiful; she took care of the king and waited on
him, but the king had no intimate relations with her.
5Now Adonijah, whose mother was Haggith, put himself forward and said, "I will be king." So he got chariots and horses[d]
ready, with fifty men to run ahead of him. 6(His father had never
interfered with him by asking, "Why do you behave as you do?"
He was also very handsome and was born next after Absalom.)
7Adonijah conferred with Joab son of Zeruiah and with Abiathar the priest, and they gave him their support. 8But Zadok the
priest, Benaiah son of Jehoiada, Nathan the prophet, Shimei and
Rei[e] and David's special guard did not join Adonijah.
9Adonijah then sacrificed sheep, cattle and fattened calves at
the Stone of Zoheleth near En Rogel. He invited all his brothers,
the king's sons, and all the men of Judah who were royal officials,
10but he did not invite Nathan the prophet or Benaiah or the
special guard or his brother Solomon.
11Then Nathan asked Bathsheba, Solomon's mother, "Have
you not heard that Adonijah, the son of Haggith, has become king
without our lord David's knowing it? 12Now then, let me advise
you how you can save your own life and the life of your son
Solomon. 13Go in to King David and say to him, 'My lord the king,
did you not swear to me your servant: "Surely Solomon your son
shall be king after me, and he will sit on my throne"? Why then
has Adonijah become king?' 14While you are still there talking to
the king, I will come in and confirm what you have said."
15So Bathsheba went to see the aged king in his room, where
Abishag the Shunammite was attending him. 16Bathsheba bowed
low and knelt before the king.
"What is it you want?" the king asked.
17She said to him, "My lord, you yourself swore to me your
servant by the LORD your God: 'Solomon your son shall be king
after me, and he will sit on my throne.' 18But now Adonijah has
become king, and you, my lord the king, do not know about it.

NIV [d] 5 Or *charioteers* [e] 8 Or *and his friends*

## King James

19And he hath slain oxen and fat cattle and sheep in abundance, and hath called all the sons of the king, and Abiathar the priest, and Joab the captain of the host: but Solomon thy servant hath he not called.

20And thou, my lord, O king, the eyes of all Israel *are* upon thee, that thou shouldest tell them who shall sit on the throne of my lord the king after him.

21Otherwise it shall come to pass, when my lord the king shall sleep with his fathers, that I and my son Solomon shall be counted offenders.

22¶ And, lo, while she yet talked with the king, Nathan the prophet also came in.

23And they told the king, saying, Behold Nathan the prophet. And when he was come in before the king, he bowed himself before the king with his face to the ground.

24And Nathan said, My lord, O king, hast thou said, Adonijah shall reign after me, and he shall sit upon my throne?

25For he is gone down this day, and hath slain oxen and fat cattle and sheep in abundance, and hath called all the king's sons, and the captains of the host, and Abiathar the priest; and, behold, they eat and drink before him, and say, God save king Adonijah.

26But me, *even* me thy servant, and Zadok the priest, and Benaiah the son of Jehoiada, and thy servant Solomon, hath he not called.

27Is this thing done by my lord the king, and thou hast not showed *it* unto thy servant, who should sit on the throne of my lord the king after him?

28¶ Then king David answered and said, Call me Bath-sheba. And she came into the king's presence, and stood before the king.

29And the king sware, and said, *As* the LORD liveth, that hath redeemed my soul out of all distress,

30Even as I sware unto thee by the LORD God of Israel, saying, Assuredly Solomon thy son shall reign after me, and he shall sit upon my throne in my stead; even so will I certainly do this day.

31Then Bath-sheba bowed with *her* face to the earth, and did reverence to the king, and said, Let my lord king David live for ever.

32¶ And king David said, Call me Zadok the priest, and Nathan the prophet, and Benaiah the son of Jehoiada. And they came before the king.

33The king also said unto them, Take with you the servants of your lord, and cause Solomon my son to ride upon mine own mule, and bring him down to Gihon:

34And let Zadok the priest and Nathan the prophet anoint him there king over Israel: and blow ye with the trumpet, and say, God save king Solomon.

35Then ye shall come up after him, that he may come and sit upon my throne; for he shall be king in my stead: and I have appointed him to be ruler over Israel and over Judah.

36And Benaiah the son of Jehoiada answered the king, and said, Amen: the LORD God of my lord the king say so *too*.

37As the LORD hath been with my lord the king, even so be he with Solomon, and make his throne greater than the throne of my lord king David.

38So Zadok the priest, and Nathan the prophet, and Benaiah the son of Jehoiada, and the Cherethites, and the Pelethites, went down, and caused Solomon to ride upon king David's mule, and brought him to Gihon.

39And Zadok the priest took an horn of oil out of the tabernacle, and anointed Solomon. And they blew the trumpet; and all the people said, God save king Solomon.

40And all the people came up after him, and the people piped with pipes, and rejoiced with great joy, so that the earth rent with the sound of them.

## Amplified

19He has sacrificed oxen and fatlings and sheep in abundance, and has invited all the king's sons, and Abiathar the priest and Joab the commander of the army. But he did not invite Solomon your servant.

20Now, my lord, O king, the eyes of all Israel are on you to tell who shall sit on the throne of my lord the king after you.

21Otherwise when my lord the king shall sleep with his fathers, I and my son Solomon shall be counted offenders.

22While she was still talking with the king, Nathan the prophet also came in.

23The king was told, Here is Nathan the prophet. And when he came before the king, he bowed himself before him with his face to the ground.

24And Nathan said, My lord the king, have you said, Adonijah shall reign after me, and he shall sit on my throne?

25He has gone this day, and sacrificed oxen, fatlings, and sheep in abundance, and has invited all the king's sons, the captains of the host, and Abiathar the priest; and they eat and drink before him, and say, Long live King Adonijah!

26But me, your servant, and Zadok the priest, and Benaiah son of Jehoiada, and your servant Solomon, he has not invited.

27Is this done by my lord the king, and you have not shown your servants who shall succeed my lord the king?

28Then King David answered, Call Bathsheba. And she came into the king's presence, and stood before him.

29And the king took an oath and said, As the Lord lives Who has redeemed my soul out of all distress,

30Even as I swore to you by the Lord, the God of Israel, saying, Assuredly Solomon your son shall reign after me, and he shall sit upon my throne in my stead; even so will I certainly do this day.

31Bathsheba bowed with her face to the ground, and did obeisance to the king, and said, Let my lord King David live for ever!

32King David said, Call Zadok the priest, Nathan the prophet, and Benaiah son of Jehoiada. And they came before the king.

33The king told them, Take the servants of your lord, and cause Solomon my son to ride on my own mule, and bring him down to Gihon [in the Kidron Valley];

34And let Zadok the priest and Nathan the prophet anoint him there king over Israel. Then blow the trumpet, and say, Long live King Solomon!

35Then you shall come up after him, and he shall come and sit on my throne; for he shall be king in my stead; I have appointed him ruler over Israel and Judah.

36And Benaiah son of Jehoiada answered the king, and said, Amen! May the Lord God of my lord the king say so too.

37As the Lord has been with my lord the king, even so may He be with Solomon, and make his throne greater than the throne of my lord King David.

38So Zadok the priest, Nathan the prophet, Benaiah son of Jehoiada, the Cherethites and Pelethites [the king's bodyguard], went down and caused Solomon to ride upon King David's mule, and brought him to Gihon.

39Zadok the priest took a horn of oil out of the tent and anointed Solomon. They blew the trumpet; and all the people said, Long live King Solomon!

40All the people followed him; they played on pipes and rejoiced greatly, so that the earth [resounded] with the joyful sound.

## New American Standard

19"And he has sacrificed oxen and fatlings and sheep in abundance, and has invited all the sons of the king and Abiathar the
priest and Joab the commander of the army; but he has not invited
Solomon your servant.
20"And as for you now, my lord the king, the eyes of all Israel
are on you, to tell them who shall sit on the throne of my lord the
king after him.
21"Otherwise it will come about, as soon as my lord the king
sleeps with his fathers, that I and my son Solomon will be considered offenders."
22¶ And behold, while she was still speaking with the king,
Nathan the prophet came in.
23And they told the king, saying, "Here is Nathan the
prophet." And when he came in before the king, he prostrated
himself before the king with his face to the ground.
24Then Nathan said, "My lord the king, have you said, 'Adonijah shall be king after me, and he shall sit on my throne'?
25"For he has gone down today and has sacrificed oxen and
fatlings and sheep in abundance, and has invited all the king's
sons and the commanders of the army and Abiathar the priest, and
behold, they are eating and drinking before him; and they say, '
*Long* live King Adonijah!'
26"But me, *even* me your servant, and Zadok the priest and
Benaiah the son of Jehoiada and your servant Solomon, he has not
invited.
27"Has this thing been done by my lord the king, and you have
not shown to your servants who should sit on the throne of my
lord the king after him?"
28¶ Then King David answered and said, "Call Bathsheba to
me." And she came into the king's presence and stood before the
king.
29And the king vowed and said, "As the LORD lives, who has
redeemed my life from all distress,
30surely as I vowed to you by the LORD the God of Israel, saying,
'Your son Solomon shall be king after me, and he shall sit on my
throne in my place'; I will indeed do so this day."
31Then Bathsheba bowed with her face to the ground, and
prostrated herself before the king and said, "May my lord King
David live forever."
32¶ Then King David said, "Call to me Zadok the priest, Nathan
the prophet, and Benaiah the son of Jehoiada." And they came into
the king's presence.
33And the king said to them, "Take with you the servants of
your lord, and have my son Solomon ride on my own mule, and
bring him down to Gihon.
34"And let Zadok the priest and Nathan the prophet anoint him
there as king over Israel, and blow the trumpet and say, '*Long* live
King Solomon!'
35"Then you shall come up after him, and he shall come and sit
on my throne and be king in my place; for I have appointed him
to be ruler over Israel and Judah."
36And Benaiah the son of Jehoiada answered the king and said,
"Amen! Thus may the LORD, the God of my lord the king, say.
37"As the LORD has been with my lord the king, so may He be
with Solomon, and make his throne greater than the throne of my
lord King David!"

*Solomon Anointed King*

38¶ So Zadok the priest, Nathan the prophet, Benaiah the son
of Jehoiada, the Cherethites, and the Pelethites went down and
had Solomon ride on King David's mule, and brought him to
Gihon.
39Zadok the priest then took the horn of oil from the tent and
anointed Solomon. Then they blew the trumpet, and all the people
said, "*Long* live King Solomon!"
40And all the people went up after him, and the people were
playing on flutes and rejoicing with great joy, so that the earth
shook at their noise.

## New International

19He has sacrificed great numbers of cattle, fattened calves, and
sheep, and has invited all the king's sons, Abiathar the priest and
Joab the commander of the army, but he has not invited Solomon
your servant. 20My lord the king, the eyes of all Israel are on you,
to learn from you who will sit on the throne of my lord the king
after him. 21Otherwise, as soon as my lord the king is laid to rest
with his fathers, I and my son Solomon will be treated as criminals."
22While she was still speaking with the king, Nathan the
prophet arrived. 23And they told the king, "Nathan the prophet
is here." So he went before the king and bowed with his face to
the ground.
24Nathan said, "Have you, my lord the king, declared that
Adonijah shall be king after you, and that he will sit on your
throne? 25Today he has gone down and sacrificed great numbers
of cattle, fattened calves, and sheep. He has invited all the king's
sons, the commanders of the army and Abiathar the priest. Right
now they are eating and drinking with him and saying, 'Long live
King Adonijah!' 26But me your servant, and Zadok the priest, and
Benaiah son of Jehoiada, and your servant Solomon he did not
invite. 27Is this something my lord the king has done without
letting his servants know who should sit on the throne of my lord
the king after him?"

*David Makes Solomon King*

28Then King David said, "Call in Bathsheba." So she came into
the king's presence and stood before him.
29The king then took an oath: "As surely as the LORD lives, who
has delivered me out of every trouble, 30I will surely carry out
today what I swore to you by the LORD, the God of Israel: Solomon
your son shall be king after me, and he will sit on my throne in
my place."
31Then Bathsheba bowed low with her face to the ground and,
kneeling before the king, said, "May my lord King David live
forever!"
32King David said, "Call in Zadok the priest, Nathan the
prophet and Benaiah son of Jehoiada." When they came before the
king, 33he said to them: "Take your lord's servants with you and
set Solomon my son on my own mule and take him down to
Gihon. 34There have Zadok the priest and Nathan the prophet
anoint him king over Israel. Blow the trumpet and shout, 'Long
live King Solomon!' 35Then you are to go up with him, and he is
to come and sit on my throne and reign in my place. I have
appointed him ruler over Israel and Judah."
36Benaiah son of Jehoiada answered the king, "Amen! May the
LORD, the God of my lord the king, so declare it. 37As the LORD
was with my lord the king, so may he be with Solomon to make
his throne even greater than the throne of my lord King David!"
38So Zadok the priest, Nathan the prophet, Benaiah son of
Jehoiada, the Kerethites and the Pelethites went down and put
Solomon on King David's mule and escorted him to Gihon.
39Zadok the priest took the horn of oil from the sacred tent and
anointed Solomon. Then they sounded the trumpet and all the
people shouted, "Long live King Solomon!" 40And all the people
went up after him, playing flutes and rejoicing greatly, so that the
ground shook with the sound.

## King James

41¶ And Adonijah and all the guests that *were* with him heard *it* as they had made an end of eating. And when Joab heard the sound of the trumpet, he said, Wherefore *is this* noise of the city being in an uproar?

42And while he yet spake, behold, Jonathan the son of Abiathar the priest came: and Adonijah said unto him, Come in; for thou *art* a valiant man, and bringest good tidings.

43And Jonathan answered and said to Adonijah, Verily our lord king David hath made Solomon king.

44And the king hath sent with him Zadok the priest, and Nathan the prophet, and Benaiah the son of Jehoiada, and the Cherethites, and the Pelethites, and they have caused him to ride upon the king's mule:

45And Zadok the priest and Nathan the prophet have anointed him king in Gihon: and they are come up from thence rejoicing, so that the city rang again. This *is* the noise that ye have heard.

46And also Solomon sitteth on the throne of the kingdom.

47And moreover the king's servants came to bless our lord king David, saying, God make the name of Solomon better than thy name, and make his throne greater than thy throne. And the king bowed himself upon the bed.

48And also thus said the king, Blessed *be* the LORD God of Israel, which hath given *one* to sit on my throne this day, mine eyes even seeing *it*.

49And all the guests that *were* with Adonijah were afraid, and rose up, and went every man his way.

50¶ And Adonijah feared because of Solomon, and arose, and went, and caught hold on the horns of the altar.

51And it was told Solomon, saying, Behold, Adonijah feareth king Solomon: for, lo, he hath caught hold on the horns of the altar, saying, Let king Solomon swear unto me today that he will not slay his servant with the sword.

52And Solomon said, If he will show himself a worthy man, there shall not an hair of him fall to the earth: but if wickedness shall be found in him, he shall die.

53So king Solomon sent, and they brought him down from the altar. And he came and bowed himself to king Solomon: and Solomon said unto him, Go to thine house.

**2** NOW THE days of David drew nigh that he should die; and he charged Solomon his son, saying,

2I go the way of all the earth: be thou strong therefore, and show thyself a man;

3And keep the charge of the LORD thy God, to walk in his ways, to keep his statutes, and his commandments, and his judgments, and his testimonies, as it is written in the law of Moses, that thou mayest prosper in all that thou doest, and whithersoever thou turnest thyself:

4That the LORD may continue his word which he spake concerning me, saying, If thy children take heed to their way, to walk before me in truth with all their heart and with all their soul, there shall not fail thee (said he) a man on the throne of Israel.

5Moreover thou knowest also what Joab the son of Zeruiah did to me, *and* what he did to the two captains of the hosts of Israel, unto Abner the son of Ner, and unto Amasa the son of Jether, whom he slew, and shed the blood of war in peace, and put the blood of war upon his girdle that *was* about his loins, and in his shoes that *were* on his feet.

6Do therefore according to thy wisdom, and let not his hoar head go down to the grave in peace.

7But show kindness unto the sons of Barzillai the Gileadite, and let them be of those that eat at thy table: for so they came to me when I fled because of Absalom thy brother.

## Amplified

41And Adonijah and all the guests with him heard it as they finished feasting. When Joab heard the trumpet sound, he said, What does this uproar in the city mean?

42While he was still speaking, behold, Jonathan son of Abiathar the priest came; and Adonijah said, Come in, for you are a trustworthy man and bring good news.

43Jonathan replied, Adonijah, truly our lord King David has made Solomon king!

44The king has sent him with Zadok the priest, Nathan the prophet, Benaiah son of Jehoiada, the Cherethites and Pelethites, and they have caused him to ride upon the king's mule;

45Zadok the priest and Nathan the prophet have anointed him king in Gihon; they have come up from there rejoicing, so the city resounds. This is the noise you heard.

46Solomon sits on the royal throne.

47Moreover the king's servants came to congratulate our lord King David, saying, God make the name of Solomon better than your name, and make his throne greater than your throne. And the king bowed himself upon the bed,

48And said, Blessed be the Lord God of Israel, Who has granted me to see one of my offspring sitting on my throne this day.

49And all the guests that were with Adonijah were afraid, and rose up, and went every man his way.

50And Adonijah feared because of Solomon, and arose and went [to the tabernacle tent on Mt. Zion] and caught hold of the horns of the altar [as a fugitive's refuge].

51And it was told Solomon, Behold, Adonijah fears King Solomon; for, lo, he has caught hold of the horns of the altar, saying, Let King Solomon swear to me first that he will not slay his servant with the sword.

52Solomon said, If he will show himself to be a worthy man, not a hair of him shall fall to the ground; but if wickedness is found in him, he shall die.

53So King Solomon sent, and they brought Adonijah down from the altar [in front of the tabernacle]. He came and bowed himself to King Solomon, and Solomon said to him, Go to your house.

**2** WHEN DAVID'S time to die was near, he charged Solomon his son, saying,

2I go the way of all the earth. Be strong, and show yourself a man;

3Keep the charge of the Lord your God, walk in His ways, keep His statutes, His commandments, His precepts, and His testimonies, as it is written in the law of Moses, that you may do wisely *and* prosper in all that you do and wherever you turn;

4That the Lord may fulfill His promise to me saying, If your sons take heed to their way, to walk before Me in truth with all their heart *and* mind and with all their soul, there shall not fail you a man on the throne of Israel.

5You know also what Joab son of Zeruiah did to me, and what he did to the two captains of the hosts of Israel, Abner son of Ner, and Amasa son of Jether, whom he murdered, avenging in time of peace blood shed in war, and putting innocent blood of war on the girdle on his loins, and on the sandals of his feet.

6Do therefore according to your wisdom, but let not his hoary head go down to Sheol [the place of the dead] in peace.

7But show kindness to the sons of Barzillai the Gileadite, and let them be among those who eat at your table, for with such kindness they met me when I fled because of Absalom your brother. [II Sam. 17:27-29.]

## New American Standard

41¶ Now Adonijah and all the guests who were with him heard
*it*, as they finished eating. When Joab heard the sound of the
trumpet, he said, "Why is the city making such an uproar?"
42While he was still speaking, behold, Jonathan the son of
Abiathar the priest came. Then Adonijah said, "Come in, for you
are a valiant man and bring good news."
43But Jonathan answered and said to Adonijah, "No! Our lord
King David has made Solomon king.
44"The king has also sent with him Zadok the priest, Nathan the
prophet, Benaiah the son of Jehoiada, the Cherethites, and the
Pelethites; and they have made him ride on the king's mule.
45"And Zadok the priest and Nathan the prophet have anointed
him king in Gihon, and they have come up from there rejoicing,
so that the city is in an uproar. This is the noise which you have
heard.
46"Besides, Solomon has even taken his seat on the throne of
the kingdom.
47"And moreover, the king's servants came to bless our lord
King David, saying, 'May your God make the name of Solomon
better than your name and his throne greater than your throne!'
And the king bowed himself on the bed.
48"The king has also said thus, 'Blessed be the LORD, the God
of Israel, who has granted one to sit on my throne today while my
own eyes see *it*.' "
49¶ Then all the guests of Adonijah were terrified; and they
arose and each went on his way.
50And Adonijah was afraid of Solomon, and he arose, went and
took hold of the horns of the altar.
51Now it was told Solomon, saying, "Behold, Adonijah is afraid
of King Solomon, for behold, he has taken hold of the horns of the
altar, saying, 'Let King Solomon swear to me today that he will not
put his servant to death with the sword.' "
52And Solomon said, "If he will be a worthy man, not one of
his hairs will fall to the ground; but if wickedness is found in him,
he will die."
53So King Solomon sent, and they brought him down from the
altar. And he came and prostrated himself before King Solomon,
and Solomon said to him, "Go to your house."

*David's Charge to Solomon*

**2** AS DAVID'S time to die drew near, he charged Solomon his
son, saying,
2"I am going the way of all the earth. Be strong, therefore, and
show yourself a man.
3"And keep the charge of the LORD your God, to walk in His
ways, to keep His statutes, His commandments, His ordinances,
and His testimonies, according to what is written in the law of
Moses, that you may succeed in all that you do and wherever you
turn,
4so that the LORD may carry out His promise which He spoke
concerning me, saying, 'If your sons are careful of their way, to
walk before Me in [a]truth with all their heart and with all their soul,
you shall not lack a man on the throne of Israel.'
5"Now you also know what Joab the son of Zeruiah did to me,
what he did to the two commanders of the armies of Israel, to
Abner the son of Ner, and to Amasa the son of Jether, whom he
killed; he also shed the blood of war in peace. And he put the blood
of war on his belt about his waist, and on his sandals on his feet.
6"So act according to your wisdom, and do not let his gray hair
go down to Sheol in peace.
7"But show kindness to the sons of Barzillai the Gileadite, and
let them be among those who eat at your table; for they assisted
me when I fled from Absalom your brother.

NAS [a] Or, *faithfulness*

## New International

41Adonijah and all the guests who were with him heard it as
they were finishing their feast. On hearing the sound of the trumpet, Joab asked, "What's the meaning of all the noise in the city?"
42Even as he was speaking, Jonathan son of Abiathar the priest
arrived. Adonijah said, "Come in. A worthy man like you must be
bringing good news."
43"Not at all!" Jonathan answered. "Our lord King David has
made Solomon king. 44The king has sent with him Zadok the
priest, Nathan the prophet, Benaiah son of Jehoiada, the Kerethites and the Pelethites, and they have put him on the king's
mule, 45and Zadok the priest and Nathan the prophet have anointed him king at Gihon. From there they have gone up cheering, and
the city resounds with it. That's the noise you hear. 46Moreover,
Solomon has taken his seat on the royal throne. 47Also, the royal
officials have come to congratulate our lord King David, saying,
'May your God make Solomon's name more famous than yours
and his throne greater than yours!' And the king bowed in worship
on his bed 48and said, 'Praise be to the LORD, the God of Israel,
who has allowed my eyes to see a successor on my throne today.' "
49At this, all Adonijah's guests rose in alarm and dispersed.
50But Adonijah, in fear of Solomon, went and took hold of the
horns of the altar. 51Then Solomon was told, "Adonijah is afraid
of King Solomon and is clinging to the horns of the altar. He says,
'Let King Solomon swear to me today that he will not put his
servant to death with the sword.' "
52Solomon replied, "If he shows himself to be a worthy man,
not a hair of his head will fall to the ground; but if evil is found
in him, he will die." 53Then King Solomon sent men, and they
brought him down from the altar. And Adonijah came and bowed
down to King Solomon, and Solomon said, "Go to your home."

*David's Charge to Solomon*

**2** WHEN THE time drew near for David to die, he gave a charge
to Solomon his son.
2"I am about to go the way of all the earth," he said. "So be
strong, show yourself a man, 3and observe what the LORD your
God requires: Walk in his ways, and keep his decrees and commands, his laws and requirements, as written in the Law of Moses,
so that you may prosper in all you do and wherever you go, 4and
that the LORD may keep his promise to me: 'If your descendants
watch how they live, and if they walk faithfully before me with all
their heart and soul, you will never fail to have a man on the throne
of Israel.'
5"Now you yourself know what Joab son of Zeruiah did to
me—what he did to the two commanders of Israel's armies, Abner
son of Ner and Amasa son of Jether. He killed them, shedding
their blood in peacetime as if in battle, and with that blood stained
the belt around his waist and the sandals on his feet. 6Deal with
him according to your wisdom, but do not let his gray head go
down to the grave[b] in peace.
7"But show kindness to the sons of Barzillai of Gilead and let
them be among those who eat at your table. They stood by me
when I fled from your brother Absalom.

NIV [b] 6 Hebrew *Sheol;* also in verse 9

## King James

8And, behold, *thou hast* with thee Shimei the son of Gera, a Benjamite of Bahurim, which cursed me with a grievous curse in the day when I went to Mahanaim: but he came down to meet me at Jordan, and I sware to him by the LORD, saying, I will not put thee to death with the sword.

9Now therefore hold him not guiltless: for thou *art* a wise man, and knowest what thou oughtest to do unto him; but his hoar head bring thou down to the grave with blood.

10So David slept with his fathers, and was buried in the city of David.

11And the days that David reigned over Israel *were* forty years: seven years reigned he in Hebron, and thirty and three years reigned he in Jerusalem.

12¶ Then sat Solomon upon the throne of David his father; and his kingdom was established greatly.

13¶ And Adonijah the son of Haggith came to Bath-sheba the mother of Solomon. And she said, Comest thou peaceably? And he said, Peaceably.

14He said moreover, I have somewhat to say unto thee. And she said, Say on.

15And he said, Thou knowest that the kingdom was mine, and *that* all Israel set their faces on me, that I should reign: howbeit the kingdom is turned about, and is become my brother's: for it was his from the LORD.

16And now I ask one petition of thee, deny me not. And she said unto him, Say on.

17And he said, Speak, I pray thee, unto Solomon the king, (for he will not say thee nay,) that he give me Abishag the Shunammite to wife.

18And Bath-sheba said, Well; I will speak for thee unto the king.

19¶ Bath-sheba therefore went unto king Solomon, to speak unto him for Adonijah. And the king rose up to meet her, and bowed himself unto her, and sat down on his throne, and caused a seat to be set for the king's mother; and she sat on his right hand.

20Then she said, I desire one small petition of thee; *I pray thee,* say me not nay. And the king said unto her, Ask on, my mother: for I will not say thee nay.

21And she said, Let Abishag the Shunammite be given to Adonijah thy brother to wife.

22And king Solomon answered and said unto his mother, And why dost thou ask Abishag the Shunammite for Adonijah? ask for him the kingdom also; for he *is* mine elder brother; even for him, and for Abiathar the priest, and for Joab the son of Zeruiah.

23Then king Solomon sware by the LORD, saying, God do so to me, and more also, if Adonijah have not spoken this word against his own life.

24Now therefore, *as* the LORD liveth, which hath established me, and set me on the throne of David my father, and who hath made me an house, as he promised, Adonijah shall be put to death this day.

25And king Solomon sent by the hand of Benaiah the son of Jehoiada; and he fell upon him that he died.

26¶ And unto Abiathar the priest said the king, Get thee to Anathoth, unto thine own fields; for thou *art* worthy of death: but I will not at this time put thee to death, because thou barest the ark of the Lord GOD before David my father, and because thou hast been afflicted in all wherein my father was afflicted.

27So Solomon thrust out Abiathar from being priest unto the LORD; that he might fulfil the word of the LORD, which he spake concerning the house of Eli in Shiloh.

## Amplified

8And you have with you Shimei son of Gera, the Benjamite of Bahurim, who cursed me with a grievous curse in the day when I went to Mahanaim. But he came down to meet me at Jordan [on my return], and I swore to him by the Lord, saying, I will not put you to death with the sword.

9So do not hold him guiltless, for you are a wise man and know what you should do to him; his hoary head bring down to the grave with blood.

10So David slept with his fathers, and was buried in the city of David.

11David reigned over Israel forty years; seven years in Hebron, and thirty-three years in Jerusalem.

12Then Solomon sat on the throne of David his father, and his kingdom was firmly established.

13Adonijah the son of [David and] Haggith came to Bathsheba the mother of Solomon. She said, Do you come peaceably? And he said, Peaceably.

14He said, I have something to say to you. And she said, Say on.

15He said, You know that the kingdom belonged to me [as the eldest living son], and all Israel looked to me to reign. However the kingdom has passed from me to my brother, for it was his from the Lord.

16Now I make one request of you; do not deny me. And she said, Say on.

17He said, Pray ask King Solomon, for he will not refuse you, to give me Abishag the Shunammite to be my wife. [I Kings 1:1-4.]

18And Bathsheba said, Well; I will speak for you to the king.

19So Bathsheba went to King Solomon to speak to him for Adonijah. The king rose to meet her, bowed to her, sat down on his throne, and caused a seat to be set at his right hand for her, the king's mother.

20Then she said, I have one small request to make of you; do not refuse me. The king said to her, Ask on, my mother; for I will not refuse you.

21She said, Give Abishag the Shunammite to Adonijah your brother to be his wife.

22King Solomon answered his mother, And why do you ask Abishag the Shunammite for Adonijah? Ask for him the kingdom also, for he is my elder brother, [ask it] even for him, and for [his supporters] Abiathar the priest and Joab son of Zeruiah.

23Then King Solomon swore by the Lord, saying, God do so to me and more also if Adonijah has not requested this against his own life.

24Therefore as the Lord lives, Who has established me, and set me on the throne of David my father, and Who has made me a house, as He promised, Adonijah shall be put to death this day.

25So King Solomon sent Benaiah son of Jehoiada, who attacked [Adonijah], and he died.

26And to Abiathar the priest the king said, Get to Anathoth, to your own estate, for you deserve death; but I will not put you to death now, because you bore the ark of the Lord God before my father David, and were afflicted in all my father endured.

27So Solomon expelled Abiathar [descendant of Eli] from being priest to the Lord; fulfilling the word of the Lord which He spoke concerning the house of Eli in Shiloh. [I Sam. 2:27-36.]

## New American Standard

8"And behold, there is with you Shimei the son of Gera the
Benjamite, of Bahurim; now it was he who cursed me with a
violent curse on the day I went to Mahanaim. But when he came
down to me at the Jordan, I swore to him by the LORD, saying, 'I
will not put you to death with the sword.'
9"Now therefore, do not let him go unpunished, for you are
a wise man; and you will know what you ought to do to him, and
you will bring his gray hair down to Sheol with blood."

*Death of David*

10¶ Then David slept with his fathers and was buried in the city
of David.
11And the days that David reigned over Israel *were* forty years:
seven years he reigned in Hebron, and thirty-three years he
reigned in Jerusalem.
12And Solomon sat on the throne of David his father, and his
kingdom was firmly established.
13¶ Now Adonijah the son of Haggith came to Bathsheba the
mother of Solomon. And she said, "Do you come peacefully?"
And he said, "Peacefully."
14Then he said, "I have something *to say* to you." And she said,
"Speak."
15So he said, "You know that the kingdom was mine and that
all Israel expected me to be king; however, the kingdom has turned
about and become my brother's, for it was his from the LORD.
16"And now I am making one request of you; do not [a]refuse
me." And she said to him, "Speak."
17Then he said, "Please speak to Solomon the king, for he will
not refuse you, that he may give me Abishag the Shunammite as
a wife."
18And Bathsheba said, "Very well; I will speak to the king for
you."

*Adonijah Executed*

19¶ So Bathsheba went to King Solomon to speak to him for
Adonijah. And the king arose to meet her, bowed before her, and
sat on his throne; then he had a throne set for the king's mother,
and she sat on his right.
20Then she said, "I am making one small request of you; do not
refuse me." And the king said to her, "Ask, my mother, for I will
not refuse you."
21So she said, "Let Abishag the Shunammite be given to Adonijah your brother as a wife."
22And King Solomon answered and said to his mother, "And
why are you asking Abishag the Shunammite for Adonijah? Ask
for him also the kingdom—for he is my older brother—even for
him, for Abiathar the priest, and for Joab the son of Zeruiah!"
23Then King Solomon swore by the LORD, saying, "May God do
so to me and more also, if Adonijah has not spoken this word
against his own life.
24"Now therefore, as the LORD lives, who has established me
and set me on the throne of David my father, and who has made
me a house as He promised, surely Adonijah will be put to death
today."
25So King Solomon sent Benaiah the son of Jehoiada; and he fell
upon him so that he died.
26¶ Then to Abiathar the priest the king said, "Go to Anathoth
to your own field, for you deserve to die; but I will not put you to
death at this time, because you carried the ark of the Lord GOD
before my father David, and because you were afflicted in everything with which my father was afflicted."
27So Solomon dismissed Abiathar from being priest to the
LORD, in order to fulfill the word of the LORD, which He had
spoken concerning the house of Eli in Shiloh.

NAS [a] Lit., *turn away my (your) face,* and so in vv. 17, 20

## New International

8"And remember, you have with you Shimei son of Gera, the
Benjamite from Bahurim, who called down bitter curses on me the
day I went to Mahanaim. When he came down to meet me at the
Jordan, I swore to him by the LORD: 'I will not put you to death
by the sword.' 9But now, do not consider him innocent. You are
a man of wisdom; you will know what to do to him. Bring his gray
head down to the grave in blood."
10Then David rested with his fathers and was buried in the City
of David. 11He had reigned forty years over Israel—seven years in
Hebron and thirty-three in Jerusalem. 12So Solomon sat on the
throne of his father David, and his rule was firmly established.

*Solomon's Throne Established*

13Now Adonijah, the son of Haggith, went to Bathsheba, Solomon's mother. Bathsheba asked him, "Do you come peacefully?"
He answered, "Yes, peacefully." 14Then he added, "I have
something to say to you."
"You may say it," she replied.
15"As you know," he said, "the kingdom was mine. All Israel
looked to me as their king. But things changed, and the kingdom
has gone to my brother; for it has come to him from the LORD.
16Now I have one request to make of you. Do not refuse me."
"You may make it," she said.
17So he continued, "Please ask King Solomon—he will not
refuse you—to give me Abishag the Shunammite as my wife."
18"Very well," Bathsheba replied, "I will speak to the king for
you."
19When Bathsheba went to King Solomon to speak to him for
Adonijah, the king stood up to meet her, bowed down to her and
sat down on his throne. He had a throne brought for the king's
mother, and she sat down at his right hand.
20"I have one small request to make of you," she said. "Do not
refuse me."
The king replied, "Make it, my mother; I will not refuse you."
21So she said, "Let Abishag the Shunammite be given in marriage to your brother Adonijah."
22King Solomon answered his mother, "Why do you request
Abishag the Shunammite for Adonijah? You might as well request
the kingdom for him—after all, he is my older brother—yes, for
him and for Abiathar the priest and Joab son of Zeruiah!"
23Then King Solomon swore by the LORD: "May God deal with
me, be it ever so severely, if Adonijah does not pay with his life
for this request! 24And now, as surely as the LORD lives—he who
has established me securely on the throne of my father David and
has founded a dynasty for me as he promised—Adonijah shall be
put to death today!" 25So King Solomon gave orders to Benaiah
son of Jehoiada, and he struck down Adonijah and he died.
26To Abiathar the priest the king said, "Go back to your fields
in Anathoth. You deserve to die, but I will not put you to death
now, because you carried the ark of the Sovereign LORD before my
father David and shared all my father's hardships." 27So Solomon
removed Abiathar from the priesthood of the LORD, fulfilling the
word the LORD had spoken at Shiloh about the house of Eli.

## King James

28¶ Then tidings came to Joab: for Joab had turned after Adonijah, though he turned not after Absalom. And Joab fled unto the
tabernacle of the LORD, and caught hold on the horns of the altar.
29And it was told king Solomon that Joab was fled unto the
tabernacle of the LORD; and, behold, *he is* by the altar. Then Solomon sent Benaiah the son of Jehoiada, saying, Go, fall upon him.
30And Benaiah came to the tabernacle of the LORD, and said
unto him, Thus saith the king, Come forth. And he said, Nay; but
I will die here. And Benaiah brought the king word again, saying,
Thus said Joab, and thus he answered me.
31And the king said unto him, Do as he hath said, and fall upon
him, and bury him; that thou mayest take away the innocent
blood, which Joab shed, from me, and from the house of my
father.
32And the LORD shall return his blood upon his own head, who
fell upon two men more righteous and better than he, and slew
them with the sword, my father David not knowing *thereof, to wit,*
Abner the son of Ner, captain of the host of Israel, and Amasa the
son of Jether, captain of the host of Judah.
33Their blood shall therefore return upon the head of Joab, and
upon the head of his seed for ever: but upon David, and upon his
seed, and upon his house, and upon his throne, shall there be
peace for ever from the LORD.
34So Benaiah the son of Jehoiada went up, and fell upon him,
and slew him: and he was buried in his own house in the wilderness.
35¶ And the king put Benaiah the son of Jehoiada in his room
over the host: and Zadok the priest did the king put in the room
of Abiathar.
36¶ And the king sent and called for Shimei, and said unto him,
Build thee an house in Jerusalem, and dwell there, and go not forth
thence any whither.
37For it shall be, *that* on the day thou goest out, and passest over
the brook Kidron, thou shalt know for certain that thou shalt surely
die: thy blood shall be upon thine own head.
38And Shimei said unto the king, The saying *is* good: as my lord
the king hath said, so will thy servant do. And Shimei dwelt in
Jerusalem many days.
39And it came to pass at the end of three years, that two of the
servants of Shimei ran away unto Achish son of Maachah king of
Gath. And they told Shimei, saying, Behold, thy servants *be* in
Gath.
40And Shimei arose, and saddled his ass, and went to Gath to
Achish to seek his servants: and Shimei went, and brought his
servants from Gath.
41And it was told Solomon that Shimei had gone from Jerusalem
to Gath, and was come again.
42And the king sent and called for Shimei, and said unto him,
Did I not make thee to swear by the LORD, and protested unto thee,
saying, Know for a certain, on the day thou goest out, and walkest
abroad any whither, that thou shalt surely die? and thou saidst
unto me, The word *that* I have heard *is* good.
43Why then hast thou not kept the oath of the LORD, and the
commandment that I have charged thee with?
44The king said moreover to Shimei, Thou knowest all the
wickedness which thine heart is privy to, that thou didst to David
my father: therefore the LORD shall return thy wickedness upon
thine own head;
45And king Solomon *shall be* blessed, and the throne of David
shall be established before the LORD for ever.
46So the king commanded Benaiah the son of Jehoiada; which
went out, and fell upon him, that he died. And the kingdom was
established in the hand of Solomon.

## Amplified

28When the news came to Joab, for Joab had followed Adonijah,
though he had not followed Absalom [he] fled to the tent [taber-
nacle] of the Lord, and caught hold of the horns of the altar [before
it].
29King Solomon was told that Joab had fled to the tent of the
Lord, and was at the altar. Then Solomon sent Benaiah son of
Jehoiada, saying, Go, strike him down.
30So Benaiah came to the tent of the Lord and told Joab, The
king commands, Come forth. But Joab said, No; I will die here.
Then Benaiah brought the king word again, Thus said Joab, and
thus he answered me.
31The king said to him, Do as he has said; strike him down and
bury him, that you may take away from [me and from] my father's
house the innocent blood which Joab shed.
32The Lord shall return his bloody deeds upon his own head,
for he fell upon two men more [uncompromisingly] righteous and
honorable than he, and slew them with the sword, without my
father knowing of it: Abner son of Ner, captain of the host of Israel,
and Amasa son of Jether, captain of the host of Judah.
33So shall their blood return upon the head of Joab and of his
descendants for ever. But upon David, his descendants, his house,
and his throne, there shall be peace from the Lord for ever.
34So Benaiah son of Jehoiada went up, and struck and killed
Joab, and he was buried at his own house in the wilderness.
35The king put Benaiah son of Jehoiada in Joab's place over the
army, and put Zadok the priest in place of Abiathar.
36The king sent for Shimei, and said to him, Build yourself a
house in Jerusalem and dwell there, and do not leave there.
37For on the day you go out, and pass over the brook Kidron,
know for a certainty that you shall die; your blood shall be upon
your own head.
38And Shimei said to the king, The saying is good; as my lord
the king has said, so your servant will do. And Shimei dwelt in
Jerusalem many days.
39But after three years, two of Shimei's servants ran away to
Achish son of Maacah king of Gath. And Shimei was told, Behold,
your [runaway] servants are in Gath.
40So Shimei arose, saddled his donkey, and went to Gath to
King Achish to seek his servants, and brought them from Gath.
41It was told Solomon that Shimei went from Jerusalem to Gath,
and had returned.
42And the king sent for Shimei, and said to him, Did I not make
you swear by the Lord, and warn you, saying, Know for a certainty, on the day you go out and walk abroad anywhere you shall
surely die? And you said to me, I have heard your word; it is
accepted.
43Why then have you not kept the oath of the Lord, and the
command with which I have charged you?
44The king also said to Shimei, You are aware in your own heart
of all the evil you did to my father David; so the Lord will return
your evil upon your own head.
45But King Solomon shall be blessed, and the throne of David
shall be established before the Lord for ever.
46So the king commanded Benaiah son of Jehoiada, who went
out and struck down Shimei, and he died. And the kingdom was
established in the hand of Solomon.

## New American Standard

*Joab Executed*

28¶ Now the news came to Joab, for Joab had followed Adonijah, although he had not followed Absalom. And Joab fled to the
tent of the LORD and took hold of the horns of the altar.
29And it was told King Solomon that Joab had fled to the tent
of the LORD, and behold, he is beside the altar. Then Solomon sent
Benaiah the son of Jehoiada, saying, "Go, fall upon him."
30So Benaiah came to the tent of the LORD, and said to him,
"Thus the king has said, 'Come out.' " But he said, "No, for I will
die here." And Benaiah brought the king word again, saying,
"Thus spoke Joab, and thus he answered me."
31And the king said to him, "Do as he has spoken and fall upon
him and bury him, that you may remove from me and from my
father's house the blood which Joab shed without cause.
32"And the LORD will return his blood on his own head, because
he fell upon two men more righteous and better than he and killed
them with the sword, while my father David did not know *it:*
Abner the son of Ner, commander of the army of Israel, and
Amasa the son of Jether, commander of the army of Judah.
33"So shall their blood return on the head of Joab and on the
head of his descendants forever; but to David and his descendants
and his house and his throne, may there be peace from the LORD
forever."
34Then Benaiah the son of Jehoiada went up and fell upon him
and put him to death, and he was buried at his own house in the
wilderness.
35And the king appointed Benaiah the son of Jehoiada over the
army in his place, and the king appointed Zadok the priest in the
place of Abiathar.

*Shimei Executed*

36¶ Now the king sent and called for Shimei and said to him,
"Build for yourself a house in Jerusalem and live there, and do not
go out from there to any place.
37"For it will happen on the day you go out and cross over the
brook Kidron, you will know for certain that you shall surely die;
your blood shall be on your own head."
38Shimei then said to the king, "The word is good. As my lord
the king has said, so your servant will do." So Shimei lived in
Jerusalem many days.
39¶ But it came about at the end of three years, that two of the
servants of Shimei ran away to Achish son of Maacah, king of
Gath. And they told Shimei, saying, "Behold, your servants are in
Gath."
40Then Shimei arose and saddled his donkey, and went to Gath
to Achish to look for his servants. And Shimei went and brought
his servants from Gath.
41And it was told Solomon that Shimei had gone from Jerusalem
to Gath, and had returned.
42So the king sent and called for Shimei and said to him, "Did
I not make you swear by the LORD and solemnly warn you, saying,
'You will know for certain that on the day you depart and go
anywhere, you shall surely die'? And you said to me, 'The word
which I have heard is good.'
43"Why then have you not kept the oath of the LORD, and the
command which I have laid on you?"
44The king also said to Shimei, "You know all the evil which you
acknowledge in your heart, which you did to my father David;
therefore the LORD shall return your evil on your own head.
45"But King Solomon shall be blessed, and the throne of David
shall be established before the LORD forever."
46So the king commanded Benaiah the son of Jehoiada, and he
went out and fell upon him so that he died. Thus the kingdom was
established in the hands of Solomon.

## New International

28When the news reached Joab, who had conspired with Adonijah though not with Absalom, he fled to the tent of the LORD and
took hold of the horns of the altar. 29King Solomon was told that
Joab had fled to the tent of the LORD and was beside the altar. Then
Solomon ordered Benaiah son of Jehoiada, "Go, strike him down!"
30So Benaiah entered the tent of the LORD and said to Joab, "The
king says, 'Come out!' "
But he answered, "No, I will die here."
Benaiah reported to the king, "This is how Joab answered me."
31Then the king commanded Benaiah, "Do as he says. Strike
him down and bury him, and so clear me and my father's house
of the guilt of the innocent blood that Joab shed. 32The LORD will
repay him for the blood he shed, because without the knowledge
of my father David he attacked two men and killed them with the
sword. Both of them—Abner son of Ner, commander of Israel's
army, and Amasa son of Jether, commander of Judah's army—
were better men and more upright than he. 33May the guilt of their
blood rest on the head of Joab and his descendants forever. But on
David and his descendants, his house and his throne, may there
be the LORD's peace forever."
34So Benaiah son of Jehoiada went up and struck down Joab and
killed him, and he was buried on his own land[a] in the desert.
35The king put Benaiah son of Jehoiada over the army in Joab's
position and replaced Abiathar with Zadok the priest.
36Then the king sent for Shimei and said to him, "Build yourself
a house in Jerusalem and live there, but do not go anywhere else.
37The day you leave and cross the Kidron Valley, you can be sure
you will die; your blood will be on your own head."
38Shimei answered the king, "What you say is good. Your
servant will do as my lord the king has said." And Shimei stayed
in Jerusalem for a long time.
39But three years later, two of Shimei's slaves ran off to Achish
son of Maacah, king of Gath, and Shimei was told, "Your slaves
are in Gath." 40At this, he saddled his donkey and went to Achish
at Gath in search of his slaves. So Shimei went away and brought
the slaves back from Gath.
41When Solomon was told that Shimei had gone from Jerusalem
to Gath and had returned, 42the king summoned Shimei and said
to him, "Did I not make you swear by the LORD and warn you, 'On
the day you leave to go anywhere else, you can be sure you will
die'? At that time you said to me, 'What you say is good. I will
obey.' 43Why then did you not keep your oath to the LORD and
obey the command I gave you?"
44The king also said to Shimei, "You know in your heart all the
wrong you did to my father David. Now the LORD will repay you
for your wrongdoing. 45But King Solomon will be blessed, and
David's throne will remain secure before the LORD forever."
46Then the king gave the order to Benaiah son of Jehoiada, and
he went out and struck Shimei down and killed him.
The kingdom was now firmly established in Solomon's hands.

NIV [a] 34 Or *buried in his tomb*

## King James

3 AND SOLOMON made affinity with Pharaoh king of Egypt,
and took Pharaoh's daughter, and brought her into the city
of David, until he had made an end of building his own house, and
the house of the LORD, and the wall of Jerusalem round about.
2Only the people sacrificed in high places, because there was
no house built unto the name of the LORD, until those days.
3And Solomon loved the LORD, walking in the statutes of David
his father: only he sacrificed and burnt incense in high places.
4And the king went to Gibeon to sacrifice there; for that *was* the
great high place: a thousand burnt offerings did Solomon offer
upon that altar.
5¶ In Gibeon the LORD appeared to Solomon in a dream by
night: and God said, Ask what I shall give thee.
6And Solomon said, Thou hast shown unto thy servant David
my father great mercy, according as he walked before thee in truth,
and in righteousness, and in uprightness of heart with thee; and
thou hast kept for him this great kindness, that thou hast given
him a son to sit on his throne, as *it is* this day.
7And now, O LORD my God, thou hast made thy servant king
instead of David my father: and I *am but* a little child: I know not
*how* to go out or come in.
8And thy servant *is* in the midst of thy people which thou hast
chosen, a great people, that cannot be numbered nor counted for
multitude.
9Give therefore thy servant an understanding heart to judge thy
people, that I may discern between good and bad: for who is able
to judge this thy so great a people?
10And the speech pleased the Lord, that Solomon had asked
this thing.
11And God said unto him, Because thou hast asked this thing,
and hast not asked for thyself long life; neither hast asked riches
for thyself, nor hast asked the life of thine enemies; but hast asked
for thyself understanding to discern judgment;
12Behold, I have done according to thy words: lo, I have given
thee a wise and an understanding heart; so that there was none
like thee before thee, neither after thee shall any arise like unto
thee.
13And I have also given thee that which thou hast not asked,
both riches, and honour: so that there shall not be any among the
kings like unto thee all thy days.
14And if thou wilt walk in my ways, to keep my statutes and
my commandments, as thy father David did walk, then I will
lengthen thy days.
15And Solomon awoke; and, behold, *it was* a dream. And he
came to Jerusalem, and stood before the ark of the covenant of the
LORD, and offered up burnt offerings, and offered peace offerings,
and made a feast to all his servants.
16¶ Then came there two women, *that were* harlots, unto the
king, and stood before him.
17And the one woman said, O my lord, I and this woman dwell
in one house; and I was delivered of a child with her in the house.
18And it came to pass the third day after that I was delivered,
that this woman was delivered also: and we *were* together; *there was*
no stranger with us in the house, save we two in the house.
19And this woman's child died in the night; because she overlaid it.
20And she arose at midnight, and took my son from beside me,
while thine handmaid slept, and laid it in her bosom, and laid her
dead child in my bosom.

## Amplified

3 AND SOLOMON made an alliance with Pharaoh king of
Egypt, and took Pharaoh's daughter, and brought her into
the city of David, until he had finished building his own house,
and the house of the Lord, and the wall around Jerusalem.
2But the people sacrificed [to God] in the high places [as the
heathen did to their idols], for there was no house yet built to the
name of the Lord.
3Solomon loved the Lord, walking [at first] in the statutes *and*
practices of David his father; only he sacrificed and burned incense
in high places.
4The king went to Gibeon [near Jerusalem, where stood the
tabernacle and the bronze altar] to sacrifice there, for that was the
great high place. One thousand burnt offerings Solomon offered
on that altar.
5In Gibeon the Lord appeared to Solomon in a dream by night.
And God said, [a]Ask what I shall give you.
6Solomon said, You have shown to Your servant David my
father great mercy *and* loving-kindness according as he walked
before You in faithfulness, righteousness, and uprightness of heart
with You; and You have kept for him this great kindness *and*
steadfast love, that you have given him a son to sit on his throne
this day.
7Now, O Lord my God, You have made Your servant king
instead of David my father, and I am [b]but a lad [in wisdom and
experience]; I know not how to go out [begin] or come in [finish].
8Your servant is in the midst of Your people whom You have
chosen, a great people that are not counted for multitude.
9So give Your servant an understanding mind *and* a hearing
heart to judge Your people, that I may discern between good and
bad; for who is able to judge *and* rule this Your great people? [James
1:5.]
10It pleased the Lord that Solomon had asked this.
11God said to him, Because you have asked this, and have not
asked for long life, or for riches, or for the life of your enemies, but
have asked for yourself understanding to recognize what is just
and right,
12Behold, I have done as you asked. I have given you a wise,
discerning mind so that no one before you was your equal, nor
shall any arise after you equal to you.
13I have also given you what you have not asked, both riches
and honor; so that there shall not be any among the kings equal
to you all your days.
14And if you will go My way, keep My statutes and My commandments as your father David did, then I will lengthen your
days.
15Solomon awoke, and behold, it was a dream. He came to
Jerusalem, stood before the ark of the covenant of the Lord, and
offered burnt offerings and peace offerings, and made a feast for
all his servants.
16Then two women who had become mothers out of wedlock
came and stood before the king.
17And one woman said, O my lord, I and this woman dwell in
one house, and I was delivered of a child with her in the house.
18And the third day after I was delivered, this woman also was
delivered; and we were together; no stranger was with us, just we
two in the house.
19And this woman's child died in the night, because she lay on
it.
20And she arose at midnight, and took my son from beside me,
while your handmaid slept, and laid it in her bosom, and laid her
dead child in my bosom.

**AMP** [a] This is the high privilege of the child of God. Each one's life tells what he has asked for—"in Heaven above or in the earth beneath." Which shall it be, God's will and glory, or our own? [b] Solomon was already a father. Cp. I Kings 11:42 and 14:21.

## New American Standard

*Solomon's Rule Consolidated*

**3** THEN SOLOMON formed a marriage alliance with Pharaoh king of Egypt, and took Pharaoh's daughter and brought her to the city of David, until he had finished building his own house and the house of the LORD and the wall around Jerusalem.

2The people were still sacrificing on the high places, because there was no house built for the name of the LORD until those days.

3¶ Now Solomon loved the LORD, walking in the statutes of his father David, except he sacrificed and burned incense on the high places.

4And the king went to Gibeon to sacrifice there, for that was the great high place; Solomon offered a thousand burnt offerings on that altar.

5In Gibeon the LORD appeared to Solomon in a dream at night; and God said, "Ask what *you wish* me to give you."

*Solomon's Prayer*

6Then Solomon said, "Thou hast shown great lovingkindness to Thy servant David my father, according as he walked before Thee in [c]truth and righteousness and uprightness of heart toward Thee; and Thou hast reserved for him this great lovingkindness, that Thou hast given him a son to sit on his throne, as *it is* this day.

7"And now, O LORD my God, Thou hast made Thy servant king in place of my father David, yet I am but a little child; I do not know how to go out or come in.

8"And Thy servant is in the midst of Thy people which Thou hast chosen, a great people who cannot be numbered or counted for multitude.

9"So give Thy servant an understanding heart to judge Thy people to discern between good and evil. For who is able to judge this great people of Thine?"

*God's Answer*

10¶ And it was pleasing in the sight of the Lord that Solomon had asked this thing.

11And God said to him, "Because you have asked this thing and have not asked for yourself long life, nor have asked riches for yourself, nor have you asked for the life of your enemies, but have asked for yourself discernment to understand justice,

12behold, I have done according to your words. Behold, I have given you a wise and discerning heart, so that there has been no one like you before you, nor shall one like you arise after you.

13"And I have also given you what you have not asked, both riches and honor, so that there will not be any among the kings like you all your days.

14"And if you walk in My ways, keeping My statutes and commandments, as your father David walked, then I will prolong your days."

15¶ Then Solomon awoke, and behold, it was a dream. And he came to Jerusalem and stood before the ark of the covenant of the Lord, and offered burnt offerings and made peace offerings, and made a feast for all his servants.

*Solomon Wisely Judges*

16¶ Then two women who were harlots came to the king and stood before him.

17And the one woman said, "Oh, my lord, this woman and I live in the same house; and I gave birth to a child while she *was* in the house.

18"And it happened on the third day after I gave birth, that this woman also gave birth to a child, and we were together. There was no stranger with us in the house, only the two of us in the house.

19"And this woman's son died in the night, because she lay on it.

20"So she arose in the middle of the night and took my son from beside me while your maidservant slept, and laid him in her bosom, and laid her dead son in my bosom.

NAS [c] Or, *faithfulness*

## New International

*Solomon Asks for Wisdom*

**3** SOLOMON MADE an alliance with Pharaoh king of Egypt and married his daughter. He brought her to the City of David until he finished building his palace and the temple of the LORD, and the wall around Jerusalem. 2The people, however, were still sacrificing at the high places, because a temple had not yet been built for the Name of the LORD. 3Solomon showed his love for the LORD by walking according to the statutes of his father David, except that he offered sacrifices and burned incense on the high places.

4The king went to Gibeon to offer sacrifices, for that was the most important high place, and Solomon offered a thousand burnt offerings on that altar. 5At Gibeon the LORD appeared to Solomon during the night in a dream, and God said, "Ask for whatever you want me to give you."

6Solomon answered, "You have shown great kindness to your servant, my father David, because he was faithful to you and righteous and upright in heart. You have continued this great kindness to him and have given him a son to sit on his throne this very day.

7"Now, O LORD my God, you have made your servant king in place of my father David. But I am only a little child and do not know how to carry out my duties. 8Your servant is here among the people you have chosen, a great people, too numerous to count or number. 9So give your servant a discerning heart to govern your people and to distinguish between right and wrong. For who is able to govern this great people of yours?"

10The Lord was pleased that Solomon had asked for this. 11So God said to him, "Since you have asked for this and not for long life or wealth for yourself, nor have asked for the death of your enemies but for discernment in administering justice, 12I will do what you have asked. I will give you a wise and discerning heart, so that there will never have been anyone like you, nor will there ever be. 13Moreover, I will give you what you have not asked for—both riches and honor—so that in your lifetime you will have no equal among kings. 14And if you walk in my ways and obey my statutes and commands as David your father did, I will give you a long life." 15Then Solomon awoke—and he realized it had been a dream.

He returned to Jerusalem, stood before the ark of the Lord's covenant and sacrificed burnt offerings and fellowship offerings.[d] Then he gave a feast for all his court.

*A Wise Ruling*

16Now two prostitutes came to the king and stood before him. 17One of them said, "My lord, this woman and I live in the same house. I had a baby while she was there with me. 18The third day after my child was born, this woman also had a baby. We were alone; there was no one in the house but the two of us.

19"During the night this woman's son died because she lay on him. 20So she got up in the middle of the night and took my son from my side while I your servant was asleep. She put him by her breast and put her dead son by my breast. 21The next morning, I

NIV [d] *15* Traditionally *peace offerings*

## King James

21And when I rose in the morning to give my child suck, behold, it was dead: but when I had considered it in the morning,
behold, it was not my son, which I did bear.
22And the other woman said, Nay; but the living *is* my son, and
the dead *is* thy son. And this said, No; but the dead *is* thy son, and
the living *is* my son. Thus they spake before the king.
23Then said the king, The one saith, This *is* my son that liveth,
and thy son *is* the dead: and the other saith, Nay; but thy son *is*
the dead, and my son *is* the living.
24And the king said, Bring me a sword. And they brought a
sword before the king.
25And the king said, Divide the living child in two, and give half
to the one, and half to the other.
26Then spake the woman whose the living child *was* unto the
king, for her bowels yearned upon her son, and she said, O my
lord, give her the living child, and in no wise slay it. But the other
said, Let it be neither mine nor thine, *but* divide *it*.
27Then the king answered and said, Give her the living child,
and in no wise slay it: she *is* the mother thereof.
28And all Israel heard of the judgment which the king had
judged; and they feared the king: for they saw that the wisdom of
God *was* in him, to do judgment.

4 SO KING Solomon was king over all Israel.
2And these *were* the princes which he had; Azariah the son
of Zadok the priest,
3Elihoreph and Ahiah, the sons of Shisha, scribes; Jehoshaphat
the son of Ahilud, the recorder.
4And Benaiah the son of Jehoiada *was* over the host: and Zadok
and Abiathar *were* the priests:
5And Azariah the son of Nathan *was* over the officers: and
Zabud the son of Nathan *was* principal officer, *and* the king's
friend:
6And Ahishar *was* over the household: and Adoniram the son
of Abda *was* over the tribute.
7¶ And Solomon had twelve officers over all Israel, which provided victuals for the king and his household: each man his month
in a year made provision.
8And these *are* their names: The son of Hur, in mount Ephraim:
9The son of Dekar, in Makaz, and in Shaalbim, and Beth-
shemesh, and Elon-beth-hanan:
10The son of Hesed, in Aruboth; to him *pertained* Sochoh, and
all the land of Hepher:
11The son of Abinadab, in all the region of Dor; which had
Taphath the daughter of Solomon to wife:
12Baana the son of Ahilud; *to him pertained* Taanach and Megiddo, and all Beth-shean, which *is* by Zartanah beneath Jezreel, from
Beth-shean to Abel-meholah, *even* unto *the place that is* beyond
Jokneam:
13The son of Geber, in Ramoth-gilead; to him *pertained* the
towns of Jair the son of Manasseh, which *are* in Gilead; to him *also*
*pertained* the region of Argob, which *is* in Bashan, threescore great
cities with walls and brasen bars:
14Ahinadab the son of Iddo *had* Mahanaim:
15Ahimaaz *was* in Naphtali; he also took Basmath the daughter
of Solomon to wife:
16Baanah the son of Hushai *was* in Asher and in Aloth:
17Jehoshaphat the son of Paruah, in Issachar:
18Shimei the son of Elah, in Benjamin:
19Geber the son of Uri *was* in the country of Gilead, *in* the
country of Sihon king of the Amorites, and of Og king of Bashan;
and *he was* the only officer which *was* in the land.

## Amplified

21And when I rose to nurse my child, behold, it was dead: but
when I had considered it in the morning, behold, it was not the
son I had borne.
22But the other woman said, No, but the living is my son, and
the dead is your son! And this one said, No, but the dead son is
your son, and the living is my son. Thus they spoke before the
king.
23The king said, One says, This is my son that is alive, and yours
is the dead one. The other woman says, No, but your son is the
dead one, and mine is the living one.
24And the king said, Bring me a sword. And they brought a
sword to the king.
25And the king said, Divide the living child in two, and give half
to the one, and half to the other.
26Then the mother of the living child said to the king, for she
yearned over her son, O my lord, give her the living baby, and by
no means slay it. But the other said, Let it not be mine or yours,
but divide it.
27Then the king said, Give her [who pleads for his life] the living
baby and by no means slay it. She is the child's mother.
28And all Israel heard of the judgment which the king had
made, and they stood in awe of him, for they saw that the wisdom
of God was in him, to do justice.

4 KING SOLOMON was king over all Israel.
2These were his chief officials: Azariah son of Zadok was the
[high] priest;
3Elihoreph and Ahijah sons of Shisha were secretaries; Jehoshaphat son of Ahilud was recorder;
4Benaiah son of Jehoiada commanded the army; Zadok and
Abiathar were priests;
5Azariah son of Nathan was over the officers; Zabud son of
Nathan was priest and the king's friend *and* private advisor.
6Ahishar was in charge of the palace; and Adoniram son of
Abda was in charge of the forced labor.
7Solomon had twelve officers over all Israel, who secured provisions for the king and his household; each man had to provide for
a month in a year.
8These were their names: Ben-hur, in the hill country of
Ephraim;
9Ben-deker, in Makaz, Sha-albim, Beth-shemesh, and
Elonbeth-hanan;
10Ben-hesed, in Arubboth (to him belonged Soco and all the
land of Hepher);
11Ben-abinadab, in all Naphath-Dor (he had Taphath Solomon's
daughter as wife);
12Baana son of Ahilud, in Taanach, Megiddo, and all Beth-
shean which is beside Zarethan below Jezreel, from Beth-shean to
Abel-meholah, as far as beyond Jokmeam;
13Ben-geber, in Ramoth-gilead (to him belonged the villages of
Jair son of Manasseh, which are in Gilead, also the region of
Argob, which is in Bashan, sixty great cities with walls and bronze
bars);
14Ahinadab son of Iddo, in Mahanaim;
15Ahima-az was in Naphtali (he had taken Basemath Solomon's
daughter as his wife);
16Baana son of Hushai, in Asher and Bealoth;
17Jehoshaphat son of Paruah, in Issachar;
18Shimei son of Ela, in Benjamin;
19Geber son of Uri, in Gilead, the country of Sihon king of the
Amorites and Og king of Bashan; only one officer was over all the
country [at one time, each serving for one month].

## New American Standard

21“And when I rose in the morning to nurse my son, behold, he was dead; but when I looked at him carefully in the morning, behold, he was not my son, whom I had borne.”

22Then the other woman said, “No! For the living one is my son, and the dead one is your son.” But the first woman said, “No! For the dead one is your son, and the living one is my son.” Thus they spoke before the king.

23¶ Then the king said, “The one says, ‘This is my son who is living, and your son is the dead one’; and the other says, ‘No! For your son is the dead one, and my son is the living one.’ ”

24And the king said, “Get me a sword.” So they brought a sword before the king.

25And the king said, “Divide the living child in two, and give half to the one and half to the other.”

26Then the woman whose child *was* the living one spoke to the king, for she was deeply stirred over her son and said, “Oh, my lord, give her the living child, and by no means kill him.” But the other said, “He shall be neither mine nor yours; divide *him!*”

27Then the king answered and said, “Give the first woman the living child, and by no means kill him. She is his mother.”

28When all Israel heard of the judgment which the king had handed down, they feared the king; for they saw that the wisdom of God was in him to administer justice.

*Solomon's Officials*

4 NOW KING Solomon was king over all Israel.

2And these were his officials: Azariah the son of Zadok *was* the priest;

3Elihoreph and Ahijah, the sons of Shisha *were* secretaries; Jehoshaphat the son of Ahilud *was* the recorder;

4and Benaiah the son of Jehoiada *was* over the army; and Zadok and Abiathar *were* priests;

5and Azariah the son of Nathan *was* over the deputies; and Zabud the son of Nathan, a priest, *was* the king's friend;

6and Ahishar was over the household; and Adoniram the son of Abda *was* over the men subject to forced labor.

7¶ And Solomon had twelve deputies over all Israel, who provided for the king and his household; each man had to provide for a month in the year.

8And these are their names: Ben-hur, in the hill country of Ephraim;

9Ben-deker in Makaz and Shaalbim and Beth-shemesh and Elonbeth-hanan;

10Ben-hesed, in Arubboth (Socoh *was* his and all the land of Hepher);

11Ben-abinadab, *in* all the height of Dor (Taphath the daughter of Solomon was his wife);

12Baana the son of Ahilud, *in* Taanach and Megiddo, and all Beth-shean which is beside Zarethan below Jezreel, from Beth-shean to Abel-meholah as far as the other side of Jokmeam;

13Ben-geber, in Ramoth-gilead (the towns of Jair, the son of Manasseh, which are in Gilead were his: the region of Argob, which is in Bashan, sixty great cities with walls and bronze bars *were* his);

14Ahinadab the son of Iddo, *in* Mahanaim;

15Ahimaaz, in Naphtali (he also married Basemath the daughter of Solomon);

16Baana the son of Hushai, in Asher and Bealoth;

17Jehoshaphat the son of Paruah, in Issachar;

18Shimei the son of Ela, in Benjamin;

19Geber the son of Uri, in the land of Gilead, the country of Sihon king of the Amorites and of Og king of Bashan; and *he was* the only deputy who *was* in the land.

## New International

got up to nurse my son—and he was dead! But when I looked at him closely in the morning light, I saw that it wasn't the son I had borne.”

22The other woman said, “No! The living one is my son; the dead one is yours.”

But the first one insisted, “No! The dead one is yours; the living one is mine.” And so they argued before the king.

23The king said, “This one says, ‘My son is alive and your son is dead,’ while that one says, ‘No! Your son is dead and mine is alive.’ ”

24Then the king said, “Bring me a sword.” So they brought a sword for the king. 25He then gave an order: “Cut the living child in two and give half to one and half to the other.”

26The woman whose son was alive was filled with compassion for her son and said to the king, “Please, my lord, give her the living baby! Don't kill him!”

But the other said, “Neither I nor you shall have him. Cut him in two!”

27Then the king gave his ruling: “Give the living baby to the first woman. Do not kill him; she is his mother.”

28When all Israel heard the verdict the king had given, they held the king in awe, because they saw that he had wisdom from God to administer justice.

*Solomon's Officials and Governors*

4 SO KING Solomon ruled over all Israel. 2And these were his chief officials:

Azariah son of Zadok—the priest;
3Elihoreph and Ahijah, sons of Shisha—secretaries;
Jehoshaphat son of Ahilud—recorder;
4Benaiah son of Jehoiada—commander in chief;
Zadok and Abiathar—priests;
5Azariah son of Nathan—in charge of the district officers;
Zabud son of Nathan—a priest and personal adviser to the king;
6Ahishar—in charge of the palace;
Adoniram son of Abda—in charge of forced labor.

7Solomon also had twelve district governors over all Israel, who supplied provisions for the king and the royal household. Each one had to provide supplies for one month in the year. 8These are their names:

Ben-Hur—in the hill country of Ephraim;
9Ben-Deker—in Makaz, Shaalbim, Beth Shemesh and Elon Bethhanan;
10Ben-Hesed—in Arubboth (Socoh and all the land of Hepher were his);
11Ben-Abinadab—in Naphoth Dor[a] (he was married to Taphath daughter of Solomon);
12Baana son of Ahilud—in Taanach and Megiddo, and in all of Beth Shan next to Zarethan below Jezreel, from Beth Shan to Abel Meholah across to Jokmeam;
13Ben-Geber—in Ramoth Gilead (the settlements of Jair son of Manasseh in Gilead were his, as well as the district of Argob in Bashan and its sixty large walled cities with bronze gate bars);
14Ahinadab son of Iddo—in Mahanaim;
15Ahimaaz—in Naphtali (he had married Basemath daughter of Solomon);
16Baana son of Hushai—in Asher and in Aloth;
17Jehoshaphat son of Paruah—in Issachar;
18Shimei son of Ela—in Benjamin;
19Geber son of Uri—in Gilead (the country of Sihon king of the Amorites and the country of Og king of Bashan). He was the only governor over the district.

NIV [a] 11 *Or in the heights of Dor*

## King James

20¶ Judah and Israel *were* many, as the sand which *is* by the sea in multitude, eating and drinking, and making merry.

21And Solomon reigned over all kingdoms from the river unto the land of the Philistines, and unto the border of Egypt: they brought presents, and served Solomon all the days of his life.

22¶ And Solomon's provision for one day was thirty measures of fine flour, and threescore measures of meal,

23Ten fat oxen, and twenty oxen out of the pastures, and an hundred sheep, beside harts, and roebucks, and fallowdeer, and fatted fowl.

24For he had dominion over all *the region* on this side the river, from Tiphsah even to Azzah, over all the kings on this side the river: and he had peace on all sides round about him.

25And Judah and Israel dwelt safely, every man under his vine and under his fig tree, from Dan even to Beer-sheba, all the days of Solomon.

26¶ And Solomon had forty thousand stalls of horses for his chariots, and twelve thousand horsemen.

27And those officers provided victual for king Solomon, and for all that came unto king Solomon's table, every man in his month: they lacked nothing.

28Barley also and straw for the horses and dromedaries brought they unto the place where *the officers* were, every man according to his charge.

29¶ And God gave Solomon wisdom and understanding exceeding much, and largeness of heart, even as the sand that *is* on the sea shore.

30And Solomon's wisdom excelled the wisdom of all the children of the east country, and all the wisdom of Egypt.

31For he was wiser than all men; than Ethan the Ezrahite, and Heman, and Chalcol, and Darda, the sons of Mahol: and his fame was in all nations round about.

32And he spake three thousand proverbs: and his songs were a thousand and five.

33And he spake of trees, from the cedar tree that *is* in Lebanon even unto the hyssop that springeth out of the wall: he spake also of beasts, and of fowl, and of creeping things, and of fishes.

34And there came of all people to hear the wisdom of Solomon, from all kings of the earth, which had heard of his wisdom.

**5** AND HIRAM king of Tyre sent his servants unto Solomon; for he had heard that they had anointed him king in the room of his father: for Hiram was ever a lover of David.

2And Solomon sent to Hiram, saying,

3Thou knowest how that David my father could not build an house unto the name of the LORD his God for the wars which were about him on every side, until the LORD put them under the soles of his feet.

4But now the LORD my God hath given me rest on every side, *so that there is* neither adversary nor evil occurrent.

5And, behold, I purpose to build an house unto the name of the LORD my God, as the LORD spake unto David my father, saying, Thy son, whom I will set upon thy throne in thy room, he shall build an house unto my name.

6Now therefore command thou that they hew me cedar trees out of Lebanon; and my servants shall be with thy servants: and unto thee will I give hire for thy servants according to all that thou shalt appoint: for thou knowest that *there is* not among us any that can skill to hew timber like unto the Sidonians.

## Amplified

20Judah and Israel were many, like the sand which is by the sea in multitude; they ate, drank, and rejoiced.

21Solomon reigned [a]over all the kingdoms from the [Euphrates] River to the land of the Philistines and to the border of Egypt; they brought tribute and served Solomon all the days of his life.

22Solomon's provision for one day was thirty measures of fine flour, sixty measures of meal,

23Ten fat oxen, twenty pasture-fed cattle, a hundred sheep, besides harts, gazelles, roebucks, and fatted fowl—of choice kinds.

24For he had dominion over all the region west of the [Euphrates] River, from Tiphsah to Gaza, over all the kings west of the River; and he had peace on all sides around him.

25Judah and Israel dwelt safely, every man under his vine and fig tree, from Dan to Beersheba, all of Solomon's days.

26Solomon also had 40,000 stalls of horses for his chariots, and 12,000 horsemen.

27And those officers provided food for King Solomon, and for all who came to his table, every man in his month; they let nothing be lacking.

28Barley also and straw for the horses and swift steeds they brought to the place where it was needed, each according to his assignment.

29And God gave Solomon exceptionally much wisdom and understanding, and breadth of mind like the sand of the seashore.

30Solomon's wisdom excelled the wisdom of all the people of the east, and all the wisdom of Egypt.

31For he was wiser [b]than all other men; than Ethan the Ezrahite, and Heman, Calcol, and Darda, the sons of Mahol; his fame was in all the nations round about.

32He also originated 3,000 proverbs, and his songs were 1,005.

33He spoke of trees, from the cedar that is in Lebanon to the hyssop that grows out of the wall; he spoke also of beasts, of birds, of creeping things, and of fish.

34Men came from all peoples to hear the wisdom of Solomon, and from all kings of the earth who had heard of his wisdom.

**5** HIRAM KING of Tyre sent his servants to Solomon, when he heard that he was anointed king in place of his father, for Hiram always loved David.

2And Solomon sent to Hiram, saying,

3You know how David my father could not build a house to the name of the Lord his God because wars were about him on every side, until the Lord put his foes under his feet. [Cp. I Chron. 22:8; II Sam. 7:4ff.]

4But now the Lord my God has given me rest on every side, so that there is neither adversary nor evil confronting me.

5And I purpose to build a house to the name of the Lord my God, as the Lord said to David my father, Your son, whom I will set on your throne in your place, shall build the house to My name *and* presence.

6So, Hiram, command them to hew me cedar trees out of Lebanon; my servants shall join yours, and I will give you whatever wages you set for your servants; for you know that no one among us can equal the skill of the Sidon men in cutting timber.

**AMP** [a] That King Solomon's empire was as great as is definitely indicated here and in II Chron. 9:26 has frequently been questioned, because of the great empires of Assyria on the Euphrates and Egypt on the Nile. But archaeological discoveries prove that "precisely during the period 1100-900 when the kingdom of Israel was being built up, 'the weak and inglorious twenty-first dynasty' was ruling in Egypt and at the same time Assyria went into a period of decline" (J. P. Free in *Archaeology and Bible History*, citing A. T. Olmstead's *History of Assyria*, chap. 7). [b] "Wiser than all other men," until Christ came. Jesus said, "Something more *and* greater than Solomon is here" (Matt. 12:42).

## New American Standard

*Solomon's Power, Wealth and Wisdom*

20¶ Judah and Israel *were* as numerous as the sand that is on the
seashore in abundance; *they* were eating and drinking and rejoicing.
21¶ Now Solomon ruled over all the kingdoms from the [c]River
*to* the land of the Philistines and to the border of Egypt; *they*
brought tribute and served Solomon all the days of his life.
22And Solomon's provision for one day was thirty [d]kors of fine
flour and sixty kors of meal,
23ten fat oxen, twenty pasture-fed oxen, a hundred sheep besides deer, gazelles, roebucks, and fattened fowl.
24For he had dominion over everything west of the River, from
Tiphsah even to Gaza, over all the kings west of the River; and he
had peace on all sides around about him.
25So Judah and Israel lived in safety, every man under his vine
and his fig tree, from Dan even to Beersheba, all the days of
Solomon.
26And Solomon had [e]40,000 stalls of horses for his chariots, and
12,000 horsemen.
27And those deputies provided for King Solomon and all who
came to King Solomon's table, each in his month; they left nothing
lacking.
28They also brought barley and straw for the horses and swift
steeds to the place where it should be, each according to his
charge.
29¶ Now God gave Solomon wisdom and very great discernment and breadth of mind, like the sand that is on the seashore.
30And Solomon's wisdom surpassed the wisdom of all the sons
of the east and all the wisdom of Egypt.
31For he was wiser than all men, than Ethan the Ezrahite,
Heman, Calcol and Darda, the sons of Mahol; and his fame was
*known* in all the surrounding nations.
32He also spoke 3,000 proverbs, and his songs were 1,005.
33And he spoke of trees, from the cedar that is in Lebanon even
to the hyssop that grows on the wall; he spoke also of animals and
birds and creeping things and fish.
34And men came from all peoples to hear the wisdom of Solomon, from all the kings of the earth who had heard of his wisdom.

*Alliance with King Hiram*

5 NOW HIRAM king of Tyre sent his servants to Solomon,
when he heard that they had anointed him king in place of
his father, for Hiram had always been a friend of David.
2Then Solomon sent *word* to Hiram, saying,
3"You know that David my father was unable to build a house
for the name of the LORD his God because of the wars which
surrounded him, until the LORD put them under the soles of his
feet.
4"But now the LORD my God has given me rest on every side;
there is neither adversary nor misfortune.
5"And behold, I intend to build a house for the name of the
LORD my God, as the LORD spoke to David my father, saying,
'Your son, whom I will set on your throne in your place, he will
build the house for My name.'
6"Now therefore, command that they cut for me cedars from
Lebanon, and my servants will be with your servants; and I will
give you wages for your servants according to all that you say, for
you know that there is no one among us who knows how to cut
timber like the Sidonians."

NAS [c] I.e., Euphrates, and so through v. 24 [d] I.e., One kor equals approx. 10 bushels [e] One ms. reads 4,000, cf. 2 Chr. 9:25

## New International

*Solomon's Daily Provisions*

20The people of Judah and Israel were as numerous as the sand
on the seashore; they ate, they drank and they were happy. 21And
Solomon ruled over all the kingdoms from the River[f] to the land
of the Philistines, as far as the border of Egypt. These countries
brought tribute and were Solomon's subjects all his life.
22Solomon's daily provisions were thirty cors[g] of fine flour and
sixty cors[h] of meal, 23ten head of stall-fed cattle, twenty of pasture-
fed cattle and a hundred sheep and goats, as well as deer, gazelles,
roebucks and choice fowl. 24For he ruled over all the kingdoms
west of the River, from Tiphsah to Gaza, and had peace on all
sides. 25During Solomon's lifetime Judah and Israel, from Dan to
Beersheba, lived in safety, each man under his own vine and fig
tree.
26Solomon had four[i] thousand stalls for chariot horses, and
twelve thousand horses.[j]
27The district officers, each in his month, supplied provisions
for King Solomon and all who came to the king's table. They saw
to it that nothing was lacking. 28They also brought to the proper
place their quotas of barley and straw for the chariot horses and
the other horses.

*Solomon's Wisdom*

29God gave Solomon wisdom and very great insight, and a
breadth of understanding as measureless as the sand on the seashore. 30Solomon's wisdom was greater than the wisdom of all the
men of the East, and greater than all the wisdom of Egypt. 31He
was wiser than any other man, including Ethan the Ezrahite—wiser than Heman, Calcol and Darda, the sons of Mahol. And his
fame spread to all the surrounding nations. 32He spoke three
thousand proverbs and his songs numbered a thousand and five.
33He described plant life, from the cedar of Lebanon to the hyssop
that grows out of walls. He also taught about animals and birds,
reptiles and fish. 34Men of all nations came to listen to Solomon's
wisdom, sent by all the kings of the world, who had heard of his
wisdom.

*Preparations for Building the Temple*

5 WHEN HIRAM king of Tyre heard that Solomon had been
anointed king to succeed his father David, he sent his envoys
to Solomon, because he had always been on friendly terms with
David. 2Solomon sent back this message to Hiram:

3"You know that because of the wars waged against my
father David from all sides, he could not build a temple for the
Name of the LORD his God until the LORD put his enemies
under his feet. 4But now the LORD my God has given me rest
on every side, and there is no adversary or disaster. 5I intend,
therefore, to build a temple for the Name of the LORD my God,
as the LORD told my father David, when he said, 'Your son
whom I will put on the throne in your place will build the
temple for my Name.'
6"So give orders that cedars of Lebanon be cut for me. My
men will work with yours, and I will pay you for your men
whatever wages you set. You know that we have no one so
skilled in felling timber as the Sidonians."

NIV [f] *21* That is, the Euphrates; also in verse 24 [g] *22* That is, probably about 185 bushels (about 6.6 kiloliters) [h] *22* That is, probably about 375 bushels (about 13.2 kiloliters) [i] *26* Some Septuagint manuscripts (see also 2 Chron. 9:25); Hebrew *forty* [j] *26* Or *charioteers*

## King James

7¶ And it came to pass, when Hiram heard the words of Solomon, that he rejoiced greatly, and said, Blessed *be* the LORD this day, which hath given unto David a wise son over this great people.

8And Hiram sent to Solomon, saying, I have considered the things which thou sentest to me for: *and* I will do all thy desire concerning timber of cedar, and concerning timber of fir.

9My servants shall bring *them* down from Lebanon unto the sea: and I will convey them by sea in floats unto the place that thou shalt appoint me, and will cause them to be discharged there, and thou shalt receive *them:* and thou shalt accomplish my desire, in giving food for my household.

10So Hiram gave Solomon cedar trees and fir trees *according to* all his desire.

11And Solomon gave Hiram twenty thousand measures of wheat *for* food to his household, and twenty measures of pure oil: thus gave Solomon to Hiram year by year.

12And the LORD gave Solomon wisdom, as he promised him: and there was peace between Hiram and Solomon; and they two made a league together.

13¶ And king Solomon raised a levy out of all Israel; and the levy was thirty thousand men.

14And he sent them to Lebanon, ten thousand a month by courses: a month they were in Lebanon, *and* two months at home: and Adoniram *was* over the levy.

15And Solomon had threescore and ten thousand that bare burdens, and fourscore thousand hewers in the mountains;

16Beside the chief of Solomon's officers which *were* over the work, three thousand and three hundred, which ruled over the people that wrought in the work.

17And the king commanded, and they brought great stones, costly stones, *and* hewed stones, to lay the foundation of the house.

18And Solomon's builders and Hiram's builders did hew *them*, and the stonesquarers: so they prepared timber and stones to build the house.

6 AND IT came to pass in the four hundred and eightieth year after the children of Israel were come out of the land of Egypt, in the fourth year of Solomon's reign over Israel, in the month Zif, which *is* the second month, that he began to build the house of the LORD.

2And the house which king Solomon built for the LORD, the length thereof *was* threescore cubits, and the breadth thereof twenty *cubits,* and the height thereof thirty cubits.

3And the porch before the temple of the house, twenty cubits *was* the length thereof, according to the breadth of the house; *and* ten cubits *was* the breadth thereof before the house.

4And for the house he made windows of narrow lights.

5¶ And against the wall of the house he built chambers round about, *against* the walls of the house round about, *both* of the temple and of the oracle: and he made chambers round about:

6The nethermost chamber *was* five cubits broad, and the middle *was* six cubits broad, and the third *was* seven cubits broad: for without *in the wall* of the house he made narrowed rests round about, that *the beams* should not be fastened in the walls of the house.

7And the house, when it was in building, was built of stone made ready before it was brought thither: so that there was neither hammer nor axe *nor* any tool of iron heard in the house, while it was in building.

## Amplified

7When Hiram heard the words of Solomon, he rejoiced greatly, and said, Blessed be the Lord this day, Who has given David a wise son to be over this great people.

8And Hiram sent to Solomon, saying, I have considered the things for which you sent to me. I will do all you wish concerning cedar and cypress timber.

9My servants shall bring the logs down from Lebanon to the sea, make them into rafts and float them by sea to the place that you direct; I will have them released there, and you shall take them away. And you shall fulfill my desire by providing food for my household.

10So Hiram gave Solomon all the cedar and cypress trees he desired.

11And Solomon gave Hiram 20,000 measures of wheat for food for his household, and 20 measures of pure, beaten oil. He gave these to Hiram yearly.

12The Lord gave Solomon wisdom, as He promised him; and there was peace between Hiram and Solomon, and they made a treaty.

13King Solomon raised a levy [of forced labor] out of all Israel; and the levy was 30,000 men.

14He sent them to Lebanon, 10,000 a month by divisions; one month they were in Lebanon, and two months at home. Adoniram was over the levy.

15And Solomon had 70,000 burdenbearers, and 80,000 hewers [of stone] in the hill country of Judah,

16Besides Solomon's 3,300 overseers in charge of the people doing the work.

17The king commanded, and they hewed *and* brought out [a]great, costly stones in order to lay the foundation of the house with dressed stone.

18Solomon's and Hiram's builders and the men of Gebal did the hewing and prepared the timber and stones to build the house.

6 AND 480 years after the Israelites came out of the land of Egypt, in the fourth year of Solomon's reign over Israel, in the second month, Ziv, he began to build the Lord's house.

2The length of the house Solomon built for the Lord was sixty cubits, its breadth twenty, and its height thirty cubits.

3The length of the vestibule in front of the temple was twenty cubits, equal to the width of the house, and its depth in front of the house was ten cubits.

4For the house he made narrow [latticed] windows.

5Against the wall of the house he built chambers, running round the walls of the house, both of the holy place and of the holy of holies; and he made side chambers all around.

6The first story side chambers were five cubits wide, those of the middle story six cubits wide, and of the third story seven cubits wide; for around the outside of the wall of the house he made offsets, in order that the supporting beams should not be thrust into the walls of the house.

7When the house was being built, its stone was made ready at the quarry, and no hammer, ax, or tool of iron was heard in the house while it was in building.

**AMP** [a] These great foundation stones remain to this day. One of them is almost thirty-nine feet long, one of the most interesting stones of the world. It is the chief cornerstone of the Mosque of Omar's massive wall, placed in its present position 3,000 years ago. Markings on the stones are Phoenician, as was Tyre from which Solomon received building materials for the temple.

## New American Standard

7¶ And it came about when Hiram heard the words of Solomon, that he rejoiced greatly and said, "Blessed be the LORD today,
who has given to David a wise son over this great people."
8So Hiram sent *word* to Solomon, saying, "I have heard *the*
*message* which you have sent me; I will do what you desire concerning the cedar and cypress timber.
9"My servants will bring *them* down from Lebanon to the sea;
and I will make them into rafts *to go* by sea to the place where you
direct me, and I will have them broken up there, and you shall
carry *them* away. Then you shall accomplish my desire by giving
food to my household."
10So Hiram gave Solomon as much as he desired of the cedar
and cypress timber.
11Solomon then gave Hiram 20,000 kors of wheat as food for his
household, and twenty kors of beaten oil; thus Solomon would
give Hiram year by year.
12And the LORD gave wisdom to Solomon, just as He promised
him; and there was peace between Hiram and Solomon, and the
two of them made a covenant.

*Conscription of Laborers*

13¶ Now King Solomon levied forced laborers from all Israel;
and the forced laborers numbered 30,000 men.
14And he sent them to Lebanon, 10,000 a month in relays; they
were in Lebanon a month *and* two months at home. And Adoniram
*was* over the forced laborers.
15Now Solomon had 70,000 transporters, and 80,000 hewers *of*
*stone* in the mountains,
16besides Solomon's 3,300 chief deputies who *were* over the
project *and* who ruled over the people who were doing the work.
17Then the king commanded, and they quarried great stones,
costly stones, to lay the foundation of the house with cut stones.
18So Solomon's builders and Hiram's builders and the Gebalites
cut them, and prepared the timbers and the stones to build the
house.

*The Building of the Temple*

6 NOW IT came about in the four hundred and eightieth year
after the sons of Israel came out of the land of Egypt, in the
fourth year of Solomon's reign over Israel, in the month of Ziv
which is the second month, that he began to build the house of the
LORD.
2As for the house which King Solomon built for the LORD, its
length *was* sixty [b]cubits and its width twenty *cubits* and its height
thirty cubits.
3And the porch in front of the nave of the house *was* twenty
cubits in length, corresponding to the width of the house, *and* its
depth along the front of the house *was* ten cubits.
4Also for the house he made windows with *artistic* frames.
5And against the wall of the house he built stories encompass-
ing the walls of the house around both the nave and the inner
sanctuary; thus he made side chambers all around.
6The lowest story *was* five cubits wide, and the middle *was* six
cubits wide, and the third *was* seven cubits wide; for on the outside
he made offsets *in the wall* of the house all around in order that *the*
*beams* should not be inserted in the walls of the house.
7And the house, while it was being built, was built of stone
prepared at the quarry, and there was neither hammer nor axe nor
any iron tool heard in the house while it was being built.

NAS [b] I.e., One cubit equals approx. 18 in.

## New International

7When Hiram heard Solomon's message, he was greatly
pleased and said, "Praise be to the LORD today, for he has given
David a wise son to rule over this great nation."
8So Hiram sent word to Solomon:

"I have received the message you sent me and will do all
you want in providing the cedar and pine logs. 9My men will
haul them down from Lebanon to the sea, and I will float them
in rafts by sea to the place you specify. There I will separate
them and you can take them away. And you are to grant my
wish by providing food for my royal household."

10In this way Hiram kept Solomon supplied with all the cedar
and pine logs he wanted, 11and Solomon gave Hiram twenty thousand cors[c] of wheat as food for his household, in addition to
twenty thousand baths[d,e] of pressed olive oil. Solomon continued
to do this for Hiram year after year. 12The LORD gave Solomon
wisdom, just as he had promised him. There were peaceful relations between Hiram and Solomon, and the two of them made a
treaty.
13King Solomon conscripted laborers from all Israel—thirty
thousand men. 14He sent them off to Lebanon in shifts of ten
thousand a month, so that they spent one month in Lebanon and
two months at home. Adoniram was in charge of the forced labor.
15Solomon had seventy thousand carriers and eighty thousand
stonecutters in the hills, 16as well as thirty-three hundred[f] foremen who supervised the project and directed the workmen. 17At
the king's command they removed from the quarry large blocks of
quality stone to provide a foundation of dressed stone for the
temple. 18The craftsmen of Solomon and Hiram and the men of
Gebal[g] cut and prepared the timber and stone for the building of
the temple.

*Solomon Builds the Temple*

6 IN THE four hundred and eightieth[h] year after the Israelites
had come out of Egypt, in the fourth year of Solomon's reign
over Israel, in the month of Ziv, the second month, he began to
build the temple of the LORD.
2The temple that King Solomon built for the LORD was sixty
cubits long, twenty wide and thirty high.[i] 3The portico at the front
of the main hall of the temple extended the width of the temple,
that is twenty cubits,[j] and projected ten cubits[k] from the front of
the temple. 4He made narrow clerestory windows in the temple.
5Against the walls of the main hall and inner sanctuary he built a
structure around the building, in which there were side rooms.
6The lowest floor was five cubits[l] wide, the middle floor six cubits[m] and the third floor seven.[n] He made offset ledges around the
outside of the temple so that nothing would be inserted into the
temple walls.
7In building the temple, only blocks dressed at the quarry were
used, and no hammer, chisel or any other iron tool was heard at
the temple site while it was being built.

NIV [c] *11* That is, probably about 125,000 bushels (about 4,400 kiloliters) [d] *11* Septuagint (see also 2 Chron. 2:10); Hebrew *twenty cors* [e] *11* That is, about 115,000 gallons (about 440 kiloliters) [f] *16* Hebrew; some Septuagint manuscripts (see also 2 Chron. 2:2, 18) *thirty-six hundred* [g] *18* That is, Byblos [h] *1* Hebrew; Septuagint *four hundred and fortieth* [i] *2* That is, about 90 feet (about 27 meters) long and 30 feet (about 9 meters) wide and 45 feet (about 13.5 meters) high [j] *3* That is, about 30 feet (about 9 meters) [k] *3* That is, about 15 feet (about 4.5 meters) [l] *6* That is, about 7 1/2 feet (about 2.3 meters); also in verses 10 and 24 [m] *6* That is, about 9 feet (about 2.7 meters) [n] *6* That is, about 10 1/2 feet (about 3.1 meters)

## King James

8 The door for the middle chamber *was* in the right side of the house: and they went up with winding stairs into the middle *chamber,* and out of the middle into the third.

9 So he built the house, and finished it; and covered the house with beams and boards of cedar.

10 And *then* he built chambers against all the house, five cubits high: and they rested on the house with timber of cedar.

11 ¶ And the word of the LORD came to Solomon, saying,

12 *Concerning* this house which thou art in building, if thou wilt walk in my statutes, and execute my judgments, and keep all my commandments to walk in them; then will I perform my word with thee, which I spake unto David thy father:

13 And I will dwell among the children of Israel, and will not forsake my people Israel.

14 So Solomon built the house, and finished it.

15 And he built the walls of the house within with boards of cedar, both the floor of the house, and the walls of the ceiling: *and* he covered *them* on the inside with wood, and covered the floor of the house with planks of fir.

16 And he built twenty cubits on the sides of the house, both the floor and the walls with boards of cedar: he even built *them* for it within, *even* for the oracle, *even* for the most holy *place.*

17 And the house, that *is,* the temple before it, was forty cubits *long.*

18 And the cedar of the house within *was* carved with knobs and open flowers: all *was* cedar; there was no stone seen.

19 And the oracle he prepared in the house within, to set there the ark of the covenant of the LORD.

20 And the oracle in the forepart *was* twenty cubits in length, and twenty cubits in breadth, and twenty cubits in the height thereof: and he overlaid it with pure gold; and *so* covered the altar *which was of* cedar.

21 So Solomon overlaid the house within with pure gold: and he made a partition by the chains of gold before the oracle; and he overlaid it with gold.

22 And the whole house he overlaid with gold, until he had finished all the house: also the whole altar that *was* by the oracle he overlaid with gold.

23 ¶ And within the oracle he made two cherubims *of* olive tree, *each* ten cubits high.

24 And five cubits *was* the one wing of the cherub, and five cubits the other wing of the cherub: from the uttermost part of the one wing unto the uttermost part of the other *were* ten cubits.

25 And the other cherub *was* ten cubits: both the cherubims *were* of one measure and one size.

26 The height of the one cherub *was* ten cubits, and so *was it* of the other cherub.

27 And he set the cherubims within the inner house: and they stretched forth the wings of the cherubims, so that the wing of the one touched the *one* wall, and the wing of the other cherub touched the other wall; and their wings touched one another in the midst of the house.

28 And he overlaid the cherubims with gold.

29 And he carved all the walls of the house round about with carved figures of cherubims and palm trees and open flowers, within and without.

30 And the floor of the house he overlaid with gold, within and without.

31 ¶ And for the entering of the oracle he made doors *of* olive tree: the lintel *and* side posts *were* a fifth part *of the wall.*

32 The two doors also *were of* olive tree; and he carved upon them carvings of cherubims and palm trees and open flowers, and overlaid *them* with gold, and spread gold upon the cherubims, and upon the palm trees.

33 So also made he for the door of the temple posts *of* olive tree, a fourth part *of the wall.*

## Amplified

8 The entrance to the lowest side chamber was on the right [or south] side of the house, and one went up winding stairs into the middle chamber, and from the middle into the third.

9 So Solomon built the temple building, and finished it, and roofed the house with beams and boards of cedar.

10 Then he built the stories of chambers [the lean-to] against all the house, each *story* five cubits high; and it was joined to the house with timbers of cedar.

11 Now the word of the Lord came to Solomon, saying,

12 Concerning this house which you are building, if you will walk in My statutes, execute My precepts, and keep all My commandments to walk in them, then I will fulfill to you My promises, which I made to David your father.

13 And I will dwell among the Israelites, and will not forsake My people Israel.

14 So Solomon built the house, and finished it.

15 He built the walls of the house [the holy place and the holy of holies] within with boards of cedar, from the floor of the house to the rafters of the ceiling. He covered the inside with wood, and the floor of the house with boards of cypress.

16 He built twenty cubits of the rear of the house with boards of cedar from the floor to the rafters; he built it within for the sanctuary, the holy of holies.

17 The [rest of the] house, that is, the temple in front of the holy of holies, was forty cubits long.

18 The cedar on the house within was carved with gourds and open flowers; all was cedar, no stone was visible.

19 And he prepared the holy of holies in the inner room in which to set the ark of the covenant of the Lord.

20 The holy of holies was twenty cubits in length, in breadth, and in height. He overlaid it with pure gold; he also overlaid the cedar altar.

21 Solomon overlaid the house within with pure gold, and he drew chains of gold across in front of the holy of holies, and overlaid it with gold.

22 And the whole house he overlaid with gold, until all the house was finished. Also the whole [incense] altar that [stood outside the door but] belonged to the holy of holies he overlaid with gold.

23 Within the holy of holies he made two cherubim of olive wood, each ten cubits high.

24 Five cubits was the length of one wing of the cherub and five cubits its other wing; from the tip of one wing to the tip of the other was ten cubits.

25 The wings of the other cherub were also ten cubits. Both cherubim were the same,

26 The height of one cherub ten cubits, as was the other.

27 He put the cherubim within the inner sanctuary. Their wings were stretched out, so that the wing of one touched one wall, and the wing of the other cherub touched the other wall, and their inner wings touched in the midst of the room.

28 Solomon overlaid the cherubim with gold.

29 He carved all the walls of the house [these two holy rooms] round about with figures of cherubim, palm trees, and open flowers, within and without.

30 The floor of the house he overlaid with gold, inside and out.

31 For the holy of holies he made [folding] doors of olive wood; their entire width was one-fifth that of the wall.

32 On the two doors of olive wood he carved cherubim, palm trees, and open flowers; he overlaid them with gold, and spread gold on the cherubim and palm trees.

33 Also he made for the door of the holy place foursided posts of olive wood.

## New American Standard

8The doorway for the [a]lowest side chamber *was* on the right side of the house; and they would go up by winding stairs to the middle *story,* and from the middle to the third.

9So he built the house and finished it; and he covered the house with beams and planks of cedar.

10He also built the stories against the whole house, each five cubits high; and they were fastened to the house with timbers of cedar.

**11**¶ Now the word of the LORD came to Solomon saying,

12"*Concerning* this house which you are building, if you will walk in My statutes and execute My ordinances and keep all My commandments by walking in them, then I will carry out My word with you which I spoke to David your father.

13"And I will dwell among the sons of Israel, and will not forsake My people Israel."

**14**¶ So Solomon built the house and finished it.

15Then he built the walls of the house on the inside with boards of cedar; from the floor of the house to the ceiling he overlaid *the walls* on the inside with wood, and he overlaid the floor of the house with boards of cypress.

16And he built twenty cubits on the rear part of the house with boards of cedar from the floor to the ceiling; he built *them* for it on the inside as an inner sanctuary, *even* as the most holy place.

17And the house, that is, the nave in front of *the inner sanctuary,* was forty cubits *long.*

18And there was cedar on the house within, carved *in the shape* of gourds and open flowers; all was cedar, there was no stone seen.

19Then he prepared an inner sanctuary within the house in order to place there the ark of the covenant of the LORD.

20And the inner sanctuary *was* twenty cubits in length, twenty cubits in width, and twenty cubits in height, and he overlaid it with pure gold. He also overlaid the altar with cedar.

21So Solomon overlaid the inside of the house with pure gold. And he drew chains of gold across the front of the inner sanctuary; and he overlaid it with gold.

22And he overlaid the whole house with gold, until all the house was finished. Also the whole altar which was by the inner sanctuary he overlaid with gold.

**23**¶ Also in the inner sanctuary he made two cherubim of olive wood, each ten cubits high.

24And five cubits *was* the one wing of the cherub and five cubits the other wing of the cherub; from the end of one wing to the end of the other wing *were* ten cubits.

25And the other cherub *was* ten cubits; both the cherubim were of the same measure and the same form.

26The height of the one cherub *was* ten cubits, and so *was* the other cherub.

27And he placed the cherubim in the midst of the inner house, and the wings of the cherubim were spread out, so that the wing of the one was touching the *one* wall, and the wing of the other cherub was touching the other wall. So their wings were touching each other in the center of the house.

28He also overlaid the cherubim with gold.

**29**¶ Then he carved all the walls of the house round about with carved engravings of cherubim, palm trees, and open flowers, inner and outer *sanctuaries.*

30And he overlaid the floor of the house with gold, inner and outer *sanctuaries.*

31And for the entrance of the inner sanctuary he made doors of olive wood, the lintel *and* five-sided doorposts.

32So *he made* two doors of olive wood, and he carved on them carvings of cherubim, palm trees, and open flowers, and overlaid them with gold; and he spread the gold on the cherubim and on the palm trees.

33So also he made for the entrance of the nave four-sided doorposts of olive wood

**NAS** [a] So with Gr. and versions; M.T., *middle*

## New International

8The entrance to the lowest[b] floor was on the south side of the
temple; a stairway led up to the middle level and from there to the
third. 9So he built the temple and completed it, roofing it with
beams and cedar planks. 10And he built the side rooms all along
the temple. The height of each was five cubits, and they were
attached to the temple by beams of cedar.
11The word of the LORD came to Solomon: 12"As for this temple
you are building, if you follow my decrees, carry out my regulations
and keep all my commands and obey them, I will fulfill
through you the promise I gave to David your father. 13And I will
live among the Israelites and will not abandon my people Israel."
14So Solomon built the temple and completed it. 15He lined its
interior walls with cedar boards, paneling them from the floor of
the temple to the ceiling, and covered the floor of the temple with
planks of pine. 16He partitioned off twenty cubits[c] at the rear of
the temple with cedar boards from floor to ceiling to form within
the temple an inner sanctuary, the Most Holy Place. 17The main
hall in front of this room was forty cubits[d] long. 18The inside of
the temple was cedar, carved with gourds and open flowers.
Everything was cedar; no stone was to be seen.
19He prepared the inner sanctuary within the temple to set the
ark of the covenant of the LORD there. 20The inner sanctuary was
twenty cubits long, twenty wide and twenty high.[e] He overlaid
the inside with pure gold, and he also overlaid the altar of cedar.
21Solomon covered the inside of the temple with pure gold, and
he extended gold chains across the front of the inner sanctuary,
which was overlaid with gold. 22So he overlaid the whole interior
with gold. He also overlaid with gold the altar that belonged to the
inner sanctuary.
23In the inner sanctuary he made a pair of cherubim of olive
wood, each ten cubits[f] high. 24One wing of the first cherub was
five cubits long, and the other wing five cubits—ten cubits from
wing tip to wing tip. 25The second cherub also measured ten
cubits, for the two cherubim were identical in size and shape.
26The height of each cherub was ten cubits. 27He placed the cherubim
inside the innermost room of the temple, with their wings
spread out. The wing of one cherub touched one wall, while the
wing of the other touched the other wall, and their wings touched
each other in the middle of the room. 28He overlaid the cherubim
with gold.
29On the walls all around the temple, in both the inner and
outer rooms, he carved cherubim, palm trees and open flowers.
30He also covered the floors of both the inner and outer rooms of
the temple with gold.
31For the entrance of the inner sanctuary he made doors of olive
wood with five-sided jambs. 32And on the two olive wood doors
he carved cherubim, palm trees and open flowers, and overlaid the
cherubim and palm trees with beaten gold. 33In the same way he
made four-sided jambs of olive wood for the entrance to the main
hall. 34He also made two pine doors, each having two leaves that

**NIV** [b] *8* Septuagint; Hebrew *middle* [c] *16* That is, about 30 feet (about 9 meters) [d] *17* That is, about 60 feet (about 18 meters) [e] *20* That is, about 30 feet (about 9 meters) long, wide and high [f] *23* That is, about 15 feet (about 4.5 meters)

## King James

34 And the two doors *were of* fir tree: the two leaves of the one
door *were* folding, and the two leaves of the other door *were* folding.
35 And he carved *thereon* cherubims and palm trees and open
flowers: and covered *them* with gold fitted upon the carved work.
36 ¶ And he built the inner court with three rows of hewed stone,
and a row of cedar beams.
37 ¶ In the fourth year was the foundation of the house of the
LORD laid, in the month Zif:
38 And in the eleventh year, in the month Bul, which *is* the
eighth month, was the house finished throughout all the parts
thereof, and according to all the fashion of it. So was he seven
years in building it.

**7** BUT SOLOMON was building his own house thirteen years,
and he finished all his house.
2 ¶ He built also the house of the forest of Lebanon; the length
thereof *was* an hundred cubits, and the breadth thereof fifty cubits,
and the height thereof thirty cubits, upon four rows of cedar
pillars, with cedar beams upon the pillars.
3 And *it was* covered with cedar above upon the beams, that *lay*
on forty-five pillars, fifteen *in* a row.
4 And *there were* windows *in* three rows, and light *was* against
light *in* three ranks.
5 And all the doors and posts *were* square, with the windows:
and light *was* against light *in* three ranks.
6 ¶ And he made a porch of pillars; the length thereof *was* fifty
cubits, and the breadth thereof thirty cubits: and the porch *was*
before them: and the *other* pillars and the thick beam *were* before
them.
7 ¶ Then he made a porch for the throne where he might judge,
*even* the porch of judgment: and *it was* covered with cedar from one
side of the floor to the other.
8 ¶ And his house where he dwelt *had* another court within the
porch, *which* was of the like work. Solomon made also an house
for Pharaoh's daughter, whom he had taken *to wife*, like unto this
porch.
9 All these *were of* costly stones, according to the measures of
hewed stones, sawed with saws, within and without, even from
the foundation unto the coping, and *so* on the outside toward the
great court.
10 And the foundation *was of* costly stones, even great stones,
stones of ten cubits, and stones of eight cubits.
11 And above *were* costly stones, after the measures of hewed
stones, and cedars.
12 And the great court round about *was* with three rows of
hewed stones, and a row of cedar beams, both for the inner court
of the house of the LORD, and for the porch of the house.
13 ¶ And king Solomon sent and fetched Hiram out of Tyre.
14 He *was* a widow's son of the tribe of Naphtali, and his father
*was* a man of Tyre, a worker in brass: and he was filled with
wisdom, and understanding, and cunning to work all works in
brass. And he came to king Solomon, and wrought all his work.
15 For he cast two pillars of brass, of eighteen cubits high apiece:
and a line of twelve cubits did compass either of them about.
16 And he made two chapiters *of* molten brass, to set upon the
tops of the pillars: the height of the one chapiter *was* five cubits,
and the height of the other chapiter *was* five cubits:
17 *And* nets of checker work, and wreaths of chain work, for the
chapiters which *were* upon the top of the pillars; seven for the one
chapiter, and seven for the other chapiter.

## Amplified

34 The two doors were of cypress wood; the two leaves of each
door were folding.
35 He carved on them cherubim, palm trees, and open flowers,
covered with gold evenly applied on the carved work.
36 He built the inner court with three rows of hewn stone, and
a row of cedar beams.
37 The fourth year the foundation of the Lord's house was laid,
in the [second] month, Ziv;
38 The eleventh year, in Bul, the eighth month, the house was
finished throughout, according to all its specifications. So he was
seven years in building it.

**7** SOLOMON WAS building his own house [a]thirteen years,
and he finished all of it.
2 He built also the Forest of Lebanon House; its length was a
hundred cubits, its breadth fifty, and its height thirty cubits, upon
four rows of cedar pillars, with cedar beams upon the pillars.
3 And it was covered with cedar above over the side chambers
that were upon the forty-five pillars, fifteen in a row.
4 There were window frames in three rows, and window opposite window in three tiers.
5 All the doorways and windows were square cut, and window
was opposite window in three tiers.
6 He also made the Hall of Pillars; its length fifty cubits and its
breadth thirty cubits. There was a porch in front, and pillars, and
a cornice before them.
7 He made the porch for the throne where he was to judge, the
Porch of Judgment; it was covered with cedar from floor to ceiling.
8 His house where he was to dwell had another court behind the
Porch of Judgment, of similar work. Solomon also made a house
like this porch for Pharaoh's daughter, whom he had married.
9 All were of costly stones, hewn according to measure, sawed
with saws, back and front, even from foundation to coping, and
from the outside to the great court.
10 The foundation was of costly stones, even great stones of
eight and ten cubits.
11 And above were costly stones, hewn according to measure,
and cedar timbers.
12 Also the great encircling court had three courses of hewn
stone, and a course of cedar beams, like was around the inner
court, of the house of the Lord and the porch of the house.
13 King Solomon brought Hiram from Tyre.
14 He was the son of a widow of the tribe of Naphtali, and his
father was a man of Tyre, a worker in bronze. He was full of
wisdom, understanding, and skill to do any kind of work in
bronze. So he came to King Solomon and did all his [bronze] work.
15 He fashioned the two pillars of bronze, each eighteen cubits
high, and a line of twelve cubits measured its circumference.
16 He made two capitals of molten bronze to set upon the tops
of the pillars; the height of each capital was five cubits.
17 Nets of checker work and wreaths of chain work for the
capitals were on the tops of the pillars, seven for each capital.

**AMP** [a] Solomon built God's house first, then his own. That his took much longer is no reflection on Solomon, for David had made every possible preparation for building the temple, greatly reducing the time needed to finish it. (Cp. I Chron. 22:2-5). David even left for Solomon plans and patterns for the temple, and loyal friends eager to help. (Cp. 1 Chron. 28:14-19, and 1 Kings 5:1.)

## New American Standard

34and two doors of cypress wood; the two leaves of the one door
turned on pivots, and the two leaves of the other door turned on
pivots.
35And he carved *on it* cherubim, palm trees, and open flowers;
and he overlaid *them* with gold evenly applied on the engraved
work.
36And he built the inner court with three rows of cut stone and
a row of cedar beams.
37¶ In the fourth year the foundation of the house of the LORD
was laid, in the month of Ziv.
38And in the eleventh year, in the month of Bul, which is the
eighth month, the house was finished throughout all its parts and
according to all its plans. So he was seven years in building it.

*Solomon's Palace*

7 NOW SOLOMON was building his own house thirteen
years, and he finished all his house.
2And he built the house of the forest of Lebanon; its length was
100 [b]cubits and its width 50 cubits and its height 30 cubits, on four
rows of cedar pillars with cedar beams on the pillars.
3And it was paneled with cedar above the side chambers which
were on the 45 pillars, 15 in each row.
4And *there were artistic window* frames in three rows, and window was opposite window in three ranks.
5And all the doorways and doorposts *had* squared *artistic*
frames, and window was opposite window in three ranks.
6Then he made the hall of pillars; its length was 50 cubits and
its width 30 cubits, and a porch *was* in front of them and pillars and
a threshold in front of them.
7And he made the hall of the throne where he was to judge,
the hall of judgment, and it was paneled with cedar from floor to
floor.
8And his house where he was to live, the other court inward
from the hall, was of the same workmanship. He also made a
house like this hall for Pharaoh's daughter, whom Solomon had
married.
9¶ All these were of costly stones, of stone cut according to
measure, sawed with saws, inside and outside; even from the
foundation to the coping, and so on the outside to the great court.
10¶ And the foundation was of costly stones, *even* large stones,
stones of ten cubits and stones of eight cubits.
11And above were costly stones, stone cut according to measure, and cedar.
12So the great court all around *had* three rows of cut stone and
a row of cedar beams even as the inner court of the house of the
LORD, and the porch of the house.

*Hiram's Work in the Temple*

13¶ Now King Solomon sent and brought Hiram from Tyre.
14He was a widow's son from the tribe of Naphtali, and his
father was a man of Tyre, a worker in bronze; and he was filled
with wisdom and understanding and skill for doing any work in
bronze. So he came to King Solomon and performed all his work.
15¶ And he fashioned the two pillars of bronze; eighteen cubits
was the height of one pillar, and a line of twelve cubits measured
the circumference of both.
16He also made two capitals of molten bronze to set on the tops
of the pillars; the height of the one capital was five cubits and the
height of the other capital was five cubits.
17*There were* nets of network and twisted threads of chainwork
for the capitals which were on the top of the pillars; seven for the
one capital and seven for the other capital.

NAS [b] I.e., One cubit equals approx. 18 in.

## New International

turned in sockets. 35He carved cherubim, palm trees and open
flowers on them and overlaid them with gold hammered evenly
over the carvings.
36And he built the inner courtyard of three courses of dressed
stone and one course of trimmed cedar beams.
37The foundation of the temple of the LORD was laid in the
fourth year, in the month of Ziv. 38In the eleventh year in the
month of Bul, the eighth month, the temple was finished in all its
details according to its specifications. He had spent seven years
building it.

*Solomon Builds His Palace*

7 IT TOOK Solomon thirteen years, however, to complete the
construction of his palace. 2He built the Palace of the Forest
of Lebanon a hundred cubits long, fifty wide and thirty high,[c]
with four rows of cedar columns supporting trimmed cedar beams.
3It was roofed with cedar above the beams that rested on the
columns—forty-five beams, fifteen to a row. 4Its windows were
placed high in sets of three, facing each other. 5All the doorways
had rectangular frames; they were in the front part in sets of three,
facing each other.[d]
6He made a colonnade fifty cubits long and thirty wide.[e] In
front of it was a portico, and in front of that were pillars and an
overhanging roof.
7He built the throne hall, the Hall of Justice, where he was to
judge, and he covered it with cedar from floor to ceiling.[f] 8And
the palace in which he was to live, set farther back, was similar in
design. Solomon also made a palace like this hall for Pharaoh's
daughter, whom he had married.
9All these structures, from the outside to the great courtyard
and from foundation to eaves, were made of blocks of high-grade
stone cut to size and trimmed with a saw on their inner and outer
faces. 10The foundations were laid with large stones of good quality, some measuring ten cubits[g] and some eight.[h] 11Above were
high-grade stones, cut to size, and cedar beams. 12The great courtyard was surrounded by a wall of three courses of dressed stone
and one course of trimmed cedar beams, as was the inner courtyard of the temple of the LORD with its portico.

*The Temple's Furnishings*

13King Solomon sent to Tyre and brought Huram,[i] 14whose
mother was a widow from the tribe of Naphtali and whose father
was a man of Tyre and a craftsman in bronze. Huram was highly
skilled and experienced in all kinds of bronze work. He came to
King Solomon and did all the work assigned to him.
15He cast two bronze pillars, each eighteen cubits high and
twelve cubits around,[j] by line. 16He also made two capitals of cast
bronze to set on the tops of the pillars; each capital was five cubits[k]
high. 17A network of interwoven chains festooned the capitals on
top of the pillars, seven for each capital. 18He made pomegranates

NIV [c] 2 That is, about 150 feet (about 46 meters) long, 75 feet (about 23 meters) wide and 45 feet (about 13.5 meters) high [d] *5* The meaning of the Hebrew for this verse is uncertain. [e] *6* That is, about 75 feet (about 23 meters) long and 45 feet (about 13.5 meters) wide [f] *7* Vulgate and Syriac; Hebrew *floor* [g] *10* That is, about 15 feet (about 4.5 meters) [h] *10* That is, about 12 feet (about 3.6 meters) [i] *13* Hebrew *Hiram,* a variant of *Huram;* also in verses 40 and 45 [j] *15* That is, about 27 feet (about 8.1 meters) high and 18 feet (about 5.4 meters) around [k] *16* That is, about 7 1/2 feet (about 2.3 meters); also in verse 23

## King James

18And he made the pillars, and two rows round about upon the one network, to cover the chapiters that *were* upon the top, with pomegranates: and so did he for the other chapiter.

19And the chapiters that *were* upon the top of the pillars *were* of lily work in the porch, four cubits.

20And the chapiters upon the two pillars *had pomegranates* also above, over against the belly which *was* by the network: and the pomegranates *were* two hundred in rows round about upon the other chapiter.

21And he set up the pillars in the porch of the temple: and he set up the right pillar, and called the name thereof Jachin: and he set up the left pillar, and called the name thereof Boaz.

22And upon the top of the pillars *was* lily work: so was the work of the pillars finished.

23¶ And he made a molten sea, ten cubits from the one brim to the other: *it was* round all about, and his height *was* five cubits: and a line of thirty cubits did compass it round about.

24And under the brim of it round about *there were* knobs compassing it, ten in a cubit, compassing the sea round about: the knobs *were* cast in two rows, when it was cast.

25It stood upon twelve oxen, three looking toward the north, and three looking toward the west, and three looking toward the south, and three looking toward the east: and the sea *was set* above upon them, and all their hinder parts *were* inward.

26And it *was* an handbreadth thick, and the brim thereof was wrought like the brim of a cup, with flowers of lilies: it contained two thousand baths.

27¶ And he made ten bases of brass; four cubits *was* the length of one base, and four cubits the breadth thereof, and three cubits the height of it.

28And the work of the bases *was* on this *manner:* they had borders, and the borders *were* between the ledges:

29And on the borders that *were* between the ledges *were* lions, oxen, and cherubims: and upon the ledges *there was* a base above: and beneath the lions and oxen *were* certain additions made of thin work.

30And every base had four brasen wheels, and plates of brass: and the four corners thereof had undersetters: under the laver *were* undersetters molten, at the side of every addition.

31And the mouth of it within the chapiter and above *was* a cubit: but the mouth thereof *was* round *after* the work of the base, a cubit and an half: and also upon the mouth of it *were* gravings with their borders, foursquare, not round.

32And under the borders *were* four wheels; and the axletrees of the wheels *were joined* to the base: and the height of a wheel *was* a cubit and half a cubit.

33And the work of the wheels *was* like the work of a chariot wheel: their axletrees, and their naves, and their felloes, and their spokes, *were* all molten.

34And *there were* four undersetters to the four corners of one base: *and* the undersetters *were* of the very base itself.

35And in the top of the base *was there* a round compass of half a cubit high: and on the top of the base the ledges thereof and the borders thereof *were* of the same.

36For on the plates of the ledges thereof, and on the borders thereof, he graved cherubims, lions, and palm trees, according to the proportion of every one, and additions round about.

37After this *manner* he made the ten bases: all of them had one casting, one measure, *and* one size.

38¶ Then made he ten lavers of brass: one laver contained forty baths: *and* every laver was four cubits: *and* upon every one of the ten bases one laver.

39And he put five bases on the right side of the house, and five on the left side of the house: and he set the sea on the right side of the house eastward over against the south.

40¶ And Hiram made the lavers, and the shovels, and the basins. So Hiram made an end of doing all the work that he made king Solomon for the house of the LORD:

## Amplified

18So Hiram made the pillars. There were two rows of pomegranates encircling each network, to cover the capitals that were upon the top.

19The capitals that were upon the top of the pillars in the porch were of lily-work, four cubits.

20The capitals were upon the two pillars and also above the rounded projection beside the network. There were 200 pomegranates in two rows round about; and so with the other capital.

21Hiram set up the pillars of the porch of the temple; he set up the right pillar and called its name Jachin [he will establish], and he set up the left pillar and called its name Boaz [in strength].

22On the tops of the pillars was lily-work. So the work of the pillars was finished.

23He made a round molten sea, ten cubits from brim to brim, five cubits high and thirty cubits in circumference.

24Under its brim were gourds encircling the sea, ten to a cubit; the gourds were in two rows, cast in one piece with it.

25It stood upon twelve oxen, three facing north, three west, three south, and three east; the sea was set upon them and all their rears pointed inward.

26It was a handbreadth thick, and its brim was made like the brim of a cup, like a lily blossom. It held 2,000 baths [Hebrew liquid measurement].

27Hiram made ten bronze bases [for the lavers]; their length and breadth was four cubits, and the height three cubits.

28This is the way the bases were made; they had panels between the ledges.

29On the panels between the ledges were lions, oxen, and cherubim; and upon the ledges there was a pedestal above. Beneath the lions and oxen were wreaths of hanging work.

30And every base had four bronze wheels and axles of bronze; and at the four corners were supports for a laver. Beneath the laver the supports were cast, with wreaths at the side of each.

31Its mouth within the capital projected upward a cubit, and its mouth was round like the work of a pedestal, a cubit and a half; also upon its mouth were carvings, and their borders were square, not round.

32Under the borders were four wheels; and the axles of the wheels were one piece with the base; and the height of a wheel was a cubit and a half.

33The wheels were made like a chariot wheel: their axles, their rims, their spokes, and their hubs, were all cast.

34There were four supports to the four corners of each base; the supports were part of the base itself.

35On the top of the base there was a circular elevation half a cubit high, and on the top of the base its stays and panels were of one piece with it.

36And on the surface of its stays and its panels Hiram carved cherubim, lions, and palm trees, according to the space of each, with wreaths round about.

37Thus he made the ten bases; they all had one casting, one measure, and one form.

38Then he made ten lavers of bronze; each laver held forty baths and measured four cubits, and there was one laver on each of the ten bases.

39He put the bases five on the south side of the house, and five on the north side; and he set the sea at the southeast corner of the house.

40Hiram made the lavers, the shovels, and the basins. So Hiram finished all the work that he did for King Solomon on the house of the Lord:

## New American Standard

18So he made the pillars, and two rows around on the one
network to cover the capitals which were on the top of the pomegranates; and so he did for the other capital.
19And the capitals which *were* on the top of the pillars in the
porch were of lily design, four cubits.
20And *there were* capitals on the two pillars, even above *and* close
to the rounded projection which was beside the network; and the
pomegranates *numbered* two hundred in rows around both capitals.
21Thus he set up the pillars at the porch of the nave; and he set
up the right pillar and named it [a]Jachin, and he set up the left pillar
and named it [b]Boaz.
22And on the top of the pillars was lily design. So the work of
the pillars was finished.
23¶ Now he made the sea of cast *metal* ten cubits from brim to
brim, circular in form, and its height was five cubits, and thirty
cubits in circumference.
24And under its brim gourds went around encircling it ten to a
cubit, completely surrounding the sea; the gourds were in two
rows, cast with the rest.
25It stood on twelve oxen, three facing north, three facing west,
three facing south, and three facing east; and the sea *was set* on top
of them, and all their rear parts *turned* inward.
26And it was a handbreadth thick, and its brim was made like
the brim of a cup, *as* a lily blossom; it could hold two thousand
baths.
27¶ Then he made the ten stands of bronze; the length of each
stand was four cubits and its width four cubits and its height three
cubits.
28And this was the design of the stands: they had borders, even
borders between the [c]frames,
29and on the borders which were between the [d]frames *were*
lions, oxen and cherubim; and on the [e]frames there *was* a pedestal
above, and beneath the lions and oxen *were* wreaths of hanging
work.
30Now each stand had four bronze wheels with bronze axles,
and its four feet had supports; beneath the basin *were* cast supports
with wreaths at each side.
31And its opening inside the crown at the top *was* a cubit, and
its opening *was* round like the design of a pedestal, a cubit and a
half; and also on its opening *there were* engravings, and their borders were square, not round.
32And the four wheels *were* underneath the borders, and the
axles of the wheels *were* on the stand. And the height of a wheel
*was* a cubit and a half.
33And the workmanship of the wheels *was* like the workmanship of a chariot wheel. Their axles, their rims, their spokes, and
their hubs *were* all cast.
34Now *there were* four supports at the four corners of each stand;
its supports *were* part of the stand itself.
35And on the top of the stand *there was* a circular form half a
cubit high, and on the top of the stand its stays and its borders *were*
part of it.
36And he engraved on the plates of its stays and on its borders,
cherubim, lions and palm trees, according to the clear space on
each, with wreaths *all* around.
37He made the ten stands like this: all of them had one casting,
one measure and one form.
38And he made ten basins of bronze, one basin held forty baths;
each basin *was* four cubits, *and* on each of the ten stands *was* one
basin.
39Then he set the stands, five on the right side of the house and
five on the left side of the house; and he set the sea *of cast metal*
on the right side of the house eastward toward the south.
40¶ Now Hiram made the basins and the shovels and the bowls.
So Hiram finished doing all the work which he performed for King
Solomon *in* the house of the LORD:

**NAS** [a] I.e., he shall establish [b] I.e., in it is strength [c] Or, *crossbars* [d] Or, *crossbars* [e] Or, *crossbars*

## New International

in two rows[f] encircling each network to decorate the capitals on
top of the pillars.[g] He did the same for each capital. 19The capitals
on top of the pillars in the portico were in the shape of lilies, four
cubits[h] high. 20On the capitals of both pillars, above the bowl-
shaped part next to the network, were the two hundred pomegranates in rows all around. 21He erected the pillars at the portico
of the temple. The pillar to the south he named Jakin[i] and the one
to the north Boaz.[j] 22The capitals on top were in the shape of lilies.
And so the work on the pillars was completed.
23He made the Sea of cast metal, circular in shape, measuring
ten cubits[k] from rim to rim and five cubits high. It took a line of
thirty cubits[l] to measure around it. 24Below the rim, gourds encircled it—ten to a cubit. The gourds were cast in two rows in one
piece with the Sea.
25The Sea stood on twelve bulls, three facing north, three facing
west, three facing south and three facing east. The Sea rested on
top of them, and their hindquarters were toward the center. 26It
was a handbreadth[m] in thickness, and its rim was like the rim of
a cup, like a lily blossom. It held two thousand baths.[n]
27He also made ten movable stands of bronze; each was four
cubits long, four wide and three high.[o] 28This is how the stands
were made: They had side panels attached to uprights. 29On the
panels between the uprights were lions, bulls and cherubim—and
on the uprights as well. Above and below the lions and bulls were
wreaths of hammered work. 30Each stand had four bronze wheels
with bronze axles, and each had a basin resting on four supports,
cast with wreaths on each side. 31On the inside of the stand there
was an opening that had a circular frame one cubit[p] deep. This
opening was round, and with its basework it measured a cubit and
a half.[q] Around its opening there was engraving. The panels of the
stands were square, not round. 32The four wheels were under the
panels, and the axles of the wheels were attached to the stand. The
diameter of each wheel was a cubit and a half. 33The wheels were
made like chariot wheels; the axles, rims, spokes and hubs were
all of cast metal.
34Each stand had four handles, one on each corner, projecting
from the stand. 35At the top of the stand there was a circular band
half a cubit[r] deep. The supports and panels were attached to the
top of the stand. 36He engraved cherubim, lions and palm trees on
the surfaces of the supports and on the panels, in every available
space, with wreaths all around. 37This is the way he made the ten
stands. They were all cast in the same molds and were identical
in size and shape.
38He then made ten bronze basins, each holding forty baths[s]
and measuring four cubits across, one basin to go on each of the
ten stands. 39He placed five of the stands on the south side of the
temple and five on the north. He placed the Sea on the south side,
at the southeast corner of the temple. 40He also made the basins
and shovels and sprinkling bowls.

So Huram finished all the work he had undertaken for King
Solomon in the temple of the LORD:

**NIV** [f] *18* Two Hebrew manuscripts and Septuagint; most Hebrew manuscripts *made the pillars, and there were two rows* [g] *18* Many Hebrew manuscripts and Syriac; most Hebrew manuscripts *pomegranates* [h] *19* That is, about 6 feet (about 1.8 meters); also in verse 38 [i] *21 Jakin* probably means *he establishes.* [j] *21 Boaz* probably means *in him is strength.* [k] *23* That is, about 15 feet (about 4.5 meters) [l] *23* That is, about 45 feet (about 13.5 meters) [m] *26* That is, about 3 inches (about 8 centimeters) [n] *26* That is, probably about 11,500 gallons (about 44 kiloliters); the Septuagint does not have this sentence. [o] *27* That is, about 6 feet (about 1.8 meters) long and wide and about 4 1/2 feet (about 1.3 meters) high [p] *31* That is, about 1 1/2 feet (about 0.5 meter) [q] *31* That is, about 2 1/4 feet (about 0.7 meter); also in verse 32 [r] *35* That is, about 3/4 foot (about 0.2 meter) [s] *38* That is, about 230 gallons (about 880 liters)

## King James

41The two pillars, and the *two* bowls of the chapiters that *were*
on the top of the two pillars; and the two networks, to cover the
two bowls of the chapiters which *were* upon the top of the pillars;
42And four hundred pomegranates for the two networks, *even*
two rows of pomegranates for one network, to cover the two bowls
of the chapiters that *were* upon the pillars;
43And the ten bases, and ten lavers on the bases;
44And one sea, and twelve oxen under the sea;
45And the pots, and the shovels, and the basins: and all these
vessels, which Hiram made to king Solomon for the house of the
LORD, *were of* bright brass.
46In the plain of Jordan did the king cast them, in the clay
ground between Succoth and Zarthan.
47And Solomon left all the vessels *unweighed,* because they were
exceeding many: neither was the weight of the brass found out.
48And Solomon made all the vessels that *pertained* unto the
house of the LORD: the altar of gold, and the table of gold, whereupon the showbread *was,*
49And the candlesticks of pure gold, five on the right *side,* and
five on the left, before the oracle, with the flowers, and the lamps,
and the tongs *of* gold,
50And the bowls, and the snuffers, and the basins, and the
spoons, and the censers *of* pure gold; and the hinges *of* gold, *both*
for the doors of the inner house, the most holy *place, and* for the
doors of the house, *to wit,* of the temple.
51So was ended all the work that king Solomon made for the
house of the LORD. And Solomon brought in the things which
David his father had dedicated; *even* the silver, and the gold, and
the vessels, did he put among the treasures of the house of the
LORD.

**8** THEN SOLOMON assembled the elders of Israel, and all the
heads of the tribes, the chief of the fathers of the children of
Israel, unto king Solomon in Jerusalem, that they might bring up
the ark of the covenant of the LORD out of the city of David, which
*is* Zion.
2And all the men of Israel assembled themselves unto king
Solomon at the feast in the month Ethanim, which *is* the seventh
month.
3And all the elders of Israel came, and the priests took up the
ark.
4And they brought up the ark of the LORD, and the tabernacle
of the congregation, and all the holy vessels that *were* in the tabernacle, even those did the priests and the Levites bring up.
5And king Solomon, and all the congregation of Israel, that
were assembled unto him, *were* with him before the ark, sacrificing
sheep and oxen, that could not be told nor numbered for multitude.
6And the priests brought in the ark of the covenant of the LORD
unto his place, into the oracle of the house, to the most holy *place,*
*even* under the wings of the cherubims.
7For the cherubims spread forth *their* two wings over the place
of the ark, and the cherubims covered the ark and the staves
thereof above.
8And they drew out the staves, that the ends of the staves were
seen out in the holy *place* before the oracle, and they were not seen
without: and there they are unto this day.
9 *There was* nothing in the ark save the two tables of stone, which
Moses put there at Horeb, when the LORD made *a covenant* with
the children of Israel, when they came out of the land of Egypt.
10And it came to pass, when the priests were come out of the
holy *place,* that the cloud filled the house of the LORD,
11So that the priests could not stand to minister because of the
cloud: for the glory of the LORD had filled the house of the LORD.

## Amplified

41The two pillars, and the two bowls of the capitals that were
on the tops of the two pillars, and the two networks to cover the
two bowls;
42And the 400 pomegranates for the two networks, two rows of
pomegranates for each network, to cover the two bowls of the
capitals that were upon the pillars;
43The ten bases, and the ten lavers on the bases;
44One sea, and the twelve oxen under it.
45Now the pots, the shovels, and the basins, all these vessels
which Hiram made for King Solomon in the house of the Lord,
were of burnished bronze.
46In the Jordan plain the king cast them, in clay ground between
Succoth and Zarethan.
47Solomon left all the vessels unweighed, because they were so
many; the weight of the bronze was not found out.
48Solomon made all the other vessels of the Lord's house: the
[incense] altar of gold, the table of gold for the showbread,
49The lampstands of pure gold, five on the right side, and five
on the left, in front of the holy of holies, with the flowers, the
lamps, and the tongs of gold,
50The cups, snuffers, basins, spoons, firepans, of pure gold;
and the hinges of gold, for the doors of the innermost room, the
holy of holies, and for the doors of the holy place.
51So all the work that King Solomon did on the house of the
Lord was completed. Solomon brought in the things which David
his father had dedicated, the silver, the gold, and the vessels, and
put them in the treasuries of the Lord's house.

**8** THEN SOLOMON assembled the elders of Israel and all the
heads of the tribes, the chiefs of the fathers' houses of the
Israelites, before the king in Jerusalem, to bring up the ark of the
covenant of the Lord out of Zion the city of David.
2All the men of Israel assembled themselves before King Solomon at the feast in the seventh month, Ethanim.
3All the elders of Israel came, and the priests took up the ark.
4And they brought up the ark of the Lord, the tent of meeting,
and all the holy vessels that were in the tent; the priests and the
Levites brought them up.
5King Solomon, and all the congregation of Israel, who had
assembled before him, were with him before the ark, sacrificing
sheep and oxen, so many that they could not be reported or
counted.
6And the priests brought the ark of the covenant of the Lord to
its place in the holy of holies of the house, under the wings of the
cherubim.
7For the cherubim spread forth their two wings over the place
of the ark, and the cherubim covered the ark and its poles.
8The poles were so long that the ends of them were seen from
the holy place before the holy of holies, but they were not seen
outside; they are there to this day.
9There was nothing in the ark except the two tables of stone,
which Moses put there at Horeb, where the Lord made a covenant
with the Israelites when they came out of the land of Egypt. [Deut.
10:2-5.]
10When the priests had come out of the holy place, the cloud
filled the Lord's house,
11So the priests could not stand to minister because of the cloud,
for the glory of the Lord had filled the Lord's house.

## New American Standard

41 the two pillars and the *two* bowls of the capitals which *were*
on the top of the two pillars, and the two networks to cover the
two bowls of the capitals which *were* on the top of the pillars;
42 and the four hundred pomegranates for the two networks,
two rows of pomegranates for each network to cover the two bowls
of the capitals which *were* on the tops of the pillars;
43 and the ten stands with the ten basins on the stands;
44 and the one sea and the twelve oxen under the sea;
45 and the pails and the shovels and the bowls; even all these
utensils which Hiram made for King Solomon *in* the house of the
LORD *were* of polished bronze.
46 In the plain of the Jordan the king cast them, in the clay
ground between Succoth and Zarethan.
47 And Solomon left all the utensils *unweighed,* because *they were*
too many; the weight of the bronze could not be ascertained.
48 ¶ And Solomon made all the furniture which *was in* the house
of the LORD: the golden altar and the golden table on which *was*
the bread of the Presence;
49 and the lampstands, five on the right side and five on the left,
in front of the inner sanctuary, of pure gold; and the flowers and
the lamps and the tongs, of gold;
50 and the cups and the snuffers and the bowls and the spoons
and the firepans, of pure gold; and the hinges both for the doors
of the inner house, the most holy place, *and* for the doors of the
house, *that is,* of the nave, of gold.
51 ¶ Thus all the work that King Solomon performed *in* the house
of the LORD was finished. And Solomon brought in the things
dedicated by his father David, the silver and the gold and the
utensils, *and* he put them in the treasuries of the house of the LORD.

*The Ark Brought into the Temple*

8 THEN SOLOMON assembled the elders of Israel and all the
heads of the tribes, the leaders of the fathers' *households* of the
sons of Israel, to King Solomon in Jerusalem, to bring up the ark
of the covenant of the LORD from the city of David, which is Zion.
2 And all the men of Israel assembled themselves to King Solomon at the feast, in the month Ethanim, which is the seventh
month.
3 Then all the elders of Israel came, and the priests took up the
ark.
4 And they brought up the ark of the LORD and the tent of
meeting and all the holy utensils, which were in the tent, and the
priests and the Levites brought them up.
5 And King Solomon and all the congregation of Israel, who
were assembled to him, were with him before the ark, sacrificing
so many sheep and oxen they could not be counted or numbered.
6 Then the priests brought the ark of the covenant of the LORD
to its place, into the inner sanctuary of the house, to the most holy
place, under the wings of the cherubim.
7 For the cherubim spread *their* wings over the place of the ark,
and the cherubim made a covering over the ark and its poles from
above.
8 But the poles were so long that the ends of the poles could be
seen from the holy place before the inner sanctuary, but they could
not be seen outside; they are there to this day.
9 There was nothing in the ark except the two tablets of stone
which Moses put there at Horeb, where the LORD made a covenant
with the sons of Israel, when they came out of the land of Egypt.
10 And it came about when the priests came from the holy place,
that the cloud filled the house of the LORD,
11 so that the priests could not stand to minister because of the
cloud, for the glory of the LORD filled the house of the LORD.

## New International

41 the two pillars;
the two bowl-shaped capitals on top of the pillars;
the two sets of network decorating the two bowl-shaped
capitals on top of the pillars;
42 the four hundred pomegranates for the two sets of network
(two rows of pomegranates for each network, decorating
the bowl-shaped capitals on top of the pillars);
43 the ten stands with their ten basins;
44 the Sea and the twelve bulls under it;
45 the pots, shovels and sprinkling bowls.

All these objects that Huram made for King Solomon for the
temple of the LORD were of burnished bronze. 46 The king had
them cast in clay molds in the plain of the Jordan between Succoth
and Zarethan. 47 Solomon left all these things unweighed, because
there were so many; the weight of the bronze was not determined.
48 Solomon also made all the furnishings that were in the LORD's
temple:

the golden altar;
the golden table on which was the bread of the Presence;
49 the lampstands of pure gold (five on the right and five on the
left, in front of the inner sanctuary);
the gold floral work and lamps and tongs;
50 the pure gold basins, wick trimmers, sprinkling bowls,
dishes and censers;
and the gold sockets for the doors of the innermost room, the
Most Holy Place, and also for the doors of the main hall
of the temple.

51 When all the work King Solomon had done for the temple of
the LORD was finished, he brought in the things his father David
had dedicated—the silver and gold and the furnishings—and he
placed them in the treasuries of the LORD's temple.

*The Ark Brought to the Temple*

8 THEN KING Solomon summoned into his presence at Jerusalem the elders of Israel, all the heads of the tribes and the
chiefs of the Israelite families, to bring up the ark of the LORD's
covenant from Zion, the City of David. 2 All the men of Israel came
together to King Solomon at the time of the festival in the month
of Ethanim, the seventh month.
3 When all the elders of Israel had arrived, the priests took up
the ark, 4 and they brought up the ark of the LORD and the Tent of
Meeting and all the sacred furnishings in it. The priests and Levites
carried them up, 5 and King Solomon and the entire assembly of
Israel that had gathered about him were before the ark, sacrificing
so many sheep and cattle that they could not be recorded or
counted.
6 The priests then brought the ark of the LORD's covenant to its
place in the inner sanctuary of the temple, the Most Holy Place,
and put it beneath the wings of the cherubim. 7 The cherubim
spread their wings over the place of the ark and overshadowed the
ark and its carrying poles. 8 These poles were so long that their
ends could be seen from the Holy Place in front of the inner
sanctuary, but not from outside the Holy Place; and they are still
there today. 9 There was nothing in the ark except the two stone
tablets that Moses had placed in it at Horeb, where the LORD made
a covenant with the Israelites after they came out of Egypt.
10 When the priests withdrew from the Holy Place, the cloud
filled the temple of the LORD. 11 And the priests could not perform
their service because of the cloud, for the glory of the LORD filled
his temple.

## King James

12¶ Then spake Solomon, The LORD said that he would dwell in the thick darkness.

13I have surely built thee an house to dwell in, a settled place for thee to abide in for ever.

14And the king turned his face about, and blessed all the congregation of Israel: (and all the congregation of Israel stood;)

15And he said, Blessed *be* the LORD God of Israel, which spake with his mouth unto David my father, and hath with his hand fulfilled *it*, saying,

16Since the day that I brought forth my people Israel out of Egypt, I chose no city out of all the tribes of Israel to build an house, that my name might be therein; but I chose David to be over my people Israel.

17And it was in the heart of David my father to build an house for the name of the LORD God of Israel.

18And the LORD said unto David my father, Whereas it was in thine heart to build an house unto my name, thou didst well that it was in thine heart.

19Nevertheless thou shalt not build the house; but thy son that shall come forth out of thy loins, he shall build the house unto my name.

20And the LORD hath performed his word that he spake, and I am risen up in the room of David my father, and sit on the throne of Israel, as the LORD promised, and have built an house for the name of the LORD God of Israel.

21And I have set there a place for the ark, wherein *is* the covenant of the LORD, which he made with our fathers, when he brought them out of the land of Egypt.

22¶ And Solomon stood before the altar of the LORD in the presence of all the congregation of Israel, and spread forth his hands toward heaven:

23And he said, LORD God of Israel, *there is* no God like thee, in heaven above, or on earth beneath, who keepest covenant and mercy with thy servants that walk before thee with all their heart:

24Who hast kept with thy servant David my father that thou promisedst him: thou spakest also with thy mouth, and hast fulfilled *it* with thine hand, as *it is* this day.

25Therefore now, LORD God of Israel, keep with thy servant David my father that thou promisedst him, saying, There shall not fail thee a man in my sight to sit on the throne of Israel; so that thy children take heed to their way, that they walk before me as thou hast walked before me.

26And now, O God of Israel, let thy word, I pray thee, be verified, which thou spakest unto thy servant David my father.

27But will God indeed dwell on the earth? behold, the heaven and heaven of heavens cannot contain thee; how much less this house that I have builded?

28Yet have thou respect unto the prayer of thy servant, and to his supplication, O LORD my God, to hearken unto the cry and to the prayer, which thy servant prayeth before thee today:

29That thine eyes may be open toward this house night and day, *even* toward the place of which thou hast said, My name shall be there: that thou mayest hearken unto the prayer which thy servant shall make toward this place.

30And hearken thou to the supplication of thy servant, and of thy people Israel, when they shall pray toward this place: and hear thou in heaven thy dwellingplace: and when thou hearest, forgive.

31¶ If any man trespass against his neighbour, and an oath be laid upon him to cause him to swear, and the oath come before thine altar in this house:

32Then hear thou in heaven, and do, and judge thy servants, condemning the wicked, to bring his way upon his head; and justifying the righteous, to give him according to his righteousness.

## Amplified

12Then Solomon said, The Lord said that He would dwell in the thick darkness.

13I have surely built You a house of habitation, a settled place for You to dwell in for ever.

14And the king turned his face about, and blessed all the assembly of Israel; and all the assembly of Israel stood.

15He said, Blessed be the Lord God of Israel, Who spoke with His mouth to David my father, and has with his hand fulfilled it, saying,

16Since the day that I brought forth My people Israel out of Egypt, I chose no city out of all the tribes of Israel in which to build a house, that My name [and My presence] might be in it; but I chose David to be over My people Israel.

17Now it was in the heart of David my father to build a house for the name [the presence] of the Lord, the God of Israel.

18And the Lord said to David my father, Whereas it was in your heart to build a house for My name, you did well that it was in your heart;

19Yet you shall not build the house; but your son who shall be born to you shall build *it* to My name [and My actively present person].

20And the Lord has fulfilled His promise which He made; I have risen up in the place of David my father, and sit on the throne of Israel, as the Lord promised, and have built a house for the name [renown] of the Lord, the God of Israel.

21And I have made there a place for the ark [the token of His presence], in which is the covenant [the ten commandments] of the Lord which He made with our fathers, when He brought them out of the land of Egypt. [Exod. 34:28.]

22Then Solomon stood [in the court] before the Lord's burnt offering altar in the presence of all the assembly of Israel, and spread forth his hands toward Heaven;

23And he said, O Lord, the God of Israel, there is no God like You, in Heaven above or on earth beneath, keeping covenant and showing mercy *and* loving-kindness to Your servants who walk before You with all their heart;

24You have kept what You promised Your servant David my father. You also spoke with Your mouth, and have fulfilled it with Your hand, as this day.

25Therefore now, O Lord, the God of Israel, keep with Your servant David my father what You promised him when You said, There shall not fail you a man before Me to sit on the throne of Israel, if only your children take heed to their way, that they walk before Me as you have done.

26Now, O God of Israel, let Your word, which You spoke to Your servant David my father, be confirmed [by experience].

27But will God indeed dwell with men on the earth? Behold, the heaven and Heaven of heavens [in its most extended compass] cannot contain You; how much less this house that I have built?

28Yet graciously consider the prayer and supplication of Your servant, O Lord my God, to hearken to the (loud) cry and prayer, which he prays before You today.

29That Your eyes may be open toward this house night and day, toward the place of which You have said, My name [and the token of My presence] shall be there; that You may hearken to the prayer which Your servant shall make in [or facing toward] this place.

30Hearken to the prayer of Your servant and of Your people Israel, when they pray in *or* toward this place. Hear in Heaven Your dwelling place, and when You hear, forgive.

31Whenever a man sins against his neighbor and is made to take an oath, and comes and swears the oath before Your altar in this house,

32Then hear in Heaven, and do, and judge Your servants, condemning the wicked by bringing his guilt upon his own head, and justifying the [uncompromisingly] righteous by rewarding him according to his righteousness—his uprightness, right standing with God.

## New American Standard

*Solomon Addresses the People*

12¶ Then Solomon said,
"The LORD has said that He would dwell in the thick
cloud.
13 "I have surely built Thee a lofty house,
A place for Thy dwelling forever."
14Then the king faced about and blessed all the assembly of
Israel, while all the assembly of Israel was standing.
15And he said, "Blessed be the LORD, the God of Israel, who
spoke with His mouth to my father David and has fulfilled *it* with
His hand, saying,
16'Since the day that I brought My people Israel from Egypt, I
did not choose a city out of all the tribes of Israel *in which* to build
a house that My name might be there, but I chose David to be over
My people Israel.'
17"Now it was in the heart of my father David to build a house
for the name of the LORD, the God of Israel.
18"But the LORD said to my father David, 'Because it was in your
heart to build a house for My name, you did well that it was in your
heart.
19'Nevertheless you shall not build the house, but your son who
shall be born to you, he shall build the house for My name.'
20"Now the LORD has fulfilled His word which He spoke; for I
have risen in place of my father David and sit on the throne of
Israel, as the LORD promised, and have built the house for the
name of the LORD, the God of Israel.
21"And there I have set a place for the ark, in which is the
covenant of the LORD, which He made with our fathers when He
brought them from the land of Egypt."

*The Prayer of Dedication*

22¶ Then Solomon stood before the altar of the LORD in the
presence of all the assembly of Israel and spread out his hands
toward heaven.
23And he said, "O LORD, the God of Israel, there is no God like
Thee in heaven above or on earth beneath, who art keeping covenant and *showing* lovingkindness to Thy servants who walk before Thee with all their heart,
24who hast kept with Thy servant, my father David, that which
Thou hast promised him; indeed, Thou hast spoken with Thy
mouth and hast fulfilled it with Thy hand as it is this day.
25"Now therefore, O LORD, the God of Israel, keep with Thy
servant David my father that which Thou hast promised him,
saying, 'You shall not lack a man to sit on the throne of Israel, if
only your sons take heed to their way to walk before Me as you
have walked.'
26"Now therefore, O God of Israel, let Thy word, I pray Thee,
be confirmed which Thou hast spoken to Thy servant, my father
David.
27¶ "But will God indeed dwell on the earth? Behold, heaven
and the highest heaven cannot contain Thee, how much less this
house which I have built!
28"Yet have regard to the prayer of Thy servant and to his
supplication, O LORD my God, to listen to the cry and to the prayer
which Thy servant prays before Thee today;
29that Thine eyes may be open toward this house night and day,
toward the place of which Thou hast said, 'My name shall be
there,' to listen to the prayer which Thy servant shall pray toward
this place.
30"And listen to the supplication of Thy servant and of Thy
people Israel, when they pray toward this place; hear Thou in
heaven Thy dwelling place; hear and forgive.
31¶ "If a man sins against his neighbor and is made to take an
oath, and he comes *and* takes an oath before Thine altar in this
house,
32then hear Thou in heaven and act and judge Thy servants,
condemning the wicked by bringing his way on his own head and
justifying the righteous by giving him according to his righteousness.

## New International

12Then Solomon said, "The LORD has said that he would dwell
in a dark cloud; 13I have indeed built a magnificent temple for you,
a place for you to dwell forever."
14While the whole assembly of Israel was standing there, the
king turned around and blessed them. 15Then he said:

"Praise be to the LORD, the God of Israel, who with his own
hand has fulfilled what he promised with his own mouth to
my father David. For he said, 16'Since the day I brought my
people Israel out of Egypt, I have not chosen a city in any tribe
of Israel to have a temple built for my Name to be there, but
I have chosen David to rule my people Israel.'
17"My father David had it in his heart to build a temple for
the Name of the LORD, the God of Israel. 18But the LORD said
to my father David, 'Because it was in your heart to build a
temple for my Name, you did well to have this in your heart.
19Nevertheless, you are not the one to build the temple, but
your son, who is your own flesh and blood—he is the one
who will build the temple for my Name.'
20"The LORD has kept the promise he made: I have succeeded David my father and now I sit on the throne of Israel,
just as the LORD promised, and I have built the temple for the
Name of the LORD, the God of Israel. 21I have provided a place
there for the ark, in which is the covenant of the LORD that
he made with our fathers when he brought them out of
Egypt."

*Solomon's Prayer of Dedication*

22Then Solomon stood before the altar of the LORD in front of
the whole assembly of Israel, spread out his hands toward heaven
23and said:

"O LORD, God of Israel, there is no God like you in heaven
above or on earth below—you who keep your covenant of
love with your servants who continue wholeheartedly in your
way. 24You have kept your promise to your servant David my
father; with your mouth you have promised and with your
hand you have fulfilled it—as it is today.
25"Now LORD, God of Israel, keep for your servant David
my father the promises you made to him when you said, 'You
shall never fail to have a man to sit before me on the throne
of Israel, if only your sons are careful in all they do to walk
before me as you have done.' 26And now, O God of Israel, let
your word that you promised your servant David my father
come true.
27"But will God really dwell on earth? The heavens, even
the highest heaven, cannot contain you. How much less this
temple I have built! 28Yet give attention to your servant's
prayer and his plea for mercy, O LORD my God. Hear the cry
and the prayer that your servant is praying in your presence
this day. 29May your eyes be open toward this temple night
and day, this place of which you said, 'My Name shall be
there,' so that you will hear the prayer your servant prays
toward this place. 30Hear the supplication of your servant and
of your people Israel when they pray toward this place. Hear
from heaven, your dwelling place, and when you hear, forgive.
31"When a man wrongs his neighbor and is required to
take an oath and he comes and swears the oath before your
altar in this temple, 32then hear from heaven and act. Judge
between your servants, condemning the guilty and bringing
down on his own head what he has done. Declare the innocent not guilty, and so establish his innocence.

## King James

33¶ When thy people Israel be smitten down before the enemy, because they have sinned against thee, and shall turn again to thee, and confess thy name, and pray, and make supplication unto thee in this house:

34Then hear thou in heaven, and forgive the sin of thy people Israel, and bring them again unto the land which thou gavest unto their fathers.

35¶ When heaven is shut up, and there is no rain, because they have sinned against thee; if they pray toward this place, and confess thy name, and turn from their sin, when thou afflictest them:

36Then hear thou in heaven, and forgive the sin of thy servants, and of thy people Israel, that thou teach them the good way wherein they should walk, and give rain upon thy land, which thou hast given to thy people for an inheritance.

37¶ If there be in the land famine, if there be pestilence, blasting, mildew, locust, *or* if there be caterpillar; if their enemy besiege them in the land of their cities; whatsoever plague, whatsoever sickness *there be;*

38What prayer and supplication soever be *made* by any man, *or* by all thy people Israel, which shall know every man the plague of his own heart, and spread forth his hands toward this house:

39Then hear thou in heaven thy dwellingplace, and forgive, and do, and give to every man according to his ways, whose heart thou knowest; (for thou, *even* thou only, knowest the hearts of all the children of men;)

40That they may fear thee all the days that they live in the land which thou gavest unto our fathers.

41Moreover concerning a stranger, that *is* not of thy people Israel, but cometh out of a far country for thy name's sake;

42(For they shall hear of thy great name, and of thy strong hand, and of thy stretched out arm;) when he shall come and pray toward this house;

43Hear thou in heaven thy dwellingplace, and do according to all that the stranger calleth to thee for: that all people of the earth may know thy name, to fear thee, as *do* thy people Israel; and that they may know that this house, which I have builded, is called by thy name.

44¶ If thy people go out to battle against their enemy, whithersoever thou shalt send them, and shall pray unto the LORD toward the city which thou hast chosen, and *toward* the house that I have built for thy name:

45Then hear thou in heaven their prayer and their supplication, and maintain their cause.

46If they sin against thee, (for *there is* no man that sinneth not,) and thou be angry with them, and deliver them to the enemy, so that they carry them away captives unto the land of the enemy, far or near;

47 *Yet* if they shall bethink themselves in the land whither they were carried captives, and repent, and make supplication unto thee in the land of them that carried them captives, saying, We have sinned, and have done perversely, we have committed wickedness;

48And *so* return unto thee with all their heart, and with all their soul, in the land of their enemies, which led them away captive, and pray unto thee toward their land, which thou gavest unto their fathers, the city which thou hast chosen, and the house which I have built for thy name:

49Then hear thou their prayer and their supplication in heaven thy dwellingplace, and maintain their cause,

## Amplified

33When Your people Israel are struck down before the enemy because they have sinned against You, and they turn again to You, confess Your name [Your revelation of Yourself] and pray, beseeching You in this house;

34Then hear in Heaven, and forgive the sin of Your people Israel, and return them to the land You gave to their fathers.

35When Heaven is shut up and no rain falls because they have sinned against You, if they pray in [or toward] this place, and confess Your name [Your revelation of Yourself] and turn from their sin, when You afflict them,

36Then hear in Heaven, and forgive the sin of Your servants, Your people Israel, when You teach them the good way in which they should walk; and give rain upon Your land which You have given to Your people as an inheritance.

37If there is famine in the land, or pestilence, blight, mildew, locust, or caterpillar; if their enemy besieges them in the land of their cities; whatever plague, whatever sickness there is;

38Whatever prayer and supplication is made by any or all of Your people Israel, each man knowing the affliction of his own heart and spreading forth his hands toward this house [and its pledge of Your presence];

39Then hear in Heaven Your dwelling place, and forgive, and act, and give to every man according to his ways, whose heart You know; for You and You only know the hearts of all the children of men;

40That they may fear *and* revere You all the days that they live in the land which You gave to our fathers.

41Moreover concerning a stranger, who is not of Your people Israel, but comes from a far country for the sake of Your name [and Your active presence]—

42For they will hear of Your great name [Your revelation of Yourself], Your strong hand and stretched out arm; when he shall pray in [or toward] this house,

43Hear in Heaven Your dwelling place, and do according to all that the stranger asks of You; that all people of the earth may know Your name [and [a]Your revelation of Your presence], and fear *and* revere You, as do Your people Israel, and may know *and* comprehend that this house which I have built is called by Your name [and contains the token of [b]Your presence].

44If Your people go out to battle against their enemy, wherever You shall send them, and shall pray to the Lord toward the city which You have chosen and the house that I have built for Your name [and Your revelation of Yourself];

45Then hear in Heaven their prayer and supplication, and defend their cause *and* maintain their right.

46If they sin against You—for there is no man who does not sin—and You are angry with them, and deliver them to the enemy, so that they are carried away captive to the enemy's land, far or near;

47Yet if they think *and* consider in the land where they were carried captive, and repent, and make supplication to You there, saying, We have sinned, and have done perversely and wickedly;

48If they repent *and* turn to You with all their mind and with all their heart in the land of their enemies, who took them captive, and pray to You toward their land, which You gave to their fathers, the city which You have chosen and the house which I have built for Your name;

49Then hear their prayer and their supplication in Heaven Your dwelling place, and defend their cause *and* maintain their right.

**AMP** [a] To know the *name* of God is to witness the manifestation of those attributes and apprehend that character which the name denotes. (Exod. 6:3 with 7; Ps. 91:14; Isa. 52:6; 64:2; Jer. 16:21—*Davis Dictionary of the Bible.* God's *name,* that is, His self-revelation *(Ellicott's Commentary on the Whole Bible).* The name signifies the active presence of the person in the fulness of the revealed character *(The New Bible Dictionary).* [b] God . . . [acknowledged] the ark as a token of His presence *(Matthew Henry's Commentary in One Volume).* The ark of the covenant, *the pledge of the divine gracious* presence; and the cloud that filled the house . . . is the sign that Jehovah will dwell here (*Lange's Commentary, Kings,* p. 98).

## New American Standard

33¶ "When Thy people Israel are defeated before an enemy, because they have sinned against Thee, if they turn to Thee again and confess Thy name and pray and make supplication to Thee in this house,
34then hear Thou in heaven, and forgive the sin of Thy people Israel, and bring them back to the land which Thou didst give to their fathers.
35¶ "When the heavens are shut up and there is no rain, because they have sinned against Thee, and they pray toward this place and confess Thy name and turn from their sin when Thou dost afflict them,
36then hear Thou in heaven and forgive the sin of Thy servants and of Thy people Israel, indeed, teach them the good way in which they should walk. And send rain on Thy land, which Thou hast given Thy people for an inheritance.
37¶ "If there is famine in the land, if there is pestilence, if there is blight *or* mildew, locust *or* grasshopper, if their enemy besieges them in the land of their cities, whatever plague, whatever sickness there is,
38whatever prayer or supplication is made by any man *or* by all Thy people Israel, each knowing the affliction of his own heart, and spreading his hands toward this house;
39then hear Thou in heaven Thy dwelling place, and forgive and act and render to each according to all his ways, whose heart Thou knowest, for Thou alone dost know the hearts of all the sons of men,
40that they may [c]fear Thee all the days that they live in the land which Thou hast given to our fathers.
41¶ "Also concerning the foreigner who is not of Thy people Israel, when he comes from a far country for Thy name's sake
42(for they will hear of Thy great name and Thy mighty hand, and of Thine outstretched arm); when he comes and prays toward this house,
43hear Thou in heaven Thy dwelling place, and do according to all for which the foreigner calls to Thee, in order that all the peoples of the earth may know Thy name, to [d]fear Thee, as *do* Thy people Israel, and that they may know that this house which I have built is called by Thy name.
44¶ "When Thy people go out to battle against their enemy, by whatever way Thou shalt send them, and they pray to the LORD toward the city which Thou hast chosen and the house which I have built for Thy name,
45then hear in heaven their prayer and their supplication, and maintain their cause.
46¶ "When they sin against Thee (for there is no man who does not sin) and Thou art angry with them and dost deliver them to an enemy, so that they take them away captive to the land of the enemy, far off or near;
47if they take thought in the land where they have been taken captive, and repent and make supplication to Thee in the land of those who have taken them captive, saying, 'We have sinned and have committed iniquity, we have acted wickedly';
48if they return to Thee with all their heart and with all their soul in the land of their enemies who have taken them captive, and pray to Thee toward their land which Thou hast given to their fathers, the city which Thou hast chosen, and the house which I have built for Thy name;
49then hear their prayer and their supplication in heaven Thy dwelling place, and maintain their cause,

NAS [c] Or, *revere* [d] Or, *revere*

## New International

33"When your people Israel have been defeated by an
enemy because they have sinned against you, and when they
turn back to you and confess your name, praying and making
supplication to you in this temple, 34then hear from heaven
and forgive the sin of your people Israel and bring them back
to the land you gave to their fathers.
35"When the heavens are shut up and there is no rain
because your people have sinned against you, and when they
pray toward this place and confess your name and turn from
their sin because you have afflicted them, 36then hear from
heaven and forgive the sin of your servants, your people
Israel. Teach them the right way to live, and send rain on the
land you gave your people for an inheritance.
37"When famine or plague comes to the land, or blight or
mildew, locusts or grasshoppers, or when an enemy besieges
them in any of their cities, whatever disaster or disease may
come, 38and when a prayer or plea is made by any of your
people Israel—each one aware of the afflictions of his own
heart, and spreading out his hands toward this temple—
39then hear from heaven, your dwelling place. Forgive and
act; deal with each man according to all he does, since you
know his heart (for you alone know the hearts of all men), 40so
that they will fear you all the time they live in the land you
gave our fathers.
41"As for the foreigner who does not belong to your people
Israel but has come from a distant land because of your
name— 42for men will hear of your great name and your
mighty hand and your outstretched arm—when he comes
and prays toward this temple, 43then hear from heaven, your
dwelling place, and do whatever the foreigner asks of you, so
that all the peoples of the earth may know your name and fear
you, as do your own people Israel, and may know that this
house I have built bears your Name.
44"When your people go to war against their enemies,
wherever you send them, and when they pray to the LORD
toward the city you have chosen and the temple I have built
for your Name, 45then hear from heaven their prayer and
their plea, and uphold their cause.
46"When they sin against you—for there is no one who
does not sin—and you become angry with them and give
them over to the enemy, who takes them captive to his own
land, far away or near; 47and if they have a change of heart
in the land where they are held captive, and repent and plead
with you in the land of their conquerors and say, 'We have
sinned, we have done wrong, we have acted wickedly'; 48and
if they turn back to you with all their heart and soul in the land
of their enemies who took them captive, and pray to you
toward the land you gave their fathers, toward the city you
have chosen and the temple I have built for your Name; 49then
from heaven, your dwelling place, hear their prayer and their
plea, and uphold their cause. 50And forgive your people, who

## King James

50And forgive thy people that have sinned against thee, and all
their transgressions wherein they have transgressed against thee,
and give them compassion before them who carried them captive,
that they may have compassion on them:
51For they *be* thy people, and thine inheritance, which thou
broughtest forth out of Egypt, from the midst of the furnace of
iron:
52That thine eyes may be open unto the supplication of thy
servant, and unto the supplication of thy people Israel, to hearken
unto them in all that they call for unto thee.
53For thou didst separate them from among all the people of the
earth, *to be* thine inheritance, as thou spakest by the hand of Moses
thy servant, when thou broughtest our fathers out of Egypt, O
Lord GOD.
54And it was *so*, that when Solomon had made an end of praying all this prayer and supplication unto the LORD, he arose from
before the altar of the LORD, from kneeling on his knees with his
hands spread up to heaven.
55And he stood, and blessed all the congregation of Israel with
a loud voice, saying,
56Blessed *be* the LORD, that hath given rest unto his people
Israel, according to all that he promised: there hath not failed one
word of all his good promise, which he promised by the hand of
Moses his servant.
57The LORD our God be with us, as he was with our fathers: let
him not leave us, nor forsake us:
58That he may incline our hearts unto him, to walk in all his
ways, and to keep his commandments, and his statutes, and his
judgments, which he commanded our fathers.
59And let these my words, wherewith I have made supplication
before the LORD, be nigh unto the LORD our God day and night,
that he maintain the cause of his servant, and the cause of his
people Israel at all times, as the matter shall require:
60That all the people of the earth may know that the LORD *is*
God, *and that there is* none else.
61Let your heart therefore be perfect with the LORD our God, to
walk in his statutes, and to keep his commandments, as at this
day.
62¶ And the king, and all Israel with him, offered sacrifice before
the LORD.
63And Solomon offered a sacrifice of peace offerings, which he
offered unto the LORD, two and twenty thousand oxen, and an
hundred and twenty thousand sheep. So the king and all the
children of Israel dedicated the house of the LORD.
64The same day did the king hallow the middle of the court that
*was* before the house of the LORD: for there he offered burnt offerings, and meat offerings, and the fat of the peace offerings: because
the brasen altar that *was* before the LORD *was* too little to receive
the burnt offerings, and meat offerings, and the fat of the peace
offerings.
65And at that time Solomon held a feast, and all Israel with him,
a great congregation, from the entering in of Hamath unto the river
of Egypt, before the LORD our God, seven days and seven days,
*even* fourteen days.
66On the eighth day he sent the people away: and they blessed
the king, and went unto their tents joyful and glad of heart for all
the goodness that the LORD had done for David his servant, and
for Israel his people.

9 AND IT came to pass, when Solomon had finished the building of the house of the LORD, and the king's house, and all
Solomon's desire which he was pleased to do,

## Amplified

50And forgive Your people who have sinned against You, and
all their transgressions against You, and grant them compassion
before those who carried them captive, that they may have pity
and be merciful to them—
51For they are Your people and Your heritage which You
brought out of Egypt, from the midst of the iron furnace.
52Let Your eyes be open to the supplication of Your servant, and
of Your people Israel, to hearken to them in all that they call for
to You.
53For You separated them from among all the people of the
earth to be Your heritage, as You declared through Moses your
servant when You brought our fathers out of Egypt, O Lord God.
54When Solomon finished offering all this prayer and supplication to the Lord, he arose from before the Lord's altar, where he
had knelt with hands stretched toward Heaven.
55And he stood and blessed all the assembly of Israel with a
loud voice, saying,
56Blessed be the Lord Who has given rest to His people Israel,
according to all that He promised. Not one word has failed of all
His good promise which He promised through Moses His servant.
57The Lord our God be with us as He was with our fathers; may
He not leave us or forskae us;
58That He may incline our hearts to Him, to walk in all His ways
and to keep His commandments, His statutes, and His precepts,
which He commanded our fathers.
59Let these my words, with which I have made supplication
before the Lord, be near to the Lord our God day and night, that
He may maintain the cause *and* right of His servant and of His
people Israel as each day requires,
60That all the earth's people may know that the Lord is God,
there is no other.
61Let your heart therefore be blameless *and* wholly true with the
Lord our God, to walk in His statutes and to keep His commandments, as today.
62And the king and all Israel with him offered sacrifice before
the Lord.
63Solomon offered as peace offerings to the Lord, 22,000 oxen
and 120,000 sheep. So the king and all the Israelites dedicated the
house of the Lord.
64The same day the king consecrated the middle of the court
that was before the Lord's house; there he offered burnt offerings,
cereal offerings, and the fat of the peace offerings, because the
bronze altar that was before the Lord was too small to receive [all]
the offerings.
65So at that time Solomon held the feast, and all Israel with him,
a great assembly, from the entrance of Hamath to the Brook of
Egypt, before the Lord our God, seven days [for the dedication]
and seven days [for the feast of tabernacles], fourteen days in all.
66The eighth day he sent the people away; they blessed the
king, and went to their tents with greatest joy and gratitude for all
the goodness the Lord had shown to David His servant and Israel
His people.

9 WHEN SOLOMON finished the building of the Lord's
house, and the king's house and all he desired and was
pleased to do,

# New American Standard

50and forgive Thy people who have sinned against Thee and all
their transgressions which they have transgressed against Thee,
and make them *objects of* compassion before those who have taken
them captive, that they may have compassion on them
51(for they are Thy people and Thine inheritance which Thou
hast brought forth from Egypt, from the midst of the iron furnace),
52that Thine eyes may be open to the supplication of Thy servant and to the supplication of Thy people Israel, to listen to them
whenever they call to Thee.
53"For Thou hast separated them from all the peoples of the
earth as Thine inheritance, as Thou didst speak through Moses
Thy servant, when Thou didst bring our fathers forth from Egypt,
O Lord GOD."

*Solomon's Benediction*

54¶ And it came about that when Solomon had finished praying
this entire prayer and supplication to the LORD, he arose from
before the altar of the LORD, from kneeling on his knees with his
hands spread toward heaven.
55And he stood and blessed all the assembly of Israel with a
loud voice, saying,
56"Blessed be the LORD, who has given rest to His people Israel,
according to all that He promised; not one word has failed of all
His good promise, which He promised through Moses His servant.
57"May the LORD our God be with us, as He was with our
fathers; may He not leave us or forsake us,
58that He may incline our hearts to Himself, to walk in all His
ways and to keep His commandments and His statutes and His
ordinances, which He commanded our fathers.
59"And may these words of mine, with which I have made
supplication before the LORD, be near to the LORD our God day and
night, that He may maintain the cause of His servant and the cause
of His people Israel, as each day requires,
60so that all the peoples of the earth may know that the LORD
is God; there is no one else.
61"Let your heart therefore be wholly devoted to the LORD our
God, to walk in His statutes and to keep His commandments, as
at this day."

*Dedicatory Sacrifices*

62¶ Now the king and all Israel with him offered sacrifice before
the LORD.
63And Solomon offered for the sacrifice of peace offerings,
which he offered to the LORD, 22,000 oxen and 120,000 sheep. So
the king and all the sons of Israel dedicated the house of the LORD.
64On the same day the king consecrated the middle of the court
that *was* before the house of the LORD, because there he offered the
burnt offering and the grain offering and the fat of the peace
offerings; for the bronze altar that *was* before the LORD *was* too
small to hold the burnt offering and the grain offering and the fat
of the peace offerings.
65So Solomon observed the feast at that time, and all Israel with
him, a great assembly from the entrance of Hamath to the brook
of Egypt, before the LORD our God, for seven days and seven *more*
days, *even* fourteen days.
66On the eighth day he sent the people away and they blessed
the king. Then they went to their tents joyful and glad of heart for
all the goodness that the LORD had shown to David His servant
and to Israel His people.

*God's Promise and Warning*

9 NOW IT came about when Solomon had finished building
the house of the LORD, and the king's house, and all that
Solomon desired to do,

# New International

have sinned against you; forgive all the offenses they have
committed against you, and cause their conquerors to show
them mercy; 51for they are your people and your inheritance,
whom you brought out of Egypt, out of that iron-smelting
furnace.
52"May your eyes be open to your servant's plea and to the
plea of your people Israel, and may you listen to them whenever they cry out to you. 53For you singled them out from all
the nations of the world to be your own inheritance, just as
you declared through your servant Moses when you, O Sovereign LORD, brought our fathers out of Egypt."

54When Solomon had finished all these prayers and supplications to the LORD, he rose from before the altar of the LORD, where
he had been kneeling with his hands spread out toward heaven.
55He stood and blessed the whole assembly of Israel in a loud
voice, saying:

56"Praise be to the LORD, who has given rest to his people
Israel just as he promised. Not one word has failed of all the
good promises he gave through his servant Moses. 57May the
LORD our God be with us as he was with our fathers; may he
never leave us nor forsake us. 58May he turn our hearts to
him, to walk in all his ways and to keep the commands,
decrees and regulations he gave our fathers. 59And may these
words of mine, which I have prayed before the LORD, be near
to the LORD our God day and night, that he may uphold the
cause of his servant and the cause of his people Israel according to each day's need, 60so that all the peoples of the earth
may know that the LORD is God and that there is no other.
61But your hearts must be fully committed to the LORD our
God, to live by his decrees and obey his commands, as at this
time."

*The Dedication of the Temple*

62Then the king and all Israel with him offered sacrifices before
the LORD. 63Solomon offered a sacrifice of fellowship offerings[a] to
the LORD: twenty-two thousand cattle and a hundred and twenty
thousand sheep and goats. So the king and all the Israelites dedicated the temple of the LORD.
64On that same day the king consecrated the middle part of the
courtyard in front of the temple of the LORD, and there he offered
burnt offerings, grain offerings and the fat of the fellowship offerings, because the bronze altar before the LORD was too small to
hold the burnt offerings, the grain offerings and the fat of the
fellowship offerings.
65So Solomon observed the festival at that time, and all Israel
with him—a vast assembly, people from Lebo[b] Hamath to the
Wadi of Egypt. They celebrated it before the LORD our God for
seven days and seven days more, fourteen days in all. 66On the
following day he sent the people away. They blessed the king and
then went home, joyful and glad in heart for all the good things
the LORD had done for his servant David and his people Israel.

*The LORD Appears to Solomon*

9 WHEN SOLOMON had finished building the temple of the
LORD and the royal palace, and had achieved all he had

**NIV** [a] *63* Traditionally *peace offerings;* also in verse 64 [b] *65* Or *from the entrance to*

## King James

2That the LORD appeared to Solomon the second time, as he had
appeared unto him at Gibeon.
3And the LORD said unto him, I have heard thy prayer and thy
supplication, that thou hast made before me: I have hallowed this
house, which thou hast built, to put my name there for ever; and
mine eyes and mine heart shall be there perpetually.
4And if thou wilt walk before me, as David thy father walked,
in integrity of heart, and in uprightness, to do according to all that
I have commanded thee, *and* wilt keep my statutes and my judgments:
5Then I will establish the throne of thy kingdom upon Israel for
ever, as I promised to David thy father, saying, There shall not fail
thee a man upon the throne of Israel.
6 *But* if ye shall at all turn from following me, ye or your
children, and will not keep my commandments *and* my statutes
which I have set before you, but go and serve other gods, and
worship them:
7Then will I cut off Israel out of the land which I have given
them; and this house, which I have hallowed for my name, will I
cast out of my sight; and Israel shall be a proverb and a byword
among all people:
8And at this house, *which* is high, every one that passeth by it
shall be astonished, and shall hiss; and they shall say, Why hath
the LORD done thus unto this land, and to this house?
9And they shall answer, Because they forsook the LORD their
God, who brought forth their fathers out of the land of Egypt, and
have taken hold upon other gods, and have worshipped them, and
served them: therefore hath the LORD brought upon them all this
evil.
10¶ And it came to pass at the end of twenty years, when
Solomon had built the two houses, the house of the LORD, and the
king's house,
11( *Now* Hiram the king of Tyre had furnished Solomon with
cedar trees and fir trees, and with gold, according to all his desire,)
that then king Solomon gave Hiram twenty cities in the land of
Galilee.
12And Hiram came out from Tyre to see the cities which Solomon had given him; and they pleased him not.
13And he said, What cities *are* these which thou hast given me,
my brother? And he called them the land of Cabul unto this day.
14And Hiram sent to the king sixscore talents of gold.
15¶ And this *is* the reason of the levy which king Solomon
raised; for to build the house of the LORD, and his own house, and
Millo, and the wall of Jerusalem, and Hazor, and Megiddo, and
Gezer.
16 *For* Pharaoh king of Egypt had gone up, and taken Gezer, and
burnt it with fire, and slain the Canaanites that dwelt in the city,
and given it *for* a present unto his daughter, Solomon's wife.
17And Solomon built Gezer, and Beth-horon the nether,
18And Baalath, and Tadmor in the wilderness, in the land,
19And all the cities of store that Solomon had, and cities for his
chariots, and cities for his horsemen, and that which Solomon
desired to build in Jerusalem, and in Lebanon, and in all the land
of his dominion.
20 *And* all the people *that were* left of the Amorites, Hittites,
Perizzites, Hivites, and Jebusites, which *were* not of the children
of Israel,

## Amplified

2The Lord appeared to Solomon the second time, as He had
appeared to him at Gibeon.
3The Lord told him, I have heard your prayer and supplication
which you have made before Me; I have hallowed this house which
you have built, and I have put My name [and My presence] there
for ever; My eyes and My heart shall be there perpetually.
4And if you will walk before Me, as David your father walked,
in integrity of heart and uprightness, doing according to all that
I have commanded you, keeping My statutes and My precepts,
5Then I will establish your royal throne over Israel for ever, as
I promised David your father, saying, There shall not fail you a
man upon the throne of Israel.
6But if you turn away from following Me, you or your children,
and will not keep My commandments and My statutes which I
have set before you, but go and serve other gods and worship
them,
7Then I will cut off Israel from the land I have given them; and
this house I have hallowed for My name [renown] I will cast from
My sight; and Israel shall be a proverb and a byword among all
peoples.
8This house shall become a heap of ruins; every passerby shall
be astonished and shall hiss [with surprise] and say, Why has the
Lord done thus to this land and to this house?
9Then they will answer, Because they forsook the Lord their
God, Who brought their fathers out of the land of Egypt, and have
laid hold of other gods, and have worshiped and served them;
therefore the Lord has brought on them all this evil.
10At the end of twenty years, in which Solomon had built the
two houses, the Lord's house and the king's house,
11For which Hiram king of Tyre had furnished Solomon with as
much cedar and cypress timber and gold as he desired, King
Solomon gave Hiram twenty cities in the land of Galilee.
12And Hiram came from Tyre to see the cities which Solomon
had given him, and they did not please him.
13He said, What are these cities worth which you have given
me, my brother? So they are called the Cabul [unproductive] land
to this day.
14And Hiram sent to the king 120 talents of gold.
15This is the account of the levy [of forced labor] which King
Solomon raised to build the house of the Lord, his own house,
Millo, the wall of Jerusalem, Hazor, Megiddo, and Gezer.
16For Pharaoh king of Egypt had gone up and taken Gezer,
burned it with fire, slain the Canaanites who dwelt in the city, and
given it as dowry to his daughter, Solomon's wife.
17So Solomon rebuilt Gezer and Beth-horon the lower,
18Baalath and Tamar [Tadmor] in the wilderness, in the land of
Judah,
19And all the store-cities which Solomon had, and cities for his
chariots, and cities for his horsemen, and whatever Solomon desired to build [a]for his pleasure in Jerusalem, in Lebanon, and in
all the land of his dominion.
20As for all the people who were left of the Amorites, Hittites,
Perizzites, Hivites, and Jebusites, who were not Israelites,

**AMP** [a] Once on the throne, Solomon became a thorough-going despot. All political power was taken out of the hands of the [tribal] sheiks . . . and placed in the hands of officers who were simply creatures of Solomon. The resources of the nation were expended, not on works of public utility, but on the personal aggrandizement of the monarch. In the means he took to gratify his passions he showed himself to be little better than a savage *(International Standard Bible Encyclopedia)*. The division of the nation [at Solomon's death] with all the weakness and misery that it caused [idolatry, ignoring God, captivity, exile, the loss of the ten tribes] through the coming centuries was the direct outgrowth of Solomon's unholy self-indulgence (Amos R. Wells in *Bible Miniatures*). Because of his extensive building program and his extravagant expenditures in the maintenance of his luxurious court, he resorted to forced labor, and heavy taxation. Bitter opposition to his rule thus engendered the division of the United Kingdom after his death *(The New Jewish Encyclopedia)*.

## New American Standard

2that the LORD appeared to Solomon a second time, as He had
appeared to him at Gibeon.
3And the LORD said to him, "I have heard your prayer and your
supplication, which you have made before Me; I have consecrated
this house which you have built by putting My name there forever,
and My eyes and My heart will be there perpetually.
4"And as for you, if you will walk before Me as your father
David walked, in integrity of heart and uprightness, doing according to all that I have commanded you *and* will keep My statutes and
My ordinances,
5then I will establish the throne of your kingdom over Israel
forever, just as I promised to your father David, saying, 'You shall
not lack a man on the throne of Israel.'
6"But if you or your sons shall indeed turn away from following Me, and shall not keep My commandments and My statutes
which I have set before you and shall go and serve other gods and
worship them,
7then I will cut off Israel from the land which I have given
them, and the house which I have consecrated for My name, I will
cast out of My sight. So Israel will become a proverb and a byword
among all peoples.
8"And this house will become a heap of ruins; everyone who
passes by will be astonished and hiss and say, 'Why has the LORD
done thus to this land and to this house?'
9"And they will say, 'Because they forsook the LORD their God,
who brought their fathers out of the land of Egypt, and adopted
other gods and worshiped them and served them, therefore the
LORD has brought all this adversity on them.' "

*Cities Given to Hiram*

**10¶** And it came about at the end of twenty years in which
Solomon had built the two houses, the house of the LORD and the
king's house
11(Hiram king of Tyre had supplied Solomon with cedar and
cypress timber and gold according to all his desire), then King
Solomon gave Hiram twenty cities in the land of Galilee.
12So Hiram came out from Tyre to see the cities which Solomon
had given him, and they did not please him.
13And he said, "What are these cities which you have given me,
my brother?" So they were called the land of [b]Cabul to this day.
14And Hiram sent to the king 120 talents of gold.
**15¶** Now this is the account of the forced labor which King
Solomon levied to build the house of the LORD, his own house, the
[c]Millo, the wall of Jerusalem, Hazor, Megiddo, and Gezer.
16*For* Pharaoh king of Egypt had gone up and captured Gezer,
and burned it with fire, and killed the Canaanites who lived in the
city, and had given it *as* a dowry to his daughter, Solomon's wife.
17So Solomon rebuilt Gezer and the lower Beth-horon
18and Baalath and Tamar in the wilderness, in the land *of Judah,*
19and all the storage cities which Solomon had, even the cities
for his chariots and the cities for his horsemen, and all that it
pleased Solomon to build in Jerusalem, in Lebanon, and in all the
land under his rule.
20*As for* all the people who were left of the Amorites, the
Hittites, the Perizzites, the Hivites and the Jebusites, who were not
of the sons of Israel,

**NAS** [b] I.e., as good as nothing [c] I.e., citadel

## New International

desired to do, 2the LORD appeared to him a second time, as he had
appeared to him at Gibeon. 3The LORD said to him:
"I have heard the prayer and plea you have made before
me; I have consecrated this temple, which you have built, by
putting my Name there forever. My eyes and my heart will
always be there.
4"As for you, if you walk before me in integrity of heart and
uprightness, as David your father did, and do all I command
and observe my decrees and laws, 5I will establish your royal
throne over Israel forever, as I promised David your father
when I said, 'You shall never fail to have a man on the throne
of Israel.'
6"But if you[d] or your sons turn away from me and do not
observe the commands and decrees I have given you[e] and go
off to serve other gods and worship them, 7then I will cut off
Israel from the land I have given them and will reject this
temple I have consecrated for my Name. Israel will then
become a byword and an object of ridicule among all peoples.
8And though this temple is now imposing, all who pass by
will be appalled and will scoff and say, 'Why has the LORD
done such a thing to this land and to this temple?' 9People will
answer, 'Because they have forsaken the LORD their God, who
brought their fathers out of Egypt, and have embraced other
gods, worshiping and serving them—that is why the LORD
brought all this disaster on them.' "

*Solomon's Other Activities*

10At the end of twenty years, during which Solomon built these
two buildings—the temple of the LORD and the royal palace—
11King Solomon gave twenty towns in Galilee to Hiram king of
Tyre, because Hiram had supplied him with all the cedar and pine
and gold he wanted. 12But when Hiram went from Tyre to see the
towns that Solomon had given him, he was not pleased with them.
13"What kind of towns are these you have given me, my brother?"
he asked. And he called them the Land of Cabul,[f] a name they
have to this day. 14Now Hiram had sent to the king 120 talents[g]
of gold.
15Here is the account of the forced labor King Solomon conscripted to build the LORD's temple, his own palace, the supporting terraces,[h] the wall of Jerusalem, and Hazor, Megiddo and
Gezer. 16(Pharaoh king of Egypt had attacked and captured Gezer.
He had set it on fire. He killed its Canaanite inhabitants and then
gave it as a wedding gift to his daughter, Solomon's wife. 17And
Solomon rebuilt Gezer.) He built up Lower Beth Horon, 18Baalath,
and Tadmor[i] in the desert, within his land, 19as well as all his store
cities and the towns for his chariots and for his horses[j] —whatever
he desired to build in Jerusalem, in Lebanon and throughout all
the territory he ruled.
20All the people left from the Amorites, Hittites, Perizzites,
Hivites and Jebusites (these peoples were not Israelites), 21that is,

**NIV** [d] *6* The Hebrew is plural. [e] *6* The Hebrew is plural. [f] *13 Cabul* sounds like the Hebrew for *good-for-nothing.* [g] *14* That is, about 4 1/2 tons (about 4 metric tons) [h] *15* Or *the Millo;* also in verse 24 [i] *18* The Hebrew may also be read *Tamar.* [j] *19* Or *charioteers*

# King James

21 Their children that were left after them in the land, whom the children of Israel also were not able utterly to destroy, upon those did Solomon levy a tribute of bondservice unto this day.

22 But of the children of Israel did Solomon make no bondmen: but they *were* men of war, and his servants, and his princes, and his captains, and rulers of his chariots, and his horsemen.

23 These *were* the chief of the officers that *were* over Solomon's work, five hundred and fifty, which bare rule over the people that wrought in the work.

24 ¶ But Pharaoh's daughter came up out of the city of David unto her house which *Solomon* had built for her: then did he build Millo.

25 ¶ And three times in a year did Solomon offer burnt offerings and peace offerings upon the altar which he built unto the LORD, and he burnt incense upon the altar that *was* before the LORD. So he finished the house.

26 ¶ And king Solomon made a navy of ships in Ezion-geber, which *is* beside Eloth, on the shore of the Red sea, in the land of Edom.

27 And Hiram sent in the navy his servants, shipmen that had knowledge of the sea, with the servants of Solomon.

28 And they came to Ophir, and fetched from thence gold, four hundred and twenty talents, and brought *it* to king Solomon.

10 AND WHEN the queen of Sheba heard of the fame of Solomon concerning the name of the LORD, she came to prove him with hard questions.

2 And she came to Jerusalem with a very great train, with camels that bare spices, and very much gold, and precious stones: and when she was come to Solomon, she communed with him of all that was in her heart.

3 And Solomon told her all her questions: there was not *any* thing hid from the king, which he told her not.

4 And when the queen of Sheba had seen all Solomon's wisdom, and the house that he had built,

5 And the meat of his table, and the sitting of his servants, and the attendance of his ministers, and their apparel, and his cupbearers, and his ascent by which he went up unto the house of the LORD; there was no more spirit in her.

6 And she said to the king, It was a true report that I heard in mine own land of thy acts and of thy wisdom.

7 Howbeit I believed not the words, until I came, and mine eyes had seen *it:* and, behold, the half was not told me: thy wisdom and prosperity exceedeth the fame which I heard.

8 Happy *are* thy men, happy *are* these thy servants, which stand continually before thee, *and* that hear thy wisdom.

9 Blessed be the LORD thy God, which delighted in thee, to set thee on the throne of Israel: because the LORD loved Israel for ever, therefore made he thee king, to do judgment and justice.

10 And she gave the king an hundred and twenty talents of gold, and of spices very great store, and precious stones: there came no more such abundance of spices as these which the queen of Sheba gave to king Solomon.

11 And the navy also of Hiram, that brought gold from Ophir, brought in from Ophir great plenty of almug trees, and precious stones.

12 And the king made of the almug trees pillars for the house of the LORD, and for the king's house, harps also and psalteries for singers: there came no such almug trees, nor were seen unto this day.

13 And king Solomon gave unto the queen of Sheba all her desire, whatsoever she asked, beside *that* which Solomon gave her of his royal bounty. So she turned and went to her own country, she and her servants.

# Amplified

21 Their children who were left after them in the land, whom the Israelites were not able utterly to destroy, of them Solomon made a forced levy of slaves to this day.

22 But Solomon made no slaves of the Israelites; they were the soldiers, his officials, attendants, commanders, captains, chariot officers, and horsemen.

23 These were the chief officers over Solomon's work, 550 who had charge of the people who did the work.

24 But Pharaoh's daughter came up out of the city of David to her house which Solomon had built for her; then he built Millo.

25 Three times a year Solomon offered burnt offerings and peace offerings on the altar he built to the Lord, and he burned incense with them before the Lord. So he finished the house.

26 And King Solomon made a fleet of ships in Ezion-geber, which is beside Eloth, on the shore of the Red Sea, in Edom.

27 And Hiram sent with the fleet his servants, shipmen who had knowledge of the sea, with the servants of Solomon.

28 They came to Ophir, and got 420 talents of gold, and brought it to King Solomon.

10 WHEN THE queen of Sheba heard of [the constant connection of] the fame of Solomon with the name of the Lord, she came to prove him with hard questions—problems and riddles.

2 She came to Jerusalem with a very great train, with camels bearing spices, very much gold, and precious stones. When she had come to Solomon, she communed with him of all that was in her mind.

3 Solomon answered all her questions; there was nothing hidden from the king, which he failed to explain to her.

4 When the queen of Sheba had seen all Solomon's wisdom *and* skill, the house he had built,

5 The food of his table, the seating of his officials, the standing at attention of his servants, their apparel, his cupbearers, his ascent by which he went up to the house of the Lord [or the burnt offerings he sacrificed], she was breathless *and* overcome.

6 She said to the king, It was a true report I heard in my own land of your acts *and* sayings and wisdom.

7 I did not believe it until I came and my eyes had seen. Behold, the half was not told me. You have added wisdom and goodness exceeding the fame I heard.

8 Happy are your men! Happy are these your servants who stand continually before you, hearing your wisdom!

9 Blessed be the Lord your God, Who delighted in you and set you on the throne of Israel! Because the Lord loved Israel forever, He made you king to execute justice and righteousness.

10 And she gave the king 120 talents of gold, and of spices a very great store, and precious stones. No more came such abundance of spices as these the queen of Sheba gave King Solomon.

11 The navy also of Hiram, brought from Ophir gold and a great plenty of almug [algum] wood and precious stones.

12 Of the almug wood the king made pillars for the house of the Lord, and for the king's house, lyres also and harps for the singers. No such almug wood came or was seen to this day.

13 King Solomon gave to the queen of Sheba all she wanted, whatever she asked, besides his gifts to her from his royal bounty. So she returned to her own country, she and her servants.

## New American Standard

21their descendants who were left after them in the land whom
the sons of Israel were unable to destroy utterly, from them Solomon levied forced laborers, even to this day.
22But Solomon did not make slaves of the sons of Israel; for they
were men of war, his servants, his princes, his captains, his chariot
commanders, and his horsemen.
23¶ These *were* the chief officers who were over Solomon's work,
five hundred and fifty, who ruled over the people doing the work.
24¶ As soon as Pharaoh's daughter came up from the city of
David to her house which *Solomon* had built for her, then he built
the Millo.
25¶ Now three times in a year Solomon offered burnt offerings
and peace offerings on the altar which he built to the LORD, burning incense with them *on the altar* which *was* before the LORD. So
he finished the house.
26¶ King Solomon also built a fleet of ships in Ezion-geber,
which is near Eloth on the shore of the Red Sea, in the land of
Edom.
27And Hiram sent his servants with the fleet, sailors who knew
the sea, along with the servants of Solomon.
28And they went to Ophir, and took four hundred and twenty
talents of gold from there, and brought *it* to King Solomon.

*The Queen of Sheba*

10 NOW WHEN the queen of Sheba heard about the fame of
Solomon concerning the name of the LORD, she came to
test him with difficult questions.
2So she came to Jerusalem with a very large retinue, with
camels carrying spices and very much gold and precious stones.
When she came to Solomon, she spoke with him about all that was
in her heart.
3And Solomon answered all her questions; nothing was hidden from the king which he did not explain to her.
4When the queen of Sheba perceived all the wisdom of Solomon, the house that he had built,
5the food of his table, the seating of his servants, the attendance of his waiters and their attire, his cupbearers, and his stairway by which he went up to the house of the LORD, there was no
more spirit in her.
6Then she said to the king, "It was a true report which I heard
in my own land about your words and your wisdom.
7"Nevertheless I did not believe the reports, until I came and
my eyes had seen it. And behold, the half was not told me. You
exceed *in* wisdom and prosperity the report which I heard.
8"How blessed are your men, how blessed are these your
servants who stand before you continually *and* hear your wisdom.
9"Blessed be the LORD your God who delighted in you to set
you on the throne of Israel; because the LORD loved Israel forever,
therefore He made you king, to do justice and righteousness."
10And she gave the king a hundred and twenty talents of gold,
and a very great *amount* of spices and precious stones. Never again
did such abundance of spices come in as that which the queen of
Sheba gave King Solomon.
11¶ And also the ships of Hiram, which brought gold from
Ophir, brought in from Ophir a very great *number of* almug trees
and precious stones.
12And the king made of the almug trees supports for the house
of the LORD and for the king's house, also lyres and harps for the
singers; such almug trees have not come in *again*, nor have they
been seen to this day.
13¶ And King Solomon gave to the queen of Sheba all her desire
which she requested, besides what he gave her according to his
royal bounty. Then she turned and went to her own land together
with her servants.

## New International

their descendants remaining in the land, whom the Israelites could
not exterminate[a] —these Solomon conscripted for his slave labor
force, as it is to this day. 22But Solomon did not make slaves of any
of the Israelites; they were his fighting men, his government officials, his officers, his captains, and the commanders of his chariots
and charioteers. 23They were also the chief officials in charge of
Solomon's projects—550 officials supervising the men who did the
work.
24After Pharaoh's daughter had come up from the City of David
to the palace Solomon had built for her, he constructed the supporting terraces.
25Three times a year Solomon sacrificed burnt offerings and
fellowship offerings[b] on the altar he had built for the LORD, burning incense before the LORD along with them, and so fulfilled the
temple obligations.
26King Solomon also built ships at Ezion Geber, which is near
Elath in Edom, on the shore of the Red Sea.[c] 27And Hiram sent
his men—sailors who knew the sea—to serve in the fleet with
Solomon's men. 28They sailed to Ophir and brought back 420
talents[d] of gold, which they delivered to King Solomon.

*The Queen of Sheba Visits Solomon*

10 WHEN THE queen of Sheba heard about the fame of
Solomon and his relation to the name of the LORD, she
came to test him with hard questions. 2Arriving at Jerusalem with
a very great caravan—with camels carrying spices, large quantities
of gold, and precious stones—she came to Solomon and talked
with him about all that she had on her mind. 3Solomon answered
all her questions; nothing was too hard for the king to explain to
her. 4When the queen of Sheba saw all the wisdom of Solomon and
the palace he had built, 5the food on his table, the seating of his
officials, the attending servants in their robes, his cupbearers, and
the burnt offerings he made at[e] the temple of the LORD, she was
overwhelmed.
6She said to the king, "The report I heard in my own country
about your achievements and your wisdom is true. 7But I did not
believe these things until I came and saw with my own eyes.
Indeed, not even half was told me; in wisdom and wealth you have
far exceeded the report I heard. 8How happy your men must be!
How happy your officials, who continually stand before you and
hear your wisdom! 9Praise be to the LORD your God, who has
delighted in you and placed you on the throne of Israel. Because
of the LORD's eternal love for Israel, he has made you king, to
maintain justice and righteousness."
10And she gave the king 120 talents[f] of gold, large quantities
of spices, and precious stones. Never again were so many spices
brought in as those the queen of Sheba gave to King Solomon.
11(Hiram's ships brought gold from Ophir; and from there they
brought great cargoes of almugwood[g] and precious stones. 12The
king used the almugwood to make supports for the temple of the
LORD and for the royal palace, and to make harps and lyres for the
musicians. So much almugwood has never been imported or seen
since that day.)
13King Solomon gave the queen of Sheba all she desired and
asked for, besides what he had given her out of his royal bounty.
Then she left and returned with her retinue to her own country.

NIV [a] *21* The Hebrew term refers to the irrevocable giving over of things or persons to the LORD, often by totally destroying them. [b] *25* Traditionally *peace offerings* [c] *26* Hebrew *Yam Suph;* that is, Sea of Reeds [d] *28* That is, about 16 tons (about 14.5 metric tons) [e] *5* Or *the ascent by which he went up to* [f] *10* That is, about 4 1/2 tons (about 4 metric tons) [g] *11* Probably a variant of *algumwood;* also in verse 12

## King James

14¶ Now the weight of gold that came to Solomon in one year was six hundred threescore and six talents of gold,

15Beside *that he had* of the merchantmen, and of the traffic of the spice merchants, and of all the kings of Arabia, and of the governors of the country.

16¶ And king Solomon made two hundred targets *of* beaten gold: six hundred *shekels* of gold went to one target.

17And *he made* three hundred shields *of* beaten gold; three pound of gold went to one shield: and the king put them in the house of the forest of Lebanon.

18¶ Moreover the king made a great throne of ivory, and overlaid it with the best gold.

19The throne had six steps, and the top of the throne *was* round behind: and *there were* stays on either side on the place of the seat, and two lions stood beside the stays.

20And twelve lions stood there on the one side and on the other upon the six steps: there was not the like made in any kingdom.

21¶ And all king Solomon's drinking vessels *were of* gold, and all the vessels of the house of the forest of Lebanon *were of* pure gold; none *were of* silver: it was nothing accounted of in the days of Solomon.

22For the king had at sea a navy of Tharshish with the navy of Hiram: once in three years came the navy of Tharshish, bringing gold, and silver, ivory, and apes, and peacocks.

23So king Solomon exceeded all the kings of the earth for riches and for wisdom.

24¶ And all the earth sought to Solomon, to hear his wisdom, which God had put in his heart.

25And they brought every man his present, vessels of silver, and vessels of gold, and garments, and armour, and spices, horses, and mules, a rate year by year.

26¶ And Solomon gathered together chariots and horsemen: and he had a thousand and four hundred chariots, and twelve thousand horsemen, whom he bestowed in the cities for chariots, and with the king at Jerusalem.

27And the king made silver *to be* in Jerusalem as stones, and cedars made he *to be* as the sycamore trees that *are* in the vale, for abundance.

28¶ And Solomon had horses brought out of Egypt, and linen yarn: the king's merchants received the linen yarn at a price.

29And a chariot came up and went out of Egypt for six hundred *shekels* of silver, and an horse for an hundred and fifty: and so for all the kings of the Hittites, and for the kings of Syria, did they bring *them* out by their means.

**11** BUT KING Solomon loved many strange women, together with the daughter of Pharaoh, women of the Moabites, Ammonites, Edomites, Zidonians, *and* Hittites;

2Of the nations *concerning* which the LORD said unto the children of Israel, Ye shall not go in to them, neither shall they come in unto you: *for* surely they will turn away your heart after their gods: Solomon clave unto these in love.

3And he had seven hundred wives, princesses, and three hundred concubines: and his wives turned away his heart.

4For it came to pass, when Solomon was old, *that* his wives turned away his heart after other gods: and his heart was not perfect with the LORD his God, as *was* the heart of David his father.

5For Solomon went after Ashtoreth the goddess of the Zidonians, and after Milcom the abomination of the Ammonites.

6And Solomon did evil in the sight of the LORD, and went not fully after the LORD, as *did* David his father.

## Amplified

14Now the weight of gold that came to Solomon in one [particular] year was 666 talents of gold,

15Besides what the traders brought and the traffic of the merchants, and from all the [tributary] kings and governors of the land of Arabia.

16King Solomon made 200 large shields of beaten gold; 600 shekels of gold went into each shield;

17And 300 shields of beaten gold; three minas of gold went into each shield. The king put them in the House of the Forest of Lebanon.

18Also the king made a great throne of ivory, and overlaid it with the finest gold.

19The throne had six steps, and attached at the rear of the top of the throne was a round covering *or* canopy. On either side of the seat were arm rests, and two lions stood beside the arm rests.

20Twelve lions stood there, one on either end of each of the six steps; there was not the like ever made in any kingdom.

21All King Solomon's drinking vessels were of gold, and all vessels of the House of the Forest of Lebanon were of pure gold; none were of silver; it was accounted as nothing in the days of Solomon.

22For the king had a fleet of ships of Tarshish at sea with the fleet of Hiram. Once every three years the fleet of Tarshish came bringing gold, silver, ivory, apes, and peacocks.

23So King Solomon exceeded all the kings of the earth in riches and in wisdom [skill].

24And all the earth sought the presence of Solomon, to hear his wisdom, which God had put in his mind.

25Every man brought tribute: vessels of silver and gold, garments, equipment, spices, horses, and mules, so much year by year.

26Solomon collected chariots and horsemen; he had 1,400 chariots, and 12,000 horsemen whom he stationed in the chariot cities and with the king in Jerusalem.

27The king made silver as common in Jerusalem as stones, and cedars as plentiful as the sycamore trees in the lowland.

28Solomon's horses were brought out of Egypt, and the king's merchants received them in droves, each at a price. [Deut. 17:15, 16.]

29A chariot could be brought out of Egypt for 600 shekels of silver, and a horse for 150. And so for all the kings of the Hittites and of Syria they were exported by the king's merchants.

**11** BUT KING Solomon [defiantly] loved many foreign women: the [a]daughter of Pharaoh, women of the Moabites, Ammonites, Edomites, Zidonians, and Hittites.

2Of the very nations of whom the Lord said to the Israelites, You shall not mingle with them, neither shall they mingle with you; for surely they will turn away your hearts after their gods. Yet Solomon clung to these in love. [Deut. 17:17.]

3He had 700 wives, princesses, and 300 concubines; and his wives turned away his heart from God.

4For when Solomon was old, his wives turned away his heart after other gods, and his heart was not perfect (complete and whole) with the Lord his God, as was the heart of David his father.

5For Solomon went after Ashtoreth the goddess of the Sidonians, and after Milcom the abominable idol of the Ammonites! [I Kings 9:6-9.]

6Solomon did evil in the sight of the Lord, and went not fully after the Lord, as David his father did.

**AMP** [a] "Solomon brought the daughter of Pharaoh out of the city of David into the house that he had built for her, for he said, My wife shall not dwell in the house of David king of Israel, because the places are holy to which the ark of the Lord has come" (II Chron. 8:11). God had given Solomon the name "Jedidiah—beloved of the Lord" (II Sam. 12:25); yet he chose to be the beloved of heathen women instead, in defiance of God's covenant with him.

## New American Standard

*Wealth, Splendor and Wisdom*

14¶ Now the weight of gold which came in to Solomon in one year *was* 666 talents of gold,

15 besides *that* from the traders and the [b]wares of the merchants and all the kings of the Arabs and the governors of the country.

16 And King Solomon made 200 large shields of beaten gold, using 600 *shekels of* gold on each large shield.

17 And *he made* 300 shields of beaten gold, using three minas of gold on each shield, and the king put them in the house of the forest of Lebanon.

18 Moreover, the king made a great throne of ivory and overlaid it with refined gold.

19 There *were* six steps to the throne and a round top to the throne at its rear, and arms on each side of the seat, and two lions standing beside the arms.

20 And twelve lions were standing there on the six steps on the one side and on the other; nothing like *it* was made for any other kingdom.

21 And all King Solomon's drinking vessels *were* of gold, and all the vessels of the house of the forest of Lebanon *were* of pure gold. None was of silver; it was not considered [c]valuable in the days of Solomon.

22 For the king had at sea the ships of Tarshish with the ships of Hiram; once every three years the ships of Tarshish came bringing gold and silver, ivory and apes and peacocks.

23¶ So King Solomon became greater than all the kings of the earth in riches and in wisdom.

24 And all the earth was seeking the presence of Solomon, to hear his wisdom which God had put in his heart.

25 And they brought every man his gift, articles of silver and gold, garments, weapons, spices, horses, and mules, so much year by year.

26¶ Now Solomon gathered chariots and horsemen; and he had 1,400 chariots and 12,000 horsemen, and he stationed them in the chariot cities and with the king in Jerusalem.

27 And the king made silver *as common* as stones in Jerusalem, and he made cedars as plentiful as sycamore trees that are in the [d]lowland.

28 Also Solomon's import of horses was from Egypt and Kue, and the king's merchants procured *them* from Kue for a price.

29 And a chariot was imported from Egypt for 600 *shekels* of silver, and a horse for 150; and by the same means they exported them to all the kings of the Hittites and to the kings of the Arameans.

*Solomon Turns from God*

**11** NOW KING Solomon loved many foreign women along with the daughter of Pharaoh: Moabite, Ammonite, Edomite, Sidonian, and Hittite women,

2 from the nations concerning which the LORD had said to the sons of Israel, "You shall not associate with them, neither shall they associate with you, *for* they will surely turn your heart away after their gods." Solomon held fast to these in love.

3 And he had seven hundred wives, princesses, and three hundred concubines, and his wives turned his heart away.

4 For it came about when Solomon was old, his wives turned his heart away after other gods; and his heart was not [e]wholly devoted to the LORD his God, as the heart of David his father *had been*.

5 For Solomon went after Ashtoreth the goddess of the Sidonians and after Milcom the detestable idol of the Ammonites.

6 And Solomon did what was evil in the sight of the LORD, and did not follow the LORD fully, as David his father *had done*.

NAS [b] Or, *traffic* [c] Lit., *anything* [d] Or, *Shephelah* [e] Lit., *complete with*

## New International

*Solomon's Splendor*

14 The weight of the gold that Solomon received yearly was 666
talents,[f] 15 not including the revenues from merchants and traders
and from all the Arabian kings and the governors of the land.
16 King Solomon made two hundred large shields of hammered
gold; six hundred bekas[g] of gold went into each shield. 17 He also
made three hundred small shields of hammered gold, with three
minas[h] of gold in each shield. The king put them in the Palace of
the Forest of Lebanon.
18 Then the king made a great throne inlaid with ivory and
overlaid with fine gold. 19 The throne had six steps, and its back
had a rounded top. On both sides of the seat were armrests, with
a lion standing beside each of them. 20 Twelve lions stood on the
six steps, one at either end of each step. Nothing like it had ever
been made for any other kingdom. 21 All King Solomon's goblets
were gold, and all the household articles in the Palace of the Forest
of Lebanon were pure gold. Nothing was made of silver, because
silver was considered of little value in Solomon's days. 22 The king
had a fleet of trading ships[i] at sea along with the ships of Hiram.
Once every three years it returned, carrying gold, silver and ivory,
and apes and baboons.
23 King Solomon was greater in riches and wisdom than all the
other kings of the earth. 24 The whole world sought audience with
Solomon to hear the wisdom God had put in his heart. 25 Year after
year, everyone who came brought a gift—articles of silver and
gold, robes, weapons and spices, and horses and mules.
26 Solomon accumulated chariots and horses; he had fourteen
hundred chariots and twelve thousand horses,[j] which he kept in
the chariot cities and also with him in Jerusalem. 27 The king made
silver as common in Jerusalem as stones, and cedar as plentiful as
sycamore-fig trees in the foothills. 28 Solomon's horses were imported from Egypt[k] and from Kue[l] —the royal merchants purchased them from Kue. 29 They imported a chariot from Egypt for
six hundred shekels[m] of silver, and a horse for a hundred and
fifty.[n] They also exported them to all the kings of the Hittites and
of the Arameans.

*Solomon's Wives*

**11** KING SOLOMON, however, loved many foreign women
besides Pharaoh's daughter—Moabites, Ammonites,
Edomites, Sidonians and Hittites. 2 They were from nations about
which the LORD had told the Israelites, "You must not intermarry
with them, because they will surely turn your hearts after their
gods." Nevertheless, Solomon held fast to them in love. 3 He had
seven hundred wives of royal birth and three hundred concubines,
and his wives led him astray. 4 As Solomon grew old, his wives
turned his heart after other gods, and his heart was not fully
devoted to the LORD his God, as the heart of David his father had
been. 5 He followed Ashtoreth the goddess of the Sidonians, and
Molech[o] the detestable god of the Ammonites. 6 So Solomon did
evil in the eyes of the LORD; he did not follow the LORD completely,
as David his father had done.

NIV [f] *14* That is, about 25 tons (about 23 metric tons) [g] *16* That is, about 7 1/2 pounds (about 3.5 kilograms) [h] *17* That is, about 3 3/4 pounds (about 1.7 kilograms) [i] *22* Hebrew *of ships of Tarshish* [j] *26* Or *charioteers* [k] *28* Or possibly *Muzur*, a region in Cilicia; also in verse 29 [l] *28* Probably *Cilicia* [m] *29* That is, about 15 pounds (about 7 kilograms) [n] *29* That is, about 3 3/4 pounds (about 1.7 kilograms) [o] *5* Hebrew *Milcom*; also in verse 33

## King James

7Then did Solomon build an high place for Chemosh, the abomination of Moab, in the hill that *is* before Jerusalem, and for Molech, the abomination of the children of Ammon.

8And likewise did he for all his strange wives, which burnt incense and sacrificed unto their gods.

9¶ And the LORD was angry with Solomon, because his heart was turned from the LORD God of Israel, which had appeared unto him twice,

10And had commanded him concerning this thing, that he should not go after other gods: but he kept not that which the LORD commanded.

11Wherefore the LORD said unto Solomon, Forasmuch as this is done of thee, and thou hast not kept my covenant and my statutes, which I have commanded thee, I will surely rend the kingdom from thee, and will give it to thy servant.

12Notwithstanding in thy days I will not do it for David thy father's sake: *but* I will rend it out of the hand of thy son.

13Howbeit I will not rend away all the kingdom; *but* will give one tribe to thy son for David my servant's sake, and for Jerusalem's sake which I have chosen.

14¶ And the LORD stirred up an adversary unto Solomon, Hadad the Edomite: he *was* of the king's seed in Edom.

15For it came to pass, when David was in Edom, and Joab the captain of the host was gone up to bury the slain, after he had smitten every male in Edom;

16(For six months did Joab remain there with all Israel, until he had cut off every male in Edom:)

17That Hadad fled, he and certain Edomites of his father's servants with him, to go into Egypt; Hadad *being* yet a little child.

18And they arose out of Midian, and came to Paran: and they took men with them out of Paran, and they came to Egypt, unto Pharaoh king of Egypt; which gave him an house, and appointed him victuals, and gave him land.

19And Hadad found great favour in the sight of Pharaoh, so that he gave him to wife the sister of his own wife, the sister of Tahpenes the queen.

20And the sister of Tahpenes bare him Genubath his son, whom Tahpenes weaned in Pharaoh's house: and Genubath was in Pharaoh's household among the sons of Pharaoh.

21And when Hadad heard in Egypt that David slept with his fathers, and that Joab the captain of the host was dead, Hadad said to Pharaoh, Let me depart, that I may go to mine own country.

22Then Pharaoh said unto him, But what hast thou lacked with me, that, behold, thou seekest to go to thine own country? And he answered, Nothing: howbeit let me go in any wise.

23¶ And God stirred him up *another* adversary, Rezon the son of Eliadah, which fled from his lord Hadadezer king of Zobah:

24And he gathered men unto him, and became captain over a band, when David slew them *of Zobah:* and they went to Damascus, and dwelt therein, and reigned in Damascus.

25And he was an adversary to Israel all the days of Solomon, beside the mischief that Hadad *did:* and he abhorred Israel, and reigned over Syria.

26¶ And Jeroboam the son of Nebat, an Ephrathite of Zereda, Solomon's servant, whose mother's name *was* Zeruah, a widow woman, even he lifted up *his* hand against the king.

27And this *was* the cause that he lifted up *his* hand against the king: Solomon built Millo, *and* repaired the breaches of the city of David his father.

## Amplified

7Then Solomon built a high place for Chemosh the abominable idol of Moab, on the hill opposite Jerusalem! and for Molech the abominable idol of the Ammonites.

8And he did so [a]for all of his foreign wives, who burned incense and sacrificed to their gods.

9And the Lord was angry with Solomon, because his heart was turned from the Lord God of Israel, Who had appeared to him twice,

10And had commanded him concerning this thing, that he should not go after other gods; but he did not do what the Lord commanded.

11Therefore the Lord said to Solomon, Because you are doing this and have not kept My covenant and My statutes, which I have commanded you, I will surely rend the kingdom from you, and will give it to your servant!

12However in your days I will not do it, for David your father's sake; but I will rend it out of the hand of your son!

13However I will not tear away all the kingdom; but will give one tribe to your son for David My servant's sake, and for the sake of Jerusalem which I have chosen.

14The Lord stirred up an adversary against Solomon, Hadad the Edomite. He was of royal descent in Edom.

15For when David was in Edom, and Joab the commander of Israel's army went up to bury the slain, he slew every male in Edom

16(For Joab and all Israel remained there for six months, until he had cut off every male in Edom);

17But Hadad fled, he and certain Edomites of his father's servants, to Egypt, Hadad being yet a little child.

18They set out from Midian, and came to Paran; and took men with them out of Paran and came to Egypt, to Pharaoh king of Egypt, who gave [young] Hadad a house and land and ordered provisions for him.

19Hadad found great favor with Pharaoh, so that he gave him in marriage the sister of his own wife Tahpenes the queen.

20The sister of Tahpenes bore Hadad Genubath his son, whom Tahpenes weaned in Pharaoh's house; and Genubath was in Pharaoh's household among the sons of Pharaoh.

21But when Hadad heard in Egypt that David slept with his fathers, and that Joab the commander of Israel's army was dead, Hadad said to Pharaoh, Let me depart, that I may go to my own country.

22Then Pharaoh said to him, But what have you lacked with me, that now you want to go to your own country? He replied, Nothing. However, let me go anyhow.

23God raised up for [Hadad] another adversary, Rezon son of Eliadah, who had fled from his master Hadadezer king of Zobah.

24Rezon gathered men about him and became leader of a marauding band, after the slaughter by David. They went to Damascus and dwelt, and made [Rezon] king in Damascus.

25And Rezon was an adversary to Israel all the days of Solomon, besides the mischief that Hadad did. Rezon abhorred Israel and reigned over Syria.

26Jeroboam the son of Nebat, an Ephrathite of Zereda, Solomon's servant, whose mother's name was Zeruah, a widow woman, rebelled against the king,

27And for this reason: Solomon built Millo, and repaired the breaches of the city of David his father.

**AMP** [a] What all this did to Solomon's sweet fellowship with God is to be seen in Ecclesiastes. Take the sun out of the sky and all earth's beauty and fruitfulness will go also. Take God out of your sky and life's joys will be turned to dregs, bitterness, and futility. Solomon had deliberately chosen to live "under the sun" instead of under God. In the awareness of his own unquestionable greatness, he had become indifferent to the fact that "here is more than Solomon" (Luke 11:31) and that to scorn or ignore God is fatal. With all his wisdom he failed to recognize that, "God will not allow Himself to be sneered at—scorned, disdained or mocked [by mere pretensions or professions, or by His precepts being set aside] . . . For whatever a man sows, that *and* that only is what he will reap" (Gal. 6:7).

## New American Standard

7Then Solomon built a high place for Chemosh the detestable idol of Moab, on the mountain which is east of Jerusalem, and for Molech the detestable idol of the sons of Ammon.

8Thus also he did for all his foreign wives, who burned incense and sacrificed to their gods.

9¶ Now the LORD was angry with Solomon because his heart was turned away from the LORD, the God of Israel, who had appeared to him twice,

10and had commanded him concerning this thing, that he should not go after other gods; but he did not observe what the LORD had commanded.

11So the LORD said to Solomon, "Because you have done this, and you have not kept My covenant and My statutes, which I have commanded you, I will surely tear the kingdom from you, and will give it to your servant.

12"Nevertheless I will not do it in your days for the sake of your father David, *but* I will tear it out of the hand of your son.

13"However, I will not tear away all the kingdom, *but* I will give one tribe to your son for the sake of My servant David and for the sake of Jerusalem which I have chosen."

*God Raises Adversaries*

14¶ Then the LORD raised up an adversary to Solomon, Hadad the Edomite; he was of the royal line in Edom.

15For it came about, when David was in Edom, and Joab the commander of the army had gone up to bury the slain, and had struck down every male in Edom

16(for Joab and all Israel stayed there six months, until he had cut off every male in Edom),

17that Hadad fled to Egypt, he and certain Edomites of his father's servants with him, while Hadad *was* a young boy.

18And they arose from Midian and came to Paran; and they took men with them from Paran and came to Egypt, to Pharaoh king of Egypt, who gave him a house and assigned him food and gave him land.

19Now Hadad found great favor before Pharaoh, so that he gave him in marriage the sister of his own wife, the sister of Tahpenes the queen.

20And the sister of Tahpenes bore his son Genubath, whom Tahpenes weaned in Pharaoh's house; and Genubath was in Pharaoh's house among the sons of Pharaoh.

21But when Hadad heard in Egypt that David slept with his fathers, and that Joab the commander of the army was dead, Hadad said to Pharaoh, "Send me away, that I may go to my own country."

22Then Pharaoh said to him, "But what have you lacked with me, that behold, you are seeking to go to your own country?" And he answered, "Nothing; nevertheless you must surely let me go."

23¶ God also raised up *another* adversary to him, Rezon the son of Eliada, who had fled from his lord Hadadezer king of Zobah.

24And he gathered men to himself and became leader of a marauding band, after David slew them of *Zobah;* and they went to Damascus and stayed there, and reigned in Damascus.

25So he was an adversary to Israel all the days of Solomon, along with the evil that Hadad *did;* and he abhorred Israel and reigned over Aram.

26¶ Then Jeroboam the son of Nebat, an Ephraimite of Zeredah, Solomon's servant, whose mother's name was Zeruah, a widow, also rebelled against the king.

27Now this was the reason why he rebelled against the king: Solomon built the Millo, *and* closed up the breach of the city of his father David.

## New International

7On a hill east of Jerusalem, Solomon built a high place for
Chemosh the detestable god of Moab, and for Molech the detestable god of the Ammonites. 8He did the same for all his foreign
wives, who burned incense and offered sacrifices to their gods.
9The LORD became angry with Solomon because his heart had
turned away from the LORD, the God of Israel, who had appeared
to him twice. 10Although he had forbidden Solomon to follow
other gods, Solomon did not keep the LORD's command. 11So the
LORD said to Solomon, "Since this is your attitude and you have
not kept my covenant and my decrees, which I commanded you,
I will most certainly tear the kingdom away from you and give it
to one of your subordinates. 12Nevertheless, for the sake of David
your father, I will not do it during your lifetime. I will tear it out
of the hand of your son. 13Yet I will not tear the whole kingdom
from him, but will give him one tribe for the sake of David my
servant and for the sake of Jerusalem, which I have chosen."

*Solomon's Adversaries*

14Then the LORD raised up against Solomon an adversary,
Hadad the Edomite, from the royal line of Edom. 15Earlier when
David was fighting with Edom, Joab the commander of the army,
who had gone up to bury the dead, had struck down all the men
in Edom. 16Joab and all the Israelites stayed there for six months,
until they had destroyed all the men in Edom. 17But Hadad, still
only a boy, fled to Egypt with some Edomite officials who had
served his father. 18They set out from Midian and went to Paran.
Then taking men from Paran with them, they went to Egypt, to
Pharaoh king of Egypt, who gave Hadad a house and land and
provided him with food.
19Pharaoh was so pleased with Hadad that he gave him a sister
of his own wife, Queen Tahpenes, in marriage. 20The sister of
Tahpenes bore him a son named Genubath, whom Tahpenes
brought up in the royal palace. There Genubath lived with Pharaoh's own children.
21While he was in Egypt, Hadad heard that David rested with
his fathers and that Joab the commander of the army was also
dead. Then Hadad said to Pharaoh, "Let me go, that I may return
to my own country."
22"What have you lacked here that you want to go back to your
own country?" Pharaoh asked.
"Nothing," Hadad replied, "but do let me go!"
23And God raised up against Solomon another adversary, Rezon son of Eliada, who had fled from his master, Hadadezer king
of Zobah. 24He gathered men around him and became the leader
of a band of rebels when David destroyed the forces[b] ⌊of Zobah⌋;
the rebels went to Damascus, where they settled and took control.
25Rezon was Israel's adversary as long as Solomon lived, adding
to the trouble caused by Hadad. So Rezon ruled in Aram and was
hostile toward Israel.

*Jeroboam Rebels Against Solomon*

26Also, Jeroboam son of Nebat rebelled against the king. He was
one of Solomon's officials, an Ephraimite from Zeredah, and his
mother was a widow named Zeruah.
27Here is the account of how he rebelled against the king: Solomon had built the supporting terraces[c] and had filled in the gap
in the wall of the city of David his father. 28Now Jeroboam was a

NIV [b] 24 Hebrew *destroyed them* [c] 27 Or *the Millo*

## King James

28And the man Jeroboam *was* a mighty man of valour: and Solomon seeing the young man that he was industrious, he made him ruler over all the charge of the house of Joseph.
29And it came to pass at that time when Jeroboam went out of Jerusalem, that the prophet Ahijah the Shilonite found him in the way; and he had clad himself with a new garment; and they two *were* alone in the field:
30And Ahijah caught the new garment that *was* on him, and rent it *in* twelve pieces:
31And he said to Jeroboam, Take thee ten pieces: for thus saith the LORD, the God of Israel, Behold, I will rend the kingdom out of the hand of Solomon, and will give ten tribes to thee:
32(But he shall have one tribe for my servant David's sake, and for Jerusalem's sake, the city which I have chosen out of all the tribes of Israel:)
33Because that they have forsaken me, and have worshipped Ashtoreth the goddess of the Zidonians, Chemosh the god of the Moabites, and Milcom the god of the children of Ammon, and have not walked in my ways, to do *that which is* right in mine eyes, and *to keep* my statutes and my judgments, as *did* David his father.
34Howbeit I will not take the whole kingdom out of his hand: but I will make him prince all the days of his life for David my servant's sake, whom I chose, because he kept my commandments and my statutes:
35But I will take the kingdom out of his son's hand, and will give it unto thee, *even* ten tribes.
36And unto his son will I give one tribe, that David my servant may have a light always before me in Jerusalem, the city which I have chosen me to put my name there.
37And I will take thee, and thou shalt reign according to all that thy soul desireth, and shalt be king over Israel.
38And it shall be, if thou wilt hearken unto all that I command thee, and wilt walk in my ways, and do *that is* right in my sight, to keep my statutes and my commandments, as David my servant did; that I will be with thee, and build thee a sure house, as I built for David, and will give Israel unto thee.
39And I will for this afflict the seed of David, but not for ever.
40Solomon sought therefore to kill Jeroboam. And Jeroboam arose, and fled into Egypt, unto Shishak king of Egypt, and was in Egypt until the death of Solomon.
41¶ And the rest of the acts of Solomon, and all that he did, and his wisdom, *are* they not written in the book of the acts of Solomon?
42And the time that Solomon reigned in Jerusalem over all Israel *was* forty years.
43And Solomon slept with his fathers, and was buried in the city of David his father: and Rehoboam his son reigned in his stead.

**12** AND REHOBOAM went to Shechem: for all Israel were come to Shechem to make him king.
2And it came to pass, when Jeroboam the son of Nebat, who was yet in Egypt, heard *of it*, (for he was fled from the presence of king Solomon, and Jeroboam dwelt in Egypt;)
3That they sent and called him. And Jeroboam and all the congregation of Israel came, and spake unto Rehoboam, saying,
4Thy father made our yoke grievous: now therefore make thou the grievous service of thy father, and his heavy yoke which he put upon us, lighter, and we will serve thee.
5And he said unto them, Depart yet *for* three days, then come again to me. And the people departed.
6¶ And king Rehoboam consulted with the old men, that stood before Solomon his father while he yet lived, and said, How do ye advise that I may answer this people?

## Amplified

28The man Jeroboam was a mighty man of courage; Solomon seeing the young man was industrious, put him in charge over all the [forced] labor of the house of Joseph.
29At that time, when Jeroboam went out of Jerusalem, the prophet Ahijah the Shilonite met him in the way. Ahijah had clad himself with a new garment, and they two were alone in the field.
30Ahijah caught the new garment he wore and tore it into twelve pieces;
31He said to Jeroboam, You take ten pieces; for thus says the Lord, the God of Israel, Behold, I will tear the kingdom from the hand of Solomon, and will give you ten tribes.
32(But he shall have one tribe for My servant David's sake and for Jerusalem's sake, the city which I have chosen out of all the tribes of Israel),
33Because they have forsaken Me, and have worshiped Ashtoreth, goddess of the Sidonians, Chemosh, god of the Moabites, and Milcom, god of the Ammonites, and have not walked in My ways to do what is right in My sight, keeping My statutes and My ordinances, as did David his father.
34However I will not take the whole kingdom out of his hand; but I will make him ruler all the days of his life for David My servant's sake, whom I chose, because he kept My commandments and My statutes;
35But I will take the kingdom out of his son's hand, and give it to you, ten tribes.
36Yet to his son I will give one tribe, that David My servant may always have a light before Me in Jerusalem, the city where I have chosen to put My name.
37And I will take you, and you shall reign according to all that your soul desires, and shall be king over Israel.
38And if you will hearken to all I command you, and will walk in My ways, and do right in My sight, keeping My statutes and My commandments, as David My servant did, I will be with you and build you a sure house, as I built for David, and will give Israel to you.
39And I will for this afflict the descendants of David, but not for ever.
40Solomon sought therefore to kill Jeroboam. But Jeroboam arose and fled into Egypt, to Shishak king of Egypt, and was in Egypt until Solomon died.
41The rest of the acts of Solomon, and all that he did, and his wisdom (skill), are they not written in the book of the acts of Solomon?
42The time Solomon reigned in Jerusalem over all Israel was forty years.
43And Solomon slept with his fathers, and was buried in the city of David his father; Rehoboam his son reigned in his stead.

**12** REHOBOAM WENT to Shechem, for all Israel had come to Shechem to make him king.
2And when Jeroboam son of Nebat heard of it, (for he still dwelt in Egypt where he fled from King Solomon) [he] returned from Egypt,
3And they sent and called him. And Jeroboam and all the assembly of Israel came and said to Rehoboam,
4Your father made our yoke heavy. Now therefore lighten the hard service and the heavy yoke your father put upon us, and we will serve you.
5He replied, Go away for three days, then return to me. So the people departed.
6And King Rehoboam consulted with the old men, who stood before Solomon his father while he yet lived, and said, How do you advise me to answer this people?

## New American Standard

28Now the man Jeroboam was a valiant warrior, and when
Solomon saw that the young man was industrious, he appointed
him over all the forced labor of the house of Joseph.
29And it came about at that time, when Jeroboam went out of
Jerusalem, that the prophet Ahijah the Shilonite found him on the
road. Now Ahijah had clothed himself with a new cloak; and both
of them were alone in the field.
30Then Ahijah took hold of the new cloak which was on him,
and tore it into twelve pieces.
31And he said to Jeroboam, "Take for yourself ten pieces; for
thus says the LORD, the God of Israel, 'Behold, I will tear the
kingdom out of the hand of Solomon and give you ten tribes
32(but he will have one tribe, for the sake of My servant David
and for the sake of Jerusalem, the city which I have chosen from
all the tribes of Israel),
33because they have forsaken Me, and have worshiped Ashtoreth the goddess of the Sidonians, Chemosh the god of Moab,
and Milcom the god of the sons of Ammon; and they have not
walked in My ways, doing what is right in My sight and *observing*
My statutes and My ordinances, as his father David *did*.
34'Nevertheless I will not take the whole kingdom out of his
hand, but I will make him ruler all the days of his life, for the sake
of My servant David whom I chose, who observed My commandments and My statutes;
35but I will take the kingdom from his son's hand and give it
to you, *even* ten tribes.
36'But to his son I will give one tribe, that My servant David may
have a lamp always before Me in Jerusalem, the city where I have
chosen for Myself to put My name.
37'And I will take you, and you shall reign over whatever you
desire, and you shall be king over Israel.
38'Then it will be, that if you listen to all that I command you
and walk in My ways, and do what is right in My sight by observing My statutes and My commandments, as My servant David did,
then I will be with you and build you an enduring house as I built
for David, and I will give Israel to you.
39'Thus I will afflict the descendants of David for this, but not
always.'"
40Solomon sought therefore to put Jeroboam to death; but Jeroboam arose and fled to Egypt to Shishak king of Egypt, and he was
in Egypt until the death of Solomon.

*The Death of Solomon*

41¶ Now the rest of the acts of Solomon and whatever he did,
and his wisdom, are they not written in the book of the acts of
Solomon?
42Thus the time that Solomon reigned in Jerusalem over all
Israel was forty years.
43And Solomon slept with his fathers and was buried in the city
of his father David, and his son Rehoboam reigned in his place.

*King Rehoboam Acts Foolishly*

**12** THEN REHOBOAM went to Shechem, for all Israel had
come to Shechem to make him king.
2Now it came about when Jeroboam the son of Nebat heard *of*
*it*, that he was living in Egypt (for he was yet in Egypt, where he
had fled from the presence of King Solomon).
3Then they sent and called him, and Jeroboam and all the
assembly of Israel came and spoke to Rehoboam, saying,
4"Your father made our yoke hard; now therefore lighten the
hard service of your father and his heavy yoke which he put on
us, and we will serve you."
5Then he said to them, "Depart for three days, then return to
me." So the people departed.
6¶ And King Rehoboam consulted with the elders who had
served his father Solomon while he was still alive, saying, "How
do you counsel *me* to answer this people?"

## New International

man of standing, and when Solomon saw how well the young man
did his work, he put him in charge of the whole labor force of the
house of Joseph.
29About that time Jeroboam was going out of Jerusalem, and
Ahijah the prophet of Shiloh met him on the way, wearing a new
cloak. The two of them were alone out in the country, 30and Ahijah
took hold of the new cloak he was wearing and tore it into twelve
pieces. 31Then he said to Jeroboam, "Take ten pieces for yourself,
for this is what the LORD, the God of Israel, says: 'See, I am going
to tear the kingdom out of Solomon's hand and give you ten tribes.
32But for the sake of my servant David and the city of Jerusalem,
which I have chosen out of all the tribes of Israel, he will have one
tribe. 33I will do this because they have[a] forsaken me and worshiped Ashtoreth the goddess of the Sidonians, Chemosh the god
of the Moabites, and Molech the god of the Ammonites, and have
not walked in my ways, nor done what is right in my eyes, nor kept
my statutes and laws as David, Solomon's father, did.
34" 'But I will not take the whole kingdom out of Solomon's
hand; I have made him ruler all the days of his life for the sake of
David my servant, whom I chose and who observed my commands and statutes. 35I will take the kingdom from his son's hands
and give you ten tribes. 36I will give one tribe to his son so that
David my servant may always have a lamp before me in Jerusalem,
the city where I chose to put my Name. 37However, as for you, I
will take you, and you will rule over all that your heart desires; you
will be king over Israel. 38If you do whatever I command you and
walk in my ways and do what is right in my eyes by keeping my
statutes and commands, as David my servant did, I will be with
you. I will build you a dynasty as enduring as the one I built for
David and will give Israel to you. 39I will humble David's descendants because of this, but not forever.' "
40Solomon tried to kill Jeroboam, but Jeroboam fled to Egypt,
to Shishak the king, and stayed there until Solomon's death.

*Solomon's Death*

41As for the other events of Solomon's reign—all he did and the
wisdom he displayed—are they not written in the book of the
annals of Solomon? 42Solomon reigned in Jerusalem over all Israel
forty years. 43Then he rested with his fathers and was buried in
the city of David his father. And Rehoboam his son succeeded him
as king.

*Israel Rebels Against Rehoboam*

**12** REHOBOAM WENT to Shechem, for all the Israelites had
gone there to make him king. 2When Jeroboam son of
Nebat heard this (he was still in Egypt, where he had fled from
King Solomon), he returned from[b] Egypt. 3So they sent for Jeroboam, and he and the whole assembly of Israel went to Rehoboam
and said to him: 4"Your father put a heavy yoke on us, but now
lighten the harsh labor and the heavy yoke he put on us, and we
will serve you."
5Rehoboam answered, "Go away for three days and then come
back to me." So the people went away.
6Then King Rehoboam consulted the elders who had served his
father Solomon during his lifetime. "How would you advise me
to answer these people?" he asked.

**NIV** [a] 33 Hebrew; Septuagint, Vulgate and Syriac *because he has* [b] 2 Or *he remained in*

## King James

7And they spake unto him, saying, If thou wilt be a servant unto this people this day, and wilt serve them, and answer them, and speak good words to them, then they will be thy servants for ever.

8But he forsook the counsel of the old men, which they had given him, and consulted with the young men that were grown up with him, *and* which stood before him:

9And he said unto them, What counsel give ye that we may answer this people, who have spoken to me, saying, Make the yoke which thy father did put upon us lighter?

10And the young men that were grown up with him spake unto him, saying, Thus shalt thou speak unto this people that spake unto thee, saying, Thy father made our yoke heavy, but make thou *it* lighter unto us; thus shalt thou say unto them, My little *finger* shall be thicker than my father's loins.

11And now whereas my father did lade you with a heavy yoke, I will add to your yoke: my father hath chastised you with whips, but I will chastise you with scorpions.

12¶ So Jeroboam and all the people came to Rehoboam the third day, as the king had appointed, saying, Come to me again the third day.

13And the king answered the people roughly, and forsook the old men's counsel that they gave him;

14And spake to them after the counsel of the young men, saying, My father made your yoke heavy, and I will add to your yoke: my father *also* chastised you with whips, but I will chastise you with scorpions.

15Wherefore the king hearkened not unto the people; for the cause was from the LORD, that he might perform his saying, which the LORD spake by Ahijah the Shilonite unto Jeroboam the son of Nebat.

16¶ So when all Israel saw that the king hearkened not unto them, the people answered the king, saying, What portion have we in David? neither *have we* inheritance in the son of Jesse: to your tents, O Israel: now see to thine own house, David. So Israel departed unto their tents.

17But *as for* the children of Israel which dwelt in the cities of Judah, Rehoboam reigned over them.

18Then king Rehoboam sent Adoram, who *was* over the tribute; and all Israel stoned him with stones, that he died. Therefore king Rehoboam made speed to get him up to his chariot, to flee to Jerusalem.

19So Israel rebelled against the house of David unto this day.

20And it came to pass, when all Israel heard that Jeroboam was come again, that they sent and called him unto the congregation, and made him king over all Israel: there was none that followed the house of David, but the tribe of Judah only.

21¶ And when Rehoboam was come to Jerusalem, he assembled all the house of Judah, with the tribe of Benjamin, an hundred and fourscore thousand chosen men, which were warriors, to fight against the house of Israel, to bring the kingdom again to Rehoboam the son of Solomon.

22But the word of God came unto Shemaiah the man of God, saying,

23Speak unto Rehoboam, the son of Solomon, king of Judah, and unto all the house of Judah and Benjamin, and to the remnant of the people, saying,

24Thus saith the LORD, Ye shall not go up, nor fight against your brethren the children of Israel: return every man to his house; for this thing is from me. They hearkened therefore to the word of the LORD, and returned to depart, according to the word of the LORD.

25¶ Then Jeroboam built Shechem in mount Ephraim, and dwelt therein; and went out from thence, and built Penuel.

## Amplified

7And they said to him, If you will be a servant to this people today and serve them, and answer them with good words, they will be your servants for ever.

8But he forsook the counsel the old men gave him, and consulted the young men who grew up with him and stood before him.

9He said to them, What do you advise that we answer this people who have said, Make the yoke your father put on us lighter?

10The young men who grew up with him answered, To the people who told you, Your father made our yoke heavy, but you make it lighter for us, say this, My little finger shall be thicker than my father's loins.

11And now whereas my father loaded you with a heavy yoke, I will add to your yoke. My father chastised you with whips, but I will chastise you with scorpions.

12So Jeroboam and all the people came to Rehoboam the third day, as the king had appointed.

13And the king answered the people roughly, and forsook the counsel the old men had given him,

14And spoke to them after the counsel of the young men, saying, My father made your yoke heavy, but I will add to your yoke; he chastised you with whips, but I will chastise you with scorpions.

15So the king did not hearken to the people; for the situation was from the Lord, that He might fulfill His word, which He spoke by Ahijah the Shilonite to Jeroboam the son of Nebat. [11:29-33.]

16So when all Israel saw the king did not heed them, they answered the king, What portion have we in David? We have no inheritance in the son of Jesse. To your tents, O Israel! Look now to your own house, David! So Israel went to their tents.

17But Rehoboam reigned over the Israelites who dwelt in the cities of Judah.

18Then King Rehoboam sent Adoram, who was over the tribute [taskmaster over the forced labor], and all Israel stoned him to death with stones. So King Rehoboam hastened to get into his chariot to flee to Jerusalem.

19So Israel rebelled against the house of David to this day.

20When all Israel heard that Jeroboam had returned, they sent and called him to the assembly, and made him king over all Israel. None followed the house of David except the tribe of Judah only.

21And when Rehoboam was come to Jerusalem, he assembled all the house of Judah, with the tribe of Benjamin, 180,000 chosen warriors, to fight against the house of Israel, to bring the kingdom back to Rehoboam son of Solomon.

22But the word of God came to Shemaiah the man of God, saying,

23Tell Rehoboam son of Solomon, king of Judah, and all the house of Judah and Benjamin, and the remnant of the people,

24Thus says the Lord, You shall not go up, or fight against your brethren the Israelites. Return every man to his house, for this thing is from Me. So they hearkened to the Lord's word, and returned home, according to the Lord's word.

25Then Jeroboam built Shechem in the hill country of Ephraim, and lived there; he went out from there and built Penuel.

## New American Standard

7 Then they spoke to him, saying, "If you will be a servant to
this people today, will serve them, grant them their petition, and
speak good words to them, then they will be your servants forever."
8 But he forsook the counsel of the elders which they had given
him, and consulted with the young men who grew up with him
and served him.
9 So he said to them, "What counsel do you give that we may
answer this people who have spoken to me, saying, 'Lighten the
yoke which your father put on us'?"
10 And the young men who grew up with him spoke to him,
saying, "Thus you shall say to this people who spoke to you,
saying, 'Your father made our yoke heavy, now you make it lighter
for us!' But you shall speak to them, 'My little finger is thicker than
my father's loins!
11 'Whereas my father loaded you with a heavy yoke, I will add
to your yoke; my father disciplined you with whips, but I will
discipline you with scorpions.'"
**12**¶ Then Jeroboam and all the people came to Rehoboam on the
third day as the king had directed, saying, "Return to me on the
third day."
13 And the king answered the people harshly, for he forsook the
advice of the elders which they had given him,
14 and he spoke to them according to the advice of the young
men, saying, "My father made your yoke heavy, but I will add to
your yoke; my father disciplined you with whips, but I will discipline you with scorpions."
15 So the king did not listen to the people; for it was a turn *of
events* from the LORD, that He might establish His word, which the
LORD spoke through Ahijah the Shilonite to Jeroboam the son of
Nebat.

*The Kingdom Divided Jeroboam Rules Israel*

**16**¶ When all Israel *saw* that the king did not listen to them, the
people answered the king, saying,
"What portion do we have in David?
*We have* no inheritance in the son of Jesse;
To your tents, O Israel!
Now look after your own house, David!"
So Israel departed to their tents.
17 But as for the sons of Israel who lived in the cities of Judah,
Rehoboam reigned over them.
18 Then King Rehoboam sent Adoram, who was over the forced
labor, and all Israel stoned him to death. And King Rehoboam
made haste to mount his chariot to flee to Jerusalem.
19 So Israel has been in rebellion against the house of David to
this day.
20 And it came about when all Israel heard that Jeroboam had
returned, that they sent and called him to the assembly and made
him king over all Israel. None but the tribe of Judah followed the
house of David.
**21**¶ Now when Rehoboam had come to Jerusalem, he assembled
all the house of Judah and the tribe of Benjamin, 180,000 chosen
men who were warriors, to fight against the house of Israel to
restore the kingdom to Rehoboam the son of Solomon.
22 But the word of God came to Shemaiah the man of God,
saying,
23 "Speak to Rehoboam the son of Solomon, king of Judah, and
to all the house of Judah and Benjamin and to the rest of the
people, saying,
24 'Thus says the LORD, "You must not go up and fight against
your relatives the sons of Israel; return every man to his house, for
this thing has come from Me."'" So they listened to the word of
the LORD, and returned and went *their way* according to the word
of the LORD.

*Jeroboam's Idolatry*

**25**¶ Then Jeroboam built Shechem in the hill country of
Ephraim, and lived there. And he went out from there and built
Penuel.

## New International

7 They replied, "If today you will be a servant to these people
and serve them and give them a favorable answer, they will always
be your servants."
8 But Rehoboam rejected the advice the elders gave him and
consulted the young men who had grown up with him and were
serving him. 9 He asked them, "What is your advice? How should
we answer these people who say to me, 'Lighten the yoke your
father put on us'?"
10 The young men who had grown up with him replied, "Tell
these people who have said to you, 'Your father put a heavy yoke
on us, but make our yoke lighter'—tell them, 'My little finger is
thicker than my father's waist. 11 My father laid on you a heavy
yoke; I will make it even heavier. My father scourged you with
whips; I will scourge you with scorpions.'"
12 Three days later Jeroboam and all the people returned to
Rehoboam, as the king had said, "Come back to me in three days."
13 The king answered the people harshly. Rejecting the advice
given him by the elders, 14 he followed the advice of the young men
and said, "My father made your yoke heavy; I will make it even
heavier. My father scourged you with whips; I will scourge you
with scorpions." 15 So the king did not listen to the people, for this
turn of events was from the LORD, to fulfill the word the LORD had
spoken to Jeroboam son of Nebat through Ahijah the Shilonite.
16 When all Israel saw that the king refused to listen to them,
they answered the king:

"What share do we have in David,
what part in Jesse's son?
To your tents, O Israel!
Look after your own house, O David!"

So the Israelites went home. 17 But as for the Israelites who were
living in the towns of Judah, Rehoboam still ruled over them.
18 King Rehoboam sent out Adoniram,[a] who was in charge of
forced labor, but all Israel stoned him to death. King Rehoboam,
however, managed to get into his chariot and escape to Jerusalem.
19 So Israel has been in rebellion against the house of David to this
day.
20 When all the Israelites heard that Jeroboam had returned,
they sent and called him to the assembly and made him king over
all Israel. Only the tribe of Judah remained loyal to the house of
David.
21 When Rehoboam arrived in Jerusalem, he mustered the
whole house of Judah and the tribe of Benjamin—a hundred and
eighty thousand fighting men—to make war against the house of
Israel and to regain the kingdom for Rehoboam son of Solomon.
22 But this word of God came to Shemaiah the man of God:
23 "Say to Rehoboam son of Solomon king of Judah, to the whole
house of Judah and Benjamin, and to the rest of the people, 24 'This
is what the LORD says: Do not go up to fight against your brothers,
the Israelites. Go home, every one of you, for this is my doing.'"
So they obeyed the word of the LORD and went home again, as the
LORD had ordered.

*Golden Calves at Bethel and Dan*

25 Then Jeroboam fortified Shechem in the hill country of
Ephraim and lived there. From there he went out and built up
Peniel.[b]

**NIV** [a] *18* Some Septuagint manuscripts and Syriac (see also 1 Kings 4:6 and 5:14); Hebrew *Adoram* [b] *25* Hebrew *Penuel,* a variant of *Peniel*

## King James

26 And Jeroboam said in his heart, Now shall the kingdom return to the house of David:
27 If this people go up to do sacrifice in the house of the LORD
at Jerusalem, then shall the heart of this people turn again unto
their lord, *even* unto Rehoboam king of Judah, and they shall kill
me, and go again to Rehoboam king of Judah.
28 Whereupon the king took counsel, and made two calves *of*
gold, and said unto them, It is too much for you to go up to
Jerusalem: behold thy gods, O Israel, which brought thee up out
of the land of Egypt.
29 And he set the one in Beth-el, and the other put he in Dan.
30 And this thing became a sin: for the people went *to worship*
before the one, *even* unto Dan.
31 And he made an house of high places, and made priests of
the lowest of the people, which were not of the sons of Levi.
32 And Jeroboam ordained a feast in the eighth month, on the
fifteenth day of the month, like unto the feast that *is* in Judah, and
he offered upon the altar. So did he in Beth-el, sacrificing unto the
calves that he had made: and he placed in Beth-el the priests of the
high places which he had made.
33 So he offered upon the altar which he had made in Beth-el the
fifteenth day of the eighth month, *even* in the month which he had
devised of his own heart; and ordained a feast unto the children
of Israel: and he offered upon the altar, and burnt incense.

**13** AND, BEHOLD, there came a man of God out of Judah
by the word of the LORD unto Beth-el: and Jeroboam stood
by the altar to burn incense.
2 And he cried against the altar in the word of the LORD, and
said, O altar, altar, thus saith the LORD; Behold, a child shall be
born unto the house of David, Josiah by name; and upon thee shall
he offer the priests of the high places that burn incense upon thee,
and men's bones shall be burnt upon thee.
3 And he gave a sign the same day, saying, This *is* the sign which
the LORD hath spoken; Behold, the altar shall be rent, and the
ashes that *are* upon it shall be poured out.
4 And it came to pass, when king Jeroboam heard the saying of
the man of God, which had cried against the altar in Beth-el, that
he put forth his hand from the altar, saying, Lay hold on him. And
his hand, which he put forth against him, dried up, so that he
could not pull it in again to him.
5 The altar also was rent, and the ashes poured out from the
altar, according to the sign which the man of God had given by the
word of the LORD.
6 And the king answered and said unto the man of God, Entreat
now the face of the LORD thy God, and pray for me, that my hand
may be restored me again. And the man of God besought the
LORD, and the king's hand was restored him again, and became
as *it was* before.
7 And the king said unto the man of God, Come home with me,
and refresh thyself, and I will give thee a reward.
8 And the man of God said unto the king, If thou wilt give me
half thine house, I will not go in with thee, neither will I eat bread
nor drink water in this place:
9 For so was it charged me by the word of the LORD, saying, Eat
no bread, nor drink water, nor turn again by the same way that
thou camest.
10 So he went another way, and returned not by the way that
he came to Beth-el.

## Amplified

26 Jeroboam said in his heart, Now the kingdom will return to
the house of David;
27 If this people goes up to the house of the Lord at Jerusalem
to sacrifice, then the heart of this people will turn again to their
lord, to Rehoboam king of Judah, and they will kill me and go back
to Rehoboam king of Judah.
28 So the king took counsel, and made two calves of gold. And
he said to the people, It is too much for you to go [all the way] up
to Jerusalem. Behold your gods, O Israel, which brought you up
out of the land of Egypt.
29 And he set the one golden calf in Bethel, and the other he put
in Dan.
30 And this thing became a sin; for the people went to worship
each of them, even as far as Dan.
31 Jeroboam also made houses on high places, and made priests
of the people, who were not Levites.
32 And Jeroboam appointed a feast on the fifteenth day of the
eighth month like the feast kept in Judah, and he offered sacrifices
upon the altar. So he did in Bethel, sacrificing to the calves he had
made; and he placed in Bethel the priests of the high places he had
made.
33 So he offered upon the altar he had made in Bethel on the
fifteenth day of the eighth month, a date which he chose individually, and he appointed a feast for the Israelites, and he went up
to the altar to burn incense [in defiance of God's law.]

**13** AND, BEHOLD, there came a man of God out of Judah
by the word of the Lord to Bethel. Jeroboam stood by the
altar to burn incense.
2 The man cried against the altar by the word of the Lord, O
altar, altar, thus says the Lord: Behold, a son shall be born to the
house of David, Josiah by name; and on you shall he offer the
priests of the high places that burn incense on you, and men's
bones shall be burned on you.
3 And he gave a sign the same day, saying, This is the sign which
the Lord has spoken: Behold, the altar shall be split, and the ashes
that are upon it shall be poured out. [Fulfilled in II Kings 23:15, 16.]
4 When King Jeroboam heard the words the man of God cried
against the altar in Bethel, he thrust out his hand, saying, Lay hold
on him! And his hand, which he put forth against him, dried up,
so that he could not draw it to him again.
5 The altar also was split, and the ashes poured out from the
altar, according to the sign which the man of God had given by the
word of the Lord. [v. 3.]
6 And the king said to the man of God, Entreat now the favor
of the Lord your God, and pray for me, that my hand may be
restored to me. And the man of God entreated the Lord, and the
king's hand was restored, and became as it was before.
7 And the king said to the man of God, Come home with me,
and refresh yourself, and I will give you a reward.
8 And the man of God said to the king, If you give me half your
house, I will not go in with you. And I will not eat bread or drink
water in this place.
9 For I was commanded by the word of the Lord, You shall eat
no bread, or drink water, or return by the way you came.
10 So he went another way, and did not return by the way that
he came to Bethel.

## New American Standard

26And Jeroboam said in his heart, "Now the kingdom will return to the house of David.
27"If this people go up to offer sacrifices in the house of the
LORD at Jerusalem, then the heart of this people will return to their
lord, *even* to Rehoboam king of Judah; and they will kill me and
return to Rehoboam king of Judah."
28So the king consulted, and made two golden calves, and he
said to them, "It is too much for you to go up to Jerusalem; behold
your gods, O Israel, that brought you up from the land of Egypt."
29And he set one in Bethel, and the other he put in Dan.
30Now this thing became a sin, for the people went *to worship*
before the one as far as Dan.
31And he made houses on high places, and made priests from
among all the people who were not of the sons of Levi.
32And Jeroboam instituted a feast in the eighth month on the
fifteenth day of the month, like the feast which is in Judah, and
he went up to the altar; thus he did in Bethel, sacrificing to the
calves which he had made. And he stationed in Bethel the priests
of the high places which he had made.
33Then he went up to the altar which he had made in Bethel on
the fifteenth day in the eighth month, even in the month which
he had devised in his own heart; and he instituted a feast for the
sons of Israel, and went up to the altar to burn incense.

*Jeroboam Warned, Stricken*

13 NOW BEHOLD, there came a man of God from Judah to
Bethel by the word of the LORD, while Jeroboam was
standing by the altar to burn incense.
2And he cried against the altar by the word of the LORD, and
said, "O altar, altar, thus says the LORD, 'Behold, a son shall be
born to the house of David, Josiah by name; and on you he shall
sacrifice the priests of the high places who burn incense on you,
and human bones shall be burned on you.' "
3Then he gave a sign the same day, saying, "This is the sign
which the LORD has spoken, 'Behold, the altar shall be split apart
and the ashes which are on it shall be poured out.' "
4Now it came about when the king heard the saying of the man
of God, which he cried against the altar in Bethel, that Jeroboam
stretched out his hand from the altar, saying, "Seize him." But his
hand which he stretched out against him dried up, so that he could
not draw it back to himself.
5The altar also was split apart and the ashes were poured out
from the altar, according to the sign which the man of God had
given by the word of the LORD.
6And the king answered and said to the man of God, "Please
[a]entreat the LORD your God, and pray for me, that my hand may
be restored to me." So the man of God [b]entreated the LORD, and
the king's hand was restored to him, and it became as it was
before.
7Then the king said to the man of God, "Come home with me
and refresh yourself, and I will give you a reward."
8But the man of God said to the king, "If you were to give me
half your house I would not go with you, nor would I eat bread
or drink water in this place.
9"For so it was commanded me by the word of the LORD,
saying, 'You shall eat no bread, nor drink water, nor return by the
way which you came.' "
10So he went another way, and did not return by the way which
he came to Bethel.

NAS [a] Lit., *soften(ed) the face of* [b] Lit., *soften(ed) the face of*

## New International

26Jeroboam thought to himself, "The kingdom will now likely
revert to the house of David. 27If these people go up to offer
sacrifices at the temple of the LORD in Jerusalem, they will again
give their allegiance to their lord, Rehoboam king of Judah. They
will kill me and return to King Rehoboam."
28After seeking advice, the king made two golden calves. He
said to the people, "It is too much for you to go up to Jerusalem.
Here are your gods, O Israel, who brought you up out of Egypt."
29One he set up in Bethel, and the other in Dan. 30And this thing
became a sin; the people went even as far as Dan to worship the
one there.
31Jeroboam built shrines on high places and appointed priests
from all sorts of people, even though they were not Levites. 32He
instituted a festival on the fifteenth day of the eighth month, like
the festival held in Judah, and offered sacrifices on the altar. This
he did in Bethel, sacrificing to the calves he had made. And at
Bethel he also installed priests at the high places he had made.
33On the fifteenth day of the eighth month, a month of his own
choosing, he offered sacrifices on the altar he had built at Bethel.
So he instituted the festival for the Israelites and went up to the
altar to make offerings.

*The Man of God From Judah*

13 BY THE word of the LORD a man of God came from Judah
to Bethel, as Jeroboam was standing by the altar to make
an offering. 2He cried out against the altar by the word of the LORD:
"O altar, altar! This is what the LORD says: 'A son named Josiah
will be born to the house of David. On you he will sacrifice the
priests of the high places who now make offerings here, and
human bones will be burned on you.' " 3That same day the man
of God gave a sign: "This is the sign the LORD has declared: The
altar will be split apart and the ashes on it will be poured out."
4When King Jeroboam heard what the man of God cried out
against the altar at Bethel, he stretched out his hand from the altar
and said, "Seize him!" But the hand he stretched out toward the
man shriveled up, so that he could not pull it back. 5Also, the altar
was split apart and its ashes poured out according to the sign given
by the man of God by the word of the LORD.
6Then the king said to the man of God, "Intercede with the
LORD your God and pray for me that my hand may be restored."
So the man of God interceded with the LORD, and the king's hand
was restored and became as it was before.
7The king said to the man of God, "Come home with me and
have something to eat, and I will give you a gift."
8But the man of God answered the king, "Even if you were to
give me half your possessions, I would not go with you, nor would
I eat bread or drink water here. 9For I was commanded by the word
of the LORD: 'You must not eat bread or drink water or return by
the way you came.' " 10So he took another road and did not return
by the way he had come to Bethel.

## King James

11¶ Now there dwelt an old prophet in Beth-el; and his sons came and told him all the works that the man of God had done that day in Beth-el: the words which he had spoken unto the king, them they told also to their father.

12And their father said unto them, What way went he? For his sons had seen what way the man of God went, which came from Judah.

13And he said unto his sons, Saddle me the ass. So they saddled him the ass; and he rode thereon,

14And went after the man of God, and found him sitting under an oak: and he said unto him, *Art* thou the man of God that camest from Judah? And he said, I *am*.

15Then he said unto him, Come home with me, and eat bread.

16And he said, I may not return with thee, nor go in with thee: neither will I eat bread nor drink water with thee in this place:

17For it was said to me by the word of the LORD, Thou shalt eat no bread nor drink water there, nor turn again to go by the way that thou camest.

18He said unto him, I *am* a prophet also as thou *art;* and an angel spake unto me by the word of the LORD, saying, Bring him back with thee into thine house, that he may eat bread and drink water. *But* he lied unto him.

19So he went back with him, and did eat bread in his house, and drank water.

20¶ And it came to pass, as they sat at the table, that the word of the LORD came unto the prophet that brought him back:

21And he cried unto the man of God that came from Judah, saying, Thus saith the LORD, Forasmuch as thou hast disobeyed the mouth of the LORD, and hast not kept the commandment which the LORD thy God commanded thee,

22But camest back, and hast eaten bread and drunk water in the place, of the which *the* LORD did say to thee, Eat no bread, and drink no water; thy carcase shall not come unto the sepulchre of thy fathers.

23¶ And it came to pass, after he had eaten bread, and after he had drunk, that he saddled for him the ass, *to wit,* for the prophet whom he had brought back.

24And when he was gone, a lion met him by the way, and slew him: and his carcase was cast in the way, and the ass stood by it, the lion also stood by the carcase.

25And, behold, men passed by, and saw the carcase cast in the way, and the lion standing by the carcase: and they came and told *it* in the city where the old prophet dwelt.

26And when the prophet that brought him back from the way heard *thereof,* he said, It *is* the man of God, who was disobedient unto the word of the LORD: therefore the LORD hath delivered him unto the lion, which hath torn him, and slain him, according to the word of the LORD, which he spake unto him.

27And he spake to his sons, saying, Saddle me the ass. And they saddled *him.*

28And he went and found his carcase cast in the way, and the ass and the lion standing by the carcase: the lion had not eaten the carcase, nor torn the ass.

29And the prophet took up the carcase of the man of God, and laid it upon the ass, and brought it back: and the old prophet came to the city, to mourn and to bury him.

30And he laid his carcase in his own grave; and they mourned over him, *saying,* Alas, my brother!

31And it came to pass, after he had buried him, that he spake to his sons, saying, When I am dead, then bury me in the sepulchre wherein the man of God *is* buried; lay my bones beside his bones:

32For the saying which he cried by the word of the LORD against the altar in Beth-el, and against all the houses of the high places which *are* in the cities of Samaria, shall surely come to pass.

33¶ After this thing Jeroboam returned not from his evil way, but made again of the lowest of the people priests of the high places: whosoever would, he consecrated him, and he became *one* of the priests of the high places.

## Amplified

11Now there dwelt an old prophet in Bethel; and his sons came and told him all that the man of God had done that day in Bethel; the words which he had spoken to the king they told also to their father.

12Their father asked them, Which way did he go? For his sons had seen which way the man of God went, who came from Judah.

13He said to his sons, Saddle the donkey for me. So they saddled the donkey and he rode on it,

14And went after the man of God, and found him sitting under an oak; and he said to him, Are you the man of God who came from Judah? And he said, I am.

15Then he said to him, Come home with me, and eat bread.

16He said, I may not return with you, or go in with you; neither will I eat bread or drink water with you in this place;

17For I was told by the word of the Lord, You shall not eat bread or drink water there, or return by the way that you came.

18He answered, I am a prophet also as you are; and an angel spoke to me by the word of the Lord, saying, Bring him back with you to your house, that he may eat bread and drink water. But he lied to him.

19So the man from Judah went back with him, and ate and drank water in his house.

20And as they sat at the table, the word of the Lord came to the prophet who brought him back,

21And he cried to the man of God who came from Judah, Thus says the Lord, Because you have disobeyed the word of the Lord, and have not kept the command which the Lord your God commanded you,

22But came back, and have eaten bread and drunk water in the place of which the Lord said to you, Eat no bread, and drink no water; your corpse shall not come to the tomb of your fathers.

23And after the prophet of the house had eaten bread and drunk, he saddled the donkey for the man he had brought back;

24And when he was gone, a lion met him by the road and slew him; and his corpse was cast in the way, and the donkey stood by it; the lion also stood by the corpse.

25And behold, men passed by, and saw the corpse thrown in the road, and the lion standing by the corpse, and they came and told it in the city where the old prophet dwelt.

26When the prophet who brought him back from the way heard of it, he said, It is the man of God, who was disobedient to the word of the Lord; therefore the Lord has given him to the lion, which has torn him, and slain him, according to the word of the Lord, which He spoke to him.

27And he said to his sons, Saddle the donkey for me. And they saddled it.

28And he went and found the corpse thrown in the road, and the donkey and the lion stood by the body; the lion had not eaten the corpse or torn the donkey.

29The prophet took up the corpse of the man of God and laid it upon the donkey and brought it back; and the old prophet came into the city, to mourn and to bury him.

30And he laid the body in his own grave; and they mourned over him, saying, Alas, my brother!

31After he had buried him, he said to his sons, When I am dead, bury me in the grave in which the man of God is buried; lay my bones beside his bones;

32For the saying which he cried by the word of the Lord against the altar in Bethel, and against all the houses of the high places which are in the cities of Samaria, shall surely come to pass.

33After this thing Jeroboam turned not from his evil way, but made priests for the high places again from among all the people. Whoever would, he consecrated, that there might be priests of the high places.

## New American Standard

*The Disobedient Prophet*
11¶ Now an old prophet was living in Bethel; and his sons came
and told him all the deeds which the man of God had done that
day in Bethel; the words which he had spoken to the king, these
also they related to their father.
12And their father said to them, "Which way did he go?" Now
his sons had seen the way which the man of God who came from
Judah had gone.
13Then he said to his sons, "Saddle the donkey for me." So they
saddled the donkey for him and he rode away on it.
14So he went after the man of God and found him sitting under
an oak; and he said to him, "Are you the man of God who came
from Judah?" And he said, "I am."
15Then he said to him, "Come home with me and eat bread."
16And he said, "I cannot return with you, nor go with you, nor
will I eat bread or drink water with you in this place.
17"For a command *came* to me by the word of the LORD, 'You
shall eat no bread, nor drink water there; do not return by going
the way which you came.' "
18And he said to him, "I also am a prophet like you, and an
angel spoke to me by the word of the LORD, saying, 'Bring him
back with you to your house, that he may eat bread and drink
water.' " *But* he lied to him.
19So he went back with him, and ate bread in his house and
drank water.
20¶ Now it came about, as they were sitting down at the table,
that the word of the LORD came to the prophet who had brought
him back;
21and he cried to the man of God who came from Judah, saying,
"Thus says the LORD, 'Because you have disobeyed the command
of the LORD, and have not observed the commandment which the
LORD your God commanded you,
22but have returned and eaten bread and drunk water in the
place of which He said to you, "Eat no bread and drink no water";
your body shall not come to the grave of your fathers.' "
23And it came about after he had eaten bread and after he had
drunk, that he saddled the donkey for him, for the prophet whom
he had brought back.
24Now when he had gone, a lion met him on the way and killed
him, and his body was thrown on the road, with the donkey
standing beside it; the lion also was standing beside the body.
25And behold, men passed by and saw the body thrown on the
road, and the lion standing beside the body; so they came and told
*it* in the city where the old prophet lived.
26¶ Now when the prophet who brought him back from the way
heard *it*, he said, "It is the man of God, who disobeyed the command of the LORD; therefore the LORD has given him to the lion,
which has torn him and killed him, according to the word of the
LORD which He spoke to him."
27Then he spoke to his sons, saying, "Saddle the donkey for
me." And they saddled *it*.
28And he went and found his body thrown on the road with the
donkey and the lion standing beside the body; the lion had not
eaten the body nor torn the donkey.
29So the prophet took up the body of the man of God and laid
it on the donkey, and brought it back and he came to the city of
the old prophet to mourn and to bury him.
30And he laid his body in his own grave, and they mourned
over him, *saying*, "Alas, my brother!"
31And it came about after he had buried him, that he spoke to
his sons, saying, "When I die, bury me in the grave in which the
man of God is buried; lay my bones beside his bones.
32"For the thing shall surely come to pass which he cried by the
word of the LORD against the altar in Bethel and against all the
houses of the high places which are in the cities of Samaria."
33¶ After this event Jeroboam did not return from his evil way,
but again he made priests of the high places from among all the
people; any who would, he ordained, to be priests of the high
places.

## New International

11Now there was a certain old prophet living in Bethel, whose
sons came and told him all that the man of God had done there
that day. They also told their father what he had said to the king.
12Their father asked them, "Which way did he go?" And his sons
showed him which road the man of God from Judah had taken.
13So he said to his sons, "Saddle the donkey for me." And when
they had saddled the donkey for him, he mounted it 14and rode
after the man of God. He found him sitting under an oak tree and
asked, "Are you the man of God who came from Judah?"
"I am," he replied.
15So the prophet said to him, "Come home with me and eat."
16The man of God said, "I cannot turn back and go with you,
nor can I eat bread or drink water with you in this place. 17I have
been told by the word of the LORD: 'You must not eat bread or
drink water there or return by the way you came.' "
18The old prophet answered, "I too am a prophet, as you are.
And an angel said to me by the word of the LORD: 'Bring him back
with you to your house so that he may eat bread and drink
water.' " (But he was lying to him.) 19So the man of God returned
with him and ate and drank in his house.
20While they were sitting at the table, the word of the LORD
came to the old prophet who had brought him back. 21He cried out
to the man of God who had come from Judah, "This is what the
LORD says: 'You have defied the word of the LORD and have not
kept the command the LORD your God gave you. 22You came back
and ate bread and drank water in the place where he told you not
to eat or drink. Therefore your body will not be buried in the tomb
of your fathers.' "
23When the man of God had finished eating and drinking, the
prophet who had brought him back saddled his donkey for him.
24As he went on his way, a lion met him on the road and killed
him, and his body was thrown down on the road, with both the
donkey and the lion standing beside it. 25Some people who passed
by saw the body thrown down there, with the lion standing beside
the body, and they went and reported it in the city where the old
prophet lived.
26When the prophet who had brought him back from his journey heard of it, he said, "It is the man of God who defied the word
of the LORD. The LORD has given him over to the lion, which has
mauled him and killed him, as the word of the LORD had warned
him."
27The prophet said to his sons, "Saddle the donkey for me,"
and they did so. 28Then he went out and found the body thrown
down on the road, with the donkey and the lion standing beside
it. The lion had neither eaten the body nor mauled the donkey.
29So the prophet picked up the body of the man of God, laid it on
the donkey, and brought it back to his own city to mourn for him
and bury him. 30Then he laid the body in his own tomb, and they
mourned over him and said, "Oh, my brother!"
31After burying him, he said to his sons, "When I die, bury me
in the grave where the man of God is buried; lay my bones beside
his bones. 32For the message he declared by the word of the LORD
against the altar in Bethel and against all the shrines on the high
places in the towns of Samaria will certainly come true."
33Even after this, Jeroboam did not change his evil ways, but
once more appointed priests for the high places from all sorts of
people. Anyone who wanted to become a priest he consecrated for
the high places. 34This was the sin of the house of Jeroboam that

## King James

34And this thing became sin unto the house of Jeroboam, even
to cut *it* off, and to destroy *it* from off the face of the earth.

**14** AT THAT time Abijah the son of Jeroboam fell sick.
2And Jeroboam said to his wife, Arise, I pray thee, and
disguise thyself, that thou be not known to be the wife of Jeroboam; and get thee to Shiloh: behold, there *is* Ahijah the prophet,
which told me that *I should be* king over this people.
3And take with thee ten loaves, and cracknels, and a cruse of
honey, and go to him: he shall tell thee what shall become of the
child.
4And Jeroboam's wife did so, and arose, and went to Shiloh,
and came to the house of Ahijah. But Ahijah could not see; for his
eyes were set by reason of his age.
5¶ And the LORD said unto Ahijah, Behold, the wife of Jeroboam
cometh to ask a thing of thee for her son; for he *is* sick: thus and
thus shalt thou say unto her: for it shall be, when she cometh in,
that she shall feign herself *to be* another *woman*.
6And it was *so*, when Ahijah heard the sound of her feet, as she
came in at the door, that he said, Come in, thou wife of Jeroboam;
why feignest thou thyself *to be* another? for I *am* sent to thee *with*
heavy *tidings*.
7Go, tell Jeroboam, Thus saith the LORD God of Israel, Forasmuch as I exalted thee from among the people, and made thee
prince over my people Israel,
8And rent the kingdom away from the house of David, and
gave it thee: and *yet* thou hast not been as my servant David, who
kept my commandments, and who followed me with all his heart,
to do *that* only *which was* right in mine eyes;
9But hast done evil above all that were before thee: for thou hast
gone and made thee other gods, and molten images, to provoke
me to anger, and hast cast me behind thy back:
10Therefore, behold, I will bring evil upon the house of Jeroboam, and will cut off from Jeroboam him that pisseth against the
wall, *and* him that is shut up and left in Israel, and will take away
the remnant of the house of Jeroboam, as a man taketh away dung,
till it be all gone.
11Him that dieth of Jeroboam in the city shall the dogs eat; and
him that dieth in the field shall the fowls of the air eat: for the LORD
hath spoken *it*.
12Arise thou therefore, get thee to thine own house: *and* when
thy feet enter into the city, the child shall die.
13And all Israel shall mourn for him, and bury him: for he only
of Jeroboam shall come to the grave, because in him there is found
*some* good thing toward the LORD God of Israel in the house of
Jeroboam.
14Moreover the LORD shall raise him up a king over Israel, who
shall cut off the house of Jeroboam that day: but what? even now.
15For the LORD shall smite Israel, as a reed is shaken in the
water, and he shall root up Israel out of this good land, which he
gave to their fathers, and shall scatter them beyond the river,
because they have made their groves, provoking the LORD to anger.
16And he shall give Israel up because of the sins of Jeroboam,
who did sin, and who made Israel to sin.

**AMP** [a] The Hebrew text gives no particulars about the background of Jeroboam's wife; but there is an insertion in the Septuagint version, found in the Vatican Manuscript after chapter 12:24, and recorded in *Ellicott's Commentary*, in which we find further information about her. When Jeroboam, then taskmaster over the forced labor of the house of Joseph, fled to Egypt to escape death at the hands of King Solomon, he went to King Shishak of Egypt, and was with him until the death of Solomon. Then when Jeroboam asked permission of King Shishak to return to his own land, the king told him, "Ask of me a request, and I will give it to you." And he gave to Jeroboam Ano, the elder sister of his own wife Thekemina [Tahpenes] to be his wife. She was great among the daughters of the king, and bore to Jeroboam Abias [Abijah] his son [who now lies dying in the palace of Jeroboam, while Queen Ano, his mother, is about to hear what the old prophet has been required by God to tell her].

## Amplified

34And this thing became the sin of the dynasty of Jeroboam,
that caused it to be abolished and destroyed from the face of the
earth.

**14** THEN ABIJAH the [little] son of Jeroboam became sick.
2And Jeroboam said to his wife, Arise, I pray you, and
disguise yourself, that you may not be recognized as Jeroboam's
wife, and go to Shiloh. Behold, Ahijah the prophet is there, who
told me that I should be king over this people.
3Take ten loaves, some cakes, and a bottle of honey, and go to
him. He will tell you what shall happen to the child.
4Jeroboam's wife did so. She arose and went [twenty miles] to
Shiloh, and came to the house of Ahijah. Ahijah could not see; for
his eyes were dim because of his age.
5And the Lord said to Ahijah, Behold, the [a]wife of Jeroboam
is coming to ask you concerning her son; for he is sick. Thus and
thus shall you say to her. When she came, she pretended to be
another woman.
6But when Ahijah heard the sound of her feet, as she came in
at the door, he said, Come in, wife of Jeroboam. Why do you
pretend to be another? For I am charged with heavy news for you.
7Go, tell Jeroboam, Thus says the Lord, the God of Israel,
Because I exalted you from among the people, and made you
leader over My people Israel,
8And rent the kingdom away from the house of David, and
gave it to you; and yet you have not been as My servant David,
who kept My commandments and followed Me with all his heart,
to do only what was right in My eyes,
9But have done evil above all who were before you, for you have
made yourself other gods, molten images, to provoke Me to anger,
and have cast Me behind your back;
10Therefore behold, I will bring evil upon the house of Jeroboam, and will cut off from [him] every male, both bond and free
in Israel, and will utterly sweep away the house of Jeroboam, as
a man sweeps away dung, till it is all gone.
11Any one of Jeroboam who dies in the city the dogs shall eat;
and any who dies in the field the birds of the heavens shall eat;
for the Lord has spoken it.
12Arise therefore [Ano], get to your own house. When your feet
enter the city, the child shall die.
13And all Israel shall mourn for him, and bury him; for he only
of Jeroboam shall come to the grave, because in him there is found
something good *and* pleasing to the Lord, the God of Israel, in the
house of Jeroboam.
14Moreover the Lord will raise up for Himself a king over Israel,
who shall cut off the house of Jeroboam this day. From now on
15The Lord will smite Israel, as a reed is shaken in the water,
and He will root up Israel out of this good land, which He gave
to their fathers, and will scatter them beyond the [Euphrates]
River, because they have made their Asherim [idolatrous sym-
bols], provoking the Lord to anger.
16He will give Israel up because of the sins of Jeroboam, which
he has sinned and made Israel to sin.

## New American Standard

34And this event became sin to the house of Jeroboam, even to
blot *it* out and destroy *it* from off the face of the earth.

*Ahijah Prophesies against the King*

**14** AT THAT time Abijah the son of Jeroboam became sick.
2And Jeroboam said to his wife, "Arise now, and disguise
yourself so that they may not know that you are the wife of
Jeroboam, and go to Shiloh; behold, Ahijah the prophet is there,
who spoke concerning me *that I would be* king over this people.
3"And take ten loaves with you, *some* cakes and a jar of honey,
and go to him. He will tell you what will happen to the boy."
4And Jeroboam's wife did so, and arose and went to Shiloh,
and came to the house of Ahijah. Now Ahijah could not see, for
his eyes were dim because of his age.
5Now the LORD had said to Ahijah, "Behold, the wife of Jeroboam is coming to inquire of you concerning her son, for he is sick.
You shall say thus and thus to her, for it will be when she arrives
that she will pretend to be another woman."
6¶ And it came about when Ahijah heard the sound of her feet
coming in the doorway, that he said, "Come in, wife of Jeroboam,
why do you pretend to be another woman? For I am sent to you
*with* a harsh *message.*
7"Go, say to Jeroboam, 'Thus says the LORD God of Israel,
"Because I exalted you from among the people and made you
leader over My people Israel,
8and tore the kingdom away from the house of David and gave
it to you—yet you have not been like My servant David, who kept
My commandments and who followed Me with all his heart, to do
only that which was right in My sight;
9you also have done more evil than all who were before you,
and have gone and made for yourself other gods and molten
images to provoke Me to anger, and have cast Me behind your
back—
10therefore behold, I am bringing calamity on the house of
Jeroboam, and will cut off from Jeroboam every male person, both
bond and free in Israel, and I will make a clean sweep of the house
of Jeroboam, as one sweeps away dung until it is all gone.
11"Anyone belonging to Jeroboam who dies in the city the dogs
will eat. And he who dies in the field the birds of the heavens will
eat; for the LORD has spoken *it.*" '
12"Now you arise, go to your house. When your feet enter the
city the child will die.
13"And all Israel shall mourn for him and bury him, for he alone
of Jeroboam's *family* shall come to the grave, because in him something good was found toward the LORD God of Israel in the house
of Jeroboam.
14"Moreover, the LORD will raise up for Himself a king over
Israel who shall cut off the house of Jeroboam this day and from
now on.
15"For the LORD will strike Israel, as a reed is shaken in the
water; and He will uproot Israel from this good land which He
gave to their fathers, and will scatter them beyond the *Euphrates*
River, because they have made their [b]Asherim, provoking the
LORD to anger.
16"And He will give up Israel on account of the sins of Jeroboam, which he committed and with which he made Israel to sin."

NAS [b] I.e., wooden symbols of a female deity. Also v. 23

## New International

led to its downfall and to its destruction from the face of the earth.

*Ahijah's Prophecy Against Jeroboam*

**14** AT THAT time Abijah son of Jeroboam became ill, 2and
Jeroboam said to his wife, "Go, disguise yourself, so you
won't be recognized as the wife of Jeroboam. Then go to Shiloh.
Ahijah the prophet is there—the one who told me I would be king
over this people. 3Take ten loaves of bread with you, some cakes
and a jar of honey, and go to him. He will tell you what will happen
to the boy." 4So Jeroboam's wife did what he said and went to
Ahijah's house in Shiloh.
Now Ahijah could not see; his sight was gone because of his
age. 5But the LORD had told Ahijah, "Jeroboam's wife is coming
to ask you about her son, for he is ill, and you are to give her such
and such an answer. When she arrives, she will pretend to be
someone else."
6So when Ahijah heard the sound of her footsteps at the door,
he said, "Come in, wife of Jeroboam. Why this pretense? I have
been sent to you with bad news. 7Go, tell Jeroboam that this is
what the LORD, the God of Israel, says: 'I raised you up from
among the people and made you a leader over my people Israel.
8I tore the kingdom away from the house of David and gave it to
you, but you have not been like my servant David, who kept my
commands and followed me with all his heart, doing only what
was right in my eyes. 9You have done more evil than all who lived
before you. You have made for yourself other gods, idols made of
metal; you have provoked me to anger and thrust me behind your
back.
10" 'Because of this, I am going to bring disaster on the house
of Jeroboam. I will cut off from Jeroboam every last male in Israel—
slave or free. I will burn up the house of Jeroboam as one burns
dung, until it is all gone. 11Dogs will eat those belonging to Jeroboam who die in the city, and the birds of the air will feed on those
who die in the country. The LORD has spoken!'
12"As for you, go back home. When you set foot in your city,
the boy will die. 13All Israel will mourn for him and bury him. He
is the only one belonging to Jeroboam who will be buried, because
he is the only one in the house of Jeroboam in whom the LORD,
the God of Israel, has found anything good.
14"The LORD will raise up for himself a king over Israel who will
cut off the family of Jeroboam. This is the day! What? Yes, even
now.[c] 15And the LORD will strike Israel, so that it will be like a reed
swaying in the water. He will uproot Israel from this good land
that he gave to their forefathers and scatter them beyond the
River,[d] because they provoked the LORD to anger by making
Asherah poles.[e] 16And he will give Israel up because of the sins
Jeroboam has committed and has caused Israel to commit."

NIV [c] *14* The meaning of the Hebrew for this sentence is uncertain. [d] *15* That is, the Euphrates [e] *15* That is, symbols of the goddess Asherah; here and elsewhere in 1 Kings

## King James

17¶ And Jeroboam's wife arose, and departed, and came to Tirzah: *and* when she came to the threshold of the door, the child died;

18And they buried him; and all Israel mourned for him, according to the word of the LORD, which he spake by the hand of his servant Ahijah the prophet.

19And the rest of the acts of Jeroboam, how he warred, and how he reigned, behold, they *are* written in the book of the chronicles of the kings of Israel.

20And the days which Jeroboam reigned *were* two and twenty years: and he slept with his fathers, and Nadab his son reigned in his stead.

21¶ And Rehoboam the son of Solomon reigned in Judah. Rehoboam *was* forty and one years old when he began to reign, and he reigned seventeen years in Jerusalem, the city which the LORD did choose out of all the tribes of Israel, to put his name there. And his mother's name *was* Naamah an Ammonitess.

22And Judah did evil in the sight of the LORD, and they provoked him to jealousy with their sins which they had committed, above all that their fathers had done.

23For they also built them high places, and images, and groves, on every high hill, and under every green tree.

24And there were also sodomites in the land: *and* they did according to all the abominations of the nations which the LORD cast out before the children of Israel.

25¶ And it came to pass in the fifth year of king Rehoboam, *that* Shishak king of Egypt came up against Jerusalem:

26And he took away the treasures of the house of the LORD, and the treasures of the king's house; he even took away all: and he took away all the shields of gold which Solomon had made.

27And king Rehoboam made in their stead brasen shields, and committed *them* unto the hands of the chief of the guard, which kept the door of the king's house.

28And it was *so*, when the king went into the house of the LORD, that the guard bare them, and brought them back into the guard chamber.

29¶ Now the rest of the acts of Rehoboam, and all that he did, *are* they not written in the book of the chronicles of the kings of Judah?

30And there was war between Rehoboam and Jeroboam all *their* days.

31And Rehoboam slept with his fathers, and was buried with his fathers in the city of David. And his mother's name *was* Naamah an Ammonitess. And Abijam his son reigned in his stead.

**15** NOW IN the eighteenth year of king Jeroboam the son of Nebat reigned Abijam over Judah.

2Three years reigned he in Jerusalem. And his mother's name *was* Maachah, the daughter of Abishalom.

3And he walked in all the sins of his father, which he had done before him: and his heart was not perfect with the LORD his God, as the heart of David his father.

4Nevertheless for David's sake did the LORD his God give him a lamp in Jerusalem, to set up his son after him, and to establish Jerusalem:

5Because David did *that which was* right in the eyes of the LORD, and turned not aside from any *thing* that he commanded him all the days of his life, save only in the matter of Uriah the Hittite.

6And there was war between Rehoboam and Jeroboam all the days of his life.

## Amplified

17So Jeroboam's wife departed, and came to Tirzah. When she came to the threshold of the house, the child died.

18And all Israel buried him and mourned for him, according to the word of the Lord, spoken by His servant Ahijah the prophet.

19The rest of the acts of Jeroboam, how he warred and how he reigned, behold, they are written in the Book of the Chronicles of the Kings of Israel.

20Jeroboam reigned twenty-two years; and he slept with his fathers, and Nadab his son reigned in his stead.

21And Rehoboam the son of Solomon reigned in Judah. Rehoboam was forty-one years old when he began to reign, and he reigned seventeen years in Jerusalem, the city the Lord chose out of all the tribes of Israel, to put His name [and the pledge of His presence] there. His mother's name was Naamah the Ammonitess.

22And Judah did evil in the sight of the Lord, Whom they provoked to jealousy with the sins they committed, above all that their fathers had done.

23For they also built themselves [idolatrous] high places, pillars and [Asherim] groves, on every high hill and under every green tree;

24There were also sodomites [male cult prostitutes] in the land. They did all the abominations of the nations whom the Lord cast out before the Israelites.

25In the fifth year of King Rehoboam, Shishak king of Egypt [Jeroboam's brother-in-law] came up against Jerusalem;

26He took away the treasures of the house of the Lord and of the king's house; he took away all, including all the shields of gold which Solomon had made.

27King Rehoboam made in their stead bronze shields, and committed them to the hands of the captains of the guard, who kept the door of the king's house.

28And as often as the king went into the house of the Lord, the guard bore them, and brought them back into the guardroom.

29The rest of the acts of Rehoboam, and all that he did, are they not written in the Book of the Chronicles of the Kings of Judah?

30There was war between Rehoboam and Jeroboam continually.

31Rehoboam slept with his fathers, and was buried with them in the city of David. His mother's name was Naamah the Ammonitess. Abijam [Abijah] his son reigned in his stead.

**15** IN THE eighteenth year of King Jeroboam son of Nebat, Abijam began to reign over Judah.

2He reigned three years in Jerusalem. His mother was Maachah [Micaiah] the daughter [granddaughter] of Abishalom [Absalom].

3He walked in all the sins of his father [Rehoboam] before him; and his heart was not blameless with the Lord his God, as the heart of David his father [forefather].

4Nevertheless for David's sake the Lord his God gave him a lamp in Jerusalem, setting up his son after him and establishing Jerusalem;

5Because David did what was right in the eyes of the Lord, and turned not aside from anything that He commanded him all the days of his life, except only in the matter of Uriah the Hittite.

6There was war between [Abijam's father] Rehoboam and Jeroboam all the days of [Rehoboam's] life.

## New American Standard

17¶ Then Jeroboam's wife arose and departed and came to Tirzah. As she was entering the threshold of the house, the child
died.
18And all Israel buried him and mourned for him, according to
the word of the LORD which He spoke through His servant Ahijah
the prophet.
19¶ Now the rest of the acts of Jeroboam, how he made war and
how he reigned, behold, they are written in the Book of the
Chronicles of the Kings of Israel.
20And the time that Jeroboam reigned *was* twenty-two years;
and he slept with his fathers, and Nadab his son reigned in his
place.

*Rehoboam Misleads Judah*

21¶ Now Rehoboam the son of Solomon reigned in Judah. Rehoboam was forty-one years old when he became king, and he
reigned seventeen years in Jerusalem, the city which the LORD had
chosen from all the tribes of Israel to put His name there. And his
mother's name was Naamah the Ammonitess.
22And Judah did evil in the sight of the LORD, and they provoked Him to jealousy more than all that their fathers had done,
with the sins which they committed.
23For they also built for themselves high places and *sacred* pillars
and Asherim on every high hill and beneath every luxuriant tree.
24And there were also male cult prostitutes in the land. They
did according to all the abominations of the nations which the
LORD dispossessed before the sons of Israel.
25¶ Now it came about in the fifth year of King Rehoboam, that
Shishak the king of Egypt came up against Jerusalem.
26And he took away the treasures of the house of the LORD and
the treasures of the king's house, and he took everything, even
taking all the shields of gold which Solomon had made.
27So King Rehoboam made shields of bronze in their place, and
committed them to the care of the commanders of the [a]guard who
guarded the doorway of the king's house.
28Then it happened as often as the king entered the house of
the LORD, that the [b]guards would carry them and would bring
them back into the guards' room.
29¶ Now the rest of the acts of Rehoboam and all that he did,
are they not written in the Book of the Chronicles of the Kings of
Judah?
30And there was war between Rehoboam and Jeroboam continually.
31And Rehoboam slept with his fathers, and was buried with
his fathers in the city of David; and his mother's name was Naamah the Ammonitess. And Abijam his son became king in his
place.

*Abijam Reigns over Judah*

15 NOW IN the eighteenth year of King Jeroboam, the son
of Nebat, Abijam became king over Judah.
2He reigned three years in Jerusalem; and his mother's name
was Maacah the daughter of Abishalom.
3And he walked in all the sins of his father which he had
committed before him; and his heart was not wholly devoted to the
LORD his God, like the heart of his father David.
4But for David's sake the LORD his God gave him a lamp in
Jerusalem, to raise up his son after him and to establish Jerusalem;
5because David did what was right in the sight of the LORD,
and had not turned aside from anything that He commanded him
all the days of his life, except in the case of Uriah the Hittite.
6And there was war between Rehoboam and Jeroboam all the
days of his life.

NAS [a] Lit., *runner(s)* [b] Lit., *runner(s)*

## New International

17Then Jeroboam's wife got up and left and went to Tirzah. As
soon as she stepped over the threshold of the house, the boy died.
18They buried him, and all Israel mourned for him, as the LORD
had said through his servant the prophet Ahijah.
19The other events of Jeroboam's reign, his wars and how he
ruled, are written in the book of the annals of the kings of Israel.
20He reigned for twenty-two years and then rested with his fathers. And Nadab his son succeeded him as king.

*Rehoboam King of Judah*

21Rehoboam son of Solomon was king in Judah. He was forty-
one years old when he became king, and he reigned seventeen
years in Jerusalem, the city the LORD had chosen out of all the
tribes of Israel in which to put his Name. His mother's name was
Naamah; she was an Ammonite.
22Judah did evil in the eyes of the LORD. By the sins they
committed they stirred up his jealous anger more than their fathers
had done. 23They also set up for themselves high places, sacred
stones and Asherah poles on every high hill and under every
spreading tree. 24There were even male shrine prostitutes in the
land; the people engaged in all the detestable practices of the
nations the LORD had driven out before the Israelites.
25In the fifth year of King Rehoboam, Shishak king of Egypt
attacked Jerusalem. 26He carried off the treasures of the temple of
the LORD and the treasures of the royal palace. He took everything,
including all the gold shields Solomon had made. 27So King Rehoboam made bronze shields to replace them and assigned these to
the commanders of the guard on duty at the entrance to the royal
palace. 28Whenever the king went to the LORD's temple, the
guards bore the shields, and afterward they returned them to the
guardroom.
29As for the other events of Rehoboam's reign, and all he did,
are they not written in the book of the annals of the kings of Judah?
30There was continual warfare between Rehoboam and Jeroboam.
31And Rehoboam rested with his fathers and was buried with them
in the City of David. His mother's name was Naamah; she was an
Ammonite. And Abijah[c] his son succeeded him as king.

*Abijah King of Judah*

15 IN THE eighteenth year of the reign of Jeroboam son of
Nebat, Abijah[d] became king of Judah, 2and he reigned in
Jerusalem three years. His mother's name was Maacah daughter
of Abishalom.[e]
3He committed all the sins his father had done before him; his
heart was not fully devoted to the LORD his God, as the heart of
David his forefather had been. 4Nevertheless, for David's sake the
LORD his God gave him a lamp in Jerusalem by raising up a son
to succeed him and by making Jerusalem strong. 5For David had
done what was right in the eyes of the LORD and had not failed to
keep any of the LORD's commands all the days of his life—except
in the case of Uriah the Hittite.
6There was war between Rehoboam[f] and Jeroboam throughout
⌞Abijah's⌟ lifetime. 7As for the other events of Abijah's reign, and

NIV [c] *31* Some Hebrew manuscripts and Septuagint (see also 2 Chron. 12:16); most Hebrew manuscripts *Abijam* [d] *1* Some Hebrew manuscripts and Septuagint (see also 2 Chron. 12:16); most Hebrew manuscripts *Abijam;* also in verses 7 and 8 [e] *2* A variant of *Absalom;* also in verse 10 [f] *6* Most Hebrew manuscripts; some Hebrew manuscripts and Syriac *Abijam* (that is, Abijah)

## King James

7Now the rest of the acts of Abijam, and all that he did, *are* they not written in the book of the chronicles of the kings of Judah? And there was war between Abijam and Jeroboam.

8And Abijam slept with his fathers; and they buried him in the city of David: and Asa his son reigned in his stead.

9¶ And in the twentieth year of Jeroboam king of Israel reigned Asa over Judah.

10And forty and one years reigned he in Jerusalem. And his mother's name *was* Maachah, the daughter of Abishalom.

11And Asa did *that which was* right in the eyes of the LORD, as *did* David his father.

12And he took away the sodomites out of the land, and removed all the idols that his fathers had made.

13And also Maachah his mother, even her he removed from *being* queen, because she had made an idol in a grove; and Asa destroyed her idol, and burnt *it* by the brook Kidron.

14But the high places were not removed: nevertheless Asa's heart was perfect with the LORD all his days.

15And he brought in the things which his father had dedicated, and the things which himself had dedicated, into the house of the LORD, silver, and gold, and vessels.

16¶ And there was war between Asa and Baasha king of Israel all their days.

17And Baasha king of Israel went up against Judah, and built Ramah, that he might not suffer any to go out or come in to Asa king of Judah.

18Then Asa took all the silver and the gold *that were* left in the treasures of the house of the LORD, and the treasures of the king's house, and delivered them into the hand of his servants: and king Asa sent them to Ben-hadad, the son of Tabrimon, the son of Hezion, king of Syria, that dwelt at Damascus, saying,

19 *There is* a league between me and thee, *and* between my father and thy father: behold, I have sent unto thee a present of silver and gold; come and break thy league with Baasha king of Israel, that he may depart from me.

20So Ben-hadad hearkened unto king Asa, and sent the captains of the hosts which he had against the cities of Israel, and smote Ijon, and Dan, and Abel-beth-maachah, and all Cinneroth, with all the land of Naphtali.

21And it came to pass, when Baasha heard *thereof*, that he left off building of Ramah, and dwelt in Tirzah.

22Then king Asa made a proclamation throughout all Judah; none *was* exempted: and they took away the stones of Ramah, and the timber thereof, wherewith Baasha had builded; and king Asa built with them Geba of Benjamin, and Mizpah.

23The rest of all the acts of Asa, and all his might, and all that he did, and the cities which he built, *are* they not written in the book of the chronicles of the kings of Judah? Nevertheless in the time of his old age he was diseased in his feet.

24And Asa slept with his fathers, and was buried with his fathers in the city of David his father: and Jehoshaphat his son reigned in his stead.

25¶ And Nadab the son of Jeroboam began to reign over Israel in the second year of Asa king of Judah, and reigned over Israel two years.

26And he did evil in the sight of the LORD, and walked in the way of his father, and in his sin wherewith he made Israel to sin.

27¶ And Baasha the son of Ahijah, of the house of Issachar, conspired against him; and Baasha smote him at Gibbethon, which *belonged* to the Philistines; for Nadab and all Israel laid siege to Gibbethon.

28Even in the third year of Asa king of Judah did Baasha slay him, and reigned in his stead.

## Amplified

7The rest of the acts of Abijam, and all that he did, are they not written in the Book of the Chronicles of the Kings of Judah? And there was war between Abijam and Jeroboam.

8Abijam slept with his fathers, and they buried him in the city of David. Asa his son reigned in his stead.

9In the twentieth year of Jeroboam king of Israel Asa began to reign over Judah.

10Forty-one years he reigned in Jerusalem. His mother was [also named] Maacah [Micaiah], the daughter of Abishalom [Absalom]. [Cp. v. 2.]

11And Asa did right in the eyes of the Lord, as did David his father [forefather].

12He put away the sodomites [male cult prostitutes] out of the land, and removed all the idols that his fathers [Solomon, Rehoboam, and Abijam] had made *or* promoted. [11:5-11; 14:22.]

13Also Maacah his mother he removed from being queen mother, because she had an image made for [the goddess] Asherah. Asa destroyed her image, burning it by the brook Kidron.

14But the high places were not removed. Yet Asa's heart was blameless with the Lord all his days.

15He brought the things which his father had dedicated and the things which he himself had dedicated into the house of the Lord, silver, gold, and vessels.

16There was war between Asa and Baasha king of Israel all their days.

17Baasha king of Israel went up against Judah, and built Ramah, that he might allow no one to go out or come in to Asa king of Judah.

18Then Asa took all the silver and gold left in the treasuries of the house of the Lord and of the king's house, and delivered them into the hands of his servants; and King Asa sent them to Benhadad son of Tabrimmon, son of Hezion, king of Syria, who dwelt at Damascus, saying,

19Let there be a league between me and you, as between my father and your father. Behold, I am sending you a present of silver and gold; go, break your league with Baasha king of Israel, that he may withdraw from me.

20So Benhadad hearkened to king Asa, and sent the commanders of his armies against the cities of Israel, and smote Ijon, Dan, and Abel-beth-maacah, and all Chinneroth, with all the land of Naphtali.

21When Baasha heard of it, he quit building Ramah, and dwelt in Tirzah.

22Then King Asa made a proclamation to all Judah; none was exempted. They carried away the stones of Ramah and its timber, with which Baasha had been building; and King Asa built with them Geba of Benjamin, and Mizpah.

23The rest of all the acts of Asa, all his might, all that he did, and the cities which he built, are they not written in the Book of the Chronicles of the Kings of Judah? But in the time of his old age he was diseased in his feet.

24Asa slept with his fathers, and was buried with *them* in the city of David his father. Jehoshaphat his son reigned in his stead.

25Nadab son of Jeroboam began to reign over Israel in the second year of Asa king of Judah, and reigned two years.

26He did evil in the sight of the Lord, and walked in the way of his father, and in his sin with which he made Israel sin.

27Baasha son of Ahijah, of the house of Issachar, conspired against Nadab; and Baasha smote him at Gibbethon, which belonged to the Philistines; for Nadab and all Israel were laying siege to Gibbethon.

28In the third year of Asa king of Judah Baasha slew Nadab and reigned in his stead.

## New American Standard

7¶ Now the rest of the acts of Abijam and all that he did, are they not written in the Book of the Chronicles of the Kings of Judah? And there was war between Abijam and Jeroboam.

*Asa Succeeds Abijam*

8And Abijam slept with his fathers and they buried him in the city of David; and Asa his son became king in his place.

9¶ So in the twentieth year of Jeroboam the king of Israel, Asa began to reign as king of Judah.

10And he reigned forty-one years in Jerusalem; and his mother's name was Maacah the daughter of Abishalom.

11And Asa did what was right in the sight of the LORD, like David his father.

12He also put away the male cult prostitutes from the land, and removed all the idols which his fathers had made.

13And he also removed Maacah his mother from *being* queen mother, because she had made a horrid image as an Asherah; and Asa cut down her horrid image and burned *it* at the brook Kidron.

14But the high places were not taken away; nevertheless the heart of Asa was wholly devoted to the LORD all his days.

15And he brought into the house of the LORD the dedicated things of his father and his own dedicated things: silver and gold and utensils.

16¶ Now there was war between Asa and Baasha king of Israel all their days.

17And Baasha king of Israel went up against Judah and fortified Ramah in order to prevent *anyone* from going out or coming in to Asa king of Judah.

18Then Asa took all the silver and the gold which were left in the treasuries of the house of the LORD and the treasuries of the king's house, and delivered them into the hand of his servants. And King Asa sent them to Ben-hadad the son of Tabrimmon, the son of Hezion, king of Aram, who lived in Damascus, saying,

19" *Let there be* a treaty between you and me, *as* between my father and your father. Behold, I have sent you a present of silver and gold; go, break your treaty with Baasha king of Israel so that he will withdraw from me."

20So Ben-hadad listened to King Asa and sent the commanders of his armies against the cities of Israel, and conquered Ijon, Dan, Abel-beth-maacah and all Chinneroth, besides all the land of Naphtali.

21And it came about when Baasha heard *of it* that he ceased fortifying Ramah, and remained in Tirzah.

22Then King Asa made a proclamation to all Judah—none was exempt—and they carried away the stones of Ramah and its timber with which Baasha had built. And King Asa built with them Geba of Benjamin and Mizpah.

*Jehoshaphat Succeeds Asa*

23¶ Now the rest of all the acts of Asa and all his might and all that he did and the cities which he built, are they not written in the Book of the Chronicles of the Kings of Judah? But in the time of his old age he was diseased in his feet.

24And Asa slept with his fathers and was buried with his fathers in the city of David his father; and Jehoshaphat his son reigned in his place.

*Nadab, then Baasha, Rules over Israel*

25Now Nadab the son of Jeroboam became king over Israel in the second year of Asa king of Judah, and he reigned over Israel two years.

26And he did evil in the sight of the LORD, and walked in the way of his father and in his sin which he made Israel sin.

27Then Baasha the son of Ahijah of the house of Issachar conspired against him, and Baasha struck him down at Gibbethon, which belonged to the Philistines, while Nadab and all Israel were laying siege to Gibbethon.

28So Baasha killed him in the third year of Asa king of Judah, and reigned in his place.

## New International

all he did, are they not written in the book of the annals of the kings
of Judah? There was war between Abijah and Jeroboam. 8And
Abijah rested with his fathers and was buried in the City of David.
And Asa his son succeeded him as king.

*Asa King of Judah*

9In the twentieth year of Jeroboam king of Israel, Asa became
king of Judah, 10and he reigned in Jerusalem forty-one years. His
grandmother's name was Maacah daughter of Abishalom.
11Asa did what was right in the eyes of the LORD, as his father
David had done. 12He expelled the male shrine prostitutes from
the land and got rid of all the idols his fathers had made. 13He even
deposed his grandmother Maacah from her position as queen
mother, because she had made a repulsive Asherah pole. Asa cut
the pole down and burned it in the Kidron Valley. 14Although he
did not remove the high places, Asa's heart was fully committed
to the LORD all his life. 15He brought into the temple of the LORD
the silver and gold and the articles that he and his father had
dedicated.

16There was war between Asa and Baasha king of Israel
throughout their reigns. 17Baasha king of Israel went up against
Judah and fortified Ramah to prevent anyone from leaving or
entering the territory of Asa king of Judah.

18Asa then took all the silver and gold that was left in the
treasuries of the LORD's temple and of his own palace. He entrusted it to his officials and sent them to Ben-Hadad son of Tabrimmon, the son of Hezion, the king of Aram, who was ruling in
Damascus. 19"Let there be a treaty between me and you," he said,
"as there was between my father and your father. See, I am sending you a gift of silver and gold. Now break your treaty with
Baasha king of Israel so he will withdraw from me."

20Ben-Hadad agreed with King Asa and sent the commanders
of his forces against the towns of Israel. He conquered Ijon, Dan,
Abel Beth Maacah and all Kinnereth in addition to Naphtali.
21When Baasha heard this, he stopped building Ramah and withdrew to Tirzah. 22Then King Asa issued an order to all Judah—no
one was exempt—and they carried away from Ramah the stones
and timber Baasha had been using there. With them King Asa built
up Geba in Benjamin, and also Mizpah.

23As for all the other events of Asa's reign, all his achievements,
all he did and the cities he built, are they not written in the book
of the annals of the kings of Judah? In his old age, however, his
feet became diseased. 24Then Asa rested with his fathers and was
buried with them in the city of his father David. And Jehoshaphat
his son succeeded him as king.

*Nadab King of Israel*

25Nadab son of Jeroboam became king of Israel in the second
year of Asa king of Judah, and he reigned over Israel two years.
26He did evil in the eyes of the LORD, walking in the ways of his
father and in his sin, which he had caused Israel to commit.

27Baasha son of Ahijah of the house of Issachar plotted against
him, and he struck him down at Gibbethon, a Philistine town,
while Nadab and all Israel were besieging it. 28Baasha killed Nadab
in the third year of Asa king of Judah and succeeded him as king.

## King James

29 And it came to pass, when he reigned, *that* he smote all the house of Jeroboam; he left not to Jeroboam any that breathed, until he had destroyed him, according unto the saying of the LORD, which he spake by his servant Ahijah the Shilonite:

30 Because of the sins of Jeroboam which he sinned, and which he made Israel sin, by his provocation wherewith he provoked the LORD God of Israel to anger.

31 ¶ Now the rest of the acts of Nadab, and all that he did, *are* they not written in the book of the chronicles of the kings of Israel?

32 And there was war between Asa and Baasha king of Israel all their days.

33 In the third year of Asa king of Judah began Baasha the son of Ahijah to reign over all Israel in Tirzah, twenty and four years.

34 And he did evil in the sight of the LORD, and walked in the way of Jeroboam, and in his sin wherewith he made Israel to sin.

**16** THEN THE word of the LORD came to Jehu the son of Hanani against Baasha, saying,

2 Forasmuch as I exalted thee out of the dust, and made thee prince over my people Israel; and thou hast walked in the way of Jeroboam, and hast made my people Israel to sin, to provoke me to anger with their sins;

3 Behold, I will take away the posterity of Baasha, and the posterity of his house; and will make thy house like the house of Jeroboam the son of Nebat.

4 Him that dieth of Baasha in the city shall the dogs eat; and him that dieth of his in the fields shall the fowls of the air eat.

5 Now the rest of the acts of Baasha, and what he did, and his might, *are* they not written in the book of the chronicles of the kings of Israel?

6 So Baasha slept with his fathers, and was buried in Tirzah: and Elah his son reigned in his stead.

7 And also by the hand of the prophet Jehu the son of Hanani came the word of the LORD against Baasha, and against his house, even for all the evil that he did in the sight of the LORD, in provoking him to anger with the work of his hands, in being like the house of Jeroboam; and because he killed him.

8 ¶ In the twenty and sixth year of Asa king of Judah began Elah the son of Baasha to reign over Israel in Tirzah, two years.

9 And his servant Zimri, captain of half *his* chariots, conspired against him, as he was in Tirzah, drinking himself drunk in the house of Arza steward of *his* house in Tirzah.

10 And Zimri went in and smote him, and killed him, in the twenty and seventh year of Asa king of Judah, and reigned in his stead.

11 ¶ And it came to pass, when he began to reign, as soon as he sat on his throne, *that* he slew all the house of Baasha: he left him not one that pisseth against a wall, neither of his kinsfolks, nor of his friends.

12 Thus did Zimri destroy all the house of Baasha, according to the word of the LORD, which he spake against Baasha by Jehu the prophet,

13 For all the sins of Baasha, and the sins of Elah his son, by which they sinned, and by which they made Israel to sin, in provoking the LORD God of Israel to anger with their vanities.

14 Now the rest of the acts of Elah, and all that he did, *are* they not written in the book of the chronicles of the kings of Israel?

15 ¶ In the twenty and seventh year of Asa king of Judah did Zimri reign seven days in Tirzah. And the people *were* encamped against Gibbethon, which *belonged* to the Philistines.

## Amplified

29 As soon as he was king, Baasha killed all the household of Jeroboam; he left to [it] not one who breathed, until he had destroyed it, according to the word of the Lord, which He spoke by His servant Ahijah the Shilonite; [I Kings 14:9-16.]

30 Because of the sins of Jeroboam which he sinned and by which he made Israel to sin, and because of his provocation of the Lord, the God of Israel, to anger.

31 The rest of Nadab's acts, and all that he did, are they not written in the Book of the Chronicles of the Kings of Israel?

32 There was war between Asa and Baasha king of Israel all their days.

33 In the third year of Asa king of Judah, Baasha son of Ahijah began his reign of twenty-four years over all Israel in Tirzah.

34 He did evil in the sight of the Lord, and walked in the way of Jeroboam, and in his sin with which he made Israel sin.

**16** AND THE word of the Lord came to Jehu the son of Hanani against Baasha, saying,

2 Because I exalted you [Baasha] out of the dust and made you leader over My people Israel, and you have walked in the way of Jeroboam and have made My people Israel sin, to provoke Me to anger with their sins,

3 Behold, I will utterly sweep away Baasha and his house, and will make your house like [that] of Jeroboam son of Nebat.

4 Any of Baasha's family who dies in the city the dogs shall eat, and any of his who dies in the field the birds of the heavens shall eat.

5 Now the rest of the acts of Baasha, what he did, and his might, are they not written in the Book of the Chronicles of the Kings of Israel?

6 Baasha slept with his fathers, and was buried in Tirzah. Elah his son reigned in his stead.

7 Also the word of the Lord against Baasha and his house came by the prophet Jehu son of Hanani for all the evil that Baasha did in the sight of the Lord, in provoking Him to anger with [idols] the work of his hands, in being like the house of Jeroboam, and also because he destroyed it [the family of Jeroboam, of his own accord].

8 In the twenty-sixth year of Asa king of Judah, Elah son of Baasha began his reign of two years over Israel in Tirzah.

9 Elah's servant Zimri, captain of half his chariots, conspired against Elah. He was in Tirzah, drinking himself drunk in the house of Arza, who was over the household in Tirzah.

10 Zimri came in and smote and killed him, in the twenty-seventh year of Asa king of Judah, and reigned in his stead.

11 When he began to reign, as soon as he sat on his throne, he killed all the household of Baasha; he left not one male of his kinsmen or his friends.

12 Thus Zimri destroyed all the house of Baasha, according to the word of the Lord, which He spoke against Baasha by Jehu the prophet, [v. 3.]

13 For all the sins of Baasha and of Elah his son, by which they sinned and made Israel sin, in provoking the Lord God of Israel to anger with their idols.

14 The rest of the acts of Elah, and all he did, are they not written in the Book of the Chronicles of the Kings of Israel?

15 In the twenty-seventh year of Asa king of Judah Zimri reigned seven days in Tirzah. The troops were encamped against Gibbethon, which belonged to the Philistines,

## New American Standard

29 And it came about, as soon as he was king, he struck down
all the household of Jeroboam. He did not leave to Jeroboam any
persons alive, until he had destroyed them, according to the word
of the LORD, which He spoke by His servant Ahijah the Shilonite,
30 *and* because of the sins of Jeroboam which he sinned, and
which he made Israel sin, because of his provocation with which
he provoked the LORD God of Israel to anger.
31 ¶ Now the rest of the acts of Nadab and all that he did, are
they not written in the Book of the Chronicles of the Kings of
Israel?

*War with Judah*

32 And there was war between Asa and Baasha king of Israel all
their days.
33 ¶ In the third year of Asa king of Judah, Baasha the son of
Ahijah became king over all Israel at Tirzah, *and reigned* twenty-
four years.
34 And he did evil in the sight of the LORD, and walked in the
way of Jeroboam and in his sin which he made Israel sin.

*Prophecy against Baasha*

**16** NOW THE word of the LORD came to Jehu the son of
Hanani against Baasha, saying,
2 "Inasmuch as I exalted you from the dust and made you
leader over My people Israel, and you have walked in the way of
Jeroboam and have made My people Israel sin, provoking Me to
anger with their sins,
3 behold, I will consume Baasha and his house, and I will make
your house like the house of Jeroboam the son of Nebat.
4 "Anyone of Baasha who dies in the city the dogs shall eat, and
anyone of his who dies in the field the birds of the heavens will
eat."
5 ¶ Now the rest of the acts of Baasha and what he did and his
might, are they not written in the Book of the Chronicles of the
Kings of Israel?

*The Israelite Kings*

6 And Baasha slept with his fathers and was buried in Tirzah,
and Elah his son became king in his place.
7 Moreover, the word of the LORD through the prophet Jehu the
son of Hanani also came against Baasha and his household, both
because of all the evil which he did in the sight of the LORD,
provoking Him to anger with the work of his hands, in being like
the house of Jeroboam, and because he struck it.
8 ¶ In the twenty-sixth year of Asa king of Judah, Elah the son
of Baasha became king over Israel at Tirzah, *and reigned* two years.
9 And his servant Zimri, commander of half his chariots, conspired against him. Now he *was* at Tirzah drinking himself drunk
in the house of Arza, who *was* over the household at Tirzah.
10 Then Zimri went in and struck him and put him to death, in
the twenty-seventh year of Asa king of Judah, and became king in
his place.
11 And it came about, when he became king, as soon as he sat
on his throne, that he killed all the household of Baasha; he did
not leave a single male, neither of his relatives nor of his friends.
12 Thus Zimri destroyed all the household of Baasha, according
to the word of the LORD, which He spoke against Baasha through
Jehu the prophet,
13 for all the sins of Baasha and the sins of Elah his son, which
they sinned and which they made Israel sin, provoking the LORD
God of Israel to anger with their idols.
14 Now the rest of the acts of Elah and all that he did, are they
not written in the Book of the Chronicles of the Kings of Israel?
15 ¶ In the twenty-seventh year of Asa king of Judah, Zimri
reigned seven days at Tirzah. Now the people were camped
against Gibbethon, which belonged to the Philistines.

## New International

29 As soon as he began to reign, he killed Jeroboam's whole
family. He did not leave Jeroboam anyone that breathed, but destroyed them all, according to the word of the LORD given through
his servant Ahijah the Shilonite— 30 because of the sins Jeroboam
had committed and had caused Israel to commit, and because he
provoked the LORD, the God of Israel, to anger.
31 As for the other events of Nadab's reign, and all he did, are
they not written in the book of the annals of the kings of Israel?
32 There was war between Asa and Baasha king of Israel throughout their reigns.

*Baasha King of Israel*

33 In the third year of Asa king of Judah, Baasha son of Ahijah
became king of all Israel in Tirzah, and he reigned twenty-four
years. 34 He did evil in the eyes of the LORD, walking in the ways
of Jeroboam and in his sin, which he had caused Israel to commit.

**16** THEN THE word of the LORD came to Jehu son of Hanani
against Baasha: 2 "I lifted you up from the dust and made
you leader of my people Israel, but you walked in the ways of
Jeroboam and caused my people Israel to sin and to provoke me
to anger by their sins. 3 So I am about to consume Baasha and his
house, and I will make your house like that of Jeroboam son of
Nebat. 4 Dogs will eat those belonging to Baasha who die in the
city, and the birds of the air will feed on those who die in the
country."
5 As for the other events of Baasha's reign, what he did and his
achievements, are they not written in the book of the annals of the
kings of Israel? 6 Baasha rested with his fathers and was buried in
Tirzah. And Elah his son succeeded him as king.
7 Moreover, the word of the LORD came through the prophet
Jehu son of Hanani to Baasha and his house, because of all the evil
he had done in the eyes of the LORD, provoking him to anger by
the things he did, and becoming like the house of Jeroboam—and
also because he destroyed it.

*Elah King of Israel*

8 In the twenty-sixth year of Asa king of Judah, Elah son of
Baasha became king of Israel, and he reigned in Tirzah two years.
9 Zimri, one of his officials, who had command of half his chariots, plotted against him. Elah was in Tirzah at the time, getting
drunk in the home of Arza, the man in charge of the palace at
Tirzah. 10 Zimri came in, struck him down and killed him in the
twenty-seventh year of Asa king of Judah. Then he succeeded him
as king.
11 As soon as he began to reign and was seated on the throne,
he killed off Baasha's whole family. He did not spare a single male,
whether relative or friend. 12 So Zimri destroyed the whole family
of Baasha, in accordance with the word of the LORD spoken against
Baasha through the prophet Jehu— 13 because of all the sins Baasha
and his son Elah had committed and had caused Israel to commit,
so that they provoked the LORD, the God of Israel, to anger by their
worthless idols.
14 As for the other events of Elah's reign, and all he did, are they
not written in the book of the annals of the kings of Israel?

*Zimri King of Israel*

15 In the twenty-seventh year of Asa king of Judah, Zimri
reigned in Tirzah seven days. The army was encamped near
Gibbethon, a Philistine town. 16 When the Israelites in the camp

## King James

16And the people *that were* encamped heard say, Zimri hath
conspired, and hath also slain the king: wherefore all Israel made
Omri, the captain of the host, king over Israel that day in the camp.
17And Omri went up from Gibbethon, and all Israel with him,
and they besieged Tirzah.
18And it came to pass, when Zimri saw that the city was taken,
that he went into the palace of the king's house, and burnt the
king's house over him with fire, and died,
19For his sins which he sinned in doing evil in the sight of the
LORD, in walking in the way of Jeroboam, and in his sin which he
did, to make Israel to sin.
20Now the rest of the acts of Zimri, and his treason that he
wrought, *are* they not written in the book of the chronicles of the
kings of Israel?
21¶ Then were the people of Israel divided into two parts: half
of the people followed Tibni the son of Ginath, to make him king;
and half followed Omri.
22But the people that followed Omri prevailed against the
people that followed Tibni the son of Ginath: so Tibni died, and
Omri reigned.
23¶ In the thirty and first year of Asa king of Judah began Omri
to reign over Israel, twelve years: six years reigned he in Tirzah.
24And he bought the hill Samaria of Shemer for two talents of
silver, and built on the hill, and called the name of the city which
he built, after the name of Shemer, owner of the hill, Samaria.
25¶ But Omri wrought evil in the eyes of the LORD, and did
worse than all that *were* before him.
26For he walked in all the way of Jeroboam the son of Nebat,
and in his sin wherewith he made Israel to sin, to provoke the
LORD God of Israel to anger with their vanities.
27Now the rest of the acts of Omri which he did, and his might
that he showed, *are* they not written in the book of the chronicles
of the kings of Israel?
28So Omri slept with his fathers, and was buried in Samaria:
and Ahab his son reigned in his stead.
29¶ And in the thirty and eighth year of Asa king of Judah began
Ahab the son of Omri to reign over Israel: and Ahab the son of
Omri reigned over Israel in Samaria twenty and two years.
30And Ahab the son of Omri did evil in the sight of the LORD
above all that *were* before him.
31And it came to pass, as if it had been a light thing for him to
walk in the sins of Jeroboam the son of Nebat, that he took to wife
Jezebel the daughter of Ethbaal king of the Zidonians, and went
and served Baal, and worshipped him.
32And he reared up an altar for Baal in the house of Baal, which
he had built in Samaria.
33And Ahab made a grove; and Ahab did more to provoke the
LORD God of Israel to anger than all the kings of Israel that were
before him.
34¶ In his days did Hiel the Beth-elite build Jericho: he laid the
foundation thereof in Abiram his firstborn, and set up the gates
thereof in his youngest *son* Segub, according to the word of the
LORD, which he spake by Joshua the son of Nun.

17 AND ELIJAH the Tishbite, *who was* of the inhabitants of
Gilead, said unto Ahab, *As* the LORD God of Israel liveth,
before whom I stand, there shall not be dew nor rain these years,
but according to my word.
2And the word of the LORD came unto him, saying,
3Get thee hence, and turn thee eastward, and hide thyself by
the brook Cherith, that *is* before Jordan.
4And it shall be, *that* thou shalt drink of the brook; and I have
commanded the ravens to feed thee there.

## Amplified

16And they heard the rumor, Zimri has conspired and slain the
king! So all Israel made Omri, the commander of the army, king
over Israel that day in the camp.
17So Omri went up from Gibbethon, and all Israel with him, and
they besieged Tirzah.
18And when Zimri saw that the city was taken, he went into the
stronghold of the king's house, and burned the king's house over
him with fire, and died,
19Because of his sins committed in doing evil in the sight of the
Lord, in walking in the way of Jeroboam, and his sin in causing
Israel to sin.
20The rest of the acts of Zimri, and his deeds of treason, are they
not written in the Book of the Chronicles of the Kings of Israel?
21Then the people of Israel were divided into two factions. Half
of the people followed Tibni son of Ginath, to make him king, and
half followed Omri.
22But the people who followed Omri prevailed against those
who followed Tibni son of Ginath; so Tibni died, and Omri
reigned.
23In the thirty-first year of Asa king of Judah, Omri began his
reign of twelve years over Israel. He reigned six years in Tirzah.
24Omri bought the hill Samaria of Shemer for two talents of
silver. He built a city on the hill *and* fortified it and called it Samaria
[Shomeron] after the owner of the hill, Shemer.
25But Omri did evil in the eyes of the Lord, worse than all who
were before him.
26He walked in all the way of Jeroboam son of Nebat, and in his
sin by which he made Israel sin, to provoke the Lord God of Israel
to anger with their idols.
27The rest of the acts of Omri and his might that he showed, are
they not written in the Book of the Chronicles of the Kings of
Israel?
28So Omri slept with his fathers, and was buried in Samaria.
Ahab his son reigned in his stead.
29In the thirty-eighth year of Asa king of Judah, Ahab son of
Omri began his reign of twenty-two years over Israel in Samaria.
30And Ahab son of Omri did evil in the sight of the Lord above
all before him.
31As if it had been a light thing for Ahab to walk in the sins of
Jeroboam son of Nebat, he took for wife Jezebel daughter of Ethbaal king of the Sidonians, and served Baal and worshiped him.
32He erected an altar for Baal in the house of Baal, which he built
in Samaria.
33And Ahab made an Asherah. Ahab did more to provoke the
Lord God of Israel to anger than all the kings of Israel before him.
34In his days Hiel the Bethelite built Jericho. He laid its foundation at the cost of the life of Abiram his first-born, and set up its
gates with the loss of his youngest son Segub, according to the
word of the Lord, which He spoke by Joshua the son of Nun. [Josh.
6:26.]

17 ELIJAH THE Tishbite, of the temporary residents of Gilead, said to Ahab, As the Lord, the God of Israel lives,
before Whom I stand, there shall not be dew or rain these years,
but according to My word.
2And the word of the Lord came to him, saying,
3Go from here and turn east, and hide yourself by the brook
Cherith, that is east of the Jordan.
4You shall drink of the brook, and I have commanded the
ravens to feed you there.

## New American Standard

16And the people who were camped heard it said, "Zimri has
conspired and has also struck down the king." Therefore all Israel
made Omri, the commander of the army, king over Israel that day
in the camp.
17Then Omri and all Israel with him went up from Gibbethon,
and they besieged Tirzah.
18And it came about, when Zimri saw that the city was taken,
that he went into the citadel of the king's house and burned the
king's house over him with fire, and died,
19because of his sins which he sinned, doing evil in the sight
of the LORD, walking in the way of Jeroboam, and in his sin which
he did, making Israel sin.
20Now the rest of the acts of Zimri and his conspiracy which he
carried out, are they not written in the Book of the Chronicles of
the Kings of Israel?
**21**¶ Then the people of Israel were divided into two parts: half
of the people followed Tibni the son of Ginath, to make him king;
the *other* half followed Omri.
22But the people who followed Omri prevailed over the people
who followed Tibni the son of Ginath. And Tibni died and Omri
became king.
23In the thirty-first year of Asa king of Judah, Omri became king
over Israel, *and reigned* twelve years; he reigned six years at Tirzah.
24And he bought the hill Samaria from Shemer for two talents
of silver; and he built on the hill, and named the city which he built
Samaria, after the name of Shemer, the owner of the hill.
25And Omri did evil in the sight of the LORD, and acted more
wickedly than all who *were* before him.
26For he walked in all the way of Jeroboam the son of Nebat and
in his sins which he made Israel sin, provoking the LORD God of
Israel with their idols.
27Now the rest of the acts of Omri which he did and his might
which he showed, are they not written in the Book of the Chronicles of the Kings of Israel?
28So Omri slept with his fathers, and was buried in Samaria;
and Ahab his son became king in his place.
**29**¶ Now Ahab the son of Omri became king over Israel in the
thirty-eighth year of Asa king of Judah, and Ahab the son of Omri
reigned over Israel in Samaria twenty-two years.
30And Ahab the son of Omri did evil in the sight of the LORD
more than all who were before him.
31And it came about, as though it had been a trivial thing for
him to walk in the sins of Jeroboam the son of Nebat, that he
married Jezebel the daughter of Ethbaal king of the Sidonians, and
went to serve Baal and worshiped him.
32So he erected an altar for Baal in the house of Baal, which he
built in Samaria.
33And Ahab also made the [a]Asherah. Thus Ahab did more to
provoke the LORD God of Israel than all the kings of Israel who
were before him.
34In his days Hiel the Bethelite built Jericho; he laid its foundations with the *loss of* Abiram his first-born, and set up its gates with
the *loss of* his youngest son Segub, according to the word of the
LORD, which He spoke by Joshua the son of Nun.

*Elijah Predicts Drought*

**17** NOW ELIJAH the Tishbite, who was of the settlers of
Gilead, said to Ahab, "As the LORD, the God of Israel
lives, before whom I stand, surely there shall be neither dew nor
rain these years, except by my word."
2And the word of the LORD came to him, saying,
3"Go away from here and turn eastward, and hide yourself by
the brook Cherith, which is east of the Jordan.
4"And it shall be that you shall drink of the brook, and I have
commanded the ravens to provide for you there."

NAS [a] I.e., wooden symbol of a female deity

## New International

heard that Zimri had plotted against the king and murdered him,
they proclaimed Omri, the commander of the army, king over
Israel that very day there in the camp. 17Then Omri and all the
Israelites with him withdrew from Gibbethon and laid siege to
Tirzah. 18When Zimri saw that the city was taken, he went into the
citadel of the royal palace and set the palace on fire around him.
So he died, 19because of the sins he had committed, doing evil in
the eyes of the LORD and walking in the ways of Jeroboam and in
the sin he had committed and had caused Israel to commit.
20As for the other events of Zimri's reign, and the rebellion he
carried out, are they not written in the book of the annals of the
kings of Israel?

*Omri King of Israel*

21Then the people of Israel were split into two factions; half
supported Tibni son of Ginath for king, and the other half supported Omri. 22But Omri's followers proved stronger than those
of Tibni son of Ginath. So Tibni died and Omri became king.
23In the thirty-first year of Asa king of Judah, Omri became king
of Israel, and he reigned twelve years, six of them in Tirzah. 24He
bought the hill of Samaria from Shemer for two talents[b] of silver
and built a city on the hill, calling it Samaria, after Shemer, the
name of the former owner of the hill.
25But Omri did evil in the eyes of the LORD and sinned more
than all those before him. 26He walked in all the ways of Jeroboam
son of Nebat and in his sin, which he had caused Israel to commit,
so that they provoked the LORD, the God of Israel, to anger by their
worthless idols.
27As for the other events of Omri's reign, what he did and the
things he achieved, are they not written in the book of the annals
of the kings of Israel? 28Omri rested with his fathers and was
buried in Samaria. And Ahab his son succeeded him as king.

*Ahab Becomes King of Israel*

29In the thirty-eighth year of Asa king of Judah, Ahab son of
Omri became king of Israel, and he reigned in Samaria over Israel
twenty-two years. 30Ahab son of Omri did more evil in the eyes
of the LORD than any of those before him. 31He not only considered
it trivial to commit the sins of Jeroboam son of Nebat, but he also
married Jezebel daughter of Ethbaal king of the Sidonians, and
began to serve Baal and worship him. 32He set up an altar for Baal
in the temple of Baal that he built in Samaria. 33Ahab also made
an Asherah pole and did more to provoke the LORD, the God of
Israel, to anger than did all the kings of Israel before him.
34In Ahab's time, Hiel of Bethel rebuilt Jericho. He laid its
foundations at the cost of his firstborn son Abiram, and he set up
its gates at the cost of his youngest son Segub, in accordance with
the word of the LORD spoken by Joshua son of Nun.

*Elijah Fed by Ravens*

**17** NOW ELIJAH the Tishbite, from Tishbe[c] in Gilead, said
to Ahab, "As the LORD, the God of Israel, lives, whom I
serve, there will be neither dew nor rain in the next few years
except at my word."
2Then the word of the LORD came to Elijah: 3"Leave here, turn
eastward and hide in the Kerith Ravine, east of the Jordan. 4You
will drink from the brook, and I have ordered the ravens to feed
you there."

NIV [b] 24 That is, about 150 pounds (about 70 kilograms) [c] 1 Or *Tishbite, of the settlers*

## King James

5 So he went and did according unto the word of the LORD: for he went and dwelt by the brook Cherith, that *is* before Jordan.

6 And the ravens brought him bread and flesh in the morning, and bread and flesh in the evening; and he drank of the brook.

7 And it came to pass after a while, that the brook dried up, because there had been no rain in the land.

8 ¶ And the word of the LORD came unto him, saying,

9 Arise, get thee to Zarephath, which *belongeth* to Zidon, and dwell there: behold, I have commanded a widow woman there to sustain thee.

10 So he arose and went to Zarephath. And when he came to the gate of the city, behold, the widow woman *was* there gathering of sticks: and he called to her, and said, Fetch me, I pray thee, a little water in a vessel, that I may drink.

11 And as she was going to fetch *it*, he called to her, and said, Bring me, I pray thee, a morsel of bread in thine hand.

12 And she said, *As* the LORD thy God liveth, I have not a cake, but an handful of meal in a barrel, and a little oil in a cruse: and, behold, I *am* gathering two sticks, that I may go in and dress it for me and my son, that we may eat it, and die.

13 And Elijah said unto her, Fear not; go *and* do as thou hast said: but make me thereof a little cake first, and bring *it* unto me, and after make for thee and for thy son.

14 For thus saith the LORD God of Israel, The barrel of meal shall not waste, neither shall the cruse of oil fail, until the day *that* the LORD sendeth rain upon the earth.

15 And she went and did according to the saying of Elijah: and she, and he, and her house, did eat *many* days.

16 *And* the barrel of meal wasted not, neither did the cruse of oil fail, according to the word of the LORD, which he spake by Elijah.

17 ¶ And it came to pass after these things, *that* the son of the woman, the mistress of the house, fell sick; and his sickness was so sore, that there was no breath left in him.

18 And she said unto Elijah, What have I to do with thee, O thou man of God? art thou come unto me to call my sin to remembrance, and to slay my son?

19 And he said unto her, Give me thy son. And he took him out of her bosom, and carried him up into a loft, where he abode, and laid him upon his own bed.

20 And he cried unto the LORD, and said, O LORD my God, hast thou also brought evil upon the widow with whom I sojourn, by slaying her son?

21 And he stretched himself upon the child three times, and cried unto the LORD, and said, O LORD my God, I pray thee, let this child's soul come into him again.

22 And the LORD heard the voice of Elijah; and the soul of the child came into him again, and he revived.

23 And Elijah took the child, and brought him down out of the chamber into the house, and delivered him unto his mother: and Elijah said, See, thy son liveth.

24 ¶ And the woman said to Elijah, Now by this I know that thou *art* a man of God, *and* that the word of the LORD in thy mouth *is* truth.

**18** AND IT came to pass *after* many days, that the word of the LORD came to Elijah in the third year, saying, Go, show thyself unto Ahab; and I will send rain upon the earth.

2 And Elijah went to show himself unto Ahab. And *there was* a sore famine in Samaria.

3 And Ahab called Obadiah, which *was* the governor of *his* house. (Now Obadiah feared the LORD greatly:

## Amplified

5 So he did according to the word of the Lord; he went and dwelt by the brook Cherith, that is east of Jordan.

6 And the ravens brought him bread and flesh in the morning and bread and flesh in the evening, and he drank of the brook.

7 After a while the brook dried up, because there was no rain in the land.

8 And the word of the Lord came to him,

9 Arise, go to Zarephath, which belongs to Sidon, and dwell there. Behold, I have commanded a widow there to provide for you.

10 So he arose and went to Zarephath. When he came to the gate of the city, behold, a widow was there gathering sticks. He called to her, Bring me a little water in a vessel that I may drink.

11 As she was going to get it, he called to her and said, Bring me a morsel of bread in your hand.

12 And she said, As the Lord your God lives, I have not a loaf baked but only a handful of meal in the jar and a little oil in the bottle. See, I am gathering two sticks, that I may go in and bake it for me and my son, that we may eat it, and die.

13 Elijah said to her, Fear not; go and do as you have said; but make me a little cake of [it] first and bring it to me, and afterward prepare for yourself and your son.

14 For thus says the Lord, the God of Israel, The jar of meal shall not waste away, or the bottle of oil fail, until the day that the Lord sends rain on the earth.

15 She did as Elijah said; and she, and he, and her household ate many days.

16 The jar of meal was not spent nor did the bottle of oil fail, according to the word which the Lord spoke by Elijah.

17 After these things the son of the woman, the mistress of the house, became sick; and his sickness was so severe that there was no breath left in him.

18 And she said to Elijah, What have you against me, O man of God? Have you come to me to call my sin to remembrance and to slay my son?

19 He said to her, Give me your son. And he took him from her bosom and carried him up into the chamber where he stayed, and laid him upon his own bed.

20 And Elijah cried to the Lord and said, O Lord my God, have You brought further calamity upon the widow with whom I sojourn, by slaying her son?

21 And he stretched himself upon the child three times, and cried to the Lord, and said, O Lord my God, I pray You, let this child's soul come back into him.

22 And the Lord heard the voice of Elijah, and the soul of the child came into him again, and he revived.

23 And Elijah took the child, and brought him down out of the chamber into the [lower part of the] house, and gave him to his mother: and Elijah said, See, your son is alive!

24 And the woman said to Elijah, By this I know that you are a man of God, and that the word of the Lord in your mouth is truth.

**18** AFTER MANY days, the word of the Lord came to Elijah in the third year, saying, Go, show yourself to Ahab, and I will send rain upon the earth.

2 So Elijah went to show himself to Ahab. Now the famine was severe in Samaria.

3 And Ahab called Obadiah, who was the governor of his house. (Now Obadiah feared the Lord greatly;

## New American Standard

5So he went and did according to the word of the LORD, for he
went and lived by the brook Cherith, which is east of the Jordan.
6And the ravens brought him bread and meat in the morning
and bread and meat in the evening, and he would drink from the
brook.
7And it happened after a while, that the brook dried up, because there was no rain in the land.
8¶ Then the word of the LORD came to him, saying,
9"Arise, go to Zarephath, which belongs to Sidon, and stay
there; behold, I have commanded a widow there to provide for
you."
10So he arose and went to Zarephath, and when he came to the
gate of the city, behold, a widow was there gathering sticks; and
he called to her and said, "Please get me a little water in a jar, that
I may drink."
11And as she was going to get *it*, he called to her and said,
"Please bring me a piece of bread in your hand."
12But she said, "As the LORD your God lives, I have no bread,
only a handful of flour in the bowl and a little oil in the jar; and
behold, I am gathering a few sticks that I may go in and prepare
for me and my son, that we may eat it and die."
13Then Elijah said to her, "Do not fear; go, do as you have said,
but make me a little bread cake from it first, and bring *it* out to me,
and afterward you may make *one* for yourself and for your son.
14"For thus says the LORD God of Israel, 'The bowl of flour shall
not be exhausted, nor shall the jar of oil be empty, until the day
that the LORD sends rain on the face of the earth.' "
15So she went and did according to the word of Elijah, and she
and he and her household ate for *many* days.
16The bowl of flour was not exhausted nor did the jar of oil
become empty, according to the word of the LORD which He spoke
through Elijah.

*Elijah Raises Widow's Son*

17¶ Now it came about after these things, that the son of the
woman, the mistress of the house, became sick; and his sickness
was so severe, that there was no breath left in him.
18So she said to Elijah, "What do I have to do with you, O man
of God? You have come to me to bring my iniquity to remembrance, and to put my son to death!"
19And he said to her, "Give me your son." Then he took him
from her bosom and carried him up to the upper room where he
was living, and laid him on his own bed.
20And he called to the LORD and said, "O LORD my God, hast
Thou also brought calamity to the widow with whom I am staying,
by causing her son to die?"
21Then he stretched himself upon the child three times, and
called to the LORD, and said, "O LORD my God, I pray Thee, let
this child's life return to him."
22And the LORD heard the voice of Elijah, and the life of the
child returned to him and he revived.
23And Elijah took the child, and brought him down from the
upper room into the house and gave him to his mother; and Elijah
said, "See, your son is alive."
24Then the woman said to Elijah, "Now I know that you are a
man of God, and that the word of the LORD in your mouth is
truth."

*Obadiah Meets Elijah*

**18** NOW IT came about *after* many days, that the word of the
LORD came to Elijah in the third year, saying, "Go, show
yourself to Ahab, and I will send rain on the face of the earth."
2So Elijah went to show himself to Ahab. Now the famine *was*
severe in Samaria.
3And Ahab called Obadiah who *was* over the household. (Now
Obadiah [a]feared the LORD greatly;

NAS [a] Or, *revered*

## New International

5So he did what the LORD had told him. He went to the Kerith
Ravine, east of the Jordan, and stayed there. 6The ravens brought
him bread and meat in the morning and bread and meat in the
evening, and he drank from the brook.

*The Widow at Zarephath*

7Some time later the brook dried up because there had been no
rain in the land. 8Then the word of the LORD came to him: 9"Go
at once to Zarephath of Sidon and stay there. I have commanded
a widow in that place to supply you with food." 10So he went to
Zarephath. When he came to the town gate, a widow was there
gathering sticks. He called to her and asked, "Would you bring me
a little water in a jar so I may have a drink?" 11As she was going
to get it, he called, "And bring me, please, a piece of bread."
12"As surely as the LORD your God lives," she replied, "I don't
have any bread—only a handful of flour in a jar and a little oil in
a jug. I am gathering a few sticks to take home and make a meal
for myself and my son, that we may eat it—and die."
13Elijah said to her, "Don't be afraid. Go home and do as you
have said. But first make a small cake of bread for me from what
you have and bring it to me, and then make something for yourself
and your son. 14For this is what the LORD, the God of Israel, says:
'The jar of flour will not be used up and the jug of oil will not run
dry until the day the LORD gives rain on the land.' "
15She went away and did as Elijah had told her. So there was
food every day for Elijah and for the woman and her family. 16For
the jar of flour was not used up and the jug of oil did not run dry,
in keeping with the word of the LORD spoken by Elijah.
17Some time later the son of the woman who owned the house
became ill. He grew worse and worse, and finally stopped breathing. 18She said to Elijah, "What do you have against me, man of
God? Did you come to remind me of my sin and kill my son?"
19"Give me your son," Elijah replied. He took him from her
arms, carried him to the upper room where he was staying, and
laid him on his bed. 20Then he cried out to the LORD, "O LORD my
God, have you brought tragedy also upon this widow I am staying
with, by causing her son to die?" 21Then he stretched himself out
on the boy three times and cried to the LORD, "O LORD my God,
let this boy's life return to him!"
22The LORD heard Elijah's cry, and the boy's life returned to
him, and he lived. 23Elijah picked up the child and carried him
down from the room into the house. He gave him to his mother
and said, "Look, your son is alive!"
24Then the woman said to Elijah, "Now I know that you are a
man of God and that the word of the LORD from your mouth is the
truth."

*Elijah and Obadiah*

**18** AFTER A long time, in the third year, the word of the
LORD came to Elijah: "Go and present yourself to Ahab,
and I will send rain on the land." 2So Elijah went to present himself
to Ahab.
Now the famine was severe in Samaria, 3and Ahab had summoned Obadiah, who was in charge of his palace. (Obadiah was
a devout believer in the LORD. 4While Jezebel was killing off the

## King James

4For it was *so*, when Jezebel cut off the prophets of the LORD,
that Obadiah took an hundred prophets, and hid them by fifty in
a cave, and fed them with bread and water.)
5And Ahab said unto Obadiah, Go into the land, unto all fountains of water, and unto all brooks: peradventure we may find
grass to save the horses and mules alive, that we lose not all the
beasts.
6So they divided the land between them to pass throughout it:
Ahab went one way by himself, and Obadiah went another way
by himself.
7¶ And as Obadiah was in the way, behold, Elijah met him: and
he knew him, and fell on his face, and said, *Art* thou that my lord
Elijah?
8And he answered him, I *am:* go, tell thy lord, Behold, Elijah
*is here.*
9And he said, What have I sinned, that thou wouldest deliver
thy servant into the hand of Ahab, to slay me?
10 *As* the LORD thy God liveth, there is no nation or kingdom,
whither my lord hath not sent to seek thee: and when they said,
*He is* not *there;* he took an oath of the kingdom and nation, that they
found thee not.
11And now thou sayest, Go, tell thy lord, Behold, Elijah *is here.*
12And it shall come to pass, *as soon as* I am gone from thee, that
the spirit of the LORD shall carry thee whither I know not; and *so*
when I come and tell Ahab, and he cannot find thee, he shall slay
me: but I thy servant fear the LORD from my youth.
13Was it not told my lord what I did when Jezebel slew the
prophets of the LORD, how I hid an hundred men of the LORD's
prophets by fifty in a cave, and fed them with bread and water?
14And now thou sayest, Go, tell thy lord, Behold, Elijah *is here:*
and he shall slay me.
15And Elijah said, *As* the LORD of hosts liveth, before whom I
stand, I will surely show myself unto him today.
16So Obadiah went to meet Ahab, and told him: and Ahab went
to meet Elijah.
17¶ And it came to pass, when Ahab saw Elijah, that Ahab said
unto him, *Art* thou he that troubleth Israel?
18And he answered, I have not troubled Israel; but thou, and
thy father's house, in that ye have forsaken the commandments
of the LORD, and thou hast followed Baalim.
19Now therefore send, *and* gather to me all Israel unto mount
Carmel, and the prophets of Baal four hundred and fifty, and the
prophets of the groves four hundred, which eat at Jezebel's table.
20So Ahab sent unto all the children of Israel, and gathered the
prophets together unto mount Carmel.
21And Elijah came unto all the people, and said, How long halt
ye between two opinions? if the LORD *be* God, follow him: but if
Baal, *then* follow him. And the people answered him not a word.
22Then said Eliajah unto the people, I, *even* I only, remain a
prophet of the LORD; but Baal's prophets *are* four hundred and fifty
men.
23Let them therefore give us two bullocks; and let them choose
one bullock for themselves, and cut it in pieces, and lay *it* on wood,
and put no fire *under:* and I will dress the other bullock, and lay
*it* on wood, and put no fire *under:*
24And call ye on the name of your gods, and I will call on the
name of the LORD: and the God that answereth by fire, let him be
God. And all the people answered and said, It is well spoken.
25And Elijah said unto the prophets of Baal, Choose you one
bullock for yourselves, and dress *it* first; for ye *are* many; and call
on the name of your gods, but put no fire *under.*

## Amplified

4For when Jezebel cut off the prophets of the Lord, Obadiah
took a hundred prophets, and hid them by fifties in a cave, and
fed them with bread and water.)
5And Ahab said to Obadiah, Go into the land, to all fountains
of water and to all brooks; perhaps we may find grass to save the
horses and mules alive, that we lose none of the beasts.
6So they divided the land between them to pass through it.
Ahab went one way and Obadiah went another way, each by
himself.
7As Obadiah was on the way, lo, Elijah met him. He recognized
him, and fell on his face, and said, Are you my lord Elijah?
8He answered him, It is I; go tell your lord, Behold, Elijah is
here.
9And he said, What sin have I committed that you would deliver your servant into the hand of Ahab to be slain?
10As the Lord your God lives, there is no nation or kingdom,
where my lord has not sent to seek you. And when they said, He
is not here, he took an oath of the kingdom and nation that they
had not found you.
11And now you say, Go, tell your lord, Behold, Elijah is here.
12And as soon as I have gone from you, the Spirit of the Lord
will carry you I know not where; so when I come and tell Ahab,
and he cannot find you, he will kill me. But I your servant have
feared *and* revered the Lord from my youth.
13Was it not told my lord what I did when Jezebel slew the
prophets of the Lord, how I hid a hundred men of the Lord's
prophets by fifties in a cave, and fed them with bread and water?
14And now you say, Go, tell your lord, Behold, Elijah is here;
and he will kill me.
15Elijah said, As the Lord of hosts lives, before Whom I stand,
I will surely show myself to Ahab today.
16So Obadiah went to meet Ahab and told him, and Ahab went
to meet Elijah.
17When Ahab saw Elijah, Ahab said to him, Are you he who
troubles Israel?
18Elijah replied, I have not troubled Israel; but you have, and
your father's house, by forsaking the commandments of the Lord
and by following the Baals.
19Therefore send and gather to me all Israel at Mount Carmel,
and the 450 prophets of Baal, and the 400 prophets of the Asherah,
who eat at [Queen] Jezebel's table.
20So Ahab sent to all the Israelites, and assembled the prophets
at Mount Carmel.
21Elijah came near to all the people, and said, How long will you
halt *and* limp between two opinions? If the Lord is God, follow
Him! But if Baal, then follow him. And the people did not answer
him a word.
22Then Elijah said to the people, I, I only, remain a prophet of
the Lord; but Baal's prophets are 450 men.
23Let two bulls be given us; let them choose one bull for themselves, and cut it in pieces and lay it on the wood, but put no fire
to it. I will dress the other bull, lay it on the wood, and put no fire
to it.
24Then you call on the name of your god, and I will call on the
name of the Lord; and the *one* Who answers by fire, let him be God.
And all the people answered, It is well spoken.
25Elijah said to the prophets of Baal, Choose one bull for yourselves, and dress it first, for you are many; and call on the name
of your god, but put no fire under.

## New American Standard

4for it came about, when Jezebel destroyed the prophets of the
LORD, that Obadiah took a hundred prophets and hid them by
fifties in a cave, and provided them with bread and water.)
5Then Ahab said to Obadiah, "Go through the land to all the
springs of water and to all the valleys; perhaps we will find grass
and keep the horses and mules alive, and not have to kill some of
the cattle."
6So they divided the land between them to survey it; Ahab
went one way by himself and Obadiah went another way by
himself.
7¶ Now as Obadiah was on the way, behold, Elijah met him,
and he recognized him and fell on his face and said, "Is this you,
Elijah my master?"
8And he said to him, "It is I. Go, say to your master, 'Behold,
Elijah *is here*.'"
9And he said, "What sin have I committed, that you are giving
your servant into the hand of Ahab, to put me to death?
10"As the LORD your God lives, there is no nation or kingdom
where my master has not sent to search for you; and when they
said, 'He is not *here*,' he made the kingdom or nation swear that
they could not find you.
11"And now you are saying, 'Go, say to your master, "Behold,
Elijah *is here*."'
12"And it will come about when I leave you that the Spirit of
the LORD will carry you where I do not know; so when I come and
tell Ahab and he cannot find you, he will kill me, although *I* your
servant have feared the LORD from my youth.
13"Has it not been told to my master what I did when Jezebel
killed the prophets of the LORD, that I hid a hundred prophets of
the LORD by fifties in a cave, and provided them with bread and
water?
14"And now you are saying, 'Go, say to your master, "Behold,
Elijah *is here*"'; he will then kill me."
15And Elijah said, "As the LORD of hosts lives, before whom I
stand, I will surely show myself to him today."
16¶ So Obadiah went to meet Ahab, and told him; and Ahab
went to meet Elijah.
17And it came about, when Ahab saw Elijah that Ahab said to
him, "Is this you, you troubler of Israel?"
18And he said, "I have not troubled Israel, but you and your
father's house *have*, because you have forsaken the commandments of the LORD, and you have followed the Baals.
19"Now then send *and* gather to me all Israel at Mount Carmel,
*together* with 450 prophets of Baal and 400 prophets of the Asherah,
who eat at Jezebel's table."

*God or Baal on Mount Carmel*

20¶ So Ahab sent *a message* among all the sons of Israel, and
brought the prophets together at Mount Carmel.
21And Elijah came near to all the people and said, "How long
*will* you hesitate between two opinions? If the LORD is God, follow
Him; but if Baal, follow him." But the people did not answer him
a word.
22Then Elijah said to the people, "I alone am left a prophet of
the LORD, but Baal's prophets are 450 men.
23"Now let them give us two oxen; and let them choose one ox
for themselves and cut it up, and place it on the wood, but put no
fire *under it*; and I will prepare the other ox, and lay it on the wood,
and I will not put a fire *under it*.
24"Then you call on the name of your god, and I will call on the
name of the LORD, and the God who answers by fire, He is God."
And all the people answered and said, "[a]That is a good idea."
25¶ So Elijah said to the prophets of Baal, "Choose one ox for
yourselves and prepare it first for you are many, and call on the
name of your god, but put no fire *under it*."

NAS [a] Lit., *The matter is good*

## New International

LORD's prophets, Obadiah had taken a hundred prophets and
hidden them in two caves, fifty in each, and had supplied them
with food and water.) 5Ahab had said to Obadiah, "Go through
the land to all the springs and valleys. Maybe we can find some
grass to keep the horses and mules alive so we will not have to kill
any of our animals." 6So they divided the land they were to cover,
Ahab going in one direction and Obadiah in another.
7As Obadiah was walking along, Elijah met him. Obadiah
recognized him, bowed down to the ground, and said, "Is it really
you, my lord Elijah?"
8"Yes," he replied. "Go tell your master, 'Elijah is here.'"
9"What have I done wrong," asked Obadiah, "that you are
handing your servant over to Ahab to be put to death? 10As surely
as the LORD your God lives, there is not a nation or kingdom where
my master has not sent someone to look for you. And whenever
a nation or kingdom claimed you were not there, he made them
swear they could not find you. 11But now you tell me to go to my
master and say, 'Elijah is here.' 12I don't know where the Spirit of
the LORD may carry you when I leave you. If I go and tell Ahab
and he doesn't find you, he will kill me. Yet I your servant have
worshiped the LORD since my youth. 13Haven't you heard, my
lord, what I did while Jezebel was killing the prophets of the LORD?
I hid a hundred of the LORD's prophets in two caves, fifty in each,
and supplied them with food and water. 14And now you tell me
to go to my master and say, 'Elijah is here.' He will kill me!"
15Elijah said, "As the LORD Almighty lives, whom I serve, I will
surely present myself to Ahab today."

*Elijah on Mount Carmel*

16So Obadiah went to meet Ahab and told him, and Ahab went
to meet Elijah. 17When he saw Elijah, he said to him, "Is that you,
you troubler of Israel?"
18"I have not made trouble for Israel," Elijah replied. "But you
and your father's family have. You have abandoned the LORD's
commands and have followed the Baals. 19Now summon the
people from all over Israel to meet me on Mount Carmel. And
bring the four hundred and fifty prophets of Baal and the four
hundred prophets of Asherah, who eat at Jezebel's table."
20So Ahab sent word throughout all Israel and assembled the
prophets on Mount Carmel. 21Elijah went before the people and
said, "How long will you waver between two opinions? If the LORD
is God, follow him; but if Baal is God, follow him."
But the people said nothing.
22Then Elijah said to them, "I am the only one of the LORD's
prophets left, but Baal has four hundred and fifty prophets. 23Get
two bulls for us. Let them choose one for themselves, and let them
cut it into pieces and put it on the wood but not set fire to it. I will
prepare the other bull and put it on the wood but not set fire to
it. 24Then you call on the name of your god, and I will call on the
name of the LORD. The god who answers by fire—he is God."
Then all the people said, "What you say is good."
25Elijah said to the prophets of Baal, "Choose one of the bulls
and prepare it first, since there are so many of you. Call on the

## King James

26And they took the bullock which was given them, and they
dressed *it,* and called on the name of Baal from morning even until
noon, saying, O Baal, hear us. But *there was* no voice, nor any that
answered. And they leaped upon the altar which was made.
27And it came to pass at noon, that Elijah mocked them, and
said, Cry aloud: for he *is* a god; either he is talking, or he is
pursuing, or he is in a journey, *or* peradventure he sleepeth, and
must be awaked.
28And they cried aloud, and cut themselves after their manner
with knives and lancets, till the blood gushed out upon them.
29And it came to pass, when midday was past, and they prophesied until the *time* of the offering of the *evening* sacrifice, that *there
was* neither voice, nor any to answer, nor any that regarded.
30And Elijah said unto all the people, Come near unto me. And
all the people came near unto him. And he repaired the altar of the
LORD *that was* broken down.
31And Elijah took twelve stones, according to the number of the
tribes of the sons of Jacob, unto whom the word of the LORD came,
saying, Israel shall be thy name:
32And with the stones he built an altar in the name of the LORD:
and he made a trench about the altar, as great as would contain
two measures of seed.
33And he put the wood in order, and cut the bullock in pieces,
and laid *him* on the wood, and said, Fill four barrels with water,
and pour *it* on the burnt sacrifice, and on the wood.
34And he said, Do *it* the second time. And they did *it* the second
time. And he said, Do *it* the third time. And they did *it* the third
time.
35And the water ran round about the altar; and he filled the
trench also with water.
36And it came to pass at *the time of* the offering of the *evening*
sacrifice, that Elijah the prophet came near, and said, LORD God
of Abraham, Isaac, and of Israel, let it be known this day that thou
*art* God in Israel, and *that* I *am* thy servant, and *that* I have done
all these things at thy word.
37Hear me, O LORD, hear me, that this people may know that
thou *art* the LORD God, and *that* thou hast turned their heart back
again.
38Then the fire of the LORD fell, and consumed the burnt sacrifice, and the wood, and the stones, and the dust, and licked up
the water that *was* in the trench.
39And when all the people saw *it,* they fell on their faces: and
they said, The LORD, he *is* the God; the LORD, he *is* the God.
40And Elijah said unto them, Take the prophets of Baal; let not
one of them escape. And they took them: and Elijah brought them
down to the brook Kishon, and slew them there.
41¶ And Elijah said unto Ahab, Get thee up, eat and drink; for
*there is* a sound of abundance of rain.
42So Ahab went up to eat and to drink. And Elijah went up to
the top of Carmel; and he cast himself down upon the earth, and
put his face between his knees,
43And said to his servant, Go up now, look toward the sea. And
he went up, and looked, and said, *There is* nothing. And he said,
Go again seven times.
44And it came to pass at the seventh time, that he said, Behold,
there ariseth a little cloud out of the sea, like a man's hand. And
he said, Go up, say unto Ahab, Prepare *thy chariot,* and get thee
down, that the rain stop thee not.
45And it came to pass in the mean while, that the heaven was
black with clouds and wind, and there was a great rain. And Ahab
rode, and went to Jezreel.
46And the hand of the LORD was on Elijah; and he girded up
his loins, and ran before Ahab to the entrance of Jezreel.

## Amplified

26So they took the bull given them, dressed it, and called on the
name of Baal from morning until noon, saying, O Baal, hear *and*
answer us! But there was no voice; no one answered. And they
leaped upon *or* limped about the altar they had made.
27At noon Elijah mocked them, saying, Cry aloud, for he is a
god; either he is musing, or he has gone aside, or he is on a
journey, or perhaps he is asleep and must be awakened.
28And they cried aloud, and cut themselves after their custom
with knives and lances, until the blood gushed out upon them.
29Midday passed, and they did the part of prophets until time
for offering the evening sacrifice, but there was no voice, no answer, no one who paid attention.
30Then Elijah said to all the people, Come near to me. And all
the people came near him. And he repaired the [old] altar of the
Lord that had been broken down [by Jezebel]. [Cp. 18:13; 19:10.]
31Then Elijah took twelve stones, according to the number of
the tribes of the sons of Jacob to whom the word of the Lord came,
saying, Israel shall be your name. [Gen. 32:28.]
32And with the stones Elijah built an altar in the name [and
self-revelation] of the Lord. He made a trench about the altar, as
great as would contain two measures of seed.
33He put the wood in order, and cut the bull in pieces and laid
it on the wood, and said, Fill four jars with water, and pour it on
the burnt offering and the wood.
34And he said, Do it the second time. And they did it the second
time. And he said, Do it the third time. And they did it the third
time.
35The water ran round about the altar; and he filled the trench
also with water.
36At the time of the offering of the evening sacrifice, Elijah the
prophet came near, and said, O Lord, the God of Abraham, Isaac,
and Israel, let it be known this day that You are God in Israel, and
that I am Your servant, and that I have done all these things at Your
word.
37Hear me, O Lord, hear me, that this people may know that
You, the Lord, are God, and have turned their hearts back [to
You].
38Then the fire of the Lord fell, and consumed the burnt sacrifice, and the wood, and the stones, and the dust, and licked up
the water that was in the trench.
39When all the people saw it, they fell on their faces; and they
said, The Lord, He is God! The Lord, He is God!
40And Elijah said, Seize the prophets of Baal; let not one escape.
They seized them, and Elijah brought them down to the brook
Kishon, and [as God's law required] slew them there. [Deut. 13:5;
18:20.]
41And Elijah said to Ahab, Go up, eat and drink; for there is the
sound of abundance of rain.
42So Ahab went up to eat and to drink. And Elijah went up to
the top of Carmel; and he bowed himself down upon the earth,
and put his face between his knees,
43And said to his servant, Go up now, look toward the sea. And
he went up, and looked, and said, There is nothing. Elijah said,
Go again seven times.
44And at the seventh time the servant said, A cloud, small as
a man's hand is arising out of the sea. And Elijah said, Go up, say
to Ahab, Hitch your chariot and go down, lest the rain stop you.
45In a little while the heavens were black with wind-swept
clouds, and there was a great rain. And Ahab went to Jezreel.
46The hand of the Lord was on Elijah. He girded up his loins,
and ran before Ahab to the entrance of Jezreel [nearly twenty
miles].

## New American Standard

26 Then they took the ox which was given them and they prepared it and called on the name of Baal from morning until noon
saying, "O Baal, answer us." But there was no voice and no one
answered. And they leaped about the altar which they made.
27 And it came about at noon, that Elijah mocked them and said,
"Call out with a loud voice, for he is a god; either he is occupied
or gone aside, or is on a journey, or perhaps he is asleep and needs
to be awakened."
28 So they cried with a loud voice and cut themselves according
to their custom with swords and lances until the blood gushed out
on them.
29 And it came about when midday was past, that they raved
until the time of the offering of the *evening* sacrifice; but there was
no voice, no one answered, and no one paid attention.
30 ¶ Then Elijah said to all the people, "Come near to me." So
all the people came near to him. And he repaired the altar of the
LORD which had been torn down.
31 And Elijah took twelve stones according to the number of the
tribes of the sons of Jacob, to whom the word of the LORD had
come, saying, "Israel shall be your name."
32 So with the stones he built an altar in the name of the LORD,
and he made a trench around the altar, large enough to hold two
measures of seed.
33 Then he arranged the wood and cut the ox in pieces and laid
*it* on the wood. And he said, "Fill four pitchers with water and
pour *it* on the burnt offering and on the wood."
34 And he said, "Do it a second time," and they did it a second
time. And he said, "Do it a third time," and they did it a third time.
35 And the water flowed around the altar, and he also filled the
trench with water.
36 Then it came about at the time of the offering of the *evening*
sacrifice, that Elijah the prophet came near and said, "O LORD, the
God of Abraham, Isaac and Israel, today let it be known that Thou
art God in Israel, and that I am Thy servant, and that I have done
all these things at Thy word.

*Elijah's Prayer*

37 "Answer me, O LORD, answer me, that this people may know
that Thou, O LORD, art God, and *that* Thou hast turned their heart
back again."
38 Then the fire of the LORD fell, and consumed the burnt offering and the wood and the stones and the dust, and licked up the
water that was in the trench.
39 And when all the people saw it, they fell on their faces; and
they said, "The LORD, He is God; the LORD, He is God."
40 Then Elijah said to them, "Seize the prophets of Baal; do not
let one of them escape." So they seized them; and Elijah brought
them down to the brook Kishon, and slew them there.
41 ¶ Now Elijah said to Ahab, "Go up, eat and drink; for there
is the sound of the roar of a *heavy* shower."
42 So Ahab went up to eat and drink. But Elijah went up to the
top of Carmel; and he crouched down on the earth, and put his
face between his knees.
43 And he said to his servant, "Go up now, look toward the sea."
So he went up and looked and said, "There is nothing." And he
said, "Go back" seven times.
44 And it came about at the seventh *time,* that he said, "Behold,
a cloud as small as a man's hand is coming up from the sea." And
he said, "Go up, say to Ahab, 'Prepare *your chariot* and go down,
so that the *heavy* shower does not stop you.' "
45 So it came about in a little while, that the sky grew black with
clouds and wind, and there was a heavy shower. And Ahab rode
and went to Jezreel.
46 Then the hand of the LORD was on Elijah, and he girded up
his loins and outran Ahab to Jezreel.

## New International

name of your god, but do not light the fire." 26 So they took the bull
given them and prepared it.
Then they called on the name of Baal from morning till noon.
"O Baal, answer us!" they shouted. But there was no response; no
one answered. And they danced around the altar they had made.
27 At noon Elijah began to taunt them. "Shout louder!" he said.
"Surely he is a god! Perhaps he is deep in thought, or busy, or
traveling. Maybe he is sleeping and must be awakened." 28 So they
shouted louder and slashed themselves with swords and spears,
as was their custom, until their blood flowed. 29 Midday passed,
and they continued their frantic prophesying until the time for the
evening sacrifice. But there was no response, no one answered, no
one paid attention.
30 Then Elijah said to all the people, "Come here to me." They
came to him, and he repaired the altar of the LORD, which was in
ruins. 31 Elijah took twelve stones, one for each of the tribes descended from Jacob, to whom the word of the LORD had come,
saying, "Your name shall be Israel." 32 With the stones he built an
altar in the name of the LORD, and he dug a trench around it large
enough to hold two seahs[a] of seed. 33 He arranged the wood, cut
the bull into pieces and laid it on the wood. Then he said to them,
"Fill four large jars with water and pour it on the offering and on
the wood."
34 "Do it again," he said, and they did it again.
"Do it a third time," he ordered, and they did it the third time.
35 The water ran down around the altar and even filled the trench.
36 At the time of sacrifice, the prophet Elijah stepped forward
and prayed: "O LORD, God of Abraham, Isaac and Israel, let it be
known today that you are God in Israel and that I am your servant
and have done all these things at your command. 37 Answer me,
O LORD, answer me, so these people will know that you, O LORD,
are God, and that you are turning their hearts back again."
38 Then the fire of the LORD fell and burned up the sacrifice, the
wood, the stones and the soil, and also licked up the water in the
trench.
39 When all the people saw this, they fell prostrate and cried,
"The LORD—he is God! The LORD—he is God!"
40 Then Elijah commanded them, "Seize the prophets of Baal.
Don't let anyone get away!" They seized them, and Elijah had
them brought down to the Kishon Valley and slaughtered there.
41 And Elijah said to Ahab, "Go, eat and drink, for there is the
sound of a heavy rain." 42 So Ahab went off to eat and drink, but
Elijah climbed to the top of Carmel, bent down to the ground and
put his face between his knees.
43 "Go and look toward the sea," he told his servant. And he
went up and looked.
"There is nothing there," he said.
Seven times Elijah said, "Go back."
44 The seventh time the servant reported, "A cloud as small as
a man's hand is rising from the sea."
So Elijah said, "Go and tell Ahab, 'Hitch up your chariot and
go down before the rain stops you.' "
45 Meanwhile, the sky grew black with clouds, the wind rose,
a heavy rain came on and Ahab rode off to Jezreel. 46 The power
of the LORD came upon Elijah and, tucking his cloak into his belt,
he ran ahead of Ahab all the way to Jezreel.

NIV [a] 32 That is, probably about 13 quarts (about 15 liters)

## King James

19 AND AHAB told Jezebel all that Elijah had done, and
withal how he had slain all the prophets with the sword.
2Then Jezebel sent a messenger unto Elijah, saying, So let the
gods do *to me,* and more also, if I make not thy life as the life of
one of them by tomorrow about this time.
3And when he saw *that,* he arose, and went for his life, and
came to Beer-sheba, which *belongeth* to Judah, and left his servant
there.
4¶ But he himself went a day's journey into the wilderness, and
came and sat down under a juniper tree: and he requested for
himself that he might die; and said, It is enough; now, O LORD,
take away my life; for I *am* not better than my fathers.
5And as he lay and slept under a juniper tree, behold, then an
angel touched him, and said unto him, Arise *and* eat.
6And he looked, and, behold, *there was* a cake baken on the
coals, and a cruse of water at his head. And he did eat and drink,
and laid him down again.
7And the angel of the LORD came again the second time, and
touched him, and said, Arise *and* eat; because the journey *is* too
great for thee.
8And he arose, and did eat and drink, and went in the strength
of that meat forty days and forty nights unto Horeb the mount of
God.
9¶ And he came thither unto a cave, and lodged there; and,
behold, the word of the LORD *came* to him, and he said unto him,
What doest thou here, Elijah?
10And he said, I have been very jealous for the LORD God of
hosts: for the children of Israel have forsaken thy covenant,
thrown down thine altars, and slain thy prophets with the sword;
and I, *even* I only, am left; and they seek my life, to take it away.
11And he said, Go forth, and stand upon the mount before the
LORD. And, behold, the LORD passed by, and a great and strong
wind rent the mountains, and brake in pieces the rocks before the
LORD; *but* the LORD *was* not in the wind: and after the wind an
earthquake; *but* the LORD *was* not in the earthquake:
12And after the earthquake a fire; *but* the LORD *was* not in the
fire: and after the fire a still small voice.
13And it was *so,* when Elijah heard *it,* that he wrapped his face
in his mantle, and went out, and stood in the entering in of the
cave. And, behold, *there came* a voice unto him, and said, What
doest thou here, Elijah?
14And he said, I have been very jealous for the LORD God of
hosts: because the children of Israel have forsaken thy covenant,
thrown down thine altars, and slain thy prophets with the sword;
and I, *even* I only, am left; and they seek my life, to take it away.
15And the LORD said unto him, Go, return on thy way to the
wilderness of Damascus: and when thou comest, anoint Hazael *to
be* king over Syria:
16And Jehu the son of Nimshi shalt thou anoint *to be* king over
Israel: and Elisha the son of Shaphat of Abel-meholah shalt thou
anoint *to be* prophet in thy room.
17And it shall come to pass, *that* him that escapeth the sword
of Hazael shall Jehu slay: and him that escapeth from the sword
of Jehu shall Elisha slay.
18Yet I have left *me* seven thousand in Israel, all the knees which
have not bowed unto Baal, and every mouth which hath not kissed
him.

## Amplified

19 AHAB TOLD Jezebel all that Elijah had done, and how he
had slain all the prophets [of Baal] with the sword.
2Then Jezebel sent a messenger to Elijah, saying, So let the gods
do to me, and more also, if I make not your life as the life of one
of them by this time tomorrow.
3Then he was afraid, and arose and went for his life, and came
to Beersheba of Judah [over eighty miles, and out of Jezebel's
realm] and left his servant there.
4But he himself went a day's journey into the wilderness, and
came and sat down under a lone broom *or* juniper tree, and asked
that he might die. He said, It is enough; now, O Lord, take away
my life; for I am no better than my fathers.
5As he lay asleep under the broom *or* juniper tree, behold, an
angel touched him, and said to him, Arise and eat.
6He looked, and, behold, there was a cake baked on the coals,
and a bottle of water at his head. And he ate and drank, and lay
down again.
7The Angel of the Lord came the second time, and touched him,
and said, Arise and eat, for the journey is too great for you.
8So he arose, and ate and drank, and went in the strength of
that food forty days and nights to Horeb the mount of God.
9There he came to a cave, and lodged in it; and, behold, the
word of the Lord came and He said to him, What are you doing
here, Elijah?
10He replied, I have been very jealous for the Lord God of hosts;
for the Israelites have forsaken Your covenant, thrown down Your
altars, and killed Your prophets with the sword; and I, I only, am
left; and they seek my life, to take it away.
11And He said, Go out and stand on the mount before the Lord.
And behold, the Lord passed by, and a great and strong wind rent
the mountains, and broke in pieces the rocks before the Lord, but
the Lord was not in the wind; and after the wind an earthquake,
but the Lord was not in the earthquake;
12And after the earthquake a fire, but the Lord was not in the
fire; and after the fire [a sound of gentle stillness and] a still, small
voice.
13When Elijah heard the voice, he wrapped his face in his
mantle and went out and stood in the entrance of the cave. And
behold, there came a voice to him, and said, What are you doing
here, Elijah?
14He said, I have been very jealous for the Lord God of hosts;
because the Israelites have forsaken Your covenant, thrown down
Your altars, and slain Your prophets with the sword; and I, I only,
am left, and they seek my life, to destroy it.
15And the Lord said to him, Go, return on your way to the
wilderness of Damascus; and when you arrive, anoint Hazael to
be king over Syria;
16And anoint Jehu son of Nimshi to be king over Israel; and
anoint Elisha son of Shaphat of Abel-meholah to be prophet in
your place.
17And him who escapes from the sword of [a]Hazael Jehu shall
slay; and him who escapes the sword of Jehu Elisha shall slay.
18Yet I will leave Myself 7,000 in Israel, all the knees that have
not bowed to Baal, and every mouth that has not kissed him.

**AMP** [a] Ahab had again fallen under the sway of Jezebel. Therefore, Baal-worship would recover from the blow dealt it by Elijah. Elijah is accordingly instructed to take the necessary steps for the destruction of Baal-worship. They were three. First, Ahab was to be attacked from without by the Syrians, and for that purpose warlike Hazael was to take the Syrian throne. Second, when Ahab was thus weakened, Jehu was to seize his throne, since Jehu was a known opponent of Baal-worship and also a ruthless soldier. Third, Elijah was to appoint as his own successor the vigorous and whole-hearted Elisha, who might be trusted under Jehu to complete the destruction of the adherents of Baal (*Cambridge Bible,* condensed).

## New American Standard

*Elijah Flees from Jezebel*

**19** NOW AHAB told Jezebel all that Elijah had done, and
how he had killed all the prophets with the sword.
2Then Jezebel sent a messenger to Elijah, saying, "So may the
gods do to me and even more, if I do not make your [b]life as the
life of one of them by tomorrow about this time."
3And he was afraid and arose and ran for his [c]life and came
to Beersheba, which belongs to Judah, and left his servant there.
4But he himself went a day's journey into the wilderness, and
came and sat down under a juniper tree; and he requested for
himself that he might die, and said, "It is enough; now, O LORD,
take my [d]life, for I am not better than my fathers."
5And he lay down and slept under a juniper tree; and behold,
there was an angel touching him, and he said to him, "Arise, eat."
6Then he looked and behold, there was at his head a bread cake
*baked on* hot stones, and a jar of water. So he ate and drank and
lay down again.
7And the angel of the LORD came again a second time and
touched him and said, "Arise, eat, because the journey is too great
for you."
8So he arose and ate and drank, and went in the strength of
that food forty days and forty nights to Horeb, the mountain of
God.

*Elijah at Horeb*

9¶ Then he came there to a cave, and lodged there; and behold,
the word of the LORD *came* to him, and He said to him, "What are
you doing here, Elijah?"
10And he said, "I have been very zealous for the LORD, the God
of hosts; for the sons of Israel have forsaken Thy covenant, torn
down Thine altars and killed Thy prophets with the sword. And
I alone am left; and they seek my life, to take it away."
11So He said, "Go forth, and stand on the mountain before the
LORD." And behold, the LORD was passing by! And a great and
strong wind was rending the mountains and breaking in pieces the
rocks before the LORD; *but* the LORD *was* not in the wind. And after
the wind an earthquake, *but* the LORD *was* not in the earthquake.
12And after the earthquake a fire, *but* the LORD *was* not in the
fire; and after the fire a sound of a gentle blowing.
13And it came about when Elijah heard *it*, that he wrapped his
face in his mantle, and went out and stood in the entrance of the
cave. And behold, a voice *came* to him and said, "What are you
doing here, Elijah?"
14Then he said, "I have been very zealous for the LORD, the God
of hosts; for the sons of Israel have forsaken Thy covenant, torn
down Thine altars and killed Thy prophets with the sword. And
I alone am left; and they seek my life, to take it away."
15¶ And the LORD said to him, "Go, return on your way to the
wilderness of Damascus, and when you have arrived, you shall
anoint Hazael king over Aram;
16and Jehu the son of Nimshi you shall anoint king over Israel;
and Elisha the son of Shaphat of Abel-meholah you shall anoint
as prophet in your place.
17"And it shall come about, the one who escapes from the
sword of Hazael, Jehu shall put to death, and the one who escapes
from the sword of Jehu, Elisha shall put to death.
18"Yet I will leave 7,000 in Israel, all the knees that have not
bowed to Baal and every mouth that has not kissed him."

NAS [b] Lit., *soul* [c] Lit., *soul* [d] Lit., *soul*

## New International

*Elijah Flees to Horeb*

**19** NOW AHAB told Jezebel everything Elijah had done and
how he had killed all the prophets with the sword. 2So
Jezebel sent a messenger to Elijah to say, "May the gods deal with
me, be it ever so severely, if by this time tomorrow I do not make
your life like that of one of them."
3Elijah was afraid[e] and ran for his life. When he came to Beer-
sheba in Judah, he left his servant there, 4while he himself went
a day's journey into the desert. He came to a broom tree, sat down
under it and prayed that he might die. "I have had enough, LORD,"
he said. "Take my life; I am no better than my ancestors." 5Then
he lay down under the tree and fell asleep.
All at once an angel touched him and said, "Get up and eat."
6He looked around, and there by his head was a cake of bread
baked over hot coals, and a jar of water. He ate and drank and then
lay down again.
7The angel of the LORD came back a second time and touched
him and said, "Get up and eat, for the journey is too much for
you." 8So he got up and ate and drank. Strengthened by that food,
he traveled forty days and forty nights until he reached Horeb, the
mountain of God. 9There he went into a cave and spent the night.

*The LORD Appears to Elijah*

And the word of the LORD came to him: "What are you doing
here, Elijah?"
10He replied, "I have been very zealous for the LORD God
Almighty. The Israelites have rejected your covenant, broken
down your altars, and put your prophets to death with the sword.
I am the only one left, and now they are trying to kill me too."
11The LORD said, "Go out and stand on the mountain in the
presence of the LORD, for the LORD is about to pass by."
Then a great and powerful wind tore the mountains apart and
shattered the rocks before the LORD, but the LORD was not in the
wind. After the wind there was an earthquake, but the LORD was
not in the earthquake. 12After the earthquake came a fire, but the
LORD was not in the fire. And after the fire came a gentle whisper.
13When Elijah heard it, he pulled his cloak over his face and went
out and stood at the mouth of the cave.
Then a voice said to him, "What are you doing here, Elijah?"
14He replied, "I have been very zealous for the LORD God
Almighty. The Israelites have rejected your covenant, broken
down your altars, and put your prophets to death with the sword.
I am the only one left, and now they are trying to kill me too."
15The LORD said to him, "Go back the way you came, and go
to the Desert of Damascus. When you get there, anoint Hazael
king over Aram. 16Also, anoint Jehu son of Nimshi king over
Israel, and anoint Elisha son of Shaphat from Abel Meholah to
succeed you as prophet. 17Jehu will put to death any who escape
the sword of Hazael, and Elisha will put to death any who escape
the sword of Jehu. 18Yet I reserve seven thousand in Israel—all
whose knees have not bowed down to Baal and all whose mouths
have not kissed him."

NIV [e] 3 Or *Elijah saw*

## King James

19¶ So he departed thence, and found Elisha the son of Shaphat,
who *was* plowing *with* twelve yoke *of oxen* before him, and he with
the twelfth: and Elijah passed by him, and cast his mantle upon
him.
20And he left the oxen, and ran after Elijah, and said, Let me,
I pray thee, kiss my father and my mother, and *then* I will follow
thee. And he said unto him, Go back again: for what have I done
to thee?
21And he returned back from him, and took a yoke of oxen, and
slew them, and boiled their flesh with the instruments of the oxen,
and gave unto the people, and they did eat. Then he arose, and
went after Elijah, and ministered unto him.

**20** AND BEN-HADAD the king of Syria gathered all his host
together: and *there were* thirty and two kings with him,
and horses, and chariots: and he went up and besieged Samaria,
and warred against it.
2And he sent messengers to Ahab king of Israel into the city,
and said unto him, Thus saith Ben-hadad,
3Thy silver and thy gold *is* mine; thy wives also and thy children, *even* the goodliest, *are* mine.
4And the king of Israel answered and said, My lord, O king,
according to thy saying, I *am* thine, and all that I have.
5And the messengers came again, and said, Thus speaketh
Ben-hadad, saying, Although I have sent unto thee, saying, Thou
shalt deliver me thy silver, and thy gold, and thy wives, and thy
children;
6Yet I will send my servants unto thee tomorrow about this
time, and they shall search thine house, and the houses of thy
servants; and it shall be, *that* whatsoever is pleasant in thine eyes,
they shall put *it* in their hand, and take *it* away.
7Then the king of Israel called all the elders of the land, and
said, Mark, I pray you, and see how this *man* seeketh mischief: for
he sent unto me for my wives, and for my children, and for my
silver, and for my gold; and I denied him not.
8And all the elders and all the people said unto him, Hearken
not *unto him,* nor consent.
9Wherefore he said unto the messengers of Ben-hadad, Tell my
lord the king, All that thou didst send for to thy servant at the first
I will do: but this thing I may not do. And the messengers departed, and brought him word again.
10And Ben-hadad sent unto him, and said, The gods do so unto
me, and more also, if the dust of Samaria shall suffice for handfuls
for all the people that follow me.
11And the king of Israel answered and said, Tell *him,* Let not
him that girdeth on *his harness* boast himself as he that putteth it
off.
12And it came to pass, when *Ben-hadad* heard this message, as
he *was* drinking, he and the kings in the pavilions, that he said
unto his servants, Set *yourselves in array.* And they set *themselves
in array* against the city.
13¶ And, behold, there came a prophet unto Ahab king of Israel,
saying, Thus saith the LORD, Hast thou seen all this great multitude? behold, I will deliver it into thine hand this day; and thou
shalt know that I *am* the LORD.
14And Ahab said, By whom? And he said, Thus saith the LORD,
*Even* by the young men of the princes of the provinces. Then he
said, Who shall order the battle? And he answered, Thou.
15Then he numbered the young men of the princes of the provinces, and they were two hundred and thirty two: and after them
he numbered all the people, *even* all the children of Israel, *being*
seven thousand.
16And they went out at noon. But Ben-hadad *was* drinking
himself drunk in the pavilions, he and the kings, the thirty and two
kings that helped him.

## Amplified

19So Elijah left there and found Elisha son of Shaphat, whose
plowing was being done with twelve yoke of oxen, and he drove
the twelfth. Elijah crossed over to him and cast his mantle upon
him.
20He left the oxen, and ran after Elijah, and said, Let me kiss
my father and mother, and then I will follow you. And he [testing
Elisha] said, Go on back. What have I done to you? [Settle it for
yourself.]
21So Elisha went back from him. Then he took a yoke of oxen,
slew them, boiled their flesh with the oxen's yoke [as fuel], and
gave to the people, and they ate. Then he arose, followed Elijah
and served him. [II Kings 3:11.]

**20** BENHADAD KING of Syria gathered all his army together; thirty-two kings were with him, and horses and
chariots; and he went up and besieged Samaria, warring against
it.
2He sent messengers into Samaria to Ahab king of Israel, and
said to him, Thus says Benhadad:
3Your silver and your gold are mine; your wives and your
children, even the fairest, also are mine.
4And the king of Israel answered and said, My lord, O king,
according to what you say, I am yours, and all that I have.
5The messengers came again and said, Thus says Benhadad,
Although I have sent to you, saying, You shall deliver to me your
silver, your gold, your wives and your children;
6Yet I will send my servants to you tomorrow about this time,
and they shall search your house and the houses of your servants;
and all the desire of your eyes they shall lay hands upon and take
it away.
7Then the king of Israel called all the elders of the land, and
said, Notice now and see how this man is seeking our destruction.
He sent to me for my wives, my children, my silver, and my gold,
and I did not refuse him.
8And all the elders and all the people said to him, Do not heed
him or consent.
9So he said to Benhadad's messengers, Tell my lord the king,
All you first sent for to your servant I will do; but this thing I cannot
do. And the messengers left; then they brought him word again.
10Benhadad sent to him, and said, The gods do so to me, and
more also, if the rubbish of Samaria shall be enough for each of all
the people who are at my feet *and* follow me to get a handful.
11The king of Israel answered, Tell him, Let not him who girds
on his harness boast as he who puts it off.
12When Benhadad heard this messsage, as he and the kings
were drinking in the booths, he said to his servants, Set the army
in array. And they set themselves in array against [Samaria].
13Then a prophet came to Ahab king of Israel, and said, Thus
says the Lord, Have you seen all this great multitude? Behold, I
will deliver it into your hand today; and you shall know *and* realize
that I am the Lord.
14Ahab said, By whom? And he said, Thus says the Lord, By
the young men [the attendants or bodyguard] of the governors of
the districts. Then Ahab said, Who shall order the battle? And he
answered, You.
15Ahab numbered the attendants of the governors of the districts and they were 232. After them he numbered all the people
[the army of] Israel, 7,000. [I Kings 19:18.]
16And they went out at noon. But Benhadad was drinking
himself drunk in the booths, he and the thirty-two kings who
helped him.

## New American Standard

19¶ So he departed from there and found Elisha the son of Shaphat, while he was plowing with twelve pairs *of oxen* before him, and he with the twelfth. And Elijah passed over to him and threw his mantle on him.

20And he left the oxen and ran after Elijah and said, "Please let me kiss my father and my mother, then I will follow you." And he said to him, "Go back again, for what have I done to you?"

21So he returned from following him, and took the pair of oxen and sacrificed them and boiled their flesh with the implements of the oxen, and gave *it* to the people and they ate. Then he arose and followed Elijah and ministered to him.

*War with Aram*

**20** NOW BEN-HADAD king of Aram gathered all his army, and there *were* thirty-two kings with him, and horses and chariots. And he went up and besieged Samaria, and fought against it.

2Then he sent messengers to the city to Ahab king of Israel, and said to him, "Thus says Ben-hadad,

3'Your silver and your gold are mine; your most beautiful wives and children are also mine.' "

4And the king of Israel answered and said, "It is according to your word, my lord, O king; I am yours, and all that I have."

5Then the messengers returned and said, "Thus says Ben-hadad, 'Surely, I sent to you saying, "You shall give me your silver and your gold and your wives and your children,"

6but about this time tomorrow I will send my servants to you, and they will search your house and the houses of your servants; and it shall come about, whatever is desirable in your eyes, they will take in their hand and carry away.' "

7¶ Then the king of Israel called all the elders of the land and said, "Please observe and see how this man is looking for trouble; for he sent to me for my wives and my children and my silver and my gold, and I did not refuse him."

8And all the elders and all the people said to him, "Do not listen or consent."

9So he said to the messengers of Ben-hadad, "Tell my lord the king, 'All that you sent for to your servant at the first I will do, but this thing I cannot do.' " And the messengers departed and brought him word again.

10And Ben-hadad sent to him and said, "May the gods do so to me and more also, if the dust of Samaria shall suffice for handfuls for all the people who follow me."

11Then the king of Israel answered and said, "Tell *him*, 'Let not him who girds on *his armor* boast like him who takes *it* off.' "

12And it came about when *Ben-hadad* heard this message, as he was drinking with the kings in the temporary shelters, that he said to his servants, "Station *yourselves*." So they stationed *themselves* against the city.

*Ahab Victorious*

13¶ Now behold, a prophet approached Ahab king of Israel and said, "Thus says the LORD, 'Have you seen all this great multitude? Behold, I will deliver them into your hand today, and you shall know that I am the LORD.' "

14And Ahab said, "By whom?" So he said, "Thus says the LORD, 'By the young men of the rulers of the provinces.' " Then he said, "Who shall begin the battle?" And he answered, "You."

15Then he mustered the young men of the rulers of the provinces, and there were 232; and after them he mustered all the people, *even* all the sons of Israel, 7,000.

16¶ And they went out at noon, while Ben-hadad was drinking himself drunk in the temporary shelters with the thirty-two kings who helped him.

## New International

*The Call of Elisha*

19So Elijah went from there and found Elisha son of Shaphat. He was plowing with twelve yoke of oxen, and he himself was driving the twelfth pair. Elijah went up to him and threw his cloak around him. 20Elisha then left his oxen and ran after Elijah. "Let me kiss my father and mother good-by," he said, "and then I will come with you."

"Go back," Elijah replied. "What have I done to you?"

21So Elisha left him and went back. He took his yoke of oxen and slaughtered them. He burned the plowing equipment to cook the meat and gave it to the people, and they ate. Then he set out to follow Elijah and became his attendant.

*Ben-Hadad Attacks Samaria*

**20** NOW BEN-HADAD king of Aram mustered his entire army. Accompanied by thirty-two kings with their horses and chariots, he went up and besieged Samaria and attacked it. 2He sent messengers into the city to Ahab king of Israel, saying, "This is what Ben-Hadad says: 3'Your silver and gold are mine, and the best of your wives and children are mine.' "

4The king of Israel answered, "Just as you say, my lord the king. I and all I have are yours."

5The messengers came again and said, "This is what Ben-Hadad says: 'I sent to demand your silver and gold, your wives and your children. 6But about this time tomorrow I am going to send my officials to search your palace and the houses of your officials. They will seize everything you value and carry it away.' "

7The king of Israel summoned all the elders of the land and said to them, "See how this man is looking for trouble! When he sent for my wives and my children, my silver and my gold, I did not refuse him."

8The elders and the people all answered, "Don't listen to him or agree to his demands."

9So he replied to Ben-Hadad's messengers, "Tell my lord the king, 'Your servant will do all you demanded the first time, but this demand I cannot meet.' " They left and took the answer back to Ben-Hadad.

10Then Ben-Hadad sent another message to Ahab: "May the gods deal with me, be it ever so severely, if enough dust remains in Samaria to give each of my men a handful."

11The king of Israel answered, "Tell him: 'One who puts on his armor should not boast like one who takes it off.' "

12Ben-Hadad heard this message while he and the kings were drinking in their tents,[a] and he ordered his men: "Prepare to attack." So they prepared to attack the city.

*Ahab Defeats Ben-Hadad*

13Meanwhile a prophet came to Ahab king of Israel and announced, "This is what the LORD says: 'Do you see this vast army? I will give it into your hand today, and then you will know that I am the LORD.' "

14"But who will do this?" asked Ahab.

The prophet replied, "This is what the LORD says: 'The young officers of the provincial commanders will do it.' "

"And who will start the battle?" he asked.

The prophet answered, "You will."

15So Ahab summoned the young officers of the provincial commanders, 232 men. Then he assembled the rest of the Israelites, 7,000 in all. 16They set out at noon while Ben-Hadad and the 32

NIV [a] 12 Or *in Succoth;* also in verse 16

## King James

17And the young men of the princes of the provinces went out first; and Ben-hadad sent out, and they told him, saying, There are men come out of Samaria.

18And he said, Whether they be come out for peace, take them alive; or whether they be come out for war, take them alive.

19So these young men of the princes of the provinces came out of the city, and the army which followed them.

20And they slew every one his man: and the Syrians fled; and Israel pursued them: and Ben-hadad the king of Syria escaped on an horse with the horsemen.

21And the king of Israel went out, and smote the horses and chariots, and slew the Syrians with a great slaughter.

22¶ And the prophet came to the king of Israel, and said unto him, Go, strengthen thyself, and mark, and see what thou doest: for at the return of the year the king of Syria will come up against thee.

23And the servants of the king of Syria said unto him, Their gods *are* gods of the hills; therefore they were stronger than we; but let us fight against them in the plain, and surely we shall be stronger than they.

24And do this thing, Take the kings away, every man out of his place, and put captains in their rooms:

25And number thee an army, like the army that thou hast lost, horse for horse, and chariot for chariot: and we will fight against them in the plain, *and* surely we shall be stronger than they. And he hearkened unto their voice, and did so.

26And it came to pass at the return of the year, that Ben-hadad numbered the Syrians, and went up to Aphek, to fight against Israel.

27And the children of Israel were numbered, and were all present, and went against them: and the children of Israel pitched before them like two little flocks of kids; but the Syrians filled the country.

28¶ And there came a man of God, and spake unto the king of Israel, and said, Thus saith the LORD, Because the Syrians have said, The LORD *is* God of the hills, but he *is* not God of the valleys, therefore will I deliver all this great multitude into thine hand, and ye shall know that I *am* the LORD.

29And they pitched one over against the other seven days. And *so* it was, that in the seventh day the battle was joined: and the children of Israel slew of the Syrians an hundred thousand footmen in one day.

30But the rest fled to Aphek, into the city; and *there* a wall fell upon twenty and seven thousand of the men *that were* left. And Ben-hadad fled, and came into the city, into an inner chamber.

31¶ And his servants said unto him, Behold now, we have heard that the kings of the house of Israel *are* merciful kings: let us, I pray thee, put sackcloth on our loins, and ropes upon our heads, and go out to the king of Israel: peradventure he will save thy life.

32So they girded sackcloth on their loins, and *put* ropes on their heads, and came to the king of Israel, and said, Thy servant Ben-hadad saith, I pray thee, let me live. And he said, *Is* he yet alive? he *is* my brother.

33Now the men did diligently observe whether *any thing would come* from him, and did hastily catch *it:* and they said, Thy brother Ben-hadad. Then he said, Go ye, bring him. Then Ben-hadad came forth to him; and he caused him to come up into the chariot.

34And *Ben-hadad* said unto him, The cities, which my father took from thy father, I will restore; and thou shalt make streets for thee in Damascus, as my father made in Samaria. Then *said Ahab,* I will send thee away with this covenant. So he made a covenant with him, and sent him away.

35¶ And a certain man of the sons of the prophets said unto his neighbour in the word of the LORD, Smite me, I pray thee. And the man refused to smite him.

36Then said he unto him, Because thou hast not obeyed the voice of the LORD, behold, as soon as thou art departed from me, a lion shall slay thee. And as soon as he was departed from him, a lion found him, and slew him.

## Amplified

17The servants of the governors of the districts went out first; and Benhadad sent out, and they told him, saying, There are men come out of Samaria.

18And he said, Whether they have come out for peace or for war, take them alive.

19So these [strong young guards] of the governors of the districts went out of [Samaria], and the army followed them.

20And each one killed his man; the Syrians fled, and Israel pursued them. Benhadad king of Syria escaped on a horse with the horsemen.

21The king of Israel went out, and smote [the riders of] the horses and chariots, and slew the Syrians with a great slaughter.

22The prophet came to the king of Israel, and said to him, Go, fortify yourself and become strong, and give attention to what you must do; for the first of next year the king of Syria will return against you.

23And the servants of the king of Syria said to him, Israel's gods are gods of the hills, therefore they were stronger than we; but let us fight against them in the plain, and surely we shall be stronger than they.

24And do this thing: Remove the kings, each from his place, and put governors in their stead.

25And muster yourself an army, like the army you have lost, horse for horse, and chariot for chariot; and we will fight against them in the plain, and surely we shall be stronger than they. And he heeded their speech and did so.

26And at the return of the year, Benhadad mustered the Syrians, and went up to Aphek to fight against Israel.

27The Israelites were counted and, all present, went against them. The Israelites encamped before the enemy like two little flocks of lost kids [absolutely everything against them but Almighty God]; but the Syrians filled the country.

28A man of God came and said to the king of Israel, Thus says the Lord, Because the Syrians have said, The Lord is God of the hills, but He is not God of the valleys, therefore I will deliver all this great multitude into your hand, and you shall know *and* recognize by experience that I am the Lord. [Phil. 4:13.]

29They encamped opposite each other seven days. Then the battle was joined; and the Israelites slew of the Syrians 100,000 foot soldiers in one day.

30But the rest fled to the city of Aphek; and the wall fell upon 27,000 men that were left. Benhadad fled into the city *and* from chamber to chamber.

31His servants said to him, We have heard that the kings of the house of Israel are merciful kings. Let us put sackcloth on our loins, and ropes about our [necks], and go out to the king of Israel; perhaps he will spare your life.

32So they girded sackcloth on their loins, and put ropes on their necks, and came to the king of Israel, and said, Your servant Benhadad says, I pray you, let me live. And King [Ahab] said, Is he yet alive? He is my brother.

33Now the men took it as an omen and they hastily took it up and said, Yes, your brother, Benhadad. Then the king said, Go, bring him. Then Benhadad came forth to him, and the victorious king caused him to come up into the chariot.

34Benhadad [tempting him] said, The cities which my father took from your father, I will restore; and you may maintain bazaars of your own in Damascus, as my father did in Samaria. Then, said Ahab, I will send you away on these terms. So he made a covenant with him and sent him away.

35And a certain man of the sons of the prophets said to his neighbor, At the command of the Lord, strike me, I pray you. And the man refused to strike him.

36Then said he to him, Because you have not obeyed the voice of the Lord, behold, as soon as you have left me a lion will slay you. And as soon as he departed from him, a lion found him and killed him.

## New American Standard

17And the young men of the rulers of the provinces went out first; and Ben-hadad sent out and they told him, saying, "Men have come out from Samaria."

18Then he said, "If they have come out for peace, take them alive; or if they have come out for war, take them alive."

19So these went out from the city, the young men of the rulers of the provinces, and the army which followed them.

20And they killed each his man; and the Arameans fled, and Israel pursued them, and Ben-hadad king of Aram escaped on a horse with horsemen.

21And the king of Israel went out and struck the horses and chariots, and killed the Arameans with a great slaughter.

**22**¶ Then the prophet came near to the king of Israel, and said to him, "Go, strengthen yourself and observe and see what you have to do; for at the turn of the year the king of Aram will come up against you."

23Now the servants of the king of Aram said to him, "Their gods are gods of the mountains, therefore they were stronger than we; but rather let us fight against them in the plain, *and* surely we shall be stronger than they.

24"And do this thing: remove the kings, each from his place, and put captains in their place,

25and muster an army like the army that you have lost, horse for horse, and chariot for chariot. Then we will fight against them in the plain, and surely we shall be stronger than they." And he listened to their voice and did so.

*Another Aramean War*

**26**¶ So it came about at the turn of the year, that Ben-hadad mustered the Arameans and went up to Aphek to fight against Israel.

27And the sons of Israel were mustered and were provisioned and went to meet them; and the sons of Israel camped before them like two little flocks of goats, but the Arameans filled the country.

28Then a man of God came near and spoke to the king of Israel and said, "Thus says the LORD, 'Because the Arameans have said, "The LORD is a god of *the* mountains, but He is not a god of *the* valleys"; therefore I will give all this great multitude into your hand, and you shall know that I am the LORD.' "

29So they camped one over against the other seven days. And it came about that on the seventh day, the battle was joined, and the sons of Israel killed *of* the Arameans 100,000 foot soldiers in one day.

30But the rest fled to Aphek into the city, and the wall fell on 27,000 men who were left. And Ben-hadad fled and came into the city into an inner chamber.

**31**¶ And his servants said to him, "Behold now, we have heard that the kings of the house of Israel are merciful kings, please let us put sackcloth on our loins and ropes on our heads, and go out to the king of Israel; perhaps he will save your life."

32So they girded sackcloth on their loins and *put* ropes on their heads, and came to the king of Israel and said, "Your servant Ben-hadad says, 'Please let me live.' " And he said, "Is he still alive? He is my brother."

33Now the men took this as an omen, and quickly catching his word said, "Your brother Ben-hadad." Then he said, "Go, bring him." Then Ben-hadad came out to him, and he took him up into the chariot.

34And *Ben-hadad* said to him, "The cities which my father took from your father I will restore, and you shall make streets for yourself in Damascus, as my father made in Samaria." *Ahab said,* "And I will let you go with this covenant." So he made a covenant with him and let him go.

**35**¶ Now a certain man of the sons of the prophets said to another by the word of the LORD, "Please strike me." But the man refused to strike him.

36Then he said to him, "Because you have not listened to the voice of the LORD, behold, as soon as you have departed from me, a lion will kill you." And as soon as he had departed from him a lion found him, and killed him.

## New International

kings allied with him were in their tents getting drunk. 17The
young officers of the provincial commanders went out first.
Now Ben-Hadad had dispatched scouts, who reported, "Men
are advancing from Samaria."
18He said, "If they have come out for peace, take them alive; if
they have come out for war, take them alive."
19The young officers of the provincial commanders marched
out of the city with the army behind them 20and each one struck
down his opponent. At that, the Arameans fled, with the Israelites
in pursuit. But Ben-Hadad king of Aram escaped on horseback
with some of his horsemen. 21The king of Israel advanced and
overpowered the horses and chariots and inflicted heavy losses on
the Arameans.
22Afterward, the prophet came to the king of Israel and said,
"Strengthen your position and see what must be done, because
next spring the king of Aram will attack you again."
23Meanwhile, the officials of the king of Aram advised him,
"Their gods are gods of the hills. That is why they were too strong
for us. But if we fight them on the plains, surely we will be stronger
than they. 24Do this: Remove all the kings from their commands
and replace them with other officers. 25You must also raise an
army like the one you lost—horse for horse and chariot for chariot—so we can fight Israel on the plains. Then surely we will be
stronger than they." He agreed with them and acted accordingly.
26The next spring Ben-Hadad mustered the Arameans and
went up to Aphek to fight against Israel. 27When the Israelites
were also mustered and given provisions, they marched out to
meet them. The Israelites camped opposite them like two small
flocks of goats, while the Arameans covered the countryside.
28The man of God came up and told the king of Israel, "This is
what the LORD says: 'Because the Arameans think the LORD is a
god of the hills and not a god of the valleys, I will deliver this vast
army into your hands, and you will know that I am the LORD.' "
29For seven days they camped opposite each other, and on the
seventh day the battle was joined. The Israelites inflicted a hundred thousand casualties on the Aramean foot soldiers in one day.
30The rest of them escaped to the city of Aphek, where the wall
collapsed on twenty-seven thousand of them. And Ben-Hadad
fled to the city and hid in an inner room.
31His officials said to him, "Look, we have heard that the kings
of the house of Israel are merciful. Let us go to the king of Israel
with sackcloth around our waists and ropes around our heads.
Perhaps he will spare your life."
32Wearing sackcloth around their waists and ropes around their
heads, they went to the king of Israel and said, "Your servant
Ben-Hadad says: 'Please let me live.' "
The king answered, "Is he still alive? He is my brother."
33The men took this as a good sign and were quick to pick up
his word. "Yes, your brother Ben-Hadad!" they said.
"Go and get him," the king said. When Ben-Hadad came out,
Ahab had him come up into his chariot.
34"I will return the cities my father took from your father,"
Ben-Hadad offered. "You may set up your own market areas in
Damascus, as my father did in Samaria."
⌞Ahab said,⌟ "On the basis of a treaty I will set you free." So he
made a treaty with him, and let him go.

*A Prophet Condemns Ahab*

35By the word of the LORD one of the sons of the prophets said
to his companion, "Strike me with your weapon," but the man
refused.
36So the prophet said, "Because you have not obeyed the LORD,
as soon as you leave me a lion will kill you." And after the man
went away, a lion found him and killed him.

## King James

37 Then he found another man, and said, Smite me, I pray thee. And the man smote him, so that in smiting he wounded *him*.

38 So the prophet departed, and waited for the king by the way, and disguised himself with ashes upon his face.

39 And as the king passed by, he cried unto the king: and he said, Thy servant went out into the midst of the battle; and, behold, a man turned aside, and brought a man unto me, and said, Keep this man: if by any means he be missing, then shall thy life be for his life, or else thou shalt pay a talent of silver.

40 And as thy servant was busy here and there, he was gone. And the king of Israel said unto him, So *shall* thy judgment *be;* thyself hast decided *it*.

41 And he hasted, and took the ashes away from his face; and the king of Israel discerned him that he *was* of the prophets.

42 And he said unto him, Thus saith the LORD, Because thou hast let go out of *thy* hand a man whom I appointed to utter destruction, therefore thy life shall go for his life, and thy people for his people.

43 And the king of Israel went to his house heavy and displeased, and came to Samaria.

**21** AND IT came to pass after these things, *that* Naboth the Jezreelite had a vineyard, which *was* in Jezreel, hard by the palace of Ahab king of Samaria.

2 And Ahab spake unto Naboth, saying, Give me thy vineyard, that I may have it for a garden of herbs, because it *is* near unto my house: and I will give thee for it a better vineyard than it; *or*, if it seem good to thee, I will give thee the worth of it in money.

3 And Naboth said to Ahab, The LORD forbid it me, that I should give the inheritance of my fathers unto thee.

4 And Ahab came into his house heavy and displeased because of the word which Naboth the Jezreelite had spoken to him: for he had said, I will not give thee the inheritance of my fathers. And he laid him down upon his bed, and turned away his face, and would eat no bread.

5 ¶ But Jezebel his wife came to him, and said unto him, Why is thy spirit so sad, that thou eatest no bread?

6 And he said unto her, Because I spake unto Naboth the Jezreelite, and said unto him, Give me thy vineyard for money; or else, if it please thee, I will give thee *another* vineyard for it: and he answered, I will not give thee my vineyard.

7 And Jezebel his wife said unto him, Dost thou now govern the kingdom of Israel? arise, *and* eat bread, and let thine heart be merry: I will give thee the vineyard of Naboth the Jezreelite.

8 So she wrote letters in Ahab's name, and sealed *them* with his seal, and sent the letters unto the elders and to the nobles that *were* in his city, dwelling with Naboth.

9 And she wrote in the letters, saying, Proclaim a fast, and set Naboth on high among the people:

10 And set two men, sons of Belial, before him, to bear witness against him, saying, Thou didst blaspheme God and the king. And *then* carry him out, and stone him, that he may die.

11 And the men of his city, *even* the elders and the nobles who were the inhabitants in his city, did as Jezebel had sent unto them, *and* as it *was* written in the letters which she had sent unto them.

12 They proclaimed a fast, and set Naboth on high among the people.

13 And there came in two men, children of Belial, and sat before him: and the men of Belial witnessed against him, *even* against Naboth, in the presence of the people, saying, Naboth did blaspheme God and the king. Then they carried him forth out of the city, and stoned him with stones, that he died.

14 Then they sent to Jezebel, saying, Naboth is stoned, and is dead.

## Amplified

37 Then [the prophet] found another man, and said, Strike me, I pray you. And the man struck him, so that in striking he wounded him.

38 So the prophet departed, and waited for King Ahab by the way, and disguised himself with ashes upon his face.

39 And as the king passed by, the [prophet] cried out to him, Your servant went out into the midst of the battle, and behold, a man turned aside and brought a man to me, and said, Keep this man. If for any reason he is missing, then your life shall be required for his life, or else you shall pay a talent of silver.

40 But as your servant was busy here and there, he was gone. And the king of Israel said to him, Such is your own verdict; you yourself have decided it.

41 The man hastily removed the ashes from his face, and Ahab king of Israel recognized him as one of the prophets.

42 And he said to the king, Thus says the Lord, Because you have let go out of your hand the man I had devoted to destruction, therefore your life shall go for his life, and your people for his people.

43 And King [Ahab] of Israel went to his house resentful and sullen, and came to Samaria. [I Kings 22:34-36.]

**21** NOW NABOTH the Jezreelite had a vineyard in Jezreel, close beside the palace of Ahab king of Samaria, and after these things,

2 Ahab said to Naboth, Give me your vineyard, that I may have it for a garden of herbs, because it is near my house. I will give you a better vineyard for it; or, if you prefer, I will give you its worth in money.

3 Naboth said to Ahab, The Lord forbid that I should give the inheritance of my fathers to you.

4 And Ahab [already depressed by the Lord's message to him] came into his house *more* resentful and sullen because of what Naboth the Jezreelite had said to him; for he had said, I will not give you the inheritance of my fathers. And he lay down on his bed, turned away his face and would eat no food.

5 But Jezebel his wife came and said to him, Why is your spirit so troubled that you eat no food?

6 And he said to her, Because I spoke to Naboth the Jezreelite, and said to him, Give me your vineyard for money, or if you prefer, I will give you another vineyard for it; and he answered, I will not give you my vineyard.

7 Jezebel his wife said to him, Do you not govern Israel? Arise, eat food, and let your heart be happy. I will give you the vineyard of Naboth the Jezreelite.

8 So she wrote letters in Ahab's name, and sealed them with his seal, and sent them to the elders and nobles who dwelt with Naboth in his city.

9 And in the letters she said, Proclaim a fast, and set Naboth up high among the people;

10 And set two men, base fellows, before him, and let them bear witness against him, saying, You cursed *and* renounced God and the king. Then carry him out and stone him to death.

11 And the men of his city, the elders and the nobles who dwelt there, did as Jezebel had directed in the letters sent them.

12 They proclaimed a fast and set Naboth on high among the people.

13 Two base fellows came in and sat opposite him, and they charged Naboth before the people, saying, Naboth cursed *and* renounced God and the king. Then he was carried out of the city and stoned to death.

14 Then they sent to Jezebel, saying, Naboth is stoned and is dead.

# New American Standard

37Then he found another man and said, "Please strike me."
And the man struck him, wounding him.
38So the prophet departed and waited for the king by the way,
and disguised himself with a bandage over his eyes.
39And as the king passed by, he cried to the king and said,
"Your servant went out into the midst of the battle; and behold,
a man turned aside and brought a man to me and said, 'Guard this
man; if for any reason he is missing, then your life shall be for his
life, or else you shall pay a talent of silver.'
40"And while your servant was busy here and there, he was
gone." And the king of Israel said to him, "So shall your judgment
be; you yourself have decided *it*."
41Then he hastily took the bandage away from his eyes, and the
king of Israel recognized him that he was of the prophets.
42And he said to him, "Thus says the LORD, 'Because you have
let go out of *your* hand the man whom I had devoted to destruction, therefore your life shall go for his life, and your people for
his people.' "
43So the king of Israel went to his house sullen and vexed, and
came to Samaria.

*Ahab Covets Naboth's Vineyard*

21 NOW IT came about after these things, that Naboth the
Jezreelite had a vineyard which *was* in Jezreel beside the
palace of Ahab king of Samaria.
2And Ahab spoke to Naboth, saying, "Give me your vineyard,
that I may have it for a vegetable garden because it is close beside
my house, and I will give you a better vineyard than it in its place;
if you like, I will give you the price of it in money."
3But Naboth said to Ahab, "The LORD forbid me that I should
give you the inheritance of my fathers."
4So Ahab came into his house sullen and vexed because of the
word which Naboth the Jezreelite had spoken to him; for he said,
"I will not give you the inheritance of my fathers." And he lay
down on his bed and turned away his face and ate no food.
5¶ But Jezebel his wife came to him and said to him, "How is
it that your spirit is so sullen that you are not eating food?"
6So he said to her, "Because I spoke to Naboth the Jezreelite,
and said to him, 'Give me your vineyard for money; or else, if it
pleases you, I will give you a vineyard in its place.' But he said,
'I will not give you my vineyard.' "
7And Jezebel his wife said to him, "Do you now reign over
Israel? Arise, eat bread, and let your heart be joyful; I will give you
the vineyard of Naboth the Jezreelite."
8So she wrote letters in Ahab's name and sealed them with his
seal, and sent letters to the elders and to the nobles who were
living with Naboth in his city.
9Now she wrote in the letters, saying, "Proclaim a fast, and
seat Naboth at the head of the people;
10and seat two worthless men before him, and let them testify
against him, saying, 'You cursed God and the king.' Then take him
out and stone him to death."

*Jezebel's Plot*

11¶ So the men of his city, the elders and the nobles who lived
in his city, did as Jezebel had sent *word* to them, just as it was
written in the letters which she had sent them.
12They proclaimed a fast and seated Naboth at the head of the
people.
13Then the two worthless men came in and sat before him; and
the worthless men testified against him, even against Naboth,
before the people, saying, "Naboth cursed God and the king." So
they took him outside the city and stoned him to death with
stones.
14Then they sent *word* to Jezebel, saying, "Naboth has been
stoned, and is dead."

# New International

37The prophet found another man and said, "Strike me,
please." So the man struck him and wounded him. 38Then the
prophet went and stood by the road waiting for the king. He
disguised himself with his headband down over his eyes. 39As the
king passed by, the prophet called out to him, "Your servant went
into the thick of the battle, and someone came to me with a captive
and said, 'Guard this man. If he is missing, it will be your life for
his life, or you must pay a talent[a] of silver.' 40While your servant
was busy here and there, the man disappeared."
"That is your sentence," the king of Israel said. "You have
pronounced it yourself."
41Then the prophet quickly removed the headband from his
eyes, and the king of Israel recognized him as one of the prophets.
42He said to the king, "This is what the LORD says: 'You have set
free a man I had determined should die.[b] Therefore it is your life
for his life, your people for his people.' " 43Sullen and angry, the
king of Israel went to his palace in Samaria.

*Naboth's Vineyard*

21 SOME TIME later there was an incident involving a vineyard belonging to Naboth the Jezreelite. The vineyard was
in Jezreel, close to the palace of Ahab king of Samaria. 2Ahab said
to Naboth, "Let me have your vineyard to use for a vegetable
garden, since it is close to my palace. In exchange I will give you
a better vineyard or, if you prefer, I will pay you whatever it is
worth."
3But Naboth replied, "The LORD forbid that I should give you
the inheritance of my fathers."
4So Ahab went home, sullen and angry because Naboth the
Jezreelite had said, "I will not give you the inheritance of my
fathers." He lay on his bed sulking and refused to eat.
5His wife Jezebel came in and asked him, "Why are you so
sullen? Why won't you eat?"
6He answered her, "Because I said to Naboth the Jezreelite, 'Sell
me your vineyard; or if you prefer, I will give you another vineyard
in its place.' But he said, 'I will not give you my vineyard.' "
7Jezebel his wife said, "Is this how you act as king over Israel?
Get up and eat! Cheer up. I'll get you the vineyard of Naboth the
Jezreelite."
8So she wrote letters in Ahab's name, placed his seal on them,
and sent them to the elders and nobles who lived in Naboth's city
with him. 9In those letters she wrote:

> "Proclaim a day of fasting and seat Naboth in a prominent
> place among the people. 10But seat two scoundrels opposite
> him and have them testify that he has cursed both God and
> the king. Then take him out and stone him to death."

11So the elders and nobles who lived in Naboth's city did as
Jezebel directed in the letters she had written to them. 12They
proclaimed a fast and seated Naboth in a prominent place among
the people. 13Then two scoundrels came and sat opposite him and
brought charges against Naboth before the people, saying,
"Naboth has cursed both God and the king." So they took him
outside the city and stoned him to death. 14Then they sent word
to Jezebel: "Naboth has been stoned and is dead."

**NIV** [a] *39* That is, about 75 pounds (about 34 kilograms) [b] *42* The Hebrew term refers to the irrevocable giving over of things or persons to the LORD, often by totally destroying them.

## King James

15¶ And it came to pass, when Jezebel heard that Naboth was
stoned, and was dead, that Jezebel said to Ahab, Arise, take
possession of the vineyard of Naboth the Jezreelite, which he
refused to give thee for money: for Naboth is not alive, but dead.
16And it came to pass, when Ahab heard that Naboth was dead,
that Ahab rose up to go down to the vineyard of Naboth the
Jezreelite, to take possession of it.
17¶ And the word of the LORD came to Elijah the Tishbite,
saying,
18Arise, go down to meet Ahab king of Israel, which *is* in
Samaria: behold, *he is* in the vineyard of Naboth, whither he is
gone down to possess it.
19And thou shalt speak unto him, saying, Thus saith the LORD,
Hast thou killed, and also taken possession? And thou shalt speak
unto him, saying, Thus saith the LORD, In the place where dogs
licked the blood of Naboth shall dogs lick thy blood, even thine.
20And Ahab said to Elijah, Hast thou found me, O mine enemy?
And he answered, I have found *thee:* because thou hast sold thyself
to work evil in the sight of the LORD.
21Behold, I will bring evil upon thee, and will take away thy
posterity, and will cut off from Ahab him that pisseth against the
wall, and him that is shut up and left in Israel,
22And will make thine house like the house of Jeroboam the son
of Nebat, and like the house of Baasha the son of Ahijah, for the
provocation wherewith thou hast provoked *me* to anger, and made
Israel to sin.
23And of Jezebel also spake the LORD, saying, The dogs shall eat
Jezebel by the wall of Jezreel.
24Him that dieth of Ahab in the city the dogs shall eat; and him
that dieth in the field shall the fowls of the air eat.
25¶ But there was none like unto Ahab, which did sell himself
to work wickedness in the sight of the LORD, whom Jezebel his
wife stirred up.
26And he did very abominably in following idols, according to
all *things* as did the Amorites, whom the LORD cast out before the
children of Israel.
27And it came to pass, when Ahab heard those words, that he
rent his clothes, and put sackcloth upon his flesh, and fasted, and
lay in sackcloth, and went softly.
28And the word of the LORD came to Elijah the Tishbite, saying,
29Seest thou how Ahab humbleth himself before me? because
he humbleth himself before me, I will not bring the evil in his days:
*but* in his son's days will I bring the evil upon his house.

22 AND THEY continued three years without war between
Syria and Israel.
2And it came to pass in the third year, that Jehoshaphat the king
of Judah came down to the king of Israel.
3And the king of Israel said unto his servants, Know ye that
Ramoth in Gilead *is* ours, and we *be* still, *and* take it not out of the
hand of the king of Syria?
4And he said unto Jehoshaphat, Wilt thou go with me to battle
to Ramoth-gilead? And Jehoshaphat said to the king of Israel, I *am*
as thou *art*, my people as thy people, my horses as thy horses.
5And Jehoshaphat said unto the king of Israel, Inquire, I pray
thee, at the word of the LORD today.
6Then the king of Israel gathered the prophets together, about
four hundred men, and said unto them, Shall I go against Ramoth-
gilead to battle, or shall I forbear? And they said, Go up; for the
Lord shall deliver *it* into the hand of the king.
7And Jehoshaphat said, *Is there* not here a prophet of the LORD
besides, that we might inquire of him?

## Amplified

15Then Jezebel said to Ahab, Arise, take possession of the vineyard of Naboth the Jezreelite, which he refused to sell you, for
Naboth is not alive, but dead.
16When Ahab heard that, he arose to go down to the vineyard
of Naboth the Jezreelite, to take possession of it.
17Then the word of the Lord came to Elijah the Tishbite, saying,
18Arise, go down to meet Ahab king of Israel, in Samaria. He
is in the vineyard of Naboth, which he has gone to possess.
19Say to him, Thus says the Lord, Have you killed, and also
taken possession? Thus says the Lord, In the place where dogs
licked the blood of Naboth shall dogs lick your blood, even yours.
20And Ahab said to Elijah, Have you found me, O my enemy?
And he answered, I have found you, because you have sold yourself to do evil in the sight of the Lord.
21Lo [says the Lord], I will bring evil on you and utterly sweep
away and cut off from Ahab every male, bond and free;
22And will make your household like that of Jeroboam son of
Nebat, and like the household of Baasha son of Ahijah, for the
provocation with which you have provoked Me to anger, and
made Israel to sin.
23Also the Lord said of Jezebel, The dogs shall eat Jezebel by the
wall of Jezreel.
24Him of Ahab who dies in the city the dogs shall eat, and him
who dies in the field the birds of the air shall eat.
25For there was no one who sold himself to do evil in the sight
of the Lord as did Ahab, incited by his wife Jezebel.
26He did very abominably in going after idols, as had the Amorites, whom the Lord cast out before the Israelites.
27When Ahab heard those words of Elijah, he tore his clothes,
put sackcloth on his flesh, fasted, lay in sackcloth, and went
quietly.
28And the word of the Lord came to Elijah the Tishbite, saying,
29Do you see how Ahab humbles himself before Me? Because
he humbles himself before Me, I will not bring the evil in his
lifetime; but in his son's day I will bring the evil upon his house.

22 SYRIA AND Israel continued without war for three years.
2In the third year, Jehoshaphat king of Judah came down
to the king of Israel.
3And [Ahab] king of Israel said to his servants, Do you know
that Ramoth in Gilead is ours, and we keep silence and do not take
it from the king of Syria?
4And [Ahab] said to Jehoshaphat, Will you go with me to
Ramoth-gilead to battle? Jehoshaphat said to the king of Israel, I
am as you are, my people as your people, my horses as your
horses.
5But Jehoshaphat said to the king of Israel, Inquire first, I pray
you, for the word of the Lord today.
6Then [Ahab] king of Israel gathered the prophets together,
about 400 men, and said to them, Shall I go against Ramoth-gilead
to battle or shall I hold back? And they said, Go up; for the Lord
will deliver it into the hand of the king.
7Jehoshaphat said, Is there not another prophet of the Lord here
whom we may ask?

## New American Standard

15And it came about when Jezebel heard that Naboth had been
stoned and was dead, that Jezebel said to Ahab, "Arise, take
possession of the vineyard of Naboth, the Jezreelite, which he
refused to give you for money; for Naboth is not alive, but dead."
16And it came about when Ahab heard that Naboth was dead,
that Ahab arose to go down to the vineyard of Naboth the Jezreelite, to take possession of it.
17¶ Then the word of the LORD came to Elijah the Tishbite,
saying,
18"Arise, go down to meet Ahab king of Israel, who is in Samaria; behold, he is in the vineyard of Naboth where he has gone
down to take possession of it.
19"And you shall speak to him, saying, 'Thus says the LORD,
"Have you murdered, and also taken possession?"' And you shall
speak to him, saying, 'Thus says the LORD, "In the place where the
dogs licked up the blood of Naboth the dogs shall lick up your
blood, even yours."'"
20And Ahab said to Elijah, "Have you found me, O my enemy?" And he answered, "I have found *you,* because you have sold
yourself to do evil in the sight of the LORD.
21"Behold, I will bring evil upon you, and will utterly sweep
you away, and will cut off from Ahab every male, both bond and
free in Israel;
22and I will make your house like the house of Jeroboam the son
of Nebat, and like the house of Baasha the son of Ahijah, because
of the provocation with which you have provoked *Me* to anger,
and *because* you have made Israel sin.
23"And of Jezebel also has the LORD spoken, saying, 'The dogs
shall eat Jezebel in the district of Jezreel.'
24"The one belonging to Ahab, who dies in the city, the dogs
shall eat, and the one who dies in the field the birds of heaven shall
eat."
25¶ Surely there was no one like Ahab who sold himself to do
evil in the sight of the LORD, because Jezebel his wife incited him.
26And he acted very abominably in following idols, according
to all that the Amorites had done, whom the LORD cast out before
the sons of Israel.
27¶ And it came about when Ahab heard these words, that he
tore his clothes and put on sackcloth and fasted, and he lay in
sackcloth and went about despondently.
28Then the word of the LORD came to Elijah the Tishbite, saying,
29"Do you see how Ahab has humbled himself before Me?
Because he has humbled himself before Me, I will not bring the evil
in his days, *but* I will bring the evil upon his house in his son's
days."

*Ahab's Third Campaign against Aram*

22 AND THREE years passed without war between Aram
and Israel.
2And it came about in the third year, that Jehoshaphat the king
of Judah came down to the king of Israel.
3Now the king of Israel said to his servants, "Do you know that
Ramoth-gilead belongs to us, and we are still doing nothing to take
it out of the hand of the king of Aram?"
4And he said to Jehoshaphat, "Will you go with me to battle
at Ramoth-gilead?" And Jehoshaphat said to the king of Israel, "I
am as you are, my people as your people, my horses as your
horses."
5¶ Moreover, Jehoshaphat said to the king of Israel, "Please
inquire first for the word of the LORD."
6Then the king of Israel gathered the prophets together, about
four hundred men, and said to them, "Shall I go against Ramoth-
gilead to battle or shall I refrain?" And they said, "Go up, for the
Lord will give *it* into the hand of the king."
7But Jehoshaphat said, "Is there not yet a prophet of the LORD
here, that we may inquire of him?"

## New International

15As soon as Jezebel heard that Naboth had been stoned to
death, she said to Ahab, "Get up and take possession of the
vineyard of Naboth the Jezreelite that he refused to sell you. He
is no longer alive, but dead." 16When Ahab heard that Naboth was
dead, he got up and went down to take possession of Naboth's
vineyard.
17Then the word of the LORD came to Elijah the Tishbite: 18"Go
down to meet Ahab king of Israel, who rules in Samaria. He is now
in Naboth's vineyard, where he has gone to take possession of it.
19Say to him, 'This is what the LORD says: Have you not murdered
a man and seized his property?' Then say to him, 'This is what the
LORD says: In the place where dogs licked up Naboth's blood, dogs
will lick up your blood—yes, yours!'"
20Ahab said to Elijah, "So you have found me, my enemy!"
"I have found you," he answered, "because you have sold
yourself to do evil in the eyes of the LORD. 21'I am going to bring
disaster on you. I will consume your descendants and cut off from
Ahab every last male in Israel—slave or free. 22I will make your
house like that of Jeroboam son of Nebat and that of Baasha son
of Ahijah, because you have provoked me to anger and have
caused Israel to sin.'
23"And also concerning Jezebel the LORD says: 'Dogs will devour Jezebel by the wall of[a] Jezreel.'
24"Dogs will eat those belonging to Ahab who die in the city,
and the birds of the air will feed on those who die in the country."
25(There was never a man like Ahab, who sold himself to do evil
in the eyes of the LORD, urged on by Jezebel his wife. 26He behaved
in the vilest manner by going after idols, like the Amorites the
LORD drove out before Israel.)
27When Ahab heard these words, he tore his clothes, put on
sackcloth and fasted. He lay in sackcloth and went around meekly.
28Then the word of the LORD came to Elijah the Tishbite:
29"Have you noticed how Ahab has humbled himself before me?
Because he has humbled himself, I will not bring this disaster in
his day, but I will bring it on his house in the days of his son."

*Micaiah Prophesies Against Ahab*

22 FOR THREE years there was no war between Aram and
Israel. 2But in the third year Jehoshaphat king of Judah
went down to see the king of Israel. 3The king of Israel had said
to his officials, "Don't you know that Ramoth Gilead belongs to us
and yet we are doing nothing to retake it from the king of Aram?"
4So he asked Jehoshaphat, "Will you go with me to fight against
Ramoth Gilead?"
Jehoshaphat replied to the king of Israel, "I am as you are, my
people as your people, my horses as your horses." 5But Jehoshaphat also said to the king of Israel, "First seek the counsel of the
LORD."
6So the king of Israel brought together the prophets—about
four hundred men—and asked them, "Shall I go to war against
Ramoth Gilead, or shall I refrain?"
"Go," they answered, "for the Lord will give it into the king's
hand."
7But Jehoshaphat asked, "Is there not a prophet of the LORD
here whom we can inquire of?"

**NIV** [a] 23 Most Hebrew manuscripts; a few Hebrew manuscripts, Vulgate and Syriac (see also 2 Kings 9:26) *the plot of ground at*

## King James

8 And the king of Israel said unto Jehoshaphat, *There is* yet one man, Micaiah the son of Imlah, by whom we may inquire of the LORD: but I hate him; for he doth not prophesy good concerning me, but evil. And Jehoshaphat said, Let not the king say so.

9 Then the king of Israel called an officer, and said, Hasten *hither* Micaiah the son of Imlah.

10 And the king of Israel and Jehoshaphat the king of Judah sat each on his throne, having put on their robes, in a void place in the entrance of the gate of Samaria; and all the prophets prophesied before them.

11 And Zedekiah the son of Chenaanah made him horns of iron: and he said, Thus saith the LORD, With these shalt thou push the Syrians, until thou have consumed them.

12 And all the prophets prophesied so, saying, Go up to Ramoth-gilead, and prosper: for the LORD shall deliver *it* into the king's hand.

13 And the messenger that was gone to call Micaiah spake unto him, saying, Behold now, the words of the prophets *declare* good unto the king with one mouth: let thy word, I pray thee, be like the word of one of them, and speak *that which is* good.

14 And Micaiah said, *As* the LORD liveth, what the LORD saith unto me, that will I speak.

15 ¶ So he came to the king. And the king said unto him, Micaiah, shall we go against Ramoth-gilead to battle, or shall we forbear? And he answered him, Go, and prosper: for the LORD shall deliver *it* into the hand of the king.

16 And the king said unto him, How many times shall I adjure thee that thou tell me nothing but *that which is* true in the name of the LORD?

17 And he said, I saw all Israel scattered upon the hills, as sheep that have not a shepherd: and the LORD said, These have no master: let them return every man to his house in peace.

18 And the king of Israel said unto Jehoshaphat, Did I not tell thee that he would prophesy no good concerning me, but evil?

19 And he said, Hear thou therefore the word of the LORD: I saw the LORD sitting on his throne, and all the host of heaven standing by him on his right hand and on his left.

20 And the LORD said, Who shall persuade Ahab, that he may go up and fall at Ramoth-gilead? And one said on this manner, and another said on that manner.

21 And there came forth a spirit, and stood before the LORD, and said, I will persuade him.

22 And the LORD said unto him, Wherewith? And he said, I will go forth, and I will be a lying spirit in the mouth of all his prophets. And he said, Thou shalt persuade *him*, and prevail also: go forth, and do so.

23 Now therefore, behold, the LORD hath put a lying spirit in the mouth of all these thy prophets, and the LORD hath spoken evil concerning thee.

24 But Zedekiah the son of Chenaanah went near, and smote Micaiah on the cheek, and said, Which way went the spirit of the LORD from me to speak unto thee?

25 And Micaiah said, Behold, thou shalt see in that day, when thou shalt go into an inner chamber to hide thyself.

26 And the king of Israel said, Take Micaiah, and carry him back unto Amon the governor of the city, and to Joash the king's son;

27 And say, Thus saith the king, Put this *fellow* in the prison, and feed him with bread of affliction and with water of affliction, until I come in peace.

28 And Micaiah said, If thou return at all in peace, the LORD hath not spoken by me. And he said, Hearken, O people, every one of you.

29 So the king of Israel and Jehoshaphat the king of Judah went up to Ramoth-gilead.

30 And the king of Israel said unto Jehoshaphat, I will disguise myself, and enter into the battle; but put thou on thy robes. And the king of Israel disguised himself, and went into the battle.

## Amplified

8 [Ahab] king of Israel said to Jehoshaphat, There is yet one man, Micaiah son of Imlah, by whom we may inquire of the Lord, but I hate him; for he never prophesies good for me, but evil. Jehoshaphat said, Let not the king say that.

9 Then [Ahab] king of Israel told an officer, Bring quickly Micaiah son of Imlah.

10 Now the king of Israel and Jehoshaphat king of Judah were sitting in [royal] robes [or armor], each on his throne in an open place (on a threshing floor) at the entrance of the gate of Samaria; and all the prophets prophesied before them.

11 And Zedekiah son of Chenaanah made him horns of iron, and said, Thus says the Lord, With these you shall push the Syrians, until they are destroyed.

12 And all the prophets agreed, saying, Go up to Ramoth-gilead and prosper; for the Lord will deliver it into the king's hand.

13 The messenger who went to call Micaiah said to him, Behold now, the prophets unanimously declare good to the king. Let your answer, I pray you, be like theirs, and say what is good.

14 But Micaiah said, As the Lord lives, I will speak what the Lord says to me.

15 So he came to the king. King [Ahab] said, Micaiah, shall we go against Ramoth-gilead to battle, or shall we hold back? And he answered, Go, and prosper; for the Lord will deliver it into the king's hand.

16 And the king said to him, How many times must I charge you to tell me nothing but the truth in the name of the Lord?

17 And he said, I saw all Israel scattered upon the hills, as sheep that have no shepherd; and the Lord said, These have no master. Let them return every man to his house in peace.

18 Then the king of Israel said to Jehoshaphat, Did I not tell you that he would prophesy no good concerning me, but evil?

19 And Micaiah said, Hear the word of the Lord: I saw the Lord sitting on His throne, and all the host of Heaven standing by Him on His right hand and on His left.

20 And the Lord said, Who will entice Ahab to go up and fall at Ramoth-gilead? One said this way, another said that way.

21 Then there came forth the spirit [of whom I am about to tell], and stood before the Lord, and said, I will entice him.

22 The Lord said to him, By what means? And he said, I will go forth and be a lying spirit in the mouth of all his prophets. [The Lord] said, You shall entice him, and succeed also; go forth and do it.

23 So the Lord has put a lying spirit in the mouth of all these prophets, and the Lord has spoken evil concerning you.

24 But Zedekiah the son of Chenaanah went near and struck Micaiah on the cheek, and said, Which way went the Spirit of the Lord from me to speak to you?

25 Micaiah said, Behold, you shall see on that day when you go into an inner chamber to hide yourself.

26 [Ahab] king of Israel said, Take Micaiah, carry him back to Amon the governor of the city and to Joash the king's son;

27 And say, The king says, Put this fellow in prison, and feed him with bread and water of affliction until I come in peace.

28 Micaiah said, If you return at all in peace, the Lord has not spoken by me. He [added], Hear, O people, every one of you!

29 So [Ahab] king of Israel and Jehoshaphat the king of Judah went up to Ramoth-gilead.

30 And the king of Israel said to Jehoshaphat, I will disguise myself and enter the battle; but you put on your [royal] clothing. And the king of Israel disguised himself and went into the battle.

## New American Standard

8And the king of Israel said to Jehoshaphat, "There is yet one
man by whom we may inquire of the LORD, but I hate him, because
he does not prophesy good concerning me, but evil. *He is* Micaiah
son of Imlah." But Jehoshaphat said, "Let not the king say so."
9Then the king of Israel called an officer and said, "Bring
quickly Micaiah son of Imlah."
10Now the king of Israel and Jehoshaphat king of Judah were
sitting each on his throne, arrayed in *their* robes, at the threshing
floor at the entrance of the gate of Samaria; and all the prophets
were prophesying before them.
11Then Zedekiah the son of Chenaanah made horns of iron for
himself and said, "Thus says the LORD, 'With these you shall gore
the Arameans until they are consumed.' "
12And all the prophets were prophesying thus, saying, "Go up
to Ramoth-gilead and prosper, for the LORD will give *it* into the
hand of the king."

*Micaiah Predicts Defeat*

**13**¶ Then the messenger who went to summon Micaiah spoke
to him saying, "Behold now, the words of the prophets are uniformly favorable to the king. Please let your word be like the word
of one of them, and speak favorably."
14But Micaiah said, "As the LORD lives, what the LORD says to
me, that I will speak."
15When he came to the king, the king said to him, "Micaiah,
shall we go to Ramoth-gilead to battle, or shall we refrain?" And
he answered him, "Go up and succeed, and the LORD will give *it*
into the hand of the king."
16Then the king said to him, "How many times must I adjure
you to speak to me nothing but the truth in the name of the LORD?"
17So he said,

"I saw all Israel
Scattered on the mountains,
Like sheep which have no shepherd.
And the LORD said, 'These have no master.
Let each of them return to his house in peace.' "

18Then the king of Israel said to Jehoshaphat, "Did I not tell you
that he would not prophesy good concerning me, but evil?"
19And Micaiah said, "Therefore, hear the word of the LORD. I
saw the LORD sitting on His throne, and all the host of heaven
standing by Him on His right and on His left.
20"And the LORD said, 'Who will entice Ahab to go up and fall
at Ramoth-gilead?' And one said this while another said that.
21"Then a spirit came forward and stood before the LORD and
said, 'I will entice him.'
22"And the LORD said to him, 'How?' And he said, 'I will go out
and be a deceiving spirit in the mouth of all his prophets.' Then
He said, 'You are to entice *him* and also prevail. Go and do so.'
23"Now therefore, behold, the LORD has put a deceiving spirit
in the mouth of all these your prophets; and the LORD has proclaimed disaster against you."
**24**¶ Then Zedekiah the son of Chenaanah came near and struck
Micaiah on the cheek and said, "How did the Spirit of the LORD
pass from me to speak to you?"
25And Micaiah said, "Behold, you shall see on that day when
you enter an inner room to hide yourself."
26Then the king of Israel said, "Take Micaiah and return him to
Amon the governor of the city and to Joash the king's son;
27and say, 'Thus says the king, "Put this man in prison, and
feed him sparingly with bread and water until I return safely." ' "
28And Micaiah said, "If you indeed return safely the LORD has
not spoken by me." And he said, "Listen, all you people."

*Defeat and Death of Ahab*

**29**¶ So the king of Israel and Jehoshaphat king of Judah went up
against Ramoth-gilead.
30And the king of Israel said to Jehoshaphat, "I will disguise
myself and go into the battle, but you put on your robes." So the
king of Israel disguised himself and went into the battle.

## New International

8The king of Israel answered Jehoshaphat, "There is still one
man through whom we can inquire of the LORD, but I hate him
because he never prophesies anything good about me, but always
bad. He is Micaiah son of Imlah."
"The king should not say that," Jehoshaphat replied.
9So the king of Israel called one of his officials and said, "Bring
Micaiah son of Imlah at once."
10Dressed in their royal robes, the king of Israel and Jehoshaphat king of Judah were sitting on their thrones at the threshing
floor by the entrance of the gate of Samaria, with all the prophets
prophesying before them. 11Now Zedekiah son of Kenaanah had
made iron horns and he declared, "This is what the LORD says:
'With these you will gore the Arameans until they are destroyed.' "
12All the other prophets were prophesying the same thing.
"Attack Ramoth Gilead and be victorious," they said, "for the
LORD will give it into the king's hand."
13The messenger who had gone to summon Micaiah said to
him, "Look, as one man the other prophets are predicting success
for the king. Let your word agree with theirs, and speak favorably."
14But Micaiah said, "As surely as the LORD lives, I can tell him
only what the LORD tells me."
15When he arrived, the king asked him, "Micaiah, shall we go
to war against Ramoth Gilead, or shall I refrain?"
"Attack and be victorious," he answered, "for the LORD will
give it into the king's hand."
16The king said to him, "How many times must I make you
swear to tell me nothing but the truth in the name of the LORD?"
17Then Micaiah answered, "I saw all Israel scattered on the hills
like sheep without a shepherd, and the LORD said, 'These people
have no master. Let each one go home in peace.' "
18The king of Israel said to Jehoshaphat, "Didn't I tell you that
he never prophesies anything good about me, but only bad?"
19Micaiah continued, "Therefore hear the word of the LORD: I
saw the LORD sitting on his throne with all the host of heaven
standing around him on his right and on his left. 20And the LORD
said, 'Who will entice Ahab into attacking Ramoth Gilead and
going to his death there?'
"One suggested this, and another that. 21Finally, a spirit came
forward, stood before the LORD and said, 'I will entice him.'
22" 'By what means?' the LORD asked.
" 'I will go out and be a lying spirit in the mouths of all his
prophets,' he said.
" 'You will succeed in enticing him,' said the LORD. 'Go and do
it.'
23"So now the LORD has put a lying spirit in the mouths of all
these prophets of yours. The LORD has decreed disaster for you."
24Then Zedekiah son of Kenaanah went up and slapped Micaiah in the face. "Which way did the spirit from[a] the LORD go
when he went from me to speak to you?" he asked.
25Micaiah replied, "You will find out on the day you go to hide
in an inner room."
26The king of Israel then ordered, "Take Micaiah and send him
back to Amon the ruler of the city and to Joash the king's son 27and
say, 'This is what the king says: Put this fellow in prison and give
him nothing but bread and water until I return safely.' "
28Micaiah declared, "If you ever return safely, the LORD has not
spoken through me." Then he added, "Mark my words, all you
people!"

*Ahab Killed at Ramoth Gilead*

29So the king of Israel and Jehoshaphat king of Judah went up
to Ramoth Gilead. 30The king of Israel said to Jehoshaphat, "I will
enter the battle in disguise, but you wear your royal robes." So the
king of Israel disguised himself and went into battle.

**NIV** [a] 24 Or *Spirit of*

## King James

31But the king of Syria commanded his thirty and two captains
that had rule over his chariots, saying, Fight neither with small nor
great, save only with the king of Israel.
32And it came to pass, when the captains of the chariots saw
Jehoshaphat, that they said, Surely it *is* the king of Israel. And they
turned aside to fight against him: and Jehoshaphat cried out.
33And it came to pass, when the captains of the chariots perceived that it *was* not the king of Israel, that they turned back from
pursuing him.
34And a *certain* man drew a bow at a venture, and smote the
king of Israel between the joints of the harness: wherefore he said
unto the driver of his chariot, Turn thine hand, and carry me out
of the host; for I am wounded.
35And the battle increased that day: and the king was stayed up
in his chariot against the Syrians, and died at even: and the blood
ran out of the wound into the midst of the chariot.
36And there went a proclamation throughout the host about the
going down of the sun, saying, Every man to his city, and every
man to his own country.
37¶ So the king died, and was brought to Samaria; and they
buried the king in Samaria.
38And *one* washed the chariot in the pool of Samaria; and the
dogs licked up his blood; and they washed his armour; according
unto the word of the LORD which he spake.
39Now the rest of the acts of Ahab, and all that he did, and the
ivory house which he made, and all the cities that he built, *are* they
not written in the book of the chronicles of the kings of Israel?
40So Ahab slept with his fathers; and Ahaziah his son reigned
in his stead.
41¶ And Jehoshaphat the son of Asa began to reign over Judah
in the fourth year of Ahab king of Israel.
42Jehoshaphat *was* thirty and five years old when he began to
reign; and he reigned twenty and five years in Jerusalem. And his
mother's name *was* Azubah the daughter of Shilhi.
43And he walked in all the ways of Asa his father; he turned not
aside from it, doing *that which was* right in the eyes of the LORD:
nevertheless the high places were not taken away; *for* the people
offered and burnt incense yet in the high places.
44And Jehoshaphat made peace with the king of Israel.
45Now the rest of the acts of Jehoshaphat, and his might that
he showed, and how he warred, *are* they not written in the book
of the chronicles of the kings of Judah?
46And the remnant of the sodomites, which remained in the
days of his father Asa, he took out of the land.
47 *There was* then no king in Edom: a deputy *was* king.
48Jehoshaphat made ships of Tharshish to go to Ophir for gold:
but they went not; for the ships were broken at Ezion-geber.
49Then said Ahaziah the son of Ahab unto Jehoshaphat, Let my
servants go with thy servants in the ships. But Jehoshaphat would
not.
50¶ And Jehoshaphat slept with his fathers, and was buried with
his fathers in the city of David his father: and Jehoram his son
reigned in his stead.
51¶ Ahaziah the son of Ahab began to reign over Israel in Samaria the seventeenth year of Jehoshaphat king of Judah, and
reigned two years over Israel.
52And he did evil in the sight of the LORD, and walked in the
way of his father, and in the way of his mother, and in the way
of Jeroboam the son of Nebat, who made Israel to sin:
53For he served Baal, and worshipped him, and provoked to
anger the LORD God of Israel, according to all that his father had
done.

## Amplified

31But the king of Syria had commanded the thirty-two captains
of his chariots, Fight neither with small nor great, but only with
*Ahab* king of Israel.
32And when the captains of the chariots saw Jehoshaphat, they
said, Surely it is the king of Israel. They turned to fight against him,
but Jehoshaphat cried out.
33And when the captains of the chariots saw that it was not the
king of Israel, they turned back from pursuing him.
34But a certain man drew a bow at a venture, and smote [Ahab]
king of Israel between the joints of the armor. So he said to the
driver of his chariot, Turn around and carry me out of the army,
for I am wounded.
35The battle increased that day, and [Ahab] the king was
propped up in his chariot facing the Syrians, and at nightfall he
died. And the blood of his wound flowed onto the floor of the
chariot.
36And there went a cry throughout the army about sundown,
saying, Every man to his city and his own country,
37For the king is dead! And [Ahab] was brought to Samaria,
where they buried him.
38And they washed *his* chariot by the pool of Samaria, where
the harlots bathed, and the dogs licked up his blood, as the Lord
had predicted. [I Kings 21:19.]
39The rest of Ahab's acts, all he did, the ivory palace and all the
cities he built, are they not written in the Book of the Chronicles
of the Kings of Israel?
40So Ahab slept with his fathers; Ahaziah his son reigned in his
stead.
41Jehoshaphat son of Asa began to reign over Judah in the
fourth year of Ahab king of Israel.
42Jehoshaphat was thirty-five years old when he began to reign;
and he reigned twenty-five years in Jerusalem. His mother was
Azubah daughter of Shilhi.
43He walked in all the way *or* custom of Asa his father, never
swerving from it, doing right in the sight of the Lord. However,
the [idolatrous] high places were not taken away; for the people
still sacrificed and burned incense in the high places.
44And Jehoshaphat made peace with Israel's king.
45The rest of the acts of Jehoshaphat, his might that he showed,
and how he warred, are they not written in the Book of the Chronicles of the Kings of Judah?
46And the remnant of the sodomites [the male cult prostitutes],
who remained in the days of his father Asa, *Jehoshaphat* expelled
from the country.
47There was no king in Edom; a deputy was acting king.
48Jehoshaphat ordered ships of Tarshish to go to Ophir for gold,
but they did not, for the ships were wrecked at Ezion-geber.
49When Ahaziah son of Ahab said to Jehoshaphat, Let my
servants go with your servants in the ships, Jehoshaphat refused.
50Jehoshaphat slept with his fathers, and was buried with them
in the city of David his father [forefather]; and Jehoram his son
reigned in his stead.
51Ahaziah son of Ahab began his two year reign over Israel in
Samaria the seventeenth year of Jehoshaphat king of Judah.
52He did evil in the sight of the Lord, and walked in the way
of his father [Ahab] and of his mother [Jezebel] and of Jeroboam
son of Nebat, who made Israel sin.
53He served Baal and worshiped him, and provoked the Lord,
the God of Israel, to anger in all the ways his father had done.

## New American Standard

31Now the king of Aram had commanded the thirty-two captains of his chariots, saying, "Do not fight with small or great, but
with the king of Israel alone."
32So it came about, when the captains of the chariots saw Jehoshaphat, that they said, "Surely it is the king of Israel," and they
turned aside to fight against him, and Jehoshaphat cried out.
33Then it happened, when the captains of the chariots saw that
it was not the king of Israel, that they turned back from pursuing
him.
34¶ Now a certain man drew his bow at random and struck the
king of Israel in a joint of the armor. So he said to the driver of his
chariot, "Turn around, and take me out of the fight; for I am
severely wounded."
35And the battle raged that day, and the king was propped up
in his chariot in front of the Arameans, and died at evening, and
the blood from the wound ran into the bottom of the chariot.
36Then a cry passed throughout the army close to sunset, saying, "Every man to his city and every man to his country."
37¶ So the king died and was brought to Samaria, and they
buried the king in Samaria.
38And they washed the chariot by the pool of Samaria, and the
dogs licked up his blood (now the harlots bathed themselves *there*),
according to the word of the LORD which He spoke.
39Now the rest of the acts of Ahab and all that he did and the
ivory house which he built and all the cities which he built, are they
not written in the Book of the Chronicles of the Kings of Israel?
40So Ahab slept with his fathers, and Ahaziah his son became
king in his place.

*The New Rulers*

41¶ Now Jehoshaphat the son of Asa became king over Judah
in the fourth year of Ahab king of Israel.
42Jehoshaphat was thirty-five years old when he became king,
and he reigned twenty-five years in Jerusalem. And his mother's
name was Azubah the daughter of Shilhi.
43And he walked in all the way of Asa his father; he did not turn
aside from it, doing right in the sight of the LORD. However, the
high places were not taken away; the people still sacrificed and
burnt incense on the high places.
44Jehoshaphat also made peace with the king of Israel.
45¶ Now the rest of the acts of Jehoshaphat, and his might which
he showed and how he warred, are they not written in the Book
of the Chronicles of the Kings of Judah?
46And the remnant of the sodomites who remained in the days
of his father Asa, he expelled from the land.
47Now there was no king in Edom; a deputy was king.
48Jehoshaphat made ships of Tarshish to go to Ophir for gold,
but they did not go for the ships were broken at Ezion-geber.
49Then Ahaziah the son of Ahab said to Jehoshaphat, "Let my
servants go with your servants in the ships." But Jehoshaphat was
not willing.
50And Jehoshaphat slept with his fathers and was buried with
his fathers in the city of his father David, and Jehoram his son
became king in his place.
51¶ Ahaziah the son of Ahab became king over Israel in Samaria
in the seventeenth year of Jehoshaphat king of Judah, and he
reigned two years over Israel.
52And he did evil in the sight of the LORD and walked in the way
of his father and in the way of his mother and in the way of
Jeroboam the son of Nebat, who caused Israel to sin.
53So he served Baal and worshiped him and provoked the LORD
God of Israel to anger according to all that his father had done.

## New International

31Now the king of Aram had ordered his thirty-two chariot
commanders, "Do not fight with anyone, small or great, except the
king of Israel." 32When the chariot commanders saw Jehoshaphat,
they thought, "Surely this is the king of Israel." So they turned to
attack him, but when Jehoshaphat cried out, 33the chariot commanders saw that he was not the king of Israel and stopped pursuing him.
34But someone drew his bow at random and hit the king of
Israel between the sections of his armor. The king told his chariot
driver, "Wheel around and get me out of the fighting. I've been
wounded." 35All day long the battle raged, and the king was
propped up in his chariot facing the Arameans. The blood from his
wound ran onto the floor of the chariot, and that evening he died.
36As the sun was setting, a cry spread through the army: "Every
man to his town; everyone to his land!"
37So the king died and was brought to Samaria, and they buried
him there. 38They washed the chariot at a pool in Samaria (where
the prostitutes bathed),[a] and the dogs licked up his blood, as the
word of the LORD had declared.
39As for the other events of Ahab's reign, including all he did,
the palace he built and inlaid with ivory, and the cities he fortified,
are they not written in the book of the annals of the kings of Israel?
40Ahab rested with his fathers. And Ahaziah his son succeeded
him as king.

*Jehoshaphat King of Judah*

41Jehoshaphat son of Asa became king of Judah in the fourth
year of Ahab king of Israel. 42Jehoshaphat was thirty-five years old
when he became king, and he reigned in Jerusalem twenty-five
years. His mother's name was Azubah daughter of Shilhi. 43In
everything he walked in the ways of his father Asa and did not
stray from them; he did what was right in the eyes of the LORD.
The high places, however, were not removed, and the people
continued to offer sacrifices and burn incense there. 44Jehoshaphat
was also at peace with the king of Israel.
45As for the other events of Jehoshaphat's reign, the things he
achieved and his military exploits, are they not written in the book
of the annals of the kings of Judah? 46He rid the land of the rest
of the male shrine prostitutes who remained there even after the
reign of his father Asa. 47There was then no king in Edom; a
deputy ruled.
48Now Jehoshaphat built a fleet of trading ships[b] to go to Ophir
for gold, but they never set sail—they were wrecked at Ezion
Geber. 49At that time Ahaziah son of Ahab said to Jehoshaphat,
"Let my men sail with your men," but Jehoshaphat refused.
50Then Jehoshaphat rested with his fathers and was buried with
them in the city of David his father. And Jehoram his son succeeded him.

*Ahaziah King of Israel*

51Ahaziah son of Ahab became king of Israel in Samaria in the
seventeenth year of Jehoshaphat king of Judah, and he reigned
over Israel two years. 52He did evil in the eyes of the LORD, because
he walked in the ways of his father and mother and in the ways
of Jeroboam son of Nebat, who caused Israel to sin. 53He served
and worshiped Baal and provoked the LORD, the God of Israel, to
anger, just as his father had done.

NIV [a] 38 Or *Samaria and cleaned the weapons* [b] 48 Hebrew *of ships of Tarshish*

## King James

THE SECOND BOOK OF THE

# Kings

COMMONLY CALLED

THE FOURTH BOOK OF THE KINGS

**1** THEN MOAB rebelled against Israel after the death of Ahab.
2And Ahaziah fell down through a lattice in his upper chamber that *was* in Samaria, and was sick: and he sent messengers, and
said unto them, Go, inquire of Baal-zebub the god of Ekron
whether I shall recover of this disease.
3But the angel of the LORD said to Elijah the Tishbite, Arise, go
up to meet the messengers of the king of Samaria, and say unto
them, *Is it* not because *there is* not a God in Israel, *that* ye go to
inquire of Baal-zebub the god of Ekron?
4Now therefore thus saith the LORD, Thou shalt not come down
from that bed on which thou art gone up, but shalt surely die. And
Elijah departed.
5¶ And when the messengers turned back unto him, he said
unto them, Why are ye now turned back?
6And they said unto him, There came a man up to meet us, and
said unto us, Go, turn again unto the king that sent you, and say
unto him, Thus saith the LORD, *Is it* not because *there is* not a God
in Israel, *that* thou sendest to inquire of Baal-zebub the god of
Ekron? therefore thou shalt not come down from that bed on
which thou art gone up, but shalt surely die.
7And he said unto them, What manner of man *was he* which
came up to meet you, and told you these words?
8And they answered him, *He was* an hairy man, and girt with
a girdle of leather about his loins. And he said, It *is* Elijah the
Tishbite.
9Then the king sent unto him a captain of fifty with his fifty.
And he went up to him: and, behold, he sat on the top of an hill.
And he spake unto him, Thou man of God, the king hath said,
Come down.
10And Elijah answered and said to the captain of fifty, If I *be* a
man of God, then let fire come down from heaven, and consume
thee and thy fifty. And there came down fire from heaven, and
consumed him and his fifty.
11Again also he sent unto him another captain of fifty with his
fifty. And he answered and said unto him, O man of God, thus
hath the king said, Come down quickly.
12And Elijah answered and said unto them, If I *be* a man of God,
let fire come down from heaven, and consume thee and thy fifty.
And the fire of God came down from heaven, and consumed him
and his fifty.
13¶ And he sent again a captain of the third fifty with his fifty.
And the third captain of fifty went up, and came and fell on his
knees before Elijah, and besought him, and said unto him, O man
of God, I pray thee, let my life, and the life of these fifty thy
servants, be precious in thy sight.
14Behold, there came fire down from heaven, and burnt up the
two captains of the former fifties with their fifties: therefore let my
life now be precious in thy sight.
15And the angel of the LORD said unto Elijah, Go down with
him: be not afraid of him. And he arose, and went down with him
unto the king.

## Amplified

THE SECOND BOOK OF THE

# Kings

**1** MOAB REBELLED against Israel after the death of Ahab.
2[King] Ahaziah fell down through a lattice in his upper
chamber in Samaria, and lay sick. He sent messengers, saying, Go,
ask Baal-zebub the god of [Philistine] Ekron if I shall recover from
this illness.
3But the Angel of the Lord said to Elijah the Tishbite, Arise, go
up to meet the messengers of the king in Samaria, and say to them,
Is it because there is no God in Israel, that you are going to inquire
of Baal-zebub, the god of Ekron?
4Therefore the Lord says, You [Ahaziah] shall not leave the bed
on which you lie, but shall surely die. And Elijah departed.
5When the messengers returned to Ahaziah, he said, Why have
you turned back?
6They replied, A man came up to meet us who said, Go back
to the king who sent you and tell him, Thus says the Lord, Is there
no God in Israel, that you send to inquire of Baal-zebub, the god
of Ekron? Therefore you shall not leave the bed on which you lie,
but shall surely die.
7The king asked, What was the man like who came to meet you
saying these things?
8They answered, He was a hairy man, with a girdle of leather
about his loins. And he said, It is Elijah the Tishbite.
9Then the king sent to Elijah a captain of fifty men with his fifty
[to seize him]. He found Elijah sitting on a hilltop, and said, Man
of God, the king says, Come down.
10Elijah said to the captain of fifty, If I am a man of God, then
let fire come down from Heaven, and consume you and your fifty.
And fire fell from Heaven and consumed him and his fifty.
11Again King [Ahaziah] sent to him another captain of fifty with
his fifty. And he said to Elijah, Man of God, the king has said,
Come down quickly!
12And Elijah answered, If I am a man of God, let fire come down
from Heaven, and consume you and your fifty. And the fire of God
came down from Heaven and consumed him and his fifty.
13Ahaziah sent again a captain of a third fifty with his fifty. And
the third captain of fifty went up, and fell on his knees before
Elijah, and besought him, and said to him, O man of God, I pray
you, let my life, and the life of these fifty your servants, be precious
in your sight.
14Behold, fire came down from Heaven, and burned up the two
captains of the former fifties with their fifties. Therefore let my life
now be precious in your sight.
15The Angel of the Lord said to Elijah, Go down with him; do
not be afraid of him. So he arose, and went with him to the king.

## New American Standard

# 2 Kings

*Ahaziah's Messengers Meet Elijah*

1 NOW MOAB rebelled against Israel after the death of Ahab.
2And Ahaziah fell through the lattice in his upper chamber
which *was* in Samaria, and became ill. So he sent messengers and
said to them, "Go, inquire of Baal-zebub, the god of Ekron,
whether I shall recover from this sickness."
3But the angel of the LORD said to Elijah the Tishbite, "Arise,
go up to meet the messengers of the king of Samaria and say to
them, 'Is it because there is no God in Israel *that* you are going to
inquire of Baal-zebub, the god of Ekron?'
4"Now therefore thus says the LORD, 'You shall not come
down from the bed where you have gone up, but you shall surely
die.'" Then Elijah departed.
5¶ When the messengers returned to him he said to them,
"Why have you returned?"
6And they said to him, "A man came up to meet us and said
to us, 'Go, return to the king who sent you and say to him, "Thus
says the LORD, 'Is it because there is no God in Israel *that* you are
sending to inquire of Baal-zebub, the god of Ekron? Therefore you
shall not come down from the bed where you have gone up, but
shall surely die.'"'"
7And he said to them, "What kind of man was he who came
up to meet you and spoke these words to you?"
8And they answered him, "*He was* a hairy man with a leather
girdle bound about his loins." And he said, "It is Elijah the Tishbite."
9¶ Then *the king* sent to him a captain of fifty with his fifty. And
he went up to him, and behold, he was sitting on the top of the
hill. And he said to him, "O man of God, the king says, 'Come
down.'"
10And Elijah answered and said to the captain of fifty, "If I am
a man of God, let fire come down from heaven and consume you
and your fifty." Then fire came down from heaven and consumed
him and his fifty.
11So he again sent to him another captain of fifty with his fifty.
And he answered and said to him, "O man of God, thus says the
king, 'Come down quickly.'"
12And Elijah answered and said to them, "If I am a man of God,
let fire come down from heaven and consume you and your fifty."
Then the fire of God came down from heaven and consumed him
and his fifty.
13So he again sent the captain of a third fifty with his fifty. When
the third captain of fifty went up, he came and bowed down on
his knees before Elijah, and begged him and said to him, "O man
of God, please let my life and the lives of these fifty servants of
yours be precious in your sight.
14"Behold fire came down from heaven, and consumed the first
two captains of fifty with their fifties; but now let my life be
precious in your sight."
15And the angel of the LORD said to Elijah, "Go down with him;
do not be afraid of him." So he arose and went down with him to
the king.

## New International

# 2 Kings

*The LORD's Judgment on Ahaziah*

1 AFTER AHAB'S death, Moab rebelled against Israel. 2Now
Ahaziah had fallen through the lattice of his upper room in
Samaria and injured himself. So he sent messengers, saying to
them, "Go and consult Baal-Zebub, the god of Ekron, to see if I
will recover from this injury."
3But the angel of the LORD said to Elijah the Tishbite, "Go up
and meet the messengers of the king of Samaria and ask them, 'Is
it because there is no God in Israel that you are going off to consult
Baal-Zebub, the god of Ekron?' 4Therefore this is what the LORD
says: 'You will not leave the bed you are lying on. You will certainly die!'" So Elijah went.
5When the messengers returned to the king, he asked them,
"Why have you come back?"
6"A man came to meet us," they replied. "And he said to us,
'Go back to the king who sent you and tell him, "This is what the
LORD says: Is it because there is no God in Israel that you are
sending men to consult Baal-Zebub, the god of Ekron? Therefore
you will not leave the bed you are lying on. You will certainly
die!"'"
7The king asked them, "What kind of man was it who came to
meet you and told you this?"
8They replied, "He was a man with a garment of hair and with
a leather belt around his waist."
The king said, "That was Elijah the Tishbite."
9Then he sent to Elijah a captain with his company of fifty men.
The captain went up to Elijah, who was sitting on the top of a hill,
and said to him, "Man of God, the king says, 'Come down!'"
10Elijah answered the captain, "If I am a man of God, may fire
come down from heaven and consume you and your fifty men!"
Then fire fell from heaven and consumed the captain and his men.
11At this the king sent to Elijah another captain with his fifty
men. The captain said to him, "Man of God, this is what the king
says, 'Come down at once!'"
12"If I am a man of God," Elijah replied, "may fire come down
from heaven and consume you and your fifty men!" Then the fire
of God fell from heaven and consumed him and his fifty men.
13So the king sent a third captain with his fifty men. This third
captain went up and fell on his knees before Elijah. "Man of God,"
he begged, "please have respect for my life and the lives of these
fifty men, your servants! 14See, fire has fallen from heaven and
consumed the first two captains and all their men. But now have
respect for my life!"
15The angel of the LORD said to Elijah, "Go down with him; do
not be afraid of him." So Elijah got up and went down with him
to the king.

## King James

16And he said unto him, Thus saith the LORD, Forasmuch as thou hast sent messengers to inquire of Baal-zebub the god of Ekron, *is it* not because *there is* no God in Israel to inquire of his word? therefore thou shalt not come down off that bed on which thou art gone up, but shalt surely die.

17¶ So he died according to the word of the LORD which Elijah had spoken. And Jehoram reigned in his stead in the second year of Jehoram the son of Jehoshaphat king of Judah; because he had no son.

18Now the rest of the acts of Ahaziah which he did, *are* they not written in the book of the chronicles of the kings of Israel?

**2** AND IT came to pass, when the LORD would take up Elijah into heaven by a whirlwind, that Elijah went with Elisha from Gilgal.

2And Elijah said unto Elisha, Tarry here, I pray thee; for the LORD hath sent me to Beth-el. And Elisha said *unto him, As* the LORD liveth, and *as* thy soul liveth, I will not leave thee. So they went down to Beth-el.

3And the sons of the prophets that *were* at Beth-el came forth to Elisha, and said unto him, Knowest thou that the LORD will take away thy master from thy head today? And he said, Yea, I know *it;* hold ye your peace.

4And Elijah said unto him, Elisha, tarry here, I pray thee; for the LORD hath sent me to Jericho. And he said, *As* the LORD liveth, and *as* thy soul liveth, I will not leave thee. So they came to Jericho.

5And the sons of the prophets that *were* at Jericho came to Elisha, and said unto him, Knowest thou that the LORD will take away thy master from thy head today? And he answered, Yea, I know *it;* hold ye your peace.

6And Elijah said unto him, Tarry, I pray thee, here; for the LORD hath sent me to Jordan. And he said, *As* the LORD liveth, and *as* thy soul liveth, I will not leave thee. And they two went on.

7And fifty men of the sons of the prophets went, and stood to view afar off: and they two stood by Jordan.

8And Elijah took his mantle, and wrapped *it* together, and smote the waters, and they were divided hither and thither, so that they two went over on dry ground.

9¶ And it came to pass, when they were gone over, that Elijah said unto Elisha, Ask what I shall do for thee, before I be taken away from thee. And Elisha said, I pray thee, let a double portion of thy spirit be upon me.

10And he said, Thou hast asked a hard thing: *nevertheless,* if thou see me *when I am* taken from thee, it shall be so unto thee; but if not, it shall not be *so.*

11And it came to pass, as they still went on, and talked, that, behold, *there appeared* a chariot of fire, and horses of fire, and parted them both asunder; and Elijah went up by a whirlwind into heaven.

12¶ And Elisha saw *it,* and he cried, My father, my father, the chariot of Israel, and the horsemen thereof. And he saw him no more: and he took hold of his own clothes, and rent them in two pieces.

13He took up also the mantle of Elijah that fell from him, and went back, and stood by the bank of Jordan;

14And he took the mantle of Elijah that fell from him, and smote the waters, and said, Where *is* the LORD God of Elijah? and when he also had smitten the waters, they parted hither and thither: and Elisha went over.

## Amplified

16Elijah said to [King] Ahaziah, Thus says the Lord, Since you have sent messengers to inquire of Baal-zebub, god of Ekron, is it because there is no God in Israel of Whom to inquire His word? Therefore you shall not leave the bed on which you lie, but shall surely die.

17So Ahaziah died according to the word of the Lord which Elijah had spoken. J(eh)oram [also a son of Ahab] reigned in Israel in his stead in the second year of Jehoram son of Jehoshaphat king of Judah; because Ahaziah had no son [but his brother].

18Now the rest of the acts of Ahaziah, are they not written in the Book of the Chronicles of the Kings of Israel?

**2** WHEN THE Lord was about to take Elijah up to Heaven by a whirlwind, Elijah and Elisha were going from Gilgal,

2And Elijah said to Elisha, Tarry here, I pray you, for the Lord has sent me to Bethel. But Elisha replied, As the Lord lives, and as your soul lives, I will not leave you. So they went down to Bethel.

3The prophets' sons who were at Bethel came to Elisha and said, Do you know the Lord will take your master from you today? He said, Yes, I know it; hold your peace.

4Elijah said to him, Elisha, tarry here, I pray you, for the Lord has sent me to Jericho. But he said, As the Lord lives, and as your soul lives, I will not leave you. So they came to Jericho.

5The sons of the prophets who were at Jericho came to Elisha, and said, Do you know that the Lord will take your master away from you today? And he answered, Yes, I know it; hold your peace.

6Elijah said to him, Tarry here, I pray you; for the Lord has sent me to Jordan. But he said, As the Lord lives, and as your soul lives, I will not leave you. And they two went on.

7Fifty men of the sons of the prophets also went, and stood [to watch] afar off; and they two stood by the Jordan.

8And Elijah took his mantle and rolled it up and struck the waters, and they divided this way and that, so that they two went over on dry ground.

9And when they had gone over, Elijah said to Elisha, Ask what I shall do for you before I am taken from you. And Elisha said, I pray you, let a double portion of your spirit be upon me.

10He said, You have asked a hard thing. However, if you see me when I am taken from you, it shall be so for you; but if not, it shall not be so.

11As they still went on, and talked, behold, a chariot of fire and horses of fire parted the two of them; and Elijah went up by a whirlwind into Heaven.

12And Elisha saw it, and he cried, My father, my father! The chariot of Israel and its horsemen! And he saw him no more. And he took hold of his own clothes and tore them in two pieces.

13He took up also the mantle of Elijah that fell from him, and went back and stood by the bank of Jordan.

14And he took the mantle that fell from Elijah, and struck the waters, and said, Where is the Lord God of Elijah? And when he had struck the waters, they parted this way and that, and Elisha went over.

## New American Standard

16Then he said to him, "Thus says the LORD, 'Because you have
sent messengers to inquire of Baal-zebub, the god of Ekron—is it
because there is no God in Israel to inquire of His word?—therefore
you shall not come down from the bed where you have gone up,
but shall surely die.' "

*Jehoram Reigns over Israel*

17¶ So Ahaziah died according to the word of the LORD which
Elijah had spoken. And because he had no son, Jehoram became
king in his place in the second year of Jehoram the son of Jehoshaphat, king of Judah.

18Now the rest of the acts of Ahaziah which he did, are they not
written in the Book of the Chronicles of the Kings of Israel?

*Elijah Taken to Heaven*

2 AND IT came about when the LORD was about to take up
Elijah by a whirlwind to heaven, that Elijah went with Elisha
from Gilgal.

2And Elijah said to Elisha, "Stay here please, for the LORD has
sent me as far as Bethel." But Elisha said, "As the LORD lives and
as you yourself live, I will not leave you." So they went down to
Bethel.

3Then the sons of the prophets who *were at* Bethel came out to
Elisha and said to him, "Do you know that the LORD will take away
your master from over you today?" And he said, "Yes, I know; be
still."

4And Elijah said to him, "Elisha, please stay here, for the LORD
has sent me to Jericho." But he said, "As the LORD lives, and as
you yourself live, I will not leave you." So they came to Jericho.
5And the sons of the prophets who *were* at Jericho approached
Elisha and said to him, "Do you know that the LORD will take away
your master from over you today?" And he answered, "Yes, I
know; be still."

6Then Elijah said to him, "Please stay here, for the LORD has
sent me to the Jordan." And he said, "As the LORD lives, and as
you yourself live, I will not leave you." So the two of them went
on.

7¶ Now fifty men of the sons of the prophets went and stood
opposite *them* at a distance, while the two of them stood by the
Jordan.

8And Elijah took his mantle and folded it together and struck
the waters, and they were divided here and there, so that the two
of them crossed over on dry ground.

9Now it came about when they had crossed over, that Elijah
said to Elisha, "Ask what I shall do for you before I am taken from
you." And Elisha said, "Please, let a double portion of your spirit
be upon me."

10And he said, "You have asked a hard thing. *Nevertheless*, if
you see me when I am taken from you, it shall be so for you; but
if not, it shall not be *so*."

11Then it came about as they were going along and talking, that
behold, *there appeared* a chariot of fire and horses of fire which
separated the two of them. And Elijah went up by a whirlwind to
heaven.

12And Elisha saw *it* and cried out, "My father, my father, the
chariots of Israel and its horsemen!" And he saw him no more.
Then he took hold of his own clothes and tore them in two pieces.

13He also took up the mantle of Elijah that fell from him, and
returned and stood by the bank of the Jordan.

14And he took the mantle of Elijah that fell from him, and struck
the waters and said, "Where is the LORD, the God of Elijah?" And
when he also had struck the waters, they were divided here and
there; and Elisha crossed over.

## New International

16He told the king, "This is what the LORD says: Is it because
there is no God in Israel for you to consult that you have sent
messengers to consult Baal-Zebub, the god of Ekron? Because you
have done this, you will never leave the bed you are lying on. You
will certainly die!" 17So he died, according to the word of the LORD
that Elijah had spoken.

Because Ahaziah had no son, Joram[a] succeeded him as king in
the second year of Jehoram son of Jehoshaphat king of Judah. 18As
for all the other events of Ahaziah's reign, and what he did, are
they not written in the book of the annals of the kings of Israel?

*Elijah Taken Up to Heaven*

2 WHEN THE LORD was about to take Elijah up to heaven in
a whirlwind, Elijah and Elisha were on their way from Gilgal.
2Elijah said to Elisha, "Stay here; the LORD has sent me to Bethel."

But Elisha said, "As surely as the LORD lives and as you live,
I will not leave you." So they went down to Bethel.

3The company of the prophets at Bethel came out to Elisha and
asked, "Do you know that the LORD is going to take your master
from you today?"

"Yes, I know," Elisha replied, "but do not speak of it."

4Then Elijah said to him, "Stay here, Elisha; the LORD has sent
me to Jericho."

And he replied, "As surely as the LORD lives and as you live,
I will not leave you." So they went to Jericho.

5The company of the prophets at Jericho went up to Elisha and
asked him, "Do you know that the LORD is going to take your
master from you today?"

"Yes, I know," he replied, "but do not speak of it."

6Then Elijah said to him, "Stay here; the LORD has sent me to
the Jordan."

And he replied, "As surely as the LORD lives and as you live,
I will not leave you." So the two of them walked on.

7Fifty men of the company of the prophets went and stood at
a distance, facing the place where Elijah and Elisha had stopped
at the Jordan. 8Elijah took his cloak, rolled it up and struck the
water with it. The water divided to the right and to the left, and
the two of them crossed over on dry ground.

9When they had crossed, Elijah said to Elisha, "Tell me, what
can I do for you before I am taken from you?"

"Let me inherit a double portion of your spirit," Elisha replied.

10"You have asked a difficult thing," Elijah said, "yet if you see
me when I am taken from you, it will be yours—otherwise not."

11As they were walking along and talking together, suddenly
a chariot of fire and horses of fire appeared and separated the two
of them, and Elijah went up to heaven in a whirlwind. 12Elisha saw
this and cried out, "My father! My father! The chariots and horsemen of Israel!" And Elisha saw him no more. Then he took hold
of his own clothes and tore them apart.

13He picked up the cloak that had fallen from Elijah and went
back and stood on the bank of the Jordan. 14Then he took the cloak
that had fallen from him and struck the water with it. "Where now
is the LORD, the God of Elijah?" he asked. When he struck the
water, it divided to the right and to the left, and he crossed over.

NIV [a] 17 Hebrew *Jehoram*, a variant of *Joram*

# King James

15And when the sons of the prophets which *were* to view at Jericho saw him, they said, The spirit of Elijah doth rest on Elisha. And they came to meet him, and bowed themselves to the ground before him.

16¶ And they said unto him, Behold now, there be with thy servants fifty strong men; let them go, we pray thee, and seek thy master: lest peradventure the spirit of the LORD hath taken him up, and cast him upon some mountain, or into some valley. And he said, Ye shall not send.

17And when they urged him till he was ashamed, he said, Send. They sent therefore fifty men; and they sought three days, but found him not.

18And when they came again to him, (for he tarried at Jericho,) he said unto them, Did I not say unto you, Go not?

19¶ And the men of the city said unto Elisha, Behold, I pray thee, the situation of this city *is* pleasant, as my lord seeth: but the water *is* naught, and the ground barren.

20And he said, Bring me a new cruse, and put salt therein. And they brought *it* to him.

21And he went forth unto the spring of the waters, and cast the salt in there, and said, Thus saith the LORD, I have healed these waters; there shall not be from thence any more death or barren *land*.

22So the waters were healed unto this day, according to the saying of Elisha which he spake.

23¶ And he went up from thence unto Beth-el: and as he was going up by the way, there came forth little children out of the city, and mocked him, and said unto him, Go up, thou bald head; go up, thou bald head.

24And he turned back, and looked on them, and cursed them in the name of the LORD. And there came forth two she bears out of the wood, and tare forty and two children of them.

25And he went from thence to mount Carmel, and from thence he returned to Samaria.

**3** NOW JEHORAM the son of Ahab began to reign over Israel in Samaria the eighteenth year of Jehoshaphat king of Judah, and reigned twelve years.

2And he wrought evil in the sight of the LORD; but not like his father, and like his mother: for he put away the image of Baal that his father had made.

3Nevertheless he cleaved unto the sins of Jeroboam the son of Nebat, which made Israel to sin; he departed not therefrom.

4¶ And Mesha king of Moab was a sheepmaster, and rendered unto the king of Israel an hundred thousand lambs, and an hundred thousand rams, with the wool.

5But it came to pass, when Ahab was dead, that the king of Moab rebelled against the king of Israel.

6¶ And king Jehoram went out of Samaria the same time, and numbered all Israel.

7And he went and sent to Jehoshaphat the king of Judah, saying, The king of Moab hath rebelled against me: wilt thou go with me against Moab to battle? And he said, I will go up: I *am* as thou *art*, my people as thy people, *and* my horses as thy horses.

8And he said, Which way shall we go up? And he answered, The way through the wilderness of Edom.

# Amplified

15When the sons of the prophets who were [watching] at Jericho saw him, they said, The spirit of Elijah rests on Elisha. And they came to meet him, and bowed themselves to the ground before him.

16And they said to him, Behold now, there are among your servants fifty strong men; let them go, we pray you, and seek your master; it may be the Spirit of the Lord has taken him up and cast him on some mountain or into some valley. And he said, You shall not send.

17But when they urged him till he was embarrassed, he said, Send. So they sent fifty men, who sought three days, but did not find him.

18When they returned to Elisha, who had waited at Jericho, he said to them, Did I not tell you, Do not go?

19And the men of the city said to Elisha, Behold, inhabiting of this city is pleasant, as my lord sees, but the water is bad, and the locality causes miscarriage *and* barrenness [in all animals].

20He said, Bring me a new bowl, and put salt [the symbol of God's purifying power] in it. And they brought it to him.

21Then Elisha went to the spring of the waters, and cast the salt in it, and said, Thus says the Lord, I [not the salt] have healed these waters; there shall not be any more death, miscarriage *or* barrenness [and bereavement] because of it.

22So the waters were healed to this day, as Elisha had said.

23He went up from Jericho to Bethel. On the way, [a]young [maturing and accountable] boys came out of the city and mocked him, and said to him, Go up [in a whirlwind], you baldhead! Go up, you baldhead!

24And he turned around and looked at them, and called a curse down on them in the name of the Lord. And two she-bears came out of the wood, and ripped up forty-two of the boys.

25Elisha went from there to Mount Carmel, and from there he returned to Samaria.

**3** J(EH)ORAM SON of Ahab began to reign over Israel in Samaria the eighteenth year of Jehoshaphat king of Judah, and reigned twelve years.

2He did evil in the sight of the Lord, but not like his father and mother, for he put away the pillar of Baal that his father had made.

3Yet he clung to the sins of Jeroboam son of Nebat, which made Israel to sin; he departed not from them.

4 [b]Mesha king of Moab was a sheepmaster, and paid in tribute to the king of Israel [annually] 100,000 lambs and 100,000 rams, with the wool.

5But when Ahab died, the king of Moab rebelled against the king of Israel.

6So King J(eh)oram went out of Samaria at that time and mustered all Israel.

7And he sent to Jehoshaphat king of Judah, saying, The king of Moab has rebelled against me. Will you go with me to war against Moab? And he said, I will go; I am as you are, my people as your people, my horses as your horses.

8Jehoram said, Which way shall we go up? Jehoshaphat answered, The way through the wilderness of Edom.

**AMP** [a] This incident has long been misunderstood because the Hebrew word "naar," used here, was translated "little boys." That these characteristic juvenile delinquents were old enough to be fully accountable is obvious from the use of the word elsewhere. For example, it was used by David of his son Solomon and translated "young *and inexperienced*," when Solomon was a father (I Chron. 22:5; cp. II Chron. 9:30 and I Kings 14:21). It was used of Joseph when he was seventeen (Gen. 37:2). In fact, not less than seventy times in the *Authorized Version* this word "naar" is translated "young man" or "young men." [b] This name of the king of Moab occurs in the first line of the Moabite Stone. In that inscription the Moabite king mentions his successes against Omri and Omri's successor [I Kings 16:23].

## New American Standard

*Elisha Succeeds Elijah*

15¶ Now when the sons of the prophets who *were* at Jericho
opposite *him* saw him, they said, "The spirit of Elijah rests on
Elisha." And they came to meet him and bowed themselves to the
ground before him.
16And they said to him, "Behold now, there are with your
servants fifty strong men, please let them go and search for your
master; perhaps the Spirit of the LORD has taken him up and cast
him on some mountain or into some valley." And he said, "You
shall not send."
17But when they urged him until he was ashamed, he said,
"Send." They sent therefore fifty men; and they searched three
days, but did not find him.
18And they returned to him while he was staying at Jericho; and
he said to them, "Did I not say to you, 'Do not go'?"
19¶ Then the men of the city said to Elisha, "Behold now, the
situation of this city is pleasant, as my lord sees; but the water is
bad, and the land is unfruitful."
20And he said, "Bring me a new jar, and put salt in it." So they
brought *it* to him.
21And he went out to the spring of water, and threw salt in it
and said, "Thus says the LORD, 'I have purified these waters; there
shall not be from there death or unfruitfulness any longer.'"
22So the waters have been purified to this day, according to the
word of Elisha which he spoke.
23¶ Then he went up from there to Bethel; and as he was going
up by the way, young lads came out from the city and mocked him
and said to him, "Go up, you baldhead; go up, you baldhead!"
24When he looked behind him and saw them, he cursed them
in the name of the LORD. Then two female bears came out of the
woods and tore up forty-two lads of their number.
25And he went from there to Mount Carmel, and from there he
returned to Samaria.

*Jehoram Meets Moab Rebellion*

3 NOW JEHORAM the son of Ahab became king over Israel at
Samaria in the eighteenth year of Jehoshaphat king of Judah,
and reigned twelve years.
2And he did evil in the sight of the LORD, though not like his
father and his mother; for he put away the *sacred* pillar of Baal
which his father had made.
3Nevertheless, he clung to the sins of Jeroboam the son of
Nebat, which he made Israel sin; he did not depart from them.
4¶ Now Mesha king of Moab was a sheep breeder, and used
to pay the king of Israel 100,000 lambs and the wool of 100,000
rams.
5But it came about, when Ahab died, the king of Moab rebelled
against the king of Israel.
6And King Jehoram went out of Samaria at that time and
mustered all Israel.
7Then he went and sent *word* to Jehoshaphat the king of Judah,
saying, "The king of Moab has rebelled against me. Will you go
with me to fight against Moab?" And he said, "I will go up; I am
as you are, my people as your people, my horses as your horses."
8And he said, "Which way shall we go up?" And he answered,
"The way of the wilderness of Edom."

## New International

15The company of the prophets from Jericho, who were watching, said, "The spirit of Elijah is resting on Elisha." And they went
to meet him and bowed to the ground before him. 16"Look," they
said, "we your servants have fifty able men. Let them go and look
for your master. Perhaps the Spirit of the LORD has picked him up
and set him down on some mountain or in some valley."
"No," Elisha replied, "do not send them."
17But they persisted until he was too ashamed to refuse. So he
said, "Send them." And they sent fifty men, who searched for
three days but did not find him. 18When they returned to Elisha,
who was staying in Jericho, he said to them, "Didn't I tell you not
to go?"

*Healing of the Water*

19The men of the city said to Elisha, "Look, our lord, this town
is well situated, as you can see, but the water is bad and the land
is unproductive."
20"Bring me a new bowl," he said, "and put salt in it." So they
brought it to him.
21Then he went out to the spring and threw the salt into it,
saying, "This is what the LORD says: 'I have healed this water.
Never again will it cause death or make the land unproductive.'"
22And the water has remained wholesome to this day, according
to the word Elisha had spoken.

*Elisha Is Jeered*

23From there Elisha went up to Bethel. As he was walking along
the road, some youths came out of the town and jeered at him. "Go
on up, you baldhead!" they said. "Go on up, you baldhead!" 24He
turned around, looked at them and called down a curse on them
in the name of the LORD. Then two bears came out of the woods
and mauled forty-two of the youths. 25And he went on to Mount
Carmel and from there returned to Samaria.

*Moab Revolts*

3 JORAM[c] SON of Ahab became king of Israel in Samaria in
the eighteenth year of Jehoshaphat king of Judah, and he
reigned twelve years. 2He did evil in the eyes of the LORD, but not
as his father and mother had done. He got rid of the sacred stone
of Baal that his father had made. 3Nevertheless he clung to the sins
of Jeroboam son of Nebat, which he had caused Israel to commit;
he did not turn away from them.
4Now Mesha king of Moab raised sheep, and he had to supply
the king of Israel with a hundred thousand lambs and with the
wool of a hundred thousand rams. 5But after Ahab died, the king
of Moab rebelled against the king of Israel. 6So at that time King
Joram set out from Samaria and mobilized all Israel. 7He also sent
this message to Jehoshaphat king of Judah: "The king of Moab has
rebelled against me. Will you go with me to fight against Moab?"
"I will go with you," he replied. "I am as you are, my people
as your people, my horses as your horses."
8"By what route shall we attack?" he asked.
"Through the Desert of Edom," he answered.

**NIV** [c] *1* Hebrew *Jehoram,* a variant of *Joram;* also in verse 6

## King James

9 So the king of Israel went, and the king of Judah, and the king of Edom: and they fetched a compass of seven days' journey: and there was no water for the host, and for the cattle that followed them.

10 And the king of Israel said, Alas! that the LORD hath called these three kings together, to deliver them into the hand of Moab!

11 But Jehoshaphat said, *Is there* not here a prophet of the LORD, that we may inquire of the LORD by him? And one of the king of Israel's servants answered and said, Here *is* Elisha the son of Shaphat, which poured water on the hands of Elijah.

12 And Jehoshaphat said, The word of the LORD is with him. So the king of Israel and Jehoshaphat and the king of Edom went down to him.

13 And Elisha said unto the king of Israel, What have I to do with thee? get thee to the prophets of thy father, and to the prophets of thy mother. And the king of Israel said unto him, Nay: for the LORD hath called these three kings together, to deliver them into the hand of Moab.

14 And Elisha said, *As* the LORD of hosts liveth, before whom I stand, surely, were it not that I regard the presence of Jehoshaphat the king of Judah, I would not look toward thee, nor see thee.

15 But now bring me a minstrel. And it came to pass, when the minstrel played, that the hand of the LORD came upon him.

16 And he said, Thus saith the LORD, Make this valley full of ditches.

17 For thus saith the LORD, Ye shall not see wind, neither shall ye see rain; yet that valley shall be filled with water, that ye may drink, both ye, and your cattle, and your beasts.

18 And this is *but* a light thing in the sight of the LORD: he will deliver the Moabites also into your hand.

19 And ye shall smite every fenced city, and every choice city, and shall fell every good tree, and stop all wells of water, and mar every good piece of land with stones.

20 And it came to pass in the morning, when the meat offering was offered, that, behold, there came water by the way of Edom, and the country was filled with water.

21 ¶ And when all the Moabites heard that the kings were come up to fight against them, they gathered all that were able to put on armour, and upward, and stood in the border.

22 And they rose up early in the morning, and the sun shone upon the water, and the Moabites saw the water on the other side *as* red as blood:

23 And they said, This *is* blood: the kings are surely slain, and they have smitten one another: now therefore, Moab, to the spoil.

24 And when they came to the camp of Israel, the Israelites rose up and smote the Moabites, so that they fled before them: but they went forward smiting the Moabites, even in *their* country.

25 And they beat down the cities, and on every good piece of land cast every man his stone, and filled it; and they stopped all the wells of water, and felled all the good trees: only in Kir-haraseth left they the stones thereof; howbeit the slingers went about *it*, and smote it.

26 ¶ And when the king of Moab saw that the battle was too sore for him, he took with him seven hundred men that drew swords, to break through *even* unto the king of Edom: but they could not.

27 Then he took his eldest son that should have reigned in his stead, and offered him *for* a burnt offering upon the wall. And there was great indignation against Israel: and they departed from him, and returned to *their own* land.

## Amplified

9 So the king of Israel went with the king of Judah and the king of Edom. They made a circuit of seven days' journey, but there was no water for the army nor for the animals following them.

10 Then the king of Israel said, Alas! The Lord has called [us] three kings together, to be delivered into Moab's hand!

11 But Jehoshaphat said, Is there no prophet of the Lord here by whom we may inquire of the Lord? One of the king of Israel's servants answered, Elisha son of Shaphat, who served Elijah, is here.

12 Jehoshaphat said, The word of the Lord is with him. So Jehoram king of Israel and Jehoshaphat and the king of Edom went down to Elisha.

13 And Elisha said to the king of Israel, What have I to do with you? Go to the prophets of your [wicked] father Ahab and your [wicked] mother Jezebel. But the king of Israel said to him, No, for the Lord has called [us] three kings together, to be delivered into the hand of Moab.

14 And Elisha said, As the Lord of hosts lives, before Whom I stand, surely, were it not that I respect the presence of Jehoshaphat king of Judah, I would neither look at you nor see you [King Jehoram].

15 But now bring me a minstrel. And while the minstrel played the hand *and* power of the Lord came upon [Elisha].

16 And he said, Thus says the Lord, Make this [dry] brook-bed full of trenches.

17 For says the Lord, You shall not see wind or rain; yet that ravine shall be filled with water, so you, your cattle, and your beasts [of burden] may drink.

18 This is but a light thing in the sight of the Lord. He will deliver the Moabites also into your hand.

19 You shall smite every fenced city and every choice city, and shall fell every good tree, and stop all wells of water, and mar every good piece of land with stones.

20 In the morning when the sacrifice was offered, behold, there came water by the way of Edom, and the country was filled with water.

21 When all the Moabites heard that the kings had come up to fight against them, all who were able to put on armor, young and old, gathered and drew up at the border.

22 When they rose up early next morning, and the sun shone upon the water, the Moabites saw the water across from them as red as blood.

23 And they said, This is blood; the kings have surely been fighting and have slain one another. Now then, Moab, to the spoil!

24 But when they came to the camp of Israel, the Israelites rose up and smote the Moabites, so that they fled before them. And they went forward, slaying the Moabites as they went.

25 They beat down the cities' [walls], and on every good piece of land every man cast a stone, covering it [with stones]; and they stopped all the springs of water, and felled all the good trees, until only the stones [of the walls of Moab's capital city] of Kir-hareseth were left standing, and the slingers surrounded and took it.

26 And when the king of Moab saw that the battle was against him, he took with him 700 swordsmen to break through to the king of Edom; but they could not.

27 Then he [Moab's king] took his eldest son who was to reign in his stead, and offered him for a burnt offering on the wall [in full view of the horrified enemy kings]. And there was great indignation, wrath, *and* bitterness against Israel; and they [his allies, Judah and Edom] withdrew from [Jehoram], and returned to their own land.

## New American Standard

9So the king of Israel went with the king of Judah and the king of Edom; and they made a circuit of seven days' journey, and there was no water for the army or for the cattle that followed them.

10Then the king of Israel said, "Alas! For the LORD has called these three kings to give them into the hand of Moab."

11But Jehoshaphat said, "Is there not a prophet of the LORD here, that we may inquire of the LORD by him?" And one of the king of Israel's servants answered and said, "Elisha the son of Shaphat is here, who used to pour water on the hands of Elijah."

12And Jehoshaphat said, "The word of the LORD is with him." So the king of Israel and Jehoshaphat and the king of Edom went down to him.

13¶ Now Elisha said to the king of Israel, "What do I have to do with you? Go to the prophets of your father and to the prophets of your mother." And the king of Israel said to him, "No, for the LORD has called these three kings *together* to give them into the hand of Moab."

14And Elisha said, "As the LORD of hosts lives, before whom I stand, were it not that I regard the presence of Jehoshaphat the king of Judah, I would not look at you nor see you.

15"But now bring me a minstrel." And it came about, when the minstrel played, that the hand of the LORD came upon him.

16And he said, "Thus says the LORD, 'Make this valley full of trenches.'

17"For thus says the LORD, 'You shall not see wind nor shall you see rain; yet that valley shall be filled with water, so that you shall drink, both you and your cattle and your beasts.

18'And this is but a slight thing in the sight of the LORD; He shall also give the Moabites into your hand.

19'Then you shall strike every fortified city and every choice city, and fell every good tree and stop all springs of water, and mar every good piece of land with stones.' "

20And it happened in the morning about the time of offering the sacrifice, that behold, water came by the way of Edom, and the country was filled with water.

21¶ Now all the Moabites heard that the kings had come up to fight against them. And all who were able to put on armor and older were summoned, and stood on the border.

22And they rose early in the morning, and the sun shone on the water, and the Moabites saw the water opposite *them* as red as blood.

23Then they said, "This is blood; the kings have surely fought together, and they have slain one another. Now therefore, Moab, to the spoil!"

24But when they came to the camp of Israel, the Israelites arose and struck the Moabites, so that they fled before them; and they went forward into the land, slaughtering the Moabites.

25Thus they destroyed the cities; and each one threw a stone on every piece of good land and filled it. So they stopped all the springs of water and felled all the good trees, until in Kir-hareseth *only* they left its stones; however, the slingers went about *it* and struck it.

26When the king of Moab saw that the battle was too fierce for him, he took with him 700 men who drew swords, to break through to the king of Edom; but they could not.

27Then he took his oldest son who was to reign in his place, and offered him as a burnt offering on the wall. And there came great wrath against Israel, and they departed from him and returned to their own land.

## New International

9So the king of Israel set out with the king of Judah and the king
of Edom. After a roundabout march of seven days, the army had
no more water for themselves or for the animals with them.
10"What!" exclaimed the king of Israel. "Has the LORD called us
three kings together only to hand us over to Moab?"
11But Jehoshaphat asked, "Is there no prophet of the LORD here,
that we may inquire of the LORD through him?"
An officer of the king of Israel answered, "Elisha son of Shaphat
is here. He used to pour water on the hands of Elijah.[a]"
12Jehoshaphat said, "The word of the LORD is with him." So the
king of Israel and Jehoshaphat and the king of Edom went down
to him.
13Elisha said to the king of Israel, "What do we have to do with
each other? Go to the prophets of your father and the prophets of
your mother."
"No," the king of Israel answered, "because it was the LORD
who called us three kings together to hand us over to Moab."
14Elisha said, "As surely as the LORD Almighty lives, whom I
serve, if I did not have respect for the presence of Jehoshaphat king
of Judah, I would not look at you or even notice you. 15But now
bring me a harpist."
While the harpist was playing, the hand of the LORD came upon
Elisha 16and he said, "This is what the LORD says: Make this valley
full of ditches. 17For this is what the LORD says: You will see neither
wind nor rain, yet this valley will be filled with water, and you,
your cattle and your other animals will drink. 18This is an easy
thing in the eyes of the LORD; he will also hand Moab over to you.
19You will overthrow every fortified city and every major town.
You will cut down every good tree, stop up all the springs, and
ruin every good field with stones."
20The next morning, about the time for offering the sacrifice,
there it was—water flowing from the direction of Edom! And the
land was filled with water.
21Now all the Moabites had heard that the kings had come to
fight against them; so every man, young and old, who could bear
arms was called up and stationed on the border. 22When they got
up early in the morning, the sun was shining on the water. To the
Moabites across the way, the water looked red—like blood.
23"That's blood!" they said. "Those kings must have fought and
slaughtered each other. Now to the plunder, Moab!"
24But when the Moabites came to the camp of Israel, the Israelites rose up and fought them until they fled. And the Israelites
invaded the land and slaughtered the Moabites. 25They destroyed
the towns, and each man threw a stone on every good field until
it was covered. They stopped up all the springs and cut down
every good tree. Only Kir Hareseth was left with its stones in
place, but men armed with slings surrounded it and attacked it as
well.
26When the king of Moab saw that the battle had gone against
him, he took with him seven hundred swordsmen to break
through to the king of Edom, but they failed. 27Then he took his
firstborn son, who was to succeed him as king, and offered him
as a sacrifice on the city wall. The fury against Israel was great; they
withdrew and returned to their own land.

NIV [a] *11* That is, he was Elijah's personal servant.

## King James

4 NOW THERE cried a certain woman of the wives of the sons
of the prophets unto Elisha, saying, Thy servant my husband
is dead; and thou knowest that thy servant did fear the LORD: and
the creditor is come to take unto him my two sons to be bondmen.
2And Elisha said unto her, What shall I do for thee? tell me,
what hast thou in the house? And she said, Thine handmaid hath
not any thing in the house, save a pot of oil.
3Then he said, Go, borrow thee vessels abroad of all thy neighbours, *even* empty vessels; borrow not a few.
4And when thou art come in, thou shalt shut the door upon
thee and upon thy sons, and shalt pour out into all those vessels,
and thou shalt set aside that which is full.
5So she went from him, and shut the door upon her and upon
her sons, who brought *the vessels* to her; and she poured out.
6And it came to pass, when the vessels were full, that she said
unto her son, Bring me yet a vessel. And he said unto her, *There
is* not a vessel more. And the oil stayed.
7Then she came and told the man of God. And he said, Go, sell
the oil, and pay thy debt, and live thou and thy children of the rest.
8¶ And it fell on a day, that Elisha passed to Shunem, where *was*
a great woman; and she constrained him to eat bread. And *so* it
was, *that* as oft as he passed by, he turned in thither to eat bread.
9And she said unto her husband, Behold now, I perceive that
this *is* an holy man of God, which passeth by us continually.
10Let us make a little chamber, I pray thee, on the wall; and let
us set for him there a bed, and a table, and a stool, and a candlestick: and it shall be, when he cometh to us, that he shall turn in
thither.
11And it fell on a day, that he came thither, and he turned into
the chamber, and lay there.
12And he said to Gehazi his servant, Call this Shunammite. And
when he had called her, she stood before him.
13And he said unto him, Say now unto her, Behold, thou hast
been careful for us with all this care; what *is* to be done for thee?
wouldest thou be spoken for to the king, or to the captain of the
host? And she answered, I dwell among mine own people.
14And he said, What then *is* to be done for her? And Gehazi
answered, Verily she hath no child, and her husband is old.
15And he said, Call her. And when he had called her, she stood
in the door.
16And he said, About this season, according to the time of life,
thou shalt embrace a son. And she said, Nay, my lord, *thou* man
of God, do not lie unto thine handmaid.
17And the woman conceived, and bare a son at that season that
Elisha had said unto her, according to the time of life.
18¶ And when the child was grown, it fell on a day, that he went
out to his father to the reapers.
19And he said unto his father, My head, my head. And he said
to a lad, Carry him to his mother.
20And when he had taken him, and brought him to his mother,
he sat on her knees till noon, and *then* died.
21And she went up, and laid him on the bed of the man of God,
and shut *the door* upon him, and went out.
22And she called unto her husband, and said, Send me, I pray
thee, one of the young men, and one of the asses, that I may run
to the man of God, and come again.
23And he said, Wherefore wilt thou go to him today? *it is* neither
new moon, nor sabbath. And she said, *It shall be* well.
24Then she saddled an ass, and said to her servant, Drive, and
go forward; slack not *thy* riding for me, except I bid thee.
25So she went and came unto the man of God to mount Carmel.
And it came to pass, when the man of God saw her afar off, that
he said to Gehazi his servant, Behold, *yonder is* that Shunammite:

## Amplified

4 NOW THE wife of a son of the prophets cried to Elisha, Your
servant my husband is dead; and you know that your servant
feared the Lord; but the creditor has come to take my two sons to
be his slaves.
2Elisha said to her, What shall I do for you? Tell me, what have
you [of sale value] in the house? She said, Your handmaid has
nothing in the house, except a jar of oil.
3Then he said, Go around and borrow vessels of all your neighbors, empty vessels and not a few.
4And when you come in, shut the door upon you and your
sons. Then pour out [the oil you have] into all those vessels, setting
aside each one when it is full.
5So she went from him, and shut the door upon herself and her
sons, who brought to her the vessels as she poured the oil.
6When the vessels were all full, she said to her son, Bring me
another vessel. And he said to her, There is not *one* left. Then the
oil stopped multiplying.
7Then she came and told the man of God. He said, Go, sell the
oil, and pay your debt, and you and your sons live on the rest.
8One day Elisha went on to Shunem, where a rich and influential woman lived who insisted on his eating a meal. Afterward
whenever he passed by he stopped there for a meal.
9And she said to her husband, Behold now, I perceive that this
is a holy man of God, who passes by continually.
10Let us make a small chamber on the [housetop], and put there
for him a bed, a table, a chair, and a lamp. Then whenever he
comes to us, he can go [up the outside stairs and rest] here.
11One day he came and turned into the chamber and lay there.
12And he said to Gehazi his servant, Call this Shunammite.
When he had called her, she stood before him.
13And he said to Gehazi, Say now to her, You have been most
painstaking *and* reverently concerned for us; what is to be done for
you? Would you like to be spoken for to the king or to the commander of the army? She answered, I dwell among my own people
[they are sufficient].
14Later Elisha said, What then is to be done for her? Gehazi
answered, She has no child, and her husband is old.
15He said, Call her. [Gehazi] called her, and she stood in the
doorway.
16Elisha said, At this season, when the time comes round, you
shall embrace a son. She said, No, my lord, you man of God, do
not lie to your handmaid.
17But the woman conceived, and bore a son at that season the
following year, as Elisha had said to her.
18When the child had grown, he went out one day to his father
with the reapers.
19But he said to his father, My head, my head! The man said
to his servant, Carry him to his mother.
20And when he was brought to his mother, he sat on her knees
till noon, then died.
21And she went up and laid him on the bed of the man of God,
and shut the door upon him, and went out.
22And she called to her husband, and said, Send me one of the
servants and one of the donkeys, that I may go quickly to the man
of God, and come again.
23And he said, Why go to him today? It is neither new moon
nor sabbath. And she said, It will be all right.
24Then she saddled the donkey, and said to her servant, Ride
fast. Do not slacken your pace for me unless I tell you.
25So she set out and came to the man of God at Mount Carmel.
When the man of God saw her afar off, he said to Gehazi his
servant, Behold, yonder is that Shunammite.

## New American Standard

*The Widow's Oil*

**4** NOW A certain woman of the wives of the sons of the prophets cried out to Elisha, "Your servant my husband is dead,
and you know that your servant feared the LORD; and the creditor
has come to take my two children to be his slaves."
2And Elisha said to her, "What shall I do for you? Tell me, what
do you have in the house?" And she said, "Your maidservant has
nothing in the house except a jar of oil."
3Then he said, "Go, borrow vessels at large for yourself from
all your neighbors, *even* empty vessels; do not get a few.
4"And you shall go in and shut the door behind you and your
sons, and pour out into all these vessels; and you shall set aside
what is full."
5So she went from him and shut the door behind her and her
sons; they were bringing *the vessels* to her and she poured.
6And it came about when the vessels were full, that she said
to her son, "Bring me another vessel." And he said to her, "There
is not one vessel more." And the oil stopped.
7Then she came and told the man of God. And he said, "Go,
sell the oil and pay your debt, and you *and* your sons can live on
the rest."

*The Shunammite Woman*

8¶ Now there came a day when Elisha passed over to Shunem,
where there was a prominent woman, and she persuaded him to
eat food. And so it was, as often as he passed by, he turned in there
to eat food.
9And she said to her husband, "Behold now, I perceive that
this is a holy man of God passing by us continually.
10"Please, let us make a little walled upper chamber and let us
set a bed for him there, and a table and a chair and a lampstand;
and it shall be, when he comes to us, *that* he can turn in there."
11One day he came there and turned in to the upper chamber
and rested.
12Then he said to Gehazi his servant, "Call this Shunammite."
And when he had called her, she stood before him.
13And he said to him, "Say now to her, 'Behold, you have been
careful for us with all this care; what can I do for you? Would you
be spoken for to the king or to the captain of the army?' " And she
answered, "I live among my own people."
14So he said, "What then is to be done for her?" And Gehazi
answered, "Truly she has no son and her husband is old."
15And he said, "Call her." When he had called her, she stood
in the doorway.
16Then he said, "At this season next year you shall embrace a
son." And she said, "No, my lord, O man of God, do not lie to
your maidservant."
17And the woman conceived and bore a son at that season the
next year, as Elisha had said to her.

*The Shunammite's Son*

18¶ When the child was grown, the day came that he went out
to his father to the reapers.
19And he said to his father, "My head, my head." And he said
to his servant, "Carry him to his mother."
20When he had taken him and brought him to his mother, he
sat on her lap until noon, and *then* died.
21And she went up and laid him on the bed of the man of God,
and shut *the door* behind him, and went out.
22Then she called to her husband and said, "Please send me one
of the servants and one of the donkeys, that I may run to the man
of God and return."
23And he said, "Why will you go to him today? It is neither new
moon nor sabbath." And she said, " *It will be* well."
24Then she saddled a donkey and said to her servant, "Drive
and go forward; do not slow down the pace for me unless I tell
you."
25So she went and came to the man of God to Mount Carmel.
And it came about when the man of God saw her at a distance, that
he said to Gehazi his servant, "Behold, yonder is the Shunammite.

## New International

*The Widow's Oil*

**4** THE WIFE of a man from the company of the prophets cried
out to Elisha, "Your servant my husband is dead, and you
know that he revered the LORD. But now his creditor is coming to
take my two boys as his slaves."
2Elisha replied to her, "How can I help you? Tell me, what do
you have in your house?"
"Your servant has nothing there at all," she said, "except a little
oil."
3Elisha said, "Go around and ask all your neighbors for empty
jars. Don't ask for just a few. 4Then go inside and shut the door
behind you and your sons. Pour oil into all the jars, and as each
is filled, put it to one side."
5She left him and afterward shut the door behind her and her
sons. They brought the jars to her and she kept pouring. 6When
all the jars were full, she said to her son, "Bring me another one."
But he replied, "There is not a jar left." Then the oil stopped
flowing.
7She went and told the man of God, and he said, "Go, sell the
oil and pay your debts. You and your sons can live on what is left."

*The Shunammite's Son Restored to Life*

8One day Elisha went to Shunem. And a well-to-do woman was
there, who urged him to stay for a meal. So whenever he came by,
he stopped there to eat. 9She said to her husband, "I know that
this man who often comes our way is a holy man of God. 10Let's
make a small room on the roof and put in it a bed and a table, a
chair and a lamp for him. Then he can stay there whenever he
comes to us."
11One day when Elisha came, he went up to his room and lay
down there. 12He said to his servant Gehazi, "Call the Shunammite." So he called her, and she stood before him. 13Elisha said to
him, "Tell her, 'You have gone to all this trouble for us. Now what
can be done for you? Can we speak on your behalf to the king or
the commander of the army?' "
She replied, "I have a home among my own people."
14"What can be done for her?" Elisha asked.
Gehazi said, "Well, she has no son and her husband is old."
15Then Elisha said, "Call her." So he called her, and she stood
in the doorway. 16"About this time next year," Elisha said, "you
will hold a son in your arms."
"No, my lord," she objected. "Don't mislead your servant, O
man of God!"
17But the woman became pregnant, and the next year about that
same time she gave birth to a son, just as Elisha had told her.
18The child grew, and one day he went out to his father, who
was with the reapers. 19"My head! My head!" he said to his father.
His father told a servant, "Carry him to his mother." 20After the
servant had lifted him up and carried him to his mother, the boy
sat on her lap until noon, and then he died. 21She went up and laid
him on the bed of the man of God, then shut the door and went
out.
22She called her husband and said, "Please send me one of the
servants and a donkey so I can go to the man of God quickly and
return."
23"Why go to him today?" he asked. "It's not the New Moon
or the Sabbath."
"It's all right," she said.
24She saddled the donkey and said to her servant, "Lead on;
don't slow down for me unless I tell you." 25So she set out and
came to the man of God at Mount Carmel.
When he saw her in the distance, the man of God said to his
servant Gehazi, "Look! There's the Shunammite! 26Run to meet

## King James

26Run now, I pray thee, to meet her, and say unto her, *Is it* well
with thee? *is it* well with thy husband? *is it* well with the child? And
she answered, *It is* well.
27And when she came to the man of God to the hill, she caught
him by the feet: but Gehazi came near to thrust her away. And the
man of God said, Let her alone; for her soul *is* vexed within her:
and the LORD hath hid *it* from me, and hath not told me.
28Then she said, Did I desire a son of my lord? did I not say,
Do not deceive me?
29Then he said to Gehazi, Gird up thy loins, and take my staff
in thine hand, and go thy way: if thou meet any man, salute him
not; and if any salute thee, answer him not again: and lay my staff
upon the face of the child.
30And the mother of the child said, *As* the LORD liveth, and *as*
thy soul liveth, I will not leave thee. And he arose, and followed
her.
31And Gehazi passed on before them, and laid the staff upon
the face of the child; but *there was* neither voice, nor hearing.
Wherefore he went again to meet him, and told him, saying, The
child is not awaked.
32And when Elisha was come into the house, behold, the child
was dead, *and* laid upon his bed.
33He went in therefore, and shut the door upon them twain,
and prayed unto the LORD.
34And he went up, and lay upon the child, and put his mouth
upon his mouth, and his eyes upon his eyes, and his hands upon
his hands: and he stretched himself upon the child; and the flesh
of the child waxed warm.
35Then he returned, and walked in the house to and fro; and
went up, and stretched himself upon him: and the child sneezed
seven times, and the child opened his eyes.
36And he called Gehazi, and said, Call this Shunammite. So he
called her. And when she was come in unto him, he said, Take up
thy son.
37Then she went in, and fell at his feet, and bowed herself to
the ground, and took up her son, and went out.
38¶ And Elisha came again to Gilgal: and *there was* a dearth in
the land; and the sons of the prophets *were* sitting before him: and
he said unto his servant, Set on the great pot, and seethe pottage
for the sons of the prophets.
39And one went out into the field to gather herbs, and found
a wild vine, and gathered thereof wild gourds his lap full, and
came and shred *them* into the pot of pottage: for they knew *them*
not.
40So they poured out for the men to eat. And it came to pass,
as they were eating of the pottage, that they cried out, and said,
O *thou* man of God, *there is* death in the pot. And they could not
eat *thereof*.
41But he said, Then bring meal. And he cast *it* into the pot; and
he said, Pour out for the people, that they may eat. And there was
no harm in the pot.
42¶ And there came a man from Baal-shalisha, and brought the
man of God bread of the firstfruits, twenty loaves of barley, and
full ears of corn in the husk thereof. And he said, Give unto the
people, that they may eat.
43And his servitor said, What, should I set this before an hundred men? He said again, Give the people, that they may eat: for
thus saith the LORD, They shall eat, and shall leave *thereof*.
44So he set *it* before them, and they did eat, and left *thereof*,
according to the word of the LORD.

## Amplified

26Run to meet her, and say, Is it well with you? Well with your
husband? Well with the child? And she answered, It is well.
27When she came to the mountain to the man of God, she clung
to his feet. Gehazi came to thrust her away, but the man of God
said, Let her alone, for her soul is bitter *and* vexed within her; and
the Lord has hid it from me, and has not told me.
28Then she said, Did I desire a son of my lord? Did I not say,
Do not deceive me?
29Then he said to Gehazi, Gird up your loins, and take my staff
in your hand and go, lay my staff on the face of the child. If you
meet any man, do not salute him. If he salutes you, do not answer
him.
30The mother of the child said, As the Lord lives and as my soul
lives, I will not leave you. And he arose, and followed her.
31Gehazi passed on before them and laid the staff on the child's
face, but the boy neither spoke nor heard. So he went back to meet
Elisha and said to him, The child has not awakened.
32When Elisha arrived in the house, the child was dead, and
laid upon his bed.
33So he went in, shut the door upon the two of them, and
prayed to the Lord.
34He went up and lay on the child, put his mouth on his mouth,
his eyes on his eyes, and his hands on his hands. And as he
stretched himself on him *and* embraced him, the child's flesh
became warm.
35Then he returned, and walked in the house to and fro; and
went up again and stretched himself upon him; and the child
sneezed seven times, then opened his eyes.
36Then [Elisha] called Gehazi and said, Call this Shunammite.
So he called her. And when she came, he said, Take up your son.
37She came and fell at his feet, bowing herself to the ground;
then took up her son and went out.
38Elisha came back to Gilgal during a famine in the land. The
sons of the prophets were sitting before him, and he said to his
servant, Set on the big pot and cook pottage for the sons of the
prophets.
39Then one went into the field to gather herbs and gathered
from a wild vine his lap full of wild gourds, and returned and cut
them up into the pot of pottage; for they were unknown to them.
40So they poured out for the men to eat. But as they ate of the
pottage, they cried out, O man of God, there is death in the pot!
And they could not eat it.
41But he said, Bring meal [as a symbol of God's healing power].
And he cast it into the pot and said, Pour out for the people that
they may eat. Then there was no harm in the pot.
42[At another time] a man from Baal-shalisha came and brought
the man of God bread of the first fruits, twenty loaves of barley,
and fresh ears of grain [in the husk] in his sack. And Elisha said,
Give to the men that they may eat.
43His servant said, How am I to set [only] this before a hundred
[hungry] men? He said, Give to the men that they may eat; for thus
says the Lord, They shall be fed and have some left.
44So he set it before them, and they ate, and left some as the
Lord had said.

## New American Standard

26"Please run now to meet her and say to her, 'Is it well with
you? Is it well with your husband? Is it well with the child?' " And
she answered, "It is well."
27When she came to the man of God to the hill, she caught hold
of his feet. And Gehazi came near to push her away; but the man
of God said, "Let her alone, for her soul is troubled within her; and
the LORD has hidden it from me and has not told me."
28Then she said, "Did I ask for a son from my lord? Did I not
say, 'Do not deceive me'?"
29¶ Then he said to Gehazi, "Gird up your loins and take my
staff in your hand, and go your way; if you meet any man, do not
salute him, and if anyone salutes you, do not answer him; and lay
my staff on the lad's face."
30And the mother of the lad said, "As the LORD lives and as you
yourself live, I will not leave you." And he arose and followed her.
31Then Gehazi passed on before them and laid the staff on the
lad's face, but there was neither sound nor response. So he returned to meet him and told him, "The lad has not awakened."
32When Elisha came into the house, behold the lad was dead
and laid on his bed.
33So he entered and shut the door behind them both, and
prayed to the LORD.
34And he went up and lay on the child, and put his mouth on
his mouth and his eyes on his eyes and his hands on his hands,
and he stretched himself on him; and the flesh of the child became
warm.
35Then he returned and walked in the house once back and
forth, and went up and stretched himself on him; and the lad
sneezed seven times and the lad opened his eyes.
36And he called Gehazi and said, "Call this Shunammite." So
he called her. And when she came in to him, he said, "Take up
your son."
37Then she went in and fell at his feet and bowed herself to the
ground, and she took up her son and went out.

*The Poisonous Stew*

38¶ When Elisha returned to Gilgal, *there was* a famine in the
land. As the sons of the prophets were sitting before him, he said
to his servant, "Put on the large pot and boil stew for the sons of
the prophets."
39Then one went out into the field to gather herbs, and found
a wild vine and gathered from it his lap full of wild gourds, and
came and sliced them into the pot of stew, for they did not know
*what they were.*
40So they poured *it* out for the men to eat. And it came about
as they were eating of the stew, that they cried out and said, "O
man of God, there is death in the pot." And they were unable to
eat.
41But he said, "Now bring meal." And he threw it into the pot,
and he said, "Pour *it* out for the people that they may eat." Then
there was no harm in the pot.
42¶ Now a man came from Baal-shalishah, and brought the man
of God bread of the first fruits, twenty loaves of barley and fresh
ears of grain in his sack. And he said, "Give *them* to the people that
they may eat."
43And his attendant said, "What, shall I set this before a hundred men?" But he said, "Give *them* to the people that they may
eat, for thus says the LORD, 'They shall eat and have *some* left
over.' "
44So he set *it* before them, and they ate and had *some* left over,
according to the word of the LORD.

## New International

her and ask her, 'Are you all right? Is your husband all right? Is
your child all right?' "
"Everything is all right," she said.
27When she reached the man of God at the mountain, she took
hold of his feet. Gehazi came over to push her away, but the man
of God said, "Leave her alone! She is in bitter distress, but the
LORD has hidden it from me and has not told me why."
28"Did I ask you for a son, my lord?" she said. "Didn't I tell you,
'Don't raise my hopes'?"
29Elisha said to Gehazi, "Tuck your cloak into your belt, take my
staff in your hand and run. If you meet anyone, do not greet him,
and if anyone greets you, do not answer. Lay my staff on the boy's
face."
30But the child's mother said, "As surely as the LORD lives and
as you live, I will not leave you." So he got up and followed her.
31Gehazi went on ahead and laid the staff on the boy's face, but
there was no sound or response. So Gehazi went back to meet
Elisha and told him, "The boy has not awakened."
32When Elisha reached the house, there was the boy lying dead
on his couch. 33He went in, shut the door on the two of them and
prayed to the LORD. 34Then he got on the bed and lay upon the
boy, mouth to mouth, eyes to eyes, hands to hands. As he
stretched himself out upon him, the boy's body grew warm. 35Eli-
sha turned away and walked back and forth in the room and then
got on the bed and stretched out upon him once more. The boy
sneezed seven times and opened his eyes.
36Elisha summoned Gehazi and said, "Call the Shunammite."
And he did. When she came, he said, "Take your son." 37She came
in, fell at his feet and bowed to the ground. Then she took her son
and went out.

*Death in the Pot*

38Elisha returned to Gilgal and there was a famine in that region. While the company of the prophets was meeting with him,
he said to his servant, "Put on the large pot and cook some stew
for these men."
39One of them went out into the fields to gather herbs and
found a wild vine. He gathered some of its gourds and filled the
fold of his cloak. When he returned, he cut them up into the pot
of stew, though no one knew what they were. 40The stew was
poured out for the men, but as they began to eat it, they cried out,
"O man of God, there is death in the pot!" And they could not eat
it.
41Elisha said, "Get some flour." He put it into the pot and said,
"Serve it to the people to eat." And there was nothing harmful in
the pot.

*Feeding of a Hundred*

42A man came from Baal Shalishah, bringing the man of God
twenty loaves of barley bread baked from the first ripe grain, along
with some heads of new grain. "Give it to the people to eat," Elisha
said.
43"How can I set this before a hundred men?" his servant
asked.
But Elisha answered, "Give it to the people to eat. For this is
what the LORD says: 'They will eat and have some left over.' "
44Then he set it before them, and they ate and had some left over,
according to the word of the LORD.

## King James

5 NOW NAAMAN, captain of the host of the king of Syria, was
a great man with his master, and honourable, because by him
the Lord had given deliverance unto Syria: he was also a mighty
man in valour, *but he was* a leper.
2And the Syrians had gone out by companies, and had brought
away captive out of the land of Israel a little maid; and she waited
on Naaman's wife.
3And she said unto her mistress, Would God my lord *were* with
the prophet that *is* in Samaria! for he would recover him of his
leprosy.
4And *one* went in, and told his lord, saying, Thus and thus said
the maid that *is* of the land of Israel.
5And the king of Syria said, Go to, go, and I will send a letter
unto the king of Israel. And he departed, and took with him ten
talents of silver, and six thousand *pieces* of gold, and ten changes
of raiment.
6And he brought the letter to the king of Israel, saying, Now
when this letter is come unto thee, behold, I have *therewith* sent
Naaman my servant to thee, that thou mayest recover him of his
leprosy.
7And it came to pass, when the king of Israel had read the letter,
that he rent his clothes, and said, *Am* I God, to kill and to make
alive, that this man doth send unto me to recover a man of his
leprosy? wherefore consider, I pray you, and see how he seeketh
a quarrel against me.
8¶ And it was *so*, when Elisha the man of God had heard that
the king of Israel had rent his clothes, that he sent to the king,
saying, Wherefore hast thou rent thy clothes? let him come now
to me, and he shall know that there is a prophet in Israel.
9So Naaman came with his horses and with his chariot, and
stood at the door of the house of Elisha.
10And Elisha sent a messenger unto him, saying, Go and wash
in Jordan seven times, and thy flesh shall come again to thee, and
thou shalt be clean.
11But Naaman was wroth, and went away, and said, Behold,
I thought, He will surely come out to me, and stand, and call on
the name of the Lord his God, and strike his hand over the place,
and recover the leper.
12 *Are* not Abana and Pharpar, rivers of Damascus, better than
all the waters of Israel? may I not wash in them, and be clean? So
he turned and went away in a rage.
13And his servants came near, and spake unto him, and said,
My father, *if* the prophet had bid thee *do some* great thing, wouldest
thou not have done *it?* how much rather then, when he saith to
thee, Wash, and be clean?
14Then went he down, and dipped himself seven times in Jordan, according to the saying of the man of God: and his flesh came
again like unto the flesh of a little child, and he was clean.
15¶ And he returned to the man of God, he and all his company,
and came, and stood before him: and he said, Behold, now I know
that *there is* no God in all the earth, but in Israel: now therefore,
I pray thee, take a blessing of thy servant.
16But he said, *As* the Lord liveth, before whom I stand, I will
receive none. And he urged him to take *it;* but he refused.
17And Naaman said, Shall there not then, I pray thee, be given
to thy servant two mules' burden of earth? for thy servant will
henceforth offer neither burnt offering nor sacrifice unto other
gods, but unto the Lord.
18In this thing the Lord pardon thy servant, *that* when my
master goeth into the house of Rimmon to worship there, and he
leaneth on my hand, and I bow myself in the house of Rimmon:
when I bow down myself in the house of Rimmon, the Lord
pardon thy servant in this thing.
19And he said unto him, Go in peace. So he departed from him
a little way.
20¶ But Gehazi, the servant of Elisha the man of God, said,
Behold, my master hath spared Naaman this Syrian, in not receiving at his hands that which he brought: but, *as* the Lord liveth, I
will run after him, and take somewhat of him.

## Amplified

5 NAAMAN, COMMANDER of the army of the king of Syria,
was a great man with his master, accepted [and acceptable],
because by him the Lord had given victory to Syria; he was also
a mighty man of valor, but he was a leper.
2The Syrians had gone out in bands and had brought away
captive out of the land of Israel a little maid; and she waited on
Naaman's wife.
3She said to her mistress, Would that my lord were with the
prophet who is in Samaria! For he would heal him of his leprosy.
4[Naaman] went in, and told his king, Thus and thus said the
maid from Israel.
5And the king of Syria said, Go now, and I will send a letter to
the king of Israel. And he departed, and took with him ten talents
of silver, 6,000 shekels of gold, and ten changes of raiment.
6And he brought the letter to the king of Israel. It said, When
this letter comes to you, I will with it have sent to you my servant
Naaman, that you may cure him of leprosy.
7When the king of Israel read the letter, he rent his clothes and
said, Am I God, to kill and to make alive, that this man sends to
me to heal a man of his leprosy? Just consider, and see how he is
seeking a quarrel with me.
8When Elisha the man of God heard that the king of Israel had
rent his clothes, he sent to the king, asking, Why have you rent
your clothes? Let Naaman come now to me, and he shall know that
there is a prophet in Israel.
9So Naaman came with his horses and chariots and stopped at
Elisha's door.
10Elisha sent a messenger to him, saying, Go and wash in
Jordan seven times, and your flesh shall be restored, and you shall
be clean.
11But Naaman was angry, and went away, and said, Behold, I
thought he would surely come out to me, and stand, and call on
the name of the Lord his God, and wave his hand over the place,
and heal the leper.
12Are not Abana and Pharpar, rivers of Damascus, better than
all the waters of Israel? May I not wash in them, and be clean? So
he turned and went away in a rage.
13And his servants came near, and said to him, My father, if the
prophet had bid you to do some great thing, would you not have
done it? How much rather then, when he says to you, Wash, and
be clean?
14Then he went down and dipped himself seven times in the
Jordan, as the man of God had said; and his flesh was restored like
that of a little child, and he was clean.
15Then Naaman returned to the man of God, he and all his
company, and stood before him. He said, Behold, now I know that
there is no God in all the earth but in Israel. So now accept a gift
from your servant.
16Elisha said, As the Lord lives, before Whom I stand, I will
accept none. He urged him to take it, but Elisha refused.
17Naaman said, Then, I pray you, let there be given to me your
servant two mules' burden of earth? For your servant will henceforth offer neither burnt offering nor sacrifice to other gods, but
only to the Lord.
18In this thing the Lord pardon your servant: when my master
[the king] goes into the house of [his god] Rimmon to worship
there, and he leans on my hand, and I bow myself in the house
of Rimmon, when I bow down myself in the house of Rimmon, the
Lord pardon your servant in this thing.
19Elisha said to him, Go in peace. So Naaman departed from
him a little way.
20But Gehazi, servant of Elisha the man of God, said, Behold,
my master spared this Naaman the Syrian, in not receiving from
his hands what he brought; but, as the Lord lives, I will run after
him and get something from him.

# New American Standard

*Naaman Is Healed*

5 NOW NAAMAN, captain of the army of the king of Aram, was a great man with his master, and highly respected, because by him the LORD had given victory to Aram. The man was also a valiant warrior, *but he was* a leper.

2Now the Arameans had gone out in bands, and had taken captive a little girl from the land of Israel; and she waited on Naaman's wife.

3And she said to her mistress, "I wish that my master were with the prophet who is in Samaria! Then he would cure him of his leprosy."

4And Naaman went in and told his master, saying, "Thus and thus spoke the girl who is from the land of Israel."

5Then the king of Aram said, "Go now, and I will send a letter to the king of Israel." And he departed and took with him ten talents of silver and six thousand *shekels* of gold and ten changes of clothes.

6And he brought the letter to the king of Israel, saying, "And now as this letter comes to you, behold, I have sent Naaman my servant to you, that you may cure him of his leprosy."

7And it came about when the king of Israel read the letter, that he tore his clothes and said, "Am I God, to kill and to make alive, that this man is sending *word* to me to cure a man of his leprosy? But consider now, and see how he is seeking a quarrel against me."

8¶ And it happened when Elisha the man of God heard that the king of Israel had torn his clothes, that he sent *word* to the king, saying, "Why have you torn your clothes? Now let him come to me, and he shall know that there is a prophet in Israel."

9So Naaman came with his horses and his chariots, and stood at the doorway of the house of Elisha.

10And Elisha sent a messenger to him, saying, "Go and wash in the Jordan seven times, and your flesh shall be restored to you and *you shall* be clean."

11But Naaman was furious and went away and said, "Behold, I thought, 'He will surely come out to me, and stand and call on the name of the LORD his God, and wave his hand over the place, and cure the leper.'

12"Are not Abanah and Pharpar, the rivers of Damascus, better than all the waters of Israel? Could I not wash in them and be clean?" So he turned and went away in a rage.

13Then his servants came near and spoke to him and said, "My father, had the prophet told you *to do some* great thing, would you not have done *it*? How much more *then*, when he says to you, 'Wash, and be clean'?"

14So he went down and dipped *himself* seven times in the Jordan, according to the word of the man of God; and his flesh was restored like the flesh of a little child, and he was clean.

*Gehazi's Greed*

15¶ When he returned to the man of God with all his company, and came and stood before him, he said, "Behold now, I know that there is no God in all the earth, but in Israel; so please take a present from your servant now."

16But he said, "As the LORD lives, before whom I stand, I will take nothing." And he urged him to take *it*, but he refused.

17And Naaman said, "If not, please let your servant at least be given two mules' load of earth; for your servant will no more offer burnt offering nor will he sacrifice to other gods, but to the LORD.

18"In this matter may the LORD pardon your servant: when my master goes into the house of Rimmon to worship there, and he leans on my hand and I bow myself in the house of Rimmon, when I bow myself in the house of Rimmon, the LORD pardon your servant in this matter."

19And he said to him, "Go in peace." So he departed from him some distance.

20¶ But Gehazi, the servant of Elisha the man of God, thought, "Behold, my master has spared this Naaman the Aramean, by not receiving from his hands what he brought. As the LORD lives, I will run after him and take something from him."

# New International

*Naaman Healed of Leprosy*

5 NOW NAAMAN was commander of the army of the king of Aram. He was a great man in the sight of his master and highly regarded, because through him the LORD had given victory to Aram. He was a valiant soldier, but he had leprosy.[a]

2Now bands from Aram had gone out and had taken captive a young girl from Israel, and she served Naaman's wife. 3She said to her mistress, "If only my master would see the prophet who is in Samaria! He would cure him of his leprosy."

4Naaman went to his master and told him what the girl from Israel had said. 5"By all means, go," the king of Aram replied. "I will send a letter to the king of Israel." So Naaman left, taking with him ten talents[b] of silver, six thousand shekels[c] of gold and ten sets of clothing. 6The letter that he took to the king of Israel read: "With this letter I am sending my servant Naaman to you so that you may cure him of his leprosy."

7As soon as the king of Israel read the letter, he tore his robes and said, "Am I God? Can I kill and bring back to life? Why does this fellow send someone to me to be cured of his leprosy? See how he is trying to pick a quarrel with me!"

8When Elisha the man of God heard that the king of Israel had torn his robes, he sent him this message: "Why have you torn your robes? Have the man come to me and he will know that there is a prophet in Israel." 9So Naaman went with his horses and chariots and stopped at the door of Elisha's house. 10Elisha sent a messenger to say to him, "Go, wash yourself seven times in the Jordan, and your flesh will be restored and you will be cleansed."

11But Naaman went away angry and said, "I thought that he would surely come out to me and stand and call on the name of the LORD his God, wave his hand over the spot and cure me of my leprosy. 12Are not Abana and Pharpar, the rivers of Damascus, better than any of the waters of Israel? Couldn't I wash in them and be cleansed?" So he turned and went off in a rage.

13Naaman's servants went to him and said, "My father, if the prophet had told you to do some great thing, would you not have done it? How much more, then, when he tells you, 'Wash and be cleansed'!" 14So he went down and dipped himself in the Jordan seven times, as the man of God had told him, and his flesh was restored and became clean like that of a young boy.

15Then Naaman and all his attendants went back to the man of God. He stood before him and said, "Now I know that there is no God in all the world except in Israel. Please accept now a gift from your servant."

16The prophet answered, "As surely as the LORD lives, whom I serve, I will not accept a thing." And even though Naaman urged him, he refused.

17"If you will not," said Naaman, "please let me, your servant, be given as much earth as a pair of mules can carry, for your servant will never again make burnt offerings and sacrifices to any other god but the LORD. 18But may the LORD forgive your servant for this one thing: When my master enters the temple of Rimmon to bow down and he is leaning on my arm and I bow there also—when I bow down in the temple of Rimmon, may the LORD forgive your servant for this."

19"Go in peace," Elisha said.

After Naaman had traveled some distance, 20Gehazi, the servant of Elisha the man of God, said to himself, "My master was too easy on Naaman, this Aramean, by not accepting from him what he brought. As surely as the LORD lives, I will run after him and get something from him."

**NIV** [a] *1* The Hebrew word was used for various diseases affecting the skin—not necessarily leprosy; also in verses 3, 6, 7, 11 and 27. [b] *5* That is, about 750 pounds (about 340 kilograms) [c] *5* That is, about 150 pounds (about 70 kilograms)

## King James

21So Gehazi followed after Naaman. And when Naaman saw
*him* running after him, he lighted down from the chariot to meet
him, and said, *Is* all well?
22And he said, All *is* well. My master hath sent me, saying,
Behold, even now there be come to me from mount Ephraim two
young men of the sons of the prophets: give them, I pray thee, a
talent of silver, and two changes of garments.
23And Naaman said, Be content, take two talents. And he urged
him, and bound two talents of silver in two bags, with two changes
of garments, and laid *them* upon two of his servants; and they bare
*them* before him.
24And when he came to the tower, he took *them* from their
hand, and bestowed *them* in the house: and he let the men go, and
they departed.
25But he went in, and stood before his master. And Elisha said
unto him, Whence *comest thou,* Gehazi? And he said, Thy servant
went no whither.
26And he said unto him, Went not mine heart *with thee,* when
the man turned again from his chariot to meet thee? *Is it* a time to
receive money, and to receive garments, and oliveyards, and vineyards, and sheep, and oxen, and menservants, and maidservants?
27The leprosy therefore of Naaman shall cleave unto thee, and
unto thy seed for ever. And he went out from his presence a leper
*as white* as snow.

6 AND THE sons of the prophets said unto Elisha, Behold now,
the place where we dwell with thee is too strait for us.
2Let us go, we pray thee, unto Jordan, and take thence every
man a beam, and let us make us a place there, where we may
dwell. And he answered, Go ye.
3And one said, Be content, I pray thee, and go with thy servants. And he answered, I will go.
4So he went with them. And when they came to Jordan, they
cut down wood.
5But as one was felling a beam, the axe head fell into the water:
and he cried, and said, Alas, master! for it was borrowed.
6And the man of God said, Where fell it? And he showed him
the place. And he cut down a stick, and cast *it* in thither; and the
iron did swim.
7Therefore said he, Take *it* up to thee. And he put out his hand,
and took it.
8¶ Then the king of Syria warred against Israel, and took counsel with his servants, saying, In such and such a place *shall be* my
camp.
9And the man of God sent unto the king of Israel, saying,
Beware that thou pass not such a place; for thither the Syrians are
come down.
10And the king of Israel sent to the place which the man of God
told him and warned him of, and saved himself there, not once nor
twice.
11Therefore the heart of the king of Syria was sore troubled for
this thing; and he called his servants, and said unto them, Will ye
not show me which of us *is* for the king of Israel?
12And one of his servants said, None, my lord, O king: but
Elisha, the prophet that *is* in Israel, telleth the king of Israel the
words that thou speakest in thy bedchamber.
13¶ And he said, Go and spy where he *is,* that I may send and
fetch him. And it was told him, saying, Behold, *he is* in Dothan.
14Therefore sent he thither horses, and chariots, and a great
host: and they came by night, and compassed the city about.
15And when the servant of the man of God was risen early, and
gone forth, behold, an host compassed the city both with horses
and chariots. And his servant said unto him, Alas, my master! how
shall we do?

## Amplified

21So Gehazi followed after Naaman. When Naaman saw one
running after him, he lighted down from the chariot to meet him,
and said, Is all well?
22And he said, All is well. My master has sent me to say, There
have just come to me from the hill country of Ephraim two young
men of the sons of the prophets; pray, give them a talent of silver
and two changes of garments.
23And Naaman said, Be pleased to take two talents. And he
urged him, and bound two talents of silver in two bags with two
changes of garments and laid them upon two of his servants, and
they bore them before Gehazi.
24When he came to the hill, he took them from their hand, and
put them in the house; and he sent the men away, and they left.
25He went in, and stood before his master. Elisha said, Where
have you been, Gehazi? He said, Your servant went nowhere.
26Elisha said to him, Did not my spirit go with you, when the
man turned from his chariot to meet you? Was it a time to accept
money, garments, olive orchards, vineyards, sheep, oxen, menservants, and maidservants?
27Therefore the leprosy of Naaman shall cleave to you and to
your offspring for ever. And Gehazi went from his presence a leper
as white as snow.

6 THE SONS of the prophets said to Elisha, Look now, the
place where we live before you is too small for us.
2Let us go to the Jordan, and each man get there a [house] beam,
and let us make us a place there where we may dwell. And he
answered, Go.
3One said, Be pleased to go with your servants. He answered,
I will go.
4So he went with them. And when they came to the Jordan,
they cut down trees.
5But as one was felling his beam, the axe head fell into the
water; and he cried, Alas, my master, for it was borrowed!
6The man of God said, Where did it fall? When shown the place,
Elisha cut off a stick and threw it in there, and the iron floated.
7He said, Pick it up. And he put out his hand, and took it.
8When the king of Syria was warring against Israel, counseling
with his servants he said, In such and such a place shall be my
camp.
9Then the man of God sent to the king of Israel, saying, Beware
that you pass not such a place; for the Syrians are coming down
there.
10Then the king of Israel sent to the place of which [Elisha] told
*and* warned him, and thus protected *and* saved himself there repeatedly.
11Therefore the mind of the king of Syria was greatly troubled
by this thing. He called his servants and said, Will you show me
who of us is for the king of Israel?
12One of his servants said, None, my lord, O king; but Elisha,
the prophet who is in Israel, tells the king of Israel the words that
you speak in your bedchamber.
13He said, Go and see where he is, that I may send and seize
him. And it was told him, He is in Dothan.
14So [the Syrian king] sent there horses, chariots, and a great
army. They came by night, and surrounded the city.
15When the servant of the man of God rose early and went out,
behold, an army with horses and chariots was around the city.
Elisha's servant said to him, Alas, my master! What shall we do?

## New American Standard

21So Gehazi pursued Naaman. When Naaman saw one running
after him, he came down from the chariot to meet him and said,
"Is all well?"
22And he said, "All is well. My master has sent me, saying,
'Behold, just now two young men of the sons of the prophets have
come to me from the hill country of Ephraim. Please give them a
talent of silver and two changes of clothes.'"
23And Naaman said, "Be pleased to take two talents." And he
urged him, and bound two talents of silver in two bags with two
changes of clothes, and gave them to two of his servants; and they
carried *them* before him.
24When he came to the hill, he took them from their hand and
deposited them in the house, and he sent the men away, and they
departed.
25But he went in and stood before his master. And Elisha said
to him, "Where have you been, Gehazi?" And he said, "Your
servant went nowhere."
26Then he said to him, "Did not my heart go *with you*, when the
man turned from his chariot to meet you? Is it a time to receive
money and to receive clothes and olive groves and vineyards and
sheep and oxen and male and female servants?
27"Therefore, the leprosy of Naaman shall cleave to you and to
your descendants forever." So he went out from his presence a
leper *as white* as snow.

*The Axe Head Recovered*

6 NOW THE sons of the prophets said to Elisha, "Behold now,
the place before you where we are living is too limited for us.
2"Please let us go to the Jordan, and each of us take from there
a beam, and let us make a place there for ourselves where we may
live." So he said, "Go."
3Then one said, "Please be willing to go with your servants."
And he answered, "I shall go."
4So he went with them; and when they came to the Jordan,
they cut down trees.
5But as one was felling a beam, the axe head fell into the water;
and he cried out and said, "Alas, my master! For it was borrowed."
6Then the man of God said, "Where did it fall?" And when he
showed him the place, he cut off a stick, and threw *it* in there, and
made the iron float.
7And he said, "Take it up for yourself." So he put out his hand
and took it.

*The Arameans Plot to Capture Elisha*

8¶ Now the king of Aram was warring against Israel; and he
counseled with his servants saying, "In such and such a place shall
be my camp."
9And the man of God sent *word* to the king of Israel saying,
"Beware that you do not pass this place, for the Arameans are
coming down there."
10And the king of Israel sent to the place about which the man
of God had told him; thus he warned him, so that he guarded
himself there, more than once or twice.
11Now the heart of the king of Aram was enraged over this
thing; and he called his servants and said to them, "Will you tell
me which of us is for the king of Israel?"
12And one of his servants said, "No, my lord, O king; but
Elisha, the prophet who is in Israel, tells the king of Israel the
words that you speak in your bedroom."
13So he said, "Go and see where he is, that I may send and take
him." And it was told him, saying, "Behold, he is in Dothan."
14And he sent horses and chariots and a great army there, and
they came by night and surrounded the city.
15¶ Now when the attendant of the man of God had risen early
and gone out, behold, an army with horses and chariots was
circling the city. And his servant said to him, "Alas, my master!
What shall we do?"

## New International

21So Gehazi hurried after Naaman. When Naaman saw him
running toward him, he got down from the chariot to meet him.
"Is everything all right?" he asked.
22"Everything is all right," Gehazi answered. "My master sent
me to say, 'Two young men from the company of the prophets
have just come to me from the hill country of Ephraim. Please give
them a talent[a] of silver and two sets of clothing.'"
23"By all means, take two talents," said Naaman. He urged
Gehazi to accept them, and then tied up the two talents of silver
in two bags, with two sets of clothing. He gave them to two of his
servants, and they carried them ahead of Gehazi. 24When Gehazi
came to the hill, he took the things from the servants and put them
away in the house. He sent the men away and they left. 25Then
he went in and stood before his master Elisha.
"Where have you been, Gehazi?" Elisha asked.
"Your servant didn't go anywhere," Gehazi answered.
26But Elisha said to him, "Was not my spirit with you when the
man got down from his chariot to meet you? Is this the time to take
money, or to accept clothes, olive groves, vineyards, flocks, herds,
or menservants and maidservants? 27Naaman's leprosy will cling
to you and to your descendants forever." Then Gehazi went from
Elisha's presence and he was leprous, as white as snow.

*An Axhead Floats*

6 THE COMPANY of the prophets said to Elisha, "Look, the
place where we meet with you is too small for us. 2Let us go
to the Jordan, where each of us can get a pole; and let us build a
place there for us to live."
And he said, "Go."
3Then one of them said, "Won't you please come with your
servants?"
"I will," Elisha replied. 4And he went with them.
They went to the Jordan and began to cut down trees. 5As one
of them was cutting down a tree, the iron axhead fell into the
water. "Oh, my lord," he cried out, "it was borrowed!"
6The man of God asked, "Where did it fall?" When he showed
him the place, Elisha cut a stick and threw it there, and made the
iron float. 7"Lift it out," he said. Then the man reached out his
hand and took it.

*Elisha Traps Blinded Arameans*

8Now the king of Aram was at war with Israel. After conferring
with his officers, he said, "I will set up my camp in such and such
a place."
9The man of God sent word to the king of Israel: "Beware of
passing that place, because the Arameans are going down there."
10So the king of Israel checked on the place indicated by the man
of God. Time and again Elisha warned the king, so that he was on
his guard in such places.
11This enraged the king of Aram. He summoned his officers and
demanded of them, "Will you not tell me which of us is on the side
of the king of Israel?"
12"None of us, my lord the king," said one of his officers, "but
Elisha, the prophet who is in Israel, tells the king of Israel the very
words you speak in your bedroom."
13"Go, find out where he is," the king ordered, "so I can send
men and capture him." The report came back: "He is in Dothan."
14Then he sent horses and chariots and a strong force there. They
went by night and surrounded the city.
15When the servant of the man of God got up and went out early
the next morning, an army with horses and chariots had surrounded the city. "Oh, my lord, what shall we do?" the servant asked.

**NIV** [a] 22 That is, about 75 pounds (about 34 kilograms)

## King James

16 And he answered, Fear not: for they that *be* with us *are* more than they that *be* with them.

17 And Elisha prayed, and said, LORD, I pray thee, open his eyes, that he may see. And the LORD opened the eyes of the young man; and he saw: and, behold, the mountain *was* full of horses and chariots of fire round about Elisha.

18 And when they came down to him, Elisha prayed unto the LORD, and said, Smite this people, I pray thee, with blindness. And he smote them with blindness according to the word of Elisha.

19 ¶ And Elisha said unto them, This *is* not the way, neither *is* this the city: follow me, and I will bring you to the man whom ye seek. But he led them to Samaria.

20 And it came to pass, when they were come into Samaria, that Elisha said, LORD, open the eyes of these *men*, that they may see. And the LORD opened their eyes, and they saw; and, behold, *they were* in the midst of Samaria.

21 And the king of Israel said unto Elisha, when he saw them, My father, shall I smite *them*? shall I smite *them?*

22 And he answered, Thou shalt not smite *them:* wouldest thou smite those whom thou hast taken captive with thy sword and with thy bow? set bread and water before them, that they may eat and drink, and go to their master.

23 And he prepared great provision for them: and when they had eaten and drunk, he sent them away, and they went to their master. So the bands of Syria came no more into the land of Israel.

24 ¶ And it came to pass after this, that Ben-hadad king of Syria gathered all his host, and went up, and besieged Samaria.

25 And there was a great famine in Samaria: and, behold, they besieged it, until an ass's head was *sold* for fourscore *pieces* of silver, and the fourth part of a cab of dove's dung for five *pieces* of silver.

26 And as the king of Israel was passing by upon the wall, there cried a woman unto him, saying, Help, my lord, O king.

27 And he said, If the LORD do not help thee, whence shall I help thee? out of the barnfloor, or out of the winepress?

28 And the king said unto her, What aileth thee? And she answered, This woman said unto me, Give thy son, that we may eat him today, and we will eat my son tomorrow.

29 So we boiled my son, and did eat him: and I said unto her on the next day, Give thy son, that we may eat him: and she hath hid her son.

30 ¶ And it came to pass, when the king heard the words of the woman, that he rent his clothes; and he passed by upon the wall, and the people looked, and, behold, *he had* sackcloth within upon his flesh.

31 Then he said, God do so and more also to me, if the head of Elisha the son of Shaphat shall stand on him this day.

32 But Elisha sat in his house, and the elders sat with him; and *the king* sent a man from before him: but ere the messenger came to him, he said to the elders, See ye how this son of a murderer hath sent to take away mine head? look, when the messenger cometh, shut the door, and hold him fast at the door: *is* not the sound of his master's feet behind him?

33 And while he yet talked with them, behold, the messenger came down unto him: and he said, Behold, this evil *is* of the LORD; what should I wait for the LORD any longer?

## Amplified

16 *Elisha* answered, Fear not; for those with us are more than those with them.

17 Then Elisha prayed, Lord, I pray You, open his eyes that he may see. And the Lord opened the young man's eyes, and he saw; and behold, the mountain was full of horses and chariots of fire round about Elisha.

18 And when the Syrians came down to him, Elisha prayed to the Lord, Smite this people with blindness, I pray You. And God smote them with blindness as Elisha asked.

19 Elisha said to the Syrians, This is not the way nor the city. Follow me, and I will bring you to the man whom you seek. And he led them to Samaria.

20 And when they had come into Samaria, Elisha said, Lord, open the eyes of these men, that they may see. And the Lord opened their eyes, and they saw. Lo, they were in the midst of Samaria!

21 When the king of Israel saw them, he said to Elisha, My father, shall I slay them? Shall I slay them?

22 [Elisha] answered, You shall not slay them. Would you slay those you have taken captive with your sword and bow? Set bread and water before them, that they may eat and drink, and return to their master.

23 So [the king] prepared great provision for them; and when they had eaten and drunk, he sent them away, and they went to their master. And the bands of Syria came no more into the land of Israel.

24 Afterward Benhadad king of Syria gathered his whole army and went up and besieged Samaria,

25 And a great famine came to Samaria. They besieged it, until a donkey's head was sold for eighty shekels of silver, and the fourth of a kab of dove's dung [a wild vegetable] for five shekels of silver.

26 As the king of Israel was passing by upon the wall, a woman cried to him, Help, my lord, O king!

27 He said, *For* if he does not help you [No, let the Lord help you!], from where can I get you help? Out of the threshing floor, or out of the wine press?

28 And the king said to her, What ails you? She answered, This woman said to me, Give me your son, so we may eat him today, and we will eat my son tomorrow.

29 So we boiled my son, and ate him. The next day I said to her, Give your son, that we may eat him, but she had hidden her son.

30 When the king heard the woman's words he rent his clothes. As he went on upon the wall, the people looked and lo, he wore sackcloth inside on his flesh.

31 Then he said, God do so and more also to me, if the head of Elisha son of Shaphat shall stand on him this day!

32 Now Elisha sat in his house, and the elders sat with him; and the king sent a man from before him [to behead Elisha]. But before the messenger arrived, Elisha said to the elders, See how this son of [Jezebel] a murderer is sending to remove my head? Look, when the messenger comes, shut the door, and hold it fast against him. Is not the sound of his master's feet [just] behind him?

33 And while Elisha was talking with them, lo, *the messenger* came to him [and then the king came also]. And [the relenting king] said, This evil is from the Lord! Why should I longer wait [expecting Him to withdraw His punishment? What, Elisha, can be done now]?

## New American Standard

16 So he answered, "Do not fear, for those who are with us are
more than those who are with them."
17 Then Elisha prayed and said, "O LORD, I pray, open his eyes
that he may see." And the LORD opened the servant's eyes, and
he saw; and behold, the mountain was full of horses and chariots
of fire all around Elisha.
18 And when they came down to him, Elisha prayed to the LORD
and said, "Strike this people with blindness, I pray." So He struck
them with blindness according to the word of Elisha.
19 Then Elisha said to them, "This is not the way, nor is this the
city; follow me and I will bring you to the man whom you seek."
And he brought them to Samaria.
20¶ And it came about when they had come into Samaria, that
Elisha said, "O LORD, open the eyes of these *men*, that they may
see." So the LORD opened their eyes, and they saw; and behold,
they were in the midst of Samaria.
21 Then the king of Israel when he saw them, said to Elisha, "My
father, shall I kill them? Shall I kill them?"
22 And he answered, "You shall not kill *them*. Would you kill
those you have taken captive with your sword and with your bow?
Set bread and water before them, that they may eat and drink and
go to their master."
23 So he prepared a great feast for them; and when they had
eaten and drunk he sent them away, and they went to their master. And the marauding bands of Arameans did not come again
into the land of Israel.

*The Siege of Samaria—Cannibalism*

24¶ Now it came about after this, that Ben-hadad king of Aram
gathered all his army and went up and besieged Samaria.
25 And there was a great famine in Samaria; and behold, they
besieged it, until a donkey's head was sold for eighty *shekels* of
silver, and a fourth of a [a]kab of dove's dung for five *shekels* of
silver.
26 And as the king of Israel was passing by on the wall a woman
cried out to him, saying, "Help, my lord, O king!"
27 And he said, "If the LORD does not help you, from where shall
I help you? From the threshing floor, or from the wine press?"
28 And the king said to her, "What is the matter with you?" And
she answered, "This woman said to me, 'Give your son that we
may eat him today, and we will eat my son tomorrow.'
29 "So we boiled my son and ate him; and I said to her on the
next day, 'Give your son, that we may eat him'; but she has hidden
her son."
30 And it came about when the king heard the words of the
woman, that he tore his clothes—now he was passing by on the
wall—and the people looked, and behold, he had sackcloth
beneath on his body.
31 Then he said, "May God do so to me and more also, if the
head of Elisha the son of Shaphat remains on him today."
32¶ Now Elisha was sitting in his house, and the elders were
sitting with him. And *the king* sent a man from his presence; but
before the messenger came to him, he said to the elders, "Do you
see how this son of a murderer has sent to take away my head?
Look, when the messenger comes, shut the door and hold the door
shut against him. Is not the sound of his master's feet behind
him?"
33 And while he was still talking with them, behold, the messenger came down to him, and he said, "Behold, this evil is from the
LORD; why should I wait for the LORD any longer?"

NAS [a] I.e., One kab equals approx. 2 quarts

## New International

16 "Don't be afraid," the prophet answered. "Those who are
with us are more than those who are with them."
17 And Elisha prayed, "O LORD, open his eyes so he may see."
Then the LORD opened the servant's eyes, and he looked and saw
the hills full of horses and chariots of fire all around Elisha.
18 As the enemy came down toward him, Elisha prayed to the
LORD, "Strike these people with blindness." So he struck them
with blindness, as Elisha had asked.
19 Elisha told them, "This is not the road and this is not the city.
Follow me, and I will lead you to the man you are looking for."
And he led them to Samaria.
20 After they entered the city, Elisha said, "LORD, open the eyes
of these men so they can see." Then the LORD opened their eyes
and they looked, and there they were, inside Samaria.
21 When the king of Israel saw them, he asked Elisha, "Shall I
kill them, my father? Shall I kill them?"
22 "Do not kill them," he answered. "Would you kill men you
have captured with your own sword or bow? Set food and water
before them so that they may eat and drink and then go back to
their master." 23 So he prepared a great feast for them, and after
they had finished eating and drinking, he sent them away, and
they returned to their master. So the bands from Aram stopped
raiding Israel's territory.

*Famine in Besieged Samaria*

24 Some time later, Ben-Hadad king of Aram mobilized his entire
army and marched up and laid siege to Samaria. 25 There was a
great famine in the city; the siege lasted so long that a donkey's
head sold for eighty shekels[b] of silver, and a quarter of a cab[c] of
seed pods[d] for five shekels.[e]
26 As the king of Israel was passing by on the wall, a woman
cried to him, "Help me, my lord the king!"
27 The king replied, "If the LORD does not help you, where can
I get help for you? From the threshing floor? From the winepress?"
28 Then he asked her, "What's the matter?"
She answered, "This woman said to me, 'Give up your son so
we may eat him today, and tomorrow we'll eat my son.' 29 So we
cooked my son and ate him. The next day I said to her, 'Give up
your son so we may eat him,' but she had hidden him."
30 When the king heard the woman's words, he tore his robes.
As he went along the wall, the people looked, and there, underneath, he had sackcloth on his body. 31 He said, "May God deal
with me, be it ever so severely, if the head of Elisha son of Shaphat
remains on his shoulders today!"
32 Now Elisha was sitting in his house, and the elders were
sitting with him. The king sent a messenger ahead, but before he
arrived, Elisha said to the elders, "Don't you see how this murderer is sending someone to cut off my head? Look, when the
messenger comes, shut the door and hold it shut against him. Is
not the sound of his master's footsteps behind him?"
33 While he was still talking to them, the messenger came down
to him. And ⌊the king⌋ said, "This disaster is from the LORD. Why
should I wait for the LORD any longer?"

NIV [b] *25* That is, about 2 pounds (about 1 kilogram) [c] *25* That is, probably about 1/2 pint (about 0.3 liter) [d] *25* Or *of dove's dung* [e] *25* That is, about 2 ounces (about 55 grams)

## King James

7 THEN ELISHA said, Hear ye the word of the LORD; Thus saith the LORD, Tomorrow about this time *shall* a measure of fine flour *be sold* for a shekel, and two measures of barley for a shekel, in the gate of Samaria.

2 Then a lord on whose hand the king leaned answered the man of God, and said, Behold, *if* the LORD would make windows in heaven, might this thing be? And he said, Behold, thou shalt see *it* with thine eyes, but shalt not eat thereof.

3 ¶ And there were four leprous men at the entering in of the gate: and they said one to another, Why sit we here until we die?

4 If we say, We will enter into the city, then the famine *is* in the city, and we shall die there: and if we sit still here, we die also. Now therefore come, and let us fall unto the host of the Syrians: if they save us alive, we shall live; and if they kill us, we shall but die.

5 And they rose up in the twilight, to go unto the camp of the Syrians: and when they were come to the uttermost part of the camp of Syria, behold, *there was* no man there.

6 For the Lord had made the host of the Syrians to hear a noise of chariots, and a noise of horses, *even* the noise of a great host: and they said one to another, Lo, the king of Israel hath hired against us the kings of the Hittites, and the kings of the Egyptians, to come upon us.

7 Wherefore they arose and fled in the twilight, and left their tents, and their horses, and their asses, even the camp as it *was*, and fled for their life.

8 And when these lepers came to the uttermost part of the camp, they went into one tent, and did eat and drink, and carried thence silver, and gold, and raiment, and went and hid *it;* and came again, and entered into another tent, and carried thence *also*, and went and hid *it*.

9 Then they said one to another, We do not well: this day *is* a day of good tidings, and we hold our peace: if we tarry till the morning light, some mischief will come upon us: now therefore come, that we may go and tell the king's household.

10 So they came and called unto the porter of the city: and they told them, saying, We came to the camp of the Syrians, and, behold, *there was* no man there, neither voice of man, but horses tied, and asses tied, and the tents as they *were*.

11 And he called the porters; and they told *it* to the king's house within.

12 ¶ And the king arose in the night, and said unto his servants, I will now show you what the Syrians have done to us. They know that we *be* hungry; therefore are they gone out of the camp to hide themselves in the field, saying, When they come out of the city, we shall catch them alive, and get into the city.

13 And one of his servants answered and said, Let *some* take, I pray thee, five of the horses that remain, which are left in the city, (behold, they *are* as all the multitude of Israel that are left in it: behold, *I say*, they *are* even as all the multitude of the Israelites that are consumed:) and let us send and see.

14 They took therefore two chariot horses; and the king sent after the host of the Syrians, saying, Go and see.

15 And they went after them unto Jordan: and, lo, all the way *was* full of garments and vessels, which the Syrians had cast away in their haste. And the messengers returned, and told the king.

16 And the people went out, and spoiled the tents of the Syrians. So a measure of fine flour was *sold* for a shekel, and two measures of barley for a shekel, according to the word of the LORD.

17 ¶ And the king appointed the lord on whose hand he leaned to have the charge of the gate: and the people trode upon him in the gate, and he died, as the man of God had said, who spake when the king came down to him.

## Amplified

7 THEN ELISHA said, Hear the word of the Lord: Thus says the Lord, Tomorrow about this time a measure of fine flour will sell for a shekel, and two measures of barley for a shekel, in the gate of Samaria!

2 Then the captian on whose hand the king leaned answered the man of God, and said, If the Lord would make windows in Heaven, could this thing be? But Elisha said, You shall see it with your own eyes, but you shall not eat of it.

3 Now four men who were lepers were at the entrance of the city's gate; and they said to one another, Why do we sit here until we die?

4 If we say, We will enter the city, then the famine is in the city, and we shall die there; and if we sit still here, we die also. So now come, let us go over to the army of the Syrians. If they save us alive we shall live, and if they kill us we shall but die.

5 So they arose in the twilight and went to the Syrian camp. But when they came to the edge of the camp, no man was there.

6 For the Lord had made the Syrian army hear a noise of chariots and horses, the noise of a great army. They had said to one another, The king of Israel has hired the Hittite and Egyptian kings to come upon us.

7 So the Syrians arose and fled in the twilight, and left their tents, horses, donkeys, even the camp as it was, and fled for their lives.

8 And when these lepers came to the edge of the camp, they went into one tent, and ate and drank, and carried away silver, gold, and clothing, and went and hid them [in the darkness]. Then they entered another tent and carried from there also, and went and hid it.

9 Then they said one to another, We are not doing right. This is a day of (glad) good news, and we are silent *and* do not speak up! If we wait until daylight, some punishment will come upon us [for not reporting at once]. So now come, let us go and tell the king's household.

10 So they came and called to the gatekeepers of the city. They told them, We came to the camp of the Syrians, and, behold, there was neither sight nor sound of man there, only the horses and donkeys tied and the tents as they were.

11 Then the gatekeepers called out, and it was told to the king's household within.

12 And the king rose in the night, and said to his servants, I will tell you what the Syrians have done to us. They know that we are hungry; therefore they have gone out of the camp to hide themselves in the open country, thinking, When they come out of the city, we shall take them alive and get into the city.

13 One of his servants said, Let some men take five of the remaining horses; [if they are caught and killed] they will be no worse off than all the multitude of Israel left in the city to be consumed. Let us send and see.

14 So they took two chariot horses; and the king sent them after the Syrian army, saying, Go and see.

15 They went after them to the Jordan. All the way was strewn with clothing and equipment which the Syrians had cast away in their flight. And the messengers returned and told the king.

16 Then the people went out and plundered the tents of the Syrians. So a measure of fine flour was sold for a shekel, and two measures of barley for a shekel, as the Lord had spoken [through Elisha]. [v. 1.]

17 The king had appointed the captain on whose hand he leaned to have charge of the gate; and the [starving] people trampled him in the gate [as they struggled to get through for food], and he died, as the man of God had foretold when the king came down to him.

## New American Standard

*Elisha Promises Food*

7 THEN ELISHA said, "Listen to the word of the LORD; thus
says the LORD, 'Tomorrow about this time a measure of fine
flour shall be *sold* for a shekel, and two measures of barley for a
shekel, in the gate of Samaria.' "
2And the royal officer on whose hand the king was leaning
answered the man of God and said, "Behold, if the LORD should
make windows in heaven, could this thing be?" Then he said,
"Behold you shall see it with your own eyes, but you shall not eat
of it."

*Four Lepers Relate Arameans' Flight*

3¶ Now there were four leprous men at the entrance of the gate;
and they said to one another, "Why do we sit here until we die?
4"If we say, 'We will enter the city,' then the famine is in the
city and we shall die there; and if we sit here, we die also. Now
therefore come, and let us go over to the camp of the Arameans.
If they spare us, we shall live; and if they kill us, we shall but die."
5And they arose at twilight to go to the camp of the Arameans;
when they came to the outskirts of the camp of the Arameans,
behold, there was no one there.
6For the Lord had caused the army of the Arameans to hear a
sound of chariots and a sound of horses, *even* the sound of a great
army, so that they said to one another, "Behold, the king of Israel
has hired against us the kings of the Hittites and the kings of the
Egyptians, to come upon us."
7Therefore they arose and fled in the twilight, and left their
tents and their horses and their donkeys, even the camp just as it
was, and fled for their life.
8When these lepers came to the outskirts of the camp, they
entered one tent and ate and drank, and carried from there silver
and gold and clothes, and went and hid *them*; and they returned
and entered another tent and carried from there *also*, and went and
hid *them*.
9¶ Then they said to one another, "We are not doing right. This
day is a day of good news, but we are keeping silent; if we wait
until morning light, punishment will overtake us. Now therefore
come, let us go and tell the king's household."
10So they came and called to the gatekeepers of the city, and
they told them, saying, "We came to the camp of the Arameans,
and behold, there was no one there, nor the voice of man, only the
horses tied and the donkeys tied, and the tents just as they were."
11And the gatekeepers called, and told *it* within the king's
household.
12Then the king arose in the night and said to his servants, "I
will now tell you what the Arameans have done to us. They know
that we are hungry; therefore they have gone from the camp to
hide themselves in the field, saying, 'When they come out of the
city, we shall capture them alive and get into the city.' "
13And one of his servants answered and said, "Please, let some
*men* take five of the horses which remain, which are left in the city.
Behold, they *will be in any case* like all the multitude of Israel who
are left in it; behold, they *will be in any case* like all the multitude
of Israel who have already perished, so let us send and see."
14They took therefore two chariots with horses, and the king
sent after the army of the Arameans, saying, "Go and see."

*The Promise Fulfilled*

15And they went after them to the Jordan, and behold, all the
way was full of clothes and equipment, which the Arameans had
thrown away in their haste. Then the messengers returned and
told the king.
16¶ So the people went out and plundered the camp of the
Arameans. Then a measure of fine flour *was sold* for a shekel and
two measures of barley for a shekel, according to the word of the
LORD.
17Now the king appointed the royal officer on whose hand he
leaned to have charge of the gate; but the people trampled on him
at the gate, and he died just as the man of God had said, who spoke
when the king came down to him.

## New International

7 ELISHA SAID, "Hear the word of the LORD. This is what the
LORD says: About this time tomorrow, a seah[a] of flour will
sell for a shekel[b] and two seahs[c] of barley for a shekel at the gate
of Samaria."
2The officer on whose arm the king was leaning said to the man
of God, "Look, even if the LORD should open the floodgates of the
heavens, could this happen?"
"You will see it with your own eyes," answered Elisha, "but
you will not eat any of it!"

*The Siege Lifted*

3Now there were four men with leprosy[d] at the entrance of the
city gate. They said to each other, "Why stay here until we die?
4If we say, 'We'll go into the city'—the famine is there, and we will
die. And if we stay here, we will die. So let's go over to the camp
of the Arameans and surrender. If they spare us, we live; if they
kill us, then we die."
5At dusk they got up and went to the camp of the Arameans.
When they reached the edge of the camp, not a man was there,
6for the Lord had caused the Arameans to hear the sound of
chariots and horses and a great army, so that they said to one
another, "Look, the king of Israel has hired the Hittite and Egyptian kings to attack us!" 7So they got up and fled in the dusk and
abandoned their tents and their horses and donkeys. They left the
camp as it was and ran for their lives.
8The men who had leprosy reached the edge of the camp and
entered one of the tents. They ate and drank, and carried away
silver, gold and clothes, and went off and hid them. They returned
and entered another tent and took some things from it and hid
them also.
9Then they said to each other, "We're not doing right. This is
a day of good news and we are keeping it to ourselves. If we wait
until daylight, punishment will overtake us. Let's go at once and
report this to the royal palace."
10So they went and called out to the city gatekeepers and told
them, "We went into the Aramean camp and not a man was
there—not a sound of anyone—only tethered horses and donkeys,
and the tents left just as they were." 11The gatekeepers shouted
the news, and it was reported within the palace.
12The king got up in the night and said to his officers, "I will
tell you what the Arameans have done to us. They know we are
starving; so they have left the camp to hide in the countryside,
thinking, 'They will surely come out, and then we will take them
alive and get into the city.' "
13One of his officers answered, "Have some men take five of the
horses that are left in the city. Their plight will be like that of all
the Israelites left here—yes, they will only be like all these Israelites
who are doomed. So let us send them to find out what happened."
14So they selected two chariots with their horses, and the king
sent them after the Aramean army. He commanded the drivers,
"Go and find out what has happened." 15They followed them as
far as the Jordan, and they found the whole road strewn with the
clothing and equipment the Arameans had thrown away in their
headlong flight. So the messengers returned and reported to the
king. 16Then the people went out and plundered the camp of the
Arameans. So a seah of flour sold for a shekel, and two seahs of
barley sold for a shekel, as the LORD had said.
17Now the king had put the officer on whose arm he leaned in
charge of the gate, and the people trampled him in the gateway,
and he died, just as the man of God had foretold when the king
came down to his house. 18It happened as the man of God had said

**NIV** [a] *1* That is, probably about 7 quarts (about 7.3 liters); also in verses 16 and 18 [b] *1* That is, about 2/5 ounce (about 11 grams); also in verses 16 and 18 [c] *1* That is, probably about 13 quarts (about 15 liters); also in verses 16 and 18 [d] *3* The Hebrew word is used for various diseases affecting the skin—not necessarily leprosy; also in verse 8.

## King James

18 And it came to pass as the man of God had spoken to the king,
saying, Two measures of barley for a shekel, and a measure of fine
flour for a shekel, shall be tomorrow about this time in the gate of
Samaria:
19 And that lord answered the man of God, and said, Now,
behold, *if* the LORD should make windows in heaven, might such
a thing be? And he said, Behold, thou shalt see it with thine eyes,
but shalt not eat thereof.
20 And so it fell out unto him: for the people trode upon him in
the gate, and he died.

**8** THEN SPAKE Elisha unto the woman, whose son he had
restored to life, saying, Arise, and go thou and thine household, and sojourn wheresoever thou canst sojourn: for the LORD
hath called for a famine; and it shall also come upon the land seven
years.
2 And the woman arose, and did after the saying of the man of
God: and she went with her household, and sojourned in the land
of the Philistines seven years.
3 And it came to pass at the seven years' end, that the woman
returned out of the land of the Philistines: and she went forth to
cry unto the king for her house and for her land.
4 And the king talked with Gehazi the servant of the man of
God, saying, Tell me, I pray thee, all the great things that Elisha
hath done.
5 And it came to pass, as he was telling the king how he had
restored a dead body to life, that, behold, the woman, whose son
he had restored to life, cried to the king for her house and for her
land. And Gehazi said, My lord, O king, this *is* the woman, and
this *is* her son, whom Elisha restored to life.
6 And when the king asked the woman, she told him. So the
king appointed unto her a certain officer, saying, Restore all that
*was* hers, and all the fruits of the field since the day that she left
the land, even until now.
7 ¶ And Elisha came to Damascus; and Ben-hadad the king of
Syria was sick; and it was told him, saying, The man of God is come
hither.
8 And the king said unto Hazael, Take a present in thine hand,
and go, meet the man of God, and inquire of the LORD by him,
saying, Shall I recover of this disease?
9 So Hazael went to meet him, and took a present with him,
even of every good thing of Damascus, forty camels' burden, and
came and stood before him, and said, Thy son Ben-hadad king of
Syria hath sent me to thee, saying, Shall I recover of this disease?
10 And Elisha said unto him, Go, say unto him, Thou mayest
certainly recover: howbeit the LORD hath shown me that he shall
surely die.
11 And he settled his countenance stedfastly, until he was
ashamed: and the man of God wept.
12 And Hazael said, Why weepeth my lord? And he answered,
Because I know the evil that thou wilt do unto the children of
Israel: their strong holds wilt thou set on fire, and their young men
wilt thou slay with the sword, and wilt dash their children, and
rip up their women with child.
13 And Hazael said, But what, *is* thy servant a dog, that he
should do this great thing? And Elisha answered, The LORD hath
shown me that thou *shalt be* king over Syria.
14 So he departed from Elisha, and came to his master; who said
to him, What said Elisha to thee? And he answered, He told me
*that* thou shouldest surely recover.
15 And it came to pass on the morrow, that he took a thick cloth,
and dipped *it* in water, and spread *it* on his face, so that he died:
and Hazael reigned in his stead.

## Amplified

18 When the man of God had told the king, Two measures of
barley shall sell for a shekel, and a measure of fine flour for a shekel
tomorrow about this time in the gate of Samaria,
19 The captain had told the man of God, If the Lord should make
windows in Heaven, could such a thing be? And he said, You shall
see it with your own eyes, but you shall not eat of it. [v. 2.]
20 And so it was fulfilled to him, for the people trampled on him
in the gate, and he died.

**8** NOW ELISHA had said to the woman, whose son he had
restored to life, Arise, and go with your household, and
sojourn wherever you can, for the Lord has called for a famine, and
moreover, it will come upon the land seven years.
2 So the woman arose, and did as the man of God had said; she
went with her household and sojourned in the land of the Philistines seven years.
3 At the end of the seven years the woman returned from the
land of the Philistines; and she went to appeal to the king for her
house and land.
4 The king talked with Gehazi the servant of the man of God,
saying, Tell me, all the great things Elisha has done.
5 And as Gehazi was telling the king how [Elisha] had restored
the dead to life, behold, the woman whose son he had restored to
life appealed to the king for her house and land. And Gehazi said,
My lord, O king, this is the woman, and this is her son whom
Elisha brought back to life.
6 When the king asked the woman, she told him. So the king
appointed to her a certain officer, saying, Restore all that was hers,
and all the fruits of the field since the day that she left the land,
even until now.
7 Elisha came to Damascus, and Benhadad king of Syria was
sick; and he was told, The man of God has come here.
8 And the king said to Hazael, Take a present in your hand, and
go, meet the man of God, and inquire of the Lord by him, saying,
Shall I recover of this disease?
9 So Hazael went to meet Elisha, and took a present with him,
of every good thing of Damascus, forty camel loads, and came and
stood before him, and said, Your son Benhadad king of Syria has
sent me to you, asking, Shall I recover from this disease?
10 And Elisha said, Go, say to him, You shall certainly recover.
But the Lord has shown me that he shall certainly die.
11 Elisha stared steadily at him until Hazael was embarrassed.
And the man of God wept.
12 And Hazael said, Why do you weep, my lord? He answered,
Because I know the evil that you will do to the Israelites. You will
burn their strongholds, slay their young men with the sword, dash
their infants in pieces, and rip up their pregnant women.
13 And Hazael said, What is your servant, only a dog, that he
should do this monstrous thing? And Elisha answered, The Lord
has shown me that you will be king over Syria.
14 Then [Hazael] departed from Elisha, and came to his master,
who said to him, What did Elisha say to you? And he answered,
He told me you would surely recover.
15 But the next day Hazael took the bedspread and dipped it in
water, and spread it on [the Syrian king's] face, so that he died.
And Hazael reigned in his stead.

## New American Standard

18And it came about just as the man of God had spoken to the
king, saying, "Two measures of barley for a shekel and a measure
of fine flour for a shekel, shall be *sold* tomorrow about this time at
the gate of Samaria."
19Then the royal officer answered the man of God and said,
"Now behold, if the LORD should make windows in heaven, could
such a thing be?" And he said, "Behold, you shall see it with your
own eyes, but you shall not eat of it."
20And so it happened to him, for the people trampled on him
at the gate, and he died.

*Jehoram Restores the Shunammite's Land*

8 NOW ELISHA spoke to the woman whose son he had restored to life, saying, "Arise and go with your household,
and sojourn wherever you can sojourn; for the LORD has called for
a famine, and it shall even come on the land for seven years."
2So the woman arose and did according to the word of the man
of God, and she went with her household and sojourned in the
land of the Philistines seven years.
3And it came about at the end of seven years, that the woman
returned from the land of the Philistines; and she went out to
appeal to the king for her house and for her field.
4Now the king was talking with Gehazi, the servant of the man
of God, saying, "Please relate to me all the great things that Elisha
has done."
5And it came about, as he was relating to the king how he had
restored to life the one who was dead, that behold, the woman
whose son he had restored to life, appealed to the king for her
house and for her field. And Gehazi said, "My lord, O king, this
is the woman and this is her son, whom Elisha restored to life."
6When the king asked the woman, she related *it* to him. So the
king appointed for her a certain officer, saying, "Restore all that
was hers and all the produce of the field from the day that she left
the land even until now."

*Elisha Predicts Evil from Hazael*

7¶ Then Elisha came to Damascus. Now Ben-hadad king of
Aram was sick, and it was told him, saying, "The man of God has
come here."
8And the king said to Hazael, "Take a gift in your hand and
go to meet the man of God, and inquire of the LORD by him, saying,
'Will I recover from this sickness?' "
9So Hazael went to meet him and took a gift in his hand, even
every kind of good thing of Damascus, forty camels' loads; and he
came and stood before him and said, "Your son Ben-hadad king
of Aram has sent me to you, saying, 'Will I recover from this
sickness?' "
10Then Elisha said to him, "Go, say to him, 'You shall surely
recover,' but the LORD has shown me that he will certainly die."
11And he fixed his gaze steadily *on him* until he was ashamed,
and the man of God wept.
12And Hazael said, "Why does my lord weep?" Then he answered, "Because I know the evil that you will do to the sons of
Israel: their strongholds you will set on fire, and their young men
you will kill with the sword, and their little ones you will dash in
pieces, and their women with child you will rip up."
13Then Hazael said, "But what is your servant, *who is but* a dog,
that he should do this great thing?" And Elisha answered, "The
LORD has shown me that you will be king over Aram."
14So he departed from Elisha and returned to his master, who
said to him, "What did Elisha say to you?" And he answered, "He
told me that you would surely recover."
15And it came about on the morrow, that he took the cover and
dipped it in water and spread it on his face, so that he died. And
Hazael became king in his place.

## New International

to the king: "About this time tomorrow, a seah of flour will sell for
a shekel and two seahs of barley for a shekel at the gate of Samaria."
19The officer had said to the man of God, "Look, even if the
LORD should open the floodgates of the heavens, could this happen?" The man of God had replied, "You will see it with your own
eyes, but you will not eat any of it!" 20And that is exactly what
happened to him, for the people trampled him in the gateway, and
he died.

*The Shunammite's Land Restored*

8 NOW ELISHA had said to the woman whose son he had
restored to life, "Go away with your family and stay for a
while wherever you can, because the LORD has decreed a famine
in the land that will last seven years." 2The woman proceeded to
do as the man of God said. She and her family went away and
stayed in the land of the Philistines seven years.
3At the end of the seven years she came back from the land of
the Philistines and went to the king to beg for her house and land.
4The king was talking to Gehazi, the servant of the man of God,
and had said, "Tell me about all the great things Elisha has done."
5Just as Gehazi was telling the king how Elisha had restored the
dead to life, the woman whose son Elisha had brought back to life
came to beg the king for her house and land.
Gehazi said, "This is the woman, my lord the king, and this is
her son whom Elisha restored to life." 6The king asked the woman
about it, and she told him.
Then he assigned an official to her case and said to him, "Give
back everything that belonged to her, including all the income
from her land from the day she left the country until now."

*Hazael Murders Ben-Hadad*

7Elisha went to Damascus, and Ben-Hadad king of Aram was
ill. When the king was told, "The man of God has come all the way
up here," 8he said to Hazael, "Take a gift with you and go to meet
the man of God. Consult the LORD through him; ask him, 'Will I
recover from this illness?' "
9Hazael went to meet Elisha, taking with him as a gift forty
camel-loads of all the finest wares of Damascus. He went in and
stood before him, and said, "Your son Ben-Hadad king of Aram
has sent me to ask, 'Will I recover from this illness?' "
10Elisha answered, "Go and say to him, 'You will certainly
recover'; but[a] the LORD has revealed to me that he will in fact die."
11He stared at him with a fixed gaze until Hazael felt ashamed.
Then the man of God began to weep.
12"Why is my lord weeping?" asked Hazael.
"Because I know the harm you will do to the Israelites," he
answered. "You will set fire to their fortified places, kill their
young men with the sword, dash their little children to the ground,
and rip open their pregnant women."
13Hazael said, "How could your servant, a mere dog, accomplish such a feat?"
"The LORD has shown me that you will become king of Aram,"
answered Elisha.
14Then Hazael left Elisha and returned to his master. When
Ben-Hadad asked, "What did Elisha say to you?" Hazael replied,
"He told me that you would certainly recover." 15But the next day
he took a thick cloth, soaked it in water and spread it over the
king's face, so that he died. Then Hazael succeeded him as king.

**NIV** [a] 10 The Hebrew may also be read *Go and say, 'You will certainly not recover,' for.*

## King James

16¶ And in the fifth year of Joram the son of Ahab king of Israel,
Jehoshaphat *being* then king of Judah, Jehoram the son of Jehoshaphat king of Judah began to reign.
17Thirty and two years old was he when he began to reign; and
he reigned eight years in Jerusalem.
18And he walked in the way of the kings of Israel, as did the
house of Ahab: for the daughter of Ahab was his wife: and he did
evil in the sight of the LORD.
19Yet the LORD would not destroy Judah for David his servant's
sake, as he promised him to give him always a light, *and* to his
children.
20¶ In his days Edom revolted from under the hand of Judah,
and made a king over themselves.
21So Joram went over to Zair, and all the chariots with him: and
he rose by night, and smote the Edomites which compassed him
about, and the captains of the chariots: and the people fled into
their tents.
22Yet Edom revolted from under the hand of Judah unto this
day. Then Libnah revolted at the same time.
23And the rest of the acts of Joram, and all that he did, *are* they
not written in the book of the chronicles of the kings of Judah?
24And Joram slept with his fathers, and was buried with his
fathers in the city of David: and Ahaziah his son reigned in his
stead.
25¶ In the twelfth year of Joram the son of Ahab king of Israel
did Ahaziah the son of Jehoram king of Judah begin to reign.
26Two and twenty years old *was* Ahaziah when he began to
reign; and he reigned one year in Jerusalem. And his mother's
name *was* Athaliah, the daughter of Omri king of Israel.
27And he walked in the way of the house of Ahab, and did evil
in the sight of the LORD, as *did* the house of Ahab: for he *was* the
son-in-law of the house of Ahab.
28¶ And he went with Joram the son of Ahab to the war against
Hazael king of Syria in Ramoth-gilead; and the Syrians wounded
Joram.
29And king Joram went back to be healed in Jezreel of the
wounds which the Syrians had given him at Ramah, when he
fought against Hazael king of Syria. And Ahaziah the son of Jehoram king of Judah went down to see Joram the son of Ahab in
Jezreel, because he was sick.

**9** AND ELISHA the prophet called one of the children of the
prophets, and said unto him, Gird up thy loins, and take this
box of oil in thine hand, and go to Ramoth-gilead:
2And when thou comest thither, look out there Jehu the son of
Jehoshaphat the son of Nimshi, and go in, and make him arise up
from among his brethren, and carry him to an inner chamber;
3Then take the box of oil, and pour *it* on his head, and say, Thus
saith the LORD, I have anointed thee king over Israel. Then open
the door, and flee, and tarry not.
4¶ So the young man, *even* the young man the prophet, went
to Ramoth-gilead.
5And when he came, behold, the captains of the host *were*
sitting; and he said, I have an errand to thee, O captain. And Jehu
said, Unto which of all us? And he said, To thee, O captain.
6And he arose, and went into the house; and he poured the oil
on his head, and said unto him, Thus saith the LORD God of Israel,
I have anointed thee king over the people of the LORD, *even* over
Israel.
7And thou shalt smite the house of Ahab thy master, that I may
avenge the blood of my servants the prophets, and the blood of
all the servants of the LORD, at the hand of Jezebel.

## Amplified

16In the fifth year of Joram son of Ahab king of Israel, Jehoshaphat being then king of Judah, Jehoram son of Jehoshaphat king
of Judah began to reign.
17He was thirty-two years old when he began to reign, and he
reigned eight years in Jerusalem.
18He walked in the way of the kings of Israel, as did the house
of Ahab, for [Athaliah] the daughter of Ahab was his wife. He did
evil in the sight of the Lord.
19Yet for David His servant's sake, the Lord would not destroy
Judah, for He promised to give him and his sons a lamp for ever.
20In his days Edom revolted from the rule of Judah, and set up
a king over themselves.
21So Jehoram [of Judah] went over to Zair with all his chariots.
He and his chariot commanders rose up by night and slew the
Edomites who had surrounded them, and [escaping], his army
fled home.
22So Edom revolted from the rule of Judah to this day. Then
Libnah revolted at the same time.
23The rest of the acts of J(eh)oram, and all that he did, are they
not written in the Book of the Chronicles of the Kings of Judah?
24J(eh)oram slept with his fathers, and was buried with [them]
in the city of David. Ahaziah his son reigned in his stead.
25In the twelfth year of Joram son of Ahab, king of Israel,
Ahaziah son of Jehoram king of Judah began to reign.
26Ahaziah was twenty-two years old when he began to reign,
and he reigned one year in Jerusalem. His mother's name was
Athaliah, the granddaughter of Omri king of Israel.
27He walked in the way of the house of Ahab, and did evil in
the sight of the Lord, as did the house of Ahab, for his father was
son-in-law of Ahab.
28Ahaziah went with Joram the son of Ahab to war against
Hazael king of Syria in Ramoth-gilead; and the Syrians wounded
Joram.
29King Joram returned to Jezreel to be healed of the wounds
which the Syrians had given him at Ramah, when he fought
against Hazael king of Syria. And Ahaziah son of Jehoram king of
Judah went down to see Joram son of Ahab in Jezreel, because he
was sick.

**9** AND ELISHA the prophet called one of the sons of the prophets, and said to him, Gird up your loins, take this flask of oil
in your hand, and go to Ramoth-gilead.
2When you arrive, look there for Jehu son of Jehoshaphat son
of Nimshi; and go in and have him arise from among his brethren
and lead him to an inner chamber.
3Then take the cruse of oil, and pour it on his head, and say,
Thus says the Lord, I have anointed you king over Israel. Then
open the door and flee; do not tarry.
4So the young man, the young prophet, went to Ramoth-gilead.
5And when he came, the captains of the army were sitting
outside; and he said, I have an errand to you, O captain. Jehu said,
To which of us all? And he said, To you, O captain.
6And Jehu arose, and they went into the house; and the prophet
poured the oil on Jehu's head, and said to him, Thus says the Lord
God of Israel, I have anointed you king over the people of the Lord,
even over Israel.
7You shall strike down the house of Ahab your master, that I
may avenge the blood of My servants the prophets and of all the
servants of the Lord [who have died] at the hand of Jezebel.

## New American Standard

*Another Jehoram Reigns in Judah*

**16**¶ Now in the fifth year of Joram the son of Ahab king of Israel, Jehoshaphat being then the king of Judah, Jehoram the son of Jehoshaphat king of Judah became king.

17He was thirty-two years old when he became king, and he reigned eight years in Jerusalem.

18And he walked in the way of the kings of Israel, just as the house of Ahab had done, for the daughter of Ahab became his wife; and he did evil in the sight of the LORD.

19However, the LORD was not willing to destroy Judah, for the sake of David His servant, since He had promised him to give a lamp to him through his sons always.

**20**¶ In his days Edom revolted from under the hand of Judah, and made a king over themselves.

21Then Joram crossed over to Zair, and all his chariots with him. And it came about that he arose by night and struck the Edomites who had surrounded him and the captains of the chariots; but *his* army fled to their tents.

22So Edom revolted against Judah to this day. Then Libnah revolted at the same time.

23And the rest of the acts of Joram and all that he did, are they not written in the Book of the Chronicles of the Kings of Judah?

*Ahaziah Succeeds Jehoram in Judah*

24So Joram slept with his fathers, and was buried with his fathers in the city of David; and Ahaziah his son became king in his place.

**25**¶ In the twelfth year of Joram the son of Ahab king of Israel, Ahaziah the son of Jehoram king of Judah began to reign.

26Ahaziah *was* twenty-two years old when he became king, and he reigned one year in Jerusalem. And his mother's name *was* Athaliah the granddaughter of Omri king of Israel.

27And he walked in the way of the house of Ahab, and did evil in the sight of the LORD, like the house of Ahab *had done,* because he was a son-in-law of the house of Ahab.

28Then he went with Joram the son of Ahab to war against Hazael king of Aram at Ramoth-gilead, and the Arameans wounded Joram.

29So King Joram returned to be healed in Jezreel of the wounds which the Arameans had inflicted on him at Ramah, when he fought against Hazael king of Aram. Then Ahaziah the son of Jehoram king of Judah went down to see Joram the son of Ahab in Jezreel because he was sick.

*Jehu Reigns over Israel*

**9** NOW ELISHA the prophet called one of the sons of the prophets, and said to him, "Gird up your loins, and take this flask of oil in your hand, and go to Ramoth-gilead.

2"When you arrive there, search out Jehu the son of Jehoshaphat the son of Nimshi, and go in and bid him arise from among his brothers, and bring him to an inner room.

3"Then take the flask of oil and pour it on his head and say, 'Thus says the LORD, "I have anointed you king over Israel."' Then open the door and flee and do not wait."

4So the young man, the servant of the prophet, went to Ramoth-gilead.

5When he came, behold, the captains of the army were sitting, and he said, "I have a word for you, O captain." And Jehu said, "For which *one* of us?" And he said, "For you, O captain."

6And he arose and went into the house, and he poured the oil on his head and said to him, "Thus says the LORD, the God of Israel, 'I have anointed you king over the people of the LORD, *even* over Israel.

7'And you shall strike the house of Ahab your master, that I may avenge the blood of My servants the prophets, and the blood of all the servants of the LORD, at the hand of Jezebel.

## New International

*Jehoram King of Judah*

16In the fifth year of Joram son of Ahab king of Israel, when
Jehoshaphat was king of Judah, Jehoram son of Jehoshaphat began
his reign as king of Judah. 17He was thirty-two years old when he
became king, and he reigned in Jerusalem eight years. 18He walked
in the ways of the kings of Israel, as the house of Ahab had done,
for he married a daughter of Ahab. He did evil in the eyes of the
LORD. 19Nevertheless, for the sake of his servant David, the LORD
was not willing to destroy Judah. He had promised to maintain a
lamp for David and his descendants forever.
20In the time of Jehoram, Edom rebelled against Judah and set
up its own king. 21So Jehoram[a] went to Zair with all his chariots.
The Edomites surrounded him and his chariot commanders, but
he rose up and broke through by night; his army, however, fled
back home. 22To this day Edom has been in rebellion against
Judah. Libnah revolted at the same time.
23As for the other events of Jehoram's reign, and all he did, are
they not written in the book of the annals of the kings of Judah?
24Jehoram rested with his fathers and was buried with them in the
City of David. And Ahaziah his son succeeded him as king.

*Ahaziah King of Judah*

25In the twelfth year of Joram son of Ahab king of Israel, Ahaziah son of Jehoram king of Judah began to reign. 26Ahaziah was
twenty-two years old when he became king, and he reigned in
Jerusalem one year. His mother's name was Athaliah, a granddaughter of Omri king of Israel. 27He walked in the ways of the
house of Ahab and did evil in the eyes of the LORD, as the house
of Ahab had done, for he was related by marriage to Ahab's family.
28Ahaziah went with Joram son of Ahab to war against Hazael
king of Aram at Ramoth Gilead. The Arameans wounded Joram;
29so King Joram returned to Jezreel to recover from the wounds the
Arameans had inflicted on him at Ramoth[b] in his battle with
Hazael king of Aram.
Then Ahaziah son of Jehoram king of Judah went down to
Jezreel to see Joram son of Ahab, because he had been wounded.

*Jehu Anointed King of Israel*

**9** THE PROPHET Elisha summoned a man from the company
of the prophets and said to him, "Tuck your cloak into your
belt, take this flask of oil with you and go to Ramoth Gilead. 2When
you get there, look for Jehu son of Jehoshaphat, the son of Nimshi.
Go to him, get him away from his companions and take him into
an inner room. 3Then take the flask and pour the oil on his head
and declare, 'This is what the LORD says: I anoint you king over
Israel.' Then open the door and run; don't delay!"
4So the young man, the prophet, went to Ramoth Gilead.
5When he arrived, he found the army officers sitting together. "I
have a message for you, commander," he said.
"For which of us?" asked Jehu.
"For you, commander," he replied.
6Jehu got up and went into the house. Then the prophet poured
the oil on Jehu's head and declared, "This is what the LORD, the
God of Israel, says: 'I anoint you king over the LORD's people
Israel. 7You are to destroy the house of Ahab your master, and I
will avenge the blood of my servants the prophets and the blood
of all the LORD's servants shed by Jezebel. 8The whole house of

NIV [a] 21 Hebrew *Joram,* a variant of *Jehoram;* also in verses 23 and 24
[b] 29 Hebrew *Ramah,* a variant of *Ramoth*

## King James

8For the whole house of Ahab shall perish: and I will cut off from Ahab him that pisseth against the wall, and him that is shut up and left in Israel:

9And I will make the house of Ahab like the house of Jeroboam the son of Nebat, and like the house of Baasha the son of Ahijah:

10And the dogs shall eat Jezebel in the portion of Jezreel, and *there shall be* none to bury *her*. And he opened the door, and fled.

11¶ Then Jehu came forth to the servants of his lord: and *one* said unto him, *Is* all well? wherefore came this mad *fellow* to thee? And he said unto them, Ye know the man, and his communication.

12And they said, *It is* false; tell us now. And he said, Thus and thus spake he to me, saying, Thus saith the LORD, I have anointed thee king over Israel.

13Then they hasted, and took every man his garment, and put *it* under him on the top of the stairs, and blew with trumpets, saying, Jehu is king.

14So Jehu the son of Jehoshaphat the son of Nimshi conspired against Joram. (Now Joram had kept Ramoth-gilead, he and all Israel, because of Hazael king of Syria.

15But king Joram was returned to be healed in Jezreel of the wounds which the Syrians had given him, when he fought with Hazael king of Syria.) And Jehu said, If it be your minds, *then* let none go forth *nor* escape out of the city to go to tell *it* in Jezreel.

16So Jehu rode in a chariot, and went to Jezreel; for Joram lay there. And Ahaziah king of Judah was come down to see Joram.

17And there stood a watchman on the tower in Jezreel, and he spied the company of Jehu as he came, and said, I see a company. And Joram said, Take an horseman, and send to meet them, and let him say, *Is it* peace?

18So there went one on horseback to meet him, and said, Thus saith the king, *Is it* peace? And Jehu said, What hast thou to do with peace? turn thee behind me. And the watchman told, saying, The messenger came to them, but he cometh not again.

19Then he sent out a second on horseback, which came to them, and said, Thus saith the king, *Is it* peace? And Jehu answered, What hast thou to do with peace? turn thee behind me.

20And the watchman told, saying, He came even unto them, and cometh not again: and the driving *is* like the driving of Jehu the son of Nimshi; for he driveth furiously.

21And Joram said, Make ready. And his chariot was made ready. And Joram king of Israel and Ahaziah king of Judah went out, each in his chariot, and they went out against Jehu, and met him in the portion of Naboth the Jezreelite.

22And it came to pass, when Joram saw Jehu, that he said, *Is it* peace, Jehu? And he answered, What peace, so long as the whoredoms of thy mother Jezebel and her witchcrafts *are so* many?

23And Joram turned his hands, and fled, and said to Ahaziah, *There is* treachery, O Ahaziah.

24And Jehu drew a bow with his full strength, and smote Jehoram between his arms, and the arrow went out at his heart, and he sunk down in his chariot.

25Then said *Jehu* to Bidkar his captain, Take up, *and* cast him in the portion of the field of Naboth the Jezreelite: for remember how that, when I and thou rode together after Ahab his father, the LORD laid this burden upon him;

26Surely I have seen yesterday the blood of Naboth, and the blood of his sons, saith the LORD; and I will requite thee in this plat, saith the LORD. Now therefore take *and* cast him into the plat *of ground*, according to the word of the LORD.

## Amplified

8For the whole house of Ahab shall perish, and I will cut off from Ahab every male, bond or free, in Israel.

9I will make the house of Ahab like the house of Jeroboam son of Nebat, and like the house of Baasha son of Ahijah.

10And the dogs shall eat Jezebel in the portion of Jezreel, and none shall bury her. And he opened the door, and fled. [Fulfilled, 9:33-37.]

11When Jehu came out to the servants of his master, one said to him, Is all well? Why did this mad fellow come to you? And he said to them, You know that class of man and what he would say.

12And they said, That is false; tell us now. And he said, Thus and thus he spoke to me, saying, Thus says the Lord, I have anointed you king over Israel.

13Then they hastily took every man his garment, and put it [for a cushion] under Jehu on the top of the [outside] stairs, and blew with trumpets, saying, Jehu is king!

14So Jehu son of Jehoshaphat son of Nimshi conspired against Joram [to dethrone and slay him]. Now Joram was holding Ramoth-gilead, he and all Israel, against Hazael king of Syria.

15But King Joram had returned to be healed in Jezreel of the wounds which the Syrians had given him, when he fought with Hazael king of Syria. And Jehu said, If it be your mind, let no one make his escape from the city [Ramoth-gilead] to go and tell it in Jezreel [the capital].

16So Jehu rode in a chariot, and went to Jezreel, for Joram lay there. And Ahaziah king of Judah had come down to see Joram.

17A watchman on the tower in Jezreel spied the company of Jehu as he came, and said, I see a company. And Joram said, Send a horseman to meet them, and have him ask, Do you come in peace?

18So one on horseback went to meet him, and said, Thus says the king, Is it peace? And Jehu said, What have you to do with peace? Rein in behind me. And the watchman reported, The messenger came to them, but he does not return.

19Then Joram sent out a second on horseback, who came to them and said, Thus says the king, Is it peace? Jehu replied, What have you to do with peace? Ride behind me.

20And the watchman reported, He came to them, but does not return; also the driving is like the driving of Jehu son of Nimshi, for he drives furiously.

21Joram said, Make ready. When his chariot was made ready, Joram king of Israel and Ahaziah king of Judah went out, each in his chariot. Thus they went out to meet Jehu, and met him in the field of Naboth the Jezreelite.

22When Joram saw Jehu, he said, Is it peace, Jehu? And he answered, How can peace exist, as long as the fornications of your mother Jezebel and her witchcrafts are so many?

23Then Joram reined about and fled, and he said to Ahaziah, Treachery, Ahaziah!

24But Jehu drew his bow with his full strength, and shot Joram between his shoulders, and the arrow went out through his heart, and he sank down in his chariot.

25Then said Jehu to Bidkar his captain, Take [Joram] up, and cast him in the plot of Naboth the Jezreelite's field; for remember how, when I and you rode together after Ahab his father, the Lord uttered this prophecy against him:

26As surely as I saw yesterday the blood of Naboth, and the blood of his sons, says the Lord, I will repay you on this plot of ground, says the Lord. Now therefore take and cast Joram into the plot of ground [of Naboth] as the word of the Lord said. [I Kings 21:15-29.]

## New American Standard

8'For the whole house of Ahab shall perish, and I will cut off
from Ahab every male person both bond and free in Israel.
9'And I will make the house of Ahab like the house of Jeroboam
the son of Nebat, and like the house of Baasha the son of Ahijah.
10'And the dogs shall eat Jezebel in the territory of Jezreel, and
none shall bury *her*.' " Then he opened the door and fled.
11¶ Now Jehu came out to the servants of his master, and one
said to him, "Is all well? Why did this mad fellow come to you?"
And he said to them, "You know *very well* the man and his talk."
12And they said, "It is a lie, tell us now." And he said, "Thus
and thus he said to me, 'Thus says the LORD, "I have anointed you
king over Israel." ' "
13Then they hurried and each man took his garment and placed
it under him on the bare steps, and blew the trumpet, saying,
"Jehu is king!"

*Jehoram (Joram) Is Assassinated*

14¶ So Jehu the son of Jehoshaphat the son of Nimshi conspired
against Joram. Now Joram with all Israel was defending Ramoth-
gilead against Hazael king of Aram,
15but King [a]Joram had returned to Jezreel to be healed of the
wounds which the Arameans had inflicted on him when he fought
with Hazael king of Aram. So Jehu said, "If this is your mind, *then*
let no one escape *or* leave the city to go tell *it* in Jezreel."
16Then Jehu rode in a chariot and went to Jezreel, for Joram was
lying there. And Ahaziah king of Judah had come down to see
Joram.
17¶ Now the watchman was standing on the tower in Jezreel
and he saw the company of Jehu as he came, and said, "I see a
company." And Joram said, "Take a horseman and send him to
meet them and let him say, 'Is it peace?' "
18So a horseman went to meet him and said, "Thus says the
king, 'Is it peace?' " And Jehu said, "What have you to do with
peace? Turn behind me." And the watchman reported, "The messenger came to them, but he did not return."
19Then he sent out a second horseman, who came to them and
said, "Thus says the king, 'Is it peace?' " And Jehu answered,
"What have you to do with peace? Turn behind me."
20And the watchman reported, "He came even to them, and he
did not return; and the driving is like the driving of Jehu the son
of Nimshi, for he drives furiously."
21¶ Then Joram said, "Get ready." And they made his chariot
ready. And Joram king of Israel and Ahaziah king of Judah went
out, each in his chariot, and they went out to meet Jehu and found
him in the property of Naboth the Jezreelite.
22And it came about, when Joram saw Jehu, that he said, "Is
it peace, Jehu?" And he answered, "What peace, so long as the
harlotries of your mother Jezebel and her witchcrafts are so
many?"
23So Joram reined about and fled and said to Ahaziah, " *There
is* treachery, O Ahaziah!"
24And Jehu drew his bow with his full strength and shot Joram
between his arms; and the arrow went through his heart, and he
sank in his chariot.
25Then *Jehu* said to Bidkar his officer, "Take *him* up and cast him
into the [b]property of the field of Naboth the Jezreelite, for I remember when you and I were riding together after Ahab his father, that
the LORD laid this oracle against him:
26'Surely I have seen yesterday the blood of Naboth and the
blood of his sons,' says the LORD, 'and I will repay you in this
[c]property,' says the LORD. Now then, take and cast him into the
property, according to the word of the LORD."

NAS [a] Heb., *Jehoram*, and so throughout this context [b] Lit., *portion*, and so throughout this context [c] Lit., *portion*, and so throughout this context

## New International

Ahab will perish. I will cut off from Ahab every last male in
Israel—slave or free. 9I will make the house of Ahab like the house
of Jeroboam son of Nebat and like the house of Baasha son of
Ahijah. 10As for Jezebel, dogs will devour her on the plot of ground
at Jezreel, and no one will bury her.' " Then he opened the door
and ran.
11When Jehu went out to his fellow officers, one of them asked
him, "Is everything all right? Why did this madman come to you?"
"You know the man and the sort of things he says," Jehu
replied.
12"That's not true!" they said. "Tell us."
Jehu said, "Here is what he told me: 'This is what the LORD says:
I anoint you king over Israel.' "
13They hurried and took their cloaks and spread them under
him on the bare steps. Then they blew the trumpet and shouted,
"Jehu is king!"

*Jehu Kills Joram and Ahaziah*

14So Jehu son of Jehoshaphat, the son of Nimshi, conspired
against Joram. (Now Joram and all Israel had been defending
Ramoth Gilead against Hazael king of Aram, 15but King Joram[d]
had returned to Jezreel to recover from the wounds the Arameans
had inflicted on him in the battle with Hazael king of Aram.) Jehu
said, "If this is the way you feel, don't let anyone slip out of the
city to go and tell the news in Jezreel." 16Then he got into his
chariot and rode to Jezreel, because Joram was resting there and
Ahaziah king of Judah had gone down to see him.
17When the lookout standing on the tower in Jezreel saw Jehu's
troops approaching, he called out, "I see some troops coming."
"Get a horseman," Joram ordered. "Send him to meet them and
ask, 'Do you come in peace?' "
18The horseman rode off to meet Jehu and said, "This is what
the king says: 'Do you come in peace?' "
"What do you have to do with peace?" Jehu replied. "Fall in
behind me."
The lookout reported, "The messenger has reached them, but
he isn't coming back."
19So the king sent out a second horseman. When he came to
them he said, "This is what the king says: 'Do you come in
peace?' "
Jehu replied, "What do you have to do with peace? Fall in
behind me."
20The lookout reported, "He has reached them, but he isn't
coming back either. The driving is like that of Jehu son of Nimshi—
he drives like a madman."
21"Hitch up my chariot," Joram ordered. And when it was
hitched up, Joram king of Israel and Ahaziah king of Judah rode
out, each in his own chariot, to meet Jehu. They met him at the
plot of ground that had belonged to Naboth the Jezreelite. 22When
Joram saw Jehu he asked, "Have you come in peace, Jehu?"
"How can there be peace," Jehu replied, "as long as all the
idolatry and witchcraft of your mother Jezebel abound?"
23Joram turned about and fled, calling out to Ahaziah, "Treachery, Ahaziah!"
24Then Jehu drew his bow and shot Joram between the shoulders. The arrow pierced his heart and he slumped down in his
chariot. 25Jehu said to Bidkar, his chariot officer, "Pick him up and
throw him on the field that belonged to Naboth the Jezreelite.
Remember how you and I were riding together in chariots behind
Ahab his father when the LORD made this prophecy about him:
26'Yesterday I saw the blood of Naboth and the blood of his sons,
declares the LORD, and I will surely make you pay for it on this plot
of ground, declares the LORD.'[e] Now then, pick him up and throw
him on that plot, in accordance with the word of the LORD."

NIV [d] 15 Hebrew *Jehoram*, a variant of *Joram*; also in verses 17 and 21-24
[e] 26 See 1 Kings 21:19.

## King James

27¶ But when Ahaziah the king of Judah saw *this,* he fled by the way of the garden house. And Jehu followed after him, and said, Smite him also in the chariot. *And they did so* at the going up to Gur, which *is* by Ibleam. And he fled to Megiddo, and died there.
28And his servants carried him in a chariot to Jerusalem, and buried him in his sepulchre with his fathers in the city of David.
29And in the eleventh year of Joram the son of Ahab began Ahaziah to reign over Judah.
30¶ And when Jehu was come to Jezreel, Jezebel heard *of it;* and she painted her face, and tired her head, and looked out at a window.
31And as Jehu entered in at the gate, she said, *Had* Zimri peace, who slew his master?
32And he lifted up his face to the window, and said, Who *is* on my side? who? And there looked out to him two *or* three eunuchs.
33And he said, Throw her down. So they threw her down: and *some* of her blood was sprinkled on the wall, and on the horses: and he trode her under foot.
34And when he was come in, he did eat and drink, and said, Go, see now this cursed *woman,* and bury her: for she *is* a king's daughter.
35And they went to bury her: but they found no more of her than the skull, and the feet, and the palms of *her* hands.
36Wherefore they came again, and told him. And he said, This *is* the word of the LORD, which he spake by his servant Elijah the Tishbite, saying, In the portion of Jezreel shall dogs eat the flesh of Jezebel:
37And the carcase of Jezebel shall be as dung upon the face of the field in the portion of Jezreel; *so* that they shall not say, This *is* Jezebel.

10 AND AHAB had seventy sons in Samaria. And Jehu wrote letters, and sent to Samaria, unto the rulers of Jezreel, to the elders, and to them that brought up Ahab's *children,* saying,
2Now as soon as this letter cometh to you, seeing your master's sons *are* with you, and *there are* with you chariots and horses, a fenced city also, and armour;
3Look even out the best and meetest of your master's sons, and set *him* on his father's throne, and fight for your master's house.
4But they were exceedingly afraid, and said, Behold, two kings stood not before him: how then shall we stand?
5And he that *was* over the house, and he that *was* over the city, the elders also, and the bringers up *of the children,* sent to Jehu, saying, *We are* thy servants, and will do all that thou shalt bid us; we will not make any king: do thou *that which is* good in thine eyes.
6Then he wrote a letter the second time to them, saying, If ye *be* mine, and *if* ye will hearken unto my voice, take ye the heads of the men your master's sons, and come to me to Jezreel by tomorrow this time. Now the king's sons, *being* seventy persons, *were* with the great men of the city, which brought them up.
7And it came to pass, when the letter came to them, that they took the king's sons, and slew seventy persons, and put their heads in baskets, and sent him *them* to Jezreel.
8¶ And there came a messenger, and told him, saying, They have brought the heads of the king's sons. And he said, Lay ye them in two heaps at the entering in of the gate until the morning.
9And it came to pass in the morning, that he went out, and stood, and said to all the people, Ye *be* righteous: behold, I conspired against my master, and slew him: but who slew all these?

## Amplified

27When Ahaziah king of Judah saw this, he fled by the way of the garden house. Jehu followed him, and said, Smite him also in the chariot. And they did so at the ascent to Gur, which is by Ibleam. And [Ahaziah] fled to Megiddo, and died there.
28His servants took him in a chariot to Jerusalem, and buried him in his sepulcher with his fathers in the city of David;
29In the eleventh year of Joram son of Ahab Ahaziah's reign over Judah began.
30Now when Jehu came to Jezreel, Jezebel heard of it; and she painted her eyes, and beautified her head, and looked out at [an upper] window.
31And as Jehu entered in at the gate, she said, [Have you come in] peace, you Zimri, who slew his master? [I Kings 16:9, 10.]
32Jehu lifted up his face to the window, and said, Who is on my side? Who? And two or three eunuchs looked out at him.
33And he said, Throw her down! So they threw her down, and some of her blood splattered on the wall, and on the horses; and he drove over her.
34When he came in, he ate and drank, and said, See now to this cursed woman, and bury her, for she is a king's daughter.
35They went to bury her, but they found nothing left of her except the skull, feet, and palms of her hands.
36They came again, and told Jehu. He said, This is the word of the Lord, which He spoke by His servant Elijah the Tishbite, In the portion of Jezreel shall dogs eat the flesh of Jezebel. [I Kings 21:23.]
37The corpse of Jezebel shall be as dung upon the face of the field in the portion of Jezreel, so that they shall not say, This is Jezebel.

10 AHAB HAD seventy [grandsons] in Samaria. So Jehu wrote letters, and sent from Jezreel to the rulers of Samaria, to the elders, and to those who brought up Ahab's [grandsons], saying,
2Now as soon as this letter comes to you, seeing your master [Joram's] sons are with you, and also chariots and horses, a fortified city and weapons,
3Select the best and most fit of your master's sons, and set him on his father's throne, and fight for your master's house.
4But they were exceedingly afraid, and reasoned, The two kings could not stand before [Jehu]; how then can we stand?
5And he who was over the household, and he who was over the city, the elders also, and the guardians *and* tutors, sent to Jehu, saying, We are your servants and will do all that you bid us; [but] we will not make any man king; do what is good in your eyes.
6Then [Jehu] wrote a second letter to them, saying, If you are with me, and will obey me, take the heads of your master [Joram's] sons and come to me to Jezreel by tomorrow this time. Now the [dead] king's sons, seventy persons, were with the great men of the city, who were bringing them up.
7When the letter came to these men, they took the king's sons and slew them, seventy persons, and put their heads in baskets and sent them to Jehu at Jezreel.
8When a messenger came and told him, They have brought the heads of the king's sons, he said, Lay them in two heaps at the entrance of the city gate until morning.
9Next morning he went out, and stood, and said to all the people, You are just *and* innocent. Behold, I conspired against my master, and slew him; but who smote all these?

## New American Standard

*Jehu Assassinates Ahaziah*

27¶ When Ahaziah the king of Judah saw *this,* he fled by the way
of the garden house. And Jehu pursued him and said, "Shoot him
too, in the chariot." *So they shot him* at the ascent of Gur, which
is at Ibleam. But he fled to Megiddo and died there.
28Then his servants carried him in a chariot to Jerusalem, and
buried him in his grave with his fathers in the city of David.
29¶ Now in the eleventh year of Joram, the son of Ahab, Ahaziah became king over Judah.
30¶ When Jehu came to Jezreel, Jezebel heard *of it,* and she
painted her eyes and adorned her head, and looked out the window.
31And as Jehu entered the gate, she said, "Is it well, Zimri, your
master's murderer?"
32Then he lifted up his face to the window and said, "Who is
on my side? Who?" And two or three officials looked down at him.

*Jezebel Is Slain*

33And he said, "Throw her down." So they threw her down,
and some of her blood was sprinkled on the wall and on the
horses, and he trampled her under foot.
34When he came in, he ate and drank; and he said, "See now
to this cursed woman and bury her, for she is a king's daughter."
35And they went to bury her, but they found no more of her
than the skull and the feet and the palms of her hands.
36Therefore they returned and told him. And he said, "This is
the word of the LORD, which He spoke by His servant Elijah the
Tishbite, saying, 'In the property of Jezreel the dogs shall eat the
flesh of Jezebel;
37and the corpse of Jezebel shall be as dung on the face of the
field in the property of Jezreel, so they cannot say, "This is Jezebel."'"

*Judgment upon Ahab's House*

**10** NOW AHAB had seventy sons in Samaria. And Jehu
wrote letters and sent *them* to Samaria, to the rulers of
Jezreel, the elders, and to the guardians of *the children of* Ahab,
saying,
2"And now, when this letter comes to you, since your master's
sons are with you, as well as the chariots and horses and a fortified
city and the weapons,
3select the best and [a]fittest of your master's sons, and set *him*
on his father's throne, and fight for your master's house."
4But they feared greatly and said, "Behold, the two kings did
not stand before him; how then can we stand?"
5And the one who *was* over the household, and he who *was*
over the city, the elders, and the guardians of *the children,* sent *word*
to Jehu, saying, "We are your servants, all that you say to us we
will do, we will not make any man king; do what is good in your
sight."
6Then he wrote a letter to them a second time saying, "If you
are on my side, and you will listen to my voice, take the heads of
the men, your master's sons, and come to me at Jezreel tomorrow
about this time." Now the king's sons, seventy persons, *were* with
the great men of the city, *who* were rearing them.
7And it came about when the letter came to them, that they
took the king's sons, and slaughtered *them,* seventy persons, and
put their heads in baskets, and sent *them* to him at Jezreel.
8When the messenger came and told him, saying, "They have
brought the heads of the king's sons," he said, "Put them in two
heaps at the entrance of the gate until morning."
9Now it came about in the morning, that he went out and
stood, and said to all the people, "You are innocent; behold, I
conspired against my master and killed him, but who killed all
these?

NAS [a] Lit., *most upright*

## New International

27When Ahaziah king of Judah saw what had happened, he fled
up the road to Beth Haggan.[b] Jehu chased him, shouting, "Kill
him too!" They wounded him in his chariot on the way up to Gur
near Ibleam, but he escaped to Megiddo and died there. 28His
servants took him by chariot to Jerusalem and buried him with his
fathers in his tomb in the City of David. 29(In the eleventh year of
Joram son of Ahab, Ahaziah had become king of Judah.)

*Jezebel Killed*

30Then Jehu went to Jezreel. When Jezebel heard about it, she
painted her eyes, arranged her hair and looked out of a window.
31As Jehu entered the gate, she asked, "Have you come in peace,
Zimri, you murderer of your master?"[c]
32He looked up at the window and called out, "Who is on my
side? Who?" Two or three eunuchs looked down at him. 33"Throw
her down!" Jehu said. So they threw her down, and some of her
blood spattered the wall and the horses as they trampled her
underfoot.
34Jehu went in and ate and drank. "Take care of that cursed
woman," he said, "and bury her, for she was a king's daughter."
35But when they went out to bury her, they found nothing except
her skull, her feet and her hands. 36They went back and told Jehu,
who said, "This is the word of the LORD that he spoke through his
servant Elijah the Tishbite: On the plot of ground at Jezreel dogs
will devour Jezebel's flesh.[d] 37Jezebel's body will be like refuse on
the ground in the plot at Jezreel, so that no one will be able to say,
'This is Jezebel.'"

*Ahab's Family Killed*

**10** NOW THERE were in Samaria seventy sons of the house
of Ahab. So Jehu wrote letters and sent them to Samaria:
to the officials of Jezreel,[e] to the elders and to the guardians of
Ahab's children. He said, 2"As soon as this letter reaches you,
since your master's sons are with you and you have chariots and
horses, a fortified city and weapons, 3choose the best and most
worthy of your master's sons and set him on his father's throne.
Then fight for your master's house."
4But they were terrified and said, "If two kings could not resist
him, how can we?"
5So the palace administrator, the city governor, the elders and
the guardians sent this message to Jehu: "We are your servants
and we will do anything you say. We will not appoint anyone as
king; you do whatever you think best."
6Then Jehu wrote them a second letter, saying, "If you are on
my side and will obey me, take the heads of your master's sons
and come to me in Jezreel by this time tomorrow."
Now the royal princes, seventy of them, were with the leading
men of the city, who were rearing them. 7When the letter arrived,
these men took the princes and slaughtered all seventy of them.
They put their heads in baskets and sent them to Jehu in Jezreel.
8When the messenger arrived, he told Jehu, "They have brought
the heads of the princes."
Then Jehu ordered, "Put them in two piles at the entrance of
the city gate until morning."
9The next morning Jehu went out. He stood before all the
people and said, "You are innocent. It was I who conspired against
my master and killed him, but who killed all these? 10Know then,

NIV [b] 27 Or *fled by way of the garden house* [c] 31 Or *"Did Zimri have peace, who murdered his master?"* [d] 36 See 1 Kings 21:23. [e] 1 Hebrew; some Septuagint manuscripts and Vulgate *of the city*

## King James

10 Know now that there shall fall unto the earth nothing of the word of the LORD, which the LORD spake concerning the house of Ahab: for the LORD hath done *that* which he spake by his servant Elijah.

11 So Jehu slew all that remained of the house of Ahab in Jezreel, and all his great men, and his kinsfolks, and his priests, until he left him none remaining.

12 ¶ And he arose and departed, and came to Samaria. *And* as he *was* at the shearing house in the way,

13 Jehu met with the brethren of Ahaziah king of Judah, and said, Who *are* ye? And they answered, We *are* the brethren of Ahaziah; and we go down to salute the children of the king and the children of the queen.

14 And he said, Take them alive. And they took them alive, and slew them at the pit of the shearing house, *even* two and forty men: neither left he any of them.

15 ¶ And when he was departed thence, He lighted on Jehonadab the son of Rechab *coming* to meet him: and he saluted him, and said to him, Is thine heart right, as my heart *is* with thy heart? And Jehonadab answered, It is. If it be, give *me* thine hand. And he gave *him* his hand; and he took him up to him into the chariot.

16 And he said, Come with me, and see my zeal for the LORD. So they made him ride in his chariot.

17 And when he came to Samaria, he slew all that remained unto Ahab in Samaria, till he had destroyed him, according to the saying of the LORD, which he spake to Elijah.

18 ¶ And Jehu gathered all the people together, and said unto them, Ahab served Baal a little; *but* Jehu shall serve him much.

19 Now therefore call unto me all the prophets of Baal, all his servants, and all his priests; let none be wanting: for I have a great sacrifice *to do* to Baal; whosoever shall be wanting, he shall not live. But Jehu did *it* in subtlety, to the intent that he might destroy the worshippers of Baal.

20 And Jehu said, Proclaim a solemn assembly for Baal. And they proclaimed *it*.

21 And Jehu sent through all Israel: and all the worshippers of Baal came, so that there was not a man left that came not. And they came into the house of Baal; and the house of Baal was full from one end to another.

22 And he said unto him that *was* over the vestry, Bring forth vestments for all the worshippers of Baal. And he brought them forth vestments.

23 And Jehu went, and Jehonadab the son of Rechab, into the house of Baal, and said unto the worshippers of Baal, Search, and look that there be here with you none of the servants of the LORD, but the worshippers of Baal only.

24 And when they went in to offer sacrifices and burnt offerings, Jehu appointed fourscore men without, and said, *If* any of the men whom I have brought into your hands escape, *he that letteth him go*, his life *shall be* for the life of him.

25 And it came to pass, as soon as he had made an end of offering the burnt offering, that Jehu said to the guard and to the captains, Go in, *and* slay them; let none come forth. And they smote them with the edge of the sword; and the guard and the captains cast *them* out, and went to the city of the house of Baal.

26 And they brought forth the images out of the house of Baal, and burned them.

27 And they brake down the image of Baal, and brake down the house of Baal, and made it a draught house unto this day.

28 Thus Jehu destroyed Baal out of Israel.

29 ¶ Howbeit *from* the sins of Jeroboam the son of Nebat, who made Israel to sin, Jehu departed not from after them, *to wit*, the golden calves that *were* in Beth-el, and that *were* in Dan.

## Amplified

10 Know now that nothing which the Lord spoke concerning the house of Ahab shall be unfulfilled *or* ineffective; for the Lord has done what He said by His servant Elijah.

11 So Jehu slew all that remained of the house of Ahab in Jezreel, and all his great men, his familiar friends, and his priests, until he left him none remaining.

12 And he arose and went to Samaria. And as he was at the shearing house of the shepherds on the way,

13 Jehu met the kinsmen of Ahaziah king of Judah, and said, Who are you? They answered, We are the kinsmen of Ahaziah, and we came down to visit the royal princes and the sons of [Jezebel] the queen mother.

14 He said, Take them alive. And they did so, and slew them at the cistern of the shearing house, forty-two men; he left none of them.

15 When Jehu left there, he met Jehonadab son of Rechab coming to meet him. He saluted him, and said to him, Is your heart right, as my heart is with yours? Jehonadab answered, It is. [Jehu said], If it is, give me your hand. He gave him his hand and Jehu took him up into the chariot.

16 And he said, Come with me, and see my zeal for the Lord. So they made [the Rechabite] ride in Jehu's chariot.

17 When Jehu came to Samaria, he slew all who remained to Ahab in Samaria, till he had destroyed them all, according to what the Lord said to Elijah.

18 Jehu assembled all the people and said to them, Ahab served Baal a little; but Jehu will serve him much.

19 So call to me all the prophets of Baal, all his worshipers and all his priests; let none be missing, for I have a great sacrifice to make to Baal; whoever is missing shall not live. But Jehu did it with trickery intending to destroy the Baal worshipers.

20 Jehu said, Sanctify a solemn assembly for Baal. And they proclaimed it.

21 Jehu sent through all Israel; and all the worshipers of Baal came; not a man failed to come. They went to the house *or* temple of Baal, filling it from one end to the other.

22 And he said to the man over the vestry, Bring vestments for all the worshipers of Baal. And he brought them vestments.

23 Then Jehu with Jehonadab son of Rechab went into the house of Baal, and said to the worshipers of Baal, Search, and see that there are here with you none of the servants of the Lord, but Baal worshipers only.

24 And when they two went in to offer sacrifices and burnt offerings, Jehu appointed eighty men outside, and said, If any of the men whom I have brought into your hands escape, he who lets him go shall forfeit his own life for his life.

25 As soon as he had finished offering the burnt offering, Jehu said to the guard and to the officers, Go in and slay them; let none escape. And they smote them with the sword; and the guard *or* runners [before the king] and the officers threw their bodies out and went into the inner dwelling of the house of Baal.

26 They brought out the pillars *or* obelisks of the house of Baal, and burned them.

27 They broke down the pillars of Baal, and the house of Baal and made it [for ever unclean] a privy to this day.

28 Thus Jehu rooted Baal out of Israel.

29 But Jehu did not give up the sins of Jeroboam son of Nebat, by which he made Israel to sin, that is, the golden calves at Bethel and Dan.

## New American Standard

10"Know then that there shall fall to the earth nothing of the
word of the LORD, which the LORD spoke concerning the house of
Ahab, for the LORD has done what He spoke through His servant
Elijah."
11So Jehu killed all who remained of the house of Ahab in
Jezreel, and all his great men and his acquaintances and his priests,
until he left him without a survivor.
12¶ Then he arose and departed, and went to Samaria. On the
way while he was at [a]Beth-eked of the shepherds,
13Jehu met the relatives of Ahaziah king of Judah and said,
"Who are you?" And they answered, "We are the relatives of
Ahaziah; and we have come down to greet the sons of the king and
the sons of the queen mother."
14And he said, "Take them alive." So they took them alive, and
killed them at the pit of Beth-eked, forty-two men; and he left none
of them.
15¶ Now when he had departed from there, he met Jehonadab
the son of Rechab *coming* to meet him; and he greeted him and said
to him, "Is your heart right, as my heart is with your heart?" And
Jehonadab answered, "It is." *Jehu said,* "If it is, give *me* your
hand." And he gave him his hand, and he took him up to him into
the chariot.
16And he said, "Come with me and see my zeal for the LORD."
So he made him ride in his chariot.
17And when he came to Samaria, he killed all who remained to
Ahab in Samaria, until he had destroyed him, according to the
word of the LORD, which He spoke to Elijah.

*Jehu Destroys Baal Worshipers*

18¶ Then Jehu gathered all the people and said to them, "Ahab
served Baal a little; Jehu will serve him much.
19"And now, summon all the prophets of Baal, all his worshipers and all his priests; let no one be missing, for I have a great
sacrifice for Baal; whoever is missing shall not live." But Jehu did
it in cunning, in order that he might destroy the worshipers of
Baal.
20And Jehu said, "Sanctify a solemn assembly for Baal." And
they proclaimed *it*.
21Then Jehu sent throughout Israel and all the worshipers of
Baal came, so that there was not a man left who did not come. And
when they went into the house of Baal, the house of Baal was filled
from one end to the other.
22And he said to the one who *was* in charge of the wardrobe,
"Bring out garments for all the worshipers of Baal." So he brought
out garments for them.
23And Jehu went into the house of Baal with Jehonadab the son
of Rechab; and he said to the worshipers of Baal, "Search and see
that there may be here with you none of the servants of the LORD,
but only the worshipers of Baal."
24Then they went in to offer sacrifices and burnt offerings. Now
Jehu had stationed for himself eighty men outside, and he had
said, "The one who permits any of the men whom I bring into your
hands to escape, shall give up his life in exchange."
25¶ Then it came about, as soon as he had finished offering the
burnt offering, that Jehu said to the guard and to the royal officers,
"Go in, kill them; let none come out." And they killed them with
the edge of the sword; and the guard and the royal officers threw
*them* out, and went to the inner room of the house of Baal.
26And they brought out the *sacred* pillars of the house of Baal,
and burned them.
27They also broke down the *sacred* pillar of Baal and broke down
the house of Baal, and made it a latrine to this day.
28Thus Jehu eradicated Baal out of Israel.
29¶ However, *as for* the sins of Jeroboam the son of Nebat, which
he made Israel sin, from these Jehu did not depart, *even* the golden
calves that *were* at Bethel and that *were* at Dan.

NAS [a] I.e., house of binding

## New International

that not a word the LORD has spoken against the house of Ahab
will fail. The LORD has done what he promised through his servant
Elijah." 11So Jehu killed everyone in Jezreel who remained of the
house of Ahab, as well as all his chief men, his close friends and
his priests, leaving him no survivor.
12Jehu then set out and went toward Samaria. At Beth Eked of
the Shepherds, 13he met some relatives of Ahaziah king of Judah
and asked, "Who are you?"
They said, "We are relatives of Ahaziah, and we have come
down to greet the families of the king and of the queen mother."
14"Take them alive!" he ordered. So they took them alive and
slaughtered them by the well of Beth Eked—forty-two men. He left
no survivor.
15After he left there, he came upon Jehonadab son of Recab,
who was on his way to meet him. Jehu greeted him and said, "Are
you in accord with me, as I am with you?"
"I am," Jehonadab answered.
"If so," said Jehu, "give me your hand." So he did, and Jehu
helped him up into the chariot. 16Jehu said, "Come with me and
see my zeal for the LORD." Then he had him ride along in his
chariot.
17When Jehu came to Samaria, he killed all who were left there
of Ahab's family; he destroyed them, according to the word of the
LORD spoken to Elijah.

*Ministers of Baal Killed*

18Then Jehu brought all the people together and said to them,
"Ahab served Baal a little; Jehu will serve him much. 19Now summon all the prophets of Baal, all his ministers and all his priests.
See that no one is missing, because I am going to hold a great
sacrifice for Baal. Anyone who fails to come will no longer live."
But Jehu was acting deceptively in order to destroy the ministers
of Baal.
20Jehu said, "Call an assembly in honor of Baal." So they proclaimed it. 21Then he sent word throughout Israel, and all the
ministers of Baal came; not one stayed away. They crowded into
the temple of Baal until it was full from one end to the other. 22And
Jehu said to the keeper of the wardrobe, "Bring robes for all the
ministers of Baal." So he brought out robes for them.
23Then Jehu and Jehonadab son of Recab went into the temple
of Baal. Jehu said to the ministers of Baal, "Look around and see
that no servants of the LORD are here with you—only ministers of
Baal." 24So they went in to make sacrifices and burnt offerings.
Now Jehu had posted eighty men outside with this warning: "If
one of you lets any of the men I am placing in your hands escape,
it will be your life for his life."
25As soon as Jehu had finished making the burnt offering, he
ordered the guards and officers: "Go in and kill them; let no one
escape." So they cut them down with the sword. The guards and
officers threw the bodies out and then entered the inner shrine of
the temple of Baal. 26They brought the sacred stone out of the
temple of Baal and burned it. 27They demolished the sacred stone
of Baal and tore down the temple of Baal, and people have used
it for a latrine to this day.
28So Jehu destroyed Baal worship in Israel. 29However, he did
not turn away from the sins of Jeroboam son of Nebat, which he
had caused Israel to commit—the worship of the golden calves at
Bethel and Dan.

## King James

30And the LORD said unto Jehu, Because thou hast done well in executing *that which is* right in mine eyes, *and* hast done unto the house of Ahab according to all that *was* in mine heart, thy children of the fourth *generation* shall sit on the throne of Israel.

31But Jehu took no heed to walk in the law of the LORD God of Israel with all his heart: for he departed not from the sins of Jeroboam, which made Israel to sin.

32¶ In those days the LORD began to cut Israel short: and Hazael smote them in all the coasts of Israel;

33From Jordan eastward, all the land of Gilead, the Gadites, and the Reubenites, and the Manassites, from Aroer, which *is* by the river Arnon, even Gilead and Bashan.

34Now the rest of the acts of Jehu, and all that he did, and all his might, *are* they not written in the book of the chronicles of the kings of Israel?

35And Jehu slept with his fathers: and they buried him in Samaria. And Jehoahaz his son reigned in his stead.

36And the time that Jehu reigned over Israel in Samaria *was* twenty and eight years.

**11** AND WHEN Athaliah the mother of Ahaziah saw that her son was dead, she arose and destroyed all the seed royal.

2But Jehosheba, the daughter of king Joram, sister of Ahaziah, took Joash the son of Ahaziah, and stole him from among the king's sons *which were* slain; and they hid him, *even* him and his nurse, in the bedchamber from Athaliah, so that he was not slain.

3And he was with her hid in the house of the LORD six years. And Athaliah did reign over the land.

4¶ And the seventh year Jehoiada sent and fetched the rulers over hundreds, with the captains and the guard, and brought them to him into the house of the LORD, and made a covenant with them, and took an oath of them in the house of the LORD, and showed them the king's son.

5And he commanded them, saying, This *is* the thing that ye shall do; A third part of you that enter in on the sabbath shall even be keepers of the watch of the king's house;

6And a third part *shall be* at the gate of Sur; and a third part at the gate behind the guard: so shall ye keep the watch of the house, that it be not broken down.

7And two parts of all you that go forth on the sabbath, even they shall keep the watch of the house of the LORD about the king.

8And ye shall compass the king round about, every man with his weapons in his hand: and he that cometh within the ranges, let him be slain: and be ye with the king as he goeth out and as he cometh in.

9And the captains over the hundreds did according to all *things* that Jehoiada the priest commanded: and they took every man his men that were to come in on the sabbath, with them that should go out on the sabbath, and came to Jehoiada the priest.

10And to the captains over hundreds did the priest give king David's spears and shields, that *were* in the temple of the LORD.

11And the guard stood, every man with his weapons in his hand, round about the king, from the right corner of the temple to the left corner of the temple, *along* by the altar and the temple.

12And he brought forth the king's son, and put the crown upon him, and *gave him* the testimony; and they made him king, and anointed him; and they clapped their hands, and said, God save the king.

13¶ And when Athaliah heard the noise of the guard *and* of the people, she came to the people into the temple of the LORD.

## Amplified

30And the Lord said to Jehu, Because you have executed well what is right in My eyes and have done to the house of Ahab as I willed, your sons of the fourth generation shall sit on Israel's throne. [Fulfilled, 15:12.]

31But Jehu paid no attention to walking in the law of the Lord God of Israel with all his heart. He did not quit the sins with which Jeroboam made Israel to sin.

32 *So* in those days the Lord began to cut off parts of Israel. Hazael [of Syria] defeated them in all the [across Jordan] territory of Israel:

33From Jordan east, all the land of Gilead, the Gadites, Reubenites, and Manassites, from Aroer, which is by the valley of the Arnon, even Gilead and Bashan.

34The rest of the acts of Jehu, and all that he did, and all his might, are they not written in the Book of the Chronicles of the Kings of Israel?

35Jehu slept with his fathers. They buried him in Samaria. Jehoahaz his son reigned in his stead.

36The time that Jehu reigned over Israel in Samaria was twenty-eight years.

**11** WHEN ATHALIAH mother of [King] Ahaziah [of Judah] saw that her son was dead, she arose and destroyed all the royal descendants.

2But Jehosheba daughter of king Jehoram, [half] sister of Ahaziah, stole Joash son of Ahaziah from among the king's sons who were to be slain, even him and his nurse, and hid them from Athaliah in an inner storeroom for beds, so he was not slain.

3Joash was with his nurse hid in the house of the Lord six years. And Athaliah reigned over the land.

4In the seventh year Jehoiada [the priest, Jehosheba's husband] sent for the captains over hundreds of the Carites and of the guard (or runners, and brought them to him to the house of the Lord, and made a covenant with them, and took an oath of them in the house of the Lord, and showed them the king's [hidden] son.

5And he commanded them, saying, This is the thing you shall do: a third of you who come in on the sabbath shall keep watch of the king's house,

6A third shall be at the gate Sur, and a third at the gate behind the guard. So you shall keep watch of the palace [from three places] and be a barrier.

7And two divisions of all you who go on duty on the sabbath shall keep the watch of the house of the Lord to [protect] the king.

8You shall surround the *little* king, every man with his weapons in his hand. And let any one who breaks through the ranks be put to death. You be with the king when he goes out and when he comes in.

9The captains over the hundreds did all Jehoiada the priest commanded; and they took every man his men who were to come on duty on the sabbath, with those who should go off duty on the sabbath, and came to Jehoiada the priest.

10To the captains over hundreds the priest gave the spears and shields that had been King David's, which were in the house of the Lord.

11And the guard stood, every man with his weapons in his hand, from the right corner to the left corner of the temple area along by the altar [in the court] and the temple proper.

12And Jehoiada brought out the king's son, and put the crown on him, and gave him the testimony [the Mosaic law]; and they proclaimed him king, and anointed him; and they clapped their hands, and said, Long live the king!

13When Athaliah heard the noise of the guard and the people, she went into the house of the Lord to the people.

## New American Standard

30And the LORD said to Jehu, "Because you have done well in executing what is right in My eyes, *and* have done to the house of Ahab according to all that *was* in My heart, your sons of the fourth generation shall sit on the throne of Israel."

31But Jehu was not careful to walk in the law of the LORD, the God of Israel, with all his heart; he did not depart from the sins of Jeroboam, which he made Israel sin.

32¶ In those days the LORD began to cut off *portions* from Israel; and Hazael defeated them throughout the territory of Israel:

33from the Jordan eastward, all the land of Gilead, the Gadites and the Reubenites and the Manassites, from Aroer, which is by the valley of the Arnon, even Gilead and Bashan.

*Jehoahaz Succeeds Jehu*

34Now the rest of the acts of Jehu and all that he did and all his might, are they not written in the Book of the Chronicles of the Kings of Israel?

35And Jehu slept with his fathers, and they buried him in Samaria. And Jehoahaz his son became king in his place.

36Now the time which Jehu reigned over Israel in Samaria *was* twenty-eight years.

*Athaliah Queen of Judah*

**11** WHEN ATHALIAH the mother of Ahaziah saw that her son was dead, she rose and destroyed all the royal offspring.

2But Jehosheba, the daughter of King Joram, sister of Ahaziah, took Joash the son of Ahaziah and stole him from among the king's sons who were being put to death, and placed him and his nurse in the bedroom. So they hid him from Athaliah, and he was not put to death.

3So he was hidden with her in the house of the LORD six years, while Athaliah was reigning over the land.

4¶ Now in the seventh year Jehoiada sent and brought the captains of hundreds of the Carites and of the [a]guard, and brought them to him in the house of the LORD. Then he made a covenant with them and put them under oath in the house of the LORD, and showed them the king's son.

5And he commanded them, saying, "This is the thing that you shall do: one third of you, who come in on the sabbath and keep watch over the king's house

6(one third also *shall be* at the gate Sur, and one third at the gate behind the [b]guards), shall keep watch over the house for defense.

7"And two parts of you, *even* all who go out on the sabbath, shall also keep watch over the house of the LORD for the king.

8"Then you shall surround the king, each with his weapons in his hand; and whoever comes within the ranks shall be put to death. And be with the king when he goes out and when he comes in."

9¶ So the captains of hundreds did according to all that Jehoiada the priest commanded. And each one of them took his men who were to come in on the sabbath, with those who were to go out on the sabbath, and came to Jehoiada the priest.

10And the priest gave to the captains of hundreds the spears and shields that had been King David's, which *were* in the house of the LORD.

11And the guards stood each with his weapons in his hand, from the right side of the house to the left side of the house, by the altar and by the house, around the king.

12Then he brought the king's son out and put the crown on him, and *gave him* the testimony; and they made him king and anointed him, and they clapped their hands and said, "*Long* live the king!"

13¶ When Athaliah heard the noise of the guard *and of* the people, she came to the people in the house of the LORD.

NAS [a] Lit., *runners* [b] Lit., *runners*

## New International

30The LORD said to Jehu, "Because you have done well in accomplishing what is right in my eyes and have done to the house
of Ahab all I had in mind to do, your descendants will sit on the
throne of Israel to the fourth generation." 31Yet Jehu was not
careful to keep the law of the LORD, the God of Israel, with all his
heart. He did not turn away from the sins of Jeroboam, which he
had caused Israel to commit.
32In those days the LORD began to reduce the size of Israel.
Hazael overpowered the Israelites throughout their territory 33east
of the Jordan in all the land of Gilead (the region of Gad, Reuben
and Manasseh), from Aroer by the Arnon Gorge through Gilead
to Bashan.
34As for the other events of Jehu's reign, all he did, and all his
achievements, are they not written in the book of the annals of the
kings of Israel?
35Jehu rested with his fathers and was buried in Samaria. And
Jehoahaz his son succeeded him as king. 36The time that Jehu
reigned over Israel in Samaria was twenty-eight years.

*Athaliah and Joash*

**11** WHEN ATHALIAH the mother of Ahaziah saw that her
son was dead, she proceeded to destroy the whole royal
family. 2But Jehosheba, the daughter of King Jehoram[c] and sister
of Ahaziah, took Joash son of Ahaziah and stole him away from
among the royal princes, who were about to be murdered. She put
him and his nurse in a bedroom to hide him from Athaliah; so he
was not killed. 3He remained hidden with his nurse at the temple
of the LORD for six years while Athaliah ruled the land.
4In the seventh year Jehoiada sent for the commanders of units
of a hundred, the Carites and the guards and had them brought
to him at the temple of the LORD. He made a covenant with them
and put them under oath at the temple of the LORD. Then he
showed them the king's son. 5He commanded them, saying, "This
is what you are to do: You who are in the three companies that are
going on duty on the Sabbath—a third of you guarding the royal
palace, 6a third at the Sur Gate, and a third at the gate behind the
guard, who take turns guarding the temple— 7and you who are
in the other two companies that normally go off Sabbath duty are
all to guard the temple for the king. 8Station yourselves around the
king, each man with his weapon in his hand. Anyone who approaches your ranks[d] must be put to death. Stay close to the king
wherever he goes."
9The commanders of units of a hundred did just as Jehoiada the
priest ordered. Each one took his men—those who were going on
duty on the Sabbath and those who were going off duty—and
came to Jehoiada the priest. 10Then he gave the commanders the
spears and shields that had belonged to King David and that were
in the temple of the LORD. 11The guards, each with his weapon in
his hand, stationed themselves around the king—near the altar
and the temple, from the south side to the north side of the temple.
12Jehoiada brought out the king's son and put the crown on
him; he presented him with a copy of the covenant and proclaimed
him king. They anointed him, and the people clapped their hands
and shouted, "Long live the king!"
13When Athaliah heard the noise made by the guards and the
people, she went to the people at the temple of the LORD. 14She

NIV [c] 2 Hebrew *Joram*, a variant of *Jehoram* [d] 8 Or *approaches the precincts*

## King James

14 And when she looked, behold, the king stood by a pillar, as the manner *was*, and the princes and the trumpeters by the king, and all the people of the land rejoiced, and blew with trumpets: and Athaliah rent her clothes, and cried, Treason, Treason.

15 But Jehoiada the priest commanded the captains of the hundreds, the officers of the host, and said unto them, Have her forth without the ranges: and him that followeth her kill with the sword. For the priest had said, Let her not be slain in the house of the LORD.

16 And they laid hands on her; and she went by the way by the which the horses came into the king's house: and there was she slain.

17 ¶ And Jehoiada made a covenant between the LORD and the king and the people, that they should be the LORD's people; between the king also and the people.

18 And all the people of the land went into the house of Baal, and brake it down; his altars and his images brake they in pieces thoroughly, and slew Mattan the priest of Baal before the altars. And the priest appointed officers over the house of the LORD.

19 And he took the rulers over hundreds, and the captains, and the guard, and all the people of the land; and they brought down the king from the house of the LORD, and came by the way of the gate of the guard to the king's house. And he sat on the throne of the kings.

20 And all the people of the land rejoiced, and the city was in quiet: and they slew Athaliah with the sword *beside* the king's house.

21 Seven years old *was* Jehoash when he began to reign.

**12** IN THE seventh year of Jehu Jehoash began to reign; and forty years reigned he in Jerusalem. And his mother's name *was* Zibiah of Beer-sheba.

2 And Jehoash did *that which was* right in the sight of the LORD all his days wherein Jehoiada the priest instructed him.

3 But the high places were not taken away: the people still sacrificed and burnt incense in the high places.

4 ¶ And Jehoash said to the priests, All the money of the dedicated things that is brought into the house of the LORD, *even* the money of every one that passeth *the account*, the money that every man is set at, *and* all the money that cometh into any man's heart to bring into the house of the LORD,

5 Let the priests take *it* to them, every man of his acquaintance: and let them repair the breaches of the house, wheresoever any breach shall be found.

6 But it was *so, that* in the three and twentieth year of king Jehoash the priests had not repaired the breaches of the house.

7 Then king Jehoash called for Jehoiada the priest, and the *other* priests, and said unto them, Why repair ye not the breaches of the house? now therefore receive no *more* money of your acquaintance, but deliver it for the breaches of the house.

8 And the priests consented to receive no *more* money of the people, neither to repair the breaches of the house.

9 But Jehoiada the priest took a chest, and bored a hole in the lid of it, and set it beside the altar, on the right side as one cometh into the house of the LORD: and the priests that kept the door put therein all the money *that was* brought into the house of the LORD.

10 And it was *so*, when they saw that *there was* much money in the chest, that the king's scribe and the high priest came up, and they put up in bags, and told the money that was found in the house of the LORD.

## Amplified

14 When she looked, there stood the king [on the platform] by the pillar, as was customary [on such occasions], and the captains and the trumpeters beside the king, with all the people of the land rejoicing and blowing trumpets. And Athaliah rent her clothes, and cried, Treason! treason!

15 Then Jehoiada the priest commanded the captains of the hundreds set over the army and said to them, Take her forth outside the ranks, and him who follows her kill with the sword. For the priest had said, Let her not be slain in the house of the Lord.

16 They seized her, and she went through the horses' entrance to the king's house, and there she was slain.

17 And Jehoiada made a covenant between the Lord, the king and the people, that they would be the Lord's people; also between the king and the people.

18 Then all the people of the land went to the house of Baal and destroyed it. His altar and his images they broke completely in pieces, and Mattan the priest of Baal they slew before the altars. And [Jehoiada] the priest appointed watchmen to guard the house of the Lord.

19 Then he took the rulers over hundreds, the captains, the guard, and all the people of the land, and they brought the king down from the house of the Lord, and came by way of the guards' gate to the king's house. And [little] Joash was seated on the throne of the kings.

20 So all the people of the land rejoiced, and the city was quiet after Athaliah had been slain with the sword beside the king's house.

21 Joash was seven years old when he began to reign.

**12** IN THE seventh year of Jehu [a]Joash began to reign, and he reigned forty years in Jerusalem. His mother was Zibiah of Beer-sheba.

2 Joash did right in the sight of the Lord all his days in which Jehoiada the priest instructed him.

3 Yet the high places were not taken away; the people still sacrificed and burned incense in the high places.

4 And Joash said to the priests, All the current money brought into the house of the Lord to provide the dedicated things, also the money [which the priests by command have] assessed on all those bound by vows, also all the money that it comes into any man's heart voluntarily to bring into the house of the Lord,

5 Let the priests solicit *and* receive such contributions, every man from his acquaintance; and let them repair the Lord's house wherever any such need may be found.

6 But in the twenty-third year of King Joash's reign the priests had not made the needed repairs on the Lord's house.

7 Then king Joash called for Jehoiada the priest, and the other priests, and said to them, Why are you not repairing the [Lord's] house? Do not take any more money from your acquaintances, but turn it all over for the repair of the house. [You are no longer responsible for this work. I will take it into my own hands.]

8 And the priests consented to receive no more money of the people, neither to repair the breaches of the house.

9 Then Jehoiada the priest took a chest, and bored a hole in the lid of it, and set it beside the altar on the right side as one entered the house of the Lord; and the priests who guarded the door put in the chest all the money that was brought into the house of the Lord.

10 And whenever they saw that there was much money in the chest, the king's scribe and the high priest came up and counted the money that was found in the house of the Lord and tied it up in bags.

**AMP** [a] Judah and Israel each had a king named *Joash* or *Jehoash*, and the Hebrew uses the two forms of the name interchangeably. Since the time of their reigns overlapped, it became difficult not to confuse them. So this version will call the first one, the king of Judah who began his reign at seven years of age, *Joash;* and the king of Israel, who began his reign thirty-seven years later, *Jehoash*, as the Hebrew does in 13:10 and 14:17.

## New American Standard

14And she looked and behold, the king was standing by the
pillar, according to the custom, with the captains and the trumpeters beside the king; and all the people of the land rejoiced and blew
trumpets. Then Athaliah tore her clothes and cried, "Treason!
Treason!"
15And Jehoiada the priest commanded the captains of hundreds
who were appointed over the army, and said to them, "Bring her
out between the ranks, and whoever follows her put to death with
the sword." For the priest said, "Let her not be put to death in the
house of the LORD."
16So they seized her, and when she arrived at the horses' entrance of the king's house, she was put to death there.
17¶ Then Jehoiada made a covenant between the LORD and the
king and the people, that they should be the LORD's people, also
between the king and the people.
18And all the people of the land went to the house of Baal, and
tore it down; his altars and his images they broke in pieces
thoroughly, and killed Mattan the priest of Baal before the altars.
And the priest appointed officers over the house of the LORD.
19And he took the captains of hundreds and the Carites and the
guards and all the people of the land; and they brought the king
down from the house of the LORD, and came by the way of the gate
of the guards to the king's house. And he sat on the throne of the
kings.
20So all the people of the land rejoiced and the city was quiet.
For they had put Athaliah to death with the sword at the king's
house.
21¶ Jehoash was seven years old when he became king.

*Joash (Jehoash) Reigns over Judah*

**12** IN THE seventh year of Jehu, Jehoash became king, and
he reigned forty years in Jerusalem; and his mother's
name was Zibiah of Beersheba.
2And Jehoash did right in the sight of the LORD all his days in
which Jehoiada the priest instructed him.
3Only the high places were not taken away; the people still
sacrificed and burned incense on the high places.

*The Temple to Be Repaired*

4¶ Then Jehoash said to the priests, "All the money of the
sacred things which is brought into the house of the LORD, in
current money, *both* the money of each man's assessment *and* all
the money which any man's heart prompts him to bring into the
house of the LORD,
5let the priests take it for themselves, each from his acquaintance; and they shall repair the [b]damages of the house wherever
any damage may be found.
6¶ But it came about that in the twenty-third year of King
Jehoash the priests had not repaired the damages of the house.
7Then King Jehoash called for Jehoiada the priest, and for the
*other* priests and said to them, "Why do you not repair the damages of the house? Now therefore take no *more* money from your
acquaintances, but pay it for the damages of the house."
8So the priests agreed that they should take no *more* money
from the people, nor repair the damages of the house.
9¶ But Jehoiada the priest took a chest and bored a hole in its
lid, and put it beside the altar, on the right side as one comes into
the house of the LORD; and the priests who guarded the threshold
put in it all the money which was brought into the house of the
LORD.
10And when they saw that there was much money in the chest,
the king's scribe and the high priest came up and tied *it* in bags
and counted the money which was found in the house of the LORD.

NAS [b] Lit., *breaches,* and so through v. 12

## New International

looked and there was the king, standing by the pillar, as the
custom was. The officers and the trumpeters were beside the king,
and all the people of the land were rejoicing and blowing trumpets.
Then Athaliah tore her robes and called out, "Treason! Treason!"
15Jehoiada the priest ordered the commanders of units of a
hundred, who were in charge of the troops: "Bring her out between the ranks[c] and put to the sword anyone who follows her."
For the priest had said, "She must not be put to death in the temple
of the LORD." 16So they seized her as she reached the place where
the horses enter the palace grounds, and there she was put to
death.
17Jehoiada then made a covenant between the LORD and the
king and people that they would be the LORD's people. He also
made a covenant between the king and the people. 18All the
people of the land went to the temple of Baal and tore it down.
They smashed the altars and idols to pieces and killed Mattan the
priest of Baal in front of the altars.
Then Jehoiada the priest posted guards at the temple of the
LORD. 19He took with him the commanders of hundreds, the Carites, the guards and all the people of the land, and together they
brought the king down from the temple of the LORD and went into
the palace, entering by way of the gate of the guards. The king then
took his place on the royal throne, 20and all the people of the land
rejoiced. And the city was quiet, because Athaliah had been slain
with the sword at the palace.
21Joash[d] was seven years old when he began to reign.

*Joash Repairs the Temple*

**12** IN THE seventh year of Jehu, Joash[e] became king, and he
reigned in Jerusalem forty years. His mother's name was
Zibiah; she was from Beersheba. 2Joash did what was right in the
eyes of the LORD all the years Jehoiada the priest instructed him.
3The high places, however, were not removed; the people continued to offer sacrifices and burn incense there.
4Joash said to the priests, "Collect all the money that is brought
as sacred offerings to the temple of the LORD—the money collected
in the census, the money received from personal vows and the
money brought voluntarily to the temple. 5Let every priest receive
the money from one of the treasurers, and let it be used to repair
whatever damage is found in the temple."
6But by the twenty-third year of King Joash the priests still had
not repaired the temple. 7Therefore King Joash summoned Jehoiada the priest and the other priests and asked them, "Why aren't
you repairing the damage done to the temple? Take no more
money from your treasurers, but hand it over for repairing the
temple." 8The priests agreed that they would not collect any more
money from the people and that they would not repair the temple
themselves.
9Jehoiada the priest took a chest and bored a hole in its lid. He
placed it beside the altar, on the right side as one enters the temple
of the LORD. The priests who guarded the entrance put into the
chest all the money that was brought to the temple of the LORD.
10Whenever they saw that there was a large amount of money in
the chest, the royal secretary and the high priest came, counted the
money that had been brought into the temple of the LORD and put
it into bags. 11When the amount had been determined, they gave

NIV [c] *15* Or *out from the precincts* [d] *21* Hebrew *Jehoash,* a variant of *Joash*
[e] *1* Hebrew *Jehoash,* a variant of *Joash;* also in verses 2, 4, 6, 7 and 18

## King James

11And they gave the money, being told, into the hands of them that did the work that had the oversight of the house of the LORD: and they laid it out to the carpenters and builders, that wrought upon the house of the LORD,

12And to masons, and hewers of stone, and to buy timber and hewed stone to repair the breaches of the house of the LORD, and for all that was laid out for the house to repair *it*.

13Howbeit there were not made for the house of the LORD bowls of silver, snuffers, basins, trumpets, any vessels of gold, or vessels of silver, of the money *that was* brought into the house of the LORD:

14But they gave that to the workmen, and repaired therewith the house of the LORD.

15Moreover they reckoned not with the men, into whose hand they delivered the money to be bestowed on workmen: for they dealt faithfully.

16The trespass money and sin money was not brought into the house of the LORD: it was the priests'.

17¶ Then Hazael king of Syria went up, and fought against Gath, and took it: and Hazael set his face to go up to Jerusalem.

18And Jehoash king of Judah took all the hallowed things that Jehoshaphat, and Jehoram, and Ahaziah, his fathers, kings of Judah, had dedicated, and his own hallowed things, and all the gold *that was* found in the treasures of the house of the LORD, and in the king's house, and sent *it* to Hazael king of Syria: and he went away from Jerusalem.

19¶ And the rest of the acts of Joash, and all that he did, *are* they not written in the book of the chronicles of the kings of Judah?

20And his servants arose, and made a conspiracy, and slew Joash in the house of Millo, which goeth down to Silla.

21For Jozachar the son of Shimeath, and Jehozabad the son of Shomer, his servants, smote him, and he died; and they buried him with his fathers in the city of David: and Amaziah his son reigned in his stead.

**13** IN THE three and twentieth year of Joash the son of Ahaziah king of Judah Jehoahaz the son of Jehu began to reign over Israel in Samaria, *and reigned* seventeen years.

2And he did *that which was* evil in the sight of the LORD, and followed the sins of Jeroboam the son of Nebat, which made Israel to sin; he departed not therefrom.

3¶ And the anger of the LORD was kindled against Israel, and he delivered them into the hand of Hazael king of Syria, and into the hand of Ben-hadad the son of Hazael, all *their* days.

4And Jehoahaz besought the LORD, and the LORD hearkened unto him: for he saw the oppression of Israel, because the king of Syria oppressed them.

5(And the LORD gave Israel a saviour, so that they went out from under the hand of the Syrians: and the children of Israel dwelt in their tents, as beforetime.

6Nevertheless they departed not from the sins of the house of Jeroboam, who made Israel sin, *but* walked therein: and there remained the grove also in Samaria.)

7Neither did he leave of the people to Jehoahaz but fifty horsemen, and ten chariots, and ten thousand footmen; for the king of Syria had destroyed them, and had made them like the dust by threshing.

8¶ Now the rest of the acts of Jehoahaz, and all that he did, and his might, *are* they not written in the book of the chronicles of the kings of Israel?

9And Jehoahaz slept with his fathers; and they buried him in Samaria: and Joash his son reigned in his stead.

## Amplified

11Then they gave the money, when it was weighed, into the hands of those who were doing the work, who had the oversight of the house of the Lord; and they paid it out to the carpenters and builders who worked on the house of the Lord,

12And to the masons, and stonecutters, and to buy timber and hewn stone for making the repairs on the house of the Lord, and for all that was outlay for repairing the house.

13However there were not made for the house of the Lord basins of silver, snuffers, bowls, trumpets, any vessels of gold, or of silver, from the money that was brought into the house of the Lord.

14But they gave that to the workmen, and repaired with it the house of the Lord.

15Moreover they did not require an accounting of the men into whose hand they delivered the money to be paid to the workmen, for they dealt faithfully.

16The money from the guilt and sin offerings was not brought into the house of the Lord; it was the priests'.

17Then Hazael king of Syria went up, fought against Gath [in Philistia] and took it; and Hazael set his face to go up to Jerusalem.

18And Joash king of Judah took all the hallowed things that Jehoshaphat, Jehoram, and Ahaziah, his [forefathers], kings of Judah, had dedicated, and his own hallowed things, and all the gold that was found in the treasuries of the house of the Lord and in the king's house, and sent them to Hazael king of Syria; and Hazael went away from Jerusalem.

19The rest of the acts of Joash, and all that he did, are they not written in the Book of the Chronicles of the Kings of Judah?

20His servants arose and made a conspiracy, and slew Joash [in revenge] in the house of Millo, on the way that goes down to Silla. [II Chron. 24:22-25.]

21It was Jozachar son of Shimeath, and Jehozabad son of Shomer, his servants, who smote him, so that he died. They buried [Joash] with his fathers in the city of David. Amaziah his son reigned in his stead.

**13** IN THE twenty-third year of Joash son of Ahaziah, king of Judah, Jehoahaz son of Jehu began to reign over Israel in Samaria, and reigned seventeen years.

2He did evil in the sight of the Lord, and followed the sins of Jeroboam son of Nebat, which made Israel to sin, and did not depart from them.

3The anger of the Lord was kindled against Israel, and He delivered them into the hand of Hazael king of Syria and of Ben-hadad son of Hazael, continually.

4But Jehoahaz besought the Lord, and the Lord hearkened to him; for He saw the oppression of Israel, how the king of Syria burdened them.

5(Then the Lord gave Israel a savior [one to rescue and give them peace] so that they escaped from under the hand of the Syrians; and the Israelites dwelt in their tents *or* homes as before.

6Yet they did not depart from the sins of the house of Jeroboam, who made Israel sin, but the nation walked in them, and the Asherah remained in Samaria.)

7[Benhadad] of Syria did not leave to Jehoahaz of [Israel] an army of more than fifty horsemen, ten chariots, and 10,000 footmen; for the Syrian king had destroyed them, and made them like dust to be trampled.

8The rest of the acts of Jehoahaz, all that he did, and his might, are they not written in the Book of the Chronicles of the Kings of Israel?

9Jehoahaz slept with his fathers, and they buried him in Samaria. Jehoash his son reigned in his stead.

## New American Standard

11And they gave the money which was weighed out into the
hands of those who did the work, who had the oversight of
the house of the LORD; and they paid it out to the carpenters and
the builders, who worked on the house of the LORD;
12and to the masons and the stonecutters, and for buying timber
and hewn stone to repair the damages to the house of the LORD,
and for all that was laid out for the house to repair it.
13But there were not made for the house of the LORD silver cups,
snuffers, bowls, trumpets, any vessels of gold, or vessels of silver
from the money which was brought into the house of the LORD;
14for they gave that to those who did the work, and with it they
repaired the house of the LORD.
15Moreover, they did not require an accounting from the men
into whose hand they gave the money to pay to those who did the
work, for they dealt faithfully.
16The money from the guilt offerings and the money from the
sin offerings, was not brought into the house of the LORD; it was
for the priests.
17¶ Then Hazael king of Aram went up and fought against Gath
and captured it, and Hazael set his face to go up to Jerusalem.
18And Jehoash king of Judah took all the sacred things that
Jehoshaphat and Jehoram and Ahaziah, his fathers, kings of
Judah, had dedicated, and his own sacred things and all the gold
that was found among the treasuries of the house of the LORD and
of the king's house, and sent *them* to Hazael king of Aram. Then
he went away from Jerusalem.

*Joash (Jehoash) Succeeded by Amaziah in Judah*

19¶ Now the rest of the acts of Joash and all that he did, are they
not written in the Book of the Chronicles of the Kings of Judah?
20And his servants arose and made a conspiracy, and struck
down Joash at the house of Millo *as he was* going down to Silla.
21For Jozacar the son of Shimeath, and Jehozabad the son of
Shomer, his servants, struck *him,* and he died; and they buried him
with his fathers in the city of David, and Amaziah his son became
king in his place.

*Kings of Israel: Jehoahaz and Jehoash*

**13** IN THE twenty-third year of Joash the son of Ahaziah,
king of Judah, Jehoahaz the son of Jehu became king over
Israel at Samaria, *and he reigned* seventeen years.
2And he did evil in the sight of the LORD, and followed the sins
of Jeroboam the son of Nebat, with which he made Israel sin; he
did not turn from them.
3So the anger of the LORD was kindled against Israel, and He
gave them continually into the hand of Hazael king of Aram, and
into the hand of Ben-hadad the son of Hazael.
4Then Jehoahaz entreated the favor of the LORD, and the LORD
listened to him; for He saw the oppression of Israel, how the king
of Aram oppressed them.
5And the LORD gave Israel a [a]deliverer, so that they escaped
from under the hand of the Arameans; and the sons of Israel lived
in their tents as formerly.
6Nevertheless they did not turn away from the sins of the
house of Jeroboam, with which he made Israel sin, but walked in
them; and the Asherah also remained standing in Samaria.
7For he left to Jehoahaz of the army not more than fifty horsemen and ten chariots and 10,000 footmen, for the king of Aram had
destroyed them and made them like the dust at threshing.
8Now the rest of the acts of Jehoahaz, and all that he did and
his might, are they not written in the Book of the Chronicles of the
Kings of Israel?
9And Jehoahaz slept with his fathers, and they buried him in
Samaria; and Joash his son became king in his place.

**NAS** [a] Or, *savior*

## New International

the money to the men appointed to supervise the work on the
temple. With it they paid those who worked on the temple of the
LORD—the carpenters and builders, 12the masons and stonecutters. They purchased timber and dressed stone for the repair of the
temple of the LORD, and met all the other expenses of restoring the
temple.
13The money brought into the temple was not spent for making
silver basins, wick trimmers, sprinkling bowls, trumpets or any
other articles of gold or silver for the temple of the LORD; 14it was
paid to the workmen, who used it to repair the temple. 15They did
not require an accounting from those to whom they gave the
money to pay the workers, because they acted with complete
honesty. 16The money from the guilt offerings and sin offerings
was not brought into the temple of the LORD; it belonged to the
priests.
17About this time Hazael king of Aram went up and attacked
Gath and captured it. Then he turned to attack Jerusalem. 18But
Joash king of Judah took all the sacred objects dedicated by his
fathers—Jehoshaphat, Jehoram and Ahaziah, the kings of Judah—
and the gifts he himself had dedicated and all the gold found in
the treasuries of the temple of the LORD and of the royal palace,
and he sent them to Hazael king of Aram, who then withdrew
from Jerusalem.
19As for the other events of the reign of Joash, and all he did,
are they not written in the book of the annals of the kings of Judah?
20His officials conspired against him and assassinated him at Beth
Millo, on the road down to Silla. 21The officials who murdered him
were Jozabad son of Shimeath and Jehozabad son of Shomer. He
died and was buried with his fathers in the City of David. And
Amaziah his son succeeded him as king.

*Jehoahaz King of Israel*

**13** IN THE twenty-third year of Joash son of Ahaziah king of
Judah, Jehoahaz son of Jehu became king of Israel in Samaria, and he reigned seventeen years. 2He did evil in the eyes of
the LORD by following the sins of Jeroboam son of Nebat, which
he had caused Israel to commit, and he did not turn away from
them. 3So the LORD's anger burned against Israel, and for a long
time he kept them under the power of Hazael king of Aram and
Ben-Hadad his son.
4Then Jehoahaz sought the LORD's favor, and the LORD listened
to him, for he saw how severely the king of Aram was oppressing
Israel. 5The LORD provided a deliverer for Israel, and they escaped
from the power of Aram. So the Israelites lived in their own homes
as they had before. 6But they did not turn away from the sins of
the house of Jeroboam, which he had caused Israel to commit; they
continued in them. Also, the Asherah pole[b] remained standing in
Samaria.
7Nothing had been left of the army of Jehoahaz except fifty
horsemen, ten chariots and ten thousand foot soldiers, for the king
of Aram had destroyed the rest and made them like the dust at
threshing time.
8As for the other events of the reign of Jehoahaz, all he did and
his achievements, are they not written in the book of the annals
of the kings of Israel? 9Jehoahaz rested with his fathers and was
buried in Samaria. And Jehoash[c] his son succeeded him as king.

**NIV** [b] 6 That is, a symbol of the goddess Asherah; here and elsewhere in
2 Kings [c] 9 Hebrew *Joash;* a variant of *Jehoash* also in verses 12-14 and 25

## King James

10¶ In the thirty and seventh year of Joash king of Judah began
Jehoash the son of Jehoahaz to reign over Israel in Samaria, *and
reigned* sixteen years.
11And he did *that which was* evil in the sight of the LORD; he
departed not from all the sins of Jeroboam the son of Nebat, who
made Israel sin: *but* he walked therein.
12And the rest of the acts of Joash, and all that he did, and his
might wherewith he fought against Amaziah king of Judah, *are*
they not written in the book of the chronicles of the kings of Israel?
13And Joash slept with his fathers; and Jeroboam sat upon his
throne: and Joash was buried in Samaria with the kings of Israel.
14¶ Now Elisha was fallen sick of his sickness whereof he died.
And Joash the king of Israel came down unto him, and wept over
his face, and said, O my father, my father, the chariot of Israel, and
the horsemen thereof.
15And Elisha said unto him, Take bow and arrows. And he took
unto him bow and arrows.
16And he said to the king of Israel, Put thine hand upon the
bow. And he put his hand *upon it:* and Elisha put his hands upon
the king's hands.
17And he said, Open the window eastward. And he opened *it*.
Then Elisha said, Shoot. And he shot. And he said, The arrow of
the LORD's deliverance, and the arrow of deliverance from Syria:
for thou shalt smite the Syrians in Aphek, till thou have consumed
*them*.
18And he said, Take the arrows. And he took *them*. And he said
unto the king of Israel, Smite upon the ground. And he smote
thrice, and stayed.
19And the man of God was wroth with him, and said, Thou
shouldest have smitten five or six times; then hadst thou smitten
Syria till thou hadst consumed *it:* whereas now thou shalt smite
Syria *but* thrice.
20¶ And Elisha died, and they buried him. And the bands of the
Moabites invaded the land at the coming in of the year.
21And it came to pass, as they were burying a man, that, behold, they spied a band *of men;* and they cast the man into the
sepulchre of Elisha: and when the man was let down, and touched
the bones of Elisha, he revived, and stood up on his feet.
22¶ But Hazael king of Syria oppressed Israel all the days of
Jehoahaz.
23And the LORD was gracious unto them, and had compassion
on them, and had respect unto them, because of his covenant with
Abraham, Isaac, and Jacob, and would not destroy them, neither
cast he them from his presence as yet.
24So Hazael king of Syria died; and Ben-hadad his son reigned
in his stead.
25And Jehoash the son of Jehoahaz took again out of the hand
of Ben-hadad the son of Hazael the cities, which he had taken out
of the hand of Jehoahaz his father by war. Three times did Joash
beat him, and recovered the cities of Israel.

**14** IN THE second year of Joash son of Jehoahaz king of Israel
reigned Amaziah the son of Joash king of Judah.
2He was twenty and five years old when he began to reign, and
reigned twenty and nine years in Jerusalem. And his mother's
name *was* Jehoaddan of Jerusalem.
3And he did *that which was* right in the sight of the LORD, yet
not like David his father: he did according to all things as Joash his
father did.
4Howbeit the high places were not taken away: as yet the
people did sacrifice and burnt incense on the high places.

## Amplified

10In the thirty-seventh year of Joash king of Judah, Jehoash son
of Jehoahaz began to reign over Israel in Samaria, and reigned
sixteen years.
11He did evil in the sight of the Lord; he departed not from all
the sins of Jeroboam the son of Nebat, who made Israel sin; he
walked in them.
12The rest of the acts of Jehoash, all that he did, and his might
with which he fought against Amaziah king of Judah, are they not
written in the Book of the Chronicles of the Kings of Israel?
13Jehoash slept with his fathers, and Jeroboam[II] sat on his
throne. Jehoash was buried in Samaria with the kings of Israel.
14Now Elisha [previously] had become ill of the illness of which
he died. And Jehoash the king of Israel came down to him, and
wept over him and said, O my father, my father, the chariot of
Israel, and the horsemen of it! [II Kings 2:12.]
15And Elisha said to him, Take bow and arrows. And he took
bow and arrows.
16And he said to the king of Israel, Put your hand upon the bow.
And he put his hand upon it; and Elisha put his hands upon the
king's hands.
17And he said, Open the window to the east. And he opened
it. Then Elisha said, Shoot. And he shot. And he said, The Lord's
arrow of victory, the arrow of victory over Syria. For you shall
smite the Syrians in Aphek, till you have destroyed them.
18Then he said, Take the arrows. And he took them. And he
said to the king of Israel, Strike on the ground. And he struck three
times and stopped.
19And the man of God was angry with him, and said, You
should have struck five or six times; then you would have struck
down Syria until you had destroyed it; but now you shall strike
Syria down only three times.
20Elisha died, and they buried him. Bands of the Moabites
invaded the land in the spring of the next year.
21As a man was being buried [on an open bier], such a band was
seen coming, and the man was cast into Elisha's grave. And when
the man being let down touched the bones of Elisha, he revived
and stood on his feet.
22Hazael king of Syria oppressed Israel all the days of Jehoahaz.
23But the Lord was gracious to them, and had compassion on
them, and returned toward them, because of [a]His covenant with
Abraham, Isaac, and Jacob, and would not destroy them, or cast
them from His presence, yet. [Mal. 3:6]
24Hazael king of Syria died; Benhadad his son reigned in his
stead.
25Jehoash son of Jehoahaz recovered from Benhadad son of
Hazael the cities which he had taken from Jehoahaz his father by
war. Three times Jehoash defeated him, and recovered the cities
of Israel. [Verse 19.]

**14** IN THE second year of Jehoash son of Jehoahaz king of
Israel, Amaziah son of Joash king of Judah reigned.
2He was twenty-five years old when he began his twenty-nine
years' reign in Jerusalem. His mother was Jeho-addin of Jerusalem.
3He did right in the sight of the Lord, yet not like David his
[forefather]. He did all things as Joash his father did.
4But the high places were not removed; the people still sacrificed and burned incense on the high places.

**AMP** [a] Abraham, Isaac and Jacob had been dead a thousand years, yet God's covenant with them was undiminishingly effective.

## New American Standard

10¶ In the thirty-seventh year of Joash king of Judah, Jehoash
the son of Jehoahaz, became king over Israel in Samaria, *and reigned*
sixteen years.
11And he did evil in the sight of the LORD; he did not turn away
from all the sins of Jeroboam the son of Nebat, with which he made
Israel sin, but he walked in them.
12Now the rest of the acts of Joash and all that he did and his
might with which he fought against Amaziah king of Judah, are
they not written in the Book of the Chronicles of the Kings of
Israel?
13So Joash slept with his fathers, and Jeroboam sat on his
throne; and Joash was buried in Samaria with the kings of Israel.

*Death of Elisha*

14¶ When Elisha became sick with the illness of which he was
to die, Joash the king of Israel came down to him and wept over
him and said, "My father, my father, the chariots of Israel and its
horsemen!"
15And Elisha said to him, "Take a bow and arrows." So he took
a bow and arrows.
16Then he said to the king of Israel, "Put your hand on the
bow." And he put his hand *on it*, then Elisha laid his hands on the
king's hands.
17And he said, "Open the window toward the east," and he
opened *it*. Then Elisha said, "Shoot!" And he shot. And he said,
"The LORD's arrow of victory, even the arrow of victory over Aram;
for you shall defeat the Arameans at Aphek until you have destroyed *them*."
18Then he said, "Take the arrows," and he took them. And he
said to the king of Israel, "Strike the ground," and he struck *it*
three times and stopped.
19So the man of God was angry with him and said, "You should
have struck five or six times, then you would have struck Aram
until you would have destroyed *it*. But now you shall strike Aram
*only* three times."
20¶ And Elisha died, and they buried him. Now the bands of
the Moabites would invade the land in the spring of the year.
21And as they were burying a man, behold, they saw a marauding band; and they cast the man into the grave of Elisha. And when
the man touched the bones of Elisha he revived and stood up on
his feet.
22¶ Now Hazael king of Aram had oppressed Israel all the days
of Jehoahaz.
23But the LORD was gracious to them and had compassion on
them and turned to them because of His covenant with Abraham,
Isaac, and Jacob, and would not destroy them or cast them from
His presence until now.
24When Hazael king of Aram died, Ben-hadad his son became
king in his place.
25Then Jehoash the son of Jehoahaz took again from the hand
of Ben-hadad the son of Hazael the cities which he had taken in
war from the hand of Jehoahaz his father. Three times Joash defeated him and recovered the cities of Israel.

*Amaziah Reigns over Judah*

**14** IN THE second year of Joash son of Joahaz king of Israel,
Amaziah the son of Joash king of Judah became king.
2He was twenty-five years old when he became king, and he
reigned twenty-nine years in Jerusalem. And his mother's name
was Jehoaddin of Jerusalem.
3And he did right in the sight of the LORD, yet not like David
his father; he did according to all that Joash his father had done.
4Only the high places were not taken away; the people still
sacrificed and burned incense on the high places.

## New International

*Jehoash King of Israel*

10In the thirty-seventh year of Joash king of Judah, Jehoash son
of Jehoahaz became king of Israel in Samaria, and he reigned
sixteen years. 11He did evil in the eyes of the LORD and did not turn
away from any of the sins of Jeroboam son of Nebat, which he had
caused Israel to commit; he continued in them.
12As for the other events of the reign of Jehoash, all he did and
his achievements, including his war against Amaziah king of
Judah, are they not written in the book of the annals of the kings
of Israel? 13Jehoash rested with his fathers, and Jeroboam succeeded him on the throne. Jehoash was buried in Samaria with the
kings of Israel.
14Now Elisha was suffering from the illness from which he died.
Jehoash king of Israel went down to see him and wept over him.
"My father! My father!" he cried. "The chariots and horsemen of
Israel!"
15Elisha said, "Get a bow and some arrows," and he did so.
16"Take the bow in your hands," he said to the king of Israel.
When he had taken it, Elisha put his hands on the king's hands.
17"Open the east window," he said, and he opened it. "Shoot!"
Elisha said, and he shot. "The LORD's arrow of victory, the arrow
of victory over Aram!" Elisha declared. "You will completely destroy the Arameans at Aphek."
18Then he said, "Take the arrows," and the king took them.
Elisha told him, "Strike the ground." He struck it three times and
stopped. 19The man of God was angry with him and said, "You
should have struck the ground five or six times; then you would
have defeated Aram and completely destroyed it. But now you will
defeat it only three times."
20Elisha died and was buried.
Now Moabite raiders used to enter the country every spring.
21Once while some Israelites were burying a man, suddenly they
saw a band of raiders; so they threw the man's body into Elisha's
tomb. When the body touched Elisha's bones, the man came to life
and stood up on his feet.
22Hazael king of Aram oppressed Israel throughout the reign of
Jehoahaz. 23But the LORD was gracious to them and had compassion and showed concern for them because of his covenant with
Abraham, Isaac and Jacob. To this day he has been unwilling to
destroy them or banish them from his presence.
24Hazael king of Aram died, and Ben-Hadad his son succeeded
him as king. 25Then Jehoash son of Jehoahaz recaptured from
Ben-Hadad son of Hazael the towns he had taken in battle from
his father Jehoahaz. Three times Jehoash defeated him, and so he
recovered the Israelite towns.

*Amaziah King of Judah*

**14** IN THE second year of Jehoash[b] son of Jehoahaz king of
Israel, Amaziah son of Joash king of Judah began to reign.
2He was twenty-five years old when he became king, and he
reigned in Jerusalem twenty-nine years. His mother's name was
Jehoaddin; she was from Jerusalem. 3He did what was right in the
eyes of the LORD, but not as his father David had done. In everything he followed the example of his father Joash. 4The high
places, however, were not removed; the people continued to offer
sacrifices and burn incense there.

NIV [b] 1 Hebrew *Joash*, a variant of *Jehoash*; also in verses 13, 23 and 27

## King James

5¶ And it came to pass, as soon as the kingdom was confirmed in his hand, that he slew his servants which had slain the king his father.

6But the children of the murderers he slew not: according unto that which is written in the book of the law of Moses, wherein the LORD commanded, saying, The fathers shall not be put to death for the children, nor the children be put to death for the fathers; but every man shall be put to death for his own sin.

7He slew of Edom in the valley of salt ten thousand, and took Selah by war, and called the name of it Joktheel unto this day.

8¶ Then Amaziah sent messengers to Jehoash, the son of Jehoahaz son of Jehu, king of Israel, saying, Come, let us look one another in the face.

9And Jehoash the king of Israel sent to Amaziah king of Judah, saying, The thistle that *was* in Lebanon sent to the cedar that *was* in Lebanon, saying, Give thy daughter to my son to wife: and there passed by a wild beast that *was* in Lebanon, and trode down the thistle.

10Thou hast indeed smitten Edom, and thine heart hath lifted thee up: glory *of this*, and tarry at home: for why shouldest thou meddle to *thy* hurt, that thou shouldest fall, *even* thou, and Judah with thee?

11But Amaziah would not hear. Therefore Jehoash king of Israel went up; and he and Amaziah king of Judah looked one another in the face at Beth-shemesh, which *belongeth* to Judah.

12And Judah was put to the worse before Israel; and they fled every man to their tents.

13And Jehoash king of Israel took Amaziah king of Judah, the son of Jehoash the son of Ahaziah, at Beth-shemesh, and came to Jerusalem, and brake down the wall of Jerusalem from the gate of Ephraim unto the corner gate, four hundred cubits.

14And he took all the gold and silver, and all the vessels that were found in the house of the LORD, and in the treasures of the king's house, and hostages, and returned to Samaria.

15¶ Now the rest of the acts of Jehoash which he did, and his might, and how he fought with Amaziah king of Judah, *are* they not written in the book of the chronicles of the kings of Israel?

16And Jehoash slept with his fathers, and was buried in Samaria with the kings of Israel; and Jeroboam his son reigned in his stead.

17¶ And Amaziah the son of Joash king of Judah lived after the death of Jehoash son of Jehoahaz king of Israel fifteen years.

18And the rest of the acts of Amaziah, *are* they not written in the book of the chronicles of the kings of Judah?

19Now they made a conspiracy against him in Jerusalem: and he fled to Lachish; but they sent after him to Lachish, and slew him there.

20And they brought him on horses: and he was buried at Jerusalem with his fathers in the city of David.

21¶ And all the people of Judah took Azariah, which *was* sixteen years old, and made him king instead of his father Amaziah.

22He built Elath, and restored it to Judah, after that the king slept with his fathers.

23¶ In the fifteenth year of Amaziah the son of Joash king of Judah Jeroboam the son of Joash king of Israel began to reign in Samaria, *and reigned* forty and one years.

24And he did *that which was* evil in the sight of the LORD: he departed not from all the sins of Jeroboam the son of Nebat, who made Israel to sin.

25He restored the coast of Israel from the entering of Hamath unto the sea of the plain, according to the word of the LORD God of Israel, which he spake by the hand of his servant Jonah, the son of Amittai, the prophet, which *was* of Gath-hepher.

26For the LORD saw the affliction of Israel, *that it was* very bitter: for *there was* not any shut up, nor any left, nor any helper for Israel.

## Amplified

5As soon as the kingdom was established in Amaziah's hand, he slew his servants who had slain the king his father. [12:20.]

6But he did not slay the children of the murderers; in compliance with what is written in the book of the law of Moses, in which the Lord commanded, The fathers shall not be put to death for the children, nor the children for the fathers; but every man shall die for his own sin only.

7Amaziah slew of Edom in the Valley of Salt 10,000, and took Sela [Petra, the Rock] by war, and called it Joktheel, which is the name of it to this day.

8Then Amaziah sent messengers to Jehoash son of Jehoahaz son of Jehu, king of Israel, saying, Come, let us look one another in the face *and* test each other.

9Jehoash king of Israel replied to Amaziah king of Judah, The thistle in Lebanon sent to the cedar in Lebanon, saying, Give your daughter to my son as wife; and a wild beast of Lebanon passed by and trampled the thistle [leaving the cedar unharmed].

10You have indeed smitten Edom, and your heart has lifted you up. Glory in that and stay at home; for why should you meddle to your hurt *and* provoke calamity, causing you to fall, you and Judah with you?

11But Amaziah would not hear. So Jehoash king of Israel went up; and he and Amaziah king of Judah measured swords at Beth-shemesh, which belongs to Judah.

12But Judah was defeated by Israel and every man fled home.

13And Jehoash king of Israel captured Amaziah king of Judah, son of Joash son of Ahaziah, at Beth-shemesh, and came to Jerusalem, and broke down the wall of Jerusalem from the Ephraim Gate to the Corner Gate, 400 cubits.

14He seized all the gold and silver, and all the vessels found in the Lord's house and in the treasuries of the king's house, also hostages, and returned to Samaria.

15The rest of the acts of Jehoash, his might, and how he fought with Amaziah king of Judah, are they not written in the Book of the Chronicles of Israel's Kings?

16Jehoash slept with his fathers, and was buried in Samaria with Israel's kings. Jeroboam [II] reigned in his stead.

17Amaziah son of Joash king of Judah lived after the death of Jehoash son of Jehoahaz king of Israel fifteen years.

18The rest of the acts of Amaziah, are they not written in the Book of the Chronicles of the Kings of Judah?

19Now a conspiracy was made against him in Jerusalem, and Amaziah fled to Lachish; but they sent after him to Lachish and slew him there.

20They brought him on horses; and he was buried at Jerusalem with his fathers in the city of David.

21And all the people of Judah took Azariah, sixteen years old, and made him king instead of his father Amaziah.

22He built Elath and restored it to Judah, after the king [his father] died.

23In the fifteenth year of Amaziah son of Joash king of Judah Jeroboam [II] son of Jehoash king of Israel began to reign in Samaria, and reigned forty-one years.

24He did evil in the sight of the Lord; he did not depart from all the sins of Jeroboam [I] son of Nebat, with which he made Israel to sin.

25Jeroboam restored Israel's border from the entrance of Hamath to the [Dead] Sea of the Arabah, according to the word of the Lord, the God of Israel, which He spoke by His servant Jonah son of Amittai, the prophet from Gath-hepher.

26For the Lord saw as very bitter the affliction of Israel; there was no one left, bond or free, nor any helper for Israel.

# New American Standard

5Now it came about, as soon as the kingdom was firmly in his
hand, that he killed his servants who had slain the king his father.
6But the sons of the slayers he did not put to death, according
to what is written in the book of the law of Moses, as the LORD
commanded, saying, "The fathers shall not be put to death for the
sons, nor the sons be put to death for the fathers; but each shall
be put to death for his own sin."
7He killed *of* Edom in the Valley of Salt 10,000 and took Sela
by war, and named it Joktheel to this day.
8Then Amaziah sent messengers to Jehoash, the son of Jehoahaz son of Jehu, king of Israel, saying, "Come, let us face each
other."
9And Jehoash king of Israel sent to Amaziah king of Judah,
saying, "The thorn bush which was in Lebanon sent to the cedar
which was in Lebanon, saying, 'Give your daughter to my son in
marriage.' But there passed by a wild beast that was in Lebanon,
and trampled the thorn bush.
10"You have indeed defeated Edom, and your heart has become
proud. Enjoy your glory and stay at home; for why should you
provoke trouble so that you, even you, should fall, and Judah with
you?"
11¶ But Amaziah would not listen. So Jehoash king of Israel
went up; and he and Amaziah king of Judah faced each other at
Beth-shemesh, which belongs to Judah.
12And Judah was defeated by Israel, and they fled each to his
tent.
13Then Jehoash king of Israel captured Amaziah king of Judah,
the son of Jehoash the son of Ahaziah, at Beth-shemesh, and came
to Jerusalem and tore down the wall of Jerusalem from the Gate
of Ephraim to the Corner Gate, 400 cubits.
14And he took all the gold and silver and all the utensils which
were found in the house of the LORD, and in the treasuries of the
king's house, the hostages also, and returned to Samaria.

*Jeroboam II Succeeds Jehoash in Israel*

15¶ Now the rest of the acts of Jehoash which he did, and his
might and how he fought with Amaziah king of Judah, are they
not written in the Book of the Chronicles of the Kings of Israel?
16So Jehoash slept with his fathers and was buried in Samaria
with the kings of Israel; and Jeroboam his son became king in his
place.

*Azariah (Uzziah) Succeeds Amaziah in Judah*

17¶ And Amaziah the son of Joash king of Judah lived fifteen
years after the death of Jehoash son of Jehoahaz king of Israel.
18Now the rest of the acts of Amaziah, are they not written in
the Book of the Chronicles of the Kings of Judah?
19And they conspired against him in Jerusalem, and he fled to
Lachish; but they sent after him to Lachish and killed him there.
20Then they brought him on horses and he was buried at Jerusalem with his fathers in the city of David.
21And all the people of Judah took Azariah, who *was* sixteen
years old, and made him king in the place of his father Amaziah.
22He built Elath and restored it to Judah, after the king slept
with his fathers.
23¶ In the fifteenth year of Amaziah the son of Joash king of
Judah, Jeroboam the son of Joash king of Israel became king in
Samaria, *and reigned* forty-one years.
24And he did evil in the sight of the LORD; he did not depart
from all the sins of Jeroboam the son of Nebat, which he made
Israel sin.
25He restored the border of Israel from the entrance of Hamath
as far as the Sea of the Arabah, according to the word of the LORD,
the God of Israel, which He spoke through His servant Jonah the
son of Amittai, the prophet, who was of Gath-hepher.
26For the LORD saw the affliction of Israel, *which was* very bitter;
for there was neither bond nor free, nor was there any helper for
Israel.

# New International

5After the kingdom was firmly in his grasp, he executed the
officials who had murdered his father the king. 6Yet he did not put
the sons of the assassins to death, in accordance with what is
written in the Book of the Law of Moses where the LORD commanded: "Fathers shall not be put to death for their children, nor
children put to death for their fathers; each is to die for his own
sins."[a]
7He was the one who defeated ten thousand Edomites in the
Valley of Salt and captured Sela in battle, calling it Joktheel, the
name it has to this day.
8Then Amaziah sent messengers to Jehoash son of Jehoahaz,
the son of Jehu, king of Israel, with the challenge: "Come, meet
me face to face."
9But Jehoash king of Israel replied to Amaziah king of Judah:
"A thistle in Lebanon sent a message to a cedar in Lebanon, 'Give
your daughter to my son in marriage.' Then a wild beast in Lebanon came along and trampled the thistle underfoot. 10You have
indeed defeated Edom and now you are arrogant. Glory in your
victory, but stay at home! Why ask for trouble and cause your own
downfall and that of Judah also?"
11Amaziah, however, would not listen, so Jehoash king of Israel
attacked. He and Amaziah king of Judah faced each other at Beth
Shemesh in Judah. 12Judah was routed by Israel, and every man
fled to his home. 13Jehoash king of Israel captured Amaziah king
of Judah, the son of Joash, the son of Ahaziah, at Beth Shemesh.
Then Jehoash went to Jerusalem and broke down the wall of
Jerusalem from the Ephraim Gate to the Corner Gate—a section
about six hundred feet long.[b] 14He took all the gold and silver and
all the articles found in the temple of the LORD and in the treasuries
of the royal palace. He also took hostages and returned to Samaria.
15As for the other events of the reign of Jehoash, what he did
and his achievements, including his war against Amaziah king of
Judah, are they not written in the book of the annals of the kings
of Israel? 16Jehoash rested with his fathers and was buried in
Samaria with the kings of Israel. And Jeroboam his son succeeded
him as king.
17Amaziah son of Joash king of Judah lived for fifteen years after
the death of Jehoash son of Jehoahaz king of Israel. 18As for the
other events of Amaziah's reign, are they not written in the book
of the annals of the kings of Judah?
19They conspired against him in Jerusalem, and he fled to Lachish, but they sent men after him to Lachish and killed him there.
20He was brought back by horse and was buried in Jerusalem with
his fathers, in the City of David.
21Then all the people of Judah took Azariah,[c] who was sixteen
years old, and made him king in place of his father Amaziah. 22He
was the one who rebuilt Elath and restored it to Judah after Amaziah rested with his fathers.

*Jeroboam II King of Israel*

23In the fifteenth year of Amaziah son of Joash king of Judah,
Jeroboam son of Jehoash king of Israel became king in Samaria,
and he reigned forty-one years. 24He did evil in the eyes of the
LORD and did not turn away from any of the sins of Jeroboam son
of Nebat, which he had caused Israel to commit. 25He was the one
who restored the boundaries of Israel from Lebo[d] Hamath to the
Sea of the Arabah,[e] in accordance with the word of the LORD, the
God of Israel, spoken through his servant Jonah son of Amittai, the
prophet from Gath Hepher.
26The LORD had seen how bitterly everyone in Israel, whether
slave or free, was suffering; there was no one to help them. 27And

NIV [a] 6 Deut. 24:16 [b] *13* Hebrew *four hundred cubits* (about 180 meters) [c] *21* Also called *Uzziah* [d] *25* Or *from the entrance to* [e] *25* That is, the Dead Sea

## King James

27And the LORD said not that he would blot out the name of Israel from under heaven: but he saved them by the hand of Jeroboam the son of Joash.

28¶ Now the rest of the acts of Jeroboam, and all that he did, and his might, how he warred, and how he recovered Damascus, and Hamath, *which belonged* to Judah, for Israel, *are* they not written in the book of the chronicles of the kings of Israel?

29And Jeroboam slept with his fathers, *even* with the kings of Israel; and Zachariah his son reigned in his stead.

**15** IN THE twenty and seventh year of Jeroboam king of Israel began Azariah son of Amaziah king of Judah to reign.

2Sixteen years old was he when he began to reign, and he reigned two and fifty years in Jerusalem. And his mother's name *was* Jecholiah of Jerusalem.

3And he did *that which was* right in the sight of the LORD, according to all that his father Amaziah had done;

4Save that the high places were not removed: the people sacrificed and burnt incense still on the high places.

5¶ And the LORD smote the king, so that he was a leper unto the day of his death, and dwelt in a several house. And Jotham the king's son *was* over the house, judging the people of the land.

6And the rest of the acts of Azariah, and all that he did, *are* they not written in the book of the chronicles of the kings of Judah?

7So Azariah slept with his fathers; and they buried him with his fathers in the city of David: and Jotham his son reigned in his stead.

8¶ In the thirty and eighth year of Azariah king of Judah did Zachariah the son of Jeroboam reign over Israel in Samaria six months.

9And he did *that which was* evil in the sight of the LORD, as his fathers had done: he departed not from the sins of Jeroboam the son of Nebat, who made Israel to sin.

10And Shallum the son of Jabesh conspired against him, and smote him before the people, and slew him, and reigned in his stead.

11And the rest of the acts of Zachariah, behold, they *are* written in the book of the chronicles of the kings of Israel.

12This *was* the word of the LORD which he spake unto Jehu, saying, Thy sons shall sit on the throne of Israel unto the fourth *generation*. And so it came to pass.

13¶ Shallum the son of Jabesh began to reign in the nine and thirtieth year of Uzziah king of Judah; and he reigned a full month in Samaria.

14For Menahem the son of Gadi went up from Tirzah, and came to Samaria, and smote Shallum the son of Jabesh in Samaria, and slew him, and reigned in his stead.

15And the rest of the acts of Shallum, and his conspiracy which he made, behold, they *are* written in the book of the chronicles of the kings of Israel.

16¶ Then Menahem smote Tiphsah, and all that *were* therein, and the coasts thereof from Tirzah: because they opened not *to him*, therefore he smote *it; and* all the women therein that were with child he ripped up.

17In the nine and thirtieth year of Azariah king of Judah began Menahem the son of Gadi to reign over Israel, *and reigned* ten years in Samaria.

18And he did *that which was* evil in the sight of the LORD: he departed not all his days from the sins of Jeroboam the son of Nebat, who made Israel to sin.

**AMP** [a] This savage conduct was among the enormities that a heathen ruler might perpetrate, but only here do we find such cruelty employed by an Israelite. It shows the great degradation and barbarity of the times (*Cambridge Bible*, condensed).

## Amplified

27But the Lord had not said that He would blot out the name of Israel from under the heavens, so He saved them by the hand of Jeroboam [II] son of Jehoash.

28The rest of the acts of Jeroboam [II], all that he did, his might, how he warred, and how he recovered for Israel Damascus and Hamath, which had belonged to Judah, are they not written in the Book of the Chronicles of the Kings of Israel?

29Jeroboam [II] slept with his fathers, the kings of Israel. Zechariah his son reigned in his stead.

**15** IN THE twenty-seventh year of Jeroboam [II] king of Israel Azariah [Uzziah] son of Amaziah, king of Judah, began to reign.

2He was sixteen years old when he began his fifty-two years' reign in Jerusalem. His mother was Jecoliah of Jerusalem.

3He did right in the Lord's sight, in keeping with all his father Amaziah had done,

4Except the high places were not removed; the people sacrificed and burned incense still on the high places.

5And the Lord smote the king, so that he was a leper to his dying day, and dwelt in a separate house. Jotham the king's son was over the household, judging the people of the land. [II Chron. 26:16-21.]

6The rest of Azariah's acts, all that he did, are they not written in the Book of the Chronicles of the Kings of Judah?

7Azariah slept with his fathers, and they buried him with them in the city of David. Jotham his son reigned in his stead.

8In the thirty-eighth year of Azariah king of Judah Zachariah son of Jeroboam [II] reigned over Israel in Samaria six months.

9He did evil in the sight of the Lord, as his fathers had done; he departed not from the sins of Jeroboam [I] son of Nebat, with which he made Israel to sin.

10Shallum son of Jabesh conspired against Zachariah and struck and killed him before the people, and reigned in his stead.

11The rest of the acts of Zachariah, see, they are written in the Book of the Chronicles of the Kings of Israel.

12This was the fulfillment of the promise to Jehu from the Lord, Your sons shall sit on the throne of Israel to the fourth generation. And so it came to pass. [II Kings 10:30.]

13Shallum son of Jabesh, in the thirty-ninth year of Uzziah king of Judah, began his reign of a full month in Samaria.

14For Menahem son of Gadi went up from Tirzah, and came to Samaria, and smote and killed Shallum son of Jabesh in Samaria and reigned in his stead.

15The rest of Shallum's acts, his conspiracy, see, they are written in the Book of the Chronicles of the Kings of Israel.

16Then Menahem smote Tiphsah, and all who were in it, and its territory from Tirzah on; he attacked it because they did not open to him; and all [a]the women there who were with child he ripped up.

17In the thirty-ninth year of Azariah king of Judah Menahem son of Gadi began his ten years' reign over Israel in Samaria.

18He did evil in the sight of the Lord; he did not depart all his days from the sins of Jeroboam son of Nebat, which he caused Israel to sin.

## New American Standard

27And the LORD did not say that He would blot out the name
of Israel from under heaven, but He saved them by the hand of
Jeroboam the son of Joash.

*Zechariah Reigns over Israel*

28¶ Now the rest of the acts of Jeroboam and all that he did and
his might, how he fought and how he recovered for Israel, Damascus and Hamath, *which had belonged* to Judah, are they not written
in the Book of the Chronicles of the Kings of Israel?
29And Jeroboam slept with his fathers, even with the kings of
Israel, and Zechariah his son became king in his place.

*Series of Kings: Azariah (Uzziah) over Judah*

**15** IN THE twenty-seventh year of Jeroboam king of Israel,
Azariah son of Amaziah king of Judah became king.
2He was sixteen years old when he became king, and he
reigned fifty-two years in Jerusalem; and his mother's name was
Jecoliah of Jerusalem.
3And he did right in the sight of the LORD, according to all that
his father Amaziah had done.
4Only the high places were not taken away; the people still
sacrificed and burned incense on the high places.
5And the LORD struck the king, so that he was a leper to the
day of his death. And he lived in a separate house, while Jotham
the king's son was over the household, judging the people of the
land.
6Now the rest of the acts of Azariah and all that he did, are they
not written in the Book of the Chronicles of the Kings of Judah?
7And Azariah slept with his fathers, and they buried him with
his fathers in the city of David, and Jotham his son became king
in his place.

*Zechariah over Israel*

8¶ In the thirty-eighth year of Azariah king of Judah, Zechariah
the son of Jeroboam became king over Israel in Samaria *for* six
months.
9And he did evil in the sight of the LORD, as his fathers had
done; he did not depart from the sins of Jeroboam the son of Nebat,
which he made Israel sin.
10Then Shallum the son of Jabesh conspired against him and
struck him before the people and killed him, and reigned in his
place.
11Now the rest of the acts of Zechariah, behold they are written
in the Book of the Chronicles of the Kings of Israel.
12This is the word of the LORD which He spoke to Jehu, saying,
"Your sons to the fourth generation shall sit on the throne of
Israel." And so it was.
13¶ Shallum son of Jabesh became king in the thirty-ninth year
of Uzziah king of Judah, and he reigned one month in Samaria.
14Then Menahem son of Gadi went up from Tirzah and came
to Samaria, and struck Shallum son of Jabesh in Samaria, and killed
him and became king in his place.
15Now the rest of the acts of Shallum and his conspiracy which
he made, behold they are written in the Book of the Chronicles of
the Kings of Israel.
16Then Menahem struck Tiphsah and all who were in it and its
borders from Tirzah, because they did not open *to him,* therefore
he struck *it;* and he ripped up all its women who were with child.

*Menahem over Israel*

17¶ In the thirty-ninth year of Azariah king of Judah, Menahem
son of Gadi became king over Israel *and reigned* ten years in Samaria.
18And he did evil in the sight of the LORD; he did not depart all
his days from the sins of Jeroboam the son of Nebat, which he
made Israel sin.

## New International

since the LORD had not said he would blot out the name of Israel
from under heaven, he saved them by the hand of Jeroboam son
of Jehoash.
28As for the other events of Jeroboam's reign, all he did, and his
military achievements, including how he recovered for Israel both
Damascus and Hamath, which had belonged to Yaudi,[b] are they
not written in the book of the annals of the kings of Israel? 29Jero-
boam rested with his fathers, the kings of Israel. And Zechariah
his son succeeded him as king.

*Azariah King of Judah*

**15** IN THE twenty-seventh year of Jeroboam king of Israel,
Azariah son of Amaziah king of Judah began to reign. 2He
was sixteen years old when he became king, and he reigned in
Jerusalem fifty-two years. His mother's name was Jecoliah; she
was from Jerusalem. 3He did what was right in the eyes of the
LORD, just as his father Amaziah had done. 4The high places,
however, were not removed; the people continued to offer sacrifices and burn incense there.
5The LORD afflicted the king with leprosy[c] until the day he died,
and he lived in a separate house.[d] Jotham the king's son had
charge of the palace and governed the people of the land.
6As for the other events of Azariah's reign, and all he did, are
they not written in the book of the annals of the kings of Judah?
7Azariah rested with his fathers and was buried near them in the
City of David. And Jotham his son succeeded him as king.

*Zechariah King of Israel*

8In the thirty-eighth year of Azariah king of Judah, Zechariah
son of Jeroboam became king of Israel in Samaria, and he reigned
six months. 9He did evil in the eyes of the LORD, as his fathers had
done. He did not turn away from the sins of Jeroboam son of
Nebat, which he had caused Israel to commit.
10Shallum son of Jabesh conspired against Zechariah. He attacked him in front of the people,[e] assassinated him and succeeded him as king. 11The other events of Zechariah's reign are
written in the book of the annals of the kings of Israel. 12So the
word of the LORD spoken to Jehu was fulfilled: "Your descendants
will sit on the throne of Israel to the fourth generation."[f]

*Shallum King of Israel*

13Shallum son of Jabesh became king in the thirty-ninth year of
Uzziah king of Judah, and he reigned in Samaria one month.
14Then Menahem son of Gadi went from Tirzah up to Samaria. He
attacked Shallum son of Jabesh in Samaria, assassinated him and
succeeded him as king.
15The other events of Shallum's reign, and the conspiracy he
led, are written in the book of the annals of the kings of Israel.
16At that time Menahem, starting out from Tirzah, attacked
Tiphsah and everyone in the city and its vicinity, because they
refused to open their gates. He sacked Tiphsah and ripped open
all the pregnant women.

*Menahem King of Israel*

17In the thirty-ninth year of Azariah king of Judah, Menahem
son of Gadi became king of Israel, and he reigned in Samaria ten
years. 18He did evil in the eyes of the LORD. During his entire reign
he did not turn away from the sins of Jeroboam son of Nebat,
which he had caused Israel to commit.

**NIV** [b] *28* Or *Judah* [c] *5* The Hebrew word was used for various diseases affecting the skin—not necessarily leprosy. [d] *5* Or *in a house where he was relieved of responsibility* [e] *10* Hebrew; some Septuagint manuscripts *in Ibleam* [f] *12* 2 Kings 10:30

## King James

19 *And* Pul the king of Assyria came against the land: and
Menahem gave Pul a thousand talents of silver, that his hand
might be with him to confirm the kingdom in his hand.
20 And Menahem exacted the money of Israel, *even* of all the
mighty men of wealth, of each man fifty shekels of silver, to give
to the king of Assyria. So the king of Assyria turned back, and
stayed not there in the land.
21 ¶ And the rest of the acts of Menahem, and all that he did,
*are* they not written in the book of the chronicles of the kings of
Israel?
22 And Menahem slept with his fathers; and Pekahiah his son
reigned in his stead.
23 ¶ In the fiftieth year of Azariah king of Judah Pekahiah the son
of Menahem began to reign over Israel in Samaria, *and reigned* two
years.
24 And he did *that which was* evil in the sight of the LORD: he
departed not from the sins of Jeroboam the son of Nebat, who
made Israel to sin.
25 But Pekah the son of Remaliah, a captain of his, conspired
against him, and smote him in Samaria, in the palace of the king's
house, with Argob and Arieh, and with him fifty men of the
Gileadites: and he killed him, and reigned in his room.
26 And the rest of the acts of Pekahiah, and all that he did,
behold, they *are* written in the book of the chronicles of the kings
of Israel.
27 ¶ In the two and fiftieth year of Azariah king of Judah Pekah
the son of Remaliah began to reign over Israel in Samaria, *and
reigned* twenty years.
28 And he did *that which was* evil in the sight of the LORD: he
departed not from the sins of Jeroboam the son of Nebat, who
made Israel to sin.
29 In the days of Pekah king of Israel came Tiglath-pileser king
of Assyria, and took Ijon, and Abel-beth-maachah, and Janoah,
and Kedesh, and Hazor, and Gilead, and Galilee, all the land of
Naphtali, and carried them captive to Assyria.
30 And Hoshea the son of Elah made a conspiracy against Pekah
the son of Remaliah, and smote him, and slew him, and reigned
in his stead, in the twentieth year of Jotham the son of Uzziah.
31 And the rest of the acts of Pekah, and all that he did, behold,
they *are* written in the book of the chronicles of the kings of Israel.
32 ¶ In the second year of Pekah the son of Remaliah king of
Israel began Jotham the son of Uzziah king of Judah to reign.
33 Five and twenty years old was he when he began to reign, and
he reigned sixteen years in Jerusalem. And his mother's name *was*
Jerusha, the daughter of Zadok.
34 And he did *that which was* right in the sight of the LORD: he
did according to all that his father Uzziah had done.
35 ¶ Howbeit the high places were not removed: the people
sacrificed and burned incense still in the high places. He built the
higher gate of the house of the LORD.
36 ¶ Now the rest of the acts of Jotham, and all that he did, *are*
they not written in the book of the chronicles of the kings of Judah?
37 In those days the LORD began to send against Judah Rezin the
king of Syria, and Pekah the son of Remaliah.
38 And Jotham slept with his fathers, and was buried with his
fathers in the city of David his father: and Ahaz his son reigned
in his stead.

**16** IN THE seventeenth year of Pekah the son of Remaliah
Ahaz the son of Jotham king of Judah began to reign.

## Amplified

19 There came against the land Pul king of Assyria; and Menahem gave Pul 1,000 talents of silver, that he might help him to
confirm his kingship.
20 Menahem exacted the money from Israel, from all the men of
wealth, of each man fifty shekels of silver, to give to the king of
Assyria. So the king of Assyria turned back, and did not stay in
the land.
21 The rest of Menahem's acts, all that he did, are they not
written in the Book of the Chronicles of the Kings of Israel?
22 Menahem slept with his fathers; Pekahiah his son reigned in
his stead.
23 In the fiftieth year of Azariah king of Judah Pekahiah son of
Menahem began his two years' reign over Israel in Samaria.
24 He did evil in the sight of the Lord; he did not depart from
the sins of Jeroboam [I] son of Nebat, which he made Israel sin.
25 But Pekah son of Remaliah, his captain, conspired against
[Pekahiah], and attacked him in Samaria, in the citadel of the
king's house, with Argob and Arieh; [for] with [Pekah] were fifty
Gileadites; and he killed him, and reigned in his stead.
26 The rest of the acts of Pekahiah, all he did, see, they are
written in the Book of Chronicles of the Kings of Israel.
27 In the fifty-second year of Azariah king of Judah Pekah son
of Remaliah began his twenty-year reign over Israel in Samaria.
28 He did evil in the Lord's sight; he did not depart from the sins
of Jeroboam [I] son of Nebat, which he made Israel sin.
29 In the days of Pekah king of Israel Tiglath-pileser king of
Assyria came and took Ijon, Abel-beth-maacah, Janoah, Kedesh,
Hazor, Gilead, and Galilee, all the land of Naphtali; and carried the
people captive to Assyria.
30 Hoshea son of Elah conspired against Pekah son of Remaliah
[of Israel]; he smote and killed him, and reigned in his stead, in
the twentieth year of Jotham son of Uzziah, king of Judah.
31 The rest of Pekah's acts, all that he did, behold, they are
written in the Book of the Chronicles of Israel's Kings.
32 In the second year of Pekah son of Remaliah king of Israel
Jotham son of Uzziah, king of Judah, became king.
33 When twenty-five years old he began his reign of sixteen
years in Jerusalem. His mother was Jerusha daughter of Zadok.
34 He did right in the Lord's sight, according to all his father
Uzziah had done.
35 Yet the high places were not removed; the people sacrificed
and burned incense still on the high places. He built the upper gate
of the house of the Lord.
36 The rest of the acts of Jotham, all he did, are they not written
in the Book of the Chronicles of Judah's Kings?
37 In those days the Lord began sending Rezin king of Syria and
Pekah son of Remaliah against Judah.
38 Jotham slept with his fathers, and was buried [with them] in
the city of David his [forefather]; Ahaz his son succeeded him.

**16** IN THE seventeenth year of Pekah son of Remaliah, Ahaz
son of Jotham, king of Judah, became king.

## New American Standard

19¶ Pul, king of Assyria, came against the land, and Menahem gave Pul a thousand talents of silver so that his hand might be with him to strengthen the kingdom under his rule.
20 Then Menahem exacted the money from Israel, even from all the mighty men of wealth, from each man fifty shekels of silver to pay the king of Assyria. So the king of Assyria returned and did not remain there in the land.
21 Now the rest of the acts of Menahem and all that he did, are they not written in the Book of the Chronicles of the Kings of Israel?
22 And Menahem slept with his fathers, and Pekahiah his son became king in his place.

*Pekahiah over Israel*

23¶ In the fiftieth year of Azariah king of Judah, Pekahiah son of Menahem became king over Israel in Samaria, *and reigned* two years.
24 And he did evil in the sight of the LORD; he did not depart from the sins of Jeroboam son of Nebat, which he made Israel sin.
25 Then Pekah son of Remaliah, his officer, conspired against him and struck him in Samaria, in the castle of the king's house with Argob and Arieh; and with him were fifty men of the Gileadites, and he killed him and became king in his place.
26 Now the rest of the acts of Pekahiah and all that he did, behold they are written in the Book of the Chronicles of the Kings of Israel.

*Pekah over Israel*

27¶ In the fifty-second year of Azariah king of Judah, Pekah son of Remaliah became king over Israel in Samaria, *and reigned* twenty years.
28 And he did evil in the sight of the LORD; he did not depart from the sins of Jeroboam son of Nebat, which he made Israel sin.
29¶ In the days of Pekah king of Israel, Tiglath-pileser king of Assyria came and captured Ijon and Abel-beth-maacah and Janoah and Kedesh and Hazor and Gilead and Galilee, all the land of Naphtali; and he carried them captive to Assyria.
30 And Hoshea the son of Elah made a conspiracy against Pekah the son of Remaliah, and struck him and put him to death and became king in his place, in the twentieth year of Jotham the son of Uzziah.
31 Now the rest of the acts of Pekah and all that he did, behold, they are written in the Book of the Chronicles of the Kings of Israel.

*Jotham over Judah*

32¶ In the second year of Pekah the son of Remaliah king of Israel, Jotham the son of Uzziah king of Judah became king.
33 He was twenty-five years old when he became king, and he reigned sixteen years in Jerusalem; and his mother's name *was* Jerusha the daughter of Zadok.
34 And he did what was right in the sight of the LORD; he did according to all that his father Uzziah had done.
35 Only the high places were not taken away; the people still sacrificed and burned incense on the high places. He built the upper gate of the house of the LORD.
36 Now the rest of the acts of Jotham and all that he did, are they not written in the Book of the Chronicles of the Kings of Judah?
37 In those days the LORD began to send Rezin king of Aram and Pekah the son of Remaliah against Judah.
38 And Jotham slept with his fathers, and he was buried with his fathers in the city of David his father; and Ahaz his son became king in his place.

*Ahaz Reigns over Judah*

**16** IN THE seventeenth year of Pekah the son of Remaliah, Ahaz the son of Jotham, king of Judah, became king.

## New International

19 Then Pul[a] king of Assyria invaded the land, and Menahem
gave him a thousand talents[b] of silver to gain his support and
strengthen his own hold on the kingdom. 20 Menahem exacted this
money from Israel. Every wealthy man had to contribute fifty
shekels[c] of silver to be given to the king of Assyria. So the king
of Assyria withdrew and stayed in the land no longer.
21 As for the other events of Menahem's reign, and all he did,
are they not written in the book of the annals of the kings of Israel?
22 Menahem rested with his fathers. And Pekahiah his son succeeded him as king.

*Pekahiah King of Israel*

23 In the fiftieth year of Azariah king of Judah, Pekahiah son of
Menahem became king of Israel in Samaria, and he reigned two
years. 24 Pekahiah did evil in the eyes of the LORD. He did not turn
away from the sins of Jeroboam son of Nebat, which he had caused
Israel to commit. 25 One of his chief officers, Pekah son of Remaliah, conspired against him. Taking fifty men of Gilead with him,
he assassinated Pekahiah, along with Argob and Arieh, in the
citadel of the royal palace at Samaria. So Pekah killed Pekahiah and
succeeded him as king.
26 The other events of Pekahiah's reign, and all he did, are
written in the book of the annals of the kings of Israel.

*Pekah King of Israel*

27 In the fifty-second year of Azariah king of Judah, Pekah son
of Remaliah became king of Israel in Samaria, and he reigned
twenty years. 28 He did evil in the eyes of the LORD. He did not turn
away from the sins of Jeroboam son of Nebat, which he had caused
Israel to commit.
29 In the time of Pekah king of Israel, Tiglath-Pileser king of
Assyria came and took Ijon, Abel Beth Maacah, Janoah, Kedesh
and Hazor. He took Gilead and Galilee, including all the land of
Naphtali, and deported the people to Assyria. 30 Then Hoshea son
of Elah conspired against Pekah son of Remaliah. He attacked and
assassinated him, and then succeeded him as king in the twentieth
year of Jotham son of Uzziah.
31 As for the other events of Pekah's reign, and all he did, are
they not written in the book of the annals of the kings of Israel?

*Jotham King of Judah*

32 In the second year of Pekah son of Remaliah king of Israel,
Jotham son of Uzziah king of Judah began to reign. 33 He was
twenty-five years old when he became king, and he reigned in
Jerusalem sixteen years. His mother's name was Jerusha daughter
of Zadok. 34 He did what was right in the eyes of the LORD, just as
his father Uzziah had done. 35 The high places, however, were not
removed; the people continued to offer sacrifices and burn incense
there. Jotham rebuilt the Upper Gate of the temple of the LORD.
36 As for the other events of Jotham's reign, and what he did,
are they not written in the book of the annals of the kings of Judah?
37 (In those days the LORD began to send Rezin king of Aram and
Pekah son of Remaliah against Judah.) 38 Jotham rested with his
fathers and was buried with them in the City of David, the city of
his father. And Ahaz his son succeeded him as king.

*Ahaz King of Judah*

**16** IN THE seventeenth year of Pekah son of Remaliah, Ahaz
son of Jotham king of Judah began to reign. 2 Ahaz was

NIV [a] *19* Also called *Tiglath-Pileser* [b] *19* That is, about 37 tons (about 34 metric tons) [c] *20* That is, about 1 1/4 pounds (about 0.6 kilogram)

## King James

2 Twenty years old *was* Ahaz when he began to reign, and reigned sixteen years in Jerusalem, and did not *that which was* right in the sight of the LORD his God, like David his father.

3 But he walked in the way of the kings of Israel, yea, and made his son to pass through the fire, according to the abominations of the heathen, whom the LORD cast out from before the children of Israel.

4 And he sacrificed and burnt incense in the high places, and on the hills, and under every green tree.

5 ¶ Then Rezin king of Syria and Pekah son of Remaliah king of Israel came up to Jerusalem to war: and they besieged Ahaz, but could not overcome *him*.

6 At that time Rezin king of Syria recovered Elath to Syria, and drave the Jews from Elath: and the Syrians came to Elath, and dwelt there unto this day.

7 So Ahaz sent messengers to Tiglath-pileser king of Assyria, saying, I *am* thy servant and thy son: come up, and save me out of the hand of the king of Syria, and out of the hand of the king of Israel, which rise up against me.

8 And Ahaz took the silver and gold that was found in the house of the LORD, and in the treasures of the king's house, and sent *it for* a present to the king of Assyria.

9 And the king of Assyria hearkened unto him: for the king of Assyria went up against Damascus, and took it, and carried *the people of* it captive to Kir, and slew Rezin.

10 ¶ And king Ahaz went to Damascus to meet Tiglath-pileser king of Assyria, and saw an altar that *was* at Damascus: and king Ahaz sent to Urijah the priest the fashion of the altar, and the pattern of it, according to all the workmanship thereof.

11 And Urijah the priest built an altar according to all that king Ahaz had sent from Damascus: so Urijah the priest made *it* against king Ahaz came from Damascus.

12 And when the king was come from Damascus, the king saw the altar: and the king approached to the altar, and offered thereon.

13 And he burnt his burnt offering and his meat offering, and poured his drink offering, and sprinkled the blood of his peace offerings, upon the altar.

14 And he brought also the brasen altar, which *was* before the LORD, from the forefront of the house, from between the altar and the house of the LORD, and put it on the north side of the altar.

15 And king Ahaz commanded Urijah the priest, saying, Upon the great altar burn the morning burnt offering, and the evening meat offering, and the king's burnt sacrifice, and his meat offering, with the burnt offering of all the people of the land, and their meat offering, and their drink offerings; and sprinkle upon it all the blood of the burnt offering, and all the blood of the sacrifice: and the brasen altar shall be for me to inquire *by*.

16 Thus did Urijah the priest, according to all that king Ahaz commanded.

17 ¶ And king Ahaz cut off the borders of the bases, and removed the laver from off them; and took down the sea from off the brasen oxen that *were* under it, and put it upon a pavement of stones.

18 And the covert for the sabbath that they had built in the house, and the king's entry without, turned he from the house of the LORD for the king of Assyria.

19 ¶ Now the rest of the acts of Ahaz which he did, *are* they not written in the book of the chronicles of the kings of Judah?

20 And Ahaz slept with his fathers, and was buried with his fathers in the city of David: and Hezekiah his son reigned in his stead.

## Amplified

2 Ahaz was twenty years old when he began his sixteen years' reign in Jerusalem. He did not do right in the sight of the Lord his God, like David his [forefather].

3 But he walked in the way of Israel's kings, yes, and made his son pass through the fire [and offered him as a sacrifice] in accord with the abominable [idolatrous] practices of the [heathen] nations, whom the Lord drove out before the Israelites.

4 He sacrificed and burned incense in the high places, on the hills, and under every green tree.

5 Then Rezin king of Syria and Pekah son of Remaliah, king of Israel, came up to Jerusalem to wage war; they besieged Ahaz but could not conquer him.

6 At that time Rezin king of Syria got back Elath [in Edom] for Syria and drove the Jews from [it]. The Syrians came to Elath, and dwell there to this day.

7 So Ahaz sent messengers to Tiglath-pileser king of Assyria, saying, I am your servant and son: come up, and save me out of the hand of the kings of Syria and of Israel, who are attacking me.

8 And Ahaz took the silver and gold in the house of the Lord and in the treasuries of the king's house, and sent a present to the king of Assyria.

9 Assyria's king hearkened to him; he went up against Damascus, took it, carried its people captive to Kir, and slew Rezin.

10 King Ahaz went to Damascus to meet Tiglath-pileser king of Assyria, and saw there their [heathen] altar. King Ahaz sent to Urijah the priest a model of the altar, and an exact pattern for its construction.

11 So Urijah the priest built an altar according to all that King Ahaz had sent from Damascus, finishing it before King Ahaz returned.

12 When the king came from Damascus he looked at the altar, and offered on it.

13 King Ahaz burned his burnt offering, his cereal offering, poured his drink offering, and dashed the blood of his peace offerings upon that altar.

14 The bronze altar which was before the Lord he removed from the front of the house, from between his [new] altar and the house of the Lord, and put it on the north side of his altar.

15 And King Ahaz commanded Urijah the priest, Upon the principal [the new] altar burn the morning burnt offering, the evening cereal offering, the king's burnt sacrifice and his cereal offering, with the burnt offering and cereal offering and drink offering of all the people of the land; and dash upon the [new] altar all the blood of the burnt offering and the sacrifice. But the [old] bronze altar shall be kept for me to use to inquire by of the Lord.

16 Urijah the priest did all this as King Ahaz commanded.

17 [To keep Assyria's king from getting them] King Ahaz cut off the panels of the bases [of the ten lavers] and removed the laver from each of them; and he took down the sea from off the bronze oxen that were under it, and put it upon stone supports.

18 And the covered way for the sabbath that they had built in the temple court, and the king's outer entrance, he removed from the house of the Lord because of the king of Assyria [who if he heard of them might seize them].

19 The rest of the acts of Ahaz, are they not written in the book of the Chronicles of the Kings of Judah?

20 Ahaz slept with his fathers, and was buried [with them] in the city of David. Hezekiah his son reigned in his stead.

## New American Standard

2Ahaz *was* twenty years old when he became king, and he reigned sixteen years in Jerusalem; and he did not do what was right in the sight of the LORD his God, as his father David *had done.*

3But he walked in the way of the kings of Israel, and even made his son pass through the fire, according to the abominations of the nations whom the LORD had driven out from before the sons of Israel.

4And he sacrificed and burned incense on the high places and on the hills and under every green tree.

5¶ Then Rezin king of Aram and Pekah son of Remaliah, king of Israel, came up to Jerusalem to *wage* war; and they besieged Ahaz, but could not overcome him.

6At that time Rezin king of Aram recovered Elath for Aram, and cleared the Judeans out of Elath entirely; and the Arameans came to Elath, and have lived there to this day.

*Ahaz Seeks Help of Aram*

7¶ So Ahaz sent messengers to Tiglath-pileser king of Assyria, saying, "I am your servant and your son; come up and deliver me from the hand of the king of Aram, and from the hand of the king of Israel, who are rising up against me."

8And Ahaz took the silver and gold that was found in the house of the LORD and in the treasuries of the king's house, and sent a present to the king of Assyria.

9So the king of Assyria listened to him; and the king of Assyria went up against Damascus and captured it, and carried *the people of* it away into exile to Kir, and put Rezin to death.

*Damascus Falls*

10¶ Now King Ahaz went to Damascus to meet Tiglath-pileser king of Assyria, and saw the altar which *was* at Damascus; and King Ahaz sent to Urijah the priest the pattern of the altar and its model, according to all its workmanship.

11So Urijah the priest built an altar; according to all that King Ahaz had sent from Damascus, thus Urijah the priest made *it,* before the coming of King Ahaz from Damascus.

12And when the king came from Damascus, the king saw the altar; then the king approached the altar and went up to it,

13and burned his burnt offering and his meal offering, and poured his libation and sprinkled the blood of his peace offerings on the altar.

14And the bronze altar, which *was* before the LORD, he brought from the front of the house, from between *his* altar and the house of the LORD, and he put it on the north side of *his* altar.

15Then King Ahaz commanded Urijah the priest, saying, "Upon the great altar burn the morning burnt offering and the evening meal offering and the king's burnt offering and his meal offering, with the burnt offering of all the people of the land and their meal offering and their libations; and sprinkle on it all the blood of the burnt offering and all the blood of the sacrifice. But the bronze altar shall be for me to inquire *by.*"

16So Urijah the priest did according to all that King Ahaz commanded.

17¶ Then King Ahaz cut off the borders of the stands, and removed the laver from them; he also took down the sea from the bronze oxen which were under it, and put it on a pavement of stone.

18And the covered way for the sabbath which they had built in the house, and the outer entry of the king, he removed from the house of the LORD because of the king of Assyria.

*Hezekiah Reigns over Judah*

19Now the rest of the acts of Ahaz which he did, are they not written in the Book of the Chronicles of the Kings of Judah?

20So Ahaz slept with his fathers, and was buried with his fathers in the city of David; and his son Hezekiah reigned in his place.

## New International

twenty years old when he became king, and he reigned in Jerusalem sixteen years. Unlike David his father, he did not do what was
right in the eyes of the LORD his God. 3He walked in the ways of
the kings of Israel and even sacrificed his son in[a] the fire, following
the detestable ways of the nations the LORD had driven out before
the Israelites. 4He offered sacrifices and burned incense at the high
places, on the hilltops and under every spreading tree.
5Then Rezin king of Aram and Pekah son of Remaliah king of
Israel marched up to fight against Jerusalem and besieged Ahaz,
but they could not overpower him. 6At that time, Rezin king of
Aram recovered Elath for Aram by driving out the men of Judah.
Edomites then moved into Elath and have lived there to this day.
7Ahaz sent messengers to say to Tiglath-Pileser king of Assyria,
"I am your servant and vassal. Come up and save me out of the
hand of the king of Aram and of the king of Israel, who are
attacking me." 8And Ahaz took the silver and gold found in the
temple of the LORD and in the treasuries of the royal palace and
sent it as a gift to the king of Assyria. 9The king of Assyria complied
by attacking Damascus and capturing it. He deported its inhabitants to Kir and put Rezin to death.
10Then King Ahaz went to Damascus to meet Tiglath-Pileser
king of Assyria. He saw an altar in Damascus and sent to Uriah
the priest a sketch of the altar, with detailed plans for its construction. 11So Uriah the priest built an altar in accordance with all the
plans that King Ahaz had sent from Damascus and finished it
before King Ahaz returned. 12When the king came back from
Damascus and saw the altar, he approached it and presented
offerings[b] on it. 13He offered up his burnt offering and grain
offering, poured out his drink offering, and sprinkled the blood of
his fellowship offerings[c] on the altar. 14The bronze altar that stood
before the LORD he brought from the front of the temple—from
between the new altar and the temple of the LORD—and put it on
the north side of the new altar.
15King Ahaz then gave these orders to Uriah the priest: "On the
large new altar, offer the morning burnt offering and the evening
grain offering, the king's burnt offering and his grain offering, and
the burnt offering of all the people of the land, and their grain
offering and their drink offering. Sprinkle on the altar all the blood
of the burnt offerings and sacrifices. But I will use the bronze altar
for seeking guidance." 16And Uriah the priest did just as King
Ahaz had ordered.
17King Ahaz took away the side panels and removed the basins
from the movable stands. He removed the Sea from the bronze
bulls that supported it and set it on a stone base. 18He took away
the Sabbath canopy[d] that had been built at the temple and removed the royal entryway outside the temple of the LORD, in
deference to the king of Assyria.
19As for the other events of the reign of Ahaz, and what he did,
are they not written in the book of the annals of the kings of Judah?
20Ahaz rested with his fathers and was buried with them in the
City of David. And Hezekiah his son succeeded him as king.

NIV [a] 3 Or *even made his son pass through* [b] 12 Or *and went up* [c] 13 Traditionally *peace offerings* [d] 18 Or *the dais of his throne* (see Septuagint)

## King James

**17** IN THE twelfth year of Ahaz king of Judah began Hoshea the son of Elah to reign in Samaria over Israel nine years.

2 And he did *that which was* evil in the sight of the LORD, but not as the kings of Israel that were before him.

3 ¶ Against him came up Shalmaneser king of Assyria; and Hoshea became his servant, and gave him presents.

4 And the king of Assyria found conspiracy in Hoshea: for he had sent messengers to So king of Egypt, and brought no present to the king of Assyria, as *he had done* year by year: therefore the king of Assyria shut him up, and bound him in prison.

5 ¶ Then the king of Assyria came up throughout all the land, and went up to Samaria, and besieged it three years.

6 ¶ In the ninth year of Hoshea the king of Assyria took Samaria, and carried Israel away into Assyria, and placed them in Halah and in Habor *by* the river of Gozan, and in the cities of the Medes.

7 For *so* it was, that the children of Israel had sinned against the LORD their God, which had brought them up out of the land of Egypt, from under the hand of Pharaoh king of Egypt, and had feared other gods,

8 And walked in the statutes of the heathen, whom the LORD cast out from before the children of Israel, and of the kings of Israel, which they had made.

9 And the children of Israel did secretly *those* things that *were* not right against the LORD their God, and they built them high places in all their cities, from the tower of the watchmen to the fenced city.

10 And they set them up images and groves in every high hill, and under every green tree:

11 And there they burnt incense in all the high places, as *did* the heathen whom the LORD carried away before them; and wrought wicked things to provoke the LORD to anger:

12 For they served idols, whereof the LORD had said unto them, Ye shall not do this thing.

13 Yet the LORD testified against Israel, and against Judah, by all the prophets, *and by* all the seers, saying, Turn ye from your evil ways, and keep my commandments *and* my statutes, according to all the law which I commanded your fathers, and which I sent to you by my servants the prophets.

14 Notwithstanding they would not hear, but hardened their necks, like to the neck of their fathers, that did not believe in the LORD their God.

15 And they rejected his statutes, and his covenant that he made with their fathers, and his testimonies which he testified against them; and they followed vanity, and became vain, and went after the heathen that *were* round about them, *concerning* whom the LORD had charged them, that they should not do like them.

16 And they left all the commandments of the LORD their God, and made them molten images, *even* two calves, and made a grove, and worshipped all the host of heaven, and served Baal.

17 And they caused their sons and their daughters to pass through the fire, and used divination and enchantments, and sold themselves to do evil in the sight of the LORD, to provoke him to anger.

18 Therefore the LORD was very angry with Israel, and removed them out of his sight: there was none left but the tribe of Judah only.

19 Also Judah kept not the commandments of the LORD their God, but walked in the statutes of Israel which they made.

20 And the LORD rejected all the seed of Israel, and afflicted them, and delivered them into the hand of spoilers, until he had cast them out of his sight.

## Amplified

**17** IN THE twelfth year of Ahaz king of Judah Hoshea son of Elah began his nine year reign in Samaria over Israel.

2 He did evil in the sight of the Lord, but not as Israel's kings before him did.

3 Against him came up Shalmaneser king of Assyria; and Hoshea became his servant, and brought him tribute.

4 But the king of Assyria found treachery in Hoshea; for he had sent messengers to So king of Egypt, and offered no tribute to the king of Assyria, as he had done year by year; therefore the king of Assyria shut him up, and bound him in prison.

5 Then the king of Assyria invaded all the land, and went up to Samaria, and besieged it three years.

6 In the ninth year of Hoshea the king of Assyria took Samaria, and carried the Israelites away into Assyria, and placed them in Halah and in Habor by the river of Gozan, and in the cities of the Medes.

7 This was so because the Israelites had sinned against the Lord their God, Who had brought them out of the land of Egypt, from under the hand of Pharaoh king of Egypt, and they had feared other gods,

8 And walked in the customs of the [heathen] nations, whom the Lord drove out before the Israelites, customs the kings of Israel had introduced.

9 The Israelites did secretly against the Lord their God things not right. They built for themselves high places in all their towns, from [lonely] watchtower to [populous] fortified city.

10 They set up for themselves pillars and Asherim on every high hill and under every green tree.

11 There they burned incense on all the high places, as did the nations whom the Lord carried away before them; and did wicked things provoking the Lord to anger.

12 And they served idols, of which the Lord had said to them, You shall not do this thing.

13 Yet the Lord warned Israel and Judah by all the prophets and all the seers, saying, Turn from your evil ways, and keep My commandments and My statutes, according to all the law which I commanded your fathers, and which I sent to you by My servants the prophets.

14 Yet they would not hear, but hardened their necks, as did their fathers who did not believe [trust in, rely on and remain steadfast] to the Lord their God.

15 They despised *and* rejected His statutes, and His covenant which He made with their fathers, and His warnings to them, and they followed vanity (that is, false gods) [falsehood, emptiness, and futility; and they themselves and their prayers] became false [empty and futile]. They went after the heathen round about them, of whom the Lord had charged them, that they should not do as they did.

16 And they forsook all the commandments of the Lord their God, and made them molten images, even two calves, and made an Asherah, and worshiped all the [starry] host of the heavens, and served Baal.

17 They caused their sons and their daughters to pass through the fire, and used divination and enchantments, and sold themselves to do evil in the sight of the Lord, provoking Him to anger.

18 Therefore the Lord was very angry with Israel, and removed them out of His sight. None was left but the tribe of Judah only.

19 Judah also did not keep the commandments of the Lord their God, but walked in the customs which Israel introduced.

20 The Lord rejected all the descendants of Israel, and afflicted them, and delivered them into the hand of spoilers, until He had cast them out of His sight.

## New American Standard

*Hoshea Reigns over Israel*

**17** IN THE twelfth year of Ahaz king of Judah, Hoshea the son of Elah became king over Israel in Samaria, *and reigned* nine years.

2And he did evil in the sight of the LORD, only not as the kings of Israel who were before him.

3Shalmaneser king of Assyria came up against him, and Hoshea became his servant and paid him tribute.

4But the king of Assyria found conspiracy in Hoshea, who had sent messengers to So king of Egypt and had offered no tribute to the king of Assyria, as *he had done* year by year; so the king of Assyria shut him up and bound him in prison.

5Then the king of Assyria invaded the whole land and went up to Samaria and besieged it three years.

*Israel Captive*

6In the ninth year of Hoshea, the king of Assyria captured Samaria and carried Israel away into exile to Assyria, and settled them in Halah and Habor, *on* the river of Gozan, and in the cities of the Medes.

*Why Israel Fell*

7¶ Now *this* came about, because the sons of Israel had sinned against the LORD their God, who had brought them up from the land of Egypt from under the hand of Pharaoh, king of Egypt, and they had [a]feared other gods

8and walked in the customs of the nations whom the LORD had driven out before the sons of Israel, and *in the customs* of the kings of Israel which they had introduced.

9And the sons of Israel did things secretly which were not right, against the LORD their God. Moreover, they built for themselves high places in all their towns, from watchtower to fortified city.

10And they set for themselves *sacred* pillars and [b]Asherim on every high hill and under every green tree,

11and there they burned incense on all the high places as the nations *did* which the LORD had carried away to exile before them; and they did evil things provoking the LORD.

12And they served idols, concerning which the LORD had said to them, "You shall not do this thing."

13Yet the LORD warned Israel and Judah, through all His prophets *and* every seer, saying, "Turn from your evil ways and keep My commandments, My statutes according to all the law which I commanded your fathers, and which I sent to you through My servants the prophets."

14However, they did not listen, but stiffened their neck like their fathers, who did not believe in the LORD their God.

15And they rejected His statutes and His covenant which He made with their fathers, and His warnings with which He warned them. And they followed vanity and became vain, and *went* after the nations which surrounded them, concerning which the LORD had commanded them not to do like them.

16And they forsook all the commandments of the LORD their God and made for themselves molten images, *even* two calves, and made an Asherah and worshiped all the host of heaven and served Baal.

17Then they made their sons and their daughters pass through the fire, and practiced divination and enchantments, and sold themselves to do evil in the sight of the LORD, provoking Him.

18So the LORD was very angry with Israel, and removed them from His sight; none was left except the tribe of Judah.

19¶ Also Judah did not keep the commandments of the LORD their God, but walked in the customs which Israel had introduced.

20And the LORD rejected all the descendants of Israel and afflicted them and gave them into the hand of plunderers, until He had cast them out of His sight.

NAS [a] Lit., *revered,* and so throughout this context [b] I.e., wooden symbols of a female deity

## New International

*Hoshea Last King of Israel*

**17** IN THE twelfth year of Ahaz king of Judah, Hoshea son
of Elah became king of Israel in Samaria, and he reigned
nine years. 2He did evil in the eyes of the LORD, but not like the
kings of Israel who preceded him.
3Shalmaneser king of Assyria came up to attack Hoshea, who
had been Shalmaneser's vassal and had paid him tribute. 4But the
king of Assyria discovered that Hoshea was a traitor, for he had
sent envoys to So[c] king of Egypt, and he no longer paid tribute
to the king of Assyria, as he had done year by year. Therefore
Shalmaneser seized him and put him in prison. 5The king of Assyria invaded the entire land, marched against Samaria and laid
siege to it for three years. 6In the ninth year of Hoshea, the king
of Assyria captured Samaria and deported the Israelites to Assyria.
He settled them in Halah, in Gozan on the Habor River and in the
towns of the Medes.

*Israel Exiled Because of Sin*

7All this took place because the Israelites had sinned against the
LORD their God, who had brought them up out of Egypt from
under the power of Pharaoh king of Egypt. They worshiped other
gods 8and followed the practices of the nations the LORD had
driven out before them, as well as the practices that the kings of
Israel had introduced. 9The Israelites secretly did things against
the LORD their God that were not right. From watchtower to fortified city they built themselves high places in all their towns. 10They
set up sacred stones and Asherah poles on every high hill and
under every spreading tree. 11At every high place they burned
incense, as the nations whom the LORD had driven out before them
had done. They did wicked things that provoked the LORD to
anger. 12They worshiped idols, though the LORD had said, "You
shall not do this."[d] 13The LORD warned Israel and Judah through
all his prophets and seers: "Turn from your evil ways. Observe my
commands and decrees, in accordance with the entire Law that I
commanded your fathers to obey and that I delivered to you
through my servants the prophets."
14But they would not listen and were as stiff-necked as their
fathers, who did not trust in the LORD their God. 15They rejected
his decrees and the covenant he had made with their fathers and
the warnings he had given them. They followed worthless idols
and themselves became worthless. They imitated the nations
around them although the LORD had ordered them, "Do not do as
they do," and they did the things the LORD had forbidden them
to do.
16They forsook all the commands of the LORD their God and
made for themselves two idols cast in the shape of calves, and an
Asherah pole. They bowed down to all the starry hosts, and they
worshiped Baal. 17They sacrificed their sons and daughters in[e] the
fire. They practiced divination and sorcery and sold themselves to
do evil in the eyes of the LORD, provoking him to anger.
18So the LORD was very angry with Israel and removed them
from his presence. Only the tribe of Judah was left, 19and even
Judah did not keep the commands of the LORD their God. They
followed the practices Israel had introduced. 20Therefore the LORD
rejected all the people of Israel; he afflicted them and gave them
into the hands of plunderers, until he thrust them from his presence.

NIV [c] 4 Or *to Sais, to the; So* is possibly an abbreviation for *Osorkon.* [d] *12* Exodus 20:4, 5 [e] *17* Or *They made their sons and daughters pass through*

## King James

21 For he rent Israel from the house of David; and they made Jeroboam the son of Nebat king: and Jeroboam drave Israel from following the LORD, and made them sin a great sin.

22 For the children of Israel walked in all the sins of Jeroboam which he did; they departed not from them;

23 Until the LORD removed Israel out of his sight, as he had said by all his servants the prophets. So was Israel carried away out of their own land to Assyria unto this day.

24 ¶ And the king of Assyria brought *men* from Babylon, and from Cuthah, and from Ava, and from Hamath, and from Sepharvaim, and placed *them* in the cities of Samaria instead of the children of Israel: and they possessed Samaria, and dwelt in the cities thereof.

25 And *so* it was at the beginning of their dwelling there, *that* they feared not the LORD: therefore the LORD sent lions among them, which slew *some* of them.

26 Wherefore they spake to the king of Assyria, saying, The nations which thou hast removed, and placed in the cities of Samaria, know not the manner of the God of the land: therefore he hath sent lions among them, and, behold, they slay them, because they know not the manner of the God of the land.

27 Then the king of Assyria commanded, saying, Carry thither one of the priests whom ye brought from thence; and let them go and dwell there, and let him teach them the manner of the God of the land.

28 Then one of the priests whom they had carried away from Samaria came and dwelt in Beth-el, and taught them how they should fear the LORD.

29 Howbeit every nation made gods of their own, and put *them* in the houses of the high places which the Samaritans had made, every nation in their cities wherein they dwelt.

30 And the men of Babylon made Succoth-benoth, and the men of Cuth made Nergal, and the men of Hamath made Ashima,

31 And the Avites made Nibhaz and Tartak, and the Sepharvites burnt their children in fire to Adrammelech and Anammelech, the gods of Sepharvaim.

32 So they feared the LORD, and made unto themselves of the lowest of them priests of the high places, which sacrificed for them in the houses of the high places.

33 They feared the LORD, and served their own gods, after the manner of the nations whom they carried away from thence.

34 Unto this day they do after the former manners: they fear not the LORD, neither do they after their statutes, or after their ordinances, or after the law and commandment which the LORD commanded the children of Jacob, whom he named Israel;

35 With whom the LORD had made a covenant, and charged them, saying, Ye shall not fear other gods, nor bow yourselves to them, nor serve them, nor sacrifice to them:

36 But the LORD, who brought you up out of the land of Egypt with great power and a stretched out arm, him shall ye fear, and him shall ye worship, and to him shall ye do sacrifice.

37 And the statutes, and the ordinances, and the law, and the commandment, which he wrote for you, ye shall observe to do for evermore; and ye shall not fear other gods.

38 And the covenant that I have made with you ye shall not forget; neither shall ye fear other gods.

39 But the LORD your God ye shall fear; and he shall deliver you out of the hand of all your enemies.

40 Howbeit they did not hearken, but they did after their former manner.

41 So these nations feared the LORD, and served their graven images, both their children, and their children's children: as did their fathers, so do they unto this day.

## Amplified

21 For He tore Israel from the house of David; and they made Jeroboam son of Nebat king; and Jeroboam drew *and* drove Israel away from following the Lord, and made them sin a great sin.

22 For the Israelites walked in all the sins Jeroboam committed; they departed not from them,

23 Until the Lord removed Israel from His sight, as He had foretold by all His servants the prophets. So Israel was carried away from their own land to Assyria to this day.

24 The king of Assyria brought men from Babylon, Cuthah, Avva, Hamath, and Sepharvaim, and placed them in the cities of Samaria instead of the Israelites. They possessed Samaria, and dwelt in its cities.

25 At the beginning of their dwelling there, they did not fear *and* revere the Lord. Therefore the Lord sent lions among them, which killed some of them.

26 So the king of Assyria was told, The nations you removed and placed in the cities of Samaria, do not know the manner in which the God of the land requires their worship; therefore He has sent lions among them, and behold, they are killing them, because they do not know the manner of [worship demanded by] the God of the land.

27 Then the king of Assyria commanded, Take to Samaria one of the priests you brought from there, and let him [and his helpers] go and live there, and let him teach the people the law of the God of the land.

28 So one of the priests they had carried away from Samaria came and dwelt in Bethel, and taught them how they should fear *and* revere the Lord.

29 But every nationality still made gods of their own, and put them in the shrines of the high places which the Samaritans had made, every nationality in the city in which they dwelt.

30 The men of Babylon made [and worhiped their deity] Succoth-benoth, the men of Cuth made Nergal, the men of Hamath made Ashima,

31 The Avvites made Nibhaz and Tartak; the Sepharvites burned their children in the fire to Adrammelech and Anammelech, the gods of Sepharvaim.

32 So they feared the Lord, yet appointed from among themselves, whether high or low, priests of the high places, who sacrificed for them in the shrines of the high places.

33 They feared the Lord, yet served their own gods, as did the nations from among whom they had been carried away.

34 Unto this day they do after their former custom: they do not fear the Lord [as God sees it], neither do they obey the statutes, or the ordinances, or the law and commandment which the Lord commanded the children of Jacob whom He named Israel;

35 With whom the Lord had made a covenant, and commanded them, You shall not fear other gods or bow yourselves to them or serve them or sacrifice to them.

36 But you shall (reverently) fear, bow yourselves to, and sacrifice to the Lord, Who brought you out of the land of Egypt with great power and an outstretched arm;

37 And the statutes, ordinances, law, and commandment, which He wrote for you, you shall observe and do for evermore; you shall not fear other gods.

38 And the covenant that I have made with you you shall not forget. You shall not fear other gods,

39 But the Lord your God you shall (reverently) fear; then He will deliver you out of the hand of all your enemies.

40 However they did not listen, but they did as they had done formerly.

41 So these nations [vainly] feared the Lord, and also served their graven images, as did their children, and their children's children. As their fathers did, so do they to this day.

## New American Standard

21When He had torn Israel from the house of David, they made
Jeroboam the son of Nebat king. Then Jeroboam drove Israel away
from following the LORD, and made them commit a great sin.
22And the sons of Israel walked in all the sins of Jeroboam which
he did; they did not depart from them,
23until the LORD removed Israel from His sight, as He spoke
through all His servants the prophets. So Israel was carried away
into exile from their own land to Assyria until this day.

*Cities of Israel Filled with Strangers*

24¶ And the king of Assyria brought *men* from Babylon and from
Cuthah and from Avva and from Hamath and Sephar-vaim, and
settled *them* in the cities of Samaria in place of the sons of Israel.
So they possessed Samaria and lived in its cities.
25And it came about at the beginning of their living there, that
they did not fear the LORD; therefore the LORD sent lions among
them which killed some of them.
26So they spoke to the king of Assyria, saying, "The nations
whom you have carried away into exile in the cities of Samaria do
not know the custom of the god of the land; so he has sent lions
among them, and behold, they kill them because they do not know
the custom of the god of the land."
27¶ Then the king of Assyria commanded, saying, "Take there
one of the priests whom you carried away into exile, and let him
go and live there; and let him teach them the custom of the god
of the land."
28So one of the priests whom they had carried away into exile
from Samaria came and lived at Bethel, and taught them how they
should fear the LORD.
29But every nation still made gods of its own and put them in
the houses of the high places which the people of Samaria had
made, every nation in their cities in which they lived.
30And the men of Babylon made Succoth-benoth, the men of
Cuth made Nergal, the men of Hamath made Ashima,
31and the Avvites made Nibhaz and Tartak; and the Sepharvites
burned their children in the fire to Adrammelech and Anammelech the gods of Sepharvaim.
32They also feared the LORD and appointed from among themselves priests of the high places, who acted for them in the houses
of the high places.
33They feared the LORD and served their own gods according
to the custom of the nations from among whom they had been
carried away into exile.
34¶ To this day they do according to the earlier customs: they
do not fear the LORD, nor do they follow their statutes or their
ordinances or the law, or the commandments which the LORD
commanded the sons of Jacob, whom He named Israel;
35with whom the LORD made a covenant and commanded
them, saying, "You shall not fear other gods, nor bow down
yourselves to them nor serve them nor sacrifice to them.
36"But the LORD, who brought you up from the land of Egypt
with great power and with an outstretched arm, Him you shall
fear, and to Him you shall bow yourselves down, and to Him you
shall sacrifice.
37"And the statutes and the ordinances and the law and the
commandment, which He wrote for you, you shall observe to do
forever; and you shall not fear other gods.
38"And the covenant that I have made with you, you shall not
forget, nor shall you fear other gods.
39"But the LORD your God you shall fear; and He will deliver
you from the hand of all your enemies."
40However, they did not listen, but they did according to their
earlier custom.
41So while these nations feared the LORD, they also served their
idols; their children likewise and their grandchildren, as their fathers did, so they do to this day.

## New International

21When he tore Israel away from the house of David, they made
Jeroboam son of Nebat their king. Jeroboam enticed Israel away
from following the LORD and caused them to commit a great sin.
22The Israelites persisted in all the sins of Jeroboam and did not
turn away from them 23until the LORD removed them from his
presence, as he had warned through all his servants the prophets.
So the people of Israel were taken from their homeland into exile
in Assyria, and they are still there.

*Samaria Resettled*

24The king of Assyria brought people from Babylon, Cuthah,
Avva, Hamath and Sepharvaim and settled them in the towns of
Samaria to replace the Israelites. They took over Samaria and lived
in its towns. 25When they first lived there, they did not worship
the LORD; so he sent lions among them and they killed some of the
people. 26It was reported to the king of Assyria: "The people you
deported and resettled in the towns of Samaria do not know what
the god of that country requires. He has sent lions among them,
which are killing them off, because the people do not know what
he requires."
27Then the king of Assyria gave this order: "Have one of the
priests you took captive from Samaria go back to live there and
teach the people what the god of the land requires." 28So one of
the priests who had been exiled from Samaria came to live in Bethel
and taught them how to worship the LORD.
29Nevertheless, each national group made its own gods in the
several towns where they settled, and set them up in the shrines
the people of Samaria had made at the high places. 30The men from
Babylon made Succoth Benoth, the men from Cuthah made Nergal, and the men from Hamath made Ashima; 31the Avvites made
Nibhaz and Tartak, and the Sepharvites burned their children in
the fire as sacrifices to Adrammelech and Anammelech, the gods
of Sepharvaim. 32They worshiped the LORD, but they also appointed all sorts of their own people to officiate for them as priests
in the shrines at the high places. 33They worshiped the LORD, but
they also served their own gods in accordance with the customs
of the nations from which they had been brought.
34To this day they persist in their former practices. They neither
worship the LORD nor adhere to the decrees and ordinances, the
laws and commands that the LORD gave the descendants of Jacob,
whom he named Israel. 35When the LORD made a covenant with
the Israelites, he commanded them: "Do not worship any other
gods or bow down to them, serve them or sacrifice to them. 36But
the LORD, who brought you up out of Egypt with mighty power
and outstretched arm, is the one you must worship. To him you
shall bow down and to him offer sacrifices. 37You must always be
careful to keep the decrees and ordinances, the laws and commands he wrote for you. Do not worship other gods. 38Do not
forget the covenant I have made with you, and do not worship
other gods. 39Rather, worship the LORD your God; it is he who will
deliver you from the hand of all your enemies."
40They would not listen, however, but persisted in their former
practices. 41Even while these people were worshiping the LORD,
they were serving their idols. To this day their children and grandchildren continue to do as their fathers did.

## King James

**18** NOW IT came to pass in the third year of Hoshea son of Elah king of Israel, *that* Hezekiah the son of Ahaz king of Judah began to reign.

2 Twenty and five years old was he when he began to reign; and he reigned twenty and nine years in Jerusalem. His mother's name also *was* Abi, the daughter of Zachariah.

3 And he did *that which was* right in the sight of the LORD, according to all that David his father did.

4 ¶ He removed the high places, and brake the images, and cut down the groves, and brake in pieces the brasen serpent that Moses had made: for unto those days the children of Israel did burn incense to it: and he called it Nehushtan.

5 He trusted in the LORD God of Israel; so that after him was none like him among all the kings of Judah, nor *any* that were before him.

6 For he clave to the LORD, *and* departed not from following him, but kept his commandments, which the LORD commanded Moses.

7 And the LORD was with him; *and* he prospered whithersoever he went forth: and he rebelled against the king of Assyria, and served him not.

8 He smote the Philistines, *even* unto Gaza, and the borders thereof, from the tower of the watchmen to the fenced city.

9 ¶ And it came to pass in the fourth year of king Hezekiah, which *was* the seventh year of Hoshea son of Elah king of Israel, *that* Shalmaneser king of Assyria came up against Samaria, and besieged it.

10 And at the end of three years they took it: *even* in the sixth year of Hezekiah, that *is* the ninth year of Hoshea king of Israel, Samaria was taken.

11 And the king of Assyria did carry away Israel unto Assyria, and put them in Halah and in Habor *by* the river of Gozan, and in the cities of the Medes:

12 Because they obeyed not the voice of the LORD their God, but transgressed his covenant, *and* all that Moses the servant of the LORD commanded, and would not hear *them*, nor do *them*.

13 ¶ Now in the fourteenth year of king Hezekiah did Sennacherib king of Assyria come up against all the fenced cities of Judah, and took them.

14 And Hezekiah king of Judah sent to the king of Assyria to Lachish, saying, I have offended; return from me: that which thou puttest on me will I bear. And the king of Assyria appointed unto Hezekiah king of Judah three hundred talents of silver and thirty talents of gold.

15 And Hezekiah gave *him* all the silver that was found in the house of the LORD, and in the treasures of the king's house.

16 At that time did Hezekiah cut off *the gold from* the doors of the temple of the LORD, and *from* the pillars which Hezekiah king of Judah had overlaid, and gave it to the king of Assyria.

17 ¶ And the king of Assyria sent Tartan and Rabsaris and Rabshakeh from Lachish to king Hezekiah with a great host against Jerusalem. And they went up and came to Jerusalem. And when they were come up, they came and stood by the conduit of the upper pool, which *is* in the highway of the fuller's field.

18 And when they had called to the king, there came out to them Eliakim the son of Hilkiah, which *was* over the household, and Shebna the scribe, and Joah the son of Asaph the recorder.

19 And Rab-shakeh said unto them, Speak ye now to Hezekiah, Thus saith the great king, the king of Assyria, What confidence *is* this wherein thou trustest?

20 Thou sayest, (but *they are but* vain words,) *I have* counsel and strength for the war. Now on whom dost thou trust, that thou rebellest against me?

## Amplified

**18** IN THE third year of Hoshea son of Elah, king of Israel, Hezekiah son of Ahaz, king of Judah, began to reign.

2 He was twenty-five years old when he began his twenty-nine years' reign in Jerusalem. His mother was Abi daughter of Zechariah.

3 Hezekiah did right in the sight of the Lord, according to all that David his [forefather] had done.

4 He removed the high places, broke the images, cut down the Asherah, and broke in pieces the bronze serpent that Moses had made; for until then the Israelites had burned incense to it; but he called it Nehushtan [a brazen trifle].

5 Hezekiah trusted in, leaned on *and* was confident in the Lord God of Israel; so that neither after him nor before him was any of all the kings of Judah like him.

6 For he clung *and* held fast to the Lord, and ceased not to follow Him, but kept His commandments, as the Lord commanded Moses.

7 And the Lord was with Hezekiah; he prospered wherever he went. And he rebelled against the king of Assyria and refused to serve him.

8 He smote the Philistines, even to Gaza [the most distant city], and its borders, from the [isolated] watchtower to the [populous] fortified city.

9 In the fourth year of King Hezekiah, which was the seventh of Hoshea son of Elah, king of Israel, Shalmaneser king of Assyria came up against Samaria and besieged it.

10 After three years it was taken; in the sixth year of Hezekiah, that is the ninth year of Hoshea king of Israel, Samaria was taken.

11 The king of Assyria carried Israel away to Assyria, and put them in Halah, and on the Habor, the river of Gozan, and in the cities of the Medes;

12 Because they did not obey the voice of the Lord their God, but transgressed His covenant, even all that Moses the servant of the Lord commanded, and would not hear it or do it.

13 In the fourteenth year of Hezekiah, Sennacherib king of Assyria came up against all the fortified cities of Judah and took them.

14 Then Hezekiah king of Judah sent to the king of Assyria to Lachish, saying, I have done wrong; depart from me. What you put on me I will bear. And the king of Assyria exacted of Hezekiah king of Judah 300 talents of silver and thirty talents of gold.

15 And Hezekiah gave him all the silver that was found in the house of the Lord and in the treasuries of the king's house.

16 Then Hezekiah stripped off the gold from the doors of the temple of the Lord and from the doorposts which he as king of Judah had overlaid, and gave it to the king of Assyria.

17 And the king of Assyria sent [the high officials] the Tartan, the Rabsaris, and the Rabshakeh from Lachish to King Hezekiah at Jerusalem with a great army. They went up to Jerusalem, and when they arrived, they came and stood by the canal of the upper pool, which is on the highway to the fuller's field.

18 When they called for the king, there came out to them Eliakim son of Hilkiah, who was over the king's household, and Shebna the scribe, and Joah son of Asaph, the recorder.

19 The Rabshakeh told them, Say to Hezekiah, Thus says the great king of Assyria: What justifies this confidence of yours?

20 You say (but they are empty words), There is counsel and strength for war. Now on whom do you rely, that you rebel against me?

## New American Standard

*Hezekiah Reigns over Judah*

**18** NOW IT came about in the third year of Hoshea, the son of Elah king of Israel, that Hezekiah the son of Ahaz king of Judah became king.

2He was twenty-five years old when he became king, and he reigned twenty-nine years in Jerusalem; and his mother's name was Abi the daughter of Zechariah.

3And he did right in the sight of the LORD, according to all that his father David had done.

4He removed the high places and broke down the *sacred* pillars and cut down the [a]Asherah. He also broke in pieces the bronze serpent that Moses had made, for until those days the sons of Israel burned incense to it; and it was called [b]Nehushtan.

5He trusted in the LORD, the God of Israel; so that after him there was none like him among all the kings of Judah, nor *among those* who were before him.

6For he clung to the LORD; he did not depart from following Him, but kept His commandments, which the LORD had commanded Moses.

*Hezekiah Victorious*

7And the LORD was with him; wherever he went he prospered. And he rebelled against the king of Assyria and did not serve him.

8He defeated the Philistines as far as Gaza and its territory, from watchtower to fortified city.

9¶ Now it came about in the fourth year of King Hezekiah, which was the seventh year of Hoshea son of Elah king of Israel, that Shalmaneser king of Assyria came up against Samaria and besieged it.

10And at the end of three years they captured it; in the sixth year of Hezekiah, which was the ninth year of Hoshea king of Israel, Samaria was captured.

11Then the king of Assyria carried Israel away into exile to Assyria, and put them in Halah and on the Habor, the river of Gozan, and in the cities of the Medes,

12because they did not obey the voice of the LORD their God, but transgressed His covenant, even all that Moses the servant of the LORD commanded; they would neither listen, nor do *it*.

*Invasion of Judah*

13¶ Now in the fourteenth year of King Hezekiah, Sennacherib king of Assyria came up against all the fortified cities of Judah and seized them.

14Then Hezekiah king of Judah sent to the king of Assyria at Lachish, saying, "I have done wrong. Withdraw from me; whatever you impose on me I will bear." So the king of Assyria required of Hezekiah king of Judah three hundred talents of silver and thirty talents of gold.

15And Hezekiah gave *him* all the silver which was found in the house of the LORD, and in the treasuries of the king's house.

16At that time Hezekiah cut off *the gold from* the doors of the temple of the LORD, and *from* the doorposts which Hezekiah king of Judah had overlaid, and gave it to the king of Assyria.

17¶ Then the king of Assyria sent Tartan and Rab-saris and Rabshakeh from Lachish to King Hezekiah with a large army to Jerusalem. So they went up and came to Jerusalem. And when they went up, they came and stood by the conduit of the upper pool, which is on the highway of the [c]fuller's field.

18When they called to the king, Eliakim the son of Hilkiah, who was over the household, and Shebnah the scribe and Joah the son of Asaph the recorder, came out to them.

19Then Rabshakeh said to them, "Say now to Hezekiah, 'Thus says the great king, the king of Assyria, "What is this confidence that you have?

20"You say (but *they are* only empty words), '*I have* counsel and strength for the war.' Now on whom do you rely, that you have rebelled against me?

**NAS** [a] I.e., wooden symbol of a female deity [b] I.e., a piece of bronze [c] I.e., launderer's

## New International

*Hezekiah King of Judah*

**18** IN THE third year of Hoshea son of Elah king of Israel,
Hezekiah son of Ahaz king of Judah began to reign. 2He
was twenty-five years old when he became king, and he reigned
in Jerusalem twenty-nine years. His mother's name was Abijah[d]
daughter of Zechariah. 3He did what was right in the eyes of the
LORD, just as his father David had done. 4He removed the high
places, smashed the sacred stones and cut down the Asherah
poles. He broke into pieces the bronze snake Moses had made, for
up to that time the Israelites had been burning incense to it. (It was
called[e] Nehushtan.[f])
5Hezekiah trusted in the LORD, the God of Israel. There was no
one like him among all the kings of Judah, either before him or
after him. 6He held fast to the LORD and did not cease to follow
him; he kept the commands the LORD had given Moses. 7And the
LORD was with him; he was successful in whatever he undertook.
He rebelled against the king of Assyria and did not serve him.
8From watchtower to fortified city, he defeated the Philistines, as
far as Gaza and its territory.
9In King Hezekiah's fourth year, which was the seventh year
of Hoshea son of Elah king of Israel, Shalmaneser king of Assyria
marched against Samaria and laid siege to it. 10At the end of three
years the Assyrians took it. So Samaria was captured in Hezekiah's
sixth year, which was the ninth year of Hoshea king of Israel. 11The
king of Assyria deported Israel to Assyria and settled them in
Halah, in Gozan on the Habor River and in towns of the Medes.
12This happened because they had not obeyed the LORD their God,
but had violated his covenant—all that Moses the servant of the
LORD commanded. They neither listened to the commands nor
carried them out.
13In the fourteenth year of King Hezekiah's reign, Sennacherib
king of Assyria attacked all the fortified cities of Judah and captured them. 14So Hezekiah king of Judah sent this message to the
king of Assyria at Lachish: "I have done wrong. Withdraw from
me, and I will pay whatever you demand of me." The king of
Assyria exacted from Hezekiah king of Judah three hundred talents[g] of silver and thirty talents[h] of gold. 15So Hezekiah gave him
all the silver that was found in the temple of the LORD and in the
treasuries of the royal palace.
16At this time Hezekiah king of Judah stripped off the gold with
which he had covered the doors and doorposts of the temple of the
LORD, and gave it to the king of Assyria.

*Sennacherib Threatens Jerusalem*

17The king of Assyria sent his supreme commander, his chief
officer and his field commander with a large army, from Lachish
to King Hezekiah at Jerusalem. They came up to Jerusalem and
stopped at the aqueduct of the Upper Pool, on the road to the
Washerman's Field. 18They called for the king; and Eliakim son of
Hilkiah the palace administrator, Shebna the secretary, and Joah
son of Asaph the recorder went out to them.
19The field commander said to them, "Tell Hezekiah:

"'This is what the great king, the king of Assyria, says: On
what are you basing this confidence of yours? 20You say you
have strategy and military strength—but you speak only empty words. On whom are you depending, that you rebel
against me? 21Look now, you are depending on Egypt, that

**NIV** [d] 2 Hebrew *Abi*, a variant of *Abijah* [e] 4 Or *He called it* [f] 4 *Nehushtan* sounds like the Hebrew for *bronze* and *snake* and *unclean thing.* [g] *14* That is, about 11 tons (about 10 metric tons) [h] *14* That is, about 1 ton (about 1 metric ton)

## King James

21Now, behold, thou trustest upon the staff of this bruised reed, *even* upon Egypt, on which if a man lean, it will go into his hand, and pierce it: so *is* Pharaoh king of Egypt unto all that trust on him.

22But if ye say unto me, We trust in the LORD our God: *is* not that he, whose high places and whose altars Hezekiah hath taken away, and hath said to Judah and Jerusalem, Ye shall worship before this altar in Jerusalem?

23Now therefore, I pray thee, give pledges to my lord the king of Assyria, and I will deliver thee two thousand horses, if thou be able on thy part to set riders upon them.

24How then wilt thou turn away the face of one captain of the least of my master's servants, and put thy trust on Egypt for chariots and for horsemen?

25Am I now come up without the LORD against this place to destroy it? The LORD said to me, Go up against this land, and destroy it.

26Then said Eliakim the son of Hilkiah, and Shebna, and Joah, unto Rab-shakeh, Speak, I pray thee, to thy servants in the Syrian language; for we understand *it:* and talk not with us in the Jews' language in the ears of the people that *are* on the wall.

27But Rab-shakeh said unto them, Hath my master sent me to thy master, and to thee, to speak these words? *hath he* not *sent me* to the men which sit on the wall, that they may eat their own dung, and drink their own piss with you?

28Then Rab-shakeh stood and cried with a loud voice in the Jews' language, and spake, saying, Hear the word of the great king, the king of Assyria:

29Thus saith the king, Let not Hezekiah deceive you: for he shall not be able to deliver you out of his hand:

30Neither let Hezekiah make you trust in the LORD, saying, The LORD will surely deliver us, and this city shall not be delivered into the hand of the king of Assyria.

31Hearken not to Hezekiah: for thus saith the king of Assyria, Make *an agreement* with me by a present, and come out to me, and *then* eat ye every man of his own vine, and every one of his fig tree, and drink ye every one the waters of his cistern:

32Until I come and take you away to a land like your own land, a land of corn and wine, a land of bread and vineyards, a land of oil olive and of honey, that ye may live, and not die: and hearken not unto Hezekiah, when he persuadeth you, saying, The LORD will deliver us.

33Hath any of the gods of the nations delivered at all his land out of the hand of the king of Assyria?

34Where *are* the gods of Hamath, and of Arpad? where *are* the gods of Sepharvaim, Hena, and Ivah? have they delivered Samaria out of mine hand?

35Who *are* they among all the gods of the countries, that have delivered their country out of mine hand, that the LORD should deliver Jerusalem out of mine hand?

36But the people held their peace, and answered him not a word: for the king's commandment was, saying, Answer him not.

37Then came Eliakim the son of Hilkiah, which *was* over the household, and Shebna the scribe, and Joah the son of Asaph the recorder, to Hezekiah with *their* clothes rent, and told him the words of Rab-shakeh.

**19** AND IT came to pass, when king Hezekiah heard *it,* that he rent his clothes, and covered himself with sackcloth, and went into the house of the LORD.

2And he sent Eliakim, which *was* over the household, and Shebna the scribe, and the elders of the priests, covered with sackcloth, to Isaiah the prophet the son of Amoz.

3And they said unto him, Thus saith Hezekiah, This day *is* a day of trouble, and of rebuke, and blasphemy: for the children are come to the birth, and *there is* not strength to bring forth.

## Amplified

21Behold, you are relying on Egypt, that broken reed of a staff; if a man leans on it, it will pierce his hand. So is Pharaoh king of Egypt to all who trust *and* rely on him.

22But if you tell me, We trust in *and* rely on the Lord our God, is it not He, Whose high places and altars Hezekiah has removed, saying to Judah and Jerusalem, You shall worship before this altar in Jerusalem?

23So now, make a wager *and* give pledges to my lord the king of Assyria: I will deliver you 2,000 horses, if you can on your part put riders on them.

24How then can you beat back one captain among the least of my master's servants, when your trust is put on Egypt for chariots and horsemen?

25Have I come up without the Lord against this place to destroy it? The Lord said to me, Go up against this land and destroy it.

26Then Eliakim son of Hilkiah, and Shebna, and Joah said to the Rabshakeh, Pray, speak to your servants in the Aramaic (Syrian) language, for we understand it; and do not speak to us in the Jews' language in the hearing of the people on the wall.

27But the Rabshakeh said to them, Has my master sent me to your master and you only, to say these things? Has he not sent me to the men who sit on the wall [whom Hezekiah has doomed to be forced] to eat their own dung and drink their own urine along with you?

28Then the Rabshakeh stood and cried with a loud voice in the Jews' language, Hear the word of the great king of Assyria!

29Thus says the king, Let not Hezekiah deceive you; for he will not be able to deliver you out of my hand.

30Nor let Hezekiah make you trust in *and* rely on the Lord, saying, The Lord will surely deliver us, and this city will not be given into the hand of Assyria's king.

31Hearken not to Hezekiah, for thus says the king of Assyria: Make your peace with me and come out to me, and eat every man from his own vine and fig tree, and drink every one the waters of his own cistern;

32Until I come and take you away to a land like your own, a land of grain and vintage fruit, of bread and vineyards, of olive trees and honey, that you may live, and not die. Do not listen to Hezekiah when he urges you, saying, The Lord will deliver us.

33Has any of the gods of the nations ever delivered his land out of the hand of the king of Assyria?

34Where are the gods of Hamath and Arpad [in Syria]? Where are the gods of Sepharvaim, Hena, and Ivvah [in the Euphrates valley]? Have they delivered Samaria [Israel's capital] out of my hand?

35Who of all the gods of the countries have delivered their country out of my hand, that the Lord should deliver Jerusalem out of my hand?

36But the people were silent and answered him not a word, for Hezekiah had commanded, Do not answer him.

37Then Eliakim son of Hilkiah, who was over the royal household, and Shebna the scribe, and Joah son of Asaph the recorder, came to Hezekiah with their clothes rent, and told him what the Rabshakeh had said.

**19** WHEN KING Hezekiah heard it, he rent his clothes, and covered himself with sackcloth, and went into the house of the Lord.

2And he sent Eliakim, who was over his household, Shebna the scribe, and the older priests, covered with sackcloth, to Isaiah the prophet, son of Amoz.

3They said to him, Hezekiah says, This is a day of [extreme danger and] distress, of rebuke *and* chastisement, and blasphemous *and* insolent insult; for children have come to the birth, and there is not strength to bring them forth.

## New American Standard

21"Now behold, you rely on the staff of this crushed reed, *even*
on Egypt; on which if a man leans, it will go into his hand and
pierce it. So is Pharaoh king of Egypt to all who rely on him.
22"But if you say to me, 'We trust in the LORD our God,' is it
not He whose high places and whose altars Hezekiah has taken
away, and has said to Judah and to Jerusalem, 'You shall worship
before this altar in Jerusalem'?
23"Now therefore, come, make a bargain with my master the
king of Assyria, and I will give you two thousand horses, if you
are able on your part to set riders on them.
24"How then can you repulse one official of the least of my
master's servants, and rely on Egypt for chariots and for horsemen?
25"Have I now come up without the LORD's approval against
this place to destroy it? The LORD said to me, 'Go up against this
land and destroy it.' " ' "
26¶ Then Eliakim the son of Hilkiah, and Shebnah and Joah, said
to Rabshakeh, "Speak now to your servants in Aramaic, for we
understand *it;* and do not speak with us in Judean, in the hearing
of the people who are on the wall."
27But Rabshakeh said to them, "Has my master sent me only
to your master and to you to speak these words, *and* not to the men
who sit on the wall, *doomed* to eat their own dung and drink their
own urine with you?"
28Then Rabshakeh stood and cried with a loud voice in Judean,
saying, "Hear the word of the great king, the king of Assyria.
29"Thus says the king, 'Do not let Hezekiah deceive you, for he
will not be able to deliver you from my hand;
30nor let Hezekiah make you trust in the LORD, saying, "The
LORD will surely deliver us, and this city shall not be given into the
hand of the king of Assyria."
31'Do not listen to Hezekiah, for thus says the king of Assyria,
"Make your peace with me and come out to me, and eat each of
his vine and each of his fig tree and drink each of the waters of his
own cistern,
32until I come and take you away to a land like your own land,
a land of grain and new wine, a land of bread and vineyards, a land
of olive trees and honey, that you may live and not die." But do
not listen to Hezekiah, when he misleads you, saying, "The LORD
will deliver us."
33'Has any one of the gods of the nations delivered his land
from the hand of the king of Assyria?
34'Where are the gods of Hamath and Arpad? Where are the
gods of Sepharvaim, Hena and Ivvah? Have they delivered Samaria from my hand?
35'Who among all the gods of the lands have delivered their
land from my hand, that the LORD should deliver Jerusalem from
my hand?' "
36But the people were silent and answered him not a word, for
the king's commandment was, "Do not answer him."
37Then Eliakim the son of Hilkiah, who was over the household, and Shebna the scribe and Joah the son of Asaph, the
recorder, came to Hezekiah with their clothes torn and told him
the words of Rabshakeh.

*Isaiah Encourages Hezekiah*

19 AND WHEN King Hezekiah heard *it,* he tore his clothes,
covered himself with sackcloth and entered the house of
the LORD.
2Then he sent Eliakim who was over the household with Shebna the scribe and the elders of the priests, covered with sackcloth,
to Isaiah the prophet the son of Amoz.
3And they said to him, "Thus says Hezekiah, 'This day is a day
of distress, rebuke, and rejection; for children have come to birth,
and there is no strength to *deliver.*

## New International

splintered reed of a staff, which pierces a man's hand and
wounds him if he leans on it! Such is Pharaoh king of Egypt
to all who depend on him. 22And if you say to me, "We are
depending on the LORD our God"—isn't he the one whose
high places and altars Hezekiah removed, saying to Judah
and Jerusalem, "You must worship before this altar in Jerusalem"?
23" 'Come now, make a bargain with my master, the king
of Assyria: I will give you two thousand horses—if you can
put riders on them! 24How can you repulse one officer of the
least of my master's officials, even though you are depending
on Egypt for chariots and horsemen[a]? 25Furthermore, have I
come to attack and destroy this place without word from the
LORD? The LORD himself told me to march against this country
and destroy it.' "

26Then Eliakim son of Hilkiah, and Shebna and Joah said to the
field commander, "Please speak to your servants in Aramaic, since
we understand it. Don't speak to us in Hebrew in the hearing of
the people on the wall."
27But the commander replied, "Was it only to your master and
you that my master sent me to say these things, and not to the men
sitting on the wall—who, like you, will have to eat their own filth
and drink their own urine?"
28Then the commander stood and called out in Hebrew: "Hear
the word of the great king, the king of Assyria! 29This is what the
king says: Do not let Hezekiah deceive you. He cannot deliver you
from my hand. 30Do not let Hezekiah persuade you to trust in the
LORD when he says, 'The LORD will surely deliver us; this city will
not be given into the hand of the king of Assyria.'
31"Do not listen to Hezekiah. This is what the king of Assyria
says: Make peace with me and come out to me. Then every one
of you will eat from his own vine and fig tree and drink water from
his own cistern, 32until I come and take you to a land like your
own, a land of grain and new wine, a land of bread and vineyards,
a land of olive trees and honey. Choose life and not death!
"Do not listen to Hezekiah, for he is misleading you when he
says, 'The LORD will deliver us.' 33Has the god of any nation ever
delivered his land from the hand of the king of Assyria? 34Where
are the gods of Hamath and Arpad? Where are the gods of Sepharvaim, Hena and Ivvah? Have they rescued Samaria from my hand?
35Who of all the gods of these countries has been able to save his
land from me? How then can the LORD deliver Jerusalem from my
hand?"
36But the people remained silent and said nothing in reply,
because the king had commanded, "Do not answer him."
37Then Eliakim son of Hilkiah the palace administrator, Shebna
the secretary and Joah son of Asaph the recorder went to Hezekiah, with their clothes torn, and told him what the field commander had said.

*Jerusalem's Deliverance Foretold*

19 WHEN KING Hezekiah heard this, he tore his clothes and
put on sackcloth and went into the temple of the LORD.
2He sent Eliakim the palace administrator, Shebna the secretary
and the leading priests, all wearing sackcloth, to the prophet Isaiah
son of Amoz. 3They told him, "This is what Hezekiah says: This
day is a day of distress and rebuke and disgrace, as when children
come to the point of birth and there is no strength to deliver them.

NIV [a] 24 Or *charioteers*

## King James

4It may be the LORD thy God will hear all the words of Rabshakeh, whom the king of Assyria his master hath sent to reproach
the living God; and will reprove the words which the LORD thy
God hath heard: wherefore lift up *thy* prayer for the remnant that
are left.
5So the servants of king Hezekiah came to Isaiah.
6¶ And Isaiah said unto them, Thus shall ye say to your master,
Thus saith the LORD, Be not afraid of the words which thou hast
heard, with which the servants of the king of Assyria have blasphemed me.
7Behold, I will send a blast upon him, and he shall hear a
rumour, and shall return to his own land; and I will cause him to
fall by the sword in his own land.
8¶ So Rab-shakeh returned, and found the king of Assyria warring against Libnah: for he had heard that he was departed from
Lachish.
9And when he heard say of Tirhakah king of Ethiopia, Behold,
he is come out to fight against thee: he sent messengers again unto
Hezekiah, saying,
10Thus shall ye speak to Hezekiah king of Judah, saying, Let not
thy God in whom thou trustest deceive thee, saying, Jerusalem
shall not be delivered into the hand of the king of Assyria.
11Behold, thou hast heard what the kings of Assyria have done
to all lands, by destroying them utterly: and shalt thou be delivered?
12Have the gods of the nations delivered them which my fathers
have destroyed; *as* Gozan, and Haran, and Rezeph, and the children of Eden which *were* in Thelasar?
13Where *is* the king of Hamath, and the king of Arpad, and the
king of the city of Sepharvaim, of Hena, and Ivah?
14¶ And Hezekiah received the letter of the hand of the messengers, and read it: and Hezekiah went up into the house of the
LORD, and spread it before the LORD.
15And Hezekiah prayed before the LORD, and said, O LORD God
of Israel, which dwellest *between* the cherubims, thou art the God,
*even* thou alone, of all the kingdoms of the earth; thou hast made
heaven and earth.
16LORD, bow down thine ear, and hear: open, LORD, thine eyes,
and see: and hear the words of Sennacherib, which hath sent him
to reproach the living God.
17Of a truth, LORD, the kings of Assyria have destroyed the
nations and their lands,
18And have cast their gods into the fire: for they *were* no gods,
but the work of men's hands, wood and stone: therefore they have
destroyed them.
19Now therefore, O LORD our God, I beseech thee, save thou
us out of his hand, that all the kingdoms of the earth may know
that thou *art* the LORD God, *even* thou only.
20¶ Then Isaiah the son of Amoz sent to Hezekiah, saying, Thus
saith the LORD God of Israel, *That* which thou hast prayed to me
against Sennacherib king of Assyria I have heard.
21This *is* the word that the LORD hath spoken concerning him;
The virgin the daughter of Zion hath despised thee, *and* laughed
thee to scorn; the daughter of Jerusalem hath shaken her head at
thee.
22Whom hast thou reproached and blasphemed? and against
whom hast thou exalted *thy* voice, and lifted up thine eyes on
high? *even* against the Holy *One* of Israel.

## Amplified

4It may be the Lord your God will hear all the words of the
Rabshakeh, whom the king of Assyria has sent to mock, reproach,
insult *and* defy the living God, and will rebuke the words which
the Lord your God has heard. So raise your prayer for the remnant
[of His people] that is left.
5So the servants of King Hezekiah came to Isaiah.
6Isaiah said to them, Say to your master, Thus says the Lord,
Do not be afraid because of the words you have heard, with which
the servants of the king of Assyria have reviled *and* blasphemed
Me.
7Behold, I will put a spirit in him so that he shall hear a rumor,
and return to his own land; and I will cause him to fall by the sword
in his own country.
8So the Rabshakeh returned, and found the king of Assyria
fighting against Libnah [a fortified city of Judah]; for he had heard
that the king had left Lachish.
9And Sennacherib king of Assyria heard concerning Tirhakah
king of Ethiopia, He has come to make war against you. And when
he heard it, he sent messengers again to Hezekiah, saying,
10Say this to Hezekiah king of Judah, Let not your God on
Whom you rely deceive you by saying, Jerusalem shall not be
delivered into the hand of the king of Assyria.
11Behold, you have heard what the Assyrian kings have done
to all lands, destroying them utterly. And shall you be delivered?
12Have the gods of the nations delivered those whom my ancestors have destroyed, as Gozan, Haran [of Mesopotamia], Rezeph,
and the people of Eden who were in Telassar?
13Where are the kings of Hamath, of Aphad [of northern Syria],
of the city of Sepharvaim, of Hena, and Ivvah?
14Hezekiah received the letter from the hand of the messengers,
and read it. And he went up into the house of the Lord, and spread
it before the Lord.
15And Hezekiah prayed: O Lord the God of Israel, Who [in
symbol] are enthroned above the cherubim [of the ark in the tem-
ple], You are the God, You alone, of all the kingdoms of the earth;
You have made the heavens and the earth.
16Lord, bow down Your ear and hear; Lord, open Your eyes and
see; hear the words of Sennacherib, which he has sent to mock,
reproach, insult *and* defy the living God.
17It is true, Lord, the Assyrian kings have laid waste the nations
and their lands,
18And have cast the gods of those peoples into the fire; for they
were no gods, but the work of men's hands, wood and stone; so
they [could and] have destroyed them.
19Now therefore, O Lord our God, I beseech You, save us out
of his hand, that all the kingdoms of the earth may know *and*
understand that You, O Lord, are God alone.
20Then Isaiah son of Amoz sent to Hezekiah, saying, Thus says
the Lord God of Israel: Your prayer to Me about Sennacherib king
of Assyria I have heard.
21This is the word that the Lord has spoken concerning him:
The virgin daughter of Zion has despised you and laughed you to
scorn; the daughter of Jerusalem has wagged her head behind you.
22Whom have you mocked *and* reviled, insulted *and* blasphemed? Against whom have you raised your voice and haughtily
lifted your eyes? Against the Holy One of Israel!

## New American Standard

4'Perhaps the LORD your God will hear all the words of Rabshakeh, whom his master the king of Assyria has sent to reproach
the living God, and will rebuke the words which the LORD your
God has heard. Therefore, offer a prayer for the remnant that is
left.' "
5So the servants of King Hezekiah came to Isaiah.
6And Isaiah said to them, "Thus you shall say to your master,
'Thus says the LORD, "Do not be afraid because of the words that
you have heard, with which the servants of the king of Assyria
have blasphemed Me.
7"Behold, I will put a spirit in him so that he shall hear a rumor
and return to his own land. And I will make him fall by the sword
in his own land." ' "

*Sennacherib Defies God*

8¶ Then Rabshakeh returned and found the king of Assyria
fighting against Libnah, for he had heard that the king had left
Lachish.
9When he heard *them* say concerning Tirhakah king of Cush,
"Behold, he has come out to fight against you," he sent messengers again to Hezekiah saying,
10"Thus you shall say to Hezekiah king of Judah, 'Do not let
your God in whom you trust deceive you saying, "Jerusalem shall
not be given into the hand of the king of Assyria."
11'Behold, you have heard what the kings of Assyria have done
to all the lands, destroying them completely. So will you be
spared?
12'Did the gods of those nations which my fathers destroyed
deliver them, *even* Gozan and Haran and Rezeph and the sons of
Eden who *were* in Telassar?
13'Where is the king of Hamath, the king of Arpad, the king of
the city of Sepharvaim, and *of* Hena and Ivvah?' "

*Hezekiah's Prayer*

14¶ Then Hezekiah took the letter from the hand of the messengers and read it, and he went up to the house of the LORD and
spread it out before the LORD.
15And Hezekiah prayed before the LORD and said, "O LORD, the
God of Israel, who art enthroned *above* the cherubim, Thou art the
God, Thou alone, of all the kingdoms of the earth. Thou hast made
heaven and earth.
16"Incline Thine ear, O LORD, and hear; open Thine eyes, O
LORD, and see; and listen to the words of Sennacherib, which he
has sent to reproach the living God.
17"Truly, O LORD, the kings of Assyria have devastated the
nations and their lands
18and have cast their gods into the fire, for they were not gods
but the work of men's hands, wood and stone. So they have
destroyed them.
19"And now, O LORD our God, I pray, deliver us from his hand
that all the kingdoms of the earth may know that Thou alone, O
LORD, art God."

*God's Answer through Isaiah*

20¶ Then Isaiah the son of Amoz sent to Hezekiah saying, "Thus
says the LORD, the God of Israel, 'Because you have prayed to Me
about Sennacherib king of Assyria, I have heard *you*.'
21"This is the word that the LORD has spoken against him:
'She has despised you and mocked you,
The virgin daughter of Zion;
She has shaken *her* head behind you,
The daughter of Jerusalem!
22 'Whom have you reproached and blasphemed?
And against whom have you raised *your* voice,
And haughtily lifted up your eyes?
Against the Holy One of Israel!

## New International

4It may be that the LORD your God will hear all the words of the
field commander, whom his master, the king of Assyria, has sent
to ridicule the living God, and that he will rebuke him for the
words the LORD your God has heard. Therefore pray for the remnant that still survives."
5When King Hezekiah's officials came to Isaiah, 6Isaiah said to
them, "Tell your master, 'This is what the LORD says: Do not be
afraid of what you have heard—those words with which the un-
derlings of the king of Assyria have blasphemed me. 7Listen! I am
going to put such a spirit in him that when he hears a certain
report, he will return to his own country, and there I will have him
cut down with the sword.' "
8When the field commander heard that the king of Assyria had
left Lachish, he withdrew and found the king fighting against
Libnah.
9Now Sennacherib received a report that Tirhakah, the Cushite[a] king ⌞of Egypt⌟, was marching out to fight against him. So he
again sent messengers to Hezekiah with this word: 10"Say to Hezekiah king of Judah: Do not let the god you depend on deceive you
when he says, 'Jerusalem will not be handed over to the king of
Assyria.' 11Surely you have heard what the kings of Assyria have
done to all the countries, destroying them completely. And will
you be delivered? 12Did the gods of the nations that were destroyed by my forefathers deliver them: the gods of Gozan, Haran,
Rezeph and the people of Eden who were in Tel Assar? 13Where
is the king of Hamath, the king of Arpad, the king of the city of
Sepharvaim, or of Hena or Ivvah?"

*Hezekiah's Prayer*

14Hezekiah received the letter from the messengers and read it.
Then he went up to the temple of the LORD and spread it out before
the LORD. 15And Hezekiah prayed to the LORD: "O LORD, God of
Israel, enthroned between the cherubim, you alone are God over
all the kingdoms of the earth. You have made heaven and earth.
16Give ear, O LORD, and hear; open your eyes, O LORD, and see;
listen to the words Sennacherib has sent to insult the living God.
17"It is true, O LORD, that the Assyrian kings have laid waste
these nations and their lands. 18They have thrown their gods into
the fire and destroyed them, for they were not gods but only wood
and stone, fashioned by men's hands. 19Now, O LORD our God,
deliver us from his hand, so that all kingdoms on earth may know
that you alone, O LORD, are God."

*Isaiah Prophesies Sennacherib's Fall*

20Then Isaiah son of Amoz sent a message to Hezekiah: "This
is what the LORD, the God of Israel, says: I have heard your prayer
concerning Sennacherib king of Assyria. 21This is the word that the
LORD has spoken against him:

" 'The Virgin Daughter of Zion
despises you and mocks you.
The Daughter of Jerusalem
tosses her head as you flee.
22Who is it you have insulted and blasphemed?
Against whom have you raised your voice
and lifted your eyes in pride?
Against the Holy One of Israel!

NIV [a] 9 That is, from the upper Nile region

## King James

23 By thy messengers thou hast reproached the Lord, and hast said, With the multitude of my chariots I am come up to the height of the mountains, to the sides of Lebanon, and will cut down the tall cedar trees thereof, *and* the choice fir trees thereof: and I will enter into the lodgings of his borders, *and into* the forest of his Carmel.

24 I have digged and drunk strange waters, and with the sole of my feet have I dried up all the rivers of besieged places.

25 Hast thou not heard long ago *how* I have done it, *and* of ancient times that I have formed it? now have I brought it to pass, that thou shouldest be to lay waste fenced cities *into* ruinous heaps.

26 Therefore their inhabitants were of small power, they were dismayed and confounded; they were *as* the grass of the field, and *as* the green herb, *as* the grass on the housetops, and *as corn* blasted before it be grown up.

27 But I know thy abode, and thy going out, and thy coming in, and thy rage against me.

28 Because thy rage against me and thy tumult is come up into mine ears, therefore I will put my hook in thy nose, and my bridle in thy lips, and I will turn thee back by the way by which thou camest.

29 And this *shall be* a sign unto thee, Ye shall eat this year such things as grow of themselves, and in the second year that which springeth of the same; and in the third year sow ye, and reap, and plant vineyards, and eat the fruits thereof.

30 And the remnant that is escaped of the house of Judah shall yet again take root downward, and bear fruit upward.

31 For out of Jerusalem shall go forth a remnant, and they that escape out of mount Zion: the zeal of the LORD *of hosts* shall do this.

32 Therefore thus saith the LORD concerning the king of Assyria, He shall not come into this city, nor shoot an arrow there, nor come before it with shield, nor cast a bank against it.

33 By the way that he came, by the same shall he return, and shall not come into this city, saith the LORD.

34 For I will defend this city, to save it, for mine own sake, and for my servant David's sake.

35 ¶ And it came to pass that night, that the angel of the LORD went out, and smote in the camp of the Assyrians an hundred fourscore and five thousand: and when they arose early in the morning, behold, they *were* all dead corpses.

36 So Sennacherib king of Assyria departed, and went and returned, and dwelt at Nineveh.

37 And it came to pass, as he was worshipping in the house of Nisroch his god, that Adrammelech and Sharezer his sons smote him with the sword: and they escaped into the land of Armenia. And Esar-haddon his son reigned in his stead.

## Amplified

23 By your messengers you have mocked, reproached, insulted *and* defied the Lord, and have said, With my many chariots I have gone up to the height of the mountains, to the far recesses of Lebanon; I cut down its tall cedar trees, and its choicest cypress trees; I entered its most distant retreat, its densest forest.

24 I dug wells and drank foreign waters, and with the sole of my feet have I dried up all [the defense and] the streams of Egypt.

25 But, says the God of Israel, Have you not heard how I ordained long ago what now I have brought to pass? I planned it in olden times that you [king of Assyria] should be My instrument to lay waste fortified cities, making them ruinous heaps.

26 That is why their inhabitants had little power; they were dismayed and confounded; they were like plants of the field, the green herb, the grass on the house tops, blasted before grown up.

27 But [O Sennacherib] I the Lord know your sitting down, your going out, your coming in, and your raging against Me.

28 Because your raging against Me and your arrogance *and* careless ease have come to My ears, therefore I will put My hook in your nose and My bridle in your lips, and I will turn you back by the way on which you came, O king of Assyria.

29 And [Hezekiah, says the Lord] this shall be a sign of these things to you: you shall eat this year what grows of itself, also in the second year what springs up voluntarily; but the third year sow and reap, plant vineyards and eat their fruit.

30 And the remnant that has survived of the house of Judah shall again take root downward, and bear fruit upward.

31 For out of Jerusalem shall go forth a remnant, and a band of survivors out of Mount Zion. The zeal of the Lord of hosts shall perform this.

32 Therefore thus says the Lord concerning the king of Assyria, He shall not come into this city, or shoot an arrow here, or come before it with shield, or cast a siege mound against it.

33 By the way that he came, by that way shall he return, and shall not come into this city, says the Lord.

34 For I will defend this city, to save it, for My own sake, and for My servant David's sake.

35 And it all came to pass, for that night the Angel of the Lord went forth and slew 185,000 in the camp of the Assyrians; and when the living arose early in the morning, behold, all these were dead bodies.

36 So Sennacherib king of Assyria departed, and returned and dwelt at Nineveh.

37 And as he was worshiping in the house of Nisroch his god, Adrammelech and Sharezer his sons killed him with the sword, and escaped to the land of Armenia *or* Ararat. Esarhaddon his son reigned in his stead.

## New American Standard

23 'Through your messengers you have reproached the
Lord,
And you have said, "With my many chariots
I came up to the heights of the mountains,
To the remotest parts of Lebanon;
And I cut down its tall cedars *and* its choice cypresses.
And I entered its farthest lodging place, its thickest
forest.
24 "I dug *wells* and drank foreign waters,
And with the sole of my feet I dried up
All the rivers of Egypt."

25 ¶ 'Have you not heard?
Long ago I did it;
From ancient times I planned it.
Now I have brought it to pass,
That you should turn fortified cities into ruinous heaps.
26 Therefore their inhabitants were short of strength,
They were dismayed and put to shame;
They were as the vegetation of the field and as the
green herb,
As grass on the housetops is scorched before it is
grown up.
27 'But I know your sitting down,
And your going out and your coming in,
And your raging against Me.
28 'Because of your raging against Me,
And because your arrogance has come up to My ears,
Therefore I will put My hook in your nose,
And My bridle in your lips,
And I will turn you back by the way which you came.

29¶ 'Then this shall be the sign for you: you shall eat this year
what grows of itself, in the second year what springs from the
same, and in the third year sow, reap, plant vineyards, and eat
their fruit.
30'And the surviving remnant of the house of Judah shall again
take root downward and bear fruit upward.
31'For out of Jerusalem shall go forth a remnant, and out of
Mount Zion survivors. The zeal of [a]the LORD shall perform this.
32'Therefore thus says the LORD concerning the king of Assyria,
"He shall not come to this city or shoot an arrow there; neither
shall he come before it with a shield, nor throw up a mound against
it.
33"By the way that he came, by the same he shall return, and
he shall not come to this city," ' declares the LORD.
34'For I will defend this city to save it for My own sake and for
My servant David's sake.' "
35¶ Then it happened that night that the angel of the LORD went
out, and struck 185,000 in the camp of the Assyrians; and when
men rose early in the morning, behold, all of them were dead.
36So Sennacherib king of Assyria departed and returned *home*,
and lived at Nineveh.
37And it came about as he was worshiping in the house of
Nisroch his god, that Adrammelech and Sharezer killed him with
the sword; and they escaped into the land of Ararat. And Esarhaddon his son became king in his place.

NAS [a] Some ancient mss. read *the LORD of hosts*

## New International

23By your messengers
you have heaped insults on the Lord.
And you have said,
"With my many chariots
I have ascended the heights of the mountains,
the utmost heights of Lebanon.
I have cut down its tallest cedars,
the choicest of its pines.
I have reached its remotest parts,
the finest of its forests.
24I have dug wells in foreign lands
and drunk the water there.
With the soles of my feet
I have dried up all the streams of Egypt."
25" 'Have you not heard?
Long ago I ordained it.
In days of old I planned it;
now I have brought it to pass,
that you have turned fortified cities
into piles of stone.
26Their people, drained of power,
are dismayed and put to shame.
They are like plants in the field,
like tender green shoots,
like grass sprouting on the roof,
scorched before it grows up.
27" 'But I know where you stay
and when you come and go
and how you rage against me.
28Because you rage against me
and your insolence has reached my ears,
I will put my hook in your nose
and my bit in your mouth,
and I will make you return
by the way you came.'

29"This will be the sign for you, O Hezekiah:

"This year you will eat what grows by itself,
and the second year what springs from that.
But in the third year sow and reap,
plant vineyards and eat their fruit.
30Once more a remnant of the house of Judah
will take root below and bear fruit above.
31For out of Jerusalem will come a remnant,
and out of Mount Zion a band of survivors.

The zeal of the LORD Almighty will accomplish this.

32"Therefore this is what the LORD says concerning the king of
Assyria:

"He will not enter this city
or shoot an arrow here.
He will not come before it with shield
or build a siege ramp against it.
33By the way that he came he will return;
he will not enter this city,
declares the LORD.
34I will defend this city and save it,
for my sake and for the sake of David my servant."

35That night the angel of the LORD went out and put to death
a hundred and eighty-five thousand men in the Assyrian camp.
When the people got up the next morning—there were all the dead
bodies! 36So Sennacherib king of Assyria broke camp and withdrew. He returned to Nineveh and stayed there.
37One day, while he was worshiping in the temple of his god
Nisroch, his sons Adrammelech and Sharezer cut him down with
the sword, and they escaped to the land of Ararat. And Esarhaddon his son succeeded him as king.

## King James

**20** IN THOSE days was Hezekiah sick unto death. And the prophet Isaiah the son of Amoz came to him, and said unto him, Thus saith the LORD, Set thine house in order; for thou shalt die, and not live.

2 Then he turned his face to the wall, and prayed unto the LORD, saying,

3 I beseech thee, O LORD, remember now how I have walked before thee in truth and with a perfect heart, and have done *that which is* good in thy sight. And Hezekiah wept sore.

4 And it came to pass, afore Isaiah was gone out into the middle court, that the word of the LORD came to him, saying,

5 Turn again, and tell Hezekiah the captain of my people, Thus saith the LORD, the God of David thy father, I have heard thy prayer, I have seen thy tears: behold, I will heal thee: on the third day thou shalt go up unto the house of the LORD.

6 And I will add unto thy days fifteen years; and I will deliver thee and this city out of the hand of the king of Assyria; and I will defend this city for mine own sake, and for my servant David's sake.

7 And Isaiah said, Take a lump of figs. And they took and laid *it* on the boil, and he recovered.

8 ¶ And Hezekiah said unto Isaiah, What *shall be* the sign that the LORD will heal me, and that I shall go up into the house of the LORD the third day?

9 And Isaiah said, This sign shalt thou have of the LORD, that the LORD will do the thing that he hath spoken: shall the shadow go forward ten degrees, or go back ten degrees?

10 And Hezekiah answered, It is a light thing for the shadow to go down ten degrees: nay, but let the shadow return backward ten degrees.

11 And Isaiah the prophet cried unto the LORD: and he brought the shadow ten degrees backward, by which it had gone down in the dial of Ahaz.

12 ¶ At that time Berodach-baladan, the son of Baladan, king of Babylon, sent letters and a present unto Hezekiah: for he had heard that Hezekiah had been sick.

13 And Hezekiah hearkened unto them, and showed them all the house of his precious things, the silver, and the gold, and the spices, and the precious ointment, and *all* the house of his armour, and all that was found in his treasures: there was nothing in his house, nor in all his dominion, that Hezekiah showed them not.

14 ¶ Then came Isaiah the prophet unto king Hezekiah, and said unto him, What said these men? and from whence came they unto thee? And Hezekiah said, They are come from a far country, *even* from Babylon.

15 And he said, What have they seen in thine house? And Hezekiah answered, All *the things* that *are* in mine house have they seen: there is nothing among my treasures that I have not showed them.

16 And Isaiah said unto Hezekiah, Hear the word of the LORD.

17 Behold, the days come, that all that *is* in thine house, and that which thy fathers have laid up in store unto this day, shall be carried into Babylon: nothing shall be left, saith the LORD.

## Amplified

**20** IN THOSE days Hezekiah became deadly ill. The prophet Isaiah son of Amoz came and said to him, Thus says the Lord, Set your house in order, for you shall die, you shall not recover.

2 Then Hezekiah turned his face to the wall and prayed to the Lord, saying,

3 I beseech You, O Lord, [earnestly] remember now how I have walked before You in faithfulness *and* truth, and with a whole heart [entirely devoted to You], and have done what is good in Your sight. And Hezekiah wept bitterly.

4 Before Isaiah had gone out of the middle court the word of the Lord came to him,

5 Turn back and tell Hezekiah the leader of My people, Thus says the Lord, the God of David, your [forefather], I have heard your prayer, I have seen your tears. Behold, I will heal you; on the third day you shall go up to the house of the Lord.

6 I will [a]add to your lifetime fifteen years, and deliver you and this city [Jerusalem] out of the hand of the king of Assyria; and I will defend this city for My own sake and for My servant David's sake.

7 And Isaiah said, Bring a cake of figs; let them lay it on the burning inflammation that he may recover.

8 Hezekiah said to Isaiah, What shall be the sign that the Lord will heal me, and that I shall go up into the house of the Lord the third day?

9 And Isaiah said, This is the sign to you from the Lord that He will do the thing He has promised: shall the shadow [denoting the time of day] go forward ten steps, or go back ten steps?

10 Hezekiah answered, It is an easy matter for the shadow to go forward ten steps, so let the shadow go back ten steps.

11 So Isaiah the prophet cried to the Lord, and He brought the shadow ten steps backward, by which it had gone down on the sun-dial of Ahaz.

12 At that time Merodach-baladan son of Baladan, king of Babylon, sent letters and a present to Hezekiah, for he had heard of Hezekiah's illness.

13 And Hezekiah rejoiced *and* welcomed the embassy, and showed them all his treasure house, the silver, gold, spices, precious ointment, his armory, and all that was found in his treasuries; there was nothing in his house or in all his realm that Hezekiah did not show them.

14 Then Isaiah the prophet came to King Hezekiah, and said, What did these men say? From where did they come to you? Hezekiah said, They are from a far country, Babylon.

15 Isaiah said, What have they seen in your house? Hezekiah answered, They have seen all that is in my house. There is no treasure of mine that I have not shown them.

16 Then Isaiah said to Hezekiah, Hear the word of the Lord!

17 Behold, the time is coming, when [b]all that is in your house, and what your [forefathers] have stored up till this day, shall be carried to Babylon; nothing shall be left, says the Lord.

**AMP** [a] Good King Hezekiah's prayer life holds a mighty challenge and a clear and terrible warning for every believer. In his nation's darkest hour (18:13-17), he prayed and God performed a miracle, one He had foretold (19:20, 32-37). It is a wonderful thing to have such power as that with God! But in this chapter (20) and the next, that power has become a terrible thing; for Hezekiah had put himself on God's "ways and means committee," as chairman, in fact. God virtually said, "Your time has come to die" (20:1). But Hezekiah's words and tears implied, "No! I want to live [and have sons to do mighty things, and I myself have my best years ahead of me]!" Read this chapter and the next and note at least ten (numbered) *terrible* things that resulted, that only God could foresee, and that only Hezekiah's death, when God intended it, would have prevented. But Hezekiah interfered. The only safe prayer policy is "God's will; nothing more; nothing less; nothing else; at any cost" [Luke 22:42]. It pays triumphantly! Martin Luther is quoted as saying, "Blessed is he who submits to the will of God; he can never be unhappy. Men may deal with him as they will . . . ; he is without care; he knows that 'all things work together for good' for him," Rom. 8:28 (quoted in *Lange's Commentary*, on Acts 21:14). [b] This is the first of ten consecutively numbered tragic results of Hezekiah's self-willed prayer, mentioned in footnote on verse 6, which God's plan for Hezekiah's death would have prevented. See verses 20:18; 21:1, 3, 4, 6, 9, 14, 16, 20.

## New American Standard

*Hezekiah's Illness and Recovery*

**20** IN THOSE days Hezekiah became mortally ill. And Isaiah
the prophet the son of Amoz came to him and said to him,
"Thus says the LORD, 'Set your house in order, for you shall die
and not live.' "
2Then he turned his face to the wall, and prayed to the LORD,
saying,
3"Remember now, O LORD, I beseech Thee, how I have walked
before Thee in truth and with a whole heart, and have done what
is good in Thy sight." And Hezekiah wept bitterly.
4And it came about before Isaiah had gone out of the middle
court, that the word of the LORD came to him, saying,
5"Return and say to Hezekiah the leader of My people, 'Thus
says the LORD, the God of your father David, "I have heard your
prayer, I have seen your tears; behold, I will heal you. On the third
day you shall go up to the house of the LORD.
6"And I will add fifteen years to your life, and I will deliver you
and this city from the hand of the king of Assyria; and I will defend
this city for My own sake and for My servant David's sake." ' "
7Then Isaiah said, "Take a cake of figs." And they took and laid
*it* on the boil, and he recovered.
8¶ Now Hezekiah said to Isaiah, "What will be the sign that the
LORD will heal me, and that I shall go up to the house of the LORD
the third day?"
9And Isaiah said, "This shall be the sign to you from the LORD,
that the LORD will do the thing that He has spoken: shall the
shadow go forward ten steps or go back ten steps?"
10So Hezekiah answered, "It is easy for the shadow to decline
ten steps; no, but let the shadow turn backward ten steps."
11And Isaiah the prophet cried to the LORD, and He brought the
shadow on the stairway back ten steps by which it had gone down
on the stairway of Ahaz.

*Hezekiah Shows Babylon His Treasures*

12¶ At that time Berodach-baladan a son of Baladan, king of
Babylon, sent letters and a present to Hezekiah, for he heard that
Hezekiah had been sick.
13And Hezekiah listened to them, and showed them all his
treasure house, the silver and the gold and the spices and the
precious oil and the house of his armor and all that was found in
his treasuries. There was nothing in his house, nor in all his
dominion, that Hezekiah did not show them.
14Then Isaiah the prophet came to King Hezekiah and said to
him, "What did these men say, and from where have they come
to you?" And Hezekiah said, "They have come from a far country,
from Babylon."
15And he said, "What have they seen in your house?" So Hezekiah answered, "They have seen all that is in my house; there is
nothing among my treasuries that I have not shown them."
16¶ Then Isaiah said to Hezekiah, "Hear the word of the LORD.
17'Behold, the days are coming when all that is in your house,
and all that your fathers have laid up in store to this day shall be
carried to Babylon; nothing shall be left,' says the LORD.

## New International

*Hezekiah's Illness*

**20** IN THOSE days Hezekiah became ill and was at the point
of death. The prophet Isaiah son of Amoz went to him and
said, "This is what the LORD says: Put your house in order, because
you are going to die; you will not recover."
2Hezekiah turned his face to the wall and prayed to the LORD,
3"Remember, O LORD, how I have walked before you faithfully
and with wholehearted devotion and have done what is good in
your eyes." And Hezekiah wept bitterly.
4Before Isaiah had left the middle court, the word of the LORD
came to him: 5"Go back and tell Hezekiah, the leader of my people,
'This is what the LORD, the God of your father David, says: I have
heard your prayer and seen your tears; I will heal you. On the third
day from now you will go up to the temple of the LORD. 6I will add
fifteen years to your life. And I will deliver you and this city from
the hand of the king of Assyria. I will defend this city for my sake
and for the sake of my servant David.' "
7Then Isaiah said, "Prepare a poultice of figs." They did so and
applied it to the boil, and he recovered.
8Hezekiah had asked Isaiah, "What will be the sign that the
LORD will heal me and that I will go up to the temple of the LORD
on the third day from now?"
9Isaiah answered, "This is the LORD's sign to you that the LORD
will do what he has promised: Shall the shadow go forward ten
steps, or shall it go back ten steps?"
10"It is a simple matter for the shadow to go forward ten steps,"
said Hezekiah. "Rather, have it go back ten steps."
11Then the prophet Isaiah called upon the LORD, and the LORD
made the shadow go back the ten steps it had gone down on the
stairway of Ahaz.

*Envoys From Babylon*

12At that time Merodach-Baladan son of Baladan king of Babylon sent Hezekiah letters and a gift, because he had heard of
Hezekiah's illness. 13Hezekiah received the messengers and
showed them all that was in his storehouses—the silver, the gold,
the spices and the fine oil—his armory and everything found
among his treasures. There was nothing in his palace or in all his
kingdom that Hezekiah did not show them.
14Then Isaiah the prophet went to King Hezekiah and asked,
"What did those men say, and where did they come from?"
"From a distant land," Hezekiah replied. "They came from
Babylon."
15The prophet asked, "What did they see in your palace?"
"They saw everything in my palace," Hezekiah said. "There is
nothing among my treasures that I did not show them."
16Then Isaiah said to Hezekiah, "Hear the word of the LORD:
17The time will surely come when everything in your palace, and
all that your fathers have stored up until this day, will be carried
off to Babylon. Nothing will be left, says the LORD. 18And some of

## King James

18 And of thy sons that shall issue from thee, which thou shalt
beget, shall they take away; and they shall be eunuchs in the palace
of the king of Babylon.
19 Then said Hezekiah unto Isaiah, Good *is* the word of the LORD
which thou hast spoken. And he said, *Is it* not *good,* if peace and
truth be in my days?
20 ¶ And the rest of the acts of Hezekiah, and all his might, and
how he made a pool, and a conduit, and brought water into the
city, *are* they not written in the book of the chronicles of the kings
of Judah?
21 And Hezekiah slept with his fathers: and Manasseh his son
reigned in his stead.

**21** MANASSEH *WAS* twelve years old when he began to
reign, and reigned fifty and five years in Jerusalem. And
his mother's name *was* Hephzibah.
2 And he did *that which was* evil in the sight of the LORD, after
the abominations of the heathen, whom the LORD cast out before
the children of Israel.
3 For he built up again the high places which Hezekiah his father
had destroyed; and he reared up altars for Baal, and made a grove,
as did Ahab king of Israel; and worshipped all the host of heaven,
and served them.
4 And he built altars in the house of the LORD, of which the LORD
said, In Jerusalem will I put my name.
5 And he built altars for all the host of heaven in the two courts
of the house of the LORD.
6 And he made his son pass through the fire, and observed
times, and used enchantments, and dealt with familiar spirits and
wizards: he wrought much wickedness in the sight of the LORD,
to provoke *him* to anger.
7 And he set a graven image of the grove that he had made in
the house, of which the LORD said to David, and to Solomon his
son, In this house, and in Jerusalem, which I have chosen out of
all tribes of Israel, will I put my name for ever:
8 Neither will I make the feet of Israel move any more out of the
land which I gave their fathers; only if they will observe to do
according to all that I have commanded them, and according to all
the law that my servant Moses commanded them.
9 But they hearkened not: and Manasseh seduced them to do
more evil than did the nations whom the LORD destroyed before
the children of Israel.
10 ¶ And the LORD spake by his servants the prophets, saying,
11 Because Manasseh king of Judah hath done these abominations, *and* hath done wickedly above all that the Amorites did,
which *were* before him, and hath made Judah also to sin with his
idols:
12 Therefore thus saith the LORD God of Israel, Behold, I *am*
bringing *such* evil upon Jerusalem and Judah, that whosoever
heareth of it, both his ears shall tingle.
13 And I will stretch over Jerusalem the line of Samaria, and the
plummet of the house of Ahab: and I will wipe Jerusalem as *a man*
wipeth a dish, wiping *it,* and turning *it* upside down.
14 And I will forsake the remnant of mine inheritance, and deliver them into the hand of their enemies; and they shall become
a prey and a spoil to all their enemies;
15 Because they have done *that which was* evil in my sight, and
have provoked me to anger, since the day their fathers came forth
out of Egypt, even unto this day.
16 Moreover Manasseh shed innocent blood very much, till he
had filled Jerusalem from one end to another; beside his sin wherewith he made Judah to sin, in doing *that which was* evil in the sight
of the LORD.
17 ¶ Now the rest of the acts of Manasseh, and all that he did,
and his sin that he sinned, *are* they not written in the book of the
chronicles of the kings of Judah?

## Amplified

18 And some of your sons, who shall be born to you, shall be
taken away, and shall be eunuchs in the palace of Babylon's king.
19 Then said Hezekiah to Isaiah, The word of the Lord you have
spoken is good. For he thought, Is it not good, if [all this evil is for
the future and] peace and security shall be in my days?
20 The rest of the acts of Hezekiah, and all his might, and how
he made the pool and the canal and brought water into the city,
are they not written in the Book of the Chronicles of the Kings of
Judah?
21 Hezekiah slept with his fathers. Manasseh his son reigned in
his stead.

**21** MANASSEH WAS twelve years old when he began his
fifty-five years' [wicked] reign in Jerusalem. His mother's
name was Hephzibah.
2 He [Hezekiah's son] did evil in the sight of the Lord, after the
[idolatrous] practices of the [heathen] nations, whom the Lord cast
out before the Israelites.
3 For he built up again the high places which Hezekiah his
father had destroyed; and he reared up altars for Baal, and made
an Asherah, as did Ahab king of Israel; and worshiped all the
[starry] host of the heavens and served them!
4 And he built [heathen] altars in the house of the Lord, of
which the Lord said, In Jerusalem will I put My name [and the
pledge of My presence].
5 And he [good Hezekiah's son] built altars for all the host of the
heavens in the two courts of the house of the Lord!
6 And he made his son pass through the fire *and* burned him as
an offering [to Molech]; he practiced soothsaying and augury, and
dealt with mediums and wizards! He did much wickedness in the
sight of the Lord, provoking Him to anger.
7 He made a graven image of Asherah and set it in the house of
which the Lord said to David and to Solomon his son, In this house
and in Jerusalem, which I have chosen out of all tribes of Israel,
will I put My name [and the pledge of My presence] for ever;
8 And I will not cause the feet of Israel to wander any more out
of the land which I gave their fathers, if only they will observe to
do according to all that I have commanded them, and according
to all the law that My servant Moses commanded them.
9 But they would not listen; and Manasseh seduced them to do
more evil than the nations did whom the Lord destroyed before
the Israelites!
10 And the Lord said by His servants the prophets,
11 Because Manasseh king of Judah has committed these abominations, and has done wickedly above all that the Amorites did
who were before him, and has made Judah also to sin with his
idols;
12 Therefore thus says the Lord, the God of Israel, Behold, I am
bringing such evil upon Jerusalem and Judah, that whoever hears
of it, both his ears shall tingle!
13 And I will stretch over Jerusalem the measuring line of Samaria, and the plummet of the house of Ahab; and I will wipe
Jerusalem as one wipes a dish, wiping it and turning it upside
down.
14 And I will cast off the rest of My inheritance, and deliver them
into the hand of their enemies; and they shall become a prey and
a spoil to all their enemies,
15 For they have done evil in My sight and have provoked Me
to anger, since their fathers came out of Egypt to this day.
16 Moreover Manasseh shed very much innocent blood, filling
Jerusalem from one end to another; besides his sin in making
Judah sin, by doing evil in the sight of the Lord! [Cp. II Chron.
33:10-19.]
17 The rest of the acts of Manasseh, all that he did, and his sin
that he committed, are they not written in the Book of the Chronicles of the Kings of Judah?

## New American Standard

18'And some of your sons who shall issue from you, whom you
shall beget, shall be taken away; and they shall become officials in
the palace of the king of Babylon.' "
19Then Hezekiah said to Isaiah, "The word of the LORD which
you have spoken is good." For he thought, "Is it not so, if there
shall be peace and truth in my days?"
20Now the rest of the acts of Hezekiah and all his might, and
how he made the pool and the conduit, and brought water into the
city, are they not written in the Book of the Chronicles of the Kings
of Judah?
21So Hezekiah slept with his fathers, and Manasseh his son
became king in his place.

*Manasseh Succeeds Hezekiah*

**21** MANASSEH WAS twelve years old when he became
king, and he reigned fifty-five years in Jerusalem; and his
mother's name was Hephzibah.
2And he did evil in the sight of the LORD, according to the
abominations of the nations whom the LORD dispossessed before
the sons of Israel.
3For he rebuilt the high places which Hezekiah his father had
destroyed; and he erected altars for Baal and made an Asherah, as
Ahab king of Israel had done, and worshiped all the host of heaven
and served them.
4And he built altars in the house of the LORD, of which the
LORD had said, "In Jerusalem I will put My name."
5For he built altars for all the host of heaven in the two courts
of the house of the LORD.
6And he made his son pass through the fire, practiced witchcraft and used divination, and dealt with mediums and spiritists.
He did much evil in the sight of the LORD provoking *Him to anger*.
7Then he set the carved image of Asherah that he had made,
in the house of which the LORD said to David and to his son
Solomon, "In this house and in Jerusalem, which I have chosen
from all the tribes of Israel, I will put My name forever.
8"And I will not make the feet of Israel wander anymore from
the land which I gave their fathers, if only they will observe to do
according to all that I have commanded them, and according to all
the law that My servant Moses commanded them."
9But they did not listen, and Manasseh seduced them to do evil
more than the nations whom the LORD destroyed before the sons
of Israel.

*The King's Idolatries Rebuked*

10¶ Now the LORD spoke through His servants the prophets,
saying,
11"Because Manasseh king of Judah has done these abominations, having done wickedly more than all the Amorites did who
*were* before him, and has also made Judah sin with his idols;
12therefore thus says the LORD, the God of Israel, 'Behold, I am
bringing *such* calamity on Jerusalem and Judah, that whoever
hears of it, both his ears shall tingle.
13'And I will stretch over Jerusalem the line of Samaria and the
plummet of the house of Ahab, and I will wipe Jerusalem as one
wipes a dish, wiping it and turning it upside down.
14'And I will abandon the remnant of My inheritance and deliver them into the hand of their enemies, and they shall become
as plunder and spoil to all their enemies;
15because they have done evil in My sight, and have been
provoking Me to anger, since the day their fathers came from
Egypt, even to this day.' "
16¶ Moreover, Manasseh shed very much innocent blood until
he had filled Jerusalem from one end to another; besides his sin
with which he made Judah sin, in doing evil in the sight of the
LORD.
17Now the rest of the acts of Manasseh and all that he did and
his sin which he committed, are they not written in the Book of
the Chronicles of the Kings of Judah?

## New International

your descendants, your own flesh and blood, that will be born to
you, will be taken away, and they will become eunuchs in the
palace of the king of Babylon."
19"The word of the LORD you have spoken is good," Hezekiah
replied. For he thought, "Will there not be peace and security in
my lifetime?"
20As for the other events of Hezekiah's reign, all his achievements and how he made the pool and the tunnel by which he
brought water into the city, are they not written in the book of the
annals of the kings of Judah? 21Hezekiah rested with his fathers.
And Manasseh his son succeeded him as king.

*Manasseh King of Judah*

**21** MANASSEH WAS twelve years old when he became
king, and he reigned in Jerusalem fifty-five years. His
mother's name was Hephzibah. 2He did evil in the eyes of the
LORD, following the detestable practices of the nations the LORD
had driven out before the Israelites. 3He rebuilt the high places his
father Hezekiah had destroyed; he also erected altars to Baal and
made an Asherah pole, as Ahab king of Israel had done. He bowed
down to all the starry hosts and worshiped them. 4He built altars
in the temple of the LORD, of which the LORD had said, "In Jerusalem I will put my Name." 5In both courts of the temple of the LORD,
he built altars to all the starry hosts. 6He sacrificed his own son in[a]
the fire, practiced sorcery and divination, and consulted mediums
and spiritists. He did much evil in the eyes of the LORD, provoking
him to anger.
7He took the carved Asherah pole he had made and put it in
the temple, of which the LORD had said to David and to his son
Solomon, "In this temple and in Jerusalem, which I have chosen
out of all the tribes of Israel, I will put my Name forever. 8I will
not again make the feet of the Israelites wander from the land I
gave their forefathers, if only they will be careful to do everything
I commanded them and will keep the whole Law that my servant
Moses gave them." 9But the people did not listen. Manasseh led
them astray, so that they did more evil than the nations the LORD
had destroyed before the Israelites.
10The LORD said through his servants the prophets: 11"Manasseh king of Judah has committed these detestable sins. He has
done more evil than the Amorites who preceded him and has led
Judah into sin with his idols. 12Therefore this is what the LORD, the
God of Israel, says: I am going to bring such disaster on Jerusalem
and Judah that the ears of everyone who hears of it will tingle. 13I
will stretch out over Jerusalem the measuring line used against
Samaria and the plumb line used against the house of Ahab. I will
wipe out Jerusalem as one wipes a dish, wiping it and turning it
upside down. 14I will forsake the remnant of my inheritance and
hand them over to their enemies. They will be looted and plundered by all their foes, 15because they have done evil in my eyes
and have provoked me to anger from the day their forefathers
came out of Egypt until this day."
16Moreover, Manasseh also shed so much innocent blood that
he filled Jerusalem from end to end—besides the sin that he had
caused Judah to commit, so that they did evil in the eyes of the
LORD.
17As for the other events of Manasseh's reign, and all he did,
including the sin he committed, are they not written in the book
of the annals of the kings of Judah? 18Manasseh rested with his

**NIV** [a] 6 Or *He made his own son pass through*

## King James

18 And Manasseh slept with his fathers, and was buried in the garden of his own house, in the garden of Uzza: and Amon his son reigned in his stead.

19 ¶ Amon *was* twenty and two years old when he began to reign, and he reigned two years in Jerusalem. And his mother's name *was* Meshullemeth, the daughter of Haruz of Jotbah.

20 And he did *that which was* evil in the sight of the LORD, as his father Manasseh did.

21 And he walked in all the way that his father walked in, and served the idols that his father served, and worshipped them:

22 And he forsook the LORD God of his fathers, and walked not in the way of the LORD.

23 ¶ And the servants of Amon conspired against him, and slew the king in his own house.

24 And the people of the land slew all them that had conspired against king Amon; and the people of the land made Josiah his son king in his stead.

25 Now the rest of the acts of Amon which he did, *are* they not written in the book of the chronicles of the kings of Judah?

26 And he was buried in his sepulchre in the garden of Uzza: and Josiah his son reigned in his stead.

**22** JOSIAH *WAS* eight years old when he began to reign, and he reigned thirty and one years in Jerusalem. And his mother's name *was* Jedidah, the daughter of Adaiah of Boscath.

2 And he did *that which was* right in the sight of the LORD, and walked in all the way of David his father, and turned not aside to the right hand or to the left.

3 ¶ And it came to pass in the eighteenth year of king Josiah, *that* the king sent Shaphan the son of Azaliah, the son of Meshullam, the scribe, to the house of the LORD, saying,

4 Go up to Hilkiah the high priest, that he may sum the silver which is brought into the house of the LORD, which the keepers of the door have gathered of the people:

5 And let them deliver it into the hand of the doers of the work, that have the oversight of the house of the LORD: and let them give it to the doers of the work which *is* in the house of the LORD, to repair the breaches of the house,

6 Unto carpenters, and builders, and masons, and to buy timber and hewn stone to repair the house.

7 Howbeit there was no reckoning made with them of the money that was delivered into their hand, because they dealt faithfully.

8 ¶ And Hilkiah the high priest said unto Shaphan the scribe, I have found the book of the law in the house of the LORD. And Hilkiah gave the book to Shaphan, and he read it.

9 And Shaphan the scribe came to the king, and brought the king word again, and said, Thy servants have gathered the money that was found in the house, and have delivered it into the hand of them that do the work, that have the oversight of the house of the LORD.

10 And Shaphan the scribe showed the king, saying, Hilkiah the priest hath delivered me a book. And Shaphan read it before the king.

11 And it came to pass, when the king had heard the words of the book of the law, that he rent his clothes.

12 And the king commanded Hilkiah the priest, and Ahikam the son of Shaphan, and Achbor the son of Michaiah, and Shaphan the scribe, and Asahiah a servant of the king's, saying,

13 Go ye, inquire of the LORD for me, and for the people, and for all Judah, concerning the words of this book that is found: for great *is* the wrath of the LORD that is kindled against us, because our fathers have not hearkened unto the words of this book, to do according unto all that which is written concerning us.

## Amplified

18 Manasseh slept with his fathers, and was buried in the garden of his own house, in the garden of Uzza. Amon his son reigned in his stead.

19 Amon was twenty-two years old when he began his two years' reign in Jerusalem. His mother was Meshullemeth daughter of Haruz of Jotbah.

20 [But] he also did evil in the sight of the Lord as his father Manasseh had done. [See also, 23:26, 27; 24:3, 4.]

21 He walked in all the way of his father, and served the idols that his father served, and worshiped them;

22 He forsook the Lord, the God of his [forefathers], and did not walk in the way of the Lord.

23 The servants of Amon conspired against him, and killed *him* in his own house.

24 But the people of the land killed all those who had conspired against King Amon, and made Josiah his son king in his stead.

25 The rest of the acts of Amon, are they not written in the Book of the Chronicles of the Kings of Judah?

26 He was buried in his tomb in the garden of Uzza. Josiah his son succeeded him.

**22** JOSIAH WAS eight years old when he began his thirty-one years' reign in Jerusalem. His mother was Jedidah daughter of Adaiah of Bozkath.

2 He did right in the sight of the Lord, and walked in all the way of David his [forefather], and turned not aside to the right hand or to the left.

3 In the eighteenth year of King Josiah, he sent Shaphan son of Azaliah, son of Meshullam, the scribe, to the Lord's house, saying,

4 Go up to Hilkiah the high priest, that he may count the money brought into the house of the Lord, which the keepers of the door have gathered from the people:

5 And let them deliver it into the hand of the workmen who have oversight of the Lord's house, to give to the laborers engaged in the repairing of the Lord's house,

6 That is, to the carpenters, builders, and masons, and to buy timber and hewn stone to repair the house.

7 However there was no accounting required of them for the money delivered into their hand, because they dealt faithfully.

8 Hilkiah the high priest said to Shaphan the scribe, I have found the book of the law in the house of the Lord! Hilkiah gave the book to Shaphan, and he read it.

9 And Shaphan the scribe came to the king, and reported to him, Your servants have gathered the money that was found in the house, and have delivered it into the hand of the workmen who have oversight of the house of the Lord.

10 Then Shaphan the scribe told the king, Hilkiah the priest has given me a book. And Shaphan read it before the king.

11 And when the king heard the words of the book of the law, he rent his clothes.

12 And the king commanded Hilkiah the priest, Ahikam son of Shaphan, Achbor son of Micaiah, Shaphan the scribe, and Asaiah servant of the king,

13 Go, inquire of the Lord for me, and for the people, and for all Judah, concerning the words of this book that has been found; for great is the wrath of the Lord that is kindled against us, because our fathers have not listened *and* obeyed the words of this book, to do according to all that is written concerning us.

## New American Standard

18And Manasseh slept with his fathers and was buried in the
garden of his own house, in the garden of Uzza, and Amon his son
became king in his place.

*Amon Succeeds Manasseh*

19¶ Amon was twenty-two years old when he became king, and
he reigned two years in Jerusalem; and his mother's name *was*
Meshullemeth the daughter of Haruz of Jotbah.
20And he did evil in the sight of the LORD, as Manasseh his
father had done.
21For he walked in all the way that his father had walked, and
served the idols that his father had served and worshiped them.
22So he forsook the LORD, the God of his fathers, and did not
walk in the way of the LORD.
23And the servants of Amon conspired against him and killed
the king in his own house.
24Then the people of the land killed all those who had conspired
against King Amon, and the people of the land made Josiah his son
king in his place.
25Now the rest of the acts of Amon which he did, are they not
written in the Book of the Chronicles of the Kings of Judah?
26And he was buried in his grave in the garden of Uzza, and
Josiah his son became king in his place.

*Josiah Succeeds Amon*

**22** JOSIAH WAS eight years old when he became king, and
he reigned thirty-one years in Jerusalem; and his mother's
name *was* Jedidah the daughter of Adaiah of Bozkath.
2And he did right in the sight of the LORD and walked in all
the way of his father David, nor did he turn aside to the right or
to the left.
3¶ Now it came about in the eighteenth year of King Josiah that
the king sent Shaphan, the son of Azaliah the son of Meshullam
the scribe, to the house of the LORD saying,
4"Go up to Hilkiah the high priest that he may count the
money brought in to the house of the LORD which the doorkeepers
have gathered from the people.
5"And let them deliver it into the hand of the workmen who
have the oversight of the house of the LORD, and let them give it
to the workmen who are in the house of the LORD to repair the
damages of the house,
6to the carpenters and the builders and tne masons and for
buying timber and hewn stone to repair the house.
7"Only no accounting shall be made with them for the money
delivered into their hands, for they deal faithfully."

*The Lost Book*

8¶ Then Hilkiah the high priest said to Shaphan the scribe, "I
have found the book of the law in the house of the LORD." And
Hilkiah gave the book to Shaphan who read it.
9And Shaphan the scribe came to the king and brought back
word to the king and said, "Your servants have emptied out the
money that was found in the house, and have delivered it into
the hand of the workmen who have the oversight of the house on
the LORD."
10Moreover, Shaphan the scribe told the king saying, "Hilkiah
the priest has given me a book." And Shaphan read it in the
presence of the king.
11And it came about when the king heard the words of the book
of the law, that he tore his clothes.
12Then the king commanded Hilkiah the priest, Ahikam the son
of Shaphan, Achbor the son of Micaiah, Shaphan the scribe, and
Asaiah the king's servant saying,
13"Go, inquire of the LORD for me and the people and all Judah
concerning the words of this book that has been found, for great
is the wrath of the LORD that burns against us, because our fathers
have not listened to the words of this book, to do according to all
that is written concerning us."

## New International

fathers and was buried in his palace garden, the garden of Uzza.
And Amon his son succeeded him as king.

*Amon King of Judah*

19Amon was twenty-two years old when he became king, and
he reigned in Jerusalem two years. His mother's name was Meshullemeth daughter of Haruz; she was from Jotbah. 20He did evil
in the eyes of the LORD, as his father Manasseh had done. 21He
walked in all the ways of his father; he worshiped the idols his
father had worshiped, and bowed down to them. 22He forsook the
LORD, the God of his fathers, and did not walk in the way of the
LORD.
23Amon's officials conspired against him and assassinated the
king in his palace. 24Then the people of the land killed all who had
plotted against King Amon, and they made Josiah his son king in
his place.
25As for the other events of Amon's reign, and what he did, are
they not written in the book of the annals of the kings of Judah?
26He was buried in his grave in the garden of Uzza. And Josiah his
son succeeded him as king.

*The Book of the Law Found*

**22** JOSIAH WAS eight years old when he became king, and
he reigned in Jerusalem thirty-one years. His mother's
name was Jedidah daughter of Adaiah; she was from Bozkath. 2He
did what was right in the eyes of the LORD and walked in all the
ways of his father David, not turning aside to the right or to the
left.
3In the eighteenth year of his reign, King Josiah sent the secretary, Shaphan son of Azaliah, the son of Meshullam, to the temple
of the LORD. He said: 4"Go up to Hilkiah the high priest and have
him get ready the money that has been brought into the temple of
the LORD, which the doorkeepers have collected from the people.
5Have them entrust it to the men appointed to supervise the work
on the temple. And have these men pay the workers who repair
the temple of the LORD— 6the carpenters, the builders and the
masons. Also have them purchase timber and dressed stone to
repair the temple. 7But they need not account for the money entrusted to them, because they are acting faithfully."
8Hilkiah the high priest said to Shaphan the secretary, "I have
found the Book of the Law in the temple of the LORD." He gave
it to Shaphan, who read it. 9Then Shaphan the secretary went to
the king and reported to him: "Your officials have paid out the
money that was in the temple of the LORD and have entrusted it
to the workers and supervisors at the temple." 10Then Shaphan
the secretary informed the king, "Hilkiah the priest has given me
a book." And Shaphan read from it in the presence of the king.
11When the king heard the words of the Book of the Law, he
tore his robes. 12He gave these orders to Hilkiah the priest, Ahikam son of Shaphan, Acbor son of Micaiah, Shaphan the secretary
and Asaiah the king's attendant: 13"Go and inquire of the LORD for
me and for the people and for all Judah about what is written in
this book that has been found. Great is the LORD's anger that burns
against us because our fathers have not obeyed the words of this
book; they have not acted in accordance with all that is written
there concerning us."

## King James

14 So Hilkiah the priest, and Ahikam, and Achbor, and Shaphan, and Asahiah, went unto Huldah the prophetess, the wife of Shallum the son of Tikvah, the son of Harhas, keeper of the wardrobe; (now she dwelt in Jerusalem in the college;) and they communed with her.

15 ¶ And she said unto them, Thus saith the LORD God of Israel, Tell the man that sent you to me,

16 Thus saith the LORD, Behold, I will bring evil upon this place, and upon the inhabitants thereof, *even* all the words of the book which the king of Judah hath read:

17 Because they have forsaken me, and have burned incense unto other gods, that they might provoke me to anger with all the works of their hands; therefore my wrath shall be kindled against this place, and shall not be quenched.

18 But to the king of Judah which sent you to inquire of the LORD, thus shall ye say to him, Thus saith the LORD God of Israel, *As touching* the words which thou hast heard;

19 Because thine heart was tender, and thou hast humbled thyself before the LORD, when thou heardest what I spake against this place, and against the inhabitants thereof, that they should become a desolation and a curse, and hast rent thy clothes, and wept before me; I also have heard *thee*, saith the LORD.

20 Behold therefore, I will gather thee unto thy fathers, and thou shalt be gathered into thy grave in peace; and thine eyes shall not see all the evil which I will bring upon this place. And they brought the king word again.

## Amplified

14 So Hilkiah the priest, Ahikam, Achbor, Shaphan, and Asaiah went to Huldah the prophetess, the wife of Shallum son of Tikvah, son of Harhas, keeper of the wardrobe (now she dwelt in Jerusalem in the Second Quarter); and they talked with her.

15 She said to them, Thus says the Lord, the God of Israel: Tell the man who sent you to me,

16 Thus says the Lord, Behold, I will bring evil upon this place and upon its inhabitants, all the words of the book which the king of Judah has read.

17 Because they have forsaken Me and have burned incense to other gods, provoking Me to anger with all the work of their hands, therefore My wrath will be kindled against this place and will not be quenched.

18 But to the king of Judah who sent you to inquire of the Lord, say this, Thus says the Lord, the God of Israel: Regarding the words you have heard,

19 Because your heart was [tender and] penitent, and you humbled yourself before the Lord when you heard what I said against this place and against its inhabitants, that they should become a desolation, [an astonishment and] a curse, and have rent your clothes and wept before Me, I also have heard you, says the Lord.

20 Behold therefore [King Josiah], I will gather you to your fathers, taken to your grave in peace, and your eyes shall not see all the evil which I will bring on this place. And they brought the king word.

## King James

**23** AND THE king sent, and they gathered unto him all the elders of Judah and of Jerusalem.

2 And the king went up into the house of the LORD, and all the men of Judah and all the inhabitants of Jerusalem with him, and the priests, and the prophets, and all the people, both small and great: and he read in their ears all the words of the book of the covenant which was found in the house of the LORD.

3 ¶ And the king stood by a pillar, and made a covenant before the LORD, to walk after the LORD, and to keep his commandments and his testimonies and his statutes with all *their* heart and all *their* soul, to perform the words of this covenant that were written in this book. And all the people stood to the covenant.

4 And the king commanded Hilkiah the high priest, and the priests of the second order, and the keepers of the door, to bring forth out of the temple of the LORD all the vessels that were made for Baal, and for the grove, and for all the host of heaven: and he burned them without Jerusalem in the fields of Kidron, and carried the ashes of them unto Beth-el.

5 And he put down the idolatrous priests, whom the kings of Judah had ordained to burn incense in the high places in the cities of Judah, and in the places round about Jerusalem; them also that burned incense unto Baal, to the sun, and to the moon, and to the planets, and to all the hosts of heaven.

6 And he brought out the grove from the house of the LORD, without Jerusalem, unto the brook Kidron, and burned it at the brook Kidron, and stamped *it* small to powder, and cast the powder thereof upon the graves of the children of the people.

7 And he brake down the houses of the sodomites, that *were* by the house of the LORD, where the women wove hangings for the grove.

8 And he brought all the priests out of the cities of Judah, and defiled the high places where the priests had burned incense, from Geba to Beer-sheba, and brake down the high places of the gates that *were* in the entering in of the gate of Joshua the governor of the city, which *were* on a man's left hand at the gate of the city.

## Amplified

**23** KING JOSIAH sent and gathered to him all the elders of Judah and of Jerusalem.

2 The king went up to the house of the Lord, and with him all the men of Judah, all the inhabitants of Jerusalem, the priests, the prophets, and all the people, both small and great. And he read in their ears all the words of the book of the covenant which was found in the Lord's house.

3 The king stood [on the platform] by the pillar and made a covenant before the Lord, to walk after the Lord and to keep His commandments, His testimonies and His statutes with all his heart and soul, to confirm the words of this covenant that were written in this book. And all the people stood to join in the covenant.

4 And the king commanded Hilkiah the high priest, and the priests of the second rank, and the keepers of the threshold, to bring out of the temple of the Lord all the vessels made for Baal, for the Asherah, and for all the host of the heavens, and he burned them outside Jerusalem in the fields of the Kidron, and carried their ashes to Bethel [where Israel's idolatry began]. [I Kings 12:28, 29.]

5 He put out the idolatrous priests, whom the kings of Judah had ordained to burn incense in the high places in Judah's cities and round about Jerusalem; also those who burned incense to Baal, to the sun, to the moon, to the constellation [or twelve signs of the Zodiac], and to all the host of the heavens.

6 And Josiah brought the Asherah from the house of the Lord, outside Jerusalem to the brook Kidron, and burned it there, and beat it to dust and cast its dust upon the graves of the common people [who had sacrificed to it].

7 And be broke down the houses of the male cult prostitutes, that were by the house of the Lord, where the women wove [tent] hangings for the Asherah [shrines].

8 And [Josiah] brought all the [idolatrous] priests out of the city of Judah, and defiled the high places where the priests had burned incense, from Geba to Beer-sheba [north to south], and broke down the high places both at the entrance of the gate of Joshua the governor of the city, and that which was on one's left at the city's gate.

## New American Standard

*Huldah Predicts*

14¶ So Hilkiah the priest, Ahikam, Achbor, Shaphan, and Asaiah went to Huldah the prophetess, the wife of Shallum the son of Tikvah, the son of Harhas, keeper of the wardrobe (now she lived in Jerusalem in the Second Quarter); and they spoke to her.

15And she said to them, "Thus says the LORD God of Israel, 'Tell the man who sent you to me,

16thus says the LORD, "Behold, I bring evil on this place and on its inhabitants, *even* all the words of the book which the king of Judah has read.

17"Because they have forsaken Me and have burned incense to other gods that they might provoke Me to anger with all the work of their hands, therefore My wrath burns against this place, and it shall not be quenched." '

18"But to the king of Judah who sent you to inquire of the LORD thus shall you say to him, 'Thus says the LORD God of Israel, " *Regarding* the words which you have heard,

19because your heart was tender and you humbled yourself before the LORD when you heard what I spoke against this place and against its inhabitants that they should become a desolation and a curse, and you have torn your clothes and wept before Me, I truly have heard you," declares the LORD.

20"Therefore, behold, I will gather you to your fathers, and you shall be gathered to your grave in peace, neither shall your eyes see all the evil which I will bring on this place." ' " So they brought back word to the king.

*Josiah's Covenant*

**23** THEN THE king sent, and they gathered to him all the elders of Judah and of Jerusalem.

2And the king went up to the house of the LORD and all the men of Judah and all the inhabitants of Jerusalem with him, and the priests and the prophets and all the people, both small and great; and he read in their hearing all the words of the book of the covenant, which was found in the house of the LORD.

3And the king stood by the pillar and made a covenant before the LORD, to walk after the LORD, and to keep His commandments and His testimonies and His statutes with all *his* heart and all *his* soul, to carry out the words of this covenant that were written in this book. And all the people entered into the covenant.

*Reforms under Josiah*

4¶ Then the king commanded Hilkiah the high priest and the priests of the second order and the doorkeepers, to bring out of the temple of the LORD all the vessels that were made for Baal, for [a]Asherah, and for all the host of heaven; and he burned them outside Jerusalem in the fields of the Kidron, and carried their ashes to Bethel.

5And he did away with the idolatrous priests whom the kings of Judah had appointed to burn incense in the high places in the cities of Judah and in the surrounding area of Jerusalem, also those who burned incense to Baal, to the sun and to the moon and to the constellations and to all the host of heaven.

6And he brought out the Asherah from the house of the LORD outside Jerusalem to the brook Kidron, and burned it at the brook Kidron, and ground *it* to dust, and threw its dust on the graves of the common people.

7He also broke down the houses of the *male* cult prostitutes which *were* in the house of the LORD, where the women were weaving hangings for the Asherah.

8Then he brought all the priests from the cities of Judah, and defiled the high places where the priests had burned incense, from Geba to Beersheba; and he broke down the high places of the gates which *were* at the entrance of the gate of Joshua the governor of the city, which *were* on one's left at the city gate.

NAS [a] I.e., wooden symbol of a female deity

## New International

14Hilkiah the priest, Ahikam, Acbor, Shaphan and Asaiah went
to speak to the prophetess Huldah, who was the wife of Shallum
son of Tikvah, the son of Harhas, keeper of the wardrobe. She
lived in Jerusalem, in the Second District.
15She said to them, "This is what the LORD, the God of Israel,
says: Tell the man who sent you to me, 16'This is what the LORD
says: I am going to bring disaster on this place and its people,
according to everything written in the book the king of Judah has
read. 17Because they have forsaken me and burned incense to
other gods and provoked me to anger by all the idols their hands
have made,[b] my anger will burn against this place and will not be
quenched.' 18Tell the king of Judah, who sent you to inquire of the
LORD, 'This is what the LORD, the God of Israel, says concerning
the words you heard: 19Because your heart was responsive and
you humbled yourself before the LORD when you heard what I
have spoken against this place and its people, that they would
become accursed and laid waste, and because you tore your robes
and wept in my presence, I have heard you, declares the LORD.
20Therefore I will gather you to your fathers, and you will be buried
in peace. Your eyes will not see all the disaster I am going to bring
on this place.' "

So they took her answer back to the king.

*Josiah Renews the Covenant*

**23** THEN THE king called together all the elders of Judah and
Jerusalem. 2He went up to the temple of the LORD with the
men of Judah, the people of Jerusalem, the priests and the prophets—all the people from the least to the greatest. He read in their
hearing all the words of the Book of the Covenant, which had been
found in the temple of the LORD. 3The king stood by the pillar and
renewed the covenant in the presence of the LORD—to follow the
LORD and keep his commands, regulations and decrees with all his
heart and all his soul, thus confirming the words of the covenant
written in this book. Then all the people pledged themselves to the
covenant.
4The king ordered Hilkiah the high priest, the priests next in
rank and the doorkeepers to remove from the temple of the LORD
all the articles made for Baal and Asherah and all the starry hosts.
He burned them outside Jerusalem in the fields of the Kidron
Valley and took the ashes to Bethel. 5He did away with the pagan
priests appointed by the kings of Judah to burn incense on the high
places of the towns of Judah and on those around Jerusalem—
those who burned incense to Baal, to the sun and moon, to the
constellations and to all the starry hosts. 6He took the Asherah
pole from the temple of the LORD to the Kidron Valley outside
Jerusalem and burned it there. He ground it to powder and scattered the dust over the graves of the common people. 7He also tore
down the quarters of the male shrine prostitutes, which were in
the temple of the LORD and where women did weaving for
Asherah.
8Josiah brought all the priests from the towns of Judah and
desecrated the high places, from Geba to Beersheba, where the
priests had burned incense. He broke down the shrines[c] at the
gates—at the entrance to the Gate of Joshua, the city governor,
which is on the left of the city gate. 9Although the priests of the

NIV [b] 17 Or *by everything they have done* [c] 8 Or *high places*

## King James

9Nevertheless the priests of the high places came not up to the altar of the LORD in Jerusalem, but they did eat of the unleavened bread among their brethren.

10And he defiled Topheth, which *is* in the valley of the children of Hinnom, that no man might make his son or his daughter to pass through the fire to Molech.

11And he took away the horses that the kings of Judah had given to the sun, at the entering in of the house of the LORD, by the chamber of Nathan-melech the chamberlain, which *was* in the suburbs, and burned the chariots of the sun with fire.

12And the altars that *were* on the top of the upper chamber of Ahaz, which the kings of Judah had made, and the altars which Manasseh had made in the two courts of the house of the LORD, did the king beat down, and brake *them* down from thence, and cast the dust of them into the brook Kidron.

13And the high places that *were* before Jerusalem, which *were* on the right hand of the mount of corruption, which Solomon the king of Israel had builded for Ashtoreth the abomination of the Zidonians, and for Chemosh the abomination of the Moabites, and for Milcom the abomination of the children of Ammon, did the king defile.

14And he brake in pieces the images, and cut down the groves, and filled their places with the bones of men.

15¶ Moreover the altar that *was* at Beth-el, *and* the high place which Jeroboam the son of Nebat, who made Israel to sin, had made, both that altar and the high place he brake down, and burned the high place, *and* stamped *it* small to powder, and burned the grove.

16And as Josiah turned himself, he spied the sepulchres that *were* there in the mount, and sent, and took the bones out of the sepulchres, and burned *them* upon the altar, and polluted it, according to the word of the LORD which the man of God proclaimed, who proclaimed these words.

17Then he said, What title *is* that that I see? And the men of the city told him, *It is* the sepulchre of the man of God, which came from Judah, and proclaimed these things that thou hast done against the altar of Beth-el.

18And he said, Let him alone; let no man move his bones. So they let his bones alone, with the bones of the prophet that came out of Samaria.

19And all the houses also of the high places that *were* in the cities of Samaria, which the kings of Israel had made to provoke *the* LORD to anger, Josiah took away, and did to them according to all the acts that he had done in Beth-el.

20And he slew all the priests of the high places that *were* there upon the altars, and burned men's bones upon them, and returned to Jerusalem.

21¶ And the king commanded all the people, saying, Keep the passover unto the LORD your God, as *it is* written in the book of this covenant.

22Surely there was not holden such a passover from the days of the judges that judged Israel, nor in all the days of the kings of Israel, nor of the kings of Judah;

23But in the eighteenth year of king Josiah, *wherein* this passover was holden to the LORD in Jerusalem.

24¶ Moreover the *workers with* familiar spirits, and the wizards, and the images, and the idols, and all the abominations that were spied in the land of Judah and in Jerusalem, did Josiah put away, that he might perform the words of the law which were written in the book that Hilkiah the priest found in the house of the LORD.

25And like unto him was there no king before him, that turned to the LORD with all his heart, and with all his soul, and with all his might, according to all the law of Moses; neither after him arose there *any* like him.

26¶ Notwithstanding the LORD turned not from the fierceness of his great wrath, wherewith his anger was kindled against Judah, because of all the provocations that Manasseh had provoked him withal.

## Amplified

9However, the priests of the high places were not allowed to sacrifice upon the Lord's altar in Jerusalem, but they ate unleavened bread among their brethren.

10And Josiah defiled Topheth, which is in the valley of the sons of Hinnom, that no man might ever burn there his son or his daughter as an offering to Molech. [Ezek. 16:21.]

11And he removed the horses that the kings of Judah had devoted to the sun, at the entrance of the house of the Lord, by the chamber of Nathan-melech the chamberlain, which was in the area, and he burned the chariots of the sun with fire.

12And the altars on the roof of the upper chamber of Ahaz, which the kings of Judah had made, and the altars which Manasseh had made in the two courts of the house of the Lord, [Josiah] pulled down and beat them in pieces, and he [ran and] cast their dust into the brook Kidron.

13And the king defiled the high places east of Jerusalem, south of the mount of corruption, which Solomon the king of Israel had built for Ashtoreth the abominable [goddess] of the Sidonians, for Chemosh the abominable god of the Moabites, and for Milcom the abominable [god] of the Ammonites.

14He broke in pieces the pillars [images], and cut down the Asherim, and replaced them with the bones of men [to defile the places forever].

15Moreover the altar at Bethel, the high place made by Jeroboam son of Nebat, who made Israel to sin, that altar with the high place Josiah tore down *and* broke in pieces its stones, beating them to dust, and burned the Asherah.

16And as Josiah turned, he saw the tombs across on the mount, and he sent and brought the bones out of the tombs, and burned them upon the altar, and defiled it, in fulfillment of the word of the Lord which the man of God prophesied, who predicted these things [about this altar, naming Josiah before he was born]. [I Kings 13:2-5.]

17Josiah said, What is that monument I see? The men of the city told him, It is the tomb of the man of God who came from Judah, and foretold these things that you have just done against the altar of Bethel.

18He said, Let him alone; let no man move his bones. So they let his bones alone, with the bones of the prophet that came out of Samaria. [I Kings 13:31, 32.]

19Also Josiah took away all the houses of the high places in the cities of Samaria, which the kings of Israel had made provoking the Lord to anger, and he did to them all that he had done in Bethel.

20He slew all the priests of the high places that were there, upon the altars, and burned men's bones upon them [to defile the places forever]. Then he returned to Jerusalem.

21The king commanded all the people, Keep the passover to the Lord your God, as it is written in the book of this covenant.

22Surely such a passover was not held from the days of Israel's judges, even in all the days of the kings of Israel or Judah;

23But in the eighteenth year of King Josiah, this passover was kept to the Lord in Jerusalem.

24Moreover, Josiah put away the mediums, the wizards, the teraphim [household gods], the idols and all the abominations that were seen in Judah and in Jerusalem, that he might establish the words of the law written in the book found by Hilkiah the priest in the house of the Lord.

25There was no king like him before or after [Josiah], who turned to the Lord with all his heart and all his soul and all his might, according to all the law of Moses.

26Still the Lord did not turn from the fierceness of His great wrath, kindled against Judah, because of all the provocations with which Manasseh had provoked Him.

## New American Standard

9Nevertheless the priests of the high places did not go up to
the altar of the LORD in Jerusalem, but they ate unleavened bread
among their brothers.
10He also defiled [a]Topheth, which is in the valley of the son of
Hinnom, that no man might make his son or his daughter pass
through the fire for Molech.
11And he did away with the horses which the kings of Judah
had given to the sun, at the entrance of the house of the LORD, by
the chamber of Nathan-melech the official, which *was* in the precincts; and he burned the chariots of the sun with fire.
12And the altars which *were* on the roof, the upper chamber of
Ahaz, which the kings of Judah had made, and the altars which
Manasseh had made in the two courts of the house of the LORD,
the king broke down; and he [b]smashed them there, and threw
their dust into the brook Kidron.
13And the high places which *were* before Jerusalem, which *were*
on the right of the mount of destruction which Solomon the king
of Israel had built for Ashtoreth the abomination of the Sidonians,
and for Chemosh the abomination of Moab, and for Milcom the
abomination of the sons of Ammon, the king defiled.
14And he broke in pieces the *sacred* pillars and cut down the
Asherim and filled their places with human bones.
**15**¶ Furthermore, the altar that *was* at Bethel *and* the high place
which Jeroboam the son of Nebat, who made Israel sin, had made,
even that altar and the high place he broke down. Then he demolished its stones, ground them to dust, and burned the Asherah.
16Now when Josiah turned, he saw the graves that *were* there
on the mountain, and he sent and took the bones from the graves
and burned *them* on the altar and defiled it according to the word
of the LORD which the man of God proclaimed, who proclaimed
these things.
17Then he said, "What is this monument that I see?" And the
men of the city told him, "It is the grave of the man of God who
came from Judah and proclaimed these things which you have
done against the altar of Bethel."
18And he said, "Let him alone; let no one disturb his bones."
So they left his bones undisturbed with the bones of the prophet
who came from Samaria.
19And Josiah also removed all the houses of the high places
which *were* in the cities of Samaria, which the kings of Israel had
made provoking the LORD; and he did to them just as he had done
in Bethel.
20And all the priests of the high places who *were* there he
slaughtered on the altars and burned human bones on them; then
he returned to Jerusalem.

*Passover Reinstituted*

**21**¶ Then the king commanded all the people saying, "Celebrate
the Passover to the LORD your God as it is written in this book of
the covenant."
22Surely such a Passover had not been celebrated from the days
of the judges who judged Israel, nor in all the days of the kings
of Israel and of the kings of Judah.
23But in the eighteenth year of King Josiah, this Passover was
observed to the LORD in Jerusalem.
**24**¶ Moreover, Josiah removed the mediums and the spiritists
and the teraphim and the idols and all the abominations that were
seen in the land of Judah and in Jerusalem, that he might confirm
the words of the law which were written in the book that Hilkiah
the priest found in the house of the LORD.
25And before him there was no king like him who turned to the
LORD with all his heart and with all his soul and with all his might,
according to all the law of Moses; nor did any like him arise after
him.
**26**¶ However, the LORD did not turn from the fierceness of His
great wrath with which His anger burned against Judah, because
of all the provocations with which Manasseh had provoked Him.

NAS [a] I.e., place of burning [b] Or, *ran from there*

## New International

high places did not serve at the altar of the LORD in Jerusalem, they
ate unleavened bread with their fellow priests.
10He desecrated Topheth, which was in the Valley of Ben Hinnom, so no one could use it to sacrifice his son or daughter in[c] the
fire to Molech. 11He removed from the entrance to the temple of
the LORD the horses that the kings of Judah had dedicated to the
sun. They were in the court near the room of an official named
Nathan-Melech. Josiah then burned the chariots dedicated to the
sun.
12He pulled down the altars the kings of Judah had erected on
the roof near the upper room of Ahaz, and the altars Manasseh had
built in the two courts of the temple of the LORD. He removed them
from there, smashed them to pieces and threw the rubble into the
Kidron Valley. 13The king also desecrated the high places that were
east of Jerusalem on the south of the Hill of Corruption—the ones
Solomon king of Israel had built for Ashtoreth the vile goddess of
the Sidonians, for Chemosh the vile god of Moab, and for Molech[d]
the detestable god of the people of Ammon. 14Josiah smashed the
sacred stones and cut down the Asherah poles and covered the
sites with human bones.
15Even the altar at Bethel, the high place made by Jeroboam son
of Nebat, who had caused Israel to sin—even that altar and high
place he demolished. He burned the high place and ground it to
powder, and burned the Asherah pole also. 16Then Josiah looked
around, and when he saw the tombs that were there on the hillside, he had the bones removed from them and burned on the altar
to defile it, in accordance with the word of the LORD proclaimed
by the man of God who foretold these things.
17The king asked, "What is that tombstone I see?"
The men of the city said, "It marks the tomb of the man of God
who came from Judah and pronounced against the altar of Bethel
the very things you have done to it."
18"Leave it alone," he said. "Don't let anyone disturb his
bones." So they spared his bones and those of the prophet who
had come from Samaria.
19Just as he had done at Bethel, Josiah removed and defiled all
the shrines at the high places that the kings of Israel had built in
the towns of Samaria that had provoked the LORD to anger. 20Jo-
siah slaughtered all the priests of those high places on the altars
and burned human bones on them. Then he went back to Jerusalem.
21The king gave this order to all the people: "Celebrate the
Passover to the LORD your God, as it is written in this Book of the
Covenant." 22Not since the days of the judges who led Israel, nor
throughout the days of the kings of Israel and the kings of Judah,
had any such Passover been observed. 23But in the eighteenth year
of King Josiah, this Passover was celebrated to the LORD in Jerusalem.
24Furthermore, Josiah got rid of the mediums and spiritists, the
household gods, the idols and all the other detestable things seen
in Judah and Jerusalem. This he did to fulfill the requirements of
the law written in the book that Hilkiah the priest had discovered
in the temple of the LORD. 25Neither before nor after Josiah was
there a king like him who turned to the LORD as he did—with all
his heart and with all his soul and with all his strength, in accordance with all the Law of Moses.
26Nevertheless, the LORD did not turn away from the heat of his
fierce anger, which burned against Judah because of all that Manasseh had done to provoke him to anger. 27So the LORD said, "I

NIV [c] 10 Or *to make his son or daughter pass through* [d] 13 Hebrew *Milcom*

## King James

27 And the LORD said, I will remove Judah also out of my sight, as I have removed Israel, and will cast off this city Jerusalem which I have chosen, and the house of which I said, My name shall be there.

28 Now the rest of the acts of Josiah, and all that he did, *are* they not written in the book of the chronicles of the kings of Judah?

29 ¶ In his days Pharaoh-nechoh king of Egypt went up against the king of Assyria to the river Euphrates: and king Josiah went against him; and he slew him at Megiddo, when he had seen him.

30 And his servants carried him in a chariot dead from Megiddo, and brought him to Jerusalem, and buried him in his own sepulchre. And the people of the land took Jehoahaz the son of Josiah, and anointed him, and made him king in his father's stead.

31 ¶ Jehoahaz *was* twenty and three years old when he began to reign; and he reigned three months in Jerusalem. And his mother's name *was* Hamutal, the daughter of Jeremiah of Libnah.

32 And he did *that which was* evil in the sight of the LORD, according to all that his fathers had done.

33 And Pharaoh-nechoh put him in bands at Riblah in the land of Hamath, that he might not reign in Jerusalem; and put the land to a tribute of an hundred talents of silver, and a talent of gold.

34 And Pharaoh-nechoh made Eliakim the son of Josiah king in the room of Josiah his father, and turned his name to Johoiakim, and took Jehoahaz away: and he came to Egypt, and died there.

35 And Jehoiakim gave the silver and the gold to Pharaoh; but he taxed the land to give the money according to the commandment of Pharaoh: he exacted the silver and the gold of the people of the land, of every one according to his taxation, to give *it* unto Pharaoh-nechoh.

36 ¶ Jehoiakim *was* twenty and five years old when he began to reign; and he reigned eleven years in Jerusalem. And his mother's name was Zebudah, the daughter of Pedaiah of Rumah.

37 And he did *that which was* evil in the sight of the LORD, according to all that his fathers had done.

**24** IN HIS days Nebuchadnezzar king of Babylon came up, and Jehoiakim became his servant three years: then he turned and rebelled against him.

2 And the LORD sent against him bands of the Chaldees, and bands of the Syrians, and bands of the Moabites, and bands of the children of Ammon, and sent them against Judah to destroy it, according to the word of the LORD, which he spake by his servants the prophets.

3 Surely at the commandment of the LORD came *this* upon Judah, to remove *them* out of his sight, for the sins of Manasseh, according to all that he did;

4 And also for the innocent blood that he shed: for he filled Jerusalem with innocent blood; which the LORD would not pardon.

5 ¶ Now the rest of the acts of Jehoiakim, and all that he did, *are* they not written in the book of the chronicles of the kings of Judah?

6 So Jehoiakim slept with his fathers: and Jehoiachin his son reigned in his stead.

7 And the king of Egypt came not again any more out of his land: for the king of Babylon had taken from the river of Egypt unto the river Euphrates all that pertained to the king of Egypt.

8 ¶ Jehoiachin *was* eighteen years old when he began to reign, and he reigned in Jerusalem three months. And his mother's name *was* Nehushta, the daughter of Elnathan of Jerusalem.

## Amplified

27 And the Lord said, I will remove Judah also out of My sight, as I have removed Israel, and will cast off this city, Jerusalem, which I have chosen, and the house of which I said, My name [and the pledge of My presence] shall be there.

28 The rest of the acts of Josiah, all that he did, are they not written in the Book of the Chronicles of Judah's Kings?

29 In his days Pharaoh Necho king of Egypt went up against the king of Assyria to the river Euphrates. King Josiah went out against him, but he slew Josiah at Megiddo when he saw him.

30 Josiah's servants carried him dead in a chariot from Megiddo, brought him to Jerusalem, and buried him in his own tomb. The people of the land anointed Jehoahaz son of Josiah king in his stead.

31 Jehoahaz was twenty-three years old when he began his three months' reign in Jerusalem. His mother was Hamutal, daughter of Jeremiah of Libnah.

32 He did evil in the sight of the Lord, according to all [the evil] his forefathers had done.

33 And Pharaoh Necho put him in bonds at Riblah in the land of Hamath, that he might not reign in Jerusalem, and laid a tribute of a hundred talents of silver and a talent of gold upon the land.

34 Pharaoh Necho made Eliakim son of Josiah king in place of Josiah, and changed his name to Jehoiakim. But he took Jehoahaz away to Egypt, where he died.

35 Jehoiakim gave the silver and the gold to Pharaoh, but he taxed the land to give the money as Pharaoh commanded. He exacted the silver and gold of the people of the land, from every one according to his assessment, to give it to Pharaoh Necho.

36 Jehoiakim was twenty-five years old when he began his eleven years' reign in Jerusalem. His mother was Zebidah daughter of Pedaiah of Rumah.

37 He did evil in the sight of the Lord, like all his [forefathers] had done.

**24** IN HIS days Nebuchadnezzar king of Babylon came up, and Jehoiakim became his servant for three years; then he turned and rebelled against him.

2 The Lord sent against Jehoiakim bands of Chaldeans, of Syrians, of Moabites, and of Ammonites, and sent them against Judah to destroy it, according to the word of the Lord, which He spoke by His servants the prophets.

3 Surely this came upon Judah at the command of the Lord, to remove them out of His sight, for the sins of Manasseh, according to all he had done;

4 And also for the innocent blood that he shed; for he filled Jerusalem with innocent blood, and the Lord would not pardon.

5 The rest of the acts of Jehoiakim, all that he did, are they not written in the Book of the Chronicles of Judah's Kings?

6 So Jehoiakim slept with his fathers. Jehoiachin his son reigned in his stead.

7 The king of Egypt came no more out of his land, for the king of Babylon had taken all that belonged to Egypt's king from the river of Egypt to the river Euphrates.

8 Jehoiachin was eighteen years old when he began his three months' reign in Jerusalem. His mother was Nehushta daughter of Elnathan of Jerusalem.

# New American Standard

27And the LORD said, "I will remove Judah also from My sight, as I have removed Israel. And I will cast off Jerusalem, this city which I have chosen, and the temple of which I said, 'My name shall be there.'"

## Jehoahaz Succeeds Josiah

28¶ Now the rest of the acts of Josiah and all that he did, are they not written in the Book of the Chronicles of the Kings of Judah? 29In his days Pharaoh Neco king of Egypt went up to the king of Assyria to the river Euphrates. And King Josiah went to meet him, and when *Pharaoh Neco* saw him he killed him at Megiddo. 30And his servants drove his body in a chariot from Megiddo, and brought him to Jerusalem and buried him in his own tomb. Then the people of the land took Jehoahaz the son of Josiah and anointed him and made him king in place of his father.

31¶ Jehoahaz was twenty-three years old when he became king, and he reigned three months in Jerusalem; and his mother's name was Hamutal the daughter of Jeremiah of Libnah.

32And he did evil in the sight of the LORD, according to all that his fathers had done.

33And Pharaoh Neco imprisoned him at Riblah in the land of Hamath, that he might not reign in Jerusalem; and he imposed on the land a fine of one hundred talents of silver and a talent of gold.

## Jehoiakim Made King by Pharaoh

34And Pharaoh Neco made Eliakim the son of Josiah king in the place of Josiah his father, and changed his name to Jehoiakim. But he took Jehoahaz away and brought *him* to Egypt, and he died there.

35So Jehoiakim gave the silver and gold to Pharaoh, but he taxed the land in order to give the money at the command of Pharaoh. He exacted the silver and gold from the people of the land, each according to his valuation, to give it to Pharaoh Neco.

36¶ Jehoiakim was twenty-five years old when he became king, and he reigned eleven years in Jerusalem; and his mother's name *was* Zebidah the daughter of Pedaiah of Rumah.

37And he did evil in the sight of the LORD, according to all that his fathers had done.

## Babylon Controls Jehoiakim

**24** IN HIS days Nebuchadnezzar king of Babylon came up, and Jehoiakim became his servant *for* three years; then he turned and rebelled against him.

2And the LORD sent against him bands of Chaldeans, bands of Arameans, bands of Moabites, and bands of Ammonites. So He sent them against Judah to destroy it, according to the word of the LORD, which He had spoken through His servants the prophets.

3Surely at the command of the LORD it came upon Judah, to remove *them* from His sight because of the sins of Manasseh, according to all that he had done,

4and also for the innocent blood which he shed, for he filled Jerusalem with innocent blood; and the LORD would not forgive.

5Now the rest of the acts of Jehoiakim and all that he did, are they not written in the Book of the Chronicles of the Kings of Judah?

## Jehoiachin Reigns

6So Jehoiakim slept with his fathers, and Jehoiachin his son became king in his place.

7And the king of Egypt did not come out of his land again, for the king of Babylon had taken all that belonged to the king of Egypt from the brook of Egypt to the river Euphrates.

8¶ Jehoiachin was eighteen years old when he became king, and he reigned three months in Jerusalem; and his mother's name *was* Nehushta the daughter of Elnathan of Jerusalem.

# New International

will remove Judah also from my presence as I removed Israel, and I will reject Jerusalem, the city I chose, and this temple, about which I said, 'There shall my Name be.'ª "

28As for the other events of Josiah's reign, and all he did, are they not written in the book of the annals of the kings of Judah? 29While Josiah was king, Pharaoh Neco king of Egypt went up to the Euphrates River to help the king of Assyria. King Josiah marched out to meet him in battle, but Neco faced him and killed him at Megiddo. 30Josiah's servants brought his body in a chariot from Megiddo to Jerusalem and buried him in his own tomb. And the people of the land took Jehoahaz son of Josiah and anointed him and made him king in place of his father.

## Jehoahaz King of Judah

31Jehoahaz was twenty-three years old when he became king, and he reigned in Jerusalem three months. His mother's name was Hamutal daughter of Jeremiah; she was from Libnah. 32He did evil in the eyes of the LORD, just as his fathers had done. 33Pharaoh Neco put him in chains at Riblah in the land of Hamathᵇ so that he might not reign in Jerusalem, and he imposed on Judah a levy of a hundred talentsᶜ of silver and a talentᵈ of gold. 34Pharaoh Neco made Eliakim son of Josiah king in place of his father Josiah and changed Eliakim's name to Jehoiakim. But he took Jehoahaz and carried him off to Egypt, and there he died. 35Jehoiakim paid Pharaoh Neco the silver and gold he demanded. In order to do so, he taxed the land and exacted the silver and gold from the people of the land according to their assessments.

## Jehoiakim King of Judah

36Jehoiakim was twenty-five years old when he became king, and he reigned in Jerusalem eleven years. His mother's name was Zebidah daughter of Pedaiah; she was from Rumah. 37And he did evil in the eyes of the LORD, just as his fathers had done.

**24** DURING JEHOIAKIM'S reign, Nebuchadnezzar king of Babylon invaded the land, and Jehoiakim became his vassal for three years. But then he changed his mind and rebelled against Nebuchadnezzar. 2The LORD sent Babylonian,ᵉ Aramean, Moabite and Ammonite raiders against him. He sent them to destroy Judah, in accordance with the word of the LORD proclaimed by his servants the prophets. 3Surely these things happened to Judah according to the LORD's command, in order to remove them from his presence because of the sins of Manasseh and all he had done, 4including the shedding of innocent blood. For he had filled Jerusalem with innocent blood, and the LORD was not willing to forgive.

5As for the other events of Jehoiakim's reign, and all he did, are they not written in the book of the annals of the kings of Judah? 6Jehoiakim rested with his fathers. And Jehoiachin his son succeeded him as king.

7The king of Egypt did not march out from his own country again, because the king of Babylon had taken all his territory, from the Wadi of Egypt to the Euphrates River.

## Jehoiachin King of Judah

8Jehoiachin was eighteen years old when he became king, and he reigned in Jerusalem three months. His mother's name was Nehushta daughter of Elnathan; she was from Jerusalem. 9He did

**NIV** ª 27 1 Kings 8:29   ᵇ 33 Hebrew; Septuagint (see also 2 Chron. 36:3) *Neco at Riblah in Hamath removed him*   ᶜ 33 That is, about 3 3/4 tons (about 3.4 metric tons)   ᵈ 33 That is, about 75 pounds (about 34 kilograms)   ᵉ 2 Or *Chaldean*

# King James

9And he did *that which was* evil in the sight of the LORD, according to all that his father had done.

10¶ At that time the servants of Nebuchadnezzar king of Babylon came up against Jerusalem, and the city was besieged.

11And Nebuchadnezzar king of Babylon came against the city, and his servants did besiege it.

12And Jehoiachin the king of Judah went out to the king of Babylon, he, and his mother, and his servants, and his princes, and his officers: and the king of Babylon took him in the eighth year of his reign.

13And he carried out thence all the treasures of the house of the LORD, and the treasures of the king's house, and cut in pieces all the vessels of gold which Solomon king of Israel had made in the temple of the LORD, as the LORD had said.

14And he carried away all Jerusalem, and all the princes, and all the mighty men of valour, *even* ten thousand captives, and all the craftsmen and smiths: none remained, save the poorest sort of the people of the land.

15And he carried away Jehoiachin to Babylon, and the king's mother, and the king's wives, and his officers, and the mighty of the land, *those* carried he into captivity from Jerusalem to Babylon.

16And all the men of might, *even* seven thousand, and craftsmen and smiths a thousand, all *that were* strong *and* apt for war, even them the king of Babylon brought captive to Babylon.

17¶ And the king of Babylon made Mattaniah his father's brother king in his stead, and changed his name to Zedekiah.

18Zedekiah *was* twenty and one years old when he began to reign, and he reigned eleven years in Jerusalem. And his mother's name *was* Hamutal, the daughter of Jeremiah of Libnah.

19And he did *that which was* evil in the sight of the LORD, according to all that Jehoiakim had done.

20For through the anger of the LORD it came to pass in Jerusalem and Judah, until he had cast them out from his presence, that Zedekiah rebelled against the king of Babylon.

**25** AND IT came to pass in the ninth year of his reign, in the tenth month, in the tenth *day* of the month, *that* Nebuchadnezzar king of Babylon came, he, and all his host, against Jerusalem, and pitched against it; and they built forts against it round about.

2And the city was besieged unto the eleventh year of king Zedekiah.

3And on the ninth *day* of the *fourth* month the famine prevailed in the city, and there was no bread for the people of the land.

4¶ And the city was broken up, and all the men of war *fled* by night by the way of the gate between two walls, which *is* by the king's garden: (now the Chaldees *were* against the city round about:) and *the king* went the way toward the plain.

5And the army of the Chaldees pursued after the king, and overtook him in the plains of Jericho: and all his army were scattered from him.

6So they took the king, and brought him up to the king of Babylon to Riblah; and they gave judgment upon him.

7And they slew the sons of Zedekiah before his eyes, and put out the eyes of Zedekiah, and bound him with fetters of brass, and carried him to Babylon.

8¶ And in the fifth month, on the seventh *day* of the month, which *is* the nineteenth year of king Nebuchadnezzar king of Babylon, came Nebuzar-adan, captain of the guard, a servant of the king of Babylon, unto Jerusalem:

# Amplified

9And he did evil in the sight of the Lord, in keeping with all his father had done.

10At that time the servants of Nebuchadnezzar king of Babylon came up to Jerusalem, and the city was besieged.

11Nebuchadnezzar king of Babylon came to the city, while his servants were besieging it.

12Jehoiachin king of Judah surrendered to the king of Babylon, himself, his mother, his servants, princes, and palace officials. The king of Babylon took him prisoner in the eighth year of Nebuchadnezzar's reign.

13He carried off all the treasures of the Lord's house and the king's house, and cut in pieces all the vessels of gold in the temple of the Lord, which Solomon king of Israel had made as the Lord had said.

14He carried away all Jerusalem, all the princes, all the mighty men of valor, 10,000 captives, and all the craftsmen and smiths; none remained, except the poorest of the land.

15Nebuchadnezzar took captive to Babylon King Jehoiachin; his mother, his wives, his officials, and the chief *and* mighty men of the land [the prophet Ezekiel included], he took from Jerusalem to Babylon into exile. [Ezek. 1:1.]

16And the king of Babylon brought captive to Babylon all the men of valor, 7,000, and craftsmen and smiths, 1,000, all strong and fit for war.

17And the king of Babylon made Mattaniah, Jehoiachin's uncle, king in his stead, and changed his name to Zedekiah.

18Zedekiah was twenty-one years old when he began his eleven years' reign in Jerusalem. His mother was Hamutal daughter of Jeremiah of Libnah.

19He did evil in the sight of the Lord, in keeping with all Jehoiakim had done.

20For because of the anger of the Lord it came to the point in Jerusalem and Judah that He cast them out of His presence. Zedekiah rebelled against the king of Babylon.

**25** IN THE ninth year of Zedekiah's reign, on the tenth day of the tenth month, Nebuchadnezzar king of Babylon came with all his army against Jerusalem and laid siege to it, and they built siege works against it round about.

2The city was besieged [nearly two years] until the eleventh year of King Zedekiah.

3On the ninth day of the fourth month the famine was complete in the city; there was no food for the people of the land.

4Then the city was broken through; the king and all the warriors fled by night by way of the gate between the two walls by the king's garden; though the Chaldeans were round about the city. [The king] went by the way toward Arabah (the plain).

5The Chaldean army pursued the king, and overtook him in the plains of Jericho; all his army was scattered from him.

6So they captured Zedekiah, and brought him to the king of Babylon at Riblah, and sentence was passed on him.

7And they slew the sons of Zedekiah before his eyes, and put out the eyes of Zedekiah, and bound him in double fetters [hands and feet], and carried him to Babylon. [Foretold, Jer. 34:3; Ezek. 12:13.]

8On the seventh day of the fifth month of the nineteenth year of King Nebuchadnezzar of Babylon, Nebuzaradan, captain of the Babylonian king's guard, came to Jerusalem.

## New American Standard

9And he did evil in the sight of the LORD, according to all that
his father had done.

*Deportation to Babylon*

10¶ At that time the servants of Nebuchadnezzar king of Babylon went up to Jerusalem, and the city came under siege.
11And Nebuchadnezzar the king of Babylon came to the city,
while his servants were besieging it.
12And Jehoiachin the king of Judah went out to the king of
Babylon, he and his mother and his servants and his captains and
his officials. So the king of Babylon took him captive in the eighth
year of his reign.
13And he carried out from there all the treasures of the house
of the LORD, and the treasures of the king's house, and cut in
pieces all the vessels of gold which Solomon king of Israel had
made in the temple of the LORD, just as the LORD had said.
14Then he led away into exile all Jerusalem and all the captains
and all the mighty men of valor, ten thousand captives, and all the
craftsmen and the smiths. None remained except the poorest
people of the land.
15So he led Jehoiachin away into exile to Babylon; also the king's
mother and the king's wives and his officials and the leading men
of the land, he led away into exile from Jerusalem to Babylon.
16And all the men of valor, seven thousand, and the craftsmen
and the smiths, one thousand, all strong and fit for war, and these
the king of Babylon brought into exile to Babylon.

*Zedekiah Made King*

17Then the king of Babylon made his uncle Mattaniah, king in
his place, and changed his name to Zedekiah.
18¶ Zedekiah was twenty-one years old when he became king,
and he reigned eleven years in Jerusalem; and his mother's name
*was* Hamutal the daughter of Jeremiah of Libnah.
19And he did evil in the sight of the LORD, according to all that
Jehoiakim had done.
20For through the anger of the LORD *this* came about in Jerusalem and Judah until He cast them out from His presence. And
Zedekiah rebelled against the king of Babylon.

*Nebuchadnezzar Besieges Jerusalem*

**25** NOW IT came about in the ninth year of his reign, on the
tenth day of the tenth month, that Nebuchadnezzar king
of Babylon came, he and all his army, against Jerusalem, camped
against it, and built a siege wall all around it.
2So the city was under siege until the eleventh year of King
Zedekiah.
3On the ninth day of the *fourth* month the famine was so severe
in the city that there was no food for the people of the land.
4Then the city was broken into, and all the men of war *fled* by
night by way of the gate between the two walls beside the king's
garden, though the Chaldeans were all around the city. And they
went by way of the Arabah.
5But the army of the Chaldeans pursued the king and overtook
him in the plains of Jericho and all his army was scattered from
him.
6Then they captured the king and brought him to the king of
Babylon at Riblah, and he passed sentence on him.
7And they slaughtered the sons of Zedekiah before his eyes,
then put out the eyes of Zedekiah and bound him with bronze
fetters and brought him to Babylon.

*Jerusalem Burned and Plundered*

8¶ Now on the seventh day of the fifth month, which was the
nineteenth year of King Nebuchadnezzar, king of Babylon, Nebuzaradan the captain of the guard, a servant of the king of Babylon,
came to Jerusalem.

## New International

evil in the eyes of the LORD, just as his father had done.
10At that time the officers of Nebuchadnezzar king of Babylon
advanced on Jerusalem and laid siege to it, 11and Nebuchadnezzar
himself came up to the city while his officers were besieging it.
12Jehoiachin king of Judah, his mother, his attendants, his nobles
and his officials all surrendered to him.
In the eighth year of the reign of the king of Babylon, he took
Jehoiachin prisoner. 13As the LORD had declared, Nebuchadnezzar
removed all the treasures from the temple of the LORD and from
the royal palace, and took away all the gold articles that Solomon
king of Israel had made for the temple of the LORD. 14He carried
into exile all Jerusalem: all the officers and fighting men, and all
the craftsmen and artisans—a total of ten thousand. Only the
poorest people of the land were left.
15Nebuchadnezzar took Jehoiachin captive to Babylon. He also
took from Jerusalem to Babylon the king's mother, his wives, his
officials and the leading men of the land. 16The king of Babylon
also deported to Babylon the entire force of seven thousand fighting men, strong and fit for war, and a thousand craftsmen and
artisans. 17He made Mattaniah, Jehoiachin's uncle, king in his
place and changed his name to Zedekiah.

*Zedekiah King of Judah*

18Zedekiah was twenty-one years old when he became king,
and he reigned in Jerusalem eleven years. His mother's name was
Hamutal daughter of Jeremiah; she was from Libnah. 19He did evil
in the eyes of the LORD, just as Jehoiakim had done. 20It was
because of the LORD's anger that all this happened to Jerusalem
and Judah, and in the end he thrust them from his presence.

*The Fall of Jerusalem*

Now Zedekiah rebelled against the king of Babylon.

**25** SO IN the ninth year of Zedekiah's reign, on the tenth day
of the tenth month, Nebuchadnezzar king of Babylon
marched against Jerusalem with his whole army. He encamped
outside the city and built siege works all around it. 2The city was
kept under siege until the eleventh year of King Zedekiah. 3By the
ninth day of the ⌞fourth⌟[a] month the famine in the city had become
so severe that there was no food for the people to eat. 4Then the
city wall was broken through, and the whole army fled at night
through the gate between the two walls near the king's garden,
though the Babylonians[b] were surrounding the city. They fled
toward the Arabah,[c] 5but the Babylonian[d] army pursued the king
and overtook him in the plains of Jericho. All his soldiers were
separated from him and scattered, 6and he was captured. He was
taken to the king of Babylon at Riblah, where sentence was pronounced on him. 7They killed the sons of Zedekiah before his eyes.
Then they put out his eyes, bound him with bronze shackles and
took him to Babylon.
8On the seventh day of the fifth month, in the nineteenth year
of Nebuchadnezzar king of Babylon, Nebuzaradan commander of
the imperial guard, an official of the king of Babylon, came to
Jerusalem. 9He set fire to the temple of the LORD, the royal palace

**NIV** [a] 3 See Jer. 52:6. [b] 4 Or *Chaldeans;* also in verses 13, 25 and 26 [c] 4 Or *the Jordan Valley* [d] 5 Or *Chaldean;* also in verses 10 and 24

## King James

9And he burnt the house of the LORD, and the king's house, and all the houses of Jerusalem, and every great *man's* house burnt he with fire.

10And all the army of the Chaldees, that *were with* the captain of the guard, brake down the walls of Jerusalem round about.

11Now the rest of the people *that were* left in the city, and the fugitives that fell away to the king of Babylon, with the remnant of the multitude, did Nebuzar-adan the captain of the guard carry away.

12But the captain of the guard left of the poor of the land *to be* vinedressers and husbandmen.

13And the pillars of brass that *were* in the house of the LORD, and the bases, and the brasen sea that *was* in the house of the LORD, did the Chaldees break in pieces, and carried the brass of them to Babylon.

14And the pots, and the shovels, and the snuffers, and the spoons, and all the vessels of brass wherewith they ministered, took they away.

15And the firepans, and the bowls, *and* such things as *were* of gold, *in* gold, and of silver, *in* silver, the captain of the guard took away.

16The two pillars, one sea, and the bases which Solomon had made for the house of the LORD; the brass of all these vessels was without weight.

17The height of the one pillar *was* eighteen cubits, and the chapiter upon it *was* brass: and the height of the chapiter three cubits; and the wreathen work, and pomegranates upon the chapiter round about, all of brass: and like unto these had the second pillar with wreathen work.

18¶ And the captain of the guard took Seraiah the chief priest, and Zephaniah the second priest, and the three keepers of the door:

19And out of the city he took an officer that was set over the men of war, and five men of them that were in the king's presence, which were found in the city, and the principal scribe of the host, which mustered the people of the land, and threescore men of the people of the land *that were* found in the city:

20And Nebuzar-adan captain of the guard took these, and brought them to the king of Babylon to Riblah:

21And the king of Babylon smote them, and slew them at Riblah in the land of Hamath. So Judah was carried away out of their land.

22¶ And *as for* the people that remained in the land of Judah, whom Nebuchadnezzar king of Babylon had left, even over them he made Gedaliah the son of Ahikam, the son of Shaphan, ruler.

23And when all the captains of the armies, they and their men, heard that the king of Babylon had made Gedaliah governor, there came to Gedaliah to Mizpah, even Ishmael the son of Nethaniah, and Johanan the son of Careah, and Seraiah the son of Tanhumeth the Netophathite, and Jaazaniah the son of a Maachathite, they and their men.

24And Gedaliah sware to them, and to their men, and said unto them, Fear not to be the servants of the Chaldees: dwell in the land, and serve the king of Babylon; and it shall be well with you.

25But it came to pass in the seventh month, that Ishmael the son of Nethaniah, the son of Elishama, of the seed royal, came, and ten men with him, and smote Gedaliah, that he died, and the Jews and the Chaldees that were with him at Mizpah.

26And all the people, both small and great, and the captains of the armies, arose, and came to Egypt: for they were afraid of the Chaldees.

27¶ And it came to pass in the seven and thirtieth year of the captivity of Jehoiachin king of Judah, in the twelfth month, on the seven and twentieth *day* of the month, *that* Evil-merodach king of Babylon in the year that he began to reign did lift up the head of Jehoiachin king of Judah out of prison;

28And he spake kindly to him, and set his throne above the throne of the kings that *were* with him in Babylon;

## Amplified

9He burned the house of the Lord, the king's house, and all the houses of Jerusalem; every great house he burned down.

10All the army of the Chaldeans who were with the captain of the [Babylonian] guard, broke down the walls around Jerusalem.

11Now the rest of the people left in the city, and the deserters who fell away to the king of Babylon, with the rest of the multitude, Nebuzaradan the captain of the guard carried into exile.

12But the captain of the guard left some of the poorest of the land to be vinedressers and soil tillers.

13The bronze pillars in the Lord's house, and [its] bases and bronze sea, the Chaldeans smashed, and carried the bronze to Babylon.

14And they took away the pots, shovels, snuffers, dishes for incense, all the bronze vessels used in the temple service,

15The firepans, and bowls. Such things as were of gold, the captain of the guard took away as gold, and what was of silver [he took away] as silver.

16The two pillars, the one sea, and the bases, which Solomon had made for the house of the Lord, the bronze of all these articles was incalculable.

17The height of the one pillar was eighteen cubits, and upon it was a capital of bronze. The height of the capital was three cubits; a network and pomegranates round about the capital were all of bronze. And the second pillar had the same as these with a network.

18The captain of the guard took Seraiah the chief priest, Zephaniah the second priest, and the three keepers of the threshold;

19And out of the city he took an officer who was in command of the men of war, and five men of the king's personal advisors, who were found in the city, and the scribe of the captain of the army, who mustered the people of the land, and sixty men of the people who were found in the city.

20Nebuzaradan captain of the guard took these, and brought them to the king of Babylon at Riblah:

21The king of Babylon smote and killed them at Riblah in the land of Hamath [north of Damascus]. So Judah was taken into exile.

22Over the people whom Nebuchadnezzar king of Babylon had left in the land of Judah, he appointed as governor Gedaliah son of Ahikam, son of Shaphan.

23And when all the captains of the forces and their men, heard that the king of Babylon had made Gedaliah governor, they came with their men to Gedaliah at Mizpah, namely, Ishmael son of Nethaniah, Johanan son of Kareah, Seraiah son of Tanhumeth the Netophathite, and Ja-azaniah son of the Ma-acathite.

24And Gedaliah swore to them and their men, saying, Do not be afraid of the Chaldean officials. Dwell in the land, and serve the king of Babylon, and it shall be well with you.

25But in the seventh month, Ishmael son of Nethaniah, son of Elishama, of the royal family [so having a claim to be governor], came with ten men and smote and killed Gedaliah and the Jews and the Chaldeans who were with him at Mizpah.

26Then all the people, both small and great, and the captains of the forces arose and went to Egypt; for they were afraid of the Chaldeans.

27And in the thirty-seventh year of the captivity of Jehoiachin king of Judah, on the twenty-seventh day of the twelfth month, Evil-merodach king of Babylon, in the year that he began to reign, showed favor to Jehoiachin king of Judah *and* released him from prison;

28He spoke kindly to him, and ranked him above the kings with him in Babylon.

## New American Standard

9 And he burned the house of the LORD, the king's house, and all the houses of Jerusalem; even every great house he burned with fire.

10 So all the army of the Chaldeans who *were with* the captain of the guard broke down the walls around Jerusalem.

11 Then the rest of the people who were left in the city and the deserters who had deserted to the king of Babylon and the rest of the multitude, Nebuzaradan the captain of the guard carried away into exile.

12 But the captain of the guard left some of the poorest of the land to be vinedressers and plowmen.

13¶ Now the bronze pillars which were in the house of the LORD, and the stands and the bronze sea which were in the house of the LORD, the Chaldeans broke in pieces and carried the bronze to Babylon.

14 And they took away the pots, the shovels, the snuffers, the spoons, and all the bronze vessels which were used in *temple* service.

15 The captain of the guard also took away the firepans and the basins, what was fine gold and what was fine silver.

16 The two pillars, the one sea, and the stands which Solomon had made for the house of the LORD—the bronze of all these vessels was beyond weight.

17 The height of the one pillar was eighteen cubits, and a bronze capital was on it; the height of the capital was three cubits, with a network and pomegranates on the capital all around, all of bronze. And the second pillar was like these with network.

18¶ Then the captain of the guard took Seraiah the chief priest and Zephaniah the second priest, with the three officers of the temple.

19 And from the city he took one official who was overseer of the men of war, and five of the king's advisers who were found in the city; and the scribe of the captain of the army, who mustered the people of the land; and sixty men of the people of the land who were found in the city.

20 And Nebuzaradan the captain of the guard took them and brought them to the king of Babylon at Riblah.

21 Then the king of Babylon struck them down and put them to death at Riblah in the land of Hamath. So Judah was led away into exile from its land.

*Gedaliah Made Governor*

22¶ Now *as for* the people who were left in the land of Judah, whom Nebuchadnezzar king of Babylon had left, he appointed Gedaliah the son of Ahikam, the son of Shaphan over them.

23 When all the captains of the forces, they and *their* men, heard that the king of Babylon had appointed Gedaliah *governor*, they came to Gedaliah to Mizpah, namely, Ishmael the son of Nethaniah, and Johanan the son of Kareah, and Seraiah the son of Tanhumeth the Netophathite, and Jaazaniah the son of the Maacathite, they and their men.

24 And Gedaliah swore to them and their men and said to them, "Do not be afraid of the servants of the Chaldeans; live in the land and serve the king of Babylon, and it will be well with you."

25¶ But it came about in the seventh month, that Ishmael the son of Nethaniah, the son of Elishama, of the royal family, came with ten men and struck Gedaliah down so that he died along with the Jews and the Chaldeans who were with him at Mizpah.

26 Then all the people, both small and great, and the captains of the forces arose and went to Egypt; for they were afraid of the Chaldeans.

27¶ Now it came about in the thirty-seventh year of the exile of Jehoiachin king of Judah, in the twelfth month, on the twenty-seventh *day* of the month, that Evil-merodach king of Babylon, in the year that he became king, released Jehoiachin king of Judah from prison;

28 and he spoke kindly to him and set his throne above the throne of the kings who *were* with him in Babylon.

## New International

and all the houses of Jerusalem. Every important building he
burned down. 10 The whole Babylonian army, under the commander of the imperial guard, broke down the walls around
Jerusalem. 11 Nebuzaradan the commander of the guard carried
into exile the people who remained in the city, along with the rest
of the populace and those who had gone over to the king of
Babylon. 12 But the commander left behind some of the poorest
people of the land to work the vineyards and fields.

13 The Babylonians broke up the bronze pillars, the movable
stands and the bronze Sea that were at the temple of the LORD and
they carried the bronze to Babylon. 14 They also took away the pots,
shovels, wick trimmers, dishes and all the bronze articles used in
the temple service. 15 The commander of the imperial guard took
away the censers and sprinkling bowls—all that were made of pure
gold or silver.

16 The bronze from the two pillars, the Sea and the movable
stands, which Solomon had made for the temple of the LORD, was
more than could be weighed. 17 Each pillar was twenty-seven feet[a]
high. The bronze capital on top of one pillar was four and a half
feet[b] high and was decorated with a network and pomegranates
of bronze all around. The other pillar, with its network, was similar.

18 The commander of the guard took as prisoners Seraiah the
chief priest, Zephaniah the priest next in rank and the three doorkeepers. 19 Of those still in the city, he took the officer in charge
of the fighting men and five royal advisers. He also took the
secretary who was chief officer in charge of conscripting the people
of the land and sixty of his men who were found in the city.
20 Nebuzaradan the commander took them all and brought them
to the king of Babylon at Riblah. 21 There at Riblah, in the land of
Hamath, the king had them executed.

So Judah went into captivity, away from her land.

22 Nebuchadnezzar king of Babylon appointed Gedaliah son of
Ahikam, the son of Shaphan, to be over the people he had left
behind in Judah. 23 When all the army officers and their men heard
that the king of Babylon had appointed Gedaliah as governor, they
came to Gedaliah at Mizpah—Ishmael son of Nethaniah, Johanan
son of Kareah, Seraiah son of Tanhumeth the Netophathite, Jaazaniah the son of the Maacathite, and their men. 24 Gedaliah took an
oath to reassure them and their men. "Do not be afraid of the
Babylonian officials," he said. "Settle down in the land and serve
the king of Babylon, and it will go well with you."

25 In the seventh month, however, Ishmael son of Nethaniah,
the son of Elishama, who was of royal blood, came with ten men
and assassinated Gedaliah and also the men of Judah and the
Babylonians who were with him at Mizpah. 26 At this, all the
people from the least to the greatest, together with the army officers, fled to Egypt for fear of the Babylonians.

*Jehoiachin Released*

27 In the thirty-seventh year of the exile of Jehoiachin king of
Judah, in the year Evil-Merodach[c] became king of Babylon, he
released Jehoiachin from prison on the twenty-seventh day of the
twelfth month. 28 He spoke kindly to him and gave him a seat of
honor higher than those of the other kings who were with him in

**NIV** [a] *17* Hebrew *eighteen cubits* (about 8.1 meters) [b] *17* Hebrew *three cubits* (about 1.3 meters) [c] *27* Also called *Amel-Marduk*

## King James

29And changed his prison garments: and he did eat bread continually before him all the days of his life.
30And his allowance *was* a continual allowance given him of the king, a daily rate for every day, all the days of his life.

## Amplified

29Jehoiachin put off his prison garments, and he dined regularly at the king's table the remainder of his life.
30And his allowance, a continual one, was given him by the king, every day a portion, the rest of his life.

## New American Standard

29And Jehoiachin changed his prison clothes, and had his meals
in the king's presence regularly all the days of his life;
30and for his allowance, a regular allowance was given him by
the king, a portion for each day, all the days of his life.

## New International

Babylon. 29So Jehoiachin put aside his prison clothes and for the
rest of his life ate regularly at the king's table. 30Day by day the
king gave Jehoiachin a regular allowance as long as he lived.

## King James

THE FIRST BOOK OF THE

# Chronicles

1 ADAM, SHETH, Enosh,
2 Kenan, Mahalaleel, Jered,
3 Henoch, Methuselah, Lamech,
4 Noah, Shem, Ham, and Japheth.
5 ¶ The sons of Japheth; Gomer, and Magog, and Madai, and Javan, and Tubal, and Meshech, and Tiras.
6 And the sons of Gomer; Ashchenaz, and Riphath, and Togarmah.
7 And the sons of Javan; Elishah, and Tarshish, Kittim, and Dodanim.
8 ¶ The sons of Ham; Cush, and Mizraim, Put, and Canaan.
9 And the sons of Cush; Seba, and Havilah, and Sabta, and Raamah, and Sabtecha. And the sons of Raamah; Sheba, and Dedan.
10 And Cush begat Nimrod: he began to be mighty upon the earth.
11 And Mizraim begat Ludim, and Anamim, and Lehabim, and Naphtuhim,
12 And Pathrusim, and Casluhim, (of whom came the Philistines,) and Caphthorim.
13 And Canaan begat Zidon his firstborn, and Heth,
14 The Jebusite also, and the Amorite, and the Girgashite,
15 And the Hivite, and the Arkite, and the Sinite,
16 And the Arvadite, and the Zemarite, and the Hamathite.
17 ¶ The sons of Shem; Elam, and Asshur, and Arphaxad, and Lud, and Aram, and Uz, and Hul, and Gether, and Meshech.
18 And Arphaxad begat Shelah, and Shelah begat Eber.
19 And unto Eber were born two sons: the name of the one *was* Peleg; because in his days the earth was divided: and his brother's name *was* Joktan.
20 And Joktan begat Almodad, and Sheleph, and Hazarmaveth, and Jerah,
21 Hadoram also, and Uzal, and Diklah,
22 And Ebal, and Abimael, and Sheba,

## Amplified

THE FIRST BOOK OF THE

# Chronicles

1 ADAM [HIS genealogical line], Seth, Enosh,
2 Kenan, Mahalalel, Jared,
3 Enoch, Methuselah, Lamech,
4 Noah, Shem, Ham, and Japheth.
5 The sons of Japheth: Gomer, Magog, Madai, Javan, Tubal, Meshech, and Tiras.
6 The sons of Gomer: Ashikenaz, Diphath, and Togarmah.
7 The sons of Javan: Elishah, Tarshish, Kittim, and Rodanim.
8 The sons of Ham: Cush, Mizraim (Egypt), Put, and Canaan.
9 The sons of Cush: Seba, Havilah, Sabta, Raama, and Sabteca. The sons of Raamah: Sheba and Dedan.
10 Cush was the father of Nimrod; he began to be a mighty one upon the earth.
11 Mizraim (Egypt) was the father of Ludim, Anamim, Lehabim, Naphtuhim,
12 Pathrusim, Casluhim, of whom came the Philistines, and Caphtorim.
13 Canaan was the father of Zidon his first-born, and Heth,
14 The Jebusites, Amorites, Girgashites,
15 Hivites, Arkites, Sinites,
16 Arvadites, Zemarites, and Hamathites.
17 The sons of Shem: Elam, Asshur, Arpachshad, Lud, Aram, Uz, Hul, Gether, and Meshech.
18 Arpachshad was the father of Shelah, Shelah of Eber.
19 To Eber were born two sons: the name of the one was Peleg, because in his days [the population of] the earth was divided [according to its languages], and his brother's name was Joktan.
20 Joktan was the father of Almodad, Sheleph, Hazar-maveth, Jerah,
21 Hadoram, Uzal, Diklah,
22 Ebal, Abimael, Sheba,

## New American Standard

# 1 Chronicles

*Genealogy from Adam*

**1** ADAM, SETH, Enosh,
2Kenan, Mahalalel, Jared,
3Enoch, Methuselah, Lamech,
4Noah, Shem, Ham and Japheth.
5¶ The sons of Japheth *were* Gomer, Magog, Madai, Javan,
Tubal, Meshech, and Tiras.
6And the sons of Gomer *were* Ashkenaz, Diphath, and Togarmah.
7And the sons of Javan *were* Elishah, Tarshish, Kittim, and
Rodanim.
8¶ The sons of Ham *were* Cush, Mizraim, Put, and Canaan.
9And the sons of Cush *were* Seba, Havilah, Sabta, Raama, and
Sabteca; and the sons of Raamah *were* Sheba and Dedan.
10And Cush became the father of Nimrod; he began to be a
mighty one in the earth.
11And Mizraim became the father of the people of Lud, Anam,
Lehab, Naphtuh,
12Pathrus, Casluh, from which the Philistines came, and Caphtor.
13¶ And Canaan became the father of Sidon, his first-born,
Heth,
14and the Jebusites, the Amorites, the Girgashites,
15the Hivites, the Arkites, the Sinites,
16the Arvadites, the Zemarites, and the Hamathites.
17¶ The sons of Shem *were* Elam, Asshur, Arpachshad, Lud,
Aram, Uz, Hul, Gether, and Meshech.
18And Arpachshad became the father of Shelah and Shelah
became the father of Eber.
19And two sons were born to Eber, the name of the one was
Peleg, for in his days the earth was divided, and his brother's name
was Joktan.
20And Joktan became the father of Almodad, Sheleph, Hazarmaveth, Jerah,
21Hadoram, Uzal, Diklah,
22Ebal, Abimael, Sheba,

## New International

# 1 Chronicles

*Historical Records From Adam to Abraham*

*To Noah's Sons*

**1** ADAM, SETH, Enosh, 2Kenan, Mahalalel, Jared, 3Enoch,
Methuselah, Lamech, Noah.

4The sons of Noah:[a]
Shem, Ham and Japheth.

*The Japhethites*

5The sons[b] of Japheth:
Gomer, Magog, Madai, Javan, Tubal, Meshech and Tiras.
6The sons of Gomer:
Ashkenaz, Riphath[c] and Togarmah.
7The sons of Javan:
Elishah, Tarshish, the Kittim and the Rodanim.

*The Hamites*

8The sons of Ham:
Cush, Mizraim,[d] Put and Canaan.
9The sons of Cush:
Seba, Havilah, Sabta, Raamah and Sabteca.
The sons of Raamah:
Sheba and Dedan.
10Cush was the father[e] of
Nimrod, who grew to be a mighty warrior on earth.
11Mizraim was the father of
the Ludites, Anamites, Lehabites, Naphtuhites, 12Pathrusites, Casluhites (from whom the Philistines came) and
Caphtorites.
13Canaan was the father of
Sidon his firstborn,[f] and of the Hittites, 14Jebusites, Amorites, Girgashites, 15Hivites, Arkites, Sinites, 16Arvadites,
Zemarites and Hamathites.

*The Semites*

17The sons of Shem:
Elam, Asshur, Arphaxad, Lud and Aram.
The sons of Aram[g]:
Uz, Hul, Gether and Meshech.
18Arphaxad was the father of Shelah,
and Shelah the father of Eber.
19Two sons were born to Eber:
One was named Peleg,[h] because in his time the earth was divided; his brother was named Joktan.
20Joktan was the father of
Almodad, Sheleph, Hazarmaveth, Jerah, 21Hadoram,
Uzal, Diklah, 22Obal,[i] Abimael, Sheba, 23Ophir, Havilah

**NIV** a *4* Septuagint; Hebrew does not have *The sons of Noah:* b *5 Sons* may mean *descendants* or *successors* or *nations;* also in verses 6-10, 17 and 20. c *6* Many Hebrew manuscripts and Vulgate (see also Septuagint and Gen. 10:3); most Hebrew manuscripts *Diphath* d *8* That is, Egypt; also in verse 11 e *10 Father* may mean *ancestor* or *predecessor* or *founder;* also in verses 11, 13, 18 and 20. f *13* Or *of the Sidonians, the foremost* g *17* One Hebrew manuscript and some Septuagint manuscripts (see also Gen. 10:23); most Hebrew manuscripts do not have this line. h *19 Peleg* means *division.* i *22* Some Hebrew manuscripts and Syriac (see also Gen. 10:28); most Hebrew manuscripts *Ebal*

## King James

23And Ophir, and Havilah, and Jobab. All these *were* the sons
of Joktan.
24¶ Shem, Arphaxad, Shelah,
25Eber, Peleg, Reu,
26Serug, Nahor, Terah,
27Abram; the same *is* Abraham.
28The sons of Abraham; Isaac, and Ishmael.
29¶ These *are* their generations: The firstborn of Ishmael,
Nebaioth; then Kedar, and Adbeel, and Mibsam,
30Mishma, and Dumah, Massa, Hadad, and Tema,
31Jetur, Naphish, and Kedemah. These are the sons of Ishmael.
32¶ Now the sons of Keturah, Abraham's concubine: she bare
Zimran, and Jokshan, and Medan, and Midian, and Ishbak, and
Shuah. And the sons of Jokshan; Sheba, and Dedan.
33And the sons of Midian; Ephah, and Epher, and Henoch, and
Abida, and Eldaah. All these *are* the sons of Keturah.
34And Abraham begat Isaac. The sons of Isaac; Esau and Israel.
35¶ The sons of Esau; Eliphaz, Reuel, and Jeush, and Jaalam,
and Korah.
36The sons of Eliphaz; Teman, and Omar, Zephi, and Gatam,
Kenaz, and Timna, and Amalek.
37The sons of Reuel; Nahath, Zerah, Shammah, and Mizzah.
38And the sons of Seir; Lotan, and Shobal, and Zibeon, and
Anah, and Dishon, and Ezar, and Dishan.
39And the sons of Lotan; Hori, and Homam: and Timna *was*
Lotan's sister.
40The sons of Shobal; Alian, and Manahath, and Ebal, Shephi,
and Onam. And the sons of Zibeon; Aiah, and Anah.
41The sons of Anah; Dishon. And the sons of Dishon; Amram,
and Eshban, and Ithran, and Cheran.
42The sons of Ezer; Bilhan, and Zavan, *and* Jakan. The sons of
Dishan; Uz, and Aran.

## Amplified

23Ophir, Havilah, and Jobab. All these were the sons of Joktan.
24Shem, Arpachshad, Shelah,
25Eber, Peleg, Reu,
26Serug, Nahor, Terah,
27Abram, the same is Abraham.
28The sons of Abraham: Isaac and Ishmael.
29These are their descendants: The first-born of Ishmael,
Nebaioth; Kedar, Adbeel, Mibsam,
30Mishma, Dumah, Massa, Hadad, Tema,
31Jetur, Naphish, and Kedemah. These are the sons of Ishmael.
32Now the sons of Keturah, Abraham's concubine: she bore
Zimran, Jokshan, Medan, Midian, Ishbak, and Shuah. The sons of
Jokshan: Sheba and Dedan.
33The sons of Midian: Ephah, Epher, Hanoch, Abida, and Eldaah. All these are the sons [and grandsons] of Keturah.
34Abraham was the father of Isaac. The sons of Isaac: Esau and
Israel.
35The sons of Esau: Eliphaz, Reuel, Jeush, Jalam, and Korah.
36The sons of Eliphaz: Teman, Omar, Zephi, Gatam, Kenaz,
Timna, and Amalek.
37The sons of Reuel: Nahath, Zerah, Shammah, and Mizzah.
38The sons of Seir: Lotan, Shobal, Zibeon, Anah, Dishon, Ezer,
and Dishan.
39The sons of Lotan: Hori and Homam; and Timna was Lotan's
sister.
40The sons of Shobal: Alian, Manahath, Ebal, Shephi, and
Onam. The sons of Zibeon: Aiah and Anah.
41The sons of Anah: Dishon. The sons of Dishon: Hamran,
Eshban, Ithran, and Cheran.
42The sons of Ezer: Bilhan, Zaavan, [and] Jaakan. The sons of
Dishan: Uz and Aran.

## New American Standard

23Ophir, Havilah, and Jobab; all these *were* the sons of Joktan.
**24**¶ Shem, Arpachshad, Shelah,
25Eber, Peleg, Reu,
26Serug, Nahor, Terah,

*Descendants of Abraham*

27Abram, that is Abraham.
**28**¶ The sons of Abraham *were* Isaac and Ishmael.
29These are their genealogies: the first-born of Ishmael *was*
Nebaioth, then Kedar, Adbeel, Mibsam,
30Mishma, Dumah, Massa, Hadad, Tema,
31Jetur, Naphish and Kedemah; these *were* the sons of Ishmael.
32And the sons of Keturah, Abraham's concubine, *whom* she
bore, *were* Zimran, Jokshan, Medan, Midian, Ishbak, and Shuah.
And the sons of Jokshan *were* Sheba and Dedan.
33And the sons of Midian *were* Ephah, Epher, Hanoch, Abida,
and Eldaah. All these were the sons of Keturah.
34And Abraham became the father of Isaac. The sons of Isaac
*were* Esau and Israel.
35The sons of Esau *were* Eliphaz, Reuel, Jeush, Jalam, and
Korah.
36The sons of Eliphaz *were* Teman, Omar, Zephi, Gatam,
Kenaz, Timna, and Amalek.
37The sons of Reuel *were* Nahath, Zerah, Shammah, and Mizzah.
38And the sons of Seir *were* Lotan, Shobal, Zibeon, Anah, Dishon, Ezer, and Dishan.
39And the sons of Lotan *were* Hori and Homam; and Lotan's
sister *was* Timna.
40The sons of Shobal *were* Alian, Manahath, Ebal, Shephi, and
Onam. And the sons of Zibeon *were* Aiah and Anah.
41The son of Anah *was* Dishon. And the sons of Dishon *were*
Hamran, Eshban, Ithran, and Cheran.
42The sons of Ezer *were* Bilhan, Zaavan and Jaakan. The sons of
Dishan *were* Uz and Aran.

## New International

and Jobab. All these were sons of Joktan.
24Shem, Arphaxad,[a] Shelah,
25Eber, Peleg, Reu,
26Serug, Nahor, Terah
27and Abram (that is, Abraham).

*The Family of Abraham*

28The sons of Abraham:
Isaac and Ishmael.

*Descendants of Hagar*

29These were their descendants:
Nebaioth the firstborn of Ishmael, Kedar, Adbeel, Mib-
sam, 30Mishma, Dumah, Massa, Hadad, Tema, 31Jetur,
Naphish and Kedemah. These were the sons of Ishmael.

*Descendants of Keturah*

32The sons born to Keturah, Abraham's concubine:
Zimran, Jokshan, Medan, Midian, Ishbak and Shuah.
The sons of Jokshan:
Sheba and Dedan.
33The sons of Midian:
Ephah, Epher, Hanoch, Abida and Eldaah.
All these were descendants of Keturah.

*Descendants of Sarah*

34Abraham was the father of Isaac.
The sons of Isaac:
Esau and Israel.

*Esau's Sons*

35The sons of Esau:
Eliphaz, Reuel, Jeush, Jalam and Korah.
36The sons of Eliphaz:
Teman, Omar, Zepho,[b] Gatam and Kenaz;
by Timna: Amalek.[c]
37The sons of Reuel:
Nahath, Zerah, Shammah and Mizzah.

*The People of Seir in Edom*

38The sons of Seir:
Lotan, Shobal, Zibeon, Anah, Dishon, Ezer and Dishan.
39The sons of Lotan:
Hori and Homam. Timna was Lotan's sister.
40The sons of Shobal:
Alvan,[d] Manahath, Ebal, Shepho and Onam.
The sons of Zibeon:
Aiah and Anah.
41The son of Anah:
Dishon.
The sons of Dishon:
Hemdan,[e] Eshban, Ithran and Keran.
42The sons of Ezer:
Bilhan, Zaavan and Akan.[f]
The sons of Dishan[g]:
Uz and Aran.

**NIV** [a] *24* Hebrew; some Septuagint manuscripts *Arphaxad, Cainan* (see also note at Gen. 11:10) [b] *36* Many Hebrew manuscripts, some Septuagint manuscripts and Syriac (see also Gen. 36:11); most Hebrew manuscripts *Zephi* [c] *36* Some Septuagint manuscripts (see also Gen. 36:12); Hebrew *Gatam, Kenaz, Timna and Amalek* [d] *40* Many Hebrew manuscripts and some Septuagint manuscripts (see also Gen. 36:23); most Hebrew manuscripts *Alian* [e] *41* Many Hebrew manuscripts and some Septuagint manuscripts (see also Gen. 36:26); most Hebrew manuscripts *Hamran* [f] *42* Many Hebrew and Septuagint manuscripts (see also Gen. 36:27); most Hebrew manuscripts *Zaavan, Jaakan* [g] *42* Hebrew *Dishon,* a variant of *Dishan*

## King James

43¶ Now these *are* the kings that reigned in the land of Edom before *any* king reigned over the children of Israel; Bela the son of Beor: and the name of his city *was* Dinhabah.
44And when Bela was dead, Jobab the son of Zerah of Bozrah reigned in his stead.
45And when Jobab was dead, Husham of the land of the Temanites reigned in his stead.
46And when Husham was dead, Hadad the son of Bedad, which smote Midian in the field of Moab, reigned in his stead: and the name of his city *was* Avith.
47And when Hadad was dead, Samlah of Masrekah reigned in his stead.
48And when Samlah was dead, Shaul of Rehoboth by the river reigned in his stead.
49And when Shaul was dead, Baal-hanan the son of Achbor reigned in his stead.
50And when Baal-hanan was dead, Hadad reigned in his stead: and the name of his city *was* Pai; and his wife's name *was* Mehetabel, the daughter of Matred, the daughter of Mezahab.
51¶ Hadad died also. And the dukes of Edom were; duke Timnah, duke Aliah, duke Jetheth,
52Duke Aholibamah, duke Elah, duke Pinon,
53Duke Kenaz, duke Teman, duke Mibzar,
54Duke Magdiel, duke Iram. These *are* the dukes of Edom.

**2** THESE *ARE* the sons of Israel; Reuben, Simeon, Levi, and Judah, Issachar, and Zebulun,
2Dan, Joseph, and Benjamin, Naphtali, Gad, and Asher.
3¶ The sons of Judah; Er, and Onan, and Shelah: *which* three were born unto him of the daughter of Shua the Canaanitess. And Er, the firstborn of Judah, was evil in the sight of the LORD; and he slew him.
4And Tamar his daughter-in-law bare him Pharez and Zerah. All the sons of Judah *were* five.
5The sons of Pharez; Hezron, and Hamul.
6And the sons of Zerah; Zimri, and Ethan, and Heman, and Calcol, and Dara: five of them in all.
7And the sons of Carmi; Achar, the troubler of Israel, who transgressed in the thing accursed.
8And the sons of Ethan; Azariah.
9The sons also of Hezron, that were born unto him; Jerahmeel, and Ram, and Chelubai.
10And Ram begat Amminadab; and Amminadab begat Nahshon, prince of the children of Judah;
11And Nahshon begat Salma, and Salma begat Boaz,
12And Boaz begat Obed, and Obed begat Jesse.

## Amplified

43These are the kings who reigned in the land of Edom before any king reigned over the Israelites: Bela son of Beor; the name of his city was Dinhabah.
44When Bela died, Jobab son of Zerah of Bozrah reigned in his stead.
45When Jobab died, Husham of the land of the Temanites reigned in his stead.
46When Husham died, Hadad [I of Edom] son of Bedad, who defeated Midian in the field of Moab, reigned in his stead; his city was Avith.
47When Hadad [I] died, Samlah of Masrekah reigned in his stead.
48When Samlah died, Shaul of Rehoboth on the River [Euphrates] reigned in his stead.
49When Shaul died, Baal-hanan son of Achbor reigned in his stead.
50When Baal-hanan died, Hadad [II] reigned in his stead; his city was Pai; his wife was Mehetabel daughter of Matred, daughter of Mezahab.
51Hadad died also. The chiefs of Edom were: chiefs Timna, Aliah, Jetheth,
52Oholibamah, Elah, Pinon,
53Kenaz, Teman, Mibzar,
54Magdiel, and Iram. These are the chiefs of Edom.

**2** THESE ARE the sons of Israel: Reuben, Simeon, Levi, Judah, Issachar, Zebulun,
2Dan, Joseph, Benjamin, Naphtali, Gad, and Asher.
3The sons of Judah: Er, Onan, and Shelah, which three Shua's daughter the Canaanitess bore him. Er, Judah's eldest, was evil in the Lord's sight and He slew him.
4Tamar Judah's daughter-in-law bore him Pharez and Zerah. All Judah's sons were five.
5The sons of Pharez: Hezron and Hamul.
6The sons of Zerah: Zimri, Ethan, Heman, Calcol, and Dara; five in all. [I Kings 4:31.]
7The sons of Carmi: Achar, the troubler of Israel, who transgressed in the matter of the devoted thing. [Josh. 7:1.]
8The sons of Ethan: Azariah.
9The sons of Hezron, that were born to him: Jerahmeel, Ram, and Chelubai [that is, Caleb].
10Ram was the father of Amminadab, and Amminadab of Nahshon, prince of the sons of Judah;
11Nahshon was the father of Salma, Salma of Boaz,
12Boaz of Obed, and Obed of Jesse.

## New American Standard

43¶ Now these are the kings who reigned in the land of Edom
before any king of the sons of Israel reigned. Bela *was* the son of
Beor, and the name of his city was Dinhabah.
44When Bela died, Jobab the son of Zerah of Bozrah became
king in his place.
45When Jobab died, Husham of the land of the Temanites
became king in his place.
46When Husham died, Hadad the son of Bedad, who defeated
Midian in the field of Moab, became king in his place; and the
name of his city *was* Avith.
47When Hadad died, Samlah of Masrekah became king in his
place.
48When Samlah died, Shaul of Rehoboth by the River became
king in his place.
49When Shaul died, Baal-hanan the son of Achbor became king
in his place.
50When Baal-hanan died, Hadad became king in his place; and
the name of his city was Pai, and his wife's name was Mehetabel,
the daughter of Matred, the daughter of Mezahab.
51Then Hadad died. Now the chiefs of Edom were: chief Timna,
chief Aliah, chief Jetheth,
52chief Oholibamah, chief Elah, chief Pinon,
53chief Kenaz, chief Teman, chief Mibzar,
54chief Magdiel, chief Iram. These *were* the chiefs of Edom.

*Genealogy: Twelve Sons of Jacob (Israel)*

**2** THESE ARE the sons of Israel: Reuben, Simeon, Levi, Judah,
Issachar, Zebulun,
2Dan, Joseph, Benjamin, Naphtali, Gad, and Asher.
3¶ The sons of Judah *were* Er, Onan, and Shelah; *these* three
were born to him by Bath-shua the Canaanitess. And Er, Judah's
first-born, was wicked in the sight of the LORD, so He put him to
death.
4And Tamar his daughter-in-law bore him Perez and Zerah.
Judah had five sons in all.
5¶ The sons of Perez *were* Hezron and Hamul.
6And the sons of Zerah *were* Zimri, Ethan, Heman, Calcol, and
Dara; five of them in all.
7And the son of Carmi *was* Achar, the troubler of Israel, who
violated the ban.
8And the son of Ethan *was* Azariah.
9¶ Now the sons of Hezron, who were born to him *were* Jerahmeel, Ram, and Chelubai.
10And Ram became the father of Amminadab, and Amminadab
became the father of Nahshon, leader of the sons of Judah;
11Nahshon became the father of Salma, Salma became the father of Boaz,

*Genealogy of David*

12Boaz became the father of Obed, and Obed became the father
of Jesse;

## New International

*The Rulers of Edom*

43These were the kings who reigned in Edom before any Israelite king reigned[a]:
Bela son of Beor, whose city was named Dinhabah.
44When Bela died, Jobab son of Zerah from Bozrah succeeded
him as king.
45When Jobab died, Husham from the land of the Temanites
succeeded him as king.
46When Husham died, Hadad son of Bedad, who defeated
Midian in the country of Moab, succeeded him as king.
His city was named Avith.
47When Hadad died, Samlah from Masrekah succeeded him as
king.
48When Samlah died, Shaul from Rehoboth on the river[b] succeeded him as king.
49When Shaul died, Baal-Hanan son of Acbor succeeded him
as king.
50When Baal-Hanan died, Hadad succeeded him as king. His
city was named Pau,[c] and his wife's name was Mehetabel
daughter of Matred, the daughter of Me-Zahab. 51Hadad
also died.
The chiefs of Edom were:
Timna, Alvah, Jetheth, 52Oholibamah, Elah, Pinon,
53Kenaz, Teman, Mibzar, 54Magdiel and Iram. These were
the chiefs of Edom.

*Israel's Sons*

**2** THESE WERE the sons of Israel:
Reuben, Simeon, Levi, Judah, Issachar, Zebulun, 2Dan,
Joseph, Benjamin, Naphtali, Gad and Asher.

*Judah*

*To Hezron's Sons*

3The sons of Judah:
Er, Onan and Shelah. These three were born to him by a
Canaanite woman, the daughter of Shua. Er, Judah's first-
born, was wicked in the LORD's sight; so the LORD put him
to death. 4Tamar, Judah's daughter-in-law, bore him
Perez and Zerah. Judah had five sons in all.
5The sons of Perez:
Hezron and Hamul.
6The sons of Zerah:
Zimri, Ethan, Heman, Calcol and Darda[d]—five in all.
7The son of Carmi:
Achar,[e] who brought trouble on Israel by violating the
ban on taking devoted things.[f]
8The son of Ethan:
Azariah.
9The sons born to Hezron were:
Jerahmeel, Ram and Caleb.[g]

*From Ram Son of Hezron*

10Ram was the father of
Amminadab, and Amminadab the father of Nahshon, the
leader of the people of Judah. 11Nahshon was the father
of Salmon,[h] Salmon the father of Boaz, 12Boaz the father
of Obed and Obed the father of Jesse.

**NIV** [a] 43 Or *before an Israelite king reigned over them* [b] 48 Possibly the Euphrates [c] *50* Many Hebrew manuscripts, some Septuagint manuscripts, Vulgate and Syriac (see also Gen. 36:39); most Hebrew manuscripts *Pai* [d] *6* Many Hebrew manuscripts, some Septuagint manuscripts and Syriac (see also 1 Kings 4:31); most Hebrew manuscripts *Dara* [e] *7 Achar* means *trouble; Achar* is called *Achan* in Joshua. [f] *7* The Hebrew term refers to the irrevocable giving over of things or persons to the LORD, often by totally destroying them. [g] *9* Hebrew *Kelubai,* a variant of *Caleb* [h] *11* Septuagint (see also Ruth 4:21); Hebrew *Salma*

## King James

13¶ And Jesse begat his firstborn Eliab, and Abinadab the second, and Shimma the third,
14Nethaneel the fourth, Raddai the fifth,
15Ozem the sixth, David the seventh:
16Whose sisters *were* Zeruiah, and Abigail. And the sons of Zeruiah; Abishai, and Joab, and Asahel, three.
17And Abigail bare Amasa: and the father of Amasa *was* Jether the Ishmaelite.
18¶ And Caleb the son of Hezron begat *children* of Azubah *his* wife, and of Jerioth: her sons *are* these; Jesher, and Shobab, and Ardon.
19And when Azubah was dead, Caleb took unto him Ephrath, which bare him Hur.
20And Hur begat Uri, and Uri begat Bezaleel.
21¶ And afterward Hezron went in to the daughter of Machir the father of Gilead, whom he married when he *was* threescore years old; and she bare him Segub.
22And Segub begat Jair, who had three and twenty cities in the land of Gilead.
23And he took Geshur, and Aram, with the towns of Jair, from them, with Kenath, and the towns thereof, *even* threescore cities. All these *belonged to* the sons of Machir the father of Gilead.
24And after that Hezron was dead in Caleb-ephratah, then Abiah Hezron's wife bare him Ashur the father of Tekoa.
25¶ And the sons of Jerahmeel the firstborn of Hezron were, Ram the firstborn, and Bunah, and Oren, and Ozem, *and* Ahijah.
26Jerahmeel had also another wife, whose name *was* Atarah; she *was* the mother of Onam.
27And the sons of Ram the firstborn of Jerahmeel were, Maaz, and Jamin, and Eker.
28And the sons of Onam were, Shammai, and Jada. And the sons of Shammai; Nadab, and Abishur.
29And the name of the wife of Abishur *was* Abihail, and she bare him Ahban, and Molid.
30And the sons of Nadab; Seled, and Appaim: but Seled died without children.
31And the sons of Appaim; Ishi. And the sons of Ishi; Sheshan. And the children of Sheshan; Ahlai.
32And the sons of Jada the brother of Shammai; Jether, and Jonathan: and Jether died without children.
33And the sons of Jonathan; Peleth, and Zaza. These were the sons of Jerahmeel.
34¶ Now Sheshan had no sons, but daughters. And Sheshan had a servant, an Egyptian, whose name *was* Jarha.
35And Sheshan gave his daughter to Jarha his servant to wife; and she bare him Attai.
36And Attai begat Nathan, and Nathan begat Zabad,
37And Zabad begat Ephlal, and Ephlal begat Obed,
38And Obed begat Jehu, and Jehu begat Azariah,
39And Azariah begat Helez, and Helez begat Eleasah,
40And Eleasah begat Sisamai, and Sisamai begat Shallum,
41And Shallum begat Jekamiah, and Jekamiah begat Elishama.

## Amplified

13Jesse was the father of Eliab his first-born, Abinadab second, Shima third,
14Nethanel fourth, Raddai fifth,
15Ozem sixth, David seventh;
16Their sisters were Zeruiah and Abigail. The sons of Zeruiah: Abishai, Joab, and Asahel, three.
17Abigail bore Amasa, and the father of Amasa was Jether the Ishmaelite.
18And Caleb the son of Hezron had sons by his wife Azubah and by Jerioth. [Azubah's] sons were: Jesher, Shobab, and Ardon.
19Azubah died, and Caleb married Ephrath, who bore him Hur.
20Hur was the father of Uri, and Uri of Bezalel [the skillful craftsman who made the furnishings of the tabernacle]. [Exod. 31:2-5.]
21Later, when Hezron was sixty years old, he married the daughter of Machir father of Gilead, and she bore him Segub.
22Segub was the father of Jair, who had twenty-three cities in the land of Gilead.
23But Geshur and Aram took from them Havvoth-jair, Kenath and its villages, sixty towns. All these were the descendants of Machir, father of Gilead.
24After Hezron was dead in Caleb-ephrathah, Abiah Hezron's wife bore to him Ashhur father of Tekoa.
25The sons of Jerahmeel the first-born of Hezron: Ram the first-born, Bunah, Oren, Ozem, and Ahijah.
26Jerahmeel had another wife, named Atarah; she was the mother of Onam.
27The sons of Ram, the first-born of Jerahmeel, were Maaz, Jamin, and Eker.
28The sons of Onam: Shammai and Jada. The sons of Shammai: Nadab and Abishur.
29Abishur's wife was Abihail; she bore him Ahban and Molid.
30The sons of Nadab: Seled and Appa-im. Seled died childless.
31The sons of Appa-im: Ishi. The sons of Ishi: Sheshan. The sons of Sheshan: Ahlai.
32The sons of Jada, brother of Shammai: Jether and Jonathan; Jether died childless.
33The sons of Jonathan: Peleth and Zaza. These were the descendants of Jerahmeel.
34Sheshan had no sons, only daughters. But Sheshan had a servant, an Egyptian, whose name was Jarha.
35Sheshan gave his daughter to Jarha his servant as wife; she bore him Attai.
36Attai was the father of Nathan, and Nathan of Zabad,
37Zabad was the father of Ephlal, and Ephlal of Obed,
38Obed was the father of Jehu, and Jehu of Azariah,
39Azariah was the father of Helez, and Helez of Eleasah,
40Eleasah was the father of Sismai, and Sismai of Shallum;
41Shallum was the father of Jekamiah, and Jekamiah of Elishama.

## New American Standard

13and Jesse became the father of Eliab his first-born, then Abinadab the second, Shimea the third,
14Nethanel the fourth, Raddai the fifth,
15Ozem the sixth, David the seventh;
16and their sisters *were* Zeruiah and Abigail. And the three sons
of Zeruiah *were* Abshai, Joab, and Asahel.
17And Abigail bore Amasa, and the father of Amasa was Jether
the Ishmaelite.
18¶ Now Caleb the son of Hezron had sons by Azubah *his* wife,
and by Jerioth; and these were her sons: Jesher, Shobab, and
Ardon.
19When Azubah died, Caleb married Ephrath, who bore him
Hur.
20And Hur became the father of Uri, and Uri became the father
of Bezalel.
21¶ Afterward Hezron went in to the daughter of Machir the
father of Gilead, whom he married when he was sixty years old;
and she bore him Segub.
22And Segub became the father of Jair, who had twenty-three
cities in the land of Gilead.
23But Geshur and Aram took the towns of Jair from them, with
Kenath and its villages, *even* sixty cities. All these were the sons
of Machir, the father of Gilead.
24And after the death of Hezron in Caleb-ephrathah, Abijah,
Hezron's wife, bore him Ashhur the father of Tekoa.
25¶ Now the sons of Jerahmeel the first-born of Hezron *were*
Ram the first-born, then Bunah, Oren, Ozem, *and* Ahijah.
26And Jerahmeel had another wife, whose name was Atarah;
she was the mother of Onam.
27And the sons of Ram, the first-born of Jerahmeel, were Maaz,
Jamin, and Eker.
28And the sons of Onam were Shammai and Jada. And the sons
of Shammai *were* Nadab and Abishur.
29And the name of Abishur's wife *was* Abihail, and she bore him
Ahban and Molid.
30And the sons of Nadab *were* Seled and Appaim, and Seled
died without sons.
31And the son of Appaim *was* Ishi. And the son of Ishi *was*
Sheshan. And the son of Sheshan *was* Ahlai.
32And the sons of Jada the brother of Shammai *were* Jether and
Jonathan, and Jether died without sons.
33And the sons of Jonathan *were* Peleth and Zaza. These were
the sons of Jerahmeel.
34Now Sheshan had no sons, only daughters. And Sheshan had
an Egyptian servant whose name was Jarha.
35And Sheshan gave his daughter to Jarha his servant in marriage, and she bore him Attai.
36And Attai became the father of Nathan, and Nathan became
the father of Zabad,
37and Zabad became the father of Ephlal, and Ephlal became the
father of Obed,
38and Obed became the father of Jehu, and Jehu became the
father of Azariah,
39and Azariah became the father of Helez, and Helez became
the father of Eleasah,
40and Eleasah became the father of Sismai, and Sismai became
the father of Shallum,
41and Shallum became the father of Jekamiah, and Jekamiah
became the father of Elishama.

## New International

13Jesse was the father of
Eliab his firstborn; the second son was Abinadab, the third
Shimea, 14the fourth Nethanel, the fifth Raddai, 15the
sixth Ozem and the seventh David. 16Their sisters were
Zeruiah and Abigail. Zeruiah's three sons were Abishai,
Joab and Asahel. 17Abigail was the mother of Amasa,
whose father was Jether the Ishmaelite.

*Caleb Son of Hezron*

18Caleb son of Hezron had children by his wife Azubah (and
by Jerioth). These were her sons: Jesher, Shobab and Ardon. 19When Azubah died, Caleb married Ephrath, who
bore him Hur. 20Hur was the father of Uri, and Uri the
father of Bezalel.
21Later, Hezron lay with the daughter of Makir the father of
Gilead (he had married her when he was sixty years old),
and she bore him Segub. 22Segub was the father of Jair,
who controlled twenty-three towns in Gilead. 23(But Geshur and Aram captured Havvoth Jair,[a] as well as Kenath
with its surrounding settlements—sixty towns.) All these
were descendants of Makir the father of Gilead.
24After Hezron died in Caleb Ephrathah, Abijah the wife of
Hezron bore him Ashhur the father[b] of Tekoa.

*Jerahmeel Son of Hezron*

25The sons of Jerahmeel the firstborn of Hezron:
Ram his firstborn, Bunah, Oren, Ozem and[c] Ahijah.
26Jerahmeel had another wife, whose name was Atarah;
she was the mother of Onam.
27The sons of Ram the firstborn of Jerahmeel:
Maaz, Jamin and Eker.
28The sons of Onam:
Shammai and Jada.
The sons of Shammai:
Nadab and Abishur.
29Abishur's wife was named Abihail, who bore him Ahban and
Molid.
30The sons of Nadab:
Seled and Appaim. Seled died without children.
31The son of Appaim:
Ishi, who was the father of Sheshan.
Sheshan was the father of Ahlai.
32The sons of Jada, Shammai's brother:
Jether and Jonathan. Jether died without children.
33The sons of Jonathan:
Peleth and Zaza.
These were the descendants of Jerahmeel.
34Sheshan had no sons—only daughters.
He had an Egyptian servant named Jarha. 35Sheshan gave
his daughter in marriage to his servant Jarha, and she bore
him Attai.
36Attai was the father of Nathan,
Nathan the father of Zabad,
37Zabad the father of Ephlal,
Ephlal the father of Obed,
38Obed the father of Jehu,
Jehu the father of Azariah,
39Azariah the father of Helez,
Helez the father of Eleasah,
40Eleasah the father of Sismai,
Sismai the father of Shallum,
41Shallum the father of Jekamiah,
and Jekamiah the father of Elishama.

**NIV** [a] 23 Or *captured the settlements of Jair* [b] 24 *Father* may mean *civic leader or military leader;* also in verses 42, 45, 49-52 and possibly elsewhere. [c] 25 Or *Oren and Ozem, by*

## King James

42¶ Now the sons of Caleb the brother of Jerahmeel *were*, Mesha
his firstborn, which *was* the father of Ziph; and the sons of Mareshah the father of Hebron.
43And the sons of Hebron; Korah, and Tappuah, and Rekem,
and Shema.
44And Shema begat Raham, the father of Jorkoam: and Rekem
begat Shammai.
45And the son of Shammai *was* Maon: and Maon *was* the father
of Beth-zur.
46And Ephah, Caleb's concubine, bare Haran, and Moza, and
Gazez: and Haran begat Gazez.
47And the sons of Jahdai; Regem, and Jotham, and Gesham,
and Pelet, and Ephah, and Shaaph.
48Maachah, Caleb's concubine, bare Sheber, and Tirhanah.
49She bare also Shaaph the father of Madmannah, Sheva the
father of Machbenah, and the father of Gibea: and the daughter of
Caleb *was* Achsah.
50¶ These were the sons of Caleb the son of Hur, the firstborn
of Ephratah; Shobal the father of Kirjath-jearim,
51Salma the father of Bethlehem, Hareph the father of Beth-
gader.
52And Shobal the father of Kirjath-jearim had sons; Haroeh, *and*
half of the Manahethites.
53And the families of Kirjath-jearim; the Ithrites, and the Pu-
hites, and the Shumathites, and the Mishraites; of them came the
Zareathites, and the Eshtaulites.
54The sons of Salma; Bethlehem, and the Netophathites,
Ataroth, the house of Joab, and half of the Manahethites, the
Zorites.
55And the families of the scribes which dwelt at Jabez; the
Tirathites, the Shimeathites, *and* Suchathites. These *are* the Kenites
that came of Hemath, the father of the house of Rechab.

3 NOW THESE were the sons of David, which were born unto
him in Hebron; the firstborn Amnon, of Ahinoam the Jezreelitess; the second Daniel, of Abigail the Carmelitess:
2The third, Absalom the son of Maachah the daughter of Talmai
king of Geshur: the fourth, Adonijah the son of Haggith:
3The fifth, Shephatiah of Abital: the sixth, Ithream by Eglah his
wife.
4 *These* six were born unto him in Hebron; and there he reigned
seven years and six months: and in Jerusalem he reigned thirty and
three years.
5And these were born unto him in Jerusalem; Shimea, and
Shobab, and Nathan, and Solomon, four, of Bath-shua the daughter of Ammiel:
6Ibhar also, and Elishama, and Eliphelet,
7And Nogah, and Nepheg, and Japhia,
8And Elishama, and Eliada, and Eliphelet, nine.
9 *These were* all the sons of David, beside the sons of the concubines, and Tamar their sister.
10¶ And Solomon's son *was* Rehoboam, Abia his son, Asa his
son, Jehoshaphat his son,
11Joram his son, Ahaziah his son, Joash his son,

## Amplified

42The sons of Caleb brother of Jerahmeel: Mesha [Mareshah] his
first-born was the father of Ziph. The sons of Mareshah: [he was]
father of Hebron.
43The sons of Hebron: Korah, Tappuah, Rekem, and Shema.
44Shema was the father of Raham, the father of Jorke-am; and
Rekem was the father of Shammai.
45The son of Shammai was Maon; Maon's son was Beth-zur.
46Ephah, Caleb's concubine, bore Haran, Moza, Gazez; Haran
was the father of Gazez.
47The sons of Jahdai: Regem, Jotham, Geshan, Pelet, Ephah,
and Shaaph.
48Maacah, Caleb's concubine, bore Sheber and Tirhanah; also
49Shaaph father of Madmannah, Sheva father of Machbenah
and of Gibea; and the daughter of Caleb was Achsah.
50These were the descendants of Caleb. The sons of Hur, the
first-born of Ephrathah: Shobal the father of Kiriath-jearim,
51Salma the father of Bethlehem, and Hareph the father of
Beth-gader.
52Shobal father of Kiriath-jearim had [other] descendants: Haroeh, and half [the inhabitants] of Menuhoth [in Judah].
53And the families of Kiriath-jearim: the Ithrites, Puthites, Shumathites, and Mishraites; of them came the Zorathites and the
Eshtaolites.
54The descendants of Salma: Bethlehem, the Netophathites,
Atroth-beth-joab, and half of the Manahathites, [and] the Zorites.
55The families of scribes who dwelt at Jabez: the Tirathites,
Shimeathites, and Sucathites. These are the Kenites who came
from Hammath, father of the house of Rechab.

3 THESE SONS of David were born to him in Hebron: the
first-born Amnon, of Ahinoam the Jezreelitess; second Daniel
[Chileab], of Abigail the Carmelitess;
2Third Absalom, son of Maacah daughter of Talmai, king of
Geshur; fourth Adonijah of Haggith;
3Fifth Shephatiah of Abital; sixth Ithream of his wife Eglah.
4These six were born to David in Hebron; there he reigned
seven years and six months, and in Jerusalem he reigned thirty-
three years.
5These were born to [David] in Jerusalem: Shimea, Shobab,
Nathan, Solomon, four of Bathshua [Bathsheba] daughter of Ammiel [Eliam];
6Then Ibhar, Elishama, Eliphelet,
7Nogah, Nepheg, Japhia,
8Elishama, Eliada, and Eliphelet, nine.
9These were all the sons of David, besides the sons of the
concubines, and Tamar was their sister.
10Solomon's descendants [omitting non-reigning offspring]
were his son Rehoboam; Abijah was his son, Asa his son, Jehoshaphat his son,
11Joram his son, Ahaziah his son, Joash his son,

## New American Standard

42¶ Now the sons of Caleb, the brother of Jerahmeel, *were* Mesha
his first-born, who was the father of Ziph; and his son was Mareshah, the father of Hebron.
43And the sons of Hebron *were* Korah and Tappuah and Rekem
and Shema.
44And Shema became the father of Raham, the father of Jorkeam; and Rekem became the father of Shammai.
45And the son of Shammai was Maon, and Maon *was* the father
of Bethzur.
46And Ephah, Caleb's concubine, bore Haran, Moza, and
Gazez; and Haran became the father of Gazez.
47And the sons of Jahdai *were* Regem, Jotham, Geshan, Pelet,
Ephah, and Shaaph.
48Maacah, Caleb's concubine, bore Sheber and Tirhanah.
49She also bore Shaaph the father of Madmannah, Sheva the
father of Machbena and the father of Gibea; and the daughter of
Caleb *was* Achsah.
50These were the sons of Caleb.
¶The sons of Hur, the first-born of Ephrathah, *were* Shobal the
father of Kiriath-jearim,
51Salma the father of Bethlehem *and* Hareph the father of Beth-
gader.
52And Shobal the father of Kiriath-jearim had sons: Haroeh,
half of the Manahathites,
53and the families of Kiriath-jearim: the Ithrites, the Puthites,
the Shumathites, and the Mishraites; from these came the Zorathites and the Eshtaolites.
54The sons of Salma *were* Bethlehem and the Netophathites,
Atroth-beth-joab and half of the Manahathites, the Zorites.
55And the families of scribes who lived at Jabez *were* the Tirathites, the Shimeathites, *and* the Sucathites. Those are the Kenites
who came from Hammath, the father of the house of Rechab.

*Family of David*

3 NOW THESE were the sons of David who were born to him
in Hebron: the first-born *was* Amnon, by Ahinoam the Jezreelitess; the second *was* Daniel, by Abigail the Carmelitess;
2the third *was* Absalom the son of Maacah, the daughter of
Talmai king of Geshur; the fourth *was* Adonijah the son of Haggith;
3the fifth *was* Shephatiah, by Abital; the sixth *was* Ithream, by
his wife Eglah.
4Six were born to him in Hebron, and there he reigned seven
years and six months. And in Jerusalem he reigned thirty-three
years.
5And these were born to him in Jerusalem: Shimea, Shobab,
Nathan, and Solomon, four, by Bath-shua the daughter of Ammiel;
6and Ibhar, Elishama, Eliphelet,
7Nogah, Nepheg, and Japhia,
8Elishama, Eliada, and Eliphelet, nine.
9All *these were* the sons of David, besides the sons of the concubines; and Tamar *was* their sister.
10¶ Now Solomon's son *was* Rehoboam, Abijah *was* his son, Asa
his son, Jehoshaphat his son,
11Joram his son, Ahaziah his son, Joash his son,

## New International

*The Clans of Caleb*

42The sons of Caleb the brother of Jerahmeel:
Mesha his firstborn, who was the father of Ziph, and his
son Mareshah,[a] who was the father of Hebron.
43The sons of Hebron:
Korah, Tappuah, Rekem and Shema. 44Shema was the
father of Raham, and Raham the father of Jorkeam. Rekem
was the father of Shammai. 45The son of Shammai was
Maon, and Maon was the father of Beth Zur.
46Caleb's concubine Ephah was the mother of Haran, Moza
and Gazez. Haran was the father of Gazez.
47The sons of Jahdai:
Regem, Jotham, Geshan, Pelet, Ephah and Shaaph.
48Caleb's concubine Maacah was the mother of Sheber and
Tirhanah. 49She also gave birth to Shaaph the father of
Madmannah and to Sheva the father of Macbenah and
Gibea. Caleb's daughter was Acsah. 50These were the de-
scendants of Caleb.
The sons of Hur the firstborn of Ephrathah:
Shobal the father of Kiriath Jearim, 51Salma the father of
Bethlehem, and Hareph the father of Beth Gader.
52The descendants of Shobal the father of Kiriath Jearim were:
Haroeh, half the Manahathites, 53and the clans of Kiriath
Jearim: the Ithrites, Puthites, Shumathites and Mishraites.
From these descended the Zorathites and Eshtaolites.
54The descendants of Salma:
Bethlehem, the Netophathites, Atroth Beth Joab, half the
Manahathites, the Zorites, 55and the clans of scribes[b] who
lived at Jabez: the Tirathites, Shimeathites and Sucathites.
These are the Kenites who came from Hammath, the fa-
ther of the house of Recab.[c]

*The Sons of David*

3 THESE WERE the sons of David born to him in Hebron:
The firstborn was Amnon the son of Ahinoam of Jezreel;
the second, Daniel the son of Abigail of Carmel;
2the third, Absalom the son of Maacah daughter of Talmai
king of Geshur;
the fourth, Adonijah the son of Haggith;
3the fifth, Shephatiah the son of Abital;
and the sixth, Ithream, by his wife Eglah.
4These six were born to David in Hebron, where he reigned
seven years and six months.
David reigned in Jerusalem thirty-three years, 5and these were the
children born to him there:
Shammua,[d] Shobab, Nathan and Solomon. These four
were by Bathsheba[e] daughter of Ammiel. 6There were
also Ibhar, Elishua,[f] Eliphelet, 7Nogah, Nepheg, Japhia,
8Elishama, Eliada and Eliphelet—nine in all. 9All these
were the sons of David, besides his sons by his concubines. And Tamar was their sister.

*The Kings of Judah*

10Solomon's son was Rehoboam,
Abijah his son,
Asa his son,
Jehoshaphat his son,
11Jehoram[g] his son,
Ahaziah his son,
Joash his son,

**NIV** [a] *42* The meaning of the Hebrew for this phrase is uncertain. [b] *55* Or *of the Sopherites* [c] *55* Or *father of Beth Recab* [d] *5* Hebrew *Shimea,* a variant of *Shammua* [e] *5* One Hebrew manuscript and Vulgate (see also Septuagint and 2 Samuel 11:3); most Hebrew manuscripts *Bathshua* [f] *6* Two Hebrew manuscripts (see also 2 Samuel 5:15 and 1 Chron. 14:5); most Hebrew manuscripts *Elishama* [g] *11* Hebrew *Joram,* a variant of *Jehoram*

## King James

12Amaziah his son, Azariah his son, Jotham his son,
13Ahaz his son, Hezekiah his son, Manasseh his son,
14Amon his son, Josiah his son.
15And the sons of Josiah *were,* the firstborn Johanan, the second
Jehoiakim, the third Zedekiah, the fourth Shallum.
16And the sons of Jehoiakim: Jeconiah his son, Zedekiah his
son.
17¶ And the sons of Jeconiah; Assir, Salathiel his son,
18Malchiram also, and Pedaiah, and Shenazar, Jecamiah, Hoshama, and Nedabiah.
19And the sons of Pedaiah *were,* Zerubbabel, and Shimei: and
the sons of Zerubbabel; Meshullam, and Hananiah, and Shelomith
their sister:
20And Hashubah, and Ohel, and Berechiah, and Hasadiah,
Jushab-hesed, five.
21And the sons of Hananiah; Pelatiah, and Jesaiah: the sons of
Rephaiah, the sons of Arnan, the sons of Obadiah, the sons of
Shechaniah.
22And the sons of Shechaniah; Shemaiah: and the sons of Shemaiah; Hattush, and Igeal, and Bariah, and Neariah, and Shaphat,
six.
23And the sons of Neariah; Elioenai, and Hezekiah, and Azrikam, three.
24And the sons of Elioenai *were,* Hodaiah, and Eliashib, and
Pelaiah, and Akkub, and Johanan, and Dalaiah, and Anani, seven.

4 THE SONS of Judah; Pharez, Hezron, and Carmi, and Hur,
and Shobal.
2And Reaiah the son of Shobal begat Jahath; and Jahath begat
Ahumai, and Lahad. These *are* the families of the Zorathites.
3And these *were of* the father of Etam; Jezreel, and Ishma, and
Idbash: and the name of their sister *was* Hazelelponi:
4And Penuel the father of Gedor, and Ezer the father of Hushah. These *are* the sons of Hur, the firstborn of Ephratah, the
father of Bethlehem.
5¶ And Ashur the father of Tekoa had two wives, Helah and
Naarah.
6And Naarah bare him Ahuzam, and Hepher, and Temeni, and
Haahashtari. These *were* the sons of Naarah.
7And the sons of Helah *were,* Zereth, and Jezoar, and Ethnan.
8And Coz begat Anub, and Zobebah, and the families of Aharhel the son of Harum.
9¶ And Jabez was more honourable than his brethren: and his
mother called his name Jabez, saying, Because I bare him with
sorrow.

## Amplified

12Amaziah his son, Azariah his son, Jotham his son,
13Ahaz his son, Hezekiah his son, Manasseh his son,
14Amon his son, Josiah his son.
15The descendants of Josiah: first-born Johanan, second Jehoiakim, third Zedekiah, fourth Shallum.
16The descendants of Jehoiakim: Jeconiah his son, Zedekiah his
son.
17The descendants of Jeconiah, the captive: Shealtiel his son,
18Malchiram, Pedaiah, Shenazzar, Jekamiah, Hoshama, and
Nedabiah.
19The sons of Pedaiah: Zerubbabel and Shimei; the sons of
Zerubbabel: Meshullam, Hananiah, and Shelomith was their sister;
20And Hashubah, Ohel, Berechiah, Hasadiah, [and] Jushabhesed, five [the sons of Meshullam?].
21The sons of Hananiah: Pelatiah, and Jeshaiah, whose son was
Rephaiah, his son Arnan, his son Obadiah, his son Shecaniah.
22The sons of Shecaniah: Shemaiah. The sons of Shemaiah:
Hattush, Igal, Bariah, Neariah, and Shaphat, six.
23The sons of Neariah: Elioenai, Hizkiah, and Azrikam, three.
24The sons of Elioenai: Hodaviah, Eliashib, Pelaiah, Akkub,
Johanan, Dolaiah, and Anani, seven.

4 THE SONS of Judah: Perez, Hezron, Carmi, Hur, and Shobal.
2Reaiah the son of Shobal was the father of Jahath, and Jahath
of Ahumai and Lahad. These were the families of the Zorathites.
3These were the sons of [Hur] the father of Etam: Jezreel, Ishma, Idbash, and their sister was Hazzelelponi;
4And Penuel the father of Gedor, and Ezer the father of Hushah. These were the sons of Hur, the eldest of Ephrathah
[Ephrath], the father of Bethlehem.
5Ashur, the father of Tekoa, had two wives, Helah and Naarah;
6Naarah bore him Ahuzzam, Hepher, Temeni, and Ha-ahashtari. These were Naarah's sons.
7The sons of Helah: Zereth, Izhar, and Ethnan.
8Koz was the father of Anub, Zobebah, and the families of
Aharhel son of Harum.
9Jabez was honorable above his brothers; but his mother named
him Jabez (sorrow maker), saying, Because I bore him in pain.

## New American Standard

12Amaziah his son, Azariah his son, Jotham his son,
13Ahaz his son, Hezekiah his son, Manasseh his son,
14Amon his son, Josiah his son.
15And the sons of Josiah *were* Johanan the first-born, and the
second *was* Jehoiakim, the third Zedekiah, the fourth Shallum.
16And the sons of Jehoiakim *were* Jeconiah his son, Zedekiah his
son.
17And the sons of Jeconiah, the prisoner, *were* Shealtiel his son,
18and Malchiram, Pedaiah, Shenazzar, Jekamiah, Hoshama,
and Nedabiah.
19And the sons of Pedaiah *were* Zerubbabel and Shimei. And the
sons of Zerubbabel *were* Meshullam and Hananiah, and Shelomith
*was* their sister;
20and Hashubah, Ohel, Berechiah, Hasadiah, and Jushab-hesed, five.
21And the sons of Hananiah *were* Pelatiah and Jeshaiah, the
sons of Rephaiah, the sons of Arnan, the sons of Obadiah, the sons
of Shecaniah.
22And the [a]son of Shecaniah *was* Shemaiah, and the sons of
Shemaiah *were* Hattush, Igal, Bariah, Neariah, and Shaphat, six.
23And the sons of Neariah *were* Elioenai, Hizkiah, and Azrikam,
three.
24And the sons of Elioenai *were* Hodaviah, Eliashib, Pelaiah,
Akkub, Johanan, Delaiah, and Anani, seven.

*Line of Hur, Asher*

4 THE SONS of Judah *were* Perez, Hezron, Carmi, Hur, and
Shobal.
2And Reaiah the son of Shobal became the father of Jahath, and
Jahath became the father of Ahumai and Lahad. These *were* the
families of the Zorathites.
3And these *were* the sons of Etam: Jezreel, Ishma, and Idbash;
and the name of their sister *was* Hazzelelponi.
4And Penuel *was* the father of Gedor, and Ezer the father of
Hushah. These *were* the sons of Hur, the first-born of Ephrathah,
the father of Bethlehem.
5And Ashhur, the father of Tekoa, had two wives, Helah and
Naarah.
6And Naarah bore him Ahuzzam, Hepher, Temeni, and Haahashtari. These were the sons of Naarah.
7And the sons of Helah *were* Zereth, Izhar and Ethnan.
8And Koz became the father of Anub and Zobebah, and the
families of Aharhel the son of Harum.
9And Jabez was more honorable than his brothers, and his
mother named him Jabez saying, "Because I bore *him* with pain."

NAS [a] Lit., *sons*

## New International

12Amaziah his son,
Azariah his son,
Jotham his son,
13Ahaz his son,
Hezekiah his son,
Manasseh his son,
14Amon his son,
Josiah his son.
15The sons of Josiah:
Johanan the firstborn,
Jehoiakim the second son,
Zedekiah the third,
Shallum the fourth.
16The successors of Jehoiakim:
Jehoiachin[b] his son,
and Zedekiah.

*The Royal Line After the Exile*

17The descendants of Jehoiachin the captive:
Shealtiel his son, 18Malkiram, Pedaiah, Shenazzar, Jeka-
miah, Hoshama and Nedabiah.
19The sons of Pedaiah:
Zerubbabel and Shimei.
The sons of Zerubbabel:
Meshullam and Hananiah.
Shelomith was their sister.
20There were also five others:
Hashubah, Ohel, Berekiah, Hasadiah and Jushab-Hesed.
21The descendants of Hananiah:
Pelatiah and Jeshaiah, and the sons of Rephaiah, of Ar-
nan, of Obadiah and of Shecaniah.
22The descendants of Shecaniah:
Shemaiah and his sons:
Hattush, Igal, Bariah, Neariah and Shaphat—six in all.
23The sons of Neariah:
Elioenai, Hizkiah and Azrikam—three in all.
24The sons of Elioenai:
Hodaviah, Eliashib, Pelaiah, Akkub, Johanan, Delaiah
and Anani—seven in all.

*Other Clans of Judah*

4 THE DESCENDANTS of Judah:
Perez, Hezron, Carmi, Hur and Shobal.
2Reaiah son of Shobal was the father of Jahath, and Jahath the
father of Ahumai and Lahad. These were the clans of the
Zorathites.
3These were the sons[c] of Etam:
Jezreel, Ishma and Idbash. Their sister was named Hazzelelponi. 4Penuel was the father of Gedor, and Ezer the
father of Hushah.
These were the descendants of Hur, the firstborn of Ephrathah and father[d] of Bethlehem.
5Ashhur the father of Tekoa had two wives, Helah and Naarah.
6Naarah bore him Ahuzzam, Hepher, Temeni and Haahashtari. These were the descendants of Naarah.
7The sons of Helah:
Zereth, Zohar, Ethnan, 8and Koz, who was the father of
Anub and Hazzobebah and of the clans of Aharhel son of
Harum.

9Jabez was more honorable than his brothers. His mother had
named him Jabez,[e] saying, "I gave birth to him in pain." 10Jabez

NIV [b] *16* Hebrew *Jeconiah,* a variant of *Jehoiachin;* also in verse 17 [c] *3* Some Septuagint manuscripts (see also Vulgate); Hebrew *father* [d] *4 Father* may mean *civic leader* or *military leader;* also in verses 12, 14, 17, 18 and possibly elsewhere. [e] *9 Jabez* sounds like the Hebrew for *pain.*

## King James

10 And Jabez called on the God of Israel, saying, Oh that thou wouldest bless me indeed, and enlarge my coast, and that thine hand might be with me, and that thou wouldest keep *me* from evil, that it may not grieve me! And God granted him that which he requested.

11 ¶ And Chelub the brother of Shuah begat Mehir, which *was* the father of Eshton.

12 And Eshton begat Beth-rapha, and Paseah, and Tehinnah the father of Ir-nahash. These *are* the men of Rechah.

13 And the sons of Kenaz; Othniel, and Seraiah: and the sons of Othniel; Hathath.

14 And Meonothai begat Ophrah: and Seraiah begat Joab, the father of the valley of Charashim; for they were craftsmen.

15 And the sons of Caleb the son of Jephunneh; Iru, Elah, and Naam: and the sons of Elah, even Kenaz.

16 And the sons of Jehaleleel; Ziph, and Ziphah, Tiria, and Asareel.

17 And the sons of Ezra *were,* Jether, and Mered, and Epher, and Jalon: and she bare Miriam, and Shammai, and Ishbah the father of Eshtemoa.

18 And his wife Jehudijah bare Jered the father of Gedor, and Heber the father of Socho, and Jekuthiel the father of Zanoah. And these *are* the sons of Bithiah the daughter of Pharaoh, which Mered took.

19 And the sons of *his* wife Hodiah the sister of Naham, the father of Keilah the Garmite, and Eshtemoa the Maachathite.

20 And the sons of Shimon *were,* Amnon, and Rinnah, Ben-hanan, and Tilon. And the sons of Ishi *were,* Zoheth, and Ben-zoheth.

21 ¶ The sons of Shelah the son of Judah *were,* Er the father of Lecah, and Laadah the father of Mareshah, and the families of the house of them that wrought fine linen, of the house of Ashbea,

22 And Jokim, and the men of Chozeba, and Joash, and Saraph, who had the dominion in Moab, and Jashubi-lehem. And *these are* ancient things.

23 These *were* the potters, and those that dwelt among plants and hedges: there they dwelt with the king for his work.

24 ¶ The sons of Simeon *were,* Nemuel, and Jamin, Jarib, Zerah, *and* Shaul:

25 Shallum his son, Mibsam his son, Mishma his son.

26 And the sons of Mishma; Hamuel his son, Zacchur his son, Shimei his son.

27 And Shimei had sixteen sons and six daughters; but his brethren had not many children, neither did all their family multiply, like to the children of Judah.

28 And they dwelt at Beer-sheba, and Moladah, and Hazar-shual,

29 And at Bilhah, and at Ezem, and at Tolad,

30 And at Bethuel, and at Hormah, and at Ziklag,

31 And at Beth-marcaboth, and Hazar-susim, and at Beth-birei, and at Shaaraim. These *were* their cities unto the reign of David.

32 And their villages *were,* Etam, and Ain, Rimmon, and Tochen, and Ashan, five cities:

33 And all their villages that *were* round about the same cities, unto Baal. These *were* their habitations, and their genealogy.

34 And Meshobab, and Jamlech, and Joshah the son of Amaziah,

35 And Joel, and Jehu the son of Josibiah, the son of Seraiah, the son of Asiel,

## Amplified

10 Jabez cried to the God of Israel, saying, Oh that You would bless me and enlarge my border, and that Your hand might be with me, and You would keep me from evil so it might not hurt me! And God granted his request.

11 Chelub brother of Shuhah was the father of Mehir, the father of Eshton.

12 Eshton was the father of Bethrapha, Paseah, and Tehinnah father of Irnahash. These are the men of Recah.

13 The sons of Kenaz: Othniel and Seraiah; the sons of Othniel: Hathath [and Meonothai].

14 Meonothai was father of Ophrah; and Seraiah of Joab, father of Geharashim (the valley of craftsmen), [so named] because they were craftsmen.

15 The sons of Caleb [Joshua's companion] son of Jephunneh: Iru, Elah, and Naam. The sons of Elah: Kenaz.

16 The sons of Jehallel: Ziph, Ziphah, Tiria, and Asarel.

17 The sons of Ezrah: Jether, Mered, Epher, and Jalon. [a]These are the sons of Bithiah daughter of Pharaoh, whom Mered married: she bore Miriam, Shammai, and Ishbah, the father of Eshtemoa.

18 And Mered's Jewish wife bore Jered father of Gedor, Heber father of Soco, and Jekuthiel father of Zanoah.

19 The sons of the wife of Hodiah, the sister of Naham, were the fathers of Keilah the Garmite, and Eshtemoa the Ma-acathite.

20 The sons of Shimon: Amnon, Rinnah, Ben-hanan, and Tilon. The sons of Ishi: Zoheth and Ben-zoheth.

21 The sons of Shelah son of Judah: Er father of Lecah, and Laadah father of Mareshah, and the families of the house of linen workers at Bath-ashbea;

22 And Jokim, the men of Cozeba, Joash, and Saraph, who ruled in Moab, and returned to [Bethlehem]. These are ancient matters.

23 These were the potters and those who dwelt among plantations and hedges—at Netaim and Gederah; there they dwelt with the king for his work.

24 The sons of Simeon: Nemuel, Jamin, Jarib, Zerah, and Shaul;

25 Shallum was his son, Mibsam his son, Mishma his son.

26 The sons of Mishma: Hammuel his son, Zaccur his son, Shimei his son.

27 Shimei had sixteen sons and six daughters; but his brothers did not have many children, neither did all their family multiply like the children of Judah.

28 They dwelt at Beer-sheba, Moladah, Hazar-shual,

29 Bilhah, Ezem, Tolad,

30 Bethuel, Hormah, Ziklag,

31 Beth-marcaboth, Hazar-susim, Beth-biri, and at Sha-araim. These were their towns [and villages] until the reign of David.

32 There were also Etam, Ain, Rimmon, Tochen, and Ashan, five towns,

33 And all their villages that were round about these towns, as far as Baal[-ath-beer]. These were their settlements and they had their genealogical record.

34 Meshobab, Jamlech, Joshah son of Amaziah,

35 Joel, Jehu son of Joshibiah, son of Seraiah, son of Asiel,

AMP [a] This clause, to the colon, is transposed from verse 18.

## New American Standard

10Now Jabez called on the God of Israel, saying, "Oh that Thou wouldst bless me indeed, and enlarge my border, and that Thy hand might be with me, and that Thou wouldst keep *me* from harm, that *it* may not pain me!" And God granted him what he requested.

11¶ And Chelub the brother of Shuhah became the father of Mehir, who was the father of Eshton.

12And Eshton became the father of Beth-rapha and Paseah, and Tehinnah the father of Ir-nahash. These are the men of Recah.

13¶ Now the sons of Kenaz *were* Othniel and Seraiah. And the son of Othniel *was* Hathath.

14And Meonothai became the father of Ophrah, and Seraiah became the father of Joab the father of Ge-harashim, for they were craftsmen.

15And the sons of Caleb the son of Jephunneh *were* Iru, Elah and Naam; and the son of Elah *was* Kenaz.

16And the sons of Jehallelel *were* Ziph and Ziphah, Tiria and Asarel.

17And the sons of Ezrah *were* Jether, Mered, Epher, and Jalon. (And these are the sons of Bithia the daughter of Pharaoh, whom Mered took) and she conceived *and bore* Miriam, Shammai, and Ishbah the father of Eshtemoa.

18And his Jewish wife bore Jered the father of Gedor, and Heber the father of Soco, and Jekuthiel the father of Zanoah.

19And the sons of the wife of Hodiah, the sister of Naham, *were* the fathers of Keilah the Garmite and Eshtemoa the Maacathite.

20And the sons of Shimon *were* Amnon and Rinnah, Benhanan and Tilon. And the sons of Ishi *were* Zoheth and Ben-zoheth.

21The sons of Shelah the son of Judah *were* Er the father of Lecah and Laadah the father of Mareshah, and the families of the house of the linen workers at Beth-ashbea;

22and Jokim, the men of Cozeba, Joash, Saraph, who ruled in Moab, and Jashubi-lehem. And the records are ancient.

23These were the potters and the inhabitants of Netaim and Gederah; they lived there with the king for his work.

*Descendants of Simeon*

24¶ The sons of Simeon *were* Nemuel and Jamin, Jarib, Zerah, Shaul;

25Shallum his son, Mibsam his son, Mishma his son.

26And the sons of Mishma *were* Hammuel his son, Zaccur his son, Shimei his son.

27Now Shimei had sixteen sons and six daughters; but his brothers did not have many sons, nor did all their family multiply like the sons of Judah.

28And they lived at Beersheba, Moladah, and Hazar-shual,

29at Bilhah, Ezem, Tolad,

30Bethuel, Hormah, Ziklag,

31Beth-marcaboth, Hazar-susim, Beth-biri, and Shaaraim. These *were* their cities until the reign of David.

32And their villages *were* Etam, Ain, Rimmon, Tochen, and Ashan, five cities;

33and all their villages that *were* around the same cities as far as Baal. These *were* their settlements, and they have their genealogy.

34And Meshobab and Jamlech and Joshah the son of Amaziah,

35and Joel and Jehu the son of Joshibiah, the son of Seraiah, the son of Asiel,

## New International

cried out to the God of Israel, "Oh, that you would bless me and enlarge my territory! Let your hand be with me, and keep me from harm so that I will be free from pain." And God granted his request.

11Kelub, Shuhah's brother, was the father of Mehir, who was the father of Eshton. 12Eshton was the father of Beth Rapha, Paseah and Tehinnah the father of Ir Nahash.[b] These were the men of Recah.

13The sons of Kenaz:
Othniel and Seraiah.
The sons of Othniel:
Hathath and Meonothai.[c] 14Meonothai was the father of Ophrah.
Seraiah was the father of Joab,
the father of Ge Harashim.[d] It was called this because its people were craftsmen.

15The sons of Caleb son of Jephunneh:
Iru, Elah and Naam.
The son of Elah:
Kenaz.

16The sons of Jehallelel:
Ziph, Ziphah, Tiria and Asarel.

17The sons of Ezrah:
Jether, Mered, Epher and Jalon. One of Mered's wives gave birth to Miriam, Shammai and Ishbah the father of Eshtemoa. 18(His Judean wife gave birth to Jered the father of Gedor, Heber the father of Soco, and Jekuthiel the father of Zanoah.) These were the children of Pharaoh's daughter Bithiah, whom Mered had married.

19The sons of Hodiah's wife, the sister of Naham:
the father of Keilah the Garmite, and Eshtemoa the Maacathite.

20The sons of Shimon:
Amnon, Rinnah, Ben-Hanan and Tilon.
The descendants of Ishi:
Zoheth and Ben-Zoheth.

21The sons of Shelah son of Judah:
Er the father of Lecah, Laadah the father of Mareshah and the clans of the linen workers at Beth Ashbea, 22Jokim, the men of Cozeba, and Joash and Saraph, who ruled in Moab and Jashubi Lehem. (These records are from ancient times.) 23They were the potters who lived at Netaim and Gederah; they stayed there and worked for the king.

*Simeon*

24The descendants of Simeon:
Nemuel, Jamin, Jarib, Zerah and Shaul;
25Shallum was Shaul's son, Mibsam his son and Mishma his son.

26The descendants of Mishma:
Hammuel his son, Zaccur his son and Shimei his son.

27Shimei had sixteen sons and six daughters, but his brothers did not have many children; so their entire clan did not become as numerous as the people of Judah. 28They lived in Beersheba, Moladah, Hazar Shual, 29Bilhah, Ezem, Tolad, 30Bethuel, Hormah, Ziklag, 31Beth Marcaboth, Hazar Susim, Beth Biri and Shaaraim. These were their towns until the reign of David. 32Their surrounding villages were Etam, Ain, Rimmon, Token and Ashan—five towns— 33and all the villages around these towns as far as Baalath.[e] These were their settlements. And they kept a genealogical record.

34Meshobab, Jamlech, Joshah son of Amaziah, 35Joel, Jehu son of Joshibiah, the son of Seraiah, the son of Asiel, 36also

NIV [b] 12 Or *of the city of Nahash* [c] 13 Some Septuagint manuscripts and Vulgate; Hebrew does not have *and Meonothai.* [d] 14 *Ge Harashim* means *valley of craftsmen.* [e] 33 Some Septuagint manuscripts (see also Joshua 19:8); Hebrew *Baal*

## King James

36And Elioenai, and Jaakobah, and Jeshohaiah, and Asaiah, and Adiel, and Jesimiel, and Benaiah,

37And Ziza the son of Shiphi, the son of Allon, the son of Jedaiah, the son of Shimri, the son of Shemaiah;

38These mentioned by *their* names *were* princes in their families: and the house of their fathers increased greatly.

39¶ And they went to the entrance of Gedor, *even* unto the east side of the valley, to seek pasture for their flocks.

40And they found fat pasture and good, and the land *was* wide, and quiet, and peaceable; for *they* of Ham had dwelt there of old.

41And these written by name came in the days of Hezekiah king of Judah, and smote their tents, and the habitations that were found there, and destroyed them utterly unto this day, and dwelt in their rooms: because *there was* pasture there for their flocks.

42And *some* of them, *even* of the sons of Simeon, five hundred men, went to mount Seir, having for their captains Pelatiah, and Neariah, and Rephaiah, and Uzziel, the sons of Ishi.

43And they smote the rest of the Amalekites that were escaped, and dwelt there unto this day.

5 NOW THE sons of Reuben the firstborn of Israel, (for he *was* the firstborn; but, forasmuch as he defiled his father's bed, his birthright was given unto the sons of Joseph the son of Israel: and the genealogy is not to be reckoned after the birthright.

2For Judah prevailed above his brethren, and of him *came* the chief ruler; but the birthright *was* Joseph's:)

3The sons, *I say*, of Reuben the firstborn of Israel *were*, Hanoch, and Pallu, Hezron, and Carmi.

4The sons of Joel; Shemaiah his son, Gog his son, Shimei his son,

5Micah his son, Reaia his son, Baal his son,

6Beerah his son, whom Tilgath-pilneser king of Assyria carried away *captive:* he *was* prince of the Reubenites.

7And his brethren by their families, when the genealogy of their generations was reckoned, *were* the chief, Jeiel, and Zechariah,

8And Bela the son of Azaz, the son of Shema, the son of Joel, who dwelt in Aroer, even unto Nebo and Baal-meon:

9And eastward he inhabited unto the entering in of the wilderness from the river Euphrates: because their cattle were multiplied in the land of Gilead.

10And in the days of Saul they made war with the Hagarites, who fell by their hand: and they dwelt in their tents throughout all the east *land* of Gilead.

11¶ And the children of Gad dwelt over against them, in the land of Bashan unto Salcah:

12Joel the chief, and Shapham the next, and Jaanai, and Shaphat in Bashan.

13And their brethren of the house of their fathers *were*, Michael, and Meshullam, and Sheba, and Jorai, and Jachan, and Zia, and Heber, seven.

14These *are* the children of Abihail the son of Huri, the son of Jaroah, the son of Gilead, the son of Michael, the son of Jeshishai, the son of Jahdo, the son of Buz;

15Ahi the son of Abdiel, the son of Guni, chief of the house of their fathers.

## Amplified

36Eli-oenai, Ja-akobah, Jeshohaiah, Asaiah, Adiel, Jesimiel, Benaiah,

37Ziza son of Shiphi, son of Allon, son of Jedaiah, son of Shimri, son of Shemaiah.

38These mentioned by name were princes in their families, and their fathers' houses increased greatly [so they needed more room].

39And they journeyed to the entrance of Gedor, to the east side of the valley, to seek pasture for their flocks.

40And they found rich, good pasture, and the [cleared] land was wide, quiet, and peaceful; because people of Ham had dwelt there of old [and had left it a better place for those who came after them].

41And these registered by name came in the days of Hezekiah king of Judah, and destroyed their tents and the Meunim [foreigners] who were found there, and exterminated them to this day, and settled in their stead, because there was pasture for their flocks.

42And some of them of the sons of Simeon, 500 men, went to Mount Seir, having for their leaders Pelatiah, and Neariah, Rephaiah, and Uzziel, the sons of Ishi.

43They destroyed the remnant of the Amalekites that had escaped, and they have dwelt there to this day.

5 NOW [WE come to] the sons of Reuben the first-born of Israel. For [Reuben] was the eldest; but because he polluted his father's couch [with Bilhah his father's concubine] his birthright was given to the sons of Joseph the [favorite] son of Israel; so the genealogy is not to be reckoned according to the birthright. [Gen. 35:22; 49:3, 4; 48:15-22.]

2Judah prevailed above his brethren, and of him came the prince *and* leader [and eventually the Messiah], yet the birthright was Joseph's. [Gen. 49:10; Mic. 5:2.]

3The sons of Reuben the first-born of Israel: Hanoch, Pallu, Hezron, and Carmi.

4The sons of Joel: Shemaiah his son, Gog his son, Shimei his son,

5Micah his son, Reaiah his son, Baal his son,

6Beerah his son, whom Tilgath-pilneser king of Assyria carried away captive; he was a prince of the Reubenites.

7And his brethren by their families, when the genealogy of their generations was reckoned: the chief, Jeiel, and Zechariah,

8Bela son of Azaz, son of Shema, son of Joel, who dwelt in Aroer as far as Nebo and Baal-meon;

9Eastward [Bela] inhabited the land as far as the entrance into the desert this [west] side of the river Euphrates; because their cattle had multiplied in the land of Gilead.

10In the days of [King] Saul they made war with the Hagrites *or* Ishmaelites, who fell by their hand; they dwelt in their tents in all the land east of Gilead.

11The children of Gad who dwelt over opposite them in the land of Bashan as far as Salecah:

12Joel the chief, Shapham the next, Janai, and Shaphat in Bashan.

13Their kinsmen of the houses of their fathers: Michael, Meshullam, Sheba, Jorai, Jacan, Zia, and Eber, seven.

14These were the sons of Abihail son of Huri, son of Jaroah, son of Gilead, son of Michael, son of Jeshishai, son of Jahdo, son of Buz;

15Ahi son of Abdiel, son of Guni, was chief in their fathers' houses.

## New American Standard

36and Elioenai, Jaakobah, Jeshohaiah, Asaiah, Adiel, Jesimiel,
Benaiah,
37Ziza the son of Shiphi, the son of Allon, the son of Jedaiah,
the son of Shimri, the son of Shemaiah;
38these mentioned by name *were* leaders in their families; and
their fathers' houses increased greatly.
39And they went to the entrance of Gedor, even to the east side
of the valley, to seek pasture for their flocks.
40And they found rich and good pasture, and the land was
broad and quiet and peaceful; for those who lived there formerly
*were* Hamites.
41And these, recorded by name, came in the days of Hezekiah
king of Judah, and attacked their tents, and the Meunites who
were found there, and destroyed them utterly to this day, and
lived in their place; because there was pasture there for their flocks.
42And from them, from the sons of Simeon, five hundred men
went to Mount Seir, with Pelatiah, Neariah, Rephaiah, and Uzziel,
the sons of Ishi, as their leaders.
43And they destroyed the remnant of the Amalekites who escaped, and have lived there to this day.

*Genealogy from Reuben*

5 NOW THE sons of Reuben the first-born of Israel (for he was
the first-born, but because he defiled his father's bed, his
birthright was given to the sons of Joseph the son of Israel; so that
he is not enrolled in the genealogy according to the birthright.
2Though Judah prevailed over his brothers, and from him *came*
the leader, yet the birthright belonged to Joseph),
3the sons of Reuben the first-born of Israel *were* Hanoch and
Pallu, Hezron and Carmi.
4The sons of Joel *were* Shemaiah his son, Gog his son, Shimei
his son,
5Micah his son, Reaiah his son, Baal his son,
6Beerah his son, whom Tilgath-pilneser king of Assyria carried
away into exile; he was leader of the Reubenites.
7And his kinsmen by their families, in the genealogy of their
generations, *were* Jeiel the chief, then Zechariah
8and Bela the son of Azaz, the son of Shema, the son of Joel,
who lived in Aroer, even to Nebo and Baal-meon.
9And to the east he settled as far as the entrance of the wilderness from the river Euphrates, because their cattle had increased
in the land of Gilead.
10And in the days of Saul they made war with the Hagrites, who
fell by their hand, so that they occupied their tents throughout all
the land east of Gilead.
11¶ Now the sons of Gad lived opposite them in the land of
Bashan as far as Salecah.
12Joel *was* the chief, and Shapham the second, then Janai and
Shaphat in Bashan.
13And their kinsmen of their fathers' households *were* Michael,
Meshullam, Sheba, Jorai, Jacan, Zia, and Eber, seven.
14These *were* the sons of Abihail, the son of Huri, the son of
Jaroah, the son of Gilead, the son of Michael, the son of Jeshishai,
the son of Jahdo, the son of Buz;
15Ahi the son of Abdiel, the son of Guni, *was* head of their
fathers' households.

## New International

Elioenai, Jaakobah, Jeshohaiah, Asaiah, Adiel, Jesimiel, Benaiah, 37and Ziza son of Shiphi, the son of Allon, the son of
Jedaiah, the son of Shimri, the son of Shemaiah.

38The men listed above by name were leaders of their clans.
Their families increased greatly, 39and they went to the outskirts
of Gedor to the east of the valley in search of pasture for their
flocks. 40They found rich, good pasture, and the land was spacious, peaceful and quiet. Some Hamites had lived there formerly.
41The men whose names were listed came in the days of Hezekiah king of Judah. They attacked the Hamites in their dwellings
and also the Meunites who were there and completely destroyed[a]
them, as is evident to this day. Then they settled in their place,
because there was pasture for their flocks. 42And five hundred of
these Simeonites, led by Pelatiah, Neariah, Rephaiah and Uzziel,
the sons of Ishi, invaded the hill country of Seir. 43They killed the
remaining Amalekites who had escaped, and they have lived there
to this day.

*Reuben*

5 THE SONS of Reuben the firstborn of Israel (he was the
firstborn, but when he defiled his father's marriage bed, his
rights as firstborn were given to the sons of Joseph son of Israel;
so he could not be listed in the genealogical record in accordance
with his birthright, 2and though Judah was the strongest of his
brothers and a ruler came from him, the rights of the firstborn
belonged to Joseph)— 3the sons of Reuben the firstborn of Israel:
Hanoch, Pallu, Hezron and Carmi.
4The descendants of Joel:
Shemaiah his son, Gog his son,
Shimei his son, 5Micah his son,
Reaiah his son, Baal his son,
6and Beerah his son, whom Tiglath-Pileser[b] king of Assyria
took into exile. Beerah was a leader of the Reubenites.
7Their relatives by clans, listed according to their genealogical
records:
Jeiel the chief, Zechariah, 8and Bela son of Azaz, the son
of Shema, the son of Joel. They settled in the area from
Aroer to Nebo and Baal Meon. 9To the east they occupied
the land up to the edge of the desert that extends to the
Euphrates River, because their livestock had increased in
Gilead.
10During Saul's reign they waged war against the
Hagrites, who were defeated at their hands; they occupied
the dwellings of the Hagrites throughout the entire region
east of Gilead.

*Gad*

11The Gadites lived next to them in Bashan, as far as Salecah:
12Joel was the chief, Shapham the second, then Janai and
Shaphat, in Bashan.
13Their relatives, by families, were:
Michael, Meshullam, Sheba, Jorai, Jacan, Zia and Eber—
seven in all.
14These were the sons of Abihail son of Huri, the son of
Jaroah, the son of Gilead, the son of Michael, the son of
Jeshishai, the son of Jahdo, the son of Buz.
15Ahi son of Abdiel, the son of Guni, was head of their
family.

**NIV** [a] *41* The Hebrew term refers to the irrevocable giving over of things or persons to the LORD, often by totally destroying them. [b] *6* Hebrew *Tilgath-Pilneser,* a variant of *Tiglath-Pileser;* also in verse 26

## King James

16And they dwelt in Gilead in Bashan, and in her towns, and
in all the suburbs of Sharon, upon their borders.
17All these were reckoned by genealogies in the days of Jotham
king of Judah, and in the days of Jeroboam king of Israel.
18¶ The sons of Reuben, and the Gadites, and half the tribe of
Manasseh, of valiant men, men able to bear buckler and sword,
and to shoot with bow, and skilful in war, *were* four and forty
thousand seven hundred and threescore, that went out to the war.
19And they made war with the Hagarites, with Jetur, and Neph-
ish, and Nodab.
20And they were helped against them, and the Hagarites were
delivered into their hand, and all that *were* with them: for they
cried to God in the battle, and he was entreated of them; because
they put their trust in him.
21And they took away their cattle; of their camels fifty thousand, and of sheep two hundred and fifty thousand, and of asses
two thousand, and of men an hundred thousand.
22For there fell down many slain, because the war *was* of God.
And they dwelt in their steads until the captivity.
23¶ And the children of the half tribe of Manasseh dwelt in the
land: they increased from Bashan unto Baal-hermon and Senir,
and unto mount Hermon.
24And these *were* the heads of the house of their fathers, even
Epher, and Ishi, and Eliel, and Azriel, and Jeremiah, and Hodaviah, and Jahdiel, mighty men of valour, famous men, *and* heads
of the house of their fathers.
25¶ And they transgressed against the God of their fathers, and
went a-whoring after the gods of the people of the land, whom
God destroyed before them.
26And the God of Israel stirred up the spirit of Pul king of
Assyria, and the spirit of Tilgath-pilneser king of Assyria, and he
carried them away, even the Reubenites, and the Gadites, and the
half tribe of Manasseh, and brought them unto Halah, and Habor,
and Hara, and to the river Gozan, unto this day.

6 THE SONS of Levi; Gershon, Kohath, and Merari.
2And the sons of Kohath; Amram, Izhar, and Hebron, and
Uzziel.
3And the children of Amram; Aaron, and Moses, and Miriam.
The sons also of Aaron; Nadab, and Abihu, Eleazar, and Ithamar.
4¶ Eleazar begat Phinehas, Phinehas begat Abishua,
5And Abishua begat Bukki, and Bukki begat Uzzi,
6And Uzzi begat Zerahiah, and Zerahiah begat Meraioth,
7Meraioth begat Amariah, and Amariah begat Ahitub,
8And Ahitub begat Zadok, and Zadok begat Ahimaaz,
9And Ahimaaz begat Azariah, and Azariah begat Johanan,
10And Johanan begat Azariah, (he *it is* that executed the priest's
office in the temple that Solomon built in Jerusalem:)
11And Azariah begat Amariah, and Amariah begat Ahitub,
12And Ahitub begat Zadok, and Zadok begat Shallum,

## Amplified

16They dwelt in Gilead, in Bashan and in its towns, and in all
the suburbs *and* pasture lands of Sharon to their limits.
17All these were enrolled by genealogies in the days of Jotham
king of Judah, and in the days of Jeroboam [II] king of Israel.
18The sons of Reuben, the Gadites, and the half tribe of Manasseh, of valiant men, able to bear buckler and sword, and to
shoot with bow, and skillful in war were 44,760 able *and* ready to
go forth to war.
19And [these Israelites, on the east side of the Jordan River]
made war with the Hagrites [a tribe of northern Arabia], with Jetur,
Naphish, and Nodab.
20They were given help against them, and the Hagrites *or* Ishmaelites were delivered into their hand, and all that were allied
with them, for they cried to God in the battle, and He granted their
entreaty because they relied on, clung to *and* trusted in Him.
21And [these Israelites] took away their adversaries' herds: of
their camels 50,000, and of sheep 250,000, and of donkeys 2,000,
and of the lives of men 100,000.
22For a great number fell mortally wounded, because the battle
was God's. And [these Israelites] dwelt in their territory until the
captivity [by Assyria more than five centuries later]. [II Kings
15:29.]
23And the people of the half-tribe of Manasseh dwelt in the
land; their settlements spread from Bashan to Baal-hermon, Senir,
and Mount Hermon.
24And these were the heads of their fathers' houses: Epher, Ishi,
Eliel, Azriel, Jeremiah, Hodaviah, and Jahdiel, mighty men of
strength of mind *and* spirit (enabling them to encounter danger
with firmness and personal bravery), famous men, and heads of
the houses of their fathers.
25They transgressed against the God of their fathers, and
played the harlot [by unfaithfulness to their own God and run-
ning] after the gods of the native peoples whom God had destroyed before them.
26So the God of Israel stirred up the spirit of Pul king of Assyria,
[that is,] the spirit of Tilgath-pilneser king of Assyria, and he
carried them away, the Reubenites, Gadites, and half-tribe of Manasseh, and brought them to Halah, Habor, Hara, and the river
Gozan, to this day.

6 THE SONS of Levi: Gershom, Kohath, and Merari.
2The sons of Kohath: Amram, Izhar, Hebron, and Uzziel.
3The children of Amram: Aaron, Moses, and Miriam. The sons
also of Aaron: Nadab, Abihu, Eleazar, and Ithamar.
4Eleazar was the father of Phinehas, Phinehas of Abishua,
5Abishua was the father of Bukki, and Bukki of Uzzi,
6Uzzi of Zerahiah, and Zerahiah of Meraioth,
7Meraioth of Amariah, and Amariah of Ahitub,
8Ahitub of Zadok, and Zadok of Ahimaaz,
9Ahimaaz of Azariah, and Azariah of Johanan,
10Johanan of Azariah, who was priest in the temple Solomon
built in Jerusalem;
11Azariah of Amariah, and Amariah of Ahitub,
12Ahitub of Zadok, and Zadok of Shallum,

## New American Standard

16 And they lived in Gilead, in Bashan and in its towns, and in
all the pasture lands of Sharon, as far as their borders.
17 All of these were enrolled in the genealogies in the days of
Jotham king of Judah and in the days of Jeroboam king of Israel.
18 ¶ The sons of Reuben and the Gadites and the half-tribe of
Manasseh, *consisting* of valiant men, men who bore shield and
sword and shot with bow, and *were* skillful in battle, *were* 44,760,
who went to war.
19 And they made war against the Hagrites, Jetur, Naphish, and
Nodab.
20 And they were helped against them, and the Hagrites and all
who *were* with them were given into their hand; for they cried out
to God in the battle, and He was entreated for them, because they
trusted in Him.
21 And they took away their cattle: their 50,000 camels, 250,000
sheep, 2,000 donkeys, and 100,000 men.
22 For many fell slain, because the war *was* of God. And they
settled in their place until the exile.
23 ¶ Now the sons of the half-tribe of Manasseh lived in the land;
from Bashan to Baal-hermon and Senir and Mount Hermon they
were numerous.
24 And these were the heads of their fathers' households, even
Epher, Ishi, Eliel, Azriel, Jeremiah, Hodaviah, and Jahdiel, mighty
men of valor, famous men, heads of their fathers' households.
25 ¶ But they acted treacherously against the God of their fathers,
and played the harlot after the gods of the peoples of the land,
whom God had destroyed before them.
26 So the God of Israel stirred up the spirit of Pul, king of Assyria, even the spirit of Tilgath-pilneser king of Assyria, and he
carried them away into exile, namely the Reubenites, the Gadites,
and the half-tribe of Manasseh, and brought them to Halah, Habor, Hara, and to the river of Gozan, to this day.

*Genealogy: The Priestly Line*

**6** THE SONS of Levi *were* Gershon, Kohath and Merari.
2 And the sons of Kohath *were* Amram, Izhar, Hebron, and
Uzziel.
3 And the children of Amram *were* Aaron, Moses, and Miriam.
And the sons of Aaron *were* Nadab, Abihu, Eleazar, and Ithamar.
4 Eleazar became the father of Phinehas, *and* Phinehas became
the father of Abishua,
5 and Abishua became the father of Bukki, and Bukki became
the father of Uzzi,
6 and Uzzi became the father of Zerahiah, and Zerahiah became
the father of Meraioth,
7 Meraioth became the father of Amariah, and Amariah became
the father of Ahitub,
8 and Ahitub became the father of Zadok, and Zadok became
the father of Ahimaaz,
9 and Ahimaaz became the father of Azariah, and Azariah
became the father of Johanan,
10 and Johanan became the father of Azariah (it was he who
served as the priest in the house which Solomon built in Jerusalem),
11 and Azariah became the father of Amariah, and Amariah
became the father of Ahitub,
12 and Ahitub became the father of Zadok, and Zadok became
the father of Shallum,

## New International

16 The Gadites lived in Gilead, in Bashan and its outlying villages, and on all the pasturelands of Sharon as far as they
extended.
17 All these were entered in the genealogical records during the
reigns of Jotham king of Judah and Jeroboam king of Israel.

18 The Reubenites, the Gadites and the half-tribe of Manasseh
had 44,760 men ready for military service—able-bodied men who
could handle shield and sword, who could use a bow, and who
were trained for battle. 
19 They waged war against the Hagrites,
Jetur, Naphish and Nodab. 
20 They were helped in fighting them,
and God handed the Hagrites and all their allies over to them,
because they cried out to him during the battle. He answered their
prayers, because they trusted in him. 
21 They seized the livestock
of the Hagrites—fifty thousand camels, two hundred fifty thousand sheep and two thousand donkeys. They also took one hundred thousand people captive, 
22 and many others fell slain, be-
cause the battle was God's. And they occupied the land until the
exile.

*The Half-Tribe of Manasseh*

23 The people of the half-tribe of Manasseh were numerous; they
settled in the land from Bashan to Baal Hermon, that is, to Senir
(Mount Hermon).
24 These were the heads of their families: Epher, Ishi, Eliel,
Azriel, Jeremiah, Hodaviah and Jahdiel. They were brave warriors,
famous men, and heads of their families. 
25 But they were unfaith-
ful to the God of their fathers and prostituted themselves to the
gods of the peoples of the land, whom God had destroyed before
them. 
26 So the God of Israel stirred up the spirit of Pul king of
Assyria (that is, Tiglath-Pileser king of Assyria), who took the
Reubenites, the Gadites and the half-tribe of Manasseh into exile.
He took them to Halah, Habor, Hara and the river of Gozan, where
they are to this day.

*Levi*

**6** THE SONS of Levi:
Gershon, Kohath and Merari.
2 The sons of Kohath:
Amram, Izhar, Hebron and Uzziel.
3 The children of Amram:
Aaron, Moses and Miriam.
The sons of Aaron:
Nadab, Abihu, Eleazar and Ithamar.
4 Eleazar was the father of Phinehas,
Phinehas the father of Abishua,
5 Abishua the father of Bukki,
Bukki the father of Uzzi,
6 Uzzi the father of Zerahiah,
Zerahiah the father of Meraioth,
7 Meraioth the father of Amariah,
Amariah the father of Ahitub,
8 Ahitub the father of Zadok,
Zadok the father of Ahimaaz,
9 Ahimaaz the father of Azariah,
Azariah the father of Johanan,
10 Johanan the father of Azariah (it was he who served as
priest in the temple Solomon built in Jerusalem),
11 Azariah the father of Amariah,
Amariah the father of Ahitub,
12 Ahitub the father of Zadok,
Zadok the father of Shallum,

## King James

13 And Shallum begat Hilkiah, and Hilkiah begat Azariah,

14 And Azariah begat Seraiah, and Seraiah begat Jehozadak,

15 And Jehozadak went *into captivity,* when the LORD carried away Judah and Jerusalem by the hand of Nebuchadnezzar.

16 ¶ The sons of Levi; Gershom, Kohath, and Merari.

17 And these *be* the names of the sons of Gershom; Libni, and Shimei.

18 And the sons of Kohath *were,* Amram, and Izhar, and Hebron, and Uzziel.

19 The sons of Merari; Mahli, and Mushi. And these *are* the families of the Levites according to their fathers.

20 Of Gershom; Libni his son, Jahath his son, Zimmah his son,

21 Joah his son, Iddo his son, Zerah his son, Jeaterai his son.

22 The sons of Kohath; Amminadab his son, Korah his son, Assir his son,

23 Elkanah his son, and Ebiasaph his son, and Assir his son,

24 Tahath his son, Uriel his son, Uzziah his son, and Shaul his son.

25 And the sons of Elkanah; Amasai, and Ahimoth.

26 *As for* Elkanah: the sons of Elkanah; Zophai his son, and Nahath his son,

27 Eliab his son, Jeroham his son, Elkanah his son.

28 And the sons of Samuel; the firstborn Vashni, and Abiah.

29 The sons of Merari; Mahli, Libni his son, Shimei his son, Uzza his son,

30 Shimea his son, Haggiah his son, Asaiah his son.

31 And these *are they* whom David set over the service of song in the house of the LORD, after that the ark had rest.

32 And they ministered before the dwellingplace of the tabernacle of the congregation with singing, until Solomon had built the house of the LORD in Jerusalem: and *then* they waited on their office according to their order.

33 And these *are* they that waited with their children. Of the sons of the Kohathites: Heman a singer, the son of Joel, the son of Shemuel,

34 The son of Elkanah, the son of Jeroham, the son of Eliel, the son of Toah,

35 The son of Zuph, the son of Elkanah, the son of Mahath, the son of Amasai,

36 The son of Elkanah, the son of Joel, the son of Azariah, the son of Zephaniah,

37 The son of Tahath, the son of Assir, the son of Ebiasaph, the son of Korah,

38 The son of Izhar, the son of Kohath, the son of Levi, the son of Israel.

## Amplified

13 Shallum of Hilkiah, and Hilkiah of Azariah,

14 Azariah of Seraiah, and Seraiah of Jehozadak;

15 Jehozadak went into captivity when the Lord sent Judah and Jerusalem into exile by the hand of Nebuchadnezzar.

16 The sons of Levi: Gershom, Kohath, and Merari.

17 These are the names of the sons of Gershom: Libni and Shimei.

18 The sons of Kohath: Amram, Izhar, Hebron, and Uzziel.

19 The sons of Merari: Mahli and Mushi. These are the families of the Levites according to their fathers.

20 Of Gershom: Libni his son, Jahath his son, Zimmah his son,

21 Joah his son, Iddo his son, Zerah his son, Jeatherai his son.

22 The sons of Kohath: Amminadab his son, Korah his son, Assir his son,

23 Elkanah his son, Ebiasaph his son, Assir his son,

24 Tahath his son, Uriel his son, Uzziah his son, and Shaul his son.

25 And the sons of Elkanah: Amasai and Ahimoth.

26 Elkanah his son, Zophai his son, Nahath his son,

27 Eliab his son, Jeroham his son, Elkanah [Samuel's father] his son.

28 The sons of Samuel: the first-born [Joel] and Abijah.

29 The sons of Merari: Mahli, Libni his son, Shimei his son, Uzza his son,

30 Shimea his son, Haggiah his son, Asaiah his son.

31 These David put over the service of song in the house of the Lord, after the ark of the covenant rested there [after being taken by the Philistines and later placed in the house of Abinadab, where it remained for nearly 100 years during the rest of Samuel's judgeship, and Saul's entire reign, and into David's reign].

32 They ministered before the tabernacle of the tent of meeting with singing, until Solomon had built the Lord's house in Jerusalem, performing their service in due order.

33 These and their sons served of the Kohathites: Heman the singer, son of Joel, son of Samuel [the great prophet and judge],

34 Son of Elkanah [III], son of Jeroham, son of Eliel, son of Toah,

35 Son of Zuph, son of Elkanah [II], son of Mahath, son of Amasai,

36 Son of Elkanah [I], son of Joel, son of Azariah, son of Zephaniah,

37 Son of Tahath, son of Assir, son of Ebiasaph, son of Korah,

38 Son of Izhar, son of Kohath, son of Levi, son of Israel (Jacob).

## New American Standard

13and Shallum became the father of Hilkiah, and Hilkiah
became the father of Azariah,
14and Azariah became the father of Seraiah, and Seraiah became
the father of Jehozadak;
15and Jehozadak went *along* when the LORD carried Judah and
Jerusalem away into exile by Nebuchadnezzar.
16¶ The sons of Levi *were* Gershom, Kohath, and Merari.
17And these are the names of the sons of Gershom: Libni and
Shimei.
18And the sons of Kohath *were* Amram, Izhar, Hebron, and
Uzziel.
19The sons of Merari *were* Mahli and Mushi. And these are the
families of the Levites according to their fathers' *households*.
20Of Gershom: Libni his son, Jahath his son, Zimmah his son,
21Joah his son, Iddo his son, Zerah his son, Jeatherai his son.
22The sons of Kohath *were* Amminadab his son, Korah his son,
Assir his son,
23Elkanah his son, Ebiasaph his son, and Assir his son,
24Tahath his son, Uriel his son, Uzziah his son, and Shaul his
son.
25And the sons of Elkanah *were* Amasai and Ahimoth.
26 *As for* Elkanah, the sons of Elkanah *were* Zophai his son and
Nahath his son,
27Eliab his son, Jeroham his son, Elkanah his son.
28And the sons of Samuel *were* Joel, the first-born and Abijah,
the second.
29The sons of Merari *were* Mahli, Libni his son, Shimei his son,
Uzzah his son,
30Shimea his son, Haggiah his son, Asaiah his son.
31¶ Now these are those whom David appointed over the service of song in the house of the LORD, after the ark rested *there*.
32And they ministered with song before the tabernacle of the
tent of meeting, until Solomon had built the house of the LORD in
Jerusalem; and they served in their office according to their order.
33And these are those who served with their sons. From the
sons of the Kohathites *were* Heman the singer, the son of Joel, the
son of Samuel,
34the son of Elkanah, the son of Jeroham, the son of Eliel, the
son of Toah,
35the son of Zuph, the son of Elkanah, the son of Mahath, the
son of Amasai,
36the son of Elkanah, the son of Joel, the son of Azariah, the son
of Zephaniah,
37the son of Tahath, the son of Assir, the son of Ebiasaph, the
son of Korah,
38the son of Izhar, the son of Kohath, the son of Levi, the son
of Israel.

## New International

13Shallum the father of Hilkiah,
Hilkiah the father of Azariah,
14Azariah the father of Seraiah,
and Seraiah the father of Jehozadak.
15Jehozadak was deported when the LORD sent Judah and
Jerusalem into exile by the hand of Nebuchadnezzar.
16The sons of Levi:
Gershon,[a] Kohath and Merari.
17These are the names of the sons of Gershon:
Libni and Shimei.
18The sons of Kohath:
Amram, Izhar, Hebron and Uzziel.
19The sons of Merari:
Mahli and Mushi.
These are the clans of the Levites listed according to their
fathers:
20Of Gershon:
Libni his son, Jehath his son,
Zimmah his son, 21Joah his son,
Iddo his son, Zerah his son
and Jeatherai his son.
22The descendants of Kohath:
Amminadab his son, Korah his son,
Assir his son, 23Elkanah his son,
Ebiasaph his son, Assir his son,
24Tahath his son, Uriel his son,
Uzziah his son and Shaul his son.
25The descendants of Elkanah:
Amasai, Ahimoth,
26Elkanah his son,[b] Zophai his son,
Nahath his son, 27Eliab his son,
Jeroham his son, Elkanah his son
and Samuel his son.[c]
28The sons of Samuel:
Joel[d] the firstborn
and Abijah the second son.
29The descendants of Merari:
Mahli, Libni his son,
Shimei his son, Uzzah his son,
30Shimea his son, Haggiah his son
and Asaiah his son.

*The Temple Musicians*

31These are the men David put in charge of the music in the
house of the LORD after the ark came to rest there. 32They ministered with music before the tabernacle, the Tent of Meeting, until
Solomon built the temple of the LORD in Jerusalem. They performed their duties according to the regulations laid down for
them.
33Here are the men who served, together with their sons:
From the Kohathites:
Heman, the musician,
the son of Joel, the son of Samuel,
34the son of Elkanah, the son of Jeroham,
the son of Eliel, the son of Toah,
35the son of Zuph, the son of Elkanah,
the son of Mahath, the son of Amasai,
36the son of Elkanah, the son of Joel,
the son of Azariah, the son of Zephaniah,
37the son of Tahath, the son of Assir,
the son of Ebiasaph, the son of Korah,
38the son of Izhar, the son of Kohath,
the son of Levi, the son of Israel;

**NIV** [a] *16* Hebrew *Gershom,* a variant of *Gershon;* also in verses 17, 20, 43, 62 and 71 [b] *26* Some Hebrew manuscripts, Septuagint and Syriac; most Hebrew manuscripts *Ahimoth 26and Elkanah. The sons of Elkanah:* [c] *27* Some Septuagint manuscripts (see also 1 Samuel 1:19,20 and 1 Chron. 6:33,34); Hebrew does not have *and Samuel his son.* [d] *28* Some Septuagint manuscripts and Syriac (see also 1 Samuel 8:2 and 1 Chron. 6:33); Hebrew does not have *Joel.*

## King James

39And his brother Asaph, who stood on his right hand, *even*
Asaph the son of Berachiah, the son of Shimea,
40The son of Michael, the son of Baaseiah, the son of Malchiah,
41The son of Ethni, the son of Zerah, the son of Adaiah,
42The son of Ethan, the son of Zimmah, the son of Shimei,
43The son of Jahath, the son of Gershom, the son of Levi.
44And their brethren the sons of Merari *stood* on the left hand:
Ethan the son of Kishi, the son of Abdi, the son of Malluch,
45The son of Hashabiah, the son of Amaziah, the son of Hilkiah,
46The son of Amzi, the son of Bani, the son of Shamer,
47The son of Mahli, the son of Mushi, the son of Merari, the son
of Levi.
48Their brethren also the Levites *were* appointed unto all manner of service of the tabernacle of the house of God.
49¶ But Aaron and his sons offered upon the altar of the burnt offering, and on the altar of incense, *and were appointed* for all the work of the *place* most holy, and to make an atonement for Israel, according to all that Moses the servant of God had commanded.
50And these *are* the sons of Aaron; Eleazar his son, Phinehas his
son, Abishua his son,
51Bukki his son, Uzzi his son, Zerahiah his son,
52Meraioth his son, Amariah his son, Ahitub his son,
53Zadok his son, Ahimaaz his son.
54¶ Now these *are* their dwelling places throughout their castles in their coasts, of the sons of Aaron, of the families of the Kohathites: for theirs was the lot.
55And they gave them Hebron in the land of Judah, and the suburbs thereof round about it.
56But the fields of the city, and the villages thereof, they gave to Caleb the son of Jephunneh.
57And to the sons of Aaron they gave the cities of Judah, *namely*, Hebron, *the city* of refuge, and Libnah with her suburbs, and Jattir, and Eshtemoa, with their suburbs,
58And Hilen with her suburbs, Debir with her suburbs,
59And Ashan with her suburbs, and Beth-shemesh with her
suburbs:
60And out of the tribe of Benjamin; Geba with her suburbs, and Alemeth with her suburbs, and Anathoth with her suburbs. All their cities throughout their families *were* thirteen cities.
61And unto the sons of Kohath, *which were* left of the family of that tribe, *were cities given* out of the half tribe, *namely, out of* the half *tribe* of Manasseh, by lot, ten cities.
62And to the sons of Gershom throughout their families out of the tribe of Issachar, and out of the tribe of Asher, and out of the tribe of Naphtali, and out of the tribe of Manasseh in Bashan, thirteen cities.
63Unto the sons of Merari *were given* by lot, throughout their families, out of the tribe of Reuben, and out of the tribe of Gad, and out of the tribe of Zebulun, twelve cities.
64And the children of Israel gave to the Levites *these* cities with their suburbs.
65And they gave by lot out of the tribe of the children of Judah, and out of the tribe of the children of Simeon, and out of the tribe of the children of Benjamin, these cities, which are called by *their* names.
66And *the residue* of the families of the sons of Kohath had cities of their coasts out of the tribe of Ephraim.
67And they gave unto them, *of* the cities of refuge, Shechem in mount Ephraim with her suburbs; *they gave* also Gezer with her
suburbs,
68And Jokmeam with her suburbs, and Beth-horon with her
suburbs,
69And Aijalon with her suburbs, and Gath-rimmon with her
suburbs:
70And out of the half tribe of Manasseh; Aner with her suburbs, and Bileam with her suburbs, for the family of the remnant of the sons of Kohath.

## Amplified

39Heman's [tribal] brother Asaph, stood on his right hand:
Asaph son of Berechiah, son of Shimea,
40Son of Michael, son of Ba-aseiah, son of Malchijah,
41Son of Ethni, son of Zerah, son of Adaiah,
42Son of Ethan, son of Zimmah, son of Shimei,
43Son of Jahath, son of Gershom, son of Levi.
44Their kinsmen the sons of Merari stood on the left hand:
Ethan son of Kishi, son of Abdi, son of Malluch,
45Son of Hashabiah, son of Amaziah, son of Hilkiah,
46Son of Amzi, son of Bani, son of Shemer,
47Son of Mahli, son of Mushi, son of Merari, son of Levi.
48And their brethren the Levites [who were not descended from Aaron] were appointed for all other kinds of service of the tabernacle of the house of God.
49But [the line of] Aaron and his sons offered upon the altars of burnt offering and of incense, ministering for all the work of the holy of holies and to make atonement for Israel, according to all Moses God's servant had commanded.
50The sons of Aaron: Eleazar his son, Phinehas his son, Abishua
his son,
51Bukki his son, Uzzi his son, Zerahiah his son,
52Meraioth his son, Amariah his son, Ahitub his son,
53Zadok his son, Ahimaaz his son.
54Their dwelling places are according to their settlements within their borders: to the sons of Aaron, of the families of Kohathites, for theirs was the [first] lot, [Josh. 21:10.]
55To them they gave Hebron in the land of Judah and its surrounding suburbs;
56But the fields of the city and its villages, they gave to Caleb
the son of Jephunneh.
57To the sons of Aaron they gave the city of refuge, Hebron; also Libnah with its pasture lands, Jattir, Eshtemoa with its pasture lands, [Josh. 21:13.]
58Hilen with its pasture lands, Debir with its pasture lands,
59Ashan with its pasture lands, and Beth-shemesh with its pasture lands.
60And out of the tribe of Benjamin: Geba, Alemeth and Anathoth with their pasture lands. All their cities according to their families were thirteen.
61And to the rest of the Kohathites ten cities were given by lot out of the family of the tribe [of Ephraim and of Dan and] of the half-tribe, the half of Manasseh. [Supplying from Josh. 21:5.]
62To the Gershomites according to their families [were allotted] thirteen cities out of the tribes of Issachar, Asher, Naphtali, and Manasseh in Bashan.
63To the Merarites were given by lot, according to their families, twelve cities out of the tribes of Reuben, Gad, and Zebulun.
64And the Israelites gave to the Levites these cities with their pasture lands.
65They gave by lot out of the tribes of Judah, Simeon, and Benjamin these cities whose names are mentioned.
66Some of the families of the Kohathites had cities in the allotted territory out of the tribe of Ephraim.
67And [the Ephraimites] gave to [the Levites] the city of refuge, Shechem in the hill country of Ephraim; also Gezer, [both] with their suburbs *and* pasture lands;
68Jokmeam, Beth-horon,
69Aijalon, and Gath-rimmon, with their suburbs *and* pasture
lands;
70And out of the half-tribe of Manasseh [these cities] with their suburbs *and* pasture lands: Aner and Bileam, for the rest of the families of the sons of Kohath.

## New American Standard

39And *Heman's* brother Asaph stood at his right hand, even
Asaph the son of Berechiah, the son of Shimea,
40the son of Michael, the son of Baaseiah, the son of Malchijah,
41the son of Ethni, the son of Zerah, the son of Adaiah,
42the son of Ethan, the son of Zimmah, the son of Shimei,
43the son of Jahath, the son of Gershom, the son of Levi.
44And on the left hand *were* their kinsmen the sons of Merari:
Ethan the son of Kishi, the son of Abdi, the son of Malluch,
45the son of Hashabiah, the son of Amaziah, the son of Hilkiah,
46the son of Amzi, the son of Bani, the son of Shemer,
47the son of Mahli, the son of Mushi, the son of Merari, the son
of Levi.
48And their kinsmen the Levites were appointed for all the
service of the tabernacle of the house of God.
**49**¶ But Aaron and his sons offered on the altar of burnt offering
and on the altar of incense, for all the work of the most holy place,
and to make atonement for Israel, according to all that Moses the
servant of God had commanded.
50And these are the sons of Aaron: Eleazar his son, Phinehas
his son, Abishua his son,
51Bukki his son, Uzzi his son, Zerahiah his son,
52Meraioth his son, Amariah his son, Ahitub his son,
53Zadok his son, Ahimaaz his son.
**54**¶ Now these are their settlements according to their camps
within their borders. To the sons of Aaron of the families of the
Kohathites (for theirs was the *first* lot),
55to them they gave Hebron in the land of Judah, and its pasture
lands around it;
56but the fields of the city and its villages, they gave to Caleb
the son of Jephunneh.
57And to the sons of Aaron they gave the *following* cities of
refuge: Hebron, Libnah also with its pasture lands, Jattir, Eshtemoa with its pasture lands,
58Hilen with its pasture lands, Debir with its pasture lands,
59Ashan with its pasture lands, and Beth-shemesh with its pasture lands;
60and from the tribe of Benjamin: Geba with its pasture lands,
Allemeth with its pasture lands, and Anathoth with its pasture
lands. All their cities throughout their families were thirteen cities.
**61**¶ Then to the rest of the sons of Kohath *were given* by lot, from
the family of the tribe, from the half-tribe, the half of Manasseh,
ten cities.
62And to the sons of Gershom, according to their families, *were
given* from the tribe of Issachar and from the tribe of Asher, the
tribe of Naphtali, and the tribe of Manasseh, thirteen cities in
Bashan.
63To the sons of Merari *were given* by lot, according to their
families, from the tribe of Reuben, the tribe of Gad, and the tribe
of Zebulun, twelve cities.
64So the sons of Israel gave to the Levites the cities with their
pasture lands.
65And they gave by lot from the tribe of the sons of Judah, the
tribe of the sons of Simeon, and the tribe of the sons of Benjamin,
these cities which are mentioned by name.
**66**¶ Now some of the families of the sons of Kohath had cities
of their territory from the tribe of Ephraim.
67And they gave to them the *following* cities of refuge: Shechem
in the hill country of Ephraim with its pasture lands, Gezer also
with its pasture lands,
68Jokmeam with its pasture lands, Beth-horon with its pasture
lands,
69Aijalon with its pasture lands, and Gath-rimmon with its
pasture lands;
70and from the half-tribe of Manasseh: Aner with its pasture
lands and Bileam with its pasture lands, for the rest of the family
of the sons of Kohath.

## New International

39and Heman's associate Asaph, who served at his right hand:
Asaph son of Berekiah, the son of Shimea,
40the son of Michael, the son of Baaseiah,[a]
the son of Malkijah, 41the son of Ethni,
the son of Zerah, the son of Adaiah,
42the son of Ethan, the son of Zimmah,
the son of Shimei, 43the son of Jahath,
the son of Gershon, the son of Levi;
44and from their associates, the Merarites, at his left hand:
Ethan son of Kishi, the son of Abdi,
the son of Malluch, 45the son of Hashabiah,
the son of Amaziah, the son of Hilkiah,
46the son of Amzi, the son of Bani,
the son of Shemer, 47the son of Mahli,
the son of Mushi, the son of Merari,
the son of Levi.

48Their fellow Levites were assigned to all the other duties of
the tabernacle, the house of God. 49But Aaron and his descendants
were the ones who presented offerings on the altar of burnt offering and on the altar of incense in connection with all that was done
in the Most Holy Place, making atonement for Israel, in accordance
with all that Moses the servant of God had commanded.
50These were the descendants of Aaron:
Eleazar his son, Phinehas his son,
Abishua his son, 51Bukki his son,
Uzzi his son, Zerahiah his son,
52Meraioth his son, Amariah his son,
Ahitub his son, 53Zadok his son
and Ahimaaz his son.

54These were the locations of their settlements allotted as their
territory (they were assigned to the descendants of Aaron who
were from the Kohathite clan, because the first lot was for them):
55They were given Hebron in Judah with its surrounding
pasturelands. 56But the fields and villages around the city
were given to Caleb son of Jephunneh.
57So the descendants of Aaron were given Hebron (a city
of refuge), and Libnah,[b] Jattir, Eshtemoa, 58Hilen, Debir,
59Ashan, Juttah[c] and Beth Shemesh, together with their pasturelands. 60And from the tribe of Benjamin they were given
Gibeon,[d] Geba, Alemeth and Anathoth, together with their
pasturelands.
These towns, which were distributed among the Kohathite
clans, were thirteen in all.
61The rest of Kohath's descendants were allotted ten towns
from the clans of half the tribe of Manasseh.
62The descendants of Gershon, clan by clan, were allotted thirteen towns from the tribes of Issachar, Asher and Naphtali, and
from the part of the tribe of Manasseh that is in Bashan.
63The descendants of Merari, clan by clan, were allotted twelve
towns from the tribes of Reuben, Gad and Zebulun.
64So the Israelites gave the Levites these towns and their pasturelands. 65From the tribes of Judah, Simeon and Benjamin they
allotted the previously named towns.
66Some of the Kohathite clans were given as their territory
towns from the tribe of Ephraim.
67In the hill country of Ephraim they were given Shechem
(a city of refuge), and Gezer,[e] 68Jokmeam, Beth Horon,
69Aijalon and Gath Rimmon, together with their pasturelands.
70And from half the tribe of Manasseh the Israelites gave
Aner and Bileam, together with their pasturelands, to the rest
of the Kohathite clans.

**NIV** [a] *40* Most Hebrew manuscripts; some Hebrew manuscripts, one Septuagint manuscript and Syriac *Maaseiah* [b] *57* See Joshua 21:13; Hebrew *given the cities of refuge: Hebron, Libnah.* [c] *59* Syriac (see also Septuagint and Joshua 21:16); Hebrew does not have *Juttah.* [d] *60* See Joshua 21:17; Hebrew does not have *Gibeon.* [e] *67* See Joshua 21:21; Hebrew *given the cities of refuge: Shechem, Gezer.*

## King James

71Unto the sons of Gershom *were given* out of the family of the
half tribe of Manasseh, Golan in Bashan with her suburbs, and
Ashtaroth with her suburbs:
72And out of the tribe of Issachar; Kedesh with her suburbs,
Daberath with her suburbs,
73And Ramoth with her suburbs, and Anem with her suburbs:
74And out of the tribe of Asher; Mashal with her suburbs, and
Abdon with her suburbs,
75And Hukok with her suburbs, and Rehob with her suburbs:
76And out of the tribe of Naphtali; Kedesh in Galilee with her
suburbs, and Hammon with her suburbs, and Kirjathaim with her
suburbs.
77Unto the rest of the children of Merari *were given* out of the
tribe of Zebulun, Rimmon with her suburbs, Tabor with her suburbs:
78And on the other side Jordan by Jericho, on the east side of
Jordan, *were given them* out of the tribe of Reuben, Bezer in the
wilderness with her suburbs, and Jahzah with her suburbs,
79Kedemoth also with her suburbs, and Mephaath with her
suburbs:
80And out of the tribe of Gad; Ramoth in Gilead with her suburbs, and Mahanaim with her suburbs,
81And Heshbon with her suburbs, and Jazer with her suburbs.

7 NOW THE sons of Issachar *were,* Tola, and Puah, Jashub, and
Shimrom, four.
2And the sons of Tola; Uzzi, and Rephaiah, and Jeriel, and
Jahmai, and Jibsam, and Shemuel, heads of their father's house,
*to wit,* of Tola: *they were* valiant men of might in their generations;
whose number *was* in the days of David two and twenty thousand
and six hundred.
3And the sons of Uzzi; Izrahiah: and the sons of Izrahiah; Michael and Obadiah, and Joel, Ishiah, five: all of them chief men.
4And with them, by their generations, after the house of their
fathers, *were* bands of soldiers for war, six and thirty thousand *men:*
for they had many wives and sons.
5And their brethren among all the families of Issachar *were*
valiant men of might, reckoned in all by their genealogies fourscore and seven thousand.
6¶ *The sons* of Benjamin: Bela, and Becher, and Jediael, three.
7And the sons of Bela; Ezbon, and Uzzi, and Uzziel, and Jerimoth, and Iri, five; heads of the house of *their* fathers, mighty men
of valour; and were reckoned by their genealogies twenty and two
thousand and thirty and four.
8And the sons of Becher; Zemira, and Joash, and Eliezer, and
Elioenai, and Omri, and Jerimoth, and Abiah, and Anathoth, and
Alameth. All these *are* the sons of Becher.
9And the number of them, after their genealogy by their generations, heads of the house of their fathers, mighty men of valour,
*was* twenty thousand and two hundred.
10The sons also of Jediael; Bilhan: and the sons of Bilhan; Jeush,
and Benjamin, and Ehud, and Chenaanah, and Zethan, and Tharshish, and Ahishahar.
11All these the sons of Jediael, by the heads of their fathers,
mighty men of valour, *were* seventeen thousand and two hundred
*soldiers,* fit to go out for war *and* battle.

## Amplified

71To the Gershomites were given out of the half-tribe of Manasseh, Golan in Bashan and Ashtaroth with their suburbs *and*
pasture lands.
72Out of the tribe of Issachar with their suburbs *and* pasture
lands: Kedesh, Daberath,
73Ramoth, and Anem.
74Out of the tribe of Asher with their suburbs *and* pasture lands:
Mashal, Abdon,
75Hukok, and Rehob.
76And out of the tribe of Naphtali with their suburbs *and* pasture
lands: Kedesh in Galilee, Hammon, and Kiriathaim.
77To the rest of the Merarites were given from the tribe of
Zebulun, Rimmono and Tabor with their suburbs *and* pasture
lands.
78On the other side of Jordan, on the east side by Jericho the
Levites were given out of the tribe of Reuben [these cities] with
their suburbs *and* pasture lands: Bezer in the wilderness, Jahzah,
79Kedemoth, and Mephaath;
80Out of the tribe of Gad [these cities] with their suburbs *and*
pasture lands: Ramoth in Gilead, Mahanaim,
81Heshbon, and Jazer.

7 THE SONS of Issachar were Tola, Puah, Jashub, and Shimron, four.
2The sons of Tola: Uzzi, Rephaiah, Jeriel, Jahmai, Ibsam, Shemuel, heads of their fathers' houses, descendants of Tola; mighty
men of valor in their generations; their number in David's days
was 22,600.
3The sons of Uzzi: Izrahiah. The sons of Izrahiah: Michael,
Obadiah, Joel, Isshiah, five, all of them chief men.
4And with them, by their generations, according to their fathers' houses, were units of the army for war, 36,000, for they had
many wives and children [with them].
5Their kinsmen from all the families of Issachar, mighty men of
valor, registered by genealogies were in all 87,000.
6The sons of Benjamin: Bela, Becher, and Jediael, three.
7The sons of Bela: Ezbon, Uzzi, Uzziel, Jerimoth, and Iri, five,
heads of the houses of their fathers, mighty men of valor; by their
genealogies they numbered 22,034.
8The sons of Becher: Zemirah, Joash, Eliezer, Elioenai, Omri,
Jeremoth, Abijah, Anathoth, and Alemeth, all sons of Becher.
9The number of them by their genealogies by generations, as
heads of their fathers' houses, mighty warriors, was 20,200.
10The sons of Jediael: Bilhan. The sons of Bilhan: Jeush, Benjamin, Ehud, Chenaanah, Zethan, Tarshish, and Ahishahar.
11All these were the sons of Jediael, according to the heads of
their fathers' houses, mighty men of valor, 17,200 able *and* fit for
service in war.

## New American Standard

71¶ To the sons of Gershom *were given,* from the family of the
half-tribe of Manasseh: Golan in Bashan with its pasture lands and
Ashtaroth with its pasture lands;
72and from the tribe of Issachar: Kedesh with its pasture lands,
Daberath with its pasture lands,
73and Ramoth with its pasture lands, Anem with its pasture
lands;
74and from the tribe of Asher: Mashal with its pasture lands,
Abdon with its pasture lands,
75Hukok with its pasture lands, and Rehob with its pasture
lands;
76and from the tribe of Naphtali: Kedesh in Galilee with its
pasture lands, Hammon with its pasture lands, and Kiriathaim
with its pasture lands.
77¶ To the rest of *the Levites,* the sons of Merari, *were given,* from
the tribe of Zebulun: Rimmono with its pasture lands, Tabor with
its pasture lands;
78and beyond the Jordan at Jericho, on the east side of the
Jordan, *were given them,* from the tribe of Reuben: Bezer in the
wilderness with its pasture lands, Jahzah with its pasture lands,
79Kedemoth with its pasture lands, and Mephaath with its pasture lands;
80and from the tribe of Gad: Ramoth in Gilead with its pasture
lands, Mahanaim with its pasture lands,
81Heshbon with its pasture lands, and Jazer with its pasture
lands.

*Genealogy from Issachar*

7 NOW THE sons of Issachar *were* four: Tola, Puah, Jashub, and
Shimron.
2And the sons of Tola *were* Uzzi, Rephaiah, Jeriel, Jahmai,
Ibsam, and Samuel, heads of their fathers' households. *The sons* of
Tola *were* mighty men of valor in their generations; their number
in the days of David was 22,600.
3And the son of Uzzi *was* Izrahiah. And the sons of Izrahiah
*were* Michael, Obadiah, Joel, Isshiah; all five of them *were* chief
men.
4And with them by their generations according to their fathers'
households were 36,000 troops of the army for war, for they had
many wives and sons.
5And their relatives among all the families of Issachar *were*
mighty men of valor, enrolled by genealogy, in all 87,000.

*Descendants of Benjamin*

6¶ *The sons of* Benjamin *were* three: Bela and Becher and Jediael.
7And the sons of Bela were five: Ezbon, Uzzi, Uzziel, Jerimoth,
and Iri. They *were* heads of fathers' households, mighty men of
valor, and were 22,034 enrolled by genealogy.
8And the sons of Becher *were* Zemirah, Joash, Eliezer, Elioenai,
Omri, Jeremoth, Abijah, Anathoth, and Alemeth. All these *were*
the sons of Becher.
9And they were enrolled by genealogy, according to their generations, heads of their fathers' households, 20,200 mighty men of
valor.
10And the son of Jediael *was* Bilhan. And the sons of Bilhan *were*
Jeush, Benjamin, Ehud, Chenaanah, Zethan, Tarshish, and Ahishahar.
11All these *were* sons of Jediael, according to the heads of their
fathers' households, 17,200 mighty men of valor, who were ready
to go out with the army to war.

## New International

71The Gershonites received the following:
From the clan of the half-tribe of Manasseh
they received Golan in Bashan and also Ashtaroth, together with their pasturelands;
72from the tribe of Issachar
they received Kedesh, Daberath, 73Ramoth and Anem,
together with their pasturelands;
74from the tribe of Asher
they received Mashal, Abdon, 75Hukok and Rehob, together with their pasturelands;
76and from the tribe of Naphtali
they received Kedesh in Galilee, Hammon and Kiriathaim, together with their pasturelands.

77The Merarites (the rest of the Levites) received the following:
From the tribe of Zebulun
they received Jokneam, Kartah,[a] Rimmono and Tabor,
together with their pasturelands;
78from the tribe of Reuben across the Jordan east of Jericho
they received Bezer in the desert, Jahzah, 79Kedemoth and
Mephaath, together with their pasturelands;
80and from the tribe of Gad
they received Ramoth in Gilead, Mahanaim, 81Heshbon
and Jazer, together with their pasturelands.

*Issachar*

7 THE SONS of Issachar:
Tola, Puah, Jashub and Shimron—four in all.
2The sons of Tola:
Uzzi, Rephaiah, Jeriel, Jahmai, Ibsam and Samuel—heads
of their families. During the reign of David, the descendants of Tola listed as fighting men in their genealogy numbered 22,600.
3The son of Uzzi:
Izrahiah.
The sons of Izrahiah:
Michael, Obadiah, Joel and Isshiah. All five of them were
chiefs. 4According to their family genealogy, they had
36,000 men ready for battle, for they had many wives and
children.
5The relatives who were fighting men belonging to all the
clans of Issachar, as listed in their genealogy, were 87,000
in all.

*Benjamin*

6Three sons of Benjamin:
Bela, Beker and Jediael.
7The sons of Bela:
Ezbon, Uzzi, Uzziel, Jerimoth and Iri, heads of families—
five in all. Their genealogical record listed 22,034 fighting
men.
8The sons of Beker:
Zemirah, Joash, Eliezer, Elioenai, Omri, Jeremoth, Abijah, Anathoth and Alemeth. All these were the sons of
Beker. 9Their genealogical record listed the heads of families and 20,200 fighting men.
10The son of Jediael:
Bilhan.
The sons of Bilhan:
Jeush, Benjamin, Ehud, Kenaanah, Zethan, Tarshish and
Ahishahar. 11All these sons of Jediael were heads of families. There were 17,200 fighting men ready to go out to
war.

NIV [a] *77* See Septuagint and Joshua 21:34; Hebrew does not have *Jokneam, Kartah.*

## King James

12Shuppim also, and Huppim, the children of Ir, *and* Hushim, the sons of Aher.

13¶ The sons of Naphtali; Jahziel, and Guni, and Jezer, and Shallum, the sons of Bilhah.

14¶ The sons of Manasseh; Ashriel, whom she bare: ( *but* his concubine the Aramitess bare Machir the father of Gilead:

15And Machir took to wife *the sister* of Huppim and Shuppim, whose sister's name *was* Maachah;) and the name of the second *was* Zelophehad: and Zelophehad had daughters.

16And Maachah the wife of Machir bare a son, and she called his name Peresh; and the name of his brother *was* Sheresh; and his sons *were* Ulam and Rakem.

17And the sons of Ulam; Bedan. These *were* the sons of Gilead, the son of Machir, the son of Manasseh.

18And his sister Hammoleketh bare Ishod, and Abiezer, and Mahalah.

19And the sons of Shemidah were, Ahian, and Shechem, and Likhi, and Aniam.

20¶ And the sons of Ephraim; Shuthelah, and Bered his son, and Tahath his son, and Eladah his son, and Tahath his son,

21¶ And Zabad his son, and Shuthelah his son, and Ezer, and Elead, whom the men of Gath *that were* born in *that* land slew, because they came down to take away their cattle.

22And Ephraim their father mourned many days, and his brethren came to comfort him.

23¶ And when he went in to his wife, she conceived, and bare a son, and he called his name Beriah, because it went evil with his house.

24(And his daughter *was* Sherah, who built Beth-horon the nether, and the upper, and Uzzen-sherah.)

25And Rephah *was* his son, also Resheph, and Telah his son, and Tahan his son,

26Laadan his son, Ammihud his son, Elishama his son,

27Non his son, Jehoshuah his son.

28¶ And their possessions and habitations *were*, Beth-el and the towns thereof, and eastward Naaran, and westward Gezer, with the towns thereof; Shechem also and the towns thereof, unto Gaza and the towns thereof:

29And by the borders of the children of Manasseh, Beth-shean and her towns, Taanach and her towns, Megiddo and her towns, Dor and her towns. In these dwelt the children of Joseph the son of Israel.

30¶ The sons of Asher; Imnah, and Isuah, and Ishuai, and Beriah, and Serah their sister.

31And the sons of Beriah; Heber, and Malchiel, who *is* the father of Birzavith.

32And Heber begat Japhlet, and Shomer, and Hotham, and Shua their sister.

33And the sons of Japhlet; Pasach, and Bimhal, and Ashvath. These *are* the children of Japhlet.

34And the sons of Shamer; Ahi, and Rohgah, Jehubbah, and Aram.

## Amplified

12Shuppim and Huppim were the sons of Ir, Hushim the son of Aher.

13The sons of Naphtali: Jahziel, Guni, Jezer, and Shallum, whose [grandmother] was Bilhah.

14The sons of Manasseh: Ashriel, whom his concubine the Aramitess bore; she bore Machir the father of Gilead.

15And Machir took as wife the sister of Huppim and Shuppim; her name was Maacah; the name of a second [and later descendant; the first being Gilead], was Zelophehad; and Zelophehad had daughters [only]. [Num. 27:1-7.]

16Maacah the wife of Machir bore a son; she called his name Peresh; the name of his brother was Sheresh; his sons were Ulam and Rakem.

17The sons of Ulam: Bedan. These were the sons of Gilead son of Machir, son of Manasseh.

18His sister Hammolecheth bore Ishbod, Abiezer, and Mahlah.

19The sons of Shemida were Ahian, Shechem, Likhi, and Aniam.

20The sons of Ephraim: Shuthelah, Bered his son, Tahath [I] his son, Eleadah his son, Tahath [II] his son,

21Zabad his son, and Shuthelah his son. [During Ephraim's lifetime, his sons] Ezer and Elead, were slain by men of Gath born in the land, who had come down to steal the cattle [of the Ephraimites, probably before the Israelites left Egypt].

22And Ephraim their father mourned many days, and his brethren came to comfort him.

23Then his wife conceived and bore a son, and he called his name Beriah [meaning, in evil], because calamity had befallen his house.

24[Beriah's] daughter was Sheerah, who built both lower and upper Beth-horon, and Uzzen-sheerah.

25Rephah was his son, and Resheph [his son]; Resheph's son was Telah, Tahan his son,

26Ladan his son, Ammihud his son, Elishama his son,

27Nun his son, Joshua [Moses' sucessor] his son.

28And their possessions and settlements were Bethel and its towns, and eastward Naaran, and westward Gezer, Shechem, and as far as Azzah (Gaza) with all their towns.

29And along the borders of the Manassites, Beth-shean, Taanach, Megiddo, Dor, and all their towns. In these dwelt the sons of Joseph son of Israel.

30The sons of Asher: Imnah, Ishvah, Ishvi, Beriah, and Serah their sister.

31The sons of Beriah: Heber, and Malchiel, who was the father of Birzaith.

32Heber was the father of Japhlet, Shomer, Hotham, and Shua their sister.

33The sons of Japhlet: Pasach, Bimhal, and Ashvath. These are the sons of Japhlet.

34The sons of Shemer (Shomer) his brother: Rohgah, Jehubbah, and Aram.

## New American Standard

12 And Shuppim and Huppim *were* the sons of Ir; Hushim *was*
the son of Aher.

*Sons of Naphtali*

13 ¶ The sons of Naphtali *were* Jahziel, Guni, Jezer, and Shallum,
the sons of Bilhah.

*Descendants of Manasseh*

14 ¶ The sons of Manasseh *were* Asriel, whom his Aramean
concubine bore; she bore Machir the father of Gilead.
15 And Machir took a wife for Huppim and Shuppim, whose
sister's name was Maacah. And the name of the second was Zelophehad, and Zelophehad had daughters.
16 And Maacah the wife of Machir bore a son, and she named
him Peresh; and the name of his brother *was* Sheresh, and his sons
*were* Ulam and Rakem.
17 And the son of Ulam *was* Bedan. These *were* the sons of Gilead
the son of Machir, the son of Manasseh.
18 And his sister Hammolecheth bore Ishhod and Abiezer and
Mahlah.
19 And the sons of Shemida were Ahian and Shechem and Likhi
and Aniam.

*Descendants of Ephraim*

20 ¶ And the sons of Ephraim *were* Shuthelah and Bered his son,
Tahath his son, Eleadah his son, Tahath his son,
21 Zabad his son, Shuthelah his son, and Ezer and Elead whom
the men of Gath who were born in the land killed, because they
came down to take their livestock.
22 And their father Ephraim mourned many days, and his relatives came to comfort him.
23 Then he went in to his wife, and she conceived and bore a son,
and he named him Beriah, because misfortune had come upon his
house.
24 And his daughter was Sheerah, who built lower and upper
Beth-horon, also Uzzen-sheerah.
25 And Rephah was his son *along* with Resheph, Telah his son,
Tahan his son,
26 Ladan his son, Ammihud his son, Elishama his son,
27 Non his son, and Joshua his son.
28 ¶ And their possessions and settlements *were* Bethel with its
towns, and to the east Naaran, and to the west Gezer with its
towns, and Shechem with its towns as far as Ayyah with its towns,
29 and along the borders of the sons of Manasseh, Beth-shean
with its towns, Taanach with its towns, Megiddo with its towns,
Dor with its towns. In these lived the sons of Joseph the son of
Israel.

*Descendants of Asher*

30 ¶ The sons of Asher *were* Imnah, Ishvah, Ishvi and Beriah, and
Serah their sister.
31 And the sons of Beriah *were* Heber and Malchiel, who was the
father of Birzaith.
32 And Heber became the father of Japhlet, Shomer and Hotham, and Shua their sister.
33 And the sons of Japhlet *were* Pasach, Bimhal, and Ashvath.
These were the sons of Japhlet.
34 And the sons of Shemer *were* Ahi and Rohgah, Jehubbah and
Aram.

## New International

12 The Shuppites and Huppites were the descendants of Ir, and
the Hushites the descendants of Aher.

*Naphtali*

13 The sons of Naphtali:
Jahziel, Guni, Jezer and Shillem[a] —the descendants of Bilhah.

*Manasseh*

14 The descendants of Manasseh:
Asriel was his descendant through his Aramean
concubine. She gave birth to Makir the father of Gilead.
15 Makir took a wife from among the Huppites and
Shuppites. His sister's name was Maacah.
Another descendant was named Zelophehad, who had
only daughters.
16 Makir's wife Maacah gave birth to a son and named him
Peresh. His brother was named Sheresh, and his sons were
Ulam and Rakem.
17 The son of Ulam:
Bedan.
These were the sons of Gilead son of Makir, the son of Ma-
nasseh. 18 His sister Hammoleketh gave birth to Ishhod,
Abiezer and Mahlah.
19 The sons of Shemida were:
Ahian, Shechem, Likhi and Aniam.

*Ephraim*

20 The descendants of Ephraim:
Shuthelah, Bered his son,
Tahath his son, Eleadah his son,
Tahath his son, 21 Zabad his son
and Shuthelah his son.
Ezer and Elead were killed by the native-born men of
Gath, when they went down to seize their livestock. 22 Their
father Ephraim mourned for them many days, and his
relatives came to comfort him. 23 Then he lay with his wife
again, and she became pregnant and gave birth to a son. He
named him Beriah,[b] because there had been misfortune in
his family. 24 His daughter was Sheerah, who built Lower
and Upper Beth Horon as well as Uzzen Sheerah.
25 Rephah was his son, Resheph his son,[c]
Telah his son, Tahan his son,
26 Ladan his son, Ammihud his son,
Elishama his son, 27 Nun his son
and Joshua his son.
28 Their lands and settlements included Bethel and its surrounding villages, Naaran to the east, Gezer and its villages to the west,
and Shechem and its villages all the way to Ayyah and its villages.
29 Along the borders of Manasseh were Beth Shan, Taanach,
Megiddo and Dor, together with their villages. The descendants
of Joseph son of Israel lived in these towns.

*Asher*

30 The sons of Asher:
Imnah, Ishvah, Ishvi and Beriah. Their sister was Serah.
31 The sons of Beriah:
Heber and Malkiel, who was the father of Birzaith.
32 Heber was the father of Japhlet, Shomer and Hotham and of
their sister Shua.
33 The sons of Japhlet:
Pasach, Bimhal and Ashvath.
These were Japhlet's sons.
34 The sons of Shomer:
Ahi, Rohgah,[d] Hubbah and Aram.

**NIV** [a] *13* Some Hebrew and Septuagint manuscripts (see also Gen. 46:24 and Num. 26:49); most Hebrew manuscripts *Shallum* [b] *23 Beriah* sounds like the Hebrew for *misfortune.* [c] *25* Some Septuagint manuscripts; Hebrew does not have *his son.* [d] *34* Or *of his brother Shomer: Rohgah*

## King James

35And the sons of his brother Helem; Zophah, and Imna, and Shelesh, and Amal.

36The sons of Zophah; Suah, and Harnepher, and Shual, and Beri, and Imrah,

37Bezer, and Hod, and Shamma, and Shilshah, and Ithran, and Beera.

38And the sons of Jether; Jephunneh, and Pispah, and Ara.

39And the sons of Ulla; Arah, and Haniel, and Rezia.

40All these *were* the children of Asher, heads of *their* father's house, choice *and* mighty men of valour, chief of the princes. And the number throughout the genealogy of them that were apt to the war *and* to battle *was* twenty and six thousand men.

8 NOW BENJAMIN begat Bela his firstborn, Ashbel the second, and Aharah the third,

2Nohah the fourth, and Rapha the fifth.

3And the sons of Bela were, Addar, and Gera, and Abihud,

4And Abishua, and Naaman, and Ahoah,

5And Gera, and Shephuphan, and Huram.

6And these *are* the sons of Ehud: these are the heads of the fathers of the inhabitants of Geba, and they removed them to Manahath:

7And Naaman, and Ahiah, and Gera, he removed them, and begat Uzza, and Ahihud.

8And Shaharaim begat *children* in the country of Moab, after he had sent them away; Hushim and Baara *were* his wives.

9And he begat of Hodesh his wife, Jobab, and Zibia, and Mesha, and Malcham,

10And Jeuz, and Shachia, and Mirma. These *were* his sons, heads of the fathers.

11And of Hushim he begat Abitub, and Elpaal.

12The sons of Elpaal; Eber, and Misham, and Shamed, who built Ono, and Lod, with the towns thereof:

13Beriah also, and Shema, who *were* heads of the fathers of the inhabitants of Aijalon, who drove away the inhabitants of Gath:

14And Ahio, Shashak, and Jeremoth,

15And Zebadiah, and Arad, and Ader,

16And Michael, and Ispah, and Joha, the sons of Beriah;

17And Zebadiah, and Meshullam, and Hezeki, and Heber,

18Ishmerai also, and Jezliah, and Jobab, the sons of Elpaal;

19And Jakim, and Zichri, and Zabdi,

20And Elienai, and Zilthai, and Eliel,

21And Adaiah, and Beraiah, and Shimrath, the sons of Shimhi;

22And Ishpan, and Heber, and Eliel,

23And Abdon, and Zichri, and Hanan,

24And Hananiah, and Elam, and Antothijah,

25And Iphedeiah, and Penuel, the sons of Shashak;

26And Shamsherai, and Shehariah, and Athaliah,

27And Jaresiah, and Eliah, and Zichri, the sons of Jeroham.

28These *were* heads of the fathers, by their generations, chief *men*. These dwelt in Jerusalem.

29And at Gibeon dwelt the father of Gibeon; whose wife's name *was* Maachah:

30And his firstborn son Abdon, and Zur, and Kish, and Baal, and Nadab,

31And Gedor, and Ahio, and Zacher.

32And Mikloth begat Shimeah. And these also dwelt with their brethren in Jerusalem, over against them.

33¶ And Ner begat Kish, and Kish begat Saul, and Saul begat Jonathan, and Malchi-shua, and Abinadab, and Esh-baal.

34And the son of Jonathan *was* Merib-baal; and Merib-baal begat Micah.

35And the sons of Micah *were*, Pithon, and Melech, and Tarea, and Ahaz.

## Amplified

35The sons of his brother Helem [Hotham]: Zophah, Imna, Shelesh, and Amal.

36The sons of Zophah: Suah, Harnepher, Shual, Beri, Imrah,

37Bezer, Hod, Shamma, Shilshah, Ithran, and Beera.

38The sons of Jether: Jephunneh, Pispa, and Ara.

39The sons of Ulla: Arah, Hanniel, and Rizia.

40All these were offspring of Asher, heads of their fathers' houses, approved, mighty warriors, chief of the princes. Their number, enrolled by genealogies, for service in war, was 26,000 men.

8 BENJAMIN WAS the father of Bela his first-born, Ashbel, second, Aharah third,

2Nohah fourth, and Rapha fifth.

3Bela's sons were, Addar, Gera, Abihud,

4Abishua, Naaman, Ahoah,

5Gera, Shephuphan, and Huram.

6The sons of Ehud: These are the heads of the fathers' houses of the inhabitants of Geba; they were exiled to Manahath:

7Naaman, Ahijah, and Gera, that is, Heglam, who was the father of Uzza and Ahihud.

8Shaharaim had sons in the country of Moab, after he had [divorced and] sent away Hushim and Baara his wives.

9And by Hodesh his [Moabitish] wife he was the father of Jobab, Zibia, Mesha, Malcam,

10Jeuz, Sachia, and Mirmah. These were his sons, heads of fathers' houses.

11By Hushim [divorced] he had had sons: Abitub and Elpaal.

12The sons of Elpaal: Eber, Misham, and Shemed, who built Ono and Lod with its towns;

13Also Beriah and Shema, who were heads of fathers' houses of the inhabitants of Aijalon, who put to flight the inhabitants of Gath;

14And Ahio, Shashak, and Jeremoth.

15The sons of Beriah: Zebadiah, Arad, Eder,

16Michael, Ishpah, and Joha.

17Zebadiah, Meshullam, Hizki, Heber,

18Ishmerai, Izliah, and Jobab were the sons of Elpaal.

19Jakim, Zichri, Zabdi,

20Elienai, Zille-thai, Eliel,

21Adaiah, Beraiah, and Shimrath were the sons of Shimei.

22Ishpan, Eber, Eliel,

23Abdon, Zichri, Hanan,

24Hananiah, Elam, Anthothijah,

25Iphdeiah, and Penuel were the sons of Shashak.

26Shamsherai, Shehariah, Athaliah,

27Ja-areshiah, Elijah, and Zichri were the sons of Jeroham.

28These were heads of the fathers' houses, according to their generations, chief men. These dwelt in Jerusalem.

29At Gibeon dwelt [Jeiel] the father of Gibeon, whose wife's name was Maacah.

30His first-born son was Abdon, then Zur, Kish, Baal, Nadab,

31Gedor, Ahio, Zecher.

32And Mikloth father of Shimeah. These dwelt together opposite their kinsmen in Jerusalem.

33Ner was the father of Kish, and Kish of [King] Saul the father of Jonathan, Malchishua, Abinadab, and Eshbaal (Ishbosheth).

34The son of Jonathan was Merib-baal (Mephibosheth), the father of Micah.

35The sons of Micah: Pithon, Melech, Tarea, and Ahaz.

## New American Standard

35And the sons of his brother Helem *were* Zophah, Imna, Shelesh, and Amal.
36The sons of Zophah *were* Suah, Harnepher, Shual, Beri, and Imrah,
37Bezer, Hod, Shamma, Shilshah, Ithran, and Beera.
38And the sons of Jether *were* Jephunneh, Pispa, and Ara.
39And the sons of Ulla *were* Arah, Hanniel, and Rizia.
40All these *were* the sons of Asher, heads of the fathers' houses, choice and mighty men of valor, heads of the princes. And the number of them enrolled by genealogy for service in war was 26,000 men.

*Genealogy from Benjamin*

8 AND BENJAMIN became the father of Bela his first-born, Ashbel the second, Aharah the third,
2Nohah the fourth, and Rapha the fifth.
3And Bela had sons: Addar, Gera, Abihud,
4Abishua, Naaman, Ahoah,
5Gera, Shephuphan, and Huram.
6And these are the sons of Ehud: these are the heads of fathers' *households* of the inhabitants of Geba, and they carried them into exile to Manahath,
7namely, Naaman, Ahijah, and Gera—he carried them into exile; and he became the father of Uzza and Ahihud.
8And Shaharaim became the father of children in the country of Moab, after he had sent away Hushim and Baara his wives.
9And by Hodesh his wife he became the father of Jobab, Zibia, Mesha, Malcam,
10Jeuz, Sachia, Mirmah. These were his sons, heads of fathers' *households*.
11And by Hushim he became the father of Abitub and Elpaal.
12And the sons of Elpaal *were* Eber, Misham, and Shemed, who built Ono and Lod, with its towns;
13and Beriah and Shema, who were heads of fathers' *households* of the inhabitants of Aijalon, who put to flight the inhabitants of Gath;
14and Ahio, Shashak, and Jeremoth.
15And Zebadiah, Arad, Eder,
16Michael, Ishpah, and Joha *were* the sons of Beriah.
17And Zebadiah, Meshullam, Hizki, Heber,
18Ishmerai, Izliah, and Jobab *were* the sons of Elpaal.
19And Jakim, Zichri, Zabdi,
20Elienai, Zillethai, Eliel,
21Adaiah, Beraiah, and Shimrath *were* the sons of Shimei.
22And Ishpan, Eber, Eliel,
23Abdon, Zichri, Hanan,
24Hananiah, Elam, Anthothijah,
25Iphdeiah, and Penuel *were* the sons of Shashak.
26And Shamsherai, Shehariah, Athaliah,
27Jaareshiah, Elijah, and Zichri *were* the sons of Jeroham.
28These were heads of the fathers' *households* according to their generations, chief men, who lived in Jerusalem.
**29**¶ Now in Gibeon, *Jeiel,* the father of Gibeon lived, and his wife's name was Maacah;
30and his first-born son *was* Abdon, then Zur, Kish, Baal, Nadab,
31Gedor, Ahio, and Zecher.
32And Mikloth became the father of Shimeah. And they also lived with their relatives in Jerusalem opposite their *other* relatives.

*Genealogy from King Saul*

33And Ner became the father of Kish, and Kish became the father of Saul, and Saul became the father of Jonathan, Malchishua, Abinadab, and Eshbaal.
34And the son of Jonathan *was* Merib-baal, and Merib-baal became the father of Micah.
35And the sons of Micah *were* Pithon, Melech, Tarea, and Ahaz.

## New International

35The sons of his brother Helem:
Zophah, Imna, Shelesh and Amal.
36The sons of Zophah:
Suah, Harnepher, Shual, Beri, Imrah, 37Bezer, Hod,
Shamma, Shilshah, Ithran[a] and Beera.
38The sons of Jether:
Jephunneh, Pispah and Ara.
39The sons of Ulla:
Arah, Hanniel and Rizia.
40All these were descendants of Asher—heads of families, choice men, brave warriors and outstanding leaders. The number of men ready for battle, as listed in their genealogy, was 26,000.

*The Genealogy of Saul the Benjamite*

8 BENJAMIN WAS the father of Bela his firstborn,
Ashbel the second son, Aharah the third,
2Nohah the fourth and Rapha the fifth.
3The sons of Bela were:
Addar, Gera, Abihud,[b] 4Abishua, Naaman, Ahoah,
5Gera, Shephuphan and Huram.
6These were the descendants of Ehud, who were heads of families of those living in Geba and were deported to Manahath:
7Naaman, Ahijah, and Gera, who deported them and who was the father of Uzza and Ahihud.
8Sons were born to Shaharaim in Moab after he had divorced his wives Hushim and Baara. 9By his wife Hodesh he had
Jobab, Zibia, Mesha, Malcam, 10Jeuz, Sakia and Mirmah.
These were his sons, heads of families. 11By Hushim he
had Abitub and Elpaal.
12The sons of Elpaal:
Eber, Misham, Shemed (who built Ono and Lod with its surrounding villages), 13and Beriah and Shema, who were heads of families of those living in Aijalon and who drove out the inhabitants of Gath.
14Ahio, Shashak, Jeremoth, 15Zebadiah, Arad, Eder, 16Michael, Ishpah and Joha were the sons of Beriah.
17Zebadiah, Meshullam, Hizki, Heber, 18Ishmerai, Izliah and Jobab were the sons of Elpaal.
19Jakim, Zicri, Zabdi, 20Elienai, Zillethai, Eliel, 21Adaiah, Beraiah and Shimrath were the sons of Shimei.
22Ishpan, Eber, Eliel, 23Abdon, Zicri, Hanan, 24Hananiah,
Elam, Anthothijah, 25Iphdeiah and Penuel were the sons of Shashak.
26Shamsherai, Shehariah, Athaliah, 27Jaareshiah, Elijah and Zicri were the sons of Jeroham.
28All these were heads of families, chiefs as listed in their genealogy, and they lived in Jerusalem.

29Jeiel[c] the father[d] of Gibeon lived in Gibeon.
His wife's name was Maacah, 30and his firstborn son was
Abdon, followed by Zur, Kish, Baal, Ner,[e] Nadab, 31Ge-
dor, Ahio, Zeker 32and Mikloth, who was the father of Shimeah. They too lived near their relatives in Jerusalem.
33Ner was the father of Kish, Kish the father of Saul, and Saul the father of Jonathan, Malki-Shua, Abinadab and Esh-Baal.[f]
34The son of Jonathan:
Merib-Baal,[g] who was the father of Micah.
35The sons of Micah:
Pithon, Melech, Tarea and Ahaz.

**NIV** [a] 37 Possibly a variant of *Jether* [b] 3 Or *Gera the father of Ehud* [c] 29 Some Septuagint manuscripts (see also 1 Chron. 9:35); Hebrew does not have *Jeiel.* [d] 29 *Father* may mean *civic leader* or *military leader.* [e] 30 Some Septuagint manuscripts (see also 1 Chron. 9:36); Hebrew does not have *Ner.* [f] 33 Also known as *Ish-Bosheth* [g] 34 Also known as *Mephibosheth*

## King James

36And Ahaz begat Jehoadah; and Jehoadah begat Alemeth, and Azmaveth, and Zimri; and Zimri begat Moza,

37And Moza begat Binea: Rapha *was* his son, Eleasah his son, Azel his son:

38And Azel had six sons, whose names *are* these, Azrikam, Bocheru, and Ishmael, and Sheariah, and Obadiah, and Hanan. All these *were* the sons of Azel.

39And the sons of Eshek his brother *were*, Ulam his firstborn, Jehush the second, and Eliphelet the third.

40And the sons of Ulam were mighty men of valour, archers, and had many sons, and sons' sons, an hundred and fifty. All these *are* of the sons of Benjamin.

## Amplified

36Ahaz was the father of Jehoaddah; and Jehoaddah of Alemeth, Azmaveth, and Zimri; Zimri was the father of Moza.

37Moza was the father of Binea; Raphah was his son, Eleasah his son, Azel his son.

38Azel had six sons: Azrikam, Bocheru, Ishmael, Sheariah, Obadiah, and Hanan. All these were the sons of Azel.

39The sons of Eshek his brother: Ulam his first-born, Jehush second, Eliphelet third.

40The sons of Ulam were mighty warriors, archers, with many sons and grandsons, 150. All these were Benjamites.

## King James

9 SO ALL Israel were reckoned by genealogies; and, behold, they *were* written in the book of the kings of Israel and Judah, *who* were carried away to Babylon for their transgression.

2¶ Now the first inhabitants that *dwelt* in their possessions in their cities *were*, the Israelites, the priests, Levites, and the Nethinims.

3And in Jerusalem dwelt of the children of Judah, and of the children of Benjamin, and of the children of Ephraim, and Manasseh;

4Uthai the son of Ammihud, the son of Omri, the son of Imri, the son of Bani, of the children of Pharez the son of Judah.

5And of the Shilonites; Asaiah the firstborn, and his sons.

6And of the sons of Zerah; Jeuel, and their brethren, six hundred and ninety.

7And of the sons of Benjamin; Sallu the son of Meshullam, the son of Hodaviah, the son of Hasenuah,

8And Ibneiah the son of Jeroham, and Elah the son of Uzzi, the son of Michri, and Meshullam the son of Shephathiah, the son of Reuel, the son of Ibnijah;

9And their brethren, according to their generations, nine hundred and fifty and six. All these men *were* chief of the fathers in the house of their fathers.

10¶ And of the priests; Jedaiah, and Jehoiarib, and Jachin,

11And Azariah the son of Hilkiah, the son of Meshullam, the son of Zadok, the son of Meraioth, the son of Ahitub, the ruler of the house of God;

12And Adaiah the son of Jeroham, the son of Pashur, the son of Malchijah, and Maasiai the son of Adiel, the son of Jahzerah, the son of Meshullam, the son of Meshillemith, the son of Immer;

13And their brethren, heads of the house of their fathers, a thousand and seven hundred and threescore; very able men for the work of the service of the house of God.

14And of the Levites; Shemaiah the son of Hasshub, the son of Azrikam, the son of Hashabiah, of the sons of Merari;

15And Bakbakkar, Heresh, and Galal, and Mattaniah the son of Micah, the son of Zichri, the son of Asaph;

16And Obadiah the son of Shemaiah, the son of Galal, the son of Jeduthun, and Berechiah the son of Asa, the son of Elkanah, that dwelt in the villages of the Netophathites.

17And the porters *were*, Shallum, and Akkub, and Talmon, and Ahiman, and their brethren: Shallum *was* the chief;

18Who hitherto *waited* in the king's gate eastward: they *were* porters in the companies of the children of Levi.

## Amplified

9 SO ALL Israel was enrolled by genealogies; and they are written in the Book of the Kings of Israel. And Judah was carried away captive to Babylon for their unfaithfulness to God.

2Now the first [of the returned exiles] to dwell again in their possessions in the cities of Israel were the priests, Levites, and the Nethinim [the temple servants].

3In Jerusalem dwelt some of the people of Judah, Benjamin, Ephraim, and Manasseh:

4Uthai the son of Ammihud, son of Omri, son of Imri, son of Bani, of the sons of Pharez the son of Judah.

5Of the Shilonites: Asaiah the first-born, and his sons.

6Of the sons of Zerah: Jeuel, and their kinsmen, 690.

7Of the Benjamites: Sallu son of Meshullam, son of Hodaviah, son of Hassenuah,

8Ibneiah son of Jeroham, Elah son of Uzzi, son of Michri, and Meshullam son of Shephatiah, son of Reuel, son of Ibnijah;

9And their kinsmen according to their generations, 956. All these were heads of fathers' houses according to their fathers' houses.

10Of the priests: Jedaiah, Jehoiarib, Jachin,

11Azariah son of Hilkiah, son of Meshullam, son of Zadok, son of Meraioth, son of Ahitub, the chief officer of God's house;

12And Adaiah son of Jeroham, son of Pashhur, son of Malchijab, Massai son of Adiel, son of Jahzerah, son of Meshullam, son of Meshillemith, son of Immer;

13And their kinsmen, heads of their fathers' houses, 1,760; very able men for the work of the service of the house of God.

14Of the Levites: Shemaiah son of Hasshub, son of Azrikam, son of Hashabiah, of the sons of Merari;

15And Bakbakkar, Heresh, Galal, and Mattaniah son of Mica, son of Zichri, son of Asaph;

16Obadiah son of Shemaiah, son of Galal, son of Jeduthun, and Berechiah son of Asa, son of Elkanah, who dwelt in the villages of the Netophathites [near Jerusalem].

17The gatekeepers were: Shallum, Akkub, Talmon, Ahiman, and their kinsmen, Shallum being the chief,

18Who hitherto were assigned to the king's east side gate. They were the gatekeepers of the camp of the Levites.

## New American Standard

36And Ahaz became the father of Jehoaddah, and Jehoaddah
became the father of Alemeth, Azmaveth, and Zimri; and Zimri
became the father of Moza.
37And Moza became the father of Binea; Raphah *was* his son,
Eleasah his son, Azel his son.
38And Azel had six sons, and these *were* their names: Azrikam,
Bocheru, Ishmael, Sheariah, Obadiah and Hanan. All these *were*
the sons of Azel.
39And the sons of Eshek his brother *were* Ulam his first-born,
Jeush the second, and Eliphelet the third.
40And the sons of Ulam were mighty men of valor, archers, and
had many sons and grandsons, 150 *of them*. All these *were* of the
sons of Benjamin.

*People of Jerusalem*

9 SO ALL Israel was enrolled by genealogies; and behold, they
are written in the Book of the Kings of Israel. And Judah was
carried away into exile to Babylon for their unfaithfulness.
2¶ Now the first who lived in their possessions in their cities
*were* Israel, the priests, the Levites and the temple servants.
3And some of the sons of Judah, of the sons of Benjamin, and
of the sons of Ephraim and Manasseh lived in Jerusalem:
4Uthai the son of Ammihud, the son of Omri, the son of Imri,
the son of Bani, from the sons of Perez the son of Judah.
5And from the Shilonites *were* Asaiah the first-born and his
sons.
6And from the sons of Zerah *were* Jeuel and their relatives, 690
*of them*.
7And from the sons of Benjamin *were* Sallu the son of Meshullam, the son of Hodaviah, the son of Hassenuah,
8and Ibneiah the son of Jeroham, and Elah the son of Uzzi, the
son of Michri, and Meshullam the son of Shephatiah, the son of
Reuel, the son of Ibnijah;
9and their relatives according to their generations, 956. All
these *were* heads of fathers' *households* according to their fathers'
houses.
10¶ And from the priests *were* Jedaiah, Jehoiarib, Jachin,
11and Azariah the son of Hilkiah, the son of Meshullam, the son
of Zadok, the son of Meraioth, the son of Ahitub, the chief officer
of the house of God;
12and Adaiah the son of Jeroham, the son of Pashhur, the son
of Malchijah, and Maasai the son of Adiel, the son of Jahzerah, the
son of Meshullam, the son of Meshillemith, the son of Immer;
13and their relatives, heads of their fathers' households, 1,760
very able men for the work of the service of the house of God.
14¶ And of the Levites *were* Shemaiah the son of Hasshub, the
son of Azrikam, the son of Hashabiah, of the sons of Merari;
15and Bakbakkar, Heresh and Galal and Mattaniah the son of
Mica, the son of Zichri, the son of Asaph,
16and Obadiah the son of Shemaiah, the son of Galal, the son
of Jeduthun, and Berechiah the son of Asa, the son of Elkanah,
who lived in the villages of the Netophathites.
17¶ Now the gatekeepers *were* Shallum and Akkub and Talmon
and Ahiman and their relatives (Shallum the chief
18*being stationed* until now at the king's gate to the east). These
*were* the gatekeepers for the camp of the sons of Levi.

## New International

36Ahaz was the father of Jehoaddah, Jehoaddah was the
father of Alemeth, Azmaveth and Zimri, and Zimri was
the father of Moza. 37Moza was the father of Binea; Raphah was his son, Eleasah his son and Azel his son.
38Azel had six sons, and these were their names:
Azrikam, Bokeru, Ishmael, Sheariah, Obadiah and Hanan. All these were the sons of Azel.
39The sons of his brother Eshek:
Ulam his firstborn, Jeush the second son and Eliphelet the
third. 40The sons of Ulam were brave warriors who could
handle the bow. They had many sons and grandsons—
150 in all.
All these were the descendants of Benjamin.

9 ALL ISRAEL was listed in the genealogies recorded in the
book of the kings of Israel.

*The People in Jerusalem*

The people of Judah were taken captive to Babylon because of
their unfaithfulness. 2Now the first to resettle on their own property in their own towns were some Israelites, priests, Levites and
temple servants.
3Those from Judah, from Benjamin, and from Ephraim and
Manasseh who lived in Jerusalem were:
4Uthai son of Ammihud, the son of Omri, the son of Imri, the
son of Bani, a descendant of Perez son of Judah.
5Of the Shilonites:
Asaiah the firstborn and his sons.
6Of the Zerahites:
Jeuel.
The people from Judah numbered 690.
7Of the Benjamites:
Sallu son of Meshullam, the son of Hodaviah, the son of
Hassenuah;
8Ibneiah son of Jeroham; Elah son of Uzzi, the son of Micri;
and Meshullam son of Shephatiah, the son of Reuel, the
son of Ibnijah.
9The people from Benjamin, as listed in their genealogy,
numbered 956. All these men were heads of their families.
10Of the priests:
Jedaiah; Jehoiarib; Jakin;
11Azariah son of Hilkiah, the son of Meshullam, the son of
Zadok, the son of Meraioth, the son of Ahitub, the official
in charge of the house of God;
12Adaiah son of Jeroham, the son of Pashhur, the son of
Malkijah; and Maasai son of Adiel, the son of Jahzerah,
the son of Meshullam, the son of Meshillemith, the son of
Immer.
13The priests, who were heads of families, numbered 1,760.
They were able men, responsible for ministering in the
house of God.
14Of the Levites:
Shemaiah son of Hasshub, the son of Azrikam, the son of
Hashabiah, a Merarite; 15Bakbakkar, Heresh, Galal and
Mattaniah son of Mica, the son of Zicri, the son of Asaph;
16Obadiah son of Shemaiah, the son of Galal, the son of
Jeduthun; and Berekiah son of Asa, the son of Elkanah,
who lived in the villages of the Netophathites.
17The gatekeepers:
Shallum, Akkub, Talmon, Ahiman and their brothers,
Shallum their chief 18being stationed at the King's Gate on
the east, up to the present time. These were the gatekeepers belonging to the camp of the Levites. 19Shallum

## King James

19And Shallum the son of Kore, the son of Ebiasaph, the son of Korah, and his brethren, of the house of his father, the Korahites, *were* over the work of the service, keepers of the gates of the tabernacle: and their fathers, *being* over the host of the LORD, *were* keepers of the entry.

20And Phinehas the son of Eleazar was the ruler over them in time past, *and* the LORD *was* with him.

21 *And* Zechariah the son of Meshelemiah *was* porter of the door of the tabernacle of the congregation.

22All these *which were* chosen to be porters in the gates *were* two hundred and twelve. These were reckoned by their genealogy in their villages, whom David and Samuel the seer did ordain in their set office.

23So they and their children *had* the oversight of the gates of the house of the LORD, *namely*, the house of the tabernacle, by wards.

24In four quarters were the porters, toward the east, west, north, and south.

25And their brethren, *which were* in their villages, *were* to come after seven days from time to time with them.

26For these Levites, the four chief porters, were in *their* set office, and were over the chambers and treasuries of the house of God.

27¶ And they lodged round about the house of God, because the charge *was* upon them, and the opening thereof every morning *pertained* to them.

28And *certain* of them had the charge of the ministering vessels, that they should bring them in and out by tale.

29 *Some* of them also *were* appointed to oversee the vessels, and all the instruments of the sanctuary, and the fine flour, and the wine, and the oil, and the frankincense, and the spices.

30And *some* of the sons of the priests made the ointment of the spices.

31And Mattithiah, *one* of the Levites, who *was* the firstborn of Shallum the Korahite, had the set office over the things that were made in the pans.

32And *other* of their brethren, of the sons of the Kohathites, *were* over the showbread, to prepare *it* every sabbath.

33And these *are* the singers, chief of the fathers of the Levites, *who remaining* in the chambers *were* free: for they were employed in *that* work day and night.

34These chief fathers of the Levites *were* chief throughout their generations; these dwelt at Jerusalem.

35¶ And in Gibeon dwelt the father of Gibeon, Jehiel, whose wife's name *was* Maachah:

36And his firstborn son Abdon, then Zur, and Kish, and Baal, and Ner, and Nadab,

37And Gedor, and Ahio, and Zechariah, and Mikloth.

38And Mikloth begat Shimeam. And they also dwelt with their brethren at Jerusalem, over against their brethren.

39And Ner begat Kish; and Kish begat Saul; and Saul begat Jonathan, and Malchi-shua, and Abinadab, and Esh-baal.

40And the son of Jonathan *was* Merib-baal: and Merib-baal begat Micah.

41And the sons of Micah *were*, Pithon, and Melech, and Tahrea, *and Ahaz*.

42And Ahaz begat Jarah; and Jarah begat Alemeth, and Azmaveth, and Zimri; and Zimri begat Moza;

43And Moza begat Binea; and Rephaiah his son, Eleasah his son, Azel his son.

44And Azel had six sons, whose names *are* these, Azrikam, Bocheru, and Ishmael, and Sheariah, and Obadiah, and Hanan: these *were* the sons of Azel.

## Amplified

19Shallum son of Kore, son of Ebiasaph, son of Korah, and his kinsmen of his father's house, the Korahites, were in charge of the work of the service, keepers of the thresholds of the tent, as their fathers had been in charge of the camp of the Lord, keepers of the entrance.

20Phinehas son of Eleazar was ruler over them in time past, and the Lord was with him.

21Zechariah son of Meshelemiah was gatekeeper at the entrance of the tent of meeting.

22All these chosen to be keepers at the thresholds were 212. These were enrolled by their genealogies in their villages [around Jerusalem], these men [whose grandfathers] David and Samuel the seer had established to their office of trust.

23So they and their sons had oversight of the gates of the Lord's house, that is, the house of the tabernacle, by wards.

24The gatekeepers were stationed on the four sides [of the house of the Lord], on the east, west, north, and south.

25Their brethren in their villages were to come in every seven days to be with them.

26For these Levites, the four chief gatekeepers, were in charge of the chambers and treasures of the house of God.

27They lodged round about God's house, for the duty [of watching] was theirs, also the opening of the house every morning.

28Some of them had charge of the serving utensils, being required to count them when they brought them in or took them out.

29Some of them also were appointed over the furniture and over all the sacred utensils, also over the fine flour, wine, oil, frankincense, and spices.

30Other sons of the priests prepared the ointment of spices.

31Mattithiah, one of the Levites, the first-born of Shallum the Korahite, was responsible for the things baked in pans.

32Of their Kohathite kinsmen, some were to prepare the showbread every Sabbath.

33These are the singers, heads of the fathers' houses of the Levites, dwelling in the temple chambers, free from other service, because on duty day and night.

34These were heads of fathers' houses of the Levites, according to their generations, chief men, who lived in Jerusalem.

35In Gibeon dwelt the father of Gibeon, Jeiel, whose wife's name was Maacah,

36His first-born son Abdon, then Zur, Kish, Baal, Ner, Nadab,

37Gedor, Ahio, Zechariah, and Mikloth.

38Mikloth was the father of Shimeam. They also dwelt beside their brethren, opposite their kinsmen in Jerusalem.

39Ner was the father of Kish, Kish of [King] Saul, Saul of Jonathan, Malchishua, Abinadab, and Eshbaal.

40The son of Jonathan was Merib-baal [Mephibosheth]; Merib-baal was the father of Micah.

41The sons of Micah: Pithon, Melech, Tahrea, and Ahaz.

42Ahaz was the father of Jarah, and Jarah of Alemeth, Azmaveth, and Zimri; Zimri was the father of Moza;

43Moza of Binea; Rephaiah was his son, Eleasah his son, Azel his son.

44Azel had six sons: Azrikam, Bocheru, Ishmael, Sheariah, Obadiah, and Hanan; these were the sons of Azel.

## New American Standard

19And Shallum the son of Kore, the son of Ebiasaph, the son
of Korah, and his relatives, of his father's house, the Korahites,
*were* over the work of the service, keepers of the thresholds of the
tent; and their fathers had been over the camp of the LORD, keepers
of the entrance.
20And Phinehas the son of Eleazar was ruler over them previously, *and* the LORD was with him.
21Zechariah the son of Meshelemiah was gatekeeper of the
entrance of the tent of meeting.
22All these who were chosen to be gatekeepers in the thresholds
were 212. These were enrolled by genealogy in their villages,
whom David and Samuel the seer appointed in their office of trust.
23So they and their sons had charge of the gates of the house
of the LORD, *even* the house of the tent, as guards.
24The gatekeepers were on the four sides, to the east, west,
north, and south.
25And their relatives in their villages *were* to come in every
seven days from time to time *to be* with them;
26for the four chief gatekeepers who *were* Levites, were in an
office of trust, and were over the chambers and over the treasuries
in the house of God.
27And they spent the night around the house of God, because
the watch was committed to them; and they *were* in charge of
opening *it* morning by morning.
28¶ Now some of them had charge of the utensils of service, for
they counted them when they brought them in and when they
took them out.
29Some of them also were appointed over the furniture and over
all the utensils of the sanctuary and over the fine flour and the wine
and the oil and the frankincense and the spices.
30And some of the sons of the priests prepared the mixing of
the spices.
31And Mattithiah, one of the Levites, who was the first-born of
Shallum the Korahite, had the responsibility over the things which
were baked in pans.
32And some of their relatives of the sons of the Kohathites *were*
over the showbread to prepare it every sabbath.
33¶ Now these are the singers, heads of fathers' *households* of the
Levites, *who lived* in the chambers *of the temple* free *from other service;*
for they were engaged in their work day and night.
34These were heads of fathers' *households* of the Levites according to their generations, chief men, who lived in Jerusalem.

*Ancestry and Descendants of Saul*

35¶ And in Gibeon Jeiel the father of Gibeon lived, and his wife's
name was Maacah,
36and his first-born son *was* Abdon, then Zur, Kish, Baal, Ner,
Nadab,
37Gedor, Ahio, Zechariah, and Mikloth.
38And Mikloth became the father of Shimeam. And they also
lived with their relatives in Jerusalem opposite their *other* relatives.
39And Ner became the father of Kish, and Kish became the
father of Saul, and Saul became the father of Jonathan, Malchi-
shua, Abinadab, and Eshbaal.
40And the son of Jonathan *was* Merib-baal; and Merib-baal
became the father of Micah.
41And the sons of Micah *were* Pithon, Melech, Tahrea, *and Ahaz.*
42And Ahaz became the father of Jarah, and Jarah became the
father of Alemeth, Azmaveth, and Zimri; and Zimri became the
father of Moza,
43and Moza became the father of Binea and Rephaiah his son,
Eleasah his son, Azel his son.
44And Azel had six sons whose names are these: Azrikam,
Bocheru and Ishmael and Sheariah and Obadiah and Hanan.
These were the sons of Azel.

## New International

son of Kore, the son of Ebiasaph, the son of Korah, and
his fellow gatekeepers from his family (the Korahites)
were responsible for guarding the thresholds of the Tent[a]
just as their fathers had been responsible for guarding the
entrance to the dwelling of the LORD. 20In earlier times
Phinehas son of Eleazar was in charge of the gatekeepers,
and the LORD was with him. 21Zechariah son of Meshelemiah was the gatekeeper at the entrance to the Tent of
Meeting.
22Altogether, those chosen to be gatekeepers at the thresholds
numbered 212. They were registered by genealogy in their villages. The gatekeepers had been assigned to their positions of trust
by David and Samuel the seer. 23They and their descendants were
in charge of guarding the gates of the house of the LORD—the
house called the Tent. 24The gatekeepers were on the four sides:
east, west, north and south. 25Their brothers in their villages had
to come from time to time and share their duties for seven-day
periods. 26But the four principal gatekeepers, who were Levites,
were entrusted with the responsibility for the rooms and treasuries
in the house of God. 27They would spend the night stationed
around the house of God, because they had to guard it; and they
had charge of the key for opening it each morning.
28Some of them were in charge of the articles used in the temple
service; they counted them when they were brought in and when
they were taken out. 29Others were assigned to take care of the
furnishings and all the other articles of the sanctuary, as well as
the flour and wine, and the oil, incense and spices. 30But some of
the priests took care of mixing the spices. 31A Levite named Mattithiah, the firstborn son of Shallum the Korahite, was entrusted
with the responsibility for baking the offering bread. 32Some of
their Kohathite brothers were in charge of preparing for every
Sabbath the bread set out on the table.
33Those who were musicians, heads of Levite families, stayed
in the rooms of the temple and were exempt from other duties
because they were responsible for the work day and night.
34All these were heads of Levite families, chiefs as listed in their
genealogy, and they lived in Jerusalem.

*The Genealogy of Saul*

35Jeiel the father[b] of Gibeon lived in Gibeon.
His wife's name was Maacah, 36and his firstborn son was
Abdon, followed by Zur, Kish, Baal, Ner, Nadab, 37Ge-
dor, Ahio, Zechariah and Mikloth. 38Mikloth was the father of Shimeam. They too lived near their relatives in
Jerusalem.
39Ner was the father of Kish, Kish the father of Saul, and Saul
the father of Jonathan, Malki-Shua, Abinadab and Esh-
Baal.[c]
40The son of Jonathan:
Merib-Baal,[d] who was the father of Micah.
41The sons of Micah:
Pithon, Melech, Tahrea and Ahaz.[e]
42Ahaz was the father of Jadah, Jadah[f] was the father of
Alemeth, Azmaveth and Zimri, and Zimri was the father
of Moza. 43Moza was the father of Binea; Rephaiah was his
son, Eleasah his son and Azel his son.
44Azel had six sons, and these were their names:
Azrikam, Bokeru, Ishmael, Sheariah, Obadiah and Hanan. These were the sons of Azel.

**NIV** [a] 19 That is, the temple; also in verses 21 and 23 [b] 35 *Father* may mean *civic leader* or *military leader.* [c] 39 Also known as *Ish-Bosheth* [d] 40 Also known as *Mephibosheth* [e] 41 Vulgate and Syriac (see also Septuagint and 1 Chron. 8:35); Hebrew does not have *and Ahaz.* [f] 42 Some Hebrew manuscripts and Septuagint (see also 1 Chron. 8:36); most Hebrew manuscripts *Jarah, Jarah*

## King James

**10** NOW THE Philistines fought against Israel; and the men of Israel fled from before the Philistines, and fell down slain in mount Gilboa.

2And the Philistines followed hard after Saul, and after his sons; and the Philistines slew Jonathan, and Abinadab, and Malchi-shua, the sons of Saul.

3And the battle went sore against Saul, and the archers hit him, and he was wounded of the archers.

4Then said Saul to his armourbearer, Draw thy sword, and thrust me through therewith; lest these uncircumcised come and abuse me. But his armourbearer would not; for he was sore afraid. So Saul took a sword, and fell upon it.

5And when his armourbearer saw that Saul was dead, he fell likewise on the sword, and died.

6So Saul died, and his three sons, and all his house died together.

7And when all the men of Israel that *were* in the valley saw that they fled, and that Saul and his sons were dead, then they forsook their cities, and fled: and the Philistines came and dwelt in them.

8¶ And it came to pass on the morrow, when the Philistines came to strip the slain, that they found Saul and his sons fallen in mount Gilboa.

9And when they had stripped him, they took his head, and his armour, and sent into the land of the Philistines round about, to carry tidings unto their idols, and to the people.

10And they put his armour in the house of their gods, and fastened his head in the temple of Dagon.

11¶ And when all Jabesh-gilead heard all that the Philistines had done to Saul,

12They arose, all the valiant men, and took away the body of Saul, and the bodies of his sons, and brought them to Jabesh, and buried their bones under the oak in Jabesh, and fasted seven days.

13¶ So Saul died for his transgression which he committed against the LORD, *even* against the word of the LORD, which he kept not, and also for asking *counsel* of *one that had* a familiar spirit, to inquire *of it;*

14And inquired not of the LORD: therefore he slew him, and turned the kingdom unto David the son of Jesse.

**11** THEN ALL Israel gathered themselves to David unto Hebron, saying, Behold, we *are* thy bone and thy flesh.

2And moreover in time past, even when Saul was king, thou *wast* he that leddest out and broughtest in Israel: and the LORD thy God said unto thee, Thou shalt feed my people Israel, and thou shalt be ruler over my people Israel.

3Therefore came all the elders of Israel to the king to Hebron; and David made a covenant with them in Hebron before the LORD; and they anointed David king over Israel, according to the word of the LORD by Samuel.

4¶ And David and all Israel went to Jerusalem, which *is* Jebus; where the Jebusites *were,* the inhabitants of the land.

5And the inhabitants of Jebus said to David, Thou shalt not come hither. Nevertheless David took the castle of Zion, which *is* the city of David.

6And David said, Whosoever smiteth the Jebusites first shall be chief and captain. So Joab the son of Zeruiah went first up, and was chief.

7And David dwelt in the castle; therefore they called it the city of David.

8And he built the city round about, even from Millo round about: and Joab repaired the rest of the city.

## Amplified

**10** NOW THE Philistines fought against Israel; and the men of Israel fled from before them and fell slain on Mount Gilboa.

2And the Philistines followed close after Saul and his sons *and* overtook them; and the Philistines slew Jonathan, Abinadab, and Malchishua, the sons of Saul.

3And the battle raged about Saul, and the archers found and wounded him.

4Then Saul said to his armor-bearer, Draw your sword, and thrust me through with it; lest these uncircumcised come and abuse *and* make sport of me. But his armor-bearer would not, for he was terrified. So Saul took his own sword and fell on it.

5When his armor-bearer saw that Saul was dead, he also fell on his sword and died.

6So Saul died; he and his three sons and all his house died together.

7And when all the men of Israel who were in the valley saw that the army fled and that Saul and his sons were dead, they forsook their cities and fled; and the Philistines came and dwelt in them.

8Next day, when the Philistines came to strip the slain, they found Saul and his sons fallen on Mount Gilboa.

9They stripped [Saul], and took his head and his armor, and sent [them] round about in Philistia to carry the news to their idols and to the people.

10And they put [Saul's] armor in the house of their gods, and fastened his head in the temple of Dagon.

11When all Jabesh-gilead heard all that the Philistines had done to Saul,

12All the brave men arose, took away the bodies of Saul and his sons, brought them to Jabesh, and buried their bones under the oak in Jabesh; then fasted seven days. [I Sam. 31:12.]

13So Saul died for his trespass against the Lord [in sparing Amalek], for his unfaithfulness in not keeping God's word, and also for consulting [a medium with] a spirit of the dead, to inquire pleadingly of it,

14And inquired not so of the Lord [in earnest penitence]; therefore the Lord slew him, and turned the kingdom over to David son of Jesse. [I Sam. 28:6.]

**11** THEN [AFTER the death of Ishbosheth, Saul's son, who ruled over eleven tribes of Israel for two troubled years after Saul's death], all Israel gathered at Hebron and said to David, Behold, we are your bone and your flesh. [II Sam. 2:8-10.]

2In times past, even when Saul was king, it was you who led out and brought in Israel; and the Lord your God said to you, You shall be shepherd of My people Israel, and you shall be prince *and* leader over [them].

3So all the elders of Israel came to the king at Hebron; and David made a covenant with them there before the Lord, and they anointed [him] king over Israel, according to the word of the Lord by Samuel. [I Sam. 16:1, 12, 13.]

4And David and all Israel went to Jerusalem, that is Jebus, where the Jebusites, the inhabitants of the land, were.

5Then the Jebusites said to David, You shall not come in here! But David took the stronghold of Zion, that is, the city of David.

6And David said, Whoever smites the Jebusites first shall be chief and commander. Joab the son of Zeruiah [David's half sister] went up first, so was made chief.

7David dwelt in the stronghold; so it was called the city of David.

8He built the city from Millo [a fortification] on around; and Joab repaired *and* revived the rest of the [old Jebusite] city.

## New American Standard

*Defeat and Death of Saul and His Sons*

**10** NOW THE Philistines fought against Israel; and the men of Israel fled before the Philistines, and fell slain on Mount Gilboa.

2And the Philistines closely pursued Saul and his sons, and the Philistines struck down Jonathan, Abinadab and Malchi-shua, the sons of Saul.

3And the battle became heavy against Saul, and the archers overtook him; and he was wounded by the archers.

4Then Saul said to his armor bearer, "Draw your sword and thrust me through with it, lest these uncircumcised come and abuse me." But his armor bearer would not, for he was greatly afraid. Therefore Saul took his sword and fell on it.

5And when his armor bearer saw that Saul was dead, he likewise fell on his sword and died.

6Thus Saul died with his three sons, and all *those* of his house died together.

7¶ When all the men of Israel who were in the valley saw that they had fled, and that Saul and his sons were dead, they forsook their cities and fled; and the Philistines came and lived in them.

8And it came about the next day, when the Philistines came to strip the slain, that they found Saul and his sons fallen on Mount Gilboa.

9So they stripped him and took his head and his armor and sent *messengers* around the land of the Philistines, to carry the good news to their idols and to the people.

10And they put his armor in the house of their gods and fastened his head in the house of Dagon.

*Jabesh-gilead's Tribute to Saul*

11When all Jabesh-gilead heard all that the Philistines had done to Saul,

12all the valiant men arose and took away the body of Saul and the bodies of his sons, and brought them to Jabesh and buried their bones under the oak in Jabesh, and fasted seven days.

13¶ So Saul died for his trespass which he committed against the LORD, because of the word of the LORD which he did not keep; and also because he asked counsel of a medium, making inquiry *of it*,

14and did not inquire of the LORD. Therefore He killed him, and turned the kingdom to David the son of Jesse.

*David Made King over All Israel*

**11** THEN ALL Israel gathered to David at Hebron and said, "Behold, we are your bone and your flesh.

2"In times past, even when Saul was king, you *were* the one who led out and brought in Israel; and the LORD your God said to you, 'You shall shepherd My people Israel, and you shall be prince over My people Israel.' "

3So all the elders of Israel came to the king at Hebron, and David made a covenant with them in Hebron before the LORD; and they anointed David king over Israel, according to the word of the LORD through Samuel.

*Jerusalem, Capital City*

4¶ Then David and all Israel went to Jerusalem (that is, Jebus); and the Jebusites, the inhabitants of the land, *were* there.

5And the inhabitants of Jebus said to David, "You shall not enter here." Nevertheless David captured the stronghold of Zion (that is, the city of David).

6Now David had said, "Whoever strikes down a Jebusite first shall be chief and commander." And Joab the son of Zeruiah went up first, so he became chief.

7Then David dwelt in the stronghold; therefore it was called the city of David.

8And he built the city all around, from the [a]Millo even to the surrounding area; and Joab repaired the rest of the city.

NAS [a] I.e., citadel

## New International

*Saul Takes His Life*

**10** NOW THE Philistines fought against Israel; the Israelites fled before them, and many fell slain on Mount Gilboa. 2The Philistines pressed hard after Saul and his sons, and they killed his sons Jonathan, Abinadab and Malki-Shua. 3The fighting grew fierce around Saul, and when the archers overtook him, they wounded him.

4Saul said to his armor-bearer, "Draw your sword and run me through, or these uncircumcised fellows will come and abuse me."

But his armor-bearer was terrified and would not do it; so Saul took his own sword and fell on it. 5When the armor-bearer saw that Saul was dead, he too fell on his sword and died. 6So Saul and his three sons died, and all his house died together.

7When all the Israelites in the valley saw that the army had fled and that Saul and his sons had died, they abandoned their towns and fled. And the Philistines came and occupied them.

8The next day, when the Philistines came to strip the dead, they found Saul and his sons fallen on Mount Gilboa. 9They stripped him and took his head and his armor, and sent messengers throughout the land of the Philistines to proclaim the news among their idols and their people. 10They put his armor in the temple of their gods and hung up his head in the temple of Dagon.

11When all the inhabitants of Jabesh Gilead heard of everything the Philistines had done to Saul, 12all their valiant men went and took the bodies of Saul and his sons and brought them to Jabesh. Then they buried their bones under the great tree in Jabesh, and they fasted seven days.

13Saul died because he was unfaithful to the LORD; he did not keep the word of the LORD and even consulted a medium for guidance, 14and did not inquire of the LORD. So the LORD put him to death and turned the kingdom over to David son of Jesse.

*David Becomes King Over Israel*

**11** ALL ISRAEL came together to David at Hebron and said, "We are your own flesh and blood. 2In the past, even while Saul was king, you were the one who led Israel on their military campaigns. And the LORD your God said to you, 'You will shepherd my people Israel, and you will become their ruler.' "

3When all the elders of Israel had come to King David at Hebron, he made a compact with them at Hebron before the LORD, and they anointed David king over Israel, as the LORD had promised through Samuel.

*David Conquers Jerusalem*

4David and all the Israelites marched to Jerusalem (that is, Jebus). The Jebusites who lived there 5said to David, "You will not get in here." Nevertheless, David captured the fortress of Zion, the City of David.

6David had said, "Whoever leads the attack on the Jebusites will become commander-in-chief." Joab son of Zeruiah went up first, and so he received the command.

7David then took up residence in the fortress, and so it was called the City of David. 8He built up the city around it, from the supporting terraces[b] to the surrounding wall, while Joab restored

NIV [b] 8 Or *the Millo*

## King James

9 So David waxed greater and greater: for the LORD of hosts *was*
with him.
10 ¶ These also *are* the chief of the mighty men whom David had,
who strengthened themselves with him in his kingdom, *and* with
all Israel, to make him king, according to the word of the LORD
concerning Israel.
11 And this *is* the number of the mighty men whom David had;
Jashobeam, an Hachmonite, the chief of the captains: he lifted up
his spear against three hundred slain *by him* at one time.
12 And after him *was* Eleazar the son of Dodo, the Ahohite, who
*was one* of the three mighties.
13 He was with David at Pas-dammim, and there the Philistines
were gathered together to battle, where was a parcel of ground full
of barley; and the people fled from before the Philistines.
14 And they set themselves in the midst of *that* parcel, and
delivered it, and slew the Philistines; and the LORD saved *them* by
a great deliverance.
15 ¶ Now three of the thirty captains went down to the rock to
David, into the cave of Adullam; and the host of the Philistines
encamped in the valley of Rephaim.
16 And David *was* then in the hold, and the Philistines' garrison
*was* then at Bethlehem.
17 And David longed, and said, Oh that one would give me
drink of the water of the well of Bethlehem, that *is* at the gate!
18 And the three brake through the host of the Philistines, and
drew water out of the well of Bethlehem, that *was* by the gate, and
took *it*, and brought *it* to David: but David would not drink *of* it,
but poured it out to the LORD,
19 And said, My God forbid it me, that I should do this thing:
shall I drink the blood of these men that have put their lives in
jeopardy? for with *the jeopardy of* their lives they brought it. Therefore he would not drink it. These things did these three mightiest.
20 ¶ And Abishai the brother of Joab, he was chief of the three:
for lifting up his spear against three hundred, he slew *them*, and
had a name among the three.
21 Of the three, he was more honourable than the two; for he
was their captain: howbeit he attained not to the *first* three.
22 Benaiah the son of Jehoiada, the son of a valiant man of
Kabzeel, who had done many acts; he slew two lionlike men of
Moab: also he went down and slew a lion in a pit in a snowy day.
23 And he slew an Egyptian, a man of *great* stature, five cubits
high; and in the Egyptian's hand *was* a spear like a weaver's beam;
and he went down to him with a staff, and plucked the spear out
of the Egyptian's hand, and slew him with his own spear.
24 These *things* did Benaiah the son of Jehoiada, and had the
name among the three mighties.
25 Behold, he was honourable among the thirty, but attained not
to the *first* three: and David set him over his guard.
26 ¶ Also the valiant men of the armies *were*, Asahel the brother
of Joab, Elhanan the son of Dodo of Bethlehem,
27 Shammoth the Harorite, Helez the Pelonite,
28 Ira the son of Ikkesh the Tekoite, Abiezer the Antothite,
29 Sibbecai the Hushathite, Ilai the Ahohite,
30 Maharai the Netophathite, Heled the son of Baanah the Netophathite,
31 Ithai the son of Ribai of Gibeah, *that pertained* to the children
of Benjamin, Benaiah the Pirathonite,
32 Hurai of the brooks of Gaash, Abiel the Arbathite,
33 Azmaveth the Baharumite, Eliahba the Shaalbonite,
34 The sons of Hashem the Gizonite, Jonathan the son of Shage
the Hararite,

## Amplified

9 And David became greater and greater, for the Lord of hosts
was with him.
10 Now these are the chiefs of David's mighty men, who
strongly supported him in his kingdom, together with all Israel,
to make him king, according to the word of the Lord concerning
Israel.
11 And this is the number [thirty, and list] of David's mighty
men: Jashobeam, a Hachmonite, the chief of the thirty (captains).
He lifted up his spear against 300 whom he slew at one time.
12 Next to him in rank was Eleazar son of Dodo, the Ahohite,
of the three mighty men.
13 He was with David at Pas-dammim [where David had long
before slain Goliath], and there the Philistines were gathered for
battle, where was a plot of ground full of barley *or* lentils; and the
men [of Israel] fled before the Philistines.
14 And Eleazar [one of the three] stood in the midst of that plot
and defended it, and slew the Philistines [until his hand was
weary, and his hand cleaved to the sword]; and the Lord saved by
a great victory *and* deliverance. [Cp. II Sam. 23:9, 10.]
15 Three of the thirty chief men went down to the rock to David,
into the cave of Adullam; and the army of the Philistines was
encamped in the valley of Rephaim.
16 David was then in the stronghold, and the Philistines' garrison was in Bethlehem.
17 And David longingly said, Oh, that someone would give me
water to drink from the well of Bethlehem which is by the gate!
18 Then the three [mighty men] broke through the camp of the
Philistines, and drew water out of the well of Bethlehem, which
was by the gate, and brought it to David. But David would not
drink it; he poured it out to the Lord,
19 And said, My God forbid that I should do this thing. Shall I
drink the blood of these men that have put their lives in jeopardy?
For at the risk of their lives they brought it. So he would not drink
it. These things did these three mighty men.
20 Abishai brother of Joab was chief of the three; for he lifted up
his spear against 300 *and* slew them, and was named among the
three.
21 Of the three (in the second rank) he was more renowned than
the two, and became their captain; however he attained not to the
first three.
22 Benaiah the son of Jehoiada, whose father was a valiant man
of Kabzeel, had done mighty deeds; he slew the two sons of Ariel
of Moab; also he went down and slew a lion in a pit in time of
snow.
23 He slew an Egyptian also, a man of great stature, five cubits
tall. The Egyptian held a spear like a weaver's beam, and [Benaiah]
went to him with a staff and plucked the spear out of the Egyptian's hand, and slew him with the man's own spear.
24 These things did Benaiah son of Jehoiada, and won a name
beside the three mighty men.
25 He was renowned among the thirty, but he did not attain to
the rank of the first three. David put him over his guard *and*
council.
26 Also the mighty men of the armies were Asahel brother of
Joab, Elhanan son of Dodo of Bethlehem,
27 Shammoth of Harod, Helez the Pelonite,
28 Ira son of Ikkesh of Tekoa, Abiezer of Anathoth,
29 Sibbecai the Hushathite, Ilai the Ahohite,
30 Maharai of Netophah, Heled son of Baanah of Netophah,
31 Ithai son of Ribai of Gibeah of the Benjamites, Benaiah of
Pirathon,
32 Hurai of the brooks of Gaash, Abiel the Arbathite,
33 Azmaveth of Baharum, Eliahba of Sha-albon,
34 The sons of Hashem the Gizonite, Jonathan son of Shagee the
Hararite,

## New American Standard

9And David became greater and greater, for the LORD of hosts *was* with him.

*David's Mighty Men*

**10**¶ Now these are the heads of the mighty men whom David had, who gave him strong support in his kingdom, together with all Israel, to make him king, according to the word of the LORD concerning Israel.

11And these *constitute* the list of the mighty men whom David had: Jashobeam, the son of a Hachmonite, the chief of the thirty; he lifted up his spear against three hundred whom he killed at one time.

12And after him was Eleazar the son of Dodo, the Ahohite, who *was* one of the three mighty men.

13He was with David at Pasdammim when the Philistines were gathered together there to battle, and there was a plot of ground full of barley; and the people fled before the Philistines.

14And they took their stand in the midst of the plot, and defended it, and struck down the Philistines; and the LORD saved them by a great victory.

**15**¶ Now three of the thirty chief men went down to the rock to David, into the cave of Adullam, while the army of the Philistines was camping in the valley of Rephaim.

16And David was then in the stronghold, while the garrison of the Philistines *was* then in Bethlehem.

17And David had a craving and said, "Oh that someone would give me water to drink from the well of Bethlehem, which is by the gate!"

18So the three broke through the camp of the Philistines, and drew water from the well of Bethlehem which *was* by the gate, and took *it* and brought *it* to David; nevertheless David would not drink it, but poured it out to the LORD;

19and he said, "Be it far from me before my God that I should do this. Shall I drink the blood of these men *who went* at the risk of their lives? For at the risk of their lives they brought it." Therefore he would not drink it. These things the three mighty men did.

**20**¶ As for Abshai the brother of Joab, he was chief of the thirty, and he swung his spear against three hundred and killed them; and he had a name as well as the thirty.

21Of the three in the second *rank* he was the most honored, and became their commander; however, he did not attain to the *first* three.

**22**¶ Benaiah the son of Jehoiada, the son of a valiant man of Kabzeel, mighty in deeds, struck down the two *sons of* Ariel of Moab. He also went down and killed a lion inside a pit on a snowy day.

23And he killed an Egyptian, a man of *great* stature five cubits tall. Now in the Egyptian's hand *was* a spear like a weaver's beam, but he went down to him with a club and snatched the spear from the Egyptian's hand, and killed him with his own spear.

24These *things* Benaiah the son of Jehoiada did, and had a name as well as the three mighty men.

25Behold, he was honored among the thirty, but he did not attain to the three; and David appointed him over his guard.

**26**¶ Now the mighty men of the armies *were* Asahel the brother of Joab, Elhanan the son of Dodo of Bethlehem,

27Shammoth the Harorite, Helez the Pelonite,

28Ira the son of Ikkesh the Tekoite, Abiezer the Anathothite,

29Sibbecai the Hushathite, Ilai the Ahohite,

30Maharai the Netophathite, Heled the son of Baanah the Netophathite,

31Ithai the son of Ribai of Gibeah of the sons of Benjamin, Benaiah the Pirathonite,

32Hurai of the brooks of Gaash, Abiel the Arbathite,

33Azmaveth the Baharumite, Eliahba the Shaalbonite,

34the sons of Hashem the Gizonite, Jonathan the son of Shagee the Hararite,

## New International

the rest of the city. 9And David became more and more powerful, because the LORD Almighty was with him.

*David's Mighty Men*

10These were the chiefs of David's mighty men—they, together with all Israel, gave his kingship strong support to extend it over the whole land, as the LORD had promised— 11this is the list of David's mighty men:

Jashobeam,[a] a Hacmonite, was chief of the officers[b]; he raised his spear against three hundred men, whom he killed in one encounter.

12Next to him was Eleazar son of Dodai the Ahohite, one of the three mighty men. 13He was with David at Pas Dammim when the Philistines gathered there for battle. At a place where there was a field full of barley, the troops fled from the Philistines. 14But they took their stand in the middle of the field. They defended it and struck the Philistines down, and the LORD brought about a great victory.

15Three of the thirty chiefs came down to David to the rock at the cave of Adullam, while a band of Philistines was encamped in the Valley of Rephaim. 16At that time David was in the stronghold, and the Philistine garrison was at Bethlehem. 17David longed for water and said, "Oh, that someone would get me a drink of water from the well near the gate of Bethlehem!" 18So the Three broke through the Philistine lines, drew water from the well near the gate of Bethlehem and carried it back to David. But he refused to drink it; instead, he poured it out before the LORD. 19"God forbid that I should do this!" he said. "Should I drink the blood of these men who went at the risk of their lives?" Because they risked their lives to bring it back, David would not drink it.

Such were the exploits of the three mighty men.

20Abishai the brother of Joab was chief of the Three. He raised his spear against three hundred men, whom he killed, and so he became as famous as the Three. 21He was doubly honored above the Three and became their commander, even though he was not included among them.

22Benaiah son of Jehoiada was a valiant fighter from Kabzeel, who performed great exploits. He struck down two of Moab's best men. He also went down into a pit on a snowy day and killed a lion. 23And he struck down an Egyptian who was seven and a half feet[c] tall. Although the Egyptian had a spear like a weaver's rod in his hand, Benaiah went against him with a club. He snatched the spear from the Egyptian's hand and killed him with his own spear. 24Such were the exploits of Benaiah son of Jehoiada; he too was as famous as the three mighty men. 25He was held in greater honor than any of the Thirty, but he was not included among the Three. And David put him in charge of his bodyguard.

26The mighty men were:
Asahel the brother of Joab,
Elhanan son of Dodo from Bethlehem,
27Shammoth the Harorite,
Helez the Pelonite,
28Ira son of Ikkesh from Tekoa,
Abiezer from Anathoth,
29Sibbecai the Hushathite,
Ilai the Ahohite,
30Maharai the Netophathite,
Heled son of Baanah the Netophathite,
31Ithai son of Ribai from Gibeah in Benjamin,
Benaiah the Pirathonite,
32Hurai from the ravines of Gaash,
Abiel the Arbathite,
33Azmaveth the Baharumite,
Eliahba the Shaalbonite,
34the sons of Hashem the Gizonite,
Jonathan son of Shagee the Hararite,

**NIV** [a] *11* Possibly a variant of *Jashob-Baal* [b] *11* Or *Thirty;* some Septuagint manuscripts *Three* (see also 2 Samuel 23:8) [c] *23* Hebrew *five cubits* (about 2.3 meters)

## King James

35Ahiam the son of Sacar the Hararite, Eliphal the son of Ur,
36Hepher the Mecherathite, Ahijah the Pelonite,
37Hezro the Carmelite, Naarai the son of Ezbai,
38Joel the brother of Nathan, Mibhar the son of Haggeri,
39Zelek the Ammonite, Naharai the Berothite, the armourbearer of Joab the son of Zeruiah,
40Ira the Ithrite, Gareb the Ithrite,
41Uriah the Hittite, Zabad the son of Ahlai,
42Adina the son of Shiza the Reubenite, a captain of the Reubenites, and thirty with him,
43Hanan the son of Maachah, and Joshaphat the Mithnite,
44Uzzia the Ashterathite, Shama and Jehiel the sons of Hothan the Aroerite,
45Jediael the son of Shimri, and Joha his brother, the Tizite,
46Eliel the Mahavite, and Jeribai, and Joshaviah, the sons of Elnaam, and Ithmah the Moabite,
47Eliel, and Obed, and Jasiel the Mesobaite.

12 NOW THESE *are* they that came to David to Ziklag, while he yet kept himself close because of Saul the son of Kish: and they *were* among the mighty men, helpers of the war.
2 *They were* armed with bows, and could use both the right hand and the left in *hurling* stones and *shooting* arrows out of a bow, *even* of Saul's brethren of Benjamin.
3The chief *was* Ahiezer, then Joash, the sons of Shemaah the Gibeathite; and Jeziel, and Pelet, the sons of Azmaveth; and Berachah, and Jehu the Antothite,
4And Ismaiah the Gibeonite, a mighty man among the thirty, and over the thirty; and Jeremiah, and Jahaziel, and Johanan, and Josabad the Gederathite,
5Eluzai, and Jerimoth, and Bealiah, and Shemariah, and Shephatiah the Haruphite,
6Elkanah, and Jesiah, and Azareel, and Joezer, and Jashobeam, the Korhites,
7And Joelah, and Zebadiah, the sons of Jeroham of Gedor.
8And of the Gadites there separated themselves unto David into the hold to the wilderness men of might, *and* men of war *fit* for the battle, that could handle shield and buckler, whose faces *were like* the faces of lions, and *were* as swift as the roes upon the mountains;
9Ezer the first, Obadiah the second, Eliab the third,
10Mishmannah the fourth, Jeremiah the fifth,
11Attai the sixth, Eliel the seventh,
12Johanan the eighth, Elzabad the ninth,
13Jeremiah the tenth, Machbanai the eleventh.
14These *were* of the sons of Gad, captains of the host: one of the least *was* over an hundred, and the greatest over a thousand.
15These *are* they that went over Jordan in the first month, when it had overflown all his banks; and they put to flight all *them* of the valleys, *both* toward the east, and toward the west.
16And there came of the children of Benjamin and Judah to the hold unto David.
17And David went out to meet them, and answered and said unto them, If ye be come peaceably unto me to help me, mine heart shall be knit unto you: but if *ye be come* to betray me to mine enemies, seeing *there is* no wrong in mine hands, the God of our fathers look *thereon,* and rebuke *it.*

## Amplified

35Ahiam son of Sachar the Hararite, Eliphal son of Ur,
36Hepher the Mecherathite, Ahijah the Pelonite,
37Hezro of Carmel, Naarai son of Ezbai,
38Joel brother of Nathan, Mibhar son of Hagri,
39Zelek the Ammonite, Naharai the Berothite, the armor-bearer of Joab son of Zeruiah [David's half sister],
40Ira the Ithrite, Gareb the Ithrite,
41Uriah the Hittite [Bathsheba's husband], Zabad son of Ahlai,
42Adina son of Shiza, a leader of the Reubenites, and thirty heroes with him,
43Hanan son of Maacah, and Joshaphat the Mithnite,
44Uzzia the Ashterathite, Shama and Jeiel sons of Hotham the Aroerite,
45Jediael son of Shimri, and Joha his brother, the Tizite,
46Eliel the Mahavite, Jeribai and Joshaviah sons of Elnaam, Ithmah the Moabite,
47Eliel, Obed, and Ja-asiel the Mezobaite.

12 THESE ARE they that came to David to Ziklag, while he yet concealed himself because of Saul the son of Kish; they were among the mighty men, his helpers in war.
2They were bowmen, and could use the right hand or the left to sling stones or shoot arrows from the bow; they were of Saul's kinsmen of Benjamin.
3The chief was Ahiezer, then Joash, sons of Shemaah of Gibeah; Jeziel and Pelet sons of Azmaveth; Beracah, and Jehu of Anathoth,
4Ishmaiah of Gibeon, a mighty man among the thirty and a [leader] over them; Jeremiah, Jahaziel, Johanan, Jozabad of Gederah,
5Eluzai, Jerimoth, Bealiah, Shemariah, Shephatiah the Haruphite,
6Elkanah, Isshiah, Azarel, Joezer, and Jashobeam, the Korahites;
7Joelah and Zebadiah sons of Jeroham of Gedor.
8Of Gadites there went over to David to the stronghold in the wilderness men of might, men trained for war, who could handle shield and spear, whose faces were like the faces of lions, and who were swift as gazelles on the mountains:
9Ezer chief, Obadiah second, Eliab third,
10Mishmannah fourth, Jeremiah fifth,
11Attai sixth, Eliel seventh,
12Johanan eighth, Elzabad ninth,
13Jeremiah tenth, Mach-bannai eleventh.
14These Gadites were officers of the army. The lesser was equal to *and* over 100, and the greater equal to *and* over 1,000.
15These are the men who went over Jordan in the first month, when it had overflowed all its banks, and put to flight all those in the valleys, east and west.
16There came some of the men of Benjamin and Judah to the stronghold to David.
17David went out to meet them and said to them, If you have come peaceably to me to help me, my heart shall be knit to you; but if you have come to betray me to my adversaries, although there is no violence *or* wrong in my hands, the God of our fathers look upon and rebuke you.

## New American Standard

35Ahiam the son of Sacar the Hararite, Eliphal the son of Ur,
36Hepher the Mecherathite, Ahijah the Pelonite,
37Hezro the Carmelite, Naarai the son of Ezbai,
38Joel the brother of Nathan, Mibhar the son of Hagri,
39Zelek the Ammonite, Naharai the Berothite, the armor bearer of Joab the son of Zeruiah,
40Ira the Ithrite, Gareb the Ithrite,
41Uriah the Hittite, Zabad the son of Ahlai,
42Adina the son of Shiza the Reubenite, a chief of the Reubenites, and thirty with him,
43Hanan the son of Maacah and Joshaphat the Mithnite,
44Uzzia the Ashterathite, Shama and Jeiel the sons of Hotham the Aroerite,
45Jediael the son of Shimri and Joha his brother, the Tizite,
46Eliel the Mahavite and Jeribai and Joshaviah, the sons of Elnaam, and Ithmah the Moabite,
47Eliel and Obed and Jaasiel the Mezobaite.

*David's Supporters in Ziklag*

12 NOW THESE are the ones who came to David at Ziklag, while he was still restricted because of Saul the son of Kish; and they were among the mighty men who helped *him* in war.

2They were equipped with bows, using both the right hand and the left *to sling* stones and *to shoot* arrows from the bow; *they were* Saul's kinsmen from Benjamin.

3The chief was Ahiezer, then Joash, the sons of Shemaah the Gibeathite; and Jeziel and Pelet, the sons of Azmaveth, and Beracah and Jehu the Anathothite,

4and Ishmaiah the Gibeonite, a mighty man among the thirty, and over the thirty. Then Jeremiah, Jahaziel, Johanan, Jozabad the Gederathite,

5Eluzai, Jerimoth, Bealiah, Shemariah, Shephatiah the Haruphite,

6Elkanah, Isshiah, Azarel, Joezer, Jashobeam, the Korahites,
7and Joelah and Zebadiah, the sons of Jeroham of Gedor.
8¶ And from the Gadites there came over to David in the stronghold in the wilderness, mighty men of valor, men trained for war, who could handle shield and spear, and whose faces were like the faces of lions, and *they were* as swift as the gazelles on the mountains.

9Ezer *was* the first, Obadiah the second, Eliab the third,
10Mishmannah the fourth, Jeremiah the fifth,
11Attai the sixth, Eliel the seventh,
12Johanan the eighth, Elzabad the ninth,
13Jeremiah the tenth, Machbannai the eleventh.
14These of the sons of Gad were captains of the army; he who was least was equal to a hundred and the greatest to a thousand.

15These are the ones who crossed the Jordan in the first month when it was overflowing all its banks and they put to flight all those in the valleys, both to the east and to the west.

16¶ Then some of the sons of Benjamin and Judah came to the stronghold to David.

17And David went out to meet them, and answered and said to them, "If you come peacefully to me to help me, my heart shall be united with you; but if to betray me to my adversaries, since there is no wrong in my hands, may the God of our fathers look on *it* and decide."

## New International

35Ahiam son of Sacar the Hararite,
Eliphal son of Ur,
36Hepher the Mekerathite,
Ahijah the Pelonite,
37Hezro the Carmelite,
Naarai son of Ezbai,
38Joel the brother of Nathan,
Mibhar son of Hagri,
39Zelek the Ammonite,
Naharai the Berothite, the armor-bearer of Joab son of Zeruiah,
40Ira the Ithrite,
Gareb the Ithrite,
41Uriah the Hittite,
Zabad son of Ahlai,
42Adina son of Shiza the Reubenite, who was chief of the Reubenites, and the thirty with him,
43Hanan son of Maacah,
Joshaphat the Mithnite,
44Uzzia the Ashterathite,
Shama and Jeiel the sons of Hotham the Aroerite,
45Jediael son of Shimri,
his brother Joha the Tizite,
46Eliel the Mahavite,
Jeribai and Joshaviah the sons of Elnaam,
Ithmah the Moabite,
47Eliel, Obed and Jaasiel the Mezobaite.

*Warriors Join David*

12 THESE WERE the men who came to David at Ziklag, while he was banished from the presence of Saul son of Kish (they were among the warriors who helped him in battle;
2they were armed with bows and were able to shoot arrows or to sling stones right-handed or left-handed; they were kinsmen of Saul from the tribe of Benjamin):

3Ahiezer their chief and Joash the sons of Shemaah the Gibeathite; Jeziel and Pelet the sons of Azmaveth; Beracah, Jehu the Anathothite,
4and Ishmaiah the Gibeonite, a mighty man among the Thirty, who was a leader of the Thirty; Jeremiah, Jahaziel, Johanan, Jozabad the Gederathite,
5Eluzai, Jerimoth, Bealiah, Shemariah and Shephatiah the Haruphite;
6Elkanah, Isshiah, Azarel, Joezer and Jashobeam the Korahites;
7and Joelah and Zebadiah the sons of Jeroham from Gedor.

8Some Gadites defected to David at his stronghold in the desert. They were brave warriors, ready for battle and able to handle the shield and spear. Their faces were the faces of lions, and they were as swift as gazelles in the mountains.

9Ezer was the chief,
Obadiah the second in command, Eliab the third,
10Mishmannah the fourth, Jeremiah the fifth,
11Attai the sixth, Eliel the seventh,
12Johanan the eighth, Elzabad the ninth,
13Jeremiah the tenth and Macbannai the eleventh.

14These Gadites were army commanders; the least was a match for a hundred, and the greatest for a thousand.
15It was they who crossed the Jordan in the first month when it was overflowing all its banks, and they put to flight everyone living in the valleys, to the east and to the west.

16Other Benjamites and some men from Judah also came to David in his stronghold.
17David went out to meet them and said to them, "If you have come to me in peace, to help me, I am ready to have you unite with me. But if you have come to betray me to my enemies when my hands are free from violence, may the God of our fathers see it and judge you."

## King James

18 Then the spirit came upon Amasai, *who was* chief of the captains, *and he said,* Thine *are we,* David, and on thy side, thou son of Jesse: peace, peace *be* unto thee, and peace *be* to thine helpers; for thy God helpeth thee. Then David received them, and made them captains of the band.

19 And there fell *some* of Manasseh to David, when he came with the Philistines against Saul to battle: but they helped them not: for the lords of the Philistines upon advisement sent him away, saying, He will fall to his master Saul to *the jeopardy of* our heads.

20 As he went to Ziklag, there fell to him of Manasseh, Adnah, and Jozabad, and Jediael, and Michael, and Jozabad, and Elihu, and Zilthai, captains of the thousands that *were* of Manasseh.

21 And they helped David against the band *of the rovers:* for they *were* all mighty men of valour, and were captains in the host.

22 For at *that* time day by day there came to David to help him, until *it was* a great host, like the host of God.

23 ¶ And these *are* the numbers of the bands *that were* ready armed to the war, *and* came to David to Hebron, to turn the kingdom of Saul to him, according to the word of the LORD.

24 The children of Judah that bare shield and spear *were* six thousand and eight hundred, ready armed to the war.

25 Of the children of Simeon, mighty men of valour for the war, seven thousand and one hundred.

26 Of the children of Levi four thousand and six hundred.

27 And Jehoiada *was* the leader of the Aaronites, and with him *were* three thousand and seven hundred;

28 And Zadok, a young man mighty of valour, and of his father's house twenty and two captains.

29 And of the children of Benjamin, the kindred of Saul, three thousand: for hitherto the greatest part of them had kept the ward of the house of Saul.

30 And of the children of Ephraim twenty thousand and eight hundred, mighty men of valour, famous throughout the house of their fathers.

31 And of the half tribe of Manasseh eighteen thousand, which were expressed by name, to come and make David king.

32 And of the children of Issachar, *which were men* that had understanding of the times, to know what Israel ought to do; the heads of them *were* two hundred; and all their brethren *were* at their commandment.

33 Of Zebulun, such as went forth to battle, expert in war, with all instruments of war, fifty thousand, which could keep rank: *they were* not of double heart.

34 And of Naphtali a thousand captains, and with them with shield and spear thirty and seven thousand.

35 And of the Danites expert in war twenty and eight thousand and six hundred.

36 And of Asher, such as went forth to battle, expert in war, forty thousand.

37 And on the other side of Jordan, of the Reubenites, and the Gadites, and of the half tribe of Manasseh, with all manner of instruments of war for the battle, an hundred and twenty thousand.

38 All these men of war, that could keep rank, came with a perfect heart to Hebron, to make David king over all Israel: and all the rest also of Israel *were* of one heart to make David king.

39 And there they were with David three days, eating and drinking: for their brethren had prepared for them.

40 Moreover they that were nigh them, *even* unto Issachar and Zebulun and Naphtali, brought bread on asses, and on camels, and on mules, and on oxen, *and* meat, meal, cakes of figs, and bunches of raisins, and wine, and oil, and oxen, and sheep abundantly: for *there was* joy in Israel.

## Amplified

18 Then the Spirit came upon Amasai, who was chief of the captains, and he said, Yours we are, David, and on your side, you son of Jesse! Peace, peace be to you, and peace be to your helpers, for your God helps you. Then David received them, and made them officers of his troops.

19 Some of the men of Manasseh deserted to David when he came with the Philistines for the battle against Saul. But [David's] men did not actually fight with them, for the lords of the Philistines upon advisement sent him away, saying, He will desert to his master Saul at the risk of our heads. [I Sam. 29:2-9.]

20 As David went to Ziklag, there deserted to him of Manasseh, Adnah, Jozabad, Jediael, Michael, Jozabad, Elihu, and Zillethai, chiefs of thousands in Manasseh.

21 They helped David against the band of raiders; for they were all mighty men of courage, and [all seven] became commanders in [his] army.

22 For at that time day by day men kept coming to David to help him, until there was a great army, like the army of God.

23 These are the numbers of the armed divisions who came to David at Hebron, to turn the kingdom of Saul to him, according to the word of the Lord.

24 Those of Judah who bore shield and spear were 6,800, armed for war.

25 Those of Simeon, mighty and brave warriors, 7,100.

26 Those of Levi, 4,600.

27 Jehoiada was the leader of the Aaronite [priests], and with him were 3,700.

28 And Zadok, a young man mighty in valor, and twenty-two captains from his own father's house.

29 Of the Benjamites, the kindred of [King] Saul, 3,000; hitherto the majority of them had kept their allegiance [to Saul] *and* the charge of the house of Saul.

30 Of the Ephraimites 20,800, mighty in valor, famous in their fathers' houses.

31 Of the half-tribe of Manasseh 18,000 who were mentioned by name to come and make David king.

32 And of Issachar men who had understanding of the times, to know what Israel ought to do, 200 chiefs, and all their kinsmen were under their command.

33 Of Zebulun 50,000 experienced troops, fitted out with all kinds of weapons *and* instruments of war, that could order and set the battle in array; not of double purpose *but* stable and trusty.

34 Of Naphtali 1,000 captains, and with them 37,000 [of the rank and file armed] with shield and spear.

35 Of Dan 28,600 that could set the battle in array.

36 Of Asher, able to go forth to battle, fit for active service, 40,000.

37 On the other [the east] side of the Jordan River, of Reuben, and Gad, and the half-tribe of Manasseh, 120,000 men armed with all the weapons *and* instruments of war.

38 All these being men of war arrayed in battle order, came with a perfect *and* sincere heart to Hebron, to make David king over all Israel; and all the rest also of Israel were of one mind to make David king.

39 And they were there with David for three days, eating and drinking; for their brethren had prepared for them.

40 Also those who were near them, from as far as Issachar, Zebulun and Naphtali, brought food on donkeys, camels, mules, and oxen; abundant supplies of meal, cakes of figs, bunches of raisins, wine, oil, oxen and sheep; for there was joy in Israel.

## New American Standard

18 Then the Spirit came upon Amasai, who was the chief of the
thirty, *and he said,*

> " *We* are yours, O David,
> And with you, O son of Jesse!
> Peace, peace to you,
> And peace to him who helps you;
> Indeed, your God helps you!"

Then David received them and made them captains of the band.

19 ¶ From Manasseh also some defected to David, when he was
about to go to battle with the Philistines against Saul. But they did
not help them, for the lords of the Philistines after consultation
sent him away, saying, "At *the cost of* our heads he may defect to
his master Saul."

20 As he went to Ziklag, there defected to him from Manasseh:
Adnah, Jozabad, Jediael, Michael, Jozabad, Elihu, and Zillethai,
captains of thousands who belonged to Manasseh.

21 And they helped David against the band of raiders, for they
were all mighty men of valor, and were captains in the army.

22 For day by day *men* came to David to help him, until there was
a great army like the army of God.

*Supporters Gathered at Hebron*

23 ¶ Now these are the numbers of the divisions equipped for
war, who came to David at Hebron, to turn the kingdom of Saul
to him, according to the word of the LORD.

24 The sons of Judah who bore shield and spear *were* 6,800,
equipped for war.

25 Of the sons of Simeon, mighty men of valor for war, 7,100.

26 Of the sons of Levi 4,600.

27 Now Jehoiada was the leader of *the house of* Aaron, and with
him were 3,700,

28 also Zadok, a young man mighty of valor, and of his father's
house twenty-two captains.

29 And of the sons of Benjamin, Saul's kinsmen, 3,000; for until
now the greatest part of them had kept their allegiance to the
house of Saul.

30 And of the sons of Ephraim 20,800, mighty men of valor,
famous men in their fathers' households.

31 And of the half-tribe of Manasseh 18,000, who were designated by name to come and make David king.

32 And of the sons of Issachar, men who understood the times,
with knowledge of what Israel should do, their chiefs were two
hundred; and all their kinsmen were at their command.

33 Of Zebulun, there were 50,000 who went out in the army,
who could draw up in battle formation with all kinds of weapons
of war and helped *David* with an undivided heart.

34 And of Naphtali *there were* 1,000 captains, and with them
37,000 with shield and spear.

35 And of the Danites who could draw up in battle formation,
*there were* 28,600.

36 And of Asher *there were* 40,000 who went out in the army to
draw up in battle formation.

37 And from the other side of the Jordan, of the Reubenites and
the Gadites and of the half-tribe of Manasseh, *there were* 120,000
with all *kinds* of weapons of war for the battle.

38 ¶ All these, being men of war, who could draw up in battle
formation, came to Hebron with a perfect heart, to make David
king over all Israel; and all the rest also of Israel were of one mind
to make David king.

39 And they were there with David three days, eating and drinking; for their kinsmen had prepared for them.

40 Moreover those who were near to them, *even* as far as Issachar
and Zebulun and Naphtali, brought food on donkeys, camels,
mules, and on oxen, great quantities of flour cakes, fig cakes and
bunches of raisins, wine, oil, oxen and sheep. There was joy
indeed in Israel.

## New International

18 Then the Spirit came upon Amasai, chief of the Thirty, and
he said:

> "We are yours, O David!
> We are with you, O son of Jesse!
> Success, success to you,
> and success to those who help you,
> for your God will help you."

So David received them and made them leaders of his raiding
bands.

19 Some of the men of Manasseh defected to David when he
went with the Philistines to fight against Saul. (He and his men did
not help the Philistines because, after consultation, their rulers
sent him away. They said, "It will cost us our heads if he deserts
to his master Saul.")
20 When David went to Ziklag, these were the
men of Manasseh who defected to him: Adnah, Jozabad, Jediael,
Michael, Jozabad, Elihu and Zillethai, leaders of units of a thousand in Manasseh.
21 They helped David against raiding bands, for
all of them were brave warriors, and they were commanders in his
army.
22 Day after day men came to help David, until he had a great
army, like the army of God.[a]

*Others Join David at Hebron*

23 These are the numbers of the men armed for battle who came
to David at Hebron to turn Saul's kingdom over to him, as the
LORD had said:

24 men of Judah, carrying shield and spear—6,800 armed for battle;

25 men of Simeon, warriors ready for battle—7,100;

26 men of Levi—4,600,
27 including Jehoiada, leader of the family of Aaron, with 3,700 men,
28 and Zadok, a brave young warrior, with 22 officers from his family;

29 men of Benjamin, Saul's kinsmen—3,000, most of whom had remained loyal to Saul's house until then;

30 men of Ephraim, brave warriors, famous in their own clans—20,800;

31 men of half the tribe of Manasseh, designated by name to come and make David king—18,000;

32 men of Issachar, who understood the times and knew what Israel should do—200 chiefs, with all their relatives under their command;

33 men of Zebulun, experienced soldiers prepared for battle with every type of weapon, to help David with undivided loyalty—50,000;

34 men of Naphtali—1,000 officers, together with 37,000 men carrying shields and spears;

35 men of Dan, ready for battle—28,600;

36 men of Asher, experienced soldiers prepared for battle—40,000;

37 and from east of the Jordan, men of Reuben, Gad and the half-tribe of Manasseh, armed with every type of weap-on—120,000.

38 All these were fighting men who volunteered to serve in the
ranks. They came to Hebron fully determined to make David king
over all Israel. All the rest of the Israelites were also of one mind
to make David king.
39 The men spent three days there with David,
eating and drinking, for their families had supplied provisions for
them.
40 Also, their neighbors from as far away as Issachar, Zebulun and Naphtali came bringing food on donkeys, camels, mules
and oxen. There were plentiful supplies of flour, fig cakes, raisin
cakes, wine, oil, cattle and sheep, for there was joy in Israel.

NIV [a] 22 Or *a great and mighty army*

## King James

**13** AND DAVID consulted with the captains of thousands and hundreds, *and* with every leader.

2 And David said unto all the congregation of Israel, If *it seem* good unto you, and *that it be* of the LORD our God, let us send abroad unto our brethren every where, *that are* left in all the land of Israel, and with them *also* to the priests and Levites *which are* in their cities *and* suburbs, that they may gather themselves unto us:

3 And let us bring again the ark of our God to us: for we inquired not at it in the days of Saul.

4 And all the congregation said that they would do so: for the thing was right in the eyes of all the people.

5 So David gathered all Israel together, from Shihor of Egypt even unto the entering of Hemath, to bring the ark of God from Kirjath-jearim.

6 And David went up, and all Israel, to Baalah, *that is,* to Kirjath-jearim, which *belonged* to Judah, to bring up thence the ark of God the LORD, that dwelleth *between* the cherubims, whose name is called *on it.*

7 And they carried the ark of God in a new cart out of the house of Abinadab: and Uzza and Ahio drave the cart.

8 And David and all Israel played before God with all *their* might, and with singing, and with harps, and with psalteries, and with timbrels, and with cymbals, and with trumpets.

9 ¶ And when they came unto the threshingfloor of Chidon, Uzza put forth his hand to hold the ark; for the oxen stumbled.

10 And the anger of the LORD was kindled against Uzza, and he smote him, because he put his hand to the ark: and there he died before God.

11 And David was displeased, because the LORD had made a breach upon Uzza: wherefore that place is called Perez-uzza to this day.

12 And David was afraid of God that day, saying, How shall I bring the ark of God *home* to me?

13 So David brought not the ark *home* to himself to the city of David, but carried it aside into the house of Obed-edom the Gittite.

14 And the ark of God remained with the family of Obed-edom in his house three months. And the LORD blessed the house of Obed-edom, and all that he had.

**14** NOW HIRAM king of Tyre sent messengers to David, and timber of cedars, with masons and carpenters, to build him an house.

2 And David perceived that the LORD had confirmed him king over Israel, for his kingdom was lifted up on high, because of his people Israel.

3 ¶ And David took more wives at Jerusalem: and David begat more sons and daughters.

4 Now these *are* the names of *his* children which he had in Jerusalem; Shammua, and Shobab, Nathan, and Solomon,

5 And Ibhar, and Elishua, and Elpalet,

6 And Nogah, and Nepheg, and Japhia,

7 And Elishama, and Beeliada, and Eliphalet.

8 ¶ And when the Philistines heard that David was anointed king over all Israel, all the Philistines went up to seek David. And David heard *of it,* and went out against them.

9 And the Philistines came and spread themselves in the valley of Rephaim.

## Amplified

**13** DAVID CONSULTED the captains of thousands and hundreds, even with every leader.

2 And David said to all the assembly of Israel, If it seems good to you, and if it is of the Lord our God, let us send abroad everywhere to our brethren who are left in all the land of Israel, and with them to the priests and Levites in their cities that have suburbs *and* pasture lands, that they may gather together with us.

3 And let us bring again the ark of our God to us; for we did not seek it during the days of Saul.

4 And all the assembly agreed to do so, for the thing seemed right in the eyes of all the people.

5 So David gathered all Israel together from the Shihor, the brook of Egypt [that marked the southeast border of Palestine] to the entrance of Hemath, to bring the ark of God from Kiriath-jearim.

6 And David and all Israel went up to Baalah, that is, to Kiriath-jearim which belonged to Judah, to bring up from there the ark of God the Lord, which is called by the name of Him Who sits (enthroned) above the cherubim.

7 And they carried the ark of God on a new cart, and brought it out of the house of Abinadab; and Uzza and Ahio (his brother) drove the cart.

8 And David and all Israel merrily celebrated before God with all their might, with songs and lyres and harps and tambourines and cymbals and trumpets.

9 And when they came to the threshing floor of Chidon, Uzza put out his hand to steady the ark, for the oxen [that were drawing the cart] stumbled *and* were restive.

10 And the anger of the Lord was kindled against Uzza, and He smote him, because he touched the ark, and there he died before God. [Num. 4:15.]

11 And David was offended because the Lord had broken forth upon Uzza; that place to this day is called Perez-uzza—the breaking forth upon Uzza.

12 And David was afraid of God that day; and he said, How can I bring the ark of God home to me?

13 So David did not bring the ark home to the city of David, but carried it aside into the house of Obed-edom the Gittite [a Levitical porter, born in Gath-rimmon]. [Cp. 15:24; Josh. 21:20, 24.]

14 And the ark of God remained with the family of Obed-edom in his house three months. And the Lord blessed the house of Obed-edom, and all that he had.

**14** AND HIRAM King of Tyre sent messengers to David, and cedar timbers, with masons and carpenters to build him a house.

2 And David perceived that the Lord had established *and* confirmed him king over Israel, for his kingdom was exalted highly for His people Israel's sake.

3 And David took more wives to Jerusalem; and [he] became the father of more sons and daughters.

4 Now these are the names of the children whom he had in Jerusalem: Shammua, Shobab, Nathan, Solomon,

5 Ibhar, Elishua, Elpelet,

6 Nogah, Nepheg, Japhia,

7 Elishama, Beeliada, and Eliphelet.

8 And when the Philistines heard that David was anointed king over all Israel, [they] all went up to seek David. And [he] heard of it and went out before them.

9 Now the Philistines had come and made a raid in the valley of Rephaim.

## New American Standard

*Peril in Transporting the Ark*

**13** THEN DAVID consulted with the captains of the thousands and the hundreds, even with every leader.
2And David said to all the assembly of Israel, "If it seems good
to you, and if it is from the LORD our God, let us send everywhere
to our kinsmen who remain in all the land of Israel, also to the
priests and Levites who are with them in their cities with pasture
lands, that they may meet with us;
3and let us bring back the ark of our God to us, for we did not
seek it in the days of Saul."
4Then all the assembly said that they would do so, for the thing
was right in the eyes of all the people.
5So David assembled all Israel together, from the Shihor of
Egypt even to the entrance of Hamath, to bring the ark of God from
Kiriath-jearim.
6And David and all Israel went up to Baalah, *that is,* to Kiriath-
jearim, which belongs to Judah, to bring up from there the ark of
God, the LORD who is enthroned *above* the cherubim, where His
name is called.
7And they carried the ark of God on a new cart from the house
of Abinadab, and Uzza and Ahio drove the cart.
8And David and all Israel were celebrating before God with all
*their* might, even with songs and with lyres, harps, tambourines,
cymbals, and with trumpets.
9¶ When they came to the threshing floor of Chidon, Uzza put
out his hand to hold the ark, because the oxen nearly upset *it.*
10And the anger of the LORD burned against Uzza, so He struck
him down because he put out his hand to the ark; and he died there
before God.
11Then David became angry because of the LORD'S outburst
against Uzza; and he called that place [a]Perez-uzza to this day.
12And David was afraid of God that day, saying, "How can I
bring the ark of God *home* to me?"
13So David did not take the ark with him to the city of David,
but took it aside to the house of Obed-edom the Gittite.
14Thus the ark of God remained with the family of Obed-edom
in his house three months; and the LORD blessed the family of
Obed-edom with all that he had.

*David's Family Enlarged*

**14** NOW HIRAM king of Tyre sent messengers to David with
cedar trees, masons, and carpenters, to build a house for
him.
2And David realized that the LORD had established him as king
over Israel, *and* that his kingdom was highly exalted, for the sake
of His people Israel.
3¶ Then David took more wives at Jerusalem, and David
became the father of more sons and daughters.
4And these are the names of the children born *to him* in Jerusalem: Shammua, Shobab, Nathan, Solomon,
5Ibhar, Elishua, Elpelet,
6Nogah, Nepheg, Japhia,
7Elishama, Beeliada and Eliphelet.

*Philistines Defeated*

8¶ When the Philistines heard that David had been anointed
king over all Israel, all the Philistines went up in search of David;
and David heard of it and went out against them.
9Now the Philistines had come and made a raid in the valley
of Rephaim.

NAS [a] I.e., the breakthrough of Uzza

## New International

*Bringing Back the Ark*

**13** DAVID CONFERRED with each of his officers, the commanders of thousands and commanders of hundreds. 2He
then said to the whole assembly of Israel, "If it seems good to you
and if it is the will of the LORD our God, let us send word far and
wide to the rest of our brothers throughout the territories of Israel,
and also to the priests and Levites who are with them in their
towns and pasturelands, to come and join us. 3Let us bring the ark
of our God back to us, for we did not inquire of[b] it[c] during the
reign of Saul." 4The whole assembly agreed to do this, because it
seemed right to all the people.
5So David assembled all the Israelites, from the Shihor River in
Egypt to Lebo[d] Hamath, to bring the ark of God from Kiriath
Jearim. 6David and all the Israelites with him went to Baalah of
Judah (Kiriath Jearim) to bring up from there the ark of God the
LORD, who is enthroned between the cherubim—the ark that is
called by the Name.
7They moved the ark of God from Abinadab's house on a new
cart, with Uzzah and Ahio guiding it. 8David and all the Israelites
were celebrating with all their might before God, with songs and
with harps, lyres, tambourines, cymbals and trumpets.
9When they came to the threshing floor of Kidon, Uzzah
reached out his hand to steady the ark, because the oxen stumbled.
10The LORD's anger burned against Uzzah, and he struck him
down because he had put his hand on the ark. So he died there
before God.
11Then David was angry because the LORD's wrath had broken
out against Uzzah, and to this day that place is called Perez Uzzah.[e]
12David was afraid of God that day and asked, "How can I ever
bring the ark of God to me?" 13He did not take the ark to be with
him in the City of David. Instead, he took it aside to the house of
Obed-Edom the Gittite. 14The ark of God remained with the family
of Obed-Edom in his house for three months, and the LORD
blessed his household and everything he had.

*David's House and Family*

**14** NOW HIRAM king of Tyre sent messengers to David,
along with cedar logs, stonemasons and carpenters to
build a palace for him. 2And David knew that the LORD had established him as king over Israel and that his kingdom had been
highly exalted for the sake of his people Israel.
3In Jerusalem David took more wives and became the father of
more sons and daughters. 4These are the names of the children
born to him there: Shammua, Shobab, Nathan, Solomon, 5Ibhar,
Elishua, Elpelet, 6Nogah, Nepheg, Japhia, 7Elishama, Beeliada[f]
and Eliphelet.

*David Defeats the Philistines*

8When the Philistines heard that David had been anointed king
over all Israel, they went up in full force to search for him, but
David heard about it and went out to meet them. 9Now the Philistines had come and raided the Valley of Rephaim; 10so David

NIV [b] 3 Or *we neglected* [c] 3 Or *him* [d] 5 Or *to the entrance to* [e] 11 *Perez Uzzah* means *outbreak against Uzzah.* [f] 7 A variant of *Eliada*

## King James

10 And David inquired of God, saying, Shall I go up against the
Philistines? and wilt thou deliver them into mine hand? And the
LORD said unto him, Go up; for I will deliver them into thine hand.
11 So they came up to Baal-perazim; and David smote them
there. Then David said, God hath broken in upon mine enemies
by mine hand like the breaking forth of waters: therefore they
called the name of that place Baal-perazim.
12 And when they had left their gods there, David gave a commandment, and they were burned with fire.
13 And the Philistines yet again spread themselves abroad in the
valley.
14 Therefore David inquired again of God; and God said unto
him, Go not up after them; turn away from them, and come upon
them over against the mulberry trees.
15 And it shall be, when thou shalt hear a sound of going in the
tops of the mulberry trees, *that* then thou shalt go out to battle: for
God is gone forth before thee to smite the host of the Philistines.
16 David therefore did as God commanded him: and they smote
the host of the Philistines from Gibeon even to Gazer.
17 And the fame of David went out into all lands; and the LORD
brought the fear of him upon all nations.

15 AND *DAVID* made him houses in the city of David, and
prepared a place for the ark of God, and pitched for it a
tent.
2 Then David said, None ought to carry the ark of God but the
Levites: for them hath the LORD chosen to carry the ark of God,
and to minister unto him for ever.
3 And David gathered all Israel together to Jerusalem, to bring
up the ark of the LORD unto his place, which he had prepared for
it.
4 And David assembled the children of Aaron, and the Levites:
5 Of the sons of Kohath; Uriel the chief, and his brethren an
hundred and twenty:
6 Of the sons of Merari; Asaiah the chief, and his brethren two
hundred and twenty:
7 Of the sons of Gershom; Joel the chief, and his brethren an
hundred and thirty:
8 Of the sons of Elizaphan; Shemaiah the chief, and his brethren
two hundred:
9 Of the sons of Hebron; Eliel the chief, and his brethren fourscore:
10 Of the sons of Uzziel; Amminadab the chief, and his brethren
an hundred and twelve.
11 And David called for Zadok and Abiathar the priests, and for
the Levites, for Uriel, Asaiah, and Joel, Shemaiah, and Eliel, and
Amminadab,
12 And said unto them, Ye *are* the chief of the fathers of the
Levites: Sanctify yourselves, *both* ye and your brethren, that ye
may bring up the ark of the LORD God of Israel unto *the place that*
I have prepared for it.
13 For because ye *did it* not at the first, the LORD our God made
a breach upon us, for that we sought him not after the due order.
14 So the priests and the Levites sanctified themselves to bring
up the ark of the LORD God of Israel.
15 And the children of the Levites bare the ark of God upon their
shoulders with the staves thereon, as Moses commanded according to the word of the LORD.
16 And David spake to the chief of the Levites to appoint their
brethren *to be* the singers with instruments of music, psalteries and
harps and cymbals, sounding, by lifting up the voice with joy.
17 So the Levites appointed Heman the son of Joel; and of his
brethren, Asaph the son of Berechiah; and of the sons of Merari
their brethren, Ethan the son of Kushaiah;

## Amplified

10 David asked God, Shall I go up against the Philistines? And
will You deliver them into my hand? And the Lord said, Go up,
and I will deliver them into your hand.
11 So [Israel] came up to Baal-perazim, and David smote *the*
[Philistines] there. Then David said, God has broken my enemies
by my hand, like the bursting forth of waters; therefore they called
the name of that place Baal-perazim (Lord of breaking through).
12 [The Philistines] left their gods there; David commanded and
they were burned.
13 And the Philistines again made a raid in the valley.
14 And David inquired again of God; and God said to him, Do
not go up after them; turn away from them, and come [around]
upon them over opposite the mulberry trees.
15 And when you hear a sound of marching in the tops of the
mulberry *or* balsam trees, then go out to battle; for God has gone
out before you to smite the Philistine host.
16 So David did as God commanded him, and they smote the
army of the Philistines from Gibeon even to Gezer.
17 And the fame of David went out into all lands, and the Lord
brought the fear of him upon all nations.

15 DAVID MADE him houses in the city of David, and he
prepared a place for the ark of God, and pitched a tent
for it.
2 Then David said, None should carry the ark of God but the
Levites; for the Lord chose them to carry the ark of God and to
minister to Him for ever.
3 And David assembled all Israel at Jerusalem, to bring up the
ark of the Lord to its place, which he had prepared for it.
4 And David gathered together the sons of Aaron and the Levites:
5 Of the sons of Kohath, Uriel the chief, with 120 kinsmen.
6 Of the sons of Merari, Asaiah the chief, with 220 kinsmen.
7 Of the sons of Gershom, Joel the chief, with 130 kinsmen.
8 Of the sons of Elizaphan, Shemaiah the chief, with 200 kinsmen.
9 Of the sons of Hebron, Eliel the chief, with eighty kinsmen.
10 Of the sons of Uzziel, Amminadab the chief, with 112 kinsmen.
11 And David called for Zadok and Abiathar the priests, and for
the Levites, Uriel, Asaiah, Joel, Shemaiah, Eliel, and Amminadab,
12 And said to them, You are the heads of the fathers' houses
of the Levites; sanctify yourselves, both you and your brethren,
that you may bring up the ark of the Lord, the God of Israel, to
the place that I have prepared for it.
13 For because you bore it not [as God directed] at the first, the
Lord our God broke forth upon us, because we did not seek Him
in the way He ordained. [Num. 1:50; I Chron. 13:7-10.]
14 So the priests and the Levites sanctified themselves to bring
up the ark of the Lord, the God of Israel.
15 The Levites carried the ark of God on their shoulders with the
poles, as Moses commanded by the word of the Lord.
16 David told the chief Levites to appoint their brethren the
singers with instruments of music, harps, lyres and cymbals, to
play loudly and lift up their voices with joy.
17 So the Levites appointed Heman son of Joel, and of his brethren, Asaph son of Berechiah; and of the sons of Merari, their
brethren, Ethan son of Kushaiah;

## New American Standard

10 And David inquired of God, saying, "Shall I go up against the Philistines? And wilt Thou give them into my hand?" Then the LORD said to him, "Go up, for I will give them into your hand."

11 So they came up to Baal-perazim, and David defeated them there; and David said, "God has broken through my enemies by my hand, like the breakthrough of waters." Therefore they named that place [a]Baal-perazim.

12 And they abandoned their gods there; so David gave the order and they were burned with fire.

13¶ And the Philistines made yet another raid in the valley.

14 And David inquired again of God, and God said to him, "You shall not go up after them; circle around behind them, and come at them in front of the balsam trees.

15 "And it shall be when you hear the sound of marching in the tops of the balsam trees, then you shall go out to battle, for God will have gone out before you to strike the army of the Philistines."

16 And David did just as God had commanded him, and they struck down the army of the Philistines from Gibeon even as far as Gezer.

17 Then the fame of David went out into all the lands; and the LORD brought the fear of him on all the nations.

*Plans to Move the Ark to Jerusalem*

**15** NOW *DAVID* built houses for himself in the city of David; and he prepared a place for the ark of God, and pitched a tent for it.

2 Then David said, "No one is to carry the ark of God but the Levites; for the LORD chose them to carry the ark of God, and to minister to Him forever."

3 And David assembled all Israel at Jerusalem, to bring up the ark of the LORD to its place, which he had prepared for it.

4 And David gathered together the sons of Aaron, and the Levites:

5 of the sons of Kohath, Uriel the chief, and 120 of his relatives;

6 of the sons of Merari, Asaiah the chief, and 220 of his relatives;

7 of the sons of Gershom, Joel the chief, and 130 of his relatives;

8 of the sons of Elizaphan, Shemaiah the chief, and 200 of his relatives;

9 of the sons of Hebron, Eliel the chief, and 80 of his relatives;

10 of the sons of Uzziel, Amminadab the chief, and 112 of his relatives.

11 Then David called for Zadok and Abiathar the priests, and for the Levites, for Uriel, Asaiah, Joel, Shemaiah, Eliel, and Amminadab,

12 and said to them, "You are the heads of the fathers' *households* of the Levites; consecrate yourselves both you and your relatives, that you may bring up the ark of the LORD God of Israel, to *the place* that I have prepared for it.

13 "Because you did not *carry it* at the first, the LORD our God made an outburst on us, for we did not seek Him according to the ordinance."

14 So the priests and the Levites consecrated themselves to bring up the ark of the LORD God of Israel.

15 And the sons of the Levites carried the ark of God on their shoulders, with the poles thereon as Moses had commanded according to the word of the LORD.

16¶ Then David spoke to the chiefs of the Levites to appoint their relatives the singers, with instruments of music, harps, lyres, loud-sounding cymbals, to raise sounds of joy.

17 So the Levites appointed Heman the son of Joel, and from his relatives, Asaph the son of Berechiah; and from the sons of Merari their relatives, Ethan the son of Kushaiah,

NAS [a] I.e., the master of breakthrough

## New International

inquired of God: "Shall I go and attack the Philistines? Will you hand them over to me?"

The LORD answered him, "Go, I will hand them over to you."

11 So David and his men went up to Baal Perazim, and there he defeated them. He said, "As waters break out, God has broken out against my enemies by my hand." So that place was called Baal Perazim.[b] 12 The Philistines had abandoned their gods there, and David gave orders to burn them in the fire.

13 Once more the Philistines raided the valley; 14 so David inquired of God again, and God answered him, "Do not go straight up, but circle around them and attack them in front of the balsam trees. 15 As soon as you hear the sound of marching in the tops of the balsam trees, move out to battle, because that will mean God has gone out in front of you to strike the Philistine army." 16 So David did as God commanded him, and they struck down the Philistine army, all the way from Gibeon to Gezer.

17 So David's fame spread throughout every land, and the LORD made all the nations fear him.

*The Ark Brought to Jerusalem*

**15** AFTER DAVID had constructed buildings for himself in the City of David, he prepared a place for the ark of God and pitched a tent for it. 2 Then David said, "No one but the Levites may carry the ark of God, because the LORD chose them to carry the ark of the LORD and to minister before him forever."

3 David assembled all Israel in Jerusalem to bring up the ark of the LORD to the place he had prepared for it. 4 He called together the descendants of Aaron and the Levites:

5 From the descendants of Kohath,
Uriel the leader and 120 relatives;
6 from the descendants of Merari,
Asaiah the leader and 220 relatives;
7 from the descendants of Gershon,[c]
Joel the leader and 130 relatives;
8 from the descendants of Elizaphan,
Shemaiah the leader and 200 relatives;
9 from the descendants of Hebron,
Eliel the leader and 80 relatives;
10 from the descendants of Uzziel,
Amminadab the leader and 112 relatives.

11 Then David summoned Zadok and Abiathar the priests, and Uriel, Asaiah, Joel, Shemaiah, Eliel and Amminadab the Levites. 12 He said to them, "You are the heads of the Levitical families; you and your fellow Levites are to consecrate yourselves and bring up the ark of the LORD, the God of Israel, to the place I have prepared for it. 13 It was because you, the Levites, did not bring it up the first time that the LORD our God broke out in anger against us. We did not inquire of him about how to do it in the prescribed way." 14 So the priests and Levites consecrated themselves in order to bring up the ark of the LORD, the God of Israel. 15 And the Levites carried the ark of God with the poles on their shoulders, as Moses had commanded in accordance with the word of the LORD.

16 David told the leaders of the Levites to appoint their brothers as singers to sing joyful songs, accompanied by musical instruments: lyres, harps and cymbals.

17 So the Levites appointed Heman son of Joel; from his brothers, Asaph son of Berekiah; and from their brothers the Merarites, Ethan son of Kushaiah; 18 and with them their brothers next in

NIV [b] 11 *Baal Perazim* means *the lord who breaks out.* [c] 7 Hebrew *Gershom,* a variant of *Gershon*

## King James

18 And with them their brethren of the second *degree,* Zechariah, Ben, and Jaaziel, and Shemiramoth, and Jehiel, and Unni, Eliab, and Benaiah, and Maaseiah, and Mattithiah, and Elipheleh, and Mikneiah, and Obed-edom, and Jeiel, the porters.

19 So the singers, Heman, Asaph, and Ethan, *were appointed* to sound with cymbals of brass;

20 And Zechariah, and Aziel, and Shemiramoth, and Jehiel, and Unni, and Eliab, and Maaseiah, and Benaiah, with psalteries on Alamoth;

21 And Mattithiah, and Elipheleh, and Mikneiah, and Obed-edom, and Jeiel, and Azaziah, with harps on the Sheminith to excel.

22 And Chenaniah, chief of the Levites, *was* for song: he instructed about the song, because he *was* skilful.

23 And Berechiah and Elkanah *were* doorkeepers for the ark.

24 And Shebaniah, and Jehoshaphat, and Nethaneel, and Amasai, and Zechariah, and Benaiah, and Eliezer, the priests, did blow with the trumpets before the ark of God: and Obed-edom and Jehiah *were* doorkeepers for the ark.

25 ¶ So David, and the elders of Israel, and the captains over thousands, went to bring up the ark of the covenant of the LORD out of the house of Obed-edom with joy.

26 And it came to pass, when God helped the Levites that bare the ark of the covenant of the LORD, that they offered seven bullocks and seven rams.

27 And David *was* clothed with a robe of fine linen, and all the Levites that bare the ark, and the singers, and Chenaniah the master of the song with the singers: David also *had* upon him an ephod of linen.

28 Thus all Israel brought up the ark of the covenant of the LORD with shouting, and with sound of the cornet, and with trumpets, and with cymbals, making a noise with psalteries and harps.

29 ¶ And it came to pass, *as* the ark of the covenant of the LORD came to the city of David, that Michal the daughter of Saul looking out at a window saw king David dancing and playing: and she despised him in her heart.

**16** SO THEY brought the ark of God, and set it in the midst of the tent that David had pitched for it: and they offered burnt sacrifices and peace offerings before God.

2 And when David had made an end of offering the burnt offerings and the peace offerings, he blessed the people in the name of the LORD.

3 And he dealt to every one of Israel, both man and woman, to every one a loaf of bread, and a good piece of flesh, and a flagon *of wine.*

4 ¶ And he appointed *certain* of the Levites to minister before the ark of the LORD, and to record, and to thank and praise the LORD God of Israel:

5 Asaph the chief, and next to him Zechariah, Jeiel, and Shemiramoth, and Jehiel, and Mattithiah, and Eliab, and Benaiah, and Obed-edom: and Jeiel with psalteries and with harps; but Asaph made a sound with cymbals;

6 Benaiah also and Jahaziel the priests with trumpets continually before the ark of the covenant of God.

7 ¶ Then on that day David delivered first *this psalm* to thank the LORD into the hand of Asaph and his brethren.

8 Give thanks unto the LORD, call upon his name, make known his deeds among the people.

9 Sing unto him, sing psalms unto him, talk ye of all his wondrous works.

## Amplified

18 And with them their brethren of the second class, Zechariah, Ben, Jaaziel, Shemiramoth, Jehiel, Unni, Eliab, Benaiah, Maaseiah, Mattithiah, Eliphelehu and Mikneiah, also the gatekeepers, Obed-edom and Jeiel.

19 So the singers, Heman, Asaph, and Ethan, were appointed to sound bronze cymbals;

20 Zechariah, Aziel, Shemiramoth, Jehiel, Unni, Eliab, Maaseiah, and Benaiah, were to play harps [resembling guitars] set to Alamoth [probably the treble voice].

21 Mattithiah, Eliphelehu, Mikneiah, Obed-edom, Jeiel, and Azaziah were to lead with lyres set to Sheminith [the bass voice].

22 Chenaniah, leader of the Levites in singing, was put in charge of carrying the ark *and* lifting up song. He instructed about these matters, because he was skilled *and* able.

23 Berechiah and Elkanah were gatekeepers for the ark.

24 Shebaniah, Joshaphat, Nethanel, Amasai, Zechariah, Benaiah, and Eliezer, the priests, were to blow the trumpets before the ark of God; and Obed-edom and Jehiah (Jeiel) were also gatekeepers for the ark.

25 So David, the elders of Israel, and the captains over thousands, went to bring up the ark of the covenant of the Lord out of the house of Obed-edom with joy.

26 And when God helped the Levites who carried the ark of the covenant of the Lord [with a safe start], they offered seven bulls and seven rams.

27 David was clothed with a robe of fine linen, as were the Levites who bore the ark, and the singers, and Chenaniah, director of the music of the singers. David also wore an ephod [a priestly upper garment] of linen.

28 Thus all Israel brought up the ark of the covenant of the Lord with shouting, sound of the cornet, trumpets, and cymbals, sounding aloud with harps and lyres.

29 As the ark of the covenant of the Lord came to the city of David, Michal [David's wife], daughter of Saul, from a window saw King David leaping as in sport, and she despised him in her heart.

**16** SO THEY brought the ark of God, and set it in the midst of the tent which David had pitched for it; and they offered burnt offerings and peace offerings before God.

2 And when David had finished offering the burnt offerings and the peace offerings, he blessed the people in the name of the Lord.

3 And he distributed to every one of Israel, both man and woman, to every one a loaf of bread, a portion of meat, and a cake of raisins.

4 He appointed Levites to minister before the ark of the Lord, and to celebrate (by calling to mind), thanking and praising the Lord, the God of Israel;

5 Asaph was the chief, next to him Zechariah, Jeiel (Jaaziel), Shemiramoth, Jehiel, Mattithiah, Eliab, and Benaiah, Obed-edom and Jeiel, who were to play harps and lyres; Asaph was to sound the cymbals;

6 Benaiah and Jahaziel the priests were to blow trumpets continually before the ark of the covenant of God.

7 Then on that day David first entrusted to Asaph and his brethren the singing of thanks to the Lord—as their chief task.

8 O give thanks to the Lord; call on His name; make known His doings among the peoples!

9 Sing to Him, sing praises to Him; meditate *and* talk of all His wondrous works *and* devoutly praise them!

## New American Standard

18 and with them their relatives of the second rank, Zechariah,
Ben, Jaaziel, Shemiramoth, Jehiel, Unni, Eliab, Benaiah, Maaseiah,
Mattithiah, Eliphelehu, Mikneiah, Obed-edom, and Jeiel, the gatekeepers.
19 So the singers, Heman, Asaph, and Ethan *were appointed* to
sound aloud cymbals of bronze;
20 and Zechariah, Aziel, Shemiramoth, Jehiel, Unni, Eliab, Maaseiah, and Benaiah, with harps *tuned* to alamoth;
21 and Mattithiah, Eliphelehu, Mikneiah, Obed-edom, Jeiel, and
Azaziah, to lead with lyres tuned to the sheminith.
22 And Chenaniah, chief of the Levites, was *in charge of* the
singing; he gave instruction in singing because he was skillful.
23 And Berechiah and Elkanah were gatekeepers for the ark.
24 And Shebaniah, Joshaphat, Nethanel, Amasai, Zechariah,
Benaiah, and Eliezer, the priests, blew the trumpets before the ark
of God. Obed-edom and Jehiah also *were* gatekeepers for the ark.
**25**¶ So *it was* David, with the elders of Israel and the captains
over thousands, who went to bring up the ark of the covenant of
the LORD from the house of Obed-edom with joy.
26 And it came about because God was helping the Levites who
were carrying the ark of the covenant of the LORD, that they
sacrificed seven bulls and seven rams.
27 Now David was clothed with a robe of fine linen with all the
Levites who were carrying the ark, and the singers and Chenaniah
the leader of the singing *with* the singers. David also wore an
ephod of linen.
28 Thus all Israel brought up the ark of the covenant of the LORD
with shouting, and with sound of the horn, with trumpets, with
loud-sounding cymbals, with harps and lyres.
**29**¶ And it happened when the ark of the covenant of the LORD
came to the city of David, that Michal the daughter of Saul looked
out of the window, and saw King David leaping and making
merry; and she despised him in her heart.

*A Tent for the Ark*

**16** AND THEY brought in the ark of God and placed it inside
the tent which David had pitched for it, and they offered
burnt offerings and peace offerings before God.
2 When David had finished offering the burnt offering and the
peace offerings, he blessed the people in the name of the LORD.
3 And he distributed to everyone of Israel, both man and
woman, to everyone a loaf of bread and a portion *of meat* and a
raisin cake.
**4**¶ And he appointed some of the Levites *as* ministers before
the ark of the LORD, even to celebrate and to thank and praise the
LORD God of Israel:
5 Asaph the chief, and second to him Zechariah, *then* Jeiel,
Shemiramoth, Jehiel, Mattithiah, Eliab, Benaiah, Obed-edom, and
Jeiel, with musical instruments, harps, lyres; also Asaph *played*
loud-sounding cymbals,
6 and Benaiah and Jahaziel the priests *blew* trumpets continually before the ark of the covenant of God.
**7**¶ Then on that day David first assigned Asaph and his relatives to give thanks to the LORD.

*Psalm of Thanksgiving*

8 Oh give thanks to the LORD, call upon His name;
Make known His deeds among the peoples.
9 Sing to Him, sing praises to Him;
[a]Speak of all His wonders.

**NAS** [a] Or, *Meditate on*

## New International

rank: Zechariah,[b] Jaaziel, Shemiramoth, Jehiel, Unni, Eliab, Benaiah, Maaseiah, Mattithiah, Eliphelehu, Mikneiah, Obed-Edom
and Jeiel,[c] the gatekeepers.
19 The musicians Heman, Asaph and Ethan were to sound the
bronze cymbals; 20 Zechariah, Aziel, Shemiramoth, Jehiel, Unni,
Eliab, Maaseiah and Benaiah were to play the lyres according to
*alamoth*,[d] 21 and Mattithiah, Eliphelehu, Mikneiah, Obed-Edom,
Jeiel and Azaziah were to play the harps, directing according to
*sheminith*.[e] 22 Kenaniah the head Levite was in charge of the singing; that was his responsibility because he was skillful at it.
23 Berekiah and Elkanah were to be doorkeepers for the ark.
24 Shebaniah, Joshaphat, Nethanel, Amasai, Zechariah, Benaiah
and Eliezer the priests were to blow trumpets before the ark of
God. Obed-Edom and Jehiah were also to be doorkeepers for the
ark.
25 So David and the elders of Israel and the commanders of units
of a thousand went to bring up the ark of the covenant of the LORD
from the house of Obed-Edom, with rejoicing. 26 Because God had
helped the Levites who were carrying the ark of the covenant of
the LORD, seven bulls and seven rams were sacrificed. 27 Now
David was clothed in a robe of fine linen, as were all the Levites
who were carrying the ark, and as were the singers, and Kenaniah,
who was in charge of the singing of the choirs. David also wore
a linen ephod. 28 So all Israel brought up the ark of the covenant
of the LORD with shouts, with the sounding of rams' horns and
trumpets, and of cymbals, and the playing of lyres and harps.
29 As the ark of the covenant of the LORD was entering the City
of David, Michal daughter of Saul watched from a window. And
when she saw King David dancing and celebrating, she despised
him in her heart.

**16** THEY BROUGHT the ark of God and set it inside the tent
that David had pitched for it, and they presented burnt
offerings and fellowship offerings[f] before God. 2 After David had
finished sacrificing the burnt offerings and fellowship offerings, he
blessed the people in the name of the LORD. 3 Then he gave a loaf
of bread, a cake of dates and a cake of raisins to each Israelite man
and woman.
4 He appointed some of the Levites to minister before the ark of
the LORD, to make petition, to give thanks, and to praise the LORD,
the God of Israel: 5 Asaph was the chief, Zechariah second, then
Jeiel, Shemiramoth, Jehiel, Mattithiah, Eliab, Benaiah, Obed-
Edom and Jeiel. They were to play the lyres and harps, Asaph was
to sound the cymbals, 6 and Benaiah and Jahaziel the priests were
to blow the trumpets regularly before the ark of the covenant of
God.

*David's Psalm of Thanks*

7 That day David first committed to Asaph and his associates
this psalm of thanks to the LORD:

8 Give thanks to the LORD, call on his name;
make known among the nations what he has done.
9 Sing to him, sing praise to him;
tell of all his wonderful acts.

**NIV** [b] *18* Three Hebrew manuscripts and most Septuagint manuscripts (see also verse 20 and 1 Chron. 16:5); most Hebrew manuscripts *Zechariah son and* or *Zechariah, Ben and* [c] *18* Hebrew; Septuagint (see also verse 21) *Jeiel and Azaziah* [d] *20* Probably a musical term [e] *21* Probably a musical term [f] *1* Traditionally *peace offerings;* also in verse 2

## King James

10 Glory ye in his holy name: let the heart of them rejoice that seek the LORD.

11 Seek the LORD and his strength, seek his face continually.

12 Remember his marvellous works that he hath done, his wonders, and the judgments of his mouth;

13 O ye seed of Israel his servant, ye children of Jacob, his chosen ones.

14 He *is* the LORD our God; his judgments *are* in all the earth.

15 Be ye mindful always of his covenant; the word *which* he commanded to a thousand generations;

16 *Even of the covenant* which he made with Abraham, and of his oath unto Isaac;

17 And hath confirmed the same to Jacob for a law, *and* to Israel *for* an everlasting covenant,

18 Saying, Unto thee will I give the land of Canaan, the lot of your inheritance;

19 When ye were but few, even a few, and strangers in it.

20 And *when* they went from nation to nation, and from *one* kingdom to another people;

21 He suffered no man to do them wrong: yea, he reproved kings for their sakes,

22 *Saying*, Touch not mine anointed, and do my prophets no harm.

23 Sing unto the LORD, all the earth; show forth from day to day his salvation.

24 Declare his glory among the heathen; his marvellous works among all nations.

25 For great *is* the LORD, and greatly to be praised: he also *is* to be feared above all gods.

26 For all the gods of the people *are* idols: but the LORD made the heavens.

27 Glory and honour *are* in his presence; strength and gladness *are* in his place.

28 Give unto the LORD, ye kindreds of the people, give unto the LORD glory and strength.

29 Give unto the LORD the glory *due* unto his name: bring an offering, and come before him: worship the LORD in the beauty of holiness.

30 Fear before him, all the earth: the world also shall be stable, that it be not moved.

31 Let the heavens be glad, and let the earth rejoice: and let *men* say among the nations, The LORD reigneth.

32 Let the sea roar, and the fulness thereof: let the fields rejoice, and all that *is* therein.

33 Then shall the trees of the wood sing out at the presence of the LORD, because he cometh to judge the earth.

34 O give thanks unto the LORD; for *he is* good; for his mercy *endureth* for ever.

35 And say ye, Save us, O God of our salvation, and gather us together, and deliver us from the heathen, that we may give thanks to thy holy name, *and* glory in thy praise.

36 Blessed *be* the LORD God of Israel for ever and ever. And all the people said, Amen, and praised the LORD.

37 ¶ So he left there before the ark of the covenant of the LORD Asaph and his brethren, to minister before the ark continually, as every day's work required:

## Amplified

10 Glory in His holy name; let the heart of those rejoice who seek the Lord!

11 Seek the Lord and His strength, yearn for *and* seek His face *and* to be in His presence continually!

12 (Earnestly) remember the marvelous deeds which He has done, His miracles, and the judgments He uttered [as in Egypt],

13 O you offspring of [Abraham and] of Israel His servants, you children of Jacob, His chosen ones!

14 He is the Lord our God; His judgments are in all the earth.

15 Be mindful of His covenant forever, the promise which He commanded *and* established to a thousand generations,

16 Of the covenant which He made with Abraham, and of His sworn promise to Isaac;

17 He confirmed it as a statute to Jacob, and to Israel for an everlasting covenant, [Gen. 35:11, 12.]

18 Saying, To you I will give the land of Canaan, the measured portion of your possession *and* inheritance.

19 When they were but few, even a very few, and only temporary residents *and* strangers in it.

20 When they went from nation to nation, and from kingdom to another people,

21 He allowed no man to do them wrong; yes, He reproved kings for their sakes, [Gen. 12:17; 20:3; Exod. 7:15-18.]

22 Saying, Touch not My anointed, and do My prophets no harm. [Gen. 20:7.]

23 Sing to the Lord, all the earth; show forth from day to day His salvation.

24 Declare His glory among the nations, His marvelous works among all peoples.

25 For great is the Lord, and greatly to be praised; He also is to be (reverently) feared above all so-called gods.

26 For all the gods of the people are [lifeless] idols, but the Lord made the heavens.

27 Honor and majesty are [found] in His presence; strength and joy are [found] in His sanctuary.

28 Ascribe to the Lord, you families of the people, ascribe to the Lord glory and strength.

29 Ascribe to the Lord the glory due His name; bring an offering, and come before Him; worship the Lord in the beauty of holiness *and* in holy array.

30 Tremble *and* reverently fear before Him, all the earth's peoples; the world also shall be established so it cannot be moved.

31 Let the heavens be glad, and let the earth rejoice, and let men say among the nations, The Lord reigns!

32 Let the sea roar, and all the things that fill it; let the fields rejoice, and all that is in them.

33 Then shall the trees of the wood sing out for joy before the Lord, for He comes to judge *and* govern the earth.

34 O give thanks to the Lord, for He is good; for His mercy *and* loving-kindness endure for ever!

35 And say, Save us, O God of our salvation; gather us together, and deliver us from the nations, that we may give thanks to Your holy name, and glory in Your praise.

36 Blessed be the Lord, the God of Israel for ever and ever! And all the people said, Amen! and praised the Lord.

37 So David left Asaph and his brethren before the ark of the covenant of the Lord to minister before the ark continually, as each day's work required,

## New American Standard

10 Glory in His holy name;
Let the heart of those who seek the LORD be glad.
11 Seek the LORD and His strength;
Seek His face continually.
12 Remember His wonderful deeds which He has done,
His marvels and the judgments from His mouth,
13 O seed of Israel His servant,
Sons of Jacob, His chosen ones!
14 He is the LORD our God;
His judgments are in all the earth.
15 Remember His covenant forever,
The word which He commanded to a thousand generations,
16 *The covenant* which He made with Abraham,
And His oath to Isaac.
17 He also confirmed it to Jacob for a statute,
To Israel as an everlasting covenant,
18 Saying, "To you I will give the land of Canaan,
As the portion of your inheritance."
19 When they were only a few in number,
Very few, and strangers in it,
20 And they wandered about from nation to nation,
And from *one* kingdom to another people,
21 He permitted no man to oppress them,
And He reproved kings for their sakes, *saying*,
22 "Do not touch My anointed ones,
And do My prophets no harm."
23 Sing to the LORD, all the earth;
Proclaim good tidings of His salvation from day to day.
24 Tell of His glory among the nations,
His wonderful deeds among all the peoples.
25 For great is the LORD, and greatly to be praised;
He also is to be feared above all gods.
26 For all the gods of the peoples are idols,
But the LORD made the heavens.
27 Splendor and majesty are before Him,
Strength and joy are in His place.
28 Ascribe to the LORD, O families of the peoples,
Ascribe to the LORD glory and strength.
29 Ascribe to the LORD the glory due His name;
Bring an offering, and come before Him;
Worship the LORD in holy array.
30 Tremble before Him, all the earth;
Indeed, the world is firmly established, it will not be moved.
31 Let the heavens be glad, and let the earth rejoice;
And let them say among the nations, "The LORD reigns."
32 Let the sea roar, and all it contains;
Let the field exult, and all that is in it.
33 Then the trees of the forest will sing for joy before the LORD;
For He is coming to judge the earth.
34 O give thanks to the LORD, for *He is* good;
For His lovingkindness is everlasting.
35 Then say, "Save us, O God of our salvation,
And gather us and deliver us from the nations,
To give thanks to Thy holy name,
And glory in Thy praise."
36 Blessed be the LORD, the God of Israel,
From everlasting even to everlasting.
Then all the people said, "Amen," and praised the LORD.

*Worship before the Ark*

37¶ So he left Asaph and his relatives there before the ark of the covenant of the LORD, to minister before the ark continually, as every day's work required;

## New International

10Glory in his holy name;
let the hearts of those who seek the LORD rejoice.
11Look to the LORD and his strength;
seek his face always.
12Remember the wonders he has done,
his miracles, and the judgments he pronounced,
13O descendants of Israel his servant,
O sons of Jacob, his chosen ones.

14He is the LORD our God;
his judgments are in all the earth.
15He remembers[a] his covenant forever,
the word he commanded, for a thousand generations,
16the covenant he made with Abraham,
the oath he swore to Isaac.
17He confirmed it to Jacob as a decree,
to Israel as an everlasting covenant:
18"To you I will give the land of Canaan
as the portion you will inherit."

19When they were but few in number,
few indeed, and strangers in it,
20they[b] wandered from nation to nation,
from one kingdom to another.
21He allowed no man to oppress them;
for their sake he rebuked kings:
22"Do not touch my anointed ones;
do my prophets no harm."

23Sing to the LORD, all the earth;
proclaim his salvation day after day.
24Declare his glory among the nations,
his marvelous deeds among all peoples.
25For great is the LORD and most worthy of praise;
he is to be feared above all gods.
26For all the gods of the nations are idols,
but the LORD made the heavens.
27Splendor and majesty are before him;
strength and joy in his dwelling place.
28Ascribe to the LORD, O families of nations,
ascribe to the LORD glory and strength,
29 ascribe to the LORD the glory due his name.
Bring an offering and come before him;
worship the LORD in the splendor of his[c] holiness.
30Tremble before him, all the earth!
The world is firmly established; it cannot be moved.
31Let the heavens rejoice, let the earth be glad;
let them say among the nations, "The LORD reigns!"
32Let the sea resound, and all that is in it;
let the fields be jubilant, and everything in them!
33Then the trees of the forest will sing,
they will sing for joy before the LORD,
for he comes to judge the earth.
34Give thanks to the LORD, for he is good;
his love endures forever.
35Cry out, "Save us, O God our Savior;
gather us and deliver us from the nations,
that we may give thanks to your holy name,
that we may glory in your praise."
36Praise be to the LORD, the God of Israel,
from everlasting to everlasting.

Then all the people said "Amen" and "Praise the LORD."

37David left Asaph and his associates before the ark of the
covenant of the LORD to minister there regularly, according to each
day's requirements. 38He also left Obed-Edom and his sixty-eight

**NIV** [a] *15* Some Septuagint manuscripts (see also Psalm 105:8); Hebrew *Remember* [b] *18-20* One Hebrew manuscript, Septuagint and Vulgate (see also Psalm 105:12); most Hebrew manuscripts *inherit, / [19]though you are but few in number, / few indeed, and strangers in it." / [20]They* [c] *29* Or *LORD with the splendor of*

## King James

38And Obed-edom with their brethren, threescore and eight; Obed-edom also the son of Jeduthun and Hosah *to be* porters:
39And Zadok the priest, and his brethren the priests, before the tabernacle of the LORD in the high place that *was* at Gibeon,
40To offer burnt offerings unto the LORD upon the altar of the burnt offering continually morning and evening, and *to do* according to all that is written in the law of the LORD, which he commanded Israel;
41And with them Heman and Jeduthun, and the rest that were chosen, who were expressed by name, to give thanks to the LORD, because his mercy *endureth* for ever;
42And with them Heman and Jeduthun with trumpets and cymbals for those that should make a sound, and with musical instruments of God. And the sons of Jeduthun *were* porters.
43And all the people departed every man to his house: and David returned to bless his house.

17 NOW IT came to pass, as David sat in his house, that David said to Nathan the prophet, Lo, I dwell in an house of cedars, but the ark of the covenant of the LORD *remaineth* under curtains.
2Then Nathan said unto David, Do all that *is* in thine heart; for God *is* with thee.
3¶ And it came to pass the same night, that the word of God came to Nathan, saying,
4Go and tell David my servant, Thus saith the LORD, Thou shalt not build me an house to dwell in:
5For I have not dwelt in an house since the day that I brought up Israel unto this day; but have gone from tent to tent, and from *one* tabernacle *to another*.
6Wheresoever I have walked with all Israel, spake I a word to any of the judges of Israel, whom I commanded to feed my people, saying, Why have ye not built me an house of cedars?
7Now therefore thus shalt thou say unto my servant David, Thus saith the LORD of hosts, I took thee from the sheepcote, *even* from following the sheep, that thou shouldest be ruler over my people Israel:
8And I have been with thee whithersoever thou hast walked, and have cut off all thine enemies from before thee, and have made thee a name like the name of the great men that *are* in the earth.
9Also I will ordain a place for my people Israel, and will plant them, and they shall dwell in their place, and shall be moved no more; neither shall the children of wickedness waste them any more, as at the beginning,
10And since the time that I commanded judges *to be* over my people Israel. Moreover I will subdue all thine enemies. Furthermore I tell thee that the LORD will build thee an house.
11¶ And it shall come to pass, when thy days be expired that thou must go *to be* with thy fathers, that I will raise up thy seed after thee, which shall be of thy sons; and I will establish his kingdom.
12He shall build me an house, and I will establish his throne for ever.
13I will be his father, and he shall be my son: and I will not take my mercy away from him, as I took *it* from *him* that was before thee:

## Amplified

38And Obed-edom with [his] sixty-eight kinsmen. Also Obed-edom son of Jeduthun, and Hosah were to be gatekeepers.
39And David left Zadok the priest and his brethren the priests before the tabernacle of the Lord in the high place that was at Gibeon,
40To offer burnt offerings to the Lord upon the altar of burnt offering continually morning and evening, and to do all that is written in the law of the Lord which He commanded Israel;
41With them were Heman and Jeduthun, and the rest who were chosen and expressly named to give thanks to the Lord, for His mercy *and* loving-kindness endure for ever.
42With them were Heman and Jeduthun with trumpets and cymbals for those who should sound aloud, and instruments for accompanying the songs of God. And the sons of Jeduthun were to be at the gate.
43Then all the people departed each man to his house, and David returned home to bless his household.

17 AS DAVID sat in his house he said to Nathan the prophet, Lo, I dwell in a house of cedars, but the ark of the covenant of the Lord remains under tent curtains.
2Then Nathan said to David, Do all that is in your heart; for God is with you.
3And that same night the word of God came to Nathan, saying,
4Go and tell David My servant, Thus says the Lord, You shall not build Me a house to dwell in,
5For I have not dwelt in a house since the day that I brought up Israel from Egypt until this day; but I have gone from tent to tent, and from one tabernacle to another.
6Wherever I have walked with all Israel, did I say a word to any of the judges of Israel, whom I commanded to feed My people, saying, Why have you not built Me a house of cedar?
7Now therefore thus shall you say to My servant David, Thus says the Lord of hosts, I took you from the sheepfold, from following the sheep, that you should be prince over My people Israel.
8And I have been with you wherever you have gone, and I have cut off all your enemies from before you, and I will make you a name like the name of the great ones of the earth.
9Also I will appoint a place for My people Israel, and will plant them, that they may dwell in their own place and be moved no more; neither shall the children of wickedness waste them any more, as at the first,
10Since the time that I commanded judges to be over My people Israel. Moreover I will subdue all your enemies. Furthermore I foretell to you that the Lord will build you a house—a blessed posterity.
11And it shall come to pass, when your days are fulfilled to go to be with your fathers, I will raise up your offspring after you, one of your own sons, and I will establish his kingdom.
12He shall build Me a house, and I will establish his throne for ever. [Cp. I Chron. 28:7.]
13I will be his father, and he shall be My son: and I will not take My mercy *and* steadfast love away from him, as I took it from him [King Saul] who was before you. [Heb. 1:5, 6.

## New American Standard

38and Obed-edom with his 68 relatives; Obed-edom, also the
son of Jeduthun, and Hosah as gatekeepers.
39And *he left* Zadok the priest and his relatives the priests before
the tabernacle of the LORD in the high place which *was* at Gibeon,
40to offer burnt offerings to the LORD on the altar of burnt
offering continually morning and evening, even according to all
that is written in the law of the LORD, which He commanded Israel.
41And with them *were* Heman and Jeduthun, and the rest who
were chosen, who were designated by name, to give thanks to the
LORD, because His lovingkindness is everlasting.
42And with them *were* Heman and Jeduthun *with* trumpets and
cymbals for those who should sound aloud, and *with* instruments
*for* the songs of God, and the sons of Jeduthun for the gate.
43Then all the people departed each to his house, and David
returned to bless his household.

*God's Covenant with David*

17 AND IT came about, when David dwelt in his house, that
David said to Nathan the prophet, "Behold, I am dwelling
in a house of cedar, but the ark of the covenant of the LORD is under
curtains."
2Then Nathan said to David, "Do all that is in your heart, for
God is with you."
3And it came about the same night, that the word of God came
to Nathan, saying,
4"Go and tell David My servant, 'Thus says the LORD, "You
shall not build a house for Me to dwell in;
5for I have not dwelt in a house since the day that I brought
up Israel to this day, but I have gone from tent to tent and from
*one* dwelling place *to another.*
6"In all places where I have walked with all Israel, have I
spoken a word with any of the judges of Israel, whom I commanded to shepherd My people, saying, 'Why have you not built
for Me a house of cedar?' " '
7"Now, therefore, thus shall you say to My servant David,
'Thus says the LORD of hosts, "I took you from the pasture, from
following the sheep, that you should be leader over My people
Israel.
8"And I have been with you wherever you have gone, and
have cut off all your enemies from before you; and I will make you
a name like the name of the great ones who are in the earth.
9"And I will appoint a place for My people Israel, and will plant
them, that they may dwell in their own place and be moved no
more; neither shall the wicked waste them anymore as formerly,
10even from the day that I commanded judges *to be* over My
people Israel. And I will subdue all your enemies. Moreover, I tell
you that the LORD will build a house for you.
11"And it shall come about when your days are fulfilled that you
must go *to be* with your fathers, that I will set up *one of* your
descendants after you, who shall be of your sons; and I will establish his kingdom.
12"He shall build for Me a house, and I will establish his throne
forever.
13"I will be his father, and he shall be My son; and I will not
take My lovingkindness away from him, as I took it from him who
was before you.

## New International

associates to minister with them. Obed-Edom son of Jeduthun,
and also Hosah, were gatekeepers.
39David left Zadok the priest and his fellow priests before the
tabernacle of the LORD at the high place in Gibeon 40to present
burnt offerings to the LORD on the altar of burnt offering regularly,
morning and evening, in accordance with everything written in
the Law of the LORD, which he had given Israel. 41With them were
Heman and Jeduthun and the rest of those chosen and designated
by name to give thanks to the LORD, "for his love endures forever."
42Heman and Jeduthun were responsible for the sounding of the
trumpets and cymbals and for the playing of the other instruments
for sacred song. The sons of Jeduthun were stationed at the gate.
43Then all the people left, each for his own home, and David
returned home to bless his family.

*God's Promise to David*

17 AFTER DAVID was settled in his palace, he said to Nathan the prophet, "Here I am, living in a palace of cedar,
while the ark of the covenant of the LORD is under a tent."
2Nathan replied to David, "Whatever you have in mind, do it,
for God is with you."
3That night the word of God came to Nathan, saying:
4"Go and tell my servant David, 'This is what the LORD
says: You are not the one to build me a house to dwell in. 5I
have not dwelt in a house from the day I brought Israel up out
of Egypt to this day. I have moved from one tent site to
another, from one dwelling place to another. 6Wherever I
have moved with all the Israelites, did I ever say to any of their
leaders[a] whom I commanded to shepherd my people, "Why
have you not built me a house of cedar?" '
7"Now then, tell my servant David, 'This is what the LORD
Almighty says: I took you from the pasture and from following the flock, to be ruler over my people Israel. 8I have been
with you wherever you have gone, and I have cut off all your
enemies from before you. Now I will make your name like the
names of the greatest men of the earth. 9And I will provide
a place for my people Israel and will plant them so that they
can have a home of their own and no longer be disturbed.
Wicked people will not oppress them anymore, as they did at
the beginning 10and have done ever since the time I appointed
leaders over my people Israel. I will also subdue all your
enemies.
" 'I declare to you that the LORD will build a house for you:
11When your days are over and you go to be with your fathers,
I will raise up your offspring to succeed you, one of your own
sons, and I will establish his kingdom. 12He is the one who
will build a house for me, and I will establish his throne
forever. 13I will be his father, and he will be my son. I will
never take my love away from him, as I took it away from your

NIV [a] 6 Traditionally *judges*; also in verse 10

## King James

14 But I will settle him in mine house and in my kingdom for ever: and his throne shall be established for evermore.

15 According to all these words, and according to all this vision, so did Nathan speak unto David.

16 ¶ And David the king came and sat before the LORD, and said, Who *am* I, O LORD God, and what *is* mine house, that thou hast brought me hitherto?

17 And *yet* this was a small thing in thine eyes, O God; for thou hast *also* spoken of thy servant's house for a great while to come, and hast regarded me according to the estate of a man of high degree, O LORD God.

18 What can David *speak* more to thee for the honour of thy servant? for thou knowest thy servant.

19 O LORD, for thy servant's sake, and according to thine own heart, hast thou done all this greatness, in making known all *these* great things.

20 O LORD, *there is* none like thee, neither *is there any* God beside thee, according to all that we have heard with our ears.

21 And what one nation in the earth *is* like thy people Israel, whom God went to redeem *to be* his own people, to make thee a name of greatness and terribleness, by driving out nations from before thy people, whom thou hast redeemed out of Egypt?

22 For thy people Israel didst thou make thine own people for ever; and thou, LORD, becamest their God.

23 Therefore now, LORD, let the thing that thou hast spoken concerning thy servant and concerning his house be established for ever, and do as thou hast said.

24 Let it even be established, that thy name may be magnified for ever, saying, The LORD of hosts *is* the God of Israel, *even* a God to Israel: and *let* the house of David thy servant *be* established before thee.

25 For thou, O my God, hast told thy servant that thou wilt build him an house: therefore thy servant hath found *in his heart* to pray before thee.

26 And now, LORD, thou art God, and hast promised this goodness unto thy servant:

27 Now therefore let it please thee to bless the house of thy servant, that it may be before thee for ever: for thou blessest, O LORD, and *it shall be* blessed for ever.

**18** NOW AFTER this it came to pass, that David smote the Philistines, and subdued them, and took Gath and her towns out of the hand of the Philistines.

2 And he smote Moab; and the Moabites became David's servants, *and* brought gifts.

3 ¶ And David smote Hadarezer king of Zobah unto Hamath, as he went to stablish his dominion by the river Euphrates.

4 And David took from him a thousand chariots, and seven thousand horsemen, and twenty thousand footmen: David also houghed all the chariot *horses*, but reserved of them an hundred chariots.

5 And when the Syrians of Damascus came to help Hadarezer king of Zobah, David slew of the Syrians two and twenty thousand men.

6 Then David put *garrisons* in Syria-damascus; and the Syrians became David's servants, *and* brought gifts. Thus the LORD preserved David whithersoever he went.

## Amplified

14 But I will settle [a]Him in My house and in My kingdom for ever; and His throne shall be established for evermore. [Isa. 9:7.]

15 According to all these words, and according to all this vision, so Nathan spoke to David.

16 And David the king went in and sat before the Lord, and said, Who am I, O Lord God, and what is my house *and* family that You have brought me up to this?

17 And yet this was a small thing in Your eyes, O God; for You have spoken of Your servant's house for a great while to come, and have regarded me according to the estate of a man of high degree, O Lord God!

18 What more can David say to You for thus honoring Your servant? For You know Your servant.

19 O Lord, for Your servant's sake, and in accord with Your own heart You have wrought all this greatness, to make known all these great things.

20 O Lord, there is none like You, nor is there any God beside You, according to all that our ears have heard.

21 And what nation on the earth is like Your people Israel, whom God went to redeem to Himself for a people, making Yourself a name by great and terrible things, by driving out nations from before Your people whom You redeemed out of Egypt?

22 You made Your people Israel Your own forever, and You, Lord, became their God.

23 Therefore now, Lord, let the word which You have spoken concerning Your servant and his house be established for ever, and do as You have said.

24 Let it be established, and let Your name [and the character that name denotes] be magnified for ever, saying, The Lord of hosts, the God of Israel, is Israel's God; and the house of David Your servant will be established before You.

25 For You, O my God, have told Your servant that You will build him a house (a blessed posterity); therefore Your servant has found courage *and* confidence to pray before You.

26 And now, Lord, You are God, and have promised this good thing to Your servant;

27 Therefore may it please You to bless the house (posterity) of Your servant that it may continue before You for ever; for what You bless, O Lord, is blessed for ever.

**18** AFTER THIS David smote and subdued the Philistines, and took Gath and its villages out of the hand of the Philistines.

2 He smote Moab, and the Moabites became David's servants and brought tribute.

3 Also David defeated Hadadezer king of Zobah toward Hamath, as he went to establish his dominion by the river Euphrates.

4 David took from him 1,000 chariots, 7,000 horsemen, and 20, 000 foot soldiers. David also hamstrung all the chariot horses, but reserved enough for 100 chariots.

5 When the Syrians of Damascus came to help Hadadezer king of Zobah, David slew of the Syrians 22,000 men.

6 Then David put garrisons in Syria, [whose capital was] Damascus; the Syrians became David's servants and brought tribute. Thus the Lord preserved *and* gave victory to David wherever he went.

**AMP** [a] The "house" or "kingdom of God," in which this preservation or confirming of the seed of David is to take place, is first the Old Testament theocracy [government of a state by the immediate direction of God], then the Messianic kingdom of the new covenant. The text of II Samuel 7:16 differs: "and thy house and thy kingdom shall endure forever before thee, and thy throne shall be established for ever." The sense of both is Messianic [though the writer in earlier verses definitely referred not to Christ, but to Solomon. Cp. verses 11 to 13 and II Samuel 7:13, 14] (adapted from *Lange's Commentary*). "The reference in this prophecy looks beyond Solomon to Him of whom the greatest princes of the house of David were but imperfect types" *(Ellicott's Commentary)*.

## New American Standard

14"But I will settle him in My house and in My kingdom forever,
and his throne shall be established forever."'"
15According to all these words and according to all this vision,
so Nathan spoke to David.

*David's Prayer in Response*

16¶ Then David the king went in and sat before the LORD and
said, "Who am I, O LORD God, and what is my house that Thou
hast brought me this far?
17"And this was a small thing in Thine eyes, O God; but Thou
hast spoken of Thy servant's house for a great while to come, and
hast regarded me according to the standard of a man of high
degree, O LORD God.
18"What more can David still *say* to Thee concerning the honor
*bestowed* on Thy servant? For Thou knowest Thy servant.
19"O LORD, for Thy servant's sake, and according to Thine own
heart, Thou hast wrought all this greatness, to make known all
these great things.
20"O LORD, there is none like Thee, neither is there any God
besides Thee, according to all that we have heard with our ears.
21"And what one nation in the earth is like Thy people Israel,
whom God went to redeem for Himself *as* a people, to make Thee
a name by great and terrible things, in driving out nations from
before Thy people, whom Thou didst redeem out of Egypt?
22"For Thy people Israel Thou didst make Thine own people
forever, and Thou, O LORD, didst become their God.
23"And now, O LORD, let the word that Thou hast spoken
concerning Thy servant and concerning his house, be established
forever, and do as Thou hast spoken.
24"And let Thy name be established and magnified forever,
saying, 'The LORD of hosts is the God of Israel, *even* a God to Israel;
and the house of David Thy servant is established before Thee.'
25"For Thou, O my God, hast revealed to Thy servant that Thou
wilt build for him a house; therefore Thy servant hath found
*courage* to pray before Thee.
26"And now, O LORD, Thou art God, and hast promised this
good thing to Thy servant.
27"And now it hath pleased Thee to bless the house of Thy
servant, that it may continue forever before Thee; for Thou, O
LORD, hast blessed, and it is blessed forever."

*David's Kingdom Strengthened*

18 NOW AFTER this it came about that David defeated the
Philistines and subdued them and took Gath and its towns
from the hand of the Philistines.
2And he defeated Moab, and the Moabites became servants to
David, bringing tribute.
3David also defeated Hadadezer king of Zobah *as far as*
Hamath, as he went to establish his rule to the Euphrates River.
4And David took from him 1,000 chariots and 7,000 horsemen
and 20,000 foot soldiers, and David hamstrung all the chariot
horses, but reserved *enough* of them for 100 chariots.
5¶ When the Arameans of Damascus came to help Hadadezer
king of Zobah, David killed 22,000 men of the Arameans.
6Then David put *garrisons* among the Arameans of Damascus;
and the Arameans became servants to David, bringing tribute.
And the LORD helped David wherever he went.

## New International

predecessor. 14I will set him over my house and my kingdom
forever; his throne will be established forever.'"
15Nathan reported to David all the words of this entire revelation.

*David's Prayer*

16Then King David went in and sat before the LORD, and he
said:
"Who am I, O LORD God, and what is my family, that you
have brought me this far? 17And as if this were not enough
in your sight, O God, you have spoken about the future of the
house of your servant. You have looked on me as though I
were the most exalted of men, O LORD God.
18"What more can David say to you for honoring your
servant? For you know your servant, 19O LORD. For the sake
of your servant and according to your will, you have done this
great thing and made known all these great promises.
20"There is no one like you, O LORD, and there is no God
but you, as we have heard with our own ears. 21And who is
like your people Israel—the one nation on earth whose God
went out to redeem a people for himself, and to make a name
for yourself, and to perform great and awesome wonders by
driving out nations from before your people, whom you redeemed from Egypt? 22You made your people Israel your very
own forever, and you, O LORD, have become their God.
23"And now, LORD, let the promise you have made concerning your servant and his house be established forever. Do
as you promised, 24so that it will be established and that your
name will be great forever. Then men will say, 'The LORD
Almighty, the God over Israel, is Israel's God!' And the house
of your servant David will be established before you.
25"You, my God, have revealed to your servant that you
will build a house for him. So your servant has found courage
to pray to you. 26O LORD, you are God! You have promised
these good things to your servant. 27Now you have been
pleased to bless the house of your servant, that it may continue forever in your sight; for you, O LORD, have blessed it,
and it will be blessed forever."

*David's Victories*

18 IN THE course of time, David defeated the Philistines and
subdued them, and he took Gath and its surrounding
villages from the control of the Philistines.
2David also defeated the Moabites, and they became subject to
him and brought tribute.
3Moreover, David fought Hadadezer king of Zobah, as far as
Hamath, when he went to establish his control along the Euphrates River. 4David captured a thousand of his chariots, seven thousand charioteers and twenty thousand foot soldiers. He hamstrung all but a hundred of the chariot horses.
5When the Arameans of Damascus came to help Hadadezer
king of Zobah, David struck down twenty-two thousand of them.
6He put garrisons in the Aramean kingdom of Damascus, and the
Arameans became subject to him and brought tribute. The LORD
gave David victory everywhere he went.

## King James

7And David took the shields of gold that were on the servants of Hadarezer, and brought them to Jerusalem.

8Likewise from Tibhath, and from Chun, cities of Hadarezer, brought David very much brass, wherewith Solomon made the brasen sea, and the pillars, and the vessels of brass.

9¶ Now when Tou king of Hamath heard how David had smitten all the host of Hadarezer king of Zobah;

10He sent Hadoram his son to king David, to inquire of his welfare, and to congratulate him, because he had fought against Hadarezer, and smitten him; (for Hadarezer had war with Tou;) and *with him* all manner of vessels of gold and silver and brass.

11¶ Them also king David dedicated unto the LORD, with the silver and the gold that he brought from all *these* nations; from Edom, and from Moab, and from the children of Ammon, and from the Philistines, and from Amalek.

12Moreover Abishai the son of Zeruiah slew of the Edomites in the valley of salt eighteen thousand.

13¶ And he put garrisons in Edom; and all the Edomites became David's servants. Thus the LORD preserved David whithersoever he went.

14¶ So David reigned over all Israel, and executed judgment and justice among all his people.

15And Joab the son of Zeruiah *was* over the host; and Jehoshaphat the son of Ahilud, recorder.

16And Zadok the son of Ahitub, and Abimelech the son of Abiathar, *were* the priests; and Shavsha was scribe;

17And Benaiah the son of Jehoiada *was* over the Cherethites and the Pelethites; and the sons of David *were* chief about the king.

**19** NOW IT came to pass after this, that Nahash the king of the children of Ammon died, and his son reigned in his stead.

2And David said, I will show kindness unto Hanun the son of Nahash, because his father showed kindness to me. And David sent messengers to comfort him concerning his father. So the servants of David came into the land of the children of Ammon to Hanun, to comfort him.

3But the princes of the children of Ammon said to Hanun, Thinkest thou that David doth honour thy father, that he hath sent comforters unto thee? are not his servants come unto thee for to search, and to overthrow, and to spy out the land?

4Wherefore Hanun took David's servants, and shaved them, and cut off their garments in the midst hard by their buttocks, and sent them away.

5Then there went *certain,* and told David how the men were served. And he sent to meet them: for the men were greatly ashamed. And the king said, Tarry at Jericho until your beards be grown, and *then* return.

6¶ And when the children of Ammon saw that they had made themselves odious to David, Hanun and the children of Ammon sent a thousand talents of silver to hire them chariots and horsemen out of Mesopotamia, and out of Syria-maachah, and out of Zobah.

7So they hired thirty and two thousand chariots, and the king of Maachah and his people; who came and pitched before Medeba. And the children of Ammon gathered themselves together from their cities, and came to battle.

8And when David heard *of it,* he sent Joab, and all the host of the mighty men.

9And the children of Ammon came out, and put the battle in array before the gate of the city: and the kings that were come *were* by themselves in the field.

10Now when Joab saw that the battle was set against him before and behind, he chose out of all the choice of Israel, and put *them* in array against the Syrians.

## Amplified

7David took the shields of gold that were carried by the servants of Hadadezer, and brought them to Jerusalem.

8Likewise from Tibhath, and from Cun, cities of Hadadezer, David brought very much bronze, with which Solomon later made the bronze laver, the pillars, and the vessels of bronze.

9When Tou king of Hamath heard how David had defeated all the host of Hadadezer king of Zobah,

10He sent Hadoram his son to King David, to salute him and to congratulate him because he had fought and defeated Hadadezer, for Hadadezer had had wars with Tou; and Hadoram brought with him all manner of vessels of gold, silver, and bronze.

11King David dedicated them also to the Lord, with the silver and the gold he brought from all these nations: Edom, Moab, the Ammonites, the Philistines, and the Amalekites.

12Also Abishai son of Zeruiah slew 18,000 of the Edomites in the Valley of Salt.

13He put garrisons in Edom, and all the Edomites became David's servants. Thus the Lord preserved *and* gave victory to David wherever he went.

14So David reigned over all Israel, and executed judgment and justice among all his people.

15Joab son of Zeruiah [David's half sister] was over the army; and Jehoshaphat son of Ahilud, recorder.

16Zadok son of Ahitub and Abimelech son of Abiathar were the priests, and Shavsha was secretary [of state].

17Benaiah son of Jehoiada was over [David's bodyguard] the Cherethites and the Pelethites; and David's sons were chiefs next to the king.

**19** AFTER THIS, Nahash king of the Ammonites died, and his son reigned in his stead.

2David said, I will show kindness to Hanun son of Nahash, because his father showed kindness to me. And David sent messengers to comfort him concerning his father's death. So the servants of David came into the land of the Ammonites to comfort Hanun.

3But the princes of the Ammonites said to Hanun, Do you think that David has sent comforters to you because he honors your father? Have his servants not come to you to search, to overthrow, and to spy out the land?

4Therefore Hanun took David's servants, shaved them, cut off their garments in the middle near their buttocks, and sent them away.

5When David was told how the men were served, he sent to meet them; for *they* were greatly shamed *and* embarrassed. The king said, Stay in Jericho until your beards are grown, then return.

6When the Ammonites saw that they had made themselves hateful to David, Hanun and [his people] sent 1,000 talents of silver to hire chariots and horsemen from Mesopotamia, and Aram-maacah, and Zobah.

7So they hired 32,000 chariots, and the king of Maacah and his troops, who came and pitched before Medeba. And the Ammonites gathered from their cities, and came to battle.

8When David heard of it, he sent Joab, and all the army of mighty men.

9And the Ammonites came out and lined up in battle array before the entrance of the city [Medeba], and the kings who had come were by themselves in the open country.

10When Joab saw that the battle was set against him before and behind, he chose from all the choice men of Israel, and put them in array against the Syrians.

## New American Standard

7And David took the shields of gold which were carried by the
servants of Hadadezer, and brought them to Jerusalem.
8Also from Tibhath and from Cun, cities of Hadadezer, David
took a very large amount of bronze, with which Solomon made the
bronze sea and the pillars and the bronze utensils.
9¶ Now when Tou king of Hamath heard that David had defeated all the army of Hadadezer king of Zobah,
10he sent Hadoram his son to King David, to greet him and to
bless him, because he had fought against Hadadezer and had
defeated him; for Hadadezer had been at war with Tou. And
*Hadoram brought* all kinds of articles of gold and silver and bronze.
11King David also dedicated these to the LORD with the silver
and the gold which he had carried away from all the nations: from
Edom, Moab, the sons of Ammon, the Philistines, and from
Amalek.
12¶ Moreover Abishai the son of Zeruiah defeated 18,000 Edomites in the Valley of Salt.
13Then he put garrisons in Edom, and all the Edomites became
servants to David. And the LORD helped David wherever he went.
14¶ So David reigned over all Israel; and he administered justice
and righteousness for all his people.
15And Joab the son of Zeruiah *was* over the army, and Jehoshaphat the son of Ahilud *was* recorder;
16and Zadok the son of Ahitub and Abimelech the son of Abiathar *were* priests, and Shavsha *was* secretary;
17and Benaiah the son of Jehoiada *was* over the Cherethites and
the Pelethites, and the sons of David *were* chiefs at the king's side.

*David's Messengers Abused*

**19** NOW IT came about after this, that Nahash the king of the
sons of Ammon died, and his son became king in his
place.
2Then David said, "I will show kindness to Hanun the son of
Nahash, because his father showed kindness to me." So David
sent messengers to console him concerning his father. And David's servants came into the land of the sons of Ammon to Hanun,
to console him.
3But the princes of the sons of Ammon said to Hanun, "Do you
think that David is honoring your father, in that he has sent
comforters to you? Have not his servants come to you to search
and to overthrow and to spy out the land?"
4So Hanun took David's servants and shaved them, and cut off
their garments in the middle as far as their hips, and sent them
away.
5Then *certain persons* went and told David about the men. And
he sent to meet them, for the men were greatly humiliated. And
the king said, "Stay at Jericho until your beards grow, and *then*
return."
6¶ When the sons of Ammon saw that they had made themselves odious to David, Hanun and the sons of Ammon sent 1,000
talents of silver to hire for themselves chariots and horsemen from
Mesopotamia, from Aram-maacah, and from Zobah.
7So they hired for themselves 32,000 chariots, and the king of
Maacah and his people, who came and camped before Medeba.
And the sons of Ammon gathered together from their cities and
came to battle.
8When David heard *of it,* he sent Joab and all the army, the
mighty men.
9And the sons of Ammon came out and drew up in battle array
at the entrance of the city, and the kings who had come were by
themselves in the field.

*Ammon and Aram Defeated*

10¶ Now when Joab saw that the battle was set against him in
front and in the rear, he selected from all the choice men of Israel
and they arrayed themselves against the Arameans.

## New International

7David took the gold shields carried by the officers of Hadadezer and brought them to Jerusalem.
8From Tebah[a] and Cun, towns
that belonged to Hadadezer, David took a great quantity of bronze,
which Solomon used to make the bronze Sea, the pillars and
various bronze articles.
9When Tou king of Hamath heard that David had defeated the
entire army of Hadadezer king of Zobah,
10he sent his son Hadoram to King David to greet him and congratulate him on his
victory in battle over Hadadezer, who had been at war with Tou.
Hadoram brought all kinds of articles of gold and silver and
bronze.
11King David dedicated these articles to the LORD, as he had
done with the silver and gold he had taken from all these nations:
Edom and Moab, the Ammonites and the Philistines, and Amalek.
12Abishai son of Zeruiah struck down eighteen thousand
Edomites in the Valley of Salt.
13He put garrisons in Edom, and
all the Edomites became subject to David. The LORD gave David
victory everywhere he went.

*David's Officials*

14David reigned over all Israel, doing what was just and right
for all his people.
15Joab son of Zeruiah was over the army; Jehoshaphat son of Ahilud was recorder;
16Zadok son of Ahitub and
Ahimelech[b] son of Abiathar were priests; Shavsha was secretary;
17Benaiah son of Jehoiada was over the Kerethites and Pelethites;
and David's sons were chief officials at the king's side.

*The Battle Against the Ammonites*

**19** IN THE course of time, Nahash king of the Ammonites
died, and his son succeeded him as king.
2David thought,
"I will show kindness to Hanun son of Nahash, because his father
showed kindness to me." So David sent a delegation to express his
sympathy to Hanun concerning his father.
When David's men came to Hanun in the land of the Ammonites to express sympathy to him,
3the Ammonite nobles said to
Hanun, "Do you think David is honoring your father by sending
men to you to express sympathy? Haven't his men come to you
to explore and spy out the country and overthrow it?"
4So Hanun
seized David's men, shaved them, cut off their garments in the
middle at the buttocks, and sent them away.
5When someone came and told David about the men, he sent
messengers to meet them, for they were greatly humiliated. The
king said, "Stay at Jericho till your beards have grown, and then
come back."
6When the Ammonites realized that they had become a stench
in David's nostrils, Hanun and the Ammonites sent a thousand
talents[c] of silver to hire chariots and charioteers from Aram Naharaim,[d] Aram Maacah and Zobah.
7They hired thirty-two thousand
chariots and charioteers, as well as the king of Maacah with his
troops, who came and camped near Medeba, while the Ammonites were mustered from their towns and moved out for battle.
8On hearing this, David sent Joab out with the entire army of
fighting men.
9The Ammonites came out and drew up in battle
formation at the entrance to their city, while the kings who had
come were by themselves in the open country.
10Joab saw that there were battle lines in front of him and
behind him; so he selected some of the best troops in Israel and
deployed them against the Arameans.
11He put the rest of the men

**NIV** [a] *8* Hebrew *Tibhath,* a variant of *Tebah* [b] *16* Some Hebrew manuscripts, Vulgate and Syriac (see also 2 Samuel 8:17); most Hebrew manuscripts *Abimelech* [c] *6* That is, about 37 tons (about 34 metric tons) [d] *6* That is, Northwest Mesopotamia

# King James

11 And the rest of the people he delivered unto the hand of Abishai his brother, and they set *themselves* in array against the children of Ammon.

12 And he said, If the Syrians be too strong for me, then thou shalt help me: but if the children of Ammon be too strong for thee, then I will help thee.

13 Be of good courage, and let us behave ourselves valiantly for our people, and for the cities of our God: and let the LORD do *that which is* good in his sight.

14 So Joab and the people that *were* with him drew nigh before the Syrians unto the battle; and they fled before him.

15 And when the children of Ammon saw that the Syrians were fled, they likewise fled before Abishai his brother, and entered into the city. Then Joab came to Jerusalem.

16 ¶ And when the Syrians saw that they were put to the worse before Israel, they sent messengers, and drew forth the Syrians that *were* beyond the river: and Shophach the captain of the host of Hadarezer *went* before them.

17 And it was told David; and he gathered all Israel, and passed over Jordan, and came upon them, and set *the battle* in array against them. So when David had put the battle in array against the Syrians, they fought with him.

18 But the Syrians fled before Israel; and David slew of the Syrians seven thousand *men which fought in* chariots, and forty thousand footmen, and killed Shophach the captain of the host.

19 And when the servants of Hadarezer saw that they were put to the worse before Israel, they made peace with David, and became his servants: neither would the Syrians help the children of Ammon any more.

**20** AND IT came to pass, that after the year was expired, at the time that kings go out *to battle*, Joab led forth the power of the army, and wasted the country of the children of Ammon, and came and besieged Rabbah. But David tarried at Jerusalem. And Joab smote Rabbah, and destroyed it.

2 And David took the crown of their king from off his head, and found it to weigh a talent of gold, and *there were* precious stones in it; and it was set upon David's head: and he brought also exceeding much spoil out of the city.

3 And he brought out the people that *were* in it, and cut *them* with saws, and with harrows of iron, and with axes. Even so dealt David with all the cities of the children of Ammon. And David and all the people returned to Jerusalem.

4 ¶ And it came to pass after this, that there arose war at Gezer with the Philistines; at which time Sibbechai the Hushathite slew Sippai, *that was* of the children of the giant: and they were subdued.

5 And there was war again with the Philistines; and Elhanan the son of Jair slew Lahmi the brother of Goliath the Gittite, whose spear staff *was* like a weaver's beam.

6 And yet again there was war at Gath, where was a man of *great* stature, whose fingers and toes *were* four and twenty, six *on each hand,* and six *on each foot:* and he also was the son of the giant.

7 But when he defied Israel, Jonathan the son of Shimea David's brother slew him.

8 These were born unto the giant in Gath; and they fell by the hand of David, and by the hand of his servants.

**21** AND SATAN stood up against Israel, and provoked David to number Israel.

# Amplified

11 The rest of the soldiers he delivered to Abishai his brother, and they were arrayed against the Ammonites.

12 And he said, If the Syrians are too strong for me, then you help me; but if the Ammonites are too strong for you, I will help you.

13 Be of good courage, and let us behave ourselves courageously for our people, and for the cities of our God; and may the Lord do what is good in His sight.

14 So Joab and the people who were with him drew near before the Syrians for battle; and they fled before him.

15 And when the Ammonites saw that the Syrians fled, they likewise fled before Abishai, Joab's brother, and entered into the city [Medeba]. Then Joab came to Jerusalem.

16 When the Syrians saw that they were defeated by Israel, they sent messengers and drew forth the Syrians who were beyond the Euphrates River, with Shophach the commander of the army of Hadadezer at their head.

17 It was told David, and he gathered all Israel, and crossed Jordan, and drew up his army against them. So when David set the battle in array against the Syrians, they fought with him.

18 But the Syrians fled before Israel, and David slew of the Syrians 7,000 men in chariots and 40,000 foot soldiers, and killed Shophach the commander of the army.

19 When the servants of Hadadezer saw that they were defeated before Israel, they made peace with David and became subject to him; nor would the Syrians longer help the Ammonites.

**20** AFTER THE end of the year, when kings go out to battle, Joab led forth the army, and devastated the land of the Ammonites, and came and besieged Rabbah. But David tarried at Jerusalem. Joab smote Rabbah, and overthrew it.

2 David took their king's crown from off his head, and found it weighed a talent of gold, and precious stones were in it. It was set upon David's head. He brought also very much spoil out of the city of Rabbah.

3 He brought out the people in it, and set them at cutting with saws, iron wedges, and axes. So David dealt with all the Ammonite cities. And David and all the army returned to Jerusalem.

4 After this there arose war at Gezer with the Philistines; then Sibbecai the Hushathite slew Sippai, of the sons of the giant; and they were subdued.

5 There was war again with the Philistines; and Elhanan son of Jair slew Lahmi brother of Goliath the Gittite, the staff of whose spear was like a weaver's beam.

6 And again there was war at Gath, where was a man of great stature, who had twenty-four fingers and toes, six on each hand and each foot. He also was born to the giant.

7 And when he reproached *and* defied Israel, Jonathan son of Shimea, David's brother, slew him.

8 These were born to the giant [clan] in Gath, and they fell by the hand of David and his servants.

**21** SATAN (an adversary) STOOD up against Israel, and stirred up David to number Israel.

## New American Standard

11But the remainder of the people he placed in the hand of
Abshai his brother; and they arrayed themselves against the sons
of Ammon.
12And he said, "If the Arameans are too strong for me, then you
shall help me; but if the sons of Ammon are too strong for you,
then I will help you.
13"Be strong, and let us show ourselves courageous for the sake
of our people and for the cities of our God; and may the LORD do
what is good in His sight."
14So Joab and the people who were with him drew near to the
battle against the Arameans, and they fled before him.
15When the sons of Ammon saw that the Arameans fled, they
also fled before Abshai his brother, and entered the city. Then Joab
came to Jerusalem.
16¶ When the Arameans saw that they had been defeated by
Israel, they sent messengers, and brought out the Arameans who
were beyond the [a]River, with Shophach the commander of the
army of Hadadezer leading them.
17When it was told David, he gathered all Israel together and
crossed the Jordan, and came upon them and drew up in formation
against them. And when David drew up in battle array against the
Arameans, they fought against him.
18And the Arameans fled before Israel, and David killed of the
Arameans 7,000 charioteers and 40,000 foot soldiers, and put to
death Shophach the commander of the army.
19So when the servants of Hadadezer saw that they were defeated by Israel, they made peace with David and served him.
Thus the Arameans were not willing to help the sons of Ammon
anymore.

*War with Philistine Giants*

**20** THEN IT happened in the spring, at the time when kings
go out *to battle,* that Joab led out the army and ravaged the
land of the sons of Ammon, and came and besieged Rabbah. But
David stayed at Jerusalem. And Joab struck Rabbah and overthrew
it.
2And David took the crown of their king from his head, and
he found it to weigh a talent of gold, and there was a precious stone
in it; and it was placed on David's head. And he brought out the
spoil of the city, a very great amount.
3And he brought out the people who *were* in it, and cut *them*
with saws and with sharp instruments and with axes. And thus
David did to all the cities of the sons of Ammon. Then David and
all the people returned *to* Jerusalem.
4¶ Now it came about after this, that war broke out at Gezer
with the Philistines; then Sibbecai the Hushathite killed Sippai,
one of the descendants of the giants, and they were subdued.
5And there was war with the Philistines again, and Elhanan
the son of Jair killed Lahmi the brother of Goliath the Gittite, the
shaft of whose spear *was* like a weaver's beam.
6And again there was war at Gath, where there was a man of
*great* stature who had twenty-four fingers and toes, six *fingers on
each hand* and six *toes on each foot;* and he also was descended from
the giants.
7And when he taunted Israel, Jonathan the son of Shimea,
David's brother, killed him.
8These were descended from the giants in Gath, and they fell
by the hand of David and by the hand of his servants.

*Census Brings Pestilence*

**21** THEN SATAN stood up against Israel and moved David
to number Israel.

NAS [a] I.e., Euphrates

## New International

under the command of Abishai his brother, and they were deployed against the Ammonites. 12Joab said, "If the Arameans are
too strong for me, then you are to rescue me; but if the Ammonites
are too strong for you, then I will rescue you. 13Be strong and let
us fight bravely for our people and the cities of our God. The LORD
will do what is good in his sight."
14Then Joab and the troops with him advanced to fight the
Arameans, and they fled before him. 15When the Ammonites saw
that the Arameans were fleeing, they too fled before his brother
Abishai and went inside the city. So Joab went back to Jerusalem.
16After the Arameans saw that they had been routed by Israel,
they sent messengers and had Arameans brought from beyond the
River,[b] with Shophach the commander of Hadadezer's army leading them.
17When David was told of this, he gathered all Israel and
crossed the Jordan; he advanced against them and formed his
battle lines opposite them. David formed his lines to meet the
Arameans in battle, and they fought against him. 18But they fled
before Israel, and David killed seven thousand of their charioteers
and forty thousand of their foot soldiers. He also killed Shophach
the commander of their army.
19When the vassals of Hadadezer saw that they had been defeated by Israel, they made peace with David and became subject
to him.
So the Arameans were not willing to help the Ammonites anymore.

*The Capture of Rabbah*

**20** IN THE spring, at the time when kings go off to war, Joab
led out the armed forces. He laid waste the land of the
Ammonites and went to Rabbah and besieged it, but David remained in Jerusalem. Joab attacked Rabbah and left it in ruins.
2David took the crown from the head of their king[c]—its weight
was found to be a talent[d] of gold, and it was set with precious
stones—and it was placed on David's head. He took a great quantity of plunder from the city 3and brought out the people who were
there, consigning them to labor with saws and with iron picks and
axes. David did this to all the Ammonite towns. Then David and
his entire army returned to Jerusalem.

*War With the Philistines*

4In the course of time, war broke out with the Philistines, at
Gezer. At that time Sibbecai the Hushathite killed Sippai, one of
the descendants of the Rephaites, and the Philistines were subjugated.
5In another battle with the Philistines, Elhanan son of Jair killed
Lahmi the brother of Goliath the Gittite, who had a spear with a
shaft like a weaver's rod.
6In still another battle, which took place at Gath, there was a
huge man with six fingers on each hand and six toes on each
foot—twenty-four in all. He also was descended from Rapha.
7When he taunted Israel, Jonathan son of Shimea, David's brother,
killed him.
8These were descendants of Rapha in Gath, and they fell at the
hands of David and his men.

*David Numbers the Fighting Men*

**21** SATAN ROSE up against Israel and incited David to take
a census of Israel. 2So David said to Joab and the com-

NIV [b] *16* That is, the Euphrates [c] *2* Or *of Milcom,* that is, Molech [d] *2* That
is, about 75 pounds (about 34 kilograms)

## King James

2And David said to Joab and to the rulers of the people, Go, number Israel from Beer-sheba even to Dan; and bring the number of them to me, that I may know *it*.

3And Joab answered, The LORD make his people an hundred times so many more as they *be:* but, my lord the king, *are* they not all my lord's servants? why then doth my lord require this thing? why will he be a cause of trespass to Israel?

4Nevertheless the king's word prevailed against Joab. Wherefore Joab departed, and went throughout all Israel, and came to Jerusalem.

5¶ And Joab gave the sum of the number of the people unto David. And all *they of* Israel were a thousand thousand and an hundred thousand men that drew sword: and Judah *was* four hundred threescore and ten thousand men that drew sword.

6But Levi and Benjamin counted he not among them: for the king's word was abominable to Joab.

7And God was displeased with this thing; therefore he smote Israel.

8And David said unto God, I have sinned greatly, because I have done this thing: but now, I beseech thee, do away the iniquity of thy servant; for I have done very foolishly.

9¶ And the LORD spake unto Gad, David's seer, saying,

10Go and tell David, saying, Thus saith the LORD, I offer thee three *things:* choose thee one of them, that I may do *it* unto thee.

11So Gad came to David, and said unto him, Thus saith the LORD, Choose thee

12Either three years' famine; or three months to be destroyed before thy foes, while that the sword of thine enemies overtaketh *thee;* or else three days the sword of the LORD, even the pestilence, in the land, and the angel of the LORD destroying throughout all the coasts of Israel. Now therefore advise thyself what word I shall bring again to him that sent me.

13And David said unto Gad, I am in a great strait: let me fall now into the hand of the LORD; for very great *are* his mercies: but let me not fall into the hand of man.

14¶ So the LORD sent pestilence upon Israel: and there fell of Israel seventy thousand men.

15And God sent an angel unto Jerusalem to destroy it: and as he was destroying, the LORD beheld, and he repented him of the evil, and said to the angel that destroyed, It is enough, stay now thine hand. And the angel of the LORD stood by the threshingfloor of Ornan the Jebusite.

16And David lifted up his eyes, and saw the angel of the LORD stand between the earth and the heaven, having a drawn sword in his hand stretched out over Jerusalem. Then David and the elders *of Israel, who were* clothed in sackcloth, fell upon their faces.

17And David said unto God, *Is it* not I *that* commanded the people to be numbered? even I it is that have sinned and done evil indeed; but *as for* these sheep, what have they done? let thine hand, I pray thee, O LORD my God, be on me, and on my father's house; but not on thy people, that they should be plagued.

18¶ Then the angel of the LORD commanded Gad to say to David, that David should go up, and set up an altar unto the LORD in the threshingfloor of Ornan the Jebusite.

19And David went up at the saying of Gad, which he spake in the name of the LORD.

20And Ornan turned back, and saw the angel; and his four sons with him hid themselves. Now Ornan was threshing wheat.

21And as David came to Ornan, Ornan looked and saw David, and went out of the threshingfloor, and bowed himself to David with *his* face to the ground.

22Then David said to Ornan, Grant me the place of *this* threshingfloor, that I may build an altar therein unto the LORD: thou shalt grant it me for the full price: that the plague may be stayed from the people.

## Amplified

2David said to Joab and the rulers of the people, Go, number Israel from Beer-sheba to Dan; and bring me the total, that I may know it.

3And Joab answered, The Lord multiply His people a hundred times! But, my lord the king, are they not all my lord's servants? Why then does my lord require this? Why will he bring guilt upon Israel?

4But the king's word prevailed against Joab. So Joab departed, and went throughout all Israel, and came to Jerusalem.

5Joab gave the total number of the people to David. And all of Israel were 1,100,000 who drew the sword, and of Judah 470,000 who drew the sword.

6But Levi and Benjamin he did not include among them, for the king's order was detestable to Joab.

7And God was displeased with this [reliance on human resources], and He smote Israel.

8And David said to God, I have sinned greatly, because I have done this thing. But now, I beseech You, take away the hateful wickedness of Your servant; for I have done very foolishly.

9And the Lord said to Gad, David's seer,

10Go and tell David, Thus says the Lord, I offer you three things; choose one of them, that I may do it to you.

11So Gad came to David, and said to him, Thus says the Lord, Take which you will:

12Either three years famine, or three months of devastation before your foes, while the sword of your enemies overtakes you; or else three days of the sword of the Lord and pestilence in the land, and the Angel of the Lord destroying throughout all the borders of Israel. Now therefore consider what answer I shall return to Him Who sent me.

13And David said to Gad, I am in great *and* distressing perplexity; let me fall, I pray, into the hand of the Lord, for very great *and* many are His mercies; but let me not fall into the hand of man.

14So the Lord sent a pestilence upon Israel; and there fell of Israel 70,000 men.

15God sent an angel to Jerusalem to destroy it; and as he was destroying, the Lord beheld, and He regretted *and* relented of the evil, and said to the destroying angel, It is enough, now stay your hand. And the Angel of the Lord stood by the threshing floor of Ornan the Jebusite.

16David lifted up his eyes, and saw the Angel of the Lord standing between earth and the heavens, having a drawn sword in his hand stretched out over Jerusalem. Then David and the elders, clothed in sackcloth, fell upon their faces.

17And David said to God, Is it not I who commanded the people to be numbered? I it is who has sinned and done evil indeed; but as for these sheep, what have they done? Let Your hand, I pray You, O Lord my God, be on me, and on my father's house; but not on Your people, that they should be plagued.

18Then the Angel of the Lord commanded Gad to say to David, that David should go up, and set up an altar to the Lord in the threshing floor of Ornan the Jebusite.

19So David went up at Gad's word, which he spoke in the name of the Lord.

20Now Ornan was threshing wheat, and he turned back and saw the Angel; and his four sons hid themselves.

21And as David came to Ornan, Ornan looked and saw him, and went out from the threshing floor and bowed himself to David with his face to the ground.

22Then David said to Ornan, Grant me the site of this threshing floor, that I may build an altar on it to the Lord. You shall charge me the full price for it, that the plague may be averted from the people.

## New American Standard

2So David said to Joab and to the princes of the people, "Go,
number Israel from Beersheba even to Dan, and bring me *word* that
I may know their number."
3And Joab said, "May the LORD add to His people a hundred
times as many as they are! But, my lord the king, are they not all
my lord's servants? Why does my lord seek this thing? Why should
he be a cause of guilt to Israel?"
4Nevertheless, the king's word prevailed against Joab. Therefore, Joab departed and went throughout all Israel, and came to
Jerusalem.
5And Joab gave the number of the census of *all* the people to
David. And all Israel were 1,100,000 men who drew the sword; and
Judah *was* 470,000 men who drew the sword.
6But he did not number Levi and Benjamin among them, for
the king's command was abhorrent to Joab.
7And God was displeased with this thing, so He struck Israel.
8And David said to God, "I have sinned greatly, in that I have
done this thing. But now, please take away the iniquity of Thy
servant, for I have done very foolishly."
9¶ And the LORD spoke to Gad, David's seer, saying,
10"Go and speak to David, saying, 'Thus says the LORD, "I offer
you three things; choose for yourself one of them, that I may do
*it* to you." ' "
11So Gad came to David and said to him, "Thus says the LORD,
'Take for yourself
12either three years of famine, or three months to be swept
away before your foes, while the sword of your enemies overtakes
*you*, or else three days of the sword of the LORD, even pestilence
in the land, and the angel of the LORD destroying throughout all
the territory of Israel.' Now, therefore, consider what answer I
shall return to Him who sent me."
13And David said to Gad, "I am in great distress; please let me
fall into the hand of the LORD, for His mercies are very great. But
do not let me fall into the hand of man."
14So the LORD sent a pestilence on Israel; 70,000 men of Israel
fell.
15And God sent an angel to Jerusalem to destroy it; but as he
was about to destroy *it*, the LORD saw and was sorry over the
calamity, and said to the destroying angel, "It is enough; now relax
your hand." And the angel of the LORD was standing by the
threshing floor of Ornan the Jebusite.
16Then David lifted up his eyes and saw the angel of the LORD
standing between earth and heaven, with his drawn sword in his
hand stretched out over Jerusalem. Then David and the elders,
covered with sackcloth, fell on their faces.
17And David said to God, "Is it not I who commanded to count
the people? Indeed, I am the one who has sinned and done very
wickedly, but these sheep, what have they done? O LORD my God,
please let Thy hand be against me and my father's household, but
not against Thy people that they should be plagued."

*David's Altar*

18¶ Then the angel of the LORD commanded Gad to say to
David, that David should go up and build an altar to the LORD on
the threshing floor of Ornan the Jebusite.
19So David went up at the word of Gad, which he spoke in the
name of the LORD.
20Now Ornan turned back and saw the angel, and his four sons
*who were* with him hid themselves. And Ornan was threshing
wheat.
21And as David came to Ornan, Ornan looked and saw David,
and went out from the threshing floor, and prostrated himself
before David with his face to the ground.
22Then David said to Ornan, "Give me the site of *this* threshing
floor, that I may build on it an altar to the LORD; for the full price
you shall give it to me, that the plague may be restrained from the
people."

## New International

manders of the troops, "Go and count the Israelites from Beer-
sheba to Dan. Then report back to me so that I may know how
many there are."
3But Joab replied, "May the LORD multiply his troops a hundred
times over. My lord the king, are they not all my lord's subjects?
Why does my lord want to do this? Why should he bring guilt on
Israel?"
4The king's word, however, overruled Joab; so Joab left and
went throughout Israel and then came back to Jerusalem. 5Joab
reported the number of the fighting men to David: In all Israel
there were one million one hundred thousand men who could
handle a sword, including four hundred and seventy thousand in
Judah.
6But Joab did not include Levi and Benjamin in the numbering,
because the king's command was repulsive to him. 7This command was also evil in the sight of God; so he punished Israel.
8Then David said to God, "I have sinned greatly by doing this.
Now, I beg you, take away the guilt of your servant. I have done
a very foolish thing."
9The LORD said to Gad, David's seer, 10"Go and tell David, 'This
is what the LORD says: I am giving you three options. Choose one
of them for me to carry out against you.' "
11So Gad went to David and said to him, "This is what the LORD
says: 'Take your choice: 12three years of famine, three months of
being swept away[a] before your enemies, with their swords over-
taking you, or three days of the sword of the LORD—days of plague
in the land, with the angel of the LORD ravaging every part of
Israel.' Now then, decide how I should answer the one who sent
me."
13David said to Gad, "I am in deep distress. Let me fall into the
hands of the LORD, for his mercy is very great; but do not let me
fall into the hands of men."
14So the LORD sent a plague on Israel, and seventy thousand
men of Israel fell dead. 15And God sent an angel to destroy Jerusalem. But as the angel was doing so, the LORD saw it and was
grieved because of the calamity and said to the angel who was
destroying the people, "Enough! Withdraw your hand." The angel
of the LORD was then standing at the threshing floor of Araunah[b]
the Jebusite.
16David looked up and saw the angel of the LORD standing
between heaven and earth, with a drawn sword in his hand extended over Jerusalem. Then David and the elders, clothed in
sackcloth, fell facedown.
17David said to God, "Was it not I who ordered the fighting men
to be counted? I am the one who has sinned and done wrong.
These are but sheep. What have they done? O LORD my God, let
your hand fall upon me and my family, but do not let this plague
remain on your people."
18Then the angel of the LORD ordered Gad to tell David to go
up and build an altar to the LORD on the threshing floor of Araunah
the Jebusite. 19So David went up in obedience to the word that Gad
had spoken in the name of the LORD.
20While Araunah was threshing wheat, he turned and saw the
angel; his four sons who were with him hid themselves. 21Then
David approached, and when Araunah looked and saw him, he
left the threshing floor and bowed down before David with his face
to the ground.
22David said to him, "Let me have the site of your threshing
floor so I can build an altar to the LORD, that the plague on the
people may be stopped. Sell it to me at the full price."

**NIV** [a] *12* Hebrew; Septuagint and Vulgate (see also 2 Samuel 24:13) *of fleeing*
[b] *15* Hebrew *Ornan*, a variant of *Araunah*; also in verses 18-28

## King James

23 And Ornan said unto David, Take *it* to thee, and let my lord the king do *that which is* good in his eyes: lo, I give *thee* the oxen *also* for burnt offerings, and the threshing instruments for wood, and the wheat for the meat offering; I give it all.

24 And king David said to Ornan, Nay; but I will verily buy it for the full price: for I will not take *that* which *is* thine for the LORD, nor offer burnt offerings without cost.

25 So David gave to Ornan for the place six hundred shekels of gold by weight.

26 And David built there an altar unto the LORD, and offered burnt offerings and peace offerings, and called upon the LORD; and he answered him from heaven by fire upon the altar of burnt offering.

27 And the LORD commanded the angel; and he put up his sword again into the sheath thereof.

28 ¶ At that time when David saw that the LORD had answered him in the threshingfloor of Ornan the Jebusite, then he sacrificed there.

29 For the tabernacle of the LORD, which Moses made in the wilderness, and the altar of the burnt offering, *were* at that season in the high place at Gibeon.

30 But David could not go before it to inquire of God: for he was afraid because of the sword of the angel of the LORD.

**22** THEN DAVID said, This *is* the house of the LORD God, and this *is* the altar of the burnt offering for Israel.

2 And David commanded to gather together the strangers that *were* in the land of Israel; and he set masons to hew wrought stones to build the house of God.

3 And David prepared iron in abundance for the nails for the doors of the gates, and for the joinings; and brass in abundance without weight;

4 Also cedar trees in abundance: for the Zidonians and they of Tyre brought much cedar wood to David.

5 And David said, Solomon my son *is* young and tender, and the house *that is* to be builded for the LORD *must be* exceeding magnifical, of fame and of glory throughout all countries: I will *therefore* now make preparation for it. So David prepared abundantly before his death.

6 ¶ Then he called for Solomon his son, and charged him to build an house for the LORD God of Israel.

7 And David said to Solomon, My son, as for me, it was in my mind to build an house unto the name of the LORD my God:

8 But the word of the LORD came to me, saying, Thou hast shed blood abundantly, and hast made great wars: thou shalt not build an house unto my name, because thou hast shed much blood upon the earth in my sight.

9 Behold, a son shall be born to thee, who shall be a man of rest; and I will give him rest from all his enemies round about: for his name shall be Solomon, and I will give peace and quietness unto Israel in his days.

10 He shall build an house for my name; and he shall be my son, and I *will be* his father; and I will establish the throne of his kingdom over Israel for ever.

11 Now, my son, the LORD be with thee; and prosper thou, and build the house of the LORD thy God, as he hath said of thee.

12 Only the LORD give thee wisdom and understanding, and give thee charge concerning Israel, that thou mayest keep the law of the LORD thy God.

## Amplified

23 Ornan said to David, Take it, and let my lord the king do what is good in his eyes. I give you the oxen also for burnt offerings, and the threshing sledges for wood, and the wheat for the meal offering. I give it all.

24 And King David said to Ornan, No, but I will pay the full price; I will not take what is yours for the Lord, nor offer burnt offerings which cost me nothing.

25 So David gave to Ornan for the site 600 shekels of gold by weight.

26 And David built there an altar to the Lord, and offered burnt offerings and peace offerings, and called upon the Lord; and He answered him by fire from Heaven upon the altar of burnt offering.

27 Then the Lord commanded the [avenging] angel, and he put his sword back into its sheath.

28 When David saw that the Lord had answered him at the threshing floor of Ornan the Jebusite, he sacrificed there.

29 For the tabernacle of the Lord, which Moses made in the wilderness, and the altar of burnt offering were at that time in the high place at Gibeon.

30 But David could not go before it to inquire of God; for he was afraid of the sword of the Angel of the Lord.

**22** THEN DAVID said, Here shall be the house of the Lord God and here the altar of the burnt offering for Israel.

2 David commanded to gather together the strangers who were in the land of Israel, and he set stonecutters to hew out stones to build the house of God.

3 David prepared iron in abundance for nails for the doors of the gates and for the couplings, and bronze in abundance without weighing,

4 Also cedar trees without number; for the Sidonians and they of Tyre brought much cedar timber to David.

5 David said, Solomon my son is young and inexperienced, and the house that is to be built for the Lord must be exceedingly magnificent, of fame and glory throughout all lands; I will therefore make preparation for it. So David prepared abundantly before his death.

6 Then he called for Solomon his son, and charged him to build a house for the Lord God of Israel.

7 David said to Solomon, My son, it was in my heart to build a house to the name *and* [for the symbol of] the presence of the Lord my God.

8 But the word of the Lord came to me, saying, You have shed much blood and have waged great wars; you shall not build a house to My name, because you have shed much blood on the earth in My sight.

9 Behold, a son shall be born to you who shall be a man of peace. I will give him rest from all his enemies round about; for his name shall be Solomon (peaceable), and I will give peace and quiet to Israel in his days. [II Sam. 12:24, 25.]

10 He shall build a house for My name *and* [the symbol of My] presence. He shall be My son, and I will be his father, and I will establish his royal throne over Israel for ever.

11 Now, my son, the Lord be with and prosper you in building the house of the Lord your God as He has spoken concerning you.

12 Only the Lord give you wisdom and understanding, as you are put in charge of Israel, that you may keep the law of the Lord your God.

## New American Standard

23 And Ornan said to David, "Take *it* for yourself; and let my
lord the king do what is good in his sight. See, I will give the oxen
for burnt offerings and the threshing sledges for wood and the
wheat for the grain offering; I will give *it* all."
24 But King David said to Ornan, "No, but I will surely buy *it*
for the full price; for I will not take what is yours for the LORD, or
offer a burnt offering which costs me nothing."
25 So David gave Ornan 600 shekels of gold by weight for the
site.
26 Then David built an altar to the LORD there, and offered burnt
offerings and peace offerings. And he called to the LORD and He
answered him with fire from heaven on the altar of burnt offering.
27 And the LORD commanded the angel, and he put his sword
back in its sheath.
28 ¶ At that time, when David saw that the LORD had answered
him on the threshing floor of Ornan the Jebusite, he offered sacrifice there.
29 For the tabernacle of the LORD, which Moses had made in the
wilderness, and the altar of burnt offering *were* in the high place
at Gibeon at that time.
30 But David could not go before it to inquire of God, for he was
terrified by the sword of the angel of the LORD.

*David Prepares for Temple Building*

22 THEN DAVID said, "This is the house of the LORD God,
and this is the altar of burnt offering for Israel."
2 ¶ So David gave orders to gather the foreigners who were in
the land of Israel, and he set stonecutters to hew out stones to build
the house of God.
3 And David prepared large quantities of iron to make the nails
for the doors of the gates and for the clamps, and more bronze than
could be weighed;
4 and timbers of cedar logs beyond number, for the Sidonians
and Tyrians brought large quantities of cedar timber to David.
5 And David said, "My son Solomon is young and inexperienced, and the house that is to be built for the LORD shall be
exceedingly magnificent, famous and glorious throughout all
lands. *Therefore* now I will make preparation for it." So David made
ample preparations before his death.

*Solomon Charged with the Task*

6 ¶ Then he called for his son Solomon, and charged him to
build a house for the LORD God of Israel.
7 And David said to Solomon, "My son, I had intended to build
a house to the name of the LORD my God.
8 "But the word of the LORD came to me, saying, 'You have
shed much blood, and have waged great wars; you shall not build
a house to My name, because you have shed *so* much blood on the
earth before Me.
9 'Behold, a son shall be born to you, who shall be a man of rest;
and I will give him rest from all his enemies on every side; for his
name shall be [a]Solomon, and I will give peace and quiet to Israel
in his days.
10 'He shall build a house for My name, and he shall be My son,
and I will be his father; and I will establish the throne of his
kingdom over Israel forever.'
11 "Now, my son, the LORD be with you that you may be successful, and build the house of the LORD your God just as He has
spoken concerning you.
12 "Only the LORD give you discretion and understanding, and
give you charge over Israel, so that you may keep the law of the
LORD your God.

NAS [a] I.e., peaceful

## New International

23 Araunah said to David, "Take it! Let my lord the king do
whatever pleases him. Look, I will give the oxen for the burnt
offerings, the threshing sledges for the wood, and the wheat for
the grain offering. I will give all this."
24 But King David replied to Araunah, "No, I insist on paying
the full price. I will not take for the LORD what is yours, or sacrifice
a burnt offering that costs me nothing."
25 So David paid Araunah six hundred shekels[b] of gold for the
site. 26 David built an altar to the LORD there and sacrificed burnt
offerings and fellowship offerings.[c] He called on the LORD, and
the LORD answered him with fire from heaven on the altar of burnt
offering.
27 Then the LORD spoke to the angel, and he put his sword back
into its sheath. 28 At that time, when David saw that the LORD had
answered him on the threshing floor of Araunah the Jebusite, he
offered sacrifices there. 29 The tabernacle of the LORD, which Moses
had made in the desert, and the altar of burnt offering were at that
time on the high place at Gibeon. 30 But David could not go before
it to inquire of God, because he was afraid of the sword of the angel
of the LORD.

22 THEN DAVID said, "The house of the LORD God is to be
here, and also the altar of burnt offering for Israel."

*Preparations for the Temple*

2 So David gave orders to assemble the aliens living in Israel,
and from among them he appointed stonecutters to prepare
dressed stone for building the house of God. 3 He provided a large
amount of iron to make nails for the doors of the gateways and for
the fittings, and more bronze than could be weighed. 4 He also
provided more cedar logs than could be counted, for the Sidonians
and Tyrians had brought large numbers of them to David.
5 David said, "My son Solomon is young and inexperienced,
and the house to be built for the LORD should be of great magnificence and fame and splendor in the sight of all the nations. Therefore I will make preparations for it." So David made extensive
preparations before his death.
6 Then he called for his son Solomon and charged him to build
a house for the LORD, the God of Israel. 7 David said to Solomon:
"My son, I had it in my heart to build a house for the Name of the
LORD my God. 8 But this word of the LORD came to me: 'You have
shed much blood and have fought many wars. You are not to build
a house for my Name, because you have shed much blood on the
earth in my sight. 9 But you will have a son who will be a man of
peace and rest, and I will give him rest from all his enemies on
every side. His name will be Solomon,[d] and I will grant Israel
peace and quiet during his reign. 10 He is the one who will build
a house for my Name. He will be my son, and I will be his father.
And I will establish the throne of his kingdom over Israel forever.'
11 "Now, my son, the LORD be with you, and may you have
success and build the house of the LORD your God, as he said you
would. 12 May the LORD give you discretion and understanding
when he puts you in command over Israel, so that you may keep
the law of the LORD your God. 13 Then you will have success if you

NIV [b] 25 That is, about 15 pounds (about 7 kilograms) [c] 26 Traditionally *peace offerings* [d] 9 *Solomon* sounds like and may be derived from the Hebrew for *peace*.

## King James

13Then shalt thou prosper, if thou takest heed to fulfil the statutes and judgments which the LORD charged Moses with concerning Israel: be strong, and of good courage; dread not, nor be dismayed.
14Now, behold, in my trouble I have prepared for the house of the LORD an hundred thousand talents of gold, and a thousand thousand talents of silver; and of brass and iron without weight; for it is in abundance: timber also and stone have I prepared; and thou mayest add thereto.
15Moreover *there are* workmen with thee in abundance, hewers and workers of stone and timber, and all manner of cunning men for every manner of work.
16Of the gold, the silver, and the brass, and the iron, *there is* no number. Arise *therefore,* and be doing, and the LORD be with thee.
17¶ David also commanded all the princes of Israel to help Solomon his son, *saying,*
18 *Is* not the LORD your God with you? and hath he *not* given you rest on every side? for he hath given the inhabitants of the land into mine hand; and the land is subdued before the LORD, and before his people.
19Now set your heart and your soul to seek the LORD your God; arise therefore, and build ye the sanctuary of the LORD God, to bring the ark of the covenant of the LORD, and the holy vessels of God, into the house that is to be built to the name of the LORD.

23 SO WHEN David was old and full of days, he made Solomon his son king over Israel.
2¶ And he gathered together all the princes of Israel, with the priests and the Levites.
3Now the Levites were numbered from the age of thirty years and upward: and their number by their polls, man by man, was thirty and eight thousand.
4Of which, twenty and four thousand *were* to set forward the work of the house of the LORD; and six thousand *were* officers and judges:
5Moreover four thousand *were* porters; and four thousand praised the LORD with the instruments which I made, *said David,* to praise *therewith.*
6And David divided them into courses among the sons of Levi, *namely,* Gershon, Kohath, and Merari.
7¶ Of the Gershonites *were,* Laadan, and Shimei.
8The sons of Laadan; the chief *was* Jehiel, and Zetham, and Joel, three.
9The sons of Shimei; Shelomith, and Haziel, and Haran, three. These *were* the chief of the fathers of Laadan.
10And the sons of Shimei *were,* Jahath, Zina, and Jeush, and Beriah. These four *were* the sons of Shimei.
11And Jahath was the chief, and Zizah the second: but Jeush and Beriah had not many sons; therefore they were in one reckoning, according to *their* father's house.
12¶ The sons of Kohath; Amram, Izhar, Hebron, and Uzziel, four.
13The sons of Amram; Aaron and Moses: and Aaron was separated, that he should sanctify the most holy things, he and his sons for ever, to burn incense before the LORD, to minister unto him, and to bless in his name for ever.
14Now *concerning* Moses the man of God, his sons were named of the tribe of Levi.

## Amplified

13Then you will prosper, if you are careful to keep *and* fulfill the statutes and ordinances with which the Lord charged Moses concerning Israel. Be strong and of good courage; dread not *and* fear not; be not dismayed.
14In my affliction *and* trouble I have provided for the house of the Lord 100,000 talents of gold, 1,000,000 talents of silver, and bronze and iron without weighing. I have also provided timber and stone; you must add to them.
15You have workmen in abundance: hewers, workers of stone and timber, and all kinds of craftsmen without number, skillful in doing every kind of work
16With gold, silver, bronze, and iron. So arise and be doing, and the Lord be with you!
17David also commanded all the princes of Israel to help Solomon his son, saying,
18Is not the Lord your God with you? And has He not given you peace on every side? For He has given the inhabitants of the land into my hand; and the land is subdued before the Lord and His people.
19Now set your mind and heart to seek—inquire of and require as your vital necessity—the Lord your God. Arise and build the sanctuary of the Lord God, so that the ark of the covenant of the Lord and the holy vessels of God may be brought into the house built to the name *and* renown of the Lord.

23 WHEN DAVID was old and full of days, he made Solomon his son king over Israel.
2David assembled all the leaders of Israel, with the priests and Levites.
3The Levites thirty years old and upward numbered, man by man, 38,000.
4Of whom [a]24,000 were to oversee the work of the house of the Lord, and 6,000 were to be officers and judges,
5And, said David, 4,000 shall be gatekeepers, and 4,000 are to praise the Lord with the instruments which I made for praise.
6And David organized them in sections according to the sons of Levi: Gershon, Kohath, and Merari.
7Of the Gershonites: Ladan [Libni], and Shimei.
8The sons of Ladan: Jehiel the chief, Zetham, and Joel, three.
9The sons of Shimei: Shelomoth, Haziel, and Haran, three. These were the heads of the fathers' houses of Ladan.
10And the sons of Shimei: Jahath, Zina [Zizah], Jeush, and Beriah. Of these four sons of Shimei,
11Jahath was chief, and Zizah second; but Jeush and Beriah had not many sons [not enough for a father's house or clan], so they were counted together as one father's house.
12The sons of Kohath: Amram, Izhar, Hebron, and Uzziel, four.
13The sons of Amram: Aaron and Moses. Aaron was set apart to sanctify him as most holy, *and* to consecrate the most holy things, that he and his sons forever might burn incense before the Lord, minister to Him, and bless in His name [and the character which that name denotes] for ever.
14But the sons of Moses the man of God were named among the tribe of Levi.

**AMP** [a] The reader may be tempted to consider these figures absurdly high, if he does not get the whole picture. Note these features of it: (1) The Levites were divided into twenty-four rotating divisions. (2) One thousand workers on duty at one time for Solomon's temple, considering the many purposes and cost of the building, its ornate ritual, and the scale of the work, is not unreasonable according to authorities. (3) In the primitive simplicity of the wilderness, the worshiper killed the animal he brought for an offering, skinned, cut it in pieces, and washed the entrails and legs. But now all these services were the duty of the Levites or Nethinim (servants of the temple), also the number of worshipers had greatly increased.

## New American Standard

13"Then you shall prosper, if you are careful to observe the
statutes and the ordinances which the LORD commanded Moses
concerning Israel. Be strong and courageous, do not fear nor be
dismayed.
14"Now behold, with great pains I have prepared for the house
of the LORD 100,000 talents of gold and 1,000,000 talents of silver,
and bronze and iron beyond weight, for they are in great quantity;
also timber and stone I have prepared, and you may add to them.
15"Moreover, there are many workmen with you, stonecutters
and masons of stone and carpenters, and all men who are skillful
in every kind of work.
16"Of the gold, the silver and the bronze and the iron, there is
no limit. Arise and work, and may the LORD be with you."
17¶ David also commanded all the leaders of Israel to help his
son Solomon, *saying,*
18"Is not the LORD your God with you? And has He not given
you rest on every side? For He has given the inhabitants of the land
into my hand, and the land is subdued before the LORD and before
His people.
19"Now set your heart and your soul to seek the LORD your
God; arise, therefore, and build the sanctuary of the LORD God, so
that you may bring the ark of the covenant of the LORD, and the
holy vessels of God into the house that is to be built for the name
of the LORD."

*Solomon Reigns*

**23** NOW WHEN David reached old age, he made his son
Solomon king over Israel.
2And he gathered together all the leaders of Israel with the
priests and the Levites.

*Offices of the Levites*

3And the Levites were numbered from thirty years old and
upward, and their number by census of men was 38,000.
4Of these, 24,000 were to oversee the work of the house of the
LORD; and 6,000 *were* officers and judges,
5and 4,000 *were* gatekeepers, and 4,000 *were* praising the LORD
with the instruments which David made for giving praise.
6And David divided them into divisions according to the sons
of Levi: Gershon, Kohath, and Merari.

*Gershonites*

7¶ Of the Gershonites *were* Ladan and Shimei.
8The sons of Ladan *were* Jehiel the first and Zetham and Joel,
three.
9The sons of Shimei *were* Shelomoth and Haziel and Haran,
three. These were the heads of the fathers' *households* of Ladan.
10And the sons of Shimei *were* Jahath, Zina, Jeush, and Beriah.
These four *were* the sons of Shimei.
11And Jahath was the first, and Zizah the second; but Jeush and
Beriah did not have many sons, so they became a father's household, one class.

*Kohathites*

12¶ The sons of Kohath were four: Amram, Izhar, Hebron and
Uzziel.
13The sons of Amram were Aaron and Moses. And Aaron was
set apart to sanctify him as most holy, he and his sons forever, to
burn incense before the LORD, to minister to Him and to bless in
His name forever.
14But *as for* Moses the man of God, his sons were named among
the tribe of Levi.

## New International

are careful to observe the decrees and laws that the LORD gave
Moses for Israel. Be strong and courageous. Do not be afraid or
discouraged.
14"I have taken great pains to provide for the temple of the LORD
a hundred thousand talents[b] of gold, a million talents[c] of silver,
quantities of bronze and iron too great to be weighed, and wood
and stone. And you may add to them. 15You have many workmen:
stonecutters, masons and carpenters, as well as men skilled in
every kind of work 16in gold and silver, bronze and iron—craftsmen beyond number. Now begin the work, and the LORD be with
you."
17Then David ordered all the leaders of Israel to help his son
Solomon. 18He said to them, "Is not the LORD your God with you?
And has he not granted you rest on every side? For he has handed
the inhabitants of the land over to me, and the land is subject to
the LORD and to his people. 19Now devote your heart and soul to
seeking the LORD your God. Begin to build the sanctuary of the
LORD God, so that you may bring the ark of the covenant of the
LORD and the sacred articles belonging to God into the temple that
will be built for the Name of the LORD."

*The Levites*

**23** WHEN DAVID was old and full of years, he made his son
Solomon king over Israel.
2He also gathered together all the leaders of Israel, as well as
the priests and Levites. 3The Levites thirty years old or more were
counted, and the total number of men was thirty-eight thousand.
4David said, "Of these, twenty-four thousand are to supervise the
work of the temple of the LORD and six thousand are to be officials
and judges. 5Four thousand are to be gatekeepers and four thousand are to praise the LORD with the musical instruments I have
provided for that purpose."
6David divided the Levites into groups corresponding to the
sons of Levi: Gershon, Kohath and Merari.

*Gershonites*

7Belonging to the Gershonites:
Ladan and Shimei.
8The sons of Ladan:
Jehiel the first, Zetham and Joel—three in all.
9The sons of Shimei:
Shelomoth, Haziel and Haran—three in all.
These were the heads of the families of Ladan.
10And the sons of Shimei:
Jahath, Ziza,[d] Jeush and Beriah.
These were the sons of Shimei—four in all.
11Jahath was the first and Ziza the second, but Jeush and
Beriah did not have many sons; so they were counted as
one family with one assignment.

*Kohathites*

12The sons of Kohath:
Amram, Izhar, Hebron and Uzziel—four in all.
13The sons of Amram:
Aaron and Moses.
Aaron was set apart, he and his descendants forever, to
consecrate the most holy things, to offer sacrifices before
the LORD, to minister before him and to pronounce blessings in his name forever. 14The sons of Moses the man of
God were counted as part of the tribe of Levi.

**NIV** [b] *14* That is, about 3,750 tons (about 3,450 metric tons) [c] *14* That is, about 37,500 tons (about 34,500 metric tons) [d] *10* One Hebrew manuscript, Septuagint and Vulgate (see also verse 11); most Hebrew manuscripts *Zina*

## King James

15The sons of Moses *were*, Gershom, and Eliezer.
16Of the sons of Gershom, Shebuel *was* the chief.
17And the sons of Eliezer *were*, Rehabiah the chief. And Eliezer had none other sons; but the sons of Rehabiah were very many.
18Of the sons of Izhar; Shelomith the chief.
19Of the sons of Hebron; Jeriah the first, Amariah the second, Jahaziel the third, and Jekameam the fourth.
20Of the sons of Uzziel; Michah the first, and Jesiah the second.
21¶ The sons of Merari; Mahli, and Mushi. The sons of Mahli; Eleazar, and Kish.
22And Eleazar died, and had no sons, but daughters: and their brethren the sons of Kish took them.
23The sons of Mushi; Mahli, and Eder, and Jeremoth, three.
24¶ These *were* the sons of Levi after the house of their fathers; *even* the chief of the fathers, as they were counted by number of names by their polls, that did the work for the service of the house of the LORD, from the age of twenty years and upward.
25For David said, The LORD God of Israel hath given rest unto his people, that they may dwell in Jerusalem for ever:
26And also unto the Levites; they shall no *more* carry the tabernacle, nor any vessels of it for the service thereof.
27For by the last words of David the Levites *were* numbered from twenty years old and above:
28Because their office *was* to wait on the sons of Aaron for the service of the house of the LORD, in the courts, and in the chambers, and in the purifying of all holy things, and the work of the service of the house of God;
29Both for the showbread, and for the fine flour for meat offering, and for the unleavened cakes, and for *that which is baked in* the pan, and for that which is fried, and for all manner of measure and size;
30And to stand every morning to thank and praise the LORD, and likewise at even;
31And to offer all burnt sacrifices unto the LORD in the sabbaths, in the new moons, and on the set feasts, by number, according to the order commanded unto them, continually before the LORD:
32And that they should keep the charge of the tabernacle of the congregation, and the charge of the holy *place*, and the charge of the sons of Aaron their brethren, in the service of the house of the LORD.

**24** NOW *THESE are* the divisions of the sons of Aaron. The sons of Aaron; Nadab, and Abihu, Eleazar, and Ithamar.
2But Nadab and Abihu died before their father, and had no children: therefore Eleazar and Ithamar executed the priest's office.
3And David distributed them, both Zadok of the sons of Eleazar, and Ahimelech of the sons of Ithamar, according to their offices in their service.
4And there were more chief men found of the sons of Eleazar than of the sons of Ithamar; and *thus* were they divided. Among the sons of Eleazar *there were* sixteen chief men of the house of *their* fathers, and eight among the sons of Ithamar according to the house of their fathers.
5Thus were they divided by lot, one sort with another; for the governors of the sanctuary, and governors *of the house* of God, were of the sons of Eleazar, and of the sons of Ithamar.

## Amplified

15The sons of Moses: Gershom and Eliezer.
16The sons of Gershom, Shebuel the chief.
17The sons of Eliezer: Rehabiah the chief. Eliezer had no other sons, but Rehabiah's sons were very many.
18The sons of Izhar: Shelomith the chief.
19The sons of Hebron: Jeriah first, Amariah second, Jahaziel third, and Jekameam fourth.
20The sons of Uzziel: Micah first, and Isshiah second.
21The sons of Merari: Mahli and Mushi. The sons of Mahli: Eleazar and Kish.
22Eleazar died, and had no sons, but daughters only, and their kinsmen, sons of Kish, took them as wives.
23The sons of Mushi: Mahli, Eder, and Jeremoth, three.
24These were the Levites by their fathers' houses, the heads of fathers' houses of those registered according to the number of names of the individuals who were the servants of the house of the Lord, from twenty years old and upward.
25For David said, The Lord, the God of Israel has given peace *and* rest to His people; and He dwells in Jerusalem for ever.
26So the Levites no more have need to carry the tabernacle and all its vessels for its service;
27For by the last words *and* acts of David these were the number of the Levites from twenty years old and above,
28But their duty should be to wait on (the priests) the sons of Aaron in the service of the house of the Lord, caring for the courts, the chambers, the cleansing of all holy things, and any work of the service of God's house;
29For the showbread also, and for the fine flour for a cereal offering, whether of unleavened wafers, or of what is baked on the griddle, or soaked [in oil], and for all measuring of amount and size [as the law of Moses required];
30To stand every morning to thank and praise the Lord, and likewise at evening;
31To assist in offering all burnt sacrifices to the Lord on sabbaths, new moons, and set feast days by number according to the ordinance concerning them, continually before the Lord.
32So they shall keep charge of the tent of meeting and the holy place and shall attend the sons of Aaron their kinsmen for the service of the house of the Lord.

**24** THE COURSES *or* divisions of the priests, the sons of Aaron, were these. The sons of Aaron: Nadab and Abihu, Eleazar and Ithamar.
2But Nadab and Abihu died before their father, and had no children; therefore Eleazar and Ithamar executed the priest's office.
3And David with Zadok of the sons of Eleazar, and Ahimelech of the sons of Ithamar, divided *and* distributed them according to their assigned duties.
4Since there were more chief men found among the sons of Eleazar [because of the misfortunes of Eli, and Saul's slaughter of the priests at Nob] than among the sons of Ithamar, they were divided thus: sixteen heads of fathers' houses of the sons of Eleazar and eight of the sons of Ithamar according to their fathers' houses.
5Thus were they divided by lot, one group with the other, for there were chiefs of the sanctuary, and chiefs of God [high priests], drawn both from the sons of Eleazar and from the sons of Ithamar.

## New American Standard

15The sons of Moses *were* Gershom and Eliezer.
16The son of Gershom *was* Shebuel the chief.
17And the son of Eliezer was Rehabiah the chief; and Eliezer had no other sons, but the sons of Rehabiah were very many.
18The son of Izhar was Shelomith the chief.
19The sons of Hebron *were* Jeriah the first, Amariah the second, Jahaziel the third and Jekameam the fourth.
20The sons of Uzziel *were* Micah the first and Isshiah the second.

*Merarites*

21¶ The sons of Merari were Mahli and Mushi. The sons of Mahli *were* Eleazar and Kish.
22And Eleazar died and had no sons, but daughters only, so their brothers, the sons of Kish, took them *as wives.*
23The sons of Mushi *were* three: Mahli, Eder, and Jeremoth.

*Duties Revised*

24¶ These were the sons of Levi according to their fathers' households, *even* the heads of the fathers' *households* of those of them who were counted, in the number of names by their census, doing the work for the service of the house of the LORD, from twenty years old and upward.
25For David said, "The LORD God of Israel has given rest to His people, and He dwells in Jerusalem forever.
26"And also, the Levites will no longer need to carry the tabernacle and all its utensils for its service."
27For by the last words of David the sons of Levi *were* numbered, from twenty years old and upward.
28For their office is to assist the sons of Aaron with the service of the house of the LORD, in the courts and in the chambers and in the purifying of all holy things, even the work of the service of the house of God,
29and with the showbread, and the fine flour for a grain offering, and unleavened wafers, or *what is baked in* the pan, or what is well-mixed, and all measures of volume and size.
30And they are to stand every morning to thank and to praise the LORD, and likewise at evening,
31and to offer all burnt offerings to the LORD, on the sabbaths, the new moons and the fixed festivals in the number *set* by the ordinance concerning them, continually before the LORD.
32Thus they are to keep charge of the tent of meeting, and charge of the holy place, and charge of the sons of Aaron their relatives, for the service of the house of the LORD.

## New International

15The sons of Moses:
Gershom and Eliezer.
16The descendants of Gershom:
Shubael was the first.
17The descendants of Eliezer:
Rehabiah was the first.
Eliezer had no other sons, but the sons of Rehabiah were very numerous.
18The sons of Izhar:
Shelomith was the first.
19The sons of Hebron:
Jeriah the first, Amariah the second, Jahaziel the third and Jekameam the fourth.
20The sons of Uzziel:
Micah the first and Isshiah the second.

*Merarites*

21The sons of Merari:
Mahli and Mushi.
The sons of Mahli:
Eleazar and Kish.
22Eleazar died without having sons: he had only daughters.
Their cousins, the sons of Kish, married them.
23The sons of Mushi:
Mahli, Eder and Jerimoth—three in all.

24These were the descendants of Levi by their families—the heads of families as they were registered under their names and counted individually, that is, the workers twenty years old or more who served in the temple of the LORD.
25For David had said, "Since the LORD, the God of Israel, has granted rest to his people and has come to dwell in Jerusalem forever,
26the Levites no longer need to carry the tabernacle or any of the articles used in its service."
27According to the last instructions of David, the Levites were counted from those twenty years old or more.
28The duty of the Levites was to help Aaron's descendants in the service of the temple of the LORD: to be in charge of the courtyards, the side rooms, the purification of all sacred things and the performance of other duties at the house of God.
29They were in charge of the bread set out on the table, the flour for the grain offerings, the unleavened wafers, the baking and the mixing, and all measurements of quantity and size.
30They were also to stand every morning to thank and praise the LORD. They were to do the same in the evening
31and whenever burnt offerings were presented to the LORD on Sabbaths and at New Moon festivals and at appointed feasts. They were to serve before the LORD regularly in the proper number and in the way prescribed for them.
32And so the Levites carried out their responsibilities for the Tent of Meeting, for the Holy Place and, under their brothers the descendants of Aaron, for the service of the temple of the LORD.

*Divisions of Levites*

**24** NOW THE divisions of the descendants of Aaron *were these:* the sons of Aaron *were* Nadab, Abihu, Eleazar, and Ithamar.
2But Nadab and Abihu died before their father and had no sons. So Eleazar and Ithamar served as priests.
3And David, with Zadok of the sons of Eleazar and Ahimelech of the sons of Ithamar, divided them according to their offices for their ministry.
4Since more chief men were found from the descendants of Eleazar than the descendants of Ithamar, they divided them thus: *there were* sixteen heads of fathers' households of the descendants of Eleazar, and eight of the descendants of Ithamar according to their fathers' households.
5Thus they were divided by lot, the one as the other; for they were officers of the sanctuary and officers of God, both from the descendants of Eleazar and the descendants of Ithamar.

*The Divisions of Priests*

**24** THESE WERE the divisions of the sons of Aaron:
The sons of Aaron were Nadab, Abihu, Eleazar and Ithamar.
2But Nadab and Abihu died before their father did, and they had no sons; so Eleazar and Ithamar served as the priests.
3With the help of Zadok a descendant of Eleazar and Ahimelech a descendant of Ithamar, David separated them into divisions for their appointed order of ministering.
4A larger number of leaders were found among Eleazar's descendants than among Ithamar's, and they were divided accordingly: sixteen heads of families from Eleazar's descendants and eight heads of families from Ithamar's descendants.
5They divided them impartially by drawing lots, for there were officials of the sanctuary and officials of God among the descendants of both Eleazar and Ithamar.

## King James

6 And Shemaiah the son of Nethaneel the scribe, *one* of the
Levites, wrote them before the king, and the princes, and Zadok
the priest, and Ahimelech the son of Abiathar, and *before* the chief
of the fathers of the priests and Levites: one principal household
being taken for Eleazar, and *one* taken for Ithamar.
7 Now the first lot came forth to Jehoiarib, the second to Jedaiah,
8 The third to Harim, the fourth to Seorim,
9 The fifth to Malchijah, the sixth to Mijamin,
10 The seventh to Hakkoz, the eighth to Abijah,
11 The ninth to Jeshuah, the tenth to Shecaniah,
12 The eleventh to Eliashib, the twelfth to Jakim,
13 The thirteenth to Huppah, the fourteenth to Jeshebeab,
14 The fifteenth to Bilgah, the sixteenth to Immer,
15 The seventeenth to Hezir, the eighteenth to Aphses,
16 The nineteenth to Pethahiah, the twentieth to Jehezekel,
17 The one and twentieth to Jachin, the two and twentieth to
Gamul,
18 The three and twentieth to Delaiah, the four and twentieth to
Maaziah.
19 These *were* the orderings of them in their service to come into
the house of the LORD, according to their manner, under Aaron
their father, as the LORD God of Israel had commanded him.
20 ¶ And the rest of the sons of Levi *were these:* Of the sons of
Amram; Shubael: of the sons of Shubael; Jehdeiah.
21 Concerning Rehabiah: of the sons of Rehabiah, the first *was*
Isshiah.
22 Of the Izharites; Shelomoth: of the sons of Shelomoth; Jahath.
23 And the sons *of Hebron;* Jeriah *the first,* Amariah the second,
Jahaziel the third, Jekameam the fourth.
24 *Of* the sons of Uzziel; Michah: of the sons of Michah; Shamir.
25 The brother of Michah *was* Isshiah: of the sons of Isshiah;
Zechariah.
26 The sons of Merari *were* Mahli and Mushi: the sons of Jaaziah;
Beno.
27 ¶ The sons of Merari by Jaaziah; Beno, and Shoham, and
Zaccur, and Ibri.
28 Of Mahli *came* Eleazar, who had no sons.
29 Concerning Kish: the son of Kish *was* Jerahmeel.
30 The sons also of Mushi; Mahli, and Eder, and Jerimoth. These
*were* the sons of the Levites after the house of their fathers.
31 These likewise cast lots over against their brethren the sons
of Aaron in the presence of David the king, and Zadok, and
Ahimelech, and the chief of the fathers of the priests and Levites,
even the principal fathers over against their younger brethren.

## Amplified

6 Shemaiah the scribe, son of Nethanel, a Levite, recorded them
in the presence of the king, the princes, Zadok the priest, Ahimelech son of Abiathar [the priest who escaped being killed at Nob
by Saul and fled to David], and the heads of the fathers' houses
of the priests and Levites; one father's house being taken alternately for Eleazar and one for Ithamar.
7 The lots fell, first one to Jehoiarib, second to Jedaiah,
8 Third to Harim, fourth to Se-orim,
9 Fifth to Malchijah, sixth to Mijamin,
10 Seventh to Hakkoz, eighth to Abijah,
11 Ninth to Jeshua, tenth to Shecaniah,
12 Eleventh to Eliashib, twelfth to Jakim,
13 Thirteenth to Huppah, fourteenth to Jeshebe-ab,
14 Fifteenth to Bilgah, sixteenth to Immer,
15 Seventeenth to Hezir, eighteenth to Happizzez,
16 Nineteenth to Pethahiah, twentieth to Jehezkel,
17 Twenty-first to Jachin, twenty-second to Gamul,
18 Twenty-third to Delaiah, twenty-fourth to Maaziah.
19 This was their order for coming on duty to serve in the house
of the Lord, according to the procedure ordered for them by their
[forefather] Aaron, as the Lord God of Israel had commanded him.
20 The rest of the sons of Levi: of the sons of Amram, Shuba-el;
of the sons of Shuba-el, Jehdeiah.
21 Of Rehabiah: of the sons of Rehabiah, Isshiah the chief.
22 Of the Izharites, Shelomoth; of the sons of Shelomoth, Jahath.
23 The sons of Hebron: Jeriah first, Amariah second, Jahaziel
third, Jekameam fourth.
24 The sons of Uzziel, Micah; of the sons of Micah, Shamir.
25 The brother of Micah, Isshiah; of the sons of Isshiah, Zechariah.
26 The sons of Merari: Mahli and Mushi. The sons of Jaaziah:
Beno.
27 The sons of Merari by Jaaziah: Beno, Shoham, Zaccur, and
Ibri.
28 Of Mahli: Eleazar, who had no sons.
29 Of Kish, the sons of Kish: Jerahmeel.
30 The sons of Mushi: Mahli, Eder, and Jerimoth. These were the
sons of the Levites according to their fathers' houses.
31 These likewise cast lots as did their kinsmen the sons of Aaron
in the presence of David the king, Zadok, Ahimelech, and the
heads of the fathers' houses of the priests and Levites; the head
of each father's house and his younger brother alike.

# New American Standard

6And Shemaiah, the son of Nethanel the scribe, from the Levites, recorded them in the presence of the king, the princes,
Zadok the priest, Ahimelech the son of Abiathar, and the heads
of the fathers' *households* of the priests and of the Levites; one
father's household taken for Eleazar and one taken for Ithamar.
7¶ Now the first lot came out for Jehoiarib, the second for
Jedaiah,
8the third for Harim, the fourth for Seorim,
9the fifth for Malchijah, the sixth for Mijamin,
10the seventh for Hakkoz, the eighth for Abijah,
11the ninth for Jeshua, the tenth for Shecaniah,
12the eleventh for Eliashib, the twelfth for Jakim,
13the thirteenth for Huppah, the fourteenth for Jeshebeab,
14the fifteenth for Bilgah, the sixteenth for Immer,
15the seventeenth for Hezir, the eighteenth for Happizzez,
16the nineteenth for Pethahiah, the twentieth for Jehezkel,
17the twenty-first for Jachin, the twenty-second for Gamul,
18the twenty-third for Delaiah, the twenty-fourth for Maaziah.
19These were their offices for their ministry, when *they* came in
to the house of the LORD according to the ordinance *given* to them
through Aaron their father, just as the LORD God of Israel had
commanded him.
20¶ Now for the rest of the sons of Levi: of the sons of Amram,
Shubael; of the sons of Shubael, Jehdeiah.
21Of Rehabiah: of the sons of Rehabiah, Isshiah the first.
22Of the Izharites, Shelomoth; of the sons of Shelomoth, Jahath.
23And the sons *of Hebron:* Jeriah *the first,* Amariah the second,
Jahaziel the third, Jekameam the fourth.
24 *Of* the sons of Uzziel, Micah; of the sons of Micah, Shamir.
25The brother of Micah, Isshiah; of the sons of Isshiah, Zechariah.
26The sons of Merari, Mahli and Mushi; the sons of Jaaziah,
Beno.
27The sons of Merari: by Jaaziah *were* Beno, Shoham, Zaccur,
and Ibri.
28By Mahli: Eleazar, who had no sons.
29By Kish: the sons of Kish, Jerahmeel.
30And the sons of Mushi: Mahli, Eder, and Jerimoth. These *were*
the sons of the Levites according to their fathers' households.
31These also cast lots just as their relatives the sons of Aaron in
the presence of David the king, Zadok, Ahimelech, and the heads
of the fathers' *households* of the priests and of the Levites—the head
of fathers' *households* as well as those of his younger brother.

# New International

6The scribe Shemaiah son of Nethanel, a Levite, recorded their
names in the presence of the king and of the officials: Zadok the
priest, Ahimelech son of Abiathar and the heads of families of the
priests and of the Levites—one family being taken from Eleazar
and then one from Ithamar.

7The first lot fell to Jehoiarib,
the second to Jedaiah,
8the third to Harim,
the fourth to Seorim,
9the fifth to Malkijah,
the sixth to Mijamin,
10the seventh to Hakkoz,
the eighth to Abijah,
11the ninth to Jeshua,
the tenth to Shecaniah,
12the eleventh to Eliashib,
the twelfth to Jakim,
13the thirteenth to Huppah,
the fourteenth to Jeshebeab,
14the fifteenth to Bilgah,
the sixteenth to Immer,
15the seventeenth to Hezir,
the eighteenth to Happizzez,
16the nineteenth to Pethahiah,
the twentieth to Jehezkel,
17the twenty-first to Jakin,
the twenty-second to Gamul,
18the twenty-third to Delaiah
and the twenty-fourth to Maaziah.

19This was their appointed order of ministering when they
entered the temple of the LORD, according to the regulations prescribed for them by their forefather Aaron, as the LORD, the God
of Israel, had commanded him.

*The Rest of the Levites*

20As for the rest of the descendants of Levi:
from the sons of Amram: Shubael;
from the sons of Shubael: Jehdeiah.
21As for Rehabiah, from his sons:
Isshiah was the first.
22From the Izharites: Shelomoth;
from the sons of Shelomoth: Jahath.
23The sons of Hebron: Jeriah the first,[a] Amariah the second,
Jahaziel the third and Jekameam the fourth.
24The son of Uzziel: Micah;
from the sons of Micah: Shamir.
25The brother of Micah: Isshiah;
from the sons of Isshiah: Zechariah.
26The sons of Merari: Mahli and Mushi.
The son of Jaaziah: Beno.
27The sons of Merari:
from Jaaziah: Beno, Shoham, Zaccur and Ibri.
28From Mahli: Eleazar, who had no sons.
29From Kish: the son of Kish:
Jerahmeel.
30And the sons of Mushi: Mahli, Eder and Jerimoth.

These were the Levites, according to their families. 31They also
cast lots, just as their brothers the descendants of Aaron did, in the
presence of King David and of Zadok, Ahimelech, and the heads
of families of the priests and of the Levites. The families of the
oldest brother were treated the same as those of the youngest.

**NIV** [a] 23 Two Hebrew manuscripts and some Septuagint manuscripts (see also 1 Chron. 23:19); most Hebrew manuscripts *The sons of Jeriah:*

## King James

**25** MOREOVER DAVID and the captains of the host separated to the service of the sons of Asaph, and of Heman, and of Jeduthun, who should prophesy with harps, with psalteries, and with cymbals: and the number of the workmen according to their service was:

2 Of the sons of Asaph; Zaccur, and Joseph, and Nethaniah, and Asarelah, the sons of Asaph under the hands of Asaph, which prophesied according to the order of the king.

3 Of Jeduthun: the sons of Jeduthun; Gedaliah, and Zeri, and Jeshaiah, Hashabiah, and Mattithiah, six, under the hands of their father Jeduthun, who prophesied with a harp, to give thanks and to praise the LORD.

4 Of Heman: the sons of Heman; Bukkiah, Mattaniah, Uzziel, Shebuel, and Jerimoth, Hananiah, Hanani, Eliathah, Giddalti, and Romamti-ezer, Joshbekashah, Mallothi, Hothir, *and* Mahazioth:

5 All these *were* the sons of Heman the king's seer in the words of God, to lift up the horn. And God gave to Heman fourteen sons and three daughters.

6 All these *were* under the hands of their father for song *in* the house of the LORD, with cymbals, psalteries, and harps, for the service of the house of God, according to the king's order to Asaph, Jeduthun, and Heman.

7 So the number of them, with their brethren that were instructed in the songs of the LORD, *even* all that were cunning, was two hundred fourscore and eight.

8 ¶ And they cast lots, ward against *ward,* as well the small as the great, the teacher as the scholar.

9 Now the first lot came forth for Asaph to Joseph: the second to Gedaliah, who with his brethren and sons *were* twelve:

10 The third to Zaccur, *he,* his sons, and his brethren, *were* twelve:

11 The fourth to Izri, *he,* his sons, and his brethren, *were* twelve:

12 The fifth to Nethaniah, *he,* his sons, and his brethren, *were* twelve:

13 The sixth to Bukkiah, *he,* his sons, and his brethren, *were* twelve:

14 The seventh to Jesharelah, *he,* his sons, and his brethren, *were* twelve:

15 The eighth to Jeshaiah, *he,* his sons, and his brethren, *were* twelve:

16 The ninth to Mattaniah, *he,* his sons, and his brethren, *were* twelve:

17 The tenth to Shimei, *he,* his sons, and his brethren, *were* twelve:

18 The eleventh to Azareel, *he,* his sons, and his brethren, *were* twelve:

19 The twelfth to Hashabiah, *he,* his sons, and his brethren, *were* twelve:

20 The thirteenth to Shubael, *he,* his sons, and his brethren, *were* twelve:

21 The fourteenth to Mattithiah, *he,* his sons, and his brethren, *were* twelve:

22 The fifteenth to Jeremoth, *he,* his sons, and his brethren, *were* twelve:

23 The sixteenth to Hananiah, *he,* his sons, and his brethren, *were* twelve:

24 The seventeenth to Joshbekashah, *he,* his sons, and his brethren, *were* twelve:

## Amplified

**25** ALSO DAVID and the chiefs of the host [of the Lord] separated to the [temple] service some of the sons of Asaph, Heman, and Jeduthun, who should prophesy—being inspired—with lyres, harps, and cymbals. The list of the musicians according to their service was:

2 Of the sons of Asaph: Zaccur, Joseph, Nethaniah, and Asharelah, the sons of Asaph under the direction of Asaph, who prophesied—witnessed and testified under divine inspiration—in keeping with the king's order.

3 Of the sons of Jeduthun: Gedaliah, Zeri, Jeshaiah, Shimei, Hashabiah, and Mattithiah, six, under direction of their father Jeduthun, who witnessed *and* prophesied under divine inspiration with the lyre in thanksgiving and praise to the Lord.

4 Of Heman, the sons of Heman: Bukkiah, Mattaniah, Uzziel, Shebuel, Jerimoth, Hananiah, Hanani, Eliathah, Giddalti, Romamti-ezer, Joshbekashah, Mallothi, Hothir, and Mahazi-oth.

5 All these were the sons of Heman the king's seer [his mediator] in the words *and* things of God to exalt Him; for God gave to Heman fourteen sons and three daughters, [Ps. 68:25.]

6 All of whom were [in the choir] under the direction of their father for song in the house of the Lord, with cymbals, harps, and lyres, for the service of the house of God. Asaph, Jeduthun, and Heman were under the order of the king.

7 So the number of them [who led the remainder of the 4,000], with their kinsmen who were specially trained in songs to the Lord, all who were talented singers, was 288. [Cp. 23:5.]

8 [The musicians] cast lots for their duties, small and great, teacher and scholar alike.

9 The first lot fell for Asaph to Joseph; the second to Gedaliah, to him, his brethren and his sons, twelve;

10 The third to Zaccur, his sons and his brethren, twelve;

11 The fourth to Izri, his sons and his brethren, twelve;

12 The fifth to Nethaniah, his sons and his brethren, twelve;

13 The sixth to Bukkiah, his sons and his brethren, twelve;

14 The seventh to Jesharelah, his sons and his brethren, twelve;

15 The eighth to Jeshaiah, his sons and his brethren, twelve;

16 The ninth to Mattaniah, his sons and his brethren, twelve;

17 The tenth to Shimei, his sons and his brethren, twelve;

18 The eleventh to Azarel, his sons and his brethren, twelve;

19 The twelfth to Hashabiah, his sons and his brethren, twelve;

20 The thirteenth to Shuba-el, his sons and his brethren, twelve;

21 The fourteenth to Mattithiah, his sons and his brethren, twelve;

22 The fifteenth to Jeremoth, his sons and his brethren, twelve;

23 The sixteenth to Hananiah, his sons and his brethren, twelve;

24 The seventeenth of Joshbekashah, his sons and his brethren, twelve;

## New American Standard

*Number and Services of Musicians*

**25** MOREOVER, DAVID and the commanders of the army set apart for the service *some* of the sons of Asaph and of Heman and of Jeduthun, who *were* to prophesy with lyres, harps, and cymbals; and the number of those who performed their service was:

2Of the sons of Asaph: Zaccur, Joseph, Nethaniah, and Asharelah; the sons of Asaph *were* under the direction of Asaph, who prophesied under the direction of the king.

3Of Jeduthun, the sons of Jeduthun: Gedaliah, Zeri, Jeshaiah, Shimei, Hashabiah, and Mattithiah, six, under the direction of their father Jeduthun with the harp, who prophesied in giving thanks and praising the LORD.

4Of Heman, the sons of Heman: Bukkiah, Mattaniah, Uzziel, Shebuel and Jerimoth, Hananiah, Hanani, Eliathah, Giddalti and Romamti-ezer, Joshbekashah, Mallothi, Hothir, Mahazioth.

5All these *were* the sons of Heman the king's seer to exalt him according to the words of God, for God gave fourteen sons and three daughters to Heman.

6All these were under the direction of their father to sing in the house of the LORD, with cymbals, harps and lyres, for the service of the house of God. Asaph, Jeduthun and Heman *were* under the direction of the king.

7And their number who were trained in singing to the LORD, with their [a]relatives, all who were skillful, *was* 288.

*Divisions of Musicians*

8And they cast lots for their duties, all alike, the small as well as the great, the teacher *as well* as the pupil.

9¶ Now the first lot came out for Asaph to Joseph, the second for Gedaliah, he with his relatives and sons *were* twelve;
10the third to Zaccur, his sons and his relatives, twelve;
11the fourth to Izri, his sons and his relatives, twelve;
12the fifth to Nethaniah, his sons and his relatives, twelve;
13the sixth to Bukkiah, his sons and his relatives, twelve;
14the seventh to Jesharelah, his sons and his relatives, twelve;
15the eighth to Jeshaiah, his sons and his relatives, twelve;
16the ninth to Mattaniah, his sons and his relatives, twelve;
17the tenth to Shimei, his sons and his relatives, twelve;
18the eleventh to Azarel, his sons and his relatives, twelve;
19the twelfth to Hashabiah, his sons and his relatives, twelve;
20for the thirteenth, Shubael, his sons and his relatives, twelve;
21for the fourteenth, Mattithiah, his sons and his relatives, twelve;
22for the fifteenth to Jeremoth, his sons and his relatives, twelve;
23for the sixteenth to Hananiah, his sons and his relatives, twelve;
24for the seventeenth to Joshbekashah, his sons and his relatives, twelve;

NAS [a] Lit., *brothers*, and so throughout this context

## New International

*The Singers*

**25** DAVID, TOGETHER with the commanders of the army, set apart some of the sons of Asaph, Heman and Jeduthun for the ministry of prophesying, accompanied by harps, lyres and cymbals. Here is the list of the men who performed this service:

2From the sons of Asaph:
Zaccur, Joseph, Nethaniah and Asarelah. The sons of Asaph were under the supervision of Asaph, who prophesied under the king's supervision.

3As for Jeduthun, from his sons:
Gedaliah, Zeri, Jeshaiah, Shimei,[b] Hashabiah and Mattithiah, six in all, under the supervision of their father Jeduthun, who prophesied, using the harp in thanking and praising the LORD.

4As for Heman, from his sons:
Bukkiah, Mattaniah, Uzziel, Shubael and Jerimoth; Hananiah, Hanani, Eliathah, Giddalti and Romamti-Ezer; Joshbekashah, Mallothi, Hothir and Mahazioth. 5All these were sons of Heman the king's seer. They were given him through the promises of God to exalt him.[c] God gave Heman fourteen sons and three daughters.

6All these men were under the supervision of their fathers for the music of the temple of the LORD, with cymbals, lyres and harps, for the ministry at the house of God. Asaph, Jeduthun and Heman were under the supervision of the king. 7Along with their relatives—all of them trained and skilled in music for the LORD—they numbered 288. 8Young and old alike, teacher as well as student, cast lots for their duties.

9The first lot, which was for Asaph, fell to Joseph,
his sons and relatives,[d] 12[e]
the second to Gedaliah,
he and his relatives and sons, 12
10the third to Zaccur,
his sons and relatives, 12
11the fourth to Izri,[f]
his sons and relatives, 12
12the fifth to Nethaniah,
his sons and relatives, 12
13the sixth to Bukkiah,
his sons and relatives, 12
14the seventh to Jesarelah,[g]
his sons and relatives, 12
15the eighth to Jeshaiah,
his sons and relatives, 12
16the ninth to Mattaniah,
his sons and relatives, 12
17the tenth to Shimei,
his sons and relatives, 12
18the eleventh to Azarel,[h]
his sons and relatives, 12
19the twelfth to Hashabiah,
his sons and relatives, 12
20the thirteenth to Shubael,
his sons and relatives, 12
21the fourteenth to Mattithiah,
his sons and relatives, 12
22the fifteenth to Jerimoth,
his sons and relatives, 12
23the sixteenth to Hananiah,
his sons and relatives, 12
24the seventeenth to Joshbekashah,
his sons and relatives, 12

NIV [b] 3 One Hebrew manuscript and some Septuagint manuscripts (see also verse 17); most Hebrew manuscripts do not have *Shimei*. [c] 5 Hebrew *exalt the horn* [d] 9 See Septuagint; Hebrew does not have *his sons and relatives*. [e] 9 See the total in verse 7; Hebrew does not have *twelve*. [f] 11 A variant of *Zeri* [g] 14 A variant of *Asarelah* [h] 18 A variant of *Uzziel*

## King James

25The eighteenth to Hanani, *he*, his sons, and his brethren, *were* twelve:
26The nineteenth to Mallothi, *he*, his sons, and his brethren, *were* twelve:
27The twentieth to Eliathah, *he*, his sons, and his brethren, *were* twelve:
28The one and twentieth to Hothir, *he*, his sons, and his brethren, *were* twelve:
29The two and twentieth to Giddalti, *he*, his sons, and his brethren, *were* twelve:
30The three and twentieth to Mahazioth, *he*, his sons, and his brethren, *were* twelve:
31The four and twentieth to Romamti-ezer, *he*, his sons, and his brethren, *were* twelve.

**26** CONCERNING THE divisions of the porters: Of the Korhites *was* Meshelemiah the son of Kore, of the sons of Asaph.
2And the sons of Meshelemiah *were*, Zechariah the firstborn, Jediael the second, Zebadiah the third, Jathniel the fourth,
3Elam the fifth, Jehohanan the sixth, Elioenai the seventh.
4Moreover the sons of Obed-edom *were*, Shemaiah the firstborn, Jehozabad the second, Joah the third, and Sacar the fourth, and Nethaneel the fifth,
5Ammiel the sixth, Issachar the seventh, Peulthai the eighth: for God blessed him.
6Also unto Shemaiah his son were sons born, that ruled throughout the house of their father: for they *were* mighty men of valour.
7The sons of Shemaiah; Othni, and Rephael, and Obed, Elzabad, whose brethren *were* strong men, Elihu, and Semachiah.
8All these of the sons of Obed-edom: they and their sons and their brethren, able men for strength for the service, *were* threescore and two of Obed-edom.
9And Meshelemiah had sons and brethren, strong men, eighteen.
10Also Hosah, of the children of Merari, had sons; Simri the chief, (for *though* he was not the firstborn, yet his father made him the chief;)
11Hilkiah the second, Tebaliah the third, Zechariah the fourth: all the sons and brethren of Hosah *were* thirteen.
12Among these *were* the divisions of the porters, *even* among the chief men, *having* wards one against another, to minister in the house of the LORD.
13¶ And they cast lots, as well the small as the great, according to the house of their fathers, for every gate.
14And the lot eastward fell to Shelemiah. Then for Zechariah his son, a wise counsellor, they cast lots; and his lot came out northward.
15To Obed-edom southward; and to his sons the house of Asuppim.
16To Shuppim and Hosah *the lot came forth* westward, with the gate Shallecheth, by the causeway of the going up, ward against ward.

## Amplified

25The eighteenth to Hanani, his sons and his brethren, twelve;
26The nineteenth to Mallothi, his sons and his brethren, twelve;
27The twentieth to Eliathah, his sons and his brethren, twelve;
28The twenty-first to Hothir, his sons and his brethren, twelve;
29The twenty-second to Giddalti, his sons and his brethren, twelve;
30The twenty-third to Mahazioth, his sons and his brethren, twelve;
31The twenty-fourth to Romamti-ezer, his sons and his brethren, twelve.

**26** FOR THE divisions of the gatekeepers: Of the Korahites was Meshelemiah son of Kore, of the sons of Asaph.
2And Meshelemiah had sons: Zechariah the first-born, Jediael second, Zebadiah third, Jathniel fourth,
3Elam fifth, Jehohanan sixth, Eliehoenai seventh.
4Obed-edom had sons: Shemaiah the first-born, Jehozabad second, Joah third, Sachar fourth, Nethanel fifth,
5Ammiel sixth, Issachar seventh, Pe-ullethai eighth; for God blessed him.
6Also to Shemaiah his son were sons born who were rulers in their fathers' houses, for they were mighty men of ability *and* courage.
7The sons of Shemaiah: Othni, Rephael, Obed, and Elzabad, whose brethren were strong *and* able men, Elihu and Semachiah.
8All these were sons of Obed-edom [in whose house the ark was kept] with their sons and brethren, strong *and* able men for the service, sixty-two. [Cp. 13:13, 14.]
9Meshelemiah had sons and brethren, strong *and* able men, eighteen.
10Also Hosah, of the sons of Merari, had sons: Shimri the chief; he was not the first-born, yet his father made him chief,
11Hilkiah second, Tebaliah third, Zechariah fourth; all the sons and brethren of Hosah, thirteen.
12Of these were the divisions of the gatekeepers, even of the chief men, having duties as did their brethren, to minister in the house of the Lord;
13And they cast lots by fathers' houses, small and great alike, for every gate.
14The lot for the east fell to Shelemiah. They cast lots also for Zechariah his son, a wise counselor, and his lot came out for the north;
15To Obed-edom for the south, and to his sons the storehouse was allotted.
16To Shuppim and Hosah the lot fell for the west, by the refuse gate that goes into the ascending highway, post opposite post.

## New American Standard

25for the eighteenth to Hanani, his sons and his relatives,
twelve;
26for the nineteenth to Mallothi, his sons and his relatives,
twelve;
27for the twentieth to Eliathah, his sons and his relatives,
twelve;
28for the twenty-first to Hothir, his sons and his relatives,
twelve;
29for the twenty-second to Giddalti, his sons and his relatives,
twelve;
30for the twenty-third to Mahazioth, his sons and his relatives,
twelve;
31for the twenty-fourth to Romamti-ezer, his sons and his relatives, twelve.

*Divisions of the Gatekeepers*

**26** FOR THE divisions of the gatekeepers *there were* of the Korahites, Meshelemiah the son of Kore, of the sons of Asaph.
2And Meshelemiah had sons: Zechariah the first-born, Jediael
the second, Zebadiah the third, Jathniel the fourth,
3Elam the fifth, Johanan the sixth, Eliehoenai the seventh.
4And Obed-edom had sons: Shemaiah the first-born, Jehozabad the second, Joah the third, Sacar the fourth, Nethanel the fifth,
5Ammiel the sixth, Issachar the seventh, *and* Peullethai the eighth; God had indeed blessed him.
6Also to his son Shemaiah sons were born who ruled over the house of their father, for they were mighty men of valor.
7The sons of Shemaiah *were* Othni, Rephael, Obed, and Elzabad, whose brothers, Elihu and Semachiah, were valiant men.
8All these *were* of the sons of Obed-edom; they and their sons and their relatives *were* able men with strength for the service, 62 from Obed-edom.
9And Meshelemiah had sons and relatives, 18 valiant men.
10Also Hosah, *one* of the sons of Merari had sons: Shimri the first (although he was not the first-born, his father made him first),
11Hilkiah the second, Tebaliah the third, Zechariah the fourth; all the sons and relatives of Hosah *were* 13.
12¶ To these divisions of the gatekeepers, the chief men, *were given* duties like their relatives to minister in the house of the LORD.
13And they cast lots, the small and the great alike, according to their fathers' households, for every gate.
14And the lot to the east fell to Shelemiah. Then they cast lots *for* his son Zechariah, a counselor with insight, and his lot came out to the north.
15For Obed-edom *it fell* to the south, and to his sons went the storehouse.
16For Shuppim and Hosah *it was* to the west, by the gate of Shallecheth, on the ascending highway. Guard corresponded to guard.

## New International

25the eighteenth to Hanani,
his sons and relatives, 12
26the nineteenth to Mallothi,
his sons and relatives, 12
27the twentieth to Eliathah,
his sons and relatives, 12
28the twenty-first to Hothir,
his sons and relatives, 12
29the twenty-second to Giddalti,
his sons and relatives, 12
30the twenty-third to Mahazioth,
his sons and relatives, 12
31the twenty-fourth to Romamti-Ezer,
his sons and relatives, 12

*The Gatekeepers*

**26** THE DIVISIONS of the gatekeepers:
From the Korahites: Meshelemiah son of Kore, one of the sons of Asaph.
2Meshelemiah had sons:
Zechariah the firstborn,
Jediael the second,
Zebadiah the third,
Jathniel the fourth,
3Elam the fifth,
Jehohanan the sixth
and Eliehoenai the seventh.
4Obed-Edom also had sons:
Shemaiah the firstborn,
Jehozabad the second,
Joah the third,
Sacar the fourth,
Nethanel the fifth,
5Ammiel the sixth,
Issachar the seventh
and Peullethai the eighth.
(For God had blessed Obed-Edom.)
6His son Shemaiah also had sons, who were leaders in their father's family because they were very capable men. 7The
sons of Shemaiah: Othni, Rephael, Obed and Elzabad; his relatives Elihu and Semakiah were also able men. 8All
these were descendants of Obed-Edom; they and their sons and their relatives were capable men with the strength to do the work—descendants of Obed-Edom, 62 in all.
9Meshelemiah had sons and relatives, who were able men—18 in all.
10Hosah the Merarite had sons: Shimri the first (although he was not the firstborn, his father had appointed him the first), 11Hilkiah the second, Tabaliah the third and Zechariah the fourth. The sons and relatives of Hosah were 13 in all.
12These divisions of the gatekeepers, through their chief men, had duties for ministering in the temple of the LORD, just as their relatives had. 13Lots were cast for each gate, according to their families, young and old alike.
14The lot for the East Gate fell to Shelemiah.[a] Then lots were cast for his son Zechariah, a wise counselor, and the lot for the North Gate fell to him. 15The lot for the South Gate fell to Obed-Edom, and the lot for the storehouse fell to his sons. 16The lots for the West Gate and the Shalleketh Gate on the upper road fell to Shuppim and Hosah.
Guard was alongside of guard: 17There were six Levites a day

NIV [a] 14 A variant of *Meshelemiah*

## King James

17Eastward *were* six Levites, northward four a day, southward four a day, and toward Asuppim two *and* two.
18At Parbar westward, four at the causeway, *and* two at Parbar.
19These *are* the divisions of the porters among the sons of Kore, and among the sons of Merari.
20¶ And of the Levites, Ahijah *was* over the treasures of the house of God, and over the treasures of the dedicated things.
21 *As concerning* the sons of Laadan; the sons of the Gershonite Laadan, chief fathers, *even* of Laadan the Gershonite, *were* Jehieli.
22The sons of Jehieli; Zetham, and Joel his brother, *which were* over the treasures of the house of the LORD.
23Of the Amramites, *and* the Izharites, the Hebronites, *and* the Uzzielites:
24And Shebuel the son of Gershom, the son of Moses, *was* ruler of the treasures.
25And his brethren by Eliezer; Rehabiah his son, and Jeshaiah his son, and Joram his son, and Zichri his son, and Shelomith his son.
26Which Shelomith and his brethren *were* over all the treasures of the dedicated things, which David the king, and the chief fathers, the captains over thousands and hundreds, and the captains of the host, had dedicated.
27Out of the spoils won in battles did they dedicate to maintain the house of the LORD.
28And all that Samuel the seer, and Saul the son of Kish, and Abner the son of Ner, and Joab the son of Zeruiah, had dedicated; *and* whosoever had dedicated *any thing, it was* under the hand of Shelomith, and of his brethren.
29¶ Of the Izharites, Chenaniah and his sons *were* for the outward business over Israel, for officers and judges.
30 *And* of the Hebronites, Hashabiah and his brethren, men of valour, a thousand and seven hundred, *were* officers among them of Israel on this side Jordan westward in all the business of the LORD, and in the service of the king.
31Among the Hebronites *was* Jerijah the chief, *even* among the Hebronites, according to the generations of his fathers. In the fortieth year of the reign of David they were sought for, and there were found among them mighty men of valour at Jazer of Gilead.
32And his brethren, men of valour, *were* two thousand and seven hundred chief fathers, whom king David made rulers over the Reubenites, the Gadites, and the half tribe of Manasseh, for every matter pertaining to God, and affairs of the king.

**27** NOW THE children of Israel after their number, *to wit*, the chief fathers and captains of thousands and hundreds, and their officers that served the king in any matter of the courses, which came in and went out month by month throughout all the months of the year, of every course *were* twenty and four thousand.
2Over the first course for the first month *was* Jashobeam the son of Zabdiel: and in his course *were* twenty and four thousand.
3Of the children of Perez *was* the chief of all the captains of the host for the first month.
4And over the course of the second month *was* Dodai an Ahohite, and of his course *was* Mikloth also the ruler: in his course likewise *were* twenty and four thousand.
5The third captain of the host for the third month *was* Benaiah the son of Jehoiada, a chief priest: and in his course *were* twenty and four thousand.

## Amplified

17On the east were six Levites, on the north four a day, on the south four a day, and two and two at the storehouse.
18At the colonnade [?] on the west side [of the outer court of the temple] were four at the road and two at the colonnade.
19These were the divisions of the gatekeepers among the Korahites and the sons of Merari.
20Of the Levites, Ahijah was over the treasuries of the house of God and the treasuries of the dedicated gifts.
21The sons of Ladan, the descendants of Gershon through Ladan, the heads of families of Ladan the Gershonite: Jehieli.
22The sons of Jehieli, Zetham and Joel his brother, were over the treasuries of the house of the Lord.
23Of the Amramites, Izharites, Hebronites, and Uzzielites:
24Shebuel son of Gershom, son of Moses, was ruler over the treasuries.
25His brethren: from Eliezer were his son Rehabiah, his son was Jeshaiah, his son Joram, his son Zichri, and his son Shelomoth.
26This Shelomoth and his brethren were over all the treasuries of the dedicated gifts, which King David, the heads of the fathers' houses, the officers over thousands and hundreds, and the commanders of the army, had dedicated.
27From spoil won in battles they dedicated gifts to maintain the house of the Lord.
28Also all that Samuel the seer, Saul son of Kish, Abner son of Ner, and Joab son of Zeruiah had dedicated, and whatever any one had dedicated, it was in charge of Shelomoth and his brethren.
29Of the Izharites, Chenaniah and his sons were appointed to outside duties for Israel, as officers and judges.
30Of the Hebronites, Hashabiah and his brethren, men of courage *and* ability, 1,700, were officers over Israel on the west side of Jordan in all the Lord's business and the king's service.
31Of the Hebronites Jerijah was the chief, according to their generations by fathers' houses. In the fortieth year of David's reign search was made, and men of great courage *and* ability were found among them at Jazer in Gilead.
32Jerijah's kinsmen, men of courage *and* ability, were 2,700 heads of fathers' houses; King David made them overseers of the Reubenites, the Gadites, and the half-tribe of Manasseh, for everything pertaining to God, and affairs of the king.

**27** THIS IS the list of the Israelites, the heads of fathers' houses, the commanders of thousands and hundreds, and their officers who served the king in all matters of the divisions that came and went, month by month throughout the year, each division numbering 24,000.
2Over the first division for the first month was Jashobeam son of Zabdiel. In his division were 24,000.
3He was descended from Perez, and was chief of all the commanders of the army for the first month.
4Over the division for the second month was Dodai the Ahohite, and of his division Mikloth the chief officer. In his division were 24,000.
5The third commander of the army for the third month was Benaiah, son of Jehoiada the priest, as chief. In his division were 24,000.

## New American Standard

17On the east there were six Levites, on the north four daily, on
the south four daily, and at the storehouse two by two.
18At the [a]Parbar on the west *there were* four at the highway and
two at the Parbar.
19These were the divisions of the gatekeepers of the sons of
Korah and of the sons of Merari.

*Keepers of the Treasure*

20¶ [b]And the Levites, their relatives, had charge of the treasures
of the house of God, and of the treasures of the dedicated gifts.
21The sons of Ladan, the sons of the Gershonites belonging to
Ladan, *namely,* the Jehielites, *were* the heads of the fathers'
*households,* belonging to Ladan the Gershonite.
22The sons of Jehieli, Zetham and Joel his brother, had charge
of the treasures of the house of the LORD.
23As for the Amramites, the Izharites, the Hebronites, and the
Uzzielites,
24Shebuel the son of Gershom, the son of Moses, was officer
over the treasures.
25And his relatives by Eliezer *were* Rehabiah his son, Jeshaiah
his son, Joram his son, Zichri his son, and Shelomoth his son.
26This Shelomoth and his relatives had charge of all the treasures of the dedicated gifts, which King David and the heads of
the fathers' *households,* the commanders of thousands and hundreds, and commanders of the army, had dedicated.
27They dedicated part of the spoil won in battles to repair the
house of the LORD.
28And all that Samuel the seer had dedicated and Saul the son
of Kish, Abner the son of Ner and Joab the son of Zeruiah, everyone who had dedicated *anything, all of this* was in the care of
Shelomoth and his relatives.

*Outside Duties*

29As for the Izharites, Chenaniah and his sons were *assigned* to
outside duties for Israel, as officers and judges.
30As for the Hebronites, Hashabiah and his relatives, 1,700
capable men, had charge of the affairs of Israel west of the Jordan,
for all the work of the LORD and the service of the king.
31As for the Hebronites, Jerijah the chief (these Hebronites were
investigated according to their genealogies and fathers' *households,*
in the fortieth year of David's reign, and men of outstanding
capability were found among them at Jazer of Gilead)
32and his relatives, capable men, *were* 2,700 in number, heads
of fathers' *households.* And King David made them overseers of the
Reubenites, the Gadites and the half-tribe of the Manassites concerning all the affairs of God and of the king.

*Commanders of the Army*

27 NOW *THIS is* the enumeration of the sons of Israel, the
heads of fathers' *households,* the commanders of thousands and of hundreds, and their officers who served the king in
all the affairs of the divisions which came in and went out month
by month throughout all the months of the year, each division
*numbering* 24,000.
2Jashobeam the son of Zabdiel [c]had charge of the first division
for the first month; and in his division *were* 24,000.
3 *He was* from the sons of Perez, *and was* chief of all the commanders of the army for the first month.
4Dodai the Ahohite and his division had charge of the division
for the second month, Mikloth *being* the chief officer; and in his
division *were* 24,000.
5The third commander of the army for the third month *was*
Benaiah, the son of Jehoiada the priest, *as* chief; and in his division
*were* 24,000.

NAS [a] Possibly *court* or *colonnade* [b] So Gr.; Heb., *As for the Levites, Ahijah had* [c] Lit., *was over,* and so throughout the ch.

## New International

on the east, four a day on the north, four a day on the south and
two at a time at the storehouse. 18As for the court to the west, there
were four at the road and two at the court itself.
19These were the divisions of the gatekeepers who were descendants of Korah and Merari.

*The Treasurers and Other Officials*

20Their fellow Levites were[d] in charge of the treasuries of the
house of God and the treasuries for the dedicated things.
21The descendants of Ladan, who were Gershonites through
Ladan and who were heads of families belonging to Ladan the
Gershonite, were Jehieli, 22the sons of Jehieli, Zetham and his
brother Joel. They were in charge of the treasuries of the temple
of the LORD.
23From the Amramites, the Izharites, the Hebronites and the
Uzzielites:
24Shubael, a descendant of Gershom son of Moses, was the
officer in charge of the treasuries. 25His relatives through
Eliezer: Rehabiah his son, Jeshaiah his son, Joram his son,
Zicri his son and Shelomith his son. 26Shelomith and his
relatives were in charge of all the treasuries for the things
dedicated by King David, by the heads of families who
were the commanders of thousands and commanders of
hundreds, and by the other army commanders. 27Some of
the plunder taken in battle they dedicated for the repair
of the temple of the LORD. 28And everything dedicated by
Samuel the seer and by Saul son of Kish, Abner son of Ner
and Joab son of Zeruiah, and all the other dedicated things
were in the care of Shelomith and his relatives.
29From the Izharites: Kenaniah and his sons were assigned
duties away from the temple, as officials and judges over
Israel.
30From the Hebronites: Hashabiah and his relatives—seventeen hundred able men—were responsible in Israel west
of the Jordan for all the work of the LORD and for the king's
service. 31As for the Hebronites, Jeriah was their chief
according to the genealogical records of their families. In
the fortieth year of David's reign a search was made in the
records, and capable men among the Hebronites were
found at Jazer in Gilead. 32Jeriah had twenty-seven hundred relatives, who were able men and heads of families,
and King David put them in charge of the Reubenites, the
Gadites and the half-tribe of Manasseh for every matter
pertaining to God and for the affairs of the king.

*Army Divisions*

27 THIS IS the list of the Israelites—heads of families, commanders of thousands and commanders of hundreds, and
their officers, who served the king in all that concerned the army
divisions that were on duty month by month throughout the year.
Each division consisted of 24,000 men.
2In charge of the first division, for the first month, was Jashobeam
son of Zabdiel. There were 24,000 men in his division. 3He
was a descendant of Perez and chief of all the army officers
for the first month.
4In charge of the division for the second month was Dodai the
Ahohite; Mikloth was the leader of his division. There were
24,000 men in his division.
5The third army commander, for the third month, was Benaiah
son of Jehoiada the priest. He was chief and there were
24,000 men in his division. 6This was the Benaiah who was

NIV [d] 20 Septuagint; Hebrew *As for the Levites, Ahijah was*

## King James

6 This *is that* Benaiah, *who was* mighty *among* the thirty, and above the thirty: and in his course *was* Ammizabad his son.

7 The fourth *captain* for the fourth month *was* Asahel the brother of Joab, and Zebadiah his son after him: and in his course *were* twenty and four thousand.

8 The fifth captain for the fifth month *was* Shamhuth the Izrahite: and in his course *were* twenty and four thousand.

9 The sixth *captain* for the sixth month *was* Ira the son of Ikkesh the Tekoite: and in his course *were* twenty and four thousand.

10 The seventh *captain* for the seventh month *was* Helez the Pelonite, of the children of Ephraim: and in his course *were* twenty and four thousand.

11 The eighth *captain* for the eighth month *was* Sibbecai the Hushathite, of the Zarhites: and in his course *were* twenty and four thousand.

12 The ninth *captain* for the ninth month *was* Abiezer the Anetothite, of the Benjamites: and in his course *were* twenty and four thousand.

13 The tenth *captain* for the tenth month *was* Maharai the Netophathite, of the Zarhites: and in his course *were* twenty and four thousand.

14 The eleventh *captain* for the eleventh month *was* Benaiah the Pirathonite, of the children of Ephraim: and in his course *were* twenty and four thousand.

15 The twelfth *captain* for the twelfth month *was* Heldai the Netophathite, of Othniel: and in his course *were* twenty and four thousand.

16 ¶ Furthermore over the tribes of Israel: the ruler of the Reubenites *was* Eliezer the son of Zichri: of the Simeonites, Shephatiah the son of Maachah:

17 Of the Levites, Hashabiah the son of Kemuel: of the Aaronites, Zadok:

18 Of Judah, Elihu, *one* of the brethren of David: of Issachar, Omri the son of Michael:

19 Of Zebulun, Ishmaiah the son of Obadiah: of Naphtali, Jerimoth the son of Azriel:

20 Of the children of Ephraim, Hoshea the son of Azaziah: of the half tribe of Manasseh, Joel the son of Pedaiah:

21 Of the half *tribe* of Manasseh in Gilead, Iddo the son of Zechariah: of Benjamin, Jaasiel the son of Abner:

22 Of Dan, Azareel the son of Jeroham. These *were* the princes of the tribes of Israel.

23 ¶ But David took not the number of them from twenty years old and under: because the LORD had said he would increase Israel like to the stars of the heavens.

24 Joab the son of Zeruiah began to number, but he finished not, because there fell wrath for it against Israel; neither was the number put in the account of the chronicles of king David.

25 ¶ And over the king's treasures *was* Azmaveth the son of Adiel: and over the storehouses in the fields, in the cities, and in the villages, and in the castles, *was* Jehonathan the son of Uzziah:

26 And over them that did the work of the field for tillage of the ground *was* Ezri the son of Chelub:

27 And over the vineyards *was* Shimei the Ramathite: over the increase of the vineyards for the wine cellars *was* Zabdi the Shiphmite:

28 And over the olive trees and the sycamore trees that *were* in the low plains *was* Baal-hanan the Gederite: and over the cellars of oil *was* Joash:

29 And over the herds that fed in Sharon *was* Shitrai the Sharonite: and over the herds *that were* in the valleys *was* Shaphat the son of Adlai:

30 Over the camels also *was* Obil the Ishmaelite: and over the asses *was* Jehdeiah the Meronothite:

31 And over the flocks *was* Jaziz the Hagerite. All these *were* the rulers of the substance which *was* king David's.

## Amplified

6 This is that Benaiah, who was a mighty man of the thirty and over the thirty; and in his division was Ammizabad his son.

7 Fourth, for the fourth month, Asahel brother of Joab, and Zebadiah his son after him. In his division were 24,000.

8 Fifth, for the fifth month, Shamhuth the Izrahite. In his division were 24,000.

9 Sixth, for the sixth month, Ira son of Ikkesh the Tekoite. In his division were 24,000.

10 Seventh, for the seventh month, Helez the Pelonite, of the Ephraimites. In his division were 24,000.

11 Eighth, for the eighth month, Sibbecai the Hushathite, of the Zarahites. In his division were 24,000.

12 Ninth, for the ninth month, Abiezer of Anathoth, a Benjamite. In his division were 24,000.

13 Tenth, for the tenth month, Maharai from Netophah, of the Zerahites. In his division were 24,000.

14 Eleventh, for the eleventh month, Benaiah the Pirathonite, of the sons of Ephraim. In his division were 24,000.

15 Twelfth, for the twelfth month, Heldai the Netophathite, of Othniel. In his division were 24,000.

16 Also over the tribes of Israel: of the Reubenites Eliezer the son of Zichri was chief officer; of the Simeonites, Shephatiah son of Maachah;

17 Of Levi, Hashabiah son of Kemuel; of Aaron, Zadok;

18 Of Judah, Elihu, one of David's brothers; of Issachar, Omri son of Michael;

19 Of Zebulun, Ishmaiah son of Obadiah; of Naphtali, Jerimoth son of Azriel;

20 Of the Ephraimites, Hoshea son of Azaziah; of the half-tribe of Manasseh, Joel son of Pedaiah;

21 Of the half-tribe of Manasseh in Gilead, Iddo son of Zechariah; of Benjamin, Ja-asiel son of Abner;

22 Of Dan, Azarel son of Jeroham. These were the leaders of the tribes of Israel.

23 But David did not number those under twenty years of age, for the Lord had promised to make Israel as the stars of the heavens.

24 Joab son of Zeruiah began a census, but did not finish; because the census brought wrath upon Israel, and the number was not recorded in the chronicles of King David.

25 Over the king's treasuries was Azmaveth son of Adiel; and over the treasuries in the country, cities, villages, and towers *or* forts was Jonathan son of Uzziah.

26 Over those who did the work of the field for tilling the soil, Ezri son of Chelub;

27 Over the vineyards was Shimei the Ramathite; over the produce of the vineyards for the wine cellars, Zabdi the Shiphmite;

28 Over the olive and sycamore trees in the low plains, Baal-hanan the Gederite; over the stores of oil, Joash;

29 Over the herds pasturing in Sharon, Shitrai the Sharonite; over the herds in the valleys, Shaphat son of Adlai;

30 Over the camels, Obil the Ishmaelite; over the she-donkeys, Jehdeiah the Meronothite;

31 And over the flocks, Jaziz the Hagrite. All these were stewards of King David's property.

## New American Standard

6This Benaiah *was* the mighty man of the thirty, and had charge of thirty; and over his division was Ammizabad his son.
7The fourth for the fourth month *was* Asahel the brother of Joab, and Zebadiah his son after him; and in his division *were* 24,000.
8The fifth for the fifth month *was* the commander Shamhuth the Izrahite; and in his division *were* 24,000.
9The sixth for the sixth month *was* Ira the son of Ikkesh the Tekoite; and in his division *were* 24,000.
10The seventh for the seventh month *was* Helez the Pelonite of the sons of Ephraim; and in his division *were* 24,000.
11The eighth for the eighth month *was* Sibbecai the Hushathite of the Zerahites; and in his division *were* 24,000.
12The ninth for the ninth month *was* Abiezer the Anathothite of the Benjamites; and in his division *were* 24,000.
13The tenth for the tenth month *was* Maharai the Netophathite of the Zerahites; and in his division *were* 24,000.
14The eleventh for the eleventh month *was* Benaiah the Pirathonite of the sons of Ephraim; and in his division *were* 24,000.
15The twelfth for the twelfth month *was* Heldai the Netophathite of Othniel; and in his division *were* 24,000.

*Chief Officers of the Tribes*

16¶ Now in charge of the tribes of Israel: chief officer for the Reubenites was Eliezer the son of Zichri; for the Simeonites, Shephatiah the son of Maacah;
17for Levi, Hashabiah the son of Kemuel; for Aaron, Zadok;
18for Judah, Elihu, *one* of David's brothers; for Issachar, Omri the son of Michael;
19for Zebulun, Ishmaiah the son of Obadiah; for Naphtali, Jeremoth the son of Azriel;
20for the sons of Ephraim, Hoshea the son of Azaziah; for the half-tribe of Manasseh, Joel the son of Pedaiah;
21for the half-tribe of Manasseh in Gilead, Iddo the son of Zechariah; for Benjamin, Jaasiel the son of Abner;
22for Dan, Azarel the son of Jeroham. These *were* the princes of the tribes of Israel.
23But David did not count those twenty years of age and under, because the LORD had said He would multiply Israel as the stars of heaven.
24Joab the son of Zeruiah had begun to count *them,* but did not finish; and because of this, wrath came upon Israel, and the number was not included in the account of the chronicles of King David.

*Various Overseers*

25¶ Now Azmaveth the son of Adiel had charge of the king's storehouses. And Jonathan the son of Uzziah had charge of the storehouses in the country, in the cities, in the villages, and in the towers.
26And Ezri the son of Chelub had charge of the agricultural workers who tilled the soil.
27And Shimei the Ramathite had charge of the vineyards; and Zabdi the Shiphmite had charge of the produce of the vineyards *stored* in the wine cellars.
28And Baal-hanan the Gederite had charge of the olive and sycamore trees in the [a]Shephelah; and Joash had charge of the stores of oil.
29And Shitrai the Sharonite had charge of the cattle which were grazing in Sharon; and Shaphat the son of Adlai had charge of the cattle in the valleys.
30And Obil the Ishmaelite had charge of the camels; and Jehdeiah the Meronothite had charge of the donkeys.
31And Jaziz the Hagrite had charge of the flocks. All these were overseers of the property which belonged to King David.

NAS [a] Or, *lowlands*

## New International

a mighty man among the Thirty and was over the Thirty. His son Ammizabad was in charge of his division.
7The fourth, for the fourth month, was Asahel the brother of Joab; his son Zebadiah was his successor. There were 24,000 men in his division.
8The fifth, for the fifth month, was the commander Shamhuth the Izrahite. There were 24,000 men in his division.
9The sixth, for the sixth month, was Ira the son of Ikkesh the Tekoite. There were 24,000 men in his division.
10The seventh, for the seventh month, was Helez the Pelonite, an Ephraimite. There were 24,000 men in his division.
11The eighth, for the eighth month, was Sibbecai the Hushathite, a Zerahite. There were 24,000 men in his division.
12The ninth, for the ninth month, was Abiezer the Anathothite, a Benjamite. There were 24,000 men in his division.
13The tenth, for the tenth month, was Maharai the Netophathite, a Zerahite. There were 24,000 men in his division.
14The eleventh, for the eleventh month, was Benaiah the Pirathonite, an Ephraimite. There were 24,000 men in his division.
15The twelfth, for the twelfth month, was Heldai the Netophathite, from the family of Othniel. There were 24,000 men in his division.

*Officers of the Tribes*

16The officers over the tribes of Israel:

over the Reubenites: Eliezer son of Zicri;
over the Simeonites: Shephatiah son of Maacah;
17over Levi: Hashabiah son of Kemuel;
over Aaron: Zadok;
18over Judah: Elihu, a brother of David;
over Issachar: Omri son of Michael;
19over Zebulun: Ishmaiah son of Obadiah;
over Naphtali: Jerimoth son of Azriel;
20over the Ephraimites: Hoshea son of Azaziah;
over half the tribe of Manasseh: Joel son of Pedaiah;
21over the half-tribe of Manasseh in Gilead: Iddo son of Zechariah;
over Benjamin: Jaasiel son of Abner;
22over Dan: Azarel son of Jeroham.
These were the officers over the tribes of Israel.

23David did not take the number of the men twenty years old
or less, because the LORD had promised to make Israel as numerous as the stars in the sky. 24Joab son of Zeruiah began to count
the men but did not finish. Wrath came on Israel on account of this numbering, and the number was not entered in the book[b] of the annals of King David.

*The King's Overseers*

25Azmaveth son of Adiel was in charge of the royal storehouses.
Jonathan son of Uzziah was in charge of the storehouses in the outlying districts, in the towns, the villages and the watchtowers.
26Ezri son of Kelub was in charge of the field workers who farmed the land.
27Shimei the Ramathite was in charge of the vineyards.
Zabdi the Shiphmite was in charge of the produce of the vineyards for the wine vats.
28Baal-Hanan the Gederite was in charge of the olive and sycamore-fig trees in the western foothills.
Joash was in charge of the supplies of olive oil.
29Shitrai the Sharonite was in charge of the herds grazing in Sharon.
Shaphat son of Adlai was in charge of the herds in the valleys.
30Obil the Ishmaelite was in charge of the camels.
Jehdeiah the Meronothite was in charge of the donkeys.
31Jaziz the Hagrite was in charge of the flocks.
All these were the officials in charge of King David's property.

NIV [b] 24 Septuagint; Hebrew *number*

## King James

32Also Jonathan David's uncle was a counsellor, a wise man, and a scribe: and Jehiel the son of Hachmoni *was* with the king's sons:

33And Ahithophel *was* the king's counsellor: and Hushai the Archite *was* the king's companion:

34And after Ahithophel *was* Jehoiada the son of Benaiah, and Abiathar: and the general of the king's army *was* Joab.

28 AND DAVID assembled all the princes of Israel, the princes of the tribes, and the captains of the companies that ministered to the king by course, and the captains over the thousands, and captains over the hundreds, and the stewards over all the substance and possession of the king, and of his sons, with the officers, and with the mighty men, and with all the valiant men, unto Jerusalem.

2Then David the king stood up upon his feet, and said, Hear me, my brethren, and my people: *As for me*, I *had* in mine heart to build an house of rest for the ark of the covenant of the LORD, and for the footstool of our God, and had made ready for the building:

3But God said unto me, Thou shalt not build an house for my name, because thou *hast been* a man of war, and hast shed blood.

4Howbeit the LORD God of Israel chose me before all the house of my father to be king over Israel for ever: for he hath chosen Judah *to be* the ruler; and of the house of Judah, the house of my father; and among the sons of my father he liked me to make *me* king over all Israel:

5And of all my sons, (for the LORD hath given me many sons,) he hath chosen Solomon my son to sit upon the throne of the kingdom of the LORD over Israel.

6And he said unto me, Solomon thy son, he shall build my house and my courts: for I have chosen him *to be* my son, and I will be his father.

7Moreover I will establish his kingdom for ever, if he be constant to do my commandments and my judgments, as at this day.

8Now therefore in the sight of all Israel the congregation of the LORD, and in the audience of our God, keep and seek for all the commandments of the LORD your God: that ye may possess this good land, and leave *it* for an inheritance for your children after you for ever.

9¶ And thou, Solomon my son, know thou the God of thy father, and serve him with a perfect heart and with a willing mind: for the LORD searcheth all hearts, and understandeth all the imaginations of the thoughts: if thou seek him, he will be found of thee; but if thou forsake him, he will cast thee off for ever.

10Take heed now; for the LORD hath chosen thee to build an house for the sanctuary: be strong, and do *it*.

AMP [a] God's promises to men invariably are dependent upon the other party to the covenant meeting His conditions, whether He says so at the time or not. In verse 7 we find Him promising to establish Solomon's kingdom for ever. Yet in I Kings 11:9-11 we find that God became angry with Solomon for all his later degenerate and abominable conduct and his treachery of heart toward Him, and without mercy, except for David's sake, God declared the kingdom would be torn from him. Was God breaking His covenant with Solomon? No, Solomon had broken and nullified that covenant long before; it no longer existed. There was now no promise for God to keep. Christians are prone to think that God will keep His part of a bargain whether they do or not, but the wisest man who ever lived died knowing that God is not mocked; "he inevitably deludes himself who attempts to delude God. For whatever a man sows, that and that only is what he will reap." (Gal. 6:7). "If you seek Him—inquiring for and of Him, and requiring Him as your first and vital necessity—you will find Him; but if you forsake Him, He will cast you off for ever!" David was telling Solomon all this, but as the new king grew in power, popularity, and personal aggrandizement, step by step he set himself up as privileged to ignore God. In all his wisdom he failed to comprehend that, "Something greater, *and* more exalted *and* more majestic than the temple is here! . . . Something more *and* greater than Solomon is here" (Matt. 12:6, 42).

## Amplified

32Also Jonathan, David's uncle was a counselor, a wise man and a scribe; he and Jehiel son of Hachmoni attended the king's sons [as tutors]. [II Kings 10:6.]

33Ahithophel was the king's counselor; Hushai the Archite was the king's companion *and* friend.

34Ahithophel was succeeded by Jehoiada son of Benaiah, and Abiathar. Joab was the commander of the king's army.

28 DAVID ASSEMBLED at Jerusalem all the leaders of Israel and of the tribes, the officers of the divisions that served the king in courses, and those over thousands and hundreds, and the stewards over all the property and livestock of the king and his sons, with the palace officers, the mighty men, and all the mighty warriors.

2Then David the king rose to his feet and said, Hear me, my brethren and my people: I myself intended to build a house of rest for the ark of the covenant of the Lord, as a footstool for our God, and I prepared materials for the building;

3But God said to me, You shall not build a house for My name [and presence], because you have been a man of war and have shed blood.

4However, the Lord, the God of Israel chose me before all my father's house to be king over Israel for ever; for He chose Judah to be the ruler; and of the house of Judah, the house of my father; and among the sons of my father He was pleased to make me king over all Israel;

5And of all my sons, for the Lord has given me many sons, He has chosen Solomon my son to sit upon the throne of the kingdom of the Lord over Israel.

6And He said to me, Solomon your son shall build My house and My courts; for I have chosen him to be My son, and I will be his father.

7I will establish his kingdom for ever, if he loyally *and* continuously obeys My commandments and My ordinances, as he does today.

8Now therefore in the sight of all Israel, the assembly of the Lord and the hearing of our God, keep and seek [to be familiar with] all the commandments of the Lord your God, that you may possess this good land, and leave it as an inheritance for your children after you for ever.

9And you, Solomon my son, know the God of your father—have personal knowledge of Him, be acquainted with and understand Him; appreciate, heed and cherish Him—and serve Him with a blameless heart and a willing mind. For the Lord searches all hearts *and* minds, and understands all the wanderings of the thoughts. If you seek Him—inquiring for and of Him, and requiring Him as your first and vital necessity—you will find Him; but [a]if you forsake Him, He will cast you off for ever!

10Take heed now; for the Lord has chosen you to build a house for the sanctuary. Be strong and do it!

## New American Standard

*Counselors*

32¶ Also Jonathan, David's uncle, *was* a counselor, a man of
understanding, and a scribe; and Jehiel the son of Hachmoni tu-
tored the king's sons.
33And Ahithophel was counselor to the king; and Hushai the
Archite was the king's friend.
34And Jehoiada the son of Benaiah, and Abiathar succeeded
Ahithophel; and Joab was the commander of the king's army.

*David's Address about the Temple*

**28** NOW DAVID assembled at Jerusalem all the officials of
Israel, the princes of the tribes, and the commanders of
the divisions that served the king, and the commanders of thousands, and the commanders of hundreds, and the overseers of all
the property and livestock belonging to the king and his sons, with
the officials and the mighty men, even all the valiant men.
2Then King David rose to his feet and said, "Listen to me, my
brethren and my people; I *had* [b]intended to build a [c]permanent
home for the ark of the covenant of the LORD and for the footstool
of our God. So I had made preparations to build *it*.
3"But God said to me, 'You shall not build a house for My name
because you are a man of war and have shed blood.'
4"Yet, the LORD, the God of Israel, chose me from all the house
of my father to be king over Israel forever. For He has chosen Judah
to be a leader; and in the house of Judah, my father's house, and
among the sons of my father He took pleasure in me to make *me*
king over all Israel.
5"And of all my sons (for the LORD has given me many sons),
He has chosen my son Solomon to sit on the throne of the kingdom
of the LORD over Israel.
6"And He said to me, 'Your son Solomon is the one who shall
build My house and My courts; for I have chosen him to be a son
to Me, and I will be a father to him.
7'And I will establish his kingdom forever, if he resolutely
performs My commandments and My ordinances, as is done
now.'
8"So now, in the sight of all Israel, the assembly of the LORD,
and in the hearing of our God, observe and seek after all the
commandments of the LORD your God in order that you may
possess the good land and bequeath *it* to your sons after you
forever.
9¶ "As for you, my son Solomon, know the God of your father,
and serve Him with a whole heart and a willing mind; for the LORD
searches all hearts, and understands every intent of the thoughts.
If you seek Him, He will let you find Him; but if you forsake Him,
He will reject you forever.
10"Consider now, for the LORD has chosen you to build a house
for the sanctuary; be courageous and act."

NAS [b] Lit., *in my heart* [c] Lit., *house of rest*

## New International

32Jonathan, David's uncle, was a counselor, a man of insight
and a scribe. Jehiel son of Hacmoni took care of the king's sons.
33Ahithophel was the king's counselor.
Hushai the Arkite was the king's friend. 34Ahithophel was
succeeded by Jehoiada son of Benaiah and by Abiathar.
Joab was the commander of the royal army.

*David's Plans for the Temple*

**28** DAVID SUMMONED all the officials of Israel to assemble
at Jerusalem: the officers over the tribes, the commanders
of the divisions in the service of the king, the commanders of
thousands and commanders of hundreds, and the officials in
charge of all the property and livestock belonging to the king and
his sons, together with the palace officials, the mighty men and all
the brave warriors.
2King David rose to his feet and said: "Listen to me, my brothers and my people. I had it in my heart to build a house as a place
of rest for the ark of the covenant of the LORD, for the footstool of
our God, and I made plans to build it. 3But God said to me, 'You
are not to build a house for my Name, because you are a warrior
and have shed blood.'
4"Yet the LORD, the God of Israel, chose me from my whole
family to be king over Israel forever. He chose Judah as leader, and
from the house of Judah he chose my family, and from my father's
sons he was pleased to make me king over all Israel. 5Of all my
sons—and the LORD has given me many—he has chosen my son
Solomon to sit on the throne of the kingdom of the LORD over
Israel. 6He said to me: 'Solomon your son is the one who will build
my house and my courts, for I have chosen him to be my son, and
I will be his father. 7I will establish his kingdom forever if he is
unswerving in carrying out my commands and laws, as is being
done at this time.'
8"So now I charge you in the sight of all Israel and of the
assembly of the LORD, and in the hearing of our God: Be careful
to follow all the commands of the LORD your God, that you may
possess this good land and pass it on as an inheritance to your
descendants forever.
9"And you, my son Solomon, acknowledge the God of your
father, and serve him with wholehearted devotion and with a
willing mind, for the LORD searches every heart and understands
every motive behind the thoughts. If you seek him, he will be
found by you; but if you forsake him, he will reject you forever.
10Consider now, for the LORD has chosen you to build a temple as
a sanctuary. Be strong and do the work."

# King James

11¶ Then David gave to Solomon his son the pattern of the porch, and of the houses thereof, and of the treasuries thereof, and of the upper chambers thereof, and of the inner parlours thereof, and of the place of the mercy seat,

12And the pattern of all that he had by the spirit, of the courts of the house of the Lord, and of all the chambers round about, of the treasuries of the house of God, and of the treasuries of the dedicated things:

13Also for the courses of the priests and the Levites, and for all the work of the service of the house of the Lord, and for all the vessels of service in the house of the Lord.

14 *He gave* of gold by weight for *things* of gold, for all instruments of all manner of service; *silver also* for all instruments of silver by weight, for all instruments of every kind of service:

15Even the weight for the candlesticks of gold, and for their lamps of gold, by weight for every candlestick, and for the lamps thereof: and for the candlesticks of silver by weight, *both* for the candlestick, and *also* for the lamps thereof, according to the use of every candlestick.

16And by weight *he gave* gold for the tables of showbread, for every table; and *likewise* silver for the tables of silver:

17Also pure gold for the fleshhooks, and the bowls, and the cups: and for the golden basins *he gave gold* by weight for every basin; and *likewise silver* by weight for every basin of silver:

18And for the altar of incense refined gold by weight; and gold for the pattern of the chariot of the cherubims, that spread out *their wings*, and covered the ark of the covenant of the Lord.

19All *this, said David,* the Lord made me understand in writing by *his* hand upon me, *even* all the works of this pattern.

20And David said to Solomon his son, Be strong and of good courage, and do *it:* fear not, nor be dismayed: for the Lord God, *even* my God, *will be* with thee; he will not fail thee, nor forsake thee, until thou hast finished all the work for the service of the house of the Lord.

21And, behold, the courses of the priests and the Levites, *even they shall be with thee* for all the service of the house of God: and *there shall be* with thee for all manner of workmanship every willing skilful man, for any manner of service: also the princes and all the people *will be* wholly at thy commandment.

**29** FURTHERMORE DAVID the king said unto all the congregation, Solomon my son, whom alone God hath chosen, *is yet* young and tender, and the work *is* great: for the palace *is* not for man, but for the Lord God.

2Now I have prepared with all my might for the house of my God the gold for *things to be made* of gold, and the silver for *things* of silver, and the brass for *things* of brass, the iron for *things* of iron, and wood for *things* of wood; onyx stones, and *stones* to be set, glistering stones, and of divers colours, and all manner of precious stones, and marble stones in abundance.

3Moreover, because I have set my affection to the house of my God, I have of mine own proper good, of gold and silver, *which* I have given to the house of my God, over and above all that I have prepared for the holy house,

4 *Even* three thousand talents of gold, of the gold of Ophir, and seven thousand talents of refined silver, to overlay the walls of the houses *withal:*

5The gold for *things* of gold, and the silver for *things* of silver, and for all manner of work *to be made* by the hands of artificers. And who *then* is willing to consecrate his service this day unto the Lord?

6¶ Then the chief of the fathers and princes of the tribes of Israel, and the captains of thousands and of hundreds, with the rulers of the king's work, offered willingly,

# Amplified

11Then David gave Solomon his son the plan of the vestibule of the temple, its houses, its treasuries, its upper chambers, its inner rooms, and of the place for the [ark and its] mercy seat.

12And the plan of all that he had in mind (by the Spirit) for the courts of the house of the Lord, all the surrounding chambers, the treasuries of the house of God, and the treasuries for the dedicated gifts;

13The plan for the divisions of the priests and the Levites, for all the work of the service in the house of the Lord; for all the vessels for service in the house of the Lord,

14The weight of gold and silver for all the gold and silver articles of every kind of service;

15The weight of the golden lampstands and their lamps, the weight of gold or silver for each lampstand and its lamps, according to the use of each lampstand;

16The gold by weight for each table of showbread, and the silver for the tables of silver;

17Also pure gold for the forks, basins, and cups; for the golden bowls by weight of each; for the silver bowls by weight of each;

18For the incense altar refined gold by weight, and gold for the plan of the chariot of the cherubim that spread their wings and covered the ark of the Lord's covenant.

19All this the Lord made me understand by the writing by His hand upon me, all the work to be done according to the plan.

20Also David told Solomon his son, Be strong and courageous, and do it. Fear not; be not dismayed; for the Lord God, my God, is with you. He will not fail or forsake you, until you have finished all the work for the service of the house of the Lord.

21And see, [you have] the divisions of the priests and Levites for all the service of God's house; and with you in all the kinds of work will be every willing, skillful man for any kind of service; also the officers and all the people will be wholly at your command.

**29** AND KING David said to all the assembly, Solomon my son, whom alone God has chosen, is yet young, tender *and* inexperienced and the work is great; for the palace is not to be for man but for the Lord God.

2So I have provided with all my might for the house of my God the gold for things to be of gold, silver for things of silver, bronze for things of bronze, iron for things of iron, and wood for things of wood; onyx *or* beryl stones, stones to be set, stones of antimony, stones of various colors, and all sorts of precious stones, and marble stones in abundance.

3Moreover, because I have set my affection on the house of my God, in addition to all I have prepared for the holy house, I have a private treasure of gold and silver which I give for the house of my God:

4It is 3,000 talents of gold, gold of Ophir; 7,000 talents of refined silver for overlaying the walls of the house.

5Gold for the uses of gold, silver for the uses of silver, and for every work to be done by craftsmen. Now who will offer willingly to fill his hand [and consecrate it] today to the Lord [like one consecrating himself to the priesthood]?

6Then the chief of the fathers and princes of the tribes of Israel, and the captains of thousands and of hundreds, with the rulers of the king's work, offered willingly,

## New American Standard

11¶ Then David gave to his son Solomon the plan of the porch *of the temple,* its buildings, its storehouses, its upper rooms, its inner rooms, and the room for the mercy seat;

12and the plan of all that he had in mind, for the courts of the house of the LORD, and for all the surrounding rooms, for the storehouses of the house of God, and for the storehouses of the dedicated things;

13also for the divisions of the priests and the Levites and for all the work of the service of the house of the LORD and for all the utensils of service in the house of the LORD;

14for the golden *utensils,* the weight of gold for all utensils for every kind of service; for the silver utensils, the weight *of silver* for all utensils for every kind of service;

15and the weight *of gold* for the golden lampstands and their golden lamps, with the weight of each lampstand and its lamps; and *the weight of silver* for the silver lampstands, with the weight of each lampstand and its lamps according to the use of each lampstand;

16and the gold by weight for the tables of showbread, for each table; and silver for the silver tables;

17and the forks, the basins, and the pitchers of pure gold; and for the golden bowls with the weight for each bowl; and for the silver bowls with the weight for each bowl;

18and for the altar of incense refined gold by weight; and gold for the model of the chariot, *even* the cherubim, that spread out *their wings,* and covered the ark of the covenant of the LORD.
19"All *this," said David,* "the LORD made me understand in writing by His hand upon me, all the details of this pattern."

20¶ Then David said to his son Solomon, "Be strong and courageous, and act; do not fear nor be dismayed, for the LORD God, my God, is with you. He will not fail you nor forsake you until all the work for the service of the house of the LORD is finished.

21"Now behold, *there are* the divisions of the priests and the Levites for all the service of the house of God, and every willing man of any skill will be with you in all the work for all kinds of service. The officials also and all the people will be entirely at your command."

*Offerings for the Temple*

**29** THEN KING David said to the entire assembly, "My son Solomon, whom alone God has chosen, is still young and inexperienced and the work is great; for the temple is not for man, but for the LORD God.

2"Now with all my ability I have provided for the house of my God the gold for the *things of* gold, and the silver for the *things of* silver, and the bronze for the *things of* bronze, the iron for the *things of* iron, and wood for the *things of* wood, onyx stones and inlaid *stones,* stones of antimony, and stones of various colors, and all kinds of precious stones, and alabaster in abundance.

3"And moreover, in my delight in the house of my God, the treasure I have of gold and silver, I give to the house of my God, over and above all that I have already provided for the holy [a]temple,

4 *namely,* 3,000 talents of gold, of the gold of Ophir, and 7,000 talents of refined silver, to overlay the walls of the buildings;

5of gold for the *things of* gold, and of silver for the *things of* silver, that is, for all the work done by the craftsmen. Who then is willing to consecrate himself this day to the LORD?"

6¶ Then the rulers of the fathers' *households,* and the princes of the tribes of Israel, and the commanders of thousands and of hundreds, with the overseers over the king's work, offered willingly;

NAS [a] Lit., *house*

## New International

11Then David gave his son Solomon the plans for the portico of
the temple, its buildings, its storerooms, its upper parts, its inner
rooms and the place of atonement. 12He gave him the plans of all
that the Spirit had put in his mind for the courts of the temple of
the LORD and all the surrounding rooms, for the treasuries of the
temple of God and for the treasuries for the dedicated things. 13He
gave him instructions for the divisions of the priests and Levites,
and for all the work of serving in the temple of the LORD, as well
as for all the articles to be used in its service. 14He designated the
weight of gold for all the gold articles to be used in various kinds
of service, and the weight of silver for all the silver articles to be
used in various kinds of service: 15the weight of gold for the gold
lampstands and their lamps, with the weight for each lampstand
and its lamps; and the weight of silver for each silver lampstand
and its lamps, according to the use of each lampstand; 16the weight
of gold for each table for consecrated bread; the weight of silver for
the silver tables; 17the weight of pure gold for the forks, sprinkling
bowls and pitchers; the weight of gold for each gold dish; the
weight of silver for each silver dish; 18and the weight of the refined
gold for the altar of incense. He also gave him the plan for the
chariot, that is, the cherubim of gold that spread their wings and
shelter the ark of the covenant of the LORD.
19"All this," David said, "I have in writing from the hand of the
LORD upon me, and he gave me understanding in all the details
of the plan."
20David also said to Solomon his son, "Be strong and courageous, and do the work. Do not be afraid or discouraged, for the
LORD God, my God, is with you. He will not fail you or forsake
you until all the work for the service of the temple of the LORD is
finished. 21The divisions of the priests and Levites are ready for all
the work on the temple of God, and every willing man skilled in
any craft will help you in all the work. The officials and all the
people will obey your every command."

*Gifts for Building the Temple*

**29** THEN KING David said to the whole assembly: "My son
Solomon, the one whom God has chosen, is young and
inexperienced. The task is great, because this palatial structure is
not for man but for the LORD God. 2With all my resources I have
provided for the temple of my God—gold for the gold work, silver
for the silver, bronze for the bronze, iron for the iron and wood
for the wood, as well as onyx for the settings, turquoise,[b] stones
of various colors, and all kinds of fine stone and marble—all of
these in large quantities. 3Besides, in my devotion to the temple
of my God I now give my personal treasures of gold and silver for
the temple of my God, over and above everything I have provided
for this holy temple: 4three thousand talents[c] of gold (gold of
Ophir) and seven thousand talents[d] of refined silver, for the overlaying of the walls of the buildings, 5for the gold work and the
silver work, and for all the work to be done by the craftsmen. Now,
who is willing to consecrate himself today to the LORD?"
6Then the leaders of families, the officers of the tribes of Israel,
the commanders of thousands and commanders of hundreds, and
the officials in charge of the king's work gave willingly. 7They gave

NIV [b] 2 The meaning of the Hebrew for this word is uncertain. [c] 4 That is, about 110 tons (about 100 metric tons) [d] 4 That is, about 260 tons (about 240 metric tons)

## King James

7And gave for the service of the house of God of gold five thousand talents and ten thousand drams, and of silver ten thousand talents, and of brass eighteen thousand talents, and one hundred thousand talents of iron.

8And they with whom *precious* stones were found gave *them* to the treasure of the house of the LORD, by the hand of Jehiel the Gershonite.

9Then the people rejoiced, for that they offered willingly, because with perfect heart they offered willingly to the LORD: and David the king also rejoiced with great joy.

10¶ Wherefore David blessed the LORD before all the congregation: and David said, Blessed *be* thou, LORD God of Israel our father, for ever and ever.

11Thine, O LORD, *is* the greatness, and the power, and the glory, and the victory, and the majesty: for all *that is* in the heaven and in the earth *is thine;* thine *is* the kingdom, O LORD, and thou art exalted as head above all.

12Both riches and honour *come* of thee, and thou reignest over all; and in thine hand *is* power and might; and in thine hand *it is* to make great, and to give strength unto all.

13Now therefore, our God, we thank thee, and praise thy glorious name.

14But who *am* I, and what *is* my people, that we should be able to offer so willingly after this sort? for all things *come* of thee, and of thine own have we given thee.

15For we *are* strangers before thee, and sojourners, as *were* all our fathers: our days on the earth *are* as a shadow, and *there is* none abiding.

16O LORD our God, all this store that we have prepared to build thee an house for thine holy name *cometh* of thine hand, and *is* all thine own.

17I know also, my God, that thou triest the heart, and hast pleasure in uprightness. As for me, in the uprightness of mine heart I have willingly offered all these things: and now have I seen with joy thy people, which are present here, to offer willingly unto thee.

18O LORD God of Abraham, Isaac, and of Israel, our fathers, keep this for ever in the imagination of the thoughts of the heart of thy people, and prepare their heart unto thee:

19And give unto Solomon my son a perfect heart, to keep thy commandments, thy testimonies, and thy statutes, and to do all *these things,* and to build the palace, *for* the which I have made provision.

20¶ And David said to all the congregation, Now bless the LORD your God. And all the congregation blessed the LORD God of their fathers, and bowed down their heads, and worshipped the LORD, and the king.

21And they sacrificed sacrifices unto the LORD, and offered burnt offerings unto the LORD, on the morrow after that day, *even* a thousand bullocks, a thousand rams, *and* a thousand lambs, with their drink offerings, and sacrifices in abundance for all Israel:

22And did eat and drink before the LORD on that day with great gladness. And they made Solomon the son of David king the second time, and anointed *him* unto the LORD *to be* the chief governor, and Zadok *to be* priest.

23Then Solomon sat on the throne of the LORD as king instead of David his father, and prospered; and all Israel obeyed him.

24And all the princes, and the mighty men, and all the sons likewise of king David, submitted themselves unto Solomon the king.

25And the LORD magnified Solomon exceedingly in the sight of all Israel, and bestowed upon him *such* royal majesty as had not been on any king before him in Israel.

26¶ Thus David the son of Jesse reigned over all Israel.

27And the time that he reigned over Israel *was* forty years; seven years reigned he in Hebron, and thirty and three *years* reigned he in Jerusalem.

## Amplified

7And gave for the service of the house of God of gold 5,000 talents and 10,000 darics, of silver 10,000 talents, of bronze 18,000 talents, and 100,000 talents of iron.

8And whoever had precious stones gave them to the treasury of the house of the Lord, in the care of Jehiel the Gershonite.

9Then the people rejoiced because these had given willingly, for with a whole *and* blameless heart they had offered freely to the Lord. King David also rejoiced greatly.

10Therefore David blessed the Lord before all the assembly, and said, Be praised, adored *and* thanked, O Lord, the God of Israel our [forefather], for ever and ever.

11Yours, O Lord, is the greatness, and the power, and the glory, and the victory, and the majesty; for all that is in the heavens and the earth is Yours; Yours is the kingdom, O Lord, and Yours it is to be exalted as head over all.

12Both riches and honor come from You, and You reign over all. In Your hand are power and might; in Your hand it is to make great and to give strength to all.

13Now therefore, our God, we thank You and praise Your glorious name *and* those attributes which that name denotes.

14But who am I, and what is my people, that we should retain strength *and* be able to offer thus so willingly? For all things come from You, and of Your own (hand) we have given You.

15For we are strangers before You, and sojourners, as all our fathers were; our days on the earth are like a shadow, and there is no hope *or* expectation of remaining.

16O Lord our God, all this store that we have prepared to build You a house for Your holy name *and* the token of Your presence comes from Your hand and is all Your own.

17I know also, my God, that You try the heart, and delight in uprightness. In the uprightness of my heart I have freely offered all these things. And now I have seen with joy Your people, present here, offer voluntarily *and* freely to You.

18O Lord God of Abraham, Isaac, and Israel our fathers, keep for ever such purposes *and* thoughts in the minds of Your people, and direct *and* establish their hearts toward You.

19And give to Solomon my son a blameless heart to keep Your commandments, testimonies, and statutes, and to do all necessary to build the palace [for You] for which I have made provision.

20And David said to all the assembly, Now adore (praise, and thank) the Lord your God! And all the assembly blessed the Lord the God of their fathers, and bowed down and did obeisance to the Lord, and to the king [as His earthly representative].

21The next day they offered sacrifices and burnt offerings to the Lord, 1,000 bulls, 1,000 rams, and 1,000 lambs, with their drink offerings, and sacrifices in abundance for all Israel;

22They ate and drank before the Lord on that day with great rejoicing. They made Solomon the son of David king the second time, and anointed him as prince for the Lord, and Zadok to be high priest.

23Then Solomon sat on the throne of the Lord as king instead of David his father, and prospered; and all Israel obeyed him.

24All the leaders and mighty men, and also all the sons of King David, pledged allegiance to King Solomon.

25And the Lord magnified Solomon exceedingly in the sight of all Israel, and bestowed upon him such royal majesty as had not been on any king before him in Israel.

26Thus David son of Jesse reigned over all Israel.

27The time he reigned over Israel was forty years; he reigned seven years in Hebron and thirty-three years in Jerusalem.

## New American Standard

7and for the service for the house of God they gave 5,000 talents and 10,000 darics of gold, and 10,000 talents of silver, and 18,000 talents of brass, and 100,000 talents of iron.

8And whoever possessed *precious* stones gave them to the treasury of the house of the LORD, in care of Jehiel the Gershonite.

9Then the people rejoiced because they had offered so willingly, for they made their offering to the LORD with a whole heart, and King David also rejoiced greatly.

*David's Prayer*

10¶ So David blessed the LORD in the sight of all the assembly; and David said, "Blessed art Thou, O LORD God of Israel our father, forever and ever.

11"Thine, O LORD, is the greatness and the power and the glory and the victory and the majesty, indeed everything that is in the heavens and the earth; Thine is the dominion, O LORD, and Thou dost exalt Thyself as head over all.

12"Both riches and honor *come* from Thee, and Thou dost rule over all, and in Thy hand is power and might; and it lies in Thy hand to make great, and to strengthen everyone.

13"Now therefore, our God, we thank Thee, and praise Thy glorious name.

14"But who am I and who are my people that we should be able to offer as generously as this? For all things come from Thee, and from Thy hand we have given Thee.

15"For we are sojourners before Thee, and tenants, as all our fathers were; our days on the earth are like a shadow, and there is no hope.

16"O LORD our God, all this abundance that we have provided to build Thee a house for Thy holy name, it is from Thy hand, and all is Thine.

17"Since I know, O my God, that Thou triest the heart and delightest in uprightness, I, in the integrity of my heart, have willingly offered all these *things;* so now with joy I have seen Thy people, who are present here, make *their* offerings willingly to Thee.

18"O LORD, the God of Abraham, Isaac, and Israel, our fathers, preserve this forever in the intentions of the heart of Thy people, and direct their heart to Thee;

19"and give to my son Solomon a perfect heart to keep Thy commandments, Thy testimonies, and Thy statutes, and to do *them* all, and to build the temple, for which I have made provision."

20Then David said to all the assembly, "Now bless the LORD your God." And all the assembly blessed the LORD, the God of their fathers, and bowed low and did homage to the LORD and to the king.

*Sacrifices*

21And on the next day they made sacrifices to the LORD and offered burnt offerings to the LORD, 1,000 bulls, 1,000 rams *and* 1,000 lambs, with their libations and sacrifices in abundance for all Israel.

22So they ate and drank that day before the LORD with great gladness.

*Solomon Again Made King*

And they made Solomon the son of David king a second time, and they anointed *him* as ruler for the LORD and Zadok as priest.

23Then Solomon sat on the throne of the LORD as king instead of David his father; and he prospered, and all Israel obeyed him.

24And all the officials, the mighty men, and also all the sons of King David pledged allegiance to King Solomon.

25And the LORD highly exalted Solomon in the sight of all Israel, and bestowed on him royal majesty which had not been on any king before him in Israel.

26¶ Now David the son of Jesse reigned over all Israel.

27And the period which he reigned over Israel *was* forty years; he reigned in Hebron seven years and in Jerusalem thirty-three *years.*

## New International

toward the work on the temple of God five thousand talents[a] and
ten thousand darics[b] of gold, ten thousand talents[c] of silver,
eighteen thousand talents[d] of bronze and a hundred thousand
talents[e] of iron. 8Any who had precious stones gave them to the
treasury of the temple of the LORD in the custody of Jehiel the
Gershonite. 9The people rejoiced at the willing response of their
leaders, for they had given freely and wholeheartedly to the LORD.
David the king also rejoiced greatly.

*David's Prayer*

10David praised the LORD in the presence of the whole assembly, saying,

"Praise be to you, O LORD,
God of our father Israel,
from everlasting to everlasting.
11Yours, O LORD, is the greatness and the power
and the glory and the majesty and the splendor,
for everything in heaven and earth is yours.
Yours, O LORD, is the kingdom;
you are exalted as head over all.
12Wealth and honor come from you;
you are the ruler of all things.
In your hands are strength and power
to exalt and give strength to all.
13Now, our God, we give you thanks,
and praise your glorious name.

14"But who am I, and who are my people, that we should be
able to give as generously as this? Everything comes from you, and
we have given you only what comes from your hand. 15We are
aliens and strangers in your sight, as were all our forefathers. Our
days on earth are like a shadow, without hope. 16O LORD our God,
as for all this abundance that we have provided for building you
a temple for your Holy Name, it comes from your hand, and all
of it belongs to you. 17I know, my God, that you test the heart and
are pleased with integrity. All these things have I given willingly
and with honest intent. And now I have seen with joy how willingly your people who are here have given to you. 18O LORD, God
of our fathers Abraham, Isaac and Israel, keep this desire in the
hearts of your people forever, and keep their hearts loyal to you.
19And give my son Solomon the wholehearted devotion to keep
your commands, requirements and decrees and to do everything
to build the palatial structure for which I have provided."
20Then David said to the whole assembly, "Praise the LORD
your God." So they all praised the LORD, the God of their fathers;
they bowed low and fell prostrate before the LORD and the king.

*Solomon Acknowledged as King*

21The next day they made sacrifices to the LORD and presented
burnt offerings to him: a thousand bulls, a thousand rams and a
thousand male lambs, together with their drink offerings, and
other sacrifices in abundance for all Israel. 22They ate and drank
with great joy in the presence of the LORD that day.
Then they acknowledged Solomon son of David as king a second time, anointing him before the LORD to be ruler and Zadok to
be priest. 23So Solomon sat on the throne of the LORD as king in
place of his father David. He prospered and all Israel obeyed him.
24All the officers and mighty men, as well as all of King David's
sons, pledged their submission to King Solomon.
25The LORD highly exalted Solomon in the sight of all Israel and
bestowed on him royal splendor such as no king over Israel ever
had before.

*The Death of David*

26David son of Jesse was king over all Israel. 27He ruled over
Israel forty years—seven in Hebron and thirty-three in Jerusalem.

**NIV** [a] 7 That is, about 190 tons (about 170 metric tons) [b] 7 That is, about 185 pounds (about 84 kilograms) [c] 7 That is, about 375 tons (about 345 metric tons) [d] 7 That is, about 675 tons (about 610 metric tons) [e] 7 That is, about 3,750 tons (about 3,450 metric tons)

## King James

28And he died in a good old age, full of days, riches, and
honour: and Solomon his son reigned in his stead.
29Now the acts of David the king, first and last, behold, they
*are* written in the book of Samuel the seer, and in the book of
Nathan the prophet, and in the book of Gad the seer,
30With all his reign and his might, and the times that went over
him, and over Israel, and over all the kingdoms of the countries.

## Amplified

28He died in a good old age [his seventy-first year] full *and*
satisfied with days, riches, and honor; Solomon his son reigned in
his stead.
29Now the acts of King David, from first to last, are written in
the recorded words of Samuel the seer, Nathan the prophet, and
Gad the seer,
30With accounts of all his reign and his might, and the times
through which he and Israel passed, as did all the kingdoms of the
countries.

## New American Standard

*Death of David*

28Then he died in a ripe old age, full of days, riches and honor; and his son Solomon reigned in his place.

29Now the acts of King David, from first to last, are written in the chronicles of Samuel the seer, in the chronicles of Nathan the prophet, and in the chronicles of Gad the seer,

30with all his reign, his power, and the circumstances which came on him, on Israel, and on all the kingdoms of the lands.

## New International

28He died at a good old age, having enjoyed long life, wealth and honor. His son Solomon succeeded him as king.

29As for the events of King David's reign, from beginning to end, they are written in the records of Samuel the seer, the records of Nathan the prophet and the records of Gad the seer,
30together with the details of his reign and power, and the circumstances that surrounded him and Israel and the kingdoms of all the other lands.

## King James

THE SECOND BOOK OF THE

# Chronicles

**1** AND SOLOMON the son of David was strengthened in his kingdom, and the LORD his God *was* with him, and magnified him exceedingly.

2 Then Solomon spake unto all Israel, to the captains of thousands and of hundreds, and to the judges, and to every governor in all Israel, the chief of the fathers.

3 So Solomon, and all the congregation with him, went to the high place that *was* at Gibeon; for there was the tabernacle of the congregation of God, which Moses the servant of the LORD had made in the wilderness.

4 But the ark of God had David brought up from Kirjath-jearim to *the place which* David had prepared for it: for he had pitched a tent for it at Jerusalem.

5 Moreover the brasen altar, that Bezaleel the son of Uri, the son of Hur, had made, he put before the tabernacle of the LORD: and Solomon and the congregation sought unto it.

6 And Solomon went up thither to the brasen altar before the LORD, which *was* at the tabernacle of the congregation, and offered a thousand burnt offerings upon it.

7 ¶ In that night did God appear unto Solomon, and said unto him, Ask what I shall give thee.

8 And Solomon said unto God, Thou hast shown great mercy unto David my father, and hast made me to reign in his stead.

9 Now, O LORD God, let thy promise unto David my father be established: for thou hast made me king over a people like the dust of the earth in multitude.

10 Give me now wisdom and knowledge, that I may go out and come in before this people: for who can judge this thy people, *that is so* great?

11 And God said to Solomon, Because this was in thine heart, and thou hast not asked riches, wealth, or honour, nor the life of thine enemies, neither yet hast asked long life; but hast asked wisdom and knowledge for thyself, that thou mayest judge my people, over whom I have made thee king:

12 Wisdom and knowledge *is* granted unto thee; and I will give thee riches, and wealth, and honour, such as none of the kings have had that *have been* before thee, neither shall there any after thee have the like.

13 ¶ Then Solomon came *from his journey* to the high place that *was* at Gibeon to Jerusalem, from before the tabernacle of the congregation, and reigned over Israel.

14 And Solomon gathered chariots and horsemen: and he had a thousand and four hundred chariots, and twelve thousand horsemen, which he placed in the chariot cities, and with the king at Jerusalem.

15 And the king made silver and gold at Jerusalem *as plenteous* as stones, and cedar trees made he as the sycamore trees that *are* in the vale for abundance.

16 And Solomon had horses brought out of Egypt, and linen yarn: the king's merchants received the linen yarn at a price.

## Amplified

THE SECOND BOOK OF THE

# Chronicles

**1** SOLOMON SON of David was strengthened in his kingdom, and the Lord his God was with him and made him exceedingly great.

2 Solomon spoke to all Israel, to the captains of thousands and of hundreds, and to the judges, and to every prince in all Israel, the heads of the fathers' houses.

3 And Solomon, and all the assembly [a united nation] with him, went to the high place that was at Gibeon; for the tent of meeting of God, which Moses the servant of the Lord had made in the wilderness, was there [where the Canaanites had habitually worshiped].

4 But David had brought up the ark of God from Kiriath-jearim to the place which David had prepared for it, for he had pitched a tent for it at Jerusalem.

5 Moreover the bronze altar, that Bezalel son of Uri, son of Hur, had made, was there before the tabernacle of the Lord, and Solomon and the assembly sought [the Lord].

6 Solomon went up there to the bronze altar before the Lord, at the tent of meeting, and offered 1,000 burnt offerings on it.

7 That night God appeared to Solomon and said to him, Ask what I shall give you.

8 And Solomon said to God, You have shown great mercy *and* loving-kindness to David my father, and have made me king in his place.

9 Now, O Lord God, let Your promise to David my father be fulfilled, for you have made me king over a people like the dust of the earth in multitude.

10 Give me now wisdom and knowledge to go out and come in before this people; for who can rule this Your people, that is so great?

11 God replied to Solomon, Because this was in your heart, and you have not asked riches, possessions, honor *and* glory, or the life of your foes, or even for long life, but have asked wisdom and knowledge for yourself that you may rule *and* judge My people over whom I have made you king,

12 Wisdom and knowledge are granted you, and I will give you riches, possessions, honor *and* glory, such as none of the kings had before you, and none after you shall have their equal.

13 Then Solomon came from the high place at Gibeon, from before the tent of meeting, to Jerusalem. And he reigned over Israel.

14 Solomon gathered chariots and horsemen; he had 1,400 chariots and 12,000 horsemen, which he placed in the cities [suited for the use] of chariots, and with the king at Jerusalem.

15 And the king made silver and gold in Jerusalem as common as stones, and he made cedar as plentiful as the sycamores of the lowland.

16 Solomon's horses were brought out of Egypt; the king's merchants received them in droves, each drove at a price. [Contrary to Deut. 17:16, 17.]

## New American Standard

# 2 Chronicles

*Solomon Worships at Gibeon*

1 NOW SOLOMON the son of David established himself securely over his kingdom, and the LORD his God *was* with him
and exalted him greatly.
2And Solomon spoke to all Israel, to the commanders of thousands and of hundreds and to the judges and to every leader in
all Israel, the heads of the fathers' *households.*
3Then Solomon, and all the assembly with him, went to the
high place which was at Gibeon; for God's tent of meeting was
there, which Moses the servant of the LORD had made in the
wilderness.
4However, David had brought up the ark of God from Kiriath-
jearim to the place he had prepared for it; for he had pitched a tent
for it in Jerusalem.
5Now the bronze altar, which Bezalel the son of Uri, the son
of Hur, had made, was there before the tabernacle of the LORD,
and Solomon and the assembly sought it out.
6And Solomon went up there before the LORD to the bronze
altar which *was* at the tent of meeting, and offered a thousand
burnt offerings on it.
7¶ In that night God appeared to Solomon and said to him,
"Ask what I shall give you."

*Solomon's Prayer for Wisdom*

8And Solomon said to God, "Thou hast dealt with my father
David with great lovingkindness, and hast made me king in his
place.
9"Now, O LORD God, Thy promise to my father David is
fulfilled; for Thou hast made me king over a people as numerous
as the dust of the earth.
10"Give me now wisdom and knowledge, that I may go out and
come in before this people; for who can rule this great people of
Thine?"
11And God said to Solomon, "Because you had this in mind,
and did not ask for riches, wealth, or honor, or the life of those who
hate you, nor have you even asked for long life, but you have
asked for yourself wisdom and knowledge, that you may rule My
people, over whom I have made you king,
12wisdom and knowledge have been granted to you. And I will
give you riches and wealth and honor, such as none of the kings
who were before you has possessed, nor those who will come after
you."
13So Solomon went from the high place which was at Gibeon,
from the tent of meeting, to Jerusalem, and he reigned over Israel.

*Solomon's Wealth*

14¶ And Solomon amassed chariots and horsemen. He had
1,400 chariots, and 12,000 horsemen, and he stationed them in the
chariot cities and with the king at Jerusalem.
15And the king made silver and gold as plentiful in Jerusalem
as stones, and he made cedars as plentiful as sycamores in the
lowland.
16And Solomon's horses were imported from Egypt and from
Kue; the king's traders procured them from Kue for a price.

## New International

# 2 Chronicles

*Solomon Asks for Wisdom*

1 SOLOMON SON of David established himself firmly over his
kingdom, for the LORD his God was with him and made him
exceedingly great.
2Then Solomon spoke to all Israel—to the commanders of thousands and commanders of hundreds, to the judges and to all the
leaders in Israel, the heads of families— 3and Solomon and the
whole assembly went to the high place at Gibeon, for God's Tent
of Meeting was there, which Moses the LORD's servant had made
in the desert. 4Now David had brought up the ark of God from
Kiriath Jearim to the place he had prepared for it, because he had
pitched a tent for it in Jerusalem. 5But the bronze altar that Bezalel
son of Uri, the son of Hur, had made was in Gibeon in front of the
tabernacle of the LORD; so Solomon and the assembly inquired of
him there. 6Solomon went up to the bronze altar before the LORD
in the Tent of Meeting and offered a thousand burnt offerings on
it.
7That night God appeared to Solomon and said to him, "Ask
for whatever you want me to give you."
8Solomon answered God, "You have shown great kindness to
David my father and have made me king in his place. 9Now, LORD
God, let your promise to my father David be confirmed, for you
have made me king over a people who are as numerous as the dust
of the earth. 10Give me wisdom and knowledge, that I may lead
this people, for who is able to govern this great people of yours?"
11God said to Solomon, "Since this is your heart's desire and
you have not asked for wealth, riches or honor, nor for the death
of your enemies, and since you have not asked for a long life but
for wisdom and knowledge to govern my people over whom I have
made you king, 12therefore wisdom and knowledge will be given
you. And I will also give you wealth, riches and honor, such as no
king who was before you ever had and none after you will have."
13Then Solomon went to Jerusalem from the high place at Gibeon, from before the Tent of Meeting. And he reigned over Israel.
14Solomon accumulated chariots and horses; he had fourteen
hundred chariots and twelve thousand horses,[a] which he kept in
the chariot cities and also with him in Jerusalem. 15The king made
silver and gold as common in Jerusalem as stones, and cedar as
plentiful as sycamore-fig trees in the foothills. 16Solomon's horses
were imported from Egypt[b] and from Kue[c] —the royal merchants
purchased them from Kue. 17They imported a chariot from Egypt

**NIV** [a] *14* Or *charioteers* [b] *16* Or possibly *Muzur,* a region in Cilicia; also in verse 17 [c] *16* Probably Cilicia

## King James

17And they fetched up, and brought forth out of Egypt a chariot
for six hundred *shekels* of silver, and an horse for an hundred and
fifty: and so brought they out *horses* for all the kings of the Hittites,
and for the kings of Syria, by their means.

**2** AND SOLOMON determined to build an house for the name
of the LORD, and an house for his kingdom.
2And Solomon told out threescore and ten thousand men to
bear burdens, and fourscore thousand to hew in the mountain,
and three thousand and six hundred to oversee them.
3¶ And Solomon sent to Huram the king of Tyre, saying, As
thou didst deal with David my father, and didst send him cedars
to build him an house to dwell therein, *even so deal with me*.
4Behold, I build an house to the name of the LORD my God, to
dedicate *it* to him, *and* to burn before him sweet incense, and for
the continual showbread, and for the burnt offerings morning and
evening, on the sabbaths, and on the new moons, and on the
solemn feasts of the LORD our God. This *is an ordinance* for ever to
Israel.
5And the house which I build *is* great: for great *is* our God above
all gods.
6But who is able to build him an house, seeing the heaven and
heaven of heavens cannot contain him? who *am* I then, that I
should build him an house, save only to burn sacrifice before him?
7Send me now therefore a man cunning to work in gold, and
in silver, and in brass, and in iron, and in purple, and crimson, and
blue, and that can skill to grave with the cunning men that *are* with
me in Judah and in Jerusalem, whom David my father did provide.
8Send me also cedar trees, fir trees, and algum trees, out of
Lebanon: for I know that thy servants can skill to cut timber in
Lebanon; and, behold, my servants *shall be* with thy servants,
9Even to prepare me timber in abundance: for the house which
I am about to build *shall be* wonderful great.
10And, behold, I will give to thy servants, the hewers that cut
timber, twenty thousand measures of beaten wheat, and twenty
thousand measures of barley, and twenty thousand baths of wine,
and twenty thousand baths of oil.
11¶ Then Huram the king of Tyre answered in writing, which
he sent to Solomon, Because the LORD hath loved his people, he
hath made thee king over them.
12Huram said moreover, Blessed *be* the LORD God of Israel, that
made heaven and earth, who hath given to David the king a wise
son, endued with prudence and understanding, that might build
an house for the LORD, and an house for his kingdom.
13And now I have sent a cunning man, endued with understanding, of Huram my father's,
14The son of a woman of the daughters of Dan, and his father
*was* a man of Tyre, skilful to work in gold, and in silver, in brass,
in iron, in stone, and in timber, in purple, in blue, and in fine linen,
and in crimson; also to grave any manner of graving, and to find
out every device which shall be put to him, with thy cunning men,
and with the cunning men of my lord David thy father.
15Now therefore the wheat, and the barley, the oil, and the
wine, which my lord hath spoken of, let him send unto his servants:
16And we will cut wood out of Lebanon, as much as thou shalt
need: and we will bring it to thee in floats by sea to Joppa; and thou
shalt carry it up to Jerusalem.

## Amplified

17They imported from Egypt a chariot for 600 shekels of silver,
and a horse for 150; so they brought out horses for all the Hittite
and Syrian kings as export agents.

**2** SOLOMON DETERMINED to build a temple for the name of
the Lord, and a royal capitol.
2And Solomon counted out 70,000 men to bear burdens, 80,000
to be stonecutters in the hill country, and 3,600 overseers.
3And Solomon sent to Hiram king of Tyre, saying, As you dealt
with David my father, and sent him cedars to build him a house
in which to dwell, even so deal with me.
4Behold, I am about to build a house for the name of the Lord
my God, dedicated to Him for the burning of incense of sweet
spices before Him, for the continual showbread, and for the burnt
offerings morning and evening, on the sabbaths, new moons, and
on the solemn feasts of the Lord our God, as ordained for ever for
Israel.
5The house which I am to build is great, for our God is greater
than all gods.
6But who is able to build Him a house, since Heaven, even
highest Heaven, cannot contain Him? Who am I to build Him a
house, except as a place to burn incense in worship before Him?
7Now therefore send a man skilled to work in gold, silver,
bronze, and iron, and in purple, crimson, and blue colors, who is
a trained engraver, to work with the skilled men who are with me
in Judah and Jerusalem, whom David my father provided.
8Send me also from Lebanon, cedar, cypress and algum timber,
for I know your servants can skillfully cut timber in Lebanon, and
my servants will be with your servants,
9To prepare me timber in abundance; for the house I am about
to build shall be great and wonderful.
10And I will give to your servants who cut timber, 20,000 measures of crushed wheat and also of barley, and 20,000 baths of wine
and also of oil.
11Then Hiram the king of Tyre replied in writing sent to Solomon, Because the Lord loves His people, He has made you king
over them.
12Hiram said also, Blessed be the Lord God of Israel, Who made
Heaven and earth, Who has given to David the king a wise son,
endued with prudence and understanding, who should build a
house for the Lord, and a royal palace for his capital.
13Now I have sent a skilled man, endued with understanding,
even Huram-abi, my trusted counselor,
14The son of a woman of the daughters of [a]Dan; his father was
a man of Tyre. He is a trained worker in gold, silver, bronze, iron,
stone, and wood, in purple, blue, and crimson colors, and in fine
linen; also to engrave any type of engraving, and to carry out any
design given him, with your skilled men, and those of my lord
David your father.
15Now therefore the wheat, barley, oil, and wine, of which my
lord has spoken, let him send them to his servants;
16And we will cut whatever timber you need from Lebanon,
and bring it to you in rafts by sea to Joppa, so you may take it up
to Jerusalem.

**AMP** [a] I Kings 7:14 says this woman was of the tribe of Naphtali. Doubtless her mother's marriage identified her with a tribe of which she was not native.

## New American Standard

17 And they imported chariots from Egypt for 600 *shekels* of silver
apiece, and horses for 150 apiece, and by the same means they
exported them to all the kings of the Hittites and the kings of
Aram.

*Solomon Will Build a Temple and Palace*

**2** NOW SOLOMON decided to build a house for the name of
the LORD, and a royal palace for himself.
2 So Solomon assigned 70,000 men to carry loads, and 80,000
men to quarry *stone* in the mountains, and 3,600 to supervise them.
3 Then Solomon sent *word* to Huram the king of Tyre, saying,
"As you dealt with David my father, and sent him cedars to build
him a house to dwell in, so do for me.
4 "Behold, I am about to build a house for the name of the LORD
my God, dedicating it to Him, to burn fragrant incense before Him,
and *to set out* the showbread continually, and to offer burnt offerings morning and evening, on sabbaths and on new moons and
on the appointed feasts of the LORD our God, this *being required*
forever in Israel.
5 "And the house which I am about to build *will be* great; for
greater is our God than all the gods.
6 "But who is able to build a house for Him, for the heavens and
the highest heavens cannot contain Him? So who am I, that I
should build a house for Him, except to [b]burn *incense* before Him?
7 "And now send me a skilled man to work in gold, silver, brass
and iron, and in purple, crimson and violet *fabrics*, and who knows
how to make engravings, to *work* with the skilled men whom I
have in Judah and Jerusalem, whom David my father provided.
8 "Send me also cedar, cypress and algum timber from Lebanon, for I know that your servants know how to cut timber of
Lebanon; and indeed, my servants *will work* with your servants,
9 to prepare timber in abundance for me, for the house which
I am about to build *will be* great and wonderful.
10 "Now behold, I will give to your servants, the woodsmen
who cut the timber, 20,000 [c]kors of crushed wheat, and 20,000
kors of barley, and 20,000 baths of wine, and 20,000 baths of oil."

*Huram to Assist*

11 ¶ Then Huram, king of Tyre, answered in a letter sent to
Solomon: "Because the LORD loves His people, He has made you
king over them."
12 Then Huram continued, "Blessed be the LORD, the God of
Israel, who has made heaven and earth, who has given King David
a wise son, endowed with discretion and understanding, who will
build a house for the LORD and a royal palace for himself.
13 "And now I am sending a skilled man, endowed with understanding, Huram-abi,
14 the son of a Danite woman and a Tyrian father, who knows
how to work in gold, silver, bronze, iron, stone and wood, *and* in
purple, violet, linen and crimson fabrics, and *who knows how* to
make all kinds of engravings and to execute any design which may
be assigned to him, *to work* with your skilled men, and with those
of my lord David your father.
15 "Now then, let my lord send to his servants wheat and barley,
oil and wine, of which he has spoken.
16 "And we will cut whatever timber you need from Lebanon,
and bring it to you on rafts by sea to Joppa, so that you may carry
it up to Jerusalem."

NAS [b] Lit., *offer up in smoke* [c] I.e., A kor equals approx. 10 bushels

## New International

for six hundred shekels[d] of silver, and a horse for a hundred and
fifty.[e] They also exported them to all the kings of the Hittites and
of the Arameans.

*Preparations for Building the Temple*

**2** SOLOMON GAVE orders to build a temple for the Name of
the LORD and a royal palace for himself. 2 He conscripted
seventy thousand men as carriers and eighty thousand as stonecutters in the hills and thirty-six hundred as foremen over them.
3 Solomon sent this message to Hiram[f] king of Tyre:

"Send me cedar logs as you did for my father David when
you sent him cedar to build a palace to live in. 4 Now I am
about to build a temple for the Name of the LORD my God and
to dedicate it to him for burning fragrant incense before him,
for setting out the consecrated bread regularly, and for making burnt offerings every morning and evening and on Sabbaths and New Moons and at the appointed feasts of the LORD
our God. This is a lasting ordinance for Israel.
5 "The temple I am going to build will be great, because our
God is greater than all other gods. 6 But who is able to build
a temple for him, since the heavens, even the highest heavens, cannot contain him? Who then am I to build a temple for
him, except as a place to burn sacrifices before him?
7 "Send me, therefore, a man skilled to work in gold and
silver, bronze and iron, and in purple, crimson and blue yarn,
and experienced in the art of engraving, to work in Judah and
Jerusalem with my skilled craftsmen, whom my father David
provided.
8 "Send me also cedar, pine and algum[g] logs from Lebanon, for I know that your men are skilled in cutting timber
there. My men will work with yours 9 to provide me with
plenty of lumber, because the temple I build must be large and
magnificent. 10 I will give your servants, the woodsmen who
cut the timber, twenty thousand cors[h] of ground wheat,
twenty thousand cors of barley, twenty thousand baths[i] of
wine and twenty thousand baths of olive oil."

11 Hiram king of Tyre replied by letter to Solomon:

"Because the LORD loves his people, he has made you their
king."

12 And Hiram added:

"Praise be to the LORD, the God of Israel, who made
heaven and earth! He has given King David a wise son, endowed with intelligence and discernment, who will build a
temple for the LORD and a palace for himself.
13 "I am sending you Huram-Abi, a man of great skill,
14 whose mother was from Dan and whose father was from
Tyre. He is trained to work in gold and silver, bronze and
iron, stone and wood, and with purple and blue and crimson
yarn and fine linen. He is experienced in all kinds of engraving and can execute any design given to him. He will work
with your craftsmen and with those of my lord, David your
father.
15 "Now let my lord send his servants the wheat and barley
and the olive oil and wine he promised, 16 and we will cut all
the logs from Lebanon that you need and will float them in
rafts by sea down to Joppa. You can then take them up to
Jerusalem."

NIV [d] *17* That is, about 15 pounds (about 7 kilograms) [e] *17* That is, about 3 3/4 pounds (about 1.7 kilograms) [f] *3* Hebrew *Huram,* a variant of *Hiram;* also in verses 11 and 12 [g] *8* Probably a variant of *almug;* possibly juniper [h] *10* That is, probably about 125,000 bushels (about 4,400 kiloliters) [i] *10* That is, probably about 115,000 gallons (about 440 kiloliters)

## King James

17¶ And Solomon numbered all the strangers that *were* in the land of Israel, after the numbering wherewith David his father had numbered them; and they were found an hundred and fifty thousand and three thousand and six hundred.

18And he set threescore and ten thousand of them *to be* bearers of burdens, and fourscore thousand *to be* hewers in the mountain, and three thousand and six hundred overseers to set the people awork.

**3** THEN SOLOMON began to build the house of the LORD at Jerusalem in mount Moriah, where *the* LORD appeared unto David his father, in the place that David had prepared in the threshingfloor of Ornan the Jebusite.

2And he began to build in the second *day* of the second month, in the fourth year of his reign.

3¶ Now these *are the things wherein* Solomon was instructed for the building of the house of God. The length by cubits after the first measure *was* threescore cubits, and the breadth twenty cubits.

4And the porch that *was* in the front *of the house*, the length *of it was* according to the breadth of the house, twenty cubits, and the height *was* an hundred and twenty: and he overlaid it within with pure gold.

5And the greater house he ceiled with fir tree, which he overlaid with fine gold, and set thereon palm trees and chains.

6And he garnished the house with precious stones for beauty: and the gold *was* gold of Parvaim.

7He overlaid also the house, the beams, the posts, and the walls thereof, and the doors thereof, with gold; and graved cherubims on the walls.

8And he made the most holy house, the length whereof *was* according to the breadth of the house, twenty cubits, and the breadth thereof twenty cubits: and he overlaid it with fine gold, *amounting* to six hundred talents.

9And the weight of the nails *was* fifty shekels of gold. And he overlaid the upper chambers with gold.

10And in the most holy house he made two cherubims of image work, and overlaid them with gold.

11¶ And the wings of the cherubims *were* twenty cubits long: one wing *of the one cherub was* five cubits, reaching to the wall of the house: and the other wing *was likewise* five cubits, reaching to the wing of the other cherub.

12And *one* wing of the other cherub *was* five cubits, reaching to the wall of the house: and the other wing *was* five cubits *also*, joining to the wing of the other cherub.

13The wings of these cherubims spread themselves forth twenty cubits: and they stood on their feet, and their faces *were* inward.

14¶ And he made the veil *of* blue, and purple, and crimson, and fine linen, and wrought cherubims thereon.

15Also he made before the house two pillars of thirty and five cubits high, and the chapiter that *was* on the top of each of them *was* five cubits.

16And he made chains, *as* in the oracle, and put *them* on the heads of the pillars; and made an hundred pomegranates, and put *them* on the chains.

17And he reared up the pillars before the temple, one on the right hand, and the other on the left; and called the name of that on the right hand Jachin, and the name of that on the left Boaz.

## Amplified

17Then Solomon took a census of all the aliens in the land of Israel, like the census of them which his father David had taken. They were found to be 153,600.

18And he assigned 70,000 of them to be burden-bearers, 80,000 to work in the mountain quarries, and 3,600 as overseers to direct the people's work.

**3** THEN SOLOMON began to build the house of the Lord at Jerusalem on Mount Moriah, where the Lord appeared to David his father, in the place that David had appointed, on the threshingfloor of Ornan the Jebusite. [I Chron. 21:20-22.]

2And Solomon began to build on the second day of the second month, in the fourth year of his reign.

3Now these are the measurements for the foundations which Solomon laid for the house of God. The length in cubits by the former measure was sixty cubits, and the breadth twenty cubits.

4The porch *or* vestibule across the front of the house was the same length as the house's breadth, twenty cubits, and the [a]height 120 cubits. He overlaid it inside with pure gold.

5And the greater house [the holy place] he lined with cypress, and overlaid it with fine gold, and made palm trees and chains on it.

6And he adorned the house with precious stones for beauty; and the gold was gold of Parvaim.

7He lined the house [the holy place], its beams, thresholds, walls, and doors with gold, and engraved cherubim on the walls.

8He made the most holy place; its length equaling the breadth of the house, twenty cubits, and its breadth twenty cubits; he overlaid it with 600 talents of fine gold.

9The weight of the nails was fifty shekels of gold. And he lined the upper chambers with gold.

10And in the most holy place he made two cherubim of image work, and they were overlaid with gold.

11And the wings of the cherubim [combined] extended twenty cubits: one wing of one cherub was five cubits, reaching to the wall of the house; and its other wing of five cubits touched the other cherub's wing.

12And of the other cherub one wing of five cubits touched the wall of the house, and the other wing, also five cubits, joined the wing of the first cherub.

13The wings of these cherubim extended twenty cubits; the cherubim stood on their feet, their faces toward the holy place.

14And he made the veil [between the holy place and the most holy place] of blue, purple, crimson, and fine linen, and embroidered cherubim on it.

15Before the house he made two pillars 35 cubits high, with a capital on the top of each of five cubits.

16He made chains like a necklace and put them on the heads of the pillars, and he made 100 pomegranates and put them on the chains.

17He erected the pillars before the temple, one on the right, the other on the left; and called the one on the right Jachin [meaning, he shall establish], and the one on the left Boaz [meaning, in it is strength].

**AMP** [a] This extreme height is believed by most scholars to be a copyist's error, but II Chron. 7:21 seems to confirm it. It reads, ". . . This house, which was so high . . ." (before its destruction).

# New American Standard

17¶ And Solomon numbered all the aliens who *were* in the land of Israel, following the census which his father David had taken; and 153,600 were found.

18And he appointed 70,000 of them to carry loads, and 80,000 to quarry *stones* in the mountains, and 3,600 supervisors to make the people work.

*The Temple Construction in Jerusalem*

**3** THEN SOLOMON began to build the house of the LORD in Jerusalem on Mount Moriah, where *the* LORD had appeared to his father David, at the place that David had prepared, on the threshing floor of Ornan the Jebusite.

2And he began to build on the second *day* in the second month of the fourth year of his reign.

*Dimensions and Materials of the Temple*

3Now these are the foundations which Solomon laid for building the house of God. The length in [b]cubits, according to the old standard *was* sixty cubits, and the width twenty cubits.

4And the porch which was in front of the house was as long as the width of the house, twenty cubits, and the height 120; and inside he overlaid it with pure gold.

5And he overlaid the main room with cypress wood and overlaid it with fine gold, and ornamented it with palm trees and chains.

6Further, he adorned the house with precious stones; and the gold was gold from Parvaim.

7He also overlaid the house with gold—the beams, the thresholds, and its walls, and its doors; and he carved cherubim on the walls.

8¶ Now he made the room of the holy of holies: its length, across the width of the house, *was* twenty cubits, and its width *was* twenty cubits; and he overlaid it with fine gold, *amounting* to 600 talents.

9And the weight of the nails was fifty shekels of gold. He also overlaid the upper rooms with gold.

10¶ Then he made two sculptured cherubim in the room of the holy of holies and overlaid them with gold.

11And the wingspan of the cherubim *was* twenty cubits; the wing of one, of five cubits, touched the wall of the house, and *its* other wing, of five cubits, touched the wing of the other cherub.

12And the wing of the other cherub, of five cubits, touched the wall of the house; and *its* other wing of five cubits, was attached to the wing of the first cherub.

13The wings of these cherubim extended twenty cubits, and they stood on their feet facing the *main* room.

14And he made the veil of violet, purple, crimson and fine linen, and he worked cherubim on it.

15¶ He also made two pillars for the front of the house, thirty-five cubits high, and the capital on the top of each *was* five cubits.

16And he made chains in the inner sanctuary, and placed *them* on the tops of the pillars; and he made one hundred pomegranates and placed *them* on the chains.

17And he erected the pillars in front of the temple, one on the right and the other on the left, and named the one on the right Jachin and the one on the left Boaz.

**NAS** [b] I.e., One cubit equals approx. 18 in.

# New International

17Solomon took a census of all the aliens who were in Israel, after the census his father David had taken; and they were found to be 153,600. 18He assigned 70,000 of them to be carriers and 80,000 to be stonecutters in the hills, with 3,600 foremen over them to keep the people working.

*Solomon Builds the Temple*

**3** THEN SOLOMON began to build the temple of the LORD in Jerusalem on Mount Moriah, where the LORD had appeared to his father David. It was on the threshing floor of Araunah[c] the Jebusite, the place provided by David. 2He began building on the second day of the second month in the fourth year of his reign.

3The foundation Solomon laid for building the temple of God was sixty cubits long and twenty cubits wide[d] (using the cubit of the old standard). 4The portico at the front of the temple was twenty cubits[e] long across the width of the building and twenty cubits[f] high.

He overlaid the inside with pure gold. 5He paneled the main hall with pine and covered it with fine gold and decorated it with palm tree and chain designs. 6He adorned the temple with precious stones. And the gold he used was gold of Parvaim. 7He overlaid the ceiling beams, doorframes, walls and doors of the temple with gold, and he carved cherubim on the walls.

8He built the Most Holy Place, its length corresponding to the width of the temple—twenty cubits long and twenty cubits wide. He overlaid the inside with six hundred talents[g] of fine gold. 9The gold nails weighed fifty shekels.[h] He also overlaid the upper parts with gold.

10In the Most Holy Place he made a pair of sculptured cherubim and overlaid them with gold. 11The total wingspan of the cherubim was twenty cubits. One wing of the first cherub was five cubits[i] long and touched the temple wall, while its other wing, also five cubits long, touched the wing of the other cherub. 12Similarly one wing of the second cherub was five cubits long and touched the other temple wall, and its other wing, also five cubits long, touched the wing of the first cherub. 13The wings of these cherubim extended twenty cubits. They stood on their feet, facing the main hall.[j]

14He made the curtain of blue, purple and crimson yarn and fine linen, with cherubim worked into it.

15In the front of the temple he made two pillars, which ⌊together⌋ were thirty-five cubits[k] long, each with a capital on top measuring five cubits. 16He made interwoven chains[l] and put them on top of the pillars. He also made a hundred pomegranates and attached them to the chains. 17He erected the pillars in the front of the temple, one to the south and one to the north. The one to the south he named Jakin[m] and the one to the north Boaz.[n]

**NIV** [c] *1* Hebrew *Ornan,* a variant of *Araunah* [d] *3* That is, about 90 feet (about 27 meters) long and 30 feet (about 9 meters) wide [e] *4* That is, about 30 feet (about 9 meters); also in verses 8, 11 and 13 [f] *4* Some Septuagint and Syriac manuscripts; Hebrew *and a hundred and twenty* [g] *8* That is, about 23 tons (about 21 metric tons) [h] *9* That is, about 1 1/4 pounds (about 0.6 kilogram) [i] *11* That is, about 7 1/2 feet (about 2.3 meters); also in verse 15 [j] *13* Or *facing inward* [k] *15* That is, about 52 feet (about 16 meters) [l] *16* Or possibly *made chains in the inner sanctuary;* the meaning of the Hebrew for this phrase is uncertain. [m] *17* *Jakin* probably means *he establishes.* [n] *17* *Boaz* probably means *in him is strength.*

## King James

4 MOREOVER HE made an altar of brass, twenty cubits the length thereof, and twenty cubits the breadth thereof, and ten cubits the height thereof.

2¶ Also he made a molten sea of ten cubits from brim to brim, round in compass, and five cubits the height thereof; and a line of thirty cubits did compass it round about.

3And under it *was* the similitude of oxen, which did compass it round about: ten in a cubit, compassing the sea round about. Two rows of oxen *were* cast, when it was cast.

4It stood upon twelve oxen, three looking toward the north, and three looking toward the west, and three looking toward the south, and three looking toward the east: and the sea *was set* above upon them, and all their hinder parts *were* inward.

5And the thickness of it *was* an handbreadth, and the brim of it like the work of the brim of a cup, with flowers of lilies; *and* it received and held three thousand baths.

6¶ He made also ten lavers, and put five on the right hand, and five on the left, to wash in them: such things as they offered for the burnt offering they washed in them; but the sea *was* for the priests to wash in.

7And he made ten candlesticks of gold according to their form, and set *them* in the temple, five on the right hand, and five on the left.

8He made also ten tables, and placed *them* in the temple, five on the right side, and five on the left. And he made an hundred basins of gold.

9¶ Furthermore he made the court of the priests, and the great court, and doors for the court, and overlaid the doors of them with brass.

10And he set the sea on the right side of the east end, over against the south.

11And Huram made the pots, and the shovels, and the basins. And Huram finished the work that he was to make for king Solomon for the house of God;

12 *To wit*, the two pillars, and the pommels, and the chapiters *which were* on the top of the two pillars, and the two wreaths to cover the two pommels of the chapiters which *were* on the top of the pillars;

13And four hundred pomegranates on the two wreaths; two rows of pomegranates on each wreath, to cover the two pommels of the chapiters which *were* upon the pillars.

14He made also bases, and lavers made he upon the bases;

15One sea, and twelve oxen under it.

16The pots also, and the shovels, and the fleshhooks, and all their instruments, did Huram his father make to king Solomon for the house of the LORD of bright brass.

17In the plain of Jordan did the king cast them, in the clay ground between Succoth and Zeredathah.

18Thus Solomon made all these vessels in great abundance: for the weight of the brass could not be found out.

19¶ And Solomon made all the vessels that *were for* the house of God, the golden altar also, and the tables whereon the shewbread *was set;*

20Moreover the candlesticks with their lamps, that they should burn after the manner before the oracle, of pure gold;

21And the flowers, and the lamps, and the tongs, *made he of* gold, *and* that perfect gold;

22And the snuffers, and the basins, and the spoons, and the censers, *of* pure gold: and the entry of the house, the inner doors thereof for the most holy *place*, and the doors of the house of the temple, *were of* gold.

## Amplified

4 ALSO SOLOMON made an altar of bronze, its top twenty by twenty cubits and its height ten cubits.

2Also he made a round sea of molten metal, ten cubits from brim to brim, and five cubits high, and a line of thirty cubits measured around it.

3Under it were figures of oxen encircling it, ten to a cubit. The oxen were in two rows, cast in one piece with it.

4It stood upon twelve oxen, three looking north, three west, three south, three east; and the sea rested upon them, and all their hinder parts were inward.

5Its thickness was a handbreadth; its brim was like the brim of a cup, like the flower of a lily; it held 3,000 baths [measures].

6He made also ten lavers in which to wash, and put five on the right (south) side and five on the left (north); such things as they offered for the burnt offering they washed in them, but the sea was for the priests to wash in.

7And he made ten golden lampstands as directed, and set them in the temple, five on the right side and five on the left.

8He made also ten tables, and placed them in the temple, five each on the right and left sides, and 100 basins of gold.

9Moreover he made the priests' court, and the great court, and doors for the court, and overlaid their doors with bronze.

10And he set the sea at the southeast corner of the house.

11And Huram made the pots, shovels, and basins. So Huram finished the work of God's house that he did for King Solomon:

12The two pillars, the bowls, the capitals on top of the two pillars, and the two networks to cover the two bowls of the capitals on top of the pillars,

13And 400 pomegranates for the two networks, two rows of pomegranates for each network, to cover the two bowls of the capitals upon the pillars.

14He made also bases *or* stands, and lavers upon the bases,

15One sea, and the twelve oxen under it,

16The pots, shovels, and fleshhooks, and all their equipment Huram his trusted counselor made of burnished bronze for King Solomon for the house of the Lord.

17In the plain of Jordan the king cast them, in the clay ground between Succoth and Zeredah.

18Solomon made all these things in such great numbers that the weight of the bronze was not computed.

19And Solomon made all the vessels for the house of God, the golden altar also, and the tables for the showbread [the bread of the Presence],

20And the lampstands with their lamps of pure gold, to burn before the inner sanctuary [the holy of holies], as directed;

21The flowers, lamps, and tongs, of purest gold;

22The snuffers, basins, dishes for incense, and firepans, of pure gold; and for the temple entry, the inner doors for its most holy place and the doors of the holy place were of gold.

## New American Standard

*Furnishings of the Temple*

**4** THEN HE made a bronze altar, twenty cubits in length and
twenty cubits in width and ten cubits in height.
2Also he made the cast *metal* sea, ten cubits from brim to brim,
circular in form, and its height *was* five cubits and its circumference
thirty cubits.
3Now figures like oxen *were* under it *and* all around it, ten
cubits, entirely encircling the sea. The oxen *were* in two rows, cast
in one piece.
4It stood on twelve oxen, three facing the north, three facing
west, three facing south, and three facing east; and the sea *was set*
on top of them, and all their hindquarters turned inwards.
5And it was a handbreadth thick, and its brim was made like
the brim of a cup, *like* a lily blossom; it could hold 3,000 baths.
6He also made ten basins in which to wash, and he set five on
the right side and five on the left, to rinse things for the burnt
offering; but the sea *was* for the priests to wash in.
7¶ Then he made the ten golden lampstands in the way prescribed for them, and he set them in the temple, five on the right
side and five on the left.
8He also made ten tables and placed them in the temple, five
on the right side and five on the left. And he made one hundred
golden bowls.
9Then he made the court of the priests and the great court and
doors for the court, and overlaid their doors with bronze.
10And he set the sea on the right side *of the house* toward the
southeast.
11¶ Huram also made the pails, the shovels, and the bowls. So
Huram finished doing the work which he performed for King
Solomon in the house of God:
12the two pillars, the bowls and the two capitals on top of the
pillars, and the two networks to cover the two bowls of the capitals
which were on top of the pillars,
13and the four hundred pomegranates for the two networks,
two rows of pomegranates for each network to cover the two bowls
of the capitals which were on the pillars.
14He also made the stands and he made the basins on the
stands,
15*and* the one sea with the twelve oxen under it.
16And the pails, the shovels, the forks, and all its utensils,
Huram-abi made of polished bronze for King Solomon for the
house of the LORD.
17On the plain of the Jordan the king cast them, in the clay
ground between Succoth and Zeredah.
18Thus Solomon made all these utensils in great quantities, for
the weight of the bronze could not be found out.
19¶ Solomon also made all the things that *were* in the house of
God: even the golden altar, the tables with the bread of the Presence on them,
20the lampstands with their lamps of pure gold, to burn in front
of the inner sanctuary in the way prescribed;
21the flowers, the lamps, and the tongs of gold, of purest gold;
22and the snuffers, the bowls, the spoons, and the firepans of
pure gold; and the entrance of the house, its inner doors for the
holy of holies, and the doors of the house, *that is*, of the nave, of
gold.

## New International

*The Temple's Furnishings*

**4** HE MADE a bronze altar twenty cubits long, twenty cubits
wide and ten cubits high.[a] 2He made the Sea of cast metal,
circular in shape, measuring ten cubits from rim to rim and five
cubits[b] high. It took a line of thirty cubits[c] to measure around it.
3Below the rim, figures of bulls encircled it—ten to a cubit.[d] The
bulls were cast in two rows in one piece with the Sea.
4The Sea stood on twelve bulls, three facing north, three facing
west, three facing south and three facing east. The Sea rested on
top of them, and their hindquarters were toward the center. 5It
was a handbreadth[e] in thickness, and its rim was like the rim of
a cup, like a lily blossom. It held three thousand baths.[f]
6He then made ten basins for washing and placed five on the
south side and five on the north. In them the things to be used for
the burnt offerings were rinsed, but the Sea was to be used by the
priests for washing.
7He made ten gold lampstands according to the specifications
for them and placed them in the temple, five on the south side and
five on the north.
8He made ten tables and placed them in the temple, five on the
south side and five on the north. He also made a hundred gold
sprinkling bowls.
9He made the courtyard of the priests, and the large court and
the doors for the court, and overlaid the doors with bronze. 10He
placed the Sea on the south side, at the southeast corner.
11He also made the pots and shovels and sprinkling bowls.
So Huram finished the work he had undertaken for King Solomon in the temple of God:

12the two pillars;
the two bowl-shaped capitals on top of the pillars;
the two sets of network decorating the two bowl-shaped
capitals on top of the pillars;
13the four hundred pomegranates for the two sets of network
(two rows of pomegranates for each network, decorating
the bowl-shaped capitals on top of the pillars);
14the stands with their basins;
15the Sea and the twelve bulls under it;
16the pots, shovels, meat forks and all related articles.

All the objects that Huram-Abi made for King Solomon for the
temple of the LORD were of polished bronze. 17The king had them
cast in clay molds in the plain of the Jordan between Succoth and
Zarethan.[g] 18All these things that Solomon made amounted to so
much that the weight of the bronze was not determined.
19Solomon also made all the furnishings that were in God's
temple:

the golden altar;
the tables on which was the bread of the Presence;
20the lampstands of pure gold with their lamps, to burn in front
of the inner sanctuary as prescribed;
21the gold floral work and lamps and tongs (they were solid
gold);
22the pure gold wick trimmers, sprinkling bowls, dishes and
censers; and the gold doors of the temple: the inner doors
to the Most Holy Place and the doors of the main hall.

**NIV** [a] *1* That is, about 30 feet (about 9 meters) long and wide, and about 15 feet (about 4.5 meters) high [b] *2* That is, about 7 1/2 feet (about 2.3 meters) [c] *2* That is, about 45 feet (about 13.5 meters) [d] *3* That is, about 1 1/2 feet (about 0.5 meter) [e] *5* That is, about 3 inches (about 8 centimeters) [f] *5* That is, about 17,500 gallons (about 66 kiloliters) [g] *17* Hebrew *Zeredatha*, a variant of *Zarethan*

## King James

5 THUS ALL the work that Solomon made for the house of the LORD was finished: and Solomon brought in *all* the things that David his father had dedicated; and the silver, and the gold, and all the instruments, put he among the treasures of the house of God.

2¶ Then Solomon assembled the elders of Israel, and all the heads of the tribes, the chief of the fathers of the children of Israel, unto Jerusalem, to bring up the ark of the covenant of the LORD out of the city of David, which *is* Zion.

3Wherefore all the men of Israel assembled themselves unto the king in the feast which *was* in the seventh month.

4And all the elders of Israel came; and the Levites took up the ark.

5And they brought up the ark, and the tabernacle of the congregation, and all the holy vessels that *were* in the tabernacle, these did the priests *and* the Levites bring up.

6Also king Solomon, and all the congregation of Israel that were assembled unto him before the ark, sacrificed sheep and oxen, which could not be told nor numbered for multitude.

7And the priests brought in the ark of the covenant of the LORD unto his place, to the oracle of the house, into the most holy *place*, *even* under the wings of the cherubims:

8For the cherubims spread forth *their* wings over the place of the ark, and the cherubims covered the ark and the staves thereof above.

9And they drew out the staves *of the ark*, that the ends of the staves were seen from the ark before the oracle; but they were not seen without. And there it is unto this day.

10 *There was* nothing in the ark save the two tables which Moses put *therein* at Horeb, when the LORD made *a covenant* with the children of Israel, when they came out of Egypt.

11¶ And it came to pass, when the priests were come out of the holy *place*: (for all the priests *that were* present were sanctified, *and* did not *then* wait by course:

12Also the Levites *which were* the singers, all of them of Asaph, of Heman, of Jeduthun, with their sons and their brethren, *being* arrayed in white linen, having cymbals and psalteries and harps, stood at the east end of the altar, and with them an hundred and twenty priests sounding with trumpets:)

13It came even to pass, as the trumpeters and singers *were* as one, to make one sound to be heard in praising and thanking the LORD; and when they lifted up *their* voice with the trumpets and cymbals and instruments of music, and praised the LORD, *saying*, For *he is* good; for his mercy *endureth* for ever: that *then* the house was filled with a cloud, *even* the house of the LORD;

14So that the priests could not stand to minister by reason of the cloud: for the glory of the LORD had filled the house of God.

6 THEN SAID Solomon, The LORD hath said that he would dwell in the thick darkness.

2But I have built an house of habitation for thee, and a place for thy dwelling for ever.

3And the king turned his face, and blessed the whole congregation of Israel: and all the congregation of Israel stood.

4And he said, Blessed *be* the LORD God of Israel, who hath with his hands fulfilled *that* which he spake with his mouth to my father David, saying,

## Amplified

5 THUS ALL the work that Solomon did for the house of the Lord was finished. He brought in all the things that David his father had dedicated, and the silver, the gold, and all the vessels he put in the treasuries of the house of God.

2Then Solomon assembled the elders of Israel and all the heads of the tribes, the chiefs of the fathers' houses of the Israelites, to Jerusalem to bring up the ark of the covenant of the Lord out of the city of David, which is Zion.

3All the men of Israel gathered to the king at the feast in the seventh month.

4And all the elders of Israel came, and the Levites took up the ark.

5And the priests and Levites brought up the ark, the tent of meeting, and all the holy vessels that were in the tent.

6Also King Solomon and all the assembly of Israel who were gathered to him before the ark, sacrificed sheep and oxen, so numerous that they could not be counted or reported.

7And the priests brought the ark of the covenant of the Lord to its place, to the sanctuary of the house, into the holy of holies, under the wings of the cherubim;

8For the cherubim spread out their wings over the place of the ark, making a covering above the ark and its poles.

9And they drew out the poles of the ark, so that the ends of the poles protruding from the ark were visible from the front of the holy of holies, but were not visible from without. It is there to this day.

10There was nothing in the ark except the two tables [the ten commandments] which Moses put in it at Mount Horeb, when the Lord made a covenant with the Israelites, when they came out of Egypt.

11And when the priests had come out of the holy place (for all the priests present had sanctified themselves—separating themselves from everything that defiles—without regard to their divisions;

12And all the Levites who were singers, all of those of Asaph, Heman, and Jeduthun, with their sons and kinsmen, arrayed in fine linen, having cymbals, harps, and lyres stood at the east end of the altar, and with them 120 priests blowing trumpets);

13And when the trumpeters and singers were in unison, making one sound to be heard in praising and thanking the Lord, and when they lifted up their voice with the trumpets and cymbals and other instruments for song, and praised the Lord, saying, For He is good, for His mercy *and* loving-kindness endure for ever, then the house of the Lord was filled with a cloud,

14So that the priests could not stand to minister because of the cloud; for the glory of the Lord filled the house of God.

6 THEN SOLOMON said, The Lord has said that He would dwell in the thick darkness;

2I have built You a house, [in which the dark holy of holies seems] a *fitting* abode for You, a place for You to dwell in for ever.

3And the king turned his face, and blessed all the assembly of Israel, and they all stood.

4And he said, Blessed be the Lord, the God of Israel, Who has fulfilled with His hands what He promised with His mouth to David my father, saying,

## New American Standard

*The Ark Is Brought into the Temple*

**5** THUS ALL the work that Solomon performed for the house of the LORD was finished. And Solomon brought in the things that David his father had dedicated, even the silver and the gold and all the utensils, *and* put *them* in the treasuries of the house of God.

2¶ Then Solomon assembled to Jerusalem the elders of Israel and all the heads of the tribes, the leaders of the fathers' *households* of the sons of Israel, to bring up the ark of the covenant of the LORD out of the city of David, which is Zion.

3And all the men of Israel assembled themselves to the king at the feast, that is *in* the seventh month.

4Then all the elders of Israel came, and the Levites took up the ark.

5And they brought up the ark and the tent of meeting and all the holy utensils which *were* in the tent; the Levitical priests brought them up.

6And King Solomon and all the congregation of Israel who were assembled with him before the ark were sacrificing so many sheep and oxen, that they could not be counted or numbered.

7Then the priests brought the ark of the covenant of the LORD to its place, into the inner sanctuary of the house, to the holy of holies, under the wings of the cherubim.

8For the cherubim spread their wings over the place of the ark, so that the cherubim made a covering over the ark and its poles.

9And the poles were so long that the ends of the poles of the ark could be seen in front of the inner sanctuary, but they could not be seen outside; and they are there to this day.

10There was nothing in the ark except the two tablets which Moses put *there* at Horeb, where the LORD made a covenant with the sons of Israel, when they came out of Egypt.

*The Glory of God Fills the Temple*

11¶ And when the priests came forth from the holy place (for all the priests who were present had sanctified themselves, without regard to divisions),

12and all the Levitical singers, Asaph, Heman, Jeduthun, and their sons and kinsmen, clothed in fine linen, with cymbals, harps, and lyres, standing east of the altar, and with them one hundred and twenty priests blowing trumpets

13in unison when the trumpeters and the singers were to make themselves heard with one voice to praise and to glorify the LORD, and when they lifted up their voice accompanied by trumpets and cymbals and instruments of music, and when they praised the LORD *saying,* "*He* indeed is good for His lovingkindness is everlasting," then the house, the house of the LORD, was filled with a cloud,

14so that the priests could not stand to minister because of the cloud, for the glory of the LORD filled the house of God.

*Solomon's Dedication*

**6** THEN SOLOMON said,
"The LORD has said that He would dwell in the thick cloud.
2 "I have built Thee a lofty house,
And a place for Thy dwelling forever."

3Then the king faced about and blessed all the assembly of Israel, while all the assembly of Israel was standing.

4¶ And he said, "Blessed be the LORD, the God of Israel, who spoke with His mouth to my father David and has fulfilled *it* with His hands, saying,

## New International

**5** WHEN ALL the work Solomon had done for the temple of the LORD was finished, he brought in the things his father David had dedicated—the silver and gold and all the furnishings—and he placed them in the treasuries of God's temple.

*The Ark Brought to the Temple*

2Then Solomon summoned to Jerusalem the elders of Israel, all the heads of the tribes and the chiefs of the Israelite families, to bring up the ark of the LORD's covenant from Zion, the City of David. 3And all the men of Israel came together to the king at the time of the festival in the seventh month.

4When all the elders of Israel had arrived, the Levites took up the ark, 5and they brought up the ark and the Tent of Meeting and all the sacred furnishings in it. The priests, who were Levites, carried them up; 6and King Solomon and the entire assembly of Israel that had gathered about him were before the ark, sacrificing so many sheep and cattle that they could not be recorded or counted.

7The priests then brought the ark of the LORD's covenant to its place in the inner sanctuary of the temple, the Most Holy Place, and put it beneath the wings of the cherubim. 8The cherubim spread their wings over the place of the ark and covered the ark and its carrying poles. 9These poles were so long that their ends, extending from the ark, could be seen from in front of the inner sanctuary, but not from outside the Holy Place; and they are still there today. 10There was nothing in the ark except the two tablets that Moses had placed in it at Horeb, where the LORD made a covenant with the Israelites after they came out of Egypt.

11The priests then withdrew from the Holy Place. All the priests who were there had consecrated themselves, regardless of their divisions. 12All the Levites who were musicians—Asaph, Heman, Jeduthun and their sons and relatives—stood on the east side of the altar, dressed in fine linen and playing cymbals, harps and lyres. They were accompanied by 120 priests sounding trumpets. 13The trumpeters and singers joined in unison, as with one voice, to give praise and thanks to the LORD. Accompanied by trumpets, cymbals and other instruments, they raised their voices in praise to the LORD and sang:

"He is good;
his love endures forever."

Then the temple of the LORD was filled with a cloud, 14and the priests could not perform their service because of the cloud, for the glory of the LORD filled the temple of God.

**6** THEN SOLOMON said, "The LORD has said that he would dwell in a dark cloud; 2I have built a magnificent temple for you, a place for you to dwell forever."

3While the whole assembly of Israel was standing there, the king turned around and blessed them. 4Then he said:

"Praise be to the LORD, the God of Israel, who with his hands has fulfilled what he promised with his mouth to my father David. For he said, 5'Since the day I brought my people

# King James

5Since the day that I brought forth my people out of the land of Egypt I chose no city among all the tribes of Israel to build an house in, that my name might be there; neither chose I any man to be a ruler over my people Israel:

6But I have chosen Jerusalem, that my name might be there; and have chosen David to be over my people Israel.

7Now it was in the heart of David my father to build an house for the name of the LORD God of Israel.

8But the LORD said to David my father, Forasmuch as it was in thine heart to build an house for my name, thou didst well in that it was in thine heart:

9Notwithstanding thou shalt not build the house; but thy son which shall come forth out of thy loins, he shall build the house for my name.

10The LORD therefore hath performed his word that he hath spoken: for I am risen up in the room of David my father, and am set on the throne of Israel, as the LORD promised, and have built the house for the name of the LORD God of Israel.

11And in it have I put the ark, wherein *is* the covenant of the LORD, that he made with the children of Israel.

12¶ And he stood before the altar of the LORD in the presence of all the congregation of Israel, and spread forth his hands:

13For Solomon had made a brasen scaffold, of five cubits long, and five cubits broad, and three cubits high, and had set it in the midst of the court: and upon it he stood, and kneeled down upon his knees before all the congregation of Israel, and spread forth his hands toward heaven,

14And said, O LORD God of Israel, *there is* no God like thee in the heaven, nor in the earth; which keepest covenant, and *showest* mercy unto thy servants, that walk before thee with all their hearts:

15Thou which hast kept with thy servant David my father that which thou hast promised him; and spakest with thy mouth, and hast fulfilled *it* with thine hand, as *it is* this day.

16Now therefore, O LORD God of Israel, keep with thy servant David my father that which thou hast promised him, saying, There shall not fail thee a man in my sight to sit upon the throne of Israel; yet so that thy children take heed to their way to walk in my law, as thou hast walked before me.

17Now then, O LORD God of Israel, let thy word be verified, which thou hast spoken unto thy servant David.

18But will God in very deed dwell with men on the earth? behold, heaven and the heaven of heavens cannot contain thee; how much less this house which I have built!

19Have respect therefore to the prayer of thy servant, and to his supplication, O LORD my God, to hearken unto the cry and the prayer which thy servant prayeth before thee:

20That thine eyes may be open upon this house day and night, upon the place whereof thou hast said that thou wouldest put thy name there; to hearken unto the prayer which thy servant prayeth toward this place.

21Hearken therefore unto the supplications of thy servant, and of thy people Israel, which they shall make toward this place: hear thou from thy dwelling place, *even* from heaven; and when thou hearest, forgive.

22¶ If a man sin against his neighbour, and an oath be laid upon him to make him swear, and the oath come before thine altar in this house;

23Then hear thou from heaven, and do, and judge thy servants, by requiting the wicked, by recompensing his way upon his own head; and by justifying the righteous, by giving him according to his righteousness.

# Amplified

5Since the day that I brought My people out of the land of Egypt I chose no city among all the tribes of Israel to build a house in, that My name might be there; [a]neither chose I any man to be a ruler over My people Israel;

6But I have chosen Jerusalem, that My name [and the symbol of My presence] might be there, and have chosen David to be over My people Israel.

7Now it was in the heart of David my father to build a house for the name *and* renown of the Lord the God of Israel.

8But the Lord said to David my father, Since it was in your heart to build a house for My name *and* renown, you did well that it was in your heart.

9Yet you shall not build the house, but your son who shall be born to you, he shall build the house for My name.

10The Lord therefore has performed His word that He has spoken, for I have risen up in the place of David my father, and sit on the throne of Israel, as the Lord promised, and have built the house for the name of the Lord the God of Israel.

11In it have I put the ark [the symbol of His presence], in which is the covenant of the Lord [the ten commandments] which He made with the people of Israel.

12And Solomon stood before the altar of the Lord in the presence of all the assembly of Israel and spread forth his hands.

13(For he had made a bronze scaffold, five cubits square and three cubits high, and had set it in the midst of the court; upon it he stood, and he knelt upon his knees before all the assembly of Israel and spread forth his hands toward Heaven),

14And said, O Lord God of Israel, there is no God like You in the heavens or in the earth, keeping covenant and showing mercy *and* loving-kindness to Your servants who walk before You with all their hearts;

15You Who have kept Your promises to my father David, and fulfilled with Your hand what You spoke with Your mouth, as it is today.

16Now therefore, O Lord God of Israel, keep with Your servant David my father that which You promised him, saying, There shall not fail a man in My sight to sit on the throne of Israel, provided your children are careful to walk in My law as you, David, have walked before Me.

17Now then, O Lord God of Israel, let Your word to Your servant David be verified.

18But will God actually dwell with men on the earth? Behold, Heaven and the Heaven of heavens cannot contain You; how much less this house which I have built!

19Yet have respect for the prayer of Your servant, and to his supplication, O Lord my God, to listen to the cry and the prayer which Your servant prays before You;

20That Your eyes may be open upon this house day and night, toward the place in which You have said You would put Your name [and the symbol of your presence] to listen to *and* heed the prayer which Your servant prays facing this place.

21So listen to *and* heed the requests of Your servant and Your people Israel, which they shall make facing this place; hear from Your dwelling place, Heaven, and when You hear, forgive.

22If a man sins against his neighbor, and he is required to take an oath, and the oath comes before Your altar in this house;

23Then hear from Heaven, and do, and judge Your servants, requiting the wicked by bringing his conduct upon his own head, and by justifying the [uncompromisingly] righteous by giving him according to his righteousness [his uprightness and right standing with God].

**AMP** [a] God is plainly saying here that it was not His desire for Israel to have a king. To be sure, when to Samuel's attempt to dissuade the people they replied, "No, but we will have a king over us, that we may be like other nations," God said to Samuel, "They have rejected Me from being king over them . . . Make them a king" (I Sam. 8:7, 22). But Saul was originally the people's, not God's choice. The Bible nowhere teaches that "the voice of the people is the voice of God." But it does teach that when people make demands of God that are not in harmony with His will, He may grant them to their sorrow, and send "leanness into their soul" (Ps. 106:15).

## New American Standard

5'Since the day that I brought My people from the land of
Egypt, I did not choose a city out of all the tribes of Israel *in which*
to build a house that My name might be there, nor did I choose
any man for a leader over My people Israel;

6but I have chosen Jerusalem that My name might be there,
and I have chosen David to be over My people Israel.'

7"Now it was in the heart of my father David to build a house
for the name of the LORD, the God of Israel.

8"But the LORD said to my father David, 'Because it was in your
heart to build a house for My name, you did well that it was in your
heart.

9'Nevertheless you shall not build the house, but your son who
shall be born to you, he shall build the house for My name.'

10"Now the LORD has fulfilled His word which He spoke; for I
have risen in the place of my father David and sit on the throne
of Israel, as the LORD promised, and have built the house for the
name of the LORD, the God of Israel.

11"And there I have set the ark, in which is the covenant of the
LORD, which He made with the sons of Israel."

*Solomon's Prayer of Dedication*

12¶ Then he stood before the altar of the LORD in the presence
of all the assembly of Israel and spread out his hands.

13Now Solomon had made a bronze platform, five cubits long,
five cubits wide, and three cubits high, and had set it in the midst
of the court; and he stood on it, knelt on his knees in the presence
of all the assembly of Israel, and spread out his hands toward
heaven.

14And he said, "O LORD, the God of Israel, there is no god like
Thee in heaven or on earth, keeping covenant and *showing* loving-
kindness to Thy servants who walk before Thee with all their heart;

15who has kept with Thy servant David, my father, that which
Thou hast promised him; indeed, Thou hast spoken with Thy
mouth, and hast fulfilled it with Thy hand, as it is this day.

16"Now therefore, O LORD, the God of Israel, keep with Thy
servant David, my father, that which Thou hast promised him,
saying, 'You shall not lack a man to sit on the throne of Israel, if
only your sons take heed to their way, to walk in My law as you
have walked before Me.'

17"Now therefore, O LORD, the God of Israel, let Thy word be
confirmed which Thou hast spoken to Thy servant David.

18¶ "But will God indeed dwell with mankind on the earth?
Behold, heaven and the highest heaven cannot contain Thee; how
much less this house which I have built.

19"Yet have regard to the prayer of Thy servant and to his
supplication, O LORD my God, to listen to the cry and to the prayer
which Thy servant prays before Thee;

20that Thine eyes may be open toward this house day and night,
toward the place of which Thou hast said that *Thou wouldst* put Thy
name there, to listen to the prayer which Thy servant shall pray
toward this place.

21"And listen to the supplications of Thy servant and of Thy
people Israel, when they pray toward this place; hear Thou from
Thy dwelling place, from heaven; hear Thou and forgive.

22¶ "If a man sins against his neighbor, and is made to take an
oath, and he comes *and* takes an oath before Thine altar in this
house,

23then hear Thou from heaven and act and judge Thy servants,
punishing the wicked by bringing his way on his own head and
justifying the righteous by giving him according to his righteousness.

## New International

out of Egypt, I have not chosen a city in any tribe of Israel to
have a temple built for my Name to be there, nor have I
chosen anyone to be the leader over my people Israel. 6But
now I have chosen Jerusalem for my Name to be there, and
I have chosen David to rule my people Israel.'

7"My father David had it in his heart to build a temple for
the Name of the LORD, the God of Israel. 8But the LORD said
to my father David, 'Because it was in your heart to build a
temple for my Name, you did well to have this in your heart.
9Nevertheless, you are not the one to build the temple, but
your son, who is your own flesh and blood—he is the one
who will build the temple for my Name.'

10"The LORD has kept the promise he made. I have succeeded David my father and now I sit on the throne of Israel,
just as the LORD promised, and I have built the temple for the
Name of the LORD, the God of Israel. 11There I have placed
the ark, in which is the covenant of the LORD that he made
with the people of Israel."

*Solomon's Prayer of Dedication*

12Then Solomon stood before the altar of the LORD in front of
the whole assembly of Israel and spread out his hands. 13Now he
had made a bronze platform, five cubits[b] long, five cubits wide
and three cubits[c] high, and had placed it in the center of the outer
court. He stood on the platform and then knelt down before the
whole assembly of Israel and spread out his hands toward heaven.
14He said:

"O LORD, God of Israel, there is no God like you in heaven
or on earth—you who keep your covenant of love with your
servants who continue wholeheartedly in your way. 15You
have kept your promise to your servant David my father; with
your mouth you have promised and with your hand you have
fulfilled it—as it is today.

16"Now LORD, God of Israel, keep for your servant David
my father the promises you made to him when you said, 'You
shall never fail to have a man to sit before me on the throne
of Israel, if only your sons are careful in all they do to walk
before me according to my law, as you have done.' 17And
now, O LORD, God of Israel, let your word that you promised
your servant David come true.

18"But will God really dwell on earth with men? The heavens, even the highest heavens, cannot contain you. How
much less this temple I have built! 19Yet give attention to your
servant's prayer and his plea for mercy, O LORD my God.
Hear the cry and the prayer that your servant is praying in
your presence. 20May your eyes be open toward this temple
day and night, this place of which you said you would put
your Name there. May you hear the prayer your servant prays
toward this place. 21Hear the supplications of your servant
and of your people Israel when they pray toward this place.
Hear from heaven, your dwelling place; and when you hear,
forgive.

22"When a man wrongs his neighbor and is required to
take an oath and he comes and swears the oath before your
altar in this temple, 23then hear from heaven and act. Judge
between your servants, repaying the guilty by bringing down
on his own head what he has done. Declare the innocent not
guilty and so establish his innocence.

**NIV** [b] *13* That is, about 7 1/2 feet (about 2.3 meters) [c] *13* That is, about 4 1/2 feet (about 1.3 meters)

# King James

24¶ And if thy people Israel be put to the worse before the enemy, because they have sinned against thee; and shall return and confess thy name, and pray and make supplication before thee in this house;

25Then hear thou from the heavens, and forgive the sin of thy people Israel, and bring them again unto the land which thou gavest to them and to their fathers.

26¶ When the heaven is shut up, and there is no rain, because they have sinned against thee; *yet* if they pray toward this place, and confess thy name, and turn from their sin, when thou dost afflict them;

27Then hear thou from heaven, and forgive the sin of thy servants, and of thy people Israel, when thou hast taught them the good way, wherein they should walk; and send rain upon thy land, which thou hast given unto thy people for an inheritance.

28¶ If there be dearth in the land, if there be pestilence, if there be blasting, or mildew, locusts, or caterpillars; if their enemies besiege them in the cities of their land; whatsoever sore or whatsoever sickness *there be:*

29 *Then* what prayer *or* what supplication soever shall be made of any man, or of all thy people Israel, when every one shall know his own sore and his own grief, and shall spread forth his hands in this house:

30Then hear thou from heaven thy dwellingplace, and forgive, and render unto every man according unto all his ways, whose heart thou knowest; (for thou only knowest the hearts of the children of men:)

31That they may fear thee, to walk in thy ways, so long as they live in the land which thou gavest unto our fathers.

32¶ Moreover concerning the stranger, which is not of thy people Israel, but is come from a far country for thy great name's sake, and thy mighty hand, and thy stretched out arm; if they come and pray in this house;

33Then hear thou from the heavens, *even* from thy dwellingplace, and do according to all that the stranger calleth to thee for; that all people of the earth may know thy name, and fear thee, as *doth* thy people Israel, and may know that this house which I have built is called by thy name.

34If thy people go out to war against their enemies by the way that thou shalt send them, and they pray unto thee toward this city which thou hast chosen, and the house which I have built for thy name;

35Then hear thou from the heavens their prayer and their supplication, and maintain their cause.

36If they sin against thee, (for *there is* no man which sinneth not,) and thou be angry with them, and deliver them over before *their* enemies, and they carry them away captives unto a land far off or near;

37Yet *if* they bethink themselves in the land whither they are carried captive, and turn and pray unto thee in the land of their captivity, saying, We have sinned, we have done amiss, and have dealt wickedly;

38If they return to thee with all their heart and with all their soul in the land of their captivity, whither they have carried them captives, and pray toward their land, which thou gavest unto their fathers, and *toward* the city which thou hast chosen, and toward the house which I have built for thy name:

39Then hear thou from the heavens, *even* from thy dwellingplace, their prayer and their supplications, and maintain their cause, and forgive thy people which have sinned against thee.

40Now, my God, let, I beseech thee, thine eyes be open, and *let* thine ears *be* attent unto the prayer *that is made* in this place.

41Now therefore arise, O LORD God, into thy resting place, thou, and the ark of thy strength: let thy priests, O LORD God, be clothed with salvation, and let thy saints rejoice in goodness.

# Amplified

24If Your people Israel be defeated before the enemy because they have sinned against You, and shall return, confess Your name [and You Yourself], and pray and make supplication before You in this house,

25Then hear from Heaven, and forgive the sin of Your people Israel, and bring them again to the land which You gave to them and their fathers.

26When the heavens are shut up, and there is no rain because Your people have sinned against You, yet if they pray toward this place, confess your name [and You Yourself], and turn from their sin when You afflict them,

27Then hear from Heaven and forgive the sin of Your servants, *all* of Your people Israel, when You have taught them the good way in which they should walk; and send rain upon Your land, which You have given to Your people for an inheritance.

28If there is famine in the land, if there be pestilence, blight, mildew, locusts, or caterpillars; if their enemies besiege them in any of their cities; whatever plague or sickness there may be;

29Then whatever prayer or supplication any man or all of Your people Israel shall make, each knowing his own affliction and his own sorrow and stretching out his hands toward this house;

30Then hear from Heaven Your dwelling place, and forgive, and render to every man according to all his ways, whose heart You know; for You, You only, know men's hearts;

31That they may fear You and walk in Your ways as long as they live in the land which You gave to our fathers.

32Also concerning the stranger, who is not of Your people Israel, but has come from a far country for Your great name's sake, and Your mighty power, and Your stretched out arm; if he comes and prays toward this house,

33Hear from Heaven, from Your dwelling place, and do all that the stranger calls for to You; that all people of the earth may know Your name and fear You [reverently and worshipfully], as do Your people Israel, and may know that this house which I have built is called by Your name.

34If Your people go out to war against their enemies by the way that You send them, and they pray to You facing this city [Jerusalem] which You have chosen, and the house which I have built for Your name,

35Then hear from Heaven their prayer and supplication, and maintain their cause.

36If they sin against You—for there is no man who does not sin—and You are angry with them, and give them to enemies who take them captive to a land far or near;

37Yet if they repent in the land to which they have been carried captive, and turn and pray there, saying, We have sinned, we have done wrong, and have dealt wickedly;

38If they return to You with all their heart and soul in the land of their captivity, and pray facing their land which You gave to their fathers, and toward the city which You have chosen and the house which I have built for Your name,

39Then hear from Heaven Your dwelling place their prayer and supplications, and maintain their cause, and forgive Your people who have sinned against You.

40Now, O my God, I beseech You, let Your eyes be open and Your ears attentive to the prayer offered in this temple.

41So now arise, O Lord God, and come into Your resting place, You and the ark of Your strength *and* power. Let Your priests, O Lord God, be clothed with salvation, and let Your saints [Your zealous ones] rejoice in good *and* in Your goodness.

## New American Standard

24¶ "And if Thy people Israel are defeated before an enemy,
because they have sinned against Thee, and they return *to Thee* and
confess Thy name, and pray and make supplication before Thee
in this house,
25then hear Thou from heaven and forgive the sin of Thy people
Israel, and bring them back to the land which Thou hast given to
them and to their fathers.
26¶ "When the heavens are shut up and there is no rain because
they have sinned against Thee, and they pray toward this place
and confess Thy name, and turn from their sin when Thou dost
afflict them;
27then hear Thou in heaven and forgive the sin of Thy servants
and Thy people Israel, indeed, teach them the good way in which
they should walk. And send rain on Thy land, which Thou hast
given to Thy people for an inheritance.
28¶ "If there is famine in the land, if there is pestilence, if there
is blight or mildew, if there is locust or grasshopper, if their enemies besiege them in the land of their cities, whatever plague or
whatever sickness *there is*,
29whatever prayer or supplication is made by any man or by all
Thy people Israel, each knowing his own affliction and his own
pain, and spreading his hands toward this house,
30then hear Thou from heaven Thy dwelling place, and forgive,
and render to each according to all his ways, whose heart Thou
knowest for Thou alone dost know the hearts of the sons of men,
31that they may [a]fear Thee, to walk in Thy ways as long as they
live in the land which Thou hast given to our fathers.
32¶ "Also concerning the foreigner who is not from Thy people
Israel, when he comes from a far country for Thy great name's sake
and Thy mighty hand and Thine outstretched arm, when they
come and pray toward this house,
33then hear Thou from heaven, from Thy dwelling place, and
do according to all for which the foreigner calls to Thee, in order
that all the peoples of the earth may know Thy name, and [b]fear
Thee, as *do* Thy people Israel, and that they may know that this
house which I have built is called by Thy name.
34¶ "When Thy people go out to battle against their enemies,
by whatever way Thou shalt send them, and they pray to Thee
toward this city which Thou hast chosen, and the house which I
have built for Thy name,
35then hear Thou from heaven their prayer and their supplication, and maintain their cause.
36¶ "When they sin against Thee (for there is no man who does
not sin) and Thou art angry with them and dost deliver them to
an enemy, so that they take them away captive to a land far off or
near,
37if they take thought in the land where they are taken captive,
and repent and make supplication to Thee in the land of their
captivity, saying, 'We have sinned, we have committed iniquity,
and have acted wickedly';
38if they return to Thee with all their heart and with all their soul
in the land of their captivity, where they have been taken captive,
and pray toward their land which Thou hast given to their fathers,
and the city which Thou hast chosen, and toward the house which
I have built for Thy name,
39then hear from heaven, from Thy dwelling place, their prayer
and supplications, and maintain their cause, and forgive Thy
people who have sinned against Thee.
40¶ "Now, O my God, I pray Thee, let Thine eyes be open, and
Thine ears attentive to the prayer *offered* in this place.
41"Now therefore arise, O LORD God, to Thy resting place,
Thou and the ark of Thy might; let Thy priests, O LORD God, be
clothed with salvation, and let Thy godly ones rejoice in what is
good.

NAS [a] Or, *reverence* [b] Or, *reverence*

## New International

24"When your people Israel have been defeated by an
enemy because they have sinned against you and when they
turn back and confess your name, praying and making supplication before you in this temple, 25then hear from heaven
and forgive the sin of your people Israel and bring them back
to the land you gave to them and their fathers.
26"When the heavens are shut up and there is no rain
because your people have sinned against you, and when they
pray toward this place and confess your name and turn from
their sin because you have afflicted them, 27then hear from
heaven and forgive the sin of your servants, your people
Israel. Teach them the right way to live, and send rain on the
land you gave your people for an inheritance.
28"When famine or plague comes to the land, or blight or
mildew, locusts or grasshoppers, or when enemies besiege
them in any of their cities, whatever disaster or disease may
come, 29and when a prayer or plea is made by any of your
people Israel—each one aware of his afflictions and pains, and
spreading out his hands toward this temple— 30then hear
from heaven, your dwelling place. Forgive, and deal with
each man according to all he does, since you know his heart
(for you alone know the hearts of men), 31so that they will fear
you and walk in your ways all the time they live in the land
you gave our fathers.
32"As for the foreigner who does not belong to your people
Israel but has come from a distant land because of your great
name and your mighty hand and your outstretched arm—
when he comes and prays toward this temple, 33then hear
from heaven, your dwelling place, and do whatever the foreigner asks of you, so that all the peoples of the earth may
know your name and fear you, as do your own people Israel,
and may know that this house I have built bears your Name.
34"When your people go to war against their enemies,
wherever you send them, and when they pray to you toward
this city you have chosen and the temple I have built for your
Name, 35then hear from heaven their prayer and their plea,
and uphold their cause.
36"When they sin against you—for there is no one who
does not sin—and you become angry with them and give
them over to the enemy, who takes them captive to a land far
away or near; 37and if they have a change of heart in the land
where they are held captive, and repent and plead with you
in the land of their captivity and say, 'We have sinned, we
have done wrong and acted wickedly'; 38and if they turn back
to you with all their heart and soul in the land of their captivity
where they were taken, and pray toward the land you gave
their fathers, toward the city you have chosen and toward the
temple I have built for your Name; 39then from heaven, your
dwelling place, hear their prayer and their pleas, and uphold
their cause. And forgive your people, who have sinned
against you.
40"Now, my God, may your eyes be open and your ears
attentive to the prayers offered in this place.

41"Now arise, O LORD God, and come to your resting
place,
you and the ark of your might.
May your priests, O LORD God, be clothed with
salvation,
may your saints rejoice in your goodness.

## King James

42 O LORD God, turn not away the face of thine anointed: remember the mercies of David thy servant.

# 7

NOW WHEN Solomon had made an end of praying, the fire came down from heaven, and consumed the burnt offering and the sacrifices; and the glory of the LORD filled the house.

2 And the priests could not enter into the house of the LORD, because the glory of the LORD had filled the LORD'S house.

3 And when all the children of Israel saw how the fire came down, and the glory of the LORD upon the house, they bowed themselves with their faces to the ground upon the pavement, and worshipped, and praised the LORD, *saying*, For *he is* good; for his mercy *endureth* for ever.

4 ¶ Then the king and all the people offered sacrifices before the LORD.

5 And king Solomon offered a sacrifice of twenty and two thousand oxen, and an hundred and twenty thousand sheep: so the king and all the people dedicated the house of God.

6 And the priests waited on their offices: the Levites also with instruments of music of the LORD, which David the king had made to praise the LORD, because his mercy *endureth* for ever, when David praised by their ministry; and the priests sounded trumpets before them, and all Israel stood.

7 Moreover Solomon hallowed the middle of the court that *was* before the house of the LORD: for there he offered burnt offerings, and the fat of the peace offerings, because the brasen altar which Solomon had made was not able to receive the burnt offerings, and the meat offerings, and the fat.

8 ¶ Also at the same time Solomon kept the feast seven days, and all Israel with him, a very great congregation, from the entering in of Hamath unto the river of Egypt.

9 And in the eighth day they made a solemn assembly: for they kept the dedication of the altar seven days, and the feast seven days.

10 And on the three and twentieth day of the seventh month he sent the people away into their tents, glad and merry in heart for the goodness that the LORD had shown unto David, and to Solomon, and to Israel his people.

11 Thus Solomon finished the house of the LORD, and the king's house: and all that came into Solomon's heart to make in the house of the LORD, and in his own house, he prosperously effected.

12 ¶ And the LORD appeared to Solomon by night, and said unto him, I have heard thy prayer, and have chosen this place to myself for an house of sacrifice.

13 If I shut up heaven that there be no rain, or if I command the locusts to devour the land, or if I send pestilence among my people;

## Amplified

42 O Lord God, [a]turn not away the face *of* [me] Your anointed one; [earnestly] remember Your good deeds, mercy *and* steadfast love for David Your servant.

# 7

WHEN SOLOMON had finished praying, the fire came down from Heaven and consumed the burnt offering and the sacrifices, and the glory of the Lord filled the house.

2 The priests could not enter the house of the Lord, because the glory of the Lord had filled the Lord's house.

3 And when all the people of Israel saw how the fire came down and the glory of the Lord upon the house, they bowed with their faces upon the pavement, and worshiped and praised the Lord, saying, For He is good, for His mercy *and* loving-kindness endure for ever.

4 Then the king and all the people offered sacrifices before the Lord.

5 King Solomon offered a sacrifice of 22,000 oxen, and 120,000 sheep. So the king and all the people dedicated God's house.

6 The priests stood at their posts; the Levites also, with instruments of music to the Lord which King David had made to praise *and* give thanks to the Lord—for His mercy *and* loving-kindness endure for ever—whenever David praised by their ministry; the priests blew trumpets before them, and all Israel stood.

7 Moreover Solomon consecrated the middle of the court that was before the house of the Lord; for there he offered burnt offerings and the fat of the peace offerings, because the brazen altar which [he] had made was not sufficient to receive the burnt offerings, cereal offerings, and the fat.

8 At that time Solomon held the feast for seven days, and all Israel with him, a very great assembly, from the entrance of Hamath to the brook of Egypt.

9 The eighth day they made a solemn assembly; for they had kept the dedication of the altar and the feast each seven days.

10 And on the twenty-third day of the seventh month he sent the people away to their homes, glad and merry in heart for the goodness that the Lord had shown to David, to Solomon, and to Israel His people.

11 Thus Solomon finished the Lord's house and the king's house; all that [he] had planned to do in the Lord's house and his own house he accomplished successfully.

12 And the Lord appeared to Solomon by night and said to him: I have heard your prayer, and have chosen this place for Myself as a house of sacrifice.

13 If I shut up Heaven so no rain falls, or if I command locusts to devour the land, or if I send pestilence among My people,

**AMP** [a] Young Solomon seems, and doubtless is, utterly sincere as he offers this prayer of which God shows His approval by His miraculous demonstration of His presence, in the next verse. It raises the ever-present question, How could Solomon have begun his career like this, and have written his unquestionably divinely inspired books, and yet have fallen eventually into utter defiance of God's will? Not as the result of one false step, as with David, but as the habit of his life for the remainder of his days! Not broken with unspeakable sorrow for his awful sin, as was his penitent father (Ps. 51), but without ever apparently repenting or confessing his awful defiance of God and His explicit commands and warnings, given to Solomon personally (II Chron. 7:17-22). Possibly in this closing sentence of Solomon's prayer, we detect the fallacy in the young king's thinking. He seems to be saying in substance, "O Lord God, *I am Your responsibility* now; it will be for *You to see that my face does not turn* away from You; and not for my sake, but [since my name is identified with this temple as well as Yours, You must keep my face turned toward You] for Your own sake!" God lost no unnecessary time in attempting to set the young man straight as to whose is the responsibility for sin—in his case specifically (7:12, 17-22). But there is no evidence that Solomon applied it to himself, though he preached a bit to others, he seems to have *considered himself exempt* from obeying God's commands—an attitude which has brought disaster upon every person who has ever taken it, however great, or wise, or rich, or otherwise sufficient.

## New American Standard

42"O LORD God, do not turn away the face of Thine anointed;
remember *Thy* lovingkindness to Thy servant David."

*The Shekinah Glory*

7 NOW WHEN Solomon had finished praying, fire came down
from heaven and consumed the burnt offering and the sacrifices; and the glory of the LORD filled the house.
2And the priests could not enter into the house of the LORD,
because the glory of the LORD filled the LORD's house.
3And all the sons of Israel, seeing the fire come down and the
glory of the LORD upon the house, bowed down on the pavement
with their faces to the ground, and they worshiped and gave praise
to the LORD, *saying*, "Truly He is good, truly His lovingkindness
is everlasting."

*Sacrifices Offered*

4¶ Then the king and all the people offered sacrifice before the
LORD.
5And King Solomon offered a sacrifice of 22,000 oxen, and
120,000 sheep. Thus the king and all the people dedicated the
house of God.
6And the priests stood at their posts and the Levites, with the
instruments of music to the LORD, which King David had made for
giving praise to the LORD—"for His lovingkindness is everlasting"—whenever he gave praise by their means, while the priests
on the other side blew trumpets; and all Israel was standing.
7Then Solomon consecrated the middle of the court that *was*
before the house of the LORD, for there he offered the burnt offerings and the fat of the peace offerings, because the bronze altar
which Solomon had made was not able to contain the burnt offering, the grain offering, and the fat.

*The Feast of Dedication*

8¶ So Solomon observed the feast at that time for seven days,
and all Israel with him, a very great assembly, *who came* from the
entrance of Hamath to the brook of Egypt.
9And on the eighth day they held a solemn assembly, for the
dedication of the altar they observed seven days, and the feast
seven days.
10Then on the twenty-third day of the seventh month he sent
the people to their tents, rejoicing and happy of heart because of
the goodness that the LORD had shown to David and to Solomon
and to His people Israel.

*God's Promise and Warning*

11¶ Thus Solomon finished the house of the LORD and the king's
palace, and successfully completed all that he had planned on
doing in the house of the LORD and in his palace.
12Then the LORD appeared to Solomon at night and said to him,
"I have heard your prayer, and have chosen this place for Myself
as a house of sacrifice.
13"If I shut up the heavens so that there is no rain, or if I
command the locust to devour the land, or if I send pestilence
among My people,

## New International

42O LORD God, do not reject your anointed one.
Remember the great love promised to David your
servant."

*The Dedication of the Temple*

7 WHEN SOLOMON finished praying, fire came down from
heaven and consumed the burnt offering and the sacrifices,
and the glory of the LORD filled the temple. 2The priests could not
enter the temple of the LORD because the glory of the LORD filled
it. 3When all the Israelites saw the fire coming down and the glory
of the LORD above the temple, they knelt on the pavement with
their faces to the ground, and they worshiped and gave thanks to
the LORD, saying,

"He is good;
his love endures forever."

4Then the king and all the people offered sacrifices before the
LORD. 5And King Solomon offered a sacrifice of twenty-two thousand head of cattle and a hundred and twenty thousand sheep and
goats. So the king and all the people dedicated the temple of God.
6The priests took their positions, as did the Levites with the LORD's
musical instruments, which King David had made for praising the
LORD and which were used when he gave thanks, saying, "His
love endures forever." Opposite the Levites, the priests blew their
trumpets, and all the Israelites were standing.
7Solomon consecrated the middle part of the courtyard in front
of the temple of the LORD, and there he offered burnt offerings and
the fat of the fellowship offerings,[b] because the bronze altar he had
made could not hold the burnt offerings, the grain offerings and
the fat portions.
8So Solomon observed the festival at that time for seven days,
and all Israel with him—a vast assembly, people from Lebo[c]
Hamath to the Wadi of Egypt. 9On the eighth day they held an
assembly, for they had celebrated the dedication of the altar for
seven days and the festival for seven days more. 10On the twenty-
third day of the seventh month he sent the people to their homes,
joyful and glad in heart for the good things the LORD had done for
David and Solomon and for his people Israel.

*The LORD Appears to Solomon*

11When Solomon had finished the temple of the LORD and the
royal palace, and had succeeded in carrying out all he had in mind
to do in the temple of the LORD and in his own palace, 12the LORD
appeared to him at night and said:

"I have heard your prayer and have chosen this place for
myself as a temple for sacrifices.
13"When I shut up the heavens so that there is no rain, or
command locusts to devour the land or send a plague among
my people, 14if my people, who are called by my name, will

NIV [b] 7 Traditionally *peace offerings* [c] 8 Or *from the entrance to*

## King James

14 If my people, which are called by my name, shall humble themselves, and pray, and seek my face, and turn from their wicked ways; then will I hear from heaven, and will forgive their sin, and will heal their land.

15 Now mine eyes shall be open, and mine ears attent unto the prayer *that is made* in this place.

16 For now have I chosen and sanctified this house, that my name may be there for ever: and mine eyes and mine heart shall be there perpetually.

17 And as for thee, if thou wilt walk before me, as David thy father walked, and do according to all that I have commanded thee, and shalt observe my statutes and my judgments;

18 Then will I stablish the throne of thy kingdom, according as I have covenanted with David thy father, saying, There shall not fail thee a man *to be* ruler in Israel.

19 But if ye turn away, and forsake my statutes and my commandments, which I have set before you, and shall go and serve other gods, and worship them;

20 Then will I pluck them up by the roots out of my land which I have given them; and this house, which I have sanctified for my name, will I cast out of my sight, and will make it *to be* a proverb and a byword among all nations.

21 And this house, which is high, shall be an astonishment to every one that passeth by it; so that he shall say, Why hath the LORD done thus unto this land, and unto this house?

22 And it shall be answered, Because they forsook the LORD God of their fathers, which brought them forth out of the land of Egypt, and laid hold on other gods, and worshipped them, and served them: therefore hath he brought all this evil upon them.

**8** AND IT came to pass at the end of twenty years, wherein Solomon had built the house of the LORD, and his own house,

2 That the cities which Huram had restored to Solomon, Solomon built them, and caused the children of Israel to dwell there.

3 And Solomon went to Hamath-zobah, and prevailed against it.

4 And he built Tadmor in the wilderness, and all the store cities, which he built in Hamath.

5 Also he built Beth-horon the upper, and Beth-horon the nether, fenced cities, with walls, gates, and bars;

6 And Baalath, and all the store cities that Solomon had, and all the chariot cities, and the cities of the horsemen, and all that Solomon desired to build in Jerusalem, and in Lebanon, and throughout all the land of his dominion.

7 ¶ *As for* all the people *that were* left of the Hittites, and the Amorites, and the Perizzites, and the Hivites, and the Jebusites, which *were* not of Israel,

8 *But* of their children, who were left after them in the land, whom the children of Israel consumed not, them did Solomon make to pay tribute until this day.

9 But of the children of Israel did Solomon make no servants for his work; but they *were* men of war, and chief of his captains, and captains of his chariots and horsemen.

10 And these *were* the chief of king Solomon's officers, *even* two hundred and fifty, that bare rule over the people.

11 ¶ And Solomon brought up the daughter of Pharaoh out of the city of David unto the house that he had built for her: for he said, My wife shall not dwell in the house of David king of Israel, because *the places are* holy, whereunto the ark of the LORD hath come.

12 ¶ Then Solomon offered burnt offerings unto the LORD on the altar of the LORD, which he had built before the porch,

13 Even after a certain rate every day, offering according to the commandment of Moses, on the sabbaths, and on the new moons, and on the solemn feasts, three times in the year, *even* in the feast of unleavened bread, and in the feast of weeks, and in the feast of tabernacles.

## Amplified

14 If My people who are called by My name shall humble themselves, pray, seek, crave *and* require of necessity My face, and turn from their wicked ways, then will I hear from Heaven, forgive their sin, and heal their land.

15 Now My eyes will be open, and My ears attentive to prayer offered in this place.

16 For I have chosen and sanctified [set apart for holy use] this house, that My name may be here for ever, and My eyes and My heart will be here perpetually.

17 As for you [Solomon], if you will walk before me as David your father walked, and do all I have commanded you and observe My statutes and My ordinances, [Cp. I Kings 11:1-11.]

18 Then I will establish the throne of your kingdom, as I covenanted with David your father, saying, There shall not fail you a man to be ruler in Israel.

19 But if you [people] turn away, and forsake My statutes and My commandments which I have set before you, and go and serve other gods, and worship them;

20 Then will I pluck [Israel] up by the roots out of My land which I have given [them]; and this house, which I have hallowed for My name, will I cast out of My sight, and will make it to be a proverb and a byword among all nations. [Jer. 24:9, 10.]

21 And this house, which was so high, shall be an astonishment to every one passing it, and he will say, Why has the Lord done thus to this land and to this house?

22 Then men will say, Because they forsook the Lord God of their fathers, Who brought them out of Egypt, and they laid hold of other gods, and worshiped and served them; therefore has He brought all this evil upon them.

**8** AT THE end of twenty years, in which Solomon had built the house of the Lord and his own house,

2 The cities which Huram had given to *him,* Solomon rebuilt *and* fortified and caused the Israelites to dwell there.

3 And Solomon took Hamath-zobah.

4 He built Tadmor in the wilderness and all his store cities in Hamath.

5 Also he built Upper Beth-horon and Lower Beth-horon, fortified cities with walls, gates, and bars,

6 And Baalath, and all the store-cities [he] had, and all the cities for his chariots, and the cities for his horsemen, and all that Solomon desired to build in Jerusalem, in Lebanon, and in all his dominion.

7 All the people who were left of the Hittites, Amorites, Perizzites, Hivites, and Jebusites, who were not of Israel,

8 But descendants of those who were left in the land, whom the Israelites had not destroyed, of them Solomon made a levy for *forced* labor to this day.

9 But of the Israelites Solomon made no slaves for his work; but they were men of war, chief of his captains, and captains of his chariots and horsemen.

10 These were the chief of King Solomon's officers, 250 in authority over the people.

11 Solomon brought the daughter of Pharaoh out of the city of David into the house he had built for her, for he said, My wife shall not dwell in the house of David king of Israel, because the places are holy to which the ark of the Lord has come.

12 Then Solomon offered burnt offerings to the Lord on the Lord's altar which he had built before the [temple] porch *or* vestibule,

13 A certain number every day, offering as Moses commanded, on the sabbaths, the new moons, and the solemn feast days three times in the year—the feasts of unleavened bread, of weeks, and of tabernacles.

## New American Standard

14and My people who are called by My name humble themselves and pray, and seek My face and turn from their wicked ways, then I will hear from heaven, will forgive their sin, and will heal their land.

15"Now My eyes shall be open and My ears attentive to the prayer *offered* in this place.

16"For now I have chosen and consecrated this house that My name may be there forever, and My eyes and My heart will be there perpetually.

17"And as for you, if you walk before Me as your father David walked even to do according to all that I have commanded you and will keep My statutes and My ordinances,

18then I will establish your royal throne as I covenanted with your father David, saying, 'You shall not lack a man *to be* ruler in Israel.'

19¶ "But if you turn away and forsake My statutes and My commandments which I have set before you and shall go and serve other gods and worship them,

20then I will uproot you from My land which I have given you, and this house which I have consecrated for My name I will cast out of My sight, and I will make it a proverb and a byword among all peoples.

21"As for this house, which was exalted, everyone who passes by it will be astonished and say, 'Why has the LORD done thus to this land and to this house?'

22"And they will say, 'Because they forsook the LORD, the God of their fathers, who brought them from the land of Egypt, and they adopted other gods and worshiped them and served them, therefore He has brought all this adversity on them.' "

*Solomon's Activities and Accomplishments*

8 NOW IT came about at the end of the twenty years in which Solomon had built the house of the LORD and his own house

2that he built the cities which Huram had given to him, and settled the sons of Israel there.

3Then Solomon went to Hamath-zobah and captured it.

4And he built Tadmor in the wilderness and all the storage cities which he had built in Hamath.

5He also built upper Beth-horon and lower Beth-horon, fortified cities *with* walls, gates, and bars;

6and Baalath and all the storage cities that Solomon had, and all the cities for his chariots and cities for his horsemen, and all that it pleased Solomon to build in Jerusalem, in Lebanon, and in all the land under his rule.

7¶ All of the people who were left of the Hittites, the Amorites, the Perizzites, the Hivites, and the Jebusites, who were not of Israel,

8namely, from their descendants who were left after them in the land whom the sons of Israel had not destroyed, them Solomon raised as forced laborers to this day.

9But Solomon did not make slaves for his work from the sons of Israel; they were men of war, his chief captains, and commanders of his chariots and his horsemen.

10And these were the chief officers of King Solomon, two hundred and fifty who ruled over the people.

11¶ Then Solomon brought Pharaoh's daughter up from the city of David to the house which he had built for her; for he said, "My wife shall not dwell in the house of David king of Israel, because the places are holy where the ark of the LORD has entered."

12¶ Then Solomon offered burnt offerings to the LORD on the altar of the LORD which he had built before the porch;

13and *did so* according to the daily rule, offering *them* up according to the commandment of Moses, for the sabbaths, the new moons, and the three annual feasts—the Feast of Unleavened Bread, the Feast of Weeks, and the Feast of Booths.

## New International

humble themselves and pray and seek my face and turn from their wicked ways, then will I hear from heaven and will forgive their sin and will heal their land. 15Now my eyes will be open and my ears attentive to the prayers offered in this place. 16I have chosen and consecrated this temple so that my Name may be there forever. My eyes and my heart will always be there.

17"As for you, if you walk before me as David your father did, and do all I command, and observe my decrees and laws, 18I will establish your royal throne, as I covenanted with David your father when I said, 'You shall never fail to have a man to rule over Israel.'

19"But if you[a] turn away and forsake the decrees and commands I have given you[b] and go off to serve other gods and worship them, 20then I will uproot Israel from my land, which I have given them, and will reject this temple I have consecrated for my Name. I will make it a byword and an object of ridicule among all peoples. 21And though this temple is now so imposing, all who pass by will be appalled and say, 'Why has the LORD done such a thing to this land and to this temple?' 22People will answer, 'Because they have forsaken the LORD, the God of their fathers, who brought them out of Egypt, and have embraced other gods, worshiping and serving them—that is why he brought all this disaster on them.' "

*Solomon's Other Activities*

8 AT THE end of twenty years, during which Solomon built the temple of the LORD and his own palace, 2Solomon rebuilt the villages that Hiram[c] had given him, and settled Israelites in them. 3Solomon then went to Hamath Zobah and captured it. 4He also built up Tadmor in the desert and all the store cities he had built in Hamath. 5He rebuilt Upper Beth Horon and Lower Beth Horon as fortified cities, with walls and with gates and bars, 6as well as Baalath and all his store cities, and all the cities for his chariots and for his horses[d]—whatever he desired to build in Jerusalem, in Lebanon and throughout all the territory he ruled.

7All the people left from the Hittites, Amorites, Perizzites, Hivites and Jebusites (these peoples were not Israelites), 8that is, their descendants remaining in the land, whom the Israelites had not destroyed—these Solomon conscripted for his slave labor force, as it is to this day. 9But Solomon did not make slaves of the Israelites for his work; they were his fighting men, commanders of his captains, and commanders of his chariots and charioteers. 10They were also King Solomon's chief officials—two hundred and fifty officials supervising the men.

11Solomon brought Pharaoh's daughter up from the City of David to the palace he had built for her, for he said, "My wife must not live in the palace of David king of Israel, because the places the ark of the LORD has entered are holy."

12On the altar of the LORD that he had built in front of the portico, Solomon sacrificed burnt offerings to the LORD, 13according to the daily requirement for offerings commanded by Moses for Sabbaths, New Moons and the three annual feasts—the Feast of Unleavened Bread, the Feast of Weeks and the Feast of Tabernacles. 14In keeping with the ordinance of his father David, he

NIV [a] *19* The Hebrew is plural. [b] *19* The Hebrew is plural. [c] *2* Hebrew *Huram,* a variant of *Hiram;* also in verse 18 [d] *6* Or *charioteers*

## King James

14¶ And he appointed, according to the order of David his father, the courses of the priests to their service, and the Levites to their charges, to praise and minister before the priests, as the duty of every day required: the porters also by their courses at every gate: for so had David the man of God commanded.

15And they departed not from the commandment of the king unto the priests and Levites concerning any matter, or concerning the treasures.

16Now all the work of Solomon was prepared unto the day of the foundation of the house of the LORD, and until it was finished. *So* the house of the LORD was perfected.

17¶ Then went Solomon to Ezion-geber, and to Eloth, at the sea side in the land of Edom.

18And Huram sent him by the hands of his servants ships, and servants that had knowledge of the sea; and they went with the servants of Solomon to Ophir, and took thence four hundred and fifty talents of gold, and brought *them* to king Solomon.

9 AND WHEN the queen of Sheba heard of the fame of Solomon, she came to prove Solomon with hard questions at Jerusalem, with a very great company, and camels that bare spices, and gold in abundance, and precious stones: and when she was come to Solomon, she communed with him of all that was in her heart.

2And Solomon told her all her questions: and there was nothing hid from Solomon which he told her not.

3And when the queen of Sheba had seen the wisdom of Solomon, and the house that he had built,

4And the meat of his table, and the sitting of his servants, and the attendance of his ministers, and their apparel; his cupbearers also, and their apparel; and his ascent by which he went up into the house of the LORD; there was no more spirit in her.

5And she said to the king, *It was* a true report which I heard in mine own land of thine acts, and of thy wisdom:

6Howbeit I believed not their words, until I came, and mine eyes had seen *it*: and, behold, the one half of the greatness of thy wisdom was not told me: *for* thou exceedest the fame that I heard.

7Happy *are* thy men, and happy *are* these thy servants, which stand continually before thee, and hear thy wisdom.

8Blessed be the LORD thy God, which delighted in thee to set thee on his throne, *to be* king for the LORD thy God: because thy God loved Israel, to establish them for ever, therefore made he thee king over them, to do judgment and justice.

9And she gave the king an hundred and twenty talents of gold, and of spices great abundance, and precious stones: neither was there any such spice as the queen of Sheba gave king Solomon.

10And the servants also of Huram, and the servants of Solomon, which brought gold from Ophir, brought algum trees and precious stones.

11And the king made *of* the algum trees terraces to the house of the LORD, and to the king's palace, and harps and psalteries for singers: and there were none such seen before in the land of Judah.

12And king Solomon gave to the queen of Sheba all her desire, whatsoever she asked, beside *that* which she had brought unto the king. So she turned, and went away to her own land, she and her servants.

13¶ Now the weight of gold that came to Solomon in one year was six hundred and threescore and six talents of gold;

14Beside *that which* chapmen and merchants brought. And all the kings of Arabia and governors of the country brought gold and silver to Solomon.

15¶ And king Solomon made two hundred targets *of* beaten gold: six hundred *shekels* of beaten gold went to one target.

## Amplified

14And he appointed, as ordered by David his father, the divisions of the priests for their service, and the Levites to their offices to praise, and to serve before the priests as the duty of every day required, and the gatekeepers also by their divisions at every gate; for so had David the man of God commanded.

15And they did not turn from the command of the king to the priests and Levites in any respect or concerning the treasures.

16Thus all the work of Solomon was prepared from the day the foundation of the Lord's house was laid until it was finished. So the house of the Lord was completed.

17Then Solomon went to Ezion-geber and to Eloth on the shore of the [Red] Sea in the land of Edom,

18And Huram sent him by his servants ships and servants familiar with the sea; and they went with the servants of Solomon to Ophir, and took from there 450 talents of gold and brought them to King Solomon.

9 WHEN THE queen of Sheba heard of the fame of Solomon, she came to Jerusalem to test him with hard questions, accompanied by very many attendants and camels bearing spices, much gold, and precious stones. And when she came to Solomon she talked with him of all that was on her mind.

2And Solomon answered all her questions; there was nothing hidden from [him] which he was unable to make clear to her.

3And when the queen of Sheba had seen Solomon's wisdom, the house he had built,

4The food of his table, the seating of his officials, the [standing at] attention of his servants, their apparel, his cupbearers also and their apparel, and his burnt offerings which he offered at the house of the Lord, there was no more spirit in her.

5She said to the king, The report which I heard in my own land of your acts *and* sayings, and of your wisdom was true,

6But I did not believe their words until I came, and my eyes had seen it. Behold, the half of the greatness of your wisdom was not told me; you surpass the fame that I heard of you.

7Happy are your wives *and* men, and happy are these your servants who stand continually before you and hear your wisdom!

8Blessed be the Lord your God, Who delighted in you and set you on His throne to be king for the Lord your God! Because your God loved Israel and would establish them for ever, He made you king over them to do justice and righteousness.

9She gave the king 120 talents of gold, a very large quantity of spices, and precious stones; such spice was not anywhere as the queen of Sheba gave King Solomon.

10The servants of Huram, and [those] of Solomon, who brought gold from Ophir, also brought algum trees and precious stones.

11The king made of the algum trees terraces *or* walks to the house of the Lord and to the king's palace, and lyres and harps for the singers; none such were ever seen before in the land of Judah.

12And King Solomon gave to the queen of Sheba all her desire, whatever she asked, besides what she had brought to the king. So she with her servants returned to her own land.

13Now the weight of gold that came to Solomon in one year was 666 talents,

14Besides what traders and merchants brought; and all the kings of Arabia and governors of the country brought gold and silver to Solomon.

15And King Solomon made 200 large shields *or* bucklers of beaten gold; 600 shekels of beaten gold went to each shield.

## New American Standard

14¶ Now according to the ordinance of his father David, he
appointed the divisions of the priests for their service, and the
Levites for their duties of praise and ministering before the priests
according to the daily rule, and the gatekeepers by their divisions
at every gate; for David the man of God had so commanded.
15And they did not depart from the commandment of the king
to the priests and Levites in any manner or concerning the storehouses.
16¶ Thus all the work of Solomon was carried out from the day
of the foundation of the house of the LORD, and until it was
finished. So the house of the LORD was completed.
17¶ Then Solomon went to Ezion-geber and to Eloth on the
seashore in the land of Edom.
18And Huram by his servants sent him ships and servants who
knew the sea; and they went with Solomon's servants to Ophir,
and took from there four hundred and fifty talents of gold, and
brought them to King Solomon.

*Visit of the Queen of Sheba*

9 NOW WHEN the queen of Sheba heard of the fame of Solomon, she came to Jerusalem to test Solomon with difficult
questions. She had a very large retinue, with camels carrying
spices, and a large amount of gold and precious stones; and when
she came to Solomon, she spoke with him about all that was on
her heart.
2And Solomon answered all her questions; nothing was hidden from Solomon which he did not explain to her.
3And when the queen of Sheba had seen the wisdom of Solomon, the house which he had built,
4the food at his table, the seating of his servants, the attendance of his ministers and their attire, his cupbearers and their
attire, and his stairway by which he went up to the house of the
LORD, she was breathless.
5Then she said to the king, "It was a true report which I heard
in my own land about your words and your wisdom.
6"Nevertheless I did not believe their reports until I came and
my eyes had seen it. And behold, the half of the greatness of your
wisdom was not told me. You surpass the report that I heard.
7"How blessed are your men, how blessed are these your
servants who stand before you continually and hear your wisdom.
8"Blessed be the LORD your God who delighted in you, setting
you on His throne as king for the LORD your God; because your
God loved Israel establishing them forever, therefore He made you
king over them, to do justice and righteousness."
9Then she gave the king one hundred and twenty talents of
gold, and a very great *amount of* spices and precious stones; there
had never been spice like that which the queen of Sheba gave to
King Solomon.
10And the servants of Huram and the servants of Solomon who
brought gold from Ophir, also brought algum trees and precious
stones.
11And from the algum the king made steps for the house of the
LORD and for the king's palace, and lyres and harps for the singers;
and none like that was seen before in the land of Judah.
12And King Solomon gave to the queen of Sheba all her desire
which she requested besides *a return for* what she had brought to
the king. Then she turned and went to her own land with her
servants.

*Solomon's Wealth and Power*

13¶ Now the weight of gold which came to Solomon in one year
was 666 talents of gold,
14besides that which the traders and merchants brought; and all
the kings of Arabia and the governors of the country brought gold
and silver to Solomon.
15And King Solomon made 200 large shields of beaten gold,
using 600 *shekels of* beaten gold on each large shield.

## New International

appointed the divisions of the priests for their duties, and the
Levites to lead the praise and to assist the priests according to each
day's requirement. He also appointed the gatekeepers by divisions
for the various gates, because this was what David the man of God
had ordered. 15They did not deviate from the king's commands to
the priests or to the Levites in any matter, including that of the
treasuries.
16All Solomon's work was carried out, from the day the foundation of the temple of the LORD was laid until its completion. So the
temple of the LORD was finished.
17Then Solomon went to Ezion Geber and Elath on the coast of
Edom. 18And Hiram sent him ships commanded by his own officers, men who knew the sea. These, with Solomon's men, sailed
to Ophir and brought back four hundred and fifty talents[a] of gold,
which they delivered to King Solomon.

*The Queen of Sheba Visits Solomon*

9 WHEN THE queen of Sheba heard of Solomon's fame, she
came to Jerusalem to test him with hard questions. Arriving
with a very great caravan—with camels carrying spices, large
quantities of gold, and precious stones—she came to Solomon and
talked with him about all she had on her mind. 2Solomon answered all her questions; nothing was too hard for him to explain
to her. 3When the queen of Sheba saw the wisdom of Solomon,
as well as the palace he had built, 4the food on his table, the seating
of his officials, the attending servants in their robes, the cupbearers
in their robes and the burnt offerings he made at[b] the temple of
the LORD, she was overwhelmed.
5She said to the king, "The report I heard in my own country
about your achievements and your wisdom is true. 6But I did not
believe what they said until I came and saw with my own eyes.
Indeed, not even half the greatness of your wisdom was told me;
you have far exceeded the report I heard. 7How happy your men
must be! How happy your officials, who continually stand before
you and hear your wisdom! 8Praise be to the LORD your God, who
has delighted in you and placed you on his throne as king to rule
for the LORD your God. Because of the love of your God for Israel
and his desire to uphold them forever, he has made you king over
them, to maintain justice and righteousness."
9Then she gave the king 120 talents[c] of gold, large quantities
of spices, and precious stones. There had never been such spices
as those the queen of Sheba gave to King Solomon.
10(The men of Hiram and the men of Solomon brought gold
from Ophir; they also brought algumwood[d] and precious stones.
11The king used the algumwood to make steps for the temple of
the LORD and for the royal palace, and to make harps and lyres for
the musicians. Nothing like them had ever been seen in Judah.)
12King Solomon gave the queen of Sheba all she desired and
asked for; he gave her more than she had brought to him. Then
she left and returned with her retinue to her own country.

*Solomon's Splendor*

13The weight of the gold that Solomon received yearly was 666
talents,[e] 14not including the revenues brought in by merchants
and traders. Also all the kings of Arabia and the governors of the
land brought gold and silver to Solomon.
15King Solomon made two hundred large shields of hammered
gold; six hundred bekas[f] of hammered gold went into each shield.

**NIV** [a] *18* That is, about 17 tons (about 16 metric tons) [b] *4* Or *the ascent by which he went up to* [c] *9* That is, about 4 1/2 tons (about 4 metric tons) [d] *10* Probably a variant of *almugwood* [e] *13* That is, about 25 tons (about 23 metric tons) [f] *15* That is, about 7 1/2 pounds (about 3.5 kilograms)

## King James

16 And three hundred shields *made he of* beaten gold: three hundred *shekels* of gold went to one shield. And the king put them in the house of the forest of Lebanon.

17 Moreover the king made a great throne of ivory, and overlaid it with pure gold.

18 And *there were* six steps to the throne, with a footstool of gold, *which were* fastened to the throne, and stays on each side of the sitting place, and two lions standing by the stays:

19 And twelve lions stood there on the one side and on the other upon the six steps. There was not the like made in any kingdom.

20 ¶ And all the drinking vessels of king Solomon *were of* gold, and all the vessels of the house of the forest of Lebanon *were of* pure gold: none *were of* silver; it was *not* any thing accounted of in the days of Solomon.

21 For the king's ships went to Tarshish with the servants of Huram: every three years once came the ships of Tarshish bringing gold, and silver, ivory, and apes, and peacocks.

22 And king Solomon passed all the kings of the earth in riches and wisdom.

23 ¶ And all the kings of the earth sought the presence of Solomon, to hear his wisdom, that God had put in his heart.

24 And they brought every man his present, vessels of silver, and vessels of gold, and raiment, harness, and spices, horses, and mules, a rate year by year.

25 ¶ And Solomon had four thousand stalls for horses and chariots, and twelve thousand horsemen; whom he bestowed in the chariot cities, and with the king at Jerusalem.

26 ¶ And he reigned over all the kings from the river even unto the land of the Philistines, and to the border of Egypt.

27 And the king made silver in Jerusalem as stones, and cedar trees made he as the sycamore trees that *are* in the low plains in abundance.

28 And they brought unto Solomon horses out of Egypt, and out of all lands.

29 ¶ Now the rest of the acts of Solomon, first and last, *are* they not written in the book of Nathan the prophet, and in the prophecy of Ahijah the Shilonite, and in the visions of Iddo the seer against Jeroboam the son of Nebat?

30 And Solomon reigned in Jerusalem over all Israel forty years.

31 And Solomon slept with his fathers, and he was buried in the city of David his father: and Rehoboam his son reigned in his stead.

**10** AND REHOBOAM went to Shechem: for to Shechem were all Israel come to make him king.

2 And it came to pass, when Jeroboam the son of Nebat, who *was* in Egypt, whither he had fled from the presence of Solomon the king, heard *it*, that Jeroboam returned out of Egypt.

3 And they sent and called him. So Jeroboam and all Israel came and spake to Rehoboam, saying,

4 Thy father made our yoke grievous: now therefore ease thou somewhat the grievous servitude of thy father, and his heavy yoke that he put upon us, and we will serve thee.

5 And he said unto them, Come again unto me after three days. And the people departed.

6 ¶ And king Rehoboam took counsel with the old men that had stood before Solomon his father while he yet lived, saying, What counsel give ye *me* to return answer to this people?

7 And they spake unto him, saying, If thou be kind to this people, and please them, and speak good words to them, they will be thy servants for ever.

## Amplified

16 And he made 300 shields of beaten gold, 300 shekels of gold spread on each shield. And the king put them in the House of the Forest of Lebanon.

17 Moreover [he] made a great throne of ivory, and overlaid it with pure gold.

18 There were six steps to the throne and a gold footstool attached to the throne, and arms on each side of the seat, and two lions standing beside the arms.

19 And twelve lions stood there one on either end of each of the six steps. The like of it was never made in any kingdom before.

20 King Solomon's drinking vessels were all of gold, and all the vessels of the House of the Forest of Lebanon were of pure gold; silver was not counted as anything in the days of Solomon.

21 For the king's ships went to Tarshish with Huram's servants; once every three years the ships of Tarshish came bringing gold, silver, ivory, apes, and peacocks.

22 King Solomon surpassed all the kings of the earth in riches and wisdom.

23 And all the kings of the earth sought the presence of Solomon to hear his wisdom, which God had put into his mind.

24 And every man brought his tribute: silver and gold articles, robes, armor, spices, horses, and mules, so much year by year.

25 Solomon had 4,000 stalls for horses and chariots, and 12,000 horsemen, stationed in chariot cities or at Jerusalem with the king. [Deut. 17:16, 17.]

26 And he ruled over [a]all the kings from the [Euphrates] River to the land of Philistia and to the frontier of Egypt.

27 The king made silver in Jerusalem as common as stones, and cedar wood as plentiful as sycamore trees in the lowlands.

28 And they imported horses for Solomon from Egypt and from all lands.

29 Now the rest of the acts of Solomon, from first to last, are they not written in the history of Nathan the prophet, and in the prophecy of Ahijah, the Shilonite, and in the visions of Iddo the seer concerning Jeroboam the son of Nebat?

30 Solomon reigned in Jerusalem over all Israel forty years.

31 Then Solomon slept with his fathers; he was buried in the city of David his father. Rehoboam his son reigned in his stead.

**10** REHOBOAM WENT to Shechem, for all Israel had gone to Shechem to make him king.

2 Jeroboam the son of Nebat was in Egypt, where he had fled from the presence of King Solomon, when he heard about the new king; so Jeroboam returned from Egypt.

3 And the people sent for him. So Jeroboam and all Israel came to Rehoboam, saying,

4 [King Solomon] made our yoke grievous. So now make lighter the grievous service of your father and his heavy yoke that he put upon us, and we will serve you.

5 Rehoboam replied, Come again to me after three days. And the people departed.

6 King Rehoboam took counsel with the old men who stood before Solomon his father while he was alive, saying, What counsel do you give me in reply to the people?

7 And they answered him, If you are kind to [these] people, and please them, and speak good words to them, they will be your servants for ever.

**AMP** [a] See footnote on I Kings 4:21 for proof of this statement.

## New American Standard

16And *he made* 300 shields of beaten gold, using three hundred shekels of gold on each shield, and the king put them in the house of the forest of Lebanon.

17¶ Moreover, the king made a great throne of ivory and overlaid it with pure gold.

18And *there were* six steps to the throne and a footstool in gold attached to the throne, and arms on each side of the seat, and two lions standing beside the arms.

19And twelve lions were standing there on the six steps on the one side and on the other; nothing like *it* was made for any *other* kingdom.

20And all King Solomon's drinking vessels *were* of gold, and all the vessels of the house of the forest of Lebanon *were* of pure gold; silver was not considered valuable in the days of Solomon.

21For the king had ships which went to Tarshish with the servants of Huram; once every three years the ships of Tarshish came bringing gold and silver, ivory and apes and peacocks.

22¶ So King Solomon became greater than all the kings of the earth in riches and wisdom.

23And all the kings of the earth were seeking the presence of Solomon, to hear his wisdom which God had put in his heart.

24And they brought every man his gift, articles of silver and gold, garments, weapons, spices, horses, and mules, so much year by year.

25¶ Now Solomon had 4,000 stalls for horses and chariots and 12,000 horsemen, and he stationed them in the chariot cities and with the king in Jerusalem.

26And he was the ruler over all the kings from the Euphrates River even to the land of the Philistines, and as far as the border of Egypt.

27And the king made silver *as common* as stones in Jerusalem, and he made cedars as plentiful as sycamore trees that are in the lowland.

28And they were bringing horses for Solomon from Egypt and from all countries.

29¶ Now the rest of the acts of Solomon, from first to last, are they not written in the records of Nathan the prophet, and in the prophecy of Ahijah the Shilonite, and in the visions of Iddo the seer concerning Jeroboam the son of Nebat?

30And Solomon reigned forty years in Jerusalem over all Israel.

*Death of Solomon*

31And Solomon slept with his fathers and was buried in the city of his father David; and his son Rehoboam reigned in his place.

*Rehoboam's Reign of Folly*

**10** THEN REHOBOAM went to Shechem, for all Israel had come to Shechem to make him king.

2And it came about when Jeroboam the son of Nebat heard *of it* (for he was in Egypt where he had fled from the presence of King Solomon), that Jeroboam returned from Egypt.

3So they sent and summoned him. When Jeroboam and all Israel came, they spoke to Rehoboam, saying,

4"Your father made our yoke hard; now therefore lighten the hard service of your father and his heavy yoke which he put on us, and we will serve you."

5And he said to them, "Return to me again in three days." So the people departed.

6¶ Then King Rehoboam consulted with the elders who had served his father Solomon while he was still alive, saying, "How do you counsel *me* to answer this people?"

7And they spoke to him, saying, "If you will be kind to this people and please them and speak good words to them, then they will be your servants forever."

## New International

16He also made three hundred small shields of hammered gold,
with three hundred bekas[b] of gold in each shield. The king put
them in the Palace of the Forest of Lebanon.
17Then the king made a great throne inlaid with ivory and
overlaid with pure gold. 18The throne had six steps, and a footstool
of gold was attached to it. On both sides of the seat were armrests,
with a lion standing beside each of them. 19Twelve lions stood on
the six steps, one at either end of each step. Nothing like it had
ever been made for any other kingdom. 20All King Solomon's
goblets were gold, and all the household articles in the Palace of
the Forest of Lebanon were pure gold. Nothing was made of silver,
because silver was considered of little value in Solomon's day.
21The king had a fleet of trading ships[c] manned by Hiram's[d] men.
Once every three years it returned, carrying gold, silver and ivory,
and apes and baboons.
22King Solomon was greater in riches and wisdom than all the
other kings of the earth. 23All the kings of the earth sought audience with Solomon to hear the wisdom God had put in his heart.
24Year after year, everyone who came brought a gift—articles of
silver and gold, and robes, weapons and spices, and horses and
mules.
25Solomon had four thousand stalls for horses and chariots, and
twelve thousand horses,[e] which he kept in the chariot cities and
also with him in Jerusalem. 26He ruled over all the kings from the
River[f] to the land of the Philistines, as far as the border of Egypt.
27The king made silver as common in Jerusalem as stones, and
cedar as plentiful as sycamore-fig trees in the foothills. 28Solo-
mon's horses were imported from Egypt[g] and from all other countries.

*Solomon's Death*

29As for the other events of Solomon's reign, from beginning to
end, are they not written in the records of Nathan the prophet, in
the prophecy of Ahijah the Shilonite and in the visions of Iddo the
seer concerning Jeroboam son of Nebat? 30Solomon reigned in
Jerusalem over all Israel forty years. 31Then he rested with his
fathers and was buried in the city of David his father. And Rehoboam his son succeeded him as king.

*Israel Rebels Against Rehoboam*

**10** REHOBOAM WENT to Shechem, for all the Israelites had
gone there to make him king. 2When Jeroboam son of
Nebat heard this (he was in Egypt, where he had fled from King
Solomon), he returned from Egypt. 3So they sent for Jeroboam,
and he and all Israel went to Rehoboam and said to him: 4"Your
father put a heavy yoke on us, but now lighten the harsh labor and
the heavy yoke he put on us, and we will serve you."
5Rehoboam answered, "Come back to me in three days." So the
people went away.
6Then King Rehoboam consulted the elders who had served his
father Solomon during his lifetime. "How would you advise me
to answer these people?" he asked.
7They replied, "If you will be kind to these people and please
them and give them a favorable answer, they will always be your
servants."

**NIV** [b] *16* That is, about 3 3/4 pounds (about 1.7 kilograms) [c] *21* Hebrew *of ships that could go to Tarshish* [d] *21* Hebrew *Huram,* a variant of *Hiram* [e] *25* Or *charioteers* [f] *26* That is, the Euphrates [g] *28* Or possibly *Muzur,* a region in Cilicia

## King James

8But he forsook the counsel which the old men gave him, and took counsel with the young men that were brought up with him, that stood before him.
9And he said unto them, What advice give ye that we may return answer to this people, which have spoken to me, saying, Ease somewhat the yoke that thy father did put upon us?
10And the young men that were brought up with him spake unto him, saying, Thus shalt thou answer the people that spake unto thee, saying, Thy father made our yoke heavy, but make thou *it* somewhat lighter for us; thus shalt thou say unto them, My little *finger* shall be thicker than my father's loins.
11For whereas my father put a heavy yoke upon you, I will put more to your yoke: my father chastised you with whips, but I *will chastise you* with scorpions.
12So Jeroboam and all the people came to Rehoboam on the third day, as the king bade, saying, Come again to me on the third day.
13And the king answered them roughly; and king Rehoboam forsook the counsel of the old men,
14And answered them after the advice of the young men, saying, My father made your yoke heavy, but I will add thereto: my father chastised you with whips, but I *will chastise you* with scorpions.
15So the king hearkened not unto the people: for the cause was of God, that the LORD might perform his word, which he spake by the hand of Ahijah the Shilonite to Jeroboam the son of Nebat.
16¶ And when all Israel *saw* that the king would not hearken unto them, the people answered the king, saying, What portion have we in David? and *we have* none inheritance in the son of Jesse: every man to your tents, O Israel: *and* now, David, see to thine own house. So all Israel went to their tents.
17But *as for* the children of Israel that dwelt in the cities of Judah, Rehoboam reigned over them.
18Then king Rehoboam sent Hadoram that *was* over the tribute; and the children of Israel stoned him with stones, that he died. But king Rehoboam made speed to get him up to *his* chariot, to flee to Jerusalem.
19And Israel rebelled against the house of David unto this day.

11 AND WHEN Rehoboam was come to Jerusalem, he gathered of the house of Judah and Benjamin an hundred and fourscore thousand chosen *men,* which were warriors, to fight against Israel, that he might bring the kingdom again to Rehoboam.
2But the word of the LORD came to Shemaiah the man of God, saying,
3Speak unto Rehoboam the son of Solomon, king of Judah, and to all Israel in Judah and Benjamin, saying,
4Thus saith the LORD, Ye shall not go up, nor fight against your brethren: return every man to his house: for this thing is done of me. And they obeyed the words of the LORD, and returned from going against Jeroboam.
5¶ And Rehoboam dwelt in Jerusalem, and built cities for defence in Judah.
6He built even Bethlehem, and Etam, and Tekoa,
7And Beth-zur, and Shoco, and Adullam,
8And Gath, and Mareshah, and Ziph,
9And Adoraim, and Lachish, and Azekah,
10And Zorah, and Aijalon, and Hebron, which *are* in Judah and in Benjamin fenced cities.

## Amplified

8But the king forsook the counsel which the old men gave him, and took counsel with the young men who were brought up with him and stood before him.
9And he said to them, What answer do you advise that we give to the demand of [these] people, Make the yoke your father put upon us lighter?
10The young men who were brought up with him said to him, Tell the people who said to you, Your father made our yoke heavy, but you make it lighter: My little finger is thicker than my father's loins.
11For whereas my father put a heavy yoke upon you, I will add to your yoke. My father chastised you with whips, but I will chastise you with scorpions.
12The third day Jeroboam and all the people returned to Rehoboam as he had said.
13And the king answered them harshly, forsaking the counsel of the old men,
14And answered them after the advice of the young men, saying, My father made your yoke heavy, but I will add to it; my father chastised you with whips, but I will chastise you with scorpions.
15So the king did not heed the people; for it was [a]brought about of God, that the Lord might perform His word which He spoke by Ahijah the Shilonite to Jeroboam the son of Nebat. [I Kings 11:29-39.]
16And when all Israel saw that the king would not listen *and* heed them, they answered [him], What portion have we in David? We have no inheritance in the son of Jesse. Every man to your tents, O Israel! Now, David [tribe of Judah], see to your own house [under your tyrant King Rehoboam]! So all Israel went to their homes.
17But as to the Israelites who dwelt in Judah's cities, Rehoboam ruled over them.
18Then King Rehoboam sent Hadoram who was over the forced labor, and the Israelites stoned him, and he died. But King Rehoboam hastened to get up to his royal chariot to flee to Jerusalem.
19And Israel rebelled against the house of David to this day.

11 AND WHEN Rehoboam came to Jerusalem, he assembled of the house of Judah and Benjamin 180,000 chosen warriors to fight against [the ten rebellious tribes of] Israel, to bring the kingdom again to Rehoboam.
2But the word of the Lord came to Shemaiah the man of God, saying,
3Say to Rehoboam son of Solomon, king of Judah, and to all Israel in Judah and Benjamin,
4Thus says the Lord, You shall not go up or fight against your brethren. Return every man to his house, for this thing is from Me. And they obeyed the Lord, and returned from going against Jeroboam.
5Rehoboam dwelt in Jerusalem, and built cities for defense in Judah.
6He built Bethlehem, Etam, Tekoa,
7Beth-zur, Soco, Adullam,
8Gath, Mareshah, Ziph,
9Adoraim, Lachish, Azekah,
10Zorah, Aijalon, and Hebron, which are fortified cities in Judah and Benjamin.

**AMP** [a] God permitted the revolt of the northern tribes, intending it as a punishment of the house of David for Solomon's apostasy *(Jamieson, Fausset and Brown Bible Commentary).*

## New American Standard

8But he forsook the counsel of the elders which they had given
him, and consulted with the young men who grew up with him
and served him.
9So he said to them, "What counsel do you give that we may
answer this people, who have spoken to me, saying, 'Lighten the
yoke which your father put on us'?"
10And the young men who grew up with him spoke to him,
saying, "Thus you shall say to the people who spoke to you,
saying, 'Your father made our yoke heavy, but you make it lighter
for us.' Thus you shall say to them, 'My little finger is thicker than
my father's loins!
11'Whereas my father loaded you with a heavy yoke, I will add
to your yoke; my father disciplined you with whips, but I *will
discipline you* with scorpions.' "
12¶ So Jeroboam and all the people came to Rehoboam on the
third day as the king had directed, saying, "Return to me on the
third day."
13And the king answered them harshly, and King Rehoboam
forsook the counsel of the elders.
14And he spoke to them according to the advice of the young
men, saying, "My father made your yoke heavy, but I will add to
it; my father disciplined you with whips, but I *will discipline you*
with scorpions."
15So the king did not listen to the people, for it was a turn *of
events* from God that the LORD might establish His word, which He
spoke through Ahijah the Shilonite to Jeroboam the son of Nebat.
16¶ And when all Israel *saw* that the king did not listen to them
the people answered the king, saying,

"What portion do we have in David?
*We have* no inheritance in the son of Jesse.
Every man to your tents, O Israel;
Now look after your own house, David."

So all Israel departed to their tents.
17But as for the sons of Israel who lived in the cities of Judah,
Rehoboam reigned over them.
18Then King Rehoboam sent Hadoram, who was over the
forced labor, and the sons of Israel stoned him to death. And King
Rehoboam made haste to mount his chariot to flee to Jerusalem.
19So Israel has been in rebellion against the house of David to
this day.

*Rehoboam Reigns over Judah and Builds Cities*

11 NOW WHEN Rehoboam had come to Jerusalem, he assembled the house of Judah and Benjamin, 180,000 chosen
men who were warriors, to fight against Israel to restore the kingdom to Rehoboam.
2But the word of the LORD came to Shemaiah the man of God,
saying,
3"Speak to Rehoboam the son of Solomon, king of Judah, and
to all Israel in Judah and Benjamin, saying,
4'Thus says the LORD, "You shall not go up or fight against
your relatives; return every man to his house, for this thing is from
Me." ' " So they listened to the words of the LORD and returned
from going against Jeroboam.
5¶ Rehoboam lived in Jerusalem and built cities for defense in
Judah.
6Thus he built Bethlehem, Etam, Tekoa,
7Beth-zur, Soco, Adullam,
8Gath, Mareshah, Ziph,
9Adoraim, Lachish, Azekah,
10Zorah, Aijalon, and Hebron, which are fortified cities in Judah
and in Benjamin.

## New International

8But Rehoboam rejected the advice the elders gave him and
consulted the young men who had grown up with him and were
serving him. 9He asked them, "What is your advice? How should
we answer these people who say to me, 'Lighten the yoke your
father put on us'?"
10The young men who had grown up with him replied, "Tell
the people who have said to you, 'Your father put a heavy yoke
on us, but make our yoke lighter'—tell them, 'My little finger is
thicker than my father's waist. 11My father laid on you a heavy
yoke; I will make it even heavier. My father scourged you with
whips; I will scourge you with scorpions.' "
12Three days later Jeroboam and all the people returned to
Rehoboam, as the king had said, "Come back to me in three days."
13The king answered them harshly. Rejecting the advice of the
elders, 14he followed the advice of the young men and said, "My
father made your yoke heavy; I will make it even heavier. My
father scourged you with whips; I will scourge you with scorpions." 15So the king did not listen to the people, for this turn of
events was from God, to fulfill the word the LORD had spoken to
Jeroboam son of Nebat through Ahijah the Shilonite.
16When all Israel saw that the king refused to listen to them,
they answered the king:

"What share do we have in David,
what part in Jesse's son?
To your tents, O Israel!
Look after your own house, O David!"

So all the Israelites went home. 17But as for the Israelites who were
living in the towns of Judah, Rehoboam still ruled over them.
18King Rehoboam sent out Adoniram,[b] who was in charge of
forced labor, but the Israelites stoned him to death. King Rehoboam, however, managed to get into his chariot and escape to
Jerusalem. 19So Israel has been in rebellion against the house of
David to this day.

11 WHEN REHOBOAM arrived in Jerusalem, he mustered
the house of Judah and Benjamin—a hundred and eighty
thousand fighting men—to make war against Israel and to regain
the kingdom for Rehoboam.
2But this word of the LORD came to Shemaiah the man of God:
3"Say to Rehoboam son of Solomon king of Judah and to all the
Israelites in Judah and Benjamin, 4'This is what the LORD says: Do
not go up to fight against your brothers. Go home, every one of
you, for this is my doing.' " So they obeyed the words of the LORD
and turned back from marching against Jeroboam.

*Rehoboam Fortifies Judah*

5Rehoboam lived in Jerusalem and built up towns for defense
in Judah: 6Bethlehem, Etam, Tekoa, 7Beth Zur, Soco, Adullam,
8Gath, Mareshah, Ziph, 9Adoraim, Lachish, Azekah, 10Zorah,
Aijalon and Hebron. These were fortified cities in Judah and Benjamin. 11He strengthened their defenses and put commanders in

NIV [b] 18 Hebrew *Hadoram,* a variant of *Adoniram*

## King James

11And he fortified the strong holds, and put captains in them,
and store of victual, and of oil and wine.
12And in every several city *he put* shields and spears, and made
them exceeding strong, having Judah and Benjamin on his side.
13¶ And the priests and the Levites that *were* in all Israel resorted
to him out of all their coasts.
14For the Levites left their suburbs and their possession, and
came to Judah and Jerusalem: for Jeroboam and his sons had cast
them off from executing the priest's office unto the LORD:
15And he ordained him priests for the high places, and for the
devils, and for the calves which he had made.
16And after them out of all the tribes of Israel such as set their
hearts to seek the LORD God of Israel came to Jerusalem, to sacrifice
unto the LORD God of their fathers.
17So they strengthened the kingdom of Judah, and made Rehoboam the son of Solomon strong, three years: for three years they
walked in the way of David and Solomon.
18¶ And Rehoboam took him Mahalath the daughter of Jerimoth
the son of David to wife, *and* Abihail the daughter of Eliab the son
of Jesse;
19Which bare him children; Jeush, and Shamariah, and Zaham.
20And after her he took Maachah the daughter of Absalom;
which bare him Abijah, and Attai, and Ziza, and Shelomith.
21And Rehoboam loved Maachah the daughter of Absalom
above all his wives and his concubines: (for he took eighteen
wives, and threescore concubines; and begat twenty and eight
sons, and threescore daughters.)
22And Rehoboam made Abijah the son of Maachah the chief,
*to be* ruler among his brethren: for *he thought* to make him king.
23And he dealt wisely, and dispersed of all his children
throughout all the countries of Judah and Benjamin, unto every
fenced city: and he gave them victual in abundance. And he desired many wives.

## Amplified

11He fortified the strongholds, put captains in them, and stores
of food, oil, and vintage fruits.
12And in each city he put shields and spears, and made them
very strong. So he held Judah and Benjamin.
13And the priests and the Levites who were in all Israel came
over to Rehoboam from wherever they lived.
14For the Levites left their suburbs and their possessions and
came to Judah and Jerusalem, for Jeroboam and his sons had cast
them out from executing the priest's office to the Lord,
15And he appointed his own priests for the high places and the
[idols of demon] he-goats, and calves he had made. [I Kings 12:28.]
16And after them out of all the tribes of Israel there came to
Jerusalem those who set their hearts to seek, *and* inquire of the
Lord God of Israel, to sacrifice to the Lord, the God of their fathers.
17So they strengthened the kingdom of Judah, and upheld
Rehoboam son of Solomon for three years; for they walked in the
way of David and Solomon three years.
18Rehoboam took as wife Mahalath, whose father was Jerimoth
son of David; her mother was Abihail daughter of Eliab son of
Jesse.
19She bore him sons, Jeush, Shamariah, and Zaham.
20And after her he took Maacah daughter [granddaughter] of
Absalom, who bore him Abijah, Attai, Ziza, and Shelomith.
21And Rehoboam loved Maacah the daughter [granddaughter]
of Absalom more than all his wives and concubines (for he took
eighteen wives, and sixty concubines, and he had twenty-eight
sons and sixty daughters).
22And Rehoboam made Abijah son of Maacah the chief prince
among his brethren, for he intended to make him king.
23And he dealt understandingly and dispersed his children
throughout all Judah and Benjamin to every fortified city. He gave
them abundant supplies, and he sought many wives for them.

## King James

**12** AND IT came to pass, when Rehoboam had established
the kingdom, and had strengthened himself, he forsook
the law of the LORD, and all Israel with him.
2And it came to pass, *that* in the fifth year of king Rehoboam
Shishak king of Egypt came up against Jerusalem, because they
had transgressed against the LORD,
3With twelve hundred chariots, and threescore thousand horsemen: and the people *were* without number that came with him out
of Egypt; the Lubims, the Sukkiims, and the Ethiopians.
4And he took the fenced cities which *pertained* to Judah, and
came to Jerusalem.
5¶ Then came Shemaiah the prophet to Rehoboam, and *to* the
princes of Judah, that were gathered together to Jerusalem because
of Shishak, and said unto them, Thus saith the LORD, Ye have
forsaken me, and therefore have I also left you in the hand of
Shishak.
6Whereupon the princes of Israel and the king humbled themselves; and they said, The LORD *is* righteous.
7And when the LORD saw that they humbled themselves, the
word of the LORD came to Shemaiah, saying, They have humbled
themselves; *therefore* I will not destroy them, but I will grant them
some deliverance; and my wrath shall not be poured out upon
Jerusalem by the hand of Shishak.
8Nevertheless they shall be his servants; that they may know
my service, and the service of the kingdoms of the countries.

## Amplified

**12** WHEN REHOBOAM had established the kingdom and
had strengthened himself, he forsook the law of the Lord,
and all Israel with him.
2And in the fifth year of King Rehoboam, because they had
transgressed *and* been unfaithful to the Lord, Shishak king of
Egypt came up against Jerusalem.
3With 1,200 chariots and 60,000 horsemen, and the people were
without number who came with him from Egypt—Libyans, Sukkiim, and Ethiopians.
4And he took the fortified cities of Judah and came on to Jerusalem.
5Then Shemaiah the prophet came to Rehoboam and the
princes of Judah who had gathered at Jerusalem because of Shishak, and said to them, Thus says the Lord, You have forsaken
Me, so I have abandoned you to the hand of Shishak.
6Then the princes of Israel and the king humbled themselves,
and said, The Lord is righteous.
7And when the Lord saw that they humbled themselves, the
word of the Lord came to Shemaiah, saying, They have humbled
themselves, so I will not destroy them, but I will grant them some
deliverance, and My wrath shall not be poured out upon Jerusalem
by the hand of Shishak.
8Nevertheless they shall be his servants, that they may know
[the difference between] My service and the service of the kingdoms of the countries.

## New American Standard

11He also strengthened the fortresses and put officers in them
and stores of food, oil and wine.
12And *he put* shields and spears in every city and strengthened
them greatly. So he held Judah and Benjamin.
13¶ Moreover, the priests and the Levites who were in all Israel
stood with him from all their districts.

*Jeroboam Appoints False Priests*

14For the Levites left their pasture lands and their property and
came to Judah and Jerusalem, for Jeroboam and his sons had
excluded them from serving as priests to the LORD.
15And he set up priests of his own for the high places, for the
satyrs, and for the calves which he had made.
16And those from all the tribes of Israel who set their hearts on
seeking the LORD God of Israel, followed them to Jerusalem to
sacrifice to the LORD God of their fathers.
17And they strengthened the kingdom of Judah and supported
Rehoboam the son of Solomon for three years, for they walked in
the way of David and Solomon for three years.

*Rehoboam's Family*

18¶ Then Rehoboam took as a wife Mahalath the daughter of
Jerimoth the son of David *and of* Abihail the daughter of Eliab the
son of Jesse,
19and she bore him sons: Jeush, Shemariah, and Zaham.
20And after her he took Maacah the daughter of Absalom, and
she bore him Abijah, Attai, Ziza, and Shelomith.
21And Rehoboam loved Maacah the daughter of Absalom more
than all his *other* wives and concubines. For he had taken eighteen
wives and sixty concubines and fathered twenty-eight sons and
sixty daughters.
22And Rehoboam appointed Abijah the son of Maacah as head
and leader among his brothers, for he *intended* to make him king.
23And he acted wisely and distributed some of his sons through
all the territories of Judah and Benjamin to all the fortified cities,
and he gave them food in abundance. And he sought many wives
*for them.*

*Shishak of Egypt Invades Judah*

**12** IT TOOK place when the kingdom of Rehoboam was
established and strong that he and all Israel with him
forsook the law of the LORD.
2And it came about in King Rehoboam's fifth year, because
they had been unfaithful to the LORD, that Shishak king of Egypt
came up against Jerusalem
3with 1,200 chariots and 60,000 horsemen. And the people
who came with him from Egypt were without number: the Lubim,
the Sukkiim, and the Ethiopians.
4And he captured the fortified cities of Judah and came as far
as Jerusalem.
5Then Shemaiah the prophet came to Rehoboam and the
princes of Judah who had gathered at Jerusalem because of Shishak, and he said to them, "Thus says the LORD, 'You have forsak-
en Me, so I also have forsaken you to Shishak.' "
6So the princes of Israel and the king humbled themselves and
said, "The LORD is righteous."
7¶ And when the LORD saw that they humbled themselves, the
word of the LORD came to Shemaiah, saying, "They have humbled
themselves so I will not destroy them, but I will grant them some
*measure* of deliverance, and My wrath shall not be poured out on
Jerusalem by means of Shishak.
8"But they will become his slaves so that they may learn *the
difference between* My service and the service of the kingdoms of the
countries."

## New International

them, with supplies of food, olive oil and wine. 12He put shields
and spears in all the cities, and made them very strong. So Judah
and Benjamin were his.
13The priests and Levites from all their districts throughout
Israel sided with him. 14The Levites even abandoned their pasturelands and property, and came to Judah and Jerusalem because
Jeroboam and his sons had rejected them as priests of the LORD.
15And he appointed his own priests for the high places and for the
goat and calf idols he had made. 16Those from every tribe of Israel
who set their hearts on seeking the LORD, the God of Israel, followed the Levites to Jerusalem to offer sacrifices to the LORD, the
God of their fathers. 17They strengthened the kingdom of Judah
and supported Rehoboam son of Solomon three years, walking in
the ways of David and Solomon during this time.

*Rehoboam's Family*

18Rehoboam married Mahalath, who was the daughter of David's son Jerimoth and of Abihail, the daughter of Jesse's son Eliab.
19She bore him sons: Jeush, Shemariah and Zaham. 20Then he
married Maacah daughter of Absalom, who bore him Abijah, Attai, Ziza and Shelomith. 21Rehoboam loved Maacah daughter of
Absalom more than any of his other wives and concubines. In all,
he had eighteen wives and sixty concubines, twenty-eight sons
and sixty daughters.
22Rehoboam appointed Abijah son of Maacah to be the chief
prince among his brothers, in order to make him king. 23He acted
wisely, dispersing some of his sons throughout the districts of
Judah and Benjamin, and to all the fortified cities. He gave them
abundant provisions and took many wives for them.

*Shishak Attacks Jerusalem*

**12** AFTER REHOBOAM'S position as king was established
and he had become strong, he and all Israel[a] with him
abandoned the law of the LORD. 2Because they had been unfaithful
to the LORD, Shishak king of Egypt attacked Jerusalem in the fifth
year of King Rehoboam. 3With twelve hundred chariots and sixty
thousand horsemen and the innumerable troops of Libyans, Suk-
kites and Cushites[b] that came with him from Egypt, 4he captured
the fortified cities of Judah and came as far as Jerusalem.
5Then the prophet Shemaiah came to Rehoboam and to the
leaders of Judah who had assembled in Jerusalem for fear of Shishak, and he said to them, "This is what the LORD says, 'You have
abandoned me; therefore, I now abandon you to Shishak.' "
6The leaders of Israel and the king humbled themselves and
said, "The LORD is just."
7When the LORD saw that they humbled themselves, this word
of the LORD came to Shemaiah: "Since they have humbled themselves, I will not destroy them but will soon give them deliverance.
My wrath will not be poured out on Jerusalem through Shishak.
8They will, however, become subject to him, so that they may
learn the difference between serving me and serving the kings of
other lands."

NIV [a] *1* That is, Judah, as frequently in 2 Chronicles [b] 3 That is, people from the upper Nile region

## King James

9 So Shishak king of Egypt came up against Jerusalem, and took away the treasures of the house of the LORD, and the treasures of the king's house; he took all: he carried away also the shields of gold which Solomon had made.

10 Instead of which king Rehoboam made shields of brass, and committed *them* to the hands of the chief of the guard, that kept the entrance of the king's house.

11 And when the king entered into the house of the LORD, the guard came and fetched them, and brought them again into the guard chamber.

12 And when he humbled himself, the wrath of the LORD turned from him, that he would not destroy *him* altogether: and also in Judah things went well.

13 ¶ So king Rehoboam strengthened himself in Jerusalem, and reigned: for Rehoboam *was* one and forty years old when he began to reign, and he reigned seventeen years in Jerusalem, the city which the LORD had chosen out of all the tribes of Israel, to put his name there. And his mother's name *was* Naamah an Ammonitess.

14 And he did evil, because he prepared not his heart to seek the LORD.

15 Now the acts of Rehoboam, first and last, *are* they not written in the book of Shemaiah the prophet, and of Iddo the seer concerning genealogies? And *there were* wars between Rehoboam and Jeroboam continually.

16 And Rehoboam slept with his fathers, and was buried in the city of David: and Abijah his son reigned in his stead.

**13** NOW IN the eighteenth year of king Jeroboam began Abijah to reign over Judah.

2 He reigned three years in Jerusalem. His mother's name also *was* Michaiah the daughter of Uriel of Gibeah. And there was war between Abijah and Jeroboam.

3 And Abijah set the battle in array with an army of valiant men of war, *even* four hundred thousand chosen men: Jeroboam also set the battle in array against him with eight hundred thousand chosen men, *being* mighty men of valour.

4 ¶ And Abijah stood up upon mount Zemaraim, which *is* in mount Ephraim, and said, Hear me, thou Jeroboam, and all Israel;

5 Ought ye not to know that the LORD God of Israel gave the kingdom over Israel to David for ever, *even* to him and to his sons by a covenant of salt?

6 Yet Jeroboam the son of Nebat, the servant of Solomon the son of David, is risen up, and hath rebelled against his lord.

7 And there are gathered unto him vain men, the children of Belial, and have strengthened themselves against Rehoboam the son of Solomon, when Rehoboam was young and tender-hearted, and could not withstand them.

8 And now ye think to withstand the kingdom of the LORD in the hand of the sons of David; and ye *be* a great multitude, and *there are* with you golden calves, which Jeroboam made you for gods.

9 Have ye not cast out the priests of the LORD, the sons of Aaron, and the Levites, and have made you priests after the manner of the nations of *other* lands? so that whosoever cometh to consecrate himself with a young bullock and seven rams, *the same* may be a priest of *them that are* no gods.

10 But as for us, the LORD *is* our God, and we have not forsaken him; and the priests, which minister unto the LORD, *are* the sons of Aaron, and the Levites *wait* upon *their* business:

11 And they burn unto the LORD every morning and every evening burnt sacrifices and sweet incense: the showbread also *set they in order* upon the pure table; and the candlestick of gold with the lamps thereof, to burn every evening: for we keep the charge of the LORD our God; but ye have forsaken him.

## Amplified

9 So Shishak king of Egypt came up against Jerusalem; he took away the treasures of the house of the Lord and of the king's house; he took everything. He took away also the shields of gold Solomon had made.

10 Instead of them King Rehoboam made shields of bronze and committed them to the hands of the officers of the guard, who kept the door of the king's house.

11 And whenever the king entered the Lord's house, the guard came and got the shields of bronze and brought them again into the guard chamber.

12 When Rehoboam humbled himself the wrath of the Lord turned from him, so as not to destroy him entirely; also in Judah conditions were good.

13 So King Rehoboam established *and* strengthened himself in Jerusalem, and reigned. Rehoboam was forty-one years old when he began to reign, and he reigned seventeen years in Jerusalem, the city which the Lord had chosen out of all the tribes of Israel to put His name [and the symbol of His presence] there. His mother was Naamah an Ammonitess.

14 And he did evil, for he did not set his heart to seek (inquire of, yearn for) the Lord with all his desire.

15 Now the acts of Rehoboam, from first to last, are they not written in the histories of Shemaiah the prophet and of Iddo the seer regarding genealogies? There were wars between Rehoboam of Judah and Jeroboam of Israel continually.

16 And Rehoboam slept with his fathers, and was buried in the city of David; and Abijah his son reigned in his stead.

**13** IN THE eighteenth year of King Jeroboam Abijah began to reign over Judah.

2 He reigned three years in Jerusalem. His mother was Micaiah the daughter of Uriel of Gibeah. And there was war between Abijah and Jeroboam of Israel.

3 And Abijah prepared for battle with an army of valiant men of war, 400,000 chosen men. Jeroboam set the battle in array against him with 800,000 chosen men, mighty men of valor.

4 And Abijah stood on Mount Zemaraim, in the hill country of Ephraim, and said, Hear me, O Jeroboam and all Israel!

5 Ought you not to know that the Lord, the God of Israel, gave the kingship over Israel to David for ever, even to him and to his sons by a covenant of salt?

6 Yet Jeroboam son of Nebat, servant of Solomon son of David, rose up and rebelled against his lord [the king].

7 And there gathered to him worthless men, base fellows, who strengthened themselves against Rehoboam son of Solomon, when Rehoboam was young [as king], irresolute *and* inexperienced and did not withstand them with firmness and strength.

8 And now you think to withstand the kingdom of the Lord in the hand of the sons of David, because you are a great multitude and you have with you golden calves which Jeroboam made you for gods.

9 Have you not driven out the priests of the Lord, the sons of Aaron, and the Levites, and made priests for yourselves like the peoples of other lands? So whoever comes to consecrate himself with a young bull and seven rams may be a priest of idols that are not gods.

10 But as for us, the Lord is our God, and we have not forsaken Him. We have priests ministering to the Lord who are sons of Aaron, and Levites for their service.

11 They offer to the Lord every morning and every evening burnt sacrifices and incense of sweet spices; they set in order the showbread on the table of pure gold, and attend to the golden lampstand that its lamps may be lighted every evening; for we keep the charge of the Lord our God, but you have forsaken Him.

## New American Standard

*Plunder Impoverishes Judah*

9¶ So Shishak king of Egypt came up against Jerusalem, and took the treasures of the house of the LORD and the treasures of the king's palace. He took everything; he even took the golden shields which Solomon had made.

10Then King Rehoboam made shields of bronze in their place, and committed them to the care of the commanders of the guard who guarded the door of the king's house.

11And it happened as often as the king entered the house of the LORD, the guards came and carried them and *then* brought them back into the guards' room.

12And when he humbled himself, the anger of the LORD turned away from him, so as not to destroy *him* completely; and also conditions were good in Judah.

13¶ So King Rehoboam strengthened himself in Jerusalem, and reigned. Now Rehoboam was forty-one years old when he began to reign, and he reigned seventeen years in Jerusalem, the city which the LORD had chosen from all the tribes of Israel, to put His name there. And his mother's name was Naamah the Ammonitess.

14And he did evil because he did not set his heart to seek the LORD.

15¶ Now the acts of Rehoboam, from first to last, are they not written in the records of Shemaiah the prophet and of Iddo the seer, according to genealogical enrollment? And *there were* wars between Rehoboam and Jeroboam continually.

16And Rehoboam slept with his fathers, and was buried in the city of David; and his son Abijah became king in his place.

*Abijah Succeeds Rehoboam*

**13** IN THE eighteenth year of King Jeroboam, Abijah became king over Judah.

2He reigned three years in Jerusalem; and his mother's name was Micaiah the daughter of Uriel of Gibeah. And there was war between Abijah and Jeroboam.

3And Abijah began the battle with an army of valiant warriors, 400,000 chosen men, while Jeroboam drew up in battle formation against him with 800,000 chosen men *who were* valiant warriors.

*Civil War*

4¶ Then Abijah stood on Mount Zemaraim, which is in the hill country of Ephraim, and said, "Listen to me, Jeroboam and all Israel:

5"Do you not know that the LORD God of Israel gave the rule over Israel forever to David and his sons by a covenant of salt?

6"Yet Jeroboam the son of Nebat, the servant of Solomon the son of David, rose up and rebelled against his master,

7and worthless men gathered about him, scoundrels, who proved too strong for Rehoboam, the son of Solomon, when he was young and timid and could not hold his own against them.

8"So now you intend to resist the kingdom of the LORD through the sons of David, being a great multitude and *having* with you the golden calves which Jeroboam made for gods for you.

9"Have you not driven out the priests of the LORD, the sons of Aaron and the Levites, and made for yourselves priests like the peoples of *other* lands? Whoever comes to consecrate himself with a young bull and seven rams, even he may become a priest of *what are* no gods.

10"But as for us, the LORD is our God, and we have not forsaken Him; and the sons of Aaron are ministering to the LORD as priests, and the Levites attend to their work.

11"And every morning and evening they burn to the LORD burnt offerings and fragrant incense, and the showbread is *set* on the clean table, and the golden lampstand with its lamps is *ready* to light every evening; for we keep the charge of the LORD our God, but you have forsaken Him.

## New International

9When Shishak king of Egypt attacked Jerusalem, he carried off
the treasures of the temple of the LORD and the treasures of the
royal palace. He took everything, including the gold shields Solomon had made. 10So King Rehoboam made bronze shields to
replace them and assigned these to the commanders of the guard
on duty at the entrance to the royal palace. 11Whenever the king
went to the LORD's temple, the guards went with him, bearing the
shields, and afterward they returned them to the guardroom.
12Because Rehoboam humbled himself, the LORD's anger
turned from him, and he was not totally destroyed. Indeed, there
was some good in Judah.
13King Rehoboam established himself firmly in Jerusalem and
continued as king. He was forty-one years old when he became
king, and he reigned seventeen years in Jerusalem, the city the
LORD had chosen out of all the tribes of Israel in which to put his
Name. His mother's name was Naamah; she was an Ammonite.
14He did evil because he had not set his heart on seeking the LORD.
15As for the events of Rehoboam's reign, from beginning to
end, are they not written in the records of Shemaiah the prophet
and of Iddo the seer that deal with genealogies? There was continual warfare between Rehoboam and Jeroboam. 16Rehoboam
rested with his fathers and was buried in the City of David. And
Abijah his son succeeded him as king.

*Abijah King of Judah*

**13** IN THE eighteenth year of the reign of Jeroboam, Abijah
became king of Judah, 2and he reigned in Jerusalem three
years. His mother's name was Maacah,[a] a daughter[b] of Uriel of
Gibeah.
There was war between Abijah and Jeroboam. 3Abijah went
into battle with a force of four hundred thousand able fighting
men, and Jeroboam drew up a battle line against him with eight
hundred thousand able troops.
4Abijah stood on Mount Zemaraim, in the hill country of
Ephraim, and said, "Jeroboam and all Israel, listen to me! 5Don't
you know that the LORD, the God of Israel, has given the kingship
of Israel to David and his descendants forever by a covenant of
salt? 6Yet Jeroboam son of Nebat, an official of Solomon son of
David, rebelled against his master. 7Some worthless scoundrels
gathered around him and opposed Rehoboam son of Solomon
when he was young and indecisive and not strong enough to resist
them.
8"And now you plan to resist the kingdom of the LORD, which
is in the hands of David's descendants. You are indeed a vast army
and have with you the golden calves that Jeroboam made to be
your gods. 9But didn't you drive out the priests of the LORD, the
sons of Aaron, and the Levites, and make priests of your own as
the peoples of other lands do? Whoever comes to consecrate himself with a young bull and seven rams may become a priest of what
are not gods.
10"As for us, the LORD is our God, and we have not forsaken
him. The priests who serve the LORD are sons of Aaron, and the
Levites assist them. 11Every morning and evening they present
burnt offerings and fragrant incense to the LORD. They set out the
bread on the ceremonially clean table and light the lamps on the
gold lampstand every evening. We are observing the requirements
of the LORD our God. But you have forsaken him. 12God is with

**NIV** [a] 2 Most Septuagint manuscripts and Syriac (see also 2 Chron. 11:20 and 1 Kings 15:2); Hebrew *Micaiah* [b] 2 Or *granddaughter*

## King James

12And, behold, God himself *is* with us for *our* captain, and his priests with sounding trumpets to cry alarm against you. O children of Israel, fight ye not against the LORD God of your fathers; for ye shall not prosper.

13¶ But Jeroboam caused an ambushment to come about behind them: so they were before Judah, and the ambushment *was* behind them.

14And when Judah looked back, behold, the battle *was* before and behind: and they cried unto the LORD, and the priests sounded with the trumpets.

15Then the men of Judah gave a shout: and as the men of Judah shouted, it came to pass, that God smote Jeroboam and all Israel before Abijah and Judah.

16And the children of Israel fled before Judah: and God delivered them into their hand.

17And Abijah and his people slew them with a great slaughter: so there fell down slain of Israel five hundred thousand chosen men.

18Thus the children of Israel were brought under at that time, and the children of Judah prevailed, because they relied upon the LORD God of their fathers.

19And Abijah pursued after Jeroboam, and took cities from him, Beth-el with the towns thereof, and Jeshanah with the towns thereof, and Ephrain with the towns thereof.

20Neither did Jeroboam recover strength again in the days of Abijah: and the LORD struck him, and he died.

21¶ But Abijah waxed mighty, and married fourteen wives, and begat twenty and two sons, and sixteen daughters.

22And the rest of the acts of Abijah, and his ways, and his sayings, *are* written in the story of the prophet Iddo.

**14** SO ABIJAH slept with his fathers, and they buried him in the city of David: and Asa his son reigned in his stead. In his days the land was quiet ten years.

2And Asa did *that which was* good and right in the eyes of the LORD his God:

3For he took away the altars of the strange *gods,* and the high places, and brake down the images, and cut down the groves:

4And commanded Judah to seek the LORD God of their fathers, and to do the law and the commandment.

5Also he took away out of all the cities of Judah the high places and the images: and the kingdom was quiet before him.

6¶ And he built fenced cities in Judah: for the land had rest, and he had no war in those years; because the LORD had given him rest.

7Therefore he said unto Judah, Let us build these cities, and make about *them* walls, and towers, gates, and bars, *while* the land *is* yet before us; because we have sought the LORD our God, we have sought *him,* and he hath given us rest on every side. So they built and prospered.

8And Asa had an army *of men* that bare targets and spears, out of Judah three hundred thousand; and out of Benjamin, that bare shields and drew bows, two hundred and fourscore thousand: all these *were* mighty men of valour.

9¶ And there came out against them Zerah the Ethiopian with an host of a thousand thousand, and three hundred chariots; and came unto Mareshah.

10Then Asa went out against him, and they set the battle in array in the valley of Zephathah at Mareshah.

## Amplified

12Behold, God Himself is with us at our head, and His priests with their battle trumpets to sound an alarm against you. O Israelites, fight not against the Lord, the God of your fathers, for you can not prosper.

13But Jeroboam caused an ambushment to come around them from behind, so his troops were before Judah, and the ambush behind.

14When Judah looked, lo, the battle was before and behind; and they cried to the Lord, and the priests blew the trumpets.

15Then the men of Judah gave a shout; and as they shouted, God smote Jeroboam and all Israel before Abijah and Judah.

16And the Israelites fled before Judah, and God delivered them into their hand.

17And Abijah and his people slew them with a great slaughter, so there fell of Israel 500,000 chosen men.

18Thus the Israelites were brought low at that time, and the people of Judah prevailed, because they relied upon the Lord, the God of their fathers.

19And Abijah pursued Jeroboam, and took some cities from him, Bethel, Jeshanah, and Ephraim (Ephron) with their towns.

20Jeroboam did not recover strength again in the days of Abijah; and the Lord smote him, and he died.

21But Abijah became mighty. He married fourteen wives, and had twenty-two sons and sixteen daughters.

22And the rest of the acts of Abijah, his ways and his sayings, are written in the story of the prophet Iddo.

**14** SO ABIJAH slept with his fathers, and they buried him in the city of David; and Asa his son reigned in his stead. In his days the land was at rest for ten years.

2And Asa did what was good and right in the eyes of the Lord his God.

3He took away the foreign altars and high places, and broke down the idol pillars *or* obelisks, and cut down the Asherim,

4And commanded Judah to seek the Lord, the God of their fathers [to inquire of and for Him and crave Him as a vital necessity], and to obey the law and commandment.

5Also Asa took out of all the cities of Judah the idolatrous high places and the incense altars. And the kingdom had rest under his reign.

6And he built fortified cities in Judah, for the land had rest. He had no war in those years, for the Lord gave him peace.

7Therefore he said to Judah, Let us build these cities, and surround them with walls, towers, gates, and bars; the land is still ours, because we sought the Lord our God; we have sought Him [yearning for Him with all our desire], and He has given us rest *and* peace on every side. So they built and prospered.

8Asa had an army of 300,000 men out of Judah who bore bucklers and spears, and 280,000 out of Benjamin who bore shields and drew bows, all mighty men of courage.

9There came out against Judah Zerah the Ethiopian with a host of a million [that is, too many to be numbered], and 300 chariots, and came as far as Mareshah.

10Then Asa went out against him, and they set up their lines of battle in the valley of Zephathah at Mareshah.

## New American Standard

12"Now behold, God is with us at *our* head and His priests with
the signal trumpets to sound the alarm against you. O sons of
Israel, do not fight against the LORD God of your fathers, for you
will not succeed."
13¶ But Jeroboam had set an ambush to come from the rear, so
that *Israel* was in front of Judah, and the ambush was behind them.
14When Judah turned around, behold, they were attacked both
front and rear; so they cried to the LORD, and the priests blew the
trumpets.
15Then the men of Judah raised a war cry, and when the men
of Judah raised the war cry, then it was that God routed Jeroboam
and all Israel before Abijah and Judah.
16And when the sons of Israel fled before Judah, God gave them
into their hand.
17And Abijah and his people defeated them with a great slaughter, so that 500,000 chosen men of Israel fell slain.
18Thus the sons of Israel were subdued at that time, and the
sons of Judah conquered because they trusted in the LORD, the
God of their fathers.
19And Abijah pursued Jeroboam, and captured from him *several*
cities, Bethel with its villages, Jeshanah with its villages, and
Ephron with its villages.

*Death of Jeroboam*

20And Jeroboam did not again recover strength in the days of
Abijah; and the LORD struck him and he died.
21¶ But Abijah became powerful, and took fourteen wives to
himself; and became the father of twenty-two sons and sixteen
daughters.
22Now the rest of the acts of Abijah, and his ways and his words
are written in the treatise of the prophet Iddo.

*Asa Succeeds Abijah in Judah*

**14** SO ABIJAH slept with his fathers, and they buried him in
the city of David, and his son Asa became king in his
place. The land was undisturbed for ten years during his days.
2¶ And Asa did good and right in the sight of the LORD his God,
3for he removed the foreign altars and high places, tore down
the *sacred* pillars, cut down the [a]Asherim,
4and commanded Judah to seek the LORD God of their fathers
and to observe the law and the commandment.
5He also removed the high places and the incense altars from
all the cities of Judah. And the kingdom was undisturbed under
him.
6And he built fortified cities in Judah, since the land was undisturbed, and there was no one at war with him during those years,
because the LORD had given him rest.
7For he said to Judah, "Let us build these cities and surround
*them* with walls and towers, gates and bars. The land is still ours,
because we have sought the LORD our God; we have sought Him,
and He has given us rest on every side." So they built and prospered.
8Now Asa had an army of 300,000 from Judah, bearing large
shields and spears, and 280,000 from Benjamin, bearing shields
and wielding bows; all of them were valiant warriors.
9¶ Now Zerah the Ethiopian came out against them with an
army of a million men and 300 chariots, and he came to Mareshah.
10So Asa went out to meet him, and they drew up in battle
formation in the valley of Zephathah at Mareshah.

NAS [a] I.e., wooden symbols of a female deity

## New International

us; he is our leader. His priests with their trumpets will sound the
battle cry against you. Men of Israel, do not fight against the LORD,
the God of your fathers, for you will not succeed."
13Now Jeroboam had sent troops around to the rear, so that
while he was in front of Judah the ambush was behind them.
14Judah turned and saw that they were being attacked at both front
and rear. Then they cried out to the LORD. The priests blew their
trumpets 15and the men of Judah raised the battle cry. At the
sound of their battle cry, God routed Jeroboam and all Israel before
Abijah and Judah. 16The Israelites fled before Judah, and God
delivered them into their hands. 17Abijah and his men inflicted
heavy losses on them, so that there were five hundred thousand
casualties among Israel's able men. 18The men of Israel were subdued on that occasion, and the men of Judah were victorious
because they relied on the LORD, the God of their fathers.
19Abijah pursued Jeroboam and took from him the towns of
Bethel, Jeshanah and Ephron, with their surrounding villages.
20Jeroboam did not regain power during the time of Abijah. And
the LORD struck him down and he died.
21But Abijah grew in strength. He married fourteen wives and
had twenty-two sons and sixteen daughters.
22The other events of Abijah's reign, what he did and what he
said, are written in the annotations of the prophet Iddo.

**14** AND ABIJAH rested with his fathers and was buried in
the City of David. Asa his son succeeded him as king, and
in his days the country was at peace for ten years.

*Asa King of Judah*

2Asa did what was good and right in the eyes of the LORD his
God. 3He removed the foreign altars and the high places, smashed
the sacred stones and cut down the Asherah poles.[b] 4He commanded Judah to seek the LORD, the God of their fathers, and to
obey his laws and commands. 5He removed the high places and
incense altars in every town in Judah, and the kingdom was at
peace under him. 6He built up the fortified cities of Judah, since
the land was at peace. No one was at war with him during those
years, for the LORD gave him rest.
7"Let us build up these towns," he said to Judah, "and put
walls around them, with towers, gates and bars. The land is still
ours, because we have sought the LORD our God; we sought him
and he has given us rest on every side." So they built and prospered.
8Asa had an army of three hundred thousand men from Judah,
equipped with large shields and with spears, and two hundred
and eighty thousand from Benjamin, armed with small shields and
with bows. All these were brave fighting men.
9Zerah the Cushite marched out against them with a vast army[c]
and three hundred chariots, and came as far as Mareshah. 10Asa
went out to meet him, and they took up battle positions in the
Valley of Zephathah near Mareshah.

NIV [b] 3 That is, symbols of the goddess Asherah; here and elsewhere in 2 Chronicles [c] 9 Hebrew *with an army of a thousand thousands* or *with an army of thousands upon thousands*

## King James

11 And Asa cried unto the LORD his God, and said, LORD, *it is* nothing with thee to help, whether with many, or with them that have no power: help us, O LORD our God; for we rest on thee, and in thy name we go against this multitude. O LORD, thou *art* our God; let not man prevail against thee.

12 So the LORD smote the Ethiopians before Asa, and before Judah; and the Ethiopians fled.

13 And Asa and the people that *were* with him pursued them unto Gerar: and the Ethiopians were overthrown, that they could not recover themselves; for they were destroyed before the LORD, and before his host; and they carried away very much spoil.

14 And they smote all the cities round about Gerar; for the fear of the LORD came upon them: and they spoiled all the cities; for there was exceeding much spoil in them.

15 They smote also the tents of cattle, and carried away sheep and camels in abundance, and returned to Jerusalem.

**15** AND THE spirit of God came upon Azariah the son of Oded:

2 And he went out to meet Asa, and said unto him, Hear ye me, Asa, and all Judah and Benjamin; The LORD *is* with you, while ye be with him; and if ye seek him, he will be found of you; but if ye forsake him, he will forsake you.

3 Now for a long season Israel *hath been* without the true God, and without a teaching priest, and without law.

4 But when they in their trouble did turn unto the LORD God of Israel, and sought him, he was found of them.

5 And in those times *there was* no peace to him that went out, nor to him that came in, but great vexations *were* upon all the inhabitants of the countries.

6 And nation was destroyed of nation, and city of city: for God did vex them with all adversity.

7 Be ye strong therefore, and let not your hands be weak: for your work shall be rewarded.

8 And when Asa heard these words, and the prophecy of Oded the prophet, he took courage, and put away the abominable idols out of all the land of Judah and Benjamin, and out of the cities which he had taken from mount Ephraim, and renewed the altar of the LORD, that *was* before the porch of the LORD.

9 And he gathered all Judah and Benjamin, and the strangers with them out of Ephraim and Manasseh, and out of Simeon: for they fell to him out of Israel in abundance, when they saw that the LORD his God *was* with him.

10 So they gathered themselves together at Jerusalem in the third month, in the fifteenth year of the reign of Asa.

11 And they offered unto the LORD the same time, of the spoil *which* they had brought, seven hundred oxen and seven thousand sheep.

12 And they entered into a covenant to seek the LORD God of their fathers with all their heart and with all their soul;

13 That whosoever would not seek the LORD God of Israel should be put to death, whether small or great, whether man or woman.

14 And they sware unto the LORD with a loud voice, and with shouting, and with trumpets, and with cornets.

15 And all Judah rejoiced at the oath: for they had sworn with all their heart, and sought him with their whole desire; and he was found of them: and the LORD gave them rest round about.

16 ¶ And also *concerning* Maachah the mother of Asa the king, he removed her from *being* queen, because she had made an idol in a grove: and Asa cut down her idol, and stamped *it*, and burnt *it* at the brook Kidron.

## Amplified

11 Asa cried to the Lord his God, O Lord, there is none besides You to help, and no difference to You whether him You help is mighty or powerless. Help us, O Lord our God! For we rely on You, and we go against this multitude in Your name. O Lord, You are our God; let no man prevail against You!

12 So the Lord smote the Ethiopians before Asa and Judah, and the Ethiopians fled.

13 Asa and the people with him pursued them to Gerar, and the Ethiopians were overthrown, so that none remained alive; for they were destroyed before the Lord, and His host, who carried away very much booty.

14 And they smote all the cities round about Gerar, for the fear of the Lord came upon them. They plundered all the cities, for there was much plunder in them.

15 They smote also the cattle encampments, and carried away sheep in abundance, and camels, and returned to Jerusalem.

**15** THE SPIRIT of God came upon Azariah the son of Oded,

2 And he went out to meet Asa, and said to him, Hear me, Asa, and all Judah and Benjamin: The Lord is with you while you are with Him. If you seek Him [inquiring for and of Him, craving Him as your soul's first necessity], He will be found of you; but if you [become indifferent and] forsake Him, He will forsake you.

3 Now for a long time Israel was without the true God, without a teaching priest, and without law.

4 But when they in their trouble turned to the Lord God of Israel, and [in desperation earnestly] sought Him, He was found by them.

5 And in those times there was no peace to him who went out, nor to him who came in, but great *and* vexing afflictions *and* disturbances were upon all the inhabitants of the countries.

6 Nation was broke in pieces against nation, and city against city, for God vexed *and* troubled them with all sorts of adversity.

7 Be strong therefore, and let not your hands be weak *and* slack, for your work shall be rewarded.

8 And when Asa heard these words, the prophecy of Oded the prophet, he took courage, and put away the abominable idols from all the land of Judah and Benjamin and from the cities which he had taken in the hill country of Ephraim, and he repaired the altar [of burnt offering] of the Lord which was in front of the porch *or* vestibule [of the house] of the Lord.

9 And he gathered all Judah and Benjamin and the strangers with them out of Ephraim, Manasseh and Simeon; for they came over to Asa out of Israel in large numbers, when they saw that the Lord his God was with him.

10 So they gathered at Jerusalem in the third month of the fifteenth year of the reign of Asa,

11 And they sacrificed to the Lord on that day from the spoil which they had brought, 700 oxen and 7,000 sheep.

12 And they entered into a covenant to seek the Lord the God of their fathers *and* to yearn for Him with all their heart's desire and with all their soul,

13 And that whoever would not seek the Lord the God of Israel should be put to death, whether young or old, man or woman.

14 They took an oath to the Lord with a loud voice, with shouting, with trumpets, and with cornets.

15 And all Judah rejoiced at the oath, for they had sworn with all their heart, and sought Him [yearning for Him] with their whole desire, and He was found by them, and the Lord gave them rest *and* peace round about.

16 Also Maacah, King Asa's mother, he removed from being queen mother, because she had made an abominable image for Asherah. Asa cut down her idol, crushed it, and burned it at the brook Kidron.

## New American Standard

11Then Asa called to the LORD his God, and said, "LORD, there
is no one besides Thee to help *in the battle* between the powerful
and those who have no strength; so help us, O LORD our God, for
we trust in Thee, and in Thy name have come against this multitude. O LORD, Thou art our God; let not man prevail against
Thee."
12So the LORD routed the Ethiopians before Asa and before
Judah, and the Ethiopians fled.
13And Asa and the people who *were* with him pursued them as
far as Gerar; and so many Ethiopians fell that they could not
recover, for they were shattered before the LORD, and before His
army. And they carried away very much plunder.
14And they destroyed all the cities around Gerar, for the dread
of the LORD had fallen on them; and they despoiled all the cities,
for there was much plunder in them.
15They also struck down those who owned livestock, and they
carried away large numbers of sheep and camels. Then they returned to Jerusalem.

*The Prophet Azariah Warns Asa*

**15** NOW THE Spirit of God came on Azariah the son of
Oded,
2and he went out to meet Asa and said to him, "Listen to me,
Asa, and all Judah and Benjamin: the LORD is with you when you
are with Him. And if you seek Him, He will let you find Him; but
if you forsake Him, He will forsake you.
3"And for many days Israel was without the true God and
without a teaching priest and without law.
4"But in their distress they turned to the LORD God of Israel,
and they sought Him, and He let them find Him.
5"And in those times there was no peace to him who went out
or to him who came in, for many disturbances afflicted all the
inhabitants of the lands.
6"And nation was crushed by nation, and city by city, for God
troubled them with every kind of distress.
7"But you, be strong and do not lose courage, for there is
reward for your work."

*Asa's Reforms*

8¶ Now when Asa heard these words and the prophecy which
Azariah the son of Oded the prophet spoke, he took courage and
removed the abominable idols from all the land of Judah and
Benjamin and from the cities which he had captured in the hill
country of Ephraim. He then restored the altar of the LORD which
was in front of the porch of the LORD.
9And he gathered all Judah and Benjamin and those from
Ephraim, Manasseh, and Simeon who resided with them, for
many defected to him from Israel when they saw that the LORD his
God was with him.
10So they assembled at Jerusalem in the third month of the
fifteenth year of Asa's reign.
11And they sacrificed to the LORD that day 700 oxen and 7,000
sheep from the spoil they had brought.
12And they entered into the covenant to seek the LORD God of
their fathers with all their heart and soul;
13and whoever would not seek the LORD God of Israel should
be put to death, whether small or great, man or woman.
14Moreover, they made an oath to the LORD with a loud voice,
with shouting, with trumpets, and with horns.
15And all Judah rejoiced concerning the oath, for they had
sworn with their whole heart and had sought Him earnestly, and
He let them find Him. So the LORD gave them rest on every side.
16¶ And he also removed Maacah, the mother of King Asa, from
the *position of* queen mother, because she had made a horrid image
as an Asherah, and Asa cut down her horrid image, crushed *it* and
burned *it* at the brook Kidron.

## New International

11Then Asa called to the LORD his God and said, "LORD, there
is no one like you to help the powerless against the mighty. Help
us, O LORD our God, for we rely on you, and in your name we have
come against this vast army. O LORD, you are our God; do not let
man prevail against you."
12The LORD struck down the Cushites before Asa and Judah.
The Cushites fled, 13and Asa and his army pursued them as far as
Gerar. Such a great number of Cushites fell that they could not
recover; they were crushed before the LORD and his forces. The
men of Judah carried off a large amount of plunder. 14They destroyed all the villages around Gerar, for the terror of the LORD had
fallen upon them. They plundered all these villages, since there
was much booty there. 15They also attacked the camps of the
herdsmen and carried off droves of sheep and goats and camels.
Then they returned to Jerusalem.

*Asa's Reform*

**15** THE SPIRIT of God came upon Azariah son of Oded. 2He
went out to meet Asa and said to him, "Listen to me, Asa
and all Judah and Benjamin. The LORD is with you when you are
with him. If you seek him, he will be found by you, but if you
forsake him, he will forsake you. 3For a long time Israel was
without the true God, without a priest to teach and without the
law. 4But in their distress they turned to the LORD, the God of
Israel, and sought him, and he was found by them. 5In those days
it was not safe to travel about, for all the inhabitants of the lands
were in great turmoil. 6One nation was being crushed by another
and one city by another, because God was troubling them with
every kind of distress. 7But as for you, be strong and do not give
up, for your work will be rewarded."
8When Asa heard these words and the prophecy of Azariah son
of[a] Oded the prophet, he took courage. He removed the detestable idols from the whole land of Judah and Benjamin and from
the towns he had captured in the hills of Ephraim. He repaired the
altar of the LORD that was in front of the portico of the LORD's
temple.
9Then he assembled all Judah and Benjamin and the people
from Ephraim, Manasseh and Simeon who had settled among
them, for large numbers had come over to him from Israel when
they saw that the LORD his God was with him.
10They assembled at Jerusalem in the third month of the fifteenth year of Asa's reign. 11At that time they sacrificed to the
LORD seven hundred head of cattle and seven thousand sheep and
goats from the plunder they had brought back. 12They entered into
a covenant to seek the LORD, the God of their fathers, with all their
heart and soul. 13All who would not seek the LORD, the God of
Israel, were to be put to death, whether small or great, man or
woman. 14They took an oath to the LORD with loud acclamation,
with shouting and with trumpets and horns. 15All Judah rejoiced
about the oath because they had sworn it wholeheartedly. They
sought God eagerly, and he was found by them. So the LORD gave
them rest on every side.
16King Asa also deposed his grandmother Maacah from her
position as queen mother, because she had made a repulsive
Asherah pole. Asa cut the pole down, broke it up and burned it
in the Kidron Valley. 17Although he did not remove the high

NIV [a] *8* Vulgate and Syriac (see also Septuagint and verse 1); Hebrew does not have *Azariah son of.*

## King James

17But the high places were not taken away out of Israel: nevertheless the heart of Asa was perfect all his days.
18¶ And he brought into the house of God the things that his
father had dedicated, and that he himself had dedicated, silver,
and gold, and vessels.
19And there was no *more* war unto the five and thirtieth year of
the reign of Asa.

16 IN THE six and thirtieth year of the reign of Asa Baasha
king of Israel came up against Judah, and built Ramah, to
the intent that he might let none go out or come in to Asa king of
Judah.
2Then Asa brought out silver and gold out of the treasures of
the house of the LORD and of the king's house, and sent to Ben-
hadad king of Syria, that dwelt at Damascus, saying,
3 *There is* a league between me and thee, as *there was* between
my father and thy father: behold, I have sent thee silver and gold;
go, break thy league with Baasha king of Israel, that he may depart
from me.
4And Ben-hadad hearkened unto king Asa, and sent the captains of his armies against the cities of Israel; and they smote Ijon,
and Dan, and Abel-maim, and all the store cities of Naphtali.
5And it came to pass, when Baasha heard *it*, that he left off
building of Ramah, and let his work cease.
6Then Asa the king took all Judah; and they carried away the
stones of Ramah, and the timber thereof, wherewith Baasha was
building; and he built therewith Geba and Mizpah.
7¶ And at that time Hanani the seer came to Asa king of Judah,
and said unto him, Because thou hast relied on the king of Syria,
and not relied on the LORD thy God, therefore is the host of the
king of Syria escaped out of thine hand.
8Were not the Ethiopians and the Lubims a huge host, with
very many chariots and horsemen? yet, because thou didst rely on
the LORD, he delivered them into thine hand.
9For the eyes of the LORD run to and fro throughout the whole
earth, to shew himself strong in the behalf of *them* whose heart *is*
perfect toward him. Herein thou hast done foolishly: therefore
from henceforth thou shalt have wars.
10Then Asa was wroth with the seer, and put him in a prison
house; for *he was* in a rage with him because of this *thing*. And Asa
oppressed *some* of the people the same time.
11¶ And, behold, the acts of Asa, first and last, lo, they *are*
written in the book of the kings of Judah and Israel.
12And Asa in the thirty and ninth year of his reign was diseased
in his feet, until his disease *was* exceeding *great*: yet in his disease
he sought not to the LORD, but to the physicians.
13¶ And Asa slept with his fathers, and died in the one and
fortieth year of his reign.
14And they buried him in his own sepulchres, which he had
made for himself in the city of David, and laid him in the bed which
was filled with sweet odours and divers kinds *of spices* prepared by
the apothecaries' art: and they made a very great burning for him.

17 AND JEHOSHAPHAT his son reigned in his stead, and
strengthened himself against Israel.
2And he placed forces in all the fenced cities of Judah, and set
garrisons in the land of Judah, and in the cities of Ephraim, which
Asa his father had taken.
3And the LORD was with Jehoshaphat, because he walked in the
first ways of his father David, and sought not unto Baalim;

## Amplified

17But the high places were not taken out of Israel. Nevertheless
the heart of Asa was blameless all his days.
18And he brought into the house of God the things that his
father [Abijah] had dedicated, and those he himself had dedicated,
silver, and gold, and vessels.
19And there was no more war until the thirty-fifth year of the
reign of Asa.

16 IN THE thirty-sixth year of Asa's reign, Baasha king of
Israel came up against Judah, and built [fortified] Ramah
intending to intercept any one going out or coming in to Asa king
of Judah.
2Then Asa brought silver and gold out of the treasures of the
house of the Lord and of the king's house, and sent them to
Benhadad king of Syria, who dwelt at Damascus, saying,
3Let there be a league between me and you, as was between my
father and your father. Behold, I am sending you silver and gold;
go, break your league with Baasha king of Israel, that he may
withdraw from me.
4And Benhadad hearkened to King Asa, and sent the captains
of his armies against the cities of Israel; and they smote Ijon, Dan,
Abel-maim, and all the store-cities of Naphtali.
5And when Baasha heard it, he stopped building Ramah, and
let his work cease.
6Then King Asa took all Judah, and they carried away the
stones of Ramah and its timber, with which Baasha had been
building, and with them he built Geba and Mizpah.
7At that time Hanani the seer came to Asa king of Judah, and
said to him, Because you relied on the king of Syria, and not on
the Lord your God, the army of the king of Syria has escaped you.
8Were not the Ethiopians and Libyans a huge host, with very
many chariots and horsemen? Yet, because you relied then on the
Lord, He gave them into your hand.
9For the eyes of the Lord run to and fro throughout the whole
earth, to show Himself strong in behalf of those whose heart is
blameless toward Him. You have done foolishly in this; therefore
from now on you shall have wars.
10Then Asa was angry with the seer, and put him in prison—in
the stocks—for he was enraged with him because of this. Asa
oppressed some of the people at the same time.
11The acts of Asa, first to last, are written in the Book of the
Kings of Judah and Israel.
12In the thirty-ninth year of his reign Asa was diseased in his
feet, until his disease became very severe; yet in his disease he did
not seek the Lord, but relied on the physicians.
13And Asa slept with his fathers, dying in the forty-first year of
his reign.
14And they buried him in his own tomb which he had hewn out
for himself in the city of David, and laid him on a bier which was
filled with sweet odors and various kinds [of spices] prepared by
the perfumers' art; and they made a very great burning [of spices]
in his honor.

17 JEHOSHAPHAT HIS son reigned in Asa's stead and
strengthened himself against Israel.
2And he placed forces in all the fortified cities of Judah, and set
garrisons in the land of Judah and in the cities of Ephraim which
Asa his father had taken.
3The Lord was with Jehoshaphat, because he walked in the first
ways of his father; he did not seek the Baals,

## New American Standard

17But the high places were not removed from Israel; nevertheless Asa's heart was blameless all his days.
18And he brought into the house of God the dedicated things
of his father and his own dedicated things: silver and gold and
utensils.
19And there was no more war until the thirty-fifth year of Asa's
reign.

*Asa Wars against Baasha*

**16** IN THE thirty-sixth year of Asa's reign Baasha king of
Israel came up against Judah and fortified Ramah in order
to prevent *anyone* from going out or coming in to Asa king of Judah.
2Then Asa brought out silver and gold from the treasuries of
the house of the LORD and the king's house, and sent them to
Ben-hadad king of Aram, who lived in Damascus, saying,
3" *Let there be* a treaty between you and me, *as* between my
father and your father. Behold, I have sent you silver and gold; go,
break your treaty with Baasha king of Israel so that he will withdraw from me."
4So Ben-hadad listened to King Asa and sent the commanders
of his armies against the cities of Israel, and they conquered Ijon,
Dan, Abel-maim, and all the store cities of Naphtali.
5And it came about when Baasha heard *of it* that he ceased
fortifying Ramah and stopped his work.
6Then King Asa brought all Judah, and they carried away the
stones of Ramah and its timber with which Baasha had been building, and with them he fortified Geba and Mizpah.

*Asa Imprisons the Prophet*

7¶ At that time Hanani the seer came to Asa king of Judah and
said to him, "Because you have relied on the king of Aram and
have not relied on the LORD your God, therefore the army of the
king of Aram has escaped out of your hand.
8"Were not the Ethiopians and the Lubim an immense army
with very many chariots and horsemen? Yet, because you relied
on the LORD, He delivered them into your hand.
9"For the eyes of the LORD move to and fro throughout the
earth that He may strongly support those whose heart is completely His. You have acted foolishly in this. Indeed, from now on you
will surely have wars."
10Then Asa was angry with the seer and put him in prison, for
he was enraged at him for this. And Asa oppressed some of the
people at the same time.
11¶ And now, the acts of Asa from first to last, behold, they are
written in the Book of the Kings of Judah and Israel.
12And in the thirty-ninth year of his reign Asa became diseased
in his feet. His disease was severe, yet even in his disease he did
not seek the LORD, but the physicians.
13So Asa slept with his fathers, having died in the forty-first
year of his reign.
14And they buried him in his own tomb which he had cut out
for himself in the city of David, and they laid him in the resting
place which he had filled with spices of various kinds blended by
the perfumers' art; and they made a very great fire for him.

*Jehoshaphat Succeeds Asa*

**17** JEHOSHAPHAT HIS son then became king in his place,
and made his position over Israel firm.
2He placed troops in all the fortified cities of Judah, and set
garrisons in the land of Judah, and in the cities of Ephraim which
Asa his father had captured.

*His Good Reign*

3And the LORD was with Jehoshaphat because he followed the
example of his father David's earlier days and did not seek the
Baals,

## New International

places from Israel, Asa's heart was fully committed ⌊to the LORD⌋
all his life. 18He brought into the temple of God the silver and gold
and the articles that he and his father had dedicated.
19There was no more war until the thirty-fifth year of Asa's
reign.

*Asa's Last Years*

**16** IN THE thirty-sixth year of Asa's reign Baasha king of
Israel went up against Judah and fortified Ramah to prevent anyone from leaving or entering the territory of Asa king of
Judah.
2Asa then took the silver and gold out of the treasuries of the
LORD's temple and of his own palace and sent it to Ben-Hadad king
of Aram, who was ruling in Damascus. 3"Let there be a treaty
between me and you," he said, "as there was between my father
and your father. See, I am sending you silver and gold. Now break
your treaty with Baasha king of Israel so he will withdraw from
me."
4Ben-Hadad agreed with King Asa and sent the commanders of
his forces against the towns of Israel. They conquered Ijon, Dan,
Abel Maim[a] and all the store cities of Naphtali. 5When Baasha
heard this, he stopped building Ramah and abandoned his work.
6Then King Asa brought all the men of Judah, and they carried
away from Ramah the stones and timber Baasha had been using.
With them he built up Geba and Mizpah.
7At that time Hanani the seer came to Asa king of Judah and
said to him: "Because you relied on the king of Aram and not on
the LORD your God, the army of the king of Aram has escaped from
your hand. 8Were not the Cushites[b] and Libyans a mighty army
with great numbers of chariots and horsemen[c]? Yet when you
relied on the LORD, he delivered them into your hand. 9For the
eyes of the LORD range throughout the earth to strengthen those
whose hearts are fully committed to him. You have done a foolish
thing, and from now on you will be at war."
10Asa was angry with the seer because of this; he was so enraged that he put him in prison. At the same time Asa brutally
oppressed some of the people.
11The events of Asa's reign, from beginning to end, are written
in the book of the kings of Judah and Israel. 12In the thirty-ninth
year of his reign Asa was afflicted with a disease in his feet.
Though his disease was severe, even in his illness he did not seek
help from the LORD, but only from the physicians. 13Then in the
forty-first year of his reign Asa died and rested with his fathers.
14They buried him in the tomb that he had cut out for himself in
the City of David. They laid him on a bier covered with spices and
various blended perfumes, and they made a huge fire in his honor.

*Jehoshaphat King of Judah*

**17** JEHOSHAPHAT HIS son succeeded him as king and
strengthened himself against Israel. 2He stationed troops
in all the fortified cities of Judah and put garrisons in Judah and
in the towns of Ephraim that his father Asa had captured.
3The LORD was with Jehoshaphat because in his early years he
walked in the ways his father David had followed. He did not
consult the Baals 4but sought the God of his father and followed

**NIV** [a] *4* Also known as *Abel Beth Maacah* [b] *8* That is, people from the upper Nile region [c] *8* Or *charioteers*

## King James

4 But sought to the *Lord* God of his father, and walked in his commandments, and not after the doings of Israel.

5 Therefore the LORD stablished the kingdom in his hand; and all Judah brought to Jehoshaphat presents; and he had riches and honour in abundance.

6 And his heart was lifted up in the ways of the LORD: moreover he took away the high places and groves out of Judah.

7 ¶ Also in the third year of his reign he sent to his princes, *even* to Ben-hail, and to Obadiah, and to Zechariah, and to Nethaneel, and to Michaiah, to teach in the cities of Judah.

8 And with them *he sent* Levites, *even* Shemaiah, and Nethaniah, and Zebadiah, and Asahel, and Shemiramoth, and Jehonathan, and Adonijah, and Tobijah, and Tob-adonijah, Levites; and with them Elishama and Jehoram, priests.

9 And they taught in Judah, and *had* the book of the law of the LORD with them, and went about throughout all the cities of Judah, and taught the people.

10 ¶ And the fear of the LORD fell upon all the kingdoms of the lands that *were* round about Judah, so that they made no war against Jehoshaphat.

11 Also *some* of the Philistines brought Jehoshaphat presents, and tribute silver; and the Arabians brought him flocks, seven thousand and seven hundred rams, and seven thousand and seven hundred he goats.

12 ¶ And Jehoshaphat waxed great exceedingly; and he built in Judah castles, and cities of store.

13 And he had much business in the cities of Judah: and the men of war, mighty men of valour, *were* in Jerusalem.

14 And these *are* the numbers of them according to the house of their fathers: Of Judah, the captains of thousands; Adnah the chief, and with him mighty men of valour three hundred thousand.

15 And next to him *was* Jehohanan the captain, and with him two hundred and fourscore thousand.

16 And next him *was* Amasiah the son of Zichri, who willingly offered himself unto the LORD; and with him two hundred thousand mighty men of valour.

17 And of Benjamin; Eliada a mighty man of valour, and with him armed men with bow and shield two hundred thousand.

18 And next him *was* Jehozabad, and with him an hundred and fourscore thousand ready prepared for the war.

19 These waited on the king, beside *those* whom the king put in the fenced cities throughout all Judah.

**18** NOW JEHOSHAPHAT had riches and honour in abundance, and joined affinity with Ahab.

2 And after *certain* years he went down to Ahab to Samaria. And Ahab killed sheep and oxen for him in abundance, and for the people that *he had* with him, and persuaded him to go up *with him* to Ramoth-gilead.

3 And Ahab king of Israel said unto Jehoshaphat king of Judah, Wilt thou go with me to Ramoth-gilead? And he answered him, I *am* as thou *art*, and my people as thy people; and *we will be* with thee in the war.

4 ¶ And Jehoshaphat said unto the king of Israel, Inquire, I pray thee, at the word of the LORD today.

5 Therefore the king of Israel gathered together of prophets four hundred men, and said unto them, Shall we go to Ramoth-gilead to battle, or shall I forbear? And they said, Go up; for God will deliver *it* into the king's hand.

6 But Jehoshaphat said, *Is there* not here a prophet of the LORD besides, that we might inquire of him?

7 And the king of Israel said unto Jehoshaphat, *There is* yet one man, by whom we may inquire of the LORD: but I hate him; for he never prophesied good unto me, but always evil: the same *is* Micaiah the son of Imla. And Jehoshaphat said, Let not the king say so.

## Amplified

4 But sought *and* yearned with all his desire for the Lord the God of his father and walked in His commandments, and not after the ways of Israel.

5 Therefore the Lord established the kingdom in his hand; and all Judah brought tribute to Jehoshaphat; and he had great riches and honor.

6 His heart was cheered *and* his courage was high in the ways of the Lord; moreover he took away the high places and the Asherim out of Judah.

7 Also in the third year of his reign he sent to his princes, Ben-hail, Obadiah, Zechariah, Nethanel, and Micaiah, to teach in the cities of Judah.

8 And with them the Levites, Shemaiah, Nethaniah, Zebadiah, Asahel, Shemiramoth, Jehonathan, Adonijah, Tobijah, and Tobadonijah; and with these Levites, the priests Elishama and Jehoram.

9 And they taught in Judah, and had the book of the law of the Lord with them; they went about throughout all the cities of Judah and taught among the people.

10 And a terror from the Lord fell upon all the kingdoms of the lands that were round about Judah, so that they made no war against Jehoshaphat.

11 And some of the Philistines brought Jehoshaphat gifts, and tribute silver; and the Arabs brought him flocks, 7,700 each of rams and of he-goats.

12 And Jehoshaphat became very great. He built in Judah fortresses and store-cities;

13 And he had many works in the cities of Judah, and soldiers, mighty men of courage, in Jerusalem.

14 This was the number of them by fathers' houses: Of Judah, the captains of thousands; Adnah the chief, with 300,000 mighty men of valor.

15 Next to him was Jeho-hanan the captain, with 280,000.

16 And next to him Amasiah son of Zichri, who willingly offered himself to the Lord, with 200,000 mighty men of valor.

17 Of Benjamin: Eliada, a mighty man of valor, with 200,000 men armed with bow and shield.

18 Next to him was Jehozabad with 180,000 armed for war.

19 These were in the king's service, besides those [he] had placed in fortified cities throughout all Judah.

**18** NOW JEHOSHAPHAT had great riches and honor, but was allied [by marriage] with Ahab.

2 After some years he went down to Ahab in Samaria. And Ahab killed sheep and oxen for him in abundance, and for the people with him, and persuaded him to go up with him against Ramoth-gilead.

3 Ahab king of Israel said to Jehoshaphat king of Judah, Will you go with me to Ramoth-gilead? He answered, I am as you are, and my people as your people; we will be with you in the war.

4 And Jehoshaphat said to the king of Israel, Inquire first, I pray you, for the word of the Lord today.

5 So King [Ahab] of Israel gathered together the prophets, 400 men, and said to them, Shall we go to Ramoth-gilead to battle, or shall I forbear? And they said, Go up; for God will deliver it into the king's hand.

6 But Jehoshaphat said, Is there not another prophet of the Lord here, by whom we may inquire?

7 King [Ahab] of Israel said to Jehoshaphat, There is another man, Micaiah son of Imla, by whom we may inquire of the Lord, but I hate him, for he never has prophesied good for me, but always evil. And Jehoshaphat said, Let not the king say so.

## New American Standard

4but sought the God of his father, followed His commandments, and did not act as Israel did.
5So the LORD established the kingdom in his control, and all
Judah brought tribute to Jehoshaphat, and he had great riches and
honor.
6And he took great pride in the ways of the LORD and again
removed the high places and the Asherim from Judah.
7¶ Then in the third year of his reign he sent his officials,
Ben-hail, Obadiah, Zechariah, Nethanel, and Micaiah, to teach in
the cities of Judah;
8and with them the Levites, Shemaiah, Nethaniah, Zebadiah,
Asahel, Shemiramoth, Jehonathan, Adonijah, Tobijah, and
Tobadonijah, the Levites; and with them Elishama and Jehoram,
the priests.
9And they taught in Judah, *having* the book of the law of the
LORD with them; and they went throughout all the cities of Judah
and taught among the people.
10¶ Now the dread of the LORD was on all the kingdoms of the
lands which *were* around Judah, so that they did not make war
against Jehoshaphat.
11And some of the Philistines brought gifts and silver as tribute
to Jehoshaphat; the Arabians also brought him flocks, 7,700 rams
and 7,700 male goats.
12So Jehoshaphat grew greater and greater, and he built fortresses and store cities in Judah.
13And he had large supplies in the cities of Judah, and warriors,
valiant men, in Jerusalem.
14And this was their muster according to their fathers'
households: of Judah, commanders of thousands, Adnah *was* the
commander, and with him 300,000 valiant warriors;
15and next to him *was* Johanan the commander, and with him
280,000;
16and next to him Amasiah the son of Zichri, who volunteered
for the LORD, and with him 200,000 valiant warriors;
17and of Benjamin, Eliada a valiant warrior, and with him
200,000 armed with bow and shield;
18and next to him Jehozabad, and with him 180,000 equipped
for war.
19These are they who served the king, apart from those whom
the king put in the fortified cities through all Judah.

*Jehoshaphat Allies with Ahab*

**18** NOW JEHOSHAPHAT had great riches and honor; and
he allied himself by marriage with Ahab.
2And some years later he went down to *visit* Ahab at Samaria.
And Ahab slaughtered many sheep and oxen for him and the
people who were with him, and induced him to go up against
Ramoth-gilead.
3And Ahab king of Israel said to Jehoshaphat king of Judah,
"Will you go with me *against* Ramoth-gilead?" And he said to him,
"I am as you are, and my people as your people, and *we will be* with
you in the battle."
4¶ Moreover, Jehoshaphat said to the king of Israel, "Please
inquire first for the word of the LORD."
5Then the king of Israel assembled the prophets, four hundred
men, and said to them, "Shall we go against Ramoth-gilead to
battle, or shall I refrain?" And they said, "Go up, for God will give
*it* into the hand of the king."
6But Jehoshaphat said, "Is there not yet a prophet of the LORD
here that we may inquire of him?"
7And the king of Israel said to Jehoshaphat, "There is yet one
man by whom we may inquire of the LORD, but I hate him, for he
never prophesies good concerning me but always evil. He is Micaiah, son of Imla." But Jehoshaphat said, "Let not the king say
so."

## New International

his commands rather than the practices of Israel. 5The LORD established the kingdom under his control; and all Judah brought gifts
to Jehoshaphat, so that he had great wealth and honor. 6His heart
was devoted to the ways of the LORD; furthermore, he removed the
high places and the Asherah poles from Judah.
7In the third year of his reign he sent his officials Ben-Hail,
Obadiah, Zechariah, Nethanel and Micaiah to teach in the towns
of Judah. 8With them were certain Levites—Shemaiah, Nethaniah,
Zebadiah, Asahel, Shemiramoth, Jehonathan, Adonijah, Tobijah
and Tob-Adonijah—and the priests Elishama and Jehoram. 9They
taught throughout Judah, taking with them the Book of the Law
of the LORD; they went around to all the towns of Judah and taught
the people.
10The fear of the LORD fell on all the kingdoms of the lands
surrounding Judah, so that they did not make war with Jehoshaphat. 11Some Philistines brought Jehoshaphat gifts and silver as
tribute, and the Arabs brought him flocks: seven thousand seven
hundred rams and seven thousand seven hundred goats.
12Jehoshaphat became more and more powerful; he built forts
and store cities in Judah 13and had large supplies in the towns of
Judah. He also kept experienced fighting men in Jerusalem.
14Their enrollment by families was as follows:

From Judah, commanders of units of 1,000:
Adnah the commander, with 300,000 fighting men;
15next, Jehohanan the commander, with 280,000;
16next, Amasiah son of Zicri, who volunteered himself for
the service of the LORD, with 200,000.
17From Benjamin:
Eliada, a valiant soldier, with 200,000 men armed with
bows and shields;
18next, Jehozabad, with 180,000 men armed for battle.

19These were the men who served the king, besides those he
stationed in the fortified cities throughout Judah.

*Micaiah Prophesies Against Ahab*

**18** NOW JEHOSHAPHAT had great wealth and honor, and
he allied himself with Ahab by marriage. 2Some years later
he went down to visit Ahab in Samaria. Ahab slaughtered many
sheep and cattle for him and the people with him and urged him
to attack Ramoth Gilead. 3Ahab king of Israel asked Jehoshaphat
king of Judah, "Will you go with me against Ramoth Gilead?"
Jehoshaphat replied, "I am as you are, and my people as your
people; we will join you in the war." 4But Jehoshaphat also said
to the king of Israel, "First seek the counsel of the LORD."
5So the king of Israel brought together the prophets—four hundred men—and asked them, "Shall we go to war against Ramoth
Gilead, or shall I refrain?"
"Go," they answered, "for God will give it into the king's
hand."
6But Jehoshaphat asked, "Is there not a prophet of the LORD
here whom we can inquire of?"
7The king of Israel answered Jehoshaphat, "There is still one
man through whom we can inquire of the LORD, but I hate him
because he never prophesies anything good about me, but always
bad. He is Micaiah son of Imlah."
"The king should not say that," Jehoshaphat replied.

# King James

8And the king of Israel called for one *of his* officers, and said, Fetch quickly Micaiah the son of Imla.

9And the king of Israel and Jehoshaphat king of Judah sat either of them on his throne, clothed in *their* robes, and they sat in a void place at the entering in of the gate of Samaria; and all the prophets prophesied before them.

10And Zedekiah the son of Chenaanah had made him horns of iron, and said, Thus saith the LORD, With these thou shalt push Syria until they be consumed.

11And all the prophets prophesied so, saying, Go up to Ramoth-gilead, and prosper: for the LORD shall deliver *it* into the hand of the king.

12And the messenger that went to call Micaiah spake to him, saying, Behold, the words of the prophets *declare* good to the king with one assent; let thy word therefore, I pray thee, be like one of theirs, and speak thou good.

13And Micaiah said, *As* the LORD liveth, even what my God saith, that will I speak.

14And when he was come to the king, the king said unto him, Micaiah, shall we go to Ramoth-gilead to battle, or shall I forbear? And he said, Go ye up, and prosper, and they shall be delivered into your hand.

15And the king said to him, How many times shall I adjure thee that thou say nothing but the truth to me in the name of the LORD?

16Then he said, I did see all Israel scattered upon the mountains, as sheep that have no shepherd: and the LORD said, These have no master; let them return *therefore* every man to his house in peace.

17And the king of Israel said to Jehoshaphat, Did I not tell thee *that* he would not prophesy good unto me, but evil?

18Again he said, Therefore hear the word of the LORD; I saw the LORD sitting upon his throne, and all the host of heaven standing on his right hand and *on* his left.

19And the LORD said, Who shall entice Ahab king of Israel, that he may go up and fall at Ramoth-gilead? And one spake saying after this manner, and another saying after that manner.

20Then there came out a spirit, and stood before the LORD, and said, I will entice him. And the LORD said unto him, Wherewith?

21And he said, I will go out, and be a lying spirit in the mouth of all his prophets. And *the LORD* said, Thou shalt entice *him*, and thou shalt also prevail: go out, and do *even* so.

22Now therefore, behold, the LORD hath put a lying spirit in the mouth of these thy prophets, and the LORD hath spoken evil against thee.

23Then Zedekiah the son of Chenaanah came near, and smote Micaiah upon the cheek, and said, Which way went the spirit of the LORD from me to speak unto thee?

24And Micaiah said, Behold, thou shalt see on that day when thou shalt go into an inner chamber to hide thyself.

25Then the king of Israel said, Take ye Micaiah, and carry him back to Amon the governor of the city, and to Joash the king's son;

26And say, Thus saith the king, Put this *fellow* in the prison, and feed him with bread of affliction and with water of affliction, until I return in peace.

27And Micaiah said, If thou certainly return in peace, *then* hath not the LORD spoken by me. And he said, Hearken, all ye people.

28So the king of Israel and Jehoshaphat the king of Judah went up to Ramoth-gilead.

29And the king of Israel said unto Jehoshaphat, I will disguise myself, and will go to the battle; but put thou on thy robes. So the king of Israel disguised himself; and they went to the battle.

# Amplified

8And King [Ahab] of Israel called for one of his officers, and said, Bring quickly Micaiah son of Imla.

9The king of Israel and Jehoshaphat king of Judah sat each on his throne, arrayed in their robes; they were sitting in an open place (at the threshing floor) at the entrance of the gate of Samaria; all the prophets were prophesying before them.

10And Zedekiah son of Chenaanah had made himself horns of iron, and said, Thus says the Lord, With these you shall push the Syrians until they are destroyed.

11All the prophets prophesied so, saying, Go up to Ramoth-gilead and prosper; the Lord will deliver it into the king's hand.

12The messenger who went to call Micaiah said to him, Behold, the words of the prophets foretell good to the king with one accord. So let your word be like one of them, and speak favorably.

13But Micaiah said, As the Lord lives, what my God says, that will I speak.

14And when he had come to the king, King [Ahab] said to him, Micaiah, shall we go to Ramoth-gilead to battle, or shall I forbear? And he said, Go up and prosper, and they shall be delivered into your hand.

15And the king said to him, How many times shall I warn you to tell nothing but the truth to me in the name of the Lord?

16Then Micaiah said, I did see all Israel scattered upon the mountains, as sheep that have no shepherd; and the Lord said, These have no master; let each return to his house in peace.

17And King [Ahab] of Israel said to Jehoshaphat, Did I not tell you that he would not prophesy good to me, but evil?

18[Micaiah] said, Therefore hear the word of the Lord: I saw the Lord sitting on His throne, and all the host of Heaven standing at His right hand and His left.

19And the Lord said, Who shall entice Ahab king of Israel, that he may go up and fall at Ramoth-gilead? And one said this thing, and another that.

20Then there came a spirit and stood before the Lord, and said, I will entice him. The Lord said to him, By what means?

21And he said, I will go out, and be a lying spirit in the mouth of all his prophets. And the Lord said, You shall entice him, and also succeed; go forth and do so.

22Now you see, the Lord put a lying spirit in the mouth of your prophets, and the Lord has spoken evil concerning you.

23Then Zedekiah the son of Chenaanah came near, and smote Micaiah upon the cheek, and said, Which way went the Spirit of the Lord from me to speak to you?

24And Micaiah said, Behold, you shall see on that day when you shall go into an inner chamber to hide yourself.

25Then King [Ahab] of Israel said, Take Micaiah back to Amon the governor of the city, and to Joash the king's son;

26And say, Thus says the king, Put this fellow in the prison, and feed him with bread and water of affliction, until I return in peace.

27Micaiah said, If you return at all in peace, the Lord has not spoken by me. And he *added*, Hear it, you people, all of you!

28So Ahab king of Israel and Jehoshaphat king of Judah went up to Ramoth-gilead.

29And [Ahab] king of Israel said to Jehoshaphat, I will disguise myself and will go to the battle; but you put on your royal robes. So King Ahab of Israel disguised himself, and they went into the battle.

## New American Standard

*Ahab's False Prophets Assure Victory*

8Then the king of Israel called an officer and said, "Bring
quickly Micaiah, Imla's son."
9Now the king of Israel and Jehoshaphat the king of Judah
were sitting each on his throne, arrayed in *their* robes, and *they*
were sitting at the threshing floor at the entrance of the gate of
Samaria; and all the prophets were prophesying before them.
10And Zedekiah the son of Chenaanah made horns of iron for
himself and said, "Thus says the LORD, 'With these you shall gore
the Arameans, until they are consumed.' "
11And all the prophets were prophesying thus, saying, "Go up
to Ramoth-gilead and succeed, for the LORD will give *it* into the
hand of the king."

*Micaiah Brings Word from God*

12¶ Then the messenger who went to summon Micaiah spoke
to him saying, "Behold, the words of the prophets are uniformly
favorable to the king. So please let your word be like one of them
and speak favorably."
13But Micaiah said, "As the LORD lives, what my God says, that
I will speak."
14And when he came to the king, the king said to him, "Micaiah, shall we go to Ramoth-gilead to battle, or shall I refrain?"
He said, "Go up and succeed, for they will be given into your
hand."
15Then the king said to him, "How many times must I adjure
you to speak to me nothing but the truth in the name of the LORD?"
16So he said,
"I saw all Israel
Scattered on the mountains,
Like sheep which have no shepherd;
And the LORD said,
'These have no master.
Let each of them return to his house in peace.' "
17Then the king of Israel said to Jehoshaphat, "Did I not tell you
that he would not prophesy good concerning me, but evil?"
18And Micaiah said, "Therefore, hear the word of the LORD. I
saw the LORD sitting on His throne, and all the host of heaven
standing on His right and on His left.
19"And the LORD said, 'Who will entice Ahab king of Israel to
go up and fall at Ramoth-gilead?' And one said this while another
said that.
20"Then a spirit came forward and stood before the LORD and
said, 'I will entice him.' And the LORD said to him, 'How?'
21"And he said, 'I will go and be a deceiving spirit in the mouth
of all his prophets.' Then He said, 'You are to entice *him* and
prevail also. Go and do so.'
22"Now therefore, behold, the LORD has put a deceiving spirit
in the mouth of these your prophets; for the LORD has proclaimed
disaster against you."
23¶ Then Zedekiah the son of Chenaanah came near and struck
Micaiah on the cheek and said, "How did the Spirit of the LORD
pass from me to speak to you?"
24And Micaiah said, "Behold, you shall see on that day, when
you enter an inner room to hide yourself."
25Then the king of Israel said, "Take Micaiah and return him to
Amon the governor of the city, and to Joash the king's son;
26and say, 'Thus says the king, "Put this *man* in prison, and feed
him sparingly with bread and water until I return safely." ' "
27And Micaiah said, "If you indeed return safely, the LORD has
not spoken by me." And he said, "Listen, all you people."

*Ahab's Defeat and Death*

28¶ So the king of Israel and Jehoshaphat king of Judah went up
against Ramoth-gilead.
29And the king of Israel said to Jehoshaphat, "I will disguise
myself and go into battle, but you put on your robes." So the king
of Israel disguised himself, and they went into battle.

## New International

8So the king of Israel called one of his officials and said, "Bring
Micaiah son of Imlah at once."
9Dressed in their royal robes, the king of Israel and Jehoshaphat
king of Judah were sitting on their thrones at the threshing floor
by the entrance to the gate of Samaria, with all the prophets
prophesying before them. 10Now Zedekiah son of Kenaanah had
made iron horns, and he declared, "This is what the LORD says:
'With these you will gore the Arameans until they are destroyed.' "
11All the other prophets were prophesying the same thing.
"Attack Ramoth Gilead and be victorious," they said, "for the
LORD will give it into the king's hand."
12The messenger who had gone to summon Micaiah said to
him, "Look, as one man the other prophets are predicting success
for the king. Let your word agree with theirs, and speak favorably."
13But Micaiah said, "As surely as the LORD lives, I can tell him
only what my God says."
14When he arrived, the king asked him, "Micaiah, shall we go
to war against Ramoth Gilead, or shall I refrain?"
"Attack and be victorious," he answered, "for they will be
given into your hand."
15The king said to him, "How many times must I make you
swear to tell me nothing but the truth in the name of the LORD?"
16Then Micaiah answered, "I saw all Israel scattered on the hills
like sheep without a shepherd, and the LORD said, 'These people
have no master. Let each one go home in peace.' "
17The king of Israel said to Jehoshaphat, "Didn't I tell you that
he never prophesies anything good about me, but only bad?"
18Micaiah continued, "Therefore hear the word of the LORD: I
saw the LORD sitting on his throne with all the host of heaven
standing on his right and on his left. 19And the LORD said, 'Who
will lure Ahab king of Israel into attacking Ramoth Gilead and
going to his death there?'
"One suggested this, and another that. 20Finally, a spirit came
forward, stood before the LORD and said, 'I will lure him.'
" 'By what means?' the LORD asked.
21" 'I will go and be a lying spirit in the mouths of all his
prophets,' he said.
" 'You will succeed in luring him,' said the LORD. 'Go and do
it.'
22"So now the LORD has put a lying spirit in the mouths of these
prophets of yours. The LORD has decreed disaster for you."
23Then Zedekiah son of Kenaanah went up and slapped Micaiah in the face. "Which way did the spirit from[a] the LORD go
when he went from me to speak to you?" he asked.
24Micaiah replied, "You will find out on the day you go to hide
in an inner room."
25The king of Israel then ordered, "Take Micaiah and send him
back to Amon the ruler of the city and to Joash the king's son,
26and say, 'This is what the king says: Put this fellow in prison and
give him nothing but bread and water until I return safely.' "
27Micaiah declared, "If you ever return safely, the LORD has not
spoken through me." Then he added, "Mark my words, all you
people!"

*Ahab Killed at Ramoth Gilead*

28So the king of Israel and Jehoshaphat king of Judah went up
to Ramoth Gilead. 29The king of Israel said to Jehoshaphat, "I will
enter the battle in disguise, but you wear your royal robes." So the
king of Israel disguised himself and went into battle.

NIV [a] 23 Or *Spirit of*

## King James

30 Now the king of Syria had commanded the captains of the chariots that *were* with him, saying, Fight ye not with small or great, save only with the king of Israel.

31 And it came to pass, when the captains of the chariots saw Jehoshaphat, that they said, It *is* the king of Israel. Therefore they compassed about him to fight: but Jehoshaphat cried out, and the LORD helped him; and God moved them *to depart* from him.

32 For it came to pass, that, when the captains of the chariots perceived that it was not the king of Israel, they turned back again from pursuing him.

33 And a *certain* man drew a bow at a venture, and smote the king of Israel between the joints of the harness: therefore he said to his chariot man, Turn thine hand, that thou mayest carry me out of the host; for I am wounded.

34 And the battle increased that day: howbeit the king of Israel stayed *himself* up in *his* chariot against the Syrians until the even: and about the time of the sun going down he died.

**19** AND JEHOSHAPHAT the king of Judah returned to his house in peace to Jerusalem.

2 And Jehu the son of Hanani the seer went out to meet him, and said to king Jehoshaphat, Shouldest thou help the ungodly, and love them that hate the LORD? therefore *is* wrath upon thee from before the LORD.

3 Nevertheless there are good things found in thee, in that thou hast taken away the groves out of the land, and hast prepared thine heart to seek God.

4 And Jehoshaphat dwelt at Jerusalem: and he went out again through the people from Beer-sheba to mount Ephraim, and brought them back unto the LORD God of their fathers.

5 ¶ And he set judges in the land throughout all the fenced cities of Judah, city by city,

6 And said to the judges, Take heed what ye do: for ye judge not for man, but for the LORD, who *is* with you in the judgment.

7 Wherefore now let the fear of the LORD be upon you; take heed and do *it:* for *there is* no iniquity with the LORD our God, nor respect of persons, nor taking of gifts.

8 ¶ Moreover in Jerusalem did Jehoshaphat set of the Levites, and *of* the priests, and of the chief of the fathers of Israel, for the judgment of the LORD, and for controversies, when they returned to Jerusalem.

9 And he charged them, saying, Thus shall ye do in the fear of the LORD, faithfully, and with a perfect heart.

10 And what cause soever shall come to you of your brethren that dwell in their cities, between blood and blood, between law and commandment, statutes and judgments, ye shall even warn them that they trespass not against the LORD, and *so* wrath come upon you, and upon your brethren: this do, and ye shall not trespass.

11 And, behold, Amariah the chief priest *is* over you in all matters of the LORD; and Zebadiah the son of Ishmael, the ruler of the house of Judah, for all the king's matters: also the Levites *shall be* officers before you. Deal courageously, and the LORD shall be with the good.

**20** IT CAME to pass after this also, *that* the children of Moab, and the children of Ammon, and with them *other* beside the Ammonites, came against Jehoshaphat to battle.

## Amplified

30 Now Syria's king had commanded his chariot captains, Fight not with small or great, but only with the king of Israel.

31 And when the captains of the chariots saw Jehoshaphat [of Judah], they said, It is the king of Israel. So they turned to fight against him; but Jehoshaphat cried out, and the Lord helped him; and God moved them to depart from him.

32 For when the captains of the chariots saw that it was not the king of Israel, they turned back from pursuing him.

33 A certain man drew his bow at a venture, and smote King [Ahab] of Israel between the lower armor and the breastplate; so Ahab said to his chariot driver, Turn, carry me out of the battle, for I am wounded.

34 And the battle increased that day; however King [Ahab] of Israel propped himself up in his chariot opposite the Syrians until evening, and about sunset he died.

**19** JEHOSHAPHAT THE king of Judah returned safely to his house in Jerusalem.

2 Jehu son of Hanani the seer went out to meet him, and said to Jehoshaphat, Should you help the ungodly, and love those who hate the Lord? Because of this, wrath has gone out against you from the Lord.

3 But there are good things found in you, for you have destroyed the Asheroth out of the land, and have set your heart to seek God [with all your soul's desire].

4 Jehoshaphat dwelt at Jerusalem; and he went out again among the people from Beer-sheba to the hill country of Ephraim, and brought them back to the Lord the God of their fathers.

5 He appointed judges throughout all the fortified cities of Judah, city by city,

6 And said to the judges, Be careful what you do, for you judge not for man, but for the Lord, and He is with you in the matter of judgment.

7 So now let the reverence *and* fear of the Lord be upon you; take heed what you do, for there is no injustice with the Lord our God, or partiality, or taking of bribes.

8 Also in Jerusalem Jehoshaphat set certain Levites, priests, and heads of families of Israel to give judgment for the Lord, and decide controversies. When they [of the commission] returned to Jerusalem,

9 The king charged them, Do this in the fear of the Lord, faithfully, with integrity *and* a blameless heart;

10 Whenever any controversy shall come to you from your brethren who dwell in their cities, between blood and blood, between law and commandment, statutes and judgments, you shall warn *and* instruct them that they may not be guilty before the Lord, and wrath come upon you and your brethren. Do this and you will not be guilty.

11 And behold, Amariah the chief priest is over you in all matters of the Lord; and Zebadiah son of Ishmael, the governor of the house of Judah, in all the king's matters; also the Levites will serve you as officers. Deal courageously (be strong and do), and the Lord be with the good!

**20** AFTER THIS the Moabites, the Ammonites, and with them the Meunites, came against Jehoshaphat to battle.

## New American Standard

30Now the king of Aram had commanded the captains of his
chariots, saying, "Do not fight with small or great, but with the
king of Israel alone."
31So it came about when the captains of the chariots saw Jehoshaphat, that they said, "It is the king of Israel," and they turned
aside to fight against him. But Jehoshaphat cried out, and the LORD
helped him, and God diverted them from him.
32Then it happened when the captains of the chariots saw that
it was not the king of Israel, that they turned back from pursuing
him.
33And a certain man drew his bow at random and struck the
king of Israel in a joint of the armor. So he said to the driver of the
chariot, "Turn around, and take me out of the fight; for I am
severely wounded."
34And the battle raged that day, and the king of Israel propped
himself up in his chariot in front of the Arameans until the evening; and at sunset he died.

*Jehu Rebukes Jehoshaphat*

**19** THEN JEHOSHAPHAT the king of Judah returned in
safety to his house in Jerusalem.
2And Jehu the son of Hanani the seer went out to meet him
and said to King Jehoshaphat, "Should you help the wicked and
love those who hate the LORD and so *bring* wrath on yourself from
the LORD?
3"But there is *some* good in you, for you have removed the
Asheroth from the land and you have set your heart to seek God."
4So Jehoshaphat lived in Jerusalem and went out again among
the people from Beersheba to the hill country of Ephraim and
brought them back to the LORD, the God of their fathers.

*Reforms Instituted*

5And he appointed judges in the land in all the fortified cities
of Judah, city by city.
6And he said to the judges, "Consider what you are doing, for
you do not judge for man but for the LORD who is with you when
you render judgment.
7"Now then let the fear of the LORD be upon you; be very
careful what you do, for the LORD our God will have no part in
unrighteousness, or partiality, or the taking of a bribe."
8¶ And in Jerusalem also Jehoshaphat appointed some of the
Levites and priests, and some of the heads of the fathers'
*households* of Israel, for the judgment of the LORD and to judge
disputes among the inhabitants of Jerusalem.
9Then he charged them saying, "Thus you shall do in the fear
of the LORD, faithfully and wholeheartedly.
10"And whenever any dispute comes to you from your brethren
who live in their cities, between blood and blood, between law and
commandment, statutes and ordinances, you shall warn them that
they may not be guilty before the LORD, and wrath may *not* come
on you and your brethren. Thus you shall do and you will not be
guilty.
11"And behold, Amariah the chief priest will be over you in all
that pertains to the LORD; and Zebadiah the son of Ishmael, the
ruler of the house of Judah, in all that pertains to the king. Also
the Levites shall be officers before you. Act resolutely, and the
LORD be with the upright."

*Judah Invaded*

**20** NOW IT came about after this that the sons of Moab and
the sons of Ammon, together with some of the Meunites,
came to make war against Jehoshaphat.

## New International

30Now the king of Aram had ordered his chariot commanders,
"Do not fight with anyone, small or great, except the king of
Israel." 31When the chariot commanders saw Jehoshaphat, they
thought, "This is the king of Israel." So they turned to attack him,
but Jehoshaphat cried out, and the LORD helped him. God drew
them away from him, 32for when the chariot commanders saw that
he was not the king of Israel, they stopped pursuing him.
33But someone drew his bow at random and hit the king of
Israel between the sections of his armor. The king told the chariot
driver, "Wheel around and get me out of the fighting. I've been
wounded." 34All day long the battle raged, and the king of Israel
propped himself up in his chariot facing the Arameans until evening. Then at sunset he died.

**19** WHEN JEHOSHAPHAT king of Judah returned safely to
his palace in Jerusalem, 2Jehu the seer, the son of Hanani,
went out to meet him and said to the king, "Should you help the
wicked and love[a] those who hate the LORD? Because of this, the
wrath of the LORD is upon you. 3There is, however, some good in
you, for you have rid the land of the Asherah poles and have set
your heart on seeking God."

*Jehoshaphat Appoints Judges*

4Jehoshaphat lived in Jerusalem, and he went out again among
the people from Beersheba to the hill country of Ephraim and
turned them back to the LORD, the God of their fathers. 5He appointed judges in the land, in each of the fortified cities of Judah.
6He told them, "Consider carefully what you do, because you are
not judging for man but for the LORD, who is with you whenever
you give a verdict. 7Now let the fear of the LORD be upon you.
Judge carefully, for with the LORD our God there is no injustice or
partiality or bribery."
8In Jerusalem also, Jehoshaphat appointed some of the Levites,
priests and heads of Israelite families to administer the law of the
LORD and to settle disputes. And they lived in Jerusalem. 9He gave
them these orders: "You must serve faithfully and wholeheartedly
in the fear of the LORD. 10In every case that comes before you from
your fellow countrymen who live in the cities—whether bloodshed
or other concerns of the law, commands, decrees or ordinances—
you are to warn them not to sin against the LORD; otherwise his
wrath will come on you and your brothers. Do this, and you will
not sin.
11"Amariah the chief priest will be over you in any matter
concerning the LORD, and Zebadiah son of Ishmael, the leader of
the tribe of Judah, will be over you in any matter concerning the
king, and the Levites will serve as officials before you. Act with
courage, and may the LORD be with those who do well."

*Jehoshaphat Defeats Moab and Ammon*

**20** AFTER THIS, the Moabites and Ammonites with some of
the Meunites[b] came to make war on Jehoshaphat.

**NIV** [a] 2 Or *and make alliances with* [b] *1* Some Septuagint manuscripts; Hebrew *Ammonites*

## King James

2 Then there came some that told Jehoshaphat, saying, There cometh a great multitude against thee from beyond the sea on this side Syria; and, behold, they *be* in Hazazon-tamar, which *is* En-gedi.

3 And Jehoshaphat feared, and set himself to seek the LORD, and proclaimed a fast throughout all Judah.

4 And Judah gathered themselves together, to ask *help* of the LORD: even out of all the cities of Judah they came to seek the LORD.

5 ¶ And Jehoshaphat stood in the congregation of Judah and Jerusalem, in the house of the LORD, before the new court,

6 And said, O LORD God of our fathers, *art* not thou God in heaven? and rulest *not* thou over all the kingdoms of the heathen? and in thine hand *is there not* power and might, so that none is able to withstand thee?

7 *Art* not thou our God, *who* didst drive out the inhabitants of this land before thy people Israel, and gavest it to the seed of Abraham thy friend for ever?

8 And they dwelt therein, and have built thee a sanctuary therein for thy name, saying,

9 If, *when* evil cometh upon us, *as* the sword, judgment, or pestilence, or famine, we stand before this house, and in thy presence, (for thy name *is* in this house,) and cry unto thee in our affliction, then thou wilt hear and help.

10 And now, behold, the children of Ammon and Moab and mount Seir, whom thou wouldest not let Israel invade, when they came out of the land of Egypt, but they turned from them, and destroyed them not;

11 Behold, *I say, how* they reward us, to come to cast us out of thy possession, which thou hast given us to inherit.

12 O our God, wilt thou not judge them? for we have no might against this great company that cometh against us; neither know we what to do: but our eyes *are* upon thee.

13 And all Judah stood before the LORD, with their little ones, their wives, and their children.

14 ¶ Then upon Jahaziel the son of Zechariah, the son of Benaiah, the son of Jeiel, the son of Mattaniah, a Levite of the sons of Asaph, came the spirit of the LORD in the midst of the congregation;

15 And he said, Hearken ye, all Judah, and ye inhabitants of Jerusalem, and thou king Jehoshaphat, Thus saith the LORD unto you, Be not afraid nor dismayed by reason of this great multitude; for the battle *is* not yours, but God's.

16 Tomorrow go ye down against them: behold, they come up by the cliff of Ziz; and ye shall find them at the end of the brook, before the wilderness of Jeruel.

17 Ye shall not *need* to fight in this *battle:* set yourselves, stand ye *still,* and see the salvation of the LORD with you, O Judah and Jerusalem: fear not, nor be dismayed; tomorrow go out against them: for the LORD *will be* with you.

18 And Jehoshaphat bowed his head with *his* face to the ground: and all Judah and the inhabitants of Jerusalem fell before the LORD, worshipping the LORD.

19 And the Levites, of the children of the Kohathites, and of the children of the Korhites, stood up to praise the LORD God of Israel with a loud voice on high.

20 ¶ And they rose early in the morning, and went forth into the wilderness of Tekoa: and as they went forth, Jehoshaphat stood and said, Hear me, O Judah, and ye inhabitants of Jerusalem; Believe in the LORD your God, so shall ye be established; believe his prophets, so shall ye prosper.

21 And when he had consulted with the people, he appointed singers unto the LORD, and that should praise the beauty of holiness, as they went out before the army, and to say, Praise the LORD; for his mercy *endureth* for ever.

## Amplified

2 It was told Jehoshaphat, A great multitude has come against you from beyond the [Dead] Sea from Edom; and behold they are in Hazazon-tamar, which is En-gedi.

3 Then Jehoshaphat feared, and set himself [determinedly, as his vital need] to seek the Lord; he proclaimed a fast in all Judah.

4 And Judah gathered together to ask help of the Lord; even out of all the cities of Judah they came to seek the Lord [yearning for Him with all their desire].

5 And Jehoshaphat stood in the assembly of Judah and Jerusalem, in the house of the Lord, before the new court,

6 And said, O Lord, God of our fathers, are You not God in Heaven? And do You not rule over all the kingdoms of the nations? In Your hand are power and might, so that none is able to withstand You.

7 Did not You, O our God, drive out the inhabitants of this land before Your people Israel, and give it for ever to the descendants of Abraham Your friend?

8 They dwelt in it, and have built You a sanctuary in it for Your name, saying,

9 If evil comes upon us, the sword of judgment, or pestilence, or famine, we will stand before this house and before You, for Your name [and the symbol of Your presence] is in this house, and cry to You in our affliction, and You will hear and save.

10 And now behold, the men of Ammon, Moab, and Mount Seir, whom You would not let Israel invade when they came from the land of Egypt, and whom they turned from and did not destroy—[Deut. 2:9.]

11 Behold, they reward us by coming to drive us out of Your possession, which You have given us to inherit.

12 O our God, will You not exercise judgment upon them? For we have no might to stand against this great company that is coming against us. We do not know what to do, but our eyes are upon You.

13 And all Judah stood before the Lord, with their children and their wives.

14 Then the Spirit of the Lord came upon Jahaziel son of Zechariah, son of Benaiah, son of Jeiel, son of Mattaniah, a Levite of the sons of Asaph, in the midst of the assembly.

15 He said, Hearken, all Judah, you inhabitants of Jerusalem and you King Jehoshaphat, the Lord says this to you: Be not afraid or dismayed at this great multitude; for the battle is not yours but God's.

16 Tomorrow go down to them; behold, they will come up by the ascent of Ziz; and you will find them at the end of the ravine before the wilderness of Jeruel.

17 You shall not need to fight in this battle; take your position, stand still, and see the deliverance of the Lord [Who is] with you, O Judah and Jerusalem. Fear not, nor be dismayed; tomorrow go out against them, for the Lord is with you.

18 And Jehoshaphat bowed his head with his face to the ground, and all Judah and the inhabitants of Jerusalem fell down before the Lord, worshiping Him.

19 And the Levites, of the Kohathites and Korahites, stood up to praise the Lord God of Israel with a very loud voice.

20 And they rose early in the morning and went out into the wilderness of Tekoa; and as they went out, Jehoshaphat stood and said, Hear me, O Judah, and you inhabitants of Jerusalem! Believe in the Lord your God, and you shall be established; believe *and* remain steadfast to His prophets, and you shall prosper.

21 When he had consulted with the people, he appointed singers to sing to the Lord and praise Him in their holy [priestly] garments, as they went out before the army, saying, Give thanks to the Lord, for His mercy *and* loving-kindness endure for ever!

## New American Standard

2Then some came and reported to Jehoshaphat, saying, "A great multitude is coming against you from beyond the sea, out of Aram and behold, they are in Hazazon-tamar (that is Engedi)."

3And Jehoshaphat was afraid and turned his attention to seek the LORD; and proclaimed a fast throughout all Judah.

4So Judah gathered together to seek help from the LORD; they even came from all the cities of Judah to seek the LORD.

5¶ Then Jehoshaphat stood in the assembly of Judah and Jerusalem, in the house of the LORD before the new court,

*Jehoshaphat's Prayer*

6and he said, "O LORD, the God of our fathers, art Thou not God in the heavens? And art Thou not ruler over all the kingdoms of the nations? Power and might are in Thy hand so that no one can stand against Thee.

7"Didst Thou not, O our God, drive out the inhabitants of this land before Thy people Israel, and give it to the descendants of Abraham Thy friend forever?

8"And they lived in it, and have built Thee a sanctuary there for Thy name, saying,

9'Should evil come upon us, the sword, *or* judgment, or pestilence, or famine, we will stand before this house and before Thee (for Thy name is in this house) and cry to Thee in our distress, and Thou wilt hear and deliver *us*.'

10"And now behold, the sons of Ammon and Moab and Mount Seir, whom Thou didst not let Israel invade when they came out of the land of Egypt (they turned aside from them and did not destroy them),

11behold *how* they are rewarding us, by coming to drive us out from Thy possession which Thou hast given us as an inheritance.

12"O our God, wilt Thou not judge them? For we are powerless before this great multitude who are coming against us; nor do we know what to do, but our eyes are on Thee."

13And all Judah was standing before the LORD, with their infants, their wives, and their children.

*Jahaziel Answers the Prayer*

14¶ Then in the midst of the assembly the Spirit of the LORD came upon Jahaziel the son of Zechariah, the son of Benaiah, the son of Jeiel, the son of Mattaniah, the Levite of the sons of Asaph;

15and he said, "Listen, all Judah and the inhabitants of Jerusalem and King Jehoshaphat: thus says the LORD to you, 'Do not fear or be dismayed because of this great multitude, for the battle is not yours but God's.

16'Tomorrow go down against them. Behold, they will come up by the ascent of Ziz, and you will find them at the end of the valley in front of the wilderness of Jeruel.

17'You *need* not fight in this *battle;* station yourselves, stand and see the salvation of the LORD on your behalf, O Judah and Jerusalem.' Do not fear or be dismayed; tomorrow go out to face them, for the LORD is with you."

18And Jehoshaphat bowed his head with *his* face to the ground, and all Judah and the inhabitants of Jerusalem fell down before the LORD, worshiping the LORD.

19And the Levites, from the sons of the Kohathites and of the sons of the Korahites, stood up to praise the LORD God of Israel, with a very loud voice.

*Enemies Destroy Themselves*

20¶ And they rose early in the morning and went out to the wilderness of Tekoa; and when they went out, Jehoshaphat stood and said, "Listen to me, O Judah and inhabitants of Jerusalem, put your trust in the LORD your God, and you will be established. Put your trust in His prophets and succeed."

21And when he had consulted with the people, he appointed those who sang to the LORD and those who praised *Him* in holy attire, as they went out before the army and said, "Give thanks to the LORD, for His lovingkindness is everlasting."

## New International

2Some men came and told Jehoshaphat, "A vast army is coming
against you from Edom,[a] from the other side of the Sea.[b] It is
already in Hazazon Tamar" (that is, En Gedi). 3Alarmed, Jehoshaphat resolved to inquire of the LORD, and he proclaimed a fast for
all Judah. 4The people of Judah came together to seek help from
the LORD; indeed, they came from every town in Judah to seek
him.
5Then Jehoshaphat stood up in the assembly of Judah and
Jerusalem at the temple of the LORD in the front of the new courtyard 6and said:

"O LORD, God of our fathers, are you not the God who is
in heaven? You rule over all the kingdoms of the nations.
Power and might are in your hand, and no one can withstand
you. 7O our God, did you not drive out the inhabitants of this
land before your people Israel and give it forever to the descendants of Abraham your friend? 8They have lived in it and
have built in it a sanctuary for your Name, saying, 9'If calamity comes upon us, whether the sword of judgment, or plague
or famine, we will stand in your presence before this temple
that bears your Name and will cry out to you in our distress,
and you will hear us and save us.'
10"But now here are men from Ammon, Moab and Mount
Seir, whose territory you would not allow Israel to invade
when they came from Egypt; so they turned away from them
and did not destroy them. 11See how they are repaying us by
coming to drive us out of the possession you gave us as an
inheritance. 12O our God, will you not judge them? For we
have no power to face this vast army that is attacking us. We
do not know what to do, but our eyes are upon you."

13All the men of Judah, with their wives and children and little
ones, stood there before the LORD.
14Then the Spirit of the LORD came upon Jahaziel son of Zechariah, the son of Benaiah, the son of Jeiel, the son of Mattaniah, a
Levite and descendant of Asaph, as he stood in the assembly.
15He said: "Listen, King Jehoshaphat and all who live in Judah
and Jerusalem! This is what the LORD says to you: 'Do not be afraid
or discouraged because of this vast army. For the battle is not
yours, but God's. 16Tomorrow march down against them. They
will be climbing up by the Pass of Ziz, and you will find them at
the end of the gorge in the Desert of Jeruel. 17You will not have
to fight this battle. Take up your positions; stand firm and see the
deliverance the LORD will give you, O Judah and Jerusalem. Do not
be afraid; do not be discouraged. Go out to face them tomorrow,
and the LORD will be with you.' "
18Jehoshaphat bowed with his face to the ground, and all the
people of Judah and Jerusalem fell down in worship before the
LORD. 19Then some Levites from the Kohathites and Korahites
stood up and praised the LORD, the God of Israel, with very loud
voice.
20Early in the morning they left for the Desert of Tekoa. As they
set out, Jehoshaphat stood and said, "Listen to me, Judah and
people of Jerusalem! Have faith in the LORD your God and you will
be upheld; have faith in his prophets and you will be successful."
21After consulting the people, Jehoshaphat appointed men to sing
to the LORD and to praise him for the splendor of his[c] holiness as
they went out at the head of the army, saying:

"Give thanks to the LORD,
for his love endures forever."

**NIV** [a] 2 One Hebrew manuscript; most Hebrew manuscripts, Septuagint and Vulgate *Aram* [b] 2 That is, the Dead Sea [c] 21 Or *him with the splendor of*

## King James

22¶ And when they began to sing and to praise, the LORD set ambushments against the children of Ammon, Moab, and mount Seir, which were come against Judah; and they were smitten.

23For the children of Ammon and Moab stood up against the inhabitants of mount Seir, utterly to slay and destroy *them:* and when they had made an end of the inhabitants of Seir, every one helped to destroy another.

24And when Judah came toward the watchtower in the wilderness, they looked unto the multitude, and, behold, they *were* dead bodies fallen to the earth, and none escaped.

25And when Jehoshaphat and his people came to take away the spoil of them, they found among them in abundance both riches with the dead bodies, and precious jewels, which they stripped off for themselves, more than they could carry away: and they were three days in gathering of the spoil, it was so much.

26¶ And on the fourth day they assembled themselves in the valley of Berachah; for there they blessed the LORD: therefore the name of the same place was called, The valley of Berachah, unto this day.

27Then they returned, every man of Judah and Jerusalem, and Jehoshaphat in the forefront of them, to go again to Jerusalem with joy; for the LORD had made them to rejoice over their enemies.

28And they came to Jerusalem with psalteries and harps and trumpets unto the house of the LORD.

29And the fear of God was on all the kingdoms of *those* countries, when they had heard that the LORD fought against the enemies of Israel.

30So the realm of Jehoshaphat was quiet: for his God gave him rest round about.

31¶ And Jehoshaphat reigned over Judah: *he was* thirty and five years old when he began to reign, and he reigned twenty and five years in Jerusalem. And his mother's name *was* Azubah the daughter of Shilhi.

32And he walked in the way of Asa his father, and departed not from it, doing *that which was* right in the sight of the LORD.

33Howbeit the high places were not taken away: for as yet the people had not prepared their hearts unto the God of their fathers.

34Now the rest of the acts of Jehoshaphat, first and last, behold, they *are* written in the book of Jehu the son of Hanani, who *is* mentioned in the book of the kings of Israel.

35¶ And after this did Jehoshaphat king of Judah join himself with Ahaziah king of Israel, who did very wickedly:

36And he joined himself with him to make ships to go to Tarshish: and they made the ships in Ezion-geber.

37Then Eliezer the son of Dodavah of Mareshah prophesied against Jehoshaphat, saying, Because thou hast joined thyself with Ahaziah, the LORD hath broken thy works. And the ships were broken, that they were not able to go to Tarshish.

**21** NOW JEHOSHAPHAT slept with his fathers, and was buried with his fathers in the city of David. And Jehoram his son reigned in his stead.

2And he had brethren the sons of Jehoshaphat, Azariah, and Jehiel, and Zechariah, and Azariah, and Michael, and Shephatiah: all these *were* the sons of Jehoshaphat king of Israel.

3And their father gave them great gifts of silver, and of gold, and of precious things, with fenced cities in Judah: but the kingdom gave he to Jehoram; because he *was* the firstborn.

## Amplified

22And when they began to sing and to praise, the Lord set ambushments against the men of Ammon, Moab, and Mount Seir, who had come against Judah, and they were [self-] slaughtered;

23For [suspecting betrayal] the men of Ammon and Moab rose against those of Mount Seir, utterly destroying them. And when they had made an end of the men of Seir, they all helped to destroy one another.

24And when Judah came to the watchtower of the wilderness, they looked at the multitude, and behold, they were dead bodies fallen to the earth, and none had escaped!

25When Jehoshaphat and his people came to take the spoil, they found among them much cattle, goods, garments, and precious things, which they took for themselves, more than they could carry away, so much they were three days in gathering the spoil.

26On the fourth day they assembled in the Valley of Beracah. There they blessed the Lord; so the name of the place is still called the Valley of Beracah [blessing].

27Then they returned, every man of Judah and Jerusalem, Jehoshaphat leading them, to Jerusalem with joy; for the Lord had made them to rejoice over their enemies.

28They came to Jerusalem with harps, lyres, and trumpets to the house of the Lord.

29And the fear of God came upon all the kingdoms of those countries, when they heard that the Lord had fought against the enemies of Israel.

30So the realm of Jehoshaphat was quiet, for his God gave him rest round about.

31Thus Jehoshaphat reigned over Judah. He was thirty-five years old when he began his twenty-five year reign in Jerusalem. His mother was Azubah daughter of Shilhi.

32And he walked in the way of Asa his father, and departed not from it, doing what was right in the sight of the Lord.

33But the high places [of idolatry] were not taken away, for the people had not yet set their hearts on their fathers' God.

34Now the rest of the acts of Jehoshaphat, from first to last, they are written in the records of Jehu the son of Hanani, which are in the Book of the Kings of Israel.

35After this Jehoshaphat king of Judah joined with Ahaziah king of Israel, who did very wickedly.

36He joined him in building ships to go to Tarshish, building them in Ezion-geber.

37Then Eliezer son of Dodavahu of Mareshah prophesied against Jehoshaphat, saying, Because you have joined Ahaziah, the Lord will destroy your works. So the ships were wrecked and unable to go to Tarshish.

**21** JEHOSHAPHAT SLEPT with his fathers, and was buried with [them] in the city of David. Jehoram his son reigned in his stead.

2He had brothers: Azariah, Jehiel, Zechariah, Azariah, Michael, and Shephatiah, all the sons of Jehoshaphat king of Israel.

3Their father gave them great gifts of silver, gold, and precious things, together with fortified cities in Judah; but the kingdom he gave to Jehoram, the first-born.

## New American Standard

22 And when they began singing and praising, the LORD set ambushes against the sons of Ammon, Moab, and Mount Seir, who had come against Judah; so they were routed.

23 For the sons of Ammon and Moab rose up against the inhabitants of Mount Seir destroying *them* completely, and when they had finished with the inhabitants of Seir, they helped to destroy one another.

24¶ When Judah came to the lookout of the wilderness, they looked toward the multitude; and behold, they *were* corpses lying on the ground, and no one had escaped.

25 And when Jehoshaphat and his people came to take their spoil, they found much among them, *including* goods, garments, and valuable things which they took for themselves, more than they could carry. And they were three days taking the spoil because there was so much.

*Triumphant Return to Jerusalem*

26 Then on the fourth day they assembled in the valley of Beracah, for there they blessed the LORD. Therefore they have named that place "The Valley of [a]Beracah" until today.

27 And every man of Judah and Jerusalem returned with Jehoshaphat at their head, returning to Jerusalem with joy, for the LORD had made them to rejoice over their enemies.

28 And they came to Jerusalem with harps, lyres, and trumpets to the house of the LORD.

29 And the dread of God was on all the kingdoms of the lands when they heard that the LORD had fought against the enemies of Israel.

30 So the kingdom of Jehoshaphat was at peace, for his God gave him rest on all sides.

31¶ Now Jehoshaphat reigned over Judah. He *was* thirty-five years old when he became king, and he reigned in Jerusalem twenty-five years. And his mother's name *was* Azubah the daughter of Shilhi.

32 And he walked in the way of his father Asa and did not depart from it, doing right in the sight of the LORD.

33 The high places, however, were not removed; the people had not yet directed their hearts to the God of their fathers.

34 Now the rest of the acts of Jehoshaphat, first to last, behold, they are written in the annals of Jehu the son of Hanani, which is recorded in the Book of the Kings of Israel.

*Alliance Displeases God*

35¶ And after this Jehoshaphat king of Judah allied himself with Ahaziah king of Israel. He acted wickedly in so doing.

36 So he allied himself with him to make ships to go to Tarshish, and they made the ships in Ezion-geber.

37 Then Eliezer the son of Dodavahu of Mareshah prophesied against Jehoshaphat saying, "Because you have allied yourself with Ahaziah, the LORD has destroyed your works." So the ships were broken and could not go to Tarshish.

*Jehoram Succeeds Jehoshaphat in Judah*

**21** THEN JEHOSHAPHAT slept with his fathers and was buried with his fathers in the city of David, and Jehoram his son became king in his place.

2 And he had brothers, the sons of Jehoshaphat: Azariah, Jehiel, Zechariah, Azaryahu, Michael, and Shephatiah. All these *were* the sons of Jehoshaphat king of Israel.

3 And their father gave them many gifts of silver, gold and precious things, with fortified cities in Judah, but he gave the kingdom to Jehoram because he was the first-born.

NAS [a] I.e., blessing

## New International

22 As they began to sing and praise, the LORD set ambushes against the men of Ammon and Moab and Mount Seir who were invading Judah, and they were defeated. 23 The men of Ammon and Moab rose up against the men from Mount Seir to destroy and annihilate them. After they finished slaughtering the men from Seir, they helped to destroy one another.

24 When the men of Judah came to the place that overlooks the desert and looked toward the vast army, they saw only dead bodies lying on the ground; no one had escaped. 25 So Jehoshaphat and his men went to carry off their plunder, and they found among them a great amount of equipment and clothing[b] and also articles of value—more than they could take away. There was so much plunder that it took three days to collect it. 26 On the fourth day they assembled in the Valley of Beracah, where they praised the LORD. This is why it is called the Valley of Beracah[c] to this day.

27 Then, led by Jehoshaphat, all the men of Judah and Jerusalem returned joyfully to Jerusalem, for the LORD had given them cause to rejoice over their enemies. 28 They entered Jerusalem and went to the temple of the LORD with harps and lutes and trumpets.

29 The fear of God came upon all the kingdoms of the countries when they heard how the LORD had fought against the enemies of Israel. 30 And the kingdom of Jehoshaphat was at peace, for his God had given him rest on every side.

*The End of Jehoshaphat's Reign*

31 So Jehoshaphat reigned over Judah. He was thirty-five years old when he became king of Judah, and he reigned in Jerusalem twenty-five years. His mother's name was Azubah daughter of Shilhi. 32 He walked in the ways of his father Asa and did not stray from them; he did what was right in the eyes of the LORD. 33 The high places, however, were not removed, and the people still had not set their hearts on the God of their fathers.

34 The other events of Jehoshaphat's reign, from beginning to end, are written in the annals of Jehu son of Hanani, which are recorded in the book of the kings of Israel.

35 Later, Jehoshaphat king of Judah made an alliance with Ahaziah king of Israel, who was guilty of wickedness. 36 He agreed with him to construct a fleet of trading ships.[d] After these were built at Ezion Geber, 37 Eliezer son of Dodavahu of Mareshah prophesied against Jehoshaphat, saying, "Because you have made an alliance with Ahaziah, the LORD will destroy what you have made." The ships were wrecked and were not able to set sail to trade.[e]

**21** THEN JEHOSHAPHAT rested with his fathers and was buried with them in the City of David. And Jehoram his son succeeded him as king. 2 Jehoram's brothers, the sons of Jehoshaphat, were Azariah, Jehiel, Zechariah, Azariahu, Michael and Shephatiah. All these were sons of Jehoshaphat king of Israel.[f] 3 Their father had given them many gifts of silver and gold and articles of value, as well as fortified cities in Judah, but he had given the kingdom to Jehoram because he was his firstborn son.

**NIV** [b] 25 Some Hebrew manuscripts and Vulgate; most Hebrew manuscripts *corpses* [c] 26 *Beracah* means *praise.* [d] 36 Hebrew *of ships that could go to Tarshish* [e] 37 Hebrew *sail for Tarshish* [f] 2 That is, Judah, as frequently in 2 Chronicles

## King James

4Now when Jehoram was risen up to the kingdom of his father,
he strengthened himself, and slew all his brethren with the sword,
and *divers* also of the princes of Israel.
5¶ Jehoram *was* thirty and two years old when he began to reign,
and he reigned eight years in Jerusalem.
6And he walked in the way of the kings of Israel, like as did the
house of Ahab: for he had the daughter of Ahab to wife: and he
wrought *that which was* evil in the eyes of the LORD.
7Howbeit the LORD would not destroy the house of David,
because of the covenant that he had made with David, and as he
promised to give a light to him and to his sons for ever.
8¶ In his days the Edomites revolted from under the dominion
of Judah, and made themselves a king.
9Then Jehoram went forth with his princes, and all his chariots
with him: and he rose up by night, and smote the Edomites which
compassed him in, and the captains of the chariots.
10So the Edomites revolted from under the hand of Judah unto
this day. The same time *also* did Libnah revolt from under his
hand; because he had forsaken the LORD God of his fathers.
11Moreover he made high places in the mountains of Judah, and
caused the inhabitants of Jerusalem to commit fornication, and
compelled Judah *thereto*.
12¶ And there came a writing to him from Elijah the prophet,
saying, Thus saith the LORD God of David thy father, Because thou
hast not walked in the ways of Jehoshaphat thy father, nor in the
ways of Asa king of Judah,
13But hast walked in the way of the kings of Israel, and hast
made Judah and the inhabitants of Jerusalem to go a-whoring, like
to the whoredoms of the house of Ahab, and also hast slain thy
brethren of thy father's house, *which were* better than thyself:
14Behold, with a great plague will the LORD smite thy people,
and thy children, and thy wives, and all thy goods:
15And thou *shalt have* great sickness by disease of thy bowels,
until thy bowels fall out by reason of the sickness day by day.
16¶ Moreover the LORD stirred up against Jehoram the spirit of
the Philistines, and of the Arabians, that *were* near the Ethiopians:
17And they came up into Judah, and brake into it, and carried
away all the substance that was found in the king's house, and his
sons also, and his wives; so that there was never a son left him,
save Jehoahaz, the youngest of his sons.
18¶ And after all this the LORD smote him in his bowels with an
incurable disease.
19And it came to pass, that in process of time, after the end of
two years, his bowels fell out by reason of his sickness: so he died
of sore diseases. And his people made no burning for him, like the
burning of his fathers.
20Thirty and two years old was he when he began to reign, and
he reigned in Jerusalem eight years, and departed without being
desired. Howbeit they buried him in the city of David, but not in
the sepulchres of the kings.

**22** AND THE inhabitants of Jerusalem made Ahaziah his
youngest son king in his stead: for the band of men that
came with the Arabians to the camp had slain all the eldest. So
Ahaziah the son of Jehoram king of Judah reigned.
2Forty and two years old *was* Ahaziah when he began to reign,
and he reigned one year in Jerusalem. His mother's name also *was*
Athaliah the daughter of Omri.
3He also walked in the ways of the house of Ahab: for his
mother was his counsellor to do wickedly.

## Amplified

4When Jehoram had ascended to the kingship of his father, he
strengthened himself, and slew all his brethren with the sword,
and also some of Israel's princes.
5Jehoram at thirty-two years of age began his eight year reign
in Jerusalem.
6He walked in the way of the kings of Israel, as did the house
of Ahab; for he married the daughter of Ahab, and did what was
evil in the eyes of the Lord.
7But the Lord would not destroy the house of David, because
He had made a covenant with David and promised to give a light
to him and to his sons for ever.
8In Jehoram's days the Edomites revolted from the rule of
Judah, and set up for themselves a king.
9Then Jehoram passed over [the Jordan] with his captains and
all his chariots, and rose up by night and smote the Edomites who
had surrounded him and his chariot captains.
10So Edom revolted from the rule of Judah to this day. Then
Libnah also revolted from Jehoram's rule, because he had forsaken
the Lord, the God of his fathers.
11Moreover he made idolatrous high places in the hill country
of Judah, and debauched spiritually the inhabitants of Jerusalem,
and led Judah astray [compelling the people's cooperation].
12And there came a letter to Jehoram from Elijah the prophet,
saying, Thus says the Lord God of David your father [forefather],
Because you have not walked in the ways of Jehoshaphat your
father, nor in the ways of Asa king of Judah,
13But have walked in the way of Israel's kings, and made Judah
and the inhabitants of Jerusalem play the harlot like the [spiritual]
harlotry of Ahab's house, and also have slain your brothers of your
father's house, who were better than you,
14Behold, the Lord will smite your people, and your children,
your wives, and all your possessions with a great plague.
15And you yourself shall have a severe illness because of an
intestinal disease, until your bowels fall out because of the sickness, day after day.
16And the Lord stirred up against Jehoram the anger of the
Philistines and of the Arabs who were near the Ethiopians.
17They came against Judah, invaded it, and carried away all the
possessions found in *and* around the king's house, also his sons
and his wives; so there was not a son left him except Jehoahaz, the
youngest.
18And after all this the Lord smote [Jehoram] with an incurable
intestinal disease.
19In process of time, after two years, his bowels fell out because
of his disease. So he died in severe distress. And his people made
no funeral fire to honor him, like the fires for his fathers.
20Thirty-two years old was Jehoram when he began to reign,
and he reigned in Jerusalem eight years, and departed without
being wanted. Yet they buried him in the city of David, but not in
the tombs of the kings.

**22** THE PEOPLE of Jerusalem made Ahaziah his youngest
son king in his stead; for the troop that came with the
Arabs to the camp had slain all the older sons. So Ahaziah son of
Jehoram king of Judah reigned.
2Forty-two years old was Ahaziah when he began his one year
reign in Jerusalem. His mother was Athaliah granddaughter of
Omri.
3He also walked in the ways of the house of Ahab, for his
mother was his counselor to do wickedly.

## New American Standard

4¶ Now when Jehoram had taken over the kingdom of his father and made himself secure, he killed all his brothers with the sword, and some of the rulers of Israel also.

5 Jehoram *was* thirty-two years old when he became king, and he reigned eight years in Jerusalem.

6 And he walked in the way of the kings of Israel, just as the house of Ahab did (for Ahab's daughter was his wife), and he did evil in the sight of the LORD.

7 Yet the LORD was not willing to destroy the house of David because of the covenant which He had made with David, and since He had promised to give a lamp to him and his sons forever.

*Revolt against Judah*

8¶ In his days Edom revolted [a]against the rule of Judah, and set up a king over themselves.

9 Then Jehoram crossed over with his commanders and all his chariots with him. And it came about that he arose by night and struck down the Edomites who were surrounding him and the commanders of the chariots.

10 So Edom revolted [b]against Judah to this day. Then Libnah revolted at the same time against his rule, because he had forsaken the LORD God of his fathers.

11 Moreover, he made high places in the mountains of Judah, and caused the inhabitants of Jerusalem to play the harlot and led Judah astray.

12 Then a letter came to him from Elijah the prophet saying, "Thus says the LORD God of your father David, 'Because you have not walked in the ways of Jehoshaphat your father and the ways of Asa king of Judah,

13 but have walked in the way of the kings of Israel, and have caused Judah and the inhabitants of Jerusalem to play the harlot as the house of Ahab played the harlot, and you have also killed your brothers, your own family, who were better than you,

14 behold, the LORD is going to strike your people, your sons, your wives, and all your possessions with a great calamity;

15 and you will suffer severe sickness, a disease of your bowels, until your bowels come out because of the sickness, day by day.' "

16¶ Then the LORD stirred up against Jehoram the spirit of the Philistines and the Arabs who bordered the Ethiopians;

17 and they came against Judah and invaded it, and carried away all the possessions found in the king's house together with his sons and his wives, so that no son was left to him except Jehoahaz, the youngest of his sons.

18 So after all this the LORD smote him in his bowels with an incurable sickness.

19 Now it came about in the course of time, at the end of two years, that his bowels came out because of his sickness and he died in great pain. And his people made no fire for him like the fire for his fathers.

20 He was thirty-two years old when he became king, and he reigned in Jerusalem eight years; and he departed with no one's regret, and they buried him in the city of David, but not in the tombs of the kings.

*Ahaziah Succeeds Jehoram in Judah*

**22** THEN THE inhabitants of Jerusalem made Ahaziah, his youngest son, king in his place, for the band of men who came with the Arabs to the camp had slain all the older *sons*. So Ahaziah the son of Jehoram king of Judah began to reign.

2 Ahaziah *was* twenty-two years old when he became king, and he reigned one year in Jerusalem. And his mother's name was Athaliah, the granddaughter of Omri.

3 He also walked in the ways of the house of Ahab, for his mother was his counselor to do wickedly.

NAS [a] Lit., *from under the hand of* [b] Lit., *from under the hand of*

## New International

*Jehoram King of Judah*

4 When Jehoram established himself firmly over his father's
kingdom, he put all his brothers to the sword along with some of
the princes of Israel. 5 Jehoram was thirty-two years old when he
became king, and he reigned in Jerusalem eight years. 6 He walked
in the ways of the kings of Israel, as the house of Ahab had done,
for he married a daughter of Ahab. He did evil in the eyes of the
LORD. 7 Nevertheless, because of the covenant the LORD had made
with David, the LORD was not willing to destroy the house of
David. He had promised to maintain a lamp for him and his
descendants forever.

8 In the time of Jehoram, Edom rebelled against Judah and set
up its own king. 9 So Jehoram went there with his officers and all
his chariots. The Edomites surrounded him and his chariot commanders, but he rose up and broke through by night. 10 To this day
Edom has been in rebellion against Judah.

Libnah revolted at the same time, because Jehoram had forsak-
en the LORD, the God of his fathers. 11 He had also built high places
on the hills of Judah and had caused the people of Jerusalem to
prostitute themselves and had led Judah astray.

12 Jehoram received a letter from Elijah the prophet, which said:
"This is what the LORD, the God of your father David, says:
'You have not walked in the ways of your father Jehoshaphat
or of Asa king of Judah. 13 But you have walked in the ways
of the kings of Israel, and you have led Judah and the people
of Jerusalem to prostitute themselves, just as the house of
Ahab did. You have also murdered your own brothers, members of your father's house, men who were better than you.
14 So now the LORD is about to strike your people, your sons,
your wives and everything that is yours, with a heavy blow.
15 You yourself will be very ill with a lingering disease of the
bowels, until the disease causes your bowels to come out.' "

16 The LORD aroused against Jehoram the hostility of the Philistines and of the Arabs who lived near the Cushites. 17 They attacked Judah, invaded it and carried off all the goods found in the
king's palace, together with his sons and wives. Not a son was left
to him except Ahaziah,[c] the youngest.

18 After all this, the LORD afflicted Jehoram with an incurable
disease of the bowels. 19 In the course of time, at the end of the
second year, his bowels came out because of the disease, and he
died in great pain. His people made no fire in his honor, as they
had for his fathers.

20 Jehoram was thirty-two years old when he became king, and
he reigned in Jerusalem eight years. He passed away, to no one's
regret, and was buried in the City of David, but not in the tombs
of the kings.

*Ahaziah King of Judah*

**22** THE PEOPLE of Jerusalem made Ahaziah, Jehoram's
youngest son, king in his place, since the raiders, who
came with the Arabs into the camp, had killed all the older sons.
So Ahaziah son of Jehoram king of Judah began to reign.
2 Ahaziah was twenty-two[d] years old when he became king,
and he reigned in Jerusalem one year. His mother's name was
Athaliah, a granddaughter of Omri.
3 He too walked in the ways of the house of Ahab, for his mother
encouraged him in doing wrong. 4 He did evil in the eyes of the

NIV [c] 17 Hebrew *Jehoahaz,* a variant of *Ahaziah* [d] 2 Some Septuagint manuscripts and Syriac (see also 2 Kings 8:26); Hebrew *forty-two*

## King James

4 Wherefore he did evil in the sight of the LORD like the house of Ahab: for they were his counsellors after the death of his father to his destruction.

5 ¶ He walked also after their counsel, and went with Jehoram the son of Ahab king of Israel to war against Hazael king of Syria at Ramoth-gilead: and the Syrians smote Joram.

6 And he returned to be healed in Jezreel because of the wounds which were given him at Ramah, when he fought with Hazael king of Syria. And Azariah the son of Jehoram king of Judah went down to see Jehoram the son of Ahab at Jezreel, because he was sick.

7 And the destruction of Ahaziah was of God by coming to Joram: for when he was come, he went out with Jehoram against Jehu the son of Nimshi, whom the LORD had anointed to cut off the house of Ahab.

8 And it came to pass, that, when Jehu was executing judgment upon the house of Ahab, and found the princes of Judah, and the sons of the brethren of Ahaziah, that ministered to Ahaziah, he slew them.

9 And he sought Ahaziah: and they caught him, (for he was hid in Samaria,) and brought him to Jehu: and when they had slain him, they buried him: Because, said they, he *is* the son of Jehoshaphat, who sought the LORD with all his heart. So the house of Ahaziah had no power to keep still the kingdom.

10 ¶ But when Athaliah the mother of Ahaziah saw that her son was dead, she arose and destroyed all the seed royal of the house of Judah.

11 But Jehoshabeath, the daughter of the king, took Joash the son of Ahaziah, and stole him from among the king's sons that were slain, and put him and his nurse in a bedchamber. So Jehoshabeath, the daughter of king Jehoram, the wife of Jehoiada the priest, (for she was the sister of Ahaziah,) hid him from Athaliah, so that she slew him not.

12 And he was with them hid in the house of God six years: and Athaliah reigned over the land.

**23** AND IN the seventh year Jehoiada strengthened himself, and took the captains of hundreds, Azariah the son of Jeroham, and Ishmael the son of Jehohanan, and Azariah the son of Obed, and Maaseiah the son of Adaiah, and Elishaphat the son of Zichri, into covenant with him.

2 And they went about in Judah, and gathered the Levites out of all the cities of Judah, and the chief of the fathers of Israel, and they came to Jerusalem.

3 And all the congregation made a covenant with the king in the house of God. And he said unto them, Behold, the king's son shall reign, as the LORD hath said of the sons of David.

4 This *is* the thing that ye shall do; A third part of you entering on the sabbath, of the priests and of the Levites, *shall be* porters of the doors;

5 And a third part *shall be* at the king's house; and a third part at the gate of the foundation: and all the people *shall be* in the courts of the house of the LORD.

6 But let none come into the house of the LORD, save the priests, and they that minister of the Levites; they shall go in, for they *are* holy: but all the people shall keep the watch of the LORD.

7 And the Levites shall compass the king round about, every man with his weapons in his hand; and whosoever *else* cometh into the house, he shall be put to death: but be ye with the king when he cometh in, and when he goeth out.

## Amplified

4 So he did evil in the sight of the Lord like the house of Ahab; for they were his counselors after his father's death, to his destruction.

5 He followed their counsel and even went with Jehoram son of Ahab king of Israel to war against Hazael king of Syria at Ramoth-gilead; and the Syrians wounded Je[ho]ram,

6 And he returned to be healed in Jezreel of the wounds given him at Ramah, when he fought against Hazael king of Syria. Azariah son of Jehoram king of Judah went down to see Je[ho]ram son of Ahab in Jezreel, because he was sick.

7 But the destruction of Ahaziah was ordained of God in his coming to visit J[eh]oram. For when he got there he went out with Jehoram against Jehu son of Nimshi, whom the Lord had anointed to destroy the house of Ahab.

8 And when Jehu was executing judgment upon the house of Ahab, he met the princes of Judah and the sons of Ahaziah's slain brothers, who attended Ahaziah, and he slew them.

9 And [Jehu] sought Ahaziah, who was hidden in Samaria; he was captured, brought to Jehu, and slain. They buried him, for they said, After all, he is the grandson of Jehoshaphat, who sought the Lord with all his heart. So the house of Ahaziah had no one left able to rule the kingdom.

10 But when Athaliah mother of Ahaziah saw that her son was dead, she arose and destroyed all the royal family of Judah.

11 But Jehosheba, daughter of the king, took Joash the [infant] son of Ahaziah, and stole him away from among the king's sons who were to be slain, and she put him and his nurse in a bedchamber. So Jehosheba daughter of King Jehoram, sister of Ahaziah, and wife of Jehoiada the priest, hid [Joash] from [his grandmother] Athaliah, so that she did not slay him.

12 And Joash was with them hidden in the house of God six years, and Athaliah reigned over the land.

**23** IN THE seventh year Jehoiada [the priest] took strength *and* courage and made a covenant with the captains of hundreds, Azariah son of Jeroham, Ishmael son of Jeho-hanan, Azariah son of Obed, Ma-aseiah son of Adaiah, and Elishaphat son of Zichri.

2 And they went about in Judah, and gathered the Levites out of all the cities, and the chief of the fathers' houses of Israel, and they came to Jerusalem.

3 And all the assembly made a covenant in the house of God with the king [little Joash, to suddenly proclaim his sovereignty and overthrow Athaliah's tyranny]. And Jehoiada the priest said to them, Behold, the king's son shall reign, as the Lord has said of the offspring of David.

4 This is what you shall do: a third of you priests, and Levites, resuming service on the sabbath, shall be doorkeepers;

5 A [second] third shall be at the king's house, and [the final] third at the Foundation Gate; and all the people shall be in the courts [only] of the house of the Lord.

6 But let none come into the [main] house of the Lord, except the priests, and those of the Levites who minister; they may go in, for they are holy, but let all the rest of the people carefully observe the law against entering the holy place of the Lord.

7 And the Levites shall surround the young king, every man with his weapons in his hand; and whoever comes into the house [break through the ranks of the guard to get near Joash] shall be put to death; but you be with the king when he comes in [from the temple chamber where he is hiding] and when he goes out.

## New American Standard

4And he did evil in the sight of the LORD like the house of
Ahab, for they were his counselors after the death of his father, to
his destruction.

*Ahaziah Allies with Jehoram of Israel*

5He also walked according to their counsel, and went with
Jehoram the son of Ahab king of Israel to wage war against Hazael
king of Aram at Ramoth-gilead. But the Arameans wounded
Joram.

6So he returned to be healed in Jezreel of the wounds which
they had inflicted on him at Ramah, when he fought against Hazael king of Aram. And Ahaziah, the son of Jehoram king of Judah,
went down to see Jehoram the son of Ahab in Jezreel, because he
was sick.

7¶ Now the destruction of Ahaziah was from God, in that he
went to Joram. For when he came, he went out with Jehoram
against Jehu the son of Nimshi, whom the LORD had anointed to
cut off the house of Ahab.

*Jehu Murders Princes of Judah*

8And it came about when Jehu was executing judgment on the
house of Ahab, he found the princes of Judah and the sons of
Ahaziah's brothers, ministering to Ahaziah, and slew them.

9He also sought Ahaziah, and they caught him while he was
hiding in Samaria; they brought him to Jehu, put him to death, and
buried him. For they said, "He is the son of Jehoshaphat, who
sought the LORD with all his heart." So there was no one of the
house of Ahaziah to retain the power of the kingdom.

10¶ Now when Athaliah the mother of Ahaziah saw that her son
was dead, she rose and destroyed all the royal offspring of the
house of Judah.

11But Jehoshabeath the king's daughter took Joash the son of
Ahaziah, and stole him from among the king's sons who were
being put to death, and placed him and his nurse in the bedroom.
So Jehoshabeath, the daughter of King Jehoram, the wife of Jehoi-
ada the priest (for she was the sister of Ahaziah), hid him from
Athaliah so that she would not put him to death.

12And he was hidden with them in the house of God six years
while Athaliah reigned over the land.

*Jehoiada Sets Joash on the Throne of Judah*

**23** NOW IN the seventh year Jehoiada strengthened himself,
and took captains of hundreds: Azariah the son of Jeroham, Ishmael the son of Johanan, Azariah the son of Obed, Maaseiah the son of Adaiah, and Elishaphat the son of Zichri, *and they
entered* into a covenant with him.

2And they went throughout Judah and gathered the Levites
from all the cities of Judah, and the heads of the fathers' *households*
of Israel, and they came to Jerusalem.

3Then all the assembly made a covenant with the king in the
house of God. And Jehoiada said to them, "Behold, the king's son
shall reign, as the LORD has spoken concerning the sons of David.

4"This is the thing which you shall do: one third of you, of the
priests and Levites who come in on the sabbath, *shall be* gatekeepers,

5and one third *shall be* at the king's house, and a third at the
Gate of the Foundation; and all the people *shall be* in the courts of
the house of the LORD.

6"But let no one enter the house of the LORD except the priests
and the ministering Levites; they may enter, for they are holy. And
let all the people keep the charge of the LORD.

7"And the Levites will surround the king, each man with his
weapons in his hand; and whoever enters the house, let him be
killed. Thus be with the king when he comes in and when he goes
out."

## New International

LORD, as the house of Ahab had done, for after his father's death
they became his advisers, to his undoing. 5He also followed their
counsel when he went with Joram[a] son of Ahab king of Israel to
war against Hazael king of Aram at Ramoth Gilead. The Arameans
wounded Joram; 6so he returned to Jezreel to recover from the
wounds they had inflicted on him at Ramoth[b] in his battle with
Hazael king of Aram.

Then Ahaziah[c] son of Jehoram king of Judah went down to
Jezreel to see Joram son of Ahab because he had been wounded.

7Through Ahaziah's visit to Joram, God brought about Ahaziah's downfall. When Ahaziah arrived, he went out with Joram
to meet Jehu son of Nimshi, whom the LORD had anointed to
destroy the house of Ahab. 8While Jehu was executing judgment
on the house of Ahab, he found the princes of Judah and the sons
of Ahaziah's relatives, who had been attending Ahaziah, and he
killed them. 9He then went in search of Ahaziah, and his men
captured him while he was hiding in Samaria. He was brought to
Jehu and put to death. They buried him, for they said, "He was
a son of Jehoshaphat, who sought the LORD with all his heart." So
there was no one in the house of Ahaziah powerful enough to
retain the kingdom.

*Athaliah and Joash*

10When Athaliah the mother of Ahaziah saw that her son was
dead, she proceeded to destroy the whole royal family of the house
of Judah. 11But Jehosheba,[d] the daughter of King Jehoram, took
Joash son of Ahaziah and stole him away from among the royal
princes who were about to be murdered and put him and his nurse
in a bedroom. Because Jehosheba,[e] the daughter of King Jehoram
and wife of the priest Jehoiada, was Ahaziah's sister, she hid the
child from Athaliah so she could not kill him. 12He remained
hidden with them at the temple of God for six years while Athaliah
ruled the land.

**23** IN THE seventh year Jehoiada showed his strength. He
made a covenant with the commanders of units of a hundred: Azariah son of Jeroham, Ishmael son of Jehohanan, Azariah
son of Obed, Maaseiah son of Adaiah, and Elishaphat son of Zicri.
2They went throughout Judah and gathered the Levites and the
heads of Israelite families from all the towns. When they came to
Jerusalem, 3the whole assembly made a covenant with the king at
the temple of God.

Jehoiada said to them, "The king's son shall reign, as the LORD
promised concerning the descendants of David. 4Now this is what
you are to do: A third of you priests and Levites who are going on
duty on the Sabbath are to keep watch at the doors, 5a third of you
at the royal palace and a third at the Foundation Gate, and all the
other men are to be in the courtyards of the temple of the LORD.
6No one is to enter the temple of the LORD except the priests and
Levites on duty; they may enter because they are consecrated, but
all the other men are to guard what the LORD has assigned to
them.[f] 7The Levites are to station themselves around the king,
each man with his weapons in his hand. Anyone who enters the
temple must be put to death. Stay close to the king wherever he
goes."

**NIV** [a] 5 Hebrew *Jehoram,* a variant of *Joram;* also in verses 6 and 7 [b] 6 Hebrew *Ramah,* a variant of *Ramoth* [c] 6 Some Hebrew manuscripts, Septuagint, Vulgate and Syriac (see also 2 Kings 8:29); most Hebrew manuscripts *Azariah* [d] 11 Hebrew *Jehoshabeath,* a variant of *Jehosheba* [e] 11 Hebrew *Jehoshabeath,* a variant of *Jehosheba* [f] 6 Or *to observe the LORD's command* ⌊*not to enter*⌋

## King James

8 So the Levites and all Judah did according to all things that Jehoiada the priest had commanded, and took every man his men that were to come in on the sabbath, with them that were to go *out* on the sabbath: for Jehoiada the priest dismissed not the courses.

9 Moreover Jehoiada the priest delivered to the captains of hundreds spears, and bucklers, and shields, that *had been* king David's, which *were* in the house of God.

10 And he set all the people, every man having his weapon in his hand, from the right side of the temple to the left side of the temple, along by the altar and the temple, by the king round about.

11 Then they brought out the king's son, and put upon him the crown, and *gave him* the testimony, and made him king. And Jehoiada and his sons anointed him, and said, God save the king.

12 ¶ Now when Athaliah heard the noise of the people running and praising the king, she came to the people into the house of the LORD:

13 And she looked, and, behold, the king stood at his pillar at the entering in, and the princes and the trumpets by the king: and all the people of the land rejoiced, and sounded with trumpets, also the singers with instruments of music, and such as taught to sing praise. Then Athaliah rent her clothes, and said, Treason, Treason.

14 Then Jehoiada the priest brought out the captains of hundreds that were set over the host, and said unto them, Have her forth of the ranges: and whoso followeth her, let him be slain with the sword. For the priest said, Slay her not in the house of the LORD.

15 So they laid hands on her; and when she was come to the entering of the horse gate by the king's house, they slew her there.

16 ¶ And Jehoiada made a covenant between him, and between all the people, and between the king, that they should be the LORD'S people.

17 Then all the people went to the house of Baal, and brake it down, and brake his altars and his images in pieces, and slew Mattan the priest of Baal before the altars.

18 Also Jehoiada appointed the offices of the house of the LORD by the hand of the priests the Levites, whom David had distributed in the house of the LORD, to offer the burnt offerings of the LORD, as *it is* written in the law of Moses, with rejoicing and with singing, *as it was ordained* by David.

19 And he set the porters at the gates of the house of the LORD, that none *which was* unclean in any thing should enter in.

20 And he took the captains of hundreds, and the nobles, and the governors of the people, and all the people of the land, and brought down the king from the house of the LORD: and they came through the high gate into the king's house, and set the king upon the throne of the kingdom.

21 And all the people of the land rejoiced: and the city was quiet, after that they had slain Athaliah with the sword.

**24** JOASH *WAS* seven years old when he began to reign, and he reigned forty years in Jerusalem. His mother's name also *was* Zibiah of Beer-sheba.

2 And Joash did *that which was* right in the sight of the LORD all the days of Jehoiada the priest.

3 And Jehoiada took for him two wives; and he begat sons and daughters.

4 ¶ And it came to pass after this, *that* Joash was minded to repair the house of the LORD.

## Amplified

8 So the Levites and all Judah did according to all that Jehoiada the priest had commanded, and took every man his men who were to resume duty on the sabbath, with those who were to go out on the sabbath; for Jehoiada the priest did not dismiss the divisions [of priests and Levites].

9 Also Jehoiada the priest gave the captains of hundreds spears, bucklers, and shields, that had been King David's, which were in the house of God.

10 And he set all the people as a guard for the king, every man having his (missile) weapon in his hand, from the right side to the left side of the temple, around the altar and the temple.

11 Then they brought out the king's son, and put the crown on him, and gave him the testimony *or* law, and made him king. And Jehoiada and his sons anointed him, and said, Long live the king!

12 When Athaliah heard the noise of the people running and praising the king, she went into the Lord's house to the people;

13 And behold, there the king stood by his pillar at the entrance, the captains and the trumpeters beside him, and all the people of the land rejoicing and blowing trumpets, and the singers with musical instruments led in singing of praise. Athaliah rent her clothes, and cried, Treason! Treason!

14 Then Jehoiada the priest commanded the captains of hundreds who were over the army, Bring her out between the ranks, and whoever follows her, let him be slain with the sword. For the priest said, Do not slay her in the Lord's house.

15 So they made way for Athaliah, and she went into the entrance of the horse gate of the king's house; there they slew her.

16 Then Jehoiada made a covenant between himself, all the people, and the king, that they should be the Lord's people.

17 Then all the people went to the house of Baal, tore it down, and broke its altars and its images in pieces, and slew Mattan the priest of Baal before the altars.

18 Also Jehoiada appointed the offices *and* officers [for the care] of the house of the Lord under the direction of the priests *and* the Levites, whom David had distributed [in his day] in the house of the Lord, to offer the burnt offerings of the Lord, as written in the law of Moses, with rejoicing and singing, as ordered by David.

19 Jehoiada set the gatekeepers at the gates of the house of the Lord so that no one should enter who was in any way unclean.

20 And he took the captains of hundreds, and the nobles and governors of the people, and all the people of the land, and brought down the king from the house of the Lord; and they came through the upper gate to the king's house, and set the king upon the throne of the kingdom.

21 So all the people of the land rejoiced, and the city was quiet, after Athaliah had been slain with the sword.

**24** JOASH WAS seven years old when he began his forty-years' reign in Jerusalem. His mother was Zibiah of Beer-sheba.

2 And Joash did what was right in the sight of the Lord all the days of Jehoiada the priest [his uncle].

3 And Jehoiada took for him two wives; and he had sons and daughters.

4 After this Joash decided to repair the Lord's house.

## New American Standard

8So the Levites and all Judah did according to all that Jehoiada the priest commanded. And each one of them took his men who were to come in on the sabbath, with those who were to go out on the sabbath, for Jehoiada the priest did not dismiss *any of* the divisions.

9Then Jehoiada the priest gave to the captains of hundreds the spears and the large and small shields which had been King David's, which *were* in the house of God.

10And he stationed all the people, each man with his weapon in his hand, from the right side of the house to the left side of the house, by the altar and by the house, around the king.

11Then they brought out the king's son and put the crown on him, and *gave him* the testimony, and made him king. And Jehoiada and his sons anointed him and said, "*Long* live the king!"

*Athaliah Murdered*

12¶ When Athaliah heard the noise of the people running and praising the king, she came into the house of the LORD to the people.

13And she looked, and behold, the king was standing by his pillar at the entrance, and the captains and the trumpeters *were* beside the king. And all the people of the land rejoiced and blew trumpets, the singers with *their* musical instruments leading the praise. Then Athaliah tore her clothes and said, "Treason! Treason!"

14And Jehoiada the priest brought out the captains of hundreds who were appointed over the army, and said to them, "Bring her out between the ranks; and whoever follows her, put to death with the sword." For the priest said, "Let her not be put to death in the house of the LORD."

15So they seized her, and when she arrived at the entrance of the Horse Gate of the king's house, they put her to death there.

*Reforms Carried Out*

16¶ Then Jehoiada made a covenant between himself and all the people and the king, that they should be the LORD's people.

17And all the people went to the house of Baal, and tore it down, and they broke in pieces his altars and his images, and killed Mattan the priest of Baal before the altars.

18Moreover, Jehoiada placed the offices of the house of the LORD under the authority of the Levitical priests, whom David had assigned over the house of the LORD, to offer the burnt offerings of the LORD, as it is written in the law of Moses—with rejoicing and singing according to the order of David.

19And he stationed the gatekeepers of the house of the LORD, so that no one should enter *who was* in any way unclean.

20And he took the captains of hundreds, the nobles, the rulers of the people, and all the people of the land, and brought the king down from the house of the LORD, and came through the upper gate to the king's house. And they placed the king upon the royal throne.

21So all of the people of the land rejoiced and the city was quiet. For they had put Athaliah to death with the sword.

*Young Joash Influenced by Jehoiada*

**24** JOASH *WAS* seven years old when he became king, and he reigned forty years in Jerusalem; and his mother's name *was* Zibiah from Beersheba.

2And Joash did what was right in the sight of the LORD all the days of Jehoiada the priest.

3And Jehoiada took two wives for him, and he became the father of sons and daughters.

*Faithless Priests*

4¶ Now it came about after this that Joash decided to restore the house of the LORD.

## New International

8The Levites and all the men of Judah did just as Jehoiada the
priest ordered. Each one took his men—those who were going on
duty on the Sabbath and those who were going off duty—for
Jehoiada the priest had not released any of the divisions. 9Then he
gave the commanders of units of a hundred the spears and the
large and small shields that had belonged to King David and that
were in the temple of God. 10He stationed all the men, each with
his weapon in his hand, around the king—near the altar and the
temple, from the south side to the north side of the temple.
11Jehoiada and his sons brought out the king's son and put the
crown on him; they presented him with a copy of the covenant and
proclaimed him king. They anointed him and shouted, "Long live
the king!"
12When Athaliah heard the noise of the people running and
cheering the king, she went to them at the temple of the LORD.
13She looked, and there was the king, standing by his pillar at the
entrance. The officers and the trumpeters were beside the king,
and all the people of the land were rejoicing and blowing trumpets,
and singers with musical instruments were leading the praises.
Then Athaliah tore her robes and shouted, "Treason! Treason!"
14Jehoiada the priest sent out the commanders of units of a
hundred, who were in charge of the troops, and said to them:
"Bring her out between the ranks[a] and put to the sword anyone
who follows her." For the priest had said, "Do not put her to death
at the temple of the LORD." 15So they seized her as she reached the
entrance of the Horse Gate on the palace grounds, and there they
put her to death.
16Jehoiada then made a covenant that he and the people and the
king[b] would be the LORD's people. 17All the people went to the
temple of Baal and tore it down. They smashed the altars and idols
and killed Mattan the priest of Baal in front of the altars.
18Then Jehoiada placed the oversight of the temple of the LORD
in the hands of the priests, who were Levites, to whom David had
made assignments in the temple, to present the burnt offerings of
the LORD as written in the Law of Moses, with rejoicing and
singing, as David had ordered. 19He also stationed doorkeepers at
the gates of the LORD's temple so that no one who was in any way
unclean might enter.
20He took with him the commanders of hundreds, the nobles,
the rulers of the people and all the people of the land and brought
the king down from the temple of the LORD. They went into the
palace through the Upper Gate and seated the king on the royal
throne, 21and all the people of the land rejoiced. And the city was
quiet, because Athaliah had been slain with the sword.

*Joash Repairs the Temple*

**24** JOASH WAS seven years old when he became king, and
he reigned in Jerusalem forty years. His mother's name
was Zibiah; she was from Beersheba. 2Joash did what was right in
the eyes of the LORD all the years of Jehoiada the priest. 3Jehoiada
chose two wives for him, and he had sons and daughters.
4Some time later Joash decided to restore the temple of the
LORD. 5He called together the priests and Levites and said to them,

**NIV** [a] 14 Or *out from the precincts* [b] 16 Or *covenant between* ⌊*the* LORD⌋ *and the people and the king that they* (see 2 Kings 11:17)

## King James

5 And he gathered together the priest and the Levites, and said
to them, Go out unto the cities of Judah, and gather of all Israel
money to repair the house of your God from year to year, and see
that ye hasten the matter. Howbeit the Levites hastened *it* not.
6 And the king called for Jehoiada the chief, and said unto him,
Why hast thou not required of the Levites to bring in out of Judah
and out of Jerusalem the collection, *according to the commandment*
of Moses the servant of the LORD, and of the congregation of Israel,
for the tabernacle of witness?
7 For the sons of Athaliah, that wicked woman, had broken up
the house of God; and also all the dedicated things of the house
of the LORD did they bestow upon Baalim.
8 And at the king's commandment they made a chest, and set
it without at the gate of the house of the LORD.
9 And they made a proclamation through Judah and Jerusalem,
to bring in to the LORD the collection *that* Moses the servant of God
*laid* upon Israel in the wilderness.
10 And all the princes and all the people rejoiced, and brought
in, and cast into the chest, until they had made an end.
11 Now it came to pass, that at what time the chest was brought
unto the king's office by the hand of the Levites, and when they
saw that *there was* much money, the king's scribe and the high
priest's officer came and emptied the chest, and took it, and carried
it to his place again. Thus they did day by day, and gathered
money in abundance.
12 And the king and Jehoiada gave it to such as did the work of
the service of the house of the LORD, and hired masons and carpenters to repair the house of the LORD, and also such as wrought iron
and brass to mend the house of the LORD.
13 So the workmen wrought, and the work was perfected by
them, and they set the house of God in his state, and strengthened
it.
14 And when they had finished *it*, they brought the rest of the
money before the king and Jehoiada, whereof were made vessels
for the house of the LORD, *even* vessels to minister, and to offer
*withal*, and spoons, and vessels of gold and silver. And they offered burnt offerings in the house of the LORD continually all the
days of Jehoiada.
15 ¶ But Jehoiada waxed old, and was full of days when he died;
an hundred and thirty years old *was he* when he died.
16 And they buried him in the city of David among the kings,
because he had done good in Israel, both toward God, and toward
his house.
17 Now after the death of Jehoiada came the princes of Judah,
and made obeisance to the king. Then the king hearkened unto
them.
18 And they left the house of the LORD God of their fathers, and
served groves and idols: and wrath came upon Judah and Jerusalem for this their trespass.
19 Yet he sent prophets to them, to bring them again unto the
LORD; and they testified against them: but they would not give ear.
20 And the spirit of God came upon Zechariah the son of Jehoiada the priest, which stood above the people, and said unto them,
Thus saith God, Why transgress ye the commandments of the
LORD, that ye cannot prosper? because ye have forsaken the LORD,
he hath also forsaken you.
21 And they conspired against him, and stoned him with stones
at the commandment of the king in the court of the house of the
LORD.
22 Thus Joash the king remembered not the kindness which
Jehoiada his father had done to him, but slew his son. And when
he died, he said, The LORD look upon *it*, and require *it*.

## Amplified

5 He gathered the priests and the Levites, and said to them, Go
out to the cities of Judah, and gather from all Israel money to repair
the house of your God from year to year, and see that you hasten
the matter. But the Levites did not hasten it.
6 So the king called for Jehoiada the high priest, and said to him,
Why have you not required the Levites to bring in from Judah and
Jerusalem the tax authorized by Moses the servant of the Lord and
of the assembly of Israel, for the tent of testimony?
7 For the sons of Athaliah, that wicked woman, had broken into
the house of God; and also had used for the Baals all the dedicated
things of the house of the Lord.
8 And at the king's command they made a chest, and set it
outside the gate of the house of the Lord.
9 And they made a proclamation through Judah and Jerusalem,
to bring in for the Lord the tax that Moses the servant of God laid
upon Israel in the wilderness.
10 And all the princes and people rejoiced and brought their tax
and dropped it into the chest until they had finished.
11 When the Levites brought the chest to the king's office, and
whenever they saw that there was much money, the king's secretary and the high priest's officer came and emptied the chest, and
carried it to its place again. Thus they did day by day, and collected
money in abundance.
12 And the king and Jehoiada gave it to those who did the work
of the temple service, and hired masons and carpenters and also
those who worked in iron and bronze, to repair the house of the
Lord.
13 So the workmen labored and the work of repairing went
forward in their hands, and they set up the house of God according
to its design, and strengthened it.
14 When they had finished it, they brought the rest of the money
before the king and Jehoiada; from it were made utensils for the
Lord's house, vessels for ministering and for offering, and cups
and vessels of gold and silver. And they offered burnt offerings in
the house of the Lord continually all the days of Jehoiada.
15 But Jehoiada became old and full of [the handicaps of great]
age, and he died. He was 130 years old at his death.
16 They buried him in the city of David among the kings, because he had done good in Israel, and toward God and His house.
17 Now after the death of Jehoiada *the priest* [who had hidden
Joash] the princes of Judah came and made obeisance to King
Joash; then the king hearkened to them.
18 They forsook the house of the Lord the God of their fathers,
and served the Asherim and idols; and wrath came upon Judah
and Jerusalem for their sin [guilt].
19 Yet [God] sent prophets to them, to bring them again to the
Lord; these testified against them, but they would not listen.
20 Then the Spirit of God came upon Zechariah son of Jehoiada
the priest, who stood over the people, and he said to them, Thus
says God, Why do you transgress the commandments of the Lord,
so that you cannot prosper? Because you have forsaken the Lord,
He also has forsaken you.
21 They conspired against Zechariah the priest and stoned him
at the command of the king in the court of the Lord's house!
22 Thus Joash the king did not remember the kindness which
Jehoiada, Zechariah's father, had done him, but slew his son. And
when [Zechariah the priest] was dying he said, May the Lord see
and avenge!

## New American Standard

5 And he gathered the priests and Levites, and said to them, "Go out to the cities of Judah, and collect money from all Israel to repair the house of your God annually, and you shall do the matter quickly." But the Levites did not act quickly.

6 So the king summoned Jehoiada the chief *priest* and said to him, "Why have you not required the Levites to bring in from Judah and from Jerusalem the levy *fixed by* Moses the servant of the LORD on the congregation of Israel for the tent of the testimony?"

7 For the sons of the wicked Athaliah had broken into the house of God and even used the holy things of the house of the LORD for the Baals.

*Temple Repaired*

8 ¶ So the king commanded, and they made a chest and set it outside by the gate of the house of the LORD.

9 And they made a proclamation in Judah and Jerusalem to bring to the LORD the levy *fixed by* Moses the servant of God on Israel in the wilderness.

10 And all the officers and all the people rejoiced and brought in their levies and dropped *them* into the chest until they had finished.

11 And it came about whenever the chest was brought in to the king's officer by the Levites, and when they saw that there was much money, then the king's scribe and the chief priest's officer would come, empty the chest, take it, and return it to its place. Thus they did daily and collected much money.

12 And the king and Jehoiada gave it to those who did the work of the service of the house of the LORD; and they hired masons and carpenters to restore the house of the LORD, and also workers in iron and bronze to repair the house of the LORD.

13 So the workmen labored, and the repair work progressed in their hands, and they restored the house of God according to its specifications, and strengthened it.

14 And when they had finished, they brought the rest of the money before the king and Jehoiada; and it was made into utensils for the house of the LORD, utensils for the service and the burnt offering, and pans and utensils of gold and silver. And they offered burnt offerings in the house of the LORD continually all the days of Jehoiada.

15 ¶ Now when Jehoiada reached a ripe old age he died; he was one hundred and thirty years old at his death.

16 And they buried him in the city of David among the kings, because he had done well in Israel and to God and His house.

17 But after the death of Jehoiada the officials of Judah came and bowed down to the king, and the king listened to them.

18 And they abandoned the house of the LORD, the God of their fathers, and served the [a]Asherim and the idols; so wrath came upon Judah and Jerusalem for this their guilt.

19 Yet He sent prophets to them to bring them back to the LORD; though they testified against them, they would not listen.

*Joash Murders Son of Jehoiada*

20 Then the Spirit of God came on Zechariah the son of Jehoiada the priest; and he stood above the people and said to them, "Thus God has said, 'Why do you transgress the commandments of the LORD and do not prosper? Because you have forsaken the LORD, He has also forsaken you.' "

21 So they conspired against him and at the command of the king they stoned him to death in the court of the house of the LORD.

22 Thus Joash the king did not remember the kindness which his father Jehoiada had shown him, but he murdered his son. And as he died he said, "May the LORD see and avenge!"

NAS [a] I.e., wooden symbols of a female deity

## New International

"Go to the towns of Judah and collect the money due annually
from all Israel, to repair the temple of your God. Do it now." But
the Levites did not act at once.
6 Therefore the king summoned Jehoiada the chief priest and
said to him, "Why haven't you required the Levites to bring in
from Judah and Jerusalem the tax imposed by Moses the servant
of the LORD and by the assembly of Israel for the Tent of the
Testimony?"
7 Now the sons of that wicked woman Athaliah had broken into
the temple of God and had used even its sacred objects for the
Baals.
8 At the king's command, a chest was made and placed outside,
at the gate of the temple of the LORD. 9 A proclamation was then
issued in Judah and Jerusalem that they should bring to the LORD
the tax that Moses the servant of God had required of Israel in the
desert. 10 All the officials and all the people brought their contributions gladly, dropping them into the chest until it was full.
11 Whenever the chest was brought in by the Levites to the king's
officials and they saw that there was a large amount of money, the
royal secretary and the officer of the chief priest would come and
empty the chest and carry it back to its place. They did this regularly and collected a great amount of money. 12 The king and Jehoiada
gave it to the men who carried out the work required for the temple
of the LORD. They hired masons and carpenters to restore the
LORD's temple, and also workers in iron and bronze to repair the
temple.
13 The men in charge of the work were diligent, and the repairs
progressed under them. They rebuilt the temple of God according
to its original design and reinforced it. 14 When they had finished,
they brought the rest of the money to the king and Jehoiada, and
with it were made articles for the LORD's temple: articles for the
service and for the burnt offerings, and also dishes and other
objects of gold and silver. As long as Jehoiada lived, burnt offerings were presented continually in the temple of the LORD.
15 Now Jehoiada was old and full of years, and he died at the
age of a hundred and thirty. 16 He was buried with the kings in the
City of David, because of the good he had done in Israel for God
and his temple.

*The Wickedness of Joash*

17 After the death of Jehoiada, the officials of Judah came and
paid homage to the king, and he listened to them. 18 They abandoned the temple of the LORD, the God of their fathers, and worshiped Asherah poles and idols. Because of their guilt, God's anger
came upon Judah and Jerusalem. 19 Although the LORD sent prophets to the people to bring them back to him, and though they
testified against them, they would not listen.
20 Then the Spirit of God came upon Zechariah son of Jehoiada
the priest. He stood before the people and said, "This is what God
says: 'Why do you disobey the LORD's commands? You will not
prosper. Because you have forsaken the LORD, he has forsaken
you.' "
21 But they plotted against him, and by order of the king they
stoned him to death in the courtyard of the LORD's temple. 22 King
Joash did not remember the kindness Zechariah's father Jehoiada
had shown him but killed his son, who said as he lay dying, "May
the LORD see this and call you to account."

## King James

23¶ And it came to pass at the end of the year, *that* the host of Syria came up against him: and they came to Judah and Jerusalem, and destroyed all the princes of the people from among the people, and sent all the spoil of them unto the king of Damascus.

24For the army of the Syrians came with a small company of men, and the LORD delivered a very great host into their hand, because they had forsaken the LORD God of their fathers. So they executed judgment against Joash.

25And when they were departed from him, (for they left him in great diseases,) his own servants conspired against him for the blood of the sons of Jehoiada the priest, and slew him on his bed, and he died: and they buried him in the city of David, but they buried him not in the sepulchres of the kings.

26And these are they that conspired against him; Zabad the son of Shimeath an Ammonitess, and Jehozabad the son of Shimrith a Moabitess.

27¶ Now *concerning* his sons, and the greatness of the burdens *laid* upon him, and the repairing of the house of God, behold, they *are* written in the story of the book of the kings. And Amaziah his son reigned in his stead.

**25** AMAZIAH *WAS* twenty and five years old *when* he began to reign, and he reigned twenty and nine years in Jerusalem. And his mother's name *was* Jehoaddan of Jerusalem.

2And he did *that which was* right in the sight of the LORD, but not with a perfect heart.

3¶ Now it came to pass, when the kingdom was established to him, that he slew his servants that had killed the king his father.

4But he slew not their children, but *did* as *it is* written in the law in the book of Moses, where the LORD commanded, saying, The fathers shall not die for the children, neither shall the children die for the fathers, but every man shall die for his own sin.

5¶ Moreover Amaziah gathered Judah together, and made them captains over thousands, and captains over hundreds, according to the houses of *their* fathers, throughout all Judah and Benjamin: and he numbered them from twenty years old and above, and found them three hundred thousand choice *men, able* to go forth to war, that could handle spear and shield.

6He hired also an hundred thousand mighty men of valour out of Israel for an hundred talents of silver.

7But there came a man of God to him, saying, O king, let not the army of Israel go with thee; for the LORD *is* not with Israel, *to wit, with* all the children of Ephraim.

8But if thou wilt go, do *it*, be strong for the battle: God shall make thee fall before the enemy: for God hath power to help, and to cast down.

9And Amaziah said to the man of God, But what shall we do for the hundred talents which I have given to the army of Israel? And the man of God answered, The LORD is able to give thee much more than this.

10Then Amaziah separated them, *to wit*, the army that was come to him out of Ephraim, to go home again: wherefore their anger was greatly kindled against Judah, and they returned home in great anger.

11¶ And Amaziah strengthened himself, and led forth his people, and went to the valley of salt, and smote of the children of Seir ten thousand.

12And *other* ten thousand *left* alive did the children of Judah carry away captive, and brought them unto the top of the rock, and cast them down from the top of the rock, that they all were broken in pieces.

13¶ But the soldiers of the army which Amaziah sent back, that they should not go with him to battle, fell upon the cities of Judah, from Samaria even unto Beth-horon, and smote three thousand of them, and took much spoil.

## Amplified

23At the end of the year the army of Syria came up against Joash. They came to Judah and Jerusalem, and destroyed all the princes from among the people, and sent all their spoil to the king of Damascus.

24Though the army of the Syrians came with a small company of men, the Lord delivered a very great host into their hand, because Joash and Judah had forsaken the Lord God of their fathers. So the Syrians executed judgment against Joash.

25And when they had departed from Joash, leaving him very ill, his own servants conspired against him for the blood of the sons of Jehoiada the priest, and they slew him on his bed. So he died and they buried him in the city of David, but not in the tombs of the kings.

26The conspirators against Joash were Zabad son of Shime-ath the Ammonitess, and Jehozabad son of Shimrith the Moabitess.

27Now concerning his sons, and the greatness of the prophecies uttered against him, and the rebuilding of the house of God, they are written in the Commentary on the Book of Kings. And Amaziah son [of Joash] reigned in his stead.

**25** AMAZIAH WAS twenty-five years old when he began to reign, and he reigned twenty-nine years in Jerusalem. His mother was Jeho-addan of Jerusalem.

2He did right in the Lord's sight, but not with a perfect *or* blameless heart.

3When his kingdom was firmly established he slew his servants who had killed the king his father.

4But he did not slay their children; he did as it is written in the law in the book of Moses, where the Lord commanded, The fathers shall not die for the children, or the children die for the fathers; but every man shall die for his own sin.

5Amaziah assembled the men of Judah, and set them by fathers' houses under commanders of thousands and of hundreds for all Judah and Benjamin. He numbered them from twenty years old and over, and found them to be 300,000 choice men, fit for war and able to handle spear and shield.

6He hired also 100,000 mighty men of valor from Israel for 100 talents of silver.

7But a man of God came to him, saying, O king, do not let all this army of Ephraimites of Israel go with you of Judah for the Lord is not with you,

8For if you go [in spite of warning], no matter how strong you are for battle, God will cast you down before the enemy; for God has power to help and to cast down.

9And Amaziah said to the man of God, But what shall we do about the 100 talents which I have given to the army of Israel? The man of God answered, The Lord is able to give you much more than this.

10So Amaziah discharged the army that came to him from Ephraim, to go home; so their anger was greatly kindled against Judah; they returned home in fierce wrath.

11And Amaziah took courage and led forth his people to the Valley of Salt, and smote 10,000 of the men of Seir [Edom].

12Another 10,000 the men of Judah captured alive, and brought them to the top of a crag, and cast them down from it, and they were all dashed to pieces.

13But the soldiers of the band which Amaziah sent back, not allowing them to go with him to battle, fell upon the cities of Judah, from Samaria even to Bethhoron, and smote 3,000 [men], and took much spoil.

## New American Standard

*Aram Invades and Defeats Judah*

23¶ Now it came about at the turn of the year that the army of
the Arameans came up against him; and they came to Judah and
Jerusalem, destroyed all the officials of the people from among the
people, and sent all their spoil to the king of Damascus.
24Indeed the army of the Arameans came with a small number
of men; yet the LORD delivered a very great army into their hands,
because they had forsaken the LORD, the God of their fathers. Thus
they executed judgment on Joash.
25And when they had departed from him (for they left him very
sick), his own servants conspired against him because of the blood
of the son of Jehoiada the priest, and murdered him on his bed.
So he died, and they buried him in the city of David, but they did
not bury him in the tombs of the kings.
26Now these are those who conspired against him: Zabad the
son of Shimeath the Ammonitess, and Jehozabad the son of Shimrith the Moabitess.
27As to his sons and the many oracles against him and the
rebuilding of the house of God, behold, they are written in the
treatise of the Book of the Kings. Then Amaziah his son became
king in his place.

*Amaziah Succeeds Joash in Judah*

25 AMAZIAH WAS twenty-five years old when he became
king, and he reigned twenty-nine years in Jerusalem. And
his mother's name was Jehoaddan of Jerusalem.
2And he did right in the sight of the LORD, yet not with a whole
heart.
3Now it came about as soon as the kingdom was firmly in his
grasp, that he killed his servants who had slain his father the king.
4However, he did not put their children to death, but *did* as it
is written in the law in the book of Moses, which the LORD commanded, saying, "Fathers shall not be put to death for sons, nor
sons be put to death for fathers, but each shall be put to death for
his own sin."

*Amaziah Defeats Edomites*

5¶ Moreover, Amaziah assembled Judah and appointed them
according to *their* fathers' households under commanders of thousands and commanders of hundreds throughout Judah and Benjamin; and he took a census of those from twenty years old and
upward, and found them to be 300,000 choice men, *able* to go to
war *and* handle spear and shield.
6He hired also 100,000 valiant warriors out of Israel for one
hundred talents of silver.
7But a man of God came to him saying, "O king, do not let the
army of Israel go with you, for the LORD is not with Israel *nor with*
any of the sons of Ephraim.
8"But if you do go, do *it*, be strong for the battle; *yet* God will
bring you down before the enemy, for God has power to help and
to bring down."
9And Amaziah said to the man of God, "But what *shall we* do
for the hundred talents which I have given to the troops of Israel?"
And the man of God answered, "The LORD has much more to give
you than this."
10Then Amaziah dismissed them, the troops which came to him
from Ephraim, to go home; so their anger burned against Judah
and they returned home in fierce anger.
11¶ Now Amaziah strengthened himself, and led his people
forth, and went to the Valley of Salt, and struck down 10,000 of
the sons of Seir.
12The sons of Judah also captured 10,000 alive and brought
them to the top of the cliff, and threw them down from the top of
the cliff so that they were all dashed to pieces.
13But the troops whom Amaziah sent back from going with him
to battle, raided the cities of Judah, from Samaria to Beth-horon,
and struck down 3,000 of them, and plundered much spoil.

## New International

23At the turn of the year,[a] the army of Aram marched against
Joash; it invaded Judah and Jerusalem and killed all the leaders of
the people. They sent all the plunder to their king in Damascus.
24Although the Aramean army had come with only a few men, the
LORD delivered into their hands a much larger army. Because
Judah had forsaken the LORD, the God of their fathers, judgment
was executed on Joash. 25When the Arameans withdrew, they left
Joash severely wounded. His officials conspired against him for
murdering the son of Jehoiada the priest, and they killed him in
his bed. So he died and was buried in the City of David, but not
in the tombs of the kings.
26Those who conspired against him were Zabad,[b] son of Shimeath an Ammonite woman, and Jehozabad, son of Shimrith[c] a
Moabite woman. 27The account of his sons, the many prophecies
about him, and the record of the restoration of the temple of God
are written in the annotations on the book of the kings. And
Amaziah his son succeeded him as king.

*Amaziah King of Judah*

25 AMAZIAH WAS twenty-five years old when he became
king, and he reigned in Jerusalem twenty-nine years. His
mother's name was Jehoaddin[d]; she was from Jerusalem. 2He did
what was right in the eyes of the LORD, but not wholeheartedly.
3After the kingdom was firmly in his control, he executed the
officials who had murdered his father the king. 4Yet he did not put
their sons to death, but acted in accordance with what is written
in the Law, in the Book of Moses, where the LORD commanded:
"Fathers shall not be put to death for their children, nor children
put to death for their fathers; each is to die for his own sins."[e]
5Amaziah called the people of Judah together and assigned
them according to their families to commanders of thousands and
commanders of hundreds for all Judah and Benjamin. He then
mustered those twenty years old or more and found that there
were three hundred thousand men ready for military service, able
to handle the spear and shield. 6He also hired a hundred thousand
fighting men from Israel for a hundred talents[f] of silver.
7But a man of God came to him and said, "O king, these troops
from Israel must not march with you, for the LORD is not with
Israel—not with any of the people of Ephraim. 8Even if you go and
fight courageously in battle, God will overthrow you before the
enemy, for God has the power to help or to overthrow."
9Amaziah asked the man of God, "But what about the hundred
talents I paid for these Israelite troops?"
The man of God replied, "The LORD can give you much more
than that."
10So Amaziah dismissed the troops who had come to him from
Ephraim and sent them home. They were furious with Judah and
left for home in a great rage.
11Amaziah then marshaled his strength and led his army to the
Valley of Salt, where he killed ten thousand men of Seir. 12The
army of Judah also captured ten thousand men alive, took them
to the top of a cliff and threw them down so that all were dashed
to pieces.
13Meanwhile the troops that Amaziah had sent back and had
not allowed to take part in the war raided Judean towns from
Samaria to Beth Horon. They killed three thousand people and
carried off great quantities of plunder.

**NIV** [a] *23* Probably in the spring [b] *26* A variant of *Jozabad* [c] *26* A variant of *Shomer* [d] *1* Hebrew *Jehoaddan,* a variant of *Jehoaddin* [e] *4* Deut. 24:16 [f] *6* That is, about 3 3/4 tons (about 3.4 metric tons); also in verse 9

## King James

14¶ Now it came to pass, after that Amaziah was come from the slaughter of the Edomites, that he brought the gods of the children of Seir, and set them up *to be* his gods, and bowed down himself before them, and burned incense unto them.

15Wherefore the anger of the LORD was kindled against Amaziah, and he sent unto him a prophet, which said unto him, Why hast thou sought after the gods of the people, which could not deliver their own people out of thine hand?

16And it came to pass, as he talked with him, that *the king* said unto him, Art thou made of the king's counsel? forbear; why shouldest thou be smitten? Then the prophet forbare, and said, I know that God hath determined to destroy thee, because thou hast done this, and hast not hearkened unto my counsel.

17¶ Then Amaziah king of Judah took advice, and sent to Joash, the son of Jehoahaz, the son of Jehu, king of Israel, saying, Come, let us see one another in the face.

18And Joash king of Israel sent to Amaziah king of Judah, saying, The thistle that *was* in Lebanon sent to the cedar that *was* in Lebanon, saying, Give thy daughter to my son to wife: and there passed by a wild beast that *was* in Lebanon, and trode down the thistle.

19Thou sayest, Lo, thou hast smitten the Edomites; and thine heart lifteth thee up to boast: abide now at home; why shouldest thou meddle to *thine* hurt, that thou shouldest fall, *even* thou, and Judah with thee?

20But Amaziah would not hear; for it *came* of God, that he might deliver them into the hand *of their enemies,* because they sought after the gods of Edom.

21So Joash the king of Israel went up; and they saw one another in the face, *both* he and Amaziah king of Judah, at Beth-shemesh, which *belongeth* to Judah.

22And Judah was put to the worse before Israel, and they fled every man to his tent.

23And Joash the king of Israel took Amaziah king of Judah, the son of Joash, the son of Jehoahaz, at Beth-shemesh, and brought him to Jerusalem, and brake down the wall of Jerusalem from the gate of Ephraim to the corner gate, four hundred cubits.

24And *he took* all the gold and the silver, and all the vessels that were found in the house of God with Obed-edom, and the treasures of the king's house, the hostages also, and returned to Samaria.

25¶ And Amaziah the son of Joash king of Judah lived after the death of Joash son of Jehoahaz king of Israel fifteen years.

26Now the rest of the acts of Amaziah, first and last, behold, *are* they not written in the book of the kings of Judah and Israel?

27¶ Now after the time that Amaziah did turn away from following the LORD they made a conspiracy against him in Jerusalem; and he fled to Lachish: but they sent to Lachish after him, and slew him there.

28And they brought him upon horses, and buried him with his fathers in the city of Judah.

**26** THEN ALL the people of Judah took Uzziah, who *was* sixteen years old, and made him king in the room of his father Amaziah.

2He built Eloth, and restored it to Judah, after that the king slept with his fathers.

3Sixteen years old *was* Uzziah when he began to reign, and he reigned fifty and two years in Jerusalem. His mother's name also *was* Jecoliah of Jerusalem.

4And he did *that which was* right in the sight of the LORD, according to all that his father Amaziah did.

## Amplified

14After Amaziah came from the slaughter of the Edomites, he brought their gods and set them up to be his gods, and bowed before them, and burned incense to them.

15So the anger of the Lord was kindled against Amaziah, and He sent to him a prophet, who said, Why have you sought after the gods of the people, which could not deliver their own people out of your hand?

16As he was talking the king said to him, Have we made you the king's counselor? Stop it! Why should you be put to death? The prophet stopped, but said, I know that God has determined to destroy you, because you have done this and ignored my counsel.

17Then Amaziah king of Judah took counsel and sent to J[eh]oash son of Jehoahaz, son of Jehu, king of Israel, saying, Come [to battle], let us look one another in the face.

18J[eh]oash king of Israel sent to Amaziah king of Judah, saying, A little thistle on Lebanon sent to a great cedar on Lebanon, saying, Give your daughter to my son as wife; and a wild beast of Lebanon passed by and trampled down the thistle.

19You say, See, *I* have smitten Edom! Your heart lifts you up to boast. Stay at home; why should you meddle [and court disaster], so you will fall and Judah with you?

20But Amaziah would not hear; for it came from God, that He might deliver Judah into the hand of their enemies, because they sought after the gods of Edom.

21So J[eh]oash the king of Israel went up; and he and Amaziah king of Judah faced one another at Beth-shemesh of Judah.

22And Judah was defeated before Israel, and they fled every man to his tent.

23And J[eh]oash the king of Israel took Amaziah king of Judah son of Joash, son of Jehoahaz, at Beth-shemesh, and brought him to Jerusalem, and broke down the wall of Jerusalem from the Ephraim Gate to the Corner Gate, 400 cubits.

24And he took all the gold, the silver, and all the vessels found in God's house with [the doorkeeper] Obed-edom, and the treasures of the king's house, and hostages also, and returned to Samaria.

25And Amaziah son of Joash king of Judah lived after the death of J[eh]oash son of Jehoahaz king of Israel fifteen years.

26The rest of the acts of Amaziah, from first to last, are they not written in the Book of the Kings of Judah and Israel?

27Now after Amaziah turned away from the Lord they made a conspiracy against him in Jerusalem, and he fled to Lachish. But they sent to Lachish and slew him there.

28And they brought him upon horses, and buried him with his fathers in the city of (David in) Judah.

**26** THEN ALL the people of Judah took Uzziah, who was sixteen years old, and made him king in place of his father Amaziah.

2He built Eloth, and restored it to Judah after Amaziah slept with his fathers.

3Uzziah was sixteen years old when he began his fifty-two years' reign in Jerusalem. His mother was Jecoliah of Jerusalem.

4He did right in the Lord's sight, to the extent of all that his father Amaziah did.

## New American Standard

*Amaziah Rebuked for Idolatry*

14¶ Now it came about after Amaziah came from slaughtering
the Edomites that he brought the gods of the sons of Seir, set them
up as his gods, bowed down before them, and burned incense to
them.

15Then the anger of the LORD burned against Amaziah, and He
sent him a prophet who said to him, "Why have you sought the
gods of the people who have not delivered their own people from
your hand?"

16And it came about as he was talking with him that the king
said to him, "Have we appointed you a royal counselor? Stop! Why
should you be struck down?" Then the prophet stopped and said,
"I know that God has planned to destroy you, because you have
done this, and have not listened to my counsel."

*Amaziah Defeated by Joash of Israel*

17¶ Then Amaziah king of Judah took counsel and sent to Joash
the son of Jehoahaz the son of Jehu, the king of Israel, saying,
"Come, let us face each other."

18And Joash the king of Israel sent to Amaziah king of Judah,
saying, "The thorn bush which was in Lebanon sent to the cedar
which was in Lebanon, saying, 'Give your daughter to my son in
marriage.' But there passed by a wild beast that was in Lebanon,
and trampled the thorn bush.

19"You said, 'Behold, you have defeated Edom.' And your
heart has become proud in boasting. Now stay at home; for why
should you provoke trouble that you, even you, should fall and
Judah with you?"

20But Amaziah would not listen, for it was from God, that He
might deliver them into the hand *of Joash* because they had sought
the gods of Edom.

21So Joash king of Israel went up, and he and Amaziah king of
Judah faced each other at Beth-shemesh, which belonged to Judah.

22And Judah was defeated by Israel, and they fled each to his
tent.

23Then Joash king of Israel captured Amaziah king of Judah, the
son of Joash the son of Jehoahaz, at Beth-shemesh, and brought
him to Jerusalem, and tore down the wall of Jerusalem from the
Gate of Ephraim to the Corner Gate, 400 cubits.

24And *he took* all the gold and silver, and all the utensils which
were found in the house of God with Obed-edom, and the treasures of the king's house, the hostages also, and returned to Samaria.

25¶ And Amaziah, the son of Joash king of Judah, lived fifteen
years after the death of Joash, son of Jehoahaz, king of Israel.

26Now the rest of the acts of Amaziah, from first to last, behold,
are they not written in the Book of the Kings of Judah and Israel?

27And from the time that Amaziah turned away from following
the LORD they conspired against him in Jerusalem, and he fled to
Lachish; but they sent after him to Lachish and killed him there.

28Then they brought him on horses and buried him with his
fathers in the city of Judah.

*Uzziah Succeeds Amaziah in Judah*

**26** AND ALL the people of Judah took Uzziah, who *was*
sixteen years old, and made him king in the place of his
father Amaziah.

2He built Eloth and restored it to Judah after the king slept with
his fathers.

3Uzziah was sixteen years old when he became king, and he
reigned fifty-two years in Jerusalem; and his mother's name was
Jechiliah of Jerusalem.

4And he did right in the sight of the LORD according to all that
his father Amaziah had done.

## New International

14When Amaziah returned from slaughtering the Edomites, he
brought back the gods of the people of Seir. He set them up as his
own gods, bowed down to them and burned sacrifices to them.
15The anger of the LORD burned against Amaziah, and he sent a
prophet to him, who said, "Why do you consult this people's
gods, which could not save their own people from your hand?"

16While he was still speaking, the king said to him, "Have we
appointed you an adviser to the king? Stop! Why be struck down?"

So the prophet stopped but said, "I know that God has determined to destroy you, because you have done this and have not
listened to my counsel."

17After Amaziah king of Judah consulted his advisers, he sent
this challenge to Jehoash[a] son of Jehoahaz, the son of Jehu, king
of Israel: "Come, meet me face to face."

18But Jehoash king of Israel replied to Amaziah king of Judah:
"A thistle in Lebanon sent a message to a cedar in Lebanon, 'Give
your daughter to my son in marriage.' Then a wild beast in Lebanon came along and trampled the thistle underfoot. 19You say to
yourself that you have defeated Edom, and now you are arrogant
and proud. But stay at home! Why ask for trouble and cause your
own downfall and that of Judah also?"

20Amaziah, however, would not listen, for God so worked that
he might hand them over to ⌊Jehoash⌋, because they sought the
gods of Edom. 21So Jehoash king of Israel attacked. He and Amaziah king of Judah faced each other at Beth Shemesh in Judah.
22Judah was routed by Israel, and every man fled to his home.
23Jehoash king of Israel captured Amaziah king of Judah, the son
of Joash, the son of Ahaziah,[b] at Beth Shemesh. Then Jehoash
brought him to Jerusalem and broke down the wall of Jerusalem
from the Ephraim Gate to the Corner Gate—a section about six
hundred feet[c] long. 24He took all the gold and silver and all the
articles found in the temple of God that had been in the care of
Obed-Edom, together with the palace treasures and the hostages,
and returned to Samaria.

25Amaziah son of Joash king of Judah lived for fifteen years after
the death of Jehoash son of Jehoahaz king of Israel. 26As for the
other events of Amaziah's reign, from beginning to end, are they
not written in the book of the kings of Judah and Israel? 27From
the time that Amaziah turned away from following the LORD, they
conspired against him in Jerusalem and he fled to Lachish, but they
sent men after him to Lachish and killed him there. 28He was
brought back by horse and was buried with his fathers in the City
of Judah.

*Uzziah King of Judah*

**26** THEN ALL the people of Judah took Uzziah,[d] who was
sixteen years old, and made him king in place of his father
Amaziah. 2He was the one who rebuilt Elath and restored it to
Judah after Amaziah rested with his fathers.

3Uzziah was sixteen years old when he became king, and he
reigned in Jerusalem fifty-two years. His mother's name was Jecoliah; she was from Jerusalem. 4He did what was right in the eyes
of the LORD, just as his father Amaziah had done. 5He sought God

NIV [a] 17 Hebrew *Joash,* a variant of *Jehoash;* also in verses 18, 21, 23 and 25
[b] 23 Hebrew *Jehoahaz,* a variant of *Ahaziah* [c] 23 Hebrew *four hundred cubits*
(about 180 meters) [d] 1 Also called *Azariah*

## King James

5And he sought God in the days of Zechariah, who had understanding in the visions of God: and as long as he sought the LORD, God made him to prosper.

6And he went forth and warred against the Philistines, and brake down the wall of Gath, and the wall of Jabneh, and the wall of Ashdod, and built cities about Ashdod, and among the Philistines.

7And God helped him against the Philistines, and against the Arabians that dwelt in Gur-baal, and the Mehunims.

8And the Ammonites gave gifts to Uzziah: and his name spread abroad *even* to the entering in of Egypt; for he strengthened *himself* exceedingly.

9Moreover Uzziah built towers in Jerusalem at the corner gate, and at the valley gate, and at the turning *of the wall*, and fortified them.

10Also he built towers in the desert, and digged many wells: for he had much cattle, both in the low country, and in the plains: husbandmen *also*, and vine dressers in the mountains, and in Carmel: for he loved husbandry.

11Moreover Uzziah had an host of fighting men, that went out to war by bands, according to the number of their account by the hand of Jeiel the scribe and Maaseiah the ruler, under the hand of Hananiah, *one* of the king's captains.

12The whole number of the chief of the fathers of the mighty men of valour *were* two thousand and six hundred.

13And under their hand *was* an army, three hundred thousand and seven thousand and five hundred, that made war with mighty power, to help the king against the enemy.

14And Uzziah prepared for them throughout all the host shields, and spears, and helmets, and habergeons, and bows, and slings *to cast* stones.

15And he made in Jerusalem engines, invented by cunning men, to be on the towers and upon the bulwarks, to shoot arrows and great stones withal. And his name spread far abroad; for he was marvellously helped, till he was strong.

16¶ But when he was strong, his heart was lifted up to *his* destruction: for he transgressed against the LORD his God, and went into the temple of the LORD to burn incense upon the altar of incense.

17And Azariah the priest went in after him, and with him fourscore priests of the LORD, *that were* valiant men:

18And they withstood Uzziah the king, and said unto him, *It appertaineth* not unto thee, Uzziah, to burn incense unto the LORD, but to the priests the sons of Aaron, that are consecrated to burn incense: go out of the sanctuary; for thou hast trespassed; neither *shall it be* for thine honour from the LORD God.

19Then Uzziah was wroth, and *had* a censer in his hand to burn incense: and while he was wroth with the priests, the leprosy even rose up in his forehead before the priests in the house of the LORD, from beside the incense altar.

20And Azariah the chief priest, and all the priests, looked upon him, and, behold, he *was* leprous in his forehead, and they thrust him out from thence; yea, himself hasted also to go out, because the LORD had smitten him.

21And Uzziah the king was a leper unto the day of his death, and dwelt in a several house, *being* a leper; for he was cut off from the house of the LORD: and Jotham his son *was* over the king's house, judging the people of the land.

22¶ Now the rest of the acts of Uzziah, first and last, did Isaiah the prophet, the son of Amoz, write.

23So Uzziah slept with his fathers, and they buried him with his fathers in the field of the burial which *belonged* to the kings; for they said, He *is* a leper: and Jotham his son reigned in his stead.

## Amplified

5He set himself to seek God in the days of Zechariah who instructed him in the things of God; and as long as he sought [inquired of, yearned for] the Lord, God made him prosper.

6He went out against the Philistines, and broke down the walls of Gath, of Jabneh, and of Ashdod, and built cities near Ashdod and elsewhere among the Philistines.

7And God helped him against the Philistines, and the Arabs who dwelt in Gurbaal, and the Meunim.

8The Ammonites paid tribute to Uzziah, and his fame spread abroad even to the border of Egypt, for he became very strong.

9Also Uzziah built towers in Jerusalem at the Corner Gate, the Valley Gate, and the Angle of the Wall, and fortified them.

10Also he built towers in the wilderness and hewed out many cisterns, for he had much livestock, both in the lowland and in the tableland; and he had farmers and vinedressers in the hills and in the fertile fields [of Carmel], for he loved farming.

11And Uzziah had a combat army for waging war by regiments according to the number as recorded by Jeiel the secretary and Ma-aseiah the officer, under the direction of Hananiah, of the king's commanders.

12The whole number of the heads of fathers' houses of mighty men of valor was 2,600.

13Under their command was an army of 307,500, who could fight with mighty power to help the king against the enemy.

14Uzziah prepared for all the army shields, spears, helmets, coats of mail, bows, and stones to sling.

15In Jerusalem he made machines invented by skillful men, to be on the towers and the (corner) bulwarks, with which to shoot arrows and great stones. And his fame spread far, for he was marvelously helped, till he was strong.

16But when [King Uzziah] was strong, he became proud, to his destruction; and he trespassed against the Lord his God, for he went [a]into the temple of the Lord to burn incense on the altar of incense.

17And Azariah the priest went in after him, and with him eighty priests of the Lord, men of courage.

18They opposed King Uzziah and said to him, It is not for you, Uzziah, to burn incense to the Lord, but for the priests the sons of Aaron, who are set apart to burn incense. Withdraw from the sanctuary; you have trespassed, and that will not be to your credit *and* honor before the Lord God.

19Then Uzziah was enraged, and he had a censer in his hand to burn incense. And while he was enraged with the priests, leprosy broke out on his forehead before the priests in the house of the Lord, beside the incense altar.

20And as Azariah the chief priest and all the priests looked upon him, behold, he was leprous on his forehead! So they forced him out of there, and he also made haste to get out, because the Lord had smitten him.

21And King Uzziah was a leper to the day of his death, and being a leper he dwelt in a separate house, for he was excluded from the Lord's house. And Jotham his son took charge of the king's household, ruling the people of the land.

22Now the rest of the acts of Uzziah, from first to last, Isaiah the prophet, son of Amoz, wrote. [Isa. 1:1.]

23So Uzziah slept with his fathers, and they buried him in the burial field of the kings [outside the royal tombs], for they said, He is a leper. Jotham his son reigned in his stead.

**AMP** [a] No one but an ordained priest was permitted by law to enter the tabernacle, or later the temple proper, even in Jesus' time. See footnote on Num. 3:38.

## New American Standard

5And he continued to seek God in the days of Zechariah, who had understanding through the vision of God; and as long as he sought the LORD, God prospered him.

*Uzziah Succeeds in War*

6¶ Now he went out and warred against the Philistines, and broke down the wall of Gath and the wall of Jabneh and the wall of Ashdod; and he built cities in *the area of* Ashdod and among the Philistines.

7And God helped him against the Philistines, and against the Arabians who lived in Gur-baal, and the Meunites.

8The Ammonites also gave tribute to Uzziah, and his fame extended to the border of Egypt, for he became very strong.

9Moreover, Uzziah built towers in Jerusalem at the Corner Gate and at the Valley Gate and at the corner buttress and fortified them.

10And he built towers in the wilderness and hewed many cisterns, for he had much livestock, both in the lowland and in the plain. *He also had* plowmen and vinedressers in the hill country and the fertile fields, for he loved the soil.

11Moreover, Uzziah had an army ready for battle, which entered combat by divisions, according to the number of their muster, prepared by Jeiel the scribe and Maaseiah the official, under the direction of Hananiah, one of the king's officers.

12The total number of the heads of the households, of valiant warriors, was 2,600.

13And under their direction was an elite army of 307,500, who could wage war with great power, to help the king against the enemy.

14Moreover, Uzziah prepared for all the army shields, spears, helmets, body armor, bows and sling stones.

15And in Jerusalem he made engines *of war* invented by skillful men to be on the towers and on the corners, for the purpose of shooting arrows and great stones. Hence his fame spread afar, for he was marvelously helped until he *was* strong.

*Pride Is Uzziah's Undoing*

16¶ But when he became strong, his heart was so proud that he acted corruptly, and he was unfaithful to the LORD his God, for he entered the temple of the LORD to burn incense on the altar of incense.

17Then Azariah the priest entered after him and with him eighty priests of the LORD, valiant men.

18And they opposed Uzziah the king and said to him, "It is not for you, Uzziah, to burn incense to the LORD, but for the priests, the sons of Aaron who are consecrated to burn incense. Get out of the sanctuary, for you have been unfaithful, and will have no honor from the LORD God."

19But Uzziah, with a censer in his hand for burning incense, was enraged; and while he was enraged with the priests, the leprosy broke out on his forehead before the priests in the house of the LORD, beside the altar of incense.

20And Azariah the chief priest and all the priests looked at him, and behold, he *was* leprous on his forehead; and they hurried him out of there, and he himself also hastened to get out because the LORD had smitten him.

21And King Uzziah was a leper to the day of his death; and he lived in a separate house, being a leper, for he was cut off from the house of the LORD. And Jotham his son *was* over the king's house judging the people of the land.

22Now the rest of the acts of Uzziah, first to last, the prophet Isaiah, the son of Amoz, has written.

23So Uzziah slept with his fathers, and they buried him with his fathers in the field of the grave which belonged to the kings, for they said, "He is a leper." And Jotham his son became king in his place.

## New International

during the days of Zechariah, who instructed him in the fear[b] of
God. As long as he sought the LORD, God gave him success.
6He went to war against the Philistines and broke down the
walls of Gath, Jabneh and Ashdod. He then rebuilt towns near
Ashdod and elsewhere among the Philistines. 7God helped him
against the Philistines and against the Arabs who lived in Gur Baal
and against the Meunites. 8The Ammonites brought tribute to
Uzziah, and his fame spread as far as the border of Egypt, because
he had become very powerful.
9Uzziah built towers in Jerusalem at the Corner Gate, at the
Valley Gate and at the angle of the wall, and he fortified them. 10He
also built towers in the desert and dug many cisterns, because he
had much livestock in the foothills and in the plain. He had people
working his fields and vineyards in the hills and in the fertile
lands, for he loved the soil.
11Uzziah had a well-trained army, ready to go out by divisions
according to their numbers as mustered by Jeiel the secretary and
Maaseiah the officer under the direction of Hananiah, one of the
royal officials. 12The total number of family leaders over the fighting men was 2,600. 13Under their command was an army of 307,
500 men trained for war, a powerful force to support the king
against his enemies. 14Uzziah provided shields, spears, helmets,
coats of armor, bows and slingstones for the entire army. 15In
Jerusalem he made machines designed by skillful men for use on
the towers and on the corner defenses to shoot arrows and hurl
large stones. His fame spread far and wide, for he was greatly
helped until he became powerful.
16But after Uzziah became powerful, his pride led to his downfall. He was unfaithful to the LORD his God, and entered the
temple of the LORD to burn incense on the altar of incense. 17Aza-
riah the priest with eighty other courageous priests of the LORD
followed him in. 18They confronted him and said, "It is not right
for you, Uzziah, to burn incense to the LORD. That is for the priests,
the descendants of Aaron, who have been consecrated to burn
incense. Leave the sanctuary, for you have been unfaithful; and
you will not be honored by the LORD God."
19Uzziah, who had a censer in his hand ready to burn incense,
became angry. While he was raging at the priests in their presence
before the incense altar in the LORD's temple, leprosy[c] broke out
on his forehead. 20When Azariah the chief priest and all the other
priests looked at him, they saw that he had leprosy on his forehead, so they hurried him out. Indeed, he himself was eager to
leave, because the LORD had afflicted him.
21King Uzziah had leprosy until the day he died. He lived in a
separate house[d] —leprous, and excluded from the temple of the
LORD. Jotham his son had charge of the palace and governed the
people of the land.
22The other events of Uzziah's reign, from beginning to end, are
recorded by the prophet Isaiah son of Amoz. 23Uzziah rested with
his fathers and was buried near them in a field for burial that
belonged to the kings, for people said, "He had leprosy." And
Jotham his son succeeded him as king.

**NIV** [b] *5* Many Hebrew manuscripts, Septuagint and Syriac; other Hebrew manuscripts *vision* [c] *19* The Hebrew word was used for various diseases affecting the skin—not necessarily leprosy; also in verses 20, 21 and 23. [d] *21* Or *in a house where he was relieved of responsibilities*

## King James

**27** JOTHAM *WAS* twenty and five years old when he began to reign, and he reigned sixteen years in Jerusalem. His mother's name also *was* Jerushah, the daughter of Zadok.

2And he did *that which was* right in the sight of the LORD, according to all that his father Uzziah did: howbeit he entered not into the temple of the LORD. And the people did yet corruptly.

3He built the high gate of the house of the LORD, and on the wall of Ophel he built much.

4Moreover he built cities in the mountains of Judah, and in the forests he built castles and towers.

5¶ He fought also with the king of the Ammonites, and prevailed against them. And the children of Ammon gave him the same year an hundred talents of silver, and ten thousand measures of wheat, and ten thousand of barley. So much did the children of Ammon pay unto him, both the second year, and the third.

6So Jotham became mighty, because he prepared his ways before the LORD his God.

7¶ Now the rest of the acts of Jotham, and all his wars, and his ways, lo, they *are* written in the book of the kings of Israel and Judah.

8He was five and twenty years old when he began to reign, and reigned sixteen years in Jerusalem.

9¶ And Jotham slept with his fathers, and they buried him in the city of David: and Ahaz his son reigned in his stead.

**28** AHAZ *WAS* twenty years old when he began to reign, and he reigned sixteen years in Jerusalem: but he did not *that which was* right in the sight of the LORD, like David his father:

2For he walked in the ways of the kings of Israel, and made also molten images for Baalim.

3Moreover he burnt incense in the valley of the son of Hinnom, and burnt his children in the fire, after the abominations of the heathen whom the LORD had cast out before the children of Israel.

4He sacrificed also and burnt incense in the high places, and on the hills, and under every green tree.

5Wherefore the LORD his God delivered him into the hand of the king of Syria; and they smote him, and carried away a great multitude of them captives, and brought *them* to Damascus. And he was also delivered into the hand of the king of Israel, who smote him with a great slaughter.

6¶ For Pekah the son of Remaliah slew in Judah an hundred and twenty thousand in one day, *which were* all valiant men; because they had forsaken the LORD God of their fathers.

7And Zichri, a mighty man of Ephraim, slew Maaseiah the king's son, and Azrikam the governor of the house, and Elkanah *that was* next to the king.

8And the children of Israel carried away captive of their brethren two hundred thousand, women, sons, and daughters, and took also away much spoil from them, and brought the spoil to Samaria.

9But a prophet of the LORD was there, whose name *was* Oded: and he went out before the host that came to Samaria, and said unto them, Behold, because the LORD God of your fathers was wroth with Judah, he hath delivered them into your hand, and ye have slain them in a rage *that* reacheth up unto heaven.

10And now ye purpose to keep under the children of Judah and Jerusalem for bondmen and bondwomen unto you: *but are there* not with you, even with you, sins against the LORD your God?

11Now hear me therefore, and deliver the captives again, which ye have taken captive of your brethren: for the fierce wrath of the LORD *is* upon you.

## Amplified

**27** JOTHAM WAS twenty-five years old when he began to reign, and he reigned sixteen years in Jerusalem. His mother was Jerushah daughter of Zadok.

2He did right in the sight of the Lord, to the extent that his father Uzziah had done. However, he did not invade the temple of the Lord. But the people still did corruptly.

3He built the upper gate of the Lord's house, and did much building on the wall of Ophel.

4Moreover he built cities in the hill country of Judah, and in the forests he built forts and towers.

5He fought with the king of the Ammonites, and prevailed against them. The Ammonites gave him that year 100 talents of silver, and 10,000 measures each of wheat and of barley. That much the Ammonites paid to him also the second year and third year.

6So Jotham grew mighty, for he ordered his ways in the sight of the Lord his God.

7Now the rest of Jotham's acts, and all his wars, and his ways, behold, they are written in the Book of the Kings of Israel and Judah.

8He was twenty-five years old when he began to reign, and he reigned sixteen years in Jerusalem.

9And Jotham slept with his fathers, and they buried him in the city of David. Ahaz his son reigned in his stead.

**28** AHAZ WAS twenty years old when he began his sixteen years' reign in Jerusalem. He did not do right in the sight of the Lord, like David his father [forefather];

2But he walked in the ways of the kings of Israel, and even made molten images for the Baals.

3And he burned incense in the valley of the son of Hinnom, and burned his sons as an offering, after the abominable customs of the [heathen] nations whom the Lord drove out before the Israelites.

4He sacrificed also and burnt incense in the high places, on the hills, and under every green tree.

5Therefore the Lord his God gave Ahaz into the power of the king of Syria, who defeated him and carried away a great multitude of the Jews captive, taking them to Damascus. And he was also delivered into the hand of the king of Israel, who smote Judah with a great slaughter.

6For Pekah son of Remaliah slew in Judah 120,000 in one day, all courageous men, because they had forsaken the Lord, the God of their fathers.

7And Zichri, a mighty man of Ephraim, slew Maaseiah King Ahaz' son, and Azrikam the governor of the house, and Elkanah who was second to the king.

8And the Israelites carried away captive 200,000 of their kinsmen [of Judah], women, sons, and daughters, and also took much plunder from them and brought it to Samaria.

9But a prophet of the Lord was there, whose name was Oded; and he went out to meet the army that was returning to Samaria, and said to them, Behold, because the Lord, the God of your fathers was angry with Judah, He delivered them into your hand, but you have slain them in a fury that reaches up to Heaven.

10And now you intend to suppress the people of Judah and Jerusalem, both men and women, as your slaves. But are not you yourselves guilty of crimes against the Lord your God?

11Now hear me therefore, and set the prisoners free again, whom you have taken captive of your kinsmen, for the fierce wrath of the Lord is upon you.

## New American Standard

*Jotham Succeeds Uzziah in Judah*

**27** JOTHAM WAS twenty-five years old when he became
king, and he reigned sixteen years in Jerusalem. And his
mother's name was Jerushah the daughter of Zadok.
2And he did right in the sight of the LORD, according to all that
his father Uzziah had done; however he did not enter the temple
of the LORD. But the people continued acting corruptly.
3He built the upper gate of the house of the LORD, and he built
extensively the wall of Ophel.
4Moreover, he built cities in the hill country of Judah, and he
built fortresses and towers on the wooded *hills*.
5He fought also with the king of the Ammonites and prevailed
over them so that the Ammonites gave him during that year one
hundred talents of silver, ten thousand [a]kors of wheat and ten
thousand of barley. The Ammonites also paid him this *amount* in
the second and in the third year.
6So Jotham became mighty because he ordered his ways before
the LORD his God.
7Now the rest of the acts of Jotham, even all his wars and his
acts, behold, they are written in the Book of the Kings of Israel and
Judah.
8He was twenty-five years old when he became king, and he
reigned sixteen years in Jerusalem.
9And Jotham slept with his fathers, and they buried him in the
city of David; and Ahaz his son became king in his place.

*Ahaz Succeeds Jotham in Judah*

**28** AHAZ *WAS* twenty years old when he became king, and
he reigned sixteen years in Jerusalem; and he did not do
right in the sight of the LORD as David his father *had done*.
2But he walked in the ways of the kings of Israel; he also made
molten images for the Baals.
3Moreover, he burned incense in the valley of Ben-hinnom,
and burned his sons in fire, according to the abominations of the
nations whom the LORD had driven out before the sons of Israel.
4And he sacrificed and burned incense on the high places, on
the hills, and under every green tree.

*Judah Is Invaded*

5¶ Wherefore, the LORD his God delivered him into the hand
of the king of Aram; and they defeated him and carried away from
him a great number of captives, and brought *them* to Damascus.
And he was also delivered into the hand of the king of Israel, who
inflicted him with heavy casualties.
6For Pekah the son of Remaliah slew in Judah 120,000 in one
day, all valiant men, because they had forsaken the LORD God of
their fathers.
7And Zichri, a mighty man of Ephraim, slew Maaseiah the
king's son, and Azrikam the ruler of the house and Elkanah the
second to the king.
8¶ And the sons of Israel carried away captive of their brethren
200,000 women, sons, and daughters; and took also a great deal
of spoil from them, and they brought the spoil to Samaria.
9But a prophet of the LORD was there, whose name *was* Oded;
and he went out to meet the army which came to Samaria and said
to them, "Behold, because the LORD, the God of your fathers, was
angry with Judah, He has delivered them into your hand, and you
have slain them in a rage *which* has even reached heaven.
10"And now you are proposing to subjugate for yourselves the
people of Judah and Jerusalem for male and female slaves. Surely,
*do* you not *have* transgressions of your own against the LORD your
God?
11"Now therefore, listen to me and return the captives whom
you captured from your brothers, for the burning anger of the
LORD is against you."

NAS [a] I.e., A kor equals approx. 10 bushels

## New International

*Jotham King of Judah*

**27** JOTHAM WAS twenty-five years old when he became
king, and he reigned in Jerusalem sixteen years. His
mother's name was Jerusha daughter of Zadok. 2He did what was
right in the eyes of the LORD, just as his father Uzziah had done,
but unlike him he did not enter the temple of the LORD. The
people, however, continued their corrupt practices. 3Jotham rebuilt the Upper Gate of the temple of the LORD and did extensive
work on the wall at the hill of Ophel. 4He built towns in the Judean
hills and forts and towers in the wooded areas.
5Jotham made war on the king of the Ammonites and conquered them. That year the Ammonites paid him a hundred talents[b] of silver, ten thousand cors[c] of wheat and ten thousand cors
of barley. The Ammonites brought him the same amount also in
the second and third years.
6Jotham grew powerful because he walked steadfastly before
the LORD his God.
7The other events in Jotham's reign, including all his wars and
the other things he did, are written in the book of the kings of Israel
and Judah. 8He was twenty-five years old when he became king,
and he reigned in Jerusalem sixteen years. 9Jotham rested with his
fathers and was buried in the City of David. And Ahaz his son
succeeded him as king.

*Ahaz King of Judah*

**28** AHAZ WAS twenty years old when he became king, and
he reigned in Jerusalem sixteen years. Unlike David his
father, he did not do what was right in the eyes of the LORD. 2He
walked in the ways of the kings of Israel and also made cast idols
for worshiping the Baals. 3He burned sacrifices in the Valley of Ben
Hinnom and sacrificed his sons in the fire, following the detestable
ways of the nations the LORD had driven out before the Israelites.
4He offered sacrifices and burned incense at the high places, on the
hilltops and under every spreading tree.
5Therefore the LORD his God handed him over to the king of
Aram. The Arameans defeated him and took many of his people
as prisoners and brought them to Damascus.
He was also given into the hands of the king of Israel, who
inflicted heavy casualties on him. 6In one day Pekah son of Remaliah killed a hundred and twenty thousand soldiers in Judah—
because Judah had forsaken the LORD, the God of their fathers.
7Zicri, an Ephraimite warrior, killed Maaseiah the king's son, Azrikam the officer in charge of the palace, and Elkanah, second to
the king. 8The Israelites took captive from their kinsmen two hundred thousand wives, sons and daughters. They also took a great
deal of plunder, which they carried back to Samaria.
9But a prophet of the LORD named Oded was there, and he went
out to meet the army when it returned to Samaria. He said to them,
"Because the LORD, the God of your fathers, was angry with
Judah, he gave them into your hand. But you have slaughtered
them in a rage that reaches to heaven. 10And now you intend to
make the men and women of Judah and Jerusalem your slaves. But
aren't you also guilty of sins against the LORD your God? 11Now
listen to me! Send back your fellow countrymen you have taken
as prisoners, for the LORD's fierce anger rests on you."

NIV [b] *5* That is, about 3 3/4 tons (about 3.4 metric tons) [c] *5* That is,
probably about 62,000 bushels (about 2,200 kiloliters)

## King James

12Then certain of the heads of the children of Ephraim, Azariah the son of Johanan, Berechiah the son of Meshillemoth, and Jehizkiah the son of Shallum, and Amasa the son of Hadlai, stood up against them that came from the war,

13And said unto them, Ye shall not bring in the captives hither: for whereas we have offended against the LORD *already*, ye intend to add *more* to our sins and to our trespass: for our trespass is great, and *there is* fierce wrath against Israel.

14So the armed men left the captives and the spoil before the princes and all the congregation.

15And the men which were expressed by name rose up, and took the captives, and with the spoil clothed all that were naked among them, and arrayed them, and shod them, and gave them to eat and to drink, and anointed them, and carried all the feeble of them upon asses, and brought them to Jericho, the city of palm trees, to their brethren: then they returned to Samaria.

16¶ At that time did king Ahaz send unto the kings of Assyria to help him.

17For again the Edomites had come and smitten Judah, and carried away captives.

18The Philistines also had invaded the cities of the low country, and of the south of Judah, and had taken Beth-shemesh, and Ajalon, and Gederoth, and Shocho with the villages thereof, and Timnah with the villages thereof, Gimzo also and the villages thereof: and they dwelt there.

19For the LORD brought Judah low because of Ahaz king of Israel; for he made Judah naked, and transgressed sore against the LORD.

20And Tilgath-pilneser king of Assyria came unto him, and distressed him, but strengthened him not.

21For Ahaz took away a portion *out* of the house of the LORD, and *out* of the house of the king, and of the princes, and gave *it* unto the king of Assyria: but he helped him not.

22¶ And in the time of his distress did he trespass yet more against the LORD: this *is that* king Ahaz.

23For he sacrificed unto the gods of Damascus, which smote him: and he said, Because the gods of the kings of Syria help them, *therefore* will I sacrifice to them, that they may help me. But they were the ruin of him, and of all Israel.

24And Ahaz gathered together the vessels of the house of God, and cut in pieces the vessels of the house of God, and shut up the doors of the house of the LORD, and he made him altars in every corner of Jerusalem.

25And in every several city of Judah he made high places to burn incense unto other gods, and provoked to anger the LORD God of his fathers.

26¶ Now the rest of his acts and of all his ways, first and last, behold, they *are* written in the book of the kings of Judah and Israel.

27And Ahaz slept with his fathers, and they buried him in the city, *even* in Jerusalem: but they brought him not into the sepulchres of the kings of Israel: and Hezekiah his son reigned in his stead.

**29** HEZEKIAH BEGAN to reign *when he was* five and twenty years old, and he reigned nine and twenty years in Jerusalem. And his mother's name *was* Abijah, the daughter of Zechariah.

2And he did *that which was* right in the sight of the LORD, according to all that David his father had done.

3¶ He in the first year of his reign, in the first month, opened the doors of the house of the LORD, and repaired them.

4And he brought in the priests and the Levites, and gathered them together into the east street,

## Amplified

12Then certain of the heads of the Ephraimites [Israel], Azariah son of Johanan, Berechiah son of Meshillemoth, Jehizkiah son of Shallum, and Amasa son of Hadlai, stood up against those returning from the war,

13And said, You shall not bring the captives in here; we are guilty before the Lord already, and what you intend will add more to our sins and our guilt; for our trespass [guilt] is great, and there is fierce anger against Israel.

14So the armed men [of Israel] left the captives and the spoil [of Judah] before the princes and all the assembly.

15And the men who have been mentioned by name rose up, and took the captives and with the spoil they clothed all who were naked among them; and having clothed them, shod them, given them food and drink, anointed them [as was a host's duty], and carrying all the feeble of them upon donkeys, they brought them to Jericho, the city of palm trees, to their brethren. Then they returned to Samaria. [Luke 7:44-46.]

16At that time King Ahaz sent to the king of Assyria to help him.

17For again the Edomites had come and smitten Judah, and carried away captives.

18The Philistines had invaded the cities of the low country, and of the south of Judah, and had taken Beth-shemesh, Aijalon, Gederoth, and Soco, and also Timnah and Gimso with their villages; and they settled there.

19For the Lord brought Judah low because of Ahaz king of Israel, for Ahaz had dealt with reckless cruelty against Judah, and had been faithless [had transgressed sorely] against the Lord.

20So Tilgath-pilneser king of Assyria came to him, and distressed him without strengthening him.

21For Ahaz took [treasure] from the house of the Lord, and out of the house of the king and of the princes, and gave it as tribute to the king of Assyria; but it did not help Ahaz.

22In the time of his distress he became still more unfaithful to the Lord—this same King Ahaz.

23For he sacrificed to the gods of Damascus which defeated him, for he said, Since the gods of the kings of Syria helped them, I will sacrifice to them that they may help me. But they were the ruin of him, and of all Israel.

24And Ahaz collected the utensils of the house of God, and cut them in pieces, and shut up the doors of the Lord's temple [the holy place and the holy of holies], and he made himself altars in every corner of Jerusalem.

25In each city of Judah he made high places to burn incense to other gods, provoking to anger the Lord, the God of his fathers.

26Now the rest of his acts and of all his ways, from first to last, behold, they are written in the Book of the Kings of Judah and Israel.

27And Ahaz slept with his fathers, and they buried him in the city, in Jerusalem, but they did not bring him into the tombs of the kings of Israel. And Hezekiah his son reigned in his stead.

**29** HEZEKIAH BEGAN to reign when he was twenty-five years old, and he reigned twenty-nine years in Jerusalem. His mother was Abijah daughter of Zechariah.

2And he did right in the sight of the Lord, according to all that David his father [forefather] had done.

3In the first year of his reign, in the first month, he opened the doors of the house of the Lord [which his father had closed] and repaired them.

4He brought together the priests and Levites in the square on the east,

## New American Standard

12Then some of the heads of the sons of Ephraim—Azariah the
son of Johanan, Berechiah the son of Meshillemoth, Jehizkiah the
son of Shallum, and Amasa the son of Hadlai—arose against those
who were coming from the battle,
13and said to them, "You must not bring the captives in here,
for you are proposing *to bring* upon us guilt against the LORD
adding to our sins and our guilt; for our guilt is great so that *His*
burning anger is against Israel."
14So the armed men left the captives and the spoil before the
officers and all the assembly.
15Then the men who were designated by name arose, took the
captives, and they clothed all their naked ones from the spoil; and
they gave them clothes and sandals, fed them and gave them
drink, anointed them *with oil,* led all their feeble ones on donkeys,
and brought them to Jericho, the city of palm trees, to their brothers; then they returned to Samaria.

*Compromise with Assyria*

16¶ At that time King Ahaz sent to the [a]kings of Assyria for
help.
17For again the Edomites had come and attacked Judah, and
carried away captives.
18The Philistines also had invaded the cities of the lowland and
of the Negev of Judah, and had taken Beth-shemesh, Aijalon,
Gederoth, and Soco with its villages, Timnah with its villages, and
Gimzo with its villages, and they settled there.
19For the LORD humbled Judah because of Ahaz king of Israel,
for he had brought about a lack of restraint in Judah and was very
unfaithful to the LORD.
20So Tilgath-pilneser king of Assyria came against him and
afflicted him instead of strengthening him.
21Although Ahaz took a portion out of the house of the LORD
and out of the palace of the king and of the princes, and gave *it*
to the king of Assyria, it did not help him.
22¶ Now in the time of his distress this same King Ahaz became
yet more unfaithful to the LORD.
23For he sacrificed to the gods of Damascus which had defeated
him, and said, "Because the gods of the kings of Aram helped
them, I will sacrifice to them that they may help me." But they
became the downfall of him and all Israel.
24Moreover, when Ahaz gathered together the utensils of the
house of God, he cut the utensils of the house of God in pieces;
and he closed the doors of the house of the LORD, and made altars
for himself in every corner of Jerusalem.
25And in every city of Judah he made high places to burn
incense to other gods, and provoked the LORD, the God of his
fathers, to anger.
26Now the rest of his acts and all his ways, from first to last,
behold, they are written in the Book of the Kings of Judah and
Israel.
27So Ahaz slept with his fathers, and they buried him in the city,
in Jerusalem, for they did not bring him into the tombs of the kings
of Israel; and Hezekiah his son reigned in his place.

*Hezekiah Succeeds Ahaz in Judah*

**29** HEZEKIAH BECAME king *when he was* twenty-five years
old; and he reigned twenty-nine years in Jerusalem. And
his mother's name *was* Abijah, the daughter of Zechariah.
2And he did right in the sight of the LORD, according to all that
his father David had done.
3¶ In the first year of his reign, in the first month, he opened
the doors of the house of the LORD and repaired them.
4And he brought in the priests and the Levites, and gathered
them into the square on the east.

NAS [a] Ancient versions read *king*

## New International

12Then some of the leaders in Ephraim—Azariah son of Jehohanan, Berekiah son of Meshillemoth, Jehizkiah son of Shallum, and
Amasa son of Hadlai—confronted those who were arriving from
the war. 13"You must not bring those prisoners here," they said,
"or we will be guilty before the LORD. Do you intend to add to our
sin and guilt? For our guilt is already great, and his fierce anger
rests on Israel."
14So the soldiers gave up the prisoners and plunder in the
presence of the officials and all the assembly. 15The men designated by name took the prisoners, and from the plunder they
clothed all who were naked. They provided them with clothes and
sandals, food and drink, and healing balm. All those who were
weak they put on donkeys. So they took them back to their fellow
countrymen at Jericho, the City of Palms, and returned to Samaria.
16At that time King Ahaz sent to the king[b] of Assyria for help.
17The Edomites had again come and attacked Judah and carried
away prisoners, 18while the Philistines had raided towns in the
foothills and in the Negev of Judah. They captured and occupied
Beth Shemesh, Aijalon and Gederoth, as well as Soco, Timnah and
Gimzo, with their surrounding villages. 19The LORD had humbled
Judah because of Ahaz king of Israel,[c] for he had promoted
wickedness in Judah and had been most unfaithful to the LORD.
20Tiglath-Pileser[d] king of Assyria came to him, but he gave him
trouble instead of help. 21Ahaz took some of the things from the
temple of the LORD and from the royal palace and from the princes
and presented them to the king of Assyria, but that did not help
him.
22In his time of trouble King Ahaz became even more unfaithful
to the LORD. 23He offered sacrifices to the gods of Damascus, who
had defeated him; for he thought, "Since the gods of the kings of
Aram have helped them, I will sacrifice to them so they will help
me." But they were his downfall and the downfall of all Israel.
24Ahaz gathered together the furnishings from the temple of
God and took them away.[e] He shut the doors of the LORD's temple
and set up altars at every street corner in Jerusalem. 25In every
town in Judah he built high places to burn sacrifices to other gods
and provoked the LORD, the God of his fathers, to anger.
26The other events of his reign and all his ways, from beginning
to end, are written in the book of the kings of Judah and Israel.
27Ahaz rested with his fathers and was buried in the city of Jerusalem, but he was not placed in the tombs of the kings of Israel. And
Hezekiah his son succeeded him as king.

*Hezekiah Purifies the Temple*

**29** HEZEKIAH WAS twenty-five years old when he became
king, and he reigned in Jerusalem twenty-nine years. His
mother's name was Abijah daughter of Zechariah. 2He did what
was right in the eyes of the LORD, just as his father David had done.
3In the first month of the first year of his reign, he opened the
doors of the temple of the LORD and repaired them. 4He brought
in the priests and the Levites, assembled them in the square on the
east side 5and said: "Listen to me, Levites! Consecrate yourselves

NIV [b] *16* One Hebrew manuscript, Septuagint and Vulgate (see also 2 Kings 16:7); most Hebrew manuscripts *kings* [c] *19* That is, Judah, as frequently in 2 Chronicles [d] *20* Hebrew *Tilgath-Pilneser,* a variant of *Tiglath-Pileser* [e] *24* Or *and cut them up*

## King James

5And said unto them, Hear me, ye Levites, sanctify now yourselves, and sanctify the house of the LORD God of your fathers, and carry forth the filthiness out of the holy *place*.

6For our fathers have trespassed, and done *that which was* evil in the eyes of the LORD our God, and have forsaken him, and have turned away their faces from the habitation of the LORD, and turned *their* backs.

7Also they have shut up the doors of the porch, and put out the lamps, and have not burned incense nor offered burnt offerings in the holy *place* unto the God of Israel.

8Wherefore the wrath of the LORD was upon Judah and Jerusalem, and he hath delivered them to trouble, to astonishment, and to hissing, as ye see with your eyes.

9For, lo, our fathers have fallen by the sword, and our sons and our daughters and our wives *are* in captivity for this.

10Now *it is* in mine heart to make a covenant with the LORD God of Israel, that his fierce wrath may turn away from us.

11My sons, be not now negligent: for the LORD hath chosen you to stand before him, to serve him, and that ye should minister unto him, and burn incense.

12¶ Then the Levites arose, Mahath the son of Amasai, and Joel the son of Azariah, of the sons of the Kohathites: and of the sons of Merari, Kish the son of Abdi, and Azariah the son of Jehalelel: and of the Gershonites; Joah the son of Zimmah, and Eden the son of Joah:

13And of the sons of Elizaphan; Shimri, and Jeiel: and of the sons of Asaph; Zechariah, and Mattaniah:

14And of the sons of Heman; Jehiel, and Shimei: and of the sons of Jeduthun; Shemaiah, and Uzziel.

15And they gathered their brethren, and sanctified themselves, and came, according to the commandment of the king, by the words of the LORD, to cleanse the house of the LORD.

16And the priests went into the inner part of the house of the LORD, to cleanse *it*, and brought out all the uncleanness that they found in the temple of the LORD into the court of the house of the LORD. And the Levites took *it*, to carry *it* out abroad into the brook Kidron.

17Now they began on the first *day* of the first month to sanctify, and on the eighth day of the month came they to the porch of the LORD: so they sanctified the house of the LORD in eight days; and in the sixteenth day of the first month they made an end.

18Then they went in to Hezekiah the king, and said, We have cleansed all the house of the LORD, and the altar of burnt offering, with all the vessels thereof, and the showbread table, with all the vessels thereof.

19Moreover all the vessels, which king Ahaz in his reign did cast away in his transgression, have we prepared and sanctified, and, behold, they *are* before the altar of the LORD.

20¶ Then Hezekiah the king rose early, and gathered the rulers of the city, and went up to the house of the LORD.

21And they brought seven bullocks, and seven rams, and seven lambs, and seven he goats, for a sin offering for the kingdom, and for the sanctuary, and for Judah. And he commanded the priests the sons of Aaron to offer *them* on the altar of the LORD.

22So they killed the bullocks, and the priests received the blood, and sprinkled *it* on the altar: likewise, when they had killed the rams, they sprinkled the blood upon the altar: they killed also the lambs, and they sprinkled the blood upon the altar.

23And they brought forth the he goats *for* the sin offering before the king and the congregation; and they laid their hands upon them:

24And the priests killed them, and they made reconciliation with their blood upon the altar, to make an atonement for all Israel: for the king commanded *that* the burnt offering and the sin offering *should be made* for all Israel.

25And he set the Levites in the house of the LORD with cymbals, with psalteries, and with harps, according to the commandment of David, and of Gad the king's seer, and Nathan the prophet: for *so was* the commandment of the LORD by his prophets.

## Amplified

5And said to them, Levites, hear me! Now sanctify [purify and make free from sin] yourselves and the house of the Lord the God of your fathers, and carry out the filth from the holy place.

6For our fathers have trespassed, and done what was evil in the sight of the Lord our God, and have forsaken Him, and have turned away their faces from the dwelling place of the Lord, and turned their backs.

7Also they have closed the doors of the porch and put out the lamps, and have not burned incense or offered burnt offerings in the place holy to the God of Israel. [Cp. II Kings 16:10-16.]

8Therefore the wrath of the Lord was upon Judah and Jerusalem, and He has delivered them to be a terror *and* a cause of trembling, to be an astonishment, and a hissing, as you see with your eyes.

9For, lo, our fathers have fallen by the sword, and our sons, our daughters, and our wives are in captivity for this.

10Now it is in my heart to make a covenant with the Lord, the God of Israel, that His fierce anger may turn away from us.

11My sons, do not now be negligent, for the Lord has chosen you to stand in His presence, to serve Him, to be His ministers and burn incense to Him.

12Then the Levites arose, Mahath son of Amasai, Joel son of Azariah, of the sons of the Kohathites; of the sons of Merari, Kish son of Abdi, Azariah son of Jehallelel; of the Gershonites, Joah son of Zimmah, and Eden son of Joah;

13Of the sons of Elizaphan, Shimri and Jeuel; of the sons of Asaph, Zechariah, and Mattaniah;

14Of the sons of Heman, Jehuel and Shimei; and of the sons of Jeduthun, Shemaiah and Uzziel.

15They gathered their brethren, and sanctified themselves, and went in as the king had commanded by the words of the Lord, to cleanse the house of the Lord.

16The priests went into the inner part of the house of the Lord to cleanse it, and brought out all the uncleanness they found in the temple of the Lord into the court of the Lord's house. And the Levites carried it out to the brook Kidron.

17They began on the first day of the first month, and on the eighth day they came to the porch of the Lord; then for eight days they sanctified the house of the Lord, and on the sixteenth day they finished.

18Then they went to King Hezekiah and said, We have cleansed all the house of the Lord, and the altar of burnt offering with all its utensils and the showbread table with all its utensils.

19Moreover all the utensils which King Ahaz in his reign cast away when he was transgressing [faithless], we have made ready and sanctified; and behold, they are before the altar of the Lord.

20Then King Hezekiah rose early and gathered the officials of the city, and went up to the house of the Lord.

21They brought seven each of bulls, rams, lambs and he-goats for a sin offering for the kingdom, the sanctuary, and Judah. He commanded the priests the sons of Aaron to offer them on the Lord's altar.

22So they killed the bulls, and the priests received the blood and dashed it against the altar. Likewise, when they had killed the rams, then the lambs, they dashed the blood against the altar.

23Then the he-goats for the sin offering were brought before the king and the assembly, and they laid their hands on them,

24The priests killed them and made a sin offering with their blood upon the altar, to make atonement for all Israel; for the king commanded that the burnt offering and sin offering be made for all Israel.

25Hezekiah stationed the Levites in the Lord's house with cymbals, harps, and lyres, as David [his forefather], and Gad the king's seer, and Nathan the prophet commanded; for the commandment was from the Lord through His prophets.

## New American Standard

*Reforms Begun*

5Then he said to them, "Listen to me, O Levites. Consecrate
yourselves now, and consecrate the house of the LORD, the God
of your fathers, and carry the uncleanness out from the holy place.
6"For our fathers have been unfaithful and have done evil in
the sight of the LORD our God, and have forsaken Him and turned
their faces away from the dwelling place of the LORD, and have
turned *their* backs.
7"They have also shut the doors of the porch and put out the
lamps, and have not burned incense or offered burnt offerings in
the holy place to the God of Israel.
8"Therefore the wrath of the LORD was against Judah and
Jerusalem, and He has made them an object of terror, of horror,
and of hissing, as you see with your own eyes.
9"For behold, our fathers have fallen by the sword, and our
sons and our daughters and our wives are in captivity for this.
10"Now it is in my heart to make a covenant with the LORD God
of Israel, that His burning anger may turn away from us.
11"My sons, do not be negligent now, for the LORD has chosen
you to stand before Him, to minister to Him, and to be His ministers and burn incense."
12¶ Then the Levites arose: Mahath, the son of Amasai and Joel
the son of Azariah, from the sons of the Kohathites; and from the
sons of Merari, Kish the son of Abdi and Azariah the son of
Jehallelel; and from the Gershonites, Joah the son of Zimmah and
Eden the son of Joah;
13and from the sons of Elizaphan, Shimri and Jeiel; and from the
sons of Asaph, Zechariah and Mattaniah;
14and from the sons of Heman, Jehiel and Shimei; and from the
sons of Jeduthun, Shemaiah and Uzziel.
15And they assembled their brothers, consecrated themselves,
and went in to cleanse the house of the LORD, according to the
commandment of the king by the words of the LORD.
16So the priests went in to the inner part of the house of the
LORD to cleanse *it*, and every unclean thing which they found in
the temple of the LORD they brought out to the court of the house
of the LORD. Then the Levites received *it* to carry out to the Kidron
valley.
17Now they began the consecration on the first *day* of the first
month, and on the eighth day of the month they entered the porch
of the LORD. Then they consecrated the house of the LORD in eight
days, and finished on the sixteenth day of the first month.
18Then they went in to King Hezekiah and said, "We have
cleansed the whole house of the LORD, the altar of burnt offering
with all of its utensils, and the table of showbread with all of its
utensils.
19"Moreover, all the utensils which King Ahaz had discarded
during his reign in his unfaithfulness, we have prepared and
consecrated; and behold, they are before the altar of the LORD."

*Hezekiah Restores Temple Worship*

20¶ Then King Hezekiah arose early and assembled the princes
of the city and went up to the house of the LORD.
21And they brought seven bulls, seven rams, seven lambs, and
seven male goats for a sin offering for the kingdom, the sanctuary,
and Judah. And he ordered the priests, the sons of Aaron, to offer
*them* on the altar of the LORD.
22So they slaughtered the bulls, and the priests took the blood
and sprinkled it on the altar. They also slaughtered the rams and
sprinkled the blood on the altar; they slaughtered the lambs also
and sprinkled the blood on the altar.
23Then they brought the male goats of the sin offering before
the king and the assembly, and they laid their hands on them.
24And the priests slaughtered them and purged the altar with
their blood to atone for all Israel, for the king ordered the burnt
offering and the sin offering for all Israel.
25¶ He then stationed the Levites in the house of the LORD with
cymbals, with harps, and with lyres, according to the command
of David and of Gad the king's seer, and of Nathan the prophet;
for the command was from the LORD through His prophets.

## New International

now and consecrate the temple of the LORD, the God of your
fathers. Remove all defilement from the sanctuary. 6Our fathers
were unfaithful; they did evil in the eyes of the LORD our God and
forsook him. They turned their faces away from the LORD's dwelling place and turned their backs on him. 7They also shut the doors
of the portico and put out the lamps. They did not burn incense
or present any burnt offerings at the sanctuary to the God of Israel.
8Therefore, the anger of the LORD has fallen on Judah and Jerusalem; he has made them an object of dread and horror and scorn,
as you can see with your own eyes. 9This is why our fathers have
fallen by the sword and why our sons and daughters and our
wives are in captivity. 10Now I intend to make a covenant with the
LORD, the God of Israel, so that his fierce anger will turn away from
us. 11My sons, do not be negligent now, for the LORD has chosen
you to stand before him and serve him, to minister before him and
to burn incense."
12Then these Levites set to work:
from the Kohathites,
Mahath son of Amasai and Joel son of Azariah;
from the Merarites,
Kish son of Abdi and Azariah son of Jehallelel;
from the Gershonites,
Joah son of Zimmah and Eden son of Joah;
13from the descendants of Elizaphan,
Shimri and Jeiel;
from the descendants of Asaph,
Zechariah and Mattaniah;
14from the descendants of Heman,
Jehiel and Shimei;
from the descendants of Jeduthun,
Shemaiah and Uzziel.
15When they had assembled their brothers and consecrated
themselves, they went in to purify the temple of the LORD, as the
king had ordered, following the word of the LORD. 16The priests
went into the sanctuary of the LORD to purify it. They brought out
to the courtyard of the LORD's temple everything unclean that they
found in the temple of the LORD. The Levites took it and carried
it out to the Kidron Valley. 17They began the consecration on the
first day of the first month, and by the eighth day of the month
they reached the portico of the LORD. For eight more days they
consecrated the temple of the LORD itself, finishing on the sixteenth day of the first month.
18Then they went in to King Hezekiah and reported: "We have
purified the entire temple of the LORD, the altar of burnt offering
with all its utensils, and the table for setting out the consecrated
bread, with all its articles. 19We have prepared and consecrated all
the articles that King Ahaz removed in his unfaithfulness while he
was king. They are now in front of the LORD's altar."
20Early the next morning King Hezekiah gathered the city officials together and went up to the temple of the LORD. 21They
brought seven bulls, seven rams, seven male lambs and seven
male goats as a sin offering for the kingdom, for the sanctuary and
for Judah. The king commanded the priests, the descendants of
Aaron, to offer these on the altar of the LORD. 22So they slaughtered the bulls, and the priests took the blood and sprinkled it on
the altar; next they slaughtered the rams and sprinkled their blood
on the altar; then they slaughtered the lambs and sprinkled their
blood on the altar. 23The goats for the sin offering were brought
before the king and the assembly, and they laid their hands on
them. 24The priests then slaughtered the goats and presented their
blood on the altar for a sin offering to atone for all Israel, because
the king had ordered the burnt offering and the sin offering for all
Israel.
25He stationed the Levites in the temple of the LORD with cymbals, harps and lyres in the way prescribed by David and Gad the
king's seer and Nathan the prophet; this was commanded by the
LORD through his prophets. 26So the Levites stood ready with

## King James

26 And the Levites stood with the instruments of David, and the priests with the trumpets.

27 And Hezekiah commanded to offer the burnt offering upon the altar. And when the burnt offering began, the song of the LORD began *also* with the trumpets, and with the instruments *ordained* by David king of Israel.

28 And all the congregation worshipped, and the singers sang, and the trumpeters sounded: *and* all *this continued* until the burnt offering was finished.

29 And when they had made an end of offering, the king and all that were present with him bowed themselves, and worshipped.

30 Moreover Hezekiah the king and the princes commanded the Levites to sing praise unto the LORD with the words of David, and of Asaph the seer. And they sang praises with gladness, and they bowed their heads and worshipped.

31 Then Hezekiah answered and said, Now ye have consecrated yourselves unto the LORD, come near and bring sacrifices and thank offerings into the house of the LORD. And the congregation brought in sacrifices and thank offerings; and as many as were of a free heart burnt offerings.

32 And the number of the burnt offerings, which the congregation brought, was threescore and ten bullocks, an hundred rams, *and* two hundred lambs: all these *were* for a burnt offering to the LORD.

33 And the consecrated things *were* six hundred oxen and three thousand sheep.

34 But the priests were too few, so that they could not flay all the burnt offerings: wherefore their brethren the Levites did help them, till the work was ended, and until the *other* priests had sanctified themselves: for the Levites *were* more upright in heart to sanctify themselves than the priests.

35 And also the burnt offerings *were* in abundance, with the fat of the peace offerings, and the drink offerings for *every* burnt offering. So the service of the house of the LORD was set in order.

36 And Hezekiah rejoiced, and all the people, that God had prepared the people: for the thing was *done* suddenly.

**30** AND HEZEKIAH sent to all Israel and Judah, and wrote letters also to Ephraim and Manasseh, that they should come to the house of the LORD at Jerusalem, to keep the passover unto the LORD God of Israel.

2 For the king had taken counsel, and his princes, and all the congregation in Jerusalem, to keep the passover in the second month.

3 For they could not keep it at that time, because the priests had not sanctified themselves sufficiently, neither had the people gathered themselves together to Jerusalem.

4 And the thing pleased the king and all the congregation.

5 So they established a decree to make proclamation throughout all Israel, from Beer-sheba even to Dan, that they should come to keep the passover unto the LORD God of Israel at Jerusalem: for they had not done *it* of a long *time in such sort* as it was written.

6 So the posts went with the letters from the king and his princes throughout all Israel and Judah, and according to the commandment of the king, saying, Ye children of Israel, turn again unto the LORD God of Abraham, Isaac, and Israel, and he will return to the remnant of you, that are escaped out of the hand of the kings of Assyria.

7 And be not ye like your fathers, and like your brethren, which trespassed against the LORD God of their fathers, *who* therefore gave them up to desolation, as ye see.

8 Now be ye not stiffnecked, as your fathers *were, but* yield yourselves unto the LORD, and enter into his sanctuary, which he hath sanctified for ever: and serve the LORD your God, that the fierceness of his wrath may turn away from you.

## Amplified

26 The Levites stood with the instruments of David, and the priests with the trumpets.

27 Hezekiah commanded to offer the burnt offering upon the altar. And when the burnt offering began, the song of the Lord began also with the trumpets, and with the instruments ordained by King David of Israel.

28 And all the congregation worshiped, the singers sang, and the trumpeters sounded; all this continued until the burnt offering was finished.

29 When they had stopped offering, the king and all present with him bowed themselves and worshiped.

30 Also King Hezekiah and the princes ordered the Levites to sing praises to the Lord with the words of David and of Asaph the seer. And they sang praises with gladness, and bowed themselves and worshiped.

31 Then Hezekiah said, Now you have consecrated yourselves to the Lord; come near and bring sacrifices and thank offerings into the house of the Lord. And the assembly brought in sacrifices and thank offerings, and as many as were of a willing heart brought burnt offerings.

32 And the number of the burnt offerings, which the assembly brought was 70 bulls, 100 rams, and 200 lambs. All these were for a burnt offering to the Lord.

33 And the consecrated things were 600 oxen and 3,000 sheep.

34 But the priests were too few and could not skin all the burnt offerings. So until the other priests had sanctified themselves, their Levite kinsmen helped them, until the work was done; for the Levites were more upright in heart than the priests in sanctifying themselves.

35 Also the burnt offerings were in abundance, with the fat of the peace offerings, and the drink offering for every burnt offering. So the service of the Lord's house was set in order.

36 Thus Hezekiah rejoiced, and all the people, because of what God had prepared for the people, for *it* was done suddenly.

**30** HEZEKIAH SENT to all Israel [as well as] Judah, and wrote letters also to Ephraim and Manasseh, to come to the Lord's house at Jerusalem, to keep the passover to the Lord the God of Israel.

2 For the king and his princes and all the assembly in Jerusalem, took counsel to keep the passover in the second month. [Postponement permitted, Num. 9:10, 11.]

3 For they could not keep it at the set time, because not enough priests had sanctified themselves, neither had the people assembled in Jerusalem.

4 The new time pleased the king and all the assembly.

5 So they decreed to make a proclamation throughout all Israel, from Beer-sheba to Dan, that the people should come to keep the passover to the Lord the God of Israel, at Jerusalem; for they had not kept it collectively as prescribed for a long time.

6 So the posts went with the letters from the king and his princes throughout all Israel and Judah, as the king commanded, saying, O Israelites, return to the Lord the God of Abraham, Isaac, and Israel, that He may return to those left of you who escaped out of the hand of the kings of Assyria.

7 Do not be like your fathers and brethren who were unfaithful to the Lord the God of their fathers, so that He gave them up to desolation [to be an astonishment], as you see.

8 Now be not stiffnecked as your fathers were, but yield yourselves to the Lord, and come to His sanctuary, which He has sanctified for ever, and serve the Lord your God, that His fierce anger may turn away from you.

## New American Standard

26 And the Levites stood with the *musical* instruments of David,
and the priests with the trumpets.
27 Then Hezekiah gave the order to offer the burnt offering on
the altar. When the burnt offering began, the song to the LORD also
began with the trumpets, *accompanied* by the instruments of David,
king of Israel.
28 While the whole assembly worshiped, the singers also sang
and the trumpets sounded; all this *continued* until the burnt offering was finished.
29 ¶ Now at the completion of the burnt offerings, the king and
all who were present with him bowed down and worshiped.
30 Moreover, King Hezekiah and the officials ordered the Levites to sing praises to the LORD with the words of David and
Asaph the seer. So they sang praises with joy, and bowed down
and worshiped.
31 Then Hezekiah answered and said, "Now *that* you have consecrated yourselves to the LORD, come near and bring sacrifices
and thank offerings to the house of the LORD." And the assembly
brought sacrifices and thank offerings, and all those who were
willing *brought* burnt offerings.
32 And the number of the burnt offerings which the assembly
brought was 70 bulls, 100 rams, and 200 lambs; all these were for
a burnt offering to the LORD.
33 And the consecrated things were 600 bulls and 3,000 sheep.
34 But the priests were too few, so that they were unable to skin
all the burnt offerings; therefore their brothers the Levites helped
them until the work was completed, and until the *other* priests had
consecrated themselves. For the Levites were more conscientious
to consecrate themselves than the priests.
35 And there *were* also many burnt offerings with the fat of the
peace offerings and with the libations for the burnt offerings. Thus
the service of the house of the LORD was established *again*.
36 Then Hezekiah and all the people rejoiced over what God had
prepared for the people, because the thing came about suddenly.

*All Israel Invited to the Passover*

**30** NOW HEZEKIAH sent to all Israel and Judah and wrote
letters also to Ephraim and Manasseh, that they should
come to the house of the LORD at Jerusalem to celebrate the Passover to the LORD God of Israel.
2 For the king and his princes and all the assembly in Jerusalem
had decided to celebrate the Passover in the second month,
3 since they could not celebrate it at that time, because the
priests had not consecrated themselves in sufficient numbers, nor
had the people been gathered to Jerusalem.
4 Thus the thing was right in the sight of the king and all the
assembly.
5 So they established a decree to circulate a proclamation
throughout all Israel from Beersheba even to Dan, that they should
come to celebrate the Passover to the LORD God of Israel at Jerusalem. For they had not celebrated *it* in great numbers as it was
prescribed.
6 And the couriers went throughout all Israel and Judah with
the letters from the hand of the king and his princes, even according to the command of the king, saying, "O sons of Israel, return
to the LORD God of Abraham, Isaac, and Israel, that He may return
to those of you who escaped *and* are left from the hand of the kings
of Assyria.
7 "And do not be like your fathers and your brothers, who were
unfaithful to the LORD God of their fathers, so that He made them
a horror, as you see.
8 "Now do not stiffen your neck like your fathers, but yield to
the LORD and enter His sanctuary which He has consecrated forever, and serve the LORD your God, that His burning anger may
turn away from you.

## New International

David's instruments, and the priests with their trumpets.
27 Hezekiah gave the order to sacrifice the burnt offering on the
altar. As the offering began, singing to the LORD began also, accompanied by trumpets and the instruments of David king of
Israel. 28 The whole assembly bowed in worship, while the singers
sang and the trumpeters played. All this continued until the sacrifice of the burnt offering was completed.
29 When the offerings were finished, the king and everyone
present with him knelt down and worshiped. 30 King Hezekiah
and his officials ordered the Levites to praise the LORD with the
words of David and of Asaph the seer. So they sang praises with
gladness and bowed their heads and worshiped.
31 Then Hezekiah said, "You have now dedicated yourselves to
the LORD. Come and bring sacrifices and thank offerings to the
temple of the LORD." So the assembly brought sacrifices and thank
offerings, and all whose hearts were willing brought burnt offerings.
32 The number of burnt offerings the assembly brought was
seventy bulls, a hundred rams and two hundred male lambs—all
of them for burnt offerings to the LORD. 33 The animals consecrated
as sacrifices amounted to six hundred bulls and three thousand
sheep and goats. 34 The priests, however, were too few to skin all
the burnt offerings; so their kinsmen the Levites helped them until
the task was finished and until other priests had been consecrated,
for the Levites had been more conscientious in consecrating themselves than the priests had been. 35 There were burnt offerings in
abundance, together with the fat of the fellowship offerings[a] and
the drink offerings that accompanied the burnt offerings.
So the service of the temple of the LORD was reestablished.
36 Hezekiah and all the people rejoiced at what God had brought
about for his people, because it was done so quickly.

*Hezekiah Celebrates the Passover*

**30** HEZEKIAH SENT word to all Israel and Judah and also
wrote letters to Ephraim and Manasseh, inviting them to
come to the temple of the LORD in Jerusalem and celebrate the
Passover to the LORD, the God of Israel. 2 The king and his officials
and the whole assembly in Jerusalem decided to celebrate the
Passover in the second month. 3 They had not been able to celebrate it at the regular time because not enough priests had consecrated themselves and the people had not assembled in Jerusalem.
4 The plan seemed right both to the king and to the whole assembly. 5 They decided to send a proclamation throughout Israel, from
Beersheba to Dan, calling the people to come to Jerusalem and
celebrate the Passover to the LORD, the God of Israel. It had not
been celebrated in large numbers according to what was written.
6 At the king's command, couriers went throughout Israel and
Judah with letters from the king and from his officials, which read:

> "People of Israel, return to the LORD, the God of Abraham,
> Isaac and Israel, that he may return to you who are left, who
> have escaped from the hand of the kings of Assyria. 7 Do not
> be like your fathers and brothers, who were unfaithful to the
> LORD, the God of their fathers, so that he made them an object
> of horror, as you see. 8 Do not be stiff-necked, as your fathers
> were; submit to the LORD. Come to the sanctuary, which he
> has consecrated forever. Serve the LORD your God, so that his
> fierce anger will turn away from you. 9 If you return to the

NIV [a] 35 Traditionally *peace offerings*

## King James

9 For if ye turn again unto the LORD, your brethren and your children *shall find* compassion before them that lead them captive, so that they shall come again into this land: for the LORD your God *is* gracious and merciful, and will not turn away *his* face from you, if ye return unto him.

10 So the posts passed from city to city through the country of Ephraim and Manasseh even unto Zebulun: but they laughed them to scorn, and mocked them.

11 Nevertheless divers of Asher and Manasseh and of Zebulun humbled themselves, and came to Jerusalem.

12 Also in Judah the hand of God was to give them one heart to do the commandment of the king and of the princes, by the word of the LORD.

13 ¶ And there assembled at Jerusalem much people to keep the feast of unleavened bread in the second month, a very great congregation.

14 And they arose and took away the altars that *were* in Jerusalem, and all the altars for incense took they away, and cast *them* into the brook Kidron.

15 Then they killed the passover on the fourteenth *day* of the second month: and the priests and the Levites were ashamed, and sanctified themselves, and brought in the burnt offerings into the house of the LORD.

16 And they stood in their place after their manner, according to the law of Moses the man of God: the priests sprinkled the blood, *which they received* of the hand of the Levites.

17 For *there were* many in the congregation that were not sanctified: therefore the Levites had the charge of the killing of the passovers for every one *that was* not clean, to sanctify *them* unto the LORD.

18 For a multitude of the people, *even* many of Ephraim, and Manasseh, Issachar, and Zebulun, had not cleansed themselves, yet did they eat the passover otherwise than it was written. But Hezekiah prayed for them, saying, The good LORD pardon every one

19 *That* prepareth his heart to seek God, the LORD God of his fathers, though *he be* not *cleansed* according to the purification of the sanctuary.

20 And the LORD hearkened to Hezekiah, and healed the people.

21 And the children of Israel that were present at Jerusalem kept the feast of unleavened bread seven days with great gladness: and the Levites and the priests praised the LORD day by day, *singing* with loud instruments unto the LORD.

22 And Hezekiah spake comfortably unto all the Levites that taught the good knowledge of the LORD: and they did eat throughout the feast seven days, offering peace offerings, and making confession to the LORD God of their fathers.

23 And the whole assembly took counsel to keep other seven days: and they kept *other* seven days with gladness.

24 For Hezekiah king of Judah did give to the congregation a thousand bullocks and seven thousand sheep; and the princes gave to the congregation a thousand bullocks and ten thousand sheep: and a great number of priests sanctified themselves.

25 And all the congregation of Judah, with the priests and the Levites, and all the congregation that came out of Israel, and the strangers that came out of the land of Israel, and that dwelt in Judah, rejoiced.

26 So there was great joy in Jerusalem: for since the time of Solomon the son of David king of Israel *there was* not the like in Jerusalem.

27 ¶ Then the priests the Levites arose and blessed the people: and their voice was heard, and their prayer came *up* to his holy dwellingplace, *even* unto heaven.

## Amplified

9 For if you return to the Lord, your brethren and your children shall find compassion with their captors and return to this land. For the Lord your God is gracious and merciful, and will not turn away His face from you, if you return to Him.

10 So the posts passed from city to city through the country of Ephraim and Manasseh even to Zebulun, but the people laughed them to scorn and mocked them.

11 Yet a few of Asher, Manasseh, and Zebulun humbled themselves and came to Jerusalem.

12 Also the hand of God came upon Judah to give them one heart to do the commandment of the king and of the princes by the word of the Lord.

13 And many people came to Jerusalem to keep the feast of unleavened bread in the second month, a very great assembly.

14 They rose up and took away the altars [to idols] that were in Jerusalem, and all the altars *and* utensils for incense [to the gods] they took away and threw into the Kidron valley [dumping place for the ashes of such abominations].

15 Then they killed the passover lamb on the fourteenth day of the second month. And the priests and the Levites were ashamed and sanctified themselves, and brought burnt offerings to the Lord's house.

16 They stood in their accustomed places, as directed in the law of Moses the man of God. The priests threw [against the altar] the blood they received from the hand of the Levites.

17 For many were in the assembly who had not sanctified themselves [become clean, and free from all sin]. So the Levites had to kill the passover lambs for all who were not clean, to make them holy to the Lord.

18 For a multitude of the people, many from Ephraim, Manasseh, Issachar, and Zebulun, had not cleansed themselves, yet they ate the passover otherwise than Moses directed. For Hezekiah had prayed for them, saying, The good Lord pardon every one

19 Who sets his heart to seek *and* yearn for God, the Lord God of his fathers, even though not complying with the purification regulations of the sanctuary.

20 And the Lord hearkened to Hezekiah, and healed the people.

21 And the Israelites who were in Jerusalem kept the feast of unleavened bread seven days with great joy. The Levites and priests praised the Lord day by day, singing with instruments of much volume to the Lord.

22 Hezekiah spoke encouragingly to all the Levites who had good understanding in the Lord's work. So the people ate the seven days' appointed feast, offering peace offerings, making confession [and giving thanks] to the Lord the God of their fathers.

23 And the whole assembly took counsel to prolong the feast another seven days and they kept it another seven days with joy.

24 For Hezekiah king of Judah gave to the assembly 1,000 young bulls and 7,000 sheep, and the princes gave 1,000 young bulls and 10,000 sheep. And a great number of priests sanctified themselves [for service].

25 All the assembly of Judah, with the priests, the Levites, and all the assembly who with the sojourners came from the land of Israel to dwell in Judah, rejoiced.

26 So there was great joy in Jerusalem, for since the time of Solomon son of David king of Israel there was nothing like this in Jerusalem.

27 Then the priests and Levites arose and blessed the people, and their voice was heard, and their prayer came up to [God's] holy habitation in Heaven.

## New American Standard

9"For if you return to the LORD, your brothers and your sons *will find* compassion before those who led them captive, and will return to this land. For the LORD your God is gracious and compassionate, and will not turn *His* face away from you if you return to Him."

10So the couriers passed from city to city through the country of Ephraim and Manasseh, and as far as Zebulun, but they laughed them to scorn, and mocked them.

11Nevertheless some men of Asher, Manasseh, and Zebulun humbled themselves and came to Jerusalem.

12The hand of God was also on Judah to give them one heart to do what the king and the princes commanded by the word of the LORD.

*Passover Reinstituted*

13¶ Now many people were gathered at Jerusalem to celebrate the Feast of Unleavened Bread in the second month, a very large assembly.

14And they arose and removed the altars which *were* in Jerusalem; they also removed all the incense altars and cast *them* into the brook Kidron.

15Then they slaughtered the Passover *lambs* on the fourteenth of the second month. And the priests and Levites were ashamed of themselves and consecrated themselves, and brought burnt offerings to the house of the LORD.

16And they stood at their stations after their custom, according to the law of Moses the man of God; the priests sprinkled the blood *which they received* from the hand of the Levites.

17For *there were* many in the assembly who had not consecrated themselves; therefore, the Levites *were* over the slaughter of the Passover *lambs* for everyone who *was* unclean, in order to consecrate *them* to the LORD.

18For a multitude of the people, *even* many from Ephraim and Manasseh, Issachar and Zebulun, had not purified themselves, yet they ate the Passover otherwise than prescribed. For Hezekiah prayed for them, saying, "May the good LORD pardon

19everyone who prepares his heart to seek God, the LORD God of his fathers, though not according to the purification *rules* of the sanctuary."

20So the LORD heard Hezekiah and healed the people.

21And the sons of Israel present in Jerusalem celebrated the Feast of Unleavened Bread *for* seven days with great joy, and the Levites and the priests praised the LORD day after day with loud instruments to the LORD.

22Then Hezekiah spoke encouragingly to all the Levites who showed good insight *in the things* of the LORD. So they ate for the appointed seven days, sacrificing peace offerings and giving thanks to the LORD God of their fathers.

23¶ Then the whole assembly decided to celebrate *the feast* another seven days, so they celebrated the seven days with joy.

24For Hezekiah king of Judah had contributed to the assembly 1,000 bulls and 7,000 sheep, and the princes had contributed to the assembly 1,000 bulls and 10,000 sheep; and a large number of priests consecrated themselves.

25And all the assembly of Judah rejoiced, with the priests and the Levites, and all the assembly that came from Israel, both the sojourners who came from the land of Israel and those living in Judah.

26So there was great joy in Jerusalem, because there was nothing like this in Jerusalem since the days of Solomon the son of David, king of Israel.

27Then the Levitical priests arose and blessed the people; and their voice was heard and their prayer came to His holy dwelling place, to heaven.

## New International

LORD, then your brothers and your children will be shown compassion by their captors and will come back to this land, for the LORD your God is gracious and compassionate. He will not turn his face from you if you return to him."

10The couriers went from town to town in Ephraim and Manasseh, as far as Zebulun, but the people scorned and ridiculed them. 11Nevertheless, some men of Asher, Manasseh and Zebulun humbled themselves and went to Jerusalem. 12Also in Judah the hand of God was on the people to give them unity of mind to carry out what the king and his officials had ordered, following the word of the LORD.

13A very large crowd of people assembled in Jerusalem to celebrate the Feast of Unleavened Bread in the second month. 14They removed the altars in Jerusalem and cleared away the incense altars and threw them into the Kidron Valley.

15They slaughtered the Passover lamb on the fourteenth day of the second month. The priests and the Levites were ashamed and consecrated themselves and brought burnt offerings to the temple of the LORD. 16Then they took up their regular positions as prescribed in the Law of Moses the man of God. The priests sprinkled the blood handed to them by the Levites. 17Since many in the crowd had not consecrated themselves, the Levites had to kill the Passover lambs for all those who were not ceremonially clean and could not consecrate ⌞their lambs⌟ to the LORD. 18Although most of the many people who came from Ephraim, Manasseh, Issachar and Zebulun had not purified themselves, yet they ate the Passover, contrary to what was written. But Hezekiah prayed for them, saying, "May the LORD, who is good, pardon everyone 19who sets his heart on seeking God—the LORD, the God of his fathers—even if he is not clean according to the rules of the sanctuary." 20And the LORD heard Hezekiah and healed the people.

21The Israelites who were present in Jerusalem celebrated the Feast of Unleavened Bread for seven days with great rejoicing, while the Levites and priests sang to the LORD every day, accompanied by the LORD's instruments of praise.[a]

22Hezekiah spoke encouragingly to all the Levites, who showed good understanding of the service of the LORD. For the seven days they ate their assigned portion and offered fellowship offerings[b] and praised the LORD, the God of their fathers.

23The whole assembly then agreed to celebrate the festival seven more days; so for another seven days they celebrated joyfully. 24Hezekiah king of Judah provided a thousand bulls and seven thousand sheep and goats for the assembly, and the officials provided them with a thousand bulls and ten thousand sheep and goats. A great number of priests consecrated themselves. 25The entire assembly of Judah rejoiced, along with the priests and Levites and all who had assembled from Israel, including the aliens who had come from Israel and those who lived in Judah. 26There was great joy in Jerusalem, for since the days of Solomon son of David king of Israel there had been nothing like this in Jerusalem. 27The priests and the Levites stood to bless the people, and God heard them, for their prayer reached heaven, his holy dwelling place.

**NIV** [a] 21 Or *priests praised the* LORD *every day with resounding instruments belonging to the* LORD [b] 22 Traditionally *peace offerings*

## King James

31 NOW WHEN all this was finished, all Israel that were present went out to the cities of Judah, and brake the images in pieces, and cut down the groves, and threw down the high places and the altars out of all Judah and Benjamin, in Ephraim also and Manasseh, until they had utterly destroyed them all. Then all the children of Israel returned, every man to his possession, into their own cities.

2¶ And Hezekiah appointed the courses of the priests and the Levites after their courses, every man according to his service, the priests and Levites for burnt offerings and for peace offerings, to minister, and to give thanks, and to praise in the gates of the tents of the LORD.

3 *He appointed* also the king's portion of his substance for the burnt offerings, *to wit*, for the morning and evening burnt offerings, and the burnt offerings for the sabbaths, and for the new moons, and for the set feasts, as *it is* written in the law of the LORD.

4Moreover he commanded the people that dwelt in Jerusalem to give the portion of the priests and the Levites, that they might be encouraged in the law of the LORD.

5¶ And as soon as the commandment came abroad, the children of Israel brought in abundance the firstfruits of corn, wine, and oil, and honey, and of all the increase of the field; and the tithe of all *things* brought they in abundantly.

6And *concerning* the children of Israel and Judah, that dwelt in the cities of Judah, they also brought in the tithe of oxen and sheep, and the tithe of holy things which were consecrated unto the LORD their God, and laid *them* by heaps.

7In the third month they began to lay the foundation of the heaps, and finished *them* in the seventh month.

8And when Hezekiah and the princes came and saw the heaps, they blessed the LORD, and his people Israel.

9Then Hezekiah questioned with the priests and the Levites concerning the heaps.

10And Azariah the chief priest of the house of Zadok answered him, and said, Since *the people* began to bring the offerings into the house of the LORD, we have had enough to eat, and have left plenty: for the LORD hath blessed his people; and that which is left *is* this great store.

11¶ Then Hezekiah commanded to prepare chambers in the house of the LORD; and they prepared *them*,

12And brought in the offerings and the tithes and the dedicated *things* faithfully: over which Cononiah the Levite *was* ruler, and Shimei his brother *was* the next.

13And Jehiel, and Azaziah, and Nahath, and Asahel, and Jerimoth, and Jozabad, and Eliel, and Ismachiah, and Mahath, and Benaiah, *were* overseers under the hand of Cononiah and Shimei his brother, at the commandment of Hezekiah the king, and Azariah the ruler of the house of God.

14And Kore the son of Imnah the Levite, the porter toward the east, *was* over the freewill offerings of God, to distribute the oblations of the LORD, and the most holy things.

15And next him *were* Eden, and Miniamin, and Jeshua, and Shemaiah, Amariah, and Shecaniah, in the cities of the priests, in *their* set office, to give to their brethren by courses, as well to the great as to the small:

16Beside their genealogy of males, from three years old and upward, *even* unto every one that entereth into the house of the LORD, his daily portion for their service in their charges according to their courses;

17Both to the genealogy of the priests by the house of their fathers, and the Levites from twenty years old and upward, in their charges by their courses;

18And to the genealogy of all their little ones, their wives, and their sons, and their daughters, through all the congregation: for in their set office they sanctified themselves in holiness:

## Amplified

31 NOW WHEN all this was finished, all Israel present there went out to the cities of Judah and broke in pieces the pillars *or* obelisks, cut down the Asherim, and threw down the high places [of idolatry] and the altars in all Judah and Benjamin, in Ephraim and Manasseh, until they had utterly destroyed them all. Then all the Israelites returned to their own cities, every man to his possession.

2And Hezekiah appointed the priests and the Levites after their divisions, each man according to his service, the priests and Levites for burnt offerings and for peace offerings, to minister, to give thanks, and to praise in the gates of the camp of the Lord.

3King Hezekiah's personal contribution was for the burnt offerings: [those] of morning and evening, for the sabbaths, for the new moons, and for the appointed feasts, as written in the law of Moses.

4He commanded the people living in Jerusalem to give the portion due the priests and Levites, that they might [be free to] give themselves to the law of the Lord.

5As soon as the command went abroad, the Israelites gave in abundance the first fruits of grain, vintage fruit, oil, honey, and of all the produce of the field; and they brought in abundantly the tithe of everything.

6The people of Israel and Judah, who lived in Judah's cities also brought the tithe of cattle and sheep, and of the dedicated things which were consecrated to the Lord their God, and laid them in heaps.

7In the third month [at the end of wheat harvest] they began to lay the foundation *or* beginning of the heaps, and finished them in the seventh month.

8When Hezekiah and the princes came and saw the heaps, they blessed the Lord and His people Israel.

9Then Hezekiah questioned the priests and Levites about the heaps.

10Azariah the high priest, of the house of Zadok, answered him, Since the people began to bring the offerings into the Lord's house we have eaten and have plenty left; for the Lord has blessed His people, and what is left is this great store.

11Then Hezekiah commanded them to prepare chambers [for storage] in the house of the Lord; and they prepared them,

12And brought in the offerings, tithes, and dedicated things faithfully. Conaniah the Levite was in charge of them, and Shimei his brother came next;

13And Jehiel, Azaziah, Nahath, Asahel, Jerimoth, Jozabad, Eliel, Ismachiah, Mahath, and Benaiah were overseers directed by Conaniah and Shimei his brother, at the appointment of King Hezekiah and Azariah the chief officer of the house of God.

14Kore son of Imnah the Levite, keeper of the east gate, was over the freewill offerings to God, to apportion the contributions of the Lord and the most holy things.

15Under him were Eden, Miniamin, Jeshua, Shemaiah, Amariah, and Shecaniah, in the priests' cities, in their office of trust, faithfully to give to their brethren by divisions, to great and small alike,

16Except those [Levites] registered as males from three years old and upward, who were consecrated to the temple service [in Jerusalem] (for their daily portion) as the duty of every day required, for their service according to their offices, by their divisions.

17The registration of the priests was according to their fathers' houses; that of the Levites from twenty years old and upward, was according to their offices by their divisions;

18Also there was the registration of all their little ones, their wives, their older sons and daughters, through all the congregation; for in their office of trust they cleansed themselves *and* set themselves apart in holiness.

## New American Standard

*Idols Are Destroyed*

31 NOW WHEN all this was finished, all Israel who were
present went out to the cities of Judah, broke the pillars
in pieces, cut down the [a]Asherim, and pulled down the high
places and the altars throughout all Judah and Benjamin, as well
as in Ephraim and Manasseh, until they had destroyed them all.
Then all the sons of Israel returned to their cities, each to his
possession.
2¶ And Hezekiah appointed the divisions of the priests and the
Levites by their divisions, each according to his service, *both* the
priests and the Levites, for burnt offerings and for peace offerings,
to minister and to give thanks and to praise in the gates of the camp
of the LORD.

*Reforms Continued*

3*He* also *appointed* the king's portion of his goods for the burnt
offerings, *namely,* for the morning and evening burnt offerings,
and the burnt offerings for the sabbaths and for the new moons
and for the fixed festivals, as it is written in the law of the LORD.
4Also he commanded the people who lived in Jerusalem to give
the portion due to the priests and the Levites, that they might
devote themselves to the law of the LORD.
5And as soon as the order spread, the sons of Israel provided
in abundance the first fruits of grain, new wine, oil, honey, and
of all the produce of the field; and they brought in abundantly the
tithe of all.
6And the sons of Israel and Judah who lived in the cities of
Judah, also brought in the tithe of oxen and sheep, and the tithe
of sacred gifts which were consecrated to the LORD their God, and
placed *them* in heaps.
7In the third month they began to make the heaps, and finished *them* by the seventh month.
8And when Hezekiah and the rulers came and saw the heaps,
they blessed the LORD and His people Israel.
9Then Hezekiah questioned the priests and the Levites concerning the heaps.
10And Azariah the chief priest of the house of Zadok said to
him, "Since the contributions began to be brought into the house
of the LORD, we have had enough to eat with plenty left over, for
the LORD has blessed His people, and this great quantity is left
over."
11¶ Then Hezekiah commanded *them* to prepare rooms in the
house of the LORD, and they prepared *them.*
12And they faithfully brought in the contributions and the tithes
and the consecrated things; and Conaniah the Levite *was* the officer in charge of them and his brother Shimei *was* second.
13And Jehiel, Azaziah, Nahath, Asahel, Jerimoth, Jozabad, Eliel, Ismachiah, Mahath, and Benaiah *were* overseers under the authority of Conaniah and Shimei his brother by the appointment of
King Hezekiah, and Azariah *was* the *chief* officer of the house of
God.
14And Kore the son of Imnah the Levite, the keeper of the
eastern *gate, was* over the freewill offerings of God, to apportion
the contributions for the LORD and the most holy things.
15And under his authority *were* Eden, Miniamin, Jeshua, Shemaiah, Amariah, and Shecaniah in the cities of the priests, to distribute faithfully *their portions* to their brothers by divisions, whether
great or small,
16without regard to their genealogical enrollment, to the males
from thirty years old and upward—everyone who entered the
house of the LORD for his daily obligations—for their work in their
duties according to their divisions;
17as well as the priests who were enrolled genealogically according to their fathers' households, and the Levites from twenty
years old and upwards, by their duties *and* their divisions.
18And the genealogical enrollment *included* all their little children, their wives, their sons, and their daughters, for the whole
assembly, for they consecrated themselves faithfully in holiness.

NAS [a] I.e., wooden symbols of a female deity

## New International

31 WHEN ALL this had ended, the Israelites who were there
went out to the towns of Judah, smashed the sacred
stones and cut down the Asherah poles. They destroyed the high
places and the altars throughout Judah and Benjamin and in
Ephraim and Manasseh. After they had destroyed all of them, the
Israelites returned to their own towns and to their own property.

*Contributions for Worship*

2Hezekiah assigned the priests and Levites to divisions—each
of them according to their duties as priests or Levites—to offer
burnt offerings and fellowship offerings,[b] to minister, to give
thanks and to sing praises at the gates of the LORD's dwelling. 3The
king contributed from his own possessions for the morning and
evening burnt offerings and for the burnt offerings on the Sabbaths, New Moons and appointed feasts as written in the Law of
the LORD. 4He ordered the people living in Jerusalem to give the
portion due the priests and Levites so they could devote themselves to the Law of the LORD. 5As soon as the order went out, the
Israelites generously gave the firstfruits of their grain, new wine,
oil and honey and all that the fields produced. They brought a
great amount, a tithe of everything. 6The men of Israel and Judah
who lived in the towns of Judah also brought a tithe of their herds
and flocks and a tithe of the holy things dedicated to the LORD their
God, and they piled them in heaps. 7They began doing this in the
third month and finished in the seventh month. 8When Hezekiah
and his officials came and saw the heaps, they praised the LORD
and blessed his people Israel.
9Hezekiah asked the priests and Levites about the heaps; 10and
Azariah the chief priest, from the family of Zadok, answered,
"Since the people began to bring their contributions to the temple
of the LORD, we have had enough to eat and plenty to spare,
because the LORD has blessed his people, and this great amount
is left over."
11Hezekiah gave orders to prepare storerooms in the temple of
the LORD, and this was done. 12Then they faithfully brought in the
contributions, tithes and dedicated gifts. Conaniah, a Levite, was
in charge of these things, and his brother Shimei was next in rank.
13Jehiel, Azaziah, Nahath, Asahel, Jerimoth, Jozabad, Eliel, Is-
makiah, Mahath and Benaiah were supervisors under Conaniah
and Shimei his brother, by appointment of King Hezekiah and
Azariah the official in charge of the temple of God.
14Kore son of Imnah the Levite, keeper of the East Gate, was
in charge of the freewill offerings given to God, distributing the
contributions made to the LORD and also the consecrated gifts.
15Eden, Miniamin, Jeshua, Shemaiah, Amariah and Shecaniah assisted him faithfully in the towns of the priests, distributing to their
fellow priests according to their divisions, old and young alike.
16In addition, they distributed to the males three years old or
more whose names were in the genealogical records—all who
would enter the temple of the LORD to perform the daily duties of
their various tasks, according to their responsibilities and their
divisions. 17And they distributed to the priests enrolled by their
families in the genealogical records and likewise to the Levites
twenty years old or more, according to their responsibilities and
their divisions. 18They included all the little ones, the wives, and
the sons and daughters of the whole community listed in these
genealogical records. For they were faithful in consecrating themselves.

NIV [b] 2 Traditionally *peace offerings*

## King James

19 Also of the sons of Aaron the priests, *which were* in the fields of the suburbs of their cities, in every several city, the men that were expressed by name, to give portions to all the males among the priests, and to all that were reckoned by genealogies among the Levites.

20 ¶ And thus did Hezekiah throughout all Judah, and wrought *that which was* good and right and truth before the LORD his God.

21 And in every work that he began in the service of the house of God, and in the law, and in the commandments, to seek his God, he did *it* with all his heart, and prospered.

32 AFTER THESE things, and the establishment thereof, Sennacherib king of Assyria came, and entered into Judah, and encamped against the fenced cities, and thought to win them for himself.

2 And when Hezekiah saw that Sennacherib was come, and that he was purposed to fight against Jerusalem,

3 He took counsel with his princes and his mighty men to stop the waters of the fountains which *were* without the city: and they did help him.

4 So there was gathered much people together, who stopped all the fountains, and the brook that ran through the midst of the land, saying, Why should the kings of Assyria come, and find much water?

5 Also he strengthened himself, and built up all the wall that was broken, and raised *it* up to the towers, and another wall without, and repaired Millo *in* the city of David, and made darts and shields in abundance.

6 And he set captains of war over the people, and gathered them together to him in the street of the gate of the city, and spake comfortably to them, saying,

7 Be strong and courageous, be not afraid nor dismayed for the king of Assyria, nor for all the multitude that *is* with him: for *there be* more with us than with him:

8 With him *is* an arm of flesh; but with us *is* the LORD our God to help us, and to fight our battles. And the people rested themselves upon the words of Hezekiah king of Judah.

9 ¶ After this did Sennacherib king of Assyria send his servants to Jerusalem, (but he *himself laid siege* against Lachish, and all his power with him,) unto Hezekiah king of Judah, and unto all Judah that *were* at Jerusalem, saying,

10 Thus saith Sennacherib king of Assyria, Whereon do ye trust, that ye abide in the siege in Jerusalem?

11 Doth not Hezekiah persuade you to give over yourselves to die by famine and by thirst, saying, The LORD our God shall deliver us out of the hand of the king of Assyria?

12 Hath not the same Hezekiah taken away his high places and his altars, and commanded Judah and Jerusalem, saying, Ye shall worship before one altar, and burn incense upon it?

13 Know ye not what I and my fathers have done unto all the people of *other* lands? were the gods of the nations of those lands any ways able to deliver their lands out of mine hand?

14 Who *was there* among all the gods of those nations that my fathers utterly destroyed, that could deliver his people out of mine hand, that your God should be able to deliver you out of mine hand?

15 Now therefore let not Hezekiah deceive you, nor persuade you on this manner, neither yet believe him: for no god of any nation or kingdom was able to deliver his people out of mine hand, and out of the hand of my fathers: how much less shall your God deliver you out of mine hand?

16 And his servants spake yet *more* against the LORD God, and against his servant Hezekiah.

17 He wrote also letters to rail on the LORD God of Israel, and to speak against him, saying, As the gods of the nations of *other* lands have not delivered their people out of mine hand, so shall not the God of Hezekiah deliver his people out of mine hand.

## Amplified

19 Also for the sons of Aaron the priests, who were in the fields of the suburbs of their cities, in every city, there were men who were mentioned by name to give portions to all the males among the priests and to all who were registered among the Levites.

20 Hezekiah did this throughout all Judah, and he did what was good, right, and faithful before the Lord his God.

21 And every work that he began in the service of the house of God, in keeping with the law and the commandments to seek his God, inquiring of *and* yearning for Him, he did with all his heart, and prospered.

32 AFTER THESE things and this loyalty, Sennacherib king of Assyria came, invaded Judah, and encamped against the fortified cities, thinking to take them.

2 When Hezekiah saw that Sennacherib had come and intended to fight against Jerusalem,

3 He decided with his officers and his mighty men to stop the waters of the fountains which were without the city [by enclosing them with masonry and concealing them]; and they helped him.

4 So many people gathered, and they stopped all the springs and the brook which flowed through the land, saying, Why should the kings of Assyria come and find much water?

5 Also Hezekiah took courage and built up all the wall that was broken, and raised towers upon it, and another wall outside, and strengthened Millo in the city of David, and made weapons and shields in abundance.

6 And he set captains of war over the people, and gathered them together to him in the street of the gate of the city, and spoke encouragingly to them, saying,

7 Be strong and courageous; be not afraid or dismayed before the king of Assyria and all the horde that is with him; for there is Another with us greater than [all those] with him.

8 With him is an arm of flesh; but with us is the Lord our God to help us and to fight our battles. And the people relied on the words of Hezekiah king of Judah.

9 And this Sennacherib king of Assyria, while he himself with all his forces was before Lachish, sent his servants to Jerusalem, to Hezekiah king of Judah, and to all Judah that were at Jerusalem, saying,

10 Thus says Sennacherib king of Assyria: On what do you trust, that you remain in the strongholds in Jerusalem?

11 Is not Hezekiah leading you on in order to let you die by famine and thirst, saying, The Lord our God will deliver us out of the hand of the king of Assyria?

12 Has not the same Hezekiah taken away his high places and his altars, and commanded Judah and Jerusalem, You shall worship before one altar and burn incense upon it?

13 Do you not know what I and my fathers have done to all the people of other lands? Were the gods of the nations of those lands in any way able to deliver their lands out of my hand?

14 Who among all the gods of those nations that my fathers utterly destroyed was able to deliver his people out of my hand, that your God should be able to deliver you out of my hand?

15 So now do not let Hezekiah deceive or mislead you in this way, and do not believe him, for no god of any nation or kingdom was able to deliver his people out of my hand or the hand of my fathers. How much less will your God deliver you out of my hand!

16 And his servants said still more against the Lord God and against His servant Hezekiah.

17 The Assyrian king also wrote letters insulting to the Lord the God of Israel and speaking against Him, saying, As the gods of the nations of other lands have not delivered their people out of my hand, so shall not the God of Hezekiah deliver His people out of my hand.

## New American Standard

19Also for the sons of Aaron the priests *who were* in the pasture
lands of their cities, or in each and every city, *there were* men who
were designated by name to distribute portions to every male
among the priests and to everyone genealogically enrolled among
the Levites.
20¶ And thus Hezekiah did throughout all Judah; and he did
what *was* good, right, and true before the LORD his God.
21And every work which he began in the service of the house
of God in law and in commandment, seeking his God, he did with
all his heart and prospered.

*Sennacherib Invades Judah*

**32** AFTER THESE acts of faithfulness Sennacherib king of
Assyria came and invaded Judah and besieged the fortified cities, and thought to break into them for himself.
2Now when Hezekiah saw that Sennacherib had come, and
that he intended to make war on Jerusalem,
3he decided with his officers and his warriors to cut off the
*supply of* water from the springs which *were* outside the city, and
they helped him.
4So many people assembled and stopped up all the springs and
the stream which flowed through the region, saying, "Why should
the kings of Assyria come and find abundant water?"
5And he took courage and rebuilt all the wall that had been
broken down, and erected towers on it, and *built* another outside
wall, and strengthened the Millo *in* the city of David, and made
weapons and shields in great number.
6And he appointed military officers over the people, and gathered them to him in the square at the city gate, and spoke encouragingly to them, saying,
7"Be strong and courageous, do not fear or be dismayed because of the king of Assyria, nor because of all the multitude which
is with him; for the one with us is greater than the one with him.
8"With him is *only* an arm of flesh, but with us is the LORD our
God to help us and to fight our battles." And the people relied on
the words of Hezekiah king of Judah.

*Sennacherib Undermines Hezekiah*

9¶ After this Sennacherib king of Assyria sent his servants to
Jerusalem while he *was* besieging Lachish with all his forces with
him, against Hezekiah king of Judah and against all Judah who
*were* at Jerusalem, saying,
10"Thus says Sennacherib king of Assyria, 'On what are you
trusting that you are remaining in Jerusalem under siege?
11'Is not Hezekiah misleading you to give yourselves over to die
by hunger and by thirst, saying, "The LORD our God will deliver
us from the hand of the king of Assyria"?
12'Has not the same Hezekiah taken away His high places and
His altars, and said to Judah and Jerusalem, "You shall worship
before one altar, and on it you shall burn incense"?
13'Do you not know what I and my fathers have done to all the
peoples of the lands? Were the gods of the nations of the lands able
at all to deliver their land from my hand?
14'Who *was there* among all the gods of those nations which my
fathers utterly destroyed who could deliver his people out of my
hand, that your God should be able to deliver you from my hand?
15'Now therefore, do not let Hezekiah deceive you or mislead
you like this, and do not believe him, for no god of any nation or
kingdom was able to deliver his people from my hand or from the
hand of my fathers. How much less shall your God deliver you
from my hand?' "
16¶ And his servants spoke further against the LORD God and
against His servant Hezekiah.
17He also wrote letters to insult the LORD God of Israel, and to
speak against Him, saying, "As the gods of the nations of the lands
have not delivered their people from my hand, so the God of
Hezekiah shall not deliver His people from my hand."

## New International

19As for the priests, the descendants of Aaron, who lived on the
farm lands around their towns or in any other towns, men were
designated by name to distribute portions to every male among
them and to all who were recorded in the genealogies of the
Levites.
20This is what Hezekiah did throughout Judah, doing what was
good and right and faithful before the LORD his God. 21In everything that he undertook in the service of God's temple and in
obedience to the law and the commands, he sought his God and
worked wholeheartedly. And so he prospered.

*Sennacherib Threatens Jerusalem*

**32** AFTER ALL that Hezekiah had so faithfully done, Sennacherib king of Assyria came and invaded Judah. He laid
siege to the fortified cities, thinking to conquer them for himself.
2When Hezekiah saw that Sennacherib had come and that he
intended to make war on Jerusalem, 3he consulted with his officials and military staff about blocking off the water from the
springs outside the city, and they helped him. 4A large force of
men assembled, and they blocked all the springs and the stream
that flowed through the land. "Why should the kings[a] of Assyria
come and find plenty of water?" they said. 5Then he worked hard
repairing all the broken sections of the wall and building towers
on it. He built another wall outside that one and reinforced the
supporting terraces[b] of the City of David. He also made large
numbers of weapons and shields.
6He appointed military officers over the people and assembled
them before him in the square at the city gate and encouraged
them with these words: 7"Be strong and courageous. Do not be
afraid or discouraged because of the king of Assyria and the vast
army with him, for there is a greater power with us than with him.
8With him is only the arm of flesh, but with us is the LORD our God
to help us and to fight our battles." And the people gained confidence from what Hezekiah the king of Judah said.
9Later, when Sennacherib king of Assyria and all his forces
were laying siege to Lachish, he sent his officers to Jerusalem with
this message for Hezekiah king of Judah and for all the people of
Judah who were there:

> 10"This is what Sennacherib king of Assyria says: On what
> are you basing your confidence, that you remain in Jerusalem
> under siege? 11When Hezekiah says, 'The LORD our God will
> save us from the hand of the king of Assyria,' he is misleading
> you, to let you die of hunger and thirst. 12Did not Hezekiah
> himself remove this god's high places and altars, saying to
> Judah and Jerusalem, 'You must worship before one altar and
> burn sacrifices on it'?
> 13"Do you not know what I and my fathers have done to
> all the peoples of the other lands? Were the gods of those
> nations ever able to deliver their land from my hand? 14Who
> of all the gods of these nations that my fathers destroyed has
> been able to save his people from me? How then can your god
> deliver you from my hand? 15Now do not let Hezekiah de-
> ceive you and mislead you like this. Do not believe him, for
> no god of any nation or kingdom has been able to deliver his
> people from my hand or the hand of my fathers. How much
> less will your god deliver you from my hand!"

16Sennacherib's officers spoke further against the LORD God
and against his servant Hezekiah. 17The king also wrote letters
insulting the LORD, the God of Israel, and saying this against him:
"Just as the gods of the peoples of the other lands did not rescue
their people from my hand, so the god of Hezekiah will not rescue
his people from my hand." 18Then they called out in Hebrew to

**NIV** [a] *4* Hebrew; Septuagint and Syriac *king* [b] *5* Or *the Millo*

## King James

18Then they cried with a loud voice in the Jews' speech unto the
people of Jerusalem that *were* on the wall, to affright them, and to
trouble them; that they might take the city.
19And they spake against the God of Jerusalem, as against the
gods of the people of the earth, *which were* the work of the hands
of man.
20And for this *cause* Hezekiah the king, and the prophet Isaiah
the son of Amoz, prayed and cried to heaven.
21¶ And the LORD sent an angel, which cut off all the mighty
men of valour, and the leaders and captains in the camp of the king
of Assyria. So he returned with shame of face to his own land. And
when he was come into the house of his god, they that came forth
of his own bowels slew him there with the sword.
22Thus the LORD saved Hezekiah and the inhabitants of Jerusalem from the hand of Sennacherib the king of Assyria, and from
the hand of all *other*, and guided them on every side.
23And many brought gifts unto the LORD to Jerusalem, and
presents to Hezekiah king of Judah: so that he was magnified in
the sight of all nations from thenceforth.
24¶ In those days Hezekiah was sick to the death, and prayed
unto the LORD: and he spake unto him, and he gave him a sign.
25But Hezekiah rendered not again according to the benefit *done*
unto him; for his heart was lifted up: therefore there was wrath
upon him, and upon Judah and Jerusalem.
26Notwithstanding Hezekiah humbled himself for the pride of
his heart, *both* he and the inhabitants of Jerusalem, so that the
wrath of the LORD came not upon them in the days of Hezekiah.
27¶ And Hezekiah had exceeding much riches and honour: and
he made himself treasuries for silver, and for gold, and for precious
stones, and for spices, and for shields, and for all manner of
pleasant jewels;
28Storehouses also for the increase of corn, and wine, and oil;
and stalls for all manner of beasts, and cotes for flocks.
29Moreover he provided him cities, and possessions of flocks
and herds in abundance: for God had given him substance very
much.
30This same Hezekiah also stopped the upper watercourse of
Gihon, and brought it straight down to the west side of the city
of David. And Hezekiah prospered in all his works.
31¶ Howbeit in *the business of* the ambassadors of the princes of
Babylon, who sent unto him to inquire of the wonder that was *done*
in the land, God left him, to try him, that he might know all *that
was* in his heart.
32¶ Now the rest of the acts of Hezekiah, and his goodness,
behold, they *are* written in the vision of Isaiah the prophet, the son
of Amoz, *and* in the book of the kings of Judah and Israel.
33And Hezekiah slept with his fathers, and they buried him in
the chiefest of the sepulchres of the sons of David: and all Judah
and the inhabitants of Jerusalem did him honour at his death. And
Manasseh his son reigned in his stead.

33 MANASSEH *WAS* twelve years old when he began to
reign, and he reigned fifty and five years in Jerusalem:
2But did *that which was* evil in the sight of the LORD, like unto
the abominations of the heathen, whom the LORD had cast out
before the children of Israel.
3¶ For he built again the high places which Hezekiah his father
had broken down, and he reared up altars for Baalim, and made
groves, and worshipped all the host of heaven, and served them.
4Also he built altars in the house of the LORD, whereof the LORD
had said, In Jerusalem shall my name be for ever.
5And he built altars for all the host of heaven in the two courts
of the house of the LORD.

## Amplified

18And they shouted it loudly in the Jewish language to the
people of Jerusalem who were on the wall, to frighten and terrify
them, that they might take the city.
19And they spoke of the God of Jerusalem, as they spoke of the
gods of the people of the earth, which are the work of the hands
of men.
20For this cause Hezekiah the king and the prophet Isaiah the
son of Amoz prayed and cried to Heaven.
21And the Lord sent an angel, who cut off all the mighty warriors and commanders and officers in the camp of the king of Assyria. So the Assyrian king returned with shamed face to his own
land. And when he came into the house of his god, they who were
his own offspring slew him there with the sword. [II Kings
19:35-37.]
22Thus the Lord saved Hezekiah and the inhabitants of Jerusalem from the hand of Sennacherib the king of Assyria, and from
the hand of all his enemies, and He guided them on every side.
23And many brought gifts to Jerusalem to the Lord and presents
to Hezekiah king of Judah; so from then on he was magnified in
the sight of all nations.
24In those days Hezekiah was sick to the point of death, and he
prayed to the Lord and He answered him, and gave him a sign.
25But Hezekiah did not make return [to the Lord] according to
the benefit done to him, for his heart became proud [at such
spectacular response to his prayer]; therefore there was wrath
upon him and upon Judah and Jerusalem.
26But Hezekiah humbled himself for the pride of his heart, both
he and the inhabitants of Jerusalem, so that the wrath of the Lord
came not upon them in the days of Hezekiah.
27And Hezekiah had very great wealth and honor, and he made
himself treasuries for silver, gold, precious stones, spices, shields,
and all kinds of attractive vessels;
28Storehouses also for the increase of grain, vintage fruits, and
oil, and stalls for all kinds of cattle, and sheepfolds.
29Moreover he provided himself cities, and flocks and herds in
abundance; for God had given him very great possessions.
30This same Hezekiah also closed the upper springs of Gihon
and directed the waters down to the west side of the city of David.
And Hezekiah prospered in all his works.
31And so in the matter of the ambassadors of the princes of
Babylon, who were sent to him to inquire about the wonder that
was done in the land, God left him to himself to try him, that He
might know all that was in his heart. [Isa. 39:1-7.]
32Now the rest of the acts of Hezekiah and his good deeds,
behold, they are written in the vision of Isaiah the prophet, son of
Amoz, and in the Book of the Kings of Judah and Israel.
33And Hezekiah slept with his fathers, and was buried in the
ascent of the tombs of the descendants of David; and all Judah and
the inhabitants of Jerusalem did him honor at his death. Manasseh
his son reigned in his stead.

33 MANASSEH WAS twelve years old when he began to
reign, and he reigned fifty-five years in Jerusalem.
2But he did evil in the Lord's sight, like the abominations of the
heathen whom the Lord drove out before the Israelites.
3For he built again the [idolatrous] high places which Hezekiah
his father broke down, and he reared altars for the Baals, and made
Asheroth [fem. plur.] and worshiped all the host of the heavens
and served them.
4Also he built [heathen] altars in the Lord's house, of which the
Lord had said, In Jerusalem shall My name be for ever.
5He built altars for all the host of the heavens in the two courts
of the Lord's house.

## New American Standard

18And they called this out with a loud voice in the language of
Judah to the people of Jerusalem who were on the wall, to frighten
and terrify them, so that they might take the city.
19And they spoke of the God of Jerusalem as of the gods of the
peoples of the earth, the work of men's hands.

*Hezekiah's Prayer Is Answered*

20¶ But King Hezekiah and Isaiah the prophet, the son of Amoz,
prayed about this and cried out to heaven.
21And the LORD sent an angel who destroyed every mighty
warrior, commander and officer in the camp of the king of Assyria.
So he returned in shame to his own land. And when he had
entered the temple of his god, some of his own children killed him
there with the sword.
22So the LORD saved Hezekiah and the inhabitants of Jerusalem
from the hand of Sennacherib the king of Assyria, and from the
hand of all *others*, and guided them on every side.
23And many were bringing gifts to the LORD at Jerusalem and
choice presents to Hezekiah king of Judah, so that he was exalted
in the sight of all nations thereafter.
24¶ In those days Hezekiah became mortally ill; and he prayed
to the LORD, and the LORD spoke to him and gave him a sign.
25But Hezekiah gave no return for the benefit he received,
because his heart was proud; therefore wrath came on him and on
Judah and Jerusalem.
26However, Hezekiah humbled the pride of his heart, both he
and the inhabitants of Jerusalem, so that the wrath of the LORD did
not come on them in the days of Hezekiah.
27¶ Now Hezekiah had immense riches and honor; and he made
for himself treasuries for silver, gold, precious stones, spices,
shields and all kinds of valuable articles,
28storehouses also for the produce of grain, wine and oil, pens
for all kinds of cattle and sheepfolds for the flocks.
29And he made cities for himself, and acquired flocks and herds
in abundance; for God had given him very great wealth.
30It was Hezekiah who stopped the upper outlet of the waters
of Gihon and directed them to the west side of the city of David.
And Hezekiah prospered in all that he did.
31And even *in the matter of* the envoys of the rulers of Babylon,
who sent to him to inquire of the wonder that had happened in
the land, God left him *alone only* to test him, that He might know
all that was in his heart.
32¶ Now the rest of the acts of Hezekiah and his deeds of
devotion, behold, they are written in the vision of Isaiah the
prophet, the son of Amoz, in the Book of the Kings of Judah and
Israel.
33So Hezekiah slept with his fathers, and they buried him in the
upper section of the tombs of the sons of David; and all Judah and
the inhabitants of Jerusalem honored him at his death. And his son
Manasseh became king in his place.

*Manasseh Succeeds Hezekiah in Judah*

**33** MANASSEH WAS twelve years old when he became
king, and he reigned fifty-five years in Jerusalem.
2And he did evil in the sight of the LORD according to the
abominations of the nations whom the LORD dispossessed before
the sons of Israel.
3For he rebuilt the high places which Hezekiah his father had
broken down; he also erected altars for the Baals and made
[a]Asherim, and worshiped all the host of heaven and served them.
4And he built altars in the house of the LORD of which the LORD
had said, "My name shall be in Jerusalem forever."
5For he built altars for all the host of heaven in the two courts
of the house of the LORD.

NAS [a] I.e., wooden symbols of a female deity

## New International

the people of Jerusalem who were on the wall, to terrify them and
make them afraid in order to capture the city. 19They spoke about
the God of Jerusalem as they did about the gods of the other
peoples of the world—the work of men's hands.
20King Hezekiah and the prophet Isaiah son of Amoz cried out
in prayer to heaven about this. 21And the LORD sent an angel, who
annihilated all the fighting men and the leaders and officers in the
camp of the Assyrian king. So he withdrew to his own land in
disgrace. And when he went into the temple of his god, some of
his sons cut him down with the sword.
22So the LORD saved Hezekiah and the people of Jerusalem from
the hand of Sennacherib king of Assyria and from the hand of all
others. He took care of them[b] on every side. 23Many brought
offerings to Jerusalem for the LORD and valuable gifts for Hezekiah
king of Judah. From then on he was highly regarded by all the
nations.

*Hezekiah's Pride, Success and Death*

24In those days Hezekiah became ill and was at the point of
death. He prayed to the LORD, who answered him and gave him
a miraculous sign. 25But Hezekiah's heart was proud and he did
not respond to the kindness shown him; therefore the LORD's
wrath was on him and on Judah and Jerusalem. 26Then Hezekiah
repented of the pride of his heart, as did the people of Jerusalem;
therefore the LORD's wrath did not come upon them during the
days of Hezekiah.
27Hezekiah had very great riches and honor, and he made
treasuries for his silver and gold and for his precious stones,
spices, shields and all kinds of valuables. 28He also made buildings
to store the harvest of grain, new wine and oil; and he made stalls
for various kinds of cattle, and pens for the flocks. 29He built
villages and acquired great numbers of flocks and herds, for God
had given him very great riches.
30It was Hezekiah who blocked the upper outlet of the Gihon
spring and channeled the water down to the west side of the City
of David. He succeeded in everything he undertook. 31But when
envoys were sent by the rulers of Babylon to ask him about the
miraculous sign that had occurred in the land, God left him to test
him and to know everything that was in his heart.
32The other events of Hezekiah's reign and his acts of devotion
are written in the vision of the prophet Isaiah son of Amoz in the
book of the kings of Judah and Israel. 33Hezekiah rested with his
fathers and was buried on the hill where the tombs of David's
descendants are. All Judah and the people of Jerusalem honored
him when he died. And Manasseh his son succeeded him as king.

*Manasseh King of Judah*

**33** MANASSEH WAS twelve years old when he became
king, and he reigned in Jerusalem fifty-five years. 2He did
evil in the eyes of the LORD, following the detestable practices of
the nations the LORD had driven out before the Israelites. 3He
rebuilt the high places his father Hezekiah had demolished; he also
erected altars to the Baals and made Asherah poles. He bowed
down to all the starry hosts and worshiped them. 4He built altars
in the temple of the LORD, of which the LORD had said, "My Name
will remain in Jerusalem forever." 5In both courts of the temple of
the LORD, he built altars to all the starry hosts. 6He sacrificed his

NIV [b] 22 Hebrew; Septuagint and Vulgate *He gave them rest*

## King James

6And he caused his children to pass through the fire in the valley of the son of Hinnom: also he observed times, and used enchantments, and used witchcraft, and dealt with a familiar spirit, and with wizards: he wrought much evil in the sight of the LORD, to provoke him to anger.

7And he set a carved image, the idol which he had made, in the house of God, of which God had said to David and to Solomon his son, In this house, and in Jerusalem, which I have chosen before all the tribes of Israel, will I put my name for ever:

8Neither will I any more remove the foot of Israel from out of the land which I have appointed for your fathers; so that they will take heed to do all that I have commanded them, according to the whole law and the statutes and the ordinances by the hand of Moses.

9So Manasseh made Judah and the inhabitants of Jerusalem to err, *and* to do worse than the heathen, whom the LORD had destroyed before the children of Israel.

10And the LORD spake to Manasseh, and to his people: but they would not hearken.

11¶ Wherefore the LORD brought upon them the captains of the host of the king of Assyria, which took Manasseh among the thorns, and bound him with fetters, and carried him to Babylon.

12And when he was in affliction, he besought the LORD his God, and humbled himself greatly before the God of his fathers,

13And prayed unto him: and he was entreated of him, and heard his supplication, and brought him again to Jerusalem into his kingdom. Then Manasseh knew that the LORD he *was* God.

14Now after this he built a wall without the city of David, on the west side of Gihon, in the valley, even to the entering in at the fish gate, and compassed about Ophel, and raised it up a very great height, and put captains of war in all the fenced cities of Judah.

15And he took away the strange gods, and the idol out of the house of the LORD, and all the altars that he had built in the mount of the house of the LORD, and in Jerusalem, and cast *them* out of the city.

16And he repaired the altar of the LORD, and sacrificed thereon peace offerings and thank offerings, and commanded Judah to serve the LORD God of Israel.

17Nevertheless the people did sacrifice still in the high places, *yet* unto the LORD their God only.

18¶ Now the rest of the acts of Manasseh, and his prayer unto his God, and the words of the seers that spake to him in the name of the LORD God of Israel, behold, they *are written* in the book of the kings of Israel.

19His prayer also, and *how God* was entreated of him, and all his sins, and his trespass, and the places wherein he built high places, and set up groves and graven images, before he was humbled: behold, they *are* written among the sayings of the seers.

20¶ So Manasseh slept with his fathers, and they buried him in his own house: and Amon his son reigned in his stead.

21¶ Amon *was* two and twenty years old when he began to reign, and reigned two years in Jerusalem.

22But he did *that which was* evil in the sight of the LORD, as did Manasseh his father: for Amon sacrificed unto all the carved images which Manasseh his father had made, and served them;

23And humbled not himself before the LORD, as Manasseh his father had humbled himself; but Amon trespassed more and more.

24And his servants conspired against him, and slew him in his own house.

25¶ But the people of the land slew all them that had conspired against king Amon; and the people of the land made Josiah his son king in his stead.

## Amplified

6And he burned his children as an offering [to his god] in the valley of the son of Hinnom, and practiced soothsaying, augury, and sorcery, and dealt with mediums and wizards. He did much evil in the sight of the Lord, provoking Him to anger.

7And he set a carved image, the idol which he had made, in the house of God, of which God had said to David and to Solomon his son, In this house and in Jerusalem, which I have chosen before all the tribes of Israel, will I put My name [and presence] for ever;

8And I will no more remove Israel from the land which I appointed for your fathers, if they will only take heed to do all that I have commanded them, the whole law, the statutes, and the ordinances given by Moses.

9So Manasseh led Judah and the inhabitants of Jerusalem to do more evil than the heathen, whom the Lord had destroyed before the Israelites.

10The Lord spoke to Manasseh and to his people, but they would not hearken.

11So the Lord brought against them the commanders of the host of the king of Assyria, who took Manasseh with hooks and in fetters, and brought him to Babylon.

12When he was in affliction, he besought the Lord his God, and humbled himself greatly before the God of his fathers.

13He prayed to Him, and God, entreated by him, heard his supplication and brought him again to Jerusalem to his kingdom. Then Manasseh knew that the Lord is God.

14And he built an outer wall to the city of David west of Gihon, in the valley, to the entrance of the Fish Gate, and ran it around Ophel, raising it to a very great height; and he put commanders of the army in all the fortified cities of Judah.

15And he took away the foreign gods, and the idol out of the house of the Lord, and all the altars that he had built in the mount of the house of the Lord, and in Jerusalem, and cast them out of the city.

16And he restored the Lord's altar, and sacrificed on it offerings of peace and of thanksgiving; and he commanded Judah to serve the Lord the God of Israel.

17Yet the people still sacrificed in the high places, but only to the Lord their God.

18Now the rest of the acts of Manasseh, and his prayer to his God, and the words of the seers who spoke to him in the name of the Lord God of Israel, behold, they are written in the Book of the Kings of Israel.

19His prayer, and how God heard him, and all his sins and unfaithfulness, and the sites on which he built high places and set up Asherim and graven images before he humbled himself, behold, they are written in the Chronicles of the Seers.

20So Manasseh slept with his fathers, and they buried him in his own house [garden]; and Amon his son reigned in his stead.

21Amon was twenty-two years old when he began his two years' reign in Jerusalem.

22But he did evil in the sight of the Lord, as did Manasseh his father; for Amon sacrificed to all the images which Manasseh his father had made, and served them,

23And he did not humble himself before the Lord, as Manasseh his father [finally] did, but Amon trespassed *and* became more and more guilty.

24And his servants conspired against him and killed him in his own house.

25But the people of the land slew all those who had conspired against King Amon, and made Josiah his son king in his stead.

## New American Standard

6And he made his sons pass through the fire in the valley of
Ben-hinnom; and he practiced witchcraft, used divination, practiced sorcery, and dealt with mediums and spiritists. He did much
evil in the sight of the LORD, provoking Him *to anger*.
7Then he put the carved image of the idol which he had made
in the house of God, of which God had said to David and to
Solomon his son, "In this house and in Jerusalem, which I have
chosen from all the tribes of Israel, I will put My name forever;
8and I will not again remove the foot of Israel from the land
which I have appointed for your fathers, if only they will observe
to do all that I have commanded them according to all the law, the
statutes, and the ordinances *given* through Moses."
9Thus Manasseh misled Judah and the inhabitants of Jerusalem to do more evil than the nations whom the LORD destroyed
before the sons of Israel.

*Manasseh's Idolatry Rebuked*

10¶ And the LORD spoke to Manasseh and his people, but they
paid no attention.
11Therefore the LORD brought the commanders of the army of
the king of Assyria against them, and they captured Manasseh
with [a]hooks, bound him with bronze *chains*, and took him to
Babylon.
12And when he was in distress, he entreated the LORD his God
and humbled himself greatly before the God of his fathers.
13When he prayed to Him, He was moved by his entreaty and
heard his supplication, and brought him again to Jerusalem to his
kingdom. Then Manasseh knew that the LORD *was* God.
14¶ Now after this he built the outer wall of the city of David on
the west side of Gihon, in the valley, even to the entrance of the
Fish Gate; and he encircled the Ophel *with it* and made it very high.
Then he put army commanders in all the fortified cities of Judah.
15He also removed the foreign gods and the idol from the house
of the LORD, as well as all the altars which he had built on the
mountain of the house of the LORD and in Jerusalem, and he threw
*them* outside the city.
16And he set up the altar of the LORD and sacrificed peace
offerings and thank offerings on it; and he ordered Judah to serve
the LORD God of Israel.
17Nevertheless the people still sacrificed in the high places,
*although* only to the LORD their God.
18¶ Now the rest of the acts of Manasseh even his prayer to his
God, and the words of the seers who spoke to him in the name
of the LORD God of Israel, behold, they are among the records of
the kings of Israel.
19His prayer also and *how God* was entreated by him, and all his
sin, his unfaithfulness, and the sites on which he built high places
and erected the Asherim and the carved images, before he humbled himself, behold, they are written in the records of the Hozai.
20So Manasseh slept with his fathers, and they buried him in
his own house. And Amon his son became king in his place.

*Amon Becomes King in Judah*

21¶ Amon *was* twenty-two years old when he became king, and
he reigned two years in Jerusalem.
22And he did evil in the sight of the LORD as Manasseh his father
had done, and Amon sacrificed to all the carved images which his
father Manasseh had made, and he served them.
23Moreover, he did not humble himself before the LORD as his
father Manasseh had done, but Amon multiplied guilt.
24Finally his servants conspired against him and put him to
death in his own house.
25But the people of the land killed all the conspirators against
King Amon, and the people of the land made Josiah his son king
in his place.

**NAS** [a] I.e., thong put through the nose

## New International

sons in[b] the fire in the Valley of Ben Hinnom, practiced sorcery,
divination and witchcraft, and consulted mediums and spiritists.
He did much evil in the eyes of the LORD, provoking him to anger.
7He took the carved image he had made and put it in God's
temple, of which God had said to David and to his son Solomon,
"In this temple and in Jerusalem, which I have chosen out of all
the tribes of Israel, I will put my Name forever. 8I will not again
make the feet of the Israelites leave the land I assigned to your
forefathers, if only they will be careful to do everything I commanded them concerning all the laws, decrees and ordinances
given through Moses." 9But Manasseh led Judah and the people
of Jerusalem astray, so that they did more evil than the nations the
LORD had destroyed before the Israelites.
10The LORD spoke to Manasseh and his people, but they paid
no attention. 11So the LORD brought against them the army commanders of the king of Assyria, who took Manasseh prisoner, put
a hook in his nose, bound him with bronze shackles and took him
to Babylon. 12In his distress he sought the favor of the LORD his
God and humbled himself greatly before the God of his fathers.
13And when he prayed to him, the LORD was moved by his entreaty and listened to his plea; so he brought him back to Jerusalem
and to his kingdom. Then Manasseh knew that the LORD is God.
14Afterward he rebuilt the outer wall of the City of David, west
of the Gihon spring in the valley, as far as the entrance of the Fish
Gate and encircling the hill of Ophel; he also made it much higher.
He stationed military commanders in all the fortified cities in
Judah.
15He got rid of the foreign gods and removed the image from
the temple of the LORD, as well as all the altars he had built on the
temple hill and in Jerusalem; and he threw them out of the city.
16Then he restored the altar of the LORD and sacrificed fellowship
offerings[c] and thank offerings on it, and told Judah to serve the
LORD, the God of Israel. 17The people, however, continued to
sacrifice at the high places, but only to the LORD their God.
18The other events of Manasseh's reign, including his prayer to
his God and the words the seers spoke to him in the name of the
LORD, the God of Israel, are written in the annals of the kings of
Israel.[d] 19His prayer and how God was moved by his entreaty, as
well as all his sins and unfaithfulness, and the sites where he built
high places and set up Asherah poles and idols before he humbled
himself—all are written in the records of the seers.[e] 20Manasseh
rested with his fathers and was buried in his palace. And Amon
his son succeeded him as king.

*Amon King of Judah*

21Amon was twenty-two years old when he became king, and
he reigned in Jerusalem two years. 22He did evil in the eyes of the
LORD, as his father Manasseh had done. Amon worshiped and
offered sacrifices to all the idols Manasseh had made. 23But unlike
his father Manasseh, he did not humble himself before the LORD;
Amon increased his guilt.
24Amon's officials conspired against him and assassinated him
in his palace. 25Then the people of the land killed all who had
plotted against King Amon, and they made Josiah his son king in
his place.

**NIV** [b] *6* Or *He made his sons pass through* [c] *16* Traditionally *peace offerings*
[d] *18* That is, Judah, as frequently in 2 Chron. [e] *19* One Hebrew manuscript
and Septuagint; most Hebrew manuscripts *of Hozai*

# King James

**34** JOSIAH *WAS* eight years old when he began to reign, and
he reigned in Jerusalem one and thirty years.
2 And he did *that which was* right in the sight of the LORD, and
walked in the ways of David his father, and declined *neither* to the
right hand, nor to the left.
3 ¶ For in the eighth year of his reign, while he was yet young,
he began to seek after the God of David his father: and in the
twelfth year he began to purge Judah and Jerusalem from the high
places, and the groves, and the carved images, and the molten
images.
4 And they brake down the altars of Baalim in his presence; and
the images, that *were* on high above them, he cut down; and the
groves, and the carved images, and the molten images, he brake
in pieces, and made dust *of them,* and strewed *it* upon the graves
of them that had sacrificed unto them.
5 And he burnt the bones of the priests upon their altars, and
cleansed Judah and Jerusalem.
6 And *so did he* in the cities of Manasseh, and Ephraim, and
Simeon, even unto Naphtali, with their mattocks round about.
7 And when he had broken down the altars and the groves, and
had beaten the graven images into powder, and cut down all the
idols throughout all the land of Israel, he returned to Jerusalem.
8 ¶ Now in the eighteenth year of his reign, when he had purged
the land, and the house, he sent Shaphan the son of Azaliah, and
Maaseiah the governor of the city, and Joah the son of Joahaz the
recorder, to repair the house of the LORD his God.
9 And when they came to Hilkiah the high priest, they delivered
the money that was brought into the house of God, which the
Levites that kept the doors had gathered of the hand of Manasseh
and Ephraim, and of all the remnant of Israel, and of all Judah and
Benjamin; and they returned to Jerusalem.
10 And they put *it* in the hand of the workmen that had the
oversight of the house of the LORD, and they gave it to the workmen that wrought in the house of the LORD, to repair and amend
the house:
11 Even to the artificers and builders gave they *it,* to buy hewn
stone, and timber for couplings, and to floor the houses which the
kings of Judah had destroyed.
12 And the men did the work faithfully: and the overseers of
them *were* Jahath and Obadiah, the Levites, of the sons of Merari;
and Zechariah and Meshullam, of the sons of the Kohathites, to
set *it* forward; and *other of* the Levites, all that could skill of instruments of music.
13 Also *they were* over the bearers of burdens, and *were* overseers
of all that wrought the work in any manner of service: and of the
Levites *there were* scribes, and officers, and porters.
14 ¶ And when they brought out the money that was brought
into the house of the LORD, Hilkiah the priest found a book of the
law of the LORD *given* by Moses.
15 And Hilkiah answered and said to Shaphan the scribe, I have
found the book of the law in the house of the LORD. And Hilkiah
delivered the book to Shaphan.
16 And Shaphan carried the book to the king, and brought the
king word back again, saying, All that was committed to thy
servants, they do *it.*
17 And they have gathered together the money that was found
in the house of the LORD, and have delivered it into the hand of
the overseers, and to the hand of the workmen.
18 Then Shaphan the scribe told the king, saying, Hilkiah the
priest hath given me a book. And Shaphan read it before the king.
19 And it came to pass, when the king had heard the words of
the law, that he rent his clothes.
20 And the king commanded Hilkiah, and Ahikam the son of
Shaphan, and Abdon the son of Micah, and Shaphan the scribe,
and Asaiah a servant of the king's, saying,

# Amplified

**34** JOSIAH WAS eight years old when he began his thirty-
one years' reign in Jerusalem.
2 He did right in the sight of the Lord, and walked in the ways
of David his father [forefather], and turned aside neither to the
right hand, nor to the left.
3 For in the eighth year of his reign, while he was yet young
[sixteen], he began to seek after *and* yearn for the God of David his
father [forefather]; and in the twelfth year he began to purge Judah
and Jerusalem of the high places, the Asherim, and the carved and
molten images.
4 They broke down the altars of the Baals in his presence; the
sun-images that were high above them he hewed down; the
Asherim, and the graven images, and the molten images, he broke
in pieces, and made dust of them, and strewed it upon the graves
of those who sacrificed to them.
5 Josiah burned the bones of the [idolatrous] priests upon their
altars, and cleansed Judah and Jerusalem.
6 So he did in the cities of Manasseh, Ephraim, and Simeon,
even to Naphtali, in their ruins round about [with their axes],
7 He broke down the altars and the Asherim and beat the graven
images into powder, and hewed down all the sun-images throughout all the land of Israel. Then he returned to Jerusalem.
8 In the eighteenth year of Josiah's reign, when he had purged
the land and the [Lord's] house, he sent Shaphan son of Azaliah,
and Ma-aseiah governor of the city, and Joah son of Joahaz, the
recorder, to repair the house of the Lord his God.
9 When they came to Hilkiah the high priest, they delivered the
money that had been brought into the house of God, which the
Levites who kept the doors had collected from Manasseh,
Ephraim, all the remnant of Israel, and from all Judah, Benjamin
and Jerusalem.
10 They delivered it to the workmen who had oversight of the
Lord's house, who gave it to repair and restore the temple:
11 To the carpenters and builders to buy hewn stone, and timber
for couplings and beams for the houses which the kings of Judah
had destroyed [by neglect].
12 The men did the work faithfully. Their overseers were Jahath
and Obadiah, Levites of the sons of Merari, and Zechariah and
Meshullam of the sons of the Kohathites. The Levites, all who were
skillful with instruments of music,
13 Also had oversight of the burden bearers and all who did
work in any kind of service; and some of the Levites were scribes,
officials and gatekeepers.
14 When they were bringing out the money that was brought
into the house of the Lord, Hilkiah the priest found the book of
the law of the Lord given by Moses.
15 Hilkiah told Shaphan the scribe, I have found the book of the
law in the Lord's house. And [he] gave the book to Shaphan.
16 Shaphan took the book to King Josiah, but [first] reported to
him, All that was committed to your servants they are doing;
17 They have emptied out the money that was found in the
house of the Lord, and have delivered it into the hand of the
overseers and the workmen.
18 Then Shaphan the scribe said to the king, Hilkiah the priest
has given me a book. And Shaphan read it before the king.
19 When King Josiah had heard the words of the law, he rent his
clothes.
20 And the king commanded Hilkiah, Ahikam son of Shaphan,
Abdon son of Micah, Shaphan the scribe, and Asaiah a servant of
the king, saying,

## New American Standard

*Josiah Succeeds Amon in Judah*

**34** JOSIAH *WAS* eight years old when he became king, and
he reigned thirty-one years in Jerusalem.
2And he did right in the sight of the LORD, and walked in the
ways of his father David and did not turn aside to the right or to
the left.
3For in the eighth year of his reign while he was still a youth,
he began to seek the God of his father David; and in the twelfth
year he began to purge Judah and Jerusalem of the high places, the
Asherim, the carved images, and the molten images.
4And they tore down the altars of the Baals in his presence, and
the incense altars that were high above them he chopped down;
also the Asherim, the carved images, and the molten images he
broke in pieces and ground to powder and scattered *it* on the
graves of those who had sacrificed to them.
5Then he burned the bones of the priests on their altars, and
purged Judah and Jerusalem.
6And in the cities of Manasseh, Ephraim, Simeon, even as far
as Naphtali, in their surrounding ruins,
7he also tore down the altars and beat the Asherim and the
carved images into powder, and chopped down all the incense
altars throughout the land of Israel. Then he returned to Jerusalem.

*Josiah Repairs the Temple*

8¶ Now in the eighteenth year of his reign, when he had
purged the land and the house, he sent Shaphan the son of Azaliah, and Maaseiah an official of the city, and Joah the son of Joahaz
the recorder, to repair the house of the LORD his God.
9And they came to Hilkiah the high priest and delivered the
money that was brought into the house of God, which the Levites,
the doorkeepers, had collected from Manasseh and Ephraim, and
from all the remnant of Israel, and from all Judah and Benjamin
and the inhabitants of Jerusalem.
10Then they gave *it* into the hands of the workmen who had the
oversight of the house of the LORD, and the workmen who were
working in the house of the LORD used it to restore and repair the
house.
11They in turn gave *it* to the carpenters and to the builders to
buy quarried stone and timber for couplings and to make beams
for the houses which the kings of Judah had let go to ruin.
12And the men did the work faithfully with foremen over them
to supervise: Jahath and Obadiah, the Levites of the sons of Merari, Zechariah and Meshullam of the sons of the Kohathites, and
the Levites, all who were skillful with musical instruments.
13 *They were* also over the burden bearers, and supervised all the
workmen from job to job; and *some* of the Levites *were* scribes and
officials and gatekeepers.

*Hilkiah Discovers Lost Book of the Law*

14¶ When they were bringing out the money which had been
brought into the house of the LORD, Hilkiah the priest found the
book of the law of the LORD *given* by Moses.
15And Hilkiah responded and said to Shaphan the scribe, "I
have found the book of the law in the house of the LORD." And
Hilkiah gave the book to Shaphan.
16Then Shaphan brought the book to the king and reported
further word to the king, saying, "Everything that was entrusted
to your servants they are doing.
17"They have also emptied out the money which was found in
the house of the LORD, and have delivered it into the hands of the
supervisors and the workmen."
18Moreover, Shaphan the scribe told the king saying, "Hilkiah
the priest gave me a book." And Shaphan read from it in the
presence of the king.
19And it came about when the king heard the words of the law
that he tore his clothes.
20Then the king commanded Hilkiah, Ahikam the son of Shaphan, Abdon the son of Micah, Shaphan the scribe, and Asaiah the
king's servant, saying,

## New International

*Josiah's Reforms*

**34** JOSIAH WAS eight years old when he became king, and
he reigned in Jerusalem thirty-one years. 2He did what
was right in the eyes of the LORD and walked in the ways of his
father David, not turning aside to the right or to the left.
3In the eighth year of his reign, while he was still young, he
began to seek the God of his father David. In his twelfth year he
began to purge Judah and Jerusalem of high places, Asherah poles,
carved idols and cast images. 4Under his direction the altars of the
Baals were torn down; he cut to pieces the incense altars that were
above them, and smashed the Asherah poles, the idols and the
images. These he broke to pieces and scattered over the graves of
those who had sacrificed to them. 5He burned the bones of the
priests on their altars, and so he purged Judah and Jerusalem. 6In
the towns of Manasseh, Ephraim and Simeon, as far as Naphtali,
and in the ruins around them, 7he tore down the altars and the
Asherah poles and crushed the idols to powder and cut to pieces
all the incense altars throughout Israel. Then he went back to
Jerusalem.
8In the eighteenth year of Josiah's reign, to purify the land and
the temple, he sent Shaphan son of Azaliah and Maaseiah the ruler
of the city, with Joah son of Joahaz, the recorder, to repair the
temple of the LORD his God.
9They went to Hilkiah the high priest and gave him the money
that had been brought into the temple of God, which the Levites
who were the doorkeepers had collected from the people of Manasseh, Ephraim and the entire remnant of Israel and from all the
people of Judah and Benjamin and the inhabitants of Jerusalem.
10Then they entrusted it to the men appointed to supervise the
work on the LORD's temple. These men paid the workers who
repaired and restored the temple. 11They also gave money to the
carpenters and builders to purchase dressed stone, and timber for
joists and beams for the buildings that the kings of Judah had
allowed to fall into ruin.
12The men did the work faithfully. Over them to direct them
were Jahath and Obadiah, Levites descended from Merari, and
Zechariah and Meshullam, descended from Kohath. The Levites—
all who were skilled in playing musical instruments— 13had charge
of the laborers and supervised all the workers from job to job.
Some of the Levites were secretaries, scribes and doorkeepers.

*The Book of the Law Found*

14While they were bringing out the money that had been taken
into the temple of the LORD, Hilkiah the priest found the Book of
the Law of the LORD that had been given through Moses. 15Hilkiah
said to Shaphan the secretary, "I have found the Book of the Law
in the temple of the LORD." He gave it to Shaphan.
16Then Shaphan took the book to the king and reported to him:
"Your officials are doing everything that has been committed to
them. 17They have paid out the money that was in the temple of
the LORD and have entrusted it to the supervisors and workers."
18Then Shaphan the secretary informed the king, "Hilkiah the
priest has given me a book." And Shaphan read from it in the
presence of the king.
19When the king heard the words of the Law, he tore his robes.
20He gave these orders to Hilkiah, Ahikam son of Shaphan, Abdon
son of Micah,[a] Shaphan the secretary and Asaiah the king's attendant: 21"Go and inquire of the LORD for me and for the remnant

NIV [a] 20 Also called *Acbor son of Micaiah*

## King James

21Go, inquire of the LORD for me, and for them that are left in
Israel and in Judah, concerning the words of the book that is
found: for great *is* the wrath of the LORD that is poured out upon
us, because our fathers have not kept the word of the LORD, to do
after all that is written in this book.
22And Hilkiah, and *they* that the king *had appointed*, went to
Huldah the prophetess, the wife of Shallum the son of Tikvath, the
son of Hasrah, keeper of the wardrobe; (now she dwelt in Jerusalem in the college:) and they spake to her to that *effect*.
23¶ And she answered them, Thus saith the LORD God of Israel,
Tell ye the man that sent you to me,
24Thus saith the LORD, Behold, I will bring evil upon this place,
and upon the inhabitants thereof, *even* all the curses that are written in the book which they have read before the king of Judah:
25Because they have forsaken me, and have burned incense
unto other gods, that they might provoke me to anger with all the
works of their hands; therefore my wrath shall be poured out upon
this place, and shall not be quenched.
26And as for the king of Judah, who sent you to inquire of the
LORD, so shall ye say unto him, Thus saith the LORD God of Israel
*concerning* the words which thou hast heard;
27Because thine heart was tender, and thou didst humble thyself before God, when thou heardest his words against this place,
and against the inhabitants thereof, and humbledst thyself before
me, and didst rend thy clothes, and weep before me; I have even
heard *thee* also, saith the LORD.
28Behold, I will gather thee to thy fathers, and thou shalt be
gathered to thy grave in peace, neither shall thine eyes see all the
evil that I will bring upon this place, and upon the inhabitants of
the same. So they brought the king word again.
29¶ Then the king sent and gathered together all the elders of
Judah and Jerusalem.
30And the king went up into the house of the LORD, and all the
men of Judah, and the inhabitants of Jerusalem, and the priests,
and the Levites, and all the people, great and small: and he read
in their ears all the words of the book of the covenant that was
found in the house of the LORD.
31And the king stood in his place, and made a covenant before
the LORD, to walk after the LORD, and to keep his commandments,
and his testimonies, and his statutes, with all his heart, and with
all his soul, to perform the words of the covenant which are written
in this book.
32And he caused all that were present in Jerusalem and Benjamin to stand *to it*. And the inhabitants of Jerusalem did according
to the covenant of God, the God of their fathers.
33And Josiah took away all the abominations out of all the
countries that *pertained* to the children of Israel, and made all that
were present in Israel to serve, *even* to serve the LORD their God.
*And* all his days they departed not from following the LORD, the
God of their fathers.

35 MOREOVER JOSIAH kept a passover unto the LORD in
Jerusalem: and they killed the passover on the fourteenth
*day* of the first month.
2And he set the priests in their charges, and encouraged them
to the service of the house of the LORD,
3And said unto the Levites that taught all Israel, which were
holy unto the LORD, Put the holy ark in the house which Solomon
the son of David king of Israel did build; *it shall* not *be* a burden
upon *your* shoulders: serve now the LORD your God, and his
people Israel,

## Amplified

21Go, inquire of the Lord for me, and for those who are left in
Israel and in Judah, about the words of the book that is found. For
great is the Lord's wrath that is poured out on us, because our
fathers have not kept the word of the Lord, to do according to all
that is written in this book.
22And Hilkiah and they whom the king had appointed went to
Huldah the prophetess, wife of Shallum son of Tokhath, son of
Hasrah, keeper of the wardrobe. (She dwelt in Jerusalem in the
Second Quarter.) They spoke to her to that effect.
23And she answered them, Thus says the Lord the God of
Israel, Tell the man who sent you to me,
24Thus says the Lord, Behold, I will bring evil upon this place,
and upon its inhabitants, even all the curses that are written in the
book which they have read before the king of Judah;
25Because they have forsaken Me, and have burned incense to
other gods, that they might provoke Me to anger with all the works
of their hands; therefore My wrath shall be poured out upon this
place, and shall not be quenched.
26But say to King Josiah of Judah, who sent you to inquire of
the Lord, Thus says the Lord the God of Israel concerning the
words which you have heard:
27Because your heart was tender *and* penitent and you humbled
yourself before God when you heard His words against this place
and its inhabitants, and humbled yourself before Me, and rent
your clothes, and wept before Me, I have heard you, says the Lord.
28Behold, I will gather you to your fathers, and you shall be
gathered to your grave in peace, and your eyes shall not see all the
evil that I will bring upon this place and its inhabitants. So they
brought the king word again.
29Then King Josiah sent and gathered all the elders of Judah and
Jerusalem.
30And [he] went up into the house of the Lord, as did all the
men of Judah, the inhabitants of Jerusalem, the priests, the Levites, and all the people, great and small; and he [the king] read
in their hearing all the words of the book of the covenant that was
found in the Lord's house.
31Then the king stood in his place, and made a covenant before
the Lord, to walk after the Lord and to keep His commandments,
His testimonies, and His statutes, with all his heart and with all
his soul, to perform the words of the covenant that are written in
this book.
32And he caused all that were present in Jerusalem and Benjamin to stand in confirmation of it. And the inhabitants of Jerusalem
did according to the covenant of God, the God of their fathers.
33Josiah removed all the [idolatrous] abominations from all the
territory that belonged to the Israelites, and made all who were in
Israel serve the Lord their God. All his days they did not turn from
following the Lord the God of their fathers.

35 JOSIAH KEPT a passover to the Lord in Jerusalem; they
killed the passover lamb on the fourteenth day of the first
month.
2He appointed the priests to their positions and encouraged
them in the service of the house of the Lord.
3To the Levites who taught all Israel and were holy to the Lord,
he said, Put the holy ark in the house which Solomon son of David,
king of Israel, built; it shall no longer be a burden carried on your
shoulders. Now serve the Lord your God and His people Israel.

## New American Standard

21"Go, inquire of the LORD for me and for those who are left in
Israel and in Judah, concerning the words of the book which has
been found; for great is the wrath of the LORD which is poured out
on us because our fathers have not observed the word of the LORD,
to do according to all that is written in this book."

*Huldah, the Prophetess, Speaks*

22¶ So Hilkiah and *those* whom the king had told went to Huldah
the prophetess, the wife of Shallum the son of Tokhath, the son
of Hasrah, the keeper of the wardrobe (now she lived in Jerusalem
in the Second Quarter); and they spoke to her regarding this.
23And she said to them, "Thus says the LORD, the God of Israel,
'Tell the man who sent you to Me,
24thus says the LORD, "Behold, I am bringing evil on this place
and on its inhabitants, *even* all the curses written in the book which
they have read in the presence of the king of Judah.
25"Because they have forsaken Me and have burned incense to
other gods, that they might provoke Me to anger with all the works
of their hands, therefore My wrath will be poured out on this
place, and it shall not be quenched." '
26"But to the king of Judah who sent you to inquire of the LORD,
thus you will say to him, 'Thus says the LORD God of Israel *regard-*
*ing* the words which you have heard,
27"Because your heart was tender and you humbled yourself
before God, when you heard His words against this place and
against its inhabitants, and *because* you humbled yourself before
Me, tore your clothes, and wept before Me, I truly have heard
you," declares the LORD.
28"Behold, I will gather you to your fathers and you shall be
gathered to your grave in peace, so your eyes shall not see all the
evil which I will bring on this place and on its inhabitants." ' " And
they brought back word to the king.
29¶ Then the king sent and gathered all the elders of Judah and
Jerusalem.
30And the king went up to the house of the LORD and all the
men of Judah, the inhabitants of Jerusalem, the priests, the Levites, and all the people, from the greatest to the least; and he read
in their hearing all the words of the book of the covenant which
was found in the house of the LORD.

*Josiah's Good Reign*

31Then the king stood in his place and made a covenant before
the LORD to walk after the LORD, and to keep His commandments
and His testimonies and His statutes with all his heart and with
all his soul, to perform the words of the covenant written in this
book.
32Moreover, he made all who were present in Jerusalem and
Benjamin to stand *with him*. So the inhabitants of Jerusalem did
according to the covenant of God, the God of their fathers.
33And Josiah removed all the abominations from all the lands
belonging to the sons of Israel, and made all who were present in
Israel to serve the LORD their God. Throughout his lifetime they
did not turn from following the LORD God of their fathers.

*The Passover Observed Again*

**35** THEN JOSIAH celebrated the Passover to the LORD in
Jerusalem, and they slaughtered the Passover *animals* on
the fourteenth *day* of the first month.
2And he set the priests in their offices and encouraged them
in the service of the house of the LORD.
3He also said to the Levites who taught all Israel *and* who were
holy to the LORD, "Put the holy ark in the house which Solomon
the son of David king of Israel built; it will be a burden on *your*
shoulders no longer. Now serve the LORD your God and His
people Israel.

## New International

in Israel and Judah about what is written in this book that has been
found. Great is the LORD's anger that is poured out on us because
our fathers have not kept the word of the LORD; they have not
acted in accordance with all that is written in this book."
22Hilkiah and those the king had sent with him[a] went to speak
to the prophetess Huldah, who was the wife of Shallum son of
Tokhath,[b] the son of Hasrah,[c] keeper of the wardrobe. She lived
in Jerusalem, in the Second District.
23She said to them, "This is what the LORD, the God of Israel,
says: Tell the man who sent you to me, 24'This is what the LORD
says: I am going to bring disaster on this place and its people—all
the curses written in the book that has been read in the presence
of the king of Judah. 25Because they have forsaken me and burned
incense to other gods and provoked me to anger by all that their
hands have made,[d] my anger will be poured out on this place and
will not be quenched.' 26Tell the king of Judah, who sent you to
inquire of the LORD, 'This is what the LORD, the God of Israel, says
concerning the words you heard: 27Because your heart was responsive and you humbled yourself before God when you heard
what he spoke against this place and its people, and because you
humbled yourself before me and tore your robes and wept in my
presence, I have heard you, declares the LORD. 28Now I will gather
you to your fathers, and you will be buried in peace. Your eyes will
not see all the disaster I am going to bring on this place and on
those who live here.' "
So they took her answer back to the king.
29Then the king called together all the elders of Judah and
Jerusalem. 30He went up to the temple of the LORD with the men
of Judah, the people of Jerusalem, the priests and the Levites—all
the people from the least to the greatest. He read in their hearing
all the words of the Book of the Covenant, which had been found
in the temple of the LORD. 31The king stood by his pillar and
renewed the covenant in the presence of the LORD—to follow the
LORD and keep his commands, regulations and decrees with all his
heart and all his soul, and to obey the words of the covenant
written in this book.
32Then he had everyone in Jerusalem and Benjamin pledge
themselves to it; the people of Jerusalem did this in accordance
with the covenant of God, the God of their fathers.
33Josiah removed all the detestable idols from all the territory
belonging to the Israelites, and he had all who were present in
Israel serve the LORD their God. As long as he lived, they did not
fail to follow the LORD, the God of their fathers.

*Josiah Celebrates the Passover*

**35** JOSIAH CELEBRATED the Passover to the LORD in
Jerusalem, and the Passover lamb was slaughtered on the
fourteenth day of the first month. 2He appointed the priests to
their duties and encouraged them in the service of the LORD's
temple. 3He said to the Levites, who instructed all Israel and who
had been consecrated to the LORD: "Put the sacred ark in the
temple that Solomon son of David king of Israel built. It is not to
be carried about on your shoulders. Now serve the LORD your God
and his people Israel. 4Prepare yourselves by families in your

**NIV** [a] 22 One Hebrew manuscript, Vulgate and Syriac; most Hebrew manuscripts do not have *had sent with him.* [b] 22 Also called *Tikvah* [c] 22 Also called *Harhas* [d] 25 Or *by everything they have done*

## King James

4 And prepare *yourselves* by the houses of your fathers, after your courses, according to the writing of David king of Israel, and according to the writing of Solomon his son.

5 And stand in the holy *place* according to the divisions of the families of the fathers of your brethren the people, and *after* the division of the families of the Levites.

6 So kill the passover, and sanctify yourselves, and prepare your brethren, that *they* may do according to the word of the LORD by the hand of Moses.

7 And Josiah gave to the people, of the flock, lambs and kids, all for the passover offerings, for all that were present, to the number of thirty thousand, and three thousand bullocks: these *were* of the king's substance.

8 And his princes gave willingly unto the people, to the priests, and to the Levites: Hilkiah and Zechariah and Jehiel, rulers of the house of God, gave unto the priests for the passover offerings two thousand and six hundred *small cattle,* and three hundred oxen.

9 Conaniah also, and Shemaiah and Nethaneel, his brethren, and Hashabiah and Jeiel and Jozabad, chief of the Levites, gave unto the Levites for passover offerings five thousand *small cattle,* and five hundred oxen.

10 So the service was prepared, and the priests stood in their place, and the Levites in their courses, according to the king's commandment.

11 And they killed the passover, and the priests sprinkled *the blood* from their hands, and the Levites flayed *them.*

12 And they removed the burnt offerings, that they might give according to the divisions of the families of the people, to offer unto the LORD, as *it is* written in the book of Moses. And so *did they* with the oxen.

13 And they roasted the passover with fire according to the ordinance: but the *other* holy *offerings* sod they in pots, and in caldrons, and in pans, and divided *them* speedily among all the people.

14 And afterward they made ready for themselves, and for the priests: because the priests the sons of Aaron *were busied* in offering of burnt offerings and the fat until night; therefore the Levites prepared for themselves, and for the priests the sons of Aaron.

15 And the singers the sons of Asaph *were* in their place, according to the commandment of David, and Asaph, and Heman, and Jeduthun the king's seer; and the porters *waited* at every gate; they might not depart from their service; for their brethren the Levites prepared for them.

16 So all the service of the LORD was prepared the same day, to keep the passover, and to offer burnt offerings upon the altar of the LORD, according to the commandment of king Josiah.

17 And the children of Israel that were present kept the passover at that time, and the feast of unleavened bread seven days.

18 And there was no passover like to that kept in Israel from the days of Samuel the prophet; neither did all the kings of Israel keep such a passover as Josiah kept, and the priests, and the Levites, and all Judah and Israel that were present, and the inhabitants of Jerusalem.

19 In the eighteenth year of the reign of Josiah was this passover kept.

20 ¶ After all this, when Josiah had prepared the temple, Necho king of Egypt came up to fight against Carchemish by Euphrates: and Josiah went out against him.

21 But he sent ambassadors to him, saying, What have I to do with thee, thou king of Judah? *I come* not against thee this day, but against the house wherewith I have war: for God commanded me to make haste: forbear thee from *meddling with* God, who *is* with me, that he destroy thee not.

22 Nevertheless Josiah would not turn his face from him, but disguised himself, that he might fight with him, and hearkened not unto the words of Necho from the mouth of God, and came to fight in the valley of Megiddo.

## Amplified

4 Prepare yourselves according to your fathers' houses by your divisions, after the directions of David king of Israel and of Solomon his son.

5 And stand in the holy court of the priests according to the sections of the fathers' families of your kinsmen the common people, and let there be a section of the Levites [to attend] to each division of the families of the people.

6 Kill the passover, and sanctify yourselves, and prepare for your brethren to do according to the word of the Lord by Moses.

7 Then Josiah contributed to the lay people lambs and kids of the flock as passover offerings for all who were present, to the number of 30,000, and 3,000 young bulls, all from the king's possessions.

8 And his princes gave for a free will offering to the people, to the priests, and the Levites. Hilkiah, Zechariah, and Jehiel, chief officers of God's house, gave the priests for the passover offerings 2,600 [lambs and kids], and 300 bulls.

9 Conaniah also, and Shemaiah and Nethanel his brothers, and Hashabiah, Jeiel, and Jozabad, chiefs of the Levites, gave to the Levites for passover offerings 5,000 [lambs and kids], and 500 bulls.

10 When the service was ready, the priests stood in their place and the Levites in their divisions, as the king commanded.

11 They killed the passover lambs, and the priests sprinkled the blood they received from the Levites while skinning the animals.

12 Then they removed the burnt offerings, that they might distribute them according to the divisions of the lay families, to offer to the Lord, as directed in the book of Moses. And so they did with the bulls.

13 And they roasted the passover lambs with fire according to the ordinance; and they cooked the holy offerings in pots, in caldrons, and in pans, and carried them quickly to all the people.

14 Afterward [the Levites] prepared for themselves and the priests, because the priests the sons of Aaron were busied in offering the burnt offerings and the fat until night; so the Levites prepared for themselves and also for the priests the sons of Aaron.

15 The singers the sons of Asaph were in their place according to the command of David, and Asaph, Heman, and Jeduthun the king's seer; and the gatekeepers were at every gate; they did not need to leave their service, for their brethren the Levites prepared for them.

16 So all the Lord's service was prepared the same day, to keep the passover, and to offer burnt offerings upon the Lord's altar, as King Josiah commanded.

17 And the Israelites who were present kept the passover at that time, and the feast of unleavened bread seven days.

18 No passover like it had been kept in Israel since the days of Samuel the prophet, even by any of the kings of Israel, as was kept by Josiah and the priests, the Levites, and all Judah and Israel who were present, and the inhabitants of Jerusalem.

19 In the eighteenth year of the reign of Josiah this passover was kept.

20 After all this, when Josiah had prepared the temple, Neco king of Egypt went out to fight against Carchemish on the Euphrates, and Josiah went out against him.

21 But [Neco] sent ambassadors to [Josiah], saying, What have I to do with you, you king of Judah? I come not against you this day, but against the house with which I am at war; and God has commanded me to make haste. Refrain from opposing God, Who is with me, lest He destroy you.

22 Yet Josiah would not turn away from him, but disguised himself in order to fight with him. He did not heed the words of Neco from the mouth of God, but came to fight with him in the valley of Megiddo.

## New American Standard

4"And prepare *yourselves* by your fathers' households in your divisions, according to the writing of David king of Israel and according to the writing of his son Solomon.
5"Moreover, stand in the holy place according to the sections of the fathers' households of your brethren the lay people, and according to the Levites, by division of a father's household.
6"Now slaughter the Passover *animals*, sanctify yourselves, and prepare for your brethren to do according to the word of the LORD by Moses."
7¶ And Josiah contributed to the lay people, to all who were present, flocks of lambs and kids, all for the Passover offerings, numbering 30,000 plus 3,000 bulls; these were from the king's possessions.
8His officers also contributed a freewill offering to the people, the priests, and the Levites. Hilkiah and Zechariah and Jehiel, the officials of the house of God, gave to the priests for the Passover offerings 2,600 *from the flocks* and 300 bulls.
9Conaniah also, and Shemaiah and Nethanel, his brothers, and Hashabiah and Jeiel and Jozabad, the officers of the Levites, contributed to the Levites for the Passover offerings 5,000 *from the flocks* and 500 bulls.
10¶ So the service was prepared, and the priests stood at their stations and the Levites by their divisions according to the king's command.
11And they slaughtered the Passover *animals*, and while the priests sprinkled the blood *received* from their hand, the Levites skinned *them*.
12Then they removed the burnt offerings that *they* might give them to the sections of the fathers' households of the lay people to present to the LORD, as it is written in the book of Moses. *They did* this also with the bulls.
13So they roasted the Passover *animals* on the fire according to the ordinance, and they boiled the holy things in pots, in kettles, in pans, and carried *them* speedily to all the lay people.
14And afterwards they prepared for themselves and for the priests, because the priests, the sons of Aaron, *were* offering the burnt offerings and the fat until night; therefore the Levites prepared for themselves and for the priests, the sons of Aaron.
15The singers, the sons of Asaph, *were* also at their stations according to the command of David, Asaph, Heman, and Jeduthun the king's seer; and the gatekeepers at each gate did not have to depart from their service, because the Levites their brethren prepared for them.
16¶ So all the service of the LORD was prepared on that day to celebrate the Passover, and to offer burnt offerings on the altar of the LORD according to the command of King Josiah.
17Thus the sons of Israel who were present celebrated the Passover at that time, and the Feast of Unleavened Bread seven days.
18And there had not been celebrated a Passover like it in Israel since the days of Samuel the prophet; nor had any of the kings of Israel celebrated such a Passover as Josiah did with the priests, the Levites, all Judah and Israel who were present, and the inhabitants of Jerusalem.
19In the eighteenth year of Josiah's reign this Passover was celebrated.

*Josiah Dies in Battle*

20¶ After all this, when Josiah had set the temple in order, Neco king of Egypt came up to make war at Carchemish on the Euphrates, and Josiah went out to engage him.
21But Neco sent messengers to him, saying, "What have we to do with each other, O King of Judah? *I am* not *coming* against you today but against the house with which I am at war, and God has ordered me to hurry. Stop for your own sake from *interfering with* God who is with me, that He may not destroy you."
22However, Josiah would not turn away from him, but disguised himself in order to make war with him; nor did he listen to the words of Neco from the mouth of God, but came to make war on the plain of Megiddo.

## New International

divisions, according to the directions written by David king of Israel and by his son Solomon.
5"Stand in the holy place with a group of Levites for each subdivision of the families of your fellow countrymen, the lay
people. 6Slaughter the Passover lambs, consecrate yourselves and prepare ⌊the lambs⌋ for your fellow countrymen, doing what the LORD commanded through Moses."
7Josiah provided for all the lay people who were there a total of thirty thousand sheep and goats for the Passover offerings, and also three thousand cattle—all from the king's own possessions.
8His officials also contributed voluntarily to the people and the priests and Levites. Hilkiah, Zechariah and Jehiel, the administrators of God's temple, gave the priests twenty-six hundred Passover offerings and three hundred cattle. 9Also Conaniah along
with Shemaiah and Nethanel, his brothers, and Hashabiah, Jeiel and Jozabad, the leaders of the Levites, provided five thousand Passover offerings and five hundred head of cattle for the Levites.
10The service was arranged and the priests stood in their places with the Levites in their divisions as the king had ordered. 11The
Passover lambs were slaughtered, and the priests sprinkled the blood handed to them, while the Levites skinned the animals.
12They set aside the burnt offerings to give them to the subdivisions of the families of the people to offer to the LORD, as is written in the Book of Moses. They did the same with the cattle. 13They
roasted the Passover animals over the fire as prescribed, and boiled the holy offerings in pots, caldrons and pans and served them quickly to all the people. 14After this, they made preparations for
themselves and for the priests, because the priests, the descendants of Aaron, were sacrificing the burnt offerings and the fat portions until nightfall. So the Levites made preparations for themselves and for the Aaronic priests.
15The musicians, the descendants of Asaph, were in the places prescribed by David, Asaph, Heman and Jeduthun the king's seer. The gatekeepers at each gate did not need to leave their posts, because their fellow Levites made the preparations for them.
16So at that time the entire service of the LORD was carried out for the celebration of the Passover and the offering of burnt offerings on the altar of the LORD, as King Josiah had ordered. 17The
Israelites who were present celebrated the Passover at that time and observed the Feast of Unleavened Bread for seven days. 18The
Passover had not been observed like this in Israel since the days of the prophet Samuel; and none of the kings of Israel had ever celebrated such a Passover as did Josiah, with the priests, the Levites and all Judah and Israel who were there with the people of Jerusalem. 19This Passover was celebrated in the eighteenth year
of Josiah's reign.

*The Death of Josiah*

20After all this, when Josiah had set the temple in order, Neco king of Egypt went up to fight at Carchemish on the Euphrates, and Josiah marched out to meet him in battle. 21But Neco sent
messengers to him, saying, "What quarrel is there between you and me, O king of Judah? It is not you I am attacking at this time, but the house with which I am at war. God has told me to hurry; so stop opposing God, who is with me, or he will destroy you."
22Josiah, however, would not turn away from him, but disguised himself to engage him in battle. He would not listen to what Neco had said at God's command but went to fight him on the plain of Megiddo.

## King James

23And the archers shot at king Josiah; and the king said to his servants, Have me away; for I am sore wounded.

24His servants therefore took him out of that chariot, and put him in the second chariot that he had; and they brought him to Jerusalem, and he died, and was buried in *one of* the sepulchres of his fathers. And all Judah and Jerusalem mourned for Josiah.

25¶ And Jeremiah lamented for Josiah: and all the singing men and the singing women spake of Josiah in their lamentations to this day, and made them an ordinance in Israel: and, behold, they *are* written in the lamentations.

26Now the rest of the acts of Josiah, and his goodness, according to *that which was* written in the law of the LORD,

27And his deeds, first and last, behold, they *are* written in the book of the kings of Israel and Judah.

**36** THEN THE people of the land took Jehoahaz the son of Josiah, and made him king in his father's stead in Jerusalem.

2Jehoahaz *was* twenty and three years old when he began to reign, and he reigned three months in Jerusalem.

3And the king of Egypt put him down at Jerusalem, and condemned the land in an hundred talents of silver and a talent of gold.

4And the king of Egypt made Eliakim his brother king over Judah and Jerusalem, and turned his name to Jehoiakim. And Necho took Jehoahaz his brother, and carried him to Egypt.

5¶ Jehoiakim *was* twenty and five years old when he began to reign, and he reigned eleven years in Jerusalem: and he did *that which was* evil in the sight of the LORD his God.

6Against him came up Nebuchadnezzar king of Babylon, and bound him in fetters, to carry him to Babylon.

7Nebuchadnezzar also carried of the vessels of the house of the LORD to Babylon, and put them in his temple at Babylon.

8Now the rest of the acts of Jehoiakim, and his abominations which he did, and that which was found in him, behold, they *are* written in the book of the kings of Israel and Judah: and Jehoiachin his son reigned in his stead.

9¶ Jehoiachin *was* eight years old when he began to reign, and he reigned three months and ten days in Jerusalem: and he did *that which was* evil in the sight of the LORD.

10And when the year was expired, king Nebuchadnezzar sent, and brought him to Babylon, with the goodly vessels of the house of the LORD, and made Zedekiah his brother king over Judah and Jerusalem.

11¶ Zedekiah *was* one and twenty years old when he began to reign, and reigned eleven years in Jerusalem.

12And he did *that which was* evil in the sight of the LORD his God, *and* humbled not himself before Jeremiah the prophet *speaking* from the mouth of the LORD.

13And he also rebelled against king Nebuchadnezzar, who had made him swear by God: but he stiffened his neck, and hardened his heart from turning unto the LORD God of Israel.

14¶ Moreover all the chief of the priests, and the people, transgressed very much after all the abominations of the heathen; and polluted the house of the LORD which he had hallowed in Jerusalem.

## Amplified

23And the archers shot King Josiah; and the king said to his servants, Take me away, for I am severely wounded.

24So his servants took him out of the chariot and put him in his second chariot and brought him to Jerusalem. And he died, and was buried in the tombs of his fathers. All Judah and Jerusalem mourned for Josiah.

25Jeremiah gave a lament for Josiah; and all the singing men and women have spoken of Josiah in their laments to this day. They made them an ordinance in Israel; behold, they are written in the Laments. [Lam. 4:20.]

26Now the rest of the acts of Josiah, and his deeds according to what is written in the law of the Lord,

27And his acts, from first to last, behold, they are written in the Book of the Kings of Israel and Judah.

**36** THEN THE people of the land took Jehoahaz son of Josiah, and made him king in his father's stead in Jerusalem.

2Jehoahaz was [then] twenty-three years old; he reigned three months in Jerusalem.

3Then the king of Egypt deposed him at Jerusalem and fined the land a hundred talents of silver and a talent of gold.

4And the king of Egypt made Eliakim, Jehoahaz' brother, king over Judah and Jerusalem, and changed his name to Jehoiakim. But Neco took Jehoahaz his brother, and carried him to Egypt.

5Jehoiakim was twenty-five years old when he began to reign, and he reigned eleven years in Jerusalem. He did evil in the sight of the Lord his God.

6Against him came up Nebuchadnezzar king of Babylon, and bound him in fetters to take him to Babylon.

7Nebuchadnezzar also took some of the vessels of the house of the Lord to Babylon, and put them in his temple *or* palace there.

8Now the rest of the acts of Jehoiakim, and the abominations which he did, and what was found against him, behold, they are written in the Book of the Kings of Israel and Judah; and Jehoiachin his son reigned in his stead.

9Jehoiachin was eight[een] years old then; he reigned three months and ten days in Jerusalem. He did evil in the Lord's sight. [II Kings 24:8.]

10In the spring, King Nebuchadnezzar sent and brought him to Babylon, with the precious vessels of the house of the Lord, and made Zedekiah the [boy's] brother king over Judah and Jerusalem.

11Zedekiah was twenty-one years old when he became king, and he reigned eleven years in Jerusalem.

12He did evil in the sight of the Lord his God, and did not humble himself before Jeremiah the prophet, who spoke at the dictation of the Lord.

13He also rebelled against King Nebuchadnezzar, who made him swear by God. He stiffened his neck and hardened his heart against turning to the Lord God of Israel.

14Also all the chief of the priests and the people trespassed greatly in accord with all the abominations of the heathen, and polluted the house of the Lord which He had hallowed in Jerusalem.

## New American Standard

23And the archers shot King Josiah, and the king said to his
servants, "Take me away, for I am badly wounded."
24So his servants took him out of the chariot and carried him in
the second chariot which he had, and brought him to Jerusalem
where he died and was buried in the tombs of his fathers. And all
Judah and Jerusalem mourned for Josiah.
25Then Jeremiah chanted a lament for Josiah. And all the male
and female singers speak about Josiah in their lamentations to this
day. And they made them an ordinance in Israel; behold, they are
also written in the Lamentations.
26Now the rest of the acts of Josiah and his deeds of devotion
as written in the law of the LORD,
27and his acts, first to last, behold, they are written in the Book
of the Kings of Israel and Judah.

*Jehoahaz, Jehoiakim, then Jehoiachin Rule*

**36** THEN THE people of the land took [a]Joahaz the son of
Josiah, and made him king in place of his father in Jerusalem.
2Joahaz was twenty-three years old when he became king, and
he reigned three months in Jerusalem.
3Then the king of Egypt deposed him at Jerusalem, and imposed on the land a fine of one hundred talents of silver and one
talent of gold.
4And the king of Egypt made Eliakim his brother king over
Judah and Jerusalem, and changed his name to Jehoiakim. But
Neco took Joahaz his brother and brought him to Egypt.
5Jehoiakim was twenty-five years old when he became king,
and he reigned eleven years in Jerusalem; and he did evil in the
sight of the LORD his God.
6Nebuchadnezzar king of Babylon came up against him and
bound him with bronze *chains* to take him to Babylon.
7Nebuchadnezzar also brought *some* of the articles of the house
of the LORD to Babylon and put them in his temple at Babylon.
8Now the rest of the acts of Jehoiakim and the abominations
which he did, and what was found against him, behold, they are
written in the Book of the Kings of Israel and Judah. And Jehoiachin his son became king in his place.
9¶ Jehoiachin was eight years old when he became king, and
he reigned three months and ten days in Jerusalem, and he did evil
in the sight of the LORD.

*Captivity in Babylon Begun*

10And at the turn of the year King Nebuchadnezzar sent and
brought him to Babylon with the valuable articles of the house of
the LORD, and he made his kinsman Zedekiah king over Judah and
Jerusalem.

*Zedekiah Rules in Judah*

11Zedekiah was twenty-one years old when he became king,
and he reigned eleven years in Jerusalem.
12And he did evil in the sight of the LORD his God; he did not
humble himself before Jeremiah the prophet who spoke for the
LORD.
13And he also rebelled against King Nebuchadnezzar who had
made him swear *allegiance* by God. But he stiffened his neck and
hardened his heart against turning to the LORD God of Israel.
14Furthermore, all the officials of the priests and the people
were very unfaithful *following* all the abominations of the nations;
and they defiled the house of the LORD which He had sanctified
in Jerusalem.

NAS [a] I.e., short form of Jehoahaz

## New International

23Archers shot King Josiah, and he told his officers, "Take me
away; I am badly wounded." 24So they took him out of his chariot,
put him in the other chariot he had and brought him to Jerusalem,
where he died. He was buried in the tombs of his fathers, and all
Judah and Jerusalem mourned for him.
25Jeremiah composed laments for Josiah, and to this day all the
men and women singers commemorate Josiah in the laments.
These became a tradition in Israel and are written in the Laments.
26The other events of Josiah's reign and his acts of devotion,
according to what is written in the Law of the LORD— 27all the
events, from beginning to end, are written in the book of the kings
of Israel and Judah.

**36** AND THE people of the land took Jehoahaz son of Josiah
and made him king in Jerusalem in place of his father.

*Jehoahaz King of Judah*

2Jehoahaz[b] was twenty-three years old when he became king,
and he reigned in Jerusalem three months. 3The king of Egypt
dethroned him in Jerusalem and imposed on Judah a levy of a
hundred talents[c] of silver and a talent[d] of gold. 4The king of Egypt
made Eliakim, a brother of Jehoahaz, king over Judah and Jerusalem and changed Eliakim's name to Jehoiakim. But Neco took
Eliakim's brother Jehoahaz and carried him off to Egypt.

*Jehoiakim King of Judah*

5Jehoiakim was twenty-five years old when he became king,
and he reigned in Jerusalem eleven years. He did evil in the eyes
of the LORD his God. 6Nebuchadnezzar king of Babylon attacked
him and bound him with bronze shackles to take him to Babylon.
7Nebuchadnezzar also took to Babylon articles from the temple of
the LORD and put them in his temple[e] there.
8The other events of Jehoiakim's reign, the detestable things he
did and all that was found against him, are written in the book of
the kings of Israel and Judah. And Jehoiachin his son succeeded
him as king.

*Jehoiachin King of Judah*

9Jehoiachin was eighteen[f] years old when he became king, and
he reigned in Jerusalem three months and ten days. He did evil in
the eyes of the LORD. 10In the spring, King Nebuchadnezzar sent
for him and brought him to Babylon, together with articles of value
from the temple of the LORD, and he made Jehoiachin's uncle,[g]
Zedekiah, king over Judah and Jerusalem.

*Zedekiah King of Judah*

11Zedekiah was twenty-one years old when he became king,
and he reigned in Jerusalem eleven years. 12He did evil in the eyes
of the LORD his God and did not humble himself before Jeremiah
the prophet, who spoke the word of the LORD. 13He also rebelled
against King Nebuchadnezzar, who had made him take an oath in
God's name. He became stiff-necked and hardened his heart and
would not turn to the LORD, the God of Israel. 14Furthermore, all
the leaders of the priests and the people became more and more
unfaithful, following all the detestable practices of the nations and
defiling the temple of the LORD, which he had consecrated in
Jerusalem.

NIV [b] 2 Hebrew *Joahaz,* a variant of *Jehoahaz;* also in verse 4 [c] 3 That is, about 3 3/4 tons (about 3.4 metric tons) [d] 3 That is, about 75 pounds (about 34 kilograms) [e] *7* Or *palace* [f] *9* One Hebrew manuscript, some Septuagint manuscripts and Syriac (see also 2 Kings 24:8); most Hebrew manuscripts *eight* [g] *10* Hebrew *brother,* that is, relative (see 2 Kings 24:17)

## King James

15And the LORD God of their fathers sent to them by his messengers, rising up betimes, and sending; because he had compassion on his people, and on his dwelling place:

16But they mocked the messengers of God, and despised his words, and misused his prophets, until the wrath of the LORD arose against his people, till *there was* no remedy.

17Therefore he brought upon them the king of the Chaldees, who slew their young men with the sword in the house of their sanctuary, and had no compassion upon young man or maiden, old man, or him that stooped for age: he gave *them* all into his hand.

18And all the vessels of the house of God, great and small, and the treasures of the house of the LORD, and the treasures of the king, and of his princes; all *these* he brought to Babylon.

19And they burnt the house of God, and brake down the wall of Jerusalem, and burnt all the palaces thereof with fire, and destroyed all the goodly vessels thereof.

20And them that had escaped from the sword carried he away to Babylon; where they were servants to him and his sons until the reign of the kingdom of Persia:

21To fulfil the word of the LORD by the mouth of Jeremiah, until the land had enjoyed her sabbaths: *for* as long as she lay desolate she kept sabbath, to fulfil threescore and ten years.

22¶ Now in the first year of Cyrus king of Persia, that the word of the LORD *spoken* by the mouth of Jeremiah might be accomplished, the LORD stirred up the spirit of Cyrus king of Persia, that he made a proclamation throughout all his kingdom, and *put it* also in writing, saying,

23Thus saith Cyrus king of Persia, All the kingdoms of the earth hath the LORD God of heaven given me; and he hath charged me to build him an house in Jerusalem, which *is* in Judah. Who *is there* among you of all his people? The LORD his God *be* with him, and let him go up.

## Amplified

15And the Lord, the God of their fathers, sent to them persistently by His messengers, because He had compassion on His people and on His dwelling place;

16But they kept mocking the messengers of God, and despising His words, and scoffing at His prophets, till the wrath of the Lord rose against His people, till there was no remedy *or* healing.

17Therefore He brought against them the king of the Chaldeans, who slew their young men with the sword in the house of their sanctuary, and had no compassion on young man or virgin, old man or hoary headed; He gave them all into his hand.

18And all the vessels of the house of God, great and small, and the treasures of the Lord's house, of the king, and of his princes, all these he brought to Babylon.

19And they burned God's house, and broke down Jerusalem's wall, and burned all its palaces with fire, and destroyed all its choice vessels.

20Those who had escaped from the sword he took away to Babylon, where they were servants to him and his sons until the kingdom of Persia was established there,

21To fulfil the Lord's word by Jeremiah, till the land had enjoyed its sabbaths; for as long as it lay desolate it kept sabbath, to fulfil seventy years. [Cp. Jer. 25:11; 29:10.]

22Now in the first year of Cyrus king of Persia, that the word of the Lord by the mouth of Jeremiah might be accomplished, the Lord stirred up the spirit of Cyrus king of Persia so that he made a proclamation throughout all his kingdom, and also put it in writing:

23Thus says Cyrus king of Persia, All the kingdoms of the earth the Lord, the God of Heaven has given me; and He has charged me to build Him a house in Jerusalem, which is in Judah. Whoever there is among you of all His people, the Lord his God be with him, and let him go up [to Jerusalem].

## New American Standard

15And the LORD, the God of their fathers, sent *word* to them again and again by His messengers, because He had compassion on His people and on His dwelling place;

16but they *continually* mocked the messengers of God, despised His words and scoffed at His prophets, until the wrath of the LORD arose against His people, until there was no remedy.

17Therefore He brought up against them the king of the Chaldeans who slew their young men with the sword in the house of their sanctuary, and had no compassion on young man or virgin, old man or infirm; He gave *them* all into his hand.

18And all the articles of the house of God, great and small, and the treasures of the house of the LORD, and the treasures of the king and of his officers, he brought *them* all to Babylon.

19Then they burned the house of God, and broke down the wall of Jerusalem and burned all its fortified buildings with fire, and destroyed all its valuable articles.

20And those who had escaped from the sword he carried away to Babylon; and they were servants to him and to his sons until the rule of the kingdom of Persia,

21to fulfill the word of the LORD by the mouth of Jeremiah, until the land had enjoyed its sabbaths. All the days of its desolation it kept sabbath until seventy years were complete.

*Cyrus Permits Return*

22¶ Now in the first year of Cyrus king of Persia—in order to fulfill the word of the LORD by the mouth of Jeremiah—the LORD stirred up the spirit of Cyrus king of Persia, so that he sent a proclamation throughout his kingdom, and also *put it* in writing, saying,

23"Thus says Cyrus king of Persia, 'The LORD, the God of heaven, has given me all the kingdoms of the earth, and He has appointed me to build Him a house in Jerusalem, which is in Judah. Whoever there is among you of all His people, may the LORD his God be with him, and let him go up!' "

## New International

*The Fall of Jerusalem*

15The LORD, the God of their fathers, sent word to them
through his messengers again and again, because he had pity on
his people and on his dwelling place. 16But they mocked God's
messengers, despised his words and scoffed at his prophets until
the wrath of the LORD was aroused against his people and there
was no remedy. 17He brought up against them the king of the
Babylonians,[a] who killed their young men with the sword in the
sanctuary, and spared neither young man nor young woman, old
man or aged. God handed all of them over to Nebuchadnezzar.
18He carried to Babylon all the articles from the temple of God,
both large and small, and the treasures of the LORD's temple and
the treasures of the king and his officials. 19They set fire to God's
temple and broke down the wall of Jerusalem; they burned all the
palaces and destroyed everything of value there.
20He carried into exile to Babylon the remnant, who escaped
from the sword, and they became servants to him and his sons
until the kingdom of Persia came to power. 21The land enjoyed its
sabbath rests; all the time of its desolation it rested, until the
seventy years were completed in fulfillment of the word of the
LORD spoken by Jeremiah.
22In the first year of Cyrus king of Persia, in order to fulfill the
word of the LORD spoken by Jeremiah, the LORD moved the heart
of Cyrus king of Persia to make a proclamation throughout his
realm and to put it in writing:

23"This is what Cyrus king of Persia says:

" 'The LORD, the God of heaven, has given me all the kingdoms of the earth and he has appointed me to build a temple for him at Jerusalem in Judah. Anyone of his people among you—may the LORD his God be with him, and let him go up.' "

NIV [a] 17 Or *Chaldeans*

## King James

THE BOOK OF

# Ezra

1 NOW IN the first year of Cyrus king of Persia, that the word of the LORD by the mouth of Jeremiah might be fulfilled, the LORD stirred up the spirit of Cyrus king of Persia, that he made a proclamation throughout all his kingdom, and *put it* also in writing, saying,

2 Thus saith Cyrus king of Persia, The LORD God of heaven hath given me all the kingdoms of the earth; and he hath charged me to build him an house at Jerusalem, which *is* in Judah.

3 Who *is there* among you of all his people? his God be with him, and let him go up to Jerusalem, which *is* in Judah, and build the house of the LORD God of Israel, (he *is* the God,) which *is* in Jerusalem.

4 And whosoever remaineth in any place where he sojourneth, let the men of his place help him with silver, and with gold, and with goods, and with beasts, beside the freewill offering for the house of God that *is* in Jerusalem.

5 ¶ Then rose up the chief of the fathers of Judah and Benjamin, and the priests, and the Levites, with all *them* whose spirit God had raised, to go up to build the house of the LORD which *is* in Jerusalem.

6 And all they that *were* about them strengthened their hands with vessels of silver, with gold, with goods, and with beasts, and with precious things, beside all *that* was willingly offered.

7 ¶ Also Cyrus the king brought forth the vessels of the house of the LORD, which Nebuchadnezzar had brought forth out of Jerusalem, and had put them in the house of his gods;

8 Even those did Cyrus king of Persia bring forth by the hand of Mithredath the treasurer, and numbered them unto Sheshbazzar, the prince of Judah.

9 And this *is* the number of them: thirty chargers of gold, a thousand chargers of silver, nine and twenty knives,

10 Thirty basins of gold, silver basins of a second *sort* four hundred and ten, *and* other vessels a thousand.

11 All the vessels of gold and of silver *were* five thousand and four hundred. All *these* did Sheshbazzar bring up with *them of* the captivity that were brought up from Babylon unto Jerusalem.

## Amplified

THE BOOK OF

# Ezra

1 NOW IN the first year [a]Cyrus king of Persia [almost seventy years after the first Jewish captives were taken to Babylon], that the word of the Lord by the mouth of Jeremiah might begin to be accomplished, the Lord stirred up the spirit of Cyrus king of Persia, so that he made a proclamation throughout all his kingdom, and put it also in writing: [Jer. 29:10-14.]

2 Thus says Cyrus king of Persia, The Lord God of Heaven has given me all the kingdoms of the earth, and He has charged me to build Him a house at Jerusalem, in Judah.

3 Whoever is among you of all His people, his God be with him, and let him go up to Jerusalem in Judah and *re*build the house of the Lord, the God of Israel, in Jerusalem; He is God.

4 And in any place where a survivor [of the Babylonian captivity of the Jews] sojourns, let the men of that place assist him with silver and gold, with goods and beasts, besides freewill offerings for the house of God in Jerusalem.

5 Then rose up the heads of the fathers' houses of Judah and Benjamin, and the priests and Levites, with all those whose spirit God had stirred up, to go up to *re*build the house of the Lord in Jerusalem.

6 And all those who were around them aided them with vessels of silver, with gold, goods, beasts, and precious things, besides all that was willingly *and* freely offered.

7 Also Cyrus the king brought out the vessels of the house of the Lord, which Nebuchadnezzar had brought from Jerusalem [when he took that city] and had put them in the house of his gods.

8 These Cyrus king of Persia directed Mithredath the treasurer to bring forth and count out to Sheshbazzar [who is Zerubbabel, recognized as the legitimate heir to the throne of David], the prince of Judah.

9 And they numbered: thirty basins of gold, 1,000 basins of silver, twenty-nine sacrificial dishes,

10 Of gold bowls, thirty; another sort of silver bowls, 410, and other vessels, 1,000.

11 All the vessels of gold and of silver were 5,400. All these Sheshbazzar [the governor] brought with the people of the captivity from Babylon to Jerusalem.

**AMP** [a] Cyrus, a heathen ruler of a heathen empire (Persia) was "twice named [before his birth] in the book of Isaiah as anointed of God and predestined to conquer kings and fortified places, and set the Jews free from captivity (Isa. 44:28; 45:1-14). Daniel . . . records that during the night that followed a great feast, Belshazzar, the king of the Chaldeans, was slain and Darius the Mede received the kingdom (Dan. 5:30, 31). Darius was predecessor of Cyrus, or his regent, in Babylonia (6:28)" *(Davis' Dictionary of the Bible)*. [God gave Cyrus the resolution and the desire to execute His intention. That the Lord at this time chose a heathen as His instrument was in accordance with the new position that the empires of the world were henceforth to assume toward the kingdom of God] (*Lange's Commentary,* condensed).

## New American Standard

# Ezra

*Cyrus' Proclamation*

1 NOW IN the first year of Cyrus king of Persia, in order to
fulfill the word of the LORD by the mouth of Jeremiah, the
LORD stirred up the spirit of Cyrus king of Persia, so that he sent
a proclamation throughout all his kingdom, and also *put it* in
writing, saying,
2 "Thus says Cyrus king of Persia, 'The LORD, the God of
heaven, has given me all the kingdoms of the earth, and He has
appointed me to build Him a house in Jerusalem, which is in
Judah.
3 'Whoever there is among you of all His people, may his God
be with him! Let him go up to Jerusalem which is in Judah, and
rebuild the house of the LORD, the God of Israel; He is the God who
is in Jerusalem.
4 'And every survivor, at whatever place he may live, let the
men of that place support him with silver and gold, with goods
and cattle, together with a freewill offering for the house of God
which is in Jerusalem.' "

*Holy Vessels Restored*

5 ¶ Then the heads of fathers' *households* of Judah and Benjamin
and the priests and the Levites arose, even everyone whose spirit
God had stirred to go up and rebuild the house of the LORD which
is in Jerusalem.
6 And all those about them encouraged them with articles of
silver, with gold, with goods, with cattle, and with valuables, aside
from all that was given as a freewill offering.
7 Also King Cyrus brought out the articles of the house of the
LORD, which Nebuchadnezzar had carried away from Jerusalem
and put in the house of his gods;
8 and Cyrus, king of Persia, had them brought out by the hand
of Mithredath the treasurer, and he counted them out to Sheshbazzar, the prince of Judah.
9 Now this *was* their number: 30 gold dishes, 1,000 silver dishes,
29 duplicates;
10 30 gold bowls, 410 silver bowls of a second *kind, and* 1,000
other articles.
11 All the articles of gold and silver *numbered* 5,400. Sheshbazzar
brought them all up with the exiles who went up from Babylon to
Jerusalem.

## New International

# Ezra

*Cyrus Helps the Exiles to Return*

1 IN THE first year of Cyrus king of Persia, in order to fulfill
the word of the LORD spoken by Jeremiah, the LORD moved
the heart of Cyrus king of Persia to make a proclamation throughout his realm and to put it in writing:

2 "This is what Cyrus king of Persia says:
" 'The LORD, the God of heaven, has given me all the
kingdoms of the earth and he has appointed me to build a
temple for him at Jerusalem in Judah. 3 Anyone of his people
among you—may his God be with him, and let him go up to
Jerusalem in Judah and build the temple of the LORD, the God
of Israel, the God who is in Jerusalem. 4 And the people of any
place where survivors may now be living are to provide him
with silver and gold, with goods and livestock, and with
freewill offerings for the temple of God in Jerusalem.' "

5 Then the family heads of Judah and Benjamin, and the priests
and Levites—everyone whose heart God had moved—prepared to
go up and build the house of the LORD in Jerusalem. 6 All their
neighbors assisted them with articles of silver and gold, with
goods and livestock, and with valuable gifts, in addition to all the
freewill offerings. 7 Moreover, King Cyrus brought out the articles
belonging to the temple of the LORD, which Nebuchadnezzar had
carried away from Jerusalem and had placed in the temple of his
god.[b] 8 Cyrus king of Persia had them brought by Mithredath the
treasurer, who counted them out to Sheshbazzar the prince of
Judah.
9 This was the inventory:

| | |
|---|---|
| gold dishes | 30 |
| silver dishes | 1,000 |
| silver pans[c] | 29 |
| 10 gold bowls | 30 |
| matching silver bowls | 410 |
| other articles | 1,000 |

11 In all, there were 5,400 articles of gold and of silver. Sheshbazzar brought all these along when the exiles came up from Babylon
to Jerusalem.

NIV [b] 7 Or *gods* [c] 9 The meaning of the Hebrew for this word is uncertain.

## King James

2 NOW THESE *are* the children of the province that went up out of the captivity, of those which had been carried away, whom Nebuchadnezzar the king of Babylon had carried away unto Babylon, and came again unto Jerusalem and Judah, every one unto his city;

2Which came with Zerubbabel: Jeshua, Nehemiah, Seraiah, Reelaiah, Mordecai, Bilshan, Mizpar, Bigvai, Rehum, Baanah. The number of the men of the people of Israel:

3The children of Parosh, two thousand an hundred seventy and two.

4The children of Shephatiah, three hundred seventy and two.

5The children of Arah, seven hundred seventy and five.

6The children of Pahath-moab, of the children of Jeshua *and* Joab, two thousand eight hundred and twelve.

7The children of Elam, a thousand two hundred fifty and four.

8The children of Zattu, nine hundred forty and five.

9The children of Zaccai, seven hundred and threescore.

10The children of Bani, six hundred forty and two.

11The children of Bebai, six hundred twenty and three.

12The children of Azgad, a thousand two hundred twenty and two.

13The children of Adonikam, six hundred sixty and six.

14The children of Bigvai, two thousand fifty and six.

15The children of Adin, four hundred fifty and four.

16The children of Ater of Hezekiah, ninety and eight.

17The children of Bezai, three hundred twenty and three.

18The children of Jorah, an hundred and twelve.

19The children of Hashum, two hundred twenty and three.

20The children of Gibbar, ninety and five.

21The children of Bethlehem, an hundred twenty and three.

22The men of Netophah, fifty and six.

23The men of Anathoth, an hundred twenty and eight.

24The children of Azmaveth, forty and two.

25The children of Kirjath-arim, Chephirah, and Beeroth, seven hundred and forty and three.

26The children of Ramah and Gaba, six hundred twenty and one.

27The men of Michmas, an hundred twenty and two.

28The men of Beth-el and Ai, two hundred twenty and three.

29The children of Nebo, fifty and two.

30The children of Magbish, an hundred fifty and six.

31The children of the other Elam, a thousand two hundred fifty and four.

32The children of Harim, three hundred and twenty.

33The children of Lod, Hadid, and Ono, seven hundred twenty and five.

34The children of Jericho, three hundred forty and five.

35The children of Senaah, three thousand and six hundred and thirty.

36¶ The priests: the children of Jedaiah, of the house of Jeshua, nine hundred seventy and three.

37The children of Immer, a thousand fifty and two.

38The children of Pashur, a thousand two hundred forty and seven.

39The children of Harim, a thousand and seventeen.

40¶ The Levites: the children of Jeshua and Kadmiel, of the children of Hodaviah, seventy and four.

41¶ The singers: the children of Asaph, an hundred twenty and eight.

42¶ The children of the porters: the children of Shallum, the children of Ater, the children of Talmon, the children of Akkub, the children of Hatita, the children of Shobai, *in* all an hundred thirty and nine.

43¶ The Nethinims: the children of Ziha, the children of Hasupha, the children of Tabbaoth,

44The children of Keros, the children of Siaha, the children of Padon,

## Amplified

2 NOW THESE are the people of the province [of Judah] who went up out of the captivity of those exiles whom Nebuchadnezzar the king of Babylon had carried away to Babylon, but who came again to Jerusalem and Judah, every one to his own city.

2These came with Zerubbabel: Jeshua, Nehemiah [not the author], Seraiah, Reelaiah, Mordecai [not Esther's relative], Bilshan, Mispar, Bigvai, Rehum, Baanah. The number of the men of Israel:

3The sons [meaning male descendants] of Parosh, 2,172.

4The sons of Shephatiah, 372.

5The sons of Arah, 775.

6The sons of Pahath-moab, namely of the sons of Jeshua and Joab, 2,812.

7The sons of Elam, 1,254.

8The sons of Zattu, 945.

9The sons of Zaccai, 760.

10The sons of Bani, 642.

11The sons of Bebai, 623.

12The sons of Azgad, 1,222.

13The sons of Adonikam, 666.

14The sons of Bigvai, 2,056.

15The sons of Adin, 454.

16The sons of Ater, namely of Hezekiah, 98.

17The sons of Bezai, 323.

18The sons of Jorah, 112.

19The sons of Hashum, 223.

20The sons of Gibbar, 95.

21The sons of Bethlehem, 123.

22The men of Netophah, 56.

23The men of Anathoth, 128.

24The sons of Azmaveth, 42.

25The sons of Kiriatharim, Chephirah, and Beeroth, 743.

26The sons of Ramah and Geba, 621.

27The men of Michmas, 122.

28The men of Bethel and Ai, 223.

29The sons of Nebo, 52.

30The sons of Magbish, 156.

31The sons of the other Elam, 1,254.

32The sons of Harim, 320.

33The sons of Lod, Hadid, and Ono, 725.

34The sons of Jericho, 345.

35The sons of Senaah, 3,630.

36The priests: the sons of Jedaiah, of the house of Jeshua, 973.

37The sons of Immer, 1,052.

38The sons of Pashhur, 1,247.

39The sons of Harim, 1,017.

40The Levites: the sons of Jeshua and Kadmiel, of the house of Hodaviah, 74.

41The singers: the sons of Asaph, 128.

42The sons of the gatekeepers: of Shallum, Ater, Talmon, Akkub, Hatita, and Shobai; in all 139.

43The Nethinim [the temple servants]: the sons of Ziba, Hasupha, Tabbaoth,

44The sons of Keros, Siaha, Padon,

## New American Standard

*Number of Those Returning*

2 NOW THESE are the people of the province who came up out of the captivity of the exiles whom Nebuchadnezzar the king of Babylon had carried away to Babylon, and returned to Jerusalem and Judah, each to his city.
2These came with Zerubbabel, Jeshua, Nehemiah, Seraiah, Reelaiah, Mordecai, Bilshan, Mispar, Bigvai, Rehum, and Baanah.
¶The number of the men of the people of Israel:
3the sons of Parosh, 2,172;
4the sons of Shephatiah, 372;
5the sons of Arah, 775;
6the sons of Pahath-moab of the sons of Jeshua *and* Joab, 2,812;
7the sons of Elam, 1,254;
8the sons of Zattu, 945;
9the sons of Zaccai, 760;
10the sons of Bani, 642;
11the sons of Bebai, 623;
12the sons of Azgad, 1,222;
13the sons of Adonikam, 666;
14the sons of Bigvai, 2,056;
15the sons of Adin, 454;
16the sons of Ater of Hezekiah, 98;
17the sons of Bezai, 323;
18the sons of Jorah, 112;
19the sons of Hashum, 223;
20the sons of Gibbar, 95;
21the men of Bethlehem, 123;
22the men of Netophah, 56;
23the men of Anathoth, 128;
24the sons of Azmaveth, 42;
25the sons of Kiriath-arim, Chephirah, and Beeroth, 743;
26the sons of Ramah and Geba, 621;
27the men of Michmas, 122;
28the men of Bethel and Ai, 223;
29the sons of Nebo, 52;
30the sons of Magbish, 156;
31the sons of the other Elam, 1,254;
32the sons of Harim, 320;
33the sons of Lod, Hadid, and Ono, 725;
34the men of Jericho, 345;
35the sons of Senaah, 3,630.

*Priests Returning*

36¶ The priests: the sons of Jedaiah of the house of Jeshua, 973;
37the sons of Immer, 1,052;
38the sons of Pashhur, 1,247;
39the sons of Harim, 1,017.

*Levites Returning*

40¶ The Levites: the sons of Jeshua and Kadmiel, of the sons of Hodaviah, 74.
41The singers: the sons of Asaph, 128.
42The sons of the gatekeepers: the sons of Shallum, the sons of Ater, the sons of Talmon, the sons of Akkub, the sons of Hatita, the sons of Shobai, in all 139.
43¶ The temple servants: the sons of Ziha, the sons of Hasupha, the sons of Tabbaoth,
44the sons of Keros, the sons of Siaha, the sons of Padon,

## New International

*The List of the Exiles Who Returned*

2 NOW THESE are the people of the province who came up from the captivity of the exiles, whom Nebuchadnezzar king of Babylon had taken captive to Babylon (they returned to Jerusalem and Judah, each to his own town,
2in company with Zerubbabel, Jeshua, Nehemiah, Seraiah, Reelaiah, Mordecai, Bilshan, Mispar, Bigvai, Rehum and Baanah):

The list of the men of the people of Israel:

| | |
|---|---|
| 3the descendants of Parosh | 2,172 |
| 4of Shephatiah | 372 |
| 5of Arah | 775 |
| 6of Pahath-Moab (through the line of Jeshua and Joab) | 2,812 |
| 7of Elam | 1,254 |
| 8of Zattu | 945 |
| 9of Zaccai | 760 |
| 10of Bani | 642 |
| 11of Bebai | 623 |
| 12of Azgad | 1,222 |
| 13of Adonikam | 666 |
| 14of Bigvai | 2,056 |
| 15of Adin | 454 |
| 16of Ater (through Hezekiah) | 98 |
| 17of Bezai | 323 |
| 18of Jorah | 112 |
| 19of Hashum | 223 |
| 20of Gibbar | 95 |
| 21the men of Bethlehem | 123 |
| 22of Netophah | 56 |
| 23of Anathoth | 128 |
| 24of Azmaveth | 42 |
| 25of Kiriath Jearim,[a] Kephirah and Beeroth | 743 |
| 26of Ramah and Geba | 621 |
| 27of Micmash | 122 |
| 28of Bethel and Ai | 223 |
| 29of Nebo | 52 |
| 30of Magbish | 156 |
| 31of the other Elam | 1,254 |
| 32of Harim | 320 |
| 33of Lod, Hadid and Ono | 725 |
| 34of Jericho | 345 |
| 35of Senaah | 3,630 |

36The priests:

| | |
|---|---|
| the descendants of Jedaiah (through the family of Jeshua) | 973 |
| 37of Immer | 1,052 |
| 38of Pashhur | 1,247 |
| 39of Harim | 1,017 |

40The Levites:

| | |
|---|---|
| the descendants of Jeshua and Kadmiel (through the line of Hodaviah) | 74 |

41The singers:

| | |
|---|---|
| the descendants of Asaph | 128 |

42The gatekeepers of the temple:

| | |
|---|---|
| the descendants of Shallum, Ater, Talmon, Akkub, Hatita and Shobai | 139 |

43The temple servants:

the descendants of
Ziha, Hasupha, Tabbaoth,
44Keros, Siaha, Padon,

NIV [a] 25 See Septuagint (see also Neh. 7:29); Hebrew *Kiriath Arim.*

## King James

45The children of Lebanah, the children of Hagabah, the children of Akkub,
46The children of Hagab, the children of Shalmai, the children of Hanan,
47The children of Giddel, the children of Gahar, the children of Reaiah,
48The children of Rezin, the children of Nekoda, the children of Gazzam,
49The children of Uzza, the children of Paseah, the children of Besai,
50the children of Asnah, the children of Mehunim, the children of Nephusim,
51The children of Bakbuk, the children of Hakupha, the children of Harhur,
52The children of Bazluth, the children of Mehida, the children of Harsha,
53The children of Barkos, the children of Sisera, the children of Thamah,
54The children of Neziah, the children of Hatipha.
55¶ The children of Solomon's servants: the children of Sotai, the children of Sophereth, the children of Peruda,
56The children of Jaalah, the children of Darkon, the children of Giddel,
57The children of Shephatiah, the children of Hattil, the children of Pochereth of Zebaim, the children of Ami.
58All the Nethinims, and the children of Solomon's servants, *were* three hundred ninety and two.
59And these *were* they which went up from Tel-melah, Tel-harsa, Cherub, Addan, *and* Immer: but they could not show their father's house, and their seed, whether they *were* of Israel:
60The children of Delaiah, the children of Tobiah, the children of Nekoda, six hundred fifty and two.
61¶ And of the children of the priests: the children of Habaiah, the children of Koz, the children of Barzillai; which took a wife of the daughters of Barzillai the Gileadite, and was called after their name:
62These sought their register *among* those that were reckoned by genealogy, but they were not found: therefore were they, as polluted, put from the priesthood.
63And the Tirshatha said unto them, that they should not eat of the most holy things, till there stood up a priest with Urim and with Thummim.
64¶ The whole congregation together *was* forty and two thousand three hundred *and* threescore,
65Beside their servants and their maids, of whom *there were* seven thousand three hundred thirty and seven: and *there were* among them two hundred singing men and singing women.
66Their horses *were* seven hundred thirty and six; their mules, two hundred forty and five;
67Their camels, four hundred thirty and five; *their* asses, six thousand seven hundred and twenty.
68¶ And *some* of the chief of the fathers, when they came to the house of the LORD which *is* at Jerusalem, offered freely for the house of God to set it up in his place:
69They gave after their ability unto the treasure of the work threescore and one thousand drams of gold, and five thousand pound of silver, and one hundred priests' garments.
70So the priests, and the Levites, and *some* of the people, and the singers, and the porters, and the Nethinims, dwelt in their cities, and all Israel in their cities.

## Amplified

45The sons of Lebanah, Hagabah, Akkub,
46The sons of Hagab, Shamlai, Hanan,
47The sons of Giddel, Gahar, Reaiah,
48The sons of Rezin, Nekoda, Gazzam,
49The sons of Uzza, Paseah, Besai,
50The sons of Asnah, Meunim, Nephisim,
51The sons of Bakbuk, Hakupha, Harhur,
52The sons of Bazluth, Mehida, Harsha,
53The sons of Barkos, Sisera, Temah,
54The sons of Neziah, *and* of Hatipha.
55The sons of [King] Solomon's servants: the sons of Sotai, Sophereth (Hassorphereth), Peruda,
56The sons of Jaalah, Darkon, Giddel,
57The sons of Shephatiah, Hattil, Pochereth-hazzebaim, Ami.
58All the Nethinim [the temple servants] and the sons of Solomon's servants were 392.
59And these were they who came up from Telmelah, Telharsha, Cherub, Addan, and Immer; but they could not show a record of their fathers' houses or prove their descent, whether they were of Israel:
60The sons of Delaiah, Tobiah, and Nekoda, 652.
61And of the sons of the priests: the sons of Habaiah, of Hakkoz, and of Barzillai, who had taken a wife of the daughters of Barzillai the [noted] Gileadite, and had assumed their name. [II Sam. 17:27, 28; 19:31-39.]
62These sought their names among those enrolled in the genealogies, but they were not found; so they were excluded from the priesthood as [ceremonially] unclean.
63[Zerubbabel] the governor told them they should not eat of the most holy things [the priests' food] until there should be a priest with Urim and Thummim [who by consulting these articles in his breastplate could [a]know God's will in the matter].
64The whole congregation numbered 42,360,
65Besides their menservants and maidservants, 7,337; and among them 200 men and women singers.
66Their horses were 736; their mules, 245;
67Their camels were 435; their donkeys, 6,720.
68Some of the heads of families, when they came to the house of the Lord in Jerusalem, made freewill offerings for the house of God to *re*build it on its site.
69They gave as able to the treasury of the work 61,000 darics of gold, 5,000 minas of silver, and 100 priests' garments.
70So the priests, the Levites, some of the people, the singers, the gatekeepers, and the temple servants lived in their own towns, and all Israel [gradually settled] into their towns.

**AMP** [a] But the effort doubtless would have been in vain. Long disobedience had apparently caused Israel's priests to forfeit the divine gift of guidance through Urim and Thummim, and it was never recovered. Except for a similar incident in Nehemiah 7:65, Urim and Thummim are not again mentioned in the Scriptures, but the higher revelation by prophets superseded them as interpreters of the will of God (Exod. 28:30; Amos 3:7).

## New American Standard

45 the sons of Lebanah, the sons of Hagabah, the sons of Akkub,
46 the sons of Hagab, the sons of Shalmai, the sons of Hanan,
47 the sons of Giddel, the sons of Gahar, the sons of Reaiah,
48 the sons of Rezin, the sons of Nekoda, the sons of Gazzam,
49 the sons of Uzza, the sons of Paseah, the sons of Besai,
50 the sons of Asnah, the sons of Meunim, the sons of Nephisim,
51 the sons of Bakbuk, the sons of Hakupha, the sons of Harhur,
52 the sons of Bazluth, the sons of Mehida, the sons of Harsha,
53 the sons of Barkos, the sons of Sisera, the sons of Temah,
54 the sons of Neziah, the sons of Hatipha.
**55**¶ The sons of Solomon's servants: the sons of Sotai, the sons of Hassophereth, the sons of Peruda,
56 the sons of Jaalah, the sons of Darkon, the sons of Giddel,
57 the sons of Shephatiah, the sons of Hattil, the sons of Pochereth-hazzebaim, the sons of Ami.
58 All the temple servants, and the sons of Solomon's servants, were 392.
**59**¶ Now these are those who came up from Tel-melah, Tel-harsha, Cherub, Addan, *and* Immer, but they were not able to give evidence of their fathers' households, and their descendants, whether they were of Israel:
60 the sons of Delaiah, the sons of Tobiah, the sons of Nekoda, 652.

*Priests Removed*

61 And of the sons of the priests: the sons of Habaiah, the sons of Hakkoz, the sons of Barzillai, who took a wife from the daughters of Barzillai the Gileadite, and he was called by their name.
62 These searched *among* their ancestral registration, but they could not be located; therefore they were considered unclean *and excluded* from the priesthood.
63 And the governor said to them that they should not eat from the most holy things until a priest stood up with Urim and Thummim.
**64**¶ The whole assembly numbered 42,360,
65 besides their male and female servants, who numbered 7,337; and they had 200 singing men and women.
66 Their horses were 736; their mules, 245;
67 their camels, 435; *their* donkeys, 6,720.
**68**¶ And some of the heads of fathers' *households,* when they arrived at the house of the LORD which is in Jerusalem, offered willingly for the house of God to restore it on its foundation.
69 According to their ability they gave to the treasury for the work 61,000 gold drachmas, and 5,000 silver minas, and 100 priestly garments.
**70**¶ Now the priests and the Levites, some of the people, the singers, the gatekeepers, and the temple servants lived in their cities, and all Israel in their cities.

## New International

45 Lebanah, Hagabah, Akkub,
46 Hagab, Shalmai, Hanan,
47 Giddel, Gahar, Reaiah,
48 Rezin, Nekoda, Gazzam,
49 Uzza, Paseah, Besai,
50 Asnah, Meunim, Nephussim,
51 Bakbuk, Hakupha, Harhur,
52 Bazluth, Mehida, Harsha,
53 Barkos, Sisera, Temah,
54 Neziah and Hatipha

55 The descendants of the servants of Solomon:

the descendants of
Sotai, Hassophereth, Peruda,
56 Jaala, Darkon, Giddel,
57 Shephatiah, Hattil,
Pokereth-Hazzebaim and Ami

58 The temple servants and the descendants
of the servants of Solomon 392

59 The following came up from the towns of Tel Melah, Tel Harsha, Kerub, Addon and Immer, but they could not show that their families were descended from Israel:

60 The descendants of
Delaiah, Tobiah and Nekoda 652

61 And from among the priests:

The descendants of
Hobaiah, Hakkoz and Barzillai (a man who had married a daughter of Barzillai the Gileadite and was called by that name).

62 These searched for their family records, but they could not find them and so were excluded from the priesthood as
unclean. 63 The governor ordered them not to eat any of the most sacred food until there was a priest ministering with the Urim and Thummim.

64 The whole company numbered 42,360, 65 besides their
7,337 menservants and maidservants; and they also had 200 men and women singers. 66 They had 736 horses, 245 mules,
67 435 camels and 6,720 donkeys.

68 When they arrived at the house of the LORD in Jerusalem, some of the heads of the families gave freewill offerings toward the rebuilding of the house of God on its site. 69 According to their
ability they gave to the treasury for this work 61,000 drachmas[b] of gold, 5,000 minas[c] of silver and 100 priestly garments.
70 The priests, the Levites, the singers, the gatekeepers and the temple servants settled in their own towns, along with some of the other people, and the rest of the Israelites settled in their towns.

**NIV** [b] *69* That is, about 1,100 pounds (about 500 kilograms) [c] *69* That is, about 3 tons (about 2.9 metric tons)

## King James

**3** AND WHEN the seventh month was come, and the children of Israel *were* in the cities, the people gathered themselves together as one man to Jerusalem.

2 Then stood up Jeshua the son of Jozadak, and his brethren the priests, and Zerubbabel the son of Shealtiel, and his brethren, and builded the altar of the God of Israel, to offer burnt offerings thereon, as *it is* written in the law of Moses the man of God.

3 And they set the altar upon his bases; for fear *was* upon them because of the people of those countries: and they offered burnt offerings thereon unto the LORD, *even* burnt offerings morning and evening.

4 They kept also the feast of tabernacles, as *it is* written, and *offered* the daily burnt offerings by number, according to the custom, as the duty of every day required;

5 And afterward *offered* the continual burnt offering, both of the new moons, and of all the set feasts of the LORD that were consecrated, and of every one that willingly offered a freewill offering unto the LORD.

6 From the first day of the seventh month began they to offer burnt offerings unto the LORD. But the foundation of the temple of the LORD was not *yet* laid.

7 They gave money also unto the masons, and to the carpenters; and meat, and drink, and oil, unto them of Zidon, and to them of Tyre, to bring cedar trees from Lebanon to the sea of Joppa, according to the grant that they had of Cyrus king of Persia.

8 ¶ Now in the second year of their coming unto the house of God at Jerusalem, in the second month, began Zerubbabel the son of Shealtiel, and Jeshua the son of Jozadak, and the remnant of their brethren the priests and the Levites, and all they that were come out of the captivity unto Jerusalem; and appointed the Levites, from twenty years old and upward, to set forward the work of the house of the LORD.

9 Then stood Jeshua *with* his sons and his brethren, Kadmiel and his sons, the sons of Judah, together, to set forward the workmen in the house of God: the sons of Henadad, *with* their sons and their brethren the Levites.

10 And when the builders laid the foundation of the temple of the LORD, they set the priests in their apparel with trumpets, and the Levites the sons of Asaph with cymbals, to praise the LORD, after the ordinance of David king of Israel.

11 And they sang together by course in praising and giving thanks unto the LORD; because *he is* good, for his mercy *endureth* for ever toward Israel. And all the people shouted with a great shout, when they praised the LORD, because the foundation of the house of the LORD was laid.

12 But many of the priests and Levites and chief of the fathers, *who were* ancient men, that had seen the first house, when the foundation of this house was laid before their eyes, wept with a loud voice; and many shouted aloud for joy:

13 So that the people could not discern the noise of the shout of joy from the noise of the weeping of the people: for the people shouted with a loud shout, and the noise was heard afar off.

## Amplified

**3** WHEN THE seventh month came, and the Israelites were in the towns, the people gathered together as one man to Jerusalem.

2 Then stood up Jeshua son of Jozadak, and his brethren the priests, and Zerubbabel the son of Shealtiel, and his brethren, and they built the altar of the God of Israel, to offer burnt offerings upon it, as it is written in the [a]instructions of Moses, the man of God.

3 And they set the altar [in its place] upon its base, for fear was upon them because of the peoples of the countries; and they offered burnt offerings on it to the Lord, morning and evening.

4 They kept also the feast of tabernacles, as it is written, and offered the daily burnt offerings by number, according to the ordinances, as each day's duty required;

5 And after that the continual burnt offering, the offering at the new moon, and at all the appointed feasts of the Lord, and the offerings of every one who made a freewill offering to the Lord.

6 From the first day of the seventh month they began to offer burnt offerings to the Lord; but the foundation of the temple of the Lord was not yet laid.

7 They gave money also to the masons, and to the carpenters; and food, drink, and oil, to the Sidonians and the Tyrians, to bring cedar trees from Lebanon to the seaport of Joppa, according to the grant they had from Cyrus king of Persia.

8 In the second year of their coming to God's house at Jerusalem, in the second month, Zerubbabel son of Shealtiel and Jeshua son of Jozadak made a beginning, with the rest of their brethren the priests and Levites and all who had come to Jerusalem out of the captivity. They appointed the Levites, from twenty years old and upward, to oversee the work of the Lord's house.

9 Then Jeshua with his sons and his kinsmen, Kadmiel and his sons, sons of Judah, together took the oversight of the workmen in the house of God: the sons of Henadad, with their sons and Levite kinsmen.

10 And when the builders laid the foundation of the temple of the Lord, the priests stood in their vestments with trumpets, and the Levite sons of Asaph with their cymbals, to praise the Lord, after the order of David king of Israel.

11 They sang responsively, praising and giving thanks to the Lord, saying For He is good, for His mercy *and* loving-kindness endure for ever toward Israel. And all the people shouted with a great shout when they praised the Lord, because the foundation of the house of the Lord was laid!

12 But many of the priests and Levites and heads of fathers' houses, old men who had seen the first house [Solomon's temple], when the foundation of this house was laid before their eyes, wept with a loud voice, though many shouted aloud for joy;

13 So the people could not distinguish the shout of joy from the sound of the weeping of the people, for the people shouted with a loud shout, and the sound was heard far off.

**AMP** [a] The Hebrew word here is "torah," and although usually translated "law," that is only one phase of its meaning, and so to use it, to the exclusion of its fuller sense, may defeat its intended purpose at times. The word *torah* is used more than 200 times in the Old Testament. When capitalized, *Torah* means the whole of the Pentateuch, the five books of Moses. *Baker's Dictionary of Theology* says in part, "The Hebrew *torah* originally signified authorative instruction (Prov. 1:8); hence it most commonly means an 'oracle' or 'word' of the Lord, whether delivered through an accredited spokesman, such as Moses, or a prophet or priest. Thus *torah* comes to have the wider sense of 'instruction' (so RV margin) from God. . . . It is therefore a synonym for the whole of the revealed will of God—the word, commandments, ways, judgments, precepts, etc., of the Lord, as in Gen. 26:5, and especially throughout Ps. 119."

## New American Standard

*Altar and Sacrifices Restored*

**3** NOW WHEN the seventh month came, and the sons of Israel *were* in the cities, the people gathered together as one man to Jerusalem.

2 Then Jeshua the son of Jozadak and his brothers the priests, and Zerubbabel the son of Shealtiel, and his brothers arose and built the altar of the God of Israel, to offer burnt offerings on it, as it is written in the law of Moses, the man of God.

3 So they set up the altar on its foundation, for they were terrified because of the peoples of the lands; and they offered burnt offerings on it to the LORD, burnt offerings morning and evening.

4 And they celebrated the Feast of [b]Booths, as it is written, and *offered* the fixed number of burnt offerings daily, according to the ordinance, as each day required;

5 and afterward *there was* a continual burnt offering, also for the new moons and for all the fixed festivals of the LORD that were consecrated, and from everyone who offered a freewill offering to the LORD.

6 From the first day of the seventh month they began to offer burnt offerings to the LORD, but the foundation of the temple of the LORD had not been laid.

7 Then they gave money to the masons and carpenters, and food, drink, and oil to the Sidonians and to the Tyrians, to bring cedar wood from Lebanon to the sea at Joppa, according to the permission they had from Cyrus king of Persia.

*Temple Restoration Begun*

8 Now in the second year of their coming to the house of God at Jerusalem in the second month, Zerubbabel the son of Shealtiel and Jeshua the son of Jozadak and the rest of their brothers the priests and the Levites, and all who came from the captivity to Jerusalem, began *the work* and appointed the Levites from twenty years and older to oversee the work of the house of the LORD.

9 Then Jeshua *with* his sons and brothers stood united *with* Kadmiel and his sons, the sons of Judah *and* the sons of Henadad *with* their sons and brothers the Levites, to oversee the workmen in the temple of God.

10 Now when the builders had laid the foundation of the temple of the LORD, the priests stood in their apparel with trumpets, and the Levites, the sons of Asaph, with cymbals, to praise the LORD according to the directions of King David of Israel.

11 And they sang, praising and giving thanks to the LORD, *saying,* "For He is good, for His lovingkindness is upon Israel forever." And all the people shouted with a great shout when they praised the LORD because the foundation of the house of the LORD was laid.

12 Yet many of the priests and Levites and heads of fathers' *households,* the old men who had seen the first temple, wept with a loud voice when the foundation of this house was laid before their eyes, while many shouted aloud for joy;

13 so that the people could not distinguish the sound of the shout of joy from the sound of the weeping of the people, for the people shouted with a loud shout, and the sound was heard far away.

NAS [b] Or, *Tabernacles*

## New International

*Rebuilding the Altar*

**3** WHEN THE seventh month came and the Israelites had settled in their towns, the people assembled as one man in
Jerusalem. 2 Then Jeshua son of Jozadak and his fellow priests and
Zerubbabel son of Shealtiel and his associates began to build the
altar of the God of Israel to sacrifice burnt offerings on it, in
accordance with what is written in the Law of Moses the man of
God. 3 Despite their fear of the peoples around them, they built the
altar on its foundation and sacrificed burnt offerings on it to the
LORD, both the morning and evening sacrifices. 4 Then in accordance with what is written, they celebrated the Feast of Tabernacles with the required number of burnt offerings prescribed for
each day. 5 After that, they presented the regular burnt offerings,
the New Moon sacrifices and the sacrifices for all the appointed
sacred feasts of the LORD, as well as those brought as freewill
offerings to the LORD. 6 On the first day of the seventh month they
began to offer burnt offerings to the LORD, though the foundation
of the LORD's temple had not yet been laid.

*Rebuilding the Temple*

7 Then they gave money to the masons and carpenters, and gave
food and drink and oil to the people of Sidon and Tyre, so that they
would bring cedar logs by sea from Lebanon to Joppa, as authorized by Cyrus king of Persia.

8 In the second month of the second year after their arrival at the
house of God in Jerusalem, Zerubbabel son of Shealtiel, Jeshua son
of Jozadak and the rest of their brothers (the priests and the Levites
and all who had returned from the captivity to Jerusalem) began
the work, appointing Levites twenty years of age and older to
supervise the building of the house of the LORD. 9 Jeshua and his
sons and brothers and Kadmiel and his sons (descendants of
Hodaviah[c]) and the sons of Henadad and their sons and brothers—all Levites—joined together in supervising those working on
the house of God.

10 When the builders laid the foundation of the temple of the
LORD, the priests in their vestments and with trumpets, and the
Levites (the sons of Asaph) with cymbals, took their places to
praise the LORD, as prescribed by David king of Israel. 11 With
praise and thanksgiving they sang to the LORD:

"He is good;
his love to Israel endures forever."

And all the people gave a great shout of praise to the LORD,
because the foundation of the house of the LORD was laid. 12 But
many of the older priests and Levites and family heads, who had
seen the former temple, wept aloud when they saw the foundation
of this temple being laid, while many others shouted for joy. 13 No
one could distinguish the sound of the shouts of joy from the
sound of weeping, because the people made so much noise. And
the sound was heard far away.

NIV [c] 9 Hebrew *Yehudah,* probably a variant of *Hodaviah*

## King James

# 4

NOW WHEN the adversaries of Judah and Benjamin heard that the children of the captivity builded the temple unto the LORD God of Israel;

2Then they came to Zerubbabel, and to the chief of the fathers, and said unto them, Let us build with you: for we seek your God, as ye *do;* and we do sacrifice unto him since the days of Esar-haddon king of Assur, which brought us up hither.

3But Zerubbabel, and Jeshua, and the rest of the chief of the fathers of Israel, said unto them, Ye have nothing to do with us to build an house unto our God; but we ourselves together will build unto the LORD God of Israel, as king Cyrus the king of Persia hath commanded us.

4Then the people of the land weakened the hands of the people of Judah, and troubled them in building,

5And hired counsellors against them, to frustrate their purpose, all the days of Cyrus king of Persia, even until the reign of Darius king of Persia.

6And in the reign of Ahasuerus, in the beginning of his reign, wrote they *unto him* an accusation against the inhabitants of Judah and Jerusalem.

7¶ And in the days of Artaxerxes wrote Bishlam, Mithredath, Tabeel, and the rest of their companions, unto Artaxerxes king of Persia; and the writing of the letter *was* written in the Syrian tongue, and interpreted in the Syrian tongue.

8Rehum the chancellor and Shimshai the scribe wrote a letter against Jerusalem to Artaxerxes the king in this sort:

9Then *wrote* Rehum the chancellor, and Shimshai the scribe, and the rest of their companions; the Dinaites, the Apharsathchites, the Tarpelites, the Apharsites, the Archevites, the Babylonians, the Susanchites, the Dehavites, *and* the Elamites,

10And the rest of the nations whom the great and nobel Asnapper brought over, and set in the cities of Samaria, and the rest *that are* on this side the river, and at such a time.

11¶ This *is* the copy of the letter that they sent unto him, *even* unto Artaxerxes the king; Thy servants the men on this side the river, and at such a time.

12Be it known unto the king, that the Jews which came up from thee to us are come unto Jerusalem, building the rebellious and the bad city, and have set up the walls *thereof,* and joined the foundations.

13Be it known now unto the king, that, if this city be builded, and the walls set up *again, then* will they not pay toll, tribute, and custom, and *so* thou shalt endamage the revenue of the kings.

14Now because we have maintenance from *the king's* palace, and it was not meet for us to see the king's dishonour, therefore have we sent and certified the king;

15That search may be made in the book of the records of thy fathers: so shalt thou find in the book of the records, and know that this city *is* a rebellious city, and hurtful unto kings and provinces, and that they have moved sedition within the same of old time: for which cause was this city destroyed.

16We certify the king that, if this city be builded *again,* and the walls thereof set up, by this means thou shalt have no portion on this side the river.

17¶ *Then* sent the king an answer unto Rehum the chancellor, and *to* Shimshai the scribe, and *to* the rest of their companions that dwell in Samaria, and *unto* the rest beyond the river, Peace, and at such a time.

18The letter which ye sent unto us hath been plainly read before me.

## Amplified

# 4

NOW WHEN [the Samaritans] the adversaries of Judah and Benjamin heard that the exiles from the captivity were building a temple to the Lord, the God of Israel,

2They came to Zerubbabel [now governor] and to the heads of the fathers' houses and said, Let us build with you, for we seek *and* worship your God as you do, and we have sacrificed to Him since the days of Esarhaddon king of Assyria who brought us here. [II Kings 17:24-29.]

3But Zerubbabel and Jeshua and the rest of the heads of fathers' houses of Israel, said to them, You have nothing to do with us in building a house to our God; but we ourselves will together build to the Lord, the God of Israel, as King Cyrus, the king of Persia, has commanded us.

4Then [the Samaritans] the people of the land [continually] weakened the hands of the people of Judah, and troubled *and* terrified them in building,

5And hired counselors against them, to frustrate their purpose *and* plans all the days of Cyrus king of Persia, even until the reign of Darius [II] king of Persia.

6And in the reign of Ahasuerus [or Xerxes], in the beginning of his reign, [the Samaritans] wrote to him an accusation against the returned inhabitants of Judah and Jerusalem.

7Later, in the days of King Artaxerxes, Bishlam, Mithredath, Tabeel, and the rest of their associates wrote to Artaxerxes king of Persia; and the letter was written in the Syrian *or* Aramaic script and interpreted in that language.

8Rehum the [Persian] commander [of the Samaritans] and Shimshai the scribe wrote a letter against Jerusalem to Artaxerxes the king of this sort—

9Then wrote Rehum the [Persian] commander, Shimshai the scribe, and the rest of their associates, the Dinaites, the Apharsathchites, the Tarpelites, the Apharsites, the Achevites, the Babylonians, the Susanchites, the Dehaites, the Elamites,

10And the rest of the nations whom the great and noble Osnappar deported and settled in the city of Samaria and the rest of the country beyond [west of] the Euphrates River, and so forth.

11This is a copy of the letter which they sent to King Artaxerxes: Your servants the men beyond [that is, west of] the River [Euphrates], and so forth.

12Be it known to the king, that the Jews who came up from you to us have come to Jerusalem. This rebellious and bad city they are rebuilding, and have restored its walls and repaired the foundations.

13Be it known now to the king, that, if this city is rebuilt and the walls finished, then they will not pay tribute, custom, or toll, and the royal revenue will be diminished.

14Now because we eat the salt of the king's palace and it is not proper for us to witness the king's discredit, therefore we send to inform the king,

15In order that search may be made in the book of the records of your fathers, in which you will learn that this is a rebellious city, hurtful to kings and provinces, and that sedition was stirred up in it of old. That is why [it] was laid waste.

16We declare to the king that, if this city is rebuilt and its walls finished, it will mean that you will have no portion on this side the [Euphrates] River.

17Then the king sent an answer: To Rehum the [Persian] official, to Shimshai the scribe, to the rest of their companions who dwell in Samaria and in the rest of the country beyond the River: Greeting.

18The letter which you sent to us has been plainly read before me.

## New American Standard

*Adversaries Hinder the Work*

4 NOW WHEN the enemies of Judah and Benjamin heard that
the people of the exile were building a temple to the LORD
God of Israel,
2they approached Zerubbabel and the heads of fathers'
*households,* and said to them, "Let us build with you, for we, like
you, seek your God; and we have been sacrificing to Him since the
days of Esarhaddon king of Assyria, who brought us up here."
3But Zerubbabel and Jeshua and the rest of the heads of fathers' *households* of Israel said to them, "You have nothing in
common with us in building a house to our God; but we ourselves
will together build to the LORD God of Israel, as King Cyrus, the
king of Persia has commanded us."
4Then the people of the land discouraged the people of Judah,
and frightened them from building,
5and hired counselors against them to frustrate their counsel
all the days of Cyrus king of Persia, even until the reign of Darius
king of Persia.
6¶ Now in the reign of [a]Ahasuerus, in the beginning of his
reign, they wrote an accusation against the inhabitants of Judah
and Jerusalem.
7¶ And in the days of Artaxerxes, Bishlam, Mithredath, Tabeel,
and the rest of his colleagues, wrote to Artaxerxes king of Persia;
and the text of the letter was written in Aramaic and translated *from*
Aramaic.

*The Letter to King Artaxerxes*

8Rehum the commander and Shimshai the scribe wrote a letter
against Jerusalem to King Artaxerxes, as follows—
9then *wrote* Rehum the commander and Shimshai the scribe
and the rest of their colleagues, the judges and the lesser governors, the officials, the secretaries, the men of Erech, the Babylonians, the men of Susa, that is, the Elamites,
10and the rest of the nations which the great and honorable
Osnappar deported and settled in the city of Samaria, and in the
rest of the region beyond the [b]River. And now
11this is the copy of the letter which they sent to him: "To King
Artaxerxes: Your servants, the men in the region beyond the River,
and now
12let it be known to the king, that the Jews who came up from
you have come to us at Jerusalem; they are rebuilding the rebellious and evil city, and are finishing the walls and repairing the
foundations.
13"Now let it be known to the king, that if that city is rebuilt and
the walls are finished, they will not pay tribute, custom, or toll,
and it will damage the revenue of the kings.
14"Now because we are in the service of the palace, and it is not
fitting for us to see the king's dishonor, therefore we have sent and
informed the king,
15so that a search may be made in the record books of your
fathers. And you will discover in the record books, and learn that
that city is a rebellious city and damaging to kings and provinces,
and that they have incited revolt within it in past days; therefore
that city was laid waste.
16"We inform the king that, if that city is rebuilt and the walls
finished, as a result you will have no possession in *the province*
beyond the River."

*The King Replies and Work Stops*

17¶ *Then* the king sent an answer to Rehum the commander, to
Shimshai the scribe, and to the rest of their colleagues who live in
Samaria and in the rest of *the provinces* beyond the River: "Peace.
And now
18the document which you sent to us has been translated and
read before me.

NAS [a] Or, *Xerxes* [b] I.e., Euphrates, and so throughout this context

## New International

*Opposition to the Rebuilding*

4 WHEN THE enemies of Judah and Benjamin heard that the
exiles were building a temple for the LORD, the God of Israel,
2they came to Zerubbabel and to the heads of the families and said,
"Let us help you build because, like you, we seek your God and
have been sacrificing to him since the time of Esarhaddon king of
Assyria, who brought us here."
3But Zerubbabel, Jeshua and the rest of the heads of the families
of Israel answered, "You have no part with us in building a temple
to our God. We alone will build it for the LORD, the God of Israel,
as King Cyrus, the king of Persia, commanded us."
4Then the peoples around them set out to discourage the people
of Judah and make them afraid to go on building.[c] 5They hired
counselors to work against them and frustrate their plans during
the entire reign of Cyrus king of Persia and down to the reign of
Darius king of Persia.

*Later Opposition Under Xerxes and Artaxerxes*

6At the beginning of the reign of Xerxes,[d] they lodged an accusation against the people of Judah and Jerusalem.
7And in the days of Artaxerxes king of Persia, Bishlam, Mithredath, Tabeel and the rest of his associates wrote a letter to Artaxerxes. The letter was written in Aramaic script and in the
Aramaic language.[e,f]
8Rehum the commanding officer and Shimshai the secretary
wrote a letter against Jerusalem to Artaxerxes the king as follows:
9Rehum the commanding officer and Shimshai the secretary,
together with the rest of their associates—the judges and
officials over the men from Tripolis, Persia,[g] Erech and Babylon, the Elamites of Susa, 10and the other people whom the
great and honorable Ashurbanipal[h] deported and settled in
the city of Samaria and elsewhere in Trans-Euphrates.

11(This is a copy of the letter they sent him.)

To King Artaxerxes,

From your servants, the men of Trans-Euphrates:

12The king should know that the Jews who came up to us
from you have gone to Jerusalem and are rebuilding that
rebellious and wicked city. They are restoring the walls and
repairing the foundations.
13Furthermore, the king should know that if this city is
built and its walls are restored, no more taxes, tribute or duty
will be paid, and the royal revenues will suffer. 14Now since
we are under obligation to the palace and it is not proper for
us to see the king dishonored, we are sending this message
to inform the king, 15so that a search may be made in the
archives of your predecessors. In these records you will find
that this city is a rebellious city, troublesome to kings and
provinces, a place of rebellion from ancient times. That is why
this city was destroyed. 16We inform the king that if this city
is built and its walls are restored, you will be left with nothing
in Trans-Euphrates.

17The king sent this reply:

To Rehum the commanding officer, Shimshai the secretary
and the rest of their associates living in Samaria and elsewhere
in Trans-Euphrates:

Greetings.

18The letter you sent us has been read and translated in my
presence. 19I issued an order and a search was made, and it

NIV [c] 4 Or *and troubled them as they built* [d] 6 Hebrew *Ahasuerus,* a variant of Xerxes' name [e] 7 Or *written in Aramaic and translated* [f] 7 The text of Ezra 4:8—6:18 is in Aramaic. [g] 9 Or *officials, magistrates and governors over the men from* [h] 10 Aramaic *Osnappar,* a variant of *Ashurbanipal*

# King James

19 And I commanded, and search hath been made, and it is found that this city of old time hath made insurrection against kings, and *that* rebellion and sedition have been made therein.

20 There have been mighty kings also over Jerusalem, which have ruled over all *countries* beyond the river; and toll, tribute, and custom, was paid unto them.

21 Give ye now commandment to cause these men to cease, and that this city be not builded, until *another* commandment shall be given from me.

22 Take heed now that ye fail not to do this: why should damage grow to the hurt of the kings?

23 ¶ Now when the copy of king Artaxerxes' letter *was* read before Rehum, and Shimshai the scribe, and their companions, they went up in haste to Jerusalem unto the Jews, and made them to cease by force and power.

24 Then ceased the work of the house of God which *is* at Jerusalem. So it ceased unto the second year of the reign of Darius king of Persia.

**5** THEN THE prophets, Haggai the prophet, and Zechariah the son of Iddo, prophesied unto the Jews that *were* in Judah and Jerusalem in the name of the God of Israel, *even* unto them.

2 Then rose up Zerubbabel the son of Shealtiel, and Jeshua the son of Jozadak, and began to build the house of God which *is* at Jerusalem: and with them *were* the prophets of God helping them.

3 ¶ At the same time came to them Tatnai, governor on this side the river, and Shethar-boznai, and their companions, and said thus unto them, Who hath commanded you to build this house, and to make up this wall?

4 Then said we unto them after this manner, What are the names of the men that make this building?

5 But the eye of their God was upon the elders of the Jews, that they could not cause them to cease, till the matter came to Darius: and then they returned answer by letter concerning this *matter*.

6 ¶ The copy of the letter that Tatnai, governor on this side the river, and Shethar-boznai, and his companions the Apharsachites, which *were* on this side the river, sent unto Darius the king:

7 They sent a letter unto him, wherein was written thus; Unto Darius the king, all peace.

8 Be it known unto the king, that we went into the province of Judea, to the house of the great God, which is builded with great stones, and timber is laid in the walls, and this work goeth fast on, and prospereth in their hands.

9 Then asked we those elders, *and* said unto them thus, Who commanded you to build this house, and to make up these walls?

10 We asked their names also, to certify thee, that we might write the names of the men that *were* the chief of them.

11 And thus they returned us answer, saying, We are the servants of the God of heaven and earth, and build the house that was builded these many years ago, which a great king of Israel builded and set up.

12 But after that our fathers had provoked the God of heaven unto wrath, he gave them into the hand of Nebuchadnezzar the king of Babylon, the Chaldean, who destroyed this house, and carried the people away into Babylon.

13 But in the first year of Cyrus the king of Babylon *the same* king Cyrus made a decree to build this house of God.

# Amplified

19 I commanded, and search has been made, and it is found that this city [Jerusalem] of old time has made insurrection against kings, and that rebellion and sedition have been made in it.

20 There have been mighty kings also over Jerusalem, who have ruled over all countries beyond [west of] the [Euphrates] River; and tribute, custom, and toll were paid to them.

21 Therefore give a decree to make these men stop and that this city not be rebuilt, until a command is given by me.

22 Be sure that you do this. Why should damage grow to the hurt of the kings?

23 When the copy of King Artaxerxes' letter was read before Rehum, Shimshai the scribe, and their companions, they went up in haste to Jerusalem to the Jews, and by force and power made them cease.

24 Then the work of the house of God in Jerusalem stopped. It stopped until the second year of Darius [II] as king of Persia.

**5** NOW THE prophets, Haggai, and Zechariah son [grandson] of Iddo, prophesied to the Jews in Judah and Jerusalem in the name of the God of Israel, Whose *Spirit* was upon them.

2 Then rose up Zerubbabel son of Shealtiel, [heir to the throne of Judah] and Jeshua son of Jozadak, and began to build the house of God in Jerusalem; and with them were the prophets of God [Haggai and Zechariah] helping them. [Hag. 1:12-14; Matt. 1:12, 13.]

3 Then Tattenai, governor on the west side of the *Euphrates* River, and Shethar-bozenai and their companions came to them and said, Who [a]authorized you to build this house, and to restore this wall?

4 Then we told them [in reply] the names of the men who were building this building.

5 But the eye of their God was upon the elders of the Jews, so the enemy could not make them stop until the matter came before Darius [II] and an answer was returned by letter concerning it.

6 This is a copy of the letter that Tattenai, governor on this side the River, and Shethar-bozenai, and his associates the Apharsachites who were on this [west] side the River sent to Darius [II] the king.

7 They wrote: To Darius the king, all peace.

8 Be it known to the king, that we went to the province of Judah, to the house of the great God; it is being built with huge stones, with timber laid in the walls; this work goes on with diligence *and* care, and prospers in their hands.

9 Then we asked those elders, Who authorized you to build this house and restore these walls?

10 We asked their names also, that we might record the names of the men at their head and notify you.

11 They replied, We are servants of the God of Heaven and earth, rebuilding the house which was erected and finished many years ago, by a great king of Israel.

12 But after our fathers had provoked the God of Heaven to wrath, He gave them into the hand of Nebuchadnezzar king of Babylon, the Chaldean, who destroyed this house and carried the people away into Babylon.

13 But in the first year of Cyrus king of Babylon the same King Cyrus made a decree to rebuild this house of God.

**AMP** [a] "Seventeen or eighteen years had elapsed since Cyrus issued his decree. Two other kings had succeeded him. The third, Darius [II], was only just assuring his position upon the throne after two years of incessant warring. During this interval the affairs of a comparatively unimportant city . . . may well have been almost forgotten" *(Cambridge Bible)*.

## New American Standard

19"And a decree has been issued by me, and a search has been made and it has been discovered that that city has risen up against the kings in past days, that rebellion and revolt have been perpetrated in it,

20that mighty kings have ruled over Jerusalem, governing all *the provinces* beyond the River, and that tribute, custom, and toll were paid to them.

21"So, now issue a decree to make these men stop *work*, that the city may not be rebuilt until a decree is issued by me.

22"And beware of being negligent in carrying out this *matter*; why should damage increase to the detriment of the kings?"

**23**¶ Then as soon as the copy of King Artaxerxes' document was read before Rehum and Shimshai the scribe and their colleagues, they went in haste to Jerusalem to the Jews and stopped them by force of arms.

**24**¶ Then work on the house of God in Jerusalem ceased, and it was stopped until the second year of the reign of Darius king of Persia.

*Temple Work Resumed*

**5** WHEN THE prophets, Haggai the prophet and Zechariah the son of Iddo, prophesied to the Jews who were in Judah and Jerusalem, in the name of the God of Israel, who was over them,

2then Zerubbabel the son of Shealtiel and Jeshua the son of Jozadak arose and began to rebuild the house of God which is in Jerusalem; and the prophets of God were with them supporting them.

3At that time Tattenai, the governor of *the province* beyond the River, and Shethar-bozenai and their colleagues came to them and spoke to them thus, "Who issued you a decree to rebuild this [b]temple and to finish this structure?"

4Then we told them accordingly what the names of the men were who were reconstructing this building.

5But the eye of their God was on the elders of the Jews, and they did not stop them until a report should come to Darius, and then a written reply be returned concerning it.

*Adversaries Write to Darius*

6¶ *This is* the copy of the letter which Tattenai, the governor of *the province* beyond the River, and Shethar-bozenai and his colleagues the officials, who were beyond the River, sent to Darius the king.

7They sent a report to him in which it was written thus: "To Darius the king, all peace.

8"Let it be known to the king, that we have gone to the province of Judah, to the house of the great God, which is being built with huge stones, and beams are being laid in the walls; and this work is going on with great care and is succeeding in their hands.

9"Then we asked those elders and said to them thus, 'Who issued you a decree to rebuild this temple and to finish this structure?'

10"We also asked them their names so as to inform you, and that we might write down the names of the men who were at their head.

11"And thus they answered us, saying, 'We are the servants of the God of heaven and earth and are rebuilding the temple that was built many years ago, which a great king of Israel built and finished.

12'But because our fathers had provoked the God of heaven to wrath, He gave them into the hand of Nebuchadnezzar king of Babylon, the Chaldean, *who* destroyed this temple and deported the people to Babylon.

13'However, in the first year of Cyrus king of Babylon, King Cyrus issued a decree to rebuild this house of God.

NAS [b] Lit., *house*, and so throughout this context

## New International

was found that this city has a long history of revolt against kings and has been a place of rebellion and sedition.
20Jerusalem has had powerful kings ruling over the whole of Trans-Euphrates, and taxes, tribute and duty were paid to them.
21Now issue an order to these men to stop work, so that this city will not be rebuilt until I so order.
22Be careful not to neglect this matter. Why let this threat grow, to the detriment of the royal interests?

23As soon as the copy of the letter of King Artaxerxes was read to Rehum and Shimshai the secretary and their associates, they went immediately to the Jews in Jerusalem and compelled them by force to stop.

24Thus the work on the house of God in Jerusalem came to a standstill until the second year of the reign of Darius king of Persia.

*Tattenai's Letter to Darius*

**5** NOW HAGGAI the prophet and Zechariah the prophet, a descendant of Iddo, prophesied to the Jews in Judah and Jerusalem in the name of the God of Israel, who was over them.
2Then Zerubbabel son of Shealtiel and Jeshua son of Jozadak set to work to rebuild the house of God in Jerusalem. And the prophets of God were with them, helping them.
3At that time Tattenai, governor of Trans-Euphrates, and Shethar-Bozenai and their associates went to them and asked, "Who authorized you to rebuild this temple and restore this structure?"
4They also asked, "What are the names of the men constructing this building?"[c]
5But the eye of their God was watching over the elders of the Jews, and they were not stopped until a report could go to Darius and his written reply be received.
6This is a copy of the letter that Tattenai, governor of Trans-Euphrates, and Shethar-Bozenai and their associates, the officials of Trans-Euphrates, sent to King Darius.
7The report they sent him read as follows:

To King Darius:

Cordial greetings.

8The king should know that we went to the district of Judah, to the temple of the great God. The people are building it with large stones and placing the timbers in the walls. The work is being carried on with diligence and is making rapid progress under their direction.
9We questioned the elders and asked them, "Who authorized you to rebuild this temple and restore this structure?"
10We also asked them their names, so that we could write down the names of their leaders for your information.
11This is the answer they gave us:

"We are the servants of the God of heaven and earth, and we are rebuilding the temple that was built many years ago, one that a great king of Israel built and finished.
12But because our fathers angered the God of heaven, he handed them over to Nebuchadnezzar the Chaldean, king of Babylon, who destroyed this temple and deported the people to Babylon.
13"However, in the first year of Cyrus king of Babylon, King Cyrus issued a decree to rebuild this house of God.
14He

NIV [c] 4 See Septuagint; Aramaic 4*We told them the names of the men constructing this building.*

## King James

14 And the vessels also of gold and silver of the house of God, which Nebuchadnezzar took out of the temple that *was* in Jerusalem, and brought them into the temple of Babylon, those did Cyrus the king take out of the temple of Babylon, and they were delivered unto *one,* whose name *was* Sheshbazzar, whom he had made governor;

15 And said unto him, Take these vessels, go, carry them into the temple that *is* in Jerusalem, and let the house of God be builded in his place.

16 Then came the same Sheshbazzar, *and* laid the foundation of the house of God which *is* in Jerusalem: and since that time even until now hath it been in building, and *yet* it is not finished.

17 Now therefore, if *it seem* good to the king, let there be search made in the king's treasure house, which *is* there at Babylon, whether it be *so,* that a decree was made of Cyrus the king to build this house of God at Jerusalem, and let the king send his pleasure to us concerning this matter.

**6** THEN DARIUS the king made a decree, and search was made in the house of the rolls, where the treasures were laid up in Babylon.

2 And there was found at Achmetha, in the palace that *is* in the province of the Medes, a roll, and therein *was* a record thus written:

3 In the first year of Cyrus the king *the same* Cyrus the king made a decree *concerning* the house of God at Jerusalem, Let the house be builded, the place where they offered sacrifices, and let the foundations thereof be strongly laid; the height thereof threescore cubits, *and* the breadth thereof threescore cubits;

4 *With* three rows of great stones, and a row of new timber: and let the expenses be given out of the king's house:

5 And also let the golden and silver vessels of the house of God, which Nebuchadnezzar took forth out of the temple which *is* at Jerusalem, and brought unto Babylon, be restored, and brought again unto the temple which *is* at Jerusalem, *every one* to his place, and place *them* in the house of God.

6 Now *therefore,* Tatnai, governor beyond the river, Shethar-boznai, and your companions the Apharsachites, which *are* beyond the river, be ye far from thence:

7 Let the work of this house of God alone; let the governor of the Jews and the elders of the Jews build this house of God in his place.

8 Moreover I make a decree what ye shall do to the elders of these Jews for the building of this house of God: that of the king's goods, *even* of the tribute beyond the river, forthwith expenses be given unto these men, that they be not hindered.

9 And that which they have need of, both young bullocks, and rams, and lambs, for the burnt offerings of the God of heaven, wheat, salt, wine, and oil, according to the appointment of the priests which *are* at Jerusalem, let it be given them day by day without fail:

10 That they may offer sacrifices of sweet savours unto the God of heaven, and pray for the life of the king, and of his sons.

11 Also I have made a decree, that whosoever shall alter this word, let timber be pulled down from his house, and being set up, let him be hanged thereon; and let his house be made a dunghill for this.

12 And the God that hath caused his name to dwell there destroy all kings and people, that shall put to their hand to alter *and* to destroy this house of God which *is* at Jerusalem. I Darius have made a decree; let it be done with speed.

13 ¶ Then Tatnai, governor on this side the river, Shethar-boznai, and their companions, according to that which Darius the king had sent, so they did speedily.

## Amplified

14 And the vessels also of gold and silver of the house of God, which Nebuchadnezzar took from the temple in Jerusalem, and brought into the temple of Babylon, King Cyrus took from the temple of Babylon and delivered to a man named Shesh-bazzar, whom he had made governor;

15 And King Cyrus said to him, Go, take these vessels to Jerusalem and carry them into the temple, and let the house of God be built upon its site.

16 Then came this Shesh-bazzar and laid the foundation of the house of God in Jerusalem; and since that time until now it has been in the process of being rebuilt, and is not completed yet.

17 So now, if it seems good to the king, let search be made in the royal archives there in Babylon, to see if it is true that King Cyrus issued a decree to build this house of God at Jerusalem, and let the king send us his pleasure in this matter.

**6** THEN KING Darius [II] decreed and a search was made in Babylonia in the house where the treasured records were stored.

2 And at Ecbatana, in the capital in the province of Media, a scroll was found on which this was recorded:

3 In the first year of King Cyrus, [he] made a decree: Concerning the house of God in Jerusalem, let the house, the place where they offer sacrifices, be built, and let its foundations be strongly laid; its height and its breadth each 60 cubits,

4 With three courses of great stones and one course of new timber; let the cost be paid from the royal treasury.

5 Also let the gold and silver vessels of the house of God, which Nebuchadnezzar took from the temple in Jerusalem and brought to Babylon, be restored and brought back to the temple in Jerusalem, each put in its place in the house of God.

6 Now therefore, Tattenai, governor of the province [west of] the River, Shethar-bozenai, and your associates the Apharsachites, who are [west of] the River, keep far away from there;

7 Let the work on this house of God alone; let the governor and the elders of the Jews build this house of God on its site.

8 Moreover I make a decree as to what you shall do for these elders of the Jews for the rebuilding of this house of God: the cost is to be paid in full to these men at once from the king's revenue, the tribute of the province [west of] the River, that they may not be hindered.

9 And all they need, including young bulls, rams, and lambs for the burnt offerings to the God of Heaven, and wheat, salt, wine, and oil, according to the word of the priests at Jerusalem, let it be given them each day without fail,

10 That they may offer pleasing sacrifices to the God of Heaven, and pray for the life of the king and his sons.

11 Also I make a decree that whoever shall change *or* infringe on this order, let a beam be pulled from his house, and erected; then let him be fastened to it, and let his house be made a dunghill for this.

12 May the God Who has caused His name to dwell there overthrow all kings and peoples who put forth their hand to alter this, or to destroy this house of God in Jerusalem. I Darius make a decree; let it be executed speedily *and* exactly.

13 Then Tattenai, governor of the province this side the River, with Shethar-bozenai and their associates diligently did what King Darius had decreed.

## New American Standard

14'And also the gold and silver utensils of the house of God which Nebuchadnezzar had taken from the temple in Jerusalem, and brought them to the temple of Babylon, these King Cyrus took from the temple of Babylon, and they were given to one whose name was Sheshbazzar, whom he had appointed governor.

15'And he said to him, "Take these utensils, go *and* deposit them in the temple in Jerusalem, and let the house of God be rebuilt in its place."

16'Then that Sheshbazzar came *and* laid the foundations of the house of God in Jerusalem; and from then until now it has been under construction, and it is not *yet* completed.'

17"And now, if it pleases the king let a search be conducted in the king's treasure house, which is there in Babylon, if it be that a decree was issued by King Cyrus to rebuild this house of God at Jerusalem; and let the king send to us his decision concerning this *matter*."

*Darius Finds Cyrus' Decree*

6 THEN KING Darius issued a decree, and search was made in the [a]archives, where the treasures were stored in Babylon.

2And in [b]Ecbatana in the fortress, which is in the province of Media, a scroll was found and there was written in it as follows: "Memorandum—

3"In the first year of King Cyrus, Cyrus the king issued a decree: '*Concerning* the house of God at Jerusalem, let the temple, the place where sacrifices are offered, be rebuilt and let its foundations be retained, its height being 60 cubits and its width 60 cubits;

4with three layers of huge stones, and one layer of timbers. And let the cost be paid from the royal treasury.

5'And also let the gold and silver utensils of the temple of God, which Nebuchadnezzar took from the temple in Jerusalem and brought to Babylon, be returned and brought to their places in the temple in Jerusalem; and you shall put *them* in the house of God.'

6¶ "Now *therefore,* Tattenai, governor of *the province* beyond the River, Shethar-bozenai, and your colleagues, the officials of *the provinces* beyond the River, keep away from there.

7"Leave this work on the house of God alone; let the governor of the Jews and the elders of the Jews rebuild this house of God on its site.

8"Moreover, I issue a decree concerning what you are to do for these elders of Judah in the rebuilding of this house of God: the full cost is to be paid to these people from the royal treasury out of the taxes of *the provinces* beyond the River, and that without delay.

9"And whatever is needed, both young bulls, rams, and lambs for a burnt offering to the God of heaven, and wheat, salt, wine, and anointing oil, as the priests in Jerusalem request, *it* is to be given to them daily without fail,

10that they may offer [c]acceptable sacrifices to the God of heaven and pray for the life of the king and his sons.

11"And I issued a decree that any man who violates this edict, a timber shall be drawn from his house and he shall be impaled on it and his house shall be made a refuse heap on account of this.

12"And may the God who has caused His name to dwell there overthrow any king or people who attempts to change *it,* so as to destroy this house of God in Jerusalem. I, Darius, have issued *this* decree, let *it* be carried out with all diligence!"

*The Temple Completed and Dedicated*

13¶ Then Tattenai, the governor of *the province* beyond the River, Shethar-bozenai, and their colleagues carried out *the decree* with all diligence, just as King Darius had sent.

**NAS** [a] Lit., *house of the books* [b] Aram., *Achmetha* [c] Lit., *pleasing* or *sweet-smelling sacrifices*

## New International

even removed from the temple[d] of Babylon the gold and
silver articles of the house of God, which Nebuchadnezzar
had taken from the temple in Jerusalem and brought to the
temple[e] in Babylon.

"Then King Cyrus gave them to a man named Sheshbaz-
zar, whom he had appointed governor, 15and he told him,
'Take these articles and go and deposit them in the temple in
Jerusalem. And rebuild the house of God on its site.' 16So this
Sheshbazzar came and laid the foundations of the house of
God in Jerusalem. From that day to the present it has been
under construction but is not yet finished."

17Now if it pleases the king, let a search be made in the
royal archives of Babylon to see if King Cyrus did in fact issue
a decree to rebuild this house of God in Jerusalem. Then let
the king send us his decision in this matter.

*The Decree of Darius*

6 KING DARIUS then issued an order, and they searched in the
archives stored in the treasury at Babylon. 2A scroll was
found in the citadel of Ecbatana in the province of Media, and this
was written on it:

Memorandum:

3In the first year of King Cyrus, the king issued a decree
concerning the temple of God in Jerusalem:

Let the temple be rebuilt as a place to present sacrifices,
and let its foundations be laid. It is to be ninety feet[f] high and
ninety feet wide, 4with three courses of large stones and one
of timbers. The costs are to be paid by the royal treasury.
5Also, the gold and silver articles of the house of God, which
Nebuchadnezzar took from the temple in Jerusalem and
brought to Babylon, are to be returned to their places in the
temple in Jerusalem; they are to be deposited in the house of
God.

6Now then, Tattenai, governor of Trans-Euphrates, and
Shethar-Bozenai and you, their fellow officials of that province, stay away from there. 7Do not interfere with the work
on this temple of God. Let the governor of the Jews and the
Jewish elders rebuild this house of God on its site.

8Moreover, I hereby decree what you are to do for these
elders of the Jews in the construction of this house of God:

The expenses of these men are to be fully paid out of the
royal treasury, from the revenues of Trans-Euphrates, so that
the work will not stop. 9Whatever is needed—young bulls,
rams, male lambs for burnt offerings to the God of heaven,
and wheat, salt, wine and oil, as requested by the priests in
Jerusalem—must be given them daily without fail, 10so that
they may offer sacrifices pleasing to the God of heaven and
pray for the well-being of the king and his sons.

11Furthermore, I decree that if anyone changes this edict,
a beam is to be pulled from his house and he is to be lifted
up and impaled on it. And for this crime his house is to be
made a pile of rubble. 12May God, who has caused his Name
to dwell there, overthrow any king or people who lifts a hand
to change this decree or to destroy this temple in Jerusalem.

I Darius have decreed it. Let it be carried out with diligence.

*Completion and Dedication of the Temple*

13Then, because of the decree King Darius had sent, Tattenai,
governor of Trans-Euphrates, and Shethar-Bozenai and their associates carried it out with diligence. 14So the elders of the Jews

**NIV** [d] 14 Or *palace* [e] 14 Or *palace* [f] 3 Aramaic *sixty cubits* (about 27 meters)

## King James

14And the elders of the Jews builded, and they prospered
through the prophesying of Haggai the prophet and Zechariah the
son of Iddo. And they builded, and finished *it*, according to the
commandment of the God of Israel, and according to the commandment of Cyrus, and Darius, and Artaxerxes king of Persia.
15And this house was finished on the third day of the month
Adar, which was in the sixth year of the reign of Darius the king.
16¶ And the children of Israel, the priests, and the Levites, and
the rest of the children of the captivity, kept the dedication of this
house of God with joy,
17And offered at the dedication of this house of God an hundred
bullocks, two hundred rams, four hundred lambs; and for a sin
offering for all Israel, twelve he goats, according to the number of
the tribes of Israel.
18And they set the priests in their divisions, and the Levites in
their courses, for the service of God, which *is* at Jerusalem; as it
is written in the book of Moses.
19And the children of the captivity kept the passover upon the
fourteenth *day* of the first month.
20For the priests and the Levites were purified together, all of
them *were* pure, and killed the passover for all the children of the
captivity, and for their brethren the priests, and for themselves.
21And the children of Israel, which were come again out of
captivity, and all such as had separated themselves unto them
from the filthiness of the heathen of the land, to seek the LORD God
of Israel, did eat,
22And kept the feast of unleavened bread seven days with joy:
for the LORD had made them joyful, and turned the heart of the
king of Assyria unto them, to strengthen their hands in the work
of the house of God, the God of Israel.

**7** NOW AFTER these things, in the reign of Artaxerxes king of
Persia, Ezra the son of Seraiah, the son of Azariah, the son
of Hilkiah,
2The son of Shallum, the son of Zadok, the son of Ahitub,
3The son of Amariah, the son of Azariah, the son of Meraioth,
4The son of Zerahiah, the son of Uzzi, the son of Bukki,
5The son of Abishua, the son of Phinehas, the son of Eleazar,
the son of Aaron the chief priest:
6This Ezra went up from Babylon; and he *was* a ready scribe in
the law of Moses, which the LORD God of Israel had given: and the
king granted him all his request, according to the hand of the LORD
his God upon him.
7And there went up *some* of the children of Israel, and of the
priests, and the Levites, and the singers, and the porters, and the
Nethinims, unto Jerusalem, in the seventh year of Artaxerxes the
king.
8And he came to Jerusalem in the fifth month, which *was* in the
seventh year of the king.
9For upon the first *day* of the first month began he to go up from
Babylon, and on the first *day* of the fifth month came he to Jerusalem, according to the good hand of his God upon him.

## Amplified

14And the elders of the Jews built and prospered, through the
prophesying of Haggai the prophet and Zechariah the son of Iddo.
They finished their building as commanded by the God of Israel
and by decree of Cyrus and Darius and Artaxerxes king of Persia;
15And this house was finished on the third day of the month
of Adar, in the sixth year of the reign of King Darius.
16And the Israelites, the priests, the Levites, and the rest of the
returned exiles, celebrated the dedication of this house of God with
joy.
17They offered at the dedication of this house of God 100 young
bulls, 200 rams, 400 lambs; and for a sin offering for all Israel twelve
he-goats, according to the number of Israel's tribes.
18And they set the priests in their divisions and the Levites in
their courses, for the service of God at Jerusalem, as it is written
in the book of Moses.
19The returned exiles kept the passover on the fourteenth day
of the first month.
20For the priests and the Levites had purified themselves together; all of them were clean. So they killed the passover lamb for
all the returned exiles, for their brother priests, and for themselves.
21It was eaten by the Israelites returned from exile, and by all
who had joined them and separated themselves from the pollutions of the peoples of the land to seek the Lord, the God of Israel.
22They kept the feast of unleavened bread seven days with joy;
for the Lord had made them joyful, and had turned the heart of
the king of Assyria [referring to Darius king of Persia] to them, so
that he strengthened their hands in the work of the house of God,
the God of Israel.

**7** NOW [a]AFTER this, in the reign of Artaxerxes [son of Xerxes,
or Ahasuerus] king of Persia, Ezra the son of Seraiah, son of
Azariah, son of Hilkiah,
2Son of Shallum, son of Zadok, son of Ahitub,
3Son of Amariah, son of Azariah, son of Meraioth,
4Son of Zerahiah, son of Uzzi, son of Bukki,
5Son of Abishua, son of Phinehas, son of Eleazar, son of Aaron
the chief priest—
6This Ezra went up from Babylon. He was a skilled scribe in the
five books of Moses, which the Lord, the God of Israel, had given;
and the king granted him all he asked, for the hand of the Lord
his God was upon him.
7And also some of the Israelites, and of the priests and Levites,
the singers and gatekeepers, and the temple servants, went up
[from Babylon] to Jerusalem, in the seventh year of King Artaxerxes.
8Ezra came to Jerusalem in the fifth month of the seventh year
of the king.
9On the first of the first month he started from Babylon, and on
the first of the fifth month he arrived in Jerusalem, for upon him
was the good hand of his God.

**AMP** [a] There is about a sixty-year silence in the book of Ezra between chapters six and seven, including the years 516-458 B.C. It is during this time that events of the book of Esther took place. The Ahasuerus of the book of Esther is identified with the Xerxes who invaded Greece, was stopped at Thermopylae, defeated at the naval battle at Salamis, and nearly annihilated at Plataea (479 B.C.). The French excavations at Susa in 1880-1890 disclosed the great palace of Xerxes (Ahasuerus), where Esther would have lived. The building covered two and one-half acres. The finds at Susa from this period were so astonishing that the Louvre in Paris devoted two large rooms to the exhibition of the treasures (J. P. Free in *Archaeology and Bible History*, condensed).

## New American Standard

14And the elders of the Jews were successful in building
through the prophesying of Haggai the prophet and Zechariah the
son of Iddo. And they finished building according to the command
of the God of Israel and the decree of Cyrus, Darius, and Artaxerxes king of Persia.
15And this temple was completed on the third day of the month
Adar; it was the sixth year of the reign of King Darius.
16¶ And the sons of Israel, the priests, the Levites, and the rest
of the exiles, celebrated the dedication of this house of God with
joy.
17And they offered for the dedication of this temple of God 100
bulls, 200 rams, 400 lambs, and as a sin offering for all Israel 12
male goats, corresponding to the number of the tribes of Israel.
18Then they appointed the priests to their divisions and the
Levites in their orders for the service of God in Jerusalem, as it is
written in the book of Moses.

*The Passover Observed*

19¶ And the exiles observed the Passover on the fourteenth of
the first month.
20For the priests and the Levites had purified themselves together; all of them were pure. Then they slaughtered the Passover
*lamb* for all the exiles, both for their brothers the priests and for
themselves.
21And the sons of Israel who returned from exile and all those
who had separated themselves from the impurity of the nations of
the land to *join* them, to seek the LORD God of Israel, ate *the
Passover*.
22And they observed the Feast of Unleavened Bread seven days
with joy, for the LORD had caused them to rejoice, and had turned
the heart of the king of Assyria toward them to encourage them
in the work of the house of God, the God of Israel.

*Ezra Journeys from Babylon to Jerusalem*

**7** NOW AFTER these things, in the reign of Artaxerxes king of
Persia, *there went up* Ezra son of Seraiah, son of Azariah, son
of Hilkiah,
2son of Shallum, son of Zadok, son of Ahitub,
3son of Amariah, son of Azariah, son of Meraioth,
4son of Zerahiah, son of Uzzi, son of Bukki,
5son of Abishua, son of Phinehas, son of Eleazar, son of Aaron
the chief priest.
6This Ezra went up from Babylon, and he was a scribe skilled
in the law of Moses, which the LORD God of Israel had given; and
the king granted him all he requested because the hand of the
LORD his God *was* upon him.
7And some of the sons of Israel and some of the priests, the
Levites, the singers, the gatekeepers, and the temple servants
went up to Jerusalem in the seventh year of King Artaxerxes.
8And he came to Jerusalem in the fifth month, which was in
the seventh year of the king.
9For on the first of the first month he began to go up from
Babylon; and on the first of the fifth month he came to Jerusalem,
because the good hand of his God *was* upon him.

## New International

continued to build and prosper under the preaching of Haggai the
prophet and Zechariah, a descendant of Iddo. They finished building the temple according to the command of the God of Israel and
the decrees of Cyrus, Darius and Artaxerxes, kings of Persia. 15The
temple was completed on the third day of the month Adar, in the
sixth year of the reign of King Darius.
16Then the people of Israel—the priests, the Levites and the rest
of the exiles—celebrated the dedication of the house of God with
joy. 17For the dedication of this house of God they offered a hundred bulls, two hundred rams, four hundred male lambs and, as
a sin offering for all Israel, twelve male goats, one for each of the
tribes of Israel. 18And they installed the priests in their divisions
and the Levites in their groups for the service of God at Jerusalem,
according to what is written in the Book of Moses.

*The Passover*

19On the fourteenth day of the first month, the exiles celebrated
the Passover. 20The priests and Levites had purified themselves
and were all ceremonially clean. The Levites slaughtered the Passover lamb for all the exiles, for their brothers the priests and for
themselves. 21So the Israelites who had returned from the exile ate
it, together with all who had separated themselves from the unclean practices of their Gentile neighbors in order to seek the LORD,
the God of Israel. 22For seven days they celebrated with joy the
Feast of Unleavened Bread, because the LORD had filled them with
joy by changing the attitude of the king of Assyria, so that he
assisted them in the work on the house of God, the God of Israel.

*Ezra Comes to Jerusalem*

**7** AFTER THESE things, during the reign of Artaxerxes king of
Persia, Ezra son of Seraiah, the son of Azariah, the son of
Hilkiah, 2the son of Shallum, the son of Zadok, the son of Ahitub,
3the son of Amariah, the son of Azariah, the son of Meraioth, 4the
son of Zerahiah, the son of Uzzi, the son of Bukki, 5the son of
Abishua, the son of Phinehas, the son of Eleazar, the son of Aaron
the chief priest— 6this Ezra came up from Babylon. He was a
teacher well versed in the Law of Moses, which the LORD, the God
of Israel, had given. The king had granted him everything he
asked, for the hand of the LORD his God was on him. 7Some of the
Israelites, including priests, Levites, singers, gatekeepers and temple servants, also came up to Jerusalem in the seventh year of King
Artaxerxes.
8Ezra arrived in Jerusalem in the fifth month of the seventh year
of the king. 9He had begun his journey from Babylon on the first
day of the first month, and he arrived in Jerusalem on the first day
of the fifth month, for the gracious hand of his God was on him.

# King James

10For Ezra had prepared his heart to seek the law of the LORD, and to do *it*, and to teach in Israel statutes and judgments.

11¶ Now this *is* the copy of the letter that the king Artaxerxes gave unto Ezra the priest, the scribe, *even* a scribe of the words of the commandments of the LORD, and of his statutes to Israel.

12Artaxerxes, king of kings, unto Ezra the priest, a scribe of the law of the God of heaven, perfect *peace*, and at such a time.

13I make a decree, that all they of the people of Israel, and *of* his priests and Levites, in my realm, which are minded of their own freewill to go up to Jerusalem, go with thee.

14Forasmuch as thou art sent of the king, and of his seven counsellors, to inquire concerning Judah and Jerusalem, according to the law of thy God which *is* in thine hand;

15And to carry the silver and gold, which the king and his counsellors have freely offered unto the God of Israel, whose habitation *is* in Jerusalem,

16And all the silver and gold that thou canst find in all the province of Babylon, with the freewill offering of the people, and of the priests, offering willingly for the house of their God which *is* in Jerusalem:

17That thou mayest buy speedily with this money bullocks, rams, lambs, with their meat offerings and their drink offerings, and offer them upon the altar of the house of your God which *is* in Jerusalem.

18And whatsoever shall seem good to thee, and to thy brethren, to do with the rest of the silver and the gold, that do after the will of your God.

19The vessels also that are given thee for the service of the house of thy God, *those* deliver thou before the God of Jerusalem.

20And whatsoever more shall be needful for the house of thy God, which thou shalt have occasion to bestow, bestow *it* out of the king's treasure house.

21And I, *even* I Artaxerxes the king, do make a decree to all the treasurers which *are* beyond the river, that whatsoever Ezra the priest, the scribe of the law of the God of heaven, shall require of you, it be done speedily,

22Unto an hundred talents of silver, and to an hundred measures of wheat, and to an hundred baths of wine, and to an hundred baths of oil, and salt without prescribing *how much*.

23Whatsoever is commanded by the God of heaven, let it be diligently done for the house of the God of heaven: for why should there be wrath against the realm of the king and his sons?

24Also we certify you, that touching any of the priests and Levites, singers, porters, Nethinims, or ministers of this house of God, it shall not be lawful to impose toll, tribute, or custom, upon them.

25And thou, Ezra, after the wisdom of thy God, that *is* in thine hand, set magistrates and judges, which may judge all the people that *are* beyond the river, all such as know the laws of thy God; and teach ye them that know *them* not.

26And whosoever will not do the law of thy God, and the law of the king, let judgment be executed speedily upon him, whether *it be* unto death, or to banishment, or to confiscation of goods, or to imprisonment.

27¶ Blessed *be* the LORD God of our fathers, which hath put *such a thing* as this in the king's heart, to beautify the house of the LORD which *is* in Jerusalem:

28And hath extended mercy unto me before the king, and his counsellors, and before all the king's mighty princes. And I was strengthened as the hand of the LORD my God *was* upon me, and I gathered together out of Israel chief men to go up with me.

# Amplified

10For Ezra had [a]prepared *and* set his heart to seek the law of the Lord [to inquire for it *and* of it, to require and yearn for it], and to do and teach in Israel its statutes and its ordinances.

11Now this is the copy of the letter that King Artaxerxes gave to Ezra the priest, the scribe, even a scribe [occupied with] the words of the commands of the Lord and of His statutes to Israel:

12Artaxerxes, king of kings, to Ezra the priest, scribe of the instructions of the God of Heaven, greetings:

13I make a decree, that all of the people of Israel and of their priests and Levites in my realm, who offer freely to go up to Jerusalem, may go with you.

14For you are sent by the king and his seven counselors to inquire about Judah and Jerusalem, according to the instruction of your God which is in your hand,

15And to carry the silver and gold, which the king and his counselors have freely offered to the God of Israel, Whose dwelling is in Jerusalem;

16And all the silver and gold that you may find in all the province of Babylonia, with the freewill offerings of the people and of the priests, offered willingly for the house of their God in Jerusalem.

17Therefore you shall with all speed *and* exactness buy with this money young bulls, rams, lambs, with their cereal offerings and drink offerings, and offer them on the altar of the house of your God in Jerusalem.

18And whatever shall seem good to you and to your brethren to do with the rest of the silver and the gold, that do after the will of your God.

19The vessels also that are given you for the service of the house of your God, those deliver before the God of Jerusalem.

20And whatever more shall be needful for the house of your God, which you shall have occasion to provide, provide it out of the king's treasury.

21And I, Artaxerxes the king, make a decree to all the treasurers in the province beyond the [Euphrates] River that whatever Ezra the priest, the scribe of the instructions of the God of Heaven, shall require of you, it be done exactly *and* at once.

22Up to 100 talents of silver, 100 measures of wheat, 100 baths of wine, 100 baths of oil, and salt not specified.

23Whatever is commanded by the God of Heaven, let it be done diligently *and* honorably for the house of the God of Heaven, lest His wrath be against the realm of the king and his sons.

24Also we notify you that as to any of the priests and Levites, singers, gatekeepers, temple servants, or other servants of this house of God, it shall not be lawful to impose tribute, custom or toll on them.

25You, Ezra, after the wisdom of your God which is [in His instructions] in your hand, set magistrates and judges, who may judge all the people [west] of the River; choose those who know the instructions of your God, and teach him who does not know them.

26And whoever will not do the law of your God, and the law of the king, let judgment be executed upon him exactly *and* speedily, whether it be unto death, or banishment, or confiscation of goods, or imprisonment.

27Blessed be the Lord, the God of our fathers [said Ezra], Who put such a thing as this into the king's heart, to beautify the house of the Lord in Jerusalem;

28And Who has extended His mercy *and* steadfast love to me before the king, his counselors, and all the king's mighty officers. I was strengthened and encouraged, for the hand of the Lord my God was upon me, and I gathered together outstanding men of Israel to go with me to Jerusalem.

**AMP** [a] God can use mightily one whose whole heart craves a knowledge of Him and His Word like that. Watch Ezra through the remainder of his story, as he turns the homes of his nation back from heathendom to God—in the pouring rain! He was not merely righteous, he was "uncompromisingly righteous"; he worshiped God, Who is not merely just *and* righteous, but "rigidly just *and* righteous." [I Kings 8:32; Ezra 9:15.]

## New American Standard

10For Ezra had set his heart to study the law of the LORD, and to practice *it,* and to teach *His* statutes and ordinances in Israel.

*King's Decree on Behalf of Ezra*

11¶ Now this is the copy of the decree which King Artaxerxes gave to Ezra the priest, the scribe, learned in the words of the commandments of the LORD and His statutes to Israel:

12"Artaxerxes, king of kings, to Ezra the priest, the scribe of the law of the God of heaven, perfect *peace.* And now

13I have issued a decree that any of the people of Israel and their priests and the Levites in my kingdom who are willing to go to Jerusalem, may go with you.

14"Forasmuch as you are sent by the king and his seven counselors to inquire concerning Judah and Jerusalem according to the law of your God which is in your hand,

15and to bring the silver and gold, which the king and his counselors have freely offered to the God of Israel, whose dwelling is in Jerusalem,

16with all the silver and gold which you shall find in the whole province of Babylon, along with the freewill offering of the people and of the priests, who offered willingly for the house of their God which is in Jerusalem;

17with this money, therefore, you shall diligently buy bulls, rams, and lambs, with their grain offerings and their libations and offer them on the altar of the house of your God which is in Jerusalem.

18"And whatever seems good to you and to your brothers to do with the rest of the silver and gold, you may do according to the will of your God.

19"Also the utensils which are given to you for the service of the house of your God, deliver in full before the God of Jerusalem.

20"And the rest of the needs for the house of your God, for which you may have occasion to provide, provide *for it* from the royal treasury.

21"And I, even I King Artaxerxes, issue a decree to all the treasurers who are *in the provinces* beyond the River, that whatever Ezra the priest, the scribe of the law of the God of heaven, may require of you, it shall be done diligently,

22 *even* up to 100 talents of silver, 100 kors of wheat, 100 baths of wine, 100 baths of oil, and salt as needed.

23"Whatever is commanded by the God of heaven, let it be done with zeal for the house of the God of heaven, lest there be wrath against the kingdom of the king and his sons.

24"We also inform you that it is not allowed to impose tax, tribute or toll *on* any of the priests, Levites, singers, doorkeepers, Nethinim, or servants of this house of God.

25"And you, Ezra, according to the wisdom of your God which is in your hand, appoint magistrates and judges that they may judge all the people who are in *the province* beyond the River, *even* all those who know the laws of your God; and you may teach anyone who is ignorant *of them.*

26"And whoever will not observe the law of your God and the law of the king, let judgment be executed upon him strictly, whether for death or for banishment or for confiscation of goods or for imprisonment."

*The King's Kindness*

27¶ Blessed be the LORD, the God of our fathers, who has put *such a thing* as this in the king's heart, to adorn the house of the LORD which is in Jerusalem,

28and has extended lovingkindness to me before the king and his counselors and before all the king's mighty princes. Thus I was strengthened according to the hand of the LORD my God upon me, and I gathered leading men from Israel to go up with me.

## New International

10For Ezra had devoted himself to the study and observance of the Law of the LORD, and to teaching its decrees and laws in Israel.

*King Artaxerxes' Letter to Ezra*

11This is a copy of the letter King Artaxerxes had given to Ezra the priest and teacher, a man learned in matters concerning the commands and decrees of the LORD for Israel:

12[b] Artaxerxes, king of kings,

To Ezra the priest, a teacher of the Law of the God of heaven:

Greetings.

13Now I decree that any of the Israelites in my kingdom, including priests and Levites, who wish to go to Jerusalem with you, may go. 14You are sent by the king and his seven advisers to inquire about Judah and Jerusalem with regard to the Law of your God, which is in your hand. 15Moreover, you are to take with you the silver and gold that the king and his advisers have freely given to the God of Israel, whose dwelling is in Jerusalem, 16together with all the silver and gold you may obtain from the province of Babylon, as well as the freewill offerings of the people and priests for the temple of their God in Jerusalem. 17With this money be sure to buy bulls, rams and male lambs, together with their grain offerings and drink offerings, and sacrifice them on the altar of the temple of your God in Jerusalem.

18You and your brother Jews may then do whatever seems best with the rest of the silver and gold, in accordance with the will of your God. 19Deliver to the God of Jerusalem all the articles entrusted to you for worship in the temple of your God. 20And anything else needed for the temple of your God that you may have occasion to supply, you may provide from the royal treasury.

21Now I, King Artaxerxes, order all the treasurers of Trans-Euphrates to provide with diligence whatever Ezra the priest, a teacher of the Law of the God of heaven, may ask of you— 22up to a hundred talents[c] of silver, a hundred cors[d] of wheat, a hundred baths[e] of wine, a hundred baths[f] of olive oil, and salt without limit. 23Whatever the God of heaven has prescribed, let it be done with diligence for the temple of the God of heaven. Why should there be wrath against the realm of the king and of his sons? 24You are also to know that you have no authority to impose taxes, tribute or duty on any of the priests, Levites, singers, gatekeepers, temple servants or other workers at this house of God.

25And you, Ezra, in accordance with the wisdom of your God, which you possess, appoint magistrates and judges to administer justice to all the people of Trans-Euphrates—all who know the laws of your God. And you are to teach any who do not know them. 26Whoever does not obey the law of your God and the law of the king must surely be punished by death, banishment, confiscation of property, or imprisonment.

27Praise be to the LORD, the God of our fathers, who has put it into the king's heart to bring honor to the house of the LORD in Jerusalem in this way 28and who has extended his good favor to me before the king and his advisers and all the king's powerful officials. Because the hand of the LORD my God was on me, I took courage and gathered leading men from Israel to go up with me.

**NIV** [b] *12* The text of Ezra 7:12-26 is in Aramaic. [c] *22* That is, about 3 3/4 tons (about 3.4 metric tons) [d] *22* That is, probably about 600 bushels (about 22 kiloliters) [e] *22* That is, probably about 600 gallons (about 2.2 kiloliters) [f] *22* That is, probably about 600 gallons (about 2.2 kiloliters)

## King James

8 THESE *ARE* now the chief of their fathers, and *this is* the
genealogy of them that went up with me from Babylon, in the
reign of Artaxerxes the king.
2Of the sons of Phinehas; Gershom: of the sons of Ithamar;
Daniel: of the sons of David; Hattush.
3Of the sons of Shechaniah, of the sons of Pharosh; Zechariah:
and with him were reckoned by genealogy of the males an hundred and fifty.
4Of the sons of Pahath-moab; Elihoenai the son of Zerahiah,
and with him two hundred males.
5Of the sons of Shechaniah; the son of Jahaziel, and with him
three hundred males.
6Of the sons also of Adin; Ebed the son of Jonathan, and with
him fifty males.
7And of the sons of Elam; Jeshaiah the son of Athaliah, and with
him seventy males.
8And of the sons of Shephatiah; Zebadiah the son of Michael,
and with him fourscore males.
9Of the sons of Joab; Obadiah the son of Jehiel, and with him
two hundred and eighteen males.
10And of the sons of Shelomith; the son of Josiphiah, and with
him an hundred and threescore males.
11And of the sons of Bebai; Zechariah the son of Bebai, and with
him twenty and eight males.
12And of the sons of Azgad; Johanan the son of Hakkatan, and
with him an hundred and ten males.
13And of the last sons of Adonikam, whose names *are* these,
Eliphelet, Jeiel, and Shemaiah, and with them threescore males.
14Of the sons also of Bigvai; Uthai, and Zabbud, and with them
seventy males.
15¶ And I gathered them together to the river that runneth to
Ahava; and there abode we in tents three days: and I viewed the
people, and the priests, and found there none of the sons of Levi.
16Then sent I for Eliezer, for Ariel, for Shemaiah, and for Elnathan, and for Jarib, and for Elnathan, and for Nathan, and for
Zechariah, and for Meshullam, chief men; also for Joiarib, and for
Elnathan, men of understanding.
17And I sent them with commandment unto Iddo the chief at
the place Casiphia, and I told them what they should say unto
Iddo, *and* to his brethren the Nethinims, at the place Casiphia, that
they should bring unto us ministers for the house of our God.
18And by the good hand of our God upon us they brought us
a man of understanding, of the sons of Mahli, the son of Levi, the
son of Israel; and Sherebiah, with his sons and his brethren, eighteen;
19And Hashabiah, and with him Jeshaiah of the sons of Merari,
his brethren and their sons, twenty;
20Also of the Nethinims, whom David and the princes had
appointed for the service of the Levites, two hundred and twenty
Nethinims: all of them were expressed by name.
21¶ Then I proclaimed a fast there, at the river of Ahava, that
we might afflict ourselves before our God, to seek of him a right
way for us, and for our little ones, and for all our substance.
22For I was ashamed to require of the king a band of soldiers
and horsemen to help us against the enemy in the way: because
we had spoken unto the king, saying, The hand of our God *is* upon
all them for good that seek him; but his power and his wrath *is*
against all them that forsake him.
23So we fasted and besought our God for this: and he was
entreated of us.
24¶ Then I separated twelve of the chief of the priests, Sherebiah, Hashabiah, and ten of their brethren with them,
25And weighed unto them the silver, and the gold, and the
vessels, *even* the offering of the house of our God, which the king,
and his counsellors, and his lords, and all Israel *there* present, had
offered:

## Amplified

8 THESE ARE the heads of their fathers' houses, and this is the
genealogy of those who went up with me from Babylonia, in
the reign of King Artaxerxes.
2Of the sons of Phinehas, Gershom; of Ithamar, Daniel; of
David, Hattush;
3Of the sons of Shecaniah. Of the sons of Parosh, Zechariah,
and with him were registered 150 men by genealogy.
4Of the sons of Pahath-moab, Eliehoenai son of Zerahiah, with
200 men.
5Of the sons of Zattu, Shecaniah son of Jahaziel, with 300 men.
6Of the sons of Adin, Ebed son of Jonathan, with 50 men.
7Of the sons of Elam, Jeshaiah son of Athaliah, with 70 men.
8Of the sons of Shephatiah, Zebadiah son of Michael, with 80
men.
9Of the sons of Joab, Obadiah son of Jehiel, with 218 men.
10Of the sons of [Bani], Shelomith son of Josiphiah, with 160
men.
11Of the sons of Bebai, Zechariah son of Bebai, with 28 men.
12Of the sons of Azgad, Johanan son of Hakkatan, with 110
men.
13Of the sons of Adonikam, the last to come, their names are,
Eliphelet, Jeuel, and Shemaiah, with 60 men.
14Of the sons of Bigvai, Uthai and Zabbud [Zaccur], with 70
men.
15I, [Ezra], gathered them together at the river that runs to
Ahava, and there we encamped three days. I reviewed the people
and the priests, and found no Levites.
16Then I sent for Eliezer, Ariel, Shemaiah, Elnathan, Jarib, Elnathan, Nathan, Zechariah, Meshullam, chief men; also for Joiarib
and Elnathan, teachers.
17And I sent them to Iddo, the leading man at the place Casiphia, telling them to say to Iddo and his brethren the Nethinim
[temple servants], at the place Casiphia, Bring to us servants for
the house of our God.
18And by the good hand of our God upon us they brought us
a man of understanding, of the sons of Mahli son of Levi, son of
Israel, named Sherebiah, with his sons and his kinsmen, 18;
19And Hashabiah, and with him Jeshaiah of the sons of Merari,
with his kinsmen and their sons, 20;
20Also 220 of the Nethinim, whose forefathers David and the
officials had set apart [with their descendants] to attend the Levites. They were all mentioned by name.
21Then I proclaimed a fast there, at the river Ahava, that we
might humble ourselves before our God, to seek from Him a
straight *and* right way for us, our little ones, and all our possessions.
22For I was ashamed to request of the king a band of soldiers
and horsemen to protect us against the enemy along the way;
because we had told the king, The hand of our God is upon all
them for good who seek Him, but His power and His wrath are
against all those who forsake Him.
23So we fasted and besought our God for this, and He heard our
entreaty.
24Then I set apart twelve leading priests: Sherebiah, Hashabiah,
and ten of their kinsmen,
25And weighed out to them the silver, the gold, and the vessels,
the offering for the house of our God, which the king, his counselors, his lords, and all Israel there present had offered;

# New American Standard

*People Who Went with Ezra*

8 NOW THESE are the heads of their fathers' *households* and the
genealogical enrollment of those who went up with me from
Babylon in the reign of King Artaxerxes:
2of the sons of Phinehas, Gershom; of the sons of Ithamar,
Daniel; of the sons of David, Hattush;
3of the sons of Shecaniah *who was* of the sons of Parosh, Zechariah and with him 150 males *who were in* the genealogical list;
4of the sons of Pahath-moab, Eliehoenai the son of Zerahiah
and 200 males with him;
5of the sons of Shecaniah, the son of Jahaziel and 300 males
with him;
6and of the sons of Adin, Ebed the son of Jonathan and 50
males with him;
7and of the sons of Elam, Jeshaiah the son of Athaliah and 70
males with him;
8and of the sons of Shephatiah, Zebadiah the son of Michael
and 80 males with him;
9of the sons of Joab, Obadiah the son of Jehiel and 218 males
with him;
10and of the sons of Shelomith, the son of Josiphiah and 160
males with him;
11and of the sons of Bebai, Zechariah the son of Bebai and 28
males with him;
12and of the sons of Azgad, Johanan the son of Hakkatan and
110 males with him;
13and of the sons of Adonikam, the last ones, these being their
names, Eliphelet, Jeuel, and Shemaiah and 60 males with them;
14and of the sons of Bigvai, Uthai and Zabbud and 70 males with
them.

*Ezra Sends for Levites*

15¶ Now I assembled them at the river that runs to Ahava,
where we camped for three days; and when I observed the people
and the priests, I did not find any Levites there.
16So I sent for Eliezer, Ariel, Shemaiah, Elnathan, Jarib, Elnathan, Nathan, Zechariah, and Meshullam, leading men, and for
Joiarib and Elnathan, teachers.
17And I sent them to Iddo the leading man at the place Casiphia;
and I told them what to say to Iddo *and* his brothers, the temple
servants at the place Casiphia, *that is,* to bring ministers to us for
the house of our God.
18And according to the good hand of our God upon us they
brought us a man of insight of the sons of Mahli, the son of Levi,
the son of Israel, namely Sherebiah, and his sons and brothers, 18
men;
19and Hashabiah and Jeshaiah of the sons of Merari, with his
brothers and their sons, 20 men;
20and 220 of the temple servants, whom David and the princes
had given for the service of the Levites, all of them designated by
name.

*Protection of God Invoked*

21¶ Then I proclaimed a fast there at the river of Ahava, that we
might humble ourselves before our God to seek from Him a safe
journey for us, our little ones, and all our possessions.
22For I was ashamed to request from the king troops and horsemen to protect us from the enemy on the way, because we had said
to the king, "The hand of our God is favorably disposed to all those
who seek Him, but His power and His anger are against all those
who forsake Him."
23So we fasted and sought our God concerning this *matter,* and
He listened to our entreaty.
24¶ Then I set apart twelve of the leading priests, Sherebiah,
Hashabiah, and with them ten of their brothers;
25and I weighed out to them the silver, the gold, and the utensils, the offering for the house of our God which the king and his
counselors and his princes, and all Israel present *there,* had offered.

# New International

*List of the Family Heads Returning With Ezra*

8 THESE ARE the family heads and those registered with them
who came up with me from Babylon during the reign of King
Artaxerxes:

2of the descendants of Phinehas, Gershom;
of the descendants of Ithamar, Daniel;
of the descendants of David, Hattush 3of the descendants of
Shecaniah;
of the descendants of Parosh, Zechariah, and with him were
registered 150 men;
4of the descendants of Pahath-Moab, Eliehoenai son of Zerahiah, and with him 200 men;
5of the descendants of Zattu,[a] Shecaniah son of Jahaziel, and
with him 300 men;
6of the descendants of Adin, Ebed son of Jonathan, and with
him 50 men;
7of the descendants of Elam, Jeshaiah son of Athaliah, and
with him 70 men;
8of the descendants of Shephatiah, Zebadiah son of Michael,
and with him 80 men;
9of the descendants of Joab, Obadiah son of Jehiel, and with
him 218 men;
10of the descendants of Bani,[b] Shelomith son of Josiphiah, and
with him 160 men;
11of the descendants of Bebai, Zechariah son of Bebai, and with
him 28 men;
12of the descendants of Azgad, Johanan son of Hakkatan, and
with him 110 men;
13of the descendants of Adonikam, the last ones, whose names
were Eliphelet, Jeuel and Shemaiah, and with them 60
men;
14of the descendants of Bigvai, Uthai and Zaccur, and with
them 70 men.

*The Return to Jerusalem*

15I assembled them at the canal that flows toward Ahava, and
we camped there three days. When I checked among the people
and the priests, I found no Levites there. 16So I summoned Eliezer,
Ariel, Shemaiah, Elnathan, Jarib, Elnathan, Nathan, Zechariah
and Meshullam, who were leaders, and Joiarib and Elnathan, who
were men of learning, 17and I sent them to Iddo, the leader in
Casiphia. I told them what to say to Iddo and his kinsmen, the
temple servants in Casiphia, so that they might bring attendants
to us for the house of our God. 18Because the gracious hand of our
God was on us, they brought us Sherebiah, a capable man, from
the descendants of Mahli son of Levi, the son of Israel, and Sherebiah's sons and brothers, 18 men; 19and Hashabiah, together with
Jeshaiah from the descendants of Merari, and his brothers and
nephews, 20 men. 20They also brought 220 of the temple servants—a body that David and the officials had established to assist
the Levites. All were registered by name.
21There, by the Ahava Canal, I proclaimed a fast, so that we
might humble ourselves before our God and ask him for a safe
journey for us and our children, with all our possessions. 22I was
ashamed to ask the king for soldiers and horsemen to protect us
from enemies on the road, because we had told the king, "The
gracious hand of our God is on everyone who looks to him, but
his great anger is against all who forsake him." 23So we fasted and
petitioned our God about this, and he answered our prayer.
24Then I set apart twelve of the leading priests, together with
Sherebiah, Hashabiah and ten of their brothers, 25and I weighed
out to them the offering of silver and gold and the articles that the
king, his advisers, his officials and all Israel present there had
donated for the house of our God. 26I weighed out to them 650

**NIV** [a] *5* Some Septuagint manuscripts (also 1 Esdras 8:32); Hebrew does not have *Zattu.* [b] *10* Some Septuagint manuscripts (also 1 Esdras 8:36); Hebrew does not have *Bani.*

## King James

26I even weighed unto their hand six hundred and fifty talents of silver, and silver vessels an hundred talents, *and* of gold an hundred talents;

27Also twenty basins of gold, of a thousand drams; and two vessels of fine copper, precious as gold.

28And I said unto them, Ye *are* holy unto the LORD; the vessels *are* holy also; and the silver and the gold *are* a freewill offering unto the LORD God of your fathers.

29Watch ye, and keep *them,* until ye weigh *them* before the chief of the priests and the Levites, and chief of the fathers of Israel, at Jerusalem, in the chambers of the house of the LORD.

30So took the priests and the Levites the weight of the silver, and the gold, and the vessels, to bring *them* to Jerusalem unto the house of our God.

31¶ Then we departed from the river of Ahava on the twelfth *day* of the first month, to go unto Jerusalem: and the hand of our God was upon us, and he delivered us from the hand of the enemy, and of such as lay in wait by the way.

32And we came to Jerusalem, and abode there three days.

33¶ Now on the fourth day was the silver and the gold and the vessels weighed in the house of our God by the hand of Meremoth the son of Uriah the priest; and with him *was* Eleazar the son of Phinehas; and with them *was* Jozabad the son of Jeshua, and Noadiah the son of Binnui, Levites;

34By number *and* by weight of every one: and all the weight was written at that time.

35 *Also* the children of those that had been carried away, which were come out of the captivity, offered burnt offerings unto the God of Israel, twelve bullocks for all Israel, ninety and six rams, seventy and seven lambs, twelve he goats *for* a sin offering: all *this was* a burnt offering unto the LORD.

36¶ And they delivered the king's commissions unto the king's lieutenants, and to the governors on this side the river: and they furthered the people, and the house of God.

9 NOW WHEN these things were done, the princes came to me, saying, The people of Israel, and the priests, and the Levites, have not separated themselves from the people of the lands, *doing* according to their abominations, *even* of the Canaanites, the Hittites, the Perizzites, the Jebusites, the Ammonites, the Moabites, the Egyptians, and the Amorites.

2For they have taken of their daughters for themselves, and for their sons: so that the holy seed have mingled themselves with the people of *those* lands: yea, the hand of the princes and rulers hath been chief in this trespass.

3And when I heard this thing, I rent my garment and my mantle, and plucked off the hair of my head and of my beard, and sat down astonied.

4Then were assembled unto me every one that trembled at the words of the God of Israel, because of the transgression of those that had been carried away; and I sat astonied until the evening sacrifice.

5¶ And at the evening sacrifice I arose up from my heaviness; and having rent my garment and my mantle, I fell upon my knees, and spread out my hands unto the LORD my God,

6And said, O my God, I am ashamed and blush to lift up my face to thee, my God: for our iniquities are increased over *our* head, and our trespass is grown up unto the heavens.

7Since the days of our fathers *have* we *been* in a great trespass unto this day; and for our iniquities have we, our kings, *and* our priests, been delivered into the hand of the kings of the lands, to the sword, to captivity, and to a spoil, and to confusion of face, as *it is* this day.

## Amplified

26I weighed into their hand 650 talents of silver, and silver vessels valued at 100 talents, and 100 talents of gold;

27Also twenty basins of gold, worth 1,000 darics, and two vessels of fine bright bronze, precious as gold.

28And I said to them, You are holy to the Lord, the vessels are holy also, and the silver and the gold are a freewill offering to the Lord, the God of your fathers.

29Guard and keep them until you weigh them before the chief priests and Levites and heads of the fathers' houses of Israel in Jerusalem, in the chambers of the house of the Lord.

30So the priests and the Levites received the weight of the silver, the gold, and the vessels, to bring them to Jerusalem into the house of our God.

31We left the river Ahava on the twelfth day of the first month, to go to Jerusalem; and the hand of our God was upon us, and He delivered us from the enemy, and those who lay in wait by the way.

32And we came to Jerusalem, and [had been] there three days.

33On the fourth day the silver, the gold, and the vessels were weighed in the house of our God into the hands of Meremoth the priest, son of Uriah, and with him was Eleazar son of Phinehas, and with them were Jozabad son of Jeshua, and Noadiah son of Binnui, Levites.

34Every piece was counted and weighed, and all the weight was recorded at once.

35Also those returned exiles whose parents had been carried into captivity offered burnt offerings to the God of Israel, twelve young bulls for all Israel, ninety-six rams, seventy-seven lambs, and twelve he-goats for a sin offering. All this was a burnt offering to the Lord.

36And they delivered the king's commissions to the king's lieutenants, and to the governors west of the River; and they aided the people and God's house.

9 AFTERWARD THE officials came to me and said, The Israelites and the priests and Levites have not separated themselves from the people of the lands, but have committed the abominations of the Canaanites, Hittites, Perizzites, Jebusites, Ammonites, Moabites, Egyptians, and Amorites.

2For they have taken wives of their daughters for themselves and for their sons; so that the holy offspring have mixed themselves with the people of the lands. Indeed, the officials and chief men have been foremost in this wicked act *and* direct violation [of God's will]. [Deut. 7:3, 4.]

3When I heard this, I rent my undergarment and my mantle; I pulled hair from my head and beard, and sat down appalled.

4Then all those who trembled at the words of the God of Israel because of the offensive violation of His will by the returned exiles, gathered around me as I sat astounded until the evening sacrifice.

5At the evening sacrifice I arose from my depression, and having rent my undergarment and my mantle, I fell on my knees, and spread out my hands to the Lord my God,

6Saying, O my God, I am ashamed and blush to lift my face to You, my God; for our iniquities have risen higher than our heads, and our guilt has mounted to the heavens.

7Since the days of our fathers we have been exceedingly guilty; and for our willfulness we, our kings, and our priests, have been delivered into the hand of the kings of the lands, to the sword, captivity, plundering, and utter shame, as today.

## New American Standard

26Thus I weighed into their hands 650 talents of silver, and silver utensils *worth* 100 talents, *and* 100 gold talents,
27and 20 gold bowls, *worth* 1,000 darics; and two utensils of fine shiny bronze, precious as gold.
28Then I said to them, "You are holy to the LORD, and the utensils are holy; and the silver and the gold are a freewill offering to the LORD God of your fathers.
29"Watch and keep *them* until you weigh *them* before the leading priests, the Levites, and the heads of the fathers' *households* of Israel at Jerusalem, *in* the chambers of the house of the LORD."
30So the priests and the Levites accepted the weighed out silver and gold and the utensils, to bring *them* to Jerusalem to the house of our God.
31¶ Then we journeyed from the river Ahava on the twelfth of the first month to go to Jerusalem; and the hand of our God was over us, and He delivered us from the hand of the enemy and the ambushes by the way.
32Thus we came to Jerusalem and remained there three days.

*Treasure Placed in the Temple*

33And on the fourth day the silver and the gold and the utensils were weighed out in the house of our God into the hand of Meremoth the son of Uriah the priest, and with him *was* Eleazar the son of Phinehas; and with them *were* the Levites, Jozabad the son of Jeshua and Noadiah the son of Binnui.
34Everything *was* numbered and weighed, and all the weight was recorded at that time.
35¶ The exiles who had come from the captivity offered burnt offerings to the God of Israel: 12 bulls for all Israel, 96 rams, 77 lambs, 12 male goats for a sin offering, all as a burnt offering to the LORD.
36Then they delivered the king's edicts to the king's satraps, and to the governors *in the provinces* beyond the River, and they supported the people and the house of God.

*Mixed Marriages*

**9** NOW WHEN these things had been completed, the princes approached me, saying, "The people of Israel and the priests and the Levites have not separated themselves from the peoples of the lands, according to their abominations, *those* of the Canaanites, the Hittites, the Perizzites, the Jebusites, the Ammonites, the Moabites, the Egyptians, and the Amorites.
2"For they have taken some of their daughters *as wives* for themselves and for their sons, so that the holy race has intermingled with the peoples of the lands; indeed, the hands of the princes and the rulers have been foremost in this unfaithfulness."
3And when I heard about this matter, I tore my garment and my robe, and pulled some of the hair from my head and my beard, and sat down appalled.
4Then everyone who trembled at the words of the God of Israel on account of the unfaithfulness of the exiles gathered to me, and I sat appalled until the evening offering.

*Prayer of Confession*

5¶ But at the evening offering I arose from my humiliation, even with my garment and my robe torn, and I fell on my knees and stretched out my hands to the LORD my God;
6and I said, "O my God, I am ashamed and embarrassed to lift up my face to Thee, my God, for our iniquities have risen above our heads, and our guilt has grown even to the heavens.
7"Since the days of our fathers to this day we *have been* in great guilt, and on account of our iniquities we, our kings *and* our priests have been given into the hand of the kings of the lands, to the sword, to captivity, and to plunder and to open shame, as *it is* this day.

## New International

talents[a] of silver, silver articles weighing 100 talents,[b] 100 talents[c] of gold, 27 20 bowls of gold valued at 1,000 darics,[d] and two fine articles of polished bronze, as precious as gold.
28I said to them, "You as well as these articles are consecrated to the LORD. The silver and gold are a freewill offering to the LORD, the God of your fathers. 29Guard them carefully until you weigh them out in the chambers of the house of the LORD in Jerusalem before the leading priests and the Levites and the family heads of Israel." 30Then the priests and Levites received the silver and gold and sacred articles that had been weighed out to be taken to the house of our God in Jerusalem.
31On the twelfth day of the first month we set out from the Ahava Canal to go to Jerusalem. The hand of our God was on us, and he protected us from enemies and bandits along the way. 32So we arrived in Jerusalem, where we rested three days.
33On the fourth day, in the house of our God, we weighed out the silver and gold and the sacred articles into the hands of Meremoth son of Uriah, the priest. Eleazar son of Phinehas was with him, and so were the Levites Jozabad son of Jeshua and Noadiah son of Binnui. 34Everything was accounted for by number and weight, and the entire weight was recorded at that time.
35Then the exiles who had returned from captivity sacrificed burnt offerings to the God of Israel: twelve bulls for all Israel, ninety-six rams, seventy-seven male lambs and, as a sin offering, twelve male goats. All this was a burnt offering to the LORD. 36They also delivered the king's orders to the royal satraps and to the governors of Trans-Euphrates, who then gave assistance to the people and to the house of God.

*Ezra's Prayer About Intermarriage*

**9** AFTER THESE things had been done, the leaders came to me and said, "The people of Israel, including the priests and the Levites, have not kept themselves separate from the neighboring peoples with their detestable practices, like those of the Canaanites, Hittites, Perizzites, Jebusites, Ammonites, Moabites, Egyptians and Amorites. 2They have taken some of their daughters as wives for themselves and their sons, and have mingled the holy race with the peoples around them. And the leaders and officials have led the way in this unfaithfulness."
3When I heard this, I tore my tunic and cloak, pulled hair from my head and beard and sat down appalled. 4Then everyone who trembled at the words of the God of Israel gathered around me because of this unfaithfulness of the exiles. And I sat there appalled until the evening sacrifice.
5Then, at the evening sacrifice, I rose from my self-abasement, with my tunic and cloak torn, and fell on my knees with my hands spread out to the LORD my God 6and prayed:

"O my God, I am too ashamed and disgraced to lift up my face to you, my God, because our sins are higher than our heads and our guilt has reached to the heavens. 7From the days of our forefathers until now, our guilt has been great. Because of our sins, we and our kings and our priests have been subjected to the sword and captivity, to pillage and humiliation at the hand of foreign kings, as it is today.

NIV [a] *26* That is, about 25 tons (about 22 metric tons) [b] *26* That is, about 3 3/4 tons (about 3.4 metric tons) [c] *26* That is, about 3 3/4 tons (about 3.4 metric tons) [d] *27* That is, about 19 pounds (about 8.5 kilograms)

## King James

8And now for a little space grace hath been *shown* from the LORD our God, to leave us a remnant to escape, and to give us a nail in his holy place, that our God may lighten our eyes, and give us a little reviving in our bondage.

9For we *were* bondmen; yet our God hath not forsaken us in our bondage, but hath extended mercy unto us in the sight of the kings of Persia, to give us a reviving, to set up the house of our God, and to repair the desolations thereof, and to give us a wall in Judah and in Jerusalem.

10And now, O our God, what shall we say after this? for we have forsaken thy commandments,

11Which thou hast commanded by thy servants the prophets, saying, The land, unto which ye go to possess it, is an unclean land with the filthiness of the people of the lands, with their abominations, which have filled it from one end to another with their uncleanness.

12Now therefore give not your daughters unto their sons, neither take their daughters unto your sons, nor seek their peace or their wealth for ever: that ye may be strong, and eat the good of the land, and leave *it* for an inheritance to your children for ever.

13And after all that is come upon us for our evil deeds, and for our great trespass, seeing that thou our God hast punished us less than our iniquities *deserve*, and hast given us *such* deliverance as this;

14Should we again break thy commandments, and join in affinity with the people of these abominations? wouldest not thou be angry with us till thou hadst consumed *us*, so that *there should be* no remnant nor escaping?

15O LORD God of Israel, thou *art* righteous: for we remain yet escaped, as *it is* this day: behold, we *are* before thee in our trespasses: for we cannot stand before thee because of this.

10 NOW WHEN Ezra had prayed, and when he had confessed, weeping and casting himself down before the house of God, there assembled unto him out of Israel a very great congregation of men and women and children: for the people wept very sore.

2And Shechaniah the son of Jehiel, *one* of the sons of Elam, answered and said unto Ezra, We have trespassed against our God, and have taken strange wives of the people of the land: yet now there is hope in Israel concerning this thing.

3Now therefore let us make a covenant with our God to put away all the wives, and such as are born of them, according to the counsel of my lord, and of those that tremble at the commandment of our God; and let it be done according to the law.

4Arise; for *this* matter *belongeth* unto thee: we also *will be* with thee: be of good courage, and do *it*.

5Then arose Ezra, and made the chief priests, the Levites, and all Israel, to swear that they should do according to this word. And they sware.

6¶ Then Ezra rose up from before the house of God, and went into the chamber of Johanan the son of Eliashib: and *when* he came thither, he did eat no bread, nor drink water: for he mourned because of the transgression of them that had been carried away.

7And they made proclamation throughout Judah and Jerusalem unto all the children of the captivity, that they should gather themselves together unto Jerusalem;

8And that whosoever would not come within three days, according to the counsel of the princes and the elders, all his substance should be forfeited, and himself separated from the congregation of those that had been carried away.

9¶ Then all the men of Judah and Benjamin gathered themselves together unto Jerusalem within three days. It *was* the ninth month, on the twentieth *day* of the month; and all the people sat in the street of the house of God, trembling because of *this* matter, and for the great rain.

## Amplified

8And now for a brief moment grace has been shown us by the Lord our God, Who has left us a remnant to escape, and has given us a secure hold in His holy place, that our God may brighten our eyes and give us a little reviving in our bondage.

9For we are bondmen; yet our God has not forsaken us in our bondage, but has extended mercy *and* steadfast love to us before the kings of Persia, to give us some reviving to set up the house of our God, to repair its ruins, and to give us a wall [of protection] in Judah and Jerusalem.

10Now, O our God, what can we say after this? For we have forsaken Your commands,

11Which You have commanded by Your servants the prophets, saying, The land, which you are entering to possess, is an unclean land with the pollutions of the peoples of the lands through their abominations which have filled it from one end to the other with their filthiness.

12Therefore do not give your daughters to their sons or take their daughters to your sons, and never seek their peace or prosperity, that you may be strong, and eat the good of the land, and leave it as an inheritance to your children always.

13And after all that has come upon us for our evil deeds and for our great guilt, seeing that You, our God, have punished us less than our iniquities deserved and have given us such a remnant,

14Shall we break Your commandments again and intermarry with the peoples who practice these abominations? Would You not be angry with us till You had consumed us, so that there would be no remnant, nor any to escape? [Deut. 7:2-4.]

15O Lord, the God of Israel, You are rigidly just *and* righteous, for we are left a remnant that is escaped, as this day. Behold, we are before You in our guilt, for none can stand before You because of this.

10 NOW WHILE Ezra prayed and made confession, weeping and casting himself down before the house of God, there gathered to him out of Israel a very great assembly of men, women, and children; for the people wept bitterly.

2And Shecaniah [II] the son of Jehiel [one of the congregation], of the sons of Elam, said to Ezra: We have broken faith *and* dealt treacherously against our God, and have married foreign women of the peoples of the land; yet now there is still hope for Israel in spite of this thing.

3Therefore let us make a covenant with our God to put away all the foreign wives and their children, according to the counsel of my lord and of those who tremble at the command of our God; and let it be done according to the law.

4Arise, for it is your duty, and we are with you. Be strong *and* brave and do it.

5Then Ezra arose and made the chief of the priests, the Levites, and all Israel swear that they would do as had been said. So they took the oath.

6Then Ezra came from before the house of God, and went into the lodging place of Jeho-hanan son of Eliashib [for the night]; there he ate no bread and drank no water, for he mourned over the returned exiles' faithlessness [and violation of God's law].

7And proclamation was made throughout Judah and Jerusalem to all returned exiles, that they should assemble in Jerusalem,

8And that whoever did not come within three days, by order of the officials and the elders all his property should be forfeited, and he himself banned from the assembly of the exiles.

9Then all the men of Judah and Benjamin gathered at Jerusalem within three days. It was the twentieth day of the ninth month; and all the people sat in the open space before the house of God, trembling because of this matter and because of the heavy rain.

## New American Standard

8"But now for a brief moment grace has been *shown* from the LORD our God, to leave us an escaped remnant and to give us a peg in His holy place, that our God may enlighten our eyes and grant us a little reviving in our bondage.

9"For we are slaves; yet in our bondage, our God has not forsaken us, but has extended lovingkindness to us in the sight of the kings of Persia, to give us reviving to raise up the house of our God, to restore its ruins, and to give us a wall in Judah and Jerusalem.

10"And now, our God, what shall we say after this? For we have forsaken Thy commandments,

11which Thou hast commanded by Thy servants the prophets, saying, 'The land which you are entering to possess is an unclean land with the uncleanness of the peoples of the lands, with their abominations which have filled it from end to end *and* with their impurity.

12'So now do not give your daughters to their sons nor take their daughters to your sons, and never seek their peace or their prosperity, that you may be strong and eat the good *things* of the land and leave *it* as an inheritance to your sons forever.'

13"And after all that has come upon us for our evil deeds and our great guilt, since Thou our God hast requited *us* less than our iniquities *deserve,* and hast given us an escaped remnant as this,

14shall we again break Thy commandments and intermarry with the peoples who commit these abominations? Wouldst Thou not be angry with us to the point of destruction, until there is no remnant nor any who escape?

15"O LORD God of Israel, Thou art righteous, for we have been left an escaped remnant, as *it is* this day; behold, we are before Thee in our guilt, for no one can stand before Thee because of this."

*Reconciliation with God*

**10** NOW WHILE Ezra was praying and making confession, weeping and prostrating himself before the house of God, a very large assembly, men, women, and children, gathered to him from Israel; for the people wept bitterly.

2And Shecaniah the son of Jehiel, one of the sons of Elam, answered and said to Ezra, "We have been unfaithful to our God, and have married foreign women from the peoples of the land; yet now there is hope for Israel in spite of this.

3"So now let us make a covenant with our God to put away all the wives and their children, according to the counsel of [a]my lord and of those who tremble at the commandment of our God; and let it be done according to the law.

4"Arise! For *this* matter is your responsibility, but we will be with you; be courageous and act."

5¶ Then Ezra rose and made the leading priests, the Levites, and all Israel, take oath that they would do according to this proposal; so they took the oath.

6Then Ezra rose from before the house of God and went into the chamber of Jehohanan the son of Eliashib. Although he went there, he did not eat bread, nor drink water, for he was mourning over the unfaithfulness of the exiles.

7And they made a proclamation throughout Judah and Jerusalem to all the exiles, that they should assemble at Jerusalem,

8and that whoever would not come within three days, according to the counsel of the leaders and the elders, all his possessions should be forfeited and he himself excluded from the assembly of the exiles.

9¶ So all the men of Judah and Benjamin assembled at Jerusalem within the three days. It was the ninth month on the twentieth of the month, and all the people sat in the open square *before* the house of God, trembling because of this matter and the heavy rain.

NAS [a] Or, *the Lord*

## New International

8"But now, for a brief moment, the LORD our God has been
gracious in leaving us a remnant and giving us a firm place
in his sanctuary, and so our God gives light to our eyes and
a little relief in our bondage. 9Though we are slaves, our God
has not deserted us in our bondage. He has shown us kindness in the sight of the kings of Persia: He has granted us new
life to rebuild the house of our God and repair its ruins, and
he has given us a wall of protection in Judah and Jerusalem.
10"But now, O our God, what can we say after this? For we
have disregarded the commands 11you gave through your
servants the prophets when you said: 'The land you are entering to possess is a land polluted by the corruption of its
peoples. By their detestable practices they have filled it with
their impurity from one end to the other. 12Therefore, do not
give your daughters in marriage to their sons or take their
daughters for your sons. Do not seek a treaty of friendship
with them at any time, that you may be strong and eat the
good things of the land and leave it to your children as an
everlasting inheritance.'
13"What has happened to us is a result of our evil deeds
and our great guilt, and yet, our God, you have punished us
less than our sins have deserved and have given us a remnant
like this. 14Shall we again break your commands and intermarry with the peoples who commit such detestable practices? Would you not be angry enough with us to destroy us,
leaving us no remnant or survivor? 15O LORD, God of Israel,
you are righteous! We are left this day as a remnant. Here we
are before you in our guilt, though because of it not one of us
can stand in your presence."

*The People's Confession of Sin*

**10** WHILE EZRA was praying and confessing, weeping and throwing himself down before the house of God, a large
crowd of Israelites—men, women and children—gathered around
him. They too wept bitterly. 2Then Shecaniah son of Jehiel, one of
the descendants of Elam, said to Ezra, "We have been unfaithful
to our God by marrying foreign women from the peoples around
us. But in spite of this, there is still hope for Israel. 3Now let us
make a covenant before our God to send away all these women
and their children, in accordance with the counsel of my lord and
of those who fear the commands of our God. Let it be done according to the Law. 4Rise up; this matter is in your hands. We will
support you, so take courage and do it."
5So Ezra rose up and put the leading priests and Levites and all
Israel under oath to do what had been suggested. And they took
the oath. 6Then Ezra withdrew from before the house of God and
went to the room of Jehohanan son of Eliashib. While he was there,
he ate no food and drank no water, because he continued to mourn
over the unfaithfulness of the exiles.
7A proclamation was then issued throughout Judah and Jerusalem for all the exiles to assemble in Jerusalem. 8Anyone who failed
to appear within three days would forfeit all his property, in accordance with the decision of the officials and elders, and would
himself be expelled from the assembly of the exiles.

9Within the three days, all the men of Judah and Benjamin had
gathered in Jerusalem. And on the twentieth day of the ninth
month, all the people were sitting in the square before the house
of God, greatly distressed by the occasion and because of the rain.

## King James

10 And Ezra the priest stood up, and said unto them, Ye have transgressed, and have taken strange wives, to increase the trespass of Israel.

11 Now therefore make confession unto the LORD God of your fathers, and do his pleasure: and separate yourselves from the people of the land, and from the strange wives.

12 Then all the congregation answered and said with a loud voice, As thou hast said, so must we do.

13 But the people *are* many, and *it is* a time of much rain, and we are not able to stand without, neither *is this* a work of one day or two: for we are many that have transgressed in this thing.

14 Let now our rulers of all the congregation stand, and let all them which have taken strange wives in our cities come at appointed times, and with them the elders of every city, and the judges thereof, until the fierce wrath of our God for this matter be turned from us.

15 ¶ Only Jonathan the son of Asahel and Jahaziah the son of Tikvah were employed about this *matter:* and Meshullam and Shabbethai the Levite helped them.

16 And the children of the captivity did so. And Ezra the priest, *with* certain chief of the fathers, after the house of their fathers, and all of them by *their* names, were separated, and sat down in the first day of the tenth month to examine the matter.

17 And they made an end with all the men that had taken strange wives by the first day of the first month.

18 ¶ And among the sons of the priests there were found that had taken strange wives: *namely,* of the sons of Jeshua the son of Jozadak, and his brethren; Maaseiah, and Eliezer, and Jarib, and Gedaliah.

19 And they gave their hands that they would put away their wives; and *being* guilty, *they offered* a ram of the flock for their trespass.

20 And of the sons of Immer; Hanani, and Zebadiah.

21 And of the sons of Harim; Maaseiah, and Elijah, and Shemaiah, and Jehiel, and Uzziah.

22 And of the sons of Pashur; Elioenai, Maaseiah, Ishmael, Nethaneel, Jozabad, and Elasah.

23 Also of the Levites; Jozabad, and Shimei, and Kelaiah, (the same *is* Kelita,) Pethahiah, Judah, and Eliezer.

24 Of the singers also; Eliashib: and of the porters; Shallum, and Telem, and Uri.

25 Moreover of Israel: of the sons of Parosh; Ramiah, and Jeziah, and Malchiah, and Miamin, and Eleazar, and Malchijah, and Benaiah.

26 And of the sons of Elam; Mattaniah, Zechariah, and Jehiel, and Abdi, and Jeremoth, and Eliah.

27 And of the sons of Zattu; Elioenai, Eliashib, Mattaniah, and Jeremoth, and Zabad, and Aziza.

28 Of the sons also of Bebai; Jehohanan, Hananiah, Zabbai, *and* Athlai.

29 And of the sons of Bani; Meshullam, Malluch, and Adaiah, Jashub, and Sheal, and Ramoth.

30 And of the sons of Pahath-moab; Adna, and Chelal, Benaiah, Maaseiah, Mattaniah, Bezaleel, and Binnui, and Manasseh.

## Amplified

10 And Ezra the priest stood up and said to them, You have acted wickedly *and* broken faith [with God] and have married foreign [heathen] women, increasing the guilt of Israel.

11 So now make confession *and* give thanks to the Lord, the God of your fathers [for not consuming you], and do His will. [a]Separate yourselves from the peoples of the land, and from [your] foreign [heathen] wives.

12 Then all the assembly answered with a loud voice, As you have said, so must we do.

13 But the people are many, and it is a time of heavy rain; we cannot stand outside; nor can this work be done in a day or two; for we have greatly transgressed in this matter.

14 Let our officials stand for the whole assembly; let all in our cities who have foreign wives come by appointment, and with each group the elders of that city and its judges, until the fierce wrath of our God over this matter be turned away from us.

15 Only Jonathan son of Asahel and Jahzeiah son of Tikvah opposed this, and Meshullam and Shabbethai the Levite supported them.

16 Then the returned exiles did so. Ezra the priest and certain heads of fathers' houses were selected according to their fathers' houses, each of them by name, and they sat down on the first day of the tenth month to investigate the matter.

17 And by the first day of the first month they had come to the end of the cases of the men married to foreign wives.

18 Of the sons of the priests who had married non-Jewish women were found: of the sons of Jeshua [the high priest] son of Jozadak, and his brethren, Ma-aseiah, Eliezer, Jarib, and Gedaliah.

19 They solemnly vowed to put away their [heathen] wives; and being guilty, [each] offered a ram of the flock for [his] guilt.

20 Of the sons of Immer: Hanani and Zebadiah.

21 Of the sons of Harim: Ma-aseiah, Elijah, Shemaiah, Jehiel, and Uzziah.

22 Of the sons of Pashhur: Eli-oenai, Ma-aseiah, Ishmael, Nethanel, Jozabad, and Elasah.

23 Of the Levites: Jozabad, Shimei, Kelaiah (Kelita), Petha-hiah, Judah, and Eliezer.

24 Of the singers: Eliashib. Of the gatekeepers: Shallum, Telem, and Uri.

25 And of Israel: of the sons of Parosh: Ramiah, Izziah, Malchijah, Mijamin, Eleazar, Malchijah [Hashabiah], and Benaiah.

26 Of the sons of Elam: Mattaniah, Zechariah, Jehiel, Abdi, Jeremoth, and Elijah.

27 Of the sons of Zattu: Eli-oenai, Eliashib, Mattaniah, Jeremoth, Zabad, and Aziza.

28 Of the sons also of Bebai: Jehohanan, Hananiah, Zabbai, and Athlai.

29 Of the sons of Bani: Meshullam, Malluch, Adaiah, Jashub, Sheal, and Jeremoth.

30 Of the sons of Pahath-moab: Adna, Chelal, Benaiah, Ma-aseiah, Mattaniah, Bezalel, Binnui, and Manasseh.

**AMP** [a] The apparently great severity which characterized Ezra's divorce policy, as shown in Chapters 9 and 10, becomes thoroughly justified when Israel's tragic experiences because of marriages with heathen women are considered. The consequent idolatry, first of King Solomon, for example, and then of the whole nation, was fatal. God's wrath had been so great that He not only took the kingship from Solomon, but eventually turned the Israelites over to their enemies and left the Promised Land desolate, while the people bewailed their fate as captives in a heathen country. Ezra, to whom the keeping of God's law was of constant concern, had been born in captivity among exiles who hung their harps on the willow trees and grieved for the country, the peace and prosperity which their now justly offended God had once given them. Nothing could have been more abhorrent to Ezra than that the Jews should again fall into the snare of idolatry. His action in leading the exiles to give up their foreign wives and their children was the only way out, if God's consuming wrath was not again to be incurred. That those living of the 42,360 men who over eighty years before had made up the congregation (2:64), also saw complete separation from the foreign women as the unavoidable solution, is obvious from the fact that only four (10:15) spoke against it. However, those who were actually married to native heathen women were only 17 priests, 10 Levites, and 86 laymen—113 in all, according to the records, though the list may be incomplete.

# New American Standard

10Then Ezra the priest stood up and said to them, "You have been unfaithful and have married foreign wives adding to the guilt of Israel.

11"Now, therefore, make confession to the LORD God of your fathers, and do His will; and separate yourselves from the peoples of the land and from the foreign wives."

12Then all the assembly answered and said with a loud voice, "That's right! As you have said, so it is our duty to do.

13"But there are many people, it is the rainy season, and we are not able to stand in the open. Nor *can* the task *be done* in one or two days, for we have transgressed greatly in this matter.

14"Let our leaders represent the whole assembly and let all those in our cities who have married foreign wives come at appointed times, together with the elders and judges of each city, until the fierce anger of our God on account of this matter is turned away from us."

15Only Jonathan the son of Asahel and Jahzeiah the son of Tikvah opposed this, with Meshullam and Shabbethai the Levite supporting them.

**16**¶ But the exiles did so. And Ezra the priest selected men *who were* heads of fathers' *households* for *each of* their father's households, all of them by name. So they convened on the first day of the tenth month to investigate the matter.

17And they finished *investigating* all the men who had married foreign wives by the first of the first month.

*List of Offenders*

**18**¶ And among the sons of the priests who had married foreign wives were found of the sons of Jeshua the son of Jozadak, and his brothers: Maaseiah, Eliezer, Jarib, and Gedaliah.

19And they pledged to put away their wives, and being guilty, *they offered* a ram of the flock for their offense.

20And of the sons of Immer *there were* Hanani and Zebadiah;

21and of the sons of Harim: Maaseiah, Elijah, Shemaiah, Jehiel, and Uzziah;

22and of the sons of Pashhur: Elioenai, Maaseiah, Ishmael, Nethanel, Jozabad, and Elasah.

**23**¶ And of Levites *there were* Jozabad, Shimei, Kelaiah (that is, Kelita), Pethahiah, Judah, and Eliezer.

**24**¶ And of the singers *there was* Eliashib; and of the gatekeepers: Shallum, Telem, and Uri.

**25**¶ And of Israel, of the sons of Parosh *there were* Ramiah, Izziah, Malchijah, Mijamin, Eleazar, Malchijah, and Benaiah;

26and of the sons of Elam: Mattaniah, Zechariah, Jehiel, Abdi, Jeremoth, and Elijah;

27and of the sons of Zattu: Elioenai, Eliashib, Mattaniah, Jeremoth, Zabad, and Aziza;

28and of the sons of Bebai: Jehohanan, Hananiah, Zabbai, *and* Athlai;

29and of the sons of Bani: Meshullam, Malluch, and Adaiah, Jashub, Sheal, *and* Jeremoth;

30and of the sons of Pahath-moab: Adna, Chelal, Benaiah, Maaseiah, Mattaniah, Bezalel, Binnui, and Manasseh;

# New International

10Then Ezra the priest stood up and said to them, "You have been
unfaithful; you have married foreign women, adding to Israel's
guilt. 11Now make confession to the LORD, the God of your fathers,
and do his will. Separate yourselves from the peoples around you
and from your foreign wives."

12The whole assembly responded with a loud voice: "You are
right! We must do as you say. 13But there are many people here
and it is the rainy season; so we cannot stand outside. Besides, this
matter cannot be taken care of in a day or two, because we have
sinned greatly in this thing. 14Let our officials act for the whole
assembly. Then let everyone in our towns who has married a
foreign woman come at a set time, along with the elders and
judges of each town, until the fierce anger of our God in this matter
is turned away from us." 15Only Jonathan son of Asahel and
Jahzeiah son of Tikvah, supported by Meshullam and Shabbethai
the Levite, opposed this.

16So the exiles did as was proposed. Ezra the priest selected
men who were family heads, one from each family division, and
all of them designated by name. On the first day of the tenth
month they sat down to investigate the cases, 17and by the first day
of the first month they finished dealing with all the men who had
married foreign women.

*Those Guilty of Intermarriage*

18Among the descendants of the priests, the following had married foreign women:

From the descendants of Jeshua son of Jozadak, and his
brothers: Maaseiah, Eliezer, Jarib and Gedaliah. 19(They
all gave their hands in pledge to put away their wives, and
for their guilt they each presented a ram from the flock as
a guilt offering.)

20From the descendants of Immer:
Hanani and Zebadiah.

21From the descendants of Harim:
Maaseiah, Elijah, Shemaiah, Jehiel and Uzziah.

22From the descendants of Pashhur:
Elioenai, Maaseiah, Ishmael, Nethanel, Jozabad and Elasah.

23Among the Levites:

Jozabad, Shimei, Kelaiah (that is Kelita), Pethahiah, Judah and Eliezer.

24From the singers:
Eliashib.

From the gatekeepers:
Shallum, Telem and Uri.

25And among the other Israelites:

From the descendants of Parosh:
Ramiah, Izziah, Malkijah, Mijamin, Eleazar, Malkijah and Benaiah.

26From the descendants of Elam:
Mattaniah, Zechariah, Jehiel, Abdi, Jeremoth and Elijah.

27From the descendants of Zattu:
Elioenai, Eliashib, Mattaniah, Jeremoth, Zabad and Aziza.

28From the descendants of Bebai:
Jehohanan, Hananiah, Zabbai and Athlai.

29From the descendants of Bani:
Meshullam, Malluch, Adaiah, Jashub, Sheal and Jeremoth.

30From the descendants of Pahath-Moab:
Adna, Kelal, Benaiah, Maaseiah, Mattaniah, Bezalel, Binnui and Manasseh.

## King James

31And *of* the sons of Harim; Eliezer, Ishijah, Malchiah, Shemaiah, Shimeon,
32Benjamin, Malluch, *and* Shemariah.
33Of the sons of Hashum; Mattenai, Mattathah, Zabad, Eliphelet, Jeremai, Manasseh, *and* Shimei.
34Of the sons of Bani; Maadai, Amram, and Uel,
35Benaiah, Bedeiah, Chelluh,
36Vaniah, Meremoth, Eliashib,
37Mattaniah, Mattenai, and Jaasau,
38And Bani, and Binnui, Shimei,
39And Shelemiah, and Nathan, and Adaiah,
40Machnadebai, Shashai, Sharai,
41Azareel, and Shelemiah, Shemariah,
42Shallum, Amariah, *and* Joseph.
43Of the sons of Nebo; Jeiel, Mattithiah, Zabad, Zebina, Jadau, and Joel, Benaiah.
44All these had taken strange wives: and *some* of them had wives by whom they had children.

## Amplified

31Of the sons of Harim: Eliezer, Isshijah, Malchijah, Shemaiah, Shimeon,
32Benjamin, Malluch, and Shemariah.
33Of the sons of Hashum: Mattenai, Mattattah, Zabad, Eliphelet, Jeremai, Manasseh, and Shimei.
34Of the sons of Bani: Ma-adai, Amram, Uel,
35Benaiah, Bedeiah, Cheluhi [Cheluhu],
36Vaniah, Meremoth, Eliashib,
37Mattaniah, Mattenai, Jaasu [Jaasai],
38Bani, Binnui, Shimei,
39Shelemiah, Nathan, Adaiah,
40Machnadebai, Shashai, Sharai,
41Azarel, Shelemiah, Shemariah,
42Shallum, Amariah, and Joseph.
43Of the sons of Nebo: Jeiel, Mattithiah, Zabad, Zebina, Iddo [Jaddai], Joel, and Benaiah.
44All these had married foreign women, and some of the wives had borne children.

## New American Standard

31and *of* the sons of Harim: Eliezer, Isshijah, Malchijah, Shemaiah, Shimeon,
32Benjamin, Malluch, *and* Shemariah;
33of the sons of Hashum: Mattenai, Mattattah, Zabad, Eliphelet, Jeremai, Manasseh, *and* Shimei;
34of the sons of Bani: Maadai, Amram, Uel,
35Benaiah, Bedeiah, Cheluhi,
36Vaniah, Meremoth, Eliashib,
37Mattaniah, Mattenai, Jaasu,
38Bani, Binnui, Shimei,
39Shelemiah, Nathan, Adaiah,
40Machnadebai, Shashai, Sharai,
41Azarel, Shelemiah, Shemariah,
42Shallum, Amariah, *and* Joseph.
43Of the sons of Nebo *there were* Jeiel, Mattithiah, Zabad, Zebina, Jaddai, Joel, *and* Benaiah.
44All these had married foreign wives, and some of them had wives *by whom* they had children.

## New International

31From the descendants of Harim:
Eliezer, Ishijah, Malkijah, Shemaiah, Shimeon, 32Benjamin, Malluch and Shemariah.
33From the descendants of Hashum:
Mattenai, Mattattah, Zabad, Eliphelet, Jeremai, Manasseh and Shimei.
34From the descendants of Bani:
Maadai, Amram, Uel, 35Benaiah, Bedeiah, Keluhi, 36Vaniah, Meremoth, Eliashib, 37Mattaniah, Mattenai and Jaasu.
38From the descendants of Binnui:[a]
Shimei, 39Shelemiah, Nathan, Adaiah, 40Macnadebai, Shashai, Sharai, 41Azarel, Shelemiah, Shemariah, 42Shallum, Amariah and Joseph.
43From the descendants of Nebo:
Jeiel, Mattithiah, Zabad, Zebina, Jaddai, Joel and Benaiah.

44All these had married foreign women, and some of them had children by these wives.[b]

NIV [a] *37,38* See Septuagint (also 1 Esdras 9:34); Hebrew *Jaasu* [38]*and Bani and Binnui,* [b] *44* Or *and they sent them away with their children*

**King James**

THE BOOK OF

# Nehemiah

1 THE WORDS of Nehemiah the son of Hachaliah. And it came to pass in the month Chisleu, in the twentieth year, as I was in Shushan the palace,

2That Hanani, one of my brethren, came, he and *certain* men of Judah; and I asked them concerning the Jews that had escaped, which were left of the captivity, and concerning Jerusalem.

3And they said unto me, The remnant that are left of the captivity there in the province *are* in great affliction and reproach: the wall of Jerusalem also *is* broken down, and the gates thereof are burned with fire.

4¶ And it came to pass, when I heard these words, that I sat down and wept, and mourned *certain* days, and fasted, and prayed before the God of heaven,

5And said, I beseech thee, O LORD God of heaven, the great and terrible God, that keepeth covenant and mercy for them that love him and observe his commandments:

6Let thine ear now be attentive, and thine eyes open, that thou mayest hear the prayer of thy servant, which I pray before thee now, day and night, for the children of Israel thy servants, and confess the sins of the children of Israel, which we have sinned against thee: both I and my father's house have sinned.

7We have dealt very corruptly against thee, and have not kept the commandments, nor the statutes, nor the judgments, which thou commandest thy servant Moses.

8Remember, I beseech thee, the word that thou commandedst thy servant Moses, saying, *If* ye transgress, I will scatter you abroad among the nations:

9But *if* ye turn unto me, and keep my commandments, and do them; though there were of you cast out unto the uttermost part of the heaven, *yet* will I gather them from thence, and will bring them unto the place that I have chosen to set my name there.

10Now these *are* thy servants and thy people, whom thou hast redeemed by thy great power, and by thy strong hand.

11O Lord, I beseech thee, let now thine ear be attentive to the prayer of thy servant, and to the prayer of thy servants, who desire to fear thy name: and prosper, I pray thee, thy servant this day, and grant him mercy in the sight of this man. For I was the king's cupbearer.

**Amplified**

THE BOOK OF

# Nehemiah

1 THE WORDS *or* story of Nehemiah son of Hacaliah. Now in the month Chislev, in the twentieth year [of the Persian king], as I was in the castle of Shushan,

2Hanani, one of my kinsmen, came with certain men from Judah; and I asked them about the surviving Jews who had escaped exile, and about Jerusalem.

3And they said to me, The remnant there in the province who escaped exile are in great trouble and reproach; the wall of Jerusalem is broken down, and its [fortified] gates are destroyed by fire.

4When I heard this I sat down and wept, and mourned for days, and fasted and prayed [constantly] before the God of Heaven,

5And said, O Lord God of Heaven, the great and terrible God, Who keeps covenant, loving-kindness *and* mercy for those who love Him and keep His commandments:

6Let Your ear now be attentive, and Your eyes open, to listen to the prayer of Your servant, which I pray before You day and night for the Israelites Your servants, confessing the sins of the Israelites, which we have sinned against You. Yes, I and my father's house have sinned.

7We have acted very corruptly against You, and have not kept the commandments, statutes, and ordinances which You commanded Your servant Moses. [Deut. 6:1-9.]

8Remember [earnestly] what You commanded Your servant Moses: If you transgress *and* are unfaithful, I will scatter you abroad among the nations; [Lev. 26:33.]

9But if you return to Me and keep My commandments and do them, though your outcasts were in the farthest part of the heavens [the expanse of outer space] yet will I gather them from there, and will bring them to the place in which I have chosen to set My name. [Deut. 30:1-5.]

10Now these are Your servants and Your people, whom You have redeemed by Your great power, and by Your strong hand.

11O Lord, let Your ear be attentive to the prayer of Your servant and the prayer of Your servants, who delight to revere *and* fear Your Name [Your nature and attributes]; and prosper, I pray You, Your servant this day, and grant him mercy in the sight of this man. For I was cupbearer to the king.

2 AND IT came to pass in the month Nisan, in the twentieth year of Artaxerxes the king, *that* wine *was* before him: and I took up the wine, and gave *it* unto the king. Now I had not been *beforetime* sad in his presence.

2Wherefore the king said unto me, Why *is* thy countenance sad, seeing thou *art* not sick? this *is* nothing *else* but sorrow of heart. Then I was very sore afraid,

2 IN THE month of Nisan, in the twentieth year of King Artaxerxes, when wine was before him, I took up the wine and gave it to the king. Now I had not been sad before in his presence.

2So the king said to me, Why do you look sad, since you are not sick? This is nothing but sorrow of heart. Then I was very much afraid,

## New American Standard

# Nehemiah

*Nehemiah's Grief for the Exiles*

**1** THE WORDS of Nehemiah the son of Hacaliah.
¶Now it happened in the month Chislev, *in* the twentieth year, while I was in Susa the [a]capitol,

2that Hanani, one of my brothers, and some men from Judah came; and I asked them concerning the Jews who had escaped *and* had survived the captivity, and about Jerusalem.

3And they said to me, "The remnant there in the province who survived the captivity are in great distress and reproach, and the wall of Jerusalem is broken down and its gates are burned with fire."

4¶ Now it came about when I heard these words, I sat down and wept and mourned for days; and I was fasting and praying before the God of heaven.

5And I said, "I beseech Thee, O LORD God of heaven, the great and awesome God, who preserves the covenant and lovingkindness for those who love Him and keep His commandments,

6let Thine ear now be attentive and Thine eyes open to hear the prayer of Thy servant which I am praying before Thee now, day and night, on behalf of the sons of Israel Thy servants, confessing the sins of the sons of Israel which we have sinned against Thee; I and my father's house have sinned.

7"We have acted very corruptly against Thee and have not kept the commandments, nor the statutes, nor the ordinances which Thou didst command Thy servant Moses.

8"Remember the word which Thou didst command Thy servant Moses, saying, 'If you are unfaithful I will scatter you among the peoples;

9but if you return to Me and keep My commandments and do them, though those of you who have been scattered were in the most remote part of the heavens, I will gather them from there and will bring them to the place where I have chosen to cause My name to dwell.'

10"And they are Thy servants and Thy people whom Thou didst redeem by Thy great power and by Thy strong hand.

11"O Lord, I beseech Thee, may Thine ear be attentive to the prayer of Thy servant and the prayer of Thy servants who delight to revere Thy name, and make Thy servant successful today, and grant him compassion before this man."

¶Now I was the cupbearer to the king.

*Nehemiah's Prayer Answered*

**2** AND IT came about in the month Nisan, in the twentieth year of King Artaxerxes, that wine *was* before him, and I took up the wine and gave it to the king. Now I had not been sad in his presence.

2So the king said to me, "Why is your face sad though you are not sick? This is nothing but sadness of heart." Then I was very much afraid.

NAS [a] Or, *palace* or *citadel*

## New International

# Nehemiah

*Nehemiah's Prayer*

**1** THE WORDS of Nehemiah son of Hacaliah:

In the month of Kislev in the twentieth year, while I was in the citadel of Susa, 2Hanani, one of my brothers, came from Judah with some other men, and I questioned them about the Jewish remnant that survived the exile, and also about Jerusalem.

3They said to me, "Those who survived the exile and are back in the province are in great trouble and disgrace. The wall of Jerusalem is broken down, and its gates have been burned with fire."

4When I heard these things, I sat down and wept. For some days I mourned and fasted and prayed before the God of heaven. 5Then I said:

"O LORD, God of heaven, the great and awesome God, who keeps his covenant of love with those who love him and obey his commands, 6let your ear be attentive and your eyes open to hear the prayer your servant is praying before you day and night for your servants, the people of Israel. I confess the sins we Israelites, including myself and my father's house, have committed against you. 7We have acted very wickedly toward you. We have not obeyed the commands, decrees and laws you gave your servant Moses.

8"Remember the instruction you gave your servant Moses, saying, 'If you are unfaithful, I will scatter you among the nations, 9but if you return to me and obey my commands, then even if your exiled people are at the farthest horizon, I will gather them from there and bring them to the place I have chosen as a dwelling for my Name.'

10"They are your servants and your people, whom you redeemed by your great strength and your mighty hand. 11O Lord, let your ear be attentive to the prayer of this your servant and to the prayer of your servants who delight in revering your name. Give your servant success today by granting him favor in the presence of this man."

I was cupbearer to the king.

*Artaxerxes Sends Nehemiah to Jerusalem*

**2** IN THE month of Nisan in the twentieth year of King Artaxerxes, when wine was brought for him, I took the wine and gave it to the king. I had not been sad in his presence before; 2so the king asked me, "Why does your face look so sad when you are not ill? This can be nothing but sadness of heart."

I was very much afraid, 3but I said to the king, "May the king

## King James

3 And said unto the king, Let the king live for ever: why should not my countenance be sad, when the city, the place of my fathers' sepulchres, *lieth* waste, and the gates thereof are consumed with fire?

4 Then the king said unto me, For what dost thou make request? So I prayed to the God of heaven.

5 And I said unto the king, If it please the king, and if thy servant have found favour in thy sight, that thou wouldest send me unto Judah, unto the city of my fathers' sepulchres, that I may build it.

6 And the king said unto me, (the queen also sitting by him,) For how long shall thy journey be? and when wilt thou return? So it pleased the king to send me; and I set him a time.

7 Moreover I said unto the king, If it please the king, let letters be given me to the governors beyond the river, that they may convey me over till I come into Judah;

8 And a letter unto Asaph the keeper of the king's forest, that he may give me timber to make beams for the gates of the palace which *appertained* to the house, and for the wall of the city, and for the house that I shall enter into. And the king granted me, according to the good hand of my God upon me.

9 ¶ Then I came to the governors beyond the river, and gave them the king's letters. Now the king had sent captains of the army and horsemen with me.

10 When Sanballat the Horonite, and Tobiah the servant, the Ammonite, heard *of it*, it grieved them exceedingly that there was come a man to seek the welfare of the children of Israel.

11 So I came to Jerusalem, and was there three days.

12 ¶ And I arose in the night, I and some few men with me; neither told I *any* man what my God had put in my heart to do at Jerusalem: neither *was there any* beast with me, save the beast that I rode upon.

13 And I went out by night by the gate of the valley, even before the dragon well, and to the dung port, and viewed the walls of Jerusalem, which were broken down, and the gates thereof were consumed with fire.

14 Then I went on to the gate of the fountain, and to the king's pool: but *there was* no place for the beast *that was* under me to pass.

15 Then went I up in the night by the brook, and viewed the wall, and turned back, and entered by the gate of the valley, and *so* returned.

16 And the rulers knew not whither I went, or what I did; neither had I as yet told *it* to the Jews, nor to the priests, nor to the nobles, nor to the rulers, nor to the rest that did the work.

17 ¶ Then said I unto them, Ye see the distress that we *are* in, how Jerusalem *lieth* waste, and the gates therof are burned with fire: come, and let us build up the wall of Jerusalem, that we be no more a reproach.

18 Then I told them of the hand of my God which was good upon me; as also the king's words that he had spoken unto me. And they said, Let us rise up and build. So they strengthened their hands for *this* good *work*.

19 But when Sanballat the Horonite, and Tobiah the servant, the Ammonite, and Geshem the Arabian, heard *it*, they laughed us to scorn, and despised us, and said, What *is* this thing that ye do? will ye rebel against the king?

20 Then answered I them, and said unto them, The God of heaven, he will prosper us; therefore we his servants will arise and build: but ye have no portion, nor right, nor memorial, in Jerusalem.

**3** THEN ELIASHIB the high priest rose up with his brethren the priests, and they builded the sheep gate; they sanctified it, and set up the doors of it; even unto the tower of Meah they sanctified it, unto the tower of Hananeel.

## Amplified

3 And said to the king, Let the king live for ever! Why should I not be sad faced, when the city, the place of my fathers' sepulchers, lies waste, and its [fortified] gates are consumed by fire?

4 The king said to me, For what do you ask? So I prayed to the God of Heaven.

5 And I said to [him], If it pleases the king, and if your servant has found favor in your sight, I ask that you will send me to Judah, to the city of my fathers' sepulchers, that I may rebuild it.

6 The king, beside whom the queen was sitting, asked me, How long will your journey take, and when will you return? So it pleased [him] to send me; and I set him a time.

7 Also I said to the king, If it pleases the king, let letters be given me to the governors beyond the [Euphrates] River, that they may let me pass through to Judah;

8 And a letter to Asaph, keeper of the king's forest *or* park, that he may give me timber to make beams for the gates of the fortress of the temple, and for the city's wall, and for the house that I shall occupy. And the king granted what I asked, for the good hand of my God was upon me.

9 Then I came to the governors beyond the River, and gave them the king's letters. Now the king had sent captains of the army and horsemen with me.

10 When Sanballat the Horonite and Tobiah the servant, the Ammonite, heard this, it distressed them exceedingly that a man had come to inquire for *and* require the good *and* prosperity of the Israelites.

11 So I came to Jerusalem, and had been there three days.

12 Then I arose in the night, I and a few men with me; and I told no one what my God had put in my heart to do for Jerusalem. No beast was with me except the one I rode.

13 I went out by night by the Valley Gate toward the Dragon's Well and to the Dung Gate, and inspected the walls of Jerusalem which were broken down and its gates which had been destroyed by fire.

14 I passed over to the Fountain Gate and to the King's Pool; but there was no place for the beast that was under me to pass.

15 So [gradually] I went up by the brook [Kedron] in the night and inspected the wall; then I turned back and entered [the city] by the Valley Gate, and so returned.

16 And the magistrates knew not where I went, or what I did; nor had I yet told the Jews, the priests, the nobles, the officials, or the rest who did the work.

17 Then I said to them, You see the bad situation we are in, how Jerusalem lies waste and its gates are burned with fire. Come, let us build up the wall of Jerusalem, that we may no longer be a disgrace.

18 Then I told them of the hand of my God which was upon me for good, and also the words that the king had spoken to me. And they said, Let us rise up and build! So they strengthened their hands for the good work.

19 But when Sanballat the Horonite and Tobiah the servant, the Ammonite, and Geshem the Arab heard of it, they laughed us to scorn and despised us and said, What is this thing you are doing? Will you rebel against the king?

20 I answered them, The God of Heaven will prosper us, therefore we His servants will arise and build; but you have no portion or right or memorial in Jerusalem.

**3** THEN ELIASHIB the high priest rose up with his brethren the priests and built the Sheep Gate. They consecrated it and set up its doors; they consecrated it even to the Tower of Hammeah *or* The Hundred, as far as the Tower of Hananel.

## New American Standard

3And I said to the king, "Let the king live forever. Why should
my face not be sad when the city, the place of my fathers' tombs,
lies desolate and its gates have been consumed by fire?"
4Then the king said to me, "What would you request?" So I
prayed to the God of heaven.
5And I said to the king, "If it please the king, and if your
servant has found favor before you, send me to Judah, to the city
of my fathers' tombs, that I may rebuild it."
6Then the king said to me, the queen sitting beside him, "How
long will your journey be, and when will you return?" So it pleased
the king to send me, and I gave him a definite time.
7And I said to the king, "If it please the king, let letters be given
me for the governors *of the provinces* beyond the River, that they
may allow me to pass through until I come to Judah,
8and a letter to Asaph the keeper of the king's forest, that he
may give me timber to make beams for the gates of the fortress
which is by the [a]temple, for the wall of the city, and for the house
to which I will go." And the king granted *them* to me because the
good hand of my God *was* on me.
9¶ Then I came to the governors *of the provinces* beyond the
River and gave them the king's letters. Now the king had sent with
me officers of the army and horsemen.
10And when Sanballat the Horonite and Tobiah the Ammonite
official heard *about it*, it was very displeasing to them that someone
had come to seek the welfare of the sons of Israel.

*Nehemiah Inspects Jerusalem's Walls*

11So I came to Jerusalem and was there three days.
12And I arose in the night, I and a few men with me. I did not
tell anyone what my God was putting into my mind to do for
Jerusalem and there was no animal with me except the animal on
which I was riding.
13So I went out at night by the Valley Gate in the direction of
the Dragon's Well and *on* to the Refuse Gate, inspecting the walls
of Jerusalem which were broken down and its gates which were
consumed by fire.
14Then I passed on to the Fountain Gate and the King's Pool,
but there was no place for my mount to pass.
15So I went up at night by the ravine and inspected the wall.
Then I entered the Valley Gate again and returned.
16And the officials did not know where I had gone or what I had
done; nor had I as yet told the Jews, the priests, the nobles, the
officials, or the rest who did the work.
17¶ Then I said to them, "You see the bad situation we are in,
that Jerusalem is desolate and its gates burned by fire. Come, let
us rebuild the wall of Jerusalem that we may no longer be a
reproach."
18And I told them how the hand of my God had been favorable
to me, and also about the king's words which he had spoken to
me. Then they said, "Let us arise and build." So they put their
hands to the good *work*.
19But when Sanballat the Horonite, and Tobiah the Ammonite
official, and Geshem the Arab heard *it*, they mocked us and despised us and said, "What is this thing you are doing? Are you
rebelling against the king?"
20So I answered them and said to them, "The God of heaven
will give us success; therefore we His servants will arise and build,
but you have no portion, right, or memorial in Jerusalem."

*Builders of the Walls*

**3** THEN ELIASHIB the high priest arose with his brothers the
priests and built the Sheep Gate; they consecrated it and hung
its doors. They consecrated the wall to the Tower of the Hundred
*and* the Tower of Hananel.

NAS [a] Lit., *house*

## New International

live forever! Why should my face not look sad when the city where
my fathers are buried lies in ruins, and its gates have been destroyed by fire?"
4The king said to me, "What is it you want?"
Then I prayed to the God of heaven, 5and I answered the king,
"If it pleases the king and if your servant has found favor in his
sight, let him send me to the city in Judah where my fathers are
buried so that I can rebuild it."
6Then the king, with the queen sitting beside him, asked me,
"How long will your journey take, and when will you get back?"
It pleased the king to send me; so I set a time.
7I also said to him, "If it pleases the king, may I have letters to
the governors of Trans-Euphrates, so that they will provide me
safe-conduct until I arrive in Judah? 8And may I have a letter to
Asaph, keeper of the king's forest, so he will give me timber to
make beams for the gates of the citadel by the temple and for the
city wall and for the residence I will occupy?" And because the
gracious hand of my God was upon me, the king granted my
requests. 9So I went to the governors of Trans-Euphrates and gave
them the king's letters. The king had also sent army officers and
cavalry with me.
10When Sanballat the Horonite and Tobiah the Ammonite official heard about this, they were very much disturbed that someone
had come to promote the welfare of the Israelites.

*Nehemiah Inspects Jerusalem's Walls*

11I went to Jerusalem, and after staying there three days 12I set
out during the night with a few men. I had not told anyone what
my God had put in my heart to do for Jerusalem. There were no
mounts with me except the one I was riding on.
13By night I went out through the Valley Gate toward the Jackal[b] Well and the Dung Gate, examining the walls of Jerusalem,
which had been broken down, and its gates, which had been
destroyed by fire. 14Then I moved on toward the Fountain Gate
and the King's Pool, but there was not enough room for my mount
to get through; 15so I went up the valley by night, examining the
wall. Finally, I turned back and reentered through the Valley Gate.
16The officials did not know where I had gone or what I was doing,
because as yet I had said nothing to the Jews or the priests or
nobles or officials or any others who would be doing the work.
17Then I said to them, "You see the trouble we are in: Jerusalem
lies in ruins, and its gates have been burned with fire. Come, let
us rebuild the wall of Jerusalem, and we will no longer be in
disgrace." 18I also told them about the gracious hand of my God
upon me and what the king had said to me.
They replied, "Let us start rebuilding." So they began this good
work.
19But when Sanballat the Horonite, Tobiah the Ammonite official and Geshem the Arab heard about it, they mocked and ridiculed us. "What is this you are doing?" they asked. "Are you
rebelling against the king?"
20I answered them by saying, "The God of heaven will give us
success. We his servants will start rebuilding, but as for you, you
have no share in Jerusalem or any claim or historic right to it."

*Builders of the Wall*

**3** ELIASHIB THE high priest and his fellow priests went to
work and rebuilt the Sheep Gate. They dedicated it and set
its doors in place, building as far as the Tower of the Hundred,
which they dedicated, and as far as the Tower of Hananel. 2The

NIV [b] 13 Or *Serpent* or *Fig*

## King James

2And next unto him builded the men of Jericho. And next to them builded Zaccur the son of Imri.

3But the fish gate did the sons of Hassenaah build, who *also* laid the beams thereof, and set up the doors thereof, the locks thereof, and the bars thereof.

4And next unto them repaired Meremoth the son of Urijah, the son of Koz. And next unto them repaired Meshullam the son of Berechiah, the son of Meshezabeel. And next unto them repaired Zadok the son of Baana.

5And next unto them the Tekoites repaired; but their nobles put not their necks to the work of their Lord.

6Moreover the old gate repaired Jehoiada the son of Paseah, and Meshullam the son of Besodeiah; they laid the beams thereof, and set up the doors thereof, and the locks thereof, and the bars thereof.

7And next unto them repaired Melatiah the Gibeonite, and Jadon the Meronothite, the men of Gibeon, and of Mizpah, unto the throne of the governor on this side the river.

8Next unto him repaired Uzziel the son of Harhaiah, of the goldsmiths. Next unto him also repaired Hananiah the son of *one of* the apothecaries, and they fortified Jerusalem unto the broad wall.

9And next unto them repaired Rephaiah the son of Hur, the ruler of the half part of Jerusalem.

10And next unto them repaired Jedaiah the son of Harumaph, even over against his house. And next unto him repaired Hattush the son of Hashabniah.

11Malchijah the son of Harim, and Hashub the son of Pahath-moab, repaired the other piece, and the tower of the furnaces.

12And next unto him repaired Shallum the son of Halohesh, the ruler of the half part of Jerusalem, he and his daughters.

13The valley gate repaired Hanun, and the inhabitants of Zanoah; they built it, and set up the doors thereof, the locks thereof, and the bars thereof, and a thousand cubits on the wall unto the dung gate.

14But the dung gate repaired Malchiah the son of Rechab, the ruler of part of Beth-haccerem; he built it, and set up the doors thereof, the locks thereof, and the bars thereof.

15But the gate of the fountain repaired Shallun the son of Colhozeh, the ruler of part of Mizpah; he built it, and covered it, and set up the doors thereof, the locks thereof, and the bars thereof, and the wall of the pool of Siloah by the king's garden, and unto the stairs that go down from the city of David.

16After him repaired Nehemiah the son of Azbuk, the ruler of the half part of Beth-zur, unto *the place* over against the sepulchres of David, and to the pool that was made, and unto the house of the mighty.

17After him repaired the Levites, Rehum the son of Bani. Next unto him repaired Hashabiah, the ruler of the half part of Keilah, in his part.

18After him repaired their brethren, Bavai the son of Henadad, the ruler of the half part of Keilah.

19And next to him repaired Ezer the son of Jeshua, the ruler of Mizpah, another piece over against the going up to the armoury at the turning *of the wall*.

20After him Baruch the son of Zabbai earnestly repaired the other piece, from the turning *of the wall* unto the door of the house of Eliashib the high priest.

21After him repaired Meremoth the son of Urijah the son of Koz another piece, from the door of the house of Eliashib even to the end of the house of Eliashib.

22And after him repaired the priests, the men of the plain.

23After him repaired Benjamin and Hashub over against their house. After him repaired Azariah the son of Maaseiah the son of Ananiah by his house.

24After him repaired Binnui the son of Henadad another piece, from the house of Azariah unto the turning *of the wall*, even unto the corner.

## Amplified

2And next to him the men of Jericho built. Next to [them] Zaccur son of Imri built.

3And the Fish Gate the sons of Hassenaah built; they laid its beams and set up its doors, its bolts, and its bars.

4And next to them Meremoth son of Uriah, son of Hakkoz, repaired. Next to them Meshullam son of Berechiah, son of Meshezabel repaired. Next to them Zadok son of Baana repaired.

5Next to them the Tekoites repaired; but their nobles *or* lords did not put their necks to the work of their Lord.

6Moreover the Old Gate Joiada son of Paseah, and Meshullam son of Besodeiah repaired. They laid its beams and set up its doors, its bolts, and its bars.

7Next to them repaired Melatiah the Gibeonite and Jadon the Meronothite, the men of Gibeon and of Mizpah, [up] to the seat or residence of the governor [west of] the River [Euphrates, there in Jerusalem].

8Next to them repaired Uzziel son of Harhaiah, goldsmiths. Next to him repaired Hananiah, one of the perfumers, and they abandoned *fortification* of Jerusalem as far as the Broad Wall [omitting that part of the ancient city and reducing the area].

9Next to them repaired Rephaiah son of Hur, ruler of half the district of Jerusalem.

10Next to them repaired Jedaiah the son of Harumaph, opposite his own house. And next to him repaired Hattush the son of Hashabneiah.

11Malchijah son of Harim and Hasshub son of Pahath-moab repaired another portion and the Tower of the Furnaces.

12Next to [them] repaired Shallum son of Hallohesh, the ruler of half the district of Jerusalem, he and his daughters.

13The Valley Gate [the main entrance in the west wall, the Jaffa Gate] was repaired by Hanun and the inhabitants of Zanoah; they built it and set up its doors, its bolts, and its bars and repaired a thousand cubits of the wall, as far as the Dung Gate.

14The Dung Gate was repaired by Malchijah the son of Rechab, the ruler of the district of Beth-haccherem; he rebuilt it and set its doors, its bolts, and its bars.

15The Fountain Gate was repaired by Shallum son of Colhozeh, ruler of the district of Mizpah; he rebuilt and covered it, and set up its doors, its bolts, and its bars, and the wall of the Pool of Shelah [Siloam] of the king's garden, as far as the stairs that go down [the eastern slope] from the [portion of Jerusalem known as] the City of David.

16After him Nehemiah [III] son of Azbuk, ruler of half the district of Beth-zur, repaired [the wall] to a point opposite the sepulchers of David, and to the artificial pool and to the house of the guards.

17After him the Levites: Rehum son of Bani; next to him repaired Hashabiah, ruler of half the district of Keilah.

18After him repaired their brethren, Bavvai son of Henadad, ruler of [the other] half of the district of Keilah.

19Next to him repaired Ezer son of Jeshua, ruler of Mizpah, another district over opposite the ascent to the armory at the Angle [in the wall].

20After him Baruch son of Zabbai [Zaccai] earnestly repaired another portion [toward the hill] from the angular turning of the wall to the door of the house of Eliashib the high priest.

21After him Meremoth son of Uriah, son of Hakkoz, repaired from the door of Eliashib's house to the end of his house.

22After him the priests, men of the Plain, repaired.

23After them Benjamin and Hasshub repaired opposite their house. After them repaired Azariah son of Maaseiah, son of Ananiah beside his own house.

24After him Binnui son of Henadad repaired another section [of the wall], from the house of Azariah to the angular turn of the wall and to the corner.

## New American Standard

2And next to him the men of Jericho built, and next to them Zaccur the son of Imri built.

3¶ Now the sons of Hassenaah built the Fish Gate; they laid its beams and hung its doors with its bolts and bars.

4And next to them Meremoth the son of Uriah the son of Hakkoz made repairs. And next to him Meshullam the son of Berechiah the son of Meshezabel made repairs. And next to him Zadok the son of Baana also made repairs.

5Moreover, next to him the Tekoites made repairs, but their nobles did not support the work of their masters.

6¶ And Joiada the son of Paseah and Meshullam the son of Besodeiah repaired the Old Gate; they laid its beams and hung its doors, with its bolts and its bars.

7Next to them Melatiah the Gibeonite and Jadon the Meronothite, the men of Gibeon and of Mizpah, also made repairs for the official seat of the governor *of the province* beyond the River.

8Next to him Uzziel the son of Harhaiah of the goldsmiths made repairs. And next to him Hananiah, one of the perfumers, made repairs, and they restored Jerusalem as far as the Broad Wall.

9And next to them Rephaiah the son of Hur, the official of half the district of Jerusalem, made repairs.

10Next to them Jedaiah the son of Harumaph made repairs opposite his house. And next to him Hattush the son of Hashabneiah made repairs.

11Malchijah the son of Harim and Hasshub the son of Pahath-moab repaired another section and the Tower of Furnaces.

12And next to him Shallum the son of Hallohesh, the official of half the district of Jerusalem, made repairs, he and his daughters.

13Hanun and the inhabitants of Zanoah repaired the Valley Gate. They built it and hung its doors with its bolts and its bars, and a thousand cubits of the wall to the Refuse Gate.

14And Malchijah the son of Rechab, the official of the district of Beth-haccherem repaired the Refuse Gate. He built it and hung its doors with its bolts and its bars.

15Shallum the son of Col-hozeh, the official of the district of Mizpah, repaired the Fountain Gate. He built it, covered it, and hung its doors with its bolts and its bars, and the wall of the Pool of Shelah at the king's garden as far as the steps that descend from the city of David.

16After him Nehemiah the son of Azbuk, official of half the district of Beth-zur, made repairs as far as *a point* opposite the tombs of David, and as far as the artificial pool and the house of the mighty men.

17After him the Levites carried out repairs *under* Rehum the son of Bani. Next to him Hashabiah, the official of half the district of Keilah, carried out repairs for his district.

18After him their brothers carried out repairs *under* Bavvai the son of Henadad, official of *the other* half of the district of Keilah.

19And next to him Ezer the son of Jeshua, the official of Mizpah, repaired another section, in front of the ascent of the armory at the Angle.

20After him Baruch the son of Zabbai zealously repaired another section, from the Angle to the doorway of the house of Eliashib the high priest.

21After him Meremoth the son of Uriah the son of Hakkoz repaired another section, from the doorway of Eliashib's house even as far as the end of his house.

22And after him the priests, the men of the [a]valley, carried out repairs.

23After them Benjamin and Hasshub carried out repairs in front of their house. After them Azariah the son of Maaseiah, son of Ananiah carried out repairs beside his house.

24After him Binnui the son of Henadad repaired another section, from the house of Azariah as far as the Angle and as far as the corner.

NAS [a] Lit., *circle;* i.e., lower Jordan valley

## New International

men of Jericho built the adjoining section, and Zaccur son of Imri
built next to them.

3The Fish Gate was rebuilt by the sons of Hassenaah. They laid
its beams and put its doors and bolts and bars in place. 4Meremoth
son of Uriah, the son of Hakkoz, repaired the next section. Next
to him Meshullam son of Berekiah, the son of Meshezabel, made
repairs, and next to him Zadok son of Baana also made repairs.
5The next section was repaired by the men of Tekoa, but their
nobles would not put their shoulders to the work under their
supervisors.[b]

6The Jeshanah[c] Gate was repaired by Joiada son of Paseah and
Meshullam son of Besodeiah. They laid its beams and put its doors
and bolts and bars in place. 7Next to them, repairs were made by
men from Gibeon and Mizpah—Melatiah of Gibeon and Jadon of
Meronoth—places under the authority of the governor of Trans-
Euphrates. 8Uzziel son of Harhaiah, one of the goldsmiths, repaired the next section; and Hananiah, one of the perfume-mak-
ers, made repairs next to that. They restored[d] Jerusalem as far as
the Broad Wall. 9Rephaiah son of Hur, ruler of a half-district of
Jerusalem, repaired the next section. 10Adjoining this, Jedaiah son
of Harumaph made repairs opposite his house, and Hattush son
of Hashabneiah made repairs next to him. 11Malkijah son of Harim
and Hasshub son of Pahath-Moab repaired another section and the
Tower of the Ovens. 12Shallum son of Hallohesh, ruler of a half-
district of Jerusalem, repaired the next section with the help of his
daughters.

13The Valley Gate was repaired by Hanun and the residents of
Zanoah. They rebuilt it and put its doors and bolts and bars in
place. They also repaired five hundred yards[e] of the wall as far as
the Dung Gate.

14The Dung Gate was repaired by Malkijah son of Recab, ruler
of the district of Beth Hakkerem. He rebuilt it and put its doors and
bolts and bars in place.

15The Fountain Gate was repaired by Shallun son of Col-Hozeh,
ruler of the district of Mizpah. He rebuilt it, roofing it over and
putting its doors and bolts and bars in place. He also repaired the
wall of the Pool of Siloam,[f] by the King's Garden, as far as the
steps going down from the City of David. 16Beyond him, Nehemiah son of Azbuk, ruler of a half-district of Beth Zur, made
repairs up to a point opposite the tombs[g] of David, as far as the
artificial pool and the House of the Heroes.

17Next to him, the repairs were made by the Levites under
Rehum son of Bani. Beside him, Hashabiah, ruler of half the district of Keilah, carried out repairs for his district. 18Next to him, the
repairs were made by their countrymen under Binnui[h] son of
Henadad, ruler of the other half-district of Keilah. 19Next to him,
Ezer son of Jeshua, ruler of Mizpah, repaired another section, from
a point facing the ascent to the armory as far as the angle. 20Next
to him, Baruch son of Zabbai zealously repaired another section,
from the angle to the entrance of the house of Eliashib the high
priest. 21Next to him, Meremoth son of Uriah, the son of Hakkoz,
repaired another section, from the entrance of Eliashib's house to
the end of it.

22The repairs next to him were made by the priests from the
surrounding region. 23Beyond them, Benjamin and Hasshub made
repairs in front of their house; and next to them, Azariah son of
Maaseiah, the son of Ananiah, made repairs beside his house.
24Next to him, Binnui son of Henadad repaired another section,
from Azariah's house to the angle and the corner, 25and Palal son

NIV [b] *5* Or *their Lord* or *the governor* [c] *6* Or *Old* [d] *8* Or *They left out part of* [e] *13* Hebrew *a thousand cubits* (about 450 meters) [f] *15* Hebrew *Shelah,* a variant of *Shiloah,* that is, Siloam [g] *16* Hebrew; Septuagint, some Vulgate manuscripts and Syriac *tomb* [h] *18* Two Hebrew manuscripts and Syriac (see also Septuagint and verse 24); most Hebrew manuscripts *Bavvai*

# King James

25Palal the son of Uzai, over against the turning *of the wall*, and
the tower which lieth out from the king's high house, that *was* by
the court of the prison. After him Pedaiah the son of Parosh.
26Moreover the Nethinims dwelt in Ophel, unto *the place* over
against the water gate toward the east, and the tower that lieth out.
27After them the Tekoites repaired another piece, over against
the great tower that lieth out, even unto the wall of Ophel.
28From above the horse gate repaired the priests, every one over
against his house.
29After them repaired Zadok the son of Immer over against his
house. After him repaired also Shemaiah the son of Shechaniah,
the keeper of the east gate.
30After him repaired Hananiah the son of Shelemiah, and
Hanun the sixth son of Zalaph, another piece. After him repaired
Meshullam the son of Berechiah over against his chamber.
31After him repaired Malchiah the goldsmith's son unto the
place of the Nethinims, and of the merchants, over against the gate
Miphkad, and to the going up of the corner.
32And between the going up of the corner unto the sheep gate
repaired the goldsmiths and the merchants.

4 BUT IT came to pass, that when Sanballat heard that we
builded the wall, he was wroth, and took great indignation,
and mocked the Jews.
2And he spake before his brethren and the army of Samaria,
and said, What do these feeble Jews? will they fortify themselves?
will they sacrifice? will they make an end in a day? will they revive
the stones out of the heaps of the rubbish which are burned?
3Now Tobiah the Ammonite *was* by him, and he said, Even that
which they build, if a fox go up, he shall even break down their
stone wall.
4Hear, O our God; for we are despised: and turn their reproach
upon their own head, and give them for a prey in the land of
captivity:
5And cover not their iniquity, and let not their sin be blotted out
from before thee: for they have provoked *thee* to anger before the
builders.
6So built we the wall; and all the wall was joined together unto
the half thereof: for the people had a mind to work.
7¶ But it came to pass, *that* when Sanballat, and Tobiah, and the
Arabians, and the Ammonites, and the Ashdodites, heard that the
walls of Jerusalem were made up, *and* that the breaches began to
be stopped, then they were very wroth,
8And conspired all of them together to come *and* to fight against
Jerusalem, and to hinder it.
9Nevertheless we made our prayer unto our God, and set a
watch against them day and night, because of them.
10And Judah said, The strength of the bearers of burdens is
decayed, and *there is* much rubbish; so that we are not able to build
the wall.
11And our adversaries said, They shall not know, neither see,
till we come in the midst among them, and slay them, and cause
the work to cease.
12And it came to pass, that when the Jews which dwelt by them
came, they said unto us ten times, From all places whence ye shall
return unto us *they will be upon you.*
13¶ Therefore set I in the lower places behind the wall, *and* on
the higher places, I even set the people after their families with
their swords, their spears, and their bows.

# Amplified

25Palal son of Uzai repaired opposite the angular turn of the
wall, and the tower which stands out from the upper house of the
king, by the court of the guard. After him Pedaiah son of Parosh
26And the servants of the priests dwelling on Ophel [the hill
south of the temple] repaired to opposite the Water Gate on the
east and the projecting tower.
27After them the Tekoites repaired another portion opposite the
great projecting tower to the wall of Ophel.
28Above the Horse Gate the priests repaired, every one opposite his own house.
29After them repaired Zadok son of Immer opposite his house;
then Shemaiah son of Shecaniah, keeper of the East Gate.
30After him Hananiah son of Shelemiah, and Hanun sixth son
of Zalaph repaired another section. After him Meshullam son of
Berechiah repaired opposite his chamber.
31After him Malchijah, one of the goldsmiths, repaired as far as
the house of the temple servants and of the merchants, opposite
the Muster Gate, and to the ascent *and* upper room of the corner.
32And from the ascent *and* upper room of the corner to the
Sheep Gate the goldsmiths and merchants repaired.

4 BUT WHEN Sanballat heard that we were building the wall,
he was angry and in a great rage, and ridiculed the Jews.
2And he said before his brethren and the army of Samaria, What
are these feeble Jews doing? Will they restore things [at will and
by themselves]? Will they [try to bribe their God] with sacrifices?
Will they finish up in a day? Will they revive the stones out of the
heaps of rubbish, seeing they are burned?
3Now Tobiah the Ammonite was near him, and he said, What
they build, if a fox climbs upon it, he will break down their stone
wall.
4[And Nehemiah prayed] Hear, O our God, for we are despised; turn their taunt upon their own heads, and give them for
a prey in a land of their captivity.
5Cover not their iniquity and let not their sin be blotted out
before You; for they have vexed [with alarm] the builders *and*
provoked You.
6So we built the wall; and all [of it] was joined together to half
its height; for the people had a heart *and* mind to work.
7But when Sanballat, Tobiah, the Arabians, Ammonites, and
Ashdodites, heard that the walls of Jerusalem were going up, and
that the breaches were being closed, they were very angry;
8And they all plotted together to come and fight against Jerusalem, to injure *and* cause confusion *and* failure in it.
9But because of them we made our prayer to our God, and set
a watch against them day and night.
10And [the leaders of] Judah said, The strength of the burden-
bearers is weakening, and there is much rubbish; we are not able
to work on the wall.
11And our enemies said, They will not know or see till we come
into their midst and kill them and stop the work.
12And when the Jews who lived near them came, they said to
us ten times, You must return [to guard our little villages]; from
all places where they dwell they will be upon us.
13So I set *armed men* behind the wall in places where it was least
protection; I even thus used the people as families with their
swords, spears, and bows.

## New American Standard

25Palal the son of Uzai *made repairs* in front of the Angle and the
tower projecting from the upper house of the king, which is by the
court of the guard. After him Pedaiah the son of Parosh *made
repairs*.
26And the temple servants living in Ophel *made repairs* as far as
the front of the Water Gate toward the east and the projecting
tower.
27After him the Tekoites repaired another section in front of the
great projecting tower and as far as the wall of Ophel.
28¶ Above the Horse Gate the priests carried out repairs, each
in front of his house.
29After them Zadok the son of Immer carried out repairs in front
of his house. And after him Shemaiah the son of Shecaniah, the
keeper of the East Gate, carried out repairs.
30After him Hananiah the son of Shelemiah, and Hanun the
sixth son of Zalaph, repaired another section. After him Meshullam the son of Berechiah carried out repairs in front of his own
quarters.
31After him Malchijah one of the goldsmiths, carried out repairs
as far as the house of the temple servants and of the merchants,
in front of the Inspection Gate and as far as the upper room of the
corner.
32And between the upper room of the corner and the Sheep
Gate the goldsmiths and the merchants carried out repairs.

*Work Is Ridiculed*

4 NOW IT came about that when Sanballat heard that we were
rebuilding the wall, he became furious and very angry and
mocked the Jews.
2And he spoke in the presence of his brothers and the wealthy
*men* of Samaria and said, "What are these feeble Jews doing? Are
they going to restore *it* for themselves? Can they offer sacrifices?
Can they finish in a day? Can they revive the stones from the dusty
rubble even the burned ones?"
3Now Tobiah the Ammonite *was* near him and he said, "Even
what they are building—if a fox should jump on *it*, he would break
their stone wall down!"
4¶ Hear, O our God, how we are despised! Return their reproach on their own heads and give them up for plunder in a land
of captivity.
5Do not forgive their iniquity and let not their sin be blotted
out before Thee, for they have demoralized the builders.
6So we built the wall and the whole wall was joined together
to half its *height*, for the people had a mind to work.
7¶ Now it came about when Sanballat, Tobiah, the Arabs, the
Ammonites, and the Ashdodites heard that the repair of the walls
of Jerusalem went on, *and* that the breaches began to be closed,
they were very angry.
8And all of them conspired together to come *and* fight against
Jerusalem and to cause a disturbance in it.

*Discouragement Overcome*

9But we prayed to our God, and because of them we set up a
guard against them day and night.
10Thus in Judah it was said,
"The strength of the burden bearers is failing,
Yet there is much rubbish;
And we ourselves are unable
To rebuild the wall."
11And our enemies said, "They will not know or see until we
come among them, kill them, and put a stop to the work."
12And it came about when the Jews who lived near them came
and told us ten times, "They will come up against us from every
place where you may turn,"
13then I stationed *men* in the lowest parts of the space behind
the wall, the exposed places, and I stationed the people in families
with their swords, spears, and bows.

## New International

of Uzai worked opposite the angle and the tower projecting from
the upper palace near the court of the guard. Next to him, Pedaiah
son of Parosh 26and the temple servants living on the hill of Ophel
made repairs up to a point opposite the Water Gate toward the east
and the projecting tower. 27Next to them, the men of Tekoa repaired another section, from the great projecting tower to the wall
of Ophel.

28Above the Horse Gate, the priests made repairs, each in front
of his own house. 29Next to them, Zadok son of Immer made
repairs opposite his house. Next to him, Shemaiah son of Shecaniah, the guard at the East Gate, made repairs. 30Next to him,
Hananiah son of Shelemiah, and Hanun, the sixth son of Zalaph,
repaired another section. Next to them, Meshullam son of Berekiah made repairs opposite his living quarters. 31Next to him,
Malkijah, one of the goldsmiths, made repairs as far as the house
of the temple servants and the merchants, opposite the Inspection
Gate, and as far as the room above the corner; 32and between the
room above the corner and the Sheep Gate the goldsmiths and
merchants made repairs.

*Opposition to the Rebuilding*

4 WHEN SANBALLAT heard that we were rebuilding the wall,
he became angry and was greatly incensed. He ridiculed the
Jews, 2and in the presence of his associates and the army of Samaria, he said, "What are those feeble Jews doing? Will they
restore their wall? Will they offer sacrifices? Will they finish in a
day? Can they bring the stones back to life from those heaps of
rubble—burned as they are?"
3Tobiah the Ammonite, who was at his side, said, "What they
are building—if even a fox climbed up on it, he would break down
their wall of stones!"

4Hear us, O our God, for we are despised. Turn their insults
back on their own heads. Give them over as plunder in a land of
captivity. 5Do not cover up their guilt or blot out their sins from
your sight, for they have thrown insults in the face of[a] the builders.

6So we rebuilt the wall till all of it reached half its height, for the
people worked with all their heart.
7But when Sanballat, Tobiah, the Arabs, the Ammonites and
the men of Ashdod heard that the repairs to Jerusalem's walls had
gone ahead and that the gaps were being closed, they were very
angry. 8They all plotted together to come and fight against Jerusalem and stir up trouble against it. 9But we prayed to our God and
posted a guard day and night to meet this threat.
10Meanwhile, the people in Judah said, "The strength of the
laborers is giving out, and there is so much rubble that we cannot
rebuild the wall."
11Also our enemies said, "Before they know it or see us, we will
be right there among them and will kill them and put an end to
the work."
12Then the Jews who lived near them came and told us ten times
over, "Wherever you turn, they will attack us."
13Therefore I stationed some of the people behind the lowest
points of the wall at the exposed places, posting them by families,
with their swords, spears and bows. 14After I looked things over,

NIV [a] 5 Or *have provoked you to anger before*

## King James

14And I looked, and rose up, and said unto the nobles, and to
the rulers, and to the rest of the people, Be not ye afraid of them:
remember the Lord, *which is* great and terrible, and fight for your
brethren, your sons, and your daughters, your wives, and your
houses.
15And it came to pass, when our enemies heard that it was
known unto us, and God had brought their counsel to nought, that
we returned all of us to the wall, every one unto his work.
16And it came to pass from that time forth, *that* the half of my
servants wrought in the work, and the other half of them held both
the spears, the shields, and the bows, and the habergeons; and the
rulers *were* behind all the house of Judah.
17They which builded on the wall, and they that bare burdens,
with those that laded, *every one* with one of his hands wrought in
the work, and with the other *hand* held a weapon.
18For the builders, every one had his sword girded by his side,
and *so* builded. And he that sounded the trumpet *was* by me.
19¶ And I said unto the nobles, and to the rulers, and to the rest
of the people, The work *is* great and large, and we are separated
upon the wall, one far from another.
20In what place *therefore* ye hear the sound of the trumpet, resort
ye thither unto us: our God shall fight for us.
21So we laboured in the work: and half of them held the spears
from the rising of the morning till the stars appeared.
22Likewise at the same time said I unto the people, Let every
one with his servant lodge within Jerusalem, that in the night they
may be a guard to us, and labour on the day.
23So neither I, nor my brethren, nor my servants, nor the men
of the guard which followed me, none of us put off our clothes,
*saving that* every one put them off for washing.

**5** AND THERE was a great cry of the people and of their wives
against their brethren the Jews.
2For there were that said, We, our sons, and our daughters, *are*
many: therefore we take up corn *for them*, that we may eat, and
live.
3 *Some* also there were that said, We have mortgaged our lands,
vineyards, and houses, that we might buy corn, because of the
dearth.
4There were also that said, We have borrowed money for the
king's tribute, *and that upon* our lands and vineyards.
5Yet now our flesh *is* as the flesh of our brethren, our children
as their children: and, lo, we bring into bondage our sons and our
daughters to be servants, and *some* of our daughters are brought
unto bondage *already:* neither *is it* in our power *to redeem them;* for
other men have our lands and vineyards.
6¶ And I was very angry when I heard their cry and these
words.
7Then I consulted with myself, and I rebuked the nobles, and
the rulers, and said unto them, Ye exact usury, every one of his
brother. And I set a great assembly against them.
8And I said unto them, We after our ability have redeemed our
brethren the Jews, which were sold unto the heathen; and will ye
even sell your brethren? or shall they be sold unto us? Then held
they their peace, and found nothing *to answer*.
9Also I said, It *is* not good that ye do: ought ye not to walk in
the fear of our God because of the reproach of the heathen our
enemies?
10I likewise, *and* my brethren, and my servants, might exact of
them money and corn: I pray you, let us leave off this usury.
11Restore, I pray you, to them, even this day, their lands, their
vineyards, their oliveyards, and their houses, also the hundredth
*part* of the money, and of the corn, the wine, and the oil, that ye
exact of them.

## Amplified

14I looked [them over] and rose up, and said to the nobles and
officials and the other people, Do not be afraid of the enemy;
[earnestly] remember the Lord *and* imprint Him [on your minds],
great and terrible, and [take from Him courage to] fight for your
brethren, your sons, your daughters, your wives, and your
homes.
15And when our enemies heard that their plot was known to us,
and that God had frustrated their purpose, we all returned to the
wall, every one to his work.
16And from that time forth, half of my servants worked at the
task, and the other half held the spears, shields, bows, and coats
of mail; and the leaders stood behind all the house of Judah.
17Those who built the wall and those who bore burdens loaded
themselves so that every one worked with one hand and held a
weapon with the other hand;
18And every builder had his sword girded by his side, and so
worked. And he who sounded the trumpet was at my side.
19And I said to the nobles and officials and the rest of the
people, The work is great and scattered, and we are separated on
the wall, one far from another.
20In whatever place you hear the sound of the trumpet, rally to
us there; our God will fight for us.
21So we labored at the work, while half of them held the spears
from dawn until the stars came out.
22At that time also I said to the people, Let every one with his
servant lodge within Jerusalem, that at night they may be a guard
to us, and labor during the day.
23So none of us, I, my kinsmen, my servants, nor the men of
the guard who followed me, took off our clothes; each kept his
weapon [in his hand for days].

**5** NOW THERE arose a great cry of the [poor] people and of
their wives [driven to borrowing], against their Jewish brethren [the few who could afford to lend].
2For some said, We, our sons and daughters, are many; therefore allow us to take grain that we may eat and live! If we are not
given grain, let us take it!
3Also some said, We are mortgaging our lands, vineyards, and
houses, to buy grain because of the scarcity.
4Others said, We have borrowed money on our fields and vineyards to pay the [Persian] king's heavy tax.
5Although our flesh is the same as that of our brethren, and our
children are as theirs, yet we are forced to sell our children as
slaves; some of our daughters have already been thus sold; and we
are powerless to redeem them; for others have our lands and
vineyards.
6I [Nehemiah] was very angry when I heard their cry and these
words.
7I thought it over, then rebuked the nobles and officials. I told
them, You are exacting usury from your own kinsmen. And I held
a great assembly against them.
8I said to them, We, according to our ability, have bought back
our Jewish brethren who were sold to the nations; but will you
even sell your brethren that they may be sold to us? Then they
were silent and found not a word to say.
9Also I said, What you are doing is not good. Ought you not
to walk in the fear of our God to prevent the taunts *and* reproach
of the nations our enemies?
10I, my brethren, and my servants are lending them money and
grain. Let us stop this forbidden interest! [Exod. 22:25.]
11Return this very day to them their fields, vineyards, oliveyards, and houses, also a hundredth of all the money, grain, new
wine and oil that you have exacted from them.

## New American Standard

14When I saw *their fear,* I rose and spoke to the nobles, the
officials, and the rest of the people: "Do not be afraid of them;
remember the Lord who is great and awesome, and fight for your
brothers, your sons, your daughters, your wives, and your
houses."
15¶ And it happened when our enemies heard that it was
known to us, and that God had frustrated their plan, then all of
us returned to the wall, each one to his work.
16And it came about from that day on, that half of my servants
carried on the work while half of them held the spears, the shields,
the bows, and the breastplates; and the captains *were* behind the
whole house of Judah.
17Those who were rebuilding the wall and those who carried
burdens took *their* load with one hand doing the work and the
other holding a weapon.
18As for the builders, each *wore* his sword girded at his side as
he built, while the trumpeter *stood* near me.
19And I said to the nobles, the officials, and the rest of the
people, "The work is great and extensive, and we are separated
on the wall far from one another.
20"At whatever place you hear the sound of the trumpet, rally
to us there. Our God will fight for us."
21¶ So we carried on the work with half of them holding spears
from dawn until the stars appeared.
22At that time I also said to the people, "Let each man with his
servant spend the night within Jerusalem so that they may be a
guard for us by night and a laborer by day."
23So neither I, my brothers, my servants, nor the men of the
guard who followed me, none of us removed our clothes, each *took*
his weapon *even to* the water.

*Usury Abolished*

5 NOW THERE was a great outcry of the people and of their
wives against their Jewish brothers.
2For there were those who said, "We, our sons and our daughters, are many; therefore let us get grain that we may eat and live."
3And there were others who said, "We are mortgaging our
fields, our vineyards, and our houses that we might get grain
because of the famine."
4Also there were those who said, "We have borrowed money
for the king's tax *on* our fields and our vineyards.
5"And now our flesh is like the flesh of our brothers, our
children like their children. Yet behold, we are forcing our sons
and our daughters to be slaves, and some of our daughters are
forced into bondage *already,* and we are helpless because our fields
and vineyards belong to others."
6¶ Then I was very angry when I had heard their outcry and
these words.
7And I consulted with myself, and contended with the nobles
and the rulers and said to them, "You are exacting usury, each
from his brother!" Therefore, I held a great assembly against them.
8And I said to them, "We according to our ability have redeemed our Jewish brothers who were sold to the nations; now
would you even sell your brothers that they may be sold to us?"
Then they were silent and could not find a word *to say.*
9Again I said, "The thing which you are doing is not good;
should you not walk in the fear of our God because of the reproach
of the nations, our enemies?
10"And likewise I, my brothers and my servants, are lending
them money and grain. Please, let us leave off this usury.
11"Please, give back to them this very day their fields, their
vineyards, their olive groves, and their houses, also the hundredth
*part* of the money and of the grain, the new wine, and the oil that
you are exacting from them."

## New International

I stood up and said to the nobles, the officials and the rest of the
people, "Don't be afraid of them. Remember the Lord, who is great
and awesome, and fight for your brothers, your sons and your
daughters, your wives and your homes."
15When our enemies heard that we were aware of their plot and
that God had frustrated it, we all returned to the wall, each to his
own work.
16From that day on, half of my men did the work, while the
other half were equipped with spears, shields, bows and armor.
The officers posted themselves behind all the people of Judah
17who were building the wall. Those who carried materials did
their work with one hand and held a weapon in the other, 18and
each of the builders wore his sword at his side as he worked. But
the man who sounded the trumpet stayed with me.
19Then I said to the nobles, the officials and the rest of the
people, "The work is extensive and spread out, and we are widely
separated from each other along the wall. 20Wherever you hear the
sound of the trumpet, join us there. Our God will fight for us!"
21So we continued the work with half the men holding spears,
from the first light of dawn till the stars came out. 22At that time
I also said to the people, "Have every man and his helper stay
inside Jerusalem at night, so they can serve us as guards by night
and workmen by day." 23Neither I nor my brothers nor my men
nor the guards with me took off our clothes; each had his weapon,
even when he went for water.[a]

*Nehemiah Helps the Poor*

5 NOW THE men and their wives raised a great outcry against
their Jewish brothers. 2Some were saying, "We and our sons
and daughters are numerous; in order for us to eat and stay alive,
we must get grain."
3Others were saying, "We are mortgaging our fields, our vineyards and our homes to get grain during the famine."
4Still others were saying, "We have had to borrow money to
pay the king's tax on our fields and vineyards. 5Although we are
of the same flesh and blood as our countrymen and though our
sons are as good as theirs, yet we have to subject our sons and
daughters to slavery. Some of our daughters have already been
enslaved, but we are powerless, because our fields and our vineyards belong to others."
6When I heard their outcry and these charges, I was very angry.
7I pondered them in my mind and then accused the nobles and
officials. I told them, "You are exacting usury from your own
countrymen!" So I called together a large meeting to deal with
them 8and said: "As far as possible, we have bought back our
Jewish brothers who were sold to the Gentiles. Now you are selling
your brothers, only for them to be sold back to us!" They kept
quiet, because they could find nothing to say.
9So I continued, "What you are doing is not right. Shouldn't
you walk in the fear of our God to avoid the reproach of our Gentile
enemies? 10I and my brothers and my men are also lending the
people money and grain. But let the exacting of usury stop! 11Give
back to them immediately their fields, vineyards, olive groves and
houses, and also the usury you are charging them—the hundredth
part of the money, grain, new wine and oil."

NIV [a] 23 The meaning of the Hebrew for this clause is uncertain.

## King James

12 Then said they, We will restore *them,* and will require nothing of them; so will we do as thou sayest. Then I called the priests, and took an oath of them, that they should do according to this promise.

13 Also I shook my lap, and said, So God shake out every man from his house, and from his labour, that performeth not this promise, even thus be he shaken out, and emptied. And all the congregation said, Amen, and praised the LORD. And the people did according to this promise.

14 ¶ Moreover from the time that I was appointed to be their governor in the land of Judah, from the twentieth year even unto the two and thirtieth year of Artaxerxes the king, *that is,* twelve years, I and my brethren have not eaten the bread of the governor.

15 But the former governors that *had been* before me were chargeable unto the people, and had taken of them bread and wine, beside forty shekels of silver; yea, even their servants bare rule over the people: but so did not I, because of the fear of God.

16 Yea, also I continued in the work of this wall, neither bought we any land: and all my servants *were* gathered thither unto the work.

17 Moreover *there were* at my table an hundred and fifty of the Jews and rulers, beside those that came unto us from among the heathen that *are* about us.

18 Now *that* which was prepared *for me* daily *was* one ox *and* six choice sheep; also fowls were prepared for me, and once in ten days store of all sorts of wine: yet for all this required not I the bread of the governor, because the bondage was heavy upon this people.

19 Think upon me, my God, for good, *according* to all that I have done for this people.

6 NOW IT came to pass, when Sanballat, and Tobiah, and Geshem the Arabian, and the rest of our enemies, heard that I had builded the wall, and *that* there was no breach left therein; (though at that time I had not set up the doors upon the gates;)

2 That Sanballat and Geshem sent unto me, saying, Come, let us meet together in *some one of* the villages in the plain of Ono. But they thought to do me mischief.

3 And I sent messengers unto them, saying, I *am* doing a great work, so that I cannot come down: why should the work cease, whilst I leave it, and come down to you?

4 Yet they sent unto me four times after this sort; and I answered them after the same manner.

5 Then sent Sanballat his servant unto me in like manner the fifth time with an open letter in his hand;

6 Wherein *was* written, It is reported among the heathen, and Gashmu saith *it, that* thou and the Jews think to rebel: for which cause thou buildest the wall, that thou mayest be their king, according to these words.

7 And thou hast also appointed prophets to preach of thee at Jerusalem, saying, *There is* a king in Judah: and now shall it be reported to the king according to these words. Come now therefore, and let us take counsel together.

8 Then I sent unto him, saying, There are no such things done as thou sayest, but thou feignest them out of thine own heart.

9 For they all made us afraid, saying, Their hands shall be weakened from the work, that it be not done. Now therefore, *O God,* strengthen my hands.

## Amplified

12 Then they said, We will restore these and require nothing from them. We will do as you say. Then I called the priests, and took an oath of the lenders, that they would do according to this promise.

13 I shook my lap, and said, So may God shake out every man from his house and from [the exercise and fruits of] his labor, who does not keep this promise! So may he be shaken out and emptied. And all the assembly said, Amen, and praised the Lord. And the people did according to this promise.

14 Also in the twelve years after I was appointed to be their governor in Judah, from the twentieth to the thirty-second year of King Artaxerxes, neither I nor my kin ate food allowed to [me] the governor.

15 But the former governors lived at the expense of the people and took from them food and wine, besides forty shekels of silver [a large monthly official salary]; yes, even their servants assumed authority over the people; but I did not so, because of my [reverent] fear of God.

16 I also held fast to the work on this wall, and we bought no land; and all my servants were gathered there for the work.

17 And there were at my table 150 Jews and officials, besides those who came to us from the nations about us.

18 Now these were prepared for one day: one ox and six choice sheep; also fowls were prepared for me, and once in ten days a store of all sorts of wine. Yet for all this I did not demand [my rights], the food allowed me as governor, for the [tribute] bondage was heavy upon this people.

19 O my God, [earnestly] remember me for good for all I have done for this people. [Heb. 6:10.]

6 NOW WHEN Sanballat, Tobiah, Geshem the Arab, and the rest of our enemies heard that I had built the wall, and there was no breach left in it, although at that time I had not set up the doors in the gates,

2 Sanballat and Geshem sent to me, saying, Come, let us meet together in one of the villages in the plain of Ono. But they intended to do me harm.

3 And I sent messengers to them, saying, I am doing a great work and cannot come down. Why should the work stop while I leave to come down to you?

4 They sent to me four times this way, and I answered them as before.

5 Then Sanballat sent his servant to me again the fifth time with an open letter.

6 In it was written, It is reported among the neighboring nations, and Gashmu says it, that you and the Jews plan to rebel; therefore you are building the wall, that you may be their king, is the report.

7 Also you have set up prophets to announce concerning you in Jerusalem, There is a king in Judah. And now this will be reported to the [Persian] king. So, come now and let us take counsel together.

8 I replied to him, No such things as you say have been done; you are inventing them out of your own heart *and* mind.

9 For they all wanted to frighten us, thinking, Their hands will be so weak that the work will not be done. But now strengthen my hands!

## New American Standard

12 Then they said, "We will give *it* back and will require nothing
from them; we will do exactly as you say." So I called the priests
and took an oath from them that they would do according to this
promise.
13 I also shook out the front of my garment and said, "Thus may
God shake out every man from his house and from his possessions
who does not fulfill this promise; even thus may he be shaken out
and emptied." And all the assembly said, "Amen!" And they
praised the LORD. Then the people did according to this promise.

*Nehemiah's Example*

14 ¶ Moreover, from the day that I was appointed to be their
governor in the land of Judah, from the twentieth year to the
thirty-second year of King Artaxerxes, *for* twelve years, neither I
nor my kinsmen have eaten the governor's food *allowance*.
15 But the former governors who were before me laid burdens
on the people and took from them bread and wine besides forty
shekels of silver; even their servants domineered the people. But
I did not do so because of the fear of God.
16 And I also [a]applied myself to the work on this wall; we did
not buy any land, and all my servants were gathered there for the
work.
17 Moreover, *there were* at my table one hundred and fifty Jews
and officials, besides those who came to us from the nations that
were around us.
18 Now that which was prepared for each day was one ox *and*
six choice sheep, also birds were prepared for me; and once in ten
days all sorts of wine *were furnished* in abundance. Yet for all this
I did not demand the governor's food *allowance*, because the servitude was heavy on this people.
19 Remember me, O my God, for good, *according to* all that I have
done for this people.

## New International

12 "We will give it back," they said. "And we will not demand
anything more from them. We will do as you say."
Then I summoned the priests and made the nobles and officials
take an oath to do what they had promised. 13 I also shook out the
folds of my robe and said, "In this way may God shake out of his
house and possessions every man who does not keep this promise.
So may such a man be shaken out and emptied!"
At this the whole assembly said, "Amen," and praised the
LORD. And the people did as they had promised.
14 Moreover, from the twentieth year of King Artaxerxes, when
I was appointed to be their governor in the land of Judah, until his
thirty-second year—twelve years—neither I nor my brothers ate
the food allotted to the governor. 15 But the earlier governors—
those preceding me—placed a heavy burden on the people and
took forty shekels[c] of silver from them in addition to food and
wine. Their assistants also lorded it over the people. But out of
reverence for God I did not act like that. 16 Instead, I devoted
myself to the work on this wall. All my men were assembled there
for the work; we[d] did not acquire any land.
17 Furthermore, a hundred and fifty Jews and officials ate at my
table, as well as those who came to us from the surrounding
nations. 18 Each day one ox, six choice sheep and some poultry
were prepared for me, and every ten days an abundant supply of
wine of all kinds. In spite of all this, I never demanded the food
allotted to the governor, because the demands were heavy on
these people.
19 Remember me with favor, O my God, for all I have done for
these people.

*The Enemy's Plot*

6 NOW IT came about when it was reported to Sanballat, Tobiah, to Geshem the Arab, and to the rest of our enemies that
I had rebuilt the wall, and *that* no breach remained in it, although
at that time I had not set up the doors in the gates,
2 that Sanballat and Geshem sent *a message* to me, saying,
"Come, let us meet together at [b]Chephirim in the plain of Ono."
But they were planning to harm me.
3 So I sent messengers to them, saying, "I am doing a great
work and I cannot come down. Why should the work stop while
I leave it and come down to you?"
4 And they sent *messages* to me four times in this manner, and
I answered them in the same way.
5 Then Sanballat sent his servant to me in the same manner a
fifth time with an open letter in his hand.
6 In it was written, "It is reported among the nations, and
Gashmu says, that you and the Jews are planning to rebel; therefore you are rebuilding the wall. And you are to be their king,
according to these reports.
7 "And you have also appointed prophets to proclaim in Jerusalem concerning you, 'A king is in Judah!' And now it will be
reported to the king according to these reports. So come now, let
us take counsel together."
8 Then I sent *a message* to him saying, "Such things as you are
saying have not been done, but you are inventing them in your
own mind."
9 For all of them were *trying* to frighten us, thinking, "They will
become discouraged with the work and it will not be done." But
now, *O God*, strengthen my hands.

*Further Opposition to the Rebuilding*

6 WHEN WORD came to Sanballat, Tobiah, Geshem the Arab
and the rest of our enemies that I had rebuilt the wall and not
a gap was left in it—though up to that time I had not set the doors
in the gates— 2 Sanballat and Geshem sent me this message:
"Come, let us meet together in one of the villages[e] on the plain
of Ono."
But they were scheming to harm me; 3 so I sent messengers to
them with this reply: "I am carrying on a great project and cannot
go down. Why should the work stop while I leave it and go down
to you?" 4 Four times they sent me the same message, and each
time I gave them the same answer.
5 Then, the fifth time, Sanballat sent his aide to me with the
same message, and in his hand was an unsealed letter 6 in which
was written:

> "It is reported among the nations—and Geshem[f] says it
> is true—that you and the Jews are plotting to revolt, and
> therefore you are building the wall. Moreover, according to
> these reports you are about to become their king 7 and have
> even appointed prophets to make this proclamation about
> you in Jerusalem: 'There is a king in Judah!' Now this report
> will get back to the king; so come, let us confer together."

8 I sent him this reply: "Nothing like what you are saying is
happening; you are just making it up out of your head."
9 They were all trying to frighten us, thinking, "Their hands will
get too weak for the work, and it will not be completed."
⌞But I prayed,⌟ "Now strengthen my hands."

NAS [a] Or, *held fast* [b] Another reading is, one of *the villages*

NIV [c] *15* That is, about 1 pound (about 0.5 kilogram) [d] *16* Most Hebrew manuscripts; some Hebrew manuscripts, Septuagint, Vulgate and Syriac *I* [e] *2* Or *in Kephirim* [f] *6* Hebrew *Gashmu*, a variant of *Geshem*

# King James

10Afterward I came unto the house of Shemaiah the son of Delaiah the son of Mehetabeel, who *was* shut up; and he said, Let us meet together in the house of God, within the temple, and let us shut the doors of the temple: for they will come to slay thee; yea, in the night will they come to slay thee.

11And I said, Should such a man as I flee? and who *is there*, that, *being as I am*, would go into the temple to save his life? I will not go in.

12And, lo, I perceived that God had not sent him; but that he pronounced this prophecy against me: for Tobiah and Sanballat had hired him.

13Therefore *was* he hired, that I should be afraid, and do so, and sin, and *that* they might have *matter* for an evil report, that they might reproach me.

14My God, think thou upon Tobiah and Sanballat according to these their works, and on the prophetess Noadiah, and the rest of the prophets, that would have put me in fear.

15¶ So the wall was finished in the twenty and fifth *day of the month* Elul, in fifty and two days.

16And it came to pass, that when all our enemies heard *thereof*, and all the heathen that *were* about us saw *these things*, they were much cast down in their own eyes: for they perceived that this work was wrought of our God.

17¶ Moreover in those days the nobles of Judah sent many letters unto Tobiah, and *the letters* of Tobiah came unto them.

18For *there were* many in Judah sworn unto him, because he *was* the son-in-law of Shechaniah the son of Arah; and his son Johanan had taken the daughter of Meshullam the son of Berechiah.

19Also they reported his good deeds before me, and uttered my words to him. *And* Tobiah sent letters to put me in fear.

**7** NOW IT came to pass, when the wall was built, and I had set up the doors, and the porters and the singers and the Levites were appointed,

2That I gave my brother Hanani, and Hananiah the ruler of the palace, charge over Jerusalem: for he *was* a faithful man, and feared God above many.

3And I said unto them, Let not the gates of Jerusalem be opened until the sun be hot; and while they stand by, let them shut the doors, and bar *them*: and appoint watches of the inhabitants of Jerusalem, every one in his watch, and every one *to be* over against his house.

4Now the city *was* large and great: but the people *were* few therein, and the houses *were* not builded.

5¶ And my God put into mine heart to gather together the nobles, and the rulers, and the people, that they might be reckoned by genealogy. And I found a register of the genealogy of them which came up at the first, and found written therein,

6These *are* the children of the province, that went up out of the captivity, of those that had been carried away, whom Nebuchadnezzar the king of Babylon had carried away, and came again to Jerusalem and to Judah, every one unto his city;

7Who came with Zerubbabel, Jeshua, Nehemiah, Azariah, Raamiah, Nahamani, Mordecai, Bilshan, Mispereth, Bigvai, Nehum, Baanah. The number, *I say*, of the men of the people of Israel *was this*;

8The children of Parosh, two thousand an hundred seventy and two.

9The children of Shephatiah, three hundred seventy and two.

10The children of Arah, six hundred fifty and two.

11The children of Pahath-moab, of the children of Jeshua and Joab, two thousand and eight hundred *and* eighteen.

12The children of Elam, a thousand two hundred fifty and four.

# Amplified

10I went into the house of Shemaiah son of Delaiah son of Mehetabel, who was shut up; he said, Let us meet together in the house of God, within the temple, and let us shut the doors of the temple; for they are coming to kill you, at night they are coming to kill you.

11But I said, Should such a man as I flee? And what man such as I, could go into the temple [where only the priests are allowed to go] and yet live? I will not go in.

12And lo, I saw that God had not sent him, but he made this prophecy against me because Tobiah and Sanballat had hired him.

13He was hired that I should be made afraid and do as he said, and sin, that they might have matter for an evil report with which to taunt *and* reproach me.

14My God, think on Tobiah and Sanballat according to these their works, and on the prophetess Noadiah, and the rest of the prophets, who would have put me in fear.

15So the wall was finished the twenty-fifth day of the month Elul, in fifty-two days.

16When all our enemies heard of it, all the nations around us feared and fell far in their own esteem, for they saw that this work was done by our God.

17Moreover in those days the nobles of Judah sent many letters to Tobiah, and Tobiah's letters came to them.

18For many in Judah were bound by oath to him, because he was the son-in-law of Shecaniah son of Arah; and his son Jehohanan had married the daughter of Meshullam son of Berechiah.

19Also they spoke of [Tobiah's] good deeds before me, and told what I said to him. And Tobiah sent letters to frighten me.

**7** NOW WHEN the wall was built, and I had set up the doors, and the gatekeepers, singers, and Levites had been appointed,

2I gave my brother Hanani, and Hananiah the ruler of the castle, charge over Jerusalem; for Hananiah was a more faithful and God-fearing man than many.

3I said to them, Let not the gates of Jerusalem be opened until the sun is hot; and while the watch are still on guard, let them shut and bar the doors. Appoint guards from the people of Jerusalem, each to his watch [on the wall], and each opposite his own house.

4Now the city was wide and large, but the people in it were few, and their houses were not yet built.

5And my God put into my mind *and* heart to assemble the nobles, the officers, and the people, that they might be counted by genealogy. And I found a register of the genealogy of those who came [from Babylon] at the first, and found written in it:

6These are the people of the province, who came up out of the captivity of those exiles whom Nebuchadnezzar the king of Babylon had carried away; they returned to Jerusalem and to Judah, each to his town;

7Who came with Zerubbabel, Jeshua, Nehemiah [not the author], Azariah, Raamiah, Nahamani, Mordecai, Bilshan, Mispereth, Bigvai, Nehum, Baanah. The men of Israel numbered:

8The sons of Parosh, 2,172.

9The sons of Shephatiah, 372.

10The sons of Arah, 652.

11The sons of Pahath-moab, namely the sons of Jeshua and Joab, 2,818.

12The sons of Elam, 1,254.

## New American Standard

10¶ And when I entered the house of Shemaiah the son of
Delaiah, son of Mehetabel, who was confined at home, he said,
"Let us meet together in the house of God, within the temple, and
let us close the doors of the temple, for they are coming to kill you,
and they are coming to kill you at night."
11But I said, "Should a man like me flee? And could one such
as I go into the temple to save his life? I will not go in."
12Then I perceived that surely God had not sent him, but he
uttered *his* prophecy against me because Tobiah and Sanballat had
hired him.
13He was hired for this reason, that I might become frightened
and act accordingly and sin, so that they might have an evil report
in order that they could reproach me.
14Remember, O my God, Tobiah and Sanballat according to
these works of theirs, and also Noadiah the prophetess and the
rest of the prophets who were *trying* to frighten me.

*The Wall Is Finished*

15¶ So the wall was completed on the twenty-fifth of *the month*
Elul, in fifty-two days.
16And it came about when all our enemies heard *of it,* and all
the nations surrounding us saw *it,* they lost their confidence; for
they recognized that this work had been accomplished with the
help of our God.
17Also in those days many letters went from the nobles of Judah
to Tobiah, and Tobiah's *letters* came to them.
18For many in Judah were bound by oath to him because he was
the son-in-law of Shecaniah the son of Arah, and his son Jehohanan had married the daughter of Meshullam the son of Berechiah.
19Moreover, they were speaking about his good deeds in my
presence and reported my words to him. Then Tobiah sent letters
to frighten me.

*Census of First Returned Exiles*

7 NOW IT came about when the wall was rebuilt and I had set
up the doors, and the gatekeepers and the singers and the
Levites were appointed,
2that I put Hanani my brother, and Hananiah the commander
of the fortress, in charge of Jerusalem, for he was a faithful man
and feared God more than many.
3Then I said to them, "Do not let the gates of Jerusalem be
opened until the sun is hot, and while they are standing *guard,* let
them shut and bolt the doors. Also appoint guards from the inhabitants of Jerusalem, each at his post, and each in front of his own
house."
4Now the city was large and spacious, but the people in it were
few and the houses were not built.
5¶ Then my God put it into my heart to assemble the nobles,
the officials, and the people to be enrolled by genealogies. Then
I found the book of the genealogy of those who came up first in
which I found the following record:
6These are the people of the province who came up from the
captivity of the exiles whom Nebuchadnezzar the king of Babylon
had carried away, and who returned to Jerusalem and Judah, each
to his city,
7who came with Zerubbabel, Jeshua, Nehemiah, Azariah, Raamiah, Nahamani, Mordecai, Bilshan, Mispereth, Bigvai, Nehum,
Baanah.
¶The number of men of the people of Israel:
8the sons of Parosh, 2,172;
9the sons of Shephatiah, 372;
10the sons of Arah, 652;
11the sons of Pahath-moab of the sons of Jeshua and Joab, 2,818;
12the sons of Elam, 1,254;

## New International

10One day I went to the house of Shemaiah son of Delaiah, the
son of Mehetabel, who was shut in at his home. He said, "Let us
meet in the house of God, inside the temple, and let us close the
temple doors, because men are coming to kill you—by night they
are coming to kill you."
11But I said, "Should a man like me run away? Or should one
like me go into the temple to save his life? I will not go!" 12I realized
that God had not sent him, but that he had prophesied against me
because Tobiah and Sanballat had hired him. 13He had been hired
to intimidate me so that I would commit a sin by doing this, and
then they would give me a bad name to discredit me.
14Remember Tobiah and Sanballat, O my God, because of what
they have done; remember also the prophetess Noadiah and the
rest of the prophets who have been trying to intimidate me.

*The Completion of the Wall*

15So the wall was completed on the twenty-fifth of Elul, in
fifty-two days. 16When all our enemies heard about this, all the
surrounding nations were afraid and lost their self-confidence,
because they realized that this work had been done with the help
of our God.
17Also, in those days the nobles of Judah were sending many
letters to Tobiah, and replies from Tobiah kept coming to them.
18For many in Judah were under oath to him, since he was son-in-
law to Shecaniah son of Arah, and his son Jehohanan had married
the daughter of Meshullam son of Berekiah. 19Moreover, they kept
reporting to me his good deeds and then telling him what I said.
And Tobiah sent letters to intimidate me.

7 AFTER THE wall had been rebuilt and I had set the doors in
place, the gatekeepers and the singers and the Levites were
appointed. 2I put in charge of Jerusalem my brother Hanani, along
with[a] Hananiah the commander of the citadel, because he was a
man of integrity and feared God more than most men do. 3I said
to them, "The gates of Jerusalem are not to be opened until the sun
is hot. While the gatekeepers are still on duty, have them shut the
doors and bar them. Also appoint residents of Jerusalem as
guards, some at their posts and some near their own houses."

*The List of the Exiles Who Returned*

4Now the city was large and spacious, but there were few
people in it, and the houses had not yet been rebuilt. 5So my God
put it into my heart to assemble the nobles, the officials and the
common people for registration by families. I found the genealogical record of those who had been the first to return. This is what
I found written there:

6These are the people of the province who came up from
the captivity of the exiles whom Nebuchadnezzar king of
Babylon had taken captive (they returned to Jerusalem and
Judah, each to his own town, 7in company with Zerubbabel,
Jeshua, Nehemiah, Azariah, Raamiah, Nahamani, Mordecai,
Bilshan, Mispereth, Bigvai, Nehum and Baanah):

The list of the men of Israel:

| | |
|---|---|
| 8the descendants of Parosh | 2,172 |
| 9of Shephatiah | 372 |
| 10of Arah | 652 |
| 11of Pahath-Moab (through the line of Jeshua and Joab) | 2,818 |
| 12of Elam | 1,254 |

NIV [a] 2 Or *Hanani, that is,*

## King James

13The children of Zattu, eight hundred forty and five.
14The children of Zaccai, seven hundred and threescore.
15The children of Binnui, six hundred forty and eight.
16The children of Bebai, six hundred twenty and eight.
17The children of Azgad, two thousand three hundred twenty and two.
18The children of Adonikam, six hundred threescore and seven.
19The children of Bigvai, two thousand threescore and seven.
20The children of Adin, six hundred fifty and five.
21The children of Ater of Hezekiah, ninety and eight.
22The children of Hashum, three hundred twenty and eight.
23The children of Bezai, three hundred twenty and four.
24The children of Hariph, an hundred and twelve.
25The children of Gibeon, ninety and five.
26The men of Bethlehem and Netophah, an hundred fourscore and eight.
27The men of Anathoth, an hundred twenty and eight.
28The men of Beth-azmaveth, forty and two.
29The men of Kirjath-jearim, Chephirah, and Beeroth, seven hundred forty and three.
30The men of Ramah and Gaba, six hundred twenty and one.
31The men of Michmas, an hundred and twenty and two.
32The men of Beth-el and Ai, an hundred twenty and three.
33The men of the other Nebo, fifty and two.
34The children of the other Elam, a thousand two hundred fifty and four.
35The children of Harim, three hundred and twenty.
36The children of Jericho, three hundred forty and five.
37The children of Lod, Hadid, and Ono, seven hundred twenty and one.
38The children of Senaah, three thousand nine hundred and thirty.
39¶ The priests: the children of Jedaiah, of the house of Jeshua, nine hundred seventy and three.
40The children of Immer, a thousand fifty and two.
41The children of Pashur, a thousand two hundred forty and seven.
42The children of Harim, a thousand and seventeen.
43¶ The Levites: the children of Jeshua, of Kadmiel, *and* of the children of Hodevah, seventy and four.
44¶ The singers: the children of Asaph, an hundred forty and eight.
45¶ The porters: the children of Shallum, the children of Ater, the children of Talmon, the children of Akkub, the children of Hatita, the children of Shobai, an hundred thirty and eight.
46¶ The Nethinims: the children of Ziha, the children of Hashupha, the children of Tabbaoth,
47The children of Keros, the children of Sia, the children of Padon,
48The children of Lebana, the children of Hagaba, the children of Shalmai,
49The children of Hanan, the children of Giddel, the children of Gahar,
50The children of Reaiah, the children of Rezin, the children of Nekoda,
51The children of Gazzam, the children of Uzza, the children of Phaseah,
52The children of Besai, the children of Meunim, the children of Nephishesim,
53The children of Bakbuk, the children of Hakupha, the children of Harhur,
54The children of Bazlith, the children of Mehida, the children of Harsha,
55The children of Barkos, the children of Sisera, the children of Tamah,
56The children of Neziah, the children of Hatipha.
57¶ The children of Solomon's servants: the children of Sotai, the children of Sophereth, the children of Perida,
58The children of Jaala, the children of Darkon, the children of Giddel,

## Amplified

13The sons of Zattu, 845.
14The sons of Zaccai, 760.
15The sons of Binnui, 648.
16The sons of Bebai, 628.
17The sons of Azgad, 2,322.
18The sons of Adonikam, 667.
19The sons of Bigvai, 2,067.
20The sons of Adin, 655.
21The sons of Ater, namely of Hezekiah, 98.
22The sons of Hashum, 328.
23The sons of Bezai, 324.
24The sons of Hariph, 112.
25The sons of Gibeon, 95.
26The men of Bethlehem and Netophah, 188.
27The men of Anathoth, 128.
28The men of Beth-azmaveth, 42.
29The men of Kiriath-jearim, Chephirah, and Beeroth, 743.
30The men of Ramah and Geba, 621.
31The men of Michmas, 122.
32The men of Bethel and Ai, 123.
33The men of the other Nebo, 52.
34The sons of the other Elam, 1,254.
35The sons of Harim, 320.
36The sons of Jericho, 345.
37The sons of Lod, Hadid, and Ono, 721.
38The sons of Senaah, 3,930.
39The priests: the sons of Jedaiah, namely the house of Jeshua, 973.
40The sons of Immer, 1,052.
41The sons of Pashhur, 1,247.
42The sons of Harim, 1,017.
43The Levites: the sons of Jeshua, namely of Kadmiel, of the sons of Hodevah, 74.
44The singers: the sons of Asaph, 148.
45The gatekeepers: the sons of Shallum, of Ater, of Talmon, of Akkub, of Hatita, and of Shobai, 138.
46The Nethinim [temple servants]: the sons of Ziha, of Hasupha, of Tabbaoth,
47Of Keros, of Sia, of Padon,
48Of Lebana, of Hagaba, of Shalmai,
49Of Hanan, of Giddel, of Gahar,
50Of Reaiah, of Rezin, of Nekoda,
51Of Gazzam, of Uzza, of Paseah,
52Of Besai, of Meunim, of Nephushesim,
53Of Bakbuk, of Hakupha, of Harhur,
54Of Bazlith, of Mehida, of Harsha,
55Of Barkos, of Sisera, of Temah,
56Of Neziah, of Hatipha.
57The sons of Solomon's servants: the sons of Sotai, of Sophereth, of Perida,
58Of Jaala, of Darkon, of Giddel,

## New American Standard

13the sons of Zattu, 845;
14the sons of Zaccai, 760;
15the sons of Binnui, 648;
16the sons of Bebai, 628;
17the sons of Azgad, 2,322;
18the sons of Adonikam, 667;
19the sons of Bigvai, 2,067;
20the sons of Adin, 655;
21the sons of Ater, of Hezekiah, 98;
22the sons of Hashum, 328;
23the sons of Bezai, 324;
24the sons of Hariph, 112;
25the sons of Gibeon, 95;
26the men of Bethlehem and Netophah, 188;
27the men of Anathoth, 128;
28the men of Beth-azmaveth, 42;
29the men of Kiriath-jearim, Chephirah, and Beeroth, 743;
30the men of Ramah and Geba, 621;
31the men of Michmas, 122;
32the men of Bethel and Ai, 123;
33the men of the other Nebo, 52;
34the sons of the other Elam, 1,254;
35the sons of Harim, 320;
36the men of Jericho, 345;
37the sons of Lod, Hadid, and Ono, 721;
38the sons of Senaah, 3,930.
39¶ The priests: the sons of Jedaiah of the house of Jeshua, 973;
40the sons of Immer, 1,052;
41the sons of Pashhur, 1,247;
42the sons of Harim, 1,017.
43¶ The Levites: the sons of Jeshua, of Kadmiel, of the sons of
Hodevah, 74.
44The singers: the sons of Asaph, 148.
45The gatekeepers: the sons of Shallum, the sons of Ater, the
sons of Talmon, the sons of Akkub, the sons of Hatita, the sons
of Shobai, 138.
46¶ The temple servants: the sons of Ziha, the sons of Hasupha,
the sons of Tabbaoth,
47the sons of Keros, the sons of Sia, the sons of Padon,
48the sons of Lebana, the sons of Hagaba, the sons of Shalmai,
49the sons of Hanan, the sons of Giddel, the sons of Gahar,
50the sons of Reaiah, the sons of Rezin, the sons of Nekoda,
51the sons of Gazzam, the sons of Uzza, the sons of Paseah,
52the sons of Besai, the sons of Meunim, the sons of Nephushesim,
53the sons of Bakbuk, the sons of Hakupha, the sons of Harhur,
54the sons of Bazlith, the sons of Mehida, the sons of Harsha,
55the sons of Barkos, the sons of Sisera, the sons of Temah,
56the sons of Neziah, the sons of Hatipha.
57¶ The sons of Solomon's servants: the sons of Sotai, the sons
of Sophereth, the sons of Perida,
58the sons of Jaala, the sons of Darkon, the sons of Giddel,

## New International

13of Zattu 845
14of Zaccai 760
15of Binnui 648
16of Bebai 628
17of Azgad 2,322
18of Adonikam 667
19of Bigvai 2,067
20of Adin 655
21of Ater (through Hezekiah) 98
22of Hashum 328
23of Bezai 324
24of Hariph 112
25of Gibeon 95

26the men of Bethlehem and Netophah 188
27of Anathoth 128
28of Beth Azmaveth 42
29of Kiriath Jearim, Kephirah and Beeroth 743
30of Ramah and Geba 621
31of Micmash 122
32of Bethel and Ai 123
33of the other Nebo 52
34of the other Elam 1,254
35of Harim 320
36of Jericho 345
37of Lod, Hadid and Ono 721
38of Senaah 3,930

39The priests:

the descendants of Jedaiah (through the family of Jeshua) 973
40of Immer 1,052
41of Pashhur 1,247
42of Harim 1,017

43The Levites:

the descendants of Jeshua (through Kadmiel through the line of Hodaviah) 74

44The singers:

the descendants of Asaph 148

45The gatekeepers:

the descendants of
Shallum, Ater, Talmon, Akkub, Hatita and Shobai 138

46The temple servants:

the descendants of
Ziha, Hasupha, Tabbaoth,
47Keros, Sia, Padon,
48Lebana, Hagaba, Shalmai,
49Hanan, Giddel, Gahar,
50Reaiah, Rezin, Nekoda,
51Gazzam, Uzza, Paseah,
52Besai, Meunim, Nephussim,
53Bakbuk, Hakupha, Harhur,
54Bazluth, Mehida, Harsha,
55Barkos, Sisera, Temah,
56Neziah and Hatipha

57The descendants of the servants of Solomon:

the descendants of
Sotai, Sophereth, Perida,
58Jaala, Darkon, Giddel,

## King James

59The children of Shephatiah, the children of Hattil, the children of Pochereth of Zebaim, the children of Amon.

60All the Nethinims, and the children of Solomon's servants, *were* three hundred ninety and two.

61And these *were* they which went up *also* from Tel-melah, Tel-haresha, Cherub, Addon, and Immer: but they could not show their father's house, nor their seed, whether they *were* of Israel.

62The children of Delaiah, the children of Tobiah, the children of Nekoda, six hundred forty and two.

63¶ And of the priests: the children of Habaiah, the children of Koz, the children of Barzillai, which took *one* of the daughters of Barzillai the Gileadite to wife, and was called after their name.

64These sought their register *among* those that were reckoned by genealogy, but it was not found: therefore were they, as polluted, put from the priesthood.

65And the Tirshatha said unto them, that they should not eat of the most holy things, till there stood *up* a priest with Urim and Thummim.

66¶ The whole congregation together *was* forty and two thousand three hundred and threescore,

67Beside their manservants and their maidservants, of whom *there were* seven thousand three hundred thirty and seven: and they had two hundred forty and five singing men and singing women.

68Their horses, seven hundred thirty and six: their mules, two hundred forty and five:

69 *Their* camels, four hundred thirty and five: six thousand seven hundred and twenty asses.

70¶ And some of the chief of the fathers gave unto the work. The Tirshatha gave to the treasure a thousand drams of gold, fifty basins, five hundred and thirty priests' garments.

71And *some* of the chief of the fathers gave to the treasure of the work twenty thousand drams of gold, and two thousand and two hundred pound of silver.

72And *that* which the rest of the people gave *was* twenty thousand drams of gold, and two thousand pound of silver, and threescore and seven priests' garments.

73So the priests, and the Levites, and the porters, and the singers, and *some* of the people, and the Nethinims, and all Israel, dwelt in their cities; and when the seventh month came, the children of Israel *were* in their cities.

**8** AND ALL the people gathered themselves together as one man into the street that *was* before the water gate; and they spake unto Ezra the scribe to bring the book of the law of Moses, which the LORD had commanded to Israel.

2And Ezra the priest brought the law before the congregation both of men and women, and all that could hear with understanding, upon the first day of the seventh month.

3And he read therein before the street that *was* before the water gate from the morning until midday, before the men and the women, and those that could understand; and the ears of all the people *were attentive* unto the book of the law.

4And Ezra the scribe stood upon a pulpit of wood, which they had made for the purpose; and beside him stood Mattithiah, and Shema, and Anaiah, and Urijah, and Hilkiah, and Maaseiah, on his right hand; and on his left hand, Pedaiah, and Mishael, and Malchiah, and Hashum, and Hashbadana, Zechariah, *and* Meshullam.

5And Ezra opened the book in the sight of all the people; (for he was above all the people;) and when he opened it, all the people stood up:

## Amplified

59Of Shephatiah, of Hattil, of Pochereth-hazzebaim, of Amon.

60All the Nethinim [temple servants] and the sons of Solomon's servants, 392.

61And these were they who went up also from Telmelah, Telharsha, Cherub, Addon, and Immer: but they [had no birth records and] could not prove their father's house, nor their descent, whether they were of Israel:

62The sons of Delaiah, of Tobiah, of Nekoda, 642.

63Of the priests: the sons of Hobaiah, of Hakkoz, and of Barzillai, who [was so named because he] married one of the daughters of the [noted] Gileadite Barzillai and was called by their name.

64These sought their registration among those recorded in the genealogies, but it was not found; so they were excluded from the priesthood as [ceremonially] unclean.

65The governor told them that they should refrain from eating of the most holy food, until a priest with Urim and Thummim should arise [to determine the will of God in the matter].

66The congregation all together was 42,360.

67Besides their manservants and their maidservants, of whom there were 7,337; and they had 245 singers, men and women.

68Their horses, 736; their mules, 245;

69Their camels, 435; their donkeys, 6,720.

70And some of the heads of fathers' houses gave to the work. The Tirshatha *or* governor gave to the treasury 1,000 darics of gold, 50 basins, 530 priests' garments.

71Some of the heads of fathers' houses gave to the treasury for the work 20,000 darics of gold, and 2,200 minas of silver.

72What the rest of the people gave was 20,000 darics of gold, 2,000 minas of silver, and 67 priests' garments.

73So the priests, the Levites, the gatekeepers, the singers, some of the people, the Nethinim [the temple servants], and all Israel, dwelt in their towns, and were in them when the seventh month came.

**8** THEN ALL the people gathered together as one man in the broad place before the Water Gate; and they asked Ezra the scribe to bring the book of the law of Moses which the Lord had given Israel.

2And Ezra the priest brought the law before the assembly of both men and women and all who could hear with understanding, on the first of the seventh month.

3He read from it facing the broad place before the Water Gate from early morning until noon, to the men and women and those who could understand; and all the people were attentive to the book of the law.

4Ezra the scribe stood on a wooden pulpit, which they had made for the purpose; and beside him stood Mattithiah, Shema, Anaiah, Uriah, Hilkiah, and Maaseiah on his right hand; and on his left hand, Pedaiah, Mishael, Malchijah, Hashum, Hash-baddana, Zechariah, and Meshullam.

5Ezra opened the book in sight of all the people, for he was standing above them; and when he opened it, all the people stood.

## New American Standard

59the sons of Shephatiah, the sons of Hattil, the sons of Pochereth-hazzebaim, the sons of Amon.
60All the temple servants and the sons of Solomon's servants *were* 392.
61¶ And these *were* they who came up from Tel-melah, Tel-harsha, Cherub, Addon, and Immer; but they could not show their fathers' houses or their descendants, whether they were of Israel:
62the sons of Delaiah, the sons of Tobiah, the sons of Nekoda, 642.
63And of the priests: the sons of Hobaiah, the sons of Hakkoz, the sons of Barzillai, who took a wife of the daughters of Barzillai, the Gileadite, and was named after them.
64These searched *among* their ancestral registration, but it could not be located; therefore they were considered unclean *and excluded* from the priesthood.
65And the governor said to them that they should not eat from the most holy things until a priest arose with Urim and Thummim.

*Total of People and Gifts*

66¶ The whole assembly together *was* 42,360,
67besides their male and their female servants, of whom *there were* 7,337; and they had 245 male and female singers.
68Their horses were 736; their mules, 245;
69*their* camels, 435; *their* donkeys, 6,720.
70¶ And some from among the heads of fathers' *households* gave to the work. The governor gave to the treasury 1,000 gold drachmas, 50 basins, 530 priests' garments.
71And some of the heads of fathers' *households* gave into the treasury of the work 20,000 gold drachmas, and 2,200 silver minas.
72And that which the rest of the people gave was 20,000 gold drachmas and 2,000 silver minas, and 67 priests' garments.
73¶ Now the priests, the Levites, the gatekeepers, the singers, some of the people, the temple servants, and all Israel, lived in their cities.
¶And when the seventh month came, the sons of Israel *were* in their cities.

*Ezra Reads the Law*

8 AND ALL the people gathered as one man at the square which was in front of the Water Gate, and they asked Ezra the scribe to bring the book of the law of Moses which the LORD had given to Israel.
2Then Ezra the priest brought the law before the assembly of men, women, and all who *could* listen with understanding, on the first day of the seventh month.
3And he read from it before the square which was in front of the Water Gate from early morning until midday, in the presence of men and women, those who could understand; and all the people were attentive to the book of the law.
4And Ezra the scribe stood at a wooden podium which they had made for the purpose. And beside him stood Mattithiah, Shema, Anaiah, Uriah, Hilkiah, and Maaseiah on his right hand; and Pedaiah, Mishael, Malchijah, Hashum, Hashbaddanah, Zechariah, *and* Meshullam on his left hand.
5And Ezra opened the book in the sight of all the people for he was standing above all the people; and when he opened it, all the people stood up.

## New International

59Shephatiah, Hattil,
Pokereth-Hazzebaim and Amon
60The temple servants and the descendants of the
servants of Solomon 392
61The following came up from the towns of Tel Melah, Tel Harsha, Kerub, Addon and Immer, but they could not show that their families were descended from Israel:
62the descendants of
Delaiah, Tobiah and Nekoda 642
63And from among the priests:
the descendants of
Hobaiah, Hakkoz and Barzillai (a man who had married a daughter of Barzillai the Gileadite and was called by that name).
64These searched for their family records, but they could not find them and so were excluded from the priesthood as unclean. 65The governor, therefore, ordered them not to eat any of the most sacred food until there should be a priest ministering with the Urim and Thummim.
66The whole company numbered 42,360, 67besides their 7,337 menservants and maidservants; and they also had 245 men and women singers. 68There were 736 horses, 245 mules,[a] 69435 camels and 6,720 donkeys.
70Some of the heads of the families contributed to the work. The governor gave to the treasury 1,000 drachmas[b] of gold, 50 bowls and 530 garments for priests. 71Some of the heads of the families gave to the treasury for the work 20,000 drachmas[c] of gold and 2,200 minas[d] of silver. 72The total given by the rest of the people was 20,000 drachmas of gold, 2,000 minas[e] of silver and 67 garments for priests.
73The priests, the Levites, the gatekeepers, the singers and the temple servants, along with certain of the people and the rest of the Israelites, settled in their own towns.

*Ezra Reads the Law*

When the seventh month came and the Israelites had settled in their towns,
8 ALL THE people assembled as one man in the square before the Water Gate. They told Ezra the scribe to bring out the Book of the Law of Moses, which the LORD had commanded for Israel.
2So on the first day of the seventh month Ezra the priest brought the Law before the assembly, which was made up of men and women and all who were able to understand. 3He read it aloud from daybreak till noon as he faced the square before the Water Gate in the presence of the men, women and others who could understand. And all the people listened attentively to the Book of the Law.
4Ezra the scribe stood on a high wooden platform built for the occasion. Beside him on his right stood Mattithiah, Shema, Anaiah, Uriah, Hilkiah and Maaseiah; and on his left were Pedaiah, Mishael, Malkijah, Hashum, Hashbaddanah, Zechariah and Meshullam.
5Ezra opened the book. All the people could see him because he was standing above them; and as he opened it, the people all stood up. 6Ezra praised the LORD, the great God; and all the people

NIV [a] *68* Some Hebrew manuscripts (see also Ezra 2:66); most Hebrew manuscripts do not have this verse. [b] *70* That is, about 19 pounds (about 8.5 kilograms) [c] *71* That is, about 375 pounds (about 170 kilograms); also in verse 72 [d] *71* That is, about 1 1/3 tons (about 1.2 metric tons) [e] *72* That is, about 1 1/4 tons (about 1.1 metric tons)

## King James

6 And Ezra blessed the LORD, the great God. And all the people
answered, Amen, Amen, with lifting up their hands: and they
bowed their heads, and worshipped the LORD with *their* faces to
the ground.
7 Also Jeshua, and Bani, and Sherebiah, Jamin, Akkub, Shabbethai, Hodijah, Maaseiah, Kelita, Azariah, Jozabad, Hanan, Pelaiah, and the Levites, caused the people to understand the law: and
the people *stood* in their place.
8 So they read in the book in the law of God distinctly, and gave
the sense, and caused *them* to understand the reading.
9 ¶ And Nehemiah, which *is* the Tirshatha, and Ezra the priest
the scribe, and the Levites that taught the people, said unto all the
people, This day *is* holy unto the LORD your God; mourn not, nor
weep. For all the people wept, when they heard the words of the
law.
10 Then he said unto them, Go your way, eat the fat, and drink
the sweet, and send portions unto them for whom nothing is
prepared: for *this* day *is* holy unto our Lord: neither be ye sorry;
for the joy of the LORD is your strength.
11 So the Levites stilled all the people, saying, Hold your peace,
for the day *is* holy; neither be ye grieved.
12 And all the people went their way to eat, and to drink, and
to send portions, and to make great mirth, because they had
understood the words that were declared unto them.
13 ¶ And on the second day were gathered together the chief of
the fathers of all the people, the priests, and the Levites, unto Ezra
the scribe, even to understand the words of the law.
14 And they found written in the law which the LORD had commanded by Moses, that the children of Israel should dwell in
booths in the feast of the seventh month:
15 And that they should publish and proclaim in all their cities,
and in Jerusalem, saying, Go forth unto the mount, and fetch olive
branches, and pine branches, and myrtle branches, and palm
branches, and branches of thick trees, to make booths, as *it is*
written.
16 ¶ So the people went forth, and brought *them*, and made
themselves booths, every one upon the roof of his house, and in
their courts, and in the courts of the house of God, and in the street
of the water gate, and in the street of the gate of Ephraim.
17 And all the congregation of them that were come again out of
the captivity made booths, and sat under the booths: for since the
days of Jeshua the son of Nun unto that day had not the children
of Israel done so. And there was very great gladness.
18 Also day by day, from the first day unto the last day, he read
in the book of the law of God. And they kept the feast seven days;
and on the eighth day *was* a solemn assembly, according unto the
manner.

9 NOW IN the twenty and fourth day of this month the children of Israel were assembled with fasting, and with sack-
clothes, and earth upon them.
2 And the seed of Israel separated themselves from all strangers,
and stood and confessed their sins, and the iniquities of their
fathers.
3 And they stood up in their place, and read in the book of the
law of the LORD their God *one* fourth part of the day; and *another*
fourth part they confessed, and worshipped the LORD their God.
4 ¶ Then stood up upon the stairs, of the Levites, Jeshua, and
Bani, Kadmiel, Shebaniah, Bunni, Sherebiah, Bani, *and* Chenani,
and cried with a loud voice unto the LORD their God.

## Amplified

6 And Ezra blessed the Lord, the great God. And all the people
answered, Amen, Amen, lifting up their hands; and they bowed
their heads and worshiped the Lord with faces to the ground.
7 Also Jeshua, Bani, Sherebiah, Jamin, Akkub, Shabbethai, Hodiah, Maaseiah, Kelita, Azariah, Jozabad, Hanan, Pelaiah, the
Levites, helped the people to understand the law; and the people
[remained] in their place.
8 So they read from the book of the law of God distinctly, faithfully amplifying *and* giving the sense, so that [the people] understood the reading.
9 And Nehemiah, who was the governor, and Ezra the priest
and scribe, and the Levites who taught the people, said to all of
them, This day is holy to the Lord your God; mourn not, nor weep.
For all the people wept, when they heard the words of the law.
10 Then [Ezra] told them, Go your way, eat the fat, drink the
sweet, and send portions to him for whom nothing is prepared;
for this day is holy to our Lord; and be not grieved *and* depressed,
for the joy of the Lord is your strength *and* stronghold.
11 So the Levites quieted all the people, saying, Be still, for the
day is holy; and do not be grieved *and* sad.
12 And all the people went their way to eat, drink, send portions, and make great rejoicing, for they had understood the words
that were declared to them.
13 The second day all the heads of fathers' houses with the
priests and Levites, gathered to Ezra the scribe to study *and* understand the words of [a]divine instruction.
14 And they found written in the law which the Lord had commanded by Moses that the Israelites should dwell in booths during
the feast of the seventh month.
15 And that they should publish and proclaim in all their towns
and in Jerusalem, saying, Go out to the hills and bring branches
of olive, wild olive, myrtle, palm, and other leafy trees to make
booths, as it is written. [Lev. 23:39, 40.]
16 So the people went out and brought them and made themselves booths, each on the roof of his house, and in their courts
and the courts of God's house, and in the squares of the Water
Gate and the Gate of Ephraim.
17 All the assembly of returned exiles made booths and dwelt in
them; for since the days of Jeshua [Joshua] son of Nun to that day
the Israelites had not done so. And there was very great rejoicing.
18 Also day by day, from the first day to the last, Ezra read in
the book of the law of God. They kept the feast seven days; the
eighth day was a [closing] solemn assembly, according to the
ordinance.

9 NOW ON the twenty-fourth day of this month the Israelites
were assembled with fasting and in sackcloth, and with earth
upon their heads.
2 And the Israelites separated themselves from all foreigners,
and stood and confessed their sins and the iniquities of their
fathers.
3 And they stood in their place and read from the book of the
law of the Lord their God a fourth of the day; and for another
fourth of it they confessed and worshiped the Lord their God.
4 On the stairs of the Levites stood Jeshua, Bani, Kadmiel,
Shebaniah, Bunni, Sherebiah, Bani, and Chenani, and cried with
a loud voice to the Lord their God.

AMP [a] See footnote on Ezra 3:2.

## New American Standard

6Then Ezra blessed the LORD the great God. And all the people
answered, "Amen, Amen!" while lifting up their hands; then they
bowed low and worshiped the LORD with *their* faces to the ground.
7Also Jeshua, Bani, Sherebiah, Jamin, Akkub, Shabbethai, Hodiah, Maaseiah, Kelita, Azariah, Jozabad, Hanan, Pelaiah, and the
Levites, explained the law to the people while the people *remained*
in their place.
8And they read from the book, from the law of God, translating
to give the sense so that they understood the reading.

*"This Day Is Holy"*

9¶ Then Nehemiah, who was the governor, and Ezra the priest
*and* scribe, and the Levites who taught the people said to all the
people, "This day is holy to the LORD your God; do not mourn or
weep." For all the people were weeping when they heard the
words of the law.
10Then he said to them, "Go, eat of the fat, drink of the sweet,
and send portions to him who has nothing prepared; for this day
is holy to our Lord. Do not be grieved, for the joy of the LORD is
your strength."
11So the Levites calmed all the people, saying, "Be still, for the
day is holy; do not be grieved."
12And all the people went away to eat, to drink, to send portions and to celebrate a great festival, because they understood the
words which had been made known to them.

*Feast of Booths Restored*

13¶ Then on the second day the heads of fathers' *households* of
all the people, the priests, and the Levites were gathered to Ezra
the scribe that they might gain insight into the words of the law.
14And they found written in the law how the LORD had commanded through Moses that the sons of Israel should live in booths
during the feast of the seventh month.
15So they proclaimed and circulated a proclamation in all their
cities and in Jerusalem, saying, "Go out to the hills, and bring olive
branches, and wild olive branches, myrtle branches, palm
branches, and branches of *other* leafy trees, to make booths, as it
is written."
16So the people went out and brought *them* and made booths
for themselves, each on his roof, and in their courts, and in the
courts of the house of God, and in the square at the Water Gate,
and in the square at the Gate of Ephraim.
17And the entire assembly of those who had returned from the
captivity made booths and lived in them. The sons of Israel had
indeed not done so from the days of Joshua the son of Nun to that
day. And there was great rejoicing.
18And he read from the book of the law of God daily, from the
first day to the last day. And they celebrated the feast seven days,
and on the eighth day *there was* a solemn assembly according to the
ordinance.

## New International

lifted their hands and responded, "Amen! Amen!" Then they
bowed down and worshiped the LORD with their faces to the
ground.
7The Levites—Jeshua, Bani, Sherebiah, Jamin, Akkub, Shabbethai, Hodiah, Maaseiah, Kelita, Azariah, Jozabad, Hanan and Pelaiah—instructed the people in the Law while the people were
standing there. 8They read from the Book of the Law of God,
making it clear[b] and giving the meaning so that the people could
understand what was being read.
9Then Nehemiah the governor, Ezra the priest and scribe, and
the Levites who were instructing the people said to them all, "This
day is sacred to the LORD your God. Do not mourn or weep." For
all the people had been weeping as they listened to the words of
the Law.
10Nehemiah said, "Go and enjoy choice food and sweet drinks,
and send some to those who have nothing prepared. This day is
sacred to our Lord. Do not grieve, for the joy of the LORD is your
strength."
11The Levites calmed all the people, saying, "Be still, for this is
a sacred day. Do not grieve."
12Then all the people went away to eat and drink, to send
portions of food and to celebrate with great joy, because they now
understood the words that had been made known to them.
13On the second day of the month, the heads of all the families,
along with the priests and the Levites, gathered around Ezra the
scribe to give attention to the words of the Law. 14They found
written in the Law, which the LORD had commanded through
Moses, that the Israelites were to live in booths during the feast of
the seventh month 15and that they should proclaim this word and
spread it throughout their towns and in Jerusalem: "Go out into
the hill country and bring back branches from olive and wild olive
trees, and from myrtles, palms and shade trees, to make
booths"—as it is written.[c]
16So the people went out and brought back branches and built
themselves booths on their own roofs, in their courtyards, in the
courts of the house of God and in the square by the Water Gate
and the one by the Gate of Ephraim. 17The whole company that
had returned from exile built booths and lived in them. From the
days of Joshua son of Nun until that day, the Israelites had not
celebrated it like this. And their joy was very great.
18Day after day, from the first day to the last, Ezra read from
the Book of the Law of God. They celebrated the feast for seven
days, and on the eighth day, in accordance with the regulation,
there was an assembly.

## New American Standard

*The People Confess Their Sin*

9 NOW ON the twenty-fourth day of this month the sons of
Israel assembled with fasting, in sackcloth, and with dirt
upon them.
2And the descendants of Israel separated themselves from all
foreigners, and stood and confessed their sins and the iniquities
of their fathers.
3While they stood in their place, they read from the book of the
law of the LORD their God for a fourth of the day; and for *another*
fourth they confessed and worshiped the LORD their God.
4Now on the Levites' platform stood Jeshua, Bani, Kadmiel,
Shebaniah, Bunni, Sherebiah, Bani, *and* Chenani, and they cried
with a loud voice to the LORD their God.

## New International

*The Israelites Confess Their Sins*

9 ON THE twenty-fourth day of the same month, the Israelites
gathered together, fasting and wearing sackcloth and having
dust on their heads. 2Those of Israelite descent had separated
themselves from all foreigners. They stood in their places and
confessed their sins and the wickedness of their fathers. 3They
stood where they were and read from the Book of the Law of the
LORD their God for a quarter of the day, and spent another quarter
in confession and in worshiping the LORD their God. 4Standing on
the stairs were the Levites—Jeshua, Bani, Kadmiel, Shebaniah,
Bunni, Sherebiah, Bani and Kenani—who called with loud voices
to the LORD their God. 5And the Levites—Jeshua, Kadmiel, Bani,

NIV [b] 8 Or *God, translating it* [c] 15 See Lev. 23:37-40.

## King James

5Then the Levites, Jeshua, and Kadmiel, Bani, Hashabniah,
Sherebiah. Hodijah, Shebaniah, *and* Pethahiah, said, Stand up *and*
bless the LORD your God for ever and ever: and blessed be thy
glorious name, which is exalted above all blessing and praise.
6Thou, *even* thou, *art* LORD alone; thou hast made heaven, the
heaven of heavens, with all their host, the earth, and all *things* that
*are* therein, the seas, and all that *is* therein, and thou preservest
them all; and the host of heaven worshippeth thee.
7Thou *art* the LORD the God, who didst choose Abram, and
broughtest him forth out of Ur of the Chaldees, and gavest him the
name of Abraham;
8And foundest his heart faithful before thee, and madest a
covenant with him to give the land of the Canaanites, the Hittites,
the Amorites, and the Perizzites, and the Jebusites, and the Girgashites, to give *it, I say,* to his seed, and hast performed thy words;
for thou *art* righteous:
9And didst see the affliction of our fathers in Egypt, and heardest their cry by the Red sea;
10And showedst signs and wonders upon Pharaoh, and on all
his servants, and on all the people of his land: for thou knewest
that they dealt proudly against them. So didst thou get thee a
name, as *it is* this day.
11And thou didst divide the sea before them, so that they went
through the midst of the sea on the dry land; and their persecutors
thou threwest into the deeps, as a stone into the mighty waters.
12Moreover thou leddest them in the day by a cloudy pillar; and
in the night by a pillar of fire, to give them light in the way wherein
they should go.
13Thou camest down also upon mount Sinai, and spakest with
them from heaven, and gavest them right judgments, and true
laws, good statutes and commandments:
14And madest known unto them thy holy sabbath, and commandedst them precepts, statutes, and laws, by the hand of Moses
thy servant:
15And gavest them bread from heaven for their hunger, and
broughtest forth water for them out of the rock for their thirst, and
promisedst them that they should go in to possess the land which
thou hadst sworn to give them.
16But they and our fathers dealt proudly, and hardened their
necks, and hearkened not to thy commandments,

## Amplified

5Then the Levites, Jeshua, Kadmiel, Bani, Hashabneiah, Sherebiah, Hodiah, Shebaniah, and Pethahiah said, Stand up and bless
the Lord, your God from everlasting to everlasting. Blessed be
Your glorious name which is exalted above all blessing and praise.
6[And Ezra said], You are the Lord, You alone; You have made
Heaven, the Heaven of heavens, with all their host, the earth, and
all that is on it, the seas and all that is in them, and You preserve
them all; and the host of Heaven worship You.
7You are the Lord, the God Who chose Abram and brought him
out of Ur of the Chaldees and gave him the name Abraham;
8You found his heart faithful before You, and made the covenant with him to give his descendants the land of the Canaanite,
Hittite, Amorite, Perizzite, Jebusite, and Girgashite; and You have
fulfilled Your promise, for You are just *and* righteous.
9You saw our fathers' affliction in Egypt, and heard their cry at
the Red Sea;
10You performed signs and wonders against Pharaoh and all his
servants and all the people of his land, for You knew that they
dealt insolently against the Israelites; and You got You a name, as
it is today.
11You divided the sea before them, so that they went through
*its* midst on dry land; their persecutors You threw into the depths,
as a stone into mighty waters.
12Moreover by a pillar of cloud You led them by day, and by a
pillar of fire by night to light the way they should go.
13You came down also upon Mount Sinai, and spoke with them
from Heaven and gave them right ordinances and true laws, good
statutes and commandments.
14And You made known to them Your holy sabbath and gave
them commandments, statutes and a law by Moses Your servant.
15You gave them bread from Heaven for their hunger, and
brought water for them out of the rock for their thirst, and told
them to go in and possess the land You had sworn to give them.
[John 6:31-34.]
16But they and our fathers acted presumptuously and stiffened
their necks, and did not heed Your commandments;

## New American Standard

5¶ Then the Levites, Jeshua, Kadmiel, Bani, Hashabneiah, Sherebiah, Hodiah, Shebaniah, *and* Pethahiah, said, "Arise, bless the LORD your God forever and ever!
O may Thy glorious name be blessed
And exalted above all blessing and praise!
6 "Thou alone art the LORD.
Thou hast made the heavens,
The heaven of heavens with all their host,
The earth and all that is on it,
The seas and all that is in them.
Thou dost give life to all of them
And the heavenly host bows down before Thee.
7 "Thou art the LORD God,
Who chose Abram
And brought him out from Ur of the Chaldees,
And gave him the name Abraham.
8 "And Thou didst find his heart faithful before Thee,
And didst make a covenant with him
To give *him* the land of the Canaanite,
Of the Hittite and the Amorite,
Of the Perizzite, the Jebusite, and the Girgashite—
To give *it* to his descendants.
And Thou hast fulfilled Thy promise,
For Thou art righteous.

9¶ "Thou didst see the affliction of our fathers in Egypt,
And didst hear their cry by the Red Sea.
10 "Then Thou didst perform signs and wonders against Pharaoh,
Against all his servants and all the people of his land;
For Thou didst know that they acted arrogantly toward them,
And didst make a name for Thyself as *it is* this day.
11 "And Thou didst divide the sea before them,
So they passed through the midst of the sea on dry ground;
And their pursuers Thou didst hurl into the depths,
Like a stone into raging waters.
12 "And with a pillar of cloud Thou didst lead them by day,
And with a pillar of fire by night
To light for them the way
In which they were to go.
13 "Then Thou didst come down on Mount Sinai,
And didst speak with them from heaven;
Thou didst give to them just ordinances and true laws,
Good statutes and commandments.
14 "So Thou didst make known to them Thy holy sabbath,
And didst lay down for them commandments, statutes, and law,
Through Thy servant Moses.
15 "Thou didst provide bread from heaven for them for their hunger,
Thou didst bring forth water from a rock for them for their thirst,
And Thou didst tell them to enter in order to possess
The land which Thou didst swear to give them.

16¶ "But they, our fathers, acted arrogantly;
They [a]became stubborn and would not listen to Thy commandments.

NAS [a] Lit., *stiffened their neck*

## New International

Hashabneiah, Sherebiah, Hodiah, Shebaniah and Pethahiah—
said: "Stand up and praise the LORD your God, who is from everlasting to everlasting.[b]"

"Blessed be your glorious name, and may it be exalted
above all blessing and praise. 6You alone are the LORD. You
made the heavens, even the highest heavens, and all their starry host, the earth and all that is on it, the seas and all that is in them. You give life to everything, and the multitudes of heaven worship you.
7"You are the LORD God, who chose Abram and brought
him out of Ur of the Chaldeans and named him Abraham.
8You found his heart faithful to you, and you made a covenant
with him to give to his descendants the land of the Canaanites, Hittites, Amorites, Perizzites, Jebusites and Girgashites. You have kept your promise because you are righteous.
9"You saw the suffering of our forefathers in Egypt; you
heard their cry at the Red Sea.[c] 10You sent miraculous signs
and wonders against Pharaoh, against all his officials and all the people of his land, for you knew how arrogantly the Egyptians treated them. You made a name for yourself, which
remains to this day. 11You divided the sea before them, so that
they passed through it on dry ground, but you hurled their
pursuers into the depths, like a stone into mighty waters. 12By
day you led them with a pillar of cloud, and by night with a pillar of fire to give them light on the way they were to take.
13"You came down on Mount Sinai; you spoke to them
from heaven. You gave them regulations and laws that are just and right, and decrees and commands that are good.
14You made known to them your holy Sabbath and gave them
commands, decrees and laws through your servant Moses.
15In their hunger you gave them bread from heaven and in
their thirst you brought them water from the rock; you told them to go in and take possession of the land you had sworn with uplifted hand to give them.
16"But they, our forefathers, became arrogant and stiff-
necked, and did not obey your commands. 17They refused to

NIV [b] 5 Or *God for ever and ever* [c] 9 Hebrew *Yam Suph;* that is, Sea of Reeds

## King James

17 And refused to obey, neither were mindful of thy wonders that thou didst among them; but hardened their necks, and in their rebellion appointed a captain to return to their bondage: but thou *art* a God ready to pardon, gracious and merciful, slow to anger, and of great kindness, and forsookest them not.

18 Yea, when they had made them a molten calf, and said, This *is* thy God that brought thee up out of Egypt, and had wrought great provocations;

19 Yet thou in thy manifold mercies forsookest them not in the wilderness: the pillar of the cloud departed not from them by day, to lead them in the way; neither the pillar of fire by night, to show them light, and the way wherein they should go.

20 Thou gavest also thy good spirit to instruct them, and withheldest not thy manna from their mouth, and gavest them water for their thirst.

21 Yea, forty years didst thou sustain them in the wilderness, *so that* they lacked nothing; their clothes waxed not old, and their feet swelled not.

22 Moreover thou gavest them kingdoms and nations, and didst divide them into corners: so they possessed the land of Sihon, and the land of the king of Heshbon, and the land of Og king of Bashan.

23 Their children also multipliedst thou as the stars of heaven, and broughtest them into the land, concerning which thou hadst promised to their fathers, that they should go in to possess *it*.

24 So the children went in and possessed the land, and thou subduedst before them the inhabitants of the land, the Canaanites, and gavest them into their hands, with their kings, and the people of the land, that they might do with them as they would.

25 And they took strong cities, and a fat land, and possessed houses full of all goods, wells digged, vineyards, and oliveyards, and fruit trees in abundance: so they did eat, and were filled, and became fat, and delighted themselves in thy great goodness.

26 Nevertheless they were disobedient, and rebelled against thee, and cast thy law behind their backs, and slew thy prophets which testified against them to turn them to thee, and they wrought great provocations.

27 Therefore thou deliveredst them into the hand of their enemies, who vexed them: and in the time of their trouble, when they cried unto thee, thou heardest *them* from heaven; and according to thy manifold mercies thou gavest them saviours, who saved them out of the hand of their enemies.

## Amplified

17 They refused to obey, nor were they mindful of Your wonders *and* miracles which You did among them; but stiffened their necks, and in their rebellion appointed a captain that they might return to their bondage [in Egypt]. But You are a God ready to pardon, gracious and merciful, slow to anger, and of great steadfast love, and You did not forsake them.

18 Even when they had made them a molten calf, and said, This is your god which brought you out of Egypt, and had committed great *and* contemptible blasphemies,

19 You in Your great mercies forsook them not in the wilderness; the pillar of the cloud departed not from them by day to lead them in the way, nor the pillar of fire by night to light the way they should go.

20 You also gave Your good Spirit to instruct them, and withheld not Your manna from them and gave water for their thirst.

21 Forty years You sustained them in the wilderness; they lacked nothing; their clothes did not wear out and their feet did not swell.

22 Also You gave them kingdoms and peoples, and allotted to them every corner. So they possessed the land of Sihon king of Heshbon, and the land of Og king of Bashan.

23 Their children You also multiplied as the stars of heaven, and brought them into the land, which You told their fathers they should go in and possess.

24 So the descendants went in and possessed the land, and You subdued before them the inhabitants of the land, the Canaanites, and gave them into their hands, with their kings and the peoples of the land, that they might do with them as they would.

25 And they captured fortified cities and a rich land, and took possession of houses full of all good things, cisterns hewn out, vineyards, olive orchards, and fruit trees in abundance; so they ate and were filled and became fat, and delighted themselves in Your great goodness.

26 Yet they were disobedient, and rebelled against You and cast Your law behind their back, and killed Your prophets who accused *and* warned them to turn to You again, and they committed great *and* contemptible blasphemies.

27 Therefore You delivered them into the hand of their enemies, who distressed them. In the time of their suffering when they cried to You, You heard them from Heaven, and according to Your abundant mercies You gave them deliverers who saved them from their enemies.

## New American Standard

17 "And they refused to listen,
And did not remember Thy wondrous deeds which Thou hadst performed among them;
So they [a]became stubborn and appointed a leader to return to their slavery in Egypt.
But Thou art a God of forgiveness,
Gracious and compassionate,
Slow to anger, and abounding in lovingkindness;
And Thou didst not forsake them.
18 "Even when they made for themselves
A calf of molten metal
And said, 'This is your God
Who brought you up from Egypt,'
And committed great [b]blasphemies,
19 Thou, in Thy great compassion,
Didst not forsake them in the wilderness;
The pillar of cloud did not leave them by day,
To guide them on their way,
Nor the pillar of fire by night, to light for them the way in which they were to go.
20 "And Thou didst give Thy good Spirit to instruct them,
Thy manna Thou didst not withhold from their mouth,
And Thou didst give them water for their thirst.
21 "Indeed, forty years Thou didst provide for them in the wilderness *and* they were not in want;
Their clothes did not wear out, nor did their feet swell.
22 "Thou didst also give them kingdoms and peoples,
And Thou didst allot *them* to them as a boundary.
And they took possession of the land of Sihon the king of Heshbon,
And the land of Og the king of Bashan.
23 "And Thou didst make their sons numerous as the stars of heaven,
And Thou didst bring them into the land
Which Thou hadst told their fathers to enter and possess.
24 "So their sons entered and possessed the land.
And Thou didst subdue before them the inhabitants of the land, the Canaanites,
And Thou didst give them into their hand, with their kings, and the peoples of the land,
To do with them as they desired.
25 "And they captured fortified cities and a fertile land.
They took possession of houses full of every good thing,
Hewn cisterns, vineyards, olive groves,
Fruit trees in abundance.
So they ate, were filled, and grew fat,
And reveled in Thy great goodness.

26¶ "But they became disobedient and rebelled against Thee,
And cast Thy law behind their backs
And killed Thy prophets who had admonished them
So that they might return to Thee,
And they committed great [c]blasphemies.
27 "Therefore Thou didst deliver them into the hand of their oppressors who oppressed them,
But when they cried to Thee in the time of their distress,
Thou didst hear from heaven, and according to Thy great compassion
Thou didst give them deliverers who delivered them from the hand of their oppressors.

NAS [a] Lit., *stiffened their neck* [b] Lit., *acts of contempt* [c] Lit., *acts of contempt*

## New International

listen and failed to remember the miracles you performed among them. They became stiff-necked and in their rebellion appointed a leader in order to return to their slavery. But you are a forgiving God, gracious and compassionate, slow to anger and abounding in love. Therefore you did not desert
them, 18even when they cast for themselves an image of a calf and said, 'This is your god, who brought you up out of Egypt,' or when they committed awful blasphemies.
19"Because of your great compassion you did not abandon them in the desert. By day the pillar of cloud did not cease to guide them on their path, nor the pillar of fire by night to shine on the way they were to take.
20You gave your good Spirit to instruct them. You did not withhold your manna from their mouths, and you gave them water for their thirst.
21For forty years you sustained them in the desert; they lacked nothing, their clothes did not wear out nor did their feet become swollen.
22"You gave them kingdoms and nations, allotting to them even the remotest frontiers. They took over the country of Sihon[d] king of Heshbon and the country of Og king of Bashan.
23You made their sons as numerous as the stars in the sky, and you brought them into the land that you told their fathers to enter and possess.
24Their sons went in and took possession of the land. You subdued before them the Canaanites, who lived in the land; you handed the Canaanites over to them, along with their kings and the peoples of the land, to deal with them as they pleased.
25They captured fortified cities and fertile land; they took possession of houses filled with all kinds of good things, wells already dug, vineyards, olive groves and fruit trees in abundance. They ate to the full and were well-nourished; they reveled in your great goodness.
26"But they were disobedient and rebelled against you; they put your law behind their backs. They killed your prophets, who had admonished them in order to turn them back to you; they committed awful blasphemies.
27So you handed them over to their enemies, who oppressed them. But when they were oppressed they cried out to you. From heaven you heard them, and in your great compassion you gave them deliverers, who rescued them from the hand of their enemies.

NIV [d] 22 One Hebrew manuscript and Septuagint; most Hebrew manuscripts *Sihon, that is, the country of the*

## King James

28 But after they had rest, they did evil again before thee: therefore leftest thou them in the hand of their enemies, so that they
had the dominion over them: yet when they returned, and cried
unto thee, thou heardest *them* from heaven; and many times didst
thou deliver them according to thy mercies;
29 And testifiedst against them, that thou mightest bring them
again unto thy law: yet they dealt proudly, and hearkened not
unto thy commandments, but sinned against thy judgments,
(which if a man do, he shall live in them;) and withdrew the
shoulder, and hardened their neck, and would not hear.
30 Yet many years didst thou forbear them, and testifiedst
against them by thy spirit in thy prophets: yet would they not give
ear: therefore gavest thou them into the hand of the people of the
lands.
31 Nevertheless for thy great mercies' sake thou didst not utterly
consume them, nor forsake them; for thou *art* a gracious and
merciful God.
32 Now therefore, our God, the great, the mighty, and the terrible God, who keepest covenant and mercy, let not all the trouble
seem little before thee, that hath come upon us, on our kings, on
our princes, and on our priests, and on our prophets, and on our
fathers, and on all thy people, since the time of the kings of Assyria
unto this day.
33 Howbeit thou *art* just in all that is brought upon us; for thou
hast done right, but we have done wickedly:
34 Neither have our kings, our princes, our priests, nor our
fathers, kept thy law, nor hearkened unto thy commandments and
thy testimonies, wherewith thou didst testify against them.
35 For they have not served thee in their kingdom, and in thy
great goodness that thou gavest them, and in the large and fat land
which thou gavest before them, neither turned they from their
wicked works.
36 Behold, we *are* servants this day, and *for* the land that thou
gavest unto our fathers to eat the fruit thereof and the good thereof, behold, we *are* servants in it:
37 And it yieldeth much increase unto the kings whom thou hast
set over us because of our sins: also they have dominion over our
bodies, and over our cattle, at their pleasure, and we *are* in great
distress.
38 And because of all this we make a sure *covenant*, and write *it;*
and our princes, Levites, *and* priests, seal *unto it*.

**10** NOW THOSE that sealed *were*, Nehemiah, the Tirshatha,
the son of Hachaliah, and Zidkijah,
2 Seraiah, Azariah, Jeremiah,
3 Pashur, Amariah, Malchijah,
4 Hattush, Shebaniah, Malluch,

## Amplified

28 But after they had rest, they did evil again before You, therefore You left them in the hand of their enemies, so that they had
dominion over them; yet when they turned and cried to You, You
heard them from Heaven; and many times you delivered them
according to Your mercies,
29 And reproved *and* warned them, that You might bring them
again to Your law. Yet they acted presumptuously and did not
heed Your commandments, but sinned against Your ordinances,
by keeping which a man shall live, and they turned a stubborn
shoulder, stiffened their neck, and would not listen.
30 Yet You bore with them many years more and reproved *and*
warned them by Your Spirit through Your prophets; still they
would not listen. Therefore You gave them into the power of the
peoples of the lands.
31 Yet in Your great mercies You did not utterly consume them,
or forsake them, for You are a gracious and merciful God.
32 Now therefore, our God, the great, mighty, and terrible God,
Who keeps covenant and mercy *and* loving kindness, let not all the
trouble *and* hardship seem little to You, that has come upon us, our
kings, our princes, our priests, our prophets, our fathers, and on
all Your people, since the time of the kings of Assyria to this day.
33 However You are just in all that has come upon us, for You
have dealt faithfully, but we have done wickedly;
34 Our kings, our princes, our priests, and our fathers have not
kept Your law, or hearkened to Your commandments, Your warnings *and* reproofs which You gave them.
35 They did not serve You in their kingdom, and in Your great
goodness that You gave them, and in the large and rich land You
set before them, nor did they turn from their wicked works.
36 Behold, we are slaves this day, and as for the land that You
gave to our fathers to eat the fruit and the good of it, behold, we
are slaves in it.
37 And its rich yield goes to the kings whom You have set over
us because of our sins; they have power also over our bodies and
over our livestock at their pleasure, and we are in great distress.
38 Because of all this we make a firm *and* sure written covenant,
and our princes, Levites, and priests set their seal to it.

**10** THESE SET their seal: Nehemiah the governor, son of
Hacaliah, and Zedekiah,
2 Seraiah, Azariah, Jeremiah,
3 Pashhur, Amariah, Malchijah,
4 Hattush, Shebaniah, Malluch,

## New American Standard

28 "But as soon as they had rest, they did evil again before
Thee;
Therefore Thou didst abandon them to the hand of
their enemies, so that they ruled over them.
When they cried again to Thee, Thou didst hear from
heaven,
And many times Thou didst rescue them according to
Thy compassion,
29 And admonished them in order to turn them back to
Thy law.
Yet they acted arrogantly and did not listen to Thy
commandments but sinned against Thine ordinances,
By which if a man observes them he shall live.
And they turned a stubborn shoulder and stiffened
their neck, and would not listen.
30 "However, Thou didst bear with them for many years,
And admonished them by Thy Spirit through Thy
prophets,
Yet they would not give ear.
Therefore Thou didst give them into the hand of the
peoples of the lands.
31 "Nevertheless, in Thy great compassion Thou didst not
make an end of them or forsake them,
For Thou art a gracious and compassionate God.

32¶ "Now therefore, our God, the great, the mighty, and
the awesome God, who dost keep covenant and
lovingkindness,
Do not let all the hardship seem insignificant before
Thee,
Which has come upon us, our kings, our princes, our
priests, our prophets, our fathers, and on all Thy
people,
From the days of the kings of Assyria to this day.
33 "However, Thou art just in all that has come upon us;
For Thou hast dealt faithfully, but we have acted
wickedly.
34 "For our kings, our leaders, our priests, and our fathers
have not kept Thy law
Or paid attention to Thy commandments and Thine
admonitions with which Thou hast admonished them.
35 "But they, in their own kingdom,
With Thy great goodness which Thou didst give them,
With the broad and rich land which Thou didst set
before them,
Did not serve Thee or turn from their evil deeds.
36 "Behold, we are slaves today,
And as to the land which Thou didst give to our fathers
to eat of its fruit and its bounty,
Behold, we are slaves on it.
37 "And its abundant produce is for the kings
Whom Thou hast set over us because of our sins;
They also rule over our bodies
And over our cattle as they please,
So we are in great distress.

*A Covenant Results*

38 "Now because of all this
We are making an agreement in writing;
And on the sealed document *are the names of* our
leaders, our Levites *and* our priests."

*Signers of the Document*

**10** NOW ON the sealed document *were the names of:* Nehemiah the governor, the son of Hacaliah, and Zedekiah,
2Seraiah, Azariah, Jeremiah,
3Pashhur, Amariah, Malchijah,
4Hattush, Shebaniah, Malluch,

## New International

28"But as soon as they were at rest, they again did what
was evil in your sight. Then you abandoned them to the hand
of their enemies so that they ruled over them. And when they
cried out to you again, you heard from heaven, and in your
compassion you delivered them time after time.
29"You warned them to return to your law, but they
became arrogant and disobeyed your commands. They
sinned against your ordinances, by which a man will live if he
obeys them. Stubbornly they turned their backs on you,
became stiff-necked and refused to listen.
30For many years
you were patient with them. By your Spirit you admonished
them through your prophets. Yet they paid no attention, so
you handed them over to the neighboring peoples.
31But in
your great mercy you did not put an end to them or abandon
them, for you are a gracious and merciful God.
32"Now therefore, O our God, the great, mighty and awesome God, who keeps his covenant of love, do not let all this
hardship seem trifling in your eyes—the hardship that has
come upon us, upon our kings and leaders, upon our priests
and prophets, upon our fathers and all your people, from the
days of the kings of Assyria until today.
33In all that has
happened to us, you have been just; you have acted faithfully,
while we did wrong.
34Our kings, our leaders, our priests and
our fathers did not follow your law; they did not pay attention
to your commands or the warnings you gave them.
35Even
while they were in their kingdom, enjoying your great goodness to them in the spacious and fertile land you gave them,
they did not serve you or turn from their evil ways.
36"But see, we are slaves today, slaves in the land you gave
our forefathers so they could eat its fruit and the other good
things it produces.
37Because of our sins, its abundant harvest
goes to the kings you have placed over us. They rule over our
bodies and our cattle as they please. We are in great distress.

*The Agreement of the People*

38"In view of all this, we are making a binding agreement,
putting it in writing, and our leaders, our Levites and our priests
are affixing their seals to it."

**10** THOSE WHO sealed it were:
Nehemiah the governor, the son of Hacaliah.

Zedekiah,
2Seraiah, Azariah, Jeremiah,
3Pashhur, Amariah, Malkijah,
4Hattush, Shebaniah, Malluch,

## King James

5Harim, Meremoth, Obadiah,
6Daniel, Ginnethon, Baruch,
7Meshullam, Abijah, Mijamin,
8Maaziah, Bilgai, Shemaiah: these *were* the priests.
9And the Levites: both Jeshua the son of Azaniah, Binnui of the sons of Henadad, Kadmiel;
10And their brethren, Shebaniah, Hodijah, Kelita, Pelaiah, Hanan,
11Micha, Rehob, Hashabiah,
12Zaccur, Sherebiah, Shebaniah,
13Hodijah, Bani, Beninu.
14The chief of the people; Parosh, Pahath-moab, Elam, Zatthu, Bani,
15Bunni, Azgad, Bebai,
16Adonijah, Bigvai, Adin,
17Ater, Hizkijah, Azzur,
18Hodijah, Hashum, Bezai,
19Hariph, Anathoth, Nebai,
20Magpiash, Meshullam, Hezir,
21Meshezabeel, Zadok, Jaddua,
22Pelatiah, Hanan, Anaiah,
23Hoshea, Hananiah, Hashub,
24Hallohesh, Pileha, Shobek,
25Rehum, Hashabnah, Maaseiah,
26And Ahijah, Hanan, Anan,
27Malluch, Harim, Baanah.
28¶ And the rest of the people, the priests, the Levites, the porters, the singers, the Nethinims, and all they that had separated themselves from the people of the lands unto the law of God, their wives, their sons, and their daughters, every one having knowledge, and having understanding;
29They clave to their brethren, their nobles, and entered into a curse, and into an oath, to walk in God's law, which was given by Moses the servant of God, and to observe and do all the commandments of the LORD our Lord, and his judgments and his statutes;
30And that we would not give our daughters unto the people of the land, nor take their daughters for our sons:
31And *if* the people of the land bring ware or any victuals on the sabbath day to sell, *that* we would not buy it of them on the sabbath, or on the holy day: and *that* we would leave the seventh year, and the exaction of every debt.
32Also we made ordinances for us, to charge ourselves yearly with the third part of a shekel for the service of the house of our God;
33For the showbread, and for the continual meat offering, and for the continual burnt offering, of the sabbaths, of the new moons, for the set feasts, and for the holy *things,* and for the sin offerings to make an atonement for Israel, and *for* all the work of the house of our God.
34And we cast the lots among the priests, the Levites, and the people, for the wood offering, to bring *it* into the house of our God, after the houses of our fathers, at times appointed year by year, to burn upon the altar of the LORD our God, as *it is* written in the law:
35And to bring the firstfruits of our ground, and the firstfruits of all fruit of all trees, year by year, unto the house of the LORD:
36Also the firstborn of our sons, and of our cattle, as *it is* written in the law, and the firstlings of our herds and of our flocks, to bring to the house of our God, unto the priests that minister in the house of our God:

## Amplified

5Harim, Meremoth, Obadiah,
6Daniel, Ginnethon, Baruch,
7Meshullam, Abijah, Mijamin,
8Ma-aziah, Bilgai, Shemaiah, the priests.
9And the Levites: Jeshua son of Azaniah, Binnui of the sons of Henadad, Kadmiel;
10And their brethren, Shebaniah, Hodiah, Kelita, Pelaiah, Hanan,
11Mica, Rehob, Hashabiah,
12Zaccur, Sherebiah, Shebaniah,
13Hodiah, Bani, Beninu.
14The chiefs of the people: Parosh, Pahath-moab, Elam, Zattu, Bani,
15Bunni, Azgad, Bebai,
16Adonijah, Bigvai, Adin,
17Ater, Hezekiah, Azzur,
18Hodiah, Hashum, Bezai,
19Hariph, Anathoth, Nebai,
20Magpiash, Meshullam, Hezir,
21Meshezabel, Zadok, Jaddua,
22Pelatiah, Hanan, Anaiah,
23Hoshea, Hananiah, Hasshub,
24Hallohesh, Pilha, Shobek,
25Rehum, Hashabnah, Ma-aseiah,
26Ahiah, Hanan, Anan,
27Malluch, Harim, Baanah.
28And the rest of the people, the priests, Levites, doorkeepers, singers, Nethinim [temple servants], and all they who had separated themselves from the people of the lands to the law of God, their wives, their sons, their daughters, all who had knowledge and understanding,
29Joined with their brethren, their nobles, and entered into a curse and an oath to walk in God's law which was given to Moses the servant of God, and to observe and do all the commandments of the Lord our Lord and His ordinances and His statutes;
30We would not give our daughters to the people of the land or take their daughters for our sons;
31And if the peoples of the land brought wares or any grain on the sabbath day to sell, we would not buy it on the sabbath, or on a holy day; and we would forego raising crops the seventh year [letting the land lie fallow] and the compulsory payment of every debt. [Exod. 23:10, 11; Deut. 15:1, 2.]
32Also we pledged ourselves to pay yearly a third of a shekel for the service expenses of the house of our God [which are]:
33For the showbread, for the continual cereal and burnt offerings, the sabbaths, the new moons, the set feasts, the holy things, the sin offerings to make atonement for Israel, and for all the work of the house of our God.
34We also cast lots, the priests, the Levites, and the people, for the wood offering, to bring it into the house of our God, according to our fathers' houses, at appointed times year by year, to burn upon the altar of the Lord our God, as it is written in the law.
35And [we obligated ourselves] to bring the first fruits of our ground, and the first of all fruit of all trees, year by year, to the house of the Lord;
36Also the first-born of our sons and of our cattle, as is written in the law, and the firstlings of our herds and flocks, to bring to the house of our God, to the priests who minister in [His] house;

## New American Standard

5Harim, Meremoth, Obadiah,
6Daniel, Ginnethon, Baruch,
7Meshullam, Abijah, Mijamin,
8Maaziah, Bilgai, Shemaiah. These *were* the priests.
9And the Levites: Jeshua the son of Azaniah, Binnui of the sons of Henadad, Kadmiel;
10also their brothers Shebaniah, Hodiah, Kelita, Pelaiah, Hanan,
11Mica, Rehob, Hashabiah,
12Zaccur, Sherebiah, Shebaniah,
13Hodiah, Bani, Beninu.
14The leaders of the people: Parosh, Pahath-moab, Elam, Zattu, Bani,
15Bunni, Azgad, Bebai,
16Adonijah, Bigvai, Adin,
17Ater, Hezekiah, Azzur,
18Hodiah, Hashum, Bezai,
19Hariph, Anathoth, Nebai,
20Magpiash, Meshullam, Hezir,
21Meshezabel, Zadok, Jaddua,
22Pelatiah, Hanan, Anaiah,
23Hoshea, Hananiah, Hasshub,
24Hallohesh, Pilha, Shobek,
25Rehum, Hashabnah, Maaseiah,
26Ahiah, Hanan, Anan,
27Malluch, Harim, Baanah.

*Obligations of the Document*

28¶ Now the rest of the people, the priests, the Levites, the gatekeepers, the singers, the temple servants, and all those who had separated themselves from the peoples of the lands to the law of God, their wives, their sons and their daughters, all those who had knowledge and understanding,
29are joining with their kinsmen, their nobles, and are taking on themselves a curse and an oath to walk in God's law, which was given through Moses, God's servant, and to keep and to observe all the commandments of GOD our Lord, and His ordinances and His statutes;
30and that we will not give our daughters to the peoples of the land or take their daughters for our sons.
31As for the peoples of the land who bring wares or any grain on the sabbath day to sell, we will not buy from them on the sabbath or a holy day; and we will forego *the crops* the seventh year and the exaction of every debt.
32¶ We also placed ourselves under obligation to contribute yearly one third of a shekel for the service of the house of our God:
33for the showbread, for the continual grain offering, for the continual burnt offering, the sabbaths, the new moon, for the appointed times, for the holy things and for the sin offerings to make atonement for Israel, and all the work of the house of our God.
34¶ Likewise we cast lots for the supply of wood *among* the priests, the Levites, and the people in order that they might bring it to the house of our God, according to our fathers' households, at fixed times annually, to burn on the altar of the LORD our God as it is written in the law;
35and in order that they might bring the first fruits of our ground and the first fruits of all the fruit of every tree to the house of the LORD annually,
36and bring to the house of our God the first-born of our sons and of our cattle, and the first-born of our herds and our flocks as it is written in the law, for the priests who are ministering in the house of our God.

## New International

5Harim, Meremoth, Obadiah,
6Daniel, Ginnethon, Baruch,
7Meshullam, Abijah, Mijamin,
8Maaziah, Bilgai and Shemaiah.
These were the priests.

9The Levites:

Jeshua son of Azaniah, Binnui of the sons of Henadad, Kadmiel,
10and their associates: Shebaniah,
Hodiah, Kelita, Pelaiah, Hanan,
11Mica, Rehob, Hashabiah,
12Zaccur, Sherebiah, Shebaniah,
13Hodiah, Bani and Beninu.

14The leaders of the people:

Parosh, Pahath-Moab, Elam, Zattu, Bani,
15Bunni, Azgad, Bebai,
16Adonijah, Bigvai, Adin,
17Ater, Hezekiah, Azzur,
18Hodiah, Hashum, Bezai,
19Hariph, Anathoth, Nebai,
20Magpiash, Meshullam, Hezir,
21Meshezabel, Zadok, Jaddua,
22Pelatiah, Hanan, Anaiah,
23Hoshea, Hananiah, Hasshub,
24Hallohesh, Pilha, Shobek,
25Rehum, Hashabnah, Maaseiah,
26Ahiah, Hanan, Anan,
27Malluch, Harim and Baanah.

28"The rest of the people—priests, Levites, gatekeepers, singers, temple servants and all who separated themselves from the neighboring peoples for the sake of the Law of God, together with their wives and all their sons and daughters who are able to understand— 29all these now join their brothers the nobles, and bind themselves with a curse and an oath to follow the Law of God given through Moses the servant of God and to obey carefully all the commands, regulations and decrees of the LORD our Lord.
30"We promise not to give our daughters in marriage to the peoples around us or take their daughters for our sons.
31"When the neighboring peoples bring merchandise or grain to sell on the Sabbath, we will not buy from them on the Sabbath or on any holy day. Every seventh year we will forgo working the land and will cancel all debts.
32"We assume the responsibility for carrying out the commands to give a third of a shekel[a] each year for the service of the house of our God: 33for the bread set out on the table; for the regular grain offerings and burnt offerings; for the offerings on the Sabbaths, New Moon festivals and appointed feasts; for the holy offerings; for sin offerings to make atonement for Israel; and for all the duties of the house of our God.
34"We—the priests, the Levites and the people—have cast lots to determine when each of our families is to bring to the house of our God at set times each year a contribution of wood to burn on the altar of the LORD our God, as it is written in the Law.
35"We also assume responsibility for bringing to the house of the LORD each year the firstfruits of our crops and of every fruit tree.
36"As it is also written in the Law, we will bring the firstborn of our sons and of our cattle, of our herds and of our flocks to the house of our God, to the priests ministering there.

NIV [a] 32 That is, about 1/8 ounce (about 4 grams)

## King James

37And *that* we should bring the firstfruits of our dough, and our
offerings, and the fruit of all manner of trees, of wine and of oil,
unto the priests, to the chambers of the house of our God; and the
tithes of our ground unto the Levites, that the same Levites might
have the tithes in all the cities of our tillage.
38And the priest the son of Aaron shall be with the Levites,
when the Levites take tithes: and the Levites shall bring up the
tithe of the tithes unto the house of our God, to the chambers, into
the treasure house.
39For the children of Israel and the children of Levi shall bring
the offering of the corn, of the new wine, and the oil, unto the
chambers, where *are* the vessels of the sanctuary, and the priests
that minister, and the porters, and the singers: and we will not
forsake the house of our God.

11 AND THE rulers of the people dwelt at Jerusalem: the rest
of the people also cast lots, to bring one of ten to dwell in
Jerusalem the holy city, and nine parts *to dwell* in *other* cities.
2And the people blessed all the men, that willingly offered
themselves to dwell at Jerusalem.
3¶ Now these *are* the chief of the province that dwelt in Jerusalem: but in the cities of Judah dwelt every one in his possession
in their cities, *to wit,* Israel, the priests, and the Levites, and the
Nethinims, and the children of Solomon's servants.
4And at Jerusalem dwelt *certain* of the children of Judah, and of
the children of Benjamin. Of the children of Judah; Athaiah the son
of Uzziah, the son of Zechariah, the son of Amariah, the son of
Shephatiah, the son of Mahalaleel, of the children of Perez;
5And Maaseiah the son of Baruch, the son of Col-hozeh, the son
of Hazaiah, the son of Adaiah, the son of Joiarib, the son of
Zechariah, the son of Shiloni.
6All the sons of Perez that dwelt at Jerusalem *were* four hundred
threescore and eight valiant men.
7And these *are* the sons of Benjamin; Sallu the son of Meshullam, the son of Joed, the son of Pedaiah, the son of Kolaiah, the
son of Maaseiah, the son of Ithiel, the son of Jesaiah.
8And after him Gabbai, Sallai, nine hundred twenty and eight.
9And Joel the son of Zichri *was* their overseer: and Judah the son
of Senuah *was* second over the city.
10Of the priests: Jedaiah the son of Joiarib, Jachin.
11Seraiah the son of Hilkiah, the son of Meshullam, the son of
Zadok, the son of Meraioth, the son of Ahitub, *was* the ruler of the
house of God.
12And their brethren that did the work of the house *were* eight
hundred twenty and two: and Adaiah the son of Jeroham, the son
of Pelaliah, the son of Amzi, the son of Zechariah, the son of
Pashur, the son of Malchiah,
13And his brethren, chief of the fathers, two hundred forty and
two: and Amashai the son of Azareel, the son of Ahasai, the son
of Meshillemoth, the son of Immer,
14And their brethren, mighty men of valour, an hundred
twenty and eight: and their overseer *was* Zabdiel, the son of *one of*
the great men.
15Also of the Levites: Shemaiah the son of Hashub, the son of
Azrikam, the son of Hashabiah, the son of Bunni;
16And Shabbethai and Jozabad, of the chief of the Levites, *had*
the oversight of the outward business of the house of God.
17And Mattaniah the son of Micha, the son of Zabdi, the son
of Asaph, *was* the principal to begin the thanksgiving in prayer:
and Bakbukiah the second among his brethren, and Abda the son
of Shammua, the son of Galal, the son of Jeduthun.
18All the Levites in the holy city *were* two hundred fourscore
and four.

## Amplified

37And bring the first *and* best of our coarse meal, our contributions, the fruit of all kinds of trees, of new wine, and of oil, to the
priests, to the chambers of the house of our God; and bring the
tithes from our ground to the Levites, for they, the Levites, collect
the tithes in all our rural towns.
38And the priest, the son of Aaron, shall be with the Levites
when [they] receive tithes; and [they] shall bring one-tenth of the
tithes to the house of our God, to the chambers, into the storehouse.
39For the Israelites and the sons of Levi shall bring the offering
of grain, new wine, and oil to the chambers, where the vessels of
the sanctuary are, and the priests who minister, and the gatekeepers and singers. We will not forsake *or* neglect the house of
our God.

11 NOW THE leaders of the people dwelt at Jerusalem; the
rest of the people also cast lots, to bring one of ten to dwell
in Jerusalem the holy city, while nine tenths dwelt in other towns
*and* villages.
2And the people blessed all the men who willingly offered to
live in Jerusalem.
3These are the province chiefs who dwelt in Jerusalem; but in
the towns of Judah every one lived on his property there: Israel,
the priests, the Levites, the temple servants, and the descendants
of Solomon's servants.
4And at Jerusalem dwelt certain of the sons of Judah and Benjamin. Of Judah: Athaiah son of Uzziah, son of Zechariah, son of
Amariah, son of Shephatiah, son of Mahalalel, of the sons of Perez;
5Ma-aseiah son of Baruch, son of Col-hozeh, son of Hazaiah,
son of Adaiah, son of Joiarib, son of Zechariah, son of the Shilonite.
6All the sons of Perez who dwelt at Jerusalem were 468 valiant
men.
7These are the sons of Benjamin: Sallu son of Meshullam, son
of Joed, son of Pedaiah, son of Kolaiah, son of Ma-aseiah, son of
Ithiel, son of Jeshaiah.
8And after him Gabbai, Sallai, 928.
9Joel son of Zichri was overseer; Judah son of Hassenuah was
second over the city.
10Of the priests: Jedaiah son of Joiarib, Jachin,
11Seraiah son of Hilkiah, son of Meshullam, son of Zadok, son
of Meraioth, son of Ahitub, ruler of the house of God,
12And their brethren who did the work of the house, 822; and
Adaiah son of Jeroham, son of Pelaliah, son of Amzi, son of Zechariah, son of Pashhur, son of Malchijah,
13And his brethren, chief of fathers' houses, 242; and Amashsai
son of Azarel, son of Ahzai, son of Meshillemoth, son of Immer,
14And their brethren, mighty men of valor, 128. Their overseer
was Zabdiel son of Haggedolim [one of the great men].
15And of the Levites: Shemaiah son of Hasshub, son of Azrikam, son of Hashabiah, son of Bunni;
16And Shabbethai and Jozabad, of the chiefs of the Levites, who
had charge of the outside work of the house of God.
17Mattaniah son of Mica, son of Zabdi, son of Asaph, leader to
begin the thanksgiving in prayer, and Bakbukiah, second among
his brethren; and Abda the son of Shammua, son of Galal, son of
Jeduthun.
18The Levites in the holy city were 284.

## New American Standard

37We will also bring the first of our dough, our contributions,
the fruit of every tree, the new wine and the oil to the priests at
the chambers of the house of our God, and the tithe of our ground
to the Levites, for the Levites are they who receive the tithes in all
the rural towns.
38And the priest, the son of Aaron, shall be with the Levites
when the Levites receive tithes, and the Levites shall bring up the
tenth of the tithes to the house of our God, to the chambers of the
storehouse.
39For the sons of Israel and the sons of Levi shall bring the
contribution of the grain, the new wine and the oil, to the chambers; there are the utensils of the sanctuary, the priests who are
ministering, the gatekeepers, and the singers. Thus we will not
neglect the house of our God.

*Time Passes Heads of Provinces*

11 NOW THE leaders of the people lived in Jerusalem, but
the rest of the people cast lots to bring one out of ten to
live in Jerusalem, the holy city, while nine-tenths *remained* in the
*other* cities.
2And the people blessed all the men who volunteered to live
in Jerusalem.
3¶ Now these are the heads of the provinces who lived in
Jerusalem, but in the cities of Judah each lived on his own property
in their cities—the Israelites, the priests, the Levites, the temple
servants and the descendants of Solomon's servants.
4And some of the sons of Judah and some of the sons of
Benjamin lived in Jerusalem. From the sons of Judah: Athaiah the
son of Uzziah, the son of Zechariah, the son of Amariah, the son
of Shephatiah, the son of Mahalalel, of the sons of Perez;
5and Maaseiah the son of Baruch, the son of Col-hozeh, the
son of Hazaiah, the son of Adaiah, the son of Joiarib, the son of
Zechariah, the son of the Shilonite.
6All the sons of Perez who lived in Jerusalem were 468 able
men.
7¶ Now these are the sons of Benjamin: Sallu the son of Meshullam, the son of Joed, the son of Pedaiah, the son of Kolaiah,
the son of Maaseiah, the son of Ithiel, the son of Jeshaiah;
8and after him Gabbai *and* Sallai, 928.
9And Joel the son of Zichri was their overseer, and Judah the
son of Hassenuah was second in command of the city.
10¶ From the priests: Jedaiah the son of Joiarib, Jachin,
11Seraiah the son of Hilkiah, the son of Meshullam, the son of
Zadok, the son of Meraioth, the son of Ahitub, the leader of the
house of God,
12and their [a]kinsmen who performed the work of the temple,
822; and Adaiah the son of Jeroham, the son of Pelaliah, the son
of Amzi, the son of Zechariah, the son of Pashhur, the son of
Malchijah,
13and his kinsmen, heads of fathers' *households,* 242; and
Amashsai the son of Azarel, the son of Ahzai, the son of Meshillemoth, the son of Immer,
14and their brothers, valiant warriors, 128. And their overseer
was Zabdiel, the son of Haggedolim.
15¶ Now from the Levites: Shemaiah the son of Hasshub, the
son of Azrikam, the son of Hashabiah, the son of Bunni;
16and Shabbethai and Jozabad, from the leaders of the Levites,
who were in charge of the outside work of the house of God;
17and Mattaniah the son of Mica, the son of Zabdi, the son of
Asaph, who was the leader in beginning the thanksgiving at
prayer, and Bakbukiah, the second among his brethren; and Abda
the son of Shammua, the son of Galal, the son of Jeduthun.
18All the Levites in the holy city *were* 284.

NAS [a] Lit., *brothers,* and so throughout this context

## New International

37"Moreover, we will bring to the storerooms of the house
of our God, to the priests, the first of our ground meal, of our
⌊grain⌋ offerings, of the fruit of all our trees and of our new
wine and oil. And we will bring a tithe of our crops to the
Levites, for it is the Levites who collect the tithes in all the
towns where we work. 38A priest descended from Aaron is to
accompany the Levites when they receive the tithes, and the
Levites are to bring a tenth of the tithes up to the house of our
God, to the storerooms of the treasury. 39The people of Israel,
including the Levites, are to bring their contributions of grain,
new wine and oil to the storerooms where the articles for the
sanctuary are kept and where the ministering priests, the
gatekeepers and the singers stay.
"We will not neglect the house of our God."

*The New Residents of Jerusalem*

11 NOW THE leaders of the people settled in Jerusalem, and
the rest of the people cast lots to bring one out of every
ten to live in Jerusalem, the holy city, while the remaining nine
were to stay in their own towns. 2The people commended all the
men who volunteered to live in Jerusalem.
3These are the provincial leaders who settled in Jerusalem (now
some Israelites, priests, Levites, temple servants and descendants
of Solomon's servants lived in the towns of Judah, each on his own
property in the various towns, 4while other people from both
Judah and Benjamin lived in Jerusalem):

From the descendants of Judah:

Athaiah son of Uzziah, the son of Zechariah, the son of Amariah, the son of Shephatiah, the son of Mahalalel, a descendant of Perez; 5and Maaseiah son of Baruch, the son of Col-
Hozeh, the son of Hazaiah, the son of Adaiah, the son of
Joiarib, the son of Zechariah, a descendant of Shelah. 6The
descendants of Perez who lived in Jerusalem totaled 468 able
men.

7From the descendants of Benjamin:

Sallu son of Meshullam, the son of Joed, the son of Pedaiah,
the son of Kolaiah, the son of Maaseiah, the son of Ithiel, the
son of Jeshaiah, 8and his followers, Gabbai and Sallai—928
men. 9Joel son of Zicri was their chief officer, and Judah son
of Hassenuah was over the Second District of the city.

10From the priests:

Jedaiah; the son of Joiarib; Jakin; 11Seraiah son of Hilkiah, the
son of Meshullam, the son of Zadok, the son of Meraioth, the
son of Ahitub, supervisor in the house of God, 12and their
associates, who carried on work for the temple—822 men;
Adaiah son of Jeroham, the son of Pelaliah, the son of Amzi,
the son of Zechariah, the son of Pashhur, the son of Malkijah,
13and his associates, who were heads of families—242 men;
Amashsai son of Azarel, the son of Ahzai, the son of Meshillemoth, the son of Immer, 14and his[b] associates, who were
able men—128. Their chief officer was Zabdiel son of Haggedolim.

15From the Levites:

Shemaiah son of Hasshub, the son of Azrikam, the son of
Hashabiah, the son of Bunni; 16Shabbethai and Jozabad, two
of the heads of the Levites, who had charge of the outside
work of the house of God; 17Mattaniah son of Mica, the son
of Zabdi, the son of Asaph, the director who led in thanksgiving and prayer; Bakbukiah, second among his associates;
and Abda son of Shammua, the son of Galal, the son of
Jeduthun. 18The Levites in the holy city totaled 284.

NIV [b] *14* Most Septuagint manuscripts; Hebrew *their*

## King James

19Moreover the porters, Akkub, Talmon, and their brethren
that kept the gates, *were* an hundred seventy and two.
20¶ And the residue of Israel, of the priests, *and* the Levites, *were*
in all the cities of Judah, every one in his inheritance.
21But the Nethinims dwelt in Ophel: and Ziha and Gispa *were*
over the Nethinims.
22The overseer also of the Levites at Jerusalem *was* Uzzi the son
of Bani, the son of Hashabiah, the son of Mattaniah, the son of
Micha. Of the sons of Asaph, the singers *were* over the business
of the house of God.
23For *it was* the king's commandment concerning them, that a
certain portion should be for the singers, due for every day.
24And Pethahiah the son of Meshezabeel, of the children of
Zerah the son of Judah, *was* at the king's hand in all matters
concerning the people.
25And for the villages, with their fields, *some* of the children of
Judah dwelt at Kirjath-arba, and *in* the villages thereof, and at
Dibon, and *in* the villages thereof, and at Jekabzeel, and *in* the
villages thereof,
26And at Jeshua, and at Moladah, and at Beth-phelet,
27And at Hazar-shual, and at Beer-sheba, and *in* the villages
thereof,
28And at Ziklag, and at Mekonah, and in the villages thereof,
29And at En-rimmon, and at Zareah, and at Jarmuth,
30Zanoah, Adullam, and *in* their villages, at Lachish, and the
fields thereof, at Azekah, and *in* the villages thereof. And they
dwelt from Beer-sheba unto the valley of Hinnom.
31The children also of Benjamin from Geba *dwelt* at Michmash,
and Aija, and Beth-el, and *in* their villages,
32 *And* at Anathoth, Nob, Ananiah,
33Hazor, Ramah, Gittaim,
34Hadid, Zeboim, Neballat,
35Lod, and Ono, the valley of craftsmen.
36And of the Levites *were* divisions *in* Judah, *and* in Benjamin.

**12** NOW THESE *are* the priests and the Levites that went up
with Zerubbabel the son of Shealtiel, and Jeshua: Seraiah,
Jeremiah, Ezra,
2Amariah, Malluch, Hattush,
3Shechaniah, Rehum, Meremoth,
4Iddo, Ginnetho, Abijah,
5Miamin, Maadiah, Bilgah,
6Shemaiah, and Joiarib, Jedaiah,
7Sallu, Amok, Hilkiah, Jedaiah. These *were* the chief of the
priests and of their brethren in the days of Jeshua.
8Moreover the Levites: Jeshua, Binnui, Kadmiel, Sherebiah,
Judah, *and* Mattaniah, *which was* over the thanksgiving, he and his
brethren.
9Also Bakbukiah and Unni, their brethren, *were* over against
them in the watches.
10¶ And Jeshua begat Joiakim, Joiakim also begat Eliashib, and
Eliashib begat Joiada,
11And Joiada begat Jonathan, and Jonathan begat Jaddua.
12And in the days of Joiakim were priests, the chief of the
fathers: of Seraiah, Meraiah; of Jeremiah, Hananiah;
13Of Ezra, Meshullam; of Amariah, Jehohanan;
14Of Melicu, Jonathan; of Shebaniah, Joseph;

## Amplified

19The gatekeepers, Akkub, Talmon and their brethren who
kept watch were 172.
20And the rest of Israel, of the priests, and the Levites, were in
all the cities of Judah, each in his inheritance.
21But the temple servants dwelt on [the hill] Ophel; Ziha and
Gishpa were over [them].
22Overseer of the Levites in Jerusalem and the work of God's
house was Uzzi son of Bani, son of Hashabiah, son of Mattaniah,
son of Mica, of Asaph's sons, the singers.
23For the [Persian] king had ordered concerning them, that a
certain provision be made for the singers, as each day required.
24Pethahiah son of Meshezabel, of the sons of Zerah son of
Judah, was at the king's hand in all matters concerning the people.
25As for the villages, with their fields, some people of Judah
dwelt in Kiriath-arba, Dibon, and Jekabzeel, and their villages,
26In Jeshua, Moladah, Beth-pelet,
27Hazar-shual, Beer-sheba and its villages,
28Ziklag, Meconah and its villages,
29En-rimmon, Zorah, Jarmuth,
30Zanoah, Adullam, and their villages, Lachish and its fields,
Azekah and its villages. So they encamped from Beer-sheba to the
Hinnom Valley.
31The people of Benjamin also dwelt from Geba onward, at
Michmash, Aija, Bethel and its villages,
32At Anathoth, Nob, Ananiah,
33Hazor, Ramah, Gittaim,
34Hadid, Zeboim, Neballat,
35Lod, and Ono, the valley of craftsmen.
36And certain divisions of the Levites in Judah were joined to
Benjamin.

**12** NOW THESE are the priests and Levites who went up
with Zerubbabel son of Shealtiel, and Jeshua: Seraiah,
Jeremiah, Ezra,
2Amariah, Malluch, Hattush,
3Shecaniah, Rehum, Meremoth,
4Iddo, Ginnethoi, Abijah,
5Mijamin, Maadiah, Bilgah,
6Shemaiah, Joiarib, Jedaiah,
7Sallu, Amok, Hilkiah, and Jedaiah. These were the chiefs of the
priests and their brethren in the days of Jeshua.
8And the Levites: Jeshua, Binnui, Kadmiel, Sherebiah, Judah,
and Mattaniah, who with his brethren was over the thanksgiving
[choirs].
9Bakbukiah and Unno, their brethren, stood opposite them
according to their offices.
10And Jeshua was the father of Joiakim, Joiakim of Eliashib,
Eliashib of Joiada;
11Joiada was the father of Jonathan, and Jonathan of Jaddua.
12And in the days of Joiakim were priests, heads of fathers'
houses: of Seraiah, Meraiah; of Jeremiah, Hananiah;
13Of Ezra, Meshullam; of Amariah, Jeho-hanan;
14Of Malluchi, Jonathan; of Shebaniah, Joseph;

## New American Standard

19¶ Also the gatekeepers, Akkub, Talmon, and their brethren,
who kept watch at the gates, *were* 172.

*Outside Jerusalem*

20And the rest of Israel, of the priests, *and* of the Levites, *were*
in all the cities of Judah, each on his own inheritance.
21But the temple servants were living in Ophel, and Ziha and
Gishpa were in charge of the temple servants.
22¶ Now the overseer of the Levites in Jerusalem was Uzzi the
son of Bani, the son of Hashabiah, the son of Mattaniah, the son
of Mica, from the sons of Asaph, who were the singers for the
service of the house of God.
23For *there was* a commandment from the king concerning them
and a firm regulation for the song leaders day by day.
24And Pethahiah the son of Meshezabel, of the sons of Zerah
the son of Judah, was the king's representative in all matters
concerning the people.
25¶ Now as for the villages with their fields, some of the sons
of Judah lived in Kiriath-arba and its [a]towns, in Dibon and its
towns, and in Jekabzeel and its villages,
26and in Jeshua, in Moladah and Beth-pelet,
27and in Hazar-shual, in Beersheba and its towns,
28and in Ziklag, in Meconah and in its towns,
29and in En-rimmon, in Zorah and in Jarmuth,
30Zanoah, Adullam, and their villages, Lachish and its fields,
Azekah and its towns. So they encamped from Beersheba as far as
the valley of Hinnom.
31The sons of Benjamin also *lived* from Geba *onward,* at Michmash and Aija, at Bethel and its towns,
32at Anathoth, Nob, Ananiah,
33Hazor, Ramah, Gittaim,
34Hadid, Zeboim, Neballat,
35Lod and Ono, the valley of craftsmen.
36And from the Levites, *some* divisions in Judah belonged to
Benjamin.

*Priests and Levites Who Returned to Jerusalem with Zerubbabel*

**12** NOW THESE are the priests and the Levites who came up
with Zerubbabel the son of Shealtiel, and Jeshua: Seraiah,
Jeremiah, Ezra,
2Amariah, Malluch, Hattush,
3Shecaniah, Rehum, Meremoth,
4Iddo, Ginnethoi, Abijah,
5Mijamin, Maadiah, Bilgah,
6Shemaiah and Joiarib, Jedaiah,
7Sallu, Amok, Hilkiah, and Jedaiah. These were the heads of
the priests and their kinsmen in the days of Jeshua.
8¶ And the Levites *were* Jeshua, Binnui, Kadmiel, Sherebiah,
Judah, *and* Mattaniah *who was* in charge of the songs of thanksgiving, he and his brothers.
9Also Bakbukiah and Unni, their brothers, stood opposite
them in *their* service divisions.
10And Jeshua became the father of Joiakim, and Joiakim became
the father of Eliashib, and Eliashib became the father of Joiada,
11and Joiada became the father of Jonathan, and Jonathan
became the father of Jaddua.
12¶ Now in the days of Joiakim the priests, the heads of fathers'
*households* were: of Seraiah, Meraiah; of Jeremiah, Hananiah;
13of Ezra, Meshullam; of Amariah, Jehohanan;
14of Malluchi, Jonathan; of Shebaniah, Joseph;

NAS [a] Lit., *daughters,* and so through this ch.

## New International

19The gatekeepers:

Akkub, Talmon and their associates, who kept watch at the
gates—172 men.

20The rest of the Israelites, with the priests and Levites, were
in all the towns of Judah, each on his ancestral property.
21The temple servants lived on the hill of Ophel, and Ziha and
Gishpa were in charge of them.
22The chief officer of the Levites in Jerusalem was Uzzi son of
Bani, the son of Hashabiah, the son of Mattaniah, the son of Mica.
Uzzi was one of Asaph's descendants, who were the singers responsible for the service of the house of God. 23The singers were
under the king's orders, which regulated their daily activity.
24Pethahiah son of Meshezabel, one of the descendants of
Zerah son of Judah, was the king's agent in all affairs relating to
the people.
25As for the villages with their fields, some of the people of
Judah lived in Kiriath Arba and its surrounding settlements, in
Dibon and its settlements, in Jekabzeel and its villages, 26in Jeshua,
in Moladah, in Beth Pelet, 27in Hazar Shual, in Beersheba and its
settlements, 28in Ziklag, in Meconah and its settlements, 29in En
Rimmon, in Zorah, in Jarmuth, 30Zanoah, Adullam and their villages, in Lachish and its fields, and in Azekah and its settlements.
So they were living all the way from Beersheba to the Valley of
Hinnom.
31The descendants of the Benjamites from Geba lived in Micmash, Aija, Bethel and its settlements, 32in Anathoth, Nob and
Ananiah, 33in Hazor, Ramah and Gittaim, 34in Hadid, Zeboim and
Neballat, 35in Lod and Ono, and in the Valley of the Craftsmen.
36Some of the divisions of the Levites of Judah settled in Benjamin.

*Priests and Levites*

**12** THESE WERE the priests and Levites who returned with
Zerubbabel son of Shealtiel and with Jeshua:
Seraiah, Jeremiah, Ezra,
2Amariah, Malluch, Hattush,
3Shecaniah, Rehum, Meremoth,
4Iddo, Ginnethon,[b] Abijah,
5Mijamin,[c] Moadiah, Bilgah,
6Shemaiah, Joiarib, Jedaiah,
7Sallu, Amok, Hilkiah and Jedaiah.
These were the leaders of the priests and their associates in the
days of Jeshua.
8The Levites were Jeshua, Binnui, Kadmiel, Sherebiah, Judah,
and also Mattaniah, who, together with his associates, was in
charge of the songs of thanksgiving. 9Bakbukiah and Unni, their
associates, stood opposite them in the services.
10Jeshua was the father of Joiakim, Joiakim the father of Eliashib, Eliashib the father of Joiada, 11Joiada the father of Jonathan,
and Jonathan the father of Jaddua.
12In the days of Joiakim, these were the heads of the priestly
families:
of Seraiah's family, Meraiah;
of Jeremiah's, Hananiah;
13of Ezra's, Meshullam;
of Amariah's, Jehohanan;
14of Malluch's, Jonathan;
of Shecaniah's,[d] Joseph;

NIV [b] *4* Many Hebrew manuscripts and Vulgate (see also Neh. 12:16); most Hebrew manuscripts *Ginnethoi* [c] *5* A variant of *Miniamin* [d] *14* Very many Hebrew manuscripts, some Septuagint manuscripts and Syriac (see also Neh. 12:3); most Hebrew manuscripts *Shebaniah's*

## King James

15Of Harim, Adna; of Meraioth, Helkai;
16Of Iddo, Zechariah; of Ginnethon, Meshullam;
17Of Abijah, Zichri; of Miniamin, of Moadiah, Piltai;
18Of Bilgah, Shammua; of Shemaiah, Jehonathan;
19And of Joiarib, Mattenai; of Jedaiah, Uzzi;
20Of Sallai, Kallai; of Amok, Eber;
21Of Hilkiah, Hashabiah; of Jedaiah, Nethaneel.
22¶ The Levites in the days of Eliashib, Joiada, and Johanan, and
Jaddua, *were* recorded chief of the fathers: also the priests, to the
reign of Darius the Persian.
23The sons of Levi, the chief of the fathers, *were* written in the
book of the chronicles, even until the days of Johanan the son of
Eliashib.
24And the chief of the Levites: Hashabiah, Sherebiah, and
Jeshua the son of Kadmiel, with their brethren over against them,
to praise *and* to give thanks, according to the commandment of
David the man of God, ward over against ward.
25Mattaniah, and Bakbukiah, Obadiah, Meshullam, Talmon,
Akkub, *were* porters keeping the ward at the thresholds of the
gates.
26These *were* in the days of Joiakim the son of Jeshua, the son
of Jozadak, and in the days of Nehemiah the governor, and of Ezra
the priest, the scribe.
27¶ And at the dedication of the wall of Jerusalem they sought
the Levites out of all their places, to bring them to Jerusalem, to
keep the dedication with gladness, both with thanksgivings, and
with singing, *with* cymbals, psalteries, and with harps.
28And the sons of the singers gathered themselves together,
both out of the plain country round about Jerusalem, and from the
villages of Netophathi;
29Also from the house of Gilgal, and out of the fields of Geba
and Azmaveth: for the singers had builded them villages round
about Jerusalem.
30And the priests and the Levites purified themselves, and
purified the people, and the gates, and the wall.
31Then I brought up the princes of Judah upon the wall, and
appointed two great *companies of them that gave* thanks, *whereof one*
went on the right hand upon the wall toward the dung gate:
32And after them went Hoshaiah, and half of the princes of
Judah,
33And Azariah, Ezra, and Meshullam,
34Judah, and Benjamin, and Shemaiah, and Jeremiah,
35And *certain* of the priests' sons with trumpets; *namely,* Zechariah the son of Jonathan, the son of Shemaiah, the son of Mattaniah, the son of Michaiah, the son of Zaccur, the son of Asaph:
36And his brethren, Shemaiah, and Azarael, Milalai, Gilalai,
Maai, Nethaneel, and Judah, Hanani, with the musical instruments of David the man of God, and Ezra the scribe before them.
37And at the fountain gate, which was over against them, they
went up by the stairs of the city of David, at the going up of the
wall, above the house of David, even unto the water gate eastward.
38And the other *company of them that gave* thanks went over
against *them,* and I after them, and the half of the people upon the
wall, from beyond the tower of the furnaces even unto the broad
wall;
39And from above the gate of Ephraim, and above the old gate,
and above the fish gate, and the tower of Hananeel, and the tower
of Meah, even unto the sheep gate: and they stood still in the
prison gate.
40So stood the two *companies of them that gave* thanks in the
house of God, and I, and the half of the rulers with me:
41And the priests; Eliakim, Maaseiah, Miniamin, Michaiah, Elioenai, Zechariah, *and* Hananiah, with trumpets;
42And Maaseiah, and Shemaiah, and Eleazar, and Uzzi, and
Jehohanan, and Malchijah, and Elam, and Ezer. And the singers
sang loud, with Jezrahiah *their* overseer.

## Amplified

15Of Harim, Adna; of Meraioth, Helkai;
16Of Iddo, Zechariah; of Ginnethon, Meshullam;
17Of Abijah, Zichri; of Miniamin, of Moadiah, Piltai;
18Of Bilgah, Shammua; of Shemaiah, Jehonathan;
19Of Joiarib, Mattenai; of Jedaiah, Uzzi;
20Of Sallai, Kallai; of Amok, Eber;
21Of Hilkiah, Hashabiah; of Jedaiah, Nethanel.
22As for the Levites, in the days of Eliashib, Joiada, Johanan,
and Jaddua, the heads of fathers' houses were recorded; also the
priests until the reign of Darius the Persian.
23The sons of Levi, heads of fathers' houses, were recorded in
the Book of the Chronicles until the days of Johanan son of Eliashib.
24And the chiefs of the Levites: Hashabiah, Sherebiah, and
Jeshua son of Kadmiel, with their brethren opposite them, to
praise and to give thanks, as David, God's man, commanded,
[one] watch [singing] in response to [the men in the opposite]
watch.
25Mattaniah, Bakbukiah, Obadiah, Meshullam, Talmon, and
Akkub were gatekeepers guarding at the storehouses of the gates.
26These were in the days of Joiakim son of Jeshua, son of Jozadak, and in the days of Nehemiah the governor, and of Ezra the
priest *and* scribe.
27And for the dedication of the wall of Jerusalem they sought
the Levites in all their places, to bring them to Jerusalem, to celebrate the dedication with gladness, with thanksgivings, and with
singing, cymbals, harps, and lyres.
28And the sons of the singers gathered together from the plain
*and* circuit around Jerusalem and from the villages of the Netophathites;
29Also from Beth-gilgal and the fields of Geba and Azmaveth;
for the singers had built them villages around Jerusalem.
30And the priests and the Levites purified themselves, the
people, the gates, and the wall.
31Then I brought the princes of Judah up on the wall, and
appointed two great companies of them that gave thanks and went
in procession. One went to the right upon the wall toward the
Dung Gate;
32And after them went Hoshaiah and half of the princes of
Judah,
33And Azariah, Ezra, Meshullam,
34Judah, Benjamin, Shemaiah, and Jeremiah,
35And certain of the priests' sons with trumpets: Zechariah son
of Jonathan, son of Shemaiah, son of Mattaniah, son of Micaiah,
son of Zaccur, son of Asaph;
36And his kinsmen, Shemaiah, Azarel, Milalai, Gilalai, Maai,
Nethanel, Judah, Hanani, with the musical instruments of David,
God's man; and Ezra the scribe went before them.
37At the Fountain Gate they went up straight ahead by the stairs
of the city of David, at the wall's ascent, above David's house, to
the Water Gate on the east.
38The other company of those who gave thanks went to the left;
I followed with half of the people, upon the wall, above the Tower
of the Furnaces to the Broad Wall,
39And above the Gate of Ephraim, and by the Old Gate and by
the Fish Gate and by the tower of Hananel and the Tower of
Hammeah, even to the Sheep Gate; and they stopped at the Gate
of the Guard.
40So the two companies of those who gave thanks stood in the
house of God, and I and the half of the officials with me;
41And the priests Eliakim, Ma-aseiah, Miniamin, Micaiah, Elioenai, Zechariah, and Hananiah, with trumpets;
42And Ma-aseiah, Shemaiah, Eleazar, Uzzi, Jehohanan, Malchijah, Elam, and Ezer. And the singers sang *and* made themselves
heard, with Jezrahiah as leader.

## New American Standard

15of Harim, Adna; of Meraioth, Helkai;
16of Iddo, Zechariah; of Ginnethon, Meshullam;
17of Abijah, Zichri; of Miniamin, of Moadiah, Piltai;
18of Bilgah, Shammua; of Shemaiah, Jehonathan;
19of Joiarib, Mattenai; of Jedaiah, Uzzi;
20of Sallai, Kallai; of Amok, Eber;
21of Hilkiah, Hashabiah; of Jedaiah, Nethanel.

*The Chief Levites*

22¶ As for the Levites, the heads of fathers' *households* were registered in the days of Eliashib, Joiada, and Johanan, and Jaddua; so *were* the priests in the reign of Darius the Persian.

23The sons of Levi, the heads of fathers' *households*, were registered in the Book of the Chronicles up to the days of Johanan the son of Eliashib.

24And the heads of the Levites *were* Hashabiah, Sherebiah, and Jeshua the son of Kadmiel, with their brothers opposite them, to praise *and* give thanks, as prescribed by David the man of God, division corresponding to division.

25Mattaniah, and Bakbukiah, Obadiah, Meshullam, Talmon, *and* Akkub were gatekeepers keeping watch at the storehouses of the gates.

26These *served* in the days of Joiakim the son of Jeshua, the son of Jozadak, and in the days of Nehemiah the governor and of Ezra the priest *and* scribe.

*Dedication of the Wall*

27¶ Now at the dedication of the wall of Jerusalem they sought out the Levites from all their places, to bring them to Jerusalem so that they might celebrate the dedication with gladness, with hymns of thanksgiving and with songs *to the accompaniment* of cymbals, harps, and lyres.

28So the sons of the singers were assembled from the district around Jerusalem, and from the villages of the Netophathites,
29from Beth-gilgal, and from *their* fields in Geba and Azmaveth, for the singers had built themselves villages around Jerusalem.
30And the priests and the Levites purified themselves; they also purified the people, the gates, and the wall.

*Procedures for the Temple*

31¶ Then I had the leaders of Judah come up on top of the wall, and I appointed two great choirs, the first proceeding to the right on top of the wall toward the Refuse Gate.
32Hoshaiah and half of the leaders of Judah followed them,
33with Azariah, Ezra, Meshullam,
34Judah, Benjamin, Shemaiah, Jeremiah,
35and some of the sons of the priests with trumpets; *and* Zechariah the son of Jonathan, the son of Shemaiah, the son of Mattaniah, the son of Micaiah, the son of Zaccur, the son of Asaph,
36and his kinsmen, Shemaiah, Azarel, Milalai, Gilalai, Maai, Nethanel, Judah *and* Hanani, with the musical instruments of David the man of God. And Ezra the scribe went before them.
37And at the Fountain Gate they went directly up the steps of the city of David by the stairway of the wall above the house of David to the Water Gate on the east.
38¶ The second choir proceeded to the left, while I followed them with half of the people on the wall, above the Tower of Furnaces, to the Broad Wall,
39and above the Gate of Ephraim, by the Old Gate, by the Fish Gate, the Tower of Hananel, and the Tower of the Hundred, as far as the Sheep Gate, and they stopped at the Gate of the Guard.
40Then the two choirs took their stand in the house of God. So did I and half of the officials with me;
41and the priests, Eliakim, Maaseiah, Miniamin, Micaiah, Elioenai, Zechariah, and Hananiah, with the trumpets;
42and Maaseiah, Shemaiah, Eleazar, Uzzi, Jehohanan, Malchijah, Elam, and Ezer. And the singers sang, with Jezrahiah *their* leader,

## New International

15of Harim's, Adna;
of Meremoth's,[a] Helkai;
16of Iddo's, Zechariah;
of Ginnethon's, Meshullam;
17of Abijah's, Zicri;
of Miniamin's and of Moadiah's, Piltai;
18of Bilgah's, Shammua;
of Shemaiah's, Jehonathan;
19of Joiarib's, Mattenai;
of Jedaiah's, Uzzi;
20of Sallu's, Kallai;
of Amok's, Eber;
21of Hilkiah's, Hashabiah;
of Jedaiah's, Nethanel.

22The family heads of the Levites in the days of Eliashib, Joiada,
Johanan and Jaddua, as well as those of the priests, were recorded
in the reign of Darius the Persian. 23The family heads among the
descendants of Levi up to the time of Johanan son of Eliashib were
recorded in the book of the annals. 24And the leaders of the Levites
were Hashabiah, Sherebiah, Jeshua son of Kadmiel, and their
associates, who stood opposite them to give praise and thanksgiving, one section responding to the other, as prescribed by David
the man of God.

25Mattaniah, Bakbukiah, Obadiah, Meshullam, Talmon and
Akkub were gatekeepers who guarded the storerooms at the gates.
26They served in the days of Joiakim son of Jeshua, the son of
Jozadak, and in the days of Nehemiah the governor and of Ezra
the priest and scribe.

*Dedication of the Wall of Jerusalem*

27At the dedication of the wall of Jerusalem, the Levites were
sought out from where they lived and were brought to Jerusalem
to celebrate joyfully the dedication with songs of thanksgiving and
with the music of cymbals, harps and lyres. 28The singers also
were brought together from the region around Jerusalem—from
the villages of the Netophathites, 29from Beth Gilgal, and from the
area of Geba and Azmaveth, for the singers had built villages for
themselves around Jerusalem. 30When the priests and Levites had
purified themselves ceremonially, they purified the people, the
gates and the wall.

31I had the leaders of Judah go up on top[b] of the wall. I also
assigned two large choirs to give thanks. One was to proceed on
top[c] of the wall to the right, toward the Dung Gate. 32Hoshaiah
and half the leaders of Judah followed them, 33along with Azariah,
Ezra, Meshullam, 34Judah, Benjamin, Shemaiah, Jeremiah, 35as
well as some priests with trumpets, and also Zechariah son of
Jonathan, the son of Shemaiah, the son of Mattaniah, the son of
Micaiah, the son of Zaccur, the son of Asaph, 36and his associates—Shemaiah, Azarel, Milalai, Gilalai, Maai, Nethanel, Judah
and Hanani—with musical instruments ⌊prescribed by⌋ David the
man of God. Ezra the scribe led the procession. 37At the Fountain
Gate they continued directly up the steps of the City of David on
the ascent to the wall and passed above the house of David to the
Water Gate on the east.

38The second choir proceeded in the opposite direction. I followed them on top[d] of the wall, together with half the people—
past the Tower of the Ovens to the Broad Wall, 39over the Gate of
Ephraim, the Jeshanah[e] Gate, the Fish Gate, the Tower of Hananel
and the Tower of the Hundred, as far as the Sheep Gate. At the
Gate of the Guard they stopped.

40The two choirs that gave thanks then took their places in the
house of God; so did I, together with half the officials, 41as well
as the priests—Eliakim, Maaseiah, Miniamin, Micaiah, Elioenai,
Zechariah and Hananiah with their trumpets— 42and also Maaseiah, Shemaiah, Eleazar, Uzzi, Jehohanan, Malkijah, Elam and
Ezer. The choirs sang under the direction of Jezrahiah. 43And on

NIV [a] *15* Some Septuagint manuscripts (see also Neh. 12:3); Hebrew *Meraioth's* [b] *31* Or *go alongside* [c] *31* Or *proceed alongside* [d] *38* Or *them alongside* [e] *39* Or *Old*

## King James

43 Also that day they offered great sacrifices, and rejoiced: for God had made them rejoice with great joy: the wives also and the children rejoiced: so that the joy of Jerusalem was heard even afar off.

44 ¶ And at that time were some appointed over the chambers for the treasures, for the offerings, for the firstfruits, and for the tithes, to gather into them out of the fields of the cities the portions of the law for the priests and Levites: for Judah rejoiced for the priests and for the Levites that waited.

45 And both the singers and the porters kept the ward of their God, and the ward of the purification, according to the commandment of David, *and* of Solomon his son.

46 For in the days of David and Asaph of old *there were* chief of the singers, and songs of praise and thanksgiving unto God.

47 And all Israel in the days of Zerubbabel, and in the days of Nehemiah, gave the portions of the singers and the porters, every day his portion: and they sanctified *holy things* unto the Levites; and the Levites sanctified *them* unto the children of Aaron.

**13** ON THAT day they read in the book of Moses in the audience of the people; and therein was found written, that the Ammonite and the Moabite should not come into the congregation of God for ever;

2 Because they met not the children of Israel with bread and with water, but hired Balaam against them, that he should curse them: howbeit our God turned the curse into a blessing.

3 Now it came to pass, when they had heard the law, that they separated from Israel all the mixed multitude.

4 ¶ And before this, Eliashib the priest, having the oversight of the chamber of the house of our God, *was* allied unto Tobiah:

5 And he had prepared for him a great chamber, where aforetime they laid the meat offerings, the frankincense, and the vessels, and the tithes of the corn, the new wine, and the oil, which was commanded *to be given* to the Levites, and the singers, and the porters; and the offerings of the priests.

6 But in all this *time* was not I at Jerusalem: for in the two and thirtieth year of Artaxerxes king of Babylon came I unto the king, and after certain days obtained I leave of the king:

7 And I came to Jerusalem, and understood of the evil that Eliashib did for Tobiah, in preparing him a chamber in the courts of the house of God.

8 And it grieved me sore: therefore I cast forth all the household stuff of Tobiah out of the chamber.

9 Then I commanded, and they cleansed the chambers: and thither brought I again the vessels of the house of God, with the meat offering and the frankincense.

10 ¶ And I perceived that the portions of the Levites had not been given *them:* for the Levites and the singers, that did the work, were fled every one to his field.

11 Then contended I with the rulers, and said, Why is the house of God forsaken? And I gathered them together, and set them in their place.

12 Then brought all Judah the tithe of the corn and the new wine and the oil unto the treasuries.

13 And I made treasurers over the treasuries, Shelemiah the priest, and Zadok the scribe, and of the Levites, Pedaiah: and next to them *was* Hanan the son of Zaccur, the son of Mattaniah: for they were counted faithful, and their office *was* to distribute unto their brethren.

14 Remember me, O my God, concerning this, and wipe not out my good deeds that I have done for the house of my God, and for the offices thereof.

## Amplified

43 Also that day they offered great sacrifices and rejoiced, for God had made them rejoice with great joy; the women also and the children rejoiced. The joy of Jerusalem was heard even afar off.

44 On that day men were appointed over the chambers for the stores, the contributions, the first fruits, and the tithes, to gather into them the portions required by law for the priests and the Levites according to the fields of the towns; for Judah rejoiced over the priests and Levites who served [faithfully].

45 And they performed the due service of their God and of the purification; so did the singers and gatekeepers, as David and his son Solomon had commanded.

46 For in the days of David and Asaph of old there was a chief of singers, and songs of praise and thanksgiving to God.

47 And all Israel in the days of Zerubbabel and [later] of Nehemiah, gave the daily portions for the singers and the gatekeepers; and they set apart what was for the Levites, and the Levites set apart what was for the sons of Aaron (the priests).

**13** ON THAT day they read in the book of Moses in the audience of the people; and in it was found written that no Ammonite or Moabite should ever come into the assembly of God;

2 For they met not the Israelites with food and drink, but hired Balaam to curse them; yet our God turned the curse into a blessing. [Num. 22:3-11; Deut. 23:5, 6.]

3 When [the Jews] heard the law, they separated from Israel all of foreign descent.

4 Now before this, Eliashib the priest, who was appointed over the chambers of the house of our God, and was related [by marriage] to Tobiah [our adversary],

5 Prepared for Tobiah a large chamber where previously they had put the cereal offering, the frankincense, the vessels, and the tithes of grain, new wine, and oil, which were given by commandment to the Levites, the singers, and gatekeepers, and the contributions for the priests.

6 But in all this time I was not at Jerusalem, for in the thirty-second year of Artaxerxes [Persian] king of Babylon, I went to the king; then later I got leave of him

7 And came to Jerusalem. Then I discovered the evil that Eliashib had done for Tobiah, in preparing him [an adversary] a chamber in the courts of the house of God!

8 And it grieved me exceedingly, and I threw all the house furnishings of Tobiah out of the chamber.

9 Then I commanded, and they cleansed the chambers; and I brought back there the vessels of the house of God, with the cereal offering and frankincense.

10 And I perceived that the portions of the Levites had not been given them; so that the Levites and the singers, who did the work, [forced by necessity] had each fled to his field.

11 Then I contended with the officials and said, Why is the house of God neglected *and* forsaken? I gathered the Levites and singers and set them in their stations.

12 Then all Judah brought the tithe of the grain, the new wine, and the oil to the storerooms.

13 I set treasurers over the storerooms: Shelemiah the priest, Zadok the scribe, and Pedaiah of the Levites; assisting them was Hanan son of Zaccur, son of Mattaniah, for they were counted faithful, and their task was to distribute to their brethren.

14 O my God, [earnestly] remember me concerning this, and wipe not out my good deeds *and* kindnesses done for the house of my God, and for His service.

## New American Standard

43and on that day they offered great sacrifices and rejoiced
because God had given them great joy, even the women and
children rejoiced, so that the joy of Jerusalem was heard from afar.
44¶ On that day men were also appointed over the chambers for
the stores, the contributions, the first fruits, and the tithes, to
gather into them from the fields of the cities the portions required
by the law for the priests and Levites; for Judah rejoiced over the
priests and Levites who served.
45For they performed the worship of their God and the service
of purification, together with the singers and the gatekeepers in
accordance with the command of David *and* of his son Solomon.
46For in the days of David and Asaph, in ancient times, *there
were* leaders of the singers, songs of praise and hymns of thanksgiving to God.
47And so all Israel in the days of Zerubbabel and Nehemiah
gave the portions due the singers and the gatekeepers as each day
required, and set apart the consecrated *portion* for the Levites, and
the Levites set apart the consecrated *portion* for the sons of Aaron.

*Foreigners Excluded*

13 ON THAT day they read aloud from the book of Moses
in the hearing of the people; and there was found written
in it that no Ammonite or Moabite should ever enter the assembly
of God,
2because they did not meet the sons of Israel with bread and
water, but hired Balaam against them to curse them. However, our
God turned the curse into a blessing.
3So it came about, that when they heard the law, they excluded
all foreigners from Israel.

*Tobiah Expelled and the Temple Cleansed*

4¶ Now prior to this, Eliashib the priest, who was appointed
over the chambers of the house of our God, being related to Tobiah,
5had prepared a large room for him, where formerly they put
the grain offerings, the frankincense, the utensils, and the tithes
of grain, wine and oil prescribed for the Levites, the singers and
the gatekeepers, and the contributions for the priests.
6But during all this *time* I was not in Jerusalem, for in the
thirty-second year of Artaxerxes king of Babylon I had gone to the
king. After some time, however, I asked leave from the king,
7and I came to Jerusalem and learned about the evil that Eliashib had done for Tobiah, by preparing a room for him in the
courts of the house of God.
8And it was very displeasing to me, so I threw all of Tobiah's
household goods out of the room.
9Then I gave an order and they cleansed the rooms; and I
returned there the utensils of the house of God with the grain
offerings and the frankincense.

*Tithes Restored*

10¶ I also discovered that the portions of the Levites had not
been given *them*, so that the Levites and the singers who performed the service had gone away, each to his own field.
11So I reprimanded the officials and said, "Why is the house of
God forsaken?" Then I gathered them together and restored them
to their posts.
12All Judah then brought the tithe of the grain, wine, and oil
into the storehouses.
13And in charge of the storehouses I appointed Shelemiah the
priest, Zadok the scribe, and Pedaiah of the Levites, and in addition to them was Hanan the son of Zaccur, the son of Mattaniah;
for they were considered reliable, and it was their task to distribute
to their kinsmen.
14Remember me for this, O my God, and do not blot out my
loyal deeds which I have performed for the house of my God and
its services.

## New International

that day they offered great sacrifices, rejoicing because God had
given them great joy. The women and children also rejoiced. The
sound of rejoicing in Jerusalem could be heard far away.
44At that time men were appointed to be in charge of the storerooms for the contributions, firstfruits and tithes. From the fields
around the towns they were to bring into the storerooms the
portions required by the Law for the priests and the Levites, for
Judah was pleased with the ministering priests and Levites. 45They
performed the service of their God and the service of purification,
as did also the singers and gatekeepers, according to the commands of David and his son Solomon. 46For long ago, in the days
of David and Asaph, there had been directors for the singers and
for the songs of praise and thanksgiving to God. 47So in the days
of Zerubbabel and of Nehemiah, all Israel contributed the daily
portions for the singers and gatekeepers. They also set aside the
portion for the other Levites, and the Levites set aside the portion
for the descendants of Aaron.

*Nehemiah's Final Reforms*

13 ON THAT day the Book of Moses was read aloud in the
hearing of the people and there it was found written that
no Ammonite or Moabite should ever be admitted into the assembly of God, 2because they had not met the Israelites with food and
water but had hired Balaam to call a curse down on them. (Our
God, however, turned the curse into a blessing.) 3When the people
heard this law, they excluded from Israel all who were of foreign
descent.
4Before this, Eliashib the priest had been put in charge of the
storerooms of the house of our God. He was closely associated
with Tobiah, 5and he had provided him with a large room formerly
used to store the grain offerings and incense and temple articles,
and also the tithes of grain, new wine and oil prescribed for the
Levites, singers and gatekeepers, as well as the contributions for
the priests.
6But while all this was going on, I was not in Jerusalem, for in
the thirty-second year of Artaxerxes king of Babylon I had returned
to the king. Some time later I asked his permission 7and came back
to Jerusalem. Here I learned about the evil thing Eliashib had done
in providing Tobiah a room in the courts of the house of God. 8I
was greatly displeased and threw all Tobiah's household goods
out of the room. 9I gave orders to purify the rooms, and then I put
back into them the equipment of the house of God, with the grain
offerings and the incense.
10I also learned that the portions assigned to the Levites had not
been given to them, and that all the Levites and singers responsible
for the service had gone back to their own fields. 11So I rebuked
the officials and asked them, "Why is the house of God neglected?" Then I called them together and stationed them at their
posts.
12All Judah brought the tithes of grain, new wine and oil into
the storerooms. 13I put Shelemiah the priest, Zadok the scribe, and
a Levite named Pedaiah in charge of the storerooms and made
Hanan son of Zaccur, the son of Mattaniah, their assistant, because
these men were considered trustworthy. They were made responsible for distributing the supplies to their brothers.

14Remember me for this, O my God, and do not blot out what
I have so faithfully done for the house of my God and its services.

## King James

15¶ In those days saw I in Judah *some* treading wine presses on the sabbath, and bringing in sheaves, and lading asses; as also wine, grapes, and figs, and all *manner of* burdens, which they brought into Jerusalem on the sabbath day: and I testified *against them* in the day wherein they sold victuals.

16There dwelt men of Tyre also therein, which brought fish, and all manner of ware, and sold on the sabbath unto the children of Judah, and in Jerusalem.

17Then I contended with the nobles of Judah, and said unto them, What evil thing *is* this that ye do, and profane the sabbath day?

18Did not your fathers thus, and did not our God bring all this evil upon us, and upon this city? yet ye bring more wrath upon Israel by profaning the sabbath.

19And it came to pass, that when the gates of Jerusalem began to be dark before the sabbath, I commanded that the gates should be shut, and charged that they should not be opened till after the sabbath: and *some* of my servants set I at the gates, *that* there should no burden be brought in on the sabbath day.

20So the merchants and sellers of all kind of ware lodged without Jerusalem once or twice.

21Then I testified against them, and said unto them, Why lodge ye about the wall? if ye do *so* again, I will lay hands on you. From that time forth came they no *more* on the sabbath.

22And I commanded the Levites that they should cleanse themselves, and *that* they should come *and* keep the gates, to sanctify the sabbath day. Remember me, O my God, *concerning* this also, and spare me according to the greatness of thy mercy.

23¶ In those days also saw I Jews *that* had married wives of Ashdod, of Ammon, *and* of Moab:

24And their children spake half in the speech of Ashdod, and could not speak in the Jews' language, but according to the language of each people.

25And I contended with them, and cursed them, and smote certain of them, and plucked off their hair, and made them swear by God, *saying*, Ye shall not give your daughters unto their sons, nor take their daughters unto your sons, or for yourselves.

26Did not Solomon king of Israel sin by these things? yet among many nations was there no king like him, who was beloved of his God, and God made him king over all Israel: nevertheless even him did outlandish women cause to sin.

27Shall we then hearken unto you to do all this great evil, to transgress against our God in marrying strange wives?

28And *one* of the sons of Joiada, the son of Eliashib the high priest, *was* son-in-law to Sanballat the Horonite: therefore I chased him from me.

29Remember them, O my God, because they have defiled the priesthood, and the covenant of the priesthood, and of the Levites.

30Thus cleansed I them from all strangers, and appointed the wards of the priests and the Levites, every one in his business;

31And for the wood offering, at times appointed, and for the firstfruits. Remember me, O my God, for good.

## Amplified

15In those days I saw in Judah men treading wine presses on the sabbath, bringing in sheaves *or* heaps of grain with which they loaded donkeys; and also wine, grapes, figs, and all sorts of burdens, which they brought into Jerusalem on the sabbath day; and I protested *and* warned them on the day they sold the produce.

16There dwelt men of Tyre there also who brought fish, and all kinds of wares, and sold on the sabbath to the people of Judah, and in Jerusalem.

17Then I reproved the nobles of Judah, and said, What evil thing is this that you do, and profane the sabbath day?

18Did not your fathers thus, and did not our God bring all this evil upon us, and upon this city? Yet you bring more wrath upon Israel by profaning the sabbath.

19And when it began to get dark at the gates of Jerusalem before the sabbath [day began], I commanded that the gates should be shut and not be opened till after the sabbath; and I set some of my servants at the gates to prevent any burden being brought in on the sabbath day.

20So the merchants and sellers of all kinds of wares lodged outside Jerusalem once or twice.

21But I reproved *and* warned them, saying, Why do you lodge about the wall? If you do so again, I will lay hands on you. Then they stopped coming on the sabbath.

22And I commanded the Levites to cleanse themselves and come and guard the gates, to keep the sabbath day holy. O my God, [earnestly] remember me concerning this also, and spare me according to the greatness of Your mercy *and* loving-kindness.

23In those days also I saw Jews who had married wives of Ashdod, Ammon, and Moab;

24And their children spoke half in the speech of Ashdod, and could not speak the Hebrew, but in the language of each people.

25And I contended with them, and reviled them, and beat some of them, and pulled out their hair, and made them swear by God, saying, You shall not give your daughters to their sons, nor take their daughters for your sons, or for yourselves.

26Did not Solomon king of Israel act treacherously against God *and* miss the mark on account of such women? Among many nations there was no king like him; he was loved by his God, and God made him king over all Israel; yet strange women even caused him to sin [when he was old he turned treacherously away from the Lord to other gods, and God rent his kingdom from him]. [I Kings 11:1-11.]

27Shall we then listen to you to do all this great evil and act treacherously against our God by marrying strange [heathen] women?

28One of the sons of Joiada, son of Eliashib the high priest, was son-in-law to Sanballat the Horonite; therefore I chased him from me.

29O my God, [earnestly] remember them, because they have defiled the priesthood, and the covenant of the priests and Levites.

30Thus I cleansed them from everything foreign [heathen], and I defined the duties of the priests and Levites, every one in his work;

31And I provided for the wood offering, at appointed times, and for the first fruits. O my God, [earnestly] remember me for good *and* imprint me [on Your heart]!

## New American Standard

*Sabbath Restored*

15¶ In those days I saw in Judah some who were treading wine
presses on the sabbath, and bringing in sacks of grain and loading
*them* on donkeys, as well as wine, grapes, figs, and all kinds of
loads, and they brought *them* into Jerusalem on the sabbath day.
So I admonished *them* on the day they sold food.
16Also men of Tyre were living there *who* imported fish and all
kinds of merchandise, and sold *them* to the sons of Judah on the
sabbath, even in Jerusalem.
17Then I reprimanded the nobles of Judah and said to them,
"What is this evil thing you are doing, by profaning the sabbath
day?
18"Did not your fathers do the same so that our God brought
on us, and on this city, all this trouble? Yet you are adding to the
wrath on Israel by profaning the sabbath."
19¶ And it came about that just as it grew dark at the gates of
Jerusalem before the sabbath, I commanded that the doors should
be shut and that they should not open them until after the sabbath.
Then I stationed some of my servants at the gates *that* no load
should enter on the sabbath day.
20Once or twice the traders and merchants of every kind of
merchandise spent the night outside Jerusalem.
21Then I warned them and said to them, "Why do you spend
the night in front of the wall? If you do so again, I will use force
against you." From that time on they did not come on the sabbath.
22And I commanded the Levites that they should purify themselves and come as gatekeepers to sanctify the sabbath day. *For* this
also remember me, O my God, and have compassion on me according to the greatness of Thy lovingkindness.

*Mixed Marriages Forbidden*

23¶ In those days I also saw that the Jews had married women
from Ashdod, Ammon, *and* Moab.
24As for their children, half spoke in the language of Ashdod,
and none of them was able to speak the language of Judah, but the
language of his own people.
25So I contended with them and cursed them and struck some
of them and pulled out their hair, and made them swear by God,
"You shall not give your daughters to their sons, nor take of their
daughters for your sons or for yourselves.
26"Did not Solomon king of Israel sin regarding these things?
Yet among the many nations there was no king like him, and he
was loved by his God, and God made him king over all Israel;
nevertheless the foreign women caused even him to sin.
27"Do we then hear about you that you have committed all this
great evil by acting unfaithfully against our God by marrying foreign women?"
28Even one of the sons of Joiada, the son of Eliashib the high
priest, was a son-in-law of Sanballat the Horonite, so I drove him
away from me.
29Remember them, O my God, because they have defiled the
priesthood and the covenant of the priesthood and the Levites.
30¶ Thus I purified them from everything foreign and appointed
duties for the priests and the Levites, each in his task,
31and *I arranged* for the supply of wood at appointed times and
for the first fruits. Remember me, O my God, for good.

## New International

15In those days I saw men in Judah treading winepresses on the
Sabbath and bringing in grain and loading it on donkeys, together
with wine, grapes, figs and all other kinds of loads. And they were
bringing all this into Jerusalem on the Sabbath. Therefore I warned
them against selling food on that day. 16Men from Tyre who lived
in Jerusalem were bringing in fish and all kinds of merchandise
and selling them in Jerusalem on the Sabbath to the people of
Judah. 17I rebuked the nobles of Judah and said to them, "What
is this wicked thing you are doing—desecrating the Sabbath day?
18Didn't your forefathers do the same things, so that our God
brought all this calamity upon us and upon this city? Now you are
stirring up more wrath against Israel by desecrating the Sabbath."
19When evening shadows fell on the gates of Jerusalem before
the Sabbath, I ordered the doors to be shut and not opened until
the Sabbath was over. I stationed some of my own men at the gates
so that no load could be brought in on the Sabbath day. 20Once or
twice the merchants and sellers of all kinds of goods spent the
night outside Jerusalem. 21But I warned them and said, "Why do
you spend the night by the wall? If you do this again, I will lay
hands on you." From that time on they no longer came on the
Sabbath. 22Then I commanded the Levites to purify themselves
and go and guard the gates in order to keep the Sabbath day holy.

Remember me for this also, O my God, and show mercy to me
according to your great love.

23Moreover, in those days I saw men of Judah who had married
women from Ashdod, Ammon and Moab. 24Half of their children
spoke the language of Ashdod or the language of one of the other
peoples, and did not know how to speak the language of Judah.
25I rebuked them and called curses down on them. I beat some of
the men and pulled out their hair. I made them take an oath in
God's name and said: "You are not to give your daughters in
marriage to their sons, nor are you to take their daughters in
marriage for your sons or for yourselves. 26Was it not because of
marriages like these that Solomon king of Israel sinned? Among
the many nations there was no king like him. He was loved by his
God, and God made him king over all Israel, but even he was led
into sin by foreign women. 27Must we hear now that you too are
doing all this terrible wickedness and are being unfaithful to our
God by marrying foreign women?"
28One of the sons of Joiada son of Eliashib the high priest was
son-in-law to Sanballat the Horonite. And I drove him away from
me.

29Remember them, O my God, because they defiled the priestly
office and the covenant of the priesthood and of the Levites.

30So I purified the priests and the Levites of everything foreign,
and assigned them duties, each to his own task. 31I also made
provision for contributions of wood at designated times, and for
the firstfruits.

Remember me with favor, O my God.

## King James

THE BOOK OF

# Esther

**1** NOW IT came to pass in the days of Ahasuerus, (this *is* Ahasuerus which reigned, from India even unto Ethiopia, *over* an hundred and seven and twenty provinces:)

2 *That* in those days, when the king Ahasuerus sat on the throne of his kingdom, which *was* in Shushan the palace,

3 In the third year of his reign, he made a feast unto all his princes and his servants; the power of Persia and Media, the nobles and princes of the provinces, *being* before him:

4 When he showed the riches of his glorious kingdom and the honour of his excellent majesty many days, *even* an hundred and fourscore days.

5 And when these days were expired, the king made a feast unto all the people that were present in Shushan the palace, both unto great and small, seven days, in the court of the garden of the king's palace;

6 *Where were* white, green, and blue, *hangings*, fastened with cords of fine linen and purple to silver rings and pillars of marble: the beds *were of* gold and silver, upon a pavement of red, and blue, and white, and black, marble.

7 And they gave *them* drink in vessels of gold, (the vessels being diverse one from another,) and royal wine in abundance, according to the state of the king.

8 And the drinking *was* according to the law; none did compel: for so the king had appointed to all the officers of his house, that they should do according to every man's pleasure.

9 Also Vashti the queen made a feast for the women *in* the royal house which *belonged* to king Ahasuerus.

10 ¶ On the seventh day, when the heart of the king was merry with wine, he commanded Mehuman, Biztha, Harbona, Bigtha, and Abagtha, Zethar, and Carcas, the seven chamberlains that served in the presence of Ahasuerus the king,

11 To bring Vashti the queen before the king with the crown royal, to show the people and the princes her beauty: for she *was* fair to look on.

12 But the queen Vashti refused to come at the king's commandment by *his* chamberlains: therefore was the king very wroth, and his anger burned in him.

13 ¶ Then the king said to the wise men, which knew the times, (for so *was* the king's manner toward all that knew law and judgment:

14 And the next unto him *was* Carshena, Shethar, Admatha, Tarshish, Meres, Marsena, *and* Memucan, the seven princes of Persia and Media, which saw the king's face, *and* which sat the first in the kingdom;)

15 What shall we do unto the queen Vashti according to law, because she hath not performed the commandment of the king Ahasuerus by the chamberlains?

16 And Memucan answered before the king and the princes, Vashti the queen hath not done wrong to the king only, but also to all the princes, and to all the people that *are* in all the provinces of the king Ahasuerus.

## Amplified

THE BOOK OF

# Esther

**1** IT WAS in the days of Ahasuerus [Xerxes], the Ahasuerus who reigned from India to Ethiopia over 127 provinces.

2 In those days, when King Ahasuerus sat on his royal throne which was in Shushan *or* Susa [the capital of the Persian Empire], in the palace *or* castle,

3 In the third year of his reign he made a feast for all his princes and his courtiers; the chief officers of the Persian and Median army, and the nobles and governors of the provinces were there before him,

4 While he showed the riches of his glorious kingdom and the splendor and excellence of his majesty for many days, even 180 days.

5 And when these days were completed, the king made a feast for all the people present in Shushan the capital, both great and small, a seven days' feast in the court of the garden of the king's palace.

6 There were hangings of fine white cloth, of green and of blue [cotton], fastened with cords of fine linen and purple to silver rings *or* rods and marble pillars. The couches of gold and silver rested on a (mosaic) pavement of porphyry, white marble, mother-of-pearl, and (precious) colored stones.

7 Drinks were served in different kinds of golden goblets, and there was royal wine in abundance according to the liberality of the king.

8 And drinking was according to the law; no one was compelled to drink; for the king had directed all the officials of his palace to serve only as each guest desired.

9 Also Queen Vashti gave a banquet for the women in the royal house which belonged to King Ahasuerus.

10 On the seventh day, when the king's heart was merry with wine, he commanded Mehuman, Biztha, Harbona, Bigtha, Abagtha, Zethar, and Carkas, the seven eunuchs who ministered to King Ahasuerus as attendants,

11 To bring Queen Vashti before the king with the royal crown, to show the peoples and the princes her beauty; for she was fair to behold.

12 But Queen Vashti refused to come at the king's command by the eunuchs. Therefore the king was enraged, and his anger burned within him.

13 Then the king spoke to the wise men who knew the times; for this was the king's procedure toward all who were familiar with law and judgment,

14 Those next to him being Carshena, Shethar, Admatha, Tarshish, Meres, Marsena, and Memucan, the seven princes of Persia and Media, who were in the king's presence, and held first place in the kingdom.

15 [He said], According to the law, what is to be done to Queen Vashti because she has not done the bidding of King Ahasuerus conveyed by the eunuchs?

16 And Memucan answered before the king and the princes, Vashti the queen has not only done wrong to the king, but also to all the princes and to all the peoples who are in all the provinces of King Ahasuerus.

## New American Standard

# Esther

*The Banquets of the King*

**1** NOW IT took place in the days of Ahasuerus, the Ahasuerus who reigned from India to Ethiopia over 127 provinces,

2in those days as King Ahasuerus sat on his royal throne which *was* in Susa the capital,

3in the third year of his reign, he gave a banquet for all his princes and attendants, the army *officers* of Persia and Media, the nobles, and the princes of his provinces being in his presence.

4And he displayed the riches of his royal glory and the splendor of his great majesty for many days, 180 days.

5And when these days were completed, the king gave a banquet lasting seven days for all the people who were present in Susa the capital, from the greatest to the least, in the court of the garden of the king's palace.

6 *There were hangings of* fine white and violet linen held by cords of fine purple linen on silver rings and marble columns, *and* couches of gold and silver on a mosaic pavement of porphyry, marble, mother-of-pearl, and precious stones.

7Drinks were served in golden vessels of various kinds, and the royal wine was plentiful according to the king's bounty.

8And the drinking was *done* according to the law, there was no compulsion, for so the king had given orders to each official of his household that he should do according to the desires of each person.

9Queen Vashti also gave a banquet for the women in the palace which belonged to King Ahasuerus.

*Queen Vashti's Refusal*

10¶ On the seventh day, when the heart of the king was merry with wine, he commanded Mehuman, Biztha, Harbona, Bigtha, Abagtha, Zethar, and Carkas, the seven eunuchs who served in the presence of King Ahasuerus,

11to bring Queen Vashti before the king with *her* royal crown in order to display her beauty to the people and the princes, for she was beautiful.

12But Queen Vashti refused to come at the king's command delivered by the eunuchs. Then the king became very angry and his wrath burned within him.

13Then the king said to the wise men who understood the times—for it was the custom of the king so *to speak* before all who knew law and justice,

14and were close to him: Carshena, Shethar, Admatha, Tarshish, Meres, Marsena, and Memucan, the seven princes of Persia and Media who had access to the king's presence and sat in the first place in the kingdom—

15"According to law, what is to be done with Queen Vashti, because she did not obey the command of King Ahasuerus *delivered* by the eunuchs?"

16And in the presence of the king and the princes, Memucan said, "Queen Vashti has wronged not only the king but *also* all the princes, and all the peoples who are in all the provinces of King Ahasuerus.

## New International

# Esther

*Queen Vashti Deposed*

**1** THIS IS what happened during the time of Xerxes,[a] the Xerxes who ruled over 127 provinces stretching from India to
Cush[b]: 2At that time King Xerxes reigned from his royal throne in
the citadel of Susa, 3and in the third year of his reign he gave a banquet for all his nobles and officials. The military leaders of Persia and Media, the princes, and the nobles of the provinces were present.

4For a full 180 days he displayed the vast wealth of his kingdom
and the splendor and glory of his majesty. 5When these days were
over, the king gave a banquet, lasting seven days, in the enclosed garden of the king's palace, for all the people from the least to the
greatest, who were in the citadel of Susa. 6The garden had hang-
ings of white and blue linen, fastened with cords of white linen and purple material to silver rings on marble pillars. There were couches of gold and silver on a mosaic pavement of porphyry,
marble, mother-of-pearl and other costly stones. 7Wine was served
in goblets of gold, each one different from the other, and the royal
wine was abundant, in keeping with the king's liberality. 8By the
king's command each guest was allowed to drink in his own way, for the king instructed all the wine stewards to serve each man what he wished.

9Queen Vashti also gave a banquet for the women in the royal palace of King Xerxes.

10On the seventh day, when King Xerxes was in high spirits from wine, he commanded the seven eunuchs who served him—Mehuman, Biztha, Harbona, Bigtha, Abagtha, Zethar and Carcas— 11to bring before him Queen Vashti, wearing her royal crown, in order to display her beauty to the people and nobles, for
she was lovely to look at. 12But when the attendants delivered the
king's command, Queen Vashti refused to come. Then the king became furious and burned with anger.

13Since it was customary for the king to consult experts in matters of law and justice, he spoke with the wise men who
understood the times 14and were closest to the king—Carshena, Shethar, Admatha, Tarshish, Meres, Marsena and Memucan, the seven nobles of Persia and Media who had special access to the king and were highest in the kingdom.

15"According to law, what must be done to Queen Vashti?" he asked. "She has not obeyed the command of King Xerxes that the eunuchs have taken to her."

16Then Memucan replied in the presence of the king and the nobles, "Queen Vashti has done wrong, not only against the king but also against all the nobles and the peoples of all the provinces
of King Xerxes. 17For the queen's conduct will become known to

**NIV Esther** [a] *1* Hebrew *Ahasuerus,* a variant of Xerxes' name; here and throughout Esther [b] *1* That is, the upper Nile region

## King James

17 For *this* deed of the queen shall come abroad unto all women, so that they shall despise their husbands in their eyes, when it shall be reported, The king Ahasuerus commanded Vashti the queen to be brought in before him, but she came not.

18 *Likewise* shall the ladies of Persia and Media say this day unto all the king's princes, which have heard of the deed of the queen. Thus *shall there arise* too much contempt and wrath.

19 If it please the king, let there go a royal commandment from him, and let it be written among the laws of the Persians and the Medes, that it be not altered, That Vashti come no more before king Ahasuerus; and let the king give her royal estate unto another that is better than she.

20 And when the king's decree which he shall make shall be published throughout all his empire, (for it is great,) all the wives shall give to their husbands honour, both to great and small.

21 And the saying pleased the king and the princes; and the king did according to the word of Memucan:

22 For he sent letters into all the king's provinces, into every province according to the writing thereof, and to every people after their language, that every man should bear rule in his own house, and that *it* should be published according to the language of every people.

**2** AFTER THESE things, when the wrath of king Ahasuerus was appeased, he remembered Vashti, and what she had done, and what was decreed against her.

2 Then said the king's servants that ministered unto him, Let there be fair young virgins sought for the king:

3 And let the king appoint officers in all the provinces of his kingdom, that they may gather together all the fair young virgins unto Shushan the palace, to the house of the women, unto the custody of Hege the king's chamberlain, keeper of the women; and let their things for purification be given *them:*

4 And let the maiden which pleaseth the king be queen instead of Vashti. And the thing pleased the king; and he did so.

5 ¶ *Now* in Shushan the palace there was a certain Jew, whose name *was* Mordecai, the son of Jair, the son of Shimei, the son of Kish, a Benjamite;

6 Who had been carried away from Jerusalem with the captivity which had been carried away with Jeconiah king of Judah, whom Nebuchadnezzar the king of Babylon had carried away.

7 And he brought up Hadassah, that *is,* Esther, his uncle's daughter: for she had neither father nor mother, and the maid *was* fair and beautiful; whom Mordecai, when her father and mother were dead, took for his own daughter.

8 ¶ So it came to pass, when the king's commandment and his decree was heard, and when many maidens were gathered together unto Shushan the palace, to the custody of Hegai, that Esther was brought also unto the king's house, to the custody of Hegai, keeper of the women.

9 And the maiden pleased him, and she obtained kindness of him; and he speedily gave her her things for purification, with such things as belonged to her, and seven maidens, *which were* meet to be given her, out of the king's house: and he preferred her and her maids unto the best *place* of the house of the women.

10 Esther had not shown her people nor her kindred: for Mordecai had charged her that she should not show *it.*

11 And Mordecai walked every day before the court of the women's house, to know how Esther did, and what should become of her.

## Amplified

17 For this deed of the queen will become known to all women, making their husbands contemptible in their eyes, since they will say, King Ahasuerus commanded Queen Vashti to be brought before him, and she did not come.

18 This very day the ladies of Persia and Media who have heard of the queen's behavior will be telling it to all the king's princes. So contempt and wrath in plenty will arise.

19 If it please the king, let a royal command go forth from him, and let it be written among the laws of the Persians and Medes so that it may not be changed, that Vashti is to [be divorced, and] come no more before King Ahasuerus; and let the king give her royal position to another who is better than she.

20 So when the king's decree is made and proclaimed throughout all his kingdom, extensive as it is, all wives will give honor to their husbands, high and low.

21 This advice pleased the king and the princes, and the king did what Memucan proposed.

22 He sent letters to all the royal provinces, to each in its own script and to every people in their own language, saying that every man should rule in his own house and speak there in the language of his own people. [If he had foreign wives, let them learn his language.]

**2** AFTER THESE things, when the wrath of King Ahasuerus was pacified, he (earnestly) remembered Vashti and what she had done and what was decreed against her.

2 Then the king's servants who ministered to him said, Let beautiful young virgins be sought for the king.

3 And let the king appoint officers in all the provinces of his kingdom to gather all the beautiful young virgins to the capital in Shushan, to the harem under the custody of Hegai the king's eunuch who is in charge of the women; and let their things for purification be given them.

4 And let the maiden who pleases the king be queen instead of Vashti. This pleased the king, and he did so.

5 There was a certain Jew in the capital in Shushan whose name was Mordecai, the son of Jair, son of Shimei, son of Kish, a Benjamite,

6 Who had been carried away from Jerusalem with the captives taken away with Jeconiah king of Judah, whom Nebuchadnezzar the king of Babylon had carried into exile.

7 He had brought up Hadassah, that is Esther, his uncle's daughter, for she had neither father nor mother; the maiden was beautiful and lovely and when her father and mother died, Mordecai took her as his own daughter.

8 So when the king's command and his decree were proclaimed, and when many maidens were gathered in Shushan the capital under the custody of Hegai, Esther also was taken into the king's house to the custody of Hegai, keeper of the women.

9 And the maiden pleased [Hegai] and obtained his favor; and he speedily gave her the things for her purification and her portion of food and the seven chosen maids to be given her from the king's palace; and he removed her and her maids to the best [apartment] in the harem.

10 Esther had not made known her nationality or her kindred, for Mordecai had charged her not to do so.

11 And Mordecai [who was an [a]attendant in the king's court] walked every day before the court of the harem, to learn how Esther was and what would become of her.

AMP [a] So says the Septuagint (Greek Version), verse nineteen.

## New American Standard

17“For the queen’s conduct will become known to all the women causing them to look with contempt on their husbands by saying, ‘King Ahasuerus commanded Queen Vashti to be brought in to his presence, but she did not come.’

18“And this day the ladies of Persia and Media who have heard of the queen’s conduct will speak in *the same way* to all the king’s princes, and there will be plenty of contempt and anger.

19“If it pleases the king, let a royal edict be issued by him and let it be written in the laws of Persia and Media so that it cannot be repealed, that Vashti should come no more into the presence of King Ahasuerus, and let the king give her royal position to another who is more worthy than she.

20“And when the king’s edict which he shall make is heard throughout all his kingdom, great as it is, then all women will give honor to their husbands, great and small.”

21And *this* word pleased the king and the princes, and the king did as Memucan proposed.

22So he sent letters to all the king’s provinces, to each province according to its script and to every people according to their language, that every man should be the master in his own house and the one who speaks in the language of his own people.

*Vashti’s Successor Sought*

**2** AFTER THESE things when the anger of King Ahasuerus had subsided, he remembered Vashti and what she had done and what had been decreed against her.

2Then the king’s attendants, who served him, said, “Let beautiful young virgins be sought for the king.

3“And let the king appoint overseers in all the provinces of his kingdom that they may gather every beautiful young virgin to Susa the capital, to the harem, into the custody of Hegai, the king’s eunuch, who was in charge of the women; and let their cosmetics be given *them.*

4“Then let the young lady who pleases the king be queen in place of Vashti.” And the matter pleased the king, and he did accordingly.

5¶ *Now* there was a Jew in Susa the capital whose name was Mordecai, the son of Jair, the son of Shimei, the son of Kish, a Benjamite,

6who had been taken into exile from Jerusalem with the captives who had been exiled with Jeconiah king of Judah, whom Nebuchadnezzar the king of Babylon had exiled.

7And he was bringing up Hadassah, that is Esther, his uncle’s daughter, for she had neither father nor mother. Now the young lady was beautiful of form and face, and when her father and her mother died, Mordecai took her as his own daughter.

*Esther Finds Favor*

8¶ So it came about when the command and decree of the king were heard and many young ladies were gathered to Susa the capital into the custody of Hegai, that Esther was taken to the king’s palace into the custody of Hegai, who was in charge of the women.

9Now the young lady pleased him and found favor with him. So he quickly provided her with her cosmetics and food, gave her seven choice maids from the king’s palace, and transferred her and her maids to the best place in the harem.

10Esther did not make known her people or her kindred, for Mordecai had instructed her that she should not make *them* known.

11And every day Mordecai walked back and forth in front of the court of the harem to learn how Esther was and how she fared.

## New International

all the women, and so they will despise their husbands and say, ‘King Xerxes commanded Queen Vashti to be brought before him, but she would not come.’ 18This very day the Persian and Median women of the nobility who have heard about the queen’s conduct will respond to all the king’s nobles in the same way. There will be no end of disrespect and discord.

19“Therefore, if it pleases the king, let him issue a royal decree and let it be written in the laws of Persia and Media, which cannot be repealed, that Vashti is never again to enter the presence of King Xerxes. Also let the king give her royal position to someone else who is better than she. 20Then when the king’s edict is proclaimed throughout all his vast realm, all the women will respect their husbands, from the least to the greatest.”

21The king and his nobles were pleased with this advice, so the king did as Memucan proposed. 22He sent dispatches to all parts of the kingdom, to each province in its own script and to each people in its own language, proclaiming in each people’s tongue that every man should be ruler over his own household.

*Esther Made Queen*

**2** LATER WHEN the anger of King Xerxes had subsided, he remembered Vashti and what she had done and what he had decreed about her. 2Then the king’s personal attendants proposed, “Let a search be made for beautiful young virgins for the king. 3Let the king appoint commissioners in every province of his realm to bring all these beautiful girls into the harem at the citadel of Susa. Let them be placed under the care of Hegai, the king’s eunuch, who is in charge of the women; and let beauty treatments be given to them. 4Then let the girl who pleases the king be queen instead of Vashti.” This advice appealed to the king, and he followed it.

5Now there was in the citadel of Susa a Jew of the tribe of Benjamin, named Mordecai son of Jair, the son of Shimei, the son of Kish, 6who had been carried into exile from Jerusalem by Nebuchadnezzar king of Babylon, among those taken captive with Jehoiachin[b] king of Judah. 7Mordecai had a cousin named Hadassah, whom he had brought up because she had neither father nor mother. This girl, who was also known as Esther, was lovely in form and features, and Mordecai had taken her as his own daughter when her father and mother died.

8When the king’s order and edict had been proclaimed, many girls were brought to the citadel of Susa and put under the care of Hegai. Esther also was taken to the king’s palace and entrusted to Hegai, who had charge of the harem. 9The girl pleased him and won his favor. Immediately he provided her with her beauty treatments and special food. He assigned to her seven maids selected from the king’s palace and moved her and her maids into the best place in the harem.

10Esther had not revealed her nationality and family background, because Mordecai had forbidden her to do so. 11Every day he walked back and forth near the courtyard of the harem to find out how Esther was and what was happening to her.

**NIV** [b] 6 Hebrew *Jeconiah,* a variant of *Jehoiachin*

## King James

12¶ Now when every maid's turn was come to go in to king
Ahasuerus, after that she had been twelve months, according to
the manner of the women, (for so were the days of their purifica-
tions accomplished, *to wit*, six months with oil of myrrh, and six
months with sweet odours, and with *other* things for the purifying
of the women;)
13Then thus came *every* maiden unto the king; whatsoever she
desired was given her to go with her out of the house of the women
unto the king's house.
14In the evening she went, and on the morrow she returned into
the second house of the women, to the custody of Shaashgaz, the
king's chamberlain, which kept the concubines: she came in unto
the king no more, except the king delighted in her, and that she
were called by name.
15¶ Now when the turn of Esther, the daughter of Abihail the
uncle of Mordecai, who had taken her for his daughter, was come
to go in unto the king, she required nothing but what Hegai the
king's chamberlain, the keeper of the women, appointed. And
Esther obtained favour in the sight of all them that looked upon
her.
16So Esther was taken unto king Ahasuerus into his house royal
in the tenth month, which *is* the month Tebeth, in the seventh year
of his reign.
17And the king loved Esther above all the women, and she
obtained grace and favour in his sight more than all the virgins; so
that he set the royal crown upon her head, and made her queen
instead of Vashti.
18Then the king made a great feast unto all his princes and his
servants, *even* Esther's feast; and he made a release to the provinces, and gave gifts, according to the state of the king.
19And when the virgins were gathered together the second
time, then Mordecai sat in the king's gate.
20Esther had not *yet* shown her kindred nor her people; as
Mordecai had charged her: for Esther did the commandment of
Mordecai, like as when she was brought up with him.
21¶ In those days, while Mordecai sat in the king's gate, two of
the king's chamberlains, Bigthan and Teresh, of those which kept
the door, were wroth, and sought to lay hand on the king Ahasuerus.
22And the thing was known to Mordecai, who told *it* unto
Esther the queen; and Esther certified the king *thereof* in Mordecai's
name.
23And when inquisition was made of the matter, it was found
out; therefore they were both hanged on a tree: and it was written
in the book of the chronicles before the king.

3 AFTER THESE things did king Ahasuerus promote Haman
the son of Hammedatha the Agagite, and advanced him, and
set his seat above all the princes that *were* with him.
2And all the king's servants, that *were* in the king's gate, bowed,
and reverenced Haman: for the king had so commanded concerning him. But Mordecai bowed not, nor did *him* reverence.
3Then the king's servants, which *were* in the king's gate, said
unto Mordecai, Why transgressest thou the king's commandment?
4Now it came to pass, when they spake daily unto him, and he
hearkened not unto them, that they told Haman, to see whether
Mordecai's matters would stand: for he had told them that he *was*
a Jew.

## Amplified

12Now when the turn of each maiden came to go in to King
Ahasuerus, after the regulations for the women had been carried
out for twelve months, since this was the regular period for their
beauty treatments, six months with oil of myrrh and six months
with sweet spices *and* perfumes and the things for the purifying
of the women,
13Then in this way the maiden came to the king: whatever she
desired was given her to take with her from the harem into the
king's palace.
14In the evening she went, and next day she returned into the
second harem in the custody of Shaashgaz the king's eunuch who
was in charge of the concubines; she came to the king no more,
unless the king delighted in her and she was called for by name.
15Now when the turn for Esther the daughter of Abihail, the
uncle of Mordecai who had taken her as his own daughter, had
come to go in to the king, she required nothing but what Hegai the
king's attendant, the keeper of the women, suggested. And Esther
won favor in the sight of all who saw her.
16So Esther was taken to King Ahasuerus into his royal palace
in the tenth month, the month Tebeth, in the seventh year of his
reign.
17And the king loved Esther more than all the women, and she
obtained grace and favor in his sight more than all the maidens,
so that he set the royal crown on her head, and made her queen
instead of Vashti.
18Then the king gave a great feast for all his princes and his
servants, Esther's feast; and he gave a holiday [or a lessening of
taxes] to the provinces, and gave gifts in keeping with the generosity of the king.
19And when the maidens were gathered together the second
time, Mordecai was sitting at the king's gate.
20Now Esther had not yet revealed her nationality or her
people; for she obeyed Mordecai's command to her [ [a]to fear God
and execute His commands] just as when she was being brought
up by him.
21In those days, while Mordecai sat at the king's gate, two of
the king's eunuchs, Bigthan and Teresh, of those who guarded the
door, were angry and sought to lay hands on King Ahasuerus.
22And this was known to Mordecai, who told it to Queen Esther, and Esther told the king in Mordecai's name.
23When it was investigated and found to be true, both men
were hanged on the gallows. And it was recorded in the Book of
the Chronicles in the king's presence.

3 AFTER THESE things King [b]Ahasuerus promoted Haman
the son of Hammedatha the Agagite, and advanced him and
set his seat above all the princes who were with him.
2And all the king's servants who were at the king's gate bowed
down and did reverence to Haman; for the king had so commanded concerning him. But Mordecai did not bow down or do
him reverence.
3Then the king's servants who were at the king's gate said to
Mordecai, Why do you transgress the king's command?
4Now when they spoke to him day after day and he paid no
attention to them, they told Haman, to see whether Mordecai's
conduct would stand; for he had told them that he was a Jew.

**AMP** [a] So the Septuagint reads. The name of God is nowhere mentioned directly in the Hebrew text. [b] There seems to be little doubt that King Ahasuerus is to be identified with the well-known Xerxes, who reigned from 486 to 465 B.C. The *Zondervan Pictorial Bible Dictionary* gives four close similarities between them which support this identification. Also, "the Ahasuerus of Ezra 4:6, to whom were written accusations against the Jews of Jerusalem, is in all probability the same Xerxes, although sometimes identified with Cambyses, son of Cyrus."

## New American Standard

12¶ Now when the turn of each young lady came to go in to King Ahasuerus, after the end of her twelve months under the regulations for the women—for the days of their beautification were completed as follows: six months with oil of myrrh and six months with spices and the cosmetics for women—

13the young lady would go in to the king in this way: anything that she desired was given her to take with her from the harem to the king's palace.

14In the evening she would go in and in the morning she would return to the second harem, to the custody of Shaashgaz, the king's eunuch who was in charge of the concubines. She would not again go in to the king unless the king delighted in her and she was summoned by name.

15Now when the turn of Esther, the daughter of Abihail the uncle of Mordecai who had taken her as his daughter, came to go in to the king, she did not request anything except what Hegai, the king's eunuch who was in charge of the women, advised. And Esther found favor in the eyes of all who saw her.

16¶ So Esther was taken to King Ahasuerus to his royal palace in the tenth month which is the month Tebeth, in the seventh year of his reign.

*Esther Becomes Queen*

17And the king loved Esther more than all the women, and she found favor and kindness with him more than all the virgins, so that he set the royal crown on her head and made her queen instead of Vashti.

18Then the king gave a great banquet, Esther's banquet, for all his princes and his servants; he also made a holiday for the provinces and gave gifts according to the king's bounty.

19¶ And when the virgins were gathered together the second time, then Mordecai was sitting at the king's gate.

20Esther had not yet made known her kindred or her people, even as Mordecai had commanded her, for Esther did what Mordecai told her as she had done when under his care.

*Mordecai Saves the King*

21In those days, while Mordecai was sitting at the king's gate, Bigthan and Teresh, two of the king's officials from those who guarded the door, became angry and sought to lay hands on King Ahasuerus.

22But the plot became known to Mordecai, and he told Queen Esther, and Esther informed the king in Mordecai's name.

23Now when the plot was investigated and found *to be so*, they were both hanged on a [c]gallows; and it was written in the Book of the Chronicles in the king's presence.

*Haman's Plot against the Jews*

**3** AFTER THESE events King Ahasuerus promoted Haman, the son of Hammedatha the Agagite, and advanced him and established his authority over all the princes who *were* with him.

2And all the king's servants who were at the king's gate bowed down and paid homage to Haman; for so the king had commanded concerning him. But Mordecai neither bowed down nor paid homage.

3Then the king's servants who were at the king's gate said to Mordecai, "Why are you transgressing the king's command?"

4Now it was when they had spoken daily to him and he would not listen to them, that they told Haman to see whether Mordecai's reason would stand; for he had told them that he was a Jew.

NAS [c] Lit., *tree*

## New International

12Before a girl's turn came to go in to King Xerxes, she had to complete twelve months of beauty treatments prescribed for the women, six months with oil of myrrh and six with perfumes and cosmetics. 13And this is how she would go to the king: Anything she wanted was given her to take with her from the harem to the king's palace. 14In the evening she would go there and in the morning return to another part of the harem to the care of Shaashgaz, the king's eunuch who was in charge of the concubines. She would not return to the king unless he was pleased with her and summoned her by name.

15When the turn came for Esther (the girl Mordecai had adopted, the daughter of his uncle Abihail) to go to the king, she asked for nothing other than what Hegai, the king's eunuch who was in charge of the harem, suggested. And Esther won the favor of everyone who saw her. 16She was taken to King Xerxes in the royal residence in the tenth month, the month of Tebeth, in the seventh year of his reign.

17Now the king was attracted to Esther more than to any of the other women, and she won his favor and approval more than any of the other virgins. So he set a royal crown on her head and made her queen instead of Vashti. 18And the king gave a great banquet, Esther's banquet, for all his nobles and officials. He proclaimed a holiday throughout the provinces and distributed gifts with royal liberality.

*Mordecai Uncovers a Conspiracy*

19When the virgins were assembled a second time, Mordecai was sitting at the king's gate. 20But Esther had kept secret her family background and nationality just as Mordecai had told her to do, for she continued to follow Mordecai's instructions as she had done when he was bringing her up.

21During the time Mordecai was sitting at the king's gate, Bigthana[d] and Teresh, two of the king's officers who guarded the doorway, became angry and conspired to assassinate King Xerxes. 22But Mordecai found out about the plot and told Queen Esther, who in turn reported it to the king, giving credit to Mordecai. 23And when the report was investigated and found to be true, the two officials were hanged on a gallows.[e] All this was recorded in the book of the annals in the presence of the king.

*Haman's Plot to Destroy the Jews*

**3** AFTER THESE events, King Xerxes honored Haman son of Hammedatha, the Agagite, elevating him and giving him a seat of honor higher than that of all the other nobles. 2All the royal officials at the king's gate knelt down and paid honor to Haman, for the king had commanded this concerning him. But Mordecai would not kneel down or pay him honor.

3Then the royal officials at the king's gate asked Mordecai, "Why do you disobey the king's command?" 4Day after day they spoke to him but he refused to comply. Therefore they told Haman about it to see whether Mordecai's behavior would be tolerated, for he had told them he was a Jew.

NIV [d] 21 Hebrew *Bigthan*, a variant of *Bigthana* [e] 23 Or *were hung* (or *impaled*) *on poles*; similarly elsewhere in Esther

# King James

5And when Haman saw that Mordecai bowed not, nor did him reverence, then was Haman full of wrath.

6And he thought scorn to lay hands on Mordecai alone; for they had shown him the people of Mordecai: wherefore Haman sought to destroy all the Jews that *were* throughout the whole kingdom of Ahasuerus, *even* the people of Mordecai.

7¶ In the first month, that *is*, the month Nisan, in the twelfth year of king Ahasuerus, they cast Pur, that *is*, the lot, before Haman from day to day, and from month to month, *to* the twelfth *month*, that *is*, the month Adar.

8¶ And Haman said unto king Ahasuerus, There is a certain people scattered abroad and dispersed among the people in all the provinces of thy kingdom; and their laws *are* diverse from all people; neither keep they the king's laws: therefore it *is* not for the king's profit to suffer them.

9If it please the king, let it be written that they may be destroyed: and I will pay ten thousand talents of silver to the hands of those that have the charge of the business, to bring *it* into the king's treasuries.

10And the king took his ring from his hand, and gave it unto Haman the son of Hammedatha the Agagite, the Jews' enemy.

11And the king said unto Haman, The silver *is* given to thee, the people also, to do with them as it seemeth good to thee.

12Then were the king's scribes called on the thirteenth day of the first month, and there was written according to all that Haman had commanded unto the king's lieutenants, and to the governors that *were* over every province, and to the rulers of every people of every province according to the writing thereof, and *to* every people after their language; in the name of king Ahasuerus was it written, and sealed with the king's ring.

13And the letters were sent by posts into all the king's provinces, to destroy, to kill, and to cause to perish, all Jews, both young and old, little children and women, in one day, *even* upon the thirteenth *day* of the twelfth month, which *is* the month Adar, and *to take* the spoil of them for a prey.

14The copy of the writing for a commandment to be given in every province was published unto all people, that they should be ready against that day.

15The posts went out, being hastened by the king's commandment, and the decree was given in Shushan the palace. And the king and Haman sat down to drink; but the city Shushan was perplexed.

**4** WHEN MORDECAI perceived all that was done, Mordecai rent his clothes, and put on sackcloth with ashes, and went out into the midst of the city, and cried with a loud and a bitter cry;

2And came even before the king's gate: for none *might* enter into the king's gate clothed with sackcloth.

3And in every province, whithersoever the king's commandment and his decree came, *there was* great mourning among the Jews, and fasting, and weeping, and wailing; and many lay in sackcloth and ashes.

4¶ So Esther's maids and her chamberlains came and told *it* her. Then was the queen exceedingly grieved; and she sent raiment to clothe Mordecai, and to take away his sackcloth from him: but he received *it* not.

5Then called Esther for Hatach, *one* of the king's chamberlains, whom he had appointed to attend upon her, and gave him a commandment to Mordecai, to know what it *was*, and why it *was*.

6So Hatach went forth to Mordecai unto the street of the city, which *was* before the king's gate.

7And Mordecai told him of all that had happened unto him, and of the sum of the money that Haman had promised to pay to the king's treasuries for the Jews, to destroy them.

# Amplified

5And when Haman saw that Mordecai did not bow down or do him reverence, he was very angry.

6But he scorned laying hands only on Mordecai. So since they had told him Mordecai's nationality, Haman sought to destroy all the Jews, the people of Mordecai, throughout the whole kingdom of Ahasuerus.

7In the first month, the month of Nisan, in the twelfth year of King Ahasuerus, Haman caused Pur, that is lots, to be cast before him day after day [to find a lucky day for his venture], month after month until the twelfth, the month of Adar.

8Then Haman said to King Ahasuerus, There is a certain people scattered abroad and dispersed among the peoples in all the provinces of your kingdom; their laws are different from every other people, neither do they keep the king's laws. Therefore it is not for the king's profit to tolerate them.

9If it please the king, let it be decreed that they be destroyed, and I will pay 10,000 talents of silver into the hands of those who have charge of the king's business, that it may be brought into the king's treasuries.

10And the king took his signet ring from his hand [with which to seal his letters by the king's authority], and gave it to Haman the son of Hammedatha the Agagite, the Jews' enemy.

11And the king said to Haman, The silver is given to you, the people also, to do with them as it seems good to you.

12Then the king's secretaries were called in on the thirteenth day of the first month, and all that Haman had commanded was written to the king's chief rulers and to the governors that were over all the provinces and to the princes of each people, to every province in its own script and to each people in their own language; it was written in the name of King Ahasuerus and it was sealed with the king's [signet] ring.

13And letters were sent by special messengers to all the king's provinces, to destroy, to slay, and to do away with all Jews, both young and old, little children and women, in one day, the thirteenth day of the twelfth month, the month Adar, and to seize their belongings as spoil.

14A copy of the writing was to be published *and* given out as a decree in every province to all the peoples to be ready for that day.

15The special messengers went out in haste by order of the king, and the decree was given out in Shushan the capital. And the king and Haman sat down to drink; but the city of Shushan was perplexed [at the strange and alarming decree].

**4** NOW WHEN Mordecai learned all that was done, [he] rent his clothes, and put on sackcloth with ashes, and went out into the midst of the city, and cried with a loud and bitter cry.

2He came *and* stood before the king's gate, for no one might enter the king's gate clothed with sackcloth.

3And in every province, wherever the king's commandment and his decree came, there was great mourning among the Jews, and fasting, weeping, and wailing, and many lay in sackcloth and ashes.

4When Esther's maids and her attendants came and told it to her, the queen was exceedingly grieved *and* distressed. She sent garments to clothe Mordecai, with orders to take his sackcloth from off him; and he would not receive them.

5Then Esther called for Hathach, one of the king's attendants whom he had appointed to attend her, and ordered him to go to Mordecai, to learn what this was and why it was.

6So Hathach went out to Mordecai in the open square of the city, which was in front of the king's gate.

7And Mordecai told him of all that had happened to him, and the exact sum of money that Haman had promised to pay to the king's treasuries for the Jews to be destroyed.

## New American Standard

5When Haman saw that Mordecai neither bowed down nor
paid homage to him, Haman was filled with rage.
6But he disdained to lay hands on Mordecai alone, for they had
told him *who* the people of Mordecai *were;* therefore Haman sought
to destroy all the Jews, the people of Mordecai, who *were* throughout the whole kingdom of Ahasuerus.
7¶ In the first month, which is the month Nisan, in the twelfth
year of King Ahasuerus, Pur, that is the lot, was cast before Haman
from day to day and from month *to month,* until the twelfth month,
that is the month Adar.
8Then Haman said to King Ahasuerus, "There is a certain
people scattered and dispersed among the peoples in all the provinces of your kingdom; their laws are different from *those* of all
*other* people, and they do not observe the king's laws, so it is not
in the king's interest to let them remain.
9"If it is pleasing to the king, let it be decreed that they be
destroyed, and I will pay ten thousand talents of silver into the
hands of those who carry on the *king's* business, to put into the
king's treasuries."
10Then the king took his signet ring from his hand and gave it
to Haman, the son of Hammedatha the Agagite, the enemy of the
Jews.
11And the king said to Haman, "The silver is yours, and the
people *also,* to do with them as you please."
12Then the king's scribes were summoned on the thirteenth day
of the first month, and it was written just as Haman commanded
to the king's satraps, to the governors who were over each province, and to the princes of each people, each province according
to its script, each people according to its language, being written
in the name of King Ahasuerus and sealed with the king's signet
ring.
13And letters were sent by couriers to all the king's provinces
to destroy, to kill, and to annihilate all the Jews, both young and
old, women and children, in one day, the thirteenth *day* of the
twelfth month, which is the month Adar, and to seize their possessions as plunder.
14A copy of the edict to be issued as law in every province was
published to all the peoples so that they should be ready for this
day.
15The couriers went out impelled by the king's command while
the decree was issued in Susa the capital; and while the king and
Haman sat down to drink, the city of Susa was in confusion.

*Esther Learns of Haman's Plot*

4 WHEN MORDECAI learned all that had been done, he tore
his clothes, put on sackcloth and ashes, and went out into the
midst of the city and wailed loudly and bitterly.
2And he went as far as the king's gate, for no one was to enter
the king's gate clothed in sackcloth.
3And in each and every province where the command and
decree of the king came, there was great mourning among the
Jews, with fasting, weeping, and wailing; and many lay on sackcloth and ashes.
4¶ Then Esther's maidens and her eunuchs came and told her,
and the queen writhed in great anguish. And she sent garments
to clothe Mordecai that he might remove his sackcloth from him,
but he did not accept *them.*
5Then Esther summoned Hathach from the king's eunuchs,
whom the king had appointed to attend her, and ordered him *to
go* to Mordecai to learn what this *was* and why it *was.*
6So Hathach went out to Mordecai to the city square in front
of the king's gate.
7And Mordecai told him all that had happened to him, and the
exact amount of money that Haman had promised to pay to the
king's treasuries for the destruction of the Jews.

## New International

5When Haman saw that Mordecai would not kneel down or pay
him honor, he was enraged. 6Yet having learned who Mordecai's
people were, he scorned the idea of killing only Mordecai. Instead
Haman looked for a way to destroy all Mordecai's people, the
Jews, throughout the whole kingdom of Xerxes.
7In the twelfth year of King Xerxes, in the first month, the
month of Nisan, they cast the *pur* (that is, the lot) in the presence
of Haman to select a day and month. And the lot fell on[a] the
twelfth month, the month of Adar.
8Then Haman said to King Xerxes, "There is a certain people
dispersed and scattered among the peoples in all the provinces of
your kingdom whose customs are different from those of all other
people and who do not obey the king's laws; it is not in the king's
best interest to tolerate them. 9If it pleases the king, let a decree
be issued to destroy them, and I will put ten thousand talents[b] of
silver into the royal treasury for the men who carry out this
business."
10So the king took his signet ring from his finger and gave it to
Haman son of Hammedatha, the Agagite, the enemy of the Jews.
11"Keep the money," the king said to Haman, "and do with the
people as you please."
12Then on the thirteenth day of the first month the royal secretaries were summoned. They wrote out in the script of each province and in the language of each people all Haman's orders to the
king's satraps, the governors of the various provinces and the
nobles of the various peoples. These were written in the name of
King Xerxes himself and sealed with his own ring. 13Dispatches
were sent by couriers to all the king's provinces with the order to
destroy, kill and annihilate all the Jews—young and old, women
and little children—on a single day, the thirteenth day of the
twelfth month, the month of Adar, and to plunder their goods. 14A
copy of the text of the edict was to be issued as law in every
province and made known to the people of every nationality so
they would be ready for that day.
15Spurred on by the king's command, the couriers went out,
and the edict was issued in the citadel of Susa. The king and
Haman sat down to drink, but the city of Susa was bewildered.

*Mordecai Persuades Esther to Help*

4 WHEN MORDECAI learned of all that had been done, he tore
his clothes, put on sackcloth and ashes, and went out into the
city, wailing loudly and bitterly. 2But he went only as far as the
king's gate, because no one clothed in sackcloth was allowed to
enter it. 3In every province to which the edict and order of the king
came, there was great mourning among the Jews, with fasting,
weeping and wailing. Many lay in sackcloth and ashes.
4When Esther's maids and eunuchs came and told her about
Mordecai, she was in great distress. She sent clothes for him to put
on instead of his sackcloth, but he would not accept them. 5Then
Esther summoned Hathach, one of the king's eunuchs assigned to
attend her, and ordered him to find out what was troubling Mordecai and why.
6So Hathach went out to Mordecai in the open square of the city
in front of the king's gate. 7Mordecai told him everything that had
happened to him, including the exact amount of money Haman
had promised to pay into the royal treasury for the destruction of
the Jews. 8He also gave him a copy of the text of the edict for their

**NIV** [a] 7 Septuagint; Hebrew does not have *And the lot fell on.* [b] 9 That is, about 375 tons (about 345 metric tons)

## King James

8 Also he gave him the copy of the writing of the decree that was given at Shushan to destroy them, to show *it* unto Esther, and to declare *it* unto her, and to charge her that she should go in unto the king, to make supplication unto him, and to make request before him for her people.

9 And Hatach came and told Esther the words of Mordecai.

10 ¶ Again Esther spake unto Hatach, and gave him commandment unto Mordecai;

11 All the king's servants, and the people of the king's provinces, do know, that whosoever, whether man or woman, shall come unto the king into the inner court, who is not called, *there is* one law of his to put *him* to death, except such to whom the king shall hold out the golden sceptre, that he may live: but I have not been called to come in unto the king these thirty days.

12 And they told to Mordecai Esther's words.

13 Then Mordecai commanded to answer Esther, Think not with thyself that thou shalt escape in the king's house, more than all the Jews.

14 For if thou altogether holdest thy peace at this time, *then* shall there enlargement and deliverance arise to the Jews from another place; but thou and thy father's house shall be destroyed: and who knoweth whether thou art come to the kingdom for *such* a time as this?

15 ¶ Then Esther bade *them* return Mordecai *this answer*,

16 Go, gather together all the Jews that are present in Shushan, and fast ye for me, and neither eat nor drink three days, night or day: I also and my maidens will fast likewise; and so will I go in unto the king, which *is* not according to the law: and if I perish, I perish.

17 So Mordecai went his way, and did according to all that Esther had commanded him.

**5** NOW IT came to pass on the third day, that Esther put on *her* royal *apparel*, and stood in the inner court of the king's house, over against the king's house: and the king sat upon his royal throne in the royal house, over against the gate of the house.

2 And it was so, when the king saw Esther the queen standing in the court, *that* she obtained favour in his sight: and the king held out to Esther the golden sceptre that *was* in his hand. So Esther drew near, and touched the top of the sceptre.

3 Then said the king unto her, What wilt thou, queen Esther? and what *is* thy request? it shall be even given thee to the half of the kingdom.

4 And Esther answered, If *it seem* good unto the king, let the king and Haman come this day unto the banquet that I have prepared for him.

5 Then the king said, Cause Haman to make haste, that he may do as Esther hath said. So the king and Haman came to the banquet that Esther had prepared.

6 ¶ And the king said unto Esther at the banquet of wine, What *is* thy petition? and it shall be granted thee: and what *is* thy request? even to the half of the kingdom it shall be performed.

7 Then answered Esther, and said, My petition and my request *is:*

8 If I have found favour in the sight of the king, and if it please the king to grant my petition, and to perform my request, let the king and Haman come to the banquet that I shall prepare for them, and I will do tomorrow as the king hath said.

9 ¶ Then went Haman forth that day joyful and with a glad heart: but when Haman saw Mordecai in the king's gate, that he stood not up, nor moved for him, he was full of indignation against Mordecai.

10 Nevertheless Haman refrained himself: and when he came home, he sent and called for his friends, and Zeresh his wife.

## Amplified

8 [Mordecai] also gave him a copy of the decree to destroy them that was given out in Shushan, that he might show it to Esther, explain it to her, and charge her to go to the king, make supplication to him and plead with him for the lives of her people.

9 And Hathach came and told Esther the words of Mordecai.

10 Then Esther spoke to Hathach and gave him a message for Mordecai, saying,

11 All the king's servants and the people of the king's provinces know that any person, be it man or woman, who shall go into the inner court to the king without being called shall be put to death; there is but one law for him, except [him] to whom the king shall hold out the golden scepter that he may live. But I have not been called to come to the king these thirty days.

12 And they told Mordecai what Esther said.

13 Then Mordecai told them to return this answer to Esther, Do not flatter yourself that you shall escape in the king's palace any more than all the other Jews.

14 For if you keep silent at this time, relief and deliverance shall arise for the Jews from elsewhere, but you and your father's house will perish. And who knows but that you have come to the kingdom for such a time as this *and* for this very occasion?

15 Then Esther told them to give this answer to Mordecai,

16 Go, gather together all the Jews that are present in Shushan, and fast for me, and neither eat nor drink for three days, night or day, I also and my maids will fast as you do. Then I will go to the king, though it is against the law; and if I perish, I perish.

17 So Mordecai went away and did all that Esther had commanded him.

**5** ON THE third day [of the fast] Esther put on her royal robes and stood in the royal *or* inner court of the king's palace opposite his [throne-room]. The king was sitting on his throne, facing the main entrance of the palace.

2 And when the king saw Esther the queen standing in the court, she obtained favor in his sight and he held out to [her] the golden scepter that was in his hand. So Esther drew near, and touched the tip of the scepter.

3 Then the king said to her, What will you have, Queen Esther? What is your request? It shall be given you even to the half of the kingdom.

4 And Esther said, If it seem good to the king, let the king and Haman come this day to the dinner that I have prepared for the king.

5 Then the king said, Cause Haman to come quickly that what Esther has said may be done.

6 So the king and Haman came to the dinner that Esther had prepared.

7 And during the serving of wine the king said to Esther, What is your petition? It shall be granted you. And what is your request? Even to the half of the kingdom it shall be performed.

8 Then Esther said, My petition and my request is: If I have found favor in the sight of the king, and if it please the king to grant my petition and to perform my request, let the king and Haman come tomorrow to the dinner that I shall prepare for them, and I will do tomorrow as the king has said.

9 Haman went away that day joyful and elated in heart. But when he saw Mordecai at the king's gate, refusing to stand up or show fear before him, he was filled with wrath against Mordecai.

10 Nevertheless Haman restrained himself and went home. There he sent and called for his friends and Zeresh his wife.

## New American Standard

8He also gave him a copy of the text of the edict which had been
issued in Susa for their destruction, that he might show Esther and
inform her, and to order her to go in to the king to implore his favor
and to plead with him for her people.
9¶ And Hathach came back and related Mordecai's words to
Esther.
10Then Esther spoke to Hathach and ordered him *to reply* to
Mordecai:
11"All the king's servants and the people of the king's provinces
know that for any man or woman who comes to the king to the
inner court who is not summoned, he has but one law, that he be
put to death, unless the king holds out to him the golden scepter
so that he may live. And I have not been summoned to come to
the king for these thirty days."
12And they related Esther's words to Mordecai.
13¶ Then Mordecai told *them* to reply to Esther, "Do not imagine
that you in the king's palace can escape any more than all the Jews.
14"For if you remain silent at this time, relief and deliverance
will arise for the Jews from another place and you and your father's
house will perish. And who knows whether you have not attained
royalty for such a time as this?"

*Esther Plans to Intercede*

15Then Esther told *them* to reply to Mordecai,
16"Go, assemble all the Jews who are found in Susa, and fast
for me; do not eat or drink for three days, night or day. I and my
maidens also will fast in the same way. And thus I will go in to the
king, which is not according to the law; and if I perish, I perish."
17So Mordecai went away and did just as Esther had commanded him.

*Esther Plans a Banquet*

5 NOW IT came about on the third day that Esther put on her
royal robes and stood in the inner court of the king's palace
in front of the king's rooms, and the king was sitting on his royal
throne in the throne room, opposite the entrance to the palace.
2And it happened when the king saw Esther the queen standing in the court, she obtained favor in his sight; and the king
extended to Esther the golden scepter which was in his hand. So
Esther came near and touched the top of the scepter.
3Then the king said to her, "What is *troubling* you, Queen
Esther? And what is your request? Even to half of the kingdom it
will be given to you."
4And Esther said, "If it please the king, may the king and
Haman come this day to the banquet that I have prepared for
him."
5¶ Then the king said, "Bring Haman quickly that we may do
as Esther desires." So the king and Haman came to the banquet
which Esther had prepared.
6And, as they drank their wine at the banquet, the king said
to Esther, "What is your petition, for it shall be granted to you.
And what is your request? Even to half of the kingdom it shall be
done."
7So Esther answered and said, "My petition and my request
is:
8if I have found favor in the sight of the king, and if it please
the king to grant my petition and do what I request, may the king
and Haman come to the banquet which I shall prepare for them,
and tomorrow I will do as the king says."

*Haman's Pride*

9¶ Then Haman went out that day glad and pleased of heart;
but when Haman saw Mordecai in the king's gate, and that he did
not stand up or tremble before him, Haman was filled with anger
against Mordecai.
10Haman controlled himself, however, went to his house, and
sent for his friends and his wife Zeresh.

## New International

annihilation, which had been published in Susa, to show to Esther
and explain it to her, and he told him to urge her to go into the
king's presence to beg for mercy and plead with him for her
people.
9Hathach went back and reported to Esther what Mordecai had
said. 10Then she instructed him to say to Mordecai, 11"All the
king's officials and the people of the royal provinces know that for
any man or woman who approaches the king in the inner court
without being summoned the king has but one law: that he be put
to death. The only exception to this is for the king to extend the
gold scepter to him and spare his life. But thirty days have passed
since I was called to go to the king."
12When Esther's words were reported to Mordecai, 13he sent
back this answer: "Do not think that because you are in the king's
house you alone of all the Jews will escape. 14For if you remain
silent at this time, relief and deliverance for the Jews will arise from
another place, but you and your father's family will perish. And
who knows but that you have come to royal position for such a
time as this?"
15Then Esther sent this reply to Mordecai: 16"Go, gather together all the Jews who are in Susa, and fast for me. Do not eat
or drink for three days, night or day. I and my maids will fast as
you do. When this is done, I will go to the king, even though it
is against the law. And if I perish, I perish."
17So Mordecai went away and carried out all of Esther's instructions.

*Esther's Request to the King*

5 ON THE third day Esther put on her royal robes and stood
in the inner court of the palace, in front of the king's hall. The
king was sitting on his royal throne in the hall, facing the entrance.
2When he saw Queen Esther standing in the court, he was pleased
with her and held out to her the gold scepter that was in his hand.
So Esther approached and touched the tip of the scepter.
3Then the king asked, "What is it, Queen Esther? What is your
request? Even up to half the kingdom, it will be given you."
4"If it pleases the king," replied Esther, "let the king, together
with Haman, come today to a banquet I have prepared for him."
5"Bring Haman at once," the king said, "so that we may do
what Esther asks."
So the king and Haman went to the banquet Esther had prepared. 6As they were drinking wine, the king again asked Esther,
"Now what is your petition? It will be given you. And what is your
request? Even up to half the kingdom, it will be granted."
7Esther replied, "My petition and my request is this: 8If the king
regards me with favor and if it pleases the king to grant my petition
and fulfill my request, let the king and Haman come tomorrow to
the banquet I will prepare for them. Then I will answer the king's
question."

*Haman's Rage Against Mordecai*

9Haman went out that day happy and in high spirits. But when
he saw Mordecai at the king's gate and observed that he neither
rose nor showed fear in his presence, he was filled with rage
against Mordecai. 10Nevertheless, Haman restrained himself and
went home.
Calling together his friends and Zeresh, his wife, 11Haman

## King James

11And Haman told them of the glory of his riches, and the multitude of his children, and all *the things* wherein the king had promoted him, and how he had advanced him above the princes and servants of the king.
12Haman said moreover, Yea, Esther the queen did let no man come in with the king unto the banquet that she had prepared but myself; and tomorrow am I invited unto her also with the king.
13Yet all this availeth me nothing, so long as I see Mordecai the Jew sitting at the king's gate.
14¶ Then said Zeresh his wife and all his friends unto him, Let a gallows be made of fifty cubits high, and tomorrow speak thou unto the king that Mordecai may be hanged thereon: then go thou in merrily with the king unto the banquet. And the thing pleased Haman; and he caused the gallows to be made.

6 ON THAT night could not the king sleep, and he commanded to bring the book of records of the chronicles; and they were read before the king.
2And it was found written, that Mordecai had told of Bigthana and Teresh, two of the king's chamberlains, the keepers of the door, who sought to lay hand on the king Ahasuerus.
3And the king said, What honour and dignity hath been done to Mordecai for this? Then said the king's servants that ministered unto him, There is nothing done for him.
4¶ And the king said, Who *is* in the court? Now Haman was come into the outward court of the king's house, to speak unto the king to hang Mordecai on the gallows that he had prepared for him.
5And the king's servants said unto him, Behold, Haman standeth in the court. And the king said, Let him come in.
6So Haman came in. And the king said unto him, What shall be done unto the man whom the king delighteth to honour? Now Haman thought in his heart, To whom would the king delight to do honour more than to myself?
7And Haman answered the king, For the man whom the king delighteth to honour,
8Let the royal apparel be brought which the king *useth* to wear, and the horse that the king rideth upon, and the crown royal which is set upon his head:
9And let this apparel and horse be delivered to the hand of one of the king's most noble princes, that they may array the man *withal* whom the king delighteth to honour, and bring him on horseback through the street of the city, and proclaim before him, Thus shall it be done to the man whom the king delighteth to honour.
10Then the king said to Haman, Make haste, *and* take the apparel and the horse, as thou hast said, and do even so to Mordecai the Jew, that sitteth at the king's gate: let nothing fail of all that thou hast spoken.
11Then took Haman the apparel and the horse, and arrayed Mordecai, and brought him on horseback through the street of the city, and proclaimed before him, Thus shall it be done unto the man whom the king delighteth to honour.
12¶ And Mordecai came again to the king's gate. But Haman hasted to his house mourning, and having his head covered.
13And Haman told Zeresh his wife and all his friends every *thing* that had befallen him. Then said his wise men and Zeresh his wife unto him, If Mordecai *be* of the seed of the Jews, before whom thou hast begun to fall, thou shalt not prevail against him, but shalt surely fall before him.
14And while they *were* yet talking with him, came the king's chamberlains, and hasted to bring Haman unto the banquet that Esther had prepared.

## Amplified

11And Haman recounted to them the glory of his riches, the abundance of his [ten] sons, all the things in which the king had promoted him, and how he had advanced him above the princes and servants of the king.
12Haman added, Yes, and today Queen Esther did not let any man come with the king to the dinner she had prepared but myself; and tomorrow also I am invited by her together with the king.
13Yet all this benefits me nothing, so long as I see Mordecai the Jew sitting at the king's gate.
14Then Zeresh his wife and all his friends said to him, Let a gallows be made fifty cubits [seventy-five feet] high, and in the morning speak to the king that Mordecai may be hanged on it; then you go in merrily with the king to the dinner. And the thing pleased Haman, and he caused the gallows to be made.

6 ON THAT night the king could not sleep, and he ordered that the book of memorable deeds, the chronicles, be brought, and they were read before the king.
2And it was found written how Mordecai had told of Bigthana and Teresh, two of the king's attendants who guarded the door, who had sought to lay hands on King Ahasuerus.
3And the king said, What honor or distinction has been given Mordecai for this? Then the king's servants who ministered to him said, Nothing has been done for him.
4The king said, Who is in the court? Now Haman had just come into the outer court of the king's palace to ask the king to hang Mordecai on the gallows he had prepared for him.
5And the king's servants said to him, Behold, Haman is standing in the court. And the king said, Let him come in.
6So Haman came in. And the king said to him, What shall be done to the man whom the king delights to honor? Now Haman said to himself, To whom would the king delight to do honor more than to me?
7And Haman said to the king, For the man whom the king delights to honor,
8Let royal apparel be brought which the king has worn, and the horse which the king has ridden, and a royal crown be set on his head.
9And let the apparel and the horse be delivered to the hand of one of the king's most noble princes. Let him array the man whom the king delights to honor, and conduct him on horseback through the open square of the city and proclaim before him, Thus shall it be done to the man whom the king delights to honor.
10Then the king said to Haman, Make haste and take the apparel and the horse, as you have said, and do so to Mordecai the Jew, who sits at the king's gate. Leave out nothing that you have spoken.
11Then Haman took the apparel and the horse, and conducted Mordecai on horseback through the open square of the city, proclaiming before him, Thus shall it be done to the man whom the king delights to honor.
12Then Mordecai came again to the king's gate. But Haman hasted to his house, mourning and having his head covered.
13And Haman recounted to Zeresh his wife and all his friends everything that had happened to him. Then his wise men and Zeresh his wife said to him, If Mordecai, before whom you have begun to fall, is of the offspring of the Jews, you can not prevail against him, but shall surely fall before him.
14While they were yet talking with him the king's attendants came and hastily brought Haman to the dinner that Esther had prepared.

## New American Standard

11Then Haman recounted to them the glory of his riches, and
the number of his sons, and every *instance* where the king had
magnified him, and how he had promoted him above the princes
and servants of the king.
12Haman also said, "Even Esther the queen let no one but me
come with the king to the banquet which she had prepared; and
tomorrow also I am invited by her with the king.
13"Yet all of this does not satisfy me every time I see Mordecai
the Jew sitting at the king's gate."
14Then Zeresh his wife and all his friends said to him, "Have
a gallows fifty cubits high made and in the morning ask the king
to have Mordecai hanged on it, then go joyfully with the king to
the banquet." And the advice pleased Haman, so he had the
gallows made.

*The King Plans to Honor Mordecai*

**6** DURING THAT night the king could not sleep so he gave an
order to bring the book of records, the chronicles, and they
were read before the king.
2And it was found written what Mordecai had reported concerning Bigthana and Teresh, two of the king's eunuchs who were
doorkeepers, that they had sought to lay hands on King Ahasuerus.
3And the king said, "What honor or dignity has been bestowed
on Mordecai for this?" Then the king's servants who attended him
said, "Nothing has been done for him."
4So the king said, "Who is in the court?" Now Haman had just
entered the outer court of the king's palace in order to speak to the
king about hanging Mordecai on the gallows which he had prepared for him.
5And the king's servants said to him, "Behold, Haman is
standing in the court." And the king said, "Let him come in."
6So Haman came in and the king said to him, "What is to be
done for the man whom the king desires to honor?" And Haman
said to himself, "Whom would the king desire to honor more than
me?"
7Then Haman said to the king, "For the man whom the king
desires to honor,
8let them bring a royal robe which the king has worn, and the
horse on which the king has ridden, and on whose head a royal
crown has been placed;
9and let the robe and the horse be handed over to one of the
king's most noble princes and let them array the man whom the
king desires to honor and lead him on horseback through the city
square, and proclaim before him, 'Thus it shall be done to the man
whom the king desires to honor.' "

*Haman Must Honor Mordecai*

**10**¶ Then the king said to Haman, "Take quickly the robes and
the horse as you have said, and do so for Mordecai the Jew, who
is sitting at the king's gate; do not fall short in anything of all that
you have said."
11So Haman took the robe and the horse, and arrayed Mordecai,
and led him *on horseback* through the city square, and proclaimed
before him, "Thus it shall be done to the man whom the king
desires to honor."
12Then Mordecai returned to the king's gate. But Haman hurried home, mourning, with *his* head covered.
13And Haman recounted to Zeresh his wife and all his friends
everything that had happened to him. Then his wise men and
Zeresh his wife said to him, "If Mordecai, before whom you have
begun to fall, is of Jewish origin, you will not overcome him, but
will surely fall before him."
14While they were still talking with him, the king's eunuchs
arrived and hastily brought Haman to the banquet which Esther
had prepared.

## New International

boasted to them about his vast wealth, his many sons, and all the
ways the king had honored him and how he had elevated him
above the other nobles and officials. 12"And that's not all," Haman
added. "I'm the only person Queen Esther invited to accompany
the king to the banquet she gave. And she has invited me along
with the king tomorrow. 13But all this gives me no satisfaction as
long as I see that Jew Mordecai sitting at the king's gate."
14His wife Zeresh and all his friends said to him, "Have a
gallows built, seventy-five feet[a] high, and ask the king in the
morning to have Mordecai hanged on it. Then go with the king to
the dinner and be happy." This suggestion delighted Haman, and
he had the gallows built.

*Mordecai Honored*

**6** THAT NIGHT the king could not sleep; so he ordered the
book of the chronicles, the record of his reign, to be brought
in and read to him. 2It was found recorded there that Mordecai had
exposed Bigthana and Teresh, two of the king's officers who
guarded the doorway, who had conspired to assassinate King
Xerxes.
3"What honor and recognition has Mordecai received for this?"
the king asked.
"Nothing has been done for him," his attendants answered.
4The king said, "Who is in the court?" Now Haman had just
entered the outer court of the palace to speak to the king about
hanging Mordecai on the gallows he had erected for him.
5His attendants answered, "Haman is standing in the court."
"Bring him in," the king ordered.
6When Haman entered, the king asked him, "What should be
done for the man the king delights to honor?"
Now Haman thought to himself, "Who is there that the king
would rather honor than me?" 7So he answered the king, "For the
man the king delights to honor, 8have them bring a royal robe the
king has worn and a horse the king has ridden, one with a royal
crest placed on its head. 9Then let the robe and horse be entrusted
to one of the king's most noble princes. Let them robe the man the
king delights to honor, and lead him on the horse through the city
streets, proclaiming before him, 'This is what is done for the man
the king delights to honor!' "
10"Go at once," the king commanded Haman. "Get the robe
and the horse and do just as you have suggested for Mordecai the
Jew, who sits at the king's gate. Do not neglect anything you have
recommended."
11So Haman got the robe and the horse. He robed Mordecai,
and led him on horseback through the city streets, proclaiming
before him, "This is what is done for the man the king delights to
honor!"
12Afterward Mordecai returned to the king's gate. But Haman
rushed home, with his head covered in grief, 13and told Zeresh his
wife and all his friends everything that had happened to him.
His advisers and his wife Zeresh said to him, "Since Mordecai,
before whom your downfall has started, is of Jewish origin, you
cannot stand against him—you will surely come to ruin!" 14While
they were still talking with him, the king's eunuchs arrived and
hurried Haman away to the banquet Esther had prepared.

**NIV** [a] 14 Hebrew *fifty cubits* (about 23 meters)

## King James

7 SO THE king and Haman came to banquet with Esther the queen.

2And the king said again unto Esther on the second day at the banquet of wine, What *is* thy petition, queen Esther? and it shall be granted thee: and what *is* thy request? and it shall be performed, *even* to the half of the kingdom.

3Then Esther the queen answered and said, If I have found favour in thy sight, O king, and if it please the king, let my life be given me at my petition, and my people at my request:

4For we are sold, I and my people, to be destroyed, to be slain, and to perish. But if we had been sold for bondmen and bondwomen, I had held my tongue, although the enemy could not countervail the king's damage.

5¶ Then the king Ahasuerus answered and said unto Esther the queen, Who is he, and where is he, that durst presume in his heart to do so?

6And Esther said, The adversary and enemy *is* this wicked Haman. Then Haman was afraid before the king and the queen.

7¶ And the king arising from the banquet of wine in his wrath *went* into the palace garden: and Haman stood up to make request for his life to Esther the queen; for he saw that there was evil determined against him by the king.

8Then the king returned out of the palace garden into the place of the banquet of wine; and Haman was fallen upon the bed whereon Esther *was*. Then said the king, Will he force the queen also before me in the house? As the word went out of the king's mouth, they covered Haman's face.

9And Harbonah, one of the chamberlains, said before the king, Behold also, the gallows fifty cubits high, which Haman had made for Mordecai, who had spoken good for the king, standeth in the house of Haman. Then the king said, Hang him thereon.

10So they hanged Haman on the gallows that he had prepared for Mordecai. Then was the king's wrath pacified.

8 ON THAT day did the king Ahasuerus give the house of Haman the Jew's enemy unto Esther the queen. And Mordecai came before the king; for Esther had told what he *was* unto her.

2And the king took off his ring, which he had taken from Haman, and gave it unto Mordecai. And Esther set Mordecai over the house of Haman.

3¶ And Esther spake yet again before the king, and fell down at his feet, and besought him with tears to put away the mischief of Haman the Agagite, and his device that he had devised against the Jews.

4Then the king held out the golden sceptre toward Esther. So Esther arose, and stood before the king,

5And said, If it please the king, and if I have found favour in his sight, and the thing *seem* right before the king, and I *be* pleasing in his eyes, let it be written to reverse the letters devised by Haman the son of Hammedatha the Agagite, which he wrote to destroy the Jews which *are* in all the king's provinces:

6For how can I endure to see the evil that shall come unto my people? or how can I endure to see the destruction of my kindred?

7¶ Then the king Ahasuerus said unto Esther the queen and to Mordecai the Jew, Behold, I have given Esther the house of Haman, and him they have hanged upon the gallows, because he laid his hand upon the Jews.

8Write ye also for the Jews, as it liketh you, in the king's name, and seal *it* with the king's ring: for the writing which is written in the king's name, and sealed with the king's ring, may no man reverse.

## Amplified

7 SO THE king and Haman came to dine with Esther the queen.

2And the king said again to Esther on the second day when wine was being served, What is your petition, Queen Esther? It shall be granted. And what is your request? Even to the half of the kingdom it shall be performed.

3Then Queen Esther said, If I have found favor in your sight, O king, and if it please the king, let my life be given me at my petition and my people at my request;

4For we are sold, I and my people, to be destroyed, slain, and wiped out of existence! But if we had been sold for bondmen and bondwomen, I would have held my tongue, for our affliction is not to be compared with the damage this will do to the king.

5Then King Ahasuerus said to Queen Esther, Who is he, and where is he, who dares presume in his heart to do that?

6And Esther said, An adversary and an enemy, even this wicked Haman. Then Haman was afraid before the king and queen.

7And the king arose from the feast in his wrath and went into the palace garden; and Haman stood up to make request for his life to Queen Esther, for he saw that there was evil determined against him by the king.

8When the king returned out of the palace garden into the place of the drinking of wine, Haman was falling upon the couch where Esther was. Then said the king, Will he even forcibly assault the queen in my presence, in my own palace? As the king spoke the words, [the servants] covered Haman's face.

9Then said Harbonah, one of the attendants serving the king, Behold, the gallows fifty cubits high, which Haman has made for Mordecai, whose warning saved the king, stands at the house of Haman. And the king said, Hang him on it!

10So they hanged Haman on the gallows that he had prepared for Mordecai. Then the king's wrath was pacified.

8 ON THAT day King Ahasuerus gave the house of Haman the Jews' enemy to Queen Esther. And Mordecai came before the king, for Esther had told what he was to her.

2And the king took off his [signet] ring, which he had taken from Haman, and gave it to Mordecai. And Esther set Mordecai over the house of Haman.

3And Esther spoke yet again to the king, and fell down at his feet and besought him with tears to avert the evil plot of Haman the Agagite, and his scheme that he had devised against the Jews.

4Then the king held out to Esther the golden scepter. So Esther arose and stood before the king.

5And she said, If it please the king, and If I have found favor in his sight, and the thing seem right before the king, and I be pleasing in his eyes, let it be written to reverse the letters devised by Haman the son of Hammedatha the Agagite, which he wrote to destroy the Jews which are in all the king's provinces;

6For how can I endure to see the evil that shall come upon my people? Or how can I endure to see the destruction of my kindred?

7Then the King Ahasuerus said to Queen Esther and to Mordecai the Jew, Behold, I have given Esther the house of Haman, and him they have hanged upon the gallows, because he laid his hand upon the Jews.

8Write also concerning the Jews, as it pleases you, in the king's name, and seal it with the king's (signet) ring; for writing which is in the king's name, and sealed with the king's ring, no man can reverse.

# New American Standard

## Esther's Plea

**7** NOW THE king and Haman came to drink *wine* with Esther the queen.

2And the king said to Esther on the second day also as they drank their wine at the banquet, "What is your petition, Queen Esther? It shall be granted you. And what is your request? Even to half of the kingdom it shall be done."

3Then Queen Esther answered and said, "If I have found favor in your sight, O king, and if it please the king, let my life be given me as my petition, and my people as my request;

4for we have been sold, I and my people, to be destroyed, to be killed and to be annihilated. Now if we had only been sold as slaves, men and women, I would have remained silent, for the trouble would not be commensurate with the annoyance to the king."

5Then King Ahasuerus asked Queen Esther, "Who is he, and where is he, who would presume to do thus?"

6And Esther said, "A foe and an enemy, is this wicked Haman!" Then Haman became terrified before the king and queen.

## Haman Is Hanged

7And the king arose in his anger from drinking wine *and went* into the palace garden; but Haman stayed to beg for his life from Queen Esther, for he saw that harm had been determined against him by the king.

8Now when the king returned from the palace garden into the place where they were drinking wine, Haman was falling on the couch where Esther was. Then the king said, "Will he even assault the queen with me in the house?" As the word went out of the king's mouth, they covered Haman's face.

9Then Harbonah, one of the eunuchs who *were* before the king said, "Behold indeed, the gallows standing at Haman's house fifty cubits high, which Haman made for Mordecai who spoke good on behalf of the king!" And the king said, "Hang him on it."

10So they hanged Haman on the gallows which he had prepared for Mordecai, and the king's anger subsided.

## Mordecai Promoted

**8** ON THAT day King Ahasuerus gave the house of Haman, the enemy of the Jews, to Queen Esther; and Mordecai came before the king, for Esther had disclosed what he was to her.

2And the king took off his signet ring which he had taken away from Haman, and gave it to Mordecai. And Esther set Mordecai over the house of Haman.

3¶ Then Esther spoke again to the king, fell at his feet, wept, and implored him to avert the evil *scheme* of Haman the Agagite and his plot which he had devised against the Jews.

4And the king extended the golden scepter to Esther. So Esther arose and stood before the king.

5Then she said, "If it pleases the king and if I have found favor before him and the matter *seems* proper to the king and I am pleasing in his sight, let it be written to revoke the letters devised by Haman, the son of Hammedatha the Agagite, which he wrote to destroy the Jews who are in all the king's provinces.

6For how can I endure to see the calamity which shall befall my people, and how can I endure to see the destruction of my kindred?"

7So King Ahasuerus said to Queen Esther and to Mordecai the Jew, "Behold, I have given the house of Haman to Esther, and him they have hanged on the gallows because he had stretched out his hands against the Jews.

## The King's Decree Avenges the Jews

8"Now you write to the Jews as you see fit, in the king's name, and seal *it* with the king's signet ring; for a decree which is written in the name of the king and sealed with the king's signet ring may not be revoked."

# New International

## Haman Hanged

**7** SO THE king and Haman went to dine with Queen Esther, 2and as they were drinking wine on that second day, the king again asked, "Queen Esther, what is your petition? It will be given you. What is your request? Even up to half the kingdom, it will be granted."

3Then Queen Esther answered, "If I have found favor with you, O king, and if it pleases your majesty, grant me my life—this is my petition. And spare my people—this is my request. 4For I and my people have been sold for destruction and slaughter and annihilation. If we had merely been sold as male and female slaves, I would have kept quiet, because no such distress would justify disturbing the king.[a]"

5King Xerxes asked Queen Esther, "Who is he? Where is the man who has dared to do such a thing?"

6Esther said, "The adversary and enemy is this vile Haman."

Then Haman was terrified before the king and queen. 7The king got up in a rage, left his wine and went out into the palace garden. But Haman, realizing that the king had already decided his fate, stayed behind to beg Queen Esther for his life.

8Just as the king returned from the palace garden to the banquet hall, Haman was falling on the couch where Esther was reclining.

The king exclaimed, "Will he even molest the queen while she is with me in the house?"

As soon as the word left the king's mouth, they covered Haman's face. 9Then Harbona, one of the eunuchs attending the king, said, "A gallows seventy-five feet[b] high stands by Haman's house. He had it made for Mordecai, who spoke up to help the king."

The king said, "Hang him on it!" 10So they hanged Haman on the gallows he had prepared for Mordecai. Then the king's fury subsided.

## The King's Edict in Behalf of the Jews

**8** THAT SAME day King Xerxes gave Queen Esther the estate of Haman, the enemy of the Jews. And Mordecai came into the presence of the king, for Esther had told how he was related to her. 2The king took off his signet ring, which he had reclaimed from Haman, and presented it to Mordecai. And Esther appointed him over Haman's estate.

3Esther again pleaded with the king, falling at his feet and weeping. She begged him to put an end to the evil plan of Haman the Agagite, which he had devised against the Jews. 4Then the king extended the gold scepter to Esther and she arose and stood before him.

5"If it pleases the king," she said, "and if he regards me with favor and thinks it the right thing to do, and if he is pleased with me, let an order be written overruling the dispatches that Haman son of Hammedatha, the Agagite, devised and wrote to destroy the Jews in all the king's provinces. 6For how can I bear to see disaster fall on my people? How can I bear to see the destruction of my family?"

7King Xerxes replied to Queen Esther and to Mordecai the Jew, "Because Haman attacked the Jews, I have given his estate to Esther, and they have hanged him on the gallows. 8Now write another decree in the king's name in behalf of the Jews as seems best to you, and seal it with the king's signet ring—for no document written in the king's name and sealed with his ring can be revoked."

**NIV** a 4 Or *quiet, but the compensation our adversary offers cannot be compared with the loss the king would suffer* b 9 Hebrew *fifty cubits* (about 23 meters)

# King James

9Then were the king's scribes called at that time in the third month, that *is,* the month Sivan, on the three and twentieth *day* thereof; and it was written according to all that Mordecai commanded unto the Jews, and to the lieutenants, and the deputies and rulers of the provinces which *are* from India unto Ethiopia, an hundred twenty and seven provinces, unto every province according to the writing thereof, and unto every people after their language, and to the Jews according to their writing, and according to their language.

10And he wrote in the king Ahasuerus' name, and sealed *it* with the king's ring, and sent letters by posts on horseback, *and* riders on mules, camels, *and* young dromedaries:

11Wherein the king granted the Jews which *were* in every city to gather themselves together, and to stand for their life, to destroy, to slay, and to cause to perish, all the power of the people and province that would assault them, *both* little ones and women, and *to take* the spoil of them for a prey,

12Upon one day in all the provinces of king Ahasuerus, *namely,* upon the thirteenth *day* of the twelfth month, which *is* the month Adar.

13The copy of the writing for a commandment to be given in every province *was* published unto all people, and that the Jews should be ready against that day to avenge themselves on their enemies.

14 *So* the posts that rode upon mules *and* camels went out, being hastened and pressed on by the king's commandment. And the decree was given at Shushan the palace.

15¶ And Mordecai went out from the presence of the king in royal apparel of blue and white, and with a great crown of gold, and with a garment of fine linen and purple: and the city of Shushan rejoiced and was glad.

16The Jews had light, and gladness, and joy, and honour.

17And in every province, and in every city, whithersoever the king's commandment and his decree came, the Jews had joy and gladness, a feast and a good day. And many of the people of the land became Jews; for the fear of the Jews fell upon them.

**9** NOW IN the twelfth month, that *is,* the month Adar, on the thirteenth day of the same, when the king's commandment and his decree drew near to be put in execution, in the day that the enemies of the Jews hoped to have power over them, (though it was turned to the contrary, that the Jews had rule over them that hated them;)

2The Jews gathered themselves together in their cities throughout all the provinces of the king Ahasuerus, to lay hand on such as sought their hurt: and no man could withstand them; for the fear of them fell upon all people.

3And all the rulers of the provinces, and the lieutenants, and the deputies, and officers of the king, helped the Jews; because the fear of Mordecai fell upon them.

4For Mordecai *was* great in the king's house, and his fame went out throughout all the provinces: for this man Mordecai waxed greater and greater.

5Thus the Jews smote all their enemies with the stroke of the sword, and slaughter, and destruction, and did what they would unto those that hated them.

6And in Shushan the palace the Jews slew and destroyed five hundred men.

7And Parshandatha, and Dalphon, and Aspatha,

8And Poratha, and Adalia, and Aridatha,

9And Parmashta, and Arisai, and Aridai, and Vajezatha,

10The ten sons of Haman the sons of Hammedatha, the enemy of the Jews, slew they; but on the spoil laid they not their hand.

11On that day the number of those that were slain in Shushan the palace was brought before the king.

# Amplified

9Then the king's scribes were called, in the third month, the month Sivan, on the twenty-third day, and it was written according to all that Mordecai commanded, to the Jews, to the chief rulers, and the governors and princes of the provinces from India to Ethiopia, 127 provinces, to every province in its own script, and to every people in their own language, and to the Jews according to their writing and according to their language.

10He wrote in the name of King Ahasuerus, and sealed it with the king's ring, and sent letters by messengers on horseback, riding on swift steeds, mules and young dromedaries used in the king's service, bred from the [royal] stud.

11In it the king granted the Jews which were in every city to gather and defend their lives; to destroy, to slay and to wipe out any armed force that might attack them, their little ones and women; and they should take the enemies' goods for spoil.

12On one day in all the provinces of King Ahasuerus, the thirteenth day of the twelfth month, the month Adar,

13A copy of the writing was to be issued as a decree in every province and as a proclamation to all peoples, and the Jews should be ready on that day to avenge themselves upon their enemies.

14So the couriers who were mounted on swift beasts that were used in the king's service went out, being hurried and urged on by the king's command; and the decree was released in Shushan the capital.

15And Mordecai went forth from the presence of the king in royal apparel of blue and white, with a great crown of gold, and with a robe of fine linen and purple, and the city of Shushan shouted and rejoiced.

16The Jews had light [a dawn of new hope] and gladness and joy and honor.

17And in every province and in every city, wherever the king's command and his decree came, the Jews had gladness and joy, a feast and a holiday. And many from among the peoples of the land [submitted themselves to Jewish rite and] became Jews, for the fear of the Jews had fallen upon them.

**9** NOW IN the twelfth month, the month Adar, on the thirteenth day of Adar when the king's command and his edict were about to be executed, on the [very] day that the enemies of the Jews had planned for a massacre of them, it was turned to the contrary and the Jews had rule over those who hated them.

2The Jews gathered together in their cities throughout all the provinces of the King Ahasuerus, to lay hands on such as sought their hurt; and no man could withstand them, for the fear of them had fallen upon all the peoples.

3And all the princes of the provinces, and the chief rulers, and the governors, and they who attended to the king's business, helped the Jews; because the fear of Mordecai had fallen upon them.

4For Mordecai was great in the king's palace, and his fame went forth throughout all the provinces: for the man Mordecai became more and more powerful.

5So the Jews smote all their enemies with the sword, slaughtering and destroying them, and did as they chose with those who hated them.

6In Shushan the capital itself the Jews slew and destroyed 500 men.

7And they killed Parshandatha,

8Dalphon, Aspatha, Poratha, Adalia,

9Aridatha, Parmashta, Arisai, Aridai,

10And Vaizatha, the ten sons of Haman the son of Hammedatha, the Jews' enemy; but on the spoil they laid not their hands.

11On that day the number of those who were slain in Shushan the capital was brought before the king.

## New American Standard

9¶ So the king's scribes were called at that time in the third month (that is, the month Sivan), on the twenty-third day; and it was written according to all that Mordecai commanded to the Jews, the satraps, the governors, and the princes of the provinces which *extended* from India to Ethiopia, 127 provinces, to every province according to its script, and to every people according to their language, as well as to the Jews according to their script and their language.

10And he wrote in the name of King Ahasuerus, and sealed it with the king's signet ring, and sent letters by couriers on horses, riding on steeds sired by the royal stud.

11In them the king granted the Jews who were in each and every city *the right* to assemble and to defend their lives, to destroy, to kill, and to annihilate the entire army of any people or province which might attack them, including children and women, and to plunder their spoil,

12on one day in all the provinces of King Ahasuerus, the thirteenth *day* of the twelfth month (that is, the month Adar).

13A copy of the edict to be issued as law in each and every province, was published to all the peoples, so that the Jews should be ready for this day to avenge themselves on their enemies.

14The couriers, hastened and impelled by the king's command, went out, riding on the royal steeds; and the decree was given out in Susa the capital.

15¶ Then Mordecai went out from the presence of the king in royal robes of blue and white, with a large crown of gold and a garment of fine linen and purple; and the city of Susa shouted and rejoiced.

16For the Jews there was light and gladness and joy and honor.

17And in each and every province, and in each and every city, wherever the king's commandment and his decree arrived, there was gladness and joy for the Jews, a feast and a holiday. And many among the peoples of the land became Jews, for the dread of the Jews had fallen on them.

### *The Jews Destroy Their Enemies*

9 NOW IN the twelfth month (that is, the month Adar), on the thirteenth day when the king's command and edict were about to be executed, on the day when the enemies of the Jews hoped to gain the mastery over them, it was turned to the contrary so that the Jews themselves gained the mastery over those who hated them.

2The Jews assembled in their cities throughout all the provinces of King Ahasuerus to lay hands on those who sought their harm; and no one could stand before them, for the dread of them had fallen on all the peoples.

3Even all the princes of the provinces, the satraps, the governors, and those who were doing the king's business assisted the Jews, because the dread of Mordecai had fallen on them.

4Indeed, Mordecai was great in the king's house, and his fame spread throughout all the provinces; for the man Mordecai became greater and greater.

5Thus the Jews struck all their enemies with the sword, killing and destroying; and they did what they pleased to those who hated them.

6And in Susa the capital the Jews killed and destroyed five hundred men,

7and Parshandatha, Dalphon, Aspatha,

8Poratha, Adalia, Aridatha,

9Parmashta, Arisai, Aridai, and Vaizatha,

10the ten sons of Haman the son of Hammedatha, the Jews' enemy; but they did not lay their hands on the plunder.

11¶ On that day the number of those who were killed in Susa the capital was reported to the king.

## New International

9At once the royal secretaries were summoned—on the twenty-
third day of the third month, the month of Sivan. They wrote out
all Mordecai's orders to the Jews, and to the satraps, governors and
nobles of the 127 provinces stretching from India to Cush.[a] These
orders were written in the script of each province and the language
of each people and also to the Jews in their own script and language. 10Mordecai wrote in the name of King Xerxes, sealed the
dispatches with the king's signet ring, and sent them by mounted
couriers, who rode fast horses especially bred for the king.
11The king's edict granted the Jews in every city the right to
assemble and protect themselves; to destroy, kill and annihilate
any armed force of any nationality or province that might attack
them and their women and children; and to plunder the property
of their enemies. 12The day appointed for the Jews to do this in all
the provinces of King Xerxes was the thirteenth day of the twelfth
month, the month of Adar. 13A copy of the text of the edict was
to be issued as law in every province and made known to the
people of every nationality so that the Jews would be ready on that
day to avenge themselves on their enemies.
14The couriers, riding the royal horses, raced out, spurred on
by the king's command. And the edict was also issued in the
citadel of Susa.
15Mordecai left the king's presence wearing royal garments of
blue and white, a large crown of gold and a purple robe of fine
linen. And the city of Susa held a joyous celebration. 16For the Jews
it was a time of happiness and joy, gladness and honor. 17In every
province and in every city, wherever the edict of the king went,
there was joy and gladness among the Jews, with feasting and
celebrating. And many people of other nationalities became Jews
because fear of the Jews had seized them.

### *Triumph of the Jews*

9 ON THE thirteenth day of the twelfth month, the month of
Adar, the edict commanded by the king was to be carried out.
On this day the enemies of the Jews had hoped to overpower
them, but now the tables were turned and the Jews got the upper
hand over those who hated them. 2The Jews assembled in their
cities in all the provinces of King Xerxes to attack those seeking
their destruction. No one could stand against them, because the
people of all the other nationalities were afraid of them. 3And all
the nobles of the provinces, the satraps, the governors and the
king's administrators helped the Jews, because fear of Mordecai
had seized them. 4Mordecai was prominent in the palace; his
reputation spread throughout the provinces, and he became more
and more powerful.
5The Jews struck down all their enemies with the sword, killing
and destroying them, and they did what they pleased to those who
hated them. 6In the citadel of Susa, the Jews killed and destroyed
five hundred men. 7They also killed Parshandatha, Dalphon, Aspatha, 8Poratha, Adalia, Aridatha, 9Parmashta, Arisai, Aridai and
Vaizatha, 10the ten sons of Haman son of Hammedatha, the enemy
of the Jews. But they did not lay their hands on the plunder.
11The number of those slain in the citadel of Susa was reported
to the king that same day. 12The king said to Queen Esther, "The

NIV [a] 9 That is, the upper Nile region

## King James

12¶ And the king said unto Esther the queen, The Jews have slain and destroyed five hundred men in Shushan the palace, and the ten sons of Haman; what have they done in the rest of the king's provinces? now what *is* thy petition? and it shall be granted thee: or what *is* thy request further? and it shall be done.

13Then said Esther, If it please the king, let it be granted to the Jews which *are* in Shushan to do tomorrow also according unto this day's decree, and let Haman's ten sons be hanged upon the gallows.

14And the king commanded it so to be done: and the decree was given at Shushan; and they hanged Haman's ten sons.

15For the Jews that *were* in Shushan gathered themselves together on the fourteenth day also of the month Adar, and slew three hundred men at Shushan; but on the prey they laid not their hand.

16But the other Jews that *were* in the king's provinces gathered themselves together, and stood for their lives, and had rest from their enemies, and slew of their foes seventy and five thousand, but they laid not their hands on the prey,

17On the thirteenth day of the month Adar; and on the fourteenth day of the same rested they, and made it a day of feasting and gladness.

18But the Jews that *were* at Shushan assembled together on the thirteenth *day* thereof, and on the fourteenth thereof; and on the fifteenth *day* of the same they rested, and made it a day of feasting and gladness.

19Therefore the Jews of the villages, that dwelt in the unwalled towns, made the fourteenth day of the month Adar *a day of* gladness and feasting, and a good day, and of sending portions one to another.

20¶ And Mordecai wrote these things, and sent letters unto all the Jews that *were* in all the provinces of the king Ahasuerus, *both* nigh and far,

21To stablish *this* among them, that they should keep the fourteenth day of the month Adar, and the fifteenth day of the same, yearly,

22As the days wherein the Jews rested from their enemies, and the month which was turned unto them from sorrow to joy, and from mourning into a good day: that they should make them days of feasting and joy, and of sending portions one to another, and gifts to the poor.

23And the Jews undertook to do as they had begun, and as Mordecai had written unto them;

24Because Haman the son of Hammedatha, the Agagite, the enemy of all the Jews, had devised against the Jews to destroy them, and had cast Pur, that *is*, the lot, to consume them, and to destroy them;

25But when *Esther* came before the king, he commanded by letters that his wicked device, which he devised against the Jews, should return upon his own head, and that he and his sons should be hanged on the gallows.

26Wherefore they called these days Purim after the name of Pur. Therefore for all the words of this letter, and *of that* which they had seen concerning this matter, and which had come unto them,

27The Jews ordained, and took upon them, and upon their seed, and upon all such as joined themselves unto them, so as it should not fail, that they would keep these two days according to their writing, and according to their *appointed* time every year;

28And *that* these days *should be* remembered and kept throughout every generation, every family, every province, and every city; and *that* these days of Purim should not fail from among the Jews, nor the memorial of them perish from their seed.

29Then Esther the queen, the daughter of Abihail, and Mordecai the Jew, wrote with all authority, to confirm this second letter of Purim.

30And he sent the letters unto all the Jews, to the hundred twenty and seven provinces of the kingdom of Ahasuerus, *with* words of peace and truth,

## Amplified

12And the king said to Esther the queen, The Jews have slain and destroyed 500 men in Shushan the capital, and the ten sons of Haman; what then have they done in the rest of the king's provinces! Now what is your petition? It shall be granted to you; or what is your request further? It shall be done.

13Then said Esther, If it please the king, let it be granted to the Jews which are in Shushan to do tomorrow also according to this day's decree, and let [the dead bodies of] Haman's ten sons be hanged on the gallows. [Verse 10.]

14And the king commanded it to be done; the decree was given to Shushan, and they hanged [the bodies of] Haman's ten sons.

15And the Jews that were in Shushan gathered together on the fourteenth day also of the month Adar, and slew 300 men in Shushan; but on the spoil they laid not their hands.

16And the other Jews that were in the king's provinces gathered to defend their lives, and had relief *and* rest from their enemies, and slew of them that hated them 75,000; but on the spoil they laid not their hands.

17This was done on the thirteenth day of the month Adar; and on the fourteenth day they rested, and made it a day of feasting and gladness.

18But the Jews who were in Shushan [Susa] assembled on the thirteenth day and on the fourteenth; and on the fifteenth day they rested, and made it a day of feasting and gladness.

19Therefore the Jews of the villages who dwell in the unwalled towns make the fourteenth day of the month Adar a day of gladness and feasting, a holiday, and a day for sending choice portions to one another.

20And Mordecai recorded these things, and sent letters to all the Jews who were in all the provinces of the King Ahasuerus, both near and far,

21To command them to keep the fourteenth day of the month Adar and also the fifteenth, yearly.

22As the days on which the Jews got rest from their enemies, and as the month which was turned for them from sorrow to gladness, and from mourning into a holiday; that they should make them days of feasting and gladness, days of sending choice portions to one another and gifts to the poor.

23So the Jews undertook to do as they had begun, and as Mordecai had written to them.

24Because Haman the son of Hammedatha, the Agagite, the enemy of all the Jews, had plotted against the Jews to destroy them, and had cast Pur, that is the lot, [to find a lucky day] to crush *and* consume and destroy them;

25But when Esther brought the matter before the king, he commanded in writing that Haman's wicked scheme which he had devised against the Jews should return upon his own head, and that he and his sons should be hanged on the gallows.

26Therefore they called these days Purim, after the name Pur [lot]. Therefore, because of all that was in this letter, and what they had faced in this matter, and what had happened to them,

27The Jews ordained and took upon themselves and their descendants and all who joined them, that without fail every year they would keep these two days at the appointed time and as it was written.

28And that these days should be remembered [imprinted on their minds] and kept throughout every generation, in every family, province and city; and that these days of Purim should never cease from among the Jews, nor the commemoration of them cease among their descendants.

29Then Queen Esther the daughter of Abihail, and Mordecai the Jew gave full power [written authority], confirming this second letter about Purim.

30And letters were sent to all the Jews, to the 127 provinces of the kingdom of Ahasuerus, in words of peace and truth,

## New American Standard

12And the king said to Queen Esther, "The Jews have killed and
destroyed five hundred men and the ten sons of Haman in Susa
the capital. What then have they done in the rest of the king's
provinces! Now what is your petition? It shall even be granted you.
And what is your further request? It shall also be done."
13Then said Esther, "If it pleases the king, let tomorrow also be
granted to the Jews who are in Susa to do according to the edict
of today; and let Haman's ten sons be hanged on the gallows."
14So the king commanded that it should be done so; and an
edict was issued in Susa, and Haman's ten sons were hanged.
15And the Jews who were in Susa assembled also on the fourteenth day of the month Adar and killed three hundred men in
Susa, but they did not lay their hands on the plunder.
**16**¶ Now the rest of the Jews who *were* in the king's provinces
assembled, to defend their lives and rid themselves of their enemies, and kill 75,000 of those who hated them; but they did not
lay their hands on the plunder.
17 *This was done* on the thirteenth day of the month Adar, and
on the fourteenth day they rested and made it a day of feasting and
rejoicing.
18But the Jews who were in Susa assembled on the thirteenth
and the fourteenth of the same month, and they rested on the
fifteenth day and made it a day of feasting and rejoicing.
19Therefore the Jews of the rural areas, who live in the rural
towns, make the fourteenth day of the month Adar *a* holiday for
rejoicing and feasting and sending portions *of food* to one another.

*The Feast of Purim Instituted*

**20**¶ Then Mordecai recorded these events, and he sent letters to
all the Jews who were in all the provinces of King Ahasuerus, both
near and far,
21obliging them to celebrate the fourteenth day of the month
Adar, and the fifteenth day of the same month, annually,
22because on those days the Jews rid themselves of their enemies, and *it was a* month which was turned for them from sorrow
into gladness and from mourning into a holiday; that they should
make them days of feasting and rejoicing and sending portions *of
food* to one another and gifts to the poor.
23Thus the Jews undertook what they had started to do, and
what Mordecai had written to them.
24For Haman the son of Hammedatha, the Agagite, the adversary of all the Jews, had schemed against the Jews to destroy them,
and had cast Pur, that is the lot, to disturb them and destroy them.
25But when it came to the king's attention, he commanded by
letter that his wicked scheme which he had devised against the
Jews, should return on his own head, and that he and his sons
should be hanged on the gallows.
26Therefore they called these days Purim after the name of Pur.
And because of the instructions in this letter, both what they had
seen in this regard and what had happened to them,
27the Jews established and made a custom for themselves, and
for their descendants, and for all those who allied themselves with
them, so that they should not fail to celebrate these two days
according to their regulation, and according to their appointed
time annually.
28So these days were to be remembered and celebrated
throughout every generation, every family, every province, and
every city; and these days of Purim were not to fail from among
the Jews, or their memory fade from their descendants.
**29**¶ Then Queen Esther, daughter of Abihail, with Mordecai the
Jew, wrote with full authority to confirm this second letter about
Purim.
30And he sent letters to all the Jews, to the 127 provinces of the
kingdom of Ahasuerus, namely, words of peace and truth,

## New International

Jews have killed and destroyed five hundred men and the ten sons
of Haman in the citadel of Susa. What have they done in the rest
of the king's provinces? Now what is your petition? It will be given
you. What is your request? It will also be granted."
13"If it pleases the king," Esther answered, "give the Jews in
Susa permission to carry out this day's edict tomorrow also, and
let Haman's ten sons be hanged on gallows."
14So the king commanded that this be done. An edict was
issued in Susa, and they hanged the ten sons of Haman. 15The
Jews in Susa came together on the fourteenth day of the month of
Adar, and they put to death in Susa three hundred men, but they
did not lay their hands on the plunder.
16Meanwhile, the remainder of the Jews who were in the king's
provinces also assembled to protect themselves and get relief from
their enemies. They killed seventy-five thousand of them but did
not lay their hands on the plunder. 17This happened on the thirteenth day of the month of Adar, and on the fourteenth they rested
and made it a day of feasting and joy.

*Purim Celebrated*

18The Jews in Susa, however, had assembled on the thirteenth
and fourteenth, and then on the fifteenth they rested and made it
a day of feasting and joy.
19That is why rural Jews—those living in villages—observe the
fourteenth of the month of Adar as a day of joy and feasting, a day
for giving presents to each other.
20Mordecai recorded these events, and he sent letters to all the
Jews throughout the provinces of King Xerxes, near and far, 21to
have them celebrate annually the fourteenth and fifteenth days of
the month of Adar 22as the time when the Jews got relief from their
enemies, and as the month when their sorrow was turned into joy
and their mourning into a day of celebration. He wrote them to
observe the days as days of feasting and joy and giving presents
of food to one another and gifts to the poor.
23So the Jews agreed to continue the celebration they had
begun, doing what Mordecai had written to them. 24For Haman
son of Hammedatha, the Agagite, the enemy of all the Jews, had
plotted against the Jews to destroy them and had cast the *pur* (that
is, the lot) for their ruin and destruction. 25But when the plot came
to the king's attention,[a] he issued written orders that the evil
scheme Haman had devised against the Jews should come back
onto his own head, and that he and his sons should be hanged on
the gallows. 26(Therefore these days were called Purim, from the
word *pur*.) Because of everything written in this letter and because
of what they had seen and what had happened to them, 27the Jews
took it upon themselves to establish the custom that they and their
descendants and all who join them should without fail observe
these two days every year, in the way prescribed and at the time
appointed. 28These days should be remembered and observed in
every generation by every family, and in every province and in
every city. And these days of Purim should never cease to be
celebrated by the Jews, nor should the memory of them die out
among their descendants.
29So Queen Esther, daughter of Abihail, along with Mordecai
the Jew, wrote with full authority to confirm this second letter
concerning Purim. 30And Mordecai sent letters to all the Jews in
the 127 provinces of the kingdom of Xerxes—words of goodwill
and assurance— 31to establish these days of Purim at their desig-

**NIV** [a] 25 Or *when Esther came before the king*

## King James

31To confirm these days of Purim in their times *appointed,* according as Mordecai the Jew and Esther the queen had enjoined them, and as they had decreed for themselves and for their seed, the matters of the fastings and their cry.

32And the decree of Esther confirmed these matters of Purim; and it was written in the book.

**10** AND THE king Ahasuerus laid a tribute upon the land, and *upon* the isles of the sea.

2And all the acts of his power and of his might, and the declaration of the greatness of Mordecai, whereunto the king advanced him, *are* they not written in the book of the chronicles of the kings of Media and Persia?

3For Mordecai the Jew *was* next unto king Ahasuerus, and great among the Jews, and accepted of the multitude of his brethren, seeking the wealth of his people, and speaking peace to all his seed.

## Amplified

31To confirm that these days of Purim should be observed at their appointed times, as Mordecai the Jew and Queen Esther had commanded [the Jews], and as they had ordained for themselves and for their descendants in the matter of their fasts and their lamenting.

32And the command of Esther confirmed these observances of Purim; and it was written in the book.

**10** KING AHASUERUS laid a tribute [tax] on the land, and on the coastlands of the sea.

2And all the acts of his power and of his might, and the full account of the greatness of Mordecai, to which the king advanced him, are they not written in the Book of the Chronicles of the Kings of Media and Persia?

3For Mordecai the Jew was next to King Ahasuerus and great among the Jews, and was a favorite with the multitude of his brethren; for he sought the welfare of his people and spoke peace to his whole race.

## New American Standard

31to establish these days of Purim at their appointed times, just as Mordecai the Jew and Queen Esther had established for them, and just as they had established for themselves and for their descendants with instructions for their times of fasting and their lamentations.

32And the command of Esther established these customs for Purim, and it was written in the book.

*Mordecai's Greatness*

**10** NOW KING Ahasuerus laid a tribute on the land and on the coastlands of the sea.

2And all the accomplishments of his authority and strength, and the full account of the greatness of Mordecai, to which the king advanced him, are they not written in the Book of the Chronicles of the Kings of Media and Persia?

3For Mordecai the Jew was second *only* to King Ahasuerus and great among the Jews, and in favor with the multitude of his kinsmen, one who sought the good of his people and one who spoke for the welfare of his whole nation.

## New International

nated times, as Mordecai the Jew and Queen Esther had decreed for them, and as they had established for themselves and their descendants in regard to their times of fasting and lamentation. 32Esther's decree confirmed these regulations about Purim, and it was written down in the records.

*The Greatness of Mordecai*

**10** KING XERXES imposed tribute throughout the empire, to its distant shores. 2And all his acts of power and might, together with a full account of the greatness of Mordecai to which the king had raised him, are they not written in the book of the annals of the kings of Media and Persia? 3Mordecai the Jew was second in rank to King Xerxes, preeminent among the Jews, and held in high esteem by his many fellow Jews, because he worked for the good of his people and spoke up for the welfare of all the Jews.

## King James

THE BOOK OF

# Job

1 THERE WAS a man in the land of Uz, whose name *was* Job; and that man was perfect and upright, and one that feared God, and eschewed evil.

2And there were born unto him seven sons and three daughters.

3His substance also was seven thousand sheep, and three thousand camels, and five hundred yoke of oxen, and five hundred she asses, and a very great household; so that this man was the greatest of all the men of the east.

4And his sons went and feasted *in their* houses, every one his day; and sent and called for their three sisters to eat and to drink with them.

5And it was so, when the days of *their* feasting were gone about, that Job sent and sanctified them, and rose up early in the morning, and offered burnt offerings *according* to the number of them all: for Job said, It may be that my sons have sinned, and cursed God in their hearts. Thus did Job continually.

6¶ Now there was a day when the sons of God came to present themselves before the LORD, and Satan came also among them.

7And the LORD said unto Satan, Whence comest thou? Then Satan answered the LORD, and said, From going to and fro in the earth, and from walking up and down in it.

8And the LORD said unto Satan, Hast thou considered my servant Job, that *there is* none like him in the earth, a perfect and an upright man, one that feareth God, and escheweth evil?

9Then Satan answered the LORD, and said, Doth Job fear God for nought?

10Hast not thou made an hedge about him, and about his house, and about all that he hath on every side? thou hast blessed the work of his hands, and his substance is increased in the land.

11But put forth thine hand now, and touch all that he hath, and he will curse thee to thy face.

12And the LORD said unto Satan, Behold, all that he hath *is* in thy power; only upon himself put not forth thine hand. So Satan went forth from the presence of the LORD.

13¶ And there was a day when his sons and his daughters *were* eating and drinking wine in their eldest brother's house:

14And there came a messenger unto Job, and said, The oxen were plowing, and the asses feeding beside them:

15And the Sabeans fell *upon them,* and took them away; yea, they have slain the servants with the edge of the sword; and I only am escaped alone to tell thee.

16While he *was* yet speaking, there came also another, and said, The fire of God is fallen from heaven, and hath burned up the sheep, and the servants, and consumed them; and I only am escaped alone to tell thee.

## Amplified

THE BOOK OF

# Job

1 THERE WAS a man in the land of Uz whose name was Job; and that man was blameless and upright, and one who (reverently) feared God and abstained from *and* shunned evil [because it was wrong].

2And there were born to him seven sons and three daughters.

3He possessed seven thousand sheep, three thousand camels, five hundred yoke of oxen, five hundred female donkeys, and a very great body of servants, so that this man was the greatest of all the men of the east.

4His sons used to go and feast in the house of each on his day [birthday] in turn, and they invited their three sisters to eat and drink with them. [Gen. 40:20; 21:8.]

5And when the days of their feasting were over, Job sent for them, to purify *and* hallow them, and rose up early in the morning and offered burnt offerings according to the number of them all. For Job said, It may be that my sons have sinned, and cursed *or* disowned God in their hearts. Thus did Job at all [such] times.

6Now there was a day when the sons [the angels] of God came to present themselves before the Lord, so Satan—the adversary and accuser—also came among them. [Rev. 12:10.]

7And the Lord said to Satan, From where did you come? Then Satan answered the Lord, From going to and fro on the earth, and from walking up and down on it.

8And the Lord said to Satan, Have you considered My servant Job, that there is none like him on the earth, a blameless and upright man, one who (reverently) fears God and abstains from *and* shuns evil [because it is wrong]?

9Then Satan answered the Lord, Does Job (reverently) fear God for nothing?

10Have You not put a hedge about him and his house and all that he has, on every side? You have conferred prosperity *and* happiness upon him in the work of his hands, and his possessions have increased in the land.

11But put forth Your hand now, and touch all that he has, and he will curse You to Your face.

12And the Lord said to Satan—the adversary and the accuser—Behold, all that he has is in your power; only upon himself put not forth your hand. So Satan went forth from the presence of the Lord.

13And there was a day when [Job's] sons and his daughters were eating and drinking wine in their eldest brother's house [on his birthday];

14And there came a messenger to Job, and said, The oxen were plowing and the donkeys feeding beside them;

15And the Sabeans swooped down upon them and took away [the animals]; indeed, they have slain the servants with the edge of the sword; and I alone have escaped to tell you.

16While he was yet speaking, there came also another, and said, The fire of God [lightning] is fallen from the heavens, and has burned up the sheep and the servants, and consumed them; and I alone have escaped to tell you.

## New American Standard

# Job

*Job's Character and Wealth*

**1** THERE WAS a man in the land of Uz, whose name was Job, and that man was blameless, upright, fearing God, and turning away from evil.

2And seven sons and three daughters were born to him.

3His possessions also were 7,000 sheep, 3,000 camels, 500 yoke of oxen, 500 female donkeys, and very many servants; and that man was the greatest of all the men of the east.

4And his sons used to go and hold a feast in the house of each one on his day, and they would send and invite their three sisters to eat and drink with them.

5And it came about, when the days of feasting had completed their cycle, that Job would send and consecrate them, rising up early in the morning and offering burnt offerings *according to* the number of them all; for Job said, "Perhaps my sons have sinned and cursed God in their hearts." Thus Job did continually.

6Now there was a day when the sons of God came to present themselves before the LORD, and [a]Satan also came among them.

7And the LORD said to Satan, "From where do you come?" Then Satan answered the LORD and said, "From roaming about on the earth and walking around on it."

8And the LORD said to Satan, "Have you considered My servant Job? For there is no one like him on the earth, a blameless and upright man, fearing God and turning away from evil."

9Then Satan answered the LORD, "Does Job fear God for nothing?

10"Hast Thou not made a hedge about him and his house and all that he has, on every side? Thou hast blessed the work of his hands, and his possessions have increased in the land.

11"But put forth Thy hand now and touch all that he has; he will surely curse Thee to Thy face."

12Then the LORD said to Satan, "Behold, all that he has is in your power, only do not put forth your hand on him." So Satan departed from the presence of the LORD.

*Satan Allowed to Test Job*

13¶ Now it happened on the day when his sons and his daughters were eating and drinking wine in their oldest brother's house,

14that a messenger came to Job and said, "The oxen were plowing and the donkeys feeding beside them,

15and the Sabeans attacked and took them. They also slew the servants with the edge of the sword, and I alone have escaped to tell you."

16While he was still speaking, another also came and said, "The fire of God fell from heaven and burned up the sheep and the servants and consumed them, and I alone have escaped to tell you."

NAS [a] I.e., the adversary; so through chs. 1 and 2

## New International

# Job

*Prologue*

**1** IN THE land of Uz there lived a man whose name was Job. This man was blameless and upright; he feared God and shunned evil. 2He had seven sons and three daughters, 3and he owned seven thousand sheep, three thousand camels, five hundred yoke of oxen and five hundred donkeys, and had a large number of servants. He was the greatest man among all the people of the East.

4His sons used to take turns holding feasts in their homes, and they would invite their three sisters to eat and drink with them. 5When a period of feasting had run its course, Job would send and have them purified. Early in the morning he would sacrifice a burnt offering for each of them, thinking, "Perhaps my children have sinned and cursed God in their hearts." This was Job's regular custom.

*Job's First Test*

6One day the angels[b] came to present themselves before the LORD, and Satan[c] also came with them. 7The LORD said to Satan, "Where have you come from?"

Satan answered the LORD, "From roaming through the earth and going back and forth in it."

8Then the LORD said to Satan, "Have you considered my servant Job? There is no one on earth like him; he is blameless and upright, a man who fears God and shuns evil."

9"Does Job fear God for nothing?" Satan replied. 10"Have you not put a hedge around him and his household and everything he has? You have blessed the work of his hands, so that his flocks and herds are spread throughout the land. 11But stretch out your hand and strike everything he has, and he will surely curse you to your face."

12The LORD said to Satan, "Very well, then, everything he has is in your hands, but on the man himself do not lay a finger."

Then Satan went out from the presence of the LORD.

13One day when Job's sons and daughters were feasting and drinking wine at the oldest brother's house, 14a messenger came to Job and said, "The oxen were plowing and the donkeys were grazing nearby, 15and the Sabeans attacked and carried them off. They put the servants to the sword, and I am the only one who has escaped to tell you!"

16While he was still speaking, another messenger came and said, "The fire of God fell from the sky and burned up the sheep and the servants, and I am the only one who has escaped to tell you!"

NIV [b] 6 Hebrew *the sons of God* [c] 6 *Satan* means *accuser.*

## King James

17 While he *was* yet speaking, there came also another, and said, The Chaldeans made out three bands, and fell upon the camels, and have carried them away, yea, and slain the servants with the edge of the sword; and I only am escaped alone to tell thee.

18 While he *was* yet speaking, there came also another, and said, Thy sons and thy daughters *were* eating and drinking wine in their eldest brother's house:

19 And, behold, there came a great wind from the wilderness, and smote the four corners of the house, and it fell upon the young men, and they are dead; and I only am escaped alone to tell thee.

20 Then Job arose, and rent his mantle, and shaved his head, and fell down upon the ground, and worshipped,

21 And said, Naked came I out of my mother's womb, and naked shall I return thither: the LORD gave, and the LORD hath taken away; blessed be the name of the LORD.

22 In all this Job sinned not, nor charged God foolishly.

**2** AGAIN THERE was a day when the sons of God came to present themselves before the LORD, and Satan came also among them to present himself before the LORD.

2 And the LORD said unto Satan, From whence comest thou? And Satan answered the LORD, and said, From going to and fro in the earth, and from walking up and down in it.

3 And the LORD said unto Satan, Hast thou considered my servant Job, that *there is* none like him in the earth, a perfect and an upright man, one that feareth God, and escheweth evil? and still he holdeth fast his integrity, although thou movedst me against him, to destroy him without cause.

4 And Satan answered the LORD, and said, Skin for skin, yea, all that a man hath will he give for his life.

5 But put forth thine hand now, and touch his bone and his flesh, and he will curse thee to thy face.

6 And the LORD said unto Satan, Behold, he *is* in thine hand; but save his life.

7 ¶ So went Satan forth from the presence of the LORD, and smote Job with sore boils from the sole of his foot unto his crown.

8 And he took him a potsherd to scrape himself withal; and he sat down among the ashes.

9 ¶ Then said his wife unto him, Dost thou still retain thine integrity? curse God, and die.

10 But he said unto her, Thou speakest as one of the foolish women speaketh. What? shall we receive good at the hand of God, and shall we not receive evil? In all this did not Job sin with his lips.

11 ¶ Now when Job's three friends heard of all this evil that was come upon him, they came every one from his own place; Eliphaz the Temanite, and Bildad the Shuhite, and Zophar the Naamathite: for they had made an appointment together to come to mourn with him and to comfort him.

12 And when they lifted up their eyes afar off, and knew him not, they lifted up their voice, and wept; and they rent every one his mantle, and sprinkled dust upon their heads toward heaven.

13 So they sat down with him upon the ground seven days and seven nights, and none spake a word unto him: for they saw that *his* grief was very great.

## Amplified

17 While he was yet speaking, there came also another, and said, The Chaldeans divided into three bands, and made a raid upon the camels and have taken them away, yes, and have slain the servants with the edge of the sword; and I alone have escaped to tell you.

18 While he was yet speaking, there came also another, and said, Your sons and your daughters were eating and drinking wine in their eldest brother's house,

19 And behold, there came a great [whirlwind] from the desert, and smote the four corners of the house, and it fell upon the young people, and they are dead; and I alone have escaped to tell you.

20 Then Job arose, and rent his robe, and shaved his head, and fell down upon the ground and worshiped,

21 And said, Naked [without possessions] came I [into this world] from my mother's womb, and naked [without possessions] shall I depart. The Lord gave, and the Lord has taken away; blessed [praised and magnified in worship] be the name of the Lord!

22 In all this Job sinned not, nor charged God foolishly.

**2** AGAIN THERE was a day when the sons of God [the angels] came to present themselves before the Lord, and Satan—the adversary and the accuser—came also among them to present himself before the Lord.

2 And the Lord said to Satan, From where do you come? and Satan—the adversary and the accuser—answered the Lord, From going to and fro on the earth, and from walking up and down on it.

3 And the Lord said to Satan, Have you considered My servant Job, that there is none like him on the earth, a blameless and upright man, one who (reverently) fears God and abstains from *and* shuns all evil [because it is wrong]? And still he holds fast his integrity, although you moved Me against him, to destroy him without cause.

4 Then Satan answered the Lord, Skin for skin, yes, all that a man has will he give for his life.

5 But put forth Your hand now, and touch his bone and his flesh, and he will curse *and* renounce You to Your face.

6 And the Lord said to Satan, Behold, he is in your hand; only spare his life.

7 So Satan went forth from the presence of the Lord, and smote Job with loathsome *and* painful sores from the sole of his foot to the crown of his head.

8 And he took a piece of broken pottery with which to scrape himself, and he sat *down* among the ashes.

9 Then his wife said to him, Do you still hold fast your blameless uprightness? Renounce God, and die!

10 But he said to her, You speak as one of the impious *and* foolish women would speak. What? Shall we accept [only] good at the hand of God and shall we not accept [also] misfortune *and* what is of a bad nature? In [spite of] all this Job did not sin with his lips.

11 Now when Job's three friends heard of all this evil that was come upon him, they came each one from his own place, Eliphaz the Temanite, and Bildad the Shuhite, and Zophar the Naamathite; for they had made an appointment together to come to condole with him and to comfort him.

12 And when they looked from afar off and saw him [disfigured] beyond recognition, they lifted up their voices and wept; and they each one tore his robe, and they cast dust over their heads toward the heavens.

13 So they sat down with [Job] on the ground seven days and seven nights, and none spoke a word to him, for they saw that his grief *and* pain were very great.

## New American Standard

17While he was still speaking, another also came and said, "The
Chaldeans formed three bands and made a raid on the camels and
took them and slew the servants with the edge of the sword; and
I alone have escaped to tell you."
18While he was still speaking, another also came and said,
"Your sons and your daughters were eating and drinking wine in
their oldest brother's house,
19and behold, a great wind came from across the wilderness and
struck the four corners of the house, and it fell on the young people
and they died; and I alone have escaped to tell you."
20¶ Then Job arose and tore his robe and shaved his head, and
he fell to the ground and worshiped.
21And he said,
"Naked I came from my mother's womb,
And naked I shall return there.
The LORD gave and the LORD has taken away.
Blessed be the name of the LORD."
22Through all this Job did not sin nor did he blame God.

*Job Loses His Health*

2 AGAIN THERE was a day when the sons of God came to
present themselves before the LORD, and Satan also came
among them to present himself before the LORD.
2And the LORD said to Satan, "Where have you come from?"
Then Satan answered the LORD and said, "From roaming about on
the earth, and walking around on it."
3And the LORD said to Satan, "Have you considered My servant Job? For there is no one like him on the earth, a blameless and
upright man fearing God and turning away from evil. And he still
holds fast his integrity, although you incited Me against him, to
ruin him without cause."
4And Satan answered the LORD and said, "Skin for skin! Yes,
all that a man has he will give for his life.
5"However, put forth Thy hand, now, and touch his bone and
his flesh; he will curse Thee to Thy face."
6So the LORD said to Satan, "Behold, he is in your power, only
spare his life."
7¶ Then Satan went out from the presence of the LORD, and
smote Job with sore boils from the sole of his foot to the crown of
his head.
8And he took a potsherd to scrape himself while he was sitting
among the ashes.
9Then his wife said to him, "Do you still hold fast your integrity? Curse God and die!"
10But he said to her, "You speak as one of the foolish women
speaks. Shall we indeed accept good from God and not accept
adversity?" In all this Job did not sin with his lips.
11¶ Now when Job's three friends heard of all this adversity that
had come upon him, they came each one from his own place,
Eliphaz the Temanite, Bildad the Shuhite, and Zophar the Naamathite; and they made an appointment together to come to sympathize with him and comfort him.
12And when they lifted up their eyes at a distance, and did not
recognize him, they raised their voices and wept. And each of
them tore his robe, and they threw dust over their heads toward
the sky.
13Then they sat down on the ground with him for seven days
and seven nights with no one speaking a word to him, for they saw
that *his* pain was very great.

## New International

17While he was still speaking, another messenger came and
said, "The Chaldeans formed three raiding parties and swept
down on your camels and carried them off. They put the servants
to the sword, and I am the only one who has escaped to tell you!"
18While he was still speaking, yet another messenger came and
said, "Your sons and daughters were feasting and drinking wine
at the oldest brother's house, 19when suddenly a mighty wind
swept in from the desert and struck the four corners of the house.
It collapsed on them and they are dead, and I am the only one who
has escaped to tell you!"
20At this, Job got up and tore his robe and shaved his head.
Then he fell to the ground in worship 21and said:

"Naked I came from my mother's womb,
and naked I will depart.[a]
The LORD gave and the LORD has taken away;
may the name of the LORD be praised."

22In all this, Job did not sin by charging God with wrongdoing.

*Job's Second Test*

2 ON ANOTHER day the angels[b] came to present themselves
before the LORD, and Satan also came with them to present
himself before him. 2And the LORD said to Satan, "Where have you
come from?"
Satan answered the LORD, "From roaming through the earth
and going back and forth in it."
3Then the LORD said to Satan, "Have you considered my servant Job? There is no one on earth like him; he is blameless and
upright, a man who fears God and shuns evil. And he still maintains his integrity, though you incited me against him to ruin him
without any reason."
4"Skin for skin!" Satan replied. "A man will give all he has for
his own life. 5But stretch out your hand and strike his flesh and
bones, and he will surely curse you to your face."
6The LORD said to Satan, "Very well, then, he is in your hands;
but you must spare his life."
7So Satan went out from the presence of the LORD and afflicted
Job with painful sores from the soles of his feet to the top of his
head. 8Then Job took a piece of broken pottery and scraped himself
with it as he sat among the ashes.
9His wife said to him, "Are you still holding on to your integrity? Curse God and die!"
10He replied, "You are talking like a foolish[c] woman. Shall we
accept good from God, and not trouble?"
In all this, Job did not sin in what he said.

*Job's Three Friends*

11When Job's three friends, Eliphaz the Temanite, Bildad the
Shuhite and Zophar the Naamathite, heard about all the troubles
that had come upon him, they set out from their homes and met
together by agreement to go and sympathize with him and comfort
him. 12When they saw him from a distance, they could hardly
recognize him; they began to weep aloud, and they tore their robes
and sprinkled dust on their heads. 13Then they sat on the ground
with him for seven days and seven nights. No one said a word to
him, because they saw how great his suffering was.

**NIV** [a] 21 Or *will return there* [b] 1 Hebrew *the sons of God* [c] 10 The Hebrew word rendered *foolish* denotes moral deficiency.

## King James

**3** AFTER THIS opened Job his mouth, and cursed his day.
2 And Job spake, and said,
3 Let the day perish wherein I was born, and the night *in which* it was said, There is a man child conceived.
4 Let that day be darkness; let not God regard it from above, neither let the light shine upon it.
5 Let darkness and the shadow of death stain it; let a cloud dwell upon it; let the blackness of the day terrify it.
6 *As for* that night, let darkness seize upon it; let it not be joined unto the days of the year, let it not come into the number of the months.
7 Lo, let that night be solitary, let no joyful voice come therein.
8 Let them curse it that curse the day, who are ready to raise up their mourning.
9 Let the stars of the twilight thereof be dark; let it look for light, but *have* none; neither let it see the dawning of the day:
10 Because it shut not up the doors of my *mother's* womb, nor hid sorrow from mine eyes.
11 Why died I not from the womb? *why* did I *not* give up the ghost when I came out of the belly?
12 Why did the knees prevent me? or why the breasts that I should suck?
13 For now should I have lain still and been quiet, I should have slept: then had I been at rest,
14 With kings and counsellors of the earth, which built desolate places for themselves;
15 Or with princes that had gold, who filled their houses with silver:
16 Or as an hidden untimely birth I had not been; as infants *which* never saw light.
17 There the wicked cease *from* troubling; and there the weary be at rest.
18 *There* the prisoners rest together; they hear not the voice of the oppressor.
19 The small and great are there; and the servant *is* free from his master.
20 Wherefore is light given to him that is in misery, and life unto the bitter *in* soul;
21 Which long for death, but it *cometh* not; and dig for it more than for hid treasures;
22 Which rejoice exceedingly, *and* are glad, when they can find the grave?
23 *Why is light given* to a man whose way is hid, and whom God hath hedged in?
24 For my sighing cometh before I eat, and my roarings are poured out like the waters.
25 For the thing which I greatly feared is come upon me, and that which I was afraid of is come unto me.
26 I was not in safety, neither had I rest, neither was I quiet; yet trouble came.

**4** THEN ELIPHAZ the Temanite answered and said,
2 *If* we assay to commune with thee, wilt thou be grieved? but who can withhold himself from speaking?

## Amplified

**3** AFTER THIS Job opened his mouth, and cursed his day [birthday].
2 And Job said,
3 Let the day perish wherein I was born, and the night which announced, There is a man-child conceived.
4 Let that day be darkness! May not God above regard it, nor light shine upon it.
5 Let gloom and deep darkness claim it for their own; let a cloud dwell upon it; let all that blackens the day terrify it [the day that I was born].
6 As for that night, let thick darkness seize upon it; let it not rejoice among the days of the year; let it not come into the number of the months.
7 Yes, let that night be solitary *and* barren, let no joyful voice come into it.
8 Let those curse it who curse the day, who are skilled in rousing up Leviathan.
9 Let the stars of the early dawn of that day be dark; let [the morning] look in vain for the light, nor let it behold the day's dawning.
10 Because it shut not the doors of my mother's womb, nor hid sorrow *and* trouble from my eyes.
11 Why was I not stillborn? Why did I not give up the ghost when my mother bore me?
12 Why did the knees receive me? Or why the breasts, that I should suck?
13 For then should I have lain down and been quiet; I should have slept; then had I been at rest [in death],
14 With kings and counselors of the earth, who built up [now] desolate ruins for themselves;
15 Or with princes who had gold, who filled their houses with silver.
16 Or [why] was I not a miscarriage, hidden *and* put away, as infants who never saw light?
17 There [in death] the wicked cease from troubling, and there the weary are at rest.
18 There the [captive] prisoners rest together; they hear not the taskmaster's voice.
19 The small and the great are there, and the servant is free from his master. [Jer. 20:14-18.]
20 Why is light [of life] given to him who is in misery, and life to the bitter in soul,
21 Who long *and* wait for death, but it comes not, and dig for it more than for hid treasures;
22 Who rejoice exceedingly, and are elated when they find the grave?
23 [Why is the light of day given] to a man whose way is hidden, and whom God has hedged in?
24 For my sighing comes before my food, and my groanings are poured out like water.
25 For the thing which I greatly fear comes upon me, and that of which I am afraid befalls me.
26 I was not *or* am not at ease, nor had I *or* have I rest, nor was I *or* am I quiet, yet trouble came *and still* comes *upon me*.

**4** THEN ELIPHAZ the Temanite answered and said,
2 If we venture to converse with you, will you be offended? Yet who can restrain himself from speaking?

## New American Standard

*Job's Lament*

**3** AFTERWARD JOB opened his mouth and cursed the day of his *birth.*
2And Job said,
3 "Let the day perish on which I was to be born,
And the night *which* said, 'A boy is conceived.'
4 "May that day be darkness;
Let not God above care for it,
Nor light shine on it.
5 "Let darkness and black gloom claim it;
Let a cloud settle on it;
Let the blackness of the day terrify it.
6 "*As for* that night, let darkness seize it;
Let it not rejoice among the days of the year;
Let it not come into the number of the months.
7 "Behold, let that night be barren;
Let no joyful shout enter it.
8 "Let those curse it who curse the day,
Who are prepared to rouse Leviathan.
9 "Let the stars of its twilight be darkened;
Let it wait for light but have none,
Neither let it see the breaking dawn;
10 Because it did not shut the opening of my *mother's* womb,
Or hide trouble from my eyes.
11¶ "Why did I not die at birth,
Come forth from the womb and expire?
12 "Why did the knees receive me,
And why the breasts, that I should suck?
13 "For now I would have lain down and been quiet;
I would have slept then, I would have been at rest,
14 With kings and *with* counselors of the earth,
Who rebuilt ruins for themselves;
15 Or with princes who had gold,
Who were filling their houses *with* silver.
16 "Or like a miscarriage which is discarded, I would not be,
As infants that never saw light.
17 "There the wicked cease from raging,
And there the weary are at rest.
18 "The prisoners are at ease together;
They do not hear the voice of the taskmaster.
19 "The small and the great are there,
And the slave is free from his master.
20¶ "Why is light given to him who suffers,
And life to the bitter of soul;
21 Who long for death, but there is none,
And dig for it more than for hidden treasures;
22 Who rejoice greatly,
They exult when they find the grave?
23 " *Why is light given* to a man whose way is hidden,
And whom God has hedged in?
24 "For my groaning comes at the sight of my food,
And my cries pour out like water.
25 "For what I fear comes upon me,
And what I dread befalls me.
26 "I am not at ease, nor am I quiet,
And I am not at rest, but turmoil comes."

*Eliphaz: Innocent Do Not Suffer*

**4** THEN ELIPHAZ the Temanite answered,
2 "If one ventures a word with you, will you become impatient?
But who can refrain from speaking?

## New International

*Job Speaks*

**3** AFTER THIS, Job opened his mouth and cursed the day of his birth. 2He said:

3"May the day of my birth perish,
and the night it was said, 'A boy is born!'
4That day—may it turn to darkness;
may God above not care about it;
may no light shine upon it.
5May darkness and deep shadow[a] claim it once more;
may a cloud settle over it;
may blackness overwhelm its light.
6That night—may thick darkness seize it;
may it not be included among the days of the year
nor be entered in any of the months.
7May that night be barren;
may no shout of joy be heard in it.
8May those who curse days[b] curse that day,
those who are ready to rouse Leviathan.
9May its morning stars become dark;
may it wait for daylight in vain
and not see the first rays of dawn,
10for it did not shut the doors of the womb on me
to hide trouble from my eyes.

11"Why did I not perish at birth,
and die as I came from the womb?
12Why were there knees to receive me
and breasts that I might be nursed?
13For now I would be lying down in peace;
I would be asleep and at rest
14with kings and counselors of the earth,
who built for themselves places now lying in ruins,
15with rulers who had gold,
who filled their houses with silver.
16Or why was I not hidden in the ground like a stillborn child,
like an infant who never saw the light of day?
17There the wicked cease from turmoil,
and there the weary are at rest.
18Captives also enjoy their ease;
they no longer hear the slave driver's shout.
19The small and the great are there,
and the slave is freed from his master.

20"Why is light given to those in misery,
and life to the bitter of soul,
21to those who long for death that does not come,
who search for it more than for hidden treasure,
22who are filled with gladness
and rejoice when they reach the grave?
23Why is life given to a man
whose way is hidden,
whom God has hedged in?
24For sighing comes to me instead of food;
my groans pour out like water.
25What I feared has come upon me;
what I dreaded has happened to me.
26I have no peace, no quietness;
I have no rest, but only turmoil."

*Eliphaz*

**4** THEN ELIPHAZ the Temanite replied:

2"If someone ventures a word with you, will you be impatient?
But who can keep from speaking?

NIV [a] 5 Or *and the shadow of death* [b] 8 Or *the sea*

## King James

3Behold, thou hast instructed many, and thou hast strengthened the weak hands.
4Thy words have upholden him that was falling, and thou hast
strengthened the feeble knees.
5But now it is come upon thee, and thou faintest; it toucheth
thee, and thou art troubled.
6 *Is* not *this* thy fear, thy confidence, thy hope, and the uprightness of thy ways?
7Remember, I pray thee, who *ever* perished, being innocent? or
where were the righteous cut off ?
8Even as I have seen, they that plow iniquity, and sow wickedness, reap the same.
9By the blast of God they perish, and by the breath of his nostrils
are they consumed.
10The roaring of the lion, and the voice of the fierce lion, and
the teeth of the young lions, are broken.
11The old lion perisheth for lack of prey, and the stout lion's
whelps are scattered abroad.
12Now a thing was secretly brought to me, and mine ear received a little thereof.
13In thoughts from the visions of the night, when deep sleep
falleth on men,
14Fear came upon me, and trembling, which made all my bones
to shake.
15Then a spirit passed before my face; the hair of my flesh stood
up:
16It stood still, but I could not discern the form thereof: an image
*was* before mine eyes, *there was* silence, and I heard a voice, *saying*,
17Shall mortal man be more just than God? shall a man be more
pure than his maker?
18Behold, he put no trust in his servants; and his angels he
charged with folly:
19How much less *in* them that dwell in houses of clay, whose
foundation *is* in the dust, *which* are crushed before the moth?
20They are destroyed from morning to evening: they perish for
ever without any regarding *it*.
21Doth not their excellency *which is* in them go away? they die,
even without wisdom.

5 CALL NOW, if there be any that will answer thee; and to
which of the saints wilt thou turn?
2For wrath killeth the foolish man, and envy slayeth the silly
one.
3I have seen the foolish taking root: but suddenly I cursed his
habitation.
4His children are far from safety, and they are crushed in the
gate, neither *is there* any to deliver *them*.
5Whose harvest the hungry eateth up, and taketh it even out
of the thorns, and the robber swalloweth up their substance.
6Although affliction cometh not forth of the dust, neither doth
trouble spring out of the ground;
7Yet man is born unto trouble, as the sparks fly upward.
8I would seek unto God, and unto God would I commit my
cause:
9Which doeth great things and unsearchable; marvellous things
without number:

## Amplified

3Behold, you have instructed many, and you have strengthened the weak hands.
4Your words have held firm him who was falling, and you have
strengthened the feeble knees.
5But now it is come upon you, and you faint *and* are grieved;
it touches you, and you are troubled *and* dismayed.
6Is not your (reverent) fear of God your confidence, and the
integrity *and* uprightness of your ways your hope?
7Think (earnestly), I beg of you; who that was innocent ever
perished? Or where were those upright *and* in right standing with
God cut off?
8As I myself have seen, those who plow iniquity and sow
trouble *and* mischief reap the same.
9By the breath of God they perish, and by the blast of His anger
they are consumed.
10The roaring of the lion, and the voice of the fierce lion, and
the teeth of the young lions, are broken.
11The old *and* strong lion perishes for lack of prey, and the
whelps of the lioness are scattered abroad.
12Now a thing was secretly brought to me, and my ear received
a whisper of it.
13In thoughts from the visions of the night, when deep sleep
falls on men,
14Fear came upon me and trembling, which made all my bones
shake.
15Then a spirit passed before my face; the hair of my flesh stood
up!
16[The spirit] stood still, but I could not discern the appearance
of it. A form was before my eyes, there was silence; then I heard
a voice, saying,
17Can mortal man be just before God, *or* be more right than He
is? Can a man be pure before his Maker, *or* be more cleansed than
He is? [I John 1:7; Rev. 1:5.
18Even in His [heavenly] servants He puts no trust *or* confidence, and His angels He charges with folly *and* error;
19How much more those who dwell in houses [bodies] of clay,
whose foundation is the dust, who are crushed like the moth.
20Between morning and evening they are destroyed; without
any one noticing it they perish for ever.
21Is not their tent cord plucked up within them [so that the tent
falls]? Do they not die, and that without *acquiring* wisdom?

5 CALL NOW; is there any who will answer you? And to which
of the holy [angels] will you turn?
2For [a]vexation *and* rage kill the foolish man; jealousy *and* indignation slay the simple.
3I have seen the foolish taking root [and outwardly prospering];
but suddenly I saw his dwelling was cursed [for his doom was
certain].
4His children are far from safety; [involved in their father's ruin]
they are crushed in the [court of justice in the city's] gate, and there
is no one to deliver them.
5His harvest the hungry eat, and take it even [when it grows]
among the thorns; the snare opens for [his] wealth.
6For affliction comes not forth from the dust, neither does trouble spring forth out of the ground;
7But man is born to trouble as the sparks *and* the flame fly
upward.
8As for me, I would seek God, *and* inquire of *and* require Him
and to God would I commit my cause;
9Who does great things and unsearchable, marvelous things
without number;

**AMP** [a] This was written many centuries ago, but physicians and psychiatrists are continually emphasizing the importance today of recognizing the principle it lays down, if one would avoid being among the constantly increasing number of the mentally ill and those killed by avoidable illnesses.

## New American Standard

3 "Behold you have admonished many,
And you have strengthened weak hands.
4 "Your words have helped the tottering to stand,
And you have strengthened feeble knees.
5 "But now it has come to you, and you are impatient;
It touches you, and you are dismayed.
6 "Is not your [b]fear *of God* your confidence,
And the integrity of your ways your hope?

7¶ "Remember now, who *ever* perished being innocent?
Or where were the upright destroyed?
8 "According to what I have seen, those who plow iniquity
And those who sow trouble harvest it.
9 "By the breath of God they perish,
And by the blast of His anger they come to an end.
10 "The roaring of the lion and the voice of the *fierce* lion,
And the teeth of the young lions are broken.
11 "The lion perishes for lack of prey,
And the whelps of the lioness are scattered.

12¶ "Now a word was brought to me stealthily,
And my ear received a whisper of it.
13 "Amid disquieting thoughts from the visions of the night,
When deep sleep falls on men,
14 Dread came upon me, and trembling,
And made all my bones shake.
15 "Then a [c]spirit passed by my face;
The hair of my flesh bristled up.
16 "It stood still, but I could not discern its appearance;
A form *was* before my eyes;
*There was* silence, then I heard a voice:
17 'Can mankind be just before God?
Can a man be pure before his Maker?
18 'He puts no trust even in His servants;
And against His angels He charges error.
19 'How much more those who dwell in houses of clay,
Whose foundation is in the dust,
Who are crushed before the moth!
20 'Between morning and evening they are broken in pieces;
Unobserved, they perish forever.
21 'Is not their tent-cord plucked up within them?
They die, yet without wisdom.'

### *God Is Just*

**5** "CALL NOW, is there anyone who will answer you?
And to which of the holy ones will you turn?
2 "For vexation slays the foolish man,
And anger kills the simple.
3 "I have seen the foolish taking root,
And I cursed his abode immediately.
4 "His sons are far from safety,
They are even [d]oppressed in the gate,
Neither is there a deliverer.
5 "His harvest the hungry devour,
And take it to a *place of* thorns;
And the schemer is eager for their wealth.
6 "For affliction does not come from the dust,
Neither does trouble sprout from the ground,
7 For man is born for trouble,
As sparks fly upward.

8¶ "But as for me, I would seek God,
And I would place my cause before God;
9 Who does great and unsearchable things,
Wonders without number.

NAS [b] Or, *reverence* [c] Or, *breath passed over* [d] Lit., *crushed*

## New International

3 Think how you have instructed many,
how you have strengthened feeble hands.
4 Your words have supported those who stumbled;
you have strengthened faltering knees.
5 But now trouble comes to you, and you are discouraged;
it strikes you, and you are dismayed.
6 Should not your piety be your confidence
and your blameless ways your hope?

7 "Consider now: Who, being innocent, has ever perished?
Where were the upright ever destroyed?
8 As I have observed, those who plow evil
and those who sow trouble reap it.
9 At the breath of God they are destroyed;
at the blast of his anger they perish.
10 The lions may roar and growl,
yet the teeth of the great lions are broken.
11 The lion perishes for lack of prey,
and the cubs of the lioness are scattered.

12 "A word was secretly brought to me,
my ears caught a whisper of it.
13 Amid disquieting dreams in the night,
when deep sleep falls on men,
14 fear and trembling seized me
and made all my bones shake.
15 A spirit glided past my face,
and the hair on my body stood on end.
16 It stopped,
but I could not tell what it was.
A form stood before my eyes,
and I heard a hushed voice:
17 'Can a mortal be more righteous than God?
Can a man be more pure than his Maker?
18 If God places no trust in his servants,
if he charges his angels with error,
19 how much more those who live in houses of clay,
whose foundations are in the dust,
who are crushed more readily than a moth!
20 Between dawn and dusk they are broken to pieces;
unnoticed, they perish forever.
21 Are not the cords of their tent pulled up,
so that they die without wisdom?'[e]

**5** "CALL IF you will, but who will answer you?
To which of the holy ones will you turn?
2 Resentment kills a fool,
and envy slays the simple.
3 I myself have seen a fool taking root,
but suddenly his house was cursed.
4 His children are far from safety,
crushed in court without a defender.
5 The hungry consume his harvest,
taking it even from among thorns,
and the thirsty pant after his wealth.
6 For hardship does not spring from the soil,
nor does trouble sprout from the ground.
7 Yet man is born to trouble
as surely as sparks fly upward.

8 "But if it were I, I would appeal to God;
I would lay my cause before him.
9 He performs wonders that cannot be fathomed,
miracles that cannot be counted.

NIV [e] *21* Some interpreters end the quotation after verse 17.

## King James

10Who giveth rain upon the earth, and sendeth waters upon the fields:

11To set up on high those that be low; that those which mourn may be exalted to safety.

12He disappointeth the devices of the crafty, so that their hands cannot perform *their* enterprise.

13He taketh the wise in their own craftiness: and the counsel of the froward is carried headlong.

14They meet with darkness in the daytime, and grope in the noonday as in the night.

15But he saveth the poor from the sword, from their mouth, and from the hand of the mighty.

16So the poor hath hope, and iniquity stoppeth her mouth.

17Behold, happy *is* the man whom God correcteth: therefore despise not thou the chastening of the Almighty:

18For he maketh sore, and bindeth up: he woundeth, and his hands make whole.

19He shall deliver thee in six troubles: yea, in seven there shall no evil touch thee.

20In famine he shall redeem thee from death: and in war from the power of the sword.

21Thou shalt be hid from the scourge of the tongue: neither shalt thou be afraid of destruction when it cometh.

22At destruction and famine thou shalt laugh: neither shalt thou be afraid of the beasts of the earth.

23For thou shalt be in league with the stones of the field: and the beasts of the field shall be at peace with thee.

24And thou shalt know that thy tabernacle *shall be* in peace; and thou shalt visit thy habitation, and shalt not sin.

25Thou shalt know also that thy seed *shall be* great, and thine offspring as the grass of the earth.

26Thou shalt come to *thy* grave in a full age, like as a shock of corn cometh in in his season.

27Lo this, we have searched it, so it *is;* hear it, and know thou *it* for thy good.

6 BUT JOB answered and said,

2Oh that my grief were thoroughly weighed, and my calamity laid in the balances together!

3For now it would be heavier than the sand of the sea: therefore my words are swallowed up.

4For the arrows of the Almighty *are* within me, the poison whereof drinketh up my spirit: the terrors of God do set themselves in array against me.

5Doth the wild ass bray when he hath grass? or loweth the ox over his fodder?

6Can that which is unsavoury be eaten without salt? or is there *any* taste in the white of an egg?

7The things *that* my soul refused to touch *are* as my sorrowful meat.

8Oh that I might have my request; and that God would grant *me* the thing that I long for!

9Even that it would please God to destroy me; that he would let loose his hand, and cut me off!

10Then should I yet have comfort; yea, I would harden myself in sorrow: let him not spare; for I have not concealed the words of the Holy One.

11What *is* my strength, that I should hope? and what *is* mine end, that I should prolong my life?

## Amplified

10Who gives rain upon the earth, and sends waters upon the fields;

11So that He sets on high those who are lowly, and those who mourn He lifts to safety.

12He frustrates the devices of the crafty, so that their hands cannot perform their enterprise *or* anything of [lasting] worth.

13He catches the [so-called] wise in their own trickiness, and the counsel of the schemers is brought to a quick end. [I Cor. 3:19, 20.]

14In the daytime they meet in darkness, and at noon they grope as in the night.

15But [God] saves [the fatherless] from the sword of their mouth, and the needy from the hand of the mighty.

16So the poor have hope, and iniquity shuts her mouth.

17Happy *and* fortunate is the man whom God reproves; so do not despise *or* reject the correction of the Almighty [subjecting you to trial and suffering].

18For He wounds, but He binds up; He smites, but His hands heal.

19He will rescue you in six troubles; in seven nothing that is evil [for you] will touch you.

20In famine He will redeem you from death, and in war from the power of the sword.

21You shall be hidden from the scourge of the tongue, neither shall you be afraid of destruction when it comes.

22At destruction and famine you shall laugh, neither shall you be afraid of the living creatures of the earth.

23For you shall be in league with the stones of the field, and the beasts of the field shall be at peace with you.

24And you shall know that your tent shall be in peace, and you shall visit your fold *and* your dwelling, and miss nothing [from them].

25You shall know also that your children shall be many, and your offspring as the grass of the earth.

26You shall come to your grave in ripe old age, and as a shock of grain goes up [to the threshing floor] in its season.

27This is what we have searched out; it is true; hear *and* heed it, and know for yourself [for your good].

6 THEN JOB answered,

2Oh, that my impatience *and* vexation might be [thoroughly] weighed, and all my calamity be laid up over against them in the balances one against the other [to see if my grief is unmanly]!

3For now it would be heavier than the sand of the sea; therefore my words have been rash *and* wild;

4[But it is] because the arrows of the Almighty are within me, the poison of which my spirit drinks up; the terrors of God set themselves in array against me.

5Does the wild ass bray when he has grass? Or does the ox low over his fodder?

6Can that which has not taste to it be eaten without salt? Or is there any flavor in the white of an egg?

7[These afflictions] my soul refuses to touch! Such things are like diseased food to me [sickening and repugnant]!

8Oh, that I might have my request, and that God would grant me the thing that I long for!

9I even wish that it would please God to crush me; that He would let loose His hand and cut me off!

10Then should I still have consolation; yes, I should leap *for joy* amid unsparing pain [though I shrink from it], that I have not concealed *or* denied the words of the Holy One!

11What strength have I left, that I should wait *and* hope? And what is ahead of me, that I should be patient?

## New American Standard

10 "He gives rain on the earth,
And sends water on the fields,
11 So that He sets on high those who are lowly,
And those who mourn are lifted to safety.
12 "He frustrates the plotting of the shrewd,
So that their hands cannot attain success.
13 "He captures the wise by their own shrewdness
And the advice of the cunning is quickly thwarted.
14 "By day they meet with darkness,
And grope at noon as in the night.
15 "But He saves from the sword of their mouth,
And the poor from the hand of the mighty.
16 "So the helpless has hope,
And unrighteousness must shut its mouth.

17¶ "Behold, how happy is the man whom God reproves,
So do not despise the discipline of the Almighty.
18 "For He inflicts pain, and gives relief;
He wounds, and His hands *also* heal.
19 "From six troubles He will deliver you,
Even in seven evil will not touch you.
20 "In famine He will redeem you from death,
And in war from the power of the sword.
21 "You will be hidden from the scourge of the tongue,
Neither will you be afraid of violence when it comes.
22 "You will laugh at violence and famine,
Neither will you be afraid of wild beasts.
23 "For you will be in league with the stones of the field;
And the beasts of the field will be at peace with you.
24 "And you will know that your tent is secure,
For you will visit your abode and fear no loss.
25 "You will know also that your descendants will be many,
And your offspring as the grass of the earth.
26 "You will come to the grave in full vigor,
Like the stacking of grain in its season.
27 "Behold this, we have investigated it, thus it is;
Hear it, and know for yourself."

*Job's Friends Are No Help*

6 THEN JOB answered,
2 "Oh that my vexation were actually weighed,
And laid in the balances together with my iniquity!
3 "For then it would be heavier than the sand of the seas,
Therefore my words have been rash.
4 "For the arrows of the Almighty are within me;
Their poison my spirit drinks;
The terrors of God are arrayed against me.
5 "Does the wild donkey bray over *his* grass,
Or does the ox low over his fodder?
6 "Can something tasteless be eaten without salt,
Or is there any taste in the white of an egg?
7 "My soul refuses to touch *them;*
They are like loathsome food to me.

8¶ "Oh that my request might come to pass,
And that God would grant my longing!
9 "Would that God were willing to crush me;
That He would loose His hand and cut me off!
10 "But it is still my consolation,
And I rejoice in unsparing pain,
That I have not denied the words of the Holy One.
11 "What is my strength, that I should wait?
And what is my end, that I should endure?

## New International

10 He bestows rain on the earth;
he sends water upon the countryside.
11 The lowly he sets on high,
and those who mourn are lifted to safety.
12 He thwarts the plans of the crafty,
so that their hands achieve no success.
13 He catches the wise in their craftiness,
and the schemes of the wily are swept away.
14 Darkness comes upon them in the daytime;
at noon they grope as in the night.
15 He saves the needy from the sword in their mouth;
he saves them from the clutches of the powerful.
16 So the poor have hope,
and injustice shuts its mouth.

17 "Blessed is the man whom God corrects;
so do not despise the discipline of the Almighty.[a]
18 For he wounds, but he also binds up;
he injures, but his hands also heal.
19 From six calamities he will rescue you;
in seven no harm will befall you.
20 In famine he will ransom you from death,
and in battle from the stroke of the sword.
21 You will be protected from the lash of the tongue,
and need not fear when destruction comes.
22 You will laugh at destruction and famine,
and need not fear the beasts of the earth.
23 For you will have a covenant with the stones of the field,
and the wild animals will be at peace with you.
24 You will know that your tent is secure;
you will take stock of your property and find nothing missing.
25 You will know that your children will be many,
and your descendants like the grass of the earth.
26 You will come to the grave in full vigor,
like sheaves gathered in season.

27 "We have examined this, and it is true.
So hear it and apply it to yourself."

*Job*

6 THEN JOB replied:
2 "If only my anguish could be weighed
and all my misery be placed on the scales!
3 It would surely outweigh the sand of the seas—
no wonder my words have been impetuous.
4 The arrows of the Almighty are in me,
my spirit drinks in their poison;
God's terrors are marshaled against me.
5 Does a wild donkey bray when it has grass,
or an ox bellow when it has fodder?
6 Is tasteless food eaten without salt,
or is there flavor in the white of an egg[b]?
7 I refuse to touch it;
such food makes me ill.

8 "Oh, that I might have my request,
that God would grant what I hope for,
9 that God would be willing to crush me,
to let loose his hand and cut me off!
10 Then I would still have this consolation—
my joy in unrelenting pain—
that I had not denied the words of the Holy One.

11 "What strength do I have, that I should still hope?
What prospects, that I should be patient?

NIV [a] 17 Hebrew *Shaddai;* here and throughout Job [b] 6 The meaning of the Hebrew for this phrase is uncertain.

## King James

12 *Is* my strength the strength of stones? or *is* my flesh of brass?
13 *Is* not my help in me? and is wisdom driven quite from me?
14To him that is afflicted pity *should be shown* from his friend; but
he forsaketh the fear of the Almighty.
15My brethren have dealt deceitfully as a brook, *and* as the
stream of brooks they pass away;
16Which are blackish by reason of the ice, *and* wherein the snow
is hid:
17What time they wax warm, they vanish: when it is hot, they
are consumed out of their place.
18The paths of their way are turned aside; they go to nothing,
and perish.
19The troops of Tema looked, the companies of Sheba waited
for them.
20They were confounded because they had hoped; they came
thither, and were ashamed.
21For now ye are nothing; ye see *my* casting down, and are
afraid.
22Did I say, Bring unto me? or, Give a reward for me of your
substance?
23Or, Deliver me from the enemy's hand? or, Redeem me from
the hand of the mighty?
24Teach me, and I will hold my tongue: and cause me to understand wherein I have erred.
25How forcible are right words! but what doth your arguing
reprove?
26Do ye imagine to reprove words, and the speeches of one that
is desperate, *which are* as wind?
27Yea, ye overwhelm the fatherless, and ye dig *a pit* for your
friend.
28Now therefore be content, look upon me; for *it is* evident unto
you if I lie.
29Return, I pray you, let it not be iniquity; yea, return again, my
righteousness *is* in it.
30Is there iniquity in my tongue? cannot my taste discern perverse things?

**7** *IS THERE* not an appointed time to man upon earth? *are not*
his days also like the days of an hireling?
2As a servant earnestly desireth the shadow, and as an hireling
looketh for *the reward of* his work:
3So am I made to possess months of vanity, and wearisome
nights are appointed to me.
4When I lie down, I say, When shall I arise, and the night be
gone? and I am full of tossings to and fro unto the dawning of the
day.
5My flesh is clothed with worms and clods of dust; my skin is
broken, and become loathsome.
6My days are swifter than a weaver's shuttle, and are spent
without hope.
7O remember that my life *is* wind: mine eye shall no more see
good.
8The eye of him that hath seen me shall see me no *more:* thine
eyes *are* upon me, and I *am* not.
9 *As* the cloud is consumed and vanisheth away: so he that
goeth down to the grave shall come up no *more.*
10He shall return no more to his house, neither shall his place
know him any more.

## Amplified

12Is my strength *and* endurance that of stones? Or is my flesh
made of bronze?
13Is it not that I have no help in myself, and that wisdom is quite
driven from me?
14To him who is about to faint *and* despair, kindness is due from
his friend, lest he forsake the fear of the Almighty.
15[You] my brethren, have dealt deceitfully as a brook, as the
channel of brooks that pass away,
16Which are black *and* turbid by reason of the ice, *and* in which
the snows hides itself;
17When they get warm, they shrink *and* disappear; when it is
hot, they vanish out of their place.
18The caravans which travel by way of them turn aside; they go
into the waste places and perish. [Such is my disappointment in
you, the friends I fully trusted.]
19The caravans of Tema looked [for water], the companies of
Sheba waited for them *in vain.*
20They were confounded because they had hoped [to find
water]; they came there and were bitterly disappointed.
21Now to me you are [like a dried-up brook]; you see my dismay
*and* terror, and [believing me to be a victim of God's anger] you are
afraid [to sympathize with me].
22Did I ever say, Bring me a gift? Or, Pay a bribe on my account
from your wealth,
23To deliver me from the adversary's hand? Or, Redeem me
from the hand of the oppressors?
24Teach me, and I will hold my peace, and cause me to understand wherein I have erred.
25How forcible are words of straightforward speech! But what
does your arguing argue *or* your reproof reprove?
26Do you imagine your words to be an argument, but the
speeches of one who is desperate to be as wind?
27Yes, you would cast lots over the fatherless, and bargain for
your friend.
28Now be pleased to look upon me, that it may be evident to
you if I lie [for surely I would not lie to your face].
29Return [from your suspicion], I pray you, let there be no
injustice; yes, return again [to confidence in me], my vindication
is in it.
30Is there wrong on my tongue? Cannot my taste discern what
is destructive?

**7** IS THERE not an [appointed] warfare *and* hard labor to man
upon earth? And are not his days like the days of a hireling?
2As a servant earnestly longs for the shade *and* evening shadows, and as a hireling who looks for the reward of his work,
3So am I allotted months of futile [suffering], and [long] nights
of misery are appointed to me.
4When I lie down, I say, When shall I arise, and the night be
gone? And I am full of tossings to and fro till the dawning of the
day.
5My flesh is clothed with worms and clods of dust; my skin is
broken and become loathsome, *and* it closes up and breaks out
afresh.
6My days are swifter than a weaver's shuttle, and are spent
without hope.
7Oh, remember that my life is but wind—a puff, a breath, a sob;
my eye shall see good no more.
8The eye of him who sees me shall see me no more; while your
eyes are upon me, I shall be gone.
9As the cloud is consumed and vanishes away, so he who goes
down to Sheol [the place of the dead] shall come up no more.
10He shall return no more to his house, neither shall his place
know him any more.

## New American Standard

12 "Is my strength the strength of stones,
Or is my flesh bronze?
13 "Is it that my help is not within me,
And that deliverance is driven from me?

14¶ "For the despairing man *there should be* kindness from his friend;
Lest he forsake the fear of the Almighty.
15 "My brothers have acted deceitfully like a wadi,
Like the torrents of wadis which vanish,
16 Which are turbid because of ice,
*And* into which the snow melts.
17 "When they become waterless, they are silent,
When it is hot, they vanish from their place.
18 "The paths of their course wind along,
They go up into nothing and perish.
19 "The caravans of Tema looked,
The travelers of Sheba hoped for them.
20 "They were disappointed for they had trusted,
They came there and were confounded.
21 "Indeed, you have now become such,
You see a terror and are afraid.
22 "Have I said, 'Give me *something,*'
Or, 'Offer a bribe for me from your wealth,'
23 Or, 'Deliver me from the hand of the adversary,'
Or, 'Redeem me from the hand of the tyrants'?

24¶ "Teach me, and I will be silent;
And show me how I have erred.
25 "How painful are honest words!
But what does your argument prove?
26 "Do you intend to reprove *my* words,
When the words of one in despair belong to the wind?
27 "You would even cast *lots* for the orphans,
And barter over your friend.
28 "And now please look at me,
And *see* if I lie to your face.
29 "Desist now, let there be no injustice;
Even desist, my righteousness is yet in it.
30 "Is there injustice on my tongue?
Cannot my palate discern calamities?

### *Job's Life Seems Futile*

7 "IS NOT man forced to labor on earth,
And *are not* his days like the days of a hired man?
2 "As a slave who pants for the shade,
And as a hired man who eagerly waits for his wages,
3 So am I allotted months of vanity,
And nights of trouble are appointed me.
4 "When I lie down I say,
'When shall I arise?'
But the night continues,
And I am continually tossing until dawn.
5 "My flesh is clothed with worms and a crust of dirt;
My skin hardens and runs.
6 "My days are swifter than a weaver's shuttle,
And come to an end without hope.

7¶ "Remember that my life is *but* breath,
My eye will not again see good.
8 "The eye of him who sees me will behold me no more;
Thine eyes *will be* on me, but I will not be.
9 "When a cloud vanishes, it is gone,
So he who goes down to Sheol does not come up.
10 "He will not return again to his house,
Nor will his place know him anymore.

## New International

12 Do I have the strength of stone?
Is my flesh bronze?
13 Do I have any power to help myself,
now that success has been driven from me?

14 "A despairing man should have the devotion of his friends,
even though he forsakes the fear of the Almighty.
15 But my brothers are as undependable as intermittent streams,
as the streams that overflow
16 when darkened by thawing ice
and swollen with melting snow,
17 but that cease to flow in the dry season,
and in the heat vanish from their channels.
18 Caravans turn aside from their routes;
they go up into the wasteland and perish.
19 The caravans of Tema look for water,
the traveling merchants of Sheba look in hope.
20 They are distressed, because they had been confident;
they arrive there, only to be disappointed.
21 Now you too have proved to be of no help;
you see something dreadful and are afraid.
22 Have I ever said, 'Give something on my behalf,
pay a ransom for me from your wealth,
23 deliver me from the hand of the enemy,
ransom me from the clutches of the ruthless'?

24 "Teach me, and I will be quiet;
show me where I have been wrong.
25 How painful are honest words!
But what do your arguments prove?
26 Do you mean to correct what I say,
and treat the words of a despairing man as wind?
27 You would even cast lots for the fatherless
and barter away your friend.

28 "But now be so kind as to look at me.
Would I lie to your face?
29 Relent, do not be unjust;
reconsider, for my integrity is at stake.[a]
30 Is there any wickedness on my lips?
Can my mouth not discern malice?

7 "DOES NOT man have hard service on earth?
Are not his days like those of a hired man?
2 Like a slave longing for the evening shadows,
or a hired man waiting eagerly for his wages,
3 so I have been allotted months of futility,
and nights of misery have been assigned to me.
4 When I lie down I think, 'How long before I get up?'
The night drags on, and I toss till dawn.
5 My body is clothed with worms and scabs,
my skin is broken and festering.

6 "My days are swifter than a weaver's shuttle,
and they come to an end without hope.
7 Remember, O God, that my life is but a breath;
my eyes will never see happiness again.
8 The eye that now sees me will see me no longer;
you will look for me, but I will be no more.
9 As a cloud vanishes and is gone,
so he who goes down to the grave[b] does not return.
10 He will never come to his house again;
his place will know him no more.

NIV [a] 29 Or *my righteousness still stands* [b] 9 Hebrew *Sheol*

# King James

11Therefore I will not refrain my mouth; I will speak in the anguish of my spirit; I will complain in the bitterness of my soul.

12 *Am* I a sea, or a whale, that thou settest a watch over me?

13When I say, My bed shall comfort me, my couch shall ease my complaint;

14Then thou scarest me with dreams, and terrifiest me through visions:

15So that my soul chooseth strangling, *and* death rather than my life.

16I loathe *it;* I would not live always: let me alone; for my days *are* vanity.

17What *is* man, that thou shouldest magnify him? and that thou shouldest set thine heart upon him?

18And *that* thou shouldest visit him every morning, *and* try him every moment?

19How long wilt thou not depart from me, nor let me alone till I swallow down my spittle?

20I have sinned; what shall I do unto thee, O thou preserver of men? why hast thou set me as a mark against thee, so that I am a burden to myself?

21And why dost thou not pardon my transgression, and take away mine iniquity? for now shall I sleep in the dust; and thou shalt seek me in the morning, but I *shall* not *be.*

8 THEN ANSWERED Bildad the Shuhite, and said,

2How long wilt thou speak these *things?* and *how long shall* the words of thy mouth *be like* a strong wind?

3Doth God pervert judgment? or doth the Almighty pervert justice?

4If thy children have sinned against him, and he have cast them away for their transgression;

5If thou wouldest seek unto God betimes, and make thy supplication to the Almighty;

6If thou *wert* pure and upright; surely now he would awake for thee, and make the habitation of thy righteousness prosperous.

7Though thy beginning was small, yet thy latter end should greatly increase.

8For inquire, I pray thee, of the former age, and prepare thyself to the search of their fathers:

9(For we *are but of* yesterday, and know nothing, because our days upon earth *are* a shadow:)

10Shall not they teach thee, *and* tell thee, and utter words out of their heart?

11Can the rush grow up without mire? can the flag grow without water?

12Whilst it *is* yet in his greenness, *and* not cut down, it withereth before any *other* herb.

13So *are* the paths of all that forget God; and the hypocrite's hope shall perish:

14Whose hope shall be cut off, and whose trust *shall be* a spider's web.

15He shall lean upon his house, but it shall not stand: he shall hold it fast, but it shall not endure.

16He *is* green before the sun, and his branch shooteth forth in his garden.

# Amplified

11Therefore I will not restrain my mouth; I will speak in the anguish of my spirit; I will complain in the bitterness of my soul, [O Lord]!

12Am I a sea, or a sea monster that You set a watch over me?

13When I say, My bed shall comfort me, my couch shall ease my complaint,

14Then You scare me with dreams, and terrify me through visions;

15So that I would choose strangling *and* death rather than these my bones.

16I loathe my life; I would not live for ever. Let me alone, for my days are a breath [futility].

17What is man, that You should magnify him *and* think him important? And that You should set Your mind upon him? [Ps. 8:4.]

18And that You should visit him every morning, *and* try him every moment?

19How long will Your [plaguing] glance not look away from me, nor You let me alone till I swallow my spittle?

20If I have sinned, what [harm] have I done You, O You watcher *and* keeper of men? Why have You set me as a mark for You, so that I am a burden to myself [and You?

21And why do You not pardon my transgression and take away my iniquity? For now shall I lie down in the dust, and [even if] You will seek me diligently, [it will be too late, for] I shall not be.

8 THEN ANSWERED Bildad the Shuhite,

2How long will you say these things [Job]? And how long shall the words of your mouth be as a mighty wind?

3Does God pervert justice? Or does the Almighty pervert righteousness?

4If your children have sinned against Him, and He has delivered them into the power of their transgression,

5If you will seek diligently unto God and make your supplication to the Almighty,

6Then, if you are pure and upright, surely he will bestir Himself for you, and make your righteous dwelling prosperous again.

7And though your beginning was small, yet your latter end would greatly increase.

8For inquire, I pray you, of the former age, and apply yourself to that which their fathers have searched out;

9For we are but of yesterday, and know nothing, because our days upon earth are a shadow.

10Shall not [the forefathers] teach you, and tell you, and utter words out of their heart [the deepest part of their nature]?

11Can the rush *or* papyrus grow up without marsh? Can the flag *or* reed grass grow without water?

12While it is yet green, in flower *and* not cut down, it withers before any other herb [when without water].

13So are the ways of all who forget God; and the hope of the godless shall perish,

14For his confidence breaks, and [the object of] his trust is a spider's web.

15He shall lean upon his house, but it shall not stand; he shall hold fast to it, but it shall not last.

16He is green before the sun, and his shoots go forth over his garden.

## New American Standard

11¶ "Therefore, I will not restrain my mouth;
I will speak in the anguish of my spirit,
I will complain in the bitterness of my soul.
12 "Am I the sea, or the sea monster,
That Thou dost set a guard over me?
13 "If I say, 'My bed will comfort me,
My couch will ease my complaint,'
14 Then Thou dost frighten me with dreams
And terrify me by visions;
15 So that my soul would choose suffocation,
Death rather than my pains.
16 "I waste away; I will not live forever.
Leave me alone, for my days are *but* a breath.
17 "What is man that Thou dost magnify him,
And that Thou art concerned about him,
18 That Thou dost examine him every morning,
And try him every moment?
19 "Wilt Thou never turn Thy gaze away from me,
Nor let me alone until I swallow my spittle?
20 "Have I sinned? What have I done to Thee,
O watcher of men?
Why hast Thou set me as Thy target,
So that I am a burden to myself?
21 "Why then dost Thou not pardon my transgression
And take away my iniquity?
For now I will lie down in the dust;
And Thou wilt seek me, but I will not be."

*Bildad Says God Rewards the Good*

8 THEN BILDAD the Shuhite answered,
2 "How long will you say these *things,*
And the words of your mouth be a mighty wind?
3 "Does God pervert justice
Or does the Almighty pervert what is right?
4 "If your sons sinned against Him,
Then He delivered them into the power of their transgression.
5 "If you would seek God
And implore the compassion of the Almighty,
6 If you are pure and upright,
Surely now He would rouse Himself for you
And restore your righteous estate.
7 "Though your beginning was insignificant,
Yet your end will increase greatly.
8¶ "Please inquire of past generations,
And consider the things searched out by their fathers.
9 "For we are *only* of yesterday and know nothing,
Because our days on earth are as a shadow.
10 "Will they not teach you *and* tell you,
And bring forth words from their minds?
11¶ "Can the papyrus grow up without marsh?
Can the rushes grow without water?
12 "While it is still green *and* not cut down,
Yet it withers before any *other* plant.
13 "So are the paths of all who forget God,
And the hope of the godless will perish,
14 Whose confidence is fragile,
And whose trust a spider's web.
15 "He trusts in his house, but it does not stand;
He holds fast to it, but it does not endure.
16 "He thrives before the sun,
And his shoots spread out over his garden.

## New International

11 "Therefore I will not keep silent;
I will speak out in the anguish of my spirit,
I will complain in the bitterness of my soul.
12 Am I the sea, or the monster of the deep,
that you put me under guard?
13 When I think my bed will comfort me
and my couch will ease my complaint,
14 even then you frighten me with dreams
and terrify me with visions,
15 so that I prefer strangling and death,
rather than this body of mine.
16 I despise my life; I would not live forever.
Let me alone; my days have no meaning.

17 "What is man that you make so much of him,
that you give him so much attention,
18 that you examine him every morning
and test him every moment?
19 Will you never look away from me,
or let me alone even for an instant?
20 If I have sinned, what have I done to you,
O watcher of men?
Why have you made me your target?
Have I become a burden to you?[a]
21 Why do you not pardon my offenses
and forgive my sins?
For I will soon lie down in the dust;
you will search for me, but I will be no more."

*Bildad*

8 THEN BILDAD the Shuhite replied:

2 "How long will you say such things?
Your words are a blustering wind.
3 Does God pervert justice?
Does the Almighty pervert what is right?
4 When your children sinned against him,
he gave them over to the penalty of their sin.
5 But if you will look to God
and plead with the Almighty,
6 if you are pure and upright,
even now he will rouse himself on your behalf
and restore you to your rightful place.
7 Your beginnings will seem humble,
so prosperous will your future be.

8 "Ask the former generations
and find out what their fathers learned,
9 for we were born only yesterday and know nothing,
and our days on earth are but a shadow.
10 Will they not instruct you and tell you?
Will they not bring forth words from their understanding?
11 Can papyrus grow tall where there is no marsh?
Can reeds thrive without water?
12 While still growing and uncut,
they wither more quickly than grass.
13 Such is the destiny of all who forget God;
so perishes the hope of the godless.
14 What he trusts in is fragile[b];
what he relies on is a spider's web.
15 He leans on his web, but it gives way;
he clings to it, but it does not hold.
16 He is like a well-watered plant in the sunshine,
spreading its shoots over the garden;

**NIV** [a] *20* A few manuscripts of the Masoretic Text, an ancient Hebrew scribal tradition and Septuagint; most manuscripts of the Masoretic Text *I have become a burden to myself.* [b] *14* The meaning of the Hebrew for this word is uncertain.

# King James

17His roots are wrapped about the heap, *and* seeth the place of stones.

18If he destroy him from his place, then *it* shall deny him, *saying,* I have not seen thee.

19Behold, this *is* the joy of his way, and out of the earth shall others grow.

20Behold, God will not cast away a perfect *man,* neither will he help the evil doers:

21Till he fill thy mouth with laughing, and thy lips with rejoicing.

22They that hate thee shall be clothed with shame; and the dwellingplace of the wicked shall come to nought.

**9** THEN JOB answered and said,
2I know *it is* so of a truth: but how should man be just with God?

3If he will contend with him, he cannot answer him one of a thousand.

4 *He is* wise in heart, and mighty in strength: who hath hardened *himself* against him, and hath prospered?

5Which removeth the mountains, and they know not: which overturneth them in his anger.

6Which shaketh the earth out of her place, and the pillars thereof tremble.

7Which commandeth the sun, and it riseth not; and sealeth up the stars.

8Which alone spreadeth out the heavens, and treadeth upon the waves of the sea.

9Which maketh Arcturus, Orion, and Pleiades, and the chambers of the south.

10Which doeth great things past finding out; yea, and wonders without number.

11Lo, he goeth by me, and I see *him* not: he passeth on also, but I perceive him not.

12Behold, he taketh away, who can hinder him? who will say unto him, What doest thou?

13 *If* God will not withdraw his anger, the proud helpers do stoop under him.

14How much less shall I answer him, *and* choose out my words *to reason* with him?

15Whom, though I were righteous, *yet* would I not answer, *but* I would make supplication to my judge.

16If I had called, and he had answered me; *yet* would I not believe that he had hearkened unto my voice.

17For he breaketh me with a tempest, and multiplieth my wounds without cause.

18He will not suffer me to take my breath, but filleth me with bitterness.

19If I *speak* of strength, lo, *he is* strong: and if of judgment, who shall set me a time *to plead?*

20If I justify myself, mine own mouth shall condemn me: *if I say,* I *am* perfect, it shall also prove me perverse.

21 *Though I were* perfect, *yet* would I not know my soul: I would despise my life.

22This *is* one *thing,* therefore I said *it,* He destroyeth the perfect and the wicked.

23If the scourge slay suddenly, he will laugh at the trial of the innocent.

# Amplified

17[Godless] his roots are wrapped about the [stone] heap, *and* see their way [promisingly] among the rocks.

18But if [God] snatches him from his property, [then having passed into the hands of others] it will forget *and* deny him, [saying,] I have never seen you [before, as if ashamed of him—like his former friends].

19See, this is the joy of going the way [of the ungodly]! And from the dust others will spring up [to take his place].

20Behold, as surely as God will never uphold wrongdoers, He will never cast away a blameless man.

21He will yet fill your mouth with laughter [Job], and your lips with joyful shouting.

22Those who hate you will be clothed with shame, and the tent of the wicked shall be no more.

**9** THEN JOB answered and said,
2Yes, I know it is true; but how can mortal man be right before God?

3If one should want to contend with Him, he cannot answer one [of His questions] in a thousand.

4[God] is wise in heart and mighty in strength; who has [ever] hardened himself against Him, and prospered *or* even been safe?

5[God] who removes the mountains, and they know it not, when He overturns them in His anger;

6Who shakes the earth out of its place, and the pillars of it tremble;

7Who commands the sun and it rises not, and seals up the stars [from view];

8Who alone stretches out the heavens, and treads upon the waves *and* high places of the sea;

9Who made [the constellations] the Bear, Orion, and the [loose cluster] Pleiades, and the [vast starry] spaces of the south;

10Who does great things past finding out, yes, marvelous things without number.

11Lo, He goes by me, and I see Him not; He passes on also, but I perceive Him not.

12Behold, He snatches away; who can hinder *or* turn Him back? Who will say to Him, What are You doing?

13God will not withdraw His anger; the [proud] helpers of Rahab [arrogant monster of the sea] bow under Him.

14How much less shall I answer Him, choosing out my words to reason with Him?

15Whom, though I were righteous—upright and innocent—yet I could not answer; I must appeal for mercy to my opponent *and* judge [for my right].

16If I called, and He answered me, yet would I not believe that He listened to my voice.

17For He overwhelms *and* breaks me with a tempest, and multiplies my wounds without cause.

18He will not allow me to catch my breath, but fills me with bitterness.

19If I speak of strength, lo, He is mighty! And if of justice, Who, says He, will summon Me?

20Though I am innocent *and* in the right, my own mouth would condemn me; though I am blameless, He would prove me perverse.

21Though I am blameless, I regard not myself; I despise my life.

22It is all one; therefore I say, God [does not discriminate, but] destroys the blameless and the wicked.

23When [His] scourge slays suddenly, He mocks at the calamity *and* trial of the innocent.

## New American Standard

17 "His roots wrap around a rock pile,
He grasps a house of stones.
18 "If he is removed from his place,
Then it will deny him, *saying,* 'I never saw you.'
19 "Behold, this is the joy of His way;
And out of the dust others will spring.
20 "Lo, God will not reject *a man of* integrity,
Nor will He support the evildoers.
21 "He will yet fill your mouth with laughter,
And your lips with shouting.
22 "Those who hate you will be clothed with shame;
And the tent of the wicked will be no more."

*Job Says There Is No Arbitrator between God and Man*

9 THEN JOB answered,
2 "In truth I know that this is so,
But how can a man be in the right before God?
3 "If one wished to dispute with Him,
He could not answer Him once in a thousand *times.*
4 "Wise in heart and mighty in strength,
Who has defied Him without harm?
5 "*It is God* who removes the mountains, they know not *how,*
When He overturns them in His anger;
6 Who shakes the earth out of its place,
And its pillars tremble;
7 Who commands the sun not to shine,
And sets a seal upon the stars;
8 Who alone stretches out the heavens,
And tramples down the waves of the sea;
9 Who makes the Bear, Orion, and the Pleiades,
And the chambers of the south;
10 Who does great things, unfathomable,
And wondrous works without number.
11 "Were He to pass by me, I would not see Him;
Were He to move past *me,* I would not perceive Him.
12 "Were He to snatch away, who could restrain Him?
Who could say to Him, 'What art Thou doing?'
13¶ "God will not turn back His anger;
Beneath Him crouch the helpers of Rahab.
14 "How then can I answer Him,
*And* choose my words before Him?
15 "For though I were right, I could not answer;
I would have to implore the mercy of my judge.
16 "If I called and He answered me,
I could not believe that He was listening to my voice.
17 "For He bruises me with a tempest,
And multiplies my wounds without cause.
18 "He will not allow me to get my breath,
But saturates me with bitterness.
19 "If *it is a matter* of power, behold, *He is* the strong one!
And if *it is a matter* of justice, who can summon Him?
20 "Though I am righteous, my mouth will condemn me;
Though I am guiltless, He will declare me guilty.
21 "I am guiltless;
I do not take notice of myself;
I despise my life.
22 "It is *all* one; therefore I say,
'He destroys the guiltless and the wicked.'
23 "If the scourge kills suddenly,
He mocks the despair of the innocent.

## New International

17 it entwines its roots around a pile of rocks
and looks for a place among the stones.
18 But when it is torn from its spot,
that place disowns it and says, 'I never saw you.'
19 Surely its life withers away,
and[a] from the soil other plants grow.
20 "Surely God does not reject a blameless man
or strengthen the hands of evildoers.
21 He will yet fill your mouth with laughter
and your lips with shouts of joy.
22 Your enemies will be clothed in shame,
and the tents of the wicked will be no more."

*Job*

9 THEN JOB replied:
2 "Indeed, I know that this is true.
But how can a mortal be righteous before God?
3 Though one wished to dispute with him,
he could not answer him one time out of a thousand.
4 His wisdom is profound, his power is vast.
Who has resisted him and come out unscathed?
5 He moves mountains without their knowing it
and overturns them in his anger.
6 He shakes the earth from its place
and makes its pillars tremble.
7 He speaks to the sun and it does not shine;
he seals off the light of the stars.
8 He alone stretches out the heavens
and treads on the waves of the sea.
9 He is the Maker of the Bear and Orion,
the Pleiades and the constellations of the south.
10 He performs wonders that cannot be fathomed,
miracles that cannot be counted.
11 When he passes me, I cannot see him;
when he goes by, I cannot perceive him.
12 If he snatches away, who can stop him?
Who can say to him, 'What are you doing?'
13 God does not restrain his anger;
even the cohorts of Rahab cowered at his feet.
14 "How then can I dispute with him?
How can I find words to argue with him?
15 Though I were innocent, I could not answer him;
I could only plead with my Judge for mercy.
16 Even if I summoned him and he responded,
I do not believe he would give me a hearing.
17 He would crush me with a storm
and multiply my wounds for no reason.
18 He would not let me regain my breath
but would overwhelm me with misery.
19 If it is a matter of strength, he is mighty!
And if it is a matter of justice, who will summon him[b]?
20 Even if I were innocent, my mouth would condemn me;
if I were blameless, it would pronounce me guilty.
21 "Although I am blameless,
I have no concern for myself;
I despise my own life.
22 It is all the same; that is why I say,
'He destroys both the blameless and the wicked.'
23 When a scourge brings sudden death,
he mocks the despair of the innocent.

**NIV** [a] 19 Or *Surely all the joy it has / is that* [b] 19 See Septuagint; Hebrew *me.*

## King James

24The earth is given into the hand of the wicked: he covereth the faces of the judges thereof; if not, where, *and* who *is* he?
25Now my days are swifter than a post: they flee away, they see no good.
26They are passed away as the swift ships: as the eagle *that* hasteth to the prey.
27If I say, I will forget my complaint, I will leave off my heaviness, and comfort *myself:*
28I am afraid of all my sorrows, I know that thou wilt not hold me innocent.
29 *If* I be wicked, why then labour I in vain?
30If I wash myself with snow water, and make my hands never so clean;
31Yet shalt thou plunge me in the ditch, and mine own clothes shall abhor me.
32For *he is* not a man, as I *am, that* I should answer him, *and* we should come together in judgment.
33Neither is there any daysman betwixt us, *that* might lay his hand upon us both.
34Let him take his rod away from me, and let not his fear terrify me:
35 *Then* would I speak, and not fear him; but *it is* not so with me.

10 MY SOUL is weary of my life; I will leave my complaint upon myself; I will speak in the bitterness of my soul.
2I will say unto God, Do not condemn me; show me wherefore thou contendest with me.
3 *Is it* good unto thee that thou shouldest oppress, that thou shouldest despise the work of thine hands, and shine upon the counsel of the wicked?
4Hast thou eyes of flesh? or seest thou as man seeth?
5 *Are* thy days as the days of man? *are* thy years as man's days,
6That thou inquirest after mine iniquity, and searchest after my sin?
7Thou knowest that I am not wicked; and *there is* none that can deliver out of thine hand.
8Thine hands have made me and fashioned me together round about; yet thou dost destroy me.
9Remember, I beseech thee, that thou hast made me as the clay; and wilt thou bring me into dust again?
10Hast thou not poured me out as milk, and curdled me like cheese?
11Thou hast clothed me with skin and flesh, and hast fenced me with bones and sinews.
12Thou hast granted me life and favour, and thy visitation hath preserved my spirit.
13And these *things* hast thou hid in thine heart: I know that this *is* with thee.
14If I sin, then thou markest me, and thou wilt not acquit me from mine iniquity.
15If I be wicked, woe unto me; and *if* I be righteous, *yet* will I not lift up my head. *I am* full of confusion; therefore see thou mine affliction;
16For it increaseth. Thou huntest me as a fierce lion: and again thou showest thyself marvellous upon me.

## Amplified

24The earth is given into the hand of the wicked; He covers the faces of its judges [so that they are blinded to justice]. If it is not [God], who then is it [responsible for all this inequality]?
25Now my days are swifter than a runner; they flee away; they see no good.
26They are passed away like the swift rowboats made of reeds, or like the eagle that swoops down on the prey.
27If I say, I will forget my complaint, I will put off my sad countenance, be of good cheer *and* brighten up,
28I become afraid of all my pains *and* sorrows [yet to come], for I know You will not pronounce me innocent [by removing them].
29I shall be held guilty *and* be condemned; why then should I labor in vain [to appear innocent]?
30If I wash myself with snow, and cleanse my hands with lye,
31Yet You will plunge me into the ditch, and my own clothes will abhor me [and refuse to cover so foul a body].
32For [God] is not a *mere* man, as I am, that I should answer Him, that we should come together in court.
33There is no umpire between us, who might lay his hand upon us both [would that there were]! [I Tim. 2:5.]
34That He might take His rod away from [threatening] me, and that fear of Him might not terrify me.
35[Then] would I speak, and not fear Him, for I am not so with myself [to make me afraid, were only a fair trial given me].

10 I AM weary of my life *and* loathe it! I will give free expression to my complaint; I will speak in the bitterness of my soul.
2I will say to God, Do not condemn me—do not make me guilty! Show me why You contend with me.
3Does it seem good to You that You should oppress, that You should despise *and* reject the work of Your hands, and favor the schemes of the wicked?
4Have You eyes of flesh? Do You see as man sees?
5Are Your days as the days of man, are Your years as man's [years],
6That You inquire after my iniquity and search for my sin,
7Although You know that I am not wicked *or* guilty, and there is none who can deliver me out of Your hand?
8Your hands have formed me and made me, would You turn around and destroy me?
9Remember [earnestly], I beseech You, that You have fashioned me as clay [out of the same earth-material, exquisitely and elaborately], and will You bring me into dust again?
10Have You not poured me out as milk and curdled me like cheese?
11You have clothed me with skin and flesh, and have knit me together with bones and sinews.
12You have granted me life and favor, and Your providence has preserved my spirit.
13Yet these [the present evils] have You hid in Your heart [for me since my creation]; I know that this was with You [in Your purpose and thought].
14If I sin, then You observe me, and You will not acquit me from my iniquity *and* guilt.
15If I were wicked, woe unto me! And if I am righteous, yet must I not lift up my head, for I am filled with disgrace and the sight of my affliction.
16If I lift myself up, You hunt me like a lion, and again show Yourself [inflicting] marvelous [trials] upon me.

## New American Standard

24 "The earth is given into the hand of the wicked;
He covers the faces of its judges.
If *it is* not *He,* then who is it?
25¶ "Now my days are swifter than a runner;
They flee away, they see no good.
26 "They slip by like reed boats,
Like an eagle that swoops on its prey.
27 "Though I say, 'I will forget my complaint,
I will leave off my *sad* countenance and be cheerful,'
28 I am afraid of all my pains,
I know that Thou wilt not acquit me.
29 "I am accounted wicked,
Why then should I toil in vain?
30 "If I should wash myself with snow
And cleanse my hands with lye,
31 Yet Thou wouldst plunge me into the pit,
And my own clothes would abhor me.
32 "For *He is* not a man as I am that I may answer Him,
That we may go to court together.
33 "There is no umpire between us,
Who may lay his hand upon us both.
34 "Let Him remove His rod from me,
And let not dread of Him terrify me.
35 "*Then* I would speak and not fear Him;
But I am not like that in myself.

*Job Despairs of God's Dealings*

10 "I LOATHE my own life;
I will give full vent to my complaint;
I will speak in the bitterness of my soul.
2 "I will say to God, 'Do not condemn me;
Let me know why Thou dost contend with me.
3 'Is it right for Thee indeed to oppress,
To reject the labor of Thy hands,
And to look favorably on the schemes of the wicked?
4 'Hast Thou eyes of flesh?
Or dost Thou see as a man sees?
5 'Are Thy days as the days of a mortal,
Or Thy years as man's years,
6 That Thou shouldst seek for my guilt,
And search after my sin?
7 'According to Thy knowledge I am indeed not guilty;
Yet there is no deliverance from Thy hand.
8¶ 'Thy hands fashioned and made me altogether,
And wouldst Thou destroy me?
9 'Remember now, that Thou hast made me as clay;
And wouldst Thou turn me into dust again?
10 'Didst Thou not pour me out like milk,
And curdle me like cheese;
11 Clothe me with skin and flesh,
And knit me together with bones and sinews?
12 'Thou hast granted me life and lovingkindness;
And Thy care has preserved my spirit.
13 'Yet these things Thou hast concealed in Thy heart;
I know that this is within Thee:
14 If I sin, then Thou wouldst take note of me,
And wouldst not acquit me of my guilt.
15 'If I am wicked, woe to me!
And if I am righteous, I dare not lift up my head.
*I am* sated with disgrace and conscious of my misery.
16 'And should *my head* be lifted up, Thou wouldst hunt me like a lion;
And again Thou wouldst show Thy power against me.

## New International

24 When a land falls into the hands of the wicked,
he blindfolds its judges.
If it is not he, then who is it?
25 "My days are swifter than a runner;
they fly away without a glimpse of joy.
26 They skim past like boats of papyrus,
like eagles swooping down on their prey.
27 If I say, 'I will forget my complaint,
I will change my expression, and smile,'
28 I still dread all my sufferings,
for I know you will not hold me innocent.
29 Since I am already found guilty,
why should I struggle in vain?
30 Even if I washed myself with soap[a]
and my hands with washing soda,
31 you would plunge me into a slime pit
so that even my clothes would detest me.

32 "He is not a man like me that I might answer him,
that we might confront each other in court.
33 If only there were someone to arbitrate between us,
to lay his hand upon us both,
34 someone to remove God's rod from me,
so that his terror would frighten me no more.
35 Then I would speak up without fear of him,
but as it now stands with me, I cannot.

10 "I LOATHE my very life;
therefore I will give free rein to my complaint
and speak out in the bitterness of my soul.
2 I will say to God: Do not condemn me,
but tell me what charges you have against me.
3 Does it please you to oppress me,
to spurn the work of your hands,
while you smile on the schemes of the wicked?
4 Do you have eyes of flesh?
Do you see as a mortal sees?
5 Are your days like those of a mortal
or your years like those of a man,
6 that you must search out my faults
and probe after my sin—
7 though you know that I am not guilty
and that no one can rescue me from your hand?
8 "Your hands shaped me and made me.
Will you now turn and destroy me?
9 Remember that you molded me like clay.
Will you now turn me to dust again?
10 Did you not pour me out like milk
and curdle me like cheese,
11 clothe me with skin and flesh
and knit me together with bones and sinews?
12 You gave me life and showed me kindness,
and in your providence watched over my spirit.

13 "But this is what you concealed in your heart,
and I know that this was in your mind:
14 If I sinned, you would be watching me
and would not let my offense go unpunished.
15 If I am guilty—woe to me!
Even if I am innocent, I cannot lift my head,
for I am full of shame
and drowned in[b] my affliction.
16 If I hold my head high, you stalk me like a lion
and again display your awesome power against me.

NIV [a] 30 Or *snow* [b] 15 Or *and aware of*

## King James

17 Thou renewest thy witnesses against me, and increasest thine indignation upon me; changes and war *are* against me.
18 Wherefore then hast thou brought me forth out of the womb? Oh that I had given up the ghost, and no eye had seen me!
19 I should have been as though I had not been; I should have been carried from the womb to the grave.
20 *Are* not my days few? cease *then, and* let me alone, that I may take comfort a little,
21 Before I go *whence* I shall not return, *even* to the land of darkness and the shadow of death;
22 A land of darkness, as darkness *itself; and* of the shadow of death, without any order, and *where* the light *is* as darkness.

**11** THEN ANSWERED Zophar the Naamathite, and said,
2 Should not the multitude of words be answered? and should a man full of talk be justified?
3 Should thy lies make men hold their peace? and when thou mockest, shall no man make thee ashamed?
4 For thou hast said, My doctrine *is* pure, and I am clean in thine eyes.
5 But oh that God would speak, and open his lips against thee;
6 And that he would show thee the secrets of wisdom, that *they are* double to that which is! Know therefore that God exacteth of thee *less* than thine iniquity *deserveth.*
7 Canst thou by searching find out God? canst thou find out the Almighty unto perfection?
8 *It is* as high as heaven; what canst thou do? deeper than hell; what canst thou know?
9 The measure thereof *is* longer than the earth, and broader than the sea.
10 If he cut off, and shut up, or gather together, then who can hinder him?
11 For he knoweth vain men: he seeth wickedness also; will he not then consider *it?*
12 For vain man would be wise, though man be born *like* a wild ass's colt.
13 If thou prepare thine heart, and stretch out thine hands toward him;
14 If iniquity *be* in thine hand, put it far away, and let not wickedness dwell in thy tabernacles.
15 For then shalt thou lift up thy face without spot; yea, thou shalt be stedfast, and shalt not fear:
16 Because thou shalt forget *thy* misery, *and* remember *it* as waters *that* pass away:
17 And *thine* age shall be clearer than the noonday; thou shalt shine forth, thou shalt be as the morning.
18 And thou shalt be secure, because there is hope; yea, thou shalt dig *about thee, and* thou shalt take thy rest in safety.
19 Also thou shalt lie down, and none shall make *thee* afraid; yea, many shall make suit unto thee.
20 But the eyes of the wicked shall fail, and they shall not escape, and their hope *shall be as* the giving up of the ghost.

## Amplified

17 You renew Your witnesses against me, and increase Your indignation toward me; I am as if attacked by a troop time after time.
18 Why then did You bring me forth out of the womb? Would that I had perished, and no eye had seen me!
19 I should have been as though I had not existed; I should have been carried from the womb to the grave.
20 Are not my days few? Cease then *and* let me alone, that I may take a little comfort *and* cheer up,
21 Before I go whence I shall not return, even to the land of darkness and the shadow of death;
22 The land of sunless gloom as intense darkness; [the land] of the shadow of death, without any order, and where the light is as thick darkness.

**11** THEN ZOPHAR the Naamathite replied,
2 Should not the multitude of words be answered? And should a man full of talk [and making such great professions] be pronounced free from guilt *or* blame?
3 Should your boastings *and* babble make men keep silent? And when you mock *and* scoff, shall no man make you ashamed?
4 For you have said, My doctrine [that God afflicts the righteous knowingly] is pure, and I am clean in *God's* eyes. [Job 10:7.]
5 But oh, that God would speak, and open His lips against you;
6 And that He would show you the secrets of wisdom! For He is manifold in understanding! Know therefore that God exacts of you less than your guilt *and* iniquity [deserve].
7 Can you find out the deep things of God, *or* can you by searching find out the limit of the Almighty [explore His depths, ascend to His heights, extend to His breadths, and comprehend His infinite] perfection?
8 His wisdom is as high as the heights of Heaven! What can you do? It is deeper than Sheol [the place of the dead]! What can you know?
9 Longer in measure [and scope] is it than the earth, and broader than the sea.
10 If *God* sweeps in and arrests and calls into judgment, who can hinder Him?—If He be against a man, who shall call Him to account for it?
11 For He recognizes *and* knows hollow, wicked *and* useless men—men of falsehood; when He sees iniquity, will He not consider it?
12 But a stupid man will get wisdom [only] when a wild donkey's colt is born a man [like which he thinks himself free because he is lifted up in pride].
13 If you set your heart aright and stretch out your hands to *God;*
14 If you put sin out of your hand *and* far away from you, and let not evil dwell in your tents;
15 Then can you lift up your face to Him without stain *of sin* [and unashamed]; yes, you shall be steadfast *and* secure; you shall not fear.
16 For you shall forget your misery; you shall remember it as waters that pass away.
17 And *your* life shall be clearer than the noonday, *and* rise above it; though there be darkness, it shall be as the morning.
18 And you shall be secure *and* feel confident because there is hope; yes, you shall search about you, and you shall take your rest in safety.
19 You shall lie down and none shall make you afraid; yes, many shall sue for your favor.
20 But the eyes of the wicked shall look [for relief] in vain, and they shall not escape [the justice of God], and their hope shall be to give up the ghost.

# New American Standard

17 'Thou dost renew Thy witnesses against me,
And increase Thine anger toward me,
Hardship after hardship is with me.

18¶ 'Why then hast Thou brought me out of the womb?
Would that I had died and no eye had seen me!
19 'I should have been as though I had not been,
Carried from womb to tomb.'
20 "Would He not let my few days alone?
Withdraw from me that I may have a little cheer
21 Before I go—and I shall not return—
To the land of darkness and deep shadow;
22 The land of utter gloom as darkness *itself*,
Of deep shadow without order,
And which shines as the darkness."

*Zophar Rebukes Job*

**11** THEN ZOPHAR the Naamathite answered,
2 "Shall a multitude of words go unanswered,
And a talkative man be acquitted?
3 "Shall your boasts silence men?
And shall you scoff and none rebuke?
4 "For you have said, 'My teaching is pure,
And I am innocent in your eyes.'
5 "But would that God might speak,
And open His lips against you,
6 And show you the secrets of wisdom!
For sound wisdom has two sides.
Know then that God forgets a part of your iniquity.

7¶ "Can you discover the depths of God?
Can you discover the limits of the Almighty?
8 "*They are* high as the heavens, what can you do?
Deeper than Sheol, what can you know?
9 "Its measure is longer than the earth,
And broader than the sea.
10 "If He passes by or shuts up,
Or calls an assembly, who can restrain Him?
11 "For He knows false men,
And He sees iniquity without investigating.
12 "And an idiot will become intelligent
When the foal of a wild donkey is born a man.

13¶ "If you would direct your heart right,
And spread out your hand to Him;
14 If iniquity is in your hand, put it far away,
And do not let wickedness dwell in your tents.
15 "Then, indeed, you could lift up your face without *moral* defect,
And you would be steadfast and not fear.
16 "For you would forget *your* trouble,
As waters that have passed by, you would remember *it*.
17 "And your life would be brighter than noonday;
Darkness would be like the morning.
18 "Then you would trust, because there is hope;
And you would look around and rest securely.
19 "You would lie down and none would disturb *you*,
And many would entreat your favor.
20 "But the eyes of the wicked will fail,
And there will be no escape for them;
And their hope is to breathe their last."

# New International

17You bring new witnesses against me
and increase your anger toward me;
your forces come against me wave upon wave.

18"Why then did you bring me out of the womb?
I wish I had died before any eye saw me.
19If only I had never come into being,
or had been carried straight from the womb to the grave!
20Are not my few days almost over?
Turn away from me so I can have a moment's joy
21before I go to the place of no return,
to the land of gloom and deep shadow,[a]
22to the land of deepest night,
of deep shadow and disorder,
where even the light is like darkness."

*Zophar*

**11** THEN ZOPHAR the Naamathite replied:
2"Are all these words to go unanswered?
Is this talker to be vindicated?
3Will your idle talk reduce men to silence?
Will no one rebuke you when you mock?
4You say to God, 'My beliefs are flawless
and I am pure in your sight.'
5Oh, how I wish that God would speak,
that he would open his lips against you
6and disclose to you the secrets of wisdom,
for true wisdom has two sides.
Know this: God has even forgotten some of your sin.

7"Can you fathom the mysteries of God?
Can you probe the limits of the Almighty?
8They are higher than the heavens—what can you do?
They are deeper than the depths of the grave[b]—what can you know?
9Their measure is longer than the earth
and wider than the sea.

10"If he comes along and confines you in prison
and convenes a court, who can oppose him?
11Surely he recognizes deceitful men;
and when he sees evil, does he not take note?
12But a witless man can no more become wise
than a wild donkey's colt can be born a man.[c]

13"Yet if you devote your heart to him
and stretch out your hands to him,
14if you put away the sin that is in your hand
and allow no evil to dwell in your tent,
15then you will lift up your face without shame;
you will stand firm and without fear.
16You will surely forget your trouble,
recalling it only as waters gone by.
17Life will be brighter than noonday,
and darkness will become like morning.
18You will be secure, because there is hope;
you will look about you and take your rest in safety.
19You will lie down, with no one to make you afraid,
and many will court your favor.
20But the eyes of the wicked will fail,
and escape will elude them;
their hope will become a dying gasp."

**NIV** [a] 21 Or *and the shadow of death;* also in verse 22 [b] 8 Hebrew *than Sheol*
[c] 12 Or *wild donkey can be born tame*

## King James

**12** AND JOB answered and said,
2 No doubt but ye *are* the people, and wisdom shall die
with you.
3 But I have understanding as well as you; I *am* not inferior to
you: yea, who knoweth not such things as these?
4 I am *as* one mocked of his neighbour, who calleth upon God,
and he answereth him: the just upright *man is* laughed to scorn.
5 He that is ready to slip with *his* feet *is as* a lamp despised in
the thought of him that is at ease.
6 The tabernacles of robbers prosper, and they that provoke God
are secure; into whose hand God bringeth *abundantly.*
7 But ask now the beasts, and they shall teach thee; and the
fowls of the air, and they shall tell thee:
8 Or speak to the earth, and it shall teach thee: and the fishes
of the sea shall declare unto thee.
9 Who knoweth not in all these that the hand of the LORD hath
wrought this?
10 In whose hand *is* the soul of every living thing, and the breath
of all mankind.
11 Doth not the ear try words? and the mouth taste his meat?
12 With the ancient *is* wisdom; and in length of days understanding.
13 With him *is* wisdom and strength, he hath counsel and understanding.
14 Behold, he breaketh down, and it cannot be built again: he
shutteth up a man, and there can be no opening.
15 Behold, he withholdeth the waters, and they dry up: also he
sendeth them out, and they overturn the earth.
16 With him *is* strength and wisdom: the deceived and the deceiver *are* his.
17 He leadeth counsellors away spoiled, and maketh the judges
fools.
18 He looseth the bond of kings, and girdeth their loins with a
girdle.
19 He leadeth princes away spoiled, and overthroweth the
mighty.
20 He removeth away the speech of the trusty, and taketh away
the understanding of the aged.
21 He poureth contempt upon princes, and weakeneth the
strength of the mighty.
22 He discovereth deep things out of darkness, and bringeth out
to light the shadow of death.
23 He increaseth the nations, and destroyeth them: he enlargeth
the nations, and straiteneth them *again.*
24 He taketh away the heart of the chief of the people of the
earth, and causeth them to wander in a wilderness *where there is*
no way.
25 They grope in the dark without light, and he maketh them to
stagger like *a* drunken *man.*

**13** LO, MINE eye hath seen all *this,* mine ear hath heard and
understood it.
2 What ye know, *the same* do I know also: I *am* not inferior unto
you.

## Amplified

**12** THEN JOB answered,
2 No doubt you are the [only wise] people [in the world],
and wisdom will die with you!
3 But I have understanding as well as you; I am not inferior to
you. Who does not know such things as these [of God's wisdom
and might]?
4 I am become one who is a laughingstock to his friend; I, one
whom God answered when he called upon Him; a just, upright
(blameless) man is laughed to scorn!
5 In the thought of him who is at ease there is contempt for
misfortune; but it is ready for those whose feet slip.
6 The dwellings of robbers prosper; those who provoke God are
[apparently] secure; God supplies them abundantly [who have no
god but their own hand and power].
7 For ask now the animals and they will teach you [that God does
not deal with His creatures according to their character]; ask the
birds of the air and they will tell you.
8 Or speak to the earth [with its other forms of life], and it will
teach you; and the fish of the sea will declare [this truth] to you.
9 Who [is so blind as] not to recognize in all these [that good and
evil are promiscuously scattered throughout nature and human
life] that it is God's hand which does it [and God's way]?
10 In His hand is the life of every living thing and the breath of
all mankind.
11 Is it not the task of the ear to discriminate between [wise and
unwise] words, just as the mouth distinguishes [between desirable
and undesirable] food?
12 With the aged [you say] is wisdom; and with length of days
comes understanding.
13 But *only* with *God* is [perfect] wisdom and might; He *alone* has
[true] counsel and understanding.
14 Behold, He tears down, and it cannot be built again; He shuts
a man in, and none can open.
15 He withholds the waters, and the land dries up; again, He
sends forth [rains], and they overwhelm the land *or* transform it.
16 With Him are might and wisdom; the deceived and the deceiver are His [and in His power].
17 He leads [great and scheming] counselors away stripped *and*
barefoot, and makes the judges fools [in human estimation, by
overthrowing their plans].
18 He looses the fetters *ordered* by kings, and has *the* waistcloth
[of a slave] bound about their *own* loins.
19 He leads away priests as spoil, and men firmly seated He
overturns.
20 He deprives of speech those who are trusted, and takes away
the discernment *and* discretion of the aged.
21 He pours contempt on princes, and loosens the belt of the
strong [disabling them, bringing low the pride of the learned].
22 He uncovers deep things out of darkness, and brings out to
light black gloom *and* the shadow of death.
23 He makes nations great, and He destroys them; He enlarges
nations [and then straitens and shrinks them again], and leads
them [away captive].
24 He takes away understanding from the leaders of the people
of the land *and* of the earth, and causes them to wander in a
wilderness where there is no way.
25 They grope in the dark without light, and He makes them to
stagger *and* wander like a drunken man.

**13** [JOB CONTINUED:] Lo, my eye has seen all this, my ear
has heard and understood it.
2 What you know, I also know; I am not inferior to you.

## New American Standard

*Job Chides His Accusers*

12 THEN JOB responded,
2 "Truly then you are the people,
And with you wisdom will die!
3 "But I have intelligence as well as you;
I am not inferior to you.
And who does not know such things as these?
4 "I am a joke to my friends.
The one who called on God, and He answered him;
The just *and* blameless *man* is a joke.
5 "He who is at ease holds calamity in contempt,
As prepared for those whose feet slip.
6 "The tents of the destroyers prosper,
And those who provoke God are secure,
Whom God brings into [a]their power.

7¶ "But now ask the beasts, and let them teach you;
And the birds of the heavens, and let them tell you.
8 "Or speak to the earth, and let it teach you;
And let the fish of the sea declare to you.
9 "Who among all these does not know
That the hand of the LORD has done this,
10 In whose hand is the life of every living thing,
And the breath of all mankind?
11 "Does not the ear test words,
As the palate tastes its food?
12 "Wisdom is with aged men,
*With* long life is understanding.

*Job Speaks of the Power of God*

13¶ "With Him are wisdom and might;
To Him belong counsel and understanding.
14 "Behold, He tears down, and it cannot be rebuilt;
He imprisons a man, and there can be no release.
15 "Behold, He restrains the waters, and they dry up;
And He sends them out, and they inundate the earth.
16 "With Him are strength and sound wisdom,
The misled and the misleader belong to Him.
17 "He makes counselors walk barefoot,
And makes fools of judges.
18 "He loosens the bond of kings,
And binds their loins with a girdle.
19 "He makes priests walk barefoot,
And overthrows the secure ones.
20 "He deprives the trusted ones of speech,
And takes away the discernment of the elders.
21 "He pours contempt on nobles,
And loosens the belt of the strong.
22 "He reveals mysteries from the darkness,
And brings the deep darkness into light.
23 "He makes the nations great, then destroys them;
He enlarges the nations, then leads them away.
24 "He deprives of intelligence the chiefs of the earth's people,
And makes them wander in a pathless waste.
25 "They grope in darkness with no light,
And He makes them stagger like a drunken man.

*Job Says His Friends' Proverbs Are Ashes*

13 "BEHOLD, MY eye has seen all *this*,
My ear has heard and understood it.
2 "What you know I also know.
I am not inferior to you.

NAS [a] Lit., *his*

## New International

*Job*

12 THEN JOB replied:
2 "Doubtless you are the people,
and wisdom will die with you!
3 But I have a mind as well as you;
I am not inferior to you.
Who does not know all these things?

4 "I have become a laughingstock to my friends,
though I called upon God and he answered—
a mere laughingstock, though righteous and blameless!
5 Men at ease have contempt for misfortune
as the fate of those whose feet are slipping.
6 The tents of marauders are undisturbed,
and those who provoke God are secure—
those who carry their god in their hands.[b]

7 "But ask the animals, and they will teach you,
or the birds of the air, and they will tell you;
8 or speak to the earth, and it will teach you,
or let the fish of the sea inform you.
9 Which of all these does not know
that the hand of the LORD has done this?
10 In his hand is the life of every creature
and the breath of all mankind.
11 Does not the ear test words
as the tongue tastes food?
12 Is not wisdom found among the aged?
Does not long life bring understanding?

13 "To God belong wisdom and power;
counsel and understanding are his.
14 What he tears down cannot be rebuilt;
the man he imprisons cannot be released.
15 If he holds back the waters, there is drought;
if he lets them loose, they devastate the land.
16 To him belong strength and victory;
both deceived and deceiver are his.
17 He leads counselors away stripped
and makes fools of judges.
18 He takes off the shackles put on by kings
and ties a loincloth[c] around their waist.
19 He leads priests away stripped
and overthrows men long established.
20 He silences the lips of trusted advisers
and takes away the discernment of elders.
21 He pours contempt on nobles
and disarms the mighty.
22 He reveals the deep things of darkness
and brings deep shadows into the light.
23 He makes nations great, and destroys them;
he enlarges nations, and disperses them.
24 He deprives the leaders of the earth of their reason;
he sends them wandering through a trackless waste.
25 They grope in darkness with no light;
he makes them stagger like drunkards.

13 "MY EYES have seen all this,
my ears have heard and understood it.
2 What you know, I also know;
I am not inferior to you.

NIV [b] 6 Or *secure / in what God's hand brings them* [c] 18 Or *shackles of kings / and ties a belt*

## King James

3Surely I would speak to the Almighty, and I desire to reason with God.
4But ye *are* forgers of lies, ye *are* all physicians of no value.
5O that ye would altogether hold your peace! and it should be your wisdom.
6Hear now my reasoning, and hearken to the pleadings of my lips.
7Will ye speak wickedly for God? and talk deceitfully for him?
8Will ye accept his person? will ye contend for God?
9Is it good that he should search you out? or as one man mocketh another, do ye *so* mock him?
10He will surely reprove you, if ye do secretly accept persons.
11Shall not his excellency make you afraid? and his dread fall upon you?
12Your remembrances *are* like unto ashes, your bodies to bodies of clay.
13Hold your peace, let me alone, that I may speak, and let come on me what *will*.
14Wherefore do I take my flesh in my teeth, and put my life in mine hand?
15Though he slay me, yet will I trust in him: but I will maintain mine own ways before him.
16He also *shall be* my salvation: for an hypocrite shall not come before him.
17Hear diligently my speech, and my declaration with your ears.
18Behold now, I have ordered *my* cause; I know that I shall be justified.
19Who *is* he *that* will plead with me? for now, if I hold my tongue, I shall give up the ghost.
20Only do not two *things* unto me: then will I not hide myself from thee.
21Withdraw thine hand far from me: and let not thy dread make me afraid.
22Then call thou, and I will answer: or let me speak, and answer thou me.
23How many *are* mine iniquities and sins? make me to know my transgression and my sin.
24Wherefore hidest thou thy face, and holdest me for thine enemy?
25Wilt thou break a leaf driven to and fro? and wilt thou pursue the dry stubble?
26For thou writest bitter things against me, and makest me to possess the iniquities of my youth.
27Thou puttest my feet also in the stocks, and lookest narrowly unto all my paths; thou settest a print upon the heels of my feet.
28And he, as a rotten thing, consumeth, as a garment that is motheaten.

**14** MAN *THAT is* born of a woman *is* of few days, and full of trouble.
2He cometh forth like a flower, and is cut down: he fleeth also as a shadow, and continueth not.
3And dost thou open thine eyes upon such an one, and bringest me into judgment with thee?

## Amplified

3Surely I wish to speak to the Almighty, and I desire to argue *and* reason my case with God [that He may explain the conflict between what I believe of Him and what I see of Him].
4But you are forgers of lies [you defame my character most untruthfully]; you are all physicians of no value *and* have no remedy to offer.
5Oh, that you would altogether hold your peace! Then *you* would evidence your wisdom *and* might pass for wise men.
6Hear now my reasoning, and listen to the pleadings of my lips.
7Will you speak unrighteously for God, and talk deceitfully for Him?
8Will you show partiality to Him [be unjust to me in order to gain favor with Him]? Will you act as special pleaders for God?
9Would it be profitable for you if He should investigate your tactics [with me]? Or as one deceives *and* mocks a man, do you deceive *and* mock Him?
10He will surely reprove you, if you do secretly show partiality.
11Shall not His majesty make you afraid, and should not your awe for Him restrain you?
12Your memorable sayings are proverbs of ashes [valueless]; your defenses are defenses of clay [and will crumble].
13Hold your peace! Let me alone, so I may speak, and let come on me what will.
14Why should I take my flesh in my teeth, and put my life in my hand [incurring the danger of God's wrath]?
15[I do it because though He slay me, yet will I wait for and trust Him and] behold, He will slay me; I have no hope; nevertheless I will maintain *and* argue my ways before Him—even to His face.
16This will be my salvation, that a polluted *and* godless man shall not come before Him.
17Listen diligently to my speech, and let my declaration be in your ears.
18Behold now, I have prepared my case; I know that I shall be justified *and* vindicated.
19Who is he who will argue against *and* refute me? For then I would hold my peace and expire.
20Only [O Lord] grant two conditions to me, then will I not hide myself from You:
21Withdraw Your hand and this bodily suffering far from me; and let not my [reverent] dread of You terrify me.
22Then [Lord] call, and I will answer; or let me speak, and You answer me.
23How many are my iniquities and sins [that so much sorrow should come to me]? Make me recognize *and* know my transgression and my sin. [Rom. 8:1.]
24Why do You hide Your face [as if offended], and alienate me as if I were Your enemy?
25Will You harass *and* frighten a [poor, helpless] leaf driven to and fro, and will You pursue the chaff of the dry stubble?
26For You write bitter things against me [in Your bill of indictment], and make me inherit *and* be accountable now for the iniquities of my youth.
27You put my feet also in the stocks, and observe critically all my paths; You set a circle *and* limit around the soles of my feet [which I must not overstep].
28And he wastes away as a rotten thing, like a garment that is moth-eaten.

**14** MAN THAT is born of a woman is of few days and full of trouble.
2He comes forth like a flower, and withers; he flees also like a shadow, and continues not.
3And [Lord] do You open Your eyes upon such a one, and bring me into judgment with You?

## New American Standard

3¶ "But I would speak to the Almighty,
And I desire to argue with God.
4 "But you smear with lies;
You are all worthless physicians.
5 "O that you would be completely silent,
And that it would become your wisdom!
6 "Please hear my argument,
And listen to the contentions of my lips.
7 "Will you speak what is unjust for God,
And speak what is deceitful for Him?
8 "Will you show partiality for Him?
Will you contend for God?
9 "Will it be well when He examines you?
Or will you deceive Him as one deceives a man?
10 "He will surely reprove you,
If you secretly show partiality.
11 "Will not His majesty terrify you,
And the dread of Him fall on you?
12 "Your memorable sayings are proverbs of ashes,
Your defenses are defenses of clay.

*Job Is Sure He Will Be Vindicated*

13¶ "Be silent before me so that I may speak;
Then let come on me what may.
14 "Why should I take my flesh in my teeth,
And put my life in my hands?
15 "Though He slay me,
I will hope in Him.
Nevertheless I will argue my ways before Him.
16 "This also will be my salvation,
For a godless man may not come before His presence.
17 "Listen carefully to my speech,
And let my declaration *fill* your ears.
18 "Behold now, I have prepared my case;
I know that I will be vindicated.
19 "Who will contend with me?
For then I would be silent and die.
20¶ "Only two things do not do to me,
Then I will not hide from Thy face:
21 Remove Thy hand from me,
And let not the dread of Thee terrify me.
22 "Then call, and I will answer;
Or let me speak, then reply to me.
23 "How many are my iniquities and sins?
Make known to me my rebellion and my sin.
24 "Why dost Thou hide Thy face,
And consider me Thine enemy?
25 "Wilt Thou cause a driven leaf to tremble?
Or wilt Thou pursue the dry chaff?
26 "For Thou dost write bitter things against me,
And dost make me to inherit the iniquities of my youth.
27 "Thou dost put my feet in the stocks,
And dost watch all my paths;
Thou dost set a limit for the soles of my feet,
28 While I am decaying like a rotten thing,
Like a garment that is moth-eaten.

*Job Speaks of the Finality of Death*

**14** "MAN, WHO is born of woman,
Is short-lived and full of turmoil.
2 "Like a flower he comes forth and withers.
He also flees like a shadow and does not remain.
3 "Thou also dost open Thine eyes on him,
And bring him into judgment with Thyself.

## New International

3But I desire to speak to the Almighty
and to argue my case with God.
4You, however, smear me with lies;
you are worthless physicians, all of you!
5If only you would be altogether silent!
For you, that would be wisdom.
6Hear now my argument;
listen to the plea of my lips.
7Will you speak wickedly on God's behalf?
Will you speak deceitfully for him?
8Will you show him partiality?
Will you argue the case for God?
9Would it turn out well if he examined you?
Could you deceive him as you might deceive men?
10He would surely rebuke you
if you secretly showed partiality.
11Would not his splendor terrify you?
Would not the dread of him fall on you?
12Your maxims are proverbs of ashes;
your defenses are defenses of clay.
13"Keep silent and let me speak;
then let come to me what may.
14Why do I put myself in jeopardy
and take my life in my hands?
15Though he slay me, yet will I hope in him;
I will surely[a] defend my ways to his face.
16Indeed, this will turn out for my deliverance,
for no godless man would dare come before him!
17Listen carefully to my words;
let your ears take in what I say.
18Now that I have prepared my case,
I know I will be vindicated.
19Can anyone bring charges against me?
If so, I will be silent and die.
20"Only grant me these two things, O God,
and then I will not hide from you:
21Withdraw your hand far from me,
and stop frightening me with your terrors.
22Then summon me and I will answer,
or let me speak, and you reply.
23How many wrongs and sins have I committed?
Show me my offense and my sin.
24Why do you hide your face
and consider me your enemy?
25Will you torment a windblown leaf?
Will you chase after dry chaff?
26For you write down bitter things against me
and make me inherit the sins of my youth.
27You fasten my feet in shackles;
you keep close watch on all my paths
by putting marks on the soles of my feet.
28"So man wastes away like something rotten,
like a garment eaten by moths.

**14** "MAN BORN of woman
is of few days and full of trouble.
2He springs up like a flower and withers away;
like a fleeting shadow, he does not endure.
3Do you fix your eye on such a one?
Will you bring him[b] before you for judgment?

NIV [a] 15 Or *He will surely slay me; I have no hope — / yet I will* [b] 3 Septuagint, Vulgate and Syriac; Hebrew *me*

## King James

4Who can bring a clean *thing* out of an unclean? not one.
5Seeing his days *are* determined, the number of his months *are*
with thee, thou hast appointed his bounds that he cannot pass;
6Turn from him, that he may rest, till he shall accomplish, as
an hireling, his day.
7For there is hope of a tree, if it be cut down, that it will sprout
again, and that the tender branch thereof will not cease.
8Though the root thereof wax old in the earth, and the stock
thereof die in the ground;
9 *Yet* through the scent of water it will bud, and bring forth
boughs like a plant.
10But man dieth, and wasteth away: yea, man giveth up the
ghost, and where *is* he?
11 *As* the waters fail from the sea, and the flood decayeth and
drieth up:
12So man lieth down, and riseth not: till the heavens *be* no more,
they shall not awake, nor be raised out of their sleep.
13O that thou wouldest hide me in the grave, that thou wouldest keep me secret, until thy wrath be past, that thou wouldest
appoint me a set time, and remember me!
14If a man die, shall he live *again?* all the days of my appointed
time will I wait, till my change come.
15Thou shalt call, and I will answer thee: thou wilt have a desire
to the work of thine hands.
16For now thou numberest my steps: dost thou not watch over
my sin?
17My transgression *is* sealed up in a bag, and thou sewest up
mine iniquity.
18And surely the mountain falling cometh to nought, and the
rock is removed out of his place.
19The waters wear the stones: thou washest away the things
which grow *out* of the dust of the earth; and thou destroyest the
hope of man.
20Thou prevailest for ever against him, and he passeth: thou
changest his countenance, and sendest him away.
21His sons come to honour, and he knoweth *it* not; and they are
brought low, but he perceiveth *it* not of them.
22But his flesh upon him shall have pain, and his soul within
him shall mourn.

## Amplified

4Who can bring a clean thing out of an unclean? Not one. [Cf.
Isa. 1:18; I John 1:7.]
5Since a man's days are already determined and the number of
his months is wholly in Your control, and he cannot pass the
bounds of his allotted time;
6[O God] turn from him [and cease to watch him so pitilessly];
let him rest until he has accomplished as does a hireling the appointed time for his day.
7For there is hope of a tree, if it be cut down, that it will sprout
again, and that the tender shoots of it will not cease. [But there is
no such hope for man.]
8Though its root grows old in the earth, and its stock dies in the
ground,
9Yet through the scent [and breathing] of water [the stump of
the tree] will bud, and bring forth boughs like a young plant.
10But (the brave, strong) man must die and lie prostrate; yes,
man breathes his last, and where is he?
11As waters evaporate from the lake, and the river drains and
dries up,
12So man lies down and does not rise [to his former state]. Till
the heavens are no more, men will not awake, nor be raised
[physically] out of their sleep.
13O that You would hide me in Sheol [the unseen state], that
You would conceal me until Your wrath is past, that You would
set a definite time and then remember me earnestly [and imprint
me on your heart]!
14If a man die, shall he live again? All the days of my warfare
*and* service I will wait, till my change *and* release shall come. [John
5:25; 6:40; I Thess. 4:16.]
15 *Then* You would call and I would answer You; You would
yearn for [me] the work of Your hands.
16But now You number each of my steps; and take note of my
every sin.
17My transgression is sealed up in a bag, and You glue up my
iniquity [to preserve it in full for the day of reckoning].
18But as a mountain, if it falls, crumbles to nothing, and as the
rock is removed out of its place;
19As waters wear away the stones, and as floods wash away the
soil of the earth; so You, *O Lord,* destroy the hope of man.
20You prevail forever against him, and he passes on; You
change his appearance [in death], and send him away [from the
presence of the living].
21His sons come to honor, and he knows it not; they are brought
low, and he perceives it not.
22But his body [lamenting its decay in the grave] shall grieve
over him, and his soul shall mourn [over the body of clay which
it once enlivened].

## King James

**15** THEN ANSWERED Eliphaz the Temanite, and said,
2Should a wise man utter vain knowledge, and fill his
belly with the east wind?
3Should he reason with unprofitable talk? or with speeches
wherewith he can do no good?
4Yea, thou castest off fear, and restrainest prayer before God.
5For thy mouth uttereth thine iniquity, and thou choosest the
tongue of the crafty.
6Thine own mouth condemneth thee, and not I: yea, thine own
lips testify against thee.
7 *Art* thou the first man *that* was born? or wast thou made before
the hills?
8Hast thou heard the secret of God? and dost thou restrain
wisdom to thyself?

## Amplified

**15** THEN ELIPHAZ the Temanite answered [Job],
2Should a wise man utter such windy knowledge [as we
have just heard], and fill himself with the east wind [of withering,
parching and violent accusations]?
3Should he reason with unprofitable talk? Or with speeches
with which he can do no good?
4Indeed, you are doing away with (reverential) fear, and hindering *and* diminishing meditation *and* devotion before God.
5For your iniquity teaches your mouth, and you choose the
tongue of the crafty.
6Your own mouth condemns you, and not I; yes, your own lips
testify against you.
7Are you the first man that was born [the original wise man]?
Or were you created before the hills?
8Were you present to hear the secret counsel of God? And do
you limit [the possession of] wisdom to yourself?

## New American Standard

4 "Who can make the clean out of the unclean?
No one!
5 "Since his days are determined,
The number of his months is with Thee,
And his limits Thou hast set so that he cannot pass.
6 "Turn Thy gaze from him that he may rest,
Until he fulfills his day like a hired man.

7¶ "For there is hope for a tree,
When it is cut down, that it will sprout again,
And its shoots will not fail.
8 "Though its roots grow old in the ground,
And its stump dies in the dry soil,
9 At the scent of water it will flourish
And put forth sprigs like a plant.
10 "But man dies and lies prostrate.
Man expires, and where is he?
11 "*As* water evaporates from the sea,
And a river becomes parched and dried up,
12 So man lies down and does not rise.
Until the heavens be no more,
He will not awake nor be aroused out of his sleep.

13¶ "Oh that Thou wouldst hide me in Sheol,
That Thou wouldst conceal me until Thy wrath returns *to Thee,*
That Thou wouldst set a limit for me and remember me!
14 "If a man dies, will he live *again?*
All the days of my struggle I will wait,
Until my change comes.
15 "Thou wilt call, and I will answer Thee;
Thou wilt long for the work of Thy hands.
16 "For now Thou dost number my steps,
Thou dost not observe my sin.
17 "My transgression is sealed up in a bag,
And Thou dost wrap up my iniquity.

18¶ "But the falling mountain crumbles away,
And the rock moves from its place;
19 Water wears away stones,
Its torrents wash away the dust of the earth;
So Thou dost destroy man's hope.
20 "Thou dost forever overpower him and he departs;
*Thou* dost change his appearance and send him away.
21 "His sons achieve honor, but he does not know *it;*
Or they become insignificant, but he does not perceive it.
22 "But his body pains him,
And he mourns only for himself."

*Eliphaz Says Job Presumes Much*

15 THEN ELIPHAZ the Temanite responded,
2 "Should a wise man answer with windy knowledge,
And fill himself with the east wind?
3 "Should he argue with useless talk,
Or with words which are not profitable?
4 "Indeed, you do away with reverence,
And hinder meditation before God.
5 "For your guilt teaches your mouth,
And you choose the language of the crafty.
6 "Your own mouth condemns you, and not I;
And your own lips testify against you.

7¶ "Were you the first man to be born,
Or were you brought forth before the hills?
8 "Do you hear the secret counsel of God,
And limit wisdom to yourself?

## New International

4Who can bring what is pure from the impure?
No one!
5Man's days are determined;
you have decreed the number of his months
and have set limits he cannot exceed.
6So look away from him and let him alone,
till he has put in his time like a hired man.

7"At least there is hope for a tree:
If it is cut down, it will sprout again,
and its new shoots will not fail.
8Its roots may grow old in the ground
and its stump die in the soil,
9yet at the scent of water it will bud
and put forth shoots like a plant.
10But man dies and is laid low;
he breathes his last and is no more.
11As water disappears from the sea
or a riverbed becomes parched and dry,
12so man lies down and does not rise;
till the heavens are no more, men will not awake
or be roused from their sleep.

13"If only you would hide me in the grave[a]
and conceal me till your anger has passed!
If only you would set me a time
and then remember me!
14If a man dies, will he live again?
All the days of my hard service
I will wait for my renewal[b] to come.
15You will call and I will answer you;
you will long for the creature your hands have made.
16Surely then you will count my steps
but not keep track of my sin.
17My offenses will be sealed up in a bag;
you will cover over my sin.

18"But as a mountain erodes and crumbles
and as a rock is moved from its place,
19as water wears away stones
and torrents wash away the soil,
so you destroy man's hope.
20You overpower him once for all, and he is gone;
you change his countenance and send him away.
21If his sons are honored, he does not know it;
if they are brought low, he does not see it.
22He feels but the pain of his own body
and mourns only for himself."

*Eliphaz*

15 THEN ELIPHAZ the Temanite replied:
2"Would a wise man answer with empty notions
or fill his belly with the hot east wind?
3Would he argue with useless words,
with speeches that have no value?
4But you even undermine piety
and hinder devotion to God.
5Your sin prompts your mouth;
you adopt the tongue of the crafty.
6Your own mouth condemns you, not mine;
your own lips testify against you.

7"Are you the first man ever born?
Were you brought forth before the hills?
8Do you listen in on God's council?
Do you limit wisdom to yourself?

NIV [a] 13 Hebrew *Sheol* [b] 14 Or *release*

## King James

9What knowest thou, that we know not? *what* understandest
thou, which *is* not in us?
10With us *are* both the grayheaded and very aged men, much
elder than thy father.
11 *Are* the consolations of God small with thee? is there any
secret thing with thee?
12Why doth thine heart carry thee away? and what do thy eyes
wink at,
13That thou turnest thy spirit against God, and lettest *such*
words go out of thy mouth?
14What *is* man, that he should be clean? and *he which is* born of
a woman, that he should be righteous?
15Behold, he putteth no trust in his saints; yea, the heavens are
not clean in his sight.
16How much more abominable and filthy *is* man, which
drinketh iniquity like water?
17I will show thee, hear me; and that *which* I have seen I will
declare;
18Which wise men have told from their fathers, and have not
hid *it*:
19Unto whom alone the earth was given, and no stranger
passed among them.
20The wicked man travaileth with pain all *his* days, and the
number of years is hidden to the oppressor.
21A dreadful sound *is* in his ears: in prosperity the destroyer
shall come upon him.
22He believeth not that he shall return out of darkness, and he
is waited for of the sword.
23He wandereth abroad for bread, *saying*, Where *is it?* he
knoweth that the day of darkness is ready at his hand.
24Trouble and anguish shall make him afraid; they shall prevail
against him, as a king ready to the battle.
25For he stretcheth out his hand against God, and strengtheneth himself against the Almighty.
26He runneth upon him, *even* on *his* neck, upon the thick bosses
of his bucklers:
27Because he covereth his face with his fatness, and maketh
collops of fat on *his* flanks.
28And he dwelleth in desolate cities, *and* in houses which no
man inhabiteth, which are ready to become heaps.
29He shall not be rich, neither shall his substance continue,
neither shall he prolong the perfection thereof upon the earth.
30He shall not depart out of darkness; the flame shall dry up his
branches, and by the breath of his mouth shall he go away.
31Let not him that is deceived trust in vanity: for vanity shall be
his recompence.
32It shall be accomplished before his time, and his branch shall
not be green.
33He shall shake off his unripe grape as the vine, and shall cast
off his flower as the olive.
34For the congregation of hypocrites *shall be* desolate, and fire
shall consume the tabernacles of bribery.
35They conceive mischief, and bring forth vanity, and their belly
prepareth deceit.

## Amplified

9What do you know that we know not? What do you understand that is not equally clear to us?
10Among us are both the gray-haired and the aged, older than
your father by far.
11Are God's consolations [as we have interpreted them to you]
too trivial for you? Is there any secret thing [any bosom sin] which
you have not given up? *Or* were we too gentle [in our first speech]
toward you to be effective?
12Why does your heart carry you away [why allow yourself to
be controlled by feeling]? And why do your eyes flash [in anger
or contempt],
13That you turn your spirit against God, and let [such] words
[as you have spoken] go out of your mouth?
14What is man, that he can be pure *and* clean? And he who is
born of a woman, that he can be right *and* just?
15Behold, [God] puts no trust in His holy ones [the angels];
indeed, the heavens are not clean in His sight.
16How much less that which is abominable and corrupt, a man
who drinks iniquity like water?
17I will show you, hear me; and that which I have seen I will
relate,
18What wise men have not hid but have freely communicated;
it was told to them by their fathers,
19Unto whom alone the land was given, and no stranger intrud-
ed *or* passed among them [corrupting the truth].
20The wicked man suffers with (self-inflicted) torment all his
days, through all the years that are numbered *and* laid up for him,
the oppressor.
21A [dreadful] sound of terrors is in his ears; in prosperity the
destroyer shall come upon him [the dwellings of robbers are not
at peace].
22He believes that he will not return out of darkness, and [be-
cause of his guilt] he is waited for by the sword [of God's ven-
geance].
23He wanders abroad for food, saying, Where is it? He knows
that the day of darkness *and* destruction is already close upon him.
24Distress and anguish terrify him; [he knows] they shall prevail
against him, as a king ready for battle.
25Because he has stretched out his hand against God, and bids
defiance *and* behaves himself proudly against the Almighty,
26Running stubbornly against Him with a thickly ornamented
shield;
27Because he has covered his face with his fat, adding layers of
fat on his loins [giving himself up to animal pleasures];
28And has lived in desolate [God-forsaken] cities, *and* in houses
which no man should inhabit, which were destined to become
heaps [of ruins];
29He shall not be rich, neither shall his wealth last, neither shall
his produce bend to the earth *or* his possessions be extended on
the earth.
30He shall not depart out of darkness [and escape from calamity;
the wrath of God] shall consume him as flame consumes a dry tree,
and by the blast of His mouth he shall be swept away.
31Let him not deceive himself *and* trust in vanity—emptiness,
falseness and futility; for these shall be his recompense [for such
living].
32It shall be accomplished *and* paid in full while he still lives, and
his branch shall not be green [but shall wither away].
33He shall fail to bring his grapes to maturity [leaving them to
wither unnourished] on the vine, and shall cast off blossoms as the
olive tree [and fail of fruit].
34For the company of the godless shall be barren, and fire shall
consume the tents of bribery [wrong and injustice].
35They conceive mischief, and bring forth iniquity, and their
inmost soul hatches deceit.

## New American Standard

9 "What do you know that we do not know?
*What* do you understand that we do not?
10 "Both the gray-haired and the aged are among us,
Older than your father.
11 "Are the consolations of God too small for you,
Even the word *spoken* gently with you?
12 "Why does your heart carry you away?
And why do your eyes flash,
13 That you should turn your spirit against God,
And allow *such* words to go out of your mouth?
14 "What is man, that he should be pure,
Or he who is born of a woman, that he should be righteous?
15 "Behold, He puts no trust in His holy ones,
And the heavens are not pure in His sight;
16 How much less one who is detestable and corrupt,
Man, who drinks iniquity like water!

*What Eliphaz Has Seen of Life*

17¶ "I will tell you, listen to me;
And what I have seen I will also declare;
18 What wise men have told,
And have not concealed from their fathers,
19 To whom alone the land was given,
And no alien passed among them.
20 "The wicked man writhes in pain all *his* days,
And numbered are the years stored up for the ruthless.
21 "Sounds of terror are in his ears,
While at peace the destroyer comes upon him.
22 "He does not believe that he will return from darkness,
And he is destined for the sword.
23 "He wanders about for food, saying, 'Where is it?'
He knows that a day of darkness is at hand.
24 "Distress and anguish terrify him,
They overpower him like a king ready for the attack,
25 Because he has stretched out his hand against God,
And conducts himself arrogantly against the Almighty.
26 "He rushes headlong at Him
With his massive shield.
27 "For he has covered his face with his fat,
And made his thighs heavy with flesh.
28 "And he has lived in desolate cities,
In houses no one would inhabit,
Which are destined to become ruins.
29 "He will not become rich, nor will his wealth endure;
And his grain will not bend down to the ground.
30 "He will not escape from darkness;
The flame will wither his shoots,
And by the breath of His mouth he will go away.
31 "Let him not trust in emptiness, deceiving himself;
For emptiness will be his reward.
32 "It will be accomplished before his time,
And his palm branch will not be green.
33 "He will drop off his unripe grape like the vine,
And will cast off his flower like the olive tree.
34 "For the company of the godless is barren,
And fire consumes the tents of the corrupt.
35 "They conceive mischief and bring forth iniquity,
And their mind prepares deception."

## New International

9 What do you know that we do not know?
What insights do you have that we do not have?
10 The gray-haired and the aged are on our side,
men even older than your father.
11 Are God's consolations not enough for you,
words spoken gently to you?
12 Why has your heart carried you away,
and why do your eyes flash,
13 so that you vent your rage against God
and pour out such words from your mouth?

14 "What is man, that he could be pure,
or one born of woman, that he could be righteous?
15 If God places no trust in his holy ones,
if even the heavens are not pure in his eyes,
16 how much less man, who is vile and corrupt,
who drinks up evil like water!

17 "Listen to me and I will explain to you;
let me tell you what I have seen,
18 what wise men have declared,
hiding nothing received from their fathers
19 (to whom alone the land was given
when no alien passed among them):
20 All his days the wicked man suffers torment,
the ruthless through all the years stored up for him.
21 Terrifying sounds fill his ears;
when all seems well, marauders attack him.
22 He despairs of escaping the darkness;
he is marked for the sword.
23 He wanders about—food for vultures[a];
he knows the day of darkness is at hand.
24 Distress and anguish fill him with terror;
they overwhelm him, like a king poised to attack,
25 because he shakes his fist at God
and vaunts himself against the Almighty,
26 defiantly charging against him
with a thick, strong shield.

27 "Though his face is covered with fat
and his waist bulges with flesh,
28 he will inhabit ruined towns
and houses where no one lives,
houses crumbling to rubble.
29 He will no longer be rich and his wealth will not endure,
nor will his possessions spread over the land.
30 He will not escape the darkness;
a flame will wither his shoots,
and the breath of God's mouth will carry him away.
31 Let him not deceive himself by trusting what is worthless,
for he will get nothing in return.
32 Before his time he will be paid in full,
and his branches will not flourish.
33 He will be like a vine stripped of its unripe grapes,
like an olive tree shedding its blossoms.
34 For the company of the godless will be barren,
and fire will consume the tents of those who love bribes.
35 They conceive trouble and give birth to evil;
their womb fashions deceit."

NIV [a] 23 Or *about, looking for food*

## King James

**16** THEN JOB answered and said,

2 I have heard many such things: miserable comforters *are* ye all.

3 Shall vain words have an end? or what emboldeneth thee that thou answerest?

4 I also could speak as ye *do:* if your soul were in my soul's stead, I could heap up words against you, and shake mine head at you.

5 *But* I would strengthen you with my mouth, and the moving of my lips should assuage *your grief.*

6 Though I speak, my grief is not assuaged: and *though* I forbear, what am I eased?

7 But now he hath made me weary: thou hast made desolate all my company.

8 And thou hast filled me with wrinkles, *which* is a witness *against me:* and my leanness rising up in me beareth witness to my face.

9 He teareth *me* in his wrath, who hateth me: he gnasheth upon me with his teeth; mine enemy sharpeneth his eyes upon me.

10 They have gaped upon me with their mouth; they have smitten me upon the cheek reproachfully; they have gathered themselves together against me.

11 God hath delivered me to the ungodly, and turned me over into the hands of the wicked.

12 I was at ease, but he hath broken me asunder: he hath also taken *me* by my neck, and shaken me to pieces, and set me up for his mark.

13 His archers compass me round about, he cleaveth my reins asunder, and doth not spare; he poureth out my gall upon the ground.

14 He breaketh me with breach upon breach, he runneth upon me like a giant.

15 I have sewed sackcloth upon my skin, and defiled my horn in the dust.

16 My face is foul with weeping, and on my eyelids *is* the shadow of death;

17 Not for *any* injustice in mine hands: also my prayer *is* pure.

18 O earth, cover not thou my blood, and let my cry have no place.

19 Also now, behold, my witness *is* in heaven, and my record *is* on high.

20 My friends scorn me: *but* mine eye poureth out *tears* unto God.

21 O that one might plead for a man with God, as a man *pleadeth* for his neighbour!

22 When a few years are come, then I shall go the way *whence* I shall not return.

## Amplified

**16** THEN JOB answered,

2 I have heard many such things; wearisome *and* miserable comforters are you all!

3 Will your futile words of wind have no end? Or what makes you so bold to answer [me like this]?

4 I also could speak as you do; if you were in my stead, I could join words together against you, and shake my head at you.

5 *But* I would strengthen *and* encourage you with [the words of] my mouth, and the consolation of my lips would soothe your suffering.

6 If I speak [to you miserable comforters], my sorrow is not soothed *or* lessened; and if I refrain [from speaking], in what way am I eased? [I hardly know whether to answer you or be silent.]

7 But now [God] has taken away my strength. You [O Lord] have made desolate all my family *and* associates.

8 You have laid fast hold on me *and* have shriveled me up, which is a witness against me; and my leanness [and wretched state of body] are further evidence [against me]; [they] testify to my face.

9 [[a]My adversary Satan] has torn [me] in his wrath, and hated *and* persecuted me; he has gnashed upon me with his teeth; my adversary sharpens his eyes against me.

10 [The forces of evil] have gaped at me with their mouth; they have struck me upon the cheek insolently; they massed themselves together *and* conspired unanimously against me. [Ps. 22:13; 35:21.]

11 God has delivered me to the ungodly [to the evil one] and cast me [headlong] into the hands of the wicked [Satan's host].

12 I was living at ease, but [Satan] crushed me *and* broke me apart; yes, he seized me by the neck and dashed me in pieces, then set me up for his target.

13 [Satan's] arrows whiz around me; he slashes open my vitals, and does not spare; he pours out my gall on the ground.

14 [Satan] stabs me, making breach after breach *and* attacking again and again; he runs at me like a giant *and* irresistible warrior.

15 I have sewed sackcloth over my skin [as a sign of mourning], and have defiled my horn—my [insignia of] strength—in the dust.

16 My face is red *and* swollen with weeping, and on my eyelids is the shadow of death—my eyes are dimmed;

17 Although there is no guilt *or* violence in my hands, and my prayer is pure.

18 O earth, cover not my blood, and let my cry have no resting place [where it will cease being heard].

19 Even now, behold, my Witness is in Heaven, and He who vouches for me is on high. [Rom. 1:9.]

20 My friends scorn me, but my eye pours out tears to God.

21 O that *there were* one *who* might plead for a man with God *and* that he would maintain his right with Him, as a son of man pleads with *or* for his neighbor! [I Tim. 2:5.]

22 For when a few years are come, I shall go the way from which I shall not return.

**AMP** [a] The next six verses leave the casual reader at a loss to know of whom Job is speaking—of God, of Eliphaz, or of Satan, each of whom has been the choice of various translators and commentators. But careful study of the text itself, particularly the eleventh verse, seems to leave no question that while Job is blaming God for abandoning him to Satanic forces, nevertheless the monstrous, appalling and disgusting behavior which Job describes is by him being attributed to Satan himself. Verse eleven in any translation seems to reveal what the reader has known all along, but which Job only now sees. He still does not understand God's motive, but he is facing the facts as they are: he is at the mercy of Satan! But God's thrilling and rewarding motive is still unknown to him.

## New American Standard

*Job Says Friends Are Sorry Comforters*

**16** THEN JOB answered,
2 "I have heard many such things;
Sorry comforters are you all.
3 "Is there *no* limit to windy words?
Or what plagues you that you answer?
4 "I too could speak like you,
If I were in your place.
I could compose words against you,
And shake my head at you.
5 "I could strengthen you with my mouth,
And the solace of my lips could lessen *your pain.*

*Job Says God Shattered Him*

6¶ "If I speak, my pain is not lessened,
And if I hold back, what has left me?
7 "But now He has exhausted me;
Thou hast laid waste all my company.
8 "And Thou hast shriveled me up,
It has become a witness;
And my leanness rises up against me,
It testifies to my face.
9 "His anger has torn me and hunted me down,
He has gnashed at me with His teeth;
My adversary glares at me.
10 "They have gaped at me with their mouth,
They have slapped me on the cheek with contempt;
They have massed themselves against me.
11 "God hands me over to ruffians,
And tosses me into the hands of the wicked.
12 "I was at ease, but He shattered me,
And He has grasped me by the neck and shaken me to pieces;
He has also set me up as His target.
13 "His arrows surround me.
Without mercy He splits my kidneys open;
He pours out my gall on the ground.
14 "He breaks through me with breach after breach;
He runs at me like a warrior.
15 "I have sewed sackcloth over my skin,
And thrust my horn in the dust.
16 "My face is flushed from weeping,
And deep darkness is on my eyelids,
17 Although there is no violence in my hands,
And my prayer is pure.
18¶ "O earth, do not cover my blood,
And let there be no *resting* place for my cry.
19 "Even now, behold, my witness is in heaven,
And my advocate is on high.
20 "My friends are my scoffers;
My eye weeps to God.
21 "O that a man might plead with God
As a man with his neighbor!
22 "For when a few years are past,
I shall go the way of no return.

## New International

*Job*

**16** THEN JOB replied:

2 "I have heard many things like these;
miserable comforters are you all!
3 Will your long-winded speeches never end?
What ails you that you keep on arguing?
4 I also could speak like you,
if you were in my place;
I could make fine speeches against you
and shake my head at you.
5 But my mouth would encourage you;
comfort from my lips would bring you relief.

6 "Yet if I speak, my pain is not relieved;
and if I refrain, it does not go away.
7 Surely, O God, you have worn me out;
you have devastated my entire household.
8 You have bound me—and it has become a witness;
my gauntness rises up and testifies against me.
9 God assails me and tears me in his anger
and gnashes his teeth at me;
my opponent fastens on me his piercing eyes.
10 Men open their mouths to jeer at me;
they strike my cheek in scorn
and unite together against me.
11 God has turned me over to evil men
and thrown me into the clutches of the wicked.
12 All was well with me, but he shattered me;
he seized me by the neck and crushed me.
He has made me his target;
13 his archers surround me.
Without pity, he pierces my kidneys
and spills my gall on the ground.
14 Again and again he bursts upon me;
he rushes at me like a warrior.

15 "I have sewed sackcloth over my skin
and buried my brow in the dust.
16 My face is red with weeping,
deep shadows ring my eyes;
17 yet my hands have been free of violence
and my prayer is pure.

18 "O earth, do not cover my blood;
may my cry never be laid to rest!
19 Even now my witness is in heaven;
my advocate is on high.
20 My intercessor is my friend[b]
as my eyes pour out tears to God;
21 on behalf of a man he pleads with God
as a man pleads for his friend.

22 "Only a few years will pass
before I go on the journey of no return.

NIV [b] 20 Or *My friends treat me with scorn*

## King James

17 MY BREATH is corrupt, my days are extinct, the graves
*are ready* for me.
2 *Are there* not mockers with me? and doth not mine eye continue in their provocation?
3Lay down now, put me in a surety with thee; who *is* he *that*
will strike hands with me?
4For thou hast hid their heart from understanding: therefore
shalt thou not exalt *them*.
5He that speaketh flattery to *his* friends, even the eyes of his
children shall fail.
6He hath made me also a byword of the people; and aforetime
I was as a tabret.
7Mine eye also is dim by reason of sorrow, and all my members
*are* as a shadow.
8Upright *men* shall be astonied at this, and the innocent shall stir
up himself against the hypocrite.
9The righteous also shall hold on his way, and he that hath
clean hands shall be stronger and stronger.
10But as for you all, do ye return, and come now: for I cannot
find *one* wise *man* among you.
11My days are past, my purposes are broken off, *even* the
thoughts of my heart.
12They change the night into day: the light *is* short because of
darkness.
13If I wait, the grave *is* mine house: I have made my bed in the
darkness.
14I have said to corruption, Thou *art* my father: to the worm,
*Thou art* my mother, and my sister.
15And where *is* now my hope? as for my hope, who shall see
it?
16They shall go down to the bars of the pit, when *our* rest
together *is* in the dust.

18 THEN ANSWERED Bildad the Shuhite, and said,
2How long *will it be ere* ye make an end of words? mark,
and afterwards we will speak.
3Wherefore are we counted as beasts, *and* reputed vile in your
sight?
4He teareth himself in his anger: shall the earth be forsaken for
thee? and shall the rock be removed out of his place?
5Yea, the light of the wicked shall be put out, and the spark of
his fire shall not shine.
6The light shall be dark in his tabernacle, and his candle shall
be put out with him.
7The steps of his strength shall be straitened, and his own
counsel shall cast him down.
8For he is cast into a net by his own feet, and he walketh upon
a snare.
9The gin shall take *him* by the heel, *and* the robber shall prevail
against him.
10The snare *is* laid for him in the ground, and a trap for him in
the way.
11Terrors shall make him afraid on every side, and shall drive
him to his feet.
12His strength shall be hungerbitten, and destruction *shall be*
ready at his side.
13It shall devour the strength of his skin: *even* the firstborn of
death shall devour his strength.

## Amplified

17 MY SPIRIT is broken; my days are spent—snuffed out; the
grave is ready for me.
2Surely there are mockers *and* mockery around me, and my eye
dwells on their obstinacy, insults *and* resistance.
3Give me a pledge with Yourself [acknowledge my innocence
before my death]; who is there that will give security for me?
4But their heart [Lord] You have closed to understanding,
therefore You will not let them triumph [by giving them a verdict
against me].
5He who denounces his friends [in order to make them] a prey
*and* get a share, the eyes of his children shall fail [to find food].
6But He has made me a byword of the people, and they spit
before my face.
7My eye has grown dim because of grief, and all my members
are [wasted away] like a shadow.
8Upright men shall be astonished *and* appalled at this, and the
innocent shall stir himself up against the godless *and* polluted.
9Yet shall the righteous—those upright and in right standing
with God—hold to his way, and he who has clean hands shall
grow stronger and stronger. [Ps. 24:4.]
10But as for you, come on again, all of you, though I find not
a wise man among you.
11My days are past, my purposes *and* plans are frustrated; even
the thoughts (desires and possessions) of my heart *are broken off*.
12These [thoughts] extend from the night into the day, [so that]
the light is short because of darkness.
13But if I look to Sheol [the unseen state] as my abode, if I spread
my couch in the darkness,
14If I say to the grave *and* corruption, You are my father, and
to the worm [that feeds on decay], You are my mother and my
sister [because I will soon be closest to you],
15Where then is my hope? And, if I have hope, who will see [its
fulfillment]?
16[My hope] shall go down to the bars of Sheol [the unseen
world], when once there is rest in the dust.

18 THEN BILDAD the Shuhite answered,
2How long will you lay snares for words *and* have to hunt
for your argument? Do some clear thinking, and then we will
reply.
3Why are we counted as beasts [as if we had no sense]? Why
are we unclean in your sight?
4You who tear yourself in your anger, shall the earth be forsak-
en for you, or the rock be removed out of its place?
5Yes, the light of the wicked shall be put out, and the flame of
his fire shall not shine. [Prov. 13:9; 24:20.]
6The light shall be dark in his dwelling, and his lamp beside him
shall be put out. [Ps. 18:28.]
7The steps of his strength shall be shortened, and his own
counsel *and* the plans in which he trusted shall bring about his
downfall.
8For the wicked is cast into a net by his own feet, and he walks
upon a lattice-covered pit.
9A trap will catch him by the heel, and a snare shall lay hold
on him.
10A noose is hid for him on the ground, and a trap for him in
the way.
11Terrors shall make him afraid on every side, and shall chase
him at his heels.
12The strength [of the wicked] shall be hunger-bitten, and
calamity ready at his side *if* he halts.
13By disease his strength *and* his skin shall be devoured; the
first-born of death [the worst of diseases] shall consume his limbs.

## New American Standard

*Job Says He Has Become a Byword*

17 "MY SPIRIT is broken, my days are extinguished,
The grave is *ready* for me.
2 "Surely mockers are with me,
And my eye gazes on their provocation.

3¶ "Lay down, now, a pledge for me with Thyself;
Who is there that will be my guarantor?
4 "For Thou hast kept their heart from understanding;
Therefore Thou wilt not exalt *them.*
5 "He who informs against friends for a share *of the spoil,*
The eyes of his children also shall languish.

6¶ "But He has made me a byword of the people,
And I am one at whom men spit.
7 "My eye has also grown dim because of grief,
And all my members are as a shadow.
8 "The upright shall be appalled at this,
And the innocent shall stir up himself against the godless.
9 "Nevertheless the righteous shall hold to his way,
And he who has clean hands shall grow stronger and stronger.
10 "But come again all of you now,
For I do not find a wise man among you.
11 "My days are past, my plans are torn apart,
*Even* the wishes of my heart.
12 "They make night into day, *saying,*
'The light is near,' in the presence of darkness.
13 "If I look for Sheol as my home,
I make my bed in the darkness;
14 If I call to the pit, 'You are my father';
To the worm, 'my mother and my sister';
15 Where now is my hope?
And who regards my hope?
16 "Will it go down with me to Sheol?
Shall we together go down into the dust?"

*Bildad Speaks of the Wicked*

18 THEN BILDAD the Shuhite responded,
2 "How long will you hunt for words?
Show understanding and then we can talk.
3 "Why are we regarded as beasts,
As stupid in your eyes?
4 "O you who tear yourself in your anger—
For your sake is the earth to be abandoned,
Or the rock to be moved from its place?

5¶ "Indeed, the light of the wicked goes out,
And the flame of his fire gives no light.
6 "The light in his tent is darkened,
And his lamp goes out above him.
7 "His vigorous stride is shortened,
And his own scheme brings him down.
8 "For he is thrown into the net by his own feet,
And he steps on the webbing.
9 "A snare seizes *him* by the heel,
*And* a trap snaps shut on him.
10 "A noose for him is hidden in the ground,
And a trap for him on the path.
11 "All around terrors frighten him,
And harry him at every step.
12 "His strength is famished,
And calamity is ready at his side.
13 "His skin is devoured by disease,
The first-born of death devours his limbs.

## New International

17 MY SPIRIT is broken,
my days are cut short,
the grave awaits me.
2 Surely mockers surround me;
my eyes must dwell on their hostility.

3 "Give me, O God, the pledge you demand.
Who else will put up security for me?
4 You have closed their minds to understanding;
therefore you will not let them triumph.
5 If a man denounces his friends for reward,
the eyes of his children will fail.

6 "God has made me a byword to everyone,
a man in whose face people spit.
7 My eyes have grown dim with grief;
my whole frame is but a shadow.
8 Upright men are appalled at this;
the innocent are aroused against the ungodly.
9 Nevertheless, the righteous will hold to their ways,
and those with clean hands will grow stronger.

10 "But come on, all of you, try again!
I will not find a wise man among you.
11 My days have passed, my plans are shattered,
and so are the desires of my heart.
12 These men turn night into day;
in the face of darkness they say, 'Light is near.'
13 If the only home I hope for is the grave,[a]
if I spread out my bed in darkness,
14 if I say to corruption, 'You are my father,'
and to the worm, 'My mother' or 'My sister,'
15 where then is my hope?
Who can see any hope for me?
16 Will it go down to the gates of death[b]?
Will we descend together into the dust?"

*Bildad*

18 THEN BILDAD the Shuhite replied:
2 "When will you end these speeches?
Be sensible, and then we can talk.
3 Why are we regarded as cattle
and considered stupid in your sight?
4 You who tear yourself to pieces in your anger,
is the earth to be abandoned for your sake?
Or must the rocks be moved from their place?

5 "The lamp of the wicked is snuffed out;
the flame of his fire stops burning.
6 The light in his tent becomes dark;
the lamp beside him goes out.
7 The vigor of his step is weakened;
his own schemes throw him down.
8 His feet thrust him into a net
and he wanders into its mesh.
9 A trap seizes him by the heel;
a snare holds him fast.
10 A noose is hidden for him on the ground;
a trap lies in his path.
11 Terrors startle him on every side
and dog his every step.
12 Calamity is hungry for him;
disaster is ready for him when he falls.
13 It eats away parts of his skin;
death's firstborn devours his limbs.

NIV [a] 13 Hebrew *Sheol* [b] 16 Hebrew *Sheol*

## King James

14His confidence shall be rooted out of his tabernacle, and it shall bring him to the king of terrors.

15It shall dwell in his tabernacle, because *it is* none of his: brimstone shall be scattered upon his habitation.

16His roots shall be dried up beneath, and above shall his branch be cut off.

17His remembrance shall perish from the earth, and he shall have no name in the street.

18He shall be driven from light into darkness, and chased out of the world.

19He shall neither have son nor nephew among his people, nor any remaining in his dwellings.

20They that come after *him* shall be astonied at his day, as they that went before were affrighted.

21Surely such *are* the dwellings of the wicked, and this *is* the place *of him that* knoweth not God.

**19** THEN JOB answered and said,

2How long will ye vex my soul, and break me in pieces with words?

3These ten times have ye reproached me: ye are not ashamed *that* ye make yourselves strange to me.

4And be it indeed *that* I have erred, mine error remaineth with myself.

5If indeed ye will magnify *yourselves* against me, and plead against me my reproach:

6Know now that God hath overthrown me, and hath compassed me with his net.

7Behold, I cry out of wrong, but I am not heard: I cry aloud, but *there is* no judgment.

8He hath fenced up my way that I cannot pass, and he hath set darkness in my paths.

9He hath stripped me of my glory, and taken the crown *from* my head.

10He hath destroyed me on every side, and I am gone: and mine hope hath he removed like a tree.

11He hath also kindled his wrath against me, and he counteth me unto him as *one of* his enemies.

12His troops come together, and raise up their way against me, and encamp round about my tabernacle.

13He hath put my brethren far from me, and mine acquaintance are verily estranged from me.

14My kinsfolk have failed, and my familiar friends have forgotten me.

15They that dwell in mine house, and my maids, count me for a stranger: I am an alien in their sight.

16I called my servant, and he gave *me* no answer; I entreated him with my mouth.

17My breath is strange to my wife, though I entreated for the children's *sake* of mine own body.

18Yea, young children despised me; I arose, and they spake against me.

19All my inward friends abhorred me: and they whom I loved are turned against me.

20My bone cleaveth to my skin and to my flesh, and I am escaped with the skin of my teeth.

21Have pity upon me, have pity upon me, O ye my friends; for the hand of God hath touched me.

## Amplified

14He shall be rooted out of his dwelling place in which he trusted, and he shall be brought to [death] the king of terrors.

15There shall dwell in his tent that which is none of his [family]; sulphur shall be scattered over his dwelling [to purify it after his going].

16The roots [of the wicked] shall be dried up beneath, and above shall his branch be cut off *and* wither.

17His remembrance shall perish from the earth, and he shall have no name in the street.

18He shall be thrust from light into darkness, and driven out of the world.

19He shall neither have son nor grandson among his people, nor any remaining were he sojourned.

20They [of the west] that come after [the wicked man] shall be astonished *and* appalled at his day, as they [of the east] that went before were seized with horror.

21Surely such are the dwellings of the ungodly, and such is the place of him who knows not (recognizes not, and honors not) God.

**19** THEN JOB answered:

2How long will you vex *and* torment me, and break me in pieces with words?

3These ten times you have reproached me; you are not ashamed that you make yourselves strange [harden yourselves against me and deal severely with me].

4And if it were true that I have erred, my error would remain with me [I would be conscious of it].

5If indeed you magnify yourselves against me, and plead against me my reproach *and* humiliation,

6Know that God has overthrown *and* put me in the wrong, and has closed His net about me.

7Behold, I cry out, Violence! But I am not heard; I cry aloud for help, but there is no justice.

8He has walled up my way, so that I cannot pass, and He has set darkness upon my paths.

9He has stripped me of my glory, and taken the crown from my head.

10He has broken me down on every side, and I am gone; my hope has He pulled up like a tree.

11He has also kindled His wrath against me, and He counts me as one of His adversaries.

12His troops come together, and cast up their way *and* siege-works against me, and encamp round about my tent.

13He has put my brethren far from me, and my acquaintances are wholly estranged from me.

14My kinsfolk have failed me, and my familiar friends have forgotten me.

15Those who live temporarily in my house, and my maids, count me for a stranger; I am an alien in their sight.

16I call to my servant, and he gives me no answer, though I beseech him with words.

17I am repulsive to my wife and loathsome to the children of my own mother.

18Even young children despise me; when I get up they speak against me.

19All the men of my council *and* my familiar friends abhor me; those whom I loved are turned against me.

20My bone clings to my skin and to my flesh, and I have escaped with the skin *or* gums of my teeth.

21Have pity on me! Have pity on me, O you my friends, for the hand of God has touched me!

## New American Standard

14 "He is torn from the security of his tent,
And they march him before the king of terrors.
15 "There dwells in his tent nothing of his;
Brimstone is scattered on his habitation.
16 "His roots are dried below,
And his branch is cut off above.
17 "Memory of him perishes from the earth,
And he has no name abroad.
18 "He is driven from light into darkness,
And chased from the inhabited world.
19 "He has no offspring or posterity among his people,
Nor any survivor where he sojourned.
20 "Those in the west are appalled at his fate,
And those in the east are seized with horror.
21 "Surely such are the dwellings of the wicked,
And this is the place of him who does not know God."

*Job Feels Insulted*

**19** THEN JOB responded,
2 "How long will you torment me,
And crush me with words?
3 "These ten times you have insulted me,
You are not ashamed to wrong me.
4 "Even if I have truly erred,
My error lodges with me.
5 "If indeed you vaunt yourselves against me,
And prove my disgrace to me,
6 Know then that God has wronged me,
And has closed His net around me.

*Everything Is against Him*

7¶ "Behold, I cry, 'Violence!' but I get no answer;
I shout for help, but there is no justice.
8 "He has walled up my way so that I cannot pass;
And He has put darkness on my paths.
9 "He has stripped my honor from me,
And removed the crown from my head.
10 "He breaks me down on every side, and I am gone;
And He has uprooted my hope like a tree.
11 "He has also kindled His anger against me,
And considered me as His enemy.
12 "His troops come together,
And build up their way against me,
And camp around my tent.
13¶ "He has removed my brothers far from me,
And my acquaintances are completely estranged from me.
14 "My relatives have failed,
And my intimate friends have forgotten me.
15 "Those who live in my house and my maids consider me a stranger.
I am a foreigner in their sight.
16 "I call to my servant, but he does not answer,
I have to implore him with my mouth.
17 "My breath is offensive to my wife,
And I am loathsome to my own brothers.
18 "Even young children despise me;
I rise up and they speak against me.
19 "All my associates abhor me,
And those I love have turned against me.
20 "My bone clings to my skin and my flesh,
And I have escaped *only* by the skin of my teeth.
21 "Pity me, pity me, O you my friends,
For the hand of God has struck me.

## New International

14He is torn from the security of his tent
and marched off to the king of terrors.
15Fire resides[a] in his tent;
burning sulfur is scattered over his dwelling.
16His roots dry up below
and his branches wither above.
17The memory of him perishes from the earth;
he has no name in the land.
18He is driven from light into darkness
and is banished from the world.
19He has no offspring or descendants among his people,
no survivor where once he lived.
20Men of the west are appalled at his fate;
men of the east are seized with horror.
21Surely such is the dwelling of an evil man;
such is the place of one who knows not God."

*Job*

**19** THEN JOB replied:
2"How long will you torment me
and crush me with words?
3Ten times now you have reproached me;
shamelessly you attack me.
4If it is true that I have gone astray,
my error remains my concern alone.
5If indeed you would exalt yourselves above me
and use my humiliation against me,
6then know that God has wronged me
and drawn his net around me.

7"Though I cry, 'I've been wronged!' I get no response;
though I call for help, there is no justice.
8He has blocked my way so I cannot pass;
he has shrouded my paths in darkness.
9He has stripped me of my honor
and removed the crown from my head.
10He tears me down on every side till I am gone;
he uproots my hope like a tree.
11His anger burns against me;
he counts me among his enemies.
12His troops advance in force;
they build a siege ramp against me
and encamp around my tent.

13"He has alienated my brothers from me;
my acquaintances are completely estranged from me.
14My kinsmen have gone away;
my friends have forgotten me.
15My guests and my maidservants count me a stranger;
they look upon me as an alien.
16I summon my servant, but he does not answer,
though I beg him with my own mouth.
17My breath is offensive to my wife;
I am loathsome to my own brothers.
18Even the little boys scorn me;
when I appear, they ridicule me.
19All my intimate friends detest me;
those I love have turned against me.
20I am nothing but skin and bones;
I have escaped with only the skin of my teeth.[b]

21"Have pity on me, my friends, have pity,
for the hand of God has struck me.

NIV [a] 15 Or *Nothing he had remains* [b] 20 Or *only my gums*

## King James

22Why do ye persecute me as God, and are not satisfied with my flesh?
23Oh that my words were now written! oh that they were printed in a book!
24That they were graven with an iron pen and lead in the rock for ever!
25For I know *that* my redeemer liveth, and *that* he shall stand at the latter *day* upon the earth:
26And *though* after my skin *worms* destroy this *body*, yet in my flesh shall I see God:
27Whom I shall see for myself, and mine eyes shall behold, and not another; *though* my reins be consumed within me.
28But ye should say, Why persecute we him, seeing the root of the matter is found in me?
29Be ye afraid of the sword: for wrath *bringeth* the punishments of the sword, that ye may know *there is* a judgment.

**20** THEN ANSWERED Zophar the Naamathite, and said,
2Therefore do my thoughts cause me to answer, and for *this* I make haste.
3I have heard the check of my reproach, and the spirit of my understanding causeth me to answer.
4Knowest thou *not* this of old, since man was placed upon earth,
5That the triumphing of the wicked *is* short, and the joy of the hypocrite *but* for a moment?
6Though his excellency mount up to the heavens, and his head reach unto the clouds;
7 *Yet* he shall perish for ever like his own dung: they which have seen him shall say, Where *is* he?
8He shall fly away as a dream, and shall not be found: yea, he shall be chased away as a vision of the night.
9The eye also *which* saw him shall *see him* no more; neither shall his place any more behold him.
10His children shall seek to please the poor, and his hands shall restore their goods.
11His bones are full *of the sin* of his youth, which shall lie down with him in the dust.
12Though wickedness be sweet in his mouth, *though* he hide it under his tongue;
13 *Though* he spare it, and forsake it not; but keep it still within his mouth:
14 *Yet* his meat in his bowels is turned, *it is* the gall of asps within him.
15He hath swallowed down riches, and he shall vomit them up again: God shall cast them out of his belly.
16He shall suck the poison of asps: the viper's tongue shall slay him.
17He shall not see the rivers, the floods, the brooks of honey and butter.
18That which he laboured for shall he restore, and shall not swallow *it* down: according to *his* substance *shall* the restitution *be*, and he shall not rejoice *therein*.
19Because he hath oppressed *and* hath forsaken the poor; *because* he hath violently taken away an house which he builded not;
20Surely he shall not feel quietness in his belly, he shall not save of that which he desired.

## Amplified

22Why do you, as if God, pursue *and* persecute me? [Acting like wild beasts] why are you not satisfied with my flesh?
23Oh, that the words I now speak were written! Oh that they were inscribed in a book—carved on a tablet of stone!
24That with an iron pen and [molten] lead they were graven in the rock for ever!
25For I know that my Redeemer *and* Vindicator lives, and at last—the Last One—He will stand upon the earth; [Isa. 44:6; 48:12.]
26And after my skin, even this body, has been destroyed, then from my flesh *or* without it I shall see God,
27Whom I, even I, shall see for myself *and* on my side! And my eyes shall behold Him, and not as a stranger! My heart pines away *and* is consumed within me.
28If you say, How we will pursue him! [And continue to persecute me with the claim] that the root [cause] of all these [afflictions] is found in me,
29Then beware *and* be afraid of the sword [of divine vengeance], for wrathful are the punishments of that sword, that you may know there is a judgment.

**20** THEN ZOPHAR the Naamathite answered,
2Therefore do my thoughts give me an answer, and I make haste [to offer it] for this reason.
3I have heard the reproof which puts me to shame, but out of my understanding my spirit answers me.
4Do you not know from of old, since the time that man was placed on the earth,
5That the triumphing of the wicked is short, and the joy of the godless *and* defiled is but for a moment? [Ps. 37:35, 36.]
6Though his [proud] height mount up to the heavens, and his head reach to the clouds,
7Yet he will perish for ever like his own dung; those who have seen him will say, Where is he?
8He will fly away like a dream and will not be found; yes, he will be chased away as a vision of the night.
9The eye which saw him will see him no more, neither will his [accustomed] place any more behold him.
10The poor will oppress his children, and his hands will give back his [ill-gotten] wealth.
11His bones are full of youthful energy, but it will lie down with him in the dust.
12Though wickedness is sweet in his mouth, though he hides it under his tongue,
13Though he is loath to let it go, but keeps it still within his mouth,
14Yet his food turns [to poison] in his stomach; it is the venom of asps within him.
15He has swallowed down [his ill-gotten] riches, and he shall vomit them up again; God will cast them out of his belly.
16He shall suck the poison of asps [which ill-gotten wealth contains]; the viper's tongue shall slay him.
17He shall not look upon the rivers, the flowing streams of honey and butter [to enjoy his wealth].
18That which he labored for shall he give back, and shall not swallow it down [to enjoy it]; according to his wealth shall the restitution be, and he shall not rejoice in it.
19For he has oppressed and forsaken the poor; he has violently taken away a house which he did not build.
20Because his desire *and* greed knew no quietness within him, he will not save anything of that in which he delights.

## New American Standard

22 "Why do you persecute me as God *does,*
And are not satisfied with my flesh?

*Job Says, "My Redeemer Lives"*

23¶ "Oh that my words were written!
Oh that they were inscribed in a book!
24 "That with an iron stylus and lead
They were engraved in the rock forever!
25 "And as for me, I know that my Redeemer lives,
And at the last He will take His stand on the earth.
26 "Even after my skin is destroyed,
Yet from my flesh I shall see God;
27 Whom I myself shall behold,
And whom my eyes shall see and not another.
My heart faints within me.
28 "If you say, 'How shall we persecute him?'
And 'What pretext for a case against him can we find?'
29 *Then* be afraid of the sword for yourselves,
For wrath *brings* the punishment of the sword,
So that you may know there is judgment."

*Zophar Says, "The Triumph of the Wicked Is Short"*

20 THEN ZOPHAR the Naamathite answered,
2 "Therefore my disquieting thoughts make me respond,
Even because of my inward agitation.
3 "I listened to the reproof which insults me,
And the spirit of my understanding makes me answer.
4 "Do you know this from of old,
From the establishment of man on earth,
5 That the triumphing of the wicked is short,
And the joy of the godless momentary?
6 "Though his loftiness reaches the heavens,
And his head touches the clouds,
7 He perishes forever like his refuse;
Those who have seen him will say, 'Where is he?'
8 "He flies away like a dream, and they cannot find him;
Even like a vision of the night he is chased away.
9 "The eye which saw him sees him no more,
And his place no longer beholds him.
10 "His sons favor the poor,
And his hands give back his wealth.
11 "His bones are full of his youthful vigor,
But it lies down with him in the dust.

12¶ "Though evil is sweet in his mouth,
*And* he hides it under his tongue,
13 *Though* he desires it and will not let it go,
But holds it in his mouth,
14 *Yet* his food in his stomach is changed
To the venom of cobras within him.
15 "He swallows riches,
But will vomit them up;
God will expel them from his belly.
16 "He sucks the poison of cobras;
The viper's tongue slays him.
17 "He does not look at the streams,
The rivers flowing with honey and curds.
18 "He returns what he has attained
And cannot swallow *it;*
As to the riches of his trading,
He cannot even enjoy *them.*
19 "For he has oppressed *and* forsaken the poor;
He has seized a house which he has not built.

20¶ "Because he knew no quiet within him
He does not retain anything he desires.

## New International

22Why do you pursue me as God does?
Will you never get enough of my flesh?

23"Oh, that my words were recorded,
that they were written on a scroll,
24that they were inscribed with an iron tool on[a] lead,
or engraved in rock forever!
25I know that my Redeemer[b] lives,
and that in the end he will stand upon the earth.[c]
26And after my skin has been destroyed,
yet[d] in[e] my flesh I will see God;
27I myself will see him
with my own eyes—I, and not another.
How my heart yearns within me!

28"If you say, 'How we will hound him,
since the root of the trouble lies in him,[f]'
29you should fear the sword yourselves;
for wrath will bring punishment by the sword,
and then you will know that there is judgment.[g]"

*Zophar*

20 THEN ZOPHAR the Naamathite replied:

2"My troubled thoughts prompt me to answer
because I am greatly disturbed.
3I hear a rebuke that dishonors me,
and my understanding inspires me to reply.

4"Surely you know how it has been from of old,
ever since man[h] was placed on the earth,
5that the mirth of the wicked is brief,
the joy of the godless lasts but a moment.
6Though his pride reaches to the heavens
and his head touches the clouds,
7he will perish forever, like his own dung;
those who have seen him will say, 'Where is he?'
8Like a dream he flies away, no more to be found,
banished like a vision of the night.
9The eye that saw him will not see him again;
his place will look on him no more.
10His children must make amends to the poor;
his own hands must give back his wealth.
11The youthful vigor that fills his bones
will lie with him in the dust.

12"Though evil is sweet in his mouth
and he hides it under his tongue,
13though he cannot bear to let it go
and keeps it in his mouth,
14yet his food will turn sour in his stomach;
it will become the venom of serpents within him.
15He will spit out the riches he swallowed;
God will make his stomach vomit them up.
16He will suck the poison of serpents;
the fangs of an adder will kill him.
17He will not enjoy the streams,
the rivers flowing with honey and cream.
18What he toiled for he must give back uneaten;
he will not enjoy the profit from his trading.
19For he has oppressed the poor and left them destitute;
he has seized houses he did not build.

20"Surely he will have no respite from his craving;
he cannot save himself by his treasure.

**NIV** [a] 24 Or *and* [b] 25 Or *defender* [c] 25 Or *upon my grave* [d] 26 Or *And after I awake, / though this* ⌊*body*⌋ *has been destroyed, / then* [e] 26 Or / *apart from* [f] 28 Many Hebrew manuscripts, Septuagint and Vulgate; most Hebrew manuscripts *me* [g] 29 Or / *that you may come to know the Almighty* [h] 4 Or *Adam*

## King James

21 There shall none of his meat be left; therefore shall no man
look for his goods.
22 In the fulness of his sufficiency he shall be in straits: every
hand of the wicked shall come upon him.
23 *When* he is about to fill his belly, *God* shall cast the fury of his
wrath upon him, and shall rain *it* upon him while he is eating.
24 He shall flee from the iron weapon, *and* the bow of steel shall
strike him through.
25 It is drawn, and cometh out of the body; yea, the glittering
sword cometh out of his gall: terrors *are* upon him.
26 All darkness *shall be* hid in his secret places: a fire not blown
shall consume him; it shall go ill with him that is left in his tabernacle.
27 The heaven shall reveal his iniquity; and the earth shall rise
up against him.
28 The increase of his house shall depart, *and his goods* shall flow
away in the day of his wrath.
29 This *is* the portion of a wicked man from God, and the heritage appointed unto him by God.

**21** BUT JOB answered and said,
2 Hear diligently my speech, and let this be your consolations.
3 Suffer me that I may speak; and after that I have spoken, mock
on.
4 As for me, *is* my complaint to man? and if *it were so,* why
should not my spirit be troubled?
5 Mark me, and be astonished, and lay *your* hand upon *your*
mouth.
6 Even when I remember I am afraid, and trembling taketh hold
on my flesh.
7 Wherefore do the wicked live, become old, yea, are mighty in
power?
8 Their seed is established in their sight with them, and their
offspring before their eyes.
9 Their houses *are* safe from fear, neither *is* the rod of God upon
them.
10 Their bull gendereth, and faileth not; their cow calveth, and
casteth not her calf.
11 They send forth their little ones like a flock, and their children
dance.
12 They take the timbrel and harp, and rejoice at the sound of
the organ.
13 They spend their days in wealth, and in a moment go down
to the grave.
14 Therefore they say unto God, Depart from us; for we desire
not the knowledge of thy ways.
15 What *is* the Almighty, that we should serve him? and what
profit should we have, if we pray unto him?
16 Lo, their good *is* not in their hand: the counsel of the wicked
is far from me.
17 How oft is the candle of the wicked put out! and *how oft*
cometh their destruction upon them! *God* distributeth sorrows in
his anger.
18 They are as stubble before the wind, and as chaff that the
storm carrieth away.

## Amplified

21 There was nothing left that he did not devour; therefore his
prosperity will not endure.
22 In the fulness of his sufficiency—in the time of his great
abundance—he shall be poor and in straits; every hand of every
one who is in misery shall come upon him [he is but a wretch on
every side].
23 When he is about to fill his belly [as in the wilderness when
God sent the quails], God will cast the fierceness of His wrath upon
him, and will rain it upon him while he is eating. [Num. 11:33; Ps.
78:26-31.]
24 He will flee from the iron weapon, but the bow of bronze shall
strike him through.
25 [The arrow] is drawn forth, and it comes out after passing
through his body; yes, the glittering point comes out of his gall;
terrors march in upon him.
26 Every misfortune is laid up for his treasures; a fire not blown
by man shall devour him; it shall consume what is left in his tent
[and go ill with him who remains there].
27 The heavens shall reveal his iniquity, and the earth shall rise
up against him.
28 The produce *and* increase of his house will go into exile [with
the victors], dragged away in the day of [God's] wrath.
29 This is the wicked man's portion from God, and the heritage
appointed to him by God.

**21** THEN JOB answered,
2 Hear diligently my speech, and let this [your attention]
be your consolation [given me].
3 Allow me, and I also will speak; and after I have spoken, mock
on.
4 As for me, is my complaint to man *or* of him? And why should
I not be impatient *and* my spirit be troubled?
5 Look at me, and be astonished—appalled; and lay your hand
upon your mouth.
6 Even when I remember I am troubled *and* afraid; horror *and*
trembling take hold of my flesh.
7 Why do the wicked live, become old, and become mighty in
power?
8 Their children are established with them in their sight, and
their offspring before their eyes.
9 Their houses are safe *and* in peace, without fear, neither is the
rod of God upon them.
10 Their bull breeds and fails not; their cows calve and do not
miscarry.
11 They send forth their little ones like a flock, and their children
skip about.
12 They themselves lift up their voices *and* sing to the tambourines and the lyre, and rejoice to the sound of the pipe.
13 They spend their days in prosperity, and *peacefully* go down
to Sheol [the unseen state] in a moment.
14 Yet they say to God, Depart from us, for we do not desire the
knowledge of Your ways.
15 What is the Almighty, that we should serve Him? And what
profit do we have, if we pray to Him? [Exod. 5:2.]
16 But notice, [you say] the prosperity of the wicked is not in
their power; the mystery [of God's dealings] with the ungodly is
far from my comprehension.
17 How often *then* is it that the lamp of the wicked is put out?
That their calamity comes upon them? That God distributes pains
*and* sorrows to them in His anger? [Luke 12:46.]
18 That they are as stubble before the wind, and as chaff that the
storm steals *and* carries away?

## New American Standard

21 "Nothing remains for him to devour,
Therefore his prosperity does not endure.
22 "In the fulness of his plenty he will be cramped;
The hand of everyone who suffers will come *against* him.
23 "When he fills his belly,
*God* will send His fierce anger on him
And will rain *it* on him while he is eating.
24 "He may flee from the iron weapon,
*But* the bronze bow will pierce him.
25 "It is drawn forth and comes out of his back,
Even the glittering point from his gall.
Terrors come upon him,
26 Complete darkness is held in reserve for his treasures,
And unfanned fire will devour him;
It will consume the survivor in his tent.
27 "The heavens will reveal his iniquity,
And the earth will rise up against him.
28 "The increase of his house will depart;
*His possessions* will flow away in the day of His anger.
29 "This is the wicked man's portion from God,
Even the heritage decreed to him by God."

*Job Says God Will Deal with the Wicked*

21 THEN JOB answered,
2 "Listen carefully to my speech,
And let this be your *way of* consolation.
3 "Bear with me that I may speak;
Then after I have spoken, you may mock.
4 "As for me, is my complaint to man?
And why should I not be impatient?
5 "Look at me, and be astonished,
And put *your* hand over *your* mouth.
6 "Even when I remember, I am disturbed,
And horror takes hold of my flesh.
7 "Why do the wicked *still* live,
Continue on, also become very powerful?
8 "Their descendants are established with them in their sight,
And their offspring before their eyes,
9 Their houses are safe from fear,
Neither is the rod of God on them.
10 "His ox mates without fail;
His cow calves and does not abort.
11 "They send forth their little ones like the flock,
And their children skip about.
12 "They sing to the timbrel and harp
And rejoice at the sound of the flute.
13 "They spend their days in prosperity,
And suddenly they go down to Sheol.
14 "And they say to God, 'Depart from us!
We do not even desire the knowledge of Thy ways.
15 'Who is the Almighty, that we should serve Him,
And what would we gain if we entreat Him?'
16 "Behold, their prosperity is not in their hand;
The counsel of the wicked is far from me.

17¶ "How often is the lamp of the wicked put out,
Or *does* their calamity fall on them?
Does God apportion destruction in His anger?
18 "Are they as straw before the wind,
And like chaff which the storm carries away?

## New International

21 Nothing is left for him to devour;
his prosperity will not endure.
22 In the midst of his plenty, distress will overtake him;
the full force of misery will come upon him.
23 When he has filled his belly,
God will vent his burning anger against him
and rain down his blows upon him.
24 Though he flees from an iron weapon,
a bronze-tipped arrow pierces him.
25 He pulls it out of his back,
the gleaming point out of his liver.
Terrors will come over him;
26 total darkness lies in wait for his treasures.
A fire unfanned will consume him
and devour what is left in his tent.
27 The heavens will expose his guilt;
the earth will rise up against him.
28 A flood will carry off his house,
rushing waters[a] on the day of God's wrath.
29 Such is the fate God allots the wicked,
the heritage appointed for them by God."

*Job*

21 THEN JOB replied:
2 "Listen carefully to my words;
let this be the consolation you give me.
3 Bear with me while I speak,
and after I have spoken, mock on.

4 "Is my complaint directed to man?
Why should I not be impatient?
5 Look at me and be astonished;
clap your hand over your mouth.
6 When I think about this, I am terrified;
trembling seizes my body.
7 Why do the wicked live on,
growing old and increasing in power?
8 They see their children established around them,
their offspring before their eyes.
9 Their homes are safe and free from fear;
the rod of God is not upon them.
10 Their bulls never fail to breed;
their cows calve and do not miscarry.
11 They send forth their children as a flock;
their little ones dance about.
12 They sing to the music of tambourine and harp;
they make merry to the sound of the flute.
13 They spend their years in prosperity
and go down to the grave[b] in peace.[c]
14 Yet they say to God, 'Leave us alone!
We have no desire to know your ways.
15 Who is the Almighty, that we should serve him?
What would we gain by praying to him?'
16 But their prosperity is not in their own hands,
so I stand aloof from the counsel of the wicked.

17 "Yet how often is the lamp of the wicked snuffed out?
How often does calamity come upon them,
the fate God allots in his anger?
18 How often are they like straw before the wind,
like chaff swept away by a gale?

**NIV** [a] 28 Or *The possessions in his house will be carried off, / washed away*
[b] 13 Hebrew *Sheol* [c] 13 Or *in an instant*

## King James

19 God layeth up his iniquity for his children: he rewardeth him, and he shall know *it*.

20 His eyes shall see his destruction, and he shall drink of the wrath of the Almighty.

21 For what pleasure *hath* he in his house after him, when the number of his months is cut off in the midst?

22 Shall *any* teach God knowledge? seeing he judgeth those that are high.

23 One dieth in his full strength, being wholly at ease and quiet.

24 His breasts are full of milk, and his bones are moistened with marrow.

25 And another dieth in the bitterness of his soul, and never eateth with pleasure.

26 They shall lie down alike in the dust, and the worms shall cover them.

27 Behold, I know your thoughts, and the devices *which* ye wrongfully imagine against me.

28 For ye say, Where *is* the house of the prince? and where *are* the dwelling places of the wicked?

29 Have ye not asked them that go by the way? and do ye not know their tokens,

30 That the wicked is reserved to the day of destruction? they shall be brought forth to the day of wrath.

31 Who shall declare his way to his face? and who shall repay him *what* he hath done?

32 Yet shall he be brought to the grave, and shall remain in the tomb.

33 The clods of the valley shall be sweet unto him, and every man shall draw after him, as *there are* innumerable before him.

34 How then comfort ye me in vain, seeing in your answers there remaineth falsehood?

**22** THEN ELIPHAZ the Temanite answered and said,

2 Can a man be profitable unto God, as he that is wise may be profitable unto himself?

3 *Is it* any pleasure to the Almighty, that thou art righteous? or *is it* gain *to him*, that thou makest thy ways perfect?

4 Will he reprove thee for fear of thee? will he enter with thee into judgment?

5 *Is* not thy wickedness great? and thine iniquities infinite?

6 For thou hast taken a pledge from thy brother for nought, and stripped the naked of their clothing.

7 Thou hast not given water to the weary to drink, and thou hast withholden bread from the hungry.

8 But *as for* the mighty man, he had the earth; and the honourable man dwelt in it.

9 Thou hast sent widows away empty, and the arms of the fatherless have been broken.

10 Therefore snares *are* round about thee, and sudden fear troubleth thee;

11 Or darkness, *that* thou canst not see; and abundance of waters cover thee.

12 *Is* not God in the height of heaven? and behold the height of the stars, how high they are!

## Amplified

19 You say, God lays up [the punishment of the wicked man's] iniquity for his children. Let Him recompense it to the man himself, that he may know *and* feel it.

20 Let his own eyes see his destruction, and let him drink of the wrath of the Almighty.

21 For what pleasure *or* interest has a man in his house *and* family after he is dead, when the number of his months is cut off?

22 Shall any teach God knowledge, seeing that He judges those who are on high? [Rom. 11:34; I Cor. 2:16.]

23 One dies in his full strength, being wholly at ease and quiet;

24 His pails are full of milk [his veins are filled with nourishment] and the marrow of his bones is fresh *and* moist.

25 Whereas another man dies in bitterness of soul, and never tastes of pleasure *or* good fortune.

26 They lie down alike in the dust, and the worm spreads a covering over them.

27 Behold, I know your thoughts *and* plans, and the devices with which you would wrong me.

28 For you say, Where is the house of the rich *and* liberal prince [meaning me]? And where is the tent in which the wicked [Job] dwelt?

29 Have you not asked those who travel this way, and do you not accept their testimony and evidences,

30 That the evil man is [now] spared in the day of calamity *and* destruction; and they are led forth *and* away on the day of [God's] wrath?

31 But who declares *a man's* way [and rebukes] him to his face? And who pays him back for what he has done?

32 When he is borne to the grave, watch is kept over his tomb.

33 The clods of the valley are sweet to him, and every man shall follow him to a grave, as innumerable people [have gone] before him.

34 How then can you comfort me with empty *and* futile words, since in your replies there lurks falsehood?

**22** THEN ELIPHAZ the Temanite answered [Job],

2 Can a man be profitable to God? Surely he that is wise is profitable to himself. [Ps. 16:2; Luke 17:10.]

3 Is it any pleasure *or* advantage to the Almighty that you are righteous (upright and in right standing with Him)? Or is it gain to Him that you make your ways perfect? [Isa. 62:3; Zech. 2:8; Mal. 3:17; Acts 20:28.]

4 Is it for your [reverential] fear of Him that He [thus] reproves you, that He enters with you into judgment?

5 Is not your wickedness great? There is no end to your iniquities.

6 For you have taken pledges of your brother for nothing, and stripped the naked of their clothing.

7 You have not given water to the weary to drink, and you have withheld bread from the hungry. [Matt. 25:42.]

8 But [you, Job] the man with power possessed the land, and the favored *and* accepted man dwelt in it.

9 You have sent widows away empty-handed, and the arms of the fatherless have been broken.

10 Therefore snares are round about you, and sudden fear troubles *and* overwhelms you;

11 Your light is darkened, so that you cannot see, and a flood of waters covers you.

12 Is not God in the height of Heaven? And behold the height of the stars, how high they are!

## New American Standard

19 "*You say*, 'God stores away a man's iniquity for his sons.'
Let God repay him so that he may know *it*.
20 "Let his own eyes see his decay,
And let him drink of the wrath of the Almighty.
21 "For what does he care for his household [a]after him,
When the number of his months is cut off?
22 "Can anyone teach God knowledge,
In that He judges those on high?
23 "One dies in his full strength,
Being wholly at ease and satisfied;
24 His sides are filled out with fat,
And the marrow of his bones is moist,
25 While another dies with a bitter soul,
Never even tasting *anything* good.
26 "Together they lie down in the dust,
And worms cover them.

27 ¶ "Behold, I know your thoughts,
And the plans by which you would wrong me.
28 "For you say, 'Where is the house of the nobleman,
And where is the tent, the dwelling places of the wicked?'
29 "Have you not asked wayfaring men,
And do you not recognize their witness?
30 "For the wicked is reserved for the day of calamity;
They will be led forth at the day of fury.
31 "Who will confront him with his actions,
And who will repay him for what he has done?
32 "While he is carried to the grave,
*Men* will keep watch over *his* tomb.
33 "The clods of the valley will gently cover him;
Moreover, all men will follow after him,
While countless ones *go* before him.
34 "How then will you vainly comfort me,
For your answers remain *full of* falsehood?"

*Eliphaz Accuses and Exhorts Job*

**22** THEN ELIPHAZ the Temanite responded,
2 "Can a vigorous man be of use to God,
Or a wise man be useful to himself?
3 "Is there any pleasure to the Almighty if you are righteous,
Or profit if you make your ways perfect?
4 "Is it because of your reverence that He reproves you,
That He enters into judgment against you?
5 "Is not your wickedness great,
And your iniquities without end?
6 "For you have taken pledges of your brothers without cause,
And stripped men naked.
7 "To the weary you have given no water to drink,
And from the hungry you have withheld bread.
8 "But the earth belongs to the mighty man,
And the honorable man dwells in it.
9 "You have sent widows away empty,
And the strength of the orphans has been crushed.
10 "Therefore snares surround you,
And sudden dread terrifies you,
11 Or darkness, so that you cannot see,
And an abundance of water covers you.

12 ¶ "Is not God *in* the height of heaven?
Look also at the distant stars, how high they are!

NAS [a] I.e., after he dies

## New International

19 It is said, 'God stores up a man's punishment for his sons.'
Let him repay the man himself, so that he will know it!
20 Let his own eyes see his destruction;
let him drink of the wrath of the Almighty.[b]
21 For what does he care about the family he leaves behind
when his allotted months come to an end?

22 "Can anyone teach knowledge to God,
since he judges even the highest?
23 One man dies in full vigor,
completely secure and at ease,
24 his body[c] well nourished,
his bones rich with marrow.
25 Another man dies in bitterness of soul,
never having enjoyed anything good.
26 Side by side they lie in the dust,
and worms cover them both.

27 "I know full well what you are thinking,
the schemes by which you would wrong me.
28 You say, 'Where now is the great man's house,
the tents where wicked men lived?'
29 Have you never questioned those who travel?
Have you paid no regard to their accounts—
30 that the evil man is spared from the day of calamity,
that he is delivered from[d] the day of wrath?
31 Who denounces his conduct to his face?
Who repays him for what he has done?
32 He is carried to the grave,
and watch is kept over his tomb.
33 The soil in the valley is sweet to him;
all men follow after him,
and a countless throng goes[e] before him.

34 "So how can you console me with your nonsense?
Nothing is left of your answers but falsehood!"

*Eliphaz*

**22** THEN ELIPHAZ the Temanite replied:

2 "Can a man be of benefit to God?
Can even a wise man benefit him?
3 What pleasure would it give the Almighty if you were righteous?
What would he gain if your ways were blameless?

4 "Is it for your piety that he rebukes you
and brings charges against you?
5 Is not your wickedness great?
Are not your sins endless?
6 You demanded security from your brothers for no reason;
you stripped men of their clothing, leaving them naked.
7 You gave no water to the weary
and you withheld food from the hungry,
8 though you were a powerful man, owning land—
an honored man, living on it.
9 And you sent widows away empty-handed
and broke the strength of the fatherless.
10 That is why snares are all around you,
why sudden peril terrifies you,
11 why it is so dark you cannot see,
and why a flood of water covers you.

12 "Is not God in the heights of heaven?
And see how lofty are the highest stars!

NIV [b] 17-20 Verses 17 and 18 may be taken as exclamations and 19 and 20 as declarations. [c] 24 The meaning of the Hebrew for this word is uncertain. [d] 30 *Or man is reserved for the day of calamity, / that he is brought forth to* [e] 33 *Or / as a countless throng went*

## King James

13 And thou sayest, How doth God know? can he judge through
the dark cloud?
14 Thick clouds *are* a covering to him, that he seeth not; and he
walketh in the circuit of heaven.
15 Hast thou marked the old way which wicked men have trodden?
16 Which were cut down out of time, whose foundation was
overflown with a flood:
17 Which said unto God, Depart from us: and what can the
Almighty do for them?
18 Yet he filled their houses with good *things:* but the counsel of
the wicked is far from me.
19 The righteous see *it,* and are glad: and the innocent laugh
them to scorn.
20 Whereas our substance is not cut down, but the remnant of
them the fire consumeth.
21 Acquaint now thyself with him, and be at peace: thereby good
shall come unto thee.
22 Receive, I pray thee, the law from his mouth, and lay up his
words in thine heart.
23 If thou return to the Almighty, thou shalt be built up, thou
shalt put away iniquity far from thy tabernacles.
24 Then shalt thou lay up gold as dust, and the *gold* of Ophir as
the stones of the brooks.
25 Yea, the Almighty shall be thy defence, and thou shalt have
plenty of silver.
26 For then shalt thou have thy delight in the Almighty, and
shalt lift up thy face unto God.
27 Thou shalt make thy prayer unto him, and he shall hear thee,
and thou shalt pay thy vows.
28 Thou shalt also decree a thing, and it shall be established unto
thee: and the light shall shine upon thy ways.
29 When *men* are cast down, then thou shalt say, *There is* lifting
up; and he shall save the humble person.
30 He shall deliver the island of the innocent: and it is delivered
by the pureness of thine hands.

## Amplified

13 Therefore you say, How *and* what does God know [about me]?
Can He judge through the thick darkness?
14 Thick clouds are a covering to Him, so that He does not see,
and He walks on the vault of the heavens.
15 Will you pay attention *and* keep to the old way that wicked
men trod [in Noah's time]? [II Pet. 2:5.]
16 Men who were snatched away before their time, whose foundation was poured out as a stream [during the flood];
17 Who said to God, Depart from us, and, What can the Almighty do for *or* to us?
18 Yet He filled their houses with good [things]. But the counsel
of the ungodly is far from me.
19 The righteous see it, and are glad; and the innocent laugh
them to scorn [saying],
20 Surely those who rose up against us are cut off, and that
which remained to them the fire has consumed.
21 Acquaint now yourself with Him [agree with God and show
yourself to be conformed to His will] and be at peace; by that [you
shall prosper and great] good shall come to you.
22 Receive, I pray you, the law *and* instruction from His mouth,
and lay up His words in your heart. [Ps. 119:11.]
23 If you return to the Almighty [and submit and humble yourself before Him], you will be built up; if you put away unrighteousness far from your tents,
24 If you lay gold in the dust, and the gold of Ophir among the
stones of the brook [considering them of little worth],
25 And make the Almighty your gold and *the Lord* your precious
silver treasure,
26 Then you will have delight in the Almighty, and you will lift
up your face to God.
27 You will make your prayer to Him, and He will hear you, and
you will pay your vows.
28 You shall also decide *and* decree a thing and it shall be established for you, and the light [of God's favor] shall shine upon your
ways.
29 When they make *you* low, you will say, *There is* a lifting up;
and the humble person He lifts up *and* saves.
30 He will even deliver the one [for whom you intercede] who
is not innocent; yes, he will be delivered through the cleanness of
your hands. [Cf. Job 42:7, 8.]

## King James

**23** THEN JOB answered and said,
2 Even today *is* my complaint bitter: my stroke is heavier
than my groaning.
3 Oh that I knew where I might find him! *that* I might come *even*
to his seat!
4 I would order *my* cause before him, and fill my mouth with
arguments.
5 I would know the words *which* he would answer me, and
understand what he would say unto me.
6 Will he plead against me with *his* great power? No; but he
would put *strength* in me.
7 There the righteous might dispute with him; so should I be
delivered for ever from my judge.
8 Behold, I go forward, but he *is* not *there;* and backward, but I
cannot perceive him:
9 On the left hand, where he doth work, but I cannot behold *him:*
he hideth himself on the right hand, that I cannot see *him:*
10 But he knoweth the way that I take: *when* he hath tried me,
I shall come forth as gold.
11 My foot hath held his steps, his way have I kept, and not
declined.

## Amplified

**23** THEN JOB answered,
2 Even today is my complaint rebellious *and* bitter; my
stroke is heavier than my groaning.
3 Oh, that I knew where I might find Him, that I might come
even to His seat!
4 I would lay my cause before Him, and fill my mouth with
arguments.
5 I would learn what He would answer me, and understand
what He would say to me.
6 Would He plead against me with His great power? No; He
would give heed to me. [Isa. 27:4, 5; 57:16.]
7 There the righteous [one who is upright and in right standing
with God] could reason with Him; so I should be acquitted by my
Judge for ever.
8 Behold, I go forward [and to the east], but He is not there; or
backward [and to the west], but I cannot perceive Him;
9 On the left hand [and to the north], where He works [I seek
Him], but I cannot behold Him; He turns Himself to the right hand
[and the south], but I cannot see Him.
10 But He knows the way that I take [He has concern for it,
appreciates and pays attention to it]. When He has tried me, I shall
come forth as refined gold [pure and luminous]. [Pss. 17:3; 66:10;
James 1:12.]
11 My foot has held fast to His steps, His ways have I kept and
not turned aside.

## New American Standard

13 "And you say, 'What does God know?
Can He judge through the thick darkness?
14 'Clouds are a hiding place for Him, so that He cannot see;
And He walks on the vault of heaven.'
15 "Will you keep to the ancient path
Which wicked men have trod,
16 Who were snatched away before their time,
Whose foundations were washed away by a river?
17 "They said to God, 'Depart from us!'
And 'What can the Almighty do to them?'
18 "Yet He filled their houses with good *things;*
But the counsel of the wicked is far from me.
19 "The righteous see and are glad,
And the innocent mock them,
20 *Saying,* 'Truly our adversaries are cut off,
And their abundance the fire has consumed.'

21¶ "Yield now and be at peace with Him;
Thereby good will come to you.
22 "Please receive instruction from His mouth,
And establish His words in your heart.
23 "If you return to the Almighty, you will be restored;
If you remove unrighteousness far from your tent,
24 And place *your* gold in the dust,
And *the gold of* Ophir among the stones of the brooks,
25 Then the Almighty will be your gold
And choice silver to you.
26 "For then you will delight in the Almighty,
And lift up your face to God.
27 "You will pray to Him, and He will hear you;
And you will pay your vows.
28 "You will also decree a thing, and it will be established for you;
And light will shine on your ways.
29 "When you are cast down, you will speak with confidence
And the humble person He will save.
30 "He will deliver one who is not innocent,
And he will be delivered through the cleanness of your hands."

*Job Says He Longs for God*

**23** THEN JOB replied,
2 "Even today my complaint is rebellion;
His hand is heavy despite my groaning.
3 "Oh that I knew where I might find Him,
That I might come to His seat!
4 "I would present *my* case before Him
And fill my mouth with arguments.
5 "I would learn the words *which* He would answer,
And perceive what He would say to me.
6 "Would He contend with me by the greatness of *His* power?
No, surely He would pay attention to me.
7 "There the upright would reason with Him;
And I would be delivered forever from my Judge.

8¶ "Behold, I go forward but He is not *there,*
And backward, but I cannot perceive Him;
9 When He acts on the left, I cannot behold *Him;*
He turns on the right, I cannot see Him.
10 "But He knows the way I take;
*When* He has tried me, I shall come forth as gold.
11 "My foot has held fast to His path;
I have kept His way and not turned aside.

## New International

13 Yet you say, 'What does God know?
Does he judge through such darkness?
14 Thick clouds veil him, so he does not see us
as he goes about in the vaulted heavens.'
15 Will you keep to the old path
that evil men have trod?
16 They were carried off before their time,
their foundations washed away by a flood.
17 They said to God, 'Leave us alone!
What can the Almighty do to us?'
18 Yet it was he who filled their houses with good things,
so I stand aloof from the counsel of the wicked.

19 "The righteous see their ruin and rejoice;
the innocent mock them, saying,
20 'Surely our foes are destroyed,
and fire devours their wealth.'

21 "Submit to God and be at peace with him;
in this way prosperity will come to you.
22 Accept instruction from his mouth
and lay up his words in your heart.
23 If you return to the Almighty, you will be restored:
If you remove wickedness far from your tent
24 and assign your nuggets to the dust,
your gold of Ophir to the rocks in the ravines,
25 then the Almighty will be your gold,
the choicest silver for you.
26 Surely then you will find delight in the Almighty
and will lift up your face to God.
27 You will pray to him, and he will hear you,
and you will fulfill your vows.
28 What you decide on will be done,
and light will shine on your ways.
29 When men are brought low and you say, 'Lift them up!'
then he will save the downcast.
30 He will deliver even one who is not innocent,
who will be delivered through the cleanness of your hands."

*Job*

**23** THEN JOB replied:
2 "Even today my complaint is bitter;
his hand[a] is heavy in spite of[b] my groaning.
3 If only I knew where to find him;
if only I could go to his dwelling!
4 I would state my case before him
and fill my mouth with arguments.
5 I would find out what he would answer me,
and consider what he would say.
6 Would he oppose me with great power?
No, he would not press charges against me.
7 There an upright man could present his case before him,
and I would be delivered forever from my judge.

8 "But if I go to the east, he is not there;
if I go to the west, I do not find him.
9 When he is at work in the north, I do not see him;
when he turns to the south, I catch no glimpse of him.
10 But he knows the way that I take;
when he has tested me, I will come forth as gold.
11 My feet have closely followed his steps;
I have kept to his way without turning aside.

**NIV** [a] 2 Septuagint and Syriac; Hebrew / *the hand on me* [b] 2 Or *heavy on me in*

## King James

12Neither have I gone back from the commandment of his lips; I have esteemed the words of his mouth more than my necessary *food*.

13But he *is* in one *mind*, and who can turn him? and *what* his soul desireth, even *that* he doeth.

14For he performeth *the thing that is* appointed for me: and many such *things are* with him.

15Therefore am I troubled at his presence: when I consider, I am afraid of him.

16For God maketh my heart soft, and the Almighty troubleth me:

17Because I was not cut off before the darkness, *neither* hath he covered the darkness from my face.

**24** WHY, SEEING times are not hidden from the Almighty, do they that know him not see his days?

2 *Some* remove the landmarks; they violently take away flocks, and feed *thereof*.

3They drive away the ass of the fatherless, they take the widow's ox for a pledge.

4They turn the needy out of the way: the poor of the earth hide themselves together.

5Behold, *as* wild asses in the desert, go they forth to their work; rising betimes for a prey: the wilderness *yieldeth* food for them *and* for *their* children.

6They reap *every one* his corn in the field: and they gather the vintage of the wicked.

7They cause the naked to lodge without clothing, that *they have* no covering in the cold.

8They are wet with the showers of the mountains, and embrace the rock for want of a shelter.

9They pluck the fatherless from the breast, and take a pledge of the poor.

10They cause *him* to go naked without clothing, and they take away the sheaf *from* the hungry;

11 *Which* make oil within their walls, *and* tread *their* winepresses, and suffer thirst.

12Men groan from out of the city, and the soul of the wounded crieth out: yet God layeth not folly *to them*.

13They are of those that rebel against the light; they know not the ways thereof, nor abide in the paths thereof.

14The murderer rising with the light killeth the poor and needy, and in the night is as a thief.

15The eye also of the adulterer waiteth for the twilight, saying, No eye shall see me: and disguiseth *his* face.

16In the dark they dig through houses, *which* they had marked for themselves in the daytime: they know not the light.

17For the morning *is* to them even as the shadow of death: if *one* know *them, they are in* the terrors of the shadow of death.

18He *is* swift as the waters; their portion is cursed in the earth: he beholdeth not the way of the vineyards.

19Drought and heat consume the snow waters: *so doth* the grave *those which* have sinned.

## Amplified

12I have not gone back from the commandment of His lips; I have esteemed *and* treasured up the words of His mouth more than my necessary food.

13But He is unchangeable, and who can turn Him? And what He wants to do, that He does.

14For He performs [that which He has] planned for me, and of many such matters He is mindful.

15Therefore am I troubled *and* terrified at His presence; when I consider, I am in dread *and* afraid of Him.

16For God has made my heart faint, timid *and* broken, and the Almighty has terrified me,

17Because I was not cut off before the darkness [of these woes befell me], neither has He covered the thick darkness from my face.

**24** WHY [SEEING times are not hidden from the Almighty] does He not set seasons for judgment? Why do those who know Him not see His days [for punishment of the wicked]? [Acts 1:7.]

2Some remove the landmarks; they violently take away flocks, and pasture them [appropriating land and flocks openly].

3They drive away the donkey of the fatherless; they take the widow's ox for a pledge.

4They crowd the poor *and* needy off the road; the poor *and* meek of the earth all hide themselves.

5Behold, as wild asses in the desert, [the poor] go forth to their work, seeking diligently for prey *and* food; the wilderness yields them bread for their children [in roots and herbage].

6They reap every one his fodder in a field [that is not his own], and they glean the vintage of the wicked man.

7They lie all night naked, without clothing, and have no covering in the cold.

8They are wet with the showers of the mountains, and cling to the rock for want of shelter.

9[The violent men whose wickedness seems unnoticed] pluck the fatherless infants from the breast [to sell or make them slaves], and take [the clothing on] the poor for a pledge.

10So that the needy go about naked for lack of clothing, and though hungry they must carry [but not eat from] the sheaves.

11Among the olive rows [of the wicked, the poor] make oil; they tread [the fresh grape juice from] the presses, but suffer thirst.

12From out of the populous city men groan, and the very life of the wounded cries for help; yet God [seemingly] regards not the wrong done them.

13These wrongdoers are of those who rebel against the light; they know not its ways, nor stay in its paths.

14The murderer rises with the light; he kills the poor and the needy, and in the night becomes as a thief.

15The eye also of the adulterer waits for the twilight, saying, No eye shall see me; and he puts a disguise upon his face.

16In the dark they dig through [the penetrable walls of] houses; by day they shut themselves up; they do not know the sunlight.

17For midnight is morning to all of them; for they are familiar with the terrors of deep darkness.

18[You say,] Swiftly such men pass away on the face of the waters; their portion is cursed in the earth; [no treader] turns into their vineyards.

19Drought and heat consume the snow waters; so does Sheol [the place of the dead] those who have sinned.

## New American Standard

12 "I have not departed from the command of His lips;
I have treasured the words of His mouth more than my necessary food.
13 "But He is unique and who can turn Him?
And *what* His soul desires, that He does.
14 "For He performs what is appointed for me,
And many such *decrees* are with Him.
15 "Therefore, I would be dismayed at His presence;
*When* I consider, I am terrified of Him.
16 "*It is* God *who* has made my heart faint,
And the Almighty *who* has dismayed me,
17 But I am not silenced by the darkness,
Nor deep gloom *which* covers *me*.

*Job Says God Seems to Ignore Wrongs*

24 "WHY ARE times not stored up by the Almighty,
And why do those who know Him not see His days?
2 "Some remove the landmarks;
They seize and devour flocks.
3 "They drive away the donkeys of the orphans;
They take the widow's ox for a pledge.
4 "They push the needy aside from the road;
The poor of the land are made to hide themselves altogether.
5 "Behold, as wild donkeys in the wilderness
They go forth seeking food in their activity,
As bread for *their* children in the desert.
6 "They harvest their fodder in the field,
And they glean the vineyard of the wicked.
7 "They spend the night naked, without clothing,
And have no covering against the cold.
8 "They are wet with the mountain rains,
And they hug the rock for want of a shelter.
9 "Others snatch the orphan from the breast,
And against the poor they take a pledge.
10 "They cause *the poor* to go about naked without clothing,
And they take away the sheaves from the hungry.
11 "Within the walls they produce oil;
They tread wine presses but thirst.
12 "From the city men groan,
And the souls of the wounded cry out;
Yet God does not pay attention to folly.
13¶ "Others have been with those who rebel against the light;
They do not want to know its ways,
Nor abide in its paths.
14 "The murderer arises at dawn;
He kills the poor and the needy,
And at night he is as a thief.
15 "And the eye of the adulterer waits for the twilight,
Saying, 'No eye will see me.'
And he disguises his face.
16 "In the dark they dig into houses,
They shut themselves up by day;
They do not know the light.
17 "For the morning is the same to him as thick darkness,
For he is familiar with the terrors of thick darkness.
18¶ "They are insignificant on the surface of the water;
Their portion is cursed on the earth.
They do not turn toward the vineyards.
19 "Drought and heat consume the snow waters,
*So does* Sheol *those who* have sinned.

## New International

12 I have not departed from the commands of his lips;
I have treasured the words of his mouth more than my daily bread.
13 "But he stands alone, and who can oppose him?
He does whatever he pleases.
14 He carries out his decree against me,
and many such plans he still has in store.
15 That is why I am terrified before him;
when I think of all this, I fear him.
16 God has made my heart faint;
the Almighty has terrified me.
17 Yet I am not silenced by the darkness,
by the thick darkness that covers my face.

24 "WHY DOES the Almighty not set times for judgment?
Why must those who know him look in vain for such days?
2 Men move boundary stones;
they pasture flocks they have stolen.
3 They drive away the orphan's donkey
and take the widow's ox in pledge.
4 They thrust the needy from the path
and force all the poor of the land into hiding.
5 Like wild donkeys in the desert,
the poor go about their labor of foraging food;
the wasteland provides food for their children.
6 They gather fodder in the fields
and glean in the vineyards of the wicked.
7 Lacking clothes, they spend the night naked;
they have nothing to cover themselves in the cold.
8 They are drenched by mountain rains
and hug the rocks for lack of shelter.
9 The fatherless child is snatched from the breast;
the infant of the poor is seized for a debt.
10 Lacking clothes, they go about naked;
they carry the sheaves, but still go hungry.
11 They crush olives among the terraces[a];
they tread the winepresses, yet suffer thirst.
12 The groans of the dying rise from the city,
and the souls of the wounded cry out for help.
But God charges no one with wrongdoing.

13 "There are those who rebel against the light,
who do not know its ways
or stay in its paths.
14 When daylight is gone, the murderer rises up
and kills the poor and needy;
in the night he steals forth like a thief.
15 The eye of the adulterer watches for dusk;
he thinks, 'No eye will see me,'
and he keeps his face concealed.
16 In the dark, men break into houses,
but by day they shut themselves in;
they want nothing to do with the light.
17 For all of them, deep darkness is their morning[b];
they make friends with the terrors of darkness.[c]

18 "Yet they are foam on the surface of the water;
their portion of the land is cursed,
so that no one goes to the vineyards.
19 As heat and drought snatch away the melted snow,
so the grave[d] snatches away those who have sinned.

**NIV** [a] *11* Or *olives between the millstones;* the meaning of the Hebrew for this word is uncertain. [b] *17* Or *them, their morning is like the shadow of death* [c] *17* Or *of the shadow of death* [d] *19* Hebrew *Sheol*

## King James

20 The womb shall forget him; the worm shall feed sweetly on him; he shall be no more remembered; and wickedness shall be broken as a tree.
21 He evil entreateth the barren *that* beareth not: and doeth not good to the widow.
22 He draweth also the mighty with his power: he riseth up, and no *man* is sure of life.
23 *Though* it be given him *to be* in safety, whereon he resteth; yet his eyes *are* upon their ways.
24 They are exalted for a little while, but are gone and brought low; they are taken out of the way as all *other*, and cut off as the tops of the ears of corn.
25 And if *it be* not *so* now, who will make me a liar, and make my speech nothing worth?

**25** THEN ANSWERED Bildad the Shuhite, and said,
2 Dominion and fear *are* with him, he maketh peace in his high places.
3 Is there any number of his armies? and upon whom doth not his light arise?
4 How then can man be justified with God? or how can he be clean *that is* born of a woman?
5 Behold even to the moon, and it shineth not; yea, the stars are not pure in his sight.
6 How much less man, *that is* a worm? and the son of man, *which is* a worm?

**26** BUT JOB answered and said,
2 How hast thou helped *him that is* without power? *how* savest thou the arm *that hath* no strength?
3 How hast thou counselled *him that hath* no wisdom? and *how* hast thou plentifully declared the thing as it is?
4 To whom hast thou uttered words? and whose spirit came from thee?
5 Dead *things* are formed from under the waters, and the inhabitants thereof.
6 Hell *is* naked before him, and destruction hath no covering.
7 He stretcheth out the north over the empty place, *and* hangeth the earth upon nothing.
8 He bindeth up the waters in his thick clouds; and the cloud is not rent under them.
9 He holdeth back the face of his throne, *and* spreadeth his cloud upon it.
10 He hath compassed the waters with bounds, until the day and night come to an end.
11 The pillars of heaven tremble and are astonished at his reproof.
12 He divideth the sea with his power, and by his understanding he smiteth through the proud.
13 By his spirit he hath garnished the heavens; his hand hath formed the crooked serpent.
14 Lo, these *are* parts of his ways: but how little a portion is heard of him? but the thunder of his power who can understand?

**AMP** [a] For millenniums, various theories of what supports the earth—elephants, giants and other fantastic means—were accepted by mankind as truth; but the Bible made no such absurd error. How could Job, more than 3000 years ago, possibly have known that God "hangs the earth upon nothing," except by divine inspiration?

## Amplified

20 The womb shall forget him; the worm shall feed sweetly on him; he shall be no more remembered, and unrighteousness shall be broken as a tree [which cannot be healed]. [Prov. 10:7.]
21 [The evil man] preys upon the barren, childless woman, and does no good to the widow.
22 Yet [God] prolongs the life of the [wicked] mighty by His power; they rise up when they had despaired of life.
23 God gives them security, and they rest on it; and His eyes are upon their ways.
24 They are exalted for a little while, then are gone and brought low; they are taken out of the way as all others are, and cut off as the tops of the ears of grain.
25 And if this is not so, who will prove me a liar and make my speech worthless?

**25** THEN BILDAD the Shuhite answered,
2 Dominion and fear are with [God]; He makes peace in His high places.
3 Is there any number to His armies? And upon whom does not His light arise?
4 How then can man be justified *and* righteous before God? Or how can he who is born of a woman be pure *and* clean? [Pss. 130:3; 143:2.]
5 Behold, even the moon has no brightness [compared to God's glory] and the stars are not pure in His sight.
6 How much less man, who is a maggot! And a son of man, who is a worm!

**26** BUT JOB answered,
2 How you have helped him who is without power! How you have sustained the arm that is without strength!
3 How you have counseled him who has no wisdom! And how plentifully you have declared to him sound knowledge!
4 With whose assistance have you uttered these words? And whose spirit [inspired what] came forth from you?
5 The shades of the dead tremble underneath the waters and their inhabitants.
6 Sheol [the place of the dead] is naked before God, and Abaddon [the place of destruction] has no covering [from His eyes].
7 He it is Who spreads out the northern skies over emptiness and [a]hangs the earth upon *or* over nothing.
8 He holds the waters cloud-bound [that else would spill on earth all at once] and the cloud is not rent under them.
9 He covers the face of His throne and spreads over it His cloud.
10 He has placed an enclosing limit [the horizon] upon the waters at the boundary between light and darkness.
11 The pillars of the heavens tremble and are astonished at His rebuke.
12 He stills *or* stirs up the sea by His power, and by His understanding He smites proud Rahab.
13 By His breath the heavens are garnished; His hand pierced the [swift] fleeing serpent. [Ps. 33:6.]
14 Yet these are but [a small part of His doings] the outskirts of His ways *or* the mere fringes of His force, the faintest whisper of His voice! Who dares contemplate *or* who can understand the thunders of His full, magnificent power?

## New American Standard

20 "A mother will forget him;
The worm feeds sweetly till he is remembered no more.
And wickedness will be broken like a tree.
21 "He wrongs the barren woman,
And does no good for the widow.
22 "But He drags off the valiant by His power;
He rises, but no one has assurance of life.
23 "He provides them with security, and they are supported;
And His eyes are on their ways.
24 "They are exalted a little while, then they are gone;
Moreover, they are brought low and like everything gathered up;
Even like the heads of grain they are cut off.
25 "Now if it is not so, who can prove me a liar,
And make my speech worthless?"

*Bildad Says Man Is Inferior*

**25** THEN BILDAD the Shuhite answered,
2 "Dominion and awe belong to Him
Who establishes peace in His heights.
3 "Is there any number to His troops?
And upon whom does His light not rise?
4 "How then can a man be just with God?
Or how can he be clean who is born of woman?
5 "If even the moon has no brightness
And the stars are not pure in His sight,
6 How much less man, *that* maggot,
And the son of man, *that* worm!"

*Job Rebukes Bildad*

**26** THEN JOB responded,
2 "What a help you are to the weak!
How you have saved the arm without strength!
3 "What counsel you have given to *one* without wisdom!
What helpful insight you have abundantly provided!
4 "To whom have you uttered words?
And whose spirit was expressed through you?

*The Greatness of God*

5¶ "The departed spirits tremble
Under the waters and their inhabitants.
6 "Naked is Sheol before Him
And [b]Abaddon has no covering.
7 "He stretches out the north over empty space,
And hangs the earth on nothing.
8 "He wraps up the waters in His clouds;
And the cloud does not burst under them.
9 "He obscures the face of the full moon,
And spreads His cloud over it.
10 "He has inscribed a circle on the surface of the waters,
At the boundary of light and darkness.
11 "The pillars of heaven tremble,
And are amazed at His rebuke.
12 "He quieted the sea with His power,
And by His understanding He shattered Rahab.
13 "By His breath the heavens are cleared;
His hand has pierced the fleeing serpent.
14 "Behold, these are the fringes of His ways;
And how faint a word we hear of Him!
But His mighty thunder, who can understand?"

NAS [b] I.e., place of destruction

## New International

20 The womb forgets them,
the worm feasts on them;
evil men are no longer remembered
but are broken like a tree.
21 They prey on the barren and childless woman,
and to the widow show no kindness.
22 But God drags away the mighty by his power;
though they become established, they have no assurance of life.
23 He may let them rest in a feeling of security,
but his eyes are on their ways.
24 For a little while they are exalted, and then they are gone;
they are brought low and gathered up like all others;
they are cut off like heads of grain.

25 "If this is not so, who can prove me false
and reduce my words to nothing?"

*Bildad*

**25** THEN BILDAD the Shuhite replied:
2 "Dominion and awe belong to God;
he establishes order in the heights of heaven.
3 Can his forces be numbered?
Upon whom does his light not rise?
4 How then can a man be righteous before God?
How can one born of woman be pure?
5 If even the moon is not bright
and the stars are not pure in his eyes,
6 how much less man, who is but a maggot—
a son of man, who is only a worm!"

*Job*

**26** THEN JOB replied:
2 "How you have helped the powerless!
How you have saved the arm that is feeble!
3 What advice you have offered to one without wisdom!
And what great insight you have displayed!
4 Who has helped you utter these words?
And whose spirit spoke from your mouth?

5 "The dead are in deep anguish,
those beneath the waters and all that live in them.
6 Death[c] is naked before God;
Destruction[d] lies uncovered.
7 He spreads out the northern ⌞skies⌟ over empty space;
he suspends the earth over nothing.
8 He wraps up the waters in his clouds,
yet the clouds do not burst under their weight.
9 He covers the face of the full moon,
spreading his clouds over it.
10 He marks out the horizon on the face of the waters
for a boundary between light and darkness.
11 The pillars of the heavens quake,
aghast at his rebuke.
12 By his power he churned up the sea;
by his wisdom he cut Rahab to pieces.
13 By his breath the skies became fair;
his hand pierced the gliding serpent.
14 And these are but the outer fringe of his works;
how faint the whisper we hear of him!
Who then can understand the thunder of his power?"

NIV [c] 6 Hebrew *Sheol* [d] 6 Hebrew *Abaddon*

## King James

**27** MOREOVER JOB continued his parable, and said,

2 *As* God liveth, *who* hath taken away my judgment; and the Almighty, *who* hath vexed my soul;

3 All the while my breath *is* in me, and the spirit of God *is* in my nostrils;

4 My lips shall not speak wickedness, nor my tongue utter deceit.

5 God forbid that I should justify you: till I die I will not remove mine integrity from me.

6 My righteousness I hold fast, and will not let it go: my heart shall not reproach *me* so long as I live.

7 Let mine enemy be as the wicked, and he that riseth up against me as the unrighteous.

8 For what *is* the hope of the hypocrite, though he hath gained, when God taketh away his soul?

9 Will God hear his cry when trouble cometh upon him?

10 Will he delight himself in the Almighty? will he always call upon God?

11 I will teach you by the hand of God: *that* which *is* with the Almighty will I not conceal.

12 Behold, all ye yourselves have seen *it*; why then are ye thus altogether vain?

13 This *is* the portion of a wicked man with God, and the heritage of oppressors, *which* they shall receive of the Almighty.

14 If his children be multiplied, *it is* for the sword: and his offspring shall not be satisfied with bread.

15 Those that remain of him shall be buried in death: and his widows shall not weep.

16 Though he heap up silver as the dust, and prepare raiment as the clay;

17 He may prepare *it*, but the just shall put *it* on, and the innocent shall divide the silver.

18 He buildeth his house as a moth, and as a booth *that* the keeper maketh.

19 The rich man shall lie down, but he shall not be gathered: he openeth his eyes, and he *is* not.

20 Terrors take hold on him as waters, a tempest stealeth him away in the night.

21 The east wind carrieth him away, and he departeth: and as a storm hurleth him out of his place.

22 For *God* shall cast upon him, and not spare: he would fain flee out of his hand.

23 *Men* shall clap their hands at him, and shall hiss him out of his place.

**28** SURELY THERE is a vein for the silver, and a place for gold *where* they refine *it*.

2 Iron is taken out of the earth, and brass *is* molten *out of* the stone.

3 He setteth an end to darkness, and searcheth out all perfection: the stones of darkness, and the shadow of death.

4 The flood breaketh out from the inhabitant; *even the waters* forgotten of the foot: they are dried up, they are gone away from men.

5 *As for* the earth, out of it cometh bread: and under it is turned up as it were fire.

## Amplified

**27** JOB AGAIN took up his discourse, and said,

2 As God lives, Who has taken away my right *and* denied me justice, and the Almighty, Who has vexed *and* embittered my life;

3 As long as my life is still whole within me and the breath of God is *yet* in my nostrils,

4 My lips shall not speak untruth, nor my tongue utter deceit.

5 God forbid that I should justify you—saying you are right [in your accusations against me]; till I die I will not put away my integrity from me.

6 My uprightness *and* my right standing with God I hold fast, and will not let them go; my heart does not reproach me for any of my days, *and* it shall not reproach me as long as I live.

7 Let my enemy be as the wicked, and let him who rises up against me be as the unrighteous.

8 For what is the hope of the godless *and* polluted, even though he has gained [in this world], when God cuts him off *and* takes away his life?

9 Will God hear his cry when trouble comes upon him?

10 Will he take delight in the Almighty? Will he call upon God at all times?

11 I will teach you regarding the hand *and* handiwork of God; that which is with the Almighty [God's actual treatment of the wicked man] will I not conceal.

12 Behold, all of you have seen it yourselves; why then have you become altogether vain [cherishing foolish notions]?

13 This [I am about to tell] is the portion of a wicked man with God, and the heritage which oppressors shall receive from the Almighty.

14 If his children are multiplied, it is for the sword; and his offspring have not sufficient bread.

15 Those who survive him [the pestilence] will bury, and [their] widows will make no lamentation.

16 Though he heaps up silver like dust, and piles up clothing like clay;

17 He may prepare it, but the just will wear it, and the innocent will divide the silver.

18 He builds his house like a moth *or* a spider, like a booth which a watchman makes [to last for a season].

19 [The wicked] will lie down rich, but does it not again; he opens his eyes, and [his wealth] is gone.

20 Terrors overtake him like a [suddenly loosened] flood; a windstorm steals him away in the night.

21 The east wind lifts him up, and he is gone; it sweeps him out of his place.

22 For [God and the storm] hurl at him without pity *and* unsparingly [their thunderbolts of wrath]; he flees in haste before His power.

23 [God causes] men to clap their hands at him [in malignant joy], and hiss him out of his place.

**28** SURELY THERE is a mine for silver, and a place for gold where they refine it.

2 Iron is taken out of the earth, and copper is smelted from the stone ore.

3 Man sets an end to darkness, and searches out the farthest bounds of the ore buried in gloom and deep darkness.

4 Men break open shafts away from where people sojourn, forgotten by [human] foot; and [descend into them], hanging afar from men, they swing *or* flit to and fro.

5 As for the earth, out of it comes bread; but underneath [its surface, down deep in the mine] there is [a]blasting, turning it up as by fire.

**AMP** [a] Blasting of rocks is said to have been practiced on a large scale by the ancients. (Speaker's Commentary.)

## New American Standard

*Job Affirms His Righteousness*

**27** THEN JOB continued his discourse and said,
2 "As God lives, who has taken away my right,
And the Almighty, who has embittered my soul,
3 For as long as life is in me,
And the breath of God is in my nostrils,
4 My lips certainly will not speak unjustly,
Nor will my tongue mutter deceit.
5 "Far be it from me that I should declare you right;
Till I die I will not put away my integrity from me.
6 "I hold fast my righteousness and will not let it go.
My heart does not reproach any of my days.

*The State of the Godless*

7¶ "May my enemy be as the wicked,
And my opponent as the unjust.
8 "For what is the hope of the godless when he is cut off,
When God requires his life?
9 "Will God hear his cry,
When distress comes upon him?
10 "Will he take delight in the Almighty,
Will he call on God at all times?
11 "I will instruct you in the power of God;
What is with the Almighty I will not conceal.
12 "Behold, all of you have seen *it;*
Why then do you act foolishly?
13¶ "This is the portion of a wicked man from God,
And the inheritance *which* tyrants receive from the Almighty.
14 "Though his sons are many, they are destined for the sword;
And his descendants will not be satisfied with bread.
15 "His survivors will be buried because of the plague,
And their widows will not be able to weep.
16 "Though he piles up silver like dust,
And prepares garments as *plentiful as* the clay;
17 He may prepare *it,* but the just will wear *it,*
And the innocent will divide the silver.
18 "He has built his house like the spider's web,
Or as a hut *which* the watchman has made.
19 "He lies down rich, but never again;
He opens his eyes, and it is no more.
20 "Terrors overtake him like a flood;
A tempest steals him away in the night.
21 "The east wind carries him away, and he is gone,
For it whirls him away from his place.
22 "For it will hurl at him without sparing;
He will surely try to flee from its power.
23 "*Men* will clap their hands at him,
And will hiss him from his place.

*Job Tells of Earth's Treasures*

**28** "SURELY THERE is a [b]mine for silver,
And a place where they refine gold.
2 "Iron is taken from the dust,
And from rock copper is smelted.
3 "*Man* puts an end to darkness,
And to the farthest limit he searches out
The rock in gloom and deep shadow.
4 "He sinks a shaft far from habitation,
Forgotten by the foot;
They hang and swing to and fro far from men.
5 "The earth, from it comes food,
And underneath it is turned up as fire.

NAS [b] Or, *source*

## New International

**27** AND JOB continued his discourse:
2 "As surely as God lives, who has denied me justice,
the Almighty, who has made me taste bitterness of soul,
3 as long as I have life within me,
the breath of God in my nostrils,
4 my lips will not speak wickedness,
and my tongue will utter no deceit.
5 I will never admit you are in the right;
till I die, I will not deny my integrity.
6 I will maintain my righteousness and never let go of it;
my conscience will not reproach me as long as I live.

7 "May my enemies be like the wicked,
my adversaries like the unjust!
8 For what hope has the godless when he is cut off,
when God takes away his life?
9 Does God listen to his cry
when distress comes upon him?
10 Will he find delight in the Almighty?
Will he call upon God at all times?

11 "I will teach you about the power of God;
the ways of the Almighty I will not conceal.
12 You have all seen this yourselves.
Why then this meaningless talk?

13 "Here is the fate God allots to the wicked,
the heritage a ruthless man receives from the Almighty:
14 However many his children, their fate is the sword;
his offspring will never have enough to eat.
15 The plague will bury those who survive him,
and their widows will not weep for them.
16 Though he heaps up silver like dust
and clothes like piles of clay,
17 what he lays up the righteous will wear,
and the innocent will divide his silver.
18 The house he builds is like a moth's cocoon,
like a hut made by a watchman.
19 He lies down wealthy, but will do so no more;
when he opens his eyes, all is gone.
20 Terrors overtake him like a flood;
a tempest snatches him away in the night.
21 The east wind carries him off, and he is gone;
it sweeps him out of his place.
22 It hurls itself against him without mercy
as he flees headlong from its power.
23 It claps its hands in derision
and hisses him out of his place.

**28** "THERE IS a mine for silver
and a place where gold is refined.
2 Iron is taken from the earth,
and copper is smelted from ore.
3 Man puts an end to the darkness;
he searches the farthest recesses
for ore in the blackest darkness.
4 Far from where people dwell he cuts a shaft,
in places forgotten by the foot of man;
far from men he dangles and sways.
5 The earth, from which food comes,
is transformed below as by fire;

## King James

6The stones of it *are* the place of sapphires: and it hath dust of gold.

7 *There is* a path which no fowl knoweth, and which the vulture's eye hath not seen:

8The lion's whelps have not trodden it, nor the fierce lion passed by it.

9He putteth forth his hand upon the rock; he overturneth the mountains by the roots.

10He cutteth out rivers among the rocks; and his eye seeth every precious thing.

11He bindeth the floods from overflowing; and *the thing that is* hid bringeth he forth to light.

12But where shall wisdom be found? and where *is* the place of understanding?

13Man knoweth not the price thereof; neither is it found in the land of the living.

14The depth saith, It *is* not in me: and the sea saith, *It is* not with me.

15It cannot be gotten for gold, neither shall silver be weighed *for* the price thereof.

16It cannot be valued with the gold of Ophir, with the precious onyx, or the sapphire.

17The gold and the crystal cannot equal it: and the exchange of it *shall not be for* jewels of fine gold.

18No mention shall be made of coral, or of pearls: for the price of wisdom *is* above rubies.

19The topaz of Ethiopia shall not equal it, neither shall it be valued with pure gold.

20Whence then cometh wisdom? and where *is* the place of understanding?

21Seeing it is hid from the eyes of all living, and kept close from the fowls of the air.

22Destruction and death say, We have heard the fame thereof with our ears.

23God understandeth the way thereof, and he knoweth the place thereof.

24For he looketh to the ends of the earth, *and* seeth under the whole heaven;

25To make the weight for the winds; and he weigheth the waters by measure.

26When he made a decree for the rain, and a way for the lightning of the thunder:

27Then did he see it, and declare it; he prepared it, yea, and searched it out.

28And unto man he said, Behold, the fear of the Lord, that *is* wisdom; and to depart from evil *is* understanding.

## Amplified

6Its stones are the bed of sapphires; it holds dust of gold—which he wins.

7That path no bird of prey knows, and the falcon's eye has not seen it.

8The proud beasts [and their young] have not trodden it, nor has the fierce lion passed over it.

9Man puts forth his hand upon the flinty rock; he overturns the mountains by the roots.

10He cuts out channels *and* passages among the rocks, and his eye sees every precious thing.

11[Man] binds the streams so that they do not trickle [into the mine], and the thing that is hidden he brings forth to light.

12But where shall [a]Wisdom be found? And where is the place of understanding?

13Man knows not the price of it, neither is it found in the land of the living.

14The deep says, [Wisdom] is not in me, and the sea says, It is not with me.

15It cannot be gotten for gold, neither shall silver be weighed for the price of it.

16It cannot be valued in [terms of] the gold of Ophir, in the precious onyx *or* beryl, or the sapphire.

17Gold and glass cannot equal [Wisdom], nor can it be exchanged for jewels *or* vessels of fine gold.

18No mention shall be made of coral or of crystal, for the possession of Wisdom is even above rubies *or* pearls.

19The topaz of Ethiopia cannot compare with it, nor can it be valued in pure gold.

20From where then does Wisdom come? And where is the place of understanding?

21It is hid from the eyes of all living, and knowledge of it is withheld from the birds of the heavens.

22Abaddon (the place of destruction) and Death say, We have *only* heard the report of it with our ears.

23God understands the way [to Wisdom], and He knows the place of it [Wisdom is with God alone].

24For He looks to the ends of the earth, and sees everything under the heavens.

25When He gave to the wind weight *or* pressure, and allotted the waters by measure;

26When He made a decree for the rain, and a way for the lightning of the thunder;

27Then He saw [Wisdom] and declared it, He established it, yes, and searched it out [for His own use, and He alone possesses it].

28But to man He said, Behold, the reverential *and* worshipful fear of the Lord, that is Wisdom, and to depart from evil is understanding.

## King James

**29** MOREOVER JOB continued his parable, and said,

2Oh that I were as *in* months past, as *in* the days *when* God preserved me;

3When his candle shined upon my head, *and when* by his light I walked *through* darkness;

4As I was in the days of my youth, when the secret of God *was* upon my tabernacle;

5When the Almighty *was* yet with me, *when* my children *were* about me;

6When I washed my steps with butter, and the rock poured me out rivers of oil;

## Amplified

**29** AND JOB again took up his discussion, and said,

2Oh, that I were as in the months of old, as in the days when God watched over me; [Eccl. 7:10.]

3When His lamp shone above *and* upon my head, and by His light I walked through darkness;

4As I was in the [prime] ripeness of my days, when the friendship *and* counsel of God were over my tent;

5When the Almighty was yet with me, and my children were about me;

6When my steps [through rich pasturage] were washed with butter, and the rock poured out for me streams of oil!

**AMP** [a] Wisdom is capitalized as a reminder of its divine implications. See footnote on Proverbs 1:23.

## New American Standard

6 "Its rocks are the source of sapphires,
And its dust *contains* gold.
7 "The path no bird of prey knows,
Nor has the falcon's eye caught sight of it.
8 "The proud beasts have not trodden it,
Nor has the *fierce* lion passed over it.
9 "He puts his hand on the flint;
He overturns the mountains at the base.
10 "He hews out channels through the rocks;
And his eye sees anything precious.
11 "He dams up the streams from flowing;
And what is hidden he brings out to the light.

*The Search for Wisdom Is Harder*

12¶ "But where can wisdom be found?
And where is the place of understanding?
13 "Man does not know its value,
Nor is it found in the land of the living.
14 "The deep says, 'It is not in me';
And the sea says, 'It is not with me.'
15 "Pure gold cannot be given in exchange for it,
Nor can silver be weighed as its price.
16 "It cannot be valued in the gold of Ophir,
In precious onyx, or sapphire.
17 "Gold or glass cannot equal it,
Nor can it be exchanged for articles of fine gold.
18 "Coral and crystal are not to be mentioned;
And the acquisition of wisdom is above *that of* pearls.
19 "The topaz of Ethiopia cannot equal it,
Nor can it be valued in pure gold.
20 "Where then does wisdom come from?
And where is the place of understanding?
21 "Thus it is hidden from the eyes of all living,
And concealed from the birds of the sky.
22 "[b]Abaddon and Death say,
'With our ears we have heard a report of it.'
23¶ "God understands its way;
And He knows its place.
24 "For He looks to the ends of the earth,
And sees everything under the heavens.
25 "When He imparted weight to the wind,
And meted out the waters by measure,
26 When He set a limit for the rain,
And a course for the thunderbolt,
27 Then He saw it and declared it;
He established it and also searched it out.
28 "And to man He said, 'Behold, the fear of the Lord, that is wisdom;
And to depart from evil is understanding.'"

*Job's Past Was Glorious*

29 AND JOB again took up his discourse and said,
2 "Oh that I were as in months gone by,
As in the days when God watched over me;
3 When His lamp shone over my head,
*And* by His light I walked through darkness;
4 As I was in [c]the prime of my days,
When the friendship of God *was* over my tent;
5 When the Almighty was yet with me,
*And* my children were around me;
6 When my steps were bathed in butter,
And the rock poured out for me streams of oil!

NAS [b] I.e., Destruction [c] Lit., *the days of my autumn*

## New International

6 sapphires[d] come from its rocks,
and its dust contains nuggets of gold.
7 No bird of prey knows that hidden path,
no falcon's eye has seen it.
8 Proud beasts do not set foot on it,
and no lion prowls there.
9 Man's hand assaults the flinty rock
and lays bare the roots of the mountains.
10 He tunnels through the rock;
his eyes see all its treasures.
11 He searches[e] the sources of the rivers
and brings hidden things to light.

12 "But where can wisdom be found?
Where does understanding dwell?
13 Man does not comprehend its worth;
it cannot be found in the land of the living.
14 The deep says, 'It is not in me';
the sea says, 'It is not with me.'
15 It cannot be bought with the finest gold,
nor can its price be weighed in silver.
16 It cannot be bought with the gold of Ophir,
with precious onyx or sapphires.
17 Neither gold nor crystal can compare with it,
nor can it be had for jewels of gold.
18 Coral and jasper are not worthy of mention;
the price of wisdom is beyond rubies.
19 The topaz of Cush cannot compare with it;
it cannot be bought with pure gold.

20 "Where then does wisdom come from?
Where does understanding dwell?
21 It is hidden from the eyes of every living thing,
concealed even from the birds of the air.
22 Destruction[f] and Death say,
'Only a rumor of it has reached our ears.'
23 God understands the way to it
and he alone knows where it dwells,
24 for he views the ends of the earth
and sees everything under the heavens.
25 When he established the force of the wind
and measured out the waters,
26 when he made a decree for the rain
and a path for the thunderstorm,
27 then he looked at wisdom and appraised it;
he confirmed it and tested it.
28 And he said to man,
'The fear of the Lord—that is wisdom,
and to shun evil is understanding.'"

29 JOB CONTINUED his discourse:
2 "How I long for the months gone by,
for the days when God watched over me,
3 when his lamp shone upon my head
and by his light I walked through darkness!
4 Oh, for the days when I was in my prime,
when God's intimate friendship blessed my house,
5 when the Almighty was still with me
and my children were around me,
6 when my path was drenched with cream
and the rock poured out for me streams of olive oil.

NIV [d] 6 Or *lapis lazuli;* also in verse 16 [e] 11 Septuagint, Aquila and Vulgate; Hebrew *He dams up* [f] 22 Hebrew *Abaddon*

## King James

7When I went out to the gate through the city, *when* I prepared
my seat in the street!
8The young men saw me, and hid themselves: and the aged
arose, *and* stood up.
9The princes refrained talking, and laid *their* hand on their
mouth.
10The nobles held their peace, and their tongue cleaved to the
roof of their mouth.
11When the ear heard *me,* then it blessed me; and when the eye
saw *me,* it gave witness to me:
12Because I delivered the poor that cried, and the fatherless, and
*him that had* none to help him.
13The blessing of him that was ready to perish came upon me:
and I caused the widow's heart to sing for joy.
14I put on righteousness, and it clothed me: my judgment *was*
as a robe and a diadem.
15I was eyes to the blind, and feet *was* I to the lame.
16I *was* a father to the poor: and the cause *which* I knew not I
searched out.
17And I brake the jaws of the wicked, and plucked the spoil out
of his teeth.
18Then I said, I shall die in my nest, and I shall multiply *my* days
as the sand.
19My root *was* spread out by the waters, and the dew lay all
night upon my branch.
20My glory *was* fresh in me, and my bow was renewed in my
hand.
21Unto me *men* gave ear, and waited, and kept silence at my
counsel.
22After my words they spake not again; and my speech dropped
upon them.
23And they waited for me as for the rain; and they opened their
mouth wide *as* for the latter rain.
24 *If* I laughed on them, they believed *it* not; and the light of my
countenance they cast not down.
25I chose out their way, and sat chief, and dwelt as a king in the
army, as one *that* comforteth the mourners.

**30** BUT NOW *they that are* younger than I have me in derision, whose fathers I would have disdained to have set
with the dogs of my flock.
2Yea, whereto *might* the strength of their hands *profit* me, in
whom old age was perished?
3For want and famine *they were* solitary; fleeing into the wilderness in former time desolate and waste.
4Who cut up mallows by the bushes, and juniper roots *for* their
meat.
5They were driven forth from among *men,* (they cried after them
as *after* a thief;)
6To dwell in the cliffs of the valleys, *in* caves of the earth, and
*in* the rocks.
7Among the bushes they brayed; under the nettles they were
gathered together.
8 *They were* children of fools, yea, children of base men: they
were viler than the earth.
9And now am I their song, yea, I am their byword.

AMP [a] Blameless and upright as Job had been—and God had so pronounced him—his misunderstood afflictions had caused him to get dangerously off center. Instead of keeping his mind stayed on God and justifying Him, he is giving his whole thought to justifying himself. Instead of humility there is only self-righteousness. In this chapter he uses pronouns referring to himself fifty times. But when he was able to see himself as God saw him, he loathed himself and repented "in dust and ashes."

## Amplified

7When I went out to the gate of the city, when I prepared my
seat in the street—the broad place [for the council at the city's
gate];
8The young men saw me, and hid themselves; the aged rose up
*and* stood;
9The princes refrained from talking, and laid their hand on their
mouth;
10The voice of the nobles was hushed, and their tongue cleaved
to the roof of their mouth.
11For when the ear heard, it called me happy *and* blessed me;
and when the eye saw, it testified for me [approving];
12Because I delivered the poor who cried, the fatherless *and* him
who had none to help him.
13The blessing of him who was about to perish came upon me,
and I caused the widow's heart to sing for joy.
14I put on [a]righteousness, and it clothed me *or* clothed itself
with me; my justice was like a robe and a turban *or* a diadem *or*
a crown!
15I was eyes to the blind, and feet was I to the lame.
16I was a father to the poor *and* needy, the cause of him I did
not know I searched out.
17And I broke the jaws *or* the big teeth of the unrighteous, and
plucked the prey out of his teeth.
18Then I said, I shall die in *or* beside my nest, and I shall
multiply my days as the sand;
19My root is spread out *and* open to the waters, and the dew lies
all night upon my branch;
20My glory *and* honor are fresh in me, [being constantly
renewed] and my bow gains [ever] new strength in my hand.
21Men listened to me and waited, and kept silence for my
counsel.
22After I spoke they did not speak again, and my speech
dropped upon them [like a refreshing shower].
23And they waited for me as for the rain; and they opened their
mouths wide as for the spring rain.
24I smiled on them when they had no confidence, and their
depression did not cast down the light of my countenance.
25I chose out their way [for them], and sat as [their] chief, and
dwelt like a king among his soldiers, like one who comforts mourners.

**30** BUT NOW they who are younger than I have me in derision, whose fathers I disdained to set with the dogs of my
flock.
2Yes, how could the strength of their hands profit me? Men
whose ripe age *and* vigor have perished.
3They are gaunt with want and famine; they gnaw the dry *and*
barren ground, *or* flee into the wilderness, into the gloom of wasteness and desolation.
4They pluck saltwort *or* mallows among the bushes, and roots
of the broom for their food *or* to warm them.
5They are driven from among men, who shout after them as
after a thief.
6They must dwell in the clefts of frightful valleys [gullies made
by torrents], and in holes of the earth and of the rocks.
7Among the bushes they bray *and* howl [like wild animals];
beneath the prickly scrub they fling themselves *and* huddle together.
8Sons of the worthless and nameless, they have been scourged
*and* crushed out of the land.
9And now I have become their song; yes, I am a byword to
them.

## New American Standard

7 "When I went out to the gate of the city,
When I took my seat in the square;
8 The young men saw me and hid themselves,
And the old men arose *and* stood.
9 "The princes stopped talking,
And put *their* hands on their mouths;
10 The voice of the nobles was hushed,
And their tongue stuck to their palate.
11 "For when the ear heard, it called me blessed;
And when the eye saw, it gave witness of me,
12 Because I delivered the poor who cried for help,
And the orphan who had no helper.
13 "The blessing of the one ready to perish came upon me,
And I made the widow's heart sing for joy.
14 "I put on righteousness, and it clothed me;
My justice was like a robe and a turban.
15 "I was eyes to the blind,
And feet to the lame.
16 "I was a father to the needy,
And I investigated the case which I did not know.
17 "And I broke the jaws of the wicked,
And snatched the prey from his teeth.
18 "Then I thought, 'I shall die in my nest,
And I shall multiply *my* days as the sand.
19 'My root is spread out to the waters,
And dew lies all night on my branch.
20 'My glory is *ever* new with me,
And my bow is renewed in my hand.'

**21**¶ "To me they listened and waited,
And kept silent for my counsel.
22 "After my words they did not speak again,
And my speech dropped on them.
23 "And they waited for me as for the rain,
And opened their mouth as for the spring rain.
24 "I smiled on them when they did not believe,
And the light of my face they did not cast down.
25 "I chose a way for them and sat as chief,
And dwelt as a king among the troops,
As one who comforted the mourners.

### *Job's Present State Is Humiliating*

**30** "BUT NOW those younger than I mock me,
Whose fathers I disdained to put with the dogs of my flock.
2 "Indeed, what *good was* the strength of their hands to me?
Vigor had perished from them.
3 "From want and famine they are gaunt
Who gnaw the dry ground by night in waste and desolation,
4 Who pluck [b]mallow by the bushes,
And whose food is the root of the broom shrub.
5 "They are driven from the community;
They shout against them as *against* a thief,
6 So that they dwell in dreadful valleys,
In holes of the earth and of the rocks.
7 "Among the bushes they cry out;
Under the nettles they are gathered together.
8 "Fools, even those without a name,
They were scourged from the land.

**9**¶ "And now I have become their taunt,
I have even become a byword to them.

NAS [b] I.e., plant of the salt marshes

## New International

7 "When I went to the gate of the city
and took my seat in the public square,
8 the young men saw me and stepped aside
and the old men rose to their feet;
9 the chief men refrained from speaking
and covered their mouths with their hands;
10 the voices of the nobles were hushed,
and their tongues stuck to the roof of their mouths.
11 Whoever heard me spoke well of me,
and those who saw me commended me,
12 because I rescued the poor who cried for help,
and the fatherless who had none to assist him.
13 The man who was dying blessed me;
I made the widow's heart sing.
14 I put on righteousness as my clothing;
justice was my robe and my turban.
15 I was eyes to the blind
and feet to the lame.
16 I was a father to the needy;
I took up the case of the stranger.
17 I broke the fangs of the wicked
and snatched the victims from their teeth.

18 "I thought, 'I will die in my own house,
my days as numerous as the grains of sand.
19 My roots will reach to the water,
and the dew will lie all night on my branches.
20 My glory will remain fresh in me,
the bow ever new in my hand.'

21 "Men listened to me expectantly,
waiting in silence for my counsel.
22 After I had spoken, they spoke no more;
my words fell gently on their ears.
23 They waited for me as for showers
and drank in my words as the spring rain.
24 When I smiled at them, they scarcely believed it;
the light of my face was precious to them.[c]
25 I chose the way for them and sat as their chief;
I dwelt as a king among his troops;
I was like one who comforts mourners.

**30** "BUT NOW they mock me,
men younger than I,
whose fathers I would have disdained
to put with my sheep dogs.
2 Of what use was the strength of their hands to me,
since their vigor had gone from them?
3 Haggard from want and hunger,
they roamed[d] the parched land
in desolate wastelands at night.
4 In the brush they gathered salt herbs,
and their food[e] was the root of the broom tree.
5 They were banished from their fellow men,
shouted at as if they were thieves.
6 They were forced to live in the dry stream beds,
among the rocks and in holes in the ground.
7 They brayed among the bushes
and huddled in the undergrowth.
8 A base and nameless brood,
they were driven out of the land.

9 "And now their sons mock me in song;
I have become a byword among them.

NIV [c] *24* The meaning of the Hebrew for this clause is uncertain. [d] *3* Or *gnawed* [e] *4* Or *fuel*

## King James

10 They abhor me, they flee far from me, and spare not to spit in my face.
11 Because he hath loosed my cord, and afflicted me, they have also let loose the bridle before me.
12 Upon *my* right *hand* rise the youth; they push away my feet, and they raise up against me the ways of their destruction.
13 They mar my path, they set forward my calamity, they have no helper.
14 They came *upon me* as a wide breaking in *of waters:* in the desolation they rolled themselves *upon me.*
15 Terrors are turned upon me: they pursue my soul as the wind: and my welfare passeth away as a cloud.
16 And now my soul is poured out upon me; the days of affliction have taken hold upon me.
17 My bones are pierced in me in the night season: and my sinews take no rest.
18 By the great force *of my disease* is my garment changed: it bindeth me about as the collar of my coat.
19 He hath cast me into the mire, and I am become like dust and ashes.
20 I cry unto thee, and thou dost not hear me: I stand up, and thou regardest me *not.*
21 Thou art become cruel to me: with thy strong hand thou opposest thyself against me.
22 Thou liftest me up to the wind; thou causest me to ride *upon it,* and dissolvest my substance.
23 For I know *that* thou wilt bring me *to* death, and *to* the house appointed for all living.
24 Howbeit he will not stretch out *his* hand to the grave, though they cry in his destruction.
25 Did not I weep for him that was in trouble? was *not* my soul grieved for the poor?
26 When I looked for good, then evil came *unto me:* and when I waited for light, there came darkness.
27 My bowels boiled, and rested not: the days of affliction prevented me.
28 I went mourning without the sun: I stood up, *and* I cried in the congregation.
29 I am a brother to dragons, and a companion to owls.
30 My skin is black upon me, and my bones are burned with heat.
31 My harp also is *turned* to mourning, and my organ into the voice of them that weep.

**31** I MADE a covenant with mine eyes; why then should I think upon a maid?
2 For what portion of God *is there* from above? and *what* inheritance of the Almighty from on high?
3 *Is* not destruction to the wicked? and a strange *punishment* to the workers of iniquity?
4 Doth not he see my ways, and count all my steps?
5 If I have walked with vanity, or if my foot hath hasted to deceit;

## Amplified

10 They abhor me, they stand aloof from me, and do not refrain from spitting in my face *or* at the sight of me.
11 For God has loosed my bowstring and afflicted *and* humbled me; they have cast off the bridle [of restraint] before me.
12 On my right hand rise the rabble brood; they jostle me *and* push away my feet, and they cast up against me their ways of destruction [like an advancing army].
13 They break up *and* clutter my path [embarrassing my plans]; they urge on my calamity, even though they have no helper [and are themselves helpless].
14 As through a wide breach they come in, amid the crash [of falling walls] they roll themselves upon me.
15 Terrors are turned upon me; my honor *and* reputation they chase way like the wind, and my welfare has passed away as a cloud.
16 And now my life is poured out within me; the days of affliction have gripped hold upon me.
17 My bones are pierced [with aching] in the night season, and the pains that gnaw me take no rest.
18 By the great force [of my disease] my garment is disguised *and* disfigured; it binds me about like the collar of my coat.
19 [God] has cast me into the mire, and I am become like dust and ashes.
20 I cry to You, [Lord,] and You do not answer me; I stand up, but You [only] gaze [indifferently] at me.
21 You have become harsh *and* cruel to me; with the might of Your hand You [keep me alive only to] persecute me.
22 You lift me up on the wind; You cause me to ride upon it, and You toss me about in the tempest.
23 For I know that You will bring me to death, and to the house (of meeting) appointed for all living.
24 However, does not one falling in a heap of ruins stretch out his hand? Or in his calamity will he not therefore cry for help?
25 Did not I weep for him who was in trouble? Was not my heart grieved for the poor *and* needy?
26 But when I looked for good, then evil came to me, and when I waited for light, there came darkness.
27 My heart is troubled and does not rest; days of affliction come to meet me.
28 I go about blackened, but not by the sun. I stand up in the congregation *and* cry for help.
29 I am a brother to jackals [which howl], and a companion to ostriches [which scream dismally].
30 My skin falls from me in blackened flakes, and my bones are burned with heat.
31 Therefore my lyre is turned to mourning, and my pipe into the voice of those who weep.

**31** I DICTATED a covenant—an agreement—to my eyes; how then could I look [lustfully] upon a girl?
2 For what portion should I have from God above [if I were lewd], and what heritage from the Almighty on high?
3 Does not calamity [justly] befall the unrighteous, and disaster the workers of iniquity?
4 Does not [God] see my ways, and count all my steps?
5 If I have walked with falsehood *or* vanity, or if my foot has hastened to deceit—

## New American Standard

10 "They abhor me *and* stand aloof from me,
And they do not refrain from spitting at my face.
11 "Because He has loosed His bowstring and afflicted me,
They have cast off the bridle before me.
12 "On the right hand their brood arises;
They thrust aside my feet and build up against me their ways of destruction.
13 "They break up my path,
They profit from my destruction,
No one restrains them.
14 "As *through* a wide breach they come,
Amid the tempest they roll on.
15 "Terrors are turned against me,
They pursue my honor as the wind,
And my prosperity has passed away like a cloud.

16¶ "And now my soul is poured out within me;
Days of affliction have seized me.
17 "At night it pierces my bones within me,
And my gnawing *pains* take no rest.
18 "By a great force my garment is distorted;
It binds me about as the collar of my coat.
19 "He has cast me into the mire,
And I have become like dust and ashes.
20 "I cry out to Thee for help, but Thou dost not answer me;
I stand up, and Thou dost turn Thy attention against me.
21 "Thou hast become cruel to me;
With the might of Thy hand Thou dost persecute me.
22 "Thou dost lift me up to the wind *and* cause me to ride;
And Thou dost dissolve me in a storm.
23 "For I know that Thou wilt bring me to death
And to the house of meeting for all living.

24¶ "Yet does not one in a heap of ruins stretch out *his* hand,
Or in his disaster therefore cry out for help?
25 "Have I not wept for the one whose life is hard?
Was not my soul grieved for the needy?
26 "When I expected good, then evil came;
When I waited for light, then darkness came.
27 "I am seething within, and cannot relax;
Days of affliction confront me.
28 "I go about mourning without comfort;
I stand up in the assembly *and* cry out for help.
29 "I have become a brother to jackals,
And a companion of ostriches.
30 "My skin turns black on me,
And my bones burn with fever.
31 "Therefore my harp is turned to mourning,
And my flute to the sound of those who weep.

### *Job Asserts His Integrity*

**31** "I HAVE made a covenant with my eyes;
How then could I gaze at a virgin?
2 "And what is the portion of God from above
Or the heritage of the Almighty from on high?
3 "Is it not calamity to the unjust,
And disaster to those who work iniquity?
4 "Does He not see my ways,
And number all my steps?

5¶ "If I have walked with falsehood,
And my foot has hastened after deceit,

## New International

10They detest me and keep their distance;
they do not hesitate to spit in my face.
11Now that God has unstrung my bow and afflicted me,
they throw off restraint in my presence.
12On my right the tribe[a] attacks;
they lay snares for my feet,
they build their siege ramps against me.
13They break up my road;
they succeed in destroying me—
without anyone's helping them.[b]
14They advance as through a gaping breach;
amid the ruins they come rolling in.
15Terrors overwhelm me;
my dignity is driven away as by the wind,
my safety vanishes like a cloud.

16"And now my life ebbs away;
days of suffering grip me.
17Night pierces my bones;
my gnawing pains never rest.
18In his great power ⌞God⌟ becomes like clothing to me[c];
he binds me like the neck of my garment.
19He throws me into the mud,
and I am reduced to dust and ashes.

20"I cry out to you, O God, but you do not answer;
I stand up, but you merely look at me.
21You turn on me ruthlessly;
with the might of your hand you attack me.
22You snatch me up and drive me before the wind;
you toss me about in the storm.
23I know you will bring me down to death,
to the place appointed for all the living.

24"Surely no one lays a hand on a broken man
when he cries for help in his distress.
25Have I not wept for those in trouble?
Has not my soul grieved for the poor?
26Yet when I hoped for good, evil came;
when I looked for light, then came darkness.
27The churning inside me never stops;
days of suffering confront me.
28I go about blackened, but not by the sun;
I stand up in the assembly and cry for help.
29I have become a brother of jackals,
a companion of owls.
30My skin grows black and peels;
my body burns with fever.
31My harp is tuned to mourning,
and my flute to the sound of wailing.

**31** "I MADE a covenant with my eyes
not to look lustfully at a girl.
2For what is man's lot from God above,
his heritage from the Almighty on high?
3Is it not ruin for the wicked,
disaster for those who do wrong?
4Does he not see my ways
and count my every step?

5"If I have walked in falsehood
or my foot has hurried after deceit—

**NIV** [a] *12* The meaning of the Hebrew for this word is uncertain. [b] *13* Or *me. / 'No one can help him,' ⌞they say⌟.* [c] *18* Hebrew; Septuagint *⌞God⌟ grasps my clothing*

## King James

6Let me be weighed in an even balance, that God may know mine integrity.

7If my step hath turned out of the way, and mine heart walked after mine eyes, and if any blot hath cleaved to mine hands;

8 *Then* let me sow, and let another eat; yea, let my offspring be rooted out.

9If mine heart have been deceived by a woman, or *if* I have laid wait at my neighbour's door;

10 *Then* let my wife grind unto another, and let others bow down upon her.

11For this *is* an heinous crime; yea, it *is* an iniquity *to be punished by* the judges.

12For it *is* a fire *that* consumeth to destruction, and would root out all mine increase.

13If I did despise the cause of my manservant or of my maidservant, when they contended with me;

14What then shall I do when God riseth up? and when he visiteth, what shall I answer him?

15Did not he that made me in the womb make him? and did not one fashion us in the womb?

16If I have withheld the poor from *their* desire, or have caused the eyes of the widow to fail;

17Or have eaten my morsel myself alone, and the fatherless hath not eaten thereof;

18(For from my youth he was brought up with me, as *with* a father, and I have guided her from my mother's womb;)

19If I have seen any perish for want of clothing, or any poor without covering;

20If his loins have not blessed me, and *if* he were *not* warmed with the fleece of my sheep;

21If I have lifted up my hand against the fatherless, when I saw my help in the gate:

22 *Then* let mine arm fall from my shoulder blade, and mine arm be broken from the bone.

23For destruction *from* God *was* a terror to me, and by reason of his highness I could not endure.

24If I have made gold my hope, or have said to the fine gold, *Thou art* my confidence;

25If I rejoiced because my wealth *was* great, and because mine hand had gotten much;

26If I beheld the sun when it shined, or the moon walking *in* brightness;

27And my heart hath been secretly enticed, or my mouth hath kissed my hand:

28This also *were* an iniquity *to be punished by* the judge: for I should have denied the God *that is* above.

29If I rejoiced at the destruction of him that hated me, or lifted up myself when evil found him:

30Neither have I suffered my mouth to sin by wishing a curse to his soul.

31If the men of my tabernacle said not, Oh that we had of his flesh! we cannot be satisfied.

32The stranger did not lodge in the street: *but* I opened my doors to the traveller.

33If I covered my transgressions as Adam, by hiding mine iniquity in my bosom:

## Amplified

6Oh, let me be weighed in a just balance *and* let Him weigh me, that God may know my integrity!

7If my step has turned out of [God's] way, and my heart has gone the way my eyes [covetously] invited, and if any spot has stained my hands with guilt,

8Then let me sow, and let another eat; yes, let the produce of my field be rooted out, *or* my offspring.

9If my heart has been deceived *and* I made a fool by a woman, or if I have [covetously] laid wait at my neighbor's door [until his departure],

10Then let my wife grind [meal, as a bond slave] for another, and let others bow down upon her.

11For [adultery] is a heinous *and* chief crime, an iniquity [to demand action by] the judges, *and* punishment. [Deut. 22:22; John 8:5.]

12For [uncontrolled passion] is a fire which consumes to Abaddon [to destruction, ruin and the place of final torment]; [that fire once lighted would rage until all is consumed] and would burn to the root all my [life's] increase.

13If I have despised *and* rejected the cause of my manservant or my maidservant when they contended *or* brought a complaint against me,

14What then shall I do when God rises up [to judge]? When He visits [to inquire of me], what shall I answer Him? [Ps. 44:21.]

15Did not He Who made me in the womb make [my servant]? And did not One fashion us both in the womb? [Prov. 14:31; 22:2; Mal. 2:10.]

16If I have withheld from the poor *and* needy what they desired, or have caused the eyes of the widow to look in vain [for relief],

17Or have eaten my morsel alone, and have not shared it with the fatherless—

18No, from my youth [the fatherless] grew up with me as a father, and I have been [the widow's] guide from my mother's womb.

19If I have seen any one perish for want of clothing, or any poor person without covering;

20If his loins have not blessed me [for clothing them], and if he was not warmed with the fleece of my sheep;

21If I have lifted my hand against the fatherless, when I saw [that the judges would be favorable and be] my help at the [council] gate,

22Then let my shoulder fall away from my shoulder blade, and my arm be broken from its socket.

23For calamity from God was a terror to me, and because of His majesty I could not endure [to face Him], *and* could do nothing. [Isa. 13:6; Joel 1:15.]

24If I have made gold my trust *and* hope, or have said to fine gold, You are my confidence;

25If I rejoiced because my wealth was great and because my [powerful] hand [alone] had gotten much;

26If I beheld [as an object of worship] the sunlight when it shone, or the moon walking in its brightness;

27And my heart has been secretly enticed by them, or my mouth has kissed my hand [in homage to them];

28This also would have been [a heinous and principal] iniquity to demand the judges' action *and* punishment, for I would have denied *and* been false to the God Who is above. [Cf. Deut. 4:19; 17:2-7.]

29If I rejoiced at the destruction of him who hated me, or lifted myself up [in malicious triumph] when evil overtook him—

30No, I neither have let my mouth sin by cursing my enemy nor by praying that he might die.

31[Just ask] if the men of my tent will not say, Who can find one in need who has not been satisfied with food he gave them?

32The temporary resident has not lodged in the street, but I have opened my door to the wayfaring man.

33If like Adam *or* like [other] men I have concealed my transgressions by hiding my iniquity in my bosom,

## New American Standard

6 Let Him weigh me with accurate scales,
And let God know my integrity.
7 "If my step has turned from the way,
Or my heart followed my eyes,
Or if any spot has stuck to my hands,
8 Let me sow and another eat,
And let my crops be uprooted.

9¶ "If my heart has been enticed by a woman,
Or I have lurked at my neighbor's doorway,
10 May my wife grind for another,
And let others kneel down over her.
11 "For that would be a lustful crime;
Moreover, it would be an iniquity *punishable by* judges.
12 "For it would be fire that consumes to Abaddon,
And would uproot all my increase.

13¶ "If I have despised the claim of my male or female slaves
When they filed a complaint against me,
14 What then could I do when God arises,
And when He calls me to account, what will I answer Him?
15 "Did not He who made me in the womb make him,
And the same one fashion us in the womb?

16¶ "If I have kept the poor from *their* desire,
Or have caused the eyes of the widow to fail,
17 Or have eaten my morsel alone,
And the orphan has not shared it
18 (But from my youth he grew up with me as with a father,
And from infancy I guided her),
19 If I have seen anyone perish for lack of clothing,
Or that the needy had no covering,
20 If his loins have not thanked me,
And if he has not been warmed with the fleece of my sheep,
21 If I have lifted up my hand against the orphan,
Because I saw I had support in the gate,
22 Let my shoulder fall from the socket,
And my arm be broken off at the elbow.
23 "For calamity from God is a terror to me,
And because of His majesty I can do nothing.

24¶ "If I have put my confidence *in* gold,
And called fine gold my trust,
25 If I have gloated because my wealth was great,
And because my hand had secured *so* much;
26 If I have looked at the sun when it shone,
Or the moon going in splendor,
27 And my heart became secretly enticed,
And my hand threw a kiss from my mouth,
28 That too would have been an iniquity *calling for* judgment,
For I would have denied God above.

29¶ "Have I rejoiced at the extinction of my enemy,
Or exulted when evil befell him?
30 "No, I have not allowed my mouth to sin
By asking for his life in a curse.
31 "Have the men of my tent not said,
'Who can find one who has not been satisfied with his meat'?
32 "The alien has not lodged outside,
*For* I have opened my doors to the traveler.
33 "Have I covered my transgressions like Adam,
By hiding my iniquity in my bosom,

## New International

6 let God weigh me in honest scales
and he will know that I am blameless—
7 if my steps have turned from the path,
if my heart has been led by my eyes,
or if my hands have been defiled,
8 then may others eat what I have sown,
and may my crops be uprooted.

9 "If my heart has been enticed by a woman,
or if I have lurked at my neighbor's door,
10 then may my wife grind another man's grain,
and may other men sleep with her.
11 For that would have been shameful,
a sin to be judged.
12 It is a fire that burns to Destruction[a];
it would have uprooted my harvest.

13 "If I have denied justice to my menservants and maidservants
when they had a grievance against me,
14 what will I do when God confronts me?
What will I answer when called to account?
15 Did not he who made me in the womb make them?
Did not the same one form us both within our mothers?

16 "If I have denied the desires of the poor
or let the eyes of the widow grow weary,
17 if I have kept my bread to myself,
not sharing it with the fatherless—
18 but from my youth I reared him as would a father,
and from my birth I guided the widow—
19 if I have seen anyone perishing for lack of clothing,
or a needy man without a garment,
20 and his heart did not bless me
for warming him with the fleece from my sheep,
21 if I have raised my hand against the fatherless,
knowing that I had influence in court,
22 then let my arm fall from the shoulder,
let it be broken off at the joint.
23 For I dreaded destruction from God,
and for fear of his splendor I could not do such things.

24 "If I have put my trust in gold
or said to pure gold, 'You are my security,'
25 if I have rejoiced over my great wealth,
the fortune my hands had gained,
26 if I have regarded the sun in its radiance
or the moon moving in splendor,
27 so that my heart was secretly enticed
and my hand offered them a kiss of homage,
28 then these also would be sins to be judged,
for I would have been unfaithful to God on high.

29 "If I have rejoiced at my enemy's misfortune
or gloated over the trouble that came to him—
30 I have not allowed my mouth to sin
by invoking a curse against his life—
31 if the men of my household have never said,
'Who has not had his fill of Job's meat?'—
32 but no stranger had to spend the night in the street,
for my door was always open to the traveler—
33 if I have concealed my sin as men do,[b]
by hiding my guilt in my heart

NIV [a] 12 Hebrew *Abaddon* [b] 33 Or *as Adam did*

## King James

34 Did I fear a great multitude, or did the contempt of families
terrify me, that I kept silence, *and* went not out of the door?
35 Oh that one would hear me! behold, my desire *is, that* the
Almighty would answer me, and *that* mine adversary had written
a book.
36 Surely I would take it upon my shoulder, *and* bind it *as* a
crown to me.
37 I would declare unto him the number of my steps; as a prince
would I go near unto him.
38 If my land cry against me, or that the furrows likewise thereof
complain;
39 If I have eaten the fruits thereof without money, or have
caused the owners thereof to lose their life:
40 Let thistles grow instead of wheat, and cockle instead of barley. The words of Job are ended.

**32** SO THESE three men ceased to answer Job, because he
*was* righteous in his own eyes.
2 Then was kindled the wrath of Elihu the son of Barachel the
Buzite, of the kindred of Ram: against Job was his wrath kindled,
because he justified himself rather than God.
3 Also against his three friends was his wrath kindled, because
they had found no answer, and *yet* had condemned Job.
4 Now Elihu had waited till Job had spoken, because they *were*
elder than he.
5 When Elihu saw that *there was* no answer in the mouth of *these*
three men, then his wrath was kindled.
6 And Elihu the son of Barachel the Buzite answered and said,
I *am* young, and ye *are* very old; wherefore I was afraid, and durst
not show you mine opinion.
7 I said, Days should speak, and multitude of years should teach
wisdom.
8 But *there is* a spirit in man: and the inspiration of the Almighty
giveth them understanding.
9 Great men are not *always* wise: neither do the aged understand
judgment.
10 Therefore I said, Hearken to me; I also will show mine opinion.
11 Behold, I waited for your words; I gave ear to your reasons,
whilst ye searched out what to say.
12 Yea, I attended unto you, and, behold, *there was* none of you
that convinced Job, *or* that answered his words:
13 Lest ye should say, We have found out wisdom: God
thrusteth him down, not man.
14 Now he hath not directed *his* words against me: neither will
I answer him with your speeches.
15 They were amazed, they answered no more: they left off
speaking.
16 When I had waited, (for they spake not, but stood still, *and*
answered no more;)
17 *I said,* I will answer also my part, I also will show mine
opinion.
18 For I am full of matter, the spirit within me constraineth me.
19 Behold, my belly *is* as wine *which* hath no vent; it is ready to
burst like new bottles.

## Amplified

34 Because I feared the great multitude and the contempt of
families terrified me, so that I kept silence *and* did not go out of the
door—
35 Oh, for a hearing! Oh, for an answer from the Almighty, and
that my adversary would write out His indictment [and put His
vague accusations in tangible form] in a book!
36 Surely I would [proudly] bear it on my shoulder, *and* wind the
scroll about my head as a diadem.
37 I would count out to Him the number of my steps [with every
detail of my life], approaching His presence as a prince.
38 For if my land has cried out against me, and its furrows have
complained together with tears [that I have no right to them];
39 If I have eaten its fruits without paying for them, or have
caused its [rightful] owners to breathe their last;
40 Let thistles grow instead of wheat, and cockleburs instead of
barley. The [controversial] words of Job [with his friends] are
ended.

**32** SO THESE three men ceased to answer Job, because he
was [rigidly] righteous [upright and in right standing with
God] in his own eyes. [But there was a fifth man there also.]
2 Elihu the son of Barachel the Buzite, of the family of Ram,
became indignant. His indignation was kindled against Job because he justified himself rather than God [even made himself out
to be better than God].
3 Also against [Job's] three friends was [Elihu's] anger kindled,
because they had found no answer [were unable to show his real
error], and yet they had declared him to be in the wrong [and
responsible for his own afflictions].
4 Now Elihu had waited to speak to Job because the others were
older than he.
5 But when Elihu saw that there was no answer in the mouth of
these three men, he became angry.
6 Then Elihu the son of Barachel the Buzite said, I am young, and
you are aged; for that reason I was timid *and* restrained, and dared
not declare my opinion to you.
7 I said, Age should speak, and a multitude of years should
teach wisdom [so let it be heard].
8 But there is [a vital force] a spirit [of intelligence] in man, and
the breath of the Almighty gives men understanding. [Prov. 2:6.]
9 It is not the great [necessarily] who are wise, nor [always] the
aged who understand justice.
10 So I say, Listen to me; I also will give you my opinion [about
Job's situation] *and* my knowledge.
11 You see, I waited for your words; I listened to your wise
reasons, while you searched out what to say.
12 Yes, I paid attention to what you said, and behold, not one
of you convinced Job *or* made [satisfactory] replies to his words
[you could not refute him].
13 Beware lest you say, We have found wisdom. God thrusts
[Job] down [justly], not man [God alone is dealing with him].
14 Now [Job] has not directed his words against me [therefore I
have no cause for irritation], neither will I answer him with
speeches like yours. [I speak for truth, not for revenge.]
15 [Job's friends] are amazed *and* embarrassed; they answer no
more; they have not a thing to say [reports Elihu].
16 And shall I wait because they say nothing, but stand still *and*
answer no more?
17 I also will answer my [God-assigned] part, I also will declare
my opinion *and* my knowledge.
18 For I am full of words, the spirit within me constrains me.
19 My breast is as wine that has no vent; like new wineskins, it
is ready to burst.

## New American Standard

34 Because I feared the great multitude,
And the contempt of families terrified me,
And kept silent and did not go out of doors?
35 "Oh that I had one to hear me!
Behold, here is my signature;
Let the Almighty answer me!
And the indictment which my adversary has written,
36 Surely I would carry it on my shoulder;
I would bind it to myself like a crown.
37 "I would declare to Him the number of my steps;
Like a prince I would approach Him.
38¶ "If my land cries out against me,
And its furrows weep together;
39 If I have eaten its fruit without money,
Or have caused its owners to lose their lives,
40 Let briars grow instead of wheat,
And stinkweed instead of barley."
The words of Job are ended.

*Elihu in Anger Rebukes Job*

**32** THEN THESE three men ceased answering Job, because
he was righteous in his own eyes.
2 But the anger of Elihu the son of Barachel the Buzite, of the
family of Ram burned; against Job his anger burned, because he
justified himself before God.
3 And his anger burned against his three friends because they
had found no answer, and yet had condemned Job.
4 Now Elihu had waited to speak to Job because they were years
older than he.
5 And when Elihu saw that there was no answer in the mouth
of the three men his anger burned.
6 So Elihu the son of Barachel the Buzite spoke out and said,
"I am young in years and you are old;
Therefore I was shy and afraid to tell you what I think.
7 "I thought age should speak,
And increased years should teach wisdom.
8 "But it is a spirit in man,
And the breath of the Almighty gives them understanding.
9 "The abundant *in years* may not be wise,
Nor may elders understand justice.
10 "So I say, 'Listen to me,
I too will tell what I think.'
11¶ "Behold, I waited for your words,
I listened to your reasonings,
While you pondered what to say.
12 "I even paid close attention to you,
Indeed, there was no one who refuted Job,
Not one of you who answered his words.
13 "Do not say,
'We have found wisdom;
God will rout him, not man.'
14 "For he has not arranged *his* words against me;
Nor will I reply to him with your arguments.
15¶ "They are dismayed, they answer no more;
Words have failed them.
16 "And shall I wait, because they do not speak,
Because they stop *and* answer no more?
17 "I too will answer my share,
I also will tell my opinion.
18 "For I am full of words;
The spirit within me constrains me.
19 "Behold, my belly is like unvented wine,
Like new wineskins it is about to burst.

## New International

34 because I so feared the crowd
and so dreaded the contempt of the clans
that I kept silent and would not go outside
35 ("Oh, that I had someone to hear me!
I sign now my defense—let the Almighty answer me;
let my accuser put his indictment in writing.
36 Surely I would wear it on my shoulder,
I would put it on like a crown.
37 I would give him an account of my every step;
like a prince I would approach him.)—
38 "if my land cries out against me
and all its furrows are wet with tears,
39 if I have devoured its yield without payment
or broken the spirit of its tenants,
40 then let briers come up instead of wheat
and weeds instead of barley."
The words of Job are ended.

*Elihu*

**32** SO THESE three men stopped answering Job, because he
was righteous in his own eyes. 2 But Elihu son of Barakel
the Buzite, of the family of Ram, became very angry with Job for
justifying himself rather than God. 3 He was also angry with the
three friends, because they had found no way to refute Job, and
yet had condemned him.[a] 4 Now Elihu had waited before speaking
to Job because they were older than he. 5 But when he saw that the
three men had nothing more to say, his anger was aroused.
6 So Elihu son of Barakel the Buzite said:

"I am young in years,
and you are old;
that is why I was fearful,
not daring to tell you what I know.
7 I thought, 'Age should speak;
advanced years should teach wisdom.'
8 But it is the spirit[b] in a man,
the breath of the Almighty, that gives him understanding.
9 It is not only the old[c] who are wise,
not only the aged who understand what is right.

10 "Therefore I say: Listen to me;
I too will tell you what I know.
11 I waited while you spoke,
I listened to your reasoning;
while you were searching for words,
12 I gave you my full attention.
But not one of you has proved Job wrong;
none of you has answered his arguments.
13 Do not say, 'We have found wisdom;
let God refute him, not man.'
14 But Job has not marshaled his words against me,
and I will not answer him with your arguments.

15 "They are dismayed and have no more to say;
words have failed them.
16 Must I wait, now that they are silent,
now that they stand there with no reply?
17 I too will have my say;
I too will tell what I know.
18 For I am full of words,
and the spirit within me compels me;
19 inside I am like bottled-up wine,
like new wineskins ready to burst.

**NIV** [a] 3 Masoretic Text; an ancient Hebrew scribal tradition *Job, and so had condemned God* [b] 8 Or *Spirit;* also in verse 18 [c] 9 Or *many;* or *great*

## King James

20I will speak, that I may be refreshed: I will open my lips and
answer.
21Let me not, I pray you, accept any man's person, neither let
me give flattering titles unto man.
22For I know not to give flattering titles; *in so doing* my maker
would soon take me away.

**33** WHEREFORE, JOB, I pray thee, hear my speeches, and
hearken to all my words.
2Behold, now I have opened my mouth, my tongue hath
spoken in my mouth.
3My words *shall be of* the uprightness of my heart: and my lips
shall utter knowledge clearly.
4The spirit of God hath made me, and the breath of the Almighty hath given me life.
5If thou canst answer me, set *thy words* in order before me, stand
up.
6Behold, I *am* according to thy wish in God's stead: I also am
formed out of the clay.
7Behold, my terror shall not make thee afraid, neither shall my
hand be heavy upon thee.
8Surely thou hast spoken in mine hearing, and I have heard the
voice of *thy* words, *saying*,
9I am clean without transgression, I *am* innocent; neither *is there*
iniquity in me.
10Behold, he findeth occasions against me, he counteth me for
his enemy,
11He putteth my feet in the stocks, he marketh all my paths.
12Behold, *in* this thou art not just: I will answer thee, that God
is greater than man.
13Why dost thou strive against him? for he giveth not account
of any of his matters.
14For God speaketh once, yea twice, *yet man* perceiveth it not.
15In a dream, in a vision of the night, when deep sleep falleth
upon men, in slumberings upon the bed;
16Then he openeth the ears of men, and sealeth their instruction,
17That he may withdraw man *from his* purpose, and hide pride
from man.
18He keepeth back his soul from the pit, and his life from
perishing by the sword.
19He is chastened also with pain upon his bed, and the multitude of his bones with strong *pain:*
20So that his life abhorreth bread, and his soul dainty meat.
21His flesh is consumed away, that it cannot be seen; and his
bones *that* were not seen stick out.
22Yea, his soul draweth near unto the grave, and his life to the
destroyers.
23If there be a messenger with him, an interpreter, one among
a thousand, to show unto man his uprightness:
24Then he is gracious unto him, and saith, Deliver him from
going down to the pit: I have found a ransom.
25His flesh shall be fresher than a child's: he shall return to the
days of his youth:

## Amplified

20I must speak, that I may get relief *and* be refreshed; I will open
my lips and answer.
21I will not [I warn you] be influenced by respect for any man's
person *and* show partiality, neither will I flatter any man.
22For I know not how to flatter, [wasting my time in mere
formalities, for then] my Maker would soon take me away.

**33** BE THAT as it may, Job, I beg of you to hear what I have
to say and give heed to all my words.
2Behold, here I am with open mouth, here is my tongue talking.
3My words shall express the uprightness of my heart, and my
lips shall speak what they know with utter sincerity.
4[It is] the Spirit of God that made me [which has stirred me up],
and the breath of the Almighty that gives me life [which inspires
me].
5Answer me now if you can; set your words in order before me;
take your stand.
6Behold, I am toward God *and* before Him even as you are; I also
am formed out of the clay [though I speak with abnormal wisdom
because of a divine illumination].
7See, my terror, [for I am only a fellow-mortal, not God] I shall
not make you afraid, neither shall my pressure be heavy upon you.
8Surely you have spoken in my hearing, and I have heard the
voice of your words, saying,
9I am clean, without transgression; I am innocent, neither is
there iniquity in me;
10But lo, God finds occasions against me *and* causes of alienation
*and* indifference; He counts me for His enemy;
11He puts my feet in the stocks; He [untrustingly] watches all
my paths [you say].
12I reply to you, Behold, in this you are not just; God is superior
to man.
13Why do you contend against Him? For He does not give
account of any of His actions. [Sufficient for us it should be to know
that it is He Who does them.]
14For God [does reveal His will; He] speaks not only once, but
more than once, even though men do not regard it [including you,
Job].
15[One may hear God's voice] in a dream, in a vision of the
night, when deep sleep falls on men, while slumbering upon the
bed;
16Then He opens the ears of men, and seals their instruction
[terrifying them with warnings]
17That He may withdraw man from his purpose, and cut off
pride from him [disgusting him with his own disappointing self-
sufficiency].
18He holds him back from the pit [of destruction], and his life
from perishing by the sword [of God's destructive judgments].
19[God's voice may be heard by man when] he is chastened with
pain upon his bed, and with continual strife in his bones, *or* while
all his bones are firmly *set;*
20So that his desire makes him loathe food, and even dainty
dishes [nauseate him].
21His flesh is so wasted away that it cannot be seen, and his
bones that were not seen stick out.
22Yes, his soul draws near to corruption, and his life to the
inflicters of death—the destroyers.
23[God's voice may be heard] if there is for the hearer a messenger *or* an angel, an interpreter, one among a thousand to show to
man what is right for him [how to be upright and in right standing
with God];
24Then [God] is gracious to him, and says, Deliver him from
going down into the pit [of destruction]; I have found a ransom [a
price of redemption, an atonement]!
25[Then the man's] flesh shall be restored; it becomes fresher
*and* more tender than a child's; he returns to the days of his youth.

## New American Standard

20 "Let me speak that I may get relief;
Let me open my lips and answer.
21 "Let me now be partial to no one;
Nor flatter *any* man.
22 "For I do not know how to flatter,
*Else* my Maker would soon take me away.

*Elihu Claims to Speak for God*

33 "HOWEVER NOW, Job, please hear my speech,
And listen to all my words.
2 "Behold now, I open my mouth,
My tongue in my mouth speaks.
3 "My words are *from* the uprightness of my heart;
And my lips speak knowledge sincerely.
4 "The Spirit of God has made me,
And the breath of the Almighty gives me life.
5 "Refute me if you can;
Array yourselves before me, take your stand.
6 "Behold, I belong to God like you;
I too have been formed out of the clay.
7 "Behold, no fear of me should terrify you,
Nor should my pressure weigh heavily on you.

8¶ "Surely you have spoken in my hearing,
And I have heard the sound of *your* words:
9 'I am pure, without transgression;
I am innocent and there is no guilt in me.
10 'Behold, He invents pretexts against me;
He counts me as His enemy.
11 'He puts my feet in the stocks;
He watches all my paths.'
12 "Behold, let me tell you, you are not right in this,
For God is greater than man.
13¶ "Why do you complain against Him,
That He does not give an account of all His doings?
14 "Indeed God speaks once,
Or twice, *yet* no one notices it.
15 "In a dream, a vision of the night,
When sound sleep falls on men,
While they slumber in their beds,
16 Then He opens the ears of men,
And seals their instruction,
17 That He may turn man aside *from his* conduct,
And keep man from pride;
18 He keeps back his soul from the pit,
And his life from passing over into Sheol.
19¶ "Man is also chastened with pain on his bed,
And with unceasing complaint in his bones;
20 So that his life loathes bread,
And his soul favorite food.
21 "His flesh wastes away from sight,
And his bones which were not seen stick out.
22 "Then his soul draws near to the pit,
And his life to those who bring death.
23¶ "If there is an angel *as* mediator for him,
One out of a thousand,
To remind a man what is right for him,
24 Then let him be gracious to him, and say,
'Deliver him from going down to the pit,
I have found a ransom';
25 Let his flesh become fresher than in youth,
Let him return to the days of his youthful vigor;

## New International

20 I must speak and find relief;
I must open my lips and reply.
21 I will show partiality to no one,
nor will I flatter any man;
22 for if I were skilled in flattery,
my Maker would soon take me away.

33 "BUT NOW, Job, listen to my words;
pay attention to everything I say.
2 I am about to open my mouth;
my words are on the tip of my tongue.
3 My words come from an upright heart;
my lips sincerely speak what I know.
4 The Spirit of God has made me;
the breath of the Almighty gives me life.
5 Answer me then, if you can;
prepare yourself and confront me.
6 I am just like you before God;
I too have been taken from clay.
7 No fear of me should alarm you,
nor should my hand be heavy upon you.

8 "But you have said in my hearing—
I heard the very words—
9 'I am pure and without sin;
I am clean and free from guilt.
10 Yet God has found fault with me;
he considers me his enemy.
11 He fastens my feet in shackles;
he keeps close watch on all my paths.'

12 "But I tell you, in this you are not right,
for God is greater than man.
13 Why do you complain to him
that he answers none of man's words[a]?
14 For God does speak—now one way, now another—
though man may not perceive it.
15 In a dream, in a vision of the night,
when deep sleep falls on men
as they slumber in their beds,
16 he may speak in their ears
and terrify them with warnings,
17 to turn man from wrongdoing
and keep him from pride,
18 to preserve his soul from the pit,[b]
his life from perishing by the sword.[c]
19 Or a man may be chastened on a bed of pain
with constant distress in his bones,
20 so that his very being finds food repulsive
and his soul loathes the choicest meal.
21 His flesh wastes away to nothing,
and his bones, once hidden, now stick out.
22 His soul draws near to the pit,[d]
and his life to the messengers of death.[e]

23 "Yet if there is an angel on his side
as a mediator, one out of a thousand,
to tell a man what is right for him,
24 to be gracious to him and say,
'Spare him from going down to the pit[f];
I have found a ransom for him'—
25 then his flesh is renewed like a child's;
it is restored as in the days of his youth.

**NIV** [a] 13 Or *that he does not answer for any of his actions* [b] 18 Or *preserve him from the grave* [c] 18 Or *from crossing the River* [d] 22 Or *He draws near to the grave* [e] 22 Or *to the dead* [f] 24 Or *grave*

## King James

26He shall pray unto God, and he will be favourable unto him: and he shall see his face with joy: for he will render unto man his righteousness.

27He looketh upon men, and *if any* say, I have sinned, and perverted *that which was* right, and it profited me not;

28He will deliver his soul from going into the pit, and his life shall see the light.

29Lo, all these *things* worketh God oftentimes with man,

30To bring back his soul from the pit, to be enlightened with the light of the living.

31Mark well, O Job, hearken unto me: hold thy peace, and I will speak.

32If thou hast any thing to say, answer me: speak, for I desire to justify thee.

33If not, hearken unto me: hold thy peace, and I shall teach thee wisdom.

**34** FURTHERMORE ELIHU answered and said,

2Hear my words, O ye wise *men;* and give ear unto me, ye that have knowledge.

3For the ear trieth words, as the mouth tasteth meat.

4Let us choose to us judgment: let us know among ourselves what *is* good.

5For Job hath said, I am righteous: and God hath taken away my judgment.

6Should I lie against my right? my wound *is* incurable without transgression.

7What man *is* like Job, *who* drinketh up scorning like water?

8Which goeth in company with the workers of iniquity, and walketh with wicked men.

9For he hath said, It profiteth a man nothing that he should delight himself with God.

10Therefore hearken unto me, ye men of understanding: far be it from God, *that he should do* wickedness; and *from* the Almighty, *that he should commit* iniquity.

11For the work of a man shall he render unto him, and cause every man to find according to *his* ways.

12Yea, surely God will not do wickedly, neither will the Almighty pervert judgment.

13Who hath given him a charge over the earth? or who hath disposed the whole world?

14If he set his heart upon man, *if* he gather unto himself his spirit and his breath;

15All flesh shall perish together, and man shall turn again unto dust.

16If now *thou hast* understanding, hear this: hearken to the voice of my words.

17Shall even he that hateth right govern? and wilt thou condemn him that is most just?

18 *Is it fit* to say to a king, *Thou art* wicked? *and* to princes, *Ye are* ungodly?

19 *How much less to him* that accepteth not the persons of princes, nor regardeth the rich more than the poor? for they all *are* the work of his hands.

## Amplified

26He prays to God, and He is favorable to him, so that he sees His face with joy; for [God] restores to him his righteousness [his uprightness and right standing with God—with its joys].

27He looks upon other men *or* sings out to them, I have sinned and perverted that which was right, and it did not profit me, *or* He did not requite me [according to my iniquity]!

28[God] has redeemed my life from going down to the pit [of destruction], and my life shall see the light!

29[Elihu comments] Lo, God does all these things twice, yes, three times with a man;

30To bring back his life from the pit [of destruction], that he may be enlightened with the light of the living.

31Give heed, O Job, listen to me; hold your peace, and I will speak.

32If you have anything to say, answer me; speak, for I desire to justify you.

33If [you do] not [have anything to say], listen to me; hold your peace, and I will teach you wisdom.

**34** ELIHU ANSWERED [continued his discourse] and said,

2Hear my words, you wise men, and give ear to me, you who have [so much] knowledge.

3For the ear tries words as the palate tastes food.

4Let us choose for ourselves that which is right; let us know among ourselves what is good.

5For Job has said, I am [innocent and uncompromisingly] righteous, and God has taken away my right; [Job 33:9.]

6Would I lie against my right? Yet, notwithstanding my right, I am counted a liar. My wound is incurable, though I am without transgression.

7What man is like Job, who drinks up scoffing *and* scorning like water?

8Who goes in company with the workers of iniquity and walks with wicked men?

9For he has said, It profits a man nothing that he should delight himself with God *and* consent to Him.

10Therefore hear me, you men of understanding; far be it from God that He should do wickedness, and from the Almighty that He should commit iniquity.

11For according to the deeds of a man God will [exactly] proportion his pay, and cause every man to find [recompense] according to his ways.

12Truly God will not do wickedly, neither will the Almighty pervert justice.

13Who put [God] in charge over the earth? Or who laid on Him the whole world?

14If [God] should set His heart upon him [man], *and* withdraw His [lifegiving] spirit and His breath [from man] to Himself,

15All flesh would perish together, and man turn again to dust. [Ps. 104:29; Eccl. 12:7.]

16If now you have understanding, hear this; listen to my words.

17Is it possible that an enemy of right should govern? And will you condemn Him Who is just *and* mighty?

18[God] Who says to a king, You are worthless *and* vile, *or* to princes *and* nobles, You are ungodly *and* evil?

19[God] is not partial to princes, nor does He regard the rich more than the poor, for they all are the work of His hands.

## New American Standard

26 Then he will pray to God, and He will accept him,
That he may see His face with joy,
And He may restore His righteousness to man.
27 "He will sing to men and say,
'I have sinned and perverted what is right,
And it is not proper for me.
28 'He has redeemed my soul from going to the pit,
And my life shall see the light.'

29¶ "Behold, God does all these oftentimes with men,
30 To bring back his soul from the pit,
That he may be enlightened with the light of life.
31 "Pay attention, O Job, listen to me;
Keep silent and let me speak.
32 "*Then* if you have anything to say, answer me;
Speak, for I desire to justify you.
33 "If not, listen to me;
Keep silent, and I will teach you wisdom."

*Elihu Vindicates God's Justice*

34 THEN ELIHU continued and said,
2 "Hear my words, you wise men,
And listen to me, you who know.
3 "For the ear tests words,
As the palate tastes food.
4 "Let us choose for ourselves what is right;
Let us know among ourselves what is good.
5 "For Job has said, 'I am righteous,
But God has taken away my right;
6 Should I lie concerning my right?
My wound is incurable, *though I am* without transgression.'
7 "What man is like Job,
Who drinks up derision like water,
8 Who goes in company with the workers of iniquity,
And walks with wicked men?
9 "For he has said, 'It profits a man nothing
When he is pleased with God.'
10¶ "Therefore, listen to me, you men of understanding.
Far be it from God to do wickedness,
And from the Almighty to do wrong.
11 "For He pays a man according to his work,
And makes him find it according to his way.
12 "Surely, God will not act wickedly,
And the Almighty will not pervert justice.
13 "Who gave Him authority over the earth?
And who has laid *on Him* the whole world?
14 "If He should determine to do so,
If He should gather to Himself His spirit and His breath,
15 All flesh would perish together,
And man would return to dust.

16¶ "But if *you have* understanding, hear this;
Listen to the sound of my words.
17 "Shall one who hates justice rule?
And will you condemn a righteous mighty one,
18 Who says to a king, 'Worthless one,'
To nobles, 'Wicked ones';
19 Who shows no partiality to princes,
Nor regards the rich above the poor,
For they all are the work of His hands?

## New International

26 He prays to God and finds favor with him,
he sees God's face and shouts for joy;
he is restored by God to his righteous state.
27 Then he comes to men and says,
'I sinned, and perverted what was right,
but I did not get what I deserved.
28 He redeemed my soul from going down to the pit,[a]
and I will live to enjoy the light.'

29 "God does all these things to a man—
twice, even three times—
30 to turn back his soul from the pit,[b]
that the light of life may shine on him.

31 "Pay attention, Job, and listen to me;
be silent, and I will speak.
32 If you have anything to say, answer me;
speak up, for I want you to be cleared.
33 But if not, then listen to me;
be silent, and I will teach you wisdom."

34 THEN ELIHU said:
2 "Hear my words, you wise men;
listen to me, you men of learning.
3 For the ear tests words
as the tongue tastes food.
4 Let us discern for ourselves what is right;
let us learn together what is good.

5 "Job says, 'I am innocent,
but God denies me justice.
6 Although I am right,
I am considered a liar;
although I am guiltless,
his arrow inflicts an incurable wound.'
7 What man is like Job,
who drinks scorn like water?
8 He keeps company with evildoers;
he associates with wicked men.
9 For he says, 'It profits a man nothing
when he tries to please God.'

10 "So listen to me, you men of understanding.
Far be it from God to do evil,
from the Almighty to do wrong.
11 He repays a man for what he has done;
he brings upon him what his conduct deserves.
12 It is unthinkable that God would do wrong,
that the Almighty would pervert justice.
13 Who appointed him over the earth?
Who put him in charge of the whole world?
14 If it were his intention
and he withdrew his spirit[c] and breath,
15 all mankind would perish together
and man would return to the dust.

16 "If you have understanding, hear this;
listen to what I say.
17 Can he who hates justice govern?
Will you condemn the just and mighty One?
18 Is he not the One who says to kings, 'You are worthless,'
and to nobles, 'You are wicked,'
19 who shows no partiality to princes
and does not favor the rich over the poor,
for they are all the work of his hands?

**NIV** [a] 28 Or *redeemed me from going down to the grave* [b] 30 Or *turn him back from the grave* [c] 14 Or *Spirit*

## King James

20 In a moment shall they die, and the people shall be troubled at midnight, and pass away: and the mighty shall be taken away without hand.
21 For his eyes *are* upon the ways of man, and he seeth all his goings.
22 *There is* no darkness, nor shadow of death, where the workers of iniquity may hide themselves.
23 For he will not lay upon man more *than right;* that he should enter into judgment with God.
24 He shall break in pieces mighty men without number, and set others in their stead.
25 Therefore he knoweth their works, and he overturneth *them* in the night, so that they are destroyed.
26 He striketh them as wicked men in the open sight of others;
27 Because they turned back from him, and would not consider any of his ways:
28 So that they cause the cry of the poor to come unto him, and he heareth the cry of the afflicted.
29 When he giveth quietness, who then can make trouble? and when he hideth *his* face, who then can behold him? whether *it be done* against a nation, or against a man only:
30 That the hypocrite reign not, lest the people be ensnared.
31 Surely it is meet to be said unto God, I have borne *chastisement,* I will not offend *any more:*
32 *That which* I see not teach thou me: if I have done iniquity, I will do no more.
33 *Should it be* according to thy mind? he will recompense it, whether thou refuse, or whether thou choose; and not I: therefore speak what thou knowest.
34 Let men of understanding tell me, and let a wise man hearken unto me.
35 Job hath spoken without knowledge, and his words *were* without wisdom.
36 My desire *is that* Job may be tried unto the end because of *his* answers for wicked men.
37 For he addeth rebellion unto his sin, he clappeth *his hands* among us, and multiplieth his words against God.

**35** ELIHU SPAKE moreover, and said,
2 Thinkest thou this to be right, *that* thou saidst, My righteousness *is* more than God's?
3 For thou saidst, What advantage will it be unto thee? *and,* What profit shall I have, *if I be cleansed* from my sin?
4 I will answer thee, and thy companions with thee.
5 Look unto the heavens, and see; and behold the clouds *which* are higher than thou.
6 If thou sinnest, what doest thou against him? or *if* thy transgressions be multiplied, what doest thou unto him?
7 If thou be righteous, what givest thou him? or what receiveth he of thine hand?
8 Thy wickedness *may hurt* a man as thou *art;* and thy righteousness *may profit* the son of man.

## Amplified

20 In a moment they die; even at midnight the people are shaken and pass away, and the mighty are taken away by no [human] hand.
21 For [God's] eyes are upon the ways of a man, and He sees all his steps. [Ps. 34:15; Prov. 5:21; Jer. 16:17.]
22 There is no darkness nor thick gloom where the evildoers may hide themselves.
23 [God] sets before man no appointed time that he should appear before [Him] in judgment.
24 He breaks in pieces mighty men without inquiry [before a jury], *and* in ways past finding out, and sets others in their stead. [Dan. 2:21.]
25 Therefore He takes knowledge of their works, and He overturns them in the night, so that they are crushed *and* destroyed.
26 God strikes them down as wicked men in the open sight of beholders,
27 Because they turned aside from Him, and would not consider *or* show regard for any of His ways, [I Sam. 15:11.]
28 So that they caused the cry of the poor to come to Him, and He heard the cry of the afflicted. [James 5:4; Exod. 22:23.]
29 When He gives quietness [peace and security from oppression], who then can condemn? When He hides His face [withdrawing His favor and help], who then can behold Him [and make Him gracious], whether it be a nation or a man singly?—
30 That the godless man may not reign, that there be no one to ensnare the people.
31 For has any one said to God, I have borne my chastisement, I will not offend any more;
32 Teach me what I do not see [in regard to how I have sinned]; if I have done iniquity, I will do it no more?
33 Should [God's] recompense [for your sins] be as you will it, that you refuse to accept it? For you must do the choosing and not I. Therefore say what is your truthful conclusion.
34 Men of understanding will tell me, indeed, every wise man who hears me [will agree],
35 That Job speaks without knowledge, and his words are without wisdom *and* insight.
36 [Would that Job's afflictions be continued and] he be tried to the end, because of his answering like wicked men!
37 For he adds rebellion [in his unsubmissive, defiant attitude toward God] to his unacknowledged sin; he claps his hands [in open mockery and contempt of God] among us, and he multiplies his words of accusation against God.

**35** ELIHU SPOKE further [to Job] and said,
2 Do you think this to be your right, *or* are you saying, My righteousness is more than God's,
3 That you ask, What advantage have you? *And,* What am I profited more than if I had sinned?
4 I will answer you, and your companions with you.
5 Look to the heavens, and see; and behold the skies which are higher than you.
6 If you have sinned, how does that affect God? And if your transgressions are multiplied, What have you done to Him?
7 If you are righteous, what do you [by that] give God? Or what does He receive from your hand?
8 Your wickedness touches and affects a man such as you are, and your righteousness is for yourself, one of the human race [but it cannot touch God, Who is above such influence].

## New American Standard

20 "In a moment they die, and at midnight
People are shaken and pass away,
And the mighty are taken away without a hand.

21¶ "For His eyes are upon the ways of a man,
And He sees all his steps.
22 "There is no darkness or deep shadow
Where the workers of iniquity may hide themselves.
23 "For He does not *need to* consider a man further,
That he should go before God in judgment.
24 "He breaks in pieces mighty men without inquiry,
And sets others in their place.
25 "Therefore He knows their works,
And He overthrows *them* in the night,
And they are crushed.
26 "He strikes them like the wicked
In a public place,
27 Because they turned aside from following Him,
And had no regard for any of His ways;
28 So that they caused the cry of the poor to come to Him,
And that He might hear the cry of the afflicted—
29 When He keeps quiet, who then can condemn?
And when He hides His face, who then can behold Him,
That is, in regard to both nation and man?—
30 So that godless men should not rule,
Nor be snares of the people.

31¶ "For has anyone said to God,
'I have borne *chastisement;*
I will not offend *anymore;*
32 Teach Thou me what I do not see;
If I have done iniquity,
I will do it no more'?
33 "Shall He recompense on your terms, because you have rejected *it?*
For you must choose, and not I;
Therefore declare what you know.
34 "Men of understanding will say to me,
And a wise man who hears me,
35 'Job speaks without knowledge,
And his words are without wisdom.
36 'Job ought to be tried to the limit,
Because he answers like wicked men.
37 'For he adds rebellion to his sin;
He claps his hands among us,
And multiplies his words against God.' "

*Elihu Sharply Reproves Job*

**35** THEN ELIHU continued and said,
2 "Do you think this is according to justice?
Do you say, 'My righteousness is more than God's'?
3 "For you say, 'What advantage will it be to You?
What profit shall I have, more than if I had sinned?'
4 "I will answer you,
And your friends with you.
5 "Look at the heavens and see;
And behold the clouds—they are higher than you.
6 "If you have sinned, what do you accomplish against Him?
And if your transgressions are many, what do you do to Him?
7 "If you are righteous, what do you give to Him?
Or what does He receive from your hand?
8 "Your wickedness is for a man like yourself,
And your righteousness is for a son of man.

## New International

20 They die in an instant, in the middle of the night;
the people are shaken and they pass away;
the mighty are removed without human hand.

21 "His eyes are on the ways of men;
he sees their every step.
22 There is no dark place, no deep shadow,
where evildoers can hide.
23 God has no need to examine men further,
that they should come before him for judgment.
24 Without inquiry he shatters the mighty
and sets up others in their place.
25 Because he takes note of their deeds,
he overthrows them in the night and they are crushed.
26 He punishes them for their wickedness
where everyone can see them,
27 because they turned from following him
and had no regard for any of his ways.
28 They caused the cry of the poor to come before him,
so that he heard the cry of the needy.
29 But if he remains silent, who can condemn him?
If he hides his face, who can see him?
Yet he is over man and nation alike,
30 to keep a godless man from ruling,
from laying snares for the people.

31 "Suppose a man says to God,
'I am guilty but will offend no more.
32 Teach me what I cannot see;
if I have done wrong, I will not do so again.'
33 Should God then reward you on your terms,
when you refuse to repent?
You must decide, not I;
so tell me what you know.

34 "Men of understanding declare,
wise men who hear me say to me,
35 'Job speaks without knowledge;
his words lack insight.'
36 Oh, that Job might be tested to the utmost
for answering like a wicked man!
37 To his sin he adds rebellion;
scornfully he claps his hands among us
and multiplies his words against God."

**35** THEN ELIHU said:
2 "Do you think this is just?
You say, 'I will be cleared by God.[a]'
3 Yet you ask him, 'What profit is it to me,[b]
and what do I gain by not sinning?'

4 "I would like to reply to you
and to your friends with you.
5 Look up at the heavens and see;
gaze at the clouds so high above you.
6 If you sin, how does that affect him?
If your sins are many, what does that do to him?
7 If you are righteous, what do you give to him,
or what does he receive from your hand?
8 Your wickedness affects only a man like yourself,
and your righteousness only the sons of men.

**NIV** [a] 2 Or *My righteousness is more than God's* [b] 3 Or *you*

## King James

9By reason of the multitude of oppressions they make *the oppressed* to cry: they cry out by reason of the arm of the mighty.

10But none saith, Where *is* God my maker, who giveth songs in the night;

11Who teacheth us more than the beasts of the earth, and maketh us wiser than the fowls of heaven?

12There they cry, but none giveth answer, because of the pride of evil men.

13Surely God will not hear vanity, neither will the Almighty regard it.

14Although thou sayest thou shalt not see him, *yet* judgment *is* before him; therefore trust thou in him.

15But now, because *it is* not *so,* he hath visited in his anger; yet he knoweth *it* not in great extremity:

16Therefore doth Job open his mouth in vain; he multiplieth words without knowledge.

**36** ELIHU ALSO proceeded, and said,

2Suffer me a little, and I will show thee that *I have* yet to speak on God's behalf.

3I will fetch my knowledge from afar, and will ascribe righteousness to my Maker.

4For truly my words *shall* not *be* false: he that is perfect in knowledge *is* with thee.

5Behold, God *is* mighty, and despiseth not *any: he is* mighty in strength *and* wisdom.

6He preserveth not the life of the wicked: but giveth right to the poor.

7He withdraweth not his eyes from the righteous: but with kings *are they* on the throne; yea, he doth establish them for ever, and they are exalted.

8And if *they be* bound in fetters, *and* be holden in cords of affliction;

9Then he showeth them their work, and their transgressions that they have exceeded.

10He openeth also their ear to discipline, and commandeth that they return from iniquity.

11If they obey and serve *him,* they shall spend their days in prosperity, and their years in pleasures.

12But if they obey not, they shall perish by the sword, and they shall die without knowledge.

13But the hypocrites in heart heap up wrath: they cry not when he bindeth them.

14They die in youth, and their life *is* among the unclean.

15He delivereth the poor in his affliction, and openeth their ears in oppression.

16Even so would he have removed thee out of the strait *into* a broad place, where *there is* no straitness; and that which should be set on thy table *should be* full of fatness.

17But thou hast fulfilled the judgment of the wicked: judgment and justice take hold *on thee.*

18Because *there is* wrath, *beware* lest he take thee away with *his* stroke: then a great ransom cannot deliver thee.

## Amplified

9Because of the multitudes of oppressions the people cry out; they cry for help because of the violence of the mighty.

10But no one says, Where is God my Maker, Who gives songs of rejoicing in the night, [Acts 16:25.]

11Who teaches us more than the beasts of the earth, and makes us wiser than the birds of the heavens?

12[The people] cry out because of the pride of evil men, but He does not answer.

13Surely God will refuse to answer [the cry which is] vanity—vain and empty [instead of abiding trust]; neither will the Almighty regard it.

14How much less when [missing His righteous judgment on earth] you say that you do not see Him, that your cause is before Him, and you are waiting for Him!

15But now because God has not [speedily] punished in His anger, and seems to be unaware of the wrong *and* oppression [of which a person is guilty],

16Job uselessly opens his mouth, and multiplies words without knowledge [drawing the worthless conclusion that the righteous have no advantage more than the wicked].

**36** ELIHU PROCEEDED, and said,

2Bear with me *and* wait a little longer, and I will show you; for I have something still to say on God's behalf.

3I will bring my knowledge from afar, and will ascribe righteousness to my Maker.

4For truly my words shall not be false; He Who is perfect in knowledge is with you.

5Behold! God is mighty, and yet despises no one, nor regards anything as trivial; He is mighty in power of understanding *and* heart.

6He does not prolong the life of the wicked, but gives the needy *and* afflicted their right.

7He withdraws not His eyes from the righteous [the upright in right standing with God]; but He sets them forever with kings upon the throne, and they are exalted.

8And if they are bound in fetters [of adversity] *and* held by cords of affliction, [Ps. 107:10, 11.]

9Then He shows to them [the true character of] their deeds and their transgressions, that they have acted arrogantly [with presumption and self-sufficiency].

10He also opens their ear to instruction *and* discipline, and commands that they return from iniquity.

11If they obey and serve him, they shall spend their days in prosperity, and their years in pleasantness *and* joy.

12But if they obey not, they shall perish by the sword [of God's destructive judgments], and they shall die in ignorance of true knowledge.

13But the godless *and* profane in heart heap up anger [at the divine discipline]; they do not cry to Him when He binds them [with cords of affliction]. [Rom. 2:5.]

14They die in youth, and their life perishes among the unclean—those who are Sodomites.

15He delivers the afflicted by their affliction, and opens their ears [to His voice] by adversity.

16Indeed, God would have allured you out of the mouth of distress into a broad place where there is no situation of perplexity *or* privation, and that which would be set on your table would be full of fatness.

17But if you [Job] are filled with the judgment of the wicked, judgment and justice will keep hold on you.

18For let not wrath entice you into scorning chastisements; and let not the greatness of the ransom [the suffering, if rightly endured] turn you aside.

## New American Standard

9 ¶ "Because of the multitude of oppressions they cry out;
They cry for help because of the arm of the mighty.
10 "But no one says, 'Where is God my Maker,
Who gives songs in the night,
11 Who teaches us more than the beasts of the earth,
And makes us wiser than the birds of the heavens?'
12 "There they cry out, but He does not answer
Because of the pride of evil men.
13 "Surely God will not listen to an empty *cry*,
Nor will the Almighty regard it.
14 "How much less when you say you do not behold Him,
The case is before Him, and you must wait for Him!
15 "And now, because He has not visited *in* His anger,
Nor has He acknowledged transgression well,
16 So Job opens his mouth emptily;
He multiplies words without knowledge."

*Elihu Speaks of God's Dealings with Men*

**36** THEN ELIHU continued and said,
2 "Wait for me a little, and I will show you
That there is yet more to be said in God's behalf.
3 "I will fetch my knowledge from afar,
And I will ascribe righteousness to my Maker.
4 "For truly my words are not false;
One who is perfect in knowledge is with you.
5 "Behold, God is mighty but does not despise *any;*
*He is* mighty in strength of understanding.
6 "He does not keep the wicked alive,
But gives justice to the afflicted.
7 "He does not withdraw His eyes from the righteous;
But with kings on the throne
He has seated them forever, and they are exalted.
8 "And if they are bound in fetters,
And are caught in the cords of affliction,
9 Then he declares to them their work
And their transgressions, that they have magnified themselves.
10 "And He opens their ear to instruction,
And commands that they return from evil.
11 "If they hear and serve *Him*,
They shall end their days in prosperity,
And their years in pleasures.
12 "But if they do not hear, they shall perish by the sword,
And they shall die without knowledge.
13 "But the godless in heart lay up anger;
They do not cry for help when He binds them.
14 "They die in youth,
And their life *perishes* among the cult prostitutes.
15 "He delivers the afflicted in their affliction,
And opens their ear in *time of* oppression.
16 "Then indeed, He enticed you from the mouth of distress,
Instead of it, a broad place with no constraint;
And that which was set on your table was full of fatness.
17 ¶ "But you were full of judgment on the wicked;
Judgment and justice take hold *of you*.
18 "*Beware* lest wrath entice you to scoffing;
And do not let the greatness of the ransom turn you aside.

## New International

9 "Men cry out under a load of oppression;
they plead for relief from the arm of the powerful.
10 But no one says, 'Where is God my Maker,
who gives songs in the night,
11 who teaches more to us than to[a] the beasts of the earth
and makes us wiser than[b] the birds of the air?'
12 He does not answer when men cry out
because of the arrogance of the wicked.
13 Indeed, God does not listen to their empty plea;
the Almighty pays no attention to it.
14 How much less, then, will he listen
when you say that you do not see him,
that your case is before him
and you must wait for him,
15 and further, that his anger never punishes
and he does not take the least notice of wickedness.[c]
16 So Job opens his mouth with empty talk;
without knowledge he multiplies words."

**36** ELIHU CONTINUED:

2 "Bear with me a little longer and I will show you
that there is more to be said in God's behalf.
3 I get my knowledge from afar;
I will ascribe justice to my Maker.
4 Be assured that my words are not false;
one perfect in knowledge is with you.

5 "God is mighty, but does not despise men;
he is mighty, and firm in his purpose.
6 He does not keep the wicked alive
but gives the afflicted their rights.
7 He does not take his eyes off the righteous;
he enthrones them with kings
and exalts them forever.
8 But if men are bound in chains,
held fast by cords of affliction,
9 he tells them what they have done—
that they have sinned arrogantly.
10 He makes them listen to correction
and commands them to repent of their evil.
11 If they obey and serve him,
they will spend the rest of their days in prosperity
and their years in contentment.
12 But if they do not listen,
they will perish by the sword[d]
and die without knowledge.

13 "The godless in heart harbor resentment;
even when he fetters them, they do not cry for help.
14 They die in their youth,
among male prostitutes of the shrines.
15 But those who suffer he delivers in their suffering;
he speaks to them in their affliction.

16 "He is wooing you from the jaws of distress
to a spacious place free from restriction,
to the comfort of your table laden with choice food.
17 But now you are laden with the judgment due the wicked;
judgment and justice have taken hold of you.
18 Be careful that no one entices you by riches;
do not let a large bribe turn you aside.

**NIV** [a] 11 Or *teaches us by* [b] 11 Or *us wise by* [c] 15 Symmachus, Theodotion and Vulgate; the meaning of the Hebrew for this word is uncertain. [d] 12 Or *will cross the River*

## King James

19 Will he esteem thy riches? *no,* not gold, nor all the forces of strength.

20 Desire not the night, when people are cut off in their place.

21 Take heed, regard not iniquity: for this hast thou chosen rather than affliction.

22 Behold, God exalteth by his power: who teacheth like him?

23 Who hath enjoined him his way? or who can say, Thou hast wrought iniquity?

24 Remember that thou magnify his work, which men behold.

25 Every man may see it; man may behold *it* afar off.

26 Behold, God *is* great, and we know *him* not, neither can the number of his years be searched out.

27 For he maketh small the drops of water: they pour down rain according to the vapour thereof:

28 Which the clouds do drop *and* distil upon man abundantly.

29 Also can *any* understand the spreadings of the clouds, *or* the noise of his tabernacle?

30 Behold, he spreadeth his light upon it, and covereth the bottom of the sea.

31 For by them judgeth he the people; he giveth meat in abundance.

32 With clouds he covereth the light; and commandeth it *not to shine* by *the cloud* that cometh betwixt.

33 The noise thereof showeth concerning it, the cattle also concerning the vapour.

**37** AT THIS also my heart trembleth, and is moved out of his place.

2 Hear attentively the noise of his voice, and the sound *that* goeth out of his mouth.

3 He directeth it under the whole heaven, and his lightning unto the ends of the earth.

4 After it a voice roareth: he thundereth with the voice of his excellency; and he will not stay them when his voice is heard.

5 God thundereth marvellously with his voice; great things doeth he, which we cannot comprehend.

6 For he saith to the snow, Be thou *on* the earth; likewise to the small rain, and to the great rain of his strength.

7 He sealeth up the hand of every man; that all men may know his work.

8 Then the beasts go into dens, and remain in their places.

9 Out of the south cometh the whirlwind: and cold out of the north.

10 By the breath of God frost is given: and the breadth of the waters is straitened.

11 Also by watering he wearieth the thick cloud: he scattereth his bright cloud:

12 And it is turned round about by his counsels: that they may do whatsoever he commandeth them upon the face of the world in the earth.

13 He causeth it to come, whether for correction, or for his land, or for mercy.

## Amplified

19 Will your cry be sufficient to keep you from distress, or will all the force of your strength do it?

20 Desire not the night, when peoples are cut off in their place;

21 Take heed, turn not to iniquity, for this [the iniquity of complaining against God] you have chosen rather than [submission in] affliction.

22 Behold, God exalts *and* does loftily in His power; who is a ruler *or* a teacher like Him?

23 Who has appointed God His way? Or who can say, You have done unrighteousness?

24 Remember that [by submission] you magnify God's work, of which men have sung.

25 All men have looked upon God's work; man may behold it afar off.

26 Behold! God is great, and we know Him not; the number of His years is unsearchable. [I Cor. 13:12.]

27 For He draws up the drops of water, which distil in rain from His vapor,

28 Which the skies pour down *and* drop abundantly upon [the multitudes of] mankind.

29 Not only that, but can any one understand the spreadings of the clouds *or* the thunderings of His pavilion? [Ps. 18:11; Isa. 40:22.]

30 Behold, He spreads His lightning against the dark clouds, and covers the roots of the sea.

31 For by [His clouds] God executes judgment upon the peoples; He gives food in abundance.

32 He covers His hands with the lightning, and commands it to strike the mark.

33 His thunderings speak [awesomely] concerning Him; the cattle are told of His coming storm.

**37** INDEED, [AT His thunderings] my heart also trembles, and leaps out of its place.

2 Hear, oh, hear the roar of His voice and the sound of rumbling that goes out of His mouth!

3 Under the whole heaven He lets it loose, and His lightning to the ends of the earth.

4 After it His voice roars; He thunders with the voice of His majesty, and He restrains not [His lightnings against His adversaries] when His voice is heard.

5 God thunders marvelously with His voice; He does great things which we cannot comprehend.

6 For He says to the snow, Fall on the earth; likewise He speaks to the showers and to the downpour of His mighty rains.

7 God seals up [stops, brings to a standstill by severe weather] the hand of every man; [and now under His seal their hands are forced to inactivity], that all men whom He has made may know His doings [His sovereign power and their subjection to it].

8 Then the beasts go into dens, and remain in their lairs.

9 Out of its chamber comes the whirlwind, and cold from the scattering winds.

10 By the breath of God ice is given, and the breadth of the waters is frozen over. [Ps. 147:17, 18.]

11 He loads the thick cloud with moisture; He scatters the cloud of His lightning.

12 And it is turned round about by His guidance, that they may do whatever He commands them upon the face of the habitable earth.

13 Whether it be for correction, or for His earth *generally,* or for His mercy *and* lovingkindness, He causes it to come. [Exod. 9:18, 23; I Sam. 12:18, 19.]

## New American Standard

19 "Will your riches keep *you* from distress,
Or all the forces of *your* strength?
20 "Do not long for the night,
When people vanish in their place.
21 "Be careful, do not turn to evil;
For you have preferred this to affliction.
22 "Behold, God is exalted in His power;
Who is a teacher like Him?
23 "Who has appointed Him His way,
And who has said, 'Thou hast done wrong'?

24¶ "Remember that you should exalt His work,
Of which men have sung.
25 "All men have seen it;
Man beholds from afar.
26 "Behold, God is exalted, and we do not know *Him;*
The number of His years is unsearchable.
27 "For He draws up the drops of water,
They distill rain from the mist,
28 Which the clouds pour down,
They drip upon man abundantly.
29 "Can anyone understand the spreading of the clouds,
The thundering of His pavilion?
30 "Behold, He spreads His lightning about Him,
And He covers the depths of the sea.
31 "For by these He judges peoples;
He gives food in abundance.
32 "He covers *His* hands with the lightning,
And commands it to strike the mark.
33 "Its noise declares His presence;
The cattle also, concerning what is coming up.

*Elihu Says God Is Back of the Storm*

37 "AT THIS also my heart trembles,
And leaps from its place.
2 "Listen closely to the thunder of His voice,
And the rumbling that goes out from His mouth.
3 "Under the whole heaven He lets it loose,
And His lightning to the ends of the earth.
4 "After it, a voice roars;
He thunders with His majestic voice;
And He does not restrain the lightnings when His voice is heard.
5 "God thunders with His voice wondrously,
Doing great things which we cannot comprehend.
6 "For to the snow He says, 'Fall on the earth,'
And to the downpour and the rain, 'Be strong.'
7 "He seals the hand of every man,
That all men may know His work.
8 "Then the beast goes into its lair,
And remains in its den.
9 "Out of the south comes the storm,
And out of the north the cold.
10 "From the breath of God ice is made,
And the expanse of the waters is frozen.
11 "Also with moisture He loads the thick cloud;
He disperses the cloud of His lightning.
12 "And it changes direction, turning around by His guidance,
That it may do whatever He commands it
On the face of the inhabited earth.
13 "Whether for correction, or for His world,
Or for lovingkindness, He causes it to happen.

## New International

19 Would your wealth
or even all your mighty efforts
sustain you so you would not be in distress?
20 Do not long for the night,
to drag people away from their homes.[a]
21 Beware of turning to evil,
which you seem to prefer to affliction.

22 "God is exalted in his power.
Who is a teacher like him?
23 Who has prescribed his ways for him,
or said to him, 'You have done wrong'?
24 Remember to extol his work,
which men have praised in song.
25 All mankind has seen it;
men gaze on it from afar.
26 How great is God—beyond our understanding!
The number of his years is past finding out.

27 "He draws up the drops of water,
which distill as rain to the streams[b];
28 the clouds pour down their moisture
and abundant showers fall on mankind.
29 Who can understand how he spreads out the clouds,
how he thunders from his pavilion?
30 See how he scatters his lightning about him,
bathing the depths of the sea.
31 This is the way he governs[c] the nations
and provides food in abundance.
32 He fills his hands with lightning
and commands it to strike its mark.
33 His thunder announces the coming storm;
even the cattle make known its approach.[d]

37 "AT THIS my heart pounds
and leaps from its place.
2 Listen! Listen to the roar of his voice,
to the rumbling that comes from his mouth.
3 He unleashes his lightning beneath the whole heaven
and sends it to the ends of the earth.
4 After that comes the sound of his roar;
he thunders with his majestic voice.
When his voice resounds,
he holds nothing back.
5 God's voice thunders in marvelous ways;
he does great things beyond our understanding.
6 He says to the snow, 'Fall on the earth,'
and to the rain shower, 'Be a mighty downpour.'
7 So that all men he has made may know his work,
he stops every man from his labor.[e]
8 The animals take cover;
they remain in their dens.
9 The tempest comes out from its chamber,
the cold from the driving winds.
10 The breath of God produces ice,
and the broad waters become frozen.
11 He loads the clouds with moisture;
he scatters his lightning through them.
12 At his direction they swirl around
over the face of the whole earth
to do whatever he commands them.
13 He brings the clouds to punish men,
or to water his earth[f] and show his love.

**NIV** [a] 20 The meaning of the Hebrew for verses 18-20 is uncertain. [b] 27 Or *distill from the mist as rain* [c] 31 Or *nourishes* [d] 33 Or *announces his coming— / the One zealous against evil* [e] 7 Or / *he fills all men with fear by his power* [f] 13 Or *to favor them*

## King James

14Hearken unto this, O Job: stand still, and consider the wondrous works of God.
15Dost thou know when God disposed them, and caused the light of his cloud to shine?
16Dost thou know the balancings of the clouds, the wondrous works of him which is perfect in knowledge?
17How thy garments *are* warm, when he quieteth the earth by the south *wind?*
18Hast thou with him spread out the sky, *which is* strong, *and* as a molten lookingglass?
19Teach us what we shall say unto him; *for* we cannot order *our speech* by reason of darkness.
20Shall it be told him that I speak? if a man speak, surely he shall be swallowed up.
21And now *men* see not the bright light which *is* in the clouds: but the wind passeth, and cleanseth them.
22Fair weather cometh out of the north: with God *is* terrible majesty.
23 *Touching* the Almighty, we cannot find him out: *he is* excellent in power, and in judgment, and in plenty of justice: he will not afflict.
24Men do therefore fear him: he respecteth not any *that are* wise of heart.

**38** THEN THE LORD answered Job out of the whirlwind, and said,
2Who *is* this that darkeneth counsel by words without knowledge?
3Gird up now thy loins like a man; for I will demand of thee, and answer thou me.
4Where wast thou when I laid the foundations of the earth? declare, if thou hast understanding.
5Who hath laid the measures thereof, if thou knowest? or who hath stretched the line upon it?
6Whereupon are the foundations thereof fastened? or who laid the corner stone thereof;
7When the morning stars sang together, and all the sons of God shouted for joy?
8Or *who* shut up the sea with doors, when it brake forth, *as if* it had issued out of the womb?
9When I made the cloud the garment thereof, and thick darkness a swaddlingband for it,
10And brake up for it my decreed *place,* and set bars and doors,
11And said, Hitherto shalt thou come, but no further: and here shall thy proud waves be stayed?
12Hast thou commanded the morning since thy days; *and* caused the dayspring to know his place;
13That it might take hold of the ends of the earth, that the wicked might be shaken out of it?
14It is turned as clay *to* the seal; and they stand as a garment.
15And from the wicked their light is withholden, and the high arm shall be broken.
16Hast thou entered into the springs of the sea? or hast thou walked in the search of the depth?

## Amplified

14Hear this, O Job; stand still and consider the wondrous works of God.
15Do you know how God lays His command upon them, and causes the lightning of His [storm] cloud to shine?
16Do you know how the clouds are balanced [and poised in the heavens], the wonderful works of Him Who is perfect in knowledge?
17 *Or* why your garments are hot when He quiets the earth [in sultry summer] with the [oppressive] south *wind?*
18Can you along with Him spread out the sky, which is strong as a molten mirror?
19Tell us [Job] with what words of man we may address such a Being; we cannot state our case because we are in the dark [in the presence of the unsearchable God].
20So shall it be told Him that I wish to speak? If a man speaks, shall he be swallowed up?
21And now men cannot look upon the light when it is bright in the skies, when the wind has passed and cleared them.
22Golden brightness *and* splendor come out of the north; [if men can scarcely look upon it, how much less upon the] terrible splendor *and* majesty God has upon Him!
23Touching the Almighty, we cannot find Him out; He is excellent in power, and to justice and plenteous righteousness He does no violence [He will disregard no right]. [I Tim. 6:16.]
24Men therefore [reverently] fear Him; He regards *and* respects not any who are wise in heart [in their own understanding and conceit]. [Matt. 10:28.]

**38** THEN THE Lord answered Job out of the whirlwind, and said,
2Who is this that darkens counsel by words without knowledge? [Job 35:16.]
3Gird up now your loins like a man, and I will demand of you, and you declare to Me.
4Where were you when I laid the foundation of the earth? Declare, if you have *and* know understanding.
5Who determined the measures of the earth, if you know? Or who stretched the measuring line upon it?
6Upon what were the foundations of it fastened, or who laid its cornerstone,
7When the morning stars sang together, and all the sons of God shouted for joy?
8Or who shut up the sea with doors, when it broke forth *and* issued out of the womb?
9When I made clouds the garment of it, and thick darkness a swaddling band for it,
10And marked for it My appointed boundary, and set bars and doors, [Jer. 5:22.]
11And said, Thus far shall you come and no farther, and here shall your proud waves be stayed? [Ps. 89:9; 93:4.]
12Have you commanded the morning since your days began, *and* caused the dawn to know its place,
13So that [light] may get hold of the corners of the earth and shake the wickedness [of night] out of it?
14It is changed as clay into which a seal is pressed, and things stand out like a many-colored garment.
15From the wicked their light is withheld, and their uplifted arm is broken.
16Have you explored the springs of the sea? Or have you walked in the recesses of the deep?

## New American Standard

14¶ "Listen to this, O Job,
Stand and consider the wonders of God.
15 "Do you know how God establishes them,
And makes the lightning of His cloud to shine?
16 "Do you know about the layers of the thick clouds,
The wonders of one perfect in knowledge,
17 You whose garments are hot,
When the land is still because of the south wind?
18 "Can you, with Him, spread out the skies,
Strong as a molten mirror?
19 "Teach us what we shall say to Him;
We cannot arrange *our case* because of darkness.
20 "Shall it be told Him that I would speak?
Or should a man say that he would be swallowed up?
21¶ "And now men do not see the light which is bright in the skies;
But the wind has passed and cleared them.
22 "Out of the north comes golden *splendor;*
Around God is awesome majesty.
23 "The Almighty—we cannot find Him;
He is exalted in power;
And He will not do violence to justice and abundant righteousness.
24 "Therefore men fear Him;
He does not regard any who are wise of heart."

*God Speaks Now to Job*

38 THEN THE LORD answered Job out of the whirlwind and said,
2 "Who is this that darkens counsel
By words without knowledge?
3 "Now gird up your loins like a man,
And I will ask you, and you instruct Me!
4 "Where were you when I laid the foundation of the earth?
Tell *Me,* if you have understanding,
5 Who set its measurements, since you know?
Or who stretched the line on it?
6 "On what were its bases sunk?
Or who laid its cornerstone,
7 When the morning stars sang together,
And all the sons of God shouted for joy?
8¶ "Or *who* enclosed the sea with doors,
When, bursting forth, it went out from the womb;
9 When I made a cloud its garment,
And thick darkness its swaddling band,
10 And I placed boundaries on it,
And I set a bolt and doors,
11 And I said, 'Thus far you shall come, but no farther;
And here shall your proud waves stop'?

*God's Mighty Power*

12¶ "Have you ever in your life commanded the morning,
*And* caused the dawn to know its place;
13 That it might take hold of the ends of the earth,
And the wicked be shaken out of it?
14 "It is changed like clay *under* the seal;
And they stand forth like a garment.
15 "And from the wicked their light is withheld,
And the uplifted arm is broken.
16¶ "Have you entered into the springs of the sea?
Or have you walked in the recesses of the deep?

## New International

14"Listen to this, Job;
stop and consider God's wonders.
15Do you know how God controls the clouds
and makes his lightning flash?
16Do you know how the clouds hang poised,
those wonders of him who is perfect in knowledge?
17You who swelter in your clothes
when the land lies hushed under the south wind,
18can you join him in spreading out the skies,
hard as a mirror of cast bronze?

19"Tell us what we should say to him;
we cannot draw up our case because of our darkness.
20Should he be told that I want to speak?
Would any man ask to be swallowed up?
21Now no one can look at the sun,
bright as it is in the skies
after the wind has swept them clean.
22Out of the north he comes in golden splendor;
God comes in awesome majesty.
23The Almighty is beyond our reach and exalted in power;
in his justice and great righteousness, he does not oppress.
24Therefore, men revere him,
for does he not have regard for all the wise in heart?[a]"

*The LORD Speaks*

38 THEN THE LORD answered Job out of the storm. He said:

2"Who is this that darkens my counsel
with words without knowledge?
3Brace yourself like a man;
I will question you,
and you shall answer me.

4"Where were you when I laid the earth's foundation?
Tell me, if you understand.
5Who marked off its dimensions? Surely you know!
Who stretched a measuring line across it?
6On what were its footings set,
or who laid its cornerstone—
7while the morning stars sang together
and all the angels[b] shouted for joy?

8"Who shut up the sea behind doors
when it burst forth from the womb,
9when I made the clouds its garment
and wrapped it in thick darkness,
10when I fixed limits for it
and set its doors and bars in place,
11when I said, 'This far you may come and no farther;
here is where your proud waves halt'?

12"Have you ever given orders to the morning,
or shown the dawn its place,
13that it might take the earth by the edges
and shake the wicked out of it?
14The earth takes shape like clay under a seal;
its features stand out like those of a garment.
15The wicked are denied their light,
and their upraised arm is broken.

16"Have you journeyed to the springs of the sea
or walked in the recesses of the deep?

NIV [a]24 Or *for he does not have regard for any who think they are wise.*
[b]7 Hebrew *the sons of God*

## King James

17Have the gates of death been opened unto thee? or hast thou seen the doors of the shadow of death?

18Hast thou perceived the breadth of the earth? declare if thou knowest it all.

19Where *is* the way *where* light dwelleth? and *as for* darkness, where *is* the place thereof,

20That thou shouldest take it to the bound thereof, and that thou shouldest know the paths *to* the house thereof?

21Knowest thou *it*, because thou wast then born? or *because* the number of thy days *is* great?

22Hast thou entered into the treasures of the snow? or hast thou seen the treasures of the hail,

23Which I have reserved against the time of trouble, against the day of battle and war?

24By what way is the light parted, *which* scattereth the east wind upon the earth?

25Who hath divided a watercourse for the overflowing of waters, or a way for the lightning of thunder;

26To cause it to rain on the earth, *where* no man *is*; *on* the wilderness, wherein *there is* no man;

27To satisfy the desolate and waste *ground*; and to cause the bud of the tender herb to spring forth?

28Hath the rain a father? or who hath begotten the drops of dew?

29Out of whose womb came the ice? and the hoary frost of heaven, who hath gendered it?

30The waters are hid as *with* a stone, and the face of the deep is frozen.

31Canst thou bind the sweet influences of Pleiades, or loose the bands of Orion?

32Canst thou bring forth Mazzaroth in his season? or canst thou guide Arcturus with his sons?

33Knowest thou the ordinances of heaven? canst thou set the dominion thereof in the earth?

34Canst thou lift up thy voice to the clouds, that abundance of waters may cover thee?

35Canst thou send lightnings, that they may go, and say unto thee, Here we *are*?

36Who hath put wisdom in the inward parts? or who hath given understanding to the heart?

37Who can number the clouds in wisdom? or who can stay the bottles of heaven,

38When the dust groweth into hardness, and the clods cleave fast together?

39Wilt thou hunt the prey for the lion? or fill the appetite of the young lions,

40When they couch in *their* dens, *and* abide in the covert to lie in wait?

41Who provideth for the raven his food? when his young ones cry unto God, they wander for lack of meat.

**39** KNOWEST THOU the time when the wild goats of the rock bring forth? *or* canst thou mark when the hinds do calve?

2Canst thou number the months *that* they fulfil? or knowest thou the time when they bring forth?

## Amplified

17Have the gates of death been revealed to you? Or have you seen the doors of deep darkness?

18Have you comprehended the breadth of the earth? Tell it, if you know it all.

19Where is the [a]way where light dwells? And as for darkness, where is its abode,

20That you may conduct it to its home, and may know the paths to its house?

21You must know, since you were born then? Or because you are so extremely old!

22Have you entered the treasuries of the snow, or have you seen the treasuries of the hail,

23Which I have reserved for the time of trouble, for the day of battle and war? [Exod. 9:18; Josh. 10:11; Isa. 30:30; Rev. 16:21.]

24By what is the light distributed, *or* the east wind spread over the earth?

25Who has prepared a channel for the torrents of rain, or a path for the thunderbolt,

26To cause it to rain on the uninhabited land, *and* on the desert where no man lives,

27To satisfy the waste *and* desolate ground, and to cause the tender grass to spring forth?

28Has the rain a father? Or who has begotten the drops of dew?

29Out of whose womb came the ice? And the hoary frost of heaven, who has given it birth?

30The waters are congealed like stone, and the face of the deep is frozen.

31Can you bind the chains of [the cluster of stars called] Pleiades, or loose the cords of [the constellation] Orion?

32Can you lead forth the signs of the Zodiac in their season? Or can you guide [the stars of] the Bear with her young?

33Do you know the ordinances of the heavens? Can you establish their rule upon the earth?

34Can you lift up your voice to the clouds, so that an abundance of waters may cover you?

35Can you send lightnings, that they may go, and say to you, Here we are?

36Who has put wisdom in the inward parts [or in the dark clouds]? Or who has given understanding to the mind [or to the meteor]?

37Who can number the clouds by wisdom? Or who can pour out the [water] bottles of the heavens,

38When [heat has caused] the dust to run into a mass and the clods to cleave fast together?

39Can you [Job] hunt the prey for the lion? Or satisfy the appetite of the young lions,

40When they couch in their dens, *or* lie in wait in their hiding place?

41Who provides for the raven its prey, when its young ones cry to God *and* wander about for lack of food?

**39** DO YOU know the time when the wild goats of the rock bring forth [their young]? *Or* observe when the hinds are giving birth? [Do you attend to all this, Job?]

2Can you number the months that they carry their offspring? Or do you know the time when they are delivered,

**AMP** [a] How, except by divine inspiration, could Job have known that light does not dwell in a *place*, but a *way*? For light, as modern man has discovered, involves motion, wave motion, and traveling 186,000 miles a second it can only dwell in a *way*.

## New American Standard

17 "Have the gates of death been revealed to you?
Or have you seen the gates of deep darkness?
18 "Have you understood the expanse of the earth?
Tell *Me*, if you know all this.

19 ¶ "Where is the way to the dwelling of light?
And darkness, where is its place,
20 That you may take it to its territory,
And that you may discern the paths to its home?
21 "You know, for you were born then,
And the number of your days is great!
22 "Have you entered the storehouses of the snow,
Or have you seen the storehouses of the hail,
23 Which I have reserved for the time of distress,
For the day of war and battle?
24 "Where is the way that the light is divided,
*Or* the east wind scattered on the earth?

25 ¶ "Who has cleft a channel for the flood,
Or a way for the thunderbolt;
26 To bring rain on a land without people,
*On* a desert without a man in it,
27 To satisfy the waste and desolate land,
And to make the seeds of grass to sprout?
28 "Has the rain a father?
Or who has begotten the drops of dew?
29 "From whose womb has come the ice?
And the frost of heaven, who has given it birth?
30 "Water becomes hard like stone,
And the surface of the deep is imprisoned.

31 ¶ "Can you bind the chains of the Pleiades,
Or loose the cords of Orion?
32 "Can you lead forth a constellation in its season,
And guide the Bear with her satellites?
33 "Do you know the ordinances of the heavens,
Or fix their rule over the earth?

34 ¶ "Can you lift up your voice to the clouds,
So that an abundance of water may cover you?
35 "Can you send forth lightnings that they may go
And say to you, 'Here we are'?
36 "Who has put wisdom in the innermost being,
Or has given understanding to the mind?
37 "Who can count the clouds by wisdom,
Or tip the water jars of the heavens,
38 When the dust hardens into a mass,
And the clods stick together?

39 ¶ "Can you hunt the prey for the lion,
Or satisfy the appetite of the young lions,
40 When they crouch in *their* dens,
*And* lie in wait in *their* lair?
41 "Who prepares for the raven its nourishment,
When its young cry to God,
And wander about without food?

*God Speaks of Nature and Its Beings*

39 "DO YOU know the time the mountain goats give birth?
Do you observe the calving of the deer?
2 "Can you count the months they fulfill,
Or do you know the time they give birth?

## New International

17Have the gates of death been shown to you?
Have you seen the gates of the shadow of death[b]?
18Have you comprehended the vast expanses of the earth?
Tell me, if you know all this.

19"What is the way to the abode of light?
And where does darkness reside?
20Can you take them to their places?
Do you know the paths to their dwellings?
21Surely you know, for you were already born!
You have lived so many years!

22"Have you entered the storehouses of the snow
or seen the storehouses of the hail,
23which I reserve for times of trouble,
for days of war and battle?
24What is the way to the place where the lightning is dispersed,
or the place where the east winds are scattered over the earth?
25Who cuts a channel for the torrents of rain,
and a path for the thunderstorm,
26to water a land where no man lives,
a desert with no one in it,
27to satisfy a desolate wasteland
and make it sprout with grass?
28Does the rain have a father?
Who fathers the drops of dew?
29From whose womb comes the ice?
Who gives birth to the frost from the heavens
30when the waters become hard as stone,
when the surface of the deep is frozen?

31"Can you bind the beautiful[c] Pleiades?
Can you loose the cords of Orion?
32Can you bring forth the constellations in their seasons[d]
or lead out the Bear[e] with its cubs?
33Do you know the laws of the heavens?
Can you set up ⌊God's[f]⌋ dominion over the earth?

34"Can you raise your voice to the clouds
and cover yourself with a flood of water?
35Do you send the lightning bolts on their way?
Do they report to you, 'Here we are'?
36Who endowed the heart[g] with wisdom
or gave understanding to the mind[h]?
37Who has the wisdom to count the clouds?
Who can tip over the water jars of the heavens
38when the dust becomes hard
and the clods of earth stick together?

39"Do you hunt the prey for the lioness
and satisfy the hunger of the lions
40when they crouch in their dens
or lie in wait in a thicket?
41Who provides food for the raven
when its young cry out to God
and wander about for lack of food?

39 "DO YOU know when the mountain goats give birth?
Do you watch when the doe bears her fawn?
2Do you count the months till they bear?
Do you know the time they give birth?

**NIV** [b] 17 Or *gates of deep shadows* [c] 31 Or *the twinkling;* or *the chains of the* [d] 32 Or *the morning star in its season* [e] 32 Or *out Leo* [f] 33 Or *his;* or *their* [g] 36 The meaning of the Hebrew for this word is uncertain. [h] 36 The meaning of the Hebrew for this word is uncertain.

## King James

3They bow themselves, they bring forth their young ones, they cast out their sorrows.
4Their young ones are in good liking, they grow up with corn; they go forth, and return not unto them.
5Who hath sent out the wild ass free? or who hath loosed the bands of the wild ass?
6Whose house I have made the wilderness, and the barren land his dwellings.
7He scorneth the multitude of the city, neither regardeth he the crying of the driver.
8The range of the mountains *is* his pasture, and he searcheth after every green thing.
9Will the unicorn be willing to serve thee, or abide by thy crib?
10Canst thou bind the unicorn with his band in the furrow? or will he harrow the valleys after thee?
11Wilt thou trust him, because his strength *is* great? or wilt thou leave thy labour to him?
12Wilt thou believe him, that he will bring home thy seed, and gather *it into* thy barn?
13 *Gavest thou* the goodly wings unto the peacocks? or wings and feathers unto the ostrich?
14Which leaveth her eggs in the earth, and warmeth them in dust,
15And forgetteth that the foot may crush them, or that the wild beast may break them.
16She is hardened against her young ones, as though *they were* not hers: her labour is in vain without fear;
17Because God hath deprived her of wisdom, neither hath he imparted to her understanding.
18What time she lifteth up herself on high, she scorneth the horse and his rider.
19Hast thou given the horse strength? hast thou clothed his neck with thunder?
20Canst thou make him afraid as a grasshopper? the glory of his nostrils *is* terrible.
21He paweth in the valley, and rejoiceth in *his* strength: he goeth on to meet the armed men.
22He mocketh at fear, and is not affrighted; neither turneth he back from the sword.
23The quiver rattleth against him, the glittering spear and the shield.
24He swalloweth the ground with fierceness and rage: neither believeth he that *it is* the sound of the trumpet.
25He saith among the trumpets, Ha, ha; and he smelleth the battle afar off, the thunder of the captains, and the shouting.
26Doth the hawk fly by thy wisdom, *and* stretch her wings toward the south?
27Doth the eagle mount up at thy command, and make her nest on high?
28She dwelleth and abideth on the rock, upon the crag of the rock, and the strong place.
29From thence she seeketh the prey, *and* her eyes behold afar off.
30Her young ones also suck up blood: and where the slain *are,* there *is* she.

## Amplified

3When they bow themselves, bring forth their young ones *and* cast out their pains?
4Their young ones become strong, they grow up in the open field; they go forth, and return not to them.
5Who has sent out the wild donkey, giving him his freedom? Or who has loosed the bands of the swift donkey [by which his tame brother is bound—he, the shy, the swift-footed and the untamable],
6Whose home I have made the wilderness, and the salt land his dwelling place?
7He scorns the tumult of the city, and hears not the shoutings of the taskmaster.
8The range of the mountains is his pasture, and he searches after every green thing.
9Will the wild ox be willing to serve you, or remain beside your manger?
10Can you bind the wild ox with harness to the plow in the furrow? Or will he harrow the furrows for you?
11Will you trust him, because his strength is great, or to him will you leave your labor?
12Will you depend upon him to bring home your seed and gather the grain of your threshing floor? [Who, Job, was the author of this strange variance in disposition of animals so alike in appearance? Was it you?]
13The wings of the ostrich wave proudly, *but* are they the pinions and plumage of love?
14The ostrich leaves her eggs on the ground and warms them in the dust,
15Forgetting that a foot may crush them, or that the wild beast may trample them.
16She is hardened against her young ones, as though they were not hers; her labor is in vain because she has no sense of danger [for her unborn brood].
17For God has deprived her of wisdom, neither has He imparted to her understanding.
18Yet when she lifts up herself in flight, [so swift is she that] she can laugh to scorn the horse and his rider.
19Have you given the horse his might? Have you clothed his neck with quivering, *and* a shaking mane?
20Was it you, [Job,] who made him to leap like a locust? The majesty of his (snorting) nostrils is terrible.
21He paws in the valley, and exults in his strength; he goes out to meet the weapons [of armed men].
22He mocks at fear, and is not dismayed *or* terrified; neither does he turn back [in battle] from the sword.
23The quiver rattles upon him, as do the glittering spear and the lance [of his rider].
24[He seems in running to] devour the ground with fierceness and rage; neither can he stand still at the sound of the [war] trumpet.
25As often as the trumpet sounds he says, Ha, ha! And he smells the battle from afar, the thunder of the captains, and the shouting.
26Is it by your wisdom [Job] that the hawk soars *and* stretches her wings toward the south [as winter approaches]?
27Does the eagle mount up at your command, and make his nest on a high [inaccessible place]?
28On the cliff he dwells and remains securely, upon the point of the rock and the stronghold.
29From there he spies out the prey, and his eyes see it afar off.
30His young ones suck up blood, and where the slain are, there is he.

## New American Standard

3 "They kneel down, they bring forth their young,
They get rid of their labor pains.
4 "Their offspring become strong, they grow up in the open field;
They leave and do not return to them.

5¶ "Who sent out the wild donkey free?
And who loosed the bonds of the swift donkey,
6 To whom I gave the wilderness for a home,
And the salt land for his dwelling place?
7 "He scorns the tumult of the city,
The shoutings of the driver he does not hear.
8 "He explores the mountains for his pasture,
And he searches after every green thing.
9 "Will the wild ox consent to serve you?
Or will he spend the night at your manger?
10 "Can you bind the wild ox in a furrow with ropes?
Or will he harrow the valleys after you?
11 "Will you trust him because his strength is great
And leave your labor to him?
12 "Will you have faith in him that he will return your grain,
And gather *it from* your threshing floor?

13¶ "The ostriches' wings flap joyously
With the pinion and plumage of [a]love,
14 For she abandons her eggs to the earth,
And warms them in the dust,
15 And she forgets that a foot may crush them,
Or that a wild beast may trample them.
16 "She treats her young cruelly, as if *they* were not hers;
Though her labor be in vain, *she* is unconcerned;
17 Because God has made her forget wisdom,
And has not given her a share of understanding.
18 "When she lifts herself on high,
She laughs at the horse and his rider.

19¶ "Do you give the horse *his* might?
Do you clothe his neck with a mane?
20 "Do you make him leap like the locust?
His majestic snorting is terrible.
21 "He paws in the valley, and rejoices in *his* strength;
He goes out to meet the weapons.
22 "He laughs at fear and is not dismayed;
And he does not turn back from the sword.
23 "The quiver rattles against him,
The flashing spear and javelin.
24 "With shaking and rage he races over the ground;
And he does not stand still at the voice of the trumpet.
25 "As often as the trumpet *sounds* he says, 'Aha!'
And he scents the battle from afar,
And thunder of the captains, and the war cry.

26¶ "Is it by your understanding that the hawk soars,
Stretching his wings toward the south?
27 "Is it at your command that the eagle mounts up,
And makes his nest on high?
28 "On the cliff he dwells and lodges,
Upon the rocky crag, an inaccessible place.
29 "From there he spies out food;
His eyes see *it* from afar.
30 "His young ones also suck up blood;
And where the slain are, there is he."

NAS [a] Or, *a stork*

## New International

3They crouch down and bring forth their young;
their labor pains are ended.
4Their young thrive and grow strong in the wilds;
they leave and do not return.

5"Who let the wild donkey go free?
Who untied his ropes?
6I gave him the wasteland as his home,
the salt flats as his habitat.
7He laughs at the commotion in the town;
he does not hear a driver's shout.
8He ranges the hills for his pasture
and searches for any green thing.

9"Will the wild ox consent to serve you?
Will he stay by your manger at night?
10Can you hold him to the furrow with a harness?
Will he till the valleys behind you?
11Will you rely on him for his great strength?
Will you leave your heavy work to him?
12Can you trust him to bring in your grain
and gather it to your threshing floor?

13"The wings of the ostrich flap joyfully,
but they cannot compare with the pinions and feathers of the stork.
14She lays her eggs on the ground
and lets them warm in the sand,
15unmindful that a foot may crush them,
that some wild animal may trample them.
16She treats her young harshly, as if they were not hers;
she cares not that her labor was in vain,
17for God did not endow her with wisdom
or give her a share of good sense.
18Yet when she spreads her feathers to run,
she laughs at horse and rider.

19"Do you give the horse his strength
or clothe his neck with a flowing mane?
20Do you make him leap like a locust,
striking terror with his proud snorting?
21He paws fiercely, rejoicing in his strength,
and charges into the fray.
22He laughs at fear, afraid of nothing;
he does not shy away from the sword.
23The quiver rattles against his side,
along with the flashing spear and lance.
24In frenzied excitement he eats up the ground;
he cannot stand still when the trumpet sounds.
25At the blast of the trumpet he snorts, 'Aha!'
He catches the scent of battle from afar,
the shout of commanders and the battle cry.

26"Does the hawk take flight by your wisdom
and spread his wings toward the south?
27Does the eagle soar at your command
and build his nest on high?
28He dwells on a cliff and stays there at night;
a rocky crag is his stronghold.
29From there he seeks out his food;
his eyes detect it from afar.
30His young ones feast on blood,
and where the slain are, there is he."

## King James

# 40

MOREOVER THE LORD answered Job, and said,
2 Shall he that contendeth with the Almighty instruct *him?* he that reproveth God, let him answer it.
3 ¶ Then Job answered the LORD, and said,
4 Behold, I am vile; what shall I answer thee? I will lay mine hand upon my mouth.
5 Once have I spoken; but I will not answer: yea, twice; but I will proceed no further.
6 ¶ Then answered the LORD unto Job out of the whirlwind, and said,
7 Gird up thy loins now like a man: I will demand of thee, and declare thou unto me.
8 Wilt thou also disannul my judgment? wilt thou condemn me, that thou mayest be righteous?
9 Hast thou an arm like God? or canst thou thunder with a voice like him?
10 Deck thyself now *with* majesty and excellency; and array thyself with glory and beauty.
11 Cast abroad the rage of thy wrath: and behold every one *that is* proud, and abase him.
12 Look on every one *that is* proud, *and* bring him low; and tread down the wicked in their place.
13 Hide them in the dust together; *and* bind their faces in secret.
14 Then will I also confess unto thee that thine own right hand can save thee.
15 ¶ Behold now behemoth, which I made with thee; he eateth grass as an ox.
16 Lo now, his strength *is* in his loins, and his force *is* in the navel of his belly.
17 He moveth his tail like a cedar: the sinews of his stones are wrapped together.
18 His bones *are as* strong pieces of brass; his bones *are* like bars of iron.
19 He *is* the chief of the ways of God: he that made him can make his sword to approach *unto him.*
20 Surely the mountains bring him forth food, where all the beasts of the field play.
21 He lieth under the shady trees, in the covert of the reed, and fens.
22 The shady trees cover him *with* their shadow; the willows of the brook compass him about.
23 Behold, he drinketh up a river, *and* hasteth not: he trusteth that he can draw up Jordan into his mouth.
24 He taketh it with his eyes: *his* nose pierceth through snares.

# 41

CANST THOU draw out leviathan with an hook? or his tongue with a cord *which* thou lettest down?
2 Canst thou put an hook into his nose? or bore his jaw through with a thorn?
3 Will he make many supplications unto thee? will he speak soft *words* unto thee?
4 Will he make a covenant with thee? wilt thou take him for a servant for ever?

## Amplified

# 40

MOREOVER THE Lord said to Job,
2 Shall he who would find fault with the Almighty contend with Him? He who disputes with God, let him answer it.
3 Then Job replied to the Lord,
4 Behold, I am of small account *and* vile! What shall I answer You? I lay my hand upon my mouth. [Ezra 9:6; Ps. 51:4.]
5 I have spoken once, but I will not reply again; indeed, twice [have I answered], but I will proceed no further.
6 Then the Lord answered Job out of the whirlwind, saying,
7 Gird up your loins now like a man; I will demand of you, and you answer Me.
8 Will you also annul—set aside and render void—My judgment? Will you condemn Me [your God] that you may [appear] righteous *and* justified?
9 Have you an arm like God? Or can you thunder with a voice like His?
10 [Since you question the manner of the Almighty's rule] deck yourself now with the excellency *and* dignity [of the supreme Ruler, and yourself undertake the government of the world, if you are so wise], *and* array yourself with honor and majesty;
11 Pour forth the overflowings of your anger, and look on every one who is proud, and abase him;
12 Look on every one who is proud, *and* bring him low, and tread down the wicked where they stand [if you are so able, Job].
13 [Bury and] hide them all in the dust together, *and* shut them up [in the prison house of death].
14 [If you can do all this, Job, proving yourself of divine might] then will I, [God,] praise you also [and acknowledge that] your own right hand can save you.
15 Behold now behemoth (the hippopotamus), which I created as I did you; he eats grass as an ox.
16 See now, his strength is in his loins, and his power is in the sinews of his belly.
17 He moves his tail like a cedar tree; the tendons of his thighs are twisted together [like a rope].
18 His bones are as tubes of bronze; his limbs [or ribs] are like bars of iron.
19 [The hippopotamus] is the first [in magnitude and power] of the works of God [in animal life]; *only* He Who made him provides him with his [sword-like tusks, or God Who made him, alone can bring near His sword to master him].
20 Surely the mountains bring him forth food, where all the wild animals play.
21 He lies under the lotus trees, in the covert of the reeds and in the marsh.
22 The lotus trees cover him with their shade; the willows of the brook compass him about.
23 Behold, if a river is violent *and* overflows, he does not tremble; he is confident though a Jordan [River] swells and rushes against his mouth.
24 Can any take him when he is on the watch, or pierce through his nose with a snare?

# 41

CAN YOU draw out leviathan [the crocodile] with a fishhook? Or press down his tongue with a cord?
2 Can you put a rope into his nose? Or pierce his jaw through with a hook *or* a spike?
3 Will he make many supplications to you [begging to be spared]? Will he speak soft words to you [to coax you to treat him kindly]?
4 Will he make a covenant with you to take him for your servant forever?

## New American Standard

*Job: What Can I Say?*

40 THEN THE LORD said to Job,
2 "Will the faultfinder contend with the Almighty?
Let him who reproves God answer it."

3 ¶ Then Job answered the LORD and said,
4 "Behold, I am insignificant; what can I reply to Thee?
I lay my hand on my mouth.
5 "Once I have spoken, and I will not answer;
Even twice, and I will add no more."

*God Questions Job*

6 ¶ Then the LORD answered Job out of the storm, and said,
7 "Now gird up your loins like a man;
I will ask you, and you instruct Me.
8 "Will you really annul My judgment?
Will you condemn Me that you may be justified?
9 "Or do you have an arm like God,
And can you thunder with a voice like His?

10 ¶ "Adorn yourself with eminence and dignity;
And clothe yourself with honor and majesty.
11 "Pour out the overflowings of your anger;
And look on everyone who is proud, and make him low.
12 "Look on everyone who is proud, *and* humble him;
And tread down the wicked where they stand.
13 "Hide them in the dust together;
Bind them in the hidden *place.*
14 "Then I will also confess to you,
That your own right hand can save you.

*God's Power Shown in Creatures*

15 ¶ "Behold now, [a]Behemoth, which I made as well as you;
He eats grass like an ox.
16 "Behold now, his strength in his loins,
And his power in the muscles of his belly.
17 "He bends his tail like a cedar;
The sinews of his thighs are knit together.
18 "His bones are tubes of bronze;
His limbs are like bars of iron.

19 ¶ "He is the first of the ways of God;
Let his maker bring near his sword.
20 "Surely the mountains bring him food,
And all the beasts of the field play there.
21 "Under the lotus plants he lies down,
In the covert of the reeds and the marsh.
22 "The lotus plants cover him with shade;
The willows of the brook surround him.
23 "If a river rages, he is not alarmed;
He is confident, though the Jordan rushes to his mouth.
24 "Can anyone capture him when he is on watch,
With barbs can anyone pierce *his* nose?

*God's Power Shown in Creatures*

41 "CAN YOU draw out [b]Leviathan with a fishhook?
Or press down his tongue with a cord?
2 "Can you put a rope in his nose?
Or pierce his jaw with a hook?
3 "Will he make many supplications to you?
Or will he speak to you soft words?
4 "Will he make a covenant with you?
Will you take him for a servant forever?

NAS [a] Or, *the hippopotamus* [b] Or, *the crocodile*

## New International

40 THE LORD said to Job:
2 "Will the one who contends with the Almighty correct him?
Let him who accuses God answer him!"

3 Then Job answered the LORD:
4 "I am unworthy—how can I reply to you?
I put my hand over my mouth.
5 I spoke once, but I have no answer—
twice, but I will say no more."

6 Then the LORD spoke to Job out of the storm:
7 "Brace yourself like a man;
I will question you,
and you shall answer me.

8 "Would you discredit my justice?
Would you condemn me to justify yourself?
9 Do you have an arm like God's,
and can your voice thunder like his?
10 Then adorn yourself with glory and splendor,
and clothe yourself in honor and majesty.
11 Unleash the fury of your wrath,
look at every proud man and bring him low,
12 look at every proud man and humble him,
crush the wicked where they stand.
13 Bury them all in the dust together;
shroud their faces in the grave.
14 Then I myself will admit to you
that your own right hand can save you.

15 "Look at the behemoth,[c]
which I made along with you
and which feeds on grass like an ox.
16 What strength he has in his loins,
what power in the muscles of his belly!
17 His tail[d] sways like a cedar;
the sinews of his thighs are close-knit.
18 His bones are tubes of bronze,
his limbs like rods of iron.
19 He ranks first among the works of God,
yet his Maker can approach him with his sword.
20 The hills bring him their produce,
and all the wild animals play nearby.
21 Under the lotus plants he lies,
hidden among the reeds in the marsh.
22 The lotuses conceal him in their shadow;
the poplars by the stream surround him.
23 When the river rages, he is not alarmed;
he is secure, though the Jordan should surge against his mouth.
24 Can anyone capture him by the eyes,[e]
or trap him and pierce his nose?

41 "CAN YOU pull in the leviathan[f] with a fishhook
or tie down his tongue with a rope?
2 Can you put a cord through his nose
or pierce his jaw with a hook?
3 Will he keep begging you for mercy?
Will he speak to you with gentle words?
4 Will he make an agreement with you
for you to take him as your slave for life?

NIV [c] 15 Possibly the hippopotamus or the elephant [d] 17 Possibly trunk [e] 24 Or *by a water hole* [f] 1 Possibly the crocodile

## King James

5Wilt thou play with him as *with* a bird? or wilt thou bind him
for thy maidens?
6Shall the companions make a banquet of him? shall they part
him among the merchants?
7Canst thou fill his skin with barbed irons? or his head with fish
spears?
8Lay thine hand upon him, remember the battle, do no more.
9Behold, the hope of him is in vain: shall not *one* be cast down
even at the sight of him?
10None *is so* fierce that dare stir him up: who then is able to
stand before me?
11Who hath prevented me, that I should repay *him? whatsoever*
*is* under the whole heaven is mine.
12I will not conceal his parts, nor his power, nor his comely
proportion.
13Who can discover the face of his garment? *or* who can come
*to him* with his double bridle?
14Who can open the doors of his face? his teeth *are* terrible
round about.
15 *His* scales *are his* pride, shut up together *as with* a close seal.
16One is so near to another, that no air can come between them.
17They are joined one to another, they stick together, that they
cannot be sundered.
18By his sneezings a light doth shine, and his eyes *are* like the
eyelids of the morning.
19Out of his mouth go burning lamps, *and* sparks of fire leap
out.
20Out of his nostrils goeth smoke, as *out* of a seething pot or
caldron.
21His breath kindleth coals, and a flame goeth out of his mouth.
22In his neck remaineth strength, and sorrow is turned into joy
before him.
23The flakes of his flesh are joined together: they are firm in
themselves; they cannot be moved.
24His heart is as firm as a stone; yea, as hard as a piece of the
nether *millstone.*
25When he raiseth up himself, the mighty are afraid: by reason
of breakings they purify themselves.
26The sword of him that layeth at him cannot hold: the spear,
the dart, nor the habergeon.
27He esteemeth iron as straw, *and* brass as rotten wood.
28The arrow cannot make him flee: slingstones are turned with
him into stubble.
29Darts are counted as stubble: he laugheth at the shaking of a
spear.
30Sharp stones *are* under him: he spreadeth sharp pointed
things upon the mire.
31He maketh the deep to boil like a pot: he maketh the sea like
a pot of ointment.
32He maketh a path to shine after him; *one* would think the deep
*to be* hoary.
33Upon earth there is not his like, who is made without fear.
34He beholdeth all high *things:* he *is* a king over all the children
of pride.

## Amplified

5Will you play with [the crocodile] as with a bird? Or will you
put him on leash for your maidens?
6Will traders bargain over him? Will they divide him up among
the merchants?
7Can you fill his skin with harpoons? Or his head with fishing
spears?
8Lay your hand upon him! Remember your battle with him; you
will not do [such an ill-advised thing] again!
9Behold, the hope of [his assailant] is disappointed; one is cast
down even at the sight of him!
10No one is so fierce [and foolhardy] that he dares to stir up [the
crocodile]; who then is he who can stand before Me [the beast's
Creator, or dares to contend with Me]?
11Who has first given to Me, that I should repay him? Whatever
is under the whole heavens is Mine. [Therefore, who can have a
claim against God, God who made the unmastered crocodile?]
[Rom. 11:35.]
12I will not keep silence concerning his limbs, nor his mighty
strength, nor his goodly frame.
13Who can strip off [the crocodile's] outer garment? [Who can
penetrate his double coat of mail?] Who shall come within his
jaws?
14Who can open the doors of his [lipless] mouth? His [extended
jaws and bare] teeth are terrible round about.
15His scales are [the crocodile's] pride, [for his back is made of
rows of shields] shut up together *as with* a close seal.
16One is so near to another that no air can come between them.
17They are joined one to another, they stick together so that
they cannot be separated.
18His sneezings flash forth light, and his eyes are like the [red-
dish] eyelids of the dawn.
19Out of his mouth go burning torches, *and* sparks of fire leap
out.
20Out of his nostrils goes forth smoke, as out of a seething pot
with a fire of rushes.
21His breath kindles coals, and a flame goes forth from his
mouth.
22In [the crocodile's] neck abides strength, and terror dances
before him.
23The folds of his flesh cleave together, they are firm upon him,
they cannot shake [when he moves].
24His heart is as firm as a stone; indeed, as solid as a nether
millstone.
25When [the crocodile] raises himself up, the mighty are afraid;
because of terror *and* the crashing they are beside themselves.
26Even if one strikes at him with the sword, it cannot get any
hold, nor the spear, the dart, nor the javelin.
27He counts iron as straw, *and* bronze as rotten wood.
28The arrow cannot make [the crocodile] flee; slingstones are
treated by him as stubble.
29Clubs [also] are counted as stubble; he laughs at the rushing
*and* the rattle of the javelin.
30His underparts are like sharp pieces of broken pottery; he
spreads [grooves like] a threshing sledge upon the mire.
31He makes the deep boil like a pot; he makes the sea like a
[foaming] pot of ointment.
32[His swift darting] makes a shining track behind him; one
would think the deep to be hoary [with foam].
33Upon earth there is not [the crocodile's] like, a creature made
without fear *and* he behaves fearlessly.
34He looks all mighty [beasts of prey] in the face [without ter-
ror]; he is monarch of all the sons of pride. [And now, Job, [a]who
are you, who dares not arouse the unmastered crocodile, yet who
dares resist Me, the beast's Creator; to My face? Everything under
the heavens is Mine; therefore who can have a claim against God?]

**AMP** [a] Repeating the thought of verses ten and eleven, which are the key and climax to God's argument with Job.

## New American Standard

5 "Will you play with him as with a bird?
Or will you bind him for your maidens?
6 "Will the traders bargain over him?
Will they divide him among the merchants?
7 "Can you fill his skin with harpoons,
Or his head with fishing spears?
8 "Lay your hand on him;
Remember the battle; you will not do it again!
9 "Behold, your expectation is false;
Will you be laid low even at the sight of him?
10 "No one is so fierce that he dares to arouse him;
Who then is he that can stand before Me?
11 "Who has given to Me that I should repay *him?*
*Whatever* is under the whole heaven is Mine.

12¶ "I will not keep silence concerning his limbs,
Or his mighty strength, or his orderly frame.
13 "Who can strip off his outer armor?
Who can come within his double mail?
14 "Who can open the doors of his face?
Around his teeth there is terror.
15 "*His* strong scales are *his* pride,
Shut up *as with* a tight seal.
16 "One is so near to another,
That no air can come between them.
17 "They are joined one to another;
They clasp each other and cannot be separated.
18 "His sneezes flash forth light,
And his eyes are like the eyelids of the morning.
19 "Out of his mouth go burning torches;
Sparks of fire leap forth.
20 "Out of his nostrils smoke goes forth,
As *from* a boiling pot and *burning* rushes.
21 "His breath kindles coals,
And a flame goes forth from his mouth.
22 "In his neck lodges strength,
And dismay leaps before him.
23 "The folds of his flesh are joined together,
Firm on him and immovable.
24 "His heart is as hard as a stone;
Even as hard as a lower millstone.
25 "When he raises himself up, the mighty fear;
Because of the crashing they are bewildered.
26 "The sword that reaches him cannot avail;
Nor the spear, the dart, or the javelin.
27 "He regards iron as straw,
Bronze as rotten wood.
28 "The arrow cannot make him flee;
Slingstones are turned into stubble for him.
29 "Clubs are regarded as stubble;
He laughs at the rattling of the javelin.
30 "His underparts are *like* sharp potsherds;
He spreads out *like* a threshing sledge on the mire.
31 "He makes the depths boil like a pot;
He makes the sea like a jar of ointment.
32 "Behind him he makes a wake to shine;
One would think the deep to be gray-haired.
33 "Nothing on earth is like him,
One made without fear.
34 "He looks on everything that is high;
He is king over all the sons of pride."

## New International

5Can you make a pet of him like a bird
or put him on a leash for your girls?
6Will traders barter for him?
Will they divide him up among the merchants?
7Can you fill his hide with harpoons
or his head with fishing spears?
8If you lay a hand on him,
you will remember the struggle and never do it again!
9Any hope of subduing him is false;
the mere sight of him is overpowering.
10No one is fierce enough to rouse him.
Who then is able to stand against me?
11Who has a claim against me that I must pay?
Everything under heaven belongs to me.

12"I will not fail to speak of his limbs,
his strength and his graceful form.
13Who can strip off his outer coat?
Who would approach him with a bridle?
14Who dares open the doors of his mouth,
ringed about with his fearsome teeth?
15His back has[b] rows of shields
tightly sealed together;
16each is so close to the next
that no air can pass between.
17They are joined fast to one another;
they cling together and cannot be parted.
18His snorting throws out flashes of light;
his eyes are like the rays of dawn.
19Firebrands stream from his mouth;
sparks of fire shoot out.
20Smoke pours from his nostrils
as from a boiling pot over a fire of reeds.
21His breath sets coals ablaze,
and flames dart from his mouth.
22Strength resides in his neck;
dismay goes before him.
23The folds of his flesh are tightly joined;
they are firm and immovable.
24His chest is hard as rock,
hard as a lower millstone.
25When he rises up, the mighty are terrified;
they retreat before his thrashing.
26The sword that reaches him has no effect,
nor does the spear or the dart or the javelin.
27Iron he treats like straw
and bronze like rotten wood.
28Arrows do not make him flee;
slingstones are like chaff to him.
29A club seems to him but a piece of straw;
he laughs at the rattling of the lance.
30His undersides are jagged potsherds,
leaving a trail in the mud like a threshing sledge.
31He makes the depths churn like a boiling caldron
and stirs up the sea like a pot of ointment.
32Behind him he leaves a glistening wake;
one would think the deep had white hair.
33Nothing on earth is his equal—
a creature without fear.
34He looks down on all that are haughty;
he is king over all that are proud."

**NIV** [b] 15 Or *His pride is his*

## King James

**42** THEN JOB answered the LORD, and said,

2 I know that thou canst do every *thing,* and *that* no thought can be withholden from thee.

3 Who *is* he that hideth counsel without knowledge? therefore have I uttered that I understood not; things too wonderful for me, which I knew not.

4 Hear, I beseech thee, and I will speak: I will demand of thee, and declare thou unto me.

5 I have heard of thee by the hearing of the ear: but now mine eye seeth thee.

6 Wherefore I abhor *myself,* and repent in dust and ashes.

7 ¶ And it was *so,* that after the LORD had spoken these words unto Job, the LORD said to Eliphaz the Temanite, My wrath is kindled against thee, and against thy two friends: for ye have not spoken of me *the thing that is* right, as my servant Job *hath.*

8 Therefore take unto you now seven bullocks and seven rams, and go to my servant Job, and offer up for yourselves a burnt offering; and my servant Job shall pray for you: for him will I accept: lest I deal with you *after your* folly, in that ye have not spoken of me *the thing which is* right, like my servant Job.

9 So Eliphaz the Temanite and Bildad the Shuhite *and* Zophar the Naamathite went, and did according as the LORD commanded them: the LORD also accepted Job.

10 And the LORD turned the captivity of Job, when he prayed for his friends: also the LORD gave Job twice as much as he had before.

11 Then came there unto him all his brethren, and all his sisters, and all they that had been of his acquaintance before, and did eat bread with him in his house: and they bemoaned him, and comforted him over all the evil that the LORD had brought upon him: every man also gave him a piece of money, and every one an earring of gold.

12 So the LORD blessed the latter end of Job more than his beginning: for he had fourteen thousand sheep, and six thousand camels, and a thousand yoke of oxen, and a thousand she asses.

13 He had also seven sons and three daughters.

14 And he called the name of the first, Jemima; and the name of the second, Kezia; and the name of the third, Keren-happuch.

15 And in all the land were no women found *so* fair as the daughters of Job: and their father gave them inheritance among their brethren.

16 After this lived Job an hundred and forty years, and saw his sons, and his sons' sons, *even* four generations.

17 So Job died, *being* old and full of days.

## Amplified

**42** THEN JOB said to the Lord,

2 I know that You can do all things and that no thought *or* purpose of Yours can be restrained *or* thwarted.

3 [You said to me] Who is this that darkens *and* obscures counsel [by words] without knowledge? Therefore [I now see] I have [rashly] uttered what I did not understand, things too wonderful for me, which I did not know.

4 [I had virtually said to You what You have said to me:] Hear, I beseech You, and I will speak; I will demand of You, and You declare to me.

5 I had heard of You [only] by the hearing of the ear; but now my [spiritual] eye sees You.

6 Therefore I loathe [my words] *and* abhor myself, and repent in dust and ashes.

7 After the Lord had spoken the previous words to Job, the Lord said to Eliphaz the Temanite, My wrath is kindled against you and against your two friends; for you have not spoken of Me the thing that is right, as My servant Job has.

8 Now therefore take seven bullocks and seven rams, and go to My servant Job, and offer up for yourselves a burnt offering; and My servant Job shall pray for you, for I will accept [his prayer] that I deal not with you after your folly, in that you have not spoken of Me the thing which is right, like My servant Job.

9 So Eliphaz the Temanite and Bildad the Shuhite *and* Zophar the Naamathite went, and did according as the Lord commanded them; and the Lord accepted [Job's prayer].

10 And the Lord turned the captivity of Job *and* restored his fortunes, when he prayed for his friends; also the Lord gave Job twice as much as he had before. [Deut. 30:1-3; Ps. 126:1, 2.]

11 Then there came to him all his brothers and sisters, and all who had known him before, and they ate bread with him in his house; and they sympathized with him and comforted him over all the [distressing] calamities that the Lord had brought upon him. Every man also gave him a piece of money and every one an earring of gold.

12 And the Lord blessed the latter days of Job more than his beginning; for he had fourteen thousand sheep, six thousand camels, a thousand yoke of oxen, and a thousand female donkeys. [Cf. Job 1:3.]

13 He had also seven sons and three daughters.

14 And he called the name of the first Jemimah and the name of the second, Keziah, and the name of the third, Keren-happuch.

15 And in all the land there were no women so fair as the daughters of Job; and their father gave them inheritance among their brothers.

16 After this Job lived a hundred and forty years, and saw his sons, and his sons' sons, even four generations.

17 So Job died, an old man and full of days. [James 5:11.]

## New American Standard

*Job's Confession*

42 THEN JOB answered the LORD, and said,
2 "I know that Thou canst do all things,
And that no purpose of Thine can be thwarted.
3 'Who is this that hides counsel without knowledge?'
"Therefore I have declared that which I did not understand,
Things too wonderful for me, which I did not know."
4 'Hear, now, and I will speak;
I will ask Thee, and do Thou instruct me.'
5 "I have heard of Thee by the hearing of the ear;
But now my eye sees Thee;
6 Therefore I retract,
And I repent in dust and ashes."

*God Displeased with Job's Friends*

7¶ And it came about after the LORD had spoken these words
to Job, that the LORD said to Eliphaz the Temanite, "My wrath is
kindled against you and against your two friends, because you
have not spoken of Me what is right as My servant Job has.
8"Now therefore, take for yourselves seven bulls and seven
rams, and go to My servant Job, and offer up a burnt offering for
yourselves, and My servant Job will pray for you. For I will accept
him so that I may not do with you *according to your* folly, because
you have not spoken of Me what is right, as My servant Job has."
9So Eliphaz the Temanite and Bildad the Shuhite *and* Zophar
the Naamathite went and did as the LORD told them; and the LORD
accepted Job.

*God Restores Job's Fortunes*

10¶ And the LORD restored the fortunes of Job when he prayed
for his friends, and the LORD increased all that Job had twofold.
11Then all his brothers, and all his sisters, and all who had
known him before, came to him, and they ate bread with him in
his house; and they consoled him and comforted him for all the evil
that the LORD had brought on him. And each one gave him one
piece of money, and each a ring of gold.
12And the LORD blessed the latter *days* of Job more than his
beginning, and he had 14,000 sheep, and 6,000 camels, and 1,000
yoke of oxen, and 1,000 female donkeys.
13And he had seven sons and three daughters.
14And he named the first Jemimah, and the second Keziah, and
the third Keren-happuch.
15And in all the land no women were found so fair as Job's
daughters; and their father gave them inheritance among their
brothers.
16And after this Job lived 140 years, and saw his sons, and his
grandsons, four generations.
17And Job died, an old man and full of days.

## New International

*Job*

42 THEN JOB replied to the LORD:

2"I know that you can do all things;
no plan of yours can be thwarted.
3⌞You asked,⌟ 'Who is this that obscures my counsel without knowledge?'
Surely I spoke of things I did not understand,
things too wonderful for me to know.

4"⌞You said,⌟ 'Listen now, and I will speak;
I will question you,
and you shall answer me.'
5My ears had heard of you
but now my eyes have seen you.
6Therefore I despise myself
and repent in dust and ashes."

*Epilogue*

7After the LORD had said these things to Job, he said to Eliphaz
the Temanite, "I am angry with you and your two friends, because
you have not spoken of me what is right, as my servant Job has.
8So now take seven bulls and seven rams and go to my servant Job
and sacrifice a burnt offering for yourselves. My servant Job will
pray for you, and I will accept his prayer and not deal with you
according to your folly. You have not spoken of me what is right,
as my servant Job has." 9So Eliphaz the Temanite, Bildad the
Shuhite and Zophar the Naamathite did what the LORD told them;
and the LORD accepted Job's prayer.
10After Job had prayed for his friends, the LORD made him
prosperous again and gave him twice as much as he had before.
11All his brothers and sisters and everyone who had known him
before came and ate with him in his house. They comforted and
consoled him over all the trouble the LORD had brought upon him,
and each one gave him a piece of silver[a] and a gold ring.
12The LORD blessed the latter part of Job's life more than the
first. He had fourteen thousand sheep, six thousand camels, a
thousand yoke of oxen and a thousand donkeys. 13And he also
had seven sons and three daughters. 14The first daughter he
named Jemimah, the second Keziah and the third Keren-Happuch. 15Nowhere in all the land were there found women as
beautiful as Job's daughters, and their father granted them an
inheritance along with their brothers.
16After this, Job lived a hundred and forty years; he saw his
children and their children to the fourth generation. 17And so he
died, old and full of years.

NIV [a] 11 Hebrew *him a kesitah;* a kesitah was a unit of money of unknown weight and value.

**King James**

THE BOOK OF

# Psalms

## Book I

**1** BLESSED *IS* the man that walketh not in the counsel of the ungodly, nor standeth in the way of sinners, nor sitteth in the seat of the scornful.

2But his delight *is* in the law of the LORD; and in his law doth he meditate day and night.

3And he shall be like a tree planted by the rivers of water, that bringeth forth his fruit in his season; his leaf also shall not wither; and whatsoever he doeth shall prosper.

4The ungodly *are* not so: but *are* like the chaff which the wind driveth away.

5Therefore the ungodly shall not stand in the judgment, nor sinners in the congregation of the righteous.

6For the LORD knoweth the way of the righteous: but the way of the ungodly shall perish.

**2** WHY DO the heathen rage, and the people imagine a vain thing?

2The kings of the earth set themselves, and the rulers take counsel together, against the LORD, and against his anointed, *saying*,

3Let us break their bands asunder, and cast away their cords from us.

4He that sitteth in the heavens shall laugh: the Lord shall have them in derision.

5Then shall he speak unto them in his wrath, and vex them in his sore displeasure.

6Yet have I set my king upon my holy hill of Zion.

7I will declare the decree: the LORD hath said unto me, Thou *art* my Son; this day have I begotten thee.

8Ask of me, and I shall give *thee* the heathen *for* thine inheritance, and the uttermost parts of the earth *for* thy possession.

**Amplified**

# The Psalms

## BOOK ONE

**1**[a] BLESSED—HAPPY, fortunate, prosperous and enviable—is the man who walks *and* lives not in the counsel of the ungodly [following their advice, their plans and purposes], nor stands [submissive and inactive] in the path where sinners walk, nor sits down [to relax and rest] where the scornful [and the mockers] gather.

2But his delight *and* desire are in the law of the Lord, and on His law—the precepts, the instructions, the teachings of God—he habitually meditates (ponders and studies) by day and by night. [II Tim. 3:16; Gal. 3:1-29; Rom. 13:8-10.]

3And he shall be like a tree firmly planted [and tended] by the streams of water, ready to bring forth his fruit in its season; his leaf also shall not fade *or* wither, and everything he does shall prosper [and come to maturity]. [Jer. 17:7, 8.]

4Not so the wicked [those disobedient and living without God are not so]. But they are like the chaff [worthless, dead, without substance] which the wind drives away.

5Therefore the wicked, those disobedient [and living without God], shall not stand [justified] in the judgment; nor [b]sinners in the congregation of the righteous [those who are upright and in right standing with God].

6For the Lord knows *and* is fully acquainted with the way of the righteous; but the way of the ungodly [those living outside God's will] shall perish (end in ruin and come to nought).

**2** WHY DO the nations assemble with commotion [uproar and confusion of voices], and why do the people imagine (meditate upon and devise) an empty scheme?

2The kings of the earth take their places; the rulers take counsel together against the Lord and His Anointed One—the Messiah, the Christ. *They say,* [Acts 4:25-27.]

3Let us break Their bands [of restraint] asunder, and cast Their cords [of control] from us.

4He Who sits in the heavens laughs; the Lord has them in derision [and in supreme contempt He mocks them].

5He speaks to them in His deep anger, and troubles (terrifies and confounds) them in His displeasure *and* fury, *saying,*

6Yet have I anointed [installed and placed] My King [firmly] on My holy hill of Zion.

7I will declare the decree of the Lord: He said to Me, You are My Son; this day [I declare] I have begotten You. [Heb. 1:5; 3:5, 6; II Pet. 1:17, 18.]

8Ask of Me, and I will give You the nations as Your inheritance, and the uttermost parts of the earth for Your possession.

**AMP** [a] This has been called *The Preface Psalm,* because in some respects it may be considered "the text upon which the whole of the Psalms make up a divine sermon." It opens with a benediction, "Blessed," as does our Lord's Sermon on the Mount (Matt. 5:3). [b] Charles Haddon Spurgeon said, "Sinners cannot live in Heaven. They would be out of their element. Sooner could a fish live upon a tree than the wicked in Paradise." The only way they will ever be able to endure Heaven is to be born again and become new creatures, with pure hearts able fully to enjoy the presence of God, His holy angels and the redeemed.

## New American Standard

# The Psalms

BOOK 1

*The Righteous and the Wicked Contrasted.*

**1** HOW BLESSED is the man who does not walk in the counsel of the wicked,
Nor stand in the path of sinners,
Nor sit in the seat of scoffers!
2 But his delight is in the law of the LORD,
And in His law he meditates day and night.
3 And he will be like a tree *firmly* planted by streams of water,
Which yields its fruit in its season,
And its leaf does not wither;
And in whatever he does, he prospers.
4¶ The wicked are not so,
But they are like chaff which the wind drives away.
5 Therefore the wicked will not stand in the judgment,
Nor sinners in the assembly of the righteous.
6 For the LORD knows the way of the righteous,
But the way of the wicked will perish.

*The Reign of the LORD's Anointed.*

**2** WHY ARE the nations in an uproar,
And the peoples devising a vain thing?
2 The kings of the earth take their stand,
And the rulers take counsel together
Against the LORD and against His [c]Anointed:
3 "Let us tear their fetters apart,
And cast away their cords from us!"
4¶ He who [d]sits in the heavens laughs,
The Lord scoffs at them.
5 Then He will speak to them in His anger
And terrify them in His fury:
6 "But as for Me, I have installed My King
Upon Zion, My holy mountain."
7¶ "I will surely tell of the decree of the LORD:
He said to Me, 'Thou art My Son,
Today I have begotten Thee.
8 'Ask of Me, and I will surely give the nations as Thine inheritance,
And the *very* ends of the earth as Thy possession.

NAS [c] Or, *Messiah* [d] Or, *is enthroned*

## New International

# Psalms

BOOK I

*Psalms 1-41*

**1** BLESSED IS the man
who does not walk in the counsel of the wicked
or stand in the way of sinners
or sit in the seat of mockers.
2 But his delight is in the law of the LORD,
and on his law he meditates day and night.
3 He is like a tree planted by streams of water,
which yields its fruit in season
and whose leaf does not wither.
Whatever he does prospers.

4 Not so the wicked!
They are like chaff
that the wind blows away.
5 Therefore the wicked will not stand in the judgment,
nor sinners in the assembly of the righteous.

6 For the LORD watches over the way of the righteous,
but the way of the wicked will perish.

**2** WHY DO the nations conspire[e]
and the peoples plot in vain?
2 The kings of the earth take their stand
and the rulers gather together
against the LORD
and against his Anointed One.[f]
3 "Let us break their chains," they say,
"and throw off their fetters."
4 The One enthroned in heaven laughs;
the Lord scoffs at them.
5 Then he rebukes them in his anger
and terrifies them in his wrath, saying,
6 "I have installed my King[g]
on Zion, my holy hill."
7 I will proclaim the decree of the LORD:

He said to me, "You are my Son[h];
today I have become your Father.[i]
8 Ask of me,
and I will make the nations your inheritance,
the ends of the earth your possession.

NIV [e] *1* Hebrew; Septuagint *rage* [f] *2* Or *anointed one* [g] *6* Or *king* [h] *7* Or *son;* also in verse 12 [i] *7* Or *have begotten you*

## King James

9 Thou shalt break them with a rod of iron; thou shalt dash them
in pieces like a potter's vessel.
10 Be wise now therefore, O ye kings: be instructed, ye judges
of the earth.
11 Serve the LORD with fear, and rejoice with trembling.
12 Kiss the Son, lest he be angry, and ye perish *from* the way,
when his wrath is kindled but a little. Blessed *are* all they that put
their trust in him.

A Psalm of David, when he fled from Absalom his son.

**3** LORD, HOW are they increased that trouble me! many *are*
they that rise up against me.
2 Many *there be* which say of my soul, *There is* no help for him
in God. Selah.
3 But thou, O LORD, *art* a shield for me; my glory, and the lifter
up of mine head.
4 I cried unto the LORD with my voice, and he heard me out of
his holy hill. Selah.
5 I laid me down and slept; I awaked; for the LORD sustained me.
6 I will not be afraid of ten thousands of people, that have set
*themselves* against me round about.
7 Arise, O LORD; save me, O my God: for thou hast smitten all
mine enemies *upon* the cheek bone; thou hast broken the teeth of
the ungodly.
8 Salvation *belongeth* unto the LORD: thy blessing *is* upon thy
people. Selah.

To the chief Musician on Neginoth, A Psalm of David.

**4** HEAR ME when I call, O God of my righteousness: thou hast
enlarged me *when I was* in distress; have mercy upon me, and
hear my prayer.
2 O ye sons of men, how long *will ye turn* my glory into shame?
*how long* will ye love vanity, *and* seek after leasing? Selah.
3 But know that the LORD hath set apart him that is godly for
himself: the LORD will hear when I call unto him.
4 Stand in awe, and sin not: commune with your own heart
upon your bed, and be still. Selah.
5 Offer the sacrifices of righteousness, and put your trust in the
LORD.
6 *There be* many that say, Who will show us *any* good? LORD, lift
thou up the light of thy countenance upon us.
7 Thou hast put gladness in my heart, more than in the time *that*
their corn and their wine increased.
8 I will both lay me down in peace, and sleep: for thou, LORD,
only makest me dwell in safety.

## Amplified

9 You shall break them with a rod of iron; You shall dash them
in pieces like potter's ware. [Rev. 12:5; 19:15.]
10 Now therefore, O you kings, act wisely; be instructed *and*
warned, O you rulers of the earth.
11 Serve the Lord with reverent awe *and* worshipful fear; rejoice
*and* be in high spirits, with trembling [lest you displease Him].
12 Kiss the Son [pay homage to Him in purity] lest He be angry,
and you perish in the way, for soon shall His wrath be kindled.
O blessed—happy, fortunate and to be envied—are all those who
seek refuge *and* put their trust in Him!

A Psalm of David,
when he fled from Absalom his son.

**3** LORD, HOW they are increased who trouble me! Many are
they who rise up against me.
2 Many are saying of me, There is no help for him in God. Selah
[pause, and calmly think of that]!
3 But You, O Lord, are a shield for me, my glory, and the lifter
up of my head.
4 With my voice I cry to the Lord, and He hears and answers me
out of His holy hill. Selah [pause, and calmly think of that]!
5 I lay down and slept; I wakened again, for the Lord sustains
me.
6 I will not be afraid of ten thousands of people, who have set
themselves against me round about.
7 Arise, O Lord; save me, O my God; for You have struck all my
enemies on the cheek; You have broken the teeth of the ungodly.
8 Salvation belongs to the Lord; Your blessing be upon Your
people. Selah [pause, and calmly think of that]!

To the Chief Musician;
on stringed instruments. A Psalm of David.

**4** ANSWER ME when I call, O God of my righteousness [up-
rightness, justice and right standing with You]! You have
freed me when I was hemmed in *and* enlarged me when I was in
distress; have mercy upon me and hear my prayer.
2 O you sons of men, how long will you turn my honor *and* glory
into shame? How long will you love vanity *and* futility, *and* seek
after lies? Selah [pause, and calmly think of that]!
3 But know that the Lord has set apart for Himself [and given
distinction to] him who is godly [the man of loving-kindness]. The
Lord listens *and* heeds when I call to Him.
4 Be angry [or stand in awe] and sin not; commune with your
own heart upon your bed, and be silent [sorry for the things you
say in your heart]. Selah [pause, and calmly think of that]! [Eph.
4:26.]
5 Offer just *and* right sacrifices; trust (lean on and be confident)
in the Lord.
6 Many say, O that we might see some good! Lift up the light
of your countenance upon us, O Lord.
7 You have put more joy *and* rejoicing in my heart than [they
know] when their wheat and new wine have yielded abundantly.
8 In peace I will both lie down and sleep, for You, Lord, alone
make me dwell in safety *and* confident trust.

## New American Standard

9 'Thou shalt [a]break them with a rod of iron,
Thou shalt shatter them like earthenware.' "

10¶ Now therefore, O kings, show discernment;
Take warning, O [b]judges of the earth.
11 Worship the LORD with reverence,
And rejoice with trembling.
12 Do homage to the Son, lest He become angry, and you
perish *in* the way,
For His wrath may [c]soon be kindled.
How blessed are all who take refuge in Him!

*Morning Prayer of Trust in God.*

A Psalm of David, when he fled from Absalom his son.

**3** O LORD, how my adversaries have increased!
Many are rising up against me.
2 Many are saying of my soul,
"There is no deliverance for him in God." [d]Selah.
3¶ But Thou, O LORD, art a shield about me,
My glory, and the One who lifts my head.
4 I was crying to the LORD with my voice,
And He answered me from His holy mountain. Selah.
5 I lay down and slept;
I awoke, for the LORD sustains me.
6 I will not be afraid of ten thousands of people
Who have set themselves against me round about.
7¶ Arise, O LORD; save me, O my God!
For Thou hast smitten all my enemies on the cheek;
Thou hast shattered the teeth of the wicked.
8 Salvation belongs to the LORD;
Thy blessing *be* upon Thy people! Selah.

*Evening Prayer of Trust in God.*

For the choir director; on stringed instruments. A Psalm of David.

**4** ANSWER ME when I call, O God of my righteousness!
Thou hast relieved me in my distress;
Be gracious to me and hear my prayer.
2¶ O sons of men, how long will my honor become a
reproach?
*How long* will you love what is worthless and aim at
deception? Selah.
3 But know that the LORD has set apart the godly man for
Himself;
The LORD hears when I call to Him.
4¶ Tremble, and do not sin;
Meditate in your heart upon your bed, and be still.
Selah.
5 Offer the sacrifices of righteousness,
And trust in the LORD.
6¶ Many are saying, "Who will show us *any* good?"
Lift up the light of Thy countenance upon us, O LORD!
7 Thou hast put gladness in my heart,
More than when their grain and new wine abound.
8 In peace I will both lie down and sleep,
For Thou alone, O LORD, dost make me to dwell in
safety.

NAS [a] Another reading is *rule* [b] Or, *leaders* [c] Or, *quickly, suddenly, easily* [d] *Selah* may mean: *Pause, Crescendo* or *Musical Interlude*

## New International

9You will rule them with an iron scepter[e];
you will dash them to pieces like pottery."

10Therefore, you kings, be wise;
be warned, you rulers of the earth.
11Serve the LORD with fear
and rejoice with trembling.
12Kiss the Son, lest he be angry
and you be destroyed in your way,
for his wrath can flare up in a moment.
Blessed are all who take refuge in him.

A psalm of David. When he fled from his son Absalom.

**3** O LORD, how many are my foes!
How many rise up against me!
2Many are saying of me,
"God will not deliver him." *Selah*[f]
3But you are a shield around me, O LORD;
you bestow glory on me and lift[g] up my head.
4To the LORD I cry aloud,
and he answers me from his holy hill. *Selah*

5I lie down and sleep;
I wake again, because the LORD sustains me.
6I will not fear the tens of thousands
drawn up against me on every side.
7Arise, O LORD!
Deliver me, O my God!
Strike all my enemies on the jaw;
break the teeth of the wicked.

8From the LORD comes deliverance.
May your blessing be on your people. *Selah*

For the director of music. With stringed instruments. A psalm of David.

**4** ANSWER ME when I call to you,
O my righteous God.
Give me relief from my distress;
be merciful to me and hear my prayer.

2How long, O men, will you turn my glory into shame[h]?
How long will you love delusions and seek false gods[i]?
*Selah*
3Know that the LORD has set apart the godly for himself;
the LORD will hear when I call to him.
4In your anger do not sin;
when you are on your beds,
search your hearts and be silent. *Selah*
5Offer right sacrifices
and trust in the LORD.
6Many are asking, "Who can show us any good?"
Let the light of your face shine upon us, O LORD.
7You have filled my heart with greater joy
than when their grain and new wine abound.
8I will lie down and sleep in peace,
for you alone, O LORD,
make me dwell in safety.

NIV [e] 9 Or *will break them with a rod of iron* [f] 2 A word of uncertain meaning, occurring frequently in the Psalms; possibly a musical term [g] 3 Or *LORD, / my Glorious One, who lifts* [h] 2 Or *you dishonor my Glorious One* [i] 2 Or *seek lies*

## King James

To the chief Musician upon Nehiloth, A Psalm of David.

5 GIVE EAR to my words, O LORD, consider my meditation.
2Hearken unto the voice of my cry, my King, and my God:
for unto thee will I pray.
3My voice shalt thou hear in the morning, O LORD; in the
morning will I direct *my prayer* unto thee, and will look up.
4For thou *art* not a God that hath pleasure in wickedness:
neither shall evil dwell with thee.
5The foolish shall not stand in thy sight: thou hatest all workers
of iniquity.
6Thou shalt destroy them that speak leasing: the LORD will
abhor the bloody and deceitful man.
7But as for me, I will come *into* thy house in the multitude of
thy mercy: *and* in thy fear will I worship toward thy holy temple.
8Lead me, O LORD, in thy righteousness because of mine enemies; make thy way straight before my face.
9For *there is* no faithfulness in their mouth; their inward part *is*
very wickedness; their throat *is* an open sepulchre; they flatter
with their tongue.
10Destroy thou them, O God; let them fall by their own counsels; cast them out in the multitude of their transgressions; for they
have rebelled against thee.
11But let all those that put their trust in thee rejoice: let them
ever shout for joy, because thou defendest them: let them also that
love thy name be joyful in thee.
12For thou, LORD, wilt bless the righteous; with favour wilt thou
compass him as *with* a shield.

To the chief Musician on Neginoth upon Sheminith, A Psalm of David.

6 O LORD, rebuke me not in thine anger, neither chasten me
in thy hot displeasure.
2Have mercy upon me, O LORD; for I *am* weak: O LORD, heal
me; for my bones are vexed.
3My soul is also sore vexed: but thou, O LORD, how long?
4Return, O LORD, deliver my soul: oh save me for thy mercies'
sake.
5For in death *there is* no remembrance of thee: in the grave who
shall give thee thanks?
6I am weary with my groaning; all the night make I my bed to
swim; I water my couch with my tears.
7Mine eye is consumed because of grief; it waxeth old because
of all mine enemies.
8Depart from me, all ye workers of iniquity; for the LORD hath
heard the voice of my weeping.
9The LORD hath heard my supplication; the LORD will receive
my prayer.
10Let all mine enemies be ashamed and sore vexed: let them
return *and* be ashamed suddenly.

## Amplified

To the Chief Musician;
on wind instruments. A Psalm of David.

5 LISTEN TO my words, O Lord; give heed to my sighing *and*
groaning.
2Hear the sound of my cry, my King and my God, for to You
do I pray.
3In the morning You hear my voice, O Lord; in the morning I
prepare [a prayer, a sacrifice] for You, and watch *and* wait [for You
to speak to my heart].
4For You are not a God Who has pleasure in wickedness,
neither will the evil [man] so much as dwell [temporarily] with
You.
5Boasters can have no standing in Your sight; You abhor all
evildoers.
6You will destroy those who speak lies; the Lord abhors [and
rejects] the bloodthirsty and deceitful man.
7But as for me, I will enter Your house through the abundance
of Your steadfast love *and* mercy; I will worship toward *and* at Your
holy temple in reverent fear *and* awe of You.
8Lead me, O Lord, in Your righteousness because of my enemies; make Your way level (straight and right) before my face.
9For there is nothing trustworthy *or* steadfast *or* truthful in their
talk; their heart is destruction [or a destructive chasm, a yawning
gulf]; their throat is an open sepulcher; they make smooth *and*
flatter with their tongue. [Rom. 3:13.]
10Hold them guilty, O God; let them fall by their own designs
*and* counsels; cast them out because of the multitude of their transgressions, for they have rebelled against You.
11But let all those who take refuge *and* put their trust in You
rejoice; let them ever sing *and* shout for joy, because You make a
covering over them *and* defend them; let those also who love Your
name be joyful in You *and* be in high spirits.
12For You, Lord, will bless the [uncompromisingly] righteous
[him who is upright and in right standing with You]; as with a
shield You will surround him with good will (pleasure and favor).

To the Chief Musician; on stringed instruments,
set [*possibly*] an octave below.
A Psalm of David.

6 O LORD, rebuke me not in Your anger, nor discipline *and*
chasten me in Your hot displeasure.
2Have mercy on me *and* be gracious to me, O Lord, for I am
weak (faint and withered away). O Lord, heal me, for my bones
are troubled.
3My [inner] self [as well as my body] is also exceedingly disturbed *and* troubled. But You, O Lord, how long [until You return
and speak peace to me]?
4Return [to my relief], O Lord, deliver my life; save me for the
sake of Your steadfast love *and* mercies.
5For in death there is no remembrance of You; in Sheol [the state
of the dead] who will give You thanks?
6I am weary with my groaning; all night I soak my pillow with
tears; I drench my couch with my weeping.
7My eye grows dim because of grief; it grows old because of all
my enemies.
8Depart from me, all you workers of iniquity, for the Lord has
heard the voice of my weaping. [Matt. 7:23; Luke 13:27.]
9The Lord has heard my supplication; the Lord receives my
prayer.
10Let all my enemies be ashamed and sorely troubled; let them
turn back *and* be put to shame suddenly.

## New American Standard

*Prayer for Protection from the Wicked.*

For the choir director; for flute accompaniment. A Psalm of David.

**5** GIVE EAR to my words, O LORD, CONSIDER MY [a]groaning.
2 Heed the sound of my cry for help, my King and my God,
For to Thee do I pray.
3 In the morning, O LORD, Thou wilt hear my voice;
In the morning I will order *my prayer* to Thee and *eagerly* watch.

4¶ For Thou art not a God who takes pleasure in wickedness;
No evil dwells with Thee.
5 The boastful shall not stand before Thine eyes;
Thou dost hate all who do iniquity.
6 Thou dost destroy those who speak falsehood;
The LORD abhors the man of bloodshed and deceit.
7 But as for me, by Thine abundant lovingkindness I will enter Thy house,
At Thy holy temple I will bow in reverence for Thee.

8¶ O LORD, lead me in Thy righteousness because of my foes;
Make Thy way straight be fore me.
9 There is nothing reliable in what they say;
Their inward part is destruction *itself*;
Their throat is an open grave;
They flatter with their tongue.
10 Hold them guilty, O God;
By their own devices let them fall!
In the multitude of their transgressions thrust them out,
For they are rebellious against Thee.

11¶ But let all who take refuge in Thee be glad,
Let them ever sing for joy;
And mayest Thou shelter them,
That those who love Thy name may exult in Thee.
12 For it is Thou who dost bless the righteous man, O LORD,
Thou dost surround him with favor as with a shield.

*Prayer for Mercy in Time of Trouble.*

For the choir director; with stringed instruments, upon an eight-stringed lyre. A Psalm of David.

**6** O LORD, do not rebuke me in Thine anger,
Nor chasten me in Thy wrath.
2 Be gracious to me, O LORD, for I *am* pining away;
Heal me, O LORD, for my bones are dismayed.
3 And my soul is greatly dismayed;
But Thou, O LORD—how long?

4¶ Return, O LORD, rescue my [b]soul;
Save me because of Thy lovingkindness.
5 For there is no [c]mention of Thee in death;
In Sheol who will give Thee thanks?

6¶ I am weary with my sighing;
Every night I make my bed swim,
I dissolve my couch with my tears.
7 My eye has wasted away with grief;
It has become old because of all my adversaries.

8¶ Depart from me, all you who do iniquity,
For the LORD has heard the voice of my weeping.
9 The LORD has heard my supplication,
The LORD receives my prayer.
10 All my enemies shall be ashamed and greatly dismayed;
They shall turn back, they shall suddenly be ashamed.

NAS [a] Or, *meditation* [b] Or, *life* [c] Or, *remembrance*

## New International

For the director of music. For flutes. A psalm of David.

**5** GIVE EAR to my words, O LORD,
consider my sighing.
2 Listen to my cry for help,
my King and my God,
for to you I pray.
3 In the morning, O LORD, you hear my voice;
in the morning I lay my requests before you
and wait in expectation.

4 You are not a God who takes pleasure in evil;
with you the wicked cannot dwell.
5 The arrogant cannot stand in your presence;
you hate all who do wrong.
6 You destroy those who tell lies;
bloodthirsty and deceitful men
the LORD abhors.
7 But I, by your great mercy,
will come into your house;
in reverence will I bow down
toward your holy temple.
8 Lead me, O LORD, in your righteousness
because of my enemies—
make straight your way before me.

9 Not a word from their mouth can be trusted;
their heart is filled with destruction.
Their throat is an open grave;
with their tongue they speak deceit.
10 Declare them guilty, O God!
Let their intrigues be their downfall.
Banish them for their many sins,
for they have rebelled against you.

11 But let all who take refuge in you be glad;
let them ever sing for joy.
Spread your protection over them,
that those who love your name may rejoice in you.
12 For surely, O LORD, you bless the righteous;
you surround them with your favor as with a shield.

For the director of music. With stringed instruments. According to *sheminith*.[d] A psalm of David.

**6** O LORD, do not rebuke me in your anger
or discipline me in your wrath.
2 Be merciful to me, LORD, for I am faint;
O LORD, heal me, for my bones are in agony.
3 My soul is in anguish.
How long, O LORD, how long?

4 Turn, O LORD, and deliver me;
save me because of your unfailing love.
5 No one remembers you when he is dead.
Who praises you from the grave[e]?

6 I am worn out from groaning;
all night long I flood my bed with weeping
and drench my couch with tears.
7 My eyes grow weak with sorrow;
they fail because of all my foes.

8 Away from me, all you who do evil,
for the LORD has heard my weeping.
9 The LORD has heard my cry for mercy;
the LORD accepts my prayer.
10 All my enemies will be ashamed and dismayed;
they will turn back in sudden disgrace.

NIV [d] Title: Probably a musical term [e] 5 Hebrew *Sheol*

## King James

Shiggaion of David, which he sang unto the LORD, concerning the words
of Cush the Benjamite.

**7** O LORD my God, in thee do I put my trust: save me from all
them that persecute me, and deliver me:
2Lest he tear my soul like a lion, rending *it* in pieces, while *there*
*is* none to deliver.
3O LORD my God, if I have done this; if there be iniquity in my
hands;
4If I have rewarded evil unto him that was at peace with me;
(yea, I have delivered him that without cause is mine enemy:)
5Let the enemy persecute my soul, and take *it*; yea, let him tread
down my life upon the earth, and lay mine honour in the dust.
Selah.
6Arise, O LORD, in thine anger, lift up thyself because of the
rage of mine enemies: and awake for me *to* the judgment *that* thou
hast commanded.
7So shall the congregation of the people compass thee about: for
their sakes therefore return thou on high.
8The LORD shall judge the people: judge me, O LORD, according
to my righteousness, and according to mine integrity *that is* in me.
9Oh let the wickedness of the wicked come to an end; but
establish the just: for the righteous God trieth the hearts and reins.
10My defence *is* of God, which saveth the upright in heart.
11God judgeth the righteous, and God is angry *with the wicked*
every day.
12If he turn not, he will whet his sword; he hath bent his bow,
and made it ready.
13He hath also prepared for him the instruments of death; he
ordaineth his arrows against the persecutors.
14Behold, he travaileth with iniquity, and hath conceived mischief, and brought forth falsehood.
15He made a pit, and digged it, and is fallen into the ditch *which*
he made.
16His mischief shall return upon his own head, and his violent
dealing shall come down upon his own pate.
17I will praise the LORD according to his righteousness: and will
sing praise to the name of the LORD most high.

To the chief Musician upon Gittith, A Psalm of David.

**8** O LORD our Lord, how excellent *is* thy name in all the earth!
who hast set thy glory above the heavens.
2Out of the mouth of babes and sucklings hast thou ordained
strength because of thine enemies, that thou mightest still the
enemy and the avenger.
3When I consider thy heavens, the work of thy fingers, the
moon and the stars, which thou hast ordained;
4What is man, that thou art mindful of him? and the son of man,
that thou visitest him?

## Amplified

An Ode of David, [ *probably*] in a wild, irregular, enthusiastic strain,
which he sang to the Lord, concerning the words of Cush, a Benjamite.

**7** O LORD my God, in You I take refuge *and* put my trust; save
me from all those who pursue *and* persecute me, and deliver
me;
2Lest my foe tear my life [from my body] like a lion, dragging
*me* away, while there is none to deliver.
3O Lord my God, if I have done this, if there is wrong in my
hands,
4If I have paid back with evil him who was at peace with me,
or without cause have robbed him who was my enemy,
5Let the enemy pursue my life and take it; yes, let him trample
my life to the ground and lay my honor in the dust. Selah [pause,
and calmly think of that]!
6Arise, O Lord, in Your anger, lift up Yourself against the rage
of my enemies; and awake [and stir up] for me the justice *and*
vindication [that] You have commanded.
7Let the assembly of the peoples be gathered about You, and
return on high over it.
8The Lord judges the people; judge me, O Lord, *and* do me
justice according to my righteousness [my rightness, justice and
right standing with You] and according to the integrity that is in
me.
9O let the wickedness of the wicked come to an end, but establish the [uncompromisingly] righteous [those upright and in harmony with You]; for You, Who try the hearts and emotions *and*
thinking powers, are a righteous God. [Rev. 2:23.]
10My defense *and* shield depend on God, Who saves the upright
in heart.
11God is a righteous judge, yes, a God Who is indignant every
day.
12If a man does not turn *and* repent, [God] will whet His sword;
He has strung *and* bent His [huge] bow and made it ready [by
treading it with His foot].
13He has also prepared for him deadly weapons; He makes His
arrows fiery shafts.
14Behold, [the wicked man] conceives iniquity, and is pregnant
with mischief, and gives birth to lies.
15He made a pit, and hollowed it out, and has fallen into the
hole which he made [before the trap was completed].
16His mischief shall fall back in return upon his own head, and
his violence come down [with the loose dirt] upon his own scalp.
17I will give to the Lord the thanks due to His rightness *and*
justice, and I will sing praise to the name of the Lord Most High.

To the Chief Musician;
set to a Philistine lute, or [ *possibly*] to a particular Hittite tune. A Psalm
of David.

**8** O LORD, our Lord, how excellent (majestic and glorious) is
Your name in all the earth! You have set Your glory on [or
above] the heavens.
2Out of the mouth of babes and unweaned infants You have
established strength because of Your foes, that You might silence
the enemy and the avenger. [Matt. 21:15, 16.]
3When I view *and* consider Your heavens, the work of Your
fingers, the moon and the stars which You have ordained *and*
established;
4What is man, that You are mindful of him, and the son of
[earthborn] man, that You care for him?

## New American Standard

*The* LORD *Implored to Defend the Psalmist against the Wicked.*

A [a]Shiggaion of David, which he sang to the Lord concerning Cush, a Benjamite.

7 O LORD my God, in Thee I have taken refuge;
Save me from all those who pursue me, and deliver me,
2 Lest he tear my soul like a lion,
Dragging me away, while there is none to deliver.

3¶ O LORD my God, if I have done this,
If there is injustice in my hands,
4 If I have rewarded evil to my friend,
Or have plundered him who without cause was my adversary,
5 Let the enemy pursue my soul and overtake *it;*
And let him trample my life down to the ground,
And lay my glory in the dust. Selah.
6¶ Arise, O LORD, in Thine anger;
Lift up Thyself against the rage of my adversaries,
And arouse Thyself for me; Thou hast appointed judgment.
7 And let the assembly of the peoples encompass Thee;
And over them return Thou on high.
8 The LORD judges the peoples;
Vindicate me, O LORD, according to my righteousness and my integrity that is in me.
9 O let the evil of the wicked come to an end, but establish the righteous;
For the righteous God tries the hearts and [b]minds.
10 My shield is with God,
Who saves the upright in heart.
11 God is a righteous judge,
And a God who has indignation every day.
12¶ If a man does not repent, He will sharpen His sword;
He has bent His bow and made it ready.
13 He has also prepared for Himself deadly weapons;
He makes His arrows fiery shafts.
14 Behold, he travails with wickedness,
And he conceives mischief, and brings forth falsehood.
15 He has dug a pit and hollowed it out,
And has fallen into the hole which he made.
16 His mischief will return upon his own head,
And his violence will descend upon [c]his own pate.
17¶ I will give thanks to the LORD according to His righteousness,
And will sing praise to the name of the LORD Most High.

*The* LORD'S *Glory and Man's Dignity.*

For the choir director; on the Gittith. A Psalm of David.

8 O LORD, our Lord,
How majestic is Thy name in all the earth,
Who hast displayed Thy splendor above the heavens!
2 From the mouth of infants and nursing babes Thou hast established strength,
Because of Thine adversaries,
To make the enemy and the revengeful cease.
3¶ When I consider Thy heavens, the work of Thy fingers,
The moon and the stars, which Thou hast ordained;
4 What is man, that Thou dost take thought of him?
And the son of man, that Thou dost care for him?

NAS [a] I.e., Dithyrambic rhythm, or, wild, passionate song [b] Lit., *kidneys,* figurative for inner man [c] I.e., the crown of his own head

## New International

A *shiggaion*[d] of David, which he sang to the LORD concerning Cush, a Benjamite.

7 O LORD my God, I take refuge in you;
save and deliver me from all who pursue me,
2or they will tear me like a lion
and rip me to pieces with no one to rescue me.

3O LORD my God, if I have done this
and there is guilt on my hands—
4if I have done evil to him who is at peace with me
or without cause have robbed my foe—
5then let my enemy pursue and overtake me;
let him trample my life to the ground
and make me sleep in the dust. *Selah*

6Arise, O LORD, in your anger;
rise up against the rage of my enemies.
Awake, my God; decree justice.
7Let the assembled peoples gather around you.
Rule over them from on high;
8 let the LORD judge the peoples.
Judge me, O LORD, according to my righteousness,
according to my integrity, O Most High.
9O righteous God,
who searches minds and hearts,
bring to an end the violence of the wicked
and make the righteous secure.

10My shield[e] is God Most High,
who saves the upright in heart.
11God is a righteous judge,
a God who expresses his wrath every day.
12If he does not relent,
he[f] will sharpen his sword;
he will bend and string his bow.
13He has prepared his deadly weapons;
he makes ready his flaming arrows.

14He who is pregnant with evil
and conceives trouble gives birth to disillusionment.
15He who digs a hole and scoops it out
falls into the pit he has made.
16The trouble he causes recoils on himself;
his violence comes down on his own head.

17I will give thanks to the LORD because of his righteousness
and will sing praise to the name of the LORD Most High.

For the director of music. According to *gittith.*[g] A psalm of David.

8 O LORD, our Lord,
how majestic is your name in all the earth!

You have set your glory
above the heavens.
2From the lips of children and infants
you have ordained praise[h]
because of your enemies,
to silence the foe and the avenger.

3When I consider your heavens,
the work of your fingers,
the moon and the stars,
which you have set in place,
4what is man that you are mindful of him,
the son of man that you care for him?

NIV [d] Title: Probably a literary or musical term [e] 10 Or *sovereign* [f] 12 Or *If a man does not repent, / God* [g] Title: Probably a musical term [h] 2 Or *strength*

## King James

5For thou hast made him a little lower than the angels, and hast
crowned him with glory and honour.
6Thou madest him to have dominion over the works of thy
hands; thou hast put all *things* under his feet:
7All sheep and oxen, yea, and the beasts of the field;
8The fowl of the air, and the fish of the sea, *and whatsoever*
passeth through the paths of the seas.
9O LORD our Lord, how excellent *is* thy name in all the earth!

To the chief Musician upon Muth-labben, A Psalm of David.

**9** I WILL praise *thee*, O LORD, with my whole heart; I will show
forth all thy marvellous works.
2I will be glad and rejoice in thee: I will sing praise to thy name,
O thou most High.
3When mine enemies are turned back, they shall fall and perish
at thy presence.
4For thou hast maintained my right and my cause; thou satest
in the throne judging right.
5Thou hast rebuked the heathen, thou hast destroyed the
wicked, thou hast put out their name for ever and ever.
6O thou enemy, destructions are come to a perpetual end: and
thou hast destroyed cities; their memorial is perished with them.
7But the LORD shall endure for ever: he hath prepared his
throne for judgment.
8And he shall judge the world in righteousness, he shall minister judgment to the people in uprightness.
9The LORD also will be a refuge for the oppressed, a refuge in
times of trouble.
10And they that know thy name will put their trust in thee: for
thou, LORD, hast not forsaken them that seek thee.
11Sing praises to the LORD, which dwelleth in Zion: declare
among the people his doings.
12When he maketh inquisition for blood, he remembereth
them: he forgetteth not the cry of the humble.
13Have mercy upon me, O LORD; consider my trouble *which I*
*suffer* of them that hate me, thou that liftest me up from the gates
of death:
14That I may show forth all thy praise in the gates of the daughter of Zion: I will rejoice in thy salvation.
15The heathen are sunk down in the pit *that* they made: in the
net which they hid is their own foot taken.
16The LORD is known *by* the judgment *which* he executeth: the
wicked is snared in the work of his own hands. Higgaion. Selah.
17The wicked shall be turned into hell, *and* all the nations that
forget God.
18For the needy shall not always be forgotten: the expectation
of the poor shall *not* perish for ever.
19Arise, O LORD; let not man prevail: let the heathen be judged
in thy sight.
20Put them in fear, O LORD: *that* the nations may know themselves *to be but* men. Selah.

## Amplified

5Yet You have made him but little lower than God [or heavenly
beings], and You have crowned him with glory and honor.
6You made him to have dominion over the works of Your
hands; You have put all things under his feet. [I Cor. 15:27; Eph.
1:22, 23; Heb. 2:6-8.]
7All sheep and oxen, yes, and the beasts of the field,
8The birds of the air, and the fish of the sea, *and* whatever passes
along the paths of the seas.
9O Lord, our Lord, how excellent (majestic and glorious) is Your
name in all the earth!

To the Chief Musician;
set for [ *possibly*] soprano voices. A Psalm of David.

**9** I WILL praise You, O Lord, with my whole heart; I will show
forth (recount and tell aloud) all Your marvelous works *and*
wonderful deeds!
2I will rejoice in You and be in high spirits; I will sing praise to
Your name, O Most High!
3When my enemies turned back, they stumbled and perished
before You.
4For You have maintained my right and my cause; You sat on
the throne judging righteously.
5You have rebuked the nations, You have destroyed the
wicked, You have blotted out their name for ever and ever.
6The enemy have been cut off *and* have vanished in everlasting
ruins; You have plucked up *and* overthrown their cities; the very
memory of them has perished *and* vanished.
7But the Lord shall remain *and* continue forever; He has prepared *and* established His throne for judgment. [Heb. 1:11.]
8And He will judge the world in righteousness—rightness and
equity; He will minister justice to the peoples in uprightness. [Acts
17:31.]
9The Lord also will be a refuge *and* a high tower for the oppressed, a refuge *and* a stronghold in times of trouble [high cost,
destitution and desperation].
10And they who know Your name [who have experience and
acquaintance with Your mercy] will lean on *and* confidently put
their trust in You; for You, Lord, have not forsaken those who seek
(inquire of and for You) [on the authority of God's Word and the
right of their necessity]. [Ps. 42:1.]
11Sing praises to the Lord, Who dwells in Zion! Declare among
the peoples His doings!
12For He Who avenges the blood [of His people shed unjustly]
remembers them; He does not forget the cry of the afflicted (the
poor and the humble).
13Have mercy upon me *and* be gracious *to me*, O Lord; consider
how I am afflicted by those who hate me, You Who lift me up from
the gates of death,
14That I may show forth (recount and tell aloud) all Your
praises! In the gates of the daughter of Zion I will rejoice in Your
salvation *and* Your saving help.
15The nations have sunk down in the pit that they made; in the
net which they hid is their own foot caught.
16The Lord has made Himself known; He executes judgment;
the wicked is snared in the work of his own hands. Higgaion
[meditation]. Selah [pause, and calmly think of that]!
17The wicked shall be turned back [headlong, into premature
death] into Sheol [the place of the departed spirits of the wicked];
even all the nations that forget *or* are forgetful of God.
18For the needy shall not always be forgotten, and the expectation *and* hope of the meek *and* the poor shall not perish for ever.
19Arise, O Lord! Let not man prevail; let the nations be judged
before You.
20Put them in fear [make them realize their frail nature], O Lord,
that the nations may know themselves to be but men. Selah
[pause, and calmly think of that]!

## New American Standard

5 Yet Thou hast made him a little lower than God,
And dost crown him with glory and majesty!
6 Thou dost make him to rule over the works of Thy hands;
Thou hast put all things under his feet,
7 All sheep and oxen,
And also the beasts of the field,
8 The birds of the heavens, and the fish of the sea,
Whatever passes through the paths of the seas.

9¶ O LORD, our Lord,
How majestic is Thy name in all the earth!

*A Psalm of Thanksgiving for God's Justice.*

For the choir director; on [a]Muth-labben. A Psalm of David.

9 I WILL give thanks to the LORD with all my heart;
I will tell of all Thy wonders.
2 I will be glad and exult in Thee;
I will sing praise to Thy name, O Most High.

3¶ When my enemies turn back,
They stumble and perish before Thee.
4 For Thou hast maintained my just cause;
Thou dost sit on the throne judging righteously.
5 Thou hast rebuked the nations; Thou hast destroyed the wicked;
Thou hast blotted out their name forever and ever.
6 The enemy has come to an end in perpetual ruins,
And Thou hast uprooted the cities;
The very memory of them has perished.

7¶ But the LORD [b]abides forever;
He has established His throne for judgment,
8 And He will judge the world in righteousness;
He will execute judgment for the peoples with equity.
9 The LORD also will be a stronghold for the oppressed,
A stronghold in times of trouble,
10 And those who know Thy name will put their trust in Thee;
For Thou, O LORD, hast not forsaken those who seek Thee.

11¶ Sing praises to the LORD, who dwells in Zion;
Declare among the peoples His deeds.
12 For He who [c]requires blood remembers them;
He does not forget the cry of the afflicted.
13 Be gracious to me, O LORD;
Behold my affliction from those who hate me,
Thou who dost lift me up from the gates of death;
14 That I may tell of all Thy praises,
That in the gates of the daughter of Zion
I may rejoice in Thy salvation.
15 The nations have sunk down in the pit which they have made;
In the net which they hid, their own foot has been caught.
16 The LORD has made Himself known;
He has executed judgment.
In the work of his own hands the wicked is snared.
Higgaion Selah.

17¶ The wicked will return to Sheol,
*Even* all the nations who forget God.
18 For the needy will not always be forgotten,
Nor the hope of the afflicted perish forever.
19 Arise, O LORD, do not let man prevail;
Let the nations be judged before Thee.
20 Put them in fear, O LORD;
Let the nations know that they are but men. Selah.

NAS [a] I.e., "Death to the Son" [b] Or, *sits* as king [c] I.e., avenges bloodshed

## New International

5You made him a little lower than the heavenly beings[d]
and crowned him with glory and honor.
6You made him ruler over the works of your hands;
you put everything under his feet:
7all flocks and herds,
and the beasts of the field,
8the birds of the air,
and the fish of the sea,
all that swim the paths of the seas.

9O LORD, our Lord,
how majestic is your name in all the earth!

For[e] the director of music. To ⌊the tune of⌋ "The Death of the Son."
A psalm of David.

9 I WILL praise you, O LORD, with all my heart;
I will tell of all your wonders.
2I will be glad and rejoice in you;
I will sing praise to your name, O Most High.

3My enemies turn back;
they stumble and perish before you.
4For you have upheld my right and my cause;
you have sat on your throne, judging righteously.
5You have rebuked the nations and destroyed the wicked;
you have blotted out their name for ever and ever.
6Endless ruin has overtaken the enemy,
you have uprooted their cities;
even the memory of them has perished.
7The LORD reigns forever;
he has established his throne for judgment.
8He will judge the world in righteousness;
he will govern the peoples with justice.
9The LORD is a refuge for the oppressed,
a stronghold in times of trouble.
10Those who know your name will trust in you,
for you, LORD, have never forsaken those who seek you.
11Sing praises to the LORD, enthroned in Zion;
proclaim among the nations what he has done.
12For he who avenges blood remembers;
he does not ignore the cry of the afflicted.

13O LORD, see how my enemies persecute me!
Have mercy and lift me up from the gates of death,
14that I may declare your praises
in the gates of the Daughter of Zion
and there rejoice in your salvation.
15The nations have fallen into the pit they have dug;
their feet are caught in the net they have hidden.
16The LORD is known by his justice;
the wicked are ensnared by the work of their hands.
*Higgaion.*[f] *Selah*

17The wicked return to the grave,[g]
all the nations that forget God.
18But the needy will not always be forgotten,
nor the hope of the afflicted ever perish.

19Arise, O LORD, let not man triumph;
let the nations be judged in your presence.
20Strike them with terror, O LORD;
let the nations know they are but men. *Selah*

NIV [d] 5 Or *than God* [e] Psalms 9 and 10 may have been originally a single acrostic poem, the stanzas of which begin with the successive letters of the Hebrew alphabet. In the Septuagint they constitute one psalm. [f] *16* Or *Meditation;* possibly a musical notation [g] *17* Hebrew *Sheol*

## King James

**10** WHY STANDEST thou afar off, O LORD? *why* hidest thou *thyself* in times of trouble?

2 The wicked in *his* pride doth persecute the poor: let them be taken in the devices that they have imagined.

3 For the wicked boasteth of his heart's desire, and blesseth the covetous, *whom* the LORD abhorreth.

4 The wicked, through the pride of his countenance, will not seek *after God:* God *is* not in all his thoughts.

5 His ways are always grievous; thy judgments *are* far above out of his sight: *as for* all his enemies, he puffeth at them.

6 He hath said in his heart, I shall not be moved: for *I shall* never *be* in adversity.

7 His mouth is full of cursing and deceit and fraud: under his tongue *is* mischief and vanity.

8 He sitteth in the lurking places of the villages: in the secret places doth he murder the innocent: his eyes are privily set against the poor.

9 He lieth in wait secretly as a lion in his den: he lieth in wait to catch the poor: he doth catch the poor, when he draweth him into his net.

10 He croucheth, *and* humbleth himself, that the poor may fall by his strong ones.

11 He hath said in his heart, God hath forgotten: he hideth his face; he will never see *it*.

12 Arise, O LORD; O God, lift up thine hand: forget not the humble.

13 Wherefore doth the wicked contemn God? he hath said in his heart, Thou wilt not require *it*.

14 Thou hast seen *it;* for thou beholdest mischief and spite, to requite *it* with thy hand: the poor committeth himself unto thee; thou art the helper of the fatherless.

15 Break thou the arm of the wicked and the evil *man:* seek out his wickedness *till* thou find none.

16 The LORD *is* King for ever and ever: the heathen are perished out of his land.

17 LORD, thou hast heard the desire of the humble: thou wilt prepare their heart, thou wilt cause thine ear to hear:

18 To judge the fatherless and the oppressed, that the man of the earth may no more oppress.

To the chief Musician, *A Psalm* of David.

**11** IN THE LORD put I my trust: how say ye to my soul, Flee *as* a bird to your mountain?

2 For, lo, the wicked bend *their* bow, they make ready their arrow upon the string, that they may privily shoot at the upright in heart.

3 If the foundations be destroyed, what can the righteous do?

## Amplified

**10** WHY DO You stand afar off, O Lord? Why do You hide Yourself, [veiling Your eyes] in times of trouble (distress and desperation)?

2 The wicked in pride *and* arrogance hotly pursue *and* persecute the poor; let them be taken in the schemes which they have devised.

3 For the wicked *man* boasts (sings the praises) of his own heart's desire, and the one greedy for gain curses *and* spurns, yes, renounces *and* despises the Lord.

4 The wicked in the pride of his countenance will not seek, inquire for *and* yearn for God; all his thoughts are that there is no God [so He never punishes].

5 His ways are grievous [or persist] at all times; Your judgments [Lord] are far above *and* on high out of his sight [so he never thinks about them]; as for all his foes, he sniffs *and* sneers at them.

6 He thinks in his heart, I shall not be moved; for throughout all generations I shall not come to want *or* be in adversity.

7 His mouth is full of cursing, deceit, oppression (fraud); under his tongue are trouble and sin (mischief and iniquity).

8 He sits in ambush in the villages; in hiding places he slays the innocent; he watches stealthily for the poor (the helpless and unfortunate).

9 He lurks in secret places like a lion in his thicket; he lies in wait that he may seize the poor (the helpless and the unfortunate); he seizes the poor when he draws him into his net.

10 [The prey] is crushed, sinks down, and the helpless falls by his mighty [claws].

11 [The foe] thinks in his heart, God has quite forgotten; He has hidden His face; He will never see [my deed].

12 Arise, O Lord! O God, lift up Your hand; forget not the humble [patient and crushed].

13 Why does the wicked condemn (spurn and renounce) God? Why has he thought in his heart, You will not call to account?

14 You have seen it; yes, You note trouble and grief (vexation), to requite with Your hand. The unfortunate commits himself to You; You are helper of the fatherless.

15 Break the arm of the wicked; and as for the evil man, search out his wickedness until You find no more.

16 The Lord is King for ever and ever; the nations are perished out of His land.

17 O Lord, You have heard the desire *and* the longing of the humble *and* oppressed; You will prepare *and* strengthen *and* direct their heart, You will cause Your ear to hear,

18 To do justice to the fatherless and the oppressed, so that man who is of the earth may not terrify them any more.

To the Chief Musician *or* Choir Leader. [ *A Psalm*] of David.

**11** IN THE Lord I take refuge [and put my trust]; how can you say to me, Flee like a bird to your mountain?

2 For see, the wicked are bending the bow, they make ready their arrow upon the string, that they [furtively] in darkness may shoot at the upright in heart.

3 If the foundations are destroyed, what can the [unyieldingly] righteous do, *or* what has he wrought *or* accomplished?

## New American Standard

*A Prayer for the Overthrow of the Wicked.*

10 WHY DOST Thou stand afar off, O LORD?
Why dost Thou hide *Thyself* in times of trouble?
2 In pride the wicked hotly pursue the afflicted;
Let them be caught in the plots which they have devised.
3¶ For the wicked boasts of his heart's desire,
And [a]the greedy man curses *and* spurns the LORD.
4 The wicked, in the haughtiness of his countenance, does not seek *Him*.
All his thoughts are, "There is no God."

5¶ His ways prosper at all times;
Thy judgments are on high, out of his sight;
As for all his adversaries, he snorts at them.
6 He says to himself, "I shall not be moved;
Throughout all generations I shall not be in adversity."
7 His mouth is full of curses and deceit and oppression;
Under his tongue is mischief and wickedness.
8 He sits in the lurking places of the villages;
In the hiding places he kills the innocent;
His eyes stealthily watch for the unfortunate.
9 He lurks in a hiding place as a lion in his lair;
He lurks to catch the afflicted;
He catches the afflicted when he draws him into his net.
10 He crouches, he bows down,
And the unfortunate fall [b]by his mighty ones.
11 He says to himself, "God has forgotten;
He has hidden His face; He will never see it."

12¶ Arise, O LORD; O God, lift up Thy hand.
Do not forget the afflicted.
13 Why has the wicked spurned God?
He has said to himself, "Thou wilt not require *it*."
14 Thou hast seen *it*, for Thou hast beheld mischief and vexation to take it into Thy hand.
The unfortunate commits *himself* to Thee;
Thou hast been the helper of the orphan.
15 Break the arm of the wicked and the evildoer,
Seek out his wickedness until Thou dost find none.

16¶ The LORD is King forever and ever;
Nations have perished from His land.
17 O LORD, Thou hast heard the desire of the [c]humble;
Thou wilt strengthen their heart, Thou wilt incline Thine ear
18 To [d]vindicate the orphan and the oppressed,
That man who is of the earth may cause terror no more.

*The LORD a Refuge and Defense.*

For the choir director.
*A Psalm* of David.

11 IN THE LORD I take refuge;
How can you say to my soul, "Flee *as* a bird to your mountain;
2 For, behold, the wicked bend the bow,
They make ready their arrow upon the string,
To shoot in darkness at the upright in heart.
3 If the foundations are destroyed,
What can the righteous do?"

NAS [a] Or, *blesses the greedy man* [b] Or, *into his claws* [c] Or, *afflicted* [d] Lit., *judge*

## New International

10[e] WHY, O LORD, do you stand far off?
Why do you hide yourself in times of trouble?
2In his arrogance the wicked man hunts down the weak,
who are caught in the schemes he devises.
3He boasts of the cravings of his heart;
he blesses the greedy and reviles the LORD.
4In his pride the wicked does not seek him;
in all his thoughts there is no room for God.
5His ways are always prosperous;
he is haughty and your laws are far from him;
he sneers at all his enemies.
6He says to himself, "Nothing will shake me;
I'll always be happy and never have trouble."
7His mouth is full of curses and lies and threats;
trouble and evil are under his tongue.
8He lies in wait near the villages;
from ambush he murders the innocent,
watching in secret for his victims.
9He lies in wait like a lion in cover;
he lies in wait to catch the helpless;
he catches the helpless and drags them off in his net.
10His victims are crushed, they collapse;
they fall under his strength.
11He says to himself, "God has forgotten;
he covers his face and never sees."
12Arise, LORD! Lift up your hand, O God.
Do not forget the helpless.
13Why does the wicked man revile God?
Why does he say to himself,
"He won't call me to account"?
14But you, O God, do see trouble and grief;
you consider it to take it in hand.
The victim commits himself to you;
you are the helper of the fatherless.
15Break the arm of the wicked and evil man;
call him to account for his wickedness
that would not be found out.

16The LORD is King for ever and ever;
the nations will perish from his land.
17You hear, O LORD, the desire of the afflicted;
you encourage them, and you listen to their cry,
18defending the fatherless and the oppressed,
in order that man, who is of the earth, may terrify no more.

For the director of music. Of David.

11 IN THE LORD I take refuge.
How then can you say to me:
"Flee like a bird to your mountain.
2For look, the wicked bend their bows;
they set their arrows against the strings
to shoot from the shadows
at the upright in heart.
3When the foundations are being destroyed,
what can the righteous do[f] ?"

NIV [e] Psalms 9 and 10 may have been originally a single acrostic poem, the stanzas of which begin with the successive letters of the Hebrew alphabet. In the Septuagint they constitute one psalm. [f] 3 Or *what is the Righteous One doing*

## King James

4The LORD *is* in his holy temple, the LORD's throne *is* in heaven:
his eyes behold, his eyelids try, the children of men.
5The LORD trieth the righteous: but the wicked and him that
loveth violence his soul hateth.
6Upon the wicked he shall rain snares, fire and brimstone, and
an horrible tempest: *this shall be* the portion of their cup.
7For the righteous LORD loveth righteousness; his countenance
doth behold the upright.

To the chief Musician upon Sheminith, A Psalm of David.

**12** HELP, LORD; for the godly man ceaseth; for the faithful
fail from among the children of men.
2They speak vanity every one with his neighbour: *with* flattering lips *and* with a double heart do they speak.
3The LORD shall cut off all flattering lips, *and* the tongue that
speaketh proud things:
4Who have said, With our tongue will we prevail; our lips *are*
our own: who *is* lord over us?
5For the oppression of the poor, for the sighing of the needy,
now will I arise, saith the LORD; I will set *him* in safety *from him that*
puffeth at him.
6The words of the LORD *are* pure words: *as* silver tried in a
furnace of earth, purified seven times.
7Thou shalt keep them, O LORD, thou shalt preserve them from
this generation for ever.
8The wicked walk on every side, when the vilest men are exalted.

To the chief Musician, A Psalm of David.

**13** HOW LONG wilt thou forget me, O LORD? for ever? how
long wilt thou hide thy face from me?
2How long shall I take counsel in my soul, *having* sorrow in my
heart daily? how long shall mine enemy be exalted over me?
3Consider *and* hear me, O LORD my God: lighten mine eyes, lest
I sleep the *sleep of* death;
4Lest mine enemy say, I have prevailed against him; *and* those
that trouble me rejoice when I am moved.
5But I have trusted in thy mercy; my heart shall rejoice in thy
salvation.
6I will sing unto the LORD, because he hath dealt bountifully
with me.

To the chief Musician, *A Psalm* of David.

**14** THE FOOL hath said in his heart, *There is* no God. They
are corrupt, they have done abominable works, *there is*
none that doeth good.

## Amplified

4The Lord is in His holy temple, the Lord's throne is in Heaven;
His eyes behold, His eyelids test *and* prove the children of men.
[Acts 7:49; Rev. 4:2.]
5The Lord tests *and* proves the [unyieldingly] righteous, but His
soul abhors the wicked and him who loves violence. [James 1:12.]
6Upon the wicked He will rain quick burning coals *or* snares;
fire, brimstone and a [dreadful] scorching wind shall be the portion
of their cup.
7For the Lord is [rigidly] righteous; He loves righteous deeds;
the upright shall behold His face, *or* He beholds the upright.

To the Chief Musician;
set [ *possibly*] an octave below. A Psalm of David.

**12** HELP, LORD! For principled *and* godly people are here no
more; faithfulness *and* the faithful vanish from among the
sons of men.
2To his neighbor each one speaks words without use *or* worth
*or* truth; with flattering lips and double heart [deceitfully] they
speak.
3May the Lord cut off all flattering lips, *and* the tongue that
speaks proud boasting,
4Those who say, With our tongue we prevail, our lips are our
own [to command at our will]; who is lord *and* master over us?
5Now will I arise, says the Lord, because the poor are oppressed, because of groans of the needy; I will set him in safety *and*
in the salvation for which he pants.
6The words *and* promises of the Lord are pure words, like silver
refined in an earthen furnace, purified seven times over.
7You will keep them and preserve them, O Lord; You will guard
*and* keep us from this [evil] generation for ever.
8The wicked walk *or* prowl about on every side, as vileness is
exalted (and baseness is rated high) among the sons of men.

To the Chief Musician. A Psalm of David.

**13** HOW LONG will You forget me, O Lord? For ever? How
long will You hide Your face from me?
2How long must I lay up cares within me, and have sorrow in
my heart day after day? How long shall my enemy exalt himself
over me?
3Consider and answer me, O Lord my God; lighten the eyes [of
my faith to behold Your face in the pitch-like darkness], lest I sleep
the sleep of death;
4Lest my enemy say, I have prevailed over him, *and* those that
trouble me rejoice when I am shaken.
5But I have trusted, leaned on *and* been confident in Your mercy
*and* loving-kindness; my heart shall rejoice *and* be in high spirits
in Your salvation.
6I will sing to the Lord, because He has dealt bountifully with
me.

To the Chief Musician. [ *A Psalm*] of David.

**14** THE [EMPTY-HEADED] fool has said in his heart, There
is no God. They are corrupt, they have done abominable
deeds, there is none that does good *or* right. [Rom. 3:10.]

## New American Standard

4¶ The LORD is in His holy temple; the LORD's throne is in heaven;
His eyes behold, His eyelids test the sons of men.
5 The LORD tests the righteous and the wicked,
And the one who loves violence His soul hates.
6 Upon the wicked He will rain [a]snares;
Fire and brimstone and burning wind will be the portion of their cup.
7 For the LORD is righteous; He loves righteousness;
The upright will behold His face.

*God, a Helper against the Treacherous.*

For the choir director; upon an eight-stringed lyre. A Psalm of David.

**12** HELP, LORD, for the godly man ceases to be,
For the faithful disappear from among the sons of men.
2 They speak falsehood to one another;
With flattering lips and with a double heart they speak.
3 May the LORD cut off all flattering lips,
The tongue that speaks great things;
4 Who have said, "With our tongue we will prevail;
Our lips are our own; who is lord over us?"
5 "Because of the devastation of the afflicted, because of the groaning of the needy,
Now I will arise," says the LORD; "I will set him in the safety for which he longs."
6¶ The words of the LORD are pure words;
As silver tried in a furnace on the earth, refined seven times.
7 Thou, O LORD, wilt keep them;
Thou wilt preserve him from this generation forever.
8 The wicked strut about on every side,
When [b]vileness is exalted among the sons of men.

*Prayer for Help in Trouble.*

For the choir director.
A Psalm of David.

**13** HOW LONG, O LORD? Wilt Thou forget me forever?
How long wilt Thou hide Thy face from me?
2 How long shall I take counsel in my soul,
*Having* sorrow in my heart all the day?
How long will my enemy be exalted over me?
3¶ Consider *and* answer me, O LORD, my God;
Enlighten my eyes, lest I sleep the *sleep of* death,
4 Lest my enemy say, "I have overcome him,"
*Lest* my adversaries rejoice when I am shaken.
5¶ But I have trusted in Thy lovingkindness;
My heart shall rejoice in Thy salvation.
6 I will sing to the LORD,
Because He has dealt bountifully with me.

*Folly and Wickedness of Men.*

For the choir director.
*A Psalm* of David.

**14** THE FOOL has said in his heart, "There is no God."
They are corrupt, they have committed abominable deeds;
There is no one who does good.

**NAS** [a] Or, *coals of fire* [b] Or, *worthlessness*

## New International

4The LORD is in his holy temple;
the LORD is on his heavenly throne.
He observes the sons of men;
his eyes examine them.
5The LORD examines the righteous,
but the wicked[c] and those who love violence
his soul hates.
6On the wicked he will rain
fiery coals and burning sulfur;
a scorching wind will be their lot.

7For the LORD is righteous,
he loves justice;
upright men will see his face.

For the director of music. According to *sheminith*.[d] A psalm of David.

**12** HELP, LORD, for the godly are no more;
the faithful have vanished from among men.
2Everyone lies to his neighbor;
their flattering lips speak with deception.

3May the LORD cut off all flattering lips
and every boastful tongue
4that says, "We will triumph with our tongues;
we own our lips[e]—who is our master?"

5"Because of the oppression of the weak
and the groaning of the needy,
I will now arise," says the LORD.
"I will protect them from those who malign them."
6And the words of the LORD are flawless,
like silver refined in a furnace of clay,
purified seven times.
7O LORD, you will keep us safe
and protect us from such people forever.
8The wicked freely strut about
when what is vile is honored among men.

For the director of music. A psalm of David.

**13** HOW LONG, O LORD? Will you forget me forever?
How long will you hide your face from me?
2How long must I wrestle with my thoughts
and every day have sorrow in my heart?
How long will my enemy triumph over me?

3Look on me and answer, O LORD my God.
Give light to my eyes, or I will sleep in death;
4my enemy will say, "I have overcome him,"
and my foes will rejoice when I fall.
5But I trust in your unfailing love;
my heart rejoices in your salvation.
6I will sing to the LORD,
for he has been good to me.

For the director of music. Of David.

**14** THE FOOL[f] says in his heart,
"There is no God."
They are corrupt, their deeds are vile;
there is no one who does good.

**NIV** [c] 5 Or *The LORD, the Righteous One, examines the wicked, /* [d] Title: Probably a musical term [e] 4 Or */ our lips are our plowshares* [f] 1 The Hebrew words rendered *fool* in Psalms denote one who is morally deficient.

## King James

2The LORD looked down from heaven upon the children of men, to see if there were any that did understand, *and* seek God.

3They are all gone aside, they are *all* together become filthy: *there is* none that doeth good, no, not one.

4Have all the workers of iniquity no knowledge? who eat up my people *as* they eat bread, and call not upon the LORD.

5There were they in great fear: for God *is* in the generation of the righteous.

6Ye have shamed the counsel of the poor, because the LORD *is* his refuge.

7Oh that the salvation of Israel *were come* out of Zion! when the LORD bringeth back the captivity of his people, Jacob shall rejoice, *and* Israel shall be glad.

A Psalm of David.

15 LORD, WHO shall abide in thy tabernacle? who shall dwell in thy holy hill?

2He that walketh uprightly, and worketh righteousness, and speaketh the truth in his heart.

3 *He that* backbiteth not with his tongue, nor doeth evil to his neighbour, nor taketh up a reproach against his neighbour.

4In whose eyes a vile person is contemned; but he honoureth them that fear the LORD. *He that* sweareth to *his own* hurt, and changeth not.

5 *He that* putteth not out his money to usury, nor taketh reward against the innocent. He that doeth these *things* shall never be moved.

Michtam of David.

16 PRESERVE ME, O God: for in thee do I put my trust.

2 *O my soul,* thou hast said unto the LORD, Thou *art* my Lord: my goodness *extendeth* not to thee;

3 *But* to the saints that *are* in the earth, and *to* the excellent, in whom *is* all my delight.

4Their sorrows shall be multiplied *that* hasten *after* another *god:* their drink offerings of blood will I not offer, nor take up their names into my lips.

5The LORD *is* the portion of mine inheritance and of my cup: thou maintainest my lot.

6The lines are fallen unto me in pleasant *places;* yea, I have a goodly heritage.

7I will bless the LORD, who hath given me counsel: my reins also instruct me in the night seasons.

8I have set the LORD always before me: because *he is* at my right hand, I shall not be moved.

9Therefore my heart is glad, and my glory rejoiceth: my flesh also shall rest in hope.

## Amplified

2The Lord looked down from Heaven upon the children of men, to see if there were any who understood, dealt wisely *and* sought after God, inquiring for *and* of Him *and* requiring Him [of vital necessity].

3They are all gone aside, they are *all* together become filthy; there is none that does good *or* right, no, not one. [Rom. 3:11, 12.]

4Have all the workers of iniquity no knowledge? Who eat up my people as they eat bread, and do not call on the Lord?

5There they shall be in great fear (literally, dreading a dread), for God is with the generation of the [uncompromisingly] righteous—those upright and in right standing with Him.

6You *evildoers* would put to shame *and* confound the plans of the poor *and* patient, but the Lord is his safe refuge.

7Oh, that the salvation of Israel were come out of Zion! When the Lord shall restore the fortunes of His people, then Jacob shall rejoice, *and* Israel shall be glad. [Rom. 11:25-27.]

A Psalm of David.

15 LORD, WHO shall dwell [temporarily] in Your tabernacle? Who shall dwell [permanently] in Your holy hill?

2He who walks *and* lives uprightly *and* blamelessly, who works rightness *and* justice, and speaks *and* thinks the truth in his heart.

3He who does not slander with his tongue, nor does evil to his friend, nor takes up a reproach against his neighbor.

4In whose eyes a vile person is despised, but he honors those who fear the Lord—who revere and worship Him; who swears to his own hurt and does not change;

5 *He who* does not put out his money for [a]interest [to one of his own people], and who will not take a bribe against the innocent. He who does these things shall never be moved. [Exod. 22:25, 26.]

A Poem of David [ *probably*] intended to record memorable thoughts.

16 KEEP *AND* protect me, O God, for in You I have found refuge, *and* in You do I put my trust *and* hide myself.

2I say to the Lord, You are my Lord; I have no good beside *or* beyond You.

3As for the godly (the saints) who are in the land, they are the excellent, the noble, *and* the glorious, in whom is all my delight.

4Their sorrows shall be multiplied who choose another god; their drink offerings of blood will I not offer or take their names upon my lips.

5The Lord is my chosen *and* assigned portion, my cup; You hold *and* maintain my lot.

6The lines are fallen for me in pleasant places; yes, I have a good heritage.

7I will bless the Lord Who has given me counsel; yes, my heart instructs me in the night seasons.

8I have set the Lord continually before me; because He is at my right hand, I shall not be moved.

9Therefore my heart is glad, and my glory [my inner self] rejoices; my body too shall rest *and* confidently dwell in safety.

**AMP** [a] "Israel was originally not a mercantile people, and the law aimed at an equal diffusion of wealth, not at enriching some while others were poor. The spirit of the law still is obligatory, not to take advantage of a brother's distress to lend at interest ruinous to him; but the letter of the law is abrogated, and a loan at moderate interest is often of great service to the poor. Hence, it is referred to by our Lord in parables, apparently as a lawful as well as recognized usage. (Matt. 25:27; Luke 19:23)."—*Fausset's Bible Encyclopedia and Dictionary.*

## New American Standard

2 The LORD has looked down from heaven upon the sons
of men,
To see if there are any who understand,
Who seek after God.
3 They have all turned aside; together they have become
corrupt;
There is no one who does good, not even one.

4¶ Do all the workers of wickedness not know,
Who eat up my people *as* they eat bread,
*And* do not call upon the Lord?
5 There they are in great dread,
For God is with the righteous generation.
6 You would put to shame the counsel of the afflicted,
But the LORD is his refuge.

7¶ Oh, that the salvation of Israel would come out of Zion!
When the LORD [b]restores His captive people,
Jacob will rejoice, Israel will be glad.

*Description of a Citizen of Zion.*

A Psalm of David.

15 O LORD, who may abide in Thy tent?
Who may dwell on Thy holy hill?
2 He who walks with integrity, and works righteousness,
And speaks truth in his heart.
3 He does not slander with his tongue,
Nor does evil to his neighbor,
Nor takes up a reproach against his friend;
4 In whose eyes a reprobate is despised,
But who honors those who fear the LORD;
He swears to his own hurt, and does not change;
5 He does not put out his money [c]at interest,
Nor does he take a bribe against the innocent.
He who does these things will never be shaken.

*The LORD the Psalmist's Portion in Life and Deliverer in Death.*

A [d]Mikhtam of David.

16 PRESERVE ME, O God, for I take refuge in Thee.
2 I said to the LORD, "Thou art my Lord;
I have no good besides Thee."
3 As for the saints who are in the earth,
They are the majestic ones in whom is all my delight.
4 The sorrows of those who have bartered for another *god*
will be multiplied;
I shall not pour out their libations of blood,
Nor shall I take their names upon my lips.

5¶ The LORD is the portion of my inheritance and my cup;
Thou dost support my lot.
6 The lines have fallen to me in pleasant places;
Indeed, my heritage is beautiful to me.

7¶ I will bless the LORD who has counseled me;
Indeed, my mind instructs me in the night.
8 I have set the LORD continually before me;
Because He is at my right hand, I will not be shaken.
9 Therefore my heart is glad, and my glory rejoices;
My flesh also will dwell securely.

NAS [b] Or, *restores the fortunes of His people* [c] I.e., to a fellow Israelite
[d] Possibly Epigrammatic Poem, or, Atonement Psalm

## New International

2The LORD looks down from heaven
on the sons of men
to see if there are any who understand,
any who seek God.
3All have turned aside,
they have together become corrupt;
there is no one who does good,
not even one.

4Will evildoers never learn—
those who devour my people as men eat bread
and who do not call on the LORD?
5There they are, overwhelmed with dread,
for God is present in the company of the righteous.
6You evildoers frustrate the plans of the poor,
but the LORD is their refuge.
7Oh, that salvation for Israel would come out of Zion!
When the LORD restores the fortunes of his people,
let Jacob rejoice and Israel be glad!

A psalm of David.

15 LORD, WHO may dwell in your sanctuary?
Who may live on your holy hill?

2He whose walk is blameless
and who does what is righteous,
who speaks the truth from his heart
3 and has no slander on his tongue,
who does his neighbor no wrong
and casts no slur on his fellowman,
4who despises a vile man
but honors those who fear the LORD,
who keeps his oath
even when it hurts,
5who lends his money without usury
and does not accept a bribe against the innocent.
He who does these things
will never be shaken.

A *miktam*[e] of David.

16 KEEP ME safe, O God,
for in you I take refuge.

2I said to the LORD, "You are my Lord;
apart from you I have no good thing."
3As for the saints who are in the land,
they are the glorious ones in whom is all my delight.[f]
4The sorrows of those will increase
who run after other gods.
I will not pour out their libations of blood
or take up their names on my lips.

5LORD, you have assigned me my portion and my cup;
you have made my lot secure.
6The boundary lines have fallen for me in pleasant places;
surely I have a delightful inheritance.

7I will praise the LORD, who counsels me;
even at night my heart instructs me.
8I have set the LORD always before me.
Because he is at my right hand,
I will not be shaken.

9Therefore my heart is glad and my tongue rejoices;
my body also will rest secure,

NIV [e] Title: Probably a literary or musical term [f] 3 Or *As for the pagan priests who are in the land / and the nobles in whom all delight, I said:*

## King James

10 For thou wilt not leave my soul in hell; neither wilt thou suffer thine Holy One to see corruption.

11 Thou wilt show me the path of life: in thy presence *is* fulness of joy; at thy right hand *there are* pleasures for evermore.

A Prayer of David.

**17** HEAR THE right, O LORD, attend unto my cry, give ear unto my prayer, *that goeth* not out of feigned lips.

2 Let my sentence come forth from thy presence; let thine eyes behold the things that are equal.

3 Thou hast proved mine heart; thou hast visited *me* in the night; thou hast tried me, *and* shalt find nothing; I am purposed *that* my mouth shall not transgress.

4 Concerning the works of men, by the word of thy lips I have kept *me from* the paths of the destroyer.

5 Hold up my goings in thy paths, *that* my footsteps slip not.

6 I have called upon thee, for thou wilt hear me, O God: incline thine ear unto me, *and hear* my speech.

7 Show thy marvellous lovingkindness, O thou that savest by thy right hand them which put their trust *in thee* from those that rise up *against them*.

8 Keep me as the apple of the eye, hide me under the shadow of thy wings,

9 From the wicked that oppress me, *from* my deadly enemies, *who* compass me about.

10 They are inclosed in their own fat: with their mouth they speak proudly.

11 They have now compassed us in our steps: they have set their eyes bowing down to the earth;

12 Like as a lion *that* is greedy of his prey, and as it were a young lion lurking in secret places.

13 Arise, O LORD, disappoint him, cast him down: deliver my soul from the wicked, *which is* thy sword:

14 From men *which are* thy hand, O LORD, from men of the world, *which have* their portion in *this* life, and whose belly thou fillest with thy hid *treasure:* they are full of children, and leave the rest of their *substance* to their babes.

15 As for me, I will behold thy face in righteousness: I shall be satisfied, when I awake, with thy likeness.

To the chief Musician, *A Psalm* of David, the servant of the LORD, who spake unto the LORD the words of this song in the day *that* the LORD delivered him from the hand of all his enemies, and from the hand of Saul: And he said,

**18** I WILL love thee, O LORD, my strength.

2 The LORD *is* my rock, and my fortress, and my deliverer; my God, my strength, in whom I will trust; my buckler, and the horn of my salvation, *and* my high tower.

3 I will call upon the LORD, *who is worthy* to be praised: so shall I be saved from mine enemies.

## Amplified

10 For You will not abandon me to Sheol [the place of the dead], neither will You suffer Your holy one to see corruption. [Acts 13:35.]

11 You will show me the path of life; in Your presence is fullness of joy, at Your right hand there are pleasures for evermore. [Acts 2:25-28, 31.]

A Prayer of David.

**17** HEAR THE right (my righteous cause), O Lord; listen to my shrill, piercing cry! Give ear to my prayer, that comes from unfeigned *and* guileless lips.

2 Let my sentence of vindication come from You! Your eyes behold the things that are just *and* upright.

3 You have proved my heart; You have visited *me* in the night; You have tried me *and* find nothing—no evil purpose in me; I am purposed that my mouth shall not transgress.

4 Concerning the works of men, by the Word of Your lips I have avoided the ways of the violent—the paths of the destroyer.

5 My steps have held closely to Your paths—to the tracks of the One Who has gone on before; my feet have not slipped.

6 I have called upon You, O God, for You will hear me; incline Your ear to me *and* hear my speech.

7 Show Your marvelous loving-kindness, O You Who save by Your right hand those who trust *and* take refuge in You, from those who rise up against them.

8 Keep *and* guard me as the pupil of the eye; hide me in the shadow of Your wings,

9 From the wicked who despoil *and* oppress me, my deadly adversaries who surround me.

10 They are enclosed in their own prosperity *and* have shut up their heart to pity; with their mouth they make exorbitant claims *and* proudly *and* arrogantly speak.

11 They track us down in each step we take; now they surround us; they set their eyes to cast us to the ground,

12 Like a lion greedy *and* eager to tear his prey, and as a young lion lurking in hidden places.

13 Arise, O Lord! Confront *and* forestall him, cast him down! Deliver my life from the wicked by Your sword,

14 From men by Your hand, O Lord, from men of *this* world [these poor moths of the night], whose portion in life is idle *and* vain. Their belly is filled with Your hidden treasure—what You have stored up; their children are satiated, and they leave the rest *of their* wealth to their babes.

15 As for me, I will continue beholding Your face in righteousness—rightness, justice and right standing with You; I shall be fully satisfied, when I awake [to find myself] beholding Your form [and having sweet communion with You].

To the Chief Musician. [ *A Psalm*] of David the servant of the Lord, who spoke the words of this song to the Lord on the day when the Lord delivered him from the hand of all his enemies and from the hand of Saul. And he said:

**18** I LOVE You fervently *and* devotedly, O Lord, my strength.

2 The Lord is my rock, my fortress, and my deliverer; my God, my keen *and* firm strength in Whom I will trust *and* take refuge, my shield, and the horn of my salvation, my high tower. [Heb. 2:13.]

3 I will call upon the Lord, Who is to be praised; so shall I be saved from my enemies. [Rev. 5:12.]

## New American Standard

10 For Thou wilt not abandon my soul to Sheol;
Neither wilt Thou allow Thy Holy One to [a]undergo decay.
11 Thou wilt make known to me the path of life;
In Thy presence is fulness of joy;
In Thy right hand there are pleasures forever.

*Prayer for Protection against Oppressors.*

A Prayer of David.

**17** HEAR A just cause, O LORD, give heed to my cry;
Give ear to my prayer, which is not from deceitful lips.
2 Let my judgment come forth from Thy presence;
Let Thine eyes look with equity.
3 Thou hast tried my heart;
Thou hast visited *me* by night;
Thou hast tested me and dost find [b]nothing;
I have purposed that my mouth will not transgress.
4 As for the deeds of men, by the word of Thy lips
I have kept from the paths of the violent.
5 My steps have held fast to Thy paths.
My feet have not slipped.

6¶ I have called upon Thee, for Thou wilt answer me, O God;
Incline Thine ear to me, hear my speech.
7 Wondrously show Thy lovingkindness,
O Savior of those who take refuge at Thy right hand
From those who rise up *against them.*
8 Keep me as [c]the apple of the eye;
Hide me in the shadow of Thy wings,
9 From the wicked who despoil me,
My deadly enemies, who surround me.
10 They have closed their unfeeling *heart;*
With their mouth they speak proudly.
11 They have now surrounded us in our steps;
They set their eyes to cast *us* down to the ground.
12 He is like a lion that is eager to tear,
And as a young lion lurking in hiding places.
13¶ Arise, O LORD, confront him, bring him low;
Deliver my soul from the wicked with Thy sword,
14 From men with Thy hand, O LORD,
From men of the world, whose portion is in *this* life;
And whose belly Thou dost fill with Thy treasure;
They are satisfied with children,
And leave their abundance to their babes.
15 As for me, I shall behold Thy face in righteousness;
I will be satisfied with Thy likeness when I awake.

*The LORD Praised for Giving Deliverance.*

For the choir director. *A Psalm* of David the servant of the LORD, who spoke to the LORD the words of this song in the day that the LORD delivered him from the hand of all his enemies and from the hand of Saul. And he said,

**18** "I LOVE Thee, O LORD, my strength."
2 The LORD is my rock and my fortress and my deliverer,
My God, my rock, in whom I take refuge;
My shield and the horn of my salvation, my stronghold.
3 I call upon the LORD, who is worthy to be praised,
And I am saved from my enemies.

NAS [a] Or, *see corruption* or *the pit* [b] Or, *no evil device in me* [c] Lit., *the pupil, the daughter of the eye*

## New International

10because you will not abandon me to the grave,[d]
nor will you let your Holy One[e] see decay.
11You have made[f] known to me the path of life;
you will fill me with joy in your presence,
with eternal pleasures at your right hand.

A prayer of David.

**17** HEAR, O LORD, my righteous plea;
listen to my cry.
Give ear to my prayer—
it does not rise from deceitful lips.
2May my vindication come from you;
may your eyes see what is right.

3Though you probe my heart and examine me at night,
though you test me, you will find nothing;
I have resolved that my mouth will not sin.
4As for the deeds of men—
by the word of your lips
I have kept myself
from the ways of the violent.
5My steps have held to your paths;
my feet have not slipped.

6I call on you, O God, for you will answer me;
give ear to me and hear my prayer.
7Show the wonder of your great love,
you who save by your right hand
those who take refuge in you from their foes.
8Keep me as the apple of your eye;
hide me in the shadow of your wings
9from the wicked who assail me,
from my mortal enemies who surround me.

10They close up their callous hearts,
and their mouths speak with arrogance.
11They have tracked me down, they now surround me,
with eyes alert, to throw me to the ground.
12They are like a lion hungry for prey,
like a great lion crouching in cover.

13Rise up, O LORD, confront them, bring them down;
rescue me from the wicked by your sword.
14O LORD, by your hand save me from such men,
from men of this world whose reward is in this life.
You still the hunger of those you cherish;
their sons have plenty,
and they store up wealth for their children.
15And I—in righteousness I will see your face;
when I awake, I will be satisfied with seeing your likeness.

For the director of music. Of David the servant of the LORD. He sang to the LORD the words of this song when the LORD delivered him from the hand of all his enemies and from the hand of Saul. He said:

**18** I LOVE you, O LORD, my strength.
2The LORD is my rock, my fortress and my deliverer;
my God is my rock, in whom I take refuge.
He is my shield and the horn[g] of my salvation, my stronghold.
3I call to the LORD, who is worthy of praise,
and I am saved from my enemies.

NIV [d] 10 Hebrew *Sheol* [e] 10 Or *your faithful one* [f] 11 Or *You will make* [g] 2 *Horn* here symbolizes strength.

## King James

4 The sorrows of death compassed me, and the floods of
ungodly men made me afraid.
5 The sorrows of hell compassed me about: the snares of death
prevented me.
6 In my distress I called upon the LORD, and cried unto my God:
he heard my voice out of his temple, and my cry came before him,
*even* into his ears.
7 Then the earth shook and trembled; the foundations also of the
hills moved and were shaken, because he was wroth.
8 There went up a smoke out of his nostrils, and fire out of his
mouth devoured: coals were kindled by it.
9 He bowed the heavens also, and came down: and darkness *was*
under his feet.
10 And he rode upon a cherub, and did fly: yea, he did fly upon
the wings of the wind.
11 He made darkness his secret place; his pavilion round about
him *were* dark waters *and* thick clouds of the skies.
12 At the brightness *that was* before him his thick clouds passed,
hail *stones* and coals of fire.
13 The LORD also thundered in the heavens, and the Highest
gave his voice; hail *stones* and coals of fire.
14 Yea, he sent out his arrows, and scattered them; and he shot
out lightnings, and discomfited them.
15 Then the channels of waters were seen, and the foundations
of the world were discovered at thy rebuke, O LORD, at the blast
of the breath of thy nostrils.
16 He sent from above, he took me, he drew me out of many
waters.
17 He delivered me from my strong enemy, and from them
which hated me: for they were too strong for me.
18 They prevented me in the day of my calamity: but the LORD
was my stay.
19 He brought me forth also into a large place; he delivered me,
because he delighted in me.
20 The LORD rewarded me according to my righteousness; according to the cleanness of my hands hath he recompensed me.
21 For I have kept the ways of the LORD, and have not wickedly
departed from my God.
22 For all his judgments *were* before me, and I did not put away
his statutes from me.
23 I was also upright before him, and I kept myself from mine
iniquity.
24 Therefore hath the LORD recompensed me according to my
righteousness, according to the cleanness of my hands in his eyesight.
25 With the merciful thou wilt show thyself merciful; with an
upright man thou wilt show thyself upright;
26 With the pure thou wilt show thyself pure; and with the
froward thou wilt show thyself froward.
27 For thou wilt save the afflicted people; but wilt bring down
high looks.
28 For thou wilt light my candle: the LORD my God will enlighten
my darkness.
29 For by thee I have run through a troop; and by my God have
I leaped over a wall.

## Amplified

4 The cords *or* bands of death surrounded me, and the streams
of ungodliness *and* torrents of ruin terrified me.
5 The cords of Sheol [the place of the dead] surrounded me; the
snares of death confronted *and* came upon me.
6 In my distress [when seemingly closed in] I called upon the
Lord, and cried to my God; He heard my voice out of His temple
[heavenly dwelling place], and my cry came before Him, to His
[very] ears.
7 Then the earth quaked and rocked; the foundations also of the
mountains trembled, they moved *and* were shaken, because He
was indignant *and* angry.
8 There went up smoke from His nostrils, and lightning out of
His mouth devoured; coals were kindled by it.
9 He bowed the heavens also, and came down; and thick darkness was under His feet.
10 And He rode upon a cherub [a storm] and flew [swiftly]; yes,
He sped on with the wings of the wind.
11 He made darkness His secret hiding place; as His pavilion
[His canopy] round about Him were dark waters *and* thick clouds
of the skies.
12 Out of the brightness before Him there broke forth through
His thick clouds hailstones and coals of fire.
13 The Lord also thundered from the heavens, and the Most
High uttered His voice, hailstones and coals of fire.
14 And He sent out His arrows, and scattered them; and He
flashed forth lightnings, and put them to rout.
15 Then the beds of the sea appeared, and the foundations of the
world were laid bare at Your rebuke, O Lord, at the blast of the
breath of Your nostrils.
16 He reached from on high, He took me, He drew me out of
many waters.
17 He delivered me from my strong enemy, and from those who
hated *and* abhorred me; for they were too strong for me.
18 They confronted *and* came upon me in the day of my calamity;
but the Lord was my stay *and* support.
19 He brought me forth also into a large place; He was delivering
me, because He was pleased with me *and* delighted in me.
20 The Lord rewarded me according to my righteousness [my
conscious integrity and sincerity with Him]; according to the cleanness of my hands has He recompensed me.
21 For I have kept the ways of the Lord, and have not wickedly
departed from my God.
22 For all His ordinances were before me, and I put not away His
statutes from me.
23 I was upright before Him *and* blameless with Him, ever [on
guard] to keep myself free from my sin *and* guilt.
24 Therefore has the Lord recompensed me according to my
righteousness [my uprightness and right standing with Him], according to the cleanness of my hands in His sight.
25 With the kind *and* merciful You will show Yourself kind *and*
merciful; with an upright man You will show Yourself upright;
26 With the pure You will show Yourself pure, and with the
perverse You will show Yourself contrary.
27 For You deliver an afflicted *and* humble people, but will bring
down haughty looks.
28 For You cause my lamp to be lighted *and* shine; the Lord my
God illumines my darkness.
29 For by You I can run through a troop, and by my God I can
leap over a wall.

## New American Standard

4¶ The cords of death encompassed me,
And the torrents of [a]ungodliness terrified me.
5 The cords of Sheol surrounded me;
The snares of death confronted me.
6 In my distress I called upon the LORD,
And cried to my God for help;
He heard my voice out of His temple,
And my cry for help before Him came into His ears.

7¶ Then the earth shook and quaked;
And the foundations of the mountains were trembling
And were shaken, because He was angry.
8 Smoke went up out of His nostrils,
And fire from His mouth devoured;
Coals were kindled by it.
9 He bowed the heavens also, and came down
With thick darkness under His feet.
10 And He rode upon a cherub and flew;
And He sped upon the wings of the wind.
11 He made darkness His hiding place, His canopy around Him,
Darkness of waters, thick clouds of the skies.
12 From the brightness before Him passed His thick clouds,
Hailstones and coals of fire.
13 The LORD also thundered in the heavens,
And the Most High uttered His voice,
Hailstones and coals of fire.
14 And He sent out His arrows, and scattered them,
And lightning flashes in abundance, and routed them.
15 Then the channels of water appeared,
And the foundations of the world were laid bare
At Thy rebuke, O LORD,
At the blast of the breath of Thy nostrils.

16¶ He sent from on high, He took me;
He drew me out of many waters.
17 He delivered me from my strong enemy,
And from those who hated me, for they were too mighty for me.
18 They confronted me in the day of my calamity,
But the LORD was my stay.
19 He brought me forth also into a broad place;
He rescued me, because He delighted in me.

20¶ The LORD has rewarded me according to my righteousness;
According to the cleanness of my hands He has recompensed me.
21 For I have kept the ways of the LORD,
And have not wickedly departed from my God.
22 For all His ordinances were before me,
And I did not put away His statutes from me.
23 I was also [b]blameless with Him,
And I kept myself from my iniquity.
24 Therefore the LORD has recompensed me according to my righteousness,
According to the cleanness of my hands in His eyes.

25¶ With the kind Thou dost show Thyself kind;
With the blameless Thou dost show Thyself blameless;
26 With the pure Thou dost show Thyself pure;
And with the crooked Thou dost show Thyself [c]astute.
27 For Thou dost save an afflicted people;
But haughty eyes Thou dost abase.
28 For Thou dost light my lamp;
The LORD my God illumines my darkness.
29 For by Thee I can [d]run upon a troop;
And by my God I can leap over a wall.

NAS [a] Or, *destruction* [b] Lit., *complete;* or, *having integrity* [c] Lit., *twisted* [d] Or, *crush a troop*

## New International

4The cords of death entangled me;
the torrents of destruction overwhelmed me.
5The cords of the grave[e] coiled around me;
the snares of death confronted me.
6In my distress I called to the LORD;
I cried to my God for help.
From his temple he heard my voice;
my cry came before him, into his ears.

7The earth trembled and quaked,
and the foundations of the mountains shook;
they trembled because he was angry.
8Smoke rose from his nostrils;
consuming fire came from his mouth,
burning coals blazed out of it.
9He parted the heavens and came down;
dark clouds were under his feet.
10He mounted the cherubim and flew;
he soared on the wings of the wind.
11He made darkness his covering, his canopy around him—
the dark rain clouds of the sky.
12Out of the brightness of his presence clouds advanced,
with hailstones and bolts of lightning.
13The LORD thundered from heaven;
the voice of the Most High resounded.[f]
14He shot his arrows and scattered the enemies,
great bolts of lightning and routed them.
15The valleys of the sea were exposed
and the foundations of the earth laid bare
at your rebuke, O LORD,
at the blast of breath from your nostrils.

16He reached down from on high and took hold of me;
he drew me out of deep waters.
17He rescued me from my powerful enemy,
from my foes, who were too strong for me.
18They confronted me in the day of my disaster,
but the LORD was my support.
19He brought me out into a spacious place;
he rescued me because he delighted in me.

20The LORD has dealt with me according to my righteousness;
according to the cleanness of my hands he has rewarded me.
21For I have kept the ways of the LORD;
I have not done evil by turning from my God.
22All his laws are before me;
I have not turned away from his decrees.
23I have been blameless before him
and have kept myself from sin.
24The LORD has rewarded me according to my righteousness,
according to the cleanness of my hands in his sight.

25To the faithful you show yourself faithful,
to the blameless you show yourself blameless,
26to the pure you show yourself pure,
but to the crooked you show yourself shrewd.
27You save the humble
but bring low those whose eyes are haughty.
28You, O LORD, keep my lamp burning;
my God turns my darkness into light.
29With your help I can advance against a troop[g];
with my God I can scale a wall.

NIV [e] 5 Hebrew *Sheol* [f] 13 Some Hebrew manuscripts and Septuagint (see also 2 Samuel 22:14); most Hebrew manuscripts *resounded, / amid hailstones and bolts of lightning* [g] 29 Or *can run through a barricade*

## King James

30 *As for* God, his way *is* perfect: the word of the LORD is tried:
he *is* a buckler to all those that trust in him.
31 For who *is* God save the LORD? or who *is* a rock save our God?
32 *It is* God that girdeth me with strength, and maketh my way
perfect.
33 He maketh my feet like hinds' *feet*, and setteth me upon my
high places.
34 He teacheth my hands to war, so that a bow of steel is broken
by mine arms.
35 Thou hast also given me the shield of thy salvation: and thy
right hand hath holden me up, and thy gentleness hath made me
great.
36 Thou hast enlarged my steps under me, that my feet did not
slip.
37 I have pursued mine enemies, and overtaken them: neither
did I turn again till they were consumed.
38 I have wounded them that they were not able to rise: they are
fallen under my feet.
39 For thou hast girded me with strength unto the battle: thou
hast subdued under me those that rose up against me.
40 Thou hast also given me the necks of mine enemies; that I
might destroy them that hate me.
41 They cried, but *there was* none to save *them: even* unto the
LORD, but he answered them not.
42 Then did I beat them small as the dust before the wind: I did
cast them out as the dirt in the streets.
43 Thou hast delivered me from the strivings of the people; *and*
thou hast made me the head of the heathen: a people *whom* I have
not known shall serve me.
44 As soon as they hear of me, they shall obey me: the strangers
shall submit themselves unto me.
45 The strangers shall fade away, and be afraid out of their close
places.
46 The LORD liveth; and blessed *be* my rock; and let the God of
my salvation be exalted.
47 *It is* God that avengeth me, and subdueth the people under
me.
48 He delivereth me from mine enemies: yea, thou liftest me up
above those that rise up against me: thou hast delivered me from
the violent man.
49 Therefore will I give thanks unto thee, O LORD, among the
heathen, and sing praises unto thy name.
50 Great deliverance giveth he to his king; and showeth mercy
to his anointed, to David, and to his seed for evermore.

To the chief Musician, A Psalm of David.

19 THE HEAVENS declare the glory of God; and the firmament showeth his handiwork.
2 Day unto day uttereth speech, and night unto night showeth
knowledge.
3 *There is* no speech nor language, *where* their voice is not
heard.

## Amplified

30 As for God, His way is perfect! The Word of the Lord is tested
*and* tried; He is a shield to all those who take refuge *and* put their
trust in Him.
31 For who is God except the Lord? Or who is a rock save our
God,
32 The God who girds me with strength, and makes my way
perfect?
33 He makes my feet like hinds' feet [able to stand firmly or make
progress on the dangerous heights of testing and trouble]; He sets
me securely upon my high places.
34 He teaches my hands to war, so that my arms bend a bow of
bronze.
35 You have also given me the shield of Your salvation, and Your
right hand has held me up; Your gentleness *and* condescension
have made me great.
36 You have given plenty of room for my steps under me, that
my feet did not slip.
37 I pursued my enemies and overtook them; neither did I turn
again till they were consumed.
38 I smote them so they were not able to rise; they fell wounded
under my feet.
39 For You have girded me with strength for the battle; You have
subdued under me and caused to bow down those who rose up
against me.
40 You have also made my enemies turn their backs to me, that
I might cut off those who hate me.
41 They cried [for help], but there was none to deliver, even unto
the Lord, but He answered them not.
42 Then I beat them small as the dust before the wind; I emptied
them out as the dirt *and* mire of the streets.
43 You have delivered me from strivings of the people; You
made me the head of the nations; a people I had not known served
me.
44 As soon as they heard of me they obeyed me; foreigners
submitted themselves cringingly *and* yielded feigned obedience to
me.
45 Foreigners lost heart and came trembling out of their caves *or*
strongholds.
46 The Lord lives! Blessed be my rock, and let the God of my
salvation be exalted,
47 The God Who avenges me and subdues peoples under me;
48 Who delivers me from my enemies; yes, You lift me up above
those who rise up against me; You deliver me from the man of
violence.
49 Therefore will I give thanks *and* extol You, O Lord, among the
nations, and sing praises to Your name. [Rom. 15:9.]
50 Great deliverances *and* triumphs gives He to His king, and
shows mercy *and* steadfast love to His anointed, to David and his
offspring for ever. [II Sam. 22:2-51.]

To the Chief Musician. A Psalm of David.

19 THE HEAVENS declare the glory of God, and the firmament shows *and* proclaims His handiwork. [Rom. 1:20,
21.]
2 Day after day pours forth speech, and night after night shows
forth knowledge.
3 There is no speech nor spoken word [from the stars]; their
voice is not heard;

## New American Standard

30¶ As for God, His way is blameless;
The word of the LORD is tried;
He is a shield to all who take refuge in Him.
31 For who is God, but the LORD?
And who is a rock, except our God,
32 The God who girds me with strength,
And makes my way blameless?
33 He makes my feet like hinds' *feet*,
And sets me upon my high places.
34 He trains my hands for battle,
So that my arms can bend a bow of bronze.
35 Thou hast also given me the shield of Thy salvation,
And Thy right hand upholds me;
And Thy gentleness makes me great.
36 Thou dost enlarge my steps under me,
And my feet have not slipped.

37¶ I pursued my enemies and overtook them,
And I did not turn back until they were consumed.
38 I shattered them, so that they were not able to rise;
They fell under my feet.
39 For Thou hast girded me with strength for battle;
Thou hast subdued under me those who rose up against me.
40 Thou hast also made my enemies turn their backs to me,
And I [a]destroyed those who hated me.
41 They cried for help, but there was none to save,
*Even* to the LORD, but He did not answer them.
42 Then I beat them fine as the dust before the wind;
I emptied them out as the mire of the streets.

43¶ Thou hast delivered me from the contentions of the people;
Thou hast placed me as head of the nations;
A people whom I have not known serve me.
44 As soon as they hear, they obey me;
Foreigners [b]submit to me.
45 Foreigners fade away,
And come trembling out of their fortresses.

46¶ The LORD lives, and blessed be my rock;
And exalted be the God of my salvation,
47 The God who executes vengeance for me,
And subdues peoples under me.
48 He delivers me from my enemies;
Surely Thou dost lift me above those who rise up against me;
Thou dost rescue me from the violent man.
49 Therefore I will give thanks to Thee among the nations, O LORD,
And I will sing praises to Thy name.
50 He gives great [c]deliverance to His king,
And shows lovingkindness to His anointed,
To David and his descendants forever.

*The Works and the Word of God.*

For the choir director.
A Psalm of David.

19 THE HEAVENS are telling of the glory of God;
And their expanse is declaring the work of His hands.
2 Day to day pours forth speech,
And night to night reveals knowledge.
3 There is no speech, nor are there words;
Their voice is not heard.

NAS [a] Or, *silenced* [b] I.e., give feigned obedience [c] I.e., victories

## New International

30 As for God, his way is perfect;
the word of the LORD is flawless.
He is a shield
for all who take refuge in him.
31 For who is God besides the LORD?
And who is the Rock except our God?
32 It is God who arms me with strength
and makes my way perfect.
33 He makes my feet like the feet of a deer;
he enables me to stand on the heights.
34 He trains my hands for battle;
my arms can bend a bow of bronze.
35 You give me your shield of victory,
and your right hand sustains me;
you stoop down to make me great.
36 You broaden the path beneath me,
so that my ankles do not turn.

37 I pursued my enemies and overtook them;
I did not turn back till they were destroyed.
38 I crushed them so that they could not rise;
they fell beneath my feet.
39 You armed me with strength for battle;
you made my adversaries bow at my feet.
40 You made my enemies turn their backs in flight,
and I destroyed my foes.
41 They cried for help, but there was no one to save them—
to the LORD, but he did not answer.
42 I beat them as fine as dust borne on the wind;
I poured them out like mud in the streets.

43 You have delivered me from the attacks of the people;
you have made me the head of nations;
people I did not know are subject to me.
44 As soon as they hear me, they obey me;
foreigners cringe before me.
45 They all lose heart;
they come trembling from their strongholds.

46 The LORD lives! Praise be to my Rock!
Exalted be God my Savior!
47 He is the God who avenges me,
who subdues nations under me,
48 who saves me from my enemies.
You exalted me above my foes;
from violent men you rescued me.
49 Therefore I will praise you among the nations, O LORD;
I will sing praises to your name.
50 He gives his king great victories;
he shows unfailing kindness to his anointed,
to David and his descendants forever.

For the director of music. A psalm of David.

19 THE HEAVENS declare the glory of God;
the skies proclaim the work of his hands.
2 Day after day they pour forth speech;
night after night they display knowledge.
3 There is no speech or language
where their voice is not heard.[d]

NIV [d] 3 Or *They have no speech, there are no words; / no sound is heard from them*

## King James

4Their line is gone out through all the earth, and their words to the end of the world. In them hath he set a tabernacle for the sun,

5Which *is* as a bridegroom coming out of his chamber, *and* rejoiceth as a strong man to run a race.

6His going forth *is* from the end of the heaven, and his circuit unto the ends of it: and there is nothing hid from the heat thereof.

7The law of the LORD *is* perfect, converting the soul: the testimony of the LORD *is* sure, making wise the simple.

8The statutes of the LORD *are* right, rejoicing the heart: the commandment of the LORD *is* pure, enlightening the eyes.

9The fear of the LORD *is* clean, enduring for ever: the judgments of the LORD *are* true *and* righteous altogether.

10More to be desired *are they* than gold, yea, than much fine gold: sweeter also than honey and the honeycomb.

11Moreover by them is thy servant warned: *and* in keeping of them *there is* great reward.

12Who can understand *his* errors? cleanse thou me from secret *faults*.

13Keep back thy servant also from presumptuous *sins;* let them not have dominion over me: then shall I be upright, and I shall be innocent from the great transgression.

14Let the words of my mouth, and the meditation of my heart, be acceptable in thy sight, O LORD, my strength, and my redeemer.

To the chief Musician, A Psalm of David.

**20** THE LORD hear thee in the day of trouble; the name of the God of Jacob defend thee;

2Send thee help from the sanctuary, and strengthen thee out of Zion;

3Remember all thy offerings, and accept thy burnt sacrifice; Selah.

4Grant thee according to thine own heart, and fulfil all thy counsel.

5We will rejoice in thy salvation, and in the name of our God we will set up *our* banners: the LORD fulfil all thy petitions.

6Now know I that the LORD saveth his anointed; he will hear him from his holy heaven with the saving strength of his right hand.

7Some *trust* in chariots, and some in horses: but we will remember the name of the LORD our God.

8They are brought down and fallen: but we are risen, and stand upright.

9Save, LORD: let the king hear us when we call.

## Amplified

4Yet their voice [in evidence] goes out through all the earth, their sayings to the end of the world. Of the heavens has God made a tent for the sun, [Rom. 10:18.]

5Which is as a bridegroom coming out of his chamber, and rejoices as a strong man to run his course.

6His going forth is from the end of the heavens, and his circuit to the ends of it; and nothing [yes, no one] is hidden from the heat of it.

7The law of the Lord is perfect, restoring the [whole] person; the testimony of the Lord is sure, making wise the simple.

8The precepts of the Lord are right, rejoicing the heart; the commandment of the Lord *is* pure *and* bright, enlightening the eyes;

9The [reverent] fear of the Lord *is* clean, enduring for ever; the ordinances of the Lord are true, and righteous altogether.

10More to be desired are they than gold, even than much fine gold; sweeter also than honey and drippings from the honeycomb.

11Moreover by them is Your servant warned [reminded, illuminated and instructed]; and in keeping them there is great reward.

12Who can discern his lapses *and* errors? Clear me from hidden [and unconscious] *faults*.

13Keep back Your servant also from presumptuous sins; let them not have dominion over me! Then shall I be blameless, and I shall be innocent *and* clear of great transgression.

14Let the words of my mouth and the meditation of my heart be acceptable in Your sight, O Lord, my [firm, impenetrable] rock and my redeemer.

To the Chief Musician. A Psalm of David.

**20** THE LORD answer you in the day of trouble! The name of the God of Jacob set you up on high [and defend you];

2Send you help from the sanctuary, and support, refresh *and* strengthen you from Zion;

3Remember all your offerings, and accept your burnt sacrifice; Selah [pause, and think of that]!

4Grant you according to your heart's desire, and fulfill all your plans.

5We will (shout in) triumph at your salvation *and* victory, and in the name of our God we will set up our banners; the Lord fulfill all your petitions.

6Now I know that the Lord saves His anointed; He will answer him from His holy Heaven with the saving strength of His right hand.

7Some trust in *and* boast of chariots, and some of horses; but we will trust in *and* boast of the name of the Lord our God.

8They are bowed down and fallen; but we are risen and stand upright.

9O Lord, give victory; let the King answer us when we call.

## New American Standard

4 Their [a]line has gone out through all the earth,
And their utterances to the end of the world.
In them He has placed a tent for the sun,
5 Which is as a bridegroom coming out of his chamber;
It rejoices as a strong man to run his course.
6 Its rising is from one end of the heavens,
And its circuit to the other end of them;
And there is nothing hidden from its heat.

7¶ The law of the LORD is [b]perfect, restoring the soul;
The testimony of the LORD is sure, making wise the simple.
8 The precepts of the LORD are right, rejoicing the heart;
The commandment of the LORD is pure, enlightening the eyes.
9 The fear of the LORD is clean, enduring forever;
The judgments of the LORD are true; they are righteous altogether.
10 They are more desirable than gold, yes, than much fine gold;
Sweeter also than honey and the drippings of the honeycomb.
11 Moreover, by them Thy servant is warned;
In keeping them there is great reward.
12 Who can discern *his* errors? Acquit me of hidden *faults*.
13 Also keep back Thy servant from presumptuous *sins*;
Let them not rule over me;
Then I shall be [c]blameless,
And I shall be acquitted of great transgression.
14 Let the words of my mouth and the meditation of my heart
Be acceptable in Thy sight,
O LORD, my rock and my Redeemer.

*Prayer for Victory over Enemies.*

For the choir director. A Psalm of David.

**20** MAY THE LORD answer you in the day of trouble!
May the name of the God of Jacob set you *securely* on high!
2 May He send you help from the sanctuary,
And support you from Zion!
3 May He remember all your meal offerings,
And find your burnt offering acceptable! Selah.

4¶ May He grant you your heart's desire,
And fulfill all your [d]counsel!
5 We will sing for joy over your victory,
And in the name of our God we will set up our banners.
May the LORD fulfill all your petitions.

6¶ Now I know that the LORD saves His anointed;
He will answer him from His holy heaven,
With the saving strength of His right hand.
7 Some *boast* in chariots, and some in horses;
But we will boast in the name of the LORD, our God.
8 They have bowed down and fallen;
But we have risen and stood upright.
9 Save, O LORD;
May the King answer us in the day we call.

NAS [a] Another reading is *sound* [b] I.e., blameless [c] Lit., *complete* [d] Or, *purpose*

## New International

4Their voice[e] goes out into all the earth,
their words to the ends of the world.

In the heavens he has pitched a tent for the sun,
5 which is like a bridegroom coming forth from his pavilion,
like a champion rejoicing to run his course.
6It rises at one end of the heavens
and makes its circuit to the other;
nothing is hidden from its heat.

7The law of the LORD is perfect,
reviving the soul.
The statutes of the LORD are trustworthy,
making wise the simple.
8The precepts of the LORD are right,
giving joy to the heart.
The commands of the LORD are radiant,
giving light to the eyes.
9The fear of the LORD is pure,
enduring forever.
The ordinances of the LORD are sure
and altogether righteous.

10They are more precious than gold,
than much pure gold;
they are sweeter than honey,
than honey from the comb.
11By them is your servant warned;
in keeping them there is great reward.

12Who can discern his errors?
Forgive my hidden faults.
13Keep your servant also from willful sins;
may they not rule over me.
Then will I be blameless,
innocent of great transgression.

14May the words of my mouth and the meditation of my heart
be pleasing in your sight,
O LORD, my Rock and my Redeemer.

For the director of music. A psalm of David.

**20** MAY THE LORD answer you when you are in distress;
may the name of the God of Jacob protect you.
2May he send you help from the sanctuary
and grant you support from Zion.
3May he remember all your sacrifices
and accept your burnt offerings. *Selah*
4May he give you the desire of your heart
and make all your plans succeed.
5We will shout for joy when you are victorious
and will lift up our banners in the name of our God.
May the LORD grant all your requests.
6Now I know that the LORD saves his anointed;
he answers him from his holy heaven
with the saving power of his right hand.
7Some trust in chariots and some in horses,
but we trust in the name of the LORD our God.
8They are brought to their knees and fall,
but we rise up and stand firm.

9O LORD, save the king!
Answer[f] us when we call!

NIV [e] 4 Septuagint, Jerome and Syriac; Hebrew *line* [f] 9 Or *save! / O King, answer*

## King James

To the chief Musician, A Psalm of David.

**21** THE KING shall joy in thy strength, O LORD; and in thy
salvation how greatly shall he rejoice!
2Thou hast given him his heart's desire, and hast not withhold-
en the request of his lips. Selah.
3For thou preventest him with the blessings of goodness: thou
settest a crown of pure gold on his head.
4He asked life of thee, *and* thou gavest *it* him, *even* length of days
for ever and ever.
5His glory *is* great in thy salvation: honour and majesty hast
thou laid upon him.
6For thou hast made him most blessed for ever: thou hast made
him exceeding glad with thy countenance.
7For the king trusteth in the LORD, and through the mercy of
the most High he shall not be moved.
8Thine hand shall find out all thine enemies: thy right hand
shall find out those that hate thee.
9Thou shalt make them as a fiery oven in the time of thine anger:
the LORD shall swallow them up in his wrath, and the fire shall
devour them.
10Their fruit shalt thou destroy from the earth, and their seed
from among the children of men.
11For they intended evil against thee: they imagined a mischievous device, *which* they are not able *to perform*.
12Therefore shalt thou make them turn their back, *when* thou
shalt make ready *thine arrows* upon thy strings against the face of
them.
13Be thou exalted, LORD, in thine own strength: *so* will we sing
and praise thy power.

To the chief Musician upon Aijeleth Shahar, A Psalm of David.

**22** MY GOD, my God, why hast thou forsaken me? *why art
thou so* far from helping me, *and from* the words of my
roaring?
2O my God, I cry in the daytime, but thou hearest not; and in
the night season, and am not silent.
3But thou *art* holy, *O thou* that inhabitest the praises of Israel.
4Our fathers trusted in thee: they trusted, and thou didst deliver them.
5They cried unto thee, and were delivered: they trusted in thee,
and were not confounded.
6But I *am* a worm, and no man; a reproach of men, and despised
of the people.
7All they that see me laugh me to scorn: they shoot out the lip,
they shake the head, *saying*,
8He trusted on the LORD *that* he would deliver him: let him
deliver him, seeing he delighted in him.
9But thou *art* he that took me out of the womb: thou didst make
me hope *when I was* upon my mother's breasts.
10I was cast upon thee from the womb: thou *art* my God from
my mother's belly.

## Amplified

To the Chief Musician. A Psalm of David.

**21** THE KING [David] shall joy in Your strength, O Lord; and
in Your salvation how greatly shall he rejoice!
2You have given him his heart's desire, and have not withheld
the request of his lips. Selah [pause, and think of that]!
3For You send blessings of good things to meet him; You set a
crown of pure gold on his head.
4He asked life of You, *and* You gave it to him, long life for ever
and evermore.
5His glory is great because of Your aid; splendor and majesty
You bestow upon him.
6For You make him to be blessed *and* a blessing for ever; You
make him exceedingly glad with the joy of Your presence. [Gen.
12:2.]
7For the king trusts, relies on *and* is confident in the Lord, and
through the mercy *and* steadfast love of the Most High he will
never be moved.
8Your hand shall find all Your enemies; Your right hand shall
find all those who hate You.
9You will make them as if in a blazing oven in the time of Your
anger; the Lord will swallow them up in His wrath, and the fire
will utterly consume them.
10Their offspring You will destroy from the earth, and their sons
from among the children of men.
11For they planned evil against You; they conceived a mischievous plot which they are not able to perform.
12For You will make them turn their back; You will aim Your
bow [of divine justice] at their faces.
13Be exalted, Lord, in Your strength; we will sing and praise
Your power.

To the Chief Musician;
set to [ *the tune of*] Aijeleth Hashshahar [the hind of the morning dawn].
A Psalm of David.

**22** [a]MY GOD, my God, why have You forsaken me? Why are
You so far from helping me, and from the words of my
groaning? [Matt. 27:46.]
2O my God, I cry in the daytime, but You answer not; and by
night I am not silent *or* find no rest.
3But You are holy, O You Who dwell in [the holy place where]
the praises of Israel [are offered].
4Our fathers trusted in You; they trusted—leaned on, relied on
You and were confident—and You delivered them.
5They cried to You and were delivered; they trusted, leaned on
*and* confidently relied on You, and were not ashamed *or* confounded *or* disappointed.
6But I am a worm, and no man; I am the scorn of men, and
despised by the people. [Matt. 27:39-44.]
7All who see me laugh at me *and* mock me; they shoot out the
lip, they shake the head, saying, [Matt. 27:43.]
8He trusted *and* rolled himself on the Lord, that He would
deliver him. Let Him deliver him, seeing He delights in him! [Matt.
27:39, 43; Mark 15:29, 30; Luke 23:35.]
9Yet You are He Who took me out of the womb; You made me
hope *and* trust when I was on my mother's breasts.
10I was cast upon You from my very birth; from my mother's
womb You are my God.

**AMP** [a] "This is beyond all others 'The Psalm of the Cross.' It may have been actually repeated by our Lord when hanging on the tree; it would be too bold to say so, but even a casual reader may see that it might have been. It begins with, 'My God, my God, why hast thou forsaken me?' and ends [with the thought], 'It is finished.' For plaintive expressions uprising from unutterable depths of woe, we may say of this Psalm, 'There is none like it.' "—Charles Haddon Spurgeon in *Treasury of David.* Quoted in the Gospels as being fulfilled at Christ's crucifixion.

## New American Standard

*Praise for Deliverance.*

For the choir director. A Psalm of David.

21 O LORD, in Thy strength the king will be glad,
And in Thy [b]salvation how greatly he will rejoice!
2 Thou hast given him his heart's desire,
And Thou hast not withheld the request of his lips. Selah.
3 For Thou dost meet him with the blessings of good things;
Thou dost set a crown of fine gold on his head.
4 He asked life of Thee,
Thou didst give it to him,
Length of days forever and ever.
5 His glory is great through Thy [c]salvation,
Splendor and majesty Thou dost place upon him.
6 For Thou dost make him most blessed forever;
Thou dost make him joyful with gladness in Thy presence.

7¶ For the king trusts in the LORD,
And through the lovingkindness of the Most High he will not be shaken.
8 Your hand will find out all your enemies;
Your right hand will find out those who hate you.
9 You will make them as a fiery oven in the time of your anger;
The LORD will swallow them up in His wrath,
And fire will devour them.
10 Their [d]offspring Thou wilt destroy from the earth,
And their [e]descendants from among the sons of men.
11 Though they intended evil against Thee,
*And* devised a plot,
They will not succeed.
12 For Thou wilt make them turn their back;
Thou wilt aim with Thy bowstrings at their faces.
13 Be Thou exalted, O LORD, in Thy strength;
We will sing and praise Thy power.

*A Cry of Anguish and a Song of Praise.*

For the choir director; upon [f]Aijeleth Hashshahar. A Psalm of David.

22 MY GOD, my God, why hast Thou forsaken me?
Far from my deliverance are the words of my groaning.
2 O my God, I cry by day, but Thou dost not answer;
And by night, but I have no rest.
3 Yet Thou art holy,
O Thou who art enthroned upon the praises of Israel.
4 In Thee our fathers trusted;
They trusted, and Thou didst deliver them.
5 To Thee they cried out, and were delivered;
In Thee they trusted, and were not disappointed.

6¶ But I am a worm, and not a man,
A reproach of men, and despised by the people.
7 All who see me sneer at me;
They [g]separate with the lip, they wag the head, *saying,*
8 "[h]Commit *yourself* to the LORD; let Him deliver him;
Let Him rescue him, because He delights in him."

9¶ Yet Thou art He who didst bring me forth from the womb;
Thou didst make me trust *when* upon my mother's breasts.
10 Upon Thee I was cast from birth;
Thou hast been my God from my mother's womb.

NAS [b] Or, *victory* [c] Or, *victory* [d] Lit., *fruit* [e] Lit., *seed* [f] Lit., *the hind of the morning* [g] I.e., make mouths at me [h] Another reading is *He committed himself*

## New International

For the director of music. A psalm of David.

21 O LORD, the king rejoices in your strength.
How great is his joy in the victories you give!
2You have granted him the desire of his heart
and have not withheld the request of his lips. *Selah*
3You welcomed him with rich blessings
and placed a crown of pure gold on his head.
4He asked you for life, and you gave it to him—
length of days, for ever and ever.
5Through the victories you gave, his glory is great;
you have bestowed on him splendor and majesty.
6Surely you have granted him eternal blessings
and made him glad with the joy of your presence.
7For the king trusts in the LORD;
through the unfailing love of the Most High
he will not be shaken.

8Your hand will lay hold on all your enemies;
your right hand will seize your foes.
9At the time of your appearing
you will make them like a fiery furnace.
In his wrath the LORD will swallow them up,
and his fire will consume them.
10You will destroy their descendants from the earth,
their posterity from mankind.
11Though they plot evil against you
and devise wicked schemes, they cannot succeed;
12for you will make them turn their backs
when you aim at them with drawn bow.

13Be exalted, O LORD, in your strength;
we will sing and praise your might.

For the director of music. To ⌊the tune of⌋ "The Doe of the Morning." A psalm of David.

22 MY GOD, my God, why have you forsaken me?
Why are you so far from saving me,
so far from the words of my groaning?
2O my God, I cry out by day, but you do not answer,
by night, and am not silent.

3Yet you are enthroned as the Holy One;
you are the praise of Israel.[i]
4In you our fathers put their trust;
they trusted and you delivered them.
5They cried to you and were saved;
in you they trusted and were not disappointed.

6But I am a worm and not a man,
scorned by men and despised by the people.
7All who see me mock me;
they hurl insults, shaking their heads:
8"He trusts in the LORD;
let the LORD rescue him.
Let him deliver him,
since he delights in him."

9Yet you brought me out of the womb;
you made me trust in you
even at my mother's breast.
10From birth I was cast upon you;
from my mother's womb you have been my God.

NIV [i] 3 Or *Yet you are holy, / enthroned on the praises of Israel*

## King James

11Be not far from me; for trouble *is* near; for *there is* none to help.
12Many bulls have compassed me: strong *bulls* of Bashan have
beset me round.
13They gaped upon me *with* their mouths, *as* a ravening and a
roaring lion.
14I am poured out like water, and all my bones are out of joint:
my heart is like wax; it is melted in the midst of my bowels.
15My strength is dried up like a potsherd; and my tongue
cleaveth to my jaws; and thou hast brought me into the dust of
death.
16For dogs have compassed me: the assembly of the wicked
have inclosed me: they pierced my hands and my feet.
17I may tell all my bones: they look *and* stare upon me.
18They part my garments among them, and cast lots upon my
vesture.
19But be not thou far from me, O LORD: O my strength, haste
thee to help me.
20Deliver my soul from the sword; my darling from the power
of the dog.
21Save me from the lion's mouth: for thou hast heard me from
the horns of the unicorns.
22I will declare thy name unto my brethren: in the midst of the
congregation will I praise thee.
23Ye that fear the LORD, praise him; all ye the seed of Jacob,
glorify him; and fear him, all ye the seed of Israel.
24For he hath not despised nor abhorred the affliction of the
afflicted; neither hath he hid his face from him; but when he cried
unto him, he heard.
25My praise *shall be* of thee in the great congregation: I will pay
my vows before them that fear him.
26The meek shall eat and be satisfied: they shall praise the LORD
that seek him: your heart shall live for ever.
27All the ends of the world shall remember and turn unto the
LORD: and all the kindreds of the nations shall worship before thee.
28For the kingdom *is* the LORD's: and he *is* the governor among
the nations.
29All *they that be* fat upon earth shall eat and worship: all they
that go down to the dust shall bow before him: and none can keep
alive his own soul.
30A seed shall serve him; it shall be accounted to the Lord for
a generation.
31They shall come, and shall declare his righteousness unto a
people that shall be born, that he hath done *this*.

A Psalm of David.

23 THE LORD *is* my shepherd; I shall not want.
2He maketh me to lie down in green pastures: he leadeth
me beside the still waters.

## Amplified

11Be not far from me, for trouble is near and there is none to
help.
12Many [foes like] bulls have surrounded me; strong bulls of
Bashan have hedged me in. [Ezek. 39:18.]
13Against me they opened their mouths wide, like a ravening
and roaring lion.
14I am poured out like water, and all my bones are out of joint;
my heart is like wax, it is softened [with anguish], *and* melted
down within me.
15My strength is dried up like a fragment of clay pottery; [with
thirst] my tongue cleaves to my jaws; and You have brought me
into the dust of death. [John 19:28.]
16For [like a pack of] dogs they have encompassed me; a company of evildoers has encircled me; they pierced my hands and my
feet. [Isa. 53:7; John 19:37.]
17I can count all my bones; [the evildoers] gaze at me. [Luke
23:27, 35.]
18They part my clothing among them, and cast lots for my
raiment [a long, shirt-like garment, a seamless undertunic]. [John
19:23, 24.]
19But be not far from me, O Lord; O my help, hasten to aid me!
20Deliver my life from the sword; my dear life—my only one—
from the power of the dog [the agent of execution].
21Save me from the lion's mouth; for You have answered me
[kindly] from the horns of the wild oxen.
22I will declare Your name to my brethren; in the midst of the
congregation will I praise You. [John 20:17; Rom. 8:29; Heb. 2:12.]
23You who fear—revere and worship—the Lord, praise Him!
All you the offspring of Jacob, glorify Him. Fear—revere and worship—Him, all you offspring of Israel.
24For He has not despised or abhorred the affliction of the
afflicted, neither has He hid His face from him; but when he cried
to Him, He heard.
25My praise shall be of You in the great congregation. I will pay
to Him my vows [made in the time of trouble] before them who
fear—revere and worship—Him.
26The poor *and* afflicted shall eat and be satisfied; they shall
praise the Lord who [diligently] seek for, inquire of *and* for Him
*and* require Him [as their greatest need]. May your heart be
quickened now *and* for ever!
27All the ends of the earth shall remember and turn to the Lord,
and all the families of the nations shall bow down *and* worship
before You.
28For the kingship *and* the kingdom are the Lord's, and He is
the ruler over the nations.
29All the mighty ones upon earth shall eat [in thanksgiving] and
worship; all they that go down to the dust shall bow before Him,
even he who cannot keep himself alive.
30Posterity shall serve Him; they shall tell of the Lord to the next
generation.
31They shall come and shall declare His righteousness to a
people yet to be born, that He has done it [that it is finished]! [John
19:30.]

A Psalm of David.

23 THE LORD is my shepherd [to feed, guide and shield me];
I shall not lack.
2He makes me lie down in (fresh, tender) green pastures; He
leads me beside the still *and* restful waters. [Rev. 7:17.]

## New American Standard

11¶ Be not far from me, for trouble is near;
For there is none to help.
12 Many bulls have surrounded me;
Strong *bulls* of Bashan have encircled me.
13 They open wide their mouth at me,
As a ravening and a roaring lion.
14 I am poured out like water,
And all my bones are out of joint;
My heart is like wax;
It is melted within me.
15 My strength is dried up like a potsherd,
And my tongue cleaves to my jaws;
And Thou dost lay me in the dust of death.
16 For dogs have surrounded me;
A band of evildoers has encompassed me;
They pierced my hands and my feet.
17 I can count all my bones.
They look, they stare at me;
18 They divide my garments among them,
And for my clothing they cast lots.

19¶ But Thou, O LORD, be not far off;
O Thou my help, hasten to my assistance.
20 Deliver my soul from the sword,
My only *life* from the power of the dog.
21 Save me from the lion's mouth;
And from the horns of the wild oxen Thou dost answer me.

22¶ I will tell of Thy name to my brethren;
In the midst of the assembly I will praise Thee.
23 You who fear the LORD, praise Him;
All you descendants of Jacob, glorify Him,
And stand in awe of Him, all you descendants of Israel.
24 For He has not despised nor abhorred the affliction of the afflicted;
Neither has He hidden His face from him;
But when he cried to Him for help, He heard.

25¶ From Thee *comes* my praise in the great assembly;
I shall pay my vows before those who fear Him.
26 The [a]afflicted shall eat and be satisfied;
Those who seek Him will praise the LORD.
Let your heart live forever!
27 All the ends of the earth will remember and turn to the LORD,
And all the families of the nations will worship before Thee.
28 For the kingdom is the LORD's,
And He rules over the nations.
29 All the prosperous of the earth will eat and worship,
All those who go down to the dust will bow before Him,
Even he who cannot keep his soul alive.
30 Posterity will serve Him;
It will be told of the Lord to the *coming* generation.
31 They will come and will declare His righteousness
To a people who will be born, that He has performed *it*.

*The LORD, the Psalmist's Shepherd.*

A Psalm of David.

23 THE LORD is my shepherd,
I shall not want.
2 He makes me lie down in green pastures;
He leads me beside quiet waters.

NAS [a] Or, *poor*

## New International

11 Do not be far from me,
for trouble is near
and there is no one to help.

12 Many bulls surround me;
strong bulls of Bashan encircle me.
13 Roaring lions tearing their prey
open their mouths wide against me.
14 I am poured out like water,
and all my bones are out of joint.
My heart has turned to wax;
it has melted away within me.
15 My strength is dried up like a potsherd,
and my tongue sticks to the roof of my mouth;
you lay me[b] in the dust of death.
16 Dogs have surrounded me;
a band of evil men has encircled me,
they have pierced[c] my hands and my feet.
17 I can count all my bones;
people stare and gloat over me.
18 They divide my garments among them
and cast lots for my clothing.

19 But you, O LORD, be not far off;
O my Strength, come quickly to help me.
20 Deliver my life from the sword,
my precious life from the power of the dogs.
21 Rescue me from the mouth of the lions;
save[d] me from the horns of the wild oxen.

22 I will declare your name to my brothers;
in the congregation I will praise you.
23 You who fear the LORD, praise him!
All you descendants of Jacob, honor him!
Revere him, all you descendants of Israel!
24 For he has not despised or disdained
the suffering of the afflicted one;
he has not hidden his face from him
but has listened to his cry for help.

25 From you comes the theme of my praise in the great assembly;
before those who fear you[e] will I fulfill my vows.
26 The poor will eat and be satisfied;
they who seek the LORD will praise him—
may your hearts live forever!
27 All the ends of the earth
will remember and turn to the LORD,
and all the families of the nations
will bow down before him,
28 for dominion belongs to the LORD
and he rules over the nations.

29 All the rich of the earth will feast and worship;
all who go down to the dust will kneel before him—
those who cannot keep themselves alive.
30 Posterity will serve him;
future generations will be told about the Lord.
31 They will proclaim his righteousness
to a people yet unborn—
for he has done it.

A psalm of David.

23 THE LORD is my shepherd, I shall not be in want.
2 He makes me lie down in green pastures,
he leads me beside quiet waters,

NIV [b] 15 Or / *I am laid* [c] 16 Some Hebrew manuscripts, Septuagint and Syriac; most Hebrew manuscripts / *like the lion,* [d] 21 Or / *you have heard* [e] 25 Hebrew *him*

## King James

3 He restoreth my soul: he leadeth me in the paths of righteousness for his name's sake.

4 Yea, though I walk through the valley of the shadow of death, I will fear no evil: for thou *art* with me; thy rod and thy staff they comfort me.

5 Thou preparest a table before me in the presence of mine enemies: thou anointest my head with oil; my cup runneth over.

6 Surely goodness and mercy shall follow me all the days of my life: and I will dwell in the house of the LORD for ever.

A Psalm of David.

**24** THE EARTH *is* the LORD's, and the fulness thereof; the world, and they that dwell therein.

2 For he hath founded it upon the seas, and established it upon the floods.

3 Who shall ascend into the hill of the LORD? or who shall stand in his holy place?

4 He that hath clean hands, and a pure heart; who hath not lifted up his soul unto vanity, nor sworn deceitfully.

5 He shall receive the blessing from the LORD, and righteousness from the God of his salvation.

6 This *is* the generation of them that seek him, that seek thy face, O Jacob. Selah.

7 Lift up your heads, O ye gates; and be ye lift up, ye everlasting doors; and the King of glory shall come in.

8 Who *is* this King of glory? The LORD strong and mighty, the LORD mighty in battle.

9 Lift up your heads, O ye gates; even lift *them* up, ye everlasting doors; and the King of glory shall come in.

10 Who is this King of glory? The LORD of hosts, he *is* the King of glory. Selah.

*A Psalm* of David.

**25** UNTO THEE, O LORD, do I lift up my soul.

2 O my God, I trust in thee: let me not be ashamed, let not mine enemies triumph over me.

3 Yea, let none that wait on thee be ashamed: let them be ashamed which transgress without cause.

4 Show me thy ways, O LORD; teach me thy paths.

5 Lead me in thy truth, and teach me: for thou *art* the God of my salvation; on thee do I wait all the day.

## Amplified

3 He refreshes *and* restores my life—my self; He leads me in the paths of righteousness [uprightness and right standing with Him—not for my earning it, but] for His name's sake.

4 Yes, though I walk through the [deep, sunless] valley of the shadow of death, I will fear *or* dread no evil; for You are with me; Your rod [to protect] and Your staff [to guide], they comfort me.

5 You prepare a table before me in the presence of my enemies; You anoint my head with [a]oil; my [brimming] cup runs over.

6 Surely *or* only goodness, mercy *and* unfailing love shall follow me all the days of my life; and through the length of days the house of the Lord [and His presence] shall be my dwelling place.

A Psalm of David.

**24** THE EARTH is the Lord's, and the fullness of it, the world and they who dwell in it. [I Cor. 10:26.]

2 For He has founded it upon the seas, and established it upon the currents *and* the rivers.

3 Who shall go up into the mountain of the Lord? Or who shall stand in His holy place?

4 He who has clean hands and a pure heart, who has not lifted himself up to falsehood, *or* to what is false, nor sworn deceitfully. [Matt. 5:8.]

5 He shall receive blessing from the Lord, and righteousness from the God of his salvation.

6 This is the generation [description] of those who seek Him, who inquire of *and* for Him, *and* [of necessity] require Him, who seek Your face, [O God of] Jacob. Selah [pause, and think of that]! [Ps. 42:1.]

7 Lift up your heads, O you gates; and be lifted up, you age-abiding doors; that the King of glory may come in.

8 Who is the King of glory? The Lord, strong and mighty, the Lord, mighty in battle.

9 Lift up your heads, O you gates; yes, lift them up, you age-abiding doors, that the King of glory may come in.

10 Who is [He then], this King of glory? The Lord of hosts, He is the King of glory. Selah [pause, and think of that]!

[*A Psalm*] of David.

**25** UNTO YOU, O Lord, do I bring my life.

2 O my God, I trust, lean on, rely on *and* am confident in You; let me not be put to shame *or* [my hope in You] be disappointed; let not my enemies triumph over me.

3 Yes, let none who trust *and* hopefully wait *and* look for You be put to shame *or* be disappointed; let them be ashamed who forsake the right *or* deal treacherously without cause.

4 Show me Your ways, O Lord; teach me Your paths.

5 Guide me in Your truth *and* faithfulness and teach me, for You are the God of my salvation; for You [You only and altogether] do I wait (expectantly) all the day long.

**AMP** [a] It is difficult for those living in a temperate climate to appreciate, but it was customary in hot climates to anoint the body with oil to protect it from excessive perspiration. When mixed with perfume, the oil imparted a delightfully refreshing and invigorating sensation. Athletes anointed their bodies as a matter of course before running a race. As the body, therefore, anointed with oil was refreshed, invigorated and better fitted for action, so the Lord would anoint His "sheep" with the Holy Spirit Whom oil symbolizes, to fit them to engage more freely in His service and run in the way He directs, in heavenly fellowship with Him.

## New American Standard

3 He restores my soul;
He guides me in the paths of righteousness
For His name's sake.
4¶ Even though I walk through the [b]valley of the shadow of death,
I fear no [c]evil; for Thou art with me;
Thy rod and Thy staff, they comfort me.
5 Thou dost prepare a table before me in the presence of my enemies;
Thou hast anointed my head with oil;
My cup overflows.
6 Surely goodness and lovingkindness will follow me all the days of my life,
And I will [d]dwell in the house of the LORD forever.

*The King of Glory Entering Zion.*

A Psalm of David.

**24** THE EARTH is the LORD's, and [e]all it contains,
The world, and those who dwell in it.
2 For He has founded it upon the seas,
And established it upon the rivers.
3 Who may ascend into the hill of the LORD?
And who may stand in His holy place?
4 He who has clean hands and a pure heart,
Who has not lifted up his soul to falsehood,
And has not sworn deceitfully.
5 He shall receive a blessing from the LORD
And righteousness from the God of his salvation.
6 This is the generation of those who seek Him,
Who seek Thy face— *even* Jacob. Selah.
7¶ Lift up your heads, O gates,
And be lifted up, O [f]ancient doors,
That the King of glory may come in!
8 Who is the King of glory?
The LORD strong and mighty,
The LORD mighty in battle.
9 Lift up your heads, O gates,
And lift *them* up, O [g]ancient doors,
That the King of glory may come in!
10 Who is this King of glory?
The LORD of hosts,
He is the King of glory. Selah.

*Prayer for Protection, Guidance and Pardon.*

*A Psalm* of David.

**25** TO THEE, O LORD, I lift up my soul.
2 O my God, in Thee I trust,
Do not let me be ashamed;
Do not let my enemies exult over me.
3 Indeed, none of those who wait for Thee will be ashamed;
Those who deal treacherously without cause will be ashamed.

4¶ Make me know Thy ways, O LORD;
Teach me Thy paths.
5 Lead me in Thy truth and teach me,
For Thou art the God of my salvation;
For Thee I wait all the day.

NAS [b] Or, *valley of deep darkness* [c] Or, *harm* [d] Another reading is *return to* [e] Lit., *its fulness* [f] Lit., *everlasting* [g] Lit., *everlasting*

## New International

3 he restores my soul.
He guides me in paths of righteousness
for his name's sake.
4 Even though I walk
through the valley of the shadow of death,[h]
I will fear no evil,
for you are with me;
your rod and your staff,
they comfort me.

5 You prepare a table before me
in the presence of my enemies.
You anoint my head with oil;
my cup overflows.
6 Surely goodness and love will follow me
all the days of my life,
and I will dwell in the house of the LORD
forever.

Of David. A psalm.

**24** THE EARTH is the LORD's, and everything in it,
the world, and all who live in it;
2 for he founded it upon the seas
and established it upon the waters.
3 Who may ascend the hill of the LORD?
Who may stand in his holy place?
4 He who has clean hands and a pure heart,
who does not lift up his soul to an idol
or swear by what is false.[i]
5 He will receive blessing from the LORD
and vindication from God his Savior.
6 Such is the generation of those who seek him,
who seek your face, O God of Jacob.[j] *Selah*

7 Lift up your heads, O you gates;
be lifted up, you ancient doors,
that the King of glory may come in.
8 Who is this King of glory?
The LORD strong and mighty,
the LORD mighty in battle.
9 Lift up your heads, O you gates;
lift them up, you ancient doors,
that the King of glory may come in.
10 Who is he, this King of glory?
The LORD Almighty—
he is the King of glory. *Selah*

Of David.

**25** TO[k] YOU, O LORD, I lift up my soul;
2 in you I trust, O my God.
Do not let me be put to shame,
nor let my enemies triumph over me.
3 No one whose hope is in you
will ever be put to shame,
but they will be put to shame
who are treacherous without excuse.

4 Show me your ways, O LORD,
teach me your paths;
5 guide me in your truth and teach me,
for you are God my Savior,
and my hope is in you all day long.

NIV [h] 4 Or *through the darkest valley* [i] 4 Or *swear falsely* [j] 6 Two Hebrew manuscripts and Syriac (see also Septuagint); most Hebrew manuscripts *face, Jacob* [k] This psalm is an acrostic poem, the verses of which begin with the successive letters of the Hebrew alphabet.

## King James

6 Remember, O LORD, thy tender mercies and thy lovingkindnesses; for they *have been* ever of old.

7 Remember not the sins of my youth, nor my transgressions: according to thy mercy remember thou me for thy goodness' sake, O LORD.

8 Good and upright *is* the LORD: therefore will he teach sinners in the way.

9 The meek will he guide in judgment: and the meek will he teach his way.

10 All the paths of the LORD *are* mercy and truth unto such as keep his covenant and his testimonies.

11 For thy name's sake, O LORD, pardon mine iniquity; for it *is* great.

12 What man *is* he that feareth the LORD? him shall he teach in the way *that* he shall choose.

13 His soul shall dwell at ease; and his seed shall inherit the earth.

14 The secret of the LORD *is* with them that fear him; and he will show them his covenant.

15 Mine eyes *are* ever toward the LORD; for he shall pluck my feet out of the net.

16 Turn thee unto me, and have mercy upon me; for I *am* desolate and afflicted.

17 The troubles of my heart are enlarged: O bring thou me out of my distresses.

18 Look upon mine affliction and my pain; and forgive all my sins.

19 Consider mine enemies; for they are many; and they hate me with cruel hatred.

20 O keep my soul, and deliver me: let me not be ashamed; for I put my trust in thee.

21 Let integrity and uprightness preserve me; for I wait on thee.

22 Redeem Israel, O God, out of all his troubles.

*A Psalm* of David.

**26** JUDGE ME, O LORD; for I have walked in mine integrity: I have trusted also in the LORD; *therefore* I shall not slide.

2 Examine me, O LORD, and prove me; try my reins and my heart.

3 For thy lovingkindness *is* before mine eyes: and I have walked in thy truth.

4 I have not sat with vain persons, neither will I go in with dissemblers.

5 I have hated the congregation of evildoers; and will not sit with the wicked.

6 I will wash mine hands in innocency: so will I compass thine altar, O LORD:

7 That I may publish with the voice of thanksgiving, and tell of all thy wondrous works.

8 LORD, I have loved the habitation of thy house, and the place where thine honour dwelleth.

9 Gather not my soul with sinners, nor my life with bloody men:

10 In whose hands *is* mischief, and their right hand is full of bribes.

11 But as for me, I will walk in mine integrity: redeem me, and be merciful unto me.

## Amplified

6 Remember, O Lord, Your tender mercies and loving-kindnesses; for they have been ever of old.

7 Remember not [my lapses and frailties] the sins of my youth, nor my transgressions; according to Your mercy *and* steadfast love remember me for Your goodness' sake, O Lord.

8 Good and upright is the Lord; therefore will He instruct sinners in [His] way.

9 He leads the humble in what is right, and the humble He teaches His way.

10 All the paths of the Lord are mercy *and* steadfast love, even truth *and* faithfulness are they for those who keep His covenant and His testimonies.

11 For Your name's sake, O Lord, pardon my iniquity *and* my guilt, for *they are* great.

12 Who is the man who reverently fears *and* worships the Lord? Him shall He teach in the way that he should choose.

13 He himself shall dwell at ease, and his offspring shall inherit the land.

14 The secret [of the sweet, satisfying companionship] of the Lord have they who fear—revere and worship—Him, and He will show them His covenant, *and* reveal to them its [deep, inner] meaning. [John 7:17; 15:15.]

15 My eyes are ever toward the Lord, for He will pluck my feet out of the net.

16 *Lord,* turn to me and be gracious to me, for I am lonely and afflicted.

17 The troubles of my heart are multiplied; bring me out of my distresses.

18 Behold my affliction and my pain; and forgive all my sins [of thinking and doing].

19 Consider my enemies, for they abound; they hate me with cruel hatred.

20 O keep me, Lord, and deliver me; let me not be ashamed *or* disappointed, for my trust *and* my refuge are in You.

21 Let integrity and uprightness preserve me, for I wait for *and* expect You.

22 Redeem Israel, O God, out of all his troubles.

[*A Psalm*] of David.

**26** VINDICATE ME, O Lord, for I have walked in my integrity; I have [expectantly] trusted, leaned *and* relied on the Lord without wavering, *and* I shall not slide.

2 Examine me, O Lord, and prove me; test my heart and my mind.

3 For Your loving-kindness is before my eyes, and I have walked in Your truth [faithfully].

4 I do not sit with false persons, nor fellowship with pretenders;

5 I hate the company of evildoers, and will not sit with the wicked.

6 I will wash my hands in innocence, and go about Your altar, O Lord,

7 That I may make the voice of thanksgiving to be heard, and tell of all Your wondrous works.

8 Lord, I love the habitation of Your house, and the place where Your glory dwells.

9 Gather me not with sinners *and* sweep me not away *with them,* nor my life with bloodthirsty men,

10 In whose hands *is* wickedness, and their right hand is full of bribes.

11 But as for me, I will walk in my integrity; redeem me, and be merciful *and* gracious to me.

## New American Standard

6 Remember, O LORD, Thy compassion and Thy lovingkindnesses,
For they have been [a]from of old.
7 Do not remember the sins of my youth or my transgressions;
According to Thy lovingkindness remember Thou me,
For Thy goodness' sake, O LORD.
8¶ Good and upright is the LORD;
Therefore He instructs sinners in the way.
9 He leads the humble in justice,
And He teaches the humble His way.
10 All the paths of the LORD are lovingkindness and truth
To those who keep His covenant and His testimonies.
11 For Thy name's sake, O LORD,
Pardon my iniquity, for it is great.
12¶ Who is the man who fears the LORD?
He will instruct him in the way he should choose.
13 His soul will abide in prosperity,
And his [b]descendants will inherit the land.
14 The secret of the LORD is for those who fear Him,
And He will make them know His covenant.
15 My eyes are continually toward the LORD,
For He will pluck my feet out of the net.
16¶ Turn to me and be gracious to me,
For I am lonely and afflicted.
17 The troubles of my heart are enlarged;
Bring me out of my distresses.
18 Look upon my affliction and my [c]trouble,
And forgive all my sins.
19 Look upon my enemies, for they are many;
And they hate me with violent hatred.
20 Guard my soul and deliver me;
Do not let me be ashamed, for I take refuge in Thee.
21 Let integrity and uprightness preserve me,
For I wait for Thee.
22 Redeem Israel, O God,
Out of all his troubles.

*Protestation of Integrity and Prayer for Protection.*
*A Psalm of David.*

**26** [d]VINDICATE ME, O LORD, for I have walked in my integrity;
And I have trusted in the LORD without wavering.
2 Examine me, O LORD, and try me;
Test my [e]mind and my heart.
3 For Thy lovingkindness is before my eyes,
And I have walked in Thy truth.
4 I do not sit with [f]deceitful men,
Nor will I go with pretenders.
5 I hate the assembly of evildoers,
And I will not sit with the wicked.
6 I shall wash my hands in innocence,
And I will go about Thine altar, O LORD,
7 That I may proclaim with the voice of thanksgiving,
And declare all Thy wonders.
8¶ O LORD, I love the habitation of Thy house,
And the place where Thy glory dwells.
9 Do not take my soul away *along* with sinners,
Nor my life with men of bloodshed,
10 In whose hands is a wicked scheme,
And whose right hand is full of bribes.
11 But as for me, I shall walk in my integrity;
Redeem me, and be gracious to me.

NAS [a] Lit., *everlasting* [b] Lit., *seed* [c] Lit., *toil* [d] Lit., *Judge* [e] Lit., *kidneys,* figurative for inner man [f] Or, *worthless*

## New International

6 Remember, O LORD, your great mercy and love,
for they are from of old.
7 Remember not the sins of my youth
and my rebellious ways;
according to your love remember me,
for you are good, O LORD.
8 Good and upright is the LORD;
therefore he instructs sinners in his ways.
9 He guides the humble in what is right
and teaches them his way.
10 All the ways of the LORD are loving and faithful
for those who keep the demands of his covenant.
11 For the sake of your name, O LORD,
forgive my iniquity, though it is great.
12 Who, then, is the man that fears the LORD?
He will instruct him in the way chosen for him.
13 He will spend his days in prosperity,
and his descendants will inherit the land.
14 The LORD confides in those who fear him;
he makes his covenant known to them.
15 My eyes are ever on the LORD,
for only he will release my feet from the snare.

16 Turn to me and be gracious to me,
for I am lonely and afflicted.
17 The troubles of my heart have multiplied;
free me from my anguish.
18 Look upon my affliction and my distress
and take away all my sins.
19 See how my enemies have increased
and how fiercely they hate me!
20 Guard my life and rescue me;
let me not be put to shame,
for I take refuge in you.
21 May integrity and uprightness protect me,
because my hope is in you.

22 Redeem Israel, O God,
from all their troubles!

Of David.

**26** VINDICATE ME, O LORD,
for I have led a blameless life;
I have trusted in the LORD
without wavering.
2 Test me, O LORD, and try me,
examine my heart and my mind;
3 for your love is ever before me,
and I walk continually in your truth.
4 I do not sit with deceitful men,
nor do I consort with hypocrites;
5 I abhor the assembly of evildoers
and refuse to sit with the wicked.
6 I wash my hands in innocence,
and go about your altar, O LORD,
7 proclaiming aloud your praise
and telling of all your wonderful deeds.
8 I love the house where you live, O LORD,
the place where your glory dwells.
9 Do not take away my soul along with sinners,
my life with bloodthirsty men,
10 in whose hands are wicked schemes,
whose right hands are full of bribes.
11 But I lead a blameless life;
redeem me and be merciful to me.

## King James

12My foot standeth in an even place: in the congregations will I bless the LORD.

*A Psalm* of David.

**27** THE LORD *is* my light and my salvation; whom shall I fear? the LORD *is* the strength of my life; of whom shall I be afraid?

2When the wicked, *even* mine enemies and my foes, came upon me to eat up my flesh, they stumbled and fell.

3Though an host should encamp against me, my heart shall not fear: though war should rise against me, in this *will* I *be* confident.

4One *thing* have I desired of the LORD, that will I seek after; that I may dwell in the house of the LORD all the days of my life, to behold the beauty of the LORD, and to inquire in his temple.

5For in the time of trouble he shall hide me in his pavilion: in the secret of his tabernacle shall he hide me; he shall set me up upon a rock.

6And now shall mine head be lifted up above mine enemies round about me: therefore will I offer in his tabernacle sacrifices of joy; I will sing, yea, I will sing praises unto the LORD.

7Hear, O LORD, *when* I cry with my voice: have mercy also upon me, and answer me.

8 *When thou saidst,* Seek ye my face; my heart said unto thee, Thy face, LORD, will I seek.

9Hide not thy face *far* from me; put not thy servant away in anger: thou hast been my help; leave me not, neither forsake me, O God of my salvation.

10When my father and my mother forsake me, then the LORD will take me up.

11Teach me thy way, O LORD, and lead me in a plain path, because of mine enemies.

12Deliver me not over unto the will of mine enemies: for false witnesses are risen up against me, and such as breathe out cruelty.

13 *I had fainted,* unless I had believed to see the goodness of the LORD in the land of the living.

14Wait on the LORD: be of good courage, and he shall strengthen thine heart: wait, I say, on the LORD.

*A Psalm* of David.

**28** UNTO THEE will I cry, O LORD my rock; be not silent to me: lest, *if* thou be silent to me, I become like them that go down into the pit.

## Amplified

12My foot stands on an even place; in the congregations will I bless the Lord.

[ *A Psalm*] of David.

**27** THE LORD is my light and my salvation; whom shall I fear *or* dread? The Lord is the refuge *and* stronghold of my life; of whom shall I be afraid?

2When the wicked, even my enemies and my foes, came upon me to eat up my flesh, they stumbled and fell.

3Though a host encamp against me, my heart shall not fear; though war arise against me, (even then) in this will I be confident.

4One thing have I asked of the Lord, that will I seek after, inquire for *and* [insistently] require, that I may dwell in the house of the Lord [in His presence] all the days of my life, to behold *and* gaze upon the beauty [the sweet attractiveness and the delightful loveliness] of the Lord, and to meditate, consider *and* inquire in His temple. [Pss. 65:4; 18:6; 16:11; Luke 2:37.]

5For in the day of trouble He will hide me in His shelter; in the secret place of His tent will He hide me; He will set me high upon a rock.

6And now shall my head be lifted up above my enemies round about me; in His tent I will offer sacrifices *and* shouting of joy; I will sing, yes, I will sing praises to the Lord.

7Hear, O Lord, when I cry aloud; have mercy *and* be gracious to me and answer me!

8You have said, Seek you My face—inquire for and require My presence [as your vital need]. My heart says to You, Your face [Your presence], Lord, will I seek, inquire for *and* require [of necessity and on the authority of Your Word].

9Hide not Your face from me; turn not Your servant away in anger, You Who have been my help! Cast me not off, neither forsake me, O God of my salvation!

10Although my father and my mother have forsaken me, yet the Lord will take me up [adopt me as His child]. [Ps. 22:10.]

11Teach me Your way, O Lord, and lead me in a plain *and* even path because of my enemies—those who lie in wait for me.

12Give me not up to the will of my adversaries; for false witnesses have risen up against me; they breathe out cruelty *and* violence.

13[What, what would have become of me] had I not believed to see the Lord's goodness in the land of the living!

14Wait *and* hope for *and* expect the Lord; be brave *and* of good courage, and let your heart be stout *and* enduring. Yes, wait *and* hope for *and* expect the Lord.

[ *A Psalm*] of David.

**28** UNTO YOU do I cry, O Lord; my rock, be not deaf *and* silent to me; lest, if You be silent to me, I become like those going down to the pit [the grave].

## New American Standard

12 My foot stands on a level place;
In the congregations I shall bless the LORD.

*A Psalm of Fearless Trust in God.*
*A Psalm* of David.

**27** THE LORD is my light and my salvation;
Whom shall I fear?
The LORD is the defense of my life;
Whom shall I dread?
2 When evildoers came upon me to devour my flesh,
My adversaries and my enemies, they stumbled and fell.
3 Though a host encamp against me,
My heart will not fear;
Though war arise against me,
In *spite of* this I shall be confident.
4¶ One thing I have asked from the LORD, that I shall seek:
That I may dwell in the house of the LORD all the days of my life,
To behold the [a]beauty of the LORD,
And to [b]meditate in His temple.
5 For in the day of trouble He will conceal me in His tabernacle;
In the secret place of His tent He will hide me;
He will lift me up on a rock.
6 And now my head will be lifted up above my enemies around me;
And I will offer in His tent sacrifices with shouts of joy;
I will sing, yes, I will sing praises to the LORD.
7¶ Hear, O LORD, when I cry with my voice,
And be gracious to me and answer me.
8 *When Thou didst say,* "Seek My face," my heart said to Thee,
"Thy face, O LORD, I shall seek."
9 Do not hide Thy face from me,
Do not turn Thy servant away in anger;
Thou hast been my help;
Do not abandon me nor for sake me,
O God of my salvation!
10 For my father and my mother have forsaken me,
But the LORD will take me up.
11¶ Teach me Thy way, O LORD,
And lead me in a level path,
Because of my foes.
12 Do not deliver me over to the desire of my adversaries;
For false witnesses have risen against me,
And such as breathe out violence.
13 *I would have despaired* unless I had believed that I would see the goodness of the LORD
In the land of the living.
14 Wait for the LORD;
Be strong, and let your heart take courage;
Yes, wait for the LORD.

*A Prayer for Help, and Praise for Its Answer.*
*A Psalm* of David.

**28** TO THEE, O LORD, I call;
My rock, do not be deaf to me,
Lest, if Thou be silent to me,
I become like those who go down to the pit.

NAS [a] Lit., *delightfulness* [b] Lit., *inquire*

## New International

12 My feet stand on level ground;
in the great assembly I will praise the LORD.

Of David.

**27** THE LORD is my light and my salvation—
whom shall I fear?
The LORD is the stronghold of my life—
of whom shall I be afraid?
2 When evil men advance against me
to devour my flesh,[c]
when my enemies and my foes attack me,
they will stumble and fall.
3 Though an army besiege me,
my heart will not fear;
though war break out against me,
even then will I be confident.

4 One thing I ask of the LORD,
this is what I seek:
that I may dwell in the house of the LORD
all the days of my life,
to gaze upon the beauty of the LORD
and to seek him in his temple.
5 For in the day of trouble
he will keep me safe in his dwelling;
he will hide me in the shelter of his tabernacle
and set me high upon a rock.
6 Then my head will be exalted
above the enemies who surround me;
at his tabernacle will I sacrifice with shouts of joy;
I will sing and make music to the LORD.

7 Hear my voice when I call, O LORD;
be merciful to me and answer me.
8 My heart says of you, "Seek his[d] face!"
Your face, LORD, I will seek.
9 Do not hide your face from me,
do not turn your servant away in anger;
you have been my helper.
Do not reject me or forsake me,
O God my Savior.
10 Though my father and mother forsake me,
the LORD will receive me.
11 Teach me your way, O LORD;
lead me in a straight path
because of my oppressors.
12 Do not turn me over to the desire of my foes,
for false witnesses rise up against me,
breathing out violence.

13 I am still confident of this:
I will see the goodness of the LORD
in the land of the living.
14 Wait for the LORD;
be strong and take heart
and wait for the LORD.

Of David.

**28** TO YOU I call, O LORD my Rock;
do not turn a deaf ear to me.
For if you remain silent,
I will be like those who have gone down to the pit.

NIV [c] 2 Or *to slander me* [d] 8 Or *To you, O my heart, he has said, "Seek my*

## King James

2Hear the voice of my supplications, when I cry unto thee, when I lift up my hands toward thy holy oracle.

3Draw me not away with the wicked, and with the workers of iniquity, which speak peace to their neighbours, but mischief *is* in their hearts.

4Give them according to their deeds, and according to the wickedness of their endeavours: give them after the work of their hands; render to them their desert.

5Because they regard not the works of the LORD, nor the operation of his hands, he shall destroy them, and not build them up.

6Blessed *be* the LORD, because he hath heard the voice of my supplications.

7The LORD *is* my strength and my shield; my heart trusted in him, and I am helped: therefore my heart greatly rejoiceth; and with my song will I praise him.

8The LORD *is* their strength, and he *is* the saving strength of his anointed.

9Save thy people, and bless thine inheritance: feed them also, and lift them up for ever.

A Psalm of David.

**29** GIVE UNTO the LORD, O ye mighty, give unto the LORD glory and strength.

2Give unto the LORD the glory due unto his name; worship the LORD in the beauty of holiness.

3The voice of the LORD *is* upon the waters: the God of glory thundereth: the LORD *is* upon many waters.

4The voice of the LORD *is* powerful; the voice of the LORD *is* full of majesty.

5The voice of the LORD breaketh the cedars; yea, the LORD breaketh the cedars of Lebanon.

6He maketh them also to skip like a calf; Lebanon and Sirion like a young unicorn.

7The voice of the LORD divideth the flames of fire.

8The voice of the LORD shaketh the wilderness; the LORD shaketh the wilderness of Kadesh.

9The voice of the LORD maketh the hinds to calve, and discovereth the forests: and in his temple doth every one speak of *his* glory.

10The LORD sitteth upon the flood; yea, the LORD sitteth King for ever.

11The LORD will give strength unto his people; the LORD will bless his people with peace.

A Psalm *and* Song *at* the dedication of the house of David.

**30** I WILL extol thee, O LORD; for thou hast lifted me up, and hast not made my foes to rejoice over me.

2O LORD my God, I cried unto thee, and thou hast healed me.

3O LORD, thou hast brought up my soul from the grave: thou hast kept me alive, that I should not go down to the pit.

## Amplified

2Hear the voice of my supplication, as I cry to You for help, as I lift up my hands toward Your innermost sanctuary [the holy of holies].

3Drag me not away with the wicked, with the workers of iniquity, who speak peace with their neighbors, but malice *and* mischief are in their hearts.

4Repay them according to their work, and according to the wickedness of their doings; repay them according to the work of their hands; render to them what they deserve. [II Tim. 4:14; Rev. 18:6.]

5Because they regard not the works of the Lord, nor the operation of His hands, He will break them down and not rebuild them.

6Blessed be the Lord, because He has heard the voice of my supplications.

7The Lord is my strength and my [impenetrable] shield; my heart trusts, relies on *and* confidently leans on Him, and I am helped; therefore my heart greatly rejoices, and with my song will I praise Him.

8The Lord is their [unyielding] strength, and He is the stronghold of salvation to [me] His anointed.

9Save Your people and bless Your heritage; nourish *and* shepherd them and carry them for ever.

A Psalm of David.

**29**[a] ASCRIBE TO the Lord, O sons of the mighty, ascribe to the Lord glory and strength.

2Give to the Lord the glory due to His name; worship the Lord in the beauty of holiness *or* in holy array.

3The voice of the Lord is upon the waters; the God of glory thunders; the Lord is upon many (great) waters.

4The voice of the Lord is powerful; the voice of the Lord is full of majesty.

5The voice of the Lord breaks the cedars; yes, the Lord breaks in pieces the cedars of Lebanon.

6He makes them also to skip like a calf; Lebanon and Sirion [Mount Hermon] like a young, wild ox.

7The voice of the Lord splits *and* flashes forth forked lightning.

8The voice of the Lord makes the wilderness tremble; the Lord shakes the wilderness of Kadesh.

9The voice of the Lord makes the hinds to bring forth their young, and it strips bare the forests, while in His temple every one is saying, Glory!

10The Lord sat as King over the deluge; the Lord [still] sits as King [and] forever!

11The Lord will give [unyielding and impenetrable] strength to His people; the Lord will bless His people with peace.

A Psalm; a Song at the Dedication of the Temple. [ *A Psalm*] of David.

**30** I WILL extol You, O Lord, for You have lifted me up, and have not let my foes rejoice over me.

2O Lord my God, I cried to You and You have healed me.

3O Lord, You have brought my life up from Sheol [the place of the dead]; You have kept me alive, that I should not go down to the pit [the grave].

**AMP** [a] This psalm has been called "The Song of the Thunderstorm," a glorious psalm of praise sung during an earthshaking tempest, that reminds the psalmist of the time of Noah and the deluge (v. 10).

## New American Standard

2 Hear the voice of my supplications when I cry to Thee
for help,
When I lift up my hands toward [b]Thy holy sanctuary.
3 Do not drag me away with the wicked
And with those who work iniquity;
Who speak peace with their neighbors,
While evil is in their hearts.
4 Requite them according to their work and according to
the evil of their practices;
Requite them according to the deeds of their hands;
Repay them their [c]recompense.
5 Because they do not regard the works of the LORD
Nor the deeds of His hands,
He will tear them down and not build them up.

6¶ Blessed be the LORD,
Because He has heard the voice of my supplication.
7 The LORD is my strength and my shield;
My heart trusts in Him, and I am helped;
Therefore my heart exults,
And with my song I shall thank Him.
8 The LORD is their strength,
And He is a saving defense to His anointed.
9 Save Thy people, and bless Thine inheritance;
Be their shepherd also, and carry them forever.

*The Voice of the LORD in the Storm.*

A Psalm of David.

29 ASCRIBE TO the LORD, O sons of the mighty,
Ascribe to the LORD glory and strength.
2 Ascribe to the LORD the glory due to His name;
Worship the LORD in holy array.

3¶ The voice of the LORD is upon the waters;
The God of glory thunders,
The LORD is over many waters.
4 The voice of the LORD is powerful,
The voice of the LORD is majestic.
5 The voice of the LORD breaks the cedars;
Yes, the LORD breaks in pieces the cedars of Lebanon.
6 And He makes Lebanon skip like a calf,
And Sirion like a young wild ox.
7 The voice of the LORD hews out flames of fire.
8 The voice of the LORD shakes the wilderness;
The LORD shakes the wilderness of Kadesh.
9 The voice of the LORD makes the deer to calve,
And strips the forests bare,
And in His temple everything says, "Glory!"

10¶ The LORD sat *as King* at the flood;
Yes, the LORD sits as King forever.
11 The LORD will give strength to His people;
The LORD will bless His people with peace.

*Thanksgiving for Deliverance from Death.*

A Psalm; a Song at the Dedication of the House. *A Psalm* of David.

30 I WILL extol Thee, O LORD, for Thou hast lifted me up,
And hast not let my enemies rejoice over me.
2 O LORD my God,
I cried to Thee for help, and Thou didst heal me.
3 O LORD, Thou hast brought up my soul from Sheol;
Thou hast kept me alive, that I should not go down to
the pit.

NAS [b] Lit., *the innermost place of Thy sanctuary* [c] Or, *dealings*

## New International

2 Hear my cry for mercy
as I call to you for help,
as I lift up my hands
toward your Most Holy Place.

3 Do not drag me away with the wicked,
with those who do evil,
who speak cordially with their neighbors
but harbor malice in their hearts.
4 Repay them for their deeds
and for their evil work;
repay them for what their hands have done
and bring back upon them what they deserve.
5 Since they show no regard for the works of the LORD
and what his hands have done,
he will tear them down
and never build them up again.

6 Praise be to the LORD,
for he has heard my cry for mercy.
7 The LORD is my strength and my shield;
my heart trusts in him, and I am helped.
My heart leaps for joy
and I will give thanks to him in song.

8 The LORD is the strength of his people,
a fortress of salvation for his anointed one.
9 Save your people and bless your inheritance;
be their shepherd and carry them forever.

A psalm of David.

29 ASCRIBE TO the LORD, O mighty ones,
ascribe to the LORD glory and strength.
2 Ascribe to the LORD the glory due his name;
worship the LORD in the splendor of his[d] holiness.

3 The voice of the LORD is over the waters;
the God of glory thunders,
the LORD thunders over the mighty waters.
4 The voice of the LORD is powerful;
the voice of the LORD is majestic.
5 The voice of the LORD breaks the cedars;
the LORD breaks in pieces the cedars of Lebanon.
6 He makes Lebanon skip like a calf,
Sirion[e] like a young wild ox.
7 The voice of the LORD strikes
with flashes of lightning.
8 The voice of the LORD shakes the desert;
the LORD shakes the Desert of Kadesh.
9 The voice of the LORD twists the oaks[f]
and strips the forests bare.
And in his temple all cry, "Glory!"

10 The LORD sits[g] enthroned over the flood;
the LORD is enthroned as King forever.
11 The LORD gives strength to his people;
the LORD blesses his people with peace.

A psalm. A song. For the dedication of the temple.[h] Of David.

30 I WILL exalt you, O LORD,
for you lifted me out of the depths
and did not let my enemies gloat over me.
2 O LORD my God, I called to you for help
and you healed me.
3 O LORD, you brought me up from the grave[i];
you spared me from going down into the pit.

NIV [d] 2 Or *LORD with the splendor of* [e] 6 That is, Mount Hermon [f] 9 Or *LORD makes the deer give birth* [g] 10 Or *sat* [h] Title: Or *palace* [i] 3 Hebrew *Sheol*

## King James

4Sing unto the LORD, O ye saints of his, and give thanks at the remembrance of his holiness.
5For his anger *endureth but* a moment; in his favour *is* life: weeping may endure for a night, but joy *cometh* in the morning.
6And in my prosperity I said, I shall never be moved.
7LORD, by thy favour thou hast made my mountain to stand strong: thou didst hide thy face, *and* I was troubled.
8I cried to thee, O LORD; and unto the LORD I made supplication.
9What profit *is there* in my blood, when I go down to the pit? Shall the dust praise thee? shall it declare thy truth?
10Hear, O LORD, and have mercy upon me: LORD, be thou my helper.
11Thou hast turned for me my mourning into dancing: thou hast put off my sackcloth, and girded me with gladness;
12To the end that *my* glory may sing praise to thee, and not be silent. O LORD my God, I will give thanks unto thee for ever.

## Amplified

4Sing to the Lord, O you saints of His, and give thanks at the remembrance of His holy name.
5For His anger is but for a moment, but His favor is for a lifetime *or* in His favor is life. Weeping may endure for a night, but joy comes in the morning. [II Cor. 4:17.]
6As for me, in my prosperity I said, I shall never be moved.
7By Your favor, O Lord, You have established me as a strong mountain; You hid Your face, and I was troubled.
8I cried to You, O Lord, and to the Lord I made supplication.
9What profit is there in my blood, when I go down to the pit [the grave]? Will the dust praise You? Will it declare Your truth *and* faithfulness to men?
10Hear, O Lord, have mercy *and* be gracious to me! O Lord, be my helper!
11You have turned my mourning into dancing for me; You have put off my sackcloth and girded me with gladness,
12To the end that *my* tongue *and* my heart *and* everything glorious within me may sing praise to You, and not be silent. O Lord my God, I will give thanks to You for ever.

### King James

To the chief Musician, A Psalm of David.

**31** IN THEE, O LORD, do I put my trust; let me never be ashamed: deliver me in thy righteousness.
2Bow down thine ear to me; deliver me speedily: be thou my strong rock, for an house of defence to save me.
3For thou *art* my rock and my fortress; therefore for thy name's sake lead me, and guide me.
4Pull me out of the net that they have laid privily for me: for thou *art* my strength.
5Into thine hand I commit my spirit: thou hast redeemed me, O LORD God of truth.
6I have hated them that regard lying vanities: but I trust in the LORD.
7I will be glad and rejoice in thy mercy: for thou hast considered my trouble; thou hast known my soul in adversities;
8And hast not shut me up into the hand of the enemy: thou hast set my feet in a large room.
9Have mercy upon me, O LORD, for I am in trouble: mine eye is consumed with grief, *yea,* my soul and my belly.
10For my life is spent with grief, and my years with sighing: my strength faileth because of mine iniquity, and my bones are consumed.
11I was a reproach among all mine enemies, but especially among my neighbours, and a fear to mine acquaintance: they that did see me without fled from me.
12I am forgotten as a dead man out of mind: I am like a broken vessel.
13For I have heard the slander of many: fear *was* on every side: while they took counsel together against me, they devised to take away my life.

### Amplified

To the Chief Musician. A Psalm of David.

**31** IN YOU, O Lord, do I put my trust *and* seek refuge; let me never be put to shame *or* [have my hope in You] disappointed; deliver me in Your righteousness!
2Bow down Your ear to me, deliver me speedily! Be my rock of refuge, a strong fortress to save me!
3Yes, You are my rock and my fortress; therefore for Your name's sake lead me and guide me.
4Draw me out of the net that they have laid secretly for me; for You are my strength *and* my stronghold.
5Into Your hand I commit my spirit; You have redeemed me, O Lord God of truth *and* faithfulness. [Luke 23:46; Acts 7:59.]
6[You and] I abhor those who pay regard to vain idols; but I trust, rely on *and* confidently lean on the Lord.
7I will be glad and rejoice in Your mercy *and* steadfast love, because You have seen my affliction, You have taken note of my life in distresses,
8And You have not given me into the hand of the enemy; You have set my feet in a broad place.
9Have mercy *and* be gracious unto me, O Lord, for I am in trouble; with grief my eye is weakened, also my inner self and my body.
10For my life is spent with sorrow, and my years with sighing; my strength has failed because of my iniquity; even my bones have wasted away.
11To all my enemies I have become a reproach, but especially to my neighbors, and a dread to my acquaintances, who flee from me on the street.
12I am forgotten like a dead man, and out of mind; like a broken vessel am I.
13For I have heard the slander of many, terror on every side! While they schemed together against me, they plotted to take my life.

## New American Standard

4 Sing praise to the LORD, you His godly ones,
And give thanks to His holy name.
5 For His anger is but for a moment,
His favor is for a lifetime;
Weeping may last for the night,
But a shout of joy *comes* in the morning.

6¶ Now as for me, I said in my prosperity,
"I will never be moved."
7 O LORD, by Thy favor Thou hast made my mountain to stand strong;
Thou didst hide Thy face, I was dismayed.
8 To Thee, O LORD, I called,
And to the LORD I made supplication:
9 "What profit is there in my blood, if I go down to the pit?
Will the dust praise Thee? Will it declare Thy faithfulness?

10¶ "Hear, O LORD, and be gracious to me;
O LORD, be Thou my helper."
11 Thou hast turned for me my mourning into dancing;
Thou hast loosed my sackcloth and girded me with gladness;
12 That *my* soul may sing praise to Thee, and not be silent.
O LORD my God, I will give thanks to Thee forever.

*A Psalm of Complaint and of Praise.*

For the choir director.—A Psalm of David.

31 IN THEE, O LORD, I have taken refuge;
Let me never be ashamed;
In Thy righteousness deliver me.
2 Incline Thine ear to me, rescue me quickly;
Be Thou to me a rock of strength,
A stronghold to save me.
3 For Thou art my rock and my fortress;
For Thy name's sake Thou wilt lead me and guide me.
4 Thou wilt pull me out of the net which they have secretly laid for me;
For Thou art my strength.
5 Into Thy hand I commit my spirit;
Thou hast ransomed me, O LORD, God of truth.

6¶ I hate those who regard vain idols;
But I trust in the LORD.
7 I will rejoice and be glad in Thy lovingkindness,
Because Thou hast seen my affliction;
Thou hast known the troubles of my soul,
8 And Thou hast not given me over into the hand of the enemy;
Thou hast set my feet in a large place.

9¶ Be gracious to me, O LORD, for I am in distress;
My eye is wasted away from grief, my soul and my body *also.*
10 For my life is spent with sorrow,
And my years with sighing;
My strength has failed be cause of my iniquity,
And my body has wasted away.
11 Because of all my adversaries, I have become a reproach,
Especially to my neighbors,
And an object of dread to my acquaintances;
Those who see me in the street flee from me.
12 I am forgotten as a dead man, out of mind,
I am like a broken vessel.
13 For I have heard the slander of many,
Terror is on every side;
While they took counsel together against me,
They schemed to take away my life.

## New International

4Sing to the LORD, you saints of his;
praise his holy name.
5For his anger lasts only a moment,
but his favor lasts a lifetime;
weeping may remain for a night,
but rejoicing comes in the morning.
6When I felt secure, I said,
"I will never be shaken."
7O LORD, when you favored me,
you made my mountain[a] stand firm;
but when you hid your face,
I was dismayed.
8To you, O LORD, I called;
to the Lord I cried for mercy:
9"What gain is there in my destruction,[b]
in my going down into the pit?
Will the dust praise you?
Will it proclaim your faithfulness?
10Hear, O LORD, and be merciful to me;
O LORD, be my help."
11You turned my wailing into dancing;
you removed my sackcloth and clothed me with joy,
12that my heart may sing to you and not be silent.
O LORD my God, I will give you thanks forever.

For the director of music. A psalm of David.

31 IN YOU, O LORD, I have taken refuge;
let me never be put to shame;
deliver me in your righteousness.
2Turn your ear to me,
come quickly to my rescue;
be my rock of refuge,
a strong fortress to save me.
3Since you are my rock and my fortress,
for the sake of your name lead and guide me.
4Free me from the trap that is set for me,
for you are my refuge.
5Into your hands I commit my spirit;
redeem me, O LORD, the God of truth.
6I hate those who cling to worthless idols;
I trust in the LORD.
7I will be glad and rejoice in your love,
for you saw my affliction
and knew the anguish of my soul.
8You have not handed me over to the enemy
but have set my feet in a spacious place.
9Be merciful to me, O LORD, for I am in distress;
my eyes grow weak with sorrow,
my soul and my body with grief.
10My life is consumed by anguish
and my years by groaning;
my strength fails because of my affliction,[c]
and my bones grow weak.
11Because of all my enemies,
I am the utter contempt of my neighbors;
I am a dread to my friends—
those who see me on the street flee from me.
12I am forgotten by them as though I were dead;
I have become like broken pottery.
13For I hear the slander of many;
there is terror on every side;
they conspire against me
and plot to take my life.

NIV [a] 7 Or *hill country* [b] 9 Or *there if I am silenced* [c] 10 Or *guilt*

## King James

14But I trusted in thee, O LORD: I said, Thou *art* my God.

15My times *are* in thy hand: deliver me from the hand of mine enemies, and from them that persecute me.

16Make thy face to shine upon thy servant: save me for thy mercies' sake.

17Let me not be ashamed, O LORD; for I have called upon thee: let the wicked be ashamed, *and* let them be silent in the grave.

18Let the lying lips be put to silence; which speak grievous things proudly and contemptuously against the righteous.

19 *Oh* how great *is* thy goodness, which thou hast laid up for them that fear thee; *which* thou hast wrought for them that trust in thee before the sons of men!

20Thou shalt hide them in the secret of thy presence from the pride of man: thou shalt keep them secretly in a pavilion from the strife of tongues.

21Blessed *be* the LORD: for he hath shown me his marvellous kindness in a strong city.

22For I said in my haste, I am cut off from before thine eyes: nevertheless thou heardest the voice of my supplications when I cried unto thee.

23O love the LORD, all ye his saints: *for* the LORD preserveth the faithful, and plentifully rewardeth the proud doer.

24Be of good courage, and he shall strengthen your heart, all ye that hope in the LORD.

*A Psalm* of David, Maschil.

**32** BLESSED *IS he whose* transgression *is* forgiven, *whose* sin *is* covered.

2Blessed *is* the man unto whom the LORD imputeth not iniquity, and in whose spirit *there is* no guile.

3When I kept silence, my bones waxed old through my roaring all the day long.

4For day and night thy hand was heavy upon me: my moisture is turned into the drought of summer. Selah.

5I acknowledged my sin unto thee, and mine iniquity have I not hid. I said, I will confess my transgressions unto the LORD; and thou forgavest the iniquity of my sin. Selah.

6For this shall every one that is godly pray unto thee in a time when thou mayest be found: surely in the floods of great waters they shall not come nigh unto him.

7Thou *art* my hiding place; thou shalt preserve me from trouble; thou shalt compass me about with songs of deliverance. Selah.

## Amplified

14But I trusted, relied on *and* was confident in You, O Lord; I said, You are my God.

15My times are in Your hand; deliver me from the hand of my foes and those who pursue me *and* persecute me.

16Let Your face shine on Your servant; save me for Your mercy's sake *and* in Your loving-kindness.

17Let me not be put to shame, O Lord, *or* disappointed; for I am calling upon You; let the wicked be put to shame, let them be silent in Sheol [the place of the dead].

18Let the lying lips be silenced, which speak insolently against the [consistently] righteous, with pride and contempt.

19Oh, how great is Your goodness, which You have laid up for those who fear, revere *and* worship You, goodness which You have wrought for those who trust *and* take refuge in You before the sons of men!

20In the secret of Your presence You hide them from the plots of men; You keep them secretly in Your pavilion from the strife of tongues.

21Blessed be the Lord! For He has shown me His marvelous loving favor when beset as in a besieged city.

22As for me, I said in my haste *and* alarm, I am cut off from before Your eyes. But You heard the voice of my supplications when I cried to You for aid.

23O love the Lord, all you His saints; the Lord preserves the faithful, and plentifully pays back him who deals haughtily.

24Be strong and let your heart take courage, all you who wait *and* hope for *and* expect the Lord!

[*A Psalm of David.*] A skillful song, *or* a didactic *or* reflective poem.

**32** BLESSED—HAPPY, fortunate [to be envied]—is he who has forgiveness of his transgression continually exercised upon him, whose sin is covered.

2Blessed—happy, fortunate [to be envied]—is the man to whom the Lord imputes no iniquity, and in whose spirit there is no deceit. [Rom. 4:7, 8.]

3When I kept silence [before I confessed], my bones wasted away through my groaning all the day long.

4For day and night Your hand [of displeasure] was heavy upon me; my moisture was turned into the drought of summer. Selah [pause, and calmly think of that]!

5I acknowledged my sin to You, and my iniquity I did not hide. I said, I will confess my transgressions to the Lord [continually unfolding the past till all is told], then You [instantly] forgave me the guilt *and* iniquity of my sin. Selah [pause, and calmly think of that]!

6For this [forgiveness] let every one who is godly pray; pray to You in a time when You may be found; surely when the great waters [of trial] overflow they shall not reach [the spirit in] him.

7You are a hiding place for me; You, Lord, preserve me from trouble; You surround me with songs *and* shouts of deliverance. Selah [pause, and think calmly of that]!

## New American Standard

14¶ But as for me, I trust in Thee, O LORD,
I say, "Thou art my God."
15 My times are in Thy hand;
Deliver me from the hand of my enemies, and from those who persecute me.
16 Make Thy face to shine upon Thy servant;
Save me in Thy lovingkindness.
17 Let me not be put to shame, O LORD, for I call upon Thee;
Let the wicked be put to shame, let them be silent in Sheol.
18 Let the lying lips be dumb,
Which speak arrogantly against the righteous
With pride and contempt.

19¶ How great is Thy goodness,
Which Thou hast stored up for those who fear Thee,
Which Thou hast wrought for those who take refuge in Thee,
Before the sons of men!
20 Thou dost hide them in the secret place of Thy presence from the conspiracies of man;
Thou dost keep them secretly in a shelter from the strife of tongues.
21 Blessed be the LORD,
For He has made marvelous His lovingkindness to me in a besieged city.
22 As for me, I said in my alarm,
"I am cut off from before Thine eyes";
Nevertheless Thou didst hear the voice of my supplications
When I cried to Thee.

23¶ O love the LORD, all you His godly ones!
The LORD preserves the faithful,
And fully recompenses the proud doer.
24 Be strong, and let your heart take courage,
All you who hope in the LORD.

*Blessedness of Forgiveness and of Trust in God.*

*A Psalm* of David. A [a]Maskil.

32 HOW BLESSED is he whose transgression is forgiven,
Whose sin is covered!
2 How blessed is the man to whom the LORD does not impute iniquity,
And in whose spirit there is no deceit!

3¶ When I kept silent *about my sin*, my body wasted away
Through my groaning all day long.
4 For day and night Thy hand was heavy upon me;
My vitality was drained away *as* with the fever heat of summer. Selah.
5 I acknowledged my sin to Thee,
And my iniquity I did not hide;
I said, "I will confess my transgressions to the LORD";
And Thou didst forgive the guilt of my sin. Selah.
6 Therefore, let everyone who is godly pray to Thee in a time when Thou mayest be found;
Surely in a flood of great waters they shall not reach him.
7 Thou art my hiding place; Thou dost preserve me from trouble;
Thou dost surround me with songs of deliverance. Selah.

NAS [a] Possibly, *Contemplative* or *Didactic*, or *Skillful Psalm*

## New International

14But I trust in you, O LORD;
I say, "You are my God."
15My times are in your hands;
deliver me from my enemies
and from those who pursue me.
16Let your face shine on your servant;
save me in your unfailing love.
17Let me not be put to shame, O LORD,
for I have cried out to you;
but let the wicked be put to shame
and lie silent in the grave.[b]
18Let their lying lips be silenced,
for with pride and contempt
they speak arrogantly against the righteous.

19How great is your goodness,
which you have stored up for those who fear you,
which you bestow in the sight of men
on those who take refuge in you.
20In the shelter of your presence you hide them
from the intrigues of men;
in your dwelling you keep them safe
from accusing tongues.
21Praise be to the LORD,
for he showed his wonderful love to me
when I was in a besieged city.
22In my alarm I said,
"I am cut off from your sight!"
Yet you heard my cry for mercy
when I called to you for help.
23Love the LORD, all his saints!
The LORD preserves the faithful,
but the proud he pays back in full.
24Be strong and take heart,
all you who hope in the LORD.

Of David. A *maskil*.[c]

32 BLESSED IS he
whose transgressions are forgiven,
whose sins are covered.
2Blessed is the man
whose sin the LORD does not count against him
and in whose spirit is no deceit.

3When I kept silent,
my bones wasted away
through my groaning all day long.
4For day and night
your hand was heavy upon me;
my strength was sapped
as in the heat of summer. *Selah*
5Then I acknowledged my sin to you
and did not cover up my iniquity.
I said, "I will confess
my transgressions to the LORD"—
and you forgave
the guilt of my sin. *Selah*

6Therefore let everyone who is godly pray to you
while you may be found;
surely when the mighty waters rise,
they will not reach him.
7You are my hiding place;
you will protect me from trouble
and surround me with songs of deliverance. *Selah*

NIV [b] *17* Hebrew *Sheol* [c] Title: Probably a literary or musical term

## King James

8I will instruct thee and teach thee in the way which thou shalt go: I will guide thee with mine eye.

9Be ye not as the horse, *or* as the mule, *which* have no understanding: whose mouth must be held in with bit and bridle, lest they come near unto thee.

10Many sorrows *shall be* to the wicked: but he that trusteth in the LORD, mercy shall compass him about.

11Be glad in the LORD, and rejoice, ye righteous: and shout for joy, all *ye that are* upright in heart.

**33** REJOICE IN the LORD, O ye righteous: *for* praise is comely for the upright.

2Praise the LORD with harp: sing unto him with the psaltery *and* an instrument of ten strings.

3Sing unto him a new song; play skilfully with a loud noise.

4For the word of the LORD *is* right; and all his works *are done* in truth.

5He loveth righteousness and judgment: the earth is full of the goodness of the LORD.

6By the word of the LORD were the heavens made; and all the host of them by the breath of his mouth.

7He gathereth the waters of the sea together as an heap: he layeth up the depth in storehouses.

8Let all the earth fear the LORD: let all the inhabitants of the world stand in awe of him.

9For he spake, and it was *done;* he commanded, and it stood fast.

10The LORD bringeth the counsel of the heathen to nought: he maketh the devices of the people of none effect.

11The counsel of the LORD standeth for ever, the thoughts of his heart to all generations.

12Blessed *is* the nation whose God *is* the LORD; *and* the people *whom* he hath chosen for his own inheritance.

13The LORD looketh from heaven; he beholdeth all the sons of men.

14From the place of his habitation he looketh upon all the inhabitants of the earth.

15He fashioneth their hearts alike; he considereth all their works.

16There is no king saved by the multitude of an host: a mighty man is not delivered by much strength.

17An horse *is* a vain thing for safety: neither shall he deliver *any* by his great strength.

18Behold, the eye of the LORD *is* upon them that fear him, upon them that hope in his mercy;

19To deliver their soul from death, and to keep them alive in famine.

20Our soul waiteth for the LORD: he *is* our help and our shield.

21For our heart shall rejoice in him, because we have trusted in his holy name.

22Let thy mercy, O LORD, be upon us, according as we hope in thee.

## Amplified

8I, *the Lord,* will instruct you and teach you in the way you should go; I will counsel you with My eye upon you.

9Be not like the horse or the mule, which lack understanding; which must have their mouths held firm with bit and bridle, else they will not come with you.

10Many are the sorrows of the wicked, but he who trusts, relies on *and* confidently leans on the Lord shall be compassed about with mercy *and* with loving-kindness.

11Be glad in the Lord, and rejoice, you [uncompromisingly] righteous—you who are upright and in right standing with Him; shout for joy, all you upright in heart!

**33** REJOICE IN the Lord, O you [uncompromisingly] righteous [you upright, in right standing with God]; *for* praise is becoming *and* appropriate for those who are upright *in heart.*

2Give thanks to the Lord with the lyre, sing praises to Him with the harp of ten strings.

3Sing to Him a new song; play skillfully [on the strings] with a loud *and* joyful sound.

4For the word of the Lord *is* right; and all His work *is* done in faithfulness.

5He loves righteousness and justice; the earth is full of the loving-kindness of the Lord.

6By the word of the Lord were the heavens made, and all their host by the breath of His mouth. [Heb. 11:3; II Pet. 3:5.]

7He gathers the waters of the sea as in a bottle; He puts the deeps in storage places.

8Let all the earth fear the Lord—revere and worship Him; let all the inhabitants of the world stand in awe of Him.

9For He spoke, and it was done; He commanded, and it stood fast.

10The Lord brings the counsel of the nations to nought; He makes the thoughts *and* plans of the peoples of no effect.

11The counsel of the Lord stands for ever, the thoughts of His heart to all generations.

12Blessed—happy, fortunate [to be envied]—is the nation whose God is the Lord, the people He has chosen as His heritage.

13The Lord looks from Heaven, He beholds all the sons of men.

14From His dwelling place He looks [intently] upon all the inhabitants of the earth,

15He Who fashions the hearts of them all, Who considers all their doings.

16No king is saved by the great size *and* power of his army; a mighty man is not delivered by his much strength.

17A horse is devoid of value for victory; neither does he deliver any by his great power.

18Behold, the Lord's eye is upon those who fear Him—who revere and worship Him with awe; who wait for Him *and* hope in His mercy *and* loving-kindness,

19To deliver them from death, and keep them alive in famine.

20Our inner selves wait [earnestly] for the Lord; He is our help and our shield.

21For in Him does our heart rejoice, because we have trusted (relied on and been confident) in His holy name.

22Let Your mercy *and* loving-kindness, O Lord, be upon us in proportion to our waiting *and* hoping for You.

## New American Standard

8¶ I will instruct you and teach you in the way which you should go;
I will counsel you with My eye upon you.
9 Do not be as the horse or as the mule which have no understanding,
Whose trappings include bit and bridle to hold them in check,
*Otherwise* they will not come near to you.
10 Many are the sorrows of the wicked;
But he who trusts in the LORD, lovingkindness shall surround him.
11 Be glad in the LORD and rejoice, you righteous ones,
And shout for joy, all you who are upright in heart.

*Praise to the Creator and Preserver.*

**33** SING FOR joy in the LORD, O you righteous ones;
Praise is becoming to the upright.
2 Give thanks to the LORD with the lyre;
Sing praises to Him with a harp of ten strings.
3 Sing to Him a new song;
Play skillfully with a shout of joy.
4 For the word of the LORD is upright;
And all His work is *done* in faithfulness.
5 He loves righteousness and justice;
The earth is full of the lovingkindness of the LORD.
6¶ By the word of the LORD the heavens were made,
And by the breath of His mouth all their host.
7 He gathers the waters of the sea together as a heap;
He lays up the deeps in storehouses.
8 Let all the earth fear the LORD;
Let all the inhabitants of the world stand in awe of Him.
9 For He spoke, and it was done;
He commanded, and it stood fast.
10 The LORD nullifies the counsel of the nations;
He frustrates the plans of the peoples.
11 The counsel of the LORD stands forever,
The plans of His heart from generation to generation.
12 Blessed is the nation whose God is the LORD,
The people whom He has chosen for His own inheritance.
13¶ The LORD looks from heaven;
He sees all the sons of men;
14 From His dwelling place He looks out
On all the inhabitants of the earth,
15 He who fashions the hearts of them all,
He who understands all their works.
16 The king is not saved by a mighty army;
A warrior is not delivered by great strength.
17 A horse is a false hope for victory;
Nor does it deliver anyone by its great strength.
18¶ Behold, the eye of the LORD is on those who fear Him,
On those who hope for His lovingkindness,
19 To deliver their soul from death,
And to keep them alive in famine.
20 Our soul waits for the LORD;
He is our help and our shield.
21 For our heart rejoices in Him,
Because we trust in His holy name.
22 Let Thy lovingkindness, O LORD, be upon us,
According as we have hoped in Thee.

## New International

8I will instruct you and teach you in the way you should go;
I will counsel you and watch over you.
9Do not be like the horse or the mule,
which have no understanding
but must be controlled by bit and bridle
or they will not come to you.
10Many are the woes of the wicked,
but the LORD's unfailing love
surrounds the man who trusts in him.

11Rejoice in the LORD and be glad, you righteous;
sing, all you who are upright in heart!

**33** SING JOYFULLY to the LORD, you righteous;
it is fitting for the upright to praise him.
2Praise the LORD with the harp;
make music to him on the ten-stringed lyre.
3Sing to him a new song;
play skillfully, and shout for joy.

4For the word of the LORD is right and true;
he is faithful in all he does.
5The LORD loves righteousness and justice;
the earth is full of his unfailing love.

6By the word of the LORD were the heavens made,
their starry host by the breath of his mouth.
7He gathers the waters of the sea into jars[a];
he puts the deep into storehouses.
8Let all the earth fear the LORD;
let all the people of the world revere him.
9For he spoke, and it came to be;
he commanded, and it stood firm.
10The LORD foils the plans of the nations;
he thwarts the purposes of the peoples.
11But the plans of the LORD stand firm forever,
the purposes of his heart through all generations.

12Blessed is the nation whose God is the LORD,
the people he chose for his inheritance.
13From heaven the LORD looks down
and sees all mankind;
14from his dwelling place he watches
all who live on earth—
15he who forms the hearts of all,
who considers everything they do.
16No king is saved by the size of his army;
no warrior escapes by his great strength.
17A horse is a vain hope for deliverance;
despite all its great strength it cannot save.
18But the eyes of the LORD are on those who fear him,
on those whose hope is in his unfailing love,
19to deliver them from death
and keep them alive in famine.

20We wait in hope for the LORD;
he is our help and our shield.
21In him our hearts rejoice,
for we trust in his holy name.
22May your unfailing love rest upon us, O LORD,
even as we put our hope in you.

NIV [a] 7 Or *sea as into a heap*

## King James

*A Psalm* of David, when he changed his behaviour before Abimelech; who drove him away, and he departed.

34 I WILL bless the LORD at all times: his praise *shall* continually *be* in my mouth.
2My soul shall make her boast in the LORD: the humble shall hear *thereof*, and be glad.
3O magnify the LORD with me, and let us exalt his name together.
4I sought the LORD, and he heard me, and delivered me from all my fears.
5They looked unto him, and were lightened: and their faces were not ashamed.
6This poor man cried, and the LORD heard *him*, and saved him out of all his troubles.
7The angel of the LORD encampeth round about them that fear him, and delivereth them.
8O taste and see that the LORD *is* good: blessed *is* the man *that* trusteth in him.
9O fear the LORD, ye his saints: for *there is* no want to them that fear him.
10The young lions do lack, and suffer hunger: but they that seek the LORD shall not want any good *thing*.
11Come, ye children, hearken unto me: I will teach you the fear of the LORD.
12What man *is he that* desireth life, *and* loveth *many* days, that he may see good?
13Keep thy tongue from evil, and thy lips from speaking guile.
14Depart from evil, and do good; seek peace, and pursue it.
15The eyes of the LORD *are* upon the righteous, and his ears *are open* unto their cry.
16The face of the LORD *is* against them that do evil, to cut off the remembrance of them from the earth.
17 *The righteous* cry, and the LORD heareth, and delivereth them out of all their troubles.
18The LORD *is* nigh unto them that are of a broken heart; and saveth such as be of a contrite spirit.
19Many *are* the afflictions of the righteous: but the LORD delivereth him out of them all.
20He keepeth all his bones: not one of them is broken.
21Evil shall slay the wicked: and they that hate the righteous shall be desolate.
22The LORD redeemeth the soul of his servants: and none of them that trust in him shall be desolate.

*A Psalm* of David.

35 PLEAD *MY cause*, O LORD, with them that strive with me: fight against them that fight against me.
2Take hold of shield and buckler, and stand up for mine help.
3Draw out also the spear, and stop *the way* against them that persecute me: say unto my soul, I *am* thy salvation.

## Amplified

[ *A Psalm*] of David, when he pretended to be insane before Abimelech, who drove him out, and he went away.

34 I WILL bless the Lord at all times; His praise shall continually be in my mouth.
2My life makes its boast in the Lord; let the humble *and* afflicted hear and be glad.
3O magnify the Lord with me, and let us exalt His name together.
4I sought (inquired of) for the Lord, *and* required Him [of necessity, and on the authority of His Word], and He heard me, and delivered me from all my fears. [Ps. 73:25; Matt. 7:7.]
5They looked to Him, and were radiant; their faces shall never *blush* for shame *or* be confused.
6This poor man cried, and the Lord heard him, and saved him out of all his troubles.
7 [a]The Angel of the Lord encamps around those who fear Him—who revere and worship Him with awe; and each of them He delivers. [Pss. 145:20; 18:1.]
8O taste and see that the Lord [our God] is good! Blessed—happy, fortunate [to be envied]—is the man who trusts *and* takes refuge in Him. [I Pet. 2:2, 3.]
9O fear the Lord, you His saints—revere and worship Him! For there is no want to those who truly revere *and* worship Him *with* godly fear.
10The young lions lack food and suffer hunger, but they who seek (inquire of and require) the Lord [by right of their need and on authority of His Word] none of them shall lack any beneficial thing.
11Come, you children, listen to me; I will teach you to revere *and* worshipfully fear the Lord.
12What man is he who desires life *and* longs for many days, that he may see good?
13Keep your tongue from evil and your lips from speaking deceit.
14Depart from evil and do good; seek, inquire for *and* crave peace, and pursue—go after—it!
15The eyes of the Lord are toward the [uncompromisingly] righteous, and His ears are open to their cry.
16The face of the Lord is against those who do evil, to cut off the remembrance of them from the earth. [I Pet. 3:10-12.]
17When the *righteous* cry for help, the Lord hears, and delivers them out of all their distress *and* troubles.
18The Lord is close to those who are of a broken heart, and saves such as are crushed with sorrow for sin *and* are humbly *and* thoroughly penitent.
19Many evils confront the [consistently] righteous; but the Lord delivers him out of them all.
20He keeps all his bones; not one of them is broken.
21Evil shall cause the death of the wicked, and they who hate the just *and* righteous shall be held guilty *and* shall be condemned.
22The Lord redeems the life of His servants, and none of those who take refuge *and* trust in Him shall be condemned *or* held guilty.

[ *A Psalm*] of David.

35 CONTEND, O Lord, with those who contend with me; fight against those who fight against me!
2Take hold of shield and buckler, and stand up for my help!
3Draw out also the spear and javelin, *and* close the way of those who pursue *and* persecute me. Say to me, I am your deliverance!

AMP [a] See footnote on Isaiah 63:9.

## New American Standard

*The* Lord *a Provider and Deliverer.*

*A Psalm* of David when he feigned madness before Abimelech, who drove him away and he departed.

34 I WILL bless the LORD at all times;
His praise shall continually be in my mouth.
2 My soul shall make its boast in the LORD;
The humble shall hear it and rejoice.
3 O magnify the LORD with me,
And let us exalt His name together.

4¶ I sought the LORD, and He answered me,
And delivered me from all my fears.
5 They looked to Him and were radiant,
And their faces shall never be ashamed.
6 This poor man cried and the LORD heard him,
And saved him out of all his troubles.
7 The angel of the LORD encamps around those who fear Him,
And rescues them.

8¶ O taste and see that the LORD is good;
How blessed is the man who takes refuge in Him!
9 O fear the LORD, you His saints;
For to those who fear Him, there is no want.
10 The young lions do lack and suffer hunger;
But they who seek the LORD shall not be in want of any good thing.
11 Come, you children, listen to me;
I will teach you the fear of the LORD.
12 Who is the man who desires life,
And loves *length of* days that he may see good?
13 Keep your tongue from evil,
And your lips from speaking deceit.
14 Depart from evil, and do good;
Seek peace, and pursue it.

15¶ The eyes of the LORD are toward the righteous,
And His ears are *open* to their cry.
16 The face of the LORD is against evildoers,
To cut off the memory of them from the earth.
17 *The righteous* cry and the LORD hears,
And delivers them out of all their troubles.
18 The LORD is near to the brokenhearted,
And saves those who are [b]crushed in spirit.

19¶ Many are the afflictions of the righteous;
But the LORD delivers him out of them all.
20 He keeps all his bones;
Not one of them is broken.
21 Evil shall slay the wicked;
And those who hate the righteous will be condemned.
22 The LORD redeems the soul of His servants;
And none of those who take refuge in Him will be condemned.

*Prayer for Rescue from Enemies.*

*A Psalm* of David.

35 CONTEND, O LORD, with those who contend with me;
Fight against those who fight against me.
2 Take hold of [c]buckler and shield,
And rise up for my help.
3 Draw also the spear and the battle-axe to meet those who pursue me;
Say to my soul, "I am your salvation."

NAS [b] Or, *contrite* [c] I.e., small shield

## New International

Of David. When he pretended to be insane before Abimelech, who drove him away, and he left.

34[d] I WILL extol the LORD at all times;
his praise will always be on my lips.
2My soul will boast in the LORD;
let the afflicted hear and rejoice.
3Glorify the LORD with me;
let us exalt his name together.

4I sought the LORD, and he answered me;
he delivered me from all my fears.
5Those who look to him are radiant;
their faces are never covered with shame.
6This poor man called, and the LORD heard him;
he saved him out of all his troubles.
7The angel of the LORD encamps around those who fear him,
and he delivers them.

8Taste and see that the LORD is good;
blessed is the man who takes refuge in him.
9Fear the LORD, you his saints,
for those who fear him lack nothing.
10The lions may grow weak and hungry,
but those who seek the LORD lack no good thing.
11Come, my children, listen to me;
I will teach you the fear of the LORD.
12Whoever of you loves life
and desires to see many good days,
13keep your tongue from evil
and your lips from speaking lies.
14Turn from evil and do good;
seek peace and pursue it.

15The eyes of the LORD are on the righteous
and his ears are attentive to their cry;
16the face of the LORD is against those who do evil,
to cut off the memory of them from the earth.
17The righteous cry out, and the LORD hears them;
he delivers them from all their troubles.
18The LORD is close to the brokenhearted
and saves those who are crushed in spirit.

19A righteous man may have many troubles,
but the LORD delivers him from them all;
20he protects all his bones,
not one of them will be broken.

21Evil will slay the wicked;
the foes of the righteous will be condemned.
22The LORD redeems his servants;
no one will be condemned who takes refuge in him.

Of David.

35 CONTEND, O LORD, with those who contend with me;
fight against those who fight against me.
2Take up shield and buckler;
arise and come to my aid.
3Brandish spear and javelin[e]
against those who pursue me.
Say to my soul,
"I am your salvation."

NIV [d] This psalm is an acrostic poem, the verses of which begin with the successive letters of the Hebrew alphabet. [e] 3 Or *and block the way*

## King James

4 Let them be confounded and put to shame that seek after my
soul: let them be turned back and brought to confusion that devise
my hurt.
5 Let them be as chaff before the wind: and let the angel of the
LORD chase *them.*
6 Let their way be dark and slippery: and let the angel of the
LORD persecute them.
7 For without cause have they hid for me their net *in* a pit, *which*
without cause they have digged for my soul.
8 Let destruction come upon him at unawares; and let his net
that he hath hid catch himself: into that very destruction let him
fall.
9 And my soul shall be joyful in the LORD: it shall rejoice in his
salvation.
10 All my bones shall say, LORD, who *is* like unto thee, which
deliverest the poor from him that is too strong for him, yea, the
poor and the needy from him that spoileth him?
11 False witnesses did rise up; they laid to my charge *things* that
I knew not.
12 They rewarded me evil for good *to* the spoiling of my soul.
13 But as for me, when they were sick, my clothing *was* sackcloth: I humbled my soul with fasting; and my prayer returned into
mine own bosom.
14 I behaved myself as though *he had been* my friend *or* brother:
I bowed down heavily, as one that mourneth *for his* mother.
15 But in mine adversity they rejoiced, and gathered themselves
together: *yea,* the abjects gathered themselves together against me,
and I knew *it* not; they did tear *me,* and ceased not:
16 With hypocritical mockers in feasts, they gnashed upon me
with their teeth.
17 Lord, how long wilt thou look on? rescue my soul from their
destructions, my darling from the lions.
18 I will give thee thanks in the great congregation: I will praise
thee among much people.
19 Let not them that are mine enemies wrongfully rejoice over
me: *neither* let them wink with the eye that hate me without a
cause.
20 For they speak not peace: but they devise deceitful matters
against *them that are* quiet in the land.
21 Yea, they opened their mouth wide against me, *and* said, Aha,
aha, our eye hath seen *it.*
22 *This* thou hast seen, O LORD: keep not silence: O Lord, be not
far from me.
23 Stir up thyself, and awake to my judgment, *even* unto my
cause, my God and my Lord.
24 Judge me, O LORD my God, according to thy righteousness;
and let them not rejoice over me.
25 Let them not say in their hearts, Ah, so would we have it: let
them not say, We have swallowed him up.
26 Let them be ashamed and brought to confusion together that
rejoice at mine hurt: let them be clothed with shame and dishonour
that magnify *themselves* against me.

## Amplified

4 Let them be put to shame and dishonor who seek after *and*
require my life; let them be turned back and confounded who plan
my hurt!
5 Let them be as chaff before the wind, with the [a]Angel of the
Lord driving them on!
6 Let their way be through dark and slippery places, with the
Angel of the Lord pursuing *and* afflicting them.
7 For without cause they hid for me their net; a pit of destruction
without cause they dug for my life.
8 Let destruction befall *my foe* unawares; let the net he had hid
for me catch him; let him fall into that very destruction.
9 Then I shall be joyful in the Lord; I shall rejoice in His deliverance.
10 All my bones shall say, Lord, who is like You, You Who
deliver the poor *and* the afflicted from him who is too strong for
him, yes, the poor and the needy from him who snatches away his
goods?
11 Malicious *and* unrighteous witnesses rise up; they ask me of
things that I know not.
12 They reward me evil for good to my personal bereavement.
13 But as for me, when they were sick, my clothing was sackcloth; I afflicted myself with fasting, and I prayed with head bowed
on my breast.
14 I behaved as if grieving for my friend *or* my brother; I bowed
down in sorrow, as one who bewails his mother.
15 But in my stumbling *and* limping they rejoiced, and gathered
together *against* me; the smiters [slanderers and revilers] gathered
against me, and I knew *them* not; they ceased not to slander *and*
revile me.
16 Like the profane mockers at feasts [making sport for the price
of a cake] they gnashed at me with their teeth.
17 Lord, how long will You look on [without action]? Rescue my
life from their destructions, my dear *and* only *life* from the lions!
18 I will give You thanks in the great assembly; I will praise You
among a mighty throng.
19 Let not those who are my foes wrongfully rejoice over me;
*neither* let them wink with the eye who hate me without cause.
[John 15:24, 25.]
20 For they do not speak peace, but they devise deceitful matters
against those who are quiet in the land.
21 Yes, they open their mouths wide against me; they say, Aha,
Aha! Our eyes have seen it!
22 You have seen, O Lord; keep not silence! O Lord, be not far
from me!
23 Arouse Yourself; awake to the justice due me, even to my
cause, my God and my Lord!
24 Judge *and* vindicate me, O Lord, my God, according to Your
righteousness—Your rightness and justice; and let *my foes* not
rejoice over me!
25 Let them not say in their hearts, Aha, that is what we wanted!
Let them not say, We have swallowed him up *and* utterly destroyed him.
26 Let them be put to shame and confusion together who rejoice
at my calamity! Let them be clothed with shame and dishonor who
magnify *and* exalt themselves against me!

**AMP** [a] See footnote on Isaiah 63:9.

## New American Standard

4 Let those be ashamed and dishonored who seek my life;
Let those be turned back and humiliated who devise evil against me.
5 Let them be like chaff before the wind,
With the angel of the LORD driving *them* on.
6 Let their way be dark and slippery,
With the angel of the LORD pursuing them.
7 For without cause they hid their net for me;
Without cause they dug a pit for my soul.
8 Let destruction come upon him unawares;
And let the net which he hid catch himself;
Into that very destruction let him fall.

9¶ And my soul shall rejoice in the LORD;
It shall exult in His salvation.
10 All my bones will say, "LORD, who is like Thee,
Who delivers the afflicted from him who is too strong for him,
And the afflicted and the needy from him who robs him?"
11 Malicious witnesses rise up;
They ask me of things that I do not know.
12 They repay me evil for good,
*To* the bereavement of my soul.
13 But as for me, when they were sick, my clothing was sackcloth;
I humbled my soul with fasting;
And my prayer kept returning to my bosom.
14 I went about as though it were my friend or brother;
I bowed down mourning, as one who sorrows for a mother.
15 But at my [b]stumbling they rejoiced, and gathered them selves together;
The smiters whom I did not know gathered together against me,
They slandered me without ceasing.
16 Like godless jesters at a feast,
They gnashed at me with their teeth.

17¶ Lord, how long wilt Thou look on?
Rescue my soul from their ravages,
My only *life* from the lions.
18 I will give Thee thanks in the great congregation;
I will praise Thee among a mighty throng.
19 Do not let those who are wrongfully my enemies rejoice over me;
Neither let those who hate me without cause wink maliciously.
20 For they do not speak peace,
But they devise deceitful words against those who are quiet in the land.
21 And they opened their mouth wide against me;
They said, "Aha, aha, our eyes have seen it!"
22¶ Thou hast seen it, O LORD, do not keep silent;
O Lord, do not be far from me.
23 Stir up Thyself, and awake to my right,
And to my cause, my God and my Lord.
24 Judge me, O LORD my God, according to Thy righteousness;
And do not let them rejoice over me.
25 Do not let them say in their heart, "Aha, our desire!"
Do not let them say, "We have swallowed him up!"
26 Let those be ashamed and humiliated altogether who rejoice at my distress;
Let those be clothed with shame and dishonor who magnify themselves over me.

NAS [b] Or, *limping*

## New International

4May those who seek my life
be disgraced and put to shame;
may those who plot my ruin
be turned back in dismay.
5May they be like chaff before the wind,
with the angel of the LORD driving them away;
6may their path be dark and slippery,
with the angel of the LORD pursuing them.
7Since they hid their net for me without cause
and without cause dug a pit for me,
8may ruin overtake them by surprise—
may the net they hid entangle them,
may they fall into the pit, to their ruin.
9Then my soul will rejoice in the LORD
and delight in his salvation.
10My whole being will exclaim,
"Who is like you, O LORD?
You rescue the poor from those too strong for them,
the poor and needy from those who rob them."

11Ruthless witnesses come forward;
they question me on things I know nothing about.
12They repay me evil for good
and leave my soul forlorn.
13Yet when they were ill, I put on sackcloth
and humbled myself with fasting.
When my prayers returned to me unanswered,
14 I went about mourning
as though for my friend or brother.
I bowed my head in grief
as though weeping for my mother.
15But when I stumbled, they gathered in glee;
attackers gathered against me when I was unaware.
They slandered me without ceasing.
16Like the ungodly they maliciously mocked[c];
they gnashed their teeth at me.
17O Lord, how long will you look on?
Rescue my life from their ravages,
my precious life from these lions.
18I will give you thanks in the great assembly;
among throngs of people I will praise you.

19Let not those gloat over me
who are my enemies without cause;
let not those who hate me without reason
maliciously wink the eye.
20They do not speak peaceably,
but devise false accusations
against those who live quietly in the land.
21They gape at me and say, "Aha! Aha!
With our own eyes we have seen it."

22O LORD, you have seen this; be not silent.
Do not be far from me, O Lord.
23Awake, and rise to my defense!
Contend for me, my God and Lord.
24Vindicate me in your righteousness, O LORD my God;
do not let them gloat over me.
25Do not let them think, "Aha, just what we wanted!"
or say, "We have swallowed him up."

26May all who gloat over my distress
be put to shame and confusion;
may all who exalt themselves over me
be clothed with shame and disgrace.

NIV [c] *16* Septuagint; Hebrew may mean *ungodly circle of mockers.*

## King James

27 Let them shout for joy, and be glad, that favour my righteous cause: yea, let them say continually, Let the LORD be magnified, which hath pleasure in the prosperity of his servant.

28 And my tongue shall speak of thy righteousness *and* of thy praise all the day long.

To the chief Musician, *A Psalm* of David the servant of the LORD.

**36** THE TRANSGRESSION of the wicked saith within my heart, *that there is* no fear of God before his eyes.

2 For he flattereth himself in his own eyes, until his iniquity be found to be hateful.

3 The words of his mouth *are* iniquity and deceit: he hath left off to be wise, *and* to do good.

4 He deviseth mischief upon his bed; he setteth himself in a way *that is* not good; he abhorreth not evil.

5 Thy mercy, O LORD, *is* in the heavens; *and* thy faithfulness *reacheth* unto the clouds.

6 Thy righteousness *is* like the great mountains; thy judgments *are* a great deep: O LORD, thou preservest man and beast.

7 How excellent *is* thy lovingkindness, O God! therefore the children of men put their trust under the shadow of thy wings.

8 They shall be abundantly satisfied with the fatness of thy house; and thou shalt make them drink of the river of thy pleasures.

9 For with thee *is* the fountain of life: in thy light shall we see light.

10 O continue thy lovingkindness unto them that know thee; and thy righteousness to the upright in heart.

11 Let not the foot of pride come against me, and let not the hand of the wicked remove me.

12 There are the workers of iniquity fallen: they are cast down, and shall not be able to rise.

*A Psalm* of David.

**37** FRET NOT thyself because of evildoers, neither be thou envious against the workers of iniquity.

2 For they shall soon be cut down like the grass, and wither as the green herb.

3 Trust in the LORD, and do good; *so* shalt thou dwell in the land, and verily thou shalt be fed.

4 Delight thyself also in the LORD; and he shall give thee the desires of thine heart.

5 Commit thy way unto the LORD; trust also in him; and he shall bring *it* to pass.

6 And he shall bring forth thy righteousness as the light, and thy judgment as the noonday.

7 Rest in the LORD, and wait patiently for him: fret not thyself because of him who prospereth in his way, because of the man who bringeth wicked devices to pass.

8 Cease from anger, and forsake wrath: fret not thyself in any wise to do evil.

## Amplified

27 Let those who favor my righteous cause *and* have pleasure in my uprightness shout for joy and be glad, and say continually, Let the Lord be magnified, Who takes pleasure in the prosperity of His servant.

28 And my tongue shall talk of Your righteousness, rightness *and* justice, and [my reasons for] Your praise all the day long.

To the Chief Musician. [ *A Psalm*] of David, the servant of the Lord.

**36** TRANSGRESSION [LIKE an oracle] speaks to the wicked deep in his heart. There is no fear *or* dread of God before his eyes. [Rom. 3:18.]

2 For he flatters *and* deceives himself in his own eyes, that his iniquity will not be found out and be hated.

3 The words of his mouth are wrong and deceitful; he has ceased to be wise *and* to do good.

4 He plans wrongdoing on his bed; he sets himself in a way that is not good; he does not reject *or* despise evil.

5 Your mercy *and* loving-kindness, O Lord, extend to the skies, *and* Your faithfulness to the clouds.

6 Your righteousness is like the mountains of God; Your judgments are like the great deep; O Lord, You preserve man and beast.

7 How precious *is* Your steadfast love, O God! The children of men take refuge *and* put their trust under the shadow of Your wings.

8 They relish *and* feast on the abundance of Your house, and You cause them to drink of the stream of Your pleasures.

9 For with You is the fountain of life; in Your light do we see light. [John 4:10, 14.]

10 O continue Your loving-kindness to those who know You, Your righteousness [salvation] to the upright in heart.

11 Let not the foot of pride overtake me, and let not the hand of the wicked drive me away.

12 There the workers of iniquity fall *and* lie prostrate; they are thrust down, and shall not be able to rise.

[ *A Psalm*] of David.

**37** FRET NOT yourself because of evildoers, neither be envious against those who work unrighteousness—that which is not upright, nor in right standing with God.

2 For they shall soon be cut down like the grass, and wither as the green herb.

3 Trust (lean on, rely on and be confident) in the Lord, and do good; so shall you dwell in the land and feed surely on His faithfulness, *and* truly you shall be fed.

4 Delight yourself also in the Lord, and He will give you the desires *and* secret petitions of your heart.

5 Commit your way to the Lord—roll and repose [each care of] your load on Him; trust (lean on, rely on and be confident) also in Him, and He will bring it to pass.

6 And He will make your uprightness *and* right standing with God go forth as the light, and your justice *and* right as [the shining sun of] the noonday.

7 Be still *and* rest in the Lord; wait for Him, *and* patiently stay yourself upon Him; fret not yourself because of him who prospers in his way, because of the man who brings wicked devices to pass.

8 Cease from anger and forsake wrath; fret not yourself; it tends only to evil-doing.

## New American Standard

27¶ Let them shout for joy and rejoice, who favor my vindication;
And let them say continually, "The LORD be magnified,
Who delights in the prosperity of His servant."
28 And my tongue shall declare Thy righteousness
*And* Thy praise all day long.

*Wickedness of Men and Lovingkindness of God.*

For the choir director. *A Psalm* of David the servant of the LORD.

**36** TRANSGRESSION SPEAKS to the ungodly within his heart;
There is no fear of God before his eyes.
2 For it flatters him in his *own* eyes,
Concerning the discovery of his iniquity *and* the hatred of it.
3 The words of his mouth are wickedness and deceit;
He has ceased to be wise *and* to do good.
4 He plans wickedness upon his bed;
He sets himself on a path that is not good;
He does not despise evil.

5¶ Thy lovingkindness, O LORD, extends to the heavens,
Thy faithfulness *reaches* to the skies.
6 Thy righteousness is like the mountains of God;
Thy judgments are *like* a great deep.
O LORD, Thou preservest man and beast.
7 How precious is Thy lovingkindness, O God!
And the children of men take refuge in the shadow of Thy wings.
8 They drink their fill of the abundance of Thy house;
And Thou dost give them to drink of the river of Thy delights.
9 For with Thee is the fountain of life;
In Thy light we see light.
10¶ O continue Thy lovingkindness to those who know Thee,
And Thy righteousness to the upright in heart.
11 Let not the foot of pride come upon me,
And let not the hand of the wicked drive me away.
12 There the doers of iniquity have fallen;
They have been thrust down and cannot rise.

*Security of Those Who Trust in the LORD, and Insecurity of the Wicked.*

*A Psalm* of David.

**37** DO NOT fret because of evildoers, Be not envious toward wrongdoers.
2 For they will wither quickly like the grass,
And fade like the green herb.
3 Trust in the LORD, and do good;
Dwell in the land and [a]cultivate faithfulness.
4 Delight yourself in the LORD;
And He will give you the desires of your heart.
5 Commit your way to the LORD,
Trust also in Him, and He will do it.
6 And He will bring forth your righteousness as the light,
And your judgment as the noonday.
7¶ [b]Rest in the LORD and wait [c]patiently for Him;
Do not fret because of him who prospers in his way,
Because of the man who carries out wicked schemes.
8 Cease from anger, and forsake wrath;
Do not fret, *it leads* only to evildoing.

NAS [a] Or, *feed securely*, or, *feed on His faithfulness* [b] Or, *Be still* [c] Or, *longingly*

## New International

27May those who delight in my vindication
shout for joy and gladness;
may they always say, "The LORD be exalted,
who delights in the well-being of his servant."
28My tongue will speak of your righteousness
and of your praises all day long.

For the director of music. Of David the servant of the LORD.

**36** AN ORACLE is within my heart
concerning the sinfulness of the wicked:[d]
There is no fear of God
before his eyes.
2For in his own eyes he flatters himself
too much to detect or hate his sin.
3The words of his mouth are wicked and deceitful;
he has ceased to be wise and to do good.
4Even on his bed he plots evil;
he commits himself to a sinful course
and does not reject what is wrong.

5Your love, O LORD, reaches to the heavens,
your faithfulness to the skies.
6Your righteousness is like the mighty mountains,
your justice like the great deep.
O LORD, you preserve both man and beast.
7 How priceless is your unfailing love!
Both high and low among men
find[e] refuge in the shadow of your wings.
8They feast on the abundance of your house;
you give them drink from your river of delights.
9For with you is the fountain of life;
in your light we see light.

10Continue your love to those who know you,
your righteousness to the upright in heart.
11May the foot of the proud not come against me,
nor the hand of the wicked drive me away.
12See how the evildoers lie fallen—
thrown down, not able to rise!

Of David.

**37**[f] DO NOT fret because of evil men
or be envious of those who do wrong;
2for like the grass they will soon wither,
like green plants they will soon die away.

3Trust in the LORD and do good;
dwell in the land and enjoy safe pasture.
4Delight yourself in the LORD
and he will give you the desires of your heart.

5Commit your way to the LORD;
trust in him and he will do this:
6He will make your righteousness shine like the dawn,
the justice of your cause like the noonday sun.

7Be still before the LORD and wait patiently for him;
do not fret when men succeed in their ways,
when they carry out their wicked schemes.

8Refrain from anger and turn from wrath;
do not fret—it leads only to evil.

NIV [d] 1 Or *heart: / Sin proceeds from the wicked.* [e] 7 Or *love, O God! / Men find;* or *love! / Both heavenly beings and men / find* [f] This psalm is an acrostic poem, the stanzas of which begin with the successive letters of the Hebrew alphabet.

# King James

9For evildoers shall be cut off: but those that wait upon the LORD, they shall inherit the earth.

10For yet for a little while, and the wicked *shall* not *be:* yea, thou shalt diligently consider his place, and it *shall* not *be.*

11But the meek shall inherit the earth; and shall delight themselves in the abundance of peace.

12The wicked plotteth against the just, and gnasheth upon him with his teeth.

13The Lord shall laugh at him: for he seeth that his day is coming.

14The wicked have drawn out the sword, and have bent their bow, to cast down the poor and needy, *and* to slay such as be of upright conversation.

15Their sword shall enter into their own heart, and their bows shall be broken.

16A little that a righteous man hath *is* better than the riches of many wicked.

17For the arms of the wicked shall be broken: but the LORD upholdeth the righteous.

18The LORD knoweth the days of the upright: and their inheritance shall be for ever.

19They shall not be ashamed in the evil time: and in the days of famine they shall be satisfied.

20But the wicked shall perish, and the enemies of the LORD *shall be* as the fat of lambs: they shall consume; into smoke shall they consume away.

21The wicked borroweth, and payeth not again: but the righteous showeth mercy, and giveth.

22For *such as be* blessed of him shall inherit the earth; and *they that be* cursed of him shall be cut off.

23The steps of a *good* man are ordered by the LORD: and he delighteth in his way.

24Though he fall, he shall not be utterly cast down: for the LORD upholdeth *him with* his hand.

25I have been young, and *now* am old; yet have I not seen the righteous forsaken, nor his seed begging bread.

26 *He is* ever merciful, and lendeth; and his seed *is* blessed.

27Depart from evil, and do good; and dwell for evermore.

28For the LORD loveth judgment, and forsaketh not his saints; they are preserved for ever: but the seed of the wicked shall be cut off.

29The righteous shall inherit the land, and dwell therein for ever.

30The mouth of the righteous speaketh wisdom, and his tongue talketh of judgment.

31The law of his God *is* in his heart; none of his steps shall slide.

32The wicked watcheth the righteous, and seeketh to slay him.

33The LORD will not leave him in his hand, nor condemn him when he is judged.

34Wait on the LORD, and keep his way, and he shall exalt thee to inherit the land: when the wicked are cut off, thou shalt see *it.*

35I have seen the wicked in great power, and spreading himself like a green bay tree.

# Amplified

9For evildoers shall be cut off; but those who wait *and* hope *and* look for the Lord, [in the end] shall inherit the earth. [Isa. 57:13c.]

10For yet a little while and the evildoer will be no more; though you look with care where he used to be, he will not be found. [Rev. 21:7, 8; Heb. 10:36, 37.]

11But the meek [in the end] shall inherit the earth, and shall delight themselves in the abundance of peace. [Matt. 5:5; Ps. 37:29.]

12The wicked plots against the [uncompromisingly] righteous man—the upright in right standing with God; he gnashes at him with his teeth.

13The Lord laughs at [the wicked]; for He sees that their own day [of defeat] is coming.

14The wicked draw the sword and bend their bows to cast down the poor and needy, to slay those who walk uprightly—blameless in conduct and in conversation.

15The sword *of the wicked* shall enter their own heart, and their bows shall be broken.

16Better is a little that the [uncompromisingly] righteous man has, than the abundance [of possessions] of many who are wrong *and* wicked. [I Tim. 6:6, 7.]

17For the arms of the wicked shall be broken; but the Lord upholds the [consistently] righteous.

18The Lord knows the days of the upright *and* blameless, and their heritage will abide for ever.

19They shall not be put to shame in the time of evil, and in the days of famine they shall be satisfied.

20But the wicked shall perish, and the enemies of the Lord shall be as the fat of lambs [that is consumed in smoke], *and* as the glory of the pastures. They shall vanish; like smoke shall they consume away.

21The wicked borrows, and pays not again [for he may be unable]; but the [uncompromisingly] righteous deals kindly and gives [for he is able].

22For such as are blessed of God shall [in the end] inherit the earth; and they that are cursed of Him shall be cut off. [Isa. 57:13c.]

23The steps of a [good] man are directed *and* established of the Lord, when He delights in his way [and He busies Himself with his every step].

24Though he fall, he shall not be utterly cast down, for the Lord grasps his hand in support *and* upholds him.

25I have been young and now am old, yet have I not seen the [uncompromisingly] righteous forsaken or his seed begging bread.

26All day long he is merciful *and* deals graciously; he lends, and his offspring is blessed.

27Depart from evil, and do good; and dwell for ever [securely].

28For the Lord delights in justice and forsakes not His saints; they are preserved for ever, but the offspring of the wicked [in time] shall be cut off.

29[Then] the [consistently] righteous shall inherit the land, and dwell upon it for ever.

30The mouth of the [uncompromisingly] righteous utters wisdom, and his tongue speaks with justice.

31The law of his God is in his heart; none of his steps shall slide.

32The wicked lies in wait for the [uncompromisingly] righteous, and seeks to put him to death.

33The Lord will not leave him in his hand, or (suffer him to) condemn him when he is judged.

34Wait for *and* expect the Lord, and keep *and* heed His way, and He will exalt you to inherit the land; [in the end] when the wicked are cut off you shall see it.

35I have seen the wicked in great power, and spreading himself like a green tree in its native soil.

## New American Standard

9 For evildoers will be cut off,
But those who wait for the LORD, they will inherit the land.
10 Yet a little while and the wicked man will be no more;
And you will look carefully for his place, and he will not be *there*.
11 But the humble will inherit the land,
And will delight themselves in abundant prosperity.

12¶ The wicked plots against the righteous,
And gnashes at him with his teeth.
13 The Lord laughs at him;
For He sees his day is coming.
14 The wicked have drawn the sword and bent their bow,
To cast down the afflicted and the needy,
To slay those who are upright in conduct.
15 Their sword will enter their own heart,
And their bows will be broken.

16¶ Better is the little of the righteous
Than the abundance of many wicked.
17 For the arms of the wicked will be broken;
But the LORD sustains the righteous.
18 The LORD knows the days of the blameless;
And their inheritance will be forever.
19 They will not be ashamed in the time of evil;
And in the days of famine they will have abundance.
20 But the wicked will perish;
And the enemies of the LORD will be like the [a]glory of the pastures,
They vanish—like smoke they vanish away.
21 The wicked borrows and does not pay back,
But the righteous is gracious and gives.
22 For those blessed by Him will inherit the land;
But those cursed by Him will be cut off.

23¶ The steps of a man are established by the LORD;
And He delights in his way.
24 When he falls, he shall not be hurled headlong;
Because the LORD is the One who holds his hand.
25 I have been young, and now I am old;
Yet I have not seen the righteous forsaken,
Or his descendants begging bread.
26 All day long he is gracious and lends;
And his descendants are a blessing.

27¶ Depart from evil, and do good,
So you will abide forever.
28 For the LORD loves justice,
And does not forsake His godly ones;
They are preserved forever;
But the descendants of the wicked will be cut off.
29 The righteous will inherit the land,
And dwell in it forever.
30 The mouth of the righteous utters wisdom,
And his tongue speaks justice.
31 The law of his God is in his heart;
His steps do not slip.
32 The wicked spies upon the righteous,
And seeks to kill him.
33 The LORD will not leave him in his hand,
Or let him be condemned when he is judged.
34 Wait for the LORD, and keep His way,
And He will exalt you to inherit the land;
When the wicked are cut off, you will see it.

35¶ I have seen a violent, wicked man
Spreading himself like a luxuriant tree in its native soil.

NAS [a] I.e., flowers

## New International

9 For evil men will be cut off,
but those who hope in the LORD will inherit the land.
10 A little while, and the wicked will be no more;
though you look for them, they will not be found.
11 But the meek will inherit the land
and enjoy great peace.
12 The wicked plot against the righteous
and gnash their teeth at them;
13 but the Lord laughs at the wicked,
for he knows their day is coming.

14 The wicked draw the sword
and bend the bow
to bring down the poor and needy,
to slay those whose ways are upright.
15 But their swords will pierce their own hearts,
and their bows will be broken.

16 Better the little that the righteous have
than the wealth of many wicked;
17 for the power of the wicked will be broken,
but the LORD upholds the righteous.
18 The days of the blameless are known to the LORD,
and their inheritance will endure forever.
19 In times of disaster they will not wither;
in days of famine they will enjoy plenty.

20 But the wicked will perish:
The LORD's enemies will be like the beauty of the fields,
they will vanish—vanish like smoke.

21 The wicked borrow and do not repay,
but the righteous give generously;
22 those the LORD blesses will inherit the land,
but those he curses will be cut off.

23 If the LORD delights in a man's way,
he makes his steps firm;
24 though he stumble, he will not fall,
for the LORD upholds him with his hand.

25 I was young and now I am old,
yet I have never seen the righteous forsaken
or their children begging bread.
26 They are always generous and lend freely;
their children will be blessed.

27 Turn from evil and do good;
then you will dwell in the land forever.
28 For the LORD loves the just
and will not forsake his faithful ones.
They will be protected forever,
but the offspring of the wicked will be cut off;
29 the righteous will inherit the land
and dwell in it forever.

30 The mouth of the righteous man utters wisdom,
and his tongue speaks what is just.
31 The law of his God is in his heart;
his feet do not slip.

32 The wicked lie in wait for the righteous,
seeking their very lives;
33 but the LORD will not leave them in their power
or let them be condemned when brought to trial.

34 Wait for the LORD
and keep his way.
He will exalt you to inherit the land;
when the wicked are cut off, you will see it.

35 I have seen a wicked and ruthless man
flourishing like a green tree in its native soil,

## King James

36 Yet he passed away, and, lo, he *was* not: yea, I sought him, but he could not be found.
37 Mark the perfect *man*, and behold the upright: for the end of *that* man *is* peace.
38 But the transgressors shall be destroyed together: the end of the wicked shall be cut off.
39 But the salvation of the righteous *is* of the LORD: *he is* their strength in the time of trouble.
40 And the LORD shall help them, and deliver them: he shall deliver them from the wicked, and save them, because they trust in him.

A Psalm of David, to bring to remembrance.

**38** O LORD, rebuke me not in thy wrath: neither chasten me in thy hot displeasure.
2 For thine arrows stick fast in me, and thy hand presseth me sore.
3 *There is* no soundness in my flesh because of thine anger; neither *is there any* rest in my bones because of my sin.
4 For mine iniquities are gone over mine head: as an heavy burden they are too heavy for me.
5 My wounds stink *and* are corrupt because of my foolishness.
6 I am troubled; I am bowed down greatly; I go mourning all the day long.
7 For my loins are filled with a loathsome *disease:* and *there is* no soundness in my flesh.
8 I am feeble and sore broken: I have roared by reason of the disquietness of my heart.
9 Lord, all my desire *is* before thee; and my groaning is not hid from thee.
10 My heart panteth, my strength faileth me: as for the light of mine eyes, it also is gone from me.
11 My lovers and my friends stand aloof from my sore; and my kinsmen stand afar off.
12 They also that seek after my life lay snares *for me:* and they that seek my hurt speak mischievous things, and imagine deceits all the day long.
13 But I, as a deaf *man*, heard not; and *I was* as a dumb man *that* openeth not his mouth.
14 Thus I was as a man that heareth not, and in whose mouth *are* no reproofs.
15 For in thee, O LORD, do I hope: thou wilt hear, O Lord my God.
16 For I said, *Hear me,* lest *otherwise* they should rejoice over me: when my foot slippeth, they magnify *themselves* against me.
17 For I *am* ready to halt, and my sorrow *is* continually before me.
18 For I will declare mine iniquity; I will be sorry for my sin.
19 But mine enemies *are* lively, *and* they are strong: and they that hate me wrongfully are multiplied.
20 They also that render evil for good are mine adversaries; because I follow *the thing that* good *is*.
21 Forsake me not, O LORD: O my God, be not far from me.
22 Make haste to help me, O Lord my salvation.

## Amplified

36 Yet he passed away, and, lo, he was not; yes, I sought *and* inquired for him, but he could not be found.
37 Mark the blameless man and behold the upright, for there is a happy end for the man of peace.
38 As for transgressors, they shall be destroyed together; in the end the wicked shall be cut off.
39 But the salvation of the [consistently] righteous is of the Lord; He is their refuge *and* secure stronghold in the time of trouble.
40 And the Lord helps them and delivers them; He delivers them from the wicked, and saves them, because they trust *and* take refuge in Him.

A Psalm of David,
to bring to remembrance *and* make memorial.

**38** O LORD, rebuke me not in Your wrath, neither chasten me in Your hot displeasure.
2 For Your arrows have sunk into me *and* stick fast, and Your hand is come down upon me *and* presses me sorely.
3 There is no soundness in my flesh because of Your indignation; neither is there any health *or* rest in my bones because of my sin.
4 For my iniquities are gone over my head [like waves of a flood]; as a heavy burden they weigh too much for me.
5 My wounds are loathsome and corrupt because of my foolishness.
6 I am bent and bowed down greatly; I go about mourning all the day long.
7 For my loins are filled with burning, and there is no soundness in my flesh.
8 I am faint and sorely bruised—deadly cold and quite worn out; I groan by reason of the disquiet *and* moaning of my heart.
9 Lord, all my desire is before You, and my sighing is not hid from You.
10 My heart throbs, my strength fails me; as for the light of my eyes, it also is gone from me.
11 My lovers and my friends stand aloof from my plague; and my neighbors *and* my near ones stand afar off. [Luke 23:49.]
12 They also that seek after *and* demand my life lay snares for me; and they that seek *and* require my hurt speak crafty *and* mischievous things; they meditate treachery *and* deceit all the day long.
13 But I, like a deaf man, hear not; and I am like a dumb man who opens not his mouth.
14 Yes, I have become like a man who hears not, in whose mouth are no arguments *or* replies.
15 For in You, O Lord, do I hope; You will answer, O Lord my God.
16 For I pray, Let them not rejoice over me, who when my foot slips boast against me.
17 For I am ready to halt *and* fall; my pain *and* sorrow are continually before me.
18 For I do confess my guilt *and* iniquity; I am filled with sorrow for my sin. [II Cor. 7:9, 10.]
19 But my enemies are vigorous *and* strong, and those who hate me wrongfully are multiplied.
20 They also that render evil for good are adversaries to me, because I follow the thing that is good.
21 Forsake me not, O Lord; O my God, be not far from me.
22 Make haste to help me, O Lord, my salvation.

## New American Standard

36 Then he passed away, and lo, he was no more;
I sought for him, but he could not be found.
37 Mark the blameless man, and behold the upright;
For the man of peace will have a posterity.
38 But transgressors will be altogether destroyed;
The posterity of the wicked will be cut off.
39 But the salvation of the righteous is from the LORD;
He is their strength in time of trouble.
40 And the LORD helps them, and delivers them;
He delivers them from the wicked, and saves them,
Because they take refuge in Him.

*Prayer of a Suffering Penitent.*

A Psalm of David, for a memorial.

**38** O LORD, rebuke me not in Thy wrath;
And chasten me not in Thy burning anger.
2 For Thine arrows have sunk deep into me,
And Thy hand has pressed down on me.
3 There is no soundness in my flesh because of Thine
indignation;
There is no health in my bones because of my sin.
4 For my iniquities are gone over my head;
As a heavy burden they weigh too much for me.
5 My wounds grow foul *and* fester.
Because of my folly,
6 I am bent over and greatly bowed down;
I go mourning all day long.
7 For my loins are filled with burning;
And there is no soundness in my flesh.
8 I am benumbed and badly crushed;
I groan because of the agitation of my heart.

9¶ Lord, all my desire is before Thee;
And my sighing is not hidden from Thee.
10 My heart throbs, my strength fails me;
And the light of my eyes, even that has gone from me.
11 My loved ones and my friends stand aloof from my
plague;
And my kinsmen stand afar off.
12 Those who seek my life lay snares *for me;*
And those who seek to injure me have threatened
destruction,
And they devise treachery all day long.

13¶ But I, like a deaf man, do not hear;
And I am like a dumb man who does not open his
mouth.
14 Yes, I am like a man who does not hear,
And in whose mouth are no arguments.
15 For I hope in Thee, O LORD;
Thou wilt answer, O Lord my God.
16 For I said, "May they not rejoice over me,
*Who,* when my foot slips, would magnify themselves
against me."
17 For I am ready to fall,
And my [a]sorrow is continually before me.
18 For I confess my iniquity;
I am full of anxiety because of my sin.
19 But my enemies are vigorous *and* [b]strong;
And many are those who hate me wrongfully.
20 And those who repay evil for good,
They oppose me, because I follow what is good.
21 Do not forsake me, O LORD;
O my God, do not be far from me!
22 Make haste to help me,
O Lord, my salvation!

NAS [a] Lit., *pain* [b] Or, *numerous*

## New International

36but he soon passed away and was no more;
though I looked for him, he could not be found.

37Consider the blameless, observe the upright;
there is a future[c] for the man of peace.
38But all sinners will be destroyed;
the future[d] of the wicked will be cut off.

39The salvation of the righteous comes from the LORD;
he is their stronghold in time of trouble.
40The LORD helps them and delivers them;
he delivers them from the wicked and saves them,
because they take refuge in him.

A psalm of David. A petition.

**38** O LORD, do not rebuke me in your anger
or discipline me in your wrath.
2For your arrows have pierced me,
and your hand has come down upon me.
3Because of your wrath there is no health in my body;
my bones have no soundness because of my sin.
4My guilt has overwhelmed me
like a burden too heavy to bear.

5My wounds fester and are loathsome
because of my sinful folly.
6I am bowed down and brought very low;
all day long I go about mourning.
7My back is filled with searing pain;
there is no health in my body.
8I am feeble and utterly crushed;
I groan in anguish of heart.

9All my longings lie open before you, O Lord;
my sighing is not hidden from you.
10My heart pounds, my strength fails me;
even the light has gone from my eyes.
11My friends and companions avoid me because of my
wounds;
my neighbors stay far away.
12Those who seek my life set their traps,
those who would harm me talk of my ruin;
all day long they plot deception.

13I am like a deaf man, who cannot hear,
like a mute, who cannot open his mouth;
14I have become like a man who does not hear,
whose mouth can offer no reply.
15I wait for you, O LORD;
you will answer, O Lord my God.
16For I said, "Do not let them gloat
or exalt themselves over me when my foot slips."

17For I am about to fall,
and my pain is ever with me.
18I confess my iniquity;
I am troubled by my sin.
19Many are those who are my vigorous enemies;
those who hate me without reason are numerous.
20Those who repay my good with evil
slander me when I pursue what is good.

21O LORD, do not forsake me;
be not far from me, O my God.
22Come quickly to help me,
O Lord my Savior.

NIV [c] 37 Or *there will be posterity* [d] 38 Or *posterity*

## King James

To the chief Musician, *even to* Jeduthun, A Psalm of David.

39 I SAID, I will take heed to my ways, that I sin not with my
tongue: I will keep my mouth with a bridle, while the
wicked is before me.
2I was dumb with silence, I held my peace, *even* from good; and
my sorrow was stirred.
3My heart was hot within me, while I was musing the fire
burned: *then* spake I with my tongue,
4LORD, make me to know mine end, and the measure of my
days, what it *is; that* I may know how frail I *am.*
5Behold, thou hast made my days *as* an handbreadth; and mine
age *is* as nothing before thee: verily every man at his best state *is*
altogether vanity. Selah.
6Surely every man walketh in a vain show: surely they are
disquieted in vain: he heapeth up *riches,* and knoweth not who
shall gather them.
7And now, Lord, what wait I for? my hope *is* in thee.
8Deliver me from all my transgressions: make me not the reproach of the foolish.
9I was dumb, I opened not my mouth; because thou didst *it.*
10Remove thy stroke away from me: I am consumed by the blow
of thine hand.
11When thou with rebukes dost correct man for iniquity, thou
makest his beauty to consume away like a moth: surely every man
*is* vanity. Selah.
12Hear my prayer, O LORD, and give ear unto my cry; hold not
thy peace at my tears: for I *am* a stranger with thee, *and* a sojourner,
as all my fathers *were.*
13O spare me, that I may recover strength, before I go hence,
and be no more.

To the chief Musician, A Psalm of David.

40 I WAITED patiently for the LORD; and he inclined unto
me, and heard my cry.
2He brought me up also out of an horrible pit, out of the miry
clay, and set my feet upon a rock, *and* established my goings.
3And he hath put a new song in my mouth, *even* praise unto
our God: many shall see *it,* and fear, and shall trust in the LORD.
4Blessed *is* that man that maketh the LORD his trust, and respecteth not the proud, nor such as turn aside to lies.
5Many, O LORD my God, *are* thy wonderful works *which* thou
hast done, and thy thoughts *which are* to us-ward: they cannot be
reckoned up in order unto thee: *if* I would declare and speak *of
them,* they are more than can be numbered.

## Amplified

To the Chief Musician;
for Jeduthun [ *founder of an official musical family*]. A Psalm of David.

39 I SAID, I will take heed *and* guard my ways, that I sin not
with my tongue; I will muzzle my mouth as with a bridle,
while the wicked are before me.
2I was dumb with silence, I held my peace without profit, and
had no comfort away from good, while my distress was renewed.
3My heart was hot within me. While I was musing the fire
burned; then I spoke with my tongue:
4Lord, make me to know my end, and [to appreciate] the measure of my days, what it is; let me know *and* realize how frail I
am—how transient is my stay here.
5Behold, You have made my days as [short as] handbreadths,
and my lifetime is as nothing in Your sight. Truly every man at his
best is merely a breath! Selah [pause, and think calmly of that]!
6Surely every man walks to and fro—like a shadow in a pan-
tomime; surely for futility *and* emptiness they are in turmoil; each
one heaps up riches, not knowing who will gather them. [I Cor.
7:31; James 4:14.]
7And now, Lord, what do I wait for *and* expect? My hope *and*
expectation are in You.
8Deliver me from all my transgressions; make me not the scorn
*and* reproach of the [self-confident] fool!
9I am dumb, I open not my mouth, for it is You Who has done
it.
10Remove Your stroke away from me; I am consumed by the
conflict *and* the blow of Your hand.
11When with rebukes You correct *and* chasten man for sin, You
waste his beauty like a moth *and* what is dear to him consumes
away; surely every man is a mere breath. Selah [pause, and think
calmly of that]!
12Hear my prayer, O Lord, and give ear to my cry; hold not Your
peace at my tears! For I am Your passing guest, a temporary
resident, as all my fathers were.
13O look away from me *and* spare me, that I may recover cheerfulness *and* encouraging strength *and* know gladness before I go
and am no more!

To the Chief Musician. A Psalm of David.

40 I WAITED patiently *and* expectantly for the Lord, and He
inclined to me and heard my cry.
2He drew me up out of a horrible pit—a pit of tumult and of
destruction—out of the miry clay (froth and slime) and set my feet
upon a rock, steadying my steps *and* establishing my goings.
3And He has put a new song in my mouth, a song of praise to
our God. Many shall see and fear—revere, and worship—and put
their trust *and* confident reliance in the Lord. [Ps. 5:11.]
4Blessed—happy, fortunate [to be envied]—is the man who
makes the Lord his refuge *and* trust, and turns not to the proud
or to followers of false gods.
5Many, O Lord my God, are the wonderful works which You
have done, and Your thoughts toward us; no one can compare
with You! If I should declare and speak of them, they are too many
to be numbered.

## New American Standard

*The Vanity of Life.*

For the choir director, for Jeduthun. A Psalm of David.

**39** I SAID, "I will guard my ways,
That I may not sin with my tongue;
I will guard my mouth as with a muzzle,
While the wicked are in my presence."
2 I was dumb and silent,
I [a]refrained *even* from good;
And my [b]sorrow grew worse.
3 My heart was hot within me;
While I was musing the fire burned;
*Then* I spoke with my tongue:
4 "LORD, make me to know my end,
And what is the extent of my days,
Let me know how transient I am.
5 "Behold, Thou hast made my days *as* handbreadths,
And my lifetime as nothing in Thy sight,
Surely every man at his best is a mere breath. Selah.
6 "Surely every man walks about as [c]a phantom;
Surely they make an uproar for nothing;
He amasses *riches*, and does not know who will gather them.

7¶ "And now, Lord, for what do I wait?
My hope is in Thee.
8 "Deliver me from all my transgressions;
Make me not the reproach of the foolish.
9 "I have become dumb, I do not open my mouth,
Because it is Thou who hast done *it*.
10 "Remove Thy plague from me;
Because of the opposition of Thy hand, I am perishing.
11 "With reproofs Thou dost chasten a man for iniquity;
Thou dost consume as a moth what is precious to him;
Surely every man is a mere breath. Selah.

12¶ "Hear my prayer, O LORD, and give ear to my cry;
Do not be silent at my tears;
For I am a stranger with Thee,
A sojourner like all my fathers.
13 "Turn Thy gaze away from me, that I may [d]smile *again*,
Before I depart and am no more."

*God Sustains His Servant.*

For the choir director. A Psalm of David.

**40** I WAITED [e]patiently for the LORD;
And He inclined to me, and heard my cry.
2 He brought me up out of the pit of destruction, out of the miry clay;
And He set my feet upon a rock making my footsteps firm.
3 And He put a new song in my mouth, a song of praise to our God;
Many will see and fear,
And will trust in the LORD.

4¶ How blessed is the man who has made the LORD his trust,
And has not turned to the proud, nor to those who lapse into falsehood.
5 Many, O LORD my God, are the wonders which Thou hast done,
And Thy thoughts toward us;
There is none to compare with Thee;
If I would declare and speak of them,
They would be too numerous to count.

NAS [a] Lit., *kept silence* [b] Lit., *pain* [c] Lit., *an image* [d] Or, *become cheerful* [e] Or, *intently*

## New International

For the director of music. For Jeduthun. A psalm of David.

**39** I SAID, "I will watch my ways
and keep my tongue from sin;
I will put a muzzle on my mouth
as long as the wicked are in my presence."
2But when I was silent and still,
not even saying anything good,
my anguish increased.
3My heart grew hot within me,
and as I meditated, the fire burned;
then I spoke with my tongue:

4"Show me, O LORD, my life's end
and the number of my days;
let me know how fleeting is my life.
5You have made my days a mere handbreadth;
the span of my years is as nothing before you.
Each man's life is but a breath. *Selah*
6Man is a mere phantom as he goes to and fro:
He bustles about, but only in vain;
he heaps up wealth, not knowing who will get it.

7"But now, Lord, what do I look for?
My hope is in you.
8Save me from all my transgressions;
do not make me the scorn of fools.
9I was silent; I would not open my mouth,
for you are the one who has done this.
10Remove your scourge from me;
I am overcome by the blow of your hand.
11You rebuke and discipline men for their sin;
you consume their wealth like a moth—
each man is but a breath. *Selah*

12"Hear my prayer, O LORD,
listen to my cry for help;
be not deaf to my weeping.
For I dwell with you as an alien,
a stranger, as all my fathers were.
13Look away from me, that I may rejoice again
before I depart and am no more."

For the director of music. Of David. A psalm.

**40** I WAITED patiently for the LORD;
he turned to me and heard my cry.
2He lifted me out of the slimy pit,
out of the mud and mire;
he set my feet on a rock
and gave me a firm place to stand.
3He put a new song in my mouth,
a hymn of praise to our God.
Many will see and fear
and put their trust in the LORD.

4Blessed is the man
who makes the LORD his trust,
who does not look to the proud,
to those who turn aside to false gods.[f]
5Many, O LORD my God,
are the wonders you have done.
The things you planned for us
no one can recount to you;
were I to speak and tell of them,
they would be too many to declare.

NIV [f] 4 Or *to falsehood*

## King James

6 Sacrifice and offering thou didst not desire; mine ears hast thou opened: burnt offering and sin offering hast thou not required.

7 Then said I, Lo, I come: in the volume of the book *it is* written of me,

8 I delight to do thy will, O my God: yea, thy law *is* within my heart.

9 I have preached righteousness in the great congregation: lo, I have not refrained my lips, O LORD, thou knowest.

10 I have not hid thy righteousness within my heart; I have declared thy faithfulness and thy salvation: I have not concealed thy lovingkindness and thy truth from the great congregation.

11 Withhold not thou thy tender mercies from me, O LORD: let thy lovingkindness and thy truth continually preserve me.

12 For innumerable evils have compassed me about: mine iniquities have taken hold upon me, so that I am not able to look up; they are more than the hairs of mine head: therefore my heart faileth me.

13 Be pleased, O LORD, to deliver me: O LORD, make haste to help me.

14 Let them be ashamed and confounded together that seek after my soul to destroy it; let them be driven backward and put to shame that wish me evil.

15 Let them be desolate for a reward of their shame that say unto me, Aha, aha.

16 Let all those that seek thee rejoice and be glad in thee: let such as love thy salvation say continually, The LORD be magnified.

17 But I *am* poor and needy; *yet* the Lord thinketh upon me: thou *art* my help and my deliverer; make no tarrying, O my God.

To the chief Musician, A Psalm of David.

**41** BLESSED *IS* he that considereth the poor: the LORD will deliver him in time of trouble.

2 The LORD will preserve him, and keep him alive; *and* he shall be blessed upon the earth: and thou wilt not deliver him unto the will of his enemies.

3 The LORD will strengthen him upon the bed of languishing: thou wilt make all his bed in his sickness.

4 I said, LORD, be merciful unto me: heal my soul; for I have sinned against thee.

5 Mine enemies speak evil of me, When shall he die, and his name perish?

6 And if he come to see *me,* he speaketh vanity: his heart gathereth iniquity to itself; *when* he goeth abroad, he telleth *it.*

7 All that hate me whisper together against me: against me do they devise my hurt.

8 An evil disease, *say they,* cleaveth fast unto him: and *now* that he lieth he shall rise up no more.

## Amplified

6 Sacrifice and offering You do not desire, *nor* have You delight in them; You have given me capacity to hear *and* obey [Your law, a more valuable service than] burnt and sin offerings *which* You do not require.

7 Then said I, Lo, I come; in the volume of the book it is written of me,

8 I delight to do Your will, O my God; yes, Your law *is* within my heart. [Heb. 10:5-9.]

9 I have proclaimed glad tidings of righteousness in the great assembly—tidings of uprightness and right standing with God. Lo, I have not restrained my lips, as You know, O Lord.

10 I have not concealed Your righteousness within my heart; I have proclaimed Your faithfulness and Your salvation; I have not hid away Your steadfast love and Your truth from the great assembly. [Acts 20:20, 27.]

11 Withhold not Your tender mercies from me, O Lord; let Your loving-kindness and Your truth continually preserve me!

12 For innumerable evils have compassed me about; my iniquities have taken such hold on me that I am not able to look up; they are more than the hairs of my head, and my heart has failed me *and* forsaken me.

13 Be pleased, O Lord, to deliver me; O Lord, make haste to help me!

14 Let them be put to shame and confounded together who seek after *and* require my life to destroy it; let them be driven backward and brought to dishonor who wish me evil *and* delight in my hurt!

15 Let them be desolate by reason of their shame who say to me, Aha, aha!

16 Let all those that seek *and* require You rejoice and be glad in You; let such as love Your salvation say continually, The Lord be magnified!

17 [As for me] I am poor and needy, yet the Lord takes thought *and* plans for me. You are my help and my deliverer. O my God, do not tarry! [Ps. 70:1-5; I Pet. 5:7.]

To the Chief Musician. A Psalm of David.

**41** BLESSED—HAPPY, fortunate [to be envied]—is he who considers the weak *and* the poor; the Lord will deliver him in the time of evil *and* trouble.

2 The Lord will protect him, and keep him alive; he shall be called blessed in the land; and You will not deliver him to the will of his enemies.

3 The Lord will sustain, refresh *and* strengthen him on his bed of languishing; all his bed You, *O Lord,* will turn, change *and* transform in his illness.

4 I said, Lord, be merciful *and* gracious to me; heal my inner self, for I have sinned against You.

5 My enemies speak evil of me, *saying,* When will he die, and his name perish?

6 And if one comes to see me, he speaks falsehood *and* empty words, while his heart gathers mischievous *gossip* [against me]; when he goes away, he tells it abroad.

7 All who hate me whisper together about me; against me do they devise my hurt—imagining the worst for me.

8 An evil disease, say they, is poured out upon him *and* cleaves fast to him; and now that he is bedfast, he will not rise up again.

## New American Standard

6¶ Sacrifice and meal offering Thou hast not desired;
My ears Thou hast [a]opened;
Burnt offering and sin offering Thou hast not required.
7 Then I said, "Behold, I come;
In the scroll of the book it is written of me;
8 I delight to do Thy will, O my God;
Thy Law is within my heart."

9¶ I have proclaimed glad tidings of righteousness in the great congregation;
Behold, I will not restrain my lips,
O LORD, Thou knowest.
10 I have not hidden Thy righteousness within my heart;
I have spoken of Thy faithfulness and Thy salvation;
I have not concealed Thy lovingkindness and Thy truth from the great congregation.

11¶ Thou, O LORD, wilt not withhold Thy compassion from me;
Thy lovingkindness and Thy truth will continually preserve me.
12 For evils beyond number have surrounded me;
My iniquities have overtaken me, so that I am not able to see;
They are more numerous than the hairs of my head;
And my heart has failed me.

13¶ Be pleased, O LORD, to deliver me;
Make haste, O LORD, to help me.
14 Let those be ashamed and humiliated together
Who seek my [b]life to destroy it;
Let those be turned back and dishonored
Who delight [c]in my hurt.
15 Let those be appalled be cause of their shame
Who say to me, "Aha, aha!"
16 Let all who seek Thee rejoice and be glad in Thee;
Let those who love Thy salvation say continually,
"The LORD be magnified!"
17 Since I am afflicted and needy,
Let the Lord be mindful of me;
Thou art my help and my deliverer;
Do not delay, O my God.

*The Psalmist in Sickness Complains of Enemies and False Friends.*

For the choir director. A Psalm of David.

41 HOW BLESSED is he who considers the helpless;
The LORD will deliver him in a day of trouble.
2 The LORD will protect him, and keep him alive,
And he shall be called blessed upon the earth;
And do not give him over to the desire of his enemies.
3 The LORD will sustain him upon his sickbed;
In his illness, Thou dost [d]restore him to health.

4¶ As for me, I said, "O LORD, be gracious to me;
Heal my soul, for I have sinned against Thee."
5 My enemies speak evil against me,
"When will he die, and his name perish?"
6 And when he comes to see *me*, he speaks falsehood;
His heart gathers wickedness to itself;
When he goes outside, he tells it.
7 All who hate me whisper together against me;
Against me they devise my hurt, *saying*,
8 "A wicked thing is poured out upon him,
That when he lies down, he will not rise up again."

NAS [a] Lit., *dug*, or possibly, *pierced* [b] Or, *soul* [c] Or, *to injure me* [d] Lit., *turn all his bed*

## New International

6 Sacrifice and offering you did not desire,
but my ears you have pierced[e,f];
burnt offerings and sin offerings
you did not require.
7 Then I said, "Here I am, I have come—
it is written about me in the scroll.[g]
8 I desire to do your will, O my God;
your law is within my heart."
9 I proclaim righteousness in the great assembly;
I do not seal my lips,
as you know, O LORD.
10 I do not hide your righteousness in my heart;
I speak of your faithfulness and salvation.
I do not conceal your love and your truth
from the great assembly.

11 Do not withhold your mercy from me, O LORD;
may your love and your truth always protect me.
12 For troubles without number surround me;
my sins have overtaken me, and I cannot see.
They are more than the hairs of my head,
and my heart fails within me.

13 Be pleased, O LORD, to save me;
O LORD, come quickly to help me.
14 May all who seek to take my life
be put to shame and confusion;
may all who desire my ruin
be turned back in disgrace.
15 May those who say to me, "Aha! Aha!"
be appalled at their own shame.
16 But may all who seek you
rejoice and be glad in you;
may those who love your salvation always say,
"The LORD be exalted!"

17 Yet I am poor and needy;
may the Lord think of me.
You are my help and my deliverer;
O my God, do not delay.

For the director of music. A psalm of David.

41 BLESSED IS he who has regard for the weak;
the LORD delivers him in times of trouble.
2 The LORD will protect him and preserve his life;
he will bless him in the land
and not surrender him to the desire of his foes.
3 The LORD will sustain him on his sickbed
and restore him from his bed of illness.

4 I said, "O LORD, have mercy on me;
heal me, for I have sinned against you."
5 My enemies say of me in malice,
"When will he die and his name perish?"
6 Whenever one comes to see me,
he speaks falsely, while his heart gathers slander;
then he goes out and spreads it abroad.

7 All my enemies whisper together against me;
they imagine the worst for me, saying,
8 "A vile disease has beset him;
he will never get up from the place where he lies."

NIV [e] 6 Hebrew; Septuagint *but a body you have prepared for me* (see also Symmachus and Theodotion) [f] 6 Or *opened* [g] 7 Or *come / with the scroll written for me*

## King James

9Yea, mine own familiar friend, in whom I trusted, which did eat of my bread, hath lifted up *his* heel against me.

10But thou, O LORD, be merciful unto me, and raise me up, that I may requite them.

11By this I know that thou favourest me, because mine enemy doth not triumph over me.

12And as for me, thou upholdest me in mine integrity, and settest me before thy face for ever.

13Blessed *be* the LORD God of Israel from everlasting, and to everlasting. Amen, and Amen.

Book II

To the chief Musician, Maschil, for the sons of Korah.

**42** AS THE hart panteth after the water brooks, so panteth my soul after thee, O God.

2My soul thirsteth for God, for the living God: when shall I come and appear before God?

3My tears have been my meat day and night, while they continually say unto me, Where *is* thy God?

4When I remember these *things,* I pour out my soul in me: for I had gone with the multitude, I went with them to the house of God, with the voice of joy and praise, with a multitude that kept holyday.

5Why art thou cast down, O my soul? and *why* art thou disquieted in me? hope thou in God: for I shall yet praise him *for* the help of his countenance.

6O my God, my soul is cast down within me: therefore will I remember thee from the land of Jordan, and of the Hermonites, from the hill Mizar.

7Deep calleth unto deep at the noise of thy waterspouts: all thy waves and thy billows are gone over me.

8 *Yet* the LORD will command his lovingkindness in the daytime, and in the night his song *shall be* with me, *and* my prayer unto the God of my life.

9I will say unto God my rock, Why hast thou forgotten me? why go I mourning because of the oppression of the enemy?

10 *As* with a sword in my bones, mine enemies reproach me; while they say daily unto me, Where *is* thy God?

11Why art thou cast down, O my soul? and why art thou disquieted within me? hope thou in God: for I shall yet praise him, *who is* the health of my countenance, and my God.

## Amplified

9Even my own familiar friend in whom I trusted (relied on and was confident), who ate of my bread, has lifted up his heel against me. [John 13:18.]

10But do You, O Lord, be merciful *and* gracious to me and raise me up, that I may requite them.

11By this I know that You favor *and* delight in me, because my enemy does not triumph over me.

12And as for me, You have upheld me in my integrity, and set me in Your presence for ever.

13Blessed be the Lord God of Israel from everlasting and to everlasting—from this age to the next and forever! Amen and Amen (so be it).

BOOK TWO

To the Chief Musician. A skillful song, *or* a didactic *or* reflective poem of the sons of Korah.

**42** AS THE hart pants *and* longs for the water brooks, so I pant *and* long for You, O God.

2My inner self thirsts for God, for the living God. When shall I come and behold the face of God? [John 7:37; I Thess. 1:9, 10.]

3My tears have been my food day and night, while men say to me all day long, Where *is* your God?

4These things I [earnestly] remember, and pour myself out within me: how I went slowly before the throng and led them in procession to the house of God [like a bandmaster before his band, timing the steps to sound of music and chant of song], with the voice of shouting and praise, a throng keeping festival.

5Why are you cast down, O my inner self? And why should you moan over me *and* be disquieted within me? Hope you in God *and* wait expectantly for Him, for I shall yet praise Him, my help and my God.

6O my God, my life is cast down upon me [and I find the burden more than I can bear]; therefore will I [earnestly] remember You from the land of the Jordan *River* and the *summits of Mount* Hermon, from the little mountain Mizar.

7[Roaring] deep calls to [roaring] deep at the thunder of Your waterspouts; all Your breakers and Your rolling waves have gone over me.

8 *Yet* the Lord will command His loving-kindness in the daytime, and in the night His song shall be with me, a prayer to the God of my life.

9I will say to God my rock, Why have You forgotten me? Why go I mourning because of the oppression of the enemy?

10As with a sword [crushing] in my bones, my enemies taunt *and* reproach me; while they say continually to me, Where is your God?

11Why are you cast down, O my inner self? And why should you moan over me *and* be disquieted within me? Hope in God *and* wait expectantly for Him; for I shall yet praise Him Who is the help of my countenance, and my God.

## New American Standard

9 Even my close friend, in whom I trusted,
Who ate my bread,
Has lifted up his heel against me.

10 ¶ But Thou, O LORD, be gracious to me, and raise me up,
That I may repay them.
11 By this I know that Thou art pleased with me,
Because my enemy does not shout in triumph over me.
12 As for me, Thou dost uphold me in my integrity,
And Thou dost set me in Thy presence forever.

13 ¶ Blessed be the LORD, the God of Israel,
From everlasting to everlasting.
Amen, and Amen.

BOOK 2

*Thirsting for God in Trouble and Exile.*

For the choir director. A Maskil of the sons of Korah.

**42** AS THE deer [a]pants for the water brooks,
So my soul pants for Thee, O God.
2 My soul thirsts for God, for the living God;
When shall I come and appear before God?
3 My tears have been my food day and night,
While *they* say to me all day long, "Where is your God?"
4 These things I remember, and I pour out my soul within me.
For I used to go along with the throng *and* lead them in procession to the house of God,
With the voice of joy and thanksgiving, a multitude keeping festival.

5 ¶ Why are you in despair, O my soul?
And *why* have you become disturbed within me?
Hope in God, for I shall again praise Him
*For* the help of His presence.
6 O my God, my soul is in despair within me;
Therefore I remember Thee from the land of the Jordan,
And the peaks of Hermon, from Mount Mizar.
7 Deep calls to deep at the sound of Thy waterfalls;
All Thy breakers and Thy waves have rolled over me.
8 The LORD will command His lovingkindness in the daytime;
And His song will be with me in the night,
A prayer to the God of my life.

9 ¶ I will say to God my rock, "Why hast Thou forgotten me?
Why do I go mourning because of the oppression of the enemy?"
10 As a shattering of my bones, my adversaries revile me,
While they say to me all day long, "Where is your God?"
11 Why are you in despair, O my soul?
And why have you become disturbed within me?
Hope in God, for I shall yet praise Him,
The help of my countenance, and my God.

NAS [a] Lit., *longs for*

## New International

9 Even my close friend, whom I trusted,
he who shared my bread,
has lifted up his heel against me.

10 But you, O LORD, have mercy on me;
raise me up, that I may repay them.
11 I know that you are pleased with me,
for my enemy does not triumph over me.
12 In my integrity you uphold me
and set me in your presence forever.

13 Praise be to the LORD, the God of Israel,
from everlasting to everlasting.
Amen and Amen.

BOOK II

*Psalms 42-72*

For[b] the director of music. A *maskil*[c] of the Sons of Korah.

**42** AS THE deer pants for streams of water,
so my soul pants for you, O God.
2 My soul thirsts for God, for the living God.
When can I go and meet with God?
3 My tears have been my food
day and night,
while men say to me all day long,
"Where is your God?"
4 These things I remember
as I pour out my soul:
how I used to go with the multitude,
leading the procession to the house of God,
with shouts of joy and thanksgiving
among the festive throng.
5 Why are you downcast, O my soul?
Why so disturbed within me?
Put your hope in God,
for I will yet praise him,
my Savior and 6 my God.

My[d] soul is downcast within me;
therefore I will remember you
from the land of the Jordan,
the heights of Hermon—from Mount Mizar.
7 Deep calls to deep
in the roar of your waterfalls;
all your waves and breakers
have swept over me.
8 By day the LORD directs his love,
at night his song is with me—
a prayer to the God of my life.

9 I say to God my Rock,
"Why have you forgotten me?
Why must I go about mourning,
oppressed by the enemy?"
10 My bones suffer mortal agony
as my foes taunt me,
saying to me all day long,
"Where is your God?"

11 Why are you downcast, O my soul?
Why so disturbed within me?
Put your hope in God,
for I will yet praise him,
my Savior and my God.

NIV [b] In many Hebrew manuscripts Psalms 42 and 43 constitute one psalm. [c] Title: Probably a literary or musical term [d] 5,6 A few Hebrew manuscripts, Septuagint and Syriac; most Hebrew manuscripts *praise him for his saving help. / 6O my God, my*

## King James

**43** JUDGE ME, O God, and plead my cause against an ungodly nation: O deliver me from the deceitful and unjust man.
2For thou *art* the God of my strength: why dost thou cast me off? why go I mourning because of the oppression of the enemy?
3O send out thy light and thy truth: let them lead me; let them bring me unto thy holy hill, and to thy tabernacles.
4Then will I go unto the altar of God, unto God my exceeding joy: yea, upon the harp will I praise thee, O God my God.
5Why art thou cast down, O my soul? and why art thou disquieted within me? hope in God: for I shall yet praise him, *who is* the health of my countenance, and my God.

To the chief Musician for the sons of Korah, Maschil.

**44** WE HAVE heard with our ears, O God, our fathers have told us, *what* work thou didst in their days, in the times of old.
2 *How* thou didst drive out the heathen with thy hand, and plantedst them; *how* thou didst afflict the people, and cast them out.
3For they got not the land in possession by their own sword, neither did their own arm save them: but thy right hand, and thine arm, and the light of thy countenance, because thou hadst a favour unto them.
4Thou art my King, O God: command deliverances for Jacob.
5Through thee will we push down our enemies: through thy name will we tread them under that rise up against us.
6For I will not trust in my bow, neither shall my sword save me.
7But thou hast saved us from our enemies, and hast put them to shame that hated us.
8In God we boast all the day long, and praise thy name for ever. Selah.
9But thou hast cast off, and put us to shame; and goest not forth with our armies.
10Thou makest us to turn back from the enemy: and they which hate us spoil for themselves.
11Thou hast given us like sheep *appointed* for meat; and hast scattered us among the heathen.
12Thou sellest thy people for nought, and dost not increase *thy wealth* by their price.
13Thou makest us a reproach to our neighbours, a scorn and a derision to them that are round about us.
14Thou makest us a byword among the heathen, a shaking of the head among the people.
15My confusion *is* continually before me, and the shame of my face hath covered me,
16For the voice of him that reproacheth and blasphemeth; by reason of the enemy and avenger.

## Amplified

**43** JUDGE *AND* vindicate me, O God; plead and defend my cause against an ungodly nation. O deliver me from the deceitful and unjust man!
2For You are the God of my strength [my stronghold—in Whom I take refuge]; why have You cast me off? Why go I mourning because of the oppression of the enemy?
3O send out Your light and Your truth; let them lead me, let them bring me to Your holy hill and to Your dwelling.
4Then will I go to the altar of God, to God my exceeding joy; yes, with the lyre will I praise You, O God, my God!
5Why are you cast down, O my inner self? And why should you moan over me *and* be disquieted within me? Hope in God *and* wait expectantly for Him; for I shall yet praise Him, Who is the help of my [sad] countenance, and my God.

To the Chief Musician. [*A Psalm*] of the sons of Korah. A skillful song, *or* a didactic *or* reflective poem.

**44** WE HAVE heard with our ears, O God, our fathers have told us, *what* work You did in their days, in the days of old.
2You drove out the nations with Your hand *and* it was Your power that gave [Israel] a home by rooting out [the heathen] peoples, but [Israel] You spread out.
3For they got not the land [of Canaan] in possession by their own sword, neither did their own arm save them; but Your right hand and Your arm and the light of Your countenance [did it], because You were favorable *and* did delight in them.
4You are my King, O God; command victories *and* deliverance for Jacob (Israel).
5Through You shall we push down our enemies; through Your name shall we tread them under who rise up against us.
6For I will not trust in *and* lean on my bow, neither shall my sword save me.
7But You have saved us from our foes, and have put them to shame who hate us.
8In God we have made our boast all the day long, and we will give thanks to Your name forever. Selah [Pause, and think calmly of that]!
9But now You have cast us off and brought us to dishonor, and You go not out with our armies.
10You make us to turn back from the enemy, and they who hate us take spoil for themselves.
11You have made us like sheep intended for mutton, and have scattered us in exile among the nations.
12You sell Your people for nothing, and have not increased Your wealth by their price.
13You have made us the taunt of our neighbors, a scoffing and a derision to those who are round about us.
14You make us a byword among the nations, a shaking of the heads among the people.
15My dishonor is before me all day long, and shame has covered my face
16At the words of the taunter and reviler, by reason of the enemy and the revengeful.

## New American Standard

*Prayer for Deliverance.*

**43** VINDICATE ME, O God, and plead my case against an ungodly nation;
O deliver me from the deceitful and unjust man!
2 For Thou art the God of my strength; why hast Thou rejected me?
Why do I go mourning because of the oppression of the enemy?
3¶ O send out Thy light and Thy truth, let them lead me;
Let them bring me to Thy holy hill,
And to Thy dwelling places.
4 Then I will go to the altar of God,
To God my exceeding joy;
And upon the lyre I shall praise Thee, O God, my God.
5¶ Why are you in despair, O my soul?
And why are you disturbed within me?
Hope in God, for I shall again praise Him,
The help of my countenance, and my God.

*Former Deliverances and Present Troubles.*

For the choir director. A Maskil of the sons of Korah.

**44** O GOD, we have heard with our ears,
Our fathers have told us,
The work that Thou didst in their days,
In the days of old.
2 Thou with Thine own hand didst drive out the nations;
Then Thou didst plant them;
Thou didst afflict the peoples,
Then Thou didst spread them abroad.
3 For by their own sword they did not possess the land;
And their own arm did not save them;
But Thy right hand, and Thine arm, and the light of Thy presence,
For Thou didst favor them.
4¶ Thou art my King, O God;
Command victories for Jacob.
5 Through Thee we will push back our adversaries;
Through Thy name we will trample down those who rise up against us.
6 For I will not trust in my bow,
Nor will my sword save me.
7 But Thou hast saved us from our adversaries,
And Thou hast put to shame those who hate us.
8 In God we have boasted all day long,
And we will give thanks to Thy name forever. Selah.
9¶ Yet Thou hast rejected *us* and brought us to dishonor,
And dost not go out with our armies.
10 Thou dost cause us to turn back from the adversary;
And those who hate us have taken spoil for themselves.
11 Thou dost give us as sheep to be eaten,
And hast scattered us among the nations.
12 Thou dost sell Thy people cheaply,
And hast not [a]profited by their sale.
13 Thou dost make us a reproach to our neighbors,
A scoffing and a derision to those around us.
14 Thou dost make us a byword among the nations,
A laughingstock among the peoples.
15 All day long my dishonor is before me,
And my humiliation has overwhelmed me,
16 Because of the voice of him who reproaches and reviles,
Because of the presence of the enemy and the avenger.

**NAS** [a] Or, *set a high price on them*

## New International

**43**[b] VINDICATE ME, O God,
and plead my cause against an ungodly nation;
rescue me from deceitful and wicked men.
2You are God my stronghold.
Why have you rejected me?
Why must I go about mourning,
oppressed by the enemy?
3Send forth your light and your truth,
let them guide me;
let them bring me to your holy mountain,
to the place where you dwell.
4Then will I go to the altar of God,
to God, my joy and my delight.
I will praise you with the harp,
O God, my God.
5Why are you downcast, O my soul?
Why so disturbed within me?
Put your hope in God,
for I will yet praise him,
my Savior and my God.

For the director of music. Of the Sons of Korah. A *maskil*.[c]

**44** WE HAVE heard with our ears, O God;
our fathers have told us
what you did in their days,
in days long ago.
2With your hand you drove out the nations
and planted our fathers;
you crushed the peoples
and made our fathers flourish.
3It was not by their sword that they won the land,
nor did their arm bring them victory;
it was your right hand, your arm,
and the light of your face, for you loved them.
4You are my King and my God,
who decrees[d] victories for Jacob.
5Through you we push back our enemies;
through your name we trample our foes.
6I do not trust in my bow,
my sword does not bring me victory;
7but you give us victory over our enemies,
you put our adversaries to shame.
8In God we make our boast all day long,
and we will praise your name forever. *Selah*
9But now you have rejected and humbled us;
you no longer go out with our armies.
10You made us retreat before the enemy,
and our adversaries have plundered us.
11You gave us up to be devoured like sheep
and have scattered us among the nations.
12You sold your people for a pittance,
gaining nothing from their sale.
13You have made us a reproach to our neighbors,
the scorn and derision of those around us.
14You have made us a byword among the nations;
the peoples shake their heads at us.
15My disgrace is before me all day long,
and my face is covered with shame
16at the taunts of those who reproach and revile me,
because of the enemy, who is bent on revenge.

**NIV** [b] In many Hebrew manuscripts Psalms 42 and 43 constitute one psalm. [c] Title: Probably a literary or musical term [d] 4 Septuagint, Aquila and Syriac; Hebrew *King, O God; / command*

## King James

17 All this is come upon us; yet have we not forgotten thee, neither have we dealt falsely in thy covenant.

18 Our heart is not turned back, neither have our steps declined from thy way;

19 Though thou hast sore broken us in the place of dragons, and covered us with the shadow of death.

20 If we have forgotten the name of our God, or stretched out our hands to a strange god;

21 Shall not God search this out? for he knoweth the secrets of the heart.

22 Yea, for thy sake are we killed all the day long; we are counted as sheep for the slaughter.

23 Awake, why sleepest thou, O Lord? arise, cast *us* not off for ever.

24 Wherefore hidest thou thy face, *and* forgettest our affliction and our oppression?

25 For our soul is bowed down to the dust: our belly cleaveth unto the earth.

26 Arise for our help, and redeem us for thy mercies' sake.

To the chief Musician upon Shoshannim, for the sons of Korah, Maschil, A Song of loves.

**45** MY HEART is inditing a good matter: I speak of the things which I have made touching the king: my tongue *is* the pen of a ready writer.

2 Thou art fairer than the children of men: grace is poured into thy lips: therefore God hath blessed thee for ever.

3 Gird thy sword upon *thy* thigh, O *most* mighty, with thy glory and thy majesty.

4 And in thy majesty ride prosperously because of truth and meekness *and* righteousness; and thy right hand shall teach thee terrible things.

5 Thine arrows *are* sharp in the heart of the king's enemies; *whereby* the people fall under thee.

6 Thy throne, O God, *is* for ever and ever: the sceptre of thy kingdom *is* a right sceptre.

7 Thou lovest righteousness, and hatest wickedness: therefore God, thy God, hath anointed thee with the oil of gladness above thy fellows.

8 All thy garments *smell* of myrrh, and aloes, *and* cassia, out of the ivory palaces, whereby they have made thee glad.

9 Kings' daughters *were* among thy honourable women: upon thy right hand did stand the queen in gold of Ophir.

10 Hearken, O daughter, and consider, and incline thine ear; forget also thine own people, and thy father's house;

11 So shall the king greatly desire thy beauty: for he *is* thy Lord; and worship thou him.

12 And the daughter of Tyre *shall be there* with a gift; *even* the rich among the people shall entreat thy favour.

13 The king's daughter *is* all glorious within: her clothing *is* of wrought gold.

14 She shall be brought unto the king in raiment of needlework: the virgins her companions that follow her shall be brought unto thee.

## Amplified

17 All this is come upon us, yet have we not forgotten You, neither have we been false to Your covenant [which You made with our fathers].

18 Our heart is not turned back, neither have our steps declined from Your path,

19 Though You have distressingly broken us in the place of jackals and covered us with deep darkness, even with the shadow of death.

20 If we have forgotten the name of our God, or stretched out our hands to a strange god,

21 Would not God discover this? For He knows the secrets of the heart.

22 No, *but* for Your sake we are killed all the day long; we are accounted as sheep for the slaughter. [Rom. 8:35-39.]

23 Awake! Why do You sleep, O Lord? Arouse Yourself, cast us not off for ever!

24 Why do You hide Your face, *and* forget our affliction and our oppression?

25 For our lives are bowed down to the dust; our body cleaves to the ground.

26 Rise up! Come to our help, and deliver us for Your mercy's sake *and* because of Your steadfast love!

To the Chief Musician; set to Lilies [*probably a popular air. A Psalm*] of the sons of Korah. A skillful song, *or* a didactic *or* reflective poem. A song of loves.

**45** MY HEART overflows with a [a]goodly theme; I address my psalm to a king. My tongue is as the pen of a ready writer.

2 You are fairer than the children of men; graciousness is poured upon Your lips; therefore God has blessed You forever.

3 Gird Your sword upon Your thigh, O mighty One, in Your glory and Your majesty!

4 And in Your majesty ride on triumphantly for the cause of truth, humility *and* righteousness [uprightness and right standing with God]; and let Your right hand guide You to tremendous things.

5 Your arrows are sharp; the peoples fall under You; Your darts pierce the heart of the king's enemies.

6 Your throne, O God, is for ever and ever; the scepter of righteousness is the scepter of Your kingdom.

7 You love righteousness, uprightness *and* right standing with God, and hate wickedness; therefore God, Your God, has anointed You with the oil of gladness above Your fellows. [Heb. 1:8, 9.]

8 Your garments are all fragrant with myrrh, aloes *and* cassia; stringed instruments make you glad.

9 Kings' daughters are among your honorable women; at your right hand stands the queen in gold of Ophir.

10 Hear, O daughter, consider, submit *and* consent to my instruction; forget also your own people and your father's house;

11 So will the king desire your beauty; for he is your lord; be submissive *and* reverence *and* honor him.

12 And, O daughter of Tyre, the richest of the people shall entreat your favor with a gift.

13 The king's daughter in the inner part *of the palace* is all glorious; her clothing is inwrought with gold. [Rev. 19:7, 8.]

14 She shall be brought to the king in raiment of needlework; with the virgins, her companions that follow her, she shall be brought to you.

**AMP** [a] Jesus spoke of what was written of Him "in the Psalms." This is one such Messianic Psalm. However, the capitalization indicating Deity is offered provisionally. The chapter is written against the background of a secular royal wedding. But the New Testament reference to this psalm in Hebrews 1:8, 9, where verses 6 and 7 are quoted and applied to Christ, makes any other interpretation seem incidental in importance.

## New American Standard

17¶ All this has come upon us, but we have not forgotten
Thee,
And we have not dealt falsely with Thy covenant.
18 Our heart has not turned back,
And our steps have not deviated from Thy way,
19 Yet Thou hast crushed us in a place of jackals,
And covered us with the shadow of death.

20¶ If we had forgotten the name of our God,
Or extended our hands to a strange god;
21 Would not God find this out?
For He knows the secrets of the heart.
22 But for Thy sake we are killed all day long;
We are considered as sheep to be slaughtered.
23 Arouse Thyself, why dost Thou sleep, O Lord?
Awake, do not reject us forever.
24 Why dost Thou hide Thy face,
And forget our affliction and our oppression?
25 For our soul has sunk down into the dust;
Our body cleaves to the earth.
26 Rise up, be our help,
And redeem us for the sake of Thy lovingkindness.

*A Song Celebrating the King's Marriage.*

For the choir director; according to the [b]Shoshannim.—A Maskil of the sons of Korah. A Song of Love.

**45** MY HEART [c]overflows with a good theme;
I address my verses to the King;
My tongue is the pen of a ready writer.
2 Thou art fairer than the sons of men;
Grace is poured upon Thy lips;
Therefore God has blessed Thee forever.

3¶ Gird Thy sword on *Thy* thigh, O Mighty One,
*In* Thy splendor and Thy majesty!
4 And in Thy majesty ride on victoriously,
For the cause of truth and meekness *and* righteousness;
Let Thy right hand teach Thee awesome things.
5 Thine arrows are sharp;
The peoples fall under Thee;
*Thine arrows are* in the heart of the King's enemies.

6¶ Thy throne, O God, is forever and ever;
A scepter of uprightness is the scepter of Thy kingdom.
7 Thou hast loved righteousness, and hated wickedness;
Therefore God, Thy God, has anointed Thee
With the oil of joy above Thy fellows.
8 All Thy garments are *fragrant with* myrrh and aloes *and*
cassia;
Out of ivory palaces stringed instruments have made
Thee glad.
9 Kings' daughters are among Thy noble ladies;
At Thy right hand stands the queen in gold from
Ophir.

10¶ Listen, O daughter, give attention and incline your
ear;
Forget your people and your father's house;
11 Then the King will desire your beauty;
Because He is your Lord, bow down to Him.
12 And the daughter of Tyre *will come* with a gift;
The rich among the people will entreat your favor.
13¶ The King's daughter is all glorious within;
Her clothing is interwoven with gold.
14 She will be led to the King in embroidered work;
The virgins, her companions who follow her,
Will be brought to Thee.

NAS [b] Possibly, *Lilies* [c] Lit., *is astir*

## New International

17 All this happened to us,
though we had not forgotten you
or been false to your covenant.
18 Our hearts had not turned back;
our feet had not strayed from your path.
19 But you crushed us and made us a haunt for jackals
and covered us over with deep darkness.

20 If we had forgotten the name of our God
or spread out our hands to a foreign god,
21 would not God have discovered it,
since he knows the secrets of the heart?
22 Yet for your sake we face death all day long;
we are considered as sheep to be slaughtered.
23 Awake, O Lord! Why do you sleep?
Rouse yourself! Do not reject us forever.
24 Why do you hide your face
and forget our misery and oppression?

25 We are brought down to the dust;
our bodies cling to the ground.
26 Rise up and help us;
redeem us because of your unfailing love.

For the director of music. To ⌊the tune of⌋ "Lilies." Of the Sons of Korah. A *maskil*.[d] A wedding song.

**45** MY HEART is stirred by a noble theme
as I recite my verses for the king;
my tongue is the pen of a skillful writer.

2 You are the most excellent of men
and your lips have been anointed with grace,
since God has blessed you forever.
3 Gird your sword upon your side, O mighty one;
clothe yourself with splendor and majesty.
4 In your majesty ride forth victoriously
in behalf of truth, humility and righteousness;
let your right hand display awesome deeds.
5 Let your sharp arrows pierce the hearts of the king's
enemies;
let the nations fall beneath your feet.
6 Your throne, O God, will last for ever and ever;
a scepter of justice will be the scepter of your kingdom.
7 You love righteousness and hate wickedness;
therefore God, your God, has set you above your
companions
by anointing you with the oil of joy.
8 All your robes are fragrant with myrrh and aloes and
cassia;
from palaces adorned with ivory
the music of the strings makes you glad.
9 Daughters of kings are among your honored women;
at your right hand is the royal bride in gold of Ophir.

10 Listen, O daughter, consider and give ear:
Forget your people and your father's house.
11 The king is enthralled by your beauty;
honor him, for he is your lord.
12 The Daughter of Tyre will come with a gift,[e]
men of wealth will seek your favor.

13 All glorious is the princess within ⌊her chamber⌋;
her gown is interwoven with gold.
14 In embroidered garments she is led to the king;
her virgin companions follow her
and are brought to you.

NIV [d] Title: Probably a literary or musical term [e] *12* Or *A Tyrian robe is among the gifts*

## King James

15With gladness and rejoicing shall they be brought: they shall enter into the king's palace.
16Instead of thy fathers shall be thy children, whom thou mayest make princes in all the earth.
17I will make thy name to be remembered in all generations: therefore shall the people praise thee for ever and ever.

To the chief Musician for the sons of Korah, A Song upon Alamoth.

**46** GOD *IS* our refuge and strength, a very present help in trouble.
2Therefore will not we fear, though the earth be removed, and
though the mountains be carried into the midst of the sea;
3 *Though* the waters thereof roar *and* be troubled, *though* the
mountains shake with the swelling thereof. Selah.
4 *There is* a river, the streams whereof shall make glad the city
of God, the holy *place* of the tabernacles of the most High.
5God *is* in the midst of her; she shall not be moved: God shall
help her, *and that* right early.
6The heathen raged, the kingdoms were moved: he uttered his
voice, the earth melted.
7The LORD of hosts *is* with us; the God of Jacob *is* our refuge.
Selah.
8Come, behold the works of the LORD, what desolations he hath
made in the earth.
9He maketh wars to cease unto the end of the earth; he breaketh
the bow, and cutteth the spear in sunder; he burneth the chariot
in the fire.
10Be still, and know that I *am* God: I will be exalted among the
heathen, I will be exalted in the earth.
11The LORD of hosts *is* with us; the God of Jacob *is* our refuge.
Selah.

To the chief Musician, A Psalm for the sons of Korah.

**47** O CLAP your hands, all ye people; shout unto God with the voice of triumph.
2For the LORD most high *is* terrible; *he is* a great King over all
the earth.
3He shall subdue the people under us, and the nations under
our feet.
4He shall choose our inheritance for us, the excellency of Jacob
whom he loved. Selah.
5God is gone up with a shout, the LORD with the sound of a
trumpet.
6Sing praises to God, sing praises: sing praises unto our King,
sing praises.
7For God *is* the King of all the earth: sing ye praises with
understanding.
8God reigneth over the heathen: God sitteth upon the throne
of his holiness.
9The princes of the people are gathered together, *even* the
people of the God of Abraham: for the shields of the earth *belong*
unto God: he is greatly exalted.

## Amplified

15With gladness and rejoicing will they be brought; they will enter into the king's palace.
16Instead of your fathers shall be your sons, whom you will make princes in all the land.
17I will make your name to be remembered in all generations; therefore shall the people praise and give you thanks for ever and ever.

To the Chief Musician. [ *A Psalm*] of the sons of Korah, set to treble voices. A song.

**46** GOD IS our refuge and strength [mighty *and* impenetrable to temptation] a very present *and* well-proved help in trouble.
2Therefore we will not fear, though the earth should change,
and though the mountains be shaken into the midst of the seas;
3Though its waters roar and foam, though the mountains tremble at its swelling *and* tumult. Selah [pause, and think calmly of
that]!
4There is a river, whose streams shall make glad the city of God,
the holy place of the tabernacles of the Most High.
5God is in the midst of her; she shall not be moved. God will
help her right early [at the dawn of the morning].
6The nations raged, the kingdoms tottered *and* were moved; He
uttered His voice, the earth melted.
7The Lord of hosts is with us; the God of Jacob is our refuge [our
fortress and high tower]. Selah [pause, and think calmly of that]!
8Come, behold the works of the Lord, Who has wrought desolations *and* wonders in the earth.
9He makes wars to cease to the end of the earth; He breaks the
bow into pieces and snaps the spear in two; He burns the chariots
in the fire.
10Let be *and* be still, and know—recognize and understand—
that I am God. I will be exalted among the nations! I will be exalted
in the earth!
11The Lord of hosts is with us; the God of Jacob is our refuge
[our high tower and stronghold]. Selah [pause, and calmly think
of that]!

To the Chief Musician. A Psalm of the sons of Korah.

**47** O CLAP your hands, all you peoples! Shout to God with the voice of triumph *and* songs of joy!
2For the Lord Most High excites terror, awe *and* dread; He is a
great King over all the earth.
3He subdued peoples under us and nations under our feet.
4He chose our inheritance for us, the glory *and* pride of Jacob
whom He loves. Selah [pause, and calmly think of that]! [I Pet. 1:4,
5.]
5God has ascended amid shouting, the Lord with the sound of
a trumpet.
6Sing praises to God, sing praises! Sing praises to our King, sing
praises!
7For God is the King of all the earth; sing praises in a skillful
psalm *and* with understanding.
8God reigns over the nations; God sits upon His holy throne.
9The princes *and* nobles of the peoples are gathered together,
a [united] people for the God of Abraham; for the shields of the
earth belong to God. He is highly exalted.

## New American Standard

15 They will be led forth with gladness and rejoicing;
They will enter into the King's palace.

16¶ In place of your fathers will be your sons;
You shall make them princes in all the earth.
17 I will cause Thy name to be remembered in all generations;
Therefore the peoples will give Thee thanks forever and ever.

*God the Refuge of His People.*

For the choir director. *A Psalm* of the sons of Korah, [a]set to Alamoth. A Song.

46 GOD IS our refuge and strength, [b]A very present help in trouble.
2 Therefore we will not fear, though the earth should change,
And though the mountains slip into the heart of the sea;
3 Though its waters roar *and* foam,
Though the mountains quake at its swelling pride. Selah.

4¶ There is a river whose streams make glad the city of God,
The holy dwelling places of the Most High.
5 God is in the midst of her, she will not be moved;
God will help her when morning dawns.
6 The nations made an uproar, the kingdoms tottered;
He raised His voice, the earth melted.
7 The LORD of hosts is with us;
The God of Jacob is our stronghold. Selah.

8¶ Come, behold the works of the LORD,
Who has wrought desolations in the earth.
9 He makes wars to cease to the end of the earth;
He breaks the bow and cuts the spear in two;
He burns the chariots with fire.
10 "Cease *striving* and know that I am God;
I will be exalted among the nations, I will be exalted in the earth."
11 The LORD of hosts is with us;
The God of Jacob is our stronghold. Selah.

*God the King of the Earth.*

For the choir director. A Psalm of the sons of Korah.

47 O CLAP your hands, all peoples; Shout to God with the voice of joy.
2 For the LORD Most High is to be feared,
A great King over all the earth.
3 He subdues peoples under us,
And nations under our feet.
4 He chooses our inheritance for us,
The glory of Jacob whom He loves. Selah.

5¶ God has ascended with a shout,
The LORD, with the sound of a trumpet.
6 Sing praises to God, sing praises;
Sing praises to our King, sing praises.
7 For God is the King of all the earth;
Sing praises with a skillful psalm.
8 God reigns over the nations,
God sits on His holy throne.
9 The princes of the people have assembled themselves *as* the people of the God of Abraham;
For the shields of the earth belong to God;
He is highly exalted.

NAS [a] Possibly, *for soprano voices* [b] Or, *Abundantly available for help*

## New International

15 They are led in with joy and gladness;
they enter the palace of the king.

16 Your sons will take the place of your fathers;
you will make them princes throughout the land.
17 I will perpetuate your memory through all generations;
therefore the nations will praise you for ever and ever.

For the director of music. Of the Sons of Korah. According to *alamoth*.[c] A song.

46 GOD IS our refuge and strength,
an ever-present help in trouble.
2 Therefore we will not fear, though the earth give way
and the mountains fall into the heart of the sea,
3 though its waters roar and foam
and the mountains quake with their surging. *Selah*

4 There is a river whose streams make glad the city of God,
the holy place where the Most High dwells.
5 God is within her, she will not fall;
God will help her at break of day.
6 Nations are in uproar, kingdoms fall;
he lifts his voice, the earth melts.

7 The LORD Almighty is with us;
the God of Jacob is our fortress. *Selah*

8 Come and see the works of the LORD,
the desolations he has brought on the earth.
9 He makes wars cease to the ends of the earth;
he breaks the bow and shatters the spear,
he burns the shields[d] with fire.
10 "Be still, and know that I am God;
I will be exalted among the nations,
I will be exalted in the earth."

11 The LORD Almighty is with us;
the God of Jacob is our fortress. *Selah*

For the director of music. Of the Sons of Korah. A psalm.

47 CLAP YOUR hands, all you nations;
shout to God with cries of joy.
2 How awesome is the LORD Most High,
the great King over all the earth!
3 He subdued nations under us,
peoples under our feet.
4 He chose our inheritance for us,
the pride of Jacob, whom he loved. *Selah*

5 God has ascended amid shouts of joy,
the LORD amid the sounding of trumpets.
6 Sing praises to God, sing praises;
sing praises to our King, sing praises.

7 For God is the King of all the earth;
sing to him a psalm[e] of praise.
8 God reigns over the nations;
God is seated on his holy throne.
9 The nobles of the nations assemble
as the people of the God of Abraham,
for the kings[f] of the earth belong to God;
he is greatly exalted.

NIV [c] Title: Probably a musical term [d] 9 Or *chariots* [e] 7 Or *a maskil* (probably a literary or musical term) [f] 9 Or *shields*

## King James

A Song *and* Psalm for the sons of Korah.

**48** GREAT *IS* the LORD, and greatly to be praised in the city of our God, *in* the mountain of his holiness.

2 Beautiful for situation, the joy of the whole earth, *is* mount Zion, *on* the sides of the north, the city of the great King.

3 God is known in her palaces for a refuge.

4 For, lo, the kings were assembled, they passed by together.

5 They saw *it, and* so they marvelled; they were troubled, *and* hasted away.

6 Fear took hold upon them there, *and* pain, as of a woman in travail.

7 Thou breakest the ships of Tarshish with an east wind.

8 As we have heard, so have we seen in the city of the LORD of hosts, in the city of our God: God will establish it for ever. Selah.

9 We have thought of thy lovingkindness, O God, in the midst of thy temple.

10 According to thy name, O God, so *is* thy praise unto the ends of the earth: thy right hand is full of righteousness.

11 Let mount Zion rejoice, let the daughters of Judah be glad, because of thy judgments.

12 Walk about Zion, and go round about her: tell the towers thereof.

13 Mark ye well her bulwarks, consider her palaces; that ye may tell *it* to the generation following.

14 For this God *is* our God for ever and ever: he will be our guide *even* unto death.

To the chief Musician, A Psalm for the sons of Korah.

**49** HEAR THIS, all *ye* people; give ear, all *ye* inhabitants of the world:

2 Both low and high, rich and poor, together.

3 My mouth shall speak of wisdom; and the meditation of my heart *shall be* of understanding.

4 I will incline mine ear to a parable: I will open my dark saying upon the harp.

5 Wherefore should I fear in the days of evil, *when* the iniquity of my heels shall compass me about?

6 They that trust in their wealth, and boast themselves in the multitude of their riches;

7 None *of them* can by any means redeem his brother, nor give to God a ransom for him:

8 (For the redemption of their soul *is* precious, and it ceaseth for ever:)

9 That he should still live for ever, *and* not see corruption.

10 For he seeth *that* wise men die, likewise the fool and the brutish person perish, and leave their wealth to others.

## Amplified

A song; a Psalm of the sons of Korah.

**48** GREAT IS the Lord, and highly to be praised in the city of our God! His holy mountain,

2 Fair *and* beautiful for elevation, is the joy of all the earth! The [a]Mount Zion [the city of David], the sides of the north [Mount Moriah and the temple], the [whole] city of the great King! [Matt. 5:35.]

3 God has made Himself known in her palaces for a refuge [a high tower and a stronghold].

4 For, lo, the kings assembled, they came onward *and* they passed away together.

5 They looked; they were amazed; they were stricken with terror, *and* took to flight—affrighted *and* dismayed.

6 Trembling took hold of them there, *and* pain as of a woman in childbirth.

7 With the east wind You shattered the ships of Tarshish.

8 As we have heard, so have we seen in the city of the Lord of hosts, in the city of our God; God will establish it for ever. Selah [pause, and calmly think of that]!

9 We have thought of Your steadfast love, O God, in the midst of Your temple.

10 As is Your name, O God, so is Your praise to the ends of the earth; Your right hand is full of righteousness—rightness and justice.

11 Let Mount Zion be glad! Let the daughters of Judah rejoice because of Your *righteous* judgments!

12 Walk about Zion, and go round about her, number her towers [her lofty and noble deeds of past days];

13 Consider well her ramparts, go through her palaces *and* citadels; that you may tell the next generation [and cease recalling disappointments].

14 For this God is our God for ever and ever; He will be our guide *even* until death.

To the Chief Musician. A Psalm of the sons of Korah.

**49** HEAR THIS, all you peoples; give ear, all you inhabitants of the world,

2 Both low and high, rich and poor together.

3 My mouth shall speak wisdom; and the meditation of my heart shall be understanding.

4 I will submit *and* consent to a parable *or* proverb; to the music of a lyre I will unfold my riddle—my problem.

5 Why should I fear in the days of evil, when the iniquity of those who would supplant me surrounds me on every side,

6 Even of those who trust in *and* lean on their wealth, and boast of the abundance of their riches?

7 None of them can by any means redeem *either* himself *or* his brother, nor give to God a ransom for him;

8 For the ransom of their life is too costly, and [the price they can pay] can never suffice,

9 So that he should live on for ever *and* never see the pit [the grave] *and* corruption.

10 For he sees that even wise men die; the [self-confident] fool and the stupid alike perish and leave their wealth to others.

**AMP** [a] *Mount Zion* was not on the north side of Jerusalem, as the usual translation of this passage implies, but was the city's most southern hill. But the *temple* did lie north-northeast of the city; and to it this passage unquestionably refers.

## New American Standard

*The Beauty and Glory of Zion.*

A Song; a Psalm of the sons of Korah.

**48** GREAT IS the LORD, and greatly to be praised,
In the city of our God, His holy mountain.
2 Beautiful in elevation, the joy of the whole earth,
Is Mount Zion *in* the far north,
The city of the great King.
3 God, in her palaces,
Has made Himself known as a stronghold.

4¶ For, lo, the kings assembled themselves,
They passed by together.
5 They saw *it*, then they were amazed;
They were terrified, they fled in alarm.
6 Panic seized them there,
Anguish, as of a woman in childbirth.
7 With the east wind
Thou dost break the ships of Tarshish.
8 As we have heard, so have we seen
In the city of the LORD of hosts, in the city of our God;
God will establish her forever. Selah.
9¶ We have thought on Thy lovingkindness, O God,
In the midst of Thy temple.
10 As is Thy name, O God,
So is Thy praise to the ends of the earth;
Thy right hand is full of righteousness.
11 Let Mount Zion be glad,
Let the daughters of Judah rejoice,
Because of Thy judgments.
12 Walk about Zion, and go around her;
Count her towers;
13 Consider her ramparts;
Go through her palaces;
That you may tell *it* to the next generation.
14 For such is God,
Our God forever and ever;
He will guide us [b]until death.

*The Folly of Trusting in Riches.*

For the choir director. A Psalm of the sons of Korah.

**49** HEAR THIS, all peoples;
Give ear, all inhabitants of the world,
2 Both low and high,
Rich and poor together.
3 My mouth will speak wisdom;
And the meditation of my heart *will be* understanding.
4 I will incline my ear to a proverb;
I will express my riddle on the harp.

5¶ Why should I fear in days of adversity,
When the iniquity of my foes surrounds me,
6 Even those who trust in their wealth,
And boast in the abundance of their riches?
7 No man can by any means redeem *his* brother,
Or give to God a ransom for him—
8 For the redemption of his soul is costly,
And he should cease *trying* forever—
9 That he should live on eternally;
That he should not [c]undergo decay.

10¶ For he sees *that even* wise men die;
The stupid and the senseless alike perish,
And leave their wealth to others.

NAS [b] Some mss. and the Gr. read *forever* [c] Or, *see corruption* or *the pit*

## New International

A song. A psalm of the Sons of Korah.

**48** GREAT IS the LORD, and most worthy of praise,
in the city of our God, his holy mountain.
2 It is beautiful in its loftiness,
the joy of the whole earth.
Like the utmost heights of Zaphon[d] is Mount Zion,
the[e] city of the Great King.
3 God is in her citadels;
he has shown himself to be her fortress.

4 When the kings joined forces,
when they advanced together,
5 they saw ⌞her⌟ and were astounded;
they fled in terror.
6 Trembling seized them there,
pain like that of a woman in labor.
7 You destroyed them like ships of Tarshish
shattered by an east wind.

8 As we have heard,
so have we seen
in the city of the LORD Almighty,
in the city of our God:
God makes her secure forever. *Selah*

9 Within your temple, O God,
we meditate on your unfailing love.
10 Like your name, O God,
your praise reaches to the ends of the earth;
your right hand is filled with righteousness.
11 Mount Zion rejoices,
the villages of Judah are glad
because of your judgments.

12 Walk about Zion, go around her,
count her towers,
13 consider well her ramparts,
view her citadels,
that you may tell of them to the next generation.
14 For this God is our God for ever and ever;
he will be our guide even to the end.

For the director of music. Of the Sons of Korah. A psalm.

**49** HEAR THIS, all you peoples;
listen, all who live in this world,
2 both low and high,
rich and poor alike:
3 My mouth will speak words of wisdom;
the utterance from my heart will give understanding.
4 I will turn my ear to a proverb;
with the harp I will expound my riddle:

5 Why should I fear when evil days come,
when wicked deceivers surround me—
6 those who trust in their wealth
and boast of their great riches?
7 No man can redeem the life of another
or give to God a ransom for him—
8 the ransom for a life is costly,
no payment is ever enough—
9 that he should live on forever
and not see decay.

10 For all can see that wise men die;
the foolish and the senseless alike perish
and leave their wealth to others.

NIV [d] 2 *Zaphon* can refer to a sacred mountain or the direction north. [e] 2 Or *earth, / Mount Zion, on the northern side / of the*

## King James

11 Their inward thought *is, that* their houses *shall continue* for ever, *and* their dwelling places to all generations; they call *their* lands after their own names.

12 Nevertheless man *being* in honour abideth not: he is like the beasts *that* perish.

13 This their way *is* their folly: yet their posterity approve their sayings. Selah.

14 Like sheep they are laid in the grave; death shall feed on them; and the upright shall have dominion over them in the morning; and their beauty shall consume in the grave from their dwelling.

15 But God will redeem my soul from the power of the grave: for he shall receive me. Selah.

16 Be not thou afraid when one is made rich, when the glory of his house is increased;

17 For when he dieth he shall carry nothing away: his glory shall not descend after him.

18 Though while he lived he blessed his soul: and *men* will praise thee, when thou doest well to thyself.

19 He shall go to the generation of his fathers; they shall never see light.

20 Man *that is* in honour, and understandeth not, is like the beasts *that* perish.

A Psalm of Asaph.

**50** THE MIGHTY God, *even* the LORD, hath spoken, and called the earth from the rising of the sun unto the going down thereof.

2 Out of Zion, the perfection of beauty, God hath shined.

3 Our God shall come, and shall not keep silence: a fire shall devour before him, and it shall be very tempestuous round about him.

4 He shall call to the heavens from above, and to the earth, that he may judge his people.

5 Gather my saints together unto me; those that have made a covenant with me by sacrifice.

6 And the heavens shall declare his righteousness: for God *is* judge himself. Selah.

7 Hear, O my people, and I will speak; O Israel, and I will testify against thee: I *am* God, *even* thy God.

8 I will not reprove thee for thy sacrifices or thy burnt offerings, *to have been* continually before me.

9 I will take no bullock out of thy house, *nor* he goats out of thy folds.

10 For every beast of the forest *is* mine, *and* the cattle upon a thousand hills.

11 I know all the fowls of the mountains: and the wild beasts of the field *are* mine.

12 If I were hungry, I would not tell thee: for the world *is* mine, and the fulness thereof.

13 Will I eat the flesh of bulls, or drink the blood of goats?

14 Offer unto God thanksgiving; and pay thy vows unto the most High:

15 And call upon me in the day of trouble: I will deliver thee, and thou shalt glorify me.

AMP [a] Asaph was a Levite and one of the leaders of David's choir. He was the head of one of the three families permanently charged with the temple music. His family formed a guild which bore his name and is frequently mentioned. One hundred and twenty-eight of them, all singers, came back from Babylon and took part when the foundations of Zerubbabel's temple were laid (Ezra 2:41; 3:10).

## Amplified

11 Their inward thought is, that their houses will continue for ever, *and* their dwelling places to all generations; they call their lands their own [apart from God] *and* after their own names.

12 But man with all his honor *and* pomp does not remain; he is like the beasts that perish.

13 This is the fate of those who are foolishly confident, yet after them men approve their sayings. Selah [pause, and calmly think of that]!

14 Like sheep they are appointed for Sheol [the place of the dead]; death shall be their shepherd; and the upright shall have dominion over them in the morning; and their form *and* beauty shall be consumed, for Sheol shall be their dwelling.

15 But God will redeem me from the power of Sheol [the place of the dead], for He will receive me. Selah [pause, and calmly think of that]!

16 Be not afraid when [an ungodly] one is made rich, when the wealth *and* glory of his house are increased;

17 For when he dies he will carry nothing away; his glory will not descend after him.

18 Though while he lives he counts himself happy *and* prosperous, and though a man gets praise when he does well for *himself,*

19 He will go to the generation of his fathers, who nevermore see the light.

20 Man who is held in honor and understands not, is like the beasts that perish.

A Psalm of [a]Asaph

**50** THE MIGHTY One, God the Lord, speaks and calls the earth from the rising of the sun to its setting.

2 Out of Zion, the perfection of beauty, God shines forth.

3 Our God comes, and does not keep silence; a fire devours before Him, and round about Him a mighty tempest rages.

4 He calls to the heavens above and to the earth, that He may judge His people:

5 Gather together to Me My saints [those who have found grace in My sight], those who have made a covenant with Me by sacrifice.

6 And the heavens declare His righteousness—rightness and justice; for God, He is judge. Selah [pause, and calmly think of that]!

7 Hear, O My people, and I will speak; O Israel, I will testify to you *and* against you; I am God, your God.

8 I do not reprove you for your sacrifices; your burnt offerings are continually before Me.

9 I will accept no bull from your house, nor he-goat out of your folds.

10 For every beast of the forest is Mine *and* the cattle upon a thousand hills *or* upon the mountains where thousands are.

11 I know *and* am acquainted with all the birds of the mountains, and the wild animals of the field are Mine *and* are with Me, in My mind.

12 If I were hungry, I would not tell you, for the world and its fullness are Mine. [I Cor. 10:26.]

13 Shall I eat of the flesh of bulls, or drink the blood of goats?

14 Offer to God the sacrifice of thanksgiving; and pay your vows to the Most High,

15 And call on Me in the day of trouble; I will deliver you, and you shall honor *and* glorify Me.

## New American Standard

11 Their [b]inner thought is, *that* their houses are forever,
*And* their dwelling places to all generations;
They have called their lands after their own names.
12 But man in *his* pomp will not endure;
He is like the beasts that perish.

13¶ This is the way of those who are foolish,
And of those after them who approve their words. Selah.

14 As sheep they are appointed for Sheol;
Death shall be their shepherd;
And the upright shall rule over them in the morning;
And their form shall be for Sheol to consume,
So that they have no habitation.
15 But God will redeem my soul from the power of Sheol;
For He will receive me. Selah.

16¶ Do not be afraid when a man becomes rich,
When the [c]glory of his house is increased;
17 For when he dies he will carry nothing away;
His [d]glory will not descend after him.
18 Though while he lives he congratulates himself—
And though *men* praise you when you do well for yourself—
19 He shall go to the generation of his fathers;
They shall never see the light.
20 Man in *his* pomp, yet with out understanding,
Is like the beasts that perish.

*God the Judge of the Righteous and the Wicked.*

A Psalm of Asaph.

**50** THE MIGHTY One, God, the LORD, has spoken,
And summoned the earth from the rising of the sun to its setting.
2 Out of Zion, the perfection of beauty,
God has shone forth.
3 May our God come and not keep silence;
Fire devours before Him,
And it is very tempestuous around Him.
4 He summons the heavens above,
And the earth, to judge His people:
5 "Gather My godly ones to Me,
Those who have made a covenant with Me by sacrifice."
6 And the heavens declare His righteousness,
For God Himself is judge. Selah.

7¶ "Hear, O My people, and I will speak;
O Israel, I will testify against you;
I am God, your God.
8 "I do not reprove you for your sacrifices,
And your burnt offerings are continually before Me.
9 "I shall take no young bull out of your house,
Nor male goats out of your folds.
10 "For every beast of the forest is Mine,
The cattle on a thousand hills.
11 "I know every bird of the mountains,
And everything that moves in the field is [e]Mine.
12 "If I were hungry, I would not tell you;
For the world is Mine, and all it contains.
13 "Shall I eat the flesh of bulls,
Or drink the blood of male goats?
14 "Offer to God a sacrifice of thanksgiving,
And pay your vows to the Most High;
15 And call upon Me in the day of trouble;
I shall rescue you, and you will honor Me."

NAS [b] Some versions read *graves are their houses* [c] Or, *wealth* [d] Or, *wealth* [e] Or, *in My mind*

## New International

11 Their tombs will remain their houses[f] forever,
their dwellings for endless generations,
though they had[g] named lands after themselves.
12 But man, despite his riches, does not endure;
he is[h] like the beasts that perish.

13 This is the fate of those who trust in themselves,
and of their followers, who approve their sayings. *Selah*
14 Like sheep they are destined for the grave,[i]
and death will feed on them.
The upright will rule over them in the morning;
their forms will decay in the grave,[j]
far from their princely mansions.
15 But God will redeem my life[k] from the grave;
he will surely take me to himself. *Selah*

16 Do not be overawed when a man grows rich,
when the splendor of his house increases;
17 for he will take nothing with him when he dies,
his splendor will not descend with him.
18 Though while he lived he counted himself blessed—
and men praise you when you prosper—
19 he will join the generation of his fathers,
who will never see the light ⌞of life⌟.
20 A man who has riches without understanding
is like the beasts that perish.

A psalm of Asaph.

**50** THE MIGHTY One, God, the LORD,
speaks and summons the earth
from the rising of the sun to the place where it sets.
2 From Zion, perfect in beauty,
God shines forth.
3 Our God comes and will not be silent;
a fire devours before him,
and around him a tempest rages.
4 He summons the heavens above,
and the earth, that he may judge his people:
5 "Gather to me my consecrated ones,
who made a covenant with me by sacrifice."
6 And the heavens proclaim his righteousness,
for God himself is judge. *Selah*
7 "Hear, O my people, and I will speak,
O Israel, and I will testify against you:
I am God, your God.
8 I do not rebuke you for your sacrifices
or your burnt offerings, which are ever before me.
9 I have no need of a bull from your stall
or of goats from your pens,
10 for every animal of the forest is mine,
and the cattle on a thousand hills.
11 I know every bird in the mountains,
and the creatures of the field are mine.
12 If I were hungry I would not tell you,
for the world is mine, and all that is in it.
13 Do I eat the flesh of bulls
or drink the blood of goats?
14 Sacrifice thank offerings to God,
fulfill your vows to the Most High,
15 and call upon me in the day of trouble;
I will deliver you, and you will honor me."

NIV [f] *11* Septuagint and Syriac; Hebrew *In their thoughts their houses will remain* [g] *11* Or / *for they have* [h] *12* Hebrew; Septuagint and Syriac read verse 12 the same as verse 20. [i] *14* Hebrew *Sheol;* also in verse 15 [j] *14* Hebrew *Sheol;* also in verse 15 [k] *15* Or *soul*

## King James

16But unto the wicked God saith, What hast thou to do to declare my statutes, or *that* thou shouldest take my covenant in thy mouth?
17Seeing thou hatest instruction, and castest my words behind thee.
18When thou sawest a thief, then thou consentedst with him, and hast been partaker with adulterers.
19Thou givest thy mouth to evil, and thy tongue frameth deceit.
20Thou sittest *and* speakest against thy brother; thou slanderest thine own mother's son.
21These *things* hast thou done, and I kept silence; thou thoughtest that I was altogether *such an one* as thyself: *but* I will reprove thee, and set *them* in order before thine eyes.
22Now consider this, ye that forget God, lest I tear *you* in pieces, and *there be* none to deliver.
23Whoso offereth praise glorifieth me: and to him that ordereth *his* conversation *aright* will I show the salvation of God.

To the chief Musician, A Psalm of David, when Nathan the prophet came unto him, after he had gone in to Bath-sheba.

**51** HAVE MERCY upon me, O God, according to thy lovingkindness: according unto the multitude of thy tender mercies blot out my transgressions.
2Wash me thoroughly from mine iniquity, and cleanse me from my sin.
3For I acknowledge my transgressions: and my sin *is* ever before me.
4Against thee, thee only, have I sinned, and done *this* evil in thy sight: that thou mightest be justified when thou speakest, *and* be clear when thou judgest.
5Behold, I was shapen in iniquity; and in sin did my mother conceive me.
6Behold, thou desirest truth in the inward parts: and in the hidden *part* thou shalt make me to know wisdom.
7Purge me with hyssop, and I shall be clean: wash me, and I shall be whiter than snow.
8Make me to hear joy and gladness; *that* the bones *which* thou hast broken may rejoice.
9Hide thy face from my sins, and blot out all mine iniquities.
10Create in me a clean heart, O God; and renew a right spirit within me.
11Cast me not away from thy presence; and take not thy holy spirit from me.
12Restore unto me the joy of thy salvation; and uphold me *with thy* free spirit.
13 *Then* will I teach transgressors thy ways; and sinners shall be converted unto thee.
14Deliver me from bloodguiltiness, O God, thou God of my salvation: *and* my tongue shall sing aloud of thy righteousness.
15O Lord, open thou my lips: and my mouth shall show forth thy praise.
16For thou desirest not sacrifice; else would I give *it:* thou delightest not in burnt offering.

## Amplified

16But to the wicked, God says, What right have you to recite My statutes, or to take My covenant *or* pledge on your lips,
17Seeing you hate instruction *and* correction and cast My words behind you—discarding them?
18When you see a thief you associate with him, and you have taken part with adulterers.
19You give your mouth to evil, and your tongue frames deceit.
20You sit and speak against your brother; you slander your own mother's son.
21These things you have done and I kept silent; you thought I was once entirely like yourself; but [now] I will reprove you, and put [the charge] in order before your eyes.
22Now consider this, you who forget God, lest I tear you in pieces, and there be none to deliver.
23He who brings an offering of praise *and* thanksgiving honors *and* glorifies Me; and he who orders his way aright—who prepares the way that I may show him—to him I will demonstrate the salvation of God.

To the Chief Musician. A Psalm of David, when Nathan the prophet came to him, after he had sinned with Bathsheba.

**51** HAVE MERCY upon me, O God, according to Your steadfast love; according to the multitude of Your tender mercies *and* loving-kindnesses blot out my transgressions.
2Wash me thoroughly [and repeatedly] from my iniquity *and* guilt, and cleanse me *and* make me wholly pure from my sin!
3For I am conscious of my transgressions *and* I acknowledge them; my sin is ever before me.
4Against You, You only, have I sinned, and done that which is evil in Your sight; so that You are justified in Your sentence and faultless in Your judgment. [Rom. 3:4.]
5Behold, I was brought forth in [a state of] iniquity; my mother was sinful who conceived me [and I, too, am sinful]. [John 3:6; Rom. 5:12; Eph. 2:3.]
6Behold, You desire truth in the inner being; make me therefore to know wisdom in my inmost heart.
7Purify me with hyssop, and I shall be clean [ceremonially]; wash me, and I shall [in reality] be whiter than snow.
8Make me to hear joy and gladness *and* be satisfied; let the bones which You have broken rejoice.
9Hide Your face from my sins, and blot out all my guilt *and* iniquities.
10Create in me a clean heart, O God; and renew a right, persevering *and* steadfast spirit within me.
11Cast me not away from Your presence, and take not Your Holy Spirit from me.
12Restore to me the joy of Your salvation, and uphold me with a willing spirit.
13Then will I teach transgressors Your ways, and sinners shall be converted *and* return to You.
14Deliver me from bloodguiltiness *and* death, O God, *the* God of my salvation; *and* my tongue shall sing aloud of Your righteousness—Your rightness and Your justice.
15O Lord, open my lips, and my mouth shall show forth Your praise.
16For You delight not in sacrifice, else would I give it; You find no pleasure in burnt offering. [I Sam. 15:22.]

## New American Standard

16¶ But to the wicked God says,
"What right have you to tell of My statutes,
And to take My covenant in your mouth?
17 "For you hate discipline,
And you cast My words behind you.
18 "When you see a thief, you are pleased with him,
And you associate with adulterers.
19 "You let your mouth loose in evil,
And your tongue frames deceit.
20 "You sit and speak against your brother;
You slander your own mother's son.
21 "These things you have done, and I kept silence;
You thought that I was just like you;
I will reprove you, and state *the case* in order before
your eyes.
22¶ "Now consider this, you who forget God,
Lest I tear *you* in pieces, and there be none to deliver.
23 "He who offers a sacrifice of thanksgiving honors Me;
And to him who orders *his way aright*
I shall show the salvation of God."

*A Contrite Sinner's Prayer for Pardon.*

For the choir director.—A Psalm of David, when Nathan the prophet came to him, after he had gone in to Bathsheba.

**51** BE GRACIOUS to me, O God, according to Thy loving-
kindness;
According to the greatness of Thy compassion blot out
my transgressions.
2 Wash me thoroughly from my iniquity,
And cleanse me from my sin.
3 For I know my transgressions,
And my sin is ever before me.
4 Against Thee, Thee only, I have sinned,
And done what is evil in Thy sight,
So that Thou [a]art justified when Thou dost speak,
And blameless when Thou dost judge.
5¶ Behold, I was brought forth in iniquity,
And in sin my mother conceived me.
6 Behold, Thou dost desire truth in the innermost being,
And in the hidden part Thou wilt make me know
wisdom.
7 Purify me with hyssop, and I shall be clean;
Wash me, and I shall be whiter than snow.
8 Make me to hear joy and gladness,
Let the bones which Thou hast broken rejoice.
9 Hide Thy face from my sins,
And blot out all my iniquities.
10¶ Create in me a clean heart, O God,
And renew a steadfast spirit within me.
11 Do not cast me away from Thy presence,
And do not take Thy Holy Spirit from me.
12 Restore to me the joy of Thy salvation,
And sustain me with a willing spirit.
13 *Then* I will teach transgressors Thy ways,
And sinners will [b]be converted to Thee.
14¶ Deliver me from bloodguiltiness, O God, Thou God of
my salvation;
*Then* my tongue will joyfully sing of Thy righteousness.
15 O Lord, open my lips,
That my mouth may declare Thy praise.
16 For Thou dost not delight in sacrifice, otherwise I
would give it;
Thou art not pleased with burnt offering.

NAS [a] Or, *mayest be in the right* [b] Or, *turn back*

## New International

16 But to the wicked, God says:
"What right have you to recite my laws
or take my covenant on your lips?
17 You hate my instruction
and cast my words behind you.
18 When you see a thief, you join with him;
you throw in your lot with adulterers.
19 You use your mouth for evil
and harness your tongue to deceit.
20 You speak continually against your brother
and slander your own mother's son.
21 These things you have done and I kept silent;
you thought I was altogether[c] like you.
But I will rebuke you
and accuse you to your face.

22 "Consider this, you who forget God,
or I will tear you to pieces, with none to rescue:
23 He who sacrifices thank offerings honors me,
and he prepares the way
so that I may show him[d] the salvation of God."

For the director of music. A psalm of David. When the prophet Nathan came to him after David had committed adultery with Bathsheba.

**51** HAVE MERCY on me, O God,
according to your unfailing love;
according to your great compassion
blot out my transgressions.
2 Wash away all my iniquity
and cleanse me from my sin.

3 For I know my transgressions,
and my sin is always before me.
4 Against you, you only, have I sinned
and done what is evil in your sight,
so that you are proved right when you speak
and justified when you judge.
5 Surely I was sinful at birth,
sinful from the time my mother conceived me.
6 Surely you desire truth in the inner parts[e];
you teach[f] me wisdom in the inmost place.

7 Cleanse me with hyssop, and I will be clean;
wash me, and I will be whiter than snow.
8 Let me hear joy and gladness;
let the bones you have crushed rejoice.
9 Hide your face from my sins
and blot out all my iniquity.

10 Create in me a pure heart, O God,
and renew a steadfast spirit within me.
11 Do not cast me from your presence
or take your Holy Spirit from me.
12 Restore to me the joy of your salvation
and grant me a willing spirit, to sustain me.

13 Then I will teach transgressors your ways,
and sinners will turn back to you.
14 Save me from bloodguilt, O God,
the God who saves me,
and my tongue will sing of your righteousness.
15 O Lord, open my lips,
and my mouth will declare your praise.
16 You do not delight in sacrifice, or I would bring it;
you do not take pleasure in burnt offerings.

NIV [c] 21 Or *thought the 'I AM' was* [d] 23 Or *and to him who considers his way / I will show* [e] 6 The meaning of the Hebrew for this phrase is uncertain. [f] 6 Or *you desired . . . ; / you taught*

## King James

17 The sacrifices of God *are* a broken spirit: a broken and a contrite heart, O God, thou wilt not despise.

18 Do good in thy good pleasure unto Zion: build thou the walls of Jerusalem.

19 Then shalt thou be pleased with the sacrifices of righteousness, with burnt offering and whole burnt offering: then shall they offer bullocks upon thine altar.

To the chief Musician, Maschil, *A Psalm* of David, when Doeg the Edomite came and told Saul, and said unto him, David is come to the house of Ahimelech.

**52** WHY BOASTEST thou thyself in mischief, O mighty man? the goodness of God *endureth* continually.

2 Thy tongue deviseth mischiefs; like a sharp razor, working deceitfully.

3 Thou lovest evil more than good; *and* lying rather than to speak righteousness. Selah.

4 Thou lovest all devouring words, O *thou* deceitful tongue.

5 God shall likewise destroy thee for ever, he shall take thee away, and pluck thee out of *thy* dwellingplace, and root thee out of the land of the living. Selah.

6 The righteous also shall see, and fear, and shall laugh at him:

7 Lo, *this is* the man *that* made not God his strength; but trusted in the abundance of his riches, *and* strengthened himself in his wickedness.

8 But I *am* like a green olive tree in the house of God: I trust in the mercy of God for ever and ever.

9 I will praise thee for ever, because thou hast done *it:* and I will wait on thy name; for *it is* good before thy saints.

To the chief Musician upon Mahalath, Maschil, *A Psalm* of David.

**53** THE FOOL hath said in his heart, *There is* no God. Corrupt are they, and have done abominable iniquity: *there is* none that doeth good.

2 God looked down from heaven upon the children of men, to see if there were *any* that did understand, that did seek God.

3 Every one of them is gone back: they are altogether become filthy; *there is* none that doeth good, no, not one.

4 Have the workers of iniquity no knowledge? who eat up my people *as* they eat bread: they have not called upon God.

5 There were they in great fear, *where* no fear was: for God hath scattered the bones of him that encampeth *against* thee: thou hast put *them* to shame, because God hath despised them.

## Amplified

17 My sacrifice [the sacrifice acceptable] to God is a broken spirit; a broken and a contrite heart [broken down with sorrow for sin and humbly and thoroughly penitent] such, O God, You will not despise.

18 Do good in Your good pleasure to Zion; rebuild the walls of Jerusalem.

19 Then will You delight in the sacrifices of righteousness, justice *and* right, with burnt offering and whole burnt offering; then bullocks will be offered upon Your altar.

To the Chief Musician. A skillful song, *or* a didactic *or* reflective poem. [*A Psalm*] of David, when Doeg the Edomite came and told Saul, David has come to the house of Ahimelech.

**52** WHY BOAST you of mischief done against the loving-kindness of God [and the godly], O mighty [sinful] man, day after day?

2 Your tongue devises wickedness, like a sharp razor, working deceitfully.

3 You love evil more than good, and lying rather than to speak righteousness, justice *and* right. Selah [pause, and calmly think of that]!

4 You love all destroying *and* devouring words, O deceitful tongue.

5 God will likewise break you down *and* destroy you for ever; He will lay hold of you and pluck you out of your tent, and uproot you from the land of the living. Selah [pause, and calmly think of that]!

6 The [uncompromisingly] righteous also shall see *it*, and be in reverent fear *and* awe, but about *you* will [scoffingly] laugh, saying,

7 See, this is the man who made not God his strength—his stronghold and high tower; but trusted *and* confidently relied on the abundance of his riches, seeking refuge *and* security for himself through his wickedness.

8 But I am like a green olive tree in the house of God; I trust *and* confidently rely on the loving-kindness *and* the mercy of God for ever and ever.

9 I will thank You *and* confide in You for ever, because You have done it [delivered me and kept me safe]. I will wait, hope *and* expect in Your name, for it is good, in the presence of Your saints [Your kind and pious ones].

To the Chief Musician;
in a mournful strain. A skillful song, *or* didactic *or* reflective poem of David.

**53** THE [EMPTY-HEADED] fool has said in his heart, There is no God. Corrupt *and* evil are they, and doing abominable iniquity; there is none who does good.

2 God looked down from Heaven upon the children of men, to see if there were any who understood, who sought, inquired after [and desperately required] God.

3 Every one of them is gone back—backslidden and fallen away; they are altogether become filthy *and* corrupt; there is none who does good, no, not one. [Rom. 3:10-12.]

4 Have those who work evil no knowledge—no understanding? They eat up My people as they eat bread; they do not call upon God.

5 There they are, in terror *and* dread, where there was [and had been] no terror *and* dread! For God has scattered the bones of him who encamps against you; you have put them to shame, because God has rejected them.

## New American Standard

17 The sacrifices of God are a broken spirit;
A broken and a contrite heart, O God, Thou wilt not despise.

18¶ By Thy favor do good to Zion;
Build the walls of Jerusalem.
19 Then Thou wilt delight in righteous sacrifices,
In burnt offering and whole burnt offering;
Then young bulls will be offered on Thine altar.

*Futility of Boastful Wickedness.*

For the choir director.—A Maskil of David, when Doeg the Edomite came and told Saul, and said to him, "David has come to the house of Ahimelech."

52 WHY DO you boast in evil, O mighty man?
The lovingkindness of God *endures* all day long.
2 Your tongue devises destruction,
Like a sharp razor, O worker of deceit.
3 You love evil more than good,
Falsehood more than speaking what is right. Selah.
4 You love all words that devour,
O deceitful tongue.

5¶ But God will break you down forever;
He will snatch you up, and tear you away from *your* tent,
And uproot you from the land of the living. Selah.
6 And the righteous will see and fear,
And will laugh at him, *saying,*
7 "Behold, the man who would not make God his refuge,
But trusted in the abundance of his riches,
*And* was strong in his *evil* desire."

8¶ But as for me, I am like a green olive tree in the house of God;
I trust in the lovingkindness of God forever and ever.
9 I will give Thee thanks forever, because Thou hast done *it,*
And I will wait on Thy name, for *it is* good, in the presence of Thy godly ones.

*Folly and Wickedness of Men.*

For the choir director; according to [a]Mahalath. A Maskil of David.

53 THE FOOL has said in his heart, "There is no God,"
They are corrupt, and have committed abominable injustice;
There is no one who does good.
2 God has looked down from heaven upon the sons of men,
To see if there is anyone who understands,
Who seeks after God.
3 Every one of them has turned aside; together they have become corrupt;
There is no one who does good, not even one.

4¶ Have the workers of wickedness no knowledge,
Who eat up My people *as though* they ate bread,
And have not called upon God?
5 There they were in great fear *where* no fear had been;
For God scattered the bones of him who encamped against you;
You put *them* to shame, because God had rejected them.

NAS [a] I.e., sickness, a sad tone

## New International

17 The sacrifices of God are[b] a broken spirit;
a broken and contrite heart,
O God, you will not despise.

18 In your good pleasure make Zion prosper;
build up the walls of Jerusalem.
19 Then there will be righteous sacrifices,
whole burnt offerings to delight you;
then bulls will be offered on your altar.

For the director of music. A *maskil*[c] of David. When Doeg the Edomite had gone to Saul and told him: "David has gone to the house of Ahimelech."

52 WHY DO you boast of evil, you mighty man?
Why do you boast all day long,
you who are a disgrace in the eyes of God?
2 Your tongue plots destruction;
it is like a sharpened razor,
you who practice deceit.
3 You love evil rather than good,
falsehood rather than speaking the truth. *Selah*
4 You love every harmful word,
O you deceitful tongue!

5 Surely God will bring you down to everlasting ruin:
He will snatch you up and tear you from your tent;
he will uproot you from the land of the living. *Selah*
6 The righteous will see and fear;
they will laugh at him, saying,
7 "Here now is the man
who did not make God his stronghold
but trusted in his great wealth
and grew strong by destroying others!"

8 But I am like an olive tree
flourishing in the house of God;
I trust in God's unfailing love
for ever and ever.
9 I will praise you forever for what you have done;
in your name I will hope, for your name is good.
I will praise you in the presence of your saints.

For the director of music. According to *mahalath*.[d] A *maskil*[e] of David.

53 THE FOOL says in his heart,
"There is no God."
They are corrupt, and their ways are vile;
there is no one who does good.

2 God looks down from heaven
on the sons of men
to see if there are any who understand,
any who seek God.
3 Everyone has turned away,
they have together become corrupt;
there is no one who does good,
not even one.

4 Will the evildoers never learn—
those who devour my people as men eat bread
and who do not call on God?
5 There they were, overwhelmed with dread,
where there was nothing to dread.
God scattered the bones of those who attacked you;
you put them to shame, for God despised them.

NIV [b] *17 Or My sacrifice, O God, is* [c] Title: Probably a literary or musical term [d] Title: Probably a musical term [e] Title: Probably a literary or musical term

# King James

6 Oh that the salvation of Israel *were come* out of Zion! When God bringeth back the captivity of his people, Jacob shall rejoice, *and* Israel shall be glad.

To the chief Musician on Neginoth, Maschil, *A Psalm* of David, when the Ziphims came and said to Saul, Doth not David hide himself with us?

**54** SAVE ME, O God, by thy name, and judge me by thy strength.

2 Hear my prayer, O God; give ear to the words of my mouth.

3 For strangers are risen up against me, and oppressors seek after my soul: they have not set God before them. Selah.

4 Behold, God *is* mine helper: the Lord *is* with them that uphold my soul.

5 He shall reward evil unto mine enemies: cut them off in thy truth.

6 I will freely sacrifice unto thee: I will praise thy name, O LORD; for *it is* good.

7 For he hath delivered me out of all trouble: and mine eye hath seen *his desire* upon mine enemies.

To the chief Musician on Neginoth, Maschil, *A Psalm* of David.

**55** GIVE EAR to my prayer, O God; and hide not thyself from my supplication.

2 Attend unto me, and hear me: I mourn in my complaint, and make a noise;

3 Because of the voice of the enemy, because of the oppression of the wicked: for they cast iniquity upon me, and in wrath they hate me.

4 My heart is sore pained within me: and the terrors of death are fallen upon me.

5 Fearfulness and trembling are come upon me, and horror hath overwhelmed me.

6 And I said, Oh that I had wings like a dove! *for then* would I fly away, and be at rest.

7 Lo, *then* would I wander far off, *and* remain in the wilderness. Selah.

8 I would hasten my escape from the windy storm *and* tempest.

9 Destroy, O Lord, *and* divide their tongues: for I have seen violence and strife in the city.

10 Day and night they go about it upon the walls thereof: mischief also and sorrow *are* in the midst of it.

11 Wickedness *is* in the midst thereof: deceit and guile depart not from her streets.

12 For *it was* not an enemy *that* reproached me; then I could have borne *it:* neither *was it* he that hated me *that* did magnify *himself* against me; then I would have hid myself from him:

13 But *it was* thou, a man mine equal, my guide, and mine acquaintance.

14 We took sweet counsel together, *and* walked unto the house of God in company.

# Amplified

6 O that the salvation *and* deliverance of Israel were come out of Zion! When God restores the fortunes of His people, then will Jacob rejoice and Israel be glad.

To the Chief Musician with stringed instruments. A skillful song *or* a didactic *or* reflective poem of David, when the Ziphites went and told Saul, David is hiding among us.

**54** SAVE ME, O God, by Your name; judge *and* vindicate me by Your mighty strength *and* power.

2 Hear my pleading *and* my prayer, O God; give ear to the words of my mouth.

3 For strangers *and* insolent men are risen up against me, and violent men *and* ruthless ones seek *and* demand my life; they do not set God before them. Selah [pause, and calmly think of that]!

4 Behold, God is my helper *and* ally; the Lord is my upholder *and* is with them who uphold my life.

5 He will pay back evil to my enemies; in Your faithfulness, *Lord,* put an end to them.

6 With a freewill offering I will sacrifice to You; I will give thanks *and* praise Your name, O Lord, for it is good.

7 For He has delivered me out of every trouble, and my eye has looked [in triumph] on my enemies.

To the Chief Musician, with stringed instruments. A skillful song, *or* a didactic *or* reflective poem of David.

**55** LISTEN TO my prayer, O God, and hide not Yourself from my supplication!

2 Attend to me, and answer me; I am restless *and* distraught in my complaint, and must moan;

3 [I am distracted] by the noise of the enemy, because of the oppression *and* threatenings of the wicked; for they would cast trouble upon me, and in wrath they persecute me.

4 My heart is grievously pained within me, and the terrors of death have fallen upon me.

5 Fear and trembling are come upon me; horror *and* fright have overwhelmed me.

6 And I say, O that I had wings like a dove! I would fly away and be at rest.

7 Yes, I would wander far away, I would lodge in the wilderness. Selah [pause, and calmly think of that]!

8 I would hasten to escape *and* to find me a shelter from the stormy wind and tempest.

9 Destroy [their schemes], O Lord; confuse their tongues; for I have seen violence and strife in the city.

10 Day and night they go about on its walls; iniquity and mischief are in its midst.

11 Violence *and* ruin are within it; fraud and guile do not depart from its streets *and* market place.

12 For it is not an enemy who reproaches *and* taunts me; then I might bear it; nor one who has hated me who insolently vaunts himself against me; then I might hide from him.

13 But it was you, a man my equal, my companion and my familiar friend;

14 We had sweet fellowship together, and used to walk to the house of God in company.

## New American Standard

6 Oh, that the salvation of Israel would come out of Zion!
When God restores His captive people,
Let Jacob rejoice, let Israel be glad.

*Prayer for Defense against Enemies.*

For the choir director; on stringed instruments. A Maskil of David, when the Ziphites came and said to Saul, "Is not David hiding himself among us?"

**54** SAVE ME, O God, by Thy name,
And [a]vindicate me by Thy power.
2 Hear my prayer, O God;
Give ear to the words of my mouth.
3 For strangers have risen against me,
And violent men have sought my life;
They have not set God before them. Selah.

4¶ Behold, God is my helper;
The Lord is the sustainer of my soul.
5 [b]He will recompense the evil to my foes;
Destroy them in Thy faithfulness.
6¶ Willingly I will sacrifice to Thee;
I will give thanks to Thy name, O LORD, for it is good.
7 For He has delivered me from all trouble;
And my eye has looked *with satisfaction* upon my enemies.

*Prayer for the Destruction of the Treacherous.*

For the choir director; on stringed instruments. A Maskil of David.

**55** GIVE EAR to my prayer, O God;
And do not hide Thyself from my supplication.
2 Give heed to me, and answer me;
I am restless in my complaint and [c]am surely distracted,
3 Because of the voice of the enemy,
Because of the pressure of the wicked;
For they bring down trouble upon me,
And in anger they bear a grudge against me.
4¶ My heart is in anguish within me,
And the terrors of death have fallen upon me.
5 Fear and trembling come upon me;
And horror has overwhelmed me.
6 And I said, "Oh, that I had wings like a dove!
I would fly away and [d]be at rest.
7 "Behold, I would wander far away,
I would lodge in the wilderness. Selah.
8 "I would hasten to my place of refuge
From the stormy wind *and* tempest."
9¶ Confuse, O Lord, divide their tongues,
For I have seen violence and strife in the city.
10 Day and night they go around her upon her walls;
And iniquity and mischief are in her midst.
11 Destruction is in her midst;
Oppression and deceit do not depart from her streets.
12¶ For it is not an enemy who reproaches me,
Then I could bear *it*;
Nor is it one who hates me who has exalted himself against me,
Then I could hide myself from him.
13 But it is you, a man my equal,
My companion and my familiar friend.
14 We who had sweet [e]fellowship together,
Walked in the house of God in the throng.

NAS [a] Lit., *judge* [b] Lit., *The evil will return* [c] Or, *I must moan* [d] Lit., *settle down* [e] Lit., *counsel*

## New International

6Oh, that salvation for Israel would come out of Zion!
When God restores the fortunes of his people,
let Jacob rejoice and Israel be glad!

For the director of music. With stringed instruments. A *maskil*[f] of David. When the Ziphites had gone to Saul and said, "Is not David hiding among us?"

**54** SAVE ME, O God, by your name;
vindicate me by your might.
2Hear my prayer, O God;
listen to the words of my mouth.

3Strangers are attacking me;
ruthless men seek my life—
men without regard for God. *Selah*
4Surely God is my help;
the Lord is the one who sustains me.

5Let evil recoil on those who slander me;
in your faithfulness destroy them.

6I will sacrifice a freewill offering to you;
I will praise your name, O LORD,
for it is good.
7For he has delivered me from all my troubles,
and my eyes have looked in triumph on my foes.

For the director of music. With stringed instruments. A *maskil*[g] of David.

**55** LISTEN TO my prayer, O God,
do not ignore my plea;
2 hear me and answer me.
My thoughts trouble me and I am distraught
3 at the voice of the enemy,
at the stares of the wicked;
for they bring down suffering upon me
and revile me in their anger.

4My heart is in anguish within me;
the terrors of death assail me.
5Fear and trembling have beset me;
horror has overwhelmed me.
6I said, "Oh, that I had the wings of a dove!
I would fly away and be at rest—
7I would flee far away
and stay in the desert; *Selah*
8I would hurry to my place of shelter,
far from the tempest and storm."

9Confuse the wicked, O Lord, confound their speech,
for I see violence and strife in the city.
10Day and night they prowl about on its walls;
malice and abuse are within it.
11Destructive forces are at work in the city;
threats and lies never leave its streets.

12If an enemy were insulting me,
I could endure it;
if a foe were raising himself against me,
I could hide from him.
13But it is you, a man like myself,
my companion, my close friend,
14with whom I once enjoyed sweet fellowship
as we walked with the throng at the house of God.

NIV [f] Title: Probably a literary or musical term [g] Title: Probably a literary or musical term

## King James

15Let death seize upon them, *and* let them go down quick into
hell: for wickedness *is* in their dwellings, *and* among them.
16As for me, I will call upon God; and the LORD shall save me.
17Evening, and morning, and at noon, will I pray, and cry
aloud: and he shall hear my voice.
18He hath delivered my soul in peace from the battle *that was*
against me: for there were many with me.
19God shall hear, and afflict them, even he that abideth of old.
Selah. Because they have no changes, therefore they fear not God.
20He hath put forth his hands against such as be at peace with
him: he hath broken his covenant.
21 *The words* of his mouth were smoother than butter, but war
*was* in his heart: his words were softer than oil, yet *were* they drawn
swords.
22Cast thy burden upon the LORD, and he shall sustain thee: he
shall never suffer the righteous to be moved.
23But thou, O God, shalt bring them down into the pit of destruction: bloody and deceitful men shall not live out half their
days; but I will trust in thee.

To the chief Musician upon Jonath-elem-rechokim, Michtam of David, when the Philistines took him in Gath.

56 BE MERCIFUL unto me, O God: for man would swallow
me up; he fighting daily oppresseth me.
2Mine enemies would daily swallow *me* up: for *they be* many that
fight against me, O thou most High.
3What time I am afraid, I will trust in thee.
4In God I will praise his word, in God I have put my trust; I will
not fear what flesh can do unto me.
5Every day they wrest my words: all their thoughts *are* against
me for evil.
6They gather themselves together, they hide themselves, they
mark my steps, when they wait for my soul.
7Shall they escape by iniquity? in *thine* anger cast down the
people, O God.
8Thou tellest my wanderings: put thou my tears into thy bottle:
*are they* not in thy book?
9When I cry *unto thee,* then shall mine enemies turn back: this
I know; for God *is* for me.
10In God will I praise *his* word: in the LORD will I praise *his*
word.
11In God have I put my trust: I will not be afraid what man can
do unto me.
12Thy vows *are* upon me, O God: I will render praises unto thee.

## Amplified

15Let desolations *and* death come suddenly upon them; let them
go down alive to Sheol [the place of the dead]; for evils are in their
habitations, in their hearts *and* their inmost part.
16As for me, I will call upon God; and the Lord will save me.
17Evening and morning and at noon will I utter my complaint
and moan *and* sigh, and He will hear my voice.
18He has redeemed my life in peace from the battle that was
against me [so that none came near me], for they were many who
strove with me.
19God will hear and humble them, even He Who abides of old.
Selah [pause, and calmly think of that]! Because in them there has
been no change [of heart], and they do not fear, revere *and* worship
God.
20[My companion] has put forth his hands against those who
were at peace with him; he has broken *and* profaned his agreement
[of friendship and loyalty].
21The words of his mouth were smoother than cream *or* butter,
but war was in his heart; his words were softer than oil, yet they
were drawn swords.
22Cast your burden on the Lord [releasing the weight of it] and
He will sustain you; He will never allow the [consistently] righteous to be moved—made to slip, fall or fail. [I Pet. 5:7.]
23But You, O God, will bring down the wicked to the pit of
destruction; men of blood and treachery shall not live out half their
days; but I will trust, lean on *and* confidently rely on You.

To the Chief Musician: *to the tune,* Silent Dove Among Those Far Away. Of David. A record of memorable thoughts, when the Philistines seized him in Gath.

56 BE MERCIFUL *and* gracious to me, O God, for man would
trample me *or* devour me; all the day long the adversary
oppresses me.
2They that lie in wait for me would swallow me up *or* trample
me all day long, for they are many who fight against me, O Most
High!
3What time I am afraid, I will have confidence *and* put my trust
*and* reliance on You.
4By [the help of] God I will praise His Word; on God I lean, rely
*and* confidently put my trust; I will not fear; what can man *who is*
flesh do to me?
5All day long they twist my words *and* trouble my affairs; all
their thoughts are against me for evil *and* my hurt.
6They gather themselves together, they hide themselves, they
watch my steps, even as they have (expectantly) waited for my life.
7They think to escape with iniquity, *and* shall they? In Your
indignation bring down the peoples, O God.
8You number *and* record my wanderings; put my tears into Your
bottle; are they not in Your book?
9Then shall my enemies turn back in the day that I cry out; this
I know, for God is for me. [Rom. 8:31.]
10In God Whose Word I praise, in the Lord, Whose Word I
praise,
11In God have I put my trust, *and* confident reliance; I will not
be afraid; what can man do to me?
12Your vows are upon me, O God; I will render praise to You
*and* give You thank offerings.

## New American Standard

15 Let death come deceitfully upon them;
Let them go down alive to Sheol,
For evil is in their dwelling, in their midst.

16¶ As for me, I shall call upon God,
And the LORD will save me.
17 Evening and morning and at noon, I will complain and murmur,
And He will hear my voice.
18 He will redeem my soul in peace from the battle *which is* against me,
For they are many *who strive* with me.
19 God will hear and answer them—
Even the one who sits enthroned from of old— Selah.
With whom there is no change,
And who do not fear God.
20 He has put forth his hands against those who were at peace with him;
He has [a]violated his covenant.
21 His speech was smoother than butter,
But his heart was war;
His words were softer than oil,
Yet they were drawn swords.

22¶ Cast your burden upon the LORD, and He will sustain you;
He will never allow the righteous to be shaken.
23 But Thou, O God, wilt bring them down to the pit of destruction;
Men of bloodshed and deceit will not live out half their days.
But I will trust in Thee.

*Supplication for Deliverance, and Grateful Trust in God.*

For the choir director; according to Jonath elem rehokim.
A Mikhtam of David, when the Philistines seized him in Gath.

**56** BE GRACIOUS, O God, for man has trampled upon me;
Fighting all day long he oppresses me.
2 My foes have trampled upon me all day long,
For they are many who fight proudly against me.
3 When I am afraid,
I will put my trust in Thee.
4 In God, whose word I praise,
In God I have put my trust;
I shall not be afraid.
What can *mere* man do to me?
5 All day long they [b]distort my words;
All their thoughts are against me for evil.
6 They [c]attack, they lurk,
They watch my steps,
As they have waited *to take* my life.
7 Because of wickedness, cast them forth,
In anger put down the peoples, O God!

8¶ Thou hast taken account of my wanderings;
Put my tears in Thy bottle;
Are *they* not in Thy book?
9 Then my enemies will turn back in the day when I call;
This I know, [d]that God is for me.
10 In God, *whose* word I praise,
In the LORD, *whose* word I praise,
11 In God I have put my [e]trust, I shall not be afraid.
What can man do to me?
12 Thy vows are *binding* upon me, O God;
I will render thank offerings to Thee.

**NAS** [a] Lit., *profaned* [b] Or, *trouble my affairs* [c] Or, *stir up strife* [d] Or, *because* [e] Or, *trust without fear*

## New International

15 Let death take my enemies by surprise;
let them go down alive to the grave,[f]
for evil finds lodging among them.

16 But I call to God,
and the LORD saves me.
17 Evening, morning and noon
I cry out in distress,
and he hears my voice.
18 He ransoms me unharmed
from the battle waged against me,
even though many oppose me.
19 God, who is enthroned forever,
will hear them and afflict them—
*Selah*
men who never change their ways
and have no fear of God.

20 My companion attacks his friends;
he violates his covenant.
21 His speech is smooth as butter,
yet war is in his heart;
his words are more soothing than oil,
yet they are drawn swords.

22 Cast your cares on the LORD
and he will sustain you;
he will never let the righteous fall.
23 But you, O God, will bring down the wicked
into the pit of corruption;
bloodthirsty and deceitful men
will not live out half their days.

But as for me, I trust in you.

For the director of music. To ⌞the tune of⌟ "A Dove on Distant Oaks." Of David. A *miktam*.[g] When the Philistines had seized him in Gath.

**56** BE MERCIFUL to me, O God, for men
hotly pursue me;
all day long they press their attack.
2 My slanderers pursue me all day long;
many are attacking me in their pride.

3 When I am afraid,
I will trust in you.
4 In God, whose word I praise,
in God I trust; I will not be afraid.
What can mortal man do to me?

5 All day long they twist my words;
they are always plotting to harm me.
6 They conspire, they lurk,
they watch my steps,
eager to take my life.
7 On no account let them escape;
in your anger, O God, bring down the nations.
8 Record my lament;
list my tears on your scroll[h]—
are they not in your record?

9 Then my enemies will turn back
when I call for help.
By this I will know that God is for me.
10 In God, whose word I praise,
in the LORD, whose word I praise—
11 in God I trust; I will not be afraid.
What can man do to me?

12 I am under vows to you, O God;
I will present my thank offerings to you.

**NIV** [f] *15* Hebrew *Sheol* [g] Title: Probably a literary or musical term [h] *8* Or / *put my tears in your wineskin*

## King James

13For thou hast delivered my soul from death: *wilt* not *thou deliver* my feet from falling, that I may walk before God in the light of the living?

To the chief Musician, Al-taschith, Michtam of David, when he fled from Saul in the cave.

**57** BE MERCIFUL unto me, O God, be merciful unto me: for my soul trusteth in thee: yea, in the shadow of thy wings will I make my refuge, until *these* calamities be overpast.

2I will cry unto God most high; unto God that performeth *all things* for me.

3He shall send from heaven, and save me *from* the reproach of him that would swallow me up. Selah. God shall send forth his mercy and his truth.

4My soul *is* among lions: *and* I lie *even among* them that are set on fire, *even* the sons of men, whose teeth *are* spears and arrows, and their tongue a sharp sword.

5Be thou exalted, O God, above the heavens; *let* thy glory *be* above all the earth.

6They have prepared a net for my steps; my soul is bowed down: they have digged a pit before me, into the midst whereof they are fallen *themselves*. Selah.

7My heart is fixed, O God, my heart is fixed: I will sing and give praise.

8Awake up, my glory; awake, psaltery and harp: I *myself* will awake early.

9I will praise thee, O Lord, among the people: I will sing unto thee among the nations.

10For thy mercy *is* great unto the heavens, and thy truth unto the clouds.

11Be thou exalted, O God, above the heavens: *let* thy glory *be* above all the earth.

To the chief Musician, Al-taschith, Michtam of David.

**58** DO YE indeed speak righteousness, O congregation? do ye judge uprightly, O ye sons of men?

2Yea, in heart ye work wickedness; ye weigh the violence of your hands in the earth.

3The wicked are estranged from the womb: they go astray as soon as they be born, speaking lies.

4Their poison *is* like the poison of a serpent: *they are* like the deaf adder *that* stoppeth her ear;

5Which will not hearken to the voice of charmers, charming never so wisely.

6Break their teeth, O God, in their mouth: break out the great teeth of the young lions, O LORD.

7Let them melt away as waters *which* run continually: *when* he bendeth *his bow to shoot* his arrows, let them be as cut in pieces.

8As a snail *which* melteth, let *every one of them* pass away: *like* the untimely birth of a woman, *that* they may not see the sun.

## Amplified

13For You have delivered my life from death, yes, and my feet from falling, that I may walk before God in the light of life *and* of the living.

To the Chief Musician;
*set to the tune,* Do Not Destroy. A record of memorable thoughts of David, when he fled from Saul in the cave.

**57** BE MERCIFUL *and* gracious to me, O God, be merciful *and* gracious to me; for my soul takes refuge *and* finds shelter *and* confidence in You; yes, in the shadow of Your wings will I take refuge *and* be confident until calamities *and* destructive storms are passed.

2I will cry to God Most High, Who performs on my behalf *and* rewards me—Who brings to pass [His purposes] for me *and* surely completes them!

3He will send from Heaven and save me from the slanders *and* reproaches of him who would trample me down *or* swallow me up, *and* put him to shame. Selah [pause, and calmly think of that]! God will send forth His mercy *and* loving-kindness *and* His truth *and* faithfulness.

4My life is among lions; I must lie among those who are aflame, the sons of men whose teeth are spears and arrows, their tongue a sharp sword.

5Be exalted, O God, above the heavens! Let Your glory be over all the earth!

6They set a net for my steps; my very life was bowed down; they dug a pit in my way; into the midst of it they have fallen themselves. Selah [pause, and calmly think of that]!

7My heart is fixed, O God; my heart is steadfast *and* confident! I will sing and make melody.

8Awake, my glory [my inner self]; awake, harp and lyre! I will awake right early [I will awake the dawn]!

9I will praise *and* give thanks to You, O Lord, among the peoples; I will sing praises to You among the nations.

10For Your mercy *and* loving-kindness are great, reaching to the heavens, and Your truth *and* faithfulness to the clouds.

11Be exalted, O God, above the heavens; let Your glory be over all the earth.

To the Chief Musician; *set to the tune,* Do Not Destroy.
A record of memorable thoughts of David.

**58** DO YOU indeed in silence speak righteousness? (Or is the righteousness, rightness and justice you should speak quite dumb) [O you mighty ones]? Do you judge fairly *and* uprightly, O you sons of men?

2No, in your heart you devise wickedness; you deal out in the land the violence of your hands.

3The ungodly are perverse *and* estranged from the womb; they go astray as soon as they are born, speaking lies.

4Their poison is like the venom of a serpent; they are like the deaf adder *or* asp that stops its ear,

5Which listens not to the voice of charmers, *or* of the enchanter casting spells never so cunningly.

6Break their teeth, O God, in their mouths; break out the fangs of the young lions, O Lord.

7Let them melt away as water which runs on apace; when he aims his arrows let them be as if they were headless *or* split apart.

8Let them be as a snail dissolving slime as it passes on, *or* as a festering sore which wastes away; like [the child to which] a woman gives untimely birth, that has not seen the sun.

## New American Standard

13 For Thou hast delivered my soul from death,
Indeed my feet from stumbling,
So that I may walk before God
In the light of the living.

*Prayer for Rescue from Persecutors.*

For the choir director; *set to* [a]Al-tashheth. A Mikhtam of David, when he fled from Saul, in the cave.

**57** BE GRACIOUS to me, O God, be gracious to me,
For my soul takes refuge in Thee;
And in the shadow of Thy wings I will take refuge,
Until destruction passes by.
2 I will cry to God Most High,
To God who accomplishes *all things* for me.
3 He will send from heaven and save me;
He reproaches him who tramples upon me. Selah.
God will send forth His lovingkindness and His truth.

4¶ My soul is among lions;
I must lie among those who breathe forth fire,
*Even* the sons of men, whose teeth are spears and arrows,
And their tongue a sharp sword.
5 Be exalted above the heavens, O God;
*Let* Thy glory *be* above all the earth.
6 They have [b]prepared a net for my steps;
My soul is bowed down;
They dug a pit before me;
They *themselves* have fallen into the midst of it. Selah.

7¶ My heart is steadfast, O God, my heart is steadfast;
I will sing, yes, I will sing praises!
8 Awake, my glory;
Awake, harp and lyre,
I will awaken the dawn!
9 I will give thanks to Thee, O Lord, among the peoples;
I will sing praises to Thee among the nations.
10 For Thy lovingkindness is great to the heavens,
And Thy truth to the clouds.
11 Be exalted above the heavens, O God;
*Let* Thy glory *be* above all the earth.

*Prayer for the Punishment of the Wicked.*

For the choir director; *set to* Al-tashheth. A Mikhtam of David.

**58** DO YOU indeed speak righteousness, O [c]gods?
Do you judge [d]uprightly, O sons of men?
2 No, in heart you work unrighteousness;
On earth you weigh out the violence of your hands.
3 The wicked are estranged from the womb;
These who speak lies go astray from birth.
4 They have venom like the venom of a serpent;
Like a deaf cobra that stops up its ear,
5 So that it does not hear the voice of charmers,
*Or* a skillful caster of spells.

6¶ O God, shatter their teeth in their mouth;
Break out the fangs of the young lions, O LORD.
7 Let them flow away like water that runs off;
*When* he aims his arrows, let them be as headless shafts.
8 *Let them be* as a snail which melts away as it goes along,
*Like* the miscarriages of a woman which never see the sun.

NAS [a] Lit., *Do Not Destroy* [b] Or, *spread* [c] Or, *judges* [d] Or, *uprightly the sons of men?*

## New International

13 For you have delivered me[e] from death
and my feet from stumbling,
that I may walk before God
in the light of life.[f]

For the director of music. ⌊To the tune of⌋ "Do Not Destroy." Of David. A *miktam*.[g] When he had fled from Saul into the cave.

**57** HAVE MERCY on me, O God, have mercy on me,
for in you my soul takes refuge.
I will take refuge in the shadow of your wings
until the disaster has passed.

2 I cry out to God Most High,
to God, who fulfills ⌊his purpose⌋ for me.
3 He sends from heaven and saves me,
rebuking those who hotly pursue me; *Selah*
God sends his love and his faithfulness.

4 I am in the midst of lions;
I lie among ravenous beasts—
men whose teeth are spears and arrows,
whose tongues are sharp swords.

5 Be exalted, O God, above the heavens;
let your glory be over all the earth.

6 They spread a net for my feet—
I was bowed down in distress.
They dug a pit in my path—
but they have fallen into it themselves. *Selah*
7 My heart is steadfast, O God,
my heart is steadfast;
I will sing and make music.
8 Awake, my soul!
Awake, harp and lyre!
I will awaken the dawn.

9 I will praise you, O Lord, among the nations;
I will sing of you among the peoples.
10 For great is your love, reaching to the heavens;
your faithfulness reaches to the skies.
11 Be exalted, O God, above the heavens;
let your glory be over all the earth.

For the director of music. ⌊To the tune of⌋ "Do Not Destroy." Of David. A *miktam*.[h]

**58** DO YOU rulers indeed speak justly?
Do you judge uprightly among men?
2 No, in your heart you devise injustice,
and your hands mete out violence on the earth.
3 Even from birth the wicked go astray;
from the womb they are wayward and speak lies.
4 Their venom is like the venom of a snake,
like that of a cobra that has stopped its ears,
5 that will not heed the tune of the charmer,
however skillful the enchanter may be.

6 Break the teeth in their mouths, O God;
tear out, O LORD, the fangs of the lions!
7 Let them vanish like water that flows away;
when they draw the bow, let their arrows be blunted.
8 Like a slug melting away as it moves along,
like a stillborn child, may they not see the sun.

NIV [e] *13* Or *my soul* [f] *13* Or *the land of the living* [g] Title: Probably a literary or musical term [h] Title: Probably a literary or musical term

## King James

9 Before your pots can feel the thorns, he shall take them away
as with a whirlwind, both living, and in *his* wrath.
10 The righteous shall rejoice when he seeth the vengeance: he
shall wash his feet in the blood of the wicked.
11 So that a man shall say, Verily *there is* a reward for the righteous: verily he is a God that judgeth in the earth.

To the chief Musician, Al-taschith, Michtam of David; when Saul sent,
and they watched the house to kill him.

**59** DELIVER ME from mine enemies, O my God: defend me
from them that rise up against me.
2 Deliver me from the workers of iniquity, and save me from
bloody men.
3 For, lo, they lie in wait for my soul: the mighty are gathered
against me; not *for* my transgression, nor *for* my sin, O LORD.
4 They run and prepare themselves without *my* fault: awake to
help me, and behold.
5 Thou therefore, O LORD God of hosts, the God of Israel, awake
to visit all the heathen: be not merciful to any wicked transgressors. Selah.
6 They return at evening: they make a noise like a dog, and go
round about the city.
7 Behold, they belch out with their mouth: swords *are* in their
lips: for who, *say they,* doth hear?
8 But thou, O LORD, shalt laugh at them; thou shalt have all the
heathen in derision.
9 *Because of* his strength will I wait upon thee: for God *is* my
defence.
10 The God of my mercy shall prevent me: God shall let me see
*my desire* upon mine enemies.
11 Slay them not, lest my people forget: scatter them by thy
power; and bring them down, O Lord our shield.
12 *For* the sin of their mouth *and* the words of their lips let them
even be taken in their pride: and for cursing and lying *which* they
speak.
13 Consume *them* in wrath, consume *them,* that they *may* not *be:*
and let them know that God ruleth in Jacob unto the ends of the
earth. Selah.
14 And at evening let them return; *and* let them make a noise like
a dog, and go round about the city.
15 Let them wander up and down for meat, and grudge if they
be not satisfied.
16 But I will sing of thy power; yea, I will sing aloud of thy mercy
in the morning: for thou hast been my defence and refuge in the
day of my trouble.
17 Unto thee, O my strength, will I sing: for God *is* my defence,
*and* the God of my mercy.

## Amplified

9 Before your pots can feel the thorns [that are placed under
them for fuel], He will take them away as with a whirlwind, the
green and the burning ones alike.
10 The [unyieldingly] righteous shall rejoice when he sees the
vengeance; he will bathe his feet in the blood of the wicked.
11 Men will say, Surely there is a reward for the [uncompromis-
ingly] righteous; surely there is a God Who judges on the earth.

To the Chief Musician;
*set to the tune,* Do Not Destroy. Of David, a record of memorable
thoughts, when Saul sent men to watch his house in order to kill him.

**59** DELIVER ME from my enemies, O my God; defend *and*
protect me from those who rise up against me.
2 Deliver me from *and* lift me above those who work evil, and
save me from the bloodthirsty men.
3 For, lo, they lie in wait for my life; fierce *and* mighty men are
banded together against me, not for my transgression, nor for any
sin of mine, O Lord.
4 They run and prepare themselves for no fault of mine; rouse
Yourself, *O Lord,* to meet *and* help me, and see!
5 You, O Lord God of hosts, the God of Israel, arise to visit all
the nations; spare none *and* be not merciful to any who treacherously plot evil. Selah [pause, and calmly think of that]!
6 They return at evening; they howl *and* snarl like dogs, and go
[prowling] about the city.
7 Behold, they belch out [insults] with their mouth; swords [of
sarcasm, ridicule, slander and lies] are in their lips; for who, they
think, hears us?
8 But You, O Lord, will laugh at them [in scorn]; You will hold
all the nations in derision.
9 O my Strength, I will watch *and* give heed to You *and* sing
praises; for God is my defense—my protector and high tower.
10 My God in His mercy *and* steadfast love will meet me; God will
let me look [triumphantly] on my enemies—those who lie in wait
for me.
11 Slay them not, lest my people forget; scatter them by Your
power *and* make them wander to and fro; and bring them down,
O Lord our shield!
12 For the sin of their mouth and the words of their lips let them
even be trapped *and* taken in their pride, and for the cursing and
lying which they utter.
13 Consume them in wrath, consume them so that they shall be
no more; and let them know that God rules over Jacob [Israel],
unto the ends of the earth. Selah [pause, and calmly think of that]!
14 And at evening let them return; let them howl *and* snarl like
dogs, and go prowling about the city.
15 Let them wander up and down for food, and tarry all night
if they be not satisfied—not getting their fill.
16 But I will sing of Your mighty strength *and* power; yes, I will
sing aloud of Your mercy *and* loving-kindness in the morning; for
You have been to me a defense—a fortress and a high tower—and
a refuge in the day of my distress.
17 Unto You, O my Strength, I will sing praises; for God is my
defense, my fortress *and* high tower, the God Who shows me
mercy *and* steadfast love.

## New American Standard

9 Before your pots can feel *the fire of* thorns,
He will sweep them away with a whirlwind, the green and the burning alike.
10 ¶ The righteous will rejoice when he sees the vengeance;
He will wash his feet in the blood of the wicked.
11 And men will say, "Surely there is a reward for the righteous;
Surely there is a God who judges on earth!"

*Prayer for Deliverance from Enemies.*

For the choir director; *set to* Al-tashheth. A Mikhtam of David, when Saul sent *men,* and they watched the house in order to kill him.

**59** DELIVER ME from my enemies, O my God;
Set me *securely* on high away from those who rise up against me.
2 Deliver me from those who do iniquity,
And save me from men of bloodshed.
3 For behold, they have set an ambush for my life;
Fierce men [a]launch an attack against me,
Not for my transgression nor for my sin, O LORD,
4 For no guilt of *mine,* they run and set themselves against me.
Arouse Thyself to help me, and see!
5 And Thou, O LORD God of hosts, the God of Israel,
Awake to punish all the nations;
Do not be gracious to any *who are* treacherous in iniquity. Selah.
6 They return at evening, they howl like a dog,
And go around the city.
7 Behold, they belch forth with their mouth;
Swords are in their lips,
For, *they say,* "Who hears?"
8 But Thou, O LORD, dost laugh at them;
Thou dost scoff at all the nations.

9 *Because of* [b]his strength I will watch for Thee,
For God is my stronghold.
10 My God in His lovingkindness will meet me;
God will let me look *triumphantly* upon my foes.
11 Do not slay them, lest my people forget;
Scatter them by Thy power, and bring them down,
O Lord, our shield.
12 *On account of* the sin of their mouth *and* the words of their lips,
Let them even be caught in their pride,
And on account of curses and lies which they utter.
13 [c]Destroy *them* in wrath, [d]destroy *them,* that they may be no more;
That *men* may know that God rules in Jacob,
To the ends of the earth. Selah.
14 And they return at evening, they howl like a dog,
And go around the city.
15 They wander about [e]for food,
And growl if they are not satisfied.

16 ¶ But as for me, I shall sing of Thy strength;
Yes, I shall joyfully sing of Thy lovingkindness in the morning,
For Thou hast been my stronghold,
And a refuge in the day of my distress.
17 O my strength, I will sing praises to Thee;
For God is my stronghold, the God who shows me lovingkindness.

NAS [a] Or, *stir up strife* [b] Many mss. and some ancient versions read *My strength* [c] Lit., *Bring to an end* [d] Lit., *Bring to an end* [e] Or, *to devour*

## New International

9 Before your pots can feel ⌊the heat of⌋ the thorns—
whether they be green or dry—the wicked will be swept away.[f]
10 The righteous will be glad when they are avenged,
when they bathe their feet in the blood of the wicked.
11 Then men will say,
"Surely the righteous still are rewarded;
surely there is a God who judges the earth."

For the director of music. ⌊To the tune of⌋ "Do Not Destroy." Of David. A *miktam.*[g] When Saul had sent men to watch David's house in order to kill him.

**59** DELIVER ME from my enemies, O God;
protect me from those who rise up against me.
2 Deliver me from evildoers
and save me from bloodthirsty men.
3 See how they lie in wait for me!
Fierce men conspire against me
for no offense or sin of mine, O LORD.
4 I have done no wrong, yet they are ready to attack me.
Arise to help me; look on my plight!
5 O LORD God Almighty, the God of Israel,
rouse yourself to punish all the nations;
show no mercy to wicked traitors. *Selah*
6 They return at evening,
snarling like dogs,
and prowl about the city.
7 See what they spew from their mouths—
they spew out swords from their lips,
and they say, "Who can hear us?"
8 But you, O LORD, laugh at them;
you scoff at all those nations.

9 O my Strength, I watch for you;
you, O God, are my fortress, 10 my loving God.

God will go before me
and will let me gloat over those who slander me.
11 But do not kill them, O Lord our shield,[h]
or my people will forget.
In your might make them wander about,
and bring them down.
12 For the sins of their mouths,
for the words of their lips,
let them be caught in their pride.
For the curses and lies they utter,
13 consume them in wrath,
consume them till they are no more.
Then it will be known to the ends of the earth
that God rules over Jacob. *Selah*

14 They return at evening,
snarling like dogs,
and prowl about the city.
15 They wander about for food
and howl if not satisfied.
16 But I will sing of your strength,
in the morning I will sing of your love;
for you are my fortress,
my refuge in times of trouble.

17 O my Strength, I sing praise to you;
you, O God, are my fortress, my loving God.

NIV [f] 9 The meaning of the Hebrew for this verse is uncertain. [g] Title: Probably a literary or musical term [h] 11 Or *sovereign*

## King James

To the chief Musician upon Shushan-eduth, Michtam of David, to teach;
when he strove with Aram-naharaim and with Aram-zobah, when Joab
returned, and smote of Edom in the valley of salt twelve thousand.

**60** O GOD, thou hast cast us off, thou hast scattered us, thou
hast been displeased; O turn thyself to us again.
2 Thou hast made the earth to tremble; thou hast broken it: heal
the breaches thereof; for it shaketh.
3 Thou hast shown thy people hard things: thou hast made us
to drink the wine of astonishment.
4 Thou hast given a banner to them that fear thee, that it may
be displayed because of the truth. Selah.
5 That thy beloved may be delivered; save *with* thy right hand,
and hear me.
6 God hath spoken in his holiness; I will rejoice, I will divide
Shechem, and mete out the valley of Succoth.
7 Gilead *is* mine, and Manasseh *is* mine; Ephraim also *is* the
strength of mine head; Judah *is* my lawgiver;
8 Moab *is* my washpot; over Edom will I cast out my shoe:
Philistia, triumph thou because of me.
9 Who will bring me *into* the strong city? who will lead me into
Edom?
10 *Wilt* not thou, O God, *which* hadst cast us off? and *thou*, O
God, *which* didst not go out with our armies?
11 Give us help from trouble: for vain *is* the help of man.
12 Through God we shall do valiantly: for he *it is that* shall tread
down our enemies.

To the chief Musician upon Neginah, *A Psalm* of David.

**61** HEAR MY cry, O God; attend unto my prayer.
2 From the end of the earth will I cry unto thee, when my
heart is overwhelmed: lead me to the rock *that* is higher than I.
3 For thou hast been a shelter for me, *and* a strong tower from
the enemy.
4 I will abide in thy tabernacle for ever: I will trust in the covert
of thy wings. Selah.
5 For thou, O God, hast heard my vows: thou hast given *me* the
heritage of those that fear thy name.
6 Thou wilt prolong the king's life: *and* his years as many generations.
7 He shall abide before God for ever: O prepare mercy and truth,
*which* may preserve him.
8 So will I sing praise unto thy name for ever, that I may daily
perform my vows.

To the chief Musician, to Jeduthun, A Psalm of David.

**62** TRULY MY soul waiteth upon God: from him *cometh* my
salvation.

## Amplified

To the Chief Musician;
*set to the tune of* The Lily of Testimony. A poem intended by David to
record memorable thoughts; to teach; when he had striven with the
Arameans of Mesopotamia and the Arameans of Zobah, and Joab
returned and smote twelve thousand Edomites in the Valley of Salt.

**60** O GOD, You have rejected us *and* cast us off, broken down
[our defenses] *and* scattered us; You have been angry; O
restore us *and* turn Yourself to us again!
2 You have made the land to quake *and* tremble; You have rent
it (open); repair its breaches, for it shakes *and* totters.
3 You have made Your people suffer hard things; You have
given us to drink wine that made us reel *and* be dazed.
4 [But now] You have set up a banner for those who fear *and*
worshipfully revere You—to which they may flee from the bow—a
standard displayed because of the truth. Selah [pause, and calmly
think of that]!
5 That Your beloved ones may be delivered, save with Your right
hand and answer us [or me].
6 God has spoken by His holiness [in His promises]. I will rejoice; I will divide and portion out [the land] Shechem and the
valley of Succoth [west to east].
7 Gilead is Mine, and Manasseh is Mine; Ephraim also is My
helmet [the defense of My head]; Judah is My scepter *and* My
lawgiver.
8 Moab is My washpot [reduced to vilest servitude]; upon Edom
I cast My shoe in triumph; over Philistia I raise the shout of victory.
9 Who will bring me [David] into the strong city [of Petra]? Who
will lead me into Edom?
10 Have You not rejected us, O God? And You go not forth, O
God, with our armies.
11 O give us help against the adversary, for vain—ineffectual
and to no purpose—is the help or salvation of man.
12 Through God we shall do valiantly; for He it is Who will tread
down our adversaries.

To the Chief Musician;
on stringed instruments. [ *A Psalm*] of David.

**61** HEAR MY cry, O God; listen to my prayer.
2 From the end of the earth will I cry to You, when my heart
is overwhelmed *and* fainting; lead me to the rock that is higher than
I—yes, a rock that is too high for me.
3 For You have been a shelter *and* a refuge for me, a strong tower
against the adversary.
4 I will dwell in Your tabernacle for ever; let me find refuge *and*
trust in the shelter of Your wings. Selah [pause, and calmly think
of that]!
5 For You, O God, have heard my vows; You have given me the
heritage of those who fear, revere *and* honor Your name.
6 You may prolong the [true] King's life [adding days upon
days], and may His years be to the last generation [of this world
and the generations of the world to come].
7 May He sit enthroned for ever before (the face of) God. O
ordain that loving-kindness and faithfulness may watch over Him!
8 So will I sing praise to Your name for ever, paying my vows
day by day.

To the Chief Musician;
according to Jeduthun [ *Ethan, the noted musician*]. A Psalm of David.

**62** FOR GOD alone my soul waits in silence; from Him comes
my salvation.

## New American Standard

*Lament over Defeat in Battle, and Prayer for Help.*

For the choir director; according to [a]Shushan Eduth.
A Mikhtam of David, to teach; when he struggled with Aram-naharaim and with Aram-zobah, and Joab returned, and smote twelve thousand of Edom in the Valley of Salt.

**60** O GOD, Thou hast rejected us. Thou hast broken us;
Thou hast been angry; O, restore us.
2 Thou hast made the land quake, Thou hast split it open;
Heal its breaches, for it totters.
3 Thou hast made Thy people experience hardship;
Thou hast given us wine to drink that makes us stagger.
4 Thou hast given a banner to those who fear Thee,
That it may be displayed because of the truth. Selah.
5 That Thy beloved may be delivered,
Save with Thy right hand, and answer us!

6¶ God has spoken in His [b]holiness:
"I will exult, I will portion out Shechem and measure out the valley of Succoth.
7 "Gilead is Mine, and Manasseh is Mine;
Ephraim also is the helmet of My head;
Judah is My [c]scepter.
8 "Moab is My washbowl;
Over Edom I shall throw My shoe;
Shout loud, O Philistia, because of Me!"

9¶ Who will bring me into the besieged city?
Who will lead me to Edom?
10 Hast not Thou Thyself, O God, rejected us?
And wilt Thou not go forth with our armies, O God?
11 O give us help against the adversary,
For deliverance by man is in vain.
12 Through God we shall do valiantly,
And it is He who will tread down our adversaries.

*Confidence in God's Protection.*

For the choir director; on a stringed instrument. *A Psalm* of David.

**61** HEAR MY cry, O God;
Give heed to my prayer.
2 From the end of the earth I call to Thee, when my heart is faint;
Lead me to the rock that is higher than I.
3 For Thou hast been a refuge for me,
A tower of strength against the enemy.
4 Let me dwell in Thy tent forever;
Let me take refuge in the shelter of Thy wings. Selah.

5¶ For Thou hast heard my vows, O God;
Thou hast given *me* the inheritance of those who fear Thy name.
6 Thou wilt prolong the king's life;
His years will be as many generations.
7 He will abide before God forever;
Appoint lovingkindness and truth, that they may preserve him.
8 So I will sing praise to Thy name forever,
That I may pay my vows day by day.

*God Alone a Refuge from Treachery and Oppression.*

For the choir director; according to Jeduthun. A Psalm of David.

**62** MY SOUL *waits* in silence for God only;
From Him is my salvation.

NAS [a] Lit., *The lily of testimony* [b] Or, *sanctuary* [c] Or, *lawgiver*

## New International

For the director of music. To ⌊the tune of⌋ "The Lily of the Covenant." A *miktam*[d] of David. For teaching. When he fought Aram Naharaim[e] and Aram Zobah,[f] and when Joab returned and struck down twelve thousand Edomites in the Valley of Salt.

**60** YOU HAVE rejected us, O God, and burst forth upon us;
you have been angry—now restore us!
2 You have shaken the land and torn it open;
mend its fractures, for it is quaking.
3 You have shown your people desperate times;
you have given us wine that makes us stagger.
4 But for those who fear you, you have raised a banner
to be unfurled against the bow. *Selah*
5 Save us and help us with your right hand,
that those you love may be delivered.
6 God has spoken from his sanctuary:
"In triumph I will parcel out Shechem
and measure off the Valley of Succoth.
7 Gilead is mine, and Manasseh is mine;
Ephraim is my helmet,
Judah my scepter.
8 Moab is my washbasin,
upon Edom I toss my sandal;
over Philistia I shout in triumph."

9 Who will bring me to the fortified city?
Who will lead me to Edom?
10 Is it not you, O God, you who have rejected us
and no longer go out with our armies?
11 Give us aid against the enemy,
for the help of man is worthless.
12 With God we will gain the victory,
and he will trample down our enemies.

For the director of music. With stringed instruments. Of David.

**61** HEAR MY cry, O God;
listen to my prayer.

2 From the ends of the earth I call to you,
I call as my heart grows faint;
lead me to the rock that is higher than I.
3 For you have been my refuge,
a strong tower against the foe.

4 I long to dwell in your tent forever
and take refuge in the shelter of your wings. *Selah*
5 For you have heard my vows, O God;
you have given me the heritage of those who fear your name.

6 Increase the days of the king's life,
his years for many generations.
7 May he be enthroned in God's presence forever;
appoint your love and faithfulness to protect him.

8 Then will I ever sing praise to your name
and fulfill my vows day after day.

For the director of music. For Jeduthun. A psalm of David.

**62** MY SOUL finds rest in God alone;
my salvation comes from him.

NIV [d] Title: Probably a literary or musical term [e] Title: That is, Arameans of Northwest Mesopotamia [f] Title: That is, Arameans of central Syria

## King James

2He only *is* my rock and my salvation; *he is* my defence; I shall not be greatly moved.

3How long will ye imagine mischief against a man? ye shall be slain all of you: as a bowing wall *shall ye be, and as* a tottering fence.

4They only consult to cast *him* down from his excellency: they delight in lies: they bless with their mouth, but they curse inwardly. Selah.

5My soul, wait thou only upon God; for my expectation *is* from him.

6He only *is* my rock and my salvation: *he is* my defence; I shall not be moved.

7In God *is* my salvation and my glory: the rock of my strength, *and* my refuge, *is* in God.

8Trust in him at all times; ye people, pour out your heart before him: God *is* a refuge for us. Selah.

9Surely men of low degree *are* vanity, *and* men of high degree *are* a lie: to be laid in the balance, they *are* altogether *lighter* than vanity.

10Trust not in oppression, and become not vain in robbery: if riches increase, set not your heart *upon them*.

11God hath spoken once; twice have I heard this; that power *belongeth* unto God.

12Also unto thee, O Lord, *belongeth* mercy: for thou renderest to every man according to his work.

A Psalm of David, when he was in the wilderness of Judah.

**63** O GOD, thou *art* my God; early will I seek thee: my soul thirsteth for thee, my flesh longeth for thee in a dry and thirsty land, where no water is;

2To see thy power and thy glory, so *as* I have seen thee in the sanctuary.

3Because thy lovingkindness *is* better than life, my lips shall praise thee.

4Thus will I bless thee while I live: I will lift up my hands in thy name.

5My soul shall be satisfied as *with* marrow and fatness; and my mouth shall praise *thee* with joyful lips:

6When I remember thee upon my bed, *and* meditate on thee in the *night* watches.

7Because thou hast been my help, therefore in the shadow of thy wings will I rejoice.

8My soul followeth hard after thee: thy right hand upholdeth me.

9But those *that* seek my soul, to destroy *it*, shall go into the lower parts of the earth.

10They shall fall by the sword: they shall be a portion for foxes.

11But the king shall rejoice in God; every one that sweareth by him shall glory: but the mouth of them that speak lies shall be stopped.

## Amplified

2He only is my rock and my salvation, my defense *and* my fortress; I shall not be greatly moved.

3How long will you set upon a man that you may slay him, all of you, like a leaning wall, like a tottering fence?

4They only consult to cast him down from his height [to dishonor him]; they delight in lies; they bless with their mouth, but they curse inwardly. Selah [pause, and calmly think of that]!

5My soul, wait only upon God *and* silently submit to Him; for my hope *and* expectation are from Him.

6He only is my rock and my salvation; He is my defense *and* my fortress; I shall not be moved.

7With God rests my salvation and my glory; my rock of unyielding strength *and* impenetrable hardness, and my refuge is in God!

8Trust, lean on, rely on *and* have confidence in Him at all times, you people; pour out your heart before Him. God is a refuge for us—a fortress and a high tower. Selah [pause, and calmly think of that]!

9Men of low degree [in the social scale] are emptiness—futility, a breath; *and* men of high degree [in the same scale] are a lie *and* a delusion. In the balances they go up; they are together lighter than a breath.

10Trust *and* rely confidently not on extortion *and* oppression, and do not vainly hope in robbery; if riches increase, set not your heart on them.

11God has spoken once, twice have I heard this, that power belongs to God.

12Also to You, O Lord, belong mercy *and* loving-kindness, for You render to every man according to his work. [Jer. 17:10; Rev. 22:12.]

A Psalm of David,
when he was in the Wilderness of Judah.

**63** O GOD, You are my God; earnestly will I seek You; my inner self thirsts for You, my flesh longs *and* is faint for You, in a dry and weary land, where no water is;

2So I have looked upon You in the sanctuary, to see Your power and Your glory.

3Because Your loving-kindness is better than life, my lips shall praise You.

4So will I bless You while I live; I will lift up my hands in Your name.

5My whole being shall be satisfied as with marrow and fatness; and my mouth shall praise You with joyful lips,

6When I remember You upon my bed, and meditate on You in the night watches.

7For You have been my help, and in the shadow of Your wings will I rejoice.

8My whole being follows hard after You *and* clings closely to You; Your right hand upholds me.

9But those who seek *and* demand my life, to ruin *and* destroy it, shall [themselves be destroyed and] go into the lower parts of the earth [into the underworld of the dead].

10They shall be given over to the power of the sword; they shall be a prey for foxes *and* jackals.

11But the king shall rejoice in God; every one who swears by Him [that is, who binds himself by God's authority, acknowledging His supremacy, and devoting himself to His glory and service alone] *every such one* shall glory, for the mouth of those who speak lies shall be stopped.

## New American Standard

2 He only is my rock and my salvation,
My stronghold; I shall not be greatly shaken.

3¶ How long will you assail a man,
That you may murder *him,* all of you,
Like a leaning wall, like a tottering fence?
4 They have counseled only to thrust him down from his high position;
They delight in falsehood;
They bless with their mouth,
But inwardly they curse. Selah.

5¶ My soul, wait in silence for God only,
For my hope is from Him.
6 He only is my rock and my salvation,
My stronghold; I shall not be shaken.
7 On God my salvation and my glory *rest;*
The rock of my strength, my refuge is in God.
8 Trust in Him at all times, O people;
Pour out your heart before Him;
God is a refuge for us. Selah.

9¶ Men of low degree are only vanity, and men of rank are a lie;
In the balances they go up;
They are together lighter than breath.
10 Do not trust in oppression,
And do not vainly hope in robbery;
If riches increase, do not set *your* heart *upon them.*

11¶ [a]Once God has spoken;
[b]Twice I have heard this:
That power belongs to God;
12 And lovingkindness is Thine, O Lord,
For Thou dost recompense a man according to his work.

*The Thirsting Soul Satisfied in God.*

A Psalm of David, when he was in the wilderness of Judah.

63 O GOD, Thou art my God; I shall seek Thee [c]earnestly;
My soul thirsts for Thee, my flesh yearns for Thee,
In a dry and weary land where there is no water.
2 Thus I have beheld Thee in the sanctuary,
To see Thy power and Thy glory.
3 Because Thy lovingkindness is better than life,
My lips will praise Thee.
4 So I will bless Thee as long as I live;
I will lift up my hands in Thy name.
5 My soul is satisfied as with [d]marrow and fatness,
And my mouth offers praises with joyful lips.

6¶ When I remember Thee on my bed,
I meditate on Thee in the night watches,
7 For Thou hast been my help,
And in the shadow of Thy wings I sing for joy.
8 My soul clings to Thee;
Thy right hand upholds me.

9¶ But those who seek my life, to destroy it,
Will go into the depths of the earth.
10 They will be delivered over to the power of the sword;
They will be a prey for foxes.
11 But the king will rejoice in God;
Everyone who swears by Him will glory,
For the mouths of those who speak lies will be stopped.

NAS [a] Or, *One thing* [b] Or, *These two things I have heard* [c] Lit., *early* [d] Lit., *fat*

## New International

2He alone is my rock and my salvation;
he is my fortress, I will never be shaken.

3How long will you assault a man?
Would all of you throw him down—
this leaning wall, this tottering fence?
4They fully intend to topple him
from his lofty place;
they take delight in lies.
With their mouths they bless,
but in their hearts they curse. *Selah*

5Find rest, O my soul, in God alone;
my hope comes from him.
6He alone is my rock and my salvation;
he is my fortress, I will not be shaken.
7My salvation and my honor depend on God[e];
he is my mighty rock, my refuge.
8Trust in him at all times, O people;
pour out your hearts to him,
for God is our refuge. *Selah*

9Lowborn men are but a breath,
the highborn are but a lie;
if weighed on a balance, they are nothing;
together they are only a breath.
10Do not trust in extortion
or take pride in stolen goods;
though your riches increase,
do not set your heart on them.

11One thing God has spoken,
two things have I heard:
that you, O God, are strong,
12 and that you, O Lord, are loving.
Surely you will reward each person
according to what he has done.

A psalm of David. When he was in the Desert of Judah.

63 O GOD, you are my God,
earnestly I seek you;
my soul thirsts for you,
my body longs for you,
in a dry and weary land
where there is no water.

2I have seen you in the sanctuary
and beheld your power and your glory.
3Because your love is better than life,
my lips will glorify you.
4I will praise you as long as I live,
and in your name I will lift up my hands.
5My soul will be satisfied as with the richest of foods;
with singing lips my mouth will praise you.
6On my bed I remember you;
I think of you through the watches of the night.
7Because you are my help,
I sing in the shadow of your wings.
8My soul clings to you;
your right hand upholds me.

9They who seek my life will be destroyed;
they will go down to the depths of the earth.
10They will be given over to the sword
and become food for jackals.

11But the king will rejoice in God;
all who swear by God's name will praise him,
while the mouths of liars will be silenced.

NIV [e] 7 Or / *God Most High is my salvation and my honor*

# King James

To the chief Musician, A Psalm of David.

**64** HEAR MY voice, O God, in my prayer: preserve my life from fear of the enemy.

2 Hide me from the secret counsel of the wicked; from the insurrection of the workers of iniquity:

3 Who whet their tongue like a sword, *and* bend *their bows to shoot* their arrows, *even* bitter words:

4 That they may shoot in secret at the perfect: suddenly do they shoot at him, and fear not.

5 They encourage themselves *in* an evil matter: they commune of laying snares privily; they say, Who shall see them?

6 They search out iniquities; they accomplish a diligent search: both the inward *thought* of every one *of them,* and the heart, *is* deep.

7 But God shall shoot at them *with* an arrow; suddenly shall they be wounded.

8 So they shall make their own tongue to fall upon themselves: all that see them shall flee away.

9 And all men shall fear, and shall declare the work of God; for they shall wisely consider of his doing.

10 The righteous shall be glad in the LORD, and shall trust in him; and all the upright in heart shall glory.

To the chief Musician, A Psalm *and* Song of David.

**65** PRAISE WAITETH for thee, O God, in Sion: and unto thee shall the vow be performed.

2 O thou that hearest prayer, unto thee shall all flesh come.

3 Iniquities prevail against me: *as for* our transgressions, thou shalt purge them away.

4 Blessed *is the man whom* thou choosest, and causest to approach *unto thee, that* he may dwell in thy courts: we shall be satisfied with the goodness of thy house, *even* of thy holy temple.

5 *By* terrible things in righteousness wilt thou answer us, O God of our salvation; *who art* the confidence of all the ends of the earth, and of them that are afar off *upon* the sea:

6 Which by his strength setteth fast the mountains; *being* girded with power:

7 Which stilleth the noise of the seas, the noise of their waves, and the tumult of the people.

8 They also that dwell in the uttermost parts are afraid at thy tokens: thou makest the outgoings of the morning and evening to rejoice.

9 Thou visitest the earth, and waterest it: thou greatly enrichest it with the river of God, *which* is full of water: thou preparest them corn, when thou hast so provided for it.

10 Thou waterest the ridges thereof abundantly: thou settlest the furrows thereof: thou makest it soft with showers: thou blessest the springing thereof.

# Amplified

To the Chief Musician. A Psalm of David.

**64** HEAR MY voice, O God, in my complaint; guard *and* preserve my life from the terror of the enemy.

2 Hide me from the secret counsel *and* conspiracy of the ungodly, from the scheming of evildoers,

3 Who whet their tongue like a sword, who aim venomous words like arrows,

4 Who shoot from ambush at the blameless; suddenly do they shoot at him, without self-reproach *or* fear.

5 They encourage themselves in an evil purpose; they talk of laying snares secretly; they say, Who will discover *us*?

6 They think out acts of injustice, and say, We have accomplished a well-devised thing; for the inward thought of each one [is unsearchable], and his heart is deep.

7 But God will shoot an unexpected arrow at them, *and* suddenly shall they be wounded.

8 And they will be made to stumble, their own tongue being against them; all who gaze upon them will shake the head *and* flee away.

9 And all men shall (reverently) fear *and* be in awe, and will declare the work of God; for they will wisely consider *and* acknowledge that it is His doing.

10 The [uncompromisingly] righteous shall be glad in the Lord, and shall trust *and* take refuge in Him; and all the upright in heart shall glory *and* offer praise.

To the Chief Musician. A Psalm of David. A Song.

**65** TO YOU belongs silence [the submissive wonder of reverence which bursts forth into praise], *and* praise is due *and* fitting to You, O God, in Zion; and to You shall the vow be performed.

2 O You Who hear prayer, to You shall all flesh come.

3 Iniquities *and* much varied guilt prevail against me; *yet* as for our transgressions, You forgive *and* purge them away [make atonement for them and cover them out of Your sight]!

4 Blessed—happy, fortunate [to be envied]—is the man whom You choose and cause to come near, that he may dwell in Your courts! We shall be satisfied with the goodness of Your house, Your holy temple.

5 By fearful *and* glorious things [that terrify the wicked, but make the godly sing praises] do You answer us in righteousness—rightness and justice—O God of our salvation, You Who are the confidence and hope of all the ends of the earth, and of those far off on the seas;

6 Who by *Your* might have founded the mountains, being girded with power;

7 Who still the roaring of the seas, the roaring of their waves, and the tumult of the peoples;

8 So that those who dwell in earth's farthest parts are afraid at *nature's* signs of Your presence; You make the places where morning and evening have birth to shout for joy.

9 You visit the earth and saturate it with water, You greatly enrich it; the river of God is full of water; You provide them grain when You have so prepared the earth.

10 You water the field's furrows abundantly, You settle the ridges of it, You make the soil soft with showers, blessing the sprouting of its vegetation.

## New American Standard

*Prayer for Deliverance from Secret Enemies.*

For the choir director. A Psalm of David.

64 HEAR MY voice, O God, in my [a]complaint;
Preserve my life from dread of the enemy.
2 Hide me from the secret counsel of evildoers,
From the tumult of those who do iniquity,
3 Who have sharpened their tongue like a sword.
They aimed bitter speech *as* their arrow,
4 To shoot from concealment at the blameless;
Suddenly they shoot at him, and do not fear.
5 They hold fast to themselves an evil purpose;
They talk of laying snares secretly;
They say, "Who can see them?"
6 They [b]devise injustices, *saying*,
"We are ready with a well-conceived plot";
For the inward thought and the heart of a man are [c]deep.
7¶ But God will shoot at them with an arrow;
Suddenly they will be wounded.
8 So they will make him stumble;
Their own tongue is against them;
All who see them will shake the head.
9 Then all men will fear,
And will declare the work of God,
And will consider what He has done.
10 The righteous man will be glad in the LORD, and will take refuge in Him;
And all the upright in heart will glory.

*God's Abundant Favor to Earth and Man.*

For the choir director. A Psalm of David. A Song.

65 THERE WILL be silence before Thee, *and* praise in Zion, O God;
And to Thee the vow will be performed.
2 O Thou who dost hear prayer,
To Thee all men come.
3 Iniquities prevail against me;
As for our transgressions, Thou dost forgive them.
4 How blessed is the one whom Thou dost choose, and bring near *to Thee*,
To dwell in Thy courts.
We will be satisfied with the goodness of Thy house,
Thy holy temple.
5¶ By awesome *deeds* Thou dost answer us in righteousness, O God of our salvation,
Thou who art the trust of all the ends of the earth and of the farthest sea;
6 Who dost establish the mountains by His strength,
Being girded with might;
7 Who dost still the roaring of the seas,
The roaring of their waves,
And the tumult of the peoples.
8 And they who dwell in the ends *of the earth* stand in awe of Thy signs;
Thou dost make the dawn and the sunset shout for joy.
9¶ Thou dost visit the earth, and cause it to overflow;
Thou dost greatly enrich it;
The stream of God is full of water;
Thou dost prepare their grain, for thus Thou dost prepare the earth.
10 Thou dost water its furrows abundantly;
Thou dost settle its ridges;
Thou dost soften it with showers;
Thou dost bless its growth.

NAS [a] Or, *concern* [b] Or, *search out* [c] Or, *unsearchable*

## New International

For the director of music. A psalm of David.

64 HEAR ME, O God, as I voice my complaint;
protect my life from the threat of the enemy.
2Hide me from the conspiracy of the wicked,
from that noisy crowd of evildoers.

3They sharpen their tongues like swords
and aim their words like deadly arrows.
4They shoot from ambush at the innocent man;
they shoot at him suddenly, without fear.

5They encourage each other in evil plans,
they talk about hiding their snares;
they say, "Who will see them[d]?"
6They plot injustice and say,
"We have devised a perfect plan!"
Surely the mind and heart of man are cunning.

7But God will shoot them with arrows;
suddenly they will be struck down.
8He will turn their own tongues against them
and bring them to ruin;
all who see them will shake their heads in scorn.
9All mankind will fear;
they will proclaim the works of God
and ponder what he has done.
10Let the righteous rejoice in the LORD
and take refuge in him;
let all the upright in heart praise him!

For the director of music. A psalm of David. A song.

65 PRAISE AWAITS[e] you, O God, in Zion;
to you our vows will be fulfilled.
2O you who hear prayer,
to you all men will come.
3When we were overwhelmed by sins,
you forgave[f] our transgressions.
4Blessed are those you choose
and bring near to live in your courts!
We are filled with the good things of your house,
of your holy temple.

5You answer us with awesome deeds of righteousness,
O God our Savior,
the hope of all the ends of the earth
and of the farthest seas,
6who formed the mountains by your power,
having armed yourself with strength,
7who stilled the roaring of the seas,
the roaring of their waves,
and the turmoil of the nations.
8Those living far away fear your wonders;
where morning dawns and evening fades
you call forth songs of joy.

9You care for the land and water it;
you enrich it abundantly.
The streams of God are filled with water
to provide the people with grain,
for so you have ordained it.[g]
10You drench its furrows
and level its ridges;
you soften it with showers
and bless its crops.

NIV [d] 5 Or *us* [e] 1 Or *befits;* the meaning of the Hebrew for this word is uncertain. [f] 3 Or *made atonement for* [g] 9 Or *for that is how you prepare the land*

## King James

11Thou crownest the year with thy goodness; and thy paths drop fatness.
12They drop *upon* the pastures of the wilderness: and the little hills rejoice on every side.
13The pastures are clothed with flocks; the valleys also are covered over with corn; they shout for joy, they also sing.

To the chief Musician, A Song *or* Psalm.

**66** MAKE A joyful noise unto God, all ye lands:
2Sing forth the honour of his name: make his praise glorious.
3Say unto God, How terrible *art thou in* thy works! through the greatness of thy power shall thine enemies submit themselves unto thee.
4All the earth shall worship thee, and shall sing unto thee; they shall sing *to* thy name. Selah.
5Come and see the works of God: *he is* terrible *in his* doing toward the children of men.
6He turned the sea into dry *land:* they went through the flood on foot: there did we rejoice in him.
7He ruleth by his power for ever; his eyes behold the nations: let not the rebellious exalt themselves. Selah.
8O bless our God, ye people, and make the voice of his praise to be heard:
9Which holdeth our soul in life, and suffereth not our feet to be moved.
10For thou, O God, hast proved us: thou hast tried us, as silver is tried.
11Thou broughtest us into the net; thou laidst affliction upon our loins.
12Thou hast caused men to ride over our heads; we went through fire and through water: but thou broughtest us out into a wealthy *place.*
13I will go into thy house with burnt offerings: I will pay thee my vows,
14Which my lips have uttered, and my mouth hath spoken, when I was in trouble.
15I will offer unto thee burnt sacrifices of fatlings, with the incense of rams; I will offer bullocks with goats. Selah.
16Come *and* hear, all ye that fear God, and I will declare what he hath done for my soul.
17I cried unto him with my mouth, and he was extolled with my tongue.
18If I regard iniquity in my heart, the Lord will not hear *me:*
19 *But* verily God hath heard *me;* he hath attended to the voice of my prayer.
20Blessed *be* God, which hath not turned away my prayer, nor his mercy from me.

To the chief Musician on Neginoth, A Psalm *or* Song.

**67** GOD BE merciful unto us, and bless us; *and* cause his face to shine upon us; Selah.
2That thy way may be known upon earth, thy saving health among all nations.

## Amplified

11You crown the year with Your bounty *and* goodness, the tracks of Your *chariot wheels* drip with fatness.
12The *luxuriant* pastures in the uncultivated country drip [with moisture], and the hills gird themselves with joy.
13The meadows are clothed with flocks, the valleys also are covered with grain, they shout for joy and sing together.

To the Chief Musician. A song, a Psalm.

**66** MAKE A joyful noise unto God, all the earth;
2Sing forth the honor *and* glory of His name; make His praise glorious!
3Say to God, How awesome *and* fearfully glorious are Your works! Through the greatness of Your power shall Your enemies submit themselves to You—with feigned and reluctant obedience.
4All the earth shall bow down to You and sing *praises* to You; they shall praise Your name in song. Selah [pause, and calmly think of that]!
5Come and see the works of God; see how [to save His people He smites their foes] *He is* terrible in His doing toward the children of men.
6He turned the sea into dry land; they crossed through the river on foot; there did we rejoice in Him.
7He rules by His might for ever, His eyes observe *and* keep watch *over* the nations; let not the rebellious exalt themselves. Selah [pause, and calmly think of that]!
8Bless our God, O peoples, give Him grateful thanks *and* make the voice of His praise to be heard,
9Who put *and* kept us among the living, and has not allowed our feet to slip.
10For You, O God, have proved us; You have tried us as silver is tried, refined *and* purified.
11You brought us into the net [the prison fortress, the dungeon]; You laid a heavy burden upon our loins.
12You caused men to ride over our heads [when we were prostrate]; we went through fire and through water; but You brought us out into a broad, moist place—to abundance and refreshment and the open air.
13I will come into Your house with burnt offerings [of entire consecration]; I will pay You my vows,
14Which my lips uttered, and my mouth promised, when I was in distress.
15I will offer to You burnt offerings of fat lambs, with rams consumed in sweet-smelling smoke; I will offer bullocks and he-goats. Selah [pause, and calmly think of that]!
16Come and hear, all you who reverently *and* worshipfully fear God, and I will declare what He has done for me!
17I cried aloud to Him; He was extolled *and* high praise was under my tongue.
18If I regard iniquity in my heart, the Lord will not hear me; [Prov. 15:29; 28:9; Isa. 1:15; John 9:31; James 4:3.]
19But certainly God has heard me; He has given heed to the voice of my prayer.
20Blessed be God, Who has not rejected my prayer, nor removed His mercy *and* loving-kindness from being [as it always is] with me.

To the Chief Musician;
on stringed instruments. A Psalm, a song.

**67** GOD BE merciful *and* gracious to us and bless us, and cause His face to shine upon us *and* among us, Selah [pause, and calmly think of that]!
2That Your way may be known upon earth, Your saving power [Your deliverances and Your salvation], among all nations.

## New American Standard

11 Thou hast crowned the year with Thy bounty,
And Thy paths drip *with* fatness.
12 The pastures of the wilderness drip,
And the hills gird themselves with rejoicing.
13 The meadows are clothed with flocks,
And the valleys are covered with grain;
They shout for joy, yes, they sing.

*Praise for God's Mighty Deeds and for His Answer to Prayer.*

For the choir director. A Song. A Psalm.

**66** SHOUT JOYFULLY to God, all the earth;
2 Sing the glory of His name;
Make His praise glorious.
3 Say to God, "How awesome are Thy works!
Because of the greatness of Thy power Thine enemies will give feigned obedience to Thee.
4 "All the earth will worship Thee,
And will sing praises to Thee;
They will sing praises to Thy name." Selah.

5¶ Come and see the works of God,
*Who is* awesome in *His* deeds toward the sons of men.
6 He turned the sea into dry land;
They passed through the river on foot;
There let us rejoice in Him!
7 He rules by His might forever;
His eyes keep watch on the nations;
Let not the rebellious exalt themselves. Selah.

8¶ Bless our God, O peoples,
And sound His praise abroad,
9 Who keeps us in life,
And does not allow our feet to slip.
10 For Thou hast tried us, O God;
Thou hast refined us as silver is refined.
11 Thou didst bring us into the net;
Thou didst lay an oppressive burden upon our loins.
12 Thou didst make men ride over our heads;
We went through fire and through water;
Yet Thou didst bring us out into *a place of* abundance.
13 I shall come into Thy house with burnt offerings;
I shall pay Thee my vows,
14 Which my lips uttered
And my mouth spoke when I was in distress.
15 I shall offer to Thee burnt offerings of fat beasts,
With the smoke of rams;
I shall make *an offering of* bulls with male goats. Selah.

16¶ Come *and* hear, all who [a]fear God,
And I will tell of what He has done for my soul.
17 I cried to Him with my mouth,
And He was extolled with my tongue.
18 If I [b]regard wickedness in my heart,
The Lord will not hear;
19 But certainly God has heard;
He has given heed to the voice of my prayer.
20 Blessed be God,
Who has not turned away my prayer,
Nor His lovingkindness from me.

*The Nations Exhorted to Praise God.*

For the choir director; with stringed instruments. A Psalm. A Song.

**67** GOD BE gracious to us and bless us,
*And* cause His face to shine upon us— Selah.
2 That Thy way may be known on the earth,
Thy salvation among all nations.

NAS [a] Or, *revere* [b] Or, *had regarded . . . would not have heard*

## New International

11You crown the year with your bounty,
and your carts overflow with abundance.
12The grasslands of the desert overflow;
the hills are clothed with gladness.
13The meadows are covered with flocks
and the valleys are mantled with grain;
they shout for joy and sing.

For the director of music. A song. A psalm.

**66** SHOUT WITH joy to God, all the earth!
2 Sing the glory of his name;
make his praise glorious!
3Say to God, "How awesome are your deeds!
So great is your power
that your enemies cringe before you.
4All the earth bows down to you;
they sing praise to you,
they sing praise to your name." *Selah*

5Come and see what God has done,
how awesome his works in man's behalf!
6He turned the sea into dry land,
they passed through the waters on foot—
come, let us rejoice in him.
7He rules forever by his power,
his eyes watch the nations—
let not the rebellious rise up against him. *Selah*

8Praise our God, O peoples,
let the sound of his praise be heard;
9he has preserved our lives
and kept our feet from slipping.
10For you, O God, tested us;
you refined us like silver.
11You brought us into prison
and laid burdens on our backs.
12You let men ride over our heads;
we went through fire and water,
but you brought us to a place of abundance.

13I will come to your temple with burnt offerings
and fulfill my vows to you—
14vows my lips promised and my mouth spoke
when I was in trouble.
15I will sacrifice fat animals to you
and an offering of rams;
I will offer bulls and goats. *Selah*

16Come and listen, all you who fear God;
let me tell you what he has done for me.
17I cried out to him with my mouth;
his praise was on my tongue.
18If I had cherished sin in my heart,
the Lord would not have listened;
19but God has surely listened
and heard my voice in prayer.
20Praise be to God,
who has not rejected my prayer
or withheld his love from me!

For the director of music. With stringed instruments. A psalm. A song.

**67** MAY GOD be gracious to us and bless us
and make his face shine upon us, *Selah*
2that your ways may be known on earth,
your salvation among all nations.

## King James

3 Let the people praise thee, O God; let all the people praise
thee.
4 O let the nations be glad and sing for joy: for thou shalt judge
the people righteously, and govern the nations upon earth. Selah.
5 Let the people praise thee, O God; let all the people praise
thee.
6 *Then* shall the earth yield her increase; *and* God, *even* our own
God, shall bless us.
7 God shall bless us; and all the ends of the earth shall fear him.

To the chief Musician, A Psalm *or* Song of David.

68 LET GOD arise, let his enemies be scattered: let them also
that hate him flee before him.
2 As smoke is driven away, *so* drive *them* away: as wax melteth
before the fire, *so* let the wicked perish at the presence of God.
3 But let the righteous be glad; let them rejoice before God: yea,
let them exceedingly rejoice.
4 Sing unto God, sing praises to his name: extol him that rideth
upon the heavens by his name JAH, and rejoice before him.
5 A father of the fatherless, and a judge of the widows, *is* God
in his holy habitation.
6 God setteth the solitary in families: he bringeth out those
which are bound with chains: but the rebellious dwell in a dry *land*.
7 O God, when thou wentest forth before thy people, when thou
didst march through the wilderness; Selah:
8 The earth shook, the heavens also dropped at the presence of
God: *even* Sinai itself *was moved* at the presence of God, the God
of Israel.
9 Thou, O God, didst send a plentiful rain, whereby thou didst
confirm thine inheritance, when it was weary.
10 Thy congregation hath dwelt therein: thou, O God, hast prepared of thy goodness for the poor.
11 The Lord gave the word: great *was* the company of those that
published *it*.
12 Kings of armies did flee apace: and she that tarried at home
divided the spoil.
13 Though ye have lain among the pots, *yet shall ye be as* the
wings of a dove covered with silver, and her feathers with yellow
gold.
14 When the Almighty scattered kings in it, it was *white* as snow
in Salmon.
15 The hill of God *is as* the hill of Bashan; an high hill *as* the hill
of Bashan.
16 Why leap ye, ye high hills? *this is* the hill *which* God desireth
to dwell in; yea, the LORD will dwell *in it* for ever.
17 The chariots of God *are* twenty thousand, *even* thousands of
angels: the Lord *is* among them, *as in* Sinai, in the holy *place*.

## Amplified

3 Let the peoples praise You, [turn away from their idols] *and*
give thanks to You, O God; let all the peoples praise *and* give
thanks to You.
4 O let the nations be glad and sing for joy; for You will judge
the peoples fairly, and guide, lead *or* drive the nations upon earth.
Selah [pause, and calmly think of that]!
5 Let the peoples praise You, [turn away from their idols] *and*
give thanks to You, O God; let all the peoples praise *and* give
thanks to You!
6 The earth has yielded its harvest [in evidence of God's approv-
al]; God, even our own God will bless us.
7 God will bless us, and all the ends of the earth shall reverently
fear Him.

To the Chief Musician. A Psalm of David, a song.

68 GOD IS [already] beginning to arise, and His enemies to
scatter; let them also who hate Him flee before Him!
2 As smoke is driven away, *so* drive them away; as wax melts
before the fire, *so* let the wicked perish before the presence of God.
3 But let the [uncompromisingly] righteous be glad; let them be
in high spirits *and* glory before God, yes, let them [jubilantly]
rejoice!
4 Sing to God, sing praises to His name; cast up a highway for
Him who rides through the deserts; His name is the Lord, be in
high spirits *and* glory before Him!
5 A father of the fatherless, and a judge *and* protector of the
widows, *is* God in His holy habitation.
6 God places the solitary in families *and* gives the desolate a
home in which to dwell; He leads the prisoners out to prosperity;
but the rebellious dwell in a parched land.
7 O God, when You went forth before Your people, when You
marched through the wilderness, Selah [pause, and calmly think
of that]!
8 The earth trembled, the heavens also poured down [rain] at the
presence of God; yonder Sinai quaked at the presence of God, the
God of Israel.
9 You, O God, did send a plentiful rain, You did restore *and*
confirm Your heritage when it languished *and* was weary.
10 Your flock found a dwelling place in it; You, O God, in Your
goodness did provide for the poor *and* needy.
11 The Lord gives the word [of power]; the women who bear *and*
publish (the news) are a great host.
12 The kings of the enemies' armies, they flee, they flee! She who
tarries at home divides the spoil [left behind],
13 Though you [the slackers] may lie among the sheepfolds [in
slothful ease], *yet for Israel* the wings of a dove covered with silver,
its pinions excessively green with gold [are trophies taken from the
enemy].
14 When the Almighty scattered kings in [the land], it was as
when it snows on Zalmon [a wooded hill near Shechem].
15 Is Mount Bashan, the high mountain of summits, Mount
Bashan [east of the Jordan], the mount of God?
16 Why look you with grudging *and* envy, you many-peaked
mountains, at the mountain [of the city called Zion] which God has
desired for His dwelling place? Yes, the Lord will dwell in it for
ever.
17 The chariots of God are twenty thousand, even thousands
upon thousands. The Lord is among them, as He was in Sinai, [so
also] in the holy place—the sanctuary [in Jerusalem].

## New American Standard

3 Let the peoples praise Thee, O God;
Let all the peoples praise Thee.
4 Let the nations be glad and sing for joy;
For Thou wilt judge the peoples with uprightness,
And guide the nations on the earth. Selah.
5 Let the peoples praise Thee, O God;
Let all the peoples praise Thee.
6 The earth has yielded its produce;
God, our God, blesses us.
7 God blesses us,
[a]That all the ends of the earth may fear Him.

*The God of Sinai and of the Sanctuary.*

For the choir director. A Psalm of David. A Song.

68 LET GOD arise, let His enemies be scattered;
And let those who hate Him flee before Him.
2 As smoke is driven away, *so* drive *them* away;
As wax melts before the fire,
*So* let the wicked perish before God.
3 But let the righteous be glad; let them exult before God;
Yes, let them rejoice with gladness.
4 Sing to God, sing praises to His name;
Lift up *a song* for Him who rides through the deserts,
Whose name is the LORD, and exult before Him.
5¶ A father of the fatherless and a judge [b]for the widows,
Is God in His holy habitation.
6 God makes a home for the lonely;
He leads out the prisoners into prosperity,
Only the rebellious dwell in a parched land.
7¶ O God, when Thou didst go forth before Thy people,
When Thou didst march through the wilderness, Selah.
8 The earth quaked;
The heavens also dropped *rain* at the presence of God;
Sinai itself *quaked* at the presence of God, the God of Israel.
9 Thou didst shed abroad a plentiful rain, O God;
Thou didst confirm Thine inheritance, when it was parched.
10 Thy creatures settled in it;
Thou didst provide in Thy goodness for the poor, O God.
11¶ The Lord gives the command;
The women who proclaim the *good* tidings are a great host:
12 "Kings of armies flee, they flee,
And she who remains at home will divide the spoil!"
13 [c]When you lie down among the [d]sheepfolds,
*You are like* the wings of a dove covered with silver,
And its pinions with glistening gold.
14 When the Almighty scattered the kings there,
It was snowing in Zalmon.
15¶ A mountain of God is the mountain of Bashan;
A mountain *of many* peaks is the mountain of Bashan.
16 Why do you look with envy, O mountains with *many* peaks,
At the mountain which God has desired for His abode?
Surely, the LORD will dwell *there* forever.
17 The chariots of God are [e]myriads, thousands upon thousands;
The Lord is among them *as at* Sinai, in holiness.

NAS [a] Or, *And let all . . . earth fear Him* [b] Lit., *of* [c] Lit., *If* [d] Or, *cooking stones*, or, *saddle bags* [e] Lit., *twice ten thousand*

## New International

3May the peoples praise you, O God;
may all the peoples praise you.
4May the nations be glad and sing for joy,
for you rule the peoples justly
and guide the nations of the earth. *Selah*
5May the peoples praise you, O God;
may all the peoples praise you.

6Then the land will yield its harvest,
and God, our God, will bless us.
7God will bless us,
and all the ends of the earth will fear him.

For the director of music. Of David. A psalm. A song.

68 MAY GOD arise, may his enemies be scattered;
may his foes flee before him.
2As smoke is blown away by the wind,
may you blow them away;
as wax melts before the fire,
may the wicked perish before God.
3But may the righteous be glad
and rejoice before God;
may they be happy and joyful.

4Sing to God, sing praise to his name,
extol him who rides on the clouds[f] —
his name is the LORD—
and rejoice before him.
5A father to the fatherless, a defender of widows,
is God in his holy dwelling.
6God sets the lonely in families,[g]
he leads forth the prisoners with singing;
but the rebellious live in a sun-scorched land.

7When you went out before your people, O God,
when you marched through the wasteland, *Selah*
8the earth shook,
the heavens poured down rain,
before God, the One of Sinai,
before God, the God of Israel.
9You gave abundant showers, O God;
you refreshed your weary inheritance.
10Your people settled in it,
and from your bounty, O God, you provided for the poor.

11The Lord announced the word,
and great was the company of those who proclaimed it:
12"Kings and armies flee in haste;
in the camps men divide the plunder.
13Even while you sleep among the campfires,[h]
the wings of ⌊my⌋ dove are sheathed with silver,
its feathers with shining gold."
14When the Almighty[i] scattered the kings in the land,
it was like snow fallen on Zalmon.

15The mountains of Bashan are majestic mountains;
rugged are the mountains of Bashan.
16Why gaze in envy, O rugged mountains,
at the mountain where God chooses to reign,
where the LORD himself will dwell forever?
17The chariots of God are tens of thousands
and thousands of thousands;
the Lord ⌊has come⌋ from Sinai into his sanctuary.

NIV [f] 4 Or / *prepare the way for him who rides through the deserts* [g] 6 Or *the desolate in a homeland* [h] 13 Or *saddlebags* [i] 14 Hebrew *Shaddai*

## King James

18Thou hast ascended on high, thou hast led captivity captive: thou hast received gifts for men; yea, *for* the rebellious also, that the LORD God might dwell *among them.*
19Blessed *be* the Lord, *who* daily loadeth us *with benefits, even* the God of our salvation. Selah.
20 *He that is* our God *is* the God of salvation; and unto GOD the Lord *belong* the issues from death.
21But God shall wound the head of his enemies, *and* the hairy scalp of such an one as goeth on still in his trespasses.
22The Lord said, I will bring again from Bashan, I will bring *my people* again from the depths of the sea:
23That thy foot may be dipped in the blood of *thine* enemies, *and* the tongue of thy dogs in the same.
24They have seen thy goings, O God; *even* the goings of my God, my King, in the sanctuary.
25The singers went before, the players on instruments *followed* after; among *them were* the damsels playing with timbrels.
26Bless ye God in the congregations, *even* the Lord, from the fountain of Israel.
27There *is* little Benjamin *with* their ruler, the princes of Judah *and* their council, the princes of Zebulun, *and* the princes of Naphtali.
28Thy God hath commanded thy strength: strengthen, O God, that which thou hast wrought for us.
29Because of thy temple at Jerusalem shall kings bring presents unto thee.
30Rebuke the company of spearmen, the multitude of the bulls, with the calves of the people, *till every one* submit himself with pieces of silver: scatter thou the people *that* delight in war.
31Princes shall come out of Egypt; Ethiopia shall soon stretch out her hands unto God.
32Sing unto God, ye kingdoms of the earth; O sing praises unto the Lord; Selah:
33To him that rideth upon the heavens of heavens, *which were* of old; lo, he doth send out his voice, *and that* a mighty voice.
34Ascribe ye strength unto God: his excellency *is* over Israel, and his strength *is* in the clouds.
35O God, *thou art* terrible out of thy holy places: the God of Israel *is* he that giveth strength and power unto *his* people. Blessed *be* God.

To the chief Musician upon Shoshannim, *A Psalm* of David.

**69** SAVE ME, O God; for the waters are come in unto *my* soul.
2I sink in deep mire, where *there is* no standing: I am come into deep waters, where the floods overflow me.

## Amplified

18 [a]You have ascended on high. You have led away captive a train of vanquished foes; You have received gifts of men, yes, of the rebellious also, that the Lord God might dwell there with them. [Eph. 4:8.]
19Blessed be the Lord, Who bears our burdens *and* carries us day by day, even the God Who is our salvation! Selah [pause, and calmly think of that]!
20God is to us a God of deliverances *and* salvation, and to God, the Lord, belongs escape from death [setting us free].
21But God will shatter the head of His enemies, the hairy scalp of such a one as goes on still in his trespasses *and* guilty ways.
22The Lord said, I will bring back [your enemies] from Bashan, I will bring them back from the depths of the [Red] Sea,
23That you may crush them, dipping your foot in blood, that the tongue of your dogs may have its share from the foe.
24They see Your goings, O God, even the [solemn processions] of my God, my King, into the sanctuary—in holiness.
25The singers go in front, the players on instruments last; between them the maidens playing on tambourines.
26Bless, give thanks *and* gratefully praise God in full congregations, even the Lord, O you who are from [Jacob] the fountain of Israel.
27There is little Benjamin in the lead [in the procession], the princes of Judah and their company, the princes of Zebulun, and the princes of Naphtali.
28Your God has commanded your strength [your might in His service and impenetrable hardness to temptation]. O God, display Your might *and strengthen what* You have wrought for us!
29[Out of respect] for Your temple at Jerusalem kings shall bring gifts to You.
30Rebuke the wild beasts dwelling among the reeds [in Egypt], the herd of bulls [the leaders], with the calves of the peoples; trample under foot those who lust for tribute money; scatter the peoples who delight in war.
31Princes shall come out of Egypt; Ethiopia shall hasten to stretch out her hands [with the offerings of submission] to God.
32Sing to God, O kingdoms of the earth; sing praises to the Lord! Selah [pause, and calmly think of that]!
33 *Sing praises* to Him Who rides upon the heavens, the ancient heavens; lo, He sends forth His voice, His mighty voice.
34Ascribe power *and* strength to God; His majesty is over Israel, and His strength *and* might are in the skies.
35O God, awe inspiring, profoundly impressive *and* terrible are You out of Your holy places; the God of Israel, He gives strength and fullness of might to His people. Blessed be God!

To the Chief Musician, *set to the tune of* Lilies. [ *A Psalm*] of David.

**69** SAVE ME, O God; for the waters are come up to my neck—they threaten my life.
2I sink in deep mire, where there is no foothold; I have come into deep waters, where the floods overwhelm me.

**AMP** [a] David sang of the ark of the covenant, which after a great victory was transferred or brought back to Zion. In this fact he sees the principle of the history of the kingdom of God, appearing in ever widening circles and nobler manner. The fact is to him a type of the method and course of the Messiah's kingdom. So the Apostle Paul (in Eph. 4:8) is perfectly justified in finding the psalmist's eye directed toward Christ, and so interpreting it. The "on high" in the Psalm is first of all Mount Zion, but this is a type of Heaven, as Paul makes clear. *(Lange's Commentary.)*

## New American Standard

18 Thou hast ascended on high, Thou hast led captive *Thy* captives;
Thou hast received gifts among men,
Even *among* the rebellious also, that the LORD God may dwell *there.*

19¶ Blessed be the Lord, who daily bears our burden,
The God *who* is our salvation. Selah.
20 God is to us a God of deliverances;
And to GOD the Lord belong escapes from death.
21 Surely God will shatter the head of His enemies,
The hairy crown of him who goes on in his guilty deeds.
22 The Lord said, "I will bring *them* back from Bashan.
I will bring *them* back from the depths of the sea;
23 That your foot may shatter *them* in blood,
The tongue of your dogs *may have* its portion from *your* enemies."

24¶ They have seen Thy procession, O God,
The procession of my God, my King, into the sanctuary.
25 The singers went on, the musicians after *them,*
In the midst of the maidens beating tambourines.
26 Bless God in the congregations,
*Even* the LORD, *you who are* of the fountain of Israel.
27 There is Benjamin, the youngest, ruling them,
The princes of Judah *in* their throng,
The princes of Zebulun, the princes of Naphtali.

28¶ Your God has commanded your strength;
Show Thyself strong, O God, who hast acted on our behalf.
29 Because of Thy temple at Jerusalem
Kings will bring gifts to Thee.
30 Rebuke the beasts in the reeds,
The herd of bulls with the calves of the peoples,
Trampling under foot the pieces of silver;
He has scattered the peoples who delight in war.
31 Envoys will come out of Egypt;
Ethiopia will quickly stretch out her hands to God.

32¶ Sing to God, O kingdoms of the earth;
Sing praises to the Lord, Selah.
33 To Him who rides upon the highest heavens, which are from ancient times;
Behold, He speaks forth with His voice, a mighty voice.
34 Ascribe strength to God;
His majesty is over Israel,
And His strength is in the skies.
35 O God, *Thou art* awesome from Thy sanctuary.
The God of Israel Himself gives strength and power to the people.
Blessed be God!

*A Cry of Distress and Imprecation on Adversaries.*

For the choir director; according to [b]Shoshannim. *A Psalm* of David.

69 SAVE ME, O God,
For the waters have threatened my life.
2 I have sunk in deep mire, and there is no foothold;
I have come into deep waters, and a flood overflows me.

NAS [b] Or possibly, *Lilies*

## New International

18 When you ascended on high,
you led captives in your train;
you received gifts from men,
even from[c] the rebellious—
that you,[d] O LORD God, might dwell there.

19 Praise be to the Lord, to God our Savior,
who daily bears our burdens. *Selah*
20 Our God is a God who saves;
from the Sovereign LORD comes escape from death.

21 Surely God will crush the heads of his enemies,
the hairy crowns of those who go on in their sins.
22 The Lord says, "I will bring them from Bashan;
I will bring them from the depths of the sea,
23 that you may plunge your feet in the blood of your foes,
while the tongues of your dogs have their share."

24 Your procession has come into view, O God,
the procession of my God and King into the sanctuary.
25 In front are the singers, after them the musicians;
with them are the maidens playing tambourines.
26 Praise God in the great congregation;
praise the LORD in the assembly of Israel.
27 There is the little tribe of Benjamin, leading them,
there the great throng of Judah's princes,
and there the princes of Zebulun and of Naphtali.

28 Summon your power, O God[e];
show us your strength, O God, as you have done before.
29 Because of your temple at Jerusalem
kings will bring you gifts.
30 Rebuke the beast among the reeds,
the herd of bulls among the calves of the nations.
Humbled, may it bring bars of silver.
Scatter the nations who delight in war.
31 Envoys will come from Egypt;
Cush[f] will submit herself to God.

32 Sing to God, O kingdoms of the earth,
sing praise to the Lord, *Selah*
33 to him who rides the ancient skies above,
who thunders with mighty voice.
34 Proclaim the power of God,
whose majesty is over Israel,
whose power is in the skies.
35 You are awesome, O God, in your sanctuary;
the God of Israel gives power and strength to his people.

Praise be to God!

For the director of music. To ⌊the tune of⌋ "Lilies." Of David.

69 SAVE ME, O God,
for the waters have come up to my neck.
2 I sink in the miry depths,
where there is no foothold.
I have come into the deep waters;
the floods engulf me.

NIV [c] *18* Or *gifts for men, / even* [d] *18* Or *they* [e] *28* Many Hebrew manuscripts, Septuagint and Syriac; most Hebrew manuscripts *Your God has summoned power for you* [f] *31* That is, the upper Nile region

## King James

3I am weary of my crying: my throat is dried: mine eyes fail while I wait for my God.

4They that hate me without a cause are more than the hairs of mine head: they that would destroy me, *being* mine enemies wrongfully, are mighty: then I restored *that* which I took not away.

5O God, thou knowest my foolishness; and my sins are not hid from thee.

6Let not them that wait on thee, O Lord GOD of hosts, be ashamed for my sake: let not those that seek thee be confounded for my sake, O God of Israel.

7Because for thy sake I have borne reproach; shame hath covered my face.

8I am become a stranger unto my brethren, and an alien unto my mother's children.

9For the zeal of thine house hath eaten me up; and the reproaches of them that reproached thee are fallen upon me.

10When I wept, *and chastened* my soul with fasting, that was to my reproach.

11I made sackcloth also my garment; and I became a proverb to them.

12They that sit in the gate speak against me; and I *was* the song of the drunkards.

13But as for me, my prayer *is* unto thee, O LORD, *in* an acceptable time: O God, in the multitude of thy mercy hear me, in the truth of thy salvation.

14Deliver me out of the mire, and let me not sink: let me be delivered from them that hate me, and out of the deep waters.

15Let not the waterflood overflow me, neither let the deep swallow me up, and let not the pit shut her mouth upon me.

16Hear me, O LORD; for thy lovingkindness *is* good: turn unto me according to the multitude of thy tender mercies.

17And hide not thy face from thy servant; for I am in trouble: hear me speedily.

18Draw nigh unto my soul, *and* redeem it: deliver me because of mine enemies.

19Thou hast known my reproach, and my shame, and my dishonour: mine adversaries *are* all before thee.

20Reproach hath broken my heart; and I am full of heaviness: and I looked *for some* to take pity, but *there was* none; and for comforters, but I found none.

21They gave me also gall for my meat; and in my thirst they gave me vinegar to drink.

22Let their table become a snare before them: and *that which should have been* for *their* welfare, *let it become* a trap.

23Let their eyes be darkened, that they see not; and make their loins continually to shake.

24Pour out thine indignation upon them, and let thy wrathful anger take hold of them.

25Let their habitation be desolate; *and* let none dwell in their tents.

26For they persecute *him* whom thou hast smitten; and they talk to the grief of those whom thou hast wounded.

## Amplified

3I am weary with my crying; my throat is parched; my eyes fail with (hopefully) waiting for my God.

4Those who hate me without cause are more than the hairs of my head; those who would cut me off *and* destroy me, being my enemies wrongfully, are many *and* mighty; I am [forced] to restore what I did not steal. [John 15:25.]

5O God, You know my folly *and* blundering; my sins *and* my guilt are not hid from You.

6Let not those who wait *and* hope *and* look for You, O Lord of hosts, be put to shame through me; let not those who seek *and* inquire for *and* require You [as their vital necessity] be brought to confusion *and* dishonor through me, O God of Israel.

7Because for Your sake I have borne taunt *and* reproach; confusion *and* shame have covered my face.

8I have become a stranger to my brethren, and an alien to my mother's children. [John 7:3-5.]

9For the zeal for Your house has eaten me up; and the reproaches *and* insults of those who reproach *and* insult You are fallen upon me. [John 2:17; Rom. 15:3.]

10When I wept *and* humbled myself with fasting, I was jeered at *and* humiliated.

11When I made sackcloth my clothing, I became a byword—an object of scorn—to them.

12They who sit in *the city's* gate talk about me, and I am the singsong of the drunkards.

13But as for me, my prayer is to You, O Lord. At an acceptable *and* opportune time, O God, in the multitude of Your mercy *and* the abundance of Your loving-kindness hear me; *and* in the truth *and* faithfulness of Your salvation answer me.

14Rescue me out of the mire, and let me not sink; let me be delivered from those who hate me and from out of the deep waters.

15Let not the flood waters overflow *and* overwhelm me, neither let the deep swallow me up, and let not the (dug) pit [with water perhaps in the bottom] close its mouth over me.

16Hear *and* answer me, O Lord; for Your loving-kindness is sweet *and* comforting; according to Your plenteous tender mercies *and* steadfast love, turn to me.

17Hide not Your face from Your servant, for I am in distress. O answer me speedily!

18Draw close to me and redeem me, ransom *and* set me free because of my enemies [lest they glory in my prolonged distress]!

19You know my reproach and my shame and my dishonor; my adversaries are all before You—fully known to You.

20Insults *and* reproach have broken my heart; I am full of heaviness *and* distressingly sick. I looked for pity, but there was none; and for comforters, but I found none.

21They gave me also gall (poisonous and bitter) for my food, and in my thirst they gave me vinegar [a soured wine] to drink. [Matt. 27:34, 48.]

22Let their own table [with all its abundance and luxury] become a snare to them; and when they are secure in peace [or at their sacrifical feasts,] *let it become* a trap to them.

23Let their eyes be darkened, so that they cannot see; and make their loins tremble continually [from terror, dismay, and feebleness].

24Pour out Your indignation upon them, and let the fierceness of Your burning anger catch up with them.

25Let their habitation *and* their encampment be a desolation, let no one dwell in their tents. [Matt. 23:38; Acts 1:20.]

26For they pursue *and* persecute him whom You have smitten, and they gossip about those whom You have wounded, [adding] to their grief *and* pain.

## New American Standard

3 I am weary with my crying; my throat is parched;
My eyes fail while I wait for my God.
4 Those who hate me without a cause are more than the hairs of my head;
Those who would destroy me are powerful, being wrongfully my enemies,
What I did not steal, I then have to restore.

5¶ O God, it is Thou who dost know my folly,
And my wrongs are not hidden from Thee.
6 May those who wait for Thee not be ashamed through me, O Lord GOD of hosts;
May those who seek Thee not be dishonored through me, O God of Israel,
7 Because for Thy sake I have borne reproach;
Dishonor has covered my face.
8 I have become estranged from my brothers,
And an alien to my mother's sons.
9 For zeal for Thy house has consumed me,
And the reproaches of those who reproach Thee have fallen on me.
10 When I wept in my soul with fasting,
It became my reproach.
11 When I made sackcloth my clothing,
I became a byword to them.
12 Those who sit in the gate talk about me,
And I *am* the song of the drunkards.

13¶ But as for me, my prayer is to Thee, O LORD, at an acceptable time;
O God, in the greatness of Thy lovingkindness,
Answer me with Thy saving truth.
14 Deliver me from the mire, and do not let me sink;
May I be delivered from my foes, and from the deep waters.
15 May the flood of water not overflow me,
And may the deep not swallow me up,
And may the pit not shut its mouth on me.

16¶ Answer me, O LORD, for Thy lovingkindness is good;
According to the greatness of Thy compassion, turn to me,
17 And do not hide Thy face from Thy servant,
For I am in distress; answer me quickly.
18 Oh draw near to my soul *and* redeem it;
Ransom me because of my enemies!
19 Thou dost know my reproach and my shame and my dishonor;
All my adversaries are [a]before Thee.

20¶ Reproach has broken my heart, and I am so sick.
And I looked for sympathy, but there was none,
And for comforters, but I found none.
21 They also gave me [b]gall for my food,
And for my thirst they gave me vinegar to drink.

22¶ May their table before them become a snare;
And when they are in peace, *may it become* a trap.
23 May their eyes grow dim so that they cannot see,
And make their loins shake continually.
24 Pour out Thine indignation on them,
And may Thy burning anger overtake them.
25 May their camp be desolate;
May none dwell in their tents.
26 For they have persecuted him whom Thou Thyself hast smitten,
And they tell of the pain of those whom Thou hast wounded.

NAS [a] Or, known *to Thee* [b] Or, *poison*

## New International

3 I am worn out calling for help;
my throat is parched.
My eyes fail,
looking for my God.
4 Those who hate me without reason
outnumber the hairs of my head;
many are my enemies without cause,
those who seek to destroy me.
I am forced to restore
what I did not steal.

5 You know my folly, O God;
my guilt is not hidden from you.

6 May those who hope in you
not be disgraced because of me,
O Lord, the LORD Almighty;
may those who seek you
not be put to shame because of me,
O God of Israel.
7 For I endure scorn for your sake,
and shame covers my face.
8 I am a stranger to my brothers,
an alien to my own mother's sons;
9 for zeal for your house consumes me,
and the insults of those who insult you fall on me.
10 When I weep and fast,
I must endure scorn;
11 when I put on sackcloth,
people make sport of me.
12 Those who sit at the gate mock me,
and I am the song of the drunkards.

13 But I pray to you, O LORD,
in the time of your favor;
in your great love, O God,
answer me with your sure salvation.
14 Rescue me from the mire,
do not let me sink;
deliver me from those who hate me,
from the deep waters.
15 Do not let the floodwaters engulf me
or the depths swallow me up
or the pit close its mouth over me.
16 Answer me, O LORD, out of the goodness of your love;
in your great mercy turn to me.
17 Do not hide your face from your servant;
answer me quickly, for I am in trouble.
18 Come near and rescue me;
redeem me because of my foes.

19 You know how I am scorned, disgraced and shamed;
all my enemies are before you.
20 Scorn has broken my heart
and has left me helpless;
I looked for sympathy, but there was none,
for comforters, but I found none.
21 They put gall in my food
and gave me vinegar for my thirst.

22 May the table set before them become a snare;
may it become retribution and[c] a trap.
23 May their eyes be darkened so they cannot see,
and their backs be bent forever.
24 Pour out your wrath on them;
let your fierce anger overtake them.
25 May their place be deserted;
let there be no one to dwell in their tents.
26 For they persecute those you wound
and talk about the pain of those you hurt.

NIV [c] 22 Or *snare / and their fellowship become*

## King James

27 Add iniquity unto their iniquity: and let them not come into thy righteousness.

28 Let them be blotted out of the book of the living, and not be written with the righteous.

29 But I *am* poor and sorrowful: let thy salvation, O God, set me up on high.

30 I will praise the name of God with a song, and will magnify him with thanksgiving.

31 *This* also shall please the LORD better than an ox *or* bullock that hath horns and hoofs.

32 The humble shall see *this, and* be glad: and your heart shall live that seek God.

33 For the LORD heareth the poor, and despiseth not his prisoners.

34 Let the heaven and earth praise him, the seas, and every thing that moveth therein.

35 For God will save Zion, and will build the cities of Judah: that they may dwell there, and have it in possession.

36 The seed also of his servants shall inherit it: and they that love his name shall dwell therein.

To the chief Musician, *A Psalm* of David, to bring to remembrance.

**70** *MAKE HASTE,* O God, to deliver me; make haste to help me, O LORD.

2 Let them be ashamed and confounded that seek after my soul: let them be turned backward, and put to confusion, that desire my hurt.

3 Let them be turned back for a reward of their shame that say, Aha, aha.

4 Let all those that seek thee rejoice and be glad in thee: and let such as love thy salvation say continually, Let God be magnified.

5 But I *am* poor and needy: make haste unto me, O God: thou *art* my help and my deliverer; O LORD, make no tarrying.

**71** IN THEE, O LORD, do I put my trust: let me never be put to confusion.

2 Deliver me in thy righteousness, and cause me to escape: incline thine ear unto me, and save me.

3 Be thou my strong habitation, whereunto I may continually resort: thou hast given commandment to save me; for thou *art* my rock and my fortress.

4 Deliver me, O my God, out of the hand of the wicked, out of the hand of the unrighteous and cruel man.

5 For thou *art* my hope, O Lord GOD: *thou art* my trust from my youth.

6 By thee have I been holden up from the womb: thou art he that took me out of my mother's bowels: my praise *shall be* continually of thee.

7 I am as a wonder unto many; but thou *art* my strong refuge.

8 Let my mouth be filled *with* thy praise *and with* thy honour all the day.

## Amplified

27 Let one [unforgiven] perverseness *and* iniquity accumulate upon another for them [in Your book], and let them not come into Your righteousness *or* be justified *and* acquitted by You.

28 Let them be blotted out of the book of the living *and* the book of life, and not be enrolled among the uncompromisingly righteous—those upright and in right standing with God. [Rev. 3:4, 5; 20:12, 15; 21:27.]

29 But I am poor, sorrowful, and in pain. Let Your salvation, O God, set me up on high.

30 I will praise the name of God with a song, and will magnify Him with thanksgiving,

31 And it will please the Lord better than an ox or a bullock that has horns and hoofs.

32 The humble shall see it and be glad; you who seek after God, inquiring for *and* requiring Him [as your first need], let your heart revive *and* live! [Pss. 22:26; 42:1.]

33 For the Lord hears the poor *and* needy, and despises not His prisoners [His miserable and wounded ones].

34 Let Heaven and earth praise Him, the seas and everything that moves in them.

35 For God will save Zion and rebuild the cities of Judah; and [His servants] shall remain *and* dwell there and have it in possession.

36 The children of His servants shall inherit it, and those who love His name shall dwell in it.

To the Chief Musician. [ *A Psalm*] of David, to bring to remembrance *or* make memorial.

**70** *MAKE HASTE,* O God, to deliver me; make haste to help me, O Lord!

2 Let them be put to shame *and* confounded that seek after *and* demand my life; let them be turned backward and brought to confusion *and* dishonor who desire *and* delight in my hurt.

3 Let them be turned back *and* appalled because of their shame *and* disgrace who say, Aha, aha!

4 May all those who seek, inquire of *and* for You, *and* require You [as their vital need] rejoice and be glad in You, and may those who love Your salvation say continually, Let God be magnified!

5 But I am poor and needy; hasten to me, O God! You are my help and my deliverer; O Lord, do not tarry!

**71** IN YOU, O Lord, do I put my trust *and* confidently take refuge; let me never be put to shame *or* confusion!

2 Deliver me in Your righteousness and cause me to escape; bow down Your ear to me and save me!

3 Be to me a rock of refuge in which to dwell, *and* a sheltering stronghold to which I may continually resort, which You have appointed to save me; for You are my rock and my fortress.

4 Rescue me, O my God, out of the hand of the wicked, out of the grasp of the unrighteous and ruthless man.

5 For You are my hope; O Lord God, You are my trust from my youth *and* the source of my confidence.

6 Upon You have I leaned *and* relied from birth; You are He Who took me from my mother's womb *and* have been my benefactor from that day. My praise is continually of You.

7 I am as a wonder *and* surprise to many, but You are my strong refuge.

8 My mouth shall be filled with Your praise and with Your honor all the day.

## New American Standard

27 Do Thou add iniquity to their iniquity,
And may they not come into Thy righteousness.
28 May they be blotted out of the book of life,
And may they not be recorded with the righteous.

29 ¶ But I am afflicted and in pain;
May Thy salvation, O God, set me *securely* on high.
30 I will praise the name of God with song,
And shall magnify Him with thanksgiving.
31 And it will please the LORD better than an ox
*Or* a young bull with horns and hoofs.
32 The humble have seen *it and* are glad;
You who seek God, let your heart revive.
33 For the LORD hears the needy,
And does not despise His *who are* prisoners.
34 ¶ Let heaven and earth praise Him,
The seas and everything that moves in them.
35 For God will save Zion and build the cities of Judah,
That they may dwell there and possess it.
36 And the descendants of His servants will inherit it,
And those who love His name will dwell in it.

*Prayer for Help against Persecutors.*

For the choir director. *A Psalm* of David; for a memorial.

70 O GOD, *hasten* to deliver me;
O LORD, hasten to my help!
2 Let those be ashamed and humiliated
Who seek my life;
Let those be turned back and dishonored
Who delight in my hurt.
3 Let those be turned back because of their shame
Who say, "Aha, aha!"
4 ¶ Let all who seek Thee rejoice and be glad in Thee;
And let those who love Thy salvation say continually,
"Let God be magnified."
5 But I am afflicted and needy;
Hasten to me, O God!
Thou art my help and my deliverer;
O LORD, do not delay.

*Prayer of an Old Man for Deliverance.*

71 IN THEE, O LORD, I have taken refuge;
Let me never be ashamed.
2 In Thy righteousness deliver me, and rescue me;
Incline Thine ear to me, and save me.
3 Be Thou to me a rock of habitation, to which I may
continually come;
Thou hast given commandment to save me,
For Thou art my rock and my fortress.
4 Rescue me, O my God, out of the hand of the wicked,
Out of the grasp of the wrongdoer and ruthless man,
5 For Thou art my hope;
O Lord GOD, *Thou art* my confidence from my youth.
6 By Thee I have been sustained from *my* birth;
Thou art He who took me from my mother's womb;
My praise is continually of Thee.

7 ¶ I have become a marvel to many;
For Thou art my strong refuge.
8 My mouth is filled with Thy praise,
And with Thy glory all day long.

## New International

27 Charge them with crime upon crime;
do not let them share in your salvation.
28 May they be blotted out of the book of life
and not be listed with the righteous.

29 I am in pain and distress;
may your salvation, O God, protect me.

30 I will praise God's name in song
and glorify him with thanksgiving.
31 This will please the LORD more than an ox,
more than a bull with its horns and hoofs.
32 The poor will see and be glad—
you who seek God, may your hearts live!
33 The LORD hears the needy
and does not despise his captive people.

34 Let heaven and earth praise him,
the seas and all that move in them,
35 for God will save Zion
and rebuild the cities of Judah.
Then people will settle there and possess it;
36 the children of his servants will inherit it,
and those who love his name will dwell there.

For the director of music. Of David. A petition.

70 HASTEN, O God, to save me;
O LORD, come quickly to help me.
2 May those who seek my life
be put to shame and confusion;
may all who desire my ruin
be turned back in disgrace.
3 May those who say to me, "Aha! Aha!"
turn back because of their shame.
4 But may all who seek you
rejoice and be glad in you;
may those who love your salvation always say,
"Let God be exalted!"

5 Yet I am poor and needy;
come quickly to me, O God.
You are my help and my deliverer;
O LORD, do not delay.

71 In you, O LORD, I have taken refuge;
let me never be put to shame.
2 Rescue me and deliver me in your righteousness;
turn your ear to me and save me.
3 Be my rock of refuge,
to which I can always go;
give the command to save me,
for you are my rock and my fortress.
4 Deliver me, O my God, from the hand of the wicked,
from the grasp of evil and cruel men.

5 For you have been my hope, O Sovereign LORD,
my confidence since my youth.
6 From birth I have relied on you;
you brought me forth from my mother's womb.
I will ever praise you.
7 I have become like a portent to many,
but you are my strong refuge.
8 My mouth is filled with your praise,
declaring your splendor all day long.

## King James

9Cast me not off in the time of old age; forsake me not when my strength faileth.
10For mine enemies speak against me; and they that lay wait for my soul take counsel together,
11Saying, God hath forsaken him: persecute and take him; for *there is* none to deliver *him.*
12O God, be not far from me: O my God, make haste for my help.
13Let them be confounded *and* consumed that are adversaries to my soul; let them be covered *with* reproach and dishonour that seek my hurt.
14But I will hope continually, and will yet praise thee more and more.
15My mouth shall show forth thy righteousness *and* thy salvation all the day; for I know not the numbers *thereof.*
16I will go in the strength of the Lord GOD: I will make mention of thy righteousness, *even* of thine only.
17O God, thou hast taught me from my youth: and hitherto have I declared thy wondrous works.
18Now also when I am old and grayheaded, O God, forsake me not; until I have shown thy strength unto *this* generation, *and* thy power to every one *that* is to come.
19Thy righteousness also, O God, *is* very high, who hast done great things: O God, who *is* like unto thee!
20 *Thou,* which hast shown me great and sore troubles, shalt quicken me again, and shalt bring me up again from the depths of the earth.
21Thou shalt increase my greatness, and comfort me on every side.
22I will also praise thee with the psaltery, *even* thy truth, O my God: unto thee will I sing with the harp, O thou Holy One of Israel.
23My lips shall greatly rejoice when I sing unto thee; and my soul, which thou hast redeemed.
24My tongue also shall talk of thy righteousness all the day long: for they are confounded, for they are brought unto shame, that seek my hurt.

*A Psalm* for Solomon.

**72** GIVE THE king thy judgments, O God, and thy righteousness unto the king's son.
2He shall judge thy people with righteousness, and thy poor with judgment.
3The mountains shall bring peace to the people, and the little hills, by righteousness.
4He shall judge the poor of the people, he shall save the children of the needy, and shall break in pieces the oppressor.
5They shall fear thee as long as the sun and moon endure, throughout all generations.

**AMP** [a] "This Psalm, in highly wrought figurative style, describes the reign of a king, as 'righteous, universal, beneficent, and perpetual.' By the older Jewish and most of the modern Christian interpreters it has been referred to Christ, whose reign present and prospective alone corresponds with its statements. As the imagery of the Second Psalm was drawn from the martial character of David's reign, that of this is from the peaceful and prosperous state of Solomon's."—*Jamieson, Fausset and Brown Commentary.* "Jesus is here, beyond all doubt, in the glory of His reign, both as He now is and as He shall be revealed in the latter-day glory."—Charles Haddon Spurgeon.

## Amplified

9Cast me not off *nor* send me away in the time of old age; forsake me not when my strength is spent *and* my powers fail.
10For my enemies talk against me; those who watch for my life consult together,
11Saying, God has forsaken him; pursue *and* persecute and take him, for there is none to deliver him.
12O God, be not far from me! O my God, make haste to help me!
13Let them be put to shame and consumed who are adversaries to my life; let them be covered with reproach, scorn *and* dishonor who seek *and* require my hurt.
14But I will hope continually, and will praise You yet more and more.
15My mouth shall tell of Your righteous acts *and* of Your deeds of salvation all the day, for their number is more than I know.
16I will come in the strength *and* with the mighty acts of the Lord God; I will mention *and* praise Your righteousness, even Yours alone.
17O God, You have taught me from my youth, and hitherto have I declared Your wondrous works.
18Yes, even when I am old and gray-headed, O God, forsake me not, *but* keep me alive until I have declared Your mighty strength to *this* generation, and Your might *and* power to all that are to come.
19Your righteousness also, O God, is very high [reaching to the heavens]; You Who have done great things, O God, who is like unto You, *or* who is Your equal?
20You Who have shown us [all], troubles great and sore, will quicken us again and will bring us up again from the depths of the earth.
21Increase my greatness (my honor), and turn and comfort me.
22I will also praise You with the harp, even Your truth and faithfulness, O my God; unto You will I sing praises with the lyre, O Holy One of Israel.
23My lips shall shout for joy when I sing praises to You, and my inner being, which You have redeemed.
24My tongue also shall talk of Your righteousness all the day long; for they are put to shame, for they are confounded, who seek *and* demand my hurt.

[ *A Psalm*] for Solomon.

**72**[a] GIVE THE king [knowledge of] Your *way of* judging, O God, and [the spirit of] Your righteousness to the king's son [to control all his actions].
2Let him judge *and* govern Your people with righteousness, and Your poor *and* afflicted with judgment *and* justice.
3The mountains shall bring peace to the people, and the hills, through [the general establishment of] righteousness.
4May he judge *and* defend the poor of the people, deliver the children of the needy, and crush the oppressor;
5So that they may revere *and* fear You while the sun and moon endure, throughout all generations.

## New American Standard

9 Do not cast me off in the time of old age;
Do not forsake me when my strength fails.
10 For my enemies have spoken against me;
And those who watch for my life have consulted together,
11 Saying, "God has forsaken him;
Pursue and seize him, for there is no one to deliver."

12 ¶ O God, do not be far from me;
O my God, hasten to my help!
13 Let those who are adversaries of my soul be ashamed *and* consumed;
Let them be covered with reproach and dishonor, who seek to injure me.
14 But as for me, I will hope continually,
And will praise Thee yet more and more.
15 My mouth shall tell of Thy righteousness,
*And* of Thy salvation all day long;
For I do not know the sum *of them.*
16 I will come with the mighty deeds of the Lord GOD;
I will make mention of Thy righteousness, Thine alone.

17 ¶ O God, Thou hast taught me from my youth;
And I still declare Thy wondrous deeds.
18 And even when *I am* old and gray, O God, do not forsake me,
Until I declare Thy strength to *this* generation,
Thy power to all who are to come.
19 For Thy righteousness, O God, *reaches* to the heavens,
Thou who hast done great things;
O God, who is like Thee?
20 Thou, who hast shown [b]me many troubles and distresses,
Wilt revive [c]me again,
And wilt bring [d]me up again from the depths of the earth.
21 Mayest Thou increase my greatness,
And turn *to* comfort me.

22 ¶ I will also praise Thee with a harp,
*Even* Thy truth, O my God;
To Thee I will sing praises with the lyre,
O Thou Holy One of Israel.
23 My lips will shout for joy when I sing praises to Thee;
And my soul, which Thou hast redeemed.
24 My tongue also will utter Thy righteousness all day long;
For they are ashamed, for they are humiliated who seek my hurt.

*The Reign of the Righteous King.*

*A Psalm* of Solomon.

72 GIVE THE king Thy judgments, O God,
And Thy righteousness to the king's son.
2 May he judge Thy people with righteousness,
And [e]Thine afflicted with justice.
3 Let the mountains bring peace to the people,
And the hills in righteousness.
4 May he vindicate the afflicted of the people,
Save the children of the needy,
And crush the oppressor.

5 ¶ Let them fear Thee while the sun endures,
And as long as the moon, throughout all generations.

NAS [b] Another reading is *us* [c] Another reading is *us* [d] Another reading is *us* [e] Or, *Thy humble*

## New International

9 Do not cast me away when I am old;
do not forsake me when my strength is gone.
10 For my enemies speak against me;
those who wait to kill me conspire together.
11 They say, "God has forsaken him;
pursue him and seize him,
for no one will rescue him."
12 Be not far from me, O God;
come quickly, O my God, to help me.
13 May my accusers perish in shame;
may those who want to harm me
be covered with scorn and disgrace.

14 But as for me, I will always have hope;
I will praise you more and more.
15 My mouth will tell of your righteousness,
of your salvation all day long,
though I know not its measure.
16 I will come and proclaim your mighty acts, O Sovereign LORD;
I will proclaim your righteousness, yours alone.
17 Since my youth, O God, you have taught me,
and to this day I declare your marvelous deeds.
18 Even when I am old and gray,
do not forsake me, O God,
till I declare your power to the next generation,
your might to all who are to come.

19 Your righteousness reaches to the skies, O God,
you who have done great things.
Who, O God, is like you?
20 Though you have made me see troubles, many and bitter,
you will restore my life again;
from the depths of the earth
you will again bring me up.
21 You will increase my honor
and comfort me once again.

22 I will praise you with the harp
for your faithfulness, O my God;
I will sing praise to you with the lyre,
O Holy One of Israel.
23 My lips will shout for joy
when I sing praise to you—
I, whom you have redeemed.
24 My tongue will tell of your righteous acts
all day long,
for those who wanted to harm me
have been put to shame and confusion.

Of Solomon.

72 ENDOW THE king with your justice, O God,
the royal son with your righteousness.
2 He will[f] judge your people in righteousness,
your afflicted ones with justice.
3 The mountains will bring prosperity to the people,
the hills the fruit of righteousness.
4 He will defend the afflicted among the people
and save the children of the needy;
he will crush the oppressor.

5 He will endure[g] as long as the sun,
as long as the moon, through all generations.

NIV [f] 2 Or *May he;* similarly in verses 3-11 and 17 [g] 5 Septuagint; Hebrew *You will be feared*

## King James

6He shall come down like rain upon the mown grass: as showers *that* water the earth.
7In his days shall the righteous flourish; and abundance of
peace so long as the moon endureth.
8He shall have dominion also from sea to sea, and from the river
unto the ends of the earth.
9They that dwell in the wilderness shall bow before him; and
his enemies shall lick the dust.
10The kings of Tarshish and of the isles shall bring presents: the
kings of Sheba and Seba shall offer gifts.
11Yea, all kings shall fall down before him: all nations shall serve
him.
12For he shall deliver the needy when he crieth; the poor also,
and *him* that hath no helper.
13He shall spare the poor and needy, and shall save the souls
of the needy.
14He shall redeem their soul from deceit and violence: and
precious shall their blood be in his sight.
15And he shall live, and to him shall be given of the gold of
Sheba: prayer also shall be made for him continually; *and* daily
shall he be praised.
16There shall be an handful of corn in the earth upon the top
of the mountains; the fruit thereof shall shake like Lebanon: and
*they* of the city shall flourish like grass of the earth.
17His name shall endure for ever: his name shall be continued
as long as the sun: and *men* shall be blessed in him: all nations shall
call him blessed.
18Blessed *be* the LORD God, the God of Israel, who only doeth
wondrous things.
19And blessed *be* his glorious name for ever: and let the whole
earth be filled *with* his glory; Amen, and Amen.
20The prayers of David the son of Jesse are ended.

Book III
A Psalm of Asaph.

**73** TRULY GOD *is* good to Israel, *even* to such as are of a clean
heart.
2But as for me, my feet were almost gone; my steps had well
nigh slipped.
3For I was envious at the foolish, *when* I saw the prosperity of
the wicked.
4For *there are* no bands in their death: but their strength *is* firm.
5They *are* not in trouble *as other* men; neither are they plagued
like *other* men.
6Therefore pride compasseth them about as a chain; violence
covereth them *as* a garment.
7Their eyes stand out with fatness: they have more than heart
could wish.
8They are corrupt, and speak wickedly *concerning* oppression:
they speak loftily.

## Amplified

6May he [Solomon as a type of King David's greater Son] be like
rain that comes down upon the mown grass, as showers that water
the earth.
7In His [Christ's] days shall the [uncompromisingly] righteous
flourish, and peace abound till there be a moon no longer. [Cf. Isa.
11:3-9.]
8He [Christ] shall have dominion also from sea to sea, and from
the River [Euphrates] to the ends of the earth. [Zech. 14:9.]
9Those who dwell in the wilderness shall bow before Him, and
His enemies shall lick the dust.
10The kings of Tarshish and of the coasts shall bring offerings;
the kings of Sheba and Seba shall offer gifts.
11Yes, all kings shall fall down before Him; all nations shall
serve Him. [Ps. 138:4.]
12For He delivers the needy when he calls, the poor also and
him who has no helper.
13He will have pity on the poor *and* weak and needy, and will
save the lives of the needy.
14He will redeem their life from oppression *and* fraud and violence, and precious *and* costly shall their blood be in His sight.
15And He shall live, and to Him shall be given of the gold of
Sheba; prayer also shall be made for Him *and* through Him continually, *and* they shall bless *and* praise Him all the day long.
16There shall be abundance of grain in the soil upon the top of
the mountains [the least fruitful places in the land]; the fruit of it
shall wave as *do the forests* of Lebanon, and *the inhabitants* of the
city shall flourish like grass of the earth.
17His name shall endure for ever; His name shall be continued
as long as the sun [indeed, His name continues before the sun].
And men shall be blessed *and* bless themselves by Him; all nations
shall call Him blessed!
18Blessed be the Lord God, the God of Israel, Who alone does
wondrous things!
19Blessed be His glorious name for ever; let the whole earth be
filled with His glory! Amen and Amen!
20The prayers of David, the son of Jesse, are ended.

BOOK THREE
A Psalm of Asaph.

**73** TRULY (ONLY) good is God to Israel, even to those who
are upright *and* pure in heart.
2But as for me, my feet were almost gone, my steps had well-
nigh slipped.
3For I was envious at the foolish *and* arrogant, when I saw the
prosperity of the wicked.
4For they suffer no violent pangs in their death, but their
strength is firm.
5They are not in trouble as other men; neither are they smitten
*and* plagued like other men.
6Therefore pride is about their neck as a chain; violence covers
them as a garment [as a long, luxurious robe].
7Their eyes stand out with fatness, they have more than heart
could wish, *and* the imaginations of their minds overflow [with
follies].
8They scoff and wickedly utter oppression; they speak loftily
[from on high, maliciously and blasphemously].

## New American Standard

6 May he come down like rain upon the mown grass,
Like showers that water the earth.
7 In his days may the righteous flourish,
And abundance of peace till the moon is no more.

8¶ May he also rule from sea to sea,
And from the River to the ends of the earth.
9 Let the nomads of the desert bow before him,
And his enemies lick the dust.
10 Let the kings of Tarshish and of the islands bring presents;
The kings of Sheba and Seba offer gifts.
11 And let all kings bow down before him,
All nations serve him.

12¶ For he will deliver the needy when he cries for help,
The afflicted also, and him who has no helper.
13 He will have compassion on the poor and needy,
And the lives of the needy he will save.
14 He will rescue their life from oppression and violence;
And their blood will be precious in his sight;
15 So may he live; and may the gold of Sheba be given to him;
And let them pray for him continually;
Let them bless him all day long.

16¶ May there be abundance of grain in the earth on top of the mountains;
Its fruit will wave like *the cedars of* Lebanon;
And may those from the city flourish like vegetation of the earth.
17 May his name endure forever;
May his name increase as long as the sun *shines*;
And let *men* bless themselves by him;
Let all nations call him blessed.

18¶ Blessed be the LORD God, the God of Israel,
Who alone works wonders.
19 And blessed be His glorious name forever;
And may the whole earth be filled with His glory.
Amen, and Amen.

20¶ The prayers of David the son of Jesse are ended.

### BOOK 3

*The End of the Wicked Contrasted with That of the Righteous.*

A Psalm of Asaph.

**73** SURELY GOD is good to Israel,
To those who are pure in heart!
2 But as for me, my feet came close to stumbling;
My steps had almost slipped.
3 For I was envious of the arrogant,
*As* I saw the prosperity of the wicked.
4 For there are no pains in their death;
And their body is fat.
5 They are not in trouble *as other* men;
Nor are they plagued like mankind.
6 Therefore pride is their necklace;
The garment of violence covers them.
7 Their eye bulges from fatness;
The imaginations of *their* heart run riot.
8 They mock, and wickedly speak of oppression;
They speak from on high.

## New International

6He will be like rain falling on a mown field,
like showers watering the earth.
7In his days the righteous will flourish;
prosperity will abound till the moon is no more.

8He will rule from sea to sea
and from the River[a] to the ends of the earth.[b]
9The desert tribes will bow before him
and his enemies will lick the dust.
10The kings of Tarshish and of distant shores
will bring tribute to him;
the kings of Sheba and Seba
will present him gifts.
11All kings will bow down to him
and all nations will serve him.

12For he will deliver the needy who cry out,
the afflicted who have no one to help.
13He will take pity on the weak and the needy
and save the needy from death.
14He will rescue them from oppression and violence,
for precious is their blood in his sight.

15Long may he live!
May gold from Sheba be given him.
May people ever pray for him
and bless him all day long.
16Let grain abound throughout the land;
on the tops of the hills may it sway.
Let its fruit flourish like Lebanon;
let it thrive like the grass of the field.
17May his name endure forever;
may it continue as long as the sun.
All nations will be blessed through him,
and they will call him blessed.

18Praise be to the LORD God, the God of Israel,
who alone does marvelous deeds.
19Praise be to his glorious name forever;
may the whole earth be filled with his glory.
Amen and Amen.

20This concludes the prayers of David son of Jesse.

### BOOK III

*Psalms 73-89*

A psalm of Asaph.

**73** SURELY GOD is good to Israel,
to those who are pure in heart.

2But as for me, my feet had almost slipped;
I had nearly lost my foothold.
3For I envied the arrogant
when I saw the prosperity of the wicked.

4They have no struggles;
their bodies are healthy and strong.[c]
5They are free from the burdens common to man;
they are not plagued by human ills.
6Therefore pride is their necklace;
they clothe themselves with violence.
7From their callous hearts comes iniquity[d];
the evil conceits of their minds know no limits.
8They scoff, and speak with malice;
in their arrogance they threaten oppression.

**NIV** [a] *8* That is, the Euphrates [b] *8* Or *the end of the land* [c] *4* With a different word division of the Hebrew; Masoretic Text *struggles at their death; / their bodies are healthy* [d] *7* Syriac (see also Septuagint); Hebrew *Their eyes bulge with fat*

## King James

9 They set their mouth against the heavens, and their tongue walketh through the earth.

10 Therefore his people return hither: and waters of a full *cup* are wrung out to them.

11 And they say, How doth God know? and is there knowledge in the most High?

12 Behold, these *are* the ungodly, who prosper in the world; they increase *in* riches.

13 Verily I have cleansed my heart *in* vain, and washed my hands in innocency.

14 For all the day long have I been plagued, and chastened every morning.

15 If I say, I will speak thus; behold, I should offend *against* the generation of thy children.

16 When I thought to know this, it *was* too painful for me;

17 Until I went into the sanctuary of God; *then* understood I their end.

18 Surely thou didst set them in slippery places: thou castedst them down into destruction.

19 How are they *brought* into desolation, as in a moment! they are utterly consumed with terrors.

20 As a dream when *one* awaketh; *so,* O Lord, when thou awakest, thou shalt despise their image.

21 Thus my heart was grieved, and I was pricked in my reins.

22 So foolish *was* I, and ignorant: I was *as* a beast before thee.

23 Nevertheless I *am* continually with thee: thou hast holden *me* by my right hand.

24 Thou shalt guide me with thy counsel, and afterward receive me *to* glory.

25 Whom have I in heaven *but thee?* and *there is* none upon earth *that* I desire beside thee.

26 My flesh and my heart faileth: *but* God *is* the strength of my heart, and my portion for ever.

27 For, lo, they that are far from thee shall perish: thou hast destroyed all them that go a-whoring from thee.

28 But *it is* good for me to draw near to God: I have put my trust in the Lord GOD, that I may declare all thy works.

Maschil of Asaph.

**74** O GOD, why hast thou cast *us* off for ever? *why* doth thine anger smoke against the sheep of thy pasture?

2 Remember thy congregation, *which* thou hast purchased of old; the rod of thine inheritance, *which* thou hast redeemed; this mount Zion, wherein thou hast dwelt.

3 Lift up thy feet unto the perpetual desolations; *even* all *that* the enemy hath done wickedly in the sanctuary.

4 Thine enemies roar in the midst of thy congregations; they set up their ensigns *for* signs.

5 *A man* was famous according as he had lifted up axes upon the thick trees.

6 But now they break down the carved work thereof at once with axes and hammers.

## Amplified

9 They set their mouth against *and* speak down from heaven, and their tongue swaggers through the earth [invading even heaven with blasphemy and smearing earth with slanders]. [Rev. 13:6.]

10 Therefore His people return here, and waters of a full cup [offered by the wicked] are *blindly* drained by them.

11 And they say, How does God know? Is there knowledge in the Most High?

12 Behold, these are the ungodly, who always prosper *and* are at ease in the world; they increase in riches.

13 Surely then in vain have I cleansed my heart and washed my hands in innocency.

14 For all the day long have I been smitten *and* plagued, and chastened every morning.

15 Had I spoken thus [and given expression to my feelings], I would have been untrue *and* have dealt treacherously against the generation of your children.

16 But when I considered how to understand this, it was too great an effort for me *and* too painful,

17 Until I went into the sanctuary of God; then I understood [for I considered] their end.

18 [After all] You do set the [wicked] in slippery places; You cast them down to ruin *and* destruction.

19 How are they become a desolation in a moment! They are utterly consumed with terrors.

20 As a dream [which seems real] until one awakens, so, O Lord, when You arouse Yourself [to take note of the wicked] You will despise their outward show.

21 For my heart was grieved, embittered *and* in a state of ferment, and I was pricked in my heart [as with the sharp fang of an adder].

22 So foolish, stupid *and* brutish was I, and ignorant; I was as a beast before You.

23 Nevertheless I am continually with You; You do hold my right hand.

24 You will guide me with Your counsel, and afterward receive me to honor *and* glory.

25 Whom have I in Heaven but You? And I have no delight *or* desire on earth beside You.

26 My flesh and my heart may fail, but God is the rock *and* firm strength of my heart, and my portion for ever.

27 For lo, those who are far from You shall perish; You will destroy all who are false to You *and* like [spiritual] harlots depart from You.

28 But it is good for me to draw near to God; I have put my trust in the Lord God *and* made Him my refuge, that I may tell of all Your works.

A skillful song, or a didactic or reflective poem of Asaph.

**74** O GOD, why do You cast us off for ever? Why does Your anger burn *and* smoke against the sheep of Your pasture?

2 [Earnestly] remember Your congregation, which You have acquired of old, which You have redeemed to be the tribe of Your heritage; remember Mount Zion where You have dwelt.

3 Direct Your feet [quickly] to the perpetual ruins *and* desolations; the foe has devastated *and* desecrated everything in the sanctuary.

4 In the midst of Your holy place Your enemies have roared [with their battle cry]; they set up their own [idol] emblems for signs [of victory].

5 They seemed as men who lifted up axes upon a thicket of trees to make themselves a record.

6 And then all the carved wood of the holy place they broke down with hatchets and hammers.

## New American Standard

9 They have set their mouth against the heavens,
And their tongue parades through the earth.
10¶ Therefore his people return to this place;
And waters of abundance are drunk by them.
11 And they say, "How does God know?
And is there knowledge with the Most High?"
12 Behold, these are the wicked;
And always at ease, they have increased *in* wealth.
13 Surely in vain I have kept my heart pure,
And washed my hands in innocence;
14 For I have been stricken all day long,
And chastened every morning.
15¶ If I had said, "I will speak thus,"
Behold, I should have betrayed the generation of Thy children.
16 When I pondered to understand this,
It was troublesome in my sight
17 Until I came into the sanctuary of God;
*Then* I perceived their end.
18 Surely Thou dost set them in slippery places;
Thou dost cast them down to destruction.
19 How they are destroyed in a moment!
They are utterly swept away by sudden terrors!
20 Like a dream when one awakes,
O Lord, when aroused, Thou wilt despise their form.
21¶ When my heart was embittered,
And I was pierced within,
22 Then I was senseless and ignorant;
I was *like* a beast before Thee.
23 Nevertheless I am continually with Thee;
Thou hast taken hold of my right hand.
24 With Thy counsel Thou wilt guide me,
And afterward receive me to glory.
25¶ Whom have I in heaven *but Thee*?
And besides Thee, I desire nothing on earth.
26 My flesh and my heart may fail,
But God is the strength of my heart and my portion forever.
27 For, behold, those who are far from Thee will perish;
Thou hast destroyed all those who are unfaithful to Thee.
28 But as for me, the nearness of God is my good;
I have made the Lord GOD my refuge,
That I may tell of all Thy works.

*An Appeal against the Devastation of the Land by the Enemy.*
A Maskil of Asaph.

74 O GOD, why hast Thou rejected *us* forever?
Why does Thine anger smoke against the sheep of Thy pasture?
2 Remember Thy congregation, which Thou hast purchased of old,
Which Thou hast redeemed to be the tribe of Thine inheritance;
*And* this Mount Zion, where Thou hast dwelt.
3 Turn Thy footsteps toward the perpetual ruins;
The enemy has damaged everything within the sanctuary.
4 Thine adversaries have roared in the midst of Thy meeting place;
They have set up their own standards for signs.
5 It seems as if one had lifted up
*His* axe in a forest of trees.
6 And now all its carved work
They smash with hatchet and hammers.

## New International

9 Their mouths lay claim to heaven,
and their tongues take possession of the earth.
10 Therefore their people turn to them
and drink up waters in abundance.[a]
11 They say, "How can God know?
Does the Most High have knowledge?"

12 This is what the wicked are like—
always carefree, they increase in wealth.

13 Surely in vain have I kept my heart pure;
in vain have I washed my hands in innocence.
14 All day long I have been plagued;
I have been punished every morning.

15 If I had said, "I will speak thus,"
I would have betrayed your children.
16 When I tried to understand all this,
it was oppressive to me
17 till I entered the sanctuary of God;
then I understood their final destiny.

18 Surely you place them on slippery ground;
you cast them down to ruin.
19 How suddenly are they destroyed,
completely swept away by terrors!
20 As a dream when one awakes,
so when you arise, O Lord,
you will despise them as fantasies.

21 When my heart was grieved
and my spirit embittered,
22 I was senseless and ignorant;
I was a brute beast before you.

23 Yet I am always with you;
you hold me by my right hand.
24 You guide me with your counsel,
and afterward you will take me into glory.
25 Whom have I in heaven but you?
And earth has nothing I desire besides you.
26 My flesh and my heart may fail,
but God is the strength of my heart
and my portion forever.

27 Those who are far from you will perish;
you destroy all who are unfaithful to you.
28 But as for me, it is good to be near God.
I have made the Sovereign LORD my refuge;
I will tell of all your deeds.

A *maskil*[b] of Asaph.

74 WHY HAVE you rejected us forever, O God?
Why does your anger smolder against the sheep of your pasture?
2 Remember the people you purchased of old,
the tribe of your inheritance, whom you redeemed—
Mount Zion, where you dwelt.
3 Turn your steps toward these everlasting ruins,
all this destruction the enemy has brought on the sanctuary.

4 Your foes roared in the place where you met with us;
they set up their standards as signs.
5 They behaved like men wielding axes
to cut through a thicket of trees.
6 They smashed all the carved paneling
with their axes and hatchets.

NIV [a] *10* The meaning of the Hebrew for this verse is uncertain. [b] Title: Probably a literary or musical term

## King James

7They have cast fire into thy sanctuary, they have defiled *by casting down* the dwellingplace of thy name to the ground.
8They said in their hearts, Let us destroy them together: they have burned up all the synagogues of God in the land.
9We see not our signs: *there is* no more any prophet: neither *is there* among us any that knoweth how long.
10O God, how long shall the adversary reproach? shall the enemy blaspheme thy name for ever?
11Why withdrawest thou thy hand, even thy right hand? pluck *it* out of thy bosom.
12For God *is* my King of old, working salvation in the midst of the earth.
13Thou didst divide the sea by thy strength; thou brakest the heads of the dragons in the waters.
14Thou brakest the heads of leviathan in pieces, *and* gavest him *to be* meat to the people inhabiting the wilderness.
15Thou didst cleave the fountain and the flood: thou driedst up mighty rivers.
16The day *is* thine, the night also *is* thine: thou hast prepared the light and the sun.
17Thou hast set all the borders of the earth: thou hast made summer and winter.
18Remember this, *that* the enemy hath reproached, O LORD, and *that* the foolish people have blasphemed thy name.
19O deliver not the soul of thy turtledove unto the multitude *of the wicked:* forget not the congregation of thy poor for ever.
20Have respect unto the covenant: for the dark places of the earth are full of the habitations of cruelty.
21O let not the oppressed return ashamed: let the poor and needy praise thy name.
22Arise, O God, plead thine own cause: remember how the foolish man reproacheth thee daily.
23Forget not the voice of thine enemies: the tumult of those that rise up against thee increaseth continually.

To the chief Musician, Al-taschith, A Psalm *or* Song of Asaph.

**75** UNTO THEE, O God, do we give thanks, *unto thee* do we give thanks: for *that* thy name is near thy wondrous works declare.
2When I shall receive the congregation I will judge uprightly.
3The earth and all the inhabitants thereof are dissolved: I bear up the pillars of it. Selah.
4I said unto the fools, Deal not foolishly: and to the wicked, Lift not up the horn:
5Lift not up your horn on high: speak *not with* a stiff neck.
6For promotion *cometh* neither from the east, nor from the west, nor from the south.
7But God *is* the judge: he putteth down one, and setteth up another.

## Amplified

7They have set Your sanctuary on fire; they have profaned the dwelling place of Your name by casting it to the ground.
8They said in their heart, Let us make havoc of *such places* altogether. They have burned up all God's meeting houses in the land.
9We do not see our symbols; there is no longer any prophet, neither does any among us know for how long.
10O God, how long is the adversary to scoff *and* reproach? Is the enemy to blaspheme *and* revile Your name for ever?
11Why do You hold back Your hand, even Your right hand? Draw it out of Your bosom *and* consume them—make an end!
12Yet God is my King of old, working salvation in the midst of the earth.
13You did divide the [Red] Sea by Your might; You broke the heads of the [Egyptian] dragons on the waters. [Exod. 14:21.]
14You crushed the heads of Leviathan [Egypt]; You did give him as food for the creatures inhabiting the wilderness.
15You did cleave open [the rock bringing forth] fountains and streams; You dried up mighty, ever-flowing rivers [Jordan]. [Exod. 17:6; Num. 20:11; Josh. 3:13.]
16The day is Yours, the night also is Yours; You have established the [starry] light and the sun.
17You have fixed all the borders of the earth [the divisions of land and sea, and of the nations]. You have made summer and winter. [Acts 17:26.]
18[Earnestly] remember how the enemy has scoffed, O Lord, *and* reproached Thee, and that a foolish *and* impious people has blasphemed Your name.
19O do not deliver the life of your turtledove to the wild beast—to the greedy multitude. Forget not the life [of the multitude] of Your poor for ever.
20Have regard for the covenant [You made with Abraham], for the dark places of the land are full of the habitations of violence.
21O let not the downtrodden return in shame; let the oppressed and needy praise Your name.
22Arise, O God, plead Your own cause; remember [earnestly] how the foolish *and* impious man scoffs *and* reproaches You day after day *and* all day long.
23Do not forget the [clamoring] voice of Your adversaries, the tumult of those who rise up against You which ascends continually.

To the Chief Musician;
*set to the tune of* Do Not Destroy. A Psalm of Asaph, a song.

**75** WE GIVE praise *and* thanks to You, O God, we praise *and* give thanks; that Your name is near Your wondrous works declare, *and* they who invoke Your name rehearse Your wonders.
2When the proper time is come [for executing My judgments] I will judge uprightly [says the Lord].
3When the earth totters, and all the inhabitants of it, it is I who will poise *and* keep steady its pillars. Selah [pause, and calmly think of that]!
4I said to the arrogant *and* boastful, Deal not arrogantly—do not boast; and to the wicked, Lift not up the horn [of personal aggrandizement];
5Lift not up your [aggressive] horn on high, speak not with a stiff neck *and* insolent arrogance.
6For not from the east nor from the west nor from the south come promotion *and* lifting up. [Isa. 14:13.]
7But God is the judge! He puts down one and lifts up another.

## New American Standard

7 They have burned Thy sanctuary to the ground;
They have defiled the dwelling place of Thy name.
8 They said in their heart, "Let us completely subdue them."
They have burned all the meeting places of God in the land.
9 We do not see our signs;
There is no longer any prophet,
Nor is there any among us who knows how long.
10 How long, O God, will the adversary revile,
*And* the enemy spurn Thy name forever?
11 Why dost Thou withdraw Thy hand, even Thy right hand?
From within Thy bosom, destroy *them*!

12 ¶ Yet God is my king from of old,
Who works deeds of deliverance in the midst of the earth.
13 [a]Thou didst divide the sea by Thy strength;
Thou didst break the heads of the sea monsters in the waters.
14 Thou didst crush the heads of Leviathan;
Thou didst give him as food for the creatures of the wilderness.
15 Thou didst break open springs and torrents;
Thou didst dry up ever-flowing streams.
16 Thine is the day, Thine also is the night;
Thou hast prepared the light and the sun.
17 Thou hast established all the boundaries of the earth;
Thou hast made summer and winter.

18 ¶ Remember this, O LORD, that the enemy has reviled;
And a foolish people has spurned Thy name.
19 Do not deliver the soul of Thy turtledove to the wild beast;
Do not forget the life of Thine afflicted forever.
20 Consider the covenant;
For the dark places of the land are full of the habitations of violence.
21 Let not the oppressed return dishonored;
Let the afflicted and needy praise Thy name.

22 ¶ Do arise, O God, *and* plead Thine own cause;
Remember how the foolish man reproaches Thee all day long.
23 Do not forget the voice of Thine adversaries,
The uproar of those who rise against Thee which ascends continually.

### *God Abases the Proud, but Exalts the Righteous.*

For the choir director; *set to* Al-tashheth. A Psalm of Asaph, a Song.

75 WE GIVE thanks to Thee, O God, we give thanks,
For Thy name is near;
Men declare Thy wondrous works.
2 "When I select an appointed time,
It is I who judge with equity.
3 "The earth and all who dwell in it [b]melt;
It is I who have firmly set its pillars. Selah.
4 "I said to the boastful, 'Do not boast,'
And to the wicked, 'Do not lift up the horn;
5 Do not lift up your horn on high,
Do not speak with insolent pride.' "

6 ¶ For not from the east, nor from the west,
Nor from the desert *comes* exaltation;
7 But God is the Judge;
He puts down one, and exalts another.

## New International

7 They burned your sanctuary to the ground;
they defiled the dwelling place of your Name.
8 They said in their hearts, "We will crush them completely!"
They burned every place where God was worshiped in the land.
9 We are given no miraculous signs;
no prophets are left,
and none of us knows how long this will be.

10 How long will the enemy mock you, O God?
Will the foe revile your name forever?
11 Why do you hold back your hand, your right hand?
Take it from the folds of your garment and destroy them!
12 But you, O God, are my king from of old;
you bring salvation upon the earth.
13 It was you who split open the sea by your power;
you broke the heads of the monster in the waters.
14 It was you who crushed the heads of Leviathan
and gave him as food to the creatures of the desert.
15 It was you who opened up springs and streams;
you dried up the ever flowing rivers.
16 The day is yours, and yours also the night;
you established the sun and moon.
17 It was you who set all the boundaries of the earth;
you made both summer and winter.

18 Remember how the enemy has mocked you, O LORD,
how foolish people have reviled your name.
19 Do not hand over the life of your dove to wild beasts;
do not forget the lives of your afflicted people forever.
20 Have regard for your covenant,
because haunts of violence fill the dark places of the land.
21 Do not let the oppressed retreat in disgrace;
may the poor and needy praise your name.

22 Rise up, O God, and defend your cause;
remember how fools mock you all day long.
23 Do not ignore the clamor of your adversaries,
the uproar of your enemies, which rises continually.

For the director of music. To the tune of "Do Not Destroy." A psalm of Asaph. A song.

75 WE GIVE thanks to you, O God,
we give thanks, for your Name is near;
men tell of your wonderful deeds.

2 You say, "I choose the appointed time;
it is I who judge uprightly.
3 When the earth and all its people quake,
it is I who hold its pillars firm. *Selah*
4 To the arrogant I say, 'Boast no more,'
and to the wicked, 'Do not lift up your horns.
5 Do not lift up your horns against heaven;
do not speak with outstretched neck.' "

6 No one from the east or the west
or from the desert can exalt a man.
7 But it is God who judges:
He brings one down, he exalts another.

NAS [a] Or, *Thou Thyself*, and so through v. 17 [b] Or, *totter*

## King James

8 For in the hand of the LORD *there is* a cup, and the wine is red; it is full of mixture; and he poureth out of the same: but the dregs thereof, all the wicked of the earth shall wring *them* out, *and* drink *them*.

9 But I will declare for ever; I will sing praises to the God of Jacob.

10 All the horns of the wicked also will I cut off; *but* the horns of the righteous shall be exalted.

To the chief Musician on Neginoth, A Psalm *or* Song of Asaph.

**76** IN JUDAH *is* God known: his name *is* great in Israel.

2 In Salem also is his tabernacle, and his dwellingplace in Zion.

3 There brake he the arrows of the bow, the shield, and the sword, and the battle. Selah.

4 Thou *art* more glorious *and* excellent than the mountains of prey.

5 The stout-hearted are spoiled, they have slept their sleep: and none of the men of might have found their hands.

6 At thy rebuke, O God of Jacob, both the chariot and horse are cast into a dead sleep.

7 Thou, *even* thou, *art* to be feared: and who may stand in thy sight when once thou art angry?

8 Thou didst cause judgment to be heard from heaven; the earth feared, and was still,

9 When God arose to judgment, to save all the meek of the earth. Selah.

10 Surely the wrath of man shall praise thee: the remainder of wrath shalt thou restrain.

11 Vow, and pay unto the LORD your God: let all that be round about him bring presents unto him that ought to be feared.

12 He shall cut off the spirit of princes: *he is* terrible to the kings of the earth.

To the chief Musician, to Jeduthun, A Psalm of Asaph.

**77** I CRIED unto God with my voice, *even* unto God with my voice; and he gave ear unto me.

2 In the day of my trouble I sought the Lord: my sore ran in the night, and ceased not: my soul refused to be comforted.

3 I remembered God, and was troubled: I complained, and my spirit was overwhelmed. Selah.

4 Thou holdest mine eyes waking: I am so troubled that I cannot speak.

5 I have considered the days of old, the years of ancient times.

6 I call to remembrance my song in the night: I commune with mine own heart: and my spirit made diligent search.

7 Will the Lord cast off for ever? and will he be favourable no more?

8 Is his mercy clean gone for ever? doth *his* promise fail for evermore?

## Amplified

8 For in the hand of the Lord there is a cup [of His wrath], and the wine foams *and* is red, well mixed; and He pours out from it, and all the wicked of the earth must drain it and drink its dregs. [Ps. 60:3; Jer. 25:15; Rev. 14:9, 10; 16:19.]

9 But I will declare *and* rejoice for ever; I will sing praises to the God of Jacob.

10 All the horns of the ungodly also will I cut off [says the Lord]; but the horns of the [uncompromisingly] righteous shall be exalted.

To the Chief Musician;
on stringed instruments. A Psalm of Asaph, a song.

**76** IN JUDAH God is known *and* renowned; His name is highly praised *and* is great in Israel.

2 In [Jeru-]Salem also is His tabernacle, and His dwelling place is in Zion.

3 There He broke the bow's flashing arrows, the shield, the sword, and the weapons of war. Selah [pause, and calmly think of that]!

4 Glorious *and* excellent are You from the mountains of prey—splendid and majestic, more than the everlasting mountains.

5 The stouthearted are stripped of their spoil; they have slept the sleep [of death], and none of the men of might could raise their hands.

6 At Your rebuke, O God of Jacob, both chariot [rider] and horse are cast into a dead sleep [of death]. [Exod. 15:1, 21; Nah. 2:13; Zech. 12:4.]

7 You, even You, are to be feared [with awe and reverence]! Who may stand in Your presence when once Your anger is roused?

8 You caused sentence to be heard from heaven; the earth feared and was still,

9 When God arose to (establish) judgment, to save all the meek *and* oppressed of the earth. Selah [pause, and calmly think of that]!

10 Surely the wrath of man shall praise You; the remainder of wrath shall You restrain *and* gird *and* arm Yourself with it.

11 Vow, and pay to the Lord your God; let all who are round about Him bring presents to Him Who ought to be (reverently) feared.

12 He will cut off the spirit [of pride and fury] of princes; He is terrible to the [ungodly] kings of the earth.

To the Chief Musician, after the manner of Jeduthun [*one of David's three chief musicians*]. A Psalm of Asaph.

**77** I WILL cry to God with my voice, even to God with my voice, and He will give ear *and* hearken to me.

2 In the day of my trouble I seek, [inquire of and desperately require] the Lord; in the night my hand is stretched out (in prayer) without slacking; I refuse to be comforted.

3 I [earnestly] remember God; I am disquieted *and* I groan; I muse in prayer, and my spirit faints—overwhelmed. Selah [pause, and calmly think of that]!

4 You hold my eyes from closing; I am so troubled that I cannot speak.

5 I consider the days of old, the years of bygone times [of prosperity].

6 I call to remembrance my song in the night; with my heart I meditate and my spirit searches diligently;

7 Will the Lord cast off for ever? And will He be favorable no more?

8 *Have* His mercy *and* loving-kindness ceased for ever? Are His promises ended for all time?

## New American Standard

8 For a cup is in the hand of the LORD, and the wine foams;
It is well mixed, and He pours out of this;
Surely all the wicked of the earth must drain *and* drink down its dregs.
9¶ But as for me, I will declare *it* forever;
I will sing praises to the God of Jacob.
10 And all the horns of the wicked He will cut off,
*But* the horns of the righteous will be lifted up.

*The Victorious Power of the God of Jacob.*

For the choir director; on stringed instruments.
A Psalm of Asaph, a Song.

**76** GOD IS known in Judah;
His name is great in Israel.
2 And His tabernacle is in Salem;
His dwelling place also is in Zion.
3 There He broke the flaming arrows,
The shield, and the sword, and the weapons of war. Selah.

4¶ Thou art resplendent,
More majestic than the mountains of prey.
5 The stouthearted were plundered;
They sank into sleep;
And none of the warriors could use his hands.
6 At Thy rebuke, O God of Jacob,
Both rider and horse were cast into a dead sleep.
7 Thou, even Thou, art to be feared;
And who may stand in Thy presence when once Thou art angry?

8¶ Thou didst cause judgment to be heard from heaven;
The earth feared, and was still,
9 When God arose to judgment,
To save all the humble of the earth. Selah.
10 For the wrath of man shall praise Thee;
With a remnant of wrath Thou shalt gird Thyself.

11¶ Make vows to the LORD your God and fulfill *them;*
Let all who are around Him bring gifts to Him who is to be feared.
12 He will cut off the spirit of princes;
He is feared by the kings of the earth.

*Comfort in Trouble from Recalling God's Mighty Deeds.*

For the choir director; according to Jeduthun.
A Psalm of Asaph.

**77** MY VOICE *rises* to God, and I will cry aloud;
My voice *rises* to God, and He will hear me.
2 In the day of my trouble I sought the Lord;
In the night my hand was stretched out [a]without weariness;
My soul refused to be comforted.
3 *When* I remember God, then I am disturbed;
*When* I sigh, then my spirit grows faint. Selah.
4 Thou hast held my eyelids *open;*
I am so troubled that I cannot speak.
5 I have considered the days of old,
The years of long ago.
6 I will remember my song in the night;
I will meditate with my heart;
And my spirit ponders.
7¶ Will the Lord reject forever?
And will He never be favorable again?
8 Has His lovingkindness ceased forever?
Has *His* promise come to an end forever?

NAS [a] Lit., *and did not grow numb*

## New International

8 In the hand of the LORD is a cup
full of foaming wine mixed with spices;
he pours it out, and all the wicked of the earth
drink it down to its very dregs.
9 As for me, I will declare this forever;
I will sing praise to the God of Jacob.
10 I will cut off the horns of all the wicked,
but the horns of the righteous will be lifted up.

For the director of music. With stringed instruments. A psalm of Asaph. A song.

**76** IN JUDAH God is known;
his name is great in Israel.
2 His tent is in Salem,
his dwelling place in Zion.
3 There he broke the flashing arrows,
the shields and the swords, the weapons of war. *Selah*
4 You are resplendent with light,
more majestic than mountains rich with game.
5 Valiant men lie plundered,
they sleep their last sleep;
not one of the warriors
can lift his hands.
6 At your rebuke, O God of Jacob,
both horse and chariot lie still.
7 You alone are to be feared.
Who can stand before you when you are angry?
8 From heaven you pronounced judgment,
and the land feared and was quiet—
9 when you, O God, rose up to judge,
to save all the afflicted of the land. *Selah*
10 Surely your wrath against men brings you praise,
and the survivors of your wrath are restrained.[b]
11 Make vows to the LORD your God and fulfill them;
let all the neighboring lands
bring gifts to the One to be feared.
12 He breaks the spirit of rulers;
he is feared by the kings of the earth.

For the director of music. For Jeduthun. Of Asaph. A psalm.

**77** I CRIED out to God for help;
I cried out to God to hear me.
2 When I was in distress, I sought the Lord;
at night I stretched out untiring hands
and my soul refused to be comforted.

3 I remembered you, O God, and I groaned;
I mused, and my spirit grew faint. *Selah*
4 You kept my eyes from closing;
I was too troubled to speak.
5 I thought about the former days,
the years of long ago;
6 I remembered my songs in the night.
My heart mused and my spirit inquired:

7 "Will the Lord reject forever?
Will he never show his favor again?
8 Has his unfailing love vanished forever?
Has his promise failed for all time?

NIV [b] 10 Or *Surely the wrath of men brings you praise, / and with the remainder of wrath you arm yourself*

## King James

9Hath God forgotten to be gracious? hath he in anger shut up
his tender mercies? Selah.
10And I said, This *is* my infirmity: *but I will remember* the years
of the right hand of the most High.
11I will remember the works of the LORD: surely I will remember
thy wonders of old.
12I will meditate also of all thy work, and talk of thy doings.
13Thy way, O God, *is* in the sanctuary: who *is so* great a God
as *our* God?
14Thou *art* the God that doest wonders: thou hast declared thy
strength among the people.
15Thou hast with *thine* arm redeemed thy people, the sons of
Jacob and Joseph. Selah.
16The waters saw thee, O God, the waters saw thee; they were
afraid: the depths also were troubled.
17The clouds poured out water: the skies sent out a sound: thine
arrows also went abroad.
18The voice of thy thunder *was* in the heaven: the lightnings
lightened the world: the earth trembled and shook.
19Thy way *is* in the sea, and thy path in the great waters, and
thy footsteps are not known.
20Thou leddest thy people like a flock by the hand of Moses and
Aaron.

Maschil of Asaph.

**78** GIVE EAR, O my people, *to* my law: incline your ears to
the words of my mouth.
2I will open my mouth in a parable: I will utter dark sayings of
old:
3Which we have heard and known, and our fathers have told
us.
4We will not hide *them* from their children, shewing to the
generation to come the praises of the LORD, and his strength, and
his wonderful works that he hath done.
5For he established a testimony in Jacob, and appointed a law
in Israel, which he commanded our fathers, that they should make
them known to their children:
6That the generation to come might know *them, even* the children *which* should be born; *who* should arise and declare *them* to
their children:
7That they might set their hope in God, and not forget the
works of God, but keep his commandments:
8And might not be as their fathers, a stubborn and rebellious
generation; a generation *that* set not their heart aright, and whose
spirit was not stedfast with God.
9The children of Ephraim, *being* armed, *and* carrying bows,
turned back in the day of battle.
10They kept not the covenant of God, and refused to walk in his
law;
11And forgat his works, and his wonders that he had shewn
them.
12Marvellous things did he in the sight of their fathers, in the
land of Egypt, *in* the field of Zoan.

## Amplified

9Has God [deliberately] abandoned *or* forgotten His graciousness? Has He in anger shut up His compassion? Selah [pause, and
calmly think of that]!
10And I say, This [apparent desertion of Israel by God] is my
appointed lot *and* trial, but I will recall the years of the right hand
of the Most High [in loving-kindness extended toward us] for this
is my grief, that the right hand of the Most High changes.
11I will [earnestly] recall the deeds of the Lord; yes, I will [ear-
nestly] remember the wonders [You performed for our fathers] of
old.
12I will meditate also upon all Your work and consider all Your
[mighty] deeds.
13Your way, O God, is in the sanctuary [in holiness, away from
sin and guilt]; who is a great God like our God?
14You are the God Who does wonders; You have demonstrated
Your power among the peoples.
15You have with Your [mighty] arm redeemed Your people, the
sons of Jacob and Joseph. Selah [Stop, and calmly think of that]!
16When the waters [at the Red Sea and the Jordan] saw You, O
God, they were afraid; the deep shuddered also, for [all] the waters
saw You.
17The clouds poured down water; the skies sent out a sound [of
rumbling thunder]; Your arrows went forth [in forked lightning].
18The voice of Your thunder was in the whirlwind; the lightnings illumined the world; the earth trembled and shook.
19Your way [in delivering Your people] was through the sea,
and Your paths through the great waters; yet Your footsteps were
not traceable, *but* were obliterated.
20You led Your people like a flock by the hand of Moses and
Aaron.

A skillful song, *or* a didactic *or* reflective poem of Asaph.

**78** GIVE EAR, O my people, to my teaching; incline your ears
to the words of my mouth.
2I will open my mouth in a parable—in instruction by [numer-
ous] examples; I will utter dark sayings of old [that hide important
truth], [Matt. 13:34, 35.]
3Which we have heard and known, and our fathers have told
us.
4We will not hide them from their children, but tell to the
generation to come the praiseworthy deeds of the Lord, and His
might, and the wonderful works that He has performed.
5For He established a testimony [an express precept] in Jacob,
and appointed a law in Israel commanding our fathers that they
should make [the great facts of God's dealing with Israel] known
to their children;
6That the generation to come might know them, that the children still to be born might arise and recount them to their children,
7That they might set their hope in God, and not forget the
works of God, but keep His commandments;
8And might not be as their fathers, a stubborn and rebellious
generation, a generation that set not their heart aright *nor* prepared
their heart [to know God], and whose spirit was not steadfast *and*
faithful to God.
9The children of Ephraim were armed and carrying bows, *yet*
they turned back in the day of battle.
10They kept not the convenant of God and refused to walk
according to His law,
11And forgot His works and His wonders that He had shown
them.
12Marvelous things did He in the sight of their fathers in the
land of Egypt, in the field of Zoan [where Pharaoh resided].

## New American Standard

9 Has God forgotten to be gracious?
Or has He in anger withdrawn His compassion? Selah.
10 Then I said, "It is my grief,
That the right hand of the Most High has changed."

11¶ I shall remember the deeds of the LORD;
Surely I will remember Thy wonders of old.
12 I will meditate on all Thy work,
And muse on Thy deeds.
13 Thy way, O God, is holy;
What god is great like our God?
14 Thou art the God who workest wonders;
Thou hast made known Thy strength among the peoples.
15 Thou hast by Thy power redeemed Thy people,
The sons of Jacob and Joseph. Selah.

16¶ The waters saw Thee, O God;
The waters saw Thee, they were in anguish;
The deeps also trembled.
17 The clouds poured out water;
The skies gave forth a sound;
Thy arrows flashed here and there.
18 The sound of Thy thunder was in the whirlwind;
The lightnings lit up the world;
The earth trembled and shook.
19 Thy way was in the sea,
And Thy paths in the mighty waters,
And Thy footprints may not be known.
20 Thou didst lead Thy people like a flock,
By the hand of Moses and Aaron.

*God's Guidance of His People in Spite of Their Unfaithfulness.*

A Maskil of Asaph.

**78** LISTEN, O my people, to my instruction;
Incline your ears to the words of my mouth.
2 I will open my mouth in a parable;
I will utter dark sayings of old,
3 Which we have heard and known,
And our fathers have told us.
4 We will not conceal them from their children,
But tell to the generation to come the praises of the LORD,
And His strength and His wondrous works that He has done.

5¶ For He established a testimony in Jacob,
And appointed a law in Israel,
Which He commanded our fathers,
That they should teach them to their children,
6 That the generation to come might know, *even* the children *yet* to be born,
*That* they may arise and tell *them* to their children,
7 That they should put their confidence in God,
And not forget the works of God,
But keep His commandments,
8 And not be like their fathers,
A stubborn and rebellious generation,
A generation that did not [a]prepare its heart,
And whose spirit was not faithful to God.

9¶ The sons of Ephraim were archers equipped with bows,
*Yet* they turned back in the day of battle.
10 They did not keep the covenant of God,
And refused to walk in His law;
11 And they forgot His deeds,
And His miracles that He had shown them.
12 He wrought wonders before their fathers,
In the land of Egypt, in the field of Zoan.

NAS [a] Or, *put right*

## New International

9 Has God forgotten to be merciful?
Has he in anger withheld his compassion?" *Selah*
10 Then I thought, "To this I will appeal:
the years of the right hand of the Most High."
11 I will remember the deeds of the LORD;
yes, I will remember your miracles of long ago.
12 I will meditate on all your works
and consider all your mighty deeds.

13 Your ways, O God, are holy.
What god is so great as our God?
14 You are the God who performs miracles;
you display your power among the peoples.
15 With your mighty arm you redeemed your people,
the descendants of Jacob and Joseph. *Selah*

16 The waters saw you, O God,
the waters saw you and writhed;
the very depths were convulsed.
17 The clouds poured down water,
the skies resounded with thunder;
your arrows flashed back and forth.
18 Your thunder was heard in the whirlwind,
your lightning lit up the world;
the earth trembled and quaked.
19 Your path led through the sea,
your way through the mighty waters,
though your footprints were not seen.

20 You led your people like a flock
by the hand of Moses and Aaron.

A *maskil*[b] of Asaph.

**78** O MY people, hear my teaching;
listen to the words of my mouth.
2 I will open my mouth in parables,
I will utter hidden things, things from of old—
3 what we have heard and known,
what our fathers have told us.
4 We will not hide them from their children;
we will tell the next generation
the praiseworthy deeds of the LORD,
his power, and the wonders he has done.
5 He decreed statutes for Jacob
and established the law in Israel,
which he commanded our forefathers
to teach their children,
6 so the next generation would know them,
even the children yet to be born,
and they in turn would tell their children.
7 Then they would put their trust in God
and would not forget his deeds
but would keep his commands.
8 They would not be like their forefathers—
a stubborn and rebellious generation,
whose hearts were not loyal to God,
whose spirits were not faithful to him.

9 The men of Ephraim, though armed with bows,
turned back on the day of battle;
10 they did not keep God's covenant
and refused to live by his law.
11 They forgot what he had done,
the wonders he had shown them.
12 He did miracles in the sight of their fathers
in the land of Egypt, in the region of Zoan.

NIV [b] Title: Probably a literary or musical term

## King James

13He divided the sea, and caused them to pass through; and he made the waters to stand as an heap.

14In the daytime also he led them with a cloud, and all the night with a light of fire.

15He clave the rocks in the wilderness, and gave *them* drink as *out of* the great depths.

16He brought streams also out of the rock, and caused waters to run down like rivers.

17And they sinned yet more against him by provoking the most High in the wilderness.

18And they tempted God in their heart by asking meat for their lust.

19Yea, they spake against God; they said, Can God furnish a table in the wilderness?

20Behold, he smote the rock, that the waters gushed out, and the streams overflowed; can he give bread also? can he provide flesh for his people?

21Therefore the Lord heard *this*, and was wroth: so a fire was kindled against Jacob, and anger also came up against Israel;

22Because they believed not in God, and trusted not in his salvation:

23Though he had commanded the clouds from above, and opened the doors of heaven,

24And had rained down manna upon them to eat, and had given them of the corn of heaven.

25Man did eat angels' food: he sent them meat to the full.

26He caused an east wind to blow in the heaven: and by his power he brought in the south wind.

27He rained flesh also upon them as dust, and feathered fowls like as the sand of the sea:

28And he let *it* fall in the midst of their camp, round about their habitations.

29So they did eat, and were well filled: for he gave them their own desire;

30They were not estranged from their lust. But while their meat *was* yet in their mouths,

31The wrath of God came upon them, and slew the fattest of them, and smote down the chosen *men* of Israel.

32For all this they sinned still, and believed not for his wondrous works.

33Therefore their days did he consume in vanity, and their years in trouble.

34When he slew them, then they sought him: and they returned and inquired early after God.

35And they remembered that God *was* their rock, and the high God their redeemer.

36Nevertheless they did flatter him with their mouth, and they lied unto him with their tongues.

37For their heart was not right with him, neither were they stedfast in his covenant.

38But he, *being* full of compassion, forgave *their* iniquity, and destroyed *them* not: yea, many a time turned he his anger away, and did not stir up all his wrath.

39For he remembered that they *were but* flesh; a wind that passeth away, and cometh not again.

40How oft did they provoke him in the wilderness, *and* grieve him in the desert!

41Yea, they turned back and tempted God, and limited the Holy One of Israel.

## Amplified

13He divided the [Red] Sea and caused them to pass through it, and He made the waters to stand like a heap. [Exod. 14:22.]

14In the daytime also He led them with a [pillar of] cloud, and all the night with a light of fire. [Exod. 13:21; 14:24.]

15He split rocks in the wilderness, and gave them drink abundantly as out of the deep.

16He brought streams also out of the rock [at Rephidim and Kadesh] and caused waters to run down like rivers. [Exod. 17:6; Num. 20:11.]

17Yet they went on still to sin against Him by provoking *and* rebelling against the Most High in the wilderness—in the land of drought.

18And they tempted God in their heart by asking food according to their *selfish* desire *and* appetite.

19Yes, they spoke against God; they said, Can God furnish [the food for] a table in the wilderness?

20Behold, He did smite the rock so that waters gushed out and the streams overflowed, *but* can He give bread also? Can He provide flesh for His people?

21Therefore, when the Lord heard, He was [full of] wrath; a fire was kindled against Jacob, His anger mounted up against Israel;

22Because in God they believed not (they relied not on Him, they adhered not to Him) and they trusted not in His salvation (His power to save).

23Yet He commanded the clouds above and opened the doors of Heaven,

24And He rained down upon them manna to eat and gave them Heaven's grain. [Exod. 16:14; John 6:31.]

25Everyone ate the bread of the mighty—man ate angel's food; *God* sent them meat in abundance.

26He let forth the east wind to blow in the heavens, and by His power He guided the south wind.

27He rained flesh also upon them as the dust, and winged birds [quails] like sand of the seas. [Num. 11:31.]

28And He let *the birds* fall in the midst of their camp, round about their tents.

29So they ate and were well filled; He gave them what they craved *and* lusted after.

30But scarce had they stilled their craving, and while their meat was yet in their mouths, [Num. 11:33.]

31The wrath of God came upon them and slew the strongest *and* sturdiest of them, and smote down Israel's chosen youth.

32In spite of all this they sinned still more, for they believed not in (relied not on and adhered not to Him for) His wondrous works.

33Therefore their days He consumed like a breath—in emptiness, falsity and futility—and their years in terror *and* sudden haste.

34When he slew *some* [of them, the remainder] inquired after Him diligently, and they repented *and* sincerely sought God [for a time].

35And they [earnestly] remembered that God was their rock, and the Most High God their redeemer.

36Nevertheless they flattered Him with their mouth, and lied to Him with their tongue.

37For their heart was not right *or* sincere with Him, neither were they faithful *and* steadfast to His covenant. [Acts 8:21.]

38But He, full of (merciful) compassion, forgave their iniquity, and destroyed them not; yes, many a time He turned His anger away, and did not stir up all His wrath *and* indignation.

39For He [earnestly] remembered that they were but flesh, a wind that goes and does not return.

40How often they defied *and* rebelled against Him in the wilderness *and* grieved Him in the desert!

41And time and again they turned back *and* tempted God, provoking *and* incensing the Holy One of Israel.

## New American Standard

13 He divided the sea, and caused them to pass through;
And He made the waters stand up like a heap.
14 Then He led them with the cloud by day,
And all the night with a light of fire.
15 He split the rocks in the wilderness,
And gave *them* abundant drink like the ocean depths.
16 He brought forth streams also from the rock,
And caused waters to run down like rivers.

17 ¶ Yet they still continued to sin against Him,
To rebel against the Most High in the desert.
18 And in their heart they put God to the test
By asking food according to their desire.
19 Then they spoke against God;
They said, "Can God prepare a table in the wilderness?
20 "Behold, He struck the rock, so that waters gushed out,
And streams were overflowing;
Can He give bread also?
Will He provide meat for His people?"

21 ¶ Therefore the LORD heard and was full of wrath,
And a fire was kindled against Jacob,
And anger also mounted against Israel;
22 Because they did not believe in God,
And did not trust in His salvation.
23 Yet He commanded the clouds above,
And opened the doors of heaven;
24 And He rained down manna upon them to eat,
And gave them food from heaven.
25 Man did eat the bread of angels;
He sent them food in abundance.
26 He caused the east wind to blow in the heavens;
And by His power He directed the south wind.
27 When He rained meat upon them like the dust,
Even winged fowl like the sand of the seas,
28 Then He let *them* fall in the midst of their camp,
Round about their dwellings.
29 So they ate and were well filled;
And their desire He gave to them.
30 Before they had satisfied their desire,
While their food was in their mouths,
31 The anger of God rose against them,
And killed some of their stoutest ones,
And subdued the choice men of Israel.
32 In spite of all this they still sinned,
And did not believe in His wonderful works.
33 So He brought their days to an end in futility,
And their years in sudden terror.

34 ¶ When He killed them, then they sought Him,
And returned and searched diligently for God;
35 And they remembered that God was their rock,
And the Most High God their Redeemer.
36 But they deceived Him with their mouth,
And lied to Him with their tongue.
37 For their heart was not steadfast toward Him,
Nor were they faithful in His covenant.
38 But He, being compassionate, forgave *their* iniquity, and did not destroy *them*;
And often He restrained His anger,
And did not arouse all His wrath.
39 Thus He remembered that they were but flesh,
A wind that passes and does not return.

40 ¶ How often they rebelled against Him in the wilderness,
And grieved Him in the desert!
41 And again and again they [a]tempted God,
And pained the Holy One of Israel.

NAS [a] Or, *put to the test*

## New International

13 He divided the sea and led them through;
he made the water stand firm like a wall.
14 He guided them with the cloud by day
and with light from the fire all night.
15 He split the rocks in the desert
and gave them water as abundant as the seas;
16 he brought streams out of a rocky crag
and made water flow down like rivers.

17 But they continued to sin against him,
rebelling in the desert against the Most High.
18 They willfully put God to the test
by demanding the food they craved.
19 They spoke against God, saying,
"Can God spread a table in the desert?
20 When he struck the rock, water gushed out,
and streams flowed abundantly.
But can he also give us food?
Can he supply meat for his people?"
21 When the LORD heard them, he was very angry;
his fire broke out against Jacob,
and his wrath rose against Israel,
22 for they did not believe in God
or trust in his deliverance.
23 Yet he gave a command to the skies above
and opened the doors of the heavens;
24 he rained down manna for the people to eat,
he gave them the grain of heaven.
25 Men ate the bread of angels;
he sent them all the food they could eat.
26 He let loose the east wind from the heavens
and led forth the south wind by his power.
27 He rained meat down on them like dust,
flying birds like sand on the seashore.
28 He made them come down inside their camp,
all around their tents.
29 They ate till they had more than enough,
for he had given them what they craved.
30 But before they turned from the food they craved,
even while it was still in their mouths,
31 God's anger rose against them;
he put to death the sturdiest among them,
cutting down the young men of Israel.

32 In spite of all this, they kept on sinning;
in spite of his wonders, they did not believe.
33 So he ended their days in futility
and their years in terror.
34 Whenever God slew them, they would seek him;
they eagerly turned to him again.
35 They remembered that God was their Rock,
that God Most High was their Redeemer.
36 But then they would flatter him with their mouths,
lying to him with their tongues;
37 their hearts were not loyal to him,
they were not faithful to his covenant.
38 Yet he was merciful;
he forgave their iniquities
and did not destroy them.
Time after time he restrained his anger
and did not stir up his full wrath.
39 He remembered that they were but flesh,
a passing breeze that does not return.

40 How often they rebelled against him in the desert
and grieved him in the wasteland!
41 Again and again they put God to the test;
they vexed the Holy One of Israel.

## King James

42 They remembered not his hand, *nor* the day when he delivered them from the enemy.

43 How he had wrought his signs in Egypt, and his wonders in the field of Zoan:

44 And had turned their rivers into blood; and their floods, that they could not drink.

45 He sent divers sorts of flies among them, which devoured them; and frogs, which destroyed them.

46 He gave also their increase unto the caterpillar, and their labour unto the locust.

47 He destroyed their vines with hail, and their sycamore trees with frost.

48 He gave up their cattle also to the hail, and their flocks to hot thunderbolts.

49 He cast upon them the fierceness of his anger, wrath, and indignation, and trouble, by sending evil angels *among them.*

50 He made a way to his anger; he spared not their soul from death, but gave their life over to the pestilence;

51 And smote all the firstborn in Egypt; the chief of *their* strength in the tabernacles of Ham:

52 But made his own people to go forth like sheep, and guided them in the wilderness like a flock.

53 And he led them on safely, so that they feared not: but the sea overwhelmed their enemies.

54 And he brought them to the border of his sanctuary, *even to* this mountain, *which* his right hand had purchased.

55 He cast out the heathen also before them, and divided them an inheritance by line, and made the tribes of Israel to dwell in their tents.

56 Yet they tempted and provoked the most high God, and kept not his testimonies:

57 But turned back, and dealt unfaithfully like their fathers: they were turned aside like a deceitful bow.

58 For they provoked him to anger with their high places, and moved him to jealousy with their graven images.

59 When God heard *this,* he was wroth, and greatly abhorred Israel:

60 So that he forsook the tabernacle of Shiloh, the tent *which* he placed among men;

61 And delivered his strength into captivity, and his glory into the enemy's hand.

62 He gave his people over also unto the sword; and was wroth with his inheritance.

63 The fire consumed their young men; and their maidens were not given to marriage.

64 Their priests fell by the sword; and their widows made no lamentation.

65 Then the Lord awaked as one out of sleep, *and* like a mighty man that shouteth by reason of wine.

66 And he smote his enemies in the hinder parts: he put them to a perpetual reproach.

67 Moreover he refused the tabernacle of Joseph, and chose not the tribe of Ephraim:

68 But chose the tribe of Judah, the mount Zion which he loved.

69 And he built his sanctuary like high *palaces,* like the earth which he hath established for ever.

## Amplified

42 They remembered not [seriously the miracles of the working of] His hand, nor the day when He delivered them from the enemy;

43 How He wrought His miracles in Egypt, and His wonders in the field of Zoan [where Pharaoh resided],

44 And turned their rivers into blood, and their streams, so that they could not drink from them.

45 He sent swarms of [venomous] flies among them which devoured them, and frogs which destroyed them.

46 He gave also their crops to the caterpillar and [the fruit of] their labor to the locust.

47 He destroyed their vines with hail and their sycamore trees with frost *and* [great chunks of] ice.

48 He (caused them to shut up their cattle or) gave them up also to the hail, and their flocks to hot thunderbolts. [Exod. 9:18-21.]

49 He let loose upon them the fierceness of His anger, wrath and indignation, and distress, by sending [a mission of] angels of calamity *and* woe among them.

50 He leveled *and* made a straight path for His anger [to give it free course]; He did not spare [the Egyptian families] from death, but gave their beasts over to the pestilence *and* the life [of their eldest] over to the plague.

51 He smote all the first-born in Egypt, the chief of their strength in the tents [of the land of the sons] of Ham.

52 But [God] led His own people forth like sheep, and guided them [with a shepherd's care] like a flock in the wilderness.

53 And He led them on safely *and* in confident trust, so that they feared not; but the sea overwhelmed their enemies. [Exod. 14:27, 28.]

54 And He brought them to His holy border, the border of [Canaan] His sanctuary, even to this mountain [Zion], which His right hand had acquired.

55 He drove out the nations also before [Israel], and allotted their land as a heritage, measured out *and* partitioned; and made the tribes of Israel to dwell in the tents of those dispossessed.

56 Yet they tempted and provoked *and* rebelled against the Most High God, and kept not His testimonies.

57 But turned back and dealt unfaithfully *and* treacherously like their fathers; they were twisted like a warped *and* deceitful bow [that will not respond to the archer's aim].

58 For they provoked Him to [righteous] anger with their high places [for idol worship], and moved Him to jealousy with their graven images.

59 When God heard this, He was full of [holy] wrath, and utterly rejected Israel, greatly abhorring *and* loathing [her ways],

60 So that He forsook the tabernacle at Shiloh, the tent in which He had dwelt among men [and never returned to it again],

61 And delivered His strength *and* power [the ark of the covenant] into captivity, and His glory into the hand of [the Philistines] the foe. [I Sam. 4:21.]

62 He gave His people over also to the sword, and was wroth with His heritage, *Israel.* [I Sam. 4:10.]

63 The fire [of war] devoured their young men, and their bereaved virgins were not praised in a wedding song.

64 Their priests [Hophni and Phinehas] fell by the sword, and their widows made no lamentation [for the bodies came not back from the scene of battle, and the widow of Phinehas also died that day]. [I Sam. 4:11, 19, 20.]

65 Then the Lord awakened as from sleep, as a strong man whose consciousness of power is heightened by wine.

66 And He smote His adversaries in the back [as they fled]; He put them to lasting shame *and* reproach.

67 Moreover He rejected the tent of Joseph and chose not the tribe of Ephraim [in which the tabernacle had been accustomed to stand].

68 But He chose the tribe of Judah [as Israel's leader], Mount Zion which He loves [to replace Shiloh as His capitol].

69 And He built His sanctuary [exalted] like the heights [of the heavens], and like the earth which He established forever.

## New American Standard

42 They did not remember His power,
The day when He redeemed them from the adversary,
43 When He performed His signs in Egypt,
And His marvels in the field of Zoan,
44 And turned their rivers to blood,
And their streams, they could not drink.
45 He sent among them swarms of flies, which devoured them,
And frogs which destroyed them.
46 He gave also their crops to the grasshopper,
And the product of their labor to the locust.
47 He destroyed their vines with hailstones,
And their sycamore trees with frost.
48 He gave over their cattle also to the hailstones,
And their herds to bolts of lightning.
49 He sent upon them His burning anger,
Fury, and indignation, and trouble,
A band of destroying angels.
50 He leveled a path for His anger;
He did not spare their soul from death,
But gave over their life to the plague,
51 And smote all the first-born in Egypt,
The first *issue* of their virility in the tents of Ham.
52 But He led forth His own people like sheep,
And guided them in the wilderness like a flock;
53 And He led them safely, so that they did not fear;
But the sea engulfed their enemies.

54 ¶ So He brought them to His holy land,
To this hill country which His right hand had gained.
55 He also drove out the nations before them,
And He apportioned them for an inheritance by measurement,
And made the tribes of Israel dwell in their tents.
56 Yet they [a]tempted and rebelled against the Most High God,
And did not keep His testimonies,
57 But turned back and acted treacherously like their fathers;
They turned aside like a treacherous bow.
58 For they provoked Him with their high places,
And aroused His jealousy with their graven images.
59 When God heard, He was filled with wrath,
And greatly abhorred Israel;
60 So that He abandoned the dwelling place at Shiloh,
The tent which He had pitched among men,
61 And gave up His strength to captivity,
And His glory into the hand of the adversary.
62 He also delivered His people to the sword,
And was filled with wrath at His inheritance.
63 Fire devoured His young men;
And His virgins had no wedding songs.
64 His priests fell by the sword;
And His widows could not weep.

65 ¶ Then the Lord awoke as *if from* sleep,
Like a warrior overcome by wine.
66 And He drove His adversaries backward;
He put on them an everlasting reproach.
67 He also rejected the tent of Joseph,
And did not choose the tribe of Ephraim,
68 But chose the tribe of Judah,
Mount Zion which He loved.
69 And He built His sanctuary like the heights,
Like the earth which He has founded forever.

NAS [a] Or, *put to the test*

## New International

42 They did not remember his power—
the day he redeemed them from the oppressor,
43 the day he displayed his miraculous signs in Egypt,
his wonders in the region of Zoan.
44 He turned their rivers to blood;
they could not drink from their streams.
45 He sent swarms of flies that devoured them,
and frogs that devastated them.
46 He gave their crops to the grasshopper,
their produce to the locust.
47 He destroyed their vines with hail
and their sycamore-figs with sleet.
48 He gave over their cattle to the hail,
their livestock to bolts of lightning.
49 He unleashed against them his hot anger,
his wrath, indignation and hostility—
a band of destroying angels.
50 He prepared a path for his anger;
he did not spare them from death
but gave them over to the plague.
51 He struck down all the firstborn of Egypt,
the firstfruits of manhood in the tents of Ham.
52 But he brought his people out like a flock;
he led them like sheep through the desert.
53 He guided them safely, so they were unafraid;
but the sea engulfed their enemies.
54 Thus he brought them to the border of his holy land,
to the hill country his right hand had taken.
55 He drove out nations before them
and allotted their lands to them as an inheritance;
he settled the tribes of Israel in their homes.

56 But they put God to the test
and rebelled against the Most High;
they did not keep his statutes.
57 Like their fathers they were disloyal and faithless,
as unreliable as a faulty bow.
58 They angered him with their high places;
they aroused his jealousy with their idols.
59 When God heard them, he was very angry;
he rejected Israel completely.
60 He abandoned the tabernacle of Shiloh,
the tent he had set up among men.
61 He sent the ark of his might into captivity,
his splendor into the hands of the enemy.
62 He gave his people over to the sword;
he was very angry with his inheritance.
63 Fire consumed their young men,
and their maidens had no wedding songs;
64 their priests were put to the sword,
and their widows could not weep.

65 Then the Lord awoke as from sleep,
as a man wakes from the stupor of wine.
66 He beat back his enemies;
he put them to everlasting shame.
67 Then he rejected the tents of Joseph,
he did not choose the tribe of Ephraim;
68 but he chose the tribe of Judah,
Mount Zion, which he loved.
69 He built his sanctuary like the heights,
like the earth that he established forever.

## King James

70He chose David also his servant, and took him from the
sheepfolds:
71From following the ewes great with young he brought him to
feed Jacob his people, and Israel his inheritance.
72So he fed them according to the integrity of his heart; and
guided them by the skilfulness of his hands.

A Psalm of Asaph.

**79** O GOD, the heathen are come into thine inheritance; thy
holy temple have they defiled; they have laid Jerusalem on
heaps.
2The dead bodies of thy servants have they given *to be* meat
unto the fowls of the heaven, the flesh of thy saints unto the beasts
of the earth.
3Their blood have they shed like water round about Jerusalem;
and *there was* none to bury *them*.
4We are become a reproach to our neighbours, a scorn and
derision to them that are round about us.
5How long, LORD? wilt thou be angry for ever? shall thy jealousy burn like fire?
6Pour out thy wrath upon the heathen that have not known
thee, and upon the kingdoms that have not called upon thy name.
7For they have devoured Jacob, and laid waste his dwellingplace.
8O remember not against us former iniquities: let thy tender
mercies speedily prevent us: for we are brought very low.
9Help us, O God of our salvation, for the glory of thy name: and
deliver us, and purge away our sins, for thy name's sake.
10Wherefore should the heathen say, Where *is* their God? let
him be known among the heathen in our sight *by* the revenging
of the blood of thy servants *which is* shed.
11Let the sighing of the prisoner come before thee; according to
the greatness of thy power preserve thou those that are appointed
to die;
12And render unto our neighbours sevenfold into their bosom
their reproach, wherewith they have reproached thee, O Lord.
13So we thy people and sheep of thy pasture will give thee
thanks for ever: we will show forth thy praise to all generations.

To the chief Musician upon Shoshannim-Eduth, A Psalm of Asaph.

**80** GIVE EAR, O Shepherd of Israel, thou that leadest Joseph
like a flock; thou that dwellest *between* the cherubims,
shine forth.
2Before Ephraim and Benjamin and Manasseh stir up thy
strength, and come *and* save us.
3Turn us again, O God, and cause thy face to shine; and we shall
be saved.

## Amplified

70He chose David His servant and took him from the sheepfolds; [I Sam. 16:11, 12.]
71From tending the ewes that had their young He brought him
to be the shepherd of Jacob His people, of Israel His inheritance.
[II Sam. 7:7, 8].
72So [David] was their shepherd with an upright heart; he guided them by the discernment *and* skillfulness *which controlled* his
hands.

A Psalm of Asaph.

**79** O GOD, the nations have come into [the land of Your
people] Your inheritance; Your sacred temple have they
defiled; they have made Jerusalem heaps of ruins.
2The dead bodies of Your servants they have given to be food
to the birds of the heavens, the flesh of Your saints to the beasts
of the earth.
3Their blood they have poured out like water round about
Jerusalem, and there was none to bury them.
4[Because of such humiliation] we have become a taunt *and*
reproach to our neighbors, a mocking and derision to those who
are round about us.
5How long, O Lord? Will You be angry forever? Shall Your
jealousy [which cannot endure a divided allegiance] burn like fire?
6Pour out Your wrath on the Gentile nations who do not acknowledge You, and upon the kingdoms that do not call on Your
name. [II Thess. 1:8.]
7For they have devoured Jacob, and laid waste his dwelling *and*
his pasture.
8O do not [earnestly] remember against us the iniquities *and*
guilt of our forefathers! Let Your compassion *and* tender mercies
speedily come to meet us, for we are brought very low.
9Help us, O God of our salvation, for the glory of Your name!
Deliver us, forgive us *and* purge away our sins, for Your name's
sake.
10Why should the Gentile nations say, Where is their God? Let
vengeance for the blood of Your servants which is poured out be
known among the nations in our sight [not delaying until some
future generation].
11Let the groaning *and* sighing of the prisoner come before You;
according to the greatness of Your power *and* Your arm spare those
who are appointed to die!
12And return into the bosom of our neighbors sevenfold the
taunts with which they have taunted *and* scoffed at You, O Lord!
13Then we Your people, the sheep of Your pasture, will give
You thanks for ever; we will show forth *and* publish Your praise
from generation to generation.

To the Chief Musician;
set to Lilies, a Testimony. A Psalm of Asaph.

**80** GIVE EAR, O shepherd of Israel, You Who lead Joseph
like a flock; You Who sit enthroned upon the cherubim [of
the ark of the covenant], shine forth,
2Before [a]Ephraim and Benjamin and Manasseh! Stir up Your
might, and come to save us!
3Restore us again, O God, and cause Your face to shine [in
pleasure and approval on us], and we shall be saved!

**AMP** [a] "It is supposed that these three tribes represented the whole [twelve tribes of Israel], Benjamin being incorporated with Judah, Manasseh comprehending the country beyond Jordan, and Ephraim the rest." It was natural for the Israelites to think of the three in one group, for they had camped together on the west side of the tabernacle during the years in the wilderness, and also they were the only descendants of Jacob's wife Rachel.

## New American Standard

70 He also chose David His servant,
And took him from the sheepfolds;
71 From the care of the ewes with suckling lambs He brought him,
To shepherd Jacob His people,
And Israel His inheritance.
72 So he shepherded them according to the integrity of his heart,
And guided them with his skillful hands.

*A Lament over the Destruction of Jerusalem, and Prayer for Help.*

A Psalm of Asaph.

**79** O GOD, the nations have invaded Thine inheritance;
They have defiled Thy holy temple;
They have laid Jerusalem in ruins.
2 They have given the dead bodies of Thy servants for food to the birds of the heavens,
The flesh of Thy godly ones to the beasts of the earth.
3 They have poured out their blood like water round about Jerusalem;
And there was no one to bury them.
4 We have become a reproach to our neighbors,
A scoffing and derision to those around us.
5 How long, O LORD? Wilt Thou be angry forever?
Will Thy jealousy burn like fire?
6 Pour out Thy wrath upon the nations which do not know Thee,
And upon the kingdoms which do not call upon Thy name.
7 For they have devoured Jacob,
And laid waste his habitation.
8¶ Do not remember the iniquities of *our* forefathers against us;
Let Thy compassion come quickly to meet us;
For we are brought very low.
9 Help us, O God of our salvation, for the glory of Thy name;
And deliver us, and forgive our sins, for Thy name's sake.
10 Why should the nations say, "Where is their God?"
Let there be known among the nations in our sight,
Vengeance for the blood of Thy servants, which has been shed.
11 Let the groaning of the prisoner come before Thee;
According to the greatness of Thy power preserve those who are doomed to die.
12 And return to our neighbors sevenfold into their bosom
The reproach with which they have reproached Thee, O Lord.
13 So we Thy people and the sheep of Thy pasture
Will give thanks to Thee forever;
To all generations we will tell of Thy praise.

*God Implored to Rescue His People from Their Calamities.*

For the choir director; *set to* El Shoshannim; Eduth. A Psalm of Asaph.

**80** OH, GIVE ear, Shepherd of Israel,
Thou who dost lead Joseph like a flock;
Thou who art enthroned *above* the cherubim, shine forth!
2 Before Ephraim and Benjamin and Manasseh, stir up Thy power,
And come to save us!
3 O God, restore us,
And cause Thy face to shine *upon us*, and we will be saved.

## New International

70He chose David his servant
and took him from the sheep pens;
71from tending the sheep he brought him
to be the shepherd of his people Jacob,
of Israel his inheritance.
72And David shepherded them with integrity of heart;
with skillful hands he led them.

A psalm of Asaph.

**79** O GOD, the nations have invaded your inheritance;
they have defiled your holy temple,
they have reduced Jerusalem to rubble.
2They have given the dead bodies of your servants
as food to the birds of the air,
the flesh of your saints to the beasts of the earth.
3They have poured out blood like water
all around Jerusalem,
and there is no one to bury the dead.
4We are objects of reproach to our neighbors,
of scorn and derision to those around us.

5How long, O LORD? Will you be angry forever?
How long will your jealousy burn like fire?
6Pour out your wrath on the nations
that do not acknowledge you,
on the kingdoms
that do not call on your name;
7for they have devoured Jacob
and destroyed his homeland.
8Do not hold against us the sins of the fathers;
may your mercy come quickly to meet us,
for we are in desperate need.

9Help us, O God our Savior,
for the glory of your name;
deliver us and forgive our sins
for your name's sake.
10Why should the nations say,
"Where is their God?"
Before our eyes, make known among the nations
that you avenge the outpoured blood of your servants.
11May the groans of the prisoners come before you;
by the strength of your arm
preserve those condemned to die.
12Pay back into the laps of our neighbors seven times
the reproach they have hurled at you, O Lord.
13Then we your people, the sheep of your pasture,
will praise you forever;
from generation to generation
we will recount your praise.

For the director of music. To the tune of "The Lilies of the Covenant." Of Asaph. A psalm.

**80** HEAR US, O Shepherd of Israel,
you who lead Joseph like a flock;
you who sit enthroned between the cherubim, shine forth
2 before Ephraim, Benjamin and Manasseh.
Awaken your might;
come and save us.

3Restore us, O God;
make your face shine upon us,
that we may be saved.

## King James

4 O LORD God of hosts, how long wilt thou be angry against the prayer of thy people?

5 Thou feedest them with the bread of tears; and givest them tears to drink in great measure.

6 Thou makest us a strife unto our neighbours: and our enemies laugh among themselves.

7 Turn us again, O God of hosts, and cause thy face to shine; and we shall be saved.

8 Thou hast brought a vine out of Egypt: thou hast cast out the heathen, and planted it.

9 Thou preparedst *room* before it, and didst cause it to take deep root, and it filled the land.

10 The hills were covered with the shadow of it, and the boughs thereof *were like* the goodly cedars.

11 She sent out her boughs unto the sea, and her branches unto the river.

12 Why hast thou *then* broken down her hedges, so that all they which pass by the way do pluck her?

13 The boar out of the wood doth waste it, and the wild beast of the field doth devour it.

14 Return, we beseech thee, O God of hosts: look down from heaven, and behold, and visit this vine;

15 And the vineyard which thy right hand hath planted, and the branch *that* thou madest strong for thyself.

16 *It is* burned with fire, *it is* cut down: they perish at the rebuke of thy countenance.

17 Let thy hand be upon the man of thy right hand, upon the son of man *whom* thou madest strong for thyself.

18 So will not we go back from thee: quicken us, and we will call upon thy name.

19 Turn us again, O LORD God of hosts, cause thy face to shine; and we shall be saved.

To the chief Musician upon Gittith, *A Psalm* of Asaph.

**81** SING ALOUD unto God our strength: make a joyful noise unto the God of Jacob.

2 Take a psalm, and bring hither the timbrel, the pleasant harp with the psaltery.

3 Blow up the trumpet in the new moon, in the time appointed, on our solemn feast day.

4 For this *was* a statute for Israel, *and* a law of the God of Jacob.

5 This he ordained in Joseph *for* a testimony, when he went out through the land of Egypt: *where* I heard a language *that* I understood not.

6 I removed his shoulder from the burden: his hands were delivered from the pots.

7 Thou calledst in trouble, and I delivered thee; I answered thee in the secret place of thunder: I proved thee at the waters of Meribah. Selah.

8 Hear, O my people, and I will testify unto thee: O Israel, if thou wilt hearken unto me;

9 There shall no strange god be in thee; neither shalt thou worship any strange god.

## Amplified

4 O Lord God of hosts, how long will You be angry with Your people's prayers?

5 You have fed them with the bread of tears, and given them tears to drink in large measure.

6 You make us a strife *and* scorn to our neighbors, and our enemies laugh among themselves.

7 Restore us again, O God of hosts, and cause Your face to shine [upon us with favor as of old], and we shall be saved!

8 You brought a vine [Israel] out of Egypt; You drove out the (heathen) nations and planted it [in Canaan].

9 You prepared room before it, and it took deep root, and it filled the land.

10 The mountains were covered with the shadow of it, and the boughs of it were like the great cedars—cedars of God.

11 [Israel] sent out its boughs to the [Mediterranean] Sea, and its branches to the [Euphrates] River. [I Kings 4:21.]

12 Why have You broken down its hedges *and* walls, so that all they who pass by pluck from its *fruit*?

13 The boar out of the wood wastes it, and the wild beast of the field feeds on it.

14 Turn again, we beseech You, O God of hosts! Look down from Heaven and see, visit *and* have regard for this vine!

15 [Protect and maintain] the stock which Your right hand planted, and the branch (the son) that You have reared *and* made strong for Yourself.

16 They have burned it with fire, it is cut down; may they perish at the rebuke of Your countenance.

17 Let Your hand be upon the man of Your right hand, upon the son of man whom You have made strong for Yourself.

18 Then will we not depart from You; revive us—give us life—and we will call upon Your name.

19 Restore us, O Lord God of hosts, cause Your face to shine [in pleasure, approval and favor on us], and we shall be saved!

To the Chief Musician;
set to Philistine lute, or [ *possibly*] a particular Gittite tune. [ *A Psalm*] of Asaph.

**81** SING ALOUD to God our strength! Shout for joy to the God of Jacob!

2 Raise a song, sound the timbrel, the sweet lyre with the harp.

3 Blow the trumpet at the new moon, at the full moon, on our feast day.

4 For this is a statute for Israel, an ordinance of the God of Jacob.

5 This He ordained in Joseph [the [a]savior] for a testimony, when He went out over the land of Egypt. The speech of one whom I knew not did I hear [saying],

6 I removed his shoulder from the burden; his hands were freed from the basket.

7 You called in distress, and I delivered you; I answered you in the secret place of thunder; I tested you at the waters of Meribah. Selah [pause, and calmly think of that]. [Num. 20:3, 13, 24.]

8 Hear, O My people, and I will admonish you; O Israel, if you would listen to Me!

9 There shall no strange god be among you, neither shall you worship any alien god.

**AMP** [a] Once, Joseph had gone out over Egypt with the title "Zaphenath-paneah," meaning according to some, "Savior of the Age," to bring deliverance from famine to the Egyptians (Gen. 41:45). Later they forgot their benefactor and severely oppressed his family and their descendants. "Then Joseph's God arose and went forth over the land [of Egypt] in righteous judgment, yet still as savior of that people [Israel], in whom dwelt the germ of blessing for all nations." (Kay, quoted in *Gray and Adams' Bible Commentary.*)

## New American Standard

4¶ O LORD God *of* hosts,
How long wilt Thou be angry with the prayer of Thy people?
5 Thou hast fed them with the bread of tears,
And Thou hast made them to drink tears in large measure.
6 Thou dost make us [b]an object of contention to our neighbors;
And our enemies laugh among themselves.
7 O God *of* hosts, restore us,
And cause Thy face to shine *upon us*, [c]and we will be saved.
8¶ Thou didst remove a vine from Egypt;
Thou didst drive out the nations, and didst plant it.
9 Thou didst clear *the ground* before it,
And it took deep root and filled the land.
10 The mountains were covered with its shadow;
And the cedars of God with its boughs.
11 It was sending out its branches to the sea,
And its shoots to the River.
12 Why hast Thou broken down its hedges,
So that all who pass *that* way pick its *fruit*?
13 A boar from the forest eats it away,
And whatever moves in the field feeds on it.
14¶ O God *of* hosts, turn again now, we beseech Thee;
Look down from heaven and see, and take care of this vine,
15 Even the shoot which Thy right hand has planted,
And on the son whom Thou hast strengthened for Thyself.
16 It is burned with fire, it is cut down;
They perish at the rebuke of Thy countenance.
17 Let Thy hand be upon the man of Thy right hand,
Upon the son of man whom Thou didst make strong for Thyself.
18 Then we shall not turn back from Thee;
Revive us, and we will call upon Thy name.
19 O LORD God of hosts, restore us;
Cause Thy face to shine *upon us*, and we will be saved.

*God's Goodness and Israel's Waywardness.*

For the choir director; on the Gittith.
*A Psalm* of Asaph.

**81** SING FOR joy to God our strength;
Shout joyfully to the God of Jacob.
2 Raise a song, strike the timbrel,
The sweet sounding lyre with the harp.
3 Blow the trumpet at the new moon,
At the full moon, on our feast day.
4 For it is a statute for Israel,
An ordinance of the God of Jacob.
5 He established it for a testimony in Joseph,
When he went throughout the land of Egypt.
I heard a language that I did not know:

6¶ "I relieved his shoulder of the burden,
His hands were freed from the basket.
7 "You called in trouble, and I rescued you;
I answered you in the hiding place of thunder;
I proved you at the waters of Meribah. Selah.
8 "Hear, O My people, and I will admonish you;
O Israel, if you would listen to Me!
9 "Let there be no strange god among you;
Nor shall you worship any foreign god.

NAS [b] Lit., *a strife to* [c] Or, *that we may*

## New International

4 O LORD God Almighty,
how long will your anger smolder
against the prayers of your people?
5 You have fed them with the bread of tears;
you have made them drink tears by the bowlful.
6 You have made us a source of contention to our neighbors,
and our enemies mock us.

7 Restore us, O God Almighty;
make your face shine upon us,
that we may be saved.

8 You brought a vine out of Egypt;
you drove out the nations and planted it.
9 You cleared the ground for it,
and it took root and filled the land.
10 The mountains were covered with its shade,
the mighty cedars with its branches.
11 It sent out its boughs to the Sea,[d]
its shoots as far as the River.[e]

12 Why have you broken down its walls
so that all who pass by pick its grapes?
13 Boars from the forest ravage it
and the creatures of the field feed on it.
14 Return to us, O God Almighty!
Look down from heaven and see!
Watch over this vine,
15 the root your right hand has planted,
the son[f] you have raised up for yourself.

16 Your vine is cut down, it is burned with fire;
at your rebuke your people perish.
17 Let your hand rest on the man at your right hand,
the son of man you have raised up for yourself.
18 Then we will not turn away from you;
revive us, and we will call on your name.

19 Restore us, O LORD God Almighty;
make your face shine upon us,
that we may be saved.

For the director of music. According to *gittith*.[g] Of Asaph.

**81** SING FOR joy to God our strength;
shout aloud to the God of Jacob!
2 Begin the music, strike the tambourine,
play the melodious harp and lyre.

3 Sound the ram's horn at the New Moon,
and when the moon is full, on the day of our Feast;
4 this is a decree for Israel,
an ordinance of the God of Jacob.
5 He established it as a statute for Joseph
when he went out against Egypt,
where we heard a language we did not understand.[h]

6 He says, "I removed the burden from their shoulders;
their hands were set free from the basket.
7 In your distress you called and I rescued you,
I answered you out of a thundercloud;
I tested you at the waters of Meribah. *Selah*

8 "Hear, O my people, and I will warn you—
if you would but listen to me, O Israel!
9 You shall have no foreign god among you;
you shall not bow down to an alien god.

NIV [d] *11* Probably the Mediterranean [e] *11* That is, the Euphrates [f] *15* Or *branch* [g] Title: Probably a musical term [h] *5* Or / *and we heard a voice we had not known*

## King James

10 I *am* the LORD thy God, which brought thee out of the land of Egypt: open thy mouth wide, and I will fill it.
11 But my people would not hearken to my voice; and Israel would none of me.
12 So I gave them up unto their own hearts' lust: *and* they walked in their own counsels.
13 Oh that my people had hearkened unto me, *and* Israel had walked in my ways!
14 I should soon have subdued their enemies, and turned my hand against their adversaries.
15 The haters of the LORD should have submitted themselves unto him: but their time should have endured for ever.
16 He should have fed them also with the finest of the wheat: and with honey out of the rock should I have satisfied thee.

A Psalm of Asaph.

**82** GOD STANDETH in the congregation of the mighty; he judgeth among the gods.
2 How long will ye judge unjustly, and accept the persons of the wicked? Selah.
3 Defend the poor and fatherless: do justice to the afflicted and needy.
4 Deliver the poor and needy: rid *them* out of the hand of the wicked.
5 They know not, neither will they understand; they walk on in darkness: all the foundations of the earth are out of course.
6 I have said, Ye *are* gods; and all of you *are* children of the most High.
7 But ye shall die like men, and fall like one of the princes.
8 Arise, O God, judge the earth: for thou shalt inherit all nations.

A Song *or* Psalm of Asaph.

**83** KEEP NOT thou silence, O God: hold not thy peace, and be not still, O God.
2 For, lo, thine enemies make a tumult: and they that hate thee have lifted up the head.
3 They have taken crafty counsel against thy people, and consulted against thy hidden ones.
4 They have said, Come, and let us cut them off from *being* a nation; that the name of Israel may be no more in remembrance.
5 For they have consulted together with one consent: they are confederate against thee:
6 The tabernacles of Edom, and the Ishmaelites; of Moab, and the Hagarenes;
7 Gebal, and Ammon, and Amalek; the Philistines with the inhabitants of Tyre;
8 Assur also is joined with them: they have helped the children of Lot. Selah.
9 Do unto them as *unto* the Midianites; as *to* Sisera, as *to* Jabin, at the brook of Kison:
10 *Which* perished at En-dor: they became *as* dung for the earth.
11 Make their nobles like Oreb, and like Zeeb: yea, all their princes as Zebah, and as Zalmunna:

## Amplified

10 I am the Lord your God, Who brought you up out of the land of Egypt. Open your mouth wide, and I will fill it.
11 But My people would not hearken to My voice, and Israel would have none of Me.
12 So I gave them up to their own hearts' lust *and* let them go after their own stubborn *will,* that they might follow their own counsels. [Acts 7:42, 43; 14:16; Rom. 1:24, 26.]
13 O that My people would listen to Me, that Israel would walk in My ways!
14 Speedily then I would subdue their enemies, and turn My hand against their adversaries.
15 [Had Israel listened to Me in Egypt, then] those who hated the Lord would have come cringing before Him, and their *defeat* would have lasted forever.
16 *God* would feed *Israel* [now] also with the finest of the wheat, and with honey out of the rock would I satisfy you.

A Psalm of Asaph.

**82** GOD STANDS in the assembly [of the representatives] of God; in the midst of the magistrates *or* judges He gives judgment [as] among the gods.
2 How long will you *magistrates or judges* judge unjustly, and show partiality to the wicked? Selah [pause, and calmly think of that].
3 Do justice to the weak (poor) and fatherless; maintain the right of the afflicted and needy.
4 Deliver the poor and needy; rescue them out of the hand of the wicked.
5 *The magistrates and judges* know not, neither will they understand; they walk on in the darkness [of complacent satisfaction]; all the foundations of the earth [the fundamental principles upon which rests the administration of justice] are shaking.
6 I said, You are gods [since you judge on My behalf, as My representatives]; indeed, all of you are children of the Most High. [John 10:34-36; Rom. 13:1, 2.]
7 But you shall die as men, and fall as one of the princes.
8 Arise, O God, judge the earth! For to You belong all the nations. [Rev. 11:15.]

A song, a Psalm of Asaph.

**83** KEEP NOT silence, O God; hold not Your peace or be still, O God.
2 For, lo, Your enemies are in tumult and those who hate You have raised their heads. [Acts 4:25, 26.]
3 They lay crafty schemes against Your people and consult together against Your hidden *and* precious ones.
4 They have said, Come, and let us wipe them out as a nation; let the name of Israel be in remembrance no more.
5 For they have consulted together with one consent *and* one heart; against You they make a covenant,
6 The tents of Edom and the Ishmaelites, of Moab and the Hagrites,
7 Gebal and Ammon and Amalek, the Philistines with the inhabitants of Tyre;
8 Assyria also has joined with them; they have helped the children of Lot [the Ammonites and the Moabites] *and* have been an arm to them. Selah [pause, and calmly think of that].
9 Do to them as [You did to] the Midianites, as to Sisera and Jabin at the brook of Kishon, [Judg. 4:12-24.]
10 Who perished at Endor, who became as manure for the earth.
11 Make their nobles like Oreb and Zeeb; yes, all their princes as Zebah and Zalmunna, [Judg. 7:23-25; 8:10-21.]

## New American Standard

10 "I, the LORD, am your God,
Who brought you up from the land of Egypt;
Open your mouth wide and I will fill it.

11¶ "But My people did not listen to My voice;
And Israel did not obey Me.
12 "So I gave them over to the stubbornness of their heart,
To walk in their own devices.
13 "Oh that My people would listen to Me,
That Israel would walk in My ways!
14 "I would quickly subdue their enemies,
And turn My hand against their adversaries.
15 "Those who hate the LORD would pretend obedience to Him;
And their time *of punishment* would be forever.
16 "But I would feed you with the finest of the wheat;
And with honey from the rock I would satisfy you."

*Unjust Judgments Rebuked.*

A Psalm of Asaph.

**82** GOD TAKES His stand in His own congregation;
He judges in the midst of the rulers.
2 How long will you judge unjustly,
And show partiality to the wicked? Selah.
3 Vindicate the weak and fatherless;
Do justice to the afflicted and destitute.
4 Rescue the weak and needy;
Deliver *them* out of the hand of the wicked.

5¶ They do not know nor do they understand;
They walk about in darkness;
All the foundations of the earth are shaken.
6 I said, "You are gods,
And all of you are sons of the Most High.
7 "Nevertheless you will die like men,
And fall like *any* one of the princes."
8 Arise, O God, judge the earth!
For it is Thou who dost possess all the nations.

*God Implored to Confound His Enemies.*

A Song, a Psalm of Asaph.

**83** O GOD, do not remain quiet;
Do not be silent and, O God, do not be still.
2 For, behold, Thine enemies make an uproar;
And those who hate Thee have exalted themselves.
3 They make shrewd plans against Thy people,
And conspire together against Thy treasured ones.
4 They have said, "Come, and let us wipe them out as a nation,
That the name of Israel be remembered no more."
5 For they have conspired together with one mind;
Against Thee do they make a covenant:
6 The tents of Edom and the Ishmaelites;
Moab, and the Hagrites;
7 Gebal, and Ammon, and Amalek;
Philistia with the inhabitants of Tyre;
8 Assyria also has joined with them;
They have become a help to the children of Lot. Selah.

9¶ Deal with them as with Midian,
As with Sisera *and* Jabin, at the torrent of Kishon,
10 Who were destroyed at En-dor,
Who became as dung for the ground.
11 Make their nobles like Oreb and Zeeb,
And all their princes like Zebah and Zalmunna,

## New International

10I am the LORD your God,
who brought you up out of Egypt.
Open wide your mouth and I will fill it.

11"But my people would not listen to me;
Israel would not submit to me.
12So I gave them over to their stubborn hearts
to follow their own devices.

13"If my people would but listen to me,
if Israel would follow my ways,
14how quickly would I subdue their enemies
and turn my hand against their foes!
15Those who hate the LORD would cringe before him,
and their punishment would last forever.
16But you would be fed with the finest of wheat;
with honey from the rock I would satisfy you."

A psalm of Asaph.

**82** GOD PRESIDES in the great assembly;
he gives judgment among the "gods":
2"How long will you[a] defend the unjust
and show partiality to the wicked? *Selah*
3Defend the cause of the weak and fatherless;
maintain the rights of the poor and oppressed.
4Rescue the weak and needy;
deliver them from the hand of the wicked.

5"They know nothing, they understand nothing.
They walk about in darkness;
all the foundations of the earth are shaken.

6"I said, 'You are "gods";
you are all sons of the Most High.'
7But you will die like mere men;
you will fall like every other ruler."

8Rise up, O God, judge the earth,
for all the nations are your inheritance.

A song. A psalm of Asaph.

**83** O GOD, do not keep silent;
be not quiet, O God, be not still.
2See how your enemies are astir,
how your foes rear their heads.
3With cunning they conspire against your people;
they plot against those you cherish.
4"Come," they say, "let us destroy them as a nation,
that the name of Israel be remembered no more."

5With one mind they plot together;
they form an alliance against you—
6the tents of Edom and the Ishmaelites,
of Moab and the Hagrites,
7Gebal,[b] Ammon and Amalek,
Philistia, with the people of Tyre.
8Even Assyria has joined them
to lend strength to the descendants of Lot. *Selah*

9Do to them as you did to Midian,
as you did to Sisera and Jabin at the river Kishon,
10who perished at Endor
and became like refuse on the ground.
11Make their nobles like Oreb and Zeeb,
all their princes like Zebah and Zalmunna,

NIV [a] 2 The Hebrew is plural. [b] *7* That is, Byblos

## King James

12Who said, Let us take to ourselves the houses of God in
possession.
13O my God, make them like a wheel; as the stubble before the
wind.
14As the fire burneth a wood, and as the flame setteth the
mountains on fire;
15So persecute them with thy tempest, and make them afraid
with thy storm.
16Fill their faces with shame; that they may seek thy name, O
LORD.
17Let them be confounded and troubled for ever; yea, let them
be put to shame, and perish:
18That *men* may know that thou, whose name alone *is* JEHO-
VAH, *art* the most high over all the earth.

To the chief Musician upon Gittith, A Psalm for the sons of Korah.

**84** HOW AMIABLE *are* thy tabernacles, O LORD of hosts!
2My soul longeth, yea, even fainteth for the courts of the
LORD: my heart and my flesh crieth out for the living God.
3Yea, the sparrow hath found an house, and the swallow a nest
for herself, where she may lay her young, *even* thine altars, O LORD
of hosts, my King, and my God.
4Blessed *are* they that dwell in thy house: they will be still
praising thee. Selah.
5Blessed *is* the man whose strength *is* in thee; in whose heart
*are* the ways *of them*.
6 *Who* passing through the valley of Baca make it a well; the rain
also filleth the pools.
7They go from strength to strength, *every one of them* in Zion
appeareth before God.
8O LORD God of hosts, hear my prayer: give ear, O God of Jacob.
Selah.
9Behold, O God our shield, and look upon the face of thine
anointed.
10For a day in thy courts *is* better than a thousand. I had rather
be a doorkeeper in the house of my God, than to dwell in the tents
of wickedness.
11For the LORD God *is* a sun and shield: the LORD will give grace
and glory: no good *thing* will he withhold from them that walk
uprightly.
12O LORD of hosts, blessed *is* the man that trusteth in thee.

To the chief Musician, A Psalm for the sons of Korah.

**85** LORD, THOU hast been favourable unto thy land: thou
hast brought back the captivity of Jacob.
2Thou hast forgiven the iniquity of thy people, thou hast
covered all their sin. Selah.
3Thou hast taken away all thy wrath: thou hast turned *thyself*
from the fierceness of thine anger.

## Amplified

12Who say, Let us take possession for ourselves of the pastures
of God.
13O my God, make them like whirling dust, as stubble *or* chaff
before the wind!
14As fire consumes the forest, and as the flame sets the mountains ablaze,
15So pursue *and* afflict them with Your tempest and terrify them
with Your tornado *or* hurricane.
16Fill their faces with shame, that they may seek, inquire for *and*
insistently require Your name, O Lord.
17Let them be put to shame and dismayed for ever; yes, let them
be put to shame and perish,
18That they may know that You Whose name alone is the Lord,
are the Most High over all the earth.

To the Chief Musician;
set to a Philistine lute, or [ *possibly*] a particular Gittite tune. A Psalm of
the sons of Korah.

**84** HOW LOVELY are Your tabernacles, O Lord of hosts!
2My soul yearns, yes, even pines *and* is homesick for the
courts of the Lord; my heart and my flesh cry out *and* sing for joy
to the living God.
3Yes, the sparrow has found a house, and the swallow a nest
for herself, where she may lay her young, even Your altars, O Lord
of hosts, my King and my God.
4Blessed—happy, fortunate [to be envied]—are those who
dwell in Your house *and* Your presence; they will be singing Your
praises all the day long. Selah [pause, and calmly think of that].
5Blessed—happy, fortunate [to be envied]— *is* the man whose
strength is in You; in whose heart are the highways to Zion.
6Passing through the valley of weeping they make it a place of
springs; the early rain also fills [the pools] with blessings.
7They go from strength to strength—increasing in victorious
power; each of them appears before God in Zion.
8O Lord God of hosts, hear my prayer; give ear, O God of Jacob!
Selah [pause, and calmly think of that]!
9Behold our shield [the king as Your agent], O God, and look
upon the face of Your anointed!
10For a day in Your courts *is* better than a thousand [anywhere
else]; I had rather be a doorkeeper *and* stand at the threshold in the
house of my God than to dwell [at ease] in the tents of wickedness.
11For the Lord God is a sun and shield; the Lord bestows
[present] grace *and* favor and [future] glory—honor, splendor and
heavenly bliss! No good thing will He withhold from those who
walk uprightly.
12O Lord of hosts, blessed—happy, fortunate [to be envied]—is
the man who trusts in You, (leaning and believing on You, committing all and confidently looking to You, and that without fear
or misgiving)!

To the Chief Musician;
a Psalm of the sons of Korah.

**85** LORD, YOU have [at last] been favorable *and* have dealt
graciously with Your land [of Canaan]. You have brought
back [from Babylon] the captives of Jacob.
2You have forgiven *and* taken away the iniquity of Your people,
You have covered all their sin. Selah [pause, and calmly realize
what that means]!
3You have withdrawn all Your wrath *and* indignation; You have
turned away from the blazing anger [which You had let loose].

## New American Standard

12 Who said, "Let us possess for ourselves
The pastures of God."
13¶ O my God, make them like the [a]whirling dust;
Like chaff before the wind.
14 Like fire that burns the forest,
And like a flame that sets the mountains on fire,
15 So pursue them with Thy tempest,
And terrify them with Thy storm.
16 Fill their faces with dishonor,
That they may seek Thy name, O LORD.
17 Let them be ashamed and dismayed forever;
And let them be humiliated and perish,
18 That they may know that Thou alone, whose name is the LORD,
Art the Most High over all the earth.

*Longing for the Temple Worship.*

For the choir director; on the Gittith.
A Psalm of the sons of Korah.

**84** HOW LOVELY are Thy dwelling places,
O LORD of hosts!
2 My soul longed and even yearned for the courts of the LORD;
My heart and my flesh sing for joy to the living God.
3 The bird also has found a house,
And the swallow a nest for herself, where she may lay her young,
Even Thine altars, O LORD of hosts,
My King and my God.
4 How blessed are those who dwell in Thy house!
They are ever praising Thee. Selah.
5¶ How blessed is the man whose strength is in Thee;
In whose heart are the highways *to Zion*!
6 Passing through the valley of [b]Baca, they make it a spring,
The early rain also covers it with blessings.
7 They go from strength to strength,
*Every one of them* appears before God in Zion.
8¶ O LORD God of hosts, hear my prayer;
Give ear, O God of Jacob! Selah.
9 Behold our shield, O God,
And look upon the face of Thine anointed.
10 For a day in Thy courts is better than a thousand *outside*.
I would rather stand at the threshold of the house of my God,
Than dwell in the tents of wickedness.
11 For the LORD God is a sun and shield;
The LORD gives grace and glory;
No good thing does He withhold from those who walk uprightly.
12 O LORD of hosts,
How blessed is the man who trusts in Thee!

*Prayer for God's Mercy upon the Nation.*

For the choir director.
A Psalm of the sons of Korah.

**85** O LORD, Thou didst show favor to Thy land;
Thou didst [c]restore the captivity of Jacob.
2 Thou didst forgive the iniquity of Thy people;
Thou didst cover all their sin. Selah.
3 Thou didst withdraw all Thy fury;
Thou didst turn away from Thy burning anger.

NAS [a] Or, *tumbleweed* [b] Probably, *Weeping* or *Balsam trees* [c] Or, *restore the fortunes*

## New International

12who said, "Let us take possession
of the pasturelands of God."
13Make them like tumbleweed, O my God,
like chaff before the wind.
14As fire consumes the forest
or a flame sets the mountains ablaze,
15so pursue them with your tempest
and terrify them with your storm.
16Cover their faces with shame
so that men will seek your name, O LORD.
17May they ever be ashamed and dismayed;
may they perish in disgrace.
18Let them know that you, whose name is the LORD—
that you alone are the Most High over all the earth.

For the director of music. According to *gittith*.[d] Of the Sons of Korah.
A psalm.

**84** HOW LOVELY is your dwelling place,
O LORD Almighty!
2My soul yearns, even faints,
for the courts of the LORD;
my heart and my flesh cry out
for the living God.
3Even the sparrow has found a home,
and the swallow a nest for herself,
where she may have her young—
a place near your altar,
O LORD Almighty, my King and my God.
4Blessed are those who dwell in your house;
they are ever praising you. *Selah*
5Blessed are those whose strength is in you,
who have set their hearts on pilgrimage.
6As they pass through the Valley of Baca,
they make it a place of springs;
the autumn rains also cover it with pools.[e]
7They go from strength to strength,
till each appears before God in Zion.
8Hear my prayer, O LORD God Almighty;
listen to me, O God of Jacob. *Selah*
9Look upon our shield,[f] O God;
look with favor on your anointed one.
10Better is one day in your courts
than a thousand elsewhere;
I would rather be a doorkeeper in the house of my God
than dwell in the tents of the wicked.
11For the LORD God is a sun and shield;
the LORD bestows favor and honor;
no good thing does he withhold
from those whose walk is blameless.
12O LORD Almighty,
blessed is the man who trusts in you.

For the director of music. Of the Sons of Korah. A psalm.

**85** YOU SHOWED favor to your land, O LORD;
you restored the fortunes of Jacob.
2You forgave the iniquity of your people
and covered all their sins. *Selah*
3You set aside all your wrath
and turned from your fierce anger.

NIV [d] Title: Probably a musical term [e] 6 Or *blessings* [f] 9 Or *sovereign*

## King James

4 Turn us, O God of our salvation, and cause thine anger toward us to cease.

5 Wilt thou be angry with us for ever? wilt thou draw out thine anger to all generations?

6 Wilt thou not revive us again: that thy people may rejoice in thee?

7 Show us thy mercy, O LORD, and grant us thy salvation.

8 I will hear what God the LORD will speak: for he will speak peace unto his people, and to his saints: but let them not turn again to folly.

9 Surely his salvation *is* nigh them that fear him; that glory may dwell in our land.

10 Mercy and truth are met together; righteousness and peace have kissed *each other*.

11 Truth shall spring out of the earth; and righteousness shall look down from heaven.

12 Yea, the LORD shall give *that which is* good; and our land shall yield her increase.

13 Righteousness shall go before him; and shall set *us* in the way of his steps.

A Prayer of David.

**86** BOW DOWN thine ear, O LORD, hear me: for I *am* poor and needy.

2 Preserve my soul; for I *am* holy: O thou my God, save thy servant that trusteth in thee.

3 Be merciful unto me, O Lord: for I cry unto thee daily.

4 Rejoice the soul of thy servant: for unto thee, O Lord, do I lift up my soul.

5 For thou, Lord, *art* good, and ready to forgive; and plenteous in mercy unto all them that call upon thee.

6 Give ear, O LORD, unto my prayer; and attend to the voice of my supplications.

7 In the day of my trouble I will call upon thee: for thou wilt answer me.

8 Among the gods *there is* none like unto thee, O Lord; neither *are there any works* like unto thy works.

9 All nations whom thou hast made shall come and worship before thee, O Lord; and shall glorify thy name.

10 For thou *art* great, and doest wondrous things: thou *art* God alone.

11 Teach me thy way, O LORD; I will walk in thy truth: unite my heart to fear thy name.

12 I will praise thee, O Lord my God, with all my heart: and I will glorify thy name for evermore.

13 For great *is* thy mercy toward me: and thou hast delivered my soul from the lowest hell.

14 O God, the proud are risen against me, and the assemblies of violent *men* have sought after my soul; and have not set thee before them.

15 But thou, O Lord, *art* a God full of compassion, and gracious, longsuffering, and plenteous in mercy and truth.

## Amplified

4 Restore us, O God of our salvation, and cause Your anger toward us to cease [for ever].

5 Will You be angry with us for ever? Will You prolong Your anger [and disfavor] *and* spread it out to all generations?

6 Will You not revive us again that Your people may rejoice in You?

7 Show Your mercy *and* loving-kindness, O Lord, and grant us Your salvation.

8 I will listen [with expectancy] to what God the Lord will say, for He will speak peace to His people, to His saints [those who are in right standing with Him]; but let them not turn again to [self-confident] folly.

9 Surely His salvation is near to those who reverently *and* worshipfully fear Him, *and* [is ready to be appropriated] that [the manifest presence of God, His] glory may tabernacle *and* abide in our land.

10 Mercy *and* loving-kindness and truth are met together; righteousness and peace have kissed each other.

11 Truth shall spring up from the earth, and righteousness shall look down from Heaven.

12 Yes, the Lord will give what is good, and our land will yield its increase.

13 Righteousness shall go before Him, and will make His footsteps a way in which to walk.

A Prayer of David.

**86** INCLINE YOUR ear, O Lord, and answer me, for I am poor *and* distressed, needy *and* desiring.

2 Preserve my life, for I am godly *and* dedicated; O my God, save Your servant for I trust in You (leaning and believing on You, committing all and confidently looking to You, without fear or doubt).

3 Be merciful *and* gracious to me, O Lord, for to You do I cry all the day.

4 Make me, Your servant, to rejoice, O Lord, for to You do I lift myself up.

5 For You, O Lord, are good, and ready to forgive [our trespasses]—sending them away, letting them go completely and for ever; and You are abundant in mercy *and* loving-kindness to all those who call upon You.

6 Give ear, O Lord, to my prayer, and listen to the cry of my supplications.

7 In the day of my trouble I will call on You, for You will answer me.

8 None like unto You are among the gods, O Lord, neither are their works like unto Yours.

9 All nations whom You have made shall come and fall down before You, O Lord, and they shall glorify Your name.

10 For You are great and work wonders! You alone are God.

11 Teach me Your way, O Lord, that I may walk *and* live in Your truth; direct *and* unite my heart [solely, reverently] to fear *and* honor Your name. [Pss. 5:11; 69:36.]

12 I will confess *and* praise You, O Lord my God, with my whole (united) heart; and I will glorify Your name for evermore.

13 For great is Your mercy *and* loving-kindness toward me, and You have delivered me from the depths of Sheol [from exceeding depth of affliction].

14 O God, the proud *and* insolent are risen against me; the rabble of violent *and* ruthless men have sought after *and* demanded my life, and have not set You before them.

15 But You, O Lord, are a God merciful and gracious, slow to anger and abounding in mercy *and* loving-kindness and truth.

## New American Standard

4¶ Restore us, O God of our salvation,
And cause Thine indignation toward us to cease.
5 Wilt Thou be angry with us forever?
Wilt Thou prolong Thine anger to all generations?
6 Wilt Thou not Thyself revive us again,
That Thy people may rejoice in Thee?
7 Show us Thy lovingkindness, O LORD,
And grant us Thy salvation.

8¶ I will hear what God the LORD will say;
For He will speak peace to His people, to His godly ones;
But let them not turn back to folly.
9 Surely His salvation is near to those who [a]fear Him,
That glory may dwell in our land.
10 Lovingkindness and truth have met together;
Righteousness and peace have kissed each other.
11 Truth springs from the earth;
And righteousness looks down from heaven.
12 Indeed, the LORD will give what is good;
And our land will yield its produce.
13 Righteousness will go before Him,
And will make His footsteps into a way.

*A Psalm of Supplication and Trust.*

A Prayer of David.

86 INCLINE THINE ear, O LORD, *and* answer me;
For I am afflicted and needy.
2 Do preserve my soul, for I am a godly man;
O Thou my God, save Thy servant who trusts in Thee.
3 Be gracious to me, O Lord,
For to Thee I cry all day long.
4 Make glad the soul of Thy servant,
For to Thee, O Lord, I lift up my soul.
5 For Thou, Lord, art good, and ready to forgive,
And abundant in lovingkindness to all who call upon Thee.
6 Give ear, O LORD, to my prayer;
And give heed to the voice of my supplications!
7 In the day of my trouble I shall call upon Thee,
For Thou wilt answer me.
8 There is no one like Thee among the gods, O Lord;
Nor are there any works like Thine.
9 All nations whom Thou hast made shall come and worship before Thee, O Lord;
And they shall glorify Thy name.
10 For Thou art great and doest wondrous deeds;
Thou alone art God.
11¶ Teach me Thy way, O LORD;
I will walk in Thy truth;
Unite my heart to fear Thy name.
12 I will give thanks to Thee, O Lord my God, with all my heart,
And will glorify Thy name forever.
13 For Thy lovingkindness toward me is great,
And Thou hast delivered my soul from the depths of Sheol.

14¶ O God, arrogant men have risen up against me,
And a band of violent men have sought my life,
And they have not set Thee before them.
15 But Thou, O Lord, art a God merciful and gracious,
Slow to anger and abundant in lovingkindness and truth.

NAS [a] Or, *reverence*

## New International

4Restore us again, O God our Savior,
and put away your displeasure toward us.
5Will you be angry with us forever?
Will you prolong your anger through all generations?
6Will you not revive us again,
that your people may rejoice in you?
7Show us your unfailing love, O LORD,
and grant us your salvation.

8I will listen to what God the LORD will say;
he promises peace to his people, his saints—
but let them not return to folly.
9Surely his salvation is near those who fear him,
that his glory may dwell in our land.

10Love and faithfulness meet together;
righteousness and peace kiss each other.
11Faithfulness springs forth from the earth,
and righteousness looks down from heaven.
12The LORD will indeed give what is good,
and our land will yield its harvest.
13Righteousness goes before him
and prepares the way for his steps.

A prayer of David.

86 HEAR, O LORD, and answer me,
for I am poor and needy.
2Guard my life, for I am devoted to you.
You are my God; save your servant
who trusts in you.
3Have mercy on me, O Lord,
for I call to you all day long.
4Bring joy to your servant,
for to you, O Lord,
I lift up my soul.

5You are forgiving and good, O Lord,
abounding in love to all who call to you.
6Hear my prayer, O LORD;
listen to my cry for mercy.
7In the day of my trouble I will call to you,
for you will answer me.

8Among the gods there is none like you, O Lord;
no deeds can compare with yours.
9All the nations you have made
will come and worship before you, O Lord;
they will bring glory to your name.
10For you are great and do marvelous deeds;
you alone are God.

11Teach me your way, O LORD,
and I will walk in your truth;
give me an undivided heart,
that I may fear your name.
12I will praise you, O Lord my God, with all my heart;
I will glorify your name forever.
13For great is your love toward me;
you have delivered me from the depths of the grave.[b]

14The arrogant are attacking me, O God;
a band of ruthless men seeks my life—
men without regard for you.
15But you, O Lord, are a compassionate and gracious God,
slow to anger, abounding in love and faithfulness.

NIV [b] *13* Hebrew *Sheol*

## King James

16O turn unto me, and have mercy upon me; give thy strength unto thy servant, and save the son of thine handmaid.
17Show me a token for good; that they which hate me may see *it*, and be ashamed: because thou, LORD, hast helped me, and comforted me.

A Psalm *or* Song for the sons of Korah.

87 HIS FOUNDATION *is* in the holy mountains.
2The LORD loveth the gates of Zion more than all the dwellings of Jacob.
3Glorious things are spoken of thee, O city of God. Selah.
4I will make mention of Rahab and Babylon to them that know me: behold Philistia, and Tyre, with Ethiopia; this *man* was born there.
5And of Zion it shall be said, This and that man was born in her: and the highest himself shall establish her.
6The LORD shall count, when he writeth up the people, *that* this *man* was born there. Selah.
7As well the singers as the players on instruments *shall be there:* all my springs *are* in thee.

A Song *or* Psalm for the sons of Korah, to the chief Musician upon Mahalath Leannoth, Maschil of Heman the Ezrahite.

88 O LORD God of my salvation, I have cried day *and* night before thee:
2Let my prayer come before thee: incline thine ear unto my cry;
3For my soul is full of troubles: and my life draweth nigh unto the grave.
4I am counted with them that go down into the pit: I am as a man *that hath* no strength:
5Free among the dead, like the slain that lie in the grave, whom thou rememberest no more: and they are cut off from thy hand.
6Thou hast laid me in the lowest pit, in darkness, in the deeps.
7Thy wrath lieth hard upon me, and thou hast afflicted *me* with all thy waves. Selah.
8Thou hast put away mine acquaintance far from me; thou hast made me an abomination unto them: *I am* shut up, and I cannot come forth.
9Mine eye mourneth by reason of affliction: LORD, I have called daily upon thee, I have stretched out my hands unto thee.
10Wilt thou show wonders to the dead? shall the dead arise *and* praise thee? Selah.
11Shall thy lovingkindness be declared in the grave? *or* thy faithfulness in destruction?
12Shall thy wonders be known in the dark? and thy righteousness in the land of forgetfulness?

## Amplified

16O turn to me, and have mercy *and* be gracious to me; grant strength—might and inflexibility [to temptation]—to Your servant, and save the son of Your handmaiden.
17Show me a sign of [Your evident] goodwill *and* favor, that those who hate me may see it and be put to shame because You, Lord, [will show Your approval of me when You] help and comfort me.

A Psalm of the sons of Korah; a song.

87 ON THE holy hills stands the city [of Jerusalem and the temple] God founded.
2The Lord loves the gates of Zion [through which the crowds of pilgrims enter from all nations] more than all the dwellings of Jacob [Israel].
3Glorious things are spoken of you, O city of God. Selah [pause, and calmly think what that means].
4I will make mention of Rahab [the poetic name for Egypt] and Babylon as among those who know [the city of God]; behold, Philistia and Tyre, with Ethiopia (Cush), *say,* This man was born there.
5Yes, of Zion it shall be said, This and that man *were* born in her; for the Most High Himself will establish her.
6The Lord shall count, when He registers the peoples, that this man was born there. Selah [pause, and calmly think of that].
7As well the singers as the players on instruments shall say, All my springs—my sources of life and joy—are in you [city of our God].

A song, a Psalm of the sons of Korah; to the Chief Musician; set to chant mournfully. A didactic or reflective poem of Heman the Ezrahite.

88 O LORD, the God of my salvation, I have cried to You for help by day; at night I am in Your presence. [Luke 18:7.]
2Let my prayer come before You *and* [really] enter into Your presence; incline Your ear to my cry!
3For I am full of troubles, and my life draws near to (Sheol) the place of the dead.
4I am counted among those who go down into the pit (the grave); I am as a man who has no help *or* strength—a mere shadow;
5Cast away among the dead, like the slain that lie in a [nameless] grave, whom You [seriously] remember no more, and they are cut off from Your hand.
6You have laid me in the depths of the lowest pit, in darkness, in the deeps.
7Your wrath lies hard upon me, and You have afflicted me with all Your waves. [Ps. 42:7.] Selah [pause, and calmly think of that].
8You have put my (familiar) friends far from me; You have made me an abomination to them. I am shut up, and I cannot come forth.
9My eye grows dim because of sorrow *and* affliction. Lord, I have called daily on You, I have spread forth my hands to You.
10Will You show wonders to the dead? Shall the departed arise and praise You? Selah [pause, and calmly think of that].
11Shall Your steadfast love be declared in the grave? Or Your faithfulness in Abaddon (Sheol, as a place of ruin and destruction)?
12Shall Your wonders be known in the dark? And Your righteousness in the place of forgetfulness—where the dead forget and are forgotten?

## New American Standard

16 Turn to me, and be gracious to me;
Oh grant Thy strength to Thy servant,
And save the son of Thy handmaid.
17 Show me a sign for good,
That those who hate me may see *it*, and be ashamed,
Because Thou, O LORD, hast helped me and comforted me.

*The Privileges of Citizenship in Zion.*

A Psalm of the sons of Korah. A Song.

87 HIS FOUNDATION is in the holy mountains.
2 The LORD loves the gates of Zion
More than all the *other* dwelling places of Jacob.
3 Glorious things are spoken of you,
O city of God. Selah.
4 "I shall mention [a]Rahab and Babylon among those who know Me;
Behold, Philistia and Tyre with Ethiopia:
'This one was born there.' "
5 But of Zion it shall be said, "This one and that one were born in her";
And the Most High Himself will establish her.
6 The LORD shall count when He registers the peoples,
"This one was born there." Selah.
7 Then those who sing as well as those who play the flutes *shall say*,
"All my springs *of joy* are in you."

*A Petition to Be Saved from Death.*

A Song.
A Psalm of the sons of Korah.
For the choir director; according to Mahalath Leannoth.
A Maskil of Heman the Ezrahite.

88 O LORD, the God of my salvation,
I have cried out by day and in the night before Thee.
2 Let my prayer come before Thee;
Incline Thine ear to my cry!
3 For my soul has had enough troubles,
And my life has drawn near to Sheol.
4 I am reckoned among those who go down to the pit;
I have become like a man without strength,
5 Forsaken among the dead,
Like the slain who lie in the grave,
Whom Thou dost remember no more,
And they are cut off from Thy hand.
6 Thou hast put me in the lowest pit,
In dark places, in the depths.
7 Thy wrath has rested upon me,
And Thou hast afflicted me with all Thy waves. Selah.
8 Thou hast removed my acquaintances far from me;
Thou hast made me an [b]object of loathing to them;
I am shut up and cannot go out.
9 My eye has wasted away because of affliction;
I have called upon Thee every day, O LORD;
I have spread out my hands to Thee.

10¶ Wilt Thou perform wonders for the dead?
Will the departed spirits rise *and* praise Thee? Selah.
11 Will Thy lovingkindness be declared in the grave,
Thy faithfulness in Abaddon?
12 Will Thy wonders be made known in the darkness?
And Thy righteousness in the land of forgetfulness?

NAS [a] I.e., Egypt [b] Lit., *abomination to them*

## New International

16Turn to me and have mercy on me;
grant your strength to your servant
and save the son of your maidservant.[c]
17Give me a sign of your goodness,
that my enemies may see it and be put to shame,
for you, O LORD, have helped me and comforted me.

Of the Sons of Korah. A psalm. A song.

87 HE HAS set his foundation on the holy mountain;
2 the LORD loves the gates of Zion
more than all the dwellings of Jacob.
3Glorious things are said of you,
O city of God: *Selah*
4"I will record Rahab[d] and Babylon
among those who acknowledge me—
Philistia too, and Tyre, along with Cush[e] —
and will say, 'This[f] one was born in Zion.' "
5Indeed, of Zion it will be said,
"This one and that one were born in her,
and the Most High himself will establish her."
6The LORD will write in the register of the peoples:
"This one was born in Zion." *Selah*
7As they make music they will sing,
"All my fountains are in you."

A song. A psalm of the Sons of Korah. For the director of music. According to *mahalath leannoth*.[g] A *maskil*[h] of Heman the Ezrahite.

88 O LORD, the God who saves me,
day and night I cry out before you.
2May my prayer come before you;
turn your ear to my cry.
3For my soul is full of trouble
and my life draws near the grave.[i]
4I am counted among those who go down to the pit;
I am like a man without strength.
5I am set apart with the dead,
like the slain who lie in the grave,
whom you remember no more,
who are cut off from your care.
6You have put me in the lowest pit,
in the darkest depths.
7Your wrath lies heavily upon me;
you have overwhelmed me with all your waves. *Selah*
8You have taken from me my closest friends
and have made me repulsive to them.
I am confined and cannot escape;
9 my eyes are dim with grief.
I call to you, O LORD, every day;
I spread out my hands to you.
10Do you show your wonders to the dead?
Do those who are dead rise up and praise you? *Selah*
11Is your love declared in the grave,
your faithfulness in Destruction[j] ?
12Are your wonders known in the place of darkness,
or your righteous deeds in the land of oblivion?

NIV [c] 16 Or *save your faithful son* [d] 4 A poetic name for Egypt [e] 4 That is, the upper Nile region [f] 4 Or *"O Rahab and Babylon, / Philistia, Tyre and Cush, / I will record concerning those who acknowledge me: / 'This* [g] Title: Possibly a tune, "The Suffering of Affliction" [h] Title: Probably a literary or musical term [i] 3 Hebrew *Sheol* [j] 11 Hebrew *Abaddon*

## King James

13But unto thee have I cried, O LORD; and in the morning shall
my prayer prevent thee.
14LORD, why castest thou off my soul? *why* hidest thou thy face
from me?
15I *am* afflicted and ready to die from *my* youth up: *while* I suffer
thy terrors I am distracted.
16Thy fierce wrath goeth over me; thy terrors have cut me off.
17They came round about me daily like water; they compassed
me about together.
18Lover and friend hast thou put far from me, *and* mine acquaintance into darkness.

Maschil of Ethan the Ezrahite.

**89** I WILL sing of the mercies of the LORD for ever: with my
mouth will I make known thy faithfulness to all generations.
2For I have said, Mercy shall be built up for ever: thy faithfulness shalt thou establish in the very heavens.
3I have made a covenant with my chosen, I have sworn unto
David my servant,
4Thy seed will I establish for ever, and build up thy throne to
all generations. Selah.
5And the heavens shall praise thy wonders, O LORD: thy faithfulness also in the congregation of the saints.
6For who in the heaven can be compared unto the LORD? *who*
among the sons of the mighty can be likened unto the LORD?
7God is greatly to be feared in the assembly of the saints, and
to be had in reverence of all *them that are* about him.
8O LORD God of hosts, who *is* a strong LORD like unto thee? or
to thy faithfulness round about thee?
9Thou rulest the raging of the sea: when the waves thereof
arise, thou stillest them.
10Thou hast broken Rahab in pieces, as one that is slain; thou
hast scattered thine enemies with thy strong arm.
11The heavens *are* thine, the earth also *is* thine: *as for* the world
and the fulness thereof, thou hast founded them.
12The north and the south thou hast created them: Tabor and
Hermon shall rejoice in thy name.
13Thou hast a mighty arm: strong is thy hand, *and* high is thy
right hand.
14Justice and judgment *are* the habitation of thy throne: mercy
and truth shall go before thy face.
15Blessed *is* the people that know the joyful sound: they shall
walk, O LORD, in the light of thy countenance.
16In thy name shall they rejoice all the day: and in thy righteousness shall they be exalted.
17For thou *art* the glory of their strength: and in thy favour our
horn shall be exalted.
18For the LORD *is* our defence; and the Holy One of Israel *is* our
king.
19Then thou spakest in vision to thy holy one, and saidst, I have
laid help upon *one that is* mighty; I have exalted *one* chosen out of
the people.
20I have found David my servant; with my holy oil have I
anointed him:

## Amplified

13But to You I cry, O Lord; and in the morning shall my prayer
come to meet You.
14Lord, why do You cast me off? Why do You hide Your face
from me? [Matt. 27:46.]
15I am afflicted and close to death from my youth up; while I
suffer Your terrors I am distracted—I faint.
16Your fierce wrath has swept over me; Your terrors destroy me.
17They surround me like a flood all day long; together they close
in upon me.
18Lover and friend have You put far from me; my familiar
friends are darkness *and* the grave.

A skillful song *or* a didactic *or* reflective poem of Ethan the Ezrahite.

**89** I WILL sing of the mercies *and* loving-kindness of the Lord
for ever; with my mouth will I make known Your faithfulness from generation to generation.
2For I have said, Mercy *and* loving-kindness shall be built up for
ever; Your faithfulness will You establish in the very heavens
[unchangeable and perpetual].
3[You have said] I have made a [a]covenant with My chosen one,
I have sworn to David My servant,
4Your Seed I will establish forever, and build up your throne
for all generations. Selah [pause, and calmly think of that]! [Gal.
3:16; Isa. 9:7; Luke 1:32, 33.]
5Let heaven [the angels] praise Your wonders, O Lord, Your
faithfulness also in the assembly of the holy ones [the holy angels].
6For who in the heavens can be compared to the Lord? Who
among the mighty [heavenly beings] can be likened to the Lord,
7A God greatly feared *and* revered in the council of the holy
[angelic] ones, and to be feared *and* worshipfully revered above all
those who are round about Him?
8O Lord God of hosts, who is a mighty one like unto You O
Lord? And Your faithfulness is round about You [an essential part
of You at all times].
9You rule the raging of the sea; when the waves of it arise, You
still them.
10You have broken Rahab (Egypt) in pieces; with Your mighty
arm You have scattered Your enemies.
11The heavens are Yours, the earth also is Yours; the world and
all that is in it, You have founded them.
12The north and the south, You have created them; Mount
Tabor and Mount Hermon joyously praise Your name.
13You have a mighty arm; strong is Your hand; Your right hand
is soaring high.
14Righteousness and justice are the foundation of Your throne;
mercy *and* loving-kindness and truth go before Your face.
15Blessed—happy, fortunate [to be envied]—are the people
who know the joyful sound [who understand and appreciate the
spiritual blessings symbolized by the feasts]; they walk, O Lord,
in the light *and* favor of Your countenance!
16In Your name they rejoice all the day, and in Your righteousness they are exalted.
17For You are the glory of their strength [their proud adornment], and by Your favor our horn is exalted *and* we walk with
uplifted faces!
18For our shield belongs to the Lord, and our king to the Holy
One of Israel.
19Once You spoke in a vision to Your devoted one and said, I
have endowed one who is mighty [a hero, giving him the power
to help—to be a champion for Israel]; I have exalted one chosen
from among the people.
20I have found David, My servant; with My holy oil have I
anointed him; [Acts 13:22.]

**AMP** [a] "This covenant most incontestably had Jesus Christ in view. This is the *Seed*, or Posterity, that should sit on the throne, and reign for ever and ever. David and his family are long since become extinct; none of his race has sat on the Jewish throne for more than *two thousand* years: but the Christ . . . will reign until all His enemies are put under His feet; and to this the Psalmist says, Selah." (One of many similar 19th century comments.)

## New American Standard

13¶ But I, O LORD, have cried out to Thee for help,
And in the morning my prayer comes before Thee.
14 O LORD, why dost Thou reject my soul?
*Why* dost Thou hide Thy face from me?
15 I was afflicted and about to die from my youth on;
I suffer Thy terrors; I am overcome.
16 Thy burning anger has passed over me;
Thy terrors have destroyed me.
17 They have surrounded me like water all day long;
They have encompassed me altogether.
18 Thou hast removed lover and friend far from me;
My acquaintances are *in* darkness.

*The LORD's Covenant with David, and Israel's Afflictions.*

A Maskil of Ethan the Ezrahite.

**89** I WILL sing of the lovingkindness of the LORD forever;
To all generations I will make known Thy faithfulness
with my mouth.
2 For I have said, "Lovingkindness will be built up
forever;
In the heavens Thou wilt establish Thy faithfulness."
3 "I have made a covenant with My chosen;
I have sworn to David My servant,
4 I will establish your seed forever,
And build up your throne to all generations." Selah.
5¶ And the heavens will praise Thy wonders, O LORD;
Thy faithfulness also in the assembly of the holy ones.
6 For who in the skies is comparable to the LORD?
Who among the sons of the mighty is like the LORD,
7 A God greatly feared in the council of the holy ones,
And awesome above all those who are around Him?
8 O LORD God of hosts, who is like Thee, O mighty
LORD?
Thy faithfulness also surrounds Thee.
9 Thou dost rule the swelling of the sea;
When its waves rise, Thou dost still them.
10 Thou Thyself didst crush Rahab like one who is slain;
Thou didst scatter Thine enemies with Thy mighty arm.
11¶ The heavens are Thine, the earth also is Thine;
The world and [b]all it contains, Thou hast founded
them.
12 The north and the south, Thou hast created them;
Tabor and Hermon shout for joy at Thy name.
13 Thou hast a strong arm;
Thy hand is mighty, Thy right hand is exalted.
14 Righteousness and justice are the foundation of Thy
throne;
Lovingkindness and truth go before Thee.
15 How blessed are the people who know the [c]joyful
sound!
O LORD, they walk in the light of Thy countenance.
16 In Thy name they rejoice all the day,
And by Thy righteousness they are exalted.
17 For Thou art the glory of their strength,
And by Thy favor our horn is exalted.
18 For our shield belongs to the LORD,
[d]And our king to the Holy One of Israel.
19¶ Once Thou didst speak in vision to Thy godly ones,
And didst say, "I have given help to one who is
mighty;
I have exalted one chosen from the people.
20 "I have found David My servant;
With My holy oil I have anointed him,

NAS [b] Lit., *its fulness* [c] Or, *blast of the trumpet, shout of joy* [d] Or, *Even to the Holy One of Israel our King*

## New International

13But I cry to you for help, O LORD;
in the morning my prayer comes before you.
14Why, O LORD, do you reject me
and hide your face from me?

15From my youth I have been afflicted and close to death;
I have suffered your terrors and am in despair.
16Your wrath has swept over me;
your terrors have destroyed me.
17All day long they surround me like a flood;
they have completely engulfed me.
18You have taken my companions and loved ones from me;
the darkness is my closest friend.

A *maskil*[e] of Ethan the Ezrahite.

**89** I WILL sing of the LORD's great love forever;
with my mouth I will make your faithfulness known
through all generations.
2I will declare that your love stands firm forever,
that you established your faithfulness in heaven itself.

3You said, "I have made a covenant with my chosen one,
I have sworn to David my servant,
4'I will establish your line forever
and make your throne firm through all generations.'"
*Selah*

5The heavens praise your wonders, O LORD,
your faithfulness too, in the assembly of the holy ones.
6For who in the skies above can compare with the LORD?
Who is like the LORD among the heavenly beings?
7In the council of the holy ones God is greatly feared;
he is more awesome than all who surround him.
8O LORD God Almighty, who is like you?
You are mighty, O LORD, and your faithfulness
surrounds you.

9You rule over the surging sea;
when its waves mount up, you still them.
10You crushed Rahab like one of the slain;
with your strong arm you scattered your enemies.
11The heavens are yours, and yours also the earth;
you founded the world and all that is in it.
12You created the north and the south;
Tabor and Hermon sing for joy at your name.
13Your arm is endued with power;
your hand is strong, your right hand exalted.

14Righteousness and justice are the foundation of your
throne;
love and faithfulness go before you.
15Blessed are those who have learned to acclaim you,
who walk in the light of your presence, O LORD.
16They rejoice in your name all day long;
they exult in your righteousness.
17For you are their glory and strength,
and by your favor you exalt our horn.[f]
18Indeed, our shield[g] belongs to the LORD,
our king to the Holy One of Israel.

19Once you spoke in a vision,
to your faithful people you said:
"I have bestowed strength on a warrior;
I have exalted a young man from among the people.
20I have found David my servant;
with my sacred oil I have anointed him.

NIV [e] Title: Probably a literary or musical term [f] *17 Horn* here symbolizes strong one. [g] *18* Or *sovereign*

## King James

21With whom my hand shall be established: mine arm also shall strengthen him.

22The enemy shall not exact upon him; nor the son of wickedness afflict him.

23And I will beat down his foes before his face, and plague them that hate him.

24But my faithfulness and my mercy *shall be* with him: and in my name shall his horn be exalted.

25I will set his hand also in the sea, and his right hand in the rivers.

26He shall cry unto me, Thou *art* my father, my God, and the rock of my salvation.

27Also I will make him *my* firstborn, higher than the kings of the earth.

28My mercy will I keep for him for evermore, and my covenant shall stand fast with him.

29His seed also will I make *to endure* for ever, and his throne as the days of heaven.

30If his children forsake my law, and walk not in my judgments;

31If they break my statutes, and keep not my commandments;

32Then will I visit their transgression with the rod, and their iniquity with stripes.

33Nevertheless my lovingkindness will I not utterly take from him, nor suffer my faithfulness to fail.

34My covenant will I not break, nor alter the thing that is gone out of my lips.

35Once have I sworn by my holiness that I will not lie unto David.

36His seed shall endure for ever, and his throne as the sun before me.

37It shall be established for ever as the moon, and *as* a faithful witness in heaven. Selah.

38But thou hast cast off and abhorred, thou hast been wroth with thine anointed.

39Thou hast made void the covenant of thy servant: thou hast profaned his crown *by casting it* to the ground.

40Thou hast broken down all his hedges; thou hast brought his strong holds to ruin.

41All that pass by the way spoil him: he is a reproach to his neighbours.

42Thou hast set up the right hand of his adversaries; thou hast made all his enemies to rejoice.

43Thou hast also turned the edge of his sword, and hast not made him to stand in the battle.

44Thou hast made his glory to cease, and cast his throne down to the ground.

45The days of his youth hast thou shortened: thou hast covered him with shame. Selah.

46How long, LORD? wilt thou hide thyself for ever? shall thy wrath burn like fire?

47Remember how short my time is: wherefore hast thou made all men in vain?

48What man *is he that* liveth, and shall not see death? shall he deliver his soul from the hand of the grave? Selah.

49Lord, where *are* thy former lovingkindnesses, *which* thou swarest unto David in thy truth?

50Remember, Lord, the reproach of thy servants; *how* I do bear in my bosom *the reproach of* all the mighty people;

## Amplified

21With whom My hand shall be established *and* ever abide, My arm also shall strengthen him.

22The enemy shall not exact from him *or* do him violence *or* outwit him, or the wicked afflict *and* humble him.

23I will beat down his foes before his face, and smite those who hate him.

24My faithfulness and My mercy *and* loving-kindness shall be with him, and in My name shall his horn be exalted [great power and prosperity shall be conferred upon him].

25I will set his hand in control also on the [Mediterranean] Sea and his right hand on the rivers [Euphrates with its tributaries].

26He shall cry to Me, You are my Father, my God, and the rock of my salvation!

27Also I will make him the first-born, highest of the kings of the earth. [Rev. 1:5.]

28My mercy *and* loving-kindness will I keep for him for evermore, and My covenant shall stand fast *and* be faithful with him.

29His offspring also will I make to endure for ever, and his throne as the days of heaven. [Gal. 3:16; Isa. 9:7.]

30If his children forsake My law, and walk not in My ordinances;

31If they break *or* profane My statutes and keep not My commandments,

32Then will I punish their transgression with the rod [of chastisement], and their iniquity with stripes. [II Sam. 7:14.]

33Nevertheless My loving-kindness will I not break off from him, nor allow My faithfulness to fail [to lie and be false to him].

34My covenant will I not break *or* profane, nor alter the thing that is gone out of My lips.

35Once [for all] have I sworn by My holiness that cannot be violated, I will not lie to David:

36His offspring shall endure for ever, and His throne [shall continue] as the sun before Me. [Gal. 3:16; Isa. 9:7.]

37It shall be established for ever as the moon, the faithful witness in the heavens. Selah [pause, and calmly think of that]. [Rev. 1:5; 3:14.]

38But [in apparent contradiction to all this] You [even You the faithful Lord] have cast off and rejected, You have been full of wrath against Your anointed.

39You have despised *and* loathed and renounced the covenant with Your servant; You have profaned his crown by casting it to the ground.

40You have broken down all his hedges *and* his walls; You have brought his strongholds to ruin.

41All that pass along the road spoil *and* rob him, he has become the scorn *and* reproach of his neighbors.

42You have exalted the right hand of his foes; You have made all his enemies rejoice.

43Moreover, You have turned back the edge of his sword, and have not made him to stand in battle.

44You have made his glory *and* splendor to cease, and have hurled to the ground his throne.

45The days of his youth have You shortened; You have covered him with shame. Selah [pause, and calmly think of that].

46How long, O Lord? Will You hide Yourself for ever? How long shall Your wrath burn like fire?

47O [earnestly] remember how short my time is, *and* what a mere fleeting life mine is, for what emptiness, falsity, futility *and* frailty You have created all men!

48What man can live and shall not see death, can deliver himself from the [powerful] hand of Sheol [the place of the dead]? Selah [pause, and calmly consider that].

49Lord, where are Your former loving-kindnesses [shown in the reigns of David and Solomon], which You swore to David in Your faithfulness?

50Remember, Lord, *and* earnestly imprint [on Your heart] the reproach of Your servants, scorned *and* insulted; how I bear in my bosom the reproach of all the many *and* mighty peoples,

## New American Standard

21 With whom My hand will be established;
My arm also will strengthen him.
22 "The enemy will not [a]deceive him,
Nor the son of wickedness afflict him.
23 "But I shall crush his adversaries before him,
And strike those who hate him.
24 "And My faithfulness and My lovingkindness will be with him,
And in My name his horn will be exalted.
25 "I shall also set his hand on the sea,
And his right hand on the rivers.
26 "He will cry to Me, 'Thou art my Father,
My God, and the rock of my salvation.'
27 "I also shall make him *My* first-born,
The highest of the kings of the earth.
28 "My lovingkindness I will keep for him forever,
And My covenant shall be confirmed to him.
29 "So I will establish his descendants forever,
And his throne as the days of heaven.

**30**¶ "If his sons forsake My law,
And do not walk in My judgments,
31 If they [b]violate My statutes,
And do not keep My commandments,
32 Then I will visit their transgression with the rod,
And their iniquity with stripes.
33 "But I will not break off My lovingkindness from him,
Nor deal falsely in My faithfulness.
34 "My covenant I will not violate,
Nor will I alter the utterance of My lips.
35 " [c]Once I have sworn by My holiness;
I will not lie to David.
36 "His descendants shall endure forever,
And his throne as the sun before Me.
37 "It shall be established forever like the moon,
And the witness in the sky is faithful." Selah.

**38**¶ But Thou hast cast off and rejected,
Thou hast been full of wrath against Thine anointed.
39 Thou hast spurned the covenant of Thy servant;
Thou hast profaned his crown in the dust.
40 Thou hast broken down all his walls;
Thou hast brought his strongholds to ruin.
41 All who pass along the way plunder him;
He has become a reproach to his neighbors.
42 Thou hast exalted the right hand of his adversaries;
Thou hast made all his enemies rejoice.
43 Thou dost also turn back the edge of his sword,
And hast not made him stand in battle.
44 Thou hast made his splendor to cease,
And cast his throne to the ground.
45 Thou hast shortened the days of his youth;
Thou hast covered him with shame. Selah.

**46**¶ How long, O LORD?
Wilt Thou hide Thyself forever?
Will Thy wrath burn like fire?
47 Remember what my span of life is;
For what vanity Thou hast created all the sons of men!
48 What man can live and not see death?
Can he deliver his soul from the power of Sheol? Selah.

**49**¶ Where are Thy former lovingkindnesses, O Lord,
Which Thou didst swear to David in Thy faithfulness?
50 Remember, O Lord, the reproach of Thy servants;
How I do bear in my bosom *the reproach of* all the many peoples,

**NAS** [a] Or, *exact usury from him* [b] Lit., *profane* [c] Or, *One thing*

## New International

21 My hand will sustain him;
surely my arm will strengthen him.
22 No enemy will subject him to tribute;
no wicked man will oppress him.
23 I will crush his foes before him
and strike down his adversaries.
24 My faithful love will be with him,
and through my name his horn[d] will be exalted.
25 I will set his hand over the sea,
his right hand over the rivers.
26 He will call out to me, 'You are my Father,
my God, the Rock my Savior.'
27 I will also appoint him my firstborn,
the most exalted of the kings of the earth.
28 I will maintain my love to him forever,
and my covenant with him will never fail.
29 I will establish his line forever,
his throne as long as the heavens endure.

30 "If his sons forsake my law
and do not follow my statutes,
31 if they violate my decrees
and fail to keep my commands,
32 I will punish their sin with the rod,
their iniquity with flogging;
33 but I will not take my love from him,
nor will I ever betray my faithfulness.
34 I will not violate my covenant
or alter what my lips have uttered.
35 Once for all, I have sworn by my holiness—
and I will not lie to David—
36 that his line will continue forever
and his throne endure before me like the sun;
37 it will be established forever like the moon,
the faithful witness in the sky." *Selah*

38 But you have rejected, you have spurned,
you have been very angry with your anointed one.
39 You have renounced the covenant with your servant
and have defiled his crown in the dust.
40 You have broken through all his walls
and reduced his strongholds to ruins.
41 All who pass by have plundered him;
he has become the scorn of his neighbors.
42 You have exalted the right hand of his foes;
you have made all his enemies rejoice.
43 You have turned back the edge of his sword
and have not supported him in battle.
44 You have put an end to his splendor
and cast his throne to the ground.
45 You have cut short the days of his youth;
you have covered him with a mantle of shame. *Selah*

46 How long, O LORD? Will you hide yourself forever?
How long will your wrath burn like fire?
47 Remember how fleeting is my life.
For what futility you have created all men!
48 What man can live and not see death,
or save himself from the power of the grave[e] ? *Selah*
49 O Lord, where is your former great love,
which in your faithfulness you swore to David?
50 Remember, Lord, how your servant has[f] been mocked,
how I bear in my heart the taunts of all the nations,

**NIV** [d] *24 Horn* here symbolizes strength. [e] *48* Hebrew *Sheol* [f] *50* Or *your servants have*

## King James

51Wherewith thine enemies have reproached, O LORD; wherewith they have reproached the footsteps of thine anointed.
52Blessed *be* the LORD for evermore. Amen, and Amen.

Book IV

A Prayer of Moses the man of God.

**90** LORD, THOU hast been our dwellingplace in all generations.
2Before the mountains were brought forth, or ever thou hadst formed the earth and the world, even from everlasting to everlasting, thou *art* God.
3Thou turnest man to destruction; and sayest, Return, ye children of men.
4For a thousand years in thy sight *are but* as yesterday when it is past, and *as* a watch in the night.
5Thou carriest them away as with a flood; they are *as* a sleep: in the morning *they are* like grass *which* groweth up.
6In the morning it flourisheth, and groweth up; in the evening it is cut down, and withereth.
7For we are consumed by thine anger, and by thy wrath are we troubled.
8Thou hast set our iniquities before thee, our secret *sins* in the light of thy countenance.
9For all our days are passed away in thy wrath: we spend our years as a tale *that is told*.
10The days of our years *are* threescore years and ten; and if by reason of strength *they be* fourscore years, yet *is* their strength labour and sorrow; for it is soon cut off, and we fly away.
11Who knoweth the power of thine anger? even according to thy fear, *so is* thy wrath.
12So teach *us* to number our days, that we may apply *our* hearts unto wisdom.
13Return, O LORD, how long? and let it repent thee concerning thy servants.
14O satisfy us early with thy mercy; that we may rejoice and be glad all our days.
15Make us glad according to the days *wherein* thou hast afflicted us, *and* the years *wherein* we have seen evil.
16Let thy work appear unto thy servants, and thy glory unto their children.
17And let the beauty of the LORD our God be upon us: and establish thou the work of our hands upon us; yea, the work of our hands establish thou it.

## Amplified

51With which Your enemies have taunted, O Lord; with which they have mocked the footsteps of Your anointed.
52Blessed be the Lord for evermore! Amen and Amen.

BOOK FOUR

A Prayer of Moses, the man of God.

**90** LORD, YOU have been our dwelling place *and* our refuge in all generations [says Moses].
2Before the mountains were brought forth, or ever You had formed *and* given birth to the earth and the world, even from everlasting to everlasting You are God.
3You turn man back to dust *and* corruption, and say, Return, O sons of the earthborn [to the earth]!
4For a thousand years in Your sight are but as yesterday when it is past, and as a watch in the night. [II Pet. 3:8.]
5You carry away [these disobedient people, doomed to die within forty years] as with a flood; they are as a sleep [vague and forgotten as soon as gone]. In the morning they are like grass which grows up:
6In the morning it flourishes and springs up; in the evening it is mown down and withers.
7For we [the Israelites in the wilderness] are consumed by Your anger, and by Your wrath are we troubled, overwhelmed *and* frightened away.
8Our iniquities, our secret heart *and* its sins [which we would so like to conceal even from ourselves] You have set in the [revealing] light of Your countenance.
9For all our days [out here in this wilderness, says Moses] are passed away in Your wrath; we spend our years as a tale that is told [for we adults know we are doomed to die soon, without reaching Canaan]. [Num. 14:26-35.]
10The days of our years are [a]threescore years and ten, or even if by reason of strength fourscore years, yet is their pride [in additional years] only labor and sorrow; for it is soon gone, and we fly away.
11Who knows the power of Your anger? [Who worthily connects this brevity of life with Your recognition of sin?] And Your wrath, who connects it with the reverent *and* worshipful fear that is due to You?
12So teach us to number our days that we may get us a heart of wisdom.
13Turn, O Lord [from Your fierce anger]; how long—? Revoke Your sentence *and* be comforted *and* eased toward Your servants.
14O satisfy us with Your mercy *and* loving-kindness in the morning [now, before we are older] that we may rejoice and be glad all our days.
15Make us glad in proportion to the days in which You have afflicted us, *and* to the years in which we have suffered evil.
16Let Your work [the signs of Your power] be revealed to Your servants, and Your (glorious) majesty to their children.
17And let the beauty *and* delightfulness *and* favor of the Lord our God be upon us; confirm *and* establish the work of our hands, yes, the work of our hands confirm *and* establish it.

**AMP** [a] This Psalm is credited to Moses, who is interceding with God to remove the curse which made it necessary for every Israelite over twenty years of age (when they rebelled against God at Kadesh-barnea) to die before reaching the Promised Land (Num. 14:26-35). Moses says most of them are dying at *seventy years.* This number has often been mistaken as a set span of life for all mankind. It was not intended to refer to anyone except those Israelites under the curse during that particular forty years. Seventy years never has been the average span of life for humanity. When Jacob, the father of the twelve tribes had reached 130 years (Gen. 47:9), he complained that he had not attained to the years of his immediate ancestors. In fact, Moses himself lived to be 120, Aaron 123, Miriam several years older, and Joshua 110; while in the Millennium a person dying at 100 will still be a child (Isa. 65:20).

## New American Standard

51 With which Thine enemies have reproached, O LORD,
With which they have reproached the footsteps of Thine anointed.
52¶ Blessed be the LORD forever!
Amen and Amen.

BOOK 4

*God's Eternity and Man's Transitoriness.*

A Prayer of Moses the man of God.

**90** LORD, THOU hast been our [b]dwelling place in all generations.
2 Before the mountains were born,
Or Thou didst give birth to the earth and the world,
Even from everlasting to everlasting, Thou art God.

3¶ Thou dost turn man back into dust,
And dost say, "Return, O children of men."
4 For a thousand years in Thy sight
Are like yesterday when it passes by,
Or *as* a watch in the night.
5 Thou hast swept them away like a flood, they fall asleep;
In the morning they are like grass which sprouts anew.
6 In the morning it flourishes, and sprouts anew;
Toward evening it fades, and withers away.

7¶ For we have been consumed by Thine anger,
And by Thy wrath we have been dismayed.
8 Thou hast placed our iniquities before Thee,
Our secret *sins* in the light of Thy presence.
9 For all our days have declined in Thy fury;
We have finished our years like a sigh.
10 As for the days of our life, they contain seventy years,
Or if due to strength, eighty years,
Yet their pride is *but* labor and sorrow;
For soon it is gone and we fly away.
11 Who understands the power of Thine anger,
And Thy fury, according to the fear that is due Thee?
12 So teach us to number our days,
That we may present to Thee a heart of wisdom.

13¶ Do return, O LORD; how long *will it be*?
And be sorry for Thy servants.
14 O satisfy us in the morning with Thy lovingkindness,
That we may sing for joy and be glad all our days.
15 Make us glad according to the days Thou hast afflicted us,
*And* the years we have seen [c]evil.
16 Let Thy work appear to Thy servants,
And Thy majesty to their children.
17 And let the favor of the Lord our God be upon us;
And do [d]confirm for us the work of our hands;
Yes, [e]confirm the work of our hands.

NAS [b] Or, *hiding place;* some ancient mss. read *place of refuge* [c] Or, *trouble* [d] Or, *give permanence to* [e] Or, *give permanence to*

## New International

51 the taunts with which your enemies have mocked, O LORD,
with which they have mocked every step of your anointed one.
52 Praise be to the LORD forever!
Amen and Amen.

BOOK IV

*Psalms 90-106*

A prayer of Moses the man of God.

**90** LORD, YOU have been our dwelling place throughout all generations.
2 Before the mountains were born
or you brought forth the earth and the world,
from everlasting to everlasting you are God.

3 You turn men back to dust,
saying, "Return to dust, O sons of men."
4 For a thousand years in your sight
are like a day that has just gone by,
or like a watch in the night.
5 You sweep men away in the sleep of death;
they are like the new grass of the morning—
6 though in the morning it springs up new,
by evening it is dry and withered.

7 We are consumed by your anger
and terrified by your indignation.
8 You have set our iniquities before you,
our secret sins in the light of your presence.
9 All our days pass away under your wrath;
we finish our years with a moan.
10 The length of our days is seventy years—
or eighty, if we have the strength;
yet their span[f] is but trouble and sorrow,
for they quickly pass, and we fly away.

11 Who knows the power of your anger?
For your wrath is as great as the fear that is due you.
12 Teach us to number our days aright,
that we may gain a heart of wisdom.

13 Relent, O LORD! How long will it be?
Have compassion on your servants.
14 Satisfy us in the morning with your unfailing love,
that we may sing for joy and be glad all our days.
15 Make us glad for as many days as you have afflicted us,
for as many years as we have seen trouble.
16 May your deeds be shown to your servants,
your splendor to their children.

17 May the favor[g] of the Lord our God rest upon us;
establish the work of our hands for us—
yes, establish the work of our hands.

NIV [f] *10 Or yet the best of them* [g] *17 Or beauty*

## King James

**91** HE THAT dwelleth in the secret place of the most High shall abide under the shadow of the Almighty.

2I will say of the LORD, *He is* my refuge and my fortress: my God; in him will I trust.

3Surely he shall deliver thee from the snare of the fowler, *and* from the noisome pestilence.

4He shall cover thee with his feathers, and under his wings shalt thou trust: his truth *shall be thy* shield and buckler.

5Thou shalt not be afraid for the terror by night; *nor* for the arrow *that* flieth by day;

6 *Nor* for the pestilence *that* walketh in darkness; *nor* for the destruction *that* wasteth at noonday.

7A thousand shall fall at thy side, and ten thousand at thy right hand; *but* it shall not come nigh thee.

8Only with thine eyes shalt thou behold and see the reward of the wicked.

9Because thou hast made the LORD, *which is* my refuge, *even* the most High, thy habitation;

10There shall no evil befall thee, neither shall any plague come nigh thy dwelling.

11For he shall give his angels charge over thee, to keep thee in all thy ways.

12They shall bear thee up in *their* hands, lest thou dash thy foot against a stone.

13Thou shalt tread upon the lion and adder: the young lion and the dragon shalt thou trample under feet.

14Because he hath set his love upon me, therefore will I deliver him: I will set him on high, because he hath known my name.

15He shall call upon me, and I will answer him: I *will be* with him in trouble; I will deliver him, and honour him.

16With long life will I satisfy him, and show him my salvation.

A Psalm *or* Song for the sabbath day.

**92** *IT IS a* good *thing* to give thanks unto the LORD, and to sing praises unto thy name, O most High:

2To show forth thy lovingkindness in the morning, and thy faithfulness every night,

3Upon an instrument of ten strings, and upon the psaltery; upon the harp with a solemn sound.

4For thou, LORD, hast made me glad through thy work: I will triumph in the works of thy hands.

5O LORD, how great are thy works! *and* thy thoughts are very deep.

6A brutish man knoweth not; neither doth a fool understand this.

7When the wicked spring as the grass, and when all the workers of iniquity do flourish; *it is* that they shall be destroyed for ever:

8But thou, LORD, *art most* high for evermore.

9For, lo, thine enemies, O LORD, for, lo, thine enemies shall perish; all the workers of iniquity shall be scattered.

10But my horn shalt thou exalt like *the horn of* an unicorn: I shall be anointed with fresh oil.

## Amplified

**91** HE WHO [a]dwells in the secret place of the Most High shall remain stable *and* fixed under the shadow of the Almighty [Whose power no foe can withstand].

2I will say of the Lord, He is my refuge and my fortress, my God, on Him I lean *and* rely, *and* in Him I (confidently) trust!

3For [then] He will deliver you from the snare of the fowler and from the deadly pestilence. [Then]

4He will cover you with His pinions, and under His wings shall you trust *and* find refuge; His truth *and* His faithfulness are a shield and a buckler. [Then]

5You shall not be afraid of the terror of the night, *nor* of the arrow [the evil plots and slanders of the wicked] that flies by day,

6Nor of the pestilence that stalks in darkness, nor of the destruction *and* sudden death that surprise *and* lay waste at noonday. [Then]

7A thousand may fall at your side, and ten thousand at your right hand, but it shall not come near you.

8Only a spectator shall you be [yourself inaccessible in the secret place of the Most High] as you witness the reward of the wicked.

9Because you have made the Lord your refuge, and the Most High your dwelling place, [Verses 1, 14.]

10There shall no evil befall you, nor any plague *or* calamity come near your tent.

11For He will give His angels [especial] charge over you, to accompany *and* defend *and* preserve you in all your ways [of obedience and service].

12They shall bear you up on their hands, lest you dash your foot against a stone. [Luke 4:10, 11; Heb. 1:14.]

13You shall tread upon the lion and adder, the young lion and the serpent shall you trample under foot. [Luke 10:19.]

14Because he has set his love upon Me, therefore will I deliver him; I will set him on high, because he knows *and* understands My name [has a personal knowledge of My mercy, love and kindness; trusts and relies on Me, knowing I will never forsake him, no, never].

15He shall call upon Me, and I will answer him; I will be with him in trouble, I will deliver him and honor him.

16With long life will I satisfy him, and show him My salvation.

A Psalm, a song for the Sabbath day.

**92** IT IS a good *and* delightful thing to give thanks to the Lord, to sing praises [with musical accompaniment] to Your name, O Most High;

2To show forth Your loving-kindness in the morning, and Your faithfulness by night,

3With an instrument of ten strings, and with the lute, with a solemn sound upon the lyre.

4For You, O Lord, have made me glad by Your work; of the deeds of Your hands I joyfully sing.

5How great are Your doings, O Lord! Your thoughts are very deep.

6A man in his rude *and* uncultivated state knows not; neither does a [self-confident] fool understand this:

7That though the wicked spring like grass, and all evildoers flourish, they are doomed to be destroyed for ever.

8But You, Lord, are on high for ever.

9For lo, Your adversaries, O Lord, for lo, Your enemies shall perish; all the evildoers shall be scattered.

10But my horn [emblem of excessive strength and stately grace] you have exalted like that of a wild ox; I am anointed with fresh oil.

**AMP** [a] The rich promises of this whole chapter are dependent upon one's meeting exactly the conditions of these first two verses. [Exod. 15:26.]

## New American Standard

*Security of the One Who Trusts in the* LORD.

**91** HE WHO dwells in the shelter of the Most High
Will abide in the shadow of the Almighty.
2 I will say to the LORD, "My refuge and my fortress,
My God, in whom I trust!"
3 For it is He who delivers you from the snare of the trapper,
And from the deadly pestilence.
4 He will cover you with His pinions,
And under His wings you may seek refuge;
His faithfulness is a shield and bulwark.

5¶ You will not be afraid of the terror by night,
Or of the arrow that flies by day;
6 Of the pestilence that stalks in darkness,
Or of the destruction that lays waste at noon.
7 A thousand may fall at your side,
And ten thousand at your right hand;
*But* it shall not approach you.
8 You will only look on with your eyes,
And see the recompense of the wicked.
9 For you have made the LORD, my refuge,
*Even* the Most High, your dwelling place.
10 No evil will befall you,
Nor will any plague come near your tent.
11¶ For He will give His angels charge concerning you,
To guard you in all your ways.
12 They will bear you up in their hands,
Lest you strike your foot against a stone.
13 You will tread upon the lion and cobra,
The young lion and the serpent you will trample down.

14¶ "Because he has loved Me, therefore I will deliver him;
I will set him *securely* on high, because he has known My name.
15 "He will call upon Me, and I will answer him;
I will be with him in trouble;
I will rescue him, and honor him.
16 "With a long life I will satisfy him,
And let him behold My salvation."

*Praise for the* LORD'S *Goodness.*

A Psalm, a Song for the Sabbath day.

**92** IT IS good to give thanks to the LORD,
And to sing praises to Thy name, O Most High;
2 To declare Thy lovingkindness in the morning,
And Thy faithfulness by night,
3 With the ten-stringed lute, and with the harp;
With resounding music upon the lyre.
4 For Thou, O LORD, hast made me glad by what Thou hast done,
I will sing for joy at the works of Thy hands.

5¶ How great are Thy works, O LORD!
Thy thoughts are very deep.
6 A senseless man has no knowledge;
Nor does a stupid man understand this:
7 That when the wicked sprouted up like grass,
And all who did iniquity flourished,
It *was only* that they might be destroyed forevermore.
8 But Thou, O LORD, art on high forever.
9 For, behold, Thine enemies, O LORD,
For, behold, Thine enemies will perish;
All who do iniquity will be scattered.

10¶ But Thou hast exalted my horn like *that of* the wild ox;
I have been anointed with fresh oil.

## New International

**91** HE WHO dwells in the shelter of the Most High
will rest in the shadow of the Almighty.[b]
2 I will say[c] of the LORD, "He is my refuge and my fortress,
my God, in whom I trust."
3 Surely he will save you from the fowler's snare
and from the deadly pestilence.
4 He will cover you with his feathers,
and under his wings you will find refuge;
his faithfulness will be your shield and rampart.
5 You will not fear the terror of night,
nor the arrow that flies by day,
6 nor the pestilence that stalks in the darkness,
nor the plague that destroys at midday.
7 A thousand may fall at your side,
ten thousand at your right hand,
but it will not come near you.
8 You will only observe with your eyes
and see the punishment of the wicked.

9 If you make the Most High your dwelling—
even the LORD, who is my refuge—
10 then no harm will befall you,
no disaster will come near your tent.
11 For he will command his angels concerning you
to guard you in all your ways;
12 they will lift you up in their hands,
so that you will not strike your foot against a stone.
13 You will tread upon the lion and the cobra;
you will trample the great lion and the serpent.

14 "Because he loves me," says the LORD, "I will rescue him;
I will protect him, for he acknowledges my name.
15 He will call upon me, and I will answer him;
I will be with him in trouble,
I will deliver him and honor him.
16 With long life will I satisfy him
and show him my salvation."

A psalm. A song. For the Sabbath day.

**92** IT IS good to praise the LORD
and make music to your name, O Most High,
2 to proclaim your love in the morning
and your faithfulness at night,
3 to the music of the ten-stringed lyre
and the melody of the harp.

4 For you make me glad by your deeds, O LORD;
I sing for joy at the works of your hands.
5 How great are your works, O LORD,
how profound your thoughts!
6 The senseless man does not know,
fools do not understand,
7 that though the wicked spring up like grass
and all evildoers flourish,
they will be forever destroyed.
8 But you, O LORD, are exalted forever.

9 For surely your enemies, O LORD,
surely your enemies will perish;
all evildoers will be scattered.
10 You have exalted my horn[d] like that of a wild ox;
fine oils have been poured upon me.

**NIV** [b] 1 Hebrew *Shaddai* [c] 2 Or *He says* [d] *10 Horn* here symbolizes strength.

## King James

11 Mine eye also shall see *my desire* on mine enemies, *and* mine ears shall hear *my desire* of the wicked that rise up against me.

12 The righteous shall flourish like the palm tree: he shall grow like a cedar in Lebanon.

13 Those that be planted in the house of the LORD shall flourish in the courts of our God.

14 They shall still bring forth fruit in old age; they shall be fat and flourishing;

15 To show that the LORD *is* upright: *he is* my rock, and *there is* no unrighteousness in him.

**93** THE LORD reigneth, he is clothed with majesty; the LORD is clothed with strength, *wherewith* he hath girded himself: the world also is stablished, that it cannot be moved.

2 Thy throne *is* established of old: thou *art* from everlasting.

3 The floods have lifted up, O LORD, the floods have lifted up their voice; the floods lift up their waves.

4 The LORD on high *is* mightier than the noise of many waters, *yea, than* the mighty waves of the sea.

5 Thy testimonies are very sure: holiness becometh thine house, O LORD, for ever.

**94** O LORD God, to whom vengeance belongeth; O God, to whom vengeance belongeth, show thyself.

2 Lift up thyself, thou judge of the earth: render a reward to the proud.

3 LORD, how long shall the wicked, how long shall the wicked triumph?

4 *How long* shall they utter *and* speak hard things? *and* all the workers of iniquity boast themselves?

5 They break in pieces thy people, O LORD, and afflict thine heritage.

6 They slay the widow and the stranger, and murder the fatherless.

7 Yet they say, The LORD shall not see, neither shall the God of Jacob regard *it*.

8 Understand, ye brutish among the people: and *ye* fools, when will ye be wise?

9 He that planted the ear, shall he not hear? he that formed the eye, shall he not see?

10 He that chastiseth the heathen, shall not he correct? he that teacheth man knowledge, *shall not he know?*

11 The LORD knoweth the thoughts of man, that they *are* vanity.

12 Blessed *is* the man whom thou chastenest, O LORD, and teachest him out of thy law;

13 That thou mayest give him rest from the days of adversity, until the pit be digged for the wicked.

## Amplified

11 My eye looks upon those who lie in wait for me; my ears hear the evildoers that rise up against me.

12 The [uncompromisingly] righteous shall flourish like the palm tree [be long-lived, stately, upright, useful and fruitful]; he shall grow like a cedar in Lebanon [majestic, stable, durable and incorruptible].

13 Planted in the house of the Lord, they shall flourish in the courts of our God.

14 [Growing in grace] they shall still bring forth fruit in old age; they shall be full of sap [of spiritual vitality] and *rich in the* verdure [of trust, love and contentment].

15 [They are living memorials] to show that the Lord is upright *and* faithful to His promises; He is my rock, and there is no unrighteousness in Him. [Rom. 9:14.]

**93** THE LORD reigns; He is clothed with majesty; the Lord is robed, He has girded Himself with strength *and* power; the world also is established, that it cannot be moved.

2 Your throne is established from of old; You are from everlasting.

3 The floods have lifted up, O Lord, the floods have lifted up their voice; the floods lift up the roaring of their waves.

4 The Lord on high is mightier *and* more glorious than the noise of many waters, yes, than the mighty breakers *and* waves of the sea.

5 Your testimonies are very sure; holiness [apparent in separation from sin, with simple trust and hearty obedience] is becoming to Your house, O Lord, for ever.

**94** O LORD God, You to Whom vengeance belongs; O God, You to Whom vengeance belongs, shine forth!

2 Rise up, O Judge of the earth; render to the proud a fit compensation!

3 Lord, how long shall the wicked, how long shall the wicked triumph *and* exult?

4 They pour out arrogant words, speaking hard things; all the evildoers boast loftily. [Jude 14, 15.]

5 They crush Your people, O Lord, and afflict Your heritage.

6 They slay the widow and the transient stranger, and murder the unprotected orphan.

7 Yet they say, The Lord does not see, neither does the God of Jacob notice it.

8 Consider *and* understand, you stupid ones among the people! And you [self-confident] fools, when will you become wise?

9 He Who planted the ear, shall He not hear? He Who formed the eye, shall He not see?

10 He Who disciplines *and* instructs the nations, shall He not punish, He Who teaches man knowledge?

11 The Lord knows the thoughts of man, that they are vain, empty and futile—only a breath. [I Cor. 3:20.]

12 Blessed—happy, fortunate [to be envied]—is the man whom You discipline *and* instruct, O Lord, and teach out of Your law;

13 That You may give him power to hold himself calm in the days of adversity, until the [inevitable] pit of corruption is dug for the wicked.

## New American Standard

11 And my eye has looked *exultantly* upon my foes,
My ears hear of the evildoers who rise up against me.
12 The righteous man will flourish like the palm tree,
He will grow like a cedar in Lebanon.
13 Planted in the house of the LORD,
They will flourish in the courts of our God.
14 They will still yield fruit in old age;
They shall be [a]full of sap and very green,
15 To declare that the LORD is upright;
*He is* my rock, and there is no unrighteousness in Him.

*The Majesty of the LORD.*

93 THE LORD reigns, He is clothed with majesty;
The LORD has clothed and girded Himself with strength;
Indeed, the world is firmly established, it will not be moved.
2 Thy throne is established from of old;
Thou art from everlasting.

3¶ The floods have lifted up, O LORD,
The floods have lifted up their voice;
The floods lift up their pounding waves.
4 More than the sounds of many waters,
*Than* the mighty breakers of the sea,
The LORD on high is mighty.
5 Thy testimonies are fully confirmed;
Holiness befits Thy house,
O LORD, forevermore.

*The LORD Implored to Avenge His People.*

94 O LORD, God of vengeance;
God of vengeance, shine forth!
2 Rise up, O Judge of the earth;
Render recompense to the proud.
3 How long shall the wicked, O LORD,
How long shall the wicked exult?
4 They pour forth *words*, they speak arrogantly;
All who do wickedness vaunt themselves.
5 They crush Thy people, O LORD,
And afflict Thy heritage.
6 They slay the widow and the stranger,
And murder the orphans.
7 And they have said, "The LORD does not see,
Nor does the God of Jacob pay heed."

8¶ Pay heed, you senseless among the people;
And when will you understand, stupid ones?
9 He who planted the ear, does He not hear?
He who formed the eye, does He not see?
10 He who chastens the nations, will He not rebuke,
*Even* He who teaches man knowledge?
11 The LORD knows the thoughts of man,
That they are a *mere* breath.

12¶ Blessed is the man whom Thou dost chasten, O LORD,
And dost teach out of Thy law;
13 That Thou mayest grant him relief from the days of adversity,
Until a pit is dug for the wicked.

NAS [a] Lit., *fat and*

## New International

11 My eyes have seen the defeat of my adversaries;
my ears have heard the rout of my wicked foes.
12 The righteous will flourish like a palm tree,
they will grow like a cedar of Lebanon;
13 planted in the house of the LORD,
they will flourish in the courts of our God.
14 They will still bear fruit in old age,
they will stay fresh and green,
15 proclaiming, "The LORD is upright;
he is my Rock, and there is no wickedness in him."

93 THE LORD reigns, he is robed in majesty;
the LORD is robed in majesty
and is armed with strength.
The world is firmly established;
it cannot be moved.
2 Your throne was established long ago;
you are from all eternity.

3 The seas have lifted up, O LORD,
the seas have lifted up their voice;
the seas have lifted up their pounding waves.
4 Mightier than the thunder of the great waters,
mightier than the breakers of the sea—
the LORD on high is mighty.

5 Your statutes stand firm;
holiness adorns your house
for endless days, O LORD.

94 O LORD, the God who avenges,
O God who avenges, shine forth.
2 Rise up, O Judge of the earth;
pay back to the proud what they deserve.
3 How long will the wicked, O LORD,
how long will the wicked be jubilant?

4 They pour out arrogant words;
all the evildoers are full of boasting.
5 They crush your people, O LORD;
they oppress your inheritance.
6 They slay the widow and the alien;
they murder the fatherless.
7 They say, "The LORD does not see;
the God of Jacob pays no heed."

8 Take heed, you senseless ones among the people;
you fools, when will you become wise?
9 Does he who implanted the ear not hear?
Does he who formed the eye not see?
10 Does he who disciplines nations not punish?
Does he who teaches man lack knowledge?
11 The LORD knows the thoughts of man;
he knows that they are futile.

12 Blessed is the man you discipline, O LORD,
the man you teach from your law;
13 you grant him relief from days of trouble,
till a pit is dug for the wicked.

## King James

14 For the LORD will not cast off his people, neither will he forsake his inheritance.
15 But judgment shall return unto righteousness: and all the upright in heart shall follow it.
16 Who will rise up for me against the evildoers? *or* who will stand up for me against the workers of iniquity?
17 Unless the LORD *had been* my help, my soul had almost dwelt in silence.
18 When I said, My foot slippeth; thy mercy, O LORD, held me up.
19 In the multitude of my thoughts within me thy comforts delight my soul.
20 Shall the throne of iniquity have fellowship with thee, which frameth mischief by a law?
21 They gather themselves together against the soul of the righteous, and condemn the innocent blood.
22 But the LORD is my defence; and my God *is* the rock of my refuge.
23 And he shall bring upon them their own iniquity, and shall cut them off in their own wickedness; *yea*, the LORD our God shall cut them off.

**95** O COME, let us sing unto the LORD: let us make a joyful noise to the rock of our salvation.
2 Let us come before his presence with thanksgiving, and make a joyful noise unto him with psalms.
3 For the LORD *is* a great God, and a great King above all gods.
4 In his hand *are* the deep places of the earth: the strength of the hills *is* his also.
5 The sea *is* his, and he made it: and his hands formed the dry *land*.
6 O come, let us worship and bow down: let us kneel before the LORD our maker.
7 For he *is* our God; and we *are* the people of his pasture, and the sheep of his hand. Today if ye will hear his voice,
8 Harden not your heart, as in the provocation, *and* as *in* the day of temptation in the wilderness:
9 When your fathers tempted me, proved me, and saw my work.
10 Forty years long was I grieved with *this* generation, and said, It *is* a people that do err in their heart, and they have not known my ways:
11 Unto whom I sware in my wrath that they should not enter into my rest.

**96** O SING unto the LORD a new song: sing unto the LORD, all the earth.
2 Sing unto the LORD, bless his name; show forth his salvation from day to day.
3 Declare his glory among the heathen, his wonders among all people.
4 For the LORD *is* great, and greatly to be praised: he *is* to be feared above all gods.

## Amplified

14 For the Lord will not cast off *nor* spurn His people, neither will He abandon His heritage.
15 For justice will return to the [uncompromisingly] righteous, and all the upright in heart will follow it.
16 Who will rise up for me against the evildoers? Who will stand up for me against the workers of iniquity?
17 Unless the Lord had been my help, I would soon have dwelt in [the land where is] silence.
18 When I said, My foot is slipping, Your mercy *and* loving-kindness, O Lord, held me up.
19 In the multitude of my (anxious) thoughts within me, Your comforts cheer *and* delight my soul!
20 Shall the throne of iniquity have fellowship with You, they who frame *and* hide their unrighteous doings under [the sacred name of] law?
21 They band themselves together against the life of the [consistently] righteous, and condemn the innocent to death.
22 But the Lord has become my high tower *and* defense, and my God, the rock of my refuge.
23 And He has turned back upon them their own iniquity, and will wipe them out by means of their own wickedness; the Lord our God will wipe them out.

**95** O COME, let us sing to the Lord; let us make a joyful noise to the rock of our salvation!
2 Let us come before His presence with thanksgiving; let us make a joyful noise to Him with songs of praise!
3 For the Lord is a great God, and a great King above all gods.
4 In His hand are the deep places of the earth; the heights *and* strength of the hills are His also.
5 The sea is His, for He made it; and His hands formed the dry land.
6 O come, let us worship and bow down; let us kneel before the Lord our Maker [in reverent praise and supplication].
7 For He is our God; and we are the people of His pasture, and the sheep of His hand. Today if you will hear His voice, [Heb. 3:7-11.]
8 Harden not your heart, as at Meribah, and as at Massah in the day of temptation in the wilderness; [Exod. 17:1-7; Num. 20:1-13; Deut. 6:16.]
9 When your fathers tried My patience *and* tested Me, proved Me and saw My work [of judgment].
10 Forty years long was I grieved *and* disgusted with that generation, and said, It is a people that do err in their heart, and they do not approve, acknowledge *or* regard My ways.
11 Wherefore I swore in My wrath that they should not enter [the land of promise] My rest. [Heb. 4:3-11.]

**96** O SING to the Lord a new song; sing to the Lord, all the earth!
2 Sing to the Lord, bless [affectionately praise] His name; show forth His salvation from day to day.
3 Declare His glory among the nations, His marvelous works among all the peoples.
4 For great is the Lord, and greatly to be praised; He is to be reverently feared *and* worshiped above all *so-called* gods. [Rev. 14:7; Deut. 6:5.]

## New American Standard

14 For the LORD will not abandon His people,
Nor will He forsake His inheritance.
15 For judgment will again be righteous;
And all the upright in heart will follow it.
16 Who will stand up for me against evildoers?
Who will take his stand for me against those who do wickedness?

17 ¶ If the LORD had not been my help,
My soul would soon have dwelt in *the abode of* silence.
18 If I should say, "My foot has slipped,"
Thy lovingkindness, O LORD, will hold me up.
19 When my anxious thoughts multiply within me,
Thy consolations delight my soul.
20 Can a throne of destruction be allied with Thee,
One which devises mischief by decree?
21 They band themselves together against the life of the righteous,
And condemn the innocent to death.
22 But the LORD has been my stronghold,
And my God the rock of my refuge.
23 And He has brought back their wickedness upon them,
And will destroy them in their evil;
The LORD our God will destroy them.

*Praise to the LORD, and Warning against Unbelief.*

**95** O COME, let us sing for joy to the LORD;
Let us shout joyfully to the rock of our salvation.
2 Let us come before His presence with thanksgiving;
Let us shout joyfully to Him with psalms.
3 For the LORD is a great God,
And a great King above all gods,
4 In whose hand are the depths of the earth;
The peaks of the mountains are His also.
5 The sea is His, for it was He who made it;
And His hands formed the dry land.

6 ¶ Come, let us worship and bow down;
Let us kneel before the LORD our Maker.
7 For He is our God,
And we are the people of His pasture, and the sheep of His hand.
Today, if you would hear His voice,
8 Do not harden your hearts, as at [a]Meribah,
As in the day of [b]Massah in the wilderness;
9 "When your fathers tested Me,
They tried Me, though they had seen My work.
10 "For forty years I loathed *that* generation,
And said they are a people who err in their heart,
And they do not know My ways.
11 "Therefore I swore in My anger,
Truly they shall not enter into My rest."

*A Call to Worship the LORD the Righteous Judge.*

**96** SING TO the LORD a new song;
Sing to the LORD, all the earth.
2 Sing to the LORD, bless His name;
Proclaim good tidings of His salvation from day to day.
3 Tell of His glory among the nations,
His wonderful deeds among all the peoples.
4 For great is the LORD, and greatly to be praised;
He is to be feared above all gods.

NAS [a] Or, *place of strife* [b] Or, *temptation*

## New International

14 For the LORD will not reject his people;
he will never forsake his inheritance.
15 Judgment will again be founded on righteousness,
and all the upright in heart will follow it.

16 Who will rise up for me against the wicked?
Who will take a stand for me against evildoers?
17 Unless the LORD had given me help,
I would soon have dwelt in the silence of death.
18 When I said, "My foot is slipping,"
your love, O LORD, supported me.
19 When anxiety was great within me,
your consolation brought joy to my soul.

20 Can a corrupt throne be allied with you—
one that brings on misery by its decrees?
21 They band together against the righteous
and condemn the innocent to death.
22 But the LORD has become my fortress,
and my God the rock in whom I take refuge.
23 He will repay them for their sins
and destroy them for their wickedness;
the LORD our God will destroy them.

**95** COME, LET us sing for joy to the LORD;
let us shout aloud to the Rock of our salvation.
2 Let us come before him with thanksgiving
and extol him with music and song.

3 For the LORD is the great God,
the great King above all gods.
4 In his hand are the depths of the earth,
and the mountain peaks belong to him.
5 The sea is his, for he made it,
and his hands formed the dry land.

6 Come, let us bow down in worship,
let us kneel before the LORD our Maker;
7 for he is our God
and we are the people of his pasture,
the flock under his care.
Today, if you hear his voice,
8 do not harden your hearts as you did at Meribah,[c]
as you did that day at Massah[d] in the desert,
9 where your fathers tested and tried me,
though they had seen what I did.
10 For forty years I was angry with that generation;
I said, "They are a people whose hearts go astray,
and they have not known my ways."
11 So I declared on oath in my anger,
"They shall never enter my rest."

**96** SING TO the LORD a new song;
sing to the LORD, all the earth.
2 Sing to the LORD, praise his name;
proclaim his salvation day after day.
3 Declare his glory among the nations,
his marvelous deeds among all peoples.

4 For great is the LORD and most worthy of praise;
he is to be feared above all gods.

NIV [c] *8 Meribah* means *quarreling.* [d] *8 Massah* means *testing.*

## King James

5 For all the gods of the nations *are* idols: but the LORD made the heavens.

6 Honour and majesty *are* before him: strength and beauty *are* in his sanctuary.

7 Give unto the LORD, O ye kindreds of the people, give unto the LORD glory and strength.

8 Give unto the LORD the glory *due unto* his name: bring an offering, and come into his courts.

9 O worship the LORD in the beauty of holiness: fear before him, all the earth.

10 Say among the heathen *that* the LORD reigneth: the world also shall be established that it shall not be moved: he shall judge the people righteously.

11 Let the heavens rejoice, and let the earth be glad; let the sea roar, and the fulness thereof.

12 Let the field be joyful, and all that *is* therein: then shall all the trees of the wood rejoice

13 Before the LORD: for he cometh, for he cometh to judge the earth: he shall judge the world with righteousness, and the people with his truth.

**97** THE LORD reigneth; let the earth rejoice; let the multitude of isles be glad *thereof.*

2 Clouds and darkness *are* round about him: righteousness and judgment *are* the habitation of his throne.

3 A fire goeth before him, and burneth up his enemies round about.

4 His lightnings enlightened the world: the earth saw, and trembled.

5 The hills melted like wax at the presence of the LORD, at the presence of the Lord of the whole earth.

6 The heavens declare his righteousness, and all the people see his glory.

7 Confounded be all they that serve graven images, that boast themselves of idols: worship him, all *ye* gods.

8 Zion heard, and was glad; and the daughters of Judah rejoiced because of thy judgments, O LORD.

9 For thou, LORD, *art* high above all the earth: thou art exalted far above all gods.

10 Ye that love the LORD, hate evil: he preserveth the souls of his saints; he delivereth them out of the hand of the wicked.

11 Light is sown for the righteous, and gladness for the upright in heart.

12 Rejoice in the LORD, ye righteous; and give thanks at the remembrance of his holiness.

A Psalm.

**98** O SING unto the LORD a new song; for he hath done marvellous things: his right hand, and his holy arm, hath gotten him the victory.

## Amplified

5 For all the gods of the nations are [lifeless] idols, but the Lord made the heavens.

6 Honor and majesty are before Him; strength and beauty are in His sanctuary.

7 Ascribe to the Lord, O you families of the people, ascribe to the Lord glory and strength.

8 Give to the Lord the glory due to His name; bring an offering and come (before Him) into His courts.

9 O worship the Lord in the beauty of holiness; tremble *and* reverently fear before Him, all the earth.

10 Say among the nations that the Lord reigns; the world also is established, that it cannot be moved; He shall judge *and* rule the people righteously *and* with justice. [Rev. 11:15; 19:6.]

11 Let the heavens be glad, and let the earth rejoice; let the sea roar and all the things which fill it.

12 Let the field be exultant, and all that is in it! Then shall all the trees of the wood sing for joy

13 Before the Lord; for He comes, for He comes to judge *and* govern the earth! He shall judge the world with righteousness *and* justice, and the people with His faithfulness *and* truth. [Rev. 19:11; I Chron. 16:23-33.]

**97** THE LORD reigns; let the earth rejoice; let the multitude of isles *and* coastlands be glad!

2 Clouds and darkness are round about Him [as at Sinai]; righteousness and justice are the foundation of His throne. [Exod. 19:9.]

3 Fire goes before Him and burns up His adversaries round about.

4 His lightnings illumine the world; the earth sees and trembles.

5 The hills melted like wax at the presence of the Lord, at the presence of the Lord of the whole earth.

6 The heavens declare His righteousness, and all the peoples see His glory.

7 Let all those be put to shame who serve graven images, who boast themselves of idols. Fall prostrate before Him, all you gods. [Heb. 1:6.]

8 Zion heard, and was glad, and the daughters of Judah rejoiced [in relief] because of Your judgments, O Lord.

9 For You, Lord, are high above all the earth; You are exalted far above all gods.

10 O you who love the Lord, hate evil; He preserves the lives of His saints [the children of God]; He delivers them out of the hand of the wicked. [Rom. 8:13-17.]

11 Light is sown for the [uncompromisingly] righteous *and* strewn along their pathway, and for the upright in heart [the irrepressible joy which comes from consciousness of His favor and protection].

12 Rejoice in the Lord, you [consistently] righteous—upright and in right standing with God—and give thanks at the remembrance of His holiness.

A Psalm.

**98** O SING to the Lord a new song, for He has done marvelous things; His right hand and His holy arm have wrought salvation for Him.

## New American Standard

5 For all the gods of the peoples are idols,
But the LORD made the heavens.
6 Splendor and majesty are before Him,
Strength and beauty are in His sanctuary.

7¶ [a]Ascribe to the LORD, O families of the peoples,
[b]Ascribe to the LORD glory and strength.
8 [c]Ascribe to the LORD the glory of His name;
Bring an offering, and come into His courts.
9 Worship the LORD in [d]holy attire;
Tremble before Him, all the earth.
10 Say among the nations, "The LORD reigns;
Indeed, the world is firmly established, it will not be moved;
He will judge the peoples with [e]equity."

11¶ Let the heavens be glad, and let the earth rejoice;
Let the sea roar, and all it contains;
12 Let the field exult, and all that is in it.
Then all the trees of the forest will sing for joy
13 Before the LORD, for He is coming;
For He is coming to judge the earth.
He will judge the world in righteousness,
And the peoples in His faithfulness.

*The LORD's Power and Dominion.*

97 THE LORD reigns; let the earth rejoice;
Let the many [f]islands be glad.
2 Clouds and thick darkness surround Him;
Righteousness and justice are the foundation of His throne.
3 Fire goes before Him,
And burns up His adversaries round about.
4 His lightnings lit up the world;
The earth saw and trembled.
5 The mountains melted like wax at the presence of the LORD,
At the presence of the Lord of the whole earth.
6 The heavens declare His righteousness,
And all the peoples have seen His glory.

7¶ Let all those be ashamed who serve graven images,
Who boast themselves of idols;
Worship Him, all you gods.
8 Zion heard *this* and was glad,
And the daughters of Judah have rejoiced
Because of Thy judgments, O LORD.
9 For Thou art the LORD Most High over all the earth;
Thou art exalted far above all gods.

10¶ Hate evil, you who love the LORD,
Who preserves the souls of His godly ones;
He delivers them from the hand of the wicked.
11 Light is sown *like seed* for the righteous,
And gladness for the upright in heart.
12 Be glad in the LORD, you righteous ones;
And give thanks to His holy name.

*A Call to Praise the LORD for His Righteousness.*

A Psalm.

98 O SING to the LORD a new song,
For He has done wonderful things,
His right hand and His holy arm have [g]gained the victory for Him.

NAS [a] Lit., *Give* [b] Lit., *Give* [c] Lit., *Give* [d] Or, *the splendor of holiness*
[e] Or, *uprightness* [f] Or, *coastlands* [g] Or, *accomplished salvation*

## New International

5 For all the gods of the nations are idols,
but the LORD made the heavens.
6 Splendor and majesty are before him;
strength and glory are in his sanctuary.

7 Ascribe to the LORD, O families of nations,
ascribe to the LORD glory and strength.
8 Ascribe to the LORD the glory due his name;
bring an offering and come into his courts.
9 Worship the LORD in the splendor of his[h] holiness;
tremble before him, all the earth.

10 Say among the nations, "The LORD reigns."
The world is firmly established, it cannot be moved;
he will judge the peoples with equity.
11 Let the heavens rejoice, let the earth be glad;
let the sea resound, and all that is in it;
12 let the fields be jubilant, and everything in them.
Then all the trees of the forest will sing for joy;
13 they will sing before the LORD, for he comes,
he comes to judge the earth.
He will judge the world in righteousness
and the peoples in his truth.

97 THE LORD reigns, let the earth be glad;
let the distant shores rejoice.
2 Clouds and thick darkness surround him;
righteousness and justice are the foundation of his throne.
3 Fire goes before him
and consumes his foes on every side.
4 His lightning lights up the world;
the earth sees and trembles.
5 The mountains melt like wax before the LORD,
before the Lord of all the earth.
6 The heavens proclaim his righteousness,
and all the peoples see his glory.

7 All who worship images are put to shame,
those who boast in idols—
worship him, all you gods!

8 Zion hears and rejoices
and the villages of Judah are glad
because of your judgments, O LORD.
9 For you, O LORD, are the Most High over all the earth;
you are exalted far above all gods.

10 Let those who love the LORD hate evil,
for he guards the lives of his faithful ones
and delivers them from the hand of the wicked.
11 Light is shed upon the righteous
and joy on the upright in heart.
12 Rejoice in the LORD, you who are righteous,
and praise his holy name.

A psalm.

98 SING TO the LORD a new song,
for he has done marvelous things;
his right hand and his holy arm
have worked salvation for him.

NIV [h] 9 Or *LORD with the splendor of*

## King James

2 The LORD hath made known his salvation: his righteousness hath he openly shown in the sight of the heathen.

3 He hath remembered his mercy and his truth toward the house of Israel: all the ends of the earth have seen the salvation of our God.

4 Make a joyful noise unto the LORD, all the earth: make a loud noise, and rejoice, and sing praise.

5 Sing unto the LORD with the harp; with the harp, and the voice of a psalm.

6 With trumpets and sound of cornet make a joyful noise before the LORD, the King.

7 Let the sea roar, and the fulness thereof; the world, and they that dwell therein.

8 Let the floods clap *their* hands: let the hills be joyful together

9 Before the LORD; for he cometh to judge the earth: with righteousness shall he judge the world, and the people with equity.

**99** THE LORD reigneth; let the people tremble: he sitteth *between* the cherubims; let the earth be moved.

2 The LORD *is* great in Zion; and he *is* high above all the people.

3 Let them praise thy great and terrible name; *for* it *is* holy.

4 The king's strength also loveth judgment; thou dost establish equity, thou executest judgment and righteousness in Jacob.

5 Exalt ye the LORD our God, and worship at his footstool; *for* he *is* holy.

6 Moses and Aaron among his priests, and Samuel among them that call upon his name; they called upon the LORD, and he answered them.

7 He spake unto them in the cloudy pillar: they kept his testimonies, and the ordinance *that* he gave them.

8 Thou answeredst them, O LORD our God: thou wast a God that forgavest them, though thou tookest vengeance of their inventions.

9 Exalt the LORD our God, and worship at his holy hill; for the LORD our God *is* holy.

A Psalm of praise.

**100** MAKE A joyful noise unto the LORD, all ye lands.

2 Serve the LORD with gladness: come before his presence with singing.

3 Know ye that the LORD he *is* God: *it is* he *that* hath made us, and not we ourselves; *we are* his people, and the sheep of his pasture.

## Amplified

2 The Lord has made known His salvation; His righteousness has He openly shown in the sight of the nations. [Luke 2:30, 31.]

3 He has [earnestly] remembered His mercy *and* loving-kindness, His truth *and* His faithfulness toward the house of Israel. All the ends of the earth have witnessed the salvation of our God. [Acts 13:47; 28:28.]

4 Make a joyful noise to the Lord, all the earth; break forth and sing for joy, yes, sing praises!

5 Sing praises to the Lord with the lyre; with the lyre and the voice of melody.

6 With trumpets and sound of the horn make a joyful noise before the King, the Lord!

7 Let the sea roar and all that fills it, the world and those who dwell in it!

8 Let the rivers clap their hands; together let the hills sing for joy

9 Before the Lord; for He is coming to judge [and rule] the earth; with righteousness will He judge [and rule] the world, and the peoples with equity.

**99** THE LORD reigns; let the peoples tremble [with reverential fear]! He sits [enthroned] above the cherubim; let the earth quake!

2 The Lord is great in Zion, and He is high above all the peoples.

3 Let them confess *and* praise Your great name, awesome *and* reverence inspiring! It is holy, *and* holy is He! [Rev. 15:4.]

4 The strength of the king who loves righteousness *and* equity You establish in uprightness; You execute justice and righteousness in Jacob [Israel].

5 Extol the Lord our God, and worship at His footstool! Holy is He!

6 Moses and Aaron were among His priests, and Samuel was among those who called upon His name; they called upon the Lord, and He answered them.

7 He spoke to them in the pillar of cloud; they kept His testimonies, and the statute that He gave them. [Ps. 105:9, 10.]

8 You answered them, O Lord our God. You were a forgiving God to them, although avenging their evil-doings *and* practices.

9 Extol the Lord our God, and worship at His holy hill; for the Lord our God is holy!

A Psalm of thanksgiving *and* for the thank offering.

**100** MAKE A joyful noise to the Lord, all you lands!

2 Serve the Lord with gladness! Come before His presence with singing!

3 Know—perceive, recognize and understand with approval—that the Lord is God! It is He Who has made us, not we ourselves [and we are His]! We are His people and the sheep of His pasture. [Eph. 2:10.]

## New American Standard

2 The LORD has made known His salvation;
He has revealed His righteousness in the sight of the nations.
3 He has remembered His lovingkindness and His faithfulness to the house of Israel;
All the ends of the earth have seen the salvation of our God.

4¶ Shout joyfully to the LORD, all the earth;
Break forth and sing for joy and sing praises.
5 Sing praises to the LORD with the lyre;
With the lyre and the sound of melody.
6 With trumpets and the sound of the horn
Shout joyfully before the King, the LORD.
7¶ Let the sea roar and all it contains,
The world and those who dwell in it.
8 Let the rivers clap their hands;
Let the mountains sing together for joy
9 Before the LORD; for He is coming to judge the earth;
He will judge the world with righteousness,
And the peoples with equity.

*Praise to the LORD for His Fidelity to Israel.*

**99** THE LORD reigns, let the peoples tremble;
He is enthroned *above* the cherubim, let the earth shake!
2 The LORD is great in Zion,
And He is exalted above all the peoples.
3 Let them praise Thy great and awesome name;
Holy is He.
4 And the strength of the King loves [a]justice;
Thou hast established equity;
Thou hast executed [b]justice and righteousness in Jacob.
5 Exalt the LORD our God,
And worship at His footstool;
Holy is He.

6¶ Moses and Aaron were among His priests,
And Samuel was among those who called on His name;
They called upon the LORD, and He answered them.
7 He spoke to them in the pillar of cloud;
They kept His testimonies,
And the statute that He gave them.
8 O LORD our God, Thou didst answer them;
Thou wast a forgiving God to them,
And *yet* an avenger of their *evil* deeds.
9 Exalt the LORD our God,
And worship at His holy hill;
For holy is the LORD our God.

*All Men Exhorted to Praise God.*

A Psalm for Thanksgiving.

**100** SHOUT JOYFULLY to the LORD, all the earth.
2 Serve the LORD with gladness;
Come before Him with joyful singing.
3 Know that the LORD Himself is God;
It is He who has made us, and [c]not we ourselves;
*We are* His people and the sheep of His pasture.

NAS [a] Or, *judgment* [b] Or, *judgment* [c] Some mss. read *His we are*

## New International

2The LORD has made his salvation known
and revealed his righteousness to the nations.
3He has remembered his love
and his faithfulness to the house of Israel;
all the ends of the earth have seen
the salvation of our God.

4Shout for joy to the LORD, all the earth,
burst into jubilant song with music;
5make music to the LORD with the harp,
with the harp and the sound of singing,
6with trumpets and the blast of the ram's horn—
shout for joy before the LORD, the King.

7Let the sea resound, and everything in it,
the world, and all who live in it.
8Let the rivers clap their hands,
let the mountains sing together for joy;
9let them sing before the LORD,
for he comes to judge the earth.
He will judge the world in righteousness
and the peoples with equity.

**99** THE LORD reigns,
let the nations tremble;
he sits enthroned between the cherubim,
let the earth shake.
2Great is the LORD in Zion;
he is exalted over all the nations.
3Let them praise your great and awesome name—
he is holy.

4The King is mighty, he loves justice—
you have established equity;
in Jacob you have done
what is just and right.
5Exalt the LORD our God
and worship at his footstool;
he is holy.

6Moses and Aaron were among his priests,
Samuel was among those who called on his name;
they called on the LORD
and he answered them.
7He spoke to them from the pillar of cloud;
they kept his statutes and the decrees he gave them.

8O LORD our God,
you answered them;
you were to Israel[d] a forgiving God,
though you punished their misdeeds.[e]
9Exalt the LORD our God
and worship at his holy mountain,
for the LORD our God is holy.

A psalm. For giving thanks.

**100** SHOUT FOR joy to the LORD, all the earth.
2 Worship the LORD with gladness;
come before him with joyful songs.
3Know that the LORD is God.
It is he who made us, and we are his[f];
we are his people, the sheep of his pasture.

NIV [d] 8 Hebrew *them* [e] 8 Or / *an avenger of the wrongs done to them* [f] 3 Or *and not we ourselves*

## King James

4Enter into his gates with thanksgiving, *and* into his courts with
praise: be thankful unto him, *and* bless his name.
5For the LORD *is* good; his mercy *is* everlasting; and his truth
*endureth* to all generations.

A Psalm of David.

**101** I WILL sing of mercy and judgment: unto thee, O
LORD, will I sing.
2I will behave myself wisely in a perfect way. O when wilt thou
come unto me? I will walk within my house with a perfect heart.
3I will set no wicked thing before mine eyes: I hate the work of
them that turn aside; *it* shall not cleave to me.
4A froward heart shall depart from me: I will not know a wicked
*person*.
5Whoso privily slandereth his neighbour, him will I cut off: him
that hath an high look and a proud heart will not I suffer.
6Mine eyes *shall be* upon the faithful of the land, that they may
dwell with me: he that walketh in a perfect way, he shall serve me.
7He that worketh deceit shall not dwell within my house: he
that telleth lies shall not tarry in my sight.
8I will early destroy all the wicked of the land; that I may cut
off all wicked doers from the city of the LORD.

A Prayer of the afflicted, when he is overwhelmed, and poureth out his complaint before the LORD.

**102** HEAR MY prayer, O LORD, and let my cry come unto
thee.
2Hide not thy face from me in the day *when* I am in trouble;
incline thine ear unto me: in the day *when* I call answer me speedily.
3For my days are consumed like smoke, and my bones are
burned as an hearth.
4My heart is smitten, and withered like grass; so that I forget
to eat my bread.
5By reason of the voice of my groaning my bones cleave to my
skin.
6I am like a pelican of the wilderness: I am like an owl of the
desert.
7I watch, and am as a sparrow alone upon the house top.
8Mine enemies reproach me all the day; *and* they that are mad
against me are sworn against me.
9For I have eaten ashes like bread, and mingled my drink with
weeping,

## Amplified

4Enter into His gates with thanksgiving *and* with a thank offering, and into His courts with praise! Be thankful *and* say so to Him,
bless *and* affectionately praise His name!
5For the Lord is good; His mercy *and* loving-kindness are everlasting; His faithfulness *and* truth endure to all generations.

A Psalm of David.

**101** I WILL sing of mercy *and* loving-kindness and justice;
to You, O Lord, will I sing.
2I will behave myself wisely *and* give heed to the blameless way.
O when will You come to me? I will walk within my house in my
integrity *and* with a blameless heart.
3I will set no base *or* wicked thing before my eyes. I hate the
work of them who turn aside [from the right path]; it shall not
grasp hold of me.
4A perverse heart shall depart from me. I will know no evil
person *or* thing.
5Whoso privily slanders his neighbor, him will I cut off [from
me]. He who has a haughty look and a proud *and* arrogant heart
I cannot *and* I will not tolerate.
6My eyes shall [look with favor] upon the faithful of the land,
that they may dwell with me. He who walks blamelessly, he shall
minister to me.
7He who works deceit shall not dwell in my house, he who tells
lies shall not continue in my presence.
8Morning after morning I will root up all the wicked in the land,
that I may eliminate all the evildoers from the city of the Lord.

A Prayer of the afflicted, when he is overwhelmed *and* faints, and pours out his complaint to God.

**102** HEAR MY prayer, O Lord, and let my cry come to You.
2Hide not Your face from me in the day when I am in
distress! Incline Your ear to me; in the day when I call answer me
speedily.
3For my days consume away like smoke, and my bones are
burned as a firebrand *or* as a hearth.
4My heart is smitten like grass, and withered; so that [in absorp-
tion] I forget to eat my food.
5By reason of my loud groaning [from suffering and trouble] my
flesh cleaves to my bones.
6I am like a melancholy pelican *or* vulture of the wilderness; I
am like a (desolate) owl of the waste places.
7I am sleepless *and* lie awake (mourning), like a bereaved sparrow alone on the housetop.
8My adversaries taunt *and* reproach me all the day; and they
that are angry with me use my name for a curse.
9For I have eaten of the ashes [in which I sat] as if they were
bread, and have mingled my drink with weeping,

## New American Standard

4¶ Enter His gates with thanksgiving,
*And* His courts with praise.
Give thanks to Him; bless His name.
5 For the LORD is good;
His lovingkindness is everlasting,
And His faithfulness to all generations.

*The Psalmist's Profession of Uprightness.*

A Psalm of David.

101 I WILL sing of lovingkindness and justice,
To Thee, O LORD, I will sing praises.
2 I will give heed to the [a]blameless way.
When wilt Thou come to me?
I will walk within my house in the integrity of my heart.
3 I will set no worthless thing before my eyes;
I hate the work of those who fall away;
It shall not fasten its grip on me.
4 A perverse heart shall depart from me;
I will know no evil.
5 Whoever secretly slanders his neighbor, him I will destroy;
No one who has a haughty look and an arrogant heart will I endure.

6¶ My eyes shall be upon the faithful of the land, that they may dwell with me;
He who walks in a [b]blameless way is the one who will minister to me.
7 He who practices deceit shall not dwell within my house;
He who speaks falsehood shall not maintain his position before me.
8 Every morning I will [c]destroy all the wicked of the land,
So as to cut off from the city of the LORD all those who do iniquity.

*Prayer of an Afflicted Man for Mercy on Himself and on Zion.*

A Prayer of the Afflicted, when he is faint, and pours out his complaint before the LORD.

102 HEAR MY prayer, O LORD! And let my cry for help come to Thee.
2 Do not hide Thy face from me in the day of my distress;
Incline Thine ear to me;
In the day when I call answer me quickly.
3 For my days have been consumed in smoke,
And my bones have been scorched like a hearth.
4 My heart has been smitten like grass and has withered away,
Indeed, I forget to eat my bread.
5 Because of the loudness of my groaning
My bones cling to my flesh.
6 I resemble a pelican of the wilderness;
I have become like an owl of the waste places.
7 I lie awake,
I have become like a lonely bird on a housetop.

8¶ My enemies have reproached me all day long;
Those who deride me have used my *name* as a curse.
9 For I have eaten ashes like bread,
And mingled my drink with weeping,

NAS [a] Or, *way of integrity* [b] Or, *way of integrity* [c] Or, *silence*

## New International

4Enter his gates with thanksgiving
and his courts with praise;
give thanks to him and praise his name.
5For the LORD is good and his love endures forever;
his faithfulness continues through all generations.

Of David. A psalm.

101 I WILL sing of your love and justice;
to you, O LORD, I will sing praise.
2I will be careful to lead a blameless life—
when will you come to me?
I will walk in my house
with blameless heart.
3I will set before my eyes
no vile thing.
The deeds of faithless men I hate;
they will not cling to me.
4Men of perverse heart shall be far from me;
I will have nothing to do with evil.

5Whoever slanders his neighbor in secret,
him will I put to silence;
whoever has haughty eyes and a proud heart,
him will I not endure.
6My eyes will be on the faithful in the land,
that they may dwell with me;
he whose walk is blameless
will minister to me.
7No one who practices deceit
will dwell in my house;
no one who speaks falsely
will stand in my presence.

8Every morning I will put to silence
all the wicked in the land;
I will cut off every evildoer
from the city of the LORD.

A prayer of an afflicted man. When he is faint and pours out his lament before the LORD.

102 HEAR MY prayer, O LORD;
let my cry for help come to you.
2Do not hide your face from me
when I am in distress.
Turn your ear to me;
when I call, answer me quickly.
3For my days vanish like smoke;
my bones burn like glowing embers.
4My heart is blighted and withered like grass;
I forget to eat my food.
5Because of my loud groaning
I am reduced to skin and bones.
6I am like a desert owl,
like an owl among the ruins.
7I lie awake; I have become
like a bird alone on a roof.
8All day long my enemies taunt me;
those who rail against me use my name as a curse.
9For I eat ashes as my food
and mingle my drink with tears

## King James

10Because of thine indignation and thy wrath: for thou hast lifted me up, and cast me down.

11My days *are* like a shadow that declineth; and I am withered like grass.

12But thou, O LORD, shalt endure for ever; and thy remembrance unto all generations.

13Thou shalt arise, *and* have mercy upon Zion: for the time to favour her, yea, the set time, is come.

14For thy servants take pleasure in her stones, and favour the dust thereof.

15So the heathen shall fear the name of the LORD, and all the kings of the earth thy glory.

16When the LORD shall build up Zion, he shall appear in his glory.

17He will regard the prayer of the destitute, and not despise their prayer.

18This shall be written for the generation to come: and the people which shall be created shall praise the LORD.

19For he hath looked down from the height of his sanctuary; from heaven did the LORD behold the earth;

20To hear the groaning of the prisoner; to loose those that are appointed to death;

21To declare the name of the LORD in Zion, and his praise in Jerusalem;

22When the people are gathered together, and the kingdoms, to serve the LORD.

23He weakened my strength in the way; he shortened my days.

24I said, O my God, take me not away in the midst of my days: thy years *are* throughout all generations.

25Of old hast thou laid the foundation of the earth: and the heavens *are* the work of thy hands.

26They shall perish, but thou shalt endure: yea, all of them shall wax old like a garment; as a vesture shalt thou change them, and they shall be changed:

27But thou *art* the same, and thy years shall have no end.

28The children of thy servants shall continue, and their seed shall be established before thee.

*A Psalm* of David.

**103** BLESS THE LORD, O my soul: and all that is within me, *bless* his holy name.

2Bless the LORD, O my soul, and forget not all his benefits:

3Who forgiveth all thine iniquities; who healeth all thy diseases;

4Who redeemeth thy life from destruction; who crowneth thee with lovingkindness and tender mercies;

5Who satisfieth thy mouth with good *things; so that* thy youth is renewed like the eagle's.

6The LORD executeth righteousness and judgment for all that are oppressed.

7He made known his ways unto Moses, his acts unto the children of Israel.

8The LORD *is* merciful and gracious, slow to anger, and plenteous in mercy.

9He will not always chide: neither will he keep *his anger* for ever.

## Amplified

10Because of Your indignation and Your wrath; for You have taken me up and cast me away.

11My days are like an evening shadow that stretches out *and* declines [with the sun], and I am withered like grass.

12But You, O Lord, are enthroned for ever, and the fame of Your name endures to all generations.

13You will arise *and* have mercy *and* loving-kindness *for* Zion, for it is time to have pity *and* compassion for her, yes, the set time is come—the moment designated. [Pss. 12:5; 119:126.]

14For Your servants take [melancholy] pleasure in the stones *of her ruins,* and show pity for her dust.

15So the nations shall fear *and* worshipfully revere the name of the Lord, and all the kings of the earth Your glory. [Ps. 96:9.]

16When the Lord builds up Zion, He will appear in His glory;

17He will regard the plea of the destitute, and will not despise their prayer.

18Let this be recorded for the generation yet unborn, and a people yet to be created shall praise the Lord.

19For He looked down from the height of His sanctuary, from Heaven did the Lord behold the earth,

20To hear the sighing *and* groaning of the prisoner, to loose those who are appointed to death;

21That men may declare the name of the Lord in Zion, and His praise in Jerusalem,

22When peoples are gathered together, and kingdoms, to worship *and* serve the Lord.

23He has afflicted *and* weakened my strength, humbling *and* bringing me low [with sorrow] in the way; He has shortened my days [aging me prematurely].

24I said, O my God, take me not away in the midst of my days, You Whose years continue throughout all generations.

25At the beginning You existed *and* laid the foundation of the earth; the heavens are the work of Your hands.

26They shall perish, but You shall remain *and* endure; yes, all of them shall wear out *and* become old like a garment. Like clothing You shall change them, and they shall be changed *and* pass away.

27But You remain the same, and Your years shall have no end. [Heb. 1:10-12.]

28The children of Your servants shall dwell safely *and* continue, and their descendants shall be established before You.

[*A Psalm*] of David.

**103** BLESS — AFFECTIONATELY, gratefully praise—the Lord, O my soul, and all that is [deepest] within me, bless His holy name!

2Bless—affectionately, gratefully praise—the Lord, O my soul, and forget not [one of] all His benefits,

3Who forgives [every one of] all your iniquities, Who heals [each of] all your diseases;

4Who redeems your life from the pit *and* corruption; Who beautifies, dignifies *and* crowns you with loving-kindness and tender mercies;

5Who satisfies your mouth [your necessity and desire at your personal age] with good; so that your youth, renewed, is like the eagle's [strong, overcoming, soaring]! [Isa. 40:31.]

6The Lord executes righteousness *and* justice [not for me only, but] for all who are oppressed.

7He made known His ways [of righteousness and justice] to Moses, His acts to the children of Israel.

8The Lord is merciful and gracious, slow to anger, and plenteous in mercy *and* loving-kindness. [James 5:11.]

9He will not always chide *or* be contending, neither will He keep His anger for ever *or* hold a grudge.

## New American Standard

10 Because of Thine indignation and Thy wrath;
For Thou hast lifted me up and cast me away.
11 My days are like a lengthened shadow;
And I wither away like grass.

12¶ But Thou, O LORD, dost abide forever;
And Thy name to all generations.
13 Thou wilt arise *and* have compassion on Zion;
For it is time to be gracious to her,
For the appointed time has come.
14 Surely Thy servants find pleasure in her stones,
And feel pity for her dust.
15 So the nations will fear the name of the LORD,
And all the kings of the earth Thy glory.
16 For the LORD has built up Zion;
He has appeared in His glory.
17 He has regarded the prayer of the destitute,
And has not despised their prayer.
18¶ This will be written for the generation to come;
That a people yet to be created may praise the LORD.
19 For He looked down from His holy height;
From heaven the LORD gazed upon the earth,
20 To hear the groaning of the prisoner;
To set free those who were doomed to death;
21 That *men* may tell of the name of the LORD in Zion,
And His praise in Jerusalem;
22 When the peoples are gathered together,
And the kingdoms, to serve the LORD.

23¶ He has weakened my strength in the way;
He has shortened my days.
24 I say, "O my God, do not take me away in the midst of my days,
Thy years are throughout all generations.
25 "Of old Thou didst found the earth;
And the heavens are the work of Thy hands.
26 "Even they will perish, but Thou dost endure;
And all of them will wear out like a garment;
Like clothing Thou wilt change them, and they will be changed.
27 "But Thou art the same,
And Thy years will not come to an end.
28 "The children of Thy servants will continue,
And their descendants will be established before Thee."

*Praise for the LORD's Mercies.*

*A Psalm of David.*

103 BLESS THE LORD, O my soul;
And all that is within me, *bless* His holy name.
2 Bless the LORD, O my soul,
And forget none of His benefits;
3 Who pardons all your iniquities;
Who heals all your diseases;
4 Who redeems your life from the pit;
Who crowns you with lovingkindness and compassion;
5 Who satisfies your [a]years with good things,
*So that* your youth is renewed like the eagle.

6¶ The LORD performs righteous deeds,
And judgments for all who are oppressed.
7 He made known His ways to Moses,
His acts to the sons of Israel.
8 The LORD is compassionate and gracious,
Slow to anger and abounding in lovingkindness.
9 He will not always strive *with us;*
Nor will He keep *His anger* forever.

NAS [a] Or, *desire*

## New International

10because of your great wrath,
for you have taken me up and thrown me aside.
11My days are like the evening shadow;
I wither away like grass.

12But you, O LORD, sit enthroned forever;
your renown endures through all generations.
13You will arise and have compassion on Zion,
for it is time to show favor to her;
the appointed time has come.
14For her stones are dear to your servants;
her very dust moves them to pity.
15The nations will fear the name of the LORD,
all the kings of the earth will revere your glory.
16For the LORD will rebuild Zion
and appear in his glory.
17He will respond to the prayer of the destitute;
he will not despise their plea.

18Let this be written for a future generation,
that a people not yet created may praise the LORD:
19"The LORD looked down from his sanctuary on high,
from heaven he viewed the earth,
20to hear the groans of the prisoners
and release those condemned to death."
21So the name of the LORD will be declared in Zion
and his praise in Jerusalem
22when the peoples and the kingdoms
assemble to worship the LORD.

23In the course of my life[b] he broke my strength;
he cut short my days.
24So I said:
"Do not take me away, O my God, in the midst of my days;
your years go on through all generations.
25In the beginning you laid the foundations of the earth,
and the heavens are the work of your hands.
26They will perish, but you remain;
they will all wear out like a garment.
Like clothing you will change them
and they will be discarded.
27But you remain the same,
and your years will never end.
28The children of your servants will live in your presence;
their descendants will be established before you."

Of David.

103 PRAISE THE LORD, O my soul;
all my inmost being, praise his holy name.
2Praise the LORD, O my soul,
and forget not all his benefits—
3who forgives all your sins
and heals all your diseases,
4who redeems your life from the pit
and crowns you with love and compassion,
5who satisfies your desires with good things
so that your youth is renewed like the eagle's.

6The LORD works righteousness
and justice for all the oppressed.

7He made known his ways to Moses,
his deeds to the people of Israel:
8The LORD is compassionate and gracious,
slow to anger, abounding in love.
9He will not always accuse,
nor will he harbor his anger forever;

NIV [b] 23 Or *By his power*

## King James

10He hath not dealt with us after our sins; nor rewarded us according to our iniquities.

11For as the heaven is high above the earth, *so* great is his mercy toward them that fear him.

12As far as the east is from the west, *so* far hath he removed our transgressions from us.

13Like as a father pitieth *his* children, *so* the LORD pitieth them that fear him.

14For he knoweth our frame; he remembereth that we *are* dust.

15 *As for* man, his days *are* as grass: as a flower of the field, so he flourisheth.

16For the wind passeth over it, and it is gone; and the place thereof shall know it no more.

17But the mercy of the LORD *is* from everlasting to everlasting upon them that fear him, and his righteousness unto children's children;

18To such as keep his covenant, and to those that remember his commandments to do them.

19The LORD hath prepared his throne in the heavens; and his kingdom ruleth over all.

20Bless the LORD, ye his angels, that excel in strength, that do his commandments, hearkening unto the voice of his word.

21Bless ye the LORD, all *ye* his hosts; ye ministers of his, that do his pleasure.

22Bless the LORD, all his works in all places of his dominion: bless the LORD, O my soul.

**104** BLESS THE LORD, O my soul. O LORD my God, thou art very great; thou art clothed with honour and majesty.

2Who coverest *thyself* with light as *with* a garment: who stretchest out the heavens like a curtain:

3Who layeth the beams of his chambers in the waters: who maketh the clouds his chariot: who walketh upon the wings of the wind:

4Who maketh his angels spirits; his ministers a flaming fire:

5 *Who* laid the foundations of the earth, *that* it should not be removed for ever.

6Thou coveredst it with the deep as *with* a garment: the waters stood above the mountains.

7At thy rebuke they fled; at the voice of thy thunder they hasted away.

8They go up by the mountains; they go down by the valleys unto the place which thou hast founded for them.

9Thou hast set a bound that they may not pass over; that they turn not again to cover the earth.

10He sendeth the springs into the valleys, *which* run among the hills.

11They give drink to every beast of the field: the wild asses quench their thirst.

12By them shall the fowls of the heaven have their habitation, *which* sing among the branches.

13He watereth the hills from his chambers: the earth is satisfied with the fruit of thy works.

## Amplified

10He has not dealt with us after our sins, nor rewarded us according to our iniquities.

11For as the heavens are high above the earth, so great are His mercy *and* loving-kindness toward those who reverently *and* worshipfully fear Him.

12As far as the east is from the west, so far has He removed our transgressions from us.

13As a father loves *and* pities his children, so the Lord loves *and* pities those who fear Him—with reverence, worship and awe.

14For He knows our frame; He [earnestly] remembers *and* imprints [on His heart] that we are dust.

15As for man, his days are as grass; as a flower of the field, so he flourishes.

16For the wind passes over it, and it is gone, and its place shall know it no more.

17But the mercy *and* loving-kindness of the Lord are from everlasting to everlasting upon those who reverently *and* worshipfully fear Him, and His righteousness is to children's children, [Deut. 10:12.]

18To such as keep His covenant—hearing, receiving, loving and obeying it; and to those who [earnestly] remember His commandments to do them [imprinting them on their hearts].

19The Lord has established His throne in the heavens; and His kingdom rules over all.

20Bless—affectionately, gratefully praise—the Lord, you His angels, you mighty ones who do His commandments, hearkening to the voice of His word.

21Bless—affectionately, gratefully praise—the Lord, all you His hosts, you ministers of His who do His pleasure.

22Bless the Lord, all His works in all places of His dominion; bless—affectionately, gratefully praise—the Lord, O my soul!

**104** BLESS — AFFECTIONATELY, gratefully praise—the Lord, O my soul! O Lord my God, You are very great! You are clothed with honor and majesty:

2Who cover Yourself with light as with a garment, Who has stretched out the heavens like a curtain *or* a tent,

3Who lays the beams of the upper room of His abode in the waters [above the firmament], Who makes the clouds His chariot, Who walks on the wings of the wind,

4Who makes winds His messengers, flames of fire His ministers. [Heb. 1:7.]

5You laid the foundations of the earth, that it should not be moved for ever. [Job 38:4, 6.]

6You covered it with the deep as with a garment; the waters stood above the mountains. [Gen. 1:2; II Pet. 3:5.]

7At Your rebuke they fled; at the voice of Your thunder they hasted away.

8The mountains rose, the valleys sank down to the place which You appointed for them.

9You have set a boundary [for the waters] which they may not pass over, that they turn not again to deluge the earth.

10He sends forth springs into the valleys; their waters run among the mountains.

11They give drink to every [wild] beast of the field; the wild asses quench their thirst there.

12Beside them the birds of the heavens have their nests; they sing among the branches. [Matt. 13:32.]

13He waters the mountains from His upper rooms; the earth is satisfied *and* abounds with the fruit of *His* works.

## New American Standard

10 He has not dealt with us according to our sins,
Nor rewarded us according to our iniquities.
11 For as high as the heavens are above the earth,
So great is His lovingkindness toward those who [a]fear Him.
12 As far as the east is from the west,
So far has He removed our transgressions from us.
13 Just as a father has compassion on *his* children,
So the LORD has compassion on those who fear Him.
14 For He Himself knows [b]our frame;
He is mindful that we are *but* dust.

15¶ As for man, his days are like grass;
As a flower of the field, so he flourishes.
16 When the wind has passed over it, it is no more;
And its place acknowledges it no longer.
17 But the lovingkindness of the LORD is from everlasting to everlasting on those who [c]fear Him,
And His righteousness to children's children,
18 To those who keep His covenant,
And who remember His precepts to do them.

19¶ The LORD has established His throne in the heavens;
And His [d]sovereignty rules over all.
20 Bless the LORD, you His angels,
Mighty in strength, who perform His word,
Obeying the voice of His word!
21 Bless the LORD, all you His hosts,
You who serve Him, doing His will.
22 Bless the LORD, all you works of His,
In all places of His dominion;
Bless the LORD, O my soul!

*The LORD's Care over All His Works.*

**104** BLESS THE LORD, O my soul!
O LORD my God, Thou art very great;
Thou art clothed with splendor and majesty,
2 Covering Thyself with light as with a cloak,
Stretching out heaven like a *tent* curtain.
3 [e]He lays the beams of His upper chambers in the waters;
He makes the clouds His chariot;
He walks upon the wings of the wind;
4 He makes [f]the winds His messengers,
[g]Flaming fire His ministers.

5¶ He established the earth upon its foundations,
So that it will not [h]totter forever and ever.
6 Thou didst cover it with the deep as with a garment;
The waters were standing above the mountains.
7 At Thy rebuke they fled;
At the sound of Thy thunder they hurried away.
8 The mountains rose; the valleys sank down
To the place which Thou didst establish for them.
9 Thou didst set a boundary that they may not pass over;
That they may not return to cover the earth.

10¶ He sends forth springs in the valleys;
They flow between the mountains;
11 They give drink to every beast of the field;
The wild donkeys quench their thirst.
12 Beside them the birds of the heavens dwell;
They lift up *their* voices among the branches.
13 He waters the mountains from His upper chambers;
The earth is satisfied with the fruit of His works.

NAS [a] Or, *revere* [b] I.e., what we are made of [c] Or, *revere* [d] Or, *kingdom* [e] Lit., *Who*, so through v. 4, and vv. 13, 14 [f] Or, *His angels, spirits* [g] Or, *His ministers flames of fire* [h] Or, *move out of place*

## New International

10he does not treat us as our sins deserve
or repay us according to our iniquities.
11For as high as the heavens are above the earth,
so great is his love for those who fear him;
12as far as the east is from the west,
so far has he removed our transgressions from us.
13As a father has compassion on his children,
so the LORD has compassion on those who fear him;
14for he knows how we are formed,
he remembers that we are dust.
15As for man, his days are like grass,
he flourishes like a flower of the field;
16the wind blows over it and it is gone,
and its place remembers it no more.
17But from everlasting to everlasting
the LORD's love is with those who fear him,
and his righteousness with their children's children—
18with those who keep his covenant
and remember to obey his precepts.

19The LORD has established his throne in heaven,
and his kingdom rules over all.

20Praise the LORD, you his angels,
you mighty ones who do his bidding,
who obey his word.
21Praise the LORD, all his heavenly hosts,
you his servants who do his will.
22Praise the LORD, all his works
everywhere in his dominion.

Praise the LORD, O my soul.

**104** PRAISE THE LORD, O my soul.
O LORD my God, you are very great;
you are clothed with splendor and majesty.
2He wraps himself in light as with a garment;
he stretches out the heavens like a tent
3 and lays the beams of his upper chambers on their waters.
He makes the clouds his chariot
and rides on the wings of the wind.
4He makes winds his messengers,[i]
flames of fire his servants.

5He set the earth on its foundations;
it can never be moved.
6You covered it with the deep as with a garment;
the waters stood above the mountains.
7But at your rebuke the waters fled,
at the sound of your thunder they took to flight;
8they flowed over the mountains,
they went down into the valleys,
to the place you assigned for them.
9You set a boundary they cannot cross;
never again will they cover the earth.

10He makes springs pour water into the ravines;
it flows between the mountains.
11They give water to all the beasts of the field;
the wild donkeys quench their thirst.
12The birds of the air nest by the waters;
they sing among the branches.
13He waters the mountains from his upper chambers;
the earth is satisfied by the fruit of his work.

NIV [i] 4 Or *angels*

## King James

14 He causeth the grass to grow for the cattle, and herb for the service of man: that he may bring forth food out of the earth;

15 And wine *that* maketh glad the heart of man, *and* oil to make *his* face to shine, and bread *which* strengtheneth man's heart.

16 The trees of the LORD are full *of sap;* the cedars of Lebanon, which he hath planted;

17 Where the birds make their nests: *as for* the stork, the fir trees *are* her house.

18 The high hills *are* a refuge for the wild goats; *and* the rocks for the conies.

19 He appointed the moon for seasons: the sun knoweth his going down.

20 Thou makest darkness, and it is night: wherein all the beasts of the forest do creep *forth*.

21 The young lions roar after their prey, and seek their meat from God.

22 The sun ariseth, they gather themselves together, and lay them down in their dens.

23 Man goeth forth unto his work and to his labour until the evening.

24 O LORD, how manifold are thy works! in wisdom hast thou made them all: the earth is full of thy riches.

25 *So is* this great and wide sea, wherein *are* things creeping innumerable, both small and great beasts.

26 There go the ships: *there is* that leviathan, *whom* thou hast made to play therein.

27 These wait all upon thee; that thou mayest give *them* their meat in due season.

28 *That* thou givest them they gather: thou openest thine hand, they are filled with good.

29 Thou hidest thy face, they are troubled: thou takest away their breath, they die, and return to their dust.

30 Thou sendest forth thy spirit, they are created: and thou renewest the face of the earth.

31 The glory of the LORD shall endure for ever: the LORD shall rejoice in his works.

32 He looketh on the earth, and it trembleth: he toucheth the hills, and they smoke.

33 I will sing unto the LORD as long as I live: I will sing praise to my God while I have my being.

34 My meditation of him shall be sweet: I will be glad in the LORD.

35 Let the sinners be consumed out of the earth, and let the wicked be no more. Bless thou the LORD, O my soul. Praise ye the LORD.

**105** O GIVE thanks unto the LORD; call upon his name: make known his deeds among the people.

2 Sing unto him, sing psalms unto him: talk ye of all his wondrous works.

## Amplified

14 He causes vegetation to grow for the cattle, and all that the earth produces for man to cultivate, that he may bring forth food out of the earth;

15 And wine that gladdens the heart of man, to make his face shine more than oil, and bread to support, refresh *and* strengthen man's heart.

16 The trees of the Lord are watered abundantly *and* are filled with sap, the cedars of Lebanon which He has planted,

17 Where the birds make their nests; as for the stork, the fir trees are her house.

18 The high mountains are for the wild goats; the rocks are a refuge for the conies *and* badgers.

19 *The Lord* appointed the moon for seasons; the sun knows [the exact time of] its setting.

20 You, *O Lord,* make darkness, and it becomes night, in which creeps forth every wild beast of the forest.

21 The young lions roar after their prey, and seek their food from God.

22 When the sun arises, they withdraw themselves, and lie down in their dens.

23 Man goes forth to his work and remains at his task until evening.

24 O Lord, how many *and* varied are Your works! In wisdom have You made them all; the earth is full of Your riches *and* Your creatures.

25 Yonder is the sea, great and wide, in which are swarms of innumerable creeping things, creatures both small and great.

26 There go the ships of the sea, and Leviathan (the sea monster) which You have formed to sport in it.

27 These all wait *and* are dependent upon You, that You may give them their food in due season.

28 When You give to them they gather it up; You open Your hand, and they are filled with good things.

29 When You hide Your face, they are troubled *and* dismayed; when You take away their breath, they die and return to their dust.

30 When You send forth Your Spirit *and* give them breath, they are created; and You replenish the face of the ground.

31 May the glory of the Lord endure for ever; may the Lord rejoice in His works,

32 Who looks on the earth and it quakes *and* trembles; Who touches the mountains and they smoke!

33 I will sing to the Lord as long as I live; I will sing praise to my God while I have any being.

34 May my meditation be sweet to Him; as for me, I will rejoice in the Lord.

35 Let sinners be consumed from the earth, and let the wicked be no more. Bless—affectionately, gratefully praise—the Lord, O my soul! Praise the Lord!—Hallelujah!

**105** O GIVE thanks unto the Lord, call upon His name, make known His doings among the peoples!

2 Sing to Him, sing praises to Him; meditate *and* talk of all His marvelous deeds *and* devoutly praise them.

## New American Standard

14¶ He causes the grass to grow for the cattle,
And vegetation for the labor of man,
So that he may bring forth food from the earth,
15 And wine which makes man's heart glad,
So that he may make *his* face glisten with oil,
And food which sustains man's heart.
16 The trees of the LORD drink their fill,
The cedars of Lebanon which He planted,
17 Where the birds build their nests,
*And* the stork, whose home is the fir trees.

18¶ The high mountains are for the wild goats;
The cliffs are a refuge for the rock badgers.
19 He made the moon for the seasons;
The sun knows the place of its setting.
20 Thou dost appoint darkness and it becomes night,
In which all the beasts of the forest prowl about.
21 The young lions roar after their prey,
And seek their food from God.
22 *When* the sun rises they withdraw,
And lie down in their dens.
23 Man goes forth to his work
And to his labor until evening.

24¶ O LORD, how many are Thy works!
In wisdom Thou hast made them all;
The earth is full of Thy [a]possessions.
25 There is the sea, great and broad,
In which are swarms without number,
Animals both small and great.
26 There the ships move along,
*And* [b]Leviathan, which Thou hast formed to sport in it.

27¶ They all wait for Thee,
To give them their food in [c]due season.
28 Thou dost give to them, they gather *it* up;
Thou dost open Thy hand, they are satisfied with good.
29 Thou dost hide Thy face, they are dismayed;
Thou dost take away their [d]spirit, they expire,
And return to their dust.
30 Thou dost send forth Thy [e]Spirit, they are created;
And Thou dost renew the face of the ground.

31¶ Let the glory of the LORD endure forever;
Let the LORD be glad in His works;
32 He looks at the earth, and it trembles;
He touches the mountains, and they smoke.
33 I will sing to the LORD as long as I live;
I will sing praise to my God while I have my being.
34 Let my meditation be pleasing to Him;
As for me, I shall be glad in the LORD.
35 Let sinners be consumed from the earth,
And let the wicked be no more.
Bless the LORD, O my soul.
Praise the LORD!

*The LORD's Wonderful Works in Behalf of Israel.*

**105** OH GIVE thanks to the LORD, call upon His name;
Make known His deeds among the peoples.
2 Sing to Him, sing praises to Him;
[f]Speak of all His wonders.

NAS [a] Or, *creatures* [b] Or, *a sea monster* [c] Lit., *its appointed time* [d] Or, *breath* [e] Or, *breath* [f] Or, *Meditate on*

## New International

14He makes grass grow for the cattle,
and plants for man to cultivate—
bringing forth food from the earth:
15wine that gladdens the heart of man,
oil to make his face shine,
and bread that sustains his heart.
16The trees of the LORD are well watered,
the cedars of Lebanon that he planted.
17There the birds make their nests;
the stork has its home in the pine trees.
18The high mountains belong to the wild goats;
the crags are a refuge for the coneys.[g]
19The moon marks off the seasons,
and the sun knows when to go down.
20You bring darkness, it becomes night,
and all the beasts of the forest prowl.
21The lions roar for their prey
and seek their food from God.
22The sun rises, and they steal away;
they return and lie down in their dens.
23Then man goes out to his work,
to his labor until evening.

24How many are your works, O LORD!
In wisdom you made them all;
the earth is full of your creatures.
25There is the sea, vast and spacious,
teeming with creatures beyond number—
living things both large and small.
26There the ships go to and fro,
and the leviathan, which you formed to frolic there.
27These all look to you
to give them their food at the proper time.
28When you give it to them,
they gather it up;
when you open your hand,
they are satisfied with good things.
29When you hide your face,
they are terrified;
when you take away their breath,
they die and return to the dust.
30When you send your Spirit,
they are created,
and you renew the face of the earth.

31May the glory of the LORD endure forever;
may the LORD rejoice in his works—
32he who looks at the earth, and it trembles,
who touches the mountains, and they smoke.

33I will sing to the LORD all my life;
I will sing praise to my God as long as I live.
34May my meditation be pleasing to him,
as I rejoice in the LORD.
35But may sinners vanish from the earth
and the wicked be no more.
Praise the LORD, O my soul.
Praise the LORD.[h]

**105** GIVE THANKS to the LORD, call on his name;
make known among the nations what he has done.
2Sing to him, sing praise to him;
tell of all his wonderful acts.

NIV [g] *18* That is, the hyrax or rock badger [h] *35* Hebrew *Hallelu Yah;* in the Septuagint this line stands at the beginning of Psalm 105.

## King James

3Glory ye in his holy name: let the heart of them rejoice that seek
the LORD.
4Seek the LORD, and his strength: seek his face evermore.
5Remember his marvellous works that he hath done; his wonders, and the judgments of his mouth;
6O ye seed of Abraham his servant, ye children of Jacob his
chosen.
7He *is* the LORD our God: his judgments *are* in all the earth.
8He hath remembered his covenant for ever, the word *which* he
commanded to a thousand generations.
9Which *covenant* he made with Abraham, and his oath unto
Isaac;
10And confirmed the same unto Jacob for a law, *and* to Israel *for*
an everlasting covenant:
11Saying, Unto thee will I give the land of Canaan, the lot of
your inheritance:
12When they were *but* a few men in number; yea, very few, and
strangers in it.
13When they went from one nation to another, from *one* kingdom to another people;
14He suffered no man to do them wrong: yea, he reproved kings
for their sakes;
15 *Saying*, Touch not mine anointed, and do my prophets no
harm.
16Moreover he called for a famine upon the land: he brake the
whole staff of bread.
17He sent a man before them, *even* Joseph, *who* was sold for a
servant:
18Whose feet they hurt with fetters: he was laid in iron:
19Until the time that his word came: the word of the LORD tried
him.
20The king sent and loosed him; *even* the ruler of the people, and
let him go free.
21He made him lord of his house, and ruler of all his substance:
22To bind his princes at his pleasure; and teach his senators
wisdom.
23Israel also came into Egypt; and Jacob sojourned in the land
of Ham.
24And he increased his people greatly; and made them stronger
than their enemies.
25He turned their heart to hate his people, to deal subtly with
his servants.
26He sent Moses his servant; *and* Aaron whom he had chosen.
27They showed his signs among them, and wonders in the land
of Ham.
28He sent darkness, and made it dark; and they rebelled not
against his word.
29He turned their waters into blood, and slew their fish.
30Their land brought forth frogs in abundance, in the chambers
of their kings.
31He spake, and there came divers sorts of flies, *and* lice in all
their coasts.
32He gave them hail for rain, *and* flaming fire in their land.
33He smote their vines also and their fig trees; and brake the
trees of their coasts.
34He spake, and the locusts came, and caterpillars, and that
without number,
35And did eat up all the herbs in their land, and devoured the
fruit of their ground.
36He smote also all the firstborn in their land, the chief of all
their strength.

## Amplified

3Glory in His holy name; let the heart of those rejoice who seek
*and* require the Lord [as their indispensable necessity].
4Seek, inquire of *and* for the Lord, *and* crave Him and His
strength [His might and inflexibility to temptation, seek and require His face and His presence continually] evermore.
5[Earnestly] remember the marvelous deeds that He has done,
His miracles *and* wonders, the judgments *and* sentences which He
pronounced [upon His enemies, as in Egypt]. [Ps. 78: 43-51.]
6O you offspring of Abraham His servant, you children of
Jacob, His chosen ones,
7He is the Lord our God; His judgments are in all the earth.
8He is [earnestly] mindful of His covenant, *and* for ever [it is
imprinted on His heart], the word which He commanded *and*
established to a thousand generations;
9The covenant which He made with Abraham, and His sworn
promise to Isaac, [Luke 1:72, 73.]
10Which He confirmed to Jacob as a statute, to Israel as an
everlasting covenant;
11Saying, Unto you will I give the land of Canaan, as your
measured portion, possession *and* inheritance.
12When they were but a few men in number, in fact, very few,
and were temporary residents *and* strangers in it;
13When they went from one nation to another, from one kingdom to another people,
14He allowed no man to do them wrong; in fact, He reproved
kings for their sakes, [Gen. 12:17; 20:3-7.]
15Saying, Touch not My anointed, and do My prophets no
harm. [I Chron. 16:8-22.]
16Moreover He called for a famine upon the land [of Egypt]; He
cut off every source of bread. [Gen. 41:54.]
17He sent a man before them, even Joseph, who was sold for
a servant. [Gen. 45:5; 50:20, 21.]
18His feet they hurt with fetters, he was laid in chains of iron
*and* his soul entered into the iron;
19Until his word [to his cruel brothers] came true, the word of
the Lord tried *and* tested him.
20The king sent and loosed him, even the ruler of the peoples,
and let him go free.
21He made Joseph lord of his house, and ruler of all his substance, [Gen. 41:40.]
22To bind his princes at his pleasure and teach his elders wisdom.
23Israel also came into Egypt, and Jacob sojourned in the land
of Ham. [Gen. 46:6.]
24There [the Lord] greatly increased His people, and made them
stronger than their oppressors.
25He turned the heart [of the Egyptians] to hate His people, to
deal craftily with His servants.
26He sent Moses His servant, and Aaron whom He had chosen.
27They showed His signs among them, wonders *and* miracles
in the land of Ham [Egypt].
28He sent [thick] darkness, and made the land dark, and they
[God's two servants] rebelled not against His word. [Exod. 10:22;
Ps. 99:7.]
29He turned [Egypt's] waters into blood, and caused their fish
to die. [Exod. 7:20, 21.]
30Their land brought forth frogs in abundance, even in the
chambers of their kings. [Exod. 8:6.]
31He spoke, and there came swarms of beetles *and* flies and
mosquitoes *and* lice in all their borders. [Exod. 8:17, 24.]
32He gave them hail for rain, with lightning like flaming fire on
their land. [Exod. 9:23, 25.]
33He smote their vines also and their fig trees, and broke the
[ice-laden] trees of their borders. [Ps. 78:47.]
34He spoke, and the locust came, and the grasshopper, and that
without number, [Exod. 10:4, 13, 14.]
35And ate up all the vegetation in their land, and devoured the
fruit of their ground.
36He smote also all the first-born in their land, the beginning *and*
chief substance of all their strength. [Exod. 12:29; Ps. 78:51.]

## New American Standard

3 Glory in His holy name;
Let the heart of those who seek the LORD be glad.
4 Seek the LORD and His strength;
Seek His face continually.
5 Remember His wonders which He has done,
His marvels, and the judgments uttered by His mouth,
6 O seed of Abraham, His servant,
O sons of Jacob, His chosen ones!
7 He is the LORD our God;
His judgments are in all the earth.

8¶ He has remembered His covenant forever,
The word which He commanded to a thousand generations,
9 *The covenant* which He made with Abraham,
And His oath to Isaac.
10 Then He confirmed it to Jacob for a statute,
To Israel as an everlasting covenant,
11 Saying, "To you I will give the land of Canaan
As the portion of your inheritance,"
12 When they were only a few men in number,
Very few, and strangers in it.
13 And they wandered about from nation to nation,
From *one* kingdom to another people.
14 He permitted no man to oppress them,
And He reproved kings for their sakes:
15 "Do not touch My anointed ones,
And do My prophets no harm."

16¶ And He called for a famine upon the land;
He broke the whole staff of bread.
17 He sent a man before them,
Joseph, *who* was sold as a slave.
18 They afflicted his feet with fetters,
He himself was laid in irons;
19 Until the time that his word came to pass,
The word of the LORD tested him.
20 The king sent and released him,
The ruler of peoples, and set him free.
21 He made him lord of his house,
And ruler over all his possessions,
22 To imprison his princes at will,
That he might teach his elders wisdom.
23 Israel also came into Egypt;
Thus Jacob sojourned in the land of Ham.
24 And He caused His people to be very fruitful,
And made them stronger than their adversaries.

25¶ He turned their heart to hate His people,
To deal craftily with His servants.
26 He sent Moses His servant,
*And* Aaron whom He had chosen.
27 They performed His wondrous acts among them,
And miracles in the land of Ham.
28 He sent darkness and made *it* dark;
And they did not rebel against His words.
29 He turned their waters into blood,
And caused their fish to die.
30 Their land swarmed with frogs
*Even* in the chambers of their kings.
31 He spoke, and there came a swarm of flies
*And* gnats in all their territory.
32 He gave them hail for rain,
*And* flaming fire in their land.
33 He struck down their vines also and their fig trees,
And shattered the trees of their territory.
34 He spoke, and locusts came,
And young locusts, even without number,
35 And ate up all vegetation in their land,
And ate up the fruit of their ground.
36 He also struck down all the first-born in their land,
The first fruits of all their vigor.

## New International

3Glory in his holy name;
let the hearts of those who seek the LORD rejoice.
4Look to the LORD and his strength;
seek his face always.

5Remember the wonders he has done,
his miracles, and the judgments he pronounced,
6O descendants of Abraham his servant,
O sons of Jacob, his chosen ones.
7He is the LORD our God;
his judgments are in all the earth.

8He remembers his covenant forever,
the word he commanded, for a thousand generations,
9the covenant he made with Abraham,
the oath he swore to Isaac.
10He confirmed it to Jacob as a decree,
to Israel as an everlasting covenant:
11"To you I will give the land of Canaan
as the portion you will inherit."

12When they were but few in number,
few indeed, and strangers in it,
13they wandered from nation to nation,
from one kingdom to another.
14He allowed no one to oppress them;
for their sake he rebuked kings:
15"Do not touch my anointed ones;
do my prophets no harm."

16He called down famine on the land
and destroyed all their supplies of food;
17and he sent a man before them—
Joseph, sold as a slave.
18They bruised his feet with shackles,
his neck was put in irons,
19till what he foretold came to pass,
till the word of the LORD proved him true.
20The king sent and released him,
the ruler of peoples set him free.
21He made him master of his household,
ruler over all he possessed,
22to instruct his princes as he pleased
and teach his elders wisdom.

23Then Israel entered Egypt;
Jacob lived as an alien in the land of Ham.
24The LORD made his people very fruitful;
he made them too numerous for their foes,
25whose hearts he turned to hate his people,
to conspire against his servants.
26He sent Moses his servant,
and Aaron, whom he had chosen.
27They performed his miraculous signs among them,
his wonders in the land of Ham.
28He sent darkness and made the land dark—
for had they not rebelled against his words?
29He turned their waters into blood,
causing their fish to die.
30Their land teemed with frogs,
which went up into the bedrooms of their rulers.
31He spoke, and there came swarms of flies,
and gnats throughout their country.
32He turned their rain into hail,
with lightning throughout their land;
33he struck down their vines and fig trees
and shattered the trees of their country.
34He spoke, and the locusts came,
grasshoppers without number;
35they ate up every green thing in their land,
ate up the produce of their soil.
36Then he struck down all the firstborn in their land,
the firstfruits of all their manhood.

## King James

37He brought them forth also with silver and gold: and *there was*
not one feeble *person* among their tribes.
38Egypt was glad when they departed: for the fear of them fell
upon them.
39He spread a cloud for a covering; and fire to give light in the
night.
40 *The people* asked, and he brought quails, and satisfied them
with the bread of heaven.
41He opened the rock, and the waters gushed out; they ran in
the dry places *like* a river.
42For he remembered his holy promise, *and* Abraham his servant.
43And he brought forth his people with joy, *and* his chosen with
gladness:
44And gave them the lands of the heathen: and they inherited
the labour of the people;
45That they might observe his statutes, and keep his laws.
Praise ye the LORD.

**106** PRAISE YE the LORD. O give thanks unto the LORD; for
*he is* good: for his mercy *endureth* for ever.
2Who can utter the mighty acts of the LORD? *who* can show forth
all his praise?
3Blessed *are* they that keep judgment, *and* he that doeth righteousness at all times.
4Remember me, O LORD, with the favour *that thou bearest unto*
thy people: O visit me with thy salvation;
5That I may see the good of thy chosen, that I may rejoice in the
gladness of thy nation, that I may glory with thine inheritance.
6We have sinned with our fathers, we have committed iniquity,
we have done wickedly.
7Our fathers understood not thy wonders in Egypt; they
remembered not the multitude of thy mercies; but provoked *him*
at the sea, *even* at the Red sea.
8Nevertheless he saved them for his name's sake, that he might
make his mighty power to be known.
9He rebuked the Red sea also, and it was dried up: so he led
them through the depths, as through the wilderness.
10And he saved them from the hand of him that hated *them*, and
redeemed them from the hand of the enemy.
11And the waters covered their enemies: there was not one of
them left.
12Then believed they his words; they sang his praise.
13They soon forgat his works; they waited not for his counsel:
14But lusted exceedingly in the wilderness, and tempted God
in the desert.
15And he gave them their request; but sent leanness into their
soul.
16They envied Moses also in the camp, *and* Aaron the saint of
the LORD.
17The earth opened and swallowed up Dathan, and covered the
company of Abiram.

## Amplified

37He brought [Israel] forth also with silver and gold, and there
was not one feeble person among their tribes. [Exod. 12:35.]
38Egypt was glad when they departed, for the fear of them fell
upon the people. [Exod. 12:33.]
39The Lord spread a cloud for a covering [by day], and fire to
give light in the night. [Exod. 13:21.]
40 *The Israelites* asked, and He brought quails, and satisfied them
with the bread of heaven. [Exod. 16:12-15.]
41He opened the rock, and waters gushed out; they ran in the
dry places like a river. [Exod. 17:6; Num. 20:11.]
42For He [earnestly] remembered His holy word *and* promise,
and Abraham His servant. [Gen. 15:14.]
43And He brought forth His people with joy, and His chosen
with gladness *and* singing.
44And gave them the lands of the nations [of Canaan], and they
reaped the fruits of those peoples' labor, [Deut. 6:10, 11.]
45That they might observe His statutes and keep His laws [hear-
ing, receiving, loving and obeying them]. Praise the
Lord!—Hallelujah!

**106** PRAISE THE Lord! — Hallelujah! O give thanks to the
Lord, for He is good; for His mercy *and* loving-kindness endure for ever! [I Chron. 16:34.]
2Who can put into words *and* tell the mighty deeds of the Lord?
*Or* can show forth all the praise [that is due Him]?
3Blessed (happy, fortunate) [to be envied] are those who observe justice—treating others fairly— *and* who do right *and* are in
right standing with God at all times.
4[Earnestly] remember me, O Lord, when You favor Your
people! O visit me also when You deliver them, *and* grant me Your
salvation!
5That I may see *and* share the welfare of Your chosen *ones*, that
I may rejoice in the gladness of Your nation, that I may glory with
Your heritage.
6We have sinned as did also our fathers, we have committed
iniquity, we have done wickedly. [Lev. 26:40-42.]
7Our fathers in Egypt understood not nor appreciated Your
miracles; they did not [earnestly] remember the multitude of Your
mercies, nor imprint Your loving-kindness [on their hearts], but
they were rebellious *and* provoked the Lord at the sea, even at the
Red Sea. [Exod. 14:21.]
8Nevertheless He saved them for His name's sake [to prove the
righteousness of the divine character], that He might make His
mighty power to be known.
9He rebuked the Red Sea also, and it was dried up; so He led
them through the depths, as through a pasture land. [Exod. 14:21.]
10And He saved them from the hand of him that hated them,
and redeemed them from the hand of the [Egyptian] enemy.
[Exod. 14:30.]
11And the waters covered their adversaries; not one of them
was left. [Exod. 14:27, 28; 15:5.]
12Then [Israel] believed His words—trusting in, relying on
them; they sang His praise.
13But they hastily forgot His works; they did not [earnestly] wait
for His plans [to develop] respecting them;
14But lusted exceedingly in the wilderness, and tempted *and*
tried to restrain God [with their insistent desire] in the desert.
[Num. 11:4.]
15And He gave them their request, but sent leanness into their
soul *and* [thinned their numbers by] disease and death. [Ps.
78:29-31.]
16They envied Moses also in the camp, and Aaron, *the high
priest*, the holy one of the Lord; [Num. 16:1-3.]
17Therefore the earth opened and swallowed up Dathan, and
closed over the company of Abiram. [Num. 16:31, 32.]

## New American Standard

37¶ Then He brought them out with silver and gold;
And among His tribes there was not one who stumbled.
38 Egypt was glad when they departed;
For the dread of them had fallen upon them.
39 He spread a cloud for a [a]covering,
And fire to illumine by night.
40 They asked, and He brought quail,
And satisfied them with the bread of heaven.
41 He opened the rock, and water flowed out;
It ran in the dry places *like* a river.
42 For He remembered His holy word
*With* Abraham His servant;
43 And He brought forth His people with joy,
His chosen ones with a joyful shout.
44 He gave them also the lands of the nations,
That they might take possession of *the fruit of* the peoples' labor,
45 So that they might keep His statutes,
And observe His laws,
Praise the LORD!

*Israel's Rebelliousness and the LORD's Deliverances.*

**106** PRAISE THE LORD!
Oh give thanks to the LORD, for He is good;
For His lovingkindness is everlasting.
2 Who can speak of the mighty deeds of the LORD,
Or can show forth all His praise?
3 How blessed are those who keep justice,
Who practice righteousness at all times!

4¶ Remember me, O LORD, in *Thy* favor toward Thy people;
Visit me with Thy salvation,
5 That I may see the prosperity of Thy chosen ones,
That I may rejoice in the gladness of Thy nation,
That I may glory with Thine [b]inheritance.

6¶ We have sinned like our fathers,
We have committed iniquity, we have behaved wickedly.
7 Our fathers in Egypt did not understand Thy wonders;
They did not remember Thine abundant kindnesses,
But rebelled by the sea, at the [c]Red Sea.
8 Nevertheless He saved them for the sake of His name,
That He might make His power known.
9 Thus He rebuked the [d]Red Sea and it dried up;
And He led them through the deeps, as through the wilderness.
10 So He saved them from the hand of the one who hated *them,*
And redeemed them from the hand of the enemy.
11 And the waters covered their adversaries;
Not one of them was left.
12 Then they believed His words;
They sang His praise.

13¶ They quickly forgot His works;
They did not wait for His counsel,
14 But craved intensely in the wilderness,
And tempted God in the desert.
15 So He gave them their request,
But sent a wasting disease among them.

16¶ When they became envious of Moses in the camp,
And of Aaron, the holy one of the LORD,
17 The earth opened and swallowed up Dathan,
And engulfed the company of Abiram.

NAS [a] Or, *curtain* [b] I.e., people [c] Lit., *Sea of Reeds* [d] Lit., *Sea of Reeds*

## New International

37He brought out Israel, laden with silver and gold,
and from among their tribes no one faltered.
38Egypt was glad when they left,
because dread of Israel had fallen on them.
39He spread out a cloud as a covering,
and a fire to give light at night.
40They asked, and he brought them quail
and satisfied them with the bread of heaven.
41He opened the rock, and water gushed out;
like a river it flowed in the desert.

42For he remembered his holy promise
given to his servant Abraham.
43He brought out his people with rejoicing,
his chosen ones with shouts of joy;
44he gave them the lands of the nations,
and they fell heir to what others had toiled for—
45that they might keep his precepts
and observe his laws.

Praise the LORD.[e]

**106** PRAISE THE LORD.[f]
Give thanks to the LORD, for he is good;
his love endures forever.
2Who can proclaim the mighty acts of the LORD
or fully declare his praise?
3Blessed are they who maintain justice,
who constantly do what is right.
4Remember me, O LORD, when you show favor to your people,
come to my aid when you save them,
5that I may enjoy the prosperity of your chosen ones,
that I may share in the joy of your nation
and join your inheritance in giving praise.
6We have sinned, even as our fathers did;
we have done wrong and acted wickedly.
7When our fathers were in Egypt,
they gave no thought to your miracles;
they did not remember your many kindnesses,
and they rebelled by the sea, the Red Sea.[g]
8Yet he saved them for his name's sake,
to make his mighty power known.
9He rebuked the Red Sea, and it dried up;
he led them through the depths as through a desert.
10He saved them from the hand of the foe;
from the hand of the enemy he redeemed them.
11The waters covered their adversaries;
not one of them survived.
12Then they believed his promises
and sang his praise.
13But they soon forgot what he had done
and did not wait for his counsel.
14In the desert they gave in to their craving;
in the wasteland they put God to the test.
15So he gave them what they asked for,
but sent a wasting disease upon them.

16In the camp they grew envious of Moses
and of Aaron, who was consecrated to the LORD.
17The earth opened up and swallowed Dathan;
it buried the company of Abiram.

NIV [e] *45* Hebrew *Hallelu Yah* [f] *1* Hebrew *Hallelu Yah;* also in verse 48
[g] *7* Hebrew *Yam Suph;* that is, Sea of Reeds; also in verses 9 and 22

## King James

18 And a fire was kindled in their company; the flame burned up the wicked.

19 They made a calf in Horeb, and worshipped the molten image.

20 Thus they changed their glory into the similitude of an ox that eateth grass.

21 They forgat God their saviour, which had done great things in Egypt;

22 Wondrous works in the land of Ham, *and* terrible things by the Red sea.

23 Therefore he said that he would destroy them, had not Moses his chosen stood before him in the breach, to turn away his wrath, lest he should destroy *them*.

24 Yea, they despised the pleasant land, they believed not his word:

25 But murmured in their tents, *and* hearkened not unto the voice of the LORD.

26 Therefore he lifted up his hand against them, to overthrow them in the wilderness:

27 To overthrow their seed also among the nations, and to scatter them in the lands.

28 They joined themselves also unto Baal-peor, and ate the sacrifices of the dead.

29 Thus they provoked *him* to anger with their inventions: and the plague brake in upon them.

30 Then stood up Phinehas, and executed judgment: and *so* the plague was stayed.

31 And that was counted unto him for righteousness unto all generations for evermore.

32 They angered *him* also at the waters of strife, so that it went ill with Moses for their sakes:

33 Because they provoked his spirit, so that he spake unadvisedly with his lips.

34 They did not destroy the nations, concerning whom the LORD commanded them:

35 But were mingled among the heathen, and learned their works.

36 And they served their idols: which were a snare unto them.

37 Yea, they sacrificed their sons and their daughters unto devils,

38 And shed innocent blood, *even* the blood of their sons and of their daughters, whom they sacrificed unto the idols of Canaan: and the land was polluted with blood.

39 Thus were they defiled with their own works, and went a-whoring with their own inventions.

40 Therefore was the wrath of the LORD kindled against his people, insomuch that he abhorred his own inheritance.

41 And he gave them into the hand of the heathen; and they that hated them ruled over them.

42 Their enemies also oppressed them, and they were brought into subjection under their hand.

43 Many times did he deliver them; but they provoked *him* with their counsel, and were brought low for their iniquity.

44 Nevertheless he regarded their affliction, when he heard their cry:

45 And he remembered for them his covenant, and repented according to the multitude of his mercies.

## Amplified

18 And a fire broke out in their company; the flame burned up the wicked. [Num. 16:35, 46.]

19 They made a calf in Horeb and worshiped a molten image. [Exod. 32:4.]

20 Thus they exchanged Him Who was their glory for the image of an ox that eats grass—they traded their honor for the image of a calf!

21 They forgot God, their Savior, Who had done such great things in Egypt,

22 Wonders *and* miracles in the land of Ham, dreadful *and* awesome things at the Red Sea.

23 Therefore He said He would destroy them. [And He would have done so] had not Moses, His chosen one, stepped into the breach before Him, to turn away His threatening wrath. [Exod. 32:10, 11, 32.]

24 Then they spurned *and* despised the pleasant *and* desirable land [Canaan]; they believed not His word—neither trusting, relying on nor holding to it;

25 But they murmured in their tents, *and* hearkened not to the voice of the Lord.

26 Therefore He lifted up His hand [as if taking an oath] against them, that He would cause them to fall in the wilderness,

27 Would cast out their descendants among the nations, and scatter them in the lands [of the earth].

28 They joined themselves also to the [idol] Baal of Peor, and ate sacrifices [offered] to the lifeless [gods].

29 Thus they provoked the Lord to anger with their practices, and a plague broke out among them.

30 Then stood up Phinehas [the priest] and executed judgment, and so the plague was stayed. [Num. 25:7, 8.]

31 And that was credited to him for righteousness [right doing and right standing with God] to all generations for ever.

32 They angered the Lord also at the waters of Meribah, so that it went ill with Moses for their sakes; [Num. 20:3-13.]

33 Because they provoked *Moses'* spirit, so that he spoke unadvisedly with his lips.

34 They did not destroy the (heathen) nations, as the Lord commanded them;

35 But mingled themselves with the [idolatrous] nations and learned their ways *and* works,

36 And served their idols, which were a snare to them.

37 Yes, they sacrificed their sons and their daughters to demons, [II Kings 16:3.]

38 And shed innocent blood, even the blood of their sons and of their daughters, whom they sacrificed to the idols of Canaan; and the land was polluted with blood.

39 Thus were they defiled by their own works, and played the harlot *and* practiced idolatry with their own deeds [of idolatrous rites].

40 Therefore was the wrath of the Lord kindled against His people, insomuch that He abhorred *and* rejected His own heritage. [Deut. 32:17.]

41 And He gave them into the hand of the (heathen) nations, and they that hated them ruled over them.

42 Their enemies also oppressed them, and they were brought into subjection under the hand of their foes.

43 Many times did [God] deliver them, but they were rebellious in their counsel, and sank low through their iniquity.

44 Nevertheless He regarded their distress, when He heard their cry.

45 And He [earnestly] remembered for their sake His covenant, and relented their sentence of evil—comforting and easing Himself—according to the abundance of His mercy *and* loving-kindness [when they cried out to Him].

## New American Standard

18 And a fire blazed up in their company;
The flame consumed the wicked.

19¶ They made a calf in Horeb,
And worshiped a molten image.
20 Thus they exchanged their glory
For the image of an ox that eats grass.
21 They forgot God their Savior,
Who had done great things in Egypt,
22 Wonders in the land of Ham,
*And* awesome things by the [a]Red Sea.
23 Therefore He said that He would destroy them,
Had not Moses His chosen one stood in the breach before Him,
To turn away His wrath from destroying *them.*
24 Then they despised the pleasant land;
They did not believe in His word,
25 But grumbled in their tents;
They did not listen to the voice of the LORD.
26 Therefore He swore to them,
That He would cast them down in the wilderness,
27 And that He would cast their seed among the nations,
And scatter them in the lands.

28¶ They joined themselves also to Baal-peor,
And ate sacrifices offered to the dead.
29 Thus they provoked *Him* to anger with their deeds;
And the plague broke out among them.
30 Then Phinehas stood up and interposed;
And so the plague was stayed.
31 And it was reckoned to him for righteousness,
To all generations forever.

32¶ They also provoked *Him* to wrath at the waters of [b]Meribah,
So that it went hard with Moses on their account;
33 Because they were rebellious against His Spirit,
He spoke rashly with his lips.

34¶ They did not destroy the peoples,
As the LORD commanded them,
35 But they mingled with the nations,
And learned their practices,
36 And served their idols,
Which became a snare to them.
37 They even sacrificed their sons and their daughters to the demons,
38 And shed innocent blood,
The blood of their sons and their daughters,
Whom they sacrificed to the idols of Canaan;
And the land was polluted with the blood.
39 Thus they became unclean in their practices,
And played the harlot in their deeds.

40¶ Therefore the anger of the LORD was kindled against His people,
And He abhorred His inheritance.
41 Then He gave them into the hand of the nations;
And those who hated them ruled over them.
42 Their enemies also oppressed them,
And they were subdued under their power.
43 Many times He would deliver them;
They, however, were rebellious in their counsel,
And *so* sank down in their iniquity.

44¶ Nevertheless He looked upon their distress,
When He heard their cry;
45 And He remembered His covenant for their sake,
And relented according to the greatness of His lovingkindness.

NAS [a] Lit., *Sea of Reeds* [b] Lit., *strife*

## New International

18 Fire blazed among their followers;
a flame consumed the wicked.
19 At Horeb they made a calf
and worshiped an idol cast from metal.
20 They exchanged their Glory
for an image of a bull, which eats grass.
21 They forgot the God who saved them,
who had done great things in Egypt,
22 miracles in the land of Ham
and awesome deeds by the Red Sea.
23 So he said he would destroy them—
had not Moses, his chosen one,
stood in the breach before him
to keep his wrath from destroying them.

24 Then they despised the pleasant land;
they did not believe his promise.
25 They grumbled in their tents
and did not obey the LORD.
26 So he swore to them with uplifted hand
that he would make them fall in the desert,
27 make their descendants fall among the nations
and scatter them throughout the lands.

28 They yoked themselves to the Baal of Peor
and ate sacrifices offered to lifeless gods;
29 they provoked the LORD to anger by their wicked deeds,
and a plague broke out among them.
30 But Phinehas stood up and intervened,
and the plague was checked.
31 This was credited to him as righteousness
for endless generations to come.

32 By the waters of Meribah they angered the LORD,
and trouble came to Moses because of them;
33 for they rebelled against the Spirit of God,
and rash words came from Moses' lips.[c]

34 They did not destroy the peoples
as the LORD had commanded them,
35 but they mingled with the nations
and adopted their customs.
36 They worshiped their idols,
which became a snare to them.
37 They sacrificed their sons
and their daughters to demons.
38 They shed innocent blood,
the blood of their sons and daughters,
whom they sacrificed to the idols of Canaan,
and the land was desecrated by their blood.
39 They defiled themselves by what they did;
by their deeds they prostituted themselves.

40 Therefore the LORD was angry with his people
and abhorred his inheritance.
41 He handed them over to the nations,
and their foes ruled over them.
42 Their enemies oppressed them
and subjected them to their power.
43 Many times he delivered them,
but they were bent on rebellion
and they wasted away in their sin.

44 But he took note of their distress
when he heard their cry;
45 for their sake he remembered his covenant
and out of his great love he relented.

NIV [c] 33 Or *against his spirit, / and rash words came from his lips*

## King James

46He made them also to be pitied of all those that carried them
captives.
47Save us, O LORD our God, and gather us from among the
heathen, to give thanks unto thy holy name, *and* to triumph in thy
praise.
48Blessed *be* the LORD God of Israel from everlasting to everlasting: and let all the people say, Amen. Praise ye the LORD.

### Book V

**107** O GIVE thanks unto the LORD, for *he is* good: for his
mercy *endureth* for ever.
2Let the redeemed of the LORD say *so,* whom he hath redeemed
from the hand of the enemy;
3And gathered them out of the lands, from the east, and from
the west, from the north, and from the south.
4They wandered in the wilderness in a solitary way; they found
no city to dwell in.
5Hungry and thirsty, their soul fainted in them.
6Then they cried unto the LORD in their trouble, *and* he delivered them out of their distresses.
7And he led them forth by the right way, that they might go to
a city of habitation.
8Oh that *men* would praise the LORD *for* his goodness, and *for*
his wonderful works to the children of men!
9For he satisfieth the longing soul, and filleth the hungry soul
with goodness.
10Such as sit in darkness and in the shadow of death, *being*
bound in affliction and iron;
11Because they rebelled against the words of God, and contemned the counsel of the most High:
12Therefore he brought down their heart with labour; they fell
down, and *there was* none to help.
13Then they cried unto the LORD in their trouble, *and* he saved
them out of their distresses.
14He brought them out of darkness and the shadow of death,
and brake their bands in sunder.
15Oh that *men* would praise the LORD *for* his goodness, and *for*
his wonderful works to the children of men!
16For he hath broken the gates of brass, and cut the bars of iron
in sunder.
17Fools because of their transgression, and because of their
iniquities, are afflicted.
18Their soul abhorreth all manner of meat; and they draw near
unto the gates of death.
19Then they cry unto the LORD in their trouble, *and* he saveth
them out of their distresses.
20He sent his word, and healed them, and delivered *them* from
their destructions.
21Oh that *men* would praise the LORD *for* his goodness, and *for*
his wonderful works to the children of men!
22And let them sacrifice the sacrifices of thanksgiving, and declare his works with rejoicing.

## Amplified

46He also caused *Israel* to find sympathy among those who had
carried them away captive.
47Deliver us, O Lord our God, and gather us from among the
nations, that we may give thanks to Your holy name *and* glory in
praising You.
48Blessed [affectionately and gratefully praised] be the Lord
God of Israel from everlasting to everlasting! And let all the people
say, Amen! Praise the Lord!—Hallelujah! [I Chron. 16:35, 36.]

### BOOK FIVE

**107** O GIVE thanks to the Lord for He is good, for His
mercy *and* loving-kindness endure for ever!
2Let the redeemed of the Lord say so, whom He has delivered
from the hand of the adversary,
3And gathered them out of the lands, from the east and from
the west, from the north and from the *Red* Sea in the south.
4Some wandered in the wilderness in a solitary desert track;
they found no city for habitation.
5Hungry and thirsty they fainted; their life was near being
extinguished.
6Then they cried to the Lord in their trouble, *and* He delivered
them out of their distresses.
7He led them forth by the straight *and* right way, that they might
go to a city where they might establish their homes.
8Oh, that men would praise [and confess to] the Lord His
goodness *and* loving-kindness, and His wonderful works to the
children of men!
9For He satisfies the longing soul, and fills the hungry soul with
good.
10Some sat in darkness and in the shadow of death, being
bound in affliction and in irons, [Luke 1:79.]
11Because they rebelled against the words of God, and spurned
the counsel of the Most High.
12Therefore He bowed down their heart with hard labor; they
stumbled *and* fell down, and there was none to help.
13Then they cried to the Lord in their trouble, and He saved
them out of their distresses.
14He brought them out of darkness and the shadow of death,
and broke apart the bonds that held them. [Acts 12:7; 16:26; Ps.
68:6.]
15Oh, that men would praise [and confess to] the Lord His
goodness *and* loving-kindness, and His wonderful works to the
children of men!
16For He has broken the gates of bronze, and cut the bars of iron
apart.
17Some are fools, (made ill) because of the way of their transgressions, and afflicted because of their iniquities;
18They loathe every kind of food, and they draw near to the
gates of death.
19Then they cry to the Lord in their trouble, and He delivers
them out of their distresses.
20He sends forth His word and heals them and rescues them
from the pit *and* destruction. [II Kings 20:4, 5; Matt. 8:8.]
21Oh, that men would praise [and confess to] the Lord His
goodness *and* loving-kindness, and His wonderful works to the
children of men! [Heb. 13:15.]
22And let them sacrifice the sacrifices of thanksgiving, and rehearse His deeds with shouts of joy *and* singing!

## New American Standard

46 He also made them *objects* of compassion
In the presence of all their captors.
47¶ Save us, O LORD our God,
And gather us from among the nations,
To give thanks to Thy holy name,
And glory in Thy praise.
48 Blessed be the LORD, the God of Israel,
From everlasting even to everlasting.
And let all the people say, "Amen."
Praise the LORD!

BOOK 5

*The LORD Delivers Men from Manifold Troubles.*

**107** OH GIVE thanks to the LORD, for He is good;
For His lovingkindness is everlasting.
2 Let the redeemed of the LORD say *so,*
Whom He has redeemed from the hand of the adversary,
3 And gathered from the lands,
From the east and from the west,
From the north and from the south.

4¶ They wandered in the wilderness in a desert region;
They did not find a way to an inhabited city.
5 *They were* hungry and thirsty;
Their soul fainted within them.
6 Then they cried out to the LORD in their trouble;
He delivered them out of their distresses.
7 He led them also by a straight way,
To go to an inhabited city.
8 Let them give thanks to the LORD for His lovingkindness,
And for His wonders to the sons of men!
9 For He has satisfied the thirsty soul,
And the hungry soul He has filled with what is good.

10¶ There were those who dwelt in darkness and in the shadow of death,
Prisoners in misery and chains,
11 Because they had rebelled against the words of God,
And spurned the counsel of the Most High.
12 Therefore He humbled their heart with labor;
They stumbled and there was none to help.
13 Then they cried out to the LORD in their trouble;
He saved them out of their distresses.
14 He brought them out of darkness and the shadow of death,
And broke their bands apart.
15 Let them give thanks to the LORD for His lovingkindness,
And for His wonders to the sons of men!
16 For He has shattered gates of bronze,
And cut bars of iron asunder.

17¶ Fools, because of their rebellious way,
And because of their iniquities, were afflicted.
18 Their soul abhorred all kinds of food;
And they drew near to the gates of death.
19 Then they cried out to the LORD in their trouble;
He saved them out of their distresses.
20 He sent His word and healed them,
And delivered *them* from their [a]destructions.
21 Let them give thanks to the LORD for His lovingkindness,
And for His wonders to the sons of men!
22 Let them also offer sacrifices of thanksgiving,
And tell of His works with joyful singing.

NAS [a] Or, *pits*

## New International

46He caused them to be pitied
by all who held them captive.

47Save us, O LORD our God,
and gather us from the nations,
that we may give thanks to your holy name
and glory in your praise.

48Praise be to the LORD, the God of Israel,
from everlasting to everlasting.
Let all the people say, "Amen!"
Praise the LORD.

BOOK V

*Psalms 107-150*

**107** GIVE THANKS to the LORD, for he is good;
his love endures forever.
2Let the redeemed of the LORD say this—
those he redeemed from the hand of the foe,
3those he gathered from the lands,
from east and west, from north and south.[b]

4Some wandered in desert wastelands,
finding no way to a city where they could settle.
5They were hungry and thirsty,
and their lives ebbed away.
6Then they cried out to the LORD in their trouble,
and he delivered them from their distress.
7He led them by a straight way
to a city where they could settle.
8Let them give thanks to the LORD for his unfailing love
and his wonderful deeds for men,
9for he satisfies the thirsty
and fills the hungry with good things.

10Some sat in darkness and the deepest gloom,
prisoners suffering in iron chains,
11for they had rebelled against the words of God
and despised the counsel of the Most High.
12So he subjected them to bitter labor;
they stumbled, and there was no one to help.
13Then they cried to the LORD in their trouble,
and he saved them from their distress.
14He brought them out of darkness and the deepest gloom
and broke away their chains.
15Let them give thanks to the LORD for his unfailing love
and his wonderful deeds for men,
16for he breaks down gates of bronze
and cuts through bars of iron.

17Some became fools through their rebellious ways
and suffered affliction because of their iniquities.
18They loathed all food
and drew near the gates of death.
19Then they cried to the LORD in their trouble,
and he saved them from their distress.
20He sent forth his word and healed them;
he rescued them from the grave.
21Let them give thanks to the LORD for his unfailing love
and his wonderful deeds for men.
22Let them sacrifice thank offerings
and tell of his works with songs of joy.

NIV [b] 3 Hebrew *north and the sea*

## King James

23 They that go down to the sea in ships, that do business in great waters;

24 These see the works of the LORD, and his wonders in the deep.

25 For he commandeth, and raiseth the stormy wind, which lifteth up the waves thereof.

26 They mount up to the heaven, they go down again to the depths: their soul is melted because of trouble.

27 They reel to and fro, and stagger like a drunken man, and are at their wit's end.

28 Then they cry unto the LORD in their trouble, and he bringeth them out of their distresses.

29 He maketh the storm a calm, so that the waves thereof are still.

30 Then are they glad because they be quiet; so he bringeth them unto their desired haven.

31 Oh that *men* would praise the LORD *for* his goodness, and *for* his wonderful works to the children of men!

32 Let them exalt him also in the congregation of the people, and praise him in the assembly of the elders.

33 He turneth rivers into a wilderness, and the watersprings into dry ground;

34 A fruitful land into barrenness, for the wickedness of them that dwell therein.

35 He turneth the wilderness into a standing water, and dry ground into watersprings.

36 And there he maketh the hungry to dwell, that they may prepare a city for habitation;

37 And sow the fields, and plant vineyards, which may yield fruits of increase.

38 He blesseth them also, so that they are multiplied greatly; and suffereth not their cattle to decrease.

39 Again, they are minished and brought low through oppression, affliction, and sorrow.

40 He poureth contempt upon princes, and causeth them to wander in the wilderness, *where there is* no way.

41 Yet setteth he the poor on high from affliction, and maketh *him* families like a flock.

42 The righteous shall see *it*, and rejoice: and all iniquity shall stop her mouth.

43 Whoso *is* wise, and will observe these *things*, even they shall understand the lovingkindness of the LORD.

A Song *or* Psalm of David.

**108** O GOD, my heart is fixed; I will sing and give praise, even with my glory.

2 Awake, psaltery and harp: I *myself* will awake early.

3 I will praise thee, O LORD, among the people: and I will sing praises unto thee among the nations.

4 For thy mercy *is* great above the heavens: and thy truth *reacheth* unto the clouds.

5 Be thou exalted, O God, above the heavens: and thy glory above all the earth;

6 That thy beloved may be delivered: save *with* thy right hand, and answer me.

## Amplified

23 Some go down to the sea *and* travel over it in ships, to do business in great waters;

24 These see the works of the Lord, and His wonders in the deep.

25 For He commands and raises the stormy wind, which lifts up the waves of the sea.

26 *Those aboard* mount up to the heavens, they go down again to the deeps; their courage melts away because of their plight.

27 They reel to and fro, and stagger like a drunken man, and are at their wit's end—all their wisdom has come to nothing.

28 Then they cry to the Lord in their trouble, and He brings them out of their distresses.

29 He hushes the storm to a calm *and* to a gentle whisper, so that the waves of the sea are still. [Ps. 89:9; Matt. 8:26.]

30 Then the men are glad because of the calm, and He brings them to their desired haven.

31 Oh, that men would praise [and confess to] the Lord His goodness *and* loving-kindness, and His wonderful works to the children of men!

32 Let them exalt Him also in the congregation of the people, and praise Him in the company of the elders.

33 He turns rivers into a wilderness, water springs into a thirsty ground, [I Kings 17:1, 7.]

34 A fruitful land into barren, salt waste, because of the wickedness of those who dwell in it. [Gen. 13:10; 14:3; 19:25.]

35 He turns a wilderness into a pool of water, and dry ground into water springs. [Isa. 41:18.]

36 And there He makes the hungry to dwell, that they may prepare a city for habitation;

37 And sow fields, and plant vineyards, which may yield fruits of increase.

38 He blesses them also, so that they are multiplied greatly, and allows not their cattle to decrease.

39 When they are diminished and bowed down through oppression, trouble and sorrow,

40 He pours contempt upon princes, and causes them to wander in the waste places, where there is no road.

41 Yet He raises the poor *and* needy from affliction, and makes them families like a flock.

42 The upright shall see it and be glad, and all iniquity shall shut her mouth.

43 Whoso is wise [if there be any truly wise] will observe *and* heed these things; and they will diligently consider the mercy *and* loving-kindness of the Lord.

A song, a Psalm of David.

**108** O GOD, my heart is fixed—steadfast [in the confidence of faith]; I will sing, yes, I will sing praises, even with my glory [all the faculties and powers of one created in Your image]!

2 Awake, harp and lyre; I myself will awake very early—I will waken the dawn!

3 I will praise *and* give thanks to You, O Lord, among the peoples; and I will sing praises unto You among the nations.

4 For Your mercy *and* loving-kindness are great *and* high as the heavens! Your truth *and* faithfulness reach to the skies! [Ps. 57:7-11.]

5 Be exalted, O God, above the heavens, and Your glory be over all the earth;

6 That Your beloved [followers] may be delivered, save with Your right hand, and answer us! [or me]!

## New American Standard

23¶ Those who go down to the sea in ships,
Who do business on great waters;
24 They have seen the works of the LORD,
And His wonders in the deep.
25 For He spoke and raised up a stormy wind,
Which lifted up the waves of the sea.
26 They rose up to the heavens, they went down to the depths;
Their soul melted away in *their* misery.
27 They reeled and staggered like a drunken man,
And [a]were at their wits' end.
28 Then they cried to the LORD in their trouble,
And He brought them out of their distresses.
29 He caused the storm to be still,
So that the waves of the sea were hushed.
30 Then they were glad because they were quiet;
So He guided them to their desired haven.
31 Let them give thanks to the LORD for His lovingkindness,
And for His wonders to the sons of men!
32 Let them extol Him also in the congregation of the people,
And praise Him at the seat of the elders.

33¶ He [b]changes rivers into a wilderness,
And springs of water into a thirsty ground;
34 A fruitful land into a salt waste,
Because of the wickedness of those who dwell in it.
35 He changes a wilderness into a pool of water,
And a dry land into springs of water;
36 And there He makes the hungry to dwell,
So that they may establish an inhabited city,
37 And sow fields, and plant vineyards,
And gather a fruitful harvest.
38 Also He blesses them and they multiply greatly;
And He does not let their cattle decrease.

39¶ When they are diminished and bowed down
Through oppression, misery, and sorrow,
40 He pours contempt upon princes,
And makes them wander in a pathless waste.
41 But He sets the needy securely on high away from affliction,
And makes *his* families like a flock.
42 The upright see it, and are glad;
But all unrighteousness shuts its mouth.
43 Who is wise? Let him give heed to these things;
And consider the lovingkindnesses of the LORD.

*God Praised and Supplicated to Give Victory.*

A Song, a Psalm of David.

**108** MY HEART is steadfast, O God;
I will sing, I will sing praises, even with my soul.
2 Awake, harp and lyre;
I will awaken the dawn!
3 I will give thanks to Thee, O LORD, among the peoples;
And I will sing praises to Thee among the nations.
4 For Thy lovingkindness is great above the heavens;
And Thy truth *reaches* to the skies.
5 Be exalted, O God, above the heavens,
And Thy glory above all the earth.
6 That Thy beloved may be delivered,
Save with Thy right hand, and answer me!

NAS [a] Lit., *all their wisdom was swallowed up* [b] Or, *turns rivers into a desert*

## New International

23 Others went out on the sea in ships;
they were merchants on the mighty waters.
24 They saw the works of the LORD,
his wonderful deeds in the deep.
25 For he spoke and stirred up a tempest
that lifted high the waves.
26 They mounted up to the heavens and went down to the depths;
in their peril their courage melted away.
27 They reeled and staggered like drunken men;
they were at their wits' end.
28 Then they cried out to the LORD in their trouble,
and he brought them out of their distress.
29 He stilled the storm to a whisper;
the waves of the sea were hushed.
30 They were glad when it grew calm,
and he guided them to their desired haven.
31 Let them give thanks to the LORD for his unfailing love
and his wonderful deeds for men.
32 Let them exalt him in the assembly of the people
and praise him in the council of the elders.

33 He turned rivers into a desert,
flowing springs into thirsty ground,
34 and fruitful land into a salt waste,
because of the wickedness of those who lived there.
35 He turned the desert into pools of water
and the parched ground into flowing springs;
36 there he brought the hungry to live,
and they founded a city where they could settle.
37 They sowed fields and planted vineyards
that yielded a fruitful harvest;
38 he blessed them, and their numbers greatly increased,
and he did not let their herds diminish.

39 Then their numbers decreased, and they were humbled
by oppression, calamity and sorrow;
40 he who pours contempt on nobles
made them wander in a trackless waste.
41 But he lifted the needy out of their affliction
and increased their families like flocks.
42 The upright see and rejoice,
but all the wicked shut their mouths.
43 Whoever is wise, let him heed these things
and consider the great love of the LORD.

A song. A psalm of David.

**108** MY HEART is steadfast, O God;
I will sing and make music with all my soul.
2 Awake, harp and lyre!
I will awaken the dawn.
3 I will praise you, O LORD, among the nations;
I will sing of you among the peoples.
4 For great is your love, higher than the heavens;
your faithfulness reaches to the skies.
5 Be exalted, O God, above the heavens,
and let your glory be over all the earth.

6 Save us and help us with your right hand,
that those you love may be delivered.

## King James

7 God hath spoken in his holiness; I will rejoice, I will divide Shechem, and mete out the valley of Succoth.

8 Gilead *is* mine; Manasseh *is* mine; Ephraim also *is* the strength of mine head; Judah *is* my lawgiver;

9 Moab *is* my washpot; over Edom will I cast out my shoe; over Philistia will I triumph.

10 Who will bring me into the strong city? who will lead me into Edom?

11 *Wilt* not *thou*, O God, *who* hast cast us off? and wilt not thou, O God, go forth with our hosts?

12 Give us help from trouble: for vain *is* the help of man.

13 Through God we shall do valiantly: for he *it is that* shall tread down our enemies.

To the chief Musician, A Psalm of David.

**109** HOLD NOT thy peace, O God of my praise;

2 For the mouth of the wicked and the mouth of the deceitful are opened against me: they have spoken against me with a lying tongue.

3 They compassed me about also with words of hatred; and fought against me without a cause.

4 For my love they are my adversaries: but I *give myself unto* prayer.

5 And they have rewarded me evil for good, and hatred for my love.

6 Set thou a wicked man over him: and let Satan stand at his right hand.

7 When he shall be judged, let him be condemned: and let his prayer become sin.

8 Let his days be few; *and* let another take his office.

9 Let his children be fatherless, and his wife a widow.

10 Let his children be continually vagabonds, and beg: let them seek *their bread* also out of their desolate places.

11 Let the extortioner catch all that he hath; and let the strangers spoil his labour.

12 Let there be none to extend mercy unto him: neither let there be any to favour his fatherless children.

13 Let his posterity be cut off; *and* in the generation following let their name be blotted out.

14 Let the iniquity of his fathers be remembered with the LORD; and let not the sin of his mother be blotted out.

15 Let them be before the LORD continually, that he may cut off the memory of them from the earth.

16 Because that he remembered not to show mercy, but persecuted the poor and needy man, that he might even slay the broken in heart.

17 As he loved cursing, so let it come unto him: as he delighted not in blessing, so let it be far from him.

18 As he clothed himself with cursing like as with his garment, so let it come into his bowels like water, and like oil into his bones.

## Amplified

7 God has promised in His holiness [regarding the establishment of David's dynasty]: I will rejoice, I will distribute [Canaan among My people], dividing Shechem and [the western region, and allotting the eastern region which contains] the valley of Succoth.

8 Gilead is Mine; Manasseh is Mine; Ephraim also is My stronghold *and* the defense of My head; Judah is My scepter *and* lawgiver. [Gen. 49:10.]

9 Moab is My washbasin; upon Edom [My slave] My shoe I cast [to be cleaned]; over Philistia I shout—in triumph.

10 Who will bring me [David] into the strong, fortified city [of Petra]? Who will lead me into Edom?

11 Have not You cast us off, O God? And You go not forth, O God, with our armies.

12 Give us help against the adversary, for vain is the help of man.

13 Through *and* with God we shall do valiantly, for He it is Who shall tread down our adversaries. [Ps. 60:5-12.]

To the Chief Musician. A Psalm of David.

**109** O GOD of my praise! Keep not silence,

2 For the mouth of the wicked and the mouth of deceit are opened against me, they have spoken to me *and* against me with a lying tongue.

3 They have compassed me about also with words of hatred, and fought against me without a cause.

4 In return for my love they are my adversaries; but I resort to prayer.

5 And they have rewarded *and* laid upon me evil for good, and hatred for my love.

6 Set a wicked man over him [as a judge], and let [a malicious] accuser stand at his right hand.

7 When *the wicked* shall be judged, let him be condemned, and let his prayer [for leniency] be turned into a sin.

8 Let his days be few, and let another take his office *and* charge. [Acts 1:20.]

9 Let his children be fatherless, and his wife a widow.

10 Let his children be continual vagabonds [as was Cain] and beg; let them seek their bread *and* be driven far from their ruined homes. [Gen. 4:12.]

11 Let the creditor *and* extortioner seize all that he has, and let strangers [barbarians and foreigners] plunder the fruits of his labor.

12 Let there be none to extend *or* continue mercy *and* kindness to him, neither let there be any to have pity on his fatherless children.

13 Let his posterity be cut off, and in the generation following let their name be blotted out.

14 Let the iniquity of his fathers be remembered by the Lord, and let not the sin of his mother be blotted out.

15 Let them be before the Lord continually, that He may cut off the memory of them from the earth!

16 Because the man did not [earnestly] remember to show mercy, but pursued *and* persecuted the poor and needy man, and the broken in heart *he was ready* to slay.

17 Yes, he loved cursing, and it came *back* upon him; as he delighted not in blessing, it was far from him.

18 He clothed himself also with cursing as with his garment, and it seeped into his inward [life] like water, and like oil into his bones.

## New American Standard

7¶ God has spoken in His [a]holiness:
"I will exult, I will portion out Shechem,
And measure out the valley of Succoth.
8 "Gilead is Mine, Manasseh is Mine;
Ephraim also is the helmet of My head;
Judah is My [b]scepter.
9 "Moab is My washbowl;
Over Edom I shall throw My shoe;
Over Philistia I will shout aloud."
10¶ Who will bring me into the besieged city?
Who will lead me to Edom?
11 Hast not Thou Thyself, O God, rejected us?
And wilt Thou not go forth with our armies, O God?
12 Oh give us help against the adversary,
For deliverance by man is in vain.
13 Through God we shall do valiantly;
And it is He who will tread down our adversaries.

*Vengeance Invoked upon Adversaries.*

For the choir director. A Psalm of David.

**109** O GOD of my praise,
Do not be silent!
2 For they have opened the wicked and deceitful mouth against me;
They have spoken against me with a lying tongue.
3 They have also surrounded me with words of hatred,
And fought against me without cause.
4 In return for my love they act as my accusers;
But I am *in* prayer.
5 Thus they have repaid me evil for good,
And hatred for my love.

6¶ Appoint a wicked man over him;
And let an accuser stand at his right hand.
7 When he is judged, let him come forth guilty;
And let his prayer become sin.
8 Let his days be few;
Let another take his office.
9 Let his children be fatherless,
And his wife a widow.
10 Let his children wander about and beg;
And let them seek *sustenance* far from their ruined homes.
11 Let the creditor seize all that he has;
And let strangers plunder the product of his labor.
12 Let there be none to extend lovingkindness to him,
Nor any to be gracious to his fatherless children.
13 Let his posterity be cut off;
In a following generation let their name be blotted out.
14¶ Let the iniquity of his fathers be remembered before the LORD,
And do not let the sin of his mother be blotted out.
15 Let them be before the LORD continually,
That He may cut off their memory from the earth;
16 Because he did not remember to show lovingkindness,
But persecuted the afflicted and needy man,
And the despondent in heart, to put *them* to death.
17 He also loved cursing, so it came to him;
And he did not delight in blessing, so it was far from him.
18 But he clothed himself with cursing as with his garment,
And it entered into his body like water,
And like oil into his bones.

NAS [a] Or, *sanctuary* [b] Or, *lawgiver*

## New International

7God has spoken from his sanctuary:
"In triumph I will parcel out Shechem
and measure off the Valley of Succoth.
8Gilead is mine, Manasseh is mine;
Ephraim is my helmet,
Judah my scepter.
9Moab is my washbasin,
upon Edom I toss my sandal;
over Philistia I shout in triumph."
10Who will bring me to the fortified city?
Who will lead me to Edom?
11Is it not you, O God, you who have rejected us
and no longer go out with our armies?
12Give us aid against the enemy,
for the help of man is worthless.
13With God we will gain the victory,
and he will trample down our enemies.

For the director of music. Of David. A psalm.

**109** O GOD, whom I praise,
do not remain silent,
2for wicked and deceitful men
have opened their mouths against me;
they have spoken against me with lying tongues.
3With words of hatred they surround me;
they attack me without cause.
4In return for my friendsip they accuse me,
but I am a man of prayer.
5They repay me evil for good,
and hatred for my friendship.

6Appoint[c] an evil man[d] to oppose him;
let an accuser[e] stand at his right hand.
7When he is tried, let him be found guilty,
and may his prayers condemn him.
8May his days be few;
may another take his place of leadership.
9May his children be fatherless
and his wife a widow.
10May his children be wandering beggars;
may they be driven[f] from their ruined homes.
11May a creditor seize all he has;
may strangers plunder the fruits of his labor.
12May no one extend kindness to him
or take pity on his fatherless children.
13May his descendants be cut off,
their names blotted out from the next generation.
14May the iniquity of his fathers be remembered before the LORD;
may the sin of his mother never be blotted out.
15May their sins always remain before the LORD,
that he may cut off the memory of them from the earth.

16For he never thought of doing a kindness,
but hounded to death the poor
and the needy and the brokenhearted.
17He loved to pronounce a curse—
may it[g] come on him;
he found no pleasure in blessing—
may it be[h] far from him.
18He wore cursing as his garment;
it entered into his body like water,
into his bones like oil.

NIV [c] 6 Or *They say:* "*Appoint* (with quotation marks at the end of verse 19) [d] 6 Or *the Evil One* [e] 6 Or *let Satan* [f] 10 Septuagint; Hebrew *sought* [g] 17 Or *curse, / and it has* [h] 17 Or *blessing, / and it is*

## King James

19Let it be unto him as the garment *which* covereth him, and for
a girdle wherewith he is girded continually.
20 *Let* this *be* the reward of mine adversaries from the LORD, and
of them that speak evil against my soul.
21But do thou for me, O GOD the Lord, for thy name's sake:
because thy mercy *is* good, deliver thou me.
22For I *am* poor and needy, and my heart is wounded within me.
23I am gone like the shadow when it declineth: I am tossed up
and down as the locust.
24My knees are weak through fasting; and my flesh faileth of
fatness.
25I became also a reproach unto them: *when* they looked upon
me they shaked their heads.
26Help me, O LORD my God: O save me according to thy mercy:
27That they may know that this *is* thy hand; *that* thou, LORD,
hast done it.
28Let them curse, but bless thou: when they arise, let them be
ashamed; but let thy servant rejoice.
29Let mine adversaries be clothed with shame, and let them
cover themselves with their own confusion, as with a mantle.
30I will greatly praise the LORD with my mouth; yea, I will praise
him among the multitude.
31For he shall stand at the right hand of the poor, to save *him*
from those that condemn his soul.

A Psalm of David.

**110** THE LORD said unto my Lord, Sit thou at my right
hand, until I make thine enemies thy footstool.
2The LORD shall send the rod of thy strength out of Zion: rule
thou in the midst of thine enemies.
3Thy people *shall be* willing in the day of thy power, in the
beauties of holiness from the womb of the morning: thou hast the
dew of thy youth.
4The LORD hath sworn, and will not repent, Thou *art* a priest
for ever after the order of Melchizedek.
5The Lord at thy right hand shall strike through kings in the day
of his wrath.
6He shall judge among the heathen, he shall *fill the places* with
the dead bodies; he shall wound the heads over many countries.
7He shall drink of the brook in the way: therefore shall he lift
up the head.

## Amplified

19Let it be to him as the raiment with which he covers himself,
and for the girdle with which he is girded continually.
20Let this be the reward of my adversaries from the Lord, and
of those who speak evil against my life.
21But You deal with me *and* act for me, O God the Lord, for Your
name's sake; because Your mercy *and* loving-kindness are good, O
deliver me.
22For I am poor and needy, and my heart is wounded *and*
stricken within me.
23I am gone like the shadow when it lengthens *and* declines; I
toss up and down *and* am shaken off as the locust.
24My knees are weak *and* totter through fasting, and my body
is gaunt *and* has no fatness.
25I am become also a reproach *and* a taunt to others; when they
see me they shake their heads. [Matt. 26:39.]
26Help me, O Lord my God; O save me according to Your mercy
*and* loving-kindness!
27That they may know that this is Your hand; that You, Lord,
have done it.
28Let them curse, but do You bless. When adversaries arise, let
them be put to shame, but let Your servant rejoice.
29Let my adversaries be clothed with shame *and* dishonor, and
let them cover themselves with their own disgrace *and* confusion,
as with a robe.
30I will give great praise *and* thanks to the Lord with my mouth;
yes, *and* I will praise Him among the multitude.
31For He will stand at the right hand of the poor *and* needy, to
save him from those who condemn his life.

A Psalm of David.

**110** THE LORD (God) says to my Lord [the Messiah], Sit
You at My right hand, until I make Your adversaries
Your footstool. [Matt. 26:64; Acts 2:34; I Cor. 15:25; Col. 3:1; Heb.
12:2.]
2The Lord will send forth from Zion the scepter of Your
strength; rule, then, in the midst of Your foes. [Rom. 11:26, 27.]
3Your people will offer themselves willingly in the day of Your
power, in the beauty of holiness *and* in holy array out of the womb
of the morning; to You *will spring forth* Your young men who are
as the dew.
4The Lord has sworn, and will not revoke *or* change it: You are
a priest for ever after the manner *and* order of Melchizedek. [Heb.
5:10; 7:11, 15, 21.]
5The Lord at Your right hand will shatter kings in the day of His
indignation.
6He will execute judgment [in overwhelming punishment]
upon the nations; He will fill the valleys with the dead bodies; He
will crush the chief heads over lands many *and* far extended. [Ezek.
38:21, 22; 39:11, 12.]
7He will drink of the brook by the way; therefore will He lift up
His head [triumphantly].

## New American Standard

19 Let it be to him as a garment with which he covers
himself,
And for a belt with which he constantly girds himself.
20 Let this be the reward of my accusers from the LORD,
And of those who speak evil against my soul.

21¶ But Thou, O GOD, the Lord, deal *kindly* with me for
Thy name's sake;
Because Thy lovingkindness is good, deliver me;
22 For I am afflicted and needy,
And my heart is wounded within me.
23 I am passing like a shadow when it lengthens;
I am shaken off like the locust.
24 My knees are weak from fasting;
And my flesh has grown lean, without fatness.
25 I also have become a reproach to them;
When they see me, they wag their head.

26¶ Help me, O LORD my God;
Save me according to Thy lovingkindness.
27 And let them know that this is Thy hand;
Thou, LORD, hast done it.
28 Let them curse, but do Thou bless;
When they arise, they shall be ashamed,
But Thy servant shall be glad.
29 Let my accusers be clothed with dishonor,
And let them cover themselves with their own shame
as with a robe.

30¶ With my mouth I will give thanks abundantly to the
LORD;
And in the midst of many I will praise Him.
31 For He stands at the right hand of the needy,
To save him from those who judge his soul.

*The LORD Gives Dominion to the King.*

A Psalm of David.

**110** THE LORD says to my Lord:"Sit at My right hand,
Until I make Thine enemies a footstool for Thy
feet."
2 The LORD will stretch forth Thy strong scepter from
Zion, *saying,*
"Rule in the midst of Thine enemies."
3 Thy people will volunteer freely in the day of Thy
power;
In holy array, from the womb of the dawn,
Thy youth are to Thee *as* the dew.

4¶ The LORD has sworn and will not change His mind,
"Thou art a priest forever
According to the order of Melchizedek."
5 The Lord is at Thy right hand;
He will shatter kings in the day of His wrath.
6 He will judge among the nations,
He will fill *them* with corpses,
He will shatter the chief men over a broad country.
7 He will drink from the brook by the wayside;
Therefore He will lift up *His* head.

## New International

19May it be like a cloak wrapped about him,
like a belt tied forever around him.
20May this be the LORD's payment to my accusers,
to those who speak evil of me.

21But you, O Sovereign LORD,
deal well with me for your name's sake;
out of the goodness of your love, deliver me.
22For I am poor and needy,
and my heart is wounded within me.
23I fade away like an evening shadow;
I am shaken off like a locust.
24My knees give way from fasting;
my body is thin and gaunt.
25I am an object of scorn to my accusers;
when they see me, they shake their heads.

26Help me, O LORD my God;
save me in accordance with your love.
27Let them know that it is your hand,
that you, O LORD, have done it.
28They may curse, but you will bless;
when they attack they will be put to shame,
but your servant will rejoice.
29My accusers will be clothed with disgrace
and wrapped in shame as in a cloak.

30With my mouth I will greatly extol the LORD;
in the great throng I will praise him.
31For he stands at the right hand of the needy one,
to save his life from those who condemn him.

Of David. A psalm.

**110** THE LORD says to my Lord:
"Sit at my right hand
until I make your enemies
a footstool for your feet."

2The LORD will extend your mighty scepter from Zion;
you will rule in the midst of your enemies.
3Your troops will be willing
on your day of battle.
Arrayed in holy majesty,
from the womb of the dawn
you will receive the dew of your youth.[a]

4The LORD has sworn
and will not change his mind:
"You are a priest forever,
in the order of Melchizedek."
5The Lord is at your right hand;
he will crush kings on the day of his wrath.
6He will judge the nations, heaping up the dead
and crushing the rulers of the whole earth.
7He will drink from a brook beside the way[b];
therefore he will lift up his head.

NIV [a] 3 Or / *your young men will come to you like the dew* [b] 7 Or / *The One who grants succession will set him in authority*

## King James

**111** PRAISE YE the LORD. I will praise the LORD with *my* whole heart, in the assembly of the upright, and *in* the congregation.

2 The works of the LORD *are* great, sought out of all them that have pleasure therein.

3 His work *is* honourable and glorious: and his righteousness endureth for ever.

4 He hath made his wonderful works to be remembered: the LORD *is* gracious and full of compassion.

5 He hath given meat unto them that fear him: he will ever be mindful of his covenant.

6 He hath shown his people the power of his works, that he may give them the heritage of the heathen.

7 The works of his hands *are* verity and judgment; all his commandments *are* sure.

8 They stand fast for ever and ever, *and are* done in truth and uprightness.

9 He sent redemption unto his people: he hath commanded his covenant for ever: holy and reverend *is* his name.

10 The fear of the LORD *is* the beginning of wisdom: a good understanding have all they that do *his commandments:* his praise endureth for ever.

**112** PRAISE YE the LORD. Blessed *is* the man *that* feareth the LORD, *that* delighteth greatly in his commandments.

2 His seed shall be mighty upon earth: the generation of the upright shall be blessed.

3 Wealth and riches *shall be* in his house: and his righteousness endureth for ever.

4 Unto the upright there ariseth light in the darkness: *he is* gracious, and full of compassion, and righteous.

5 A good man showeth favour, and lendeth: he will guide his affairs with discretion.

6 Surely he shall not be moved for ever: the righteous shall be in everlasting remembrance.

7 He shall not be afraid of evil tidings: his heart is fixed, trusting in the LORD.

8 His heart *is* established, he shall not be afraid, until he see *his desire* upon his enemies.

9 He hath dispersed, he hath given to the poor; his righteousness endureth for ever; his horn shall be exalted with honour.

10 The wicked shall see *it*, and be grieved; he shall gnash with his teeth, and melt away: the desire of the wicked shall perish.

## Amplified

**111** PRAISE THE Lord! — Hallelujah! I will praise *and* give thanks to the Lord with my whole heart, in the council of the upright, and in the congregation.

2 The works of the Lord are great, sought out by all those who have delight in them.

3 His work is honorable and glorious, and His righteousness endures for ever.

4 He has made His wonderful works to be remembered; the Lord is gracious, merciful *and* full of loving compassion.

5 He has given food *and* provision to those who reverently *and* worshipfully fear Him; He will remember His covenant for ever *and* imprint it [on His mind]. [Ps. 96:9; Deut. 10:12.]

6 He has declared *and* shown to His people the power of His works, in giving them the heritage of the nations [of Canaan].

7 The works of His hands are [absolute] truth and justice—faithful and right; and all His decrees *and* precepts are sure—fixed, established and trustworthy.

8 They stand fast *and* are established for ever and ever, and are done in [absolute] truth and uprightness.

9 He has sent redemption to His people; He has commanded His covenant to be for ever; holy is His name, inspiring awe, reverence *and* godly fear.

10 The reverent fear *and* worship of the Lord is the beginning of wisdom *and* skill [the preceding and the first essential, the prerequisite and the alphabet of them]. A good understanding, wisdom *and* meaning have all those who do [the will of the Lord]. *Their* praise of Him endures for ever. [Rev. 14:7; Matt. 22:37, 38.]

**112** PRAISE THE Lord! — Hallelujah! Blessed—happy, fortunate [to be envied]—is the man who fears (reveres and worships) the Lord, who delights greatly in His commandments. [Deut. 10:12.]

2 His [spiritual] offspring shall be a mighty one upon earth; the generation of the upright shall be blessed.

3 Prosperity *and* welfare are in his house, and his righteousness endures for ever.

4 Light arises in the darkness for the upright, gracious, compassionate *and* just—who are in right standing with God.

5 It is well with the man who deals generously and lends, who conducts his affairs with justice. [Ps. 37:26; Luke 6:35; Col. 4:5.]

6 He will not be moved, for ever; the [uncompromisingly] righteous—the upright, in right standing with God—shall be in everlasting remembrance. [Prov. 10:7.]

7 He shall not be afraid of evil tidings; his heart is firmly fixed, trusting (leaning on and being confident) in the Lord.

8 His heart is established *and* steady, he will not be afraid while he waits to see his desire upon his adversaries.

9 He has distributed freely, he has given to the poor *and* needy; his righteousness—uprightness and right standing with God—endures for ever; his horn shall be exalted in honor. [II Cor. 9:9.]

10 The wicked man will see it and be grieved *and* angered; he will gnash his teeth and disappear [in despair]; the desire of the wicked shall perish *and* come to nothing.

## New American Standard

*The LORD Praised for His Goodness.*

**111** PRAISE THE LORD!
I will give thanks to the LORD with all *my* heart,
In the company of the upright and in the assembly.
2 Great are the works of the LORD;
*They are* studied by all who delight in them.
3 Splendid and majestic is His work;
And His righteousness endures forever.
4 He has made His wonders to be remembered;
The LORD is gracious and compassionate.
5 He has given food to those who [a]fear Him;
He will remember His covenant forever.
6 He has made known to His people the power of His works,
In giving them the heritage of the nations.

7¶ The works of His hands are truth and justice;
All His precepts are sure.
8 They are upheld forever and ever;
They are performed in truth and uprightness.
9 He has sent redemption to His people;
He has ordained His covenant forever;
Holy and awesome is His name.
10 The [b]fear of the LORD is the beginning of wisdom;
A good understanding have all those who do *His commandments;*
His praise endures forever.

*Prosperity of the One Who Fears the LORD.*

**112** PRAISE THE LORD!
How blessed is the man who fears the LORD,
Who greatly delights in His commandments.
2 His [c]descendants will be mighty on earth;
The generation of the upright will be blessed.
3 Wealth and riches are in his house,
And his righteousness endures forever.
4 Light arises in the darkness for the upright;
*He is* gracious and compassionate and righteous.
5 It is well with the man who is gracious and lends;
He will maintain his cause in judgment.
6 For he will never be shaken;
The righteous will be remembered forever.

7¶ He will not fear evil tidings;
His heart is steadfast, trusting in the LORD.
8 His heart is upheld, he will not fear,
Until he looks *with satisfaction* on his adversaries.
9 He has given freely to the poor;
His righteousness endures forever;
His horn will be exalted in honor.

10¶ The wicked will see it and be vexed;
He will gnash his teeth and melt away;
The desire of the wicked will perish.

NAS [a] Or, *revere* [b] Or, *reverence for* [c] Lit., *seed*

## New International

**111**[d] PRAISE THE LORD.[e]
I will extol the LORD with all my heart
in the council of the upright and in the assembly.

2 Great are the works of the LORD;
they are pondered by all who delight in them.
3 Glorious and majestic are his deeds,
and his righteousness endures forever.
4 He has caused his wonders to be remembered;
the LORD is gracious and compassionate.
5 He provides food for those who fear him;
he remembers his covenant forever.
6 He has shown his people the power of his works,
giving them the lands of other nations.
7 The works of his hands are faithful and just;
all his precepts are trustworthy.
8 They are steadfast for ever and ever,
done in faithfulness and uprightness.
9 He provided redemption for his people;
he ordained his covenant forever—
holy and awesome is his name.

10 The fear of the LORD is the beginning of wisdom;
all who follow his precepts have good understanding.
To him belongs eternal praise.

**112**[f] PRAISE THE LORD.[g]
Blessed is the man who fears the LORD,
who finds great delight in his commands.

2 His children will be mighty in the land;
the generation of the upright will be blessed.
3 Wealth and riches are in his house,
and his righteousness endures forever.
4 Even in darkness light dawns for the upright,
for the gracious and compassionate and righteous man.[h]
5 Good will come to him who is generous and lends freely,
who conducts his affairs with justice.
6 Surely he will never be shaken;
a righteous man will be remembered forever.
7 He will have no fear of bad news;
his heart is steadfast, trusting in the LORD.
8 His heart is secure, he will have no fear;
in the end he will look in triumph on his foes.
9 He has scattered abroad his gifts to the poor,
his righteousness endures forever;
his horn[i] will be lifted high in honor.

10 The wicked man will see and be vexed,
he will gnash his teeth and waste away;
the longings of the wicked will come to nothing.

NIV [d] This psalm is an acrostic poem, the lines of which begin with the successive letters of the Hebrew alphabet. [e] *1* Hebrew *Hallelu Yah* [f] This psalm is an acrostic poem, the lines of which begin with the successive letters of the Hebrew alphabet. [g] *1* Hebrew *Hallelu Yah* [h] *4* Or */ for the LORD, is gracious and compassionate and righteous* [i] *9 Horn* here symbolizes dignity.

## King James

**113** PRAISE YE the LORD. Praise, O ye servants of the
LORD, praise the name of the LORD.
2Blessed be the name of the LORD from this time forth and for
evermore.
3From the rising of the sun unto the going down of the same
the LORD's name *is* to be praised.
4The LORD *is* high above all nations, *and* his glory above the
heavens.
5Who *is* like unto the LORD our God, who dwelleth on high,
6Who humbleth *himself* to behold *the things that are* in heaven,
and in the earth!
7He raiseth up the poor out of the dust, *and* lifteth the needy
out of the dunghill;
8That he may set *him* with princes, *even* with the princes of his
people.
9He maketh the barren woman to keep house, *and to be* a joyful
mother of children. Praise ye the LORD.

**114** WHEN ISRAEL went out of Egypt, the house of Jacob
from a people of strange language;
2Judah was his sanctuary, *and* Israel his dominion.
3The sea saw *it*, and fled: Jordan was driven back.
4The mountains skipped like rams, *and* the little hills like lambs.
5What *ailed* thee, O thou sea, that thou fleddest? thou Jordan,
*that* thou wast driven back?
6Ye mountains, *that* ye skipped like rams; *and* ye little hills, like
lambs?
7Tremble, thou earth, at the presence of the Lord, at the presence of the God of Jacob;
8Which turned the rock *into* a standing water, the flint into a
fountain of waters.

**115** NOT UNTO us, O LORD, not unto us, but unto thy
name give glory, for thy mercy, *and* for thy truth's
sake.
2Wherefore should the heathen say, Where *is* now their God?
3But our God *is* in the heavens: he hath done whatsoever he
hath pleased.
4Their idols *are* silver and gold, the work of men's hands.
5They have mouths, but they speak not: eyes have they, but
they see not:
6They have ears, but they hear not: noses have they, but they
smell not:
7They have hands, but they handle not: feet have they, but they
walk not: neither speak they through their throat.
8They that make them are like unto them; *so is* every one that
trusteth in them.

## Amplified

**113** PRAISE THE Lord! — Hallelujah! Praise, O servants of
the Lord, praise the name of the Lord!
2Blessed be the name of the Lord from this time forth and for
ever!
3From the rising of the sun to the going down of it, *and* from
east to west the name of the Lord is to be praised!
4The Lord is high above all nations, and His glory above the
heavens!
5Who is like the Lord our God, Who has His seat on high,
6Who humbles Himself to regard the heavens and the earth!
[Ps. 138:6; Isa. 57:15.]
7 *The Lord* raises up the poor out of the dust, *and* lifts up the
needy from the ash heap *and* the dung hill,
8That He may set them with princes, even with the princes of
His people.
9He makes the barren woman to be a homemaker, *and* a joyful
mother of [spiritual] children. Praise the Lord!—Hallelujah!

**114** WHEN ISRAEL came forth out of Egypt, the house of
Jacob from a people of strange language,
2Judah became *God's* sanctuary (the holy place of His habitation), and Israel His dominion. [Exod. 29:45, 46; Deut. 27:9.]
3The [Red] Sea looked and fled; the Jordan [River] was turned
back. [Exod. 14:21; Josh. 3:13, 16: Ps. 77:16.]
4The mountains skipped like rams, the little hills like lambs.
5What ails you, O sea, that you flee? O Jordan, that you turn
back?
6You mountains, that you skip like rams, and you little hills,
like lambs?
7Tremble, O earth, at the presence of the Lord, at the presence
of the God of Jacob;
8Who turned the rock into a pool of water, the flint into a
fountain of waters. [Exod. 17:6; Num. 20:11.]

**115** NOT TO us, O Lord, not to us, but to Your name give
glory, for Your mercy *and* loving-kindness and for the
sake of Your truth *and* faithfulness!
2Why should the nations say, Where is now their God?
3But our God is in Heaven; He does whatever He pleases.
4The idols of the nations are silver and gold, the work of men's
hands.
5They have mouths, but they speak not; eyes have they, but
they see not;
6They have ears, but they hear not; noses have they, but they
smell not;
7They have hands, but they handle not; feet have they, but they
walk not; neither can they make a sound with their throat.
8They who make idols are like them; so are all who trust *and* lean
on them. [Ps. 135:15-18.]

## New American Standard

*The* LORD *Exalts the Humble.*

**113** PRAISE THE LORD!
Praise, O servants of the LORD.
Praise the name of the LORD.
2 Blessed be the name of the LORD
From this time forth and forever.
3 From the rising of the sun to its setting
The name of the LORD is to be praised.
4 The LORD is high above all nations;
His glory is above the heavens.
5¶ Who is like the LORD our God,
Who is enthroned on high,
6 Who humbles Himself to behold
*The things that are* in heaven and in the earth?
7 He raises the poor from the dust,
And lifts the needy from the ash heap,
8 To make *them* sit with princes,
With the princes of His people.
9 He makes the barren woman abide in the house
*As* a joyful mother of children.
Praise the LORD!

*God's Deliverance of Israel from Egypt.*

**114** WHEN ISRAEL went forth from Egypt,
The house of Jacob from a people of strange language,
2 Judah became His sanctuary,
Israel, His dominion.
3¶ The sea looked and fled;
The Jordan turned back.
4 The mountains skipped like rams,
The hills, like lambs.
5 What ails you, O sea, that you flee?
O Jordan, that you turn back?
6 O mountains, that you skip like rams?
O hills, like lambs?
7¶ Tremble, O earth, before the Lord,
Before the God of Jacob,
8 Who turned the rock into a pool of water,
The flint into a fountain of water.

*Heathen Idols Contrasted with the* LORD.

**115** NOT TO us, O LORD, not to us,
But to Thy name give glory
Because of Thy lovingkindness, because of Thy truth.
2 Why should the nations say,
"Where, now, is their God?"
3 But our God is in the heavens;
He does whatever He pleases.
4 Their idols are silver and gold,
The work of man's hands.
5 They have mouths, but they cannot speak;
They have eyes, but they cannot see;
6 They have ears, but they cannot hear;
They have noses, but they cannot smell;
7 They have hands, but they cannot feel;
They have feet, but they cannot walk;
They cannot make a sound with their throat.
8 Those who make them will become like them,
Everyone who trusts in them.

## New International

**113** PRAISE THE LORD.[a]
Praise, O servants of the LORD,
praise the name of the LORD.
2 Let the name of the LORD be praised,
both now and forevermore.
3 From the rising of the sun to the place where it sets,
the name of the LORD is to be praised.

4 The LORD is exalted over all the nations,
his glory above the heavens.
5 Who is like the LORD our God,
the One who sits enthroned on high,
6 who stoops down to look
on the heavens and the earth?

7 He raises the poor from the dust
and lifts the needy from the ash heap;
8 he seats them with princes,
with the princes of their people.
9 He settles the barren woman in her home
as a happy mother of children.

Praise the LORD.

**114** WHEN ISRAEL came out of Egypt,
the house of Jacob from a people of foreign tongue,
2 Judah became God's sanctuary,
Israel his dominion.

3 The sea looked and fled,
the Jordan turned back;
4 the mountains skipped like rams,
the hills like lambs.

5 Why was it, O sea, that you fled,
O Jordan, that you turned back,
6 you mountains, that you skipped like rams,
you hills, like lambs?

7 Tremble, O earth, at the presence of the Lord,
at the presence of the God of Jacob,
8 who turned the rock into a pool,
the hard rock into springs of water.

**115** NOT TO us, O LORD, not to us
but to your name be the glory,
because of your love and faithfulness.
2 Why do the nations say,
"Where is their God?"
3 Our God is in heaven;
he does whatever pleases him.
4 But their idols are silver and gold,
made by the hands of men.
5 They have mouths, but cannot speak,
eyes, but they cannot see;
6 they have ears, but cannot hear,
noses, but they cannot smell;
7 they have hands, but cannot feel,
feet, but they cannot walk;
nor can they utter a sound with their throats.
8 Those who make them will be like them,
and so will all who trust in them.

NIV [a] *1* Hebrew *Hallelu Yah;* also in verse 9

## King James

9O Israel, trust thou in the LORD: he *is* their help and their shield.
10O house of Aaron, trust in the LORD: he *is* their help and their shield.
11Ye that fear the LORD, trust in the LORD: he *is* their help and their shield.
12The LORD hath been mindful of us: he will bless *us;* he will bless the house of Israel; he will bless the house of Aaron.
13He will bless them that fear the LORD, *both* small and great.
14The LORD shall increase you more and more, you and your children.
15Ye *are* blessed of the LORD which made heaven and earth.
16The heaven, *even* the heavens, *are* the LORD'S: but the earth hath he given to the children of men.
17The dead praise not the LORD, neither any that go down into silence.
18But we will bless the LORD from this time forth and for evermore. Praise the LORD.

**116** I LOVE the LORD, because he hath heard my voice *and* my supplications.
2Because he hath inclined his ear unto me, therefore will I call upon *him* as long as I live.
3The sorrows of death compassed me, and the pains of hell gat hold upon me: I found trouble and sorrow.
4Then called I upon the name of the LORD; O LORD, I beseech thee, deliver my soul.
5Gracious *is* the LORD, and righteous; yea, our God *is* merciful.
6The LORD preserveth the simple: I was brought low, and he helped me.
7Return unto thy rest, O my soul; for the LORD hath dealt bountifully with thee.
8For thou hast delivered my soul from death, mine eyes from tears, *and* my feet from falling.
9I will walk before the LORD in the land of the living.
10I believed, therefore have I spoken: I was greatly afflicted:
11I said in my haste, All men *are* liars.
12What shall I render unto the LORD *for* all his benefits toward me?
13I will take the cup of salvation, and call upon the name of the LORD.
14I will pay my vows unto the LORD now in the presence of all his people.
15Precious in the sight of the LORD *is* the death of his saints.
16O LORD, truly I *am* thy servant; I *am* thy servant, *and* the son of thine handmaid: thou hast loosed my bonds.

## Amplified

9O Israel, trust *and* take refuge in the Lord! (Lean on, rely on and be confident in Him!) He is their help and their shield.
10O house of Aaron [the priesthood], trust *and* lean on the Lord! He is their help and their shield.
11You who (reverently) fear the Lord, trust *and* lean on the Lord! He is their help and their shield.
12The Lord has been mindful of us; He will bless us; He will bless the house of Israel; He will bless the house of Aaron [the priesthood].
13He will bless those who reverently *and* worshipfully fear the Lord, both small and great. [Rev. 11:18; 19:5; Ps. 103:11.]
14The Lord give you increase more and more, you and your children.
15Blessed be you of the Lord, Who made Heaven and earth!
16The heavens are the Lord's heavens, but the earth has He given to the children of men.
17The dead praise not the Lord, neither any that go down into silence.
18But we will bless—affectionately and gratefully praise—the Lord from this time forth and for ever. Praise the Lord!—Hallelujah!

**116** I LOVE the Lord, because He has heard (and now hears) my voice and my supplications.
2Because He has inclined His ear to me, therefore will I call upon Him as long as I live.
3The cords *and* sorrows of death were around me, and the terrors of Sheol [the place of the dead] had laid hold of me; I suffered anguish and grief—trouble and sorrow.
4Then called I upon the name of the Lord: O Lord, I beseech You, save my life *and* deliver me!
5Gracious is the Lord, and [rigidly] righteous; yes, our God is merciful.
6The Lord preserves the simple; I was brought low, and He helped *and* saved me.
7Return to your rest, O my soul, for the Lord has dealt bountifully with you. [Matt. 11:29.]
8For You have delivered my life from death, my eyes from tears, and my feet from stumbling *and* falling.
9I will walk before the Lord in the land of the living.
10I believed—trusted in, relied on and clung to *my God*—and therefore have I spoken (even when I said), I am greatly afflicted. [II Cor. 4:13.]
11I said in my haste, All men are deceitful *and* liars.
12What shall I render to the Lord for all His benefits toward me?—How can I repay Him for all His bountiful dealings?
13I will lift up the cup of salvation *and* deliverance, and call on the name of the Lord.
14I will pay my vows to the Lord, yes, in the presence of all His people.
15Precious (important and no light matter) in the sight of the Lord is the death of His saints—His loving ones.
16O Lord, truly I am Your servant; I am Your servant, the son of Your handmaid; You have loosed my bonds.

## New American Standard

9¶ O Israel, trust in the LORD;
He is their help and their shield.
10 O house of Aaron, trust in the LORD;
He is their help and their shield.
11 You who [a]fear the LORD, trust in the LORD;
He is their help and their shield.
12 The LORD has been mindful of us; He will bless *us*;
He will bless the house of Israel;
He will bless the house of Aaron.
13 He will bless those who [b]fear the LORD,
The small together with the great.
14 May the LORD give you increase,
You and your children.
15 May you be blessed of the LORD,
Maker of heaven and earth.
16¶ The heavens are the heavens of the LORD;
But the earth He has given to the sons of men.
17 The dead do not praise the LORD,
Nor *do* any who go down into silence;
18 But as for us, we will bless the LORD
From this time forth and forever.
Praise the LORD!

*Thanksgiving for Deliverance from Death.*

**116** I LOVE the LORD, because He hears
My voice *and* my supplications.
2 Because He has inclined His ear to me,
Therefore I shall call *upon Him* as long as I live.
3 The cords of death encompassed me,
And the terrors of Sheol came upon me;
I found distress and sorrow.
4 Then I called upon the name of the LORD:
"O LORD, I beseech Thee, save my life!"
5¶ Gracious is the LORD, and righteous;
Yes, our God is compassionate.
6 The LORD preserves the simple;
I was brought low, and He saved me.
7 Return to your rest, O my soul,
For the LORD has dealt bountifully with you.
8 For Thou hast rescued my soul from death,
My eyes from tears,
My feet from stumbling.
9 I shall walk before the LORD
In the land of the living.
10 I believed when I said,
"I am greatly afflicted."
11 I said in my alarm,
"All men are liars."
12¶ What shall I render to the LORD
For all His benefits toward me?
13 I shall lift up the cup of salvation,
And call upon the name of the LORD.
14 I shall pay my vows to the LORD,
Oh *may it be* in the presence of all His people.
15 Precious in the sight of the LORD
Is the death of His godly ones.
16 O LORD, surely I am Thy servant,
I am Thy servant, the son of Thy handmaid,
Thou hast loosed my bonds.

NAS [a] Or, *revere* [b] Or, *revere*

## New International

9 O house of Israel, trust in the LORD—
he is their help and shield.
10 O house of Aaron, trust in the LORD—
he is their help and shield.
11 You who fear him, trust in the LORD—
he is their help and shield.

12 The LORD remembers us and will bless us:
He will bless the house of Israel,
he will bless the house of Aaron,
13 he will bless those who fear the LORD—
small and great alike.

14 May the LORD make you increase,
both you and your children.
15 May you be blessed by the LORD,
the Maker of heaven and earth.

16 The highest heavens belong to the LORD,
but the earth he has given to man.
17 It is not the dead who praise the LORD,
those who go down to silence;
18 it is we who extol the LORD,
both now and forevermore.

Praise the LORD.[c]

**116** I LOVE the LORD, for he heard my voice;
he heard my cry for mercy.
2 Because he turned his ear to me,
I will call on him as long as I live.

3 The cords of death entangled me,
the anguish of the grave[d] came upon me;
I was overcome by trouble and sorrow.
4 Then I called on the name of the LORD:
"O LORD, save me!"

5 The LORD is gracious and righteous;
our God is full of compassion.
6 The LORD protects the simplehearted;
when I was in great need, he saved me.

7 Be at rest once more, O my soul,
for the LORD has been good to you.

8 For you, O LORD, have delivered my soul from death,
my eyes from tears,
my feet from stumbling,
9 that I may walk before the LORD
in the land of the living.
10 I believed; therefore[e] I said,
"I am greatly afflicted."
11 And in my dismay I said,
"All men are liars."

12 How can I repay the LORD
for all his goodness to me?
13 I will lift up the cup of salvation
and call on the name of the LORD.
14 I will fulfill my vows to the LORD
in the presence of all his people.

15 Precious in the sight of the LORD
is the death of his saints.
16 O LORD, truly I am your servant;
I am your servant, the son of your maidservant[f];
you have freed me from my chains.

NIV [c] 18 Hebrew *Hallelu Yah* [d] 3 Hebrew *Sheol* [e] 10 Or *believed even when* [f] 16 Or *servant, your faithful son*

## King James

17 I will offer to thee the sacrifice of thanksgiving, and will call upon the name of the LORD.
18 I will pay my vows unto the LORD now in the presence of all his people,
19 In the courts of the LORD's house, in the midst of thee, O Jerusalem. Praise ye the LORD.

**117** O PRAISE the LORD, all ye nations: praise him, all ye people.
2 For his merciful kindness is great toward us: and the truth of the LORD *endureth* for ever. Praise ye the LORD.

**118** O GIVE thanks unto the LORD; for *he is* good: because his mercy *endureth* for ever.
2 Let Israel now say, that his mercy *endureth* for ever.
3 Let the house of Aaron now say, that his mercy *endureth* for ever.
4 Let them now that fear the LORD say, that his mercy *endureth* for ever.
5 I called upon the LORD in distress: the LORD answered me, *and set me* in a large place.
6 The LORD *is* on my side; I will not fear: what can man do unto me?
7 The LORD taketh my part with them that help me: therefore shall I see *my desire* upon them that hate me.
8 *It is* better to trust in the LORD than to put confidence in man.
9 *It is* better to trust in the LORD than to put confidence in princes.
10 All nations compassed me about: but in the name of the LORD will I destroy them.
11 They compassed me about; yea, they compassed me about: but in the name of the LORD I will destroy them.
12 They compassed me about like bees; they are quenched as the fire of thorns: for in the name of the LORD I will destroy them.
13 Thou hast thrust sore at me that I might fall: but the LORD helped me.
14 The LORD *is* my strength and song, and is become my salvation.
15 The voice of rejoicing and salvation *is* in the tabernacles of the righteous: the right hand of the LORD doeth valiantly.
16 The right hand of the LORD is exalted: the right hand of the LORD doeth valiantly.
17 I shall not die, but live, and declare the works of the LORD.
18 The LORD hath chastened me sore: but he hath not given me over unto death.
19 Open to me the gates of righteousness: I will go into them, *and* I will praise the LORD:
20 This gate of the LORD, into which the righteous shall enter.

## Amplified

17 I will offer to You the sacrifice of thanksgiving, and will call on the name of the Lord.
18 I will pay my vows unto the Lord, yes, in the presence of all His people,
19 In the courts of the Lord's house, in the midst of you, O Jerusalem. Praise the Lord!—Hallelujah!

**117** O PRAISE the Lord, all you nations! Praise Him, all you people! [Rom. 15:11.]
2 For His mercy *and* loving-kindness are great toward us, and the truth *and* faithfulness of the Lord endure for ever. Praise the Lord!—Hallelujah!

**118** O GIVE thanks to the Lord, for He is good; for His mercy *and* loving-kindness endure for ever!
2 Let Israel now say, that His mercy *and* loving-kindness endure for ever.
3 Let the house of Aaron [the priesthood] now say, that His mercy *and* loving-kindness endure for ever.
4 Let those now who reverently *and* worshipfully fear the Lord say, that His mercy *and* loving-kindness endure for ever.
5 Out of my distress I called upon the Lord; the Lord answered me, and set me free *and* in a large place.
6 The Lord is on my side; I will not fear. What can man do to me? [Heb. 13:6.]
7 The Lord is on my side *and* takes my part, He is among those who help me; therefore shall I see my desire upon those who hate me.
8 It is better to trust *and* take refuge in the Lord than to put confidence in man.
9 It is better to trust *and* take refuge in the Lord than to put confidence in princes.
10 All nations [the surrounding tribes] compassed me about, but in the name of the Lord will I cut them off!
11 They compassed me about, yes, they surrounded me on every side; but in the name of the Lord I will cut them off!
12 They swarmed about me like bees; they blaze up *and* are extinguished like a fire of thorns; in the name of the Lord I will cut them off! [Deut. 1:44.]
13 You [my adversary] thrust sorely at me that I might fall, but the Lord helped me.
14 The Lord is my strength and song, and He is become my salvation.
15 The voice of rejoicing and salvation is in the tents *and* private dwellings of the [uncompromisingly] righteous; the right hand of the Lord does valiantly *and* achieves strength!
16 The right hand of the Lord is exalted; the right hand of the Lord does valiantly *and* achieves strength!
17 I shall not die, but live, and declare the works *and* recount the illustrious acts of the Lord.
18 The Lord has chastened me sorely, but He has not given me over to death. [II Cor. 6:9.]
19 Open to me the [temple] gates of righteousness; I will enter through them, and I will confess *and* praise the Lord.
20 This is the gate of the Lord; the [uncompromisingly] righteous shall enter through it. [Ps. 24:7.]

## New American Standard

17 To Thee I shall offer a sacrifice of thanksgiving,
And call upon the name of the LORD.
18 I shall pay my vows to the LORD,
Oh *may it be* in the presence of all His people,
19 In the courts of the LORD's house,
In the midst of you, O Jerusalem.
Praise the LORD!

*A Psalm of Praise.*

**117** PRAISE THE LORD, all nations;
Laud Him, all peoples!
2 For His lovingkindness [a]is great toward us,
And the truth of the LORD is everlasting.
Praise the LORD!

*Thanksgiving for the LORD's Saving Goodness.*

**118** GIVE THANKS to the LORD, for He is good;
For His lovingkindness is everlasting.
2 Oh let Israel say,
"His lovingkindness is everlasting."
3 Oh let the house of Aaron say,
"His lovingkindness is everlasting."
4 Oh let those who [b]fear the LORD say,
"His lovingkindness is everlasting."
5¶ From *my* distress I called upon the LORD;
The LORD answered me *and set me* in a large place.
6 The LORD is for me; I will not fear;
What can man do to me?
7 The LORD is for me among those who help me;
Therefore I shall look *with satisfaction* on those who hate me.
8 It is better to take refuge in the LORD
Than to trust in man.
9 It is better to take refuge in the LORD
Than to trust in princes.
10¶ All nations surrounded me;
In the name of the LORD I will surely cut them off.
11 They surrounded me, yes, they surrounded me;
In the name of the LORD I will surely cut them off.
12 They surrounded me like bees;
They were extinguished as a fire of thorns;
In the name of the LORD I will surely cut them off.
13 You pushed me violently so that I was falling,
But the LORD helped me.
14 The LORD is my strength and song,
And He has become my salvation.
15¶ The sound of joyful shouting and salvation is in the tents of the righteous;
The right hand of the LORD does valiantly.
16 The right hand of the LORD is exalted;
The right hand of the LORD does valiantly.
17 I shall not die, but live,
And tell of the works of the LORD.
18 The LORD has disciplined me severely,
But He has not given me over to death.
19¶ Open to me the gates of righteousness;
I shall enter through them, I shall give thanks to the LORD.
20 This is the gate of the LORD;
The righteous will enter through it.

NAS [a] Lit., *prevails over us* [b] Or, *revere*

## New International

17I will sacrifice a thank offering to you
and call on the name of the LORD.
18I will fulfill my vows to the LORD
in the presence of all his people,
19in the courts of the house of the LORD—
in your midst, O Jerusalem.

Praise the LORD.[c]

**117** PRAISE THE LORD, all you nations;
extol him, all you peoples.
2For great is his love toward us,
and the faithfulness of the LORD endures forever.

Praise the LORD.[d]

**118** GIVE THANKS to the LORD, for he is good;
his love endures forever.

2Let Israel say:
"His love endures forever."
3Let the house of Aaron say:
"His love endures forever."
4Let those who fear the LORD say:
"His love endures forever."

5In my anguish I cried to the LORD,
and he answered by setting me free.
6The LORD is with me; I will not be afraid.
What can man do to me?
7The LORD is with me; he is my helper.
I will look in triumph on my enemies.

8It is better to take refuge in the LORD
than to trust in man.
9It is better to take refuge in the LORD
than to trust in princes.
10All the nations surrounded me,
but in the name of the LORD I cut them off.
11They surrounded me on every side,
but in the name of the LORD I cut them off.
12They swarmed around me like bees,
but they died out as quickly as burning thorns;
in the name of the LORD I cut them off.

13I was pushed back and about to fall,
but the LORD helped me.
14The LORD is my strength and my song;
he has become my salvation.

15Shouts of joy and victory
resound in the tents of the righteous:
"The LORD's right hand has done mighty things!
16 The LORD's right hand is lifted high;
the LORD's right hand has done mighty things!"

17I will not die but live,
and will proclaim what the LORD has done.
18The LORD has chastened me severely,
but he has not given me over to death.

19Open for me the gates of righteousness;
I will enter and give thanks to the LORD.
20This is the gate of the LORD
through which the righteous may enter.

NIV [c] 19 Hebrew *Hallelu Yah* [d] 2 Hebrew *Hallelu Yah*

## King James

21I will praise thee: for thou hast heard me, and art become my salvation.

22The stone *which* the builders refused is become the head *stone* of the corner.

23This is the LORD's doing; it *is* marvellous in our eyes.

24This *is* the day *which* the LORD hath made; we will rejoice and be glad in it.

25Save now, I beseech thee, O LORD: O LORD, I beseech thee, send now prosperity.

26Blessed *be* he that cometh in the name of the LORD: we have blessed you out of the house of the LORD.

27God *is* the LORD, which hath shown us light: bind the sacrifice with cords, *even* unto the horns of the altar.

28Thou *art* my God, and I will praise thee: *thou art* my God, I will exalt thee.

29O give thanks unto the LORD; for *he is* good: for his mercy *endureth* for ever.

ALEPH.

119 BLESSED *ARE* the undefiled in the way, who walk in the law of the LORD.

2Blessed *are* they that keep his testimonies, *and that* seek him with the whole heart.

3They also do no iniquity: they walk in his ways.

4Thou hast commanded *us* to keep thy precepts diligently.

5O that my ways were directed to keep thy statutes!

6Then shall I not be ashamed, when I have respect unto all thy commandments.

7I will praise thee with uprightness of heart, when I shall have learned thy righteous judgments.

8I will keep thy statutes: O forsake me not utterly.

BETH.

9Wherewithal shall a young man cleanse his way? by taking heed *thereto* according to thy word.

10With my whole heart have I sought thee: O let me not wander from thy commandments.

11Thy word have I hid in mine heart, that I might not sin against thee.

12Blessed *art* thou, O LORD: teach me thy statutes.

13With my lips have I declared all the judgments of thy mouth.

14I have rejoiced in the way of thy testimonies, as *much as* in all riches.

15I will meditate in thy precepts, and have respect unto thy ways.

16I will delight myself in thy statutes: I will not forget thy word.

GIMEL.

17Deal bountifully with thy servant, *that* I may live, and keep thy word.

## Amplified

21I will confess, praise *and* give thanks to You, for You have heard *and* answered me, and have become my salvation *and* deliverer.

22The stone which the builders rejected is become the chief corner stone.

23This is from the Lord *and* is His doing; it is marvelous in our eyes. [Matt. 21:42; Acts 4:11; I Pet. 2:7.]

24This is the day which the Lord has brought about; we will rejoice and be glad in it.

25Save now, we beseech You, O Lord; send now prosperity, O Lord, we beseech You, *and* give to us success!

26Blessed be he who comes in the name of the Lord; we bless you from the house of the Lord [you who come into His sanctuary under His guardianship]. [Mark 11:9, 10.]

27The Lord is God, Who has shown *and* given us light—He has illuminated us [with grace, freedom and joy]. Decorate the festival with leafy boughs *and* bind the sacrifices to be offered with thick cords [all over the priest's court, right up] to the horns of the altar.

28You are my God, and I will confess, praise *and* give thanks to You; You are my God, I will extol You.

29O give thanks to the Lord, for He is good; for His mercy *and* loving-kindness endure for ever.

119 BLESSED, HAPPY, fortunate [to be envied] are the undefiled—the upright, truly sincere and blameless—in the way [of the revealed will of God]; who walk—that is, order their conduct and conversation—in [the whole of God's revealed will] the law of the Lord.

2Blessed, happy, fortunate [to be envied] are they who keep His testimonies, and who seek, inquire for *and* of Him *and* crave Him with the whole heart.

3Yes, they do no unrighteousness—no willful wandering from His precepts; they walk in His ways. [I John 3:9; 5:18.]

4You have commanded us to keep Your precepts, that we should observe them diligently.

5O that my ways were directed *and* established to observe Your statutes—hearing, receiving, loving and obeying them!

6Then shall I not be put to shame [by failing to inherit Your promises], when I have respect to all Your commandments.

7I will praise *and* give thanks to You with uprightness of heart, when I shall have learned [by sanctified experiences] Your righteous judgments [Your decisions against and punishments for particular lines of thought and conduct].

8I will keep Your statutes; O forsake me not utterly.

9Wherewith shall a young man cleanse his way? By taking heed *and* keeping watch [on himself] according to Your word [conforming his life to it].

10With my whole heart have I sought You, inquiring for *and* of You, *and* yearning for You; O let me not wander *or* step aside [either in ignorance or willfully] from Your commandments. [II Chron. 15:15.]

11Your word have I laid up in my heart, that I might not sin against You.

12Blessed are You, O Lord; teach me Your statutes.

13With my lips have I declared *and* recounted all the ordinances of Your mouth.

14I have rejoiced in the way of Your testimonies, as much as in all riches.

15I will meditate on Your precepts, and have respect to Your ways [the paths of life marked out by Your law]. [Ps. 104:34.]

16I will delight myself in Your statutes; I will not forget Your Word.

17Deal bountifully with Your servant, that I may live; and I will observe Your word [hearing, receiving, loving and obeying it]. [Ps. 119:97-101.]

## New American Standard

21 I shall give thanks to Thee, for Thou hast answered me;
And Thou hast become my salvation.
22¶ The stone which the builders rejected
Has become the chief corner *stone.*
23 This is [a]the LORD's doing;
It is marvelous in our eyes.
24 This is the day which the LORD has made;
Let us rejoice and be glad in it.
25 O LORD, do save, we beseech Thee;
O LORD, we beseech Thee, do send prosperity!
26 Blessed is the one who comes in the name of the LORD;
We have blessed you from the house of the LORD.
27 The LORD is God, and He has given us light;
Bind the festival sacrifice with cords to the horns of the altar.
28 Thou art my God, and I give thanks to Thee;
*Thou art* my God, I extol Thee.
29 Give thanks to the LORD, for He is good;
For His lovingkindness is everlasting.

*Meditations and Prayers Relating to the Law of God.*

א Aleph.

**119** HOW BLESSED are those whose way is [b]blameless,
Who walk in the law of the LORD.
2 How blessed are those who observe His testimonies,
Who seek Him with all *their* heart.
3 They also do no unrighteousness;
They walk in His ways.
4 Thou hast ordained Thy precepts,
That we should keep *them* diligently.
5 Oh that my ways may be established
To keep Thy statutes!
6 Then I shall not be ashamed
When I look upon all Thy commandments.
7 I shall give thanks to Thee with uprightness of heart,
When I learn Thy righteous judgments.
8 I shall keep Thy statutes;
Do not forsake me utterly!

ב Beth.

9¶ How can a young man keep his way pure?
By keeping *it* according to Thy word.
10 With all my heart I have sought Thee;
Do not let me wander from Thy commandments.
11 Thy word I have treasured in my heart,
That I may not sin against Thee.
12 Blessed art Thou, O LORD;
Teach me Thy statutes.
13 With my lips I have told of
All the ordinances of Thy mouth.
14 I have rejoiced in the way of Thy testimonies,
As much as in all riches.
15 I will meditate on Thy precepts,
And regard Thy ways.
16 I shall delight in Thy statutes;
I shall not forget Thy word.

ג Gimel.

17¶ Deal bountifully with Thy servant,
That I may live and keep Thy word.

NAS [a] Lit., *from the LORD* [b] Lit., *complete,* or, *having integrity*

## New International

21 I will give you thanks, for you answered me;
you have become my salvation.
22 The stone the builders rejected
has become the capstone;
23 the LORD has done this,
and it is marvelous in our eyes.
24 This is the day the LORD has made;
let us rejoice and be glad in it.
25 O LORD, save us;
O LORD, grant us success.
26 Blessed is he who comes in the name of the LORD.
From the house of the LORD we bless you.[c]
27 The LORD is God,
and he has made his light shine upon us.
With boughs in hand, join in the festal procession
up[d] to the horns of the altar.
28 You are my God, and I will give you thanks;
you are my God, and I will exalt you.
29 Give thanks to the LORD, for he is good;
his love endures forever.

א Aleph

**119**[e] BLESSED ARE they whose ways are blameless,
who walk according to the law of the LORD.
2 Blessed are they who keep his statutes
and seek him with all their heart.
3 They do nothing wrong;
they walk in his ways.
4 You have laid down precepts
that are to be fully obeyed.
5 Oh, that my ways were steadfast
in obeying your decrees!
6 Then I would not be put to shame
when I consider all your commands.
7 I will praise you with an upright heart
as I learn your righteous laws.
8 I will obey your decrees;
do not utterly forsake me.

ב Beth

9 How can a young man keep his way pure?
By living according to your word.
10 I seek you with all my heart;
do not let me stray from your commands.
11 I have hidden your word in my heart
that I might not sin against you.
12 Praise be to you, O LORD;
teach me your decrees.
13 With my lips I recount
all the laws that come from your mouth.
14 I rejoice in following your statutes
as one rejoices in great riches.
15 I meditate on your precepts
and consider your ways.
16 I delight in your decrees;
I will not neglect your word.

ג Gimel

17 Do good to your servant, and I will live;
I will obey your word.

NIV [c] 26 The Hebrew is plural. [d] 27 Or *Bind the festal sacrifice with ropes / and take it* [e] This psalm is an acrostic poem; the verses of each stanza begin with the same letter of the Hebrew alphabet.

## King James

18 Open thou mine eyes, that I may behold wondrous things out of thy law.

19 I *am* a stranger in the earth: hide not thy commandments from me.

20 My soul breaketh for the longing *that it hath* unto thy judgments at all times.

21 Thou hast rebuked the proud *that are* cursed, which do err from thy commandments.

22 Remove from me reproach and contempt; for I have kept thy testimonies.

23 Princes also did sit *and* speak against me: *but* thy servant did meditate in thy statutes.

24 Thy testimonies also *are* my delight *and* my counsellors.

DALETH.

25 My soul cleaveth unto the dust: quicken thou me according to thy word.

26 I have declared my ways, and thou heardest me: teach me thy statutes.

27 Make me to understand the way of thy precepts: so shall I talk of thy wondrous works.

28 My soul melteth for heaviness: strengthen thou me according unto thy word.

29 Remove from me the way of lying: and grant me thy law graciously.

30 I have chosen the way of truth: thy judgments have I laid *before me*.

31 I have stuck unto thy testimonies: O Lord, put me not to shame.

32 I will run the way of thy commandments, when thou shalt enlarge my heart.

HE.

33 Teach me, O Lord, the way of thy statutes; and I shall keep it *unto* the end.

34 Give me understanding, and I shall keep thy law; yea, I shall observe it with *my* whole heart.

35 Make me to go in the path of thy commandments; for therein do I delight.

36 Incline my heart unto thy testimonies, and not to covetousness.

37 Turn away mine eyes from beholding vanity; *and* quicken thou me in thy way.

38 Stablish thy word unto thy servant, who *is devoted* to thy fear.

39 Turn away my reproach which I fear: for thy judgments *are* good.

40 Behold, I have longed after thy precepts: quicken me in thy righteousness.

VAU.

41 Let thy mercies come also unto me, O Lord, *even* thy salvation, according to thy word.

42 So shall I have wherewith to answer him that reproacheth me: for I trust in thy word.

43 And take not the word of truth utterly out of my mouth; for I have hoped in thy judgments.

44 So shall I keep thy law continually for ever and ever.

45 And I will walk at liberty: for I seek thy precepts.

46 I will speak of thy testimonies also before kings, and will not be ashamed.

47 And I will delight myself in thy commandments, which I have loved.

## Amplified

18 Open my eyes, that I may behold wondrous things out of Your law.

19 I am a stranger *and* a temporary resident on the earth; hide not Your commandments from me. [Ps. 39:12; Gen. 47:9; I Chron. 29:15; II Cor. 5:6; Heb. 11:13.]

20 My heart is breaking with longing that it has for Your ordinances *and* judgments at all times.

21 You rebuke the proud *and* arrogant, the accursed ones, who err *and* wander from Your commandments.

22 Take away from me reproach and contempt, for I have kept Your testimonies.

23 Princes also sat *and* talked against me, but Your servant meditated on Your statutes.

24 Your testimonies also are my delight and my counselors.

25 My earthly life cleaves to the dust; revive *and* stimulate me according to Your word! [Ps. 143:11.]

26 I have declared my ways *and* opened my griefs to You, and You listened to me; teach me Your statutes.

27 Make me to understand the way of Your precepts; so shall I meditate *and* talk of Your wondrous works. [Ps. 145:5, 6.]

28 My life dissolves *and* weeps itself away for heaviness; raise me up *and* strengthen me according to [the promises of] Your Word.

29 Remove from me the way of falsehood *and* unfaithfulness [to You], and graciously impart Your law to me.

30 I have chosen the way of truth *and* faithfulness; Your ordinances have I set before me.

31 I cleave to Your testimonies; O Lord, put me not to shame!

32 I will [not merely walk, but] run the way of Your commandments, when You give me a heart that is willing.

33 Teach me, O Lord, the way of Your statutes, and I will keep it unto the end—steadfastly.

34 Give me understanding, that I may keep Your law; yes, I will observe it with my whole heart. [Prov. 2:6; James 1:5.]

35 Make me to go in the path of Your commandments, for in them do I delight.

36 Incline my heart to Your testimonies, and not to covetousness [robbery, sensuality, unworthy riches]. [Ezek. 33:31; Mark 7:21, 22; I Tim. 6:10; Heb. 13:5.]

37 Turn away my eyes from beholding vanity [idols and idolatry]; and restore me to vigorous life *and* health in Your ways.

38 Establish Your word *and* confirm Your promise to Your servant, which is for those who reverently fear *and* devotedly worship You. [Ps. 96:9; Deut. 10:12.]

39 Turn away my reproach which I fear *and* dread, for Your ordinances are good.

40 Behold, I long for Your precepts; in Your righteousness give me renewed life.

41 Let Your mercies *and* loving-kindness come also to me, O Lord, even Your salvation, according to Your promise.

42 Then shall I have an answer for those who taunt *and* reproach me, for I lean on, rely on *and* trust in Your word.

43 And take not the word of truth utterly out of my mouth, for I hope in Your ordinances.

44 I will keep Your law continually for ever and ever [hearing, receiving, loving and obeying it].

45 And I will walk at liberty *and* at ease, for I have sought, inquired for [and desperately required] Your precepts.

46 I will speak of Your testimonies also before kings, and will not be put to shame. [Ps. 138:1; Matt. 10:18, 19; Acts 26:1, 2.]

47 For I will delight myself in Your commandments, which I love.

## New American Standard

18 Open my eyes, that I may behold
Wonderful things from Thy law.
19 I am a stranger in the earth;
Do not hide Thy commandments from me.
20 My soul is crushed with longing
After Thine ordinances at all times.
21 Thou dost rebuke the arrogant, the cursed,
Who wander from Thy commandments.
22 Take away reproach and contempt from me,
For I observe Thy testimonies.
23 Even though princes sit and talk against me,
Thy servant meditates on Thy statutes.
24 Thy testimonies also are my delight;
*They are* my counselors.

ד Daleth.

25¶ My soul cleaves to the dust;
Revive me according to Thy word.
26 I have told of my ways, and Thou hast answered me;
Teach me Thy statutes.
27 Make me understand the way of Thy precepts,
So I will meditate on Thy wonders.
28 My soul weeps because of grief;
Strengthen me according to Thy word.
29 Remove the false way from me,
And graciously grant me Thy law.
30 I have chosen the faithful way;
I have placed Thine ordinances *before me.*
31 I cleave to Thy testimonies;
O LORD, do not put me to shame!
32 I shall run the way of Thy commandments,
For Thou wilt enlarge my heart.

ה He.

33¶ Teach me, O LORD, the way of Thy statutes,
And I shall observe it to the end.
34 Give me understanding, that I may observe Thy law,
And keep it with all *my* heart.
35 Make me walk in the path of Thy commandments,
For I delight in it.
36 Incline my heart to Thy testimonies,
And not to *dishonest* gain.
37 Turn away my eyes from looking at vanity,
And revive me in Thy ways.
38 Establish Thy word to Thy servant,
As that which produces reverence for Thee.
39 Turn away my reproach which I dread,
For Thine ordinances are good.
40 Behold, I long for Thy precepts;
Revive me through Thy righteousness.

ו Vav.

41¶ May Thy lovingkindnesses also come to me, O LORD,
Thy salvation according to Thy word;
42 So I shall have an answer for him who reproaches me,
For I trust in Thy word.
43 And do not take the word of truth utterly out of my mouth,
For I wait for Thine ordinances.
44 So I will keep Thy law continually,
Forever and ever.
45 And I will walk at liberty,
For I seek Thy precepts.
46 I will also speak of Thy testimonies before kings,
And shall not be ashamed.
47 And I shall delight in Thy commandments,
Which I love.

## New International

18 Open my eyes that I may see
wonderful things in your law.
19 I am a stranger on earth;
do not hide your commands from me.
20 My soul is consumed with longing
for your laws at all times.
21 You rebuke the arrogant, who are cursed
and who stray from your commands.
22 Remove from me scorn and contempt,
for I keep your statutes.
23 Though rulers sit together and slander me,
your servant will meditate on your decrees.
24 Your statutes are my delight;
they are my counselors.

ד Daleth

25 I am laid low in the dust;
preserve my life according to your word.
26 I recounted my ways and you answered me;
teach me your decrees.
27 Let me understand the teaching of your precepts;
then I will meditate on your wonders.
28 My soul is weary with sorrow;
strengthen me according to your word.
29 Keep me from deceitful ways;
be gracious to me through your law.
30 I have chosen the way of truth;
I have set my heart on your laws.
31 I hold fast to your statutes, O LORD;
do not let me be put to shame.
32 I run in the path of your commands,
for you have set my heart free.

ה He

33 Teach me, O LORD, to follow your decrees;
then I will keep them to the end.
34 Give me understanding, and I will keep your law
and obey it with all my heart.
35 Direct me in the path of your commands,
for there I find delight.
36 Turn my heart toward your statutes
and not toward selfish gain.
37 Turn my eyes away from worthless things;
preserve my life according to your word.[a]
38 Fulfill your promise to your servant,
so that you may be feared.
39 Take away the disgrace I dread,
for your laws are good.
40 How I long for your precepts!
Preserve my life in your righteousness.

ו Waw

41 May your unfailing love come to me, O LORD,
your salvation according to your promise;
42 then I will answer the one who taunts me,
for I trust in your word.
43 Do not snatch the word of truth from my mouth,
for I have put my hope in your laws.
44 I will always obey your law,
for ever and ever.
45 I will walk about in freedom,
for I have sought out your precepts.
46 I will speak of your statutes before kings
and will not be put to shame,
47 for I delight in your commands
because I love them.

NIV [a] 37 Two manuscripts of the Masoretic Text and Dead Sea Scrolls; most manuscripts of the Masoretic Text *life in your way*

## King James

48My hands also will I lift up unto thy commandments, which
I have loved; and I will meditate in thy statutes.

ZAIN.

49Remember the word unto thy servant, upon which thou hast
caused me to hope.
50This *is* my comfort in my affliction: for thy word hath
quickened me.
51The proud have had me greatly in derision: *yet* have I not
declined from thy law.
52I remembered thy judgments of old, O LORD; and have comforted myself.
53Horror hath taken hold upon me because of the wicked that
forsake thy law.
54Thy statutes have been my songs in the house of my pilgrimage.
55I have remembered thy name, O LORD, in the night, and have
kept thy law.
56This I had, because I kept thy precepts.

CHETH.

57 *Thou art* my portion, O LORD: I have said that I would keep
thy words.
58I entreated thy favour with *my* whole heart: be merciful unto
me according to thy word.
59I thought on my ways, and turned my feet unto thy testimonies.
60I made haste, and delayed not to keep thy commandments.
61The bands of the wicked have robbed me: *but* I have not
forgotten thy law.
62At midnight I will rise to give thanks unto thee because of thy
righteous judgments.
63I *am* a companion of all *them* that fear thee, and of them that
keep thy precepts.
64The earth, O LORD, is full of thy mercy: teach me thy statutes.

TETH.

65Thou hast dealt well with thy servant, O LORD, according
unto thy word.
66Teach me good judgment and knowledge: for I have believed
thy commandments.
67Before I was afflicted I went astray: but now have I kept thy
word.
68Thou *art* good, and doest good; teach me thy statutes.
69The proud have forged a lie against me: *but* I will keep thy
precepts with *my* whole heart.
70Their heart is as fat as grease; *but* I delight in thy law.
71 *It is* good for me that I have been afflicted; that I might learn
thy statutes.
72The law of thy mouth *is* better unto me than thousands of gold
and silver.

JOD.

73Thy hands have made me and fashioned me: give me understanding, that I may learn thy commandments.
74They that fear thee will be glad when they see me; because
I have hoped in thy word.
75I know, O LORD, that thy judgments *are* right, and *that* thou
in faithfulness hast afflicted me.

## Amplified

48My hands also will I lift up (in fervent supplication) to Your
commandments, which I love, and I will meditate on Your statutes.
49Remember [fervently] the word *and* promise to Your servant,
on which You have caused me to hope.
50This is my comfort *and* consolation in my affliction, that Your
word has revived me *and* given me life. [Rom. 15:4.]
51The proud have had me greatly in derision, yet have I not
declined in my interest *or* turned aside from Your law.
52When I have [earnestly] recalled Your ordinances from of old,
O Lord, I have taken comfort.
53Burning indignation, terror *and* sadness seize upon me because of the wicked who forsake Your law.
54Your statutes have been my songs in the house of my pilgrimage.
55I have [earnestly] remembered Your name, O Lord, in the
night, and have observed Your law.
56This I have had [as the gift of Your grace and as my reward],
that I have kept Your precepts [hearing, receiving, loving and
obeying them].
57You are my portion, O Lord; I have promised to keep Your
words.
58I entreat Your favor with my whole heart; be merciful *and*
gracious to me according to Your promise.
59I considered my ways; I turned my feet *to obey* Your testimonies.
60I made haste and delayed not to keep Your commandments.
61Though the cords of the wicked have enclosed *and* ensnared
me, I have not forgotten Your law.
62At midnight I will rise to give thanks to You because of Your
righteous ordinances.
63I am a companion of all those who fear, revere, *and* worship
You, and of those who observe *and* give heed to Your precepts.
64The earth, O Lord, is full of Your mercy *and* loving-kindness;
teach me Your statutes.
65You have dealt well with Your servant, O Lord, according to
Your promise.
66Teach me good judgment, wise *and* right discernment and
knowledge, for I have believed [trusted, relied on and clung to]
Your commandments.
67Before I was afflicted I went astray, but now Your word do I
keep [hearing, receiving, loving and obeying it].
68You are good *and* kind and do good; teach me Your statutes.
69The arrogant *and* godless have put together a lie against me,
but I will keep Your precepts with my whole heart.
70Their heart is as fat as grease [their minds are dull and brutal];
but I delight in Your law.
71It is good for me that I have been afflicted, that I might learn
Your statutes.
72The law from Your mouth is better to me than thousands of
gold and silver.
73Your hands have made me, cunningly fashioned *and* established me; give me understanding, that I may learn Your commandments.
74Those who reverently *and* worshipfully fear You will see me
and be glad, because I have hoped in Your word *and* tarried for it.
75I know, O Lord, that Your judgments are right *and* righteous,
and that in faithfulness You have afflicted me. [Heb. 12:10.]

## New American Standard

48 And I shall lift up my hands to Thy commandments,
Which I love;
And I will meditate on Thy statutes.

ז Zayin.

49¶ Remember the word to Thy servant,
In which Thou hast made me hope.
50 This is my comfort in my affliction,
That Thy word has revived me.
51 The arrogant utterly deride me,
*Yet* I do not turn aside from Thy law.
52 I have remembered Thine ordinances from [a]of old,
O LORD,
And comfort myself.
53 Burning indignation has seized me because of the
wicked,
Who forsake Thy law.
54 Thy statutes are my songs
In the house of my pilgrimage.
55 O LORD, I remember Thy name in the night,
And keep Thy law.
56 This has become mine,
That I observe Thy precepts.

ח Heth.

57¶ The LORD is my portion;
I have promised to keep Thy words.
58 I entreated Thy favor with all *my* heart;
Be gracious to me according to Thy word.
59 I considered my ways,
And turned my feet to Thy testimonies.
60 I hastened and did not delay
To keep Thy commandments.
61 The cords of the wicked have encircled me,
*But* I have not forgotten Thy law.
62 At midnight I shall rise to give thanks to Thee
Because of Thy righteous ordinances.
63 I am a companion of all those who fear Thee,
And of those who keep Thy precepts.
64 The earth is full of Thy lovingkindness, O LORD;
Teach me Thy statutes.

ט Teth.

65¶ Thou hast dealt well with Thy servant,
O LORD, according to Thy word.
66 Teach me good discernment and knowledge,
For I believe in Thy commandments.
67 Before I was afflicted I went astray,
But now I keep Thy word.
68 Thou art good and doest good;
Teach me Thy statutes.
69 The arrogant [b]have forged a lie against me;
With all *my* heart I will observe Thy precepts.
70 Their heart is covered with fat,
*But* I delight in Thy law.
71 It is good for me that I was afflicted,
That I may learn Thy statutes.
72 The law of Thy mouth is better to me
Than thousands of gold and silver *pieces*.

י Yodh.

73¶ Thy hands made me and [c]fashioned me;
Give me understanding, that I may learn Thy
commandments.
74 May those who fear Thee see me and be glad,
Because I wait for Thy word.
75 I know, O LORD, that Thy judgments are righteous,
And that in faithfulness Thou hast afflicted me.

NAS [a] Or, *everlasting* [b] Lit., *besmear me with lies* [c] Lit., *established*

## New International

48 I lift up my hands to[d] your commands, which I love,
and I meditate on your decrees.

ז Zayin

49 Remember your word to your servant,
for you have given me hope.
50 My comfort in my suffering is this:
Your promise preserves my life.
51 The arrogant mock me without restraint,
but I do not turn from your law.
52 I remember your ancient laws, O LORD,
and I find comfort in them.
53 Indignation grips me because of the wicked,
who have forsaken your law.
54 Your decrees are the theme of my song
wherever I lodge.
55 In the night I remember your name, O LORD,
and I will keep your law.
56 This has been my practice:
I obey your precepts.

ח Heth

57 You are my portion, O LORD;
I have promised to obey your words.
58 I have sought your face with all my heart;
be gracious to me according to your promise.
59 I have considered my ways
and have turned my steps to your statutes.
60 I will hasten and not delay
to obey your commands.
61 Though the wicked bind me with ropes,
I will not forget your law.
62 At midnight I rise to give you thanks
for your righteous laws.
63 I am a friend to all who fear you,
to all who follow your precepts.
64 The earth is filled with your love, O LORD;
teach me your decrees.

ט Teth

65 Do good to your servant
according to your word, O LORD.
66 Teach me knowledge and good judgment,
for I believe in your commands.
67 Before I was afflicted I went astray,
but now I obey your word.
68 You are good, and what you do is good;
teach me your decrees.
69 Though the arrogant have smeared me with lies,
I keep your precepts with all my heart.
70 Their hearts are callous and unfeeling,
but I delight in your law.
71 It was good for me to be afflicted
so that I might learn your decrees.
72 The law from your mouth is more precious to me
than thousands of pieces of silver and gold.

י Yodh

73 Your hands made me and formed me;
give me understanding to learn your commands.
74 May those who fear you rejoice when they see me,
for I have put my hope in your word.
75 I know, O LORD, that your laws are righteous,
and in faithfulness you have afflicted me.

NIV [d] *48* Or *for*

## King James

76Let, I pray thee, thy merciful kindness be for my comfort, according to thy word unto thy servant.
77Let thy tender mercies come unto me, that I may live: for thy law *is* my delight.
78Let the proud be ashamed; for they dealt perversely with me without a cause: *but* I will meditate in thy precepts.
79Let those that fear thee turn unto me, and those that have known thy testimonies.
80Let my heart be sound in thy statutes; that I be not ashamed.

CAPH.

81My soul fainteth for thy salvation: *but* I hope in thy word.
82Mine eyes fail for thy word, saying, When wilt thou comfort me?
83For I am become like a bottle in the smoke; *yet* do I not forget thy statutes.
84How many *are* the days of thy servant? when wilt thou execute judgment on them that persecute me?
85The proud have digged pits for me, which *are* not after thy law.
86All thy commandments *are* faithful: they persecute me wrongfully; help thou me.
87They had almost consumed me upon earth; but I forsook not thy precepts.
88Quicken me after thy lovingkindness; so shall I keep the testimony of thy mouth.

LAMED.

89For ever, O LORD, thy word is settled in heaven.
90Thy faithfulness *is* unto all generations: thou hast established the earth, and it abideth.
91They continue this day according to thine ordinances: for all *are* thy servants.
92Unless thy law *had been* my delights, I should then have perished in mine affliction.
93I will never forget thy precepts: for with them thou hast quickened me.
94I *am* thine, save me; for I have sought thy precepts.
95The wicked have waited for me to destroy me: *but* I will consider thy testimonies.
96I have seen an end of all perfection: *but* thy commandment *is* exceeding broad.

MEM.

97O how love I thy law! it *is* my meditation all the day.
98Thou through thy commandments hast made me wiser than mine enemies: for they *are* ever with me.
99I have more understanding than all my teachers: for thy testimonies *are* my meditation.
100I understand more than the ancients, because I keep thy precepts.
101I have refrained my feet from every evil way, that I might keep thy word.
102I have not departed from thy judgments: for thou hast taught me.
103How sweet are thy words unto my taste! *yea, sweeter* than honey to my mouth!
104Through thy precepts I get understanding: therefore I hate every false way.

## Amplified

76Let, I pray You, Your merciful kindness *and* steadfast love be for my comfort, according to Your promise to Your servant.
77Let Your tender mercies *and* loving-kindness come to me, that I may live; for Your law is my delight!
78Let the proud be put to shame, for they dealt perversely with me without a cause; but I will meditate on Your precepts.
79Let those who reverently *and* worshipfully fear You turn to me, and those who have known Your testimonies.
80Let my heart be sound—sincere and wholehearted and blameless—in Your statutes, that I be not put to shame.
81My soul languishes *and* grows faint for Your salvation, but I hope in Your word.
82My eyes fail with watching for [the fulfillment of] Your promise. I say, When will You comfort me?
83For I have become like a bottle [a wineskin blackened and shriveled] in the smoke [in which it hangs], yet do I not forget Your statutes.
84How many are the days Your servant *must endure*? When will You judge those who pursue and persecute me? [Rev. 6:10.]
85The godless *and* arrogant have dug pitfalls for me, men who do not conform to Your law.
86All Your commandments are faithful *and* sure. *The godless* pursue *and* persecute me with falsehood; help me, *Lord*!
87They had almost consumed me upon earth, but I forsook not Your precepts.
88According to Your steadfast love give life to me; then I will keep the testimony of Your mouth [hearing, receiving, loving and obeying it].
89For ever, O Lord, Your Word [stands firm as the heavens] is settled in Heaven. [Ps. 89:2; Matt. 24:34, 35; I Pet. 1:25.]
90Your faithfulness is from generation to generation; You have established the earth, and it stands fast.
91All [the whole universe] are Your servants; therefore they continue this day according to Your ordinances. [Jer. 33:25.]
92Unless Your law had been my delight, I would have perished in my affliction.
93I will never forget Your precepts; [how can I?] for it is by them You have quickened me—granted me life.
94I am Yours, therefore save me—Your own; for I have sought (inquired of and for) Your precepts, *and* required them [as my urgent need]. [Ps. 42:1.]
95The wicked waited for me to destroy me, but I considered Your testimonies.
96I have seen that everything [human] has its limits *and* end, [no matter how extensive, noble and excellent] *but* Your commandment is exceedingly broad *and* extends without limits [into eternity]. [Rom. 3:10-19.]
97Oh, how love I Your law! It is my meditation all the day. [Ps. 1:2.]
98You through Your commandments make me wiser than my enemies; for *Your words* are ever before me.
99I have better understanding *and* deeper insight than all my teachers, because Your testimonies are my meditation. [II Tim. 3:15.]
100I understand more than the aged, because I keep Your precepts [hearing, receiving, loving and obeying them].
101I have restrained my feet from every evil way, that I might keep Your Word [hearing, receiving, loving and obeying it]. [Prov. 1:15.]
102I have not turned aside from Your ordinances, for You have taught me.
103How sweet are Your words to my taste, sweeter than honey to my mouth! [Ps. 19:10; Prov. 8:11.]
104Through Your precepts I get understanding; therefore I hate every false way.

## New American Standard

76 O may Thy lovingkindness comfort me,
According to Thy word to Thy servant.
77 May Thy compassion come to me that I may live,
For Thy law is my delight.
78 May the arrogant be ashamed, for they subvert me with a lie;
*But* I shall meditate on Thy precepts.
79 May those who fear Thee turn to me,
Even those who know Thy testimonies.
80 May my heart be blameless in Thy statutes,
That I may not be ashamed.

### כ Kaph.

81¶ My soul languishes for Thy salvation;
I wait for Thy word.
82 My eyes fail *with longing* for Thy word,
While I say, "When wilt Thou comfort me?"
83 Though I have become like a wineskin in the smoke,
I do not forget Thy statutes.
84 How many are the days of Thy servant?
When wilt Thou execute judgment on those who persecute me?
85 The arrogant have dug pits for me,
*Men* who are not in accord with Thy law.
86 All Thy commandments are faithful;
They have persecuted me with a lie; help me!
87 They almost destroyed me on earth,
But as for me, I did not forsake Thy precepts.
88 Revive me according to Thy lovingkindness,
So that I may keep the testimony of Thy mouth.

### ל Lamedh.

89¶ Forever, O LORD,
Thy word [a]is settled in heaven.
90 Thy faithfulness *continues* throughout all generations;
Thou didst establish the earth, and it stands.
91 They stand this day according to Thine ordinances,
For all things are Thy servants.
92 If Thy law had not been my delight,
Then I would have perished in my affliction.
93 I will never forget Thy precepts,
For by them Thou hast revived me.
94 I am Thine, save me;
For I have sought Thy precepts.
95 The wicked wait for me to destroy me;
I shall diligently consider Thy testimonies.
96 I have seen a limit to all perfection;
Thy commandment is exceedingly broad.

### מ Mem.

97¶ O how I love Thy law!
It is my meditation all the day.
98 Thy commandments make me wiser than my enemies,
For they are ever mine.
99 I have more insight than all my teachers,
For Thy testimonies are my meditation.
100 I understand more than the aged,
Because I have observed Thy precepts.
101 I have restrained my feet from every evil way,
That I may keep Thy word.
102 I have not turned aside from Thine ordinances,
For Thou Thyself hast taught me.
103 How sweet are Thy words to my taste!
*Yes, sweeter* than honey to my mouth!
104 From Thy precepts I get understanding;
Therefore I hate every false way.

NAS [a] Lit., *stands firm*

## New International

76 May your unfailing love be my comfort,
according to your promise to your servant.
77 Let your compassion come to me that I may live,
for your law is my delight.
78 May the arrogant be put to shame for wronging me without cause;
but I will meditate on your precepts.
79 May those who fear you turn to me,
those who understand your statutes.
80 May my heart be blameless toward your decrees,
that I may not be put to shame.

### כ Kaph

81 My soul faints with longing for your salvation,
but I have put my hope in your word.
82 My eyes fail, looking for your promise;
I say, "When will you comfort me?"
83 Though I am like a wineskin in the smoke,
I do not forget your decrees.
84 How long must your servant wait?
When will you punish my persecutors?
85 The arrogant dig pitfalls for me,
contrary to your law.
86 All your commands are trustworthy;
help me, for men persecute me without cause.
87 They almost wiped me from the earth,
but I have not forsaken your precepts.
88 Preserve my life according to your love,
and I will obey the statutes of your mouth.

### ל Lamedh

89 Your word, O LORD, is eternal;
it stands firm in the heavens.
90 Your faithfulness continues through all generations;
you established the earth, and it endures.
91 Your laws endure to this day,
for all things serve you.
92 If your law had not been my delight,
I would have perished in my affliction.
93 I will never forget your precepts,
for by them you have preserved my life.
94 Save me, for I am yours;
I have sought out your precepts.
95 The wicked are waiting to destroy me,
but I will ponder your statutes.
96 To all perfection I see a limit;
but your commands are boundless.

### מ Mem

97 Oh, how I love your law!
I meditate on it all day long.
98 Your commands make me wiser than my enemies,
for they are ever with me.
99 I have more insight than all my teachers,
for I meditate on your statutes.
100 I have more understanding than the elders,
for I obey your precepts.
101 I have kept my feet from every evil path
so that I might obey your word.
102 I have not departed from your laws,
for you yourself have taught me.
103 How sweet are your words to my taste,
sweeter than honey to my mouth!
104 I gain understanding from your precepts;
therefore I hate every wrong path.

# King James

NUN.

105 Thy word *is* a lamp unto my feet, and a light unto my path.

106 I have sworn, and I will perform *it*, that I will keep thy righteous judgments.

107 I am afflicted very much: quicken me, O LORD, according unto thy word.

108 Accept, I beseech thee, the freewill offerings of my mouth, O LORD, and teach me thy judgments.

109 My soul *is* continually in my hand: yet do I not forget thy law.

110 The wicked have laid a snare for me: yet I erred not from thy precepts.

111 Thy testimonies have I taken as an heritage for ever: for they *are* the rejoicing of my heart.

112 I have inclined mine heart to perform thy statutes always, *even unto* the end.

SAMECH.

113 I hate *vain* thoughts: but thy law do I love.

114 Thou *art* my hiding place and my shield: I hope in thy word.

115 Depart from me, ye evildoers: for I will keep the commandments of my God.

116 Uphold me according unto thy word, that I may live: and let me not be ashamed of my hope.

117 Hold thou me up, and I shall be safe: and I will have respect unto thy statutes continually.

118 Thou hast trodden down all them that err from thy statutes: for their deceit *is* falsehood.

119 Thou puttest away all the wicked of the earth *like* dross: therefore I love thy testimonies.

120 My flesh trembleth for fear of thee; and I am afraid of thy judgments.

AIN.

121 I have done judgment and justice: leave me not to mine oppressors.

122 Be surety for thy servant for good: let not the proud oppress me.

123 Mine eyes fail for thy salvation, and for the word of thy righteousness.

124 Deal with thy servant according unto thy mercy, and teach me thy statutes.

125 I *am* thy servant; give me understanding, that I may know thy testimonies.

126 *It is* time for *thee*, LORD, to work: *for* they have made void thy law.

127 Therefore I love thy commandments above gold; yea, above fine gold.

128 Therefore I esteem all *thy* precepts *concerning* all *things to be* right; *and* I hate every false way.

PE.

129 Thy testimonies *are* wonderful: therefore doth my soul keep them.

130 The entrance of thy words giveth light; it giveth understanding unto the simple.

131 I opened my mouth, and panted: for I longed for thy commandments.

132 Look thou upon me, and be merciful unto me, as thou usest to do unto those that love thy name.

133 Order my steps in thy word: and let not any iniquity have dominion over me.

# Amplified

105 Your word is a lamp to my feet and a light to my path. [Prov. 6:23.]

106 I have sworn [an oath] and have confirmed it, that I will keep Your righteous ordinances—hearing, receiving, loving and obeying them. [Neh. 10:29.]

107 I am sorely afflicted; renew *and* quicken me—give me life—O Lord, according to Your Word!

108 Accept, I beseech You, the freewill offerings of my mouth, O Lord, and teach me Your ordinances. [Hos. 14:2; Heb. 13:15.]

109 My life is continually in my hand, yet do I not forget Your law.

110 The wicked have laid a snare for me, yet I do not stray from Your precepts.

111 Your testimonies have I taken as a heritage for ever, for they are the rejoicing of my heart. [Deut. 33:4.]

112 I have inclined my heart to perform Your statutes for ever, even to the end.

113 I hate the thoughts of the undecided [in religion] double-minded people; but Your law do I love.

114 You are my hiding place and my shield; I hope in Your word. [Pss. 32:7; 91:1.]

115 Depart from me, you evildoers; that I may keep the commandments of my God [hearing, receiving, loving and obeying them]. [Pss. 6:8; 139:19; Matt. 7:23.]

116 Uphold me according to Your promise, that I may live, and let me not be put to shame in my hope! [Ps. 25:2; Rom. 5:5; 9:33; 10:11.]

117 Hold me up, that I may be safe and have regard for Your statutes continually!

118 You spurn *and* set at nought all those who stray from Your statutes, for their own lying deceives them *and* their tricks are in vain.

119 You put away *and* count as dross all the wicked of the earth [for there is no true metal in them]; therefore I love Your testimonies.

120 My flesh trembles *and* shudders for fear *and* reverential, worshipful awe of You, and I am afraid *and* in dread of Your judgments.

121 I have done justice and righteousness; leave me not to those who would oppress me.

122 Be surety for Your servant for good [as Judah was surety for the safety of Benjamin]; let not the proud oppress me. [Gen. 43:9.]

123 My eyes fail with watching for Your salvation, and for the fulfillment of Your righteous promise.

124 Deal with Your servant according to Your mercy *and* loving-kindness, and teach me Your statutes.

125 I am Your servant; give me understanding—discernment and comprehension—that I may know (discern and be familiar with the character of) Your testimonies.

126 It is time for the Lord to act; they have frustrated Your law.

127 Therefore I love Your commandments more than [resplendent] gold; yes, more than [perfectly] refined gold.

128 Therefore I esteem as right all, yes, all Your precepts; I hate every false way.

129 Your testimonies are wonderful—far exceeding anything conceived by man; therefore my [penitent] self keeps them [hearing, receiving, loving and obeying them.]

130 The entrance *and* unfolding of Your words gives light; it gives understanding—discernment and comprehension—to the simple.

131 I opened my mouth and panted (with eager desire), for I longed for Your commandments.

132 Look upon me, be merciful unto me *and* show me favor, as is Your way to those who love Your name.

133 Establish my steps *and* direct them by (means of) Your word; let not any iniquity have dominion over me.

## New American Standard

נ Nun.

105¶ Thy word is a lamp to my feet,
And a light to my path.
106 I have sworn, and I will confirm it,
That I will keep Thy righteous ordinances.
107 I am exceedingly afflicted;
Revive me, O LORD, according to Thy word.
108 O accept the freewill offerings of my mouth, O LORD,
And teach me Thine ordinances.
109 My life is continually [a]in my hand,
Yet I do not forget Thy law.
110 The wicked have laid a snare for me,
Yet I have not gone astray from Thy precepts.
111 I have inherited Thy testimonies forever,
For they are the joy of my heart.
112 I have inclined my heart to perform Thy statutes
Forever, *even* to the end.

ס Samekh.

113¶ I hate those who are double-minded,
But I love Thy law.
114 Thou art my hiding place and my shield;
I wait for Thy word.
115 Depart from me, evildoers,
That I may observe the commandments of my God.
116 Sustain me according to Thy word, that I may live;
And do not let me be ashamed of my hope.
117 Uphold me that I may be safe,
That I may have regard for Thy statutes continually.
118 Thou hast rejected all those who wander from Thy statutes,
For their deceitfulness is useless.
119 Thou hast removed all the wicked of the earth *like* dross;
Therefore I love Thy testimonies.
120 My flesh trembles for fear of Thee,
And I am afraid of Thy judgments.

ע Ayin.

121¶ I have done justice and righteousness;
Do not leave me to my oppressors.
122 Be surety for Thy servant for good;
Do not let the arrogant oppress me.
123 My eyes fail *with longing* for Thy salvation,
And for Thy righteous word.
124 Deal with Thy servant according to Thy lovingkindness,
And teach me Thy statutes.
125 I am Thy servant; give me understanding,
That I may know Thy testimonies.
126 It is time for the LORD to act,
*For* they have broken Thy law.
127 Therefore I love Thy commandments
Above gold, yes, above fine gold.
128 Therefore I esteem right all *Thy* precepts concerning everything,
I hate every false way.

פ Pe.

129¶ Thy testimonies are wonderful;
Therefore my soul observes them.
130 The unfolding of Thy words gives light;
It gives understanding to the simple.
131 I opened my mouth wide and panted,
For I longed for Thy commandments.
132 Turn to me and be gracious to me,
After Thy manner with those who love Thy name.
133 Establish my footsteps in Thy word,
And do not let any iniquity have dominion over me.

NAS [a] I.e., in danger

## New International

נ Nun

105 Your word is a lamp to my feet
and a light for my path.
106 I have taken an oath and confirmed it,
that I will follow your righteous laws.
107 I have suffered much;
preserve my life, O LORD, according to your word.
108 Accept, O LORD, the willing praise of my mouth,
and teach me your laws.
109 Though I constantly take my life in my hands,
I will not forget your law.
110 The wicked have set a snare for me,
but I have not strayed from your precepts.
111 Your statutes are my heritage forever;
they are the joy of my heart.
112 My heart is set on keeping your decrees
to the very end.

ס Samekh

113 I hate double-minded men,
but I love your law.
114 You are my refuge and my shield;
I have put my hope in your word.
115 Away from me, you evildoers,
that I may keep the commands of my God!
116 Sustain me according to your promise, and I will live;
do not let my hopes be dashed.
117 Uphold me, and I will be delivered;
I will always have regard for your decrees.
118 You reject all who stray from your decrees,
for their deceitfulness is in vain.
119 All the wicked of the earth you discard like dross;
therefore I love your statutes.
120 My flesh trembles in fear of you;
I stand in awe of your laws.

ע Ayin

121 I have done what is righteous and just;
do not leave me to my oppressors.
122 Ensure your servant's well-being;
let not the arrogant oppress me.
123 My eyes fail, looking for your salvation,
looking for your righteous promise.
124 Deal with your servant according to your love
and teach me your decrees.
125 I am your servant; give me discernment
that I may understand your statutes.
126 It is time for you to act, O LORD;
your law is being broken.
127 Because I love your commands
more than gold, more than pure gold,
128 and because I consider all your precepts right,
I hate every wrong path.

פ Pe

129 Your statutes are wonderful;
therefore I obey them.
130 The unfolding of your words gives light;
it gives understanding to the simple.
131 I open my mouth and pant,
longing for your commands.
132 Turn to me and have mercy on me,
as you always do to those who love your name.
133 Direct my footsteps according to your word;
let no sin rule over me.

## King James

134 Deliver me from the oppression of man: so will I keep thy precepts.
135 Make thy face to shine upon thy servant; and teach me thy statutes.
136 Rivers of waters run down mine eyes, because they keep not thy law.

TZADDI.

137 Righteous *art* thou, O LORD, and upright *are* thy judgments.
138 Thy testimonies *that* thou hast commanded *are* righteous and very faithful.
139 My zeal hath consumed me, because mine enemies have forgotten thy words.
140 Thy word *is* very pure: therefore thy servant loveth it.
141 I *am* small and despised: *yet* do not I forget thy precepts.
142 Thy righteousness *is* an everlasting righteousness, and thy law *is* the truth.
143 Trouble and anguish have taken hold on me: *yet* thy commandments *are* my delights.
144 The righteousness of thy testimonies *is* everlasting: give me understanding, and I shall live.

KOPH.

145 I cried with *my* whole heart; hear me, O LORD: I will keep thy statutes.
146 I cried unto thee; save me, and I shall keep thy testimonies.
147 I prevented the dawning of the morning, and cried: I hoped in thy word.
148 Mine eyes prevent the *night* watches, that I might meditate in thy word.
149 Hear my voice according unto thy lovingkindness: O LORD, quicken me according to thy judgment.
150 They draw nigh that follow after mischief: they are far from thy law.
151 Thou *art* near, O LORD; and all thy commandments *are* truth.
152 Concerning thy testimonies, I have known of old that thou hast founded them for ever.

RESH.

153 Consider mine affliction, and deliver me: for I do not forget thy law.
154 Plead my cause, and deliver me: quicken me according to thy word.
155 Salvation *is* far from the wicked: for they seek not thy statutes.
156 Great *are* thy tender mercies, O LORD: quicken me according to thy judgments.
157 Many *are* my persecutors and mine enemies; *yet* do I not decline from thy testimonies.
158 I beheld the transgressors, and was grieved; because they kept not thy word.
159 Consider how I love thy precepts: quicken me, O LORD, according to thy lovingkindness.
160 Thy word *is* true *from* the beginning: and every one of thy righteous judgments *endureth* for ever.

SCHIN.

161 Princes have persecuted me without a cause: but my heart standeth in awe of thy word.
162 I rejoice at thy word, as one that findeth great spoil.
163 I hate and abhor lying: *but* thy law do I love.

## Amplified

134 Deliver me from the oppression of man; so will I keep Your precepts [hearing, receiving, loving and obeying them]. [Luke 1:74.]
135 Make Your face to shine [with pleasure] upon Your servant, and teach me Your statutes. [Ps. 4:6.]
136 Streams of water have run down my eyes because men do not keep Your law [they hear it not, nor receive it, love it or obey it].
137 [Rigidly] righteous are You, O Lord, and upright are Your judgments *and* all expressions of Your will.
138 You have commanded *and* appointed Your testimonies in righteousness and in great faithfulness.
139 My zeal has consumed me *and* cut me off, because my adversaries have forgotton Your words.
140 Your word is very pure—tried and well-refined; therefore Your servant loves it.
141 I am small (insignificant) and despised, but I do not forget Your precepts.
142 Your righteousness is an everlasting righteousness, and Your law is truth. [Ps. 19:9; John 17:17.]
143 Trouble and anguish have found *and* taken hold on me, yet Your commandments are my delight.
144 Your righteous testimonies are everlasting *and* Your decrees are binding to eternity; give me understanding and I shall live—give me discernment and comprehension and I shall not die.
145 I cried with my whole heart; hear me, O Lord; I will keep Your statutes [I will hear, receive, love and obey them].
146 I cried to You; save me, that I may keep Your testimonies [hearing, receiving, loving and obeying them.]
147 I anticipated the dawning of the morning and cried [in child-like prayer]; I hoped in Your word.
148 My eyes anticipate the night watches *and* I am awake before the cry of the watchman, that I might meditate on Your word.
149 Hear my voice according to Your steadfast love; O Lord, quicken me *and* give me life, according to Your (righteous) decree.
150 They draw near that follow after wrong thinking *and* persecute me with wickedness; they are far from Your law.
151 You are near, O Lord, [nearer to me than my foes] and all Your commandments are truth.
152 Of old have I known Your testimonies, *and* for a long time, therefore, [it is a thoroughly established conviction] that You have founded them for ever. [Luke 21:33.]
153 Consider my affliction and deliver me, for I do not forget Your law.
154 Plead my cause and redeem me, revive me *and* give me life according to Your word.
155 Salvation is far from the wicked, for they seek not *nor* hunger for Your statutes.
156 Great are Your tender mercies *and* loving-kindness, O Lord; give me life according to Your ordinances.
157 Many are my persecutors and my adversaries, yet I do not swerve from Your testimonies.
158 I beheld the treacherous and was grieved *and* loathed them, because they do not respect Your law [neither hearing, receiving, loving nor obeying it].
159 Consider how I love Your precepts; revive me *and* give life to me, O Lord, according to Your loving-kindness!
160 The sum of Your Word is truth [the total of the full meanings of all Your individual precepts] and every one of Your righteous decrees endures for ever.
161 Princes pursue *and* persecute me without cause, but my heart stands in awe of Your words [dreading violation of them far more than the force of prince or potentate]. [I Sam. 24:11, 14; 26:18.]
162 I rejoice at Your word as one who finds great spoil.
163 I hate and abhor falsehood, but Your law do I love.

## New American Standard

134 Redeem me from the oppression of man,
That I may keep Thy precepts.
135 Make Thy face shine upon Thy servant,
And teach me Thy statutes.
136 My eyes shed streams of water,
Because they do not keep Thy law.

צ Tsadhe.

137¶ Righteous art Thou, O LORD,
And upright are Thy judgments.
138 Thou hast commanded Thy testimonies in righteousness
And exceeding faithfulness.
139 My zeal has consumed me,
Because my adversaries have forgotten Thy words.
140 Thy word is very pure,
Therefore Thy servant loves it.
141 I am small and despised,
*Yet* I do not forget Thy precepts.
142 Thy righteousness is an everlasting righteousness,
And Thy law is truth.
143 Trouble and anguish have come upon me;
*Yet* Thy commandments are my delight.
144 Thy testimonies are righteous forever;
Give me understanding that I may live.

ק Qoph.

145¶ I cried with all my heart; answer me, O LORD!
I will observe Thy statutes.
146 I cried to Thee; save me,
And I shall keep Thy testimonies.
147 I rise before dawn and cry for help;
I wait for Thy words.
148 My eyes anticipate the night watches,
That I may meditate on Thy word.
149 Hear my voice according to Thy lovingkindness;
Revive me, O LORD, according to Thine ordinances.
150 Those who follow after wickedness draw near;
They are far from Thy law.
151 Thou art near, O LORD,
And all Thy commandments are truth.
152 Of old I have known from Thy testimonies,
That Thou hast founded them forever.

ר Resh.

153¶ Look upon my affliction and rescue me,
For I do not forget Thy law.
154 Plead my cause and redeem me;
Revive me according to Thy word.
155 Salvation is far from the wicked,
For they do not seek Thy statutes.
156 Great are Thy mercies, O LORD;
Revive me according to Thine ordinances.
157 Many are my persecutors and my adversaries,
*Yet* I do not turn aside from Thy testimonies.
158 I behold the treacherous and loathe *them*,
Because they do not keep Thy word.
159 Consider how I love Thy precepts;
Revive me, O LORD, according to Thy lovingkindness.
160 The sum of Thy word is truth,
And every one of Thy righteous ordinances is
everlasting.

ש Shin.

161¶ Princes persecute me without cause,
But my heart stands in awe of Thy words.
162 I rejoice at Thy word,
As one who finds great spoil.
163 I hate and despise falsehood,
*But* I love Thy law.

## New International

134Redeem me from the oppression of men,
that I may obey your precepts.
135Make your face shine upon your servant
and teach me your decrees.
136Streams of tears flow from my eyes,
for your law is not obeyed.

צ Tsadhe

137Righteous are you, O LORD,
and your laws are right.
138The statutes you have laid down are righteous;
they are fully trustworthy.
139My zeal wears me out,
for my enemies ignore your words.
140Your promises have been thoroughly tested,
and your servant loves them.
141Though I am lowly and despised,
I do not forget your precepts.
142Your righteousness is everlasting
and your law is true.
143Trouble and distress have come upon me,
but your commands are my delight.
144Your statutes are forever right;
give me understanding that I may live.

ק Qoph

145I call with all my heart; answer me, O LORD,
and I will obey your decrees.
146I call out to you; save me
and I will keep your statutes.
147I rise before dawn and cry for help;
I have put my hope in your word.
148My eyes stay open through the watches of the night,
that I may meditate on your promises.
149Hear my voice in accordance with your love;
preserve my life, O LORD, according to your laws.
150Those who devise wicked schemes are near,
but they are far from your law.
151Yet you are near, O LORD,
and all your commands are true.
152Long ago I learned from your statutes
that you established them to last forever.

ר Resh

153Look upon my suffering and deliver me,
for I have not forgotten your law.
154Defend my cause and redeem me;
preserve my life according to your promise.
155Salvation is far from the wicked,
for they do not seek out your decrees.
156Your compassion is great, O LORD;
preserve my life according to your laws.
157Many are the foes who persecute me,
but I have not turned from your statutes.
158I look on the faithless with loathing,
for they do not obey your word.
159See how I love your precepts;
preserve my life, O LORD, according to your love.
160All your words are true;
all your righteous laws are eternal.

ש Sin and Shin

161Rulers persecute me without cause,
but my heart trembles at your word.
162I rejoice in your promise
like one who finds great spoil.
163I hate and abhor falsehood
but I love your law.

## King James

164Seven times a day do I praise thee because of thy righteous judgments.
165Great peace have they which love thy law: and nothing shall offend them.
166LORD, I have hoped for thy salvation, and done thy commandments.
167My soul hath kept thy testimonies; and I love them exceedingly.
168I have kept thy precepts and thy testimonies: for all my ways *are* before thee.

TAU

169Let my cry come near before thee, O LORD: give me understanding according to thy word.
170Let my supplication come before thee: deliver me according to thy word.
171My lips shall utter praise, when thou hast taught me thy statutes.
172My tongue shall speak of thy word: for all thy commandments *are* righteousness.
173Let thine hand help me; for I have chosen thy precepts.
174I have longed for thy salvation, O LORD; and thy law *is* my delight.
175Let my soul live, and it shall praise thee; and let thy judgments help me.
176I have gone astray like a lost sheep; seek thy servant; for I do not forget thy commandments.

A Song of degrees.

120 IN MY distress I cried unto the LORD, and he heard me.
2Deliver my soul, O LORD, from lying lips, *and* from a deceitful tongue.
3What shall be given unto thee? or what shall be done unto thee, thou false tongue?
4Sharp arrows of the mighty, with coals of juniper.
5Woe is me, that I sojourn in Mesech, *that* I dwell in the tents of Kedar!
6My soul hath long dwelt with him that hateth peace.
7I *am for* peace: but when I speak, they *are* for war.

A Song of degrees.

121 I WILL lift up mine eyes unto the hills, from whence cometh my help.
2My help *cometh* from the LORD, which made heaven and earth.
3He will not suffer thy foot to be moved: he that keepeth thee will not slumber.
4Behold, he that keepeth Israel shall neither slumber nor sleep.
5The LORD *is* thy keeper: the LORD *is* thy shade upon thy right hand.
6The sun shall not smite thee by day, nor the moon by night.
7The LORD shall preserve thee from all evil: he shall preserve thy soul.

## Amplified

164Seven times a day *and* all day long do I praise You because of Your righteous decrees.
165Great peace have they who love Your law; nothing shall offend them *or* make them stumble. [Prov. 3:2; Isa. 32:17.]
166I am hoping *and* waiting (eagerly) for Your salvation, O Lord, and I do Your commandments. [Gen. 49:18.]
167Your testimonies have I kept [hearing, receiving and obeying them]; I love them exceedingly!
168I have observed Your precepts *and* Your testimonies, for all my ways are (fully known) before You.
169Let my mournful cry *and* supplication come near before You, O Lord; give me understanding—discernment and comprehension—according to Your word [of assurance and promise].
170Let my supplication come before You; deliver me according to Your word!
171My lips pour forth praise [with thanksgiving and renewed trust] when You teach me Your statutes.
172My tongue shall sing [praise for the fulfillment] of Your word, for all Your commandments are righteous.
173Let Your hand be ready to help me, for I have chosen Your precepts.
174I have longed for Your salvation, O Lord, and Your law is my delight.
175Let me live that I may praise You, and let Your decrees help me.
176I have gone astray like a lost sheep; seek, inquire for and demand Your servant, for I do not forget Your commandments. [Isa. 53:6; Luke 15:4; I Pet. 2:25.]

A Song of [a]Ascents.

120 IN MY distress I cried to the Lord, and He answered me.
2Deliver me, O Lord, from lying lips and from a deceitful tongue.
3What shall be given to you? Or what more shall be done to you, you deceitful tongue?
4Sharp arrows of a (mighty) warrior, with (glowing) coals of the broom tree!
5Woe is me, that I sojourn with Meshech, that I dwell beside the tents of Kedar [as if among notoriously barbarous people]! [Gen. 10:2; 25:13; Jer. 49:28, 29.]
6My life has too long had its dwelling with him who hates peace.
7I am for peace; but when I speak, they are for war.

A Song of [b]Ascents.

121 I WILL lift up my eyes to the hills [around Jerusalem, to sacred Mount Zion and Mount Moriah]. From whence shall my help come? [Jer. 3:23.]
2My help comes from the Lord, Who made Heaven and earth.
3He will not allow your foot to slip *or* to be moved; He Who keeps you will not slumber. [I Sam. 2:9; Prov. 3:23, 26; Ps. 127:1; Isa. 27:3.]
4Behold, He who keeps Israel will neither slumber nor sleep.
5The Lord is your keeper; the Lord is your shade on your right hand [the side not carrying a shield]. [Isa. 25:4.]
6The sun shall not smite you by day, nor the moon by night. [Ps. 91:5; Isa. 49:10; Rev. 7:16.]
7The Lord will keep you from all evil; He will keep your life.

**AMP** [a] Possibly the fifteen Psalms known as the "Songs of Degrees or Ascents" were sung by the caravans of pilgrims going up to attend the annual feasts at Jerusalem; but it is quite as possible that the title has reference to some peculiarity in connection with the music or the manner of using it. [b] See Psalm 120 title footnote.

## New American Standard

164 Seven times a day I praise Thee,
Because of Thy righteous ordinances.
165 Those who love Thy law have great peace,
And nothing causes them to stumble.
166 I hope for Thy salvation, O LORD,
And do Thy commandments.
167 My soul keeps Thy testimonies,
And I love them exceedingly.
168 I keep Thy precepts and Thy testimonies,
For all my ways are before Thee.

ת Tav.

169¶ Let my cry come before Thee, O LORD;
Give me understanding according to Thy word.
170 Let my supplication come before Thee;
Deliver me according to Thy word.
171 Let my lips utter praise,
For Thou dost teach me Thy statutes.
172 Let my tongue sing of Thy word,
For all Thy commandments are righteousness.
173 Let Thy hand be ready to help me,
For I have chosen Thy precepts.
174 I long for Thy salvation, O LORD,
And Thy law is my delight.
175 Let my soul live that it may praise Thee,
And let Thine ordinances help me.
176 I have gone astray like a lost sheep; seek Thy servant,
For I do not forget Thy commandments.

*Prayer for Deliverance from the Treacherous.*

A Song of Ascents.

**120** IN MY trouble I cried to the LORD,
And He answered me.
2 Deliver my soul, O LORD, from lying lips,
From a deceitful tongue.
3 What shall be given to you, and what more shall be done to you,
You deceitful tongue?
4 Sharp arrows of the warrior,
With the *burning* coals of the broom tree.

5¶ Woe is me, for I sojourn in Meshech,
For I dwell among the tents of Kedar!
6 Too long has my soul had its dwelling
With those who hate peace.
7 I am *for* peace, but when I speak,
They are for war.

*The LORD the Keeper of Israel.*

A Song of Ascents.

**121** I WILL lift up my eyes to the mountains;
From whence shall my help come?
2 My help *comes* from the LORD,
Who made heaven and earth.
3 He will not allow your foot to slip;
He who keeps you will not slumber.
4 Behold, He who keeps Israel
Will neither slumber nor sleep.

5¶ The LORD is your keeper;
The LORD is your shade on your right hand.
6 The sun will not smite you by day,
Nor the moon by night.
7 The LORD will [c]protect you from all evil;
He will keep your soul.

NAS [c] Or, *keep*

## New International

164 Seven times a day I praise you
for your righteous laws.
165 Great peace have they who love your law,
and nothing can make them stumble.
166 I wait for your salvation, O LORD,
and I follow your commands.
167 I obey your statutes,
for I love them greatly.
168 I obey your precepts and your statutes,
for all my ways are known to you.

ת Taw

169 May my cry come before you, O LORD;
give me understanding according to your word.
170 May my supplication come before you;
deliver me according to your promise.
171 May my lips overflow with praise,
for you teach me your decrees.
172 May my tongue sing of your word,
for all your commands are righteous.
173 May your hand be ready to help me,
for I have chosen your precepts.
174 I long for your salvation, O LORD,
and your law is my delight.
175 Let me live that I may praise you,
and may your laws sustain me.
176 I have strayed like a lost sheep.
Seek your servant,
for I have not forgotten your commands.

A song of ascents.

**120** I CALL on the LORD in my distress,
and he answers me.
2 Save me, O LORD, from lying lips
and from deceitful tongues.

3 What will he do to you,
and what more besides, O deceitful tongue?
4 He will punish you with a warrior's sharp arrows,
with burning coals of the broom tree.

5 Woe to me that I dwell in Meshech,
that I live among the tents of Kedar!
6 Too long have I lived
among those who hate peace.
7 I am a man of peace;
but when I speak, they are for war.

A song of ascents.

**121** I LIFT up my eyes to the hills—
where does my help come from?
2 My help comes from the LORD,
the Maker of heaven and earth.
3 He will not let your foot slip—
he who watches over you will not slumber;
4 indeed, he who watches over Israel
will neither slumber nor sleep.
5 The LORD watches over you—
the LORD is your shade at your right hand;
6 the sun will not harm you by day,
nor the moon by night.

7 The LORD will keep you from all harm—
he will watch over your life;

## King James

8The LORD shall preserve thy going out and thy coming in from this time forth, and even for evermore.

A Song of degrees of David.

**122** I WAS glad when they said unto me, Let us go into the house of the LORD.
2Our feet shall stand within thy gates, O Jerusalem.
3Jerusalem is builded as a city that is compact together:
4Whither the tribes go up, the tribes of the LORD, unto the testimony of Israel, to give thanks unto the name of the LORD.
5For there are set thrones of judgment, the thrones of the house of David.
6Pray for the peace of Jerusalem: they shall prosper that love thee.
7Peace be within thy walls, *and* prosperity within thy palaces.
8For my brethren and companions' sakes, I will now say, Peace *be* within thee.
9Because of the house of the LORD our God I will seek thy good.

A Song of degrees.

**123** UNTO THEE lift I up mine eyes, O thou that dwellest in the heavens.
2Behold, as the eyes of servants *look* unto the hand of their masters, *and* as the eyes of a maiden unto the hand of her mistress; so our eyes *wait* upon the LORD our God, until that he have mercy upon us.
3Have mercy upon us, O LORD, have mercy upon us: for we are exceedingly filled with contempt.
4Our soul is exceedingly filled with the scorning of those that are at ease, *and* with the contempt of the proud.

A Song of degrees of David.

**124** IF *IT had not been* the LORD who was on our side, now may Israel say;
2If *it had not been* the LORD who was on our side, when men rose up against us:
3Then they had swallowed us up quick, when their wrath was kindled against us:
4Then the waters had overwhelmed us, the stream had gone over our soul:
5Then the proud waters had gone over our soul.
6Blessed *be* the LORD, who hath not given us *as* a prey to their teeth.
7Our soul is escaped as a bird out of the snare of the fowlers: the snare is broken, and we are escaped.
8Our help *is* in the name of the LORD, who made heaven and earth.

## Amplified

8The Lord will keep your going out and your coming in from this time forth and for evermore. [Deut. 28:6; Prov. 2:8; 3:6.]

A Song of [a]Ascents. Of David.

**122** I WAS glad when they said to me, Let us go to the house of the Lord! [Isa. 2:3; Zech. 8:21.]
2Our feet are standing within your gates, O Jerusalem!
3Jerusalem, which is built as a city that is compact together;
4To which the tribes go up, even the tribes of the Lord, as was decreed *and* as a testimony for Israel, to give thanks to the name of the Lord.
5For there thrones of judgment were set, the thrones of the house of David.
6Pray for the peace of Jerusalem! May they prosper that love you [the Holy City]!
7Peace be within your walls and prosperity within your palaces!
8For my brethren and companions' sake, I will now say, Peace be within you!
9For the sake of the house of the Lord our God I will seek, inquire for *and* require your good.

A Song of [b]Ascents.

**123** UNTO YOU do I lift up my eyes, O You who are enthroned in heaven.
2Behold, as the eyes of servants look to the hand of their master, and as the eyes of a maid to the hand of her mistress, so our eyes look to the Lord our God, until He have mercy *and* loving-kindness for us.
3Have mercy on us, O Lord, have mercy *and* loving-kindness for us; for we are exceedingly surfeited with contempt.
4Our life is exceedingly filled with the scorning *and* scoffing of those who are at ease, and with the contempt of the proud—irresponsible tyrants, who disregard God's law.

A Song of [c]Ascents. Of David.

**124** IF IT had not been the Lord Who was on our side, now may Israel say,
2If it had not been the Lord Who was on our side, when men rose up against us,
3Then they would have quickly swallowed us up alive, when their wrath was kindled against us;
4Then the waters would have overwhelmed us *and* swept us away, the torrent would have gone over us;
5Then the proud waters would have gone over us.
6Blessed be the Lord, Who has not given us as prey to their teeth!
7We are like a bird escaped from the snare of the fowlers; the snare is broken, and we have escaped!
8Our help is in the name of the Lord Who made Heaven and earth.

**AMP** [a] See Psalm 120 title footnote. [b] See Psalm 120 title footnote. [c] See Psalm 120 title footnote.

## New American Standard

8 The LORD will [d]guard your going out and your coming in
From this time forth and forever.

*Prayer for the Peace of Jerusalem.*

A Song of Ascents, of David.

**122** I WAS glad when they said to me,
"Let us go to the house of the LORD."
2 Our feet are standing
Within your gates, O Jerusalem,
3 Jerusalem, that is built
As a city that is compact together;
4 To which the tribes go up, even the tribes of the LORD—
An ordinance for Israel—
To give thanks to the name of the LORD.
5 For there thrones were set for judgment,
The thrones of the house of David.

6¶ Pray for the peace of Jerusalem:
"May they prosper who love you.
7 "May peace be within your walls,
And prosperity within your palaces."
8 For the sake of my brothers and my friends,
I will now say, "May peace be within you."
9 For the sake of the house of the LORD our God
I will seek your good.

*Prayer for the LORD's Help.*

A Song of Ascents.

**123** TO THEE I lift up my eyes,
O Thou who art enthroned in the heavens!
2 Behold, as the eyes of servants *look* to the hand of their master,
As the eyes of a maid to the hand of her mistress;
So our eyes *look* to the LORD our God,
Until He shall be gracious to us.

3¶ Be gracious to us, O LORD, be gracious to us;
For we are greatly filled with contempt.
4 Our soul is greatly filled
With the scoffing of those who are at ease,
*And* with the contempt of the proud.

*Praise for Rescue from Enemies.*

A Song of Ascents, of David.

**124** "HAD IT not been the LORD who was on our side,"
Let Israel now say,
2 "Had it not been the LORD who was on our side,
When men rose up against us;
3 Then they would have swallowed us alive,
When their anger was kindled against us;
4 Then the waters would have engulfed us,
The stream would have swept over our soul;
5 Then the raging waters would have swept over our soul."

6¶ Blessed be the LORD,
Who has not given us to be torn by their teeth.
7 Our soul has escaped as a bird out of the snare of the trapper;
The snare is broken and we have escaped.
8 Our help is in the name of the LORD,
Who made heaven and earth.

## New International

8the LORD will watch over your coming and going
both now and forevermore.

A song of ascents. Of David.

**122** I REJOICED with those who said to me,
"Let us go to the house of the LORD."
2Our feet are standing
in your gates, O Jerusalem.
3Jerusalem is built like a city
that is closely compacted together.
4That is where the tribes go up,
the tribes of the LORD,
to praise the name of the LORD
according to the statute given to Israel.
5There the thrones for judgment stand,
the thrones of the house of David.

6Pray for the peace of Jerusalem:
"May those who love you be secure.
7May there be peace within your walls
and security within your citadels."
8For the sake of my brothers and friends,
I will say, "Peace be within you."
9For the sake of the house of the LORD our God,
I will seek your prosperity.

A song of ascents.

**123** I LIFT up my eyes to you,
to you whose throne is in heaven.
2As the eyes of slaves look to the hand of their master,
as the eyes of a maid look to the hand of her mistress,
so our eyes look to the LORD our God,
till he shows us his mercy.

3Have mercy on us, O LORD, have mercy on us,
for we have endured much contempt.
4We have endured much ridicule from the proud,
much contempt from the arrogant.

A song of ascents. Of David.

**124** IF THE LORD had not been on our side—
let Israel say—
2if the LORD had not been on our side
when men attacked us,
3when their anger flared against us,
they would have swallowed us alive;
4the flood would have engulfed us,
the torrent would have swept over us,
5 the raging waters
would have swept us away.

6Praise be to the LORD,
who has not let us be torn by their teeth.
7We have escaped like a bird
out of the fowler's snare;
the snare has been broken,
and we have escaped.
8Our help is in the name of the LORD,
the Maker of heaven and earth.

NAS [d] Or, *keep*

## King James

A Song of degrees.

**125** THEY THAT trust in the LORD *shall be* as mount Zion, *which* cannot be removed, *but* abideth for ever.
2 *As* the mountains *are* round about Jerusalem, so the LORD *is* round about his people from henceforth even for ever.
3For the rod of the wicked shall not rest upon the lot of the righteous; lest the righteous put forth their hands unto iniquity.
4Do good, O LORD, unto *those that be* good, and to *them that are* upright in their hearts.
5As for such as turn aside unto their crooked ways, the LORD shall lead them forth with the workers of iniquity: *but* peace *shall be* upon Israel.

A Song of degrees.

**126** WHEN THE LORD turned again the captivity of Zion, we were like them that dream.
2Then was our mouth filled with laughter, and our tongue with singing: then said they among the heathen, The LORD hath done great things for them.
3The LORD hath done great things for us; *whereof* we are glad.
4Turn again our captivity, O LORD, as the streams in the south.
5They that sow in tears shall reap in joy.
6He that goeth forth and weepeth, bearing precious seed, shall doubtless come again with rejoicing, bringing his sheaves *with him*.

A Song of degrees for Solomon.

**127** EXCEPT THE LORD build the house, they labour in vain that build it: except the LORD keep the city, the watchman waketh *but* in vain.
2 *It is* vain for you to rise up early, to sit up late, to eat the bread of sorrows: *for* so he giveth his beloved sleep.
3Lo, children *are* an heritage of the LORD *and* the fruit of the womb *is his* reward.
4As arrows *are* in the hand of a mighty man; so *are* children of the youth.
5Happy *is* the man that hath his quiver full of them: they shall not be ashamed, but they shall speak with the enemies in the gate.

A Song of degrees.

**128** BLESSED *IS* every one that feareth the LORD; that walketh in his ways.

## Amplified

A Song of [a]Ascents.

**125** THOSE WHO trust, lean on *and* confidently hope in the Lord are as Mount Zion, which cannot be moved, but abides *and* stands fast for ever.
2As the mountains are round about Jerusalem, so the Lord is round about His people from this time forth and for ever.
3For the scepter of wickedness shall not rest upon the land of the [uncompromisingly] righteous, lest the righteous [God's people] stretch forth their hands to iniquity *and* apostasy.
4Do good, O Lord, to those who are good, and to those who are right [with You and all people] in their hearts.
5As for such as turn aside to their crooked ways [of indifference to God], the Lord will lead them forth with the workers of iniquity. Peace be upon Israel!

A Song of [b]Ascents.

**126** WHEN THE Lord brought back the captives who returned to Zion, we were like those who dream [it seemed so unreal]. [Ps. 53:6; Acts 12:9.]
2Then was our mouth filled with laughter, and our tongue was singing. Then they said among the nations, The Lord has done great things for them.
3The Lord has done great things for us! We are glad!
4Turn to freedom our captivity *and* restore our fortunes, O Lord, as the streams in the South [are restored by the torrents].
5They who sow in tears shall reap in joy *and* singing.
6He who goes forth bearing seed and weeps [at needing his precious supply of grain for sowing], shall doubtless come again with rejoicing, bringing his sheaves with him.

A Song of [c]Ascents. Of Solomon.

**127** EXCEPT THE Lord builds the house, they labor in vain who build it; except the Lord keeps the city, the watchman wakes but in vain. [Ps. 121:1, 3, 5.]
2It is vain for you to rise up early, to take rest late, to eat the bread of [anxious] toil; for He gives [blessings] to His beloved in sleep.
3Lo, children are a heritage from the Lord, the fruit of the womb a reward. [Deut. 28:4.]
4As arrows are in the hand of a warrior, so are the children of one's youth.
5Happy, blessed *and* fortunate is the man whose quiver is filled with them! They will not be put to shame when they speak with their adversaries [in gatherings] at the *city's* gate.

A Song of [d]Ascents.

**128** BLESSED—HAPPY, fortunate [to be envied]—is every one who fears, reveres *and* worships the Lord; who walks in His ways *and* lives according to His commandments. [Ps. 1:1, 2.]

**AMP** [a] See Psalm 120 title footnote. [b] See Psalm 120 title footnote. [c] See Psalm 120 title footnote. [d] See Psalm 120 title footnote.

## New American Standard

*The LORD Surrounds His People.*

A Song of Ascents.

**125** THOSE WHO trust in the LORD
Are as Mount Zion, which cannot be moved, but abides forever.
2 As the mountains surround Jerusalem,
So the LORD surrounds His people
From this time forth and forever.
3 For the scepter of wickedness shall not rest upon the land of the righteous;
That the righteous may not put forth their hands to do wrong.

4¶ Do good, O LORD, to those who are good,
And to those who are upright in their hearts.
5 But as for those who turn aside to their crooked ways,
The LORD will lead them away with the doers of iniquity.
Peace be upon Israel.

*Thanksgiving for Return from Captivity.*

A Song of Ascents.

**126** WHEN THE LORD brought back the captive ones of Zion,
We were like those who dream.
2 Then our mouth was filled with laughter,
And our tongue with joyful shouting;
Then they said among the nations,
"The LORD has done great things for them."
3 The LORD has done great things for us;
We are glad.
4¶ Restore our captivity, O LORD,
As the streams in the South.
5 Those who sow in tears shall reap with joyful shouting.
6 He who goes to and fro weeping, carrying *his* bag of seed,
Shall indeed come again with a shout of joy, bringing his sheaves *with him.*

*Prosperity Comes from the LORD.*

A Song of Ascents, of Solomon.

**127** UNLESS THE LORD builds the house,
They labor in vain who build it;
Unless the LORD guards the city,
The watchman keeps awake in vain.
2 It is vain for you to rise up early,
To retire late,
To eat the bread of painful labors;
For He gives to His beloved *even in his* sleep.

3¶ Behold, children are a gift of the LORD;
The fruit of the womb is a reward.
4 Like arrows in the hand of a warrior,
So are the children of one's youth.
5 How blessed is the man whose quiver is full of them;
They shall not be ashamed,
When they speak with their enemies in the gate.

*Blessedness of the Fear of the LORD.*

A Song of Ascents.

**128** HOW BLESSED is everyone who fears the LORD,
Who walks in His ways.

## New International

A song of ascents.

**125** THOSE WHO trust in the LORD are like Mount Zion,
which cannot be shaken but endures forever.
2As the mountains surround Jerusalem,
so the LORD surrounds his people
both now and forevermore.

3The scepter of the wicked will not remain
over the land allotted to the righteous,
for then the righteous might use
their hands to do evil.

4Do good, O LORD, to those who are good,
to those who are upright in heart.
5But those who turn to crooked ways
the LORD will banish with the evildoers.
Peace be upon Israel.

A song of ascents.

**126** WHEN THE LORD brought back the captives to[e] Zion,
we were like men who dreamed.[f]
2Our mouths were filled with laughter,
our tongues with songs of joy.
Then it was said among the nations,
"The LORD has done great things for them."
3The LORD has done great things for us,
and we are filled with joy.

4Restore our fortunes,[g] O LORD,
like streams in the Negev.
5Those who sow in tears
will reap with songs of joy.
6He who goes out weeping,
carrying seed to sow,
will return with songs of joy,
carrying sheaves with him.

A song of ascents. Of Solomon.

**127** UNLESS THE LORD builds the house,
its builders labor in vain.
Unless the LORD watches over the city,
the watchmen stand guard in vain.
2In vain you rise early
and stay up late,
toiling for food to eat—
for he grants sleep to[h] those he loves.

3Sons are a heritage from the LORD,
children a reward from him.
4Like arrows in the hands of a warrior
are sons born in one's youth.
5Blessed is the man
whose quiver is full of them.
They will not be put to shame
when they contend with their enemies in the gate.

A song of ascents.

**128** BLESSED ARE all who fear the LORD,
who walk in his ways.

NIV [e] 1 Or *LORD restored the fortunes of* [f] 1 Or *men restored to health* [g] 4 Or *Bring back our captives* [h] 2 Or *eat— / for while they sleep he provides for*

## King James

2For thou shalt eat the labour of thine hands: happy *shalt* thou
*be*, and *it shall be* well with thee.
3Thy wife *shall be* as a fruitful vine by the sides of thine house:
thy children like olive plants round about thy table.
4Behold, that thus shall the man be blessed that feareth the
LORD.
5The LORD shall bless thee out of Zion: and thou shalt see the
good of Jerusalem all the days of thy life.
6Yea, thou shalt see thy children's children, *and* peace upon
Israel.

A Song of degrees.

**129** MANY A time have they afflicted me from my youth,
may Israel now say:
2Many a time have they afflicted me from my youth: yet they
have not prevailed against me.
3The plowers plowed upon my back: they made long their
furrows.
4The LORD *is* righteous: he hath cut asunder the cords of the
wicked.
5Let them all be confounded and turned back that hate Zion.
6Let them be as the grass *upon* the housetops, which withereth
afore it groweth up:
7Wherewith the mower filleth not his hand; nor he that bindeth
sheaves his bosom.
8Neither do they which go by say, The blessing of the LORD *be*
upon you: we bless you in the name of the LORD.

A Song of degrees.

**130** OUT OF the depths have I cried unto thee, O LORD.
2Lord, hear my voice: let thine ears be attentive to the
voice of my supplications.
3If thou, LORD, shouldest mark iniquities, O Lord, who shall
stand?
4But *there is* forgiveness with thee, that thou mayest be feared.
5I wait for the LORD, my soul doth wait, and in his word do I
hope.
6My soul *waiteth* for the Lord more than they that watch for the
morning: *I say, more than* they that watch for the morning.
7Let Israel hope in the LORD: for with the LORD *there is* mercy,
and with him *is* plenteous redemption.
8And he shall redeem Israel from all his iniquities.

## Amplified

2For you shall eat [the fruit] of the labor of your hands; happy,
blessed, fortunate [enviable] shall you be, and it shall be well with
you.
3Your wife shall be as a fruitful vine in the innermost parts of
your house; your children like olive plants round about your table.
4Behold, thus shall the man be blessed who reverently *and*
worshipfully fears the Lord.
5The Lord bless you out of Zion [His sanctuary], and may you
see the prosperity of Jerusalem all the days of your life;
6Yes, may you see your children's children. Peace be upon
Israel!

A Song of [a]Ascents.

**129** MANY A time *and* much have they afflicted me from
my youth up, let Israel now say,
2Many a time *and* much have they afflicted me from my youth
up, yet they have not prevailed against me.
3The plowers plowed upon my back; they made long their
furrows.
4The Lord is [uncompromisingly] righteous; He has cut asunder
the thick cords by which the wicked [enslaved us].
5Let them all be put to shame and turned backward who hate
Zion.
6Let them be as the grass upon the housetops, which withers
before it grows up,
7With which the mower fills not his hand, nor the binder of
sheaves his bosom;
8While those who go by do not say, The blessing of the Lord
be upon you! We bless you in the name of the Lord!

A Song of [b]Ascents.

**130** OUT OF the depths have I cried to You, O Lord.
2Lord, hear my voice; let Your ears be attentive to the
voice of my supplications.
3If You, Lord, should keep account *and* treat [us according to
our] sins, O Lord, who could stand? [Ps. 143:2; Rom. 3:20; Gal.
2:16.]
4But there is forgiveness with You, [just what man needs] that
You may be reverently feared *and* worshiped. [Deut. 10:12.]
5I wait for the Lord, I expectantly wait, and in His word do I
hope.
6I am looking *and* waiting for the Lord more than watchmen for
the morning; I say, more than watchmen for the morning.
7O Israel, hope in the Lord! For with the Lord there is mercy
*and* loving-kindness, and with Him is plenteous redemption.
8And He will redeem Israel from all his iniquities.

AMP [a] See Psalm 120 title footnote. [b] See Psalm 120 title footnote.

## New American Standard

2 When you shall eat of the [c]fruit of your hands,
You will be happy and it will be well with you.
3 Your wife shall be like a fruitful vine,
Within your house,
Your children like olive plants
Around your table.
4 Behold, for thus shall the man be blessed
Who fears the LORD.

5¶ The LORD bless you from Zion,
And may you see the prosperity of Jerusalem all the days of your life.
6 Indeed, may you see your children's children.
Peace be upon Israel!

*Prayer for the Overthrow of Zion's Enemies.*

A Song of Ascents.

**129** "MANY TIMES they have persecuted me from my youth up,"
Let Israel now say,
2 "Many times they have persecuted me from my youth up;
Yet they have not prevailed against me.
3 "The plowers plowed upon my back;
They lengthened their furrows."
4 The LORD is righteous;
He has cut in two the cords of the wicked.

5¶ May all who hate Zion,
Be put to shame and turned backward,
6 Let them be like grass upon the housetops,
Which withers before it grows up;
7 With which the reaper does not fill his hand,
Or the binder of sheaves his bosom;
8 Nor do those who pass by say,
"The blessing of the LORD be upon you;
We bless you in the name of the LORD."

*Hope in the LORD's Forgiving Love.*

A Song of Ascents.

**130** OUT OF the depths I have cried to Thee, O LORD.
2 Lord, hear my voice!
Let Thine ears be attentive
To the voice of my supplications.
3 If Thou, LORD, shouldst mark iniquities,
O Lord, who could stand?
4 But there is forgiveness with Thee,
That Thou mayest be feared.

5¶ I wait for the LORD, my soul does wait,
And in His word do I hope.
6 My soul *waits* for the Lord
More than the watchmen for the morning;
*Indeed, more than* the watchmen for the morning.
7 O Israel, hope in the LORD;
For with the LORD there is lovingkindness,
And with Him is abundant redemption.
8 And He will redeem Israel
From all his iniquities.

NAS [c] Lit., *labor*

## New International

2 You will eat the fruit of your labor;
blessings and prosperity will be yours.
3 Your wife will be like a fruitful vine
within your house;
your sons will be like olive shoots
around your table.
4 Thus is the man blessed
who fears the LORD.

5 May the LORD bless you from Zion
all the days of your life;
may you see the prosperity of Jerusalem,
6 and may you live to see your children's children.

Peace be upon Israel.

A song of ascents.

**129** THEY HAVE greatly oppressed me from my youth—
let Israel say—
2 they have greatly oppressed me from my youth,
but they have not gained the victory over me.
3 Plowmen have plowed my back
and made their furrows long.
4 But the LORD is righteous;
he has cut me free from the cords of the wicked.

5 May all who hate Zion
be turned back in shame.
6 May they be like grass on the roof,
which withers before it can grow;
7 with it the reaper cannot fill his hands,
nor the one who gathers fill his arms.
8 May those who pass by not say,
"The blessing of the LORD be upon you;
we bless you in the name of the LORD."

A song of ascents.

**130** OUT OF the depths I cry to you, O LORD;
2 O Lord, hear my voice.
Let your ears be attentive
to my cry for mercy.

3 If you, O LORD, kept a record of sins,
O Lord, who could stand?
4 But with you there is forgiveness;
therefore you are feared.

5 I wait for the LORD, my soul waits,
and in his word I put my hope.
6 My soul waits for the Lord
more than watchmen wait for the morning,
more than watchmen wait for the morning.

7 O Israel, put your hope in the LORD,
for with the LORD is unfailing love
and with him is full redemption.
8 He himself will redeem Israel
from all their sins.

## King James

A Song of degrees of David.

**131** LORD, MY heart is not haughty, nor mine eyes lofty: neither do I exercise myself in great matters, or in things too high for me.

2 Surely I have behaved and quieted myself, as a child that is weaned of his mother: my soul *is* even as a weaned child.

3 Let Israel hope in the LORD from henceforth and for ever.

A Song of degrees.

**132** LORD, REMEMBER David, *and* all his afflictions:

2 How he sware unto the LORD, *and* vowed unto the mighty *God* of Jacob;

3 Surely I will not come into the tabernacle of my house, nor go up into my bed;

4 I will not give sleep to mine eyes, *or* slumber to mine eyelids,

5 Until I find out a place for the LORD, an habitation for the mighty *God* of Jacob.

6 Lo, we heard of it at Ephratah: we found it in the fields of the wood.

7 We will go into his tabernacles: we will worship at his footstool.

8 Arise, O LORD, into thy rest; thou, and the ark of thy strength.

9 Let thy priests be clothed with righteousness; and let thy saints shout for joy.

10 For thy servant David's sake turn not away the face of thine anointed.

11 The LORD hath sworn *in* truth unto David; he will not turn from it; Of the fruit of thy body will I set upon thy throne.

12 If thy children will keep my covenant and my testimony that I shall teach them, their children shall also sit upon thy throne for evermore.

13 For the LORD hath chosen Zion; he hath desired *it* for his habitation.

14 This *is* my rest for ever: here will I dwell; for I have desired it.

15 I will abundantly bless her provision: I will satisfy her poor with bread.

16 I will also clothe her priests with salvation: and her saints shall shout aloud for joy.

17 There will I make the horn of David to bud: I have ordained a lamp for mine anointed.

18 His enemies will I clothe with shame: but upon himself shall his crown flourish.

A Song of degrees of David.

**133** BEHOLD, HOW good and how pleasant *it is* for brethren to dwell together in unity!

## Amplified

A Song of [a]Ascents. Of David.

**131** LORD, MY heart is not haughty, nor my eyes lofty; neither do I exercise myself in matters too great or in things too wonderful for me.

2 Surely I have calmed and quieted my soul, like a weaned child with his mother; like a weaned child is my soul within me [ceased from fretting].

3 O Israel, hope in the Lord from this time forth and for ever.

A Song of [b]Ascents.

**132** LORD, [EARNESTLY] remember to David's credit all his humiliations *and* hardships *and* endurance.

2 How he swore to the Lord, and vowed to the mighty God of Jacob,

3 Surely I will not enter my dwelling house, or get into my bed,

4 I will not permit my eyes to sleep, *or* my eyelids to slumber,

5 Until I have found a place for the Lord, a habitation for the Mighty One of Jacob. [Acts 7:46.]

6 Lo, at Ephratah we [first] heard of [the discovered ark]; we found it in the fields of the wood—at [Kiriath-] Jearim. [I Sam. 6:21.]

7 Let us go into His tabernacle; let us worship at His footstool.

8 Arise, O Lord, to Your resting place, You and the ark [the symbol] of Your strength.

9 Let Your priests be clothed with righteousness [right living and right standing with God], and let Your saints shout for joy!

10 For Your servant David's sake turn not away the face of Your anointed *and* reject not Your own king.

11 The Lord swore to David in truth; He will not turn back from it: Of the fruit of your body will I set upon your throne. [Ps. 89:3, 4; Luke 1:69; Acts 2:30, 31.]

12 If your children will keep my covenant and My testimony that I shall teach them, their children also shall sit upon your throne for ever.

13 For the Lord has chosen Zion; He has desired it for His habitation.

14 This is My resting place for ever [says the Lord]; here will I dwell, for I have desired it.

15 I will surely *and* abundantly bless her provision; I will satisfy her poor with bread.

16 Her priests also will I clothe with salvation, and her saints shall shout aloud for joy.

17 There will I make a horn spring forth unto David *and* bud; I have ordained *and* prepared a lamp for My anointed [fulfilling the promises of old]. [I Kings 11:36; 15:4; II Chron. 21:7; Luke 1:69.]

18 His enemies will I clothe with shame, but upon himself shall his crown flourish.

A Song of [c]Ascents. Of David.

**133** BEHOLD, HOW good and how pleasant it is for brethren to dwell together in unity!

**AMP** [a] See Psalm 120 title footnote. [b] See Psalm 120 title footnote. [c] See Psalm 120 title footnote.

## New American Standard

*Childlike Trust in the* LORD.

A Song of Ascents, of David.

131 O LORD, my heart is not proud, nor my eyes haughty;
Nor do I involve myself in great matters,
Or in things too difficult for me.
2 Surely I have composed and quieted my soul;
Like a weaned child *rests* against his mother,
My soul is like a weaned child within me.
3 O Israel, hope in the LORD
From this time forth and forever.

*Prayer for the* LORD*'s Blessing upon the Sanctuary.*

A Song of Ascents.

132 REMEMBER, O LORD, on David's behalf,
All his affliction;
2 How he swore to the LORD,
And vowed to the Mighty One of Jacob,
3 "Surely I will not enter my house,
Nor lie on my bed;
4 I will not give sleep to my eyes,
Or slumber to my eyelids;
5 Until I find a place for the LORD,
A dwelling place for the Mighty One of Jacob."
6¶ Behold, we heard of it in Ephrathah;
We found it in the field of Jaar.
7 Let us go into His dwelling place;
Let us worship at His footstool.
8 Arise, O LORD, to Thy resting place;
Thou and the ark of Thy strength.
9 Let Thy priests be clothed with righteousness;
And let Thy godly ones sing for joy.
10 ¶ For the sake of David Thy servant,
Do not turn away the face of Thine anointed.
11 The LORD has sworn to David,
A truth from which He will not turn back;
"Of the fruit of your body I will set upon your throne.
12 "If your sons will keep My covenant,
And My testimony which I will teach them,
Their sons also shall sit upon your throne forever."
13¶ For the LORD has chosen Zion;
He has desired it for His habitation.
14 "This is My resting place forever;
Here I will dwell, for I have desired it.
15 "I will abundantly bless her provision;
I will satisfy her needy with bread.
16 "Her priests also I will clothe with salvation;
And her godly ones will sing aloud for joy.
17 "There I will cause the horn of David to spring forth;
I have prepared a lamp for Mine anointed.
18 "His enemies I will clothe with shame;
But upon himself his crown shall shine."

*The Excellency of Brotherly Unity.*

A Song of Ascents, of David.

133 BEHOLD, HOW good and how pleasant it is
For brothers to dwell together in unity!

## New International

A song of ascents. Of David.

131 MY HEART is not proud, O LORD,
my eyes are not haughty;
I do not concern myself with great matters
or things too wonderful for me.
2But I have stilled and quieted my soul;
like a weaned child with its mother,
like a weaned child is my soul within me.

3O Israel, put your hope in the LORD
both now and forevermore.

A song of ascents.

132 O LORD, remember David
and all the hardships he endured.

2He swore an oath to the LORD
and made a vow to the Mighty One of Jacob:
3"I will not enter my house
or go to my bed—
4I will allow no sleep to my eyes,
no slumber to my eyelids,
5till I find a place for the LORD,
a dwelling for the Mighty One of Jacob."
6We heard it in Ephrathah,
we came upon it in the fields of Jaar[d; e]
7"Let us go to his dwelling place;
let us worship at his footstool—
8arise, O LORD, and come to your resting place,
you and the ark of your might.
9May your priests be clothed with righteousness;
may your saints sing for joy."
10For the sake of David your servant,
do not reject your anointed one.
11The LORD swore an oath to David,
a sure oath that he will not revoke:
"One of your own descendants
I will place on your throne—
12if your sons keep my covenant
and the statutes I teach them,
then their sons will sit
on your throne for ever and ever."
13For the LORD has chosen Zion,
he has desired it for his dwelling:
14"This is my resting place for ever and ever;
here I will sit enthroned, for I have desired it—
15I will bless her with abundant provisions;
her poor will I satisfy with food.
16I will clothe her priests with salvation,
and her saints will ever sing for joy.

17"Here I will make a horn[f] grow for David
and set up a lamp for my anointed one.
18I will clothe his enemies with shame,
but the crown on his head will be resplendent."

A song of ascents. Of David.

133 HOW GOOD and pleasant it is
when brothers live together in unity!

NIV [d] 6 That is, Kiriath Jearim [e] 6 Or *heard of it in Ephrathah, / we found it in the fields of Jaar.* (And no quotes around verses 7-9) [f] 17 *Horn* here symbolizes strong one, that is, king.

## King James

2 *It is* like the precious ointment upon the head, that ran down upon the beard, *even* Aaron's beard: that went down to the skirts of his garments;

3 As the dew of Hermon, *and as the dew* that descended upon the mountains of Zion: for there the LORD commanded the blessing, *even* life for evermore.

A Song of degrees.

**134** BEHOLD, BLESS ye the LORD, all *ye* servants of the LORD, which by night stand in the house of the LORD.

2 Lift up your hands *in* the sanctuary, and bless the LORD.

3 The LORD that made heaven and earth bless thee out of Zion.

**135** PRAISE YE the LORD. Praise ye the name of the LORD; praise *him*, O ye servants of the LORD.

2 Ye that stand in the house of the LORD, in the courts of the house of our God,

3 Praise the LORD; for the LORD *is* good: sing praises unto his name; for *it is* pleasant.

4 For the LORD hath chosen Jacob unto himself, *and* Israel for his peculiar treasure.

5 For I know that the LORD *is* great, and *that* our Lord *is* above all gods.

6 Whatsoever the LORD pleased, *that* did he in heaven, and in earth, in the seas, and all deep places.

7 He causeth the vapours to ascend from the ends of the earth; he maketh lightnings for the rain; he bringeth the wind out of his treasuries.

8 Who smote the firstborn of Egypt, both of man and beast.

9 *Who* sent tokens and wonders into the midst of thee, O Egypt, upon Pharaoh, and upon all his servants.

10 Who smote great nations, and slew mighty kings;

11 Sihon king of the Amorites, and Og king of Bashan, and all the kingdoms of Canaan:

12 And gave their land *for* an heritage, an heritage unto Israel his people.

13 Thy name, O LORD, *endureth* for ever; *and* thy memorial, O LORD, throughout all generations.

14 For the LORD will judge his people, and he will repent himself concerning his servants.

15 The idols of the heathen *are* silver and gold, the work of men's hands.

16 They have mouths, but they speak not; eyes have they, but they see not;

17 They have ears, but they hear not; neither is there *any* breath in their mouths.

18 They that make them are like unto them: *so is* every one that trusteth in them.

## Amplified

2 It is like the precious ointment poured on the head, that ran down on the beard, even the beard of Aaron [the first high priest], that came down upon the collar *and* skirts of his garments [consecrating the whole body]; [Exod. 30:25, 30.]

3 Like the dew of [lofty] Mount Hermon, and the dew that comes on the hills of Zion; for there the Lord has commanded the blessing, even life for evermore [upon the high and the lowly].

A Song of [a]Ascents.

**134** BEHOLD, BLESS [affectionately and gratefully praise] the Lord, all you servants of the Lord, [singers] who by night stand in the house of the Lord. [I Chron. 9:33.]

2 Lift up your hands in holiness *and* to the sanctuary, and bless the Lord [affectionately and gratefully praise Him]!

3 The Lord bless you out of Zion, even He Who made Heaven and earth.

**135** PRAISE THE Lord! — Hallelujah! Praise the name of the Lord; praise Him, O you servants of the Lord!

2 You who stand in the house of the Lord, in the courts of the house of our God,

3 Praise the Lord! For the Lord is good; sing praises to His name, for He is gracious *and* lovely!

4 For the Lord has chosen [the descendants of] Jacob for Himself, Israel for His peculiar possession *and* treasure. [Deut. 7:6.]

5 For I know that the Lord is great, and that our Lord is above all gods.

6 Whatever the Lord pleased, that has He done in *the* heavens and on earth, in the seas and all deeps;

7 Who causes the vapors to arise from the ends of the earth, Who makes lightnings for the rain, Who brings the wind out of His storehouses;

8 Who smote the first-born of Egypt, both of man and beast; [Pss. 78:51; 136:10; Exod. 12:12, 29.]

9 Who sent signs and wonders into the midst of you, O Egypt, upon Pharaoh and all his servants;

10 Who smote nations many *and* great, and slew mighty kings,

11 Sihon king of the Amorites, Og king of Bashan, and all the kingdoms of Canaan.

12 *The Lord* gave their land for a heritage, a heritage to Israel His people.

13 Your name, O Lord, endures for ever; Your fame, O Lord, throughout all ages.

14 For the Lord will judge *and* vindicate His people, and He will stay His judgments [manifesting His righteousness and mercy] *and* take into favor His servants [those who meet His terms of separation to Him]. [Heb. 10:30.]

15 The idols of the nations are silver and gold, the work of men's hands.

16 *Idols* have mouths, but they speak not; eyes have they, but they see not;

17 They have ears, but they hear not, nor is there any breath in their mouths.

18 Those who make *idols* are like them; so is every one who trusts *and* relies on them. [Ps. 115:4-8.]

**AMP** [a] See Psalm 120 title footnote.

## New American Standard

2 It is like the precious oil upon the head,
Coming down upon the beard,
*Even* Aaron's beard,
Coming down upon the edge of his robes.
3 It is like the dew of Hermon,
Coming down upon the mountains of Zion;
For there the LORD commanded the blessing—life forever.

*Greetings of Night Watchers.*

A Song of Ascents.

**134** BEHOLD, BLESS the LORD, all servants of the LORD,
Who serve by night in the house of the LORD!
2 Lift up your hands to the sanctuary,
And bless the LORD.
3 May the LORD bless you from Zion,
He who made heaven and earth.

*Praise the LORD's Wonderful Works. Vanity of Idols.*

**135** PRAISE THE LORD!
Praise the name of the LORD;
Praise *Him,* O servants of the LORD,
2 You who stand in the house of the LORD,
In the courts of the house of our God!
3 Praise the LORD, for the LORD is good;
Sing praises to His name, for it is lovely.
4 For the LORD has chosen Jacob for Himself,
Israel for His own possession.

5¶ For I know that the LORD is great,
And that our Lord is above all gods.
6 Whatever the LORD pleases, He does,
In heaven and in earth, in the seas and in all deeps.
7 He causes the vapors to ascend from the ends of the earth;
Who makes lightnings for the rain;
Who brings forth the wind from His treasuries.

8¶ He smote the first-born of Egypt,
Both of man and beast.
9 He sent signs and wonders into your midst, O Egypt,
Upon Pharaoh and all his servants.
10 He smote many nations,
And slew mighty kings,
11 Sihon, king of the Amorites,
And Og, king of Bashan,
And all the kingdoms of Canaan;
12 And He gave their land as a heritage,
A heritage to Israel His people.
13 Thy name, O LORD, is everlasting,
Thy remembrance, O LORD, throughout all generations.
14 For the LORD will judge His people,
And will have compassion on His servants.
15 The idols of the nations are *but* silver and gold,
The work of man's hands.
16 They have mouths, but they do not speak;
They have eyes, but they do not see;
17 They have ears, but they do not hear;
Nor is there any breath at all in their mouths.
18 Those who make them will be like them,
*Yes,* everyone who trusts in them.

## New International

2It is like precious oil poured on the head,
running down on the beard,
running down on Aaron's beard,
down upon the collar of his robes.
3It is as if the dew of Hermon
were falling on Mount Zion.
For there the LORD bestows his blessing,
even life forevermore.

A song of ascents.

**134** PRAISE THE LORD, all you servants of the LORD
who minister by night in the house of the LORD.
2Lift up your hands in the sanctuary
and praise the LORD.

3May the LORD, the Maker of heaven and earth,
bless you from Zion.

**135** PRAISE THE LORD.[b]
Praise the name of the LORD;
praise him, you servants of the LORD,
2you who minister in the house of the LORD,
in the courts of the house of our God.

3Praise the LORD, for the LORD is good;
sing praise to his name, for that is pleasant.
4For the LORD has chosen Jacob to be his own,
Israel to be his treasured possession.

5I know that the LORD is great,
that our Lord is greater than all gods.
6The LORD does whatever pleases him,
in the heavens and on the earth,
in the seas and all their depths.
7He makes clouds rise from the ends of the earth;
he sends lightning with the rain
and brings out the wind from his storehouses.
8He struck down the firstborn of Egypt,
the firstborn of men and animals.
9He sent his signs and wonders into your midst, O Egypt,
against Pharaoh and all his servants.
10He struck down many nations
and killed mighty kings—
11Sihon king of the Amorites,
Og king of Bashan
and all the kings of Canaan—
12and he gave their land as an inheritance,
an inheritance to his people Israel.

13Your name, O LORD, endures forever,
your renown, O LORD, through all generations.
14For the LORD will vindicate his people
and have compassion on his servants.

15The idols of the nations are silver and gold,
made by the hands of men.
16They have mouths, but cannot speak,
eyes, but they cannot see;
17they have ears, but cannot hear,
nor is there breath in their mouths.
18Those who make them will be like them,
and so will all who trust in them.

NIV [b] *1* Hebrew *Hallelu Yah;* also in verses 3 and 21

## King James

19Bless the LORD, O house of Israel: bless the LORD, O house of
Aaron:
20Bless the LORD, O house of Levi: ye that fear the LORD, bless
the LORD.
21Blessed be the LORD out of Zion, which dwelleth at Jerusalem.
Praise ye the LORD.

**136** O GIVE thanks unto the LORD; for *he is* good: for his
mercy *endureth* for ever.
2O give thanks unto the God of gods: for his mercy *endureth* for
ever.
3O give thanks to the Lord of lords: for his mercy *endureth* for
ever.
4To him who alone doeth great wonders: for his mercy *endureth*
for ever.
5To him that by wisdom made the heavens: for his mercy *endureth* for ever.
6To him that stretched out the earth above the waters: for his
mercy *endureth* for ever.
7To him that made great lights: for his mercy *endureth* for ever:
8The sun to rule by day: for his mercy *endureth* for ever:
9The moon and stars to rule by night: for his mercy *endureth* for
ever.
10To him that smote Egypt in their firstborn: for his mercy
*endureth* for ever:
11And brought out Israel from among them: for his mercy *endureth* for ever:
12With a strong hand, and with a stretched out arm: for his
mercy *endureth* for ever.
13To him which divided the Red sea into parts: for his mercy
*endureth* for ever:
14And made Israel to pass through the midst of it: for his mercy
*endureth* for ever:
15But overthrew Pharaoh and his host in the Red sea: for his
mercy *endureth* for ever.
16To him which led his people through the wilderness: for his
mercy *endureth* for ever.
17To him which smote great kings: for his mercy *endureth* for
ever:
18And slew famous kings: for his mercy *endureth* for ever:
19Sihon king of the Amorites: for his mercy *endureth* for ever:
20And Og the king of Bashan: for his mercy *endureth* for ever:
21And gave their land for an heritage: for his mercy *endureth* for
ever:
22 *Even* an heritage unto Israel his servant: for his mercy *endureth*
for ever.
23Who remembered us in our low estate: for his mercy *endureth*
for ever:
24And hath redeemed us from our enemies: for his mercy *endureth* for ever.
25Who giveth food to all flesh: for his mercy *endureth* for ever.
26O give thanks unto the God of heaven: for his mercy *endureth*
for ever.

## Amplified

19Bless [affectionately and gratefully praise] the Lord, O house
of Israel; bless the Lord, O house of Aaron [God's ministers].
20Bless the Lord, O house of Levi [the dedicated tribe]; you who
reverently *and* worshipfully fear the Lord, bless the Lord [affec-
tionately and gratefully praise Him]! [Deut. 6:5; Ps. 31:23.]
21Blessed out of Zion be the Lord, Who dwells [with us] at
Jerusalem! Praise the Lord!—Hallelujah!

**136** O GIVE thanks to the Lord, for He is good; for His
mercy *and* loving-kindness endure for ever.
2O give thanks to the God of gods, for His mercy *and* loving-
kindness endure for ever.
3O give thanks to the Lord of lords, for His mercy *and* loving-
kindness endure for ever;
4To Him Who alone does great wonders, for His mercy *and*
loving-kindness endure for ever;
5To Him Who by wisdom *and* understanding made the heavens, for His mercy *and* loving-kindness endure for ever;
6To Him Who stretched out the earth upon the waters, for His
mercy *and* loving-kindness endure for ever;
7To Him Who made great lights, for His mercy *and* loving-kindness endure for ever;
8The sun to rule over the day, for His mercy *and* loving-kindness endure for ever;
9The moon and stars to rule by night, for His mercy *and* loving-
kindness endure for ever;
10To Him Who smote Egypt in their first-born, for His mercy *and*
loving-kindness endure for ever; [Exod. 12:29.]
11And brought out Israel from among them, for His mercy *and*
loving-kindness endure for ever; [Exod. 12:51; 13:3, 17.]
12With a strong hand and with a stretched-out arm, for His
mercy *and* loving-kindness endure for ever;
13To Him Who divided the Red Sea into parts, for His mercy *and*
loving-kindness endure for ever; [Exod. 14:21, 22.]
14And made Israel to pass through the midst of it, for His mercy
*and* loving-kindness endure for ever;
15But shook off *and* overthrew Pharaoh and his host in the Red
Sea, for His mercy *and* loving-kindness endure for ever;
16To Him Who led His people through the wilderness, for His
mercy *and* loving-kindness endure for ever;
17To Him Who smote great kings, for His mercy *and* loving-
kindness endure for ever;
18And slew famous kings, for His mercy *and* loving-kindness
endure for ever; [Deut. 29:7.]
19Sihon king of the Amorites, for His mercy *and* loving-kindness
endure for ever; [Num. 21:21-24.]
20And Og the king of Bashan, for His mercy *and* loving-kindness endure for ever; [Num. 21:33-35.]
21And gave their land for a heritage, for His mercy *and* loving-
kindness endure for ever;
22Even a heritage to Israel His servant, for His mercy *and* loving-
kindness endure for ever; [Josh. 12:1.]
23To Him Who [earnestly] remembered us in our low estate *and*
imprinted us [on his heart], for His mercy *and* loving-kindness
endure for ever;
24And rescued us from our enemies, for His mercy *and* loving-
kindness endure for ever;
25To Him Who gives food to all flesh, for His mercy *and* loving-
kindness endure for ever!
26O give thanks to the God of Heaven, for His mercy *and* loving-
kindness endure for ever!

## New American Standard

19¶ O house of Israel, bless the LORD;
O house of Aaron, bless the LORD;
20 O house of Levi, bless the LORD;
You who [a]revere the LORD, bless the LORD.
21 Blessed be the LORD from Zion,
Who dwells in Jerusalem.
Praise the LORD!

*Thanks for the LORD's Goodness to Israel.*

**136** GIVE THANKS to the LORD, for He is good;
For His lovingkindness is everlasting.
2 Give thanks to the God of gods,
For His lovingkindness is everlasting.
3 Give thanks to the Lord of lords,
For His lovingkindness is everlasting.
4 To Him who alone does great wonders,
For His lovingkindness is everlasting;
5 To Him who made the heavens with skill,
For His lovingkindness is everlasting;
6 To Him who spread out the earth above the waters,
For His lovingkindness is everlasting;
7 To Him who made *the* great lights,
For His lovingkindness is everlasting:
8 The sun to rule by day,
For His lovingkindness is everlasting,
9 The moon and stars to rule by night,
For His lovingkindness is everlasting.

10¶ To Him who smote the Egyptians in their first-born,
For His lovingkindness is everlasting,
11 And brought Israel out from their midst,
For His lovingkindness is everlasting,
12 With a strong hand and an outstretched arm,
For His lovingkindness is everlasting;
13 To Him who divided the Red Sea asunder,
For His lovingkindness is everlasting,
14 And made Israel pass through the midst of it,
For His lovingkindness is everlasting;
15 But He overthrew Pharaoh and his army in the Red Sea,
For His lovingkindness is everlasting.
16 To Him who led His people through the wilderness,
For His lovingkindness is everlasting;
17 To Him who smote great kings,
For His lovingkindness is everlasting,
18 And slew mighty kings,
For His lovingkindness is everlasting:
19 Sihon, king of the Amorites,
For His lovingkindness is everlasting,
20 And Og, king of Bashan,
For His lovingkindness is everlasting,
21 And gave their land as a heritage,
For His lovingkindness is everlasting,
22 Even a heritage to Israel His servant,
For His lovingkindness is everlasting.

23¶ Who remembered us in our low estate,
For His lovingkindness is everlasting,
24 And has rescued us from our adversaries,
For His lovingkindness is everlasting;
25 Who gives food to all flesh,
For His lovingkindness is everlasting.
26 Give thanks to the God of heaven,
For His lovingkindness is everlasting.

NAS [a] Or, *fear*

## New International

19 O house of Israel, praise the LORD;
O house of Aaron, praise the LORD;
20 O house of Levi, praise the LORD;
you who fear him, praise the LORD.
21 Praise be to the LORD from Zion,
to him who dwells in Jerusalem.

Praise the LORD.

**136** GIVE THANKS to the LORD, for he is good.
*His love endures forever.*
2 Give thanks to the God of gods.
*His love endures forever.*
3 Give thanks to the Lord of lords:
*His love endures forever.*

4 to him who alone does great wonders,
*His love endures forever.*
5 who by his understanding made the heavens,
*His love endures forever.*
6 who spread out the earth upon the waters,
*His love endures forever.*
7 who made the great lights—
*His love endures forever.*
8 the sun to govern the day,
*His love endures forever.*
9 the moon and stars to govern the night;
*His love endures forever.*

10 to him who struck down the firstborn of Egypt
*His love endures forever.*
11 and brought Israel out from among them
*His love endures forever.*
12 with a mighty hand and outstretched arm;
*His love endures forever.*

13 to him who divided the Red Sea[b] asunder
*His love endures forever.*
14 and brought Israel through the midst of it,
*His love endures forever.*
15 but swept Pharaoh and his army into the Red Sea;
*His love endures forever.*

16 to him who led his people through the desert,
*His love endures forever.*
17 who struck down great kings,
*His love endures forever.*
18 and killed mighty kings—
*His love endures forever.*
19 Sihon king of the Amorites
*His love endures forever.*
20 and Og king of Bashan—
*His love endures forever.*
21 and gave their land as an inheritance,
*His love endures forever.*
22 an inheritance to his servant Israel;
*His love endures forever.*

23 to the One who remembered us in our low estate
*His love endures forever.*
24 and freed us from our enemies,
*His love endures forever.*
25 and who gives food to every creature.
*His love endures forever.*
26 Give thanks to the God of heaven.
*His love endures forever.*

NIV [b] *13* Hebrew *Yam Suph;* that is, Sea of Reeds; also in verse 15

## King James

**137** BY THE rivers of Babylon, there we sat down, yea, we wept, when we remembered Zion.

2 We hanged our harps upon the willows in the midst thereof.

3 For there they that carried us away captive required of us a song; and they that wasted us *required of us* mirth, *saying,* Sing us *one* of the songs of Zion.

4 How shall we sing the LORD's song in a strange land?

5 If I forget thee, O Jerusalem, let my right hand forget *her cunning.*

6 If I do not remember thee, let my tongue cleave to the roof of my mouth; if I prefer not Jerusalem above my chief joy.

7 Remember, O LORD, the children of Edom in the day of Jerusalem; who said, Rase *it,* rase *it, even* to the foundation thereof.

8 O daughter of Babylon, who art to be destroyed; happy *shall he be,* that rewardeth thee as thou hast served us.

9 Happy *shall he be,* that taketh and dasheth thy little ones against the stones.

A *Psalm* of David.

**138** I WILL praise thee with my whole heart: before the gods will I sing praise unto thee.

2 I will worship toward thy holy temple, and praise thy name for thy lovingkindness and for thy truth: for thou hast magnified thy word above all thy name.

3 In the day when I cried thou answeredst me, *and* strengthenedst me *with* strength in my soul.

4 All the kings of the earth shall praise thee, O LORD, when they hear the words of thy mouth.

5 Yea, they shall sing in the ways of the LORD: for great *is* the glory of the LORD.

6 Though the LORD *be* high, yet hath he respect unto the lowly: but the proud he knoweth afar off.

7 Though I walk in the midst of trouble, thou wilt revive me: thou shalt stretch forth thine hand against the wrath of mine enemies, and thy right hand shall save me.

8 The LORD will perfect *that which* concerneth me: thy mercy, O LORD, *endureth* for ever: forsake not the works of thine own hands.

To the chief Musician, A Psalm of David.

**139** O LORD, thou hast searched me, and known *me.*

2 Thou knowest my downsitting and mine uprising, thou understandest my thought afar off.

3 Thou compassest my path and my lying down, and art acquainted *with* all my ways.

## Amplified

**137** BY THE rivers of Babylon, there we [captives] sat down, yes, we wept when we [earnestly] remembered Zion [city of our God imprinted on our hearts].

2 On the willow trees in the midst of *Babylon* we hung our harps.

3 For there they who led us captive required of us a song with words; and our tormentors *and* they who wasted us required of us mirth, saying, Sing us one of the songs of Zion.

4 How shall we sing the Lord's song in a strange land?

5 If I forget you, O Jerusalem, let my right hand forget her skill [with the harp].

6 Let my tongue cleave to the roof of my mouth if I remember you not, if I prefer not Jerusalem above my chief joy! [Ezek. 3:26.]

7 Remember, O Lord, against the Edomites, that they said in the day of Jerusalem's fall, Down, down to the ground with her!

8 O daughter of Babylon [you devastator, you!] who [ought to be and] shall be destroyed; happy *and* blessed shall he be who requites you as you have served us. [Isa. 13:1-22; Jer. 25:12, 13.]

9 Happy *and* blessed shall he be who takes and dashes your little ones against the rock!

[ *A Psalm*] of David.

**138** I WILL confess *and* praise You *O God,* with my whole heart; before the gods will I sing praises to You.

2 I will worship toward Your holy temple, and praise Your name for Your loving-kindness and for Your truth *and* faithfulness; for You have exalted above all else Your name and Your word, *and* You have magnified Your word above all Your name!

3 In the day when I called, You answered me, and strengthened me with strength (might and inflexibility) [to temptation] in my inner self.

4 All the kings of the land shall give You credit *and* praise You, O Lord, for they have heard of the promises of Your mouth [which were fulfilled].

5 Yes, they shall sing of the ways of the Lord, *and* joyfully celebrate His mighty acts, for great is the glory of the Lord.

6 For though the Lord is high, yet has He respect to the lowly [bringing them into fellowship with Him]; but the proud *and* haughty He knows *and* recognizes [only] at a distance. [Prov. 3:34; James 4:6; I Pet. 5:5.]

7 Though I walk in the midst of trouble, You will revive me; You will stretch forth Your hand against the wrath of my enemies, and Your right hand will save me. [Ps. 23:3, 4.]

8 The Lord will perfect that which concerns me; Your mercy *and* loving-kindness, O Lord, endure for ever; forsake not the works of Your own hands. [Ps. 57:2; Phil. 1:6.]

To the Chief Musician. A Psalm of David.

**139** O LORD, you have searched me (thoroughly) and have known me.

2 You know my downsitting and my uprising; You understand my thought afar off. [Matt. 9:4; John 2:24, 25.]

3 You sift *and* search out my path and my lying down, and are acquainted with all my ways.

## New American Standard

*An Experience of the Captivity.*

137 BY THE rivers of Babylon,
There we sat down and wept,
When we remembered Zion.
2 Upon the willows in the midst of it
We hung our harps.
3 For there our captors demanded of us songs,
And our tormentors mirth, *saying*,
"Sing us one of the songs of Zion."
4¶ How can we sing the LORD's song
In a foreign land?
5 If I forget you, O Jerusalem,
May my right hand forget *her skill*.
6 May my tongue cleave to the roof of my mouth,
If I do not remember you,
If I do not exalt Jerusalem
Above my chief joy.
7¶ Remember, O LORD, against the sons of Edom
The day of Jerusalem,
Who said, "Raze it, raze it,
To its very foundation."
8 O daughter of Babylon, you devastated one,
How blessed will be the one who repays you
With the recompense with which you have repaid us.
9 How blessed will be the one who seizes and dashes
your little ones
Against the rock.

*Thanksgiving for the LORD's Favor.*

*A Psalm* of David.

138 I WILL give Thee thanks with all my heart;
I will sing praises to Thee before the gods.
2 I will bow down toward Thy holy temple,
And give thanks to Thy name for Thy lovingkindness
and Thy truth;
For Thou hast magnified Thy word according to all Thy
name.
3 On the day I called Thou didst answer me;
Thou didst make me bold with strength in my soul.
4¶ All the kings of the earth will give thanks to Thee,
O LORD,
When they have heard the words of Thy mouth.
5 And they will sing of the ways of the LORD.
For great is the glory of the LORD.
6 For though the LORD is exalted,
Yet He regards the lowly;
But the haughty He knows from afar.
7¶ Though I walk in the midst of trouble, Thou wilt revive
me;
Thou wilt stretch forth Thy hand against the wrath of
my enemies,
And Thy right hand will save me.
8 The LORD will accomplish what concerns me;
Thy lovingkindness, O LORD, is everlasting;
Do not forsake the works of Thy hands.

*God's Omnipresence and Omniscience.*

For the choir director.
A Psalm of David.

139 O LORD, Thou hast searched me and known *me*.
2 Thou dost know when I sit down and when I
rise up;
Thou dost understand my thought from afar.
3 Thou dost scrutinize my path and my lying down,
And art intimately acquainted with all my ways.

## New International

137 BY THE rivers of Babylon we sat and wept
when we remembered Zion.
2There on the poplars
we hung our harps,
3for there our captors asked us for songs,
our tormentors demanded songs of joy;
they said, "Sing us one of the songs of Zion!"
4How can we sing the songs of the LORD
while in a foreign land?
5If I forget you, O Jerusalem,
may my right hand forget ⌊its skill⌋.
6May my tongue cling to the roof of my mouth
if I do not remember you,
if I do not consider Jerusalem
my highest joy.
7Remember, O LORD, what the Edomites did
on the day Jerusalem fell.
"Tear it down," they cried,
"tear it down to its foundations!"
8O Daughter of Babylon, doomed to destruction,
happy is he who repays you
for what you have done to us—
9he who seizes your infants
and dashes them against the rocks.

Of David.

138 I WILL praise you, O LORD, with all my heart;
before the "gods" I will sing your praise.
2I will bow down toward your holy temple
and will praise your name
for your love and your faithfulness,
for you have exalted above all things
your name and your word.
3When I called, you answered me;
you made me bold and stouthearted.
4May all the kings of the earth praise you, O LORD,
when they hear the words of your mouth.
5May they sing of the ways of the LORD,
for the glory of the LORD is great.
6Though the LORD is on high, he looks upon the lowly,
but the proud he knows from afar.
7Though I walk in the midst of trouble,
you preserve my life;
you stretch out your hand against the anger of my foes,
with your right hand you save me.
8The LORD will fulfill ⌊his purpose⌋ for me;
your love, O LORD, endures forever—
do not abandon the works of your hands.

For the director of music. Of David. A psalm.

139 O LORD, you have searched me
and you know me.
2You know when I sit and when I rise;
you perceive my thoughts from afar.
3You discern my going out and my lying down;
you are familiar with all my ways.

## King James

4For *there is* not a word in my tongue, *but,* lo, O LORD, thou knowest it altogether.

5Thou hast beset me behind and before, and laid thine hand upon me.

6 *Such* knowledge *is* too wonderful for me; it is high, I cannot *attain* unto it.

7Whither shall I go from thy spirit? or whither shall I flee from thy presence?

8If I ascend up into heaven, thou *art* there: if I make my bed in hell, behold, thou *art there.*

9 *If* I take the wings of the morning, *and* dwell in the uttermost parts of the sea;

10Even there shall thy hand lead me, and thy right hand shall hold me.

11If I say, Surely the darkness shall cover me; even the night shall be light about me.

12Yea, the darkness hideth not from thee; but the night shineth as the day: the darkness and the light *are* both alike *to thee.*

13For thou hast possessed my reins: thou hast covered me in my mother's womb.

14I will praise thee; for I am fearfully *and* wonderfully made: marvellous *are* thy works; and *that* my soul knoweth right well.

15My substance was not hid from thee, when I was made in secret, *and* curiously wrought in the lowest parts of the earth.

16Thine eyes did see my substance, yet being unperfect; and in thy book all *my members* were written, *which* in continuance were fashioned, when *as yet there was* none of them.

17How precious also are thy thoughts unto me, O God! how great is the sum of them!

18 *If* I should count them, they are more in number than the sand: when I awake, I am still with thee.

19Surely thou wilt slay the wicked, O God: depart from me therefore, ye bloody men.

20For they speak against thee wickedly, *and* thine enemies take *thy name* in vain.

21Do not I hate them, O LORD, that hate thee? and am not I grieved with those that rise up against thee?

22I hate them with perfect hatred: I count them mine enemies.

23Search me, O God, and know my heart: try me, and know my thoughts:

24And see if *there be any* wicked way in me, and lead me in the way everlasting.

To the chief Musician, A Psalm of David.

**140** DELIVER ME, O LORD, from the evil man: preserve me from the violent man;

2Which imagine mischiefs in *their* heart; continually are they gathered together *for* war.

3They have sharpened their tongues like a serpent; adders' poison *is* under their lips. Selah.

4Keep me, O LORD, from the hands of the wicked; preserve me from the violent man; who have purposed to overthrow my goings.

## Amplified

4For there is not a word in my tongue [still unuttered], but, lo, O Lord, You know it altogether. [Heb. 4:13.]

5You have beset me *and* shut me in behind and before, and have laid Your hand upon me.

6Your (infinite) knowledge is too wonderful for me; it is high above me, I cannot reach it.

7Where could I go from Your Spirit? Or where could I flee from Your presence?

8If I ascend up into Heaven, You are there; if I make my bed in Sheol [the place of the dead], behold, You are there. [Rom. 11:33.]

9If I take the wings of the morning and dwell in the uttermost parts of the sea,

10Even there shall Your hand lead me, and Your right hand shall hold me.

11If I say, Surely the darkness shall cover me, and the night shall be *the only* light about me,

12Even the darkness hides nothing from You, but the night shines as the day; the darkness and the light are both alike to You. [Dan. 2:22.]

13For You did form my inward parts, You did knit me together in my mother's womb.

14I will confess *and* praise You, for You are fearfully wonderful, *and* for the awful wonder of my birth! Wonderful are Your works, and that my inner self knows right well.

15My frame was not hidden from You, when I was being formed in secret *and* intricately *and* curiously wrought (as if embroidered with various colors) in the depths of the earth [a region of darkness and mystery].

16Your eyes saw my unformed substance, and in Your book all the days *of my life* were written, before ever they took shape, when as yet there was none of them.

17How precious *and* weighty also are Your thoughts to me, O God! How vast is the sum of them! [Ps. 40:5.]

18If I could count them, they are more in number than the sand. When I awoke [could I count to the end] I would still be with You.

19If you would [only] slay the wicked, O God, and the men of blood would depart from me; [Isa. 11:4.]

20Who speak against You wickedly, and Your enemies take Your name in vain! [Jude 15.]

21Do not I hate them, O Lord, who hate You? And am not I grieved *and* do not I loathe those who rise up against You?

22I hate them with perfect hatred; they have become my enemies.

23Search me [thoroughly], O God, and know my heart! Try me, and know my thoughts!

24And see if there is any wicked *or* hurtful way in me, and lead me in the way everlasting.

To the Chief Musician. A Psalm of David.

**140** DELIVER ME, O Lord, from the evil man; preserve me from the violent man;

2They devise mischiefs in their heart; continually are they gathered together *and* stir up wars.

3They have sharpened their tongues like a serpent's; adders' poison is under their lips. Selah [pause, and calmly think of that]. [Rom. 3:13.]

4Keep me, O Lord, from the hands of the wicked; preserve me from the violent men, who have purposed to thrust aside my steps.

## New American Standard

4 Even before there is a word on my tongue,
Behold, O LORD, Thou dost know it all.
5 Thou hast enclosed me behind and before,
And laid Thy hand upon me.
6 *Such* knowledge is too wonderful for me;
It is *too* high, I cannot attain to it.

7¶ Where can I go from Thy Spirit?
Or where can I flee from Thy presence?
8 If I ascend to heaven, Thou art there;
If I make my bed in Sheol, behold, Thou art there.
9 If I take the wings of the dawn,
If I dwell in the remotest part of the sea,
10 Even there Thy hand will lead me,
And Thy right hand will lay hold of me.
11 If I say, "Surely the darkness will overwhelm me,
And the light around me will be night,"
12 Even the darkness is not dark to Thee,
And the night is as bright as the day.
Darkness and light are alike *to Thee.*

13¶ For Thou didst form my inward parts;
Thou didst weave me in my mother's womb.
14 I will give thanks to Thee, for [a]I am fearfully and wonderfully made;
Wonderful are Thy works,
And my soul knows it very well.
15 My frame was not hidden from Thee,
When I was made in secret,
*And* skillfully wrought in the depths of the earth.
16 Thine eyes have seen my unformed substance;
And in Thy book they were all written,
The days that were ordained *for me,*
When as yet there was not one of them.

17¶ How precious also are Thy thoughts to me, O God!
How vast is the sum of them!
18 If I should count them, they would outnumber the sand.
When I awake, I am still with Thee.

19¶ O that Thou wouldst slay the wicked, O God;
Depart from me, therefore, men of bloodshed.
20 For they speak against Thee wickedly,
And Thine enemies take *Thy name* in vain.
21 Do I not hate those who hate Thee, O LORD?
And do I not loathe those who rise up against Thee?
22 I hate them with the utmost hatred;
They have become my enemies.

23¶ Search me, O God, and know my heart;
Try me and know my anxious thoughts;
24 And see if there be any hurtful way in me,
And lead me in the everlasting way.

*Prayer for Protection against the Wicked.*

For the choir director.
A Psalm of David.

**140** RESCUE ME, O LORD, from evil men;
Preserve me from violent men,
2 Who devise evil things in *their* hearts;
They continually stir up wars.
3 They sharpen their tongues as a serpent;
Poison of a viper is under their lips. Selah.

4¶ Keep me, O LORD, from the hands of the wicked;
Preserve me from violent men,
Who have purposed to [b]trip up my feet.

NAS [a] Some ancient versions read *Thou art fearfully wonderful* [b] Lit., *push violently*

## New International

4 Before a word is on my tongue
you know it completely, O LORD.
5 You hem me in—behind and before;
you have laid your hand upon me.
6 Such knowledge is too wonderful for me,
too lofty for me to attain.

7 Where can I go from your Spirit?
Where can I flee from your presence?
8 If I go up to the heavens, you are there;
if I make my bed in the depths,[c] you are there.
9 If I rise on the wings of the dawn,
if I settle on the far side of the sea,
10 even there your hand will guide me,
your right hand will hold me fast.

11 If I say, "Surely the darkness will hide me
and the light become night around me,"
12 even the darkness will not be dark to you;
the night will shine like the day,
for darkness is as light to you.

13 For you created my inmost being;
you knit me together in my mother's womb.
14 I praise you because I am fearfully and wonderfully made;
your works are wonderful,
I know that full well.
15 My frame was not hidden from you
when I was made in the secret place.
When I was woven together in the depths of the earth,
16 your eyes saw my unformed body.
All the days ordained for me
were written in your book
before one of them came to be.

17 How precious to[d] me are your thoughts, O God!
How vast is the sum of them!
18 Were I to count them,
they would outnumber the grains of sand.
When I awake,
I am still with you.

19 If only you would slay the wicked, O God!
Away from me, you bloodthirsty men!
20 They speak of you with evil intent;
your adversaries misuse your name.
21 Do I not hate those who hate you, O LORD,
and abhor those who rise up against you?
22 I have nothing but hatred for them;
I count them my enemies.

23 Search me, O God, and know my heart;
test me and know my anxious thoughts.
24 See if there is any offensive way in me,
and lead me in the way everlasting.

For the director of music. A psalm of David.

**140** RESCUE ME, O LORD, from evil men;
protect me from men of violence,
2 who devise evil plans in their hearts
and stir up war every day.
3 They make their tongues as sharp as a serpent's;
the poison of vipers is on their lips. *Selah*

4 Keep me, O LORD, from the hands of the wicked;
protect me from men of violence
who plan to trip my feet.

NIV [c] *8* Hebrew *Sheol* [d] *17* Or *concerning*

## King James

5The proud have hid a snare for me, and cords; they have spread a net by the wayside; they have set gins for me. Selah.
6I said unto the LORD, Thou *art* my God: hear the voice of my supplications, O LORD.
7O GOD the Lord, the strength of my salvation, thou hast covered my head in the day of battle.
8Grant not, O LORD, the desires of the wicked: further not his wicked device; *lest* they exalt themselves. Selah.
9 *As for* the head of those that compass me about, let the mischief of their own lips cover them.
10Let burning coals fall upon them: let them be cast into the fire; into deep pits, that they rise not up again.
11Let not an evil speaker be established in the earth: evil shall hunt the violent man to overthrow *him*.
12I know that the LORD will maintain the cause of the afflicted, *and* the right of the poor.
13Surely the righteous shall give thanks unto thy name: the upright shall dwell in thy presence.

A Psalm of David.

**141** LORD, I cry unto thee: make haste unto me; give ear unto my voice, when I cry unto thee.
2Let my prayer be set forth before thee *as* incense; *and* the lifting up of my hands *as* the evening sacrifice.
3Set a watch, O LORD, before my mouth; keep the door of my lips.
4Incline not my heart to *any* evil thing, to practise wicked works with men that work iniquity: and let me not eat of their dainties.
5Let the righteous smite me; *it shall be* a kindness: and let him reprove me; *it shall be* an excellent oil, *which* shall not break my head: for yet my prayer also *shall be* in their calamities.
6When their judges are overthrown in stony places, they shall hear my words; for they are sweet.
7Our bones are scattered at the grave's mouth, as when one cutteth and cleaveth *wood* upon the earth.
8But mine eyes *are* unto thee, O GOD the Lord: in thee is my trust; leave not my soul destitute.
9Keep me from the snares *which* they have laid for me, and the gins of the workers of iniquity.
10Let the wicked fall into their own nets, whilst that I withal escape.

Maschil of David; A Prayer when he was in the cave.

**142** I CRIED unto the LORD with my voice; with my voice unto the LORD did I make my supplication.
2I poured out my complaint before him; I showed before him my trouble.

## Amplified

5The proud have hid a snare for me; they have spread cords as a net by the wayside, they have set traps for me. Selah [pause, and calmly think of that].
6I said to the Lord, You are my God; give ear to the voice of my supplications, O Lord.
7O God the Lord, the strength of my salvation, You have covered my head in the day of battle.
8Grant not, O Lord, the desires of the wicked; further not his wicked plot *and* device, lest they exalt themselves. Selah [pause, and calmly think of that].
9Those who are fencing me in raise their head. May the mischief of their own lips *and* the very things they desire for me come upon them.
10Let burning coals fall upon them; let them be cast into the fire, into floods of water *or* deep water-pits, from which they shall not rise.
11Let not a man of slanderous tongue be established in the earth; let evil hunt the violent man to overthrow him—let calamity follow his evil-doings.
12I know, *and* rest in confidence upon it, that the Lord will maintain the cause of the afflicted, and justice for the poor *and* needy [of His believing children].
13Surely the [uncompromisingly] righteous shall give thanks to Your name; the upright shall dwell in Your presence—before Your very face.

A Psalm of David.

**141** LORD, I have called upon You; hasten to me; give ear to my voice when I cry to You.
2Let my prayer be set forth as incense before You, the lifting up of my hands as the evening sacrifice. [Rev. 8:3, 4; I Tim. 2:8.]
3Set a guard, O Lord, before my mouth; keep watch at the door of my lips.
4Incline my heart not to submit *or* consent to any evil thing, or be occupied in deeds of wickedness with men that work iniquity, and let me not eat of their dainties.
5Let the righteous man smite and correct me; it is a kindness. Oil so choice let not my head refuse *or* discourage; for even in their evils *or* calamities shall my prayer continue. [Prov. 9:8; 19:25; 25:12; Gal. 6:1.]
6When their rulers are overthrown in stony places, [their followers] shall hear my words, that they are sweet—pleasant, mild, and just.
7The unburied bones [of slaughtered rulers] shall lie scattered at the mouth of Sheol, [as unregarded] as the lumps of soil behind the plowman when he breaks open the ground. [II Cor. 1:9.]
8But my eyes are toward You, O God the Lord; in You do I trust *and* take refuge; pour not out my life *nor* leave it destitute *and* bare.
9Keep me from the trap which they have laid for me, and the snares of evildoers.
10Let the wicked fall together into their own nets, while I pass over them *and* escape.

A skillful song *or* a didactic *or* reflective poem of David, when he was in the cave. A Prayer.

**142** I CRY to the Lord with my voice; with my voice to the Lord do I make supplication.
2I pour out my complaint before Him; I tell before Him my trouble.

## New American Standard

5 The proud have hidden a trap for me, and cords;
They have spread a net by the wayside;
They have set snares for me. Selah.

6¶ I said to the LORD, "Thou art my God;
Give ear, O LORD, to the voice of my supplications.
7 "O GOD the Lord, the strength of my salvation,
Thou hast covered my head in the day of battle.
8 "Do not grant, O LORD, the desires of the wicked;
Do not promote his *evil* device, *lest* they be exalted. Selah.

9¶ "As for the head of those who surround me,
May the mischief of their lips cover them.
10 "May burning coals fall upon them;
May they be cast into the fire,
Into deep pits from which they cannot rise.
11 "May a slanderer not be established in the earth;
May evil hunt the violent man [a]speedily."

12¶ I know that the LORD will maintain the cause of the afflicted,
And justice for the poor.
13 Surely the righteous will give thanks to Thy name;
The upright will dwell in Thy presence.

*An Evening Prayer for Sanctification and Protection.*

A Psalm of David.

**141** O LORD, I call upon Thee; hasten to me!
Give ear to my voice when I call to Thee!
2 May my prayer be counted as incense before Thee;
The lifting up of my hands as the evening offering.
3 Set a guard, O LORD, over my mouth;
Keep watch over the door of my lips.
4 Do not incline my heart to any evil thing,
To practice deeds of wickedness
With men who do iniquity;
And do not let me eat of their delicacies.

5¶ Let the righteous smite me in kindness and reprove me;
It is oil upon the head;
Do not let my head refuse it,
For still my prayer is against their wicked deeds.
6 Their judges are thrown down by the sides of the rock,
And they hear my words, for they are pleasant.
7 As when one plows and breaks open the earth,
Our bones have been scattered at the mouth of Sheol.

8¶ For my eyes are toward Thee, O GOD, the Lord;
In Thee I take refuge; do not leave me defenseless.
9 Keep me from the jaws of the trap which they have set for me,
And from the snares of those who do iniquity.
10 Let the wicked fall into their own nets,
While I pass by safely.

*Prayer for Help in Trouble.*

Maskil of David, when he was in the cave. A Prayer.

**142** I CRY aloud with my voice to the LORD;
I make supplication with my voice to the LORD.
2 I pour out my complaint before Him;
I declare my trouble before Him.

NAS [a] Lit., *thrust upon thrust*

## New International

5 Proud men have hidden a snare for me;
they have spread out the cords of their net
and have set traps for me along my path. *Selah*
6 O LORD, I say to you, "You are my God."
Hear, O LORD, my cry for mercy.
7 O Sovereign LORD, my strong deliverer,
who shields my head in the day of battle—
8 do not grant the wicked their desires, O LORD;
do not let their plans succeed,
or they will become proud. *Selah*

9 Let the heads of those who surround me
be covered with the trouble their lips have caused.
10 Let burning coals fall upon them;
may they be thrown into the fire,
into miry pits, never to rise.
11 Let slanderers not be established in the land;
may disaster hunt down men of violence.

12 I know that the LORD secures justice for the poor
and upholds the cause of the needy.
13 Surely the righteous will praise your name
and the upright will live before you.

A psalm of David.

**141** O LORD, I call to you; come quickly to me.
Hear my voice when I call to you.
2 May my prayer be set before you like incense;
may the lifting up of my hands be like the evening sacrifice.
3 Set a guard over my mouth, O LORD;
keep watch over the door of my lips.
4 Let not my heart be drawn to what is evil,
to take part in wicked deeds
with men who are evildoers;
let me not eat of their delicacies.
5 Let a righteous man[b] strike me—it is a kindness;
let him rebuke me—it is oil on my head.
My head will not refuse it.

Yet my prayer is ever against the deeds of evildoers;
6 their rulers will be thrown down from the cliffs,
and the wicked will learn that my words were well spoken.
7 ⌊They will say,⌋ "As one plows and breaks up the earth,
so our bones have been scattered at the mouth of the grave.[c]"

8 But my eyes are fixed on you, O Sovereign LORD;
in you I take refuge—do not give me over to death.
9 Keep me from the snares they have laid for me,
from the traps set by evildoers.
10 Let the wicked fall into their own nets,
while I pass by in safety.

A *maskil*[d] of David. When he was in the cave. A prayer.

**142** I CRY aloud to the LORD;
I lift up my voice to the LORD for mercy.
2 I pour out my complaint before him;
before him I tell my trouble.

NIV [b] 5 Or *Let the Righteous One* [c] 7 Hebrew *Sheol* [d] Title: Probably a literary or musical term

## King James

3 When my spirit was overwhelmed within me, then thou knewest my path. In the way wherein I walked have they privily laid a snare for me.

4 I looked on *my* right hand, and beheld, but *there was* no man that would know me: refuge failed me; no man cared for my soul.

5 I cried unto thee, O LORD: I said, Thou *art* my refuge *and* my portion in the land of the living.

6 Attend unto my cry; for I am brought very low: deliver me from my persecutors; for they are stronger than I.

7 Bring my soul out of prison, that I may praise thy name: the righteous shall compass me about; for thou shalt deal bountifully with me.

A Psalm of David.

**143** HEAR MY prayer, O LORD, give ear to my supplications: in thy faithfulness answer me, *and* in thy righteousness.

2 And enter not into judgment with thy servant: for in thy sight shall no man living be justified.

3 For the enemy hath persecuted my soul; he hath smitten my life down to the ground; he hath made me to dwell in darkness, as those that have been long dead.

4 Therefore is my spirit overwhelmed within me; my heart within me is desolate.

5 I remember the days of old; I meditate on all thy works; I muse on the work of thy hands.

6 I stretch forth my hands unto thee: my soul *thirsteth* after thee, as a thirsty land. Selah.

7 Hear me speedily, O LORD: my spirit faileth: hide not thy face from me, lest I be like unto them that go down into the pit.

8 Cause me to hear thy lovingkindness in the morning; for in thee do I trust: cause me to know the way wherein I should walk; for I lift up my soul unto thee.

9 Deliver me, O LORD, from mine enemies: I flee unto thee to hide me.

10 Teach me to do thy will; for thou *art* my God: thy spirit *is* good; lead me into the land of uprightness.

11 Quicken me, O LORD, for thy name's sake: for thy righteousness' sake bring my soul out of trouble.

12 And of thy mercy cut off mine enemies, and destroy all them that afflict my soul: for I *am* thy servant.

## Amplified

3 When my spirit was overwhelmed *and* fainted [throwing all its weight] upon me, then You knew my path. In the way wherein I walk they have hidden a snare for me.

4 Look on the right hand [the point of attack] and see, for there is no man who knows me [to appear for me]; refuge has failed me *and* I have no way to flee; no man cares for my life *or* my welfare.

5 I cried to You, O Lord; I said, You are my refuge, my portion in the land of the living.

6 Attend to my loud cry, for I am brought very low; deliver me from my persecutors, for they are stronger than I.

7 Bring my life out of prison, that I may confess, praise *and* give thanks to Your name; the righteous will surround me *and* crown themselves because of me, for You will deal bountifully with me.

A Psalm of David.

**143** HEAR MY prayer, O Lord; give ear to my supplications! In Your faithfulness answer me, and in Your righteousness.

2 And enter not into judgment with Your servant, for in Your sight no man living is [in himself] righteous *or* justified. [Rom. 3:20-26; Gal. 2:16; Ps. 130:3.]

3 For the enemy has pursued *and* persecuted my soul; he has crushed my life down to the ground; he has made me to dwell in dark places, as those who have been long dead.

4 Therefore is my spirit overwhelmed *and* faints within me [wrapped in gloom]; my heart within my bosom grows numb.

5 I remember the days of old, I meditate on all Your doings; I ponder on the work of Your hands.

6 I spread forth my hands to You; my soul thirsts after You like a thirsty land [for water]. Selah [pause, and calmly think of that].

7 Answer me speedily, O Lord, for my spirit fails; hide not Your face from me, lest I become like those who go down into the pit [the grave].

8 Cause me to hear Your loving-kindness in the morning; for on You do I lean *and* in You do I trust. Cause me to know the way wherein I should walk, for I lift up my inner self to You.

9 Deliver me, O Lord, from my enemies; I flee to You to hide me.

10 Teach me to do Your will, for You are my God; let Your good Spirit lead me into a plain country *and* into the land of uprightness.

11 Save my life, O Lord, for Your name's sake; in Your righteousness bring my life out of trouble *and* free me from distress.

12 And in your mercy *and* loving-kindness cut off my enemies and destroy all those who afflict my inner self, for I am Your servant.

## New American Standard

3 When my spirit was overwhelmed within me,
Thou didst know my path.
In the way where I walk
They have hidden a trap for me.
4 Look to the right and see;
For there is no one who regards me;
There is no escape for me;
No one cares for my soul.

5¶ I cried out to Thee, O LORD;
I said, "Thou art my refuge,
My portion in the land of the living.
6 "Give heed to my cry,
For I am brought very low;
Deliver me from my persecutors,
For they are too strong for me.
7 "Bring my soul out of prison,
So that I may give thanks to Thy name;
The righteous will surround me,
For Thou wilt deal bountifully with me."

*Prayer for Deliverance and Guidance.*

A Psalm of David.

**143** HEAR MY prayer, O LORD,
Give ear to my supplications!
Answer me in Thy faithfulness, in Thy righteousness!
2 And do not enter into judgment with Thy servant,
For in Thy sight no man living is righteous.
3 For the enemy has persecuted my soul;
He has crushed my life to the ground;
He has made me dwell in dark places, like those who have long been dead.
4 Therefore my spirit is overwhelmed within me;
My heart is [a]appalled within me.

5¶ I remember the days of old;
I meditate on all Thy doings;
I muse on the work of Thy hands.
6 I stretch out my hands to Thee;
My soul *longs* for Thee, as a parched land. Selah.

7¶ Answer me quickly, O LORD, my spirit fails;
Do not hide Thy face from me,
Lest I become like those who go down to the pit.
8 Let me hear Thy lovingkindness in the morning;
For I trust in Thee;
Teach me the way in which I should walk;
For to Thee I lift up my soul.
9 Deliver me, O LORD, from my enemies;
I take refuge in Thee.

10¶ Teach me to do Thy will,
For Thou art my God;
Let Thy good Spirit lead me on level ground.
11 For the sake of Thy name, O LORD, revive me.
In Thy righteousness bring my soul out of trouble.
12 And in Thy lovingkindness cut off my enemies,
And destroy all those who afflict my soul;
For I am Thy servant.

NAS [a] Or, *desolate*

## New International

3When my spirit grows faint within me,
it is you who know my way.
In the path where I walk
men have hidden a snare for me.
4Look to my right and see;
no one is concerned for me.
I have no refuge;
no one cares for my life.

5I cry to you, O LORD;
I say, "You are my refuge,
my portion in the land of the living."
6Listen to my cry,
for I am in desperate need;
rescue me from those who pursue me,
for they are too strong for me.
7Set me free from my prison,
that I may praise your name.
Then the righteous will gather about me
because of your goodness to me.

A psalm of David.

**143** O LORD, hear my prayer,
listen to my cry for mercy;
in your faithfulness and righteousness
come to my relief.
2Do not bring your servant into judgment,
for no one living is righteous before you.

3The enemy pursues me,
he crushes me to the ground;
he makes me dwell in darkness
like those long dead.
4So my spirit grows faint within me;
my heart within me is dismayed.

5I remember the days of long ago;
I meditate on all your works
and consider what your hands have done.
6I spread out my hands to you;
my soul thirsts for you like a parched land. *Selah*

7Answer me quickly, O LORD;
my spirit fails.
Do not hide your face from me
or I will be like those who go down to the pit.
8Let the morning bring me word of your unfailing love,
for I have put my trust in you.
Show me the way I should go,
for to you I lift up my soul.
9Rescue me from my enemies, O LORD,
for I hide myself in you.
10Teach me to do your will,
for you are my God;
may your good Spirit
lead me on level ground.

11For your name's sake, O LORD, preserve my life;
in your righteousness, bring me out of trouble.
12In your unfailing love, silence my enemies;
destroy all my foes,
for I am your servant.

# King James

*A Psalm* of David.

**144** BLESSED *BE* the LORD my strength, which teacheth my hands to war, *and* my fingers to fight:

2My goodness, and my fortress; my high tower, and my deliverer; my shield, and *he* in whom I trust; who subdueth my people under me.

3LORD, what *is* man, that thou takest knowledge of him! *or* the son of man, that thou makest account of him!

4Man is like to vanity: his days *are* as a shadow that passeth away.

5Bow thy heavens, O LORD, and come down: touch the mountains, and they shall smoke.

6Cast forth lightning, and scatter them: shoot out thine arrows, and destroy them.

7Send thine hand from above; rid me, and deliver me out of great waters, from the hand of strange children;

8Whose mouth speaketh vanity, and their right hand *is* a right hand of falsehood.

9I will sing a new song unto thee, O God: upon a psaltery *and* an instrument of ten strings will I sing praises unto thee.

10 *It is he* that giveth salvation unto kings: who delivereth David his servant from the hurtful sword.

11Rid me, and deliver me from the hand of strange children, whose mouth speaketh vanity, and their right hand *is* a right hand of falsehood:

12That our sons *may be* as plants grown up in their youth; *that* our daughters *may be* as corner stones, polished *after* the similitude of a palace:

13 *That* our garners *may be* full, affording all manner of store: *that* our sheep may bring forth thousands and ten thousands in our streets:

14 *That* our oxen *may be* strong to labour; *that there be* no breaking in, nor going out; that *there be* no complaining in our streets.

15Happy *is that* people, that is in such a case: *yea,* happy *is that* people, whose God *is* the LORD.

David's *Psalm* of praise.

**145** I WILL extol thee, my God, O king; and I will bless thy name for ever and ever.

2Every day will I bless thee; and I will praise thy name for ever and ever.

3Great *is* the LORD, and greatly to be praised; and his greatness *is* unsearchable.

4One generation shall praise thy works to another, and shall declare thy mighty acts.

5I will speak of the glorious honour of thy majesty, and of thy wondrous works.

# Amplified

[ *A Psalm*] of David.

**144** BLESSED BE the Lord, my rock *and* my keen *and* firm strength, Who teaches my hands to war and my fingers to fight;

2My steadfast love and my fortress, my high tower and my deliverer, my shield and He in Whom I trust *and* take refuge, Who subdues my people under me.

3Lord, what is man, that You take notice of him? Or [a] son of man that You take account of him? [Ps. 8:4; Job 7:17; Heb. 2:6.]

4Man is like vanity *and* a breath, his days are as a shadow that passes away.

5Bow Your heavens, O Lord, and come down; touch the mountains, and they shall smoke.

6Cast forth lightning and scatter [my enemies], send out Your arrows and embarrass *and* frustrate them.

7Stretch forth Your hand from above, rescue me and deliver me out of great waters, from the hand of hostile aliens [tribes about us],

8Whose mouth speaks deceit, and whose right hand is a right hand *raised in taking* fraudulent oaths.

9I will sing a new song to You, O God; upon a harp, an instrument of ten strings, will I offer praises to You.

10You are He Who gives salvation to kings, Who rescues David His servant from the hurtful sword [of evil].

11Rescue me, and deliver me out of the power of (hostile) alien *tribes,* whose mouth speaks deceit and whose right hand is a right hand *raised in taking* fraudulent oaths.

12When our sons shall be as plants grown large in their youth, *and* our daughters as sculptured, corner pillars hewn like those of a palace;

13When our garners are full, affording all manner of store, *and* our sheep bring forth thousands and ten thousands in our pastures;

14When our oxen are well loaded; when there is no invasion [of hostile armies], and no going forth [against besiegers]—when there is no murder or manslaughter—and no outcry in our streets;

15Happy *and* blessed is the people that is in such a case; yes, happy—blessed, fortunate, prosperous [to be envied]—is the people whose God is the Lord!

[ *A Psalm*] of praise. Of David.

**145** I WILL extol You, my God, O King; and I will bless Your name for ever and ever—with grateful, affectionate praise.

2Every day [with its new reasons] will I bless You—affectionately and gratefully praise You; yes, I will praise Your name for ever and ever.

3Great is the Lord and highly to be praised, and His greatness is [so vast and deep as to be] unsearchable. [Job 5:9; 9:10; Rom. 11:33.]

4One generation shall laud Your works to another, and shall declare Your mighty acts.

5Of the glorious splendor of Your majesty, and of Your wondrous works, I will meditate.

## New American Standard

*Prayer for Rescue and Prosperity.*

*A Psalm* of David.

**144** BLESSED BE the LORD, my rock,
Who trains my hands for war,
*And* my fingers for battle;
2 My lovingkindness and my fortress,
My stronghold and my deliverer;
My shield and He in whom I take refuge;
Who subdues my people under me.
3 O LORD, what is man, that Thou dost take knowledge of him?
Or the son of man, that Thou dost think of him?
4 Man is like a mere breath;
His days are like a passing shadow.

5¶ Bow Thy heavens, O LORD, and come down;
Touch the mountains, that they may smoke.
6 Flash forth lightning and scatter them;
Send out Thine arrows and confuse them.
7 Stretch forth Thy hand from on high;
Rescue me and deliver me out of great waters,
Out of the hand of aliens
8 Whose mouths speak deceit,
And whose right hand is a right hand of falsehood.

9¶ I will sing a new song to Thee, O God;
Upon a harp of ten strings I will sing praises to Thee,
10 Who dost give salvation to kings;
Who dost rescue David His servant from the evil sword.
11 Rescue me, and deliver me out of the hand of aliens,
Whose mouth speaks deceit,
And whose right hand is a right hand of falsehood.

12¶ Let our sons in their youth be as grown-up plants,
And our daughters as corner pillars fashioned as for a palace;
13 *Let* our garners be full, furnishing every kind of produce,
*And* our flocks bring forth thousands and ten thousands in our fields;
14 *Let* our cattle bear,
Without mishap and without loss,
*Let there be* no outcry in our streets!
15 How blessed are the people who are so situated;
How blessed are the people whose God is the LORD!

*The LORD Extolled for His Goodness.*

*A Psalm of* Praise, of David.

**145** I WILL extol Thee, my God, O King;
And I will bless Thy name forever and ever.
2 Every day I will bless Thee,
And I will praise Thy name forever and ever.
3 Great is the LORD, and highly to be praised;
And His greatness is unsearchable.
4 One generation shall praise Thy works to another,
And shall declare Thy mighty acts.
5 On the glorious splendor of Thy majesty,
And on Thy wonderful works, I will meditate.

## New International

Of David.

**144** PRAISE BE to the LORD my Rock,
who trains my hands for war,
my fingers for battle.
2 He is my loving God and my fortress,
my stronghold and my deliverer,
my shield, in whom I take refuge,
who subdues peoples[a] under me.

3 O LORD, what is man that you care for him,
the son of man that you think of him?
4 Man is like a breath;
his days are like a fleeting shadow.
5 Part your heavens, O LORD, and come down;
touch the mountains, so that they smoke.
6 Send forth lightning and scatter ⌞the enemies⌟;
shoot your arrows and rout them.
7 Reach down your hand from on high;
deliver me and rescue me
from the mighty waters,
from the hands of foreigners
8 whose mouths are full of lies,
whose right hands are deceitful.

9 I will sing a new song to you, O God;
on the ten-stringed lyre I will make music to you,
10 to the One who gives victory to kings,
who delivers his servant David from the deadly sword.

11 Deliver me and rescue me
from the hands of foreigners
whose mouths are full of lies,
whose right hands are deceitful.

12 Then our sons in their youth
will be like well-nurtured plants,
and our daughters will be like pillars
carved to adorn a palace.
13 Our barns will be filled
with every kind of provision.
Our sheep will increase by thousands,
by tens of thousands in our fields;
14 our oxen will draw heavy loads.[b]
There will be no breaching of walls,
no going into captivity,
no cry of distress in our streets.
15 Blessed are the people of whom this is true;
blessed are the people whose God is the LORD.

A psalm of praise. Of David.

**145**[c] I WILL exalt you, my God the King;
I will praise your name for ever and ever.
2 Every day I will praise you
and extol your name for ever and ever.

3 Great is the LORD and most worthy of praise;
his greatness no one can fathom.
4 One generation will commend your works to another;
they will tell of your mighty acts.
5 They will speak of the glorious splendor of your majesty,
and I will meditate on your wonderful works.[d]

**NIV** [a] 2 Many manuscripts of the Masoretic Text, Dead Sea Scrolls, Aquila, Jerome and Syriac; most manuscripts of the Masoretic Text *subdues my people* [b] 14 Or *our chieftains will be firmly established* [c] This psalm is an acrostic poem, the verses of which (including verse 13b) begin with the successive letters of the Hebrew alphabet. [d] 5 Dead Sea Scrolls and Syriac (see also Septuagint); Masoretic Text *On the glorious splendor of your majesty / and on your wonderful works I will meditate*

## King James

6And *men* shall speak of the might of thy terrible acts: and I will declare thy greatness.
7They shall abundantly utter the memory of thy great goodness, and shall sing of thy righteousness.
8The LORD *is* gracious, and full of compassion; slow to anger, and of great mercy.
9The LORD *is* good to all: and his tender mercies *are* over all his works.
10All thy works shall praise thee, O LORD; and thy saints shall bless thee.
11They shall speak of the glory of thy kingdom, and talk of thy power;
12To make known to the sons of men his mighty acts, and the glorious majesty of his kingdom.
13Thy kingdom *is* an everlasting kingdom, and thy dominion *endureth* throughout all generations.
14The LORD upholdeth all that fall, and raiseth up all *those that be* bowed down.
15The eyes of all wait upon thee; and thou givest them their meat in due season.
16Thou openest thine hand, and satisfiest the desire of every living thing.
17The LORD *is* righteous in all his ways, and holy in all his works.
18The LORD *is* nigh unto all them that call upon him, to all that call upon him in truth.
19He will fulfil the desire of them that fear him: he also will hear their cry, and will save them.
20The LORD preserveth all them that love him: but all the wicked will he destroy.
21My mouth shall speak the praise of the LORD: and let all flesh bless his holy name for ever and ever.

**146** PRAISE YE the LORD. Praise the LORD, O my soul.
2While I live will I praise the LORD: I will sing praises unto my God while I have any being.
3Put not your trust in princes, *nor* in the son of man, in whom *there is* no help.
4His breath goeth forth, he returneth to his earth; in that very day his thoughts perish.
5Happy *is he* that *hath* the God of Jacob for his help, whose hope *is* in the LORD his God:
6Which made heaven, and earth, the sea, and all that therein *is:* which keepeth truth for ever:
7Which executeth judgment for the oppressed: which giveth food to the hungry. The LORD looseth the prisoners:
8The LORD openeth *the eyes of* the blind: the LORD raiseth them that are bowed down: the LORD loveth the righteous:
9The LORD preserveth the strangers; he relieveth the fatherless and widow: but the way of the wicked he turneth upside down.

## Amplified

6Men shall speak of the might of Your tremendous *and* terrible acts, and I will declare Your greatness.
7They shall pour forth [as a fountain] the fame of Your great *and* abundant goodness, and shall sing aloud of Your rightness *and* justice.
8The Lord is gracious and full of compassion, slow to anger and abounding in mercy *and* loving-kindness.
9The Lord is good to all, and His tender mercies are over all His works—the entirety of things created.
10All Your works shall praise You, O Lord, and Your loving ones shall bless You—affectionately and gratefully shall Your saints confess and praise You!
11They shall speak of the glory of Your kingdom, and talk of Your power,
12To make known to the sons of men God's mighty deeds, and the glorious majesty of His kingdom.
13Your kingdom is an everlasting kingdom, and Your dominion endures throughout all generations.
14The Lord upholds all those [of His own] who are falling, and raises up all those who are bowed down.
15The eyes of all wait for You—looking, watching and expecting; and You give them their food in due season.
16You open Your hand, and satisfy every living thing with favor.
17The Lord is [rigidly] righteous in all His ways, and gracious *and* merciful in all His works.
18The Lord is near to all who call upon Him, to all who call upon Him sincerely *and* in truth.
19He will fulfill the desire of those who reverently *and* worshipfully fear Him, He also will hear their cry, and will save them.
20The Lord preserves all those who love Him, but all the wicked will He destroy.
21My mouth shall speak the praise of the Lord, and let all flesh bless—affectionately and gratefully praise—His holy name for ever and ever.

**146** PRAISE THE Lord! — Hallelujah! Praise the Lord, O my soul!
2While I live will I praise the Lord. I will sing praises to my God while I have any being.
3Put not your trust in princes, in a son of man, in whom there is no help.
4When his breath leaves him he returns to his earth; in that very day his [previous] thoughts, plans *and* purposes perish. [I Cor. 2:6.]
5Happy—blessed, fortunate [enviable]—is he who has the God of [special revelation to] Jacob for his help, whose hope is in the Lord his God; [Gen. 32:30.]
6Who made Heaven and earth, the sea, and all that in them is, Who keeps truth *and* is faithful for ever;
7Who executes justice for the oppressed; Who gives food to the hungry. The Lord sets free the prisoners;
8The Lord opens the eyes of the blind; the Lord lifts up those who are bowed down; the Lord loves the [uncompromisingly] righteous—those upright in heart and in right standing with Him. [John 9:7, 32; Luke 13:13.]
9The Lord protects *and* preserves the strangers *and* temporary residents; He upholds the fatherless and the widow *and* sets them upright; but the way of the wicked He makes crooked—turns upside down and brings to ruin.

## New American Standard

6 And men shall speak of the power of Thine awesome acts;
And I will tell of Thy greatness.
7 They shall eagerly utter the memory of Thine abundant goodness,
And shall shout joyfully of Thy righteousness.

8¶ The LORD is gracious and merciful;
Slow to anger and great in lovingkindness.
9 The LORD is good to all,
And His mercies are over all His works.
10 All Thy works shall give thanks to Thee, O LORD,
And Thy godly ones shall bless Thee.
11 They shall speak of the glory of Thy kingdom,
And talk of Thy power;
12 To make known to the sons of men Thy mighty acts,
And the glory of the majesty of Thy kingdom.
13 Thy kingdom is an everlasting kingdom,
And Thy dominion *endures* throughout all generations.

14¶ The LORD sustains all who fall,
And raises up all who are bowed down.
15 The eyes of all look to Thee,
And Thou dost give them their food in due time.
16 Thou dost open Thy hand,
And dost satisfy the desire of every living thing.

17¶ The LORD is righteous in all His ways,
And kind in all His deeds.
18 The LORD is near to all who call upon Him,
To all who call upon Him in truth.
19 He will fulfill the desire of those who fear Him;
He will also hear their cry and will save them.
20 The LORD keeps all who love Him;
But all the wicked, He will destroy.
21 My mouth will speak the praise of the LORD;
And all flesh will bless His holy name forever and ever.

*The LORD an Abundant Helper.*

**146** PRAISE THE LORD!
Praise the LORD, O my soul!
2 I will praise the LORD while I live;
I will sing praises to my God while I have my being.
3 Do not trust in princes,
In mortal man, in whom there is no salvation.
4 His spirit departs, he returns to the earth;
In that very day his thoughts perish.
5 How blessed is he whose help is the God of Jacob,
Whose hope is in the LORD his God;
6 Who made heaven and earth,
The sea and all that is in them;
Who keeps faith forever;
7 Who executes justice for the oppressed;
Who gives food to the hungry.
The LORD sets the prisoners free.

8¶ The LORD opens *the eyes of* the blind;
The LORD raises up those who are bowed down;
The LORD loves the righteous;
9 The LORD protects the strangers;
He supports the fatherless and the widow;
But He thwarts the way of the wicked.

## New International

6 They will tell of the power of your awesome works,
and I will proclaim your great deeds.
7 They will celebrate your abundant goodness
and joyfully sing of your righteousness.

8 The LORD is gracious and compassionate,
slow to anger and rich in love.
9 The LORD is good to all;
he has compassion on all he has made.
10 All you have made will praise you, O LORD;
your saints will extol you.
11 They will tell of the glory of your kingdom
and speak of your might,
12 so that all men may know of your mighty acts
and the glorious splendor of your kingdom.
13 Your kingdom is an everlasting kingdom,
and your dominion endures through all generations.
The LORD is faithful to all his promises
and loving toward all he has made.[a]
14 The LORD upholds all those who fall
and lifts up all who are bowed down.
15 The eyes of all look to you,
and you give them their food at the proper time.
16 You open your hand
and satisfy the desires of every living thing.
17 The LORD is righteous in all his ways
and loving toward all he has made.
18 The LORD is near to all who call on him,
to all who call on him in truth.
19 He fulfills the desires of those who fear him;
he hears their cry and saves them.
20 The LORD watches over all who love him,
but all the wicked he will destroy.

21 My mouth will speak in praise of the LORD.
Let every creature praise his holy name
for ever and ever.

**146** PRAISE THE LORD.[b]
Praise the LORD, O my soul.
2 I will praise the LORD all my life;
I will sing praise to my God as long as I live.

3 Do not put your trust in princes,
in mortal men, who cannot save.
4 When their spirit departs, they return to the ground;
on that very day their plans come to nothing.

5 Blessed is he whose help is the God of Jacob,
whose hope is in the LORD his God,
6 the Maker of heaven and earth,
the sea, and everything in them—
the LORD, who remains faithful forever.
7 He upholds the cause of the oppressed
and gives food to the hungry.
The LORD sets prisoners free,
8 the LORD gives sight to the blind,
the LORD lifts up those who are bowed down,
the LORD loves the righteous.
9 The LORD watches over the alien
and sustains the fatherless and the widow,
but he frustrates the ways of the wicked.

**NIV** [a] *13* One manuscript of the Masoretic Text, Dead Sea Scrolls and Syriac (see also Septuagint); most manuscripts of the Masoretic Text do not have the last two lines of verse 13. [b] *1* Hebrew *Hallelu Yah;* also in verse 10

## King James

10 The LORD shall reign for ever, *even* thy God, O Zion, unto all generations. Praise ye the LORD.

**147** PRAISE YE the LORD: for *it is* good to sing praises unto our God; for *it is* pleasant; *and* praise is comely.
2 The LORD doth build up Jerusalem: he gathereth together the outcasts of Israel.
3 He healeth the broken in heart, and bindeth up their wounds.
4 He telleth the number of the stars; he calleth them all by *their* names.
5 Great *is* our Lord, and of great power: his understanding *is* infinite.
6 The LORD lifteth up the meek: he casteth the wicked down to the ground.
7 Sing unto the LORD with thanksgiving; sing praise upon the harp unto our God:
8 Who covereth the heaven with clouds, who prepareth rain for the earth, who maketh grass to grow upon the mountains.
9 He giveth to the beast his food, *and* to the young ravens which cry.
10 He delighteth not in the strength of the horse: he taketh not pleasure in the legs of a man.
11 The LORD taketh pleasure in them that fear him, in those that hope in his mercy.
12 Praise the LORD, O Jerusalem; praise thy God, O Zion.
13 For he hath strengthened the bars of thy gates; he hath blessed thy children within thee.
14 He maketh peace *in* thy borders, *and* filleth thee with the finest of the wheat.
15 He sendeth forth his commandment *upon* earth: his word runneth very swiftly.
16 He giveth snow like wool: he scattereth the hoarfrost like ashes.
17 He casteth forth his ice like morsels: who can stand before his cold?
18 He sendeth out his word, and melteth them: he causeth his wind to blow, *and* the waters flow.
19 He showeth his word unto Jacob, his statutes and his judgments unto Israel.
20 He hath not dealt so with any nation: and *as for his* judgments, they have not known them. Praise ye the LORD.

**148** PRAISE YE the LORD. Praise ye the LORD from the heavens: praise him in the heights.
2 Praise ye him, all his angels: praise ye him, all his hosts.
3 Praise ye him, sun and moon: praise him, all ye stars of light.

## Amplified

10 The Lord shall reign for ever, even Your God, O Zion, from generation to generation. Praise the Lord!—Hallelujah! [Ps. 10:16; Rev. 11:15.]

**147** PRAISE THE Lord! For it is good to sing praises to our God, for He is gracious *and* lovely; praise is becoming *and* appropriate.
2 The Lord is building up Jerusalem; He is gathering together the exiles of Israel.
3 He heals the brokenhearted and binds up their wounds—curing their pains and their sorrows. [Ps. 34:18; Isa. 57:15; 61:1; Luke 4:18.]
4 He determines *and* counts the number of the stars; He calls them all by their names.
5 Great is our Lord, and of great power; His understanding is inexhaustible *and* boundless.
6 The Lord lifts up the humble *and* downtrodden; He casts the wicked down to the ground.
7 Sing to the Lord with thanksgiving; sing praises with the harp *or* the lyre to our God!
8 Who covers the heavens with clouds, Who prepares rain for the earth, Who makes grass to grow on the mountains.
9 He gives to the beast his food, and to the young ravens that for which they cry.
10 He delights not in the strength of the horse; nor does He take pleasure in the legs of a man.
11 The Lord takes pleasure in those who reverently *and* worshipfully fear Him, in those who hope in His mercy *and* loving-kindness. [Ps. 145:20.]
12 Praise the Lord, O Jerusalem! Praise your God, O Zion!
13 For He has strengthened *and* made hard the bars of your gates; *and* He has blessed your children within you.
14 He makes peace in your borders; He fills you with the finest of the wheat.
15 He sends forth His commandment to the earth; His word runs very swiftly.
16 He gives [to the earth] snow like [a blanket of] wool; He scatters the hoarfrost like ashes.
17 He casts forth His ice like crumbs; who can stand before His cold?
18 He sends out His word, and melts [ice and snow]; He causes His wind to blow, and the waters flow.
19 He declares His Word to Jacob, His statutes and His ordinances to Israel. [Mal. 4:4.]
20 He has not dealt so with any (other) nation; they have not known (understood, appreciated, given heed to and cherished) His ordinances. Praise the Lord!—Hallelujah! [Ps. 79:6; Jer. 10:25.]

**148** PRAISE THE Lord! Praise the Lord from the heavens, praise Him in the heights!
2 Praise Him, all His angels, praise Him, all His host!
3 Praise Him, sun and moon, praise Him, all you stars of light!

## New American Standard

10 The LORD will reign forever,
Thy God, O Zion, to all generations.
Praise the LORD!

*Praise for Jerusalem's Restoration and Prosperity.*

**147** PRAISE THE LORD!
For it is good to sing praises to our God;
For [a]it is pleasant *and* praise is becoming.
2 The LORD builds up Jerusalem;
He gathers the outcasts of Israel.
3 He heals the brokenhearted,
And binds up their [b]wounds.
4 He counts the number of the stars;
He gives names to all of them.
5 Great is our Lord, and abundant in strength;
His understanding is infinite.
6 The LORD [c]supports the afflicted;
He brings down the wicked to the ground.
7¶ Sing to the LORD with thanksgiving;
Sing praises to our God on the lyre,
8 Who covers the heavens with clouds,
Who provides rain for the earth,
Who makes grass to grow on the mountains.
9 He gives to the beast its food,
*And* to the young ravens which cry.
10 He does not delight in the strength of the horse;
He does not take pleasure in the legs of a man.
11 The LORD favors those who fear Him,
Those who wait for His lovingkindness.
12¶ Praise the LORD, O Jerusalem!
Praise your God, O Zion!
13 For He has strengthened the bars of your gates;
He has blessed your sons within you.
14 He makes peace in your borders;
He satisfies you with the finest of the wheat.
15 He sends forth His command to the earth;
His word runs very swiftly.
16 He gives snow like wool;
He scatters the frost like ashes.
17 He casts forth His ice as fragments;
Who can stand before His cold?
18 He sends forth His word and melts them;
He causes His wind to blow and the waters to flow.
19 He declares His words to Jacob,
His statutes and His ordinances to Israel.
20 He has not dealt thus with any nation;
And as for His ordinances, they have not known them.
Praise the LORD!

*The Whole Creation Invoked to Praise the LORD.*

**148** PRAISE THE LORD!
Praise the LORD from the heavens;
Praise Him in the heights!
2 Praise Him, all His angels;
Praise Him, all His hosts!
3 Praise Him, sun and moon;
Praise Him, all stars of light!

NAS [a] Or, *He is gracious* [b] Lit., *sorrows* [c] Or, *relieves*

## New International

10The LORD reigns forever,
your God, O Zion, for all generations.

Praise the LORD.

**147** PRAISE THE LORD.[d]

How good it is to sing praises to our God,
how pleasant and fitting to praise him!

2The LORD builds up Jerusalem;
he gathers the exiles of Israel.
3He heals the brokenhearted
and binds up their wounds.
4He determines the number of the stars
and calls them each by name.
5Great is our Lord and mighty in power;
his understanding has no limit.
6The LORD sustains the humble
but casts the wicked to the ground.

7Sing to the LORD with thanksgiving;
make music to our God on the harp.
8He covers the sky with clouds;
he supplies the earth with rain
and makes grass grow on the hills.
9He provides food for the cattle
and for the young ravens when they call.

10His pleasure is not in the strength of the horse,
nor his delight in the legs of a man;
11the LORD delights in those who fear him,
who put their hope in his unfailing love.

12Extol the LORD, O Jerusalem;
praise your God, O Zion,
13for he strengthens the bars of your gates
and blesses your people within you.
14He grants peace to your borders
and satisfies you with the finest of wheat.

15He sends his command to the earth;
his word runs swiftly.
16He spreads the snow like wool
and scatters the frost like ashes.
17He hurls down his hail like pebbles.
Who can withstand his icy blast?
18He sends his word and melts them;
he stirs up his breezes, and the waters flow.

19He has revealed his word to Jacob,
his laws and decrees to Israel.
20He has done this for no other nation;
they do not know his laws.

Praise the LORD.

**148** PRAISE THE LORD.[e]

Praise the LORD from the heavens,
praise him in the heights above.
2Praise him, all his angels,
praise him, all his heavenly hosts.
3Praise him, sun and moon,
praise him, all you shining stars.

NIV [d] *1* Hebrew *Hallelu Yah;* also in verse 20 [e] *1* Hebrew *Hallelu Yah;* also in verse 14

## King James

4Praise him, ye heavens of heavens, and ye waters that *be* above the heavens.
5Let them praise the name of the LORD: for he commanded, and they were created.
6He hath also stablished them for ever and ever; he hath made a decree which shall not pass.
7Praise the LORD from the earth, ye dragons, and all deeps:
8Fire, and hail; snow, and vapour; stormy wind fulfilling his word:
9Mountains, and all hills; fruitful trees, and all cedars:
10Beasts, and all cattle; creeping things, and flying fowl:
11Kings of the earth, and all people; princes, and all judges of the earth:
12Both young men, and maidens; old men, and children:
13Let them praise the name of the LORD: for his name alone is excellent; his glory *is* above the earth and heaven.
14He also exalteth the horn of his people, the praise of all his saints; *even* of the children of Israel, a people near unto him. Praise ye the LORD.

**149** PRAISE YE the LORD. Sing unto the LORD a new song, *and* his praise in the congregation of saints.
2Let Israel rejoice in him that made him: let the children of Zion be joyful in their King.
3Let them praise his name in the dance: let them sing praises unto him with the timbrel and harp.
4For the LORD taketh pleasure in his people: he will beautify the meek with salvation.
5Let the saints be joyful in glory: let them sing aloud upon their beds.
6 *Let* the high *praises* of God *be* in their mouth, and a twoedged sword in their hand;
7To execute vengeance upon the heathen, *and* punishments upon the people;
8To bind their kings with chains, and their nobles with fetters of iron;
9To execute upon them the judgment written: this honour have all his saints. Praise ye the LORD.

**150** PRAISE YE the LORD. Praise God in his sanctuary: praise him in the firmament of his power.
2Praise him for his mighty acts; praise him according to his excellent greatness.
3Praise him with the sound of the trumpet: praise him with the psaltery and harp.
4Praise him with the timbrel and dance: praise him with stringed instruments and organs.

## Amplified

4Praise Him, you highest heavens, and you waters above the heavens!
5Let them praise the name of the Lord, for He commanded, and they were created.
6He also established them for ever and ever; He made a decree which shall not pass away—He fixed their bounds which cannot be passed over.
7Praise the Lord from the earth, you sea monsters and all deeps,
8You lightning, hail, fog *and* frost, you stormy wind fulfilling His orders!
9Mountains and all hills, fruitful trees and all cedars,
10Beasts and all cattle, creeping things and flying birds!
11Kings of the earth and all peoples, princes and all rulers *and* judges of the earth!
12Both young men and maidens, old men and children!
13Let them praise *and* exalt the name of the Lord, for His name alone is exalted *and* supreme! His glory *and* majesty are above earth and Heaven!
14He has lifted up a horn for His people [giving them power, prosperity, dignity and pre-eminence], a song of praise for all His godly ones, for the people of Israel who are near to Him. Praise the Lord!—Hallelujah! [Ps. 75:10; Eph. 2:17.]

**149** PRAISE THE Lord! Sing to the Lord a new song, praise Him in the assembly of His saints!
2Let Israel rejoice in Him, his Maker; let Zion's children triumph *and* be joyful in their King! [Zech. 9:9; Matt. 21:5.]
3Let them praise His name in chorus *and* choir *and* with the [single or group] dance, let them sing praises to Him with the tambourine and lyre!
4For the Lord takes pleasure in His people; He will beautify the humble with salvation *and* adorn the wretched with victory.
5Let the saints be joyful in the glory *and* beauty [which God confers upon them]; let them sing for joy upon their beds.
6Let the high praises of God be in their throat and a two-edged sword in their hand, [Heb. 4:12; Rev. 1:16.]
7To wreak vengeance upon the nations and chastisements upon the peoples;
8To bind their kings with chains and their nobles with fetters of iron,
9To execute upon them the judgment written. He [the Lord] is the honor of all His saints. Praise the Lord!—Hallelujah!

**150** PRAISE THE Lord! Praise God in His sanctuary; praise Him in the heavens of His power!
2Praise Him for His mighty acts; praise Him according to the abundance of His greatness! [Ps. 145:5, 6; Deut. 3:24.]
3Praise Him with trumpet sound; praise Him with lute and harp!
4Praise Him with tambourine and [single or group] dance; praise Him with stringed and wind instruments *or* flutes!

## New American Standard

4 Praise Him, highest heavens,
And the waters that are above the heavens!
5 Let them praise the name of the LORD,
For He commanded and they were created.
6 He has also established them forever and ever;
He has made a decree which will not pass away.

7¶ Praise the LORD from the earth,
Sea monsters and all deeps;
8 Fire and hail, snow and clouds;
Stormy wind, fulfilling His word;
9 Mountains and all hills;
Fruit trees and all cedars;
10 Beasts and all cattle;
Creeping things and winged fowl;
11 Kings of the earth and all peoples;
Princes and all judges of the earth;
12 Both young men and virgins;
Old men and children.

13¶ Let them praise the name of the LORD,
For His name alone is exalted;
His glory is above earth and heaven.
14 And He has lifted up a horn for His people,
Praise for all His godly ones;
*Even* for the sons of Israel, a people near to Him.
Praise the LORD!

*Israel Invoked to Praise the LORD.*

### 149

PRAISE THE LORD!
Sing to the LORD a new song,
And His praise in the congregation of the godly ones.
2 Let Israel be glad in his Maker;
Let the sons of Zion rejoice in their King.
3 Let them praise His name with dancing;
Let them sing praises to Him with timbrel and lyre.
4 For the LORD takes pleasure in His people;
He will beautify the afflicted ones with salvation.

5¶ Let the godly ones exult in glory;
Let them sing for joy on their beds.
6 *Let* the high praises of God *be* in their mouth,
And a two-edged sword in their hand,
7 To execute vengeance on the nations,
And punishment on the peoples;
8 To bind their kings with chains,
And their nobles with fetters of iron;
9 To execute on them the judgment written;
This is an honor for all His godly ones.
Praise the LORD!

*A Psalm of Praise.*

### 150

PRAISE THE LORD!
Praise God in His sanctuary;
Praise Him in His mighty expanse.
2 Praise Him for His mighty deeds;
Praise Him according to His excellent greatness.

3¶ Praise Him with trumpet sound;
Praise Him with harp and lyre.
4 Praise Him with timbrel and dancing;
Praise Him with stringed instruments and pipe.

## New International

4 Praise him, you highest heavens
and you waters above the skies.
5 Let them praise the name of the LORD,
for he commanded and they were created.
6 He set them in place for ever and ever;
he gave a decree that will never pass away.

7 Praise the LORD from the earth,
you great sea creatures and all ocean depths,
8 lightning and hail, snow and clouds,
stormy winds that do his bidding,
9 you mountains and all hills,
fruit trees and all cedars,
10 wild animals and all cattle,
small creatures and flying birds,
11 kings of the earth and all nations,
you princes and all rulers on earth,
12 young men and maidens,
old men and children.

13 Let them praise the name of the LORD,
for his name alone is exalted;
his splendor is above the earth and the heavens.
14 He has raised up for his people a horn,[a]
the praise of all his saints,
of Israel, the people close to his heart.

Praise the LORD.

### 149

PRAISE THE LORD.[b]

Sing to the LORD a new song,
his praise in the assembly of the saints.

2 Let Israel rejoice in their Maker;
let the people of Zion be glad in their King.
3 Let them praise his name with dancing
and make music to him with tambourine and harp.
4 For the LORD takes delight in his people;
he crowns the humble with salvation.
5 Let the saints rejoice in this honor
and sing for joy on their beds.

6 May the praise of God be in their mouths
and a double-edged sword in their hands,
7 to inflict vengeance on the nations
and punishment on the peoples,
8 to bind their kings with fetters,
their nobles with shackles of iron,
9 to carry out the sentence written against them.
This is the glory of all his saints.

Praise the LORD.

### 150

PRAISE THE LORD.[c]

Praise God in his sanctuary;
praise him in his mighty heavens.
2 Praise him for his acts of power;
praise him for his surpassing greatness.
3 Praise him with the sounding of the trumpet,
praise him with the harp and lyre,
4 praise him with tambourine and dancing,
praise him with the strings and flute,

**NIV** [a] *14 Horn* here symbolizes strong one, that is, king. [b] *1* Hebrew *Hallelu Yah;* also in verse 9 [c] *1* Hebrew *Hallelu Yah;* also in verse 6

## King James

5Praise him upon the loud cymbals: praise him upon the high sounding cymbals.
6Let every thing that hath breath praise the LORD. Praise ye the LORD.

## Amplified

5Praise Him with sounding cymbals; praise Him with loud clashing cymbals!
6Let everything that has breath *and* every breath of life praise the Lord! Praise you the Lord!—Hallelujah!

## New American Standard

5 Praise Him with loud cymbals;
Praise Him with resounding cymbals.
6 Let everything that has breath praise the LORD.
Praise the LORD!

## New International

5praise him with the clash of cymbals,
praise him with resounding cymbals.
6Let everything that has breath praise the LORD.

Praise the LORD.

## King James

THE

# Proverbs

1 THE PROVERBS of Solomon the son of David, king of Israel;
2To know wisdom and instruction; to perceive the words of
understanding;
3To receive the instruction of wisdom, justice, and judgment,
and equity;
4To give subtlety to the simple, to the young man knowledge
and discretion.
5A wise *man* will hear, and will increase learning; and a man of
understanding shall attain unto wise counsels:
6To understand a proverb, and the interpretation; the words of
the wise, and their dark sayings.
7¶ The fear of the LORD *is* the beginning of knowledge: *but* fools
despise wisdom and instruction.
8My son, hear the instruction of thy father, and forsake not the
law of thy mother:
9For they *shall be* an ornament of grace unto thy head, and
chains about thy neck.
10¶ My son, if sinners entice thee, consent thou not.
11If they say, Come with us, let us lay wait for blood, let us lurk
privily for the innocent without cause:
12Let us swallow them up alive as the grave; and whole, as
those that go down into the pit:
13We shall find all precious substance, we shall fill our houses
with spoil:
14Cast in thy lot among us; let us all have one purse:
15My son, walk not thou in the way with them; refrain thy foot
from their path:
16For their feet run to evil, and make haste to shed blood.
17Surely in vain the net is spread in the sight of any bird.
18And they lay wait for their *own* blood; they lurk privily for
their *own* lives.
19So *are* the ways of every one that is greedy of gain; *which*
taketh away the life of the owners thereof.
20¶ Wisdom crieth without; she uttereth her voice in the streets:

## Amplified

# The Proverbs

1 THE PROVERBS [truths obscurely expressed, maxims and
parables] of Solomon the son of David, king of Israel:
2 [a]That people may know skill *and* godly wisdom and instruction, discern *and* comprehend the words of understanding *and*
insight,
3Receive instruction in wise dealing *and* the discipline of wise
thoughtfulness, righteousness, justice and integrity;
4That prudence may be given to the simple, and knowledge,
discretion *and* discernment to the youth;
5The wise also may hear and increase in learning, and the
person of understanding acquire skill *and* attain to sound counsels
[so that he may be able to steer his course rightly]; [Prov. 9:9.]
6To understand a proverb and a figure of speech *or* an enigma
with its interpretation, and the words of the wise and their dark
sayings *or* riddles.
7The reverent *and* worshipful fear of the Lord is the beginning
*and* the principal *and* choice part of knowledge—that is, its starting
point and its essence; but fools despise skillful *and* godly wisdom,
instruction *and* discipline. [Ps. 111:10.]
8My son, hear the instruction of your father; reject not *nor*
forsake the teaching of your mother;
9For they are a [victor's] chaplet of grace upon your head, and
the chains *and* pendants [of gold worn by kings] for your neck.
10My son, if sinners entice you, do not consent. [Ps. 1:1; Eph.
5:11.]
11If they say, Come with us, let us lie in wait *to shed* blood, let
us ambush the innocent without cause [and show that his piety is
in vain];
12Let us swallow them up alive as does Sheol [the place of the
dead], and whole, as those who go down into the pit [of the dead];
13We shall find *and* take all precious goods [when our victims
are put out of the way], we shall fill our houses with plunder;
14Throw in your lot among us [they insist], *and* be a sworn
brother *and* comrade; let us all have one purse in common.
15My son, do not walk in the way with them, restrain your foot
from their path;
16For their feet run to evil, and they make haste to shed blood.
17For in vain is the net spread in the sight of any bird;
18But [when these men set a trap for others] they are lying in
wait for their own blood, they set an ambush for their own lives.
19So are the ways of every one who is greedy of gain; such
[greed for plunder] takes away the life of its possessors. [Prov.
15:27; I Tim. 6:10.]
20Wisdom cries aloud in the street; she raises her voice in the
markets.

**AMP** [a] Over the doors of the school of Plato these words were written in Greek, "Let no one enter who is not a geometrician." But Solomon opens wide the doors of his Proverbs with a special message of welcome to the unlearned, the simple, the foolish, the young, and even to the wise, that all "may increase in learning."

## New American Standard

# Proverbs

*The Usefulness of Proverbs*

**1** THE PROVERBS of Solomon the son of David, king of Israel:
2 To know wisdom and instruction,
To discern the sayings of understanding,
3 To receive instruction in wise behavior,
Righteousness, justice and equity;
4 To give prudence to the naive,
To the youth knowledge and discretion,
5 A wise man will hear and increase in learning,
And a man of understanding will acquire wise counsel,
6 To understand a proverb and a figure,
The words of the wise and their riddles.

7¶ The fear of the LORD is the beginning of knowledge;
Fools despise wisdom and instruction.

*The Enticement of Sinners*

8¶ Hear, my son, your father's instruction,
And do not forsake your mother's teaching;
9 Indeed, they are a graceful wreath to your head,
And ornaments about your neck.
10 My son, if sinners entice you,
Do not consent.
11 If they say, "Come with us,
Let us lie in wait for blood,
Let us ambush the innocent without cause;
12 Let us swallow them alive like Sheol,
Even whole, as those who go down to the pit;
13 We shall find all *kinds* of precious wealth,
We shall fill our houses with spoil;
14 Throw in your lot with us,
We shall all have one purse,"
15 My son, do not walk in the way with them.
Keep your feet from their path,
16 For their feet run to evil,
And they hasten to shed blood.
17 Indeed, it is useless to spread the net
In the eyes of any bird;
18 But they lie in wait for their own blood;
They ambush their own lives.
19 So are the ways of everyone who gains by violence;
It takes away the life of its possessors.

*Wisdom Warns*

20¶ Wisdom shouts in the street,
She lifts her voice in the square;

## New International

# Proverbs

*Prologue: Purpose and Theme*

**1** THE PROVERBS of Solomon son of David, king of Israel:
2for attaining wisdom and discipline;
for understanding words of insight;
3for acquiring a disciplined and prudent life,
doing what is right and just and fair;
4for giving prudence to the simple,
knowledge and discretion to the young—
5let the wise listen and add to their learning,
and let the discerning get guidance—
6for understanding proverbs and parables,
the sayings and riddles of the wise.

7The fear of the LORD is the beginning of knowledge,
but fools[b] despise wisdom and discipline.

*Exhortations to Embrace Wisdom*

*Warning Against Enticement*

8Listen, my son, to your father's instruction
and do not forsake your mother's teaching.
9They will be a garland to grace your head
and a chain to adorn your neck.

10My son, if sinners entice you,
do not give in to them.
11If they say, "Come along with us;
let's lie in wait for someone's blood,
let's waylay some harmless soul;
12let's swallow them alive, like the grave,[c]
and whole, like those who go down to the pit;
13we will get all sorts of valuable things
and fill our houses with plunder;
14throw in your lot with us,
and we will share a common purse"—
15my son, do not go along with them,
do not set foot on their paths;
16for their feet rush into sin,
they are swift to shed blood.
17How useless to spread a net
in full view of all the birds!
18These men lie in wait for their own blood;
they waylay only themselves!
19Such is the end of all who go after ill-gotten gain;
it takes away the lives of those who get it.

*Warning Against Rejecting Wisdom*

20Wisdom calls aloud in the street,
she raises her voice in the public squares;

**NIV** [b] *7* The Hebrew words rendered *fool* in Proverbs, and often elsewhere in the Old Testament, denote one who is morally deficient. [c] *12* Hebrew *Sheol*

## King James

21 She crieth in the chief place of concourse, in the openings of
the gates: in the city she uttereth her words, *saying*,
22 How long, ye simple ones, will ye love simplicity? and the
scorners delight in their scorning, and fools hate knowledge?
23 Turn you at my reproof: behold, I will pour out my spirit unto
you, I will make known my words unto you.
24 ¶ Because I have called, and ye refused; I have stretched out
my hand, and no man regarded;
25 But ye have set at nought all my counsel, and would none of
my reproof:
26 I also will laugh at your calamity; I will mock when your fear
cometh;
27 When your fear cometh as desolation, and your destruction
cometh as a whirlwind; when distress and anguish cometh upon
you.
28 Then shall they call upon me, but I will not answer; they shall
seek me early, but they shall not find me:
29 For that they hated knowledge, and did not choose the fear
of the LORD:
30 They would none of my counsel: they despised all my reproof.
31 Therefore shall they eat of the fruit of their own way, and be
filled with their own devices.
32 For the turning away of the simple shall slay them, and the
prosperity of fools shall destroy them.
33 But whoso hearkeneth unto me shall dwell safely, and shall
be quiet from fear of evil.

## Amplified

21 She cries at the head of the noisy intersections—in the chief
gathering places—at the entrance of the city gates she speaks:
22 How long, O simple ones *and* open [to evil], will you love
being simple? And the scoffers delight in scoffing, and [self-confi-
dent] fools hate knowledge?
23 If you will turn (repent) *and* give heed to my reproof, behold,
I [ [a]Wisdom], will pour out my spirit upon you, I will make My
words known to you. [Isa. 11:2; Eph. 1:17-20.]
24 Because I have called and you refused [to answer], have
stretched out my hand and no man heeded it, [Isa. 65:11, 12; 66:4;
Jer. 7:13, 14; Zech. 7:11-13.]
25 But you have treated as nothing all my counsel, and would
accept none of my reproof,
26 I also will laugh at your calamity; I will mock when the thing
comes that shall cause you terror *and* panic,
27 When your panic comes as a storm *and* desolation, and your
calamity comes on as a whirlwind, when distress and anguish
come upon you.
28 Then will they call upon me [Wisdom], but I will not answer;
they will seek me early *and* diligently, but they will not find me.
[Job 27:9; 35:12, 13; Isa. 1:15, 16; Jer. 11:11; Mic. 3:4; James 4:3.]
29 Because they hated knowledge, and did not choose the reverent *and* worshipful fear of the Lord, [Prov. 8:13.]
30 Would have none of my counsel, and despised all my reproof,
31 Therefore shall they eat of the fruit of their own way, and be
satiated with their own devices.
32 For the backsliding of the simple shall slay them, and the
careless ease of [self-confident] fools shall destroy them. [Isa. 32:6.]
33 But whoso hearkens to me [Wisdom], shall dwell securely *and*
in confident trust, and shall be quiet without fear *or* dread of evil.

## King James

**2** MY SON, if thou wilt receive my words, and hide my commandments with thee;
2 So that thou incline thine ear unto wisdom, *and* apply thine
heart to understanding;
3 Yea, if thou criest after knowledge, *and* liftest up thy voice for
understanding;
4 If thou seekest her as silver, and searchest for her as *for* hid
treasures;
5 Then shalt thou understand the fear of the LORD, and find the
knowledge of God.
6 For the LORD giveth wisdom: out of his mouth *cometh* knowledge and understanding.
7 He layeth up sound wisdom for the righteous: *he is* a buckler
to them that walk uprightly.
8 He keepeth the paths of judgment, and preserveth the way of
his saints.
9 Then shalt thou understand righteousness, and judgment,
and equity; *yea*, every good path.
10 ¶ When wisdom entereth into thine heart, and knowledge is
pleasant unto thy soul;
11 Discretion shall preserve thee, understanding shall keep thee:
12 To deliver thee from the way of the evil *man*, from the man
that speaketh froward things;
13 Who leave the paths of uprightness, to walk in the ways of
darkness;
14 Who rejoice to do evil, *and* delight in the frowardness of the
wicked;
15 Whose ways *are* crooked, and *they* froward in their paths:

## Amplified

**2** MY SON, if you will receive my words and treasure up my
commandments with you,
2 Making your ear attentive to skillful *and* godly Wisdom, *and*
inclining and directing your heart *and* mind to understanding—
applying all your powers to the quest for it;
3 Yes, if you cry out for insight and raise your voice for understanding,
4 If you seek *Wisdom* as silver, and search for skillful *and* godly
Wisdom as for hid treasures;
5 Then you will understand the reverent *and* worshipful fear of
the Lord and find the knowledge of [our omniscient] God. [Prov.
1:7.]
6 For the Lord gives skillful *and* godly Wisdom; from His mouth
come knowledge and understanding.
7 He hides away sound *and* godly Wisdom *and* stores it for the
righteous—those who are upright and in right standing with Him;
He is a shield to those who walk uprightly *and* in integrity,
8 That He may guard the paths of justice. Yes, He preserves the
way of His saints. [I Sam. 2:9; Ps. 66:8, 9.]
9 Then you will understand righteousness, justice and fair dealing [in every area and relation]; yes, you will understand every
good path.
10 For skillful *and* godly [b]Wisdom shall enter into your heart,
and knowledge shall be pleasant to you;
11 Discretion shall watch over you, understanding shall keep
you;
12 To deliver you from the way of evil *and* the evil man, from men
who speak perverse things *and* are liars,
13 Men who forsake the paths of uprightness to walk in the ways
of darkness,
14 Who rejoice to do evil and delight in the perverseness of evil,
15 Who are crooked in their ways, wayward *and* devious in their
paths.

**AMP** [a] Read "the Wisdom of God" instead of "Wisdom," and see the wonderful power of this book. The Apostle Paul called Christ "the wisdom of God . . . in Whom are hid all the treasures of wisdom and knowledge." (I Cor. 1:24; Col. 2:3.) [b] See footnote on chapter 1:23.

## New American Standard

21 At the head of the noisy *streets* she cries out;
At the entrance of the gates in the city, she utters her sayings:
22 "How long, O naive ones, will you love simplicity?
And scoffers delight themselves in scoffing,
And fools hate knowledge?
23 "Turn to my reproof,
Behold, I will pour out my spirit on you;
I will make my words known to you.
24 Because I called, and you refused;
I stretched out my hand, and no one paid attention;
25 And you neglected all my counsel,
And did not want my reproof;
26 I will even laugh at your calamity;
I will mock when your dread comes,
27 When your dread comes like a storm,
And your calamity comes on like a whirlwind,
When distress *and* anguish come on you.
28 "Then they will call on me, but I will not answer;
They will seek me diligently, but they shall not find me,
29 Because they hated knowledge,
And did not choose the fear of the LORD.
30 "They would not accept my counsel,
They spurned all my reproof.
31 "So they shall eat of the fruit of their own way,
And be satiated with their own devices.
32 "For the waywardness of the naive shall kill them,
And the complacency of fools shall destroy them.
33 "But he who listens to me shall live securely,
And shall be at ease from the dread of evil."

*The Pursuit of Wisdom Brings Security*

2 MY SON, if you will receive my sayings,
And treasure my commandments within you,
2 Make your ear attentive to wisdom,
Incline your heart to understanding;
3 For if you cry for discernment,
Lift your voice for understanding;
4 If you seek her as silver,
And search for her as for hidden treasures;
5 Then you will discern the fear of the LORD,
And discover the knowledge of God.
6 For the LORD gives wisdom;
From His mouth *come* knowledge and understanding.
7 He stores up sound wisdom for the upright;
*He is* a shield to those who walk in integrity,
8 Guarding the paths of justice,
And He preserves the way of His godly ones.
9 Then you will discern righteousness and justice
And equity *and* every good course.
10 For wisdom will enter your heart,
And knowledge will be pleasant to your soul;
11 Discretion will guard you,
Understanding will watch over you,
12 To deliver you from the way of evil,
From the man who speaks perverse things;
13 From those who leave the paths of uprightness,
To walk in the ways of darkness;
14 Who delight in doing evil,
And rejoice in the perversity of evil;
15 Whose paths are crooked,
And who are devious in their ways;

## New International

21 at the head of the noisy streets[c] she cries out,
in the gateways of the city she makes her speech:
22 "How long will you simple ones[d] love your simple ways?
How long will mockers delight in mockery
and fools hate knowledge?
23 If you had responded to my rebuke,
I would have poured out my heart to you
and made my thoughts known to you.
24 But since you rejected me when I called
and no one gave heed when I stretched out my hand,
25 since you ignored all my advice
and would not accept my rebuke,
26 I in turn will laugh at your disaster;
I will mock when calamity overtakes you—
27 when calamity overtakes you like a storm,
when disaster sweeps over you like a whirlwind,
when distress and trouble overwhelm you.

28 "Then they will call to me but I will not answer;
they will look for me but will not find me.
29 Since they hated knowledge
and did not choose to fear the LORD,
30 since they would not accept my advice
and spurned my rebuke,
31 they will eat the fruit of their ways
and be filled with the fruit of their schemes.
32 For the waywardness of the simple will kill them,
and the complacency of fools will destroy them;
33 but whoever listens to me will live in safety
and be at ease, without fear of harm."

*Moral Benefits of Wisdom*

2 MY SON, if you accept my words
and store up my commands within you,
2 turning your ear to wisdom
and applying your heart to understanding,
3 and if you call out for insight
and cry aloud for understanding,
4 and if you look for it as for silver
and search for it as for hidden treasure,
5 then you will understand the fear of the LORD
and find the knowledge of God.
6 For the LORD gives wisdom,
and from his mouth come knowledge and understanding.
7 He holds victory in store for the upright,
he is a shield to those whose walk is blameless,
8 for he guards the course of the just
and protects the way of his faithful ones.

9 Then you will understand what is right and just
and fair—every good path.
10 For wisdom will enter your heart,
and knowledge will be pleasant to your soul.
11 Discretion will protect you,
and understanding will guard you.

12 Wisdom will save you from the ways of wicked men,
from men whose words are perverse,
13 who leave the straight paths
to walk in dark ways,
14 who delight in doing wrong
and rejoice in the perverseness of evil,
15 whose paths are crooked
and who are devious in their ways.

NIV [c] 21 Hebrew; Septuagint / *on the tops of the walls* [d] 22 The Hebrew word rendered *simple* in Proverbs generally denotes one without moral direction and inclined to evil.

## King James

16To deliver thee from the strange woman, *even* from the stranger *which* flattereth with her words;

17Which forsaketh the guide of her youth, and forgetteth the covenant of her God.

18For her house inclineth unto death, and her paths unto the dead.

19None that go unto her return again, neither take they hold of the paths of life.

20That thou mayest walk in the way of good *men*, and keep the paths of the righteous.

21For the upright shall dwell in the land, and the perfect shall remain in it,

22But the wicked shall be cut off from the earth, and the transgressors shall be rooted out of it.

**3** MY SON, forget not my law; but let thine heart keep my commandments:

2For length of days, and long life, and peace, shall they add to thee.

3Let not mercy and truth forsake thee: bind them about thy neck; write them upon the table of thine heart:

4So shalt thou find favour and good understanding in the sight of God and man.

5¶ Trust in the LORD with all thine heart; and lean not unto thine own understanding.

6In all thy ways acknowledge him, and he shall direct thy paths.

7¶ Be not wise in thine own eyes: fear the LORD, and depart from evil.

8It shall be health to thy navel, and marrow to thy bones.

9Honour the LORD with thy substance, and with the firstfruits of all thine increase:

10So shall thy barns be filled with plenty, and thy presses shall burst out with new wine.

11¶ My son, despise not the chastening of the LORD; neither be weary of his correction:

12For whom the LORD loveth he correcteth; even as a father the son *in whom* he delighteth.

13¶ Happy *is* the man *that* findeth wisdom, and the man *that* getteth understanding.

14For the merchandise of it *is* better than the merchandise of silver, and the gain thereof than fine gold.

15She *is* more precious than rubies: and all the things thou canst desire are not to be compared unto her.

16Length of days *is* in her right hand; *and* in her left hand riches and honour.

17Her ways *are* ways of pleasantness, and all her paths *are* peace.

18She *is* a tree of life to them that lay hold upon her: and happy *is every one* that retaineth her.

19The LORD by wisdom hath founded the earth; by understanding hath he established the heavens.

20By his knowledge the depths are broken up, and the clouds drop down the dew.

21¶ My son, let not them depart from thine eyes: keep sound wisdom and discretion:

## Amplified

16[Discretion shall watch over you, understanding shall keep you] to deliver you from the alien woman, from the outsider with her flattering words, [Verse 11.]

17Who forsakes the husband *and* guide of her youth and forgets the covenant of her God;

18For her house sinks down to death, and her paths to the spirits [of the dead].

19None who go to her return again, neither do they attain *or* regain the paths of life.

20So may you walk in the way of good men, and keep to the paths of the [consistently] righteous—the upright, in right standing with God.

21For the upright shall dwell in the land, and the men of integrity, blameless *and* complete [in God's sight], shall remain in it;

22But the wicked shall be cut off from the earth, and the treacherous shall be rooted out of it.

**3** MY SON, forget not my law *or* teaching, but let your heart keep my commandments;

2For length of days, and years of a life [worth living], and tranquility [inward and outward and continuing through old age till death], these shall they add to you.

3Let not mercy and kindness [shutting out all hatred and selfishness], and truth [shutting out all deliberate hypocrisy or falsehood] forsake you. Bind them about your neck; write them upon the tablet of your heart; [Col. 3:9-12.]

4So shall you find favor, good understanding *and* high esteem in the sight [or judgment] of God and man. [Luke 2:52.]

5Lean on, trust *and* be confident in the Lord with all your heart *and* mind, and do not rely on your own insight *or* understanding.

6In all your ways know, recognize *and* acknowledge Him, and He will direct *and* make straight *and* plain your paths.

7Be not wise in your own eyes; reverently fear *and* worship the Lord, and turn [entirely] away from evil. [Prov. 8:13.]

8It shall be health to your nerves *and* sinews, and marrow *and* moistening to your bones.

9Honor the Lord with your capital *and* sufficiency [from righteous labors], and with the first fruits of all your income; [Deut. 26:2; Mal. 3:10; Luke 14:13, 14.]

10So shall your storage places be filled with plenty, and your vats be overflowing with new wine. [Deut. 28:8.]

11My son, do not despise *or* shrink from the chastening of the Lord—His correction by punishment, or by subjection to suffering or trial; neither be weary *and* impatient *and* loathe *or* abhor His reproof; [Ps. 94:12; Heb. 12:5, 6; Rev. 3:19.]

12For whom the Lord loves He corrects, even as a father corrects the son in whom he delights.

13Happy—blessed, fortunate [enviable]—is the man who finds skillful *and* godly [a]Wisdom, and the man who gets understanding—drawing it forth [from God's Word and life's experiences].

14For the gaining of it is better than the gaining of silver, and the profit of it than fine gold.

15Skillful *and* godly Wisdom is more precious than rubies, and nothing you can wish for is to be compared to her. [Job 28:12-18.]

16Length of days is in her right hand, and in her left hand are riches and honor. [Prov. 8:12-21; I Tim. 4:8.]

17Her ways are highways of pleasantness, and all her paths are peace.

18She is a tree of life to those who lay hold on her, and happy—blessed, fortunate [to be envied]—is every one who holds her fast.

19The Lord by skillful *and* godly Wisdom has founded the earth; by understanding He has established the heavens. [Col. 1:16.]

20By His knowledge the deeps were broken up, and the skies distill the dew.

21My son, let them not escape from your sight, but keep sound wisdom and discretion,

**AMP** [a] See footnote on chapter 1:23.

## New American Standard

16 To deliver you from the strange woman,
From the adulteress who flatters with her words;
17 That leaves the companion of her youth,
And forgets the covenant of her God;
18 For her house sinks down to death,
And her tracks *lead* to the dead;
19 None who go to her return again,
Nor do they reach the paths of life.
20 So you will walk in the way of good men,
And keep to the paths of the righteous.
21 For the upright will live in the land,
And the blameless will remain in it;
22 But the wicked will be cut off from the land,
And the treacherous will be uprooted from it.

*The Rewards of Wisdom*

3 MY SON, do not forget my teaching,
But let your heart keep my commandments;
2 For length of days and years of life,
And peace they will add to you.
3 Do not let kindness and truth leave you;
Bind them around your neck,
Write them on the tablet of your heart.
4 So you will find favor and good repute
In the sight of God and man.
5 Trust in the LORD with all your heart,
And do not lean on your own understanding.
6 In all your ways acknowledge Him,
And He will make your paths straight.
7 Do not be wise in your own eyes;
Fear the LORD and turn away from evil.
8 It will be healing to your body,
And refreshment to your bones.
9 Honor the LORD from your wealth,
And from the first of all your produce;
10 So your barns will be filled with plenty,
And your vats will overflow with new wine.
11 My son, do not reject the discipline of the LORD,
Or loathe His reproof,
12 For whom the LORD loves He reproves,
Even as a father, the son in whom he delights.
13¶ How blessed is the man who finds wisdom,
And the man who gains understanding.
14 For its profit is better than the profit of silver,
And its gain than fine gold.
15 She is more precious than jewels;
And nothing you desire compares with her.
16 Long life is in her right hand;
In her left hand are riches and honor.
17 Her ways are pleasant ways,
And all her paths are peace.
18 She is a tree of life to those who take hold of her,
And happy are all who hold her fast.
19 The LORD by wisdom founded the earth;
By understanding He established the heavens.
20 By His knowledge the deeps were broken up,
And the skies drip with dew.
21 My son, let them not depart from your sight;
Keep sound wisdom and discretion,

## New International

16It will save you also from the adulteress,
from the wayward wife with her seductive words,
17who has left the partner of her youth
and ignored the covenant she made before God.[b]
18For her house leads down to death
and her paths to the spirits of the dead.
19None who go to her return
or attain the paths of life.

20Thus you will walk in the ways of good men
and keep to the paths of the righteous.
21For the upright will live in the land,
and the blameless will remain in it;
22but the wicked will be cut off from the land,
and the unfaithful will be torn from it.

*Further Benefits of Wisdom*

3 MY SON, do not forget my teaching,
but keep my commands in your heart,
2for they will prolong your life many years
and bring you prosperity.

3Let love and faithfulness never leave you;
bind them around your neck,
write them on the tablet of your heart.
4Then you will win favor and a good name
in the sight of God and man.

5Trust in the LORD with all your heart
and lean not on your own understanding;
6in all your ways acknowledge him,
and he will make your paths straight.[c]

7Do not be wise in your own eyes;
fear the LORD and shun evil.
8This will bring health to your body
and nourishment to your bones.

9Honor the LORD with your wealth,
with the firstfruits of all your crops;
10then your barns will be filled to overflowing,
and your vats will brim over with new wine.

11My son, do not despise the LORD's discipline
and do not resent his rebuke,
12because the LORD disciplines those he loves,
as a father[d] the son he delights in.

13Blessed is the man who finds wisdom,
the man who gains understanding,
14for she is more profitable than silver
and yields better returns than gold.
15She is more precious than rubies;
nothing you desire can compare with her.
16Long life is in her right hand;
in her left hand are riches and honor.
17Her ways are pleasant ways,
and all her paths are peace.
18She is a tree of life to those who embrace her;
those who lay hold of her will be blessed.

19By wisdom the LORD laid the earth's foundations,
by understanding he set the heavens in place;
20by his knowledge the deeps were divided,
and the clouds let drop the dew.

21My son, preserve sound judgment and discernment,
do not let them out of your sight;

NIV [b] 17 Or *covenant of her God* [c] 6 Or *will direct your paths* [d] 12 Hebrew; Septuagint / *and he punishes*

## King James

22 So shall they be life unto thy soul, and grace to thy neck.
23 Then shalt thou walk in thy way safely, and thy foot shall not stumble.
24 When thou liest down, thou shalt not be afraid: yea, thou shalt lie down, and thy sleep shall be sweet.
25 Be not afraid of sudden fear, neither of the desolation of the wicked, when it cometh.
26 For the LORD shall be thy confidence, and shall keep thy foot from being taken.
27 ¶ Withhold not good from them to whom it is due, when it is in the power of thine hand to do *it*.
28 Say not unto thy neighbour, Go, and come again, and tomorrow I will give; when thou hast it by thee.
29 Devise not evil against thy neighbour, seeing he dwelleth securely by thee.
30 ¶ Strive not with a man without cause, if he have done thee no harm.
31 ¶ Envy thou not the oppressor, and choose none of his ways.
32 For the froward *is* abomination to the LORD: but his secret *is* with the righteous.
33 ¶ The curse of the LORD *is* in the house of the wicked: but he blesseth the habitation of the just.
34 Surely he scorneth the scorners: but he giveth grace unto the lowly.
35 The wise shall inherit glory: but shame shall be the promotion of fools.

**4** HEAR, YE children, the instruction of a father, and attend to know understanding.
2 For I give you good doctrine, forsake ye not my law.
3 For I was my father's son, tender and only *beloved* in the sight of my mother.
4 He taught me also, and said unto me, Let thine heart retain my words: keep my commandments, and live.
5 Get wisdom, get understanding: forget *it* not; neither decline from the words of my mouth.
6 Forsake her not, and she shall preserve thee: love her, and she shall keep thee.
7 Wisdom *is* the principal thing; *therefore* get wisdom: and with all thy getting get understanding.
8 Exalt her, and she shall promote thee: she shall bring thee to honour, when thou dost embrace her.
9 She shall give to thine head an ornament of grace: a crown of glory shall she deliver to thee.
10 Hear, O my son, and receive my sayings; and the years of thy life shall be many.
11 I have taught thee in the way of wisdom; I have led thee in right paths.

## Amplified

22 And they will be life to your inner self, and a gracious ornament to your neck [your outer self].
23 Then you will walk on your way securely *and* in confident trust, and your shall not dash your foot *or* stumble. [Prov. 10:9; Ps. 91:11, 12.]
24 When you lie down you shall not be afraid; yes, you shall lie down and your sleep shall be sweet.
25 Be not afraid of sudden terror *and* panic, nor of the stormy blast *or* the storm and ruin of the wicked when it comes [for you will be guiltless],
26 For the Lord shall be your confidence, firm *and* strong, and shall keep your foot from being caught [in a trap or hidden danger].
27 Withhold not good from those to whom it is due [its rightful owners], when it is in the power of your hand to do it. [Rom. 13:7; Gal. 6:10.]
28 Do not say to your neighbor, Go, and come again, and tomorrow I will give it, when you have it with you. [Lev. 19:13; Deut. 24:15.]
29 Do not contrive *or* dig up *or* cultivate evil against your neighbor, who dwells trustingly *and* confidently beside you.
30 Contend not with a man for no reason, when he has done you no wrong. [Rom. 12:18.]
31 Do not resentfully envy *and* be jealous of an unscrupulous, grasping man, and choose none of his ways. [Prov. 24:1; Pss. 37:1; 73:3.]
32 For the perverse are an abomination—extremely disgusting and detestable—to the Lord; but His confidential communion *and* secret counsel are with the uncompromisingly righteous—those who are upright and in right standing with Him. [Ps. 25:14.]
33 The curse of the Lord is in *and* on the house of the wicked, but He declares blessed—joyful and favored with blessings—the home of the just *and* consistently righteous. [Ps. 37:22; Zech. 5:4; Mal. 2:2.]
34 Though He scoffs at the scoffers *and* scorns the scorners, yet He gives His undeserved favor to the low [in rank], the humble *and* the afflicted. [James 4:6; I Pet. 5:5.]
35 The wise shall inherit glory—all honor and good; but shame is the highest rank conferred on [self-confident] fools. [Isa. 32:6.]

**4** HEAR, MY sons, the instruction of a father, and give attention to gain *and* to know intelligent discernment, comprehension *and* interpretation [of spiritual matters].
2 For I give you good doctrine—what is to be received; do not forsake my teaching.
3 When I [Solomon] was a son with my father [David], tender and the only one in the sight of my mother [Bathsheba],
4 He taught me, and said to me, Let your heart hold fast my words; keep my commandments and live. [I Chron. 28:9; Eph. 6:4.]
5 Get skillful *and* godly Wisdom, get understanding—discernment, comprehension and interpretation; do not forget, and do not turn back from the words of my mouth.
6 Forsake not [Wisdom] and she will keep, defend *and* protect you; love her and she will guard you.
7 The beginning of Wisdom is, get Wisdom—skillful and godly Wisdom! For skillful *and* godly Wisdom is the principal thing. And with all you have gotten get understanding—discernment, comprehension and interpretation. [James 1:5.]
8 Prize Wisdom highly *and* exalt her, and she will exalt *and* promote you; she will bring you to honor when you embrace her.
9 She shall give to your head a wreath of gracefulness; a crown of beauty *and* glory will she deliver to you.
10 Hear, O my son, and receive my sayings, and the years of your life shall be many.
11 I have taught you in the way of skillful *and* godly Wisdom [which is comprehensive insight into the ways and purposes of God]; I have led you in paths of uprightness.

## New American Standard

22 So they will be life to your soul,
And adornment to your neck.
23 Then you will walk in your way securely,
And your foot will not stumble.
24 When you lie down, you will not be afraid;
When you lie down, your sleep will be sweet.
25 Do not be afraid of sudden fear,
Nor of the onslaught of the wicked when it comes;
26 For the LORD will be your confidence,
And will keep your foot from being caught.

27¶ Do not withhold good from those to whom it is due,
When it is in your power to do *it*.
28 Do not say to your neighbor, "Go, and come back,
And tomorrow I will give *it*,"
When you have it with you.
29 Do not devise harm against your neighbor,
While he lives in security beside you.
30 Do not contend with a man without cause,
If he has done you no harm.
31 Do not envy a man of violence,
And do not choose any of his ways.
32 For the crooked *man* is an abomination to the LORD;
But He is intimate with the upright.
33 The curse of the LORD is on the house of the wicked,
But He blesses the dwelling of the righteous.
34 Though He scoffs at the scoffers,
Yet He gives grace to the afflicted.
35 The wise will inherit honor,
But fools display dishonor.

### *A Father's Instruction*

4 HEAR, *O* sons, the instruction of a father,
And give attention that you may gain understanding,
2 For I give you sound teaching;
Do not abandon my instruction.
3 When I was a son to my father,
Tender and the only son in the sight of my mother,
4 Then he taught me and said to me,
"Let your heart hold fast my words;
Keep my commandments and live;
5 Acquire wisdom! Acquire understanding!
Do not forget, nor turn away from the words of my mouth.
6 "Do not forsake her, and she will guard you;
Love her, and she will watch over you.
7 "The beginning of wisdom *is:* Acquire wisdom;
And with all your acquiring, get understanding.
8 "Prize her, and she will exalt you;
She will honor you if you embrace her.
9 "She will place on your head a garland of grace;
She will present you with a crown of beauty."

10¶ Hear, my son, and accept my sayings,
And the years of your life will be many.
11 I have directed you in the way of wisdom;
I have led you in upright paths.

## New International

22they will be life for you,
an ornament to grace your neck.
23Then you will go on your way in safety,
and your foot will not stumble;
24when you lie down, you will not be afraid;
when you lie down, your sleep will be sweet.
25Have no fear of sudden disaster
or of the ruin that overtakes the wicked,
26for the LORD will be your confidence
and will keep your foot from being snared.

27Do not withhold good from those who deserve it,
when it is in your power to act.
28Do not say to your neighbor,
"Come back later; I'll give it tomorrow"—
when you now have it with you.
29Do not plot harm against your neighbor,
who lives trustfully near you.
30Do not accuse a man for no reason—
when he has done you no harm.

31Do not envy a violent man
or choose any of his ways,
32for the LORD detests a perverse man
but takes the upright into his confidence.

33The LORD's curse is on the house of the wicked,
but he blesses the home of the righteous.
34He mocks proud mockers
but gives grace to the humble.
35The wise inherit honor,
but fools he holds up to shame.

### *Wisdom Is Supreme*

4 LISTEN, MY sons, to a father's instruction;
pay attention and gain understanding.
2I give you sound learning,
so do not forsake my teaching.
3When I was a boy in my father's house,
still tender, and an only child of my mother,
4he taught me and said,
"Lay hold of my words with all your heart;
keep my commands and you will live.
5Get wisdom, get understanding;
do not forget my words or swerve from them.
6Do not forsake wisdom, and she will protect you;
love her, and she will watch over you.
7Wisdom is supreme; therefore get wisdom.
Though it cost all you have,[a] get understanding.
8Esteem her, and she will exalt you;
embrace her, and she will honor you.
9She will set a garland of grace on your head
and present you with a crown of splendor."

10Listen, my son, accept what I say,
and the years of your life will be many.
11I guide you in the way of wisdom
and lead you along straight paths.

NIV [a] 7 Or *Whatever else you get*

## King James

12 When thou goest, thy steps shall not be straitened; and when
thou runnest, thou shalt not stumble.
13 Take fast hold of instruction; let *her* not go: keep her; for she
*is* thy life.
14¶ Enter not into the path of the wicked, and go not in the way
of evil *men*.
15 Avoid it, pass not by it, turn from it, and pass away.
16 For they sleep not, except they have done mischief; and their
sleep is taken away, unless they cause *some* to fall.
17 For they eat the bread of wickedness, and drink the wine of
violence.
18 But the path of the just *is* as the shining light, that shineth
more and more unto the perfect day.
19 The way of the wicked *is* as darkness: they know not at what
they stumble.
20¶ My son, attend to my words; incline thine ear unto my
sayings.
21 Let them not depart from thine eyes; keep them in the midst
of thine heart.
22 For they *are* life unto those that find them, and health to all
their flesh.
23¶ Keep thy heart with all diligence; for out of it *are* the issues
of life.
24 Put away from thee a froward mouth, and perverse lips put
far from thee.
25 Let thine eyes look right on, and let thine eyelids look straight
before thee.
26 Ponder the path of thy feet, and let all thy ways be established.
27 Turn not to the right hand nor to the left: remove thy foot from
evil.

## Amplified

12 When you walk, your steps shall not be hampered—your
path will be clear and open; and when you run you shall not
stumble.
13 Take fast hold of instruction, do not let go; guard her, for she
is your life.
14 Enter not into the path of the wicked, and go not in the way
of evil men.
15 Avoid it, do not go on it; turn from it and pass on.
16 For they cannot sleep unless they have caused trouble *or*
vexation; their sleep is taken away unless they have caused someone to fall.
17 For they eat the bread of wickedness and drink the wine of
violence.
18 But the path of the uncompromisingly just *and* righteous is
like the light of dawn, that shines more and more—brighter and
clearer—until [it reaches its full strength and glory in] the perfect
(to-be-prepared) day. [Matt. 5:14; Phil. 2:15; II Sam. 23:4.]
19 The way of the wicked is as deep darkness; they do not know
at what they stumble. [John 12:35.]
20 My son, attend to my words; consent *and* submit to my sayings.
21 Let them not depart from your sight; keep them in the center
of your heart.
22 For they are life to those who find them, healing *and* health
to all their flesh.
23 Keep your heart with all vigilance *and* above all that you
guard, for out of it flow the springs of life.
24 Put away from you false *and* dishonest speech, and willful *and*
contrary talk put far from you.
25 Let your eyes look right on [with fixed purpose], and let your
gaze be straight before you.
26 Consider well the path of your feet, and let all your ways be
established *and* ordered aright.
27 Turn not aside to the right hand or to the left; remove your
foot from evil.

**5** MY SON, attend unto my wisdom, *and* bow thine ear to my
understanding:
2 That thou mayest regard discretion, and *that* thy lips may keep
knowledge.
3¶ For the lips of a strange woman drop *as* an honeycomb, and
her mouth *is* smoother than oil:
4 But her end is bitter as wormwood, sharp as a twoedged
sword.
5 Her feet go down to death; her steps take hold on hell.
6 Lest thou shouldest ponder the path of life, her ways are
moveable, *that* thou canst not know *them*.
7 Hear me now therefore, O ye children, and depart not from the
words of my mouth.
8 Remove thy way far from her, and come not nigh the door of
her house:
9 Lest thou give thine honour unto others, and thy years unto
the cruel:
10 Lest strangers be filled with thy wealth; and thy labours *be* in
the house of a stranger;
11 And thou mourn at the last, when thy flesh and thy body are
consumed,
12 And say, How have I hated instruction, and my heart despised reproof;
13 And have not obeyed the voice of my teachers, nor inclined
mine ear to them that instructed me!

**5** MY SON, be attentive to my wisdom [learned by actual and
costly experience], and incline your ear to my understanding
[of what is becoming and prudent for you];
2 That you may exercise proper discrimination *and* discretion,
and your lips guard *and* keep knowledge *and* the wise answer [to
temptation].
3 For the lips of a loose woman drip honey as a honeycomb, and
her mouth is smoother than oil; [II Pet. 2:14-17; Ezek. 20:30; Col.
2:8-10.]
4 But in the end she is bitter as wormwood, sharp as a two-edged
*and* devouring sword.
5 Her feet go down to death; her steps take hold of Sheol
(Hades)—the place of the dead.
6 She loses sight of *and* walks not in the path of life; her ways
wind about aimlessly, and you cannot know them.
7 Now therefore, my sons, listen to me, and depart not from the
words of my mouth.
8 Let your way in life be far from her; and come not near the door
of her house—avoid the very scenes of temptation; [Prov. 4:15;
Rom. 16:17; I Thess. 5:19-22.]
9 Lest you give your honor to others, and your years to those
without mercy;
10 Lest strangers [and false teachings] take their fill of your
strength *and* wealth, and your labors go to the house of an alien
[from God];
11 And you groan *and* mourn when your end comes, when your
flesh and body are consumed,
12 And you say, How I hated instruction *and* discipline, and my
heart despised reproof!
13 I have not obeyed the voice of my teachers, nor submitted *and*
consented to those who instructed me.

## New American Standard

12 When you walk, your steps will not be impeded;
And if you run, you will not stumble.
13 Take hold of instruction; do not let go.
Guard her, for she is your life.
14 Do not enter the path of the wicked,
And do not proceed in the way of evil men.
15 Avoid it, do not pass by it;
Turn away from it and pass on.
16 For they cannot sleep unless they do evil;
And they are robbed of sleep unless they make *someone* stumble.
17 For they eat the bread of wickedness,
And drink the wine of violence.
18 But the path of the righteous is like the light of dawn,
That shines brighter and brighter until the full day.
19 The way of the wicked is like darkness;
They do not know over what they stumble.

20 ¶ My son, give attention to my words;
Incline your ear to my sayings.
21 Do not let them depart from your sight;
Keep them in the midst of your heart.
22 For they are life to those who find them,
And health to all their whole body.
23 Watch over your heart with all diligence,
For from it *flow* the springs of life.
24 Put away from you a deceitful mouth,
And put devious lips far from you.
25 Let your eyes look directly ahead,
And let your gaze be fixed straight in front of you.
26 Watch the path of your feet,
And all your ways will be established.
27 Do not turn to the right nor to the left;
Turn your foot from evil.

*Pitfalls of Immorality*

5 MY SON, give attention to my wisdom,
Incline your ear to my understanding;
2 That you may observe discretion,
And your lips may reserve knowledge.
3 For the lips of an adulteress drip honey,
And smoother than oil is her speech;
4 But in the end she is bitter as wormwood,
Sharp as a two-edged sword.
5 Her feet go down to death,
Her steps lay hold of Sheol.
6 She does not ponder the path of life;
Her ways are unstable, she does not know *it*.

7¶ Now then, *my* sons, listen to me,
And do not depart from the words of my mouth.
8 Keep your way far from her,
And do not go near the door of her house,
9 Lest you give your vigor to others,
And your years to the cruel one;
10 Lest strangers be filled with your strength,
And your hard-earned goods *go* to the house of an alien;
11 And you groan at your latter end,
When your flesh and your body are consumed;
12 And you say, "How I have hated instruction!
And my heart spurned reproof!
13 "And I have not listened to the voice of my teachers,
Nor inclined my ear to my instructors!

## New International

12When you walk, your steps will not be hampered;
when you run, you will not stumble.
13Hold on to instruction, do not let it go;
guard it well, for it is your life.
14Do not set foot on the path of the wicked
or walk in the way of evil men.
15Avoid it, do not travel on it;
turn from it and go on your way.
16For they cannot sleep till they do evil;
they are robbed of slumber till they make someone fall.
17They eat the bread of wickedness
and drink the wine of violence.

18The path of the righteous is like the first gleam of dawn,
shining ever brighter till the full light of day.
19But the way of the wicked is like deep darkness;
they do not know what makes them stumble.

20My son, pay attention to what I say;
listen closely to my words.
21Do not let them out of your sight,
keep them within your heart;
22for they are life to those who find them
and health to a man's whole body.
23Above all else, guard your heart,
for it is the wellspring of life.
24Put away perversity from your mouth;
keep corrupt talk far from your lips.
25Let your eyes look straight ahead,
fix your gaze directly before you.
26Make level[a] paths for your feet
and take only ways that are firm.
27Do not swerve to the right or the left;
keep your foot from evil.

*Warning Against Adultery*

5 MY SON, pay attention to my wisdom,
listen well to my words of insight,
2that you may maintain discretion
and your lips may preserve knowledge.
3For the lips of an adulteress drip honey,
and her speech is smoother than oil;
4but in the end she is bitter as gall,
sharp as a double-edged sword.
5Her feet go down to death;
her steps lead straight to the grave.[b]
6She gives no thought to the way of life;
her paths are crooked, but she knows it not.

7Now then, my sons, listen to me;
do not turn aside from what I say.
8Keep to a path far from her,
do not go near the door of her house,
9lest you give your best strength to others
and your years to one who is cruel,
10lest strangers feast on your wealth
and your toil enrich another man's house.
11At the end of your life you will groan,
when your flesh and body are spent.
12You will say, "How I hated discipline!
How my heart spurned correction!
13I would not obey my teachers
or listen to my instructors.

NIV [a] 26 Or *Consider the* [b] 5 Hebrew *Sheol*

## King James

14I was almost in all evil in the midst of the congregation and assembly.

15¶ Drink waters out of thine own cistern, and running waters out of thine own well.

16Let thy fountains be dispersed abroad, *and* rivers of waters in the streets.

17Let them be only thine own, and not strangers' with thee.

18Let thy fountain be blessed: and rejoice with the wife of thy youth.

19 *Let her be as* the loving hind and pleasant roe; let her breasts satisfy thee at all times; and be thou ravished always with her love.

20And why wilt thou, my son, be ravished with a strange woman, and embrace the bosom of a stranger?

21For the ways of man *are* before the eyes of the LORD, and he pondereth all his goings.

22¶ His own iniquities shall take the wicked himself, and he shall be holden with the cords of his sins.

23He shall die without instruction; and in the greatness of his folly he shall go astray.

**6** MY SON, if thou be surety for thy friend, *if* thou hast stricken thy hand with a stranger,

2Thou art snared with the words of thy mouth, thou art taken with the words of thy mouth.

3Do this now, my son, and deliver thyself, when thou art come into the hand of thy friend; go, humble thyself, and make sure thy friend.

4Give not sleep to thine eyes, nor slumber to thine eyelids.

5Deliver thyself as a roe from the hand *of the hunter,* and as a bird from the hand of the fowler.

6¶ Go to the ant, thou sluggard; consider her ways, and be wise:

7Which having no guide, overseer, or ruler,

8Provideth her meat in the summer, *and* gathereth her food in the harvest.

9How long wilt thou sleep, O sluggard? when wilt thou arise out of thy sleep?

10 *Yet* a little sleep, a little slumber, a little folding of the hands to sleep:

11So shall thy poverty come as one that travelleth, and thy want as an armed man.

12¶ A naughty person, a wicked man, walketh with a froward mouth.

13He winketh with his eyes, he speaketh with his feet, he teacheth with his fingers;

14Frowardness *is* in his heart, he deviseth mischief continually; he soweth discord.

15Therefore shall his calamity come suddenly; suddenly shall he be broken without remedy.

16¶ These six *things* doth the LORD hate: yea, seven *are* an abomination unto him:

17A proud look, a lying tongue, and hands that shed innocent blood,

**AMP** [a] All of the Ten Commandments are reflected in the Proverbs; here it is the seventh, "You shall not commit adultery." [b] The Bible consistently teaches that one is not to forsake a friend, and this passage is not to be otherwise construed. But it is one thing to lend a friend money, and quite another thing to promise to pay his debts for him if he fails to do so himself. It might cost one, under the rigid customary law for debt, his money, his land, his bed, his clothing; and if these were not sufficient he and his wife and children could be sold as slaves, not to be released until the next year of Jubilee—fifty years after the previous one. God's Word is very plain on the subject of not underwriting another person's debts. See Prov. 11:15; 17:18; 22:26.

## Amplified

14[The extent and boldness of] my sin involved almost all evil *in the estimation* of the congregation *and* the community.

15 [a]Drink waters out of your own cistern [of pure marriage relationship], and fresh running waters out of your own well.

16Should your offspring be dispersed abroad as water-brooks in the streets?

17[Confine yourself to your own wife] let your children be for you alone, and not the children of strangers with you.

18Let your fountain—of human life—be blessed [with the rewards of fidelity], and rejoice with the wife of your youth.

19Let her be as the loving hind and pleasant doe [tender, gentle, attractive]; let her bosom satisfy you at all times; and always be transported with delight in her love.

20Why should you, my son, be infatuated with a loose woman, embrace the bosom of an outsider, *and* go astray?

21For the ways of man are directly before the eyes of the Lord, and He [Who would have us live soberly, chastely and godly] carefully weighs all man's goings. [Prov. 15:3; II Chron. 16:9; Job 31:4; 34:21; Jer. 16:17; Hos. 7:2; Heb. 4:13.]

22His own iniquities shall ensnare the wicked, and he shall be held with the cords of his sin.

23He will die for lack of discipline *and* instruction, and in the greatness of his folly he will go astray *and* be lost.

**6** MY SON, if you have become security for your neighbor, if you have given your pledge for a stranger *or* another,

2You are snared with the words of your lips, you are caught in the speech of your mouth.

3Do this now [at once and earnestly], my son, and deliver yourself, when you have put yourself into the [b]power of your neighbor; go, bestir *and* humble yourself, and beg your neighbor [to pay his debt and release you].

4Give not [unnecessary] sleep to your eyes, nor slumber to your eyelids;

5Deliver yourself as a roe *or* gazelle would from the hand of the hunter, and as a bird from the hand of the fowler.

6Go to the ant, you sluggard; consider her ways, and be wise; [Job 12:7.]

7Which having no chief, overseer, or ruler,

8Provides her food in the summer, and gathers her supplies in the harvest.

9How long will you sleep, O sluggard? When will you arise out of your sleep? [Prov. 24:33, 34.]

10Yet a little sleep, a little slumber, a little folding of the hands to lie down *and* sleep;

11So will your poverty come as a robber *or* one who travels [with slow but surely approaching steps], and your want as an armed man [making you helpless]. [Prov. 10:4; 13:4; 20:4.]

12A worthless person, a wicked man is he who goes about with a perverse [contrary, wayward] mouth.

13He winks with his eyes, he speaks by shuffling *or* tapping with his feet, he makes signs [to mislead and deceive] *and* teaches with his fingers.

14Willful *and* contrary in his heart, he devises trouble, vexation *and* evil continually; he lets loose discord, *and* sows it.

15Therefore upon him shall the crushing weight of calamity come suddenly; suddenly shall he be broken and that without remedy.

16These six things the Lord hates; indeed, seven are an abomination to Him:

17A proud look [the spirit that makes one overestimate himself and underestimate others], a lying tongue, and hands that shed innocent blood, [Ps. 120:2, 3.]

## New American Standard

14 "I was almost in utter ruin
In the midst of the assembly and congregation."
15¶ Drink water from your own cistern,
And fresh water from your own well.
16 Should your springs be dispersed abroad,
Streams of water in the streets?
17 Let them be yours alone,
And not for strangers with you.
18 Let your fountain be blessed,
And rejoice in the wife of your youth.
19 *As* a loving hind and a graceful doe,
Let her breasts satisfy you at all times;
Be exhilarated always with her love.
20 For why should you, my son, be exhilarated with an adulteress,
And embrace the bosom of a foreigner?
21 For the ways of a man are before the eyes of the LORD,
And He watches all his paths.
22 His own iniquities will capture the wicked,
And he will be held with the cords of his sin.
23 He will die for lack of instruction,
And in the greatness of his folly he will go astray.

*Parental Counsel*

6 MY SON, if you have become surety for your neighbor,
Have given a pledge for a stranger,
2 *If* you have been snared with the words of your mouth,
Have been caught with the words of your mouth,
3 Do this then, my son, and deliver yourself;
Since you have come into the hand of your neighbor,
Go, humble yourself, and importune your neighbor.
4 Do not give sleep to your eyes,
Nor slumber to your eyelids;
5 Deliver yourself like a gazelle from *the hunter's* hand,
And like a bird from the hand of the fowler.
6¶ Go to the ant, O sluggard,
Observe her ways and be wise,
7 Which, having no chief,
Officer or ruler,
8 Prepares her food in the summer,
*And* gathers her provision in the harvest.
9 How long will you lie down, O sluggard?
When will you arise from your sleep?
10 "A little sleep, a little slumber,
A little folding of the hands to rest"—
11 And your poverty will come in like a vagabond,
And your need like an armed man.
12¶ A worthless person, a wicked man,
Is the one who walks with a false mouth,
13 Who winks with his eyes, who signals with his feet,
Who points with his fingers;
14 Who *with* perversity in his heart devises evil continually,
Who spreads strife.
15 Therefore his calamity will come suddenly;
Instantly he will be broken, and there will be no healing.
16¶ There are six things which the LORD hates,
Yes, seven which are an abomination to Him:
17 Haughty eyes, a lying tongue,
And hands that shed innocent blood,

## New International

14I have come to the brink of utter ruin
in the midst of the whole assembly."
15Drink water from your own cistern,
running water from your own well.
16Should your springs overflow in the streets,
your streams of water in the public squares?
17Let them be yours alone,
never to be shared with strangers.
18May your fountain be blessed,
and may you rejoice in the wife of your youth.
19A loving doe, a graceful deer—
may her breasts satisfy you always,
may you ever be captivated by her love.
20Why be captivated, my son, by an adulteress?
Why embrace the bosom of another man's wife?
21For a man's ways are in full view of the LORD,
and he examines all his paths.
22The evil deeds of a wicked man ensnare him;
the cords of his sin hold him fast.
23He will die for lack of discipline,
led astray by his own great folly.

*Warnings Against Folly*

6 MY SON, if you have put up security for your neighbor,
if you have struck hands in pledge for another,
2if you have been trapped by what you said,
ensnared by the words of your mouth,
3then do this, my son, to free yourself,
since you have fallen into your neighbor's hands:
Go and humble yourself;
press your plea with your neighbor!
4Allow no sleep to your eyes,
no slumber to your eyelids.
5Free yourself, like a gazelle from the hand of the hunter,
like a bird from the snare of the fowler.

6Go to the ant, you sluggard;
consider its ways and be wise!
7It has no commander,
no overseer or ruler,
8yet it stores its provisions in summer
and gathers its food at harvest.

9How long will you lie there, you sluggard?
When will you get up from your sleep?
10A little sleep, a little slumber,
a little folding of the hands to rest—
11and poverty will come on you like a bandit
and scarcity like an armed man.[c]

12A scoundrel and villain,
who goes about with a corrupt mouth,
13 who winks with his eye,
signals with his feet
and motions with his fingers,
14 who plots evil with deceit in his heart—
he always stirs up dissension.
15Therefore disaster will overtake him in an instant;
he will suddenly be destroyed—without remedy.

16There are six things the LORD hates,
seven that are detestable to him:
17 haughty eyes,
a lying tongue,
hands that shed innocent blood,

**NIV** [c] *11* Or *like a vagrant / and scarcity like a beggar*

## King James

18An heart that deviseth wicked imaginations, feet that be swift
in running to mischief,
19A false witness *that* speaketh lies, and he that soweth discord
among brethren.
20¶ My son, keep thy father's commandment, and forsake not
the law of thy mother:
21Bind them continually upon thine heart, *and* tie them about
thy neck.
22When thou goest, it shall lead thee; when thou sleepest, it
shall keep thee; and *when* thou awakest, it shall talk with thee.
23For the commandment *is* a lamp; and the law *is* light; and
reproofs of instruction *are* the way of life:
24To keep thee from the evil woman, from the flattery of the
tongue of a strange woman.
25Lust not after her beauty in thine heart; neither let her take
thee with her eyelids.
26For by means of a whorish woman *a man is brought* to a piece
of bread: and the adulteress will hunt for the precious life.
27Can a man take fire in his bosom, and his clothes not be
burned?
28Can one go upon hot coals, and his feet not be burned?
29So he that goeth in to his neighbour's wife; whosoever
toucheth her shall not be innocent.
30 *Men* do not despise a thief, if he steal to satisfy his soul when
he is hungry;
31But *if* he be found, he shall restore sevenfold; he shall give all
the substance of his house.
32 *But* whoso committeth adultery with a woman lacketh understanding: he *that* doeth it destroyeth his own soul.
33A wound and dishonour shall he get; and his reproach shall
not be wiped away.
34For jealousy *is* the rage of a man: therefore he will not spare
in the day of vengeance.
35He will not regard any ransom; neither will he rest content,
though thou givest many gifts.

7 MY SON, keep my words, and lay up my commandments
with thee.
2Keep my commandments, and live; and my law as the apple
of thine eye.
3Bind them upon thy fingers, write them upon the table of thine
heart.
4Say unto wisdom, Thou *art* my sister; and call understanding
*thy* kinswoman:
5That they may keep thee from the strange woman, from the
stranger *which* flattereth with her words.
6¶ For at the window of my house I looked through my case-
ment,
7And beheld among the simple ones, I discerned among the
youths, a young man void of understanding,
8Passing through the street near her corner; and he went the
way to her house,
9In the twilight, in the evening, in the black and dark night:
10And, behold, there met him a woman *with* the attire of an
harlot, and subtle of heart.

## Amplified

18A heart that manufactures wicked thought *and* plans, feet that
are swift in running to evil,
19A false witness who breathes out lies [even under oath], and
he who sows discord among his brethren.
20My son, keep your father's [God-given] commandment, and
forsake not the law of [God] your mother [taught you]. [Eph.
6:1-3.]
21Bind them continually upon your heart, and tie them about
your neck. [Prov. 3:3; 7:3.]
22When you go, [the Word of your parents' God] it shall lead
you; when you sleep, it shall keep you, and when you waken, it
shall talk with you.
23For the commandment is a lamp, and the whole teaching *of*
the law is light, and reproofs of discipline are the way of life, [Pss.
19:8; 119:105.]
24To keep you from the evil woman, from the flattery of the
tongue of a loose woman.
25Lust not after her beauty in your heart, neither let her capture
you with her eyelids.
26For on account of a harlot a man is brought to a piece of bread,
and the adulteress will stalk *and* snare [as with a hook] the precious
life *of a man.*
27Can a man take fire in his bosom and his clothes not be
burned?
28Can one go upon hot coals and his feet not be burned?
29So he who cohabits with his neighbor's wife [will be tortured
with evil consequences and just retribution]; he who touches her
shall not be innocent *or* go unpunished.
30Men do not despise a thief, if he steals to satisfy himself when
he is hungry;
31But if he is found out, he must restore seven times [what he
stole]; he must give the whole substance of his house [if necessary
to meet his fine];
32But whoever commits adultery with a woman lacks heart *and*
understanding—moral principle and prudence; he who does it is
destroying his own life.
33Wounds and disgrace will he get, and his reproach will not
be wiped away.
34For jealousy makes [the wronged] man furious; therefore he
will not spare in the day of vengeance [upon the detected ones].
35He will not consider any ransom [offered to buy him off from
demanding full punishment], neither will he be satisfied though
you offer him many gifts *and* bribes.

7 MY SON, keep my words; lay up with you my commandments [for use when needed] *and* treasure them.
2Keep my commandments and live, and keep my law *and* teaching as the apple (the pupil) of your eye.
3Bind them upon your fingers, write them on the tablet of your
heart.
4Say to skillful *and* godly Wisdom, You are my sister, and regard
understanding *or* insight as your intimate friend;
5That they may keep you from the loose woman, from the
adventuress who flatters *and* makes smooth her words.
6For at the window of my house I looked out through my lattice,
7And among the simple [empty-headed and empty-hearted]
ones, I perceived among the youths a young man void of good
sense,
8Sauntering through the street near the [loose woman's] corner;
and he went the way to her house,
9In the twilight, in the evening; night black and dense was
falling [over the young man's life].
10And lo, there met him a woman dressed as a harlot, and sly
*and* cunning of heart.

## New American Standard

18 A heart that devises wicked plans,
Feet that run rapidly to evil,
19 A false witness *who* utters lies,
And one who spreads strife among brothers.

20¶ My son, observe the commandment of your father,
And do not forsake the teaching of your mother;
21 Bind them continually on your heart;
Tie them around your neck.
22 When you walk about, they will guide you;
When you sleep, they will watch over you;
And when you awake, they will talk to you.
23 For the commandment is a lamp, and the teaching is light;
And reproofs for discipline are the way of life,
24 To keep you from the evil woman,
From the smooth tongue of the adulteress.
25 Do not desire her beauty in your heart,
Nor let her catch you with her eyelids.
26 For on account of a harlot *one is reduced* to a loaf of bread,
And an adulteress hunts for the precious life.
27 Can a man take fire in his bosom,
And his clothes not be burned?
28 Or can a man walk on hot coals,
And his feet not be scorched?
29 So is the one who goes in to his neighbor's wife;
Whoever touches her will not go unpunished.
30 Men do not despise a thief if he steals
To satisfy himself when he is hungry;
31 But when he is found, he must repay sevenfold;
He must give all the substance of his house.
32 The one who commits adultery with a woman is lacking sense;
He who would destroy himself does it.
33 Wounds and disgrace he will find,
And his reproach will not be blotted out.
34 For jealousy enrages a man,
And he will not spare in the day of vengeance.
35 He will not accept any ransom,
Nor will he be content though you give many gifts.

*The Wiles of the Harlot*

**7** MY SON, keep my words,
And treasure my commandments within you.
2 Keep my commandments and live,
And my teaching as the apple of your eye.
3 Bind them on your fingers;
Write them on the tablet of your heart.
4 Say to wisdom, "You are my sister,"
And call understanding *your* intimate friend;
5 That they may keep you from an adulteress,
From the foreigner who flatters with her words.

6¶ For at the window of my house
I looked out through my lattice,
7 And I saw among the naive,
I discerned among the youths,
A young man lacking sense,
8 Passing through the street near her corner;
And he takes the way to her house,
9 In the twilight, in the evening,
In the middle of the night and *in* the darkness.
10 And behold, a woman *comes* to meet him,
Dressed as a harlot and cunning of heart.

## New International

18 a heart that devises wicked schemes,
feet that are quick to rush into evil,
19 a false witness who pours out lies
and a man who stirs up dissension among brothers.

*Warning Against Adultery*

20 My son, keep your father's commands
and do not forsake your mother's teaching.
21 Bind them upon your heart forever;
fasten them around your neck.
22 When you walk, they will guide you;
when you sleep, they will watch over you;
when you awake, they will speak to you.
23 For these commands are a lamp,
this teaching is a light,
and the corrections of discipline
are the way to life,
24 keeping you from the immoral woman,
from the smooth tongue of the wayward wife.
25 Do not lust in your heart after her beauty
or let her captivate you with her eyes,
26 for the prostitute reduces you to a loaf of bread,
and the adulteress preys upon your very life.
27 Can a man scoop fire into his lap
without his clothes being burned?
28 Can a man walk on hot coals
without his feet being scorched?
29 So is he who sleeps with another man's wife;
no one who touches her will go unpunished.

30 Men do not despise a thief if he steals
to satisfy his hunger when he is starving.
31 Yet if he is caught, he must pay sevenfold,
though it costs him all the wealth of his house.
32 But a man who commits adultery lacks judgment;
whoever does so destroys himself.
33 Blows and disgrace are his lot,
and his shame will never be wiped away;
34 for jealousy arouses a husband's fury,
and he will show no mercy when he takes revenge.
35 He will not accept any compensation;
he will refuse the bribe, however great it is.

*Warning Against the Adulteress*

**7** MY SON, keep my words
and store up my commands within you.
2 Keep my commands and you will live;
guard my teachings as the apple of your eye.
3 Bind them on your fingers;
write them on the tablet of your heart.
4 Say to wisdom, "You are my sister,"
and call understanding your kinsman;
5 they will keep you from the adulteress,
from the wayward wife with her seductive words.

6 At the window of my house
I looked out through the lattice.
7 I saw among the simple,
I noticed among the young men,
a youth who lacked judgment.
8 He was going down the street near her corner,
walking along in the direction of her house
9 at twilight, as the day was fading,
as the dark of night set in.

10 Then out came a woman to meet him,
dressed like a prostitute and with crafty intent.

# King James

11(She *is* loud and stubborn; her feet abide not in her house:
12Now *is she* without, now in the streets, and lieth in wait at
every corner.)
13So she caught him, and kissed him, *and* with an impudent face
said unto him,
14 *I have* peace offerings with me; this day have I paid my vows.
15Therefore came I forth to meet thee, diligently to seek thy
face, and I have found thee.
16I have decked my bed with coverings of tapestry, with carved
*works,* with fine linen of Egypt.
17I have perfumed my bed with myrrh, aloes, and cinnamon.
18Come, let us take our fill of love until the morning: let us
solace ourselves with loves.
19For the goodman *is* not at home, he is gone a long journey:
20He hath taken a bag of money with him, *and* will come home
at the day appointed.
21With her much fair speech she caused him to yield, with the
flattering of her lips she forced him.
22He goeth after her straightway, as an ox goeth to the slaughter, or as a fool to the correction of the stocks;
23Till a dart strike through his liver; as a bird hasteth to the
snare, and knoweth not that it *is* for his life.
24¶ Hearken unto me now therefore, O ye children, and attend
to the words of my mouth.
25Let not thine heart decline to her ways, go not astray in her
paths.
26For she hath cast down many wounded: yea, many strong
*men* have been slain by her.
27Her house *is* the way to hell, going down to the chambers of
death.

**8** DOTH NOT wisdom cry? and understanding put forth her
voice?
2She standeth in the top of high places, by the way in the places
of the paths.
3She crieth at the gates, at the entry of the city, at the coming
in at the doors.
4Unto you, O men, I call; and my voice *is* to the sons of man.
5O ye simple, understand wisdom: and, ye fools, be ye of an
understanding heart.
6Hear; for I will speak of excellent things; and the opening of
my lips *shall be* right things.
7For my mouth shall speak truth; and wickedness *is* an abomination to my lips.
8All the words of my mouth *are* in righteousness; *there is* nothing froward or perverse in them.
9They *are* all plain to him that understandeth, and right to them
that find knowledge.
10Receive my instruction, and not silver; and knowledge rather
than choice gold.
11For wisdom *is* better than rubies; and all the things that may
be desired are not to be compared to it.
12I wisdom dwell with prudence, and find out knowledge of
witty inventions.

# Amplified

11She is turbulent *and* willful; her feet stay not in her house;
12Now in the streets, now in the market places, she sets her
ambush at every corner.
13So she caught him and kissed him, and with impudent face
she said to him,
14Sacrifices of peace offerings were due from me; this day I paid
my vows.
15So I came forth to meet you [that you might share with me the
feast from my offering]; diligently I sought your face, and I have
found you.
16I have spread my couch with rugs *and* cushions of tapestry,
with striped sheets of fine linen of Egypt;
17I have perfumed my bed with myrrh, aloes, and cinnamon.
18Come, let us take our fill of love until the morning; let us
console *and* delight ourselves with love.
19For the man is not at home, he is gone on a long journey;
20He has taken a bag of money with him, and will come home
at the day appointed—at the full moon.
21With her much justifying *and* enticing argument she persuades him, with the allurements of her lips she leads him [to
overcome his conscience and his fears] *and* forces him along.
22Suddenly he *yields, and* follows her reluctantly, like an ox
moving to the slaughter, as one in fetters to the correction *to be
given* to a fool, [or [a]as a dog enticed by food to the muzzle];
23Till a dart [of passion] pierces *and* inflames his vitals; then like
a bird fluttering straight into the net, *he hastens,* not knowing that
it will cost his life.
24Listen to me now therefore, O you sons, and be attentive to
the words of my mouth.
25Let not your heart incline toward her ways, do not stray into
her paths.
26For she has cast down many wounded; indeed, all her slain
are a mighty host. [Neh. 13:26.]
27Her house is the way to Sheol [Hades, the place of the dead]
going down to the chambers of death.

**8** DOES NOT skillful *and* godly Wisdom cry out, and understanding raise her voice? [In contrast to the loose woman.]
2On the top of the heights beside the way where the paths meet,
stands Wisdom, skillful *and* godly;
3At the gates at the entrance of the town, at the coming in at
the doors she cries out:
4To you, O men, I call, and my voice is directed to the sons of
men.
5O you simple *and* thoughtless, understand prudence; and, you
[self-confident] fools, be of an understanding heart. [Isa. 32:6.]
6Hear, for I will speak excellent *and* princely things; and the
opening of my lips shall be for right things.
7For my mouth shall utter truth, and wrong-doing is detestable
*and* loathsome to my lips.
8All the words of my mouth are righteous—upright and in right
standing with God; there is nothing contrary to truth or crooked
in them.
9They are all plain to him who understands [and opens his
heart], and right to those who find knowledge [and live by it].
10Receive my instruction in preference to [striving for] silver,
and knowledge rather than choice gold;
11For skillful *and* godly Wisdom is better than rubies *or* pearls,
and all the things that may be desired are not to be compared to
it. [Job 28:15; Pss. 19:10; 119:127.]
12I, Wisdom [from God], have made prudence my dwelling,
and I find out knowledge and discretion. [James 1:5.]

**AMP** [a] *The Septuagint Version* (Greek) so reads at this point.

## New American Standard

11 She is boisterous and rebellious;
Her feet do not remain at home;
12 *She is* now in the streets, now in the squares,
And lurks by every corner.
13 So she seizes him and kisses him,
And with a brazen face she says to him:
14 "I was due to offer peace offerings;
Today I have paid my vows.
15 "Therefore I have come out to meet you,
To seek your presence earnestly, and I have found you.
16 "I have spread my couch with coverings,
With colored linens of Egypt.
17 "I have sprinkled my bed
With myrrh, aloes and cinnamon.
18 "Come, let us drink our fill of love until morning;
Let us delight ourselves with caresses.
19 "For the man is not at home,
He has gone on a long journey;
20 He has taken a bag of money with him,
At full moon he will come home."
21 With her many persuasions she entices him;
With her flattering lips she seduces him.
22 Suddenly he follows her,
As an ox goes to the slaughter,
Or as *one in* fetters to the discipline of a fool,
23 Until an arrow pierces through his liver;
As a bird hastens to the snare,
So he does not know that it *will cost him* his life.

24¶ Now therefore, *my* sons, listen to me,
And pay attention to the words of my mouth.
25 Do not let your heart turn aside to her ways,
Do not stray into her paths.
26 For many are the victims she has cast down,
And numerous are all her slain.
27 Her house is the way to Sheol,
Descending to the chambers of death.

*The Commendation of Wisdom*

8 DOES NOT wisdom call,
And understanding lift up her voice?
2 On top of the heights beside the way,
Where the paths meet, she takes her stand;
3 Beside the gates, at the opening to the city,
At the entrance of the doors, she cries out:
4 "To you, O men, I call,
And my voice is to the sons of men.
5 "O naive ones, discern prudence;
And, O fools, discern wisdom.
6 "Listen, for I shall speak noble things;
And the opening of my lips *will produce* right things.
7 "For my mouth will utter truth;
And wickedness is an abomination to my lips.
8 "All the utterances of my mouth are in righteousness;
There is nothing crooked or perverted in them.
9 "They are all straightforward to him who understands,
And right to those who find knowledge.
10 "Take my instruction, and not silver,
And knowledge rather than choicest gold.
11 "For wisdom is better than jewels;
And all desirable things can not compare with her.

12¶ "I, wisdom, dwell with prudence,
And I find knowledge *and* discretion.

## New International

11(She is loud and defiant,
her feet never stay at home;
12now in the street, now in the squares,
at every corner she lurks.)
13She took hold of him and kissed him
and with a brazen face she said:

14"I have fellowship offerings[b] at home;
today I fulfilled my vows.
15So I came out to meet you;
I looked for you and have found you!
16I have covered my bed
with colored linens from Egypt.
17I have perfumed my bed
with myrrh, aloes and cinnamon.
18Come, let's drink deep of love till morning;
let's enjoy ourselves with love!
19My husband is not at home;
he has gone on a long journey.
20He took his purse filled with money
and will not be home till full moon."

21With persuasive words she led him astray;
she seduced him with her smooth talk.
22All at once he followed her
like an ox going to the slaughter,
like a deer[c] stepping into a noose[d]
23 till an arrow pierces his liver,
like a bird darting into a snare,
little knowing it will cost him his life.

24Now then, my sons, listen to me;
pay attention to what I say.
25Do not let your heart turn to her ways
or stray into her paths.
26Many are the victims she has brought down;
her slain are a mighty throng.
27Her house is a highway to the grave,[e]
leading down to the chambers of death.

*Wisdom's Call*

8 DOES NOT wisdom call out?
Does not understanding raise her voice?
2On the heights along the way,
where the paths meet, she takes her stand;
3beside the gates leading into the city,
at the entrances, she cries aloud:
4"To you, O men, I call out;
I raise my voice to all mankind.
5You who are simple, gain prudence;
you who are foolish, gain understanding.
6Listen, for I have worthy things to say;
I open my lips to speak what is right.
7My mouth speaks what is true,
for my lips detest wickedness.
8All the words of my mouth are just;
none of them is crooked or perverse.
9To the discerning all of them are right;
they are faultless to those who have knowledge.
10Choose my instruction instead of silver,
knowledge rather than choice gold,
11for wisdom is more precious than rubies,
and nothing you desire can compare with her.

12"I, wisdom, dwell together with prudence;
I possess knowledge and discretion.

**NIV** [b] 14 Traditionally *peace offerings* [c] 22 Syriac (see also Septuagint); Hebrew *fool* [d] 22 The meaning of the Hebrew for this line is uncertain. [e] 27 Hebrew *Sheol*

# King James

13The fear of the LORD *is* to hate evil: pride, and arrogancy, and the evil way, and the froward mouth, do I hate.
14Counsel *is* mine, and sound wisdom: I *am* understanding; I have strength.
15By me kings reign, and princes decree justice.
16By me princes rule, and nobles, *even* all the judges of the earth.
17I love them that love me; and those that seek me early shall find me.
18Riches and honour *are* with me; *yea,* durable riches and righteousness.
19My fruit *is* better than gold, yea, than fine gold; and my revenue than choice silver.
20I lead in the way of righteousness, in the midst of the paths of judgment:
21That I may cause those that love me to inherit substance; and I will fill their treasures.
22The LORD possessed me in the beginning of his way, before his works of old.
23I was set up from everlasting, from the beginning, or ever the earth was.
24When *there were* no depths, I was brought forth; when *there were* no fountains abounding with water.
25Before the mountains were settled, before the hills was I brought forth:
26While as yet he had not made the earth, nor the fields, nor the highest part of the dust of the world.
27When he prepared the heavens, I *was* there: when he set a compass upon the face of the depth:
28When he established the clouds above: when he strengthened the fountains of the deep:
29When he gave to the sea his decree, that the waters should not pass his commandment: when he appointed the foundations of the earth:
30Then I was by him, *as* one brought up *with him:* and I was daily *his* delight, rejoicing always before him;
31Rejoicing in the habitable part of his earth; and my delights *were* with the sons of men.
32Now therefore hearken unto me, O ye children: for blessed *are they that* keep my ways.
33Hear instruction, and be wise, and refuse it not.
34Blessed *is* the man that heareth me, watching daily at my gates, waiting at the posts of my doors.
35For whoso findeth me findeth life, and shall obtain favour of the LORD.
36But he that sinneth against me wrongeth his own soul: all they that hate me love death.

9 WISDOM HATH builded her house, she hath hewn out her seven pillars:
2She hath killed her beasts; she hath mingled her wine; she hath also furnished her table.

# Amplified

13The reverent fear *and* worshipful awe of the Lord *includes* the hatred of evil. Pride, arrogance, the evil way, and perverted *and* twisted speech I hate.
14I have counsel and sound knowledge, I have understanding, I have might *and* power.
15By me kings reign, and rulers decree justice. [Dan. 2:21; Rom. 13:1.]
16By me princes rule, and nobles, even all the judges *and* governors of the earth.
17I love those who love me, and those who seek me early *and* diligently shall find me. [I Sam. 2:30; Ps. 91:14; John 14:21; James 1:5.]
18Riches and honor are with me, enduring wealth, and righteousness [that is, uprightness in every area and relation, and right standing with God]. [Prov. 3:16; Matt. 6:33.]
19My fruit is better than gold, yes, than refined gold, and my increase than choice silver.
20I [Wisdom] walk in the way of righteousness [of moral and spiritual rectitude in every area and relation], in the midst of the paths of justice,
21That I may cause those who love me to inherit [true] riches, and that I may fill their treasuries.
22The Lord formed *and* brought me [Wisdom] forth at the beginning of His way, before His acts of old.
23I [Wisdom] was inaugurated *and* ordained from everlasting, from the beginning, before ever the earth existed. [John 1:1; I Cor. 1:24.]
24When there were no deeps, I was brought forth, when there were no fountains laden with water.
25Before the mountains were settled, before the hills I was brought forth; [Job 15:7, 8.]
26While as yet He had not made land, or the fields, or the first of the dust of the earth.
27When He prepared the heavens, I [Wisdom] was there; when He drew a circle upon the face of the deep *and* stretched out the firmament over it,
28When He made firm the skies above, when He established the fountains of the deep,
29When He gave to the sea its limit *and* His decree that the waters should not transgress [across the boundaries set by] His command, when He appointed the foundations of the earth; [Job 38:10, 11; Ps. 104:6-9; Jer. 5:22.]
30Then I [Wisdom] was [a]beside Him as a master *and* director of the work; and I was daily His delight, rejoicing before Him always, [John 1:2, 18; Matt. 3:17.]
31Rejoicing in His inhabited earth and delighting in the sons of men. [Ps. 16:3.]
32Now therefore listen to me, O you sons; for blessed—happy, fortunate [to be envied]—are those who keep my ways. [Pss. 119:1, 2; 128:1, 2; Luke 11:28.]
33Hear instruction and be wise, and do not refuse *or* neglect it.
34Blessed—happy, fortunate [to be envied]—is the man who listens to me, watching daily at my gates, waiting at the posts of my doors.
35For whoever finds me [Wisdom] finds life, and shall draw forth *and* obtain favor of the Lord.
36But he who misses me *or* sins against me wrongs *and* injures himself; all who hate me love *and* court death.

9 WISDOM HAS built her house, she has hewn out *and* set up her seven [perfect number of] pillars.
2She has killed her beasts, she has mixed her [spiritual] wine, she has also set her table. [Matt. 22:2-4.]

**AMP** [a] Compare footnote on Prov. 1:23.

## New American Standard

13 "The fear of the LORD is to hate evil;
Pride and arrogance and the evil way,
And the perverted mouth, I hate.
14 "Counsel is mine and sound wisdom;
I am understanding, power is mine.
15 "By me kings reign,
And rulers decree justice.
16 "By me princes rule, and nobles,
All who judge rightly.
17 "I love those who love me;
And those who diligently seek me will find me.
18 "Riches and honor are with me,
Enduring wealth and righteousness.
19 "My fruit is better than gold, even pure gold,
And my yield than choicest silver.
20 "I walk in the way of righteousness,
In the midst of the paths of justice,
21 To endow those who love me with wealth,
That I may fill their treasuries.

22¶ "The LORD possessed me at the beginning of His way,
Before His works of old.
23 "From everlasting I was established,
From the beginning, from the earliest times of the earth.
24 "When there were no depths I was brought forth,
When there were no springs abounding with water.
25 "Before the mountains were settled,
Before the hills I was brought forth;
26 While He had not yet made the earth and the fields,
Nor the first dust of the world.
27 "When He established the heavens, I was there,
When He inscribed a circle on the face of the deep,
28 When He made firm the skies above,
When the springs of the deep became fixed,
29 When He set for the sea its boundary,
So that the water should not transgress His command,
When He marked out the foundations of the earth;
30 Then I was beside Him, *as* a master workman;
And I was daily *His* delight,
Rejoicing always before Him,
31 Rejoicing in the world, His earth,
And *having* my delight in the sons of men.

32¶ "Now therefore, *O* sons, listen to me,
For blessed are they who keep my ways.
33 "Heed instruction and be wise,
And do not neglect *it*.
34 "Blessed is the man who listens to me,
Watching daily at my gates,
Waiting at my doorposts.
35 "For he who finds me finds life,
And obtains favor from the LORD.
36 "But he who sins against me injures himself;
All those who hate me love death."

*Wisdom's Invitation*

**9** WISDOM HAS built her house,
She has hewn out her seven pillars;
2 She has prepared her food, she has mixed her wine;
She has also set her table;

## New International

13 To fear the LORD is to hate evil;
I hate pride and arrogance,
evil behavior and perverse speech.
14 Counsel and sound judgment are mine;
I have understanding and power.
15 By me kings reign
and rulers make laws that are just;
16 by me princes govern,
and all nobles who rule on earth.[b]
17 I love those who love me,
and those who seek me find me.
18 With me are riches and honor,
enduring wealth and prosperity.
19 My fruit is better than fine gold;
what I yield surpasses choice silver.
20 I walk in the way of righteousness,
along the paths of justice,
21 bestowing wealth on those who love me
and making their treasuries full.

22 "The LORD brought me forth as the first of hid works,[c,d]
before his deeds of old;
23 I was appointed[e] from eternity,
from the beginning, before the world began.
24 When there were no oceans, I was given birth,
when there were no springs abounding with water;
25 before the mountains were settled in place,
before the hills, I was given birth,
26 before he made the earth or its fields
or any of the dust of the world.
27 I was there when he set the heavens in place,
when he marked out the horizon on the face of the deep,
28 when he established the clouds above
and fixed securely the fountains of the deep,
29 when he gave the sea its boundary
so the waters would not overstep his command,
and when he marked out the foundations of the earth.
30 Then I was the craftsman at his side.
I was filled with delight day after day,
rejoicing always in his presence,
31 rejoicing in his whole world
and delighting in mankind.

32 "Now then, my sons, listen to me;
blessed are those who keep my ways.
33 Listen to my instruction and be wise;
do not ignore it.
34 Blessed is the man who listens to me,
watching daily at my doors,
waiting at my doorway.
35 For whoever finds me finds life
and receives favor from the LORD.
36 But whoever fails to find me harms himself;
all who hate me love death."

*Invitations of Wisdom and of Folly*

**9** WISDOM HAS built her house;
she has hewn out its seven pillars.
2 She has prepared her meat and mixed her wine;
she has also set her table.

**NIV** [b] *16* Many Hebrew manuscripts and Septuagint; most Hebrew manuscripts *and nobles—all righteous rulers* [c] *22 Or way; or dominion* [d] *22 Or The* LORD *possessed me at the beginning of his work; or The* LORD *brought me forth at the beginning of his work* [e] *23 Or fashioned*

## King James

3She hath sent forth her maidens; she crieth upon the highest places of the city,
4Whoso *is* simple, let him turn in hither: *as for* him that wanteth understanding, she saith to him,
5Come, eat of my bread, and drink of the wine *which* I have mingled.
6Forsake the foolish, and live; and go in the way of understanding.
7He that reproveth a scorner getteth to himself shame: and he that rebuketh a wicked *man getteth* himself a blot.
8Reprove not a scorner, lest he hate thee: rebuke a wise man, and he will love thee.
9Give *instruction* to a wise *man,* and he will be yet wiser: teach a just *man,* and he will increase in learning.
10The fear of the LORD *is* the beginning of wisdom: and the knowledge of the holy *is* understanding.
11For by me thy days shall be multiplied, and the years of thy life shall be increased.
12If thou be wise, thou shalt be wise for thyself: but *if* thou scornest, thou alone shalt bear *it.*
13¶ A foolish woman *is* clamorous: *she is* simple, and knoweth nothing.
14For she sitteth at the door of her house, on a seat in the high places of the city,
15To call passengers who go right on their ways:
16Whoso *is* simple, let him turn in hither: and *as for* him that wanteth understanding, she saith to him,
17Stolen waters are sweet, and bread *eaten* in secret is pleasant.
18But he knoweth not that the dead *are* there; *and that* her guests *are* in the depths of hell.

10 THE PROVERBS of Solomon. A wise son maketh a glad father: but a foolish son *is* the heaviness of his mother.
2Treasures of wickedness profit nothing: but righteousness delivereth from death.
3The LORD will not suffer the soul of the righteous to famish: but he casteth away the substance of the wicked.
4He becometh poor that dealeth *with* a slack hand: but the hand of the diligent maketh rich.
5He that gathereth in summer *is* a wise son: *but* he that sleepeth in harvest *is* a son that causeth shame.
6Blessings *are* upon the head of the just: but violence covereth the mouth of the wicked.
7The memory of the just *is* blessed: but the name of the wicked shall rot.
8The wise in heart will receive commandments: but a prating fool shall fall.
9He that walketh uprightly walketh surely: but he that perverteth his ways shall be known.

## Amplified

3She has sent out her maids to cry from the highest places of the town,
4Whoever is simple [easily led astray, wavering], let him turn in here! As for him who lacks understanding, [God's] Wisdom says to him,
5Come, eat of my bread, and drink of the [spiritual] wine which I have mixed. [Isa. 55:1; John 6:27.]
6Leave off, simple ones—forsake the foolish and simple-minded—and live! And walk in the way of insight *and* understanding.
7He who rebukes a scorner heaps upon himself abuse, and he who reproves a wicked man gets for himself bruises.
8Reprove not a scorner, lest he hate you; reprove a wise man, and he will love you. [Ps. 141:5.]
9Give instruction to a wise man, and he will be yet wiser; teach a righteous man—one upright and in right standing with God—and he will increase in learning.
10The reverent *and* worshipful fear of the Lord is the beginning [the chief and choice part] of Wisdom, and the knowledge of the Holy One is insight *and* understanding.
11For by me [Wisdom from God], your days shall be multiplied, and the years of your life shall be increased.
12If you are wise, you are wise for yourself; if you scorn, you alone will bear it *and* pay the penalty.
13The foolish woman is noisy; she is simple *and* open to all forms of evil; she [willfully and recklessly] knows nothing whatever [of eternal value].
14For she sits at the door of her house, *or* on a seat in the conspicuous places of the town,
15Calling to those who pass by, who go uprightly on their way:
16Whoever is simple, wavering *and* easily led astray, let him turn in here! And as for him who lacks understanding, she says to him,
17Stolen waters [pleasures] are sweet [because they are forbidden], and bread eaten in secret is pleasant. [Prov. 20:17.]
18But he knows not that the shades of the dead are there [specters haunting the scene of past transgressions], and that her invited guests are [already sunk] in the depths of Sheol [the lower world, Hades].

10 THE PROVERBS of Solomon. A wise son makes a glad father, but a foolish *and* self-confident son is the grief of his mother.
2Treasures of wickedness profit nothing, but righteousness [moral and spiritual rectitude in every area and relation] delivers from death.
3The Lord will not allow the [uncompromisingly] righteous to famish, but He thwarts the desire of the wicked. [Pss. 34:9, 10; 37:25.]
4He becomes poor who works with a slack *and* idle hand, but the hand of the diligent makes rich.
5He who gathers in summer is a wise son, but he who sleeps in harvest is a son who causes shame.
6Blessings are upon the head of the [uncompromisingly] righteous—the upright, in right standing with God; but the mouth of the wicked conceals violence.
7The memory of the [uncompromisingly] righteous is a blessing, but the name of the wicked shall rot. [Pss. 112:6; 9:5.]
8The wise in heart will accept *and* obey commandments, but the foolish of lips will fall headlong.
9He who walks uprightly walks surely, but he who takes a crooked way shall be found out *and* punished.

## New American Standard

3 She has sent out her maidens, she calls
From the tops of the heights of the city:
4 "Whoever is naive, let him turn in here!"
To him who lacks understanding she says,
5 "Come, eat of my food,
And drink of the wine I have mixed.
6 "Forsake *your* folly and live,
And proceed in the way of understanding."
7¶ He who corrects a scoffer gets dishonor for himself,
And he who reproves a wicked man *gets* insults for himself.
8 Do not reprove a scoffer, lest he hate you,
Reprove a wise man, and he will love you.
9 Give *instruction* to a wise man, and he will be still wiser,
Teach a righteous man, and he will increase *his* learning.
10 The fear of the LORD is the beginning of wisdom,
And the knowledge of the Holy One is understanding.
11 For by me your days will be multiplied,
And years of life will be added to you.
12 If you are wise, you are wise for yourself,
And if you scoff, you alone will bear it.
13¶ The woman of folly is boisterous,
*She is* naive, and knows nothing.
14 And she sits at the doorway of her house,
On a seat by the high places of the city,
15 Calling to those who pass by,
Who are making their paths straight:
16 "Whoever is naive, let him turn in here,"
And to him who lacks understanding she says,
17 "Stolen water is sweet;
And bread *eaten* in secret is pleasant."
18 But he does not know that the dead are there,
*That* her guests are in the depths of Sheol.

*Contrast of the Righteous and the Wicked*

10 THE PROVERBS of Solomon.
A wise son makes a father glad,
But a foolish son is a grief to his mother.
2 Ill-gotten gains do not profit,
But righteousness delivers from death.
3 The LORD will not allow the righteous to hunger,
But He will thrust *aside* the craving of the wicked.
4 Poor is he who works with a negligent hand,
But the hand of the diligent makes rich.
5 He who gathers in summer is a son who acts wisely,
*But* he who sleeps in harvest is a son who acts shamefully.
6 Blessings are on the head of the righteous,
But the mouth of the wicked conceals violence.
7 The memory of the righteous is blessed,
But the name of the wicked will rot.
8 The wise of heart will receive commands,
But a babbling fool will be thrown down.
9 He who walks in integrity walks securely,
But he who perverts his ways will be found out.

## New International

3She has sent out her maids, and she calls
from the highest point of the city.
4"Let all who are simple come in here!"
she says to those who lack judgment.
5"Come, eat my food
and drink the wine I have mixed.
6Leave your simple ways and you will live;
walk in the way of understanding.

7"Whoever corrects a mocker invites insult;
whoever rebukes a wicked man incurs abuse.
8Do not rebuke a mocker or he will hate you;
rebuke a wise man and he will love you.
9Instruct a wise man and he will be wiser still;
teach a righteous man and he will add to his learning.

10"The fear of the LORD is the beginning of wisdom,
and knowledge of the Holy One is understanding.
11For through me your days will be many,
and years will be added to your life.
12If you are wise, your wisdom will reward you;
if you are a mocker, you alone will suffer."

13The woman Folly is loud;
she is undisciplined and without knowledge.
14She sits at the door of her house,
on a seat at the highest point of the city,
15calling out to those who pass by,
who go straight on their way.
16"Let all who are simple come in here!"
she says to those who lack judgment.
17"Stolen water is sweet;
food eaten in secret is delicious!"
18But little do they know that the dead are there,
that her guests are in the depths of the grave.[a]

*Proverbs of Solomon*

10 THE PROVERBS of Solomon:
A wise son brings joy to his father,
but a foolish son grief to his mother.

2Ill-gotten treasures are of no value,
but righteousness delivers from death.

3The LORD does not let the righteous go hungry
but he thwarts the craving of the wicked.

4Lazy hands make a man poor,
but diligent hands bring wealth.

5He who gathers crops in summer is a wise son,
but he who sleeps during harvest is a disgraceful son.

6Blessings crown the head of the righteous,
but violence overwhelms the mouth of the wicked.[b]

7The memory of the righteous will be a blessing,
but the name of the wicked will rot.

8The wise in heart accept commands,
but a chattering fool comes to ruin.

9The man of integrity walks securely,
but he who takes crooked paths will be found out.

**NIV** [a] *18* Hebrew *Sheol* [b] *6* Or *but the mouth of the wicked conceals violence;* also in verse 11

## King James

10 He that winketh with the eye causeth sorrow: but a prating fool shall fall.
11 The mouth of a righteous *man is* a well of life: but violence covereth the mouth of the wicked.
12 Hatred stirreth up strifes: but love covereth all sins.
13 In the lips of him that hath understanding wisdom is found: but a rod *is* for the back of him that is void of understanding.
14 Wise *men* lay up knowledge: but the mouth of the foolish *is* near destruction.
15 The rich man's wealth *is* his strong city: the destruction of the poor *is* their poverty.
16 The labour of the righteous *tendeth* to life: the fruit of the wicked to sin.
17 He *is in* the way of life that keepeth instruction: but he that refuseth reproof erreth.
18 He that hideth hatred *with* lying lips, and he that uttereth a slander, *is* a fool.
19 In the multitude of words there wanteth not sin: but he that refraineth his lips *is* wise.
20 The tongue of the just *is as* choice silver: the heart of the wicked *is* little worth.
21 The lips of the righteous feed many: but fools die for want of wisdom.
22 The blessing of the LORD, it maketh rich, and he addeth no sorrow with it.
23 *It is* as sport to a fool to do mischief: but a man of understanding hath wisdom.
24 The fear of the wicked, it shall come upon him: but the desire of the righteous shall be granted.
25 As the whirlwind passeth, so *is* the wicked no *more:* but the righteous *is* an everlasting foundation.
26 As vinegar to the teeth, and as smoke to the eyes, so *is* the sluggard to them that send him.
27 The fear of the LORD prolongeth days: but the years of the wicked shall be shortened.
28 The hope of the righteous *shall be* gladness: but the expectation of the wicked shall perish.
29 The way of the LORD *is* strength to the upright: but destruction *shall be* to the workers of iniquity.
30 The righteous shall never be removed: but the wicked shall not inhabit the earth.
31 The mouth of the just bringeth forth wisdom: but the froward tongue shall be cut out.
32 The lips of the righteous know what is acceptable: but the mouth of the wicked *speaketh* frowardness.

**11** A FALSE balance *is* abomination to the LORD: but a just weight *is* his delight.

## Amplified

10 He who winks with the eye [craftily and with malice] causes sorrow; the foolish of lips will fall headlong, [but [a]he who boldly reproves makes peace].
11 The mouth of an [uncompromisingly] righteous man is a well of life, but the mouth of the wicked conceals violence.
12 Hatred stirs up contentions, but love covers all transgressions.
13 In the lips of him who has discernment, skillful *and* godly [b]Wisdom is found, but discipline *and* the rod are for the back of him who is without sense *and* understanding.
14 Wise men store up knowledge [in mind and heart], but the mouth of the foolish is a present destruction.
15 The rich man's wealth is his strong city; the poverty of the poor is their ruin. [Ps. 52:7; I Tim. 6:17.]
16 The earnings of the righteous—the upright in right standing with God—lead to life; but the profit of the wicked leads to further sin. [I Tim. 6:10; Rom. 6:21.]
17 He who heeds instruction *and* correction is [not only himself] in the way of life, *but* is a way of life for others. And he who neglects *or* refuses reproof [not only himself] goes astray, *but* causes to err *and* is a path toward ruin for others.
18 He who hides hatred is of lying lips, and he who utters a slander is a [self-confident] fool. [Prov. 26:24-26.]
19 In a multitude of words transgression is not lacking, but he who restrains his lips is prudent.
20 The tongue of those who are upright *and* in right standing with God is as choice silver; the mind of those who are wicked *and* out of harmony with God is of little value.
21 The lips of the [uncompromisingly] righteous feed *and* guide many; but fools die for want of understanding *and* heart.
22 The blessing of the Lord, it makes [truly] rich, and He adds no sorrow with it, *neither* does toiling increase it.
23 It is as sport to a [self-confident] fool to do wickedness, but to have skillful *and* godly Wisdom is pleasure *and* relaxation to a man of understanding.
24 The thing a wicked man fears shall come upon him, but the desire of the [uncompromisingly] righteous shall be granted.
25 When the whirlwind passes, the wicked is no more, but the [uncompromisingly] righteous has an everlasting foundation. [Matt. 7:24-27; Ps. 125:1.]
26 As vinegar to the teeth, and as smoke to the eyes, so is the sluggard to those who employ *and* send him.
27 The reverent *and* worshipful fear of the Lord prolongs one's days, but the years of the wicked shall be made short.
28 The hope of the [uncompromisingly] righteous—the upright, in right standing with God—shall be gladness, but the expectation of the wicked [those who are out of harmony with God] shall come to nothing.
29 The way of the Lord is strength *and* a stronghold to the upright, but it is destruction to the workers of iniquity.
30 The [consistently] righteous shall never be removed, but the wicked shall not inhabit the earth *eventually*. [Pss. 37:22; 125:1.]
31 The mouth of the righteous [those harmonious with God] brings forth skillful *and* godly [c]Wisdom, but the perverse tongue shall be cut down [as a barren and rotten tree].
32 The lips of the [uncompromisingly] righteous know [and therefore utter] what is acceptable, but the mouth of the wicked knows [and therefore speaks only] what is obstinately willful *and* contrary.

**11** A FALSE balance *and* unrighteous dealings are extremely offensive *and* shamefully sinful to the Lord, but a just weight is His delight. [Prov. 16:11; Lev. 19:35, 36.]

**AMP** [a] *The Septuagint Version* (Greek) so reads at this point. [b] See footnote on chapter 1:23. [c] "Wisdom" is capitalized as a reminder of its divine implications. See note on chapter 1:23.

## New American Standard

10 He who winks the eye causes trouble,
And a babbling fool will be thrown down.
11 The mouth of the righteous is a fountain of life,
But the mouth of the wicked conceals violence.
12 Hatred stirs up strife,
But love covers all transgressions.
13 On the lips of the discerning, wisdom is found,
But a rod is for the back of him who lacks
understanding.
14 Wise men store up knowledge,
But with the mouth of the foolish, ruin is at hand.
15 The rich man's wealth is his fortress,
The ruin of the poor is their poverty.
16 The wages of the righteous is life,
The income of the wicked, punishment.
17 He is *on* the path of life who heeds instruction,
But he who forsakes reproof goes astray.
18 He who conceals hatred *has* lying lips,
And he who spreads slander is a fool.
19 When there are many words, transgression is
unavoidable,
But he who restrains his lips is wise.
20 The tongue of the righteous is *as* choice silver,
The heart of the wicked is *worth* little.
21 The lips of the righteous feed many,
But fools die for lack of understanding.
22 It is the blessing of the LORD that makes rich,
And He adds no sorrow to it.
23 Doing wickedness is like sport to a fool;
And *so is* wisdom to a man of understanding.
24 What the wicked fears will come upon him,
And the desire of the righteous will be granted.
25 When the whirlwind passes, the wicked is no more,
But the righteous *has* an everlasting foundation.
26 Like vinegar to the teeth and smoke to the eyes,
So is the lazy one to those who send him.
27 The fear of the LORD prolongs life,
But the years of the wicked will be shortened.
28 The hope of the righteous is gladness,
But the expectation of the wicked perishes.
29 The way of the LORD is a stronghold to the upright,
But ruin to the workers of iniquity.
30 The righteous will never be shaken,
But the wicked will not dwell in the land.
31 The mouth of the righteous flows with wisdom,
But the perverted tongue will be cut out.
32 The lips of the righteous bring forth what is acceptable,
But the mouth of the wicked, what is perverted.

*Contrast the Upright and the Wicked*

**11** A FALSE balance is an abomination to the LORD,
But a just weight is His delight.

## New International

10 He who winks maliciously causes grief,
and a chattering fool comes to ruin.
11 The mouth of the righteous is a fountain of life,
but violence overwhelms the mouth of the wicked.
12 Hatred stirs up dissension,
but love covers over all wrongs.
13 Wisdom is found on the lips of the discerning,
but a rod is for the back of him who lacks judgment.
14 Wise men store up knowledge,
but the mouth of a fool invites ruin.
15 The wealth of the rich is their fortified city,
but poverty is the ruin of the poor.
16 The wages of the righteous bring them life,
but the income of the wicked brings them punishment.
17 He who heeds discipline shows the way to life,
but whoever ignores correction leads others astray.
18 He who conceals his hatred has lying lips,
and whoever spreads slander is a fool.
19 When words are many, sin is not absent,
but he who holds his tongue is wise.
20 The tongue of the righteous is choice silver,
but the heart of the wicked is of little value.
21 The lips of the righteous nourish many,
but fools die for lack of judgment.
22 The blessing of the LORD brings wealth,
and he adds no trouble to it.
23 A fool finds pleasure in evil conduct,
but a man of understanding delights in wisdom.
24 What the wicked dreads will overtake him;
what the righteous desire will be granted.
25 When the storm has swept by, the wicked are gone,
but the righteous stand firm forever.
26 As vinegar to the teeth and smoke to the eyes,
so is a sluggard to those who send him.
27 The fear of the LORD adds length to life,
but the years of the wicked are cut short.
28 The prospect of the righteous is joy,
but the hopes of the wicked come to nothing.
29 The way of the LORD is a refuge for the righteous,
but it is the ruin of those who do evil.
30 The righteous will never be uprooted,
but the wicked will not remain in the land.
31 The mouth of the righteous brings forth wisdom,
but a perverse tongue will be cut out.
32 The lips of the righteous know what is fitting,
but the mouth of the wicked only what is perverse.

**11** THE LORD abhors dishonest scales,
but accurate weights are his delight.

## King James

2 *When* pride cometh, then cometh shame: but with the lowly *is* wisdom.

3 The integrity of the upright shall guide them: but the perverseness of transgressors shall destroy them.

4 Riches profit not in the day of wrath: but righteousness delivereth from death.

5 The righteousness of the perfect shall direct his way: but the wicked shall fall by his own wickedness.

6 The righteousness of the upright shall deliver them: but transgressors shall be taken in *their own* naughtiness.

7 When a wicked man dieth, *his* expectation shall perish: and the hope of unjust *men* perisheth.

8 The righteous is delivered out of trouble, and the wicked cometh in his stead.

9 An hypocrite with *his* mouth destroyeth his neighbour: but through knowledge shall the just be delivered.

10 When it goeth well with the righteous, the city rejoiceth: and when the wicked perish, *there is* shouting.

11 By the blessing of the upright the city is exalted: but it is overthrown by the mouth of the wicked.

12 He that is void of wisdom despiseth his neighbour: but a man of understanding holdeth his peace.

13 A talebearer revealeth secrets: but he that is of a faithful spirit concealeth the matter.

14 Where no counsel *is*, the people fall: but in the multitude of counsellors *there is* safety.

15 He that is surety for a stranger shall smart *for it:* and he that hateth suretyship is sure.

16 A gracious woman retaineth honour: and strong *men* retain riches.

17 The merciful man doeth good to his own soul: but *he that is* cruel troubleth his own flesh.

18 The wicked worketh a deceitful work: but to him that soweth righteousness *shall be* a sure reward.

19 As righteousness *tendeth* to life: so he that pursueth evil *pursueth it* to his own death.

20 They that are of a froward heart *are* abomination to the LORD: but *such as are* upright in *their* way *are* his delight.

21 *Though* hand *join* in hand, the wicked shall not be unpunished: but the seed of the righteous shall be delivered.

22 *As* a jewel of gold in a swine's snout, *so is* a fair woman which is without discretion.

23 The desire of the righteous *is* only good: *but* the expectation of the wicked *is* wrath.

24 There is that scattereth, and yet increaseth; and *there is* that withholdeth more than is meet, but *it tendeth* to poverty.

25 The liberal soul shall be made fat: and he that watereth shall be watered also himself.

26 He that withholdeth corn, the people shall curse him: but blessing *shall be* upon the head of him that selleth *it*.

27 He that diligently seeketh good procureth favour: but he that seeketh mischief, it shall come unto him.

## Amplified

2 When swelling *and* pride come, then emptiness *and* shame come also; but with the humble—those who are lowly, [who have been pruned or chiseled by trial] and renounce self—is skillful *and* godly Wisdom *and* soundness.

3 The integrity of the upright shall guide them, but the willful contrariness *and* crookedness of the treacherous shall destroy them.

4 Riches provide no security in any day of wrath *and* judgment, but righteousness—uprightness and right standing with God—delivers from death. [Prov. 10:2; Zeph. 1:18.]

5 The righteousness of the blameless shall rectify *and* make plain his way *and* keep it straight, but the wicked shall fall by his own wickedness.

6 The righteousness of the upright—their rectitude in every area and relation—shall deliver them; but the treacherous shall be taken in their own iniquity *and* greedy desire.

7 When the wicked dies, his hope [for the future] perishes, and the expectation of the godless comes to nothing.

8 The [uncompromisingly] righteous is delivered out of trouble, and the wicked gets into it instead.

9 With his mouth the godless man destroys his neighbor, but through knowledge *and* superior discernment shall the righteous be delivered.

10 When it goes well with the [uncompromisingly] righteous the city rejoices, but when the wicked perish there are shouts of joy.

11 By the blessing of the influence of the upright *and* God's favor [because of them] the city is exalted; but it is overthrown by the mouth of the wicked.

12 He who belittles *and* despises his neighbor lacks sense, but a man of understanding keeps silent.

13 He who goes about as a talebearer reveals secrets, but he who is trustworthy *and* faithful in spirit keeps the matter hidden.

14 Where no wise guidance is, the people fall; but in the multitude of counselors there is safety.

15 He who becomes security for an outsider shall smart for it, but he who hates suretyship is secure [from its penalties].

16 A gracious *and* good woman wins honor [for her husband], and violent men win riches; [but [a]a woman who hates righteousness is a throne of dishonor for him].

17 The merciful, kind *and* generous man benefits himself [for his deeds return to bless him], but he who is cruel *and* callous [to the wants of others] brings on himself retribution.

18 A wicked man earns deceitful wages, but he who sows righteousness [moral and spiritual rectitude in every area and relation] shall have a sure reward—permanent and satisfying. [Hos. 10:12; Gal. 6:8, 9; James 3:18.]

19 He who is steadfast in righteousness—uprightness and right standing with God—shall attain to life, and he who pursues evil does it to his own death.

20 They who are willfully contrary in heart are extremely disgusting *and* shamefully vile in the eyes of the Lord, but such as are blameless *and* whole-hearted in their ways are His delight!

21 Assuredly—I pledge it—the wicked shall not go unpunished, but the multitude of the [uncompromisingly] righteous shall be delivered.

22 As a ring of gold in a swine's snout, so is a fair woman who is without discretion.

23 The desire of the [consistently] righteous brings only good, but the expectation of the wicked brings wrath.

24 There are those who [generously] scatter abroad, and yet increase more; there are those who withhold more than is fitting *or* what is justly due, but it tends only to want.

25 The liberal person shall be enriched, and he who waters shall himself be watered. [II Cor. 9:6-10.]

26 The people will curse him who holds back grain [when the public needs it]; but a blessing [from God and man] is upon the head of him who sells it.

27 He who diligently seeks good seeks [God's] favor, but he who searches after evil, it shall come upon him.

**AMP** [a] *The Septuagint Version* (Greek) so reads at this point.

## New American Standard

2 When pride comes, then comes dishonor,
But with the humble is wisdom.
3 The integrity of the upright will guide them,
But the falseness of the treacherous will destroy them.
4 Riches do not profit in the day of wrath,
But righteousness delivers from death.
5 The righteousness of the blameless will smooth his way,
But the wicked will fall by his own wickedness.
6 The righteousness of the upright will deliver them,
But the treacherous will be caught by *their own* greed.
7 When a wicked man dies, *his* expectation will perish,
And the hope of strong men perishes.
8 The righteous is delivered from trouble,
But the wicked takes his place.
9 With *his* mouth the godless man destroys his neighbor,
But through knowledge the righteous will be delivered.
10 When it goes well with the righteous, the city rejoices,
And when the wicked perish, there is glad shouting.
11 By the blessing of the upright a city is exalted,
But by the mouth of the wicked it is torn down.
12 He who despises his neighbor lacks sense,
But a man of understanding keeps silent.
13 He who goes about as a talebearer reveals secrets,
But he who is trustworthy conceals a matter.
14 Where there is no guidance, the people fall,
But in abundance of counselors there is victory.
15 He who is surety for a stranger will surely suffer for it,
But he who hates going surety is safe.
16 A gracious woman attains honor,
And violent men attain riches.
17 The merciful man does himself good,
But the cruel man does himself harm.
18 The wicked earns deceptive wages,
But he who sows righteousness *gets* a true reward.
19 He who is steadfast in righteousness *will attain* to life,
And he who pursues evil *will bring about* his own death.
20 The perverse in heart are an abomination to the LORD,
But the blameless in *their* walk are His delight.
21 Assuredly, the evil man will not go unpunished,
But the descendants of the righteous will be delivered.
22 *As* a ring of gold in a swine's snout,
*So is* a beautiful woman who lacks [b]discretion.
23 The desire of the righteous is only good,
*But* the expectation of the wicked is wrath.
24 There is one who scatters, yet increases all the more,
And there is one who withholds what is justly due, but *it results* only in want.
25 The generous man will be prosperous,
And he who waters will himself be watered.
26 He who withholds grain, the people will curse him,
But blessing will be on the head of him who sells *it*.
27 He who diligently seeks good seeks favor,
But he who searches after evil, it will come to him.

NAS [b] Lit., *taste*

## New International

2 When pride comes, then comes disgrace,
but with humility comes wisdom.

3 The integrity of the upright guides them,
but the unfaithful are destroyed by their duplicity.

4 Wealth is worthless in the day of wrath,
but righteousness delivers from death.

5 The righteousness of the blameless makes a straight way for them,
but the wicked are brought down by their own wickedness.

6 The righteousness of the upright delivers them,
but the unfaithful are trapped by evil desires.

7 When a wicked man dies, his hope perishes;
all he expected from his power comes to nothing.

8 The righteous man is rescued from trouble,
and it comes on the wicked instead.

9 With his mouth the godless destroys his neighbor,
but through knowledge the righteous escape.

10 When the righteous prosper, the city rejoices;
when the wicked perish, there are shouts of joy.

11 Through the blessing of the upright a city is exalted,
but by the mouth of the wicked it is destroyed.

12 A man who lacks judgment derides his neighbor,
but a man of understanding holds his tongue.

13 A gossip betrays a confidence,
but a trustworthy man keeps a secret.

14 For lack of guidance a nation falls,
but many advisers make victory sure.

15 He who puts up security for another will surely suffer,
but whoever refuses to strike hands in pledge is safe.

16 A kindhearted woman gains respect,
but ruthless men gain only wealth.

17 A kind man benefits himself,
but a cruel man brings trouble on himself.

18 The wicked man earns deceptive wages,
but he who sows righteousness reaps a sure reward.

19 The truly righteous man attains life,
but he who pursues evil goes to his death.

20 The LORD detests men of perverse heart
but he delights in those whose ways are blameless.

21 Be sure of this: The wicked will not go unpunished,
but those who are righteous will go free.

22 Like a gold ring in a pig's snout
is a beautiful woman who shows no discretion.

23 The desire of the righteous ends only in good,
but the hope of the wicked only in wrath.

24 One man gives freely, yet gains even more;
another withholds unduly, but comes to poverty.

25 A generous man will prosper;
he who refreshes others will himself be refreshed.

26 People curse the man who hoards grain,
but blessing crowns him who is willing to sell.

27 He who seeks good finds goodwill,
but evil comes to him who searches for it.

## King James

28He that trusteth in his riches shall fall: but the righteous shall flourish as a branch.

29He that troubleth his own house shall inherit the wind: and the fool *shall be* servant to the wise of heart.

30The fruit of the righteous *is* a tree of life; and he that winneth souls *is* wise.

31Behold, the righteous shall be recompensed in the earth: much more the wicked and the sinner.

**12** WHOSO LOVETH instruction loveth knowledge: but he that hateth reproof *is* brutish.

2A good *man* obtaineth favour of the LORD: but a man of wicked devices will he condemn.

3A man shall not be established by wickedness: but the root of the righteous shall not be moved.

4A virtuous woman *is* a crown to her husband: but she that maketh ashamed *is* as rottenness in his bones.

5The thoughts of the righteous *are* right: *but* the counsels of the wicked *are* deceit.

6The words of the wicked *are* to lie in wait for blood: but the mouth of the upright shall deliver them.

7The wicked are overthrown, and *are* not: but the house of the righteous shall stand.

8A man shall be commended according to his wisdom: but he that is of a perverse heart shall be despised.

9 *He that is* despised, and hath a servant, *is* better than he that honoureth himself, and lacketh bread.

10A righteous *man* regardeth the life of his beast: but the tender mercies of the wicked *are* cruel.

11He that tilleth his land shall be satisfied with bread: but he that followeth vain *persons is* void of understanding.

12The wicked desireth the net of evil *men:* but the root of the righteous yieldeth *fruit*.

13The wicked is snared by the transgression of *his* lips: but the just shall come out of trouble.

14A man shall be satisfied with good by the fruit of *his* mouth: and the recompence of a man's hands shall be rendered unto him.

15The way of a fool *is* right in his own eyes: but he that hearkeneth unto counsel *is* wise.

16A fool's wrath is presently known: but a prudent *man* covereth shame.

17 *He that* speaketh truth showeth forth righteousness: but a false witness deceit.

18There is that speaketh like the piercings of a sword: but the tongue of the wise *is* health.

19The lip of truth shall be established for ever: but a lying tongue *is* but for a moment.

20Deceit *is* in the heart of them that imagine evil: but to the counsellors of peace *is* joy.

21There shall no evil happen to the just: but the wicked shall be filled with mischief.

## Amplified

28He who leans on, trusts *and* is confident in his riches shall fall, but the [uncompromisingly] righteous shall flourish like a green bough.

29He who troubles his own house shall inherit the wind, and the foolish shall be servant to the wise of heart.

30The fruit of the [uncompromisingly] righteous is a tree of life, and he who is wise captures human lives *for God* [as a fisher of men]—he gathers and receives them *for eternity*. [Matt. 4:19; I Cor. 9:19; James 5:20.]

31Behold, the [uncompromisingly] righteous shall be recompensed on earth; how much more the wicked and the sinner! [And [a]if the righteous are barely saved, what will become of the ungodly and wicked?] [I Pet. 4:18.]

**12** WHOEVER LOVES instruction *and* correction loves knowledge, but he who hates reproof is like a brute beast, stupid *and* indiscriminating.

2A good man obtains favor of the Lord, but a man of wicked devices He condemns.

3A man shall not be established by wickedness, but the root of the [uncompromisingly] righteous shall never be moved.

4A virtuous *and* worthy wife—earnest and strong in character—is a crowning joy to her husband, but she who makes ashamed is as rottenness in his bones. [Prov. 31:23; I Cor. 11:7.]

5The thoughts *and* purposes of the [consistently] righteous are honest *and* reliable, but the counsels *and* designs of the wicked are treacherous.

6The words of the wicked lie in wait for blood, but the mouth of the upright shall deliver them *and* the innocent ones [thus endangered].

7The wicked are overthrown and are not, but the house of the [uncompromisingly] righteous shall stand.

8A man shall be commended according to his wisdom, but he who is of a perverse heart shall be despised.

9Better is he who is lightly esteemed but works for his own support, than he who assumes honor for himself and lacks bread.

10A [consistently] righteous man regards the life of his beast, but the tender mercies of the wicked are cruel. [Deut. 25:4.]

11He who tills his land shall be satisfied with bread, but he who follows worthless pursuits is lacking in sense *and* without understanding.

12The wicked desires the booty of evil men, but the root of the [uncompromisingly] righteous yields [richer fruitage].

13The wicked is [dangerously] snared by the transgression of his lips, but the [uncompromisingly] righteous shall come out of trouble.

14From the fruit of his words a man shall be satisfied with good, and the work of a man's hands shall come back to him.

15The way of a fool is right in his own eyes, but he who listens to counsel is wise. [Prov. 3:7; 21:2; 9:9.]

16A fool's wrath is quickly *and* openly known; but a prudent man ignores an insult.

17He who breathes out truth shows forth righteousness—uprightness and right standing with God; but a false witness utters deceit.

18There are those who speak rashly like the piercing of a sword, but the tongue of the wise brings healing.

19Truthful lips shall be established for ever, but a lying tongue is [credited] but for a moment.

20Deceit is in the heart of those who devise evil, but to the counselors of peace is joy.

21No [actual] evil, misfortune *or* calamity shall come upon the righteous, but the wicked shall be filled with evil, misfortune *and* calamity. [Job 5:19; Prov. 12:13; Isa. 46:4; Jer. 1:8; Dan. 6:27; Ps. 91:3; II Tim. 4:18.]

**AMP** [a] *The Septuagint Version* (Greek) so reads for this verse.

## New American Standard

28 He who trusts in his riches will fall,
But the righteous will flourish like the *green* leaf.
29 He who troubles his own house will inherit wind,
And the foolish will be servant to the wisehearted.
30 The fruit of the righteous is a tree of life,
And he who is wise wins souls.
31 If the righteous will be rewarded in the earth,
How much more the wicked and the sinner!

*Contrast the Upright and the Wicked*

12 WHOEVER LOVES discipline loves knowledge,
But he who hates reproof is stupid.
2 A good man will obtain favor from the LORD,
But He will condemn a man who devises evil.
3 A man will not be established by wickedness,
But the root of the righteous will not be moved.
4 An excellent wife is the crown of her husband,
But she who shames *him* is as rottenness in his bones.
5 The thoughts of the righteous are just,
*But* the counsels of the wicked are deceitful.
6 The words of the wicked lie in wait for blood,
But the mouth of the upright will deliver them.
7 The wicked are overthrown and are no more,
But the house of the righteous will stand.
8 A man will be praised according to his insight,
But one of perverse mind will be despised.
9 Better is he who is lightly esteemed and has a servant,
Than he who honors himself and lacks bread.
10 A righteous man has regard for the life of his beast,
But the compassion of the wicked is cruel.
11 He who tills his land will have plenty of bread,
But he who pursues vain *things* lacks sense.
12 The wicked desires the booty of evil men,
But the root of the righteous yields *fruit*.
13 An evil man is ensnared by the transgression of his lips,
But the righteous will escape from trouble.
14 A man will be satisfied with good by the fruit of his words,
And the deeds of a man's hands will return to him.
15 The way of a fool is right in his own eyes,
But a wise man is he who listens to counsel.
16 A fool's vexation is known at once,
But a prudent man conceals dishonor.
17 He who speaks truth tells what is right,
But a false witness, deceit.
18 There is one who speaks rashly like the thrusts of a sword,
But the tongue of the wise brings healing.
19 Truthful lips will be established forever,
But a lying tongue is only for a moment.
20 Deceit is in the heart of those who devise evil,
But counselors of peace have joy.
21 No harm befalls the righteous,
But the wicked are filled with trouble.

## New International

28 Whoever trusts in his riches will fall,
but the righteous will thrive like a green leaf.
29 He who brings trouble on his family will inherit only wind,
and the fool will be servant to the wise.
30 The fruit of the righteous is a tree of life,
and he who wins souls is wise.
31 If the righteous receive their due on earth,
how much more the ungodly and the sinner!

12 WHOEVER LOVES discipline loves knowledge,
but he who hates correction is stupid.
2 A good man obtains favor from the LORD,
but the LORD condemns a crafty man.
3 A man cannot be established through wickedness,
but the righteous cannot be uprooted.
4 A wife of noble character is her husband's crown,
but a disgraceful wife is like decay in his bones.
5 The plans of the righteous are just,
but the advice of the wicked is deceitful.
6 The words of the wicked lie in wait for blood,
but the speech of the upright rescues them.
7 Wicked men are overthrown and are no more,
but the house of the righteous stands firm.
8 A man is praised according to his wisdom,
but men with warped minds are despised.
9 Better to be a nobody and yet have a servant
than pretend to be somebody and have no food.
10 A righteous man cares for the needs of his animal,
but the kindest acts of the wicked are cruel.
11 He who works his land will have abundant food,
but he who chases fantasies lacks judgment.
12 The wicked desire the plunder of evil men,
but the root of the righteous flourishes.
13 An evil man is trapped by his sinful talk,
but a righteous man escapes trouble.
14 From the fruit of his lips a man is filled with good things
as surely as the work of his hands rewards him.
15 The way of a fool seems right to him,
but a wise man listens to advice.
16 A fool shows his annoyance at once,
but a prudent man overlooks an insult.
17 A truthful witness gives honest testimony,
but a false witness tells lies.
18 Reckless words pierce like a sword,
but the tongue of the wise brings healing.
19 Truthful lips endure forever,
but a lying tongue lasts only a moment.
20 There is deceit in the hearts of those who plot evil,
but joy for those who promote peace.
21 No harm befalls the righteous,
but the wicked have their fill of trouble.

## King James

22 Lying lips *are* abomination to the LORD: but they that deal truly *are* his delight.

23 A prudent man concealeth knowledge: but the heart of fools proclaimeth foolishness.

24 The hand of the diligent shall bear rule: but the slothful shall be under tribute.

25 Heaviness in the heart of man maketh it stoop: but a good word maketh it glad.

26 The righteous *is* more excellent than his neighbour: but the way of the wicked seduceth them.

27 The slothful *man* roasteth not that which he took in hunting: but the substance of a diligent man *is* precious.

28 In the way of righteousness *is* life; and *in* the pathway *thereof there is* no death.

**13** A WISE son *heareth* his father's instruction: but a scorner heareth not rebuke.

2 A man shall eat good by the fruit of *his* mouth: but the soul of the transgressors *shall eat* violence.

3 He that keepeth his mouth keepeth his life: *but* he that openeth wide his lips shall have destruction.

4 The soul of the sluggard desireth, and *hath* nothing: but the soul of the diligent shall be made fat.

5 A righteous *man* hateth lying: but a wicked *man* is loathsome, and cometh to shame.

6 Righteousness keepeth *him that is* upright in the way: but wickedness overthroweth the sinner.

7 There is that maketh himself rich, yet *hath* nothing: *there is* that maketh himself poor, yet *hath* great riches.

8 The ransom of a man's life *are* his riches: but the poor heareth not rebuke.

9 The light of the righteous rejoiceth: but the lamp of the wicked shall be put out.

10 Only by pride cometh contention: but with the well advised *is* wisdom.

11 Wealth *gotten* by vanity shall be diminished: but he that gathereth by labour shall increase.

12 Hope deferred maketh the heart sick: but *when* the desire cometh, *it is* a tree of life.

13 Whoso despiseth the word shall be destroyed: but he that feareth the commandment shall be rewarded.

14 The law of the wise *is* a fountain of life, to depart from the snares of death.

15 Good understanding giveth favour: but the way of transgressors *is* hard.

16 Every prudent *man* dealeth with knowledge: but a fool layeth open *his* folly.

17 A wicked messenger falleth into mischief: but a faithful ambassador *is* health.

18 Poverty and shame *shall be to* him that refuseth instruction: but he that regardeth reproof shall be honoured.

## Amplified

22 Lying lips are extremely disgusting *and* hateful to the Lord, but they who deal truly are His delight. [Prov. 6:17; 11:20; Rev. 22:15.]

23 A prudent man is reluctant to display his knowledge, but the heart of [self-confident] fools proclaims their folly. [Isa. 32:6.]

24 The hand of the diligent will rule, but the slothful will be put to forced labor.

25 Anxiety in a man's heart weighs it down, but an encouraging word makes it glad. [Prov. 15:13; Ps. 50:4.]

26 The [consistently] righteous man is a guide to his neighbor, but the way of the wicked causes others to go astray.

27 The slothful man will not catch his game, *or* roast it if he should kill it; but the diligent man will get precious possessions.

28 Life is in the way of righteousness [moral and spiritual rectitude in every area and relation], and in its pathway there is no death, *but* immortality—perpetual, eternal life. [John 3:36; 4:36; 8:51; 11:26; I Cor. 15:54; Gal. 6:8.]

**13** A WISE son heeds [and is the fruit of] his father's instruction *and* correction, but a scoffer listens not to rebuke.

2 A good man shall eat good from the fruit of his mouth, but the desire of the treacherous is for violence.

3 He who guards his mouth keeps his life, but he who opens wide his lips will come to ruin.

4 The appetite of the sluggard craves and gets nothing, but the appetite of the diligent shall be abundantly supplied. [Prov. 10:4.]

5 A [consistently] righteous man hates lying *and* deceit, but a wicked man is loathsome [his very breath spreads pollution] and he comes *surely* to shame.

6 Righteousness [rightness and justice in every area and relation] guards him who is upright in the way, but wickedness plunges into sin *and* overthrows the sinner.

7 One man considers himself rich, yet has nothing [to keep permanently]; another man considers himself poor, yet has great [and indestructible] riches. [Prov. 12:9; Luke 12:20, 21.]

8 A rich man can buy his way out of threatened death by paying a ransom, but the poor man does not even have to listen to threats [from the envious].

9 The light of the [uncompromisingly] righteous [is within him; it grows brighter and] rejoices; but the lamp of the wicked [furnishes only a derived, temporary light and] shall be put out shortly.

10 By pride *and* insolence comes only contention, but with the well-advised is skillful *and* godly [a]Wisdom.

11 Wealth [not earned] but won in haste, *or* unjustly, *or* from the production of things for vain *or* detrimental use, [such riches] will dwindle away; but he who gathers little by little will increase *them*.

12 Hope deferred makes the heart sick, but when the desire is fulfilled, it is a tree of life.

13 Whoever despises the Word [of God] brings destruction upon himself, but he who (reverently) fears *and* respects the commandment [of God] shall be rewarded.

14 The teaching of the wise is a fountain of life, that one may avoid the snares of death.

15 Good understanding wins favor, but the way of the transgressor is hard [like the barren, dry soil or the impassable swamp].

16 Every prudent man deals with knowledge, but a [self-confident] fool exposes *and* flaunts his folly.

17 A wicked messenger falls into evil, but a faithful ambassador brings healing.

18 Poverty and shame shall be to him who refuses instruction *and* correction, but he who heeds reproof shall be honored.

**AMP** [a] See footnote on chapter 1:23.

## New American Standard

22 Lying lips are an abomination to the LORD,
But those who deal faithfully are His delight.
23 A prudent man conceals knowledge,
But the heart of fools proclaims folly.
24 The hand of the diligent will rule,
But the slack *hand* will be put to forced labor.
25 Anxiety in the heart of a man weighs it down,
But a good word makes it glad.
26 The righteous is a guide to his neighbor,
But the way of the wicked leads them astray.
27 A slothful man does not roast his prey,
But the precious possession of a man *is* diligence.
28 In the way of righteousness is life,
And in *its* pathway there is no death.

*Contrast the Upright and the Wicked*

**13** A WISE son *accepts his* father's discipline,
But a scoffer does not listen to rebuke.
2 From the fruit of a man's mouth he enjoys good,
But the desire of the treacherous is violence.
3 The one who guards his mouth preserves his life;
The one who opens wide his lips comes to ruin.
4 The soul of the sluggard craves and *gets* nothing,
But the soul of the diligent is made fat.
5 A righteous man hates falsehood,
But a wicked man acts disgustingly and shamefully.
6 Righteousness guards the one whose way is blameless,
But wickedness subverts the sinner.
7 There is one who pretends to be rich, but has nothing;
*Another* pretends to be poor, but has great wealth.
8 The ransom of a man's life is his riches,
But the poor hears no rebuke.
9 The light of the righteous [b]rejoices,
But the lamp of the wicked goes out.
10 Through presumption comes nothing but strife,
But with those who receive counsel is wisdom.
11 Wealth *obtained* by fraud dwindles,
But the one who gathers by labor increases *it*.
12 Hope deferred makes the heart sick,
But desire fulfilled is a tree of life.
13 The one who despises the word will be in debt to it,
But the one who fears the commandment will be rewarded.
14 The teaching of the wise is a fountain of life,
To turn aside from the snares of death.
15 Good understanding produces favor,
But the way of the treacherous is hard.
16 Every prudent man acts with knowledge,
But a fool displays folly.
17 A wicked messenger falls into adversity,
But a faithful envoy *brings* healing.
18 Poverty and shame *will come* to him who neglects discipline,
But he who regards reproof will be honored.

NAS [b] I.e., shines brightly

## New International

22 The LORD detests lying lips,
but he delights in men who are truthful.

23 A prudent man keeps his knowledge to himself,
but the heart of fools blurts out folly.

24 Diligent hands will rule,
but laziness ends in slave labor.

25 An anxious heart weighs a man down,
but a kind word cheers him up.

26 A righteous man is cautious in friendship,[c]
but the way of the wicked leads them astray.

27 The lazy man does not roast[d] his game,
but the diligent man prizes his possessions.

28 In the way of righteousness there is life;
along that path is immortality.

**13** A WISE son heeds his father's instruction,
but a mocker does not listen to rebuke.

2 From the fruit of his lips a man enjoys good things,
but the unfaithful have a craving for violence.

3 He who guards his lips guards his life,
but he who speaks rashly will come to ruin.

4 The sluggard craves and gets nothing,
but the desires of the diligent are fully satisfied.

5 The righteous hate what is false,
but the wicked bring shame and disgrace.

6 Righteousness guards the man of integrity,
but wickedness overthrows the sinner.

7 One man pretends to be rich, yet has nothing;
another pretends to be poor, yet has great wealth.

8 A man's riches may ransom his life,
but a poor man hears no threat.

9 The light of the righteous shines brightly,
but the lamp of the wicked is snuffed out.

10 Pride only breeds quarrels,
but wisdom is found in those who take advice.

11 Dishonest money dwindles away,
but he who gathers money little by little makes it grow.

12 Hope deferred makes the heart sick,
but a longing fulfilled is a tree of life.

13 He who scorns instruction will pay for it,
but he who respects a command is rewarded.

14 The teaching of the wise is a fountain of life,
turning a man from the snares of death.

15 Good understanding wins favor,
but the way of the unfaithful is hard.[e]

16 Every prudent man acts out of knowledge,
but a fool exposes his folly.

17 A wicked messenger falls into trouble,
but a trustworthy envoy brings healing.

18 He who ignores discipline comes to poverty and shame,
but whoever heeds correction is honored.

NIV [c] 26 Or *man is a guide to his neighbor* [d] 27 The meaning of the Hebrew for this word is uncertain. [e] 15 Or *unfaithful does not endure*

## King James

19The desire accomplished is sweet to the soul: but *it is* abomination to fools to depart from evil.

20He that walketh with wise *men* shall be wise: but a companion of fools shall be destroyed.

21Evil pursueth sinners: but to the righteous good shall be repaid.

22A good *man* leaveth an inheritance to his children's children: and the wealth of the sinner *is* laid up for the just.

23Much food *is in* the tillage of the poor: but there is *that is* destroyed for want of judgment.

24He that spareth his rod hateth his son: but he that loveth him chasteneth him betimes.

25The righteous eateth to the satisfying of his soul: but the belly of the wicked shall want.

**14** EVERY WISE woman buildeth her house: but the foolish plucketh it down with her hands.

2He that walketh in his uprightness feareth the LORD: but *he that is* perverse in his ways despiseth him.

3In the mouth of the foolish *is* a rod of pride: but the lips of the wise shall preserve them.

4Where no oxen *are,* the crib *is* clean: but much increase *is* by the strength of the ox.

5A faithful witness will not lie: but a false witness will utter lies.

6A scorner seeketh wisdom, and *findeth it* not: but knowledge *is* easy unto him that understandeth.

7Go from the presence of a foolish man, when thou perceivest not *in him* the lips of knowledge.

8The wisdom of the prudent *is* to understand his way: but the folly of fools *is* deceit.

9Fools make a mock at sin: but among the righteous *there is* favour.

10The heart knoweth his own bitterness; and a stranger doth not intermeddle with his joy.

11The house of the wicked shall be overthrown: but the tabernacle of the upright shall flourish.

12There is a way which seemeth right unto a man, but the end thereof *are* the ways of death.

13Even in laughter the heart is sorrowful; and the end of that mirth *is* heaviness.

14The backslider in heart shall be filled with his own ways: and a good man *shall be satisfied* from himself.

15The simple believeth every word: but the prudent *man* looketh well to his going.

16A wise *man* feareth, and departeth from evil: but the fool rageth, and is confident.

17 *He that is* soon angry dealeth foolishly: and a man of wicked devices is hated.

18The simple inherit folly: but the prudent are crowned with knowledge.

## Amplified

19Satisfied desire is sweet to a person; therefore it is hateful *and* exceedingly offensive to [self-confident] fools to give up evil [upon which they have set their hearts].

20He who walks [as a companion] with wise men shall be wise, but he who associates with [self-confident] fools will [be a fool himself and] shall smart for it. [Isa. 32:6.]

21Evil pursues sinners, but the consistently upright *and* in right standing with God shall be recompensed with good.

22A good man leaves an inheritance [of moral stability and goodness] to his children's children, and the wealth of the sinner [finds its way eventually] into the hands of the righteous, for whom it was laid up.

23Much food is in the tilled land of the poor, but there are those who are destroyed because of injustice.

24He who spares his rod [of discipline] hates his son, but he who loves him diligently disciplines *and* punishes him early. [Prov. 19:18; 22:15; 23:13; 29:15, 17.]

25The [uncompromisingly] righteous eats to his own satisfaction, but the stomach of the wicked shall want.

**14** EVERY WISE woman builds her house, but the foolish one tears it down with her own hands.

2He who walks in uprightness reverently *and* worshipfully fears the Lord, but he who is contrary *and* devious in his ways despises Him.

3In the [a]fool's own mouth is a rod *to shame* his pride, but the wise men's lips shall preserve them.

4Where no oxen are, the grain crib is empty, but much increase *of crops* is by the strength of the ox.

5A faithful witness will not lie, but a false witness breathes out falsehoods.

6A scoffer seeks Wisdom in vain [for his very attitude blinds and deafens him to it], but knowledge is easy to him who [being teachable] understands.

7Go from the presence of a foolish *and* self-confident man, for you will not find knowledge in his lips.

8The wisdom of the prudent is to understand his way, but the folly of [self-confident] fools is to deceive.

9Fools make a mock at sin, *and* sin mocks the fools [who are its victims]—a sin offering made by them only mocks them [bringing them disappointment and disfavor]; but among the upright there is the favor of God. [Prov. 10:23.]

10The heart knows its own bitterness, and no stranger shares its joy.

11The house of the wicked shall be overthrown, but the tent of the upright shall flourish.

12There is a way which seems right to a man *and* appears straight before him, but at the end of it are the ways of death.

13Even in laughter the heart is sorrowful, and the end of mirth is heaviness *and* grief.

14The backslider in heart [from God and God-fearing] shall be filled with [the fruit of] his own ways, and a good man shall be satisfied from himself [with the holy thoughts and actions which his heart prompts, and in which he delights].

15The simpleton believes every word he hears, but the prudent man looks *and* considers well where he is going.

16A wise man suspects danger and cautiously avoids evil, but the fool bears himself insolently and is [presumptuously] confident.

17He who foams up quickly *and* flies into a passion will deal foolishly, and a man of wicked plots *and* plans is hated.

18The simple acquire folly, but the prudent are crowned with knowledge.

**AMP** [a] The word "fool" in the Old Testament seldom, if ever, means feeble-minded, imbecile, idiot, or moron. Rather, it always has in it the meaning of *a rebel,* especially against God and the laws of order, decency and justice. Notice in Proverbs how many such characteristics are listed against the fool, and God's attitude toward them.

## New American Standard

19 Desire realized is sweet to the soul,
But it is an abomination to fools to depart from evil.
20 He who walks with wise men will be wise,
But the companion of fools will suffer harm.
21 Adversity pursues sinners,
But the righteous will be rewarded with prosperity.
22 A good man leaves an inheritance to his children's children,
And the wealth of the sinner is stored up for the righteous.
23 Abundant food *is in* the fallow ground of the poor,
But it is swept away by injustice.
24 He who spares his rod hates his son,
But he who loves him disciplines him diligently.
25 The righteous has enough to satisfy his appetite,
But the stomach of the wicked is in want.

*Contrast the Upright and the Wicked*

14 THE WISE woman builds her house,
But the foolish tears it down with her own hands.
2 He who walks in his uprightness fears the LORD,
But he who is crooked in his ways despises Him.
3 In the mouth of the foolish is a rod for *his* back,
But the lips of the wise will preserve them.
4 Where no oxen are, the manger is clean,
But much increase *comes* by the strength of the ox.
5 A faithful witness will not lie,
But a false witness speaks lies.
6 A scoffer seeks wisdom, and *finds* none,
But knowledge is easy to him who has understanding.
7 Leave the presence of a fool,
Or you will not discern words of knowledge.
8 The wisdom of the prudent is to understand his way,
But the folly of fools is deceit.
9 Fools mock at sin,
But among the upright there is good will.
10 The heart knows its own bitterness,
And a stranger does not share its joy.
11 The house of the wicked will be destroyed,
But the tent of the upright will flourish.
12 There is a way *which seems* right to a man,
But its end is the way of death.
13 Even in laughter the heart may be in pain,
And the end of joy may be grief.
14 The backslider in heart will have his fill of his own ways,
But a good man will *be satisfied* with his.
15 The naive believes everything,
But the prudent man considers his steps.
16 A wise man is cautious and turns away from evil,
But a fool is arrogant and careless.
17 A quick-tempered man acts foolishly,
And a man of evil devices is hated.
18 The naive inherit folly,
But the prudent are crowned with knowledge.

## New International

19 A longing fulfilled is sweet to the soul,
but fools detest turning from evil.

20 He who walks with the wise grows wise,
but a companion of fools suffers harm.

21 Misfortune pursues the sinner,
but prosperity is the reward of the righteous.

22 A good man leaves an inheritance for his children's children,
but a sinner's wealth is stored up for the righteous.

23 A poor man's field may produce abundant food,
but injustice sweeps it away.

24 He who spares the rod hates his son,
but he who loves him is careful to discipline him.

25 The righteous eat to their hearts' content,
but the stomach of the wicked goes hungry.

14 THE WISE woman builds her house,
but with her own hands the foolish one tears hers down.

2 He whose walk is upright fears the LORD,
but he whose ways are devious despises him.

3 A fool's talk brings a rod to his back,
but the lips of the wise protect them.

4 Where there are no oxen, the manger is empty,
but from the strength of an ox comes an abundant harvest.

5 A truthful witness does not deceive,
but a false witness pours out lies.

6 The mocker seeks wisdom and finds none,
but knowledge comes easily to the discerning.

7 Stay away from a foolish man,
for you will not find knowledge on his lips.

8 The wisdom of the prudent is to give thought to their ways,
but the folly of fools is deception.

9 Fools mock at making amends for sin,
but goodwill is found among the upright.

10 Each heart knows its own bitterness,
and no one else can share its joy.

11 The house of the wicked will be destroyed,
but the tent of the upright will flourish.

12 There is a way that seems right to a man,
but in the end it leads to death.

13 Even in laughter the heart may ache,
and joy may end in grief.

14 The faithless will be fully repaid for their ways,
and the good man rewarded for his.

15 A simple man believes anything,
but a prudent man gives thought to his steps.

16 A wise man fears the LORD and shuns evil,
but a fool is hotheaded and reckless.

17 A quick-tempered man does foolish things,
and a crafty man is hated.

18 The simple inherit folly,
but the prudent are crowned with knowledge.

## King James

19 The evil bow before the good; and the wicked at the gates of the righteous.

20 The poor is hated even of his own neighbour: but the rich *hath* many friends.

21 He that despiseth his neighbour sinneth: but he that hath mercy on the poor, happy *is* he.

22 Do they not err that devise evil? but mercy and truth *shall be* to them that devise good.

23 In all labour there is profit: but the talk of the lips *tendeth* only to penury.

24 The crown of the wise *is* their riches: *but* the foolishness of fools *is* folly.

25 A true witness delivereth souls: but a deceitful *witness* speaketh lies.

26 In the fear of the LORD *is* strong confidence: and his children shall have a place of refuge.

27 The fear of the LORD *is* a fountain of life, to depart from the snares of death.

28 In the multitude of people *is* the king's honour: but in the want of people *is* the destruction of the prince.

29 *He that is* slow to wrath *is* of great understanding: but *he that is* hasty of spirit exalteth folly.

30 A sound heart *is* the life of the flesh: but envy the rottenness of the bones.

31 He that oppresseth the poor reproacheth his Maker: but he that honoureth him hath mercy on the poor.

32 The wicked is driven away in his wickedness: but the righteous hath hope in his death.

33 Wisdom resteth in the heart of him that hath understanding: but *that which is* in the midst of fools is made known.

34 Righteousness exalteth a nation: but sin *is* a reproach to any people.

35 The king's favour *is* toward a wise servant: but his wrath is *against* him that causeth shame.

**15** A SOFT answer turneth away wrath: but grievous words stir up anger.

2 The tongue of the wise useth knowledge aright: but the mouth of fools poureth out foolishness.

3 The eyes of the LORD *are* in every place, beholding the evil and the good.

4 A wholesome tongue *is* a tree of life: but perverseness therein *is* a breach in the spirit.

5 A fool despiseth his father's instruction: but he that regardeth reproof is prudent.

6 In the house of the righteous *is* much treasure: but in the revenues of the wicked is trouble.

7 The lips of the wise disperse knowledge: but the heart of the foolish *doeth* not so.

8 The sacrifice of the wicked *is* an abomination to the LORD: but the prayer of the upright *is* his delight.

## Amplified

19 The evil bow before the good, and the wicked [stand suppliant] at the gates of the [uncompromisingly] righteous.

20 The poor is hated even by his own neighbor, but the rich has many friends.

21 He who despises his neighbor sins [against God, his fellow man and himself], but happy—blessed and fortunate—is he who is kind *and* merciful to the poor.

22 Do they not err who devise evil *and* wander from the way of life? But loving-kindness *and* mercy, loyalty *and* faithfulness shall be to those who devise good.

23 In all labor there is profit, but idle talk leads only to poverty.

24 The crown of the wise is their wealth of wisdom, but the foolishness of [self-confident] fools is [nothing but] folly.

25 A true witness saves lives, but a deceitful witness speaks lies [and endangers lives].

26 In the reverent *and* worshipful fear of the Lord is strong confidence, and His children shall always have a place of refuge.

27 Reverent *and* worshipful fear of the Lord is a fountain of life, that one may avoid the snares of death. [John 4:10, 14.]

28 In the multitude of people is the king's glory, but in a lack of people is the prince's ruin.

29 He who is slow to anger has great understanding, but he who is hasty of spirit exposes *and* exalts his folly. [Prov. 16:32; James 1:19.]

30 A calm *and* undisturbed mind *and* heart are the life *and* health of the body, but envy, jealousy *and* wrath are as rottenness of the bones.

31 He who oppresses the poor reproaches, mocks *and* insults his Maker, but he who is kind *and* merciful to the needy honors Him. [Prov. 17:5; Matt. 25:40, 45.]

32 The wicked is overthrown through his wrongdoing *and* calamity, but the [consistently] righteous has hope *and* confidence even in his death.

33 Wisdom rests [silently] in the mind *and* heart of him who has understanding, but that which is in the inward part of [self-confident] fools is made known. [Isa. 32:6.]

34 Uprightness *and* right standing with God [moral and spiritual rectitude in every area and relation] *these* elevate a nation, but sin is a reproach to any people.

35 The king's favor is toward a wise *and* discreet servant, but his wrath is against him who does shamefully. [Matt. 24:45, 47.]

**15** A SOFT answer turns away wrath; but grievous words stir up anger. [Prov. 25:15.]

2 The tongue of the wise utters knowledge rightly, but the mouth of [self-confident] fools pours out folly.

3 The eyes of the Lord are in every place, keeping watch upon the evil and the good. [Prov. 5:21; Job 34:21; Jer. 16:17; 32:19; Heb. 4:13.]

4 A gentle tongue [with its healing power] is a tree of life, but willful contrariness in it breaks down the spirit.

5 A fool despises his father's instruction *and* correction, but he who regards reproof acquires prudence.

6 In the house of the [uncompromisingly] righteous is great [priceless] treasure, but with the income of the wicked is trouble *and* vexation.

7 The lips of the wise disperse knowledge [sifting it as chaff from the grain]; not so the mind of the self-confident *and* foolish.

8 The sacrifice of the wicked is an abomination, hateful *and* exceedingly offensive to the Lord, but the prayer of the upright is His delight! [Isa. 1:11; Jer. 6:20; Amos 5:22.]

## New American Standard

19 The evil will bow down before the good,
And the wicked at the gates of the righteous.
20 The poor is hated even by his neighbor,
But those who love the rich are many.
21 He who despises his neighbor sins,
But happy is he who is gracious to the poor.
22 Will they not go astray who devise evil?
But kindness and truth *will be to* those who devise good.
23 In all labor there is profit,
But mere talk *leads* only to poverty.
24 The crown of the wise is their riches,
*But* the folly of fools is foolishness.
25 A truthful witness saves lives,
But he who speaks lies is treacherous.
26 In the [a]fear of the LORD there is strong confidence,
And his children will have refuge.
27 The [b]fear of the LORD is a fountain of life,
That one may avoid the snares of death.
28 In a multitude of people is a king's glory,
But in the dearth of people is a prince's ruin.
29 He who is slow to anger has great understanding,
But he who is quick-tempered exalts folly.
30 A tranquil heart is life to the body,
But passion is rottenness to the bones.
31 He who oppresses the poor reproaches his Maker,
But he who is gracious to the needy honors Him.
32 The wicked is thrust down by his wrongdoing,
But the righteous has a refuge when he dies.
33 Wisdom rests in the heart of one who has understanding,
But in the bosom of fools it is made known.
34 Righteousness exalts a nation,
But sin is a disgrace to *any* people.
35 The king's favor is toward a servant who acts wisely,
But his anger is toward him who acts shamefully.

*Contrast the Upright and the Wicked*

15 A GENTLE answer turns away wrath,
But a harsh word stirs up anger.
2 The tongue of the wise makes knowledge acceptable,
But the mouth of fools spouts folly.
3 The eyes of the LORD are in every place,
Watching the evil and the good.
4 A soothing tongue is a tree of life,
But perversion in it crushes the spirit.
5 A fool rejects his father's discipline,
But he who regards reproof is prudent.
6 Much wealth is *in* the house of the righteous,
But trouble is in the income of the wicked.
7 The lips of the wise spread knowledge,
But the hearts of fools are not so.
8 The sacrifice of the wicked is an abomination to the LORD,
But the prayer of the upright is His delight.

NAS [a] Or, *reverence* [b] Or, *reverence*

## New International

19 Evil men will bow down in the presence of the good,
and the wicked at the gates of the righteous.

20 The poor are shunned even by their neighbors,
but the rich have many friends.

21 He who despises his neighbor sins,
but blessed is he who is kind to the needy.

22 Do not those who plot evil go astray?
But those who plan what is good find[c] love and faithfulness.

23 All hard work brings a profit,
but mere talk leads only to poverty.

24 The wealth of the wise is their crown,
but the folly of fools yields folly.

25 A truthful witness saves lives,
but a false witness is deceitful.

26 He who fears the LORD has a secure fortress,
and for his children it will be a refuge.

27 The fear of the LORD is a fountain of life,
turning a man from the snares of death.

28 A large population is a king's glory,
but without subjects a prince is ruined.

29 A patient man has great understanding,
but a quick-tempered man displays folly.

30 A heart at peace gives life to the body,
but envy rots the bones.

31 He who oppresses the poor shows contempt for their Maker,
but whoever is kind to the needy honors God.

32 When calamity comes, the wicked are brought down,
but even in death the righteous have a refuge.

33 Wisdom reposes in the heart of the discerning
and even among fools she lets herself be known.[d]

34 Righteousness exalts a nation,
but sin is a disgrace to any people.

35 A king delights in a wise servant,
but a shameful servant incurs his wrath.

15 A GENTLE answer turns away wrath,
but a harsh word stirs up anger.

2 The tongue of the wise commends knowledge,
but the mouth of the fool gushes folly.

3 The eyes of the LORD are everywhere,
keeping watch on the wicked and the good.

4 The tongue that brings healing is a tree of life,
but a deceitful tongue crushes the spirit.

5 A fool spurns his father's discipline,
but whoever heeds correction shows prudence.

6 The house of the righteous contains great treasure,
but the income of the wicked brings them trouble.

7 The lips of the wise spread knowledge;
not so the hearts of fools.

8 The LORD detests the sacrifice of the wicked,
but the prayer of the upright pleases him.

NIV [c] 22 Or *show* [d] 33 Hebrew; Septuagint and Syriac / *but in the heart of fools she is not known*

## King James

9The way of the wicked *is* an abomination unto the LORD: but he loveth him that followeth after righteousness.

10Correction *is* grievous unto him that forsaketh the way: *and* he that hateth reproof shall die.

11Hell and destruction *are* before the LORD: how much more then the hearts of the children of men?

12A scorner loveth not one that reproveth him: neither will he go unto the wise.

13A merry heart maketh a cheerful countenance: but by sorrow of the heart the spirit is broken.

14The heart of him that hath understanding seeketh knowledge: but the mouth of fools feedeth on foolishness.

15All the days of the afflicted *are* evil: but he that is of a merry heart *hath* a continual feast.

16Better *is* little with the fear of the LORD than great treasure and trouble therewith.

17Better *is* a dinner of herbs where love is, than a stalled ox and hatred therewith.

18A wrathful man stirreth up strife: but *he that is* slow to anger appeaseth strife.

19The way of the slothful *man is* as an hedge of thorns: but the way of the righteous *is* made plain.

20A wise son maketh a glad father: but a foolish man despiseth his mother.

21Folly *is* joy to *him that is* destitute of wisdom: but a man of understanding walketh uprightly.

22Without counsel purposes are disappointed: but in the multitude of counsellors they are established.

23A man hath joy by the answer of his mouth: and a word *spoken* in due season, how good *is it!*

24The way of life *is* above to the wise, that he may depart from hell beneath.

25The LORD will destroy the house of the proud: but he will establish the border of the widow.

26The thoughts of the wicked *are* an abomination to the LORD: but *the words* of the pure *are* pleasant words.

27He that is greedy of gain troubleth his own house; but he that hateth gifts shall live.

28The heart of the righteous studieth to answer: but the mouth of the wicked poureth out evil things.

29The LORD *is* far from the wicked: but he heareth the prayer of the righteous.

30The light of the eyes rejoiceth the heart: *and* a good report maketh the bones fat.

31The ear that heareth the reproof of life abideth among the wise.

32He that refuseth instruction despiseth his own soul: but he that heareth reproof getteth understanding.

33The fear of the LORD *is* the instruction of wisdom; and before honour *is* humility.

## Amplified

9The way of the wicked is an abomination, extremely disgusting *and* shamefully vile to the Lord, but He loves him who pursues righteousness [spiritual and moral rectitude in every area and relation].

10There is severe discipline for him who forsakes God's way, *and* he who hates reproof will die [physically, morally and spiritually].

11Sheol [the place of the dead] and Abaddon [the abyss, the final place of the accuser Satan] both are before the Lord; how much more then the hearts of the children of men? [Job 26:6; Ps. 139:8; Rev. 9:2; 20:1, 2.]

12A scorner has no love for one who rebukes him, neither will he go to the wise [for counsel].

13A glad heart makes a cheerful countenance, but by sorrow of heart the spirit is broken. [Prov. 17:22.]

14The mind of him who has understanding seeks knowledge, inquires after *and* craves it, but the mouths of [self-confident] fools feed on folly. [Isa. 32:6.]

15All the days of the desponding afflicted are made evil [by anxious thoughts and foreboding], but he who has a glad heart has a continual feast [regardless of circumstances].

16Better is little with the reverent, worshipful fear of the Lord than great *and* rich treasure and trouble with it. [Prov. 16:8; Ps. 37:16; I Tim. 6:6.]

17Better is a dinner of herbs where love is, than a fatted ox and hatred with it. [Prov. 17:1.]

18A hot-tempered man stirs up strife, but he who is slow to anger appeases contention.

19The way of the sluggard is overgrown with thorns [it pricks, lacerates and entangles him], but the way of the righteous is plain *and* raised like a highway.

20A wise son makes a glad father, but a self-confident *and* foolish man despises his mother *and* puts her to shame.

21Folly is pleasure to him who is without heart *and* sense, but a man of understanding walks uprightly—making straight his going. [Eph. 5:15.]

22Where there is no counsel, purposes are frustrated, but with many counselors they are accomplished.

23A man has joy in making an apt answer, and a word spoken at the right moment, how good it is!

24The path of the wise leads upward to life, that he may avoid *the gloom* in the depths of Sheol (Hades). [Phil. 3:20; Col. 3:1, 2.]

25The Lord tears down the house of the proud, but He will make secure the boundaries of the [consecrated] widow.

26The thoughts of the wicked are shamefully vile *and* exceedingly offensive to the Lord, but the words of the pure are pleasing words to Him.

27He who is greedy for unjust gain troubles his own household, but he who hates bribes will live. [Isa. 5:8; Jer. 17:11.]

28The mind of the [uncompromisingly] righteous studies how to answer, but the mouth of the wicked pours out evil things. [I Pet. 3:15.]

29The Lord is far from the wicked, but He hears the prayer of the [consistently] righteous—the upright, in right standing with Him.

30The light in the eyes [of him whose heart is joyful] rejoices the heart of others, *and* good news nourishes the bones.

31The ear that listens to the reproof *that leads to or gives* life will remain among the wise.

32He who refuses *and* ignores instruction *and* correction despises himself, but he who heeds reproof gets understanding.

33The reverent *and* worshipful fear of the Lord *brings* instruction in Wisdom, and humility comes before honor.

## New American Standard

9 The way of the wicked is an abomination to the LORD,
But He loves him who pursues righteousness.
10 Stern discipline is for him who forsakes the way;
He who hates reproof will die.
11 Sheol and Abaddon *lie open* before the LORD,
How much more the hearts of men!
12 A scoffer does not love one who reproves him,
He will not go to the wise.
13 A joyful heart makes a cheerful face,
But when the heart is sad, the spirit is broken.
14 The mind of the intelligent seeks knowledge,
But the mouth of fools feeds on folly.
15 All the days of the afflicted are bad,
But a cheerful heart *has* a continual feast.
16 Better is a little with the fear of the LORD,
Than great treasure and turmoil with it.
17 Better is a dish of vegetables where love is,
Than a fattened ox and hatred with it.
18 A hot-tempered man stirs up strife,
But the slow to anger pacifies contention.
19 The way of the sluggard is as a hedge of thorns,
But the path of the upright is a highway.
20 A wise son makes a father glad,
But a foolish man despises his mother.
21 Folly is joy to him who lacks sense,
But a man of understanding walks straight.
22 Without consultation, plans are frustrated,
But with many counselors they succeed.
23 A man has joy in an apt answer,
And how delightful is a timely word!
24 The path of life *leads* upward for the wise,
That he may keep away from Sheol below.
25 The LORD will tear down the house of the proud,
But He will establish the boundary of the widow.
26 Evil plans are an abomination to the LORD,
But pleasant words are pure.
27 He who profits illicitly troubles his own house,
But he who hates bribes will live.
28 The heart of the righteous ponders how to answer,
But the mouth of the wicked pours out evil things.
29 The LORD is far from the wicked,
But He hears the prayer of the righteous.
30 Bright eyes gladden the heart;
Good news puts fat on the bones.
31 He whose ear listens to the life-giving reproof
Will dwell among the wise.
32 He who neglects discipline despises himself,
But he who listens to reproof acquires understanding.
33 The fear of the LORD is the instruction for wisdom,
And before honor *comes* humility.

## New International

9 The LORD detests the way of the wicked
but he loves those who pursue righteousness.

10 Stern discipline awaits him who leaves the path;
he who hates correction will die.

11 Death and Destruction[a] lie open before the LORD—
how much more the hearts of men!

12 A mocker resents correction;
he will not consult the wise.

13 A happy heart makes the face cheerful,
but heartache crushes the spirit.

14 The discerning heart seeks knowledge,
but the mouth of a fool feeds on folly.

15 All the days of the oppressed are wretched,
but the cheerful heart has a continual feast.

16 Better a little with the fear of the LORD
than great wealth with turmoil.

17 Better a meal of vegetables where there is love
than a fattened calf with hatred.

18 A hot-tempered man stirs up dissension,
but a patient man calms a quarrel.

19 The way of the sluggard is blocked with thorns,
but the path of the upright is a highway.

20 A wise son brings joy to his father,
but a foolish man despises his mother.

21 Folly delights a man who lacks judgment,
but a man of understanding keeps a straight course.

22 Plans fail for lack of counsel,
but with many advisers they succeed.

23 A man finds joy in giving an apt reply—
and how good is a timely word!

24 The path of life leads upward for the wise
to keep him from going down to the grave.[b]

25 The LORD tears down the proud man's house
but he keeps the widow's boundaries intact.

26 The LORD detests the thoughts of the wicked,
but those of the pure are pleasing to him.

27 A greedy man brings trouble to his family,
but he who hates bribes will live.

28 The heart of the righteous weighs its answers,
but the mouth of the wicked gushes evil.

29 The LORD is far from the wicked
but he hears the prayer of the righteous.

30 A cheerful look brings joy to the heart,
and good news gives health to the bones.

31 He who listens to a life-giving rebuke
will be at home among the wise.

32 He who ignores discipline despises himself,
but whoever heeds correction gains understanding.

33 The fear of the LORD teaches a man wisdom,[c]
and humility comes before honor.

**NIV** [a] *11* Hebrew *Sheol and Abaddon* [b] 24 Hebrew *Sheol* [c] 33 Or *Wisdom teaches the fear of the LORD*

## King James

**16** THE PREPARATIONS of the heart in man, and the answer of the tongue, *is* from the LORD.

2 All the ways of a man *are* clean in his own eyes; but the LORD weigheth the spirits.

3 Commit thy works unto the LORD, and thy thoughts shall be established.

4 The LORD hath made all *things* for himself: yea, even the wicked for the day of evil.

5 Every one *that is* proud in heart *is* an abomination to the LORD: *though* hand *join* in hand, he shall not be unpunished.

6 By mercy and truth iniquity is purged: and by the fear of the LORD *men* depart from evil.

7 When a man's ways please the LORD, he maketh even his enemies to be at peace with him.

8 Better *is* a little with righteousness than great revenues without right.

9 A man's heart deviseth his way: but the LORD directeth his steps.

10 A divine sentence *is* in the lips of the king: his mouth transgresseth not in judgment.

11 A just weight and balance *are* the LORD'S: all the weights of the bag *are* his work.

12 *It is* an abomination to kings to commit wickedness: for the throne is established by righteousness.

13 Righteous lips *are* the delight of kings; and they love him that speaketh right.

14 The wrath of a king *is as* messengers of death: but a wise man will pacify it.

15 In the light of the king's countenance *is* life; and his favour *is* as a cloud of the latter rain.

16 How much better *is it* to get wisdom than gold! and to get understanding rather to be chosen than silver!

17 The highway of the upright *is* to depart from evil: he that keepeth his way preserveth his soul.

18 Pride *goeth* before destruction, and an haughty spirit before a fall.

19 Better *it is to be* of an humble spirit with the lowly, than to divide the spoil with the proud.

20 He that handleth a matter wisely shall find good: and whoso trusteth in the LORD, happy *is* he.

21 The wise in heart shall be called prudent: and the sweetness of the lips increaseth learning.

22 Understanding *is* a wellspring of life unto him that hath it: but the instruction of fools *is* folly.

23 The heart of the wise teacheth his mouth, and addeth learning to his lips.

24 Pleasant words *are as* an honeycomb, sweet to the soul, and health to the bones.

25 There is a way that seemeth right unto a man, but the end thereof *are* the ways of death.

26 He that laboureth laboureth for himself; for his mouth craveth it of him.

## Amplified

**16** THE PLANS of the mind *and* orderly thinking belong to man, but from the Lord comes the [wise] answer of the tongue.

2 All the ways of a man are pure in his own eyes, but the Lord weighs the spirits—the thoughts and intents of the heart. [I Sam. 16:7; Heb. 4:12.]

3 Roll your works upon the Lord—commit and trust them wholly to Him; [He will cause your thoughts to become agreeable to His will, and] so shall your plans be established *and* succeed.

4 The Lord has made everything [to accommodate itself and contribute] to its own end *and* His own purpose; even the wicked [are fitted for their role] for the day of calamity *and* evil.

5 Every one proud *and* arrogant in heart is disgusting, hateful *and* exceedingly offensive to the Lord; be assured—I pledge it—he will not go unpunished. [Prov. 8:13.]

6 By mercy *and* love, truth *and* fidelity [to God and man, not by sacrificial offerings] iniquity is purged out of the heart, and by the reverent, worshipful fear of the Lord men depart from *and* avoid evil.

7 When a man's ways please the Lord, He makes even his enemies to be at peace with him.

8 Better is a little with righteousness—uprightness in every area and human relation and right standing with God—than great revenues with injustice. [Prov. 15:16; Ps. 37:16.]

9 A man's mind plans his way, but the Lord directs his steps *and* makes them sure. [Prov. 20:24; Ps. 37:23; Jer. 10:23.]

10 Divinely directed decisions are on the lips of the king; his mouth should not transgress in judgment.

11 A just balance *or* scales are the Lord's; all the weights of the bag are His work [established on His eternal principles].

12 It is an abomination [to God and men] for kings to commit wickedness, for the throne is established *and* made secure by righteousness—spiritual and moral rectitude in every area and relation.

13 Right *and* just lips are the delight of a king, and he loves him who speaks what is right.

14 The wrath of a king is as messengers of death, but a wise man will pacify it.

15 In the light of the king's countenance is life, and his favor is as a cloud bringing the spring rain.

16 How much better it is to get skillful *and* godly Wisdom than gold! And to get understanding is to be chosen rather than silver. [Prov. 8:10, 19.]

17 The highway of the upright turns aside from evil; he who guards his way preserves his life.

18 Pride goes before destruction, and a haughty spirit before a fall.

19 Better it is to be of a humble spirit with the meek *and* poor, than to divide the spoil with the proud.

20 He who deals wisely *and* heeds [God's] Word shall find good, and whoever leans on, trusts *and* is confident in the Lord, happy, blessed, *and* fortunate is he.

21 The wise in heart shall be called prudent, understanding *and* knowing; and winsome speech increases learning [in both speaker and listener].

22 Understanding is a wellspring of life to him who has it, but to give instruction to fools is folly.

23 The mind of the wise instructs his mouth, and adds learning *and* persuasiveness to his lips.

24 Pleasant words are as a honeycomb, sweet to the mind and healing to the body.

25 There is a way that seems right to a man *and* appears straight before him, but at the end of it are the ways of death.

26 The appetite of the laborer works for him, for *the need of* his mouth urges him on.

## New American Standard

*Contrast the Upright and the Wicked*

**16** THE PLANS of the heart belong to man,
But the answer of the tongue is from the LORD.
2 All the ways of a man are clean in his own sight,
But the LORD weighs the motives.
3 Commit your works to the LORD,
And your plans will be established.
4 The LORD has made everything for its own purpose,
Even the wicked for the day of evil.
5 Everyone who is proud in heart is an abomination to the LORD;
Assuredly, he will not be unpunished.
6 By lovingkindness and truth iniquity is atoned for,
And by the fear of the LORD one keeps away from evil.
7 When a man's ways are pleasing to the LORD,
He makes even his enemies to be at peace with him.
8 Better is a little with righteousness
Than great income with injustice.
9 The mind of man plans his way,
But the LORD directs his steps.
10 A divine decision is in the lips of the king;
His mouth should not err in judgment.
11 A just balance and scales belong to the LORD;
All the weights of the bag are His concern.
12 It is an abomination for kings to commit wickedness,
For a throne is established on righteousness.
13 Righteous lips are the delight of kings,
And he who speaks right is loved.
14 The wrath of a king is *as* messengers of death,
But a wise man will appease it.
15 In the light of a king's face is life,
And his favor is like a cloud with the spring rain.
16 How much better it is to get wisdom than gold!
And to get understanding is to be chosen above silver.
17 The highway of the upright is to depart from evil;
He who watches his way preserves his life.
18 Pride *goes* before destruction,
And a haughty spirit before stumbling.
19 It is better to be of a humble spirit with the lowly,
Than to divide the spoil with the proud.
20 He who gives attention to the word shall find good,
And blessed is he who trusts in the LORD.
21 The wise in heart will be called discerning,
And sweetness of speech increases persuasiveness.
22 Understanding is a fountain of life to him who has it,
But the discipline of fools is folly.
23 The heart of the wise teaches his mouth,
And adds persuasiveness to his lips.
24 Pleasant words are a honeycomb,
Sweet to the soul and healing to the bones.
25 There is a way *which seems* right to a man,
But its end is the way of death.
26 A worker's appetite works for him,
For his hunger urges him *on*.

## New International

**16** TO MAN belong the plans of the heart,
but from the LORD comes the reply of the tongue.

2 All a man's ways seem innocent to him,
but motives are weighed by the LORD.

3 Commit to the LORD whatever you do,
and your plans will succeed.

4 The LORD works out everything for his own ends—
even the wicked for a day of disaster.

5 The LORD detests all the proud of heart.
Be sure of this: They will not go unpunished.

6 Through love and faithfulness sin is atoned for;
through the fear of the LORD a man avoids evil.

7 When a man's ways are pleasing to the LORD,
he makes even his enemies live at peace with him.

8 Better a little with righteousness
than much gain with injustice.

9 In his heart a man plans his course,
but the LORD determines his steps.

10 The lips of a king speak as an oracle,
and his mouth should not betray justice.

11 Honest scales and balances are from the LORD;
all the weights in the bag are of his making.

12 Kings detest wrongdoing,
for a throne is established through righteousness.

13 Kings take pleasure in honest lips;
they value a man who speaks the truth.

14 A king's wrath is a messenger of death,
but a wise man will appease it.

15 When a king's face brightens, it means life;
his favor is like a rain cloud in spring.

16 How much better to get wisdom than gold,
to choose understanding rather than silver!

17 The highway of the upright avoids evil;
he who guards his way guards his life.

18 Pride goes before destruction,
a haughty spirit before a fall.

19 Better to be lowly in spirit and among the oppressed
than to share plunder with the proud.

20 Whoever gives heed to instruction prospers,
and blessed is he who trusts in the LORD.

21 The wise in heart are called discerning,
and pleasant words promote instruction.[a]

22 Understanding is a fountain of life to those who have it,
but folly brings punishment to fools.

23 A wise man's heart guides his mouth,
and his lips promote instruction.[b]

24 Pleasant words are a honeycomb,
sweet to the soul and healing to the bones.

25 There is a way that seems right to a man,
but in the end it leads to death.

26 The laborer's appetite works for him;
his hunger drives him on.

**NIV** [a] 21 Or *words make a man persuasive* [b] 23 Or *mouth / and makes his lips persuasive*

## King James

27An ungodly man diggeth up evil: and in his lips *there is* as a burning fire.

28A froward man soweth strife: and a whisperer separateth chief friends.

29A violent man enticeth his neighbour, and leadeth him into the way *that is* not good.

30He shutteth his eyes to devise froward things: moving his lips he bringeth evil to pass.

31The hoary head *is* a crown of glory, *if* it be found in the way of righteousness.

32 *He that is* slow to anger *is* better than the mighty; and he that ruleth his spirit than he that taketh a city.

33The lot is cast into the lap; but the whole disposing thereof *is* of the LORD.

**17** BETTER *IS* a dry morsel, and quietness therewith, than an house full of sacrifices *with* strife.

2A wise servant shall have rule over a son that causeth shame, and shall have part of the inheritance among the brethren.

3The refining pot *is* for silver, and the furnace for gold: but the LORD trieth the hearts.

4A wicked doer giveth heed to false lips; *and* a liar giveth ear to a naughty tongue.

5Whoso mocketh the poor reproacheth his Maker: *and* he that is glad at calamities shall not be unpunished.

6Children's children *are* the crown of old men; and the glory of children *are* their fathers.

7Excellent speech becometh not a fool: much less do lying lips a prince.

8A gift *is as* a precious stone in the eyes of him that hath it: whithersoever it turneth, it prospereth.

9He that covereth a transgression seeketh love; but he that repeateth a matter separateth *very* friends.

10A reproof entereth more into a wise man than an hundred stripes into a fool.

11An evil *man* seeketh only rebellion: therefore a cruel messenger shall be sent against him.

12Let a bear robbed of her whelps meet a man, rather than a fool in his folly.

13Whoso rewardeth evil for good, evil shall not depart from his house.

14The beginning of strife *is as* when one letteth out water: therefore leave off contention, before it be meddled with.

15He that justifieth the wicked, and he that condemneth the just, even they both *are* abomination to the LORD.

16Wherefore *is there* a price in the hand of a fool to get wisdom, seeing *he hath* no heart *to it?*

17A friend loveth at all times, and a brother is born for adversity.

18A man void of understanding striketh hands, *and* becometh surety in the presence of his friend.

## Amplified

27A worthless man devises *and* digs up mischief, and in his lips there is as a scorching fire.

28A perverse man sows strife, and a whisperer separates close friends. [Prov. 17:9.]

29The exceedingly grasping, covetous *and* violent man entices his neighbor, leading him into the way that is not good.

30He who shuts his eyes to devise perverse things, and who compresses his lips [as if in concealment] will bring evil to pass.

31The hoary head is a crown of beauty *and* glory, if it is found in the way of righteousness—of spiritual and moral rectitude in every area and relation. [Prov. 20:29.]

32He who is slow to anger is better than the mighty, and he who rules his *own* spirit than he who takes a city.

33The lot is cast into the lap, but the decision is wholly of the Lord— *even* the events [that seem accidental] are really ordered by Him.

**17** BETTER IS a dry morsel with quietness than a house full of feasting (on offered sacrifices) with strife.

2A wise servant shall have rule over a son who causes shame, and shall share in the inheritance among the brothers.

3The refining pot is for silver, and the furnace for gold, but the Lord tries the hearts. [Prov. 27:21; Ps. 26:2; Jer. 17:10; Mal. 3:3.]

4An evildoer gives heed to wicked lips, *and* a liar listens to a mischievous tongue.

5Whoever mocks the poor reproaches his Maker, and he who is glad at calamity shall not be held innocent *or* go unpunished. [Prov. 14:31; Job 31:29; Obad. 12.]

6Children's children are the crown of old men, and the glory of children is their fathers. [Pss. 127:3; 128:3.]

7Fine *or* arrogant speech does not become [an empty-headed] fool; much less do lying lips become a prince.

8A bribe is like a bright, precious stone that dazzles the eyes *and* affects the mind of him who gives it; [as if by magic] he prospers whichever way he turns.

9He who covers *and* forgives an offense seeks love, but he who repeats *or* harps on a matter separates even close friends.

10A reproof enters deeper into one of understanding than a hundred lashes into a [self-confident] fool. [Isa. 32:6.]

11An evil man seeks only rebellion; therefore a stern *and* pitiless messenger shall be sent against him.

12Let [the brute ferocity of] a bear robbed of her whelps meet a man, rather than a [self-confident] fool in his folly [when he is in a rage]. [Hos. 13:8.]

13Whoever rewards evil for good, evil shall not depart from his house. [Ps. 109:4, 5; Jer. 18:20.]

14The beginning of strife is as when water first trickles [from a crack in a dam]; therefore stop contention before it becomes worse *and* quarreling breaks out.

15He who justifies the wicked and he who condemns the righteous are both an abomination—exceedingly disgusting and hateful—to the Lord. [Prov. 24:24; Exod. 23:7; Isa. 5:23.]

16Of what use is money in the hand of a [self-confident] fool to buy skillful *and* godly Wisdom, when he has no understanding *or* heart for it?

17A friend loves at all times, and is born, as is a brother, for adversity.

18A man void of good sense gives a pledge *and* becomes security for another in the presence of his neighbor.

## New American Standard

27 A worthless man digs up evil,
While his words are as a scorching fire.
28 A perverse man spreads strife,
And a slanderer separates intimate friends.
29 A man of violence entices his neighbor,
And leads him in a way that is not good.
30 He who winks his eyes *does so* to devise perverse things;
He who compresses his lips brings evil to pass.
31 A gray head is a crown of glory;
It is found in the way of righteousness.
32 He who is slow to anger is better than the mighty,
And he who rules his spirit, than he who captures a city.
33 The lot is cast into the lap,
But its every decision is from the LORD.

*Contrast the Upright and the Wicked*

17 BETTER IS a dry morsel and quietness with it
Than a house full of feasting with strife.
2 A servant who acts wisely will rule over a son who acts shamefully,
And will share in the inheritance among brothers.
3 The refining pot is for silver and the furnace for gold,
But the LORD tests hearts.
4 An evildoer listens to wicked lips,
A liar pays attention to a destructive tongue.
5 He who mocks the poor reproaches his Maker;
He who rejoices at calamity will not go unpunished.
6 Grandchildren are the crown of old men,
And the glory of sons is their fathers.
7 Excellent speech is not fitting for a fool;
Much less are lying lips to a prince.
8 A bribe is a charm in the sight of its owner;
Wherever he turns, he prospers.
9 He who covers a transgression seeks love,
But he who repeats a matter separates intimate friends.
10 A rebuke goes deeper into one who has understanding
Than a hundred blows into a fool.
11 A rebellious man seeks only evil,
So a cruel messenger will be sent against him.
12 Let a man meet a bear robbed of her cubs,
Rather than a fool in his folly.
13 He who returns evil for good,
Evil will not depart from his house.
14 The beginning of strife is *like* letting out water,
So abandon the quarrel before it breaks out.
15 He who justifies the wicked, and he who condemns the righteous,
Both of them alike are an abomination to the LORD.
16 Why is there a price in the hand of a fool to buy wisdom,
When he has no sense?
17 A friend loves at all times,
And a brother is born for adversity.
18 A man lacking in sense pledges,
And becomes surety in the presence of his neighbor.

## New International

27A scoundrel plots evil,
and his speech is like a scorching fire.

28A perverse man stirs up dissension,
and a gossip separates close friends.

29A violent man entices his neighbor
and leads him down a path that is not good.

30He who winks with his eye is plotting perversity;
he who purses his lips is bent on evil.

31Gray hair is a crown of splendor;
it is attained by a righteous life.

32Better a patient man than a warrior,
a man who controls his temper than one who takes a city.

33The lot is cast into the lap,
but its every decision is from the LORD.

17 BETTER A dry crust with peace and quiet
than a house full of feasting,[a] with strife.

2A wise servant will rule over a disgraceful son,
and will share the inheritance as one of the brothers.

3The crucible for silver and the furnace for gold,
but the LORD tests the heart.

4A wicked man listens to evil lips;
a liar pays attention to a malicious tongue.

5He who mocks the poor shows contempt for their Maker;
whoever gloats over disaster will not go unpunished.

6Children's children are a crown to the aged,
and parents are the pride of their children.

7Arrogant[b] lips are unsuited to a fool—
how much worse lying lips to a ruler!

8A bribe is a charm to the one who gives it;
wherever he turns, he succeeds.

9He who covers over an offense promotes love,
but whoever repeats the matter separates close friends.

10A rebuke impresses a man of discernment
more than a hundred lashes a fool.

11An evil man is bent only on rebellion;
a merciless official will be sent against him.

12Better to meet a bear robbed of her cubs
than a fool in his folly.

13If a man pays back evil for good,
evil will never leave his house.

14Starting a quarrel is like breaching a dam;
so drop the matter before a dispute breaks out.

15Acquitting the guilty and condemning the innocent—
the LORD detests them both.

16Of what use is money in the hand of a fool,
since he has no desire to get wisdom?

17A friend loves at all times,
and a brother is born for adversity.

18A man lacking in judgment strikes hands in pledge
and puts up security for his neighbor.

NIV [a] 1 Hebrew *sacrifices* [b] 7 Or *Eloquent*

## King James

19 He loveth transgression that loveth strife: *and* he that exalteth
his gate seeketh destruction.
20 He that hath a froward heart findeth no good: and he that
hath a perverse tongue falleth into mischief.
21 He that begetteth a fool *doeth it* to his sorrow: and the father
of a fool hath no joy.
22 A merry heart doeth good *like* a medicine: but a broken spirit
drieth the bones.
23 A wicked *man* taketh a gift out of the bosom to pervert the
ways of judgment.
24 Wisdom *is* before him that hath understanding; but the eyes
of a fool *are* in the ends of the earth.
25 A foolish son *is* a grief to his father, and bitterness to her that
bare him.
26 Also to punish the just *is* not good, *nor* to strike princes for
equity.
27 He that hath knowledge spareth his words: *and* a man of
understanding is of an excellent spirit.
28 Even a fool, when he holdeth his peace, is counted wise: *and*
he that shutteth his lips *is esteemed* a man of understanding.

**18** THROUGH DESIRE a man, having separated himself,
seeketh *and* intermeddleth with all wisdom.
2 A fool hath no delight in understanding, but that his heart may
discover itself.
3 When the wicked cometh, *then* cometh also contempt, and
with ignominy reproach.
4 The words of a man's mouth *are as* deep waters, *and* the wellspring of wisdom *as* a flowing brook.
5 *It is* not good to accept the person of the wicked, to overthrow
the righteous in judgment.
6 A fool's lips enter into contention, and his mouth calleth for
strokes.
7 A fool's mouth *is* his destruction, and his lips *are* the snare of
his soul.
8 The words of a talebearer *are* as wounds, and they go down
into the innermost parts of the belly.
9 He also that is slothful in his work is brother to him that is a
great waster.
10 The name of the LORD *is* a strong tower: the righteous runneth
into it, and is safe.
11 The rich man's wealth *is* his strong city, and as an high wall
in his own conceit.
12 Before destruction the heart of man is haughty, and before
honour *is* humility.
13 He that answereth a matter before he heareth *it*, it *is* folly and
shame unto him.
14 The spirit of a man will sustain his infirmity; but a wounded
spirit who can bear?
15 The heart of the prudent getteth knowledge; and the ear of the
wise seeketh knowledge.
16 A man's gift maketh room for him, and bringeth him before
great men.
17 *He that is* first in his own cause *seemeth* just; but his neighbour
cometh and searcheth him.

## Amplified

19 He who loves strife *and* is quarrelsome loves transgression *and*
involves himself in guilt; he who raises high his gateway and is
boastful *and* arrogant invites destruction.
20 He who has a wayward *and* crooked mind finds no good, and
he who has a willful *and* contrary tongue will fall into calamity.
[James 3:8.]
21 He who becomes the parent of a [self-confident] fool does it
to his sorrow, and the father of [an empty-headed] fool has no joy
[in him].
22 A happy heart is a good medicine *and* a cheerful mind works
healing, but a broken spirit dries the bones. [Prov. 12:25; 15:13, 15.]
23 A wicked man receives a bribe out of the bosom [pocket] to
pervert the ways of justice.
24 A man of understanding sets skillful *and* godly Wisdom before
his face, but the eyes of a [self-confident] fool are on the ends of
the earth.
25 A self-confident *and* foolish son is a grief to his father, and
bitterness to her who bore him.
26 Also to punish *or* fine the righteous is not good, *nor* to smite
the noble for their uprightness.
27 He who has knowledge spares his words, and a man of
understanding has a cool spirit. [James 1:19.]
28 Even a fool when he holds his peace is considered wise; when
he closes his lips he is esteemed a man of understanding.

**18** HE WHO willfully separates *and* estranges himself [from
God and man] seeks his own desire *and* pretext to break
out against all wise *and* sound judgment.
2 A [self-confident] fool has no delight in understanding, but
only in revealing his personal opinions *and* himself.
3 When the wicked comes in [to the depth of evil], he becomes
a contemptuous despiser [of all that is pure and good], and with
inner baseness comes outer shame *and* reproach.
4 The words of a [discreet and wise] man's mouth are as deep
waters [plenteous and difficult to fathom]; and the fountain of
skillful *and* godly Wisdom is as a gushing stream [sparkling, fresh,
pure and life-giving].
5 To respect the person of the wicked *and* be partial, so as to
deprive the [consistently] righteous of justice, is not good.
6 A [self-confident] fool's lips bring contention, and his mouth
invites a beating.
7 A [self-confident] fool's mouth is his ruin, and his lips are a
snare to himself.
8 The words of a whisperer *or* talebearer are as dainty morsels;
they go down into the innermost parts of the body.
9 He who is loose *and* slack in his work is brother to him who
is a destroyer [ *and* [a]he who does not use his endeavors to heal
himself is brother to him who commits suicide].
10 The name of the Lord is a strong tower; the [consistently]
righteous man—upright and in right standing with God—runs
into it and is safe, high [above evil] *and* strong.
11 The rich man's wealth is his strong city, and as a high protecting wall, in his own imagination *and* conceit.
12 Haughtiness comes before disaster, and humility before hon-
or.
13 He who answers a matter before he hears the facts, it is folly
and shame to him. [John 7:51.]
14 The strong spirit of a man will sustain him in bodily pain *or*
trouble, but a weak *and* broken spirit who can raise up *or* bear?
15 The mind of the prudent is ever getting knowledge, and the
ear of the wise is ever seeking—inquiring for and craving—knowledge.
16 A man's gift makes room for him and brings him before great
men. [Prov. 17:8; 21:14; Gen. 32:20; I Sam. 25:27.]
17 He who states his case first seems right, until his rival comes
and cross-examines him.

**AMP** [a] This verse so reads in *The Septuagint Version* (the Greek translation of the Hebrew). Its statement squarely meets the problem as to whether one has a moral right to neglect his body by letting "nature take its course" unhindered in illness.

## New American Standard

19 He who loves transgression loves strife;
He who raises his door seeks destruction.
20 He who has a crooked mind finds no good,
And he who is perverted in his language falls into evil.
21 He who begets a fool *does so* to his sorrow,
And the father of a fool has no joy.
22 A joyful heart is good medicine,
But a broken spirit dries up the bones.
23 A wicked man receives a bribe from the bosom
To pervert the ways of justice.
24 Wisdom is in the presence of the one who has understanding,
But the eyes of a fool are on the ends of the earth.
25 A foolish son is a grief to his father,
And bitterness to her who bore him.
26 It is also not good to fine the righteous,
*Nor* to strike the noble for *their* uprightness.
27 He who restrains his words has knowledge,
And he who has a cool spirit is a man of understanding.
28 Even a fool, when he keeps silent, is considered wise;
When he closes his lips, he is *counted* prudent.

*Contrast the Upright and the Wicked*

18 HE WHO separates himself seeks *his own* desire,
He quarrels against all sound wisdom.
2 A fool does not delight in understanding,
But only in revealing his own mind.
3 When a wicked man comes, contempt also comes,
And with dishonor *comes* reproach.
4 The words of a man's mouth are deep waters;
The fountain of wisdom is a bubbling brook.
5 To show partiality to the wicked is not good,
*Nor* to thrust aside the righteous in judgment.
6 A fool's lips bring strife,
And his mouth calls for blows.
7 A fool's mouth is his ruin,
And his lips are the snare of his soul.
8 The words of a whisperer are like dainty morsels,
And they go down into the innermost parts of the body.
9 He also who is slack in his work
Is brother to him who destroys.
10 The name of the LORD is a strong tower;
The righteous runs into it and is safe.
11 A rich man's wealth is his strong city,
And like a high wall in his own imagination.
12 Before destruction the heart of man is haughty,
But humility *goes* before honor.
13 He who gives an answer before he hears,
It is folly and shame to him.
14 The spirit of a man can endure his sickness,
But a broken spirit who can bear?
15 The mind of the prudent acquires knowledge,
And the ear of the wise seeks knowledge.
16 A man's gift makes room for him,
And brings him before great men.
17 The first to plead his case *seems* just,
*Until* another comes and examines him.

## New International

19He who loves a quarrel loves sin;
he who builds a high gate invites destruction.
20A man of perverse heart does not prosper;
he whose tongue is deceitful falls into trouble.
21To have a fool for a son brings grief;
there is no joy for the father of a fool.

22A cheerful heart is good medicine,
but a crushed spirit dries up the bones.

23A wicked man accepts a bribe in secret
to pervert the course of justice.

24A discerning man keeps wisdom in view,
but a fool's eyes wander to the ends of the earth.

25A foolish son brings grief to his father
and bitterness to the one who bore him.

26It is not good to punish an innocent man,
or to flog officials for their integrity.

27A man of knowledge uses words with restraint,
and a man of understanding is even-tempered.

28Even a fool is thought wise if he keeps silent,
and discerning if he holds his tongue.

18 AN UNFRIENDLY man pursues selfish ends;
he defies all sound judgment.

2A fool finds no pleasure in understanding
but delights in airing his own opinions.

3When wickedness comes, so does contempt,
and with shame comes disgrace.

4The words of a man's mouth are deep waters,
but the fountain of wisdom is a bubbling brook.

5It is not good to be partial to the wicked
or to deprive the innocent of justice.

6A fool's lips bring him strife,
and his mouth invites a beating.

7A fool's mouth is his undoing,
and his lips are a snare to his soul.

8The words of a gossip are like choice morsels;
they go down to a man's inmost parts.

9One who is slack in his work
is brother to one who destroys.

10The name of the LORD is a strong tower;
the righteous run to it and are safe.

11The wealth of the rich is their fortified city;
they imagine it an unscalable wall.

12Before his downfall a man's heart is proud,
but humility comes before honor.

13He who answers before listening—
that is his folly and his shame.

14A man's spirit sustains him in sickness,
but a crushed spirit who can bear?

15The heart of the discerning acquires knowledge;
the ears of the wise seek it out.

16A gift opens the way for the giver
and ushers him into the presence of the great.

17The first to present his case seems right,
till another comes forward and questions him.

# King James

18The lot causeth contentions to cease, and parteth between the mighty.

19A brother offended *is harder to be won* than a strong city: and *their* contentions *are* like the bars of a castle.

20A man's belly shall be satisfied with the fruit of his mouth; *and* with the increase of his lips shall he be filled.

21Death and life *are* in the power of the tongue: and they that love it shall eat the fruit thereof.

22 *Whoso* findeth a wife findeth a good *thing,* and obtaineth favour of the Lord.

23The poor useth entreaties; but the rich answereth roughly.

24A man *that hath* friends must show himself friendly: and there is a friend *that* sticketh closer than a brother.

**19** BETTER *IS* the poor that walketh in his integrity, than *he that is* perverse in his lips, and is a fool.

2Also, *that* the soul *be* without knowledge, *it is* not good; and he that hasteth with *his* feet sinneth.

3The foolishness of man perverteth his way: and his heart fretteth against the Lord.

4Wealth maketh many friends; but the poor is separated from his neighbour.

5A false witness shall not be unpunished, and *he that* speaketh lies shall not escape.

6Many will entreat the favour of the prince: and every man *is* a friend to him that giveth gifts.

7All the brethren of the poor do hate him: how much more do his friends go far from him? he pursueth *them with* words, *yet* they *are* wanting *to* him.

8He that getteth wisdom loveth his own soul: he that keepeth understanding shall find good.

9A false witness shall not be unpunished, and *he that* speaketh lies shall perish.

10Delight is not seemly for a fool; much less for a servant to have rule over princes.

11The discretion of a man deferreth his anger; and *it is* his glory to pass over a transgression.

12The king's wrath *is* as the roaring of a lion; but his favour *is* as dew upon the grass.

13A foolish son *is* the calamity of his father: and the contentions of a wife *are* a continual dropping.

14House and riches *are* the inheritance of fathers: and a prudent wife *is* from the Lord.

15Slothfulness casteth into a deep sleep; and an idle soul shall suffer hunger.

16He that keepeth the commandment keepeth his own soul; *but* he that despiseth his ways shall die.

17He that hath pity upon the poor lendeth unto the Lord; and that which he hath given will he pay him again.

# Amplified

18To cast lots puts an end to disputes, and decides between powerful contenders.

19A brother offended is harder to be won than a strong city, and their contentions separate them like the bars of a castle.

20A man's *moral* self shall be filled with the fruit of his mouth, *and* with the consequence of his words he must be satisfied [whether good or evil].

21Death and life are in the power of the tongue, and they who indulge it shall eat the fruit of it [for death or life]. [Matt. 12:37.]

22He who finds a [true] wife finds a good thing, and obtains favor of the Lord. [Prov. 19:14; 31:10.]

23The poor use entreaties, but the rich answer roughly.

24The man of many friends [a friend of all the world] will prove himself a bad friend, but there is a friend who sticks closer than a brother.

**19** BETTER IS the poor who walks in his integrity, than the rich who is perverse in his speech and is a [self-confident] fool.

2Desire without knowledge is not good, and to be over-hasty is to sin and miss the mark.

3The foolishness of man subverts his way [ruins his affairs]; then his heart is resentful *and* frets against the Lord.

4Wealth makes many friends, but the poor is avoided by his neighbor. [Prov. 14:20.]

5A false witness shall not be unpunished, and he who breathes out lies shall not escape. [Prov. 6:19; 21:28; Exod. 23:1; Deut. 19:16-19.]

6Many will entreat the favor of the liberal man, and every man is a friend to him who gives gifts.

7All the brothers of the poor detest him; how much more do his friends go far from him! He pursues them with words, but they are gone.

8He who gains Wisdom loves his own life; he who keeps understanding shall prosper *and* find good.

9A false witness shall not be unpunished, and he who breathes forth lies shall perish.

10Luxury is not fitting for a [self-confident] fool, much less for a slave to rule over princes.

11Good sense makes a man restrain his anger, and it is his glory to overlook a transgression *or* an offense.

12The king's wrath is as terrifying as the roaring of a lion, but his favor is as [refreshing as] dew upon the grass. [Hos. 14:5.]

13A self-confident *and* foolish son is the [multiplied] calamity of his father, and the contentions of a wife are as a continual dropping [of water through a chink in the roof].

14House and riches are the inheritance from fathers, but a wise, understanding *and* prudent wife is from the Lord. [Prov. 18:22.]

15Slothfulness casts one into a deep sleep, and the idle person shall suffer hunger.

16He who keeps the commandment [of the Lord] keeps his own life, but he who despises His ways shall die. [Luke 10:28; 11:28.]

17He who has pity on the poor lends to the Lord, and that which he has given He will repay to him. [Prov. 28:27; Eccl. 11:1; Matt. 10:42; 25:40; II Cor. 9:6-8; Heb. 6:10.]

## New American Standard

18 The lot puts an end to contentions,
And decides between the mighty.
19 A brother offended *is harder to be won* than a strong city,
And contentions are like the bars of a castle.
20 With the fruit of a man's mouth his stomach will be satisfied;
He will be satisfied *with* the product of his lips.
21 Death and life are in the power of the tongue,
And those who love it will eat its fruit.
22 He who finds a wife finds a good thing,
And obtains favor from the LORD.
23 The poor man utters supplications,
But the rich man answers roughly.
24 A man of *many* friends *comes* to ruin,
But there is a friend who sticks closer than a brother.

*On Life and Conduct*

19 BETTER IS a poor man who walks in his integrity
Than he who is perverse in speech and is a fool.
2 Also it is not good for a person to be without knowledge,
And he who makes haste with his feet errs.
3 The foolishness of man subverts his way,
And his heart rages against the LORD.
4 Wealth adds many friends,
But a poor man is separated from his friend.
5 A false witness will not go unpunished,
And he who tells lies will not escape.
6 Many will entreat the favor of a generous man,
And every man is a friend to him who gives gifts.
7 All the brothers of a poor man hate him;
How much more do his friends go far from him!
He pursues *them with* words, *but* they are gone.
8 He who gets wisdom loves his own soul;
He who keeps understanding will find good.
9 A false witness will not go unpunished,
And he who tells lies will perish.
10 Luxury is not fitting for a fool;
Much less for a slave to rule over princes.
11 A man's discretion makes him slow to anger,
And it is his glory to overlook a transgression.
12 The king's wrath is like the roaring of a lion,
But his favor is like dew on the grass.
13 A foolish son is destruction to his father,
And the contentions of a wife are a constant dripping.
14 House and wealth are an inheritance from fathers,
But a prudent wife is from the LORD.
15 Laziness casts into a deep sleep,
And an idle man will suffer hunger.
16 He who keeps the commandment keeps his soul,
*But* he who is careless of his ways will die.
17 He who is gracious to a poor man lends to the LORD,
And He will repay him for his good deed.

## New International

18 Casting the lot settles disputes
and keeps strong opponents apart.

19 An offended brother is more unyielding than a fortified city,
and disputes are like the barred gates of a citadel.

20 From the fruit of his mouth a man's stomach is filled;
with the harvest from his lips he is satisfied.

21 The tongue has the power of life and death,
and those who love it will eat its fruit.

22 He who finds a wife finds what is good
and receives favor from the LORD.

23 A poor man pleads for mercy,
but a rich man answers harshly.

24 A man of many companions may come to ruin,
but there is a friend who sticks closer than a brother.

19 BETTER A poor man whose walk is blameless
than a fool whose lips are perverse.

2 It is not good to have zeal without knowledge,
nor to be hasty and miss the way.

3 A man's own folly ruins his life,
yet his heart rages against the LORD.

4 Wealth brings many friends,
but a poor man's friend deserts him.

5 A false witness will not go unpunished,
and he who pours out lies will not go free.

6 Many curry favor with a ruler,
and everyone is the friend of a man who gives gifts.

7 A poor man is shunned by all his relatives—
how much more do his friends avoid him!
Though he pursues them with pleading,
they are nowhere to be found.[a]

8 He who gets wisdom loves his own soul;
he who cherishes understanding prospers.

9 A false witness will not go unpunished,
and he who pours out lies will perish.

10 It is not fitting for a fool to live in luxury—
how much worse for a slave to rule over princes!

11 A man's wisdom gives him patience;
it is to his glory to overlook an offense.

12 A king's rage is like the roar of a lion,
but his favor is like dew on the grass.

13 A foolish son is his father's ruin,
and a quarrelsome wife is like a constant dripping.

14 Houses and wealth are inherited from parents,
but a prudent wife is from the LORD.

15 Laziness brings on deep sleep,
and the shiftless man goes hungry.

16 He who obeys instructions guards his life,
but he who is contemptuous of his ways will die.

17 He who is kind to the poor lends to the LORD,
and he will reward him for what he has done.

NIV [a] 7 The meaning of the Hebrew for this sentence is uncertain.

## King James

18 Chasten thy son while there is hope, and let not thy soul spare for his crying.

19 A man of great wrath shall suffer punishment: for if thou deliver *him*, yet thou must do it again.

20 Hear counsel, and receive instruction, that thou mayest be wise in thy latter end.

21 *There are* many devices in a man's heart; nevertheless the counsel of the LORD, that shall stand.

22 The desire of a man *is* his kindness: and a poor man *is* better than a liar.

23 The fear of the LORD *tendeth* to life: and *he that hath it* shall abide satisfied; he shall not be visited with evil.

24 A slothful *man* hideth his hand in *his* bosom, and will not so much as bring it to his mouth again.

25 Smite a scorner, and the simple will beware: and reprove one that hath understanding, *and* he will understand knowledge.

26 He that wasteth *his* father, *and* chaseth away *his* mother, *is* a son that causeth shame, and bringeth reproach.

27 Cease, my son, to hear the instruction *that causeth* to err from the words of knowledge.

28 An ungodly witness scorneth judgment: and the mouth of the wicked devoureth iniquity.

29 Judgments are prepared for scorners, and stripes for the back of fools.

**20** WINE *IS* a mocker, strong drink *is* raging: and whosoever is deceived thereby is not wise.

2 The fear of a king *is* as the roaring of a lion: *whoso* provoketh him to anger sinneth *against* his own soul.

3 *It is* an honour for a man to cease from strife: but every fool will be meddling.

4 The sluggard will not plow by reason of the cold; *therefore* shall he beg in harvest, and *have* nothing.

5 Counsel in the heart of man *is like* deep water; but a man of understanding will draw it out.

6 Most men will proclaim every one his own goodness: but a faithful man who can find?

7 The just *man* walketh in his integrity: his children *are* blessed after him.

8 A king that sitteth in the throne of judgment scattereth away all evil with his eyes.

9 Who can say, I have made my heart clean, I am pure from my sin?

10 Divers weights, *and* divers measures, both of them *are* alike abomination to the LORD.

11 Even a child is known by his doings, whether his work *be* pure, and whether *it be* right.

12 The hearing ear, and the seeing eye, the LORD hath made even both of them.

13 Love not sleep, lest thou come to poverty; open thine eyes, *and* thou shalt be satisfied with bread.

14 *It is* naught, *it is* naught, saith the buyer: but when he is gone his way, then he boasteth.

## Amplified

18 Discipline your son while there is hope, but do not [indulge your angry resentments by undue chastisements and] set yourself to his ruin.

19 A man of great wrath shall suffer the penalty, for if you deliver him [from the consequences], he will [feel free to] cause you to do it again.

20 Hear counsel, receive instruction *and* accept correction, that you may be wise in the time to come.

21 Many plans are in a man's mind, but it is the Lord's purpose for him that will stand. [Job 23:13; Ps. 33:10, 11; Isa. 14:26, 27; 46:10; Acts 5:39; Heb. 6:17.]

22 That which is desired in a man is loyalty *and* kindness, *and* his glory *and* delight are his giving, but a poor man is better than a liar.

23 The reverent, worshipful fear of the Lord leads to life, and he who has it shall rest satisfied; he cannot be visited with [actual] evil. [Job 5:19; Prov. 12:13; Isa. 46:4; Jer. 1:8; Dan. 6:27; Ps. 91:3; II Tim. 4:8.]

24 The sluggard buries his hand in the dish, and will not so much as bring it to his mouth again.

25 Strike a scoffer, and the simple will learn prudence; reprove a man of understanding, *and* he will increase in knowledge.

26 He who does violence to his father and chases away his mother is a son who causes shame and brings reproach.

27 Cease, my son, to hear instruction only to ignore it *and* stray from the words of knowledge.

28 A worthless witness scoffs at justice, and the mouth of the wicked swallows iniquity.

29 Judgments are prepared for scoffers, and stripes for the back of [self-confident] fools. [Isa. 32:6.]

**20** WINE IS a mocker, strong drink a riotous brawler, and whoever errs *or* reels because of it is not wise. [Prov. 23:29, 30; Isa. 28:7; Hos. 4:11.]

2 The terror of a king is as the roaring of a lion; whoever provokes him to anger *or* angers himself against him sins against his own life.

3 It is an honor for a man to cease from strife *and* keep aloof from it, but every fool will be quarreling.

4 The sluggard will not plow when winter sets in; therefore shall he beg in harvest, and have nothing.

5 Counsel in the heart of man is like water in a deep well, but a man of understanding will draw it out. [Prov. 18:4.]

6 Many a man proclaims his own loving-kindness *and* goodness, but a faithful man who can find?

7 The righteous man walks in his integrity; blessed—happy, fortunate [enviable]—are his children after him.

8 A king who sits on the throne of judgment winnows out all evil [like chaff] with his eyes.

9 Who can say, I have made my heart clean, I am pure from my sin? [I Kings 8:46; II Chron. 6:36; Job 9:30; 14:4; Ps. 51:5; I John 1:8.]

10 Diverse weights [one for buying and another for selling] and diverse measures, both of them are exceedingly offensive *and* abhorrent to the Lord. [Deut. 25:13; Mic. 6:10, 11.]

11 Even a child is known by his acts, whether *or not* what he does is pure and right.

12 The hearing ear and the seeing eye, the Lord has made both of them.

13 Love not sleep, lest you come to poverty; open your eyes *and* you will be satisfied with bread.

14 It is worthless, it is worthless! says the buyer; but when he goes his way, then he boasts [about his bargain].

## New American Standard

18 Discipline your son while there is hope,
And do not desire his death.
19 *A man of* great anger shall bear the penalty,
For if you rescue *him*, you will only have to do it again.
20 Listen to counsel and accept discipline,
That you may be wise the rest of your days.
21 Many are the plans in a man's heart,
But the counsel of the LORD, it will stand.
22 What is desirable in a man is his [a]kindness,
And *it is* better to be a poor man than a liar.
23 The fear of the LORD *leads* to life,
So that one may sleep satisfied, untouched by evil.
24 The sluggard buries his hand in the dish,
*And* will not even bring it back to his mouth.
25 Strike a scoffer and the naive may become shrewd,
But reprove one who has understanding and he will gain knowledge.
26 He who assaults *his* father *and* drives *his* mother away
Is a shameful and disgraceful son.
27 Cease listening, my son, to discipline,
*And you will* stray from the words of knowledge.
28 A rascally witness makes a mockery of justice,
And the mouth of the wicked spreads iniquity.
29 Judgments are prepared for scoffers,
And blows for the back of fools.

*On Life and Conduct*

20 WINE IS a mocker, strong drink a brawler,
And whoever is intoxicated by it is not wise.
2 The terror of a king is like the growling of a lion;
He who provokes him to anger forfeits his own life.
3 Keeping away from strife is an honor for a man,
But any fool will quarrel.
4 The sluggard does not plow after the autumn,
So he begs during the harvest and has nothing.
5 A plan in the heart of a man is *like* deep water,
But a man of understanding draws it out.
6 Many a man proclaims his own loyalty,
But who can find a trustworthy man?
7 A righteous man who walks in his integrity—
How blessed are his sons after him.
8 A king who sits on the throne of justice
Disperses all evil with his eyes.
9 Who can say, "I have cleansed my heart,
I am pure from my sin"?
10 Differing weights and differing measures,
Both of them are abominable to the LORD.
11 It is by his deeds that a lad distinguishes himself
If his conduct is pure and right.
12 The hearing ear and the seeing eye,
The LORD has made both of them.
13 Do not love sleep, lest you become poor;
Open your eyes, *and* you will be satisfied with food.
14 "Bad, bad," says the buyer;
But when he goes his way, then he boasts.

NAS [a] Or, *loyalty*

## New International

18 Discipline your son, for in that there is hope;
do not be a willing party to his death.

19 A hot-tempered man must pay the penalty;
if you rescue him, you will have to do it again.

20 Listen to advice and accept instruction,
and in the end you will be wise.

21 Many are the plans in a man's heart,
but it is the LORD's purpose that prevails.

22 What a man desires is unfailing love[b];
better to be poor than a liar.

23 The fear of the LORD leads to life:
Then one rests content, untouched by trouble.

24 The sluggard buries his hand in the dish;
he will not even bring it back to his mouth!

25 Flog a mocker, and the simple will learn prudence;
rebuke a discerning man, and he will gain knowledge.

26 He who robs his father and drives out his mother
is a son who brings shame and disgrace.

27 Stop listening to instruction, my son,
and you will stray from the words of knowledge.

28 A corrupt witness mocks at justice,
and the mouth of the wicked gulps down evil.

29 Penalties are prepared for mockers,
and beatings for the backs of fools.

20 WINE IS a mocker and beer a brawler;
whoever is led astray by them is not wise.

2 A king's wrath is like the roar of a lion;
he who angers him forfeits his life.

3 It is to a man's honor to avoid strife,
but every fool is quick to quarrel.

4 A sluggard does not plow in season;
so at harvest time he looks but finds nothing.

5 The purposes of a man's heart are deep waters,
but a man of understanding draws them out.

6 Many a man claims to have unfailing love,
but a faithful man who can find?

7 The righteous man leads a blameless life;
blessed are his children after him.

8 When a king sits on his throne to judge,
he winnows out all evil with his eyes.

9 Who can say, "I have kept my heart pure;
I am clean and without sin"?

10 Differing weights and differing measures—
the LORD detests them both.

11 Even a child is known by his actions,
by whether his conduct is pure and right.

12 Ears that hear and eyes that see—
the LORD has made them both.

13 Do not love sleep or you will grow poor;
stay awake and you will have food to spare.

14 "It's no good, it's no good!" says the buyer;
then off he goes and boasts about his purchase.

NIV [b] 22 Or *A man's greed is his shame*

## King James

15 There is gold, and a multitude of rubies: but the lips of knowledge *are* a precious jewel.

16 Take his garment that is surety *for* a stranger: and take a pledge of him for a strange woman.

17 Bread of deceit *is* sweet to a man; but afterwards his mouth shall be filled with gravel.

18 *Every* purpose is established by counsel: and with good advice make war.

19 He that goeth about *as* a talebearer revealeth secrets: therefore meddle not with him that flattereth with his lips.

20 Whoso curseth his father or his mother, his lamp shall be put out in obscure darkness.

21 An inheritance *may be* gotten hastily at the beginning; but the end thereof shall not be blessed.

22 Say not thou, I will recompense evil; *but* wait on the LORD, and he shall save thee.

23 Divers weights *are* an abomination unto the LORD; and a false balance *is* not good.

24 Man's goings *are* of the LORD; how can a man then understand his own way?

25 *It is* a snare to the man *who* devoureth *that which is* holy, and after vows to make inquiry.

26 A wise king scattereth the wicked, and bringeth the wheel over them.

27 The spirit of man *is* the candle of the LORD, searching all the inward parts of the belly.

28 Mercy and truth preserve the king: and his throne is upholden by mercy.

29 The glory of young men *is* their strength: and the beauty of old men *is* the gray head.

30 The blueness of a wound cleanseth away evil: so *do* stripes the inward parts of the belly.

**21** THE KING'S heart *is* in the hand of the LORD, *as* the rivers of water: he turneth it whithersoever he will.

2 Every way of a man *is* right in his own eyes: but the LORD pondereth the hearts.

3 To do justice and judgment *is* more acceptable to the LORD than sacrifice.

4 An high look, and a proud heart, *and* the plowing of the wicked, *is* sin.

5 The thoughts of the diligent *tend* only to plenteousness; but of every one *that is* hasty only to want.

6 The getting of treasures by a lying tongue *is* a vanity tossed to and fro of them that seek death.

7 The robbery of the wicked shall destroy them; because they refuse to do judgment.

8 The way of man *is* froward and strange: but *as for* the pure, his work *is* right.

9 *It is* better to dwell in a corner of the housetop, than with a brawling woman in a wide house.

## Amplified

15 There is gold, and a multitude of pearls; but the lips of knowledge are a vase of preciousness [the most precious of all]. [Prov. 3:15; 8:11; Job 28:12, 16-19.]

16 [The judge tells the creditor] Take his garment who is security for a stranger, and hold him in pledge when he is security for foreigners.

17 Food gained by deceit is sweet to a man, but afterward his mouth will be filled with gravel.

18 Purposes *and* plans are established by counsel, and *only* with good advice make *or* carry on war.

19 He who goes about as a talebearer reveals secrets; therefore associate not with him who talks too freely. [Rom. 16:17, 18.]

20 Whoever curses his father or his mother, his lamp shall be put out in complete darkness.

21 An inheritance hastily gotten [by greedy, unjust means] at the beginning, in the end will not be blessed. [Prov. 28:20; Hab. 2:6.]

22 Do not say, I will repay evil; wait (expectantly) for the Lord, and He will rescue you. [Rom. 12:17-19; I Thess. 5:15; I Pet. 3:9; II Sam. 16:12.]

23 Diverse *and* deceitful weights are shamefully vile *and* abhorrent to the Lord, and false scales are not good.

24 Man's steps are ordered by the Lord; how can a man then understand his way?

25 It is a snare to a man to utter a vow [of consecration] rashly, and *not until* afterward inquire [whether he can fulfill it].

26 A wise king winnows the wicked [from among the good], and brings the threshing wheel over them [to separate the chaff from the grain].

27 The spirit of man [that factor in human personality which proceeds immediately from God] is the lamp of the Lord, searching all his innermost parts. [I Cor. 2:11.]

28 Loving-kindness *and* mercy, truth *and* faithfulness preserve the king, and his throne is upheld by [the people's] loyalty.

29 The glory of young men is their strength, and the beauty of old men is their gray head [suggesting wisdom and experience].

30 Blows that wound cleanse away evil, and strokes [for correction] reach to the innermost parts.

**21** THE KING'S heart is in the hand of the Lord as are the watercourses; He turns it whichever way He will.

2 Every way of man is right in his own eyes, but the Lord weighs *and* tries the hearts. [Prov. 24:12; Luke 16:15.]

3 To do righteousness and justice is more acceptable to the Lord than sacrifice. [Prov. 15:8; I Sam. 15:22; Isa. 1:11; Hos. 6:6; Mic. 6:7, 8.]

4 Haughtiness of eyes and a proud heart, even the tillage of the wicked, *or* the lamp *of joy* to them, [whatever it may be] is sin [in the eyes of God].

5 The thoughts of the [steadily] diligent tend only to plenteousness, but every one who is impatient *and* hasty hastens only to want.

6 Securing treasures by a lying tongue is a vapor driven to and fro; those who seek them seek death.

7 The violence of the wicked shall sweep them away, because they refuse to do justice.

8 The way of the guilty is exceedingly crooked, but as for the pure, his work is right *and* his conduct is straight.

9 It is better to dwell in a corner of the housetop [on the flat oriental roof, exposed to all kinds of weather] than in a house shared with a nagging, quarrelsome *and* faultfinding woman.

## New American Standard

15 There is gold, and an abundance of jewels;
But the lips of knowledge are a more precious thing.
16 Take his garment when he becomes surety for a stranger;
And for foreigners, hold him in pledge.
17 Bread obtained by falsehood is sweet to a man,
But afterward his mouth will be filled with gravel.
18 Prepare plans by consultation,
And make war by wise guidance.
19 He who goes about as a slanderer reveals secrets,
Therefore do not associate with a gossip.
20 He who curses his father or his mother,
His lamp will go out in time of darkness.
21 An inheritance gained hurriedly at the beginning,
Will not be blessed in the end.
22 Do not say, "I will repay evil";
Wait for the LORD, and He will save you.
23 Differing weights are an abomination to the LORD,
And a false scale is not good.
24 Man's steps are *ordained* by the LORD,
How then can man understand his way?
25 It is a snare for a man to say rashly, "It is holy!"
And after the vows to make inquiry.
26 A wise king winnows the wicked,
And drives the *threshing* wheel over them.
27 The spirit of man is the lamp of the LORD,
Searching all the innermost parts of his being.
28 Loyalty and truth preserve the king,
And he upholds his throne by righteousness.
29 The glory of young men is their strength,
And the honor of old men is their gray hair.
30 Stripes that wound scour away evil,
And strokes *reach* the innermost parts.

*On Life and Conduct*

**21** THE KING'S heart is *like* channels of water in the hand of the LORD;
He turns it wherever He wishes.
2 Every man's way is right in his own eyes,
But the LORD weighs the hearts.
3 To do righteousness and justice
Is desired by the LORD rather than sacrifice.
4 Haughty eyes and a proud heart,
The lamp of the wicked, is sin.
5 The plans of the diligent *lead* surely to advantage,
But everyone who is hasty *comes* surely to poverty.
6 The getting of treasures by a lying tongue
Is a fleeting vapor, the pursuit of death.
7 The violence of the wicked will drag them away,
Because they refuse to act with justice.
8 The way of a guilty man is crooked,
But as for the pure, his conduct is upright.
9 It is better to live in a corner of a roof,
Than in a house shared with a contentious woman.

## New International

15 Gold there is, and rubies in abundance,
but lips that speak knowledge are a rare jewel.

16 Take the garment of one who puts up security for a stranger;
hold it in pledge if he does it for a wayward woman.

17 Food gained by fraud tastes sweet to a man,
but he ends up with a mouth full of gravel.

18 Make plans by seeking advice;
if you wage war, obtain guidance.

19 A gossip betrays a confidence;
so avoid a man who talks too much.

20 If a man curses his father or mother,
his lamp will be snuffed out in pitch darkness.

21 An inheritance quickly gained at the beginning
will not be blessed at the end.

22 Do not say, "I'll pay you back for this wrong!"
Wait for the LORD, and he will deliver you.

23 The LORD detests differing weights,
and dishonest scales do not please him.

24 A man's steps are directed by the LORD.
How then can anyone understand his own way?

25 It is a trap for a man to dedicate something rashly
and only later to consider his vows.

26 A wise king winnows out the wicked;
he drives the threshing wheel over them.

27 The lamp of the LORD searches the spirit of a man[a];
it searches out his inmost being.

28 Love and faithfulness keep a king safe;
through love his throne is made secure.

29 The glory of young men is their strength,
gray hair the splendor of the old.

30 Blows and wounds cleanse away evil,
and beatings purge the inmost being.

**21** THE KING'S heart is in the hand of the LORD;
he directs it like a watercourse wherever he pleases.

2 All a man's ways seem right to him,
but the LORD weighs the heart.

3 To do what is right and just
is more acceptable to the LORD than sacrifice.

4 Haughty eyes and a proud heart,
the lamp of the wicked, are sin!

5 The plans of the diligent lead to profit
as surely as haste leads to poverty.

6 A fortune made by a lying tongue
is a fleeting vapor and a deadly snare.[b]

7 The violence of the wicked will drag them away,
for they refuse to do what is right.

8 The way of the guilty is devious,
but the conduct of the innocent is upright.

9 Better to live on a corner of the roof
than share a house with a quarrelsome wife.

**NIV** [a] 27 Or *The spirit of man is the LORD's lamp* [b] 6 Some Hebrew manuscripts, Septuagint and Vulgate; most Hebrew manuscripts *vapor for those who seek death*

## King James

10The soul of the wicked desireth evil: his neighbour findeth no favour in his eyes.

11When the scorner is punished, the simple is made wise: and when the wise is instructed, he receiveth knowledge.

12The righteous *man* wisely considereth the house of the wicked: *but God* overthroweth the wicked for *their* wickedness.

13Whoso stoppeth his ears at the cry of the poor, he also shall cry himself, but shall not be heard.

14A gift in secret pacifieth anger: and a reward in the bosom strong wrath.

15 *It is* joy to the just to do judgment: but destruction *shall be* to the workers of iniquity.

16The man that wandereth out of the way of understanding shall remain in the congregation of the dead.

17He that loveth pleasure *shall be* a poor man: he that loveth wine and oil shall not be rich.

18The wicked *shall be* a ransom for the righteous, and the transgressor for the upright.

19 *It is* better to dwell in the wilderness, than with a contentious and an angry woman.

20 *There is* treasure to be desired and oil in the dwelling of the wise; but a foolish man spendeth it up.

21He that followeth after righteousness and mercy findeth life, righteousness, and honour.

22A wise *man* scaleth the city of the mighty, and casteth down the strength of the confidence thereof.

23Whoso keepeth his mouth and his tongue keepeth his soul from troubles.

24Proud *and* haughty scorner *is* his name, who dealeth in proud wrath.

25The desire of the slothful killeth him; for his hands refuse to labour.

26He coveteth greedily all the day long: but the righteous giveth and spareth not.

27The sacrifice of the wicked *is* abomination: how much more, *when* he bringeth it with a wicked mind?

28A false witness shall perish: but the man that heareth speaketh constantly.

29A wicked man hardeneth his face: but *as for* the upright, he directeth his way.

30 *There is* no wisdom nor understanding nor counsel against the LORD.

31The horse *is* prepared against the day of battle: but safety *is* of the LORD.

**22** A *GOOD* name *is* rather to be chosen than great riches, *and* loving favour rather than silver and gold.

2The rich and poor meet together: the LORD *is* the maker of them all.

3A prudent *man* foreseeth the evil, and hideth himself: but the simple pass on, and are punished.

## Amplified

10The soul *or* life of the wicked craves *and* seeks evil; his neighbor finds no favor in his eyes. [James 2:16.]

11When the scoffer is punished, the fool gets a lesson in being wise; but men of wisdom *and* good sense learn by being instructed.

12The [uncompromisingly] righteous man considers well the house of the wicked, how the wicked are cast down to ruin.

13Whoever stops his ears at the cry of the poor will cry out himself and not be heard. [Matt. 18:30-34; James 2:13.]

14A gift in secret pacifies *and* turns away anger, and a bribe in the lap, strong wrath.

15When justice is done it is a joy to the righteous [the upright, in right standing with God]; but to the evildoers it is dismay, calamity *and* ruin.

16The man who wanders out of the way of understanding shall abide in the congregation of the spirits—of the dead.

17He who loves pleasure will be a poor man; he who loves wine and oil will not be rich.

18The wicked shall be a ransom for the [uncompromisingly] righteous, and the treacherous for the upright [because the wicked fall themselves into the traps and pits they have dug for the good].

19It is better to dwell in a desert land than with a contentious woman and vexation.

20There are precious treasure and oil in the dwelling of the wise, but a self-confident *and* foolish man swallows it up *and* wastes it.

21He who earnestly seeks after *and* craves righteousness, mercy *and* loving-kindness will find life in addition to righteousness [uprightness and right standing with God] and *also* honor. [Prov. 15:9; Matt. 5:6.]

22A wise man scales the city walls of the mighty and brings down the stronghold in which they trust.

23He who guards his mouth and his tongue keeps himself from troubles. [Prov. 12:13; 13:3; 18:21; James 3:2.]

24The proud *and* haughty man—scoffer is his name—deals *and* acts with overbearing pride.

25The desire of the slothful kills him, for his hands refuse to labor.

26He covets greedily all the day long, but the [uncompromisingly] righteous gives and does not withhold. [II Cor. 9:6-10.]

27The sacrifice of the wicked is exceedingly disgusting *and* abhorrent [to the Lord]; how much more when he brings it with evil intention?

28A false witness will perish, but the word of a man who hears attentively will endure *and* be unchallenged.

29A wicked man puts on the bold, unfeeling face [of guilt], but as for the upright, he considers, directs *and* establishes his way [with the confidence of integrity].

30There is no wisdom or understanding or counsel [that can prevail] against the Lord.

31The horse is prepared for the day of battle, but deliverance *and* victory are of the Lord.

**22** A GOOD name is rather to be chosen than great riches, and loving favor rather than silver and gold.

2The rich and poor meet together; the Lord is the maker of them all. [Prov. 14:31; Job 31:15.]

3A prudent man sees the evil and hides himself, but the simple pass on and are punished (with suffering).

## New American Standard

10 The soul of the wicked desires evil;
His neighbor finds no favor in his eyes.
11 When the scoffer is punished, the naive becomes wise;
But when the wise is instructed, he receives knowledge.
12 The righteous one considers the house of the wicked,
Turning the wicked to ruin.
13 He who shuts his ear to the cry of the poor
Will also cry himself and not be answered.
14 A gift in secret subdues anger,
And a bribe in the bosom, strong wrath.
15 The execution of justice is joy for the righteous,
But is terror to the workers of iniquity.
16 A man who wanders from the way of understanding
Will rest in the assembly of the dead.
17 He who loves pleasure *will become* a poor man;
He who loves wine and oil will not become rich.
18 The wicked is a ransom for the righteous,
And the treacherous is in the place of the upright.
19 It is better to live in a desert land,
Than with a contentious and vexing woman.
20 There is precious treasure and oil in the dwelling of the wise,
But a foolish man swallows it up.
21 He who pursues righteousness and loyalty
Finds life, righteousness and honor.
22 A wise man scales the city of the mighty,
And brings down the stronghold in which they trust.
23 He who guards his mouth and his tongue,
Guards his soul from troubles.
24 "Proud," "Haughty," "Scoffer," are his names,
Who acts with insolent pride.
25 The desire of the sluggard puts him to death,
For his hands refuse to work;
26 All day long he is craving,
While the righteous gives and does not hold back.
27 The sacrifice of the wicked is an abomination,
How much more when he brings it with evil intent!
28 A false witness will perish,
But the man who listens *to the truth* will speak forever.
29 A wicked man shows a bold face,
But as for the upright, he makes his way sure.
30 There is no wisdom and no understanding
And no counsel against the LORD.
31 The horse is prepared for the day of battle,
But victory belongs to the LORD.

*On Life and Conduct*

**22** A *GOOD* name is to be more desired than great riches,
Favor is better than silver and gold.
2 The rich and the poor have a common bond,
The LORD is the maker of them all.
3 The prudent sees the evil and hides himself,
But the naive go on, and are punished for it.

## New International

10The wicked man craves evil;
his neighbor gets no mercy from him.
11When a mocker is punished, the simple gain wisdom;
when a wise man is instructed, he gets knowledge.
12The Righteous One[a] takes note of the house of the wicked
and brings the wicked to ruin.
13If a man shuts his ears to the cry of the poor,
he too will cry out and not be answered.
14A gift given in secret soothes anger,
and a bribe concealed in the cloak pacifies great wrath.
15When justice is done, it brings joy to the righteous
but terror to evildoers.
16A man who strays from the path of understanding
comes to rest in the company of the dead.
17He who loves pleasure will become poor;
whoever loves wine and oil will never be rich.
18The wicked become a ransom for the righteous,
and the unfaithful for the upright.
19Better to live in a desert
than with a quarrelsome and ill-tempered wife.
20In the house of the wise are stores of choice food and oil,
but a foolish man devours all he has.
21He who pursues righteousness and love
finds life, prosperity[b] and honor.
22A wise man attacks the city of the mighty
and pulls down the stronghold in which they trust.
23He who guards his mouth and his tongue
keeps himself from calamity.
24The proud and arrogant man—"Mocker" is his name;
he behaves with overweening pride.
25The sluggard's craving will be the death of him,
because his hands refuse to work.
26All day long he craves for more,
but the righteous give without sparing.
27The sacrifice of the wicked is detestable—
how much more so when brought with evil intent!
28A false witness will perish,
and whoever listens to him will be destroyed forever.[c]
29A wicked man puts up a bold front,
but an upright man gives thought to his ways.
30There is no wisdom, no insight, no plan
that can succeed against the LORD.
31The horse is made ready for the day of battle,
but victory rests with the LORD.

**22** A GOOD name is more desirable than great riches;
to be esteemed is better than silver or gold.

2Rich and poor have this in common:
The LORD is the Maker of them all.

3A prudent man sees danger and takes refuge,
but the simple keep going and suffer for it.

**NIV** [a] 12 Or *The righteous man* [b] 21 Or *righteousness* [c] 28 Or / *but the words of an obedient man will live on*

## King James

4By humility *and* the fear of the LORD *are* riches, and honour, and life.

5Thorns *and* snares *are* in the way of the froward: he that doth keep his soul shall be far from them.

6Train up a child in the way he should go: and when he is old, he will not depart from it.

7The rich ruleth over the poor, and the borrower *is* servant to the lender.

8He that soweth iniquity shall reap vanity: and the rod of his anger shall fail.

9He that hath a bountiful eye shall be blessed; for he giveth of his bread to the poor.

10Cast out the scorner, and contention shall go out; yea, strife and reproach shall cease.

11He that loveth pureness of heart, *for* the grace of his lips the king *shall be* his friend.

12The eyes of the LORD preserve knowledge, and he overthroweth the words of the transgressor.

13The slothful *man* saith, *There is* a lion without, I shall be slain in the streets.

14The mouth of strange women *is* a deep pit: he that is abhorred of the LORD shall fall therein.

15Foolishness *is* bound in the heart of a child; *but* the rod of correction shall drive it far from him.

16He that oppresseth the poor to increase his *riches, and* he that giveth to the rich, *shall* surely *come* to want.

17Bow down thine ear, and hear the words of the wise, and apply thine heart unto my knowledge.

18For *it is* a pleasant thing if thou keep them within thee; they shall withal be fitted in thy lips.

19That thy trust may be in the LORD, I have made known to thee this day, even to thee.

20Have not I written to thee excellent things in counsels and knowledge,

21That I might make thee know the certainty of the words of truth; that thou mightest answer the words of truth to them that send unto thee?

22Rob not the poor, because he *is* poor: neither oppress the afflicted in the gate:

23For the LORD will plead their cause, and spoil the soul of those that spoiled them.

24Make no friendship with an angry man; and with a furious man thou shalt not go:

25Lest thou learn his ways, and get a snare to thy soul.

26Be not thou *one* of them that strike hands, *or* of them that are sureties for debts.

27If thou hast nothing to pay, why should he take away thy bed from under thee?

28Remove not the ancient landmark, which thy fathers have set.

29Seest thou a man diligent in his business? he shall stand before kings; he shall not stand before mean *men*.

## Amplified

4The reward of humility *and* the reverent *and* worshipful fear of the Lord is riches and honor and life.

5Thorns and snares are in the way of the obstinate *and* willful; he who guards himself will be far from them.

6Train up a child in the way he should go [and in keeping with his individual gift or bent], and when he is old he will not depart from it. [Eph. 6:4; II Tim. 3:15.]

7The rich rules over the poor, and the borrower is servant to the lender.

8He who sows iniquity will reap calamity *and* futility, and the rod of his wrath [with which he smites others] will fail.

9He who has a bountiful eye shall be blessed, for he gives of his bread to the poor. [II Cor. 9:6-10.]

10Drive out the scoffer and contention will go out; yes, strife and abuse will cease.

11He who loves purity *and* the pure in heart, *and* who is gracious in speech, will for the grace of his lips have the king for his friend.

12The eyes of the Lord keep guard over knowledge *and* him who has it, but He overthrows the words of the treacherous.

13The sluggard says, There is a lion outside! I shall be slain in the streets!

14The mouth of loose women is a deep pit [for ensnaring wild animals]; he with whom the Lord is indignant *and* who is abhorrent to Him will fall into it.

15Foolishness is bound up in the heart of a child, but the rod of discipline will drive it far from him.

16He who oppresses the poor to get gain for himself, *and* he who gives to the rich will surely come to want.

17Listen [consent and submit] to the words of the wise, and apply your mind to my knowledge;

18For it will be pleasant if you keep them in your mind [believing them]; your lips will be accustomed to [confessing] them.

19That your trust—belief, reliance, support and confidence—may be in the Lord, I have made known these things to you today, even to you.

20Have I not written to you [long ago] excellent things in counsels and knowledge,

21To make you know the certainty of the words of truth, that you may give a true answer to those who sent you? [Luke 1:3, 4.]

22Rob not the poor [being tempted by his helplessness], neither oppress the afflicted at the gate [where the city court is held]; [Exod. 23:6; Job 31:16, 21.]

23For the Lord will plead their cause, and deprive of life those who deprive *the poor or afflicted*. [Zech. 7:10; Mal. 3:5.]

24Make no friendships with a man given to anger, and with a wrathful man do not associate,

25Lest you learn his ways and get yourself into a snare.

26Be not one of those who strike hands *and* pledge themselves, *or* of those who become security for another's debts.

27If you have nothing with which to pay, why should he take away your bed from under you?

28Remove not the ancient landmark which your fathers have set.

29Do you see a man diligent *and* skillful in his business? He will stand before kings; he will not stand before obscure men.

## New American Standard

4 The reward of humility *and* the fear of the LORD
Are riches, honor and life.
5 Thorns *and* snares are in the way of the perverse;
He who guards himself will be far from them.
6 Train up a child in the way he should go,
Even when he is old he will not depart from it.
7 The rich rules over the poor,
And the borrower *becomes* the lender's slave.
8 He who sows iniquity will reap vanity,
And the rod of his fury will perish.
9 He who is generous will be blessed,
For he gives some of his food to the poor.
10 Drive out the scoffer, and contention will go out,
Even strife and dishonor will cease.
11 He who loves purity of heart
*And* whose speech is gracious, the king is his friend.
12 The eyes of the LORD preserve knowledge,
But He overthrows the words of the treacherous man.
13 The sluggard says, "There is a lion outside;
I shall be slain in the streets!"
14 The mouth of an adulteress is a deep pit;
He who is cursed of the LORD will fall into it.
15 Foolishness is bound up in the heart of a child;
The rod of discipline will remove it far from him.
16 He who oppresses the poor to make much for himself
Or who gives to the rich, *will* only *come to* poverty.

**17** ¶ Incline your ear and hear the words of the wise,
And apply your mind to my knowledge;
18 For it will be pleasant if you keep them within you,
That they may be ready on your lips.
19 So that your trust may be in the LORD,
I have taught you today, even you.
20 Have I not written to you excellent things
Of counsels and knowledge,
21 To make you know the certainty of the words of truth
That you may correctly answer to him who sent you?

**22** ¶ Do not rob the poor because he is poor,
Or crush the afflicted at the gate;
23 For the LORD will plead their case,
And take the life of those who rob them.

**24** ¶ Do not associate with a man *given* to anger;
Or go with a hot-tempered man,
25 Lest you learn his ways,
And find a snare for yourself.

**26** ¶ Do not be among those who give pledges,
Among those who become sureties for debts.
27 If you have nothing with which to pay,
Why should he take your bed from under you?

**28** ¶ Do not move the ancient boundary
Which your fathers have set.

**29** ¶ Do you see a man skilled in his work?
He will stand before kings;
He will not stand before obscure men.

## New International

4 Humility and the fear of the LORD
bring wealth and honor and life.

5 In the paths of the wicked lie thorns and snares,
but he who guards his soul stays far from them.

6 Train[a] a child in the way he should go,
and when he is old he will not turn from it.

7 The rich rule over the poor,
and the borrower is servant to the lender.

8 He who sows wickedness reaps trouble,
and the rod of his fury will be destroyed.

9 A generous man will himself be blessed,
for he shares his food with the poor.

10 Drive out the mocker, and out goes strife;
quarrels and insults are ended.

11 He who loves a pure heart and whose speech is gracious
will have the king for his friend.

12 The eyes of the LORD keep watch over knowledge,
but he frustrates the words of the unfaithful.

13 The sluggard says, "There is a lion outside!"
or, "I will be murdered in the streets!"

14 The mouth of an adulteress is a deep pit;
he who is under the LORD's wrath will fall into it.

15 Folly is bound up in the heart of a child,
but the rod of discipline will drive it far from him.

16 He who oppresses the poor to increase his wealth
and he who gives gifts to the rich—both come to
poverty.

### *Sayings of the Wise*

17 Pay attention and listen to the sayings of the wise;
apply your heart to what I teach,
18 for it is pleasing when you keep them in your heart
and have all of them ready on your lips.
19 So that your trust may be in the LORD,
I teach you today, even you.
20 Have I not written thirty[b] sayings for you,
sayings of counsel and knowledge,
21 teaching you true and reliable words,
so that you can give sound answers
to him who sent you?

22 Do not exploit the poor because they are poor
and do not crush the needy in court,
23 for the LORD will take up their case
and will plunder those who plunder them.

24 Do not make friends with a hot-tempered man,
do not associate with one easily angered,
25 or you may learn his ways
and get yourself ensnared.

26 Do not be a man who strikes hands in pledge
or puts up security for debts;
27 if you lack the means to pay,
your very bed will be snatched from under you.

28 Do not move an ancient boundary stone
set up by your forefathers.

29 Do you see a man skilled in his work?
He will serve before kings;
he will not serve before obscure men.

**NIV** [a] 6 Or *Start* [b] 20 Or *not formerly written;* or *not written excellent*

## King James

**23** WHEN THOU sittest to eat with a ruler, consider diligently what *is* before thee:

2 And put a knife to thy throat, if thou *be* a man given to appetite.

3 Be not desirous of his dainties: for they *are* deceitful meat.

4 Labour not to be rich: cease from thine own wisdom.

5 Wilt thou set thine eyes upon that which is not? for *riches* certainly make themselves wings; they fly away as an eagle toward heaven.

6 Eat thou not the bread of *him that hath* an evil eye, neither desire thou his dainty meats:

7 For as he thinketh in his heart, so *is* he: Eat and drink, saith he to thee; but his heart *is* not with thee.

8 The morsel *which* thou hast eaten shalt thou vomit up, and lose thy sweet words.

9 Speak not in the ears of a fool: for he will despise the wisdom of thy words.

10 Remove not the old landmark; and enter not into the fields of the fatherless:

11 For their redeemer *is* mighty; he shall plead their cause with thee.

12 Apply thine heart unto instruction, and thine ears to the words of knowledge.

13 Withhold not correction from the child: for *if* thou beatest him with the rod, he shall not die.

14 Thou shalt beat him with the rod, and shalt deliver his soul from hell.

15 My son, if thine heart be wise, my heart shall rejoice, even mine.

16 Yea, my reins shall rejoice, when thy lips speak right things.

17 Let not thine heart envy sinners: but *be thou* in the fear of the LORD all the day long.

18 For surely there is an end; and thine expectation shall not be cut off.

19 Hear thou, my son, and be wise, and guide thine heart in the way.

20 Be not among winebibbers; among riotous eaters of flesh:

21 For the drunkard and the glutton shall come to poverty: and drowsiness shall clothe *a man* with rags.

22 Hearken unto thy father that begat thee, and despise not thy mother when she is old.

23 Buy the truth, and sell *it* not; *also* wisdom, and instruction, and understanding.

24 The father of the righteous shall greatly rejoice: and he that begetteth a wise *child* shall have joy of him.

25 Thy father and thy mother shall be glad, and she that bare thee shall rejoice.

26 My son, give me thine heart, and let thine eyes observe my ways.

27 For a whore *is* a deep ditch; and a strange woman *is* a narrow pit.

28 She also lieth in wait as *for* a prey, and increaseth the transgressors among men.

## Amplified

**23** WHEN YOU sit down to eat with a ruler, consider who *and* what are before you;

2 For you will put a knife to your throat, if you are a man given to desire.

3 Be not desirous of his dainties, for they are deceitful food [offered with questionable motives].

4 Weary not yourself to be rich; cease from *this* your own wisdom. [Prov. 28:20; I Tim. 6:9, 10.]

5 Will you set your eyes upon wealth, when [suddenly] it is gone? For riches certainly make themselves wings, like an eagle that flies toward the heavens.

6 Eat not the bread of him who has a hard, grudging *and* envious eye, neither desire his dainty foods;

7 For as he thinks in his heart, so is he. As one who reckons he says to you, eat and drink, yet his heart is not with you [but is grudging the cost].

8 The morsel which you have eaten you will vomit up, and your complimentary words will be wasted.

9 Speak not in the ears of a [self-confident] fool, for he will despise the wisdom of your words. [Isa. 32:6.]

10 Remove not the old landmark, and enter not into the fields of the fatherless, [Prov. 22:28; Deut. 19:14; 27:17.]

11 For their Redeemer is mighty; He will plead their cause against you.

12 Apply your mind to instruction *and* correction, and your ears to the words of knowledge.

13 Withhold not discipline from the child, for if you strike *and* punish him with the [reed-like] rod, he will not die.

14 You shall whip him with the rod and deliver his life from Sheol [Hades, the place of the dead].

15 My son, if your heart is wise, my heart will be glad, even mine.

16 Yes, my heart will rejoice when your lips speak right things.

17 Let not your heart envy sinners, but continue in the reverent *and* worshipful fear of the Lord all the day long.

18 For surely there is a latter end [a future and a reward]; and your hope *and* expectation shall not be cut off.

19 Hear, my son, and be wise, and direct your mind in the way [of the Lord].

20 Do not associate with winebibbers; be not among them *nor* among gluttonous eaters of meat; [Isa. 5:22; Luke 21:34; Rom. 13:13; Eph. 5:18.]

21 For the drunkard and the glutton shall come to poverty, and drowsiness shall clothe a man with rags.

22 Hearken to your father who begot you, and despise not your mother when she is old.

23 Buy the truth and sell it not; not only that, but, also discernment *and* judgment, instruction and understanding.

24 The father of the [uncompromisingly] righteous—the upright, in right standing with God—shall greatly rejoice, and he who becomes the father of a wise child shall have joy in him.

25 Let your father and your mother be glad, and let her who bore you rejoice.

26 My son, give me your heart, and let your eyes observe *and* delight in my ways.

27 For a harlot is a deep ditch, and a loose woman is a narrow pit.

28 She also lies in wait as a robber *or* as for prey, and she increases the treacherous among men.

## New American Standard

*On Life and Conduct*

23 WHEN YOU sit down to dine with a ruler,
Consider carefully what is before you;
2 And put a knife to your throat,
If you are a man of *great* appetite.
3 Do not desire his delicacies,
For it is deceptive food.

4¶ Do not weary yourself to gain wealth,
Cease from your consideration *of it.*
5 When you set your eyes on it, it is gone.
For *wealth* certainly makes itself wings,
Like an eagle that flies *toward* the heavens.

6¶ Do not eat the bread of a selfish man,
Or desire his delicacies;
7 For as he thinks within himself, so he is.
He says to you, "Eat and drink!"
But his heart is not with you.
8 You will vomit up the morsel you have eaten,
And waste your compliments.

9¶ Do not speak in the hearing of a fool,
For he will despise the wisdom of your words.

10¶ Do not move the ancient boundary,
Or go into the fields of the fatherless;
11 For their Redeemer is strong;
He will plead their case against you.
12 Apply your heart to discipline,
And your ears to words of knowledge.

13¶ Do not hold back discipline from the child,
Although you beat him with the rod, he will not die.
14 You shall beat him with the rod,
And deliver his soul from Sheol.

15¶ My son, if your heart is wise,
My own heart also will be glad;
16 And my inmost being will rejoice,
When your lips speak what is right.

17¶ Do not let your heart envy sinners,
But *live* in the fear of the LORD always.
18 Surely there is a future,
And your hope will not be cut off.
19 Listen, my son, and be wise,
And direct your heart in the way.
20 Do not be with heavy drinkers of wine,
*Or* with gluttonous eaters of meat;
21 For the heavy drinker and the glutton will come to poverty,
And drowsiness will clothe *a man* with rags.

22¶ Listen to your father who begot you,
And do not despise your mother when she is old.
23 Buy truth, and do not sell *it,*
*Get* wisdom and instruction and understanding.

24¶ The father of the righteous will greatly rejoice,
And he who begets a wise son will be glad in him.
25 Let your father and your mother be glad,
And let her rejoice who gave birth to you.

26¶ Give me your heart, my son,
And let your eyes delight in my ways.
27 For a harlot is a deep pit,
And an adulterous woman is a narrow well.
28 Surely she lurks as a robber,
And increases the faithless among men.

## New International

23 WHEN YOU sit to dine with a ruler,
note well what[a] is before you,
2and put a knife to your throat
if you are given to gluttony.
3Do not crave his delicacies,
for that food is deceptive.

4Do not wear yourself out to get rich;
have the wisdom to show restraint.
5Cast but a glance at riches, and they are gone,
for they will surely sprout wings
and fly off to the sky like an eagle.

6Do not eat the food of a stingy man,
do not crave his delicacies;
7for he is the kind of man
who is always thinking about the cost.[b]
"Eat and drink," he says to you,
but his heart is not with you.
8You will vomit up the little you have eaten
and will have wasted your compliments.

9Do not speak to a fool,
for he will scorn the wisdom of your words.

10Do not move an ancient boundary stone
or encroach on the fields of the fatherless,
11for their Defender is strong;
he will take up their case against you.

12Apply your heart to instruction
and your ears to words of knowledge.

13Do not withhold discipline from a child;
if you punish him with the rod, he will not die.
14Punish him with the rod
and save his soul from death.[c]

15My son, if your heart is wise,
then my heart will be glad;
16my inmost being will rejoice
when your lips speak what is right.

17Do not let your heart envy sinners,
but always be zealous for the fear of the LORD.
18There is surely a future hope for you,
and your hope will not be cut off.

19Listen, my son, and be wise,
and keep your heart on the right path.
20Do not join those who drink too much wine
or gorge themselves on meat,
21for drunkards and gluttons become poor,
and drowsiness clothes them in rags.

22Listen to your father, who gave you life,
and do not despise your mother when she is old.
23Buy the truth and do not sell it;
get wisdom, discipline and understanding.
24The father of a righteous man has great joy;
he who has a wise son delights in him.
25May your father and mother be glad;
may she who gave you birth rejoice!

26My son, give me your heart
and let your eyes keep to my ways,
27for a prostitute is a deep pit
and a wayward wife is a narrow well.
28Like a bandit she lies in wait,
and multiplies the unfaithful among men.

**NIV** [a] 1 Or *who* [b] 7 Or *for as he thinks within himself, / so he is;* or *for as he puts on a feast, / so he is* [c] 14 Hebrew *Sheol*

## King James

29 Who hath woe? who hath sorrow? who hath contentions? who hath babbling? who hath wounds without cause? who hath redness of eyes?

30 They that tarry long at the wine; they that go to seek mixed wine.

31 Look not thou upon the wine when it is red, when it giveth his colour in the cup, *when* it moveth itself aright.

32 At the last it biteth like a serpent, and stingeth like an adder.

33 Thine eyes shall behold strange women, and thine heart shall utter perverse things.

34 Yea, thou shalt be as he that lieth down in the midst of the sea, or as he that lieth upon the top of a mast.

35 They have stricken me, *shalt thou say, and* I was not sick; they have beaten me, *and* I felt *it* not: when shall I awake? I will seek it yet again.

**24** BE NOT thou envious against evil men, neither desire to be with them.

2 For their heart studieth destruction, and their lips talk of mischief.

3 Through wisdom is an house builded; and by understanding it is established:

4 And by knowledge shall the chambers be filled with all precious and pleasant riches.

5 A wise man *is* strong; yea, a man of knowledge increaseth strength.

6 For by wise counsel thou shalt make thy war: and in multitude of counsellors *there is* safety.

7 Wisdom *is* too high for a fool: he openeth not his mouth in the gate.

8 He that deviseth to do evil shall be called a mischievous person.

9 The thought of foolishness *is* sin: and the scorner *is* an abomination to men.

10 *If* thou faint in the day of adversity, thy strength *is* small.

11 If thou forbear to deliver *them that are* drawn unto death, and *those that are* ready to be slain;

12 If thou sayest, Behold, we knew it not; doth not he that pondereth the heart consider *it?* and he that keepeth thy soul, doth *not* he know *it?* and shall *not* he render to *every* man according to his works?

13 My son, eat thou honey, because *it is* good; and the honeycomb, *which is* sweet to thy taste:

14 So *shall* the knowledge of wisdom *be* unto thy soul: when thou hast found *it*, then there shall be a reward, and thy expectation shall not be cut off.

15 Lay not wait, O wicked *man*, against the dwelling of the righteous; spoil not his resting place:

16 For a just *man* falleth seven times, and riseth up again: but the wicked shall fall into mischief.

17 Rejoice not when thine enemy falleth, and let not thine heart be glad when he stumbleth:

## Amplified

29 Who has woe? Who has sorrow? Who has strife? Who has complaining? Who has wounds without cause? Who has redness *and* dimness of eyes?

30 Those who tarry long at the wine, they who go to seek *and* try mixed wine. [Prov. 20:1; Eph. 5:18.]

31 Do not look at wine when it is red, when it sparkles in the wineglass, when it goes down smoothly.

32 At the last it bites like a serpent, and stings like an adder.

33 [Under the influence of wine] your eyes will behold strange things [and loose women], and your mind will utter things turned the wrong way, untrue, incorrect *and* petulant.

34 Yes, you will be [as unsteady] as he who lies down in the midst of the sea, and [as open to disaster] as he who lies upon the top of a mast.

35 You will say, They struck me, but I was not hurt! They beat me [as with a hammer], but I did not feel it! When shall I awake? I will crave *and* seek more wine again [and escape reality].

**24** BE NOT envious of evil men, nor desire to be with them.

2 For their minds plot oppression *and* devise violence, and their lips talk of causing trouble *and* vexation.

3 Through skillful *and* godly [a]Wisdom is a house [a life, a home, a famiiy] built, and by understanding it is established [on a sound and good foundation].

4 And by knowledge shall the chambers [of its every area] be filled with all precious and pleasant riches.

5 A wise man is strong *and* [b]better than a strong man, and a man of knowledge increases *and* strengthens his power; [Prov. 21:22; Eccl. 9:16.]

6 For by wise counsel you can wage your war, and in an abundance of counselors there is victory *and* safety.

7 Wisdom is too high for a [c]fool; he opens not his mouth in the gate [where the city's rulers sit in judgment].

8 He who plans to do evil will be called a mischief-maker.

9 The plans of the foolish *and* the thought of foolishness are sin, and the scoffer is an abomination to men.

10 If you faint in the day of adversity, your strength is small.

11 Deliver those who are drawn away to death, and those who totter to the slaughter hold back [from their doom].

12 If you [profess ignorance and] say, Behold, we did not know this, does not He Who weighs *and* ponders the hearts perceive *and* consider it? And He Who guards your life, does not He know it? And shall not He render to [you and] every man according to his works?

13 My son, eat honey, because it is good, and the drippings of honeycomb are sweet to your taste.

14 So shall you know skillful *and* godly Wisdom to be to your life; if you find it, then shall there be a future *and* a reward, and your hope *and* expectation shall not be cut off.

15 Lie not in wait as a wicked man against the dwelling of the [uncompromisingly] righteous—the upright, in right standing with God; destroy not his fold *or* his resting place;

16 For a righteous man falls seven times and rises again, but the wicked are overthrown by calamity. [Job 5:19; Pss. 34:19; 37:24; Mic. 7:8.]

17 Rejoice not when your enemy falls, and let not your heart be glad when he stumbles *or* is overthrown;

**AMP** [a] See footnote on Proverbs 1:23. [b] Several other texts, including the Septuagint (Greek) so read. [c] See footnote on Proverbs 14:3.

## New American Standard

29 ¶ Who has woe? Who has sorrow?
Who has contentions? Who has complaining?
Who has wounds without cause?
Who has redness of eyes?
30 Those who linger long over wine,
Those who go to taste mixed wine.
31 Do not look on the wine when it is red,
When it sparkles in the cup,
When it goes down smoothly;
32 At the last it bites like a serpent,
And stings like a viper.
33 Your eyes will see strange things,
And your mind will utter perverse things.
34 And you will be like one who lies down in the middle of the sea,
Or like one who lies down on the top of a [d]mast.
35 "They struck me, *but* I did not become ill;
They beat me, *but* I did not know *it*.
When shall I awake?
I will seek another drink."

*Precepts and Warnings*

**24** DO NOT be envious of evil men,
Nor desire to be with them;
2 For their minds devise violence,
And their lips talk of trouble.

3 ¶ By wisdom a house is built,
And by understanding it is established;
4 And by knowledge the rooms are filled
With all precious and pleasant riches.

5 ¶ A wise man is strong,
And a man of knowledge increases power.
6 For by wise guidance you will wage war,
And in abundance of counselors there is victory.

7 ¶ Wisdom is too high for a fool,
He does not open his mouth in the gate.

8 ¶ He who plans to do evil,
Men will call him a schemer.
9 The devising of folly is sin,
And the scoffer is an abomination to men.

10 ¶ If you are slack in the day of distress,
Your strength is limited.
11 ¶ Deliver those who are being taken away to death,
And those who are staggering to slaughter, O hold *them* back.
12 If you say, "See, we did not know this,"
Does He not consider *it* who weighs the hearts?
And does He not know *it* who keeps your soul?
And will He not render to man according to his work?

13 ¶ My son, eat honey, for it is good,
Yes, the honey from the comb is sweet to your taste;
14 Know *that* wisdom is thus for your soul;
If you find *it*, then there will be a future,
And your hope will not be cut off.

15 ¶ Do not lie in wait, O wicked man, against the dwelling of the righteous;
Do not destroy his resting place;
16 For a righteous man falls seven times, and rises again,
But the wicked stumble in *time of* calamity.

17 ¶ Do not rejoice when your enemy falls,
And do not let your heart be glad when he stumbles;

NAS [d] Or, *lookout*

## New International

29 Who has woe? Who has sorrow?
Who has strife? Who has complaints?
Who has needless bruises? Who has bloodshot eyes?
30 Those who linger over wine,
who go to sample bowls of mixed wine.
31 Do not gaze at wine when it is red,
when it sparkles in the cup,
when it goes down smoothly!
32 In the end it bites like a snake
and poisons like a viper.
33 Your eyes will see strange sights
and your mind imagine confusing things.
34 You will be like one sleeping on the high seas,
lying on top of the rigging.
35 "They hit me," you will say, "but I'm not hurt!
They beat me, but I don't feel it!
When will I wake up
so I can find another drink?"

**24** DO NOT envy wicked men,
do not desire their company;
2 for their hearts plot violence,
and their lips talk about making trouble.

3 By wisdom a house is built,
and through understanding it is established;
4 through knowledge its rooms are filled
with rare and beautiful treasures.

5 A wise man has great power,
and a man of knowledge increases strength;
6 for waging war you need guidance,
and for victory many advisers.

7 Wisdom is too high for a fool;
in the assembly at the gate he has nothing to say.

8 He who plots evil
will be known as a schemer.
9 The schemes of folly are sin,
and men detest a mocker.

10 If you falter in times of trouble,
how small is your strength!
11 Rescue those being led away to death;
hold back those staggering toward slaughter.
12 If you say, "But we knew nothing about this,"
does not he who weighs the heart perceive it?
Does not he who guards your life know it?
Will he not repay each person according to what he has done?

13 Eat honey, my son, for it is good;
honey from the comb is sweet to your taste.
14 Know also that wisdom is sweet to your soul;
if you find it, there is a future hope for you,
and your hope will not be cut off.

15 Do not lie in wait like an outlaw against a righteous man's house,
do not raid his dwelling place;
16 for though a righteous man falls seven times, he rises again,
but the wicked are brought down by calamity.

17 Do not gloat when your enemy falls;
when he stumbles, do not let your heart rejoice,

## King James

18 Lest the LORD see *it*, and it displease him, and he turn away
his wrath from him.
19 Fret not thyself because of evil *men*, neither be thou envious
at the wicked;
20 For there shall be no reward to the evil *man;* the candle of the
wicked shall be put out.
21 My son, fear thou the LORD and the king: *and* meddle not with
them that are given to change:
22 For their calamity shall rise suddenly; and who knoweth the
ruin of them both?
23 These *things* also *belong* to the wise. *It is* not good to have
respect of persons in judgment.
24 He that saith unto the wicked, Thou *art* righteous; him shall
the people curse, nations shall abhor him:
25 But to them that rebuke *him* shall be delight, and a good
blessing shall come upon them.
26 *Every man* shall kiss *his* lips that giveth a right answer.
27 Prepare thy work without, and make it fit for thyself in the
field; and afterwards build thine house.
28 Be not a witness against thy neighbour without cause; and
deceive *not* with thy lips.
29 Say not, I will do so to him as he hath done to me: I will render
to the man according to his work.
30 I went by the field of the slothful, and by the vineyard of the
man void of understanding;
31 And, lo, it was all grown over with thorns, *and* nettles had
covered the face thereof, and the stone wall thereof was broken
down.
32 Then I saw, *and* considered *it* well: I looked upon *it, and*
received instruction.
33 *Yet* a little sleep, a little slumber, a little folding of the hands
to sleep:
34 So shall thy poverty come *as* one that travelleth; and thy want
as an armed man.

**25** THESE *ARE* also proverbs of Solomon, which the men of
Hezekiah king of Judah copied out.
2 *It is* the glory of God to conceal a thing: but the honour of kings
*is* to search out a matter.
3 The heaven for height, and the earth for depth, and the heart
of kings *is* unsearchable.
4 Take away the dross from the silver, and there shall come forth
a vessel for the refiner.
5 Take away the wicked *from* before the king, and his throne
shall be established in righteousness.
6 Put not forth thyself in the presence of the king, and stand not
in the place of great *men:*
7 For better *it is* that it be said unto thee, Come up hither; than
that thou shouldest be put lower in the presence of the prince
whom thine eyes have seen.
8 Go not forth hastily to strive, lest *thou know not* what to do in
the end thereof, when thy neighbour hath put thee to shame.

## Amplified

18 Lest the Lord see it, and it be evil in His eyes *and* displease
Him, and He turn away His wrath from him [to expend it upon
you, the worse offender].
19 Fret not yourself because of evildoers, neither be envious of
the wicked;
20 For there shall be no reward to the evil man; the lamp of the
wicked shall be put out.
21 My son, reverently fear the Lord and the king, and do not
associate with those who are given to change [of allegiance, and
are revolutionary];
22 For their calamity shall rise suddenly, and who knows the
punishment *and* ruin which both [the Lord and the king] will bring
upon *the rebellious*?
23 These also are sayings of the wise. To discriminate *and* be
partial, having respect of persons in judging, is not good.
24 He who says to the wicked, You are righteous *and* innocent,
peoples will curse him, nations will defy *and* abhor him.
25 But to those [upright judges] who rebuke the wicked it is well
*and* they will find delight, and a good blessing will be upon them.
26 He kisses the lips [and wins the hearts of men] who gives a
right answer.
27 [Put first things first.] Prepare your work outside, and get it
ready for yourself in the field, and afterward build your house *and*
establish a home.
28 Be not a witness against your neighbor without cause, and
deceive not with your lips. [Eph. 4:25.]
29 Say not, I will do to him as he has done to me; I will pay the
man back for his deed. [Prov. 20:22; Matt. 5:39, 44; Rom. 12:17, 19.]
30 I went by the field of the lazy man, and by the vineyard of the
man void of understanding;
31 And, lo, it was all grown over with thorns, and nettles had
covered its face, and its stone wall was broken down.
32 Then I beheld *and* considered it well; I looked *and* received
instruction.
33 Yet a little sleep, a little slumber, a little folding of the hands
to sleep;
34 So shall your poverty come as a robber, and your want as an
armed man.

**25** THESE ARE also the proverbs of Solomon, which the men
of Hezekiah king of Judah copied out. [I Kings 4:32.]
2 It is the glory of God to conceal a thing, but the glory of kings
is to search a thing out. [Deut. 29:29; Rom. 11:33.]
3 As the heaven for height, and the earth for depth, so the heart
*and* mind of kings is unsearchable.
4 Take away the dross from the silver, and there shall come forth
[the material for] a vessel for the silversmith [to work up]. [II Tim.
2:21.]
5 Take away the wicked from before the king, and his throne will
be established in righteousness [spiritual and moral rectitude in
every area and relation].
6 Be not forward [self-assertive and boastfully ambitious] in the
presence of the king, and stand not in the place of great men;
7 For better it is that it be said to you, Come up here, than that
you should be put lower in the presence of the prince whose eyes
have seen you. [Luke 14:8-10.]
8 Rush not forth soon to quarrel [before magistrates or
elsewhere], lest you know not what to do in the end, when your
neighbor has put you to shame. [Prov. 17:14; Matt. 5:25.]

## New American Standard

18 Lest the LORD see *it* and be displeased,
And He turn away His anger from him.

19¶ Do not fret because of evildoers,
Or be envious of the wicked;
20 For there will be no future for the evil man;
The lamp of the wicked will be put out.

21¶ My son, fear the LORD and the king;
Do not associate with those who are given to change;
22 For their calamity will rise suddenly,
And who knows the ruin *that comes* from both of them?

23¶ These also are sayings of the wise.
To show partiality in judgment is not good.
24 He who says to the wicked, "You are righteous,"
Peoples will curse him, nations will abhor him;
25 But to those who rebuke the *wicked* will be delight,
And a good blessing will come upon them.
26 He kisses the lips
Who gives a right answer.

27¶ Prepare your work outside,
And make it ready for yourself in the field;
Afterwards, then, build your house.

28¶ Do not be a witness against your neighbor without cause,
And do not deceive with your lips.
29 Do not say, "Thus I shall do to him as he has done to me;
I will render to the man according to his work."

30¶ I passed by the field of the sluggard,
And by the vineyard of the man lacking sense;
31 And behold, it was completely overgrown with thistles,
Its surface was covered with nettles,
And its stone wall was broken down.
32 When I saw, I reflected upon it;
I looked, *and* received instruction.
33 "A little sleep, a little slumber,
A little folding of the hands to rest,"
34 Then your poverty will come *as* a robber,
And your want like an armed man.

*Similitudes, Instructions*

25 THESE ALSO are proverbs of Solomon which the men of Hezekiah, king of Judah, transcribed.
2¶ It is the glory of God to conceal a matter,
But the glory of kings is to search out a matter.
3 *As* the heavens for height and the earth for depth,
So the heart of kings is unsearchable.
4 Take away the dross from the silver,
And there comes out a vessel for the smith;
5 Take away the wicked *from* before the king,
And his throne will be established in righteousness.
6 Do not claim honor in the presence of the king,
And do not stand in the place of great men;
7 For it is better that it be said to you, "Come up here,"
Than that you should be put lower in the presence of the prince,
Whom your eyes have seen.

8¶ Do not go out hastily to argue *your case;*
Otherwise, what will you do in the end,
When your neighbor puts you to shame?

## New International

18 or the LORD will see and disapprove
and turn his wrath away from him.

19 Do not fret because of evil men
or be envious of the wicked,
20 for the evil man has no future hope,
and the lamp of the wicked will be snuffed out.

21 Fear the LORD and the king, my son,
and do not join with the rebellious,
22 for those two will send sudden destruction upon them,
and who knows what calamities they can bring?

### *Further Sayings of the Wise*

23 These also are sayings of the wise:

To show partiality in judging is not good:
24 Whoever says to the guilty, "You are innocent"—
peoples will curse him and nations denounce him.
25 But it will go well with those who convict the guilty,
and rich blessing will come upon them.

26 An honest answer
is like a kiss on the lips.

27 Finish your outdoor work
and get your fields ready;
after that, build your house.

28 Do not testify against your neighbor without cause,
or use your lips to deceive.
29 Do not say, "I'll do to him as he has done to me;
I'll pay that man back for what he did."

30 I went past the field of the sluggard,
past the vineyard of the man who lacks judgment;
31 thorns had come up everywhere,
the ground was covered with weeds,
and the stone wall was in ruins.
32 I applied my heart to what I observed
and learned a lesson from what I saw:
33 A little sleep, a little slumber,
a little folding of the hands to rest—
34 and poverty will come on you like a bandit
and scarcity like an armed man.[a]

### *More Proverbs of Solomon*

25 THESE ARE more proverbs of Solomon, copied by the men of Hezekiah king of Judah:

2 It is the glory of God to conceal a matter;
to search out a matter is the glory of kings.

3 As the heavens are high and the earth is deep,
so the hearts of kings are unsearchable.

4 Remove the dross from the silver,
and out comes material for[b] the silversmith;
5 remove the wicked from the king's presence,
and his throne will be established through righteousness.

6 Do not exalt yourself in the king's presence,
and do not claim a place among great men;
7 it is better for him to say to you, "Come up here,"
than for him to humiliate you before a nobleman.

What you have seen with your eyes
8 do not bring[c] hastily to court,
for what will you do in the end
if your neighbor puts you to shame?

NIV [a] 34 *Or like a vagrant / and scarcity like a beggar* [b] 4 *Or comes a vessel from* [c] 7,8 *Or nobleman / on whom you had set your eyes. / 8Do not go*

## King James

9 Debate thy cause with thy neighbour *himself;* and discover not a secret to another:

10 Lest he that heareth *it* put thee to shame, and thine infamy turn not away.

11 A word fitly spoken *is like* apples of gold in pictures of silver.

12 *As* an earring of gold, and an ornament of fine gold, *so is* a wise reprover upon an obedient ear.

13 As the cold of snow in the time of harvest, *so is* a faithful messenger to them that send him: for he refresheth the soul of his masters.

14 Whoso boasteth himself of a false gift *is like* clouds and wind without rain.

15 By long forbearing is a prince persuaded, and a soft tongue breaketh the bone.

16 Hast thou found honey? eat so much as is sufficient for thee, lest thou be filled therewith, and vomit it.

17 Withdraw thy foot from thy neighbour's house; lest he be weary of thee, and *so* hate thee.

18 A man that beareth false witness against his neighbour *is* a maul, and a sword, and a sharp arrow.

19 Confidence in an unfaithful man in time of trouble *is like* a broken tooth, and a foot out of joint.

20 *As* he that taketh away a garment in cold weather, *and as* vinegar upon nitre, so *is* he that singeth songs to an heavy heart.

21 If thine enemy be hungry, give him bread to eat; and if he be thirsty, give him water to drink:

22 For thou shalt heap coals of fire upon his head, and the LORD shall reward thee.

23 The north wind driveth away rain: so *doth* an angry countenance a backbiting tongue.

24 *It is* better to dwell in the corner of the housetop, than with a brawling woman and in a wide house.

25 *As* cold waters to a thirsty soul, so *is* good news from a far country.

26 A righteous man falling down before the wicked *is as* a troubled fountain, and a corrupt spring.

27 *It is* not good to eat much honey: so *for men* to search their own glory *is not* glory.

28 He that *hath* no rule over his own spirit *is like* a city *that is* broken down, *and* without walls.

**26** AS SNOW in summer, and as rain in harvest, so honour is not seemly for a fool.

2 As the bird by wandering, as the swallow by flying, so the curse causeless shall not come.

3 A whip for the horse, a bridle for the ass, and a rod for the fool's back.

4 Answer not a fool according to his folly, lest thou also be like unto him.

**AMP** [a] This is not to be understood as a revengeful act, intended to embarrass its victim, but just the opposite. The picture is that of the high priest (Lev. 16:12), who on the Day of Atonement took his censer and filled it with "coals of fire" from off the altar of burnt offering, and then put on them incense for a pleasing, sweet-smelling fragrance. The cloud of it covered the mercy-seat and was acceptable to God for atonement. Samuel Wesley wrote: / "So artists melt the sullen ore of lead, / By heaping coals of fire upon its head: / In the kind warmth the metal learns to glow, / And pure from dross the silver runs below."

## Amplified

9 Argue your cause with your neighbor himself; discover not *and* disclose not another's secret; [Matt. 18:15.]

10 Lest he who hears you revile you *and* bring shame upon you, and your ill repute have no end.

11 A word fitly spoken *and* in due season is like apples of gold in a setting of silver. [Prov. 15:23; Isa. 50:4.]

12 As an ear *or* nose ring of gold, or an ornament of fine gold, is a wise reprover to an ear that listens *and* obeys.

13 As the cold of snow [brought from the mountains] in the time of harvest, so is a faithful messenger to those who send him; for he refreshes the life of his masters.

14 Whoever falsely boasts of gifts [he does not give] is like clouds and wind without rain. [Jude 12.]

15 By long forbearing *and* calmness of spirit a judge *or* ruler is persuaded, and soft speech breaks down the most bonelike resistance. [Prov. 15:1; 16:14; Gen. 32:4; I Sam. 25:24.]

16 Have you found [pleasure sweet like] honey? Eat only as much as is sufficient for you, lest being filled with it you vomit it up.

17 Let your foot be seldom in your neighbor's house, lest he become tired of you and hate you.

18 A man who bears false witness against his neighbor is like a heavy sledge hammer, and a sword, and a sharp arrow.

19 Confidence in an unfaithful man in time of trouble is like a broken tooth or a foot out of joint.

20 He who sings songs to a heavy heart is like him who lays off a garment in cold weather *and* as vinegar upon soda. [Dan. 6:18; Rom. 12:15.]

21 If your enemy be hungry, give him bread to eat, and if he be thirsty, give him water to drink; [Matt. 5:44; Rom. 12:20.]

22 For so doing you will [a]heap coals of fire upon his head, and the Lord will reward you.

23 The north wind brings forth rain; so does a backbiting tongue bring forth an angry countenance.

24 It is better to dwell in the corner of the housetop than to share a house with a disagreeing, quarrelsome *and* scolding woman.

25 As cold waters to a thirsty soul, so is good news from a far [home] country.

26 Like a muddied fountain and a polluted spring is a righteous man who yields, falls down *and* compromises his integrity before the wicked.

27 It is not good to eat much honey, so for men to seek glory, their own glory, causes suffering *and* is *not* glory.

28 He who has no rule over his own spirit is like a city that is broken down and without walls. [Prov. 16:32.]

**26** AS SNOW in summer and as rain in harvest, so honor is not fitting for a [self-confident] fool. [Isa. 32:6.]

2 As the sparrow in her wandering, as the swallow in her flying, so the causeless curse shall not alight. [Num. 23:8.]

3 A whip for the horse, a bridle for the donkey, and a [straight, slender] rod for the back of [self-confident] fools.

4 Answer not a [self-confident] fool according to his folly, lest you also be like him.

## New American Standard

9 Argue your case with your neighbor,
And do not reveal the secret of another,
10 Lest he who hears *it* reproach you,
And the evil report about you not pass away.
11 ¶ *Like* apples of gold in settings of silver
Is a word spoken in right circumstances.
12 *Like* an earring of gold and an ornament of fine gold
Is a wise reprover to a listening ear.
13 Like the cold of snow in the time of harvest
Is a faithful messenger to those who send him,
For he refreshes the soul of his masters.
14 *Like* clouds and wind without rain
Is a man who boasts of his gifts falsely.
15 By forbearance a ruler may be persuaded,
And a soft tongue breaks the bone.
16 Have you found honey? Eat *only* what you need,
Lest you have it in excess and vomit it.
17 Let your foot rarely be in your neighbor's house,
Lest he become weary of you and hate you.
18 *Like* a club and a sword and a sharp arrow
Is a man who bears false witness against his neighbor.
19 *Like* a bad tooth and an unsteady foot
Is confidence in a faithless man in time of trouble.
20 *Like* one who takes off a garment on a cold day, *or like* vinegar on soda,
Is he who sings songs to a troubled heart.
21 If your enemy is hungry, give him food to eat;
And if he is thirsty, give him water to drink;
22 For you will heap burning coals on his head,
And the LORD will reward you.
23 The north wind brings forth rain,
And a backbiting tongue, an angry countenance.
24 It is better to live in a corner of the roof
Than in a house shared with a contentious woman.
25 *Like* cold water to a weary soul,
So is good news from a distant land.
26 *Like* a trampled spring and a polluted well
Is a righteous man who gives way before the wicked.
27 It is not good to eat much honey,
Nor is it glory to search out one's own glory.
28 *Like* a city that is broken into *and* without walls
Is a man who has no control over his spirit.

*Similitudes, Instructions*

**26** LIKE SNOW in summer and like rain in harvest,
So honor is not fitting for a fool.
2 Like a sparrow in *its* flitting, like a swallow in *its* flying,
So a curse without cause does not alight.
3 A whip is for the horse, a bridle for the donkey,
And a rod for the back of fools.
4 Do not answer a fool according to his folly,
Lest you also be like him.

## New International

9 If you argue your case with a neighbor,
do not betray another man's confidence,
10 or he who hears it may shame you
and you will never lose your bad reputation.

11 A word aptly spoken
is like apples of gold in settings of silver.

12 Like an earring of gold or an ornament of fine gold
is a wise man's rebuke to a listening ear.

13 Like the coolness of snow at harvest time
is a trustworthy messenger to those who send him;
he refreshes the spirit of his masters.

14 Like clouds and wind without rain
is a man who boasts of gifts he does not give.

15 Through patience a ruler can be persuaded,
and a gentle tongue can break a bone.

16 If you find honey, eat just enough—
too much of it, and you will vomit.
17 Seldom set foot in your neighbor's house—
too much of you, and he will hate you.

18 Like a club or a sword or a sharp arrow
is the man who gives false testimony against his neighbor.
19 Like a bad tooth or a lame foot
is reliance on the unfaithful in times of trouble.

20 Like one who takes away a garment on a cold day,
or like vinegar poured on soda,
is one who sings songs to a heavy heart.

21 If your enemy is hungry, give him food to eat;
if he is thirsty, give him water to drink.
22 In doing this, you will heap burning coals on his head,
and the LORD will reward you.

23 As a north wind brings rain,
so a sly tongue brings angry looks.

24 Better to live on a corner of the roof
than share a house with a quarrelsome wife.

25 Like cold water to a weary soul
is good news from a distant land.

26 Like a muddied spring or a polluted well
is a righteous man who gives way to the wicked.

27 It is not good to eat too much honey,
nor is it honorable to seek one's own honor.

28 Like a city whose walls are broken down
is a man who lacks self-control.

**26** LIKE SNOW in summer or rain in harvest,
honor is not fitting for a fool.

2 Like a fluttering sparrow or a darting swallow,
an undeserved curse does not come to rest.

3 A whip for the horse, a halter for the donkey,
and a rod for the backs of fools!

4 Do not answer a fool according to his folly,
or you will be like him yourself.

## King James

5 Answer a fool according to his folly, lest he be wise in his own
conceit.
6 He that sendeth a message by the hand of a fool cutteth off the
feet, *and* drinketh damage.
7 The legs of the lame are not equal: so *is* a parable in the mouth
of fools.
8 As he that bindeth a stone in a sling, so *is* he that giveth honour
to a fool.
9 *As* a thorn goeth up into the hand of a drunkard, so *is* a parable
in the mouth of fools.
10 The great *God* that formed all *things* both rewardeth the fool,
and rewardeth transgressors.
11 As a dog returneth to his vomit, *so* a fool returneth to his folly.
12 Seest thou a man wise in his own conceit? *there is* more hope
of a fool than of him.
13 The slothful *man* saith, *There is* a lion in the way; a lion *is* in
the streets.
14 *As* the door turneth upon his hinges, so *doth* the slothful upon
his bed.
15 The slothful hideth his hand in *his* bosom; it grieveth him to
bring it again to his mouth.
16 The sluggard *is* wiser in his own conceit than seven men that
can render a reason.
17 He that passeth by, *and* meddleth with strife *belonging* not to
him, *is like* one that taketh a dog by the ears.
18 As a mad *man* who casteth firebrands, arrows, and death,
19 So *is* the man *that* deceiveth his neighbour, and saith, Am not
I in sport?
20 Where no wood is, *there* the fire goeth out: so where *there is*
no talebearer, the strife ceaseth.
21 *As* coals *are* to burning coals, and wood to fire; so *is* a contentious man to kindle strife.
22 The words of a talebearer *are* as wounds, and they go down
into the innermost parts of the belly.
23 Burning lips and a wicked heart *are like* a potsherd covered
with silver dross.
24 He that hateth dissembleth with his lips, and layeth up deceit
within him;
25 When he speaketh fair, believe him not: for *there are* seven
abominations in his heart.
26 *Whose* hatred is covered by deceit, his wickedness shall be
shown before the *whole* congregation.
27 Whoso diggeth a pit shall fall therein: and he that rolleth a
stone, it will return upon him.
28 A lying tongue hateth *those that are* afflicted by it; and a flattering mouth worketh ruin.

**27** BOAST NOT thyself of tomorrow; for thou knowest not
what a day may bring forth.
2 Let another man praise thee, and not thine own mouth; a
stranger, and not thine own lips.

## Amplified

5 Answer a [self-confident] fool according to his folly, lest he be
wise in his own eyes *and* conceit. [Matt. 16:1-4; 21:24-27.]
6 He who sends a message by the hand of a [a]fool cuts off the
feet [of satisfactory delivery], and drinks the damage.
7 Like the legs of a lame man which hang loose, so is a parable
in the mouth of fools.
8 As he who binds a stone in a sling, so is he who gives honor
to a [self-confident] fool.
9 As a thorn that goes [without being felt] into the hand of a
drunken man, so is a proverb in the mouth of [self-confident] fools.
10 *But* as an archer who wounds all, so is he who hires a fool
or chance passers-by.
11 As a dog returns to his vomit, so a fool returns to his folly.
12 Do you see a man wise in his own eyes *and* conceit? There is
more hope for a [self-confident] fool than for him. [Prov. 29:20;
Luke 18:11; Rom. 12:16; Rev. 3:17.]
13 The sluggard says, There is a lion in the way! A lion is in the
streets!
14 As the door turns on its hinges, so does the lazy man [move
not from his place] upon his bed.
15 The slothful *and* self-indulgent buries his hand in his bosom;
it distresses *and* wearies him to bring it again to his mouth. [Prov.
19:24.]
16 The sluggard is wiser in his own eyes *and* conceit than seven
men who can render a reason *and* answer discreetly.
17 He who, passing by, stops to meddle with strife that is not his
business is like one who takes a dog by the ears.
18 As a madman who casts firebrands, arrows and death,
19 So is the man who deceives his neighbor and then says, Was
I not joking? [Eph. 5:4.]
20 For lack of wood the fire goes out, and where there is no
whisperer, contention ceases.
21 As coals are to hot embers and wood to fire, so is a quarrelsome man to inflame strife. [Prov. 15:18; 29:22.]
22 The words of a whisperer *or* slanderer are as dainty morsels
*or* words of sport [to some, but to others are as deadly wounds],
and they go down into the innermost parts of the body [or of the
victim's nature].
23 Burning lips [uttering insincere words of love] and a wicked
heart are like an earthen vessel covered with the scum thrown off
from molten silver [making it appear to be solid silver].
24 He who hates, pretends with his lips, but stores up deceit
within him.
25 When he speaks kindly, do not trust him, for seven abominations are in his heart.
26 Though his hatred cover itself with guile, his wickedness shall
be shown openly before the assembly.
27 Whoever digs a pit [for another man's feet] shall fall into it
himself, and he who rolls a stone [up a height to do mischief], it
will return upon him. [Prov. 28:10; Pss. 7:15, 16; 9:15; 10:2; 57:6;
Eccl. 10:8.]
28 A lying tongue hates those whom it has wounded *and*
crushed, and a flattering mouth works ruin.

**27** DO NOT boast of [yourself and] tomorrow; for you know
not what a day may bring forth. [Luke 12:19, 20; James
4:13.]
2 Let another man praise you, and not your own mouth; a
stranger, and not your own lips.

**AMP** [a] See footnote on Proverbs 14:3.

## New American Standard

5 Answer a fool as his folly *deserves*,
Lest he be wise in his own eyes.
6 He cuts off *his own* feet, *and* drinks violence
Who sends a message by the hand of a fool.
7 *Like* the legs *which* hang down from the lame,
So is a proverb in the mouth of fools.
8 Like one who binds a stone in a sling,
So is he who gives honor to a fool.
9 *Like* a thorn *which* falls into the hand of a drunkard,
So is a proverb in the mouth of fools.
10 *Like* an archer who wounds everyone,
So is he who hires a fool or who hires those who pass by.
11 Like a dog that returns to its vomit
Is a fool who repeats his folly.
12 Do you see a man wise in his own eyes?
There is more hope for a fool than for him.
13 The sluggard says, "There is a lion in the road!
A lion is in the open square!"
14 *As* the door turns on its hinges,
So *does* the sluggard on his bed.
15 The sluggard buries his hand in the dish;
He is weary of bringing it to his mouth again.
16 The sluggard is wiser in his own eyes
Than seven men who can give a discreet answer.
17 *Like* one who takes a dog by the ears
Is he who passes by *and* meddles with strife not belonging to him.
18 Like a madman who throws
Firebrands, arrows and death,
19 So is the man who deceives his neighbor,
And says, "Was I not joking?"
20 For lack of wood the fire goes out,
And where there is no whisperer, contention quiets down.
21 *Like* charcoal to hot embers and wood to fire,
So is a contentious man to kindle strife.
22 The words of a whisperer are like dainty morsels,
And they go down into the innermost parts of the body.
23 *Like* an earthen vessel overlaid with silver dross
Are burning lips and a wicked heart.
24 He who hates disguises *it* with his lips,
But he lays up deceit in his heart.
25 When he speaks graciously, do not believe him,
For there are seven abominations in his heart.
26 *Though his* hatred covers itself with guile,
His wickedness will be revealed before the assembly.
27 He who digs a pit will fall into it,
And he who rolls a stone, it will come back on him.
28 A lying tongue hates those it crushes,
And a flattering mouth works ruin.

*Warnings and Instructions*

**27** DO NOT boast about tomorrow,
For you do not know what a day may bring forth.
2 Let another praise you, and not your own mouth;
A stranger, and not your own lips.

## New International

5Answer a fool according to his folly,
or he will be wise in his own eyes.
6Like cutting off one's feet or drinking violence
is the sending of a message by the hand of a fool.
7Like a lame man's legs that hang limp
is a proverb in the mouth of a fool.
8Like tying a stone in a sling
is the giving of honor to a fool.
9Like a thornbush in a drunkard's hand
is a proverb in the mouth of a fool.
10Like an archer who wounds at random
is he who hires a fool or any passer-by.
11As a dog returns to its vomit,
so a fool repeats his folly.
12Do you see a man wise in his own eyes?
There is more hope for a fool than for him.
13The sluggard says, "There is a lion in the road,
a fierce lion roaming the streets!"
14As a door turns on its hinges,
so a sluggard turns on his bed.
15The sluggard buries his hand in the dish;
he is too lazy to bring it back to his mouth.
16The sluggard is wiser in his own eyes
than seven men who answer discreetly.
17Like one who seizes a dog by the ears
is a passer-by who meddles in a quarrel not his own.
18Like a madman shooting
firebrands or deadly arrows
19is a man who deceives his neighbor
and says, "I was only joking!"
20Without wood a fire goes out;
without gossip a quarrel dies down.
21As charcoal to embers and as wood to fire,
so is a quarrelsome man for kindling strife.
22The words of a gossip are like choice morsels;
they go down to a man's inmost parts.
23Like a coating of glaze[b] over earthenware
are fervent lips with an evil heart.
24A malicious man disguises himself with his lips,
but in his heart he harbors deceit.
25Though his speech is charming, do not believe him,
for seven abominations fill his heart.
26His malice may be concealed by deception,
but his wickedness will be exposed in the assembly.
27If a man digs a pit, he will fall into it;
if a man rolls a stone, it will roll back on him.
28A lying tongue hates those it hurts,
and a flattering mouth works ruin.

**27** DO NOT boast about tomorrow,
for you do not know what a day may bring forth.
2Let another praise you, and not your own mouth;
someone else, and not your own lips.

**NIV** [b] 23 With a different word division of the Hebrew; Masoretic Text *of silver dross*

## King James

3 A stone *is* heavy, and the sand weighty; but a fool's wrath *is* heavier than them both.

4 Wrath *is* cruel, and anger *is* outrageous; but who *is* able to stand before envy?

5 Open rebuke *is* better than secret love.

6 Faithful *are* the wounds of a friend; but the kisses of an enemy *are* deceitful.

7 The full soul loatheth an honeycomb; but to the hungry soul every bitter thing is sweet.

8 As a bird that wandereth from her nest, so *is* a man that wandereth from his place.

9 Ointment and perfume rejoice the heart: so *doth* the sweetness of a man's friend by hearty counsel.

10 Thine own friend, and thy father's friend, forsake not; neither go into thy brother's house in the day of thy calamity: *for* better *is* a neighbour *that is* near than a brother far off.

11 My son, be wise, and make my heart glad, that I may answer him that reproacheth me.

12 A prudent *man* foreseeth the evil, *and* hideth himself; *but* the simple pass on, *and* are punished.

13 Take his garment that is surety for a stranger, and take a pledge of him for a strange woman.

14 He that blesseth his friend with a loud voice, rising early in the morning, it shall be counted a curse to him.

15 A continual dropping in a very rainy day and a contentious woman are alike.

16 Whosoever hideth her hideth the wind, and the ointment of his right hand, *which* betrayeth *itself*.

17 Iron sharpeneth iron; so a man sharpeneth the countenance of his friend.

18 Whoso keepeth the fig tree shall eat the fruit thereof: so he that waiteth on his master shall be honoured.

19 As in water face *answereth* to face, so the heart of man to man.

20 Hell and destruction are never full; so the eyes of man are never satisfied.

21 *As* the refining pot for silver, and the furnace for gold; so *is* a man to his praise.

22 Though thou shouldest bray a fool in a mortar among wheat with a pestle, *yet* will not his foolishness depart from him.

23 Be thou diligent to know the state of thy flocks, *and* look well to thy herds.

24 For riches *are* not for ever: and doth the crown *endure* to every generation?

25 The hay appeareth, and the tender grass showeth itself, and herbs of the mountains are gathered.

26 The lambs *are* for thy clothing, and the goats *are* the price of the field.

27 And *thou shalt have* goats' milk enough for thy food, for the food of thy household, and *for* the maintenance for thy maidens.

## Amplified

3 Stone is heavy, and sand weighty; but a fool's [unreasoning] wrath is heavier *and* more intolerable than them both.

4 Wrath is cruel and anger is an overwhelming flood; but who is able to stand before jealousy?

5 Open rebuke is better than love that is hidden. [Prov. 28:23; Gal. 2:14.]

6 Faithful are the wounds of a friend, but the kisses of an enemy are lavish *and* deceitful.

7 He who is satiated [with sensual pleasures] loathes *and* treads underfoot a honeycomb, but to the hungry soul every bitter thing is sweet.

8 As a bird that wanders from her nest, so is a man who strays from his home.

9 Oil and perfume rejoice the heart; so does the sweetness of a friend's counsel that comes from the heart.

10 Your own friend and your father's friend forsake not, neither go to your brother's house in the day of your calamity. Better is a neighbor who is near [in spirit] than a brother who is far off [in heart].

11 My son, be wise, and make my heart glad, that I may answer him who reproaches me [as having failed in parental duty]. [Prov. 10:1; 23:15, 24.]

12 A prudent man sees the evil and hides himself, but the simple pass on and are punished (with suffering).

13 [The judge tells the creditor] Take his garment who is security for a stranger, and hold him in pledge when he is security for foreigners.

14 The flatterer who loudly praises *and* glorifies his neighbor, rising early in the morning, it shall be counted as cursing him [for he will be suspected of sinister purpose].

15 A continual dripping on a day of violent showers and a contentious woman are alike. [Prov. 19:13.]

16 Whoever attempts to restrain *a contentious woman* might as well try to stop the wind; his right hand encounters oil [and she slips through his fingers].

17 Iron sharpens iron; so a man sharpens the countenance of his friend [to show rage or worthy purpose].

18 Whoever tends the fig tree shall eat the fruit of it; so he who patiently *and* faithfully guards *and* heeds his master shall be honored. [I Cor. 9:7, 13.]

19 As in water face answers to face, so the heart of man to man.

20 Sheol [the place of the dead] and Abaddon [the place of destruction] are never satisfied; so *the lust of* the eyes of man *is* never satisfied. [Prov. 30:16; Hab. 2:5.]

21 As the refining pot for silver and the furnace for gold [bring forth all the impurities of the metal], so let a man be in his trial of praise [ridding it of all that is base or insincere]—for a man is judged by what he praises *and* of what he boasts.

22 Even though like grain you should pound a fool in a mortar with a pestle, yet will not his foolishness depart from him.

23 Be diligent to know the state of your flocks, and look well to your herds;

24 For riches are not for ever; does a crown endure to all generations?

25 When the hay is gone, the tender grass shows itself, and herbs of the mountain are gathered.

26 The lambs are for your clothing, and the goats *furnish you* the price of a field.

27 And there will be goats' milk enough for your food, for the food of your household and the maintenance of your maids.

## New American Standard

3 A stone is heavy and the sand weighty,
But the provocation of a fool is heavier than both of them.
4 Wrath is fierce and anger is a flood,
But who can stand before jealousy?
5 Better is open rebuke
Than love that is concealed.
6 Faithful are the wounds of a friend,
But deceitful are the kisses of an enemy.
7 A sated man loathes honey,
But to a famished man any bitter thing is sweet.
8 Like a bird that wanders from her nest,
So is a man who wanders from his home.
9 Oil and perfume make the heart glad,
So a man's counsel is sweet to his friend.
10 Do not forsake your own friend or your father's friend,
And do not go to your brother's house in the day of your calamity;
Better is a neighbor who is near than a brother far away.
11 Be wise, my son, and make my heart glad,
That I may reply to him who reproaches me.
12 A prudent man sees evil *and* hides himself,
The naive proceed *and* pay the penalty.
13 Take his garment when he becomes surety for a stranger;
And for an adulterous woman hold him in pledge.
14 He who blesses his friend with a loud voice early in the morning,
It will be reckoned a curse to him.
15 A constant dripping on a day of steady rain
And a contentious woman are alike;
16 He who would restrain her restrains the wind,
And grasps oil with his right hand.
17 Iron sharpens iron,
So one man sharpens another.
18 He who tends the fig tree will eat its fruit;
And he who cares for his master will be honored.
19 As in water face *reflects* face,
So the heart of man *reflects* man.
20 Sheol and Abaddon are never satisfied,
Nor are the eyes of man ever satisfied.
21 The crucible is for silver and the furnace for gold,
And a man *is tested* by the praise accorded him.
22 Though you pound a fool in a mortar with a pestle along with crushed grain,
*Yet* his folly will not depart from him.

23 ¶ Know well the condition of your flocks,
*And* pay attention to your herds;
24 For riches are not forever,
Nor does a crown *endure* to all generations.
25 *When* the grass disappears, the new growth is seen,
And the herbs of the mountains are gathered in,
26 The lambs *will be* for your clothing,
And the goats *will bring* the price of a field,
27 And *there will be* goats' milk enough for your food,
For the food of your household,
And sustenance for your maidens.

## New International

3Stone is heavy and sand a burden,
but provocation by a fool is heavier than both.

4Anger is cruel and fury overwhelming,
but who can stand before jealousy?

5Better is open rebuke
than hidden love.

6Wounds from a friend can be trusted,
but an enemy multiplies kisses.

7He who is full loathes honey,
but to the hungry even what is bitter tastes sweet.

8Like a bird that strays from its nest
is a man who strays from his home.

9Perfume and incense bring joy to the heart,
and the pleasantness of one's friend springs from his earnest counsel.

10Do not forsake your friend and the friend of your father,
and do not go to your brother's house when disaster strikes you—
better a neighbor nearby than a brother far away.

11Be wise, my son, and bring joy to my heart;
then I can answer anyone who treats me with contempt.

12The prudent see danger and take refuge,
but the simple keep going and suffer for it.

13Take the garment of one who puts up security for a stranger;
hold it in pledge if he does it for a wayward woman.

14If a man loudly blesses his neighbor early in the morning,
it will be taken as a curse.

15A quarrelsome wife is like
a constant dripping on a rainy day;
16restraining her is like restraining the wind
or grasping oil with the hand.

17As iron sharpens iron,
so one man sharpens another.

18He who tends a fig tree will eat its fruit,
and he who looks after his master will be honored.

19As water reflects a face,
so a man's heart reflects the man.

20Death and Destruction[a] are never satisfied,
and neither are the eyes of man.

21The crucible is for silver and the furnace for gold,
but man is tested by the praise he receives.

22Though you grind a fool in a mortar,
grinding him like grain with a pestle,
you will not remove his folly from him.

23Be sure you know the condition of your flocks,
give careful attention to your herds;
24for riches do not endure forever,
and a crown is not secure for all generations.
25When the hay is removed and new growth appears
and the grass from the hills is gathered in,
26the lambs will provide you with clothing,
and the goats with the price of a field.
27You will have plenty of goats' milk
to feed you and your family
and to nourish your servant girls.

NIV [a] 20 Hebrew *Sheol and Abaddon*

## King James

**28** THE WICKED flee when no man pursueth: but the righteous are bold as a lion.

2 For the transgression of a land many *are* the princes thereof: but by a man of understanding *and* knowledge the state *thereof* shall be prolonged.

3 A poor man that oppresseth the poor *is like* a sweeping rain which leaveth no food.

4 They that forsake the law praise the wicked: but such as keep the law contend with them.

5 Evil men understand not judgment: but they that seek the LORD understand all *things*.

6 Better *is* the poor that walketh in his uprightness, than *he that is* perverse *in his* ways, though he *be* rich.

7 Whoso keepeth the law *is* a wise son: but he that is a companion of riotous *men* shameth his father.

8 He that by usury and unjust gain increaseth his substance, he shall gather it for him that will pity the poor.

9 He that turneth away his ear from hearing the law, even his prayer *shall be* abomination.

10 Whoso causeth the righteous to go astray in an evil way, he shall fall himself into his own pit: but the upright shall have good *things* in possession.

11 The rich man *is* wise in his own conceit; but the poor that hath understanding searcheth him out.

12 When righteous *men* do rejoice, *there is* great glory: but when the wicked rise, a man is hidden.

13 He that covereth his sins shall not prosper: but whoso confesseth and forsaketh *them* shall have mercy.

14 Happy *is* the man that feareth always: but he that hardeneth his heart shall fall into mischief.

15 *As* a roaring lion, and a ranging bear; *so is* a wicked ruler over the poor people.

16 The prince that wanteth understanding *is* also a great oppressor: *but* he that hateth covetousness shall prolong *his* days.

17 A man that doeth violence to the blood of *any* person shall flee to the pit; let no man stay him.

18 Whoso walketh uprightly shall be saved: but *he that is* perverse *in his* ways shall fall at once.

19 He that tilleth his land shall have plenty of bread: but he that followeth after vain *persons* shall have poverty enough.

20 A faithful man shall abound with blessings: but he that maketh haste to be rich shall not be innocent.

21 To have respect of persons *is* not good: for for a piece of bread *that* man will transgress.

22 He that hasteth to be rich *hath* an evil eye, and considereth not that poverty shall come upon him.

23 He that rebuketh a man afterwards shall find more favour than he that flattereth with the tongue.

24 Whoso robbeth his father or his mother, and saith, *It is* no transgression; the same *is* the companion of a destroyer.

## Amplified

**28** THE WICKED flee when no man pursues them, but the [uncompromisingly] righteous are bold as a lion. [Lev. 26:17, 36; Ps. 53:5.]

2 When a land transgresses, it has many rulers; but when the ruler is a man of discernment, understanding *and* knowledge, its stability will long continue.

3 A poor man who oppresses the poor is like a sweeping rain which leaves no food [plundering them of their last morsels]. [Matt. 18:28.]

4 Those who forsake the law [of God and man] praise the wicked, but such as keep the law [of God and man] contend with them. [Prov. 29:18.]

5 Evil men do not understand justice, but they who crave *and* seek the Lord understand it fully. [John 7:17; I Cor. 2:15; I John 2:20, 27.]

6 Better is the poor who walks in his integrity, then he who willfully goes in double *and* wrong ways, though he be rich.

7 Whoever keeps the law [of God and man] is a wise son, but he who is a companion of gluttons *and* the carousing, self-indulgent *and* extravagant shames his father.

8 He who by charging excessive interest *and* by unjust efforts to get gain increases his material possession, gathers it for him [to spend] who is kind *and* generous to the poor. [Prov. 13:22; Job 27:16, 17; Eccl. 2:26.]

9 He who turns away his ear from hearing the law [of God and man], even his prayer is an abomination, hateful *and* revolting *to God*. [Zech. 7:11; Prov. 15:8; Pss. 66:18; 109:7.]

10 Whoever leads the upright astray into an evil way, he shall fall himself into his own pit; but the blameless will have a goodly inheritance.

11 The rich man is wise in his own eyes *and* conceit, but the poor who has understanding will find him out.

12 When the [uncompromisingly] righteous triumph, there is great glory *and* celebration; but when the wicked rise [to power], men hide themselves.

13 He who covers his transgressions will not prosper, but whoever confesses and forsakes his sins shall obtain mercy. [Ps. 32:3, 5; I John 1:8-10.]

14 Blessed, happy, fortunate [and to be envied] is the man who reverently *and* worshipfully fears *the* Lord at all times [regardless of circumstances]; but he who hardens his heart will fall into calamity.

15 As a roaring lion or a ravenous *and* charging bear is a wicked ruler over a poor people.

16 A ruler who lacks understanding is [like a wicked one] a great oppressor, but he who hates covetousness *and* unjust gain shall prolong his days.

17 If a man willfully sheds the blood of a person [and keeps the guilt of it upon his conscience], he is fleeing to the pit [the grave] *and* hastening to his own destruction; let no man stop him!

18 He who walks uprightly shall be safe, but he who willfully goes in double *and* wrong ways shall fall in one of them.

19 He who cultivates his land shall have plenty of bread, but he who follows worthless people *and* pursuits will have poverty enough.

20 A faithful man shall abound with blessings; but he who makes haste to be rich [at any cost] shall not be unpunished. [Prov. 13:11; 20:21; 23:4; I Tim. 6:9.]

21 To have respect of persons *and* show partiality is not good, neither that man should transgress for a piece of bread.

22 He who has an evil *and* covetous eye hastens to be rich, and knows not that want will come upon him. [Prov. 21:5; 28:20.]

23 He who rebukes a man shall afterward find more favor than he who flatters with the tongue.

24 Whoever robs his father or his mother and says, That is no sin, he is in the same class as [an open, lawless robber and] a destroyer.

## New American Standard

*Warnings and Instructions*

28 THE WICKED flee when no one is pursuing,
But the righteous are bold as a lion.
2 By the transgression of a land many are its princes,
But by a man of understanding *and* knowledge, so it endures.
3 A poor man who oppresses the lowly
Is *like* a driving rain which leaves no food.
4 Those who forsake the law praise the wicked,
But those who keep the law strive with them.
5 Evil men do not understand justice,
But those who seek the LORD understand all things.
6 Better is the poor who walks in his integrity,
Than he who is crooked though he be rich.
7 He who keeps the law is a discerning son,
But he who is a companion of gluttons humiliates his father.
8 He who increases his wealth by interest and usury,
Gathers it for him who is gracious to the poor.
9 He who turns away his ear from listening to the law,
Even his prayer is an abomination.
10 He who leads the upright astray in an evil way
Will himself fall into his own pit,
But the blameless will inherit good.
11 The rich man is wise in his own eyes,
But the poor who has understanding sees through him.
12 When the righteous triumph, there is great glory,
But when the wicked rise, men hide themselves.
13 He who conceals his transgressions will not prosper,
But he who confesses and forsakes *them* will find compassion.
14 How blessed is the man who fears always,
But he who hardens his heart will fall into calamity.
15 *Like* a roaring lion and a rushing bear
Is a wicked ruler over a poor people.
16 A leader who is a great oppressor lacks understanding,
*But* he who hates unjust gain will prolong *his* days.
17 A man who is laden with the guilt of human blood
Will be a fugitive until death; let no one support him.
18 He who walks blamelessly will be delivered,
But he who is crooked will fall all at once.
19 He who tills his land will have plenty of food,
But he who follows empty *pursuits* will have poverty in plenty.
20 A faithful man will abound with blessings,
But he who makes haste to be rich will not go unpunished.
21 To show partiality is not good,
Because for a piece of bread a man will transgress.
22 A man with an evil eye hastens after wealth,
And does not know that want will come upon him.
23 He who rebukes a man will afterward find *more* favor
Than he who flatters with the tongue.
24 He who robs his father or his mother,
And says, "It is not a transgression,"
Is the companion of a man who destroys.

## New International

28 THE WICKED man flees though no one pursues,
but the righteous are as bold as a lion.

2 When a country is rebellious, it has many rulers,
but a man of understanding and knowledge maintains order.

3 A ruler[a] who oppresses the poor
is like a driving rain that leaves no crops.

4 Those who forsake the law praise the wicked,
but those who keep the law resist them.

5 Evil men do not understand justice,
but those who seek the LORD understand it fully.

6 Better a poor man whose walk is blameless
than a rich man whose ways are perverse.

7 He who keeps the law is a discerning son,
but a companion of gluttons disgraces his father.

8 He who increases his wealth by exorbitant interest
amasses it for another, who will be kind to the poor.

9 If anyone turns a deaf ear to the law,
even his prayers are detestable.

10 He who leads the upright along an evil path
will fall into his own trap,
but the blameless will receive a good inheritance.

11 A rich man may be wise in his own eyes,
but a poor man who has discernment sees through him.

12 When the righteous triumph, there is great elation;
but when the wicked rise to power, men go into hiding.

13 He who conceals his sins does not prosper,
but whoever confesses and renounces them finds mercy.

14 Blessed is the man who always fears the LORD,
but he who hardens his heart falls into trouble.

15 Like a roaring lion or a charging bear
is a wicked man ruling over a helpless people.

16 A tyrannical ruler lacks judgment,
but he who hates ill-gotten gain will enjoy a long life.

17 A man tormented by the guilt of murder
will be a fugitive till death;
let no one support him.

18 He whose walk is blameless is kept safe,
but he whose ways are perverse will suddenly fall.

19 He who works his land will have abundant food,
but the one who chases fantasies will have his fill of poverty.

20 A faithful man will be richly blessed,
but one eager to get rich will not go unpunished.

21 To show partiality is not good—
yet a man will do wrong for a piece of bread.

22 A stingy man is eager to get rich
and is unaware that poverty awaits him.

23 He who rebukes a man will in the end gain more favor
than he who has a flattering tongue.

24 He who robs his father or mother
and says, "It's not wrong"—
he is partner to him who destroys.

NIV [a] 3 Or *A poor man*

## King James

25He that is of a proud heart stirreth up strife: but he that
putteth his trust in the LORD shall be made fat.
26He that trusteth in his own heart is a fool: but whoso walketh
wisely, he shall be delivered.
27He that giveth unto the poor shall not lack: but he that hideth
his eyes shall have many a curse.
28When the wicked rise, men hide themselves: but when they
perish, the righteous increase.

**29** HE, THAT being often reproved hardeneth *his* neck, shall
suddenly be destroyed, and that without remedy.
2When the righteous are in authority, the people rejoice: but
when the wicked beareth rule, the people mourn.
3Whoso loveth wisdom rejoiceth his father: but he that keepeth
company with harlots spendeth *his* substance.
4The king by judgment establisheth the land: but he that receiveth gifts overthroweth it.
5A man that flattereth his neighbour spreadeth a net for his feet.
6In the transgression of an evil man *there is* a snare: but the
righteous doth sing and rejoice.
7The righteous considereth the cause of the poor: *but* the wicked
regardeth not to know *it*.
8Scornful men bring a city into a snare: but wise *men* turn away
wrath.
9 *If* a wise man contendeth with a foolish man, whether he rage
or laugh, *there is* no rest.
10The bloodthirsty hate the upright: but the just seek his soul.
11A fool uttereth all his mind: but a wise *man* keepeth it in till
afterwards.
12If a ruler hearken to lies, all his servants *are* wicked.
13The poor and the deceitful man meet together: the LORD
lighteneth both their eyes.
14The king that faithfully judgeth the poor, his throne shall be
established for ever.
15The rod and reproof give wisdom: but a child left *to himself*
bringeth his mother to shame.
16When the wicked are multiplied, transgression increaseth:
but the righteous shall see their fall.
17Correct thy son, and he shall give thee rest; yea, he shall give
delight unto thy soul.
18Where *there is* no vision, the people perish: but he that
keepeth the law, happy *is* he.
19A servant will not be corrected by words: for though he understand he will not answer.
20Seest thou a man *that is* hasty in his words? *there is* more hope
of a fool than of him.
21He that delicately bringeth up his servant from a child shall
have him become *his* son at the length.

## Amplified

25He who is of a greedy spirit stirs up strife, but he who puts
his trust in the Lord shall be enriched *and* blessed.
26He who leans on, trusts in *and* is confident of his own mind
*and* heart is a [self-confident] fool, but he who walks with skillful
*and* godly [a]Wisdom shall be delivered. [James 1:5.]
27He who gives to the poor will not want, but he who hides his
eyes [from their want] will have many a curse. [Prov. 19:17; 22:9;
Deut. 15:7.]
28When the wicked rise, men hide themselves; but when they
perish, the [consistently] righteous increase *and* become many.

**29** HE WHO being often reproved hardens his neck, shall
suddenly be destroyed, and that without remedy.
2When the [uncompromisingly] righteous are in authority, the
people rejoice; but when the wicked man rules, the people groan
*and* sigh.
3Whoever loves skillful *and* godly Wisdom rejoices his father,
but he who associates with harlots wastes his substance.
4The king by justice establishes the land, but he who exacts gifts
*and* tribute overthrows it.
5A man who flatters his neighbor spreads a net for his own feet.
6In the transgression of an evil man there is a snare, but the
[uncompromisingly] righteous sing and rejoice.
7The [consistently] righteous man knows *and* cares for the rights
of the poor, but the wicked man has no interest in such knowledge. [Job 29:16; 31:13; Ps. 41:1.]
8Scoffers set a city afire [inflaming the minds of the people], but
wise men turn wrath away.
9If a wise man has an argument with a foolish man, *the fool* only
rages or laughs and there is no rest.
10The bloodthirsty hate the blameless, but the upright care for
*and* seek [to save] his life. [Gen. 4:5, 8; I John 3:12.]
11A [self-confident] fool utters all his anger, but a wise man
keeps it back and stills it.
12If a ruler listens to falsehood, all his officials will be wicked.
13The poor man and the oppressor meet together; the Lord
gives light to the eyes of both.
14The king who faithfully judges the poor, his throne shall be
established continuously.
15The rod and reproof give wisdom, but a child left undisciplined brings his mother to shame.
16When the wicked are in authority transgression increases, but
the [uncompromisingly] righteous shall see the fall of the wicked.
17Correct your son, and he will give you rest; yes, he will give
delight to your heart.
18Where there is no vision [no redemptive revelations of God],
the people perish; but he who keeps the law [of God, which
includes that of man], blessed, happy, fortunate [and enviable] is
he. [I Sam. 3:1; Amos 8:11, 12.]
19A servant will not be corrected alone by words, for though he
understands, he will not answer [the master who mistreats him].
20Do you see a man who is hasty in his words? There is more
hope of a [self-confident] fool than of him.
21He who pampers his servant from a child will have him expecting the rights of a son afterward.

**AMP** [a] See note on chapter 1:23.

## New American Standard

25 An arrogant man stirs up strife,
But he who trusts in the LORD will prosper.
26 He who trusts in his own heart is a fool,
But he who walks wisely will be delivered.
27 He who gives to the poor will never want,
But he who shuts his eyes will have many curses.
28 When the wicked rise, men hide themselves;
But when they perish, the righteous increase.

*Warnings and Instructions*

**29** A MAN who hardens *his* neck after much reproof
Will suddenly be broken beyond remedy.
2 When the righteous increase, the people rejoice,
But when a wicked man rules, people groan.
3 A man who loves wisdom makes his father glad,
But he who keeps company with harlots wastes *his* wealth.
4 The king gives stability to the land by justice,
But a man who takes bribes overthrows it.
5 A man who flatters his neighbor
Is spreading a net for his steps.
6 By transgression an evil man is ensnared,
But the righteous sings and rejoices.
7 The righteous is concerned for the rights of the poor,
The wicked does not understand *such* concern.
8 Scorners set a city aflame,
But wise men turn away anger.
9 When a wise man has a controversy with a foolish man,
The foolish man either rages or laughs, and there is no rest.
10 Men of bloodshed hate the blameless,
But the upright are concerned for his life.
11 A fool always loses his temper,
But a wise man holds it back.
12 If a ruler pays attention to falsehood,
All his ministers *become* wicked.
13 The poor man and the oppressor have this in common:
The LORD gives light to the eyes of both.
14 If a king judges the poor with truth,
His throne will be established forever.
15 The rod and reproof give wisdom,
But a child who gets his own way brings shame to his mother.
16 When the wicked increase, transgression increases;
But the righteous will see their fall.
17 Correct your son, and he will give you comfort;
He will also delight your soul.
18 Where there is no vision, the people are unrestrained,
But happy is he who keeps the law.
19 A slave will not be instructed by words *alone;*
For though he understands, there will be no response.
20 Do you see a man who is hasty in his words?
There is more hope for a fool than for him.
21 He who pampers his slave from childhood
Will in the end find him to be a son.

## New International

25 A greedy man stirs up dissension,
but he who trusts in the LORD will prosper.

26 He who trusts in himself is a fool,
but he who walks in wisdom is kept safe.

27 He who gives to the poor will lack nothing,
but he who closes his eyes to them receives many curses.

28 When the wicked rise to power, people go into hiding;
but when the wicked perish, the righteous thrive.

**29** A MAN who remains stiff-necked after many rebukes
will suddenly be destroyed—without remedy.

2 When the righteous thrive, the people rejoice;
when the wicked rule, the people groan.

3 A man who loves wisdom brings joy to his father,
but a companion of prostitutes squanders his wealth.

4 By justice a king gives a country stability,
but one who is greedy for bribes tears it down.

5 Whoever flatters his neighbor
is spreading a net for his feet.

6 An evil man is snared by his own sin,
but a righteous one can sing and be glad.

7 The righteous care about justice for the poor,
but the wicked have no such concern.

8 Mockers stir up a city,
but wise men turn away anger.

9 If a wise man goes to court with a fool,
the fool rages and scoffs, and there is no peace.

10 Bloodthirsty men hate a man of integrity
and seek to kill the upright.

11 A fool gives full vent to his anger,
but a wise man keeps himself under control.

12 If a ruler listens to lies,
all his officials become wicked.

13 The poor man and the oppressor have this in common:
The LORD gives sight to the eyes of both.

14 If a king judges the poor with fairness,
his throne will always be secure.

15 The rod of correction imparts wisdom,
but a child left to himself disgraces his mother.

16 When the wicked thrive, so does sin,
but the righteous will see their downfall.

17 Discipline your son, and he will give you peace;
he will bring delight to your soul.

18 Where there is no revelation, the people cast off restraint;
but blessed is he who keeps the law.

19 A servant cannot be corrected by mere words;
though he understands, he will not respond.

20 Do you see a man who speaks in haste?
There is more hope for a fool than for him.

21 If a man pampers his servant from youth,
he will bring grief[b] in the end.

**NIV** [b] *21* The meaning of the Hebrew for this word is uncertain.

## King James

22An angry man stirreth up strife, and a furious man aboundeth
in transgression.
23A man's pride shall bring him low: but honour shall uphold
the humble in spirit.
24Whoso is partner with a thief hateth his own soul: he heareth
cursing, and betrayeth *it* not.
25The fear of man bringeth a snare: but whoso putteth his trust
in the LORD shall be safe.
26Many seek the ruler's favour; but *every* man's judgment
*cometh* from the LORD.
27An unjust man *is* an abomination to the just: and *he that is*
upright in the way *is* abomination to the wicked.

**30** THE WORDS of Agur the son of Jakeh, *even* the prophecy:
the man spake unto Ithiel, even unto Ithiel and Ucal,
2Surely I *am* more brutish than *any* man, and have not the
understanding of a man.
3I neither learned wisdom, nor have the knowledge of the holy.
4Who hath ascended up into heaven, or descended? who hath
gathered the wind in his fists? who hath bound the waters in a
garment? who hath established all the ends of the earth? what *is*
his name, and what *is* his son's name, if thou canst tell?
5Every word of God *is* pure: he *is* a shield unto them that put
their trust in him.
6Add thou not unto his words, lest he reprove thee, and thou
be found a liar.
7Two *things* have I required of thee; deny me *them* not before
I die:
8Remove far from me vanity and lies: give me neither poverty
nor riches; feed me with food convenient for me:
9Lest I be full, and deny *thee*, and say, Who *is* the LORD? or lest
I be poor, and steal, and take the name of my God *in vain*.
10Accuse not a servant unto his master, lest he curse thee, and
thou be found guilty.
11 *There is* a generation *that* curseth their father, and doth not
bless their mother.
12 *There is* a generation *that are* pure in their own eyes, and *yet*
is not washed from their filthiness.
13 *There is* a generation, O how lofty are their eyes! and their
eyelids are lifted up.
14 *There is* a generation, whose teeth *are as* swords, and their jaw
teeth *as* knives, to devour the poor from off the earth, and the
needy from *among* men.
15The horseleach hath two daughters, *crying*, Give, give. There
are three *things that* are never satisfied, *yea*, four *things* say not, *It
is* enough:

## Amplified

22A man of wrath stirs up strife, and a man given to anger
commits *and* causes much transgression.
23A man's pride will bring him low, but he who is of a humble
spirit shall obtain honor. [Prov. 15:33; 18:12; Isa. 66:2; Dan. 4:30;
Matt. 23:12; James 4:6, 10; I Pet. 5:5.]
24Whoever is partner with a thief hates his own life; he falls
under the curse [pronounced upon him who knows who the thief
is], but discloses nothing.
25The fear of man brings a snare, but whoever leans on, trusts
*and* puts his confidence in the Lord is safe *and* set on high.
26Many crave *and* seek the ruler's favor, but the wise man *waits*
for justice from the Lord.
27An unjust man is an abomination to the righteous, and he
who is upright in the way *of the Lord* is an abomination to the
wicked.

**30** THE WORDS of Agur the son of Jakeh of Massa. The man
says to Ithiel, to Ithiel and Ucal:
2Surely I am too brutish *and* stupid to be called a man, and have
not the understanding of a man [for all my secular learning is as
nothing].
3I have not learned skillful *and* godly Wisdom that I should have
the knowledge *or* burden of the Holy One.
4Who has ascended into Heaven and descended? Who has
gathered the wind in His fists? Who has bound the waters in His
garment? Who has established all the ends of the earth? What is
His name, and what is His Son's name, if you know? [John 3:13;
Rev. 19:12.]
5Every word of God is tried *and* purified; He is a shield to those
who trust *and* take refuge in Him. [Pss. 18:30; 84:11; 115:9-11.]
6Add not to His words, lest He reprove you, and you be found
a liar.
7Two things have I asked of You, *O Lord;* deny them not to me
before I die:
8Remove far from me falsehood and lies; give me neither poverty nor riches; feed me with the food that is needful for me,
9Lest I be full, and deny You, and say, Who is the Lord? Or lest
I be poor and steal, and profane the name of my God. [Deut. 8:12,
14, 17; Neh. 9:25, 26; Job 31:24; Hos. 13:6.]
10Do not accuse *and* hurt a servant to his master, lest he curse
you, and you be held guilty [of adding to the burdens of the lowly].
11There is a class of people who curse their father, and do not
bless their mother.
12There is a class of people who are pure in their own eyes, and
yet are not washed from their own filth.
13There is a class of people, Oh, how lofty are their eyes and
their raised high eyelids!
14There is a class of people whose teeth are as swords and their
fangs as knives, to devour the poor from the earth and the needy
from among men.
15The leech has two daughters, crying, Give, give! There are
three things that are never satisfied; yes, four that do not say, It
is enough:

## New American Standard

22 An angry man stirs up strife,
And a hot-tempered man abounds in transgression.
23 A man's pride will bring him low,
But a humble spirit will obtain honor.
24 He who is a partner with a thief hates his own life;
He hears the oath but tells nothing.
25 The fear of man brings a snare,
But he who trusts in the LORD will be exalted.
26 Many seek the ruler's favor,
But justice for man *comes* from the LORD.
27 An unjust man is abominable to the righteous,
And he who is upright in the way is abominable to the wicked.

*The Words of Agur*

30 THE WORDS of Agur the son of Jakeh, the oracle.
¶ The man declares to Ithiel, to Ithiel and Ucal:
2 Surely I am more stupid than any man,
And I do not have the understanding of a man.
3 Neither have I learned wisdom,
Nor do I have the knowledge of the Holy One.
4 Who has ascended into heaven and descended?
Who has gathered the wind in His fists?
Who has wrapped the waters in His garment?
Who has established all the ends of the earth?
What is His name or His son's name?
Surely you know!

5¶ Every word of God is tested;
He is a shield to those who take refuge in Him.
6 Do not add to His words
Lest He reprove you, and you be proved a liar.

7¶ Two things I asked of Thee,
Do not refuse me before I die:
8 Keep deception and lies far from me,
Give me neither poverty nor riches;
Feed me with the food that is my portion,
9 Lest I be full and deny *Thee* and say, "Who is the LORD?"
Or lest I be in want and steal,
And profane the name of my God.

10¶ Do not slander a slave to his master,
Lest he curse you and you be found guilty.

11¶ There is a [a]kind of *man* who curses his father,
And does not bless his mother.
12 There is a kind who is pure in his own eyes,
Yet is not washed from his filthiness.
13 There is a kind—oh how lofty are his eyes!
And his eyelids are raised *in arrogance*.
14 There is a kind of *man* whose teeth are *like* swords,
And his jaw teeth *like* knives,
To devour the afflicted from the earth,
And the needy from among men.

15¶ The leech has two daughters,
"Give," "Give."
There are three things that will not be satisfied,
Four that will not say, "Enough":

NAS [a] Or, *generation;* so through v. 14

## New International

22 An angry man stirs up dissension,
and a hot-tempered one commits many sins.

23 A man's pride brings him low,
but a man of lowly spirit gains honor.

24 The accomplice of a thief is his own enemy;
he is put under oath and dare not testify.

25 Fear of man will prove to be a snare,
but whoever trusts in the LORD is kept safe.

26 Many seek an audience with a ruler,
but it is from the LORD that man gets justice.

27 The righteous detest the dishonest;
the wicked detest the upright.

*Sayings of Agur*

30 THE SAYINGS of Agur son of Jakeh—an oracle[b]:
This man declared to Ithiel,
to Ithiel and to Ucal:[c]
2 "I am the most ignorant of men;
I do not have a man's understanding.
3 I have not learned wisdom,
nor have I knowledge of the Holy One.
4 Who has gone up to heaven and come down?
Who has gathered up the wind in the hollow of his hands?
Who has wrapped up the waters in his cloak?
Who has established all the ends of the earth?
What is his name, and the name of his son?
Tell me if you know!

5 "Every word of God is flawless;
he is a shield to those who take refuge in him.
6 Do not add to his words,
or he will rebuke you and prove you a liar.

7 "Two things I ask of you, O LORD;
do not refuse me before I die:
8 Keep falsehood and lies far from me;
give me neither poverty nor riches,
but give me only my daily bread.
9 Otherwise, I may have too much and disown you
and say, 'Who is the LORD?'
Or I may become poor and steal,
and so dishonor the name of my God.

10 "Do not slander a servant to his master,
or he will curse you, and you will pay for it.

11 "There are those who curse their fathers
and do not bless their mothers;
12 those who are pure in their own eyes
and yet are not cleansed of their filth;
13 those whose eyes are ever so haughty,
whose glances are so disdainful;
14 those whose teeth are swords
and whose jaws are set with knives
to devour the poor from the earth,
the needy from among mankind.

15 "The leech has two daughters.
'Give! Give!' they cry.

"There are three things that are never satisfied,
four that never say, 'Enough!':

NIV [b] 1 Or *Jakeh of Massa* [c] 1 Masoretic Text; with a different word division of the Hebrew *declared, "I am weary, O God; / I am weary, O God, and faint.*

## King James

16The grave; and the barren womb; the earth *that* is not filled with water; and the fire *that* saith not, *It is* enough.
17The eye *that* mocketh at *his* father, and despiseth to obey *his* mother, the ravens of the valley shall pick it out, and the young eagles shall eat it.
18There be three *things which* are too wonderful for me, yea, four which I know not:
19The way of an eagle in the air; the way of a serpent upon a rock; the way of a ship in the midst of the sea; and the way of a man with a maid.
20Such *is* the way of an adulterous woman; she eateth, and wipeth her mouth, and saith, I have done no wickedness.
21For three *things* the earth is disquieted, and for four *which* it cannot bear:
22For a servant when he reigneth; and a fool when he is filled with meat;
23For an odious *woman* when she is married; and an handmaid that is heir to her mistress.
24There be four *things which are* little upon the earth, but they *are* exceeding wise:
25The ants *are* a people not strong, yet they prepare their meat in the summer;
26The conies *are but* a feeble folk, yet make they their houses in the rocks;
27The locusts have no king, yet go they forth all of them by bands;
28The spider taketh hold with her hands, and is in kings' palaces.
29There be three *things* which go well, yea, four are comely in going:
30A lion *which is* strongest among beasts, and turneth not away for any;
31A greyhound; an he goat also; and a king, against whom *there is* no rising up.
32If thou hast done foolishly in lifting up thyself, or if thou hast thought evil, *lay* thine hand upon thy mouth.
33Surely the churning of milk bringeth forth butter, and the wringing of the nose bringeth forth blood: so the forcing of wrath bringeth forth strife.

31 THE WORDS of king Lemuel, the prophecy that his mother taught him.
2What, my son? and what, the son of my womb? and what, the son of my vows?
3Give not thy strength unto women, nor thy ways to that which destroyeth kings.
4 *It is* not for kings, O Lemuel, *it is* not for kings to drink wine; nor for princes strong drink:
5Lest they drink, and forget the law, and pervert the judgment of any of the afflicted.
6Give strong drink unto him that is ready to perish, and wine unto those that be of heavy hearts.

## Amplified

16Sheol [the place of the dead], the barren womb, the earth that is not satisfied with water, and the fire that says not, It is enough.
17The eye that mocks a father and scorns to obey a mother, the ravens of the valley will pick it out, and the young vultures will devour it. [Prov. 20:20; 23:22; Lev. 20:9.]
18There are three things which are too wonderful for me; yes, four which I do not understand:
19The way of an eagle in the air, the way of a serpent upon a rock, the way of a ship in the midst of the sea, and the way of a man with a maid.
20This is the way of an adulterous woman; she eats and wipes her mouth and says, I have done no wickedness.
21Under three things the earth is disquieted, and under four it cannot bear up.
22Under a servant when he reigns, and [an empty headed] fool when he is filled with food;
23An unloved *and* repugnant woman when she is married, and a maidservant when she supplants her mistress.
24There are four things which are little on the earth, but they are exceedingly wise:
25The ants are a people not strong, yet they lay up their food in the summer; [Prov. 6:6.]
26The conies are but a feeble folk, yet they make their houses in the rocks; [Ps. 104:18.]
27The locusts have no king, yet they go forth all of them by bands;
28The lizard you can seize with your hands, yet it is in kings' palaces.
29There are three things which are stately in step; yes, four are stately in their stride:
30The lion which is mightiest among beasts, and turns not back before any;
31The war horse—well-knit in the loins; the male goat also, and the king [when his army is with him and] against whom there is no rising up.
32If you have done foolishly in exalting yourself, or if you have thought evil, lay your hand upon your mouth. [Job 21:5; 40:4.]
33Surely the churning of milk brings forth butter, and the wringing of the nose brings forth blood; so the forcing of wrath brings forth strife.

31 THE WORDS of Lemuel, king of Massa, which his mother taught him:
2What, my [a]son? What, son of my womb? What *shall I advise you*, son of my vows *and* dedication to God?
3Give not your strength to [loose] women, nor your ways to those who *and* that which ruin *and* destroy kings.
4It is not for kings, O Lemuel, it is not for kings to drink wine, or for rulers to desire strong drink; [Eccl. 10:17; Hos. 4:11.]
5Lest they drink and forget the law *and* what it decrees, and pervert the justice due any of the afflicted.
6Give strong drink [as medicine] to him who is ready to pass away, and wine to those in bitter distress of heart.

**AMP** [a] It is important to the purpose of this invaluable chapter that one realize that it is first of all intended for young men. It is the mother's God-given task to provide youth with this information directly from its inspired source, letting them grow up with it in their consciousness.

## New American Standard

16 Sheol, and the barren womb,
Earth that is never satisfied with water,
And fire that never says, "Enough."
17 The eye that mocks a father,
And scorns a mother,
The ravens of the valley will pick it out,
And the young eagles will eat it.

18¶ There are three things which are too wonderful for me,
Four which I do not understand:
19 The way of an eagle in the sky,
The way of a serpent on a rock,
The way of a ship in the middle of the sea,
And the way of a man with a maid.
20 This is the way of an adulterous woman:
She eats and wipes her mouth,
And says, "I have done no wrong."

21¶ Under three things the earth quakes,
And under four, it cannot bear up:
22 Under a slave when he becomes king,
And a fool when he is satisfied with food,
23 Under an unloved woman when she gets a husband,
And a maidservant when she supplants her mistress.

24¶ Four things are small on the earth,
But they are exceedingly wise:
25 The ants are not a strong folk,
But they prepare their food in the summer;
26 The badgers are not mighty folk,
Yet they make their houses in the rocks;
27 The locusts have no king,
Yet all of them go out in ranks;
28 The lizard you may grasp with the hands,
Yet it is in kings' palaces.

29¶ There are three things which are stately in *their* march,
Even four which are stately when they walk:
30 The lion *which* is mighty among beasts
And does not retreat before any,
31 The strutting cock, the male goat also,
And a king *when his* army is with him.

32¶ If you have been foolish in exalting yourself
Or if you have plotted *evil, put your* hand on your mouth.
33 For the churning of milk produces butter,
And pressing the nose brings forth blood;
So the churning of anger produces strife.

### *The Words of Lemuel*

31 THE WORDS of King Lemuel, the oracle which his mother taught him.
2¶ What, O my son?
And what, O son of my womb?
And what, O son of my vows?
3 Do not give your strength to women,
Or your ways to that which destroys kings.
4 It is not for kings, O Lemuel,
It is not for kings to drink wine,
Or for rulers to desire strong drink,
5 Lest they drink and forget what is decreed,
And pervert the rights of all the afflicted.
6 Give strong drink to him who is perishing,
And wine to him whose life is bitter.

## New International

16the grave,[b] the barren womb,
land, which is never satisfied with water,
and fire, which never says, 'Enough!'

17"The eye that mocks a father,
that scorns obedience to a mother,
will be pecked out by the ravens of the valley,
will be eaten by the vultures.

18"There are three things that are too amazing for me,
four that I do not understand:
19the way of an eagle in the sky,
the way of a snake on a rock,
the way of a ship on the high seas,
and the way of a man with a maiden.

20"This is the way of an adulteress:
She eats and wipes her mouth
and says, 'I've done nothing wrong.'

21"Under three things the earth trembles,
under four it cannot bear up:
22a servant who becomes king,
a fool who is full of food,
23an unloved woman who is married,
and a maidservant who displaces her mistress.

24"Four things on earth are small,
yet they are extremely wise:
25Ants are creatures of little strength,
yet they store up their food in the summer;
26coneys[c] are creatures of little power,
yet they make their home in the crags;
27locusts have no king,
yet they advance together in ranks;
28a lizard can be caught with the hand,
yet it is found in kings' palaces.

29"There are three things that are stately in their stride,
four that move with stately bearing:
30a lion, mighty among beasts,
who retreats before nothing;
31a strutting rooster, a he-goat,
and a king with his army around him.[d]

32"If you have played the fool and exalted yourself,
or if you have planned evil,
clap your hand over your mouth!
33For as churning the milk produces butter,
and as twisting the nose produces blood,
so stirring up anger produces strife."

### *Sayings of King Lemuel*

31 THE SAYINGS of King Lemuel—an oracle[e] his mother taught him:

2"O my son, O son of my womb,
O son of my vows,[f]
3do not spend your strength on women,
your vigor on those who ruin kings.

4"It is not for kings, O Lemuel—
not for kings to drink wine,
not for rulers to crave beer,
5lest they drink and forget what the law decrees,
and deprive all the oppressed of their rights.
6Give beer to those who are perishing,
wine to those who are in anguish;

**NIV** [b] 16 Hebrew *Sheol* [c] 26 That is, the hyrax or rock badger [d] 31 Or *king secure against revolt* [e] 1 Or *of Lemuel king of Massa, which* [f] 2 Or */ the answer to my prayers*

## King James

7 Let him drink, and forget his poverty, and remember his misery no more.

8 Open thy mouth for the dumb in the cause of all such as are appointed to destruction.

9 Open thy mouth, judge righteously, and plead the cause of the poor and needy.

10 ¶ Who can find a virtuous woman? for her price *is* far above rubies.

11 The heart of her husband doth safely trust in her, so that he shall have no need of spoil.

12 She will do him good and not evil all the days of her life.

13 She seeketh wool, and flax, and worketh willingly with her hands.

14 She is like the merchants' ships; she bringeth her food from afar.

15 She riseth also while it is yet night, and giveth meat to her household, and a portion to her maidens.

16 She considereth a field, and buyeth it: with the fruit of her hands she planteth a vineyard.

17 She girdeth her loins with strength, and strengtheneth her arms.

18 She perceiveth that her merchandise *is* good: her candle goeth not out by night.

19 She layeth her hands to the spindle, and her hands hold the distaff.

20 She stretcheth out her hand to the poor; yea, she reacheth forth her hands to the needy.

21 She is not afraid of the snow for her household: for all her household *are* clothed with scarlet.

22 She maketh herself coverings of tapestry; her clothing *is* silk and purple.

23 Her husband is known in the gates, when he sitteth among the elders of the land.

24 She maketh fine linen, and selleth *it;* and delivereth girdles unto the merchant.

25 Strength and honour *are* her clothing; and she shall rejoice in time to come.

26 She openeth her mouth with wisdom; and in her tongue *is* the law of kindness.

27 She looketh well to the ways of her household, and eateth not the bread of idleness.

28 Her children arise up, and call her blessed; her husband *also,* and he praiseth her.

29 Many daughters have done virtuously, but thou excellest them all.

30 Favour *is* deceitful, and beauty *is* vain: *but* a woman *that* feareth the LORD, she shall be praised.

31 Give her of the fruit of her hands; and let her own works praise her in the gates.

## Amplified

7 Let him drink and forget his poverty, and [seriously] remember his want *and* misery no more.

8 Open your mouth for the dumb [those unable to speak for themselves], for the rights of all who are left desolate *and* defenseless; [Job 29:15, 16; I Sam. 19:4; Esth. 4:16.]

9 Open your mouth, judge righteously, and administer justice for the poor and needy. [Lev. 19:15; Deut. 1:16; Job 29:12; Isa. 1:17; Jer. 22:16.]

10 A capable, intelligent *and* [a]virtuous woman, who is he who can find her? She is far more precious than jewels, *and* her value is far above rubies *or* pearls. [Prov. 12:4; 18:22; 19:14.]

11 The heart of her husband trusts in her confidently *and* relies on and believes in her safely, so that he has no lack of *honest* gain or need of *dishonest* spoil.

12 She will comfort, encourage *and* do him only good as long as there is life within her.

13 She seeks out *the* wool and flax and works with willing hands to *develop it.*

14 She is like the merchant ships loaded with foodstuffs, she brings her household's food from a far [country].

15 She rises while yet it is night and gets *spiritual* food for her household and assigns her maids their tasks. [Job 23:12.]

16 She considers a *new* field before she buys *or* accepts it—expanding prudently [and not courting neglect of her present duties by assuming others]. With her savings [of time and strength] she plants fruitful vines in her vineyard. [S. of Sol. 8:12.]

17 She girds herself with strength [spiritual, mental and physical fitness for her God-given task] and makes her arms strong *and* firm.

18 She tastes *and* sees that her gain from work [with and for God] is good; her lamp goes not out; but it burns on continually through the night [of trouble, privation or sorrow, warning away fear, doubt and distrust].

19 She lays her hands to the spindle, and her hands hold the distaff.

20 She opens her hand to the poor; yes, she reaches out her filled hands to the needy [whether in body, mind or spirit].

21 She fears not *the* snow for her family, for all her household are doubly clothed in scarlet. [Josh. 2:18, 19; Heb. 9:19-22.]

22 She makes for herself coverlets, cushions *and* rugs of tapestry. Her clothing is of linen, pure white *and* fine, and of purple [such as that of which the clothing of the priests and the hallowed cloths of the temple are made]. [Isa. 61:10; I Tim. 2:9; Rev. 3:5; 19:8, 14.]

23 Her husband is known in the *city's* gates, when he sits among the elders of the land. [Prov. 12:4.]

24 She makes fine linen garments *and* leads other to buy them; she delivers to the merchants girdles [or sashes that free one for service].

25 Strength and dignity are her clothing *and* her position is strong and secure. She rejoices over the future—the latter day or time to come [knowing that she and her family are in readiness for it]!

26 She opens her mouth with skillful and godly Wisdom, and in her tongue is the law of kindness—giving counsel and instruction.

27 She looks well to how things go in her household, and the bread of idleness [gossip, discontent and self-pity] she will not eat. [I Tim. 5:14; Titus 2:5.]

28 Her children rise up and call her blessed [happy, fortunate and to be envied]; and her husband boasts of *and* praises her, *saying,*

29 [b]Many daughters have done virtuously, nobly *and* well [with the strength of character that is steadfast in goodness] but you excel them all.

30 Charm *and* grace are deceptive, and beauty is vain [because it is not lasting], but a woman who reverently *and* worshipfully fears the Lord, she shall be praised!

31 Give her of the fruit of her hands, and let her own works praise her in the gates *of the city*! [Phil. 4:8.]

---

**AMP** [a] Most unfortunately this description of God's ideal woman is usually confined in readers' minds merely to its literal sense—her ability as a homemaker, as was Martha of Bethany. But it is obvious that far more than that is meant. When the summary of what makes her price "far above rubies" is given (verse 30), it is her spiritual life only that is mentioned. One can almost hear the voice of Jesus (Luke 10:42), saying, "Mary has chosen that good portion . . . which shall not be taken from her." [b] "Many daughters have done . . . nobly and well . . . but you excel them all." This is a very great deal to be recorded of her, a woman in private life. It means she had done more than Miriam, the leader of a nation's women in praise to God, Exod. 15:20, 21; Deborah, the patriotic military advisor, Judg. 4:4-10; Huldah, the woman who revealed God's secret message to national leaders, II Kings 22:14; Ruth, the woman of constancy, Ruth 1:16; Hannah, the ideal mother, I Sam. 1:20; 2:19; the Shunammite, the hospitable woman, II Kings 4:8-10; and even more than Queen Esther, the woman who risked sacrificing her life for her people, Esth. 4:16./ In what way did she "excel them all"? In her spiritual and practical devotion to God, which permeated every area and relationship of her life. All seven of the Christian virtues (II Pet. 1:5) are there, like colored threads in a tapestry. Her secret, which is open to everyone, is the Holy Spirit's climax of the story, and of this book. In verse thirty that "reverent *and* worshipful fear of the Lord" which is "the beginning and principal part of Wisdom" (Prov. 1:7) is given the full responsibility for a life which is valued by God and her husband as "far above rubies *or* pearls."

## New American Standard

7 Let him drink and forget his poverty,
And remember his trouble no more.
8 Open your mouth for the dumb,
For the rights of all the unfortunate.
9 Open your mouth, judge righteously,
And defend the rights of the afflicted and needy.

*Description of a Worthy Woman*

10¶ An excellent wife, who can find?
For her worth is far above jewels.
11 The heart of her husband trusts in her,
And he will have no lack of gain.
12 She does him good and not evil
All the days of her life.
13 She looks for wool and flax,
And works with her hands in delight.
14 She is like merchant ships;
She brings her food from afar.
15 She rises also while it is still night,
And gives food to her household,
And portions to her maidens.
16 She considers a field and buys it;
From her earnings she plants a vineyard.
17 She girds herself with strength,
And makes her arms strong.
18 She senses that her gain is good;
Her lamp does not go out at night.
19 She stretches out her hands to the distaff,
And her hands grasp the spindle.
20 She extends her hand to the poor;
And she stretches out her hands to the needy.
21 She is not afraid of the snow for her household,
For all her household are clothed with scarlet.
22 She makes coverings for herself;
Her clothing is fine linen and purple.
23 Her husband is known in the gates,
When he sits among the elders of the land.
24 She makes linen garments and sells *them*,
And supplies belts to the tradesmen.
25 Strength and dignity are her clothing,
And she smiles at the future.
26 She opens her mouth in wisdom,
And the teaching of kindness is on her tongue.
27 She looks well to the ways of her household,
And does not eat the bread of idleness.
28 Her children rise up and bless her;
Her husband *also*, and he praises her, *saying:*
29 "Many daughters have done nobly,
But you excel them all."
30 Charm is deceitful and beauty is vain,
*But* a woman who fears the LORD, she shall be praised.
31 Give her the product of her hands,
And let her works praise her in the gates.

## New International

7 let them drink and forget their poverty
and remember their misery no more.
8 "Speak up for those who cannot speak for themselves,
for the rights of all who are destitute.
9 Speak up and judge fairly;
defend the rights of the poor and needy."

*Epilogue: The Wife of Noble Character*

10[c] A wife of noble character who can find?
She is worth far more than rubies.
11 Her husband has full confidence in her
and lacks nothing of value.
12 She brings him good, not harm,
all the days of her life.
13 She selects wool and flax
and works with eager hands.
14 She is like the merchant ships,
bringing her food from afar.
15 She gets up while it is still dark;
she provides food for her family
and portions for her servant girls.
16 She considers a field and buys it;
out of her earnings she plants a vineyard.
17 She sets about her work vigorously;
her arms are strong for her tasks.
18 She sees that her trading is profitable,
and her lamp does not go out at night.
19 In her hand she holds the distaff
and grasps the spindle with her fingers.
20 She opens her arms to the poor
and extends her hands to the needy.
21 When it snows, she has no fear for her household;
for all of them are clothed in scarlet.
22 She makes coverings for her bed;
she is clothed in fine linen and purple.
23 Her husband is respected at the city gate,
where he takes his seat among the elders of the land.
24 She makes linen garments and sells them,
and supplies the merchants with sashes.
25 She is clothed with strength and dignity;
she can laugh at the days to come.
26 She speaks with wisdom,
and faithful instruction is on her tongue.
27 She watches over the affairs of her household
and does not eat the bread of idleness.
28 Her children arise and call her blessed;
her husband also, and he praises her:
29 "Many women do noble things,
but you surpass them all."
30 Charm is deceptive, and beauty is fleeting;
but a woman who fears the LORD is to be praised.
31 Give her the reward she has earned,
and let her works bring her praise at the city gate.

**NIV** [c] *10* Verses 10-31 are an acrostic, each verse beginning with a successive letter of the Hebrew alphabet.

## King James

# Ecclesiastes

OR, THE PREACHER

1 THE WORDS of the Preacher, the son of David, king in
Jerusalem.
2Vanity of vanities, saith the Preacher, vanity of vanities; all *is*
vanity.
3What profit hath a man of all his labour which he taketh under
the sun?
4 *One* generation passeth away, and *another* generation cometh:
but the earth abideth for ever.
5The sun also ariseth, and the sun goeth down, and hasteth to
his place where he arose.
6The wind goeth toward the south, and turneth about unto the
north; it whirleth about continually, and the wind returneth again
according to his circuits.
7All the rivers run into the sea; yet the sea *is* not full; unto the
place from whence the rivers come, thither they return again.
8All things *are* full of labour; man cannot utter *it:* the eye is not
satisfied with seeing, nor the ear filled with hearing.
9The thing that hath been, it *is that* which shall be; and that
which is done *is* that which shall be done: and *there is* no new *thing*
under the sun.
10Is there *any* thing whereof it may be said, See, this *is* new? it
hath been already of old time, which was before us.
11 *There is* no remembrance of former *things;* neither shall there
be *any* remembrance of *things* that are to come with *those* that shall
come after.
12¶ I the Preacher was king over Israel in Jerusalem.
13And I gave my heart to seek and search out by wisdom concerning all *things* that are done under heaven: this sore travail hath
God given to the sons of man to be exercised therewith.
14I have seen all the works that are done under the sun; and,
behold, all *is* vanity and vexation of spirit.
15 *That which is* crooked cannot be made straight: and that which
is wanting cannot be numbered.
16I communed with mine own heart, saying, Lo, I am come to
great estate, and have gotten more wisdom than all *they* that have
been before me in Jerusalem: yea, my heart had great experience
of wisdom and knowledge.

## Amplified

# Ecclesiastes

1 THE WORDS of the Preacher, the son of David and king of
Jerusalem.
2Vapor of vapors *and* futility of futilities, says the Preacher,
vapor of vapors *and* futility of futilities, all is vanity—emptiness,
falsity and vainglory. [Rom. 8:20.]
3What profit has man left of all his toil at which he toils [a]under
the sun? [Is life worth living?]
4One generation goes, and another generation comes, but the
earth remains for ever. [Ps. 119:90.]
5The sun also rises and the sun goes down, and hastens to the
place where it rises.
6The wind goes to the south, and circles about to the north; it
circles *and* circles about continually, and on its circlings the wind
returns again. [John 3:8.]
7All the rivers run into the sea, yet the sea is not full; unto the
place from which the rivers come, to there *and* from there they
return again.
8All things are weary with toil *and* all words are feeble; man
cannot utter it; the eye is not satisfied with seeing, nor the ear filled
with hearing. [Prov. 27:20.]
9The thing that has been, it is what will be, and that which has
been done is that which will be done, and there is nothing new
under the sun.
10Is there a thing of which it may be said, See, this is new? It
has already been, in the vast ages of time [recorded or unrecorded]
which were before us.
11There is no remembrance of former happenings *or* men,
neither will there be any remembrance of happenings of generations that are to come, with those who are to come after them.
12I the Preacher have been king over Israel in Jerusalem.
13And I applied by heart *and* mind to seek and search out by
[human] [b]wisdom all human activity under heaven. It is a miserable business which [c]God has given to the sons of man with which
to be busied.
14I have seen all the works that are done under the sun, and
behold, all is vanity, a striving after wind *and* feeding on wind.
15What is crooked cannot be made straight, and what is defective *and* lacking cannot be counted.
16I entered into counsel with my own mind, saying, Lo, I have
acquired great [human] wisdom, yes, more than all who have been
over Jerusalem before me; and my mind has had great experience
of [moral] wisdom and [scientific] knowledge.

**AMP** [a] Ecclesiastes is the book of the natural man whose interests are confined to the unstable, vanishing baubles and empty satisfactions of those who live merely "under the sun." The natural man is unaware that all the affirmative answers to life are to be found in Him Who is above, not "under the sun." The natural man grovels in the dust and finds only earthworms, while the spiritual man may soar up with wings as eagles, above all that is futile and disappointing, and live in the consciousness of God's companionship, favor and incomparable, everlasting rewards. [b] The "wisdom" of Proverbs is not the "wisdom" of Ecclesiastes. The former is Godlike, the latter is usually human. [c] Throughout this book not once is the Supreme Being recognized as "Lord" [of lords and King of kings]. The word used to designate Him is invariably the one that may be applied to God or to idols—"Elohim," the God recognized "under the sun." The wisdom which is thus limited can end only in "miserable business" and vexation of spirit until it finds "the wisdom that is from above" (James 3:17), "the hidden wisdom, which God ordained before the world for our glory" (I Cor. 2:7).

## New American Standard

# Ecclesiastes

*The Futility of All Endeavor*

**1** THE WORDS of the Preacher, the son of David, king in Jerusalem.

2 "[d]Vanity of vanities," says the Preacher,
"[e]Vanity of vanities! All is vanity."

3¶ What advantage does man have in all his work
Which he does under the sun?
4 A generation goes and a generation comes,
But the earth remains forever.
5 Also, the sun rises and the sun sets;
And hastening to its place it rises there *again*.
6 Blowing toward the south,
Then turning toward the north,
The wind continues swirling along;
And on its circular courses the wind returns.
7 All the rivers flow into the sea,
Yet the sea is not full.
To the place where the rivers flow,
There they flow again.
8 All things are wearisome;
Man is not able to tell *it*.
The eye is not satisfied with seeing,
Nor is the ear filled with hearing.
9 That which has been is that which will be,
And that which has been done is that which will be done.
So, there is nothing new under the sun.
10 Is there anything of which one might say,
"See this, it is new"?
Already it has existed for ages
Which were before us.
11 There is no remembrance of earlier things;
And also of the later things which will occur,
There will be for them no remembrance
Among those who will come later *still*.

*The Futility of Wisdom*

12¶ I, the Preacher, have been king over Israel in Jerusalem.
13And I set my mind to seek and explore by wisdom concerning
all that has been done under heaven. *It* is a grievous task *which*
God has given to the sons of men to be afflicted with.
14I have seen all the works which have been done under the
sun, and behold, all is vanity and striving after wind.
15What is crooked cannot be straightened, and what is lacking
cannot be counted.
16I said to myself, "Behold, I have magnified and increased
wisdom more than all who were over Jerusalem before me; and my
mind has observed a wealth of wisdom and knowledge."

NAS [d] Or, *Futility of futilities* [e] Or, *Futility of futilities*

## New International

# Ecclesiastes

*Everything Is Meaningless*

**1** THE WORDS of the Teacher,[f] son of David, king in Jerusalem:

2"Meaningless! Meaningless!"
says the Teacher.
"Utterly meaningless!
Everything is meaningless."
3What does man gain from all his labor
at which he toils under the sun?
4Generations come and generations go,
but the earth remains forever.
5The sun rises and the sun sets,
and hurries back to where it rises.
6The wind blows to the south
and turns to the north;
round and round it goes,
ever returning on its course.
7All streams flow into the sea,
yet the sea is never full.
To the place the streams come from,
there they return again.
8All things are wearisome,
more than one can say.
The eye never has enough of seeing,
nor the ear its fill of hearing.
9What has been will be again,
what has been done will be done again;
there is nothing new under the sun.
10Is there anything of which one can say,
"Look! This is something new"?
It was here already, long ago;
it was here before our time.
11There is no remembrance of men of old,
and even those who are yet to come
will not be remembered
by those who follow.

*Wisdom Is Meaningless*

12I, the Teacher, was king over Israel in Jerusalem. 13I devoted
myself to study and to explore by wisdom all that is done under
heaven. What a heavy burden God has laid on men! 14I have seen
all the things that are done under the sun; all of them are meaningless, a chasing after the wind.

15What is twisted cannot be straightened;
what is lacking cannot be counted.

16I thought to myself, "Look, I have grown and increased in
wisdom more than anyone who has ruled over Jerusalem before
me; I have experienced much of wisdom and knowledge." 17Then

NIV [f] 1 Or *leader of the assembly;* also in verses 2 and 12

## King James

17 And I gave my heart to know wisdom, and to know madness and folly: I perceived that this also is vexation of spirit.

18 For in much wisdom *is* much grief: and he that increaseth knowledge increaseth sorrow.

**2** I SAID in mine heart, Go to now, I will prove thee with mirth, therefore enjoy pleasure: and, behold, this also *is* vanity.

2 I said of laughter, *It is* mad: and of mirth, What doeth it?

3 I sought in mine heart to give myself unto wine, yet acquainting mine heart with wisdom; and to lay hold on folly, till I might see what *was* that good for the sons of men, which they should do under the heaven all the days of their life.

4 I made me great works; I builded me houses; I planted me vineyards:

5 I made me gardens and orchards, and I planted trees in them of all *kind of* fruits:

6 I made me pools of water, to water therewith the wood that bringeth forth trees:

7 I got *me* servants and maidens, and had servants born in my house; also I had great possessions of great and small cattle above all that were in Jerusalem before me:

8 I gathered me also silver and gold, and the peculiar treasure of kings and of the provinces: I gat me men singers and women singers, and the delights of the sons of men, *as* musical instruments, and that of all sorts.

9 So I was great, and increased more than all that were before me in Jerusalem: also my wisdom remained with me.

10 And whatsoever mine eyes desired I kept not from them, I withheld not my heart from any joy; for my heart rejoiced in all my labour: and this was my portion of all my labour.

11 Then I looked on all the works that my hands had wrought, and on the labour that I had laboured to do: and, behold, all *was* vanity and vexation of spirit, and *there was* no profit under the sun.

12 ¶ And I turned myself to behold wisdom, and madness, and folly: for what *can* the man *do* that cometh after the king? *even* that which hath been already done.

13 Then I saw that wisdom excelleth folly, as far as light excelleth darkness.

14 The wise man's eyes *are* in his head; but the fool walketh in darkness: and I myself perceived also that one event happeneth to them all.

15 Then said I in my heart, As it happeneth to the fool, so it happeneth even to me; and why was I then more wise? Then I said in my heart, that this also *is* vanity.

16 For *there is* no remembrance of the wise more than of the fool for ever; seeing that which now *is* in the days to come shall all be forgotten. And how dieth the wise *man?* as the fool.

17 Therefore I hated life; because the work that is wrought under the sun *is* grievous unto me: for all *is* vanity and vexation of spirit.

18 ¶ Yea, I hated all my labour which I had taken under the sun: because I should leave it unto the man that shall be after me.

19 And who knoweth whether he shall be a wise *man* or a fool? yet shall he have rule over all my labour wherein I have laboured, and wherein I have shown myself wise under the sun. This *is* also vanity.

**AMP** [a] Solomon's reign began under most promising conditions: "he loved the Lord and walked in the statutes of David his father . . . The people feared him, for they saw that the wisdom of God was in him to do judgment." But soon his own "wisdom" alone was guiding him. He openly affronted God by taking many wives, even heathen women. They seduced him into toleration or practice of idolatry (I Kings 11:1).

## Amplified

17 And I gave my mind to know [practical] wisdom and to discern [the character of] madness and folly [in which men seem to find satisfaction]. I perceived that this also is searching after wind *and* feeding on it. [I Thess. 5:21.]

18 For in much [human] wisdom is much vexation, and he who increases knowledge increases sorrow.

**2** I SAID in my mind, Come now, I will prove you with mirth and test you with pleasure, so have a good time—enjoy pleasure. But this also was vanity—emptiness, falsity and futility! [Luke 12:19, 20.]

2 I said of laughter, It is mad, and of pleasure, What does it accomplish?

3 I searched in my mind how to cheer my body with wine, yet at the same time have my mind hold its course *and* guide me with [human] wisdom, and to lay hold of folly till I might see what was good for the sons of men to do under heaven all the days of their life.

4 I made great works; I built myself houses; I planted vineyards.

5 I made myself gardens and orchards, and I planted in them all kinds of fruit trees.

6 I made myself pools of water from which to water the forest *and* make the trees to bud.

7 I bought menservants and maidservants, and had servants born in my house; also I had great possessions of herds and flocks, more than any who had been before me in Jerusalem.

8 I also gathered for myself silver and gold and the treasure of kings and of the provinces. I got me men singers and women singers, and the delights of the sons of men, [a]concubines very many. [I Kings 9:28; 10:10, 14, 21.]

9 So I became great and increased more than all that were before me in Jerusalem; also my wisdom remained with me *and* stood by me.

10 And whatever my eyes desired I kept not from them; I withheld not my heart from any pleasure, for my heart rejoiced in all my labor, and this was my portion *and* reward for all my toil.

11 Then I looked on all that my hands had done and the labor I had spent in doing it, and behold, all was vanity and searching for wind *and* feeding on it, and there was no profit under the sun. [Matt. 16:26.]

12 So I turned to consider [human] wisdom and madness and folly; for what can the man do who succeeds the king? Nothing but what has been done already.

13 Then I saw that even [human] wisdom [that brings sorrow] is better than [the pleasures of] folly as far as light is better than darkness.

14 The wise man's eyes are in his head, but the fool walks in darkness; and yet I perceived that *in the end* one event happens to them all. [Prov. 17:24.]

15 Then said I in my heart, As it happens to the fool, so it will happen even to me; and of what use is it then for me to be more wise? Then I said in my heart, that this also is vanity—emptiness, vainglory and futility!

16 For of the wise man, the same as of the fool, there is no permanent remembrance, since in the days to come all will have been long forgotten. And how does the wise man die? Even as the fool!

17 So I hated life, because what is done under the sun was grievous to me; for all is vanity, and a striving after wind *and* feeding on it.

18 And I hated all my labor in which I had toiled under the sun; seeing that I must leave it to the man who will succeed me; [Ps. 49:10.]

19 And who knows whether he will be a wise man or a fool? Yet he will have dominion over all my labor in which I have toiled, and in which I have shown myself wise under the sun. This is also vanity—emptiness, falsity and futility!

## New American Standard

17And I set my mind to know wisdom and to know madness and folly; I realized that this also is striving after wind.
18Because in much wisdom there is much grief, and increasing knowledge *results in* increasing pain.

*The Futility of Pleasure and Possessions*

**2** I SAID to myself, "Come now, I will test you with pleasure. So enjoy yourself." And behold, it too was futility.
2I said of laughter, "It is madness," and of pleasure, "What does it accomplish?"
3I explored with my mind *how* to stimulate my body with wine while my mind was guiding *me* wisely, and how to take hold of folly, until I could see what good there is for the sons of men to do under heaven the few years of their lives.
4I enlarged my works: I built houses for myself, I planted vineyards for myself;
5I made gardens and parks for myself, and I planted in them all kinds of fruit trees;
6I made ponds of water for myself from which to irrigate a forest of growing trees.
7I bought male and female slaves, and I had homeborn slaves. Also I possessed flocks and herds larger than all who preceded me in Jerusalem.
8Also, I collected for myself silver and gold, and the treasure of kings and provinces. I provided for myself male and female singers and the pleasures of men—many concubines.
9Then I became great and increased more than all who preceded me in Jerusalem. My wisdom also stood by me.
10And all that my eyes desired I did not refuse them. I did not withhold my heart from any pleasure, for my heart was pleased because of all my labor and this was my reward for all my labor.
11Thus I considered all my activities which my hands had done and the labor which I had exerted, and behold all was [b]vanity and striving after wind and there was no profit under the sun.

*Wisdom Excels Folly*

12¶ So I turned to consider wisdom, madness and folly, for what *will* the man *do* who will come after the king *except* what has already been done?
13And I saw that wisdom excels folly as light excels darkness.
14The wise man's eyes are in his head, but the fool walks in darkness. And yet I know that one fate befalls them both.
15Then I said to myself, "As is the fate of the fool, it will also befall me. Why then have I been extremely wise?" So I said to myself, "This too is vanity."
16For there is no lasting remembrance of the wise man *as* with the fool, inasmuch as *in* the coming days all will be forgotten. And how the wise man and the fool alike die!
17So I hated life, for the work which had been done under the sun was grievous to me; because everything is futility and striving after wind.

*The Futility of Labor*

18¶ Thus I hated all the fruit of my labor for which I had labored under the sun, for I must leave it to the man who will come after me.
19And who knows whether he will be a wise man or a fool? Yet he will have control over all the fruit of my labor for which I have labored by acting wisely under the sun. This too is vanity.

NAS [b] Or, *futility*, and so throughout this context

## New International

I applied myself to the understanding of wisdom, and also of madness and folly, but I learned that this, too, is a chasing after the wind.

18For with much wisdom comes much sorrow;
the more knowledge, the more grief.

*Pleasures Are Meaningless*

**2** I THOUGHT in my heart, "Come now, I will test you with
pleasure to find out what is good." But that also proved to be
meaningless. 2"Laughter," I said, "is foolish. And what does pleasure accomplish?" 3I tried cheering myself with wine, and embracing folly—my mind still guiding me with wisdom. I wanted to see
what was worthwhile for men to do under heaven during the few
days of their lives.
4I undertook great projects: I built houses for myself and
planted vineyards. 5I made gardens and parks and planted all
kinds of fruit trees in them. 6I made reservoirs to water groves of
flourishing trees. 7I bought male and female slaves and had other
slaves who were born in my house. I also owned more herds and
flocks than anyone in Jerusalem before me. 8I amassed silver and
gold for myself, and the treasure of kings and provinces. I acquired
men and women singers, and a harem[c] as well—the delights of
the heart of man. 9I became greater by far than anyone in Jerusalem
before me. In all this my wisdom stayed with me.

10I denied myself nothing my eyes desired;
I refused my heart no pleasure.
My heart took delight in all my work,
and this was the reward for all my labor.
11Yet when I surveyed all that my hands had done
and what I had toiled to achieve,
everything was meaningless, a chasing after the wind;
nothing was gained under the sun.

*Wisdom and Folly Are Meaningless*

12Then I turned my thoughts to consider wisdom,
and also madness and folly.
What more can the king's successor do
than what has already been done?
13I saw that wisdom is better than folly,
just as light is better than darkness.
14The wise man has eyes in his head,
while the fool walks in the darkness;
but I came to realize
that the same fate overtakes them both.

15Then I thought in my heart,

"The fate of the fool will overtake me also.
What then do I gain by being wise?"
I said in my heart,
"This too is meaningless."
16For the wise man, like the fool, will not be long
remembered;
in days to come both will be forgotten.
Like the fool, the wise man too must die!

*Toil Is Meaningless*

17So I hated life, because the work that is done under the sun
was grievous to me. All of it is meaningless, a chasing after the
wind. 18I hated all the things I had toiled for under the sun,
because I must leave them to the one who comes after me. 19And
who knows whether he will be a wise man or a fool? Yet he will
have control over all the work into which I have poured my effort
and skill under the sun. This too is meaningless. 20So my heart

NIV [c] *8* The meaning of the Hebrew for this phrase is uncertain.

# King James

20Therefore I went about to cause my heart to despair of all the labour which I took under the sun.

21For there is a man whose labour *is* in wisdom, and in knowledge, and in equity; yet to a man that hath not laboured therein shall he leave it *for* his portion. This also *is* vanity and a great evil.

22For what hath man of all his labour, and of the vexation of his heart, wherein he hath laboured under the sun?

23For all his days *are* sorrows, and his travail grief; yea, his heart taketh not rest in the night. This is also vanity.

24¶ *There is* nothing better for a man, *than* that he should eat and drink, and *that* he should make his soul enjoy good in his labour. This also I saw, that it *was* from the hand of God.

25For who can eat, or who else can hasten *hereunto,* more than I?

26For *God* giveth to a man that *is* good in his sight wisdom, and knowledge, and joy: but to the sinner he giveth travail, to gather and to heap up, that he may give to *him that is* good before God. This also *is* vanity and vexation of spirit.

3 TO EVERY *thing there is* a season, and a time to every purpose under the heaven:

2A time to be born, and a time to die; a time to plant, and a time to pluck up *that which is* planted;

3A time to kill, and a time to heal; a time to break down, and a time to build up;

4A time to weep, and a time to laugh; a time to mourn, and a time to dance;

5A time to cast away stones, and a time to gather stones together; a time to embrace, and a time to refrain from embracing;

6A time to get, and a time to lose; a time to keep, and a time to cast away;

7A time to rend, and a time to sew; a time to keep silence, and a time to speak;

8A time to love, and a time to hate; a time of war, and a time of peace.

9What profit hath he that worketh in that wherein he laboureth?

10I have seen the travail, which God hath given to the sons of men to be exercised in it.

11He hath made every *thing* beautiful in his time: also he hath set the world in their heart, so that no man can find out the work that God maketh from the beginning to the end.

12I know that *there is* no good in them, but for *a man* to rejoice, and to do good in his life.

13And also that every man should eat and drink, and enjoy the good of all his labour, it *is* the gift of God.

14I know that, whatsoever God doeth, it shall be for ever: nothing can be put to it, nor anything taken from it: and God doeth *it,* that *men* should fear before him.

15That which hath been is now; and that which is to be hath already been; and God requireth that which is past.

16¶ And moreover I saw under the sun the place of judgment, *that* wickedness *was* there; and the place of righteousness, *that* iniquity *was* there.

17I said in mine heart, God shall judge the righteous and the wicked: for *there is* a time there for every purpose and for every work.

18I said in mine heart concerning the estate of the sons of men, that God might manifest them, and that they might see that they themselves are beasts.

# Amplified

20So I turned around and gave my heart up to despair over all the labor of my efforts under the sun.

21For here is a man whose labor is in wisdom and knowledge and skill; yet to a man who has not toiled for it he must leave it all as his portion. This also is vanity—emptiness, falsity, futility—and a great evil!

22For what has a man left of all his labor and of the striving *and* vexation of his heart in which he has toiled under the sun?

23For all his days are but pain *and* sorrows, and his work is a vexation *and* grief; his mind takes no rest even at night. This is also vanity—emptiness, falsity and futility!

24There is nothing better for a man, than that he should eat and drink, and make himself enjoy good in his labor. Even this, I saw, is from the hand of God.

25For who can eat, or who can have enjoyment any more than I— [a]apart from Him?

26For to the person who pleases Him God gives wisdom and knowledge and joy; but to the sinner He gives the work of gathering and heaping up, that he may give to one who pleases God. This also is vanity and striving for the wind *and* feeding on it.

3 TO EVERY thing there is a season, and a time for every matter *or* purpose under heaven:

2A time to be born, and a time to die; a time to plant, and a time to pluck up what is planted. [Heb. 9:27.]

3A time to kill, and a time to heal; a time to break down, and a time to build up;

4A time to weep, and a time to laugh; a time to mourn, and a time to dance;

5A time to cast away stones, and a time to gather stones together; a time to embrace, and a time to refrain from embracing;

6A time to get, and a time to lose; a time to keep, and a time to cast away;

7A time to rend, and a time to sew; a time to keep silence, and a time to speak; [Amos 5:13.]

8A time to love, and a time to hate; a time of war, and a time of peace. [Luke 14:26.]

9What profit remains for the worker from his toil?

10I have seen the painful labor *and* business exertion which God has given to the sons of men in which to be exercised *and* busy.

11He has made everything beautiful in its time; He also has planted eternity in men's heart *and* mind [a divinely implanted sense of a purpose working through the ages which nothing under the sun, but only God, can satisfy], yet so that man cannot find out what God has done from the beginning to the end.

12I know that there is nothing better for them than to be glad and to get *and* do good as long as they live;

13And also that every man should eat and drink and enjoy the good of all his labor; it is the gift of God.

14I know that whatever God does, it endures for ever; nothing can be added to it, nor anything taken from it; and God does it so that men will (reverently) fear Him—know that He is, revere and worship Him. [James 1:17; Ps. 19:9.]

15That which is now, already has been; and that which is to be, already has been; and God seeks out that which has passed by [so that history repeats itself].

16Moreover I saw under the sun that in the place of justice there was wickedness; and that in the place of righteousness also, wickedness was there.

17I said in my heart, God will judge the righteous and the wicked; for there is a time [appointed] for every matter *and* purpose and for every work.

18I said in my heart regarding the subject of the sons of men that God is (separating and sifting) trying them that they may see that by themselves [under the sun, without God] they are but as beasts.

**AMP** [a] (According to the Septuagint and Syriac reading.) Jesus recognized the unprecedented glory which Solomon's human wisdom had brought him, but He said that Solomon arrayed in all of it was not equal in glory to one tiny lily of the field—which God's wisdom had made. (Matt. 6:29.)

## New American Standard

20 Therefore I completely despaired of all the fruit of my labor
for which I had labored under the sun.
21 When there is a man who has labored with wisdom, knowledge and skill, then he gives his legacy to one who has not labored
with them. This too is vanity and a great evil.
22 For what does a man get in all his labor and in his striving with
which he labors under the sun?
23 Because all his days his task is painful and grievous; even at
night his mind does not rest. This too is vanity.
24 ¶ There is nothing better for a man *than* to eat and drink and
tell himself that his labor is good. This also I have seen, that it is
from the hand of God.
25 For who can eat and who can have enjoyment without Him?
26 For to a person who is good in His sight He has given wisdom
and knowledge and joy, while to the sinner He has given the task
of gathering and collecting so that he may give to one who is good
in God's sight. This too is vanity and striving after wind.

*A Time for Everything*

3 THERE IS an appointed time for everything. And there is a
time for every event under heaven—
2 A time to give birth, and a time to die;
A time to plant, and a time to uproot what is planted.
3 A time to kill, and a time to heal;
A time to tear down, and a time to build up.
4 A time to weep, and a time to laugh;
A time to mourn, and a time to dance.
5 A time to throw stones, and a time to gather stones;
A time to embrace, and a time to shun embracing.
6 A time to search, and a time to give up as lost;
A time to keep, and a time to throw away.
7 A time to tear apart, and a time to sew together;
A time to be silent, and a time to speak.
8 A time to love, and a time to hate;
A time for war, and a time for peace.
9 ¶ What profit is there to the worker from that in which he
toils?
10 I have seen the task which God has given the sons of men with
which to occupy themselves.

*God Set Eternity in the Heart of Man*

11 He has made everything [b]appropriate in its time. He has also
set eternity in their heart, yet so that man will not find out the work
which God has done from the beginning even to the end.
12 ¶ I know that there is nothing better for them than to rejoice
and to do good in one's lifetime;
13 moreover, that every man who eats and drinks sees good in
all his labor—it is the gift of God.
14 I know that everything God does will remain forever; there is
nothing to add to it and there is nothing to take from it, for God
has *so* worked that men should fear Him.
15 That which is has been already, and that which will be has
already been, for God seeks what has passed by.
16 Furthermore, I have seen under the sun *that* in the place of
justice there is wickedness, and in the place of righteousness there
is wickedness.
17 I said to myself, "God will judge both the righteous man and
the wicked man," for a time for every matter and for every deed
is there.
18 I said to myself concerning the sons of men, "God has surely
tested them in order for them to see that they are but beasts."

NAS [b] Lit., *beautiful*

## New International

began to despair over all my toilsome labor under the sun. 21 For
a man may do his work with wisdom, knowledge and skill, and
then he must leave all he owns to someone who has not worked
for it. This too is meaningless and a great misfortune. 22 What does
a man get for all the toil and anxious striving with which he labors
under the sun? 23 All his days his work is pain and grief; even at
night his mind does not rest. This too is meaningless.
24 A man can do nothing better than to eat and drink and find
satisfaction in his work. This too, I see, is from the hand of God,
25 for without him, who can eat or find enjoyment? 26 To the man
who pleases him, God gives wisdom, knowledge and happiness,
but to the sinner he gives the task of gathering and storing up
wealth to hand it over to the one who pleases God. This too is
meaningless, a chasing after the wind.

*A Time for Everything*

3 THERE IS a time for everything,
and a season for every activity under heaven:

2 a time to be born and a time to die,
a time to plant and a time to uproot,
3 a time to kill and a time to heal,
a time to tear down and a time to build,
4 a time to weep and a time to laugh,
a time to mourn and a time to dance,
5 a time to scatter stones and a time to gather them,
a time to embrace and a time to refrain,
6 a time to search and a time to give up,
a time to keep and a time to throw away,
7 a time to tear and a time to mend,
a time to be silent and a time to speak,
8 a time to love and a time to hate,
a time for war and a time for peace.

9 What does the worker gain from his toil? 10 I have seen the
burden God has laid on men. 11 He has made everything beautiful
in its time. He has also set eternity in the hearts of men; yet they
cannot fathom what God has done from beginning to end. 12 I
know that there is nothing better for men than to be happy and
do good while they live. 13 That everyone may eat and drink, and
find satisfaction in all his toil—this is the gift of God. 14 I know that
everything God does will endure forever; nothing can be added to
it and nothing taken from it. God does it so that men will revere
him.

15 Whatever is has already been,
and what will be has been before;
and God will call the past to account.[c]

16 And I saw something else under the sun:

In the place of judgment—wickedness was there,
in the place of justice—wickedness was there.

17 I thought in my heart,
"God will bring to judgment
both the righteous and the wicked,
for there will be a time for every activity,
a time for every deed."

18 I also thought, "As for men, God tests them so that they may
see that they are like the animals. 19 Man's fate is like that of the

NIV [c] *15 Or God calls back the past*

## King James

19For that which befalleth the sons of men befalleth beasts; even one thing befalleth them: as the one dieth, so dieth the other; yea, they have all one breath; so that a man hath no preeminence above a beast: for all *is* vanity.

20All go unto one place; all are of the dust, and all turn to dust again.

21Who knoweth the spirit of man that goeth upward, and the spirit of the beast that goeth downward to the earth?

22Wherefore I perceive that *there is* nothing better, than that a man should rejoice in his own works; for that *is* his portion: for who shall bring him to see what shall be after him?

4 SO I returned, and considered all the oppressions that are done under the sun: and behold the tears of *such as were* oppressed, and they had no comforter; and on the side of their oppressors *there was* power; but they had no comforter.

2Wherefore I praised the dead which are already dead more than the living which are yet alive.

3Yea, better *is he* than both they, which hath not yet been, who hath not seen the evil work that is done under the sun.

4¶ Again, I considered all travail, and every right work, that for this a man is envied of his neighbour. This *is* also vanity and vexation of spirit.

5The fool foldeth his hands together, and eateth his own flesh.

6Better *is* an handful *with* quietness, than both the hands full *with* travail and vexation of spirit.

7¶ Then I returned, and I saw vanity under the sun.

8There is one *alone,* and *there is* not a second; yea, he hath neither child nor brother: yet *is there* no end of all his labour; neither is his eye satisfied with riches; neither *saith he,* For whom do I labour, and bereave my soul of good? This *is* also vanity, yea, it *is* a sore travail.

9¶ Two *are* better than one; because they have a good reward for their labour.

10For if they fall, the one will lift up his fellow: but woe to him *that is* alone when he falleth; for *he hath* not another to help him up.

11Again, if two lie together, then they have heat: but how can one be warm *alone?*

12And if one prevail against him, two shall withstand him; and a threefold cord is not quickly broken.

13¶ Better *is* a poor and a wise child than an old and foolish king, who will no more be admonished.

14For out of prison he cometh to reign; whereas also *he that is* born in his kingdom becometh poor.

15I considered all the living which walk under the sun, with the second child that shall stand up in his stead.

## Amplified

19For that which befalls the sons of men befalls beasts, even one thing befalls them; as the one dies, so dies the other. Yes, they all have one breath *and* spirit, so that a [a]man has no pre-eminence over a beast; for all is vanity—emptiness, falsity *and* futility!

20All go to one place; all are of the dust, and all turn to dust again.

21Who knows the spirit of man whether it goes upward and the spirit of the beast whether it goes downward to the earth?

22So I saw that there is nothing better than that a man should rejoice in his own works, for that is his portion; for who shall bring him back to see what has happened after he is gone?

4 THEN I returned and considered all the oppressions that are practiced under the sun. And I beheld the tears of the oppressed, and they had no comforter; and on the side of their oppressors was power, but they *too* had no comforter.

2So I praised *and* thought more fortunate those who have been long dead than the living who are still alive.

3But better than them both *I thought him* who has not yet been born, who has not seen the evil deeds that are done under the sun.

4Then I saw that all painful effort in labor and all skill in work comes from man's rivalry with his neighbor. This is also vanity, vain striving for the wind *and* feeding on it.

5The fool folds his hands together, and eats his own flesh—by indolence destroying himself.

6Better is a handful with quietness, than both the hands full with painful effort, vain striving for the wind *and* feeding on it.

7Then I returned, and I saw vanity under the sun [in one of its peculiar forms].

8Here is one alone, no one with him; he neither has child nor brother, yet there is no end of all his labor, neither is his eye satisfied with riches, neither does he ask, For whom do I labor and deprive myself of good? This is also vanity—emptiness, falsity and futility; yes, it is painful effort *and* unhappy business. [Prov. 27:20; I John 2:16.]

9Two are better than one, because they have a good [more satisfying] reward for their labor;

10For if they fall, the one will lift up his fellow. But woe to him who is alone when he falls and has not another to lift him up!

11Again, if two lie together, then they have warmth; but how can one be warm alone?

12And though a man might prevail against him who is alone, two will withstand him. A threefold cord is not quickly broken.

13Better is a poor and wise youth than an old and foolish king, who [b]no longer knows how to receive counsel (friendly reproof and warning);

14Even though *the youth* comes out of prison to reign, while the other, born a king, becomes needy.

15I saw all the living who walk under the sun, with the youth who was to stand up in the king's stead.

**AMP** [a] Does the Bible really teach that "a man has no pre-eminence above a beast"? No! The Bible only records that the book of Ecclesiastes says it. Then why is this book in the Bible? Can it possibly be called inspired by God when it makes such "under the sun" pronouncements, some only partially true, others entirely false? Here is the tested answer: "Every scripture inspired of God is also profitable for teaching . . . reproof . . . correction, for instruction . . . in righteousness." (II Tim. 3:16 ASV.) The divine purpose in including Ecclesiastes in the Bible is obvious. It gives a startling picture of how fatal it is for even the wisest of men to substitute man's "wisdom" for God's wisdom and attempt to live by it. Solomon's reign began with God, gold and glory. It ended with bafflement, brass and bewildered acceptance of man's having "no pre-eminence above a beast"!—man, who was made "in the image of God," and "but little lower than God" or "the angels"! (Gen. 1:27; Ps. 8:5 with the margin, ASV.)
[b] "Christianity calls upon us to make our old age into an aspect of youth. There is to be no old age in the sense of spiritual exhaustion or moral decrepitude, or misanthropic isolation; old age is to be equivalent to increase of kingliness and bounty and holy influence." "The path of the righteous is as the dawning light, that shineth more and more unto the perfect day." (Prov. 4:18, ASV.)

## New American Standard

19For the fate of the sons of men and the fate of beasts is the
same. As one dies so dies the other; indeed, they all have the same
breath and there is no advantage for man over beast, for all is
vanity.
20All go to the same place. All came from the dust and all return
to the dust.
21Who knows that the breath of man ascends upward and the
breath of the beast descends downward to the earth?
22And I have seen that nothing is better than that man should
be happy in his activities, for that is his lot. For who will bring him
to see what will occur after him?

*The Evils of Oppression*

4 THEN I looked again at all the acts of oppression which were
being done under the sun. And behold *I saw* the tears of the
oppressed and *that* they had no one to comfort *them;* and on the
side of their oppressors was power, but they had no one to comfort
*them.*
2So I congratulated the dead who are already dead more than
the living who are still living.
3But better *off* than both of them is the one who has never
existed, who has never seen the evil activity that is done under the
sun.
4¶ And I have seen that every labor and every skill which is
done is *the result of* rivalry between a man and his neighbor. This
too is vanity and striving after wind.
5The fool folds his hands and consumes his own flesh.
6One hand full of rest is better than two fists full of labor and
striving after wind.
7¶ Then I looked again at vanity under the sun.
8There was a certain man without a dependent, having neither
a son nor a brother, yet there was no end to all his labor. Indeed,
his eyes were not satisfied with riches *and he never asked,* "And for
whom am I laboring and depriving myself of pleasure?" This too
is vanity and it is a grievous task.
9¶ Two are better than one because they have a good return for
their labor.
10For if either of them falls, the one will lift up his companion.
But woe to the one who falls when there is not another to lift him
up.
11Furthermore, if two lie down together they keep warm, but
how can one be warm *alone?*
12And if one can overpower him who is alone, two can resist
him. A cord of three *strands* is not quickly torn apart.
13¶ A poor, yet wise lad is better than an old and foolish king
who no longer knows *how* to receive instruction.
14For he has come out of prison to become king, even though
he was born poor in his kingdom.
15I have seen all the living under the sun throng to the side of
the second lad who replaces him.

## New International

animals; the same fate awaits them both: As one dies, so dies the
other. All have the same breath[c]; man has no advantage over the
animal. Everything is meaningless. 20All go to the same place; all
come from dust, and to dust all return. 21Who knows if the spirit
of man rises upward and if the spirit of the animal[d] goes down into
the earth?"
22So I saw that there is nothing better for a man than to enjoy
his work, because that is his lot. For who can bring him to see what
will happen after him?

*Oppression, Toil, Friendlessness*

4 AGAIN I looked and saw all the oppression that was taking
place under the sun:

I saw the tears of the oppressed—
and they have no comforter;
power was on the side of their oppressors—
and they have no comforter.
2And I declared that the dead,
who had already died,
are happier than the living,
who are still alive.
3But better than both
is he who has not yet been,
who has not seen the evil
that is done under the sun.

4And I saw that all labor and all achievement spring from man's
envy of his neighbor. This too is meaningless, a chasing after the
wind.

5The fool folds his hands
and ruins himself.
6Better one handful with tranquillity
than two handfuls with toil
and chasing after the wind.

7Again I saw something meaningless under the sun:

8There was a man all alone;
he had neither son nor brother.
There was no end to his toil,
yet his eyes were not content with his wealth.
"For whom am I toiling," he asked,
"and why am I depriving myself of enjoyment?"
This too is meaningless—
a miserable business!

9Two are better than one,
because they have a good return for their work:
10If one falls down,
his friend can help him up.
But pity the man who falls
and has no one to help him up!
11Also, if two lie down together, they will keep warm.
But how can one keep warm alone?
12Though one may be overpowered,
two can defend themselves.
A cord of three strands is not quickly broken.

*Advancement Is Meaningless*

13Better a poor but wise youth than an old but foolish king who
no longer knows how to take warning. 14The youth may have
come from prison to the kingship, or he may have been born in
poverty within his kingdom. 15I saw that all who lived and walked
under the sun followed the youth, the king's successor. 16There

**NIV** c 19 Or *spirit* d 21 Or *Who knows the spirit of man, which rises upward, or the spirit of the animal, which*

## King James

16 *There is* no end of all the people, *even* of all that have been before them: they also that come after shall not rejoice in him. Surely this also *is* vanity and vexation of spirit.

**5** KEEP THY foot when thou goest to the house of God, and be more ready to hear, than to give the sacrifice of fools: for they consider not that they do evil.

2Be not rash with thy mouth, and let not thine heart be hasty to utter *any* thing before God: for God *is* in heaven, and thou upon earth: therefore let thy words be few.

3For a dream cometh through the multitude of business; and a fool's voice *is known* by multitude of words.

4When thou vowest a vow unto God, defer not to pay it; for *he hath* no pleasure in fools: pay that which thou hast vowed.

5Better *is it* that thou shouldest not vow, than that thou shouldest vow and not pay.

6Suffer not thy mouth to cause thy flesh to sin; neither say thou before the angel, that it *was* an error: wherefore should God be angry at thy voice, and destroy the work of thine hands?

7For in the multitude of dreams and many words *there are* also *divers* vanities: but fear thou God.

8¶ If thou seest the oppression of the poor, and violent perverting of judgment and justice in a province, marvel not at the matter: for *he that is* higher than the highest regardeth; and *there be* higher than they.

9¶ Moreover the profit of the earth is for all: the king *himself* is served by the field.

10He that loveth silver shall not be satisfied with silver; nor he that loveth abundance with increase: this *is* also vanity.

11When goods increase, they are increased that eat them: and what good *is there* to the owners thereof, saving the beholding *of them* with their eyes?

12The sleep of a labouring man *is* sweet, whether he eat little or much: but the abundance of the rich will not suffer him to sleep.

13There is a sore evil *which* I have seen under the sun, *namely*, riches kept for the owners thereof to their hurt.

14But those riches perish by evil travail: and he begetteth a son, and *there is* nothing in his hand.

15As he came forth of his mother's womb, naked shall he return to go as he came, and shall take nothing of his labour, which he may carry away in his hand.

16And this also *is* a sore evil, *that* in all points as he came, so shall he go: and what profit hath he that hath laboured for the wind?

17All his days also he eateth in darkness, and *he hath* much sorrow and wrath with his sickness.

18¶ Behold *that* which I have seen: *it is* good and comely *for one* to eat and to drink, and to enjoy the good of all his labour that he taketh under the sun all the days of his life, which God giveth him: for it *is* his portion.

## Amplified

16There was no end of all the people; he was over all of them. Yet those who come later will not rejoice in him. Surely this also is vanity—emptiness, falsity, vainglory—and striving after wind *and* feeding on it.

**5** KEEP YOUR foot—give your mind to what you are doing—when you go [as Jacob to sacred Bethel] to the house of God; for to draw near to hear *and* obey is better than to give the sacrifice of fools [carelessly, irreverently], too ignorant to know that they are doing evil. [Gen. 35:1-4; Exod. 3:5.]

2Be not rash with your mouth, and let not your heart be hasty to utter a word before God; for God is in Heaven, and you upon earth; therefore let your words be few.

3For a dream comes with much business *and* painful effort, and a fool's voice with many words.

4When you vow a vow *or* make a pledge to God, do not put off paying it; for God has no pleasure in fools [those who witlessly mock Him]. Pay what you vow. [Pss. 50:14; 76:11; 66:13, 14.]

5It is better that you should not vow than that you should vow and not pay. [Prov. 20:25; Acts 5:4.]

6Do not allow your mouth to cause your body to sin, and do not say before the messenger [the priest] that it was an error *or* mistake. Why should God be [made] angry at your voice and destroy the work of your hands? [Mal. 2:7.]

7For in a multitude of dreams there is futility *and* worthlessness, and ruin in a flood of words. But do you [reverently] fear God—know He is, revere and worship Him.

8If you see the oppression of the poor, and the violent taking away justice and righteousness in the state *or* province, do not marvel at the matter. [Be sure that there are those who will attend to it] for a higher than the high is observing, and higher ones are over them.

9Moreover the profit of the earth is for all; the king himself is served by the field, *and* in all, a king is an advantage to a land with cultivated fields.

10He who loves silver will not be satisfied with silver, nor he who loves abundance with gain. This also is vanity—emptiness, falsity, futility!

11When goods increase, they who eat them increase also; and what gain is there to their owner except to see them with his eyes?

12The sleep of a laboring man is sweet, whether he eats little or much; but the fullness of the rich will not let him sleep.

13There is a serious *and* severe evil which I have seen under the sun: riches were kept by their owner to his hurt.

14But those riches are lost by a bad venture; and he becomes the father of a son, and there is nothing in his hand *with which to support the child.*

15As *the man* came forth from his mother's womb so he will go again, naked as he came, and will take away nothing for all his labor, which he may carry in his hand.

16And this also is a serious *and* severe evil, that in all points as he came, so shall he go; and what gain has he that labored for the wind? [I Tim. 6:6.]

17All his days also he eats in darkness [cheerlessly, with no sweetness and light in them], and much sorrow and sickness and wrath are his.

18Behold, what I have seen to be good and fitting is for one to eat and to drink, and find enjoyment in all the labor in which he labors under the sun all the days which God gives him, for this is his (allotted) part. [I Tim. 6:17.]

## New American Standard

16There is no end to all the people, to all who were before them,
and even the ones who will come later will not be happy with him,
for this too is vanity and striving after wind.

*Your Attitude Toward God*

**5** GUARD YOUR steps as you go to the house of God, and
draw near to listen rather than to offer the sacrifice of fools;
for they do not know they are doing evil.
2Do not be hasty in word or impulsive in thought to bring up
a matter in the presence of God. For God is in heaven and you are
on the earth; therefore let your words be few.
3For the dream comes through much effort, and the voice of
a fool through many words.
4When you make a vow to God, do not be late in paying it, for
*He takes* no delight in fools. Pay what you vow!
5It is better that you should not vow than that you should vow
and not pay.
6Do not let your speech cause you to sin and do not say in the
presence of the messenger *of God* that it was a mistake. Why should
God be angry on account of your voice and destroy the work of
your hands?
7For in many dreams and in many words there is emptiness.
Rather, fear God.
8¶ If you see oppression of the poor and denial of justice and
righteousness in the province, do not be shocked at the sight, for
one official watches over another official, and there are higher
officials over them.
9After all, a king who cultivates the field is an advantage to the
land.

*The Folly of Riches*

10¶ He who loves money will not be satisfied with money, nor
he who loves abundance *with its* income. This too is vanity.
11When good things increase, those who consume them increase. So what is the advantage to their owners except to look on?
12The sleep of the working man is pleasant, whether he eats
little or much. But the full stomach of the rich man does not allow
him to sleep.
13¶ There is a grievous evil *which* I have seen under the sun:
riches being hoarded by their owner to his hurt.
14When those riches were lost through a bad investment and he
had fathered a son, then there was nothing to support him.
15As he had come naked from his mother's womb, so will he
return as he came. He will take nothing from the fruit of his labor
that he can carry in his hand.
16And this also is a grievous evil—exactly as a man is born, thus
will he die. So, what is the advantage to him who toils for the
wind?
17Throughout his life *he* also eats in darkness with great vexation, sickness and anger.
18¶ Here is what I have seen to be good and fitting: to eat, to
drink and enjoy oneself in all one's labor in which he toils under
the sun *during* the few years of his life which God has given him;
for this is his reward.

## New International

was no end to all the people who were before them. But those who
came later were not pleased with the successor. This too is meaningless, a chasing after the wind.

*Stand in Awe of God*

**5** GUARD YOUR steps when you go to the house of God. Go
near to listen rather than to offer the sacrifice of fools, who
do not know that they do wrong.

2Do not be quick with your mouth,
do not be hasty in your heart
to utter anything before God.
God is in heaven
and you are on earth,
so let your words be few.
3As a dream comes when there are many cares,
so the speech of a fool when there are many words.

4When you make a vow to God, do not delay in fulfilling it. He
has no pleasure in fools; fulfill your vow. 5It is better not to vow
than to make a vow and not fulfill it. 6Do not let your mouth lead
you into sin. And do not protest to the ⌞temple⌟ messenger, "My
vow was a mistake." Why should God be angry at what you say
and destroy the work of your hands? 7Much dreaming and many
words are meaningless. Therefore stand in awe of God.

*Riches Are Meaningless*

8If you see the poor oppressed in a district, and justice and
rights denied, do not be surprised at such things; for one official
is eyed by a higher one, and over them both are others higher still.
9The increase from the land is taken by all; the king himself profits
from the fields.

10Whoever loves money never has money enough;
whoever loves wealth is never satisfied with his
income.
This too is meaningless.
11As goods increase,
so do those who consume them.
And what benefit are they to the owner
except to feast his eyes on them?

12The sleep of a laborer is sweet,
whether he eats little or much,
but the abundance of a rich man
permits him no sleep.

13I have seen a grievous evil under the sun:

wealth hoarded to the harm of its owner,
14 or wealth lost through some misfortune,
so that when he has a son
there is nothing left for him.
15Naked a man comes from his mother's womb,
and as he comes, so he departs.
He takes nothing from his labor
that he can carry in his hand.

16This too is a grievous evil:

As a man comes, so he departs,
and what does he gain,
since he toils for the wind?
17All his days he eats in darkness,
with great frustration, affliction and anger.

18Then I realized that it is good and proper for a man to eat and
drink, and to find satisfaction in his toilsome labor under the sun
during the few days of life God has given him—for this is his lot.

## King James

19 Every man also to whom God hath given riches and wealth, and hath given him power to eat thereof, and to take his portion, and to rejoice in his labour; this *is* the gift of God.

20 For he shall not much remember the days of his life; because God answereth *him* in the joy of his heart.

**6** THERE IS an evil which I have seen under the sun, and it *is* common among men:

2 A man to whom God hath given riches, wealth, and honour, so that he wanteth nothing for his soul of all that he desireth, yet God giveth him not power to eat thereof, but a stranger eateth it: this *is* vanity, and it *is* an evil disease.

3 ¶ If a man beget an hundred *children,* and live many years, so that the days of his years be many, and his soul be not filled with good, and also *that* he have no burial; I say, *that* an untimely birth *is* better than he.

4 For he cometh in with vanity, and departeth in darkness, and his name shall be covered with darkness.

5 Moreover he hath not seen the sun, nor known *any thing:* this hath more rest than the other.

6 ¶ Yea, though he live a thousand years twice *told,* yet hath he seen no good: do not all go to one place?

7 All the labour of man *is* for his mouth, and yet the appetite is not filled.

8 For what hath the wise more than the fool? what hath the poor, that knoweth to walk before the living?

9 ¶ Better *is* the sight of the eyes than the wandering of the desire: this *is* also vanity and vexation of spirit.

10 That which hath been is named already, and it is known that it *is* man: neither may he contend with him that is mightier than he.

11 ¶ Seeing there be many things that increase vanity, what *is* man the better?

12 For who knoweth what *is* good for man in *this* life, all the days of his vain life which he spendeth as a shadow? for who can tell a man what shall be after him under the sun?

**7** A GOOD name *is* better than precious ointment; and the day of death than the day of one's birth.

2 ¶ *It is* better to go to the house of mourning, than to go to the house of feasting: for that *is* the end of all men; and the living will lay *it* to his heart.

## Amplified

19 Also every man to whom God has given riches and possessions and power to enjoy them, and to accept his appointed lot and to rejoice in his toil, this is the gift of God *to him.*

20 For he shall not much remember [seriously] the days of his life, because God [Himself] answers *and* corresponds to the joy of his heart [the tranquillity of God is mirrored in him].

**6** THERE IS an evil which I have seen under the sun, and it lies heavily upon men:

2 A man to whom God has given riches, possessions, and honor, so that he lacks nothing for his soul of all that he might desire, yet God does not give him the power *or* capacity to enjoy them [which is the gift of God], but a stranger [in whom he has no interest succeeds him and] consumes *and* enjoys them. This is vanity—emptiness, falsity, futility; it is a sore affliction! [Luke 12:20.]

3 If a man begets a hundred children, and lives many years so that the days of his years are many, but his life is not filled with good, and also he be given no burial [honors nor be laid to rest in the sepulcher of his fathers], I say that [he who had] an untimely birth [causing death] is better off than he,

4 For *the untimely one* comes in futility and goes into darkness, and in darkness his name is covered;

5 Moreover he has not seen the sun nor had any knowledge, yet he [the stillborn child] has rest rather than he [who is aware of all that he has missed and not had to suffer].

6 Even though he lives a thousand years twice over, yet has seen no good *and* experienced no enjoyment, do not all go to one place [the place of the dead]?

7 All the labor of man is for his mouth [for self-preservation and enjoyment], and yet *his* desire is not satisfied. [Prov. 16:26.]

8 For what advantage has the wise man over the fool, [Being worldly-wise is no secret of happiness.] What advantage has the poor man who has learned how to walk before the living—publicly, with men's eyes upon him? [Being poor is not the secret of happiness, either.]

9 Better is the sight of the eyes [the enjoyment of what is available to one] than the cravings of wandering desire. This is also vanity—emptiness, falsity and futility; a striving for the wind [and feeding on it!].

10 Whatever *man* is, he has been named that long ago, and it is known that it is Adam [Adam means man, of the ground; the very name witnesses to his frailty]; nor can he contend with him who is mightier than he [whether God or death].

11 Seeing that there are *all these and* many other things *and* words that increase the emptiness, falsity, vainglory *and* futility [of living], what profit *and* what outcome is there for man?

12 For who [ [a]limited to human wisdom] knows what is good for man in his life, all the days of his vain life which he spends as a shadow [going through motions, but accomplishing nothing]? For who can tell a man what will happen [to his work, his treasure, his plans] under the sun after he is gone?

**7** A GOOD name is better than precious perfume; and the day of death than the day of one's birth.

2 It is better to go to the house of mourning than to go to the house of feasting; for that is the end of all men, and the living will lay it to heart.

**AMP** [a] How impressive throughout Ecclesiastes is the evidence that, while Solomon is doing his utmost to prove that life is futile and not worth living, the Holy Spirit is using him to show that these conclusions are the tragic effect of living "under the sun"—ignoring the Lord, away from God the Father, oblivious of the Holy Spirit—and yet face to face with the mysteries of life and nature!

## New American Standard

19Furthermore, as for every man to whom God has given riches
and wealth, He has also empowered him to eat from them and to
receive his reward and rejoice in his labor; this is the gift of God.
20For he will not often consider the years of his life, because God
keeps him occupied with the gladness of his heart.

*The Futility of Life*

**6** THERE IS an evil which I have seen under the sun and it is
prevalent among men—
2a man to whom God has given riches and wealth and honor
so that his soul lacks nothing of all that he desires, but God has
not empowered him to eat from them, for a foreigner enjoys them.
This is vanity and a severe affliction.
3If a man fathers a hundred *children* and lives many years,
however many they be, but his soul is not satisfied with good
things, and he does not even have a *proper* burial, *then* I say,
"Better the miscarriage than he,
4for it comes in futility and goes into obscurity; and its name
is covered in obscurity.
5"It never sees the sun and it never knows *anything;* it is better
off than he.
6"Even if the *other* man lives a thousand years twice and does
not enjoy good things—do not all go to one place?"
7¶ All a man's labor is for his mouth and yet the appetite is not
satisfied.
8For what advantage does the wise man have over the fool?
What *advantage* does the poor man have, knowing *how* to walk
before the living?
9What the eyes see is better than what the soul desires. This
too is futility and a striving after wind.
10¶ Whatever exists has already been named, and it is known
what man is; for he cannot dispute with him who is stronger than
he is.
11For there are many words which increase futility. What *then*
is the advantage to a man?
12For who knows what is good for a man during *his* lifetime,
*during* the few years of his futile life? He will spend them like a
shadow. For who can tell a man what will be after him under the
sun?

*Wisdom and Folly Contrasted*

**7** A GOOD name is better than a good ointment,
And the day of *one's* death is better than the day of one's
birth.
2 It is better to go to a house of mourning
Than to go to a house of feasting,
Because that is the end of every man,
And the living takes *it* to heart.

## New International

19Moreover, when God gives any man wealth and possessions,
and enables him to enjoy them, to accept his lot and be happy in
his work—this is a gift of God. 20He seldom reflects on the days
of his life, because God keeps him occupied with gladness of heart.

**6** I HAVE seen another evil under the sun, and it weighs heavily on men: 2God gives a man wealth, possessions and honor,
so that he lacks nothing his heart desires, but God does not enable
him to enjoy them, and a stranger enjoys them instead. This is
meaningless, a grievous evil.
3A man may have a hundred children and live many years; yet
no matter how long he lives, if he cannot enjoy his prosperity and
does not receive proper burial, I say that a stillborn child is better
off than he. 4It comes without meaning, it departs in darkness, and
in darkness its name is shrouded. 5Though it never saw the sun
or knew anything, it has more rest than does that man— 6even if
he lives a thousand years twice over but fails to enjoy his prosperity. Do not all go to the same place?

7All man's efforts are for his mouth,
yet his appetite is never satisfied.
8What advantage has a wise man
over a fool?
What does a poor man gain
by knowing how to conduct himself before others?
9Better what the eye sees
than the roving of the appetite.
This too is meaningless,
a chasing after the wind.

10Whatever exists has already been named,
and what man is has been known;
no man can contend
with one who is stronger than he.
11The more the words,
the less the meaning,
and how does that profit anyone?

12For who knows what is good for a man in life, during the few
and meaningless days he passes through like a shadow? Who can
tell him what will happen under the sun after he is gone?

*Wisdom*

**7** A GOOD name is better than fine perfume,
and the day of death better than the day of birth.
2It is better to go to a house of mourning
than to go to a house of feasting,
for death is the destiny of every man;
the living should take this to heart.

# King James

3 Sorrow *is* better than laughter: for by the sadness of the countenance the heart is made better.

4 The heart of the wise *is* in the house of mourning; but the heart of fools *is* in the house of mirth.

5 *It is* better to hear the rebuke of the wise, than for a man to hear the song of fools.

6 For as the crackling of thorns under a pot, so *is* the laughter of the fool: this also *is* vanity.

7 ¶ Surely oppression maketh a wise man mad; and a gift destroyeth the heart.

8 Better *is* the end of a thing than the beginning thereof: *and* the patient in spirit *is* better than the proud in spirit.

9 Be not hasty in thy spirit to be angry: for anger resteth in the bosom of fools.

10 Say not thou, What is *the cause* that the former days were better than these? for thou dost not inquire wisely concerning this.

11 ¶ Wisdom *is* good with an inheritance: and *by it there is* profit to them that see the sun.

12 For wisdom *is* a defence, *and* money *is* a defence: but the excellency of knowledge *is, that* wisdom giveth life to them that have it.

13 Consider the work of God: for who can make *that* straight, which he hath made crooked?

14 In the day of prosperity be joyful, but in the day of adversity consider: God also hath set the one over against the other, to the end that man should find nothing after him.

15 All *things* have I seen in the days of my vanity: there is a just *man* that perisheth in his righteousness, and there is a wicked *man* that prolongeth *his life* in his wickedness.

16 Be not righteous over much; neither make thyself over wise: why shouldest thou destroy thyself?

17 Be not over much wicked, neither be thou foolish: why shouldest thou die before thy time?

18 *It is* good that thou shouldest take hold of this; yea, also from this withdraw not thine hand: for he that feareth God shall come forth of them all.

19 Wisdom strengtheneth the wise more than ten mighty *men* which are in the city.

20 For *there is* not a just man upon earth, that doeth good, and sinneth not.

21 Also take no heed unto all words that are spoken; lest thou hear thy servant curse thee:

22 For oftentimes also thine own heart knoweth that thou thyself likewise hast cursed others.

23 ¶ All this have I proved by wisdom: I said, I will be wise; but it *was* far from me.

24 That which is far off, and exceeding deep, who can find it out?

# Amplified

3 Sorrow is better than laughter, for by the sadness of the countenance the heart is made better *and* gains gladness. [II Cor. 7:10.]

4 The heart of the wise is in the house of mourning, but the heart of fools is in the house of mirth *and* sensual joy.

5 It is better for a man to hear the rebuke of the wise than to hear the song of fools.

6 For as the crackling of thorns under a pot, so is the laughter of the fool. This also is vanity—emptiness, falsity, futility!

7 Surely oppression *and* extortion make a wise man foolish, and a bribe destroys the understanding *and* judgment.

8 Better is the end of a thing than the beginning of it, and the patient in spirit is better than the proud in spirit.

9 Do not be quick in spirit to be angry *or* vexed, for anger *and* vexation lodge in the bosom of fools. [James 1:19, 20.]

10 Do not say, Why were the old days better than these? For it is not wise *or* because of wisdom that you ask this.

11 Wisdom is as good as an inheritance, yes, more excellent it is for those [the living] who see the sun.

12 For wisdom is a defense even as money is a defense; but the excellency of knowledge is that wisdom shields *and* preserves the life of him who has it.

13 Consider the work of God; who can make straight what He has made crooked?

14 In the day of prosperity be joyful, but in the day of adversity consider that God has made the one side by side with the other, so that man may not find out anything that shall be after him.

15 I have seen everything in the days of my vanity—my emptiness, falsity, vainglory and futility; there is a righteous man who perishes in his righteousness, and there is a wicked man who prolongs his life in [spite of] his evil-doing.

16 Be not [morbidly exacting and externally] righteous overmuch, neither strive to make yourself [pretentiously appear] overwise; why should you [get puffed up and] destroy yourself [with presumptuous self-sufficiency]?

17 [Although all have sinned] be not wicked overmuch *or* willfully, neither be foolish; why should you die before your time?

18 It is good that you should take hold of this, and from that withdraw not your hand; for he who reverently fears *and* worships God will come forth from them all.

19 *True* wisdom is a strength to the wise man more than ten rulers *or* valiant generals who are in the city. [II Tim. 3:15; Ps. 127:1.]

20 Surely there is not a righteous man upon earth who does good and never sins. [Isa. 53:6; Rom. 3:23.]

21 Do not give heed to everything that is said, lest you hear your servant cursing you;

22 For often your own heart knows that you also have likewise cursed others.

23 All this have I tried *and* proved by wisdom; I said, I will be wise [independently of God], but it was far from me.

24 That which is, is far off, and deep, very deep; who can find it out [true wisdom independent of the fear of God]? [I Tim. 6:16.]

## New American Standard

3 Sorrow is better than laughter,
For when a face is sad a heart may be happy.
4 The mind of the wise is in the house of mourning,
While the mind of fools is in the house of pleasure.
5 It is better to listen to the rebuke of a wise man
Than for one to listen to the song of fools.
6 For as the crackling of thorn bushes under a pot,
So is the laughter of the fool,
And this too is futility.
7 For oppression makes a wise man mad,
And a bribe corrupts the heart.
8 The end of a matter is better than its beginning;
Patience of spirit is better than haughtiness of spirit.
9 Do not be eager in your heart to be angry,
For anger resides in the bosom of fools.
10 Do not say, "Why is it that the former days were better than these?"
For it is not from wisdom that you ask about this.
11 Wisdom along with an inheritance is good
And an advantage to those who see the sun.
12 For wisdom is protection *just as* money is protection.
But the advantage of knowledge is that wisdom preserves the lives of its possessors.
13 Consider the work of God,
For who is able to straighten what He has bent?
14 In the day of prosperity be happy,
But in the day of adversity consider—
God has made the one as well as the other
So that man may not discover anything *that will be* after him.

15¶ I have seen everything during my lifetime of futility; there is a righteous man who perishes in his righteousness, and there is a wicked man who prolongs *his life* in his wickedness.

16Do not be excessively righteous, and do not be overly wise. Why should you ruin yourself?

17Do not be excessively wicked, and do not be a fool. Why should you die before your time?

18It is good that you grasp one thing, and also not let go of the other; for the one who fears God comes forth with both of them.

19¶ Wisdom strengthens a wise man more than ten rulers who are in a city.

20Indeed, there is not a righteous man on earth who *continually* does good and who never sins.

21Also, do not take seriously all words which are spoken, lest you hear your servant cursing you.

22For you also have realized that you likewise have many times cursed others.

23¶ I tested all this with wisdom, *and* I said, "I will be wise," but it was far from me.

24What has been is remote and exceedingly mysterious. Who can discover it?

## New International

3Sorrow is better than laughter,
because a sad face is good for the heart.
4The heart of the wise is in the house of mourning,
but the heart of fools is in the house of pleasure.
5It is better to heed a wise man's rebuke
than to listen to the song of fools.
6Like the crackling of thorns under the pot,
so is the laughter of fools.
This too is meaningless.

7Extortion turns a wise man into a fool,
and a bribe corrupts the heart.
8The end of a matter is better than its beginning,
and patience is better than pride.
9Do not be quickly provoked in your spirit,
for anger resides in the lap of fools.

10Do not say, "Why were the old days better than these?"
For it is not wise to ask such questions.

11Wisdom, like an inheritance, is a good thing
and benefits those who see the sun.
12Wisdom is a shelter
as money is a shelter,
but the advantage of knowledge is this:
that wisdom preserves the life of its possessor.

13Consider what God has done:
Who can straighten
what he has made crooked?
14When times are good, be happy;
but when times are bad, consider:
God has made the one
as well as the other.
Therefore, a man cannot discover
anything about his future.

15In this meaningless life of mine I have seen both of these:
a righteous man perishing in his righteousness,
and a wicked man living long in his wickedness.
16Do not be overrighteous,
neither be overwise—
why destroy yourself?
17Do not be overwicked,
and do not be a fool—
why die before your time?
18It is good to grasp the one
and not let go of the other.
The man who fears God will avoid all ⌊extremes.⌋[a]

19Wisdom makes one wise man more powerful
than ten rulers in a city.

20There is not a righteous man on earth
who does what is right and never sins.
21Do not pay attention to every word people say,
or you may hear your servant cursing you—
22for you know in your heart
that many times you yourself have cursed others.

23All this I tested by wisdom and I said,
"I am determined to be wise"—
but this was beyond me.
24Whatever wisdom may be,
it is far off and most profound—
who can discover it?

NIV [a] *18* Or *will follow them both*

## King James

25I applied mine heart to know, and to search, and to seek out wisdom, and the reason *of things,* and to know the wickedness of folly, even of foolishness *and* madness:

26And I find more bitter than death the woman, whose heart *is* snares and nets, *and* her hands *as* bands: whoso pleaseth God shall escape from her; but the sinner shall be taken by her.

27Behold, this have I found, saith the preacher, *counting* one by one, to find out the account:

28Which yet my soul seeketh, but I find not: one man among a thousand have I found; but a woman among all those have I not found.

29Lo, this only have I found, that God hath made man upright; but they have sought out many inventions.

**8** WHO *IS* as the wise *man?* and who knoweth the interpretation of a thing? a man's wisdom maketh his face to shine, and the boldness of his face shall be changed.

2I *counsel thee* to keep the king's commandment, and *that* in regard of the oath of God.

3Be not hasty to go out of his sight: stand not in an evil thing; for he doeth whatsoever pleaseth him.

4Where the word of a king *is, there is* power: and who may say unto him, What doest thou?

5Whoso keepeth the commandment shall feel no evil thing: and a wise man's heart discerneth both time and judgment.

6¶ Because to every purpose there is time and judgment, therefore the misery of man *is* great upon him.

7For he knoweth not that which shall be: for who can tell him when it shall be?

8 *There is* no man that hath power over the spirit to retain the spirit; neither *hath he* power in the day of death: and *there is* no discharge in *that* war; neither shall wickedness deliver those that are given to it.

9All this have I seen, and applied my heart unto every work that is done under the sun: *there is* a time wherein one man ruleth over another to his own hurt.

10And so I saw the wicked buried, who had come and gone from the place of the holy, and they were forgotten in the city where they had so done: this *is* also vanity.

11Because sentence against an evil work is not executed speedily, therefore the heart of the sons of men is fully set in them to do evil.

12¶ Though a sinner do evil an hundred times, and his *days* be prolonged, yet surely I know that it shall be well with them that fear God, which fear before him:

13But it shall not be well with the wicked, neither shall he prolong *his* days, *which are* as a shadow; because he feareth not before God.

14There is a vanity which is done upon the earth; that there be just *men,* unto whom it happeneth according to the work of the wicked; again, there be wicked *men,* to whom it happeneth according to the work of the righteous: I said that this also *is* vanity.

## Amplified

25I turned about [penitent], and my heart was set to know and to search out and to seek [true] wisdom and the reason of things, and to know that wickedness is folly, and that foolishness is madness [and what had led me into such wickedness and madness].

26And I found that [of all sinful follies none has been so ruinous in seducing one from God as idolatrous women] more bitter than death is the woman whose heart is snares and nets and whose hands are bands. Whoever pleases God shall escape from her, but the sinner shall be taken by her.

27Behold, this I have found, says the Preacher, weighing one thing after another to find out the right estimate [and the reason],

28Which I am still seeking, but I have not found: one upright man among a thousand have I found, but an upright woman among all those [one thousand in my harem] have I not found. [I Kings 11:3.]

29Lo, this is the only *reason for it that* I have found: God made man upright, but they [men and women] have sought out many devices *for evil.*

**8** WHO IS like the wise man? And who knows the interpretation of a thing? A man's wisdom makes his face shine, and the hardness of his countenance is changed.

2I counsel you to keep the king's command, and that in regard to the oath of God [by which you swore him loyalty]. [II Sam. 21:7.]

3Be not terror-stricken *and* hasty to get out of his presence; persist not in an evil thing, for he does whatever he pleases;

4For the word of a king is authority *and* power, and who can say to him, What are you doing?

5Whoever observes the [king's] command will experience no harm, and a wise man's mind will know both when and what to do.

6For every purpose *and* matter has its *right* time and judgment, although the misery *and* wickedness of man lies heavily upon him [who rebels against the king];

7For he does not know what is to be, for who can tell him how *and* when it will be?

8There is no man who has power over the spirit to retain the breath of life, neither has he power over the day of death; and there is no discharge in battle [against death], neither will wickedness deliver those who are its possessors *and* given to it.

9All this have I seen while applying my mind to every work that is done under the sun; there is a time in which one man has power over another to his own hurt *or* to the other man's.

10And so I saw the wicked buried, who had come and gone out of the holy place [but did not thereby escape their doom], and they were [praised and] forgotten in the city where they had done such things. This also is vanity—emptiness, falsity, vainglory and futility!

11Because sentence against an evil work is not executed speedily, the heart of the sons of men is fully set to do evil.

12Though a sinner do evil a hundred times, and his days [seemingly] be prolonged [in his wickedness], yet surely I know that it will be well with those who (reverently) fear God, who revere *and* worship Him, realizing His continual presence. [Ps. 37:11, 18, 19; Isa. 3:10, 11; Matt. 25:34.]

13But it will not be well with the wicked, neither will he prolong his days like a shadow, because he does not reverently fear *and* worship God. [Matt. 25:41.]

14Here also is a futility that goes on upon the earth: there are righteous men who fare as though they were wicked, *and* wicked men who fare as though they were righteous. I said that this also is vanity—emptiness, falsity and futility!

## New American Standard

25 I directed my mind to know, to investigate, and to seek wisdom and an explanation, and to know the evil of folly and the foolishness of madness.

26 And I discovered more bitter than death the woman whose heart is snares and nets, whose hands are chains. One who is pleasing to God will escape from her, but the sinner will be captured by her.

27 ¶ "Behold, I have discovered this," says the Preacher, "*adding* one thing to another to find an explanation,

28 which I am still seeking but have not found. I have found one man among a thousand, but I have not found a woman among all these.

29 "Behold, I have found only this, that God made men upright, but they have sought out many devices."

*Obey Rulers*

**8** WHO IS like the wise man and who knows the interpretation of a matter? A man's wisdom illumines him and causes his stern face to beam.

2 ¶ I say, "Keep the command of the king because of the oath before God.

3 "Do not be in a hurry to leave him. Do not join in an evil matter, for he will do whatever he pleases."

4 Since the word of the king is authoritative, who will say to him, "What are you doing?"

5 ¶ He who keeps a *royal* command experiences no trouble, for a wise heart knows the proper time and procedure.

6 For there is a proper time and procedure for every delight, when a man's trouble is heavy upon him.

7 If no one knows what will happen, who can tell him when it will happen?

8 No man has authority to restrain the wind with the wind, or authority over the day of death; and there is no discharge in the time of war, and evil will not deliver those who practice it.

9 All this I have seen and applied my mind to every deed that has been done under the sun wherein a man has exercised authority over *another* man to his hurt.

10 ¶ So then, I have seen the wicked buried, those who used to go in and out from the holy place, and they are *soon* forgotten in the city where they did thus. This too is futility.

11 Because the sentence against an evil deed is not executed quickly, therefore the hearts of the sons of men among them are given fully to do evil.

12 Although a sinner does evil a hundred *times* and may lengthen his *life*, still I know that it will be well for those who fear God, who fear Him openly.

13 But it will not be well for the evil man and he will not lengthen his days like a shadow, because he does not fear God.

14 There is futility which is done on the earth, that is, there are righteous men to whom it happens according to the deeds of the wicked. On the other hand, there are evil men to whom it happens according to the deeds of the righteous. I say that this too is futility.

## New International

25 So I turned my mind to understand,
to investigate and to search out wisdom and the scheme of things
and to understand the stupidity of wickedness
and the madness of folly.

26 I find more bitter than death
the woman who is a snare,
whose heart is a trap
and whose hands are chains.
The man who pleases God will escape her,
but the sinner she will ensnare.

27 "Look," says the Teacher,[a] "this is what I have discovered:

"Adding one thing to another to discover the scheme of things—
28 while I was still searching
but not finding—
I found one ⌞upright⌟ man among a thousand,
but not one ⌞upright⌟ woman among them all.
29 This only have I found:
God made mankind upright,
but men have gone in search of many schemes."

**8** WHO IS like the wise man?
Who knows the explanation of things?
Wisdom brightens a man's face
and changes its hard appearance.

*Obey the King*

2 Obey the king's command, I say, because you took an oath
before God. 3 Do not be in a hurry to leave the king's presence. Do
not stand up for a bad cause, for he will do whatever he pleases.
4 Since a king's word is supreme, who can say to him, "What are
you doing?"

5 Whoever obeys his command will come to no harm,
and the wise heart will know the proper time and procedure.
6 For there is a proper time and procedure for every matter,
though a man's misery weighs heavily upon him.
7 Since no man knows the future,
who can tell him what is to come?
8 No man has power over the wind to contain it[b];
so no one has power over the day of his death.
As no one is discharged in time of war,
so wickedness will not release those who practice it.

9 All this I saw, as I applied my mind to everything done under
the sun. There is a time when a man lords it over others to his
own[c] hurt. 10 Then too, I saw the wicked buried—those who used
to come and go from the holy place and receive praise[d] in the city
where they did this. This too is meaningless.

11 When the sentence for a crime is not quickly carried out, the
hearts of the people are filled with schemes to do wrong. 12 Although a wicked man commits a hundred crimes and still lives a
long time, I know that it will go better with God-fearing men, who
are reverent before God. 13 Yet because the wicked do not fear God,
it will not go well with them, and their days will not lengthen like
a shadow.

14 There is something else meaningless that occurs on earth:
righteous men who get what the wicked deserve, and wicked men
who get what the righteous deserve. This too, I say, is meaningless. 15 So I commend the enjoyment of life, because nothing is

**NIV** [a] 27 Or *leader of the assembly* [b] 8 Or *over his spirit to retain it* [c] 9 Or *to their* [d] 10 Some Hebrew manuscripts and Septuagint (Aquila); most Hebrew manuscripts *and are forgotten*

## King James

15Then I commended mirth, because a man hath no better thing under the sun, than to eat, and to drink, and to be merry: for that shall abide with him of his labour the days of his life, which God giveth him under the sun.

16¶ When I applied mine heart to know wisdom, and to see the business that is done upon the earth: (for also *there is that* neither day nor night seeth sleep with his eyes:)

17Then I beheld all the work of God, that a man cannot find out the work that is done under the sun: because though a man labour to seek *it* out, yet he shall not find *it*; yea further; though a wise *man* think to know *it*, yet shall he not be able to find *it*.

9 FOR ALL this I considered in my heart even to declare all this, that the righteous, and the wise, and their works, *are* in the hand of God: no man knoweth either love or hatred *by* all *that is* before them.

2All *things come* alike to all: *there is* one event to the righteous, and to the wicked; to the good and to the clean, and to the unclean; to him that sacrificeth, and to him that sacrificeth not: as *is* the good, so *is* the sinner; *and* he that sweareth, as *he* that feareth an oath.

3This *is* an evil among all *things* that are done under the sun, that *there is* one event unto all: yea, also the heart of the sons of men is full of evil, and madness *is* in their heart while they live, and after that *they go* to the dead.

4¶ For to him that is joined to all the living there is hope: for a living dog is better than a dead lion.

5For the living know that they shall die: but the dead know not any thing, neither have they any more a reward; for the memory of them is forgotten.

6Also their love, and their hatred, and their envy, is now perished; neither have they any more a portion for ever in any *thing* that is done under the sun.

7¶ Go thy way, eat thy bread with joy, and drink thy wine with a merry heart; for God now accepteth thy works.

8Let thy garments be always white; and let thy head lack no ointment.

9Live joyfully with the wife whom thou lovest all the days of the life of thy vanity, which he hath given thee under the sun, all the days of thy vanity: for that *is* thy portion in *this* life, and in thy labour which thou takest under the sun.

10Whatsoever thy hand findeth to do, do *it* with thy might; for *there is* no work, nor device, nor knowledge, nor wisdom, in the grave, whither thou goest.

11¶ I returned, and saw under the sun, that the race *is* not to the swift, nor the battle to the strong, neither yet bread to the wise, nor yet riches to men of understanding, nor yet favour to men of skill; but time and chance happeneth to them all.

12For man also knoweth not his time: as the fishes that are taken in an evil net, and as the birds that are caught in the snare; so *are* the sons of men snared in an evil time, when it falleth suddenly upon them.

## Amplified

15Then I commended enjoyment, because a man has no better thing under the sun [without God] than to eat, and to drink, and to be joyful, for that will remain with him in his toil through the days of his life which God gives him under the sun.

16When I applied my mind to know wisdom, and to see the business activity [and the painful effort] that take place upon the earth, how neither day nor night some men's eyes sleep,

17Then I saw of all the work of God, that man cannot find out the work that is done under the sun; because however much a man may toil in seeking, yet he will not find it out; yes, more than that, though a wise man thinks *and* claims he knows, yet will he not be able to find it out. [Cf. Deut. 29:29; Rom. 11:33.]

9 FOR ALL this I took to heart, exploring *and* examining it all, how the righteous—the upright, in right standing with God—and the wise and their works are in the hand of God; whether it is to be love or hatred no man knows; all that is before them.

2All things come alike to all; there is one event to the righteous and to the wicked, to the good and clean and to the unclean; to him who sacrifices and to him who does not sacrifice. As is the good man, so is the sinner, *and* he who swears is as he who fears *and* shuns an oath.

3This evil is in all that is done under the sun: that one fate comes to all; also the hearts of men are full of evil, and madness is in their hearts while they live, and after that they go to the dead.

4[There is no exemption,] but he who is joined to all the living has hope, for a living dog is better than a dead lion.

5For the living know that they will die, but the dead know nothing, and they have no more reward *here,* for the memory of them is forgotten.

6Their love and their hatred and their envy have already perished; neither have they any more a share for ever in anything that is done under the sun.

7Go your way, eat your bread with joy, and drink your wine with a cheerful heart [if you are righteous, wise, and in the hand of God], for God has already accepted your works.

8Let your garments be always white [with purity], and let your head not lack *the* oil [of gladness].

9Live joyfully with the wife whom you love all the days of your vain life which He has given you under the sun—all the days of futility; for that is your portion in this life and in your work at which you toil under the sun.

10Whatever your hand finds to do, do it with your might; for there is no work or device or knowledge or wisdom in Sheol [the place of the dead], where you are going.

11I returned and saw under the sun, that the race is not to the swift, nor the battle to the strong, neither bread to the wise, nor riches to men of intelligence *and* understanding, nor favor to men of skill; but time and chance happen to them all. [Rom. 9:16; Ps. 33:16-19.]

12For man also knows not his time [of death]; as the fishes that are taken in an evil net, and as the birds that are caught in the snare, so are the sons of men snared in an evil time, when *calamity* falls suddenly upon them.

## New American Standard

15So I commended pleasure, for there is nothing good for a man under the sun except to eat and to drink and to be merry, and this will stand by him in his toils *throughout* the days of his life which God has given him under the sun.

16¶ When I gave my heart to know wisdom and to see the task which has been done on the earth (even though one should never sleep day or night),

17and I saw every work of God, *I concluded* that man cannot discover the work which has been done under the sun. Even though man should seek laboriously, he will not discover; and though the wise man should say, "I know," he cannot discover.

*Men Are in the Hand of God*

9 FOR I have taken all this to my heart and explain it that righteous men, wise men, and their deeds are in the hand of God. Man does not know whether *it will be* love or hatred; anything awaits him.

2¶ It is the same for all. There is one fate for the righteous and for the wicked; for the good, for the clean, and for the unclean; for the man who offers a sacrifice and for the one who does not sacrifice. As the good man is, so is the sinner; as the swearer is, so is the one who is afraid to swear.

3This is an evil in all that is done under the sun, that there is one fate for all men. Furthermore, the hearts of the sons of men are full of evil, and insanity is in their hearts throughout their lives. Afterwards they *go* to the dead.

4For whoever is joined with all the living, there is hope; surely a live dog is better than a dead lion.

5For the living know they will die; but the dead do not know anything, nor have they any longer a reward, for their memory is forgotten.

6Indeed their love, their hate, and their zeal have already perished, and they will no longer have a share in all that is done under the sun.

7¶ Go *then,* eat your bread in happiness, and drink your wine with a cheerful heart; for God has already approved your works.

8Let your clothes be white all the time, and let not oil be lacking on your head.

9Enjoy life with the woman whom you love all the days of your fleeting life which He has given to you under the sun; for this is your reward in life, and in your toil in which you have labored under the sun.

*Whatever Your Hand Finds to Do*

10¶ Whatever your hand finds to do, verily, do *it* with all your might; for there is no activity or planning or wisdom in Sheol where you are going.

11I again saw under the sun that the race is not to the swift, and the battle is not to the warriors, and neither is bread to the wise, nor wealth to the discerning, nor favor to men of ability; for time and chance overtake them all.

12Moreover, man does not know his time: like fish caught in a treacherous net, and birds trapped in a snare, so the sons of men are ensnared at an evil time when it suddenly falls on them.

## New International

better for a man under the sun than to eat and drink and be glad. Then joy will accompany him in his work all the days of the life God has given him under the sun.

16When I applied my mind to know wisdom and to observe man's labor on earth—his eyes not seeing sleep day or night—
17then I saw all that God has done. No one can comprehend what goes on under the sun. Despite all his efforts to search it out, man cannot discover its meaning. Even if a wise man claims he knows, he cannot really comprehend it.

*A Common Destiny for All*

9 SO I reflected on all this and concluded that the righteous and the wise and what they do are in God's hands, but no man knows whether love or hate awaits him. 2All share a common destiny—the righteous and the wicked, the good and the bad,[a] the clean and the unclean, those who offer sacrifices and those who do not.

As it is with the good man,
so with the sinner;
as it is with those who take oaths,
so with those who are afraid to take them.

3This is the evil in everything that happens under the sun: The same destiny overtakes all. The hearts of men, moreover, are full of evil and there is madness in their hearts while they live, and afterward they join the dead. 4Anyone who is among the living has hope[b]—even a live dog is better off than a dead lion!

5For the living know that they will die,
but the dead know nothing;
they have no further reward,
and even the memory of them is forgotten.
6Their love, their hate
and their jealousy have long since vanished;
never again will they have a part
in anything that happens under the sun.

7Go, eat your food with gladness, and drink your wine with a joyful heart, for it is now that God favors what you do. 8Always be clothed in white, and always anoint your head with oil. 9Enjoy life with your wife, whom you love, all the days of this meaningless life that God has given you under the sun— all your meaningless days. For this is your lot in life and in your toilsome labor under the sun. 10Whatever your hand finds to do, do it with all your might, for in the grave,[c] where you are going, there is neither working nor planning nor knowledge nor wisdom.

11I have seen something else under the sun:

The race is not to the swift
or the battle to the strong,
nor does food come to the wise
or wealth to the brilliant
or favor to the learned;
but time and chance happen to them all.

12Moreover, no man knows when his hour will come:

As fish are caught in a cruel net,
or birds are taken in a snare,
so men are trapped by evil times
that fall unexpectedly upon them.

**NIV** [a] 2 Septuagint (Aquila), Vulgate and Syriac; Hebrew does not have *and the bad.* [b] 4 Or *What then is to be chosen? With all who live, there is hope* [c] 10 Hebrew *Sheol*

# King James

13¶ This wisdom have I seen also under the sun, and it *seemed* great unto me:

14 *There was* a little city, and few men within it; and there came a great king against it, and besieged it, and built great bulwarks against it:

15Now there was found in it a poor wise man, and he by his wisdom delivered the city; yet no man remembered that same poor man.

16Then said I, Wisdom *is* better than strength: nevertheless the poor man's wisdom *is* despised, and his words are not heard.

17The words of wise *men are* heard in quiet more than the cry of him that ruleth among fools.

18Wisdom *is* better than weapons of war: but one sinner destroyeth much good.

10 DEAD FLIES cause the ointment of the apothecary to send forth a stinking savour: *so doth* a little folly him that is in reputation for wisdom *and* honour.

2A wise man's heart *is* at his right hand; but a fool's heart at his left.

3Yea also, when he that is a fool walketh by the way, his wisdom faileth *him,* and he saith to every one *that* he *is* a fool.

4If the spirit of the ruler rise up against thee, leave not thy place; for yielding pacifieth great offences.

5There is an evil *which* I have seen under the sun, as an error *which* proceedeth from the ruler:

6Folly is set in great dignity, and the rich sit in low place.

7I have seen servants upon horses, and princes walking as servants upon the earth.

8He that diggeth a pit shall fall into it; and whoso breaketh an hedge, a serpent shall bite him.

9Whoso removeth stones shall be hurt therewith; *and* he that cleaveth wood shall be endangered thereby.

10If the iron be blunt, and he do not whet the edge, then must he put to more strength: but wisdom *is* profitable to direct.

11Surely the serpent will bite without enchantment; and a babbler is no better.

12The words of a wise man's mouth *are* gracious; but the lips of a fool will swallow up himself.

13The beginning of the words of his mouth *is* foolishness: and the end of his talk *is* mischievous madness.

14A fool also is full of words: a man cannot tell what shall be; and what shall be after him, who can tell him?

15The labour of the foolish wearieth every one of them, because he knoweth not how to go to the city.

16¶ Woe to thee, O land, when thy king *is* a child, and thy princes eat in the morning!

17Blessed *art* thou, O land, when thy king *is* the son of nobles, and thy princes eat in due season, for strength, and not for drunkenness!

18¶ By much slothfulness the building decayeth; and through idleness of the hands the house droppeth through.

# Amplified

13This [illustration of] wisdom have I seen also under the sun, and it seemed great to me:

14There was a little city with few men in it; and a great king came against it and besieged it, and built great bulwarks against it.

15But there was found in it a poor wise man, and he by his wisdom delivered the city. Yet no man [seriously] remembered that poor man.

16But I say that wisdom is better than might, though the poor man's wisdom is despised and his words are not heeded.

17The words of wise men heard in quiet are better than the shouts of him who rules among fools.

18Wisdom is better than weapons of war, but one sinner destroys much good.

10 DEAD FLIES cause the ointment of the perfumer to putrefy [and] send forth a vile odor; so does a little folly [in him who is valued for wisdom] outweigh wisdom and honor.

2A wise man's heart turns him toward his right hand, but a fool's heart toward his left. [Matt. 25:31-41.]

3Even when he who is a fool walks along the road, his heart *and* understanding fail him, and he says of everyone *and* to everyone that he is a fool.

4If the temper of the ruler rises up against you, do not leave your place [or show a resisting spirit]; for gentleness *and* calmness prevent *or* put a stop to great offenses.

5There is an evil which I have seen under the sun, as an error which proceeds from the ruler:

6Folly is set in great dignity *and* in high places, and the rich sit in a low place.

7I have seen slaves on horses, and princes walking like slaves on the earth.

8He who digs a pit [for others] will fall into it, and whoever breaks through a fence *or* a *stone* wall, a serpent will bite him.

9Whoever removes [landmark] stones *or* hews out [new ones with similar intent] will be hurt with them, *and* he who fells trees will be endangered by it.

10If the axe is dull, and the man does not whet the edge, he must put forth more strength; but wisdom helps him to succeed.

11If the serpent bites before it is charmed, then it is no use to call a charmer, [and the slanderer is no better than the uncharmed snake].

12The words of a wise man's mouth are gracious *and* win him favor, but the lips of a fool will consume him.

13The beginning of the words of his mouth is foolishness, and the end of his talk is wicked madness.

14A fool also multiplies words, though no man can tell what will be; and what will happen after he is gone, who can tell him?

15The labor of fools wearies every one of them, because [he is so ignorant of the ordinary matters that] he does not even know how to get to town.

16Woe to you, O land, when your king is a child *or* a servant, and your officials feast in the morning!

17Happy, fortunate [and to be envied] are you, O land, when your king is a free man *and* of noble birth *and* character, and your officials feast at the proper time, for strength, and not for drunkenness! [Isa. 32:8.]

18Through indolence the rafters [of state affairs] decay *and* the roof sinks in, and through idleness of the hands the house leaks.

## New American Standard

13¶ Also this I came to see as wisdom under the sun, and it
impressed me.
14There was a small city with few men in it and a great king
came to it, surrounded it, and constructed large siegeworks
against it.
15But there was found in it a poor wise man and he delivered
the city by his wisdom. Yet no one remembered that poor man.
16So I said, "Wisdom is better than strength." But the wisdom
of the poor man is despised and his words are not heeded.
17The words of the wise heard in quietness are *better* than the
shouting of a ruler among fools.
18Wisdom is better than weapons of war, but one sinner destroys much good.

*A Little Foolishness*

**10** DEAD FLIES make a perfumer's oil stink, so a little foolishness is weightier than wisdom *and* honor.
2A wise man's heart *directs him* toward the right, but the foolish
man's heart *directs him* toward the left.
3Even when the fool walks along the road his sense is lacking,
and he demonstrates to everyone *that* he is a fool.
4If the ruler's temper rises against you, do not abandon your
position, because composure allays great offenses.
5¶ There is an evil I have seen under the sun, like an error
which goes forth from the ruler—
6folly is set in many exalted places while rich men sit in humble
places.
7I have seen slaves *riding* on horses and princes walking like
slaves on the land.
8¶ He who digs a pit may fall into it, and a serpent may bite
him who breaks through a wall.
9He who quarries stones may be hurt by them, and he who
splits logs may be endangered by them.
10If the axe is dull and he does not sharpen *its* edge, then he
must exert more strength. Wisdom has the advantage of giving
success.
11If the serpent bites before being charmed, there is no profit for
the charmer.
12Words from the mouth of a wise man are gracious, while the
lips of a fool consume him;
13the beginning of his talking is folly, and the end of it is wicked
madness.
14Yet the fool multiplies words. No man knows what will happen, and who can tell him what will come after him?
15The toil of a fool *so* wearies him that he does not *even* know
how to go to a city.
16Woe to you, O land, whose king is a lad and whose princes
feast in the morning.
17Blessed are you, O land, whose king is of nobility and whose
princes eat at the appropriate time—for strength, and not for
drunkenness.
18Through indolence the rafters sag, and through slackness the
house leaks.

## New International

*Wisdom Better Than Folly*

13I also saw under the sun this example of wisdom that greatly
impressed me: 14There was once a small city with only a few
people in it. And a powerful king came against it, surrounded it
and built huge siegeworks against it. 15Now there lived in that city
a man poor but wise, and he saved the city by his wisdom. But
nobody remembered that poor man. 16So I said, "Wisdom is better
than strength." But the poor man's wisdom is despised, and his
words are no longer heeded.

17The quiet words of the wise are more to be heeded
than the shouts of a ruler of fools.
18Wisdom is better than weapons of war,
but one sinner destroys much good.

**10** AS DEAD flies give perfume a bad smell,
so a little folly outweighs wisdom and honor.
2The heart of the wise inclines to the right,
but the heart of the fool to the left.
3Even as he walks along the road,
the fool lacks sense
and shows everyone how stupid he is.
4If a ruler's anger rises against you,
do not leave your post;
calmness can lay great errors to rest.

5There is an evil I have seen under the sun,
the sort of error that arises from a ruler:
6Fools are put in many high positions,
while the rich occupy the low ones.
7I have seen slaves on horseback,
while princes go on foot like slaves.

8Whoever digs a pit may fall into it;
whoever breaks through a wall may be bitten by a snake.
9Whoever quarries stones may be injured by them;
whoever splits logs may be endangered by them.

10If the ax is dull
and its edge unsharpened,
more strength is needed
but skill will bring success.

11If a snake bites before it is charmed,
there is no profit for the charmer.

12Words from a wise man's mouth are gracious,
but a fool is consumed by his own lips.
13At the beginning his words are folly;
at the end they are wicked madness—
14 and the fool multiplies words.

No one knows what is coming—
who can tell him what will happen after him?

15A fool's work wearies him;
he does not know the way to town.
16Woe to you, O land whose king was a servant[a]
and whose princes feast in the morning.
17Blessed are you, O land whose king is of noble birth
and whose princes eat at a proper time—
for strength and not for drunkenness.

18If a man is lazy, the rafters sag;
if his hands are idle, the house leaks.

NIV [a] 16 Or *king is a child*

## King James

19¶ A feast is made for laughter, and wine maketh merry: but
money answereth all *things*.
20¶ Curse not the king, no not in thy thought; and curse not the
rich in thy bedchamber: for a bird of the air shall carry the voice,
and that which hath wings shall tell the matter.

**11** CAST THY bread upon the waters: for thou shalt find it
after many days.
2Give a portion to seven, and also to eight; for thou knowest not
what evil shall be upon the earth.
3If the clouds be full of rain, they empty *themselves* upon the
earth: and if the tree fall toward the south, or toward the north,
in the place where the tree falleth, there it shall be.
4He that observeth the wind shall not sow; and he that regardeth the clouds shall not reap.
5As thou knowest not what *is* the way of the spirit, *nor* how the
bones *do grow* in the womb of her that is with child: even so thou
knowest not the works of God who maketh all.
6In the morning sow thy seed, and in the evening withhold not
thine hand: for thou knowest not whether shall prosper, either this
or that, or whether they both *shall be* alike good.
7¶ Truly the light *is* sweet, and a pleasant *thing it is* for the eyes
to behold the sun:
8But if a man live many years, *and* rejoice in them all; yet let him
remember the days of darkness; for they shall be many. All that
cometh *is* vanity.
9¶ Rejoice, O young man, in thy youth; and let thy heart cheer
thee in the days of thy youth, and walk in the ways of thine heart,
and in the sight of thine eyes: but know thou, that for all these
*things* God will bring thee into judgment.
10Therefore remove sorrow from thy heart, and put away evil
from thy flesh: for childhood and youth *are* vanity.

**12** REMEMBER NOW thy Creator in the days of thy youth,
while the evil days come not, nor the years draw nigh,
when thou shalt say, I have no pleasure in them;
2While the sun, or the light, or the moon, or the stars, be not
darkened, nor the clouds return after the rain:

## Amplified

19[Instead of repairing the breaches, the officials] make a feast
for laughter, serve wine to cheer life, and *depend on* [tax] money to
answer for all of it.
20Curse not the king, no not in your thought, and curse not the
rich in your bedchamber; for a bird of the air will carry the voice,
and a winged creature will tell the matter. [Exod. 22:28.]

**11** CAST YOUR bread upon the waters, for you will find it
after many days.
2Give a portion to seven, yes, even *divide it* to eight; for you
know not what evil may come on the earth.
3If the clouds are full of rain, they empty themselves upon the
earth; and if a tree falls toward the south or toward the north, in
the place where the tree falls, there it will lie.
4He who observes the wind [and waits for all conditions to be
favorable] will not sow, and he who regards the clouds will not
reap.
5As you know not what is the way of the wind *or* how the spirit
comes to the bones in the womb of a pregnant woman, even so
you know not the work of God Who does all.
6In the morning sow your seed, and in the evening withhold
not your hand; for you know not which shall prosper, this or that,
or whether both alike will be good.
7Truly the light is sweet, and a pleasant thing it is for the eyes
to behold the sun.
8Yes, if a man live many years, let him rejoice in them all; yet
let him [seriously] remember the days of darkness, for they will be
many. All that comes is vanity—emptiness, falsity, vainglory and
futility!
9Rejoice, O young man, in your adolescence, and let your heart
cheer you in the days of your *full-grown* youth, and walk in the
ways of your heart, and in the sight of your eyes. But know that
for all these things God will bring you into judgment.
10Therefore remove [the lusts that end in] sorrow *and* vexation
from your heart *and* mind, and put away evil from your body, for
youth and the dawn of life are vanity—transitory, idle, empty and
devoid of truth. [II Cor. 7:1; II Tim. 2:22.]

**12** REMEMBER [EARNESTLY] also your Creator [that you
are not your own, but His property], *now* in the days of
your youth, before the evil days come or the years draw near when
you will say [of physical pleasures], I have no enjoyment in them;
[II Sam. 19:35.]
2Before *sight is impaired,* and the sun and the light and the moon
and the stars are darkened and the clouds [of depression] return
after the rain [of tears];

## New American Standard

19 *Men* prepare a meal for enjoyment, and wine makes life
merry, and money is the answer to everything.
20Furthermore, in your bedchamber do not curse a king, and in
your sleeping rooms do not curse a rich man, for a bird of the
heavens will carry the sound, and the winged creature will make
the matter known.

*Cast Your Bread on the Waters*

**11** CAST YOUR bread on the surface of the waters, for you
will find it after many days.
2Divide your portion to seven, or even to eight, for you do not
know what misfortune may occur on the earth.
3If the clouds are full, they pour out rain upon the earth; and
whether a tree falls toward the south or toward the north,
wherever the tree falls, there it lies.
4He who watches the wind will not sow and he who looks at
the clouds will not reap.
5Just as you do not know the path of the wind and how bones
*are formed* in the womb of the pregnant woman, so you do not
know the activity of God who makes all things.
6Sow your seed in the morning, and do not be idle in the
evening, for you do not know whether morning or evening sowing
will succeed, or whether both of them alike will be good.
7¶ The light is pleasant, and *it is* good for the eyes to see the
sun.
8Indeed, if a man should live many years, let him rejoice in
them all, and let him remember the days of darkness, for they shall
be many. Everything that is to come *will be* futility.
9Rejoice, young man, during your childhood, and let your
heart be pleasant during the days of young manhood. And follow
the impulses of your heart and the desires of your eyes. Yet know
that God will bring you to judgment for all these things.
10So, remove vexation from your heart and put away pain from
your body, because childhood and the prime of life are fleeting.

*Remember God in Your Youth*

**12** REMEMBER ALSO your Creator in the days of your
youth, before the evil days come and the years draw near
when you will say, "I have no delight in them";
2before the sun, the light, the moon, and the stars are darkened, and clouds return after the rain;

## New International

19A feast is made for laughter,
and wine makes life merry,
but money is the answer for everything.

20Do not revile the king even in your thoughts,
or curse the rich in your bedroom,
because a bird of the air may carry your words,
and a bird on the wing may report what you say.

*Bread Upon the Waters*

**11** CAST YOUR bread upon the waters,
for after many days you will find it again.
2Give portions to seven, yes to eight,
for you do not know what disaster may come upon the land.

3If clouds are full of water,
they pour rain upon the earth.
Whether a tree falls to the south or to the north,
in the place where it falls, there will it lie.
4Whoever watches the wind will not plant;
whoever looks at the clouds will not reap.

5As you do not know the path of the wind,
or how the body is formed[a] in a mother's womb,
so you cannot understand the work of God,
the Maker of all things.

6Sow your seed in the morning,
and at evening let not your hands be idle,
for you do not know which will succeed,
whether this or that,
or whether both will do equally well.

*Remember Your Creator While Young*

7Light is sweet,
and it pleases the eyes to see the sun.
8However many years a man may live,
let him enjoy them all.
But let him remember the days of darkness,
for they will be many.
Everything to come is meaningless.

9Be happy, young man, while you are young,
and let your heart give you joy in the days of your youth.
Follow the ways of your heart
and whatever your eyes see,
but know that for all these things
God will bring you to judgment.
10So then, banish anxiety from your heart
and cast off the troubles of your body,
for youth and vigor are meaningless.

**12** REMEMBER YOUR Creator
in the days of your youth,
before the days of trouble come
and the years approach when you will say,
"I find no pleasure in them"—
2before the sun and the light
and the moon and the stars grow dark,
and the clouds return after the rain;

NIV [a] 5 Or *know how life* (or *the spirit*) / *enters the body being formed*

## King James

3In the day when the keepers of the house shall tremble, and the strong men shall bow themselves, and the grinders cease because they are few, and those that look out of the windows be darkened,

4And the doors shall be shut in the streets, when the sound of the grinding is low, and he shall rise up at the voice of the bird, and all the daughters of music shall be brought low;

5Also *when* they shall be afraid of *that which is* high, and fears *shall be* in the way, and the almond tree shall flourish, and the grasshopper shall be a burden, and desire shall fail: because man goeth to his long home, and the mourners go about the streets:

6Or ever the silver cord be loosed, or the golden bowl be broken, or the pitcher be broken at the fountain, or the wheel broken at the cistern.

7Then shall the dust return to the earth as it was: and the spirit shall return unto God who gave it.

8¶ Vanity of vanities, saith the preacher; all *is* vanity.

9And moreover, because the preacher was wise, he still taught the people knowledge; yea, he gave good heed, and sought out, *and* set in order many proverbs.

10The preacher sought to find out acceptable words: and *that which was* written *was* upright, *even* words of truth.

11The words of the wise *are* as goads, and as nails fastened *by* the masters of assemblies, *which* are given from one shepherd.

12And further, by these, my son, be admonished: of making many books *there is* no end; and much study *is* a weariness of the flesh.

13¶ Let us hear the conclusion of the whole matter: Fear God, and keep his commandments: for this *is* the whole *duty* of man.

14For God shall bring every work into judgment, with every secret thing, whether *it be* good, or whether *it be* evil.

## Amplified

3In the day when the keepers of the house [the hands and the arms] tremble, and the strong men [the feet and knees] bow themselves, and the grinders [the molar teeth] cease because they are few, and those that look out of the windows [the eyes] be darkened.

4And the doors [the lips] are shut in the streets; when the sound of the grinding *of the teeth* is low, and one rises up at the voice of a bird *and* the crowing of a cock, and all the daughters of music [the voice and ear] shall be brought low;

5Also when *the old* are afraid of danger from that which is high, and fears are in the way, and the almond tree [white hair] blooms, and the grasshopper [a little thing] is a burden, and desire *and* appetite fail, because man goes to his everlasting home, and the mourners go about the streets *or* market places. [Job 17:13.]

6 *Remember your Creator earnestly now,* before the silver cord *of life* is snapped apart, or the golden bowl is broken, or the pitcher is broken at the fountain, or the wheel broken at the cistern [and the whole circulatory system of the blood ceases to function],

7Then shall the dust [of which God made man's body] return to the earth as it was, and the spirit shall return to God Who gave it.

8Futility of futilities, says the Preacher; all is futility—emptiness, falsity, vainglory *and* transitoriness!

9And further, because the Preacher was wise, he [Solomon] still taught the people knowledge; and he pondered and sought out *and* set in order many proverbs.

10The Preacher sought out acceptable words, and to write down rightly words of truth *or* correct sentiment.

11The words of the wise are as prodding goads, and firmly fixed [in the mind] like nails are the collected sayings which are given [as proceeding] from one shepherd. [Ezek. 37:24.]

12But about going further [than words given by one shepherd], my son, be warned. Of making many books there is no end [so do not believe everything you read], and much study is a weariness of the flesh.

13All has been heard. The end of the matter is, Fear God—know that He is, revere and worship Him—and keep His commandments; for this is the whole of man [the full original purpose of his creation, the object of God's providence, the root of character, the foundation of all happiness, the adjustment to all inharmonious circumstances and conditions under the sun], *and* the whole *duty* for every man.

14For God shall bring every work into judgment, with every secret thing, whether it is good or evil. [Matt. 12:36; Acts 17:30, 31; Rom. 2:16; I Cor. 4:5.]

## New American Standard

3in the day that the watchmen of the house tremble, and
mighty men stoop, the grinding ones stand idle because they are
few, and those who look through windows grow dim;
4and the doors on the street are shut as the sound of the
grinding mill is low, and one will arise at the sound of the bird,
and all the daughters of song will sing softly.
5Furthermore, men are afraid of a high place and of terrors on
the road; the almond tree blossoms, the grasshopper drags himself
along, and the caperberry is ineffective. For man goes to his eternal
home while mourners go about in the street.
6 *Remember Him* before the silver cord is broken and the golden
bowl is crushed, the pitcher by the well is shattered and the wheel
at the cistern is crushed;
7then the dust will return to the earth as it was, and the spirit
will return to God who gave it.
8"Vanity of vanities," says the Preacher, "all is vanity!"

*Purpose of the Preacher*

9¶ In addition to being a wise man, the Preacher also taught
the people knowledge; and he pondered, searched out and arranged many proverbs.
10The Preacher sought to find delightful words and to write
words of truth correctly.
11¶ The words of wise men are like goads, and masters of *these*
collections are like well-driven nails; they are given by one Shepherd.
12But beyond this, my son, be warned: the writing of many
books is endless, and excessive devotion *to books* is wearying to the
body.
13¶ The conclusion, when all has been heard, *is:* fear God and
keep His commandments, because this *applies to* every person.
14For God will bring every act to judgment, everything which
is hidden, whether it is good or evil.

## New International

3when the keepers of the house tremble,
and the strong men stoop,
when the grinders cease because they are few,
and those looking through the windows grow dim;
4when the doors to the street are closed
and the sound of grinding fades;
when men rise up at the sound of birds,
but all their songs grow faint;
5when men are afraid of heights
and of dangers in the streets;
when the almond tree blossoms
and the grasshopper drags himself along
and desire no longer is stirred.
Then man goes to his eternal home
and mourners go about the streets.

6Remember him—before the silver cord is severed,
or the golden bowl is broken;
before the pitcher is shattered at the spring,
or the wheel broken at the well,
7and the dust returns to the ground it came from,
and the spirit returns to God who gave it.

8"Meaningless! Meaningless!" says the Teacher.[a]
"Everything is meaningless!"

*The Conclusion of the Matter*

9Not only was the Teacher wise, but also he imparted knowledge to the people. He pondered and searched out and set in order
many proverbs. 10The Teacher searched to find just the right
words, and what he wrote was upright and true.
11The words of the wise are like goads, their collected sayings
like firmly embedded nails—given by one Shepherd. 12Be warned,
my son, of anything in addition to them.
Of making many books there is no end, and much study wearies the body.

13Now all has been heard;
here is the conclusion of the matter:
Fear God and keep his commandments,
for this is the whole ⌞duty⌟ of man.
14For God will bring every deed into judgment,
including every hidden thing,
whether it is good or evil.

NIV [a] 8 Or *the leader of the assembly;* also in verses 9 and 10

## King James

THE

# Song of Solomon

1 THE SONG of songs, which *is* Solomon's.
2Let him kiss me with the kisses of his mouth: for thy love *is*
better than wine.
3Because of the savour of thy good ointments thy name *is as*
ointment poured forth, therefore do the virgins love thee.
4Draw me, we will run after thee: the king hath brought me into
his chambers: we will be glad and rejoice in thee, we will remember thy love more than wine: the upright love thee.
5I *am* black, but comely, O ye daughters of Jerusalem, as the
tents of Kedar, as the curtains of Solomon.
6Look not upon me, because I *am* black, because the sun hath
looked upon me: my mother's children were angry with me; they
made me the keeper of the vineyards; *but* mine own vineyard have
I not kept.
7Tell me, O thou whom my soul loveth, where thou feedest,
where thou makest *thy flock* to rest at noon: for why should I be
as one that turneth aside by the flocks of thy companions?
8¶ If thou know not, O thou fairest among women, go thy way
forth by the footsteps of the flock, and feed thy kids beside the
shepherds' tents.
9I have compared thee, O my love, to a company of horses in
Pharaoh's chariots.
10Thy cheeks are comely with rows *of jewels*, thy neck with
chains *of gold*.
11We will make thee borders of gold with studs of silver.

## Amplified

# The Song of Solomon

1 THE SONG of songs—the most excellent of them all—which
is Solomon's. [I Kings 4:32.]
2Let him kiss me with the kisses of his mouth! [she cries. Then
realizing that Solomon has arrived and has heard her speech,
turning to him she adds] For your love is better than wine!
3 *And she continues,* The odor of your ointments is fragrant; your
name is like perfume poured out; therefore do the maidens love
you.
4Draw me! We will run after you! The king brings me into his
apartments! We will be glad and rejoice in you! We will recall
[when we were favored with] your love, more fragrant than wine.
The upright [are not offended at your choice, but sincerely] love
you.
5I am so black. But *you are* lovely *and* pleasant [the ladies assured
her]. O you daughters of Jerusalem, *I am as dark* as the tents of *the
Bedouin tribe* Kedar! like the *beautiful* curtains of Solomon.
6[Please] do not look at me, *she said, for* I am swarthy. *I have
worked out* in the sun *and* it has left its mark upon me. My stepbrothers were angry with me, and they made me keeper of the vineyards; but my own vineyard, *my complexion,* I have not kept.
7[Addressing her shepherd, she said] Tell me, O [a]you whom
my soul loves, where you pasture your flock, where you make it
lie down at noon. For why should I *as I think of you* be as a veiled
one straying beside the flocks of your companions? [Ps. 23:1, 2.]
8If you do not know *where your lover is,* O you fairest among
women, run along, follow the tracks of the flock, and *amuse yourself
by* pasturing your kids beside the shepherds' tents.
9O my love, *he said as he saw her,* you remind me of my *favorite*
mare in my Pharaoh chariot spans.
10Your cheeks are comely with ornaments, your neck with
strings of jewels.
11We will make you chains *and* ornaments of gold, studded with
silver.

**AMP** [a] Does my spirit crave for the Divine Shepherd, even in the presence of the best that the world can offer me?

## New American Standard

# Song of Solomon

*The Young Shulammite Bride and Jerusalem's Daughters*

**1** THE [b]SONG of Songs, which is Solomon's.

2¶ " [c]May he kiss me with the kisses of his mouth!
For your love is better than wine.
3 "Your oils have a pleasing fragrance,
Your name is *like* purified oil;
Therefore the maidens love you.
4 "Draw me after you *and* let us run *together!*
The king has brought me into his chambers."
¶ "[d]We will rejoice in you and be glad;
We will extol your love more than wine.
Rightly do they love you."
5¶ " [e]I am black but lovely,
O daughters of Jerusalem,
Like the tents of Kedar,
Like the curtains of Solomon.
6 "Do not stare at me because I am swarthy,
For the sun has burned me.
My mother's sons were angry with me;
They made me caretaker of the vineyards,
*But* I have not taken care of my own vineyard.
7 "Tell me, O you whom my soul loves,
Where do you pasture *your flock,*
Where do you make *it* lie down at noon?
For why should I be like one who veils herself
Beside the flocks of your companions?"

*Solomon, the Lover, Speaks*

8¶ "[f]If you yourself do not know,
Most beautiful among women,
Go forth on the trail of the flock,
And pasture your young goats
By the tents of the shepherds.
9¶ "To me, my darling, you are like
My mare among the chariots of Pharaoh.
10 "Your cheeks are lovely with ornaments,
Your neck with strings of beads."
11¶ " [g]We will make for you ornaments of gold
With beads of silver."

NAS [b] Or, *Best of the Songs* [c] BRIDE [d] CHORUS [e] BRIDE
[f] BRIDEGROOM [g] CHORUS

## New International

# Song of Songs

**1** SOLOMON'S SONG of Songs.

*Beloved*[h]

2Let him kiss me with the kisses of his mouth—
for your love is more delightful than wine.
3Pleasing is the fragrance of your perfumes;
your name is like perfume poured out.
No wonder the maidens love you!
4Take me away with you—let us hurry!
Let the king bring me into his chambers.

*Friends*

We rejoice and delight in you[i] ;
we will praise your love more than wine.

*Beloved*

How right they are to adore you!
5Dark am I, yet lovely,
O daughters of Jerusalem,
dark like the tents of Kedar,
like the tent curtains of Solomon.[j]
6Do not stare at me because I am dark,
because I am darkened by the sun.
My mother's sons were angry with me
and made me take care of the vineyards;
my own vineyard I have neglected.
7Tell me, you whom I love, where you graze your flock
and where you rest your sheep at midday.
Why should I be like a veiled woman
beside the flocks of your friends?

*Friends*

8If you do not know, most beautiful of women,
follow the tracks of the sheep
and graze your young goats
by the tents of the shepherds.

*Lover*

9I liken you, my darling, to a mare
harnessed to one of the chariots of Pharaoh.
10Your cheeks are beautiful with earrings,
your neck with strings of jewels.
11We will make you earrings of gold,
studded with silver.

**NIV** [h] Primarily on the basis of the gender of the Hebrew pronouns used, male and female speakers are indicated in the margins by the captions *Lover* and *Beloved* respectively. The words of others are marked *Friends*. In some instances the divisions and their captions are debatable. [i] 4 The Hebrew is masculine singular. [j] 5 Or *Salma*

## King James

12¶ While the king *sitteth* at his table, my spikenard sendeth
forth the smell thereof.
13A bundle of myrrh *is* my wellbeloved unto me; he shall lie all
night betwixt my breasts.
14My beloved *is* unto me *as* a cluster of camphire in the vineyards of En-gedi.
15Behold, thou *art* fair, my love; behold, thou *art* fair; thou *hast*
doves' eyes.
16Behold, thou *art* fair, my beloved, yea, pleasant: also our bed
*is* green.
17The beams of our house *are* cedar, *and* our rafters of fir.

**2** I AM the rose of Sharon, *and* the lily of the valleys.
2As the lily among thorns, so *is* my love among the daughters.
3As the apple tree among the trees of the wood, so *is* my
beloved among the sons. I sat down under his shadow with great
delight, and his fruit *was* sweet to my taste.
4He brought me to the banqueting house, and his banner over
me *was* love.
5Stay me with flagons, comfort me with apples: for I *am* sick of
love.
6His left hand *is* under my head, and his right hand doth
embrace me.
7I charge you, O ye daughters of Jerusalem, by the roes, and
by the hinds of the field, that ye stir not up, nor awake *my* love,
till he please.
8¶ The voice of my beloved! behold, he cometh leaping upon the
mountains, skipping upon the hills.
9My beloved is like a roe or a young hart: behold, he standeth
behind our wall, he looketh forth at the windows, showing himself
through the lattice.
10My beloved spake, and said unto me, Rise up, my love, my
fair one, and come away.
11For, lo, the winter is past, the rain is over *and* gone;
12The flowers appear on the earth; the time of the singing *of birds*
is come, and the voice of the turtle is heard in our land;

## Amplified

12While the king sits at his table, *she said,* my spikenard [my
absent lover] sends forth *his* fragrance *over me.*
13My beloved [shepherd] is to me like a *scent* bag of myrrh that
lies in my bosom.
14My beloved [shepherd] is to me a cluster of henna flowers in
the vineyards of Engedi [famed for its fragrant shrubs].
15 *Behold, you are beautiful, my love; behold,* you are beautiful; you
have doves' eyes.
16[She cried,] Behold, you are beautiful my beloved [shepherd],
yes, delightful! Our arbor *and* couch are green *and* leafy;
17The beams of our house are cedars, *and* our rafters *and* panels
are cypresses *or* pines.

**2** *SHE SAID,* I am only a little rose *or* autumn crocus of the
plain of Sharon, or a *humble* lily of the valleys [that grows in
deep and difficult places].
2But Solomon replied, As the lily among thorns, so are you, my
love, among the daughters.
3As an apple tree among the trees of the wood, so is my beloved
[shepherd] among the sons! *cried the girl.* Under his shadow I
delighted to sit, and his fruit was sweet to my taste.
4He brought me to the banqueting house, and his banner over
me was love—for love waved as a *protecting and comforting* banner
over my head when I was near him.
5Sustain me with raisins, refresh me with apples, for I am sick
with love.
6 *I can feel* [a]his left hand under my head and his right hand
embraces me! [Deut. 33:27; Matt. 28:20.]
7[He said,] I charge you, O you daughters of Jerusalem, by the
gazelles or the hinds of the field [which are free to follow their own
instincts], that you not try to stir up or awaken my love until it
pleases.
8[Vividly she pictured it:] The voice of my beloved [shepherd]!
Behold, he comes leaping upon the mountains, bounding over the
hills. [John 10:27.]
9My beloved is like a gazelle or a young hart; behold, he stands
behind the wall of our house, he looks in through the windows,
he glances through the lattice.
10My beloved speaks and says to me, Rise up, my love, my fair
one, and come away.
11For, lo, the winter is past, the rain is over and gone;
12The flowers appear on the earth, the time of the singing of
birds is come, and the voice of the turtledove is heard in our land.

**AMP** [a] Have I a constant sense of my Shepherd's presence, regardless of my surroundings?

## New American Standard

12¶ "[b]While the king was at his table,
My perfume gave forth its fragrance.
13 "My beloved is to me a pouch of myrrh
Which lies all night between my breasts.
14 "My beloved is to me a cluster of henna blossoms
In the vineyards of Engedi."
15¶ "[c]How beautiful you are, my darling,
How beautiful you are!
Your eyes are *like* doves."
16¶ "[d]How handsome you are, my beloved,
*And* so pleasant!
Indeed, our couch is luxuriant!
17 "The beams of our houses are cedars,
Our rafters, cypresses."

*The Bride's Admiration*

**2** "[e]I AM the rose of Sharon,
The lily of the valleys."
2¶ "[f]Like a lily among the thorns,
So is my darling among the maidens."
3¶ "[g]Like an apple tree among the trees of the forest,
So is my beloved among the young men.
In his shade I took great delight and sat down,
And his fruit was sweet to my taste.
4 "He has brought me to *his* banquet hall,
And his banner over me is love.
5 "Sustain me with raisin cakes,
Refresh me with apples,
Because I am lovesick.
6 "*Let* his left hand be under my head
And his right hand embrace me."
7¶ "[h]I adjure you, O daughters of Jerusalem,
By the gazelles or by the hinds of the field,
That you will not arouse or awaken *my* love,
Until she pleases."
8¶ "[i]Listen! My beloved!
Behold, he is coming,
Climbing on the mountains,
Leaping on the hills!
9 "My beloved is like a gazelle or a young stag.
Behold, he is standing behind our wall,
He is looking through the windows,
He is peering through the lattice.
10¶ "My beloved responded and said to me,
'Arise, my darling, my beautiful one,
And come along.
11 'For behold, the winter is past,
The rain is over *and* gone.
12 'The flowers have *already* appeared in the land;
The time has arrived for pruning *the vines*,
And the voice of the turtledove has been heard in our land.

NAS [b] BRIDE [c] BRIDEGROOM [d] BRIDE [e] BRIDE [f] BRIDEGROOM [g] BRIDE [h] BRIDEGROOM [i] BRIDE

## New International

*Beloved*

12While the king was at his table,
my perfume spread its fragrance.
13My lover is to me a sachet of myrrh
resting between my breasts.
14My lover is to me a cluster of henna blossoms
from the vineyards of En Gedi.

*Lover*

15How beautiful you are, my darling!
Oh, how beautiful!
Your eyes are doves.

*Beloved*

16How handsome you are, my lover!
Oh, how charming!
And our bed is verdant.

*Lover*

17The beams of our house are cedars;
our rafters are firs.

*Beloved*[j]

**2** I AM a rose[k] of Sharon,
a lily of the valleys.

*Lover*

2Like a lily among thorns
is my darling among the maidens.

*Beloved*

3Like an apple tree among the trees of the forest
is my lover among the young men.
I delight to sit in his shade,
and his fruit is sweet to my taste.
4He has taken me to the banquet hall,
and his banner over me is love.
5Strengthen me with raisins,
refresh me with apples,
for I am faint with love.
6His left arm is under my head,
and his right arm embraces me.
7Daughters of Jerusalem, I charge you
by the gazelles and by the does of the field:
Do not arouse or awaken love
until it so desires.
8Listen! My lover!
Look! Here he comes,
leaping across the mountains,
bounding over the hills.
9My lover is like a gazelle or a young stag.
Look! There he stands behind our wall,
gazing through the windows,
peering through the lattice.
10My lover spoke and said to me,
"Arise, my darling,
my beautiful one, and come with me.
11See! The winter is past;
the rains are over and gone.
12Flowers appear on the earth;
the season of singing has come,
the cooing of doves
is heard in our land.

NIV [j] 1 Or *Lover* [k] 1 Possibly a member of the crocus family

## King James

13The fig tree putteth forth her green figs, and the vines *with* the tender grape give a *good* smell. Arise, my love, my fair one, and come away.

14¶ O my dove, *that art* in the clefts of the rock, in the secret *places* of the stairs, let me see thy countenance, let me hear thy voice; for sweet *is* thy voice, and thy countenance *is* comely.

15Take us the foxes, the little foxes, that spoil the vines: for our vines *have* tender grapes.

16¶ My beloved *is* mine, and I *am* his: he feedeth among the lilies.

17Until the day break, and the shadows flee away, turn, my beloved, and be thou like a roe or a young hart upon the mountains of Bether.

**3** BY NIGHT on my bed I sought him whom my soul loveth: I sought him, but I found him not.

2I will rise now, and go about the city in the streets, and in the broad ways I will seek him whom my soul loveth: I sought him, but I found him not.

3The watchmen that go about the city found me: *to whom I said,* Saw ye him whom my soul loveth?

4 *It was* but a little that I passed from them, but I found him whom my soul loveth: I held him, and would not let him go, until I had brought him into my mother's house, and into the chamber of her that conceived me.

5I charge you, O ye daughters of Jerusalem, by the roes, and by the hinds of the field, that ye stir not up, nor awake *my* love, till he please.

6¶ Who *is* this that cometh out of the wilderness like pillars of smoke, perfumed with myrrh and frankincense, with all powders of the merchant?

7Behold his bed, which *is* Solomon's; threescore valiant men *are* about it, of the valiant of Israel.

8They all hold swords, *being* expert in war: every man *hath* his sword upon his thigh because of fear in the night.

9King Solomon made himself a chariot of the wood of Lebanon.

## Amplified

13The fig tree puts forth *and* ripens her green figs, and the vines are in blossom; they give forth their fragrance. [a]Arise, my love, my fair one, and come away.

14[So I went with him, and when we were climbing the rocky steps up the hillside, my beloved shepherd said to me] O my dove, [while you are there] in the seclusion of the clefts in the solid rock, in the sheltered *and* secret place of the cliff, let me see your face, [b]let me hear your voice, for your voice is sweet and your face is lovely.

15[My heart was touched and I fervently sang to him my desire] Take us the foxes, the [c]little foxes that spoil the vineyards [of our love], for our vineyards are in blossom.

16[She said distinctly] My beloved is mine, and I am his! He pastures his flocks among the lilies. [Cf. Matt. 10:32; Acts 4:12.]

17[Then longingly addressing her absent shepherd, she cried] Until the day breaks and the shadows flee away, return hastily, O my beloved, and be like a gazelle or a young hart as you cover the mountains *which separate us.*

**3** IN THE night I dreamed that I sought for the one whom I love. *She said,* I looked for him, but could not find him. [Isa. 26:9.]

2So I decided to go out into the city, into the streets and broad ways [which are so confusing to a country girl] and seek him whom my soul loves. I sought him, but I could not find him.

3The watchmen who go about the city found me, to whom I said, Did you see him whom my soul loves?

4I had gone but a little way past them, when I found him whom my soul loves. I held him, and would not let him go until I had brought him into my mother's house, and into the chamber of her who conceived me. [Rom. 8:35; I Pet. 2:25.]

5I adjure you, O daughters of Jerusalem, by the gazelles and by the hinds of the field, that you stir not up nor awaken love until it pleases.

6Who *or* what is this, *she asked,* that comes gliding out of the wilderness like stately pillars of smoke perfumed with myrrh, frankincense and all the fragrant powders of the merchant? *Someone answered:*

7Behold, it is the traveling litter—the *bridal* car—of Solomon. Sixty mighty men are about it, of the mighty men of Israel.

8They all handle the sword and are expert in war. Every man has his sword upon his thigh, that fear be not excited in the night.

9King Solomon made himself a car *or* a palanquin of state of the *cedar* wood of Lebanon.

**AMP** [a] Do I take time to meet my Good Shepherd each day, letting Him tell me of His love, and cheering His heart with my interest in Him? [b] Do I realize that my voice in praise and song is sweet to Him, or do I withhold it? [c] What is my greatest concern, the thing about which most of all I want Christ's help? When He asks to hear my voice, what do I tell Him?

## New American Standard

13 'The fig tree has ripened its figs,
And the vines in blossom have given forth *their* fragrance.
Arise, my darling, my beautiful one,
And come along!' "
14 "O my dove, in the clefts of the rock,
In the secret place of the steep pathway,
Let me see your form,
Let me hear your voice;
For your voice is sweet,
And your form is lovely."

15¶ "Catch the foxes for us,
The little foxes that are ruining the vineyards,
While our vineyards are in blossom."
16 "My beloved is mine, and I am his;
He pastures *his flock* among the lilies.
17 "Until the cool of the day when the shadows flee away,
Turn, my beloved, and be like a gazelle
Or a young stag on the mountains of Bether."

*The Bride's Troubled Dream*

3 "[d]ON MY bed night after night I sought him
Whom my soul loves;
I sought him but did not find him.
2 'I must arise now and go about the city;
In the streets and in the squares
I must seek him whom my soul loves.'
I sought him but did not find him.
3 "The watchmen who make the rounds in the city found me,
*And I said,* 'Have you seen him whom my soul loves?'
4 "Scarcely had I left them
When I found him whom my soul loves;
I held on to him and would not let him go,
Until I had brought him to my mother's house,
And into the room of her who conceived me."
5¶ " [e]I adjure you, O daughters of Jerusalem,
By the gazelles or by the hinds of the field,
That you will not arouse or awaken *my* love,
Until she pleases."

*Solomon's Wedding Day*

6¶ "[f]What is this coming up from the wilderness
Like columns of smoke,
Perfumed with myrrh and frankincense,
With all scented powders of the merchant?
7 "Behold, it is the *traveling* couch of Solomon;
Sixty mighty men around it,
Of the mighty men of Israel.
8 "All of them are wielders of the sword,
Expert in war;
Each man has his sword at his side,
*Guarding* against the terrors of the night.
9 "King Solomon has made for himself a sedan chair
From the timber of Lebanon.

NAS [d] BRIDE [e] BRIDEGROOM [f] CHORUS

## New International

13 The fig tree forms its early fruit;
the blossoming vines spread their fragrance.
Arise, come, my darling;
my beautiful one, come with me."

*Lover*

14 My dove in the clefts of the rock,
in the hiding places on the mountainside,
show me your face,
let me hear your voice;
for your voice is sweet,
and your face is lovely.
15 Catch for us the foxes,
the little foxes
that ruin the vineyards,
our vineyards that are in bloom.

*Beloved*

16 My lover is mine and I am his;
he browses among the lilies.
17 Until the day breaks
and the shadows flee,
turn, my lover,
and be like a gazelle
or like a young stag
on the rugged hills.[g]

3 ALL NIGHT long on my bed
I looked for the one my heart loves;
I looked for him but did not find him.
2 I will get up now and go about the city,
through its streets and squares;
I will search for the one my heart loves.
So I looked for him but did not find him.
3 The watchmen found me
as they made their rounds in the city.
"Have you seen the one my heart loves?"
4 Scarcely had I passed them
when I found the one my heart loves.
I held him and would not let him go
till I had brought him to my mother's house,
to the room of the one who conceived me.
5 Daughters of Jerusalem, I charge you
by the gazelles and by the does of the field:
Do not arouse or awaken love
until it so desires.

6 Who is this coming up from the desert
like a column of smoke,
perfumed with myrrh and incense
made from all the spices of the merchant?
7 Look! It is Solomon's carriage,
escorted by sixty warriors,
the noblest of Israel,
8 all of them wearing the sword,
all experienced in battle,
each with his sword at his side,
prepared for the terrors of the night.
9 King Solomon made for himself the carriage;
he made it of wood from Lebanon.

NIV [g] 17 Or *the hills of Bether*

## King James

10 He made the pillars thereof *of* silver, the bottom thereof *of* gold, the covering of it *of* purple, the midst thereof being paved *with* love, for the daughters of Jerusalem.

11 Go forth, O ye daughters of Zion, and behold king Solomon with the crown wherewith his mother crowned him in the day of his espousals, and in the day of the gladness of his heart.

**4** BEHOLD, THOU *art* fair, my love; behold, thou *art* fair; thou *hast* doves' eyes within thy locks: thy hair *is* as a flock of goats, that appear from mount Gilead.

2 Thy teeth *are* like a flock *of sheep that are even* shorn, which came up from the washing; whereof every one bear twins, and none *is* barren among them.

3 Thy lips *are* like a thread of scarlet, and thy speech *is* comely: thy temples *are* like a piece of a pomegranate within thy locks.

4 Thy neck *is* like the tower of David builded for an armoury, whereon there hang a thousand bucklers, all shields of mighty men.

5 Thy two breasts *are* like two young roes that are twins, which feed among the lilies.

6 Until the day break, and the shadows flee away, I will get me to the mountain of myrrh, and to the hill of frankincense.

7 Thou *art* all fair, my love; *there is* no spot in thee.

8 ¶ Come with me from Lebanon, *my* spouse, with me from Lebanon: look from the top of Amana, from the top of Shenir and Hermon, from the lions' dens, from the mountains of the leopards.

9 Thou hast ravished my heart, my sister, *my* spouse; thou hast ravished my heart with one of thine eyes, with one chain of thy neck.

10 How fair is thy love, my sister, *my* spouse! how much better is thy love than wine! and the smell of thine ointments than all spices!

11 Thy lips, O *my* spouse, drop *as* the honeycomb: honey and milk *are* under thy tongue; and the smell of thy garments *is* like the smell of Lebanon.

12 A garden inclosed *is* my sister, *my* spouse; a spring shut up, a fountain sealed.

13 Thy plants *are* an orchard of pomegranates, with pleasant fruits; camphire, with spikenard,

14 Spikenard and saffron; calamus and cinnamon, with all trees of frankincense; myrrh and aloes, with all the chief spices:

## Amplified

10 He made its posts of silver, its back of gold, its seat of purple, the inside of it being lovingly *and intricately* wrought in needlework by the daughters of Jerusalem.

11 Go forth, O you daughters of Zion, and gaze upon King Solomon *wearing* the crown with which his mother [Bathsheba] crowned him on the day of his wedding, on the day of his gladness of heart.

**4** HOW FAIR you are, my love, *he said,* how very fair. Your eyes behind your veil *remind me* of those of a dove; your hair [makes me think of the black, wavy fleece] of a flock of [the Arabian] goats which one sees trailing down Mount Gilead [beyond Jordan on the frontiers of the desert].

2 Your teeth are like a flock of shorn ewes, which have come up from the washing, of which all are in pairs, and none is missing among them.

3 Your lips are like a thread of scarlet, and your mouth is lovely. Your cheeks are like halves of a pomegranate behind your veil.

4 Your neck is like the tower of David, built for an arsenal, whereon hang a thousand bucklers, all of them shields of warriors.

5 Your two breasts are like two fawns, twins of a gazelle, that feed among the lilies.

6 Until the day breaks and the shadows flee away, [in my thoughts] I will get me to the mountain of myrrh and the hill of frankincense [to him whom my soul adores].

7 [He exclaimed] O my love, how beautiful you are! There is no flaw in you! [John 14:18; Eph. 5:27.]

8 Come [a]away with me from Lebanon, my [promised] bride, come with me from Lebanon. Depart from the top of Amana, from the peak of Senir and Hermon, from the lions' dens, from the mountain of the leopards. [II Cor. 11:2, 3.]

9 You have ravished my heart *and* given me courage, my sister, my [promised] bride; you have ravished my heart *and* given me courage with one look from your eyes, with one jewel of your necklace.

10 How beautiful is your love, my sister, my [promised] bride! How much better is your love than wine! And the fragrance of your ointments than all spices! [Rom. 8:35; John 15:9.]

11 Your lips, O my [promised] bride, drop honey as the honeycomb. Honey and milk are under your tongue, and the odor of your garments is like the odor of Lebanon.

12 A garden enclosed *and* barred is my sister, my [promised] bride; a spring shut up, a fountain sealed.

13 Your shoots are an orchard of pomegranates *or* a paradise with precious fruits, henna with spikenard plants, [John 15:5; Eph. 5:9.]

14 Spikenard and saffron, calamus and cinnamon, with all trees of frankincense, myrrh and aloes, with all the chief spices.

**AMP** [a] Do I heed Christ when He bids me come away from the lions' den of temptation and dwell with Him?

## New American Standard

10 "He made its posts of silver,
Its back of gold
*And* its seat of purple fabric,
*With* its interior lovingly fitted out
By the daughters of Jerusalem.
11 "Go forth, O daughters of Zion,
And gaze on King Solomon with the crown
With which his mother has crowned him
On the day of his wedding,
And on the day of his gladness of heart."

*Solomon's Love Expressed*

4 "[b]HOW BEAUTIFUL you are, my darling,
How beautiful you are!
Your eyes are *like* doves behind your veil;
Your hair is like a flock of goats
That have descended from Mount Gilead.
2 "Your teeth are like a flock of *newly* shorn ewes
Which have come up from *their* washing,
All of which bear twins,
And not one among them has lost her young.
3 "Your lips are like a scarlet thread,
And your mouth is lovely.
Your temples are like a slice of a pomegranate
Behind your veil.
4 "Your neck is like the tower of David
Built with rows of stones,
On which are hung a thousand shields,
All the round shields of the mighty men.
5 "Your two breasts are like two fawns,
Twins of a gazelle,
Which feed among the lilies.
6 "Until the cool of the day
When the shadows flee away,
I will go my way to the mountain of myrrh
And to the hill of frankincense.
7¶ "You are altogether beautiful, my darling,
And there is no blemish in you.
8 "*Come* with me from Lebanon, *my* bride,
May you come with me from Lebanon.
Journey down from the summit of Amana,
From the summit of Senir and Hermon,
From the dens of lions,
From the mountains of leopards.
9 "You have made my heart beat faster, my sister, *my* bride;
You have made my heart beat faster with a single *glance* of your eyes,
With a single strand of your necklace.
10 "How beautiful is your love, my sister, *my* bride!
How much better is your love than wine,
And the fragrance of your oils
Than all *kinds* of spices!
11 "Your lips, *my* bride, drip honey;
Honey and milk are under your tongue,
And the fragrance of your garments is like the fragrance of Lebanon.
12 "A garden locked is my sister, *my* bride,
A rock garden locked, a spring sealed up.
13 "Your shoots are an orchard of pomegranates
With choice fruits, henna with nard plants,
14 Nard and saffron, calamus and cinnamon,
With all the trees of frankincense,
Myrrh and aloes, along with all the finest spices.

NAS [b] BRIDEGROOM

## New International

10 Its posts he made of silver,
its base of gold.
Its seat was upholstered with purple,
its interior lovingly inlaid
by[c] the daughters of Jerusalem.
11 Come out, you daughters of Zion,
and look at King Solomon wearing the crown,
the crown with which his mother crowned him
on the day of his wedding,
the day his heart rejoiced.

*Lover*

4 HOW BEAUTIFUL you are, my darling!
Oh, how beautiful!
Your eyes behind your veil are doves.
Your hair is like a flock of goats
descending from Mount Gilead.
2 Your teeth are like a flock of sheep just shorn,
coming up from the washing.
Each has its twin;
not one of them is alone.
3 Your lips are like a scarlet ribbon;
your mouth is lovely.
Your temples behind your veil
are like the halves of a pomegranate.
4 Your neck is like the tower of David,
built with elegance[d];
on it hang a thousand shields,
all of them shields of warriors.
5 Your two breasts are like two fawns,
like twin fawns of a gazelle
that browse among the lilies.
6 Until the day breaks
and the shadows flee,
I will go to the mountain of myrrh
and to the hill of incense.
7 All beautiful you are, my darling;
there is no flaw in you.
8 Come with me from Lebanon, my bride,
come with me from Lebanon.
Descend from the crest of Amana,
from the top of Senir, the summit of Hermon,
from the lions' dens
and the mountain haunts of the leopards.
9 You have stolen my heart, my sister, my bride;
you have stolen my heart
with one glance of your eyes,
with one jewel of your necklace.
10 How delightful is your love, my sister, my bride!
How much more pleasing is your love than wine,
and the fragrance of your perfume than any spice!
11 Your lips drop sweetness as the honeycomb, my bride;
milk and honey are under your tongue.
The fragrance of your garments is like that of Lebanon.
12 You are a garden locked up, my sister, my bride;
you are a spring enclosed, a sealed fountain.
13 Your plants are an orchard of pomegranates
with choice fruits,
with henna and nard,
14 nard and saffron,
calamus and cinnamon,
with every kind of incense tree,
with myrrh and aloes
and all the finest spices.

NIV [c] *10 Or its inlaid interior a gift of love / from* [d] 4 The meaning of the Hebrew for this word is uncertain.

## King James

15A fountain of gardens, a well of living waters, and streams from Lebanon.

16¶ Awake, O north wind; and come, thou south; blow upon my garden, *that* the spices thereof may flow out. Let my beloved come into his garden, and eat his pleasant fruits.

**5** I AM come into my garden, my sister, *my* spouse: I have gathered my myrrh with my spice; I have eaten my honeycomb with my honey; I have drunk my wine with my milk: eat, O friends; drink, yea, drink abundantly, O beloved.

2¶ I sleep, but my heart waketh: *it is* the voice of my beloved that knocketh, *saying*, Open to me, my sister, my love, my dove, my undefiled: for my head is filled with dew, *and* my locks with the drops of the night.

3I have put off my coat; how shall I put it on? I have washed my feet; how shall I defile them?

4My beloved put in his hand by the hole *of the door*, and my bowels were moved for him.

5I rose up to open to my beloved; and my hands dropped *with* myrrh, and my fingers *with* sweetsmelling myrrh, upon the handles of the lock.

6I opened to my beloved; but my beloved had withdrawn himself, *and* was gone: my soul failed when he spake: I sought him, but I could not find him; I called him, but he gave me no answer.

7The watchmen that went about the city found me, they smote me, they wounded me; the keepers of the walls took away my veil from me.

8I charge you, O daughters of Jerusalem, if ye find my beloved, that ye tell him, that I *am* sick of love.

9¶ What *is* thy beloved more than *another* beloved, O thou fairest among women? what *is* thy beloved more than *another* beloved, that thou dost so charge us?

10My beloved *is* white and ruddy, the chiefest among ten thousand.

## Amplified

15You are a fountain *springing up* in a garden, a well of living waters, and flowing streams from Lebanon. [John 4:10; 7:37, 38.]

16[You have called me a garden, she said.] O, I pray the *cold* [a]north wind and the *soft* south to blow upon my garden, that its spices may flow out [in abundance for you in whom my soul delights]. Let my beloved come into his garden and eat its choicest fruits.

**5** I AM come into my garden, my sister, my [promised] bride; I have gathered my myrrh with my balsam *and* spice. *From your sweet words* I have gathered the richest perfumes and spices; I have eaten my honeycomb with my honey; I have drunk my wine with my milk. Eat, O friends [feast on, O revelers of the palace; you can never make my love disloyal to me]! Drink, yes, drink abundantly of love, O precious one [for now I know you are mine, irrevocably mine! With his confident words still thrilling her being, through the lattice she saw her shepherd turn away and pass into the night]. [John 16:33.]

2I went to sleep, but my heart stayed awake. I dreamed that I heard the voice of my beloved as he knocked *at the door of my mother's cottage*. Open to me, my sister, my love, my dove, my spotless one, he said, for I am wet with the *heavy* night dew; my hair is covered with it. [Job 11:13-15.]

3 *But weary from a day in the vineyards, I had already sought my rest.* I had put off my garment; [b]how could I put it on? I had washed my feet; how could I *again* soil them? [Isa. 32:9; Heb. 3:15.]

4My beloved put in his hand by the hole of the door, and my heart was moved for him.

5I rose up to open to my beloved, and my hands dropped with myrrh, and my fingers with liquid (sweet smelling) myrrh, *which he had left* upon the handles of the bolt.

6I opened to my beloved, but my beloved had turned away *and* withdrawn himself, and was gone! My soul went forth *to him* when he spoke, but it failed me, *and now he was gone!* I sought him, but I could not find him; I called him, but he gave me no answer.

7The watchmen that went about the city found me; they struck me, they wounded me; the keepers of the walls took my veil *and* my mantle from me.

8I charge you, O daughters of Jerusalem, if you find my beloved, that you tell him that I am sick from love—simply sick *to be with him.* [Ps. 63:1.]

9What is your beloved more than another beloved, O you fairest among women? [taunted the ladies.] What is your beloved more than another beloved, that you should give us such a charge? [John 10:26.]

10[She said:] My beloved is fair and ruddy, the chief among ten thousand! [John 1:14; Ps. 45:2.]

**AMP** [a] Am I willing for the north wind of adversity to blow upon me, if it will better fit me for Christ's presence and companionship? [b] In my weariness from earthly cares, do I hesitate to answer when the Divine Shepherd knocks at my door, and so turn Him from me?

## New American Standard

15 " *You are* a garden spring,
A well of fresh water,
And streams *flowing* from Lebanon."

16¶ " [c]Awake, O north *wind*,
And come, *wind of* the south;
Make my garden breathe out *fragrance*,
Let its spices be wafted abroad.
May my beloved come into his garden
And eat its choice fruits!"

*The Torment of Separation*

5 " [d]I HAVE come into my garden, my sister, *my* bride;
I have gathered my myrrh along with my balsam.
I have eaten my honeycomb and my honey;
I have drunk my wine and my milk.
Eat, friends;
Drink and imbibe deeply, O lovers."

2¶ " [e]I was asleep, but my heart was awake.
A voice! My beloved was knocking:
'Open to me, my sister, my darling,
My dove, my perfect one!
For my head is drenched with dew,
My locks with the damp of the night.'
3 "I have taken off my dress,
How can I put it on *again?*
I have washed my feet,
How can I dirty them *again?*
4 "My beloved extended his hand through the opening,
And my feelings were aroused for him.
5 "I arose to open to my beloved;
And my hands dripped with myrrh,
And my fingers with liquid myrrh,
On the handles of the bolt.
6 "I opened to my beloved,
But my beloved had turned away *and* had gone!
My heart went out *to him* as he spoke.
I searched for him, but I did not find him;
I called him, but he did not answer me.
7 "The watchmen who make the rounds in the city found me,
They struck me *and* wounded me;
The guardsmen of the walls took away my shawl from me.
8 "I adjure you, O daughters of Jerusalem,
If you find my beloved,
As to what you will tell him:
For I am lovesick."

9¶ " [f]What kind of beloved is your beloved,
O most beautiful among women?
What kind of beloved is your beloved,
That thus you adjure us?"

*Admiration by the Bride*

10¶ " [g]My beloved is dazzling and ruddy,
Outstanding among ten thousand.

NAS [c] BRIDE [d] BRIDEGROOM [e] BRIDE [f] CHORUS [g] BRIDE

## New International

15You are[h] a garden fountain,
a well of flowing water
streaming down from Lebanon.

*Beloved*

16Awake, north wind,
and come, south wind!
Blow on my garden,
that its fragrance may spread abroad.
Let my lover come into his garden
and taste its choice fruits.

*Lover*

5 I HAVE come into my garden, my sister, my bride;
I have gathered my myrrh with my spice.
I have eaten my honeycomb and my honey;
I have drunk my wine and my milk.

*Friends*

Eat, O friends, and drink;
drink your fill, O lovers.

*Beloved*

2I slept but my heart was awake.
Listen! My lover is knocking:
"Open to me, my sister, my darling,
my dove, my flawless one.
My head is drenched with dew,
my hair with the dampness of the night."
3I have taken off my robe—
must I put it on again?
I have washed my feet—
must I soil them again?
4My lover thrust his hand through the latch-opening;
my heart began to pound for him.
5I arose to open for my lover,
and my hands dripped with myrrh,
my fingers with flowing myrrh,
on the handles of the lock.
6I opened for my lover,
but my lover had left; he was gone.
My heart sank at his departure.[i]
I looked for him but did not find him.
I called him but he did not answer.
7The watchmen found me
as they made their rounds in the city.
They beat me, they bruised me;
they took away my cloak,
those watchmen of the walls!
8O daughters of Jerusalem, I charge you—
if you find my lover,
what will you tell him?
Tell him I am faint with love.

*Friends*

9How is your beloved better than others,
most beautiful of women?
How is your beloved better than others,
that you charge us so?

*Beloved*

10My lover is radiant and ruddy,
outstanding among ten thousand.

NIV [h] 15 Or *I am* (spoken by the *Beloved*) [i] 6 Or *heart had gone out to him when he spoke*

## King James

11 His head *is as* the most fine gold, his locks *are* bushy, *and* black as a raven.

12 His eyes *are* as *the eyes* of doves by the rivers of waters, washed with milk, *and* fitly set.

13 His cheeks *are* as a bed of spices, *as* sweet flowers: his lips *like* lilies, dropping sweetsmelling myrrh.

14 His hands *are as* gold rings set with the beryl: his belly *is as* bright ivory overlaid *with* sapphires.

15 His legs *are as* pillars of marble, set upon sockets of fine gold: his countenance *is* as Lebanon, excellent as the cedars.

16 His mouth *is* most sweet: yea, he *is* altogether lovely. This *is* my beloved, and this *is* my friend, O daughters of Jerusalem.

**6** WHITHER IS thy beloved gone, O thou fairest among women? whither is thy beloved turned aside? that we may seek him with thee.

2 My beloved is gone down into his garden, to the beds of spices, to feed in the gardens, and to gather lilies.

3 I *am* my beloved's, and my beloved *is* mine: he feedeth among the lilies.

4 ¶ Thou *art* beautiful, O my love, as Tirzah, comely as Jerusalem, terrible as *an army* with banners.

5 Turn away thine eyes from me, for they have overcome me: thy hair is as a flock of goats that appear from Gilead.

6 Thy teeth *are* as a flock of sheep which go up from the washing, whereof every one beareth twins, and *there is* not one barren among them.

7 As a piece of a pomegranate *are* thy temples within thy locks.

8 There are threescore queens, and fourscore concubines, and virgins without number.

9 My dove, my undefiled is *but* one; she *is* the *only* one of her mother, she *is* the choice *one* of her that bare her. The daughters saw her, and blessed her; *yea,* the queens and the concubines, and they praised her.

10 ¶ Who *is* she *that* looketh forth as the morning, fair as the moon, clear as the sun, *and* terrible as *an army* with banners?

## Amplified

11 His head is *precious* as the most fine gold; his locks are curling *and* bushy, and black as a raven.

12 His eyes are as doves beside the water brooks, bathed in milk *and* fitly set.

13 His cheeks are as a bed of spices *or* balsam, as banks of sweet herbs yielding fragrance. His lips are like blood-red anemones or lilies, distilling liquid (sweet smelling) myrrh.

14 His hands are as rods of gold, set with [nails of] beryl *or* topaz. His body is a figure of bright ivory overlaid with [veins of] sapphire.

15 His legs are as strong and steady pillars of marble set upon bases of fine gold; his appearance is like Lebanon, excellent, stately *and* majestic as the cedars.

16 His voice *and* speech are exceedingly sweet; yes, he is altogether lovely—the whole of him delights and is precious. [a]This is my beloved, and this is my friend, O daughters of Jerusalem! [Col. 1:15; Ps. 92:15.]

**6** WHERE IS your beloved gone, O you fairest among women? [Again the ladies showed their interest in the remarkable person whom the Shulammite had championed with such unstinted praise; they too wanted to know him, they insisted.] Where is your beloved hiding himself? For we would seek him with you.

2 *She replied,* My beloved is gone down to his garden, to the beds of spices, to feed in the gardens and to gather lilies.

3 I am my beloved's [garden], and my beloved is mine! He feeds among the lilies [which grow there].

4 [*He said:*] You are as beautiful as Tirzah [capital of northern Israel's first king], my love, and as comely as Jerusalem; *but you are* as terrible as a bannered host!

5 Turn away your *flashing* eyes from me, for they have overcome me! Your hair is like a flock of goats that trail down from Mount Gilead.

6 Your teeth are like a flock of ewes coming from their washing; each is paired, not one of them is missing.

7 Your cheeks are like halves of a pomegranate behind your veil.

8 There are sixty queens, and eighty concubines, and virgins without number,

9 But my dove, my undefiled *and* perfect one, stands alone *above them all,* she is the only one of her mother, she is the choice one of her who bore her. The daughters saw her, called her blessed *and* happy, yes, the queens and the concubines, and they praised her. [Col. 2:8, 9.]

10 [The ladies asked] Who is this who looks forth as the dawn, fair as the moon, clear *and* pure as the sun, *and* terrible as a bannered host?

**AMP** [a] Is my Savior unquestionably the One altogether lovely, the One above all others most precious to me? Can I tell how and why Christ is more to me than any human being, or than all earthly possessions?

## New American Standard

11 "His head is *like* gold, pure gold;
His locks are *like* clusters of dates,
*And* black as a raven.
12 "His eyes are like doves,
Beside streams of water,
Bathed in milk,
*And* reposed in *their* setting.
13 "His cheeks are like a bed of balsam,
Banks of sweet-scented herbs;
His lips are lilies,
Dripping with liquid myrrh.
14 "His hands are rods of gold
Set with beryl;
His abdomen is carved ivory
Inlaid with sapphires.
15 "His legs are pillars of alabaster
Set on pedestals of pure gold;
His appearance is like Lebanon,
Choice as the cedars.
16 "His mouth is *full of* sweetness.
And he is wholly desirable.
This is my beloved and this is my friend,
O daughters of Jerusalem."

*Mutual Delight in Each Other*

6 "[b]WHERE HAS your beloved gone,
O most beautiful among women?
Where has your beloved turned,
That we may seek him with you?"

2¶ "[c]My beloved has gone down to his garden,
To the beds of balsam,
To pasture *his flock* in the gardens
And gather lilies.
3 "I am my beloved's and my beloved is mine,
He who pastures *his flock* among the lilies."
4¶ "[d]You are as beautiful as Tirzah, my darling,
As lovely as Jerusalem,
As awesome as an army with banners.
5 "Turn your eyes away from me,
For they have confused me;
Your hair is like a flock of goats
That have descended from Gilead.
6 "Your teeth are like a flock of ewes
Which have come up from *their* washing,
All of which bear twins,
And not one among them has lost her young.
7 "Your temples are like a slice of a pomegranate
Behind your veil.
8 "There are sixty queens and eighty concubines,
And maidens without number;
9 *But* my dove, my perfect one, is unique:
She is her mother's only *daughter;*
She is the pure *child* of the one who bore her.
The maidens saw her and called her blessed,
The queens and the concubines *also,* and they praised her, *saying,*

10¶ 'Who is this that grows like the dawn,
As beautiful as the full moon,
As pure as the sun,
As awesome as an army with banners?'

NAS [b] CHORUS [c] BRIDE [d] BRIDEGROOM

## New International

11His head is purest gold;
his hair is wavy
and black as a raven.
12His eyes are like doves
by the water streams,
washed in milk,
mounted like jewels.
13His cheeks are like beds of spice
yielding perfume.
His lips are like lilies
dripping with myrrh.
14His arms are rods of gold
set with chrysolite.
His body is like polished ivory
decorated with sapphires.[e]
15His legs are pillars of marble
set on bases of pure gold.
His appearance is like Lebanon,
choice as its cedars.
16His mouth is sweetness itself;
he is altogether lovely.
This is my lover, this my friend,
O daughters of Jerusalem.

*Friends*

6 WHERE HAS your lover gone,
most beautiful of women?
Which way did your lover turn,
that we may look for him with you?

*Beloved*

2My lover has gone down to his garden,
to the beds of spices,
to browse in the gardens
and to gather lilies.
3I am my lover's and my lover is mine;
he browses among the lilies.

*Lover*

4You are beautiful, my darling, as Tirzah,
lovely as Jerusalem,
majestic as troops with banners.
5Turn your eyes from me;
they overwhelm me.
Your hair is like a flock of goats
descending from Gilead.
6Your teeth are like a flock of sheep
coming up from the washing.
Each has its twin,
not one of them is alone.
7Your temples behind your veil
are like the halves of a pomegranate.
8Sixty queens there may be,
and eighty concubines,
and virgins beyond number;
9but my dove, my perfect one, is unique,
the only daughter of her mother,
the favorite of the one who bore her.
The maidens saw her and called her blessed;
the queens and concubines praised her.

*Friends*

10Who is this that appears like the dawn,
fair as the moon, bright as the sun,
majestic as the stars in procession?

NIV [e] 14 Or *lapis lazuli*

## King James

11I went down into the garden of nuts to see the fruits of the valley, *and* to see whether the vine flourished, *and* the pomegranates budded.

12Or ever I was aware, my soul made me *like* the chariots of Amminadib.

13Return, return, O Shulamite; return, return, that we may look upon thee. What will ye see in the Shulamite? As it were the company of two armies.

7 HOW BEAUTIFUL are thy feet with shoes, O prince's daughter! the joints of thy thighs *are* like jewels, the work of the hands of a cunning workman.

2Thy navel *is like* a round goblet, *which* wanteth not liquor: thy belly *is like* an heap of wheat set about with lilies.

3Thy two breasts *are* like two young roes *that are* twins.

4Thy neck *is* as a tower of ivory; thine eyes *like* the fishpools in Heshbon, by the gate of Bath-rabbim: thy nose *is* as the tower of Lebanon which looketh toward Damascus.

5Thine head upon thee *is* like Carmel, and the hair of thine head like purple; the king *is* held in the galleries.

6How fair and how pleasant art thou, O love, for delights!

7This thy stature is like to a palm tree, and thy breasts to clusters *of grapes*.

8I said, I will go up to the palm tree, I will take hold of the boughs thereof: now also thy breasts shall be as clusters of the vine, and the smell of thy nose like apples;

9And the roof of thy mouth like the best wine for my beloved, that goeth *down* sweetly, causing the lips of those that are asleep to speak.

10¶ I *am* my beloved's, and his desire *is* toward me.

11Come, my beloved, let us go forth into the field; let us lodge in the villages.

12Let us get up early to the vineyards; let us see if the vine flourish, *whether* the tender grape appear, *and* the pomegranates bud forth: there will I give thee my loves.

13The mandrakes give a smell, and at our gates *are* all manner of pleasant *fruits*, new and old, *which* I have laid up for thee, O my beloved.

## Amplified

11 *The Shulammite replied,* I went down into the nut orchard *one day* to look at the green plants of the valley, to see whether the *grape*vine had budded and the pomegranates were in flower.

12Before I was aware of *what was happening,* my desire *to roam about* had brought me into the area of the princes of my people—the king's retinue. [I began to flee, but they called to me]

13Return, return, O Shulammite; return, return, that we may look upon you. [I replied], What is there for you to see in the [poor, little] Shulammite? [And they answered], As upon a dance before two armies or a dance of Mahanaim.

7 [THEN HER companions began noticing and commenting on the attractiveness of her person.] How beautiful are your feet in sandals, O queenly maiden! Your rounded limbs are like jeweled chains, the work of a master hand.

2Your body is like a round goblet, in which no mixed wine is wanting; your abdomen is like a heap of wheat set about with lilies.

3Your two breasts are like two fawns, the twins of a gazelle.

4Your neck is like the tower of ivory; your eyes as the pools of Heshbon, by the gate of Bath-rabbim; your nose is like the tower of Lebanon which looks toward Damascus.

5Your head *crowns you* like *Mount* Carmel, and the hair of your head like purple. [Then seeing the king watching the girl in absorbed admiration, the speaker added] The king is held captive in its tresses.

6[The king came forward, saying] How fair and how pleasant you are, O love, for delights!

7This your stature is like to a palm tree and your bosom to its clusters *of dates, declared the king;*

8I resolve I will climb the palm tree, I will grasp its branches. Let your breasts be as clusters of the *grape*vine, and the scent of your breath like apples,

9And your kisses like the best wine—. That goes down smoothly *and* sweetly for my beloved *shepherd!* [interrupted the Shulammite], *kisses* gliding over his lips while he sleeps.

10[She proudly said] I am my beloved's, and his desire is toward me! [John 10:28.]

11[She said] Come, my beloved! Let us go forth into the field; let us lodge in the villages. [Luke 14:33.]

12Let us go out early to the vineyards and see whether the vines have budded, whether the grape blossoms have opened and the pomegranates are in bloom. There I will give you my love.

13The mandrakes give forth fragrance, and over our doors are all manner of choice fruits, new and old, which I have laid up for you, O my beloved!

## New American Standard

11 "I went down to the orchard of nut trees
To see the blossoms of the valley,
To see whether the vine had budded
*Or* the pomegranates had bloomed.
12 "Before I was aware, my soul set me
*Over* the chariots of my noble people."

13¶ "[a]Come back, come back, O Shulammite;
Come back, come back, that we may gaze at you!"

¶ "[b]Why should you gaze at the Shulammite,
As at the dance of the two companies?

*Admiration by the Bridegroom*

7 "HOW BEAUTIFUL are your feet in sandals,
O prince's daughter!
The curves of your hips are like jewels,
The work of the hands of an artist.
2 "Your navel is *like* a round goblet
Which never lacks mixed wine;
Your belly is like a heap of wheat
Fenced about with lilies.
3 "Your two breasts are like two fawns,
Twins of a gazelle.
4 "Your neck is like a tower of ivory,
Your eyes *like* the pools in Heshbon
By the gate of Bath-rabbim;
Your nose is like the tower of Lebanon,
Which faces toward Damascus.
5 "Your head crowns you like Carmel,
And the flowing locks of your head are like purple threads;
*The* king is captivated by *your* tresses.
6 "How beautiful and how delightful you are,
*My* love, with *all* your charms!
7 "Your stature is like a palm tree,
And your breasts are *like its* clusters.
8 "I said, 'I will climb the palm tree,
I will take hold of its fruit stalks.'
Oh, may your breasts be like clusters of the vine,
And the fragrance of your breath like apples,
9 And your mouth like the best wine!"

¶ "[c]It goes *down* smoothly for my beloved,
Flowing gently *through* the lips of those who fall asleep.

*The Union of Love*

10¶ "I am my beloved's,
And his desire is for me.
11 "Come, my beloved, let us go out into the country,
Let us spend the night in the villages.
12 "Let us rise early *and go* to the vineyards;
Let us see whether the vine has budded
*And its* blossoms have opened,
*And whether* the pomegranates have bloomed.
There I will give you my love.
13 "The mandrakes have given forth fragrance;
And over our doors are all choice *fruits,*
Both new and old,
Which I have saved up for you, my beloved.

NAS [a] CHORUS [b] BRIDEGROOM [c] BRIDE

## New International

*Lover*

11 I went down to the grove of nut trees
to look at the new growth in the valley,
to see if the vines had budded
or the pomegranates were in bloom.
12 Before I realized it,
my desire set me among the royal chariots of my people.[d]

*Friends*

13 Come back, come back, O Shulammite;
come back, come back, that we may gaze on you!

*Lover*

Why would you gaze on the Shulammite
as on the dance of Mahanaim?

7 HOW BEAUTIFUL your sandaled feet,
O prince's daughter!
Your graceful legs are like jewels,
the work of a craftsman's hands.
2 Your navel is a rounded goblet
that never lacks blended wine.
Your waist is a mound of wheat
encircled by lilies.
3 Your breasts are like two fawns,
twins of a gazelle.
4 Your neck is like an ivory tower.
Your eyes are the pools of Heshbon
by the gate of Bath Rabbim.
Your nose is like the tower of Lebanon
looking toward Damascus.
5 Your head crowns you like Mount Carmel.
Your hair is like royal tapestry;
the king is held captive by its tresses.
6 How beautiful you are and how pleasing,
O love, with your delights!
7 Your stature is like that of the palm,
and your breasts like clusters of fruit.
8 I said, "I will climb the palm tree;
I will take hold of its fruit."
May your breasts be like the clusters of the vine,
the fragrance of your breath like apples,
9 and your mouth like the best wine.

*Beloved*

May the wine go straight to my lover,
flowing gently over lips and teeth.[e]
10 I belong to my lover,
and his desire is for me.
11 Come, my lover, let us go to the countryside,
let us spend the night in the villages.[f]
12 Let us go early to the vineyards
to see if the vines have budded,
if their blossoms have opened,
and if the pomegranates are in bloom—
there I will give you my love.
13 The mandrakes send out their fragrance,
and at our door is every delicacy,
both new and old,
that I have stored up for you, my lover.

NIV [d] 12 Or *among the chariots of Amminadab;* or *among the chariots of the people of the prince* [e] 9 Septuagint, Aquila, Vulgate and Syriac; Hebrew *lips of sleepers* [f] 11 Or *henna bushes*

## King James

**8** O THAT thou *wert* as my brother, that sucked the breasts of my mother! *when* I should find thee without, I would kiss thee; yea, I should not be despised.

2I would lead thee, *and* bring thee into my mother's house, *who* would instruct me: I would cause thee to drink of spiced wine of the juice of my pomegranate.

3His left hand *should be* under my head, and his right hand should embrace me.

4I charge you, O daughters of Jerusalem, that ye stir not up, nor awake *my* love, until he please.

5Who *is* this that cometh up from the wilderness, leaning upon her beloved? I raised thee up under the apple tree: there thy mother brought thee forth: there she brought thee forth *that* bare thee.

6¶ Set me as a seal upon thine heart, as a seal upon thine arm: for love *is* strong as death; jealousy *is* cruel as the grave: the coals thereof *are* coals of fire, *which hath* a most vehement flame.

7Many waters cannot quench love, neither can the floods drown it: if a man would give all the substance of his house for love, it would utterly be contemned.

8¶ We have a little sister, and she hath no breasts: what shall we do for our sister in the day when she shall be spoken for?

9If she *be* a wall, we will build upon her a palace of silver: and if she *be* a door, we will inclose her with boards of cedar.

10I *am* a wall, and my breasts like towers: then was I in his eyes as one that found favour.

11Solomon had a vineyard at Baal-hamon; he let out the vineyard unto keepers; every one for the fruit thereof was to bring a thousand *pieces* of silver.

12My vineyard, which *is* mine, *is* before me: thou, O Solomon, *must have* a thousand, and those that keep the fruit thereof two hundred.

13Thou that dwellest in the gardens, the companions hearken to thy voice: cause me to hear *it*.

## Amplified

**8** [LOOKING FORWARD to the shepherd's arrival, the eager girl pictures their meeting and says:] Oh, that you were as my brother, who nursed from the breasts of my mother! When I should find you without, I would kiss you, yes, and none would despise me *for it*. [Ps. 143:6.]

2I would lead you and bring you into the house of my mother, who would instruct me; I would cause you to drink of spiced wine and of the juice of my pomegranates. [Then musingly she added]

3Oh, that his left hand were under my head, and that his right hand embraced me! [Exod. 19:4; Deut. 33:27.]

4I adjure you, O daughters of Jerusalem, that you never [again attempt to] stir up or awaken love until it pleases.

5Who is this who comes up from the wilderness leaning upon her beloved? [And as they sighted the home of her childhood, the bride said] Under the apple tree I awakened you. There your mother gave you birth; there she was in travail who bore you.

6Set me as a seal upon your heart, as a seal upon your arm; for love is strong as death; jealousy is as hard *and* cruel as Sheol (the place of the dead). Its flashes are flashes of fire, a most vehement flame—a very flame of the Lord! [Isa. 49:16; Deut. 4:24; I Cor. 10:22.]

7Many waters cannot quench love, neither can floods drown it. If a man would offer all the goods of his house for love, he would be utterly scorned *and* despised.

8[Gathered with her family and the wedding guests in her mother's cottage, the bride said to her stepbrothers, When I was a little girl, you said] We have a little sister and she has no breasts. What shall we do for our sister on the day when she is spoken for in marriage?

9If she is a wall [discreet and womanly], we will build upon her a turret [a dowry] of silver; but if she is a door [bold and flirtatious], we will enclose her with boards of cedar.

10 *Well*, I am a wall *with* battlements, and my breasts like the towers of it. Then was I in *the king's* eyes as one [to be respected and to be allowed] to find peace.

11Solomon had a vineyard at Baal-hamon; he let out the vineyard to keepers; every one for the fruit of it was to bring him a thousand pieces of silver.

12You, O Solomon, can have your thousand, and those who tend the fruit of it two hundred; but my vineyard, which is mine [with all its radiant joy] is before me!

13O you who dwell in the gardens, your companions have been listening to your voice; now cause me to hear it.

## New American Standard

*The Lovers Speak*

**8** "OH THAT you were like a brother to me
Who nursed at my mother's breasts.
*If* I found you outdoors, I would kiss you;
No one would despise me, either.
2 "I would lead you *and* bring you
Into the house of my mother, who used to instruct me;
I would give you spiced wine to drink from the juice of my pomegranates.
3 "Let his left hand be under my head,
And his right hand embrace me."

4¶ " [a]I want you to swear, O daughters of Jerusalem,
Do not arouse or awaken *my* love,
Until she pleases."

5¶ " [b]Who is this coming up from the wilderness,
Leaning on her beloved?"

¶ "[c]Beneath the apple tree I awakened you;
There your mother was in labor with you,
There she was in labor *and* gave you birth.
6 "Put me like a [d]seal over your heart,
Like a seal on your arm.
For love is as strong as death,
Jealousy is as severe as Sheol;
Its flashes are flashes of fire,
The *very* flame of the LORD.
7 "Many waters cannot quench love,
Nor will rivers overflow it;
If a man were to give all the riches of his house for love,
It would be utterly despised."

8¶ "[e]We have a little sister,
And she has no breasts;
What shall we do for our sister
On the day when she is spoken for?
9 "If she is a wall,
We shall build on her a battlement of silver;
But if she is a door,
We shall barricade her with planks of cedar."

10¶ "[f]I was a wall, and my breasts were like towers;
Then I became in his eyes as one who finds peace.
11 "Solomon had a vineyard at Baal-hamon;
He entrusted the vineyard to caretakers;
Each one was to bring a thousand *shekels* of silver for its fruit.
12 "My very own vineyard is at my disposal;
The thousand *shekels* are for you, Solomon,
And two hundred are for those who take care of its fruit."
13 " [g]O you who sit in the gardens,
*My* companions are listening for your voice—
Let me hear it!"

**NAS** [a] BRIDEGROOM [b] CHORUS [c] BRIDEGROOM [d] Or, *signet*
[e] CHORUS [f] BRIDE [g] BRIDEGROOM

## New International

**8** IF ONLY you were to me like a brother,
who was nursed at my mother's breasts!
Then, if I found you outside,
I would kiss you,
and no one would despise me.
2I would lead you
and bring you to my mother's house—
she who has taught me.
I would give you spiced wine to drink,
the nectar of my pomegranates.
3His left arm is under my head
and his right arm embraces me.
4Daughters of Jerusalem, I charge you:
Do not arouse or awaken love
until it so desires.

*Friends*

5Who is this coming up from the desert
leaning on her lover?

*Beloved*

Under the apple tree I roused you;
there your mother conceived you,
there she who was in labor gave you birth.
6Place me like a seal over your heart,
like a seal on your arm;
for love is as strong as death,
its jealousy[h] unyielding as the grave.[i]
It burns like blazing fire,
like a mighty flame.[j]
7Many waters cannot quench love;
rivers cannot wash it away.
If one were to give
all the wealth of his house for love,
it[k] would be utterly scorned.

*Friends*

8We have a young sister,
and her breasts are not yet grown.
What shall we do for our sister
for the day she is spoken for?
9If she is a wall,
we will build towers of silver on her.
If she is a door,
we will enclose her with panels of cedar.

*Beloved*

10I am a wall,
and my breasts are like towers.
Thus I have become in his eyes
like one bringing contentment.
11Solomon had a vineyard in Baal Hamon;
he let out his vineyard to tenants.
Each was to bring for its fruit
a thousand shekels[l] of silver.
12But my own vineyard is mine to give;
the thousand shekels are for you, O Solomon,
and two hundred[m] are for those who tend its fruit.

*Lover*

13You who dwell in the gardens
with friends in attendance,
let me hear your voice!

**NIV** [h] *6* Or *ardor* [i] *6* Hebrew *Sheol* [j] *6* Or / *like the very flame of the* LORD
[k] *7* Or *he* [l] *11* That is, about 25 pounds (about 11.5 kilograms); also in verse 12 [m] *12* That is, about 5 pounds (about 2.3 kilograms)

## King James

14¶ Make haste, my beloved, and be thou like to a roe or to a
young hart upon the mountains of spices.

## Amplified

14[Joyfully the radiant bride turned to him, the one altogether
lovely, the chief among ten thousand to her soul, and with uncon-
cealed eagerness to begin her life of sweet companionship with
him, she answered] Make haste, my beloved, *and* come quickly,
like a gazelle or a young hart [and take me to our waiting home]
upon the mountains of spices!

## New American Standard

14 "[a]Hurry, my beloved,
And be like a gazelle or a young stag
On the mountains of spices."

## New International

*Beloved*

14Come away, my lover,
and be like a gazelle
or like a young stag
on the spice-laden mountains.

NAS [a] BRIDE

## King James

THE BOOK

OF THE PROPHET

# Isaiah

1 THE VISION of Isaiah the son of Amoz, which he saw concerning Judah and Jerusalem in the days of Uzziah, Jotham, Ahaz, *and* Hezekiah, kings of Judah.

2 Hear, O heavens, and give ear, O earth: for the LORD hath spoken, I have nourished and brought up children, and they have rebelled against me.

3 The ox knoweth his owner, and the ass his master's crib: *but* Israel doth not know, my people doth not consider.

4 Ah sinful nation, a people laden with iniquity, a seed of evildoers, children that are corrupters: they have forsaken the LORD, they have provoked the Holy One of Israel unto anger, they are gone away backward.

5 ¶ Why should ye be stricken any more? ye will revolt more and more: the whole head is sick, and the whole heart faint.

6 From the sole of the foot even unto the head *there is* no soundness in it; *but* wounds, and bruises, and putrifying sores: they have not been closed, neither bound up, neither mollified with ointment.

7 Your country *is* desolate, your cities *are* burned with fire: your land, strangers devour it in your presence, and *it is* desolate, as overthrown by strangers.

8 And the daughter of Zion is left as a cottage in a vineyard, as a lodge in a garden of cucumbers, as a besieged city.

9 Except the LORD of hosts had left unto us a very small remnant, we should have been as Sodom, *and* we should have been like unto Gomorrah.

10 ¶ Hear the word of the LORD, ye rulers of Sodom; give ear unto the law of our God, ye people of Gomorrah.

## Amplified

THE BOOK OF

# Isaiah

1 THE VISION [seen by spiritual perception] of Isaiah the son of Amoz, which he saw concerning Judah [the kingdom] and Jerusalem [its capital] in the days of Uzziah, Jotham, Ahaz, and Hezekiah, kings of Judah.

2 Hear, O heavens, and give ear, O earth, for the lord has spoken: I have nourished and brought up sons *and* have made them great and exalted, and they have rebelled against Me *and* broken away from Me.

3 The ox *instinctively* knows his owner, and the donkey his master's crib; but Israel does not know *or* recognize Me [as Lord], My people do not consider *or* understand.

4 Ah, sinful nation, a people loaded with iniquity, offspring of evildoers, sons who deal corruptly! They have forsaken the Lord, they have despised *and* shown contempt *and* provoked the Holy One of Israel to anger, they have become utterly estranged—alienated.

5 Why should you be stricken *and* punished any more [since it brings no correction]? You will revolt more and more. The whole head is sick, and the whole heart is faint (feeble, sick and nauseated).

6 From the sole of the foot even to the head there is no soundness *or* health in *the nation's body,* but wounds and bruises and fresh *and* bleeding stripes. They have not been pressed out *and* closed up, or bound up, or softened with oil. [No one has troubled to seek a remedy.]

7 [Because of your detestable disobedience] your country lies desolate, your cities are burned with fire; your land, strangers devour it in your *very* presence, and it is desolate, as overthrown by aliens.

8 And the daughter of Zion [Jerusalem] is left like a *deserted* booth in a vineyard, like a lodge in a garden of cucumbers, like a besieged city [spared, but in the midst of desolation].

9 Except the Lord of hosts had left us a very small remnant *of survivors,* we should have been as Sodom, and we should have been like Gomorrah. [Rom. 9:29.]

10 Hear [O Jerusalem] the word of the Lord, you rulers *or* judges of [another] Sodom! Give ear to the law *and* the teaching of our God, you people of [another] Gomorrah!

## New American Standard

# Isaiah

*Rebellion of God's People*

**1** THE VISION of Isaiah the son of Amoz, concerning Judah and Jerusalem which he saw during the reigns of Uzziah, Jotham, Ahaz, *and* Hezekiah, kings of Judah.

2 Listen, O heavens, and hear, O earth;
For the LORD speaks,
"Sons I have reared and brought up,
But they have revolted against Me.
3 "An ox knows its owner,
And a donkey its master's manger,
*But* Israel does not know,
My people do not understand."

4¶ Alas, sinful nation,
People weighed down with iniquity,
Offspring of evildoers,
Sons who act corruptly!
They have abandoned the LORD,
They have despised the Holy One of Israel,
They have turned away from Him.

5¶ Where will you be stricken again,
*As* you continue in *your* rebellion?
The whole head is sick,
And the whole heart is faint.
6 From the sole of the foot even to the head
There is nothing sound in it,
*Only* bruises, welts, and raw wounds,
Not pressed out or bandaged,
Nor softened with oil.

7¶ Your land is desolate,
Your cities are burned with fire,
Your fields—strangers are devouring them in your presence;
It is desolation, as overthrown by strangers.
8 And the daughter of Zion is left like a shelter in a vineyard,
Like a watchman's hut in a cucumber field, like a besieged city.
9 Unless the LORD of hosts
Had left us a few survivors,
We would be like Sodom,
We would be like Gomorrah.

*God Has Had Enough*

10¶ Hear the word of the LORD,
You rulers of Sodom;
Give ear to the instruction of our God,
You people of Gomorrah.

## New International

# Isaiah

**1** THE VISION concerning Judah and Jerusalem that Isaiah son of Amoz saw during the reigns of Uzziah, Jotham, Ahaz and Hezekiah, kings of Judah.

*A Rebellious Nation*

2Hear, O heavens! Listen, O earth!
For the LORD has spoken:
"I reared children and brought them up,
but they have rebelled against me.
3The ox knows his master,
the donkey his owner's manger,
but Israel does not know,
my people do not understand."
4Ah, sinful nation,
a people loaded with guilt,
a brood of evildoers,
children given to corruption!
They have forsaken the LORD;
they have spurned the Holy One of Israel
and turned their backs on him.

5Why should you be beaten anymore?
Why do you persist in rebellion?
Your whole head is injured,
your whole heart afflicted.
6From the sole of your foot to the top of your head
there is no soundness—
only wounds and welts
and open sores,
not cleansed or bandaged
or soothed with oil.

7Your country is desolate,
your cities burned with fire;
your fields are being stripped by foreigners
right before you,
laid waste as when overthrown by strangers.
8The Daughter of Zion is left
like a shelter in a vineyard,
like a hut in a field of melons,
like a city under siege.
9Unless the LORD Almighty
had left us some survivors,
we would have become like Sodom,
we would have been like Gomorrah.

10Hear the word of the LORD,
you rulers of Sodom;
listen to the law of our God,
you people of Gomorrah!

## King James

11To what purpose *is* the multitude of your sacrifices unto me?
saith the LORD: I am full of the burnt offerings of rams, and the fat
of fed beasts; and I delight not in the blood of bullocks, or of lambs,
or of he goats.
12When ye come to appear before me, who hath required this
at your hand, to tread my courts?
13Bring no more vain oblations; incense is an abomination unto
me; the new moons and sabbaths, the calling of assemblies, I
cannot away with; *it is* iniquity, even the solemn meeting.
14Your new moons and your appointed feasts my soul hateth:
they are a trouble unto me; I am weary to bear *them*.
15And when ye spread forth your hands, I will hide mine eyes
from you: yea, when ye make many prayers, I will not hear: your
hands are full of blood.
16¶ Wash you, make you clean; put away the evil of your doings
from before mine eyes; cease to do evil;
17Learn to do well; seek judgment, relieve the oppressed, judge
the fatherless, plead for the widow.
18Come now, and let us reason together, saith the LORD: though
your sins be as scarlet, they shall be as white as snow; though they
be red like crimson, they shall be as wool.
19If ye be willing and obedient, ye shall eat the good of the land:
20But if ye refuse and rebel, ye shall be devoured with the
sword: for the mouth of the LORD hath spoken *it*.
21¶ How is the faithful city become an harlot! it was full of
judgment; righteousness lodged in it; but now murderers.
22Thy silver is become dross, thy wine mixed with water:
23Thy princes *are* rebellious, and companions of thieves: every
one loveth gifts, and followeth after rewards: they judge not the
fatherless, neither doth the cause of the widow come unto them.
24Therefore saith the Lord, the LORD of hosts, the mighty One
of Israel, Ah, I will ease me of mine adversaries, and avenge me
of mine enemies:
25¶ And I will turn my hand upon thee, and purely purge away
thy dross, and take away all thy tin:
26And I will restore thy judges as at the first, and thy counsellors as at the beginning: afterward thou shalt be called, The city of
righteousness, the faithful city.

## Amplified

11To what purpose is the multitude of your sacrifices to Me
[unless they are the offering of the heart]? says the Lord; I have
had enough of the burnt offerings of rams, and the fat of fed beasts
[without obedience], and I do not delight in the blood of bulls, or
of lambs, or of he-goats [without righteousness].
12When you come to appear before Me, who requires of you
that your [unholy feet] trample My courts?
13Bring no more offerings of vanity—emptiness, falsity, vainglory *and* futility; [your hollow offering of] incense is an abomination to Me; the new moons and sabbaths, the calling of assemblies
I cannot endure, *it is* iniquity *and* profanation, even the solemn
meeting.
14Your new moons and your *hypocritical* appointed feasts My
soul hates; they are an oppressive burden to Me, I am weary of
bearing them.
15And when you spread forth your hands *in prayer, imploring
help*, I will hide My eyes from you; even though you make many
prayers, I will not hear; your hands are full of blood!
16Wash yourselves; make yourselves clean; put away the evil of
your doings from before My eyes; cease to do evil,
17Learn to do right; seek justice, relieve the oppressed *and* correct the oppressor; defend the fatherless, plead for the widow.
18Come now, and let us reason together, says the Lord; though
your sins be as scarlet, they shall be as white as snow; though they
be red like crimson, they shall be as wool.
19If you are willing and obedient, you shall eat the good of the
land;
20But if you refuse and rebel, you will be devoured by the
sword, for the mouth of the Lord has spoken it.
21How the faithful city has become an *idolatrous* harlot, she who
was full of justice! Uprightness *and* right standing with God *once*
lodged in her, but now murderers.
22Your silver is become dross, your wine *is* mixed with water.
23Your princes are rebels and companions of thieves; every one
loves bribes and runs after compensation *and* rewards. They judge
not for the fatherless *nor* defend them, neither does the cause of
the widow come to them [for they delay or turn a deaf ear].
24Therefore says the Lord, the Lord of hosts, the mighty One
of Israel, Ah, I will appease Myself of My adversaries, and avenge
Myself of My enemies.
25And I will bring My hand again upon you, and thoroughly
purge away your dross [as with lye], and take away all your tin *or*
alloy.
26And I will restore your judges as at the first, and your counselors as at the beginning; afterward you shall be called the city of
righteousness, a faithful city.

## New American Standard

11 "What are your multiplied sacrifices to Me?"
Says the LORD.
"I have had enough of burnt offerings of rams,
And the fat of fed cattle.
And I take no pleasure in the blood of bulls, lambs, or
goats.
12 "When you come to appear before Me,
Who requires of you this trampling of My courts?
13 "Bring your worthless offerings no longer,
Incense is an abomination to Me.
New moon and sabbath, the calling of assemblies—
I cannot endure iniquity and the solemn assembly.
14 "I hate your new moon *festivals* and your appointed
feasts,
They have become a burden to Me.
I am weary of bearing *them.*
15 "So when you spread out your hands *in prayer,*
I will hide My eyes from you,
Yes, even though you multiply prayers,
I will not listen.
Your hands are covered with blood.
**16**¶ "Wash yourselves, make yourselves clean;
Remove the evil of your deeds from My sight.
Cease to do evil,
17 Learn to do good;
Seek justice,
Reprove the ruthless;
Defend the orphan,
Plead for the widow.

*"Let Us Reason"*

**18**¶ "Come now, and let us reason together,"
Says the LORD,
"Though your sins are as scarlet,
They will be as white as snow;
Though they are red like crimson,
They will be like wool.
19 "If you consent and obey,
You will eat the best of the land;
20 "But if you refuse and rebel,
You will be devoured by the sword."
Truly, the mouth of the LORD has spoken.

*Zion Corrupted, to be Redeemed*

**21**¶ How the faithful city has become a harlot,
She *who* was full of justice!
Righteousness once lodged in her,
But now murderers.
22 Your silver has become dross,
Your drink diluted with water.
23 Your rulers are rebels,
And companions of thieves;
Everyone loves a bribe,
And chases after rewards.
They do not defend the orphan,
Nor does the widow's plea come before them.

**24**¶ Therefore the Lord GOD of hosts,
The Mighty One of Israel declares,
"Ah, I will be relieved of My adversaries,
And avenge Myself on My foes.
25 "I will also turn My hand against you,
And will smelt away your dross as with lye,
And will remove all your alloy.
26 "Then I will restore your judges as at the first,
And your counselors as at the beginning;
After that you will be called the city of righteousness,
A faithful city."

## New International

11"The multitude of your sacrifices—
what are they to me?" says the LORD.
"I have more than enough of burnt offerings,
of rams and the fat of fattened animals;
I have no pleasure
in the blood of bulls and lambs and goats.
12When you come to appear before me,
who has asked this of you,
this trampling of my courts?
13Stop bringing meaningless offerings!
Your incense is detestable to me.
New Moons, Sabbaths and convocations—
I cannot bear your evil assemblies.
14Your New Moon festivals and your appointed feasts
my soul hates.
They have become a burden to me;
I am weary of bearing them.
15When you spread out your hands in prayer,
I will hide my eyes from you;
even if you offer many prayers,
I will not listen.
Your hands are full of blood;
16 wash and make yourselves clean.
Take your evil deeds
out of my sight!
Stop doing wrong,
17 learn to do right!
Seek justice,
encourage the oppressed.[a]
Defend the cause of the fatherless,
plead the case of the widow.
18"Come now, let us reason together,"
says the LORD.
"Though your sins are like scarlet,
they shall be as white as snow;
though they are red as crimson,
they shall be like wool.
19If you are willing and obedient,
you will eat the best from the land;
20but if you resist and rebel,
you will be devoured by the sword."
For the mouth of the LORD has spoken.

21See how the faithful city
has become a harlot!
She once was full of justice;
righteousness used to dwell in her—
but now murderers!
22Your silver has become dross,
your choice wine is diluted with water.
23Your rulers are rebels,
companions of thieves;
they all love bribes
and chase after gifts.
They do not defend the cause of the fatherless;
the widow's case does not come before them.
24Therefore the Lord, the LORD Almighty,
the Mighty One of Israel, declares:
"Ah, I will get relief from my foes
and avenge myself on my enemies.
25I will turn my hand against you;
I will thoroughly purge away your dross
and remove all your impurities.
26I will restore your judges as in days of old,
your counselors as at the beginning.
Afterward you will be called
the City of Righteousness,
the Faithful City."

NIV [a] *17 Or / rebuke the oppressor*

## King James

27Zion shall be redeemed with judgment, and her converts with righteousness.
28¶ And the destruction of the transgressors and of the sinners *shall be* together, and they that forsake the LORD shall be consumed.
29For they shall be ashamed of the oaks which ye have desired, and ye shall be confounded for the gardens that ye have chosen.
30For ye shall be as an oak whose leaf fadeth, and as a garden that hath no water.
31And the strong shall be as tow, and the maker of it as a spark, and they shall both burn together, and none shall quench *them*.

**2** THE WORD that Isaiah the son of Amoz saw concerning Judah and Jerusalem.
2And it shall come to pass in the last days, *that* the mountain of the LORD's house shall be established in the top of the mountains, and shall be exalted above the hills; and all nations shall flow unto it.
3And many people shall go and say, Come ye, and let us go up to the mountain of the LORD, to the house of the God of Jacob; and he will teach us of his ways, and we will walk in his paths: for out of Zion shall go forth the law, and the word of the LORD from Jerusalem.
4And he shall judge among the nations, and shall rebuke many people: and they shall beat their swords into plowshares, and their spears into pruninghooks: nation shall not lift up sword against nation, neither shall they learn war any more.
5O house of Jacob, come ye, and let us walk in the light of the LORD.
6¶ Therefore thou hast forsaken thy people the house of Jacob, because they be replenished from the east, and *are* soothsayers like the Philistines, and they please themselves in the children of strangers.
7Their land also is full of silver and gold, neither *is there any* end of their treasures; their land is also full of horses, neither *is there any* end of their chariots:
8Their land also is full of idols; they worship the work of their own hands, that which their own fingers have made:
9And the mean man boweth down, and the great man humbleth himself: therefore forgive them not.
10¶ Enter into the rock, and hide thee in the dust, for fear of the LORD, and for the glory of his majesty.
11The lofty looks of man shall be humbled, and the haughtiness of men shall be bowed down, and the LORD alone shall be exalted in that day.

## Amplified

27Zion shall be redeemed with justice, and her [returned] converts with righteousness—uprightness and right standing with God.
28But the crushing *and* destruction of rebels and sinners shall be together, and they that forsake the Lord shall be consumed.
29For you will be ashamed [of the folly and degradation] of the oak *or* terebinth trees in which you found *idolatrous* pleasure, and you will blush with shame for the [idolatrous worship which you practice in the passion inflaming] gardens which you have chosen.
30For you shall be as an oak *or* terebinth whose leaf withers, and as a garden that has no water.
31And the strong shall become as tow, and his work as a spark, and they shall both burn together, with none to quench them.

**2** THE WORD which Isaiah the son of Amoz saw *revealed* concerning Judah and Jerusalem.
2It shall come to pass in the latter days that the mountain of the Lord's house shall be (firmly) established as the highest of the mountains, and shall be exalted above the hills, and all nations shall flow to it.
3And many people shall come and say, Come, let us go up to the mountain of the Lord, to the house of the God of Jacob; that He may teach us His ways and that we may walk in His paths. For out of Zion shall go forth the law *and* instruction, and the word of the Lord from Jerusalem.
4And He shall judge between the nations, and shall decide [disputes] for many peoples; and they shall beat their swords into plowshares, and their spears into pruning hooks; nation shall not lift up sword against nation, neither shall they learn war any more.
5O house of Jacob, come, let us walk in the light of the Lord.
6Surely [Lord] You have rejected *and* forsaken your people, the house of Jacob, because they are filled with *customs* from the east and with soothsayers *who foretell* like the Philistines; also they strike hands *and* make pledges *and* agreements with the children of aliens. [Deut. 18:9-12.]
7Their land also is full of silver and gold, neither is there any end of their treasures; their land is also full of horses, neither is there any end to their chariots. [Deut. 17:14-17.]
8Their land also is full of idols; they worship the work of their own hands, what their own fingers have made.
9And the common man is bowed down [before idols], also the great man is brought low *and* humbles himself; therefore forgive them not [O Lord].
10Enter into the rock, and hide yourself in the dust from before the terror of the Lord, and from the glory of His majesty.
11The proud looks of man shall be brought low, and the haughtiness of men shall be humbled, and the Lord alone shall be exalted in that day.

## New American Standard

27¶ Zion will be redeemed with justice,
And her repentant ones with righteousness.
28 But transgressors and sinners will be crushed together,
And those who forsake the LORD shall come to an end.
29 Surely, you will be ashamed of the oaks which you
have desired,
And you will be embarrassed at the gardens which you
have chosen.
30 For you will be like an oak whose leaf fades away,
Or as a garden that has no water.
31 And the strong man will become tinder,
His work also a spark.
Thus they shall both burn together,
And there will be none to quench *them.*

*God's Universal Reign*

2 THE WORD which Isaiah the son of Amoz saw concerning
Judah and Jerusalem.
2 Now it will come about that
In the last days,
The mountain of the house of the LORD
Will be established as the chief of the mountains,
And will be raised above the hills;
And all the nations will stream to it.
3 And many peoples will come and say,
"Come, let us go up to the mountain of the LORD,
To the house of the God of Jacob;
That He may teach us concerning His ways,
And that we may walk in His paths."
For the law will go forth from Zion,
And the word of the LORD from Jerusalem.
4 And He will judge between the nations,
And will render decisions for many peoples;
And they will hammer their swords into plowshares,
and their spears into pruning hooks.
Nation will not lift up sword against nation,
And never again will they learn war.

5¶ Come, house of Jacob, and let us walk in the light of
the LORD.
6 For Thou hast abandoned Thy people, the house of
Jacob,
Because they are filled *with influences* from the east,
And *they are* soothsayers like the Philistines,
And they strike *bargains* with the children of foreigners.
7 Their land has also been filled with silver and gold,
And there is no end to their treasures;
Their land has also been filled with horses,
And there is no end to their chariots.
8 Their land has also been filled with idols;
They worship the work of their hands,
That which their fingers have made.
9 So the *common* man has been humbled,
And the man *of importance* has been abased,
But do not forgive them.
10 Enter the rock and hide in the dust
From the terror of the LORD and from the splendor of
His majesty.
11 The proud look of man will be abased,
And the loftiness of man will be humbled,
And the LORD alone will be exalted in that day.

## New International

27Zion will be redeemed with justice,
her penitent ones with righteousness.
28But rebels and sinners will both be broken,
and those who forsake the LORD will perish.

29"You will be ashamed because of the sacred oaks
in which you have delighted;
you will be disgraced because of the gardens
that you have chosen.
30You will be like an oak with fading leaves,
like a garden without water.
31The mighty man will become tinder
and his work a spark;
both will burn together,
with no one to quench the fire."

*The Mountain of the LORD*

2 THIS IS what Isaiah son of Amoz saw concerning Judah and
Jerusalem:
2In the last days

the mountain of the LORD's temple will be established
as chief among the mountains;
it will be raised above the hills,
and all nations will stream to it.

3Many peoples will come and say,

"Come, let us go up to the mountain of the LORD,
to the house of the God of Jacob.
He will teach us his ways,
so that we may walk in his paths."
The law will go out from Zion,
the word of the LORD from Jerusalem.
4He will judge between the nations
and will settle disputes for many peoples.
They will beat their swords into plowshares
and their spears into pruning hooks.
Nation will not take up sword against nation,
nor will they train for war anymore.

5Come, O house of Jacob,
let us walk in the light of the LORD.

*The Day of the LORD*

6You have abandoned your people,
the house of Jacob.
They are full of superstitions from the East;
they practice divination like the Philistines
and clasp hands with pagans.
7Their land is full of silver and gold;
there is no end to their treasures.
Their land is full of horses;
there is no end to their chariots.
8Their land is full of idols;
they bow down to the work of their hands,
to what their fingers have made.
9So man will be brought low
and mankind humbled—
do not forgive them.[a]

10Go into the rocks,
hide in the ground
from dread of the LORD
and the splendor of his majesty!
11The eyes of the arrogant man will be humbled
and the pride of men brought low;
the LORD alone will be exalted in that day.

NIV [a] 9 Or *not raise them up*

## King James

12 For the day of the LORD of hosts *shall be* upon every *one that is* proud and lofty, and upon every *one that is* lifted up; and he shall be brought low:

13 And upon all the cedars of Lebanon, *that are* high and lifted up, and upon all the oaks of Bashan,

14 And upon all the high mountains, and upon all the hills *that are* lifted up,

15 And upon every high tower, and upon every fenced wall,

16 And upon all the ships of Tarshish, and upon all pleasant pictures.

17 And the loftiness of man shall be bowed down, and the haughtiness of men shall be made low: and the LORD alone shall be exalted in that day.

18 And the idols he shall utterly abolish.

19 And they shall go into the holes of the rocks, and into the caves of the earth, for fear of the LORD, and for the glory of his majesty, when he ariseth to shake terribly the earth.

20 In that day a man shall cast his idols of silver, and his idols of gold, which they made *each one* for himself to worship, to the moles and to the bats;

21 To go into the clefts of the rocks, and into the tops of the ragged rocks, for fear of the LORD, and for the glory of his majesty, when he ariseth to shake terribly the earth.

22 Cease ye from man, whose breath *is* in his nostrils: for wherein is he to be accounted of?

**3** FOR, BEHOLD, the Lord, the LORD of hosts, doth take away from Jerusalem and from Judah the stay and the staff, the whole stay of bread, and the whole stay of water,

2 The mighty man, and the man of war, the judge, and the prophet, and the prudent, and the ancient,

3 The captain of fifty, and the honourable man, and the counsellor, and the cunning artificer, and the eloquent orator.

4 And I will give children *to be* their princes, and babes shall rule over them.

5 And the people shall be oppressed, every one by another, and every one by his neighbour: the child shall behave himself proudly against the ancient, and the base against the honourable.

6 When a man shall take hold of his brother of the house of his father, *saying,* Thou hast clothing, be thou our ruler, and *let* this ruin *be* under thy hand:

7 In that day shall he swear, saying, I will not be an healer; for in my house *is* neither bread nor clothing: make me not a ruler of the people.

## Amplified

12 For there shall be a day of the Lord of hosts against all that is proud and haughty and against all that is lifted up, and it shall be brought low; [Zeph. 2:3; Mal. 4:1.]

13 [The wrath of God will begin by coming down] against all the cedars of Lebanon [west of the Jordan] that are high and lifted up, and against all the oaks of Bashan [east of the Jordan];

14 And [after that] against all the high mountains and all the hills that are lifted up,

15 And against every high tower and every fenced wall,

16 And against all the ships of Tarshish and all the picturesque *and* desirable imagery [designed for mere ornament and luxury].

17 Then the loftiness of man shall be bowed down, and the haughtiness of men shall be brought low, and the Lord alone shall be exalted in that day.

18 And the idols shall utterly pass away—be abolished.

19 Then shall *the stricken* [deprived of all in which they had trusted] go into the caves of the rocks and into the holes of the earth, from before the terror *and* dread of the Lord, and from the glory of His majesty, when He arises to shake mightily *and* terribly the earth. [Luke 23:30.]

20 In that day men shall cast away to the moles and to the bats their idols of silver and their idols of gold, which they made for themselves to worship,

21 To go into the caverns of the rocks and into the clefts of the ragged rocks, from before the terror *and* dread of the Lord, and from before the glory of His majesty, when He rises to shake mightily *and* terribly the earth.

22 Cease to trust in [weak, frail and dying] man, whose breath is in his nostrils [for so short a time]; in what sense can he be counted as having intrinsic worth?

**3** FOR, BEHOLD, the Lord, the Lord of hosts, is taking away from Jerusalem and from Judah the stay and the staff—every kind of prop—the whole stay of bread, and the whole stay of water,

2 The mighty man and the man of war, the judge *and* the *professional* prophet, the one who foretells by divination and the old man,

3 The captain of fifty and the man of rank, the counselor and the expert craftsman and the skillful enchanter.

4 And I will make boys their princes, and with childishness shall they rule over them—with outrage [instead of justice].

5 And the people shall be oppressed, every one by another, and every one by his neighbor; the child shall behave himself proudly *and* with insolence against the old man, and the lowborn against the honorable *person* [of rank].

6 When a man shall take hold of his brother in the house of his father, saying, You have a robe, you shall be our judge *and* ruler, and this heap of ruins shall be under your control;

7 In that day he will answer, saying, I will not be a binder-up *and* a healer— [a]I am not a physician; for in my house is neither bread nor clothing; you shall not make me judge *and* ruler of the people.

**AMP** [a] The Vulgate (Latin) rendering.

## New American Standard

*A Day of Reckoning Coming*

12¶ For the LORD of hosts will have a day of reckoning
Against everyone who is proud and lofty,
And against everyone who is lifted up,
That he may be abased.
13 And *it will be* against all the cedars of Lebanon that are lofty and lifted up,
Against all the oaks of Bashan,
14 Against all the lofty mountains,
Against all the hills that are lifted up,
15 Against every high tower,
Against every fortified wall,
16 Against all the ships of Tarshish,
And against all the beautiful craft.
17 And the pride of man will be humbled,
And the loftiness of men will be abased,
And the LORD alone will be exalted in that day.
18 But the idols will completely vanish.
19 And *men* will go into caves of the rocks,
And into holes of the ground
Before the terror of the LORD,
And before the splendor of His majesty,
When He arises to make the earth tremble.
20 In that day men will cast away to the moles and the bats
Their idols of silver and their idols of gold,
Which they made for themselves to worship,
21 In order to go into the caverns of the rocks and the clefts of the cliffs,
Before the terror of the LORD and the splendor of His majesty,
When He arises to make the earth tremble.
22 Stop regarding man, whose breath *of life* is in his nostrils;
For why should he be esteemed?

*God Will Remove the Leaders*

3 FOR BEHOLD, the Lord GOD of hosts is going to remove from Jerusalem and Judah
Both supply and support, the whole supply of bread,
And the whole supply of water;
2 The mighty man and the warrior,
The judge and the prophet,
The diviner and the elder,
3 The captain of fifty and the honorable man,
The counselor and the expert artisan,
And the skillful enchanter.
4 And I will make mere lads their princes
And capricious children will rule over them,
5 And the people will be oppressed,
Each one by another, and each one by his neighbor;
The youth will storm against the elder,
And the inferior against the honorable.
6 When a man lays hold of his brother in his father's house, *saying,*
"You have a cloak, you shall be our ruler,
And these ruins will be under your charge,"
7 On that day will he protest, saying,
"I will not be *your* healer,
For in my house there is neither bread nor cloak;
You should not appoint me ruler of the people."

## New International

12The LORD Almighty has a day in store
for all the proud and lofty,
for all that is exalted
(and they will be humbled),
13for all the cedars of Lebanon, tall and lofty,
and all the oaks of Bashan,
14for all the towering mountains
and all the high hills,
15for every lofty tower
and every fortified wall,
16for every trading ship[b]
and every stately vessel.
17The arrogance of man will be brought low
and the pride of men humbled;
the LORD alone will be exalted in that day,
18 and the idols will totally disappear.
19Men will flee to caves in the rocks
and to holes in the ground
from dread of the LORD
and the splendor of his majesty,
when he rises to shake the earth.
20In that day men will throw away
to the rodents and bats
their idols of silver and idols of gold,
which they made to worship.
21They will flee to caverns in the rocks
and to the overhanging crags
from dread of the LORD
and the splendor of his majesty,
when he rises to shake the earth.
22Stop trusting in man,
who has but a breath in his nostrils.
Of what account is he?

*Judgment on Jerusalem and Judah*

3 SEE NOW, the Lord,
the LORD Almighty,
is about to take from Jerusalem and Judah
both supply and support:
all supplies of food and all supplies of water,
2 the hero and warrior,
the judge and prophet,
the soothsayer and elder,
3the captain of fifty and man of rank,
the counselor, skilled craftsman and clever enchanter.

4I will make boys their officials;
mere children will govern them.
5People will oppress each other—
man against man, neighbor against neighbor.
The young will rise up against the old,
the base against the honorable.

6A man will seize one of his brothers
at his father's home, and say,
"You have a cloak, you be our leader;
take charge of this heap of ruins!"
7But in that day he will cry out,
"I have no remedy.
I have no food or clothing in my house;
do not make me the leader of the people."

NIV [b] 16 Hebrew *every ship of Tarshish*

## King James

8 For Jerusalem is ruined, and Judah is fallen: because their tongue and their doings *are* against the LORD, to provoke the eyes of his glory.

9 ¶ The show of their countenance doth witness against them; and they declare their sin as Sodom, they hide *it* not. Woe unto their soul! for they have rewarded evil unto themselves.

10 Say ye to the righteous, that *it shall be* well *with him:* for they shall eat the fruit of their doings.

11 Woe unto the wicked! *it shall be* ill *with him:* for the reward of his hands shall be given him.

12 ¶ *As for* my people, children *are* their oppressors, and women rule over them. O my people, they which lead thee cause *thee* to err, and destroy the way of thy paths.

13 The LORD standeth up to plead, and standeth to judge the people.

14 The LORD will enter into judgment with the ancients of his people, and the princes thereof: for ye have eaten up the vineyard; the spoil of the poor *is* in your houses.

15 What mean ye *that* ye beat my people to pieces, and grind the faces of the poor? saith the Lord GOD of hosts.

16 ¶ Moreover the LORD saith, Because the daughters of Zion are haughty, and walk with stretched forth necks and wanton eyes, walking and mincing *as* they go, and making a tinkling with their feet:

17 Therefore the Lord will smite with a scab the crown of the head of the daughters of Zion, and the LORD will discover their secret parts.

18 In that day the Lord will take away the bravery of *their* tinkling ornaments *about their feet,* and *their* cauls, and *their* round tires like the moon,

19 The chains, and the bracelets, and the mufflers,

20 The bonnets, and the ornaments of the legs, and the headbands, and the tablets, and the earrings,

21 The rings, and nose jewels,

22 The changeable suits of apparel, and the mantles, and the wimples, and the crisping pins,

23 The glasses, and the fine linen, and the hoods, and the veils.

24 And it shall come to pass, *that* instead of sweet smell there shall be stink; and instead of a girdle a rent; and instead of well set hair baldness; and instead of a stomacher a girding of sackcloth; *and* burning instead of beauty.

25 Thy men shall fall by the sword, and thy mighty in the war.

26 And her gates shall lament and mourn; and she *being* desolate shall sit upon the ground.

## Amplified

8 For Jerusalem is ruined, and Judah is fallen; because their speech and their deeds are against the Lord, to provoke the eyes of His glory *and* defy His glorious presence.

9 Their respecting of persons *and* showing of partiality witnesses against them; they proclaim their sin like Sodom, they do not hide it. Woe to them! For they have brought evil *as a reward* upon themselves.

10 Say to the righteous that it shall be well with them, for they shall eat the fruit of their deeds.

11 Woe to the wicked! It shall be ill with him, for what his hands have done shall be done to him.

12 As for My people, children are their oppressors, and women rule over them. O My people, your leaders cause you to err, and confuse (destroy and swallow up) the course of your paths.

13 The Lord stands up to contend, and stands to judge the peoples *and His* people.

14 The Lord will enter into judgment with the elders of His people and their princes; for [by your exactions and oppressions you have robbed the people and ruined the country] you have devoured the vineyard; the spoil of the poor is in your houses.

15 What do you mean by crushing My people and grinding the face of the poor? says the Lord God of hosts.

16 Moreover the Lord said, Because the daughters of Zion are haughty and walk with outstretched necks and with undisciplined (flirtatious and alluring) eyes, tripping along with mincing *and* affected gait, and making a tinkling noise with [the anklets on] their feet;

17 Therefore the Lord will smite with a scab the crown of the heads of the daughters of Zion [making them bald], and the Lord will cause them to be [taken as captives and suffer the indignity of being] stripped naked.

18 In that day the Lord will take away the finery of their tinkling anklets, the caps of network, the crescent head ornaments,

19 The pendants, the bracelets *or* chains, and the spangled face veils *and* scarfs,

20 The headbands, the short stepping-chains [attached from one foot to the other to insure a measured gait], the sashes, the perfume boxes, the amulets *or* charms [suspended from the ears or neck],

21 The signet rings and nose rings,

22 The festal robes, the cloaks, the stoles *and* shawls, and the handbags,

23 The hand mirrors, the fine linen [undergarments], the turbans, and the [whole-body-enveloping] veils.

24 And it shall come to pass that instead of the sweet odor of spices there shall be the stench of rottenness; and instead of a girdle, a rope; and instead of well-set hair, baldness; and instead of a rich robe, a girding of sackcloth; *and* searing [of captives by the scorching heat] instead of beauty.

25 Your men shall fall by the sword, and your mighty men in battle.

26 And [Jerusalem's] gates shall lament and mourn [as those who wail for the dead]; and she, being ruined *and* desolate, shall sit upon the ground.

## New American Standard

8 For Jerusalem has stumbled, and Judah has fallen,
Because their speech and their actions are against the LORD,
To rebel against His glorious presence.
9 The expression of their faces bears witness against them.
And they display their sin like Sodom;
They do not *even* conceal *it*.
Woe to them!
For they have brought evil on themselves.
10 Say to the righteous that *it will go* well *with them*,
For they will eat the fruit of their actions.
11 Woe to the wicked! *It will go* badly *with him*,
For what he deserves will be done to him.
12 O My people! Their oppressors are children,
And women rule over them.
O My people! Those who guide you lead *you* astray,
And confuse the direction of your paths.

*God Will Judge*

13¶ The LORD arises to contend,
And stands to judge the people.
14 The LORD enters into judgment with the elders and princes of His people,
"It is you who have devoured the vineyard;
The plunder of the poor is in your houses.
15 "What do you mean by crushing My people,
And grinding the face of the poor?"
Declares the Lord GOD of hosts.

*Judah's Women Denounced*

16¶ Moreover, the LORD said, "Because the daughters of Zion are proud,
And walk with heads held high and seductive eyes,
And go along with mincing steps,
And tinkle the bangles on their feet,
17 Therefore the Lord will afflict the scalp of the daughters of Zion with scabs,
And the LORD will make their foreheads bare."
18In that day the Lord will take away the beauty of *their* anklets, headbands, crescent ornaments,
19dangling earrings, bracelets, veils,
20headdresses, ankle chains, sashes, perfume boxes, amulets,
21finger rings, nose rings,
22festal robes, outer tunics, cloaks, money purses,
23hand mirrors, undergarments, turbans, and veils.
24 Now it will come about that instead of sweet perfume there will be putrefaction;
Instead of a belt, a rope;
Instead of well-set hair, a plucked-out scalp;
Instead of fine clothes, a donning of sackcloth;
And branding instead of beauty.
25 Your men will fall by the sword,
And your mighty ones in battle.
26 And her gates will lament and mourn;
And deserted she will sit on the ground.

## New International

8Jerusalem staggers,
Judah is falling;
their words and deeds are against the LORD,
defying his glorious presence.
9The look on their faces testifies against them;
they parade their sin like Sodom;
they do not hide it.
Woe to them!
They have brought disaster upon themselves.
10Tell the righteous it will be well with them,
for they will enjoy the fruit of their deeds.
11Woe to the wicked! Disaster is upon them!
They will be paid back for what their hands have done.

12Youths oppress my people,
women rule over them.
O my people, your guides lead you astray;
they turn you from the path.

13The LORD takes his place in court;
he rises to judge the people.
14The LORD enters into judgment
against the elders and leaders of his people:
"It is you who have ruined my vineyard;
the plunder from the poor is in your houses.
15What do you mean by crushing my people
and grinding the faces of the poor?"
declares the Lord, the LORD Almighty.

16The LORD says,
"The women of Zion are haughty,
walking along with outstretched necks,
flirting with their eyes,
tripping along with mincing steps,
with ornaments jingling on their ankles.
17Therefore the Lord will bring sores on the heads of the women of Zion;
the LORD will make their scalps bald."

18In that day the Lord will snatch away their finery: the bangles
and headbands and crescent necklaces, 19the earrings and bracelets and veils, 20the headdresses and ankle chains and sashes, the
perfume bottles and charms, 21the signet rings and nose rings,
22the fine robes and the capes and cloaks, the purses 23and mirrors,
and the linen garments and tiaras and shawls.

24Instead of fragrance there will be a stench;
instead of a sash, a rope;
instead of well-dressed hair, baldness;
instead of fine clothing, sackcloth;
instead of beauty, branding.
25Your men will fall by the sword,
your warriors in battle.
26The gates of Zion will lament and mourn;
destitute, she will sit on the ground.

## King James

**4** AND IN that day seven women shall take hold of one man, saying, We will eat our own bread, and wear our own apparel: only let us be called by thy name, to take away our reproach.

2 In that day shall the branch of the LORD be beautiful and glorious, and the fruit of the earth *shall be* excellent and comely for them that are escaped of Israel.

3 And it shall come to pass, *that he that is* left in Zion, and *he that* remaineth in Jerusalem, shall be called holy, *even* every one that is written among the living in Jerusalem:

4 When the Lord shall have washed away the filth of the daughters of Zion, and shall have purged the blood of Jerusalem from the midst thereof by the spirit of judgment, and by the spirit of burning.

5 And the LORD will create upon every dwellingplace of mount Zion, and upon her assemblies, a cloud and smoke by day, and the shining of a flaming fire by night: for upon all the glory *shall be* a defence.

6 And there shall be a tabernacle for a shadow in the daytime from the heat, and for a place of refuge, and for a covert from storm and from rain.

**5** NOW WILL I sing to my wellbeloved a song of my beloved touching his vineyard. My wellbeloved hath a vineyard in a very fruitful hill:

2 And he fenced it, and gathered out the stones thereof, and planted it with the choicest vine, and built a tower in the midst of it, and also made a winepress therein: and he looked that it should bring forth grapes, and it brought forth wild grapes.

3 And now, O inhabitants of Jerusalem, and men of Judah, judge, I pray you, betwixt me and my vineyard.

4 What could have been done more to my vineyard, that I have not done in it? wherefore, when I looked that it should bring forth grapes, brought it forth wild grapes?

5 And now go to; I will tell you what I will do to my vineyard: I will take away the hedge thereof, and it shall be eaten up; *and* break down the wall thereof, and it shall be trodden down:

6 And I will lay it waste: it shall not be pruned, nor digged; but there shall come up briers and thorns: I will also command the clouds that they rain no rain upon it.

7 For the vineyard of the LORD of hosts *is* the house of Israel, and the men of Judah his pleasant plant: and he looked for judgment, but behold oppression; for righteousness, but behold a cry.

8 ¶ Woe unto them that join house to house, *that* lay field to field, till *there be* no place, that they may be placed alone in the midst of the earth!

## Amplified

**4** AND IN that day [a]seven women shall take hold of one man, saying, We will eat our own bread and provide our own apparel, only let us be called by your name to take away our reproach [of being unmarried].

2 In that day the Branch of the Lord shall be beautiful and glorious, and the fruit of the land shall be excellent and lovely to those who have escaped of Israel. [Jer. 23:5; 33:15; Zech. 3:8; 6:12.]

3 And he who is left in Zion and remains in Jerusalem will be called holy, everyone who is recorded for life in Jerusalem *and* for [b] *eternal* life, [Phil. 4:3; Joel 3:17.]

4 After the Lord has washed away the *moral* filth of the daughters of Zion [pride, vanity, haughtiness], and shall have purged the blood stains of Jerusalem from the midst of it by the spirit *and* blast of judgment and by the spirit *and blast* of burning *and* sifting.

5 And the Lord will create over the whole site, over every dwelling place of Mount Zion and over her assemblies, a cloud and smoke by day, and the shining of a flaming fire by night; for over all the glory shall be a canopy—a defense [of divine love and protection].

6 And there shall be a pavilion for a shade in the daytime from the heat, and for a place of refuge and a shelter from storm and from rain.

**5** LET ME sing of *and* for my greatly Beloved [and as His representative] a tender song of my Beloved [God, the Son] concerning His vineyard [His chosen people]. My greatly Beloved had a vineyard on a very fruitful hill. [S. of Sol. 6:3; Matt. 20:1; 21:33-40.]

2 And He dug *and* trenched the ground and gathered out the stones from it, and planted it with the choicest vine, and built a tower in the midst of it and hewed out a winepress in it. And He looked for it to bring forth grapes, and it brought forth wild grapes.

3 And now, O inhabitants of Jerusalem and men of Judah, judge, I pray you, between Me and My vineyard [My people, says the Lord].

4 What more could have been done to My vineyard, that I have not done in it? When I looked for it to bring forth grapes, why did it yield wild grapes?

5 And now I will tell you what I will do to My vineyard: I will take away its hedge, and it shall be eaten *and* burned up; and I will break down its wall, and it shall be trodden down [by enemies].

6 And I will lay it waste; it shall not be pruned or cultivated, but there shall come up briers and thorns; I will also command the clouds that they rain no rain upon it.

7 For the vineyard of the Lord of hosts is the house of Israel, and the men of Judah His pleasant planting—the plant of His delight; and He looked for justice, but behold, oppression *and* bloodshed; *He looked* for righteousness—for uprightness and right standing with God—but behold, a cry [of oppression and distress]!

8 Woe to those who join house to house [and by violently expelling the poorer occupants enclose large acreage] and join field to field, until there is no place for others, and you are made to dwell alone in the midst of the land!

**AMP** [a] Although more boy babies are born than girl babies, the number of marriageable men in the world is constantly decreasing. Over 57% of the enlisted men in World War I became casualties (—World Almanac), and the casualties in World War II have been estimated at 33,000,000. Not counting deaths in the Armed Forces, the ratio of deaths between males and females is (in 1960) nine to seven. This was not true in previous centuries. Isaiah here foresees a time when the ratio between marriageable men and women will be one to seven in Jerusalem. [b] The Chaldee translation reads "eternal life."

## New American Standard

*A Remnant Prepared*

**4** FOR SEVEN women will take hold of one man in that day, saying, "We will eat our own bread and wear our own clothes, only let us be called by your name; take away our reproach!"

2¶ In that day the Branch of the LORD will be beautiful and glorious, and the fruit of the earth *will* be the pride and the adornment of the survivors of Israel.

3And it will come about that he who is left in Zion and remains in Jerusalem will be called holy—everyone who is recorded for life in Jerusalem.

4When the Lord has washed away the filth of the daughters of Zion, and purged the bloodshed of Jerusalem from her midst, by the spirit of judgment and the spirit of burning,

5then the LORD will create over the whole area of Mount Zion and over her assemblies a cloud by day, even smoke, and the brightness of a flaming fire by night; for over all the glory will be a canopy.

6And there will be a shelter to *give* shade from the heat by day, and refuge and protection from the storm and the rain.

*Parable of the Vineyard*

**5** LET ME sing now for my well-beloved
A song of my beloved concerning His vineyard.
My well-beloved had a vineyard on a fertile hill.
2 And He dug it all around, removed its stones,
And planted it with the choicest vine.
And He built a tower in the middle of it,
And hewed out a wine vat in it;
Then He expected *it* to produce *good* grapes,
But it produced *only* worthless ones.

3¶ "And now, O inhabitants of Jerusalem and men of Judah,
Judge between Me and My vineyard.
4 "What more was there to do for My vineyard that I have not done in it?
Why, when I expected *it* to produce *good* grapes did it produce worthless ones?
5 "So now let Me tell you what I am going to do to My vineyard:
I will remove its hedge and it will be consumed;
I will break down its wall and it will become trampled ground.
6 "And I will lay it waste;
It will not be pruned or hoed,
But briars and thorns will come up.
I will also charge the clouds to rain no rain on it."

7¶ For the vineyard of the LORD of hosts is the house of Israel,
And the men of Judah His delightful plant.
Thus He looked for justice, but behold, bloodshed;
For righteousness, but behold, a cry of distress.

*Woes for the Wicked*

8¶ Woe to those who add house to house *and* join field to field,
Until there is no more room,
So that you have to live alone in the midst of the land!

## New International

**4** IN THAT day seven women
will take hold of one man
and say, "We will eat our own food
and provide our own clothes;
only let us be called by your name.
Take away our disgrace!"

*The Branch of the LORD*

2In that day the Branch of the LORD will be beautiful and glorious, and the fruit of the land will be the pride and glory of the
survivors in Israel. 3Those who are left in Zion, who remain in
Jerusalem, will be called holy, all who are recorded among the
living in Jerusalem. 4The Lord will wash away the filth of the
women of Zion; he will cleanse the bloodstains from Jerusalem by
a spirit[c] of judgment and a spirit[d] of fire. 5Then the LORD will
create over all of Mount Zion and over those who assemble there
a cloud of smoke by day and a glow of flaming fire by night; over
all the glory will be a canopy. 6It will be a shelter and shade from
the heat of the day, and a refuge and hiding place from the storm
and rain.

*The Song of the Vineyard*

**5** I WILL sing for the one I love
a song about his vineyard:
My loved one had a vineyard
on a fertile hillside.
2He dug it up and cleared it of stones
and planted it with the choicest vines.
He built a watchtower in it
and cut out a winepress as well.
Then he looked for a crop of good grapes,
but it yielded only bad fruit.

3"Now you dwellers in Jerusalem and men of Judah,
judge between me and my vineyard.
4What more could have been done for my vineyard
than I have done for it?
When I looked for good grapes,
why did it yield only bad?
5Now I will tell you
what I am going to do to my vineyard:
I will take away its hedge,
and it will be destroyed;
I will break down its wall,
and it will be trampled.
6I will make it a wasteland,
neither pruned nor cultivated,
and briers and thorns will grow there.
I will command the clouds
not to rain on it."

7The vineyard of the LORD Almighty
is the house of Israel,
and the men of Judah
are the garden of his delight.
And he looked for justice, but saw bloodshed;
for righteousness, but heard cries of distress.

*Woes and Judgments*

8Woe to you who add house to house
and join field to field
till no space is left
and you live alone in the land.

NIV [c] 4 Or *the Spirit* [d] 4 Or *the Spirit*

## King James

9 In mine ears *said* the LORD of hosts, Of a truth many houses shall be desolate, *even* great and fair, without inhabitant.

10 Yea, ten acres of vineyard shall yield one bath, and the seed of an homer shall yield an ephah.

11 ¶ Woe unto them that rise up early in the morning, *that* they may follow strong drink; that continue until night, *till* wine inflame them!

12 And the harp, and the viol, the tabret, and pipe, and wine, are in their feasts: but they regard not the work of the LORD, neither consider the operation of his hands.

13 ¶ Therefore my people are gone into captivity, because *they have* no knowledge: and their honourable men *are* famished, and their multitude dried up with thirst.

14 Therefore hell hath enlarged herself, and opened her mouth without measure: and their glory, and their multitude, and their pomp, and he that rejoiceth, shall descend into it.

15 And the mean man shall be brought down, and the mighty man shall be humbled, and the eyes of the lofty shall be humbled:

16 But the LORD of hosts shall be exalted in judgment, and God that is holy shall be sanctified in righteousness.

17 Then shall the lambs feed after their manner, and the waste places of the fat ones shall strangers eat.

18 Woe unto them that draw iniquity with cords of vanity, and sin as it were with a cart rope:

19 That say, Let him make speed, *and* hasten his work, that we may see *it:* and let the counsel of the Holy One of Israel draw nigh and come, that we may know *it!*

20 ¶ Woe unto them that call evil good, and good evil; that put darkness for light, and light for darkness; that put bitter for sweet, and sweet for bitter!

21 Woe unto *them that are* wise in their own eyes, and prudent in their own sight!

22 Woe unto *them that are* mighty to drink wine, and men of strength to mingle strong drink:

23 Which justify the wicked for reward, and take away the righteousness of the righteous from him!

24 Therefore as the fire devoureth the stubble, and the flame consumeth the chaff, *so* their root shall be as rottenness, and their blossom shall go up as dust: because they have cast away the law of the LORD of hosts, and despised the word of the Holy One of Israel.

25 Therefore is the anger of the LORD kindled against his people, and he hath stretched forth his hand against them, and hath smitten them: and the hills did tremble, and their carcases *were* torn in the midst of the streets. For all this his anger is not turned away, but his hand *is* stretched out still.

## Amplified

9 In my [Isaiah's] ears the Lord of hosts said, Of a truth many houses shall be desolate, even great and beautiful ones, without inhabitant.

10 For ten acres of vineyard shall yield only about eight gallons, and ten bushels of seed will produce but one bushel.

11 Woe unto those who rise early in the morning, that they may pursue strong drink, who tarry late into the night till wine inflames them!

12 They have lyre and harp, tambourine and flute, and wine at their feasts; but they do not regard the deeds of the Lord, neither consider the operation of His hands [in mercy and in judgment].

13 Therefore My people go into captivity [to their enemies] without knowing it *and* because they have no knowledge *of God.* And their honorable men—their glory—are famished, and their common people are parched with thirst.

14 Therefore Sheol—the unseen state, the realm of the dead—has enlarged its appetite and opened its mouth without measure, and [Jerusalem's] nobility *and* her multitude and her pomp *and* tumult and [the drunken reveler] who exults in her descend into it.

15 And the common man is bowed down, and the great man is brought low, and the eyes of the haughty are humbled.

16 But the Lord of hosts is exalted in justice, and God the Holy One shows Himself holy in righteousness *and* through righteous *judgments.*

17 Then shall the lambs feed [among the ruins] as in their pasture, and *among* the desolate places of the [exiled] rich shall sojourners *and* aliens eat.

18 Woe to those who draw *calamity* with cords of iniquity *and* falsehood, who bring *punishment* to themselves with a cart rope of wickedness;

19 Who say, Let *the Holy One* make haste *and* speed His *prophesied* vengeance, that we may see it; and let the purpose of the Holy One of Israel draw near and come, that we may know it!

20 Woe to those who call evil good and good evil, who put darkness for light and light for darkness, who put bitter for sweet and sweet for bitter!

21 Woe to those who are wise in their own eyes, and prudent *and* shrewd in their own sight!

22 Woe to those who are mighty *heroes* at drinking wine, and men of strength in mixing alcoholic drinks!

23 Who justify *and* acquit the guilty for a bribe, and take away the rights of the innocent *and* righteous from him!

24 Therefore as the tongue of fire devours the stubble, and as the dry grass sinks down in the flame, so their root shall be as rottenness and their blossom shall go up as fine dust; because they have rejected *and* cast away the law *and* the teaching of the Lord of hosts, and have not believed *but* have treated scornfully *and* have despised the word of the Holy One of Israel.

25 Therefore is the anger of the Lord kindled against His people, and He has stretched forth His hand against them and has smitten them, and the mountains trembled; and their dead bodies were as dung *and* sweepings in the midst of the streets. For all this His anger is not turned away, but His hand is stretched out still *in judgment.*

## New American Standard

9 In my ears the LORD of hosts *has sworn,* "Surely, many
houses shall become desolate,
*Even* great and fine ones, without occupants.
10 "For ten acres of vineyard will yield *only* one [a]bath *of wine,*
And a homer of seed will yield *but* an [b]ephah of
grain."
11 Woe to those who rise early in the morning that they
may pursue strong drink;
Who stay up late in the evening that wine may inflame
them!
12 And their banquets are *accompanied* by lyre and harp, by
tambourine and flute, and by wine;
But they do not pay attention to the deeds of the LORD,
Nor do they consider the work of His hands.

13¶ Therefore My people go into exile for their lack of
knowledge;
And their honorable men are famished,
And their multitude is parched with thirst.
14 Therefore Sheol has enlarged its throat and opened its
mouth without measure;
And Jerusalem's splendor, her multitude, her din *of
revelry,* and the jubilant within her, descend *into it.*
15 So the *common* man will be humbled, and the man of
*importance* abased,
The eyes of the proud also will be abased.
16 But the LORD of hosts will be exalted in judgment,
And the holy God will show Himself holy in
righteousness.
17 Then the lambs will graze as in their pasture,
And strangers will eat in the waste places of the
wealthy.

18¶ Woe to those who drag iniquity with the cords of
falsehood,
And sin as if with cart ropes;
19 Who say, "Let Him make speed, let Him hasten His
work, that we may see *it;*
And let the purpose of the Holy One of Israel draw
near
And come to pass, that we may know *it!*"
20 Woe to those who call evil good, and good evil;
Who substitute darkness for light and light for
darkness;
Who substitute bitter for sweet, and sweet for bitter!
21 Woe to those who are wise in their own eyes,
And clever in their own sight!
22 Woe to those who are heroes in drinking wine,
And valiant men in mixing strong drink;
23 Who justify the wicked for a bribe,
And take away the rights of the ones who are in the
right!

24¶ Therefore, as a tongue of fire consumes stubble,
And dry grass collapses into the flame,
So their root will become like rot and their blossom
blow away as dust;
For they have rejected the law of the LORD of hosts,
And despised the word of the Holy One of Israel.
25 On this account the anger of the LORD has burned
against His people,
And He has stretched out His hand against them and
struck them down,
And the mountains quaked; and their corpses lay like
refuse in the middle of the streets.
For all this His anger is not spent,
But His hand is still stretched out.

NAS [a] I.e., Approx. 10½ gal. [b] I.e., Approx. one bu.

## New International

9 The LORD Almighty has declared in my hearing:
"Surely the great houses will become desolate,
the fine mansions left without occupants.
10 A ten-acre[c] vineyard will produce only a bath[d] of wine,
a homer[e] of seed only an ephah[f] of grain."
11 Woe to those who rise early in the morning
to run after their drinks,
who stay up late at night
till they are inflamed with wine.
12 They have harps and lyres at their banquets,
tambourines and flutes and wine,
but they have no regard for the deeds of the LORD,
no respect for the work of his hands.
13 Therefore my people will go into exile
for lack of understanding;
their men of rank will die of hunger
and their masses will be parched with thirst.
14 Therefore the grave[g] enlarges its appetite
and opens its mouth without limit;
into it will descend their nobles and masses
with all their brawlers and revelers.
15 So man will be brought low
and mankind humbled,
the eyes of the arrogant humbled.
16 But the LORD Almighty will be exalted by his justice,
and the holy God will show himself holy by his
righteousness.
17 Then sheep will graze as in their own pasture;
lambs will feed[h] among the ruins of the rich.

18 Woe to those who draw sin along with cords of deceit,
and wickedness as with cart ropes,
19 to those who say, "Let God hurry,
let him hasten his work
so we may see it.
Let it approach,
let the plan of the Holy One of Israel come,
so we may know it."
20 Woe to those who call evil good
and good evil,
who put darkness for light
and light for darkness,
who put bitter for sweet
and sweet for bitter.
21 Woe to those who are wise in their own eyes
and clever in their own sight.
22 Woe to those who are heroes at drinking wine
and champions at mixing drinks,
23 who acquit the guilty for a bribe,
but deny justice to the innocent.
24 Therefore, as tongues of fire lick up straw
and as dry grass sinks down in the flames,
so their roots will decay
and their flowers blow away like dust;
for they have rejected the law of the LORD Almighty
and spurned the word of the Holy One of Israel.
25 Therefore the LORD's anger burns against his people;
his hand is raised and he strikes them down.
The mountains shake,
and the dead bodies are like refuse in the streets.

Yet for all this, his anger is not turned away,
his hand is still upraised.

NIV [c] *10* Hebrew *ten-yoke,* that is, the land plowed by 10 yoke of oxen in one day [d] *10* That is, probably about 6 gallons (about 22 liters) [e] *10* That is, probably about 6 bushels (about 220 liters) [f] *10* That is, probably about 3/5 bushel (about 22 liters) [g] *14* Hebrew *Sheol* [h] *17* Septuagint; Hebrew / *strangers will eat*

## King James

26¶ And he will lift up an ensign to the nations from far, and
will hiss unto them from the end of the earth: and, behold, they
shall come with speed swiftly:
27None shall be weary nor stumble among them; none shall
slumber nor sleep; neither shall the girdle of their loins be loosed,
nor the latchet of their shoes be broken:
28Whose arrows *are* sharp, and all their bows bent, their horses'
hoofs shall be counted like flint, and their wheels like a whirlwind:
29Their roaring *shall be* like a lion, they shall roar like young
lions: yea, they shall roar, and lay hold of the prey, and shall carry
*it* away safe, and none shall deliver *it*.
30And in that day they shall roar against them like the roaring
of the sea: and if *one* look unto the land, behold darkness *and*
sorrow, and the light is darkened in the heavens thereof.

6 IN THE year that king Uzziah died I saw also the Lord sitting
upon a throne, high and lifted up, and his train filled the
temple.
2Above it stood the seraphims: each one had six wings; with
twain he covered his face, and with twain he covered his feet, and
with twain he did fly.
3And one cried unto another, and said, Holy, holy, holy, *is* the
LORD of hosts: the whole earth *is* full of his glory.
4And the posts of the door moved at the voice of him that cried,
and the house was filled with smoke.
5¶ Then said I, Woe *is* me! for I am undone; because I *am* a man
of unclean lips, and I dwell in the midst of a people of unclean lips:
for mine eyes have seen the King, the LORD of hosts.
6Then flew one of the seraphims unto me, having a live coal in
his hand, *which* he had taken with the tongs from off the altar:
7And he laid *it* upon my mouth, and said, Lo, this hath touched
thy lips; and thine iniquity is taken away, and thy sin purged.
8Also I heard the voice of the Lord, saying, Whom shall I send,
and who will go for us? Then said I, Here *am* I; send me.
9¶ And he said, Go, and tell this people, Hear ye indeed, but
understand not; and see ye indeed, but perceive not.
10Make the heart of this people fat, and make their ears heavy,
and shut their eyes; lest they see with their eyes, and hear with
their ears, and understand with their heart, and convert, and be
healed.
11Then said I, Lord, how long? And he answered, Until the
cities be wasted without inhabitant, and the houses without man,
and the land be utterly desolate,
12And the LORD have removed men far away, and *there be* a
great forsaking in the midst of the land.

## Amplified

26And He will lift up a signal to call together a hostile people
from afar [to execute His judgment on Judea], and will hiss for
them from the end of the earth [as bees are hissed from their
hives], and behold, they shall come with speed swiftly!
27None shall be weary or stumble among them, none shall
slumber or sleep; nor shall the girdle of their loins be loosed or the
latchet of their shoes be broken;
28Their arrows are sharp, and all their bows bent; their horses'
hoofs shall seem like flint, and their wheels like a whirlwind.
29Their roaring shall be like a lioness', they shall roar like young
lions; they shall growl and seize their prey and carry it safely away,
and there shall be none to deliver it.
30And in that day they [the army from afar] shall roar against
*the Jews* like the roaring of the sea; and if one look to the land,
behold, darkness and distress, and the light *itself* will be darkened
by the clouds of it.

6 IN THE year that King Uzziah died, [in a vision] I saw the
Lord sitting upon a throne high and lifted up, and the skirts
of His train filled the [most holy part of the] temple. [John 12:41.]
2Above Him stood the seraphim; each had six wings; with two
*each* covered his *own* face, and with two covered his feet, and with
two he flew.
3And one cried to another and said, Holy, holy, holy, is the
Lord of hosts; the whole earth is full of His glory!
4And the foundations of the thresholds shook at the voice of
him who cried, and the house was filled with smoke.
5Then said I, Woe is me! For I am undone *and* ruined, because
I am a man of unclean lips, and I dwell in the midst of a people of
unclean lips; for my eyes have seen the King, the Lord of hosts!
6Then flew one of the seraphim [heavenly beings] to me, having
a live coal in his hand which he had taken with tongs from off the
altar;
7And with it he touched my mouth and said, Lo, this has
touched your lips; your iniquity *and* guilt *are* taken away, and your
sin is completely atoned for *and* forgiven.
8Also I heard the voice of the Lord, saying, Whom shall I send,
and who will go for Us? Then said I, Here am I; send me.
9And He said, Go, and tell this people, Hear *and* hear continually, but understand not; and see *and* see continually, but do not
apprehend with your mind.
10Make the heart of this people fat, and make their ears heavy,
and shut their eyes; lest they see with their eyes, and hear with
their ears, and understand with their hearts, and turn again and
be healed.
11Then said I, Lord, how long? And He answered, Until cities
lie waste without inhabitant, and houses without man, and the
land is utterly desolate,
12And the Lord removes *His* people far away, and the forsaken
places are many in the midst of the land.

## New American Standard

26¶ He will also lift up a standard to the distant nation,
And will whistle for it from the ends of the earth;
And behold, it will come with speed swiftly.
27 No one in it is weary or stumbles,
None slumbers or sleeps;
Nor is the belt at its waist undone,
Nor its sandal strap broken.
28 Its arrows are sharp, and all its bows are bent;
The hoofs of its horses seem like flint, and its *chariot*
wheels like a whirlwind.
29 Its roaring is like a lioness, and it roars like young lions;
It growls as it seizes the prey,
And carries *it* off with no one to deliver *it.*
30 And it shall growl over it in that day like the roaring of
the sea.
If one looks to the land, behold, there is darkness *and*
distress;
Even the light is darkened by its clouds.

*Isaiah's Vision*

6 IN THE year of King Uzziah's death, I saw the Lord sitting
on a throne, lofty and exalted, with the train of His robe filling
the temple.
2Seraphim stood above Him, each having six wings; with two
he covered his face, and with two he covered his feet, and with
two he flew.
3And one called out to another and said,
"Holy, Holy, Holy, is the LORD of hosts,
The whole earth is full of His glory."
4And the foundations of the thresholds trembled at the voice
of him who called out, while the temple was filling with smoke.
5Then I said,
"Woe is me, for I am ruined!
Because I am a man of unclean lips,
And I live among a people of unclean lips;
For my eyes have seen the King, the LORD of hosts."
6¶ Then one of the seraphim flew to me, with a burning coal
in his hand which he had taken from the altar with tongs.
7And he touched my mouth *with it* and said, "Behold, this has
touched your lips; and your iniquity is taken away, and your sin
is forgiven."

*Isaiah's Commission*

8Then I heard the voice of the Lord, saying, "Whom shall I
send, and who will go for Us?" Then I said, "Here am I. Send me!"
9 And He said, "Go, and tell this people:
'Keep on listening, but do not perceive;
Keep on looking, but do not understand.'
10 "Render the hearts of this people insensitive,
Their ears dull,
And their eyes dim,
Lest they see with their eyes,
Hear with their ears,
Understand with their hearts,
And return and be healed."
11 Then I said, "Lord, how long?" And He answered,
"Until cities are devastated *and* without inhabitant,
Houses are without people,
And the land is utterly desolate,
12 "The LORD has removed men far away,
And the forsaken places are many in the midst of the
land.

## New International

26He lifts up a banner for the distant nations,
he whistles for those at the ends of the earth.
Here they come,
swiftly and speedily!
27Not one of them grows tired or stumbles,
not one slumbers or sleeps;
not a belt is loosened at the waist,
not a sandal thong is broken.
28Their arrows are sharp,
all their bows are strung;
their horses' hoofs seem like flint,
their chariot wheels like a whirlwind.
29Their roar is like that of the lion,
they roar like young lions;
they growl as they seize their prey
and carry it off with no one to rescue.
30In that day they will roar over it
like the roaring of the sea.
And if one looks at the land,
he will see darkness and distress;
even the light will be darkened by the clouds.

*Isaiah's Commission*

6 IN THE year that King Uzziah died, I saw the Lord seated on
a throne, high and exalted, and the train of his robe filled the
temple. 2Above him were seraphs, each with six wings: With two
wings they covered their faces, with two they covered their feet,
and with two they were flying. 3And they were calling to one
another:

"Holy, holy, holy is the LORD Almighty;
the whole earth is full of his glory."

4At the sound of their voices the doorposts and thresholds shook
and the temple was filled with smoke.
5"Woe to me!" I cried. "I am ruined! For I am a man of unclean
lips, and I live among a people of unclean lips, and my eyes have
seen the King, the LORD Almighty."
6Then one of the seraphs flew to me with a live coal in his hand,
which he had taken with tongs from the altar. 7With it he touched
my mouth and said, "See, this has touched your lips; your guilt
is taken away and your sin atoned for."
8Then I heard the voice of the Lord saying, "Whom shall I send?
And who will go for us?"
And I said, "Here am I. Send me!"
9He said, "Go and tell this people:

" 'Be ever hearing, but never understanding;
be ever seeing, but never perceiving.'
10Make the heart of this people calloused;
make their ears dull
and close their eyes.[a]
Otherwise they might see with their eyes,
hear with their ears,
understand with their hearts,
and turn and be healed."

11Then I said, "For how long, O Lord?"
And he answered:

"Until the cities lie ruined
and without inhabitant,
until the houses are left deserted
and the fields ruined and ravaged,
12until the LORD has sent everyone far away
and the land is utterly forsaken.

**NIV** [a] 9,10 Hebrew; Septuagint *'You will be ever hearing, but never understanding; / you will be ever seeing, but never perceiving.' / 10This people's heart has become calloused; / they hardly hear with their ears, / and they have closed their eyes*

## King James

13¶ But yet in it *shall be* a tenth, and *it* shall return, and shall be eaten: as a teil tree, and as an oak, whose substance *is* in them, when they cast *their leaves: so* the holy seed *shall be* the substance thereof.

# 7

AND IT came to pass in the days of Ahaz the son of Jotham, the son of Uzziah, king of Judah, *that* Rezin the king of Syria, and Pekah the son of Remaliah, king of Israel, went up toward Jerusalem to war against it, but could not prevail against it.

2And it was told the house of David, saying, Syria is confederate with Ephraim. And his heart was moved, and the heart of his people, as the trees of the wood are moved with the wind.

3Then said the LORD unto Isaiah, Go forth now to meet Ahaz, thou, and Shear-jashub thy son, at the end of the conduit of the upper pool in the highway of the fuller's field;

4And say unto him, Take heed, and be quiet; fear not, neither be fainthearted for the two tails of these smoking firebrands, for the fierce anger of Rezin with Syria, and of the son of Remaliah.

5Because Syria, Ephraim, and the son of Remaliah, have taken evil counsel against thee, saying,

6Let us go up against Judah, and vex it, and let us make a breach therein for us, and set a king in the midst of it, *even* the son of Tabeal:

7Thus saith the Lord GOD, It shall not stand, neither shall it come to pass.

8For the head of Syria *is* Damascus, and the head of Damascus *is* Rezin; and within threescore and five years shall Ephraim be broken, that it be not a people.

9And the head of Ephraim *is* Samaria, and the head of Samaria *is* Remaliah's son. If ye will not believe, surely ye shall not be established.

10¶ Moreover the LORD spake again unto Ahaz, saying,

11Ask thee a sign of the LORD thy God; ask it either in the depth, or in the height above.

12But Ahaz said, I will not ask, neither will I tempt the LORD.

13And he said, Hear ye now, O house of David; *Is it* a small thing for you to weary men, but will ye weary my God also?

14Therefore the Lord himself shall give you a sign; Behold, a virgin shall conceive, and bear a son, and shall call his name Immanuel.

15Butter and honey shall he eat, that he may know to refuse the evil, and choose the good.

16For before the child shall know to refuse the evil, and choose the good, the land that thou abhorrest shall be forsaken of both her kings.

17¶ The LORD shall bring upon thee, and upon thy people, and upon thy father's house, days that have not come, from the day that Ephraim departed from Judah; *even* the king of Assyria.

18And it shall come to pass in that day, *that* the LORD shall hiss for the fly that *is* in the uttermost part of the rivers of Egypt, and for the bee that *is* in the land of Assyria.

19And they shall come, and shall rest all of them in the desolate valleys, and in the holes of the rocks, and upon all thorns, and upon all bushes.

## Amplified

13And though a tenth [of the people] remain in it, it will be for their destruction—eaten up and burned; like a terebinth tree or like an oak whose stump *and* substance remain when they are felled *or* have cast their leaves. The holy seed [the elect remnant] is the stump *and* substance [of Israel].

# 7

IN THE days of Ahaz the son of Jotham, son of Uzziah, king of Judah, Rezin the king of Syria and Pekah the son of Remaliah, the king of Israel, went up to Jerusalem to wage war against it, but they could not conquer it.

2And the house of David [Judah] was told, Syria is allied with Ephraim [Israel]. And the heart *of Ahaz* and the heart of his people trembled *and* shook as the trees of the forest tremble *and* shake with the wind.

3Then said the Lord to Isaiah, Go forth now to meet *Judah's King* Ahaz, you and your son Shearjashub [meaning, A remnant shall return], at the end of the aqueduct *or* canal of the upper pool on the highway to the fuller's field,

4And say to him, Take heed and be quiet, fear not, neither be faint-hearted because of these two stumps of smoking firebrands, at the fierce anger of [the Syrian King] Rezin and Syria, and of the son of Remaliah [Pekah, usurper of the throne of Israel].

5Because Syria, Ephraim [Israel] and the son of Remaliah have purposed evil against you, *Judah*, saying,

6Let us go up against Judah and harass *and* terrify it, and let us cleave it asunder [each of us taking a portion], and set a [vassal] king in the midst of it, namely the son of Tabeel,

7Thus says the Lord God: It shall not stand, neither shall it come to pass.

8For the head [the capital] of Syria is Damascus, and the head of Damascus is *King* Rezin. Within sixty-five years Ephraim will be broken to pieces so that it will no longer be a people.

9And the head [the capital] of Ephraim is Samaria, and the head of Samaria is Remaliah's son [Pekah]. If you will not believe *and* trust in *and* rely on *God* [and on the words of God's prophet, instead of Assyria], surely you will not be established *nor* will you remain.

10Moreover the Lord spoke again to King Ahaz, saying,

11Ask for youself a sign—a token or proof—of the Lord your God [one that will be convincing to you that God has spoken and will keep His word]; ask it either in the depth, or in the height above—let it be as deep as Sheol or as high as Heaven.

12But Ahaz said, I will not ask, neither will I tempt the Lord.

13And [Isaiah] said, Hear then, O house of David! Is it a small thing for you to weary *and* try the patience of men, but will you weary *and* try the patience of my God also?

14Therefore the Lord Himself shall give you a sign, Behold, the young woman *who* is unmarried *and* a virgin shall conceive and bear a son, and shall call his name Immanuel—God with us. [Matt. 1:22, 23; Isa. 9:6; Jer. 31:22; Mic. 5:3-5.]

15Butter *and* curds and wild honey shall he eat, when he knows to refuse the evil and choose the good.

16For before the child shall know to refuse the evil and choose the good, the land [Canaan] whose two kings you abhor, *and* of whom you are in sickening dread, shall be forsaken [both Ephraim and Syria]. [Verse 2.]

17The Lord shall bring upon you and upon your people and upon your father's house such days as have not come since the day that Ephraim [the ten northern tribes] departed from Judah, even the king of [a]Assyria.

18And in that day the Lord shall whistle for the fly [the numerous and troublesome foe] that is in the whole extent of the canal country of Egypt, and for the bee that is in the land of Assyria.

19And these [enemies like flies and bees] shall come and shall rest all of them in the desolate *and* rugged valleys *and* deep ravines, and in the clefts of the rocks, and on all thornbushes, and on all the pastures.

**AMP** [a] "Jesus was actually born in a time when the Holy Land found itself under the supremacy of [Assyria, when looked upon as] the universal Empire, and in a condition which went back to the unbelief of Ahaz as its ultimate cause" (Delitzsch, quoted in *The New Bible Commentary*).

## New American Standard

13 "Yet there will be a tenth portion in it,
And it will again be *subject* to burning,
Like a terebinth or an oak
Whose stump remains when it is felled.
The holy seed is its stump."

*War against Jerusalem*

**7** NOW IT came about in the days of Ahaz, the son of Jotham,
the son of Uzziah, king of Judah, that Rezin the king of Aram
and Pekah the son of Remaliah, king of Israel, went up to Jerusalem to *wage* war against it, but could not conquer it.
2When it was reported to the house of David, saying, "The
Arameans have camped in Ephraim," his heart and the hearts of
his people shook as the trees of the forest shake with the wind.
3¶ Then the LORD said to Isaiah, "Go out now to meet Ahaz,
you and your son Shear-jashub, at the end of the conduit of the
upper pool, on the highway to the fuller's field,
4and say to him, 'Take care, and be calm, have no fear and do
not be fainthearted because of these two stubs of smoldering firebrands, on account of the fierce anger of Rezin and Aram, and the
son of Remaliah.
5'Because Aram, *with* Ephraim and the son of Remaliah, has
planned evil against you, saying,
6"Let us go up against Judah and terrorize it, and make for
ourselves a breach in its walls, and set up the son of Tabeel as king
in the midst of it,"
7thus says the Lord GOD, "It shall not stand nor shall it come
to pass.
8"For the head of Aram is Damascus and the head of Damascus
is Rezin (now within another 65 years Ephraim will be shattered,
*so that it is* no longer a people),
9and the head of Ephraim is Samaria and the head of Samaria
is the son of Remaliah. If you will not believe, you surely shall not
last." ' "

*The Child Immanuel*

10¶ Then the LORD spoke again to Ahaz, saying,
11"Ask a sign for yourself from the LORD your God; make *it*
deep as Sheol or high as heaven."
12But Ahaz said, "I will not ask, nor will I test the LORD!"
13Then he said, "Listen now, O house of David! Is it too slight
a thing for you to try the patience of men, that you will try the
patience of my God as well?
14"Therefore the Lord Himself will give you a sign: Behold, a
virgin will be with child and bear a son, and she will call His name
[b]Immanuel.
15"He will eat curds and honey at the time He knows *enough* to
refuse evil and choose good.
16"For before the boy will know *enough* to refuse evil and choose
good, the land whose two kings you dread will be forsaken.

*Trials to Come for Judah*

17"The LORD will bring on you, on your people, and on your
father's house such days as have never come since the day that
Ephraim separated from Judah, the king of Assyria."
18And it will come about in that day, that the LORD will whistle
for the fly that is in the remotest part of the rivers of Egypt, and
for the bee that is in the land of Assyria.
19And they will all come and settle on the steep ravines, on the
ledges of the cliffs, on all the thorn bushes, and on all the watering
places.

NAS [b] I.e., God is with us

## New International

13And though a tenth remains in the land,
it will again be laid waste.
But as the terebinth and oak
leave stumps when they are cut down,
so the holy seed will be the stump in the land."

*The Sign of Immanuel*

**7** WHEN AHAZ son of Jotham, the son of Uzziah, was king of
Judah, King Rezin of Aram and Pekah son of Remaliah king
of Israel marched up to fight against Jerusalem, but they could not
overpower it.
2Now the house of David was told, "Aram has allied itself with[c]
Ephraim"; so the hearts of Ahaz and his people were shaken, as
the trees of the forest are shaken by the wind.
3Then the LORD said to Isaiah, "Go out, you and your son
Shear-Jashub,[d] to meet Ahaz at the end of the aqueduct of the
Upper Pool, on the road to the Washerman's Field. 4Say to him,
'Be careful, keep calm and don't be afraid. Do not lose heart
because of these two smoldering stubs of firewood—because of the
fierce anger of Rezin and Aram and of the son of Remaliah. 5Aram,
Ephraim and Remaliah's son have plotted your ruin, saying, 6"Let
us invade Judah; let us tear it apart and divide it among ourselves,
and make the son of Tabeel king over it." 7Yet this is what the
Sovereign LORD says:

" 'It will not take place,
it will not happen,
8for the head of Aram is Damascus,
and the head of Damascus is only Rezin.
Within sixty-five years
Ephraim will be too shattered to be a people.
9The head of Ephraim is Samaria,
and the head of Samaria is only Remaliah's son.
If you do not stand firm in your faith,
you will not stand at all.' "

10Again the LORD spoke to Ahaz, 11"Ask the LORD your God for
a sign, whether in the deepest depths or in the highest heights."
12But Ahaz said, "I will not ask; I will not put the LORD to the
test."
13Then Isaiah said, "Hear now, you house of David! Is it not
enough to try the patience of men? Will you try the patience of my
God also? 14Therefore the Lord himself will give you[e] a sign: The
virgin will be with child and will give birth to a son, and[f] will call
him Immanuel.[g] 15He will eat curds and honey when he knows
enough to reject the wrong and choose the right. 16But before the
boy knows enough to reject the wrong and choose the right, the
land of the two kings you dread will be laid waste. 17The LORD will
bring on you and on your people and on the house of your father
a time unlike any since Ephraim broke away from Judah—he will
bring the king of Assyria."
18In that day the LORD will whistle for flies from the distant
streams of Egypt and for bees from the land of Assyria. 19They will
all come and settle in the steep ravines and in the crevices in the
rocks, on all the thornbushes and at all the water holes. 20In that

NIV [c] 2 Or *has set up camp in* [d] 3 *Shear-Jashub* means *a remnant will return.* [e] 14 The Hebrew is plural. [f] 14 Masoretic Text; Dead Sea Scrolls *and he* or *and they* [g] 14 *Immanuel* means *God with us.*

## King James

20In the same day shall the Lord shave with a razor that is hired,
*namely*, by them beyond the river, by the king of Assyria, the head,
and the hair of the feet: and it shall also consume the beard.
21And it shall come to pass in that day, *that* a man shall nourish
a young cow, and two sheep;
22And it shall come to pass, for the abundance of milk *that* they
shall give he shall eat butter: for butter and honey shall every one
eat that is left in the land.
23And it shall come to pass in that day, *that* every place shall
be, where there were a thousand vines at a thousand silverlings,
it shall *even* be for briers and thorns.
24With arrows and with bows shall *men* come thither; because
all the land shall become briers and thorns.
25And *on* all hills that shall be digged with the mattock, there
shall not come thither the fear of briers and thorns: but it shall be
for the sending forth of oxen, and for the treading of lesser cattle.

**8** MOREOVER THE LORD said unto me, Take thee a great roll,
and write in it with a man's pen concerning Maher-shalal-
hash-baz.
2And I took unto me faithful witnesses to record, Uriah the
priest, and Zechariah the son of Jeberechiah.
3And I went unto the prophetess; and she conceived, and bare
a son. Then said the LORD to me, Call his name Maher-shalal-hash-
baz.
4For before the child shall have knowledge to cry, My father,
and my mother, the riches of Damascus and the spoil of Samaria
shall be taken away before the king of Assyria.
5¶ The LORD spake also unto me again, saying,
6Forasmuch as this people refuseth the waters of Shiloah that
go softly, and rejoice in Rezin and Remaliah's son;
7Now therefore, behold, the Lord bringeth up upon them the
waters of the river, strong and many, *even* the king of Assyria, and
all his glory: and he shall come up over all his channels, and go
over all his banks:
8And he shall pass through Judah; he shall overflow and go
over, he shall reach *even* to the neck; and the stretching out of his
wings shall fill the breadth of thy land, O Immanuel.
9¶ Associate yourselves, O ye people, and ye shall be broken in
pieces; and give ear, all ye of far countries: gird yourselves, and
ye shall be broken in pieces; gird yourselves, and ye shall be
broken in pieces.
10Take counsel together, and it shall come to nought; speak the
word, and it shall not stand: for God *is* with us.
11¶ For the LORD spake thus to me with a strong hand, and
instructed me that I should not walk in the way of this people,
saying,

## Amplified

20In the same day [will the people of Judah be utterly stripped
of belongings], the Lord will shave with the razor that is hired in
the parts beyond the River [Euphrates], even with the king of
Assyria; *that razor will shave* the head and the hair of the legs, and
it shall also consume the beard [leaving Judah to open shame and
scorn]. [II Kings 16:7, 8; 18:13-16.]
21And [because of desolation brought on by the invaders] in
that day a man will [be so poor that he will] keep alive only a young
milk cow and two sheep.
22And because of the abundance of milk that they will give, he
will eat butter *and* curds, for *only* butter *and* curds and *wild* honey
[no vegetables] shall everyone eat who is left in the land [these
products provided from the extensive pastures, and the plentiful
wild flowers upon which the bees depend].
23And in that day in every place where there used to be a
thousand vines, worth a thousand silver shekels, there will be
briers and thorns.
24With arrows and with bow shall a man come [to hunt] there,
because all the land will be briers and thorns;
25And *as to* all the hills that were formerly cultivated with mattock *and* hoe, you will not come there for fear of briers and thorns;
but they will have become a place where oxen are let loose to
pasture and where sheep tread.

**8** THEN THE Lord said to me, Take a large tablet [of wood,
metal or stone] and write upon it with a graving tool *and* in
ordinary characters [which the humblest man can read], Belonging
to Maher-shalal-hash-baz—They [that is, the Assyrians] hasten to
the spoil [of Syria and Israel], they speed to the prey.
2And I took faithful witnesses to record *and* attest [this proph-
ecy] for me, Uriah the priest and Zechariah the son of Jeberechiah.
3And I approached *my wife* the prophetess, and when she had
conceived and borne a son, the Lord said to me, Call his name
Maher-shalal-hash-baz [as a continual reminder to the people of
the prophecy],
4For before the child knows how to say, My father or my
mother, the riches of Damascus [Syria's capital] and the spoil of
Samaria [Israel's capital] [a]shall be carried away before the king of
Assyria.
5The Lord spoke to me yet again, and said,
6Because this people [Israel and Judah] have refused *and* despised the waters of Shiloah [Siloam, the only perennial fountain
of Jerusalem, and typical of God's protection] that go gently, and
rejoice in *and* with Rezin *the king of Syria* and Remaliah's son *Pekah
the king of Israel*,
7Now therefore, behold, the Lord brings up upon them the
waters of the River [Euphrates], strong and many, even the king
of Assyria and all the glory *of his gorgeous retinue;* and it will rise
over all its channels, brooks, valleys *and* canals, and extend far
beyond its banks; [Isa. 7:17.]
8And it will [b]sweep on into Judah; it will overflow *and* go over
[the hills], reaching even, *but only*, to the neck [of which Jerusalem
is the head], and the stretched out wings [of the armies of Assyria]
shall fill the breadth of Your land, O Immanuel
[c][Messiah]—meaning God is with us! [Num. 14:9; Ps. 46:7.]
9Make an uproar *and* be broken in pieces, O you peoples—rage,
raise the war cry, do your worst, and be utterly dismayed! Give ear
all you [our enemies] *of* far countries; gird yourselves *for war* and
be thrown into consternation; gird yourselves and be [utterly]
dismayed!
10Take counsel together [against Judah] and it shall come to
nought; speak the word, but it will not stand, for God is with
us—Immanuel!
11For the Lord spoke thus to me with *His* strong hand *upon me*,
and warned *and* instructed me not to walk in the way of this
people, saying,

**AMP** [a] Samaria was overthrown by Assyria in B.C. 722, ten years after the downfall of Damascus, fulfilling this prophecy. [b] This prophecy was literally fulfilled, and although Syria and Israel were conquered and led into captivity, the kingdom of Judah was spared and continued for over 130 years. [c] In its full sense it can apply only to the Messiah; "that Judea is His, was and still is a pledge that however sorely overwhelmed, it shall be saved at last."

## New American Standard

20¶ In that day the Lord will shave with a razor, hired from regions beyond the Euphrates (*that is,* with the king of Assyria), the head and the hair of the legs; and it will also remove the beard.
21¶ Now it will come about in that day that a man may keep alive a heifer and a pair of sheep;
22and it will happen that because of the abundance of the milk produced he will eat curds, for everyone that is left within the land will eat curds and honey.
23And it will come about in that day, that every place where there used to be a thousand vines, *valued* at a thousand *shekels* of silver, will become briars and thorns.
24*People* will come there with bows and arrows because all the land will be briars and thorns.
25And as for all the hills which used to be cultivated with the hoe, you will not go there for fear of briars and thorns; but they will become a place for pasturing oxen and for sheep to trample.

*Damascus and Samaria Fall*

8 THEN THE LORD said to me, "Take for yourself a large tablet and write on it in ordinary letters: Swift is the booty, speedy is the prey.
2"And I will take to Myself faithful witnesses for testimony, Uriah the priest and Zechariah the son of Jeberechiah."
3So I approached the prophetess, and she conceived and gave birth to a son. Then the LORD said to me, "Name him [d]Maher-shalal-hash-baz;
4for before the boy knows how to cry out 'My father' or 'My mother,' the wealth of Damascus and the spoil of Samaria will be carried away before the king of Assyria."
5¶ And again the LORD spoke to me further, saying,
6 "Inasmuch as these people have rejected the gently
flowing waters of Shiloah,
And rejoice in Rezin and the son of Remaliah;
7 "Now therefore, behold, the Lord is about to bring on
them the strong and abundant waters of the
Euphrates,
Even the king of Assyria and all his glory;
And it will rise up over all its channels and go over all
its banks.
8 "Then it will sweep on into Judah, it will overflow and
pass through,
It will reach even to the neck;
And the spread of its wings will fill the breadth of your
land, O Immanuel.

*A Believing Remnant*

9¶ "Be broken, O peoples, and be shattered;
And give ear, all remote places of the earth.
Gird yourselves, yet be shattered;
Gird yourselves, yet be shattered.
10 "Devise a plan but it will be thwarted;
State a proposal, but it will not stand,
For God is with us."
11For thus the LORD spoke to me with mighty power and instructed me not to walk in the way of this people, saying,

NAS [d] I.e., swift is the booty, speedy is the prey

## New International

day the Lord will use a razor hired from beyond the River[e]—the king of Assyria—to shave your head and the hair of your legs, and to take off your beards also. 21In that day, a man will keep alive a young cow and two goats. 22And because of the abundance of the milk they give, he will have curds to eat. All who remain in the land will eat curds and honey. 23In that day, in every place where there were a thousand vines worth a thousand silver shekels,[f] there will be only briers and thorns. 24Men will go there with bow and arrow, for the land will be covered with briers and thorns. 25As for all the hills once cultivated by the hoe, you will no longer go there for fear of the briers and thorns; they will become places where cattle are turned loose and where sheep run.

*Assyria, the LORD's Instrument*

8 THE LORD said to me, "Take a large scroll and write on it with an ordinary pen: Maher-Shalal-Hash-Baz.[g] 2And I will call in Uriah the priest and Zechariah son of Jeberekiah as reliable witnesses for me."
3Then I went to the prophetess, and she conceived and gave birth to a son. And the LORD said to me, "Name him Maher-Shalal-Hash-Baz. 4Before the boy knows how to say 'My father' or 'My mother,' the wealth of Damascus and the plunder of Samaria will be carried off by the king of Assyria."
5The LORD spoke to me again:

6"Because this people has rejected
the gently flowing waters of Shiloah
and rejoices over Rezin
and the son of Remaliah,
7therefore the Lord is about to bring against them
the mighty floodwaters of the River[h]—
the king of Assyria with all his pomp.
It will overflow all its channels,
run over all its banks
8and sweep on into Judah, swirling over it,
passing through it and reaching up to the neck.
Its outspread wings will cover the breadth of your land,
O Immanuel[i]!"
9Raise the war cry,[j] you nations, and be shattered!
Listen, all you distant lands.
Prepare for battle, and be shattered!
Prepare for battle, and be shattered!
10Devise your strategy, but it will be thwarted;
propose your plan, but it will not stand,
for God is with us.[k]

*Fear God*

11The LORD spoke to me with his strong hand upon me, warning me not to follow the way of this people. He said:

NIV [e] *20* That is, the Euphrates [f] *23* That is, about 25 pounds (about 11.5 kilograms) [g] *1 Maher-Shalal-Hash-Baz* means *quick to the plunder, swift to the spoil;* also in verse 3. [h] *7* That is, the Euphrates [i] *8 Immanuel* means *God with us.* [j] *9* Or *Do your worst* [k] *10* Hebrew *Immanuel*

## King James

12 Say ye not, A confederacy, to all *them to* whom this people shall say, A confederacy; neither fear ye their fear, nor be afraid.

13 Sanctify the LORD of hosts himself; and *let* him *be* your fear, and *let* him *be* your dread.

14 And he shall be for a sanctuary; but for a stone of stumbling and for a rock of offence to both the houses of Israel, for a gin and for a snare to the inhabitants of Jerusalem.

15 And many among them shall stumble, and fall, and be broken, and be snared, and be taken.

16 Bind up the testimony, seal the law among my disciples.

17 And I will wait upon the LORD, that hideth his face from the house of Jacob, and I will look for him.

18 Behold, I and the children whom the LORD hath given me *are* for signs and for wonders in Israel from the LORD of hosts, which dwelleth in mount Zion.

19 ¶ And when they shall say unto you, Seek unto them that have familiar spirits, and unto wizards that peep, and that mutter: should not a people seek unto their God? for the living to the dead?

20 To the law and to the testimony: if they speak not according to this word, *it is* because *there is* no light in them.

21 And they shall pass through it, hardly bestead and hungry: and it shall come to pass, that when they shall be hungry, they shall fret themselves, and curse their king and their God, and look upward.

22 And they shall look unto the earth; and behold trouble and darkness, dimness of anguish; and *they shall be* driven to darkness.

## Amplified

12 Do not call conspiracy [or hard, or holy] all that this people will call conspiracy [or hard, or holy]; neither be in fear of what they fear, nor [make others afraid and] in dread.

13 The Lord of hosts, regard Him as holy *and* honor His holy name [by regarding Him as your only hope of safety], and let Him be your fear and let Him be your dread [lest you offend Him by your fear of man and distrust of Him].

14 And He shall be for a sanctuary—a sacred and indestructible asylum [to those who reverently fear and trust in Him]; but for a stone of stumbling and for a rock of offense to both the houses of Israel, for a trap and for a snare to the inhabitants of Jerusalem.

15 And many among them shall stumble thereon, and fall and be broken, and be snared and taken.

16 Bind up the testimony, seal the law *and* the teaching among my [Isaiah's] disciples.

17 And I will wait for the Lord, Who is hiding His face from the house of Jacob, and I will look for *and* hope in Him.

18 Behold, I and the children whom the Lord has given me are [a]for signs and for wonders [that are to take place] in Israel from the Lord of hosts, Who dwells in Mount Zion.

19 And when the people [instead of putting their trust in God] shall say to you, Consult for direction mediums and wizards who chirp and mutter, should not a people seek *and* consult their God? Should they consult the dead on behalf of the living?

20 [Direct such people] to the teaching and to the testimony; if their teachings are not in accord with this word, it is surely because there is no dawn *and* no morning for them.

21 And they [who consult mediums and wizards] shall pass through *the land,* sorely distressed and hungry; and when they shall be hungry, they will fret themselves, and curse by their king and their God; and whether they look upward,

22 Or look to the earth, they will behold *only* distress and darkness, the gloom of anguish; and into thick darkness *and* widespread, obscure night they shall be driven away.

## King James

**9** NEVERTHELESS THE dimness *shall* not *be* such as *was* in her vexation, when at the first he lightly afflicted the land of Zebulun and the land of Naphtali, and afterward did more grievously afflict *her by* the way of the sea, beyond Jordan, in Galilee of the nations.

2 The people that walked in darkness have seen a great light: they that dwell in the land of the shadow of death, upon them hath the light shined.

3 Thou hast multiplied the nation, *and* not increased the joy: they joy before thee according to the joy in harvest, *and* as *men* rejoice when they divide the spoil.

4 For thou hast broken the yoke of his burden, and the staff of his shoulder, the rod of his oppressor, as in the day of Midian.

5 For every battle of the warrior *is* with confused noise, and garments rolled in blood; but *this* shall be with burning *and* fuel of fire.

## Amplified

**9** BUT [IN the midst of judgment there is the promise and the certainty of the Lord's deliverance] there shall be no gloom for her who was in anguish. In the former time the *Lord* brought into contempt the land of Zebulun and the land of Naphtali, but in the latter time He will make *it* glorious, by the way of the Sea *of Galilee, the land* beyond the Jordan, Galilee of the nations.

2 The people who walked in darkness have seen a great light; those who dwelt in the land of intense darkness *and* the shadow of death, upon them has the light shined. [Matt. 4:15, 16.]

3 You, *O Lord,* have multiplied the nation and increased their joy; they rejoice before You like the joy in harvest, as men rejoice when they divide the spoil *of battle.*

4 For the yoke of [Israel's] burden, and the staff *or* rod for [goading] his shoulder, the rod of his oppressor, You have broken as in the day of [Gideon with] Midian. [Judg. 7:8-22.]

5 For every *tramping* warrior's warboots *and* all his armor in the battle tumult and every garment rolled in blood shall be burned *as* fuel for the fire.

**AMP** [a] Isaiah's own name means, *"Salvation of the Lord"*; His two children's names were "signs" suggestive of the coming crisis and the need of God's help, *Shear-jashub* means, *"A remnant shall return,"* and *Maher-shalal-hash-baz* means: *"They hasten to the spoil; they speed to the prey,"* referring to the Assyrians. (Isa. 7:3; 8:1.)

## New American Standard

12 "You are not to say, '*It is* a conspiracy!'
In regard to all that this people call a conspiracy,
And you are not to fear what they fear or be in dread
of *it*.
13 "It is the LORD of hosts whom you should regard as
holy.
And He shall be your fear,
And He shall be your dread.
14 "Then He shall become a sanctuary;
But to both the houses of Israel, a stone to strike and a
rock to stumble over,
*And* a snare and a trap for the inhabitants of Jerusalem.
15 "And many will stumble over them,
Then they will fall and be broken;
They will even be snared and caught."
16¶ Bind up the testimony, seal the law among my disciples.
17 And I will wait for the LORD who is hiding His face from the
house of Jacob; I will even look eagerly for Him.
18 Behold, I and the children whom the LORD has given me are
for signs and wonders in Israel from the LORD of hosts, who dwells
on Mount Zion.
19¶ And when they say to you, "Consult the mediums and the
spiritists who whisper and mutter," should not a people consult
their God? *Should they consult* the dead on behalf of the living?
20 To the law and to the testimony! If they do not speak according to this word, it is because they have no dawn.
21 And they will pass through the land hard-pressed and famished, and it will turn out that when they are hungry, they will be
enraged and curse their king and their God as they face upward.
22 Then they will look to the earth, and behold, distress and
darkness, the gloom of anguish; and *they will be* driven away into
darkness.

*Birth and Reign of the Prince of Peace*

9 BUT THERE will be no *more* gloom for her who was in an-
guish; in earlier times He treated the land of Zebulun and the
land of Naphtali with contempt, but later on He shall make *it*
glorious, by the way of the sea, on the other side of Jordan, Galilee
of the Gentiles.
2 The people who walk in darkness
Will see a great light;
Those who live in a dark land,
The light will shine on them.
3 Thou shalt multiply the nation,
Thou shalt increase their gladness;
They will be glad in Thy presence
As with the gladness of harvest,
As men rejoice when they divide the spoil.
4 For Thou shalt break the yoke of their burden and the
staff on their shoulders,
The rod of their oppressor, as at the battle of Midian.
5 For every boot of the booted warrior in the *battle*
tumult,
And cloak rolled in blood, will be for burning, fuel for
the fire.

## New International

12 "Do not call conspiracy
everything that these people call conspiracy[b];
do not fear what they fear,
and do not dread it.
13 The LORD Almighty is the one you are to regard as holy,
he is the one you are to fear,
he is the one you are to dread,
14 and he will be a sanctuary;
but for both houses of Israel he will be
a stone that causes men to stumble
and a rock that makes them fall.
And for the people of Jerusalem he will be
a trap and a snare.
15 Many of them will stumble;
they will fall and be broken,
they will be snared and captured."

16 Bind up the testimony
and seal up the law among my disciples.
17 I will wait for the LORD,
who is hiding his face from the house of Jacob.
I will put my trust in him.

18 Here am I, and the children the LORD has given me. We are
signs and symbols in Israel from the LORD Almighty, who dwells
on Mount Zion.
19 When men tell you to consult mediums and spiritists, who
whisper and mutter, should not a people inquire of their God?
Why consult the dead on behalf of the living? 20 To the law and to
the testimony! If they do not speak according to this word, they
have no light of dawn. 21 Distressed and hungry, they will roam
through the land; when they are famished, they will become enraged and, looking upward, will curse their king and their God.
22 Then they will look toward the earth and see only distress and
darkness and fearful gloom, and they will be thrust into utter
darkness.

*To Us a Child Is Born*

9 NEVERTHELESS, THERE will be no more gloom for those
who were in distress. In the past he humbled the land of
Zebulun and the land of Naphtali, but in the future he will honor
Galilee of the Gentiles, by the way of the sea, along the Jordan—

2 The people walking in darkness
have seen a great light;
on those living in the land of the shadow of death[c]
a light has dawned.
3 You have enlarged the nation
and increased their joy;
they rejoice before you
as people rejoice at the harvest,
as men rejoice
when dividing the plunder.
4 For as in the day of Midian's defeat,
you have shattered
the yoke that burdens them,
the bar across their shoulders,
the rod of their oppressor.
5 Every warrior's boot used in battle
and every garment rolled in blood
will be destined for burning,
will be fuel for the fire.

NIV [b] 12 Or *Do not call for a treaty / every time these people call for a treaty*
[c] 2 Or *land of darkness*

## King James

6For unto us a child is born, unto us a son is given: and the government shall be upon his shoulder: and his name shall be called Wonderful, Counsellor, The mighty God, The everlasting Father, The Prince of Peace.
7Of the increase of *his* government and peace *there shall be* no end, upon the throne of David, and upon his kingdom, to order it, and to establish it with judgment and with justice from henceforth even for ever. The zeal of the LORD of hosts will perform this.
8¶ The Lord sent a word into Jacob, and it hath lighted upon Israel.
9And all the people shall know, *even* Ephraim and the inhabitant of Samaria, that say in the pride and stoutness of heart,
10The bricks are fallen down, but we will build with hewn stones: the sycamores are cut down, but we will change *them into* cedars.
11Therefore the LORD shall set up the adversaries of Rezin against him, and join his enemies together;
12The Syrians before, and the Philistines behind; and they shall devour Israel with open mouth. For all this his anger is not turned away, but his hand *is* stretched out still.
13¶ For the people turneth not unto him that smiteth them, neither do they seek the LORD of hosts.
14Therefore the LORD will cut off from Israel head and tail, branch and rush, in one day.
15The ancient and honourable, he *is* the head; and the prophet that teacheth lies, he *is* the tail.
16For the leaders of this people cause *them* to err; and *they that are* led of them *are* destroyed.
17Therefore the Lord shall have no joy in their young men, neither shall have mercy on their fatherless and widows: for every one *is* an hypocrite and an evildoer, and every mouth speaketh folly. For all this his anger is not turned away, but his hand *is* stretched out still.
18¶ For wickedness burneth as the fire: it shall devour the briers and thorns, and shall kindle in the thickets of the forest, and they shall mount up *like* the lifting up of smoke.
19Through the wrath of the LORD of hosts is the land darkened, and the people shall be as the fuel of the fire: no man shall spare his brother.
20And he shall snatch on the right hand, and be hungry; and he shall eat on the left hand, and they shall not be satisfied: they shall eat every man the flesh of his own arm:

## Amplified

6For to us a child is born, to us a son is given; and the government shall be upon His shoulder, and His name shall be called Wonderful Counselor, Mighty God, Everlasting Father (of Eternity), Prince of Peace. [Luke 2:11; Matt. 28:18; Heb. 1:8; Eph. 5:14.]
7Of the increase of His government and of peace there shall be no end, upon the throne of David and over His kingdom, to establish it and to uphold it with justice and with righteousness from the *latter* time forth, even for evermore. The zeal of the Lord of hosts will perform this. [Dan. 2:44; I Cor. 15:25-28.]
8The Lord has sent a word against Jacob [the ten tribes] and it has lighted upon Israel [the ten tribes, the kingdom of Ephraim].
9And all the people shall know *it*, even Ephraim and the inhabitants of Samaria [its capital], who said in pride and stoutness of heart,
10The bricks are fallen, but we will build *all the better* with hewn stones; the sycamores are cut down, but we will put *costlier* cedars in their place.
11Therefore the Lord has stirred up [the Assyrians] the adversaries of Rezin *king of Syria* against *Ephraim*, and He will stir up his enemies *and* arm *and* join them together,
12The Syrians [compelled then to fight with their enemies, going] before [on the east] and the Philistines behind [on the west]; and they will devour Israel with open mouth. For all this *God's* anger is not *then* turned away, but His hand is stretched out still *in judgment*.
13Yet the people turn not to Him Who smote them, neither do they seek [inquire for or require as their vital need] the Lord of hosts.
14Therefore the Lord will cut off from Israel head and tail [the highest and the lowest], *high* palm branch and *low* rush in one day.
15The elderly and honored man, he is the head; and the prophet who teaches lies, he is the tail.
16For they who lead this people cause them to err, and they who are led *astray* by them are swallowed up—destroyed.
17Therefore the Lord will not rejoice over their young men, neither will He have compassion on their fatherless and widows; for every one is profane and an evildoer, and every mouth speaks folly. For all this *God's* anger is not turned away, but His hand is stretched out still *in judgment*.
18For wickedness burns like a fire, it devours the briers and thorns, and kindles in the thickets of the forest; they roll upward in a column of smoke.
19Through the wrath of the Lord of hosts the land is darkened *and* burned up, and the people are like fuel for the fire; no man spares his brother.
20 *They* snatch in discord on the right hand, but are still hungry [their cruelty not diminished], and *they* devour *and* destroy on the left hand, but are not satisfied; each devours *and* destroys his own flesh [and blood] *or* his neighbor's.

## New American Standard

6 For a child will be born to us, a son will be given to us;
And the government will rest on His shoulders;
And His name will be called Wonderful Counselor,
Mighty God,
Eternal Father, Prince of Peace.
7 There will be no end to the increase of *His* government or of peace,
On the throne of David and over his kingdom,
To establish it and to uphold it with justice and righteousness
From then on and forevermore.
The zeal of the LORD of hosts will accomplish this.

*God's Anger with Israel's Arrogance*

8¶ The Lord sends a message against Jacob,
And it falls on Israel.
9 And all the people know *it*,
*That is*, Ephraim and the inhabitants of Samaria,
Asserting in pride and in arrogance of heart:
10 "The bricks have fallen down,
But we will rebuild with smooth stones;
The sycamores have been cut down,
But we will replace *them* with cedars."
11 Therefore the LORD raises against them adversaries from Rezin,
And spurs their enemies on,
12 The Arameans on the east and the Philistines on the west;
And they devour Israel with gaping jaws.
In *spite of* all this His anger does not turn away,
And His hand is still stretched out.

13¶ Yet the people do not turn back to Him who struck them,
Nor do they seek the LORD of hosts.
14 So the LORD cuts off head and tail from Israel,
*Both* palm branch and bulrush in a single day.
15 The head is the elder and honorable man,
And the prophet who teaches falsehood is the tail.
16 For those who guide this people are leading *them* astray;
And those who are guided by them are brought to confusion.
17 Therefore the Lord does not take pleasure in their young men,
Nor does He have pity on their orphans or their widows;
For every one of them is godless and an evildoer,
And every mouth is speaking foolishness.
In *spite of* all this His anger does not turn away,
And His hand is still stretched out.

18¶ For wickedness burns like a fire;
It consumes briars and thorns;
It even sets the thickets of the forest aflame,
And they roll upward in a column of smoke.
19 By the fury of the LORD of hosts the land is burned up,
And the people are like fuel for the fire;
No man spares his brother.
20 And they slice off *what is* on the right hand but *still* are hungry,
And they eat *what is* on the left hand but they are not satisfied;
Each of them eats the flesh of his own arm.

## New International

6 For to us a child is born,
to us a son is given,
and the government will be on his shoulders.
And he will be called
Wonderful Counselor,[a] Mighty God,
Everlasting Father, Prince of Peace.
7 Of the increase of his government and peace
there will be no end.
He will reign on David's throne
and over his kingdom,
establishing and upholding it
with justice and righteousness
from that time on and forever.
The zeal of the LORD Almighty
will accomplish this.

*The LORD's Anger Against Israel*

8 The Lord has sent a message against Jacob;
it will fall on Israel.
9 All the people will know it—
Ephraim and the inhabitants of Samaria—
who say with pride
and arrogance of heart,
10 "The bricks have fallen down,
but we will rebuild with dressed stone;
the fig trees have been felled,
but we will replace them with cedars."
11 But the LORD has strengthened Rezin's foes against them
and has spurred their enemies on.
12 Arameans from the east and Philistines from the west
have devoured Israel with open mouth.

Yet for all this, his anger is not turned away,
his hand is still upraised.

13 But the people have not returned to him who struck them,
nor have they sought the LORD Almighty.
14 So the LORD will cut off from Israel both head and tail,
both palm branch and reed in a single day;
15 the elders and prominent men are the head,
the prophets who teach lies are the tail.
16 Those who guide this people mislead them,
and those who are guided are led astray.
17 Therefore the Lord will take no pleasure in the young men,
nor will he pity the fatherless and widows,
for everyone is ungodly and wicked,
every mouth speaks vileness.

Yet for all this, his anger is not turned away,
his hand is still upraised.

18 Surely wickedness burns like a fire;
it consumes briers and thorns,
it sets the forest thickets ablaze,
so that it rolls upward in a column of smoke.
19 By the wrath of the LORD Almighty
the land will be scorched
and the people will be fuel for the fire;
no one will spare his brother.
20 On the right they will devour,
but still be hungry;
on the left they will eat,
but not be satisfied.
Each will feed on the flesh of his own offspring[b]:

NIV [a] 6 Or *Wonderful, Counselor* [b] 20 Or *arm*

## King James

21Manasseh, Ephraim; and Ephraim, Manasseh: *and* they together *shall be* against Judah. For all this his anger is not turned away, but his hand *is* stretched out still.

**10** WOE UNTO them that decree unrighteous decrees, and that write grievousness *which* they have prescribed;

2To turn aside the needy from judgment, and to take away the right from the poor of my people, that widows may be their prey, and *that* they may rob the fatherless!

3And what will ye do in the day of visitation, and in the desolation *which* shall come from far? to whom will ye flee for help? and where will ye leave your glory?

4Without me they shall bow down under the prisoners, and they shall fall under the slain. For all this his anger is not turned away, but his hand *is* stretched out still.

5¶ O Assyrian, the rod of mine anger, and the staff in their hand is mine indignation.

6I will send him against an hypocritical nation, and against the people of my wrath will I give him a charge, to take the spoil, and to take the prey, and to tread them down like the mire of the streets.

7Howbeit he meaneth not so, neither doth his heart think so; but *it is* in his heart to destroy and cut off nations not a few.

8For he saith, *Are* not my princes altogether kings?

9 *Is* not Calno as Carchemish? *is* not Hamath as Arpad? *is* not Samaria as Damascus?

10As my hand hath found the kingdoms of the idols, and whose graven images did excel them of Jerusalem and of Samaria;

11Shall I not, as I have done unto Samaria and her idols, so do to Jerusalem and her idols?

12Wherefore it shall come to pass, *that* when the Lord hath performed his whole work upon mount Zion and on Jerusalem, I will punish the fruit of the stout heart of the king of Assyria, and the glory of his high looks.

13For he saith, By the strength of my hand I have done *it*, and by my wisdom; for I am prudent: and I have removed the bounds of the people, and have robbed their treasures, and I have put down the inhabitants like a valiant *man:*

14And my hand hath found as a nest the riches of the people: and as one gathereth eggs *that are* left, have I gathered all the earth; and there was none that moved the wing, or opened the mouth, or peeped.

15Shall the axe boast itself against him that heweth therewith? *or* shall the saw magnify itself against him that shaketh it? as if the rod should shake *itself* against them that lift it up, *or* as if the staff should lift up *itself*, *as if it were* no wood.

## Amplified

21Manasseh [thirsts for the blood of his brother] Ephraim, and Ephraim [for that of] Manasseh; but together they are against Judah. For all this *God's* anger is not turned away, but His hand is stretched out still *in judgment*.

**10** WOE TO those *judges* who issue unrighteous decrees, and to the magistrates who keep causing unjust *and* oppressive decisions to be recorded,

2To turn aside the needy from justice and to make plunder of the rightful claim of the poor of My people, that widows may be their spoil, and that they may make the fatherless their prey!

3And what will you do in the day of visitation *of God's wrath*, and in the desolation which shall come from afar? To whom will you flee for help? And where will you deposit [for safe keeping] your wealth, *and* with whom leave your glory?

4Without Me they shall bow down among the prisoners, and they shall fall [overwhelmed] under the heaps of the slain *on the battlefield*. For all this *God's* anger is not turned away, but His hand is stretched out still *in judgment*.

5Ho, Assyrian, the rod of My anger, the staff in whose hand is My indignation *and* fury [against Israel's disobedience]!

6I will send *the Assyrian* against a hypocritical *and* godless nation, and against the people of My wrath; I command him to take the spoil and to seize the prey, and to tread them down like the mire of the streets.

7However, this is not his intention [nor is the Assyrian aware that he is doing this at My bidding], neither does his mind so think *and* plan, but it is in his mind to destroy and cut off many nations.

8For *the Assyrian* says, Are not my officers all of them either [subjugated] kings *or* their equal?

9Is not Calno *of Babylonia conquered* as is Carchemish *on the Euphrates*? Is not Hamath *in Upper Syria* as Arpad, *her neighbor*? Is not Samaria *in Israel* as Damascus *in Syria*? [Have any of these cities been able to resist Assyria? Not one!]

10As my hand has reached to the kingdoms of the idols [which were unable to defend them, and] whose graven images were more to be feared *and* dreaded *and* more mighty than those of Jerusalem and of Samaria.

11Shall I not be able to do to Jerusalem and her images as I have done to Samaria and her idols? [says the Assyrian.]

12Therefore when the Lord has completed all His work [of chastisement and purification] *to be executed* on Mount Zion and on Jerusalem, it shall be that He will inflict punishment on the fruit [the thoughts, words and deeds] of the stout *and* arrogant heart of the king of Assyria and the haughtiness of his pride.

13For *the Assyrian king* has said, I have done it solely by the power of my own hand and wisdom, for I have insight *and* understanding; I have removed the boundaries of the peoples and have robbed their treasures, and like a bull I have brought down those who sat on thrones, *and* the inhabitants.

14And my hand has found like a nest the wealth of the people, and as one gathers eggs that are forsaken, so I have gathered all the earth; and there was none that moved the wing, or that opened the mouth, or chirped.

15Shall the ax boast itself against him who chops with it? Or shall the saw magnify itself against him who wields it back and forth? As if a rod should wield those who lift it up, or as if a staff should lift itself up as if it were not wood [but a man of God]!

## New American Standard

21 Manasseh *devours* Ephraim, and Ephraim Manasseh,
*And* together they are against Judah.
In *spite of* all this His anger does not turn away,
And His hand is still stretched out.

*Assyria Is God's Instrument*

10 WOE TO those who enact evil statutes,
And to those who constantly record unjust decisions,
2 So as to deprive the needy of justice,
And rob the poor of My people of *their* rights,
In order that widows may be their spoil,
And that they may plunder the orphans.
3 Now what will you do in the day of punishment,
And in the devastation which will come from afar?
To whom will you flee for help?
And where will you leave your wealth?
4 Nothing *remains* but to crouch among the captives
Or fall among the slain.
In *spite of* all this His anger does not turn away,
And His hand is still stretched out.
5¶ Woe to Assyria, the rod of My anger
And the staff in whose hands is My indignation,
6 I send it against a godless nation
And commission it against the people of My fury
To capture booty and to seize plunder,
And to trample them down like mud in the streets.
7 Yet it does not so intend
Nor does it plan so in its heart,
But rather it is its purpose to destroy,
And to cut off many nations.
8 For it says, "Are not my princes all kings?
9 "Is not Calno like Carchemish,
Or Hamath like Arpad,
Or Samaria like Damascus?
10 "As my hand has reached to the kingdoms of the idols,
Whose graven images *were* greater than those of
Jerusalem and Samaria,
11 Shall I not do to Jerusalem and her images
Just as I have done to Samaria and her idols?"
12¶ So it will be that when the Lord has completed all His work
on Mount Zion and on Jerusalem, *He will say,* "I will punish the
fruit of the arrogant heart of the king of Assyria and the pomp of
his haughtiness."
13For he has said,
"By the power of my hand and by my wisdom I did *this,*
For I have understanding;
And I removed the boundaries of the peoples,
And plundered their treasures,
And like a mighty man I brought down *their*
inhabitants,
14 And my hand reached to the riches of the peoples like
a nest,
And as one gathers abandoned eggs, I gathered all the
earth;
And there was not one that flapped its wing or opened
*its* beak or chirped."
15¶ Is the axe to boast itself over the one who chops with
it?
Is the saw to exalt itself over the one who wields it?
*That would be* like a club wielding those who lift it,
*Or* like a rod lifting *him who* is not wood.

## New International

21 Manasseh will feed on Ephraim, and Ephraim on
Manasseh;
together they will turn against Judah.

Yet for all this, his anger is not turned away,
his hand is still upraised.

10 WOE to those who make unjust laws,
to those who issue oppressive decrees,
2to deprive the poor of their rights
and withhold justice from the oppressed of my people,
making widows their prey
and robbing the fatherless.
3What will you do on the day of reckoning,
when disaster comes from afar?
To whom will you run for help?
Where will you leave your riches?
4Nothing will remain but to cringe among the captives
or fall among the slain.

Yet for all this, his anger is not turned away,
his hand is still upraised.

*God's Judgment on Assyria*

5"Woe to the Assyrian, the rod of my anger,
in whose hand is the club of my wrath!
6I send him against a godless nation,
I dispatch him against a people who anger me,
to seize loot and snatch plunder,
and to trample them down like mud in the streets.
7But this is not what he intends,
this is not what he has in mind;
his purpose is to destroy,
to put an end to many nations.
8'Are not my commanders all kings?' he says.
9 'Has not Calno fared like Carchemish?
Is not Hamath like Arpad,
and Samaria like Damascus?
10As my hand seized the kingdoms of the idols,
kingdoms whose images excelled those of Jerusalem
and Samaria—
11shall I not deal with Jerusalem and her images
as I dealt with Samaria and her idols?' "

12When the Lord has finished all his work against Mount Zion
and Jerusalem, he will say, "I will punish the king of Assyria for
the willful pride of his heart and the haughty look in his eyes. 13For
he says:

" 'By the strength of my hand I have done this,
and by my wisdom, because I have understanding.
I removed the boundaries of nations,
I plundered their treasures;
like a mighty one I subdued[a] their kings.
14As one reaches into a nest,
so my hand reached for the wealth of the nations;
as men gather abandoned eggs,
so I gathered all the countries;
not one flapped a wing,
or opened its mouth to chirp.' "

15Does the ax raise itself above him who swings it,
or the saw boast against him who uses it?
As if a rod were to wield him who lifts it up,
or a club brandish him who is not wood!

NIV [a] 13 Or / *I subdued the mighty,*

## King James

16Therefore shall the Lord, the Lord of hosts, send among his fat ones leanness; and under his glory he shall kindle a burning like the burning of a fire.

17And the light of Israel shall be for a fire, and his Holy One for a flame: and it shall burn and devour his thorns and his briers in one day;

18And shall consume the glory of his forest, and of his fruitful field, both soul and body: and they shall be as when a standard-bearer fainteth.

19And the rest of the trees of his forest shall be few, that a child may write them.

20¶ And it shall come to pass in that day, *that* the remnant of Israel, and such as are escaped of the house of Jacob, shall no more again stay upon him that smote them; but shall stay upon the LORD, the Holy One of Israel, in truth.

21The remnant shall return, *even* the remnant of Jacob, unto the mighty God.

22For though thy people Israel be as the sand of the sea, *yet* a remnant of them shall return: the consumption decreed shall overflow with righteousness.

23For the Lord GOD of hosts shall make a consumption, even determined, in the midst of all the land.

24¶ Therefore thus saith the Lord GOD of hosts, O my people that dwellest in Zion, be not afraid of the Assyrian: he shall smite thee with a rod, and shall lift up his staff against thee, after the manner of Egypt.

25For yet a very little while, and the indignation shall cease, and mine anger in their destruction.

26And the LORD of hosts shall stir up a scourge for him according to the slaughter of Midian at the rock of Oreb: and *as* his rod *was* upon the sea, so shall he lift it up after the manner of Egypt.

27And it shall come to pass in that day, *that* his burden shall be taken away from off thy shoulder, and his yoke from off thy neck, and the yoke shall be destroyed because of the anointing.

28He is come to Aiath, he is passed to Migron; at Michmash he hath laid up his carriages:

29They are gone over the passage: they have taken up their lodging at Geba; Ramah is afraid; Gibeah of Saul is fled.

30Lift up thy voice, O daughter of Gallim: cause it to be heard unto Laish, O poor Anathoth.

31Madmenah is removed; the inhabitants of Gebim gather themselves to flee.

32As yet shall he remain at Nob that day: he shall shake his hand *against* the mount of the daughter of Zion, the hill of Jerusalem.

## Amplified

16Therefore will the Lord, the Lord of hosts, send leanness among [the Assyrian's] fat ones, and instead of his glory *or* under it He will kindle a burning like the burning of fire.

17And the light of Israel shall be for a fire and His Holy One for a flame, and it will [a]burn and devour [the Assyrian's] thorns and briers in one day;

18 *The Lord* will consume the glory of the [Assyrian's] forest and of his fruitful field, both soul and body; and it shall be as when a sick man pines away *or* a standard-bearer faints.

19And the remnant of the trees of his forest shall be few, so that a child may make a list of them.

20And it shall be in that day that the remnant of Israel, and such as are escaped of the house of Jacob, shall no more lean upon him who smote them, but will lean upon the Lord, the Holy One of Israel, in truth.

21A remnant will return [Shear-jashub, name of Isaiah's son], a remnant of Jacob, to the mighty God.

22For though your population, O Israel, be as the sand of the sea, only a remnant of it will return [and survive]. The *fully completed* destruction is decreed—decided upon and brought to an issue; it overflows with justice *and* righteousness [the infliction of just punishment]. [Rom. 9:27, 28.]

23For the Lord, the Lord of hosts, will make a full end, and whatever is determined *or* decreed *in Israel,* in the midst of all the earth.

24Therefore thus says the Lord, the Lord of hosts, O My people who dwell in Zion, do not be afraid of the Assyrian, who will smite you with a rod and will lift up his staff against you, as [the king of] Egypt did. [Exod. 5.]

25For yet a little while, and *My* indignation against you shall be accomplished, and My anger shall be directed to destruction [of the Assyrian].

26And the Lord of hosts shall stir up *and* brandish a scourge against them as when He smote Midian at the rock of Oreb; and as His rod was over the *Red* Sea, so shall He lift it up as He did *in the flight from* Egypt. [Judg. 7:24, 25; Exod. 14:26-31.]

27And it shall be in that day that the burden of *the Assyrian* shall depart from off your shoulder, and his yoke from off your neck. The yoke shall be destroyed because of fatness [which prevents it from longer going around your neck]. [Deut. 32:15.]

28 *The Assyrian with his army is come to Judah:* he has arrived at Aiath, he is passed to Migron; at Michmash he gets rid of his baggage [by storing it].

29They go through the pass, they make Geba their camping place for the night; Ramah is afraid *and* trembles, Gibeah *the city* of *King* Saul has fled.

30Cry aloud *in consternation,* O daughter of Gallim! Hearken, O Laishah! *Answer her,* O you poor Anathoth!

31Madmenah is in flight; the inhabitants of Gebim seize their belongings *and* make their households flee for safety.

32This very day *the Assyrian* will halt at Nob [the city of priests], shaking his fist at the mountain of the daughter of Zion, the hill of Jerusalem.

**AMP** [a] During a single night this prophecy was fulfilled, when "the Angel of the Lord went forth and smote in the camp of the Assyrians a hundred and eighty-five thousand men and in the morning they were all dead," just when their victory over God's people had seemed certain. (Isa. 37:38.)

## New American Standard

16 Therefore the Lord, the GOD of hosts, will send a
wasting disease among his stout warriors;
And under his glory a fire will be kindled like a
burning flame.
17 And the light of Israel will become a fire and his Holy
One a flame,
And it will burn and devour his thorns and his briars in
a single day.
18 And He will destroy the glory of his forest and of his
fruitful garden, both soul and body;
And it will be as when a sick man wastes away.
19 And the rest of the trees of his forest will be so small in
number
That a child could write them down.

*A Remnant Will Return*

**20**¶ Now it will come about in that day that the remnant of Israel,
and those of the house of Jacob who have escaped, will never again
rely on the one who struck them, but will truly rely on the LORD,
the Holy One of Israel.
21 A remnant will return, the remnant of Jacob, to the
mighty God.
22 For though your people, O Israel, may be like the sand
of the sea,
*Only* a remnant within them will return;
A destruction is determined, overflowing with
righteousness.
23For a complete destruction, one that is decreed, the Lord GOD
of hosts will execute in the midst of the whole land.
**24**¶ Therefore thus says the Lord GOD of hosts, "O My people
who dwell in Zion, do not fear the Assyrian who strikes you with
the rod and lifts up his staff against you, the way Egypt *did.*
25"For in a very little while My indignation *against you* will be
spent, and My anger *will be directed* to their destruction."
26And the LORD of hosts will arouse a scourge against him like
the slaughter of Midian at the rock of Oreb; and His staff will be
over the sea, and He will lift it up the way *He did* in Egypt.
27So it will be in that day, that his burden will be removed from
your shoulders and his yoke from your neck, and the yoke will be
broken because of fatness.
**28**¶ He has come against Aiath,
He has passed through Migron;
At Michmash he deposited his baggage.
29 They have gone through the pass, *saying,*
"Geba will be our lodging place."
Ramah is terrified, and Gibeah of Saul has fled away.
30 Cry aloud with your voice, O daughter of Gallim!
Pay attention, Laishah *and* wretched Anathoth!
31 Madmenah has fled.
The inhabitants of Gebim have sought refuge.
32 Yet today he will halt at Nob;
He shakes his fist at the mountain of the daughter of
Zion, the hill of Jerusalem.

## New International

16Therefore, the Lord, the LORD Almighty,
will send a wasting disease upon his sturdy warriors;
under his pomp a fire will be kindled
like a blazing flame.
17The Light of Israel will become a fire,
their Holy One a flame;
in a single day it will burn and consume
his thorns and his briers.
18The splendor of his forests and fertile fields
it will completely destroy,
as when a sick man wastes away.
19And the remaining trees of his forests will be so few
that a child could write them down.

*The Remnant of Israel*

20In that day the remnant of Israel,
the survivors of the house of Jacob,
will no longer rely on him
who struck them down
but will truly rely on the LORD,
the Holy One of Israel.
21A remnant will return,[b] a remnant of Jacob
will return to the Mighty God.
22Though your people, O Israel, be like the sand by the sea,
only a remnant will return.
Destruction has been decreed,
overwhelming and righteous.
23The Lord, the LORD Almighty, will carry out
the destruction decreed upon the whole land.
24Therefore, this is what the Lord, the LORD Almighty, says:

"O my people who live in Zion,
do not be afraid of the Assyrians,
who beat you with a rod
and lift up a club against you, as Egypt did.
25Very soon my anger against you will end
and my wrath will be directed to their destruction."

26The LORD Almighty will lash them with a whip,
as when he struck down Midian at the rock of Oreb;
and he will raise his staff over the waters,
as he did in Egypt.
27In that day their burden will be lifted from your
shoulders,
their yoke from your neck;
the yoke will be broken
because you have grown so fat.[c]
28They enter Aiath;
they pass through Migron;
they store supplies at Micmash.
29They go over the pass, and say,
"We will camp overnight at Geba."
Ramah trembles;
Gibeah of Saul flees.
30Cry out, O Daughter of Gallim!
Listen, O Laishah!
Poor Anathoth!
31Madmenah is in flight;
the people of Gebim take cover.
32This day they will halt at Nob;
they will shake their fist
at the mount of the Daughter of Zion,
at the hill of Jerusalem.

**NIV** [b] *21* Hebrew *shear-jashub;* also in verse 22 [c] *27* Hebrew; Septuagint *broken / from your shoulders*

## King James

33Behold, the Lord, the LORD of hosts, shall lop the bough with terror: and the high ones of stature *shall be* hewn down, and the haughty shall be humbled.

34And he shall cut down the thickets of the forest with iron, and Lebanon shall fall by a mighty one.

**11** AND THERE shall come forth a rod out of the stem of Jesse, and a Branch shall grow out of his roots:

2And the spirit of the LORD shall rest upon him, the spirit of wisdom and understanding, the spirit of counsel and might, the spirit of knowledge and of the fear of the LORD;

3And shall make him of quick understanding in the fear of the LORD: and he shall not judge after the sight of his eyes, neither reprove after the hearing of his ears:

4But with righteousness shall he judge the poor, and reprove with equity for the meek of the earth: and he shall smite the earth with the rod of his mouth, and with the breath of his lips shall he slay the wicked.

5And righteousness shall be the girdle of his loins, and faithfulness the girdle of his reins.

6The wolf also shall dwell with the lamb, and the leopard shall lie down with the kid; and the calf and the young lion and the fatling together; and a little child shall lead them.

7And the cow and the bear shall feed; their young ones shall lie down together: and the lion shall eat straw like the ox.

8And the sucking child shall play on the hole of the asp, and the weaned child shall put his hand on the cockatrice' den.

9They shall not hurt nor destroy in all my holy mountain: for the earth shall be full of the knowledge of the LORD, as the waters cover the sea.

10¶ And in that day there shall be a root of Jesse, which shall stand for an ensign of the people; to it shall the Gentiles seek: and his rest shall be glorious.

11And it shall come to pass in that day, *that* the Lord shall set his hand again the second time to recover the remnant of his people, which shall be left, from Assyria, and from Egypt, and from Pathros, and from Cush, and from Elam, and from Shinar, and from Hamath, and from the islands of the sea.

12And he shall set up an ensign for the nations, and shall assemble the outcasts of Israel, and gather together the dispersed of Judah from the four corners of the earth.

13The envy also of Ephraim shall depart, and the adversaries of Judah shall be cut off: Ephraim shall not envy Judah, and Judah shall not vex Ephraim.

14But they shall fly upon the shoulders of the Philistines toward the west; they shall spoil them of the east together: they shall lay their hand upon Edom and Moab; and the children of Ammon shall obey them.

## Amplified

33[But just when the Assyrian is in sight of his goal] behold the Lord, the Lord of hosts, will lop off the beautiful boughs with terrorizing force; the high in stature will be hewn down, and the lofty will be brought low.

34And He will cut down the thickets of the forest with an ax, and Lebanon [the Assyrian] with its majestic trees shall fall by a mighty one *and* mightily. [Isa. 9:6.]

**11** AND THERE shall come forth a Shoot out of the stock of Jesse [David's father], and a Branch out of his roots shall grow *and* bear fruit. [Rev. 5:5; 22:16.]

2And the Spirit of the Lord shall rest upon Him, the spirit of wisdom and understanding, the spirit of counsel and might, the spirit of knowledge and of the reverential *and* obedient fear of the Lord.

3And shall make Him of quick understanding, *and* His delight shall be in the reverential *and* obedient fear of the Lord. And He shall not judge by the sight of His eyes, neither decide by the hearing of His ears;

4But with righteousness *and* justice shall He judge the poor, and decide with fairness for the meek, the poor *and* downtrodden of the earth; and He shall smite the earth *and* the oppressor with the rod of His mouth, and with the breath of His lips He shall slay the wicked.

5And righteousness shall be the girdle of His waist, and faithfulness the girdle of His loins.

6And the wolf shall dwell with the lamb, and the leopard shall lie down with the kid, and the calf and the young lion and the fatted domestic animal together, and a little child shall lead them.

7And the cow and the bear shall feed side by side; their young shall lie down together; and the lion shall eat straw like the ox.

8And the sucking child shall play over the hole of the asp, and the weaned child shall put his hand on the adder's den.

9They shall not hurt or destroy in all My holy mountain, for the earth shall be full of the knowledge of the Lord as the waters cover the sea.

10And it shall be in that day that the Root of Jesse shall stand for a signal to the peoples; of Him shall the nations inquire *and* seek knowledge, and His dwelling shall be glory—His rest glorious! [John 12:32.]

11And in that day the Lord shall again lift up His hand a second time to recover—acquire and deliver—the remnant of His people which is left, from Assyria, from Lower Egypt, from Pathros, from Ethiopia, from Elam [in Persia], from Shinar, from Hamath [in Upper Syria], and from the countries bordering on the [Mediterranean] Sea. [Jer. 23:5-8.]

12And He will raise up a signal for the nations, and will assemble the outcasts of Israel, and gather together the dispersed of Judah from the four corners of the earth.

13The envy *and* jealousy of Ephraim also shall depart, and they who vex *and* harass Judah from outside *or* inside shall be cut off; Ephraim shall not envy Judah, and Judah shall not vex *and* harass Ephraim.

14But [with united forces] *Ephraim and Judah* will swoop down upon the shoulder of the Philistine's *land sloping* toward the west; together they will strip the people on the east [the Arabs]. They will lay their hand upon Edom and Moab, and the Ammonites shall obey them.

## New American Standard

33¶ Behold, the Lord, the GOD of hosts, will lop off the boughs with a terrible crash;
Those also who are tall in stature will be cut down,
And those who are lofty will be abased.
34 And He will cut down the thickets of the forest with an iron *axe*,
And Lebanon will fall by the Mighty One.

*Righteous Reign of the Branch*

**11** THEN A shoot will spring from the stem of Jesse,
And a branch from his roots will bear fruit.
2 And the Spirit of the LORD will rest on Him,
The spirit of wisdom and understanding,
The spirit of counsel and strength,
The spirit of knowledge and the fear of the LORD.
3 And He will delight in the fear of the LORD,
And He will not judge by what His eyes see,
Nor make a decision by what His ears hear;
4 But with righteousness He will judge the poor,
And decide with fairness for the afflicted of the earth;
And He will strike the earth with the rod of His mouth,
And with the breath of His lips He will slay the wicked.
5 Also righteousness will be the belt about His loins,
And faithfulness the belt about His waist.
6¶ And the wolf will dwell with the lamb,
And the leopard will lie down with the kid,
And the calf and the young lion [a]and the fatling together;
And a little boy will lead them.
7 Also the cow and the bear will graze;
Their young will lie down together;
And the lion will eat straw like the ox.
8 And the nursing child will play by the hole of the cobra,
And the weaned child will put his hand on the viper's den.
9 They will not hurt or destroy in all My holy mountain,
For the earth will be full of the knowledge of the LORD
As the waters cover the sea.
10¶ Then it will come about in that day
That the nations will resort to the root of Jesse,
Who will stand as a signal for the peoples;
And His resting place will be glorious.

*The Restored Remnant*

11¶ Then it will happen on that day that the Lord
Will again recover the second time with His hand
The remnant of His people, who will remain,
From Assyria, Egypt, Pathros, Cush, Elam, Shinar, Hamath,
And from the islands of the sea.
12 And He will lift up a standard for the nations,
And will assemble the banished ones of Israel,
And will gather the dispersed of Judah
From the four corners of the earth.
13 Then the jealousy of Ephraim will depart,
And those who harass Judah will be cut off;
Ephraim will not be jealous of Judah,
And Judah will not harass Ephraim.
14 And they will swoop down on the slopes of the Philistines on the west;
Together they will plunder the sons of the east;
They will possess Edom and Moab;
And the sons of Ammon will be subject to them.

NAS [a] Some versions read *will feed together*

## New International

33See, the Lord, the LORD Almighty,
will lop off the boughs with great power.
The lofty trees will be felled,
the tall ones will be brought low.
34He will cut down the forest thickets with an ax;
Lebanon will fall before the Mighty One.

*The Branch From Jesse*

**11** A SHOOT will come up from the stump of Jesse;
from his roots a Branch will bear fruit.
2The Spirit of the LORD will rest on him—
the Spirit of wisdom and of understanding,
the Spirit of counsel and of power,
the Spirit of knowledge and of the fear of the LORD—
3and he will delight in the fear of the LORD.

He will not judge by what he sees with his eyes,
or decide by what he hears with his ears;
4but with righteousness he will judge the needy,
with justice he will give decisions for the poor of the earth.
He will strike the earth with the rod of his mouth;
with the breath of his lips he will slay the wicked.
5Righteousness will be his belt
and faithfulness the sash around his waist.

6The wolf will live with the lamb,
the leopard will lie down with the goat,
the calf and the lion and the yearling[b] together;
and a little child will lead them.
7The cow will feed with the bear,
their young will lie down together,
and the lion will eat straw like the ox.
8The infant will play near the hole of the cobra,
and the young child put his hand into the viper's nest.
9They will neither harm nor destroy
on all my holy mountain,
for the earth will be full of the knowledge of the LORD
as the waters cover the sea.

10In that day the Root of Jesse will stand as a banner for the
peoples; the nations will rally to him, and his place of rest will be
glorious. 11In that day the Lord will reach out his hand a second
time to reclaim the remnant that is left of his people from Assyria,
from Lower Egypt, from Upper Egypt,[c] from Cush,[d] from Elam,
from Babylonia,[e] from Hamath and from the islands of the sea.

12He will raise a banner for the nations
and gather the exiles of Israel;
he will assemble the scattered people of Judah
from the four quarters of the earth.
13Ephraim's jealousy will vanish,
and Judah's enemies[f] will be cut off;
Ephraim will not be jealous of Judah,
nor Judah hostile toward Ephraim.
14They will swoop down on the slopes of Philistia to the west;
together they will plunder the people to the east.
They will lay hands on Edom and Moab,
and the Ammonites will be subject to them.

NIV [b] 6 Hebrew; Septuagint *lion will feed* [c] 11 Hebrew *from Pathros* [d] 11 That is, the upper Nile region [e] 11 Hebrew *Shinar* [f] 13 Or *hostility*

# King James

15And the LORD shall utterly destroy the tongue of the Egyptian sea; and with his mighty wind shall he shake his hand over the river, and shall smite it in the seven streams, and make *men* go over dryshod.

16And there shall be an highway for the remnant of his people, which shall be left, from Assyria; like as it was to Israel in the day that he came up out of the land of Egypt.

**12** AND IN that day thou shalt say, O LORD, I will praise thee: though thou wast angry with me, thine anger is turned away, and thou comfortedst me.

2Behold, God *is* my salvation; I will trust, and not be afraid: for the LORD JEHOVAH *is* my strength and *my* song; he also is become my salvation.

3Therefore with joy shall ye draw water out of the wells of salvation.

4And in that day shall ye say, Praise the LORD, call upon his name, declare his doings among the people, make mention that his name is exalted.

5Sing unto the LORD; for he hath done excellent things: this *is* known in all the earth.

6Cry out and shout, thou inhabitant of Zion: for great *is* the Holy One of Israel in the midst of thee.

**13** THE BURDEN of Babylon, which Isaiah the son of Amoz did see.

2Lift ye up a banner upon the high mountain, exalt the voice unto them, shake the hand, that they may go into the gates of the nobles.

3I have commanded my sanctified ones, I have also called my mighty ones for mine anger, *even* them that rejoice in my highness.

4The noise of a multitude in the mountains, like as of a great people; a tumultuous noise of the kingdoms of nations gathered together: the LORD of hosts mustereth the host of the battle.

5They come from a far country, from the end of heaven, *even* the LORD, and the weapons of his indignation, to destroy the whole land.

6¶ Howl ye; for the day of the LORD *is* at hand; it shall come as a destruction from the Almighty.

7Therefore shall all hands be faint, and every man's heart shall melt:

# Amplified

15And the Lord will utterly destroy—doom and dry up—the tongue of the Egyptian sea [the west fork of the Red Sea] and with His [mighty] scorching wind He will wave His hand over the river *Nile*, and will smite it into seven channels, and cause men to cross over dry-shod.

16And there shall be a highway from Assyria for the remnant left of His people, as there was for Israel when they came up out of the land of Egypt.

**12** AND IN that day you will say, I will give thanks to You, O Lord, for though You were angry with me, Your anger is turned away, and You comfort me.

2Behold God, my salvation! I will trust and not be afraid, for the Lord God is my strength and song; yes, He has become my salvation.

3Therefore with joy will you draw water from the wells of salvation.

4And in that day you will say, Give thanks to the Lord, call upon His name *and* by means of His name [in solemn entreaty]; declare *and* make known His deeds among the peoples of the earth, proclaim that His name is exalted!

5Sing praises to the Lord, for He has done excellent things—gloriously; let this be made known in all the earth.

6Cry aloud and shout joyfully, you women *and* inhabitants of Zion, for great in your midst is the Holy One of Israel.

**13** THE MOURNFUL prediction—a burden to be lifted up—concerning Babylon, which Isaiah the son of Amoz saw [with prophetic insight].

2Raise up a signal banner upon the high *and* bare mountain, summon [the Medes and Persians] with loud voice and beckoning hand that they may enter the gates of the *Babylonian* nobles.

3I Myself [says the Lord] have commanded My designated ones and have summoned My mighty men to execute My anger, even My proudly exulting ones [the Medes and Persians]—those who are made to triumph for My honor.

4 *Hark*, the uproar of a multitude in the mountains, as of a great people! The noise of the tumult of the kingdoms of the nations gathering together! The Lord of hosts is mustering the host for the battle.

5They come from a distant country, from the uttermost part of the heavens [the far East], even the Lord and the weapons of His indignation, to seize *and* destroy the whole land. [Cf. Ps. 19:4-6 for "heavens."]

6Wail, for the day of the Lord is at hand; as destruction from the Almighty *and* sufficient One (Shaddai) will it come! [Gen. 17:1.]

7Therefore will ªall hands be feeble and every man's heart will melt.

---

**AMP** ª Babylon was taken by surprise on the night of Belshazzar's sacrilegious feast (Dan. 5:30).

## New American Standard

15 And the LORD will utterly destroy
The tongue of the Sea of Egypt;
And He will wave His hand over the River
With His scorching wind;
And He will strike it into seven streams,
And make *men* walk over dry-shod.
16 And there will be a highway from Assyria
For the remnant of His people who will be left,
Just as there was for Israel
In the day that they came up out of the land of Egypt.

*Thanksgiving Expressed*

**12** THEN YOU will say on that day,
"I will give thanks to Thee, O LORD;
For although Thou wast angry with me,
Thine anger is turned away,
And Thou dost comfort me.
2 "Behold, God is my salvation,
I will trust and not be afraid;
For the LORD GOD is my strength and song,
And He has become my salvation."
3 Therefore you will joyously draw water
From the springs of salvation.
4 And in that day you will say,
"Give thanks to the LORD, call on His name.
Make known His deeds among the peoples;
Make *them* remember that His name is exalted."
5 Praise the LORD in song, for He has done excellent things;
Let this be known throughout the earth.
6 Cry aloud and shout for joy, O inhabitant of Zion,
For great in your midst is the Holy One of Israel.

*Prophecies about Babylon*

**13** THE ORACLE concerning Babylon which Isaiah the son of Amoz saw.
2 Lift up a standard on the [b]bare hill,
Raise your voice to them,
Wave the hand that they may enter the doors of the nobles.
3 I have commanded My consecrated ones,
I have even called My mighty warriors,
My proudly exulting ones,
To *execute* My anger.
4 A sound of tumult on the mountains,
Like that of many people!
A sound of the uproar of kingdoms,
Of nations gathered together!
The LORD of hosts is mustering the army for battle.
5 They are coming from a far country
From the farthest horizons,
The LORD and His instruments of indignation,
To destroy the whole land.

*Judgment on the Day of the LORD*

6 Wail, for the day of the LORD is near!
It will come as destruction from the Almighty.
7 Therefore all hands will fall limp,
And every man's heart will melt.

NAS [b] Or, *wind-swept mountain*

## New International

15The LORD will dry up
the gulf of the Egyptian sea;
with a scorching wind he will sweep his hand
over the Euphrates River.[c]
He will break it up into seven streams
so that men can cross over in sandals.
16There will be a highway for the remnant of his people
that is left from Assyria,
as there was for Israel
when they came up from Egypt.

*Songs of Praise*

**12** IN THAT day you will say:
"I will praise you, O LORD.
Although you were angry with me,
your anger has turned away
and you have comforted me.
2Surely God is my salvation;
I will trust and not be afraid.
The LORD, the LORD, is my strength and my song;
he has become my salvation."
3With joy you will draw water
from the wells of salvation.

4In that day you will say:
"Give thanks to the LORD, call on his name;
make known among the nations what he has done,
and proclaim that his name is exalted.
5Sing to the LORD, for he has done glorious things;
let this be known to all the world.
6Shout aloud and sing for joy, people of Zion,
for great is the Holy One of Israel among you."

*A Prophecy Against Babylon*

**13** AN ORACLE concerning Babylon that Isaiah son of Amoz saw:

2Raise a banner on a bare hilltop,
shout to them;
beckon to them
to enter the gates of the nobles.
3I have commanded my holy ones;
I have summoned my warriors to carry out my wrath—
those who rejoice in my triumph.

4Listen, a noise on the mountains,
like that of a great multitude!
Listen, an uproar among the kingdoms,
like nations massing together!
The LORD Almighty is mustering
an army for war.
5They come from faraway lands,
from the ends of the heavens—
the LORD and the weapons of his wrath—
to destroy the whole country.

6Wail, for the day of the LORD is near;
it will come like destruction from the Almighty.[d]
7Because of this, all hands will go limp,
every man's heart will melt.

NIV [c] 15 Hebrew *the River* [d] 6 Hebrew *Shaddai*

## King James

8And they shall be afraid: pangs and sorrows shall take hold of them; they shall be in pain as a woman that travaileth: they shall be amazed one at another; their faces *shall be as* flames.

9Behold, the day of the LORD cometh, cruel both with wrath and fierce anger, to lay the land desolate: and he shall destroy the sinners thereof out of it.

10For the stars of heaven and the constellations thereof shall not give their light: the sun shall be darkened in his going forth, and the moon shall not cause her light to shine.

11And I will punish the world for *their* evil, and the wicked for their iniquity; and I will cause the arrogancy of the proud to cease, and will lay low the haughtiness of the terrible.

12I will make a man more precious than fine gold; even a man than the golden wedge of Ophir.

13Therefore I will shake the heavens, and the earth shall remove out of her place, in the wrath of the LORD of hosts, and in the day of his fierce anger.

14And it shall be as the chased roe, and as a sheep that no man taketh up: they shall every man turn to his own people, and flee every one into his own land.

15Every one that is found shall be thrust through; and every one that is joined *unto them* shall fall by the sword.

16Their children also shall be dashed to pieces before their eyes; their houses shall be spoiled, and their wives ravished.

17Behold, I will stir up the Medes against them, which shall not regard silver; and *as for* gold, they shall not delight in it.

18 *Their* bows also shall dash the young men to pieces; and they shall have no pity on the fruit of the womb; their eye shall not spare children.

19¶ And Babylon, the glory of kingdoms, the beauty of the Chaldees' excellency, shall be as when God overthrew Sodom and Gomorrah.

20It shall never be inhabited, neither shall it be dwelt in from generation to generation: neither shall the Arabian pitch tent there; neither shall the shepherds make their fold there.

21But wild beasts of the desert shall lie there; and their houses shall be full of doleful creatures; and owls shall dwell there, and satyrs shall dance there.

22And the wild beasts of the islands shall cry in their desolate houses, and dragons in *their* pleasant palaces: and her time *is* near to come, and her days shall not be prolonged.

## Amplified

8And they [of Babylon] shall be dismayed and terrified; pangs and sorrows shall take hold of them; they shall be in pain as a woman in childbirth; they will gaze stupefied *and* aghast at one another, their faces will be aflame [from the effects of the unprecedented warfare].

9Behold, the day of the Lord comes! Fierce, with wrath and raging anger, to make the land *and* the *whole* earth a desolation, and to destroy out of it its sinners. [Isa. 2:10-22; Rev. 19:11-21.]

10For the stars of the heavens and their constellations will not give their light; the sun will be darkened at its rising, and the moon will not shed its light.

11And I, the Lord, will punish the world for its evil and the wicked for their guilt *and* iniquity; I will cause the arrogance of the proud to cease, and will lay low the haughtiness of the terrible *and* the boasting of the violent *and* ruthless.

12I will make a man more rare than fine gold, and mankind scarcer than the pure gold of Ophir.

13Therefore I will make the heavens tremble, and the [a]earth shall be shaken out of its place at the wrath of the Lord of hosts in the day of His fierce anger.

14And like the chased roe *or* gazelle, and like sheep that no man gathers, each [foreign resident] will turn to his own people, and flee every one to his own land.

15Every one who is found will be thrust through, and every one who is connected with the slain *and* is caught will fall by the sword.

16Their infants also will be dashed to pieces before their eyes; their houses will be plundered, and their wives ravished.

17Behold, I will stir up the Medes against them, who have no regard for silver and do not delight in gold [so cannot be bribed].

18Their bows will cut down the young men [of Babylon], and they will have no pity on the fruit of the womb; their eye will not spare children.

19And Babylon, the glory of kingdoms, the beauty of the Chaldeans' pride, shall be as Sodom and Gomorrah when God overthrew them.

20 *Babylon* shall never be inhabited or dwelt in from generation to generation; neither shall the Arab pitch his tent there, nor shall the shepherds make their sheepfolds there.

21But wild beasts of the desert will lie down there, and the peoples' houses will be full of dolefully howling creatures; and ostriches shall dwell there, and wild goats [like demons] will dance there.

22And [b]wolves *and* howling creatures will cry *and* answer in the deserted castles, and jackals in the pleasant palaces. And *Babylon's* time is nearly come, and its days will not be prolonged.

**AMP** [a] "By the outbreak of Jehovah's wrath the material universe is [to be] shaken to its foundations. Such representations are common in the descriptions of the day of the Lord, and are not to be dismissed as merely figurative." (Cambridge Bible.) See I Thess. 5:2; II Pet. 3:10; II Thess. 1:7, 8. [b] This whole prophecy is generally conceded to have been written long over a century (170 yrs. according to Ussher) before Babylon's downfall, when the circumstances necessary for its fulfillment seemed most improbable; but it has been literally fulfilled in detail. Human keenness of foresight could not possibly have foreseen that great Babylon would be wiped from the face of the earth (v. 19), become ruins infested by wild animals (vss. 21, 22), feared because of superstition by the Arabs (v. 20), with only a small village near the area to mark the place, where since the days of Nimrod mighty kings had exalted themselves above the God of Heaven. Various conquerors during the centuries contributed to Babylon's downfall until by the first century B.C. it was as utterly and hopelessly destroyed "as Sodom and Gomorrah" (v. 19).

## New American Standard

8 And they will be terrified,
Pains and anguish will take hold of *them;*
They will writhe like a woman in labor,
They will look at one another in astonishment,
Their faces aflame.
9 Behold, the day of the LORD is coming,
Cruel, with fury and burning anger,
To make the land a desolation;
And He will exterminate its sinners from it.
10 For the stars of heaven and their constellations
Will not flash forth their light;
The sun will be dark when it rises,
And the moon will not shed its light.
11 Thus I will punish the world for its evil,
And the wicked for their iniquity;
I will also put an end to the arrogance of the proud,
And abase the haughtiness of the ruthless.
12 I will make mortal man scarcer than pure gold,
And mankind than the gold of Ophir.
13 Therefore I shall make the heavens tremble,
And the earth will be shaken from its place
At the fury of the LORD of hosts
In the day of His burning anger.
14 And it will be that like a hunted gazelle,
Or like sheep with none to gather *them,*
They will each turn to his own people,
And each one flee to his own land.
15 Anyone who is found will be thrust through,
And anyone who is captured will fall by the sword.
16 Their little ones also will be dashed to pieces
Before their eyes;
Their houses will be plundered
And their wives ravished.

*Babylon Will Fall to the Medes*

17¶ Behold, I am going to stir up the Medes against them,
Who will not value silver or take pleasure in gold,
18 And *their* bows will mow down the young men,
They will not even have compassion on the fruit of the womb,
*Nor* will their eye pity children.
19 And Babylon, the beauty of kingdoms, the glory of the Chaldeans' pride,
Will be as when God overthrew Sodom and Gomorrah.
20 It will never be inhabited or lived in from generation to generation;
Nor will the Arab pitch *his* tent there,
Nor will shepherds make *their flocks* lie down there.
21 But desert creatures will lie down there,
And their houses will be full of owls,
Ostriches also will live there, and shaggy goats will frolic there.
22 And hyenas will howl in their fortified towers
And jackals in their luxurious palaces.
Her *fateful* time also will soon come
And her days will not be prolonged.

## New International

8Terror will seize them,
pain and anguish will grip them;
they will writhe like a woman in labor.
They will look aghast at each other,
their faces aflame.
9See, the day of the LORD is coming
—a cruel day, with wrath and fierce anger—
to make the land desolate
and destroy the sinners within it.
10The stars of heaven and their constellations
will not show their light.
The rising sun will be darkened
and the moon will not give its light.
11I will punish the world for its evil,
the wicked for their sins.
I will put an end to the arrogance of the haughty
and will humble the pride of the ruthless.
12I will make man scarcer than pure gold,
more rare than the gold of Ophir.
13Therefore I will make the heavens tremble;
and the earth will shake from its place
at the wrath of the LORD Almighty,
in the day of his burning anger.
14Like a hunted gazelle,
like sheep without a shepherd,
each will return to his own people,
each will flee to his native land.
15Whoever is captured will be thrust through;
all who are caught will fall by the sword.
16Their infants will be dashed to pieces before their eyes;
their houses will be looted and their wives ravished.
17See, I will stir up against them the Medes,
who do not care for silver
and have no delight in gold.
18Their bows will strike down the young men;
they will have no mercy on infants
nor will they look with compassion on children.
19Babylon, the jewel of kingdoms,
the glory of the Babylonians'[c] pride,
will be overthrown by God
like Sodom and Gomorrah.
20She will never be inhabited
or lived in through all generations;
no Arab will pitch his tent there,
no shepherd will rest his flocks there.
21But desert creatures will lie there,
jackals will fill her houses;
there the owls will dwell,
and there the wild goats will leap about.
22Hyenas will howl in her strongholds,
jackals in her luxurious palaces.
Her time is at hand,
and her days will not be prolonged.

NIV [c] 19 Or *Chaldeans'*

## King James

14 FOR THE LORD will have mercy on Jacob, and will yet choose Israel, and set them in their own land: and the strangers shall be joined with them, and they shall cleave to the house of Jacob.

2And the people shall take them, and bring them to their place: and the house of Israel shall possess them in the land of the LORD for servants and handmaids: and they shall take them captives, whose captives they were; and they shall rule over their oppressors.

3And it shall come to pass in the day that the LORD shall give thee rest from thy sorrow, and from thy fear, and from the hard bondage wherein thou wast made to serve,

4¶ That thou shalt take up this proverb against the king of Babylon, and say, How hath the oppressor ceased! the golden city ceased!

5The LORD hath broken the staff of the wicked, *and* the sceptre of the rulers.

6He who smote the people in wrath with a continual stroke, he that ruled the nations in anger, is persecuted, *and* none hindereth.

7The whole earth is at rest, *and* is quiet: they break forth into singing.

8Yea, the fir trees rejoice at thee, *and* the cedars of Lebanon, *saying*, Since thou art laid down, no feller is come up against us.

9Hell from beneath is moved for thee to meet *thee* at thy coming: it stirreth up the dead for thee, *even* all the chief ones of the earth; it hath raised up from their thrones all the kings of the nations.

10All they shall speak and say unto thee, Art thou also become weak as we? art thou become like unto us?

11Thy pomp is brought down to the grave, *and* the noise of thy viols: the worm is spread under thee, and the worms cover thee.

12How art thou fallen from heaven, O Lucifer, son of the morning! *how* art thou cut down to the ground, which didst weaken the nations!

13For thou hast said in thine heart, I will ascend into heaven, I will exalt my throne above the stars of God: I will sit also upon the mount of the congregation, in the sides of the north:

14I will ascend above the heights of the clouds: I will be like the most High.

15Yet thou shalt be brought down to hell, to the sides of the pit.

16They that see thee shall narrowly look upon thee, *and* consider thee, *saying*, *Is* this the man that made the earth to tremble, that did shake kingdoms;

17 *That* made the world as a wilderness, and destroyed the cities thereof; *that* opened not the house of his prisoners?

## Amplified

14 FOR THE Lord will have mercy on Jacob [the captive Jews in Babylon] and will again choose Israel and set them in their own land, and foreigners [who are proselytes] will join them and will cleave to the house of Jacob (Israel). [Esth. 8:17.]

2And the peoples [of Babylonia] shall [a]take them and bring them to their own country *of Judea and* aid in restoring them; and the house of Israel will possess [the foreigners who prefer to stay with] them in the land of the Lord as male and female servants; and they will take captive [not by physical, but by moral might] those whose captives they have been, and they will rule over their [former] oppressors. [Ezra 1.]

3When the Lord has given you rest from your sorrow *and* pain, and from your trouble *and* unrest, and from the hard service with which you were made to serve,

4You shall take up this [taunting] parable against the king of Babylon, and say, How the oppressor is stilled—stilled the restless insolence! The golden *and* exacting city has ceased!

5The Lord has broken the staff of the wicked, the scepter of the [tyrant] rulers,

6Who smote the peoples in anger with incessant blows *and* trod down the nations in wrath with unrelenting persecution— *until* he that smote is persecuted and no one hinders.

7The whole earth is at rest and is quiet; they break forth into singing.

8Yes, the fir trees *and* cypresses rejoice at you [O kings of Babylon] *and* the cedars of Lebanon, saying, Since you are laid low, no wood-cutter has come up against us.

9Sheol [Hades] below is stirred up to meet you at your coming [O tyrant Babylonian rulers]; it stirs up the shades of the dead to *greet* you, even all the chief ones of the earth; it raises from their thrones [in astonishment at your humbled condition] all the kings of the nations.

10All of them will [tauntingly] say to you, Have you also become weak as we are? Have you become like us?

11Your pomp *and* magnificence are brought down to Sheol [the underworld], and the sound of your harps; the maggots [which prey upon dead bodies] are spread under you, and worms cover you [O Babylonian rulers].

12How are you fallen from Heaven, O [b]light-bringer *and* day-star, son of the morning! How you are cut down to the ground, you who weakened *and* laid prostrate the nations [O blasphemous, satanic king of Babylon!]

13And you said in your heart, I will ascend to Heaven; I will exalt my throne above the stars of God; I will sit upon the mount of assembly in the uttermost north;

14I will ascend above the heights of the clouds, I will make myself like the Most High.

15Yet you shall be brought down to Sheol [Hades], to the inmost recesses of the pit [the region of the dead].

16Those who see you will gaze at you *and* consider you, saying, Is this the man who made the earth tremble, who shook kingdoms?

17Who made the world like a wilderness and overthrew its cities, who would not permit his prisoners to return home?

**AMP** [a] This prophecy (verses one and two) was fulfilled literally and in detail under King Cyrus of Persia and Babylonia. (Ezra 1.) [b] "Light-bringer" or "Shining one" was originally translated *Lucifer*, but because of the association of that name with Satan it is not now used. Some students feel that the application of the name Lucifer to Satan, in spite of the long and confident teaching to that effect, is erroneous. *Lucifer, the light-bringer*, is the Latin equivalent of the Greek word *Phosphoros*, which is used as a title of Christ in II Peter 1:19 and corresponds to the name "bright Morning Star" in Revelation 22:16, which Jesus called Himself. The application of the name has existed since the third century A.D., and is based on the supposition that Luke 10:18 is an explanation of Isaiah 14:12, which some authorities feel is not true.

## New American Standard

*Israel's Taunt*

**14** WHEN THE LORD will have compassion on Jacob, and again choose Israel, and settle them in their own land, then strangers will join them and attach themselves to the house of Jacob.

2And the peoples will take them along and bring them to their place, and the house of Israel will possess them as an inheritance in the land of the LORD as male servants and female servants; and they will take their captors captive, and will rule over their oppressors.

3¶ And it will be in the day when the LORD gives you rest from your pain and turmoil and harsh service in which you have been enslaved,

4that you will take up this taunt against the king of Babylon, and say,

"How the oppressor has ceased,
*And how* fury has ceased!
5 "The LORD has broken the staff of the wicked,
The scepter of rulers
6 Which used to strike the peoples in fury with unceasing strokes,
Which subdued the nations in anger with unrestrained persecution.
7 "The whole earth is at rest *and* is quiet;
They break forth into shouts of joy.
8 "Even the cypress trees rejoice over you, *and* the cedars of Lebanon, *saying,*
'Since you were laid low, no *tree* cutter comes up against us.'
9 "Sheol from beneath is excited over you to meet you when you come;
It arouses for you the spirits of the dead, all the leaders of the earth;
It raises all the kings of the nations from their thrones.
10 "They will all respond and say to you,
'Even you have been made weak as we,
You have become like us.
11 'Your pomp *and* the music of your harps
Have been brought down to Sheol;
Maggots are spread out *as your bed* beneath you,
And worms are your covering.'
12 "How you have fallen from heaven,
O star of the morning, son of the dawn!
You have been cut down to the earth,
You who have weakened the nations!
13 "But you said in your heart,
'I will ascend to heaven;
I will raise my throne above the stars of God,
And I will sit on the mount of assembly
In the recesses of the north.
14 'I will ascend above the heights of the clouds;
I will make myself like the Most High.'
15 "Nevertheless you will be thrust down to Sheol,
To the recesses of the pit.
16 "Those who see you will gaze at you,
They will ponder over you, *saying,*
'Is this the man who made the earth tremble,
Who shook kingdoms,
17 Who made the world like a wilderness
And overthrew its cities,
Who did not allow his prisoners to *go* home?'

## New International

**14** THE LORD will have compassion on Jacob;
once again he will choose Israel
and will settle them in their own land.
Aliens will join them
and unite with the house of Jacob.
2Nations will take them
and bring them to their own place.
And the house of Israel will possess the nations
as menservants and maidservants in the LORD's land.
They will make captives of their captors
and rule over their oppressors.

3On the day the LORD gives you relief from suffering and turmoil and cruel bondage, 4you will take up this taunt against the king of Babylon:

How the oppressor has come to an end!
How his fury[c] has ended!
5The LORD has broken the rod of the wicked,
the scepter of the rulers,
6which in anger struck down peoples
with unceasing blows,
and in fury subdued nations
with relentless aggression.
7All the lands are at rest and at peace;
they break into singing.
8Even the pine trees and the cedars of Lebanon
exult over you and say,
"Now that you have been laid low,
no woodsman comes to cut us down."
9The grave[d] below is all astir
to meet you at your coming;
it rouses the spirits of the departed to greet you—
all those who were leaders in the world;
it makes them rise from their thrones—
all those who were kings over the nations.
10They will all respond,
they will say to you,
"You also have become weak, as we are;
you have become like us."
11All your pomp has been brought down to the grave,
along with the noise of your harps;
maggots are spread out beneath you
and worms cover you.

12How you have fallen from heaven,
O morning star, son of the dawn!
You have been cast down to the earth,
you who once laid low the nations!
13You said in your heart,
"I will ascend to heaven;
I will raise my throne
above the stars of God;
I will sit enthroned on the mount of assembly,
on the utmost heights of the sacred mountain.[e]
14I will ascend above the tops of the clouds;
I will make myself like the Most High."
15But you are brought down to the grave,
to the depths of the pit.

16Those who see you stare at you,
they ponder your fate:
"Is this the man who shook the earth
and made kingdoms tremble,
17the man who made the world a desert,
who overthrew its cities
and would not let his captives go home?"

**NIV** [c] 4 Dead Sea Scrolls, Septuagint and Syriac; the meaning of the word in the Masoretic Text is uncertain. [d] 9 Hebrew *Sheol;* also in verses 11 and 15 [e] 13 Or *the north;* Hebrew *Zaphon*

## King James

18All the kings of the nations, *even* all of them, lie in glory, every one in his own house.
19But thou art cast out of thy grave like an abominable branch, *and as* the raiment of those that are slain, thrust through with a sword, that go down to the stones of the pit; as a carcase trodden under feet.
20Thou shalt not be joined with them in burial, because thou hast destroyed thy land, *and* slain thy people: the seed of evildoers shall never be renowned.
21Prepare slaughter for his children for the iniquity of their fathers; that they do not rise, nor possess the land, nor fill the face of the world with cities.
22For I will rise up against them, saith the LORD of hosts, and cut off from Babylon the name, and remnant, and son, and nephew, saith the LORD.
23I will also make it a possession for the bittern, and pools of water: and I will sweep it with the besom of destruction, saith the LORD of hosts.
24¶ The LORD of hosts hath sworn, saying, Surely as I have thought, so shall it come to pass; and as I have purposed, *so* shall it stand:
25That I will break the Assyrian in my land, and upon my mountains tread him under foot: then shall his yoke depart from off them, and his burden depart from off their shoulders.
26This *is* the purpose that is purposed upon the whole earth: and this *is* the hand that is stretched out upon all the nations.
27For the LORD of hosts hath purposed, and who shall disannul *it?* and his hand *is* stretched out, and who shall turn it back?
28In the year that king Ahaz died was this burden.
29¶ Rejoice not thou, whole Palestina, because the rod of him that smote thee is broken: for out of the serpent's root shall come forth a cockatrice, and his fruit *shall be* a fiery flying serpent.
30And the firstborn of the poor shall feed, and the needy shall lie down in safety: and I will kill thy root with famine, and he shall slay thy remnant.
31Howl, O gate; cry, O city; thou, whole Palestina, *art* dissolved: for there shall come from the north a smoke, and none *shall be* alone in his appointed times.
32What shall *one* then answer the messengers of the nation? That the LORD hath founded Zion, and the poor of his people shall trust in it.

## Amplified

18All the kings of the nations, all of them lie sleeping in glorious *array*, every one in his own sepulcher.
19But you are cast out, away from your tomb, like a loathed growth *or* premature birth *or* an abominable branch [of the family], *and* as the raiment of the slain; *and* you are clothed with the slain, those thrust through with the sword, who go down to the stones of the pit [into which carcasses are thrown], like a dead body trodden under foot.
20You shall not be joined with them in burial, because you have destroyed your land and have slain your people. May the descendants of evildoers nevermore be named!
21Prepare a slaughtering place for his sons because of the guilt *and* iniquity of their fathers, so that they may not rise, possess the earth and fill the face of the world with cities.
22And I will rise up against them, says the Lord of hosts, and cut off from Babylon name and remnant, and son and son's son, says the Lord.
23I will also make it a possession of the hedgehog *and* porcupine, and [a]marshes *and* pools of water, and I will sweep it with the broom of destruction, says the Lord of hosts.
24The Lord of hosts has sworn, saying, Surely as I have thought *and* planned, so shall it come to pass; and as I have purposed, so shall it stand:
25That I will break the Assyrian in My land, and upon My mountains tread him under foot. Then shall the [Assyrian's] [b]yoke depart from off [the people of Judah], and his burden depart from off their shoulder.
26This is the [Lord's] purpose that is purposed upon the whole earth [regarded as conquered and put under tribute by Assyria], and this is [His omnipotent] hand that is stretched out over all the nations.
27For the Lord of hosts has purposed, and who will annul it? And His hand is stretched out, and who will turn it back?
28In the year that King Ahaz *of Judah* died there came this mournful, inspired prediction—a burden to be lifted up:
29Rejoice not, O Philistia, all of you, because the rod [of Judah] that smote you is broken; for out of the serpent's root shall come forth an adder [King Hezekiah of Judah] and [the serpent's] offspring will be a fiery flying serpent. [II Kings 18:1, 3, 8.]
30And the first-born of the poor *and* the poorest of the poor [of Judah] shall feed on My meadows, and the needy will lie down in safety; but I will kill your root with famine, and your remnant shall be slain.
31Howl, O gate; cry, O city; melt away, O Philistia, all of you! For there is coming a smoke out of the north, and there is no straggler in his ranks *and* none stands aloof [in Hezekiah's battalions].
32What then shall one answer the messengers of the [Philistine] nation? That the Lord has founded Zion, and in her shall the poor *and* afflicted of His people trust *and* find refuge.

**AMP** [a] The city of Babylon was in the midst of a very fertile area, and it would have seemed reasonable to suppose that, regardless of what happened to the population, the region would always furnish pasturage for flocks. But Isaiah said it would become the possession of wild animals, and be covered with "marshes of water." This is how that prophecy was literally fulfilled: After Babylon was taken, the whole area around the city was put under water by the neglect of canals and dikes of the Euphrates River. It became stagnant "marshes of water" among ruins haunted by wild animals, and proclaiming to any who might see it that surely as the Lord has purposed, so shall it come to pass. [b] The prophecy against Assyria had by this time actually been fulfilled, but Isaiah "attached it to the still unfulfilled prophecy against Babylon to give [it] as a pledge of the fulfillment of the latter."

## New American Standard

18 "All the kings of the nations lie in glory,
Each in his own tomb.
19 "But you have been cast out of your tomb
Like a rejected branch,
Clothed with the slain who are pierced with a sword,
Who go down to the stones of the pit,
Like a trampled corpse.
20 "You will not be united with them in burial,
Because you have ruined your country,
You have slain your people.
May the offspring of evildoers not be mentioned
forever.
21 "Prepare for his sons a place of slaughter
Because of the iniquity of their fathers.
They must not arise and take possession of the earth
And fill the face of the world with cities."
22"And I will rise up against them," declares the LORD of hosts,
"and will cut off from Babylon name and survivors, offspring and
posterity," declares the LORD.
23"I will also make it a possession for the hedgehog, and
swamps of water, and I will sweep it with the broom of destruction," declares the LORD of hosts.

*Judgment on Assyria*

24The LORD of hosts has sworn saying, "Surely, just as I have
intended so it has happened, and just as I have planned so it will
stand,
25to break Assyria in My land, and I will trample him on My
mountains. Then his yoke will be removed from them, and his
burden removed from their shoulder.
26"This is the plan devised against the whole earth; and this is
the hand that is stretched out against all the nations.
27"For the LORD of hosts has planned, and who can frustrate *it*?
And as for His stretched-out hand, who can turn it back?"
28In the year that King Ahaz died this oracle came:

*Judgment on Philistia*

29 "Do not rejoice, O Philistia, all of you,
Because the rod that struck you is broken;
For from the serpent's root a viper will come out,
And its fruit will be a flying serpent.
30 "And those who are most helpless will eat,
And the needy will lie down in security;
I will destroy your root with famine,
And it will kill off your survivors.
31 "Wail, O gate; cry, O city;
Melt away, O Philistia, all of you;
For smoke comes from the north,
And there is no straggler in his ranks.
32 "How then will one answer the messengers of the
nation?
That the LORD has founded Zion,
And the afflicted of His people will seek refuge in it."

## New International

18All the kings of the nations lie in state,
each in his own tomb.
19But you are cast out of your tomb
like a rejected branch;
you are covered with the slain,
with those pierced by the sword,
those who descend to the stones of the pit.
Like a corpse trampled underfoot,
20 you will not join them in burial,
for you have destroyed your land
and killed your people.

The offspring of the wicked
will never be mentioned again.
21Prepare a place to slaughter his sons
for the sins of their forefathers;
they are not to rise to inherit the land
and cover the earth with their cities.

22"I will rise up against them,"
declares the LORD Almighty.
"I will cut off from Babylon her name and survivors,
her offspring and descendants,"
declares the LORD.
23"I will turn her into a place for owls
and into swampland;
I will sweep her with the broom of destruction,"
declares the LORD Almighty.

*A Prophecy Against Assyria*

24The LORD Almighty has sworn,

"Surely, as I have planned, so it will be,
and as I have purposed, so it will stand.
25I will crush the Assyrian in my land;
on my mountains I will trample him down.
His yoke will be taken from my people,
and his burden removed from their shoulders."

26This is the plan determined for the whole world;
this is the hand stretched out over all nations.
27For the LORD Almighty has purposed, and who can
thwart him?
His hand is stretched out, and who can turn it back?

*A Prophecy Against the Philistines*

28This oracle came in the year King Ahaz died:

29Do not rejoice, all you Philistines,
that the rod that struck you is broken;
from the root of that snake will spring up a viper,
its fruit will be a darting, venomous serpent.
30The poorest of the poor will find pasture,
and the needy will lie down in safety.
But your root I will destroy by famine;
it will slay your survivors.

31Wail, O gate! Howl, O city!
Melt away, all you Philistines!
A cloud of smoke comes from the north,
and there is not a straggler in its ranks.
32What answer shall be given
to the envoys of that nation?
"The LORD has established Zion,
and in her his afflicted people will find refuge."

## King James

**15** THE BURDEN of Moab. Because in the night Ar of Moab is laid waste, *and* brought to silence; because in the night Kir of Moab is laid waste, *and* brought to silence;

2 He is gone up to Bajith, and to Dibon, the high places, to weep: Moab shall howl over Nebo, and over Medeba: on all their heads *shall be* baldness, *and* every beard cut off.

3 In their streets they shall gird themselves with sackcloth: on the tops of their houses, and in their streets, every one shall howl, weeping abundantly.

4 And Heshbon shall cry, and Elealeh: their voice shall be heard *even* unto Jahaz: therefore the armed soldiers of Moab shall cry out; his life shall be grievous unto him.

5 My heart shall cry out for Moab; his fugitives *shall flee* unto Zoar, an heifer of three years old: for by the mounting up of Luhith with weeping shall they go it up; for in the way of Horonaim they shall raise up a cry of destruction.

6 For the waters of Nimrim shall be desolate: for the hay is withered away, the grass faileth, there is no green thing.

7 Therefore the abundance they have gotten, and that which they have laid up, shall they carry away to the brook of the willows.

8 For the cry is gone round about the borders of Moab; the howling thereof unto Eglaim, and the howling thereof unto Beer-elim.

9 For the waters of Dimon shall be full of blood: for I will bring more upon Dimon, lions upon him that escapeth of Moab, and upon the remnant of the land.

**16** SEND YE the lamb to the ruler of the land from Sela to the wilderness, unto the mount of the daughter of Zion.

2 For it shall be, *that*, as a wandering bird cast out of the nest, *so* the daughters of Moab shall be at the fords of Arnon.

3 Take counsel, execute judgment; make thy shadow as the night in the midst of the noonday; hide the outcasts; betray not him that wandereth.

4 Let mine outcasts dwell with thee, Moab; be thou a covert to them from the face of the spoiler: for the extortioner is at an end, the spoiler ceaseth, the oppressors are consumed out of the land.

## Amplified

**15** THE MOURNFUL, inspired prediction—a burden to be lifted up—concerning Moab. Because in a night Ar of Moab is laid waste and brought to silence; because in a night Kir of Moab is laid waste and brought to silence.

2 They are gone up to Bayith and to Dibon, to the high places, to weep. Moab wails over Nebo and over Medeba; on all their heads is baldness, and every beard is cut off [as a sign of deep sorrow and humiliation].

3 In their streets they gird themselves with sackcloth; on the tops of their houses and in their broad places every one wails, weeping abundantly.

4 And Heshbon and Elealeh [cities in possession of Moab] cry out; their voice is heard even to Jahaz; therefore the armed soldiers of Moab cry out; *Moab's* life is grievous *and* trembles within him.

5 My heart cries out for Moab; his nobles *and other* fugitives flee to Zoar, to Eglath-shelishiyah—like a heifer three years old. For with weeping they go up the ascent of Luhith, for on the road to Horonaim they raise a cry of destruction.

6 For the waters of Nimrim are desolations, for the grass is withered away and the new growth fails, there is no green thing.

7 Therefore the abundance [of possessions] they have acquired and that which they have stored away they [now] carry over the willow-brook *and to* the valley of the Arabians.

8 For the cry [of distress] has gone round the borders of Moab; the wailing has reached to Eglaim, and the prolonged *and* mournful cry to Beerelim.

9 For the waters of Dimon are full of blood; yet I, [the Lord], will bring even more on Dimon, a lion upon those of Moab who escape, and upon the remnant of the land.

**16** YOU [MOABITES, now fugitives in Edom which is ruled by the king of Judah, win the king's favor and protection by diverting your tribute to him, as an acknowledgment of subjection], send lambs to the ruler of the land from Selah *or* Petra through the desert *and* wilderness to the mountain of the daughter of Zion—Jerusalem. [II Kings 3:4, 5.]

2 For as wandering birds, as a brood cast out *and* a scattered nest, so shall the daughters of Moab be at the fords of the *river* Arnon. [Say to the ruler]

3 Give counsel, execute justice [for Moab, O king of Judah]; make your shade [over us] as the night in the midst of the noonday; hide the outcasts; betray not the fugitive to his pursuer.

4 Let our outcasts of Moab dwell among you; be a sheltered hiding place to them from the destroyer. When the extortion *and* the extortioner have been brought to nought, and destruction has ceased, and the oppressors *and* they who trample men down are consumed *and* have vanished out of the land,

## New American Standard

*Judgment on Moab*

**15** THE ORACLE concerning Moab.
Surely in a night Ar of Moab is devastated *and* ruined;
Surely in a night Kir of Moab is devastated *and* ruined.
2 They have gone up to the temple and *to* Dibon, *even* to the high places to weep.
Moab wails over Nebo and Medeba;
Everyone's head is bald *and* every beard is cut off.
3 In their streets they have girded themselves with sackcloth;
On their housetops and in their squares
Everyone is wailing, dissolved in tears.
4 Heshbon and Elealeh also cry out,
Their voice is heard all the way to Jahaz;
Therefore the armed men of Moab cry aloud;
His soul trembles within him.
5 My heart cries out for Moab;
His fugitives are as far as Zoar *and* Eglath-shelishiyah,
For they go up the ascent of Luhith weeping;
Surely on the road to Horonaim they raise a cry of distress over *their* ruin.
6 For the waters of Nimrim are desolate.
Surely the grass is withered, the tender grass died out,
There is no green thing.
7 Therefore the abundance *which* they have acquired and stored up
They carry off over the brook of Arabim.
8 For the cry of distress has gone around the territory of Moab,
Its wail *goes* as far as Eglaim and its wailing even to Beer-elim.
9 For the waters of Dimon are full of blood;
Surely I will bring added *woes* upon Dimon,
A lion upon the fugitives of Moab and upon the remnant of the land.

*Prophecy of Moab's Devastation*

**16** SEND THE *tribute* lamb to the ruler of the land,
From Sela by way of the wilderness to the mountain of the daughter of Zion.
2 Then, like fleeing birds *or* scattered nestlings,
The daughters of Moab will be at the fords of the Arnon.
3 "Give *us* advice, make a decision;
Cast your shadow like night at high noon;
Hide the outcasts, do not betray the fugitive.
4 "Let the outcasts of Moab stay with you;
Be a hiding place to them from the destroyer."
For the extortioner has come to an end, destruction has ceased,
Oppressors have completely *disappeared* from the land.

## New International

*A Prophecy Against Moab*

**15** AN ORACLE concerning Moab:

Ar in Moab is ruined,
destroyed in a night!
Kir in Moab is ruined,
destroyed in a night!
2Dibon goes up to its temple,
to its high places to weep;
Moab wails over Nebo and Medeba.
Every head is shaved
and every beard cut off.
3In the streets they wear sackcloth;
on the roofs and in the public squares
they all wail,
prostrate with weeping.
4Heshbon and Elealeh cry out,
their voices are heard all the way to Jahaz.
Therefore the armed men of Moab cry out,
and their hearts are faint.

5My heart cries out over Moab;
her fugitives flee as far as Zoar,
as far as Eglath Shelishiyah.
They go up the way to Luhith,
weeping as they go;
on the road to Horonaim
they lament their destruction.
6The waters of Nimrim are dried up
and the grass is withered;
the vegetation is gone
and nothing green is left.
7So the wealth they have acquired and stored up
they carry away over the Ravine of the Poplars.
8Their outcry echoes along the border of Moab;
their wailing reaches as far as Eglaim,
their lamentation as far as Beer Elim.
9Dimon's[a] waters are full of blood,
but I will bring still more upon Dimon[b]—
a lion upon the fugitives of Moab
and upon those who remain in the land.

**16** SEND LAMBS as tribute
to the ruler of the land,
from Sela, across the desert,
to the mount of the Daughter of Zion.
2Like fluttering birds
pushed from the nest,
so are the women of Moab
at the fords of the Arnon.

3"Give us counsel,
render a decision.
Make your shadow like night—
at high noon.
Hide the fugitives,
do not betray the refugees.
4Let the Moabite fugitives stay with you;
be their shelter from the destroyer."

The oppressor will come to an end,
and destruction will cease;
the aggressor will vanish from the land.

**NIV** [a] 9 Masoretic Text; Dead Sea Scrolls, some Septuagint manuscripts and Vulgate *Dibon* [b] 9 Masoretic Text; Dead Sea Scrolls, some Septuagint manuscripts and Vulgate *Dibon*

## King James

5And in mercy shall the throne be established: and he shall sit upon it in truth in the tabernacle of David, judging, and seeking judgment, and hasting righteousness.

6¶ We have heard of the pride of Moab; *he is* very proud: *even* of his haughtiness, and his pride, and his wrath: *but* his lies *shall* not *be* so.

7Therefore shall Moab howl for Moab, every one shall howl: for the foundations of Kir-hareseth shall ye mourn; surely *they are* stricken.

8For the fields of Heshbon languish, *and* the vine of Sibmah: the lords of the heathen have broken down the principal plants thereof, they are come *even* unto Jazer, they wandered *through* the wilderness: her branches are stretched out, they are gone over the sea.

9¶ Therefore I will bewail with the weeping of Jazer the vine of Sibmah: I will water thee with my tears, O Heshbon, and Elealeh: for the shouting for thy summer fruits and for thy harvest is fallen.

10And gladness is taken away, and joy out of the plentiful field; and in the vineyards there shall be no singing, neither shall there be shouting: the treaders shall tread out no wine in *their* presses; I have made *their vintage* shouting to cease.

11Wherefore my bowels shall sound like an harp for Moab, and mine inward parts for Kir-haresh.

12¶ And it shall come to pass, when it is seen that Moab is weary on the high place, that he shall come to his sanctuary to pray; but he shall not prevail.

13This *is* the word that the LORD hath spoken concerning Moab since that time.

14But now the LORD hath spoken, saying, Within three years, as the years of an hireling, and the glory of Moab shall be contemned, with all that great multitude; and the remnant *shall be* very small *and* feeble.

**17** THE BURDEN of Damascus. Behold, Damascus is taken away from *being* a city, and it shall be a ruinous heap.

2The cities of Aroer *are* forsaken: they shall be for flocks, which shall lie down, and none shall make *them* afraid.

3The fortress also shall cease from Ephraim, and the kingdom from Damascus, and the remnant of Syria: they shall be as the glory of the children of Israel, saith the LORD of hosts.

4And in that day it shall come to pass, *that* the glory of Jacob shall be made thin, and the fatness of his flesh shall wax lean.

5And it shall be as when the harvestman gathereth the corn, and reapeth the ears with his arm; and it shall be as he that gathereth ears in the valley of Rephaim.

## Amplified

5Then in mercy *and* loving-kindness shall a throne be established, and [a]One shall sit upon it in truth *and* faithfulness in the tent of David, judging and seeking justice and being swift to do righteousness. [Ps. 96:13; Jer. 48:47.]

6We have heard of the pride of Moab, that he is very proud; of his arrogance, his conceit, his wrath, his untruthful boasting.

7Moab therefore shall wail for Moab; every one shall wail. For the ruins, flagons of wine, *and* the raisin-cakes of Kirhareseth you shall sigh and mourn, utterly stricken *and* discouraged.

8For the fields of Heshbon languish, and the vine of Sibmah; the lords of the nations have broken down *Moab's* choice vine-branches, which reached even to Jazer, wandering into the wilderness; its shoots stetched out abroad, they passed over [the shores of] the *Dead* Sea.

9Therefore I [Isaiah] will weep with the weeping of Jazer for the vine of Sibmah. I will drench you with my tears, O Heshbon and Elealeh, for upon your summer fruits and your harvest the shout [of alarm and the cry of the enemy] has fallen.

10And gladness is taken away, and joy out of the plentiful field; and in the vineyards there is no singing, neither joyful sound; the treaders tread out no wine in the presses, for the shout of joy has been made to cease.

11Wherefore my heart sounds like a harp [in mourning compassion] for Moab, and my inner being *goes out* for Kirheres—for those brick-walled citadels of his.

12It shall be that when Moab presents himself, when he wearies himself [worshiping] on the high place *of idolatry*, he will come to his sanctuary [of Chemosh, god of Moab], but he will not prevail. [Then will he be ashamed of his god.] [Jer. 48:13.]

13This is the word that the Lord has spoken concerning Moab since that time [when Moab's pride and resistance to God were first known].

14But now the Lord has spoken, saying, Within [b]three years, as the years of a hireling [who will not serve longer than the allotted time], the glory of Moab shall be brought into contempt, in spite of all his mighty multitude of people; and the remnant that survives will be very small, feeble *and* no account.

**17** THE MOURNFUL, inspired prediction—a burden to be lifted up—concerning Damascus [capital of Syria, and Israel's bulwark against Assyria]. Behold, Damascus will cease to be a city, and will become a heap of ruins.

2The cities of Aroer [east of Jordan] are forsaken; they shall be for flocks, which shall lie down, and none shall make them afraid.

3His bulwark [Syria] *and* the fortress shall disappear from Ephraim, and the kingdom from Damascus; and the remnant of Syria will be as the *departed* glory of the children of Israel [her ally], says the Lord of hosts.

4And in that day the former glory of Jacob [Israel, his might, his population, his prosperity] shall be enfeebled, and the fat of his flesh shall become lean.

5And it shall be as when the reaper gathers the standing grain and his arm harvests the ears; yes, it shall be as when one gathers the ears of grain in the fertile valley of Rephaim.

**AMP** [a] Isaiah apparently puts these words in the mouths of the Moabite ambassadors to the king of Judah, but in "language so divinely framed as to apply to 'the latter days' under King Messiah, when the Lord shall bring again [reverse] the captivity of Moab." (Jamieson, Fausset and Brown Commentary.)
[b] This prophecy was fulfilled after the death of King Ahaz of Judah (chapter 14:28) and the third year of King Hezekiah, three years before the conquest of Israel by Assyria. Moab was not left completely without population at this time; there was still a "remnant." The final desolation of Moab was reserved for King Nebuchadnezzar of Babylon, five years after the taking of Jerusalem. The ruins of Elealeh, Heshbon, Medeba, Dimon, etc., still exist definitely to confirm through modern research the accuracy of the fulfillment of this prophecy.

## New American Standard

5 A throne will even be established in lovingkindness,
And a judge will sit on it in faithfulness in the tent of David;
Moreover, he will seek justice
And be prompt in righteousness.

6¶ We have heard of the pride of Moab, an excessive pride;
*Even* of his arrogance, pride, and fury;
His idle boasts are false.
7 Therefore Moab shall wail; everyone of Moab shall wail.
You shall moan for the raisin cakes of Kir-hareseth
As those who are utterly stricken.
8 For the fields of Heshbon have withered, the vines of Sibmah *as well;*
The lords of the nations have trampled down its choice clusters
Which reached as far as Jazer *and* wandered to the deserts;
Its tendrils spread themselves out *and* passed over the sea.
9 Therefore I will weep bitterly for Jazer, for the vine of Sibmah;
I will drench you with my tears, O Heshbon and Elealeh;
For the shouting over your summer fruits and your harvest has fallen away.
10 And gladness and joy are taken away from the fruitful field;
In the vineyards also there will be no cries of joy or jubilant shouting,
No treader treads out wine in the presses,
*For* I have made the shouting to cease.
11 Therefore my heart intones like a harp for Moab,
And my inward feelings for Kir-hareseth.
12 So it will come about when Moab presents himself,
When he wearies himself upon *his* high place,
And comes to his sanctuary to pray,
That he will not prevail.

13¶ This is the word which the LORD spoke earlier concerning Moab.
14But now the LORD speaks, saying, "Within three years, as a hired man would count them, the glory of Moab will be degraded along with all *his* great population, and *his* remnant will be very small *and* impotent."

*Prophecy about Damascus*

**17** THE ORACLE concerning Damascus.
"Behold, Damascus is about to be removed from being a city,
And it will become a fallen ruin.
2 "The cities of Aroer are forsaken;
They will be for flocks to lie down in,
And there will be no one to frighten *them.*
3 "The fortified city will disappear from Ephraim,
And sovereignty from Damascus
And the remnant of Aram;
They will be like the glory of the sons of Israel,"
Declares the LORD of hosts.

4¶ Now it will come about in that day that the glory of Jacob will fade,
And the fatness of his flesh will become lean.
5 It will be even like the reaper gathering the standing grain,
As his arm harvests the ears,
Or it will be like one gleaning ears of grain
In the valley of Rephaim.

## New International

5In love a throne will be established;
in faithfulness a man will sit on it—
one from the house[c] of David—
one who in judging seeks justice
and speeds the cause of righteousness.

6We have heard of Moab's pride—
her overweening pride and conceit,
her pride and her insolence—
but her boasts are empty.
7Therefore the Moabites wail,
they wail together for Moab.
Lament and grieve
for the men[d] of Kir Hareseth.
8The fields of Heshbon wither,
the vines of Sibmah also.
The rulers of the nations
have trampled down the choicest vines,
which once reached Jazer
and spread toward the desert.
Their shoots spread out
and went as far as the sea.
9So I weep, as Jazer weeps,
for the vines of Sibmah.
O Heshbon, O Elealeh,
I drench you with tears!
The shouts of joy over your ripened fruit
and over your harvests have been stilled.
10Joy and gladness are taken away from the orchards;
no one sings or shouts in the vineyards;
no one treads out wine at the presses,
for I have put an end to the shouting.
11My heart laments for Moab like a harp,
my inmost being for Kir Hareseth.
12When Moab appears at her high place,
she only wears herself out;
when she goes to her shrine to pray,
it is to no avail.

13This is the word the LORD has already spoken concerning Moab. 14But now the LORD says: "Within three years, as a servant bound by contract would count them, Moab's splendor and all her many people will be despised, and her survivors will be very few and feeble."

*An Oracle Against Damascus*

**17** AN ORACLE concerning Damascus:
"See, Damascus will no longer be a city
but will become a heap of ruins.
2The cities of Aroer will be deserted
and left to flocks, which will lie down,
with no one to make them afraid.
3The fortified city will disappear from Ephraim,
and royal power from Damascus;
the remnant of Aram will be
like the glory of the Israelites,"
declares the LORD Almighty.

4"In that day the glory of Jacob will fade;
the fat of his body will waste away.
5It will be as when a reaper gathers the standing grain
and harvests the grain with his arm—
as when a man gleans heads of grain
in the Valley of Rephaim.

NIV [c] 5 Hebrew *tent* [d] 7 Or *"raisin cakes,"* a wordplay

## King James

6¶ Yet gleaning grapes shall be left in it, as the shaking of an olive tree, two *or* three berries in the top of the uppermost bough, four *or* five in the outmost fruitful branches thereof, saith the LORD God of Israel.

7At that day shall a man look to his Maker, and his eyes shall have respect to the Holy One of Israel.

8And he shall not look to the altars, the work of his hands, neither shall respect *that* which his fingers have made, either the groves, or the images.

9¶ In that day shall his strong cities be as a forsaken bough, and an uppermost branch, which they left because of the children of Israel: and there shall be desolation.

10Because thou hast forgotten the God of thy salvation, and hast not been mindful of the rock of thy strength, therefore shalt thou plant pleasant plants, and shalt set it with strange slips:

11In the day shalt thou make thy plant to grow, and in the morning shalt thou make thy seed to flourish: *but* the harvest *shall be* a heap in the day of grief and of desperate sorrow.

12¶ Woe to the multitude of many people, *which* make a noise like the noise of the seas; and to the rushing of nations, *that* make a rushing like the rushing of mighty waters!

13The nations shall rush like the rushing of many waters: but *God* shall rebuke them, and they shall flee far off, and shall be chased as the chaff of the mountains before the wind, and like a rolling thing before the whirlwind.

14And behold at eveningtide trouble; *and* before the morning he *is* not. This *is* the portion of them that spoil us, and the lot of them that rob us.

18 WOE TO the land shadowing with wings, which *is* beyond the rivers of Ethiopia:

2That sendeth ambassadors by the sea, even in vessels of bulrushes upon the waters, *saying*, Go, ye swift messengers, to a nation scattered and peeled, to a people terrible from their beginning hitherto; a nation meted out and trodden down, whose land the rivers have spoiled!

3All ye inhabitants of the world, and dwellers on the earth, see ye, when he lifteth up an ensign on the mountains; and when he bloweth a trumpet, hear ye.

4For so the LORD said unto me, I will take my rest, and I will consider in my dwellingplace like a clear heat upon herbs, *and* like a cloud of dew in the heat of harvest.

5For afore the harvest, when the bud is perfect, and the sour grape is ripening in the flower, he shall both cut off the sprigs with pruning hooks, and take away *and* cut down the branches.

## Amplified

6Yet gleanings [of grapes] shall be left in [the land of Israel], as after the beating of an olive tree [with a stick], two or three berries in the top of the uppermost bough, four or five in the outmost branches of the fruitful tree, says the Lord God of Israel.

7In that day will men look to their Maker, and their eyes shall have respect to the Holy One of Israel.

8And they will not look to the [idolatrous] altars, the work of their hands, neither will they have respect for what their fingers have made, either the Asherim [sacred pillars or poles] or the sun-images.

9In that day will [Syria's and Israel's] strong cities be as the forsaken places in the wood and on the mountain top, as [the [a]Amorites and the Hivites] forsook their *cities* because of the children of Israel; and there will be desolation.

10Because you have forgotten the God of your salvation, [O Judah] and have not been mindful of the Rock of your strength, *and* your Stronghold; therefore you have planted pleasant nursery grounds *and* plantings [to Adonis, pots of quickly withered flowers used to set at their doors or in the courts of temples], and you have set *the grounds* with vine-slips of a strange *god*.

11In the day of your planting you hedge it in, and in the morning you make your seed to blossom, but [promising as it is] the harvest shall be a heap of ruins *and* flee away in the day of expected *possession* and of desperate sorrow *and* sickening, incurable pain.

12Hark, the uproar of a multitude of peoples! They roar *and* thunder like the noise of the seas! Ah, the roar of nations! They roar like the roaring of rushing *and* mighty waters!

13The nations will rush *and* roar like the rushing *and* roaring of many waters; but *God* will rebuke them, and they will flee far off, and will be chased like chaff on the mountains before the wind, and like rolling thistledown *or* whirling dust of the stubble before the storm.

14At evening time, behold, terror! *And* [b]before the morning [the terrorizing Assyrians] are not. This is the portion of those who strip us [the Jews] of what belongs to us, and the lot of those who rob us. [Fulfilled in Isa. 37:36.]

18 AH, THE land whirring with wings which is beyond the rivers of Cush *or* Ethiopia;

2That sends ambassadors by the Nile, and in vessels of papyrus upon the waters! Go, you swift messengers, to a nation tall and polished, to a people terrible from their beginning—feared and dreaded near and far; a nation strong and victorious, whose land the rivers divide!

3All you inhabitants of the world, you who dwell on the earth, when a signal is raised on the mountains, look! When a trumpet is blown, hear!

4For thus the Lord has said to me, I will be still and I will look on from My dwelling place like clear *and* glowing heat in sunshine, like a fine mist-cloud in the heat of harvest.

5For before the harvest, when the blossom is over and the flower becomes a ripening grape, He will cut off the sprigs with pruning hooks, and the spreading branches He will remove, cut them away.

**AMP** [a] The Septuagint (Greek) Version so reads. [b] Isaiah 14:25 foretells that God will break the Assyrian conqueror and tread him under foot. Now (in 17:14) further details seem to be furnished, terror (because the enemy has all but been victorious), but "before morning they are not." The fulfillment is found in Isaiah 37:36, immediately after a repetition of the prophecy in full, and it is also recorded in II Kings 19:35, 36. Just when an overwhelming victory by the Assyrian Sennacherib seemed inevitable, during a single night 185,000 of his army died, and Judah was spared—as the Lord through Isaiah had been promising.

## New American Standard

6 Yet gleanings will be left in it like the shaking of an
olive tree,
Two *or* three olives on the topmost bough,
Four *or* five on the branches of a fruitful tree,
Declares the LORD, the God of Israel.
7 In that day man will have regard for his Maker,
And his eyes will look to the Holy One of Israel.
8 And he will not have regard for the altars, the work of
his hands,
Nor will he look to that which his fingers have made,
Even the [c]Asherim and incense stands.
9 In that day their strong cities will be like forsaken
places in the forest,
Or like branches which they abandoned before the sons
of Israel;
And the land will be a desolation.
10 For you have forgotten the God of your salvation
And have not remembered the rock of your refuge.
Therefore you plant delightful plants
And set them with vine slips of a strange *god.*
11 In the day that you plant *it* you carefully fence *it* in,
And in the morning you bring your seed to blossom;
*But* the harvest will be a heap
In a day of sickliness and incurable pain.

12¶ Alas, the uproar of many peoples
Who roar like the roaring of the seas,
And the rumbling of nations
Who rush on like the rumbling of mighty waters!
13 The nations rumble on like the rumbling of many
waters,
But He will rebuke them and they will flee far away,
And be chased like chaff in the mountains before the
wind,
Or like whirling dust before a gale.
14 At evening time, behold, *there is* terror!
Before morning they are no more.
Such *will be* the portion of those who plunder us,
And the lot of those who pillage us.

*Message to Ethiopia*

18 ALAS, OH land of whirring wings
Which lies beyond the rivers of [d]Cush,
2 Which sends envoys by the sea,
Even in papyrus vessels on the surface of the waters.
Go, swift messengers, to a nation tall and smooth,
To a people feared far and wide,
A powerful and oppressive nation
Whose land the rivers divide.
3 All you inhabitants of the world and dwellers on earth,
As soon as a standard is raised on the mountains, you
will see *it,*
And as soon as the trumpet is blown, you will hear *it.*
4 For thus the LORD has told me,
"I will look from My dwelling place quietly
Like dazzling heat in the sunshine,
Like a cloud of dew in the heat of harvest."
5 For before the harvest, as soon as the bud blossoms
And the flower becomes a ripening grape,
Then He will cut off the sprigs with pruning knives
And remove *and* cut away the spreading branches.

NAS [c] I.e., wooden symbols of a female deity [d] Or, *Ethiopia*

## New International

6 Yet some gleanings will remain,
as when an olive tree is beaten,
leaving two or three olives on the topmost branches,
four or five on the fruitful boughs,"
declares the LORD, the God of Israel.

7 In that day men will look to their Maker
and turn their eyes to the Holy One of Israel.
8 They will not look to the altars,
the work of their hands,
and they will have no regard for the Asherah poles[e]
and the incense altars their fingers have made.

9 In that day their strong cities, which they left because of the
Israelites, will be like places abandoned to thickets and undergrowth. And all will be desolation.

10 You have forgotten God your Savior;
you have not remembered the Rock, your fortress.
Therefore, though you set out the finest plants
and plant imported vines,
11 though on the day you set them out, you make them
grow,
and on the morning when you plant them, you bring
them to bud,
yet the harvest will be as nothing
in the day of disease and incurable pain.
12 Oh, the raging of many nations—
they rage like the raging sea!
Oh, the uproar of the peoples—
they roar like the roaring of great waters!
13 Although the peoples roar like the roar of surging waters,
when he rebukes them they flee far away,
driven before the wind like chaff on the hills,
like tumbleweed before a gale.
14 In the evening, sudden terror!
Before the morning, they are gone!
This is the portion of those who loot us,
the lot of those who plunder us.

*A Prophecy Against Cush*

18 WOE TO the land of whirring wings[f]
along the rivers of Cush,[g]
2 which sends envoys by sea
in papyrus boats over the water.

Go, swift messengers,
to a people tall and smooth-skinned,
to a people feared far and wide,
an aggressive nation of strange speech,
whose land is divided by rivers.

3 All you people of the world,
you who live on the earth,
when a banner is raised on the mountains,
you will see it,
and when a trumpet sounds,
you will hear it.
4 This is what the LORD says to me:
"I will remain quiet and will look on from my dwelling
place,
like shimmering heat in the sunshine,
like a cloud of dew in the heat of harvest."
5 For, before the harvest, when the blossom is gone
and the flower becomes a ripening grape,
he will cut off the shoots with pruning knives,
and cut down and take away the spreading branches.

NIV [e] *8* That is, symbols of the goddess Asherah [f] *1* Or *of locusts*
[g] *1* That is, the upper Nile region

## King James

6They shall be left together unto the fowls of the mountains, and to the beasts of the earth: and the fowls shall summer upon them, and all the beasts of the earth shall winter upon them.

7¶ In that time shall the present be brought unto the LORD of hosts of a people scattered and peeled, and from a people terrible from their beginning hitherto; a nation meted out and trodden under foot, whose land the rivers have spoiled, to the place of the name of the LORD of hosts, the mount Zion.

**19** THE BURDEN of Egypt. Behold, the LORD rideth upon a swift cloud, and shall come into Egypt: and the idols of Egypt shall be moved at his presence, and the heart of Egypt shall melt in the midst of it.

2And I will set the Egyptians against the Egyptians: and they shall fight every one against his brother, and every one against his neighbour; city against city, *and* kingdom against kingdom.

3And the spirit of Egypt shall fail in the midst thereof; and I will destroy the counsel thereof: and they shall seek to the idols, and to the charmers, and to them that have familiar spirits, and to the wizards.

4And the Egyptians will I give over into the hand of a cruel lord; and a fierce king shall rule over them, saith the Lord, the LORD of hosts.

5And the waters shall fail from the sea, and the river shall be wasted and dried up.

6And they shall turn the rivers far away; *and* the brooks of defence shall be emptied and dried up: the reeds and flags shall wither.

7The paper reeds by the brooks, by the mouth of the brooks, and every thing sown by the brooks, shall wither, be driven away, and be no *more.*

8The fishers also shall mourn, and all they that cast angle into the brooks shall lament, and they that spread nets upon the waters shall languish.

9Moreover they that work in fine flax, and they that weave networks, shall be confounded.

10And they shall be broken in the purposes thereof, all that make sluices *and* ponds for fish.

11¶ Surely the princes of Zoan *are* fools, the counsel of the wise counsellors of Pharaoh is become brutish: how say ye unto Pharaoh, I *am* the son of the wise, the son of ancient kings?

12Where *are* they? where *are* thy wise *men?* and let them tell thee now, and let them know what the LORD of hosts hath purposed upon Egypt.

## Amplified

6They [the dead bodies of the slain warriors] shall be left together to the ravenous birds of the mountains and to the beasts of the earth; and the ravenous birds will summer upon them, and all the beasts of the earth will winter upon them.

7At that time shall a present be brought to the Lord of hosts from a people tall and polished, from a people terrible from their beginning *and* feared *and* dreaded near and far; a nation strong and victorious, whose land [south of Egypt?] the rivers *or* great channels divide, to the place *of worship* of the name of the Lord of hosts, to Mount Zion *in* Jerusalem.

**19** THE MOURNFUL, inspired prediction—a burden to be lifted up—concerning Egypt. Behold, the Lord is riding on a swift cloud and comes to Egypt, and the idols of Egypt shall tremble at His presence, and the heart of the Egyptians will melt within them.

2And I will stir up Egyptians against Egyptians, and they will fight every one against his brother and every one against his neighbor, city against city, kingdom against kingdom.

3And the spirit of the Egyptians within them will become exhausted, emptied out *and* will fail; and I will destroy their counsel *and* confound their plans; and they will seek counsel of the idols and the sorcerers, and of those having familiar spirits—the mediums—and the wizards.

4And I will give over the Egyptians into the hand of a hard *and* cruel master, and a fierce king shall rule over them, says the Lord, the Lord of hosts.

5And the waters shall fail from the Nile, and the river shall be wasted and become dry;

6And the rivers shall become foul, the stream *and* canals of Egypt shall be diminished and dried up, the reeds and the rushes shall wither *and* rot away.

7The meadows by the Nile, by the brink of the Nile, and all the sown fields of the Nile shall become dry, be blown away, and be no more.

8The fishermen shall lament, and all who cast a hook into the Nile will mourn, and they who spread nets upon the waters will languish.

9Moreover they who work in combed flax, and they who weave white [cotton] cloth will be confounded *and* in despair.

10[Those who are] the pillars *and* foundations of Egypt will be crushed, and all those who work for hire *or* who build dams will be grieved.

11The princes of Zoan [ancient capital of the Pharaohs] are utterly foolish, the counsel of the wisest counselors of Pharaoh has become witless—stupid. How can you say to Pharaoh, I am a son of the wise, a son of ancient kings?

12Where then are your wise men? Let them tell you now [if they are so wise], and let them make known what the Lord of hosts has purposed against Egypt [if they can].

## New American Standard

6 They will be left together for mountain birds of prey,
And for the beasts of the earth;
And the birds of prey will spend the summer *feeding* on them,
And all the beasts of the earth will spend harvest time on them.
7 At that time a gift of homage will be brought to the LORD of hosts
From a people tall and smooth,
Even from a people feared far and wide,
A powerful and oppressive nation,
Whose land the rivers divide—
To the place of the name of the LORD of hosts, *even* Mount Zion.

*Message to Egypt*

19 THE ORACLE concerning Egypt.
Behold, the LORD is riding on a swift cloud, and is about to come to Egypt;
The idols of Egypt will tremble at His presence,
And the heart of the Egyptians will melt within them.
2 "So I will incite Egyptians against Egyptians;
And they will each fight against his brother, and each against his neighbor,
City against city, *and* kingdom against kingdom.
3 "Then the spirit of the Egyptians will be demoralized within them;
And I will confound their strategy,
So that they will resort to idols and ghosts of the dead,
And to mediums and spiritists.
4 "Moreover, I will deliver the Egyptians into the hand of a cruel master,
And a mighty king will rule over them," declares the Lord GOD of hosts.

5¶ And the waters from the sea will dry up,
And the river will be parched and dry.
6 And the canals will emit a stench,
The streams of Egypt will thin out and dry up;
The reeds and rushes will rot away.
7 The bulrushes by the Nile, by the edge of the Nile
And all the sown fields by the Nile
Will become dry, be driven away, and be no more.
8 And the fishermen will lament,
And all those who cast a line into the Nile will mourn,
And those who spread nets on the waters will pine away.
9 Moreover, the manufacturers of linen made from combed flax
And the weavers of white cloth will be utterly dejected.
10 And the pillars *of Egypt* will be crushed;
All the hired laborers will be grieved in soul.

11¶ The princes of Zoan are mere fools;
The advice of Pharaoh's wisest advisers has become stupid.
How can you *men* say to Pharaoh,
"I am a son of the wise, a son of ancient kings"?
12 Well then, where are your wise men?
Please let them tell you,
And let them understand what the LORD of hosts
Has purposed against Egypt.

## New International

6They will all be left to the mountain birds of prey
and to the wild animals;
the birds will feed on them all summer,
the wild animals all winter.

7At that time gifts will be brought to the LORD Almighty

from a people tall and smooth-skinned,
from a people feared far and wide,
an aggressive nation of strange speech,
whose land is divided by rivers—

the gifts will be brought to Mount Zion, the place of the Name of the LORD Almighty.

*A Prophecy About Egypt*

19 AN ORACLE concerning Egypt:
See, the LORD rides on a swift cloud
and is coming to Egypt.
The idols of Egypt tremble before him,
and the hearts of the Egyptians melt within them.

2"I will stir up Egyptian against Egyptian—
brother will fight against brother,
neighbor against neighbor,
city against city,
kingdom against kingdom.
3The Egyptians will lose heart,
and I will bring their plans to nothing;
they will consult the idols and the spirits of the dead,
the mediums and the spiritists.
4I will hand the Egyptians over
to the power of a cruel master,
and a fierce king will rule over them,"
declares the Lord, the LORD Almighty.

5The waters of the river will dry up,
and the riverbed will be parched and dry.
6The canals will stink;
the streams of Egypt will dwindle and dry up.
The reeds and rushes will wither,
7 also the plants along the Nile,
at the mouth of the river.
Every sown field along the Nile
will become parched, will blow away and be no more.
8The fishermen will groan and lament,
all who cast hooks into the Nile;
those who throw nets on the water
will pine away.
9Those who work with combed flax will despair,
the weavers of fine linen will lose hope.
10The workers in cloth will be dejected,
and all the wage earners will be sick at heart.

11The officials of Zoan are nothing but fools;
the wise counselors of Pharaoh give senseless advice.
How can you say to Pharaoh,
"I am one of the wise men,
a disciple of the ancient kings"?

12Where are your wise men now?
Let them show you and make known
what the LORD Almighty
has planned against Egypt.

## King James

13 The princes of Zoan are become fools, the princes of Noph are deceived; they have also seduced Egypt, *even they that are* the stay of the tribes thereof.

14 The LORD hath mingled a perverse spirit in the midst thereof: and they have caused Egypt to err in every work thereof, as a drunken *man* staggereth in his vomit.

15 Neither shall there be *any* work for Egypt, which the head or tail, branch or rush, may do.

16 In that day shall Egypt be like unto women: and it shall be afraid and fear because of the shaking of the hand of the LORD of hosts, which he shaketh over it.

17 And the land of Judah shall be a terror unto Egypt, every one that maketh mention thereof shall be afraid in himself, because of the counsel of the LORD of hosts, which he hath determined against it.

18 ¶ In that day shall five cities in the land of Egypt speak the language of Canaan, and swear to the LORD of hosts; one shall be called, The city of destruction.

19 In that day shall there be an altar to the LORD in the midst of the land of Egypt, and a pillar at the border thereof to the LORD.

20 And it shall be for a sign and for a witness unto the LORD of hosts in the land of Egypt: for they shall cry unto the LORD because of the oppressors, and he shall send them a saviour, and a great one, and he shall deliver them.

21 And the LORD shall be known to Egypt, and the Egyptians shall know the LORD in that day, and shall do sacrifice and oblation; yea, they shall vow a vow unto the LORD, and perform *it*.

22 And the LORD shall smite Egypt: he shall smite and heal *it:* and they shall return *even* to the LORD, and he shall be entreated of them, and shall heal them.

23 ¶ In that day shall there be a highway out of Egypt to Assyria, and the Assyrian shall come into Egypt, and the Egyptian into Assyria, and the Egyptians shall serve with the Assyrians.

24 In that day shall Israel be the third with Egypt and with Assyria, *even* a blessing in the midst of the land:

25 Whom the LORD of hosts shall bless, saying, Blessed *be* Egypt my people, and Assyria the work of my hands, and Israel mine inheritance.

**20** IN THE year that Tartan came unto Ashdod, (when Sargon the king of Assyria sent him,) and fought against Ashdod, and took it;

2 At the same time spake the LORD by Isaiah the son of Amoz, saying, Go and loose the sackcloth from off thy loins, and put off thy shoe from thy foot. And he did so, walking naked and barefoot.

3 And the LORD said, Like as my servant Isaiah hath walked naked and barefoot three years *for* a sign and wonder upon Egypt and upon Ethiopia;

4 So shall the king of Assyria lead away the Egyptians prisoners, and the Ethiopians captives, young and old, naked and barefoot, even with *their* buttocks uncovered, to the shame of Egypt.

5 And they shall be afraid and ashamed of Ethiopia their expectation, and of Egypt their glory.

6 And the inhabitant of this isle shall say in that day, Behold, such *is* our expectation, whither we flee for help to be delivered from the king of Assyria: and how shall we escape?

## Amplified

13 The princes of Zoan have become fools, and the princes of Memphis are confused *and* deceived; those who are the cornerstones of her tribes have led Egypt astray.

14 The Lord has mingled a spirit of perverseness, error *and* confusion within her; *her leaders* have caused Egypt to stagger in all her doings, as a drunken man staggers in his vomit.

15 Neither can any work [done singly or by concerted action] accomplish anything for Egypt, whether by head or tail, palm branch or rush—high or low.

16 In that day will the Egyptians be like women [timid and helpless], and they will tremble and fear because of the shaking of the hand of the Lord of hosts, which He shakes over them.

17 And the land of Judah shall [allied to Assyria] become a terror to the Egyptians; everyone to whom mention of it is made will be afraid *and* everyone who mentions it, to him will they turn in fear, because of the purpose of the Lord of hosts which He purposes against Egypt.

18 In that day there shall be five cities in the land of Egypt that speak the language of *the Hebrews of* Canaan and swear allegiance to the Lord of hosts. One of them will be called the City of the Sun *or* Destruction.

19 In that day there will be an altar to the Lord in the midst of the land of Egypt, and a pillar to the Lord at its border.

20 And it shall be for a sign and for a witness to the Lord of hosts in the land of Egypt; for they will cry to the Lord because of oppressors, and He will send them a savior, even a mighty one, and he will deliver them. [Judg. 3:9, 15.]

21 And the Lord will make Himself known to Egypt, and the Egyptians will know (have knowledge of, be acquainted with, give heed to and cherish) the Lord in that day and will worship with sacrifice of animal *and* vegetable offerings; they will vow a vow to the Lord and perform it.

22 And the Lord shall smite Egypt, smiting and healing it, and they will return to the Lord, and He will listen to their entreaties and heal them.

23 In that day shall there be a highway out of Egypt to Assyria, and the Assyrian will come into Egypt, and the Egyptian into Assyria, and the Egyptians will worship [the Lord] with the Assyrians.

24 In that day Israel shall be the third with Egypt and with Assyria [in a Messianic league], a blessing in the midst of the earth,

25 Whom the Lord of hosts has blessed, saying, Blessed be Egypt My people, and Assyria the work of My hands, and Israel My heritage.

**20** IN THE year that the Tartan—Assyrian commander-in-chief—came to Ashdod in Philistia, sent by Sargon the king of Assyria, he fought against Ashdod and took it.

2 At that time the Lord had spoken by Isaiah the son of Amoz, saying, Go, loose the sackcloth from off your loins, and take your shoes from off your feet. And he had done so, walking stripped *to his loincloth* and barefoot.

3 And the Lord said, As My servant Isaiah has walked [comparatively] naked and barefoot for three years for a sign and forewarning concerning Egypt and concerning Cush, *that is*, Ethiopia,

4 So shall the king of Assyria lead away the Egyptians captives and the Ethiopians exiles, young and old, naked and barefoot, even with buttocks uncovered, to the shame of Egypt.

5 And they shall be dismayed and confounded because of Ethiopia their hope *and* expectation and of Egypt their glory *and* boast.

6 And the inhabitants of this coastland [the Israelites and their neighbors] will say in that day, See! This is what comes to those in whom we trusted *and* hoped, to whom we fled for help to deliver us from the king of Assyria! But we, how shall we escape *captivity and exile*?

## New American Standard

13 The princes of Zoan have acted foolishly,
The princes of Memphis are deluded;
*Those who are* the cornerstone of her tribes
Have led Egypt astray.
14 The LORD has mixed within her a spirit of distortion;
They have led Egypt astray in all that it does,
As a drunken man staggers in his vomit.
15 And there will be no work for Egypt
Which *its* head or tail, *its* palm branch or bulrush,
may do.

16¶ In that day the Egyptians will become like women, and they
will tremble and be in dread because of the waving of the hand of
the LORD of hosts, which He is going to wave over them.
17 And the land of Judah will become a terror to Egypt; everyone
to whom it is mentioned will be in dread of it, because of the
purpose of the LORD of hosts which He is purposing against them.
18¶ In that day five cities in the land of Egypt will be speaking
the language of Canaan and swearing *allegiance* to the LORD of
hosts; one will be called the City of [a]Destruction.
19¶ In that day there will be an altar to the LORD in the midst
of the land of Egypt, and a pillar to the LORD near its border.
20 And it will become a sign and a witness to the LORD of hosts
in the land of Egypt; for they will cry to the LORD because of
oppressors, and He will send them a Savior and a Champion, and
He will deliver them.
21 Thus the LORD will make Himself known to Egypt, and the
Egyptians will know the LORD in that day. They will even worship
with sacrifice and offering, and will make a vow to the LORD and
perform it.
22 And the LORD will strike Egypt, striking but healing; so they
will return to the LORD, and He will respond to them and will heal
them.
23¶ In that day there will be a highway from Egypt to Assyria,
and the Assyrians will come into Egypt and the Egyptians into
Assyria, and the Egyptians will worship with the Assyrians.
24¶ In that day Israel will be the third *party* with Egypt and
Assyria, a blessing in the midst of the earth,
25 whom the LORD of hosts has blessed, saying, "Blessed is
Egypt My people, and Assyria the work of My hands, and Israel
My inheritance."

*Prophecy about Egypt and Ethiopia*

20 IN THE year that the commander came to Ashdod, when
Sargon the king of Assyria sent him and he fought against
Ashdod and captured it,
2 at that time the LORD spoke through Isaiah the son of Amoz,
saying, "Go and loosen the sackcloth from your hips, and take
your shoes off your feet." And he did so, going naked and barefoot.
3 And the LORD said, "Even as My servant Isaiah has gone
naked and barefoot three years as a sign and token against Egypt
and Cush,
4 so the king of Assyria will lead away the captives of Egypt and
the exiles of Cush, young and old, naked and barefoot with buttocks uncovered, to the shame of Egypt.
5 "Then they shall be dismayed and ashamed because of Cush
their hope and Egypt their boast.
6 "So the inhabitants of this coastland will say in that day,
'Behold, such is our hope, where we fled for help to be delivered
from the king of Assyria; and we, how shall we escape?' "

NAS [a] Some ancient mss. and versions read *the Sun*

## New International

13 The officials of Zoan have become fools,
the leaders of Memphis[b] are deceived;
the cornerstones of her peoples
have led Egypt astray.
14 The LORD has poured into them
a spirit of dizziness;
they make Egypt stagger in all that she does,
as a drunkard staggers around in his vomit.
15 There is nothing Egypt can do—
head or tail, palm branch or reed.

16 In that day the Egyptians will be like women. They will shudder with fear at the uplifted hand that the LORD Almighty raises
against them. 17 And the land of Judah will bring terror to the
Egyptians; everyone to whom Judah is mentioned will be terrified,
because of what the LORD Almighty is planning against them.
18 In that day five cities in Egypt will speak the language of
Canaan and swear allegiance to the LORD Almighty. One of them
will be called the City of Destruction.[c]
19 In that day there will be an altar to the LORD in the heart of
Egypt, and a monument to the LORD at its border. 20 It will be a sign
and witness to the LORD Almighty in the land of Egypt. When they
cry out to the LORD because of their oppressors, he will send them
a savior and defender, and he will rescue them. 21 So the LORD will
make himself known to the Egyptians, and in that day they will
acknowledge the LORD. They will worship with sacrifices and
grain offerings; they will make vows to the LORD and keep them.
22 The LORD will strike Egypt with a plague; he will strike them and
heal them. They will turn to the LORD, and he will respond to their
pleas and heal them.
23 In that day there will be a highway from Egypt to Assyria. The
Assyrians will go to Egypt and the Egyptians to Assyria. The
Egyptians and Assyrians will worship together. 24 In that day Israel
will be the third, along with Egypt and Assyria, a blessing on the
earth. 25 The LORD Almighty will bless them, saying, "Blessed be
Egypt my people, Assyria my handiwork, and Israel my inheritance."

*A Prophecy Against Egypt and Cush*

20 IN THE year that the supreme commander, sent by Sargon king of Assyria, came to Ashdod and attacked and
captured it— 2 at that time the LORD spoke through Isaiah son of
Amoz. He said to him, "Take off the sackcloth from your body and
the sandals from your feet." And he did so, going around stripped
and barefoot.
3 Then the LORD said, "Just as my servant Isaiah has gone
stripped and barefoot for three years, as a sign and portent against
Egypt and Cush,[d] 4 so the king of Assyria will lead away stripped
and barefoot the Egyptian captives and Cushite exiles, young and
old, with buttocks bared—to Egypt's shame. 5 Those who trusted
in Cush and boasted in Egypt will be afraid and put to shame. 6 In
that day the people who live on this coast will say, 'See what has
happened to those we relied on, those we fled to for help and
deliverance from the king of Assyria! How then can we escape?' "

NIV [b] *13* Hebrew *Noph* [c] *18* Most manuscripts of the Masoretic Text; some manuscripts of the Masoretic Text, Dead Sea Scrolls and Vulgate *City of the Sun* (that is, Heliopolis) [d] *3* That is, the upper Nile region; also in verse 5

# King James

**21** THE BURDEN of the desert of the sea. As whirlwinds in
the south pass through; *so* it cometh from the desert, from
a terrible land.
2A grievous vision is declared unto me; the treacherous dealer
dealeth treacherously, and the spoiler spoileth. Go up, O Elam:
besiege, O Media; all the sighing thereof have I made to cease.
3Therefore are my loins filled with pain: pangs have taken hold
upon me, as the pangs of a woman that travaileth: I was bowed
down at the hearing *of it;* I was dismayed at the seeing *of it.*
4My heart panted, fearfulness affrighted me: the night of my
pleasure hath he turned into fear unto me.
5Prepare the table, watch in the watchtower, eat, drink: arise,
ye princes, *and* anoint the shield.
6For thus hath the Lord said unto me, Go, set a watchman, let
him declare what he seeth.
7And he saw a chariot *with* a couple of horsemen, a chariot of
asses, *and* a chariot of camels; and he hearkened diligently with
much heed:
8And he cried, A lion: My lord, I stand continually upon the
watchtower in the daytime, and I am set in my ward whole nights:
9And, behold, here cometh a chariot of men, *with* a couple of
horsemen. And he answered and said, Babylon is fallen, is fallen;
and all the graven images of her gods he hath broken unto the
ground.
10O my threshing, and the corn of my floor: that which I have
heard of the LORD of hosts, the God of Israel, have I declared unto
you.
11¶ The burden of Dumah. He calleth to me out of Seir, Watchman, what of the night? Watchman, what of the night?
12The watchman said, The morning cometh, and also the night:
if ye will inquire, inquire ye: return, come.
13¶ The burden upon Arabia. In the forest in Arabia shall ye
lodge, O ye travelling companies of Dedanim.

# Amplified

**21** THE MOURNFUL, inspired prediction—a burden to be
lifted up—concerning the desert of the sea [which was
Babylon after great dams were raised to control the waters of the
Euphrates River which overflowed it like a sea, and would do so
again]. As whirlwinds in the South (the Negeb) sweep through,
so it [the judgment of God by hostile armies] comes from the
desert, from a terrible land.
2A hard *and* grievous vision is declared to me; the treacherous
dealer deals treacherously, and the destroyer destroys. Go up, O
Elam [here put for Persia]! Besiege, O Media! All the sighing
[caused by Babylon's ruthless oppressions] I will cause to cease
[says the Lord].
3Therefore are my [Isaiah's] loins filled with anguish; pangs
have seized me like the pangs of a woman in childbirth; I am bent
*and* pained so that I cannot hear, I am dismayed so that I cannot
see.
4My mind reels *and* wanders, horror terrifies me. [In my mind's
eye I am at the feast of Belshazzar; I see the defilement of the
golden vessels taken from God's temple; I watch the handwriting
appear on the wall, I know that Babylon's great king is to be slain.]
The twilight I looked forward to with pleasure has been turned into
fear *and* trembling for me. [Dan. 5.]
5They prepare the table, they spread the rugs, *and having* set the
watchers [the revellers take no other precaution], they eat, they
drink. Arise, you princes, and oil your shields [for your deadly foe
is at the gates]!
6For thus has the Lord said to me, Go, set [yourself as] a watchman, let him declare what he sees.
7And when he sees a troop, horsemen in pairs, a troop of
donkeys and a troop of camels, he shall listen diligently, very
diligently.
8And *the watchman* cried like a lion: O Lord, I stand continually
on the watchtower in the daytime, and I am set in my station every
night through.
9And see! Here comes a troop of men *and* chariots, horsemen
in pairs! And he [the watchman] tells *what it foretells:* Babylon is
fallen, is fallen, and all the graven images of her gods lie shattered
to the ground [in my vision]!
10O you, my threshed and winnowed one [my own people the
Jews who must be trodden down by Babylon], that which I have
heard from the Lord of hosts, the God of Israel, I have *joyfully*
announced to you— *Babylon is to fall!*
11The mournful, inspired prediction—a burden to be lifted up—
concerning Dumah (Edom). One calls to me from Seir (Edom),
Watchman, what of the night? [How far is it spent? How long till
morning?] Guardian, what of the night?
12The watchman said, The morning comes, and also the night.
[Another time, if Edom earnestly wishes to know] if you will
inquire *of me,* inquire; return, come again.
13The mournful, inspired prediction—a burden to be lifted up—
concerning Arabia. In the forests *and* thickets of Arabia you shall
lodge, O you caravans of Dedanites [from northern Arabia].

## New American Standard

*God Commands That Babylon Be Taken*

21 THE ORACLE concerning the [a]wilderness of the sea.
As windstorms in the Negev sweep on,
It comes from the wilderness, from a terrifying land.
2 A harsh vision has been shown to me;
The treacherous one still deals treacherously, *and* the destroyer still destroys.
Go up, Elam, lay siege, Media;
I have made an end of all the groaning she has caused.
3 For this reason my loins are full of anguish;
Pains have seized me like the pains of a woman in labor.
I am so bewildered I cannot hear, so terrified I cannot see.
4 My mind reels, horror overwhelms me;
The twilight I longed for has been turned for me into trembling.
5 They set the table, they [b]spread out the cloth, they eat, they drink;
"Rise up, captains, oil the shields,"
6 For thus the Lord says to me,
"Go, station the lookout, let him report what he sees.
7 "When he sees riders, horsemen in pairs,
A train of donkeys, a train of camels,
Let him pay close attention, very close attention."
8 Then the lookout called,
"O Lord, I stand continually by day on the watchtower,
And I am stationed every night at my guard post.
9 "Now behold, here comes a troop of riders, horsemen in pairs."
And one answered and said, "Fallen, fallen is Babylon;
And all the images of her gods are shattered on the ground."
10 O my threshed *people*, and my afflicted of the threshing floor!
What I have heard from the LORD of hosts,
The God of Israel, I make known to you.

*Oracles about Edom and Arabia*

11¶ The oracle concerning Edom.
One keeps calling to me from Seir,
"Watchman, [c]how far gone is the night?
Watchman, [d]how far gone is the night?"
12 The watchman says,
"Morning comes but also night.
If you would inquire, inquire;
Come back again."

13¶ The oracle about Arabia.
In the thickets of Arabia you must spend the night,
O caravans of Dedanites.

NAS [a] Or, *sandy wastes, sea country* [b] Or, *spread out the rugs;* or possibly, *arranged the seating* [c] Lit., *what* is the time *of the night?* [d] Lit., *what* is the time *of the night?*

## New International

*A Prophecy Against Babylon*

21 AN ORACLE concerning the Desert by the Sea:
Like whirlwinds sweeping through the southland,
an invader comes from the desert,
from a land of terror.
2A dire vision has been shown to me:
The traitor betrays, the looter takes loot.
Elam, attack! Media, lay siege!
I will bring to an end all the groaning she caused.

3At this my body is racked with pain,
pangs seize me, like those of a woman in labor;
I am staggered by what I hear,
I am bewildered by what I see.
4My heart falters,
fear makes me tremble;
the twilight I longed for
has become a horror to me.

5They set the tables,
they spread the rugs,
they eat, they drink!
Get up, you officers,
oil the shields!
6This is what the Lord says to me:

"Go, post a lookout
and have him report what he sees.
7When he sees chariots
with teams of horses,
riders on donkeys
or riders on camels,
let him be alert,
fully alert."
8And the lookout[e] shouted,

"Day after day, my lord, I stand on the watchtower;
every night I stay at my post.
9Look, here comes a man in a chariot
with a team of horses.
And he gives back the answer:
'Babylon has fallen, has fallen!
All the images of its gods
lie shattered on the ground!' "
10O my people, crushed on the threshing floor,
I tell you what I have heard
from the LORD Almighty,
from the God of Israel.

*A Prophecy Against Edom*

11An oracle concerning Dumah[f] :

Someone calls to me from Seir,
"Watchman, what is left of the night?
Watchman, what is left of the night?"
12The watchman replies,
"Morning is coming, but also the night.
If you would ask, then ask;
and come back yet again."

*A Prophecy Against Arabia*

13An oracle concerning Arabia:

You caravans of Dedanites,
who camp in the thickets of Arabia,

NIV [e] *8* Dead Sea Scrolls and Syriac; Masoretic Text *A lion* [f] *11 Dumah* means *silence* or *stillness*, a wordplay on *Edom.*

## King James

14The inhabitants of the land of Tema brought water to him that was thirsty, they prevented with their bread him that fled.
15For they fled from the swords, from the drawn sword, and from the bent bow, and from the grievousness of war.
16For thus hath the Lord said unto me, Within a year, according to the years of an hireling, and all the glory of Kedar shall fail:
17And the residue of the number of archers, the mighty men of the children of Kedar, shall be diminished: for the LORD God of Israel hath spoken *it*.

22 THE BURDEN of the valley of vision. What aileth thee now, that thou art wholly gone up to the housetops?
2Thou that art full of stirs, a tumultuous city, a joyous city: thy slain *men are* not slain with the sword, nor dead in battle.
3All thy rulers are fled together, they are bound by the archers: all that are found in thee are bound together, *which* have fled from far.
4Therefore said I, Look away from me; I will weep bitterly, labour not to comfort me, because of the spoiling of the daughter of my people.
5For *it is* a day of trouble, and of treading down, and of perplexity by the Lord GOD of hosts in the valley of vision, breaking down the walls, and of crying to the mountains.
6And Elam bare the quiver with chariots of men *and* horsemen, and Kir uncovered the shield.
7And it shall come to pass, *that* thy choicest valleys shall be full of chariots, and the horsemen shall set themselves in array at the gate.
8¶ And he discovered the covering of Judah, and thou didst look in that day to the armour of the house of the forest.
9Ye have seen also the breaches of the city of David, that they are many: and ye gathered together the waters of the lower pool.
10And ye have numbered the houses of Jerusalem, and the houses have ye broken down to fortify the wall.
11Ye made also a ditch between the two walls for the water of the old pool: but ye have not looked unto the maker thereof, neither had respect unto him that fashioned it long ago.
12And in that day did the Lord GOD of hosts call to weeping, and to mourning, and to baldness, and to girding with sackcloth:
13And behold joy and gladness, slaying oxen, and killing sheep, eating flesh, and drinking wine: let us eat and drink; for tomorrow we shall die.
14And it was revealed in mine ears by the LORD of hosts, Surely this iniquity shall not be purged from you till ye die, saith the Lord GOD of hosts.

## Amplified

14To the thirsty [Dedanites] bring water, O inhabitants of the land of Tema *in Arabia*, meet the fugitive with bread [suitable] for him.
15For they have fled from the swords, from the drawn sword, and from the bent bow, and from the grievousness of war—the press of battle.
16For the Lord has said this to me, Within a year, according to the years of a hireling [who will work no longer than was agreed], all the glory of Kedar [an Arabian tribe] shall fail.
17And the remainder of the number of archers *and their* bows, the mighty men of the sons of Kedar, will be diminished *and* few; for the Lord, the God of Israel, has spoken it.

22 THE MOURNFUL, inspired prediction—a burden to be lifted up—concerning the valley of vision. What do you mean, *I wonder,* that you have all gone up to the housetops,
2You who are full of shoutings, a tumultuous city, a joyous *and* exultant city? [O Jerusalem] your slain warriors have not met [a glorious] death with the sword or in battle.
3All your *military* leaders have fled together; without the bow [which they had thrown away] they were taken captive *and* bound by the archers. All of you that were found were bound together *as captives,* though they had fled far away.
4Therefore I [Isaiah] said, Look away from me; I will weep bitterly; do not hasten *and* try to comfort me for the destruction of the daughter of my people.
5For it is a day of discomfiture *and* of tumult, of treading down, of confusion *and* perplexity from the Lord God of hosts in the valley of vision, a breaking down of the walls and of crying to the mountains.
6And [in my vision] *I saw* Elam take up the quiver, with troops in chariots, infantry *and* horsemen, and Kir [with Elam subject to Assyria] uncovered the shield.
7And it came to pass, that your choicest valleys were full of chariots, and the horsemen took their station [and set themselves in offensive array at the gate of Jerusalem]. [Fulfilled in Isa. 36; II Chron. 32.]
8Then *God* removed the protecting covering of Judah, and you looked to weapons in the house of the forest [the king's armory] in that day.
9You saw that the breaches *in the walls* of the city of David [the citadel of Zion] were many; [the water supply being still defective] you collected *within the city's walls* the waters of the lower pool;
10And you numbered the houses of Jerusalem, and you broke down the houses *to get materials* to fortify the *city* wall.
11You also made a reservoir between the two walls for the water of the old pool. But you did not look to the Maker of it, nor did you recognize Him Who planned it long ago.
12And in that day the Lord God of hosts called to weeping and mourning, to the shaving off of all hair *in humiliation,* and to girding with sackcloth.
13But instead, see the pleasure and mirth, slaying oxen and killing sheep, eating flesh and drinking wine, [with the idea] Let us eat and drink, for tomorrow we shall die.
14And the Lord of hosts revealed Himself in my ears [as He said], Surely this unatoned-for sin shall not be purged from you until [you are punished, and the punishment will be] death, says the Lord God of hosts.

## New American Standard

14 Bring water for the thirsty,
O inhabitants of the land of Tema,
Meet the fugitive with bread.
15 For they have fled from the swords,
From the drawn sword, and from the bent bow,
And from the press of battle.
16For thus the Lord said to me, "In a year, as a hired man would
count it, all the splendor of Kedar will terminate;
17and the remainder of the number of bowmen, the mighty men
of the sons of Kedar, will be few; for the LORD God of Israel has
spoken."

*The Valley of Vision*

22 THE ORACLE concerning the valley of vision.
What is the matter with you now, that you have all
gone up to the housetops?
2 You who were full of noise,
You boisterous town, you exultant city;
Your slain were not slain with the sword,
Nor did they die in battle.
3 All your rulers have fled together,
*And* have been captured without the bow;
All of you who were found were taken captive together,
Though they had fled far away.
4 Therefore I say, "Turn your eyes away from me,
Let me weep bitterly,
Do not try to comfort me concerning the destruction of
the daughter of my people."
5 For the Lord GOD of hosts has a day of panic,
subjugation, and confusion
In the valley of vision,
A breaking down of walls
And a crying to the mountain.
6 And Elam took up the quiver
With the chariots, infantry, *and* horsemen;
And Kir uncovered the shield.
7 Then your choicest valleys were full of chariots,
And the horsemen took up fixed positions at the gate.
8 And He removed the defense of Judah.
In that day you depended on the weapons of the house
of the forest,
9 And you saw that the breaches
In the *wall* of the city of David were many;
And you collected the waters of the lower pool.
10 Then you counted the houses of Jerusalem,
And you tore down houses to fortify the wall.
11 And you made a reservoir between the two walls
For the waters of the old pool.
But you did not depend on Him who made it,
Nor did you take into consideration Him who planned
it long ago.
12¶ Therefore in that day the Lord GOD of hosts, called
*you* to weeping, to wailing,
To shaving the head, and to wearing sackcloth.
13 Instead, there is gaiety and gladness,
Killing of cattle and slaughtering of sheep,
Eating of meat and drinking of wine:
"Let us eat and drink, for tomorrow we may die."
14 But the LORD of hosts revealed Himself to me,
"Surely this iniquity shall not be forgiven you
Until you die," says the Lord GOD of hosts.

## New International

14 bring water for the thirsty;
you who live in Tema,
bring food for the fugitives.
15They flee from the sword,
from the drawn sword,
from the bent bow
and from the heat of battle.

16This is what the Lord says to me: "Within one year, as a
servant bound by contract would count it, all the pomp of Kedar
will come to an end. 17The survivors of the bowmen, the warriors
of Kedar, will be few." The LORD, the God of Israel, has spoken.

*A Prophecy About Jerusalem*

22 AN ORACLE concerning the Valley of Vision:
What troubles you now,
that you have all gone up on the roofs,
2O town full of commotion,
O city of tumult and revelry?
Your slain were not killed by the sword,
nor did they die in battle.
3All your leaders have fled together;
they have been captured without using the bow.
All you who were caught were taken prisoner together,
having fled while the enemy was still far away.
4Therefore I said, "Turn away from me;
let me weep bitterly.
Do not try to console me
over the destruction of my people."

5The Lord, the LORD Almighty, has a day
of tumult and trampling and terror
in the Valley of Vision,
a day of battering down walls
and of crying out to the mountains.
6Elam takes up the quiver,
with her charioteers and horses;
Kir uncovers the shield.
7Your choicest valleys are full of chariots,
and horsemen are posted at the city gates;
8 the defenses of Judah are stripped away.

And you looked in that day
to the weapons in the Palace of the Forest;
9you saw that the City of David
had many breaches in its defenses;
you stored up water
in the Lower Pool.
10You counted the buildings in Jerusalem
and tore down houses to strengthen the wall.
11You built a reservoir between the two walls
for the water of the Old Pool,
but you did not look to the One who made it,
or have regard for the One who planned it long ago.
12The Lord, the LORD Almighty,
called you on that day
to weep and to wail,
to tear out your hair and put on sackcloth.
13But see, there is joy and revelry,
slaughtering of cattle and killing of sheep,
eating of meat and drinking of wine!
"Let us eat and drink," you say,
"for tomorrow we die!"

14The LORD Almighty has revealed this in my hearing: "Till your
dying day this sin will not be atoned for," says the Lord, the LORD
Almighty.

## King James

15¶ Thus saith the Lord GOD of hosts, Go, get thee unto this
treasurer, *even* unto Shebna, which *is* over the house, *and say,*
16What hast thou here? and whom hast thou here, that thou
hast hewed thee out a sepulchre here, *as* he that heweth him out
a sepulchre on high, *and* that graveth an habitation for himself in
a rock?
17Behold, the LORD will carry thee away with a mighty captivity,
and will surely cover thee.
18He will surely violently turn and toss thee *like* a ball into a
large country: there shalt thou die, and there the chariots of thy
glory *shall be* the shame of thy lord's house.
19And I will drive thee from thy station, and from thy state shall
he pull thee down.
20¶ And it shall come to pass in that day, that I will call my
servant Eliakim the son of Hilkiah:
21And I will clothe him with thy robe, and strengthen him with
thy girdle, and I will commit thy government into his hand: and
he shall be a father to the inhabitants of Jerusalem, and to the
house of Judah.
22And the key of the house of David will I lay upon his shoulder;
so he shall open, and none shall shut; and he shall shut, and none
shall open.
23And I will fasten him *as* a nail in a sure place; and he shall be
for a glorious throne to his father's house.
24And they shall hang upon him all the glory of his father's
house, the offspring and the issue, all vessels of small quantity,
from the vessels of cups, even to all the vessels of flagons.
25In that day, saith the LORD of hosts, shall the nail that is
fastened in the sure place be removed, and be cut down, and fall;
and the burden that *was* upon it shall be cut off: for the LORD hath
spoken *it*.

**23** THE BURDEN of Tyre. Howl, ye ships of Tarshish; for it
is laid waste, so that there is no house, no entering in:
from the land of Chittim it is revealed to them.
2Be still, ye inhabitants of the isle; thou whom the merchants
of Zidon, that pass over the sea, have replenished.
3And by great waters the seed of Sihor, the harvest of the river,
*is* her revenue; and she is a mart of nations.
4Be thou ashamed, O Zidon: for the sea hath spoken, *even* the
strength of the sea, saying, I travail not, nor bring forth children,
neither do I nourish up young men, *nor* bring up virgins.
5As at the report concerning Egypt, *so* shall they be sorely
pained at the report of Tyre.
6Pass ye over to Tarshish; howl, ye inhabitants of the isle.

## Amplified

15Come, go to this *contemptible* steward *and* treasurer, to Shebna
who is over the house [but who is presumptuous enough to be
building himself a tomb among those of the mighty], and say to
him,
16What business have you here? And whom have you en-
tombed here, that you have the right to hew you out a tomb here?
He hews him out a sepulchre on the height! He carves out a
dwelling for himself in the rock!
17Behold, the Lord will hurl you away violently, O you strong
man; yes, He will take tight hold of you *and* He will surely cover
you [with shame].
18He will surely roll you up in a bundle, *Shebna,* and toss you
like a ball into a large country; there you will die, and there shall
be your splendid chariots, you disgrace of your master's house!
19And I will thrust you from your office, and from your station
shall you be pulled down.
20And in that day I will call My servant Eliakim the son of
Hilkiah.
21And I will clothe him with your robe, and will bind your girdle
on him and I will commit your authority to his hand; he shall be
a father to the inhabitants of Jerusalem and to the house of Judah.
22And the key of the house of David I will lay upon his shoulder;
he shall open, and no one shall shut; he shall shut, and no one shall
open.
23And I will fasten him like a peg *or* nail in a firm place; and he
will become a throne of honor *and* glory to his father's house.
24And they will hang on him the honor *and* the whole weight
of *responsibility for* his father's house, the offspring and issue [of the
family, high and low], every small vessel, from the cups even to
all the flasks *and* big bulging bottles.
25In that day, says the Lord of hosts, the nail *or* peg that was
fastened in the sure place shall give way *and* be moved, and be
hewn down and fall; and the burden that was upon it shall be cut
off, for the Lord has spoken it.

**23** THE MOURNFUL, inspired prediction—a burden to be
lifted up—concerning Tyre. Wail, you ships [of Tyre returning from] *trading with* Tarshish, for *Tyre* is laid waste, so that
there is no house, no harbor; from the land of Kittim (Cyprus) they
learn of it.
2Be still, you inhabitants of the coast, you merchants of Sidon,
[a] *your messengers* passing over the sea have replenished you [with
wealth and industry],
3And on great waters, the seed *or* grain of the Shihor, the
harvest [due to the overflow] of the Nile River, was *Tyre's* revenue,
and it became the merchandise of the nations.
4Be ashamed, O Sidon [mother-city of Tyre, now a widow
bereaved of her children], for the sea has spoken, the stronghold
of the sea, saying, I have neither travailed nor brought forth children; I have neither nourished *and* reared young men nor brought
up virgins.
5When the report comes to Egypt, they will be sorely pained
over the report about Tyre.
6Pass over to Tarshish [to seek safety as exiles]! Wail, you inhabitants of the [Tyre] coast!

AMP [a] The Dead Sea Scrolls so read.

## New American Standard

15¶ Thus says the Lord GOD of hosts,
"Come, go to this steward,
To Shebna, who is in charge of the *royal* household,
16 'What right do you have here,
And whom do you have here,
That you have hewn a tomb for yourself here,
You who hew a tomb on the height,
You who carve a resting place for yourself in the rock?
17 'Behold, the LORD is about to hurl you headlong,
O man.
And He is about to grasp you firmly,
18 *And* roll you tightly like a ball,
*To be cast* into a vast country;
There you will die,
And there your splendid chariots will be,
You shame of your master's house.'
19 "And I will depose you from your office,
And I will pull you down from your station.
20 "Then it will come about in that day,
That I will summon My servant Eliakim the son of Hilkiah
21 And I will clothe him with your tunic,
And tie your sash securely about him,
I will entrust him with your authority,
And he will become a father to the inhabitants of Jerusalem and to the house of Judah.
22 "Then I will set the key of the house of David on his shoulder,
When he opens no one will shut,
When he shuts no one will open.
23 "And I will drive him *like* a peg in a firm place,
And he will become a throne of glory to his father's house.
24"So they will hang on him all the glory of his father's house,
offspring and issue, all the least of vessels, from bowls to all the
jars.
25"In that day," declares the LORD of hosts, "the peg driven in
a firm place will give way; it will even break off and fall, and the
load hanging on it will be cut off, for the LORD has spoken."

*The Fall of Tyre*

**23** THE ORACLE concerning Tyre.
Wail, O ships of Tarshish,
For *Tyre* is destroyed, without house *or* harbor;
It is reported to them from the land of Cyprus.
2 Be silent, you inhabitants of the coastland,
You merchants of Sidon;
Your messengers crossed the sea
3 And *were* on many waters.
The grain of the Nile, the harvest of the River was her revenue;
And she was the market of nations.
4 Be ashamed, O Sidon;
For the sea speaks, the stronghold of the sea, saying,
"I have neither travailed nor given birth,
I have neither brought up young men *nor* reared virgins."
5 When the report *reaches* Egypt,
They will be in anguish at the report of Tyre.
6 Pass over to Tarshish;
Wail, O inhabitants of the coastland.

## New International

15This is what the Lord, the LORD Almighty, says:
"Go, say to this steward,
to Shebna, who is in charge of the palace:
16What are you doing here and who gave you permission
to cut out a grave for yourself here,
hewing your grave on the height
and chiseling your resting place in the rock?
17"Beware, the LORD is about to take firm hold of you
and hurl you away, O you mighty man.
18He will roll you up tightly like a ball
and throw you into a large country.
There you will die
and there your splendid chariots will remain—
you disgrace to your master's house!
19I will depose you from your office,
and you will be ousted from your position.

20"In that day I will summon my servant, Eliakim son of Hilkiah. 21I will clothe him with your robe and fasten your sash
around him and hand your authority over to him. He will be a
father to those who live in Jerusalem and to the house of Judah.
22I will place on his shoulder the key to the house of David; what
he opens no one can shut, and what he shuts no one can open.
23I will drive him like a peg into a firm place; he will be a seat[b] of
honor for the house of his father. 24All the glory of his family will
hang on him: its offspring and offshoots—all its lesser vessels,
from the bowls to all the jars.

25"In that day," declares the LORD Almighty, "the peg driven
into the firm place will give way; it will be sheared off and will fall,
and the load hanging on it will be cut down." The LORD has
spoken.

*A Prophecy About Tyre*

**23** AN ORACLE concerning Tyre:

Wail, O ships of Tarshish!
For Tyre is destroyed
and left without house or harbor.
From the land of Cyprus[c]
word has come to them.

2Be silent, you people of the island
and you merchants of Sidon,
whom the seafarers have enriched.
3On the great waters
came the grain of the Shihor;
the harvest of the Nile[d] was the revenue of Tyre,
and she became the marketplace of the nations.

4Be ashamed, O Sidon, and you, O fortress of the sea,
for the sea has spoken:
"I have neither been in labor nor given birth;
I have neither reared sons nor brought up daughters."
5When word comes to Egypt,
they will be in anguish at the report from Tyre.

6Cross over to Tarshish;
wail, you people of the island.

**NIV** [b] 23 Or *throne* [c] 1,12 Hebrew *Kittim* [d] 2,3 Masoretic Text; one Dead Sea Scroll *Sidon, / who cross over the sea; / your envoys 3are on the great waters. / The grain of the Shihor, / the harvest of the Nile,*

## King James

7 *Is* this your joyous *city,* whose antiquity *is* of ancient days? her
own feet shall carry her afar off to sojourn.
8Who hath taken this counsel against Tyre, the crowning *city,*
whose merchants *are* princes, whose traffickers *are* the honourable
of the earth?
9The LORD of hosts hath purposed it, to stain the pride of all
glory, *and* to bring into contempt all the honourable of the earth.
10Pass through thy land as a river, O daughter of Tarshish: *there*
*is* no more strength.
11He stretched out his hand over the sea, he shook the kingdoms: the LORD hath given a commandment against the merchant
*city,* to destroy the strong holds thereof.
12And he said, Thou shalt no more rejoice, O thou oppressed
virgin, daughter of Zidon: arise, pass over to Chittim; there also
shalt thou have no rest.
13Behold the land of the Chaldeans; this people was not, *till* the
Assyrian founded it for them that dwell in the wilderness: they set
up the towers thereof, they raised up the palaces thereof; *and* he
brought it to ruin.
14Howl, ye ships of Tarshish: for your strength is laid waste.
15And it shall come to pass in that day, that Tyre shall be
forgotten seventy years, according to the days of one king: after
the end of seventy years shall Tyre sing as an harlot.
16Take an harp, go about the city, thou harlot that hast been
forgotten; make sweet melody, sing many songs, that thou mayest
be remembered.
17¶ And it shall come to pass after the end of seventy years, that
the LORD will visit Tyre, and she shall turn to her hire, and shall
commit fornication with all the kingdoms of the world upon the
face of the earth.
18And her merchandise and her hire shall be holiness to the
LORD: it shall not be treasured nor laid up; for her merchandise
shall be for them that dwell before the LORD, to eat sufficiently, and
for durable clothing.

## Amplified

7Is this your jubilant city, whose origin dates back into antiquity, whose own feet are accustomed to carry her far off to settle
[daughter cities]?
8Who has purposed this against Tyre, the bestower of crowns,
whose merchants were princes, whose traders were the honored
of the earth?
9The Lord of hosts has purposed it [in accordance with a fixed
principle of His government], to defile the pride of all glory and
to bring into dishonor *and* contempt all the honored of the earth.
10Overflow your land like [the overflow of] the Nile River, O
daughter of Tarshish; there is no girdle of restraint *on you* any more
[to make you pay tribute or custom duties to Tyre].
11He stretched out His hand over the sea, He shook the kingdoms; the Lord has given a command concerning Canaan to destroy her strongholds *and* fortresses [Tyre, Sidon, etc.].
12And He said, You shall no more exult, O Tyre, you oppressed
*and* extorted one, virgin daughter of Sidon. Arise, pass over to
Kittim [Cyprus]; but even there you will have no rest.
13Look at the land of the Chaldeans! That people and not the
Assyrians designed *and* assigned *Tyre* for the wild beasts *and* those
who [previously] dwelt in the wilderness. They set up their siegeworks, they overthrew its palaces, they made it a ruin!
14Howl, you ships of Tarshish, for your stronghold *of Tyre* is laid
waste—your strength has been destroyed.
15And in that day Tyre will be in obscurity *and* forgotten for
seventy years, according to the days of one dynasty. After the end
of seventy years shall Tyre sing as a harlot [who has been forgotten, but again attracts her lovers].
16Take a harp, go about the city, forgotten harlot; play skillfully
*and* make sweet melody, sing many songs, that you may be
remembered.
17And after the end of seventy years the Lord will remember
Tyre, and she will return to her hire and will play the harlot
[resume her commerce] with all the kingdoms of the world upon
the face of the earth.
18But [the profits of Tyre's new prosperity] her gain and her hire
will be [a]dedicated to the Lord [eventually]. It will not be treasured
or stored up, for her gain will be used for those who dwell in the
presence of the Lord [the ministers], that they may eat sufficiently
and have durable *and* stately clothing [suitable for those who minister at God's altar].

**24** BEHOLD, THE LORD maketh the earth empty, and
maketh it waste, and turneth it upside down, and scattereth abroad the inhabitants thereof.

**24** BEHOLD, THE Lord will make the land *and* the [b]earth
empty, and make it waste, and turn it upside down—twist
the face of it—and scatter abroad its inhabitants.

**AMP** [a] This whole prophecy (verses 14-18) was literally fulfilled in following centuries. Tyre was destroyed by Nebuchadnezzar and lay desolate for seventy years, after which a new city was built on the island, but taken by Alexander the Great. Eventually the true religion prevailed at Tyre. Jesus visited there (Matt. 15:21) and so did Paul (Acts 21:3-6). Eusebius (Hist. 10:4) says that "when the church of God was founded in Tyre . . . much of its wealth was consecrated to God . . . and was presented for the support of the ministry." Jerome, also writing in the fourth century A.D., says the wealth of the churches of Tyre "was not treasured up or hidden, but was given to those who dwelt before the Lord."
[b] "The prophet transports himself in spirit to the end of all things. He describes the destruction of the world. He sees, however, that this destruction will be gradually accomplished. He here depicts the first scene: the destruction of all that exists on the *surface* of the earth . . . as even now occurs [in limited areas] in consequence of wars . . . Jehovah empties, devastates, depopulates the *surface* of the earth . . ." (Lange's Commentary.) "The writer feels that he is living in the last days, and in the universal wretchedness and confusions of the age he seems to discern the 'beginning of sorrows.' His thoughts glide almost imperceptibly from the one point of view to the other, now describing the distress and depression which exist, and now the more terrible visitation which is imminent." (Cambridge Bible.)

## New American Standard

7 Is this your jubilant *city*,
Whose origin is from antiquity,
Whose feet used to carry her to colonize distant places?
8¶ Who has planned this against Tyre, the bestower of crowns,
Whose merchants were princes, whose traders were the honored of the earth?
9 The LORD of hosts has planned it to defile the pride of all beauty,
To despise all the honored of the earth.
10 Overflow your land like the Nile, O daughter of Tarshish,
There is no more restraint.
11 He has stretched His hand out over the sea,
He has made the kingdoms tremble;
The LORD has given a command concerning Canaan to demolish its strongholds.
12 And He has said, "You shall exult no more, O crushed virgin daughter of Sidon.
Arise, pass over to Cyprus; even there you will find no rest."
13Behold, the land of the Chaldeans—this is the people *which*
was not; Assyria appointed it for desert creatures—they erected
their siege towers, they stripped its palaces, they made it a ruin.
14 Wail, O ships of Tarshish,
For your stronghold is destroyed.
15Now it will come about in that day that Tyre will be forgotten
for seventy years like the days of one king. At the end of seventy
years it will happen to Tyre as *in* the song of the harlot:
16 Take *your* harp, walk about the city,
O forgotten harlot;
Pluck the strings skillfully, sing many songs,
That you may be remembered.
17And it will come about at the end of seventy years that the
LORD will visit Tyre. Then she will go back to her harlot's wages,
and will play the harlot with all the kingdoms on the face of the earth.
18And her gain and her harlot's wages will be set apart to the
LORD; it will not be stored up or hoarded, but her gain will become
sufficient food and choice attire for those who dwell in the presence of the LORD.

*Judgment on the Earth*

24 BEHOLD, THE LORD lays the earth waste, devastates it, distorts its surface, and scatters its inhabitants.

## New International

7Is this your city of revelry,
the old, old city,
whose feet have taken her
to settle in far-off lands?
8Who planned this against Tyre,
the bestower of crowns,
whose merchants are princes,
whose traders are renowned in the earth?
9The LORD Almighty planned it,
to bring low the pride of all glory
and to humble all who are renowned on the earth.

10Till[c] your land as along the Nile,
O Daughter of Tarshish,
for you no longer have a harbor.
11The LORD has stretched out his hand over the sea
and made its kingdoms tremble.
He has given an order concerning Phoenicia[d]
that her fortresses be destroyed.
12He said, "No more of your reveling,
O Virgin Daughter of Sidon, now crushed!

"Up, cross over to Cyprus[e];
even there you will find no rest."
13Look at the land of the Babylonians,[f]
this people that is now of no account!
The Assyrians have made it
a place for desert creatures;
they raised up their siege towers,
they stripped its fortresses bare
and turned it into a ruin.
14Wail, you ships of Tarshish;
your fortress is destroyed!
15At that time Tyre will be forgotten for seventy years, the span
of a king's life. But at the end of these seventy years, it will happen
to Tyre as in the song of the prostitute:
16"Take up a harp, walk through the city,
O prostitute forgotten;
play the harp well, sing many a song,
so that you will be remembered."
17At the end of seventy years, the LORD will deal with Tyre. She
will return to her hire as a prostitute and will ply her trade with
all the kingdoms on the face of the earth. 18Yet her profit and her
earnings will be set apart for the LORD; they will not be stored up
or hoarded. Her profits will go to those who live before the LORD,
for abundant food and fine clothes.

*The LORD's Devastation of the Earth*

24 SEE, THE LORD is going to lay waste the earth
and devastate it;
he will ruin its face
and scatter its inhabitants—

NIV [c] *10* Dead Sea Scrolls and some Septuagint manuscripts; Masoretic Text *Go through* [d] *11* Hebrew *Canaan* [e] *12* Hebrew *Kittim* [f] *13* Or *Chaldeans*

# King James

2And it shall be, as with the people, so with the priest; as with the servant, so with his master; as with the maid, so with her mistress; as with the buyer, so with the seller; as with the lender, so with the borrower; as with the taker of usury, so with the giver of usury to him.
3The land shall be utterly emptied, and utterly spoiled: for the LORD hath spoken this word.
4The earth mourneth *and* fadeth away, the world languisheth *and* fadeth away, the haughty people of the earth do languish.
5The earth also is defiled under the inhabitants thereof; because they have transgressed the laws, changed the ordinance, broken the everlasting covenant.
6Therefore hath the curse devoured the earth, and they that dwell therein are desolate: therefore the inhabitants of the earth are burned, and few men left.
7The new wine mourneth, the vine languisheth, all the merry-hearted do sigh.
8The mirth of tabrets ceaseth, the noise of them that rejoice endeth, the joy of the harp ceaseth.
9They shall not drink wine with a song; strong drink shall be bitter to them that drink it.
10The city of confusion is broken down: every house is shut up, that no man may come in.
11 *There is* a crying for wine in the streets; all joy is darkened, the mirth of the land is gone.
12In the city is left desolation, and the gate is smitten with destruction.
13¶ When thus it shall be in the midst of the land among the people, *there shall be* as the shaking of an olive tree, *and* as the gleaning grapes when the vintage is done.
14They shall lift up their voice, they shall sing for the majesty of the LORD, they shall cry aloud from the sea.
15Wherefore glorify ye the LORD in the fires, *even* the name of the LORD God of Israel in the isles of the sea.
16¶ From the uttermost part of the earth have we heard songs, *even* glory to the righteous. But I said, My leanness, my leanness, woe unto me! the treacherous dealers have dealt treacherously; yea, the treacherous dealers have dealt very treacherously.
17Fear, and the pit, and the snare, *are* upon thee, O inhabitant of the earth.
18And it shall come to pass, *that* he who fleeth from the noise of the fear shall fall into the pit; and he that cometh up out of the midst of the pit shall be taken in the snare: for the windows from on high are open, and the foundations of the earth do shake.
19The earth is utterly broken down, the earth is clean dissolved, the earth is moved exceedingly.
20The earth shall reel to and fro like a drunkard, and shall be removed like a cottage; and the transgression thereof shall be heavy upon it; and it shall fall, and not rise again.
21And it shall come to pass in that day, *that* the LORD shall punish the host of the high ones *that are* on high, and the kings of the earth upon the earth.

# Amplified

2And it shall be, as *what happens* with the people, so with the priest; as with the servant, so with his master; as with the maid, so with her mistress; as with the buyer, so with the seller; as with the lender, so with the borrower; as with the creditor, so with the debtor.
3The land *and* the earth shall be utterly laid waste and utterly pillaged; for the Lord has said this.
4The land *and* the earth mourn and wither, the world languishes and withers, the high ones of the people [and the heavens with the earth] languish.
5The land *and* the earth also *are* defiled under their inhabitants; because *they* have transgressed the laws, disregarded the statutes, broken the everlasting covenant. [Gen. 9:1-17; Deut. 29:20.]
6Therefore the curse has devoured the land *and* the earth, and they who dwell in it suffer the punishment of its guilt; therefore the inhabitants of the land *and* the earth are scorched *and* parched [under the curse of God's wrath], and few people are left. [Rom. 1:20.]
7The new wine mourns, the vine languishes, all the merry-hearted sigh.
8The mirth of the timbrels is stilled, the noise of those who rejoice ends, the joy of the lyre is stopped.
9No more will they drink wine with a song; strong drink will be bitter to them that drink it.
10The waste city of emptiness *and* confusion is broken down; every house is shut up so that no one may enter.
11There is crying in the streets for wine, all joy is darkened, the mirth of the land is gone into captivity.
12In the city is left desolation, and its gate is battered *and* destroyed.
13For so shall it be in the midst of the earth among the peoples, as the shaking *and* beating of an olive tree, and as the after-gleaning when the vintage is done [and only a small amount of the fruit remains].
14 *But* these [who have escaped and remain] will lift up their voices, they will shout; for the majesty of the Lord they will cry aloud from the [Mediterranean] Sea.
15Wherefore glorify the Lord whether in the east [in the region of daybreak's lights and fires, or in the west] *glorify* the name of the Lord God of Israel in the isles *and* coasts of the [Mediterranean] Sea.
16From the uttermost part of the earth have we heard songs: Glory to the righteous [people of Israel]! But I say, Emaciated I pine away, I pine away. Woe is me! The treacherous dealers deal treacherously; yes, the treacherous dealers deal very treacherously.
17Terror, and the pit [of destruction], and the snare are upon you, O inhabitant of the earth!
18And he who flees at the noise of the terror shall fall into the pit; and he who comes up out of the pit will be caught in the snare. For the windows of the heavens are opened [as in the deluge], and the foundations of the earth tremble *and* shake.
19The earth is utterly broken, the earth is rent asunder, the earth is shaken violently.
20The earth shall stagger like a drunken man, and shall sway to and fro like a hammock; its transgression shall lie heavily upon it, and it shall fall and not rise again.
21And in that day, the Lord will visit *and* punish the host of the high ones on high—the host of heaven, in heaven, celestial beings—and the kings of the earth, on the earth. [Eph. 3:10; 6:12; I Cor. 15:25.]

## New American Standard

2And the people will be like the priest, the servant like his
master, the maid like her mistress, the buyer like the seller, the
lender like the borrower, the creditor like the debtor.
3The earth will be completely laid waste and completely despoiled, for the LORD has spoken this word.
4The earth mourns *and* withers, the world fades *and* withers,
the exalted of the people of the earth fade away.
5The earth is also polluted by its inhabitants, for they transgressed laws, violated statutes, broke the everlasting covenant.
6Therefore, a curse devours the earth, and those who live in
it are held guilty. Therefore, the inhabitants of the earth are
burned, and few men are left.

7¶ The new wine mourns,
The vine decays,
All the merry-hearted sigh.
8 The gaiety of tambourines ceases,
The noise of revelers stops,
The gaiety of the harp ceases.
9 They do not drink wine with song;
Strong drink is bitter to those who drink it.
10 The city of chaos is broken down;
Every house is shut up so that none may enter.
11 There is an outcry in the streets concerning the wine;
All joy turns to gloom.
The gaiety of the earth is banished.
12 Desolation is left in the city,
And the gate is battered to ruins.
13 For thus it will be in the midst of the earth among the
peoples,
As the shaking of an olive tree,
As the gleanings when the grape harvest is over.
14 They raise their voices, they shout for joy.
They cry out from the west concerning the majesty of
the LORD.
15 Therefore glorify the LORD in the east,
The name of the LORD, the God of Israel
In the coastlands of the sea.
16 From the ends of the earth we hear songs, "Glory to
the Righteous One,"
But I say, "Woe to me! Woe to me! Alas for me!
The treacherous deal treacherously,
And the treacherous deal very treacherously."
17 Terror and pit and snare
Confront you, O inhabitant of the earth.
18 Then it will be that he who flees the report of disaster
will fall into the pit,
And he who climbs out of the pit will be caught in the
snare;
For the windows above are opened, and the
foundations of the earth shake.
19 The earth is broken asunder,
The earth is split through,
The earth is shaken violently.
20 The earth reels to and fro like a drunkard,
And it totters like a shack,
For its transgression is heavy upon it,
And it will fall, never to rise again.
21 So it will happen in that day,
That the LORD will punish the host of heaven, on high,
And the kings of the earth, on earth.

## New International

2it will be the same
for priest as for people,
for master as for servant,
for mistress as for maid,
for seller as for buyer,
for borrower as for lender,
for debtor as for creditor.
3The earth will be completely laid waste
and totally plundered.
The LORD has spoken this word.

4The earth dries up and withers,
the world languishes and withers,
the exalted of the earth languish.
5The earth is defiled by its people;
they have disobeyed the laws,
violated the statutes
and broken the everlasting covenant.
6Therefore a curse consumes the earth;
its people must bear their guilt.
Therefore earth's inhabitants are burned up,
and very few are left.
7The new wine dries up and the vine withers;
all the merrymakers groan.
8The gaiety of the tambourines is stilled,
the noise of the revelers has stopped,
the joyful harp is silent.
9No longer do they drink wine with a song;
the beer is bitter to its drinkers.
10The ruined city lies desolate;
the entrance to every house is barred.
11In the streets they cry out for wine;
all joy turns to gloom,
all gaiety is banished from the earth.
12The city is left in ruins,
its gate is battered to pieces.
13So will it be on the earth
and among the nations,
as when an olive tree is beaten,
or as when gleanings are left after the grape harvest.
14They raise their voices, they shout for joy;
from the west they acclaim the LORD's majesty.
15Therefore in the east give glory to the LORD;
exalt the name of the LORD, the God of Israel,
in the islands of the sea.
16From the ends of the earth we hear singing:
"Glory to the Righteous One."

But I said, "I waste away, I waste away!
Woe to me!
The treacherous betray!
With treachery the treacherous betray!"
17Terror and pit and snare await you,
O people of the earth.
18Whoever flees at the sound of terror
will fall into a pit;
whoever climbs out of the pit
will be caught in a snare.

The floodgates of the heavens are opened,
the foundations of the earth shake.
19The earth is broken up,
the earth is split asunder,
the earth is thoroughly shaken.
20The earth reels like a drunkard,
it sways like a hut in the wind;
so heavy upon it is the guilt of its rebellion
that it falls—never to rise again.

21In that day the LORD will punish
the powers in the heavens above
and the kings on the earth below.

## King James

22And they shall be gathered together, *as* prisoners are gathered in the pit, and shall be shut up in the prison, and after many days shall they be visited.

23Then the moon shall be confounded, and the sun ashamed, when the LORD of hosts shall reign in mount Zion, and in Jerusalem, and before his ancients gloriously.

**25** O LORD, thou *art* my God; I will exalt thee, I will praise thy name; for thou hast done wonderful *things; thy* counsels of old *are* faithfulness *and* truth.

2For thou hast made of a city an heap; *of* a defenced city a ruin: a palace of strangers to be no city; it shall never be built.

3Therefore shall the strong people glorify thee, the city of the terrible nations shall fear thee.

4For thou hast been a strength to the poor, a strength to the needy in his distress, a refuge from the storm, a shadow from the heat, when the blast of the terrible ones *is* as a storm *against* the wall.

5Thou shalt bring down the noise of strangers, as the heat in a dry place; *even* the heat with the shadow of a cloud: the branch of the terrible ones shall be brought low.

6¶ And in this mountain shall the LORD of hosts make unto all people a feast of fat things, a feast of wines on the lees, of fat things full of marrow, of wines on the lees well refined.

7And he will destroy in this mountain the face of the covering cast over all people, and the veil that is spread over all nations.

8He will swallow up death in victory; and the Lord GOD will wipe away tears from off all faces; and the rebuke of his people shall he take away from off all the earth: for the LORD hath spoken *it*.

9¶ And it shall be said in that day, Lo, this *is* our God; we have waited for him, and he will save us: this *is* the LORD; we have waited for him, we will be glad and rejoice in his salvation.

10For in this mountain shall the hand of the LORD rest, and Moab shall be trodden down under him, even as straw is trodden down for the dunghill.

11And he shall spread forth his hands in the midst of them, as he that swimmeth spreadeth forth *his hands* to swim: and he shall bring down their pride together with the spoils of their hands.

12And the fortress of the high fort of thy walls shall he bring down, lay low, *and* bring to the ground, *even* to the dust.

**AMP** [a] The Hebrew word used here may mean *visit in mercy* as well as *visit in punishment*, but the context does not seem to indicate the possibility of *mercy* in this case.

## Amplified

22And they will be gathered together as prisoners are gathered in a pit *or* dungeon; they will be shut up in the prison, and after many days they will be visited, inspected *and* punished *or* [a]pardoned. [II Pet. 2:4; Jude 6; Zech. 9:11, 12.]

23Then the moon will be confounded and the sun ashamed, when [they compare their ineffectual fires to the light of] the Lord of hosts Who will reign on Mount Zion and in Jerusalem, and before His elders show forth His glory.

**25** O LORD, You are my God; I will exalt You, I will praise Your name; for You have done wonderful things, even purposes planned of old *and fulfilled* in faithfulness and truth.

2For You have made of a city a heap, of a fortified city a ruin; a palace of aliens without a city—is no more a city; it will never be rebuilt.

3Therefore [many] a strong people will glorify You, [many] a city of terrible *and* ruthless nations will (reverently) fear You.

4For You have been a stronghold to the poor, a stronghold to the needy in his distress, a shelter from the storm, a shade from the heat; for the blast of the ruthless ones is like a rainstorm against a wall.

5As the heat in a dry land [is reduced by the shadow of a cloud, so] You will bring down the noise of aliens [exultant over their enemies]; *and* as the heat by the shadow of a cloud is brought low, so the song of the ruthless ones shall be brought low.

6And on this Mount [Zion] shall the Lord of hosts make for all peoples a feast of rich things [symbolical of His coronation festival inaugurating the reign of the Lord on earth, after the background of gloom, judgment and terror], a feast of wines on the lees, of fat things full of marrow, of wines on the lees well refined.

7And He will destroy on this mountain the covering of the face that is cast over the head of all people [in mourning], and the veil [of profound wretchedness] that is woven *and* spread over all nations.

8He will swallow up death *in victory*—He will abolish death forever; and the Lord God will wipe away tears from off all faces; and the reproach of His people He will take away from off all the earth; for the Lord has spoken it. [II Tim. 1:10; I Cor. 15:26, 54.]

9It shall be said in that day, Behold our God upon Whom we have waited *and* hoped that He might save us! This is the Lord; we have waited for Him, we will be glad and rejoice in His salvation.

10For the hand of the Lord shall rest on this Mount [Zion], and Moab shall be threshed *and* trodden down in his place as straw is trodden down in the (filthy) water of a [primitive] cess-pit.

11And though *Moab* stretches forth his hands in the midst of *the filthy water* as a swimmer stretches out his hands to swim, the Lord will bring down *Moab's* pride in spite of the skillfulness of his hands *and* together with it.

12And the high fortifications of your walls *the Lord* will bring down, lay low, bring to the ground, even to the dust.

## New American Standard

22 And they will be gathered together
*Like* prisoners in the dungeon,
And will be confined in prison;
And after many days they will be punished.
23 Then the moon will be abashed and the sun ashamed,
For the LORD of hosts will reign on Mount Zion and in Jerusalem,
And *His* glory will be before His elders.

*Song of Praise for God's Favor*

**25** O LORD, thou art my God;
I will exalt Thee, I will give thanks to Thy name;
For Thou hast worked wonders,
Plans *formed* long ago, with perfect faithfulness.
2 For Thou hast made a city into a heap,
A fortified city into a ruin;
A palace of strangers is a city no more,
It will never be rebuilt.
3 Therefore a strong people will glorify Thee;
Cities of ruthless nations will revere Thee.
4 For Thou hast been a defense for the helpless,
A defense for the needy in his distress,
A refuge from the storm, a shade from the heat;
For the breath of the ruthless
Is like a *rain* storm *against* a wall.
5 Like heat in drought, Thou dost subdue the uproar of aliens;
*Like* heat by the shadow of a cloud, the song of the ruthless is silenced.

6¶ And the LORD of hosts will prepare a lavish banquet for all peoples on this mountain;
A banquet of aged wine, choice pieces with marrow,
*And* refined, aged wine.
7 And on this mountain He will swallow up the covering which is over all peoples,
Even the veil which is stretched over all nations.
8 He will swallow up death for all time,
And the Lord GOD will wipe tears away from all faces,
And He will remove the reproach of His people from all the earth;
For the LORD has spoken.
9 And it will be said in that day,
"Behold, this is our God for whom we have waited that He might save us.
This is the LORD for whom we have waited;
Let us rejoice and be glad in His salvation."
10 For the hand of the LORD will rest on this mountain,
And Moab will be trodden down in his place
As straw is trodden down in the water of a manure pile.
11 And he will spread out his hands in the middle of it
As a swimmer spreads out *his hands* to swim,
But *the Lord* will lay low his pride together with the trickery of his hands.
12 And the unassailable fortifications of your walls He will bring down,
Lay low, *and* cast to the ground, even to the dust.

## New International

22They will be herded together
like prisoners bound in a dungeon;
they will be shut up in prison
and be punished[b] after many days.
23The moon will be abashed, the sun ashamed;
for the LORD Almighty will reign
on Mount Zion and in Jerusalem,
and before its elders, gloriously.

*Praise to the LORD*

**25** O LORD, you are my God;
I will exalt you and praise your name,
for in perfect faithfulness
you have done marvelous things,
things planned long ago.
2You have made the city a heap of rubble,
the fortified town a ruin,
the foreigners' stronghold a city no more;
it will never be rebuilt.
3Therefore strong peoples will honor you;
cities of ruthless nations will revere you.
4You have been a refuge for the poor,
a refuge for the needy in his distress,
a shelter from the storm
and a shade from the heat.
For the breath of the ruthless
is like a storm driving against a wall
5 and like the heat of the desert.
You silence the uproar of foreigners;
as heat is reduced by the shadow of a cloud,
so the song of the ruthless is stilled.

6On this mountain the LORD Almighty will prepare
a feast of rich food for all peoples,
a banquet of aged wine—
the best of meats and the finest of wines.
7On this mountain he will destroy
the shroud that enfolds all peoples,
the sheet that covers all nations;
8 he will swallow up death forever.
The Sovereign LORD will wipe away the tears
from all faces;
he will remove the disgrace of his people
from all the earth.
The LORD has spoken.

9In that day they will say,

"Surely this is our God;
we trusted in him, and he saved us.
This is the LORD, we trusted in him;
let us rejoice and be glad in his salvation."

10The hand of the LORD will rest on this mountain;
but Moab will be trampled under him
as straw is trampled down in the manure.
11They will spread out their hands in it,
as a swimmer spreads out his hands to swim.
God will bring down their pride
despite the cleverness[c] of their hands.
12He will bring down your high fortified walls
and lay them low;
he will bring them down to the ground,
to the very dust.

**NIV** [b] *22* Or *released* [c] *11* The meaning of the Hebrew for this word is uncertain.

## King James

**26** IN THAT day shall this song be sung in the land of Judah; We have a strong city; salvation will *God* appoint *for* walls and bulwarks.

2 Open ye the gates, that the righteous nation which keepeth the truth may enter in.

3 Thou wilt keep *him* in perfect peace, *whose* mind *is* stayed *on thee:* because he trusteth in thee.

4 Trust ye in the LORD for ever: for in the LORD JEHOVAH *is* everlasting strength:

5 ¶ For he bringeth down them that dwell on high; the lofty city, he layeth it low; he layeth it low, *even* to the ground; he bringeth it *even* to the dust.

6 The foot shall tread it down, *even* the feet of the poor, *and* the steps of the needy.

7 The way of the just *is* uprightness: thou, most upright, dost weigh the path of the just.

8 Yea, in the way of thy judgments, O LORD, have we waited for thee; the desire of *our* soul *is* to thy name, and to the remembrance of thee.

9 With my soul have I desired thee in the night; yea, with my spirit within me will I seek thee early: for when thy judgments *are* in the earth, the inhabitants of the world will learn righteousness.

10 Let favour be shown to the wicked, *yet* will he not learn righteousness: in the land of uprightness will he deal unjustly, and will not behold the majesty of the LORD.

11 LORD, *when* thy hand is lifted up, they will not see: *but* they shall see, and be ashamed for *their* envy at the people; yea, the fire of thine enemies shall devour them.

12 ¶ LORD, thou wilt ordain peace for us: for thou also hast wrought all our works in us.

13 O LORD our God, *other* lords beside thee have had dominion over us: *but* by thee only will we make mention of thy name.

14 *They are* dead, they shall not live; *they are* deceased, they shall not rise: therefore hast thou visited and destroyed them, and made all their memory to perish.

15 Thou hast increased the nation, O LORD, thou hast increased the nation: thou art glorified: thou hadst removed *it* far *unto* all the ends of the earth.

16 LORD, in trouble have they visited thee, they poured out a prayer *when* thy chastening *was* upon them.

17 Like as a woman with child, *that* draweth near the time of her delivery, is in pain, *and* crieth out in her pangs; so have we been in thy sight, O LORD.

18 We have been with child, we have been in pain, we have as it were brought forth wind; we have not wrought any deliverance in the earth; neither have the inhabitants of the world fallen.

## Amplified

**26** IN THAT day shall this song be sung in the land of Judah; [a]We have a strong city; *the Lord* sets up salvation as walls and bulwarks.

2 Open the gates, that the [uncompromisingly] righteous nation which keeps her faith *and* her troth *with God* may enter in.

3 You will guard him *and* keep him in perfect *and* constant peace whose mind [both its inclination and its character] is stayed on You, because he commits himself to You, leans on You *and* hopes confidently in You.

4 So trust in the Lord—commit yourself to Him, lean on Him, hope confidently in Him—for ever; for the Lord God is an everlasting rock—the Rock of ages.

5 For He has brought down the inhabitants of the height, the lofty city; He lays it low, lays it low to the ground; He brings it even to the dust.

6 The foot has trampled it down, even the feet of the poor, and the steps of the needy.

7 The way of the [consistently] righteous—those living in religious and moral rectitude in every area and relationship of their lives—is level *and* straight; You, O *Lord*, Who are upright, direct aright *and* level the path of the [uncompromisingly] just *and* righteous.

8 Yes, in the path of Your judgments, O Lord, we wait (expectantly) for You. Our heartfelt desire is for Your name and for the remembrance of You.

9 My soul yearns for You [O Lord] in the night; yes, my spirit within me seeks You earnestly; for *only* when Your judgments are in the earth *will* the inhabitants of the world learn righteousness—uprightness and right standing with God.

10 Though favor be shown to the wicked, yet he does not learn righteousness; in the land of uprightness he deals perversely and refuses to see the majesty of the Lord.

11 Though Your hand is lifted *high* to strike, Lord, they do not see it. Let them see Your zeal for *Your* people and be ashamed. Yes, let the fire *reserved* for Your enemies consume them.

12 Lord, You will ordain peace [God's favor and blessings, temporal and spiritual] for us, for You have also wrought in us *and* for us all our works.

13 O Lord our God, other masters besides You have ruled over us, but we will acknowledge *and* mention Your name only.

14 They [the former tyrant masters] are dead, they shall not live *and* reappear; they are powerless ghosts, they shall not rise *and* come back. Therefore You have visited and made an end of them, and caused every memorial of them [every trace of their supremacy] to perish.

15 You have increased the nation, O Lord, You have increased the nation; You are glorified; You have enlarged all the borders of the land.

16 Lord, when they were in trouble *and* distress they sought *and* visited You; they poured out a prayerful whisper when Your chastening was upon them.

17 Like a woman with child, drawing near the time of her delivery, is in pain *and* writhes and cries out in her pangs, so we have been before You—at Your presence—O Lord.

18 We have been with child, we have been writhing *and* in pain, we have as it were brought forth *only* wind. We have not wrought any deliverance in the earth, and the inhabitants of the world [of Israel] are not yet born.

**AMP** [a] The Dead Sea Scrolls here read, "You [Lord] have been to me a strong wall."

## New American Standard

*Song of Trust in God's Protection*

**26** IN THAT day this song will be sung in the land of Judah:
"We have a strong city;
He sets up walls and ramparts for security.
2 "Open the gates, that the righteous nation may enter,
The one that remains faithful.
3 "The steadfast of mind Thou wilt keep in perfect peace,
Because he trusts in Thee.
4 "Trust in the LORD forever,
For in GOD the LORD, *we have* an everlasting Rock.
5 "For He has brought low those who dwell on high, the unassailable city;
He lays it low, He lays it low to the ground, He casts it to the dust.
6 "The foot will trample it,
The feet of the afflicted, the steps of the helpless."

7¶ The way of the righteous is smooth;
O Upright One, make the path of the righteous level.
8 Indeed, *while following* the way of Thy judgments, O LORD,
We have waited for Thee eagerly;
Thy name, even Thy memory, is the desire of *our* souls.
9 At night my soul longs for Thee,
Indeed, my spirit within me seeks Thee diligently;
For when the earth experiences Thy judgments
The inhabitants of the world learn righteousness.
10 *Though* the wicked is shown favor,
He does not learn righteousness;
He deals unjustly in the land of uprightness,
And does not perceive the majesty of the LORD.
11¶ O LORD, Thy hand is lifted up *yet* they do not see it.
They see *Thy* zeal for the people and are put to shame;
Indeed, fire will devour Thine enemies.
12 LORD, Thou wilt establish peace for us,
Since Thou hast also performed for us all our works.
13 O LORD our God, other masters besides Thee have ruled us;
*But* through Thee alone we confess Thy name.
14 The dead will not live, the departed spirits will not rise;
Therefore Thou hast punished and destroyed them,
And Thou hast wiped out all remembrance of them.
15 Thou hast increased the nation, O LORD,
Thou hast increased the nation, Thou art glorified;
Thou hast extended all the borders of the land.
16 O LORD, they sought Thee in distress;
They could only whisper a prayer,
Your chastening was upon them.
17 As the pregnant woman approaches *the time* to give birth,
She writhes *and* cries out in her labor pains,
Thus were we before Thee, O LORD.
18 We were pregnant, we writhed *in labor*,
We gave birth, as it were, *only* to wind.
We could not accomplish deliverance for the earth
Nor were inhabitants of the world born.

## New International

*A Song of Praise*

**26** IN THAT day this song will be sung in the land of Judah:
We have a strong city;
God makes salvation
its walls and ramparts.
2 Open the gates
that the righteous nation may enter,
the nation that keeps faith.
3 You will keep in perfect peace
him whose mind is steadfast,
because he trusts in you.
4 Trust in the LORD forever,
for the LORD, the LORD, is the Rock eternal.
5 He humbles those who dwell on high,
he lays the lofty city low;
he levels it to the ground
and casts it down to the dust.
6 Feet trample it down—
the feet of the oppressed,
the footsteps of the poor.
7 The path of the righteous is level;
O upright One, you make the way of the righteous smooth.
8 Yes, LORD, walking in the way of your laws,[b]
we wait for you;
your name and renown
are the desire of our hearts.
9 My soul yearns for you in the night;
in the morning my spirit longs for you.
When your judgments come upon the earth,
the people of the world learn righteousness.
10 Though grace is shown to the wicked,
they do not learn righteousness;
even in a land of uprightness they go on doing evil
and regard not the majesty of the LORD.
11 O LORD, your hand is lifted high,
but they do not see it.
Let them see your zeal for your people and be put to shame;
let the fire reserved for your enemies consume them.
12 LORD, you establish peace for us;
all that we have accomplished you have done for us.
13 O LORD, our God, other lords besides you have ruled over us,
but your name alone do we honor.
14 They are now dead, they live no more;
those departed spirits do not rise.
You punished them and brought them to ruin;
you wiped out all memory of them.
15 You have enlarged the nation, O LORD;
you have enlarged the nation.
You have gained glory for yourself;
you have extended all the borders of the land.

16 LORD, they came to you in their distress;
when you disciplined them,
they could barely whisper a prayer.[c]
17 As a woman with child and about to give birth
writhes and cries out in her pain,
so were we in your presence, O LORD.
18 We were with child, we writhed in pain,
but we gave birth to wind.
We have not brought salvation to the earth;
we have not given birth to people of the world.

**NIV** [b] *8* Or *judgments* [c] *16* The meaning of the Hebrew for this clause is uncertain.

## King James

19 Thy dead *men* shall live, *together with* my dead body shall they arise. Awake and sing, ye that dwell in dust: for thy dew *is as* the dew of herbs, and the earth shall cast out the dead.

20¶ Come, my people, enter thou into thy chambers, and shut thy doors about thee: hide thyself as it were for a little moment, until the indignation be overpast.

21 For, behold, the LORD cometh out of his place to punish the inhabitants of the earth for their iniquity: the earth also shall disclose her blood, and shall no more cover her slain.

**27** IN THAT day the LORD with his sore and great and strong sword shall punish leviathan the piercing serpent, even leviathan that crooked serpent; and he shall slay the dragon that *is* in the sea.

2 In that day sing ye unto her, A vineyard of red wine.

3 I the LORD do keep it; I will water it every moment: lest *any* hurt it, I will keep it night and day.

4 Fury *is* not in me: who would set the briers *and* thorns against me in battle? I would go through them, I would burn them together.

5 Or let him take hold of my strength, *that* he may make peace with me; *and* he shall make peace with me.

6 He shall cause them that come of Jacob to take root: Israel shall blossom and bud, and fill the face of the world with fruit.

7¶ Hath he smitten him, as he smote those that smote him? *or* is he slain according to the slaughter of them that are slain by him?

8 In measure, when it shooteth forth, thou wilt debate with it: he stayeth his rough wind in the day of the east wind.

9 By this therefore shall the iniquity of Jacob be purged; and this *is* all the fruit to take away his sin; when he maketh all the stones of the altar as chalkstones that are beaten in sunder, the groves and images shall not stand up.

10 Yet the defenced city *shall be* desolate, *and* the habitation forsaken, and left like a wilderness: there shall the calf feed, and there shall he lie down, and consume the branches thereof.

11 When the boughs thereof are withered, they shall be broken off: the women come, *and* set them on fire: for it *is* a people of no understanding: therefore he that made them will not have mercy on them, and he that formed them will show them no favour.

## Amplified

19 Your dead shall live, *O Lord;* the bodies of *our* dead [saints] shall rise. You who dwell in the dust, awake and sing for joy! For Your dew is a dew of *sparkling* light, *O Lord* [heavenly, supernatural dew]; and the earth shall cast forth the dead [to life again]—for on the land of the shades *of the dead* You will let *Your dew* fall.

20 Come, my people, enter your chambers and shut your doors behind you; hide yourselves for a little while until the [Lord's] wrath is past.

21 For, behold, the Lord is coming forth out of His place [heaven] to punish the inhabitants of the earth for their iniquity; the earth also will disclose the blood shed upon her, and will no longer cover her slain *and* conceal her *guilt*.

**27** IN THAT day the Lord *will deliver Israel* [from her enemies and also the rebel powers of evil and darkness]; His sharp *and* unrelenting, great and strong sword will visit *and* punish Leviathan the swift fleeing serpent, Leviathan the twisting *and* winding serpent, and He will slay the monster that is in the sea.

2 In that day *it will be said* [of the redeemed nation of Israel], a vineyard beloved *and* lovely; sing a responsive song to it *and* about it!

3 I, the Lord, am its keeper; I water it every moment; lest anyone harm it, I guard *and* keep it night and day.

4 Wrath is not in Me. Would that the briers *and* thorns [the wicked internal foe] were lined up against Me in battle! I would stride in against them, I would burn them up together.

5 Or else [if all Israel would escape being burned up together there is but one alternative], let *them* take hold of My strength *and* make complete surrender to My protection, that *they* may make peace with Me! Yes, let *them* make peace with Me!

6 In the days *and* generations to come, Jacob shall take root; Israel shall blossom and send forth shoots, and fill the whole world with fruit [of the knowledge of the true God]. [Hos. 14:1-6; Rom. 11:12.]

7 Has *the Lord* smitten *Israel* as He smote those who smote them? *Or* have *the Israelites* been slain as their slayers were slain?

8 By driving them out of Canaan, by exile You contended with them in a measure, *O Lord*. He removed them with His rough blast *as* in the day of the east wind.

9 Only on this condition shall the iniquity of Jacob [Israel] be forgiven *and* purged, and this is the full fruit *God requires* for taking away his sin: that *Israel* should make all the stones of the *idol* altars like chalkstones crushed to pieces, so that the Asherim and the sun-images shall not remain standing *or* rise again.

10 For the fortified city is solitary, a habitation deserted and forsaken like the wilderness. There the calf grazes, and there he lies down; he strips its branches *and* eats its twigs.

11 When its boughs are withered *and* dry, they are broken off; the women come *and* set them afire. For it is a people of no understanding *or* discernment— [a]witless folk; therefore He Who made them will not have compassion on them, and He Who formed them will show them no favor.

**AMP** [a] The Dead Sea Scrolls so read.

## New American Standard

19 Your dead will live;
Their corpses will rise.
You who lie in the dust, awake and shout for joy,
For your dew is as the dew of the dawn,
And the earth will give birth to the departed spirits.
20¶ Come, my people, enter into your rooms,
And close your doors behind you;
Hide for a little while,
Until indignation runs *its* course.
21 For behold, the LORD is about to come out from His place
To punish the inhabitants of the earth for their iniquity;
And the earth will reveal her bloodshed,
And will no longer cover her slain.

*The Deliverance of Israel*

**27** IN THAT day the LORD will punish Leviathan the fleeing serpent,
With His fierce and great and mighty sword,
Even Leviathan the twisted serpent;
And He will kill the dragon who *lives* in the sea.
2¶ In that day,
"A vineyard of wine, sing of it!
3 "I, the LORD, am its keeper;
I water it every moment.
Lest anyone damage it,
I guard it night and day.
4 "I have no wrath.
Should someone give Me briars *and* thorns in battle,
*Then* I would step on them, I would burn them completely.
5 "Or let him rely on My protection,
Let him make peace with Me,
Let him make peace with Me."
6 In the days to come Jacob will take root,
Israel will blossom and sprout;
And they will fill the whole world with fruit.
7¶ Like the striking of Him who has struck them, has He struck them?
Or like the slaughter of His slain, have they been slain?
8 Thou didst contend with them by banishing them, by driving them away.
With His fierce wind He has expelled *them* on the day of the east wind.
9 Therefore through this Jacob's iniquity will be forgiven;
And this will be the full price of the pardoning of his sin:
When he makes all the altar stones like pulverized chalk stones;
*When* Asherim and incense altars will not stand.
10 For the fortified city is isolated,
A homestead forlorn and forsaken like the desert;
There the calf will graze,
And there it will lie down and feed on its branches.
11 When its limbs are dry, they are broken off;
Women come *and* make a fire with them.
For they are not a people of discernment,
Therefore their Maker will not have compassion on them.
And their Creator will not be gracious to them.

## New International

19But your dead will live;
their bodies will rise.
You who dwell in the dust,
wake up and shout for joy.
Your dew is like the dew of the morning;
the earth will give birth to her dead.
20Go, my people, enter your rooms
and shut the doors behind you;
hide yourselves for a little while
until his wrath has passed by.
21See, the LORD is coming out of his dwelling
to punish the people of the earth for their sins.
The earth will disclose the blood shed upon her;
she will conceal her slain no longer.

*Deliverance of Israel*

**27** IN THAT day,
the LORD will punish with his sword,
his fierce, great and powerful sword,
Leviathan the gliding serpent,
Leviathan the coiling serpent;
he will slay the monster of the sea.
2In that day—
"Sing about a fruitful vineyard:
3 I, the LORD, watch over it;
I water it continually.
I guard it day and night
so that no one may harm it.
4 I am not angry.
If only there were briers and thorns confronting me!
I would march against them in battle;
I would set them all on fire.
5Or else let them come to me for refuge;
let them make peace with me,
yes, let them make peace with me."
6In days to come Jacob will take root,
Israel will bud and blossom
and fill all the world with fruit.
7Has ⌞the LORD⌟ struck her
as he struck down those who struck her?
Has she been killed
as those were killed who killed her?
8By warfare[b] and exile you contend with her—
with his fierce blast he drives her out,
as on a day the east wind blows.
9By this, then, will Jacob's guilt be atoned for,
and this will be the full fruitage of the removal of his sin:
When he makes all the altar stones
to be like chalk stones crushed to pieces,
no Asherah poles[c] or incense altars
will be left standing.
10The fortified city stands desolate,
an abandoned settlement, forsaken like the desert;
there the calves graze,
there they lie down;
they strip its branches bare.
11When its twigs are dry, they are broken off
and women come and make fires with them.
For this is a people without understanding;
so their Maker has no compassion on them,
and their Creator shows them no favor.

**NIV** [b] *8* See Septuagint; the meaning of the Hebrew for this word is uncertain. [c] *9* That is, symbols of the goddess Asherah

## King James

12¶ And it shall come to pass in that day, *that* the LORD shall beat
off from the channel of the river unto the stream of Egypt, and ye
shall be gathered one by one, O ye children of Israel.
13And it shall come to pass in that day, *that* the great trumpet
shall be blown, and they shall come which were ready to perish
in the land of Assyria, and the outcasts in the land of Egypt, and
shall worship the LORD in the holy mount at Jerusalem.

**28** WOE TO the crown of pride, to the drunkards of Ephraim,
whose glorious beauty *is* a fading flower, which *are* on the
head of the fat valleys of them that are overcome with wine!
2Behold, the Lord hath a mighty and strong one, *which* as a
tempest of hail *and* a destroying storm, as a flood of mighty waters
overflowing, shall cast down to the earth with the hand.
3The crown of pride, the drunkards of Ephraim, shall be trodden under feet:
4And the glorious beauty, which *is* on the head of the fat valley,
shall be a fading flower, *and* as the hasty fruit before the summer;
which *when* he that looketh upon it seeth, while it is yet in his hand
he eateth it up.
5¶ In that day shall the LORD of hosts be for a crown of glory,
and for a diadem of beauty, unto the residue of his people,
6And for a spirit of judgment to him that sitteth in judgment,
and for strength to them that turn the battle to the gate.
7¶ But they also have erred through wine, and through strong
drink are out of the way; the priest and the prophet have erred
through strong drink, they are swallowed up of wine, they are out
of the way through strong drink; they err in vision, they stumble
*in* judgment.
8For all tables are full of vomit *and* filthiness, *so that there is* no
place *clean*.
9¶ Whom shall he teach knowledge? and whom shall he make
to understand doctrine? *them that are* weaned from the milk, *and*
drawn from the breasts.
10For precept *must be* upon precept, precept upon precept; line
upon line, line upon line; here a little, *and* there a little:
11For with stammering lips and another tongue will he speak
to this people.
12To whom he said, This *is* the rest *wherewith* ye may cause the
weary to rest; and this *is* the refreshing: yet they would not hear.

## Amplified

12And it shall be in that day that the Lord will thresh out His
grain from the flood of the river *Euphrates* to the brook of Egypt,
and you will be gathered one by one *and* one to another, O children
of Israel!
13And it shall be in that day that a great trumpet will be blown,
and they will come who were lost *and* ready to perish in the land
of Assyria and those who were driven out to the land of Egypt, and
they will worship the Lord on the holy mountain at Jerusalem.
[Matt. 24:31; Zech. 14:16; Rev. 11:15.]

**28** WOE TO [Samaria] the crown of pride of the drunkards
of Ephraim [the ten tribes], and to the fading flower of its
glorious beauty, which is on the head of the rich valley of those
overcome *and* smitten down with wine!
2Behold, the Lord has [the Assyrian] a strong and mighty one;
like a tempest of hail, a destroying storm, like a flood of mighty
overflowing waters, he will cast down to the earth with violent
hand.
3With *alien* feet [Samaria] the proud crown of the drunkards of
Ephraim will be trodden down.
4And the fading flower of its glorious beauty, which is on the
head of the rich valley, shall be like the early fig before the fruit
harvest, which when any one sees he snatches and eats up greedily at once. [So in an amazingly short time will the Assyrians devour
Samaria, Israel's capital.]
5[But] in that [future [a]Messianic] day the Lord of hosts shall
become a crown of glory and a diadem of beauty to the [converted]
remnant of His people;
6And a spirit of justice to him who sits in judgment *and* administers the law, and strength to those who turn back the battle at the
gate.
7But even these reel with wine and stagger with strong drink;
the priest and the prophet reel with strong drink, they are confused with wine, they stagger *and* are gone astray through strong
drink; they err in vision, they stumble in pronouncing judgment.
8For all tables are full of filthy vomit, so that there is no place
clean.
9Whom will He teach knowledge? [Ask the drunkards.] And
whom will He make to understand the message? Those who are
babies, just weaned from the milk and taken from the breasts? [Is
that what He thinks we are?]
10For it is [His prophets repeating over and over] precept upon
precept, precept upon precept; rule upon rule, rule upon rule; here
a little, there a little.
11No, but [the Lord will teach the rebels in a more humiliating
way] by men with stammering lips and another tongue will He
speak to this people [says Isaiah, and teach them His lessons].
12To these [complaining Jews the Lord] had said, This is the true
rest [the way to true comfort and happiness] that you shall give to
the weary, and this is the *true* refreshing. Yet they would not listen
[to His teaching],

**AMP** [a] Jonathan's Targum reads, "In that time Messiah, the Lord of hosts, shall be a crown of joy and a diadem of praise to the residue of His people." To this meaning of the passage commentators generally agree.

## New American Standard

12And it will come about in that day, that the LORD will start *His* threshing from the flowing stream of the Euphrates to the brook of Egypt; and you will be gathered up one by one, O sons of Israel.
13It will come about also in that day that a great trumpet will be blown; and those who were perishing in the land of Assyria and who were scattered in the land of Egypt will come and worship the LORD in the holy mountain at Jerusalem.

*Ephraim's Captivity Predicted*

**28** WOE TO the proud crown of the drunkards of Ephraim,
And to the fading flower of its glorious beauty,
Which is at the head of the fertile valley
Of those who are overcome with wine!
2 Behold, the Lord has a strong and mighty *agent;*
As a storm of hail, a tempest of destruction,
Like a storm of mighty overflowing waters,
He has cast *it* down to the earth with *His* hand.
3 The proud crown of the drunkards of Ephraim is trodden under foot.
4 And the fading flower of its glorious beauty,
Which is at the head of the fertile valley,
Will be like the first-ripe fig prior to summer;
Which one sees,
*And* as soon as it is in his hand,
He swallows it.
5 In that day the LORD of hosts will become a beautiful crown
And a glorious diadem to the remnant of His people;
6 A spirit of justice for him who sits in judgment,
A strength to those who repel the onslaught at the gate.
7 And these also reel with wine and stagger from strong drink:
The priest and the prophet reel with strong drink,
They are confused by wine, they stagger from strong drink;
They reel while having visions,
They totter *when rendering* judgment.
8 For all the tables are full of filthy vomit, without a *single clean* place.
9¶ "To whom would He teach knowledge?
And to whom would He interpret the message?
Those *just* weaned from milk?
Those *just* taken from the breast?
10 "For *He says,*
'Order on order, order on order,
Line on line, line on line,
A little here, a little there.' "
11 Indeed, He will speak to this people
Through stammering lips and a foreign tongue,
12 He who said to them, "Here is rest, give rest to the weary,"
And, "Here is repose," but they would not listen.

## New International

12In that day the LORD will thresh from the flowing Euphrates[b] to the Wadi of Egypt, and you, O Israelites, will be gathered up one by one. 13And in that day a great trumpet will sound. Those who were perishing in Assyria and those who were exiled in Egypt will come and worship the LORD on the holy mountain in Jerusalem.

*Woe to Ephraim*

**28** WOE TO that wreath, the pride of Ephraim's drunkards,
to the fading flower, his glorious beauty,
set on the head of a fertile valley—
to that city, the pride of those laid low by wine!
2See, the Lord has one who is powerful and strong.
Like a hailstorm and a destructive wind,
like a driving rain and a flooding downpour,
he will throw it forcefully to the ground.
3That wreath, the pride of Ephraim's drunkards,
will be trampled underfoot.
4That fading flower, his glorious beauty,
set on the head of a fertile valley,
will be like a fig ripe before harvest—
as soon as someone sees it and takes it in his hand,
he swallows it.

5In that day the LORD Almighty
will be a glorious crown,
a beautiful wreath
for the remnant of his people.
6He will be a spirit of justice
to him who sits in judgment,
a source of strength
to those who turn back the battle at the gate.

7And these also stagger from wine
and reel from beer:
Priests and prophets stagger from beer
and are befuddled with wine;
they reel from beer,
they stagger when seeing visions,
they stumble when rendering decisions.
8All the tables are covered with vomit
and there is not a spot without filth.

9"Who is it he is trying to teach?
To whom is he explaining his message?
To children weaned from their milk,
to those just taken from the breast?
10For it is:
Do and do, do and do,
rule on rule, rule on rule[c];
a little here, a little there."

11Very well then, with foreign lips and strange tongues
God will speak to this people,
12to whom he said,
"This is the resting place, let the weary rest";
and, "This is the place of repose"—
but they would not listen.

NIV [b] 12 Hebrew *River* [c] 10 Hebrew / *sav lasav sav lasav* / *kav lakav kav lakav* (possibly meaningless sounds; perhaps a mimicking of the prophet's words); also in verse 13

## King James

13 But the word of the LORD was unto them precept upon precept, precept upon precept; line upon line, line upon line; here a little, *and* there a little; that they might go, and fall backward, and be broken, and snared, and taken.

14 ¶ Wherefore hear the word of the LORD, ye scornful men, that rule this people which *is* in Jerusalem.

15 Because ye have said, We have made a covenant with death, and with hell are we at agreement; when the overflowing scourge shall pass through, it shall not come unto us: for we have made lies our refuge, and under falsehood have we hid ourselves:

16 ¶ Therefore thus saith the Lord GOD, Behold, I lay in Zion for a foundation a stone, a tried stone, a precious corner *stone*, a sure foundation: he that believeth shall not make haste.

17 Judgment also will I lay to the line, and righteousness to the plummet: and the hail shall sweep away the refuge of lies, and the waters shall overflow the hiding place.

18 ¶ And your covenant with death shall be disannulled, and your agreement with hell shall not stand; when the overflowing scourge shall pass through, then ye shall be trodden down by it.

19 From the time that it goeth forth it shall take you: for morning by morning shall it pass over, by day and by night: and it shall be a vexation only *to* understand the report.

20 For the bed is shorter than that *a man* can stretch himself *on it:* and the covering narrower than that he can wrap himself *in it.*

21 For the LORD shall rise up as *in* mount Perazim, he shall be wroth as *in* the valley of Gibeon, that he may do his work, his strange work; and bring to pass his act, his strange act.

22 Now therefore be ye not mockers, lest your bands be made strong: for I have heard from the Lord GOD of hosts a consumption, even determined upon the whole earth.

23 ¶ Give ye ear, and hear my voice; hearken, and hear my speech.

24 Doth the plowman plow all day to sow? doth he open and break the clods of his ground?

25 When he hath made plain the face thereof, doth he not cast abroad the fitches, and scatter the cummin, and cast in the principal wheat and the appointed barley and the rie in their place?

26 For his God doth instruct him to discretion, *and* doth teach him.

27 For the fitches are not threshed with a threshing instrument, neither is a cart wheel turned about upon the cummin; but the fitches are beaten out with a staff, and the cummin with a rod.

28 Bread *corn* is bruised; because he will not ever be threshing it, nor break *it with* the wheel of his cart, nor bruise it *with* his horsemen.

## Amplified

13 Therefore the word of the Lord will be to them [merely monotonous repeatings of] precept upon precept, precept upon precept; rule upon rule, rule upon rule; here a little, there a little; that they may go, and fall backward, and be broken, and snared, and taken.

14 Therefore hear the word of the Lord, you scoffers, who rule this people in Jerusalem!

15 Because you have said, We have made a covenant with death, and with Sheol [the place of the dead] we have an agreement; when the overflowing scourge passes through, it will not come to us; for we have made lies our refuge, and in falsehood we have taken shelter;

16 Therefore thus says the Lord God, Behold, I am laying in Zion for a foundation a Stone, a tested Stone, a precious Cornerstone of sure foundation; he who believes—trusts in, relies on and adheres *to that Stone*—will not [a]be ashamed *or* give way *or* make haste [in sudden panic]. [Rom. 9:33; I Pet. 2:4-6.]

17 I will make justice the line, and righteousness the plummet; and hail will sweep away the refuge of lies, and waters will overwhelm the hiding place—the shelter.

18 And your covenant with death shall be annulled, and your agreement with Sheol [the place of the dead] shall not stand; when the overwhelming scourge passes through, then you will be trodden down by it.

19 As often as it passes through, it [the enemy's scourge] will take you; for morning by morning will it pass through, by day and by night; and it will be utter terror merely to hear *and* comprehend the report *and* the message of it [but only hard treatment and dispersion will make you understand God's instruction].

20 For [they will find that] the bed is too short for a man to stretch himself on it, and the covering too narrow for him to wrap himself in it. [All their sources of confidence will fail them.]

21 For the Lord will rise up as on Mount Perazim, He will be wroth as in the valley of Gibeon, that He may do His work, His strange work, and bring to pass His act, His strange act. [II Sam. 5:20; I Chron. 14:16.]

22 Now therefore do not be scoffers, lest the bands which bind you be made strong; for a decree of destruction have I heard from the Lord God of hosts upon the whole land *and* the whole earth.

23 Give ear and hear my [Isaiah's] voice; listen and hear my words.

24 Does he who plows for sowing plow continually? Does he continue to plow and harrow his ground after it is smooth?

25 When he has leveled its surface, does he not cast abroad the seed of dill *or* fennel, and scatter cummin [a seasoning], and put the wheat in rows, and barley in its intended place, and spelt [an inferior kind of wheat] as the border?

26 And he trains each of them correctly, *for* his God instructs him correctly and teaches him.

27 For the dill is not threshed with a sharp threshing instrument, nor is a cart wheel rolled over the cummin; but the dill is beaten off with a staff and the cummin with a rod—by hand.

28 Does one crush bread grain? No, he does not thresh it continuously, but when he has driven his cart wheel and his horses over it, he scatters it—tossing it up to the wind—without having crushed it.

**AMP** [a] The Septuagint (Greek Version) reads "be ashamed."

## New American Standard

13 So the word of the LORD to them will be,
"Order on order, order on order,
Line on line, line on line,
A little here, a little there,"
That they may go and stumble backward, be broken,
snared, and taken captive.

*Judah Is Warned*

14 Therefore, hear the word of the LORD, O scoffers,
Who rule this people who are in Jerusalem,
15 Because you have said, "We have made a covenant
with death,
And with Sheol we have made a pact.
The overwhelming scourge will not reach us when it
passes by,
For we have made falsehood our refuge and we have
concealed ourselves with deception."
16 Therefore thus says the Lord GOD,
"Behold, I am laying in Zion a stone, a tested stone,
A costly cornerstone *for* the foundation, firmly placed.
He who believes *in it* will not be disturbed.
17 "And I will make justice the measuring line,
And righteousness the level;
Then hail shall sweep away the refuge of lies,
And the waters shall overflow the secret place.
18 "And your covenant with death shall be canceled,
And your pact with Sheol shall not stand;
When the overwhelming scourge passes through,
Then you become its trampling *place*.
19 "As often as it passes through, it will seize you.
For morning after morning it will pass through, *anytime*
during the day or night.
And it will be sheer terror to understand what it
means."
20 The bed is too short on which to stretch out,
And the blanket is too small to wrap oneself in.
21 For the LORD will rise up as *at* Mount Perazim,
He will be stirred up as in the valley of Gibeon;
To do His task, His unusual task,
And to work His work, His extraordinary work.
22 And now do not carry on as scoffers,
Lest your fetters be made stronger;
For I have heard from the Lord GOD of hosts,
Of decisive destruction on all the earth.

23¶ Give ear and hear my voice,
Listen and hear my words.
24 Does the farmer plow continually to plant seed?
Does he *continually* turn and harrow the ground?
25 Does he not level its surface,
And sow dill and scatter cummin,
And plant wheat in rows,
Barley in its place, and rye within its area?
26 For his God instructs and teaches him properly.
27 For dill is not threshed with a threshing sledge,
Nor is the cartwheel driven over cummin;
But dill is beaten out with a rod, and cummin with a
club.
28 *Grain for* bread is crushed,
Indeed, he does not continue to thresh it forever.
Because the wheel of *his* cart and his horses *eventually*
damage *it*,
He does not thresh it longer.

## New International

13 So then, the word of the LORD to them will become:
Do and do, do and do,
rule on rule, rule on rule;
a little here, a little there—
so that they will go and fall backward,
be injured and snared and captured.

14 Therefore hear the word of the LORD, you scoffers
who rule this people in Jerusalem.
15 You boast, "We have entered into a covenant with death,
with the grave[b] we have made an agreement.
When an overwhelming scourge sweeps by,
it cannot touch us,
for we have made a lie our refuge
and falsehood[c] our hiding place."
16 So this is what the Sovereign LORD says:

"See, I lay a stone in Zion,
a tested stone,
a precious cornerstone for a sure foundation;
the one who trusts will never be dismayed.
17 I will make justice the measuring line
and righteousness the plumb line;
hail will sweep away your refuge, the lie,
and water will overflow your hiding place.
18 Your covenant with death will be annulled;
your agreement with the grave will not stand.
When the overwhelming scourge sweeps by,
you will be beaten down by it.
19 As often as it comes it will carry you away;
morning after morning, by day and by night,
it will sweep through."
The understanding of this message
will bring sheer terror.
20 The bed is too short to stretch out on,
the blanket too narrow to wrap around you.
21 The LORD will rise up as he did at Mount Perazim,
he will rouse himself as in the Valley of Gibeon—
to do his work, his strange work,
and perform his task, his alien task.
22 Now stop your mocking,
or your chains will become heavier;
the Lord, the LORD Almighty, has told me
of the destruction decreed against the whole land.

23 Listen and hear my voice;
pay attention and hear what I say.
24 When a farmer plows for planting, does he plow
continually?
Does he keep on breaking up and harrowing the soil?
25 When he has leveled the surface,
does he not sow caraway and scatter cummin?
Does he not plant wheat in its place,[d]
barley in its plot,[e]
and spelt in its field?
26 His God instructs him
and teaches him the right way.

27 Caraway is not threshed with a sledge,
nor is a cartwheel rolled over cummin;
caraway is beaten out with a rod,
and cummin with a stick.
28 Grain must be ground to make bread;
so one does not go on threshing it forever.
Though he drives the wheels of his threshing cart over it,
his horses do not grind it.

**NIV** [b] *15* Hebrew *Sheol;* also in verse 18 [c] *15* Or *false gods* [d] *25* The meaning of the Hebrew for this word is uncertain. [e] *25* The meaning of the Hebrew for this word is uncertain.

## King James

29 This also cometh forth from the LORD of hosts, *which* is wonderful in counsel, *and* excellent in working.

# 29

WOE TO Ariel, to Ariel, the city *where* David dwelt! add ye year to year; let them kill sacrifices.

2 Yet I will distress Ariel, and there shall be heaviness and sorrow: and it shall be unto me as Ariel.

3 And I will camp against thee round about, and will lay siege against thee with a mount, and I will raise forts against thee.

4 And thou shalt be brought down, *and* shalt speak out of the ground, and thy speech shall be low out of the dust, and thy voice shall be, as of one that hath a familiar spirit, out of the ground, and thy speech shall whisper out of the dust.

5 Moreover the multitude of thy strangers shall be like small dust, and the multitude of the terrible ones *shall be* as chaff that passeth away: yea, it shall be at an instant suddenly.

6 Thou shalt be visited of the LORD of hosts with thunder, and with earthquake, and great noise, with storm and tempest, and the flame of devouring fire.

7 ¶ And the multitude of all the nations that fight against Ariel, even all that fight against her and her munition, and that distress her, shall be as a dream of a night vision.

8 It shall even be as when an hungry *man* dreameth, and, behold, he eateth; but he awaketh, and his soul is empty: or as when a thirsty man dreameth, and, behold, he drinketh; but he awaketh, and, behold, *he is* faint, and his soul hath appetite: so shall the multitude of all the nations be, that fight against mount Zion.

9 ¶ Stay yourselves, and wonder; cry ye out, and cry: they are drunken, but not with wine; they stagger, but not with strong drink.

10 For the LORD hath poured out upon you the spirit of deep sleep, and hath closed your eyes: the prophets and your rulers, the seers hath he covered.

11 And the vision of all is become unto you as the words of a book that is sealed, which *men* deliver to one that is learned, saying, Read this, I pray thee: and he saith, I cannot; for it *is* sealed:

12 And the book is delivered to him that is not learned, saying, Read this, I pray thee: and he saith, I am not learned.

13 ¶ Wherefore the Lord said, Forasmuch as this people draw near *me* with their mouth, and with their lips do honour me, but have removed their heart far from me, and their fear toward me is taught by the precept of men:

14 Therefore, behold, I will proceed to do a marvellous work among this people, *even* a marvellous work and a wonder: for the wisdom of their wise *men* shall perish, and the understanding of their prudent *men* shall be hid.

## Amplified

29 This also comes from the Lord of hosts, Who is wonderful in counsel [and] excellent in wisdom *and* effectual working.

# 29

WOE TO Ariel [Jerusalem], to Ariel, the city where David encamped! Add yet another year; let the feasts run their round [but only one year more].

2 Then will I distress Ariel, and there shall be mourning and lamentation; yet she shall be to Me like an Ariel—an altar-hearth, a hearth of burning, the altar of God.

3 And I will encamp against you round about, and will hem you in with siege works, and I will set up fortifications against you.

4 And you shall be laid low, *Jerusalem,* speaking from beneath the ground, and your speech shall come humbly from the dust; and your voice shall be like that of a ghost [produced by a medium] coming from the earth, and your speech shall whisper *and* squeak as it chatters from the dust.

5 But the multitude of your *enemy* strangers that assail you shall be like small dust, and the multitude of the ruthless *and* terrible ones like chaff that blows away. And in an instant, suddenly,

6 *You* shall be visited *and* delivered by the Lord of hosts with thunder and with earthquake and great noise, with whirlwind and tempest and the flame of a devouring fire.

7 And the multitude of all the nations that fight against Ariel [Jerusalem], even all that fight against her and her stronghold, and that distress her, shall be as a dream, a vision of the night.

8 It shall even be as when a hungry man dreams, and behold, he eats; but he wakens with his craving not satisfied; or as when a thirsty man dreams that he is drinking, but he wakens and is faint, and his thirst is not quenched. So shall the multitude of all the nations be that fight against Mount Zion.

9 Stop and wonder [at this prophecy, if you choose, whether you understand it or not; but soon you will witness the actual event] and be confounded—reluctantly! Blind yourselves [now if you choose]—take your pleasure and riot; then be blinded [at the actual occurrence]. They are drunk, but not with wine; they stagger, but not from strong drink [but from spiritual stupor].

10 For the Lord has poured out on you the spirit of deep sleep, and has closed your eyes, the prophets; and your heads, the seers, He has covered *and* muffled.

11 And the vision of all this has become to you like the words of a book that is sealed. When men give it to one who can read, saying, Read this, I pray you, he says, I cannot, for it is sealed.

12 And when the book is given to him who is not learned, saying, Read this, I pray you, he says, I cannot read.

13 And the Lord said, Forasmuch as this people draw near Me with their mouth and honor Me with their lips, but have removed their hearts *and* minds far from Me, and their fear *and* reverence for Me *are* a commandment of men that is learned by repetition [without any thought of the meaning];

14 Therefore, behold! I will again do marvelous things with this people, marvelous and astonishing things· and the wisdom of their wise men shall perish, and the understanding of their discerning men shall vanish *or* be hidden.

## New American Standard

29 This also comes from the LORD of hosts,
*Who* has made *His* counsel wonderful and *His* wisdom
great.

*Jerusalem Is Warned*

**29** WOE, O Ariel, Ariel the city *where* David *once* camped!
Add year to year, observe *your* feasts on schedule.
2 And I will bring distress to Ariel,
And she shall be *a city of* lamenting and mourning;
And she shall be like an Ariel to me.
3 And I will camp against you encircling *you*,
And I will set siegeworks against you,
And I will raise up battle towers against you.
4 Then you shall be brought low;
From the earth you shall speak,
And from the dust *where* you are prostrate,
Your words *shall come*.
Your voice shall also be like that of a spirit from the
ground,
And your speech shall whisper from the dust.

5¶ But the multitude of your enemies shall become like
fine dust,
And the multitude of the ruthless ones like the chaff
which blows away;
And it shall happen instantly, suddenly.
6 From the LORD of hosts you will be punished with
thunder and earthquake and loud noise,
*With* whirlwind and tempest and the flame of a
consuming fire.
7 And the multitude of all the nations who wage war
against Ariel,
Even all who wage war against her and her stronghold,
and who distress her,
Shall be like a dream, a vision of the night.
8 And it will be as when a hungry man dreams—
And behold, he is eating;
But when he awakens, his hunger is not satisfied,
Or as when a thirsty man dreams—
And behold, he is drinking,
But when he awakens, behold, he is faint,
And his thirst is not quenched.
Thus the multitude of all the nations shall be,
Who wage war against Mount Zion.

9¶ Be delayed and wait.
Blind yourselves and be blind.
They become drunk, but not with wine;
They stagger, but not with strong drink.
10 For the LORD has poured over you a spirit of deep
sleep,
He has shut your eyes, the prophets;
And He has covered your heads, the seers.
11 And the entire vision shall be to you like the words of a sealed
book, which when they give it to the one who is literate, saying,
"Please read this," he will say, "I cannot, for it is sealed."
12 Then the book will be given to the one who is illiterate, saying,
"Please read this." And he will say, "I cannot read."
13¶ Then the Lord said,
"Because this people draw near with their words
And honor Me with their lip service,
But they remove their hearts far from Me,
And their reverence for Me consists of tradition learned
*by rote*,
14 Therefore behold, I will once again deal marvelously
with this people, wondrously marvelous;
And the wisdom of their wise men shall perish,
And the discernment of their discerning men shall be
concealed.

## New International

29 All this also comes from the LORD Almighty,
wonderful in counsel and magnificent in wisdom.

*Woe to David's City*

**29** WOE TO you, Ariel, Ariel,
the city where David settled!
Add year to year
and let your cycle of festivals go on.
2 Yet I will besiege Ariel;
she will mourn and lament,
she will be to me like an altar hearth.[a]
3 I will encamp against you all around;
I will encircle you with towers
and set up my siege works against you.
4 Brought low, you will speak from the ground;
your speech will mumble out of the dust.
Your voice will come ghostlike from the earth;
out of the dust your speech will whisper.
5 But your many enemies will become like fine dust,
the ruthless hordes like blown chaff.
Suddenly, in an instant,
6 the LORD Almighty will come
with thunder and earthquake and great noise,
with windstorm and tempest and flames of a devouring
fire.
7 Then the hordes of all the nations that fight against Ariel,
that attack her and her fortress and besiege her,
will be as it is with a dream,
with a vision in the night—
8 as when a hungry man dreams that he is eating,
but he awakens, and his hunger remains;
as when a thirsty man dreams that he is drinking,
but he awakens faint, with his thirst unquenched.
So will it be with the hordes of all the nations
that fight against Mount Zion.

9 Be stunned and amazed,
blind yourselves and be sightless;
be drunk, but not from wine,
stagger, but not from beer.
10 The LORD has brought over you a deep sleep:
He has sealed your eyes (the prophets);
he has covered your heads (the seers).

11 For you this whole vision is nothing but words sealed in a
scroll. And if you give the scroll to someone who can read, and say
to him, "Read this, please," he will answer, "I can't; it is sealed."
12 Or if you give the scroll to someone who cannot read, and say,
"Read this, please," he will answer, "I don't know how to read."

13 The Lord says:

"These people come near to me with their mouth
and honor me with their lips,
but their hearts are far from me.
Their worship of me
is made up only of rules taught by men.[b]
14 Therefore once more I will astound these people
with wonder upon wonder;
the wisdom of the wise will perish,
the intelligence of the intelligent will vanish."

NIV [a] 2 The Hebrew for *altar hearth* sounds like the Hebrew for *Ariel*.
[b] 13 Hebrew; Septuagint *They worship me in vain; / their teachings are but rules taught by men*

## King James

15 Woe unto them that seek deep to hide their counsel from the LORD, and their works are in the dark, and they say, Who seeth us? and who knoweth us?

16 Surely your turning of things upside down shall be esteemed as the potter's clay: for shall the work say of him that made it, He made me not? or shall the thing framed say of him that framed it, He had no understanding?

17 *Is* it not yet a very little while, and Lebanon shall be turned into a fruitful field, and the fruitful field shall be esteemed as a forest?

18 ¶ And in that day shall the deaf hear the words of the book, and the eyes of the blind shall see out of obscurity, and out of darkness.

19 The meek also shall increase *their* joy in the LORD, and the poor among men shall rejoice in the Holy One of Israel.

20 For the terrible one is brought to nought, and the scorner is consumed, and all that watch for iniquity are cut off:

21 That make a man an offender for a word, and lay a snare for him that reproveth in the gate, and turn aside the just for a thing of nought.

22 Therefore thus saith the LORD, who redeemed Abraham, concerning the house of Jacob, Jacob shall not now be ashamed, neither shall his face now wax pale.

23 But when he seeth his children, the work of mine hands, in the midst of him, they shall sanctify my name, and sanctify the Holy One of Jacob, and shall fear the God of Israel.

24 They also that erred in spirit shall come to understanding, and they that murmured shall learn doctrine.

**30** WOE TO the rebellious children, saith the LORD, that take counsel, but not of me; and that cover with a covering, but not of my spirit, that they may add sin to sin:

2 That walk to go down into Egypt, and have not asked at my mouth; to strengthen themselves in the strength of Pharaoh, and to trust in the shadow of Egypt!

3 Therefore shall the strength of Pharaoh be your shame, and the trust in the shadow of Egypt *your* confusion.

4 For his princes were at Zoan, and his ambassadors came to Hanes.

5 They were all ashamed of a people *that* could not profit them, nor be an help nor profit, but a shame, and also a reproach.

6 The burden of the beasts of the south: into the land of trouble and anguish, from whence *come* the young and old lion, the viper and fiery flying serpent, they will carry their riches upon the shoulders of young asses, and their treasures upon the bunches of camels, to a people *that* shall not profit *them*.

## Amplified

15 Woe to those who *seek to* hide deep from the Lord their counsel, whose deeds are in the dark, and who say, Who sees us? Who knows us?

16 Oh, your perversity!—You turn things upside down! Shall the potter be considered of no more account than the clay? Shall the thing that is made say of its maker, He did not make me; or the thing that is formed say of him who formed it, He has no understanding?

17 Is it not yet a very little while until Lebanon shall be turned into a fruitful field, and the fruitful field shall be esteemed as a forest?

18 And in that day shall the deaf hear the words of *the* book, and out of obscurity *and* gloom and darkness the eyes of the blind shall see.

19 The meek also shall increase their joy in the Lord, and the poor among men shall rejoice *and* exult in the Holy One of Israel.

20 For the terrible one [the Assyrian enemy] shall come to nought, and the scoffer cease, and all those who watch for iniquity *as an occasion for accusation* shall be cut off;

21 That make a man an offender *and* bring condemnation upon him for a word, and lay a trap for him who upholds justice at the city gate, and thrust aside the innocent *and* truly righteous with an empty plea.

22 Therefore thus says the Lord, Who redeemed Abraham [out of Ur and idolatry], concerning the house of Jacob: Jacob shall not then be ashamed, not then shall his face become pale [with fear and disappointment because of his children's degeneracy].

23 For when he sees his children [walking in the ways of piety and virtue], the work of My hands in his midst, they will revere My name; they will revere the Holy One of Jacob and reverently fear the God of Israel.

24 Those who err in spirit will come to understanding, and those who murmur [discontentedly] will accept instruction.

**30** WOE TO the rebellious children, says the Lord, who take counsel *and* carry out a plan, but not Mine; and who make a league *and* pour out a drink offering, but not of My Spirit, thus adding sin to sin;

2 That set out to go down into Egypt, and have not asked of Me; to flee to the stronghold of Pharaoh *and* to strengthen themselves in his strength and to trust in the shadow of Egypt!

3 Therefore shall the strength *and* protection of Pharaoh turn to your shame, and the refuge in the shadow of Egypt be to your humiliation *and* confusion.

4 For though *Pharaoh's* officials are at Zoan and his ambassadors arrive at Hanes [in Egypt],

5 Yet will all be ashamed because of a people [the Egyptians] that cannot profit them, that are not a help or benefit, but a shame and disgrace.

6 A mournful, inspired prediction—a burden to be lifted up—concerning the beasts of the South [the Negeb]. Oh, the heavy burden, the load of treasures going to Egypt! Through a land of trouble and anguish, in which are the lioness and the lion, the viper and fiery flying serpent, they carry their riches upon the shoulders of young donkeys, and their treasures upon the humps of camels, to a people that will not *and* cannot profit them.

## New American Standard

15¶ Woe to those who deeply hide their plans from the LORD,
And whose deeds are *done* in a dark place,
And they say, "Who sees us?" or "Who knows us?"
16 You turn *things* around!
Shall the potter be considered as equal with the clay,
That what is made should say to its maker, "He did not make me";
Or what is formed say to him who formed it, "He has no understanding"?

*Blessing after Discipline*

17¶ Is it not yet just a little while
Before Lebanon will be turned into a fertile field,
And the fertile field will be considered as a forest?
18 And on that day the deaf shall hear words of a book,
And out of *their* gloom and darkness the eyes of the blind shall see.
19 The afflicted also shall increase their gladness in the LORD,
And the needy of mankind shall rejoice in the Holy One of Israel.
20 For the ruthless will come to an end, and the scorner will be finished,
Indeed all who are intent on doing evil will be cut off;
21 Who cause a person to be indicted by a word,
And ensnare him who adjudicates at the gate,
And defraud the one in the right with meaningless arguments.
22¶ Therefore thus says the LORD, who redeemed Abraham, concerning the house of Jacob,
"Jacob shall not now be ashamed, nor shall his face now turn pale;
23 But when he sees his children, the work of My hands, in his midst,
They will sanctify My name;
Indeed, they will sanctify the Holy One of Jacob,
And will stand in awe of the God of Israel.
24 "And those who err in mind will know the truth,
And those who criticize will accept instruction.

*Judah Warned against Egyptian Alliance*

30 "WOE TO the rebellious children," declares the LORD,
"Who execute a plan, but not Mine,
And make an alliance, but not of My Spirit,
In order to add sin to sin;
2 Who proceed down to Egypt,
Without consulting Me,
To take refuge in the safety of Pharaoh,
And to seek shelter in the shadow of Egypt!
3 "Therefore the safety of Pharaoh will be your shame,
And the shelter in the shadow of Egypt, your humiliation.
4 "For their princes are at Zoan,
And their ambassadors arrive at Hanes.
5 "Everyone will be ashamed because of a people who cannot profit them,
*Who are* not for help or profit, but for shame and also for reproach."

6¶ The oracle concerning the beasts of the Negev.
Through a land of distress and anguish,
From where *come* lioness and lion, viper and flying serpent,
They carry their riches on the backs of young donkeys
And their treasures on camels' humps,
To a people who cannot profit *them;*

## New International

15 Woe to those who go to great depths
to hide their plans from the LORD,
who do their work in darkness and think,
"Who sees us? Who will know?"
16 You turn things upside down,
as if the potter were thought to be like the clay!
Shall what is formed say to him who formed it,
"He did not make me"?
Can the pot say of the potter,
"He knows nothing"?

17 In a very short time, will not Lebanon be turned into a fertile field
and the fertile field seem like a forest?
18 In that day the deaf will hear the words of the scroll,
and out of gloom and darkness
the eyes of the blind will see.
19 Once more the humble will rejoice in the LORD;
the needy will rejoice in the Holy One of Israel.
20 The ruthless will vanish,
the mockers will disappear,
and all who have an eye for evil will be cut down—
21 those who with a word make a man out to be guilty,
who ensnare the defender in court
and with false testimony deprive the innocent of justice.

22 Therefore this is what the LORD, who redeemed Abraham, says to the house of Jacob:

"No longer will Jacob be ashamed;
no longer will their faces grow pale.
23 When they see among them their children,
the work of my hands,
they will keep my name holy;
they will acknowledge the holiness of the Holy One of Jacob,
and will stand in awe of the God of Israel.
24 Those who are wayward in spirit will gain understanding;
those who complain will accept instruction."

*Woe to the Obstinate Nation*

30 "WOE TO the obstinate children,"
declares the LORD,
"to those who carry out plans that are not mine,
forming an alliance, but not by my Spirit,
heaping sin upon sin;
2 who go down to Egypt
without consulting me;
who look for help to Pharaoh's protection,
to Egypt's shade for refuge.
3 But Pharaoh's protection will be to your shame,
Egypt's shade will bring you disgrace.
4 Though they have officials in Zoan
and their envoys have arrived in Hanes,
5 everyone will be put to shame
because of a people useless to them,
who bring neither help nor advantage,
but only shame and disgrace."

6 An oracle concerning the animals of the Negev:

Through a land of hardship and distress,
of lions and lionesses,
of adders and darting snakes,
the envoys carry their riches on donkeys' backs,
their treasures on the humps of camels,
to that unprofitable nation,

## King James

7For the Egyptians shall help in vain, and to no purpose: therefore have I cried concerning this, Their strength *is* to sit still.

8¶ Now go, write it before them in a table, and note it in a book, that it may be for the time to come for ever and ever:

9That this *is* a rebellious people, lying children, children *that* will not hear the law of the LORD:

10Which say to the seers, See not; and to the prophets, Prophesy not unto us right things, speak unto us smooth things, prophesy deceits:

11Get you out of the way, turn aside out of the path, cause the Holy One of Israel to cease from before us.

12Wherefore thus saith the Holy One of Israel, Because ye despise this word, and trust in oppression and perverseness, and stay thereon:

13Therefore this iniquity shall be to you as a breach ready to fall, swelling out in a high wall, whose breaking cometh suddenly at an instant.

14And he shall break it as the breaking of the potters' vessel that is broken in pieces; he shall not spare: so that there shall not be found in the bursting of it a sherd to take fire from the hearth, or to take water *withal* out of the pit.

15For thus saith the Lord GOD, the Holy One of Israel; In returning and rest shall ye be saved; in quietness and in confidence shall be your strength: and ye would not.

16But ye said, No; for we will flee upon horses; therefore shall ye flee: and, We will ride upon the swift; therefore shall they that pursue you be swift.

17One thousand *shall flee* at the rebuke of one; at the rebuke of five shall ye flee: till ye be left as a beacon upon the top of a mountain, and as an ensign on an hill.

18¶ And therefore will the LORD wait, that he may be gracious unto you, and therefore will he be exalted, that he may have mercy upon you: for the LORD *is* a God of judgment: blessed *are* all they that wait for him.

19For the people shall dwell in Zion at Jerusalem: thou shalt weep no more: he will be very gracious unto thee at the voice of thy cry; when he shall hear it, he will answer thee.

20And *though* the Lord give you the bread of adversity, and the water of affliction, yet shall not thy teachers be removed into a corner any more, but thine eyes shall see thy teachers:

21And thine ears shall hear a word behind thee, saying, This *is* the way, walk ye in it, when ye turn to the right hand, and when ye turn to the left.

22Ye shall defile also the covering of thy graven images of silver, and the ornament of thy molten images of gold: thou shalt cast them away as a menstruous cloth; thou shalt say unto it, Get thee hence.

23Then shall he give the rain of thy seed, that thou shalt sow the ground withal; and bread of the increase of the earth, and it shall be fat and plenteous: in that day shall thy cattle feed in large pastures.

24The oxen likewise and the young asses that ear the ground shall eat clean provender, which hath been winnowed with the shovel and with the fan.

## Amplified

7For Egypt's help is worthless and to no purpose; therefore I have called her Rahab who sits still.

8Now, go, write it before them on a tablet and inscribe it in a book, that it may be as a witness for the time to come for evermore.

9For this is a rebellious people, faithless *and* lying sons, children who will not hear the law *and* instruction of the Lord;

10Who *virtually* say to the seers [by their conduct], See not; and to the prophets, Prophesy not to us what is right; speak to us smooth things, prophesy deceitful illusions,

11Get out of the true way, turn aside out of the path, cease holding up before us the Holy One of Israel.

12Therefore thus says the Holy One of Israel, Because you despise *and* spurn this *My* word, and trust in cunning *and* oppression, in crookedness *and* perverseness, and rely on them;

13Therefore this iniquity *and* guilt shall be to you as a broken section of a high wall, bulging out and ready [at some distant day] to fall, whose crash will *then* come suddenly *and* swiftly, in an instant.

14And he shall break it as a potter's vessel is broken, breaking it in pieces without sparing; so that there cannot be found among its pieces one large enough to carry coals of fire from the hearth, or to dip water out of the cistern.

15For thus said the Lord God, the Holy One of Israel, In returning *to Me* and resting *in Me* you shall be saved; in quietness and in (trusting) confidence shall be your strength. And you would not,

16But you said, No! We will speed *our own course* on horses! Therefore you shall speed [in flight from your enemies]. You said, We will ride upon swift steeds [doing our own way]! Therefore shall they who pursue you be swift, *so swift that*

17One thousand of you will flee at the threat of one of them; at the threat of five you will flee till you are left like a beacon *or* a flagpole on the top of a mountain, and like a signal on a hill.

18And therefore the Lord [earnestly] waits—expectant, looking and longing—to be gracious to you, and therefore He lifts Himself up that He may have mercy on you *and* show loving-kindness to you; for the Lord is a God of justice. Blessed—happy, fortunate [to be envied] are all those who [earnestly] wait for Him, who expect *and* look *and* long for Him [for His victory, His favor, His love, His peace, His joy and His matchless, unbroken companionship]. [Rev. 3:5; II Cor. 12:9; I John 3:16; John 14:3, 27; Heb. 12:2.]

19O people who dwell in Zion at Jerusalem, you shall weep no more. He will surely be gracious to you at the sound of your cry; when He hears it, He will answer you.

20And though the Lord give you the bread of adversity and the water of affliction, yet your Teacher will not hide Himself any more, but your eyes shall constantly behold your Teacher.

21And your ears shall hear a word behind you, saying, This is the way, walk in it, when you turn to the right hand and when you turn to the left.

22Then you will defile your carved images overlaid with silver and your molten images plated with gold; you will cast them away as a filthy blood-stained cloth, and you will say to them, Be gone!

23Then will He give you rain for your seed with which you sow the soil, and bread grain as the produce of the ground, and it will be rich and plentiful. In that day your cattle will feed in large pastures.

24The oxen likewise and the young donkeys that till the ground will eat savory *and* salted fodder, which has been winnowed with shovel and with fork.

## New American Standard

7 Even Egypt, whose help is vain and empty.
Therefore, I have called her
"Rahab who has been exterminated."
8 Now go, write it on a tablet before them
And inscribe it on a scroll,
That it may serve in the time to come
As a witness forever.
9 For this is a rebellious people, false sons,
Sons who refuse to listen
To the instruction of the LORD;
10 Who say to the seers, "You must not see *visions*";
And to the prophets, "You must not prophesy to us what is right,
Speak to us pleasant words,
Prophesy illusions.
11 "Get out of the way, turn aside from the path,
Let us hear no more about the Holy One of Israel."
12 Therefore thus says the Holy One of Israel,
"Since you have rejected this word,
And have put your trust in oppression and guile, and have relied on them,
13 Therefore this iniquity will be to you
Like a breach about to fall,
A bulge in a high wall,
Whose collapse comes suddenly in an instant.
14 "And whose collapse is like the smashing of a potter's jar;
So ruthlessly shattered
That a sherd will not be found among its pieces
To take fire from a hearth,
Or to scoop water from a cistern."
15 For thus the Lord GOD, the Holy One of Israel, has said,
"In repentance and rest you shall be saved,
In quietness and trust is your strength."
But you were not willing,
16 And you said, "No, for we will flee on horses,"
Therefore you shall flee!
"And we will ride on swift *horses*,"
Therefore those who pursue you shall be swift.
17 One thousand *shall flee* at the threat of one *man*,
You shall flee at the threat of five;
Until you are left as a flag on a mountain top,
And as a signal on a hill.

*God Is Gracious and Just*

18¶ Therefore the LORD longs to be gracious to you,
And therefore He waits on high to have compassion on you.
For the LORD is a God of justice;
How blessed are all those who long for Him.

19O people in Zion, inhabitant in Jerusalem, you will weep no longer. He will surely be gracious to you at the sound of your cry; when He hears it, He will answer you.

20Although the Lord has given you bread of privation and water of oppression, *He,* your Teacher will no longer hide Himself, but your eyes will behold your Teacher.

21And your ears will hear a word behind you, "This is the way, walk in it," whenever you turn to the right or to the left.

22And you will defile your graven images, overlaid with silver, and your molten images plated with gold. You will scatter them as an impure thing; *and* say to them, "Be gone!"

23¶ Then He will give *you* rain for the seed which you will sow in the ground, and bread *from* the yield of the ground, and it will be rich and plenteous; on that day your livestock will graze in a roomy pasture.

24Also the oxen and the donkeys which work the ground will eat salted fodder, which has been winnowed with shovel and fork.

## New International

7 to Egypt, whose help is utterly useless.
Therefore I call her
Rahab the Do-Nothing.

8Go now, write it on a tablet for them,
inscribe it on a scroll,
that for the days to come
it may be an everlasting witness.
9These are rebellious people, deceitful children,
children unwilling to listen to the LORD's instruction.
10They say to the seers,
"See no more visions!"
and to the prophets,
"Give us no more visions of what is right!
Tell us pleasant things,
prophesy illusions.
11Leave this way,
get off this path,
and stop confronting us
with the Holy One of Israel!"

12Therefore, this is what the Holy One of Israel says:

"Because you have rejected this message,
relied on oppression
and depended on deceit,
13this sin will become for you
like a high wall, cracked and bulging,
that collapses suddenly, in an instant.
14It will break in pieces like pottery,
shattered so mercilessly
that among its pieces not a fragment will be found
for taking coals from a hearth
or scooping water out of a cistern."

15This is what the Sovereign LORD, the Holy One of Israel, says:

"In repentance and rest is your salvation,
in quietness and trust is your strength,
but you would have none of it.
16You said, 'No, we will flee on horses.'
Therefore you will flee!
You said, 'We will ride off on swift horses.'
Therefore your pursuers will be swift!
17A thousand will flee
at the threat of one;
at the threat of five
you will all flee away,
till you are left
like a flagstaff on a mountaintop,
like a banner on a hill."

18Yet the LORD longs to be gracious to you;
he rises to show you compassion.
For the LORD is a God of justice.
Blessed are all who wait for him!

19O people of Zion, who live in Jerusalem, you will weep no
more. How gracious he will be when you cry for help! As soon as
he hears, he will answer you. 20Although the Lord gives you the
bread of adversity and the water of affliction, your teachers will be
hidden no more; with your own eyes you will see them. 21Whether
you turn to the right or to the left, your ears will hear a voice
behind you, saying, "This is the way; walk in it." 22Then you will
defile your idols overlaid with silver and your images covered with
gold; you will throw them away like a menstrual cloth and say to
them, "Away with you!"

23He will also send you rain for the seed you sow in the ground,
and the food that comes from the land will be rich and plentiful.
In that day your cattle will graze in broad meadows. 24The oxen
and donkeys that work the soil will eat fodder and mash, spread
out with fork and shovel. 25In the day of great slaughter, when the

## King James

25 And there shall be upon every high mountain, and upon every high hill, rivers *and* streams of waters in the day of the great slaughter, when the towers fall.

26 Moreover the light of the moon shall be as the light of the sun, and the light of the sun shall be sevenfold, as the light of seven days, in the day that the LORD bindeth up the breach of his people, and healeth the stroke of their wound.

27 ¶ Behold, the name of the LORD cometh from far, burning *with* his anger, and the burden *thereof is* heavy: his lips are full of indignation, and his tongue as a devouring fire:

28 And his breath, as an overflowing stream, shall reach to the midst of the neck, to sift the nations with the sieve of vanity: and *there shall be* a bridle in the jaws of the people, causing *them* to err.

29 Ye shall have a song, as in the night *when* a holy solemnity is kept; and gladness of heart, as when one goeth with a pipe to come into the mountain of the LORD, to the mighty One of Israel.

30 And the LORD shall cause his glorious voice to be heard, and shall show the lighting down of his arm, with the indignation of *his* anger, and *with* the flame of a devouring fire, *with* scattering, and tempest, and hailstones.

31 For through the voice of the LORD shall the Assyrian be beaten down, *which* smote with a rod.

32 And *in* every place where the grounded staff shall pass, which the LORD shall lay upon him, *it* shall be with tabrets and harps: and in battles of shaking will he fight with it.

33 For Tophet *is* ordained of old; yea, for the king it is prepared; he hath made *it* deep *and* large: the pile thereof *is* fire and much wood; the breath of the LORD, like a stream of brimstone, doth kindle it.

## Amplified

25 And there will be upon every high mountain and upon every high hill brooks and streams of water in [the day of the Lord] the day of the great slaughter, when the towers fall [and all His enemies are destroyed].

26 Moreover the light of the moon will be as the light of the sun, and the light of the sun will be sevenfold, as the light of seven days [concentrated in one], in the day that the Lord binds up the hurt of His people, and heals their wound [inflicted by Him because of their sins].

27 Behold, the name of the Lord comes from afar, burning with His anger, and in thick, rising smoke. His lips are full of indignation, and His tongue is as a consuming fire.

28 And His breath is as an overflowing stream, that reaches even to the neck, to sift the nations with the sieve of destruction; and a bridle that causes to err will be in the jaws of the people.

29 You shall have a song, as in the night when a holy feast is kept; and gladness of heart, as when one marches in procession with a flute to come to the temple on the mountain of the Lord, to the Rock of Israel.

30 And the Lord shall cause His glorious voice to be heard, and the descending blow of His arm to be seen, in indignant anger and with flame of a devouring fire, amid crashing blast *and* cloudburst, tempest and hailstones.

31 At the voice of the Lord the Assyrians will be stricken with dismay *and* terror, when He smites them with His rod.

32 And every passing stroke of the staff of punishment *and* doom which the Lord lays upon them shall be to the sound of [Israel's] timbrels and lyres, when in battle He attacks *Assyria* with swinging *and* menacing arm.

33 For a Topheth—a place of burning and abomination—is already laid out *and* long ago prepared; yes, for the [idol-] king *and* [the god] Molech it is made ready, its pyre made deep *and* large, with fire and much wood; the breath of the Lord, like a stream of brimstone, kindles it. [Matt. 5:22; 25:41.]

## King James

**31** WOE TO them that go down to Egypt for help; and stay on horses, and trust in chariots, because *they are* many; and in horsemen, because they are very strong; but they look not unto the Holy One of Israel, neither seek the LORD!

2 Yet he also *is* wise, and will bring evil, and will not call back his words: but will arise against the house of the evildoers, and against the help of them that work iniquity.

3 Now the Egyptians *are* men, and not God; and their horses flesh, and not spirit. When the LORD shall stretch out his hand, both he that helpeth shall fall, and he that is helped shall fall down, and they all shall fail together.

## Amplified

**31** WOE TO those who go down to Egypt for help and rely on horses, and trust in chariots because they are many and in horsemen because they are very strong, but they look not to the Holy One of Israel nor seek *and* consult the Lord!

2 And yet He is wise and brings calamity, and does not recall His words; He will arise against the house [the whole race] of evildoers and against the helpers of those who work iniquity.

3 Now the Egyptians are men and not God, and their horses are flesh and not spirit; and when the Lord stretches out His hand, both *Egypt* who helps will stumble, and *Judah* who is helped will fall, and they will all perish *and* be consumed together.

## New American Standard

25And on every lofty mountain and on every high hill there will be streams running with water on the day of the great slaughter, when the towers fall.
26And the light of the moon will be as the light of the sun, and the light of the sun will be seven times *brighter*, like the light of seven days, on the day the LORD binds up the fracture of His people and heals the bruise He has inflicted.

27¶ Behold, the name of the LORD comes from a remote place;
Burning is His anger, and dense is *His* smoke;
His lips are filled with indignation,
And His tongue is like a consuming fire;
28 And His breath is like an overflowing torrent,
Which reaches to the neck,
To shake the nations back and forth in a sieve,
And to *put* in the jaws of the peoples the bridle which leads to ruin.
29 You will have songs as in the night when you keep the festival;
And gladness of heart as when one marches to *the sound of* the flute,
To go to the mountain of the LORD, to the Rock of Israel.
30 And the LORD will cause His voice of authority to be heard.
And the descending of His arm to be seen in fierce anger,
And *in* the flame of a consuming fire,
In cloudburst, downpour, and hailstones.
31 For at the voice of the LORD Assyria will be terrified,
*When* He strikes with the rod.
32 And every blow of the rod of punishment,
Which the LORD will lay on him,
Will be with *the music of* tambourines and lyres;
And in battles, brandishing weapons, He will fight them.
33 For [a]Topheth has long been ready,
Indeed, it has been prepared for the king.
He has made it deep and large,
A pyre of fire with plenty of wood;
The breath of the LORD, like a torrent of brimstone, sets it afire.

*Help Not in Egypt but in God*

**31** WOE TO those who go down to Egypt for help,
*And* rely on horses,
And trust in chariots because they are many,
And in horsemen because they are very strong,
But they do not look to the Holy One of Israel, nor seek the LORD!
2 Yet He also is wise and will bring disaster,
And does not retract His words,
But will arise against the house of evildoers,
And against the help of the workers of iniquity.
3 Now the Egyptians are men, and not God,
And their horses are flesh and not spirit;
So the LORD will stretch out His hand,
And he who helps will stumble
And he who is helped will fall,
And all of them will come to an end together.

NAS [a] I.e., the place of human sacrifice to Molech

## New International

towers fall, streams of water will flow on every high mountain and
every lofty hill. 26The moon will shine like the sun, and the sunlight will be seven times brighter, like the light of seven full days,
when the LORD binds up the bruises of his people and heals the
wounds he inflicted.

27See, the Name of the LORD comes from afar,
with burning anger and dense clouds of smoke;
his lips are full of wrath,
and his tongue is a consuming fire.
28His breath is like a rushing torrent,
rising up to the neck.
He shakes the nations in the sieve of destruction;
he places in the jaws of the peoples
a bit that leads them astray.
29And you will sing
as on the night you celebrate a holy festival;
your hearts will rejoice
as when people go up with flutes
to the mountain of the LORD,
to the Rock of Israel.
30The LORD will cause men to hear his majestic voice
and will make them see his arm coming down
with raging anger and consuming fire,
with cloudburst, thunderstorm and hail.
31The voice of the LORD will shatter Assyria;
with his scepter he will strike them down.
32Every stroke the LORD lays on them
with his punishing rod
will be to the music of tambourines and harps,
as he fights them in battle with the blows of his arm.
33Topheth has long been prepared;
it has been made ready for the king.
Its fire pit has been made deep and wide,
with an abundance of fire and wood;
the breath of the LORD,
like a stream of burning sulfur,
sets it ablaze.

*Woe to Those Who Rely on Egypt*

**31** WOE TO those who go down to Egypt for help,
who rely on horses,
who trust in the multitude of their chariots
and in the great strength of their horsemen,
but do not look to the Holy One of Israel,
or seek help from the LORD.
2Yet he too is wise and can bring disaster;
he does not take back his words.
He will rise up against the house of the wicked,
against those who help evildoers.
3But the Egyptians are men and not God;
their horses are flesh and not spirit.
When the LORD stretches out his hand,
he who helps will stumble,
he who is helped will fall;
both will perish together.

## King James

4For thus hath the LORD spoken unto me, Like as the lion and the young lion roaring on his prey, when a multitude of shepherds is called forth against him, *he* will not be afraid of their voice, nor abase himself for the noise of them: so shall the LORD of hosts come down to fight for mount Zion, and for the hill thereof.

5As birds flying, so will the LORD of hosts defend Jerusalem; defending also he will deliver *it; and* passing over he will preserve *it*.

6¶ Turn ye unto *him from* whom the children of Israel have deeply revolted.

7For in that day every man shall cast away his idols of silver, and his idols of gold, which your own hands have made unto you *for* a sin.

8¶ Then shall the Assyrian fall with the sword, not of a mighty man; and the sword, not of a mean man, shall devour him: but he shall flee from the sword, and his young men shall be discomfited.

9And he shall pass over to his strong hold for fear, and his princes shall be afraid of the ensign, saith the LORD, whose fire *is* in Zion, and his furnace in Jerusalem.

**32** BEHOLD, A king shall reign in righteousness, and princes shall rule in judgment.

2And a man shall be as an hiding place from the wind, and a covert from the tempest; as rivers of water in a dry place, as the shadow of a great rock in a weary land.

3And the eyes of them that see shall not be dim, and the ears of them that hear shall hearken.

4The heart also of the rash shall understand knowledge, and the tongue of the stammerers shall be ready to speak plainly.

5The vile person shall be no more called liberal, nor the churl said *to be* bountiful.

6For the vile person will speak villany, and his heart will work iniquity, to practise hypocrisy, and to utter error against the LORD, to make empty the soul of the hungry, and he will cause the drink of the thirsty to fail.

7The instruments also of the churl *are* evil: he deviseth wicked devices to destroy the poor with lying words, even when the needy speaketh right.

8But the liberal deviseth liberal things; and by liberal things shall he stand.

9¶ Rise up, ye women that are at ease; hear my voice, ye careless daughters; give ear unto my speech.

10Many days and years shall ye be troubled, ye careless women: for the vintage shall fail, the gathering shall not come.

11Tremble, ye women that are at ease; be troubled, ye careless ones: strip you, and make you bare, and gird *sackcloth* upon *your* loins.

## Amplified

4For the Lord has said to me, As the lion or the young lion growls over his prey, and when a large band of shepherds is called out against him will not be terrified at their voice or daunted at their noise, so the Lord of hosts will come down to fight upon Mount Zion and upon its hills.

5As birds hovering, so will the Lord of hosts defend Jerusalem, He will protect and deliver it, He will pass over *and* spare and preserve it.

6Return, O children of Israel, to Him against Whom you have so deeply plunged in revolt.

7For in that day every man *of you* will cast away [in contempt and disgust] his idols of silver and his idols of gold, which your own hands have sinfully made for you.

8Then the Assyrian shall fall by the sword, not of man; and the sword, not of men [but of God], shall devour him; and he shall flee from the sword, and his young men shall become subjected to forced labor.

9[In his flight] he shall pass beyond his rock-refuge for terror; even his officers shall desert the standard in fear *and* panic, says the Lord, Whose fire is in Zion and His furnace in Jerusalem.

**32** BEHOLD, A king will reign in righteousness, and princes will rule in justice.

2And each one of them shall be like a hiding place from the wind, and a shelter from the storm; like streams of water in a dry place, like the shade of a great rock in a weary land [to those who turn to them].

3Then the eyes of those who see will not be closed *or* dim, and the ears of those who hear will listen.

4And the mind of the rash shall understand knowledge *and* have good judgment, and the tongue of the stammerers will speak readily and plainly.

5The fool [the unbeliever and the ungodly] shall no more be called noble, nor the crafty *and* greedy of gain said to be bountiful *and* princely.

6For the fool speaks folly and his mind plans iniquity: practicing profane ungodliness and speaking error concerning the Lord, leaving the craving of the hungry unsatisfied, and causing the drink of the thirsty to fail.

7The instruments *and* methods of the fraudulent *and* greedy of gain are evil; he devises wicked devices to ruin the poor *and* the lowly with lying words, even when the plea of the needy is just *and* right.

8But the noble, open-hearted *and* liberal man devises noble things; and he stands for what is noble, open-hearted *and* generous.

9Rise up, you women who are at ease! Hear my [Isaiah's] voice, you confident *and* careless daughters, listen to what I am saying.

10In little more than a year you shall be shaken with anxiety, you careless *and* complacent women, for the vintage will fail and the ingathering shall not come.

11Tremble, you women who are at ease! Shudder with fear, you complacent ones! Strip yourselves bare and gird sackcloth upon your loins *in grief!*

## New American Standard

4¶ For thus says the LORD to me,
"As the lion or the young lion growls over his prey,
Against which a band of shepherds is called out,
Will not be terrified at their voice, nor disturbed at their noise,
So will the LORD of hosts come down to wage war on Mount Zion and on its hill."
5 Like flying birds so the LORD of hosts will protect Jerusalem.
He will protect and deliver *it;*
He will pass over and rescue *it.*
6Return to Him from whom you have deeply defected, O sons
of Israel.
7For in that day every man will cast away his silver idols and
his gold idols, which your hands have made as a sin.
8 And the Assyrian will fall by a sword not of man,
And a sword not of man will devour him.
So he will not escape the sword,
And his young men will become forced laborers.
9 "And his rock will pass away because of panic,
And his princes will be terrified at the standard,"
Declares the LORD, whose fire is in Zion and whose furnace is in Jerusalem.

*The Glorious Future*

32 BEHOLD, A king will reign righteously,
And princes will rule justly.
2 And each will be like a refuge from the wind,
And a shelter from the storm,
Like streams of water in a dry country,
Like the shade of a huge rock in a parched land.
3 Then the eyes of those who see will not be blinded,
And the ears of those who hear will listen.
4 And the mind of the hasty will discern the truth,
And the tongue of the stammerers will hasten to speak clearly.
5 No longer will the fool be called noble,
Or the rogue be spoken of *as* generous.
6 For a fool speaks nonsense,
And his heart inclines toward wickedness,
To practice ungodliness and to speak error against the LORD,
To keep the hungry person unsatisfied
And to withhold drink from the thirsty.
7 As for a rogue, his weapons are evil;
He devises wicked schemes
To destroy *the* afflicted with slander,
Even though *the* needy one speaks what is right.
8 But the noble man devises noble plans;
And by noble plans he stands.

9¶ Rise up you women who are at ease,
And hear my voice;
Give ear to my word,
You complacent daughters.
10 Within a year and *a few* days,
You will be troubled, O complacent *daughters;*
For the vintage is ended,
And the *fruit* gathering will not come.
11 Tremble, you *women* who are at ease;
Be troubled, you complacent *daughters;*
Strip, undress, and put *sackcloth* on *your* waist,

## New International

4This is what the LORD says to me:

"As a lion growls,
a great lion over his prey—
and though a whole band of shepherds
is called together against him,
he is not frightened by their shouts
or disturbed by their clamor—
so the LORD Almighty will come down
to do battle on Mount Zion and on its heights.
5Like birds hovering overhead,
the LORD Almighty will shield Jerusalem;
he will shield it and deliver it,
he will 'pass over' it and will rescue it."

6Return to him you have so greatly revolted against, O Israelites. 7For in that day every one of you will reject the idols of silver
and gold your sinful hands have made.

8"Assyria will fall by a sword that is not of man;
a sword, not of mortals, will devour them.
They will flee before the sword
and their young men will be put to forced labor.
9Their stronghold will fall because of terror;
at sight of the battle standard their commanders will panic,"
declares the LORD,
whose fire is in Zion,
whose furnace is in Jerusalem.

*The Kingdom of Righteousness*

32 SEE, A king will reign in righteousness
and rulers will rule with justice.
2Each man will be like a shelter from the wind
and a refuge from the storm,
like streams of water in the desert
and the shadow of a great rock in a thirsty land.

3Then the eyes of those who see will no longer be closed,
and the ears of those who hear will listen.
4The mind of the rash will know and understand,
and the stammering tongue will be fluent and clear.
5No longer will the fool be called noble
nor the scoundrel be highly respected.
6For the fool speaks folly,
his mind is busy with evil:
He practices ungodliness
and spreads error concerning the LORD;
the hungry he leaves empty
and from the thirsty he withholds water.
7The scoundrel's methods are wicked,
he makes up evil schemes
to destroy the poor with lies,
even when the plea of the needy is just.
8But the noble man makes noble plans,
and by noble deeds he stands.

*The Women of Jerusalem*

9You women who are so complacent,
rise up and listen to me;
you daughters who feel secure,
hear what I have to say!
10In little more than a year
you who feel secure will tremble;
the grape harvest will fail,
and the harvest of fruit will not come.
11Tremble, you complacent women;
shudder, you daughters who feel secure!
Strip off your clothes,
put sackcloth around your waists.

## King James

12 They shall lament for the teats, for the pleasant fields, for the fruitful vine.

13 Upon the land of my people shall come up thorns *and* briers; Yea, upon all the houses of joy *in* the joyous city:

14 Because the palaces shall be forsaken; the multitude of the city shall be left; the forts and towers shall be for dens for ever, a joy of wild asses, a pasture of flocks;

15 Until the spirit be poured upon us from on high, and the wilderness be a fruitful field, and the fruitful field be counted for a forest.

16 Then judgment shall dwell in the wilderness, and righteousness remain in the fruitful field.

17 And the work of righteousness shall be peace; and the effect of righteousness quietness and assurance for ever.

18 And my people shall dwell in a peaceable habitation, and in sure dwellings, and in quiet resting places;

19 When it shall hail, coming down on the forest; and the city shall be low in a low place.

20 Blessed *are* ye that sow beside all waters, that send forth *thither* the feet of the ox and the ass.

## Amplified

12 They shall beat upon their breasts for the pleasant fields, for the fruitful vine,

13 For the land of my people growing up with thorns and briers; yes, for all the houses of joy in the joyous city.

14 For the palace shall be forsaken, the populous city shall be deserted; the hill and the watchtower shall be for dens [of wild animals] endlessly, a joy of wild donkeys, a pasture of flocks;

15 Until the Spirit is poured upon us from on high, and the wilderness becomes a fruitful field, and the fruitful field is valued as a forest. [Ps. 104:30; Ezek. 36:26, 27; 39:29; Zech. 12:10.]

16 Then justice will dwell in the wilderness, and righteousness [religious and moral rectitude in every area and relation] will abide in the fruitful field.

17 And the effect of righteousness shall be peace [internal and external], and the result of righteousness, quietness and confident trust for ever.

18 My people shall dwell in a peaceable habitation, in safe dwellings, and in quiet resting places.

19 But [the wrath of the Lord] it shall hail, coming down overpoweringly on the forest [the army of the Assyrian], and the capital [a]city shall be utterly humbled *and* laid prostrate.

20 Happy *and* fortunate are you who cast your seed upon all waters [when the river overflows its banks; for the seed will sink into the mud and when the waters subside will spring up; you will find it after many days in an abundant harvest], *and* can safely send forth the ox and the donkey [to range freely].

## King James

**33** WOE TO thee that spoilest, and thou *wast* not spoiled; and dealest treacherously, and they dealt not treacherously with thee! when thou shalt cease to spoil, thou shalt be spoiled; *and* when thou shalt make an end to deal treacherously, they shall deal treacherously with thee.

2 O LORD, be gracious unto us; we have waited for thee: be thou their arm every morning, our salvation also in the time of trouble.

3 At the noise of the tumult the people fled; at the lifting up of thyself the nations were scattered.

4 And your spoil shall be gathered *like* the gathering of the caterpillar: as the running to and fro of locusts shall he run upon them.

5 The LORD is exalted; for he dwelleth on high: he hath filled Zion with judgment and righteousness.

6 And wisdom and knowledge shall be the stability of thy times, *and* strength of salvation: the fear of the LORD *is* his treasure.

7 Behold, their valiant ones shall cry without: the ambassadors of peace shall weep bitterly.

8 The highways lie waste, the wayfaring man ceaseth: he hath broken the covenant, he hath despised the cities, he regardeth no man.

9 The earth mourneth *and* languisheth: Lebanon is ashamed *and* hewn down: Sharon is like a wilderness; and Bashan and Carmel shake off *their fruits.*

## Amplified

**33** WOE TO you, destroyer, you who are not yourself destroyed; who deal treacherously though they [your victims] did not deal treacherously with you! When you have ceased to destroy, you shall be destroyed; *and* when you have stopped dealing treacherously, they will deal treacherously with you.

2 O Lord, be gracious to us; we have waited [expectantly] for You. Be the arm *of Your servants*—their strength and defense—every morning, our salvation in the time of trouble.

3 At the noise of the tumult [caused by Your voice at which the enemy is overthrown] the peoples flee; at the lifting up of Yourself nations are scattered.

4 And the spoil [of the Assyrians] shall be gathered [by the inhabitants of Jerusalem] as the caterpillar gathers; as locusts leap *and* run to and fro shall *the Jews* [spoil the Assyrians' forsaken camp as they] leap upon it.

5 The Lord is exalted, for He dwells on high; He will fill Zion with justice and righteousness [religious and moral rectitude in every area and relation].

6 And there shall be stability in your times, abundance of salvation, wisdom and knowledge; the reverent fear *and* worship of the Lord is your treasure *and* His.

7 Behold, their valiant ones cry without; the ambassadors of peace weep bitterly.

8 The highways lie waste, the wayfaring man ceases; the enemy has broken the covenant, he has despised the cities *and* [b]the witnesses, he regards no man.

9 The land mourns and languishes; Lebanon is confounded, and [its luxuriant verdure] is withered away; Sharon [a fertile pasture region south of Mount Carmel] is like a desert; Bashan [a broad, fertile plateau east of the Jordan River] and *Mount* Carmel shake off their leaves.

**AMP** [a] Authorities find it impossible to be sure whether the "city" here means Nineveh, Jerusalem, or even Babylon. [b] The Dead Sea Scrolls read "the witnesses."

## New American Standard

12 Beat your breasts for the pleasant fields, for the fruitful vine,
13 For the land of my people *in which* thorns *and* briars shall come up;
Yea, for all the joyful houses, *and for* the jubilant city.
14 Because the palace has been abandoned, the populated city forsaken.
Hill and watch-tower have become caves forever,
A delight for wild donkeys, a pasture for flocks;
15 Until the Spirit is poured out upon us from on high,
And the wilderness becomes a fertile field
And the fertile field is considered as a forest.
16 Then justice will dwell in the wilderness,
And righteousness will abide in the fertile field.
17 And the work of righteousness will be peace,
And the service of righteousness, quietness and confidence forever.
18 Then my people will live in a peaceful habitation,
And in secure dwellings and in undisturbed resting places;
19 And it will hail when the forest comes down,
And the city will be utterly laid low.
20 How blessed will you be, you who sow beside all waters,
Who let out freely the ox and the donkey.

*The Judgment of God*

33 WOE TO you, O destroyer,
While you were not destroyed;
And he who is treacherous, while *others* did not deal treacherously with him.
As soon as you shall finish destroying, you shall be destroyed;
As soon as you shall cease to deal treacherously, *others* shall deal treacherously with you.
2 O LORD, be gracious to us; we have waited for Thee.
Be Thou their strength every morning,
Our salvation also in the time of distress.
3 At the sound of the tumult peoples flee;
At the lifting up of Thyself nations disperse.
4 And your spoil is gathered *as* the caterpillar gathers;
As locusts rushing about, men rush about on it.
5 The LORD is exalted, for He dwells on high;
He has filled Zion with justice and righteousness.
6 And He shall be the stability of your times,
A wealth of salvation, wisdom, and knowledge;
The fear of the LORD is his treasure.
7 Behold, their brave men cry in the streets,
The ambassadors of peace weep bitterly.
8 The highways are desolate, the traveler has ceased,
He has broken the covenant, he has despised the cities,
He has no regard for man.
9 The land mourns and pines away,
Lebanon is shamed and withers;
Sharon is like a desert plain,
And Bashan and Carmel lose *their foliage*.

## New International

12Beat your breasts for the pleasant fields,
for the fruitful vines
13and for the land of my people,
a land overgrown with thorns and briers—
yes, mourn for all houses of merriment
and for this city of revelry.
14The fortress will be abandoned,
the noisy city deserted;
citadel and watchtower will become a wasteland forever,
the delight of donkeys, a pasture for flocks,
15till the Spirit is poured upon us from on high,
and the desert becomes a fertile field,
and the fertile field seems like a forest.
16Justice will dwell in the desert
and righteousness live in the fertile field.
17The fruit of righteousness will be peace;
the effect of righteousness will be quietness and confidence forever.
18My people will live in peaceful dwelling places,
in secure homes,
in undisturbed places of rest.
19Though hail flattens the forest
and the city is leveled completely,
20how blessed you will be,
sowing your seed by every stream,
and letting your cattle and donkeys range free.

*Distress and Help*

33 WOE TO you, O destroyer,
you who have not been destroyed!
Woe to you, O traitor,
you who have not been betrayed!
When you stop destroying,
you will be destroyed;
when you stop betraying,
you will be betrayed.

2O LORD, be gracious to us;
we long for you.
Be our strength every morning,
our salvation in time of distress.
3At the thunder of your voice, the peoples flee;
when you rise up, the nations scatter.
4Your plunder, O nations, is harvested as by young locusts;
like a swarm of locusts men pounce on it.

5The LORD is exalted, for he dwells on high;
he will fill Zion with justice and righteousness.
6He will be the sure foundation for your times,
a rich store of salvation and wisdom and knowledge;
the fear of the LORD is the key to this treasure.[c]

7Look, their brave men cry aloud in the streets;
the envoys of peace weep bitterly.
8The highways are deserted,
no travelers are on the roads.
The treaty is broken,
its witnesses[d] are despised,
no one is respected.
9The land mourns[e] and wastes away,
Lebanon is ashamed and withers;
Sharon is like the Arabah,
and Bashan and Carmel drop their leaves.

NIV [c] 6 Or *is a treasure from him* [d] 8 Dead Sea Scrolls; Masoretic Text / *the cities* [e] 9 Or *dries up*

## King James

10 Now will I rise, saith the LORD; now will I be exalted; now will I lift up myself.

11 Ye shall conceive chaff, ye shall bring forth stubble: your breath, *as* fire, shall devour you.

12 And the people shall be *as* the burnings of lime: *as* thorns cut up shall they be burned in the fire.

13 ¶ Hear, ye *that are* far off, what I have done; and, ye *that are* near, acknowledge my might.

14 The sinners in Zion are afraid; fearfulness hath surprised the hypocrites. Who among us shall dwell with the devouring fire? who among us shall dwell with everlasting burnings?

15 He that walketh righteously, and speaketh uprightly; he that despiseth the gain of oppressions, that shaketh his hands from holding of bribes, that stoppeth his ears from hearing of blood, and shutteth his eyes from seeing evil;

16 He shall dwell on high: his place of defence *shall be* the munitions of rocks: bread shall be given him; his waters *shall be* sure.

17 Thine eyes shall see the king in his beauty: they shall behold the land that is very far off.

18 Thine heart shall meditate terror. Where *is* the scribe? where *is* the receiver? where *is* he that counted the towers?

19 Thou shalt not see a fierce people, a people of a deeper speech than thou canst perceive; of a stammering tongue, *that thou canst* not understand.

20 Look upon Zion, the city of our solemnities: thine eyes shall see Jerusalem a quiet habitation, a tabernacle *that* shall not be taken down; not one of the stakes thereof shall ever be removed, neither shall any of the cords thereof be broken.

21 But there the glorious LORD *will be* unto us a place of broad rivers *and* streams; wherein shall go no galley with oars, neither shall gallant ship pass thereby.

22 For the LORD *is* our judge, the LORD *is* our lawgiver, the LORD *is* our king; he will save us.

23 Thy tacklings are loosed; they could not well strengthen their mast, they could not spread the sail: then is the prey of a great spoil divided; the lame take the prey.

24 And the inhabitant shall not say, I am sick: the people that dwell therein *shall be* forgiven *their* iniquity.

**34** COME NEAR, ye nations, to hear; and hearken, ye people: let the earth hear, and all that is therein; the world, and all things that come forth of it.

2 For the indignation of the LORD *is* upon all nations, and *his* fury upon all their armies: he hath utterly destroyed them, he hath delivered them to the slaughter.

## Amplified

10 Now will I arise, says the Lord; now will I lift up Myself; now will I be exalted.

11 You conceive chaff, you bring forth stubble; your breath is a fire that will consume you.

12 And the people will be as if burned to lime, like thorns cut down, that are burned in the fire.

13 Hear, you who are far off, *says the Lord,* what I have done; and, you who are near, acknowledge My might.

14 The sinners in Zion are afraid; trembling has seized the godless ones. *They cry,* Who among us can dwell with *that* devouring fire? Who among us can dwell with *those* everlasting burnings?

15 He who walks righteously and speaks uprightly, who despises the gain of fraud *and* of oppressions, who shakes his hand free from the taking of bribes, who stops his ears from hearing of bloodshed, and shuts his eyes to avoid looking upon evil.

16 [Such a man] will dwell on the heights; his place of defense will be the fortresses of rocks; his bread will be given him, water for him will be sure.

17 Your eyes will see the King in His beauty; *your eyes* will behold a land of wide distances that stretches afar.

18 Your mind will meditate on the terror, *asking,* Where is he who counted, where is he who weighed the tribute? Where is he who counted the towers?

19 You shall see no more the fierce *and* insolent people, a people of too deep *and* obscure a speech to be comprehended, of a strange *and* stammering tongue that you cannot understand.

20 Look upon Zion, the city of our set feasts *and* solemnities! Your eyes shall see Jerusalem a quiet habitation, a tent that shall not be taken down; not *one of* the stakes of it shall ever be pulled up, neither shall any of its cords be broken.

21 But there the Lord will be for us in majesty *and* splendor a place of broad rivers and streams, where no oar-propelled boat can go, nor mighty *and* stately ship can pass.

22 For the Lord is our judge, the Lord is our law-giver, the Lord is our king; He will save us.

23 Your hoisting ropes hang loose; they cannot strengthen *and* hold firm the foot of their mast, or keep the sail spread out. Then will prey and spoil in abundance be divided; *even* the lame will take the prey.

24 And no inhabitant will say, I am sick; the people who dwell there will be forgiven their iniquity *and* guilt.

**34** COME NEAR, you nations, to hear; and hearken, you peoples! Let the earth hear, and all that is in it; the world, and all things that come forth from it.

2 For the Lord is indignant against all nations, and His wrath is against all their host. He has utterly doomed them, He has given them over for slaughter.

## New American Standard

10 "Now I will arise," says the LORD,
"Now I will be exalted, now I will be lifted up.
11 "You have conceived chaff, you will give birth to stubble;
My breath will consume you like a fire.
12 "And the peoples will be burned to lime,
Like cut thorns which are burned in the fire.

13¶ "You who are far away, hear what I have done;
And you who are near, acknowledge My might."
14 Sinners in Zion are terrified;
Trembling has seized the godless.
"Who among us can live with the consuming fire?
Who among us can live with continual burning?"
15 He who walks righteously, and speaks with sincerity,
He who rejects unjust gain,
And shakes his hands so that they hold no bribe;
He who stops his ears from hearing about bloodshed,
And shuts his eyes from looking upon evil;
16 He will dwell on the heights;
His refuge will be the impregnable rock;
His bread will be given *him;*
His water will be sure.

17¶ Your eyes will see the King in His beauty;
They will behold a far-distant land.
18 Your heart will meditate on terror:
"Where is he who counts?
Where is he who weighs?
Where is he who counts the towers?"
19 You will no longer see a fierce people,
A people of unintelligible speech which no one comprehends,
Of a stammering tongue which no one understands.
20 Look upon Zion, the city of our appointed feasts;
Your eyes shall see Jerusalem an undisturbed habitation,
A tent which shall not be folded,
Its stakes shall never be pulled up
Nor any of its cords be torn apart.
21 But there the majestic *One,* the LORD, shall be for us
A place of rivers *and* wide canals,
On which no boat with oars shall go,
And on which no mighty ship shall pass—
22 For the LORD is our judge,
The LORD is our lawgiver,
The LORD is our king;
He will save us—
23 Your tackle hangs slack;
It cannot hold the base of its mast firmly,
Nor spread out the sail.
Then the prey of an abundant spoil will be divided;
The lame will take the plunder.
24 And no resident will say, "I am sick";
The people who dwell there will be forgiven *their* iniquity.

*God's Wrath against Nations*

34 DRAW NEAR, O nations, to hear; and listen, O peoples!
Let the earth and all it contains hear, and the world and all that springs from it.
2 For the LORD's indignation is against all the nations,
And *His* wrath against all their armies;
He has utterly destroyed them,
He has given them over to slaughter.

## New International

10 "Now will I arise," says the LORD.
"Now will I be exalted;
now will I be lifted up.
11 You conceive chaff,
you give birth to straw;
your breath is a fire that consumes you.
12 The peoples will be burned as if to lime;
like cut thornbushes they will be set ablaze."

13 You who are far away, hear what I have done;
you who are near, acknowledge my power!
14 The sinners in Zion are terrified;
trembling grips the godless:
"Who of us can dwell with the consuming fire?
Who of us can dwell with everlasting burning?"
15 He who walks righteously
and speaks what is right,
who rejects gain from extortion
and keeps his hand from accepting bribes,
who stops his ears against plots of murder
and shuts his eyes against contemplating evil—
16 this is the man who will dwell on the heights,
whose refuge will be the mountain fortress.
His bread will be supplied,
and water will not fail him.

17 Your eyes will see the king in his beauty
and view a land that stretches afar.
18 In your thoughts you will ponder the former terror:
"Where is that chief officer?
Where is the one who took the revenue?
Where is the officer in charge of the towers?"
19 You will see those arrogant people no more,
those people of an obscure speech,
with their strange, incomprehensible tongue.

20 Look upon Zion, the city of our festivals;
your eyes will see Jerusalem,
a peaceful abode, a tent that will not be moved;
its stakes will never be pulled up,
nor any of its ropes broken.
21 There the LORD will be our Mighty One.
It will be like a place of broad rivers and streams.
No galley with oars will ride them,
no mighty ship will sail them.
22 For the LORD is our judge,
the LORD is our lawgiver,
the LORD is our king;
it is he who will save us.

23 Your rigging hangs loose:
The mast is not held secure,
the sail is not spread.
Then an abundance of spoils will be divided
and even the lame will carry off plunder.
24 No one living in Zion will say, "I am ill";
and the sins of those who dwell there will be forgiven.

*Judgment Against the Nations*

34 COME NEAR, you nations, and listen;
pay attention, you peoples!
Let the earth hear, and all that is in it,
the world, and all that comes out of it!
2 The LORD is angry with all nations;
his wrath is upon all their armies.
He will totally destroy[a] them,
he will give them over to slaughter.

**NIV** [a] 2 The Hebrew term refers to the irrevocable giving over of things or persons to the LORD, often by totally destroying them; also in verse 5.

## King James

3Their slain also shall be cast out, and their stink shall come up out of their carcases, and the mountains shall be melted with their blood.

4And all the host of heaven shall be dissolved, and the heavens shall be rolled together as a scroll: and all their host shall fall down, as the leaf falleth off from the vine, and as a falling *fig* from the fig tree.

5For my sword shall be bathed in heaven: behold, it shall come down upon Idumea, and upon the people of my curse, to judgment.

6The sword of the LORD is filled with blood, it is made fat with fatness, *and* with the blood of lambs and goats, with the fat of the kidneys of rams: for the LORD hath a sacrifice in Bozrah, and a great slaughter in the land of Idumea.

7And the unicorns shall come down with them, and the bullocks with the bulls; and their land shall be soaked with blood, and their dust made fat with fatness.

8For *it is* the day of the LORD's vengeance, *and* the year of recompences for the controversy of Zion.

9And the streams thereof shall be turned into pitch, and the dust thereof into brimstone, and the land thereof shall become burning pitch.

10It shall not be quenched night nor day; the smoke thereof shall go up for ever: from generation to generation it shall lie waste; none shall pass through it for ever and ever.

11¶ But the cormorant and the bittern shall possess it; the owl also and the raven shall dwell in it: and he shall stretch out upon it the line of confusion, and the stones of emptiness.

12They shall call the nobles thereof to the kingdom, but none *shall be* there, and all her princes shall be nothing.

13And thorns shall come up in her palaces, nettles and brambles in the fortresses thereof: and it shall be an habitation of dragons, *and* a court for owls.

14The wild beasts of the desert shall also meet with the wild beasts of the island, and the satyr shall cry to his fellow; the screech owl also shall rest there, and find for herself a place of rest.

15There shall the great owl make her nest, and lay, and hatch, and gather under her shadow: there shall the vultures also be gathered, every one with her mate.

16¶ Seek ye out of the book of the LORD, and read: no one of these shall fail, none shall want her mate: for my mouth it hath commanded, and his spirit it hath gathered them.

17And he hath cast the lot for them, and his hand hath divided it unto them by line: they shall possess it for ever, from generation to generation shall they dwell therein.

## Amplified

3Their slain also shall be cast out, and the stench of their dead bodies shall rise, and the mountains shall *flow* with their blood.

4All the host of the heavens shall be dissolved *and* crumble away, and the skies shall be rolled together as a scroll; and all their host [the stars and the planets] shall drop like a faded leaf from the vine, and as a *withered fig* falls from the fig tree. [Rev. 6:13, 14.]

5Because My sword has been bathed *and* equipped in Heaven, behold, it shall come down upon Edom [the descendants of Esau], upon the people whom I have doomed for judgment. [Obad. 8-21.]

6The sword of the Lord is filled with blood *of sacrifices*, it is gorged *and* greased with fatness, with the blood of lambs and goats, with the fat of the kidneys of rams; for the Lord has a sacrifice in Bozrah [capital of Edom], and a great slaughter in the land of Edom.

7And the wild oxen shall fall with them, and the *young* bullocks with the *old and mighty* bulls, and their land shall be drunk *and* soaked with blood, and their dust made rich with fatness.

8For the Lord has a day of vengeance, a year of recompense for the cause of Zion.

9And the streams *of Edom* shall be turned into pitch, and its dust into brimstone, and its land will become burning pitch.

10 *The burning of Edom* shall not be quenched night or day; its smoke shall go up for ever; from generation to generation it shall lie waste; none shall pass through it for ever and ever. [Rev. 19:3.]

11But the pelican and the porcupine shall possess it; the owl *and* the bittern and the raven shall dwell in it; and He will stretch over it the [measuring] line of confusion, and the plummet stones of chaos *over* its nobles.

12They shall call its nobles to proclaim the kingdom, but none shall be there, and all its princes shall be no more.

13And thorns shall come up in its palaces *and* strongholds, nettles and brambles in its fortresses, and it shall be a habitation of jackals, an abode for ostriches.

14And the wild beasts of the desert will meet here with howling creatures—wolves and hyenas; and the *shaggy* wild goat will call to his fellow; the night monster will settle there and find a place of rest.

15There shall the arrow snake make her nest and lay her eggs, and hatch them and gather her young under her shade; there shall the kites be gathered *also to breed*, every one with her mate.

16Seek out of the book of the Lord, and read: no one of these [details of prophecy] shall fail, none shall want her mate [in fulfillment]; for the mouth *of the Lord* has commanded, and His Spirit has gathered them.

17And He has cast the lot for them, and His hand has portioned *Edom* to *the wild beasts* by measuring line; they shall possess it for ever, from generation to generation they shall dwell in it.

## New American Standard

3 So their slain will be thrown out,
And their corpses will give off their stench,
And the mountains will be drenched with their blood.
4 And all the host of heaven will wear away,
And the sky will be rolled up like a scroll;
All their hosts will also wither away
As a leaf withers from the vine,
Or as *one* withers from the fig tree.
5 For My sword is satiated in heaven,
Behold it shall descend for judgment upon Edom,
And upon the people whom I have devoted to
destruction.
6 The sword of the LORD is filled with blood,
It is sated with fat, with the blood of lambs and goats,
With the fat of the kidneys of rams.
For the LORD has a sacrifice in Bozrah,
And a great slaughter in the land of Edom.
7 Wild oxen shall also fall with them,
And young bulls with strong ones;
Thus their land shall be soaked with blood,
And their dust become greasy with fat.
8 For the LORD has a day of vengeance,
A year of recompense for the cause of Zion.
9 And its streams shall be turned into pitch,
And its loose earth into brimstone,
And its land shall become burning pitch.
10 It shall not be quenched night or day;
Its smoke shall go up forever;
From generation to generation it shall be desolate;
None shall pass through it forever and ever.
11 But pelican and hedgehog shall possess it,
And owl and raven shall dwell in it;
And He shall stretch over it the line of desolation
And the plumb line of emptiness.
12 Its nobles—there is no one there
*Whom* they may proclaim king—
And all its princes shall be nothing.
13 And thorns shall come up in its fortified towers,
Nettles and thistles in its fortified cities;
It shall also be a haunt of jackals
*And* an abode of ostriches.
14 And the desert creatures shall meet with the wolves,
The hairy goat also shall cry to its kind;
Yes, the night monster shall settle there
And shall find herself a resting place.
15 The tree snake shall make its nest and lay *eggs* there,
And it will hatch and gather *them* under its protection.
Yes, the hawks shall be gathered there,
Every one with its kind.

16¶ Seek from the book of the LORD, and read:
Not one of these will be missing;
None will lack its mate.
For His mouth has commanded,
And His Spirit has gathered them.
17 And He has cast the lot for them,
And His hand has divided it to them by line.
They shall possess it forever;
From generation to generation they shall dwell in it.

## New International

3Their slain will be thrown out,
their dead bodies will send up a stench;
the mountains will be soaked with their blood.
4All the stars of the heavens will be dissolved
and the sky rolled up like a scroll;
all the starry host will fall
like withered leaves from the vine,
like shriveled figs from the fig tree.

5My sword has drunk its fill in the heavens;
see, it descends in judgment on Edom,
the people I have totally destroyed.
6The sword of the LORD is bathed in blood,
it is covered with fat—
the blood of lambs and goats,
fat from the kidneys of rams.
For the LORD has a sacrifice in Bozrah
and a great slaughter in Edom.
7And the wild oxen will fall with them,
the bull calves and the great bulls.
Their land will be drenched with blood,
and the dust will be soaked with fat.

8For the LORD has a day of vengeance,
a year of retribution, to uphold Zion's cause.
9Edom's streams will be turned into pitch,
her dust into burning sulfur;
her land will become blazing pitch!
10It will not be quenched night and day;
its smoke will rise forever.
From generation to generation it will lie desolate;
no one will ever pass through it again.
11The desert owl[a] and screech owl[b] will possess it;
the great owl[c] and the raven will nest there.
God will stretch out over Edom
the measuring line of chaos
and the plumb line of desolation.
12Her nobles will have nothing there to be called a
kingdom,
all her princes will vanish away.
13Thorns will overrun her citadels,
nettles and brambles her strongholds.
She will become a haunt for jackals,
a home for owls.
14Desert creatures will meet with hyenas,
and wild goats will bleat to each other;
there the night creatures will also repose
and find for themselves places of rest.
15The owl will nest there and lay eggs,
she will hatch them, and care for her young under the
shadow of her wings;
there also the falcons will gather,
each with its mate.

16Look in the scroll of the LORD and read:

None of these will be missing,
not one will lack her mate.
For it is his mouth that has given the order,
and his Spirit will gather them together.
17He allots their portions;
his hand distributes them by measure.
They will possess it forever
and dwell there from generation to generation.

**NIV** [a] *11* The precise identification of these birds is uncertain. [b] *11* The precise identification of these birds is uncertain. [c] *11* The precise identification of these birds is uncertain.

## King James

**35** THE WILDERNESS and the solitary place shall be glad for them; and the desert shall rejoice, and blossom as the rose.

2 It shall blossom abundantly, and rejoice even with joy and singing: the glory of Lebanon shall be given unto it, the excellency of Carmel and Sharon, they shall see the glory of the LORD, *and* the excellency of our God.

3 ¶ Strengthen ye the weak hands, and confirm the feeble knees.

4 Say to them *that are* of a fearful heart, Be strong, fear not: behold, your God will come *with* vengeance, *even* God *with* a recompence; he will come and save you.

5 Then the eyes of the blind shall be opened, and the ears of the deaf shall be unstopped.

6 Then shall the lame *man* leap as an hart, and the tongue of the dumb sing: for in the wilderness shall waters break out, and streams in the desert.

7 And the parched ground shall become a pool, and the thirsty land springs of water: in the habitation of dragons, where each lay, *shall be* grass with reeds and rushes.

8 And an highway shall be there, and a way, and it shall be called The way of holiness; the unclean shall not pass over it; but it *shall be* for those: the wayfaring men, though fools, shall not err *therein.*

9 No lion shall be there, nor *any* ravenous beast shall go up thereon, it shall not be found there; but the redeemed shall walk *there:*

10 And the ransomed of the LORD shall return, and come to Zion with songs and everlasting joy upon their heads: they shall obtain joy and gladness, and sorrow and sighing shall flee away.

**36** NOW IT came to pass in the fourteenth year of king Hezekiah, *that* Sennacherib king of Assyria came up against all the defenced cities of Judah, and took them.

2 And the king of Assyria sent Rab-shakeh from Lachish to Jerusalem unto king Hezekiah with a great army. And he stood by the conduit of the upper pool in the highway of the fuller's field.

3 Then came forth unto him Eliakim, Hilkiah's son, which was over the house, and Shebna the scribe, and Joah, Asaph's son, the recorder.

4 ¶ And Rab-shakeh said unto them, Say ye now to Hezekiah, Thus saith the great king, the king of Assyria, What confidence *is* this wherein thou trustest?

5 I say, *sayest thou,* (but *they are but* vain words) *I have* counsel and strength for war: now on whom dost thou trust, that thou rebellest against me?

6 Lo, thou trustest in the staff of this broken reed, on Egypt; whereon if a man lean, it will go into his hand, and pierce it: so *is* Pharaoh king of Egypt to all that trust in him.

## Amplified

**35** THE WILDERNESS and the dry land shall be glad, the desert shall rejoice and blossom as the rose *and* the autumn crocus.

2 It shall blossom abundantly, and rejoice even with joy and singing; the glory of Lebanon shall be given to it, the excellency of *Mount* Carmel and *the plain* of Sharon. They shall see the glory of the Lord, the majesty *and* splendor *and* excellency of our God.

3 Strengthen the weak hands, and make firm the feeble *and* tottering knees. [Heb. 12:12.]

4 Say to those who are of a fearful *and* hasty heart, Be strong, fear not! Behold, your God will come with vengeance, with the recompense of God; He will come and save you.

5 Then the eyes of the blind shall be opened, and the ears of the deaf shall be unstopped;

6 Then shall the lame man leap like a hart, and the tongue of the dumb shall sing for joy; for waters shall break forth in the wilderness, and streams in the desert. [Matt. 11:5.]

7 And the burning sand *and* the mirage shall become a pool, and the thirsty ground springs of water; in the haunt of jackals, where they lay resting, shall be grass with reeds and rushes.

8 And a highway shall be there, and a way, and it shall be called The Holy Way; the unclean shall not pass over it, but it shall be for the redeemed; the wayfaring men, yes, the simple ones *and* fools, shall not err in it *and* lose their way.

9 No lion shall be there, nor shall any ravenous beast come up on it; they shall not be found there; but the redeemed shall walk on it.

10 And the ransomed of the Lord shall return, and come to Zion with singing, and everlasting joy shall be upon their heads; they shall obtain joy and gladness, and sorrow and sighing shall flee away.

**36** NOW IN the fourteenth year of King Hezekiah, Sennacherib king of Assyria came up against all the fortified cities of Judah and took them.

2 And the king of Assyria sent the Rabshakeh [the military official] from Lachish [the Judean fortress commanding the road from Egypt] to King Hezekiah at Jerusalem with a great army. And he stood by the canal of the upper pool in the highway of the fuller's field.

3 Then came out to meet him Eliakim, the son of Hilkiah, who was over the *royal* household, and Shebna the secretary, and Joah the son of Asaph, the recording *historian.*

4 And the Rabshakeh said to them, Say to Hezekiah, Thus says the great king, the king of Assyria, What reason for confidence is this in which you trust?

5 Do you suppose that mere words of the lips can pass for warlike counsel and strength? Now in whom do you trust *and* on whom do you rely that you have rebelled against me?

6 Behold, you trust on the staff of this bruised *and* broken reed, Egypt, which will pierce the hand of any man who leans on it. So is Pharaoh king of Egypt to all who trust *and* rely on him.

## New American Standard

*Zion's Happy Future*

**35** THE WILDERNESS and the desert will be glad,
And the Arabah will rejoice and blossom;
Like the crocus
2 It will blossom profusely
And rejoice with rejoicing and shout of joy.
The glory of Lebanon will be given to it,
The majesty of Carmel and Sharon.
They will see the glory of the LORD,
The majesty of our God.
3 Encourage the exhausted, and strengthen the feeble.
4 Say to those with anxious heart,
"Take courage, fear not.
Behold, your God will come *with* vengeance;
The recompense of God will come,
But He will save you."
5 Then the eyes of the blind will be opened,
And the ears of the deaf will be unstopped.
6 Then the lame will leap like a deer,
And the tongue of the dumb will shout for joy.
For waters will break forth in the wilderness
And streams in the Arabah.
7 And the scorched land will become a pool,
And the thirsty ground springs of water;
In the haunt of jackals, its resting place,
Grass *becomes* reeds and rushes.
8 And a highway will be there, a roadway,
And it will be called the Highway of Holiness.
The unclean will not travel on it,
But it *will* be for him who walks *that* way,
And fools will not wander *on it*.
9 No lion will be there,
Nor will any vicious beast go up on it;
These will not be found there.
But the redeemed will walk *there*,
10 And the ransomed of the LORD will return,
And come with joyful shouting to Zion,
With everlasting joy upon their heads.
They will find gladness and joy,
And sorrow and sighing will flee away.

*Sennacherib Invades Judah*

**36** NOW IT came about in the fourteenth year of King Hezekiah, Sennacherib king of Assyria came up against all the fortified cities of Judah and seized them.
2And the king of Assyria sent Rabshakeh from Lachish to Jerusalem to King Hezekiah with a large army. And he stood by the conduit of the upper pool on the highway of the fuller's field.
3Then Eliakim the son of Hilkiah, who was over the household, and Shebna the scribe, and Joah the son of Asaph, the recorder, came out to him.
4¶ Then Rabshakeh said to them, "Say now to Hezekiah, 'Thus says the great king, the king of Assyria, "What is this confidence that you have?
5"I say, 'Your counsel and strength for the war are only empty words.' Now on whom do you rely, that you have rebelled against me?
6"Behold, you rely on the staff of this crushed reed, *even* on Egypt; on which if a man leans, it will go into his hand and pierce it. So is Pharaoh king of Egypt to all who rely on him.

## New International

*Joy of the Redeemed*

**35** THE DESERT and the parched land will be glad;
the wilderness will rejoice and blossom.
Like the crocus, 2it will burst into bloom;
it will rejoice greatly and shout for joy.
The glory of Lebanon will be given to it,
the splendor of Carmel and Sharon;
they will see the glory of the LORD,
the splendor of our God.

3Strengthen the feeble hands,
steady the knees that give way;
4say to those with fearful hearts,
"Be strong, do not fear;
your God will come,
he will come with vengeance;
with divine retribution
he will come to save you."

5Then will the eyes of the blind be opened
and the ears of the deaf unstopped.
6Then will the lame leap like a deer,
and the mute tongue shout for joy.
Water will gush forth in the wilderness
and streams in the desert.
7The burning sand will become a pool,
the thirsty ground bubbling springs.
In the haunts where jackals once lay,
grass and reeds and papyrus will grow.
8And a highway will be there;
it will be called the Way of Holiness.
The unclean will not journey on it;
it will be for those who walk in that Way;
wicked fools will not go about on it.[a]
9No lion will be there,
nor will any ferocious beast get up on it;
they will not be found there.
But only the redeemed will walk there,
10 and the ransomed of the LORD will return.
They will enter Zion with singing;
everlasting joy will crown their heads.
Gladness and joy will overtake them,
and sorrow and sighing will flee away.

*Sennacherib Threatens Jerusalem*

**36** IN THE fourteenth year of King Hezekiah's reign, Sennacherib king of Assyria attacked all the fortified cities of Judah and captured them. 2Then the king of Assyria sent his field commander with a large army from Lachish to King Hezekiah at Jerusalem. When the commander stopped at the aqueduct of the Upper Pool, on the road to the Washerman's Field, 3Eliakim son of Hilkiah the palace administrator, Shebna the secretary, and Joah son of Asaph the recorder went out to him.
4The field commander said to them, "Tell Hezekiah,

" 'This is what the great king, the king of Assyria, says: On what are you basing this confidence of yours? 5You say you have strategy and military strength—but you speak only empty words. On whom are you depending, that you rebel against me? 6Look now, you are depending on Egypt, that splintered reed of a staff, which pierces a man's hand and wounds him if he leans on it! Such is Pharaoh king of Egypt to all who depend on him. 7And if you say to me, "We are

NIV [a] 8 Or / *the simple will not stray from it*

## King James

7But if thou say to me, We trust in the LORD our God: *is it* not he, whose high places and whose altars Hezekiah hath taken away, and said to Judah and to Jerusalem, Ye shall worship before this altar?

8Now therefore give pledges, I pray thee, to my master the king of Assyria, and I will give thee two thousand horses, if thou be able on thy part to set riders upon them.

9How then wilt thou turn away the face of one captain of the least of my master's servants, and put thy trust on Egypt for chariots and for horsemen?

10And am I now come up without the LORD against this land to destroy it? the LORD said unto me, Go up against this land, and destroy it.

11¶ Then said Eliakim and Shebna and Joah unto Rab-shakeh, Speak, I pray thee, unto thy servants in the Syrian language; for we understand *it:* and speak not to us in the Jews' language, in the ears of the people that *are* on the wall.

12¶ But Rab-shakeh said, Hath my master sent me to thy master and to thee to speak these words? *hath he* not *sent me* to the men that sit upon the wall, that they may eat their own dung, and drink their own piss with you?

13Then Rab-shakeh stood, and cried with a loud voice in the Jews' language, and said, Hear ye the words of the great king, the king of Assyria.

14Thus saith the king, Let not Hezekiah deceive you: for he shall not be able to deliver you.

15Neither let Hezekiah make you trust in the LORD, saying, The LORD will surely deliver us: this city shall not be delivered into the hand of the king of Assyria.

16Hearken not to Hezekiah: for thus saith the king of Assyria, Make *an agreement* with me *by* a present, and come out to me: and eat ye every one of his vine, and every one of his fig tree, and drink ye every one the waters of his own cistern;

17Until I come and take you away to a land like your own land, a land of corn and wine, a land of bread and vineyards.

18 *Beware* lest Hezekiah persuade you, saying, The LORD will deliver us. Hath any of the gods of the nations delivered his land out of the hand of the king of Assyria?

19Where *are* the gods of Hamath and Arphad? where *are* the gods of Sepharvaim? and have they delivered Samaria out of my hand?

20Who *are they* among all the gods of these lands, that have delivered their land out of my hand, that the LORD should deliver Jerusalem out of my hand?

21But they held their peace, and answered him not a word: for the king's commandment was, saying, Answer him not.

22¶ Then came Eliakim, the son of Hilkiah, that *was* over the household, and Shebna the scribe, and Joah, the son of Asaph, the recorder, to Hezekiah with *their* clothes rent, and told him the words of Rab-shakeh.

**37** AND IT came to pass, when king Hezekiah heard *it,* that he rent his clothes, and covered himself with sackcloth, and went into the house of the LORD.

2And he sent Eliakim, who *was* over the household, and Shebna the scribe, and the elders of the priests covered with sackcloth, unto Isaiah the prophet the son of Amoz.

3And they said unto him, Thus saith Hezekiah, This day *is* a day of trouble, and of rebuke, and of blasphemy: for the children are come to the birth, and *there is* not strength to bring forth.

## Amplified

7But if you say to me, We trust in *and* rely on the Lord our God, is it not He, whose high places and whose altars Hezekiah has taken away, and said to Judah and to Jerusalem, You shall worship before this altar? [II Kings 18:4, 5.]

8Now therefore, I pray you, make a wager with my master the king of Assyria, *and* give him pledges, and I will give you two thousand horses, if you are able on your part to put riders on them.

9How then can you repulse the attack of a single captain of the least of my master's servants when you put your reliance on Egypt for chariots and for horsemen?

10Moreover, is it without the Lord that I have now come up against this land to destroy it? The Lord said to me, Go up against this land, and destroy it.

11Then Eliakim and Shebna and Joah said to the Rabshakeh, Pray, speak to your servants in the Aramaic *or* Syrian language, for we understand it; and do not speak to us in the language of the Jews in the hearing of the people on the wall.

12But the Rabshakeh said, Has my master sent me to speak these words to your master and to you? Has he not sent me to the men sitting on the wall, who are doomed with you to eat their own dung and drink their own urine?

13Then the Rabshakeh stood and cried with a loud voice in the language of the Jews: Hear the words of the great king, the king of Assyria!

14Thus says the king, Let not Hezekiah deceive you, for he will not be able to deliver you.

15Neither let Hezekiah make you trust *and* rely on the Lord, saying, The Lord will surely deliver us; this city will not be delivered into the hand of the king of Assyria.

16Do not listen to Hezekiah; for thus says the king of Assyria: Make your peace with me and come out to me; and eat every one of his own vine and every one of his own fig tree, and drink every one the water of his own cistern;

17Until I come and take you away to a land like your own land, a land of grain and wine, a land of bread and vineyards.

18Beware lest Hezekiah persuade *and* mislead you by saying, The Lord will deliver us. Has any of the gods of the nations delivered his land out of the hand of the king of Assyria?

19Where are the gods of Hamath and Arphad [in Syria]? Where are the gods of Sepharvaim [a place from which the Assyrians brought colonists to inhabit evacuated Samaria]? And have *the gods* delivered Samaria [capital of the ten northern tribes of Israel] out of my hand?

20Who among all the gods of these lands have delivered their land out of my hand, that *you should think* the Lord can deliver Jerusalem out of my hand?

21But they kept still and answered him not a word, for the king's command was, Do not answer him.

22Then Eliakim the son of Hilkiah, who was over the household, and Shebna the secretary, and Joah the son of Asaph, the recording *historian,* came to Hezekiah with their clothes rent, and told him the words of the Rabshakeh [the Assyrian military official].

**37** AND WHEN King Hezekiah heard it, he rent his clothes, and covered himself with sackcloth, and went into the house of the Lord.

2And he sent Eliakim, who was over the *royal* household, and Shebna the secretary, and the older priests, clothed with sackcloth, to Isaiah the prophet, the son of Amoz.

3And they said to him, Thus says Hezekiah, This day is a day of trouble *and* distress, and of rebuke, and of disgrace; for the children have come to the birth, and there is not strength to bring them forth.

## New American Standard

7"But if you say to me, 'We trust in the LORD our God,' is it
not He whose high places and whose altars Hezekiah has taken
away, and has said to Judah and to Jerusalem, 'You shall worship
before this altar'?
8"Now therefore, come make a bargain with my master the
king of Assyria, and I will give you two thousand horses, if you
are able on your part to set riders on them.
9"How then can you repulse one official of the least of my
master's servants, and rely on Egypt for chariots and for horsemen?
10"And have I now come up without the LORD's approval
against this land to destroy it? The LORD said to me, 'Go up against
this land, and destroy it.' " ' "
11¶ Then Eliakim and Shebna and Joah said to Rabshakeh,
"Speak now to your servants in Aramaic, for we understand *it;* and
do not speak with us in Judean, in the hearing of the people who
are on the wall."
12But Rabshakeh said, "Has my master sent me only to your
master and to you to speak these words, *and* not to the men who
sit on the wall, *doomed* to eat their own dung and drink their own
urine with you?"
13¶ Then Rabshakeh stood and cried with a loud voice in Judean, and said, "Hear the words of the great king, the king of
Assyria.
14"Thus says the king, 'Do not let Hezekiah deceive you, for he
will not be able to deliver you;
15nor let Hezekiah make you trust in the LORD, saying, "The
LORD will surely deliver us, this city shall not be given into the
hand of the king of Assyria."
16'Do not listen to Hezekiah,' for thus says the king of Assyria,
'Make your peace with me and come out to me, and eat each of
his vine and each of his fig tree and drink each of the waters of his
own cistern,
17until I come and take you away to a land like your own land,
a land of grain and new wine, a land of bread and vineyards.
18' *Beware* lest Hezekiah misleads you, saying, "The LORD will
deliver us." Has any one of the gods of the nations delivered his
land from the hand of the king of Assyria?
19'Where are the gods of Hamath and Arpad? Where are the
gods of Sepharvaim? And when have they delivered Samaria from
my hand?
20'Who among all the gods of these lands have delivered their
land from my hand, that the LORD should deliver Jerusalem from
my hand?' "
21¶ But they were silent and answered him not a word; for the
king's commandment was, "Do not answer him."
22Then Eliakim the son of Hilkiah, who was over the household, and Shebna the scribe and Joah the son of Asaph, the
recorder, came to Hezekiah with their clothes torn and told him
the words of Rabshakeh.

*Hezekiah Seeks Isaiah's Help*

**37** AND WHEN King Hezekiah heard *it,* he tore his clothes,
covered himself with sackcloth and entered the house of
the LORD.
2Then he sent Eliakim who was over the household with Shebna the scribe and the elders of the priests, covered with sackcloth,
to Isaiah the prophet, the son of Amoz.
3And they said to him, "Thus says Hezekiah, 'This day is a day
of distress, rebuke, and rejection; for children have come to birth,
and there is no strength to deliver.

## New International

depending on the LORD our God"—isn't he the one whose
high places and altars Hezekiah removed, saying to Judah
and Jerusalem, "You must worship before this altar"?
8" 'Come now, make a bargain with my master, the king
of Assyria: I will give you two thousand horses—if you can
put riders on them! 9How then can you repulse one officer of
the least of my master's officials, even though you are depending on Egypt for chariots and horsemen? 10Furthermore,
have I come to attack and destroy this land without the LORD?
The LORD himself told me to march against this country and
destroy it.' "

11Then Eliakim, Shebna and Joah said to the field commander,
"Please speak to your servants in Aramaic, since we understand
it. Don't speak to us in Hebrew in the hearing of the people on the
wall."
12But the commander replied, "Was it only to your master and
you that my master sent me to say these things, and not to the men
sitting on the wall—who, like you, will have to eat their own filth
and drink their own urine?"
13Then the commander stood and called out in Hebrew, "Hear
the words of the great king, the king of Assyria! 14This is what the
king says: Do not let Hezekiah deceive you. He cannot deliver you!
15Do not let Hezekiah persuade you to trust in the LORD when he
says, 'The LORD will surely deliver us; this city will not be given
into the hand of the king of Assyria.'
16"Do not listen to Hezekiah. This is what the king of Assyria
says: Make peace with me and come out to me. Then every one
of you will eat from his own vine and fig tree and drink water from
his own cistern, 17until I come and take you to a land like your
own—a land of grain and new wine, a land of bread and vineyards.
18"Do not let Hezekiah mislead you when he says, 'The LORD
will deliver us.' Has the god of any nation ever delivered his land
from the hand of the king of Assyria? 19Where are the gods of
Hamath and Arpad? Where are the gods of Sepharvaim? Have
they rescued Samaria from my hand? 20Who of all the gods of these
countries has been able to save his land from me? How then can
the LORD deliver Jerusalem from my hand?"
21But the people remained silent and said nothing in reply,
because the king had commanded, "Do not answer him."
22Then Eliakim son of Hilkiah the palace administrator, Shebna
the secretary, and Joah son of Asaph the recorder went to Hezekiah, with their clothes torn, and told him what the field commander had said.

*Jerusalem's Deliverance Foretold*

**37** WHEN KING Hezekiah heard this, he tore his clothes and
put on sackcloth and went into the temple of the LORD.
2He sent Eliakim the palace administrator, Shebna the secretary,
and the leading priests, all wearing sackcloth, to the prophet Isaiah
son of Amoz. 3They told him, "This is what Hezekiah says: This
day is a day of distress and rebuke and disgrace, as when children
come to the point of birth and there is no strength to deliver them.

## King James

4 It may be the LORD thy God will hear the words of Rab-shakeh, whom the king of Assyria his master hath sent to reproach the living God, and will reprove the words which the LORD thy God hath heard: wherefore lift up *thy* prayer for the remnant that is left.

5 So the servants of king Hezekiah came to Isaiah.

6 ¶ And Isaiah said unto them, Thus shall ye say unto your master, Thus saith the LORD, Be not afraid of the words that thou hast heard, wherewith the servants of the king of Assyria have blasphemed me.

7 Behold, I will send a blast upon him, and he shall hear a rumour, and return to his own land; and I will cause him to fall by the sword in his own land.

8 ¶ So Rab-shakeh returned, and found the king of Assyria warring against Libnah: for he had heard that he was departed from Lachish.

9 And he heard say concerning Tirhakah king of Ethiopia, He is come forth to make war with thee. And when he heard *it*, he sent messengers to Hezekiah, saying,

10 Thus shall ye speak to Hezekiah king of Judah, saying, Let not thy God, in whom thou trustest, deceive thee, saying, Jerusalem shall not be given into the hand of the king of Assyria.

11 Behold, thou hast heard what the kings of Assyria have done to all lands by destroying them utterly; and shalt thou be delivered?

12 Have the gods of the nations delivered them which my fathers have destroyed, *as* Gozan, and Haran, and Rezeph, and the children of Eden which *were* in Telassar?

13 Where *is* the king of Hamath, and the king of Arphad, and the king of the city of Sepharvaim, Hena, and Ivah?

14 ¶ And Hezekiah received the letter from the hand of the messengers, and read it: and Hezekiah went up unto the house of the LORD, and spread it before the LORD.

15 And Hezekiah prayed unto the LORD, saying,

16 O LORD of hosts, God of Israel, that dwellest *between* the cherubims, thou *art* the God, *even* thou alone, of all the kingdoms of the earth: thou hast made heaven and earth.

17 Incline thine ear, O LORD, and hear; open thine eyes, O LORD, and see: and hear all the words of Sennacherib, which hath sent to reproach the living God.

18 Of a truth, LORD, the kings of Assyria have laid waste all the nations, and their countries,

19 And have cast their gods into the fire: for they *were* no gods, but the work of men's hands, wood and stone: therefore they have destroyed them.

20 Now therefore, O LORD our God, save us from his hand, that all the kingdoms of the earth may know that thou *art* the LORD, *even* thou only.

21 ¶ Then Isaiah the son of Amoz sent unto Hezekiah, saying, Thus saith the LORD God of Israel, Whereas thou hast prayed to me against Sennacherib king of Assyria:

22 This *is* the word which the LORD hath spoken concerning him; The virgin, the daughter of Zion, hath despised thee, *and* laughed thee to scorn; the daughter of Jerusalem hath shaken her head at thee.

23 Whom hast thou reproached and blasphemed? and against whom hast thou exalted *thy* voice, and lifted up thine eyes on high? *even* against the Holy One of Israel.

24 By thy servants hast thou reproached the Lord, and hast said, By the multitude of my chariots am I come up to the height of the mountains, to the sides of Lebanon; and I will cut down the tall cedars thereof, *and* the choice fir trees thereof: and I will enter into the height of his border, *and* the forest of his Carmel.

## Amplified

4 It may be the Lord your God has heard the words of the Rabshakeh, whom the king of Assyria his master has sent to mock, reproach, insult *and* defy the living God, and will rebuke the words which the Lord your God has heard. Therefore lift up your prayer for the remnant [of His people] that is left.

5 So the servants of King Hezekiah came to Isaiah.

6 And Isaiah said to them, You shall say to your master, Thus says the Lord, Do not be afraid *because* of the words which you have heard, with which the servants of the king of Assyria have reviled *and* blasphemed Me.

7 Behold, I will put a spirit in him so that he will hear a rumor, and return to his own land; and I will cause him to fall by the sword in his own land.

8 So the Rabshakeh returned, and found the king of Assyria fighting against Libnah [a fortified city of Judah]; for he had heard that *the king* had departed from Lachish.

9 And *Sennacherib the king of Assyria* heard concerning Tirhakah the king of Ethiopia, He has come forth to make war with you. And when he heard it, he sent messengers to Hezekiah, saying,

10 Thus shall you speak to Hezekiah king of Judah: Let not your God in Whom you trust deceive you by saying, Jerusalem shall not be given into the hand of the king of Assyria.

11 Behold, you have heard what the kings of Assyria have done to all lands, destroying them utterly. And shall you be delivered?

12 Have the gods of the nations delivered those whom my predecessors have destroyed, as [a]Gozan, Haran [of Mesopotamia], Rezeph, and the children of Eden that were in Telassar?

13 Where are the king of Hamath, and the king of Arpad [of northern Syria], and the king of the city of Sepharvaim, the king of Hena, or the king of Ivvah?

14 And Hezekiah received the letter from the hand of the messengers, and read it. And Hezekiah went up to the house of the Lord, and spread it before the Lord.

15 And Hezekiah prayed to the Lord:

16 O Lord of hosts, God of Israel, Who [in symbol] are enthroned above the cherubim [of the ark in the temple], You are the God, You alone, of all the kingdoms of the earth; You have made Heaven and earth.

17 Incline Your ear, O Lord, and hear; open Your eyes, O Lord, and see; and hear all the words of Sennacherib, which he has sent to mock, reproach, insult *and* defy the living God.

18 It is true, Lord, that the kings of Assyria have laid waste all the nations and their lands,

19 And have cast the gods of those peoples into the fire; for they were no gods, but the work of men's hands, wood and stone; therefore they have destroyed them.

20 Now therefore, O Lord our God, save us from his hand, that all the kingdoms of the earth may know—understand and realize—that You are the Lord, even You only.

21 Then Isaiah the son of Amoz sent to Hezekiah, saying, Thus says the Lord God of Israel, Because you have prayed to Me against Sennacherib king of Assyria,

22 This is the word which the Lord has spoken concerning him: The virgin daughter of Zion has despised you and laughed you to scorn; the daughter of Jerusalem has shaken her head behind you.

23 Whom have you mocked and reviled—insulted and blasphemed? And against whom have you raised your voice and haughtily lifted your eyes? Against the Holy One of Israel!

24 By your servants you have mocked, reproached, insulted *and* defied the Lord, and you have said, With my many chariots I have come up to the height of the mountains, to the inner recesses of Lebanon; I cut down its tallest cedars *and* its choicest cypress trees; I came to its remotest height, its most luxuriant *and* dense forest;

**AMP** [a] The place-names in this verse are all found on the Assyrian monuments. See Cuneiform Inscriptions, Schrader, on II Kings 19:12. (Cambridge Bible.)

## New American Standard

4'Perhaps the LORD your God will hear the words of Rabshakeh, whom his master the king of Assyria has sent to reproach
the living God, and will rebuke the words which the LORD your
God has heard. Therefore, offer a prayer for the remnant that is
left.' "
5So the servants of King Hezekiah came to Isaiah.
6And Isaiah said to them, "Thus you shall say to your master,
'Thus says the LORD, "Do not be afraid because of the words that
you have heard, with which the servants of the king of Assyria
have blasphemed Me.
7"Behold, I will put a spirit in him so that he shall hear a rumor
and return to his own land. And I will make him fall by the sword
in his own land." ' "
8¶ Then Rabshakeh returned and found the king of Assyria
fighting against Libnah, for he had heard that the king had left
Lachish.
9When he heard *them* say concerning Tirhakah king of Cush,
"He has come out to fight against you," and when he heard *it* he
sent messengers to Hezekiah, saying,
10"Thus you shall say to Hezekiah king of Judah, 'Do not let
your God in whom you trust deceive you, saying, "Jerusalem shall
not be given into the hand of the king of Assyria."
11'Behold, you have heard what the kings of Assyria have done
to all the lands, destroying them completely. So will you be
spared?
12'Did the gods of those nations which my fathers have destroyed deliver them, *even* Gozan and Haran and Rezeph and the
sons of Eden who *were* in Telassar?
13'Where is the king of Hamath, the king of Arpad, the king of
the city of Sepharvaim, *and of* Hena and Ivvah?' "

*Hezekiah's Prayer in the Temple*

14¶ Then Hezekiah took the letter from the hand of the messengers and read it, and he went up to the house of the LORD and
spread it out before the LORD.
15And Hezekiah prayed to the LORD saying,
16"O LORD of hosts, the God of Israel, who art enthroned *above*
the cherubim, Thou art the God, Thou alone, of all the kingdoms
of the earth. Thou hast made heaven and earth.
17"Incline Thine ear, O LORD, and hear; open Thine eyes, O
LORD, and see; and listen to all the words of Sennacherib, who sent
*them* to reproach the living God.
18"Truly, O LORD, the kings of Assyria have devastated all the
countries and their lands,
19and have cast their gods into the fire, for they were not gods
but the work of men's hands, wood and stone. So they have
destroyed them.
20"And now, O LORD our God, deliver us from his hand that
all the kingdoms of the earth may know that Thou alone, LORD,
art God."

*God Answers through Isaiah*

21Then Isaiah the son of Amoz sent *word* to Hezekiah, saying,
"Thus says the LORD, the God of Israel, 'Because you have prayed
to Me about Sennacherib king of Assyria,
22this is the word that the LORD has spoken against him:
"She has despised you and mocked you,
The virgin daughter of Zion;
She has shaken *her* head behind you,
The daughter of Jerusalem!
23 "Whom have you reproached and blasphemed?
And against whom have you raised *your* voice,
And haughtily lifted up your eyes?
Against the Holy One of Israel!
24 "Through your servants you have reproached the Lord,
And you have said, 'With my many chariots I came up
to the heights of the mountains,
To the remotest parts of Lebanon;
And I cut down its tall cedars *and* its choice cypresses.
And I will go to its highest peak, its thickest forest.

## New International

4It may be that the LORD your God will hear the words of the field
commander, whom his master, the king of Assyria, has sent to
ridicule the living God, and that he will rebuke him for the words
the LORD your God has heard. Therefore pray for the remnant that
still survives."
5When King Hezekiah's officials came to Isaiah, 6Isaiah said to
them, "Tell your master, 'This is what the LORD says: Do not be
afraid of what you have heard—those words with which the un-
derlings of the king of Assyria have blasphemed me. 7Listen! I am
going to put a spirit in him so that when he hears a certain report,
he will return to his own country, and there I will have him cut
down with the sword.' "
8When the field commander heard that the king of Assyria had
left Lachish, he withdrew and found the king fighting against
Libnah.
9Now Sennacherib received a report that Tirhakah, the Cushite[b] king of Egypt, was marching out to fight against him. When
he heard it, he sent messengers to Hezekiah with this word: 10"Say
to Hezekiah king of Judah: Do not let the god you depend on
deceive you when he says, 'Jerusalem will not be handed over to
the king of Assyria.' 11Surely you have heard what the kings of
Assyria have done to all the countries, destroying them completely. And will you be delivered? 12Did the gods of the nations that
were destroyed by my forefathers deliver them—the gods of Gozan, Haran, Rezeph and the people of Eden who were in Tel
Assar? 13Where is the king of Hamath, the king of Arpad, the king
of the city of Sepharvaim, or of Hena or Ivvah?"

*Hezekiah's Prayer*

14Hezekiah received the letter from the messengers and read it.
Then he went up to the temple of the LORD and spread it out before
the LORD. 15And Hezekiah prayed to the LORD: 16"O LORD Almighty, God of Israel, enthroned between the cherubim, you
alone are God over all the kingdoms of the earth. You have made
heaven and earth. 17Give ear, O LORD, and hear; open your eyes,
O LORD, and see; listen to all the words Sennacherib has sent to
insult the living God.
18"It is true, O LORD, that the Assyrian kings have laid waste
all these peoples and their lands. 19They have thrown their gods
into the fire and destroyed them, for they were not gods but only
wood and stone, fashioned by human hands. 20Now, O LORD our
God, deliver us from his hand, so that all kingdoms on earth may
know that you alone, O LORD, are God.[c] "

*Sennacherib's Fall*

21Then Isaiah son of Amoz sent a message to Hezekiah: "This
is what the LORD, the God of Israel, says: Because you have prayed
to me concerning Sennacherib king of Assyria, 22this is the word
the LORD has spoken against him:

"The Virgin Daughter of Zion
despises and mocks you.
The Daughter of Jerusalem
tosses her head as you flee.
23Who is it you have insulted and blasphemed?
Against whom have you raised your voice
and lifted your eyes in pride?
Against the Holy One of Israel!
24By your messengers
you have heaped insults on the Lord.
And you have said,
'With my many chariots
I have ascended the heights of the mountains,
the utmost heights of Lebanon.
I have cut down its tallest cedars,
the choicest of its pines.
I have reached its remotest heights,
the finest of its forests.

**NIV** [b] 9 That is, from the upper Nile region [c] 20 Dead Sea Scrolls (see also 2 Kings 19:19); Masoretic Text *alone are the LORD*

## King James

25I have digged, and drunk water; and with the sole of my feet have I dried up all the rivers of the besieged places.

26Hast thou not heard long ago, *how* I have done it; *and* of ancient times, that I have formed it? now have I brought it to pass, that thou shouldest be to lay waste defenced cities *into* ruinous heaps.

27Therefore their inhabitants *were* of small power, they were dismayed and confounded: they were *as* the grass of the field, and *as* the green herb, *as* the grass on the housetops, and *as corn* blasted before it be grown up.

28But I know thy abode, and thy going out, and thy coming in, and thy rage against me.

29Because thy rage against me, and thy tumult, is come up into mine ears, therefore will I put my hook in thy nose, and my bridle in thy lips, and I will turn thee back by the way by which thou camest.

30And this *shall be* a sign unto thee, Ye shall eat *this* year such as groweth of itself; and the second year that which springeth of the same: and in the third year sow ye, and reap, and plant vineyards, and eat the fruit thereof.

31And the remnant that is escaped of the house of Judah shall again take root downward, and bear fruit upward:

32For out of Jerusalem shall go forth a remnant, and they that escape out of mount Zion: the zeal of the LORD of hosts shall do this.

33Therefore thus saith the LORD concerning the king of Assyria, He shall not come into this city, nor shoot an arrow there, nor come before it with shields, nor cast a bank against it.

34By the way that he came, by the same shall he return, and shall not come into this city, saith the LORD.

35For I will defend this city to save it for mine own sake, and for my servant David's sake.

36Then the angel of the LORD went forth, and smote in the camp of the Assyrians a hundred and fourscore and five thousand: and when they arose early in the morning, behold, they *were* all dead corpses.

37¶ So Sennacherib king of Assyria departed, and went and returned, and dwelt at Nineveh.

38And it came to pass, as he was worshipping in the house of Nisroch his god, that Adrammelech and Sharezer his sons smote him with the sword; and they escaped into the land of Armenia: and Esar-haddon his son reigned in his stead.

## Amplified

25I dug wells and drank foreign waters, and with the sole of my feet I have dried up all the rivers [the Nile streams] of Egypt.

26 *But, says the God of Israel,* have you not heard that I purposed to do it long ago, that I planned it in ancient times? Now I have brought it to pass: that you [the king of Assyria] should *be My instrument* to lay waste fortified cities, making them ruinous heaps.

27Therefore their inhabitants were of small power, they were dismayed and confounded; they were as the grass of the field, and as the green herb, as the grass on the house tops, and as a field of grain blasted before it is grown *or* is in stalk.

28But I know your sitting down and your going out and your coming in, also your raging against Me.

29Because your raging against Me and your arrogance *and* careless ease have come to My ears, therefore will I put My hook in your nose and My bridle in your lips, and I will turn you back on the way by which you came.

30And [now, Hezekiah, says the Lord] this shall be the sign *of these things* to you: you shall eat this year such as grows of itself, and in the second year that which springs of the same, and in the third year sow and reap and plant vineyards, and eat the fruit of them.

31And the remnant that has survived of the house of Judah shall again take root downward, and bear fruit upward;

32For out of Jerusalem shall go forth a remnant, and a band that survives out of Mount Zion. The zeal of the Lord of hosts will perform this.

33Therefore thus says the Lord concerning the king of Assyria, He shall not come into this city, or shoot an arrow there, or come before it with shield, or cast up a siege mound against it.

34By the way that he came, by the same *way* he shall return, and he shall not come into this city, says the Lord.

35For I will defend this city to save it, for My own sake and for the sake of My servant David.

36And the Angel of the Lord went forth, and [a]slew a hundred and eighty-five thousand in the camp of the Assyrians; and when *the living* arose early in the morning, behold, all these were dead bodies.

37So Sennacherib king of Assyria departed, and returned and dwelt at Nineveh.

38And as he was worshiping in the house of Nisroch his god, Adrammelech and Sharezer his sons killed him with the sword, and they escaped into the land of Armenia *or* Ararat. And Esarhaddon his son reigned in his stead.

**AMP** [a] A startling, literal fulfillment of the prophecy made in Isaiah 31:8, 9 [See also Isa. 17:14; 14:25]. It is recorded in II Kings 19:35-37 also.

## New American Standard

25 'I dug *wells* and drank waters,
And with the sole of my feet I dried up
All the rivers of Egypt.'
26 "Have you not heard?
Long ago I did it,
From ancient times I planned it.
Now I have brought it to pass,
That you should turn fortified cities into ruinous heaps.
27 "Therefore their inhabitants were short of strength,
They were dismayed and put to shame;
They were *as* the vegetation of the field and *as* the green herb,
*As* grass on the housetops is scorched before it is grown up.
28 "But I know your sitting down,
And your going out and your coming in,
And your raging against Me.
29 "Because of your raging against Me,
And because your arrogance has come up to My ears,
Therefore I will put My hook in your nose,
And My bridle in your lips,
And I will turn you back by the way which you came.
**30**¶ "Then this shall be the sign for you: you shall eat this year
what grows of itself, in the second year what springs from the
same, and in the third year sow, reap, plant vineyards, and eat
their fruit.
31"And the surviving remnant of the house of Judah shall again
take root downward and bear fruit upward.
32"For out of Jerusalem shall go forth a remnant, and out of
Mount Zion survivors. The zeal of the LORD of hosts shall perform
this."'
33"Therefore, thus says the LORD concerning the king of Assyria, 'He shall not come to this city, or shoot an arrow there;
neither shall he come before it with a shield, nor throw up a mound
against it.
34'By the way that he came, by the same he shall return, and
he shall not come to this city,' declares the LORD.
35'For I will defend this city to save it for My own sake and for
My servant David's sake.'"

*Assyrians Destroyed*

**36**¶ Then the angel of the LORD went out, and struck 185,000 in
the camp of the Assyrians; and when men arose early in the
morning, behold, all of these were dead.
37So Sennacherib, king of Assyria, departed and returned *home*,
and lived at Nineveh.
38And it came about as he was worshiping in the house of
Nisroch his god, that Adrammelech and Sharezer his sons killed
him with the sword; and they escaped into the land of Ararat. And
Esarhaddon his son became king in his place.

## New International

25I have dug wells in foreign lands[b]
and drunk the water there.
With the soles of my feet
I have dried up all the streams of Egypt.'

26"Have you not heard?
Long ago I ordained it.
In days of old I planned it;
now I have brought it to pass,
that you have turned fortified cities
into piles of stone.
27Their people, drained of power,
are dismayed and put to shame.
They are like plants in the field,
like tender green shoots,
like grass sprouting on the roof,
scorched[c] before it grows up.
28"But I know where you stay
and when you come and go
and how you rage against me.
29Because you rage against me
and because your insolence has reached my ears,
I will put my hook in your nose
and my bit in your mouth,
and I will make you return
by the way you came.

30"This will be the sign for you, O Hezekiah:

"This year you will eat what grows by itself,
and the second year what springs from that.
But in the third year sow and reap,
plant vineyards and eat their fruit.
31Once more a remnant of the house of Judah
will take root below and bear fruit above.
32For out of Jerusalem will come a remnant,
and out of Mount Zion a band of survivors.
The zeal of the LORD Almighty
will accomplish this.

33"Therefore this is what the LORD says concerning the king of
Assyria:

"He will not enter this city
or shoot an arrow here.
He will not come before it with shield
or build a siege ramp against it.
34By the way that he came he will return;
he will not enter this city,"
declares the LORD.
35"I will defend this city and save it,
for my sake and for the sake of David my servant!"

36Then the angel of the LORD went out and put to death a
hundred and eighty-five thousand men in the Assyrian camp.
When the people got up the next morning—there were all the dead
bodies! 37So Sennacherib king of Assyria broke camp and withdrew. He returned to Nineveh and stayed there.
38One day, while he was worshiping in the temple of his god
Nisroch, his sons Adrammelech and Sharezer cut him down with
the sword, and they escaped to the land of Ararat. And Esarhaddon his son succeeded him as king.

**NIV** [b] 25 Dead Sea Scrolls (see also 2 Kings 19:24); Masoretic Text does not have *in foreign lands.* [c] 27 Some manuscripts of the Masoretic Text, Dead Sea Scrolls and some Septuagint manuscripts (see also 2 Kings 19:26); most manuscripts of the Masoretic Text *roof / and terraced fields*

## King James

**38** IN THOSE days was Hezekiah sick unto death. And Isaiah the prophet the son of Amoz came unto him, and said unto him, Thus saith the LORD, Set thine house in order: for thou shalt die, and not live.

2Then Hezekiah turned his face toward the wall, and prayed unto the LORD,

3And said, Remember now, O LORD, I beseech thee, how I have walked before thee in truth and with a perfect heart, and have done *that which is* good in thy sight. And Hezekiah wept sore.

4¶ Then came the word of the LORD to Isaiah, saying,

5Go, and say to Hezekiah, Thus saith the LORD, the God of David thy father, I have heard thy prayer, I have seen thy tears: behold, I will add unto thy days fifteen years.

6And I will deliver thee and this city out of the hand of the king of Assyria: and I will defend this city.

7And this *shall be* a sign unto thee from the LORD, that the LORD will do this thing that he hath spoken;

8Behold, I will bring again the shadow of the degrees, which is gone down in the sun dial of Ahaz, ten degrees backward. So the sun returned ten degrees, by which degrees it was gone down.

9¶ The writing of Hezekiah king of Judah, when he had been sick, and was recovered of his sickness:

10I said in the cutting off of my days, I shall go to the gates of the grave; I am deprived of the residue of my years.

11I said, I shall not see the LORD, *even* the LORD, in the land of the living: I shall behold man no more with the inhabitants of the world.

12Mine age is departed, and is removed from me as a shepherd's tent: I have cut off like a weaver my life: he will cut me off with pining sickness: from day *even* to night wilt thou make an end of me.

13I reckoned till morning, *that,* as a lion, so will he break all my bones: from day *even* to night wilt thou make an end of me.

14Like a crane *or* a swallow, so did I chatter: I did mourn as a dove: mine eyes fail *with looking* upward: O LORD, I am oppressed; undertake for me.

15What shall I say? he hath both spoken unto me, and himself hath done *it:* I shall go softly all my years in the bitterness of my soul.

16O Lord, by these *things men* live, and in all these *things is* the life of my spirit: so wilt thou recover me, and make me to live.

17Behold, for peace I had great bitterness: but thou hast in love to my soul *delivered it* from the pit of corruption: for thou hast cast all my sins behind thy back.

18For the grave cannot praise thee, death can *not* celebrate thee: they that go down into the pit cannot hope for thy truth.

19The living, the living, he shall praise thee, as I *do* this day: the father to the children shall make known thy truth.

20The LORD *was ready* to save me: therefore we will sing my songs to the stringed instruments all the days of our life in the house of the LORD.

## Amplified

**38** IN THOSE days King Hezekiah of Judah became ill and was at the point of death. And Isaiah the prophet the son of Amoz came to him, and said, Thus says the Lord: Set your house in order, for you shall die and not live.

2Then Hezekiah turned his face toward the wall, and prayed to the Lord,

3And said, Remember [earnestly] now, O Lord, I beseech You, how I have walked before You in faithfulness *and* in truth, with a whole heart [absolutely devoted to You], and have done what is good in Your sight. And Hezekiah wept bitterly.

4Then came the word of the Lord to Isaiah, saying,

5Go, and say to Hezekiah, Thus says the Lord, the God of David your father: I have heard your prayer, I have seen your tears. Behold, I will [a]add to your life fifteen years.

6And I will deliver you and this city out of the hand of the king of Assyria, and I will defend this city [Jerusalem].

7And this shall be the sign to you from the Lord, that the Lord will do this thing that He has spoken:

8Behold, I will turn the shadow of the steps *or* degrees, which the sun has gone down on the [step] sun dial of Ahaz, backward ten steps *or* degrees. And the sunlight turned back ten steps on the steps which it had gone down.

9This is the writing of Hezekiah king of Judah, when he had been sick and had recovered from his sickness:

10I said, In the noontide *and* tranquillity of my days I must depart; I am to pass through the gates of Sheol [the place of the dead], deprived of the remainder of my years.

11I said, I shall not see the Lord, even the Lord, in the land of the living; I shall behold man no more among the inhabitants of the world.

12My *fleshly* dwelling is plucked up *and* is removed from me like a shepherd's tent. I have rolled up my life as a weaver [does the finished web]; *the Lord* cuts me free from the loom; from day to night You bring me to an end.

13I thought *and* quieted myself until morning. Like a lion He breaks all my bones; from day to night You bring me to an end.

14Like a twittering swallow *or* a crane, so do I chirp *and* chatter; I moan like a dove. My eyes are weary *and* dim with looking upward. O Lord, I am oppressed; undertake for me *and* be my security [as of a debtor being sent to prison].

15But what can I say? For He has both spoken to me and He Himself has done it. I must go softly—as in solemn procession—all my years, *and* my sleep has fled, because of the bitterness of my soul.

16O Lord, by these things men live, and in all these is the life of my spirit. O give me back my health and make me live!

17Behold, that I had intense bitterness was for my peace; but You have loved back my life from the pit of corruption *and* nothingness, for You have cast all my sins behind Your back.

18For Sheol [the place of the dead] cannot confess *and* reach out the hand to You, death cannot praise *and* rejoice in You; they that go down to the pit cannot hope for Your faithfulness [to Your promises; their probation is at an end, their destiny is sealed].

19The living, the living, he shall thank *and* praise You, as I do this day; the father shall make known to the children Your faithfulness *and* Your truth.

20The Lord is ready to save (deliver) me; therefore we will sing my songs with [my] stringed instruments all the days of our life in the house of the Lord.

**AMP** [a] God's time for Hezekiah to die had come (verse 1), but he had no son. It was unthinkable to him, apparently, that he should die and leave no heir to his throne. As devout as he was, he could not trust the Lord to give His faithful servant what was best for him, but took matters in his own hands and begged to be allowed to live on. The Lord granted his request; sons were born. One, Manasseh, became Hezekiah's disgraceful and ruthless successor, not for just a few years, but for fifty-five! He undid everything reformatory that had been done, established idol worship, caused his sons to go through the fire, defied God's prophets and caused the slaughter of those who opposed him, of whom Isaiah, his father's best friend, may have been one. How little Hezekiah knew of what was best for him or for Judah! How presumptuous is any one who demands that his own shortsighted vision replace the wisdom of God's plan for his own life or for that of others!

## New American Standard

*Hezekiah Healed*

**38** IN THOSE days Hezekiah became mortally ill. And Isaiah
the prophet the son of Amoz came to him and said to him,
"Thus says the LORD, 'Set your house in order, for you shall die
and not live.' "
2Then Hezekiah turned his face to the wall, and prayed to the
LORD,
3and said, "Remember now, O LORD, I beseech Thee, how I
have walked before Thee in truth and with a whole heart, and have
done what is good in Thy sight." And Hezekiah wept bitterly.
4Then the word of the LORD came to Isaiah, saying,
5"Go and say to Hezekiah, 'Thus says the LORD, the God of
your father David, "I have heard your prayer, I have seen your
tears; behold, I will add fifteen years to your life.
6"And I will deliver you and this city from the hand of the king
of Assyria; and I will defend this city." '
7"And this shall be the sign to you from the LORD, that the
LORD will do this thing that He has spoken:
8"Behold, I will cause the shadow on the stairway, which has
gone down with the sun on the stairway of Ahaz, to go back ten
steps." So the sun's *shadow* went back ten steps on the stairway
on which it had gone down.
9¶ A writing of Hezekiah king of Judah, after his illness and
recovery:

10 I said, "In the middle of my life
I am to enter the gates of Sheol;
I am to be deprived of the rest of my years."
11 I said, "I shall not see the LORD,
The LORD in the land of the living;
I shall look on man no more among the inhabitants of
the world.
12 "Like a shepherd's tent my dwelling is pulled up and
removed from me;
As a weaver I rolled up my life.
He cuts me off from the loom;
From day until night Thou dost make an end of me.
13 "I composed *my soul* until morning.
Like a lion—so He breaks all my bones,
From day until night Thou dost make an end of me.
14 "Like a swallow, *like* a crane, so I twitter;
I moan like a dove;
My eyes look wistfully to the heights;
O Lord, I am oppressed, be my security.
15¶ "What shall I say?
For He has spoken to me, and He Himself has done it;
I shall wander about all my years because of the
bitterness of my soul.
16 "O Lord, by *these* things *men* live;
And in all these is the life of my spirit;
O restore me to health, and let me live!
17 "Lo, for *my own* welfare I had great bitterness;
It is Thou who hast kept my soul from the pit of
nothingness,
For Thou hast cast all my sins behind Thy back.
18 "For Sheol cannot thank Thee,
Death cannot praise Thee;
Those who go down to the pit cannot hope for Thy
faithfulness.
19 "It is the living who give thanks to Thee, as I do today;
A father tells his sons about Thy faithfulness.
20 "The LORD will surely save me;
So we will play my songs on stringed instruments
All *the* days of our life at the house of the LORD."

## New International

*Hezekiah's Illness*

**38** IN THOSE days Hezekiah became ill and was at the point
of death. The prophet Isaiah son of Amoz went to him and
said, "This is what the LORD says: Put your house in order, because
you are going to die; you will not recover."
2Hezekiah turned his face to the wall and prayed to the LORD,
3"Remember, O LORD, how I have walked before you faithfully
and with wholehearted devotion and have done what is good in
your eyes." And Hezekiah wept bitterly.
4Then the word of the LORD came to Isaiah: 5"Go and tell
Hezekiah, 'This is what the LORD, the God of your father David,
says: I have heard your prayer and seen your tears; I will add
fifteen years to your life. 6And I will deliver you and this city from
the hand of the king of Assyria. I will defend this city.
7" 'This is the LORD's sign to you that the LORD will do what he
has promised: 8I will make the shadow cast by the sun go back the
ten steps it has gone down on the stairway of Ahaz.' " So the
sunlight went back the ten steps it had gone down.
9A writing of Hezekiah king of Judah after his illness and recovery:

10I said, "In the prime of my life
must I go through the gates of death[b]
and be robbed of the rest of my years?"
11I said, "I will not again see the LORD,
the LORD, in the land of the living;
no longer will I look on mankind,
or be with those who now dwell in this world.[c]
12Like a shepherd's tent my house
has been pulled down and taken from me.
Like a weaver I have rolled up my life,
and he has cut me off from the loom;
day and night you made an end of me.
13I waited patiently till dawn,
but like a lion he broke all my bones;
day and night you made an end of me.
14I cried like a swift or thrush,
I moaned like a mourning dove.
My eyes grew weak as I looked to the heavens.
I am troubled; O Lord, come to my aid!"
15But what can I say?
He has spoken to me, and he himself has done this.
I will walk humbly all my years
because of this anguish of my soul.
16Lord, by such things men live;
and my spirit finds life in them too.
You restored me to health
and let me live.
17Surely it was for my benefit
that I suffered such anguish.
In your love you kept me
from the pit of destruction;
you have put all my sins
behind your back.
18For the grave[d] cannot praise you,
death cannot sing your praise;
those who go down to the pit
cannot hope for your faithfulness.
19The living, the living—they praise you,
as I am doing today;
fathers tell their children
about your faithfulness.

20The LORD will save me,
and we will sing with stringed instruments
all the days of our lives
in the temple of the LORD.

**NIV** [b] *10* Hebrew *Sheol* [c] *11* A few Hebrew manuscripts; most Hebrew manuscripts *in the place of cessation* [d] *18* Hebrew *Sheol*

## King James

21For Isaiah had said, Let them take a lump of figs, and lay *it*
for a plaster upon the boil, and he shall recover.
22Hezekiah also had said, What *is* the sign that I shall go up to
the house of the LORD?

**39** AT THAT time Merodach-baladan, the son of Baladan,
king of Babylon, sent letters and a present to Hezekiah: for
he had heard that he had been sick, and was recovered.
2And Hezekiah was glad of them, and showed them the house
of his precious things, the silver, and the gold, and the spices, and
the precious ointment, and all the house of his armour, and all that
was found in his treasures: there was nothing in his house, nor in
all his dominion, that Hezekiah showed them not.
3¶ Then came Isaiah the prophet unto king Hezekiah, and said
unto him, What said these men? and from whence came they unto
thee? And Hezekiah said, They are come from a far country unto
me, *even* from Babylon.
4Then said he, What have they seen in thine house? And Hezekiah answered, All that *is* in mine house have they seen: there is
nothing among my treasures that I have not shown them.
5Then said Isaiah to Hezekiah, Hear the word of the LORD of
hosts:
6Behold, the days come, that all that *is* in thine house, and *that*
which thy fathers have laid up in store until this day, shall be
carried to Babylon: nothing shall be left, saith the LORD.
7And of thy sons that shall issue from thee, which thou shalt
beget, shall they take away; and they shall be eunuchs in the palace
of the king of Babylon.
8Then said Hezekiah to Isaiah, Good *is* the word of the LORD
which thou hast spoken. He said moreover, For there shall be
peace and truth in my days.

**40** COMFORT YE, comfort ye my people, saith your God.
2Speak ye comfortably to Jerusalem, and cry unto her, that
her warfare is accomplished, that her iniquity is pardoned: for she
hath received of the LORD's hand double for all her sins.
3¶ The voice of him that crieth in the wilderness, Prepare ye the
way of the LORD, make straight in the desert a highway for our
God.
4Every valley shall be exalted, and every mountain and hill shall
be made low: and the crooked shall be made straight, and the
rough places plain:
5And the glory of the LORD shall be revealed, and all flesh shall
see *it* together: for the mouth of the LORD hath spoken *it*.
6The voice said, Cry. And he said, What shall I cry? All flesh
*is* grass, and all the goodliness thereof *is* as the flower of the field:

## Amplified

21Now Isaiah had said, Let them take a cake of figs, and lay it
for a plaster upon the boil, that he may recover.
22Hezekiah also had said, What is the sign that I shall go up to
the house of the Lord?

**39** AT THAT time Mero-dach-bal-adan the son of Baladan,
king of Babylon, sent *messengers with* letters and a present
to Hezekiah, for he had heard that he had been sick and had
recovered.
2And Hezekiah was glad *and* welcomed them, and showed
them the house of his spicery *and* precious things, the silver, the
gold, the spices, the precious ointment, all the house of his armor
*and* his jewels, and all that was found in his treasuries. There was
nothing in his house nor in all his dominion that Hezekiah did not
show them.
3Then came Isaiah the prophet to King Hezekiah, and said to
him, What did these men say? From where did they come to you?
And Hezekiah said, They came to me from a far country, even
from Babylon.
4Then Isaiah said, What have they seen in your house? And
Hezekiah answered, They have seen all that is in my house; there
is nothing among my treasures that I have not shown them.
5Then said Isaiah to Hezekiah, Hear the word of the Lord of
hosts:
6Behold, the days are coming when all that is in your house,
and that which your predecessors have stored up till this day, shall
be carried to Babylon. Nothing shall be left, says the Lord.
7And some of your own sons, who are born to you, shall be
taken away, and they shall be eunuchs in the palace of the king
of Babylon.
8Then said Hezekiah to Isaiah, The word of the Lord which you
have spoken is good. And he added, For there will be peace and
faithfulness [to His promises to us] in my days.

**40** COMFORT, COMFORT My people, says your God.
2Speak tenderly to the heart of Jerusalem and cry to her
that her time of service *and* her warfare are ended, that [her punishment is accepted and] her iniquity is pardoned; that she has
received punishment from the Lord's hand double for all her sins.
3A voice of one who cries, Prepare in the wilderness the way
of the Lord—clear away the obstacles—make straight *and* smooth
in the desert a highway for our God! [Mark 1:3.]
4Every valley shall be lifted *and* filled up, and every mountain
and hill shall be made low; and the crooked *and* uneven shall be
made straight *and* level, and the rough places a plain.
5And the glory—majesty and splendor—of the Lord shall be
revealed, and all flesh shall see it together, for the mouth of the
Lord has spoken it. [Luke 3:5, 6.]
6A voice of one saying, Cry [prophesy]! And I said, What shall
I cry? [The voice answered, Proclaim] All flesh is frail as grass, and
all that makes it attractive [its kindness, its goodwill, its mercy
from God, its glory and comeliness, however good] is transitory
like the flower of the field.

## New American Standard

21¶ Now Isaiah had said, "Let them take a cake of figs, and
apply it to the boil, that he may recover."
22Then Hezekiah had said, "What is the sign that I shall go up
to the house of the LORD?"

*Hezekiah Shows His Treasures*

**39** AT THAT time Merodach-baladan son of Baladan, king of
Babylon, sent letters and a present to Hezekiah, for he
heard that he had been sick and had recovered.
2And Hezekiah was pleased, and showed them all his treasure
house, the silver and the gold and the spices and the precious oil
and his whole armory and all that was found in his treasuries.
There was nothing in his house, nor in all his dominion, that
Hezekiah did not show them.
3Then Isaiah the prophet came to King Hezekiah and said to
him, "What did these men say, and from where have they come
to you?" And Hezekiah said, "They have come to me from a far
country, from Babylon."
4And he said, "What have they seen in your house?" So Hezekiah answered, "They have seen all that is in my house; there is
nothing among my treasuries that I have not shown them."
5Then Isaiah said to Hezekiah, "Hear the word of the LORD of
hosts,
6'Behold, the days are coming when all that is in your house,
and all that your fathers have laid up in store to this day shall be
carried to Babylon; nothing shall be left,' says the LORD.
7'And *some* of your sons who shall issue from you, whom you
shall beget, shall be taken away; and they shall become officials in
the palace of the king of Babylon.' "
8Then Hezekiah said to Isaiah, "The word of the LORD which
you have spoken is good." For he thought, "For there will be peace
and truth in my days."

*The Greatness of God*

**40** "COMFORT, O comfort My people," says your God.
2 "Speak kindly to Jerusalem;
And call out to her, that her warfare has ended,
That her iniquity has been removed,
That she has received of the LORD's hand
Double for all her sins."

3¶ A voice is calling,
"Clear the way for the LORD in the wilderness;
Make smooth in the desert a highway for our God.
4 "Let every valley be lifted up,
And every mountain and hill be made low;
And let the rough ground become a plain,
And the rugged terrain a broad valley;
5 Then the glory of the LORD will be revealed,
And all flesh will see *it* together;
For the mouth of the LORD has spoken."
6 A voice says, "Call out."
Then he answered, "What shall I call out?"
All flesh is grass, and all its loveliness is like the flower
of the field.

## New International

21Isaiah had said, "Prepare a poultice of figs and apply it to the
boil, and he will recover."
22Hezekiah had asked, "What will be the sign that I will go up
to the temple of the LORD?"

*Envoys From Babylon*

**39** AT THAT time Merodach-Baladan son of Baladan king of
Babylon sent Hezekiah letters and a gift, because he had
heard of his illness and recovery. 2Hezekiah received the envoys
gladly and showed them what was in his storehouses—the silver,
the gold, the spices, the fine oil, his entire armory and everything
found among his treasures. There was nothing in his palace or in
all his kingdom that Hezekiah did not show them.
3Then Isaiah the prophet went to King Hezekiah and asked,
"What did those men say, and where did they come from?"
"From a distant land," Hezekiah replied. "They came to me
from Babylon."
4The prophet asked, "What did they see in your palace?"
"They saw everything in my palace," Hezekiah said. "There is
nothing among my treasures that I did not show them."
5Then Isaiah said to Hezekiah, "Hear the word of the LORD
Almighty: 6The time will surely come when everything in your
palace, and all that your fathers have stored up until this day, will
be carried off to Babylon. Nothing will be left, says the LORD. 7And
some of your descendants, your own flesh and blood who will be
born to you, will be taken away, and they will become eunuchs in
the palace of the king of Babylon."
8"The word of the LORD you have spoken is good," Hezekiah
replied. For he thought, "There will be peace and security in my
lifetime."

*Comfort for God's People*

**40** COMFORT, COMFORT my people,
says your God.
2Speak tenderly to Jerusalem,
and proclaim to her
that her hard service has been completed,
that her sin has been paid for,
that she has received from the LORD's hand
double for all her sins.

3A voice of one calling:
"In the desert prepare
the way for the LORD[a];
make straight in the wilderness
a highway for our God.[b]
4Every valley shall be raised up,
every mountain and hill made low;
the rough ground shall become level,
the rugged places a plain.
5And the glory of the LORD will be revealed,
and all mankind together will see it.
For the mouth of the LORD has spoken."

6A voice says, "Cry out."
And I said, "What shall I cry?"

"All men are like grass,
and all their glory is like the flowers of the field.

NIV [a] 3 Or *A voice of one calling in the desert: / "Prepare the way for the LORD*
[b] 3 Hebrew; Septuagint *make straight the paths of our God*

## King James

7The grass withereth, the flower fadeth: because the spirit of the LORD bloweth upon it: surely the people *is* grass.

8The grass withereth, the flower fadeth: but the word of our God shall stand for ever.

9¶ O Zion, that bringest good tidings, get thee up into the high mountain; O Jerusalem, that bringest good tidings, lift up thy voice with strength; lift *it* up, be not afraid; say unto the cities of Judah, Behold your God!

10Behold, the Lord GOD will come with strong *hand,* and his arm shall rule for him: behold, his reward *is* with him, and his work before him.

11He shall feed his flock like a shepherd: he shall gather the lambs with his arm, and carry *them* in his bosom, *and* shall gently lead those that are with young.

12¶ Who hath measured the waters in the hollow of his hand, and meted out heaven with the span, and comprehended the dust of the earth in a measure, and weighed the mountains in scales, and the hills in a balance?

13Who hath directed the spirit of the LORD, or *being* his counsellor hath taught him?

14With whom took he counsel, and *who* instructed him, and taught him in the path of judgment, and taught him knowledge, and showed to him the way of understanding?

15Behold, the nations *are* as a drop of a bucket, and are counted as the small dust of the balance: behold, he taketh up the isles as a very little thing.

16And Lebanon *is* not sufficient to burn, nor the beasts thereof sufficient for a burnt offering.

17All nations before him *are* as nothing; and they are counted to him less than nothing, and vanity.

18¶ To whom then will ye liken God? or what likeness will ye compare unto him?

19The workman melteth a graven image, and the goldsmith spreadeth it over with gold, and casteth silver chains.

20He that *is* so impoverished that he hath no oblation chooseth a tree *that* will not rot; he seeketh unto him a cunning workman to prepare a graven image, *that* shall not be moved.

21Have ye not known? have ye not heard? hath it not been told you from the beginning? have ye not understood from the foundations of the earth?

22 *It is* he that sitteth upon the circle of the earth, and the inhabitants thereof *are* as grasshoppers; that stretcheth out the heavens as a curtain, and spreadeth them out as a tent to dwell in:

23That bringeth the princes to nothing; he maketh the judges of the earth as vanity.

## Amplified

7The grass withers, the flower fades when the breath of the Lord blows upon it; surely *all* people are as grass.

8The [a]grass withers, the flower fades, but the word of our God will stand for ever. [James 1:10, 11; I Pet. 1:24, 25.]

9O you who bring good tidings to Zion, get up to the high mountain; O you who bring good tidings to Jerusalem, lift up your voice with strength; lift it up, be not afraid; say to the cities of Judah, Behold your God! [Acts 10:36; Rom. 10:15.]

10Behold, the Lord God will come with might, and His arm will rule for Him; behold, His reward is with Him, and His recompense before Him. [Rev. 22:7, 12.]

11He will feed His flock like a shepherd, He will gather the lambs in His arm, He will carry them in His bosom, and will gently lead those that have their young.

12Who has measured the waters in the hollow of His hand, marked off the heavens with a [nine inch] span, enclosed the dust of the earth in a measure, and weighed the mountains in scales and the hills in a balance?

13Who has directed the Spirit of the Lord, or as His counselor has taught Him? [Rom. 11:34.]

14With whom did He take counsel that instruction might be given Him; who taught Him the path of justice, and taught Him knowledge, and showed Him the way of understanding?

15Behold, the nations are like a drop from a bucket, and are counted as the small dust on the scales; behold, He takes up the isles like a very little thing.

16And all Lebanon's forest would not supply sufficient fuel, nor all its wild beasts furnish victims enough to burn sacrifices [worthy of the Lord].

17All the nations are as nothing before Him; they are regarded by Him as less than nothing, and emptiness (waste, futility and worthlessness).

18To whom then will you liken God? Or with what likeness will you compare Him? [Acts 17:29.]

19The graven image! A workman casts it, and the goldsmith overlays it with gold, and casts silver chains for it.

20He who is so impoverished that he has no offering *or* oblation *or* rich gift to give [to his god, is constrained to make a wooden offering, an idol; so he] chooses a tree that will not rot; he seeks out a skillful craftsman to carve *and* set up for him an image that will not totter *or* deteriorate.

21[You worshipers of idols, you are without excuse.] Do you not know? Have you not heard? Has it not been told you from the beginning? [These things ought to convince you of God's omnipotence and of the folly of bowing to idols.] Have you not understood from the foundations of the earth? [Rom. 1:20, 21.]

22It is *God* Who sits above the circle (the horizon) of the earth, and its inhabitants are as grasshoppers; it is He Who stretches out the heavens like (gauze) curtains and spreads them out like a tent to dwell in;

23Who brings dignitaries to nothing, Who makes the judges *and* rulers of the earth as chaos—emptiness, falsity and futility.

**AMP** [a] The apostle Peter quotes this verse and then adds, "and this word is the good news [the Gospel] which was preached to you"—which confirms as fact that Isaiah is here referring to the times of Christ, the Messiah, the Anointed One.

## New American Standard

7 The grass withers, the flower fades,
When the breath of the LORD blows upon it;
Surely the people are grass.
8 The grass withers, the flower fades,
But the word of our God stands forever.

9¶ Get yourself up on a high mountain,
O Zion, bearer of good news,
Lift up your voice mightily,
O Jerusalem, bearer of good news;
Lift *it* up, do not fear.
Say to the cities of Judah,
"Here is your God!"
10 Behold, the Lord GOD will come with might,
With His arm ruling for Him.
Behold, His reward is with Him,
And His recompense before Him.
11 Like a shepherd He will tend His flock,
In His arm He will gather the lambs,
And carry *them* in His bosom;
He will gently lead the nursing *ewes*.

12¶ Who has measured the waters in the hollow of His hand,
And marked off the heavens by the span,
And calculated the dust of the earth by the measure,
And weighed the mountains in a balance,
And the hills in a pair of scales?
13 Who has directed the Spirit of the LORD,
Or as His counselor has informed Him?
14 With whom did He consult and *who* gave Him understanding?
And *who* taught Him in the path of justice and taught Him knowledge,
And informed Him of the way of understanding?
15 Behold, the nations are like a drop from a bucket,
And are regarded as a speck of dust on the scales;
Behold, He lifts up the islands like fine dust.
16 Even Lebanon is not enough to burn,
Nor its beasts enough for a burnt offering.
17 All the nations are as nothing before Him,
They are regarded by Him as less than nothing and meaningless.

18¶ To whom then will you liken God?
Or what likeness will you compare with Him?
19 *As for* the idol, a craftsman casts it,
A goldsmith plates it with gold,
And a silversmith *fashions* chains of silver.
20 He who is too impoverished for *such* an offering
Selects a tree that does not rot;
He seeks out for himself a skillful craftsman
To prepare an idol that will not totter.

21¶ Do you not know? Have you not heard?
Has it not been declared to you from the beginning?
Have you not understood from the foundations of the earth?
22 It is He who [b]sits above the [c]vault of the earth,
And its inhabitants are like grasshoppers,
Who stretches out the heavens like a curtain
And spreads them out like a tent to dwell in.
23 He *it is* who reduces rulers to nothing,
Who makes the judges of the earth meaningless.

NAS [b] Or, *is enthroned* [c] Or, *circle*

## New International

7The grass withers and the flowers fall,
because the breath of the LORD blows on them.
Surely the people are grass.
8The grass withers and the flowers fall,
but the word of our God stands forever."

9You who bring good tidings to Zion,
go up on a high mountain.
You who bring good tidings to Jerusalem,[d]
lift up your voice with a shout,
lift it up, do not be afraid;
say to the towns of Judah,
"Here is your God!"
10See, the Sovereign LORD comes with power,
and his arm rules for him.
See, his reward is with him,
and his recompense accompanies him.
11He tends his flock like a shepherd:
He gathers the lambs in his arms
and carries them close to his heart;
he gently leads those that have young.
12Who has measured the waters in the hollow of his hand,
or with the breadth of his hand marked off the heavens?
Who has held the dust of the earth in a basket,
or weighed the mountains on the scales
and the hills in a balance?
13Who has understood the mind[e] of the LORD,
or instructed him as his counselor?
14Whom did the LORD consult to enlighten him,
and who taught him the right way?
Who was it that taught him knowledge
or showed him the path of understanding?

15Surely the nations are like a drop in a bucket;
they are regarded as dust on the scales;
he weighs the islands as though they were fine dust.
16Lebanon is not sufficient for altar fires,
nor its animals enough for burnt offerings.
17Before him all the nations are as nothing;
they are regarded by him as worthless
and less than nothing.

18To whom, then, will you compare God?
What image will you compare him to?
19As for an idol, a craftsman casts it,
and a goldsmith overlays it with gold
and fashions silver chains for it.
20A man too poor to present such an offering
selects wood that will not rot.
He looks for a skilled craftsman
to set up an idol that will not topple.

21Do you not know?
Have you not heard?
Has it not been told you from the beginning?
Have you not understood since the earth was founded?
22He sits enthroned above the circle of the earth,
and its people are like grasshoppers.
He stretches out the heavens like a canopy,
and spreads them out like a tent to live in.
23He brings princes to naught
and reduces the rulers of this world to nothing.

NIV [d] 9 Or *O Zion, bringer of good tidings, / go up on a high mountain. / O Jerusalem, bringer of good tidings* [e] 13 Or *Spirit; or spirit*

## King James

24Yea, they shall not be planted; yea, they shall not be sown: yea, their stock shall not take root in the earth: and he shall also blow upon them, and they shall wither, and the whirlwind shall take them away as stubble.

25To whom then will ye liken me, or shall I be equal? saith the Holy One.

26Lift up your eyes on high, and behold who hath created these *things*, that bringeth out their host by number: he calleth them all by names by the greatness of his might, for that *he is* strong in power; not one faileth.

27Why sayest thou, O Jacob, and speakest, O Israel, My way is hid from the LORD, and my judgment is passed over from my God?

28¶ Hast thou not known? hast thou not heard, *that* the everlasting God, the LORD, the Creator of the ends of the earth, fainteth not, neither is weary? *there is* no searching of his understanding.

29He giveth power to the faint; and to *them that have* no might he increaseth strength.

30Even the youths shall faint and be weary, and the young men shall utterly fall:

31But they that wait upon the LORD shall renew *their* strength; they shall mount up with wings as eagles; they shall run, and not be weary; *and* they shall walk, and not faint.

**41** KEEP SILENCE before me, O islands; and let the people renew *their* strength: let them come near; then let them speak: let us come near together to judgment.

2Who raised up the righteous *man* from the east, called him to his foot, gave the nations before him, and made *him* rule over kings? he gave *them* as the dust to his sword, *and* as driven stubble to his bow.

3He pursued them, *and* passed safely; *even* by the way *that* he had not gone with his feet.

4Who hath wrought and done *it*, calling the generations from the beginning? I the LORD, the first, and with the last; I *am* he.

5The isles saw *it*, and feared; the ends of the earth were afraid, drew near, and came.

6They helped every one his neighbour; and *every one* said to his brother, Be of good courage.

7So the carpenter encouraged the goldsmith, *and* he that smootheth *with* the hammer him that smote the anvil, saying, It *is* ready for the soldering: and he fastened it with nails, *that* it should not be moved.

8But thou, Israel, *art* my servant, Jacob whom I have chosen, the seed of Abraham my friend.

## Amplified

24Yes, these men are scarcely planted, scarcely have they been sown, scarcely has their stock taken root in the earth, when *the Lord* blows upon them and they wither, and the whirlwind *or* tempest takes them away like stubble.

25To whom then will you liken Me, that I should be equal to him? says the Holy One.

26Lift up your eyes on high, and see! Who has created these? He Who brings out their host by number and calls them all by name; through the greatness of His might, and because He is strong in power not one is missing *or* lacks anything.

27Why, O Jacob, do you say, and declare, O Israel, My way *and* my lot are hidden from the Lord, and my right is passed over without regard from my God?

28Have you not known? Have you not heard? The everlasting God, the Lord, the Creator of the ends of the earth, does not faint or grow weary; there is no searching of His understanding.

29He gives power to the faint *and* weary, and to him who has no might He increases strength—causing it to multiply and making it abound. [II Cor. 12:9.]

30Even youths shall faint and be weary, and the *selected* young men shall feebly stumble *and* fall exhausted;

31But those who wait for the Lord—who expect, look for and hope in Him—shall change *and* renew their strength *and* power; they shall lift their wings *and* mount up [close to God] as eagles [mount up to the sun]; they shall run and not be weary; they shall walk and not faint *or* become tired. [Heb. 12:1-3.]

**41** *LISTEN* IN silence before Me, O islands *and* regions bordering on the sea, and let the people gather *and* renew their strength [for the argument; let them offer their strongest arguments]; let them come near, then let them speak; let us come near together for judgment [and decide the point at issue between us concerning the enemy advancing from the east].

2Who has roused up one [Cyrus] from the east, whom He calls in righteousness to His service *and* whom victory meets at every step? He, *the Lord*, subdues nations before him and makes him ruler over kings. He gives them as dust to the sword [of Cyrus], and as driven straw *and* chaff to his bow. [Ezra 1:2.]

3He [Cyrus] pursues them and passes safely *and* unhindered, even by a way his feet had not trod, *and* so swiftly his feet do not touch the ground.

4Who has prepared and done this, calling *and* guiding the destinies of the generations *of the nations* from the beginning? I, the Lord, the first [existing before history began] and with the last [an ever present, unchanging God]; I am He.

5The islands *and* coastlands have seen and fear, the ends of the earth tremble; they draw near and come.

6They help every one his neighbor, and say to his brother *in his tiresome idol making*, Be of good courage!

7So the carpenter encourages the goldsmith, *and* he who smooths *the metal* with the hammer him who smites the anvil, saying of the soldering, That is good! And he fastens it with nails so that it cannot be moved.

8But you, Israel, My servant, Jacob, whom I have chosen, the offspring of Abraham, My friend; [James 2:23; Heb. 2:16.]

## New American Standard

24 [a]Scarcely have they been planted,
[b]Scarcely have they been sown,
[c]Scarcely has their stock taken root in the earth,
But He merely blows on them, and they wither,
And the storm carries them away like stubble.
25 "To whom then will you liken Me
That I should be *his* equal?" says the Holy One.
26 Lift up your eyes on high
And see who has created these *stars*,
The One who leads forth their host by number,
He calls them all by name;
Because of the greatness of His might and the strength of *His* power
Not one *of them* is missing.

27¶ Why do you say, O Jacob, and assert, O Israel,
"My way is hidden from the LORD,
And the justice due me escapes the notice of my God"?
28 Do you not know? Have you not heard?
The Everlasting God, the LORD, the Creator of the ends of the earth
Does not become weary or tired.
His understanding is inscrutable.
29 He gives strength to the weary,
And to *him who* lacks might He increases power.
30 Though youths grow weary and tired,
And vigorous young men stumble badly,
31 Yet those who wait for the LORD
Will gain new strength;
They will mount up *with* wings like eagles,
They will run and not get tired,
They will walk and not become weary.

*Israel Encouraged*

**41** "COASTLANDS, LISTEN to Me in silence,
And let the peoples gain new strength;
Let them come forward, then let them speak;
Let us come together for judgment.
2 "Who has aroused one from the east
Whom He calls in righteousness to His feet?
He delivers up nations before him,
And subdues kings.
He makes them like dust with his sword,
As the wind-driven chaff with his bow.
3 "He pursues them, passing on in safety,
By a way he had not been traversing with his feet.
4 "Who has performed and accomplished *it*,
Calling forth the generations from the beginning?
'I, the LORD, am the first, and with the last. I am He.' "

5¶ The coastlands have seen and are afraid;
The ends of the earth tremble;
They have drawn near and have come.
6 Each one helps his neighbor,
And says to his brother, "Be strong!"
7 So the craftsman encourages the smelter,
*And* he who smooths *metal* with the hammer *encourages* him who beats the anvil,
Saying of the soldering, "It is good";
And he fastens it with nails,
*That* it should not totter.
8 "But you, Israel, My servant,
Jacob whom I have chosen,
Descendant of Abraham My friend,

NAS [a] Or, *Not even* [b] Or, *Not even* [c] Or, *Not even*

## New International

24 No sooner are they planted,
no sooner are they sown,
no sooner do they take root in the ground,
than he blows on them and they wither,
and a whirlwind sweeps them away like chaff.

25 "To whom will you compare me?
Or who is my equal?" says the Holy One.
26 Lift your eyes and look to the heavens:
Who created all these?
He who brings out the starry host one by one,
and calls them each by name.
Because of his great power and mighty strength,
not one of them is missing.

27 Why do you say, O Jacob,
and complain, O Israel,
"My way is hidden from the LORD;
my cause is disregarded by my God"?
28 Do you not know?
Have you not heard?
The LORD is the everlasting God,
the Creator of the ends of the earth.
He will not grow tired or weary,
and his understanding no one can fathom.
29 He gives strength to the weary
and increases the power of the weak.
30 Even youths grow tired and weary,
and young men stumble and fall;
31 but those who hope in the LORD
will renew their strength.
They will soar on wings like eagles;
they will run and not grow weary,
they will walk and not be faint.

*The Helper of Israel*

**41** "BE SILENT before me, you islands!
Let the nations renew their strength!
Let them come forward and speak;
let us meet together at the place of judgment.

2 "Who has stirred up one from the east,
calling him in righteousness to his service[d]?
He hands nations over to him
and subdues kings before him.
He turns them to dust with his sword,
to windblown chaff with his bow.
3 He pursues them and moves on unscathed,
by a path his feet have not traveled before.
4 Who has done this and carried it through,
calling forth the generations from the beginning?
I, the LORD—with the first of them
and with the last—I am he."

5 The islands have seen it and fear;
the ends of the earth tremble.
They approach and come forward;
6 each helps the other
and says to his brother, "Be strong!"
7 The craftsman encourages the goldsmith,
and he who smooths with the hammer
spurs on him who strikes the anvil.
He says of the welding, "It is good."
He nails down the idol so it will not topple.

8 "But you, O Israel, my servant,
Jacob, whom I have chosen,
you descendants of Abraham my friend,

NIV [d] 2 Or / *whom victory meets at every step*

## King James

9 *Thou* whom I have taken from the ends of the earth, and called thee from the chief men thereof, and said unto thee, Thou *art* my servant; I have chosen thee, and not cast thee away.

10¶ Fear thou not; for I *am* with thee: be not dismayed; for I *am* thy God: I will strengthen thee; yea, I will help thee; yea, I will uphold thee with the right hand of my righteousness.

11 Behold, all they that were incensed against thee shall be ashamed and confounded: they shall be as nothing; and they that strive with thee shall perish.

12 Thou shalt seek them, and shalt not find them, *even* them that contended with thee: they that war against thee shall be as nothing, and as a thing of nought.

13 For I the LORD thy God will hold thy right hand, saying unto thee, Fear not; I will help thee.

14 Fear not, thou worm Jacob, *and* ye men of Israel; I will help thee, saith the LORD, and thy redeemer, the Holy One of Israel.

15 Behold, I will make thee a new sharp threshing instrument having teeth: thou shalt thresh the mountains, and beat *them* small, and shalt make the hills as chaff.

16 Thou shalt fan them, and the wind shall carry them away, and the whirlwind shall scatter them: and thou shalt rejoice in the LORD, *and* shalt glory in the Holy One of Israel.

17 *When* the poor and needy seek water, and *there is* none, *and* their tongue faileth for thirst, I the LORD will hear them, *I* the God of Israel will not forsake them.

18 I will open rivers in high places, and fountains in the midst of the valleys: I will make the wilderness a pool of water, and the dry land springs of water.

19 I will plant in the wilderness the cedar, the shittah tree, and the myrtle, and the oil tree; I will set in the desert the fir tree, *and* the pine, and the box tree together:

20 That they may see, and know, and consider, and understand together, that the hand of the LORD hath done this, and the Holy One of Israel hath created it.

21 Produce your cause, saith the LORD; bring forth your strong *reasons,* saith the King of Jacob.

22 Let them bring *them* forth, and show us what shall happen: let them show the former things, what they *be,* that we may consider them, and know the latter end of them; or declare us things for to come.

23 Show the things that are to come hereafter, that we may know that ye *are* gods: yea, do good, or do evil, that we may be dismayed, and behold *it* together.

24 Behold, ye *are* of nothing, and your work of nought: an abomination *is he that* chooseth you.

25 I have raised up *one* from the north, and he shall come: from the rising of the sun shall he call upon my name: and he shall come upon princes as *upon* mortar, and as the potter treadeth clay.

## Amplified

9 You whom I, *the Lord,* have taken from the ends of the earth, and have called from the corners of it, and said to you, You are My servant; I have chosen you and not cast you off [even though you are exiled].

10 Fear not; [there is nothing to fear] for I am with you; do not look around you in terror *and* be dismayed, for I am your God. I will strengthen *and* harden you [to difficulties]; yes, I will help you; yes, I will hold you up *and* retain you with My *victorious* right hand of rightness *and* justice. [Acts 18:10.]

11 Behold, all they who are enraged *and* inflamed against you shall be put to shame and confounded; they who strive against you shall be as nothing and shall perish.

12 You shall seek those who contend with you, and shall not find them; they who war against you shall be as nothing, as nothing at all.

13 For I, the Lord your God, hold your right hand; I, Who say to you, Fear not, I will help you!

14 Fear not, you worm Jacob, you men of Israel! I will help you, says the Lord; your Redeemer is the Holy One of Israel.

15 Behold, I will make you to be a new, sharp, threshing instrument having teeth; you shall thresh the mountains and beat them small, and shall make the hills as chaff.

16 You shall winnow them and the wind shall carry them away, and the tempest *or* whirlwind shall scatter them. And you shall rejoice in the Lord, you shall glory in the Holy One of Israel.

17 The poor and needy are seeking water when there is none; their tongue is parched with thirst. I, the Lord, will answer them; I, the God of Israel, will not forsake them.

18 I will open rivers on the bare heights, and fountains in the midst of the valleys; I will make the wilderness a pool of water, and the dry land springs of water.

19 I will plant in the wilderness the cedar, the acacia, the myrtle, and the wild olive; I will set in the desert the cypress, the plane and the pine *trees* together;

20 That men may see, and know, and consider, and understand together, that the hand of the Lord has done this, the Holy One of Israel has created it.

21 [You idols, made by men's hands, prove your divinity!] Produce your cause—set forth your case—says the Lord; bring forth your strong proofs, says the King of Jacob.

22 Let them bring them forth, and tell us what is to happen. Let them tell us the former things, what they are, that we may consider them, and know the outcome of them; or declare to us the things to come.

23 Tell us the things that are to come hereafter, that we may know that you are gods; yes, do good or do evil, [something or other] that we may stare in astonishment *and* be dismayed as we behold *the miracle* together!

24 Behold, you [idols] are nothing, and your work is nothing! The worshiper who chooses you is an abomination—extremely disgusting and shamefully vile *in God's sight.* [I Cor. 8:4.]

25 I have raised up *and* impelled to action one from the north [Cyprus, who has now moved from the east to the north], and he is come; from the rising of the sun he calls upon My name [recognizing that his victories have been granted to him by Me]; and he shall tread upon rulers *and* deputies as upon mortar, and as the potter treads clay. [He is come with the suddenness of a comet, but none of the idol oracles of the nations has anticipated it.] [II Chron. 36:23; Ezra 1:1-3.]

## New American Standard

9 "You whom I have taken from the ends of the earth,
And called from its remotest parts,
And said to you, 'You are My servant,
I have chosen you and not rejected you.
10 'Do not fear, for I am with you;
Do not anxiously look about you, for I am your God.
I will strengthen you, surely I will help you,
Surely I will uphold you with My righteous right hand.'
11 "Behold, all those who are angered at you will be shamed and dishonored;
Those who contend with you will be as nothing, and will perish.
12 "You will seek those who quarrel with you, but will not find them,
Those who war with you will be as nothing, and non-existent.
13 "For I am the LORD your God, who upholds your right hand,
Who says to you, 'Do not fear, I will help you.'
14 "Do not fear, you worm Jacob, you men of Israel;
I will help you," declares the LORD, "and your Redeemer is the Holy One of Israel.
15 "Behold, I have made you a new, sharp threshing sledge with double edges;
You will thresh the mountains, and pulverize *them*,
And will make the hills like chaff.
16 "You will winnow them, and the wind will carry them away,
And the storm will scatter them;
But you will rejoice in the LORD,
You will glory in the Holy One of Israel.

17¶ "The afflicted and needy are seeking water, but there is none,
And their tongue is parched with thirst;
I, the LORD, will answer them Myself,
*As* the God of Israel I will not forsake them.
18 "I will open rivers on the bare heights,
And springs in the midst of the valleys;
I will make the wilderness a pool of water,
And the dry land fountains of water.
19 "I will put the cedar in the wilderness,
The acacia, and the myrtle, and the olive tree;
I will place the juniper in the desert,
Together with the box tree and the cypress,
20 That they may see and recognize,
And consider and gain insight as well,
That the hand of the LORD has done this,
And the Holy One of Israel has created it.

21¶ "Present your case," the LORD says.
"Bring forward your strong *arguments*,"
The King of Jacob says.
22 Let them bring forth and declare to us what is going to take place;
As for the former *events*, declare what they *were*,
That we may consider them, and know their outcome;
Or announce to us what is coming.
23 Declare the things that are going to come afterward,
That we may know that you are gods;
Indeed, do good or evil, that we may anxiously look about us and fear together.
24 Behold, you are of no account,
And your work amounts to nothing;
He who chooses you is an abomination.

25¶ "I have aroused one from the north, and he has come;
From the rising of the sun he will call on My name;
And he will come upon rulers as *upon* mortar,
Even as the potter treads clay."

## New International

9I took you from the ends of the earth,
from its farthest corners I called you.
I said, 'You are my servant';
I have chosen you and have not rejected you.
10So do not fear, for I am with you;
do not be dismayed, for I am your God.
I will strengthen you and help you;
I will uphold you with my righteous right hand.

11"All who rage against you
will surely be ashamed and disgraced;
those who oppose you
will be as nothing and perish.
12Though you search for your enemies,
you will not find them.
Those who wage war against you
will be as nothing at all.
13For I am the LORD, your God,
who takes hold of your right hand
and says to you, Do not fear;
I will help you.
14Do not be afraid, O worm Jacob,
O little Israel,
for I myself will help you," declares the LORD,
your Redeemer, the Holy One of Israel.
15"See, I will make you into a threshing sledge,
new and sharp, with many teeth.
You will thresh the mountains and crush them,
and reduce the hills to chaff.
16You will winnow them, the wind will pick them up,
and a gale will blow them away.
But you will rejoice in the LORD
and glory in the Holy One of Israel.

17"The poor and needy search for water,
but there is none;
their tongues are parched with thirst.
But I the LORD will answer them;
I, the God of Israel, will not forsake them.
18I will make rivers flow on barren heights,
and springs within the valleys.
I will turn the desert into pools of water,
and the parched ground into springs.
19I will put in the desert
the cedar and the acacia, the myrtle and the olive.
I will set pines in the wasteland,
the fir and the cypress together,
20so that people may see and know,
may consider and understand,
that the hand of the LORD has done this,
that the Holy One of Israel has created it.

21"Present your case," says the LORD.
"Set forth your arguments," says Jacob's King.
22"Bring in your idols, to tell us
what is going to happen.
Tell us what the former things were,
so that we may consider them
and know their final outcome.
Or declare to us the things to come,
23 tell us what the future holds,
so we may know that you are gods.
Do something, whether good or bad,
so that we will be dismayed and filled with fear.
24But you are less than nothing
and your works are utterly worthless;
he who chooses you is detestable.

25"I have stirred up one from the north, and he comes—
one from the rising sun who calls on my name.
He treads on rulers as if they were mortar,
as if he were a potter treading the clay.

## King James

26 Who hath declared from the beginning, that we may know? and beforetime, that we may say, *He is* righteous? yea, *there is* none that showeth, yea, *there is* none that declareth, yea, *there is* none that heareth your words.

27 The first *shall say* to Zion, Behold, behold them: and I will give to Jerusalem one that bringeth good tidings.

28 For I beheld, and *there was* no man; even among them, and *there was* no counsellor, that, when I asked of them, could answer a word.

29 Behold, they *are* all vanity; their works *are* nothing: their molten images *are* wind and confusion.

**42** BEHOLD MY servant, whom I uphold; mine elect, *in whom* my soul delighteth; I have put my spirit upon him: he shall bring forth judgment to the Gentiles.

2 He shall not cry, nor lift up, nor cause his voice to be heard in the street.

3 A bruised reed shall he not break, and the smoking flax shall he not quench: he shall bring forth judgment unto truth.

4 He shall not fail nor be discouraged, till he have set judgment in the earth: and the isles shall wait for his law.

5 ¶ Thus saith God the LORD, he that created the heavens, and stretched them out; he that spread forth the earth, and that which cometh out of it; he that giveth breath unto the people upon it, and spirit to them that walk therein:

6 I the LORD have called thee in righteousness, and will hold thine hand, and will keep thee, and give thee for a covenant of the people, for a light of the Gentiles;

7 To open the blind eyes, to bring out the prisoners from the prison, *and* them that sit in darkness out of the prison house.

8 I *am* the LORD: that *is* my name: and my glory will I not give to another, neither my praise to graven images.

9 Behold, the former things are come to pass, and new things do I declare: before they spring forth I tell you of them.

10 Sing unto the LORD a new song, *and* his praise from the end of the earth, ye that go down to the sea, and all that is therein; the isles, and the inhabitants thereof.

11 Let the wilderness and the cities thereof lift up *their voice*, the villages *that* Kedar doth inhabit: let the inhabitants of the rock sing, let them shout from the top of the mountains.

12 Let them give glory unto the LORD, and declare his praise in the islands.

13 The LORD shall go forth as a mighty man, he shall stir up jealousy like a man of war: he shall cry, yea, roar; he shall prevail against his enemies.

## Amplified

26 *What idol* has declared this from the beginning, that we may know? And beforetime, that we may say that he is [unquestionably] right? Yes, there is none who declares it; yes, there is none who proclaims it; yes, [for the truth is, O you dumb idols] there is none who hears you speak!

27 I, *the Lord*, first gave to Zion the announcement, Behold, [the Jews will be restored to their own land, and the man shall be raised up who will deliver them] behold them! And to Jerusalem I give a herald bringing the good news.

28 For I look [upon the heathen prophets and the priests of pagan practices], and there is no man among them [who could predict these events], and among these *idols* there is no counselor that when I ask of them can answer a word.

29 Behold, these [pagan prophets and priests] are all emptiness (falseness and futility), their works are nought; their molten images are empty wind (confusion and waste).

**42** BEHOLD MY Servant, Whom I uphold; My elect, in Whom My soul delights! I have put My Spirit upon Him; He will bring forth justice *and* right, *and* reveal truth to the nations. [Matt. 3:16, 17.]

2 He will not cry or shout aloud or cause His voice to be heard in the street.

3 A bruised reed He will not break, and a dimly burning wick He will not quench; He will bring forth justice in truth. [Matt. 12:17-21; 7:29.]

4 He will not fail *or* become weak, or be crushed *and* discouraged till He has established justice in the earth, and the islands *and* coastal regions shall hopefully wait for *and* expect His direction *and* law. [Rom. 8:22-25.]

5 Thus says God, the Lord, He Who created the heavens and stretched them forth, He Who spread abroad the earth and that which comes out of it, He Who gives breath to the people on it and spirit to those who walk in it:

6 I the Lord have called You, *the Messiah*, for a righteous purpose *and* in righteousness; I have taken You by the hand and have kept You; I have given You for a covenant to the people [Israel], for a light to the nations;

7 To open the eyes of the blind, to bring out the prisoners from the dungeon, and those who sit in darkness from the prison. [Matt. 12:18-21.]

8 I am the Lord; that is My name, and My glory I will not give to another, nor My praise to graven images.

9 Behold, the former things have come to pass, and new things I now declare; before they spring forth I tell you of them.

10 Sing to the Lord a new song, and His praise from the end of the earth! You who go down to the sea, and all that is in it, the islands *and* coastal regions and the inhabitants of them *sing* [a song such as has never been heard in the heathen world]!

11 Let the wilderness and its cities lift up their voice, the villages that Kedar inhabits; let the inhabitants of the rock [Sela or Petra] sing, let them shout from the top of the mountains!

12 Let them give glory to the Lord, and declare His praise in the islands *and* coastal regions.

13 The Lord will go forth as a mighty man; He will rouse His zealous indignation *and* vengeance like a warrior; He will cry, yes, He will shout aloud, He will do mightily against His enemies.

## New American Standard

26 Who has declared *this* from the beginning, that we might know?
Or from former times, that we may say, "*He is* right!"?
Surely there was no one who declared,
Surely there was no one who proclaimed,
Surely there was no one who heard your words.
27 "Formerly *I said* to Zion, 'Behold, here they are.'
And to Jerusalem, 'I will give a messenger of good news.'
28 "But when I look, there is no one,
And there is no counselor among them
Who, if I ask, can give an answer.
29 "Behold, all of them are [a]false;
Their works are worthless,
Their molten images are wind and emptiness.

*God's Promise concerning His Servant*

42 "BEHOLD, MY Servant, whom I uphold;
My chosen one *in whom* My soul delights.
I have put My Spirit upon Him;
He will bring forth justice to the nations.
2 "He will not cry out or raise *His voice,*
Nor make His voice heard in the street.
3 "A bruised reed He will not break,
And a dimly burning wick He will not extinguish;
He will faithfully bring forth justice.
4 "He will not be disheartened or crushed,
Until He has established justice in the earth;
And the coastlands will wait expectantly for His law."

5¶ Thus says God the LORD,
Who created the heavens and stretched them out,
Who spread out the earth and its offspring,
Who gives breath to the people on it,
And spirit to those who walk in it,
6 "I am the LORD, I have called you in righteousness,
I will also hold you by the hand and watch over you,
And I will appoint you as a covenant to the people,
As a light to the nations,
7 To open blind eyes,
To bring out prisoners from the dungeon,
And those who dwell in darkness from the prison.
8 "I am the LORD, that is My name;
I will not give My glory to another,
Nor My praise to graven images.
9 "Behold, the former things have come to pass,
Now I declare new things;
Before they spring forth I proclaim *them* to you."

10¶ Sing to the LORD a new song,
*Sing* His praise from the end of the earth!
You who go down to the sea, and all that is in it.
You islands and those who dwell on them.
11 Let the wilderness and its cities lift up *their voices,*
The settlements where Kedar inhabits.
Let the inhabitants of Sela sing aloud,
Let them shout for joy from the tops of the mountains.
12 Let them give glory to the LORD,
And declare His praise in the coastlands.
13 The LORD will go forth like a warrior,
He will arouse *His* zeal like a man of war.
He will utter a shout, yes, He will raise a war cry.
He will prevail against His enemies.

NAS [a] Another reading is *nothing*

## New International

26 Who told of this from the beginning, so we could know,
or beforehand, so we could say, 'He was right'?
No one told of this,
no one foretold it,
no one heard any words from you.
27 I was the first to tell Zion, 'Look, here they are!'
I gave to Jerusalem a messenger of good tidings.
28 I look but there is no one—
no one among them to give counsel,
no one to give answer when I ask them.
29 See, they are all false!
Their deeds amount to nothing;
their images are but wind and confusion.

*The Servant of the LORD*

42 "HERE IS my servant, whom I uphold,
my chosen one in whom I delight;
I will put my Spirit on him
and he will bring justice to the nations.
2 He will not shout or cry out,
or raise his voice in the streets.
3 A bruised reed he will not break,
and a smoldering wick he will not snuff out.
In faithfulness he will bring forth justice;
4 he will not falter or be discouraged
till he establishes justice on earth.
In his law the islands will put their hope."

5 This is what God the LORD says—
he who created the heavens and stretched them out,
who spread out the earth and all that comes out of it,
who gives breath to its people,
and life to those who walk on it:
6 "I, the LORD, have called you in righteousness;
I will take hold of your hand.
I will keep you and will make you
to be a covenant for the people
and a light for the Gentiles,
7 to open eyes that are blind,
to free captives from prison
and to release from the dungeon those who sit in darkness.

8 "I am the LORD; that is my name!
I will not give my glory to another
or my praise to idols.
9 See, the former things have taken place,
and new things I declare;
before they spring into being
I announce them to you."

*Song of Praise to the LORD*

10 Sing to the LORD a new song,
his praise from the ends of the earth,
you who go down to the sea, and all that is in it,
you islands, and all who live in them.
11 Let the desert and its towns raise their voices;
let the settlements where Kedar lives rejoice.
Let the people of Sela sing for joy;
let them shout from the mountaintops.
12 Let them give glory to the LORD
and proclaim his praise in the islands.
13 The LORD will march out like a mighty man,
like a warrior he will stir up his zeal;
with a shout he will raise the battle cry
and will triumph over his enemies.

## King James

14 I have long time holden my peace; I have been still, *and* refrained myself: *now* will I cry like a travailing woman; I will destroy and devour at once.

15 I will make waste mountains and hills, and dry up all their herbs; and I will make the rivers islands, and I will dry up the pools.

16 And I will bring the blind by a way *that* they knew not; I will lead them in paths *that* they have not known: I will make darkness light before them, and crooked things straight. These things will I do unto them, and not forsake them.

17 ¶ They shall be turned back, they shall be greatly ashamed, that trust in graven images, that say to the molten images, Ye *are* our gods.

18 Hear, ye deaf; and look, ye blind, that ye may see.

19 Who *is* blind, but my servant? or deaf, as my messenger *that* I sent? who *is* blind as *he that is* perfect, and blind as the LORD's servant?

20 Seeing many things, but thou observest not; opening the ears, but he heareth not.

21 The LORD is well pleased for his righteousness' sake; he will magnify the law, and make *it* honourable.

22 But this *is* a people robbed and spoiled; *they are* all of them snared in holes, and they are hid in prison houses: they are for a prey, and none delivereth; for a spoil, and none saith, Restore.

23 Who among you will give ear to this? *who* will hearken and hear for the time to come?

24 Who gave Jacob for a spoil, and Israel to the robbers? did not the LORD, he against whom we have sinned? for they would not walk in his ways, neither were they obedient unto his law.

25 Therefore he hath poured upon him the fury of his anger, and the strength of battle: and it hath set him on fire round about, yet he knew not; and it burned him, yet he laid *it* not to heart.

**43** BUT NOW thus saith the LORD that created thee, O Jacob, and he that formed thee, O Israel, Fear not: for I have redeemed thee, I have called *thee* by thy name; thou *art* mine.

2 When thou passest through the waters, I *will be* with thee; and through the rivers, they shall not overflow thee: when thou walkest through the fire, thou shalt not be burned; neither shall the flame kindle upon thee.

## Amplified

14 [Thus says the Lord] I have for a long time held My peace; I have been still, and restrained Myself; now I will cry out like a woman in travail, I will gasp and pant together.

15 I will lay waste mountains and hills, and dry up all their herbage; I will turn the rivers into islands, and I will dry up the pools.

16 And I will bring the blind by a way that they know not; I will lead them in paths that they have not known. I will make darkness light before them, and uneven places a plain. These things I have determined to do *for them,* and not leave them forsaken.

17 They shall be turned back, they shall be utterly put to shame, who trust in graven images, who say to molten images, You are our gods.

18 Hear, you deaf; and look, you blind, that you may see!

19 Who is blind, but My servant [Israel]? Or deaf as My messenger whom I send? Who is blind as he who is at peace with Me [who has been admitted to covenant relationship with Me]? Yes, who is blind as the Lord's servant?

20 You see many things, but you do not observe *or* apprehend their true meaning. His ears are open, but he hears not!

21 It was the Lord's pleasure for His righteousness' sake [in accordance with a steadfast and consistent purpose] to magnify instruction *and* revelation and glorify them.

22 But this is a people robbed and plundered; they are all of them snared in holes, and hidden in houses of bondage; they have become a prey with no one to deliver them, a spoil, with no one to say, Restore them! [This shows the condition that will ensue as punishment for Israel's not recognizing the Servant of Jehovah and the day of His visit among them. Luke 19:41-44.]

23 Who is there among you who will give ear to this? Who will listen and hear for the time to come?

24 Who gave up Jacob [the kingdom of Judah] for a spoil, and *the kingdom of* Israel to the robbers? Did not the Lord, He against Whom we *of Judah* have sinned and in Whose ways they *of Israel* would not walk, neither were they obedient to His law *or* His teaching?

25 Therefore He poured out upon [Israel] the fierceness of His anger and the strength of battle; and it set him on fire round about, yet he knew not [the lesson of repentance which the Assyrian conquest was intended to teach]; it burned him, but he did not lay it to heart.

**43** BUT NOW [in spite of the past judgments for Israel's sins] thus says the Lord Who created you, O Jacob, and He Who formed You, O Israel: Fear not, for I have redeemed you—ransomed you by paying a price instead of leaving you captives; I have called you by your name, you are Mine.

2 When you pass through the waters I will be with you, and through the rivers they shall not overwhelm you; when you walk through the fire you shall not be burned *or* scorched, nor shall the flame kindle upon you.

## New American Standard

*The Blindness of the People*

14¶ "I have kept silent for a long time,
I have kept still and restrained Myself.
*Now* like a woman in labor I will groan,
I will both gasp and pant.
15 "I will lay waste the mountains and hills,
And wither all their vegetation;
I will make the rivers into coastlands,
And dry up the ponds.
16 "And I will lead the blind by a way they do not know,
In paths they do not know I will guide them.
I will make darkness into light before them
And rugged places into plains.
These are the things I will do,
And I will not leave them undone."
17 They shall be turned back and be utterly put to shame,
Who trust in idols,
Who say to molten images,
"You are our gods."

18¶ Hear, you deaf!
And look, you blind, that you may see.
19 Who is blind but My servant,
Or so deaf as My messenger whom I send?
Who is so blind as he that is at peace *with Me,*
Or so blind as the servant of the LORD?
20 You have seen many things, but you do not observe *them;*
*Your* ears are open, but none hears.
21 The LORD was pleased for His righteousness' sake
To make the law great and glorious.
22 But this is a people plundered and despoiled;
All of them are trapped in caves,
Or are hidden away in prisons;
They have become a prey with none to deliver *them,*
And a spoil, with none to say, "Give *them* back!"

23¶ Who among you will give ear to this?
Who will give heed and listen hereafter?
24 Who gave Jacob up for spoil, and Israel to plunderers?
Was it not the LORD, against whom we have sinned,
And in whose ways they were not willing to walk,
And whose law they did not obey?
25 So He poured out on him the heat of His anger
And the fierceness of battle;
And it set him aflame all around,
Yet he did not recognize *it;*
And it burned him, but he paid no attention.

*Israel Redeemed*

43 BUT NOW, thus says the LORD, your Creator, O Jacob,
And He who formed you, O Israel,
"Do not fear, for I have redeemed you;
I have called you by name; you are Mine!
2 "When you pass through the waters, I will be with you;
And through the rivers, they will not overflow you.
When you walk through the fire, you will not be scorched,
Nor will the flame burn you.

## New International

14"For a long time I have kept silent,
I have been quiet and held myself back.
But now, like a woman in childbirth,
I cry out, I gasp and pant.
15I will lay waste the mountains and hills
and dry up all their vegetation;
I will turn rivers into islands
and dry up the pools.
16I will lead the blind by ways they have not known,
along unfamiliar paths I will guide them;
I will turn the darkness into light before them
and make the rough places smooth.
These are the things I will do;
I will not forsake them.
17But those who trust in idols,
who say to images, 'You are our gods,'
will be turned back in utter shame.

*Israel Blind and Deaf*

18"Hear, you deaf;
look, you blind, and see!
19Who is blind but my servant,
and deaf like the messenger I send?
Who is blind like the one committed to me,
blind like the servant of the LORD?
20You have seen many things, but have paid no attention;
your ears are open, but you hear nothing."
21It pleased the LORD
for the sake of his righteousness
to make his law great and glorious.
22But this is a people plundered and looted,
all of them trapped in pits
or hidden away in prisons.
They have become plunder,
with no one to rescue them;
they have been made loot,
with no one to say, "Send them back."
23Which of you will listen to this
or pay close attention in time to come?
24Who handed Jacob over to become loot,
and Israel to the plunderers?
Was it not the LORD,
against whom we have sinned?
For they would not follow his ways;
they did not obey his law.
25So he poured out on them his burning anger,
the violence of war.
It enveloped them in flames, yet they did not understand;
it consumed them, but they did not take it to heart.

*Israel's Only Savior*

43 BUT NOW, this is what the LORD says—
he who created you, O Jacob,
he who formed you, O Israel:
"Fear not, for I have redeemed you;
I have summoned you by name; you are mine.
2When you pass through the waters,
I will be with you;
and when you pass through the rivers,
they will not sweep over you.
When you walk through the fire,
you will not be burned;
the flames will not set you ablaze.

## King James

3For I *am* the LORD thy God, the Holy One of Israel, thy Saviour: I gave Egypt *for* thy ransom, Ethiopia and Seba for thee.

4Since thou wast precious in my sight, thou hast been honourable, and I have loved thee: therefore will I give men for thee, and people for thy life.

5Fear not: for I *am* with thee: I will bring thy seed from the east, and gather thee from the west;

6I will say to the north, Give up; and to the south, Keep not back: bring my sons from far, and my daughters from the ends of the earth;

7 *Even* every one that is called by my name: for I have created him for my glory, I have formed him; yea, I have made him.

8¶ Bring forth the blind people that have eyes, and the deaf that have ears.

9Let all the nations be gathered together, and let the people be assembled: who among them can declare this, and show us former things? let them bring forth their witnesses, that they may be justified: or let them hear, and say, *It is* truth.

10Ye *are* my witnesses, saith the LORD, and my servant whom I have chosen: that ye may know and believe me, and understand that I *am* he: before me there was no God formed, neither shall there be after me.

11I, *even* I, *am* the LORD; and beside me *there is* no saviour.

12I have declared, and have saved, and I have shown, when *there was* no strange *god* among you: therefore ye *are* my witnesses, saith the LORD, that I *am* God.

13Yea, before the day *was* I *am* he; and *there is* none that can deliver out of my hand: I will work, and who shall let it?

14¶ Thus saith the LORD, your redeemer, the Holy One of Israel; For your sake I have sent to Babylon, and have brought down all their nobles, and the Chaldeans, whose cry *is* in the ships.

15I *am* the LORD, your Holy One, the creator of Israel, your King.

16Thus saith the LORD, which maketh a way in the sea, and a path in the mighty waters;

17Which bringeth forth the chariot and horse, the army and the power; they shall lie down together, they shall not rise: they are extinct, they are quenched as tow.

18¶ Remember ye not the former things, neither consider the things of old.

## Amplified

3For I am the Lord your God, the Holy One of Israel, your Savior; I give Egypt [to the Babylonians] for your ransom, Ethiopia and Seba [a province of Ethiopia] in exchange for *your release.*

4Because you are precious in My sight, and honored, and I love you, I give men in return for you and peoples in exchange for your life.

5Fear not, for I am with you; I will bring your offspring from the east [where they are dispersed], and gather you from the west; [Acts 18:10.]

6I will say to the north, Give up, and to the south, Keep not back; bring My sons from afar and My daughters from the ends of the earth,

7Even every one who is called by My name, whom I have created for My glory, whom I have formed, whom I have made.

8Bring forth the blind people who have eyes, and the deaf who have ears.

9Let all the nations be gathered together, and let the peoples be assembled. Who among *the idolaters* could predict this [that Cyrus will be the deliverer of Israel] and show us the former things? Let them bring their witnesses, that they may be justified; or let them hear and *acknowledge,* It is the truth. [Ps. 123:3, 4.]

10You are My witnesses, says the Lord, and My servant whom I have chosen, that you may know Me, believe Me *and* remain steadfast to Me, and understand that I am He. Before Me there was no God formed, neither shall there be after Me.

11I, even I, am the Lord, and beside Me there is no Savior.

12I have declared *the future,* and have saved *the nation* [in times of danger], and I have shown *that I am God,* when there was no strange *and* alien god among you; therefore you are My witnesses, says the Lord, that I am God.

13Yes, from the time of the first existence of day *and* from this day forth I am He, and there is no one who can deliver out of My hand. I will work and who can hinder *or* reverse it?

14Thus says the Lord, your Redeemer, the Holy One of Israel: For your sake I have sent *one* to Babylon, and I will bring down all of them as fugitives, *and* all their nobles, even the Chaldeans into the ships over which they rejoiced.

15I am the Lord, your Holy One, the Creator of Israel, your King.

16Thus says the Lord, Who makes a way in the sea and a path in the mighty waters,

17Who brings forth chariot and horse, army and mighty warrior. They lie down together, they cannot rise; they are extinguished, they are quenched like a *lamp* wick.

18Do not [earnestly] remember the former things, neither consider the things of old.

## New American Standard

3 "For I am the LORD your God,
The Holy One of Israel, your Savior;
I have given Egypt as your ransom,
Cush and Seba in your place.
4 "Since you are precious in My sight,
*Since* you are honored and I love you,
I will give *other* men in your place and *other* peoples in exchange for your life.
5 "Do not fear, for I am with you;
I will bring your offspring from the east,
And gather you from the west.
6 "I will say to the north, 'Give *them* up!'
And to the south, 'Do not hold *them* back.'
Bring My sons from afar,
And My daughters from the ends of the earth,
7 Everyone who is called by My name,
And whom I have created for My glory,
Whom I have formed, even whom I have made."

*Israel Is God's Witness*

8¶ Bring out the people who are blind, even though they have eyes,
And the deaf, even though they have ears.
9 All the nations have gathered together
In order that the peoples may be assembled.
Who among them can declare this
And proclaim to us the former things?
Let them present their witnesses that they may be justified,
Or let them hear and say, "It is true."
10 "You are My witnesses," declares the LORD,
"And My servant whom I have chosen,
In order that you may know and believe Me,
And understand that I am He.
Before Me there was no God formed,
And there will be none after Me.
11 "I, even I, am the LORD;
And there is no savior besides Me.
12 "It is I who have declared and saved and proclaimed,
And there was no strange *god* among you;
So you are My witnesses," declares the LORD,
"And I am God.
13 "Even from eternity I am He;
And there is none who can deliver out of My hand;
I act and who can reverse it?"

*Babylon to Be Destroyed*

14¶ Thus says the LORD your Redeemer, the Holy One of Israel,
"For your sake I have sent to Babylon,
And will bring them all down as fugitives,
[a]Even the Chaldeans, into the ships in which they rejoice.
15 "I am the LORD, your Holy One,
The Creator of Israel, your King."
16 Thus says the LORD,
Who makes a way through the sea
And a path through the mighty waters,
17 Who brings forth the chariot and the horse,
The army and the mighty man
(They will lie down together *and* not rise again;
They have been quenched *and* extinguished like a wick):
18 "Do not call to mind the former things,
Or ponder things of the past.

NAS [a] Another reading is *As for the Chaldeans, their rejoicing is turned into lamentations*

## New International

3For I am the LORD, your God,
the Holy One of Israel, your Savior;
I give Egypt for your ransom,
Cush[b] and Seba in your stead.
4Since you are precious and honored in my sight,
and because I love you,
I will give men in exchange for you,
and people in exchange for your life.
5Do not be afraid, for I am with you;
I will bring your children from the east
and gather you from the west.
6I will say to the north, 'Give them up!'
and to the south, 'Do not hold them back.'
Bring my sons from afar
and my daughters from the ends of the earth—
7everyone who is called by my name,
whom I created for my glory,
whom I formed and made."

8Lead out those who have eyes but are blind,
who have ears but are deaf.
9All the nations gather together
and the peoples assemble.
Which of them foretold this
and proclaimed to us the former things?
Let them bring in their witnesses to prove they were right,
so that others may hear and say, "It is true."
10"You are my witnesses," declares the LORD,
"and my servant whom I have chosen,
so that you may know and believe me
and understand that I am he.
Before me no god was formed,
nor will there be one after me.
11I, even I, am the LORD,
and apart from me there is no savior.
12I have revealed and saved and proclaimed—
I, and not some foreign god among you.
You are my witnesses," declares the LORD, "that I am God.
13 Yes, and from ancient days I am he.
No one can deliver out of my hand.
When I act, who can reverse it?"

*God's Mercy and Israel's Unfaithfulness*

14This is what the LORD says—
your Redeemer, the Holy One of Israel:
"For your sake I will send to Babylon
and bring down as fugitives all the Babylonians,[c]
in the ships in which they took pride.
15I am the LORD, your Holy One,
Israel's Creator, your King."
16This is what the LORD says—
he who made a way through the sea,
a path through the mighty waters,
17who drew out the chariots and horses,
the army and reinforcements together,
and they lay there, never to rise again,
extinguished, snuffed out like a wick:
18"Forget the former things;
do not dwell on the past.

NIV [b] 3 That is, the upper Nile region [c] 14 Or *Chaldeans*

# King James

19Behold, I will do a new thing; now it shall spring forth; shall ye not know it? I will even make a way in the wilderness, *and* rivers in the desert.

20The beast of the field shall honour me, the dragons and the owls: because I give waters in the wilderness, *and* rivers in the desert, to give drink to my people, my chosen.

21This people have I formed for myself; they shall show forth my praise.

22¶ But thou hast not called upon me, O Jacob; but thou hast been weary of me, O Israel.

23Thou hast not brought me the small cattle of thy burnt offerings; neither hast thou honoured me with thy sacrifices. I have not caused thee to serve with an offering, nor wearied thee with incense.

24Thou hast bought me no sweet cane with money, neither hast thou filled me with the fat of thy sacrifices: but thou hast made me to serve with thy sins, thou hast wearied me with thine iniquities.

25I, *even* I, *am* he that blotteth out thy transgressions for mine own sake, and will not remember thy sins.

26Put me in remembrance: let us plead together: declare thou, that thou mayest be justified.

27Thy first father hath sinned, and thy teachers have transgressed against me.

28Therefore I have profaned the princes of the sanctuary, and have given Jacob to the curse, and Israel to reproaches.

**44** YET NOW hear, O Jacob my servant; and Israel, whom I have chosen:

2Thus saith the LORD that made thee, and formed thee from the womb, *which* will help thee; Fear not, O Jacob, my servant; and thou, Jesurun, whom I have chosen.

3For I will pour water upon him that is thirsty, and floods upon the dry ground: I will pour my spirit upon thy seed, and my blessing upon thine offspring:

4And they shall spring up *as* among the grass, as willows by the water courses.

5One shall say, I *am* the LORD'S; and another shall call *himself* by the name of Jacob; and another shall subscribe *with* his hand unto the LORD, and surname *himself* by the name of Israel.

6Thus saith the LORD the King of Israel, and his redeemer the LORD of hosts; I *am* the first, and I *am* the last; and beside me *there is* no God.

# Amplified

19Behold, I am doing a new thing; now it springs forth; do you not perceive *and* know it, *and* will you not give heed to it? I will even make a way in the wilderness and rivers in the desert.

20The beasts of the field shall honor Me, the jackals and the ostriches; because I give waters in the wilderness *and* rivers in the desert, to give drink to My people, My chosen, [Isa. 41:17, 18; 48:21.]

21The people I formed for Myself that they might set forth My praise [and they shall do it].

22Yet you have not called upon Me [much less toiled for Me], O Jacob; but you have been weary of Me, O Israel!

23You have not brought Me your sheep *and* goats for burnt offerings, or honored Me with your sacrifices. I have not required you to serve with an offering *or* treated you as a slave by demanding tribute, or wearied you with offering incense.

24You have not bought Me sweet cane with money, or satiated Me with the fat of your sacrifices. But you have only burdened Me with your sins, you have wearied Me with your iniquities.

25I, even I, am He Who blots out *and* cancels your transgressions for My own sake, and I will not remember your sins.

26Put Me in remembrance—remind Me of your merits; let us plead *and* argue together. Set forth your case that you may be justified—proved in the right.

27Your first father [Jacob, in particular] has sinned, and your teachers [the priests and the prophets]—your mediators—transgressed against Me.

28And so I have profaned the chief ones of the sanctuary, and have delivered Jacob to the curse [the ban, a solemn anathema or excommunication], and *have subjected* Israel to reproaches *and* reviling.

**44** YET NOW hear, O Jacob My servant and Israel whom I have chosen;

2Thus says the Lord Who made you and formed you from the womb, Who will help you: Fear not, O Jacob My servant, and you Jeshurun—the upright one [applied to Israel as type of the Messiah]—whom I have chosen.

3For I will pour water upon him who is thirsty, and floods upon the dry ground. I will pour My Spirit upon your offspring, and My blessing upon your descendants. [John 7:37-39; Isa. 35:6, 7.]

4And they shall spring up among the grass, as willows *or* poplars by the water courses.

5One shall say, I am the Lord's, and another shall call himself by the name of Jacob, and another will write [even brand or tattoo] upon his hand, I am the Lord's, and surname himself by the *honorable* name of Israel.

6Thus says the Lord, the King of Israel and his Redeemer, the Lord of hosts: I am the first, and I am the last; besides Me there is no God. [Rev. 1:17; 2:8; 22:13.]

## New American Standard

19 "Behold, I will do something new,
Now it will spring forth;
Will you not be aware of it?
I will even make a roadway in the wilderness,
Rivers in the desert.
20 "The beasts of the field will glorify Me;
The jackals and the ostriches;
Because I have given waters in the wilderness
And rivers in the desert,
To give drink to My chosen people.
21 "The people whom I formed for Myself,
Will declare My praise.

*The Shortcomings of Israel*

22¶ "Yet you have not called on Me, O Jacob;
But you have become weary of Me, O Israel.
23 "You have not brought to Me the sheep of your burnt offerings;
Nor have you honored Me with your sacrifices.
I have not burdened you with offerings,
Nor wearied you with incense.
24 "You have bought Me no sweet cane with money,
Neither have you filled Me with the fat of your sacrifices;
Rather you have burdened Me with your sins,
You have wearied Me with your iniquities.
25¶ "I, even I, am the one who wipes out your transgressions for My own sake;
And I will not remember your sins.
26 "Put Me in remembrance; let us argue our case together,
State your *cause*, that you may be proved right.
27 "Your first forefather sinned,
And your spokesmen have transgressed against Me.
28 "So I will pollute the princes of the sanctuary;
And I will consign Jacob to the ban, and Israel to revilement.

*The Blessings of Israel*

44 "BUT NOW listen, O Jacob, My servant;
And Israel, whom I have chosen:
2 Thus says the LORD who made you
And formed you from the womb, who will help you,
'Do not fear, O Jacob My servant;
And you Jeshurun whom I have chosen.
3 'For I will pour out water on the thirsty *land*
And streams on the dry ground;
I will pour out My Spirit on your offspring,
And My blessing on your descendants;
4 And they will spring up among the grass
Like poplars by streams of water.'
5 "This one will say, 'I am the LORD's';
And that one will call on the name of Jacob;
And another will write *on* his hand, 'Belonging to the LORD,'
And will name Israel's name with honor.

6¶ "Thus says the LORD, the King of Israel
And his Redeemer, the LORD of hosts:
'I am the first and I am the last,
And there is no God besides Me.

## New International

19 See, I am doing a new thing!
Now it springs up; do you not perceive it?
I am making a way in the desert
and streams in the wasteland.
20 The wild animals honor me,
the jackals and the owls,
because I provide water in the desert
and streams in the wasteland,
to give drink to my people, my chosen,
21 the people I formed for myself
that they may proclaim my praise.

22 "Yet you have not called upon me, O Jacob,
you have not wearied yourselves for me, O Israel.
23 You have not brought me sheep for burnt offerings,
nor honored me with your sacrifices.
I have not burdened you with grain offerings
nor wearied you with demands for incense.
24 You have not bought any fragrant calamus for me,
or lavished on me the fat of your sacrifices.
But you have burdened me with your sins
and wearied me with your offenses.

25 "I, even I, am he who blots out
your transgressions, for my own sake,
and remembers your sins no more.
26 Review the past for me,
let us argue the matter together;
state the case for your innocence.
27 Your first father sinned;
your spokesmen rebelled against me.
28 So I will disgrace the dignitaries of your temple,
and I will consign Jacob to destruction[a]
and Israel to scorn.

*Israel the Chosen*

44 "BUT NOW listen, O Jacob, my servant,
Israel, whom I have chosen.
2 This is what the LORD says—
he who made you, who formed you in the womb,
and who will help you:
Do not be afraid, O Jacob, my servant,
Jeshurun, whom I have chosen.
3 For I will pour water on the thirsty land,
and streams on the dry ground;
I will pour out my Spirit on your offspring,
and my blessing on your descendants.
4 They will spring up like grass in a meadow,
like poplar trees by flowing streams.
5 One will say, 'I belong to the LORD';
another will call himself by the name of Jacob;
still another will write on his hand, 'The LORD's,'
and will take the name Israel.

*The LORD, Not Idols*

6 "This is what the LORD says—
Israel's King and Redeemer, the LORD Almighty:
I am the first and I am the last;
apart from me there is no God.

**NIV** [a] *28* The Hebrew term refers to the irrevocable giving over of things or persons to the LORD, often by totally destroying them.

## King James

7 And who, as I, shall call, and shall declare it, and set it in order for me, since I appointed the ancient people? and the things that are coming, and shall come, let them show unto them.

8 Fear ye not, neither be afraid: have not I told thee from that time, and have declared *it?* ye *are* even my witnesses. Is there a God beside me? yea, *there is* no God; I know not *any.*

9 ¶ They that make a graven image *are* all of them vanity; and their delectable things shall not profit; and they *are* their own witnesses; they see not, nor know; that they may be ashamed.

10 Who hath formed a god, or molten a graven image *that* is profitable for nothing?

11 Behold, all his fellows shall be ashamed: and the workmen, they *are* of men: let them all be gathered together, let them stand up; *yet* they shall fear, *and* they shall be ashamed together.

12 The smith with the tongs both worketh in the coals, and fashioneth it with hammers, and worketh it with the strength of his arms: yea, he is hungry, and his strength faileth: he drinketh no water, and is faint.

13 The carpenter stretcheth out *his* rule; he marketh it out with a line; he fitteth it with planes, and he marketh it out with the compass, and maketh it after the figure of a man, according to the beauty of a man; that it may remain in the house.

14 He heweth him down cedars, and taketh the cypress and the oak, which he strengtheneth for himself among the trees of the forest: he planteth an ash, and the rain doth nourish *it.*

15 Then shall it be for a man to burn: for he will take thereof, and warm himself; yea, he kindleth *it,* and baketh bread; yea, he maketh a god, and worshippeth *it;* he maketh it a graven image, and falleth down thereto.

16 He burneth part thereof in the fire; with part thereof he eateth flesh; he roasteth roast, and is satisfied: yea, he warmeth *himself,* and saith, Aha, I am warm, I have seen the fire:

17 And the residue thereof he maketh a god, *even* his graven image: he falleth down unto it, and worshippeth *it,* and prayeth unto it, and saith, Deliver me; for thou *art* my god.

18 They have not known nor understood: for he hath shut their eyes, that they cannot see; *and* their hearts, that they cannot understand.

19 And none considereth in his heart, neither *is there* knowledge nor understanding to say, I have burned part of it in the fire; yea, also I have baked bread upon the coals thereof; I have roasted flesh, and eaten *it:* and shall I make the residue thereof an abomination? shall I fall down to the stock of a tree?

20 He feedeth on ashes: a deceived heart hath turned him aside, that he cannot deliver his soul, nor say, *Is there* not a lie in my right hand?

21 ¶ Remember these, O Jacob and Israel; for thou *art* my servant: I have formed thee; thou *art* my servant: O Israel, thou shalt not be forgotten of me.

## Amplified

7 Who is like Me? [Let him stand and] proclaim it, declare it, and set *his proofs* in order before Me, since I made *and* establish the people of antiquity. [Who has announced from of old] the things that are coming? Then let them declare yet future things.

8 Fear not, nor be afraid [in the coming violent upheavals]; have I not told it to you from of old and declared it? And you are My witnesses! Is there a God besides Me? There is no *other* Rock; I know not any.

9 All who make graven idols are confusion, chaos *and* worthlessness. Their [idol] objects in which they delight will not profit, and their own witnesses [worshipers] do not see or know, that they may be put to shame.

10 Who has been *such a fool as* to fashion a god or cast a graven image that is profitable for nothing?

11 Behold, all his fellows shall be put to shame, and the craftsmen, [how can they make a god?] they are but men. Let them all be gathered together, let them stand forth; they shall be terrified, they shall be put to shame together.

12 The ironsmith sharpens *and* uses a chisel and works it over the coals; he shapes *the core of the idol* with hammers and forges it with his strong arm. He becomes hungry and his strength fails; he drinks no water and is faint.

13 The carpenter stretches out a line; he marks it out with a pencil *or* red ochre; he fashions [an idol] with planes, and he marks it out with the compasses, and shapes it to have the figure of a man, with the beauty of a man, to dwell in a house.

14 He hews him down cedars, and takes the holm tree and the oak, and lets them grow strong for him among the trees of the forest; he plants a fir tree *or* an ash and the rain nourishes it.

15 Then it becomes *fuel* for a man to burn. A part of it he takes and warms himself, yes, he kindles a fire and bakes bread. [Then out of the remainder, the leavings] he makes a god and worships it! He *with his own hands* makes it into a graven image and falls down and worships it!

16 He burns part of the wood in the fire; with part of it he [cooks and] eats flesh, he roasts meat and is satisfied; also he warms himself and says, Aha, I am warm, I have seen the fire!

17 And from what is left *of the log* he makes a god, his graven idol. He falls down to it, he worships it and prays to it, and says, Deliver me, for you are my god!

18 They do not know or understand, for their eyes *God has let become* besmeared so that they cannot see, *and* their minds so that they cannot understand.

19 And not one considers in his mind, nor has he knowledge and understanding *enough* to say *to himself,* I have burned part of this log in the fire, and also I have baked bread on its coals and roasted meat and eaten it; and shall I make the remainder of it into an abomination—the very essence of what is disgusting, detestable and shamefully vile [in the eyes of a jealous God]? Shall I fall down *and* worship the stock of a tree—a block of wood [without consciousness or life]?

20 That man feeds on ashes [and finds his satisfaction in ashes]! A deluded mind has led him astray so that he cannot release *and* save himself, or ask, Is not [this thing I am holding] in my right hand a lie?

21 Remember these things [earnestly], O Jacob, Israel, for you are My servant! I formed you, you are My servant. O Israel, you shall not be forgotten by Me.

# New American Standard

7 'And who is like Me? Let him proclaim and declare it;
Yes, let him recount it to Me in order,
From the time that I established the ancient nation.
And let them declare to them the things that are coming
And the events that are going to take place.
8 'Do not tremble and do not be afraid;
Have I not long since announced it to you and declared it?
And you are My witnesses.
Is there any God besides Me,
Or is there any *other* Rock?
I know of none.' "

*The Folly of Idolatry*

9 Those who fashion a graven image are all of them futile, and their precious things are of no profit; even their own witnesses fail to see or know, so that they will be put to shame.

10 Who has fashioned a god or cast an idol to no profit?

11 Behold, all his companions will be put to shame, for the craftsmen themselves are mere men. Let them all assemble themselves, let them stand up, let them tremble, let them together be put to shame.

12 ¶ The man shapes iron into a cutting tool, and does his work over the coals, fashioning it with hammers, and working it with his strong arm. He also gets hungry and his strength fails; he drinks no water and becomes weary.

13 *Another* shapes wood, he extends a measuring line; he outlines it with red chalk. He works it with planes, and outlines it with a compass, and makes it like the form of a man, like the beauty of man, so that it may sit in a house.

14 Surely he cuts cedars for himself, and takes a cypress or an oak, and raises *it* for himself among the trees of the forest. He plants a fir, and the rain makes it grow.

15 Then it becomes *something* for a man to burn, so he takes one of them and warms himself; he also makes a fire to bake bread. He also makes a god and worships it; he makes it a graven image, and falls down before it.

16 Half of it he burns in the fire; over *this* half he eats meat as he roasts a roast, and is satisfied. He also warms himself and says, "Aha! I am warm, I have seen the fire."

17 But the rest of it he makes into a god, his graven image. He falls down before it and worships; he also prays to it and says, "Deliver me, for thou art my god."

18 ¶ They do not know, nor do they understand, for He has smeared over their eyes so that they cannot see and their hearts so that they cannot comprehend.

19 And no one recalls, nor is there knowledge or understanding to say, "I have burned half of it in the fire, and also have baked bread over its coals. I roast meat and eat *it*. Then I make the rest of it into an abomination, I fall down before a block of wood!"

20 He feeds on ashes; a deceived heart has turned him aside. And he cannot deliver himself, nor say, "Is there not a lie in my right hand?"

*God Forgives and Redeems*

21 ¶ "Remember these things, O Jacob,
And Israel, for you are My servant;
I have formed you, you are My servant,
O Israel, you will not be forgotten by Me.

# New International

7 Who then is like me? Let him proclaim it.
Let him declare and lay out before me
what has happened since I established my ancient people,
and what is yet to come—
yes, let him foretell what will come.
8 Do not tremble, do not be afraid.
Did I not proclaim this and foretell it long ago?
You are my witnesses. Is there any God besides me?
No, there is no other Rock; I know not one."

9 All who make idols are nothing,
and the things they treasure are worthless.
Those who would speak up for them are blind;
they are ignorant, to their own shame.
10 Who shapes a god and casts an idol,
which can profit him nothing?
11 He and his kind will be put to shame;
craftsmen are nothing but men.
Let them all come together and take their stand;
they will be brought down to terror and infamy.
12 The blacksmith takes a tool
and works with it in the coals;
he shapes an idol with hammers,
he forges it with the might of his arm.
He gets hungry and loses his strength;
he drinks no water and grows faint.
13 The carpenter measures with a line
and makes an outline with a marker;
he roughs it out with chisels
and marks it with compasses.
He shapes it in the form of man,
of man in all his glory,
that it may dwell in a shrine.
14 He cut down cedars,
or perhaps took a cypress or oak.
He let it grow among the trees of the forest,
or planted a pine, and the rain made it grow.
15 It is man's fuel for burning;
some of it he takes and warms himself,
he kindles a fire and bakes bread.
But he also fashions a god and worships it;
he makes an idol and bows down to it.
16 Half of the wood he burns in the fire;
over it he prepares his meal,
he roasts his meat and eats his fill.
He also warms himself and says,
"Ah! I am warm; I see the fire."
17 From the rest he makes a god, his idol;
he bows down to it and worships.
He prays to it and says,
"Save me; you are my god."
18 They know nothing, they understand nothing;
their eyes are plastered over so they cannot see,
and their minds closed so they cannot understand.
19 No one stops to think,
no one has the knowledge or understanding to say,
"Half of it I used for fuel;
I even baked bread over its coals,
I roasted meat and I ate.
Shall I make a detestable thing from what is left?
Shall I bow down to a block of wood?"
20 He feeds on ashes, a deluded heart misleads him;
he cannot save himself, or say,
"Is not this thing in my right hand a lie?"

21 "Remember these things, O Jacob,
for you are my servant, O Israel.
I have made you, you are my servant;
O Israel, I will not forget you.

## King James

22I have blotted out, as a thick cloud, thy transgressions, and, as a cloud, thy sins: return unto me; for I have redeemed thee.
23Sing, O ye heavens; for the LORD hath done *it:* shout, ye lower parts of the earth: break forth into singing, ye mountains, O forest, and every tree therein: for the LORD hath redeemed Jacob, and glorified himself in Israel.
24Thus saith the LORD, thy redeemer, and he that formed thee from the womb, I *am* the LORD that maketh all *things;* that stretcheth forth the heavens alone; that spreadeth abroad the earth by myself;
25That frustrateth the tokens of the liars, and maketh diviners mad; that turneth wise *men* backward, and maketh their knowledge foolish;
26That confirmeth the word of his servant, and performeth the counsel of his messengers; that saith to Jerusalem, Thou shalt be inhabited; and to the cities of Judah, Ye shall be built, and I will raise up the decayed places thereof:
27That saith to the deep, Be dry, and I will dry up thy rivers:
28That saith of Cyrus, *He is* my shepherd, and shall perform all my pleasure: even saying to Jerusalem, Thou shalt be built; and to the temple, Thy foundation shall be laid.

45 THUS SAITH the LORD to his anointed, to Cyrus, whose right hand I have holden, to subdue nations before him; and I will loose the loins of kings, to open before him the two leaved gates; and the gates shall not be shut;
2I will go before thee, and make the crooked places straight: I will break in pieces the gates of brass, and cut in sunder the bars of iron:
3And I will give thee the treasures of darkness, and hidden riches of secret places, that thou mayest know that I, the LORD, which call *thee* by thy name, *am* the God of Israel.
4For Jacob my servant's sake, and Israel mine elect, I have even called thee by thy name: I have surnamed thee, though thou hast not known me.
5¶ I *am* the LORD, and *there is* none else, *there is* no God beside me: I girded thee, though thou hast not known me:
6That they may know from the rising of the sun, and from the west, that *there is* none beside me. I *am* the LORD, and *there is* none else.

## Amplified

22I have blotted out as a thick cloud your transgressions, and as a cloud your sins. Return to Me, for I have redeemed you.
23Sing, O heavens, for the Lord has done it; shout, you depths of the earth; break forth into singing, you mountains, O forest, and every tree in it! For the Lord has redeemed Jacob, and will glorify Himself in Israel.
24Thus says the Lord, your Redeemer, and He Who formed you from the womb: I am the Lord Who made all things, Who alone stretched out the heavens, Who spread out the earth by Myself—who was with Me?
25[I am the Lord] Who frustrates the signs *and* confounds the omens [upon which their forecasts of the future are based by the false prophets], the [boasting] liars, and makes fools of diviners; Who turns the wise backward and makes their knowledge foolishness; [I Cor. 1:20.]
26 *The Lord* Who confirms the word of His servant, and performs the counsel of His messengers; Who says of Jerusalem, She shall [again] be inhabited; and of the cities of Judah, They shall [again] be built, and I will raise up their ruins;
27Who says to the deep, Be dry, and I will dry up your rivers;
28Who says of Cyrus, He is My shepherd (ruler), and he shall perform all My pleasure *and* fulfill all My purpose; even saying of Jerusalem, She shall *again* be built, and of the temple, Your foundation shall *again* be laid.

45 THUS SAYS the Lord to His anointed, to Cyrus, whose right hand I have held to subdue nations before him, and I will unarm *and* ungird the loins of kings to open doors before him and that gates should not be shut.
2I will go before you and level the mountains—to make the crooked places straight; I will break in pieces the doors of bronze and cut asunder the bars of iron.
3And I will give you the treasures of darkness and hidden riches of secret places, that you may know that it is I, the Lord, the God of Israel, Who calls you by your name.
4For Jacob My servant's sake, and Israel My chosen, I have called you by your name. I have surnamed you though you have not known Me.
5I am the Lord, and there is none else, there is no God besides Me. I will gird *and* arm you though you have not known Me,
6That men may know from the east *and* the rising of the sun, and from the west *and* its going down, that there is no *God* besides Me. I am the Lord, and no one else *is He.*

# New American Standard

22 "I have wiped out your transgressions like a thick cloud,
And your sins like a heavy mist.
Return to Me, for I have redeemed you."
23 Shout for joy, O heavens, for the LORD has done *it!*
Shout joyfully, you lower parts of the earth;
Break forth into a shout of joy, you mountains,
O forest, and every tree in it;
For the LORD has redeemed Jacob
And in Israel He shows forth His glory.

24 ¶ Thus says the LORD, your Redeemer, and the one who formed you from the womb,
"I, the LORD, am the maker of all things,
Stretching out the heavens by Myself,
And spreading out the earth all alone,
25 Causing the omens of boasters to fail,
Making fools out of diviners,
Causing wise men to draw back,
And turning their knowledge into foolishness,
26 Confirming the word of His servant,
And performing the purpose of His messengers.
*It is I* who says of Jerusalem, 'She shall be inhabited!'
And of the cities of Judah, 'They shall be built.'
And I will raise up her ruins *again.*
27 "*It is I* who says to the depth of the sea, 'Be dried up!'
And I will make your rivers dry.
28 "*It is I* who says of Cyrus, '*He is* My shepherd!
And he will perform all My desire.'
And he declares of Jerusalem, 'She will be built,'
And of the temple, 'Your foundation will be laid.'"

*God Uses Cyrus*

45 THUS SAYS the LORD to Cyrus His anointed,
Whom I have taken by the right hand,
To subdue nations before him,
And to loose the loins of kings;
To open doors before him so that gates will not be shut:
2 "I will go before you and make the rough places smooth;
I will shatter the doors of bronze, and cut through their iron bars.
3 "And I will give you the treasures of darkness,
And hidden wealth of secret places,
In order that you may know that it is I,
The LORD, the God of Israel, who calls you by your name.
4 "For the sake of Jacob My servant,
And Israel My chosen *one,*
I have also called you by your name;
I have given you a title of honor
Though you have not known Me.
5 "I am the LORD, and there is no other;
Besides Me there is no God.
I will gird you, though you have not known Me;
6 That men may know from the rising to the setting of the sun
That there is no one besides Me.
I am the LORD, and there is no other,

# New International

22 I have swept away your offenses like a cloud,
your sins like the morning mist.
Return to me,
for I have redeemed you."
23 Sing for joy, O heavens, for the LORD has done this;
shout aloud, O earth beneath.
Burst into song, you mountains,
you forests and all your trees,
for the LORD has redeemed Jacob,
he displays his glory in Israel.

*Jerusalem to Be Inhabited*

24 "This is what the LORD says—
your Redeemer, who formed you in the womb:

I am the LORD,
who has made all things,
who alone stretched out the heavens,
who spread out the earth by myself,

25 who foils the signs of false prophets
and makes fools of diviners,
who overthrows the learning of the wise
and turns it into nonsense,
26 who carries out the words of his servants
and fulfills the predictions of his messengers,

who says of Jerusalem, 'It shall be inhabited,'
of the towns of Judah, 'They shall be built,'
and of their ruins, 'I will restore them,'
27 who says to the watery deep, 'Be dry,
and I will dry up your streams,'
28 who says of Cyrus, 'He is my shepherd
and will accomplish all that I please;
he will say of Jerusalem, "Let it be rebuilt,"
and of the temple, "Let its foundations be laid."'

45 "THIS IS what the LORD says to his anointed,
to Cyrus, whose right hand I take hold of
to subdue nations before him
and to strip kings of their armor,
to open doors before him
so that gates will not be shut:
2 I will go before you
and will level the mountains[a];
I will break down gates of bronze
and cut through bars of iron.
3 I will give you the treasures of darkness,
riches stored in secret places,
so that you may know that I am the LORD,
the God of Israel, who summons you by name.
4 For the sake of Jacob my servant,
of Israel my chosen,
I summon you by name
and bestow on you a title of honor,
though you do not acknowledge me.
5 I am the LORD, and there is no other;
apart from me there is no God.
I will strengthen you,
though you have not acknowledged me,
6 so that from the rising of the sun
to the place of its setting
men may know there is none besides me.
I am the LORD, and there is no other.

NIV [a] 2 Dead Sea Scrolls and Septuagint; the meaning of the word in the Masoretic Text is uncertain.

## King James

7I form the light, and create darkness: I make peace, and create evil: I the LORD do all these *things*.

8Drop down, ye heavens, from above, and let the skies pour down righteousness: let the earth open, and let them bring forth salvation, and let righteousness spring up together; I the LORD have created it.

9Woe unto him that striveth with his Maker! *Let* the potsherd *strive* with the potsherds of the earth. Shall the clay say to him that fashioneth it, What makest thou? or thy work, He hath no hands?

10Woe unto him that saith unto *his* father, What begettest thou? or to the woman, What hast thou brought forth?

11Thus saith the LORD, the Holy One of Israel, and his Maker, Ask me of things to come concerning my sons, and concerning the work of my hands command ye me.

12I have made the earth, and created man upon it: I, *even* my hands, have stretched out the heavens, and all their host have I commanded.

13I have raised him up in righteousness, and I will direct all his ways: he shall build my city, and he shall let go my captives, not for price nor reward, saith the LORD of hosts.

14Thus saith the LORD, The labour of Egypt, and merchandise of Ethiopia and of the Sabeans, men of stature, shall come over unto thee, and they shall be thine: they shall come after thee; in chains they shall come over, and they shall fall down unto thee, they shall make supplication unto thee, *saying*, Surely God *is* in thee; and *there is* none else, *there is* no God.

15Verily thou *art* a God that hidest thyself, O God of Israel, the Saviour.

16They shall be ashamed, and also confounded, all of them: they shall go to confusion together *that are* makers of idols.

17 *But* Israel shall be saved in the LORD with an everlasting salvation: ye shall not be ashamed nor confounded world without end.

## Amplified

7I form the light and create darkness; I make peace [national well-being. Moral evil proceeds from the will of men, but physical evil proceeds from the will of God], and I create [physical] evil—calamity; I am the Lord Who does all these things.

8Let fall in showers, you heavens, from above, and let the skies rain down righteousness [the pure, spiritual, heavenly-life possibilities that have their foundation in the holy being of God]; let the earth open and let them, *skies and earth,* sprout forth salvation, and let righteousness germinate *and* spring up (as plants do) together; I the Lord have created it.

9Woe to him who strives with his Maker! A worthless piece of broken pottery among other pieces equally worthless [and yet presuming to strive with his Maker]! Shall the clay say to him who fashioned it, What do *you think* you are making? or, Your work has no handles? [Rom. 9:20.]

10Woe to him [who complains against his parents that they have begotten him] who says to a father, What are you begetting? or to a woman, With what are you in travail?

11Thus says the Lord, the Holy One of Israel, and his Maker: Would you question Me of things to come concerning My children, and concerning the work of My hands command Me?

12I made the earth, and created man upon it; I, with My hands, stretched out the heavens, and I commanded all their host.

13I have raised *Cyrus* up in righteousness [willing in every way that which is right and proper], and I will direct all his ways; he shall build My city, and he shall let go My captives, not for hire or for a bribe, says the Lord of hosts.

14Thus says the Lord, The labor *and* wealth of Egypt and the merchandise of Ethiopia, and the Sabeans, men of stature, shall come over to you and they shall be yours; they shall follow you; in chains [of subjection to you] they shall come over, and they shall fall down before you; they shall make supplication to you, saying, Surely God is in you, and there is no other, no God besides Him. [I Cor. 14:25.]

15Truly You are a God Who hides Yourself, O God of Israel, the Savior.

16They shall be put to shame, yes, confounded, all of them; they who are makers of idols shall go into confusion together.

17But Israel shall be saved by the Lord with an everlasting salvation; you shall not be put to shame or confounded to all eternity. [Heb. 5:9.]

## New American Standard

7 The One forming light and creating darkness,
Causing well-being and creating calamity;
I am the LORD who does all these.

*God's Supreme Power*

8¶ "Drip down, O heavens, from above,
And let the clouds pour down righteousness;
Let the earth open up and salvation bear fruit,
And righteousness spring up with it.
I, the LORD, have created it.

9¶ "Woe to *the one* who quarrels with his Maker—
An earthenware vessel among the vessels of earth!
Will the clay say to the potter, 'What are you doing?'
Or the thing you are making *say*, 'He has no hands'?
10 "Woe to him who says to a father, 'What are you begetting?'
Or to a woman, 'To what are you giving birth?' "

11¶ Thus says the LORD, the Holy One of Israel, and his Maker:
"Ask Me about the things to come concerning My sons,
And you shall commit to Me the work of My hands.
12 "It is I who made the earth, and created man upon it.
I stretched out the heavens with My hands,
And I ordained all their host.
13 "I have aroused him in righteousness,
And I will make all his ways smooth;
He will build My city, and will let My exiles go free,
Without any payment or reward," says the LORD of hosts.

14¶ Thus says the LORD,
"The products of Egypt and the merchandise of Cush
And the Sabeans, men of stature,
Will come over to you and will be yours;
They will walk behind you, they will come over in chains
And will bow down to you;
They will make supplication to you:
'Surely, God is with you, and there is none else,
No other God.' "
15 Truly, Thou art a God who hides Himself,
O God of Israel, Savior!
16 They will be put to shame and even humiliated, all of them;
The manufacturers of idols will go away together in humiliation.
17 Israel has been saved by the LORD
With an everlasting salvation;
You will not be put to shame or humiliated
To all eternity.

## New International

7I form the light and create darkness,
I bring prosperity and create disaster;
I, the LORD, do all these things.

8"You heavens above, rain down righteousness;
let the clouds shower it down.
Let the earth open wide,
let salvation spring up,
let righteousness grow with it;
I, the LORD, have created it.

9"Woe to him who quarrels with his Maker,
to him who is but a potsherd among the potsherds on the ground.
Does the clay say to the potter,
'What are you making?'
Does your work say,
'He has no hands'?
10Woe to him who says to his father,
'What have you begotten?'
or to his mother,
'What have you brought to birth?'

11"This is what the LORD says—
the Holy One of Israel, and its Maker:
Concerning things to come,
do you question me about my children,
or give me orders about the work of my hands?
12It is I who made the earth
and created mankind upon it.
My own hands stretched out the heavens;
I marshaled their starry hosts.
13I will raise up Cyrus[a] in my righteousness:
I will make all his ways straight.
He will rebuild my city
and set my exiles free,
but not for a price or reward,
says the LORD Almighty."

14This is what the LORD says:

"The products of Egypt and the merchandise of Cush,[b]
and those tall Sabeans—
they will come over to you
and will be yours;
they will trudge behind you,
coming over to you in chains.
They will bow down before you
and plead with you, saying,
'Surely God is with you, and there is no other;
there is no other god.' "

15Truly you are a God who hides himself,
O God and Savior of Israel.
16All the makers of idols will be put to shame and disgraced;
they will go off into disgrace together.
17But Israel will be saved by the LORD
with an everlasting salvation;
you will never be put to shame or disgraced,
to ages everlasting.

NIV [a] *13* Hebrew *him* [b] *14* That is, the upper Nile region

## King James

18For thus saith the LORD that created the heavens; God himself
that formed the earth and made it; he hath established it, he
created it not in vain, he formed it to be inhabited: I *am* the LORD;
and *there is* none else.
19I have not spoken in secret, in a dark place of the earth: I said
not unto the seed of Jacob, Seek ye me in vain: I the LORD speak
righteousness, I declare things that are right.
20¶ Assemble yourselves and come; draw near together, ye *that
are* escaped of the nations: they have no knowledge that set up the
wood of their graven image, and pray unto a god *that* cannot save.
21Tell ye, and bring *them* near; yea, let them take counsel together: who hath declared this from ancient time? *who* hath told
it from that time? *have* not I the LORD? and *there is* no God else
beside me; a just God and a Saviour; *there is* none beside me.
22Look unto me, and be ye saved, all the ends of the earth: for
I *am* God, and *there is* none else.
23I have sworn by myself, the word is gone out of my mouth
*in* righteousness, and shall not return, That unto me every knee
shall bow, every tongue shall swear.
24Surely, shall *one* say, in the LORD have I righteousness and
strength: *even* to him shall *men* come; and all that are incensed
against him shall be ashamed.
25In the LORD shall all the seed of Israel be justified, and shall
glory.

46 BEL BOWETH down, Nebo stoopeth, their idols were
upon the beasts, and upon the cattle: your carriages *were*
heavy laden; *they are* a burden to the weary *beast*.
2They stoop, they bow down together; they could not deliver
the burden, but themselves are gone into captivity.
3¶ Hearken unto me, O house of Jacob, and all the remnant of
the house of Israel, which are borne *by me* from the belly, which
are carried from the womb:
4And *even* to *your* old age I *am* he; and *even* to hoar hairs will
I carry *you*: I have made, and I will bear; even I will carry, and will
deliver *you*.
5¶ To whom will ye liken me, and make *me* equal, and compare
me, that we may be like?

## Amplified

18For thus says the Lord Who created the heavens, God Himself
Who formed the earth and made it, Who established it and created
it not a worthless waste; He formed it to be inhabited: I am the
Lord, and there is no one else.
19I have not spoken in secret, in a corner of the land of darkness;
I did not call the descendants of Jacob [to a fruitless service] saying,
Seek Me for nothing [but promised them a just reward]. I the Lord
speak righteousness—the truth [trustworthy, straightforward cor-
respondence between deeds and words]. I declare the things that
are right. [John 18:20.]
20Assemble yourselves and come, draw near together, you survivors of the nations! They have no knowledge who carry about
[in religious processions or into battle] their wooden idols, and
keep on praying to a god that cannot save.
21Declare and bring forward your strong arguments [for praying to gods that cannot save], yes, take counsel together. Who
announced this [the rise of Cyrus and his conquests] beforehand—
long ago? *What god* declared it of old? Have not I, the Lord? And
there is no other God besides Me, a rigidly *and* uncompromisingly
just *and* righteous God and Savior. There is none besides Me.
22Look to Me and be saved, all the ends of the earth! For I am
God, and there is no other.
23I have sworn by Myself, the word is gone out of My mouth
in righteousness and shall not return, that unto Me every knee
shall bow, every tongue shall swear *allegiance*. [Rom. 14:11; Heb.
6:13; Phil. 2:10, 11.]
24Only in the Lord shall one say, I have righteousness [salvation
and victory] and strength [to achieve]. To Him shall all come who
were incensed against Him, and shall be ashamed. [I Cor. 1:30, 31.]
25In the Lord shall all the offspring of Israel be justified [enjoy
righteousness, salvation and victory], and shall glory.

46 BEL BOWS down, Nebo stoops [gods of Babylon whose
idols are being carried off]; their idols are on the beasts *of
burden* and on the cattle; these things that you carry about are
loaded as burdens on the weary beasts.
2 *The gods* stoop, they bow down together; they could not save
*their own idols*, but are themselves gone into captivity.
3Listen to Me [says the Lord], O house of Jacob, and all the
remnant of the house of Israel, who have been borne by Me from
your birth, carried from the womb:
4Even to your old age I am He, and even to hair white with age
will I carry you. I have made, and I will bear; yes, I will carry and
will save *you*.
5To whom will you liken Me and make Me equal, and compare
Me, that we may be alike?

## New American Standard

18¶ For thus says the LORD, who created the heavens
(He is the God who formed the earth and made it,
He established it and did not create it a waste place,
*But* formed it to be inhabited),
"I am the LORD, and there is none else.
19 "I have not spoken in secret,
In some dark land;
I did not say to the offspring of Jacob,
'Seek Me in a waste place';
I, the LORD, speak righteousness
Declaring things that are upright.

20¶ "Gather yourselves and come;
Draw near together, you fugitives of the nations;
They have no knowledge,
Who carry about their wooden idol,
And pray to a god who cannot save.
21 "Declare and set forth *your case;*
Indeed, let them consult together.
Who has announced this from of old?
Who has long since declared it?
Is it not I, the LORD?
And there is no other God besides Me,
A righteous God and a Savior;
There is none except Me.
22 "Turn to Me, and be saved, all the ends of the earth;
For I am God, and there is no other.
23 "I have sworn by Myself,
The word has gone forth from My mouth in righteousness
And will not turn back,
That to Me every knee will bow, every tongue will swear *allegiance.*
24 "They will say of Me, 'Only in the LORD are righteousness and strength.'
Men will come to Him,
And all who were angry at Him shall be put to shame.
25 "In the LORD all the offspring of Israel
Will be justified, and will glory."

*Babylon's Idols and the True God*

46 BEL HAS bowed down, Nebo stoops over;
Their images are *consigned* to the beasts and the cattle.
The things that you carry are burdensome,
A load for the weary *beast.*
2 They stooped over, they have bowed down together;
They could not rescue the burden,
But have themselves gone into captivity.

3¶ "Listen to Me, O house of Jacob,
And all the remnant of the house of Israel,
You who have been borne by Me from birth,
And have been carried from the womb;
4 Even to your old age, I shall be the same,
And even to your graying years I shall bear *you!*
I have done *it,* and I shall carry *you;*
And I shall bear *you,* and I shall deliver *you.*

5¶ "To whom would you liken Me,
And make Me equal and compare Me,
That we should be alike?

## New International

18For this is what the LORD says—
he who created the heavens,
he is God;
he who fashioned and made the earth,
he founded it;
he did not create it to be empty,
but formed it to be inhabited—
he says:
"I am the LORD,
and there is no other.
19I have not spoken in secret,
from somewhere in a land of darkness;
I have not said to Jacob's descendants,
'Seek me in vain.'
I, the LORD, speak the truth;
I declare what is right.

20"Gather together and come;
assemble, you fugitives from the nations.
Ignorant are those who carry about idols of wood,
who pray to gods that cannot save.
21Declare what is to be, present it—
let them take counsel together.
Who foretold this long ago,
who declared it from the distant past?
Was it not I, the LORD?
And there is no God apart from me,
a righteous God and a Savior;
there is none but me.

22"Turn to me and be saved,
all you ends of the earth;
for I am God, and there is no other.
23By myself I have sworn,
my mouth has uttered in all integrity
a word that will not be revoked:
Before me every knee will bow;
by me every tongue will swear.
24They will say of me, 'In the LORD alone
are righteousness and strength.'"
All who have raged against him
will come to him and be put to shame.
25But in the LORD all the descendants of Israel
will be found righteous and will exult.

*Gods of Babylon*

46 BEL BOWS down, Nebo stoops low;
their idols are borne by beasts of burden.[a]
The images that are carried about are burdensome,
a burden for the weary.
2They stoop and bow down together;
unable to rescue the burden,
they themselves go off into captivity.

3"Listen to me, O house of Jacob,
all you who remain of the house of Israel,
you whom I have upheld since you were conceived,
and have carried since your birth.
4Even to your old age and gray hairs
I am he, I am he who will sustain you.
I have made you and I will carry you;
I will sustain you and I will rescue you.

5"To whom will you compare me or count me equal?
To whom will you liken me that we may be compared?

NIV [a] 1 Or *are but beasts and cattle*

## King James

6They lavish gold out of the bag, and weigh silver in the balance, *and* hire a goldsmith; and he maketh it a god: they fall down, yea, they worship.

7They bear him upon the shoulder, they carry him, and set him in his place, and he standeth; from his place shall he not remove: yea, *one* shall cry unto him, yet can he not answer, nor save him out of his trouble.

8Remember this, and show yourselves men: bring *it* again to mind, O ye transgressors.

9Remember the former things of old: for I *am* God, and *there is* none else; *I am* God, and *there is* none like me,

10Declaring the end from the beginning, and from ancient times *the things* that are not *yet* done, saying, My counsel shall stand, and I will do all my pleasure:

11Calling a ravenous bird from the east, the man that executeth my counsel from a far country: yea, I have spoken *it*, I will also bring it to pass; I have purposed *it*, I will also do it.

12¶ Hearken unto me, ye stouthearted, that *are* far from righteousness:

13I bring near my righteousness; it shall not be far off, and my salvation shall not tarry: and I will place salvation in Zion for Israel my glory.

**47** COME DOWN, and sit in the dust, O virgin daughter of Babylon, sit on the ground: *there is* no throne, O daughter of the Chaldeans: for thou shalt no more be called tender and delicate.

2Take the millstones, and grind meal: uncover thy locks, make bare the leg, uncover the thigh, pass over the rivers.

3Thy nakedness shall be uncovered, yea, thy shame shall be seen: I will take vengeance, and I will not meet *thee as* a man.

4 *As for* our redeemer, the LORD of hosts *is* his name, the Holy One of Israel.

5Sit thou silent, and get thee into darkness, O daughter of the Chaldeans: for thou shalt no more be called, The lady of kingdoms.

6¶ I was wroth with my people, I have polluted mine inheritance, and given them into thine hand: thou didst show them no mercy; upon the ancient hast thou very heavily laid thy yoke.

7¶ And thou saidst, I shall be a lady for ever: *so* that thou didst not lay these *things* to thy heart, neither didst remember the latter end of it.

## Amplified

6They lavish gold out of the cup *or* bag, weigh out silver on the scales, and hire a goldsmith, and he fashions it into a god; (then) they fall down, yes, they worship *it!*

7They bear it upon their shoulders [in processions or in battle], they carry it and set it down in its place, and there it stands; it cannot move from its place. Even if one cries to it for help, yet *the idol* cannot answer or save him out of his distress.

8[Earnestly] remember this, be ashamed *and* own yourselves guilty; bring it again to mind *and* lay it to heart, O you rebels!

9[Earnestly] remember the former things *which I did* of old; for I am God, and there is none else; I am God, and there is none like Me,

10Declaring the end *and* the result from the beginning and from ancient times the things that are not yet done, saying, My counsel shall stand, and I will do all My pleasure *and* purpose,

11Calling a ravenous bird from the east, the man [Cyrus] *who executes* My counsel from a far country. Yes, I have spoken, and I will bring it to pass; I have purposed it, and I will do it.

12Listen to Me, you stiff-hearted *and* you who have lost heart, who are far from righteousness—from uprightness and right standing with God, and His righteous deliverance.

13I bring near My righteousness [in the deliverance of Israel]; it shall not be far off, and My salvation shall not tarry; and I will put salvation in Zion, for Israel My glory—yes, give salvation in Zion and My glory to Israel.

**47** COME DOWN, and sit in the dust, O virgin daughter of Babylon, sit on the ground [in abject humiliation]; there is no throne for you, O daughter of the Chaldeans, for you shall no longer be called dainty and delicate.

2Take the millstones [like the poorest female slave of the household] and grind meal; take off your veil *and* uncover your hair; remove your skirt, bare your leg, wade through rivers [at the command of your captors].

3Your nakedness shall be exposed, and your shame shall be seen. I will take vengeance, and I will spare no man—none I encounter [will be able to resist Me],

4 *Says* our Redeemer, the Lord of hosts is His name, the Holy One of Israel.

5Sit in silence and go into darkness, O daughter of the Chaldeans; for you shall no more be called the lady *and* mistress of kingdoms.

6I was angry with My people, I profaned My inheritance [Judah] and I gave them into your hand [Babylon]. You showed them no mercy; upon the old people you made your yoke very heavy.

7And you said, I shall be mistress for ever; so you did not lay these things to heart, nor did you [seriously] remember the certain ultimate end of such conduct.

## New American Standard

6 "Those who lavish gold from the purse
And weigh silver on the scale
Hire a goldsmith, and he makes it *into* a god;
They bow down, indeed they worship it.
7 "They lift it upon the shoulder and carry it;
They set it in its place and it stands *there.*
It does not move from its place.
Though one may cry to it, it cannot answer;
It cannot deliver him from his distress.

8¶ "Remember this, and be assured;
Recall it to mind, you transgressors.
9 "Remember the former things long past,
For I am God, and there is no other;
*I am* God, and there is no one like Me,
10 Declaring the end from the beginning
And from ancient times things which have not been done,
Saying, 'My purpose will be established,
And I will accomplish all My good pleasure';
11 Calling a bird of prey from the east,
The man of My purpose from a far country.
Truly I have spoken; truly I will bring it to pass.
I have planned *it, surely* I will do it.

12¶ "Listen to Me, you stubborn-minded,
Who are far from righteousness.
13 "I bring near My righteousness, it is not far off;
And My salvation will not delay.
And I will grant salvation in Zion,
*And* My glory for Israel.

*Lament for Babylon*

47 "COME DOWN and sit in the dust,
O virgin daughter of Babylon;
Sit on the ground without a throne,
O daughter of the Chaldeans.
For you shall no longer be called tender and delicate.
2 "Take the millstones and grind meal.
Remove your veil, strip off the skirt,
Uncover the leg, cross the rivers.
3 "Your nakedness will be uncovered,
Your shame also will be exposed;
I will take vengeance and will not spare a man."
4 Our Redeemer, the LORD of hosts is His name,
The Holy One of Israel.
5 "Sit silently, and go into darkness,
O daughter of the Chaldeans;
For you will no more be called
The queen of kingdoms.
6 "I was angry with My people,
I profaned My heritage,
And gave them into your hand.
You did not show mercy to them,
On the aged you made your yoke very heavy.
7 "Yet you said, 'I shall be a queen forever.'
These things you did not consider,
Nor remember the outcome of them.

## New International

6Some pour out gold from their bags
and weigh out silver on the scales;
they hire a goldsmith to make it into a god,
and they bow down and worship it.
7They lift it to their shoulders and carry it;
they set it up in its place, and there it stands.
From that spot it cannot move.
Though one cries out to it, it does not answer;
it cannot save him from his troubles.

8"Remember this, fix it in mind,
take it to heart, you rebels.
9Remember the former things, those of long ago;
I am God, and there is no other;
I am God, and there is none like me.
10I make known the end from the beginning,
from ancient times, what is still to come.
I say: My purpose will stand,
and I will do all that I please.
11From the east I summon a bird of prey;
from a far-off land, a man to fulfill my purpose.
What I have said, that will I bring about;
what I have planned, that will I do.
12Listen to me, you stubborn-hearted,
you who are far from righteousness.
13I am bringing my righteousness near,
it is not far away;
and my salvation will not be delayed.
I will grant salvation to Zion,
my splendor to Israel.

*The Fall of Babylon*

47 "GO DOWN, sit in the dust,
Virgin Daughter of Babylon;
sit on the ground without a throne,
Daughter of the Babylonians.[a]
No more will you be called
tender or delicate.
2Take millstones and grind flour;
take off your veil.
Lift up your skirts, bare your legs,
and wade through the streams.
3Your nakedness will be exposed
and your shame uncovered.
I will take vengeance;
I will spare no one."

4Our Redeemer—the LORD Almighty is his name—
is the Holy One of Israel.

5"Sit in silence, go into darkness,
Daughter of the Babylonians;
no more will you be called
queen of kingdoms.
6I was angry with my people
and desecrated my inheritance;
I gave them into your hand,
and you showed them no mercy.
Even on the aged
you laid a very heavy yoke.
7You said, 'I will continue forever—
the eternal queen!'
But you did not consider these things
or reflect on what might happen.

NIV [a] 1 Or *Chaldeans;* also in verse 5

## King James

8 Therefore hear now this, *thou that art* given to pleasures, that dwellest carelessly, that sayest in thine heart, I *am*, and none else beside me; I shall not sit *as* a widow, neither shall I know the loss of children:

9 But these two *things* shall come to thee in a moment in one day, the loss of children, and widowhood: they shall come upon thee in their perfection for the multitude of thy sorceries, *and* for the great abundance of thine enchantments.

10 ¶ For thou hast trusted in thy wickedness: thou hast said, None seeth me. Thy wisdom and thy knowledge, it hath perverted thee; and thou hast said in thine heart, I *am*, and none else beside me.

11 ¶ Therefore shall evil come upon thee; thou shalt not know from whence it riseth: and mischief shall fall upon thee; thou shalt not be able to put it off: and desolation shall come upon thee suddenly, *which* thou shalt not know.

12 Stand now with thine enchantments, and with the multitude of thy sorceries, wherein thou hast laboured from thy youth; if so be thou shalt be able to profit, if so be thou mayest prevail.

13 Thou art wearied in the multitude of thy counsels. Let now the astrologers, the stargazers, the monthly prognosticators, stand up, and save thee from *these things* that shall come upon thee.

14 Behold, they shall be as stubble; the fire shall burn them; they shall not deliver themselves from the power of the flame: *there shall* not *be* a coal to warm at, *nor* fire to sit before it.

15 Thus shall they be unto thee with whom thou hast laboured, *even* thy merchants, from thy youth: they shall wander every one to his quarter; none shall save thee.

## Amplified

8 Therefore now hear this, you who love pleasures *and* are given up to them, who dwell safely *and* sit securely, who say in your mind, I am [mistress] and none else besides me; I shall not sit as a widow, nor shall I know the loss of children.

9 But these two things shall come to you in a moment, in one day, the loss of children and widowhood. They shall come upon you in their full measure in *spite of* the multitude of *your claims to* power given you by the assistance of evil spirits, and of the great abundance of your enchantments. [Rev. 18:7, 8.]

10 For you [Babylon] have trusted in your wickedness; you have said, No one sees me. Your wisdom and your knowledge led you astray, and you said in your heart *and* mind, I am, and there is no one besides me.

11 Therefore shall evil come upon you; you shall not know the dawning of it *or* how to charm it away; and disaster *and* evil shall fall upon you that you shall not be able to atone for [with all your offerings to your gods], and desolation shall come upon you suddenly, of which you will know nothing *or* how to avert it.

12 Persist then with your enchantments and the multitude of your sorceries [Babylon] in which you have labored from your youth, and see if perhaps you will be able to profit, if you may prevail *and* strike terror!

13 You are wearied with your many counsels *and* plans. Let now the astrologers, the stargazers, the monthly prognosticators, stand up, and make known to you *and* save you from the things that shall come upon you [Babylon].

14 Behold, they are like stubble, the fire consumes them; they cannot *even* deliver themselves from the power of the flame [much less deliver the nation]. This is no coal for warming, *or* fire before which to sit!

15 Such to you shall they [the astrologers and their kind] be with whom you have labored *and* such their fate, who have done business with you from your youth; they will wander every one to his quarter *and* in his own direction. No one will save you.

## King James

**48** HEAR YE this, O house of Jacob, which are called by the name of Israel, and are come forth out of the waters of Judah, which swear by the name of the LORD, and make mention of the God of Israel, *but* not in truth, nor in righteousness.

2 For they call themselves of the holy city, and stay themselves upon the God of Israel; The LORD of hosts *is* his name.

3 I have declared the former things from the beginning; and they went forth out of my mouth, and I showed them; I did *them* suddenly, and they came to pass.

4 Because I knew that thou *art* obstinate, and thy neck *is* an iron sinew, and thy brow brass;

5 I have even from the beginning declared *it* to thee; before it came to pass I showed *it* thee: lest thou shouldest say, Mine idol hath done them, and my graven image, and my molten image, hath commanded them.

## Amplified

**48** HEAR THIS, O house of Jacob, who are called by the name of Israel, and who came forth from the seed of Judah; who swear allegiance by the name of the Lord, and make mention of the God of Israel, but not in truth *and* sincerity, nor in righteousness—rightness and moral rectitude in every area and relation—

2 For they call themselves *citizens* of the holy city and depend on the God of Israel; the Lord of hosts is His name.

3 I have declared from the beginning the former things [which happened in times past to Israel]; they went forth from My mouth and I made them known; then suddenly I did them, and they came to pass, *says the Lord*.

4 Because I knew that you are obstinate, and your neck is an iron sinew and your brow is brass,

5 Therefore I have declared things to come to you of old; before they came to pass I announced them to you, so that you could not say, My idol has done them, and my graven image and my molten image have commanded them.

## New American Standard

8¶ "Now, then, hear this, you sensual one,
Who dwells securely,
Who says in your heart,
'I am, and there is no one besides me.
I shall not sit as a widow,
Nor shall I know loss of children.'
9 "But these two things shall come on you suddenly in one day:
Loss of children and widowhood.
They shall come on you in full measure
In spite of your many sorceries,
In spite of the great power of your spells.
10 "And you felt secure in your wickedness and said,
'No one sees me,'
Your wisdom and your knowledge, they have deluded you;
For you have said in your heart,
'I am, and there is no one besides me.'
11 "But evil will come on you
Which you will not know how to charm away;
And disaster will fall on you
For which you cannot atone,
And destruction about which you do not know
Will come on you suddenly.
12¶ "Stand *fast* now in your spells
And in your many sorceries
With which you have labored from your youth;
Perhaps you will be able to profit,
Perhaps you may cause trembling.
13 "You are wearied with your many counsels;
Let now the astrologers,
Those who prophesy by the stars,
Those who predict by the new moons,
Stand up and save you from what will come upon you.
14 "Behold, they have become like stubble,
Fire burns them;
They cannot deliver themselves from the power of the flame;
There will be no coal to warm by,
*Nor* a fire to sit before!
15 "So have those become to you with whom you have labored,
Who have trafficked with you from your youth;
Each has wandered in his own way.
There is none to save you.

*Israel's Obstinacy*

48 "HEAR THIS, O house of Jacob, who are named Israel
And who came forth from the loins of Judah,
Who swear by the name of the LORD
And invoke the God of Israel,
*But* not in truth nor in righteousness.
2 "For they call themselves after the holy city,
And lean on the God of Israel;
The LORD of hosts is His name.
3 "I declared the former things long ago
And they went forth from My mouth, and I proclaimed them.
Suddenly I acted, and they came to pass.
4 "Because I know that you are obstinate,
And your neck is an iron sinew,
And your forehead bronze,
5 Therefore I declared *them* to you long ago,
Before they took place I proclaimed *them* to you,
Lest you should say, 'My idol has done them,
And my graven image and my molten image have commanded them.'

## New International

8"Now then, listen, you wanton creature,
lounging in your security
and saying to yourself,
'I am, and there is none besides me.
I will never be a widow
or suffer the loss of children.'
9Both of these will overtake you
in a moment, on a single day:
loss of children and widowhood.
They will come upon you in full measure,
in spite of your many sorceries
and all your potent spells.
10You have trusted in your wickedness
and have said, 'No one sees me.'
Your wisdom and knowledge mislead you
when you say to yourself,
'I am, and there is none besides me.'
11Disaster will come upon you,
and you will not know how to conjure it away.
A calamity will fall upon you
that you cannot ward off with a ransom;
a catastrophe you cannot foresee
will suddenly come upon you.

12"Keep on, then, with your magic spells
and with your many sorceries,
which you have labored at since childhood.
Perhaps you will succeed,
perhaps you will cause terror.
13All the counsel you have received has only worn you out!
Let your astrologers come forward,
those stargazers who make predictions month by month,
let them save you from what is coming upon you.
14Surely they are like stubble;
the fire will burn them up.
They cannot even save themselves
from the power of the flame.
Here are no coals to warm anyone;
here is no fire to sit by.
15That is all they can do for you—
these you have labored with
and trafficked with since childhood.
Each of them goes on in his error;
there is not one that can save you.

*Stubborn Israel*

48 "LISTEN TO this, O house of Jacob,
you who are called by the name of Israel
and come from the line of Judah,
you who take oaths in the name of the LORD
and invoke the God of Israel—
but not in truth or righteousness—
2you who call yourselves citizens of the holy city
and rely on the God of Israel—
the LORD Almighty is his name:
3I foretold the former things long ago,
my mouth announced them and I made them known;
then suddenly I acted, and they came to pass.
4For I knew how stubborn you were;
the sinews of your neck were iron,
your forehead was bronze.
5Therefore I told you these things long ago;
before they happened I announced them to you
so that you could not say,
'My idols did them;
my wooden image and metal god ordained them.'

## King James

6Thou hast heard, see all this; and will not ye declare *it?* I have
shown thee new things from this time, even hidden things, and
thou didst not know them.
7They are created now, and not from the beginning; even before
the day when thou heardest them not; lest thou shouldest say,
Behold, I knew them.
8Yea, thou heardest not; yea, thou knewest not; yea, from that
time *that* thine ear was not opened: for I knew that thou wouldest
deal very treacherously, and wast called a transgressor from the
womb.
9¶ For my name's sake will I defer mine anger, and for my praise
will I refrain for thee, that I cut thee not off.
10Behold, I have refined thee, but not with silver; I have chosen
thee in the furnace of affliction.
11For mine own sake, *even* for mine own sake, will I do *it:* for
how should *my name* be polluted? and I will not give my glory unto
another.
12¶ Hearken unto me, O Jacob and Israel, my called; I *am* he; I
*am* the first, I also *am* the last.
13Mine hand also hath laid the foundation of the earth, and my
right hand hath spanned the heavens: *when* I call unto them, they
stand up together.
14All ye, assemble yourselves, and hear; which among them
hath declared these *things?* The LORD hath loved him: he will do
his pleasure on Babylon, and his arm *shall be on* the Chaldeans.
15I, *even* I, have spoken; yea, I have called him: I have brought
him, and he shall make his way prosperous.
16¶ Come ye near unto me, hear ye this; I have not spoken in
secret from the beginning; from the time that it was, there *am* I: and
now the Lord GOD, and his spirit, hath sent me.
17Thus saith the LORD, thy Redeemer, the Holy One of Israel;
I *am* the LORD thy God which teacheth thee to profit, which leadeth
thee by the way *that* thou shouldest go.
18O that thou hadst hearkened to my commandments! then had
thy peace been as a river, and thy righteousness as the waves of
the sea:
19Thy seed also had been as the sand, and the offspring of thy
bowels like the gravel thereof; his name should not have been cut
off nor destroyed from before me.
20¶ Go ye forth of Babylon, flee ye from the Chaldeans, with a
voice of singing declare ye, tell this, utter it *even* to the end of the
earth; say ye, The LORD hath redeemed his servant Jacob.

## Amplified

6You have heard [these things foretold], now you see this fulfillment; and will you not bear witness to it? I show you specified new
things from this time forth, even hidden things—kept in reserve—
which you have not known.
7They are created now [called into being by the prophetic word]
and not long ago; and before today you never heard of them, lest
you should say, Behold, I knew them!
8Yes, you have never heard; yes, you have never known; yes,
from of old your ear was not opened. For I, the Lord, knew that
you, O house of Israel, dealt very treacherously, and were called
a transgressor *and* a rebel *in* revolt from your birth.
9For My name's sake I defer My anger, and for the sake of My
praise I restrain it for you, that I may not cut you off.
10Behold, I have refined you, but not as silver; I have tried *and*
chosen you in the furnace of affliction.
11For My own sake, for My own sake, I do it [I refrain and do
not utterly destroy you], for why should I permit My name to be
polluted *and* profaned [which it would be if the Lord completely
destroyed His chosen people]? And I will not give My glory to
another [by permitting the worshipers of idols to triumph over
you].
12Listen to Me, O Jacob and Israel, My called; I am He, I am the
first, I also am the last.
13Yes, My hand has laid the foundation of the earth, and My
right hand has spread out the heavens; when I call to them, they
stand forth together [to execute My decrees].
14Assemble yourselves, all of you, and hear! Who among them
[the gods and Chaldean astrologers] has foretold these things? The
Lord has loved him [Cyrus of Persia]; he will do His pleasure *and*
purpose on Babylon, and his arm shall be against the Chaldeans.
15I, even I, have foretold it; yes, I have called him [Cyrus]; I have
brought him, and *the Lord* shall make his way prosperous.
16Come near to me and listen to this: I have not spoken in secret
from the beginning; from the time that it happened I was there.
And now the Lord God has sent His Spirit in *and* with me.
17Thus says the Lord, your Redeemer, the Holy One of Israel:
I am the Lord your God Who teaches you to profit, Who leads you
by the way that you should go.
18Oh, that you had hearkened to My commandments! Then
your peace *and* prosperity would have been like a flowing river;
and your righteousness [the holiness and purity of the nation] like
the *abundant* waves of the sea;
19Your offspring would have been as the sand, and your descendants like the offspring of the sea; their name would not be
cut off or destroyed from before Me. [Luke 19:42.]
20Go forth out of Babylon, flee from the Chaldeans! With a voice
of singing declare, tell this, cause it to go forth even to the end of
the earth; say, The Lord has redeemed His servant Jacob!

## New American Standard

6 "You have heard; look at all this.
And you, will you not declare it?
I proclaim to you new things from this time,
Even hidden things which you have not known.
7 "They are created now and not long ago;
And before today you have not heard them,
Lest you should say, 'Behold, I knew them.'
8 "You have not heard, you have not known.
Even from long ago your ear has not been open,
Because I knew that you would deal very treacherously;
And you have been called a rebel from birth.
9 "For the sake of My name I delay My wrath,
And *for* My praise I restrain *it* for you,
In order not to cut you off.
10 "Behold, I have refined you, but not as silver;
I have tested you in the furnace of affliction.
11 "For My own sake, for My own sake, I will act;
For how can *My name* be profaned?
And My glory I will not give to another.

*Deliverance Promised*

12¶ "Listen to Me, O Jacob, even Israel whom I called;
I am He, I am the first, I am also the last.
13 "Surely My hand founded the earth,
And My right hand spread out the heavens;
When I call to them, they stand together.
14 "Assemble, all of you, and listen!
Who among them has declared these things?
The LORD loves him; he shall carry out His good pleasure on Babylon,
And His arm *shall be against* the Chaldeans.
15 "I, even I, have spoken; indeed I have called him,
I have brought him, and He will make his ways successful.
16 "Come near to Me, listen to this:
From the first I have not spoken in secret,
From the time it took place, I was there.
And now the Lord GOD has sent Me, and His Spirit."

17¶ Thus says the LORD, your Redeemer, the Holy One of Israel;
"I am the LORD your God, who teaches you to profit,
Who leads you in the way you should go.
18 "If only you had paid attention to My commandments!
Then your well-being would have been like a river,
And your righteousness like the waves of the sea.
19 "Your descendants would have been like the sand,
And your offspring like its grains;
Their name would never be cut off or destroyed from My presence."

20¶ Go forth from Babylon! Flee from the Chaldeans!
Declare with the sound of joyful shouting, proclaim this,
Send it out to the end of the earth;
Say, "The LORD has redeemed His servant Jacob."

## New International

6 You have heard these things; look at them all.
Will you not admit them?

"From now on I will tell you of new things,
of hidden things unknown to you.
7 They are created now, and not long ago;
you have not heard of them before today.
So you cannot say,
'Yes, I knew of them.'
8 You have neither heard nor understood;
from of old your ear has not been open.
Well do I know how treacherous you are;
you were called a rebel from birth.
9 For my own name's sake I delay my wrath;
for the sake of my praise I hold it back from you,
so as not to cut you off.
10 See, I have refined you, though not as silver;
I have tested you in the furnace of affliction.
11 For my own sake, for my own sake, I do this.
How can I let myself be defamed?
I will not yield my glory to another.

*Israel Freed*

12 "Listen to me, O Jacob,
Israel, whom I have called:
I am he;
I am the first and I am the last.
13 My own hand laid the foundations of the earth,
and my right hand spread out the heavens;
when I summon them,
they all stand up together.

14 "Come together, all of you, and listen:
Which of ⌊the idols⌋ has foretold these things?
The LORD's chosen ally
will carry out his purpose against Babylon;
his arm will be against the Babylonians.[a]
15 I, even I, have spoken;
yes, I have called him.
I will bring him,
and he will succeed in his mission.

16 "Come near me and listen to this:
"From the first announcement I have not spoken in secret;
at the time it happens, I am there."

And now the Sovereign LORD has sent me,
with his Spirit.

17 This is what the LORD says—
your Redeemer, the Holy One of Israel:
"I am the LORD your God,
who teaches you what is best for you,
who directs you in the way you should go.
18 If only you had paid attention to my commands,
your peace would have been like a river,
your righteousness like the waves of the sea.
19 Your descendants would have been like the sand,
your children like its numberless grains;
their name would never be cut off
nor destroyed from before me."

20 Leave Babylon,
flee from the Babylonians!
Announce this with shouts of joy
and proclaim it.
Send it out to the ends of the earth;
say, "The LORD has redeemed his servant Jacob."

NIV [a] 14 Or *Chaldeans;* also in verse 20

## King James

21 And they thirsted not *when* he led them through the deserts: he caused the waters to flow out of the rock for them: he clave the rock also, and the waters gushed out.

22 *There is* no peace, saith the LORD, unto the wicked.

# 49

LISTEN, O isles, unto me; and hearken, ye people, from far; The LORD hath called me from the womb; from the bowels of my mother hath he made mention of my name.

2 And he hath made my mouth like a sharp sword; in the shadow of his hand hath he hid me, and made me a polished shaft; in his quiver hath he hid me;

3 And said unto me, Thou *art* my servant, O Israel, in whom I will be glorified.

4 Then I said, I have laboured in vain, I have spent my strength for nought, and in vain: *yet* surely my judgment *is* with the LORD, and my work with my God.

5 ¶ And now, saith the LORD that formed me from the womb *to be* his servant, to bring Jacob again to him, Though Israel be not gathered, yet shall I be glorious in the eyes of the LORD, and my God shall be my strength.

6 And he said, It is a light thing that thou shouldest be my servant to raise up the tribes of Jacob, and to restore the preserved of Israel: I will also give thee for a light to the Gentiles, that thou mayest be my salvation unto the end of the earth.

7 Thus saith the LORD, the Redeemer of Israel, *and* his Holy One, to him whom man despiseth, to him whom the nation abhorreth, to a servant of rulers, Kings shall see and arise, princes also shall worship, because of the LORD that is faithful, *and* the Holy One of Israel, and he shall choose thee.

8 Thus saith the LORD, In an acceptable time have I heard thee, and in a day of salvation have I helped thee: and I will preserve thee, and give thee for a covenant of the people, to establish the earth, to cause to inherit the desolate heritages;

9 That thou mayest say to the prisoners, Go forth; to them that *are* in darkness, Show yourselves. They shall feed in the ways, and their pastures *shall be* in all high places.

10 They shall not hunger nor thirst; neither shall the heat nor sun smite them: for he that hath mercy on them shall lead them, even by the springs of water shall he guide them.

11 And I will make all my mountains a way, and my highways shall be exalted.

## Amplified

21 And they thirsted not when He led them through the deserts; He caused the waters to flow out of the rock for them; He split the rock also, and the waters gushed out.

22 There is no peace, says the Lord, for the wicked.

# 49

LISTEN TO me, O isles *and* coastlands, and hearken, you peoples from afar; the Lord has called me from the womb, from the body of my mother He has named my name.

2 And He has made my mouth like a sharp sword; in the shadow of His hand has He hid me, and made me a polished arrow; in His quiver has He kept me close *and* concealed me.

3 And *the Lord* said to me, You are My servant, Israel—you who strive with God [and with men and prevail]—in whom I will be glorified. [Gen. 32:28; Deut. 7:6; 26:18, 19; Eph. 1:4-6.]

4 Then I said, I have labored in vain, I have spent my strength for nothing and in empty futility; yet surely my right is with the Lord, and my recompense is with my God.

5 And now, says the Lord Who formed [a]me from the womb to be His servant, to bring Jacob back to Him, and that Israel might be gathered to Him *and* not swept away, for I am honorable in the eyes of the Lord and my God has become my strength;

6 He says, It is too light a thing that you should be My servant to raise up the tribes of Jacob and to restore the survivors [of the judgments] of Israel; I will also give you for a light to the nations, that My salvation may extend to the end of the earth.

7 Thus says the Lord, the Redeemer of Israel, Israel's Holy One, to him whom man rejects *and* despises, to him whom the nations abhor, to a servant of rulers: Kings shall see you and arise: princes, and they shall prostrate themselves; because of the Lord, Who is faithful, the Holy One of Israel, Who has chosen you.

8 Thus says the Lord, In an acceptable *and* favorable time I have heard *and* answered you, and in a day of salvation I have helped you; and I will preserve you and give you for a covenant to the people, to raise up *and* establish the land [from its present state of ruin], and to apportion *and* cause them to inherit the desolate [moral wastes of heathenism, their] heritages; [II Cor. 6:2.]

9 Saying to those who are bound, Come forth; to those who are in *spiritual* darkness, Show yourselves—come into the light [of the Sun of righteousness]. They shall feed in [b]all the ways [in which they go], and their pastures shall be [not in deserts, but] on all the bare [grass covered] hills.

10 They shall not hunger or thirst, neither shall mirage *mislead* or scorching wind or sun smite them; for He Who has mercy on them will lead them, and by the springs of water will He guide them. [Rev. 7:16, 17.]

11 And I will make all My mountains a way, and My highways shall be raised up.

**AMP** [a] It is difficult to know positively to whom the Lord is speaking in these next verses, whether (1) to the Messiah, (2) to Israel, or (3) to Isaiah. The large majority of early authorities favored (1), the later ones incline toward (2). [b] The Septuagint (Greek Version that Jesus knew) here reads, "In all the highways they shall be fed, and there shall be pasture for them in all the paths."

# New American Standard

21 And they did not thirst when He led them through the
deserts.
He made the water flow out of the rock for them;
He split the rock, and the water gushed forth.
22 "There is no peace for the wicked," says the LORD.

*Salvation Reaches to the End of the Earth*

**49** LISTEN TO Me, O islands,
And pay attention, you peoples from afar.
The LORD called Me from the womb;
From the body of My mother He named Me.
2 And He has made My mouth like a sharp sword;
In the shadow of His hand He has concealed Me,
And He has also made Me a select arrow;
He has hidden Me in His quiver.
3 And He said to Me, "You are My Servant, Israel,
In Whom I will show My glory."
4 But I said, "I have toiled in vain,
I have spent My strength for nothing and vanity;
Yet surely the justice *due* to Me is with the LORD,
And My reward with My God."

5¶ And now says the LORD, who formed Me from the
womb to be His Servant,
To bring Jacob back to Him, in order that Israel might
be gathered to Him
(For I am honored in the sight of the LORD,
And My God is My strength),
6 He says, "It is too small a thing that You should be My
Servant
To raise up the tribes of Jacob, and to restore the
preserved ones of Israel;
I will also make You a light of the nations
So that My salvation may reach to the end of the
earth."
7 Thus says the LORD, the Redeemer of Israel, *and* its
Holy One,
To the despised One,
To the One abhorred by the nation,
To the Servant of rulers,
"Kings shall see and arise,
Princes shall also bow down;
Because of the LORD who is faithful, the Holy One of
Israel who has chosen You."

8¶ Thus says the LORD, "In a favorable time I have
answered You,
And in a day of salvation I have helped You;
And I will keep You and give You for a covenant of the
people,
To restore the land, to make *them* inherit the desolate
heritages;
9 Saying to those who are bound, 'Go forth,'
To those who are in darkness, 'Show yourselves.'
Along the roads they will feed,
And their pasture will be on all bare heights.
10 "They will not hunger or thirst,
Neither will the scorching heat or sun strike them
down;
For He who has compassion on them will lead them,
And will guide them to springs of water.
11 "And I will make all My mountains a road,
And My highways will be raised up.

# New International

21They did not thirst when he led them through the deserts;
he made water flow for them from the rock;
he split the rock
and water gushed out.

22"There is no peace," says the LORD, "for the wicked."

*The Servant of the LORD*

**49** LISTEN TO me, you islands;
hear this, you distant nations:
Before I was born the LORD called me;
from my birth he has made mention of my name.
2He made my mouth like a sharpened sword,
in the shadow of his hand he hid me;
he made me into a polished arrow
and concealed me in his quiver.
3He said to me, "You are my servant,
Israel, in whom I will display my splendor."
4But I said, "I have labored to no purpose;
I have spent my strength in vain and for nothing.
Yet what is due me is in the LORD's hand,
and my reward is with my God."

5And now the LORD says—
he who formed me in the womb to be his servant
to bring Jacob back to him
and gather Israel to himself,
for I am honored in the eyes of the LORD
and my God has been my strength—
6he says:
"It is too small a thing for you to be my servant
to restore the tribes of Jacob
and bring back those of Israel I have kept.
I will also make you a light for the Gentiles,
that you may bring my salvation to the ends of the
earth."

7This is what the LORD says—
the Redeemer and Holy One of Israel—
to him who was despised and abhorred by the nation,
to the servant of rulers:
"Kings will see you and rise up,
princes will see and bow down,
because of the LORD, who is faithful,
the Holy One of Israel, who has chosen you."

*Restoration of Israel*

8This is what the LORD says:

"In the time of my favor I will answer you,
and in the day of salvation I will help you;
I will keep you and will make you
to be a covenant for the people,
to restore the land
and to reassign its desolate inheritances,
9to say to the captives, 'Come out,'
and to those in darkness, 'Be free!'

"They will feed beside the roads
and find pasture on every barren hill.
10They will neither hunger nor thirst,
nor will the desert heat or the sun beat upon them.
He who has compassion on them will guide them
and lead them beside springs of water.
11I will turn all my mountains into roads,
and my highways will be raised up.

## King James

12 Behold, these shall come from far: and, lo, these from the north and from the west; and these from the land of Sinim.

13 ¶ Sing, O heavens; and be joyful, O earth; and break forth into singing, O mountains: for the LORD hath comforted his people, and will have mercy upon his afflicted.

14 But Zion said, The LORD hath forsaken me, and my Lord hath forgotten me.

15 Can a woman forget her sucking child, that she should not have compassion on the son of her womb? yea, they may forget, yet will I not forget thee.

16 Behold, I have graven thee upon the palms of *my* hands; thy walls *are* continually before me.

17 Thy children shall make haste; thy destroyers and they that made thee waste shall go forth of thee.

18 ¶ Lift up thine eyes round about, and behold: all these gather themselves together, *and* come to thee. *As* I live, saith the LORD, thou shalt surely clothe thee with them all, as with an ornament, and bind them *on thee,* as a bride *doeth.*

19 For thy waste and thy desolate places, and the land of thy destruction, shall even now be too narrow by reason of the inhabitants, and they that swallowed thee up shall be far away.

20 The children which thou shalt have, after thou hast lost the other, shall say again in thine ears, The place *is* too strait for me: give place to me that I may dwell.

21 Then shalt thou say in thine heart, Who hath begotten me these, seeing I have lost my children, and am desolate, a captive, and removing to and fro? and who hath brought up these? Behold, I was left alone; these, where *had* they *been?*

22 Thus saith the Lord GOD, Behold, I will lift up mine hand to the Gentiles, and set up my standard to the people: and they shall bring thy sons in *their* arms, and thy daughters shall be carried upon *their* shoulders.

23 And kings shall be thy nursing fathers, and their queens thy nursing mothers: they shall bow down to thee with *their* face toward the earth, and lick up the dust of thy feet; and thou shalt know that I *am* the LORD: for they shall not be ashamed that wait for me.

24 ¶ Shall the prey be taken from the mighty, or the lawful captive delivered?

25 But thus saith the LORD, Even the captives of the mighty shall be taken away, and the prey of the terrible shall be delivered: for I will contend with him that contendeth with thee, and I will save thy children.

26 And I will feed them that oppress thee with their own flesh; and they shall be drunken with their own blood, as with sweet wine: and all flesh shall know that I the LORD *am* thy Saviour and thy Redeemer, the mighty One of Jacob.

## Amplified

12 Behold, these shall come from afar; and, lo, these from the north and from the west; and these from the land of Sinim [China].

13 Sing for joy, O heavens, and be joyful, O earth, and break forth into singing, O mountains; for the Lord has comforted His people and will have compassion upon His afflicted.

14 But Zion [Jerusalem, her people seen in captivity] said, The Lord has forsaken me, and my Lord has forgotten me.

15 [And the Lord answered] Can a woman forget her nursing child, that she should not have compassion on the son of her womb? Yes, they may forget, yet will I not forget you.

16 Behold, I have indelibly imprinted (tattooed) *a picture* of you on the palm of each of My hands. O Zion, your walls are continually before Me.

17 Your children *and* your builders make haste; your destroyers and those who made you waste go forth from you.

18 Lift up your eyes round about, and see [the returning exiles, ready to rebuild Jerusalem]; all these gather together and come to you. As I live, says the Lord, you Zion, shall surely clothe yourself with them all as with an ornament, and bind them on you as a bride does.

19 For your waste and desolate places and your land [once the scene] of destruction, surely now *in coming years* will be too narrow to accommodate the population, and those who once swallowed you up will be far away.

20 The children of your bereavement [born during your captivity] shall yet say in your ears, The place is too narrow for me; make room for me that I may live.

21 Then, *Zion,* you will say in your heart, Who has borne me all these children, seeing that I lost my offspring, and am alone *and* barren *and* unfruitful, an exile put away and wandering hither and thither? And who brought them up? Behold, I was left alone [put away by the Lord, my Husband], from where then did all these children come?

22 Thus says the Lord God: Behold, I will lift up My hand to the Gentile nations, and set up My standard *and* raise high My signal banner to the peoples; and they shall bring your sons in the bosom of their garments, and your daughters shall be carried upon their shoulders.

23 And kings shall be your foster fathers *and* guardians, and their queens your nursing mothers. They shall bow down to you with their faces to the earth, and lick up the dust of your feet; and you shall know—with an acquaintance and understanding based on and grounded in personal experience—that I am the Lord: for they shall not be put to shame who wait for, look for, hope for *and* expect Me.

24 Shall the prey be taken from the mighty, or the lawful captives of the just be delivered?

25 For thus says the Lord, Even the captives of the mighty shall be taken away, and the prey of the terrible shall be delivered; for I will contend with him who contends with you, and I will give safety to your children *and* ease them.

26 And I will make those who oppress you consume themselves [in mutually destructive wars], *thus* eating their own flesh; and they shall be drunk with their own blood as with sweet wine; and all flesh shall know—with a knowledge grounded on personal experience—that I the Lord am your Savior and your Redeemer, the Mighty One of Jacob.

## New American Standard

12 "Behold, these shall come from afar;
And lo, these *will come* from the north and from the west,
And these from the land of Sinim."
13 Shout for joy, O heavens! And rejoice, O earth!
Break forth into joyful shouting, O mountains!
For the LORD has comforted His people,
And will have compassion on His afflicted.

*Promise to Zion*

**14**¶ But Zion said, "The LORD has forsaken me,
And the Lord has forgotten me."
15 "Can a woman forget her nursing child,
And have no compassion on the son of her womb?
Even these may forget, but I will not forget you.
16 "Behold, I have inscribed you on the palms *of My hands;*
Your walls are continually before Me.
17 "Your builders hurry;
Your destroyers and devastators
Will depart from you.
18 "Lift up your eyes and look around;
All of them gather together, they come to you.
As I live," declares the LORD,
"You shall surely put on all of them as jewels, and bind them on as a bride.
19 "For your waste and desolate places, and your destroyed land—
Surely now you will be too cramped for the inhabitants,
And those who swallowed you will be far away.
20 "The children of whom you were bereaved will yet say in your ears,
'The place is too cramped for me;
Make room for me that I may live *here.*'
21 "Then you will say in your heart,
'Who has begotten these for me,
Since I have been bereaved of my children,
And am barren, an exile and a wanderer?
And who has reared these?
Behold, I was left alone;
From where did these come?' "

**22**¶ Thus says the Lord GOD,
"Behold, I will lift up My hand to the nations,
And set up My standard to the peoples;
And they will bring your sons in *their* bosom,
And your daughters will be carried on *their* shoulders.
23 "And kings will be your guardians,
And their princesses your nurses.
They will bow down to you with their faces to the earth,
And lick the dust of your feet;
And *you* will know that I am the LORD;
Those who hopefully wait for Me will not be put to shame.

**24**¶ "Can the prey be taken from the mighty man,
Or the captives of a tyrant be rescued?"
25 Surely, thus says the LORD,
"Even the captives of the mighty man will be taken away,
And the prey of the tyrant will be rescued;
For I will contend with the one who contends with you,
And I will save your sons.
26 "And I will feed your oppressors with their own flesh,
And they will become drunk with their own blood as with sweet wine;
And all flesh will know that I, the LORD, am your Savior,
And your Redeemer, the Mighty One of Jacob."

## New International

12 See, they will come from afar—
some from the north, some from the west,
some from the region of Aswan.[a] "

13 Shout for joy, O heavens;
rejoice, O earth;
burst into song, O mountains!
For the LORD comforts his people
and will have compassion on his afflicted ones.

14 But Zion said, "The LORD has forsaken me,
the Lord has forgotten me."

15 "Can a mother forget the baby at her breast
and have no compassion on the child she has borne?
Though she may forget,
I will not forget you!
16 See, I have engraved you on the palms of my hands;
your walls are ever before me.
17 Your sons hasten back,
and those who laid you waste depart from you.
18 Lift up your eyes and look around;
all your sons gather and come to you.
As surely as I live," declares the LORD,
"you will wear them all as ornaments;
you will put them on, like a bride.

19 "Though you were ruined and made desolate
and your land laid waste,
now you will be too small for your people,
and those who devoured you will be far away.
20 The children born during your bereavement
will yet say in your hearing,
'This place is too small for us;
give us more space to live in.'
21 Then you will say in your heart,
'Who bore me these?
I was bereaved and barren;
I was exiled and rejected.
Who brought these up?
I was left all alone,
but these—where have they come from?' "

22 This is what the Sovereign LORD says:

"See, I will beckon to the Gentiles,
I will lift up my banner to the peoples;
they will bring your sons in their arms
and carry your daughters on their shoulders.
23 Kings will be your foster fathers,
and their queens your nursing mothers.
They will bow down before you with their faces to the ground;
they will lick the dust at your feet.
Then you will know that I am the LORD;
those who hope in me will not be disappointed."

24 Can plunder be taken from warriors,
or captives rescued from the fierce[b] ?

25 But this is what the LORD says:

"Yes, captives will be taken from warriors,
and plunder retrieved from the fierce;
I will contend with those who contend with you,
and your children I will save.
26 I will make your oppressors eat their own flesh;
they will be drunk on their own blood, as with wine.
Then all mankind will know
that I, the LORD, am your Savior,
your Redeemer, the Mighty One of Jacob."

**NIV** [a] *12* Dead Sea Scrolls; Masoretic Text *Sinim* [b] *24* Dead Sea Scrolls, Vulgate and Syriac (see also Septuagint and verse 25); Masoretic Text *righteous*

## King James

**50** THUS SAITH the LORD, Where *is* the bill of your mother's divorcement, whom I have put away? or which of my creditors *is it* to whom I have sold you? Behold, for your iniquities have ye sold yourselves, and for your transgressions is your mother put away.

2 Wherefore, when I came, *was there* no man? when I called, *was there* none to answer? Is my hand shortened at all, that it cannot redeem? or have I no power to deliver? behold, at my rebuke I dry up the sea, I make the rivers a wilderness: their fish stinketh, because *there is* no water, and dieth for thirst.

3 I clothe the heavens with blackness, and I make sackcloth their covering.

4 The Lord GOD hath given me the tongue of the learned, that I should know how to speak a word in season to *him that is* weary: he wakeneth morning by morning, he wakeneth mine ear to hear as the learned.

5 ¶ The Lord GOD hath opened mine ear, and I was not rebellious, neither turned away back.

6 I gave my back to the smiters, and my cheeks to them that plucked off the hair: I hid not my face from shame and spitting.

7 ¶ For the Lord GOD will help me; therefore shall I not be confounded: therefore have I set my face like a flint, and I know that I shall not be ashamed.

8 *He is* near that justifieth me; who will contend with me? let us stand together: who *is* mine adversary? let him come near to me.

9 Behold, the Lord GOD will help me; who *is* he *that* shall condemn me? lo, they all shall wax old as a garment; the moth shall eat them up.

10 ¶ Who *is* among you that feareth the LORD, that obeyeth the voice of his servant, that walketh *in* darkness, and hath no light? let him trust in the name of the LORD, and stay upon his God.

11 Behold, all ye that kindle a fire, that compass *yourselves* about with sparks: walk in the light of your fire, and in the sparks *that* ye have kindled. This shall ye have of mine hand; ye shall lie down in sorrow.

**51** HEARKEN TO me, ye that follow after righteousness, ye that seek the LORD: look unto the rock *whence* ye are hewn, and to the hole of the pit *whence* ye are digged.

2 Look unto Abraham your father, and unto Sarah *that* bare you: for I called him alone, and blessed him, and increased him.

## Amplified

**50** THUS SAYS the Lord, where is the bill of your mother's divorce, with which I put her away, O Israel? Or which of My creditors is it to whom I have sold you? Behold, for your iniquities you were sold, and for your transgressions was your mother put away.

2 Why, when I came, was there no man? When I called, why was there no one to answer? Is My hand shortened at all, that it cannot redeem? Or have I no power to deliver? Behold, at My rebuke I dry up the sea, I make the rivers a desert; their fish stink because there is no water, and die of thirst.

3 I clothe the heavens with *the* blackness [of murky storm clouds], and I make sackcloth *of mourning* their covering.

4 [The servant of God says] The Lord God has given me the tongue of disciples *and* of those who are taught, that I should know how to speak a word in season to him who is weary; He wakens me morning by morning, He wakens my ear to hear as disciples—as those who are taught.

5 The Lord God has opened my ear, and I have not been rebellious or turned backward.

6 I gave my back to the smiters, and my cheeks to those who plucked off the hair; I hid not my face from shame and spitting. [Matt. 26:67; 27:30.]

7 For the Lord God helps me; therefore have I not been ashamed *or* confounded; therefore have I set my face like a flint, and I know that I shall not be put to shame.

8 He is near Who declares me in the right; who will contend with me? Let us stand forth together. Who is my adversary? Let him come near to me. [Rom. 8:33-35.]

9 Behold, the Lord God will help me; who is he who will condemn me? Lo, they all shall wax old *and* be worn out as a garment; the moth shall eat them up. [Heb. 1:11, 12.]

10 Who is among you who [reverently] fears the Lord, who obeys the voice of His servant, yet who walks in darkness *and* deep trouble and has no shining splendor [in his heart]? Let him rely on, trust *and* be confident in the name of the Lord, and let him lean upon *and* be supported by His God.

11 Behold, all you [enemies of your own selves] who attempt to kindle your own fire [and work out your own plan of salvation], who surround *and* gird yourselves with momentary sparks, darts *and* firebrands that you set aflame! Walk by the light of your self-made fire, and in the sparks that you have kindled [for yourself, if you will]! But this shall you have from My hand: you shall lie down in grief *and* in torment. [Isa. 66:24.]

**51** HEARKEN TO Me, you who follow after rightness *and* justice, you who seek *and* inquire of [and require] the Lord [claiming Him by necessity and by right]; look to the rock from which you were hewn, and to the hole *in* the quarry from which you were dug.

2 Look to Abraham your father and to Sarah who bore you; for I called him when he was but one, and blessed him and made him many.

## New American Standard

*God Helps His Servant*

50 THUS SAYS the LORD,
"Where is the certificate of divorce,
By which I have sent your mother away?
Or to whom of My creditors did I sell you?
Behold, you were sold for your iniquities,
And for your transgressions your mother was sent away.
2 "Why was there no man when I came?
When I called, *why* was there none to answer?
Is My hand so short that it cannot ransom?
Or have I no power to deliver?
Behold, I dry up the sea with My rebuke,
I make the rivers a wilderness;
Their fish stink for lack of water,
And die of thirst.
3 "I clothe the heavens with blackness,
And I make sackcloth their covering."
4¶ The Lord GOD has given Me the tongue of disciples,
That I may know how to sustain the weary one with a word.
He awakens *Me* morning by morning,
He awakens My ear to listen as a disciple.
5 The Lord GOD has opened My ear;
And I was not disobedient,
Nor did I turn back.
6 I gave My back to those who strike *Me*,
And My cheeks to those who pluck out the beard;
I did not cover My face from humiliation and spitting.
7 For the Lord GOD helps Me,
Therefore, I am not disgraced;
Therefore, I have set My face like flint,
And I know that I shall not be ashamed.
8 He who vindicates Me is near;
Who will contend with Me?
Let us stand up to each other;
Who has a case against Me?
Let him draw near to Me.
9 Behold, the Lord GOD helps Me;
Who is he who condemns Me?
Behold, they will all wear out like a garment;
The moth will eat them.
10 Who is among you that fears the LORD,
That obeys the voice of His servant,
That walks in darkness and has no light?
Let him trust in the name of the LORD and rely on his God.
11 Behold, all you who kindle a fire,
Who encircle yourselves with firebrands,
Walk in the light of your fire
And among the brands you have set ablaze.
This you will have from My hand;
And you will lie down in torment.

*Israel Exhorted*

51 "LISTEN TO me, you who pursue righteousness,
Who seek the LORD:
Look to the rock from which you were hewn,
And to the quarry from which you were dug.
2 "Look to Abraham your father,
And to Sarah who gave birth to you in pain;
When *he was* one I called him,
Then I blessed him and multiplied him."

## New International

*Israel's Sin and the Servant's Obedience*

50 THIS IS what the LORD says:
"Where is your mother's certificate of divorce
with which I sent her away?
Or to which of my creditors
did I sell you?
Because of your sins you were sold;
because of your transgressions your mother was sent away.
2When I came, why was there no one?
When I called, why was there no one to answer?
Was my arm too short to ransom you?
Do I lack the strength to rescue you?
By a mere rebuke I dry up the sea,
I turn rivers into a desert;
their fish rot for lack of water
and die of thirst.
3I clothe the sky with darkness
and make sackcloth its covering."
4The Sovereign LORD has given me an instructed tongue,
to know the word that sustains the weary.
He wakens me morning by morning,
wakens my ear to listen like one being taught.
5The Sovereign LORD has opened my ears,
and I have not been rebellious;
I have not drawn back.
6I offered my back to those who beat me,
my cheeks to those who pulled out my beard;
I did not hide my face
from mocking and spitting.
7Because the Sovereign LORD helps me,
I will not be disgraced.
Therefore have I set my face like flint,
and I know I will not be put to shame.
8He who vindicates me is near.
Who then will bring charges against me?
Let us face each other!
Who is my accuser?
Let him confront me!
9It is the Sovereign LORD who helps me.
Who is he that will condemn me?
They will all wear out like a garment;
the moths will eat them up.
10Who among you fears the LORD
and obeys the word of his servant?
Let him who walks in the dark,
who has no light,
trust in the name of the LORD
and rely on his God.
11But now, all you who light fires
and provide yourselves with flaming torches,
go, walk in the light of your fires
and of the torches you have set ablaze.
This is what you shall receive from my hand:
You will lie down in torment.

*Everlasting Salvation for Zion*

51 "LISTEN TO me, you who pursue righteousness
and who seek the LORD:
Look to the rock from which you were cut
and to the quarry from which you were hewn;
2look to Abraham, your father,
and to Sarah, who gave you birth.
When I called him he was but one,
and I blessed him and made him many.

# King James

3For the LORD shall comfort Zion: he will comfort all her waste places; and he will make her wilderness like Eden, and her desert like the garden of the LORD; joy and gladness shall be found therein, thanksgiving, and the voice of melody.

4¶ Hearken unto me, my people; and give ear unto me, O my nation: for a law shall proceed from me, and I will make my judgment to rest for a light of the people.

5My righteousness *is* near; my salvation is gone forth, and mine arms shall judge the people; the isles shall wait upon me, and on mine arm shall they trust.

6Lift up your eyes to the heavens, and look upon the earth beneath: for the heavens shall vanish away like smoke, and the earth shall wax old like a garment, and they that dwell therein shall die in like manner: but my salvation shall be for ever, and my righteousness shall not be abolished.

7¶ Hearken unto me, ye that know righteousness, the people in whose heart *is* my law; fear ye not the reproach of men, neither be ye afraid of their revilings.

8For the moth shall eat them up like a garment, and the worm shall eat them like wool: but my righteousness shall be for ever, and my salvation from generation to generation.

9¶ Awake, awake, put on strength, O arm of the LORD; awake, as in the ancient days, in the generations of old. *Art* thou not it that hath cut Rahab, *and* wounded the dragon?

10 *Art* thou not it which hath dried the sea, the waters of the great deep; that hath made the depths of the sea a way for the ransomed to pass over?

11Therefore the redeemed of the LORD shall return, and come with singing unto Zion; and everlasting joy *shall be* upon their head: they shall obtain gladness and joy; *and* sorrow and mourning shall flee away.

12I, *even* I, *am* he that comforteth you: who *art* thou, that thou shouldest be afraid of a man *that* shall die, and of the son of man *which* shall be made *as* grass;

13And forgettest the LORD thy maker, that hath stretched forth the heavens, and laid the foundations of the earth; and hast feared continually every day because of the fury of the oppressor, as if he were ready to destroy? and where *is* the fury of the oppressor?

14The captive exile hasteneth that he may be loosed, and that he should not die in the pit, nor that his bread should fail.

15But I *am* the LORD thy God, that divided the sea, whose waves roared: The LORD of hosts *is* his name.

16And I have put my words in thy mouth, and I have covered thee in the shadow of mine hand, that I may plant the heavens, and lay the foundations of the earth, and say unto Zion, Thou *art* my people.

# Amplified

3For the Lord will comfort Zion; He will comfort all her waste places, and He will make her wilderness like Eden, and her desert like the garden of the Lord; joy and gladness will be found in her, thanksgiving and the voice of song *or* instrument of praise.

4Listen to Me [the Lord], O My people, and give ear to Me, O My nation; for a [divine] law will go forth from Me and I will establish My justice for a light to the peoples.

5My rightness *and* justice are near, My salvation is gone forth, and My arms shall rule the peoples; the islands shall wait for *and* expect Me, and on My arm shall they trust *and* wait with hope.

6Lift up your eyes to the heavens, and look upon the earth beneath; for the heavens shall be dissolved *and* vanish away like smoke, and the earth shall wax old like a garment, and they that dwell therein shall die in like manner—like gnats; but My salvation shall be forever, and My rightness *and* justice [and faithfully fulfilled promise] shall not be abolished. [Matt. 24:35; II Pet. 3:10; Heb. 1:11.]

7Listen to Me, you who know rightness *and* justice *and* right standing with God, the people in whose heart is My law *and* My instruction: fear not the reproach of men, neither be afraid *nor* dismayed at their revilings.

8For [in comparison with the Lord they are so weak that things as insignificant as] the moth shall eat them up like a garment, and the worm shall eat them like wool; but My rightness *and* justice [and faithfully fulfilled promise] shall be for ever, and My salvation to all generations.

9[Zion now cries to the Lord God of Israel] Awake, awake, put on strength *and* might, O arm of the Lord; awake, as in the ancient days, in the generations of long ago. Was it not You Who cut Rahab [Egypt] in pieces, Who pierced the dragon [symbol of Egypt]?

10Was it not You Who dried up the Red Sea, the waters of the great deep, Who made the depths of the sea a way for the redeemed to pass over? [Why then are we left so long in captivity?]

11[The Lord God says,] And the redeemed of the Lord shall return and come with singing to Zion; everlasting joy shall be upon their heads, they shall obtain joy and gladness, and sorrow and sighing shall flee away. [Rev. 7:17; 21:1, 4.]

12I, even I, am He Who comforts you. Who are you, that you should be afraid of man who shall die, and of *a* son of man who shall be made [as destructible] as grass,

13And have forgotten the Lord, your Maker, Who stretched forth the heavens and laid the foundations of the earth, and fear continually every day because of the fury of the oppressor, when he makes ready to destroy *or* even though he did so? And where is the fury of the oppressor?

14The captive exile *and* he who is bent down by chains shall speedily be released, and he shall not die and go down to the pit of destruction, nor shall his food fail.

15For I am the Lord your God, Who stirs up the sea so that its waves roar, *and* by rebuke restrains it. The Lord of hosts is His name.

16And I have put My words in your mouth and have covered you in the shadow of My hand, that I may fix the *new* heavens as a tabernacle, and lay the foundations of a *new* earth, and say to Zion, You are My people. [Isa. 65:17; 66:22; Rev. 21:1.]

## New American Standard

3 Indeed, the LORD will comfort Zion;
He will comfort all her waste places.
And her wilderness He will make like Eden,
And her desert like the garden of the LORD;
Joy and gladness will be found in her,
Thanksgiving and sound of a melody.
4¶ "Pay attention to Me, O My people;
And give ear to Me, O My nation;
For a law will go forth from Me,
And I will set My justice for a light of the peoples.
5 "My righteousness is near, My salvation has gone forth,
And My arms will judge the peoples;
The coastlands will wait for Me,
And for My arm they will wait expectantly.
6 "Lift up your eyes to the sky,
Then look to the earth beneath;
For the sky will vanish like smoke,
And the earth will wear out like a garment,
And its inhabitants will die in like manner,
But My salvation shall be forever,
And My righteousness shall not wane.
7 "Listen to Me, you who know righteousness,
A people in whose heart is My law;
Do not fear the reproach of man,
Neither be dismayed at their revilings.
8 "For the moth will eat them like a garment,
And the grub will eat them like wool.
But My righteousness shall be forever,
And My salvation to all generations."

9¶ Awake, awake, put on strength, O arm of the LORD;
Awake as in the days of old, the generations of long ago.
Was it not Thou who cut Rahab in pieces,
Who pierced the dragon?
10 Was it not Thou who dried up the sea,
The waters of the great deep;
Who made the depths of the sea a pathway
For the redeemed to cross over?
11 So the ransomed of the LORD will return,
And come with joyful shouting to Zion;
And everlasting joy *will be* on their heads.
They will obtain gladness and joy,
And sorrow and sighing will flee away.
12¶ "I, even I, am He who comforts you.
Who are you that you are afraid of man who dies,
And of the son of man who is made like grass;
13 That you have forgotten the LORD your Maker,
Who stretched out the heavens,
And laid the foundations of the earth;
That you fear continually all day long because of the fury of the oppressor,
As he makes ready to destroy?
But where is the fury of the oppressor?
14 "The exile will soon be set free, and will not die in the dungeon, nor will his bread be lacking.
15 "For I am the LORD your God, who stirs up the sea and its
waves roar (the LORD of hosts is His name).
16 "And I have put My words in your mouth, and have covered
you with the shadow of My hand, to establish the heavens, to
found the earth, and to say to Zion, 'You are My people.' "

## New International

3 The LORD will surely comfort Zion
and will look with compassion on all her ruins;
he will make her deserts like Eden,
her wastelands like the garden of the LORD.
Joy and gladness will be found in her,
thanksgiving and the sound of singing.
4 "Listen to me, my people;
hear me, my nation:
The law will go out from me;
my justice will become a light to the nations.
5 My righteousness draws near speedily,
my salvation is on the way,
and my arm will bring justice to the nations.
The islands will look to me
and wait in hope for my arm.
6 Lift up your eyes to the heavens,
look at the earth beneath;
the heavens will vanish like smoke,
the earth will wear out like a garment
and its inhabitants die like flies.
But my salvation will last forever,
my righteousness will never fail.

7 "Hear me, you who know what is right,
you people who have my law in your hearts:
Do not fear the reproach of men
or be terrified by their insults.
8 For the moth will eat them up like a garment;
the worm will devour them like wool.
But my righteousness will last forever,
my salvation through all generations."

9 Awake, awake! Clothe yourself with strength,
O arm of the LORD;
awake, as in days gone by,
as in generations of old.
Was it not you who cut Rahab to pieces,
who pierced that monster through?
10 Was it not you who dried up the sea,
the waters of the great deep,
who made a road in the depths of the sea
so that the redeemed might cross over?
11 The ransomed of the LORD will return.
They will enter Zion with singing;
everlasting joy will crown their heads.
Gladness and joy will overtake them,
and sorrow and sighing will flee away.

12 "I, even I, am he who comforts you.
Who are you that you fear mortal men,
the sons of men, who are but grass,
13 that you forget the LORD your Maker,
who stretched out the heavens
and laid the foundations of the earth,
that you live in constant terror every day
because of the wrath of the oppressor,
who is bent on destruction?
For where is the wrath of the oppressor?
14 The cowering prisoners will soon be set free;
they will not die in their dungeon,
nor will they lack bread.
15 For I am the LORD your God,
who churns up the sea so that its waves roar—
the LORD Almighty is his name.
16 I have put my words in your mouth
and covered you with the shadow of my hand—
I who set the heavens in place,
who laid the foundations of the earth,
and who say to Zion, 'You are my people.' "

## King James

17¶ Awake, awake, stand up, O Jerusalem, which hast drunk at the hand of the LORD the cup of his fury; thou hast drunken the dregs of the cup of trembling, *and* wrung *them* out.

18 *There is* none to guide her among all the sons *whom* she hath brought forth; neither *is there any* that taketh her by the hand of all the sons *that* she hath brought up.

19These two *things* are come unto thee; who shall be sorry for thee? desolation, and destruction, and the famine, and the sword: by whom shall I comfort thee?

20Thy sons have fainted, they lie at the head of all the streets, as a wild bull in a net: they are full of the fury of the LORD, the rebuke of thy God.

21¶ Therefore hear now this, thou afflicted, and drunken, but not with wine:

22Thus saith thy Lord the LORD, and thy God *that* pleadeth the cause of his people, Behold, I have taken out of thine hand the cup of trembling, *even* the dregs of the cup of my fury; thou shalt no more drink it again:

23But I will put it into the hand of them that afflict thee; which have said to thy soul, Bow down, that we may go over: and thou hast laid thy body as the ground, and as the street, to them that went over.

**52** AWAKE, AWAKE; put on thy strength, O Zion; put on thy beautiful garments, O Jerusalem, the holy city: for henceforth there shall no more come into thee the uncircumcised and the unclean.

2Shake thyself from the dust; arise, *and* sit down, O Jerusalem: loose thyself from the bands of thy neck, O captive daughter of Zion.

3For thus saith the LORD, Ye have sold yourselves for nought; and ye shall be redeemed without money.

4For thus saith the Lord GOD, My people went down aforetime into Egypt to sojourn there; and the Assyrian oppressed them without cause.

5Now therefore, what have I here, saith the LORD, that my people is taken away for nought? they that rule over them make them to howl, saith the LORD; and my name continually every day *is* blasphemed.

6Therefore my people shall know my name: therefore *they shall know* in that day that I *am* he that doth speak: behold, *it is* I.

## Amplified

17Arouse yourself, awake, stand up, O Jerusalem, who have drunk at the hand of the Lord the cup of His wrath, who have drunk the cup of intoxication *and* staggering to the dregs.

18There is none to guide her among all the sons she has borne, neither is there any one to take her by the hand of all the sons whom she has brought up.

19Two kinds of calamities have befallen you, but who feels sorry and commiserates you? They are desolation and destruction [on the land and city], and famine and the sword [on the inhabitants]; how shall I comfort you *or* by whom?

20Your sons have fainted, they lie [like corpses] at the head of all the streets like an antelope in a net; they are full [from drinking] of the wrath of the Lord, the rebuke of your God.

21Therefore, now hear this, you who are afflicted, and drunk, but not with wine [but thrown down by the wrath of God]:

22Thus says your Lord, the Lord, and your God Who pleads the cause of His people: Behold, I have taken from your hand the cup of intoxication *and* staggering; the cup of My wrath you shall drink no more.

23And I will put it into the hand of your tormentors *and* oppressors, those who said to you, Bow down, that we may ride *or* tread over you; and you have made your back like the ground and like the street for them to pass over.

**52** AWAKE, AWAKE, put on your strength, O Zion; put on your beautiful garments, O Jerusalem, the holy city; for henceforth there shall no more come into you the uncircumcised and the unclean. [Rev. 21:27.]

2Shake yourself from the dust; arise, sit [erect in a dignified place], O Jerusalem; loose yourself from the bonds of your neck, O captive daughter of Zion.

3For thus says the Lord, You were sold for nothing, and you shall be redeemed without money.

4For thus says the Lord God, My people went down at the first into Egypt to sojourn there; and [many years later Sennacherib] the Assyrian oppressed them for nothing. [Now I delivered you from both Egypt and Assyria; what then can prevent My delivering you from Babylon?]

5But now, what have I here, says the Lord, seeing that My people are taken away for nothing? Those who rule over them howl [with joy], says the Lord, and My name continually all day is blasphemed. [Rom. 2:24.]

6Therefore My people shall know what My name is *and* what it means; therefore they shall know in that day that I am He who speaks; behold, I AM! [Exod. 3:13, 14.]

## New American Standard

17¶ Rouse yourself! Rouse yourself! Arise, O Jerusalem,
You who have drunk from the LORD's hand the cup of His anger;
The chalice of reeling you have drained to the dregs.
18 There is none to guide her among all the sons she has borne;
Nor is there one to take her by the hand among all the sons she has reared.
19 These two things have befallen you;
Who will mourn for you?
The devastation and destruction, famine and sword;
How shall I comfort you?
20 Your sons have fainted,
They lie *helpless* at the head of every street,
Like an antelope in a net,
Full of the wrath of the LORD,
The rebuke of your God.

21¶ Therefore, please hear this, you afflicted,
Who are drunk, but not with wine:
22 Thus says your Lord, the LORD, even your God
Who contends for His people,
"Behold, I have taken out of your hand the cup of reeling;
The chalice of My anger,
You will never drink it again.
23 "And I will put it into the hand of your tormentors,
Who have said to you, 'Lie down that we may walk over you.'
You have even made your back like the ground,
And like the street for those who walk over *it*."

*Cheer for Prostrate Zion*

**52** AWAKE, AWAKE,
Clothe yourself in your strength, O Zion;
Clothe yourself in your beautiful garments,
O Jerusalem, the holy city.
For the uncircumcised and the unclean
Will no more come into you.
2 Shake yourself from the dust, rise up,
O captive Jerusalem;
Loose yourself from the chains around your neck,
O captive daughter of Zion.
3For thus says the LORD, "You were sold for nothing and you
will be redeemed without money."
4For thus says the Lord GOD, "My people went down at the
first into Egypt to reside there, then the Assyrian oppressed them
without cause.
5"Now therefore, what do I have here," declares the LORD,
"seeing that My people have been taken away without cause?"
*Again* the LORD declares, "Those who rule over them howl, and My
name is continually blasphemed all day long.
6"Therefore My people shall know My name; therefore in that
day I am the one who is speaking, 'Here I am.'"

## New International

*The Cup of the LORD's Wrath*

17Awake, awake!
Rise up, O Jerusalem,
you who have drunk from the hand of the LORD
the cup of his wrath,
you who have drained to its dregs
the goblet that makes men stagger.
18Of all the sons she bore
there was none to guide her;
of all the sons she reared
there was none to take her by the hand.
19These double calamities have come upon you—
who can comfort you?—
ruin and destruction, famine and sword—
who can[a] console you?
20Your sons have fainted;
they lie at the head of every street,
like antelope caught in a net.
They are filled with the wrath of the LORD
and the rebuke of your God.

21Therefore hear this, you afflicted one,
made drunk, but not with wine.
22This is what your Sovereign LORD says,
your God, who defends his people:
"See, I have taken out of your hand
the cup that made you stagger;
from that cup, the goblet of my wrath,
you will never drink again.
23I will put it into the hands of your tormentors,
who said to you,
'Fall prostrate that we may walk over you.'
And you made your back like the ground,
like a street to be walked over."

**52** AWAKE, AWAKE, O Zion,
clothe yourself with strength.
Put on your garments of splendor,
O Jerusalem, the holy city.
The uncircumcised and defiled
will not enter you again.
2Shake off your dust;
rise up, sit enthroned, O Jerusalem.
Free yourself from the chains on your neck,
O captive Daughter of Zion.
3For this is what the LORD says:

"You were sold for nothing,
and without money you will be redeemed."
4For this is what the Sovereign LORD says:

"At first my people went down to Egypt to live;
lately, Assyria has oppressed them.

5"And now what do I have here?" declares the LORD.
"For my people have been taken away for nothing,
and those who rule them mock,[b]"
declares the LORD.

"And all day long
my name is constantly blasphemed.
6Therefore my people will know my name;
therefore in that day they will know
that it is I who foretold it.
Yes, it is I."

NIV [a] 19 Dead Sea Scrolls, Septuagint, Vulgate and Syriac; Masoretic Text / *how can I* [b] 5 Dead Sea Scrolls and Vulgate; Masoretic Text *wail*

## King James

7¶ How beautiful upon the mountains are the feet of him that
bringeth good tidings, that publisheth peace; that bringeth good
tidings of good, that publisheth salvation; that saith unto Zion,
Thy God reigneth!
8Thy watchmen shall lift up the voice; with the voice together
shall they sing: for they shall see eye to eye, when the Lord shall
bring again Zion.
9¶ Break forth into joy, sing together, ye waste places of Jerusalem: for the Lord hath comforted his people, he hath redeemed
Jerusalem.
10The Lord hath made bare his holy arm in the eyes of all the
nations; and all the ends of the earth shall see the salvation of our
God.
11¶ Depart ye, depart ye, go ye out from thence, touch no
unclean *thing;* go ye out of the midst of her; be ye clean, that bear
the vessels of the Lord.
12For ye shall not go out with haste, nor go by flight: for the
Lord will go before you; and the God of Israel *will be* your rearward.
13¶ Behold, my servant shall deal prudently, he shall be exalted
and extolled, and be very high.
14As many were astonied at thee; his visage was so marred
more than any man, and his form more than the sons of men:
15So shall he sprinkle many nations; the kings shall shut their
mouths at him: for *that* which had not been told them shall they
see; and *that* which they had not heard shall they consider.

**53** WHO HATH believed our report? and to whom is the arm
of the Lord revealed?
2For he shall grow up before him as a tender plant, and as a root
out of a dry ground: he hath no form nor comeliness; and when
we shall see him, *there is* no beauty that we should desire him.
3He is despised and rejected of men; a man of sorrows, and
acquainted with grief: and we hid as it were *our* faces from him;
he was despised, and we esteemed him not.
4¶ Surely he hath borne our griefs, and carried our sorrows: yet
we did esteem him stricken, smitten of God, and afflicted.
5But he *was* wounded for our transgressions, *he was* bruised for
our iniquities: the chastisement of our peace *was* upon him; and
with his stripes we are healed.
6All we like sheep have gone astray; we have turned every one
to his own way; and the Lord hath laid on him the iniquity of us
all.

## Amplified

7How beautiful upon the mountains are the feet of him who
brings good tidings, who publishes peace, who brings good tidings of good, who publishes salvation, who says to Zion, Your
God reigns! [Acts 10:36; Rom. 10:15; Eph. 6:14-16.]
8Hark, your watchmen lift up their voice, together they sing for
joy; for they shall see eye to eye the return of the Lord to Zion.
9Break forth joyously, sing together, you waste places of Jerusalem; for the Lord has comforted His people, He has redeemed
Jerusalem!
10The Lord has made bare His holy arm before the eyes of all
the nations [revealing Himself as the One by Whose direction the
redemption of Israel from captivity is accomplished], and all the
ends of the earth shall witness the salvation of our God. [Luke
2:29-32; 3:6.]
11Depart, depart, go out from there [the lands of exile], touch
no unclean thing; go out of the midst of her [Babylon]; cleanse
yourselves *and* be clean, you who bear the vessels of the Lord [on
your journey from there]. [II Cor. 6:16, 17.]
12For you shall not go out with haste, nor shall you go by flight
[as was necessary when Israel left Egypt], for the Lord will go
before you, and the God of Israel will be your rear guard.
13Behold, My Servant shall deal wisely *and* shall prosper, He
shall be exalted and extolled, and shall stand very high.
14[For many the Servant of God became an object of horror;
many were astonished.] His face *and* His whole appearance were
marred more than any man's, and His form beyond that of the
sons of men; but just as many were astonished at Him,
15So shall He startle *and* sprinkle many nations; kings shall shut
their mouths because of Him; for that which has not been told
them shall they see, and that which they have not heard shall they
consider *and* understand. [Rom. 15:21.]

**53** WHO HAS believed—trusted in, relied upon and clung
to—our message of that which was revealed to us? And
to whom has the arm of the Lord been disclosed? [John 12:38-41;
Rom. 10:16.]
2For [the Servant of God] grew up before Him like a tender
plant, and as a root out of dry ground; He has no [royal, kingly
pomp] form or comeliness that we should look at Him, and no
beauty that we should desire Him.
3He was despised and rejected *and* forsaken by men, a Man of
sorrows *and* pains, and acquainted with grief *and* sickness; and as
one from Whom men hide their faces He was despised, and we did
not appreciate His worth *or* have any esteem for Him.
4Surely He has borne our griefs—sickness, weakness and distress—and carried our sorrows *and* pain [of punishment]. Yet we
*ignorantly* considered Him stricken, smitten and afflicted by God
[as if with leprosy]. [Matt. 8:17.]
5But He was wounded for our transgressions, He was bruised
for our guilt *and* iniquities; the chastisement *needful to obtain* peace
*and* well-being for us was upon Him, and with the stripes *that
wounded* Him we are healed *and* made whole.
6All we like sheep have gone astray, we have turned every one
to his own way; and the Lord has made to light on Him the guilt
*and* iniquity of us all. [I Pet. 2:24, 25.]

## New American Standard

7¶ How lovely on the mountains
Are the feet of him who brings good news,
Who announces peace
And brings good news of happiness,
Who announces salvation,
*And* says to Zion, "Your God reigns!"
8 Listen! Your watchmen lift up *their* voices,
They shout joyfully together;
For they will see with their own eyes
When the LORD restores Zion.
9 Break forth, shout joyfully together,
You waste places of Jerusalem;
For the LORD has comforted His people,
He has redeemed Jerusalem.
10 The LORD has bared His holy arm
In the sight of all the nations,
That all the ends of the earth may see
The salvation of our God.

11¶ Depart, depart, go out from there,
Touch nothing unclean;
Go out of the midst of her, purify yourselves,
You who carry the vessels of the LORD.
12 But you will not go out in haste,
Nor will you go as fugitives;
For the LORD will go before you,
And the God of Israel *will be* your rear guard.

*The Exalted Servant*

13¶ Behold, My servant will prosper,
He will be high and lifted up, and greatly exalted.
14 Just as many were astonished at you, *My people,*
So His appearance was marred more than any man,
And His form more than the sons of men.
15 Thus He will sprinkle many nations,
Kings will shut their mouths on account of Him;
For what had not been told them they will see,
And what they had not heard they will understand.

*The Suffering Servant*

**53** WHO HAS believed our message?
And to whom has the arm of the LORD been revealed?
2 For He grew up before Him like a tender shoot,
And like a root out of parched ground;
He has no *stately* form or majesty
That we should look upon Him,
Nor appearance that we should [a]be attracted to Him.
3 He was despised and forsaken of men,
A man of sorrows, and acquainted with grief;
And like one from whom men hide their face,
He was despised, and we did not esteem Him.

4¶ Surely our [b]griefs He Himself bore,
And our sorrows He carried;
Yet we ourselves esteemed Him stricken,
Smitten of God, and afflicted.
5 But He was [c]pierced through for our transgressions,
He was crushed for our iniquities;
The chastening for our well-being *fell* upon Him,
And by His scourging we are healed.
6 All of us like sheep have gone astray,
Each of us has turned to his own way;
But the LORD has caused the iniquity of us all
To fall on Him.

**NAS** [a] Lit., *desire* [b] Or, *sickness* [c] Or, *wounded*

## New International

7How beautiful on the mountains
are the feet of those who bring good news,
who proclaim peace,
who bring good tidings,
who proclaim salvation,
who say to Zion,
"Your God reigns!"
8Listen! Your watchmen lift up their voices;
together they shout for joy.
When the LORD returns to Zion,
they will see it with their own eyes.
9Burst into songs of joy together,
you ruins of Jerusalem,
for the LORD has comforted his people,
he has redeemed Jerusalem.
10The LORD will lay bare his holy arm
in the sight of all the nations,
and all the ends of the earth will see
the salvation of our God.

11Depart, depart, go out from there!
Touch no unclean thing!
Come out from it and be pure,
you who carry the vessels of the LORD.
12But you will not leave in haste
or go in flight;
for the LORD will go before you,
the God of Israel will be your rear guard.

*The Suffering and Glory of the Servant*

13See, my servant will act wisely[d];
he will be raised and lifted up and highly exalted.
14Just as there were many who were appalled at him[e]—
his appearance was so disfigured beyond that of any man
and his form marred beyond human likeness—
15so will he sprinkle many nations,[f]
and kings will shut their mouths because of him.
For what they were not told, they will see,
and what they have not heard, they will understand.

**53** WHO HAS believed our message
and to whom has the arm of the LORD been revealed?
2He grew up before him like a tender shoot,
and like a root out of dry ground.
He had no beauty or majesty to attract us to him,
nothing in his appearance that we should desire him.
3He was despised and rejected by men,
a man of sorrows, and familiar with suffering.
Like one from whom men hide their faces
he was despised, and we esteemed him not.

4Surely he took up our infirmities
and carried our sorrows,
yet we considered him stricken by God,
smitten by him, and afflicted.
5But he was pierced for our transgressions,
he was crushed for our iniquities;
the punishment that brought us peace was upon him,
and by his wounds we are healed.
6We all, like sheep, have gone astray,
each of us has turned to his own way;
and the LORD has laid on him
the iniquity of us all.

**NIV** [d] 13 Or *will prosper* [e] 14 Hebrew *you* [f] 15 Hebrew; Septuagint *so will many nations marvel at him*

## King James

7 He was oppressed, and he was afflicted, yet he opened not his mouth: he is brought as a lamb to the slaughter, and as a sheep before her shearers is dumb, so he openeth not his mouth.

8 He was taken from prison and from judgment: and who shall declare his generation? for he was cut off out of the land of the living: for the transgression of my people was he stricken.

9 And he made his grave with the wicked, and with the rich in his death; because he had done no violence, neither *was any* deceit in his mouth.

10 ¶ Yet it pleased the LORD to bruise him; he hath put *him* to grief: when thou shalt make his soul an offering for sin, he shall see *his* seed, he shall prolong *his* days, and the pleasure of the LORD shall prosper in his hand.

11 He shall see of the travail of his soul, *and* shall be satisfied: by his knowledge shall my righteous servant justify many; for he shall bear their iniquities.

12 Therefore will I divide him *a portion* with the great, and he shall divide the spoil with the strong; because he hath poured out his soul unto death: and he was numbered with the transgressors; and he bare the sin of many, and made intercession for the transgressors.

**54** SING, O barren, thou *that* didst not bear; break forth into singing, and cry aloud, thou *that* didst not travail with child: for more *are* the children of the desolate than the children of the married wife, saith the LORD.

2 Enlarge the place of thy tent, and let them stretch forth the curtains of thine habitations: spare not, lengthen thy cords, and strengthen thy stakes;

3 For thou shalt break forth on the right hand and on the left; and thy seed shall inherit the Gentiles and make the desolate cities to be inhabited.

4 Fear not; for thou shalt not be ashamed: neither be thou confounded; for thou shalt not be put to shame: for thou shalt forget the shame of thy youth, and shalt not remember the reproach of thy widowhood any more.

5 For thy Maker *is* thine husband; the LORD of hosts *is* his name; and thy Redeemer the Holy One of Israel; The God of the whole earth shall he be called.

## Amplified

7 He was oppressed, *yet when* He was afflicted He was submissive *and* opened not His mouth; as a lamb that is led to the slaughter, and as a sheep that before her shearers is dumb, so He opened not His mouth.

8 By oppression and judgment He was taken away; and as for His generation, who among them considered that He was cut off out of the land of the living for the transgression of my [Isaiah's] people, to whom the stroke was due—stricken to His death?

9 And they assigned Him a grave with the wicked and with a rich man in His death, although He had done no violence, neither was any deceit in His mouth. [Matt. 27:57-60; I Pet. 2:22, 23.]

10 Yet it was the will of the Lord to bruise Him; He has put Him to grief *and* made Him sick. When You *and* He make Him an offering for sin [and He has risen from the dead, in time to come], He shall see His *spiritual* offspring, He shall prolong His days, and the will *and* pleasure of the Lord shall prosper in His hand.

11 He shall see *the fruit* of the travail of His soul and be satisfied; by His knowledge of Himself [which He possesses and imparts to others] shall My [uncompromisingly] righteous One, My Servant, justify *and* make many righteous—upright and in right standing with God; for He shall bear their iniquities *and* their guilt [with the consequences, says the Lord].

12 Therefore will I divide Him a portion with the great [kings and rulers], and He shall divide the spoil with the mighty; because He poured out His life unto death, and *He let Himself* be regarded as a criminal *and* be numbered with the transgressors, yet He bore [and took away] the sin of many and makes intercession for the transgressors—the rebellious. [Luke 22:37.]

**54** SING, [a] O barren, you who did not bear; break forth into singing and cry aloud, you who did not travail with child! For the [spiritual] children of the desolate one will be more than the children of the married wife, says the Lord. [Gal. 4:27.]

2 Enlarge the place of your tent, and let the curtains of your habitations be stretched out; spare not, lengthen your cords and strengthen your stakes,

3 For you shall spread abroad to the right hand and to the left, and your offspring will possess the nations, and make the desolate cities to be inhabited.

4 Fear not, for you shall not be ashamed; neither be confounded *and* depressed, for you shall not be put to shame; for you shall forget the shame of your youth, and you shall not [seriously] remember the reproach of your widowhood any more.

5 For your Maker is your husband, the Lord of hosts is His name; and the Holy One of Israel is your Redeemer, the God of the whole earth He is called.

**AMP** [a] Although this chapter is primarily intended to express Zion's joy over redemption, it has also a very personal, long neglected because overlooked, message *for women*—the lonely, the disappointed, the childless, the widow. It has all the glorious confidence and assurance, the incentive and understanding for which feminine hearts have longed during the ages! Every woman who will read it every week for a year, with receptive heart and mind, will find herself not only spiritually prepared for her own childlessness or widowhood, should it come, but supplied with rich treasure with which to meet such need of countless other aching hearts to whom the Holy Spirit is here speaking.

## New American Standard

7¶ He was oppressed and He was afflicted,
Yet He did not open His mouth;
Like a lamb that is led to slaughter,
And like a sheep that is silent before its shearers,
So He did not open His mouth.
8 By oppression and judgment He was taken away;
And as for His generation, who considered
That He was cut off out of the land of the living,
For the transgression of my people to whom the stroke *was due?*
9 His grave was assigned with wicked men,
Yet He was with a rich man in His death,
Because He had done no violence,
Nor was there any deceit in His mouth.

10¶ But the LORD was pleased
To crush Him, putting *Him* to grief;
If He would render Himself *as* a guilt offering,
He will see *His* offspring,
He will prolong *His* days,
And the good pleasure of the LORD will prosper in His hand.
11 As a result of the anguish of His soul,
He will see *it* and be satisfied;
By His knowledge the Righteous One,
My Servant, will justify the many,
As He will bear their iniquities.
12 Therefore, I will allot Him a portion with the great,
And He will divide the booty with the strong;
Because He poured out Himself to death,
And was numbered with the transgressors;
Yet He Himself bore the sin of many,
And interceded for the transgressors.

*The Fertility of Zion*

54 "SHOUT FOR joy, O barren one, you who have borne no *child;*
Break forth into joyful shouting and cry aloud, you who have not travailed;
For the sons of the desolate one *will be* more numerous
Than the sons of the married woman," says the LORD.
2 "Enlarge the place of your tent;
Stretch out the curtains of your dwellings, spare not;
Lengthen your cords,
And strengthen your pegs.
3 "For you will spread abroad to the right and to the left.
And your descendants will possess nations,
And they will resettle the desolate cities.

4¶ "Fear not, for you will not be put to shame;
Neither feel humiliated, for you will not be disgraced;
But you will forget the shame of your youth,
And the reproach of your widowhood you will remember no more.
5 "For your husband is your Maker,
Whose name is the LORD of hosts;
And your Redeemer is the Holy One of Israel,
Who is called the God of all the earth.

## New International

7 He was oppressed and afflicted,
yet he did not open his mouth;
he was led like a lamb to the slaughter,
and as a sheep before her shearers is silent,
so he did not open his mouth.
8 By oppression[b] and judgment he was taken away.
And who can speak of his descendants?
For he was cut off from the land of the living;
for the transgression of my people he was stricken.[c]
9 He was assigned a grave with the wicked,
and with the rich in his death,
though he had done no violence,
nor was any deceit in his mouth.

10 Yet it was the LORD's will to crush him and cause him to suffer,
and though the LORD makes[d] his life a guilt offering,
he will see his offspring and prolong his days,
and the will of the LORD will prosper in his hand.
11 After the suffering of his soul,
he will see the light ⌊of life⌋[e] and be satisfied[f];
by his knowledge[g] my righteous servant will justify many,
and he will bear their iniquities.
12 Therefore I will give him a portion among the great,[h]
and he will divide the spoils with the strong,[i]
because he poured out his life unto death,
and was numbered with the transgressors.
For he bore the sin of many,
and made intercession for the transgressors.

*The Future Glory of Zion*

54 "SING, O barren woman,
you who never bore a child;
burst into song, shout for joy,
you who were never in labor;
because more are the children of the desolate woman
than of her who has a husband,"
says the LORD.

2 "Enlarge the place of your tent,
stretch your tent curtains wide,
do not hold back;
lengthen your cords,
strengthen your stakes.
3 For you will spread out to the right and to the left;
your descendants will dispossess nations
and settle in their desolate cities.

4 "Do not be afraid; you will not suffer shame.
Do not fear disgrace; you will not be humiliated.
You will forget the shame of your youth
and remember no more the reproach of your widowhood.
5 For your Maker is your husband—
the LORD Almighty is his name—
the Holy One of Israel is your Redeemer;
he is called the God of all the earth.

**NIV** [b] 8 Or *From arrest* [c] 8 Or *away. / Yet who of his generation considered / that he was cut off from the land of the living / for the transgression of my people, / to whom the blow was due?* [d] 10 Hebrew *though you make* [e] 11 Dead Sea Scrolls (see also Septuagint); Masoretic Text does not have *the light of life*. [f] 11 Or (with Masoretic Text) *11He will see the result of the suffering of his soul / and be satisfied* [g] 11 Or *by knowledge of him* [h] 12 Or *many* [i] 12 Or *numerous*

## King James

6For the LORD hath called thee as a woman forsaken and grieved in spirit, and a wife of youth, when thou wast refused, saith thy God.

7For a small moment have I forsaken thee; but with great mercies will I gather thee.

8In a little wrath I hid my face from thee for a moment; but with everlasting kindness will I have mercy on thee, saith the LORD thy Redeemer.

9For this *is as* the waters of Noah unto me: for *as* I have sworn that the waters of Noah should no more go over the earth; so have I sworn that I would not be wroth with thee, nor rebuke thee.

10For the mountains shall depart, and the hills be removed; but my kindness shall not depart from thee, neither shall the covenant of my peace be removed, saith the LORD that hath mercy on thee.

11¶ O thou afflicted, tossed with tempest, *and* not comforted, behold, I will lay thy stones with fair colours, and lay thy foundations with sapphires.

12And I will make thy windows of agates, and thy gates of carbuncles, and all thy borders of pleasant stones.

13And all thy children *shall be* taught of the LORD; and great *shall be* the peace of thy children.

14In righteousness shalt thou be established: thou shalt be far from oppression; for thou shalt not fear: and from terror; for it shall not come near thee.

15Behold, they shall surely gather together, *but* not by me: whosoever shall gather together against thee shall fall for thy sake.

16Behold, I have created the smith that bloweth the coals in the fire, and that bringeth forth an instrument for his work; and I have created the waster to destroy.

17¶ No weapon that is formed against thee shall prosper; and every tongue *that* shall rise against thee in judgment thou shalt condemn. This *is* the heritage of the servants of the LORD, and their righteousness *is* of me, saith the LORD.

**55** HO, EVERY one that thirsteth, come ye to the waters, and he that hath no money; come ye, buy, and eat; yea, come, buy wine and milk without money and without price.

2Wherefore do ye spend money for *that which is* not bread? and your labour for *that which* satisfieth not? hearken diligently unto me, and eat ye *that which is* good, and let your soul delight itself in fatness.

3Incline your ear, and come unto me: hear, and your soul shall live; and I will make an everlasting covenant with you, *even* the sure mercies of David.

4Behold, I have given him *for* a witness to the people, a leader and commander to the people.

## Amplified

6For the Lord has called you like a woman forsaken, grieved in spirit *and* heartsore, even a wife [wooed and won] *in* youth, when she is *later* refused *and* scorned, says your God.

7For a brief moment I forsook you, but with great compassion *and* mercies I gather you *to Me* again.

8In a little burst of wrath I hid My face from you for a moment, but with age-enduring love *and* kindness I will have compassion *and* mercy on you, says the Lord, your Redeemer.

9For this is as the days of Noah to Me; as I have sworn that the waters of Noah should no more go over the earth, so have I sworn that I will not be angry with you or rebuke you.

10For though the mountains should depart and the hills be shaken *or* removed, yet My love *and* kindness shall not depart from you, nor shall My covenant of peace *and* completeness be removed, says the Lord, Who has compassion on you.

11O you afflicted, storm-tossed and not comforted, behold, I will set your stones in fair colors—in antimony [to enhance their brilliance]—and lay your foundations with sapphires.

12And I will make your windows *and* pinnacles of [sparkling] agates *or* rubies, and your gates of [shining] carbuncles, and all the walls *of* your enclosures of precious stones. [Rev. 21:19-21.]

13And all your [spiritual] children shall be disciples—taught of the Lord [and obedient to His will]; and great shall be the peace *and* undisturbed composure of your children. [John 6:45.]

14You shall establish yourself on righteousness—right, in conformity with God's will and order; you shall be far even from the thought of oppression *or* destruction, for you shall not fear; and from terror, for it shall not come near you.

15Behold, they may gather together *and* stir up strife, but it is not from Me. Whoever stirs up strife against you shall fall away to you.

16Behold, I have created the smith who blows on the fire of coals, and who produces a weapon for its purpose, and I have created the devastator to destroy.

17 *But* no weapon that is formed against you shall prosper, and every tongue that shall rise against you in judgment you shall show to be in the wrong. This [peace, righteousness, security, triumph over opposition] is the heritage of the servants of the Lord [those in whom the ideal Servant of the Lord is reproduced]. This is the righteousness *or* the vindication which they obtain from Me—this is that which I impart to them as their justification—says the Lord.

**55** WAIT *AND* listen, every one who is thirsty! Come to the waters; and he who has no money, come, buy and eat! Yes, come, buy *priceless* [spiritual] wine and milk without money and without price [simply for the self-surrender that accepts the blessing]. [Rev. 21:6, 7; 22:17.]

2Why do you spend your money for that which is not bread? And your earnings for what does not satisfy? Hearken diligently to Me, and eat what is good, and let your soul delight itself in fatness [the profuseness of spiritual joy]. [Jer. 31:12-14.]

3Incline your ear [submit and consent to the Divine will], and come to Me; hear, and your soul shall revive; and I will make an everlasting covenant *or* league with you, even the sure mercies—kindness, good will and compassion— *promised to* David. [II Sam. 7:8-16; Acts 13:34; Heb. 13:20.]

4Behold, I have appointed Him [the Messiah, or David as representing Him] for a witness—one who shall testify of salvation—to the nations, a prince and commander to the peoples.

## New American Standard

6 "For the LORD has called you,
Like a wife forsaken and grieved in spirit,
Even like a wife of *one's* youth when she is rejected,"
Says your God.
7 "For a brief moment I forsook you,
But with great compassion I will gather you.
8 "In an outburst of anger
I hid My face from you for a moment;
But with everlasting lovingkindness I will have
compassion on you,"
Says the LORD your Redeemer.

9¶ "For this is like the days of Noah to Me;
When I swore that the waters of Noah
Should not flood the earth again,
So I have sworn that I will not be angry with you,
Nor will I rebuke you.
10 "For the mountains may be removed and the hills may
shake,
But My lovingkindness will not be removed from you,
And My covenant of peace will not be shaken,"
Says the LORD who has compassion on you.

11¶ "O afflicted one, storm-tossed, and not comforted,
Behold, I will set your stones in antimony,
And your foundations I will lay in sapphires.
12 "Moreover, I will make your battlements of rubies,
And your gates of crystal,
And your entire wall of precious stones.
13 "And all your sons will be taught of the LORD;
And the well-being of your sons will be great.
14 "In righteousness you will be established;
You will be far from oppression, for you will not fear;
And from terror, for it will not come near you.
15 "If anyone fiercely assails *you* it will not be from Me.
Whoever assails you will fall because of you.
16 "Behold, I Myself have created the smith who blows the
fire of coals,
And brings out a weapon for its work;
And I have created the destroyer to ruin.
17 "No weapon that is formed against you shall prosper;
And every tongue that accuses you in judgment you
will condemn.
This is the heritage of the servants of the LORD,
And their vindication is from Me," declares the LORD.

*The Free Offer of Mercy*

55 "HO! EVERY one who thirsts, come to the waters;
And you who have no money come, buy and eat.
Come, buy wine and milk
Without money and without cost.
2 "Why do you spend money for what is not bread,
And your wages for what does not satisfy?
Listen carefully to Me, and eat what is good,
And delight yourself in abundance.
3 "Incline your ear and come to Me.
Listen, that you may live;
And I will make an everlasting covenant with you,
*According to* the faithful mercies shown to David.
4 "Behold, I have made him a witness to the peoples,
A leader and commander for the peoples.

## New International

6 The LORD will call you back
as if you were a wife deserted and distressed in spirit—
a wife who married young,
only to be rejected," says your God.
7 "For a brief moment I abandoned you,
but with deep compassion I will bring you back.
8 In a surge of anger
I hid my face from you for a moment,
but with everlasting kindness
I will have compassion on you,"
says the LORD your Redeemer.

9 "To me this is like the days of Noah,
when I swore that the waters of Noah would never
again cover the earth.
So now I have sworn not to be angry with you,
never to rebuke you again.
10 Though the mountains be shaken
and the hills be removed,
yet my unfailing love for you will not be shaken
nor my covenant of peace be removed,"
says the LORD, who has compassion on you.

11 "O afflicted city, lashed by storms and not comforted,
I will build you with stones of turquoise,[a]
your foundations with sapphires.[b]
12 I will make your battlements of rubies,
your gates of sparkling jewels,
and all your walls of precious stones.
13 All your sons will be taught by the LORD,
and great will be your children's peace.
14 In righteousness you will be established:
Tyranny will be far from you;
you will have nothing to fear.
Terror will be far removed;
it will not come near you.
15 If anyone does attack you, it will not be my doing;
whoever attacks you will surrender to you.

16 "See, it is I who created the blacksmith
who fans the coals into flame
and forges a weapon fit for its work.
And it is I who have created the destroyer to work havoc;
17 no weapon forged against you will prevail,
and you will refute every tongue that accuses you.
This is the heritage of the servants of the LORD,
and this is their vindication from me,"
declares the LORD.

*Invitation to the Thirsty*

55 "COME, ALL you who are thirsty,
come to the waters;
and you who have no money,
come, buy and eat!
Come, buy wine and milk
without money and without cost.
2 Why spend money on what is not bread,
and your labor on what does not satisfy?
Listen, listen to me, and eat what is good,
and your soul will delight in the richest of fare.
3 Give ear and come to me;
hear me, that your soul may live.
I will make an everlasting covenant with you,
my faithful love promised to David.
4 See, I have made him a witness to the peoples,
a leader and commander of the peoples.

NIV [a] *11* The meaning of the Hebrew for this word is uncertain. [b] *11* Or *lapis lazuli*

## King James

5Behold, thou shalt call a nation *that* thou knowest not, and nations *that* knew not thee shall run unto thee because of the LORD thy God, and for the Holy One of Israel; for he hath glorified thee.

6¶ Seek ye the LORD while he may be found, call ye upon him while he is near:

7Let the wicked forsake his way, and the unrighteous man his thoughts: and let him return unto the LORD, and he will have mercy upon him; and to our God, for he will abundantly pardon.

8¶ For my thoughts *are* not your thoughts, neither *are* your ways my ways, saith the LORD.

9For *as* the heavens are higher than the earth, so are my ways higher than your ways, and my thoughts than your thoughts.

10For as the rain cometh down, and the snow from heaven, and returneth not thither, but watereth the earth, and maketh it bring forth and bud, that it may give seed to the sower, and bread to the eater:

11So shall my word be that goeth forth out of my mouth: it shall not return unto me void, but it shall accomplish that which I please, and it shall prosper *in the thing* whereto I sent it.

12For ye shall go out with joy, and be led forth with peace: the mountains and the hills shall break forth before you into singing, and all the trees of the field shall clap *their* hands.

13Instead of the thorn shall come up the fir tree, and instead of the brier shall come up the myrtle tree: and it shall be to the LORD for a name, for an everlasting sign *that* shall not be cut off.

**56** THUS SAITH the LORD, Keep ye judgment, and do justice: for my salvation *is* near to come, and my righteousness to be revealed.

2Blessed *is* the man *that* doeth this, and the son of man *that* layeth hold on it; that keepeth the sabbath from polluting it, and keepeth his hand from doing any evil.

3¶ Neither let the son of the stranger, that hath joined himself to the LORD, speak, saying, The LORD hath utterly separated me from his people: neither let the eunuch say, Behold, I *am* a dry tree.

4For thus saith the LORD unto the eunuchs that keep my sabbaths, and choose *the things* that please me, and take hold of my covenant;

5Even unto them will I give in mine house and within my walls a place and a name better than of sons and of daughters: I will give them an everlasting name, that shall not be cut off.

## Amplified

5Behold, you [a][Israel?] shall call nations that you know not, and nations that did not know you shall run to you because of the Lord your God, and of the Holy One of Israel, for He has glorified you.

6Seek, inquire for *and* require the Lord while He may be found—claiming Him by necessity and by right; call upon Him while He is near.

7Let the wicked forsake his way, and the unrighteous man his thoughts; and let him return to the Lord, and He will have love, pity *and* mercy for him; and to our God, for He will multiply to him His abundant pardon.

8For My thoughts are not your thoughts, neither are your ways My ways, says the Lord.

9For as the heavens are higher than the earth, so are My ways higher than your ways, and My thoughts than your thoughts.

10For as the rain and snow come down from the heavens, and return not there again, but water the earth and make it bring forth and sprout, that it may give seed to the sower and bread to the eater, [II Cor. 9:10.]

11So shall My word be that goes forth out of My mouth; it shall not return to Me void—without producing any effect, useless—but it shall accomplish that which I please *and* purpose, and it shall prosper in the thing for which I sent it.

12For you shall go out [from spiritual exile of sin and evil into the homeland] with joy, and be led forth [by your Leader, the Lord Himself and His word] with peace; the mountains and the hills shall break forth before you into singing, and all the trees of the field shall clap their hands.

13Instead of the thorn shall come up the cypress tree, and instead of the brier shall come up the myrtle tree; and it shall be to the Lord for a name of renown, for an everlasting sign *of jubilant exaltation and* memorial [to His praise] that shall not be cut off.

**56** THUS SAYS the Lord, Keep justice, do *and* use righteousness [conformity to the will of God which brings salvation]; for My salvation is soon to come, and My righteousness—My rightness and justice—to be revealed. [Matt. 3:2; Luke 21:31; Rom. 13:11, 12; Isa. 62:1, 11.]

2Blessed, happy, *and* fortunate is the man who does this, and the son of man who lays hold of it *and* binds himself fast to it, who keeps sacred the sabbath so as not to profane it, and keeps his hand from doing any evil.

3Let not the foreigner who has joined himself to the Lord say, The Lord will surely separate me from His people; and let not the eunuch say, Behold, I am a dry tree.

4For thus says the Lord: To the eunuchs who keep My sabbaths and choose the things which please Me and hold firmly My covenant,

5To them I will give in My house and within My walls a memorial and a name better [and more enduring] than of sons and daughters; I will give them an everlasting name that shall not be cut off.

**AMP** [a] The identification of the one here addressed is uncertain. A proportionately large number of authorities believe it to be Israel, as here indicated, but others think it is the Messiah, or David as representing Him—"the second David."

## New American Standard

5 "Behold, you will call a nation you do not know,
And a nation which knows you not will run to you,
Because of the LORD your God, even the Holy One of Israel;
For He has glorified you."

6¶ Seek the LORD while He may be found;
Call upon Him while He is near.
7 Let the wicked forsake his way,
And the unrighteous man his thoughts;
And let him return to the LORD,
And He will have compassion on him;
And to our God,
For He will abundantly pardon.
8 "For My thoughts are not your thoughts,
Neither are your ways My ways," declares the LORD.
9 "For *as* the heavens are higher than the earth,
So are My ways higher than your ways,
And My thoughts than your thoughts.
10 "For as the rain and the snow come down from heaven,
And do not return there without watering the earth,
And making it bear and sprout,
And furnishing seed to the sower and bread to the eater;
11 So shall My word be which goes forth from My mouth;
It shall not return to Me empty,
Without accomplishing what I desire,
And without succeeding *in the matter* for which I sent it.
12 "For you will go out with joy,
And be led forth with peace;
The mountains and the hills will break forth into shouts of joy before you,
And all the trees of the field will clap *their* hands.
13 "Instead of the thorn bush the cypress will come up;
And instead of the nettle the myrtle will come up;
And it will be a memorial to the LORD,
For an everlasting sign which will not be cut off."

*Rewards for Obedience to God*

**56** THUS SAYS the LORD,
"Preserve justice, and do righteousness,
For My salvation is about to come
And My righteousness to be revealed.
2 "How blessed is the man who does this,
And the son of man who takes hold of it;
Who keeps from profaning the sabbath,
And keeps his hand from doing any evil."
3 Let not the foreigner who has joined himself to the LORD say,
"The LORD will surely separate me from His people."
Neither let the eunuch say, "Behold, I am a dry tree."
4 For thus says the LORD,
"To the eunuchs who keep My sabbaths,
And choose what pleases Me,
And hold fast My covenant,
5 To them I will give in My house and within My walls a memorial,
And a name better than that of sons and daughters;
I will give them an everlasting name which will not be cut off.

## New International

5Surely you will summon nations you know not,
and nations that do not know you will hasten to you,
because of the LORD your God,
the Holy One of Israel,
for he has endowed you with splendor."

6Seek the LORD while he may be found;
call on him while he is near.
7Let the wicked forsake his way
and the evil man his thoughts.
Let him turn to the LORD, and he will have mercy on him,
and to our God, for he will freely pardon.

8"For my thoughts are not your thoughts,
neither are your ways my ways,"
declares the LORD.

9"As the heavens are higher than the earth,
so are my ways higher than your ways
and my thoughts than your thoughts.
10As the rain and the snow
come down from heaven,
and do not return to it
without watering the earth
and making it bud and flourish,
so that it yields seed for the sower and bread for the eater,
11so is my word that goes out from my mouth:
It will not return to me empty,
but will accomplish what I desire
and achieve the purpose for which I sent it.
12You will go out in joy
and be led forth in peace;
the mountains and hills
will burst into song before you,
and all the trees of the field
will clap their hands.
13Instead of the thornbush will grow the pine tree,
and instead of briers the myrtle will grow.
This will be for the LORD's renown,
for an everlasting sign,
which will not be destroyed."

*Salvation for Others*

**56** THIS IS what the LORD says:

"Maintain justice
and do what is right,
for my salvation is close at hand
and my righteousness will soon be revealed.
2Blessed is the man who does this,
the man who holds it fast,
who keeps the Sabbath without desecrating it,
and keeps his hand from doing any evil."
3Let no foreigner who has bound himself to the LORD say,
"The LORD will surely exclude me from his people."
And let not any eunuch complain,
"I am only a dry tree."

4For this is what the LORD says:

"To the eunuchs who keep my Sabbaths,
who choose what pleases me
and hold fast to my covenant—
5to them I will give within my temple and its walls
a memorial and a name
better than sons and daughters;
I will give them an everlasting name
that will not be cut off.

# King James

**6**Also the sons of the stranger, that join themselves to the Lord, to serve him, and to love the name of the Lord, to be his servants, every one that keepeth the sabbath from polluting it, and taketh hold of my covenant;

**7**Even them will I bring to my holy mountain, and make them joyful in my house of prayer: their burnt offerings and their sacrifices *shall be* accepted upon mine altar; for mine house shall be called an house of prayer for all people.

**8**The Lord God which gathereth the outcasts of Israel saith, Yet will I gather *others* to him, beside those that are gathered unto him.

**9**¶ All ye beasts of the field, come to devour, *yea*, all ye beasts in the forest.

**10**His watchmen *are* blind: they are all ignorant, they *are* all dumb dogs, they cannot bark; sleeping, lying down, loving to slumber.

**11**Yea, *they are* greedy dogs *which* can never have enough, and they *are* shepherds *that* cannot understand: they all look to their own way, every one for his gain, from his quarter.

**12**Come ye, *say they*, I will fetch wine, and we will fill ourselves with strong drink; and tomorrow shall be as this day, *and* much more abundant.

**57** THE RIGHTEOUS perisheth, and no man layeth *it* to heart: and merciful men *are* taken away, none considering that the righteous is taken away from the evil *to come*.

**2**He shall enter into peace: they shall rest in their beds, *each one* walking *in* his uprightness.

**3**¶ But draw near hither, ye sons of the sorceress, the seed of the adulterer and the whore.

**4**Against whom do ye sport yourselves? against whom make ye a wide mouth, *and* draw out the tongue? *are* ye not children of transgression, a seed of falsehood,

**5**Enflaming yourselves with idols under every green tree, slaying the children in the valleys under the clefts of the rocks?

**6**Among the smooth *stones* of the stream *is* thy portion; they, they *are* thy lot: even to them hast thou poured a drink offering, thou hast offered a meat offering. Should I receive comfort in these?

**7**Upon a lofty and high mountain hast thou set thy bed: even thither wentest thou up to offer sacrifice.

# Amplified

**6**Also the foreigners who join themselves to the Lord, to minister to Him, and to love the name of the Lord and to be His servants, every one who keeps the sabbath from profaning it and holds fast My covenant [by conscientious obedience],

**7**All these I will bring to My holy mountain, and make them joyful in My house of prayer; their burnt offerings and their sacrifices shall be accepted on My altar, for My house shall be called a house of prayer for all peoples.

**8**Thus says the Lord God Who gathers the outcasts of Israel, I will gather yet others to *Israel*, besides those already gathered.

**9**All you beasts of the field, come to devour, all you beasts [hostile nations] in the forest.

**10**[Israel's] watchmen are blind, they are all without knowledge; they are all dumb dogs, they cannot bark; dreaming, lying down, loving to slumber.

**11**Yes, the dogs are greedy, they can never have enough; and such are the shepherds who cannot understand; they have all turned to their own way, each one to his gain, from every quarter—one and all.

**12**Come, say they, I will fetch wine, and we will fill ourselves with strong drink; and tomorrow shall be as this day, a day great beyond measure.

**57** THE RIGHTEOUS man perishes, and no one lays it to heart; and merciful *and* devout men are taken away, none considering that the uncompromisingly upright *and* godly person is taken away from the calamity *and* evil to come— *even* through wickedness.

**2**He [in death] enters into peace; they rest in their beds, each one who walks straight before him *and* in his uprightness.

**3**But come close, you sons of the sorceress [nursed in witchcraft and superstition], the offspring of the adulterer and the harlot.

**4**Against whom do you make sport *and* take your delight? Against whom do you open wide *your* mouth and put out *your* tongue? Are you not yourselves the children of transgression, the offspring of deceit,

**5**You who burn with lust—inflaming yourselves with idols— among the oaks, under every green tree; who slay the children [in sacrifice] in the valleys under clefts of the rocks?

**6**Among the smooth stones of the valley is your portion; they, they are your lot; to them you have poured out a drink offering, you have offered a cereal offering. Should I be quiet in spite of all these things [and leave them unpunished]—bearing them with patience?

**7**Upon a lofty and high mountain you have openly *and* shamelessly set your [idolatrous and adulterous] bed; even there you went up to offer sacrifice [in spiritual unfaithfulness to your divine Husband].

## New American Standard

6¶ "Also the foreigners who join themselves to the LORD,
To minister to Him, and to love the name of the LORD,
To be His servants, every one who keeps from
profaning the sabbath,
And holds fast My covenant;
7 Even those I will bring to My holy mountain,
And make them joyful in My house of prayer.
Their burnt offerings and their sacrifices will be
acceptable on My altar;
For My house will be called a house of prayer for all the
peoples."
8 The Lord GOD, who gathers the dispersed of Israel,
declares,
"Yet *others* I will gather to them, to those *already*
gathered."

9¶ All you beasts of the field,
All you beasts in the forest,
Come to eat.
10 His watchmen are blind,
All of them know nothing.
All of them are dumb dogs unable to bark,
Dreamers lying down, who love to slumber;
11 And the dogs are greedy, they are not satisfied.
And they are shepherds who have no understanding;
They have all turned to their own way,
Each one to his unjust gain, to the last one.
12 "Come," *they say,* "let us get wine, and let us drink
heavily of strong drink;
And tomorrow will be like today, only more so."

*Evil Leaders Rebuked*

**57** THE RIGHTEOUS man perishes, and no man takes it to
heart;
And devout men are taken away, while no one
understands.
For the righteous man is taken away from evil,
2 He enters into peace;
They rest in their beds,
*Each one* who walked in his upright way.
3 "But come here, you sons of a sorceress,
Offspring of an adulterer and a prostitute.
4 "Against whom do you jest?
Against whom do you open wide your mouth
And stick out your tongue?
Are you not children of rebellion,
Offspring of deceit,
5 *Who* inflame yourselves among the oaks,
Under every luxuriant tree,
Who slaughter the children in the ravines,
Under the clefts of the crags?
6 "Among the smooth *stones* of the ravine
Is your portion, they are your lot;
Even to them you have poured out a libation,
You have made a grain offering.
Shall I relent concerning these things?
7 "Upon a high and lofty mountain
You have made your bed.
You also went up there to offer sacrifice.

## New International

6 And foreigners who bind themselves to the LORD
to serve him,
to love the name of the LORD,
and to worship him,
all who keep the Sabbath without desecrating it
and who hold fast to my covenant—
7 these I will bring to my holy mountain
and give them joy in my house of prayer.
Their burnt offerings and sacrifices
will be accepted on my altar;
for my house will be called
a house of prayer for all nations."
8 The Sovereign LORD declares—
he who gathers the exiles of Israel:
"I will gather still others to them
besides those already gathered."

*God's Accusation Against the Wicked*

9 Come, all you beasts of the field,
come and devour, all you beasts of the forest!
10 Israel's watchmen are blind,
they all lack knowledge;
they are all mute dogs,
they cannot bark;
they lie around and dream,
they love to sleep.
11 They are dogs with mighty appetites;
they never have enough.
They are shepherds who lack understanding;
they all turn to their own way,
each seeks his own gain.
12 "Come," each one cries, "let me get wine!
Let us drink our fill of beer!
And tomorrow will be like today,
or even far better."

**57** THE RIGHTEOUS perish,
and no one ponders it in his heart;
devout men are taken away,
and no one understands
that the righteous are taken away
to be spared from evil.
2 Those who walk uprightly
enter into peace;
they find rest as they lie in death.

3 "But you—come here, you sons of a sorceress,
you offspring of adulterers and prostitutes!
4 Whom are you mocking?
At whom do you sneer
and stick out your tongue?
Are you not a brood of rebels,
the offspring of liars?
5 You burn with lust among the oaks
and under every spreading tree;
you sacrifice your children in the ravines
and under the overhanging crags.
6 ⌊The idols⌋ among the smooth stones of the ravines are
your portion;
they, they are your lot.
Yes, to them you have poured out drink offerings
and offered grain offerings.
In the light of these things, should I relent?
7 You have made your bed on a high and lofty hill;
there you went up to offer your sacrifices.

## King James

8 Behind the doors also and the posts hast thou set up thy remembrance: for thou hast discovered *thyself to another* than me, and art gone up; thou hast enlarged thy bed, and made thee *a covenant* with them; thou lovedst their bed where thou sawest *it.*

9 And thou wentest to the king with ointment, and didst increase thy perfumes, and didst send thy messengers far off, and didst debase *thyself even* unto hell.

10 Thou art wearied in the greatness of thy way; *yet* saidst thou not, There is no hope: thou hast found the life of thine hand; therefore thou wast not grieved.

11 And of whom hast thou been afraid or feared, that thou hast lied, and hast not remembered me, nor laid *it* to thy heart? have not I held my peace even of old, and thou fearest me not?

12 I will declare thy righteousness, and thy works; for they shall not profit thee.

13 ¶ When thou criest, let thy companies deliver thee; but the wind shall carry them all away; vanity shall take *them:* but he that putteth his trust in me shall possess the land, and shall inherit my holy mountain;

14 And shall say, Cast ye up, cast ye up, prepare the way, take up the stumblingblock out of the way of my people.

15 For thus saith the high and lofty One that inhabiteth eternity, whose name *is* Holy; I dwell in the high and holy *place,* with him also *that is* of a contrite and humble spirit, to revive the spirit of the humble, and to revive the heart of the contrite ones.

16 For I will not contend for ever, neither will I be always wroth: for the spirit should fail before me, and the souls *which* I have made.

17 For the iniquity of his covetousness was I wroth, and smote him: I hid me, and was wroth, and he went on frowardly in the way of his heart.

18 I have seen his ways, and will heal him: I will lead him also, and restore comforts unto him and to his mourners.

19 I create the fruit of the lips; Peace, peace to *him that is* far off, and to *him that is* near, saith the LORD; and I will heal him.

20 But the wicked *are* like the troubled sea, when it cannot rest, whose waters cast up mire and dirt.

21 *There is* no peace, saith my God, to the wicked.

**58** CRY ALOUD, spare not, lift up thy voice like a trumpet, and show my people their transgression, and the house of Jacob their sins.

## Amplified

8 Behind the door and the doorpost you have set up your *idol* symbol [as a substitute for the scripture text God ordered]; for, deserting Me, you have uncovered and ascended and enlarged your bed, and you have made a *fresh* bargain for yourself with *the adulterers;* you loved their bed where you saw *a beckoning hand or a passion-inflaming image.* [Deut. 6:5, 6, 9; 11:18, 20.]

9 And you went to the king [of foreign lands] with gifts *or to the god* Molech with oil, and increased your perfumes *and* ointments; you sent your messengers far off, and debased yourself even to Sheol *or* Hades [symbol of an abysmal depth of degradation].

10 You were wearied with the length of your way [in trying to find rest and satisfaction in alliances apart from the true God]; yet you did not say, There is no result *or* profit. You found quickened strength, therefore you were not faint *or* heartsick [or penitent].

11 Of whom have you been afraid and in dread that you lied *and* were treacherous and did not [seriously] remember Me, did not *even* give Me a thought? Have I not been silent, even for a long time, and so you do not fear Me?

12 I will expose your [pretended] righteousness and your doings, but they will not help you.

13 When you cry out, let your (rabble) collection of idols deliver you! But the wind shall take them all, a breath shall carry them away. But he who takes refuge in Me shall possess the land [Judea] and shall inherit My holy mountain [Zion, also the heavenly inheritance and the spiritual Zion]. [Isa. 49:8; Pss. 37:9, 11; 69:35, 36; Matt. 5:5; Heb. 12:22.]

14 And the word of One shall go forth, Cast up, cast up, prepare the way, take up the stumblingblock out of the way [of the spiritual return] of My people.

15 For thus says the high and lofty One Who inhabits eternity, Whose name is Holy: I dwell in the high and holy place, with him also who is of a thoroughly penitent and humble spirit, to revive the spirit of the humble, and to revive the heart of the thoroughly penitent—bruised with sorrow for sin. [Matt. 5:3.]

16 For I will not contend for ever, neither will I be angry always, for [were it not so] the spirit [of man] would faint *and* be consumed before Me, and [My purpose in] creating the souls of men would be frustrated.

17 Because of the iniquity of his covetousness *and* unjust gain I was angry, and smote [Judah]. I hid my face and was angry, and he went on turning away *and* backsliding in the way of his [own willful] heart.

18 I have seen his [willful] ways, but I will heal him; I will lead him also, and will recompense him and restore comfort to him and to those who mourn for him. [Isa. 61:1, 2; 66:10.]

19 Peace, peace to him who is far off [both Jew and Gentile], and to him that is near! says the Lord; I create the fruit of his lips and I will heal him—make his lips blossom anew with speech [in thankful praise]. [Acts 2:39; Eph. 2:13-17, 18; Heb. 13:15.]

20 But the wicked are like the troubled sea, for it cannot rest and its waters cast up mire and dirt.

21 There is no peace, says my God, for the wicked.

**58** CRY ALOUD, spare not, lift up your voice like a trumpet and declare to My people their transgression, and to the house of Jacob their sins!

## New American Standard

8 "And behind the door and the doorpost
You have set up your sign;
Indeed, far removed from Me, you have uncovered yourself;
And have gone up and made your bed wide.
And you have made an agreement for yourselves with them,
You have loved their bed,
You have looked on *their* manhood.
9 "And you have journeyed to the king with oil
And increased your perfumes;
You have sent your envoys a great distance,
And made *them* go down to Sheol.
10 "You were tired out by the length of your road,
*Yet* you did not say, 'It is hopeless.'
You found renewed strength,
Therefore you did not faint.
11¶ "Of whom were you worried and fearful,
When you lied, and did not remember Me,
Nor give *Me* a thought?
Was I not silent even for a long time
So you do not fear Me?
12 "I will declare your righteousness and your deeds,
But they will not profit you.
13 "When you cry out, let your collection *of idols* deliver you.
But the wind will carry all of them up,
And a breath will take *them away*.
But he who takes refuge in Me shall inherit the land,
And shall possess My holy mountain."
14¶ And it shall be said,
"Build up, build up, prepare the way,
Remove *every* obstacle out of the way of My people."
15 For thus says the high and exalted One
Who lives forever, whose name is Holy,
"I dwell *on* a high and holy place,
And *also* with the contrite and lowly of spirit
In order to revive the spirit of the lowly
And to revive the heart of the contrite.
16 "For I will not contend forever,
Neither will I always be angry;
For the spirit would grow faint before Me,
And the breath *of those whom* I have made.
17 "Because of the iniquity of his unjust gain I was angry and struck him;
I hid *My face* and was angry,
And he went on turning away, in the way of his heart.
18 "I have seen his ways, but I will heal him;
I will lead him and restore comfort to him and to his mourners,
19 Creating the praise of the lips.
Peace, peace to him who is far and to him who is near,"
Says the LORD, "and I will heal him."
20 But the wicked are like the tossing sea,
For it cannot be quiet,
And its waters toss up refuse and mud.
21 "There is no peace," says my God, "for the wicked."

*Observances of Fasts*

**58** "CRY LOUDLY, do not hold back;
Raise your voice like a trumpet,
And declare to My people their transgression,
And to the house of Jacob their sins.

## New International

8Behind your doors and your doorposts
you have put your pagan symbols.
Forsaking me, you uncovered your bed,
you climbed into it and opened it wide;
you made a pact with those whose beds you love,
and you looked on their nakedness.
9You went to Molech[a] with olive oil
and increased your perfumes.
You sent your ambassadors[b] far away;
you descended to the grave[c] itself!
10You were wearied by all your ways,
but you would not say, 'It is hopeless.'
You found renewal of your strength,
and so you did not faint.

11"Whom have you so dreaded and feared
that you have been false to me,
and have neither remembered me
nor pondered this in your hearts?
Is it not because I have long been silent
that you do not fear me?
12I will expose your righteousness and your works,
and they will not benefit you.
13When you cry out for help,
let your collection of idols save you!
The wind will carry all of them off,
a mere breath will blow them away.
But the man who makes me his refuge
will inherit the land
and possess my holy mountain."

*Comfort for the Contrite*

14And it will be said:

"Build up, build up, prepare the road!
Remove the obstacles out of the way of my people."
15For this is what the high and lofty One says—
he who lives forever, whose name is holy:
"I live in a high and holy place,
but also with him who is contrite and lowly in spirit,
to revive the spirit of the lowly
and to revive the heart of the contrite.
16I will not accuse forever,
nor will I always be angry,
for then the spirit of man would grow faint before me—
the breath of man that I have created.
17I was enraged by his sinful greed;
I punished him, and hid my face in anger,
yet he kept on in his willful ways.
18I have seen his ways, but I will heal him;
I will guide him and restore comfort to him,
19 creating praise on the lips of the mourners in Israel.
Peace, peace, to those far and near,"
says the LORD. "And I will heal them."
20But the wicked are like the tossing sea,
which cannot rest,
whose waves cast up mire and mud.
21"There is no peace," says my God, "for the wicked."

*True Fasting*

**58** "SHOUT IT aloud, do not hold back.
Raise your voice like a trumpet.
Declare to my people their rebellion
and to the house of Jacob their sins.

NIV [a] 9 Or *to the king* [b] 9 Or *idols* [c] 9 Hebrew *Sheol*

## King James

2Yet they seek me daily, and delight to know my ways, as a nation that did righteousness, and forsook not the ordinance of their God: they ask of me the ordinances of justice; they take delight in approaching to God.

3¶ Wherefore have we fasted, *say they*, and thou seest not? *wherefore* have we afflicted our soul, and thou takest no knowledge? Behold, in the day of your fast ye find pleasure, and exact all your labours.

4Behold, ye fast for strife and debate, and to smite with the fist of wickedness: ye shall not fast as *ye do this* day, to make your voice to be heard on high.

5Is it such a fast that I have chosen? a day for a man to afflict his soul? *is it* to bow down his head as a bulrush, and to spread sackcloth and ashes *under him?* wilt thou call this a fast, and an acceptable day to the LORD?

6 *Is* not this the fast that I have chosen? to loose the bands of wickedness, to undo the heavy burdens, and to let the oppressed go free, and that ye break every yoke?

7 *Is it* not to deal thy bread to the hungry, and that thou bring the poor that are cast out to thy house? when thou seest the naked, that thou cover him; and that thou hide not thyself from thine own flesh?

8¶ Then shall thy light break forth as the morning, and thine health shall spring forth speedily: and thy righteousness shall go before thee; the glory of the LORD shall be thy rearward.

9Then shalt thou call, and the LORD shall answer; thou shalt cry, and he shall say, Here I *am.* If thou take away from the midst of thee the yoke, the putting forth of the finger, and speaking vanity;

10And *if* thou draw out thy soul to the hungry, and satisfy the afflicted soul; then shall thy light rise in obscurity, and thy darkness *be* as the noonday:

11And the LORD shall guide thee continually, and satisfy thy soul in drought, and make fat thy bones: and thou shalt be like a watered garden, and like a spring of water, whose waters fail not.

12And *they that shall be* of thee shall build the old waste places: thou shalt raise up the foundations of many generations; and thou shalt be called, The repairer of the breach, The restorer of paths to dwell in.

13¶ If thou turn away thy foot from the sabbath, *from* doing thy pleasure on my holy day; and call the sabbath a delight, the holy of the LORD, honourable; and shalt honour him, not doing thine own ways, nor finding thine own pleasure, nor speaking *thine own* words:

14Then shalt thou delight thyself in the LORD; and I will cause thee to ride upon the high places of the earth, and feed thee with the heritage of Jacob thy father: for the mouth of the LORD hath spoken *it*.

## Amplified

2Yet they seek, inquire for *and* require Me daily, and delight [externally] to know My ways; as [if they were in reality] a nation that did righteousness and forsook not the ordinance of their God, they ask of Me righteous judgments; they delight to draw near to God [in visible ways].

3Why have we fasted, they say, and You do not see it? Why have we afflicted ourselves, and You take no knowledge *of it*? Behold, *O Israel*, in the day of your fast [when you should be grieving for your sins] you find business profit, and [instead of stopping all work, as the Law implies you and your workmen should] you extort from your hired servants a full amount of labor. [Lev. 16:29.]

4[The facts are] you fast only for strife and debate and to smite with the fist of wickedness. Fasting as you do today will not cause your voice to be heard on high.

5Is such a fast as yours what I have chosen, a day for a man to humble himself with soul-sorrow? [Is true fasting merely mechanical?] Is it only to bow down his head like a bulrush, and to spread sackcloth and ashes under him [to indicate a condition of heart that he does not have]? Will you call this a fast and an acceptable day to the Lord?

6[Rather,] is not this the fast that I have chosen: to loose the bonds of wickedness, to undo the bands of the yoke, to let the oppressed go free, and that *you* break every [enslaving] yoke? [Acts 8:23.]

7Is it not to divide your bread with the hungry, and bring the homeless poor into your house? When you see the naked that you cover him, and that you hide not yourself from [the needs of] your own flesh *and* blood?

8Then shall your light break forth as the morning, and your healing [your restoration and the power of a new life] shall spring forth speedily; your righteousness [your rightness, your justice and your right relationship with God] shall go before you [conducting you to peace and prosperity], and the glory of the Lord shall be your rear guard. [Isa. 52:12; Exod. 14:19, 20.]

9Then you shall call, and the Lord will answer; you shall cry, and He will say, Here I am. If you take away from your midst yokes of oppression [wherever you find them], the finger pointed in scorn [toward the oppressed or the godly], and every form of false, harsh, unjust *and* wicked speaking; [Exod. 3:14.]

10And if you pour out that with which you sustain your own life for the hungry, and satisfy the need of the afflicted, then shall your light rise in darkness and your obscurity *and* gloom be as the noonday.

11And the Lord shall guide you continually, and satisfy you in drought *and* in dry places, and make strong your bones. And you shall be like a watered garden and like a spring of water, whose waters fail not.

12And your ancient ruins shall be rebuilt; you shall raise up the foundations of [buildings that have laid waste for] many generations; and you shall be called the repairer of the breach, the restorer of streets to dwell in.

13If you turn away your foot from [traveling unduly on] the sabbath, from doing your *own* pleasure on My holy day, and call the sabbath a [spiritual] delight, the holy *day* of the Lord, honorable; and shall honor Him *and* it, not going your own way or seeking *or* finding your own pleasure, or speaking with your own [idle] words;

14Then shall you delight yourself in the Lord, and I will make you to ride on the high places of the earth, and I will feed you with the heritage [promised for you to] Jacob your father; for the mouth of the Lord has spoken it. [Gen. 27:28, 29; 28:13-15.]

## New American Standard

2 "Yet they seek Me day by day, and delight to know My ways,
As a nation that has done righteousness,
And has not forsaken the ordinance of their God.
They ask Me *for* just decisions,
They delight in the nearness of God.
3 'Why have we fasted and Thou dost not see?
*Why* have we humbled ourselves and Thou dost not notice?'
Behold, on the day of your fast you find *your* desire,
And drive hard all your workers.
4 "Behold, you fast for contention and strife and to strike with a wicked fist.
You do not fast like *you do* today to make your voice heard on high.
5 "Is it a fast like this which I choose, a day for a man to humble himself?
Is it for bowing one's head like a reed,
And for spreading out sackcloth and ashes as a bed?
Will you call this a fast, even an acceptable day to the LORD?
6 "Is this not the fast which I choose,
To loosen the bonds of wickedness,
To undo the bands of the yoke,
And to let the oppressed go free,
And break every yoke?
7 "Is it not to divide your bread with the hungry,
And bring the homeless poor into the house;
When you see the naked, to cover him;
And not to hide yourself from your own flesh?
8 "Then your light will break out like the dawn,
And your recovery will speedily spring forth;
And your righteousness will go before you;
The glory of the LORD will be your rear guard.
9 "Then you will call, and the LORD will answer;
You will cry, and He will say, 'Here I am.'
If you remove the yoke from your midst,
The pointing of the finger, and speaking wickedness,
10 And if you give yourself to the hungry,
And satisfy the desire of the afflicted,
Then your light will rise in darkness,
And your gloom *will become* like midday.
11 "And the LORD will continually guide you,
And satisfy your desire in scorched places,
And give strength to your bones;
And you will be like a watered garden,
And like a spring of water whose waters do not fail.
12 "And those from among you will rebuild the ancient ruins;
You will raise up the age-old foundations;
And you will be called the repairer of the breach,
The restorer of the streets in which to dwell.

*Keeping the Sabbath*

13¶ "If because of the sabbath, you turn your foot
From doing your *own* pleasure on My holy day,
And call the sabbath a delight, the holy *day* of the LORD honorable,
And shall honor it, desisting from your *own* ways,
From seeking your *own* pleasure,
And speaking *your own* word,
14 Then you will take delight in the LORD,
And I will make you ride on the heights of the earth;
And I will feed you *with* the heritage of Jacob your father,
For the mouth of the LORD has spoken."

## New International

2For day after day they seek me out;
they seem eager to know my ways,
as if they were a nation that does what is right
and has not forsaken the commands of its God.
They ask me for just decisions
and seem eager for God to come near them.
3'Why have we fasted,' they say,
'and you have not seen it?
Why have we humbled ourselves,
and you have not noticed?'

"Yet on the day of your fasting, you do as you please
and exploit all your workers.
4Your fasting ends in quarreling and strife,
and in striking each other with wicked fists.
You cannot fast as you do today
and expect your voice to be heard on high.
5Is this the kind of fast I have chosen,
only a day for a man to humble himself?
Is it only for bowing one's head like a reed
and for lying on sackcloth and ashes?
Is that what you call a fast,
a day acceptable to the LORD?

6"Is not this the kind of fasting I have chosen:
to loose the chains of injustice
and untie the cords of the yoke,
to set the oppressed free
and break every yoke?
7Is it not to share your food with the hungry
and to provide the poor wanderer with shelter—
when you see the naked, to clothe him,
and not to turn away from your own flesh and blood?
8Then your light will break forth like the dawn,
and your healing will quickly appear;
then your righteousness[a] will go before you,
and the glory of the LORD will be your rear guard.
9Then you will call, and the LORD will answer;
you will cry for help, and he will say: Here am I.

"If you do away with the yoke of oppression,
with the pointing finger and malicious talk,
10and if you spend yourselves in behalf of the hungry
and satisfy the needs of the oppressed,
then your light will rise in the darkness,
and your night will become like the noonday.
11The LORD will guide you always;
he will satisfy your needs in a sun-scorched land
and will strengthen your frame.
You will be like a well-watered garden,
like a spring whose waters never fail.
12Your people will rebuild the ancient ruins
and will raise up the age-old foundations;
you will be called Repairer of Broken Walls,
Restorer of Streets with Dwellings.

13"If you keep your feet from breaking the Sabbath
and from doing as you please on my holy day,
if you call the Sabbath a delight
and the LORD's holy day honorable,
and if you honor it by not going your own way
and not doing as you please or speaking idle words,
14then you will find your joy in the LORD,
and I will cause you to ride on the heights of the land
and to feast on the inheritance of your father Jacob."
The mouth of the LORD has spoken.

NIV [a] 8 Or *your righteous One*

## King James

59 BEHOLD, THE LORD's hand is not shortened, that it cannot save; neither his ear heavy, that it cannot hear:

2 But your iniquities have separated between you and your God, and your sins have hid *his* face from you, that he will not hear.

3 For your hands are defiled with blood, and your fingers with iniquity; your lips have spoken lies, your tongue hath muttered perverseness.

4 None calleth for justice, nor *any* pleadeth for truth: they trust in vanity, and speak lies; they conceive mischief, and bring forth iniquity.

5 They hatch cockatrice' eggs, and weave the spider's web: he that eateth of their eggs dieth, and that which is crushed breaketh out into a viper.

6 Their webs shall not become garments, neither shall they cover themselves with their works: their works *are* works of iniquity, and the act of violence *is* in their hands.

7 Their feet run to evil, and they make haste to shed innocent blood: their thoughts *are* thoughts of iniquity; wasting and destruction *are* in their paths.

8 The way of peace they know not; and *there is* no judgment in their goings: they have made them crooked paths: whosoever goeth therein shall not know peace.

9¶ Therefore is judgment far from us, neither doth justice overtake us: we wait for light, but behold obscurity; for brightness, *but* we walk in darkness.

10 We grope for the wall like the blind, and we grope as if *we had* no eyes: we stumble at noonday as in the night; *we are* in desolate places as dead *men.*

11 We roar all like bears, and mourn sore like doves: we look for judgment, but *there is* none; for salvation, *but* it is far off from us.

12 For our transgressions are multiplied before thee, and our sins testify against us: for our transgressions *are* with us; and *as for* our iniquities, we know them;

13 In transgressing and lying against the LORD, and departing away from our God, speaking oppression and revolt, conceiving and uttering from the heart words of falsehood.

14 And judgment is turned away backward, and justice standeth afar off: for truth is fallen in the street, and equity cannot enter.

15 Yea, truth faileth; and he *that* departeth from evil maketh himself a prey: and the LORD saw *it,* and it displeased him that *there was* no judgment.

16¶ And he saw that *there was* no man, and wondered that *there was* no intercessor: therefore his arm brought salvation unto him; and his righteousness, it sustained him.

## Amplified

59 BEHOLD, THE Lord's hand is not shortened, that it cannot save; nor His ear dull with deafness that it cannot hear;

2 But your iniquities have made a separation between you and your God, and your sins have hid His face from you, so that He will not hear.

3 For your hands are defiled with blood and your fingers with iniquity; your lips have spoken lies, your tongue mutters wickedness.

4 None sues *or* calls in righteousness [but for the sake of doing injury to others, to take some undue advantage], no one goes to law honestly *and* pleads in truth; they trust in emptiness, worthlessness *and* futility, and speaking lies! They conceive mischief and bring forth evil!

5 They hatch adders' eggs, and weave the spider's web; he who eats of their eggs dies, and *from an egg* which is crushed a viper breaks out [for their nature is ruinous, deadly, evil].

6 Their webs will not serve as clothing nor will they cover themselves with what they make; their works are works of iniquity, and the act of violence is in their hands.

7 Their feet run to evil, and they make haste to shed innocent blood; their thoughts are thoughts of iniquity; desolation and destruction are in their paths *and* highways.

8 The way of peace they know not, and there is no justice *or* right in their goings; they have made them crooked paths; whoever goes in them does not know peace. [Rom. 3:15-18.]

9 Therefore are justice *and* right far from us, and righteousness *and* salvation do not overtake us; we expectantly wait for light, but [only] see darkness; for brightness, but we walk in obscurity *and* gloom.

10 We grope for the wall like the blind; yes, we grope as they who have no eyes; we stumble at noonday as in the twilight; in dark places *and* among those who are full of life *and* vigor we are as dead men.

11 We all groan *and* growl like bears, and moan plaintively like doves. We look for justice, but there is none; for salvation, but it is far from us.

12 For our transgressions are multiplied before You, *O Lord,* and our sins testify against us; for our transgressions are with us, and as for our iniquities, we know *and* recognize them as:

13 Rebelling and denying the Lord, and turning away from following our God, speaking oppression and revolt, conceiving and muttering *and* moaning from the heart words of falsehood.

14 Justice is turned away backward, and righteousness—uprightness and right standing with God—stands far off; for truth has fallen in [the city's forum], and uprightness cannot enter [the courts of justice].

15 Yes, truth is lacking, and he who departs from evil makes himself a prey. And the Lord saw it, and it displeased Him that there was no justice.

16 And He saw that there was no man, and wondered that there was no intercessor [no one to intervene on behalf of truth and right]; therefore His own arm brought Him victory, and His righteousness [having the Spirit without measure] sustained Him. [I John 2:1, 2; Isa. 53:11; Col. 2:9.]

## New American Standard

*Separation from God*

**59** BEHOLD, THE LORD's hand is not so short
That it cannot save;
Neither is His ear so dull
That it cannot hear.
2 But your iniquities have made a separation between you
and your God,
And your sins have hidden *His* face from you, so that
He does not hear.
3 For your hands are defiled with blood,
And your fingers with iniquity;
Your lips have spoken falsehood,
Your tongue mutters wickedness.
4 No one sues righteously and no one pleads honestly.
They trust in confusion, and speak lies;
They conceive mischief, and bring forth iniquity.
5 They hatch adders' eggs and weave the spider's web;
He who eats of their eggs dies,
And *from* that which is crushed a snake breaks forth.
6 Their webs will not become clothing,
Nor will they cover themselves with their works;
Their works are works of iniquity,
And an act of violence is in their hands.
7 Their feet run to evil,
And they hasten to shed innocent blood;
Their thoughts are thoughts of iniquity;
Devastation and destruction are in their highways.
8 They do not know the way of peace,
And there is no justice in their tracks;
They have made their paths crooked;
Whoever treads on them does not know peace.

*A Confession of Wickedness*

9¶ Therefore, justice is far from us,
And righteousness does not overtake us;
We hope for light, but behold, darkness;
For brightness, but we walk in gloom.
10 We grope along the wall like blind men,
We grope like those who have no eyes;
We stumble at midday as in the twilight,
Among those who are vigorous we are like dead men.
11 All of us growl like bears,
And moan sadly like doves;
We hope for justice, but there is none,
For salvation, *but* it is far from us.
12 For our transgressions are multiplied before Thee,
And our sins testify against us;
For our transgressions are with us,
And we know our iniquities:
13 Transgressing and denying the LORD,
And turning away from our God,
Speaking oppression and revolt,
Conceiving *in* and uttering from the heart lying words.
14 And justice is turned back,
And righteousness stands far away;
For truth has stumbled in the street,
And uprightness cannot enter.
15 Yes, truth is lacking;
And he who turns aside from evil makes himself a
prey.
¶ Now, the LORD saw,
And it was displeasing in His sight that there was no
justice.
16 And He saw that there was no man,
And was astonished that there was no one to intercede;
Then His own arm brought salvation to Him;
And His righteousness upheld Him.

## New International

*Sin, Confession and Redemption*

**59** SURELY THE arm of the LORD is not too short to save,
nor his ear too dull to hear.
2 But your iniquities have separated
you from your God;
your sins have hidden his face from you,
so that he will not hear.
3 For your hands are stained with blood,
your fingers with guilt.
Your lips have spoken lies,
and your tongue mutters wicked things.
4 No one calls for justice;
no one pleads his case with integrity.
They rely on empty arguments and speak lies;
they conceive trouble and give birth to evil.
5 They hatch the eggs of vipers
and spin a spider's web.
Whoever eats their eggs will die,
and when one is broken, an adder is hatched.
6 Their cobwebs are useless for clothing;
they cannot cover themselves with what they make.
Their deeds are evil deeds,
and acts of violence are in their hands.
7 Their feet rush into sin;
they are swift to shed innocent blood.
Their thoughts are evil thoughts;
ruin and destruction mark their ways.
8 The way of peace they do not know;
there is no justice in their paths.
They have turned them into crooked roads;
no one who walks in them will know peace.

9 So justice is far from us,
and righteousness does not reach us.
We look for light, but all is darkness;
for brightness, but we walk in deep shadows.
10 Like the blind we grope along the wall,
feeling our way like men without eyes.
At midday we stumble as if it were twilight;
among the strong, we are like the dead.
11 We all growl like bears;
we moan mournfully like doves.
We look for justice, but find none;
for deliverance, but it is far away.

12 For our offenses are many in your sight,
and our sins testify against us.
Our offenses are ever with us,
and we acknowledge our iniquities:
13 rebellion and treachery against the LORD,
turning our backs on our God,
fomenting oppression and revolt,
uttering lies our hearts have conceived.
14 So justice is driven back,
and righteousness stands at a distance;
truth has stumbled in the streets,
honesty cannot enter.
15 Truth is nowhere to be found,
and whoever shuns evil becomes a prey.

The LORD looked and was displeased
that there was no justice.
16 He saw that there was no one,
he was appalled that there was no one to intervene;
so his own arm worked salvation for him,
and his own righteousness sustained him.

## King James

17 For he put on righteousness as a breastplate, and an helmet of salvation upon his head; and he put on the garments of vengeance *for* clothing, and was clad with zeal as a cloak.

18 According to *their* deeds, accordingly he will repay, fury to his adversaries, recompence to his enemies; to the islands he will repay recompence.

19 So shall they fear the name of the LORD from the west, and his glory from the rising of the sun. When the enemy shall come in like a flood, the spirit of the LORD shall lift up a standard against him.

20 ¶ And the Redeemer shall come to Zion, and unto them that turn from transgression in Jacob, saith the LORD.

21 As for me, this *is* my covenant with them, saith the LORD; My spirit that *is* upon thee, and my words which I have put in thy mouth, shall not depart out of thy mouth, nor out of the mouth of thy seed, nor out of the mouth of thy seed's seed, saith the LORD, from henceforth and for ever.

**60** ARISE, SHINE; for thy light is come, and the glory of the LORD is risen upon thee.

2 For, behold, the darkness shall cover the earth, and gross darkness the people: but the LORD shall arise upon thee, and his glory shall be seen upon thee.

3 And the Gentiles shall come to thy light, and kings to the brightness of thy rising.

4 Lift up thine eyes round about, and see: all they gather themselves together, they come to thee: thy sons shall come from far, and thy daughters shall be nursed at *thy* side.

5 Then thou shalt see, and flow together, and thine heart shall fear, and be enlarged; because the abundance of the sea shall be converted unto thee, the forces of the Gentiles shall come unto thee.

6 The multitude of camels shall cover thee, the dromedaries of Midian and Ephah; all they from Sheba shall come: they shall bring gold and incense; and they shall show forth the praises of the LORD.

7 All the flocks of Kedar shall be gathered together unto thee, the rams of Nebaioth shall minister unto thee: they shall come up with acceptance on mine altar, and I will glorify the house of my glory.

8 Who *are* these *that* fly as a cloud, and as the doves to their windows?

9 Surely the isles shall wait for me, and the ships of Tarshish first, to bring thy sons from far, their silver and their gold with them, unto the name of the LORD thy God, and to the Holy One of Israel, because he hath glorified thee.

10 And the sons of strangers shall build up thy walls, and their kings shall minister unto thee: for in my wrath I smote thee, but in my favour have I had mercy on thee.

**AMP** [a] Prior to well into the twentieth century, scholars could only speculate as to what Isaiah could have meant here by "the abundant wealth of the Sea" that was one day to be turned over to Jerusalem. Of course the Dead Sea, which for ages had been considered only a place of death and desolation was ruled out. Then suddenly it was discovered that the waters of the Dead Sea contain important chemicals. In 1935 A.D. G. T. B. Davis wrote in his *Rebuilding Palestine*, "One is almost staggered by the computed wealth of the chemical salts of the Dead Sea. It is estimated that the potential value of the potash, bromine, and other chemical salts of its waters is . . . four times the wealth of the United States!" Isaiah himself did not know this, but the God who made the Dead Sea for a part in His end-time program knew all about it, and caused this record to say so.

## Amplified

17 For *the Lord* put on righteousness as a breastplate *or* coat of mail, and salvation for a helmet upon His head; He put on garments of vengeance for clothing, and was clad with zeal [and furious divine jealousy] as a cloak. [Eph. 6:14, 17; I Thess. 5:8.]

18 According as their deeds deserve, so will He repay, wrath to His adversaries, recompense to His enemies; on the foreign islands *and* coastlands He will make compensation.

19 So [as the result of the Messiah's intervention] they shall [reverently] fear the name of the Lord from the west, and His glory from the rising of the sun. When the enemy shall come in like a flood, the Spirit of the Lord will lift up a standard against him *and* put him to flight—for He will come like a rushing stream which the breath of the Lord drives. [Matt. 8:11; Luke 13:29.]

20 He shall come as a Redeemer to Zion, and to those in Jacob (Israel) who turn from transgression, says the Lord.

21 As for Me, this is My covenant *or* league with them, says the Lord: My Spirit Who is upon you [and Who writes the law of God inwardly in the heart], and My words which I have put in your mouth, shall not depart out of your mouth, or out of the mouth of your [true, spiritual] children, or out of the mouth of your children's children, says the Lord, from henceforth and for ever. [Rom. 11:26, 27; Gal. 3:29; Heb. 12:22-24.]

**60** ARISE [FROM the depression and prostration in which circumstances have kept you; rise to a new life]! Shine—be radiant with the glory of the Lord; for your light is come, and the glory of the Lord is risen upon you! [Zech. 8:23.]

2 For behold, darkness shall cover the earth, and dense darkness *all* peoples; but the Lord shall arise upon you, [O Jerusalem], and His glory shall be seen on you. [Mal. 4:2; Isa. 60:19-22; Rev. 21:2, 3.]

3 And nations shall come to your light, and kings to the brightness of your rising. [Isa. 2:2, 3; Jer. 3:17.]

4 Lift up your eyes round about you, and see! They all gather themselves together, they come to you. Your sons shall come from afar, and your daughters shall be carried *and* nursed in the arms.

5 Then you shall see and be radiant, and your heart shall thrill *and* tremble with joy [at the glorious deliverance], and be enlarged; because the abundant wealth of the [Dead] [a]Sea shall be turned to you; unto you shall the nations come with their treasures. [Ps. 119:32.]

6 A multitude of camels [from the eastern trading tribes] shall cover you [Jerusalem], the young camels of Midian and Ephah; all the men from Sheba [who once came to trade] shall come bringing gold and frankincense, and proclaiming the praises of the Lord. [Matt. 2:11.]

7 [The eastern pastoral tribes will join the trading tribes] all the flocks of Kedar shall be gathered to you, the rams of Nebaioth shall minister to you; they shall come up with acceptance on My altar, and My glorious house I will glorify.

8 Who are these who fly like a cloud, and like doves to their windows?

9 Surely the isles *and* distant coastlands shall wait for *and* expect Me, and the ships of Tarshish first, to bring your sons from far, their silver and gold with them, for the name of the Lord your God and for the Holy One of Israel, because He has beautified *and* glorified you.

10 Foreigners shall build up your walls, and their kings shall minister to you; for in My wrath I smote you, but in My favor, pleasure *and* good will I have had mercy, love *and* pity for you.

## New American Standard

17 And He put on righteousness like a breastplate,
And a helmet of salvation on His head;
And He put on garments of vengeance for clothing,
And wrapped Himself with zeal as a mantle.
18 According to *their* deeds, so He will repay,
Wrath to His adversaries, recompense to His enemies;
To the coastlands He will make recompense.
19 So they will fear the name of the LORD from the west
And His glory from the rising of the sun,
For He will come like a rushing stream,
Which the wind of the LORD drives.
20 "And a Redeemer will come to Zion,
And to those who turn from transgression in Jacob,"
declares the LORD.
21 "And as for Me, this is My covenant with them," says the
LORD: "My Spirit which is upon you, and My words which I have
put in your mouth, shall not depart from your mouth, nor from
the mouth of your offspring, nor from the mouth of your offspring's offspring," says the LORD, "from now and forever."

*A Glorified Zion*

**60** "ARISE, SHINE; for your light has come,
And the glory of the LORD has risen upon you.
2 "For behold, darkness will cover the earth,
And deep darkness the peoples;
But the LORD will rise upon you,
And His glory will appear upon you.
3 "And nations will come to your light,
And kings to the brightness of your rising.
4¶ "Lift up your eyes round about, and see;
They all gather together, they come to you.
Your sons will come from afar,
And your daughters will be carried in the arms.
5 "Then you will see and be radiant,
And your heart will thrill and rejoice;
Because the abundance of the sea will be turned to you,
The wealth of the nations will come to you.
6 "A multitude of camels will cover you,
The young camels of Midian and Ephah;
All those from Sheba will come;
They will bring gold and frankincense,
And will bear good news of the praises of the LORD.
7 "All the flocks of Kedar will be gathered together to you,
The rams of Nebaioth will minister to you;
They will go up with acceptance on My altar,
And I shall glorify My glorious house.
8 "Who are these who fly like a cloud,
And like the doves to their lattices?
9 "Surely the coastlands will wait for Me;
And the ships of Tarshish *will come* first,
To bring your sons from afar,
Their silver and their gold with them,
For the name of the LORD your God,
And for the Holy One of Israel because He has glorified
you.
10¶ "And foreigners will build up your walls,
And their kings will minister to you;
For in My wrath I struck you,
And in My favor I have had compassion on you.

## New International

17 He put on righteousness as his breastplate,
and the helmet of salvation on his head;
he put on the garments of vengeance
and wrapped himself in zeal as in a cloak.
18 According to what they have done,
so will he repay
wrath to his enemies
and retribution to his foes;
he will repay the islands their due.
19 From the west, men will fear the name of the LORD,
and from the rising of the sun, they will revere his
glory.
For he will come like a pent-up flood
that the breath of the LORD drives along.[b]

20 "The Redeemer will come to Zion,
to those in Jacob who repent of their sins,"
declares the LORD.
21 "As for me, this is my covenant with them," says the LORD.
"My Spirit, who is on you, and my words that I have put in your
mouth will not depart from your mouth, or from the mouths of
your children, or from the mouths of their descendants from this
time on and forever," says the LORD.

*The Glory of Zion*

**60** "ARISE, SHINE, for your light has come,
and the glory of the LORD rises upon you.
2 See, darkness covers the earth
and thick darkness is over the peoples,
but the LORD rises upon you
and his glory appears over you.
3 Nations will come to your light,
and kings to the brightness of your dawn.

4 "Lift up your eyes and look about you:
All assemble and come to you;
your sons come from afar,
and your daughters are carried on the arm.
5 Then you will look and be radiant,
your heart will throb and swell with joy;
the wealth on the seas will be brought to you,
to you the riches of the nations will come.
6 Herds of camels will cover your land,
young camels of Midian and Ephah.
And all from Sheba will come,
bearing gold and incense
and proclaiming the praise of the LORD.
7 All Kedar's flocks will be gathered to you,
the rams of Nebaioth will serve you;
they will be accepted as offerings on my altar,
and I will adorn my glorious temple.

8 "Who are these that fly along like clouds,
like doves to their nests?
9 Surely the islands look to me;
in the lead are the ships of Tarshish,[c]
bringing your sons from afar,
with their silver and gold,
to the honor of the LORD your God,
the Holy One of Israel,
for he has endowed you with splendor.

10 "Foreigners will rebuild your walls,
and their kings will serve you.
Though in anger I struck you,
in favor I will show you compassion.

**NIV** [b] 19 Or *When the enemy comes in like a flood, / the Spirit of the LORD will put him to flight* [c] 9 Or *the trading ships*

# King James

11 Therefore thy gates shall be open continually; they shall not be shut day nor night; that *men* may bring unto thee the forces of the Gentiles, and *that* their kings *may be* brought.

12 For the nation and kingdom that will not serve thee shall perish; yea, *those* nations shall be utterly wasted.

13 The glory of Lebanon shall come unto thee, the fir tree, the pine tree, and the box together, to beautify the place of my sanctuary; and I will make the place of my feet glorious.

14 The sons also of them that afflicted thee shall come bending unto thee; and all they that despised thee shall bow themselves down at the soles of thy feet; and they shall call thee, The city of the LORD, The Zion of the Holy One of Israel.

15 Whereas thou hast been forsaken and hated, so that no man went through *thee*, I will make thee an eternal excellency, a joy of many generations.

16 Thou shalt also suck the milk of the Gentiles, and shalt suck the breast of kings: and thou shalt know that I the LORD *am* thy Saviour and thy Redeemer, the mighty One of Jacob.

17 For brass I will bring gold, and for iron I will bring silver, and for wood brass, and for stones iron: I will also make thy officers peace, and thine exactors righteousness.

18 Violence shall no more be heard in thy land, wasting nor destruction within thy borders; but thou shalt call thy walls Salvation, and thy gates Praise.

19 The sun shall be no more thy light by day; neither for brightness shall the moon give light unto thee: but the LORD shall be unto thee an everlasting light, and thy God thy glory.

20 Thy sun shall no more go down; neither shall thy moon withdraw itself: for the LORD shall be thine everlasting light, and the days of thy mourning shall be ended.

21 Thy people also *shall be* all righteous: they shall inherit the land for ever, the branch of my planting, the work of my hands, that I may be glorified.

22 A little one shall become a thousand, and a small one a strong nation: I the LORD will hasten it in his time.

**61** THE SPIRIT of the Lord GOD *is* upon me; because the LORD hath anointed me to preach good tidings unto the meek; he hath sent me to bind up the brokenhearted, to proclaim liberty to the captives, and the opening of the prison to *them that are* bound;

2 To proclaim the acceptable year of the LORD, and the day of vengeance of our God; to comfort all that mourn;

# Amplified

11 And your gates shall be open continually, they shall not be shut day or night, that men may bring to you the wealth of the nations, and their kings led in procession [your voluntary captives]. [Rev. 21:24-27.]

12 For the nation and kingdom that will not serve you in that day [Jerusalem] shall perish; yes, those nations shall be utterly laid waste.

13 The glory of Lebanon shall come to you, the cypress, the plane, and the pine *trees* together, to beautify the place of My sanctuary; and I will make the place of My feet glorious.

14 The sons of those who afflicted you shall come bending low to you, and all those who despised you shall bow down at your feet, and they shall call you the City of the Lord, the Zion of the Holy One of Israel. [Rev. 3:9.]

15 Whereas you have been forsaken and hated, so that no man passed through you, I will make you [Jerusalem] an eternal glory, a joy from age to age.

16 You shall suck the milk of the [Gentile] nations and shall suck the breast of kings; and you shall recognize *and* know that I the Lord am your Savior and your Redeemer, the mighty One of Jacob.

17 Instead of bronze I will bring gold, and instead of iron I will bring silver; and for wood, bronze, and for stones, iron. [Instead of the tyranny of the present] I will appoint peace as your officers and righteousness as your taskmasters.

18 Violence shall no more be heard in your land, devastation or destruction within your borders, but you shall call your walls Salvation and your gates Praise.

19 The sun shall be no more your light by day, nor for brightness shall the moon give light to you; but the Lord shall be to you an everlasting light, and your God your glory *and* your beauty. [Jer. 9:23, 24; Rev. 21:23.]

20 Your sun shall no more go down, nor shall your moon withdraw itself; for the Lord shall be your everlasting light, and the days of your mourning shall be ended.

21 Your people also shall all be [uncompromisingly and consistently] righteous; they shall possess the land for ever, the branch of My planting, the work of My hands, that I may be glorified.

22 The least one shall become a thousand [a clan], and the small one a strong nation. I the Lord will hasten it in its [appointed] time.

**61** THE SPIRIT of the Lord God is upon me, because the Lord has anointed *and* qualified me to preach the Gospel *of* good tidings to the meek, the poor *and* afflicted; He has sent me to bind up *and* heal the brokenhearted, to proclaim liberty to the [physical and spiritual] captives, and the opening of the prison *and* of the eyes to those who are bound; [Rom. 10:15.]

2 To proclaim the acceptable year of the Lord—the year for His favor— [a]and the day of vengeance of our God; to comfort all who mourn; [Matt. 11:2-6; Luke 4:18, 19; 7:22.]

**AMP** [a] See footnote on Ezekiel 34:28.

## New American Standard

11 "And your gates will be open continually;
They will not be closed day or night,
So that *men* may bring to you the wealth of the nations,
With their kings led in procession.
12 "For the nation and the kingdom which will not serve
you will perish,
And the nations will be utterly ruined.
13 "The glory of Lebanon will come to you,
The juniper, the box tree, and the cypress together,
To beautify the place of My sanctuary;
And I shall make the place of My feet glorious.
14 "And the sons of those who afflicted you will come
bowing to you,
And all those who despised you will bow themselves at
the soles of your feet;
And they will call you the city of the LORD,
The Zion of the Holy One of Israel.

15¶ "Whereas you have been forsaken and hated
With no one passing through,
I will make you an everlasting pride,
A joy from generation to generation.
16 "You will also suck the milk of nations,
And will suck the breast of kings;
Then you will know that I, the LORD, am your Savior,
And your Redeemer, the Mighty One of Jacob.
17 "Instead of bronze I will bring gold,
And instead of iron I will bring silver,
And instead of wood, bronze,
And instead of stones, iron.
And I will make peace your administrators,
And righteousness your overseers.
18 "Violence will not be heard again in your land,
Nor devastation or destruction within your borders;
But you will call your walls salvation, and your gates
praise.
19 "No longer will you have the sun for light by day,
Nor for brightness will the moon give you light;
But you will have the LORD for an everlasting light,
And your God for your glory.
20 "Your sun will set no more,
Neither will your moon wane;
For you will have the LORD for an everlasting light,
And the days of your mourning will be finished.
21 "Then all your people *will be* righteous;
They will possess the land forever,
The branch of My planting,
The work of My hands,
That I may be glorified.
22 "The smallest one will become a clan,
And the least one a mighty nation.
I, the LORD, will hasten it in its time."

*Exaltation of the Afflicted*

**61** THE SPIRIT of the Lord GOD is upon me,
Because the LORD has anointed me
To bring good news to the afflicted;
He has sent me to bind up the brokenhearted,
To proclaim liberty to captives,
And freedom to prisoners;
2 To proclaim the favorable year of the LORD,
And the day of vengeance of our God;
To comfort all who mourn,

## New International

11Your gates will always stand open,
they will never be shut, day or night,
so that men may bring you the wealth of the nations—
their kings led in triumphal procession.
12For the nation or kingdom that will not serve you will
perish;
it will be utterly ruined.

13"The glory of Lebanon will come to you,
the pine, the fir and the cypress together,
to adorn the place of my sanctuary;
and I will glorify the place of my feet.
14The sons of your oppressors will come bowing before you;
all who despise you will bow down at your feet
and will call you the City of the LORD,
Zion of the Holy One of Israel.
15"Although you have been forsaken and hated,
with no one traveling through,
I will make you the everlasting pride
and the joy of all generations.
16You will drink the milk of nations
and be nursed at royal breasts.
Then you will know that I, the LORD, am your Savior,
your Redeemer, the Mighty One of Jacob.
17Instead of bronze I will bring you gold,
and silver in place of iron.
Instead of wood I will bring you bronze,
and iron in place of stones.
I will make peace your governor
and righteousness your ruler.
18No longer will violence be heard in your land,
nor ruin or destruction within your borders,
but you will call your walls Salvation
and your gates Praise.
19The sun will no more be your light by day,
nor will the brightness of the moon shine on you,
for the LORD will be your everlasting light,
and your God will be your glory.
20Your sun will never set again,
and your moon will wane no more;
the LORD will be your everlasting light,
and your days of sorrow will end.
21Then will all your people be righteous
and they will possess the land forever.
They are the shoot I have planted,
the work of my hands,
for the display of my splendor.
22The least of you will become a thousand,
the smallest a mighty nation.
I am the LORD;
in its time I will do this swiftly."

*The Year of the LORD's Favor*

**61** THE SPIRIT of the Sovereign LORD is on me,
because the LORD has anointed me
to preach good news to the poor.
He has sent me to bind up the brokenhearted,
to proclaim freedom for the captives
and release from darkness for the prisoners,[b]
2to proclaim the year of the LORD's favor
and the day of vengeance of our God,
to comfort all who mourn,

NIV [b] 1 Hebrew; Septuagint *the blind*

## King James

3To appoint unto them that mourn in Zion, to give unto them beauty for ashes, the oil of joy for mourning, the garment of praise for the spirit of heaviness; that they might be called trees of righteousness, the planting of the LORD, that he might be glorified.

4¶ And they shall build the old wastes, they shall raise up the former desolations, and they shall repair the waste cities, the desolations of many generations.

5And strangers shall stand and feed your flocks, and the sons of the alien *shall be* your plowmen and your vinedressers.

6But ye shall be named the Priests of the LORD: *men* shall call you the Ministers of our God: ye shall eat the riches of the Gentiles, and in their glory shall ye boast yourselves.

7¶ For your shame *ye shall have* double; and *for* confusion they shall rejoice in their portion: therefore in their land they shall possess the double: everlasting joy shall be unto them.

8For I the LORD love judgment, I hate robbery for burnt offering; and I will direct their work in truth, and I will make an everlasting covenant with them.

9And their seed shall be known among the Gentiles, and their offspring among the people: all that see them shall acknowledge them, that they *are* the seed *which* the LORD hath blessed.

10I will greatly rejoice in the LORD, my soul shall be joyful in my God; for he hath clothed me with the garments of salvation, he hath covered me with the robe of righteousness, as a bridegroom decketh *himself* with ornaments, and as a bride adorneth *herself* with her jewels.

11For as the earth bringeth forth her bud, and as the garden causeth the things that are sown in it to spring forth; so the Lord GOD will cause righteousness and praise to spring forth before all the nations.

**62** FOR ZION'S sake will I not hold my peace, and for Jerusalem's sake I will not rest, until the righteousness thereof go forth as brightness, and the salvation thereof as a lamp *that* burneth.

2And the Gentiles shall see thy righteousness, and all kings thy glory: and thou shalt be called by a new name, which the mouth of the LORD shall name.

3Thou shalt also be a crown of glory in the hand of the LORD, and a royal diadem in the hand of thy God.

4Thou shalt no more be termed Forsaken; neither shall thy land any more be termed Desolate: but thou shalt be called Hephzibah, and thy land Beulah: for the LORD delighteth in thee, and thy land shall be married.

## Amplified

3To grant [consolation and joy] to those who mourn in Zion, to give them an ornament—a garland or diadem—of beauty instead of ashes, the oil of joy for mourning, the garment [expressive] of praise instead of a heavy, burdened *and* failing spirit; that they may be called oaks of righteousness [lofty, strong and magnificent, distinguished for uprightness, justice and right standing with God], the planting of the Lord, that He may be glorified.

4And they shall rebuild the ancient ruins, they shall raise up the former desolations and renew the ruined cities, the devastations of many generations.

5Aliens shall stand [ready] and feed your flocks, and foreigners shall be your plowmen and your vinedressers;

6But you shall be called the priests of the Lord; people will speak of you as the ministers of our God. You shall eat the wealth of the nations, and the glory [once that of your captors] shall be yours. [Exod. 19:6; I Pet. 2:5; Rev. 1:6; 5:10; 20:6.]

7For your [former] shame you shall have a twofold recompense; instead of dishonor *and* reproach *your people* shall rejoice in their portion; therefore in their land they shall possess double [what they had forfeited]; everlasting joy shall be theirs.

8For I the Lord love justice, I hate robbery *and* wrong with violence *or* a burnt offering; and I will give them their recompense faithfully in truth, and I will make an everlasting covenant *or* league with them.

9And their offspring shall be known among the nations, and their descendants among the peoples. All who see them [in their prosperity] will recognize *and* acknowledge that they are the people whom the Lord has blessed.

10I will greatly rejoice in the Lord, my soul shall exult in my God; for He has clothed me with the garments of salvation, He has covered me with the robe of righteousness, as a bridegroom decks himself with a garland, and as a bride adorns herself with her jewels.

11For as *surely as* the earth brings forth its shoots, and as a garden causes what is sown in it to spring forth, so *surely* the Lord God will cause rightness *and* justice and praise to spring forth before all the nations [through the self-fulfilling power of His word].

**62** FOR ZION'S sake will I [Isaiah] not hold my peace, and for Jerusalem's sake I will not rest until her imputed righteousness *and* vindication go forth as brightness, and her salvation radiates as does a burning torch.

2And the nations shall see your righteousness *and* vindication—your rightness and justice [not your own, but His ascribed to you]—and all kings shall behold your salvation and glory and you shall be called by a new name, which the mouth of the Lord shall name. [Rev. 2:17.]

3You shall also be [so beautiful and prosperous as to be thought of as] a crown of glory *and* honor in the hand of the Lord, and a royal diadem [exceedingly beautiful] in the hand of your God.

4You [Judah] shall no more be termed Forsaken, nor shall your land be called Desolate any more, but you shall be called Hephzibah [My delight is in her], and your land be called Beulah [that is, Married]; for the Lord delights in you, and your land shall be married [owned and protected by the Lord].

## New American Standard

3 To grant those who mourn *in* Zion,
Giving them a garland instead of ashes,
The oil of gladness instead of mourning,
The mantle of praise instead of a spirit of fainting.
So they will be called oaks of righteousness,
The planting of the LORD, that He may be glorified.

4¶ Then they will rebuild the ancient ruins,
They will raise up the former devastations,
And they will repair the ruined cities,
The desolations of many generations.
5 And strangers will stand and pasture your flocks,
And foreigners will be your farmers and your vinedressers.
6 But you will be called the priests of the LORD;
You will be spoken of *as* ministers of our God.
You will eat the wealth of nations,
And in their riches you will boast.
7 Instead of your shame *you will have a* double *portion*,
And *instead of* humiliation they will shout for joy over their portion.
Therefore they will possess a double *portion* in their land,
Everlasting joy will be theirs.
8 For I, the LORD, love justice,
I hate robbery in the burnt offering;
And I will faithfully give them their recompense,
And I will make an everlasting covenant with them.
9 Then their offspring will be known among the nations,
And their descendants in the midst of the peoples.
All who see them will recognize them
Because they are the offspring *whom* the LORD has blessed.

10¶ I will rejoice greatly in the LORD,
My soul will exult in my God;
For He has clothed me with garments of salvation,
He has wrapped me with a robe of righteousness,
As a bridegroom decks himself with a garland,
And as a bride adorns herself with her jewels.
11 For as the earth brings forth its sprouts,
And as a garden causes the things sown in it to spring up,
So the Lord GOD will cause righteousness and praise
To spring up before all the nations.

*Zion's Glory and New Name*

**62** FOR ZION'S sake I will not keep silent,
And for Jerusalem's sake I will not keep quiet,
Until her righteousness goes forth like brightness,
And her salvation like a torch that is burning.
2 And the nations will see your righteousness,
And all kings your glory;
And you will be called by a new name,
Which the mouth of the LORD will designate.
3 You will also be a crown of beauty in the hand of the LORD,
And a royal diadem in the hand of your God.
4 It will no longer be said to you, "Forsaken,"
Nor to your land will it any longer be said, "Desolate";
But you will be called, "My delight is in her,"
And your land, "Married";
For the LORD delights in you,
And *to Him* your land will be married.

## New International

3 and provide for those who grieve in Zion—
to bestow on them a crown of beauty
instead of ashes,
the oil of gladness
instead of mourning,
and a garment of praise
instead of a spirit of despair.
They will be called oaks of righteousness,
a planting of the LORD
for the display of his splendor.

4 They will rebuild the ancient ruins
and restore the places long devastated;
they will renew the ruined cities
that have been devastated for generations.
5 Aliens will shepherd your flocks;
foreigners will work your fields and vineyards.
6 And you will be called priests of the LORD,
you will be named ministers of our God.
You will feed on the wealth of nations,
and in their riches you will boast.
7 Instead of their shame
my people will receive a double portion,
and instead of disgrace
they will rejoice in their inheritance;
and so they will inherit a double portion in their land,
and everlasting joy will be theirs.

8 "For I, the LORD, love justice;
I hate robbery and iniquity.
In my faithfulness I will reward them
and make an everlasting covenant with them.
9 Their descendants will be known among the nations
and their offspring among the peoples.
All who see them will acknowledge
that they are a people the LORD has blessed."

10 I delight greatly in the LORD;
my soul rejoices in my God.
For he has clothed me with garments of salvation
and arrayed me in a robe of righteousness,
as a bridegroom adorns his head like a priest,
and as a bride adorns herself with her jewels.
11 For as the soil makes the sprout come up
and a garden causes seeds to grow,
so the Sovereign LORD will make righteousness and praise
spring up before all nations.

*Zion's New Name*

**62** FOR ZION'S sake I will not keep silent,
for Jerusalem's sake I will not remain quiet,
till her righteousness shines out like the dawn,
her salvation like a blazing torch.
2 The nations will see your righteousness,
and all kings your glory;
you will be called by a new name
that the mouth of the LORD will bestow.
3 You will be a crown of splendor in the LORD's hand,
a royal diadem in the hand of your God.
4 No longer will they call you Deserted,
or name your land Desolate.
But you will be called Hephzibah,[a]
and your land Beulah[b];
for the LORD will take delight in you,
and your land will be married.

NIV [a] 4 *Hephzibah* means *my delight is in her.* [b] 4 *Beulah* means *married.*

## King James

5¶ For *as* a young man marrieth a virgin, *so* shall thy sons marry thee: and *as* the bridegroom rejoiceth over the bride, *so* shall thy God rejoice over thee.

6I have set watchmen upon thy walls, O Jerusalem, *which* shall never hold their peace day nor night: ye that make mention of the LORD, keep not silence,

7And give him no rest, till he establish, and till he make Jerusalem a praise in the earth.

8The LORD hath sworn by his right hand, and by the arm of his strength, Surely I will no more give thy corn *to be* meat for thine enemies; and the sons of the stranger shall not drink thy wine, for the which thou hast laboured:

9But they that have gathered it shall eat it, and praise the LORD; and they that have brought it together shall drink it in the courts of my holiness.

10¶ Go through, go through the gates; prepare ye the way of the people; cast up, cast up the highway; gather out the stones; lift up a standard for the people.

11Behold, the LORD hath proclaimed unto the end of the world, Say ye to the daughter of Zion, Behold, thy salvation cometh; behold, his reward *is* with him, and his work before him.

12And they shall call them, The holy people, The redeemed of the LORD: and thou shalt be called, Sought out, A city not forsaken.

63 WHO *IS* this that cometh from Edom, with dyed garments from Bozrah? this *that is* glorious in his apparel, travelling in the greatness of his strength? I that speak in righteousness, mighty to save.

2Wherefore *art thou* red in thine apparel, and thy garments like him that treadeth in the winevat?

3I have trodden the winepress alone; and of the people *there was* none with me: for I will tread them in mine anger, and trample them in my fury; and their blood shall be sprinkled upon my garments, and I will stain all my raiment.

4For the day of vengeance *is* in mine heart, and the year of my redeemed is come.

5And I looked, and *there was* none to help; and I wondered that *there was* none to uphold: therefore mine own arm brought salvation unto me; and my fury, it upheld me.

6And I will tread down the people in mine anger, and make them drunk in my fury, and I will bring down their strength to the earth.

## Amplified

5For as a young man marries a virgin [O Jerusalem], so shall your sons marry you; and as the bridegroom rejoices over the bride, so shall your God rejoice over you.

6I have set watchmen upon your walls, O Jerusalem, who will never hold their peace day or night; you who [are His servants and by your prayers] put the Lord in remembrance [of His promises], keep not silence,

7And give Him no rest until He establishes Jerusalem and makes it a praise in the earth.

8The Lord has sworn by His right hand and by His mighty arm: Surely I will not again give your grain to be food for your enemies, and [the invading sons of] aliens shall not drink your new wine for which you have toiled.

9But they who have gathered it shall eat it, and praise the Lord; and they who have brought in the vintage shall drink it [at the feasts celebrated] in the courts of My sanctuary—the temple of My holiness.

10Go through, go through the gates; prepare the way of the people, cast up, cast up the highway, gather out the stones; lift up a standard *or* ensign over *and* for the peoples.

11Behold, the Lord has proclaimed to the end of the earth, Say to the daughter of Zion, Behold, your salvation comes [in the person of the Lord]; behold, His reward is with Him and His work *and* recompense before Him. [Isa. 40:10.]

12And they shall call them, The holy people, The redeemed of the Lord; and you shall be called, Sought out, A city not forsaken.

63 WHO IS this Who comes from Edom, with crimson-stained garments from Bozrah [in Edom]? This One Who is glorious in His apparel, striding triumphantly in the greatness of His might? It is I, *the One* Who speaks in righteousness—proclaiming vindication—mighty to save!

2Why is Your apparel splashed with red, and Your garments like his who treads in the winepress?

3I have trodden the winepress alone, and of the peoples there was no one with Me; I trod them in My anger and trampled them in My wrath, and their life-blood is sprinkled upon My garments, and I have stained all My raiment.

4For the day of vengeance was in My heart, and My year of redemption—the year of My redeemed—has come.

5And I looked, but there was no one to help; I was amazed *and* appalled that there was no one to uphold [truth and right]. So My own arm brought Me victory, and My wrath upheld Me.

6I trod down the peoples in My anger, and made them drink of the cup of My wrath until intoxicated, and I spilled their life-blood upon the earth.

## New American Standard

5 For *as* a young man marries a virgin,
*So* your sons will marry you;
And *as* the bridegroom rejoices over the bride,
*So* your God will rejoice over you.

6¶ On your walls, O Jerusalem, I have appointed watchmen;
All day and all night they will never keep silent.
You who remind the LORD, take no rest for yourselves;
7 And give Him no rest until He establishes
And makes Jerusalem a praise in the earth.
8 The LORD has sworn by His right hand and by His strong arm,
"I will never again give your grain *as* food for your enemies;
Nor will foreigners drink your new wine, for which you have labored."
9 But those who garner it will eat it, and praise the LORD;
And those who gather it will drink it in the courts of My sanctuary.
10¶ Go through, go through the gates;
Clear the way for the people;
Build up, build up the highway;
Remove the stones, lift up a standard over the peoples.
11 Behold, the LORD has proclaimed to the end of the earth,
Say to the daughter of Zion, "Lo, your salvation comes;
Behold His reward is with Him, and His recompense before Him."
12 And they will call them, "The holy people,
The redeemed of the LORD";
And you will be called, "Sought out, a city not forsaken."

*God's Vengeance on the Nations*

63 WHO IS this who comes from Edom,
With garments of glowing colors from Bozrah,
This One who is majestic in His apparel,
Marching in the greatness of His strength?
"It is I who speak in righteousness, mighty to save."
2 Why is Your apparel red,
And Your garments like the one who treads in the wine press?
3 "I have trodden the wine trough alone,
And from the peoples there was no man with Me.
I also trod them in My anger,
And trampled them in My wrath;
And their lifeblood is sprinkled on My garments,
And I stained all My raiment.
4 "For the day of vengeance was in My heart,
And My year of redemption has come.
5 "And I looked, and there was no one to help,
And I was astonished and there was no one to uphold;
So My own arm brought salvation to Me;
And My wrath upheld Me.
6 "And I trod down the peoples in My anger,
And made them drunk in My wrath,
And I poured out their lifeblood on the earth."

## New International

5As a young man marries a maiden,
so will your sons[a] marry you;
as a bridegroom rejoices over his bride,
so will your God rejoice over you.

6I have posted watchmen on your walls, O Jerusalem;
they will never be silent day or night.
You who call on the LORD,
give yourselves no rest,
7and give him no rest till he establishes Jerusalem
and makes her the praise of the earth.

8The LORD has sworn by his right hand
and by his mighty arm:
"Never again will I give your grain
as food for your enemies,
and never again will foreigners drink the new wine
for which you have toiled;
9but those who harvest it will eat it
and praise the LORD,
and those who gather the grapes will drink it
in the courts of my sanctuary."

10Pass through, pass through the gates!
Prepare the way for the people.
Build up, build up the highway!
Remove the stones.
Raise a banner for the nations.
11The LORD has made proclamation
to the ends of the earth:
"Say to the Daughter of Zion,
'See, your Savior comes!
See, his reward is with him,
and his recompense accompanies him.'"
12They will be called the Holy People,
the Redeemed of the LORD;
and you will be called Sought After,
the City No Longer Deserted.

*God's Day of Vengeance and Redemption*

63 WHO IS this coming from Edom,
from Bozrah, with his garments stained crimson?
Who is this, robed in splendor,
striding forward in the greatness of his strength?

"It is I, speaking in righteousness,
mighty to save."

2Why are your garments red,
like those of one treading the winepress?

3"I have trodden the winepress alone;
from the nations no one was with me.
I trampled them in my anger
and trod them down in my wrath;
their blood spattered my garments,
and I stained all my clothing.
4For the day of vengeance was in my heart,
and the year of my redemption has come.
5I looked, but there was no one to help,
I was appalled that no one gave support;
so my own arm worked salvation for me,
and my own wrath sustained me.
6I trampled the nations in my anger;
in my wrath I made them drunk
and poured their blood on the ground."

NIV [a] 5 Or *Builder*

## King James

7¶ I will mention the lovingkindnesses of the LORD, *and* the praises of the LORD, according to all that the LORD hath bestowed on us, and the great goodness toward the house of Israel, which he hath bestowed on them according to his mercies, and according to the multitude of his lovingkindnesses.

8For he said, Surely they *are* my people, children *that* will not lie: so he was their Saviour.

9In all their affliction he was afflicted, and the angel of his presence saved them: in his love and in his pity he redeemed them; and he bare them, and carried them all the days of old.

10¶ But they rebelled, and vexed his holy spirit: therefore he was turned to be their enemy, *and* he fought against them.

11Then he remembered the days of old, Moses, *and* his people, *saying*, Where *is* he that brought them up out of the sea with the shepherd of his flock? where *is* he that put his holy spirit within him?

12That led *them* by the right hand of Moses with his glorious arm, dividing the water before them, to make himself an everlasting name?

13That led them through the deep, as an horse in the wilderness, *that* they should not stumble?

14As a beast goeth down into the valley, the spirit of the LORD caused him to rest: so didst thou lead thy people, to make thyself a glorious name.

15¶ Look down from heaven, and behold from the habitation of thy holiness and of thy glory: where *is* thy zeal and thy strength, the sounding of thy bowels and of thy mercies toward me? are they restrained?

16Doubtless thou *art* our father, though Abraham be ignorant of us, and Israel acknowledge us not: thou, O LORD, *art* our father, our redeemer; thy name *is* from everlasting.

17¶ O LORD, why hast thou made us to err from thy ways, *and* hardened our heart from thy fear? Return for thy servants' sake, the tribes of thine inheritance.

18The people of thy holiness have possessed *it* but a little while: our adversaries have trodden down thy sanctuary.

19We are *thine:* thou never barest rule over them; they were not called by thy name.

## Amplified

7I will recount the loving-kindnesses of the Lord, and the praiseworthy deeds of the Lord, according to all that the Lord has bestowed on us, and the great goodness to the house of Israel, which He has granted them according to His mercies, and according to the multitude of His loving-kindnesses.

8For He said, Surely they are My people, sons who will not lie—who will not deal falsely with *Me;* and so He was to them a Savior [in all their distresses].

9In all their affliction He was afflicted, and the [a]Angel of His presence saved them; in His love and in His pity He redeemed them; and He lifted them up and carried them all the days of old.

10But they rebelled and grieved His Holy Spirit; therefore He turned to be their enemy, and Himself fought against them.

11Then His people [seriously] remembered the days of old, *of* Moses and his people, and they said, Where is He Who brought [our fathers] up out of the *Red* Sea with [Moses and the other] shepherds of His flock? Where is He Who put His Holy Spirit within their midst?

12Who caused His glorious arm to go at the right hand of Moses, dividing the waters before them, to make Himself an everlasting name?

13Who led them through the depths, as a horse in the wilderness, so that they did not stumble?

14As the cattle that go down into the valley [to find better pasturage, refuge and rest], the Spirit of the Lord caused them to rest. So did You lead Your people, *Lord,* to make for Yourself a beautiful *and* glorious name [to prepare the way for its acknowledgment by all nations].

15Look down from heaven and see from the dwelling place of Your holiness and Your glory. Where are Your zeal *and* Your jealousy, and Your mighty acts [which you formerly did for Your people]? Your yearning pity and the [multitude of] compassions of Your heart are restrained *and* withheld from me.

16For *surely* You are our Father, even though [our ancestor] Abraham does not know us, and Israel [Jacob] does not acknowledge us; You, O Lord, are [still] our Father; our Redeemer from everlasting is Your name.

17O Lord, why have You made us [able] to err from Your ways, and hardened our hearts to [reverential] fear of You? Return [to bless us] for Your servants' sake, the tribes of Your heritage.

18Your holy people possessed Your sanctuary but a little while; our adversaries have trodden it down.

19We have become *to You* as they over whom You never bore rule, as they who were not called by Your name.

**AMP** [a] "The Angel of the Lord," "of God," or "of His Presence," is readily identified as the Lord God (Gen. 16:11, 13; 22:11, 12; 31:11, 13; Exod. 3:1-6, etc.). But it is obvious that the Angel of the Lord is a distinct person in Himself from God the Father (Gen. 24:7; Zech. 1:12, 13; Exod. 23:20; etc.), as this verse shows. Nor does the Angel of the Lord longer appear after Christ came in human form. He must of necessity then be One of the three-in-one Godhead. / The Angel of the Lord is the visible Lord God of the Old Testament, as Jesus Christ was of the New Testament. Thus His Deity is clearly portrayed in the Old Testament. "There is a fascinating forecast of the coming Messiah, breaking through the dimness with amazing consistency, at intervals from Genesis to Malachi. Abraham, Moses, the slave girl Hagar, the impoverished farmer Gideon, even the humble parents of Samson, had seen and talked with Him centuries before the herald angels proclaimed His birth in Bethlehem" (Cambridge Bible).

# New American Standard

*God's Ancient Mercies Recalled*

7¶ I shall make mention of the lovingkindnesses of the
LORD, the praises of the LORD,
According to all that the LORD has granted us,
And the great goodness toward the house of Israel,
Which He has granted them according to His
compassion,
And according to the multitude of His
lovingkindnesses.
8 For He said, "Surely, they are My people,
Sons who will not deal falsely."
So He became their Savior.
9 In all their affliction He was afflicted,
And the angel of His presence saved them;
In His love and in His mercy He redeemed them;
And He lifted them and carried them all the days of
old.
10 But they rebelled
And grieved His Holy Spirit;
Therefore, He turned Himself to become their enemy,
He fought against them.
11 Then His people remembered the days of old, of
Moses.
Where is He who brought them up out of the sea with
the shepherds of His flock?
Where is He who put His Holy Spirit in the midst of
them,
12 Who caused His glorious arm to go at the right hand of
Moses,
Who divided the waters before them to make for
Himself an everlasting name,
13 Who led them through the depths?
Like the horse in the wilderness, they did not stumble;
14 As the cattle which go down into the valley,
The Spirit of the LORD gave them rest.
So didst Thou lead Thy people,
To make for Thyself a glorious name.

*"Thou Art Our Father"*

15¶ Look down from heaven, and see from Thy holy and
glorious habitation;
Where are Thy zeal and Thy mighty deeds?
The stirrings of Thy heart and Thy compassion are
restrained toward me.
16 For Thou art our Father, though Abraham does not
know us,
And Israel does not recognize us.
Thou, O LORD, art our Father,
Our Redeemer from of old is Thy name.
17 Why, O LORD, dost Thou cause us to stray from Thy
ways,
And harden our heart from fearing Thee?
Return for the sake of Thy servants, the tribes of Thy
heritage.
18 Thy holy people possessed Thy sanctuary for a little
while,
Our adversaries have trodden *it* down.
19 We have become *like* those over whom Thou hast never
ruled,
*Like* those who were not called by Thy name.

# New International

*Praise and Prayer*

7I will tell of the kindnesses of the LORD,
the deeds for which he is to be praised,
according to all the LORD has done for us—
yes, the many good things he has done
for the house of Israel,
according to his compassion and many kindnesses.
8He said, "Surely they are my people,
sons who will not be false to me";
and so he became their Savior.
9In all their distress he too was distressed,
and the angel of his presence saved them.
In his love and mercy he redeemed them;
he lifted them up and carried them
all the days of old.
10Yet they rebelled
and grieved his Holy Spirit.
So he turned and became their enemy
and he himself fought against them.
11Then his people recalled[b] the days of old,
the days of Moses and his people—
where is he who brought them through the sea,
with the shepherd of his flock?
Where is he who set
his Holy Spirit among them,
12who sent his glorious arm of power
to be at Moses' right hand,
who divided the waters before them,
to gain for himself everlasting renown,
13who led them through the depths?
Like a horse in open country,
they did not stumble;
14like cattle that go down to the plain,
they were given rest by the Spirit of the LORD.
This is how you guided your people
to make for yourself a glorious name.

15Look down from heaven and see
from your lofty throne, holy and glorious.
Where are your zeal and your might?
Your tenderness and compassion are withheld from us.
16But you are our Father,
though Abraham does not know us
or Israel acknowledge us;
you, O LORD, are our Father,
our Redeemer from of old is your name.
17Why, O LORD, do you make us wander from your ways
and harden our hearts so we do not revere you?
Return for the sake of your servants,
the tribes that are your inheritance.
18For a little while your people possessed your holy place,
but now our enemies have trampled down your
sanctuary.
19We are yours from of old;
but you have not ruled over them,
they have not been called by your name.[c]

NIV [b] 11 Or *But may he recall* [c] 19 Or *We are like those you have never ruled, / like those never called by your name*

## King James

**64** OH THAT thou wouldest rend the heavens, that thou wouldest come down, that the mountains might flow down at thy presence,

2 As *when* the melting fire burneth, the fire causeth the waters to boil, to make thy name known to thine adversaries, *that* the nations may tremble at thy presence!

3 When thou didst terrible things *which* we looked not for, thou camest down, the mountains flowed down at thy presence.

4 For since the beginning of the world *men* have not heard, nor perceived by the ear, neither hath the eye seen, O God, beside thee, *what* he hath prepared for him that waiteth for him.

5 Thou meetest him that rejoiceth and worketh righteousness, *those that* remember thee in thy ways: behold, thou art wroth; for we have sinned: in those is continuance, and we shall be saved.

6 But we are all as an unclean *thing,* and all our righteousnesses *are* as filthy rags; and we all do fade as a leaf; and our iniquities, like the wind, have taken us away.

7 And *there is* none that calleth upon thy name, that stirreth up himself to take hold of thee: for thou hast hid thy face from us, and hast consumed us, because of our iniquities.

8 But now, O Lord, thou *art* our father; we *are* the clay, and thou our potter; and we all *are* the work of thy hand.

9 ¶ Be not wroth very sore, O Lord, neither remember iniquity for ever: behold, see, we beseech thee, we *are* all thy people.

10 Thy holy cities are a wilderness, Zion is a wilderness, Jerusalem a desolation.

11 Our holy and our beautiful house, where our fathers praised thee, is burned up with fire: and all our pleasant things are laid waste.

12 Wilt thou refrain thyself for these *things,* O Lord? wilt thou hold thy peace, and afflict us very sore?

**65** I AM sought of *them that* asked not *for me;* I am found of *them that* sought me not: I said, Behold me, behold me, unto a nation *that* was not called by my name.

2 I have spread out my hands all the day unto a rebellious people, which walketh in a way *that was* not good, after their own thoughts;

3 A people that provoketh me to anger continually to my face; that sacrificeth in gardens, and burneth incense upon altars of brick;

4 Which remain among the graves, and lodge in the monuments, which eat swine's flesh, and broth of abominable *things is in* their vessels;

## Amplified

**64** OH, THAT You would rend the heavens, and that You would come down, that the mountains might quake *and* flow down at Your presence,

2 As when fire kindles the brushwood and the fire causes the waters to boil; to make Your name known to Your adversaries, that the nations may tremble at Your presence!

3 When You did terrible things which we did not expect, You came down, the mountains quaked at Your presence.

4 For from of old, men have not heard, nor perceived by the ear, nor has the eye seen a God besides You, Who works *and* shows Himself active on behalf of him who [earnestly] waits for Him.

5 You meet *and* spare him who joyfully works righteousness—uprightness and justice—[earnestly] remembering You in Your ways. Behold, You were angry, for we sinned; we have long continued in our sins [prolonging Your anger], and shall we be saved?

6 For we have all become as one who is unclean [ceremonially, as a leper], and all our righteousness—our best deeds of rightness and justice—are as filthy rags *or* a polluted garment. We all fade as a leaf, and our iniquities, like the wind, take us away [far from God's favor, hurrying us to destruction]. [Lev. 13:45, 46.]

7 And no one calls upon Your name and awakens *and* bestirs himself to take *and* keep hold of You. For You have hid Your face from us and have delivered us into the [consuming] power of our iniquities. [Rom. 1:21-24.]

8 Yet, O Lord, You are our Father; we are the clay, and You our potter, and we all are the work of Your hand.

9 Do not be exceedingly angry, O Lord, or [seriously] remember iniquity for ever. Behold, consider, we beseech You, we are all Your people.

10 Your holy cities have become a wilderness, Zion has become a wilderness, Jerusalem a desolation.

11 Our holy and our beautiful house, *the temple* where our fathers praised You, is burned with fire, and all our pleasant *and* desirable places are in ruins.

12 Considering these *calamities,* will You restrain Yourself, O Lord [and not come to our aid]? Will You keep silent *and* not command our deliverance, but humble *and* afflict us exceedingly?

**65** I WAS *ready to be* inquired of by those who asked not; I was *to be* found by those who sought Me not. I said, Here I am, here I AM to a nation [Israel] that has not called on My name. [Gen. 3:14.]

2 I have spread out My hands all the day to a rebellious people, who walk in a way that is not good, after their own thoughts;

3 A people who provoke Me to My face continually, sacrificing [to idols] in gardens and burning incense upon bricks [instead of at God's prescribed altar],

4 Who sit among the graves [trying to talk with the dead], and lodge among the secret places [or caves where familiar spirits were thought to dwell], who eat swine's flesh, and broth of abominable *and* loathsome things is in their vessels;

## New American Standard

*Prayer for Mercy and Help*

64 OH, THAT Thou wouldst rend the heavens *and* come down,
That the mountains might quake at Thy presence—
2 As fire kindles the brushwood, *as* fire causes water to boil—
To make Thy name known to Thine adversaries,
*That* the nations may tremble at Thy presence!
3 When Thou didst awesome things which we did not expect,
Thou didst come down, the mountains quaked at Thy presence.
4 For from of old they have not heard nor perceived by ear,
Neither has the eye seen a God besides Thee,
Who acts in behalf of the one who waits for Him.
5 Thou dost meet him who rejoices in doing righteousness,
Who remembers Thee in Thy ways.
Behold, Thou wast angry, for we sinned,
*We continued* in them a long time;
And shall we be saved?
6 For all of us have become like one who is unclean,
And all our righteous deeds are like a filthy garment;
And all of us wither like a leaf,
And our iniquities, like the wind, take us away.
7 And there is no one who calls on Thy name,
Who arouses himself to take hold of Thee;
For Thou hast hidden Thy face from us,
And hast delivered us into the power of our iniquities.

8¶ But now, O LORD, Thou art our Father,
We are the clay, and Thou our potter;
And all of us are the work of Thy hand.
9 Do not be angry beyond measure, O LORD,
Neither remember iniquity forever;
Behold, look now, all of us are Thy people.
10 Thy holy cities have become a wilderness,
Zion has become a wilderness,
Jerusalem a desolation.
11 Our holy and beautiful house,
Where our fathers praised Thee,
Has been burned *by* fire;
And all our precious things have become a ruin.
12 Wilt Thou restrain Thyself at these things, O LORD?
Wilt Thou keep silent and afflict us beyond measure?

*A Rebellious People*

65 "I PERMITTED Myself to be sought by those who did not ask *for Me;*
I permitted Myself to be found by those who did not seek Me.
I said, 'Here am I, here am I,'
To a nation which did not call on My name.
2 "I have spread out My hands all day long to a rebellious people,
Who walk *in* the way which is not good, following their own thoughts,
3 A people who continually provoke Me to My face,
Offering sacrifices in gardens and burning incense on bricks;
4 Who sit among graves, and spend the night in secret places;
Who eat swine's flesh,
And the broth of unclean meat is *in* their pots.

## New International

64 OH, THAT you would rend the heavens and come down,
that the mountains would tremble before you!
2As when fire sets twigs ablaze
and causes water to boil,
come down to make your name known to your enemies
and cause the nations to quake before you!
3For when you did awesome things that we did not expect,
you came down, and the mountains trembled before you.
4Since ancient times no one has heard,
no ear has perceived,
no eye has seen any God besides you,
who acts on behalf of those who wait for him.
5You come to the help of those who gladly do right,
who remember your ways.
But when we continued to sin against them,
you were angry.
How then can we be saved?
6All of us have become like one who is unclean,
and all our righteous acts are like filthy rags;
we all shrivel up like a leaf,
and like the wind our sins sweep us away.
7No one calls on your name
or strives to lay hold of you;
for you have hidden your face from us
and made us waste away because of our sins.

8Yet, O LORD, you are our Father.
We are the clay, you are the potter;
we are all the work of your hand.
9Do not be angry beyond measure, O LORD;
do not remember our sins forever.
Oh, look upon us, we pray,
for we are all your people.
10Your sacred cities have become a desert;
even Zion is a desert, Jerusalem a desolation.
11Our holy and glorious temple, where our fathers praised you,
has been burned with fire,
and all that we treasured lies in ruins.
12After all this, O LORD, will you hold yourself back?
Will you keep silent and punish us beyond measure?

*Judgment and Salvation*

65 "I REVEALED myself to those who did not ask for me;
I was found by those who did not seek me.
To a nation that did not call on my name,
I said, 'Here am I, here am I.'
2All day long I have held out my hands
to an obstinate people,
who walk in ways not good,
pursuing their own imaginations—
3a people who continually provoke me
to my very face,
offering sacrifices in gardens
and burning incense on altars of brick;
4who sit among the graves
and spend their nights keeping secret vigil;
who eat the flesh of pigs,
and whose pots hold broth of unclean meat;

## King James

5Which say, Stand by thyself, come not near to me; for I am holier than thou. These *are* a smoke in my nose, a fire that burneth all the day.
6Behold, *it is* written before me: I will not keep silence, but will recompense, even recompense into their bosom,
7Your iniquities, and the iniquities of your fathers together, saith the LORD, which have burned incense upon the mountains, and blasphemed me upon the hills: therefore will I measure their former work into their bosom.
8¶ Thus saith the LORD, As the new wine is found in the cluster, and *one* saith, Destroy it not; for a blessing *is* in it: so will I do for my servants' sakes, that I may not destroy them all.
9And I will bring forth a seed out of Jacob, and out of Judah an inheritor of my mountains: and mine elect shall inherit it, and my servants shall dwell there.
10And Sharon shall be a fold of flocks, and the valley of Achor a place for the herds to lie down in, for my people that have sought me.
11¶ But ye *are* they that forsake the LORD, that forget my holy mountain, that prepare a table for that troop, and that furnish the drink offering unto that number.
12Therefore will I number you to the sword, and ye shall all bow down to the slaughter: because when I called, ye did not answer; when I spake, ye did not hear; but did evil before mine eyes, and did choose *that* wherein I delighted not.
13Therefore thus saith the Lord GOD, Behold, my servants shall eat, but ye shall be hungry: behold, my servants shall drink, but ye shall be thirsty: behold, my servants shall rejoice, but ye shall be ashamed:
14Behold, my servants shall sing for joy of heart, but ye shall cry for sorrow of heart, and shall howl for vexation of spirit.
15And ye shall leave your name for a curse unto my chosen: for the Lord GOD shall slay thee, and call his servants by another name:
16That he who blesseth himself in the earth shall bless himself in the God of truth; and he that sweareth in the earth shall swear by the God of truth; because the former troubles are forgotten, and because they are hid from mine eyes.
17¶ For, behold, I create new heavens and a new earth: and the former shall not be remembered, nor come into mind.

## Amplified

5Who say, Keep to yourself, do not come near me, for I am set apart from you *and* lest I sanctify you. These are a smoke in My nostrils, a fire that burns all the day.
6Behold, it is written before Me: I will not keep silence, but will repay; yes, I will repay into their bosom
7Both your own iniquities and the iniquities of your fathers, says the Lord; because they too burned incense upon the mountains and reviled *and* blasphemed Me upon the hills. Therefore will I measure *and* stretch out their former doings into their *own* bosom.
8Thus says the Lord: As the grape juice is found in the cluster, and one says, Do not destroy it, for there is a blessing in it, so will I do for My servants' sake, that I may not destroy them all.
9And I will bring forth an offspring from Jacob, and from Judah an inheritor of My mountains; My chosen *and* elect shall inherit it, and My servants shall dwell there.
10And [the plain of] Sharon shall be a pasture *and* fold for flocks, and the valley of Achor a place for herds to lie down in, for My people who have sought Me, inquired of Me, *and* required Me [by right of their necessity and by right of My invitation].
11But you who forsake the Lord, who forget *and* ignore My holy Mount [Zion], who prepare a table for [the Babylonian god of fortune] Gad, and who furnish mixed drinks for [the goddess of destiny] Meni;
12I will destine you [says the Lord] to the sword, and you shall all bow down to the slaughter; because when I called, you did not answer; when I spoke, you did not listen *or* obey; but you did what was evil in My eyes, and you chose that in which I did not delight.
13Therefore thus says the Lord God: Behold, My servants shall eat, but you shall be hungry; behold, My servants shall drink, but you shall be thirsty; behold, My servants shall rejoice, but you shall be put to shame;
14Behold, My servants shall sing for joy of heart, but you shall cry out for pain *and* sorrow of heart, and shall wail *and* howl for anguish, vexation *and* breaking of spirit.
15And you shall leave your name to My chosen [for those who will use it] for a curse, and the Lord God will slay you; but He will call His servants by another name [as much greater than the former name as Israel was greater than Jacob]. [Jer. 29:22; Gen. 32:28.]
16So that he who invokes a blessing on himself in the land shall do so saying, May the God of truth *and* fidelity—the Amen—bless me; and he who takes an oath in the land shall swear by the God of truth *and* faithfulness—the Amen—to His promises; because the former troubles are forgotten, and because they are hid from My eyes. [II Cor. 1:20; Rev. 3:14.]
17For, behold, I create [a]new heavens and a new earth, and the former things shall not be remembered or come into mind. [Isa. 66:22; II Pet. 3:13; Rev. 21:1.]

**AMP** [a] A new universe is here meant. The Hebrew has no single word to express the thought of cosmos, so heavens and earth are substituted.

## New American Standard

5 "Who say, 'Keep to yourself, do not come near me,
For I am holier than you!'
These are smoke in My nostrils,
A fire that burns all the day.
6 "Behold, it is written before Me,
I will not keep silent, but I will repay;
I will even repay into their bosom,
7 Both their own iniquities and the iniquities of their fathers together," says the LORD.
"Because they have burned incense on the mountains,
And scorned Me on the hills,
Therefore I will measure their former work into their bosom."

8¶ Thus says the LORD,
"As the new wine is found in the cluster,
And one says, 'Do not destroy it, for there is benefit in it,'
So I will act on behalf of My servants
In order not to destroy all of them.
9 "And I will bring forth offspring from Jacob,
And an heir of My mountains from Judah;
Even My chosen ones shall inherit it,
And My servants shall dwell there.
10 "And Sharon shall be a pasture land for flocks,
And the valley of Achor a resting place for herds,
For My people who seek Me.
11 "But you who forsake the LORD,
Who forget My holy mountain,
Who set a table for Fortune,
And who fill *cups* with mixed wine for Destiny,
12 I will destine you for the sword,
And all of you shall bow down to the slaughter.
Because I called, but you did not answer;
I spoke, but you did not hear.
And you did evil in My sight,
And chose that in which I did not delight."

13¶ Therefore, thus says the Lord GOD,
"Behold, My servants shall eat, but you shall be hungry.
Behold, My servants shall drink, but you shall be thirsty.
Behold, My servants shall rejoice, but you shall be put to shame.
14 "Behold, My servants shall shout joyfully with a glad heart,
But you shall cry out with a heavy heart,
And you shall wail with a broken spirit.
15 "And you will leave your name for a curse to My chosen ones,
And the Lord GOD will slay you.
But My servants will be called by another name.
16 "Because he who is blessed in the earth
Shall be blessed by the God of truth;
And he who swears in the earth
Shall swear by the God of truth;
Because the former troubles are forgotten,
And because they are hidden from My sight!

*New Heavens and a New Earth*

17¶ "For behold, I create new heavens and a new earth;
And the former things shall not be remembered or come to mind.

## New International

5 who say, 'Keep away; don't come near me,
for I am too sacred for you!'
Such people are smoke in my nostrils,
a fire that keeps burning all day.

6 "See, it stands written before me:
I will not keep silent but will pay back in full;
I will pay it back into their laps—
7 both your sins and the sins of your fathers,"
says the LORD.
"Because they burned sacrifices on the mountains
and defied me on the hills,
I will measure into their laps
the full payment for their former deeds."

8 This is what the LORD says:
"As when juice is still found in a cluster of grapes
and men say, 'Don't destroy it,
there is yet some good in it,'
so will I do in behalf of my servants;
I will not destroy them all.
9 I will bring forth descendants from Jacob,
and from Judah those who will possess my mountains;
my chosen people will inherit them,
and there will my servants live.
10 Sharon will become a pasture for flocks,
and the Valley of Achor a resting place for herds,
for my people who seek me.

11 "But as for you who forsake the LORD
and forget my holy mountain,
who spread a table for Fortune
and fill bowls of mixed wine for Destiny,
12 I will destine you for the sword,
and you will all bend down for the slaughter;
for I called but you did not answer,
I spoke but you did not listen.
You did evil in my sight
and chose what displeases me."

13 Therefore this is what the Sovereign LORD says:
"My servants will eat,
but you will go hungry;
my servants will drink,
but you will go thirsty;
my servants will rejoice,
but you will be put to shame.
14 My servants will sing
out of the joy of their hearts,
but you will cry out
from anguish of heart
and wail in brokenness of spirit.
15 You will leave your name
to my chosen ones as a curse;
the Sovereign LORD will put you to death,
but to his servants he will give another name.
16 Whoever invokes a blessing in the land
will do so by the God of truth;
he who takes an oath in the land
will swear by the God of truth.
For the past troubles will be forgotten
and hidden from my eyes.

*New Heavens and a New Earth*

17 "Behold, I will create
new heavens and a new earth.
The former things will not be remembered,
nor will they come to mind.

## King James

18But be ye glad and rejoice for ever *in that* which I create: for, behold, I create Jerusalem a rejoicing, and her people a joy.

19And I will rejoice in Jerusalem, and joy in my people: and the voice of weeping shall be no more heard in her, nor the voice of crying.

20There shall be no more thence an infant of days, nor an old man that hath not filled his days; for the child shall die an hundred years old; but the sinner *being* an hundred years old shall be accursed.

21And they shall build houses, and inhabit *them;* and they shall plant vineyards, and eat the fruit of them.

22They shall not build, and another inhabit; they shall not plant, and another eat: for as the days of a tree *are* the days of my people, and mine elect shall long enjoy the work of their hands.

23They shall not labour in vain, nor bring forth for trouble; for they *are* the seed of the blessed of the LORD, and their offspring with them.

24And it shall come to pass, that before they call, I will answer; and while they are yet speaking, I will hear.

25The wolf and the lamb shall feed together, and the lion shall eat straw like the bullock: and dust *shall be* the serpent's meat. They shall not hurt nor destroy in all my holy mountain, saith the LORD.

**66** THUS SAITH the LORD, The heaven *is* my throne, and the earth *is* my footstool: where *is* the house that ye build unto me? and where *is* the place of my rest?

2For all those *things* hath mine hand made, and all those *things* have been, saith the LORD: but to this *man* will I look, *even* to *him that is* poor and of a contrite spirit, and trembleth at my word.

3He that killeth an ox *is as if* he slew a man; he that sacrificeth a lamb, *as if* he cut off a dog's neck; he that offereth an oblation, *as if he offered* swine's blood; he that burneth incense, *as if* he blessed an idol. Yea, they have chosen their own ways, and their soul delighteth in their abominations.

4I also will choose their delusions, and will bring their fears upon them; because when I called, none did answer; when I spake, they did not hear: but they did evil before mine eyes, and chose *that* in which I delighted not.

## Amplified

18But be glad and rejoice for ever in that which I create; for behold, I create Jerusalem a rejoicing, and her people a joy.

19And I will rejoice in Jerusalem, and be glad in My people; and the sound of weeping shall be no more heard in it, nor the cry of distress.

20There shall no more be in it an infant that lives but a few days, or an old man who dies prematurely, for the child shall die a hundred years old, and the sinner who dies when only a hundred years old shall be [thought only a child, cut off because he is] accursed.

21They shall build houses and inhabit them, and they shall plant vineyards and eat the fruit of them.

22They shall not build and another inhabit; they shall not plant and another eat *the fruit;* for like the days of a tree shall be the days of My people, and My chosen *and* elect shall long make use of *and* enjoy the work of their hands.

23They shall not labor in vain or bring forth [children] for sudden terror *or* calamity; for they shall be the descendants of the blessed of the Lord, and their offspring with them.

24And it shall be that before they call I will answer, and while they are yet speaking I will hear.

25The wolf and the lamb shall feed together, and the lion shall eat straw like the ox; and dust shall be the serpent's food. They shall not hurt or destroy in all My holy Mount [Zion], says the Lord.

**66** THUS SAYS the Lord, Heaven is My throne and the earth is My footstool. What kind of house would you build for Me? And what kind can be My resting place? [Acts 17:24.]

2For all these things My hand has made and so all these things have come into being [for Me], says the Lord. But this is the man to whom I will look *and* have regard, he who is humble and of a broken *or* wounded spirit, and who trembles at My word *and* reveres My commands. [John 4:24.]

3[The acts of the hypocrite's worship are as abominable to God as if they were offered to idols.] He who kills an ox *then* will be guilty as if he slew *and* sacrificed a man; he who sacrifices a lamb *or* a kid, as if he broke a dog's neck *and* sacrificed him; he who offers a cereal offering, as if it were swine's blood; he who burns incense *to God,* as if he blesses an idol. *Such people* have chosen their own ways, and they delight in their abominations.

4I also will choose their delusions *and* mockings, their calamities *and* afflictions, and I will bring their fears upon them; because when I called, no one answered; when I spoke, they did not listen *or* obey; but they did what was evil in My sight, and chose that in which I did not delight.

## New American Standard

18 "But be glad and rejoice forever in what I create;
For behold, I create Jerusalem *for* rejoicing,
And her people *for* gladness.
19 "I will also rejoice in Jerusalem, and be glad in My people;
And there will no longer be heard in her
The voice of weeping and the sound of crying.
20 "No longer will there be in it an infant *who lives but a few* days,
Or an old man who does not live out his days;
For the youth will die at the age of one hundred
And the one who does not reach the age of one hundred
Shall be *thought* accursed.
21 "And they shall build houses and inhabit *them;*
They shall also plant vineyards and eat their fruit.
22 "They shall not build, and another inhabit,
They shall not plant, and another eat;
For as the lifetime of a tree, *so shall be* the days of My people,
And My chosen ones shall wear out the work of their hands.
23 "They shall not labor in vain,
Or bear *children* for calamity;
For they are the offspring of those blessed by the LORD,
And their descendants with them.
24 "It will also come to pass that before they call, I will answer;
and while they are still speaking, I will hear.
25 "The wolf and the lamb shall graze together, and the lion shall
eat straw like the ox; and dust shall be the serpent's food. They
shall do no evil or harm in all My holy mountain," says the LORD.

*Heaven Is God's Throne*

66 THUS SAYS the LORD,
"Heaven is My throne, and the earth is My footstool.
Where then is a house you could build for Me?
And where is a place that I may rest?
2 "For My hand made all these things,
Thus all these things came into being," declares the LORD.
"But to this one I will look,
To him who is humble and contrite of spirit, and who trembles at My word.

*Hypocrisy Rebuked*

3¶ "*But* he who kills an ox is *like* one who slays a man;
He who sacrifices a lamb is *like* the one who breaks a dog's neck;
He who offers a grain offering *is like one who offers* swine's blood;
He who burns incense is *like* the one who blesses an idol.
As they have chosen their *own* ways,
And their soul delights in their abominations,
4 So I will choose their punishments,
And I will bring on them what they dread.
Because I called, but no one answered;
I spoke, but they did not listen.
And they did evil in My sight,
And chose that in which I did not delight."

## New International

18 But be glad and rejoice forever
in what I will create,
for I will create Jerusalem to be a delight
and its people a joy.
19 I will rejoice over Jerusalem
and take delight in my people;
the sound of weeping and of crying
will be heard in it no more.

20 "Never again will there be in it
an infant who lives but a few days,
or an old man who does not live out his years;
he who dies at a hundred
will be thought a mere youth;
he who fails to reach[a] a hundred
will be considered accursed.
21 They will build houses and dwell in them;
they will plant vineyards and eat their fruit.
22 No longer will they build houses and others live in them,
or plant and others eat.
For as the days of a tree,
so will be the days of my people;
my chosen ones will long enjoy
the works of their hands.
23 They will not toil in vain
or bear children doomed to misfortune;
for they will be a people blessed by the LORD,
they and their descendants with them.
24 Before they call I will answer;
while they are still speaking I will hear.
25 The wolf and the lamb will feed together,
and the lion will eat straw like the ox,
but dust will be the serpent's food.
They will neither harm nor destroy
on all my holy mountain,"
says the LORD.

*Judgment and Hope*

66 THIS IS what the LORD says:
"Heaven is my throne,
and the earth is my footstool.
Where is the house you will build for me?
Where will my resting place be?
2 Has not my hand made all these things,
and so they came into being?"
declares the LORD.

"This is the one I esteem:
he who is humble and contrite in spirit,
and trembles at my word.
3 But whoever sacrifices a bull
is like one who kills a man,
and whoever offers a lamb,
like one who breaks a dog's neck;
whoever makes a grain offering
is like one who presents pig's blood,
and whoever burns memorial incense,
like one who worships an idol.
They have chosen their own ways,
and their souls delight in their abominations;
4 so I also will choose harsh treatment for them
and will bring upon them what they dread.
For when I called, no one answered,
when I spoke, no one listened.
They did evil in my sight
and chose what displeases me."

NIV [a] 20 Or / *the sinner who reaches*

## King James

5¶ Hear the word of the LORD, ye that tremble at his word; Your brethren that hated you, that cast you out for my name's sake, said, Let the LORD be glorified: but he shall appear to your joy, and they shall be ashamed.

6 A voice of noise from the city, a voice from the temple, a voice of the LORD that rendereth recompence to his enemies.

7 Before she travailed, she brought forth; before her pain came, she was delivered of a man child.

8 Who hath heard such a thing? who hath seen such things? Shall the earth be made to bring forth in one day? *or* shall a nation be born at once? for as soon as Zion travailed, she brought forth her children.

9 Shall I bring to the birth, and not cause to bring forth? saith the LORD: shall I cause to bring forth, and shut *the womb?* saith thy God.

10 Rejoice ye with Jerusalem, and be glad with her, all ye that love her: rejoice for joy with her, all ye that mourn for her:

11 That ye may suck, and be satisfied with the breasts of her consolations; that ye may milk out, and be delighted with the abundance of her glory.

12 For thus saith the LORD, Behold, I will extend peace to her like a river, and the glory of the Gentiles like a flowing stream: then shall ye suck, ye shall be borne upon *her* sides, and be dandled upon *her* knees.

13 As one whom his mother comforteth, so will I comfort you; and ye shall be comforted in Jerusalem.

14 And when ye see *this,* your heart shall rejoice, and your bones shall flourish like an herb: and the hand of the LORD shall be known toward his servants, and *his* indignation toward his enemies.

15 For, behold, the LORD will come with fire, and with his chariots like a whirlwind, to render his anger with fury, and his rebuke with flames of fire.

16 For by fire and by his sword will the LORD plead with all flesh: and the slain of the LORD shall be many.

17 They that sanctify themselves, and purify themselves in the gardens behind one *tree* in the midst, eating swine's flesh, and the abomination, and the mouse, shall be consumed together, saith the LORD.

18 For I *know* their works and their thoughts: it shall come, that I will gather all nations and tongues; and they shall come, and see my glory.

19 And I will set a sign among them, and I will send those that escape of them unto the nations, *to* Tarshish, Pul, and Lud, that draw the bow, *to* Tubal, and Javan, *to* the isles afar off, that have not heard my fame, neither have seen my glory; and they shall declare my glory among the Gentiles.

## Amplified

5 Hear the word of the Lord, you who tremble at His word: Your brethren who hate you, who cast you out for My name's sake, have said, Let the Lord be glorified that we may see your joy; but it is they who shall be put to shame.

6 [Hark!] An uproar from the city! A voice from the temple! The voice of the Lord, rendering recompense to His enemies!

7 Before *Zion* travailed she gave birth; before her pain came upon her she was delivered of a man-child.

8 Who has heard such a thing? Who has seen such things? Shall a land [a]be born in one day? *Or* shall a nation be brought forth in a moment? For as soon as Zion was in labor she brought forth her children.

9 Shall I bring to the birth and not cause to bring forth? says the Lord; shall I Who cause to bring forth shut the womb? says your God.

10 Rejoice with Jerusalem, and be glad for her, all you who love her; rejoice for joy with her, all you who mourn over her;

11 That you may nurse and be satisfied from her consoling breasts; that you may drink deeply and be delighted with the abundance *and* brightness of her glory.

12 For thus says the Lord, Behold, I will extend peace to her like a river, and the glory of the nations like an overflowing stream; then you shall be nursed, you shall be carried on her hip, and be trotted on her [God's maternal] knees.

13 As one whom his mother comforts, so will I comfort you; you shall be comforted in Jerusalem.

14 When you see this your heart shall rejoice, your bones shall flourish like green *and* tender grass, and the (powerful) hand of the Lord shall be revealed *and* known to be with His servants, and His indignation to be against His enemies.

15 For behold, the Lord will come in fire, and His chariots shall be like the stormy wind, to render His anger with fierceness, and His rebuke with flames of fire.

16 For by fire will the Lord execute judgment, and by His sword, upon all flesh; and the slain of the Lord shall be many.

17 Those who [attempt to] sanctify themselves and cleanse themselves to enter *and sacrifice* in the *idol*-gardens, following after [the image of the Syrian god Adad? meaning] one in the midst, eating hog's flesh and the abomination [creeping things] and the mouse, *their works and their thoughts* shall come to an end together, says the Lord.

18 For I know their works and their thoughts. And *the time* is coming when I will gather all nations and tongues, and they shall come and shall see My glory.

19 And I will set up a (miraculous) sign among them. And from them I will send survivors to the nations, to Tarshish, Pul *or Put,* and Lud, who draw the bow, to Tubal and Javan, to the isles *and* coastlands afar off, that have not heard My fame nor seen My glory; and they shall declare *and* proclaim My glory among the nations.

**AMP** [a] Never in the history of the world had such a thing happened before, but God keeps His word. As definitely foretold here and in Ezekiel 37:21, 22 and 38:10, 11, Israel became a recognized nation, actually "born in a day." After being away from their homeland for almost 2000 years, the Jews were given a national homeland in Palestine by the Balfour Declaration in November, 1917. In 1922 the League of Nations gave Great Britain the mandate over Palestine. On May 14, 1948, Great Britain withdrew her mandate, and immediately Israel was declared a sovereign state, and her growth and importance among nations became astonishing.

## New American Standard

5 Hear the word of the LORD, you who tremble at His word:
"Your brothers who hate you, who exclude you for My name's sake,
Have said, 'Let the LORD be glorified, that we may see your joy.'
But they will be put to shame.
6 "A voice of uproar from the city, a voice from the temple,
The voice of the LORD who is rendering recompense to His enemies.
7¶ "Before she travailed, she brought forth;
Before her pain came, she gave birth to a boy.
8 "Who has heard such a thing? Who has seen such things?
Can a land be born in one day?
Can a nation be brought forth all at once?
As soon as Zion travailed, she also brought forth her sons.
9 "Shall I bring to the point of birth, and not give delivery?" says the LORD.
"Or shall I who gives delivery shut *the womb?*" says your God.

*Joy in Jerusalem's Future*

10 "Be joyful with Jerusalem and rejoice for her, all you who love her;
Be exceedingly glad with her, all you who mourn over her,
11 That you may nurse and be satisfied with her comforting breasts,
That you may suck and be delighted with her bountiful bosom."
12 For thus says the LORD, "Behold, I extend peace to her like a river,
And the glory of the nations like an overflowing stream;
And you shall be nursed, you shall be carried on the hip and fondled on the knees.
13 "As one whom his mother comforts, so I will comfort you;
And you shall be comforted in Jerusalem."
14 Then you shall see *this,* and your heart shall be glad,
And your bones shall flourish like the new grass;
And the hand of the LORD shall be made known to His servants,
But He shall be indignant toward His enemies.
15 For behold, the LORD will come in fire
And His chariots like the whirlwind,
To render His anger with fury,
And His rebuke with flames of fire.
16 For the LORD will execute judgment by fire
And by His sword on all flesh,
And those slain by the LORD will be many.
17 "Those who sanctify and purify themselves *to go* to the gardens,
Following one in the center,
Who eat swine's flesh, detestable things, and mice,
Shall come to an end altogether," declares the LORD.

18"For I know their works and their thoughts; the time is coming to gather all nations and tongues. And they shall come and see My glory.

19"And I will set a sign among them and will send survivors from them to the nations: Tarshish, Put, Lud, Meshech, Rosh, Tubal, and Javan, to the distant coastlands that have neither heard My fame nor seen My glory. And they will declare My glory among the nations.

## New International

5Hear the word of the LORD,
you who tremble at his word:
"Your brothers who hate you,
and exclude you because of my name, have said,
'Let the LORD be glorified,
that we may see your joy!'
Yet they will be put to shame.
6Hear that uproar from the city,
hear that noise from the temple!
It is the sound of the LORD
repaying his enemies all they deserve.
7"Before she goes into labor,
she gives birth;
before the pains come upon her,
she delivers a son.
8Who has ever heard of such a thing?
Who has ever seen such things?
Can a country be born in a day
or a nation be brought forth in a moment?
Yet no sooner is Zion in labor
than she gives birth to her children.
9Do I bring to the moment of birth
and not give delivery?" says the LORD.
"Do I close up the womb
when I bring to delivery?" says your God.
10"Rejoice with Jerusalem and be glad for her,
all you who love her;
rejoice greatly with her,
all you who mourn over her.
11For you will nurse and be satisfied
at her comforting breasts;
you will drink deeply
and delight in her overflowing abundance."

12For this is what the LORD says:

"I will extend peace to her like a river,
and the wealth of nations like a flooding stream;
you will nurse and be carried on her arm
and dandled on her knees.
13As a mother comforts her child,
so will I comfort you;
and you will be comforted over Jerusalem."

14When you see this, your heart will rejoice
and you will flourish like grass;
the hand of the LORD will be made known to his servants,
but his fury will be shown to his foes.
15See, the LORD is coming with fire,
and his chariots are like a whirlwind;
he will bring down his anger with fury,
and his rebuke with flames of fire.
16For with fire and with his sword
the LORD will execute judgment upon all men,
and many will be those slain by the LORD.

17"Those who consecrate and purify themselves to go into the gardens, following the one in the midst of[b] those who eat the flesh of pigs and rats and other abominable things—they will meet their end together," declares the LORD.

18"And I, because of their actions and their imaginations, am about to come[c] and gather all nations and tongues, and they will come and see my glory.

19"I will set a sign among them, and I will send some of those who survive to the nations—to Tarshish, to the Libyans[d] and Lydians (famous as archers), to Tubal and Greece, and to the distant islands that have not heard of my fame or seen my glory.
They will proclaim my glory among the nations. 20And they will

**NIV** [b] *17* Or *gardens behind one of your temples, and* [c] *18* The meaning of the Hebrew for this clause is uncertain. [d] *19* Some Septuagint manuscripts *Put* (Libyans); Hebrew *Pul*

## King James

20And they shall bring all your brethren *for* an offering unto the
LORD out of all nations upon horses, and in chariots, and in litters,
and upon mules, and upon swift beasts, to my holy mountain
Jerusalem, saith the LORD, as the children of Israel bring an offering in a clean vessel into the house of the LORD.
21And I will also take of them for priests *and* for Levites, saith
the LORD.
22For as the new heavens and the new earth, which I will make,
shall remain before me, saith the LORD, so shall your seed and your
name remain.
23And it shall come to pass, *that* from one new moon to another,
and from one sabbath to another, shall all flesh come to worship
before me, saith the LORD.
24And they shall go forth, and look upon the carcases of the
men that have transgressed against me: for their worm shall not
die, neither shall their fire be quenched; and they shall be an
abhorring unto all flesh.

## Amplified

20And they shall bring all your brethren from all the nations as
an offering to the Lord, upon horses, and in chariots, and in litters,
and upon mules, and upon dromedaries, to My holy mountain
Jerusalem, says the Lord, just as the children of Israel bring their
cereal offering in a clean vessel to the house of the Lord.
21And I will also take some of them for priests and for Levites,
says the Lord.
22For as the new [a]heavens and the new earth which I will make
shall remain before Me, says the Lord, so shall your offspring and
your name remain.
23And it shall be that from one new moon to another new moon,
and from one sabbath to another sabbath, all flesh shall come to
worship before Me, says the Lord.
24And they shall go forth and gaze upon the dead bodies of the
[rebellious] men who have stepped over against Me; for their
worm shall not die, their fire shall not be quenched, and they shall
be an abhorrence to all mankind.

AMP [a] See footnote on Isaiah 65:17.

## New American Standard

20"Then they shall bring all your brethren from all the nations as a grain offering to the LORD, on horses, in chariots, in litters, on mules, and on camels, to My holy mountain Jerusalem," says the LORD, "just as the sons of Israel bring their grain offering in a clean vessel to the house of the LORD.

21"I will also take some of them for priests *and* for Levites," says the LORD.

22 "For just as the new heavens and the new earth
Which I make will endure before Me," declares the LORD,
"So your offspring and your name will endure.
23 "And it shall be from new moon to new moon
And from sabbath to sabbath,
All mankind will come to bow down before Me," says the LORD.
24 "Then they shall go forth and look
On the corpses of the men
Who have transgressed against Me.
For their worm shall not die,
And their fire shall not be quenched;
And they shall be an abhorrence to all mankind."

## New International

bring all your brothers, from all the nations, to my holy mountain in Jerusalem as an offering to the LORD—on horses, in chariots and wagons, and on mules and camels," says the LORD. "They will bring them, as the Israelites bring their grain offerings, to the temple of the LORD in ceremonially clean vessels.
21And I will select some of them also to be priests and Levites," says the LORD.

22"As the new heavens and the new earth that I make will endure before me," declares the LORD, "so will your name and descendants endure.
23From one New Moon to another and from one Sabbath to another, all mankind will come and bow down before me," says the LORD.
24"And they will go out and look upon the dead bodies of those who rebelled against me; their worm will not die, nor will their fire be quenched, and they will be loathsome to all mankind."

## King James

THE BOOK

OF THE PROPHET

# Jeremiah

1 THE WORDS of Jeremiah the son of Hilkiah, of the priests that *were* in Anathoth in the land of Benjamin:

2 To whom the word of the LORD came in the days of Josiah the son of Amon king of Judah, in the thirteenth year of his reign.

3 It came also in the days of Jehoiakim the son of Josiah king of Judah, unto the end of the eleventh year of Zedekiah the son of Josiah king of Judah, unto the carrying away of Jerusalem captive in the fifth month.

4 Then the word of the LORD came unto me, saying,

5 Before I formed thee in the belly I knew thee; and before thou camest forth out of the womb I sanctified thee, *and* I ordained thee a prophet unto the nations.

6 Then said I, Ah, Lord GOD! behold, I cannot speak: for I *am* a child.

7 ¶ But the LORD said unto me, Say not, I *am* a child: for thou shalt go to all that I shall send thee, and whatsoever I command thee thou shalt speak.

8 Be not afraid of their faces: for I *am* with thee to deliver thee, saith the LORD.

9 Then the LORD put forth his hand, and touched my mouth. And the LORD said unto me, Behold, I have put my words in thy mouth.

10 See, I have this day set thee over the nations and over the kingdoms, to root out, and to pull down, and to destroy, and to throw down, to build, and to plant.

11 ¶ Moreover the word of the LORD came unto me, saying, Jeremiah, what seest thou? And I said, I see a rod of an almond tree.

12 Then said the LORD unto me, Thou hast well seen: for I will hasten my word to perform it.

13 And the word of the LORD came unto me the second time, saying, What seest thou? And I said, I see a seething pot; and the face thereof *is* toward the north.

14 Then the LORD said unto me, Out of the north an evil shall break forth upon all the inhabitants of the land.

15 For, lo, I will call all the families of the kingdoms of the north, saith the LORD; and they shall come, and they shall set every one his throne at the entering of the gates of Jerusalem, and against all the walls thereof round about, and against all the cities of Judah.

16 And I will utter my judgments against them touching all their wickedness, who have forsaken me, and have burned incense unto other gods, and worshipped the works of their own hands.

17 ¶ Thou therefore gird up thy loins, and arise, and speak unto them all that I command thee: be not dismayed at their faces, lest I confound thee before them.

## Amplified

THE BOOK OF

# Jeremiah

1 THE WORDS of Jeremiah the son of Hilkiah, of the priests that were in Anathoth in the land of Benjamin [two or three miles north of Jerusalem],

2 To whom the word of the Lord came in the days of Josiah the son of Amon, king of Judah, in the thirteenth year of his reign.

3 It came also in the days of Jehoiakim the son of Josiah, king of Judah, until the end of the eleventh year of Zedekiah the son of Josiah, king of Judah, until the carrying away of Jerusalem into captivity in the fifth month.

4 Then the word of the Lord came to me [Jeremiah] saying,

5 Before I formed you in the womb I knew *and* approved of you [as My chosen instrument], and before you were born I separated *and* set you apart, consecrating you, *and* I appointed you a prophet to the nations. [Exod. 33:12; Isa. 49:1, 5; Rom. 8:29.]

6 Then said I, Ah, Lord God! Behold, I cannot speak, for I am only a youth. [Exod. 4:10; 6:12, 30; I Kings 3:7.]

7 But the Lord said to me, Say not, I am only a youth; for you shall go to all to whom I shall send you, and whatever I command you you shall speak.

8 Be not afraid of them [their faces], for I am with you to deliver you, says the Lord.

9 Then the Lord put forth His hand and touched my mouth. And the Lord said to me, Behold, I have put My words in your mouth.

10 See, I have this day appointed you to the oversight of the nations and of the kingdoms, to root out and pull down, to destroy and to overthrow, to build and to plant.

11 Moreover the word of the Lord came to me, saying, Jeremiah, what do you see? And I said, I see a branch *or* shoot of an almond tree [the emblem of alertness and activity, blossoming in late winter].

12 Then said the Lord to me, You have seen well, for I am alert *and* active, watching over My word to perform it.

13 And the word of the Lord came to me the second time, saying, What do you see? And I said, I see a boiling pot, and the face of it is [tipped away] from the north [its mouth about to pour forth on the south, Judea].

14 Then the Lord said to me, Out of the north the evil [which the prophets had foretold as the result of national sin] shall disclose itself *and* break forth upon all the inhabitants of the land.

15 For, lo, I will call all the tribes of the kingdoms of the north, says the Lord; and they shall come and set every one his throne at the entrance of the gates of Jerusalem, against all its walls round about, and against all the cities of Judah [as God's judicial act, a consequence of Judah's wickedness].

16 And I will utter My judgments against them for all the wickedness of those who have forsaken Me, burned incense to other gods, and worshiped *idols*, the works of their own hands.

17 But you [Jeremiah], gird up your loins; arise and tell them all that I command you. Do not be dismayed *and* break down at *sight of* their faces, lest I confound you before them *and* permit you to be overcome.

## New American Standard

# Jeremiah

*Jeremiah's Call and Commission*

**1** THE WORDS of Jeremiah, the son of Hilkiah, of the priests
who were in Anathoth in the land of Benjamin,
2to whom the word of the LORD came in the days of Josiah, the
son of Amon, king of Judah, in the thirteenth year of his reign.
3It came also in the days of Jehoiakim, the son of Josiah, king
of Judah, until the end of the eleventh year of Zedekiah, the son
of Josiah, king of Judah, until the exile of Jerusalem in the fifth
month.

4¶ Now the word of the LORD came to me saying,
5 "Before I formed you in the womb I knew you,
And before you were born I consecrated you;
I have appointed you a prophet to the nations."
6 Then I said, "Alas, Lord GOD!
Behold, I do not know how to speak,
Because I am a youth."
7 But the LORD said to me,
"Do not say, 'I am a youth,'
Because everywhere I send you, you shall go,
And all that I command you, you shall speak.
8 "Do not be afraid of them,
For I am with you to deliver you," declares the LORD.
9Then the LORD stretched out His hand and touched my
mouth, and the LORD said to me,
"Behold, I have put My words in your mouth.
10 "See, I have appointed you this day over the nations and
over the kingdoms,
To pluck up and to break down,
To destroy and to overthrow,
To build and to plant."

*The Almond Rod and Boiling Pot*

11¶ And the word of the LORD came to me saying, "What do you
see, Jeremiah?" And I said, "I see a rod of an almond tree."
12Then the LORD said to me, "You have seen well, for I am
watching over My word to perform it."
13¶ And the word of the LORD came to me a second time saying,
"What do you see?" And I said, "I see a boiling pot, facing away
from the north."
14Then the LORD said to me, "Out of the north the evil will break
forth on all the inhabitants of the land.
15"For, behold, I am calling all the families of the kingdoms of
the north," declares the LORD; "and they will come, and they will
set each one his throne at the entrance of the gates of Jerusalem,
and against all its walls round about, and against all the cities of
Judah.
16"And I will pronounce My judgments on them concerning all
their wickedness, whereby they have forsaken Me and have offered sacrifices to other gods, and worshiped the works of their
own hands.
17"Now, gird up your loins, and arise, and speak to them all
which I command you. Do not be dismayed before them, lest I
dismay you before them.

## New International

# Jeremiah

**1** THE WORDS of Jeremiah son of Hilkiah, one of the priests
at Anathoth in the territory of Benjamin. 2The word of the
LORD came to him in the thirteenth year of the reign of Josiah son
of Amon king of Judah, 3and through the reign of Jehoiakim son
of Josiah king of Judah, down to the fifth month of the eleventh
year of Zedekiah son of Josiah king of Judah, when the people of
Jerusalem went into exile.

*The Call of Jeremiah*

4The word of the LORD came to me, saying,
5"Before I formed you in the womb I knew[a] you,
before you were born I set you apart;
I appointed you as a prophet to the nations."
6"Ah, Sovereign LORD," I said, "I do not know how to speak;
I am only a child."
7But the LORD said to me, "Do not say, 'I am only a child.' You
must go to everyone I send you to and say whatever I command
you. 8Do not be afraid of them, for I am with you and will rescue
you," declares the LORD.
9Then the LORD reached out his hand and touched my mouth
and said to me, "Now, I have put my words in your mouth. 10See,
today I appoint you over nations and kingdoms to uproot and tear
down, to destroy and overthrow, to build and to plant."
11The word of the LORD came to me: "What do you see, Jeremiah?"
"I see the branch of an almond tree," I replied.
12The LORD said to me, "You have seen correctly, for I am
watching[b] to see that my word is fulfilled."
13The word of the LORD came to me again: "What do you see?"
"I see a boiling pot, tilting away from the north," I answered.
14The LORD said to me, "From the north disaster will be poured
out on all who live in the land. 15I am about to summon all the
peoples of the northern kingdoms," declares the LORD.

"Their kings will come and set up their thrones
in the entrance of the gates of Jerusalem;
they will come against all her surrounding walls
and against all the towns of Judah.
16I will pronounce my judgments on my people
because of their wickedness in forsaking me,
in burning incense to other gods
and in worshiping what their hands have made.

17"Get yourself ready! Stand up and say to them whatever I
command you. Do not be terrified by them, or I will terrify you
before them. 18Today I have made you a fortified city, an iron pillar

**NIV** [a] 5 Or *chose* [b] 12 The Hebrew for *watching* sounds like the Hebrew for *almond tree.*

## King James

18For, behold, I have made thee this day a defenced city, and
an iron pillar, and brasen walls against the whole land, against the
kings of Judah, against the princes thereof, against the priests
thereof, and against the people of the land.
19And they shall fight against thee; but they shall not prevail
against thee; for I *am* with thee, saith the LORD, to deliver thee.

**2** MOREOVER THE word of the LORD came to me, saying,
2Go and cry in the ears of Jerusalem, saying, Thus saith the
LORD; I remember thee, the kindness of thy youth, the love of thine
espousals, when thou wentest after me in the wilderness, in a land
*that was* not sown.
3Israel *was* holiness unto the LORD, *and* the firstfruits of his
increase: all that devour him shall offend; evil shall come upon
them, saith the LORD.
4Hear ye the word of the LORD, O house of Jacob, and all the
families of the house of Israel:
5¶ Thus saith the LORD, What iniquity have your fathers found
in me, that they are gone far from me, and have walked after
vanity, and are become vain?
6Neither said they, Where *is* the LORD that brought us up out
of the land of Egypt, that led us through the wilderness, through
a land of deserts and of pits, through a land of drought, and of the
shadow of death, through a land that no man passed through, and
where no man dwelt?
7And I brought you into a plentiful country, to eat the fruit
thereof and the goodness thereof; but when ye entered, ye defiled
my land, and made mine heritage an abomination.
8The priests said not, Where *is* the LORD? and they that handle
the law knew me not: the pastors also transgressed against me,
and the prophets prophesied by Baal, and walked after *things that*
do not profit.
9¶ Wherefore I will yet plead with you, saith the LORD, and with
your children's children will I plead.
10For pass over the isles of Chittim, and see; and send unto
Kedar, and consider diligently, and see if there be such a thing.
11Hath a nation changed *their* gods, which *are* yet no gods? but
my people have changed their glory for *that which* doth not profit.
12Be astonished, O ye heavens, at this, and be horribly afraid,
be ye very desolate, saith the LORD.

## Amplified

18For I, behold, I have made you this day a fortified city, and
an iron pillar, and brazen walls against the whole land: against the
*successive* kings of Judah, against its princes, against its priests, and
against the people of the land [giving you divine strength which
no hostile power can overcome]. [Jer. 6:27; 15:20; Isa. 50:7; 54:17;
Luke 21:15; Acts 6:10.]
19And they shall fight against you, but they shall not *finally*
prevail against you, for I am with you, says the Lord, to deliver
you.

**2** AND THE word of the Lord came to me [Jeremiah], saying,
2Go and cry in the ears of Jerusalem, saying, Thus says the
Lord, I [earnestly] remember the kindness *and* devotion of your
youth, your love after your betrothal [in Egypt] *and* marriage [at
Sinai], when you followed Me in the wilderness, in a land not
sown.
3Israel was holiness [something set apart from ordinary purposes, dedicated] to the Lord, the first fruits of His harvest [of
which no stranger was allowed to partake]; all who ate of it [injur-
ing Israel] offended *and* became guilty; evil came upon them, says
the Lord.
4Hear the word of the Lord, O house of Jacob, and all the
families of the house of Israel;
5Thus says the Lord, What unrighteousness did your fathers
find in Me that they went far from Me, and [habitually] went after
emptiness, falseness *and* futility, and *themselves* became fruitless
*and* worthless?
6Nor did they say, Where is the Lord Who brought us up out
of the land of Egypt, Who led us through the wilderness, through
a land of deserts and pits, through a land of drought and of the
shadow of death *and* deep darkness, through a land that no man
passes through, and where no man dwells?
7And I brought you into a plentiful land to enjoy its fruits and
good things; but when you entered you defiled My land and made
My heritage an abomination—detestable and loathsome.
8 *Even* the priests did not say, Where is the Lord? And those
who handle the law [given by God to Moses] knew Me not. The
rulers *and* [secular] shepherds also transgressed against Me, and
the prophets prophesied by [the authority and in the name of]
Baal, and followed after things that do not profit.
9Therefore I will still contend with you [by inflicting further
judgments on you], says the Lord, and with your children's children will I contend.
10For cross over to the coasts of Cyprus *to the west* and see; send
also to Kedar *to the east* and carefully consider, and see whether
there has been such a thing as this:
11Has a nation [ever] changed its gods, even though they are
not gods? But My people have changed *God,* their glory, for that
which does not profit.
12Be astonished *and* appalled, O heavens, at this; be shocked
*and* shrivel up with horror, says the Lord [at the behavior of the
people].

## New American Standard

18"Now behold, I have made you today as a fortified city, and as a pillar of iron and as walls of bronze against the whole land, to the kings of Judah, to its princes, to its priests and to the people of the land.

19"And they will fight against you, but they will not overcome you, for I am with you to deliver you," declares the LORD.

*Judah's Apostasy*

**2** NOW THE word of the LORD came to me saying,
2"Go and proclaim in the ears of Jerusalem, saying, 'Thus says the LORD,

"I remember concerning you the devotion of your youth,
The love of your betrothals,
Your following after Me in the wilderness,
Through a land not sown.
3 "Israel was holy to the LORD,
The first of His harvest;
All who ate of it became guilty;
Evil came upon them," declares the LORD.' "

4¶ Hear the word of the LORD, O house of Jacob, and all the families of the house of Israel.
5Thus says the LORD,
"What injustice did your fathers find in Me,
That they went far from Me
And walked after emptiness and became empty?
6 "And they did not say, 'Where is the LORD
Who brought us up out of the land of Egypt,
Who led us through the wilderness,
Through a land of deserts and of pits,
Through a land of drought and of deep darkness,
Through a land that no one crossed
And where no man dwelt?'
7 "And I brought you into the fruitful land,
To eat its fruit and its good things.
But you came and defiled My land,
And My inheritance you made an abomination.
8 "The priests did not say, 'Where is the LORD?'
And those who handle the law did not know Me;
The rulers also transgressed against Me,
And the prophets prophesied by Baal
And walked after things that did not profit.

9¶ "Therefore I will yet contend with you," declares the LORD,
"And with your sons' sons I will contend.
10 "For cross to the coastlands of Kittim and see,
And send to Kedar and observe closely,
And see if there has been such *a thing* as this!
11 "Has a nation changed gods,
When they were not gods?
But My people have changed their glory
For that which does not profit.
12 "Be appalled, O heavens, at this,
And shudder, be very desolate," declares the LORD.

## New International

and a bronze wall to stand against the whole land—against the kings of Judah, its officials, its priests and the people of the land.
19They will fight against you but will not overcome you, for I am with you and will rescue you," declares the LORD.

*Israel Forsakes God*

**2** THE WORD of the LORD came to me: 2"Go and proclaim in the hearing of Jerusalem:

" 'I remember the devotion of your youth,
how as a bride you loved me
and followed me through the desert,
through a land not sown.
3Israel was holy to the LORD,
the firstfruits of his harvest;
all who devoured her were held guilty,
and disaster overtook them,' "
declares the LORD.

4Hear the word of the LORD, O house of Jacob,
all you clans of the house of Israel.

5This is what the LORD says:
"What fault did your fathers find in me,
that they strayed so far from me?
They followed worthless idols
and became worthless themselves.
6They did not ask, 'Where is the LORD,
who brought us up out of Egypt
and led us through the barren wilderness,
through a land of deserts and rifts,
a land of drought and darkness,[a]
a land where no one travels and no one lives?'
7I brought you into a fertile land
to eat its fruit and rich produce.
But you came and defiled my land
and made my inheritance detestable.
8The priests did not ask,
'Where is the LORD?'
Those who deal with the law did not know me;
the leaders rebelled against me.
The prophets prophesied by Baal,
following worthless idols.

9"Therefore I bring charges against you again,"
declares the LORD.
"And I will bring charges against your children's
children.
10Cross over to the coasts of Kittim[b] and look,
send to Kedar[c] and observe closely;
see if there has ever been anything like this:
11Has a nation ever changed its gods?
(Yet they are not gods at all.)
But my people have exchanged their[d] Glory
for worthless idols.
12Be appalled at this, O heavens,
and shudder with great horror,"
declares the LORD.

**NIV** [a] 6 Or *and the shadow of death* [b] 10 That is, Cyprus and western coastlands [c] 10 The home of Bedouin tribes in the Syro-Arabian desert [d] 11 Masoretic Text; an ancient Hebrew scribal tradition *my*

## King James

13 For my people have committed two evils; they have forsaken me the fountain of living waters, *and* hewed them out cisterns, broken cisterns, that can hold no water.

14 ¶ *Is* Israel a servant? *is* he a homeborn *slave?* why is he spoiled?

15 The young lions roared upon him, *and* yelled, and they made his land waste: his cities are burned without inhabitant.

16 Also the children of Noph and Tahapanes have broken the crown of thy head.

17 Hast thou not procured this unto thyself, in that thou hast forsaken the LORD thy God, when he led thee by the way?

18 And now what hast thou to do in the way of Egypt, to drink the waters of Sihor? or what hast thou to do in the way of Assyria, to drink the waters of the river?

19 Thine own wickedness shall correct thee, and thy backslidings shall reprove thee: know therefore and see that *it is* an evil *thing* and bitter, that thou hast forsaken the LORD thy God, and that my fear *is* not in thee, saith the Lord GOD of hosts.

20 ¶ For of old time I have broken thy yoke, *and* burst thy bands; and thou saidst, I will not transgress; when upon every high hill and under every green tree thou wanderest, playing the harlot.

21 Yet I had planted thee a noble vine, wholly a right seed: how then art thou turned into the degenerate plant of a strange vine unto me?

22 For though thou wash thee with nitre, and take thee much soap, *yet* thine iniquity is marked before me, saith the Lord GOD.

23 How canst thou say, I am not polluted, I have not gone after Baalim? see thy way in the valley, know what thou hast done: *thou art* a swift dromedary traversing her ways;

24 A wild ass used to the wilderness, *that* snuffeth up the wind at her pleasure; in her occasion who can turn her away? all they that seek her will not weary themselves; in her month they shall find her.

25 Withhold thy foot from being unshod, and thy throat from thirst: but thou saidst, There is no hope: no; for I have loved strangers, and after them will I go.

26 As the thief is ashamed when he is found, so is the house of Israel ashamed; they, their kings, their princes, and their priests, and their prophets,

## Amplified

13 For My people have committed two evils: they have forsaken Me, the fountain of living waters, *and* they have hewn for themselves cisterns, broken cisterns, which cannot hold water.

14 Is Israel a servant? Is he a home-born slave? Why has he become a captive *and* a prey?

15 The young lions have roared over him *and* made their voices heard, and they have made his land a waste; his cities are burned ruins without inhabitant.

16 Moreover the children of Memphis and Tahpanhes [Egypt, have in times past shown their power as a foe, they] have broken *and* fed on the crown of your head, *Israel* [do not rely on them as an ally now].

17 Have you not brought this upon yourself by forsaking the Lord your God, when He led you in the way?

18 And now what have you to gain by allying yourself with Egypt *and* going her way, to drink the [black and roiled] waters of the Nile? Or what have you to gain in going the way of Assyria, to drink the waters of the Euphrates?

19 Your own wickedness shall chasten *and* correct you, and your backslidings *and* desertion of faith shall reprove you. Know therefore *and* recognize that this is an evil and bitter thing: *first,* you have forsaken the Lord your God; *second,* you are indifferent to Me, *and* the fear of Me is not in you, says the Lord of hosts.

20 For long ago [in Egypt] I broke your yoke and burst your bonds [not that you might be free, but that you might serve Me]— [a]but long since you shattered the yoke and snapped the bonds [of My law, which I put upon you]; you said, I will not serve *and* obey You! For upon every high hill and under every green tree you [eagerly] prostrated yourself *in idolatrous worship,* playing the harlot.

21 Yet I had planted you, *O house of Israel,* a choice vine, wholly of pure seed. How then have you turned into degenerate shoots of wild vine, alien to Me?

22 For though you wash yourself with lye and use much soap, yet your iniquity *and* guilt are still *upon you; you are* spotted, dirty *and* stained before Me, says the Lord.

23 How can you say, I am not defiled, I have not gone after the Baals [other gods]? Look at your way in the valley; know what you have done. You are a restive young female camel [in the uncontrollable violence of her brute passion eagerly] running hither and thither.

24 Or [you have the untamed and reckless nature of] a wild donkey used to the desert, in her heat sniffing the wind [for the scent of a male]. In her mating season who can restrain her? No *males* seeking her need weary themselves; in her month they will find her *seeking them.*

25 [Cease from your mad running after idols, from which you get nothing but bitter injury.] Keep your feet from being unshod and your throat from thirst. But you said, It is hopeless, for I have loved strangers *and* foreigners, and after them I will go.

26 As the thief is brought to shame when he is caught, so shall the house of Israel be brought to shame: they, their kings, their princes, their priests, and their prophets,

AMP [a] Another reading of the previous statement.

## New American Standard

13 "For My people have committed two evils:
They have forsaken Me,
The fountain of living waters,
To hew for themselves cisterns,
Broken cisterns,
That can hold no water.

14¶ "Is Israel a slave? Or is he a homeborn servant?
Why has he become a prey?
15 "The young lions have roared at him,
They have roared loudly.
And they have made his land a waste;
His cities have been destroyed, without inhabitant.
16 "Also the men of Memphis and Tahpanhes
Have shaved the crown of your head.
17 "Have you not done this to yourself,
By your forsaking the LORD your God,
When He led you in the way?
18 "But now what are you doing on the road to Egypt,
To drink the waters of the Nile?
Or what are you doing on the road to Assyria,
To drink the waters of the Euphrates?
19 "Your own wickedness will correct you,
And your apostasies will reprove you;
Know therefore and see that it is evil and bitter
For you to forsake the LORD your God,
And the dread of Me is not in you," declares the Lord GOD of hosts.

20¶ "For long ago I broke your yoke
*And* tore off your bonds;
But you said, 'I will not serve!'
For on every high hill
And under every green tree
You have lain down as a harlot.
21 "Yet I planted you a choice vine,
A completely faithful seed.
How then have you turned yourself before Me
Into the degenerate shoots of a foreign vine?
22 "Although you wash yourself with lye
And use much soap,
The stain of your iniquity is before Me," declares the Lord GOD.
23 "How can you say, 'I am not defiled,
I have not gone after the Baals'?
Look at your way in the valley!
Know what you have done!
You are a swift young camel entangling her ways,
24 A wild donkey accustomed to the wilderness,
That sniffs the wind in her passion.
In *the time of* her heat who can turn her away?
All who seek her will not become weary;
In her month they will find her.
25 "Keep your feet from being unshod
And your throat from thirst;
But you said, 'It is hopeless!
No! For I have loved strangers,
And after them I will walk.'

26¶ "As the thief is shamed when he is discovered,
So the house of Israel is shamed;
They, their kings, their princes,
And their priests, and their prophets,

## New International

13"My people have committed two sins:
They have forsaken me,
the spring of living water,
and have dug their own cisterns,
broken cisterns that cannot hold water.
14Is Israel a servant, a slave by birth?
Why then has he become plunder?
15Lions have roared;
they have growled at him.
They have laid waste his land;
his towns are burned and deserted.
16Also, the men of Memphis[b] and Tahpanhes
have shaved the crown of your head.[c]
17Have you not brought this on yourselves
by forsaking the LORD your God
when he led you in the way?
18Now why go to Egypt
to drink water from the Shihor[d]?
And why go to Assyria
to drink water from the River[e]?
19Your wickedness will punish you;
your backsliding will rebuke you.
Consider then and realize
how evil and bitter it is for you
when you forsake the LORD your God
and have no awe of me,"
declares the Lord, the LORD Almighty.

20"Long ago you broke off your yoke
and tore off your bonds;
you said, 'I will not serve you!'
Indeed, on every high hill
and under every spreading tree
you lay down as a prostitute.
21I had planted you like a choice vine
of sound and reliable stock.
How then did you turn against me
into a corrupt, wild vine?
22Although you wash yourself with soda
and use an abundance of soap,
the stain of your guilt is still before me,"
declares the Sovereign LORD.
23"How can you say, 'I am not defiled;
I have not run after the Baals'?
See how you behaved in the valley;
consider what you have done.
You are a swift she-camel
running here and there,
24a wild donkey accustomed to the desert,
sniffing the wind in her craving—
in her heat who can restrain her?
Any males that pursue her need not tire themselves;
at mating time they will find her.
25Do not run until your feet are bare
and your throat is dry.
But you said, 'It's no use!
I love foreign gods,
and I must go after them.'

26"As a thief is disgraced when he is caught,
so the house of Israel is disgraced—
they, their kings and their officials,
their priests and their prophets.

NIV [b] 16 Hebrew *Noph* [c] 16 Or *have cracked your skull* [d] 18 That is, a branch of the Nile [e] 18 That is, the Euphrates

## King James

27Saying to a stock, Thou *art* my father; and to a stone, Thou hast brought me forth: for they have turned *their* back unto me, and not *their* face: but in the time of their trouble they will say, Arise, and save us.

28But where *are* thy gods that thou hast made thee? let them arise, if they can save thee in the time of thy trouble: for *according to* the number of thy cities are thy gods, O Judah.

29Wherefore will ye plead with me? ye all have transgressed against me, saith the LORD.

30In vain have I smitten your children; they received no correction: your own sword hath devoured your prophets, like a destroying lion.

31¶ O generation, see ye the word of the LORD. Have I been a wilderness unto Israel? a land of darkness? wherefore say my people, We are lords; we will come no more unto thee?

32Can a maid forget her ornaments, *or* a bride her attire? yet my people have forgotten me days without number.

33Why trimmest thou thy way to seek love? therefore hast thou also taught the wicked ones thy ways.

34Also in thy skirts is found the blood of the souls of the poor innocents: I have not found it by secret search, but upon all these.

35Yet thou sayest, Because I am innocent, surely his anger shall turn from me. Behold, I will plead with thee, because thou sayest, I have not sinned.

36Why gaddest thou about so much to change thy way? thou also shalt be ashamed of Egypt, as thou wast ashamed of Assyria.

37Yea, thou shalt go forth from him, and thine hands upon thine head: for the LORD hath rejected thy confidences, and thou shalt not prosper in them.

3 THEY SAY, If a man put away his wife, and she go from him, and become another man's, shall he return unto her again? shall not that land be greatly polluted? but thou hast played the harlot with many lovers; yet return again to me, saith the LORD.

2Lift up thine eyes unto the high places, and see where thou hast not been lain with. In the ways hast thou sat for them, as the Arabian in the wilderness; and thou hast polluted the land with thy whoredoms and with thy wickedness.

## Amplified

27 *Inasmuch as* they say to a tree, You are my father, and to a stone, You gave me birth. For they have turned their back to Me, and not their face. But in the time of their trouble they say, Arise, *O Lord,* and save us!

28But where are your gods that you made for yourself? Let them arise, if they can save you in the time of your trouble! For as *many as* the number of your cities are your gods, O Judah. [Surely so many handmade idols should be able to help you!]

29Why do you complain *and* remonstrate against My wrath? You all have rebelled *and* revolted against Me, says the Lord.

30In vain have I stricken your children—your people; they received no discipline— *no* correction. Your own sword devoured your prophets like a destroying lion.

31O generation *that you are*! Behold, consider *and* regard the word of the Lord. Have I been a wilderness to Israel, *like a land without food*? A land of deep darkness, *like a way without light*? Why do My people say, We are broken loose—we are free and will roam at large; we will come no more to You?

32Can a maid forget *and* neglect [to wear] her ornaments, or a bride her *marriage* girdle [with its significance as that of a wedding ring]? Yet My people have forgotten Me days without number.

33How do you deck yourself *and* direct your way to procure *adulterous* love! Because of it even wicked women have learned *indecent* ways from you.

34Also on your skirts is found the lifeblood of the persons of the innocent poor. You did not find them house-breaking, *nor* have I found it out by secret search, but it is because of [your lust for idolatry that you have done] all these things. [That is everywhere evident.]

35Yet you keep saying, I am innocent; surely His anger has turned away from Me. Behold, I will bring you to judgment *and* will plead against you, because you say, I have not sinned.

36Why do you gad about so much to change your way? You shall be put to shame by Egypt, as you were put to shame by Assyria.

37From *Egypt* also you will come away *with* your hands upon your head, for the Lord has rejected those in whom you confide, and you shall not prosper with *respect to* them.

3 THAT IS to say, If a man puts away his wife, and she goes from him and becomes another man's, will he return to her again? [Of course not!] Will not that land be greatly polluted *that so acts*? But you have played the harlot *against Me* with many lovers; yet would you return to Me? says the Lord— *or do you even think* to return to Me?

2Lift up your eyes to the bare heights and see; where have you not been adulterously lain with? By the waysides you have sat *waiting* for *lovers* [eager for idolatry], like an Arabian [desert tribesman who waits to plunder] in the wilderness; and you have polluted the land with your vile harlotry and your wickedness [unfaithfulness and disobedience to God].

## New American Standard

27 Who say to a tree, 'You are my father,'
And to a stone, 'You gave me birth.'
For they have turned *their* back to Me,
And not *their* face;
But in the time of their trouble they will say,
'Arise and save us.'
28 "But where are your gods
Which you made for yourself?
Let them arise, if they can save you
In the time of your trouble;
For *according to* the number of your cities
Are your gods, O Judah.

29¶ "Why do you contend with Me?
You have all transgressed against Me," declares the LORD.
30 "In vain I have struck your sons;
They accepted no chastening.
Your sword has devoured your prophets
Like a destroying lion.
31 "O generation, heed the word of the LORD.
Have I been a wilderness to Israel,
Or a land of thick darkness?
Why do My people say, 'We *are free to* roam;
We will come no more to Thee'?
32 "Can a virgin forget her ornaments,
Or a bride her attire?
Yet My people have forgotten Me
Days without number.
33 "How well you prepare your way
To seek love!
Therefore even the wicked women
You have taught your ways.
34 "Also on your skirts is found
The lifeblood of the innocent poor;
You did not find them breaking in.
But in spite of all these things,
35 Yet you said, 'I am innocent;
Surely His anger is turned away from me.'
Behold, I will enter into judgment with you
Because you say, 'I have not sinned.'
36 "Why do you go around so much
Changing your way?
Also, you shall be put to shame by Egypt
As you were put to shame by Assyria.
37 "From this *place* also you shall go out
With your hands on your head;
For the LORD has rejected those in whom you trust,
And you shall not prosper with them."

*The Polluted Land*

3 GOD SAYS, "If a husband divorces his wife,
And she goes from him,
And belongs to another man,
Will he still return to her?
Will not that land be completely polluted?
But you are a harlot *with* many lovers;
Yet you turn to Me," declares the LORD.
2 "Lift up your eyes to the bare heights and see;
Where have you not been violated?
By the roads you have sat for them
Like an Arab in the desert,
And you have polluted a land
With your harlotry and with your wickedness.

## New International

27 They say to wood, 'You are my father,'
and to stone, 'You gave me birth.'
They have turned their backs to me
and not their faces;
yet when they are in trouble, they say,
'Come and save us!'
28 Where then are the gods you made for yourselves?
Let them come if they can save you
when you are in trouble!
For you have as many gods
as you have towns, O Judah.

29 "Why do you bring charges against me?
You have all rebelled against me,"
declares the LORD.
30 "In vain I punished your people;
they did not respond to correction.
Your sword has devoured your prophets
like a ravening lion.
31 "You of this generation, consider the word of the LORD:

"Have I been a desert to Israel
or a land of great darkness?
Why do my people say, 'We are free to roam;
we will come to you no more'?
32 Does a maiden forget her jewelry,
a bride her wedding ornaments?
Yet my people have forgotten me,
days without number.
33 How skilled you are at pursuing love!
Even the worst of women can learn from your ways.
34 On your clothes men find
the lifeblood of the innocent poor,
though you did not catch them breaking in.
Yet in spite of all this
35 you say, 'I am innocent;
he is not angry with me.'
But I will pass judgment on you
because you say, 'I have not sinned.'
36 Why do you go about so much,
changing your ways?
You will be disappointed by Egypt
as you were by Assyria.
37 You will also leave that place
with your hands on your head,
for the LORD has rejected those you trust;
you will not be helped by them.

3 "IF A man divorces his wife
and she leaves him and marries another man,
should he return to her again?
Would not the land be completely defiled?
But you have lived as a prostitute with many lovers—
would you now return to me?"
declares the LORD.

2 "Look up to the barren heights and see.
Is there any place where you have not been ravished?
By the roadside you sat waiting for lovers,
sat like a nomad[a] in the desert.
You have defiled the land
with your prostitution and wickedness.

NIV [a] 2 Or *an Arab*

## King James

3Therefore the showers have been withholden, and there hath been no latter rain; and thou hadst a whore's forehead, thou refusedst to be ashamed.

4Wilt thou not from this time cry unto me, My father, thou *art* the guide of my youth?

5Will he reserve *his anger* for ever? will he keep *it* to the end? Behold, thou hast spoken and done evil things as thou couldest.

6¶ The LORD said also unto me in the days of Josiah the king, Hast thou seen *that* which backsliding Israel hath done? she is gone up upon every high mountain and under every green tree, and there hath played the harlot.

7And I said after she had done all these *things,* Turn thou unto me. But she returned not. And her treacherous sister Judah saw *it.*

8And I saw, when for all the causes whereby backsliding Israel committed adultery I had put her away, and given her a bill of divorce; yet her treacherous sister Judah feared not, but went and played the harlot also.

9And it came to pass through the lightness of her whoredom, that she defiled the land, and committed adultery with stones and with stocks.

10And yet for all this her treacherous sister Judah hath not turned unto me with her whole heart, but feignedly, saith the LORD.

11And the LORD said unto me, The backsliding Israel hath justified herself more than treacherous Judah.

12¶ Go and proclaim these words toward the north, and say, Return, thou backsliding Israel, saith the LORD; *and* I will not cause mine anger to fall upon you: for I *am* merciful, saith the LORD, *and* I will not keep *anger* for ever.

13Only acknowledge thine iniquity, that thou hast transgressed against the LORD thy God, and hast scattered thy ways to the strangers under every green tree, and ye have not obeyed my voice, saith the LORD.

14Turn, O backsliding children, saith the LORD; for I am married unto you: and I will take you one of a city, and two of a family, and I will bring you to Zion:

15And I will give you pastors according to mine heart, which shall feed you with knowledge and understanding.

16And it shall come to pass, when ye be multiplied and increased in the land, in those days, saith the LORD, they shall say no more, The ark of the covenant of the LORD: neither shall it come to mind: neither shall they remember it; neither shall they visit *it;* neither shall *that* be done any more.

17At that time they shall call Jerusalem the throne of the LORD; and all the nations shall be gathered unto it, to the name of the LORD, to Jerusalem: neither shall they walk any more after the imagination of their evil heart.

18In those days the house of Judah shall walk with the house of Israel, and they shall come together out of the land of the north to the land that I have given for an inheritance unto your fathers.

19But I said, How shall I put thee among the children, and give thee a pleasant land, a goodly heritage of the hosts of nations? and I said, Thou shalt call me, My father; and shalt not turn away from me.

## Amplified

3Therefore the showers have been withheld, and there has been no spring rain; yet you have the brow of a prostitute; you refuse to be ashamed.

4Have you not just now cried to Me, My Father, You were the guide *and* companion of my youth?

5Will He retain His anger for ever? Will He keep it to the end? Behold, you have so spoken, but you have done all the evil things you could, *and* have had your way *and* have carried them through.

6Moreover the Lord said to me [Jeremiah] in the days of Josiah the king *of Judah,* Have you seen what *that* faithless *and* backsliding Israel has done, how she went up on every high hill and under every green tree, and there played the harlot?

7And I said, After she has done all these things, she will return to Me. But she did not return. And her faithless *and* treacherous sister Judah saw *it.*

8And I saw, even though *Judah knew* that for this very cause of committing adultery [idolatry] I, the Lord, had put faithless Israel away and given her a bill of divorcement; yet her faithless *and* treacherous sister Judah was not afraid, but she *also* went and played the harlot [following after idols].

9And through the infamy *and* unseemly frivolity of Israel's whoredom she polluted *and* defiled the land, [by her idolatry] committing adultery with *idols of* stones and trees.

10But in spite of all this her faithless *and* treacherous sister Judah did not return to Me in sincerity *and* with her whole heart, but in sheer hypocrisy [has she feigned obedience to King Josiah's reforms], says the Lord. [II Chron. 34:33 with Hosea 7:13, 14.]

11And the Lord said to me, Backsliding *and* faithless Israel has shown herself less guilty than false *and* treacherous Judah.

12Go and proclaim these words toward the north [where the ten tribes have been taken as captives], and say, Return, faithless Israel, says the Lord, *and* I will not cause My countenance to fall *and* look in anger upon you, for I am merciful, says the Lord; I will not keep anger for ever.

13Only know, understand *and* acknowledge your iniquity *and* guilt, that you have rebelled *and* transgressed against the Lord your God, and have scattered your favors among strangers under every green tree, and you have not obeyed My voice, says the Lord.

14Return, O faithless children [of the whole twelve tribes], says the Lord, for I am Lord *and* Master *and* Husband to you, and I will take you [not as a nation, but individually] one from a city and two from a tribal family, and I will bring you to Zion. [Luke 15:20-22.]

15And I will give you [spiritual] shepherds after My own heart [in the final time], who will feed you with knowledge and understanding *and* judgment.

16And it shall be that when you have multiplied and increased in the land in those days, says the Lord, they shall no more say, The ark of the covenant of the Lord. It shall not come to mind, nor shall they [seriously] remember it, nor shall they miss *or* visit it, nor shall it be repaired *or* made again [for instead of the ark which represented God's presence, He will show Himself present throughout the city]. [Isa. 65:17; Rev. 21:3, 22, 23.]

17At that time they shall call Jerusalem the throne of the Lord, and all the nations shall be gathered to it, in the renown *and* name of the Lord to Jerusalem, nor shall they walk any more after the stubbornness of their own evil heart.

18In those days the house of Judah shall walk with the house of Israel, and together they shall come out of the land of the north to the land that I gave for an inheritance to your fathers.

19And I thought how *gloriously and honorably* I would set you among My children and give you a pleasant land, a goodly heritage, the most beautiful *and* best among all nations! And I thought you would call Me, My Father, and would not turn away from following Me.

## New American Standard

3 "Therefore the showers have been withheld,
And there has been no spring rain.
Yet you had a harlot's forehead;
You refused to be ashamed.
4 "Have you not just now called to Me,
'My Father, Thou art the friend of my youth?
5 'Will He be angry forever?
Will He be indignant to the end?'
Behold, you have spoken
And have done evil things,
And you have had your way."

*Faithless Israel*

6¶ Then the LORD said to me in the days of Josiah the king,
"Have you seen what faithless Israel did? She went up on every
high hill and under every green tree, and she was a harlot there.
7 "And I thought, 'After she has done all these things, she will
return to Me'; but she did not return, and her treacherous sister
Judah saw it.
8 "And I saw that for all the adulteries of faithless Israel, I had
sent her away and given her a writ of divorce, yet her treacherous
sister Judah did not fear; but she went and was a harlot also.
9 "And it came about because of the lightness of her harlotry,
that she polluted the land and committed adultery with stones and
trees.
10 "And yet in spite of all this her treacherous sister Judah did
not return to Me with all her heart, but rather in deception,"
declares the LORD.

*God Invites Repentance*

11¶ And the LORD said to me, "Faithless Israel has proved
herself more righteous than treacherous Judah.
12 "Go, and proclaim these words toward the north and say,
'Return, faithless Israel,' declares the LORD;
'I will not look upon you in anger.
For I am gracious,' declares the LORD;
'I will not be angry forever.
13 'Only acknowledge your iniquity,
That you have transgressed against the LORD your God
And have scattered your favors to the strangers under
every green tree,
And you have not obeyed My voice,' declares the LORD.
14 'Return, O faithless sons,' declares the LORD;
'For I am a master to you,
And I will take you one from a city and two from a
family,
And I will bring you to Zion.'
15 "Then I will give you shepherds after My own heart, who will
feed you on knowledge and understanding.
16 "And it shall be in those days when you are multiplied and
increased in the land," declares the LORD, "they shall say no more,
'The ark of the covenant of the LORD.' And it shall not come to
mind, nor shall they remember it, nor shall they miss *it*, nor shall
it be made again.
17 "At that time they shall call Jerusalem 'The Throne of the
LORD,' and all the nations will be gathered to it, to Jerusalem, for
the name of the LORD; nor shall they walk anymore after the
stubbornness of their evil heart.
18 "In those days the house of Judah will walk with the house
of Israel, and they will come together from the land of the north
to the land that I gave your fathers as an inheritance.
19¶ "Then I said,
'How I would set you among My sons,
And give you a pleasant land,
The most beautiful inheritance of the nations!'
And I said, 'You shall call Me, My Father,
And not turn away from following Me.'

## New International

3 Therefore the showers have been withheld,
and no spring rains have fallen.
Yet you have the brazen look of a prostitute;
you refuse to blush with shame.
4 Have you not just called to me:
'My Father, my friend from my youth,
5 will you always be angry?
Will your wrath continue forever?'
This is how you talk,
but you do all the evil you can."

*Unfaithful Israel*

6 During the reign of King Josiah, the LORD said to me, "Have
you seen what faithless Israel has done? She has gone up on every
high hill and under every spreading tree and has committed adultery there. 7 I thought that after she had done all this she would
return to me but she did not, and her unfaithful sister Judah saw
it. 8 I gave faithless Israel her certificate of divorce and sent her
away because of all her adulteries. Yet I saw that her unfaithful
sister Judah had no fear; she also went out and committed adultery. 9 Because Israel's immorality mattered so little to her, she
defiled the land and committed adultery with stone and wood. 10 In
spite of all this, her unfaithful sister Judah did not return to me
with all her heart, but only in pretense," declares the LORD.
11 The LORD said to me, "Faithless Israel is more righteous than
unfaithful Judah. 12 Go, proclaim this message toward the north:

" 'Return, faithless Israel,' declares the LORD,
'I will frown on you no longer,
for I am merciful,' declares the LORD,
'I will not be angry forever.
13 Only acknowledge your guilt—
you have rebelled against the LORD your God,
you have scattered your favors to foreign gods
under every spreading tree,
and have not obeyed me,' "
declares the LORD.

14 "Return, faithless people," declares the LORD, "for I am your
husband. I will choose you—one from a town and two from a
clan—and bring you to Zion. 15 Then I will give you shepherds after
my own heart, who will lead you with knowledge and understanding. 16 In those days, when your numbers have increased greatly
in the land," declares the LORD, "men will no longer say, 'The ark
of the covenant of the LORD.' It will never enter their minds or be
remembered; it will not be missed, nor will another one be made.
17 At that time they will call Jerusalem The Throne of the LORD, and
all nations will gather in Jerusalem to honor the name of the LORD.
No longer will they follow the stubbornness of their evil hearts.
18 In those days the house of Judah will join the house of Israel, and
together they will come from a northern land to the land I gave
your forefathers as an inheritance.
19 "I myself said,

" 'How gladly would I treat you like sons
and give you a desirable land,
the most beautiful inheritance of any nation.'
I thought you would call me 'Father'
and not turn away from following me.

## King James

20¶ Surely *as* a wife treacherously departeth from her husband,
so have ye dealt treacherously with me, O house of Israel, saith the
LORD.
21A voice was heard upon the high places, weeping *and* supplications of the children of Israel: for they have perverted their
way, *and* they have forgotten the LORD their God.
22Return, ye backsliding children, *and* I will heal your backslidings. Behold, we come unto thee; for thou *art* the LORD our
God.
23Truly in vain *is salvation hoped for* from the hills, *and from* the
multitude of mountains: truly in the LORD our God *is* the salvation
of Israel.
24For shame hath devoured the labour of our fathers from our
youth; their flocks and their herds, their sons and their daughters.
25We lie down in our shame, and our confusion covereth us: for
we have sinned against the LORD our God, we and our fathers,
from our youth even unto this day, and have not obeyed the voice
of the LORD our God.

**4** IF THOU wilt return, O Israel, saith the LORD, return unto
me: and if thou wilt put away thine abominations out of my
sight, then shalt thou not remove.
2And thou shalt swear, The LORD liveth, in truth, in judgment,
and in righteousness; and the nations shall bless themselves in
him, and in him shall they glory.
3¶ For thus saith the LORD to the men of Judah and Jerusalem,
Break up your fallow ground, and sow not among thorns.
4Circumcise yourselves to the LORD, and take away the foreskins of your heart, ye men of Judah and inhabitants of Jerusalem:
lest my fury come forth like fire, and burn that none can quench
*it*, because of the evil of your doings.
5Declare ye in Judah, and publish in Jerusalem; and say, Blow
ye the trumpet in the land: cry, gather together, and say, Assemble
yourselves, and let us go into the defenced cities.
6Set up the standard toward Zion: retire, stay not: for I will
bring evil from the north, and a great destruction.
7The lion is come up from his thicket, and the destroyer of the
Gentiles is on his way; he is gone forth from his place to make thy
land desolate; *and* thy cities shall be laid waste, without an inhabitant.

## Amplified

20Surely, as a wife treacherously *and* faithlessly departs from
her husband, so have you dealt treacherously *and* faithlessly with
Me, O house of Israel, says the Lord.
21A voice is heard on the bare heights, the weeping *and* pleading of the sons of Israel; because they have perverted their way,
they have [eagerly] forgotten the Lord their God.
22Return, O faithless sons, *says the Lord, and* I will heal your
faithlessness. [And they answer] Behold, we come to You, for You
are the Lord our God.
23Truly in vain is the *hope of salvation* from the hills, *and from* the
tumult *and* noisy throng on the mountains; truly in *and* with the
Lord our God rests the salvation of Israel.
24[We have been ruined as a nation by our faithlessness and
idolatry] for the shameful thing has consumed all for which our
fathers toiled from our youth, their flocks and their herds, their
sons and their daughters.
25Let us lie prostrate in our shame, and let our dishonor *and*
confusion cover us; for we have sinned against the Lord our God,
we and our fathers, from our youth even to this day; we have not
obeyed the voice of the Lord our God.

**4** IF YOU will return, O Israel, says the Lord, if you will return
to Me, and if you will put away your abominable false gods
out of My sight, and do not stray *or* waver;
2And if you swear, As the Lord lives, in truth, in judgment *and*
justice, and in righteousness (uprightness in every area and relation), then the nations shall bless themselves in Him, and in Him
shall they glory.
3For thus says the Lord to the men of Judah and to Jerusalem,
Break up your ground left uncultivated for a season, *so that you may*
not sow among thorns.
4Circumcise yourselves to the Lord, and take away the foreskins of your heart, you men of Judah and inhabitants of Jerusalem; lest My wrath go forth like fire [consuming all that gets in its
way], and burn so that no one can quench it, because of the evil
of your doings.
5Declare in Judah and publish in Jerusalem, and say, Blow the
trumpet in the land; cry aloud and say, Assemble yourselves, and
let us go into the fortified cities.
6Raise a standard toward Zion [primarily to mark out the safest
route to those seeking safety within Jerusalem's walls]; flee for
safety, stay not, for I bring evil from the north, and great destruction.
7A lion is gone up from his thicket, and a destroyer of nations
is on his way; he is gone forth from his place to make your land
a desolate waste, and your cities shall be left in ruins without an
inhabitant.

## New American Standard

20 "Surely, as a woman treacherously departs from her
lover,
So you have dealt treacherously with Me,
O house of Israel," declares the LORD.

21¶ A voice is heard on the bare heights,
The weeping *and* the supplications of the sons of Israel;
Because they have perverted their way,
They have forgotten the LORD their God.
22 "Return, O faithless sons,
I will heal your faithlessness."
"Behold, we come to Thee;
For Thou art the LORD our God.
23 "Surely, the hills are a deception,
A tumult *on* the mountains.
Surely, in the LORD our God
Is the salvation of Israel.
24"But the shameful thing has consumed the labor of our fathers
since our youth, their flocks and their herds, their sons and their
daughters.
25"Let us lie down in our shame, and let our humiliation cover
us; for we have sinned against the LORD our God, we and our
fathers, since our youth even to this day. And we have not obeyed
the voice of the LORD our God."

*Judah Threatened with Invasion*

4 "IF YOU will return, O Israel," declares the LORD,
"*Then* you should return to Me.
And if you will put away your detested things from My
presence,
And will not waver,
2 And you will swear, 'As the LORD lives,'
In truth, in justice, and in righteousness;
Then the nations will bless themselves in Him,
And in Him they will glory."

3¶ For thus says the LORD to the men of Judah and to Jerusalem,
"Break up your fallow ground,
And do not sow among thorns.
4 "Circumcise yourselves to the LORD
And remove the foreskins of your heart,
Men of Judah and inhabitants of Jerusalem,
Lest My wrath go forth like fire
And burn with none to quench it,
Because of the evil of your deeds."

5¶ Declare in Judah and proclaim in Jerusalem, and say,
"Blow the trumpet in the land;
Cry aloud and say,
'Assemble yourselves, and let us go
Into the fortified cities.'
6 "Lift up a standard toward Zion!
Seek refuge, do not stand *still*,
For I am bringing evil from the north,
And great destruction.
7 "A lion has gone up from his thicket,
And a destroyer of nations has set out;
He has gone out from his place
To make your land a waste.
Your cities will be ruins
Without inhabitant.

## New International

20But like a woman unfaithful to her husband,
so you have been unfaithful to me, O house of Israel,"
declares the LORD.

21A cry is heard on the barren heights,
the weeping and pleading of the people of Israel,
because they have perverted their ways
and have forgotten the LORD their God.

22"Return, faithless people;
I will cure you of backsliding."

"Yes, we will come to you,
for you are the LORD our God.
23Surely the ⌊idolatrous⌋ commotion on the hills
and mountains is a deception;
surely in the LORD our God
is the salvation of Israel.
24From our youth shameful gods have consumed
the fruits of our fathers' labor—
their flocks and herds,
their sons and daughters.
25Let us lie down in our shame,
and let our disgrace cover us.
We have sinned against the LORD our God,
both we and our fathers;
from our youth till this day
we have not obeyed the LORD our God."

4 "IF YOU will return, O Israel,
return to me,"
declares the LORD.
"If you put your detestable idols out of my sight
and no longer go astray,
2and if in a truthful, just and righteous way
you swear, 'As surely as the LORD lives,'
then the nations will be blessed by him
and in him they will glory."

3This is what the LORD says to the men of Judah and to Jerusalem:

"Break up your unplowed ground
and do not sow among thorns.
4Circumcise yourselves to the LORD,
circumcise your hearts,
you men of Judah and people of Jerusalem,
or my wrath will break out and burn like fire
because of the evil you have done—
burn with no one to quench it.

*Disaster From the North*

5"Announce in Judah and proclaim in Jerusalem and say:
'Sound the trumpet throughout the land!'
Cry aloud and say:
'Gather together!
Let us flee to the fortified cities!'
6Raise the signal to go to Zion!
Flee for safety without delay!
For I am bringing disaster from the north,
even terrible destruction."

7A lion has come out of his lair;
a destroyer of nations has set out.
He has left his place
to lay waste your land.
Your towns will lie in ruins
without inhabitant.

## King James

8For this gird you with sackcloth, lament and howl: for the
fierce anger of the LORD is not turned back from us.
9And it shall come to pass at that day, saith the LORD, *that* the
heart of the king shall perish, and the heart of the princes; and the
priests shall be astonished, and the prophets shall wonder.
10Then said I, Ah, Lord GOD! surely thou hast greatly deceived
this people and Jerusalem, saying, Ye shall have peace; whereas
the sword reacheth unto the soul.
11At that time shall it be said to this people and to Jerusalem,
A dry wind of the high places in the wilderness toward the daughter of my people, not to fan, nor to cleanse,
12 *Even* a full wind from those *places* shall come unto me: now
also will I give sentence against them.
13Behold, he shall come up as clouds, and his chariots *shall be*
as a whirlwind: his horses are swifter than eagles. Woe unto us!
for we are spoiled.
14O Jerusalem, wash thine heart from wickedness, that thou
mayest be saved. How long shall thy vain thoughts lodge within
thee?
15For a voice declareth from Dan, and publisheth affliction from
mount Ephraim.
16Make ye mention to the nations; behold, publish against
Jerusalem, *that* watchers come from a far country, and give out
their voice against the cities of Judah.
17As keepers of a field, are they against her round about; because she hath been rebellious against me, saith the LORD.
18Thy way and thy doings have procured these *things* unto thee;
this *is* thy wickedness, because it is bitter, because it reacheth unto
thine heart.
19¶ My bowels, my bowels! I am pained at my very heart; my
heart maketh a noise in me; I cannot hold my peace, because thou
hast heard, O my soul, the sound of the trumpet, the alarm of war.
20Destruction upon destruction is cried; for the whole land is
spoiled: suddenly are my tents spoiled, *and* my curtains in a moment.
21How long shall I see the standard, *and* hear the sound of the
trumpet?
22For my people *is* foolish, they have not known me; they *are*
sottish children, and they have none understanding: they *are* wise
to do evil, but to do good they have no knowledge.
23I beheld the earth, and, lo, *it was* without form, and void; and
the heavens, and they *had* no light.
24I beheld the mountains, and, lo, they trembled, and all the
hills moved lightly.
25I beheld, and, lo, *there was* no man, and all the birds of the
heavens were fled.

## Amplified

8For this gird you with sackcloth, lament and wail, for the fierce
anger of the Lord has not turned back from us.
9And it shall be in that day, says the Lord, that the understanding *and* courage of the king shall fail [be paralyzed], and also that
of the princes; the priests shall be appalled and the prophets
astounded *and* dazed with horror.
10Then I [Jeremiah] said, [a]Alas, Lord God! Surely you have
greatly deceived *and* misled this people and Jerusalem, [for the
prophets represented You as] saying *to Your people,* You shall have
peace, whereas the sword has reached to *their very* life.
11At that time it will be said to this people and to Jerusalem, A
hot wind from the bare heights in the wilderness [comes at My
command] against the daughter of My people; not *a wind* to fan or
cleanse [from chaff, as when threshing], *but*
12A wind too strong *and* full for winnowing comes at My word.
Now I will also speak in judgment against *My people.*
13Behold, *the enemy* comes up like clouds, his chariots like the
whirlwind; his horses are swifter than eagles. Woe to us, for we
are ruined—destroyed!
14O Jerusalem, wash your heart from wickedness, that you may
be saved! How long shall your iniquitous *and* grossly offensive
thoughts lodge within you?
15For a voice declares from Dan [in the north] and proclaims evil
from Mount Ephraim [the range dividing Israel from Judah].
16Warn the *neighboring* nations *that our adversary is coming;* announce to Jerusalem that besiegers are coming from a far country,
and they shout against the cities of Judah.
17Like keepers of a field they are against her round about,
because she has been rebellious against Me, says the Lord.
18Your ways and your doings have brought these things down
upon you; this is your calamity *and* doom; surely it is bitter, for
surely it reaches your very heart.
19[Not only the prophet, but in thought the people cry] My
anguish, my anguish! I writhe in pain! Oh, the walls of my heart!
My heart is disquieted *and* throbs aloud to me; I cannot be silent!
For I hear the sound of the trumpet, the alarm of war.
20News of one violent disaster *and* calamity comes close after
another, for the whole land is laid waste; suddenly are my tents
spoiled *and* destroyed, and my *tent* curtains ruined in a moment.
21 *O Lord,* how long must I see the flag [marking the route for
flight], and hear the sound of the trumpet [urging the people to
flee for refuge]?
22[Their chastisement will continue until it has accomplished its
purpose] for My people are stupid, says the Lord [replying to
Jeremiah], they do not know *and* understand Me; they are thick-
headed children, and they have no understanding; they are wise
to do evil, but to do good they have no knowledge.
23[In a vision Jeremiah sees Judah laid waste by conquest *and*
captivity.] I beheld the land, and lo, it was [as at the time of
creation] a waste and vacant—void; and the heavens, and they had
no light.
24I beheld the mountains, and lo, they trembled, and all the hills
moved lightly to and fro.
25I beheld, and lo, there was no man, and all the birds of the
air had fled.

**AMP** [a] "Jeremiah could not reconcile the doom he was now commanded to pronounce, either with his own previous prophecy or with what he read in the writings of the previous prophets." We have the Apostle Peter's comment on the perplexity of the prophets in I Pet. 1:10-12. In *The Amplified New Testament* it reads, "The prophets who prophesied of the grace [divine blessing] which was intended for you, searched and inquired earnestly about this salvation. They sought [to find out] to whom or when this was to come, which the Spirit of Christ working within them indicated when He predicted the sufferings of Christ and the glories that should follow [them]. It was then disclosed to them that the services they were rendering were not meant for themselves and their period of time, but for you. . . . Into these things [the very] angels long to look!"

## New American Standard

8 "For this, put on sackcloth,
Lament and wail;
For the fierce anger of the LORD
Has not turned back from us."
9"And it shall come about in that day," declares the LORD,
"that the heart of the king and the heart of the princes will fail; and
the priests will be appalled, and the prophets will be astounded."
10¶ Then I said, "Ah, Lord GOD! Surely Thou hast utterly deceived this people and Jerusalem, saying, 'You will have peace';
whereas a sword touches the throat."
11¶ In that time it will be said to this people and to Jerusalem,
"A scorching wind from the bare heights in the wilderness in the
direction of the daughter of My people—not to winnow, and not
to cleanse,
12a wind too strong for this—will come at My command; now
I will also pronounce judgments against them.
13 "Behold, he goes up like clouds,
And his chariots like the whirlwind;
His horses are swifter than eagles.
Woe to us, for we are ruined!"

14¶ Wash your heart from evil, O Jerusalem,
That you may be saved.
How long will your wicked thoughts
Lodge within you?
15 For a voice declares from Dan,
And proclaims wickedness from Mount Ephraim.
16 "Report *it* to the nations, now!
Proclaim over Jerusalem,
'Besiegers come from a far country,
And lift their voices against the cities of Judah.
17 'Like watchmen of a field they are against her round
about,
Because she has rebelled against Me,' declares the
LORD.
18 "Your ways and your deeds
Have brought these things to you.
This is your evil. How bitter!
How it has touched your heart!"

*Lament over Judah's Devastation*

19¶ My soul, my soul! I am in anguish! Oh, my heart!
My heart is pounding in me;
I cannot be silent,
Because you have heard, O my soul,
The sound of the trumpet,
The alarm of war.
20 Disaster on disaster is proclaimed,
For the whole land is devastated;
Suddenly my tents are devastated,
My curtains in an instant.
21 How long must I see the standard,
And hear the sound of the trumpet?
22 "For My people are foolish,
They know Me not;
They are stupid children,
And they have no understanding.
They are shrewd to do evil,
But to do good they do not know."

23¶ I looked on the earth, and behold, *it was* formless and
void;
And to the heavens, and they had no light.
24 I looked on the mountains, and behold, they were
quaking,
And all the hills moved to and fro.
25 I looked, and behold, there was no man,
And all the birds of the heavens had fled.

## New International

8So put on sackcloth,
lament and wail,
for the fierce anger of the LORD
has not turned away from us.

9"In that day," declares the LORD,
"the king and the officials will lose heart,
the priests will be horrified,
and the prophets will be appalled."
10Then I said, "Ah, Sovereign LORD, how completely you have
deceived this people and Jerusalem by saying, 'You will have
peace,' when the sword is at our throats."
11At that time this people and Jerusalem will be told, "A scorching wind from the barren heights in the desert blows toward my
people, but not to winnow or cleanse; 12a wind too strong for that
comes from me.[b] Now I pronounce my judgments against them."
13Look! He advances like the clouds,
his chariots come like a whirlwind,
his horses are swifter than eagles.
Woe to us! We are ruined!
14O Jerusalem, wash the evil from your heart and be saved.
How long will you harbor wicked thoughts?
15A voice is announcing from Dan,
proclaiming disaster from the hills of Ephraim.
16"Tell this to the nations,
proclaim it to Jerusalem:
'A besieging army is coming from a distant land,
raising a war cry against the cities of Judah.
17They surround her like men guarding a field,
because she has rebelled against me,' "
declares the LORD.

18"Your own conduct and actions
have brought this upon you.
This is your punishment.
How bitter it is!
How it pierces to the heart!"

19Oh, my anguish, my anguish!
I writhe in pain.
Oh, the agony of my heart!
My heart pounds within me,
I cannot keep silent.
For I have heard the sound of the trumpet;
I have heard the battle cry.
20Disaster follows disaster;
the whole land lies in ruins.
In an instant my tents are destroyed,
my shelter in a moment.
21How long must I see the battle standard
and hear the sound of the trumpet?
22"My people are fools;
they do not know me.
They are senseless children;
they have no understanding.
They are skilled in doing evil;
they know not how to do good."

23I looked at the earth,
and it was formless and empty;
and at the heavens,
and their light was gone.
24I looked at the mountains,
and they were quaking;
all the hills were swaying.
25I looked, and there were no people;
every bird in the sky had flown away.

NIV [b] 12 Or *comes at my command*

## King James

26 I beheld, and, lo, the fruitful place *was* a wilderness, and all the cities thereof were broken down at the presence of the LORD, *and* by his fierce anger.

27 For thus hath the LORD said, The whole land shall be desolate; yet will I not make a full end.

28 For this shall the earth mourn, and the heavens above be black: because I have spoken *it*, I have purposed *it*, and will not repent, neither will I turn back from it.

29 The whole city shall flee for the noise of the horsemen and bowmen; they shall go into thickets, and climb up upon the rocks: every city *shall be* forsaken, and not a man dwell therein.

30 And *when* thou *art* spoiled, what wilt thou do? Though thou clothest thyself with crimson, though thou deckest thee with ornaments of gold, though thou rentest thy face with painting, in vain shalt thou make thyself fair; *thy* lovers will despise thee, they will seek thy life.

31 For I have heard a voice as of a woman in travail, *and* the anguish as of her that bringeth forth her first child, the voice of the daughter of Zion, *that* bewaileth herself, *that* spreadeth her hands, *saying*, Woe *is* me now! for my soul is wearied because of murderers.

5 RUN YE to and fro through the streets of Jerusalem, and see now, and know, and seek in the broad places thereof, if ye can find a man, if there be *any* that executeth judgment, that seeketh the truth; and I will pardon it.

2 And though they say, The LORD liveth; surely they swear falsely.

3 O LORD, *are* not thine eyes upon the truth? thou hast stricken them, but they have not grieved; thou hast consumed them, *but* they have refused to receive correction: they have made their faces harder than a rock; they have refused to return.

4 Therefore I said, Surely these *are* poor; they are foolish: for they know not the way of the LORD, *nor* the judgment of their God.

5 I will get me unto the great men, and will speak unto them; for they have known the way of the LORD, *and* the judgment of their God: but these have altogether broken the yoke, *and* burst the bonds.

6 Wherefore a lion out of the forest shall slay them, *and* a wolf of the evenings shall spoil them, a leopard shall watch over their cities: every one that goeth out thence shall be torn in pieces: because their transgressions are many, *and* their backslidings are increased.

## Amplified

26 I looked, and lo, the fruitful land was a desert, and all its cities were laid waste before the Lord's presence, by His fierce anger.

27 For thus says the Lord, The whole land shall be a desolation, yet I will not make a complete end of it.

28 For this shall the earth mourn, and the heavens above be black; because I have spoken, I have purposed, and I have not relented nor will I turn back *from it*.

29 Every city flees because of the noise of the horsemen and bowmen; they go into the thickets, and climb among the rocks; every city is forsaken, and not a man dwells in them.

30 And you, [plundered one] when you are made desolate what will you do? Though you clothe yourself with scarlet, though you deck yourself with ornaments of gold, though you paint your eyelids *and* make them look farther apart, in vain shall you beautify yourself. Your lovers [allies] despise you; they seek your life.

31 For I have heard a cry as of a woman in travail, anguish as of her who brings forth her first child, the cry of the daughter of Zion, who gasps for breath, who spreads her hands, saying, Woe is me now! I am fainting before the murderers.

5 RUN TO and fro through the streets of Jerusalem, and see now and take notice! Seek in her broad squares to see if you can find a man [as Abraham sought in Sodom], one who does justice, who seeks truth, sincerity *and* faithfulness; and I will pardon *Jerusalem*—for one uncompromisingly righteous person. [Gen. 18:22-32.]

2 And though they say, As the Lord lives, surely they swear falsely.

3 O Lord, do not your eyes look on the truth? [They have meant to please You outwardly, but You look on their hearts.] You have stricken them, but they have not grieved; You have consumed them, but they have refused to take correction *or* instruction; they have made their faces harder than a rock, they have refused to repent *and* return *to You*.

4 Then I said, Surely these are only the poor; they are [sinfully] foolish *and* have no understanding, for they know not the way of the Lord, the judgment—the just and righteous law—of their God.

5 I will go to the great men and will speak to them, for they must know the way of the Lord, the judgment—the just and righteous law—of their God. But [I found the very reverse to be true] these had all alike broken the yoke *of God's law* and had burst the bonds *of obedience to Him*.

6 Therefore a lion out of the forest shall slay them, a wolf of the deserts shall destroy them, a leopard *or* panther shall lie in wait against their cities. Every one who goes out of them shall be torn in pieces; because their transgressions are many, their backslidings *and* total desertion of faith are increased *and* become great *and* mighty.

## New American Standard

26 I looked, and behold, the fruitful land was a
wilderness,
And all its cities were pulled down
Before the LORD, before His fierce anger.

27¶ For thus says the LORD,
"The whole land shall be a desolation,
Yet I will not execute a complete destruction.
28 "For this the earth shall mourn,
And the heavens above be dark,
Because I have spoken, I have purposed,
And I will not change My mind, nor will I turn from
it."
29 At the sound of the horseman and bowman every city
flees;
They go into the thickets and climb among the rocks;
Every city is forsaken,
And no man dwells in them.
30 And you, O desolate one, what will you do?
Although you dress in scarlet,
Although you decorate *yourself with* ornaments of gold,
Although you enlarge your eyes with paint,
In vain you make yourself beautiful;
*Your* lovers despise you;
They seek your life.
31 For I heard a cry as of a woman in labor,
The anguish as of one giving birth to her first child,
The cry of the daughter of Zion gasping for breath,
Stretching out her hands, *saying,*
"Ah, woe is me, for I faint before murderers."

*Jerusalem's Godlessness*

5 "ROAM TO and fro through the streets of Jerusalem,
And look now, and take note.
And seek in her open squares,
If you can find a man,
If there is one who does justice, who seeks truth,
Then I will pardon her.
2 "And although they say, 'As the LORD lives,'
Surely they swear falsely."
3 O LORD, do not Thine eyes look for truth?
Thou hast smitten them,
*But* they did not weaken;
Thou hast consumed them,
But they refused to take correction.
They have made their faces harder than rock;
They have refused to repent.
4¶ Then I said, "They are only the poor,
They are foolish;
For they do not know the way of the LORD
*Or* the ordinance of their God.
5 "I will go to the great
And will speak to them,
For they know the way of the LORD,
*And* the ordinance of their God."
But they too, with one accord, have broken the yoke
*And* burst the bonds.
6 Therefore a lion from the forest shall slay them,
A wolf of the deserts shall destroy them,
A leopard is watching their cities.
Everyone who goes out of them shall be torn in pieces,
Because their transgressions are many,
Their apostasies are numerous.

## New International

26I looked, and the fruitful land was a desert;
all its towns lay in ruins
before the LORD, before his fierce anger.

27This is what the LORD says:
"The whole land will be ruined,
though I will not destroy it completely.
28Therefore the earth will mourn
and the heavens above grow dark,
because I have spoken and will not relent,
I have decided and will not turn back."

29At the sound of horsemen and archers
every town takes to flight.
Some go into the thickets;
some climb up among the rocks.
All the towns are deserted;
no one lives in them.

30What are you doing, O devastated one?
Why dress yourself in scarlet
and put on jewels of gold?
Why shade your eyes with paint?
You adorn yourself in vain.
Your lovers despise you;
they seek your life.

31I hear a cry as of a woman in labor,
a groan as of one bearing her first child—
the cry of the Daughter of Zion gasping for breath,
stretching out her hands and saying,
"Alas! I am fainting;
my life is given over to murderers."

*Not One Is Upright*

5 "GO UP and down the streets of Jerusalem,
look around and consider,
search through her squares.
If you can find but one person
who deals honestly and seeks the truth,
I will forgive this city.
2Although they say, 'As surely as the LORD lives,'
still they are swearing falsely."
3O LORD, do not your eyes look for truth?
You struck them, but they felt no pain;
you crushed them, but they refused correction.
They made their faces harder than stone
and refused to repent.
4I thought, "These are only the poor;
they are foolish,
for they do not know the way of the LORD,
the requirements of their God.
5So I will go to the leaders
and speak to them;
surely they know the way of the LORD,
the requirements of their God."
But with one accord they too had broken off the yoke
and torn off the bonds.
6Therefore a lion from the forest will attack them,
a wolf from the desert will ravage them,
a leopard will lie in wait near their towns
to tear to pieces any who venture out,
for their rebellion is great
and their backslidings many.

## King James

7¶ How shall I pardon thee for this? thy children have forsaken me, and sworn by *them that are* no gods: when I had fed them to the full, they then committed adultery, and assembled themselves by troops in the harlots' houses.

8They were *as* fed horses in the morning: every one neighed after his neighbour's wife.

9Shall I not visit for these *things?* saith the LORD: and shall not my soul be avenged on such a nation as this?

10¶ Go ye up upon her walls, and destroy; but make not a full end: take away her battlements; for they *are* not the LORD's.

11For the house of Israel and the house of Judah have dealt very treacherously against me, saith the LORD.

12They have belied the LORD, and said, *It is* not he; neither shall evil come upon us; neither shall we see sword nor famine:

13And the prophets shall become wind, and the word *is* not in them: thus shall it be done unto them.

14Wherefore thus saith the LORD God of hosts, Because ye speak this word, behold, I will make my words in thy mouth fire, and this people wood, and it shall devour them.

15Lo, I will bring a nation upon you from far, O house of Israel, saith the LORD: it *is* a mighty nation, it *is* an ancient nation, a nation whose language thou knowest not, neither understandest what they say.

16Their quiver *is* as an open sepulchre, they *are* all mighty men.

17And they shall eat up thine harvest, and thy bread, *which* thy sons and thy daughters should eat: they shall eat up thy flocks and thine herds: they shall eat up thy vines and thy fig trees: they shall impoverish thy fenced cities, wherein thou trustedst, with the sword.

18Nevertheless in those days, saith the LORD, I will not make a full end with you.

19¶ And it shall come to pass, when ye shall say, Wherefore doeth the LORD our God all these *things* unto us? then shalt thou answer them, Like as ye have forsaken me, and served strange gods in your land, so shall ye serve strangers in a land *that is* not yours.

20Declare this in the house of Jacob, and publish it in Judah, saying,

21Hear now this, O foolish people, and without understanding; which have eyes, and see not; which have ears, and hear not:

22Fear ye not me? saith the LORD: will ye not tremble at my presence, which have placed the sand *for* the bound of the sea by a perpetual decree, that it cannot pass it: and though the waves thereof toss themselves, yet can they not prevail; though they roar, yet can they not pass over it?

23But this people hath a revolting and a rebellious heart; they are revolted and gone.

## Amplified

7Why should I *and* how can I pass over this *and* forgive you for it? Your children have forsaken Me, and sworn by those that are no gods. When I had fed them to the full *and* bound them to Me by oath, they committed [spiritual] adultery, assembling themselves in troops at the houses of [idol] harlots.

8They were as fed stallions roaming at large; every one neighed after his neighbor's wife.

9Shall I not punish *them* for these things? says the Lord; and shall I not be avenged on such a nation as this?

10Go up within *Jerusalem's* walls and destroy *her vine,* but do not make a complete end. Trim away the tendrils *of her vine,* for they are not the Lord's.

11For the house of Israel and the house of Judah have dealt very faithlessly *and* treacherously against Me, says the Lord.

12They have belied *and* denied the Lord by saying, It is not He *Who speaks through His prophets;* evil shall not come upon us, nor shall we see war or famine;

13And, *say they,* the prophets will become wind [what they prophesy will not come to pass], and the word *of God* is not in them. Thus shall it be done to them [as they threatened would be done to us].

14Therefore thus says the Lord God of hosts, Because you, *the people,* speak this word, behold, I will make My words fire in your mouth, *Jeremiah,* and this people wood, and it shall devour them.

15Lo, I am bringing a nation upon you from afar, O house of Israel, says the Lord. It is a mighty *and* enduring nation, it is an ancient nation, a nation whose language you do not know, nor can you understand what they say.

16Their quiver is [filled with deadly missiles] *as* an open sepulcher *filled with dead bodies; the foe* are all mighty men—heroes.

17They shall consume your harvest and your food; they shall consume your sons and your daughters; they shall consume your flocks and your herds; they shall consume your vines and your fig trees; they shall break down *and* impoverish your fortified cities in which you trust, with the sword *they shall destroy them.*

18But even in those days, says the Lord, I will not make a full end of you.

19And when your people say, Why has the Lord our God done all these things to us? then you shall answer them, As you have forsaken Me, says the Lord, and have served strange gods in your land, so shall you serve strange gods in a land that is not yours.

20Declare this in the house of Jacob, and publish it in Judah:

21Hear now this, O foolish people, without understanding *or* heart, who have eyes and see not, who have ears and hear not: [Isa. 6:9, 10; Matt. 13:10-15; Mark 8:17, 18.]

22Do you not fear *and* reverence Me? says the Lord. Do you not tremble before Me? *I,* Who placed the sand for the boundary of the sea, a perpetual barrier which it cannot pass *and* by an everlasting ordinance beyond which it cannot go? And though the waves of the sea toss *and* shake themselves, yet they cannot prevail [against the feeble grains of sand which God has ordained by nature sufficient for His purpose]; though *the billows* roar, yet they cannot pass over that *barrier.* [Is not such a God to be reverently feared and worshiped?]

23But this people has a heart that draws back from God and a will that rebels against Him; they have revolted *and* quit His service and have gone [into idolatry].

## New American Standard

7¶ "Why should I pardon you?
Your sons have forsaken Me
And sworn by those who are not gods.
When I had fed them to the full,
They committed adultery
And trooped to the harlot's house.
8 "They were well-fed lusty horses,
Each one neighing after his neighbor's wife.
9 "Shall I not punish these *people*," declares the LORD,
"And on a nation such as this
Shall I not avenge Myself?
10¶ "Go up through her vine rows and destroy,
But do not execute a complete destruction;
Strip away her branches,
For they are not the LORD's.
11 "For the house of Israel and the house of Judah
Have dealt very treacherously with Me," declares the LORD.
12 They have lied about the LORD
And said, "[a]Not He;
Misfortune will not come on us;
And we will not see sword or famine.
13 "And the prophets are *as* wind,
And the word is not in them.
Thus it will be done to them!"

*Judgment Proclaimed*

14¶ Therefore, thus says the LORD, the God of hosts,
"Because you have spoken this word,
Behold, I am making My words in your mouth fire
And this people wood, and it will consume them.
15 "Behold, I am bringing a nation against you from afar,
O house of Israel," declares the LORD.
"It is an enduring nation,
It is an ancient nation,
A nation whose language you do not know,
Nor can you understand what they say.
16 "Their quiver is like an open grave,
All of them are mighty men.
17 "And they will devour your harvest and your food;
They will devour your sons and your daughters;
They will devour your flocks and your herds;
They will devour your vines and your fig trees;
They will demolish with the sword your fortified cities
in which you trust.
18¶ "Yet even in those days," declares the LORD, "I will not
make you a complete destruction.
19"And it shall come about when they say, 'Why has the LORD
our God done all these things to us?' then you shall say to them,
'As you have forsaken Me and served foreign gods in your land,
so you shall serve strangers in a land that is not yours.'
20¶ "Declare this in the house of Jacob
And proclaim it in Judah, saying,
21 'Hear this, O foolish and senseless people,
Who have eyes, but see not;
Who have ears, but hear not.
22 'Do you not fear Me?' declares the LORD.
'Do you not tremble in My presence?
For I have placed the sand as a boundary for the sea,
An eternal decree, so it cannot cross over it.
Though the waves toss, yet they cannot prevail;
Though they roar, yet they cannot cross over it.
23 'But this people has a stubborn and rebellious heart;
They have turned aside and departed.

NAS [a] Lit., *He is not*

## New International

7"Why should I forgive you?
Your children have forsaken me
and sworn by gods that are not gods.
I supplied all their needs,
yet they committed adultery
and thronged to the houses of prostitutes.
8They are well-fed, lusty stallions,
each neighing for another man's wife.
9Should I not punish them for this?"
declares the LORD.
"Should I not avenge myself
on such a nation as this?

10"Go through her vineyards and ravage them,
but do not destroy them completely.
Strip off her branches,
for these people do not belong to the LORD.
11The house of Israel and the house of Judah
have been utterly unfaithful to me,"
declares the LORD.

12They have lied about the LORD;
they said, "He will do nothing!
No harm will come to us;
we will never see sword or famine.
13The prophets are but wind
and the word is not in them;
so let what they say be done to them."

14Therefore this is what the LORD God Almighty says:

"Because the people have spoken these words,
I will make my words in your mouth a fire
and these people the wood it consumes.
15O house of Israel," declares the LORD,
"I am bringing a distant nation against you—
an ancient and enduring nation,
a people whose language you do not know,
whose speech you do not understand.
16Their quivers are like an open grave;
all of them are mighty warriors.
17They will devour your harvests and food,
devour your sons and daughters;
they will devour your flocks and herds,
devour your vines and fig trees.
With the sword they will destroy
the fortified cities in which you trust.

18"Yet even in those days," declares the LORD, "I will not destroy you completely. 19And when the people ask, 'Why has the
LORD our God done all this to us?' you will tell them, 'As you have
forsaken me and served foreign gods in your own land, so now
you will serve foreigners in a land not your own.'

20"Announce this to the house of Jacob
and proclaim it in Judah:
21Hear this, you foolish and senseless people,
who have eyes but do not see,
who have ears but do not hear:
22Should you not fear me?" declares the LORD.
"Should you not tremble in my presence?
I made the sand a boundary for the sea,
an everlasting barrier it cannot cross.
The waves may roll, but they cannot prevail;
they may roar, but they cannot cross it.
23But these people have stubborn and rebellious hearts;
they have turned aside and gone away.

## King James

24Neither say they in their heart, Let us now fear the LORD our God, that giveth rain, both the former and the latter, in his season: he reserveth unto us the appointed weeks of the harvest.

25¶ Your iniquities have turned away these *things*, and your sins have withholden good *things* from you.

26For among my people are found wicked *men:* they lay wait, as he that setteth snares; they set a trap, they catch men.

27As a cage is full of birds, so *are* their houses full of deceit: therefore they are become great, and waxen rich.

28They are waxen fat, they shine: yea, they overpass the deeds of the wicked: they judge not the cause, the cause of the fatherless, yet they prosper; and the right of the needy do they not judge.

29Shall I not visit for these *things?* saith the LORD: shall not my soul be avenged on such a nation as this?

30¶ A wonderful and horrible thing is committed in the land;

31The prophets prophesy falsely, and the priests bear rule by their means; and my people love *to have it* so: and what will ye do in the end thereof?

**6** O YE children of Benjamin, gather yourselves to flee out of the midst of Jerusalem, and blow the trumpet in Tekoa, and set up a sign of fire in Beth-haccerem: for evil appeareth out of the north, and great destruction.

2I have likened the daughter of Zion to a comely and delicate *woman.*

3The shepherds with their flocks shall come unto her; they shall pitch *their* tents against her round about; they shall feed every one in his place.

4Prepare ye war against her; arise, and let us go up at noon. Woe unto us! for the day goeth away, for the shadows of the evening are stretched out.

5Arise, and let us go by night, and let us destroy her palaces.

6¶ For thus hath the LORD of hosts said, Hew ye down trees, and cast a mount against Jerusalem: this *is* the city to be visited; she *is* wholly oppression in the midst of her.

7As a fountain casteth out her waters, so she casteth out her wickedness: violence and spoil is heard in her; before me continually *is* grief and wounds.

8Be thou instructed, O Jerusalem, lest my soul depart from thee; lest I make thee desolate, a land not inhabited.

## Amplified

24Nor do they say in their heart, Let us now reverently fear *and* worship the Lord our God, Who gives rain, both the autumn and the spring *rain* in its season, Who reserves *and* keeps for us the appointed weeks of the harvest.

25Your iniquities have turned these blessings away, and your sins have kept good *harvests* from you.

26For among My people are found wicked men; they watch as fowlers do who lie in wait; they set a trap, they catch men.

27As a cage is full of birds, so are their houses full of deceit *and* treachery; therefore they have become great and grown rich,

28They have grown fat *and* sleek. Yes, they surpass in deeds of wickedness. They do not judge *and* plead with justice the cause of the fatherless that it may prosper, and they do not defend the rights of the needy.

29Shall I not punish them for these things? says the Lord. Shall not I avenge Myself on such a nation as this?

30An appalling and horrible thing— *bringing* desolation and destruction—has come to pass in the land:

31The prophets prophesy falsely, and the priests bear rule at the hands *and* by means of the prophets. And My people love to have it so, but what will you do when the end comes?

**6** FLEE FOR safety, you children of Benjamin, out of the midst of Jerusalem, and blow the trumpet in Tekoa [a town far south in Judea], and raise a fire signal on Beth-haccherem [a mountain to the south]; for evil is looking forth with eagerness from the north, and great destruction.

2The comely and delicate one, *Jerusalem*, the daughter of Zion, I will destroy—to a pasturage, yes, a luxurious *pasturage* have I likened *her.*

3Shepherds with their flocks shall come against her; they shall pitch their tents round about against her; they shall pasture, each one in his place [eating up all her luxurious herbage on every side].

4Prepare yourselves for war against her, *they cry;* up, let us attack her at noon! Alas! for the day declines, the evening shadows lengthen.

5Arise! let us go by night and destroy her palaces!

6For the Lord of hosts has said, Hew down her trees, and cast up a siege mound against Jerusalem. This is the city which must be punished; there is nothing but oppression within her.

7As a fountain wells up *and* casts forth its waters *and* keeps them fresh, so she is *continually* casting out *fresh* wickedness: violence and destruction *are* heard within her; sickness and wounds are continually before Me.

8Be corrected, reformed, instructed *and* warned, O Jerusalem, lest I be alienated *and* parted from you; lest I make you a desolation, an uninhabited land.

## New American Standard

24 'They do not say in their heart,
"Let us now fear the LORD our God,
Who gives rain in its season,
Both the autumn rain and the spring rain,
Who keeps for us
The appointed weeks of the harvest."
25 'Your iniquities have turned these away,
And your sins have withheld good from you.
26 'For wicked men are found among My people,
They watch like fowlers lying in wait;
They set a trap,
They catch men.
27 'Like a cage full of birds,
So their houses are full of deceit;
Therefore they have become great and rich.
28 'They are fat, they are sleek,
They also [a]excel in deeds of wickedness;
They do not plead the cause,
The cause of the orphan, that they may prosper;
And they do not defend the rights of the poor.
29 'Shall I not punish these *people?'* declares the LORD,
'On a nation such as this
Shall I not avenge Myself?'

30¶ "An appalling and horrible thing
Has happened in the land:
31 The prophets prophesy falsely,
And the priests rule on their *own* authority;
And My people love it so!
But what will you do at the end of it?

*Destruction of Jerusalem Impending*

6 "FLEE FOR safety, O sons of Benjamin,
From the midst of Jerusalem!
Now blow a trumpet in Tekoa,
And raise a signal over [b]Beth-haccerem;
For evil looks down from the north,
And a great destruction.
2 "The comely and dainty one, the daughter of Zion, I will cut off.
3 "Shepherds and their flocks will come to her,
They will pitch *their* tents around her,
They will pasture each in his place.
4 "Prepare war against her;
Arise, and let us attack at noon.
Woe to us, for the day declines,
For the shadows of the evening lengthen!
5 "Arise, and let us attack by night
And destroy her palaces!"
6 For thus says the LORD of hosts,
"Cut down her trees,
And cast up a siege against Jerusalem.
This is the city to be punished,
In whose midst there is only oppression.
7 "As a well keeps its waters fresh,
So she keeps fresh her wickedness.
Violence and destruction are heard in her;
Sickness and wounds are ever before Me.
8 "Be warned, O Jerusalem,
Lest I be alienated from you;
Lest I make you a desolation,
A land not inhabited."

NAS [a] Or, *overlook deeds* [b] I.e., house of the vineyard

## New International

24 They do not say to themselves,
'Let us fear the LORD our God,
who gives autumn and spring rains in season,
who assures us of the regular weeks of harvest.'
25 Your wrongdoings have kept these away;
your sins have deprived you of good.

26 "Among my people are wicked men
who lie in wait like men who snare birds
and like those who set traps to catch men.
27 Like cages full of birds,
their houses are full of deceit;
they have become rich and powerful
28 and have grown fat and sleek.
Their evil deeds have no limit;
they do not plead the case of the fatherless to win it,
they do not defend the rights of the poor.
29 Should I not punish them for this?"
declares the LORD.
"Should I not avenge myself
on such a nation as this?
30 "A horrible and shocking thing
has happened in the land:
31 The prophets prophesy lies,
the priests rule by their own authority,
and my people love it this way.
But what will you do in the end?

*Jerusalem Under Siege*

6 "FLEE FOR safety, people of Benjamin!
Flee from Jerusalem!
Sound the trumpet in Tekoa!
Raise the signal over Beth Hakkerem!
For disaster looms out of the north,
even terrible destruction.
2 I will destroy the Daughter of Zion,
so beautiful and delicate.
3 Shepherds with their flocks will come against her;
they will pitch their tents around her,
each tending his own portion."

4 "Prepare for battle against her!
Arise, let us attack at noon!
But, alas, the daylight is fading,
and the shadows of evening grow long.
5 So arise, let us attack at night
and destroy her fortresses!"

6 This is what the LORD Almighty says:

"Cut down the trees
and build siege ramps against Jerusalem.
This city must be punished;
it is filled with oppression.
7 As a well pours out its water,
so she pours out her wickedness.
Violence and destruction resound in her;
her sickness and wounds are ever before me.
8 Take warning, O Jerusalem,
or I will turn away from you
and make your land desolate
so no one can live in it."

## King James

9¶ Thus saith the LORD of hosts, They shall thoroughly glean the remnant of Israel as a vine: turn back thine hand as a grapegatherer into the baskets.

10To whom shall I speak, and give warning, that they may hear? behold, their ear *is* uncircumcised, and they cannot hearken: behold, the word of the LORD is unto them a reproach; they have no delight in it.

11Therefore I am full of the fury of the LORD; I am weary with holding in: I will pour it out upon the children abroad, and upon the assembly of young men together: for even the husband with the wife shall be taken, the aged with *him that is* full of days.

12And their houses shall be turned unto others, *with their* fields and wives together: for I will stretch out my hand upon the inhabitants of the land, saith the LORD.

13For from the least of them even unto the greatest of them every one *is* given to covetousness; and from the prophet even unto the priest every one dealeth falsely.

14They have healed also the hurt *of the daughter* of my people slightly, saying, Peace, peace; when *there is* no peace.

15Were they ashamed when they had committed abomination? nay, they were not at all ashamed, neither could they blush: therefore they shall fall among them that fall: at the time *that* I visit them they shall be cast down, saith the LORD.

16Thus saith the LORD, Stand ye in the ways, and see, and ask for the old paths, where *is* the good way, and walk therein, and ye shall find rest for your souls. But they said, We will not walk *therein.*

17Also I set watchmen over you, *saying,* Hearken to the sound of the trumpet. But they said, We will not hearken.

18¶ Therefore hear, ye nations, and know, O congregation, what *is* among them.

19Hear, O earth: behold, I will bring evil upon this people, *even* the fruit of their thoughts, because they have not hearkened unto my words, nor to my law, but rejected it.

20To what purpose cometh there to me incense from Sheba, and the sweet cane from a far country? your burnt offerings *are* not acceptable, nor your sacrifices sweet unto me.

21Therefore thus saith the LORD, Behold, I will lay stumblingblocks before this people, and the fathers and the sons together shall fall upon them; the neighbour and his friend shall perish.

## Amplified

9Thus says the Lord of hosts, They shall thoroughly glean as a vine what is left of Israel. Turn back your hand again *and* again [O minister of destruction] into the baskets, like a grape gatherer, *and* strip the tendrils *of the vine.*

10To whom shall I, *Jeremiah,* speak and give warning, that they may hear? Behold, their ear is uncircumcised [never brought into covenant with God, or consecrated to His service], and they cannot hear *or* obey. Behold, the word of the Lord has become to them a reproach *and* the object of their scorn; they have no delight in it.

11Therefore I am full of the wrath of the Lord; I am weary of restraining it. I will pour it out on the children in the street, and upon the gathering of young men together; for even the husband with the wife shall be taken, the aged with the very old.

12And their houses shall be turned over to others, their fields and wives together; for I will stretch out My hand against the inhabitants of the land, says the Lord.

13For from the least of them even to the greatest of them every one is given to covetousness—to greed for unjust gain; and from the prophet even to the priest every one deals falsely.

14They have healed also the wound of the daughter of My people lightly *and* neglectfully, saying, Peace, peace, when there is no peace.

15Were they brought to shame because they had committed abominations—extremely disgusting and vile? No, they were not at all ashamed, nor could they blush [at their idolatry]. Therefore they shall fall among those who fall; at the time that I punish them they shall be overthrown, says the Lord.

16Thus says the Lord, Stand by the roads and look, and ask for the eternal paths, where is the good, old way; then walk in it, and you will find rest for your souls. But they said, We will not walk in it! [Matt. 11:29.]

17Also I set watchmen over you, saying, Hear *and* obey the sound of the trumpet. But they said, We will not listen *or* obey.

18Therefore hear, O *Gentile* nations, and know, O congregation [of believing ones], what *great things I will do* to them.

19Hear, O earth; behold, I am bringing evil upon this people, the fruit of their thoughts— *their* schemes and devices—because they have not listened *and* obeyed My words, and as for My law, they have rejected it.

20To what purpose does frankincense come to Me from Sheba [in southwest Arabia], and the sweet cane from a far country? Your burnt offerings are not acceptable, nor are your sacrifices sweet *or* pleasing to Me.

21Therefore thus says the Lord, Behold, I will lay stumblingblocks before this people, and the fathers and the sons together shall stumble against them; the neighbor and his friend shall perish.

## New American Standard

9¶ Thus says the LORD of hosts,
"They will thoroughly glean as the vine the remnant of Israel;
Pass your hand again like a grape gatherer
Over the branches."
10 To whom shall I speak and give warning,
That they may hear?
Behold, their ears are closed,
And they cannot listen.
Behold, the word of the LORD has become a reproach to them;
They have no delight in it.
11 But I am full of the wrath of the LORD:
I am weary with holding *it* in.
"Pour *it* out on the children in the street,
And on the gathering of young men together;
For both husband and wife shall be taken,
The aged and the very old.
12 "And their houses shall be turned over to others,
Their fields and their wives together;
For I will stretch out My hand
Against the inhabitants of the land," declares the LORD.
13 "For from the least of them even to the greatest of them,
Everyone is greedy for gain,
And from the prophet even to the priest
Everyone deals falsely.
14 "And they have healed the brokenness of My people superficially,
Saying, 'Peace, peace,'
But there is no peace.
15 "Were they ashamed because of the abomination they have done?
They were not even ashamed at all;
They did not even know how to blush.
Therefore they shall fall among those who fall;
At the time that I punish them,
They shall be cast down," says the LORD.

16¶ Thus says the LORD,
"Stand by the ways and see and ask for the ancient paths,
Where the good way is, and walk in it;
And you shall find rest for your souls.
But they said, 'We will not walk *in it*.'
17 "And I set watchmen over you, *saying*,
'Listen to the sound of the trumpet!'
But they said, 'We will not listen.'
18 "Therefore hear, O nations,
And know, O congregation, what is among them.
19 "Hear, O earth: behold, I am bringing disaster on this people,
The fruit of their plans,
Because they have not listened to My words,
And as for My law, they have rejected it also.
20 "For what purpose does frankincense come to Me from Sheba,
And the sweet cane from a distant land?
Your burnt offerings are not acceptable,
And your sacrifices are not pleasing to Me."
21 Therefore, thus says the LORD,
"Behold, I am laying stumbling blocks before this people.
And they will stumble against them,
Fathers and sons together;
Neighbor and friend will perish."

## New International

9This is what the LORD Almighty says:
"Let them glean the remnant of Israel
as thoroughly as a vine;
pass your hand over the branches again,
like one gathering grapes."
10To whom can I speak and give warning?
Who will listen to me?
Their ears are closed[a]
so they cannot hear.
The word of the LORD is offensive to them;
they find no pleasure in it.
11But I am full of the wrath of the LORD,
and I cannot hold it in.

"Pour it out on the children in the street
and on the young men gathered together;
both husband and wife will be caught in it,
and the old, those weighed down with years.
12Their houses will be turned over to others,
together with their fields and their wives,
when I stretch out my hand
against those who live in the land,"
declares the LORD.
13"From the least to the greatest,
all are greedy for gain;
prophets and priests alike,
all practice deceit.
14They dress the wound of my people
as though it were not serious.
'Peace, peace,' they say,
when there is no peace.
15Are they ashamed of their loathsome conduct?
No, they have no shame at all;
they do not even know how to blush.
So they will fall among the fallen;
they will be brought down when I punish them,"
says the LORD.

16This is what the LORD says:

"Stand at the crossroads and look;
ask for the ancient paths,
ask where the good way is, and walk in it,
and you will find rest for your souls.
But you said, 'We will not walk in it.'
17I appointed watchmen over you and said,
'Listen to the sound of the trumpet!'
But you said, 'We will not listen.'
18Therefore hear, O nations;
observe, O witnesses,
what will happen to them.
19Hear, O earth:
I am bringing disaster on this people,
the fruit of their schemes,
because they have not listened to my words
and have rejected my law.
20What do I care about incense from Sheba
or sweet calamus from a distant land?
Your burnt offerings are not acceptable;
your sacrifices do not please me."

21Therefore this is what the LORD says:

"I will put obstacles before this people.
Fathers and sons alike will stumble over them;
neighbors and friends will perish."

NIV [a] *10* Hebrew *uncircumcised*

## King James

22 Thus saith the LORD, Behold, a people cometh from the north country, and a great nation shall be raised from the sides of the earth.

23 They shall lay hold on bow and spear; they *are* cruel, and have no mercy; their voice roareth like the sea; and they ride upon horses, set in array as men for war against thee, O daughter of Zion.

24 We have heard the fame thereof: our hands wax feeble: anguish hath taken hold of us, *and* pain, as of a woman in travail.

25 Go not forth into the field, nor walk by the way; for the sword of the enemy *and* fear *is* on every side.

26 ¶ O daughter of my people, gird *thee* with sackcloth, and wallow thyself in ashes: make thee mourning, *as for* an only son, most bitter lamentation: for the spoiler shall suddenly come upon us.

27 I have set thee *for* a tower *and* a fortress among my people, that thou mayest know and try their way.

28 They *are* all grievous revolters, walking with slanders: *they are* brass and iron; they *are* all corrupters.

29 The bellows are burned, the lead is consumed of the fire; the founder melteth in vain: for the wicked are not plucked away.

30 Reprobate silver shall *men* call them, because the LORD hath rejected them.

**7** THE WORD that came to Jeremiah from the LORD, saying,

2 Stand in the gate of the LORD's house, and proclaim there this word, and say, Hear the word of the LORD, all *ye of* Judah, that enter in at these gates to worship the LORD.

3 Thus saith the LORD of hosts, the God of Israel, Amend your ways and your doings, and I will cause you to dwell in this place.

4 Trust ye not in lying words, saying, The temple of the LORD, The temple of the LORD, The temple of the LORD, *are* these.

5 For if ye thoroughly amend your ways and your doings; if ye thoroughly execute judgment between a man and his neighbour;

6 *If* ye oppress not the stranger, the fatherless, and the widow, and shed not innocent blood in this place, neither walk after other gods to your hurt:

7 Then will I cause you to dwell in this place, in the land that I gave to your fathers, for ever and ever.

8 ¶ Behold, ye trust in lying words, that cannot profit.

9 Will ye steal, murder, and commit adultery, and swear falsely, and burn incense unto Baal, and walk after other gods whom ye know not;

## Amplified

22 Thus says the Lord, Behold, a people is coming from the north country, and a great nation is arousing itself from the ends of the earth.

23 They lay hold on bow and spear, they are cruel (ruthless and inhuman), and have no mercy, their voice sounds like the roaring sea; they ride on horses, every one set in array as a man for battle, against you, O daughter of Zion!

24 We have heard the report of it; our hands become feeble *and* helpless; anguish has taken hold of us, *and* pangs as of a woman in childbirth.

25 Go not out into the field, nor walk on the road, for the enemy *is armed with* the sword; terror is on every side.

26 O daughter of my people [says Jeremiah], gird yourself with sackcloth, and wallow yourself in ashes; make mourning as for an only son, most bitter lamentation; for the destroyer will suddenly come upon us [on prophet and people].

27 I, *says the Lord,* have set you, *Jeremiah, as* an assayer *and* a prover of ore among My people, that you may know and try their doings, *and be* as a *watch*tower.

28 They are all the worst *kind* of rebels *and* utter revolters *against God,* going about *publishing* slanders. They are [not gold and silver ore, but] bronze and iron; they are all corrupters.

29 The bellows blow fiercely, the lead is consumed by the fire; in vain do they continue refining, for the wicked [the dross] are not removed.

30 Reprobate silver men will call them [only dross, without good metal], because the Lord has rejected them.

**7** THE WORD that came to Jeremiah from the Lord, saying,

2 Stand in the gate of the Lord's house, and proclaim there this word, and say, Hear the word of the Lord, all you of Judah, who enter in at these gates to worship the Lord.

3 Thus says the Lord of hosts, the God of Israel, Amend your ways and your doings, and I will cause you to dwell in this place.

4 Trust not in the lying words [of the false prophets, who maintain that God will protect Jerusalem because His temple is there], saying, The temple of the Lord, the temple of the Lord, the temple of the Lord is this.

5 For if you thoroughly amend your ways and your doings, if you thoroughly *and* truly execute justice between every man and his neighbor,

6 If you do not oppress the transient *and* the alien, the fatherless and the widow, or shed innocent blood [by oppression and by judicial murders] in *Jerusalem,* or go after other gods to your own hurt,

7 Then I will cause you *to dwell in* this place, in the land that I gave of old to your fathers to dwell in for ever.

8 Behold, you trust in lying words that cannot benefit—so that you do not profit.

9 Will you steal, murder, commit adultery, swear falsely, burn incense to Baal, and go after other gods that you have not known,

# New American Standard

*The Enemy from the North*

22¶ Thus says the LORD,
"Behold, a people is coming from the north land,
And a great nation will be aroused from the remote
parts of the earth.
23 "They seize bow and spear;
They are cruel and have no mercy;
Their voice roars like the sea,
And they ride on horses,
Arrayed as a man for the battle
Against you, O daughter of Zion!"
24 We have heard the report of it;
Our hands are limp.
Anguish has seized us,
Pain as of a woman in childbirth.
25 Do not go out into the field,
And do not walk on the road,
For the enemy has a sword,
Terror is on every side.
26 O daughter of my people, put on sackcloth
And roll in ashes;
Mourn as for an only son,
A lamentation most bitter.
For suddenly the destroyer
Will come upon us.
27¶ "I have made you an assayer *and* a tester among My
people,
That you may know and assay their way."
28 All of them are stubbornly rebellious,
Going about as a talebearer.
*They are* bronze and iron;
They, all of them, are corrupt.
29 The bellows blow fiercely,
The lead is consumed by the fire;
In vain the refining goes on,
But the wicked are not separated.
30 They call them rejected silver,
Because the LORD has rejected them.

*Message at the Temple Gate*

**7** THE WORD that came to Jeremiah from the LORD, saying,
2"Stand in the gate of the LORD's house and proclaim there
this word, and say, 'Hear the word of the LORD, all you of Judah,
who enter by these gates to worship the LORD!' "
3Thus says the LORD of hosts, the God of Israel, "Amend your
ways and your deeds, and I will let you dwell in this place.
4"Do not trust in deceptive words, saying, 'This is the temple
of the LORD, the temple of the LORD, the temple of the LORD.'
5"For if you truly amend your ways and your deeds, if you
truly practice justice between a man and his neighbor,
6 *if* you do not oppress the alien, the orphan, or the widow,
and do not shed innocent blood in this place, nor walk after other
gods to your own ruin,
7then I will let you dwell in this place, in the land that I gave
to your fathers forever and ever.
8¶ "Behold, you are trusting in deceptive words to no avail.
9"Will you steal, murder, and commit adultery, and swear
falsely, and offer sacrifices to Baal, and walk after other gods that
you have not known,

# New International

22This is what the LORD says:
"Look, an army is coming
from the land of the north;
a great nation is being stirred up
from the ends of the earth.
23They are armed with bow and spear;
they are cruel and show no mercy.
They sound like the roaring sea
as they ride on their horses;
they come like men in battle formation
to attack you, O Daughter of Zion."
24We have heard reports about them,
and our hands hang limp.
Anguish has gripped us,
pain like that of a woman in labor.
25Do not go out to the fields
or walk on the roads,
for the enemy has a sword,
and there is terror on every side.
26O my people, put on sackcloth
and roll in ashes;
mourn with bitter wailing
as for an only son,
for suddenly the destroyer
will come upon us.
27"I have made you a tester of metals
and my people the ore,
that you may observe
and test their ways.
28They are all hardened rebels,
going about to slander.
They are bronze and iron;
they all act corruptly.
29The bellows blow fiercely
to burn away the lead with fire,
but the refining goes on in vain;
the wicked are not purged out.
30They are called rejected silver,
because the LORD has rejected them."

*False Religion Worthless*

**7** THIS IS the word that came to Jeremiah from the LORD:
2"Stand at the gate of the LORD's house and there proclaim
this message:
" 'Hear the word of the LORD, all you people of Judah who come
through these gates to worship the LORD. 3This is what the LORD
Almighty, the God of Israel, says: Reform your ways and your
actions, and I will let you live in this place. 4Do not trust in
deceptive words and say, "This is the temple of the LORD, the
temple of the LORD, the temple of the LORD!" 5If you really change
your ways and your actions and deal with each other justly, 6if you
do not oppress the alien, the fatherless or the widow and do not
shed innocent blood in this place, and if you do not follow other
gods to your own harm, 7then I will let you live in this place, in
the land I gave your forefathers for ever and ever. 8But look, you
are trusting in deceptive words that are worthless.
9" 'Will you steal and murder, commit adultery and perjury,[a]
burn incense to Baal and follow other gods you have not known,

NIV [a] 9 Or *and swear by false gods*

## King James

10And come and stand before me in this house, which is called
by my name, and say, We are delivered to do all these abominations?
11Is this house, which is called by my name, become a den of
robbers in your eyes? Behold, even I have seen *it,* saith the LORD.
12But go ye now unto my place which *was* in Shiloh, where I set
my name at the first, and see what I did to it for the wickedness
of my people Israel.
13And now, because ye have done all these works, saith the
LORD, and I spake unto you, rising up early and speaking, but ye
heard not; and I called you, but ye answered not;
14Therefore will I do unto *this* house, which is called by my
name, wherein ye trust, and unto the place which I gave to you
and to your fathers, as I have done to Shiloh.
15And I will cast you out of my sight, as I have cast out all your
brethren, *even* the whole seed of Ephraim.
16Therefore pray not thou for this people, neither lift up cry nor
prayer for them, neither make intercession to me: for I will not hear
thee.
17¶ Seest thou not what they do in the cities of Judah and in the
streets of Jerusalem?
18The children gather wood, and the fathers kindle the fire, and
the women knead *their* dough, to make cakes to the queen of
heaven, and to pour out drink offerings unto other gods, that they
may provoke me to anger.
19Do they provoke me to anger? saith the LORD: *do they* not
*provoke* themselves to the confusion of their own faces?
20Therefore thus saith the Lord GOD; Behold, mine anger and
my fury shall be poured out upon this place, upon man, and upon
beast, and upon the trees of the field, and upon the fruit of the
ground; and it shall burn, and shall not be quenched.
21¶ Thus saith the LORD of hosts, the God of Israel; Put your
burnt offerings unto your sacrifices, and eat flesh.
22For I spake not unto your fathers, nor commanded them in
the day that I brought them out of the land of Egypt, concerning
burnt offerings or sacrifices:
23But this thing commanded I them, saying, Obey my voice,
and I will be your God, and ye shall be my people: and walk ye
in all the ways that I have commanded you, that it may be well
unto you.
24But they hearkened not, nor inclined their ear, but walked in
the counsels *and* in the imagination of their evil heart, and went
backward, and not forward.
25Since the day that your fathers came forth out of the land of
Egypt unto this day I have even sent unto you all my servants the
prophets, daily rising up early and sending *them:*
26Yet they hearkened not unto me, nor inclined their ear, but
hardened their neck: they did worse than their fathers.
27Therefore thou shalt speak all these words unto them; but
they will not hearken to thee: thou shalt also call unto them; but
they will not answer thee.
28But thou shalt say unto them, This *is* a nation that obeyeth not
the voice of the LORD their God, nor receiveth correction: truth is
perished, and is cut off from their mouth.
29¶ Cut off thine hair, *O Jerusalem,* and cast *it* away, and take
up a lamentation on high places; for the LORD hath rejected and
forsaken the generation of his wrath.
30For the children of Judah have done evil in my sight, saith the
LORD: they have set their abominations in the house which is called
by my name, to pollute it.

## Amplified

10And *then dare to* come and stand before Me in this house,
which is called by My name, and say, [By the discharge of this
religious formality] we are set free!—only to go on with this
wickedness *and* these abominations?
11Has this house, which is called by My name, become a den
of robbers in your eyes [a place of retreat for you between acts of
violence]? Behold, I Myself have seen it, says the Lord.
12But go now to My place which was in Shiloh [in Ephraim],
where I set My name at the first, and see what I did to it for the
wickedness of My people Israel. [I Sam. 4:10-18.]
13And now, because you have done all these things, says the
Lord, and *because* when I spoke to you persistently—even rising up
early and speaking—you did not listen, and when I called you, you
did not answer,
14Therefore will I do to this house [the temple], which is called
by My name *and* in which you trust, and to the place which I gave
to you and to your fathers, as I did to Shiloh.
15And I will cast you out of My sight, as I have cast out all your
brethren, even the whole posterity of Ephraim.
16Therefore do not pray for this people *of Judah,* or lift up cry
or entreaty for them, or make intercession to Me, for I will not
listen *or* hear you.
17Do you not see what they are doing in the cities of Judah and
in the streets of Jerusalem?
18The children gather wood, the fathers kindle the fire, and the
women knead the dough, to make cakes for the queen of heaven
[the moon]; and they pour out drink offerings to other gods, that
they may provoke Me to anger!
19Is it I Whom they provoke to anger? says the Lord. *Is it* not
themselves, *whom they provoke* to their own confusion *and* vexation
*and* to their own shame?
20Therefore thus says the Lord God: Behold, My anger and My
wrath will be poured out on this place, on man and beast, on the
trees of the field and the fruit of the ground; it shall burn and shall
not be quenched.
21Thus says the Lord of hosts, the God of Israel: Add your burnt
offerings to your sacrifices, and eat the flesh [if you will. It will avail
you nothing].
22For in the day that I brought them out of the land of Egypt,
I did not speak to your fathers or command them concerning burnt
offerings or sacrifices.
23But this thing I did command them: Listen to *and* obey My
voice, and I will be your God, and you shall be My people; and
walk in the whole way that I command you, that it may be well
with you.
24But they would not listen *and* obey, or bend their ear *to Me,*
but followed the counsels *and* the stubborn promptings of their
own evil hearts *and* minds, and they turned their back *and* went
in reverse instead of forward.
25Since the day that your fathers came forth out of the land of
Egypt to this day, I have persistently sent to you My servants all
the prophets, sending them daily, early and late.
26Yet the people would not listen *and* obey Me or bend their ear
*to Me,* but stiffened their neck and behaved worse than their fathers.
27Speak all these words to them, but they will not listen *and*
obey you; also call to them, but they will not answer you.
28Yet you shall say to them, This is the nation that did not obey
the voice of the Lord their God, or receive instruction *and* correction *and* warning; truth *and* faithfulness *have* perished, and *have*
completely gone from their mouths.
29Cut off your hair—your crown— *O Jerusalem,* and cast it away,
and take up a lamentation on the bare heights; for the Lord has
rejected and forsaken the generation of His wrath.
30For the children of Judah have done evil in My sight, says the
Lord; they have set their abominations—extremely disgusting and
shamefully vile—in the house which is called by My name, to
defile it.

## New American Standard

10then come and stand before Me in this house, which is called
by My name, and say, 'We are delivered!'—that you may do all
these abominations?
11"Has this house, which is called by My name, become a den
of robbers in your sight? Behold, I, even I, have seen *it*," declares
the LORD.
12¶ "But go now to My place which was in Shiloh, where I made
My name dwell at the first, and see what I did to it because of the
wickedness of My people Israel.
13"And now, because you have done all these things," declares
the LORD, "and I spoke to you, rising up early and speaking, but
you did not hear, and I called you but you did not answer,
14therefore, I will do to the house which is called by My name,
in which you trust, and to the place which I gave you and your
fathers, as I did to Shiloh.
15"And I will cast you out of My sight, as I have cast out all your
brothers, all the offspring of Ephraim.
16¶ "As for you, do not pray for this people, and do not lift up
cry or prayer for them, and do not intercede with Me; for I do not
hear you.
17"Do you not see what they are doing in the cities of Judah and
in the streets of Jerusalem?
18"The children gather wood, and the fathers kindle the fire,
and the women knead dough to make cakes for the queen of
heaven; and *they* pour out libations to other gods in order to spite
Me.
19"Do they spite Me?" declares the LORD. "Is it not themselves
*they spite*, to their own shame?"
20Therefore thus says the Lord GOD, "Behold, My anger and My
wrath will be poured out on this place, on man and on beast and
on the trees of the field and on the fruit of the ground; and it will
burn and not be quenched."
21¶ Thus says the LORD of hosts, the God of Israel, "Add your
burnt offerings to your sacrifices and eat flesh.
22"For I did not speak to your fathers, or command them in the
day that I brought them out of the land of Egypt, concerning burnt
offerings and sacrifices.
23"But this is what I commanded them, saying, 'Obey My voice,
and I will be your God, and you will be My people; and you will
walk in all the way which I command you, that it may be well with
you.'
24"Yet they did not obey or incline their ear, but walked in *their
own* counsels *and* in the stubbornness of their evil heart, and went
backward and not forward.
25"Since the day that your fathers came out of the land of Egypt
until this day, I have sent you all My servants the prophets, daily
rising early and sending *them*.
26"Yet they did not listen to Me or incline their ear, but stiffened
their neck; they did evil more than their fathers.
27¶ "And you shall speak all these words to them, but they will
not listen to you; and you shall call to them, but they will not
answer you.
28"And you shall say to them, 'This is the nation that did not
obey the voice of the LORD their God or accept correction; truth has
perished and has been cut off from their mouth.
29 'Cut off your hair and cast *it* away,
And take up a lamentation on the bare heights;
For the LORD has rejected and forsaken
The generation of His wrath.'
30"For the sons of Judah have done that which is evil in My
sight," declares the LORD, "they have set their detestable things
in the house which is called by My name, to defile it.

## New International

10and then come and stand before me in this house, which bears
my Name, and say, "We are safe"—safe to do all these detestable
things? 11Has this house, which bears my Name, become a den of
robbers to you? But I have been watching! declares the LORD.
12" 'Go now to the place in Shiloh where I first made a dwelling
for my Name, and see what I did to it because of the wickedness
of my people Israel. 13While you were doing all these things,
declares the LORD, I spoke to you again and again, but you did not
listen; I called you, but you did not answer. 14Therefore, what I did
to Shiloh I will now do to the house that bears my Name, the
temple you trust in, the place I gave to you and your fathers. 15I
will thrust you from my presence, just as I did all your brothers,
the people of Ephraim.'
16"So do not pray for this people nor offer any plea or petition
for them; do not plead with me, for I will not listen to you. 17Do
you not see what they are doing in the towns of Judah and in the
streets of Jerusalem? 18The children gather wood, the fathers light
the fire, and the women knead the dough and make cakes of bread
for the Queen of Heaven. They pour out drink offerings to other
gods to provoke me to anger. 19But am I the one they are provoking? declares the LORD. Are they not rather harming themselves,
to their own shame?
20" 'Therefore this is what the Sovereign LORD says: My anger
and my wrath will be poured out on this place, on man and beast,
on the trees of the field and on the fruit of the ground, and it will
burn and not be quenched.
21" 'This is what the LORD Almighty, the God of Israel, says: Go
ahead, add your burnt offerings to your other sacrifices and eat the
meat yourselves! 22For when I brought your forefathers out of
Egypt and spoke to them, I did not just give them commands about
burnt offerings and sacrifices, 23but I gave them this command:
Obey me, and I will be your God and you will be my people. Walk
in all the ways I command you, that it may go well with you. 24But
they did not listen or pay attention; instead, they followed the
stubborn inclinations of their evil hearts. They went backward and
not forward. 25From the time your forefathers left Egypt until now,
day after day, again and again I sent you my servants the prophets.
26But they did not listen to me or pay attention. They were stiff-
necked and did more evil than their forefathers.'
27"When you tell them all this, they will not listen to you; when
you call to them, they will not answer. 28Therefore say to them,
'This is the nation that has not obeyed the LORD its God or responded to correction. Truth has perished; it has vanished from
their lips. 29Cut off your hair and throw it away; take up a lament
on the barren heights, for the LORD has rejected and abandoned
this generation that is under his wrath.

*The Valley of Slaughter*

30" 'The people of Judah have done evil in my eyes, declares the
LORD. They have set up their detestable idols in the house that
bears my Name and have defiled it. 31They have built the high

## King James

31 And they have built the high places of Tophet, which *is* in the valley of the son of Hinnom, to burn their sons and their daughters in the fire; which I commanded *them* not, neither came it into my heart.

32 ¶ Therefore, behold, the days come, saith the LORD, that it shall no more be called Tophet, nor the valley of the son of Hinnom, but the valley of slaughter: for they shall bury in Tophet, till there be no place.

33 And the carcases of this people shall be meat for the fowls of the heaven, and for the beasts of the earth; and none shall fray *them* away.

34 Then will I cause to cease from the cities of Judah, and from the streets of Jerusalem, the voice of mirth, and the voice of gladness, the voice of the bridegroom, and the voice of the bride: for the land shall be desolate.

**8** AT THAT time, saith the LORD, they shall bring out the bones of the kings of Judah, and the bones of his princes, and the bones of the priests, and the bones of the prophets, and the bones of the inhabitants of Jerusalem, out of their graves:

2 And they shall spread them before the sun, and the moon, and all the host of heaven, whom they have loved, and whom they have served, and after whom they have walked, and whom they have sought, and whom they have worshipped: they shall not be gathered, nor be buried; they shall be for dung upon the face of the earth.

3 And death shall be chosen rather than life by all the residue of them that remain of this evil family, which remain in all the places whither I have driven them, saith the LORD of hosts.

4 ¶ Moreover thou shalt say unto them, Thus saith the LORD; Shall they fall, and not arise? shall he turn away, and not return?

5 Why *then* is this people of Jerusalem slidden back by a perpetual backsliding? they hold fast deceit, they refuse to return.

6 I hearkened and heard, *but* they spake not aright: no man repented him of his wickedness, saying, What have I done? every one turned to his course, as the horse rusheth into the battle.

7 Yea, the stork in the heaven knoweth her appointed times; and the turtle and the crane and the swallow observe the time of their coming; but my people know not the judgment of the LORD.

8 How do ye say, We *are* wise, and the law of the LORD *is* with us? Lo, certainly in vain made he *it*; the pen of the scribes *is* in vain.

9 The wise *men* are ashamed, they are dismayed and taken: lo, they have rejected the word of the LORD; and what wisdom *is* in them?

10 Therefore will I give their wives unto others, *and* their fields to them that shall inherit *them*: for every one from the least even unto the greatest is given to covetousness, from the prophet even unto the priest every one dealeth falsely.

11 For they have healed the hurt of the daughter of my people slightly, saying, Peace, peace; when *there is* no peace.

## Amplified

31 And they have built the high places of Topheth, which is in the valley of the son of Hinnom, to burn their sons and their daughters in the fire [in honor of Molech, the fire-god], which I did not command, nor did it come into My mind *or* heart.

32 Therefore, behold, the days will come, says the Lord, when it shall no more be called Topheth, or the Valley of the son of Hinnom, but the Valley of Slaughter; for [in bloody warfare] they will bury in Topheth till there is no more room *and* no place elsewhere to bury.

33 And the dead bodies of this people shall be meat for the fowls of the air, and for the beasts of the earth, and none will frighten them away.

34 Then will I cause to cease from the cities of Judah and from the streets of Jerusalem the voice of mirth and the voice of gladness, the voice of the bridegroom and the voice of the bride; for the land shall become a waste.

**8** AT THAT time, says the Lord, [the Babylonian army will break open the sepulchers, and] they shall bring out the [a]bones of the kings of Judah, the bones of its princes, the bones of the priests, the bones of the prophets, and the bones of the inhabitants of Jerusalem out of their graves.

2 And they will [carelessly] scatter the *corpses* before the sun, and the moon, and all the host of heaven, whom *the dead* have loved, and whom they have served, and after whom they have walked, and whom they have sought, inquired of *and* required, and whom they have worshiped. They shall not be gathered, or be buried; they shall be for [b]dung upon the face of the earth.

3 And death shall be chosen rather than life by all the residue of those who remain of this evil family [nation], who remain in all the places to which I have driven them, says the Lord of hosts.

4 Moreover, you, *Jeremiah*, shall say to them, Thus says the Lord: Shall men fall, and not rise up again? Shall one turn away *from God* and not repent *and* return *to Him*?

5 Why then is this people of Jerusalem turned away with a perpetual turning away *from Me*? They hold fast deceit [idolatry; false because men worship in it what is false, and it is false to the worshipers]; they refuse to repent *and* return *to God*.

6 I have listened and heard, but they have not spoken aright; no man repents of his wickedness, saying, What have I done! Every one turns to his [individual] course, as the horse rushes like a torrent into battle.

7 [Even the migratory birds are punctual to their seasons.] Yes, the stork [excelling in the great height of her flight] in the heavens knows her appointed times *of migration*. And the turtledove, the swallow and the crane observe the time of their return; but My people do not know the law of the Lord [which the lower animals instinctively recognize in so far as it applies to them].

8 How can you say, We are wise, and we have the written law of the Lord [and are learned in its language and teachings]? Lo, the truth is, the lying pen of the scribes has made of the law a falsehood [a mere code of ceremonial observances]. [Mark 7:13.]

9 The wise men shall be put to shame, they shall be dismayed and taken *captive*. Lo, they have rejected the word of the Lord, and what wisdom *and* broad, full intelligence is in them?

10 Therefore will I give their wives to others, and their fields to those who gain possession of them; for every one from the least even to the greatest is given to covetousness—is greedy for unjust gain; from the prophet even to the priest every one deals falsely.

11 For they have healed the wound of the daughter of My people only lightly *and* slightingly, saying, Peace, peace, when there is no peace.

**AMP** [a] "Of the motive of the disinterment [on the part of the Babylonian conquerors] the prophet says nothing. He had certainly no idea of its being the search for booty. He has in mind only the justice of God [which is concerned with punishment or penalties]." (Lange's Commentary.) [b] "Observe the irony. The stars look powerlessly down on the bones of their worshipers—while these send up a stench!" (Lange's Commentary.)

## New American Standard

31"And they have built the high places of Topheth, which is in the valley of the son of Hinnom, to burn their sons and their daughters in the fire, which I did not command, and it did not come into My mind.

32"Therefore, behold, days are coming," declares the LORD, "when it will no more be called Topheth, or the valley of the son of Hinnom, but the valley of the Slaughter; for they will bury in Topheth because there is no *other* place.

33"And the dead bodies of this people will be food for the birds of the sky, and for the beasts of the earth; and no one will frighten *them away*.

34"Then I will make to cease from the cities of Judah and from the streets of Jerusalem the voice of joy and the voice of gladness, the voice of the bridegroom and the voice of the bride; for the land will become a ruin.

*The Sin and Treachery of Judah*

8 "AT THAT time," declares the LORD, "they will bring out the bones of the kings of Judah, and the bones of its princes, and the bones of the priests, and the bones of the prophets, and the bones of the inhabitants of Jerusalem from their graves.

2"And they will spread them out to the sun, the moon, and to all the host of heaven, which they have loved, and which they have served, and which they have gone after, and which they have sought, and which they have worshiped. They will not be gathered or buried; they will be as dung on the face of the ground.

3"And death will be chosen rather than life by all the remnant that remains of this evil family, that remains in all the places to which I have driven them," declares the LORD of hosts.

4 "And you shall say to them, 'Thus says the LORD,
"Do *men* fall and not get up again?
Does one turn away and not repent?
5 "Why then has this people, Jerusalem,
Turned away in continual apostasy?
They hold fast to deceit,
They refuse to return.
6 "I have listened and heard,
They have spoken what is not right;
No man repented of his wickedness,
Saying, 'What have I done?'
Everyone turned to his course,
Like a horse charging into the battle.
7 "Even the stork in the sky
Knows her seasons;
And the turtledove and the swift and the thrush
Observe the time of their migration;
But My people do not know
The ordinance of the LORD.

8¶ "How can you say, 'We are wise,
And the law of the LORD is with us'?
But behold, the lying pen of the scribes
Has made *it* into a lie.
9 "The wise men are put to shame,
They are dismayed and caught;
Behold, they have rejected the word of the LORD,
And what kind of wisdom do they have?
10 "Therefore I will give their wives to others,
Their fields to new owners;
Because from the least even to the greatest
Everyone is greedy for gain;
From the prophet even to the priest
Everyone practices deceit.
11 "And they heal the brokenness of the daughter of My
people superficially,
Saying, 'Peace, peace,'
But there is no peace.

## New International

places of Topheth in the Valley of Ben Hinnom to burn their sons
and daughters in the fire—something I did not command, nor did
it enter my mind. 32So beware, the days are coming, declares the
LORD, when people will no longer call it Topheth or the Valley of
Ben Hinnom, but the Valley of Slaughter, for they will bury the
dead in Topheth until there is no more room. 33Then the carcasses
of this people will become food for the birds of the air and the
beasts of the earth, and there will be no one to frighten them away.
34I will bring an end to the sounds of joy and gladness and to the
voices of bride and bridegroom in the towns of Judah and the
streets of Jerusalem, for the land will become desolate.

8 " 'AT THAT time, declares the LORD, the bones of the kings
and officials of Judah, the bones of the priests and prophets,
and the bones of the people of Jerusalem will be removed from
their graves. 2They will be exposed to the sun and the moon and
all the stars of the heavens, which they have loved and served and
which they have followed and consulted and worshiped. They will
not be gathered up or buried, but will be like refuse lying on the
ground. 3Wherever I banish them, all the survivors of this evil
nation will prefer death to life, declares the LORD Almighty.'

*Sin and Punishment*

4"Say to them, 'This is what the LORD says:

" 'When men fall down, do they not get up?
When a man turns away, does he not return?
5Why then have these people turned away?
Why does Jerusalem always turn away?
They cling to deceit;
they refuse to return.
6I have listened attentively,
but they do not say what is right.
No one repents of his wickedness,
saying, "What have I done?"
Each pursues his own course
like a horse charging into battle.
7Even the stork in the sky
knows her appointed seasons,
and the dove, the swift and the thrush
observe the time of their migration.
But my people do not know
the requirements of the LORD.

8" 'How can you say, "We are wise,
for we have the law of the LORD,"
when actually the lying pen of the scribes
has handled it falsely?
9The wise will be put to shame;
they will be dismayed and trapped.
Since they have rejected the word of the LORD,
what kind of wisdom do they have?
10Therefore I will give their wives to other men
and their fields to new owners.
From the least to the greatest,
all are greedy for gain;
prophets and priests alike,
all practice deceit.
11They dress the wound of my people
as though it were not serious.
"Peace, peace," they say,
when there is no peace.

## King James

12Were they ashamed when they had committed abomination? nay, they were not at all ashamed, neither could they blush: therefore shall they fall among them that fall: in the time of their visitation they shall be cast down, saith the LORD.

13¶ I will surely consume them, saith the LORD: *there shall be* no grapes on the vine, nor figs on the fig tree, and the leaf shall fade; and *the things that* I have given them shall pass away from them.

14Why do we sit still? assemble yourselves, and let us enter into the defenced cities, and let us be silent there: for the LORD our God hath put us to silence, and given us water of gall to drink, because we have sinned against the LORD.

15We looked for peace, but no good *came; and* for a time of health, and behold trouble!

16The snorting of his horses was heard from Dan: the whole land trembled at the sound of the neighing of his strong ones; for they are come, and have devoured the land, and all that is in it; the city, and those that dwell therein.

17For, behold, I will send serpents, cockatrices, among you, which *will* not *be* charmed, and they shall bite you, saith the LORD.

18¶ *When* I would comfort myself against sorrow, my heart *is* faint in me.

19Behold the voice of the cry of the daughter of my people because of them that dwell in a far country: *Is* not the LORD in Zion? *is* not her king in her? Why have they provoked me to anger with their graven images, *and* with strange vanities?

20The harvest is past, the summer is ended, and we are not saved.

21For the hurt of the daughter of my people am I hurt; I am black; astonishment hath taken hold on me.

22 *Is there* no balm in Gilead; *is there* no physician there? why then is not the health of the daughter of my people recovered?

9 OH THAT my head were waters, and mine eyes a fountain of tears, that I might weep day and night for the slain of the daughter of my people!

## Amplified

12They are brought to shame because they have committed abominations—extremely disgusting and shamefully vile. And yet they were not at all ashamed, nor could they blush. Therefore they shall fall among those who fall; at the time of their punishment they shall be overthrown, says the Lord.

13I will gather *and* sweep them away, utterly consuming them, says the Lord. [I find] no grapes on the vine, nor figs on the fig tree; even the leaf is withered; and the things that I have given them shall pass away from them— *for* I have appointed to them those who shall pass over them. [Matt. 21:18, 19.]

14[Then say the people to each other] Why do we sit still? Assemble yourselves, and let us enter into the fortified cities and be silent *or* perish there; for the Lord our God has decreed our ruin, and given us bitter *and* poisonous water to drink, because we have sinned against the Lord.

15We looked for peace *and* completeness, but no good came; and for a time of healing, but behold, dismay, trouble *and* terror!

16The snorting of *Nebuchadnezzar's* horses is heard from Dan [on the northern border of Palestine]. At the sound of the neighing of his strong *war horses* the whole land quakes; for they come and devour the land and all that is in it, the city and those who dwell in it.

17For behold, I am sending among you serpents, adders which cannot be charmed, and they shall bite you, says the Lord.

18Oh, that I [ *Jeremiah*] could comfort myself against sorrow, *for* my grief is beyond healing; my heart is sick *and* faint within me!

19Behold [says the prophet], the voice of the cry of the daughter of my people *for help* because of those who dwell in a far country: Is not the Lord in Zion? Is not her King in her? [But the Lord answers] Why have they provoked Me to anger with their carved images, and with foreign idols?

20The harvest is past, the summer is ended *and* the fruit-gathering over, yet we are not saved! [comes again the voice of the people.]

21For the hurt of the daughter of my people am I, *Jeremiah,* hurt; I go mourning; dismay has taken hold on me.

22Is there no balm in Gilead? Is there no physician there? Why then is not the health of the daughter of my people restored? [Because Zion no longer had the presence of the Great Physician!] [Exod. 15:26.]

9 OH, THAT my head were waters, and my eyes a reservoir of tears, that I might weep day and night for the slain of the daughter of my people!

## New American Standard

12 "Were they ashamed because of the abomination they
had done?
They certainly were not ashamed,
And they did not know how to blush;
Therefore they shall fall among those who fall;
At the time of their punishment they shall be brought
down,"
Declares the LORD.

13¶ "I will surely snatch them away," declares the LORD;
"There will be no grapes on the vine,
And no figs on the fig tree,
And the leaf shall wither;
And what I have given them shall pass away." ' "
14 Why are we sitting still?
Assemble yourselves, and let us go into the fortified
cities,
And let us perish there,
Because the LORD our God has doomed us
And given us poisoned water to drink,
For we have sinned against the LORD.
15 *We* waited for peace, but no good *came;*
For a time of healing, but behold, terror!
16 From Dan is heard the snorting of his horses;
At the sound of the neighing of his stallions
The whole land quakes;
For they come and devour the land and its fulness,
The city and its inhabitants.
17 "For behold, I am sending serpents against you,
Adders, for which there is no charm,
And they will bite you," declares the LORD.
18¶ My sorrow is beyond healing,
My heart is faint *within me!*
19 Behold, listen! The cry of the daughter of my people
from a distant land:
"Is the LORD not in Zion? Is her King not within her?"
"Why have they provoked Me with their graven images,
with foreign idols?"
20 "Harvest is past, summer is ended,
And we are not saved."
21 For the brokenness of the daughter of my people I am
broken;
I mourn, dismay has taken hold of me.
22 Is there no balm in Gilead?
Is there no physician there?
Why then has not the health of the daughter of my
people been restored?

*A Lament over Zion*

9 OH, THAT my head were waters,
And my eyes a fountain of tears,
That I might weep day and night
For the slain of the daughter of my people!

## New International

12Are they ashamed of their loathsome conduct?
No, they have no shame at all;
they do not even know how to blush.
So they will fall among the fallen;
they will be brought down when they are punished,
says the LORD.

13" 'I will take away their harvest,
declares the LORD.
There will be no grapes on the vine.
There will be no figs on the tree,
and their leaves will wither.
What I have given them
will be taken from them.[a] ' "

14"Why are we sitting here?
Gather together!
Let us flee to the fortified cities
and perish there!
For the LORD our God has doomed us to perish
and given us poisoned water to drink,
because we have sinned against him.
15We hoped for peace
but no good has come,
for a time of healing
but there was only terror.
16The snorting of the enemy's horses
is heard from Dan;
at the neighing of their stallions
the whole land trembles.
They have come to devour
the land and everything in it,
the city and all who live there."

17"See, I will send venomous snakes among you,
vipers that cannot be charmed,
and they will bite you,"
declares the LORD.
18O my Comforter[b] in sorrow,
my heart is faint within me.
19Listen to the cry of my people
from a land far away:
"Is the LORD not in Zion?
Is her King no longer there?"

"Why have they provoked me to anger with their images,
with their worthless foreign idols?"
20"The harvest is past,
the summer has ended,
and we are not saved."

21Since my people are crushed, I am crushed;
I mourn, and horror grips me.
22Is there no balm in Gilead?
Is there no physician there?
Why then is there no healing
for the wound of my people?

9 OH, THAT my head were a spring of water
and my eyes a fountain of tears!
I would weep day and night
for the slain of my people.

NIV [a] *13* The meaning of the Hebrew for this sentence is uncertain.
[b] *18* The meaning of the Hebrew for this word is uncertain.

## King James

2 Oh that I had in the wilderness a lodging place of wayfaring men; that I might leave my people, and go from them! for they *be* all adulterers, an assembly of treacherous men.

3 And they bend their tongues *like* their bow *for* lies: but they are not valiant for the truth upon the earth; for they proceed from evil to evil, and they know not me, saith the LORD.

4 Take ye heed every one of his neighbour, and trust ye not in any brother: for every brother will utterly supplant, and every neighbour will walk with slanders.

5 And they will deceive every one his neighbour, and will not speak the truth: they have taught their tongue to speak lies, *and* weary themselves to commit iniquity.

6 Thine habitation *is* in the midst of deceit; through deceit they refuse to know me, saith the LORD.

7 Therefore thus saith the LORD of hosts, Behold, I will melt them, and try them; for how shall I do for the daughter of my people?

8 Their tongue *is as* an arrow shot out; it speaketh deceit: *one* speaketh peaceably to his neighbour with his mouth, but in heart he layeth his wait.

9 ¶ Shall I not visit them for these *things?* saith the LORD: shall not my soul be avenged on such a nation as this?

10 For the mountains will I take up a weeping and wailing, and for the habitations of the wilderness a lamentation, because they are burned up, so that none can pass through *them;* neither can *men* hear the voice of the cattle; both the fowl of the heavens and the beast are fled; they are gone.

11 And I will make Jerusalem heaps, *and* a den of dragons; and I will make the cities of Judah desolate, without an inhabitant.

12 ¶ Who *is* the wise man, that may understand this? and *who is he* to whom the mouth of the LORD hath spoken, that he may declare it, for what the land perisheth *and* is burned up like a wilderness, that none passeth through?

13 And the LORD saith, Because they have forsaken my law which I set before them, and have not obeyed my voice, neither walked therein;

14 But have walked after the imagination of their own heart, and after Baalim, which their fathers taught them:

15 Therefore thus saith the LORD of hosts, the God of Israel; Behold, I will feed them, *even* this people, with wormwood, and give them water of gall to drink.

16 I will scatter them also among the heathen, whom neither they nor their fathers have known: and I will send a sword after them, till I have consumed them.

17 ¶ Thus saith the LORD of hosts, Consider ye, and call for the mourning women, that they may come; and send for cunning *women,* that they may come:

## Amplified

2 Oh, that I had in the wilderness a lodging place (a mere shelter) for wayfaring men, that I might leave my people and go away from them! For they are all adulterers [rendering worship to idols, instead of to the Lord Who has espoused the people to Himself]; they are a gang of treacherous men—faithless *even to each other.*

3 And they bend their tongue, *which is* their bow for lies. And not according to faithfulness do they rule *and* are become strong in the land, for they proceed from evil to evil, and they do not know *and* understand *and* acknowledge Me, says the Lord.

4 Let every one beware of his neighbor and put no trust in any brother; for every brother is an utter supplanter—one who takes by the heel and trips up, a Jacob; and every neighbor goes about as a slanderer. [Gen. 25:26.]

5 And they deceive *and* mock every one his neighbor, and do not speak the truth; they have taught their tongue to speak lies; they weary themselves to commit iniquity.

6 Your habitation is in the midst of deceit (oppression upon oppression, and deceit upon deceit); through deceit they refuse to know *and* understand Me, says the Lord.

7 Therefore thus says the Lord of hosts, Behold, I will melt them [by the process of affliction to remove the dross] and test them; for how else should I deal with the daughter of My people?

8 Their tongue is a murderous arrow; it speaks deceitfully; one speaks peaceably to his neighbor with his mouth, but in his heart he lays *snares and* waits in ambush for him.

9 Shall I not punish them for these things? says the Lord. Shall I not avenge Myself on a nation such as this?

10 For the mountains I will take up a weeping and wailing, and for the pastures of the wilderness a lament, because they are burned up *and* desolated, so that no one passes through *them;* neither can men hear *any longer* the lowing of cattle; both the fowls of the air and the beasts have fled, they are gone!

11 I will make Jerusalem heaps *of ruins,* a dwelling place of jackals; and I will make the cities of Judah a desolation, without inhabitant.

12 Who is the wise man who may understand this? To whom has the mouth of the Lord spoken, that he may declare it? Why is the land ruined *and* laid waste like a wilderness, so that no one passes through it?

13 And the Lord says, Because they have forsaken My law which I set before them, and have not listened *and* obeyed My voice or walked in accordance with it,

14 But have walked stubbornly after their own heart and after the Baals, as their fathers taught them,

15 Therefore thus says the Lord of hosts, the God of Israel: Behold, I will feed them, even this people, with wormwood, and give them bitter *and* poisonous water to drink.

16 I will scatter them also among the nations whom neither they nor their fathers have known; and I will send the sword among them *and* after them, until I have consumed them.

17 Thus says the Lord of hosts: Consider, and call for the mourning women to come; send for the skillful women to come;

## New American Standard

2 O that I had in the desert
A wayfarers' lodging place;
That I might leave my people,
And go from them!
For all of them are adulterers,
An assembly of treacherous men.
3 "And they bend their tongue *like* their bow;
Lies and not truth prevail in the land;
For they proceed from evil to evil,
And they do not know Me," declares the LORD.
4 "Let everyone be on guard against his neighbor,
And do not trust any brother;
Because every brother deals craftily,
And every neighbor goes about as a slanderer.
5 "And everyone deceives his neighbor,
And does not speak the truth,
They have taught their tongue to speak lies;
They weary themselves committing iniquity.
6 "Your dwelling is in the midst of deceit;
Through deceit they refuse to know Me," declares the LORD.
7¶ Therefore thus says the LORD of hosts,
"Behold, I will refine them and assay them;
For what *else* can I do, because of the daughter of My people?
8 "Their tongue is a deadly arrow;
It speaks deceit;
With his mouth one speaks peace to his neighbor,
But inwardly he sets an ambush for him.
9 "Shall I not punish them for these things?" declares the LORD.
"On a nation such as this
Shall I not avenge Myself?
10¶ "For the mountains I will take up a weeping and wailing,
And for the pastures of the wilderness a dirge,
Because they are laid waste, so that no one passes through,
And the lowing of the cattle is not heard;
Both the birds of the sky and the beasts have fled; they are gone.
11 "And I will make Jerusalem a heap of ruins,
A haunt of jackals;
And I will make the cities of Judah a desolation,
without inhabitant."
12¶ Who is the wise man that may understand this? And *who*
*is* he to whom the mouth of the LORD has spoken, that he may
declare it? Why is the land ruined, laid waste like a desert, so that
no one passes through?
13And the LORD said, "Because they have forsaken My law
which I set before them, and have not obeyed My voice nor walked
according to it,
14but have walked after the stubbornness of their heart and after
the Baals, as their fathers taught them,"
15therefore thus says the LORD of hosts, the God of Israel,
"behold, I will feed them, this people, with wormwood and give
them poisoned water to drink.
16"And I will scatter them among the nations, whom neither
they nor their fathers have known; and I will send the sword after
them until I have annihilated them."
17¶ Thus says the LORD of hosts,
"Consider and call for the mourning women, that they may come;
And send for the wailing women, that they may come!

## New International

2Oh, that I had in the desert
a lodging place for travelers,
so that I might leave my people
and go away from them;
for they are all adulterers,
a crowd of unfaithful people.

3"They make ready their tongue
like a bow, to shoot lies;
it is not by truth
that they triumph[a] in the land.
They go from one sin to another;
they do not acknowledge me,"
declares the LORD.
4"Beware of your friends;
do not trust your brothers.
For every brother is a deceiver,[b]
and every friend a slanderer.
5Friend deceives friend,
and no one speaks the truth.
They have taught their tongues to lie;
they weary themselves with sinning.
6You[c] live in the midst of deception;
in their deceit they refuse to acknowledge me,"
declares the LORD.
7Therefore this is what the LORD Almighty says:

"See, I will refine and test them,
for what else can I do
because of the sin of my people?
8Their tongue is a deadly arrow;
it speaks with deceit.
With his mouth each speaks cordially to his neighbor,
but in his heart he sets a trap for him.
9Should I not punish them for this?"
declares the LORD.
"Should I not avenge myself
on such a nation as this?"

10I will weep and wail for the mountains
and take up a lament concerning the desert pastures.
They are desolate and untraveled,
and the lowing of cattle is not heard.
The birds of the air have fled
and the animals are gone.

11"I will make Jerusalem a heap of ruins,
a haunt of jackals;
and I will lay waste the towns of Judah
so no one can live there."

12What man is wise enough to understand this? Who has been
instructed by the LORD and can explain it? Why has the land been
ruined and laid waste like a desert that no one can cross?
13The LORD said, "It is because they have forsaken my law,
which I set before them; they have not obeyed me or followed my
law. 14Instead, they have followed the stubbornness of their
hearts; they have followed the Baals, as their fathers taught them."
15Therefore, this is what the LORD Almighty, the God of Israel,
says: "See, I will make this people eat bitter food and drink poisoned water. 16I will scatter them among nations that neither they
nor their fathers have known, and I will pursue them with the
sword until I have destroyed them."

17This is what the LORD Almighty says:

"Consider now! Call for the wailing women to come;
send for the most skillful of them.

**NIV** [a] 3 Or *lies; / they are not valiant for truth* [b] 4 Or *a deceiving Jacob*
[c] 6 That is, Jeremiah (the Hebrew is singular)

## King James

18 And let them make haste, and take up a wailing for us, that our eyes may run down with tears, and our eyelids gush out with waters.

19 For a voice of wailing is heard out of Zion, How are we spoiled! we are greatly confounded, because we have forsaken the land, because our dwellings have cast *us* out.

20 Yet hear the word of the LORD, O ye women, and let your ear receive the word of his mouth, and teach your daughters wailing, and every one her neighbour lamentation.

21 For death is come up into our windows, *and* is entered into our palaces, to cut off the children from without, *and* the young men from the streets.

22 Speak, Thus saith the LORD, Even the carcases of men shall fall as dung upon the open field, and as the handful after the harvestman, and none shall gather *them*.

23 ¶ Thus saith the LORD, Let not the wise *man* glory in his wisdom, neither let the mighty *man* glory in his might, let not the rich *man* glory in his riches:

24 But let him that glorieth glory in this, that he understandeth and knoweth me, that I *am* the LORD which exercise lovingkindness, judgment, and righteousness, in the earth: for in these *things* I delight, saith the LORD.

25 ¶ Behold, the days come, saith the LORD, that I will punish all *them which are* circumcised with the uncircumcised;

26 Egypt, and Judah, and Edom, and the children of Ammon, and Moab, and all *that are* in the utmost corners, that dwell in the wilderness: for all *these* nations *are* uncircumcised, and all the house of Israel *are* uncircumcised in the heart.

**10** HEAR YE the word which the LORD speaketh unto you, O house of Israel:

2 Thus saith the LORD, Learn not the way of the heathen, and be not dismayed at the signs of heaven; for the heathen are dismayed at them.

3 For the customs of the people *are* vain: for *one* cutteth a tree out of the forest, the work of the hands of the workman, with the axe.

4 They deck it with silver and with gold; they fasten it with nails and with hammers, that it move not.

5 They *are* upright as the palm tree, but speak not: they must needs be borne, because they cannot go. Be not afraid of them; for they cannot do evil, neither also *is it* in them to do good.

6 Forasmuch as *there is* none like unto thee, O LORD; thou *art* great, and thy name *is* great in might.

## Amplified

18 Let them make haste and raise a wailing over us *and* for us, that our eyes may run down with tears, and our eyelids gush with water.

19 For a sound of wailing is heard *coming* out of Zion, How we are plundered *and* ruined! We are greatly confounded *and* utterly put to shame, because we have forsaken the land, because they have cast down our dwellings—our dwellings that have cast us out.

20 Yet hear the word of the Lord, O you women, and let your ear receive the word of His mouth; teach your daughters a lament, and each one *teach* her neighbor a dirge.

21 For death is come up into our windows; it has entered into our palaces, cutting off the children from outdoors and the young men from the streets.

22 Speak, Thus says the Lord: The dead bodies of men shall fall like manure on the open field, and like sheaves *of grain* behind the reaper, and none shall gather them.

23 Thus says the Lord, Let not the wise *and* skillful person glory *and* boast in his wisdom *and* skill; let not the mighty *and* powerful person glory and boast in his strength *and* power; let not the person who is rich [in physical gratification and earthly wealth] glory *and* boast in his [temporal satisfactions and earthly] riches;

24 But let him who glories glory in this, that he understands and knows Me (personally and practically, directly discerning and recognizing My character), that I am the Lord Who practices loving-kindness, judgment and righteousness in the earth; for in these things I delight, says the Lord. [I Cor. 1:31; II Cor. 10:17.]

25 Behold, the days are coming, says the Lord, that I will punish all who though circumcised [outwardly] are still uncircumcised [in corresponding inward purity]:

26 Egypt, Judah, Edom, the children of Ammon, Moab [all of whom are related, except Egypt], and all who live in the desert who cut the corners of their hair; for all these nations are uncircumcised [in heart], and all the house of Israel is uncircumcised in heart.

**10** HEAR THE word which the Lord speaks to you, O house of Israel.

2 Thus says the Lord: Learn not the way of the heathen (nations), and be not dismayed at the signs of the heavens; they are dismayed at them,

3 For the customs *and* ordinances of the peoples are false, empty *and* futile. It is but a tree which one cuts out of the forest [to make for him a god], the work of the hands of the craftsman with the axe *or* other tool.

4 They deck *the idol* with silver and with gold; they fasten it with nails and with hammers, so it will not fall apart *or* move.

5 *Their idols* are like pillars of turned work—upright [and stationary] as a palm tree—like scarecrows in a cucumber field; they cannot speak; they have to be carried, for they cannot walk. Do not be afraid of them, for they cannot do evil, neither is it possible for them to do good—it is not in them.

6 None at all is like You, O Lord; You are great, and Your name is great in might.

## New American Standard

18 "And let them make haste, and take up a wailing for us,
That our eyes may shed tears,
And our eyelids flow with water.
19 "For a voice of wailing is heard from Zion,
'How are we ruined!
We are put to great shame,
For we have left the land,
Because they have cast down our dwellings.' "
20 Now hear the word of the LORD, O you women,
And let your ear receive the word of His mouth;
Teach your daughters wailing,
And everyone her neighbor a dirge.
21 For death has come up through our windows;
It has entered our palaces
To cut off the children from the streets,
The young men from the town squares.
22 Speak, "Thus declares the LORD,
'The corpses of men will fall like dung on the open field,
And like the sheaf after the reaper,
But no one will gather *them*.' "
23¶ Thus says the LORD, "Let not a wise man boast of his
wisdom, and let not the mighty man boast of his might, let not a
rich man boast of his riches;
24but let him who boasts boast of this, that he understands and
knows Me, that I am the LORD who exercises lovingkindness,
justice, and righteousness on earth; for I delight in these things,"
declares the LORD.
25¶ "Behold, the days are coming," declares the LORD, "that I
will punish all who are circumcised and yet uncircumcised—
26Egypt, and Judah, and Edom, and the sons of Ammon, and
Moab, and all those inhabiting the desert who clip the hair on their
temples; for all the nations are uncircumcised, and all the house
of Israel are uncircumcised of heart."

*A Satire on Idolatry*

10 HEAR THE word which the LORD speaks to you, O house of Israel.
2 Thus says the LORD,
"Do not learn the way of the nations,
And do not be terrified by the signs of the heavens
Although the nations are terrified by them;
3 For the customs of the peoples are delusion;
Because it is wood cut from the forest,
The work of the hands of a craftsman with a cutting tool.
4 "They decorate *it* with silver and with gold;
They fasten it with nails and with hammers
So that it will not totter.
5 "Like a scarecrow in a cucumber field are they,
And they cannot speak;
They must be carried,
Because they cannot walk!
Do not fear them,
For they can do no harm,
Nor can they do any good."

6¶ There is none like Thee, O LORD;
Thou art great, and great is Thy name in might.

## New International

18Let them come quickly
and wail over us
till our eyes overflow with tears
and water streams from our eyelids.
19The sound of wailing is heard from Zion:
'How ruined we are!
How great is our shame!
We must leave our land
because our houses are in ruins.' "

20Now, O women, hear the word of the LORD;
open your ears to the words of his mouth.
Teach your daughters how to wail;
teach one another a lament.
21Death has climbed in through our windows
and has entered our fortresses;
it has cut off the children from the streets
and the young men from the public squares.

22Say, "This is what the LORD declares:
" 'The dead bodies of men will lie
like refuse on the open field,
like cut grain behind the reaper,
with no one to gather them.' "

23This is what the LORD says:
"Let not the wise man boast of his wisdom
or the strong man boast of his strength
or the rich man boast of his riches,
24but let him who boasts boast about this:
that he understands and knows me,
that I am the LORD, who exercises kindness,
justice and righteousness on earth,
for in these I delight,"
declares the LORD.

25"The days are coming," declares the LORD, "when I will punish all who are circumcised only in the flesh— 26Egypt, Judah,
Edom, Ammon, Moab and all who live in the desert in distant
places.[a] For all these nations are really uncircumcised, and even
the whole house of Israel is uncircumcised in heart."

*God and Idols*

10 HEAR WHAT the LORD says to you, O house of Israel.
2This is what the LORD says:

"Do not learn the ways of the nations
or be terrified by signs in the sky,
though the nations are terrified by them.
3For the customs of the peoples are worthless;
they cut a tree out of the forest,
and a craftsman shapes it with his chisel.
4They adorn it with silver and gold;
they fasten it with hammer and nails
so it will not totter.
5Like a scarecrow in a melon patch,
their idols cannot speak;
they must be carried
because they cannot walk.
Do not fear them;
they can do no harm
nor can they do any good."

6No one is like you, O LORD;
you are great,
and your name is mighty in power.

NIV [a] 26 Or *desert and who clip the hair by their foreheads*

## King James

7Who would not fear thee, O King of nations? for to thee doth it appertain: forasmuch as among all the wise *men* of the nations, and in all their kingdoms, *there is* none like unto thee.

8But they are altogether brutish and foolish: the stock *is* a doctrine of vanities.

9Silver spread into plates is brought from Tarshish, and gold from Uphaz, the work of the workman, and of the hands of the founder: blue and purple *is* their clothing: they *are* all the work of cunning *men*.

10But the LORD *is* the true God, he *is* the living God, and an everlasting king: at his wrath the earth shall tremble, and the nations shall not be able to abide his indignation.

11Thus shall ye say unto them, The gods that have not made the heavens and the earth, *even* they shall perish from the earth, and from under these heavens.

12He hath made the earth by his power, he hath established the world by his wisdom, and hath stretched out the heavens by his discretion.

13When he uttereth his voice, *there is* a multitude of waters in the heavens, and he causeth the vapours to ascend from the ends of the earth; he maketh lightnings with rain, and bringeth forth the wind out of his treasures.

14Every man is brutish in *his* knowledge: every founder is confounded by the graven image: for his molten image *is* falsehood, and *there is* no breath in them.

15They *are* vanity, *and* the work of errors: in the time of their visitation they shall perish.

16The portion of Jacob *is* not like them: for he *is* the former of all *things;* and Israel *is* the rod of his inheritance: The LORD of hosts *is* his name.

17¶ Gather up thy wares out of the land, O inhabitant of the fortress.

18For thus saith the LORD, Behold, I will sling out the inhabitants of the land at this once, and will distress them, that they may find *it so*.

19¶ Woe is me for my hurt! my wound is grievous: but I said, Truly this *is* a grief, and I must bear it.

20My tabernacle is spoiled, and all my cords are broken: my children are gone forth of me, and they *are* not: *there is* none to stretch forth my tent any more, and to set up my curtains.

21For the pastors are become brutish, and have not sought the LORD: therefore they shall not prosper, and all their flocks shall be scattered.

22Behold, the noise of the bruit is come, and a great commotion out of the north country, to make the cities of Judah desolate, *and* a den of dragons.

## Amplified

7Who would not fear You, O King of the nations? For it is fitting *and* due to You, for among all the wise *men or gods* of the nations, and in all their kingdoms there is none like You.

8But they are altogether irrational *and* stupid and foolish. The instruction of idols is but wood—a teaching of falsity, emptiness, futility!

9Silver beaten *into plates* is brought from Tarshish, and gold from Uphaz, the work of the craftsman and of the hands of the goldsmith; the *idols'* clothing is of violet and purple; they are all the work of skillful men.

10But the Lord is the true God *and* the God of truth—the God Who is truth. He is the living God, and the everlasting King. At His wrath the earth quakes, and the nations are not able to bear His indignation.

11Thus shall you say to them, The gods who did not make the heavens and the earth shall perish from the earth and from under the heavens.

12 *God* has made the earth by His power, He has established the world by His wisdom, and by His understanding *and* skill has stretched out the heavens.

13When He utters His voice there is a tumult of waters in the heavens, and He causes the vapors to ascend from the ends of the earth; He makes lightnings for the rain, and brings forth the wind out of His treasuries *and* from His storehouses.

14Every man has become like a brute, irrational *and* stupid, without knowledge *of God;* every goldsmith is brought to shame by his graven idols; for his molten images are frauds *and* falsehood, and there is no breath in them.

15They are devoid of worth, use *or* truth, a work of delusion *and* mockery; in their time of trial *and* punishment they shall [helplessly] perish.

16The portion of Jacob [the true God on Whom Israel has a claim] is not like these, for He is the fashioner of all things, and Israel is the tribe of His inheritance; the Lord of hosts is His name.

17Gather up your bundle of baggage from the ground, O you who dwell under siege.

18For thus says the Lord, Behold, I will sling out the inhabitants of the land at this time, and will *bring* distress on them, that they may feel it *and* find it [as I have said, and turn to Me].

19Woe is me because of my hurt! [says Jeremiah, speaking for the nation.] My wound is grievous *and* incurable. But I said, Surely this sickness *and* suffering *and* grief are mine, and I must endure, tolerate *and* bear them.

20My tent *home* is taken by force *and* plundered, and all my *tent* cords are broken; my children have gone forth *as captives* from me, and they are not; there is no one to stretch forth my tent any more, and to set up my tent curtains.

21For the shepherds *of the people* have become like a brute, irrational *and* stupid; and have not sought the Lord *or* inquired of Him *or* required Him [by necessity, and by right of His word]. Therefore they have not dealt prudently *and* they have not prospered, and all their flocks are scattered.

22Hark, the sound of a rumor! *The invading army* comes! A great commotion out of the north country to make the cities of Judah a desolation, a dwelling place for jackals.

## New American Standard

7 Who would not fear Thee, O King of the nations?
Indeed it is Thy due!
For among all the wise men of the nations,
And in all their kingdoms,
There is none like Thee.
8 But they are altogether stupid and foolish
*In their* discipline of delusion—their idol is wood!
9 Beaten silver is brought from Tarshish,
And gold from Uphaz,
The work of a craftsman and of the hands of a goldsmith;
Violet and purple are their clothing;
They are all the work of skilled men.
10 But the LORD is the true God;
He is the living God and the everlasting King.
At His wrath the earth quakes,
And the nations cannot endure His indignation.

11¶ Thus you shall say to them, "The gods that did not make the heavens and the earth shall perish from the earth and from under the heavens."

12¶ *It is* He who made the earth by His power,
Who established the world by His wisdom;
And by His understanding He has stretched out the heavens.
13 When He utters His voice, *there is* a tumult of waters in the heavens,
And He causes the clouds to ascend from the end of the earth;
He makes lightning for the rain,
And brings out the wind from His storehouses.
14 Every man is stupid, devoid of knowledge;
Every goldsmith is put to shame by his idols;
For his molten images are deceitful,
And there is no breath in them.
15 They are worthless, a work of mockery;
In the time of their punishment they will perish.
16 The portion of Jacob is not like these;
For the Maker of all is He,
And Israel is the tribe of His inheritance;
The LORD of hosts is His name.

17¶ Pick up your bundle from the ground,
You who dwell under siege!
18 For thus says the LORD,
"Behold, I am slinging out the inhabitants of the land
At this time,
And will cause them distress,
That they may be found."

19¶ Woe is me, because of my injury!
My wound is incurable.
But I said, "Truly this is a sickness,
And I must bear it."
20 My tent is destroyed,
And all my ropes are broken;
My sons have gone from me and are no more.
There is no one to stretch out my tent again
Or to set up my curtains.
21 For the shepherds have become stupid
And have not sought the LORD;
Therefore they have not prospered,
And all their flock is scattered.
22 The sound of a report! Behold, it comes—
A great commotion out of the land of the north—
To make the cities of Judah
A desolation, a haunt of jackals.

## New International

7Who should not revere you,
O King of the nations?
This is your due.
Among all the wise men of the nations
and in all their kingdoms,
there is no one like you.
8They are all senseless and foolish;
they are taught by worthless wooden idols.
9Hammered silver is brought from Tarshish
and gold from Uphaz.
What the craftsman and goldsmith have made
is then dressed in blue and purple—
all made by skilled workers.
10But the LORD is the true God;
he is the living God, the eternal King.
When he is angry, the earth trembles;
the nations cannot endure his wrath.

11"Tell them this: 'These gods, who did not make the heavens and the earth, will perish from the earth and from under the heavens.' "[a]

12But God made the earth by his power;
he founded the world by his wisdom
and stretched out the heavens by his understanding.
13When he thunders, the waters in the heavens roar;
he makes clouds rise from the ends of the earth.
He sends lightning with the rain
and brings out the wind from his storehouses.
14Everyone is senseless and without knowledge;
every goldsmith is shamed by his idols.
His images are a fraud;
they have no breath in them.
15They are worthless, the objects of mockery;
when their judgment comes, they will perish.
16He who is the Portion of Jacob is not like these,
for he is the Maker of all things,
including Israel, the tribe of his inheritance—
the LORD Almighty is his name.

*Coming Destruction*

17Gather up your belongings to leave the land,
you who live under siege.
18For this is what the LORD says:
"At this time I will hurl out
those who live in this land;
I will bring distress on them
so that they may be captured."
19Woe to me because of my injury!
My wound is incurable!
Yet I said to myself,
"This is my sickness, and I must endure it."
20My tent is destroyed;
all its ropes are snapped.
My sons are gone from me and are no more;
no one is left now to pitch my tent
or to set up my shelter.
21The shepherds are senseless
and do not inquire of the LORD;
so they do not prosper
and all their flock is scattered.
22Listen! The report is coming—
a great commotion from the land of the north!
It will make the towns of Judah desolate,
a haunt of jackals.

NIV [a] *11* The text of this verse is in Aramaic.

## King James

23¶ O LORD, I know that the way of man *is* not in himself: *it is* not in man that walketh to direct his steps.

24O LORD, correct me, but with judgment; not in thine anger, lest thou bring me to nothing.

25Pour out thy fury upon the heathen that know thee not, and upon the families that call not on thy name: for they have eaten up Jacob, and devoured him, and consumed him, and have made his habitation desolate.

**11** THE WORD that came to Jeremiah from the LORD, saying,

2Hear ye the words of this covenant, and speak unto the men of Judah, and to the inhabitants of Jerusalem;

3And say thou unto them, Thus saith the LORD God of Israel; Cursed *be* the man that obeyeth not the words of this covenant,

4Which I commanded your fathers in the day *that* I brought them forth out of the land of Egypt, from the iron furnace, saying, Obey my voice, and do them, according to all which I command you: so shall ye be my people, and I will be your God:

5That I may perform the oath which I have sworn unto your fathers, to give them a land flowing with milk and honey, as *it is* this day. Then answered I, and said, So be it, O LORD.

6Then the LORD said unto me, Proclaim all these words in the cities of Judah, and in the streets of Jerusalem, saying, Hear ye the words of this covenant, and do them.

7For I earnestly protested unto your fathers in the day *that* I brought them up out of the land of Egypt, *even* unto this day, rising early and protesting, saying, Obey my voice.

8Yet they obeyed not, nor inclined their ear, but walked every one in the imagination of their evil heart: therefore I will bring upon them all the words of this covenant, which I commanded *them* to do; but they did *them* not.

9And the LORD said unto me, A conspiracy is found among the men of Judah, and among the inhabitants of Jerusalem.

10They are turned back to the iniquities of their forefathers, which refused to hear my words; and they went after other gods to serve them: the house of Israel and the house of Judah have broken my covenant which I made with their fathers.

11¶ Therefore thus saith the LORD, Behold, I will bring evil upon them, which they shall not be able to escape; and though they shall cry unto me, I will not hearken unto them.

12Then shall the cities of Judah and inhabitants of Jerusalem go, and cry unto the gods unto whom they offer incense: but they shall not save them at all in the time of their trouble.

13For *according to* the number of thy cities were thy gods, O Judah; and *according to* the number of the streets of Jerusalem have ye set up altars to *that* shameful thing, *even* altars to burn incense unto Baal.

14Therefore pray not thou for this people, neither lift up a cry or prayer for them: for I will not hear *them* in the time that they cry unto me for their trouble.

15What hath my beloved to do in mine house, *seeing* she hath wrought lewdness with many, and the holy flesh is passed from thee? when thou doest evil, then thou rejoicest.

16The LORD called thy name, A green olive tree, fair, *and* of goodly fruit: with the noise of a great tumult he hath kindled fire upon it, and the branches of it are broken.

## Amplified

23O Lord, [pleads Jeremiah in the name of the people] I know that [the determination of] the way of a man is not in himself. It is not in man [even in a strong man and a man at his best] to direct his *own* steps. [Ps. 37:23; Prov. 20:24.]

24O Lord, correct, instruct *and* chastise me, but with judgment *and* in just measure; not in Your anger, lest You diminish me *and* bring me to nothing.

25Pour out Your wrath upon the nations that do not know *or* recognize You, and upon the peoples that do not call upon Your name; for they have devoured Jacob; yes, devoured him and consumed him, and made his habitation a desolate waste.

**11** THE WORD that came to Jeremiah from the Lord:

2Hear the words of this covenant *or* solemn pledge, and speak to the men of Judah and the inhabitants of Jerusalem;

3Say to them, Thus says the Lord, the God of Israel: Cursed be the man who does not heed the words of this covenant *or* solemn pledge,

4Which I commanded your fathers at the time that I brought them out of the land of Egypt, from the iron furnace, saying, Listen to My voice, and do according to all that I command you. So shall you be My people, and I will be your God,

5That I may perform the oath which I swore to your fathers to give them a land flowing with milk and honey, as at this day. Then I answered, Amen, O Lord—so be it.

6And the Lord said to me, Proclaim all these words in the cities of Judah and in the streets of Jerusalem: Hear the words of this [solemn] covenant and do them.

7For I earnestly protested *and* warned your fathers at the time that I brought them up out of the land of Egypt, even to this day protesting *and* warning them persistently, saying, Obey My voice.

8Yet they did not obey or incline their ear *to Me,* but every one walked in the stubbornness of *his own* evil heart. Therefore I brought upon them all [the calamities threatened in] the words of this covenant *or* solemn pledge, which I had commanded, but they did not do.

9And the Lord said to me, A conspiracy is found among the men of Judah and among the inhabitants of Jerusalem.

10They have turned back to the iniquities of their forefathers, who refused to hear My words; they have gone after other gods to serve them; the house of Israel and the house of Judah have broken My covenant *or* solemn pledge which I made with their fathers.

11Therefore thus says the Lord, Behold, I am bringing evil *and* calamity upon them, which they shall not be able to escape; though they cry to Me, I will not listen to them.

12Then the cities of Judah and the inhabitants of Jerusalem will go and cry out to the gods to which they offer incense, but they cannot save them at all in the time of their evil trouble.

13For *as many* as the number of your cities are your gods, O Judah, and as the number of the streets of Jerusalem are the altars you have set up to the shameful thing, even altars to burn incense to Baal.

14Therefore do not pray for this people, or lift up a cry or prayer for them; for I will not listen when they cry out to Me in the time of their evil trouble.

15What right has My beloved in My house, when she has wrought lewdness *and* done treacherously many times? Can *vows and* the holy flesh [of your sacrifices] remove from you your wickedness *and* avert your calamity? Can you by these *escape your doom and* rejoice exultantly?

16The Lord [acknowledged you once to be worthy to be] called a green olive tree, fair *and* of good fruit; but with the roar of a great tempest He will set fire to it, and its branches will be consumed. [Ps. 52:8; Jer. 21:14.]

## New American Standard

23¶ I know, O LORD, that a man's way is not in himself;
Nor is it in a man who walks to direct his steps.
24 Correct me, O LORD, but with justice;
Not with Thine anger, lest Thou bring me to nothing.
25 Pour out Thy wrath on the nations that do not know
Thee,
And on the families that do not call Thy name;
For they have devoured Jacob;
They have devoured him and consumed him,
And have laid waste his habitation.

*The Broken Covenant*

11 THE WORD which came to Jeremiah from the LORD, saying,
2"Hear the words of this covenant, and speak to the men of
Judah and to the inhabitants of Jerusalem;
3and say to them, 'Thus says the LORD, the God of Israel,
"Cursed is the man who does not heed the words of this covenant
4which I commanded your forefathers in the day that I brought
them out of the land of Egypt, from the iron furnace, saying,
'Listen to My voice, and do according to all which I command you;
so you shall be My people, and I will be your God,'
5in order to confirm the oath which I swore to your forefathers,
to give them a land flowing with milk and honey, as *it is* this
day." ' " Then I answered and said, "Amen, O LORD."
6¶ And the LORD said to me, "Proclaim all these words in the
cities of Judah and in the streets of Jerusalem, saying, 'Hear the
words of this covenant and do them.
7'For I solemnly warned your fathers in the day that I brought
them up from the land of Egypt, even to this day, warning persistently, saying, "Listen to My voice."
8'Yet they did not obey or incline their ear, but walked, each
one, in the stubbornness of his evil heart; therefore I brought on
them all the words of this covenant, which I commanded *them* to
do, but they did not.' "
9¶ Then the LORD said to me, "A conspiracy has been found
among the men of Judah and among the inhabitants of Jerusalem.
10"They have turned back to the iniquities of their ancestors
who refused to hear My words, and they have gone after other
gods to serve them; the house of Israel and the house of Judah have
broken My covenant which I made with their fathers."
11Therefore thus says the LORD, "Behold I am bringing disaster
on them which they will not be able to escape; though they will
cry to Me, yet I will not listen to them.
12"Then the cities of Judah and the inhabitants of Jerusalem will
go and cry to the gods to whom they burn incense, but they surely
will not save them in the time of their disaster.
13"For your gods are as many as your cities, O Judah; and as
many as the streets of Jerusalem are the altars you have set up to
the shameful thing, altars to burn incense to Baal.
14¶ "Therefore do not pray for this people, nor lift up a cry or
prayer for them; for I will not listen when they call to Me because
of their disaster.
15 "What right has My beloved in My house
When she has done many vile deeds?
Can the sacrificial flesh take away from you your
disaster,
So *that* you can rejoice?"
16 The LORD called your name,
"A green olive tree, beautiful in fruit and form";
With the noise of a great tumult
He has kindled fire on it,
And its branches are worthless.

## New International

*Jeremiah's Prayer*

23I know, O LORD, that a man's life is not his own;
it is not for man to direct his steps.
24Correct me, LORD, but only with justice—
not in your anger,
lest you reduce me to nothing.
25Pour out your wrath on the nations
that do not acknowledge you,
on the peoples who do not call on your name.
For they have devoured Jacob;
they have devoured him completely
and destroyed his homeland.

*The Covenant Is Broken*

11 THIS IS the word that came to Jeremiah from the LORD:
2"Listen to the terms of this covenant and tell them to the
people of Judah and to those who live in Jerusalem. 3Tell them that
this is what the LORD, the God of Israel, says: 'Cursed is the man
who does not obey the terms of this covenant— 4the terms I
commanded your forefathers when I brought them out of Egypt,
out of the iron-smelting furnace.' I said, 'Obey me and do everything I command you, and you will be my people, and I will be
your God. 5Then I will fulfill the oath I swore to your forefathers,
to give them a land flowing with milk and honey'—the land you
possess today."
I answered, "Amen, LORD."
6The LORD said to me, "Proclaim all these words in the towns
of Judah and in the streets of Jerusalem: 'Listen to the terms of this
covenant and follow them. 7From the time I brought your forefathers up from Egypt until today, I warned them again and again,
saying, "Obey me." 8But they did not listen or pay attention;
instead, they followed the stubbornness of their evil hearts. So I
brought on them all the curses of the covenant I had commanded
them to follow but that they did not keep.' "
9Then the LORD said to me, "There is a conspiracy among the
people of Judah and those who live in Jerusalem. 10They have
returned to the sins of their forefathers, who refused to listen to
my words. They have followed other gods to serve them. Both the
house of Israel and the house of Judah have broken the covenant
I made with their forefathers. 11Therefore this is what the LORD
says: 'I will bring on them a disaster they cannot escape. Although
they cry out to me, I will not listen to them. 12The towns of Judah
and the people of Jerusalem will go and cry out to the gods to
whom they burn incense, but they will not help them at all when
disaster strikes. 13You have as many gods as you have towns, O
Judah; and the altars you have set up to burn incense to that
shameful god Baal are as many as the streets of Jerusalem.'
14"Do not pray for this people nor offer any plea or petition for
them, because I will not listen when they call to me in the time of
their distress.
15"What is my beloved doing in my temple
as she works out her evil schemes with many?
Can consecrated meat avert ⌞your punishment⌟?
When you engage in your wickedness,
then you rejoice.[a] "
16The LORD called you a thriving olive tree
with fruit beautiful in form.
But with the roar of a mighty storm
he will set it on fire,
and its branches will be broken.

**NIV** [a] 15 Or *Could consecrated meat avert your punishment? / Then you would rejoice*

## King James

17For the LORD of hosts, that planted thee, hath pronounced evil against thee, for the evil of the house of Israel and of the house of Judah, which they have done against themselves to provoke me to anger in offering incense unto Baal.

18¶ And the LORD hath given me knowledge *of it,* and I know *it:* then thou showedst me their doings.

19But I *was* like a lamb *or* an ox *that* is brought to the slaughter; and I knew not that they had devised devices against me, *saying,* Let us destroy the tree with the fruit thereof, and let us cut him off from the land of the living, that his name may be no more remembered.

20But, O LORD of hosts, that judgest righteously, that triest the reins and the heart, let me see thy vengeance on them: for unto thee have I revealed my cause.

21Therefore thus saith the LORD of the men of Anathoth, that seek thy life, saying, Prophesy not in the name of the LORD, that thou die not by our hand:

22Therefore thus saith the LORD of hosts, Behold, I will punish them: the young men shall die by the sword; their sons and their daughters shall die by famine:

23And there shall be no remnant of them: for I will bring evil upon the men of Anathoth, *even* the year of their visitation.

**12** RIGHTEOUS *ART* thou, O LORD, when I plead with thee: yet let me talk with thee of *thy* judgments: Wherefore doth the way of the wicked prosper? *wherefore* are all they happy that deal very treacherously?

2Thou hast planted them, yea, they have taken root: they grow, yea, they bring forth fruit: thou *art* near in their mouth, and far from their reins.

3But thou, O LORD, knowest me: thou hast seen me, and tried mine heart toward thee: pull them out like sheep for the slaughter, and prepare them for the day of slaughter.

4How long shall the land mourn, and the herbs of every field wither, for the wickedness of them that dwell therein? the beasts are consumed, and the birds; because they said, He shall not see our last end.

5¶ If thou hast run with the footmen, and they have wearied thee, then how canst thou contend with horses? and *if* in the land of peace, *wherein* thou trustedst, *they wearied thee,* then how wilt thou do in the swelling of Jordan?

6For even thy brethren, and the house of thy father, even they have dealt treacherously with thee; yea, they have called a multitude after thee: believe them not, though they speak fair words unto thee.

7¶ I have forsaken mine house, I have left mine heritage; I have given the dearly beloved of my soul into the hand of her enemies.

## Amplified

17For the Lord of hosts, Who planted you, has pronounced evil *and* calamity against you, because of the evil which the house of Israel and the house of Judah have done against themselves in provoking Me to anger by offering incense to Baal.

18And the Lord gave me [Jeremiah] knowledge of it, and I knew it. Then You, *O Lord,* showed me their doings.

19But I was like a tame lamb that is brought to the slaughter. I did not know that they had devised inventions *and* schemes against me, saying, Let us destroy the tree with its fruit, let us cut him off from the land of the living, that his name may be no more remembered.

20But, O Lord of hosts, Who judges rightly *and* justly, Who tests the heart and the mind, let me see Your vengeance on them, for to You I have revealed *and* committed my cause—rolling it upon You.

21Therefore thus says the Lord of the men of Anathoth [your home town], who seek your life [Jeremiah] and say, Prophesy not in the name of the Lord, that you die not by our hand;

22Therefore thus says the Lord of hosts, Behold, I will punish them: *their* young men shall die by the sword; their sons and their daughters shall die by famine;

23And there shall be no remnant *of the conspirators* left. For I will bring evil *and* calamity upon the men of Anathoth, in the year of their punishment.

**12** UNCOMPROMISINGLY RIGHTEOUS *and* rigidly just are You, O Lord, when I complain *and* contend with You; yet let me plead *and* reason the case with You. Why does the way of the wicked prosper? Why are all they at ease *and* thriving who deal very treacherously *and* deceitfully?

2You have planted them, yes, they have taken root; they grow, yes, they bring forth fruit. You are near in their mouth and far from their heart.

3But You, O Lord, know *and* understand me *and* my devotion to You; You have seen me and tried my heart toward You. *O Lord,* pull *these rebellious ones* out like sheep for the slaughter, and devote *and* prepare them for the day of slaughter.

4How long must the land mourn, and the grass *and* herbs of the whole country wither? Through the wickedness of those who dwell in it, the beasts and the birds are consumed *and* are swept away [by the drought], because men *mocked* me saying, He shall not *live to* see our final end.

5[But the Lord rebukes Jeremiah's impatience, saying] If you have raced with men on foot and they have tired you out, then how can you compete with horses? And if *you take to flight* in a land of peace where you feel secure, then what will you do [when you tread the tangled maze of jungle, haunted by lions] in the swelling of the Jordan?

6For even your brethren and the house of your father, even they have dealt treacherously with you; yes, even they are [like a pack of hounds] in full cry after you. Believe them not, though they speak fair words *and promise* good things to you.

7I have forsaken My house, I have cast off My heritage; I have given the dearly beloved of My life into the hand of her enemies.

## New American Standard

17And the LORD of hosts, who planted you, has pronounced evil against you because of the evil of the house of Israel and of the house of Judah, which they have done to provoke Me by offering up sacrifices to Baal.

*Plots against Jeremiah*

18¶ Moreover, the LORD made it known to me and I knew it;
Then Thou didst show me their deeds.
19 But I was like a gentle lamb led to the slaughter;
And I did not know that they had devised plots against me, *saying*,
"Let us destroy the tree with its fruit,
And let us cut him off from the land of the living,
That his name be remembered no more."
20 But, O LORD of hosts, who judges righteously,
Who tries the feelings and the heart,
Let me see Thy vengeance on them,
For to Thee have I committed my cause.

21¶ Therefore thus says the LORD concerning the men of Anathoth, who seek your life, saying, "Do not prophesy in the name of the LORD, that you might not die at our hand";
22therefore, thus says the LORD of hosts, "Behold, I am about to punish them! The young men will die by the sword, their sons and daughters will die by famine;
23and a remnant will not be left to them, for I will bring disaster on the men of Anathoth—the year of their punishment."

*Jeremiah's Prayer*

12 RIGHTEOUS ART Thou, O LORD, that I would plead *my* case with Thee;
Indeed I would discuss matters of justice with Thee:
Why has the way of the wicked prospered?
*Why* are all those who deal in treachery at ease?
2 Thou hast planted them, they have also taken root;
They grow, they have even produced fruit.
Thou art near to their lips
But far from their mind.
3 But Thou knowest me, O LORD;
Thou seest me;
And Thou dost examine my heart's *attitude* toward Thee.
Drag them off like sheep for the slaughter
And set them apart for a day of carnage!
4 How long is the land to mourn
And the vegetation of the countryside to wither?
For the wickedness of those who dwell in it,
Animals and birds have been snatched away,
Because *men* have said, "He will not see our latter ending."

5¶ "If you have run with footmen and they have tired you out,
Then how can you compete with horses?
If you fall down in a land of peace,
How will you do in the thicket of the Jordan?
6 "For even your brothers and the household of your father,
Even they have dealt treacherously with you,
Even they have cried aloud after you.
Do not believe them, although they may say nice things to you."

*God's Answer*

7¶ "I have forsaken My house,
I have abandoned My inheritance;
I have given the beloved of My soul
Into the hand of her enemies.

## New International

17The LORD Almighty, who planted you, has decreed disaster for you, because the house of Israel and the house of Judah have done evil and provoked me to anger by burning incense to Baal.

*Plot Against Jeremiah*

18Because the LORD revealed their plot to me, I knew it, for at
that time he showed me what they were doing. 19I had been like
a gentle lamb led to the slaughter; I did not realize that they had plotted against me, saying,

"Let us destroy the tree and its fruit;
let us cut him off from the land of the living,
that his name be remembered no more."
20But, O LORD Almighty, you who judge righteously
and test the heart and mind,
let me see your vengeance upon them,
for to you I have committed my cause.

21"Therefore this is what the LORD says about the men of Anathoth who are seeking your life and saying, 'Do not prophesy in the name of the LORD or you will die by our hands'— 22therefore
this is what the LORD Almighty says: 'I will punish them. Their young men will die by the sword, their sons and daughters by
famine. 23Not even a remnant will be left to them, because I will bring disaster on the men of Anathoth in the year of their punishment.'"

*Jeremiah's Complaint*

12 YOU ARE always righteous, O LORD,
when I bring a case before you.
Yet I would speak with you about your justice:
Why does the way of the wicked prosper?
Why do all the faithless live at ease?
2You have planted them, and they have taken root;
they grow and bear fruit.
You are always on their lips
but far from their hearts.
3Yet you know me, O LORD;
you see me and test my thoughts about you.
Drag them off like sheep to be butchered!
Set them apart for the day of slaughter!
4How long will the land lie parched[a]
and the grass in every field be withered?
Because those who live in it are wicked,
the animals and birds have perished.
Moreover, the people are saying,
"He will not see what happens to us."

*God's Answer*

5"If you have raced with men on foot
and they have worn you out,
how can you compete with horses?
If you stumble in safe country,[b]
how will you manage in the thickets by[c] the Jordan?
6Your brothers, your own family—
even they have betrayed you;
they have raised a loud cry against you.
Do not trust them,
though they speak well of you.

7"I will forsake my house,
abandon my inheritance;
I will give the one I love
into the hands of her enemies.

NIV [a] 4 Or *land mourn* [b] 5 Or *If you put your trust in a land of safety* [c] 5 Or *the flooding of*

## King James

8Mine heritage is unto me as a lion in the forest; it crieth out against me: therefore have I hated it.

9Mine heritage *is* unto me *as* a speckled bird, the birds round about *are* against her; come ye, assemble all the beasts of the field, come to devour.

10Many pastors have destroyed my vineyard, they have trodden my portion under foot, they have made my pleasant portion a desolate wilderness.

11They have made it desolate, *and being* desolate it mourneth unto me; the whole land is made desolate, because no man layeth *it* to heart.

12The spoilers are come upon all high places through the wilderness: for the sword of the LORD shall devour from the *one* end of the land even to the *other* end of the land: no flesh shall have peace.

13They have sown wheat, but shall reap thorns: they have put themselves to pain, *but* shall not profit: and they shall be ashamed of your revenues because of the fierce anger of the LORD.

14¶ Thus saith the LORD against all mine evil neighbours, that touch the inheritance which I have caused my people Israel to inherit; Behold, I will pluck them out of their land, and pluck out the house of Judah from among them.

15And it shall come to pass, after that I have plucked them out I will return, and have compassion on them, and will bring them again, every man to his heritage, and every man to his land.

16And it shall come to pass, if they will diligently learn the ways of my people, to swear by my name, The LORD liveth; as they taught my people to swear by Baal; then shall they be built in the midst of my people.

17But if they will not obey, I will utterly pluck up and destroy that nation, saith the LORD.

**13** THUS SAITH the LORD unto me, Go and get thee a linen girdle, and put it upon thy loins, and put it not in water.

2So I got a girdle according to the word of the LORD, and put *it* on my loins.

3And the word of the LORD came unto me the second time, saying,

4Take the girdle that thou hast got, which *is* upon thy loins, and arise, go to Euphrates, and hide it there in a hole of the rock.

5So I went, and hid it by Euphrates, as the LORD commanded me.

6And it came to pass after many days, that the LORD said unto me, Arise, go to Euphrates, and take the girdle from thence, which I commanded thee to hide there.

7Then I went to Euphrates, and digged, and took the girdle from the place where I had hid it: and, behold, the girdle was marred, it was profitable for nothing.

8Then the word of the LORD came unto me, saying,

9Thus saith the LORD, After this manner will I mar the pride of Judah, and the great pride of Jerusalem.

10This evil people, which refuse to hear my words, which walk in the imagination of their heart, and walk after other gods, to serve them, and to worship them, shall even be as this girdle, which is good for nothing.

## Amplified

8My heritage has become to Me like a lion in the forest; she has uttered her voice against Me; therefore I have [treated her as if I] hated her.

9Is My heritage to Me like a speckled bird of prey? Are the birds of prey against her round about? Go, assemble all the wild beasts of the field, bring them to devour.

10Many shepherds [of an invading host] have destroyed My vineyard, they have trampled My portion under foot, they have made My pleasant portion a desolate wilderness.

11They have made it a desolation; and desolate it mourns to Me; the whole land is made desolate, but no man lays it to heart.

12Destroyers have come upon all the bare heights in the desert; for the sword of the Lord devours from one end of the land even to the other; no flesh has peace *or* can find means to escape.

13They have sown wheat, but have reaped thorns; they have worn themselves out, but without profit; *and* they shall be ashamed of your [lack of] harvests *and* revenues because of the fierce *and* glowing anger of the Lord.

14Thus says the Lord, against all My evil neighbor *nations* who touch the inheritance which I have caused My people Israel to inherit: Behold, I will pluck them up from off their land, and I will pluck up the house of Judah from among them.

15And after I have plucked them up, I will return and have compassion on them, and will bring them again, every man to his heritage and every man to his land.

16And if these [neighbor nations] will diligently learn the ways of My people, to swear by My name, *saying*, As the Lord lives, even as they taught My people to swear by Baal, then shall they be built up in the midst of My people.

17But if *any nation* will not hear and obey, I will utterly pluck up and destroy that nation, says the Lord.

**13** THUS THE Lord said to me, Go and buy you a linen girdle and put it on your loins, and do not put it in water.

2So I bought a girdle *or* waistcloth according to the word of the Lord, and put it on my loins.

3And the word of the Lord came to me the second time, saying,

4Take the girdle which you have bought, which is on your loins, and arise, go to the *river* Euphrates, and hide it there in a cleft of the rock.

5So I went, and hid it by the Euphrates *River*, as the Lord commanded me.

6And after many days the Lord said to me, Arise, go to the Euphrates, and take from there the girdle which I commanded you to hide there.

7Then I went to the Euphrates, and dug, and took the girdle *or* waistcloth from the place where I had hidden it. And behold, the girdle was decayed *and* spoiled, it was good for nothing.

8Then the word of the Lord came to me, saying,

9Thus says the Lord, After this manner will I mar the pride of Judah and the great pride of Jerusalem.

10This evil people, who refuse to hear My words, who walk in the stubbornness of their heart and have gone after other gods to serve them and to worship them, shall even be like this girdle *or* waistcloth, which is profitable for nothing.

## New American Standard

8 "My inheritance has become to Me
Like a lion in the forest;
She has roared against Me;
Therefore I have come to hate her.
9 "Is My inheritance like a speckled bird of prey to Me?
Are the birds of prey against her on every side?
Go, gather all the beasts of the field,
Bring them to devour!
10 "Many shepherds have ruined My vineyard,
They have trampled down My field;
They have made My pleasant field
A desolate wilderness.
11 "It has been made a desolation,
Desolate, it mourns before Me;
The whole land has been made desolate,
Because no man lays it to heart.
12 "On all the bare heights in the wilderness
Destroyers have come,
For a sword of the LORD is devouring
From one end of the land even to the other;
There is no peace for anyone.
13 "They have sown wheat and have reaped thorns,
They have strained themselves to no profit.
But be ashamed of your harvest
Because of the fierce anger of the LORD."

14¶ Thus says the LORD concerning all My wicked neighbors
who strike at the inheritance with which I have endowed My
people Israel, "Behold I am about to uproot them from their land
and will uproot the house of Judah from among them.
15"And it will come about that after I have uprooted them, I will
again have compassion on them; and I will bring them back, each
one to his inheritance and each one to his land.
16"Then it will come about that if they will really learn the ways
of My people, to swear by My name, 'As the LORD lives,' even as
they taught My people to swear by Baal, then they will be built up
in the midst of My people.
17"But if they will not listen, then I will uproot that nation,
uproot and destroy it," declares the LORD.

*The Ruined Waistband*

13 THUS THE LORD said to me, "Go and buy yourself a linen
waistband, and put it around your waist, but do not put
it in water."
2So I bought the waistband in accordance with the word of the
LORD and put it around my waist.
3Then the word of the LORD came to me a second time, saying,
4"Take the waistband that you have bought, which is around
your waist, and arise, go to the Euphrates and hide it there in a
crevice of the rock."
5So I went and hid it by the Euphrates, as the LORD had
commanded me.
6And it came about after many days that the LORD said to me,
"Arise, go to the Euphrates and take from there the waistband
which I commanded you to hide there."
7Then I went to the Euphrates and dug, and I took the waistband from the place where I had hidden it; and lo, the waistband
was ruined, it was totally worthless.
8¶ Then the word of the LORD came to me, saying,
9"Thus says the LORD, 'Just so will I destroy the pride of Judah
and the great pride of Jerusalem.
10'This wicked people, who refuse to listen to My words, who
walk in the stubbornness of their hearts and have gone after other
gods to serve them and to bow down to them, let them be just like
this waistband, which is totally worthless.

## New International

8My inheritance has become to me
like a lion in the forest.
She roars at me;
therefore I hate her.
9Has not my inheritance become to me
like a speckled bird of prey
that other birds of prey surround and attack?
Go and gather all the wild beasts;
bring them to devour.
10Many shepherds will ruin my vineyard
and trample down my field;
they will turn my pleasant field
into a desolate wasteland.
11It will be made a wasteland,
parched and desolate before me;
the whole land will be laid waste
because there is no one who cares.
12Over all the barren heights in the desert
destroyers will swarm,
for the sword of the LORD will devour
from one end of the land to the other;
no one will be safe.
13They will sow wheat but reap thorns;
they will wear themselves out but gain nothing.
So bear the shame of your harvest
because of the LORD's fierce anger."

14This is what the LORD says: "As for all my wicked neighbors
who seize the inheritance I gave my people Israel, I will uproot
them from their lands and I will uproot the house of Judah from
among them. 15But after I uproot them, I will again have compassion and will bring each of them back to his own inheritance and
his own country. 16And if they learn well the ways of my people
and swear by my name, 'As surely as the LORD
lives'—even as they once taught my people to swear by Baal—then
they will be established among my people. 17But if any nation does
not listen, I will completely uproot and destroy it," declares the
LORD.

*A Linen Belt*

13 THIS IS what the LORD said to me: "Go and buy a linen
belt and put it around your waist, but do not let it touch
water." 2So I bought a belt, as the LORD directed, and put it around
my waist.
3Then the word of the LORD came to me a second time: 4"Take
the belt you bought and are wearing around your waist, and go
now to Perath[a] and hide it there in a crevice in the rocks." 5So I
went and hid it at Perath, as the LORD told me.
6Many days later the LORD said to me, "Go now to Perath and
get the belt I told you to hide there." 7So I went to Perath and dug
up the belt and took it from the place where I had hidden it, but
now it was ruined and completely useless.
8Then the word of the LORD came to me: 9"This is what the
LORD says: 'In the same way I will ruin the pride of Judah and the
great pride of Jerusalem. 10These wicked people, who refuse to
listen to my words, who follow the stubbornness of their hearts
and go after other gods to serve and worship them, will be like this
belt—completely useless! 11For as a belt is bound around a man's

NIV [a] 4 Or possibly *the Euphrates;* also in verses 5-7

## King James

11For as the girdle cleaveth to the loins of a man, so have I
caused to cleave unto me the whole house of Israel and the whole
house of Judah, saith the LORD; that they might be unto me for a
people, and for a name, and for a praise, and for a glory: but they
would not hear.
12¶ Therefore thou shalt speak unto them this word; Thus saith
the LORD God of Israel, Every bottle shall be filled with wine: and
they shall say unto thee, Do we not certainly know that every
bottle shall be filled with wine?
13Then shalt thou say unto them, Thus saith the LORD, Behold,
I will fill all the inhabitants of this land, even the kings that sit upon
David's throne, and the priests, and the prophets, and all the
inhabitants of Jerusalem, with drunkenness.
14And I will dash them one against another, even the fathers
and the sons together, saith the LORD: I will not pity, nor spare,
nor have mercy, but destroy them.
15¶ Hear ye, and give ear; be not proud: for the LORD hath
spoken.
16Give glory to the LORD your God, before he cause darkness,
and before your feet stumble upon the dark mountains, and, while
ye look for light, he turn it into the shadow of death, *and* make *it*
gross darkness.
17But if ye will not hear it, my soul shall weep in secret places
for *your* pride; and mine eye shall weep sore, and run down with
tears, because the LORD's flock is carried away captive.
18Say unto the king and to the queen, Humble yourselves, sit
down: for your principalities shall come down, *even* the crown of
your glory.
19The cities of the south shall be shut up, and none shall open
*them:* Judah shall be carried away captive all of it, it shall be wholly
carried away captive.
20Lift up your eyes, and behold them that come from the north:
where *is* the flock *that* was given thee, thy beautiful flock?
21What wilt thou say when he shall punish thee? for thou hast
taught them *to be* captains, *and* as chief over thee: shall not sorrows
take thee, as a woman in travail?
22¶ And if thou say in thine heart, Wherefore come these things
upon me? For the greatness of thine iniquity are thy skirts discovered, *and* thy heels made bare.
23Can the Ethiopian change his skin, or the leopard his spots?
*then* may ye also do good, that are accustomed to do evil.
24Therefore will I scatter them as the stubble that passeth away
by the wind of the wilderness.
25This *is* thy lot, the portion of thy measures from me, saith the
LORD; because thou hast forgotten me, and trusted in falsehood.
26Therefore will I discover thy skirts upon thy face, that thy
shame may appear.

## Amplified

11For as the girdle clings to the loins of a man, so I caused the
whole house of Israel and the whole house of Judah to cling to Me,
says the Lord, that they might be for Me a people, a name, a praise,
and a glory, but they would not listen *or* obey.
12Therefore you shall speak to them this word: Thus says the
Lord God of Israel, Every bottle *and* jar shall be filled with wine.
*The people* will say to you, Do we not certainly know that every
bottle *and* jar will be filled with wine?
13Then you shall say to them, Thus says the Lord: Behold, I will
fill with drunkenness all the inhabitants of this land; even the kings
who sit upon David's throne, the priests, the prophets, and all the
inhabitants of Jerusalem.
14And I will dash them one against another, even the fathers
and the sons together, says the Lord. I will not pity or spare or have
compassion, that I should not destroy them.
15Hear and give ear; do not be proud, for the Lord has spoken,
*says Jeremiah.*
16Give glory to the Lord your God before He brings darkness,
and before your feet stumble upon the dark *and* twilight mountains, and *before,* while you look for light, He turns it into the
shadow of death and makes it thick darkness.
17But if you will not hear *and* obey, I will weep in secret for your
pride; my eyes will weep bitterly and run down with tears, because
the Lord's flock is taken captive.
18Say to the king and the queen mother, Humble yourselves *and*
take a lowly seat, for down from your head has come your beautiful crown—the crown of your glory.
19The cities of the South [the Negeb] are shut up, and there is
no one to open them; all Judah is carried away captive, it is wholly
taken captive *and* into exile.
20Lift up your eyes and behold them [the eruption of a hostile
army] who come from the north. Where is the flock that was given
to you *to shepherd,* your beautiful flock?
21What will you say, *O Jerusalem,* when He, *the Lord,* shall set
over you for head those [tyrannical foreign nations] whom you
yourselves *at intervals* have taught to be allies with you—instructing them, even *your* friends, to be head over you? Will not pangs
take hold of you as of a woman in travail?
22And if you say in your heart, Why have these things come
upon me? *the answer is,* For the greatness of your iniquity *is* your
long robe pulled aside [showing you in the garb of a menial], *and*
you—barefooted and treated as a slave—suffer violence.
23Can the Ethiopian change his skin or the leopard his spots?
Then also can you do good who are accustomed *and* taught, *even*
trained, to do evil.
24Therefore I will scatter *you* as chaff driven away by the wind
from the desert.
25This is your lot, the portion measured to you from Me, says
the Lord, because you have forgotten Me and trusted in falsehood
[false gods and alliances with idolatrous nations].
26Therefore I Myself will *retaliate,* throwing your skirts up over
your face, that your shame [of being clad as a slave] may be
exposed.

## New American Standard

11'For as the waistband clings to the waist of a man, so I made the whole household of Israel and the whole household of Judah cling to Me,' declares the LORD, 'that they might be for Me a people, for renown, for praise, and for glory; but they did not listen.'

*Captivity Threatened*

12¶ "Therefore you are to speak this word to them, 'Thus says the LORD, the God of Israel, "Every jug is to be filled with wine." ' And when they say to you, 'Do we not very well know that every jug is to be filled with wine?'

13then say to them, 'Thus says the LORD, "Behold I am about to fill all the inhabitants of this land—the kings that sit for David on his throne, the priests, the prophets and all the inhabitants of Jerusalem—with drunkenness!

14"And I will dash them against each other, both the fathers and the sons together," declares the LORD. "I will not show pity nor be sorry nor have compassion that I should not destroy them." ' "

15¶ Listen and give heed, do not be haughty,
For the LORD has spoken.
16 Give glory to the LORD your God,
Before He brings darkness
And before your feet stumble
On the dusky mountains,
And while you are hoping for light
He makes it into deep darkness,
*And* turns *it* into gloom.
17 But if you will not listen to it,
My soul will sob in secret for *such* pride;
And my eyes will bitterly weep
And flow down with tears,
Because the flock of the LORD has been taken captive.
18 Say to the king and the queen mother,
"Take a lowly seat,
For your beautiful crown
Has come down from your head."
19 The cities of the Negev have been locked up,
And there is no one to open *them;*
All Judah has been carried into exile,
Wholly carried into exile.

20¶ "Lift up your eyes and see
Those coming from the north.
Where is the flock that was given you,
Your beautiful sheep?
21 "What will you say when He appoints over you—
And you yourself had taught them—
Former companions to be head over you?
Will not pangs take hold of you,
Like a woman in childbirth?
22 "And if you say in your heart,
'Why have these things happened to me?'
Because of the magnitude of your iniquity
Your skirts have been removed,
And your heels have been exposed.
23 "Can the Ethiopian change his skin
Or the leopard his spots?
*Then* you also can do good
Who are accustomed to do evil.
24 "Therefore I will scatter them like drifting straw
To the desert wind.
25 "This is your lot, the portion measured to you
From Me," declares the LORD,
"Because you have forgotten Me
And trusted in falsehood.
26 "So I Myself have also stripped your skirts off over your face,
That your shame may be seen.

## New International

waist, so I bound the whole house of Israel and the whole house of Judah to me,' declares the LORD, 'to be my people for my renown and praise and honor. But they have not listened.'

*Wineskins*

12"Say to them: 'This is what the LORD, the God of Israel, says: Every wineskin should be filled with wine.' And if they say to you, 'Don't we know that every wineskin should be filled with wine?'
13then tell them, 'This is what the LORD says: I am going to fill with drunkenness all who live in this land, including the kings who sit on David's throne, the priests, the prophets and all those living in Jerusalem. 14I will smash them one against the other, fathers and sons alike, declares the LORD. I will allow no pity or mercy or compassion to keep me from destroying them.' "

*Threat of Captivity*

15Hear and pay attention,
do not be arrogant,
for the LORD has spoken.
16Give glory to the LORD your God
before he brings the darkness,
before your feet stumble
on the darkening hills.
You hope for light,
but he will turn it to thick darkness
and change it to deep gloom.
17But if you do not listen,
I will weep in secret
because of your pride;
my eyes will weep bitterly,
overflowing with tears,
because the LORD's flock will be taken captive.
18Say to the king and to the queen mother,
"Come down from your thrones,
for your glorious crowns
will fall from your heads."
19The cities in the Negev will be shut up,
and there will be no one to open them.
All Judah will be carried into exile,
carried completely away.

20Lift up your eyes and see
those who are coming from the north.
Where is the flock that was entrusted to you,
the sheep of which you boasted?
21What will you say when ⌊the LORD⌋ sets over you
those you cultivated as your special allies?
Will not pain grip you
like that of a woman in labor?
22And if you ask yourself,
"Why has this happened to me?"—
it is because of your many sins
that your skirts have been torn off
and your body mistreated.
23Can the Ethiopian[a] change his skin
or the leopard its spots?
Neither can you do good
who are accustomed to doing evil.

24"I will scatter you like chaff
driven by the desert wind.
25This is your lot,
the portion I have decreed for you,"
declares the LORD,
"because you have forgotten me
and trusted in false gods.
26I will pull up your skirts over your face
that your shame may be seen—

NIV [a] 23 Hebrew *Cushite* (probably a person from the upper Nile region)

# King James

27I have seen thine adulteries, and thy neighings, the lewdness of thy whoredom, *and* thine abominations on the hills in the fields. Woe unto thee, O Jerusalem! wilt thou not be made clean? when *shall it* once *be?*

## 14

THE WORD of the LORD that came to Jeremiah concerning the dearth.

2Judah mourneth, and the gates thereof languish; they are black unto the ground; and the cry of Jerusalem is gone up.

3And their nobles have sent their little ones to the waters: they came to the pits, *and* found no water; they returned with their vessels empty; they were ashamed and confounded, and covered their heads.

4Because the ground is chapt, for there was no rain in the earth, the plowmen were ashamed, they covered their heads.

5Yea, the hind also calved in the field, and forsook *it,* because there was no grass.

6And the wild asses did stand in the high places, they snuffed up the wind like dragons; their eyes did fail, because *there was* no grass.

7¶ O LORD, though our iniquities testify against us, do thou *it* for thy name's sake: for our backslidings are many; we have sinned against thee.

8O the hope of Israel, the saviour thereof in time of trouble, why shouldest thou be as a stranger in the land, and as a wayfaring man *that* turneth aside to tarry for a night?

9Why shouldest thou be as a man astonied, as a mighty man *that* cannot save? yet thou, O LORD, *art* in the midst of us, and we are called by thy name; leave us not.

10¶ Thus saith the LORD unto this people, Thus have they loved to wander, they have not refrained their feet, therefore the LORD doth not accept them; he will now remember their iniquity, and visit their sins.

11Then said the LORD unto me, Pray not for this people for *their* good.

12When they fast, I will not hear their cry; and when they offer burnt offering and an oblation, I will not accept them: but I will consume them by the sword, and by the famine, and by the pestilence.

13¶ Then said I, Ah, Lord GOD! behold, the prophets say unto them, Ye shall not see the sword, neither shall ye have famine; but I will give you assured peace in this place.

14Then the LORD said unto me, The prophets prophesy lies in my name: I sent them not, neither have I commanded them, neither spake unto them: they prophesy unto you a false vision and divination, and a thing of nought, and the deceit of their heart.

# Amplified

27I have seen your detestable acts, even your adulteries and your lustful neighings [after idols], and the lewdness of your harlotry on the hills in the field. Woe to you, O Jerusalem! For how long a time yet will you not [meet My conditions and] be made clean?

## 14

THE WORD of the Lord that came to Jeremiah concerning the drought:

2Judah mourns and her gates languish; *her people* sit in black (mourning garb) upon the ground, and the cry of Jerusalem goes up.

3And their nobles send their little ones *and* their inferiors for water. They come to the cisterns and find no water; they return with empty vessels; they are put to shame and confounded and cover their heads.

4Because the ground is cracked *and* [the tillers are] dismayed, since there has been no rain on the land, the plowmen are put to shame, they cover their heads.

5Yes, also the hind gives birth to her calf in the field, and forsakes *it,* because there is no grass *or* herbage.

6And the wild donkeys stand on the bare heights, they pant for air like jackals *or* the crocodile; their eyesight fails because there is no grass.

7O Lord, though our iniquities testify against us [prays Jeremiah], deal *and* work *with us* for Your own name's sake [that the heathen may witness Your might and faithfulness]; for our backslidings are many, we have sinned against You.

8O hope of Israel, her Savior in the time of trouble, why should You be as a sojourner in the land and as a wayfaring man who turns aside *and* spreads his tent to tarry *only* for a night?

9Why should You be [hesitant and inactive] like a man stunned *and* confused, like a mighty man who cannot save? Yet You, O Lord, are in the midst of us, and we are called by Your name; do not leave us.

10[And the Lord replied to Jeremiah] Thus says the Lord to this people [Judah], In the manner *and* to the degree already pointed out have they loved to wander, they have not restrained their feet; therefore the Lord does not accept them; He will now [seriously] remember their iniquity and punish their sins.

11The Lord said to me: Do not pray for this people for *their* good.

12Though they fast, I will not hear their cry; and though they offer burnt offering and cereal offering [without heartfelt surrender to Me, or too late], I will not accept them; but I will consume them by the sword, by famine, and by pestilence.

13Then said I, Alas, Lord God! Behold, the [false] prophets say to them, You shall not see the sword, nor shall you have famine; but I [the Lord] will give you assured peace in this place—peace of truth.

14Then the Lord said to me, The [false] prophets prophesy lies in My name. I sent them not, neither have I commanded them, nor have I spoken to them. They prophesy to you a false *or* pretended vision, worthless divination—conjuring, and the responses supposed to be given by idols—the deceit of their own minds.

## New American Standard

27 "As for your adulteries and your *lustful* neighings,
The lewdness of your prostitution
On the hills in the field,
I have seen your abominations.
Woe to you, O Jerusalem!
How long will you remain unclean?"

*Drought and a Prayer for Mercy*

14 THAT WHICH came as the word of the LORD to Jeremiah in regard to the drought:
2 "Judah mourns,
And her gates languish
They sit on the ground in mourning,
And the cry of Jerusalem has ascended.
3 "And their nobles have sent their servants for water;
They have come to the cisterns and found no water.
They have returned with their vessels empty;
They have been put to shame and humiliated,
And they cover their heads.
4 "Because the ground is cracked,
For there has been no rain on the land;
The farmers have been put to shame,
They have covered their heads.
5 "For even the doe in the field has given birth only to abandon *her young*,
Because there is no grass.
6 "And the wild donkeys stand on the bare heights;
They pant for air like jackals,
Their eyes fail
For there is no vegetation.
7 "Although our iniquities testify against us,
O LORD, act for Thy name's sake!
Truly our apostasies have been many,
We have sinned against Thee.
8 "Thou Hope of Israel,
Its Savior in time of distress,
Why art Thou like a stranger in the land
Or like a traveler who has pitched his *tent* for the night?
9 "Why art Thou like a man dismayed,
Like a mighty man who cannot save?
Yet Thou art in our midst, O LORD,
And we are called by Thy name;
Do not forsake us!"

10¶ Thus says the LORD to this people, "Even so they have loved
to wander; they have not kept their feet in check. Therefore the
LORD does not accept them; now He will remember their iniquity
and call their sins to account."
11So the LORD said to me, "Do not pray for the welfare of this
people.
12"When they fast, I am not going to listen to their cry; and
when they offer burnt offering and grain offering, I am not going
to accept them. Rather I am going to make an end of them by the
sword, famine and pestilence."

*False Prophets*

13¶ But, "Ah, Lord GOD!" I said, "Look, the prophets are telling
them, 'You will not see the sword nor will you have famine, but
I will give you lasting peace in this place.' "
14Then the LORD said to me, "The prophets are prophesying
falsehood in My name. I have neither sent them nor commanded
them nor spoken to them; they are prophesying to you a false
vision, divination, futility and the deception of their own minds.

## New International

27your adulteries and lustful neighings,
your shameless prostitution!
I have seen your detestable acts
on the hills and in the fields.
Woe to you, O Jerusalem!
How long will you be unclean?"

*Drought, Famine, Sword*

14 THIS IS the word of the LORD to Jeremiah concerning the drought:

2"Judah mourns,
her cities languish;
they wail for the land,
and a cry goes up from Jerusalem.
3The nobles send their servants for water;
they go to the cisterns
but find no water.
They return with their jars unfilled;
dismayed and despairing,
they cover their heads.
4The ground is cracked
because there is no rain in the land;
the farmers are dismayed
and cover their heads.
5Even the doe in the field
deserts her newborn fawn
because there is no grass.
6Wild donkeys stand on the barren heights
and pant like jackals;
their eyesight fails
for lack of pasture."

7Although our sins testify against us,
O LORD, do something for the sake of your name.
For our backsliding is great;
we have sinned against you.
8O Hope of Israel,
its Savior in times of distress,
why are you like a stranger in the land,
like a traveler who stays only a night?
9Why are you like a man taken by surprise,
like a warrior powerless to save?
You are among us, O LORD,
and we bear your name;
do not forsake us!

10This is what the LORD says about this people:
"They greatly love to wander;
they do not restrain their feet.
So the LORD does not accept them;
he will now remember their wickedness
and punish them for their sins."

11Then the LORD said to me, "Do not pray for the well-being of
this people. 12Although they fast, I will not listen to their cry;
though they offer burnt offerings and grain offerings, I will not
accept them. Instead, I will destroy them with the sword, famine
and plague."
13But I said, "Ah, Sovereign LORD, the prophets keep telling
them, 'You will not see the sword or suffer famine. Indeed, I will
give you lasting peace in this place.' "
14Then the LORD said to me, "The prophets are prophesying lies
in my name. I have not sent them or appointed them or spoken
to them. They are prophesying to you false visions, divinations,
idolatries[a] and the delusions of their own minds. 15Therefore, this

NIV [a] 14 Or *visions, worthless divinations*

## King James

15Therefore thus saith the LORD concerning the prophets that prophesy in my name, and I sent them not, yet they say, Sword and famine shall not be in this land; By sword and famine shall those prophets be consumed.

16And the people to whom they prophesy shall be cast out in the streets of Jerusalem because of the famine and the sword; and they shall have none to bury them, them, their wives, nor their sons, nor their daughters: for I will pour their wickedness upon them.

17¶ Therefore thou shalt say this word unto them; Let mine eyes run down with tears night and day, and let them not cease: for the virgin daughter of my people is broken with a great breach, with a very grievous blow.

18If I go forth into the field, then behold the slain with the sword! and if I enter into the city, then behold them that are sick with famine! yea, both the prophet and the priest go about into a land that they know not.

19Hast thou utterly rejected Judah? hath thy soul loathed Zion? why hast thou smitten us, and *there is* no healing for us? we looked for peace, and *there is* no good; and for the time of healing, and behold trouble!

20We acknowledge, O LORD, our wickedness, *and* the iniquity of our fathers: for we have sinned against thee.

21Do not abhor *us*, for thy name's sake, do not disgrace the throne of thy glory: remember, break not thy covenant with us.

22Are there *any* among the vanities of the Gentiles that can cause rain? or can the heavens give showers? *art* not thou he, O LORD our God? therefore we will wait upon thee: for thou hast made all these *things*.

## Amplified

15Therefore thus says the Lord concerning the [false] prophets who prophesy in My name although I did not send them, and who say, Sword and famine shall not be in this land: By sword and famine shall those prophets be consumed.

16And the people to whom they prophesy shall be cast out in the streets of Jerusalem, victims of famine and sword, and they shall have none to bury them: them, their wives, their sons and their daughters. For I will pour out their wickedness upon them [and not on their false teachers only, for the people could not have been deceived except by their own consent].

17Therefore [Jeremiah], you shall say to them, Let my eyes run down with tears night and day, and let them not cease; for the virgin daughter of my people is smitten with a great wound, with a very grievous blow.

18If I go out into the field, then behold, those slain with the sword! And if I enter the city, then behold, those tormented with the diseases of famine! For both prophet and priest go about not knowing what to do, *or* as beggars [exiled] in a land that they know not, and have no knowledge.

19[O Lord], have You utterly rejected Judah? Do You loathe Zion? Why have You smitten us so there is no healing for us? We looked for peace *and* completeness, but no good came; and for a time of healing, but behold, dismay, disaster *and* terror!

20We know *and* acknowledge, O Lord, our wickedness, and the iniquity of our fathers; for we have sinned against You.

21Do not abhor, condemn *and* spurn us, for Your name's sake; do not dishonor, debase *and* lightly esteem Your glorious throne; [earnestly] remember, break not Your covenant *or* sacred pledge with us.

22Are there any among the false gods of the nations that can cause rain? Or can the heavens [of their own will] give showers? Are You [alone] not He, O Lord our God? Therefore we will wait for You—expectantly; for You have made [the heavens and the rain] all these things.

## King James

**15** THEN SAID the LORD unto me, Though Moses and Samuel stood before me, *yet* my mind *could* not *be* toward this people: cast *them* out of my sight, and let them go forth.

2And it shall come to pass, if they say unto thee, Whither shall we go forth? then thou shalt tell them, Thus saith the LORD; Such as *are* for death, to death; and such as *are* for the sword, to the sword; and such as *are* for the famine, to the famine; and such as *are* for the captivity, to the captivity.

3And I will appoint over them four kinds, saith the LORD: the sword to slay, and the dogs to tear, and the fowls of the heaven, and the beasts of the earth, to devour and destroy.

4And I will cause them to be removed into all kingdoms of the earth, because of Manasseh the son of Hezekiah king of Judah, for *that* which he did in Jerusalem.

5For who shall have pity upon thee, O Jerusalem? or who shall bemoan thee? or who shall go aside to ask how thou doest?

6Thou hast forsaken me, saith the LORD, thou art gone backward: therefore will I stretch out my hand against thee, and destroy thee; I am weary with repenting.

## Amplified

**15** THEN THE Lord said to me, Though Moses and Samuel stood [interceding for them] before Me, yet My mind could not be turned with favor toward this people [Judah]. Send them out of My sight, and let them go!

2And if they say to you, Where shall we go? then tell them, Thus says the Lord: Such as are for death, to death; and such as are for the sword, to the sword; and such as are for famine, to the famine; and such as are for captivity, to the captivity.

3And I will appoint over them four kinds [of destroyers], says the Lord: the sword to slay, the dogs to tear *and* drag, the birds of the air and the beasts of the earth to devour and to destroy.

4And I will cause them to be tossed to and fro among all the kingdoms of the earth, *and* be made a horror *to all nations* because of Manasseh the son of Hezekiah, king of Judah, for [the horrible wickedness] which he did in Jerusalem. [II Kings 21:3-7.]

5For who will have pity upon you, O Jerusalem, or who will bemoan you? Or who will turn aside to ask for your welfare?

6You have rejected *and* forsaken Me, says the Lord, you keep going in reverse. Therefore I have stretched out My hand against you and destroyed you; I am weary of relenting [concerning your punishment].

## New American Standard

15"Therefore thus says the LORD concerning the prophets who are prophesying in My name, although it was not I who sent them—yet they keep saying, 'There shall be no sword or famine in this land'—by sword and famine those prophets shall meet their end!

16"The people also to whom they are prophesying will be thrown out into the streets of Jerusalem because of the famine and the sword; and there will be no one to bury them— *neither* them, *nor* their wives, nor their sons, nor their daughters—for I shall pour out their *own* wickedness on them.

17 "And you will say this word to them,
'Let my eyes flow down with tears night and day,
And let them not cease;
For the virgin daughter of my people has been crushed
with a mighty blow,
With a sorely infected wound.
18 'If I go out to the country,
Behold, those slain with the sword!
Or if I enter the city,
Behold, diseases of famine!
For both prophet and priest
Have gone roving about in the land that they do not
know.' "

19¶ Hast Thou completely rejected Judah?
Or hast Thou loathed Zion?
Why hast Thou stricken us so that we are beyond
healing?
*We* waited for peace, but nothing good *came;*
And for a time of healing, but behold, terror!
20 We know our wickedness, O LORD,
The iniquity of our fathers, for we have sinned against
Thee.
21 Do not despise *us,* for Thine own name's sake;
Do not disgrace the throne of Thy glory;
Remember *and* do not annul Thy covenant with us.
22 Are there any among the idols of the nations who give
rain?
Or can the heavens grant showers?
Is it not Thou, O LORD our God?
Therefore we hope in Thee,
For Thou art the one who hast done all these things.

*Judgment Must Come*

**15** THEN THE LORD said to me, "Even though Moses and Samuel were to stand before Me, My heart would not be with this people; send them away from My presence and let them go!

2"And it shall be that when they say to you, 'Where should we go?' then you are to tell them, 'Thus says the LORD:
"Those *destined* for death, to death;
And those *destined* for the sword, to the sword;
And those *destined* for famine, to famine;
And those *destined* for captivity, to captivity." '

3"And I shall appoint over them four kinds *of doom,"* declares the LORD: "the sword to slay, the dogs to drag off, and the birds of the sky and the beasts of the earth to devour and destroy.

4"And I shall make them an object of horror among all the kingdoms of the earth because of Manasseh, the son of Hezekiah, the king of Judah, for what he did in Jerusalem.

5¶ "Indeed, who will have pity on you, O Jerusalem,
Or who will mourn for you,
Or who will turn aside to ask about your welfare?
6 "You who have forsaken Me," declares the LORD,
"You keep going backward.
So I will stretch out My hand against you and destroy
you;
I am tired of relenting!

## New International

is what the LORD says about the prophets who are prophesying in my name: I did not send them, yet they are saying, 'No sword or famine will touch this land.' Those same prophets will perish by sword and famine. 16And the people they are prophesying to will be thrown out into the streets of Jerusalem because of the famine and sword. There will be no one to bury them or their wives, their sons or their daughters. I will pour out on them the calamity they deserve.

17"Speak this word to them:
" 'Let my eyes overflow with tears
night and day without ceasing;
for my virgin daughter—my people—
has suffered a grievous wound,
a crushing blow.
18If I go into the country,
I see those slain by the sword;
if I go into the city,
I see the ravages of famine.
Both prophet and priest
have gone to a land they know not.' "

19Have you rejected Judah completely?
Do you despise Zion?
Why have you afflicted us
so that we cannot be healed?
We hoped for peace
but no good has come,
for a time of healing
but there is only terror.
20O LORD, we acknowledge our wickedness
and the guilt of our fathers;
we have indeed sinned against you.
21For the sake of your name do not despise us;
do not dishonor your glorious throne.
Remember your covenant with us
and do not break it.
22Do any of the worthless idols of the nations bring rain?
Do the skies themselves send down showers?
No, it is you, O LORD our God.
Therefore our hope is in you,
for you are the one who does all this.

**15** THEN THE LORD said to me: "Even if Moses and Samuel were to stand before me, my heart would not go out to this people. Send them away from my presence! Let them go! 2And if they ask you, 'Where shall we go?' tell them, 'This is what the LORD says:

" 'Those destined for death, to death;
those for the sword, to the sword;
those for starvation, to starvation;
those for captivity, to captivity.'

3"I will send four kinds of destroyers against them," declares the LORD, "the sword to kill and the dogs to drag away and the birds of the air and the beasts of the earth to devour and destroy. 4I will make them abhorrent to all the kingdoms of the earth because of what Manasseh son of Hezekiah king of Judah did in Jerusalem.

5"Who will have pity on you, O Jerusalem?
Who will mourn for you?
Who will stop to ask how you are?
6You have rejected me," declares the LORD.
"You keep on backsliding.
So I will lay hands on you and destroy you;
I can no longer show compassion.

## King James

7 And I will fan them with a fan in the gates of the land; I will bereave *them* of children, I will destroy my people, *since* they return not from their ways.

8 Their widows are increased to me above the sand of the seas: I have brought upon them against the mother of the young men a spoiler at noonday: I have caused *him* to fall upon it suddenly, and terrors upon the city.

9 She that hath borne seven languisheth: she hath given up the ghost; her sun is gone down while *it was* yet day: she hath been ashamed and confounded: and the residue of them will I deliver to the sword before their enemies, saith the LORD.

10 ¶ Woe is me, my mother, that thou hast borne me a man of strife and a man of contention to the whole earth! I have neither lent on usury, nor men have lent to me on usury; *yet* every one of them doth curse me.

11 The LORD said, Verily it shall be well with thy remnant; verily I will cause the enemy to entreat thee *well* in the time of evil and in the time of affliction.

12 Shall iron break the northern iron and the steel?

13 Thy substance and thy treasures will I give to the spoil without price, and *that* for all thy sins, even in all thy borders.

14 And I will make *thee* to pass with thine enemies into a land *which* thou knowest not: for a fire is kindled in mine anger, *which* shall burn upon you.

15 ¶ O LORD, thou knowest: remember me, and visit me, and revenge me of my persecutors; take me not away in thy longsuffering: know that for thy sake I have suffered rebuke.

16 Thy words were found, and I did eat them; and thy word was unto me the joy and rejoicing of mine heart: for I am called by thy name, O LORD God of hosts.

17 I sat not in the assembly of the mockers, nor rejoiced; I sat alone because of thy hand: for thou hast filled me with indignation.

18 Why is my pain perpetual, and my wound incurable, *which* refuseth to be healed? wilt thou be altogether unto me as a liar, *and as* waters *that* fail?

19 ¶ Therefore thus saith the LORD, If thou return, then will I bring thee again, *and* thou shalt stand before me: and if thou take forth the precious from the vile, thou shalt be as my mouth: let them return unto thee; but return not thou unto them.

## Amplified

7 I have winnowed them with a fan *and* a winnowing fork in the gates of the land; I have bereaved them [of children], I have destroyed My people; from their *evil* ways they did not return.

8 I have increased the number of their widows more than the sand of the seas. I have brought upon them, *both* against the mother of young men *and* the young men *themselves*, a destroyer at noonday. I have caused anguish and terrors to fall upon her [Jerusalem] suddenly.

9 She who has borne seven, languishes. She has expired; her sun has gone down while it was yet day. She has been put to shame, confounded *and* disgraced. And the rest of them I will deliver to the sword before their enemies, says the Lord.

10 Woe is me, my mother, that you bore me *to be* a man of strife and a man of contention to the whole earth! I have neither loaned, nor have men loaned to me; yet every one of them curses me. [Jer. 1:18, 19.]

11 The Lord said, Truly your release, affliction *and* strengthening shall be for good; surely [Jeremiah] I will intercede for you with the enemy *and* I will cause the enemy to ask your aid in the time of evil and in the time of affliction. [Rom. 8:28; Jer. 21:1, 2; 37:3; 42:2.]

12 Can iron break the iron from the north, and the bronze?

13 Your [nation's] substance and your treasures will I give as spoil without price, and that for all your sins, even in all your territory.

14 And I will make [your possessions] to pass with your enemies into a land which you do not know, *and* you to serve [your conquerors] there; for a fire is kindled in My anger which shall burn upon you [Israel].

15 [Jeremiah said,] O Lord, You know; [earnestly] remember me and visit me, and avenge me of my persecutors; take me not away [from joy or from life itself] in Your longsuffering [to my enemies]; know that for Your sake I suffer *and* bear reproach.

16 Your words were found, and I ate them, and Your word was to me a joy and the rejoicing of my heart; for I am called by Your name, O Lord, God of hosts.

17 I sat not in the assembly of those who make merry, nor did I rejoice; I sat alone because Your [powerful] hand *was upon me*, for You have filled me with indignation.

18 Why is my pain perpetual, and my wound incurable, refusing to be healed? Will you indeed be to me as a deceitful brook, like waters that fail *and* are uncertain?

19 Therefore thus says the Lord [to Jeremiah], If you return [give up this mistaken tone of distrust and despair], then I will give you again a settled place of quiet *and* safety, and you shall be My minister; and if you separate the precious from the vile [cleansing your own heart from unworthy suspicions concerning God's faithfulness], you shall be as My mouthpiece. [But do not yield to them.] Let them return to you—not you to *the people*.

## New American Standard

7 "And I will winnow them with a winnowing fork
At the gates of the land;
I will bereave *them* of children, I will destroy My people;
They did not repent of their ways.
8 "Their widows will be more numerous before Me
Than the sand of the seas;
I will bring against them, against the mother of a young man,
A destroyer at noonday;
I will suddenly bring down on her
Anguish and dismay.
9 "She who bore seven *sons* pines away;
Her breathing is labored.
Her sun has set while it was yet day;
She has been shamed and humiliated.
So I shall give over their survivors to the sword
Before their enemies," declares the LORD.

10¶ Woe to me, my mother, that you have borne me
As a man of strife and a man of contention to all the land!
I have neither lent, nor have men lent money to me,
*Yet* everyone curses me.
11 The LORD said, "Surely I will set you free for *purposes of* good;
Surely I will cause the enemy to make supplication to you
In a time of disaster and a time of distress.
12¶ "Can anyone smash iron,
Iron from the north, or bronze?
13 "Your wealth and your treasures
I will give for booty without cost,
Even for all your sins
And within all your borders.
14 "Then I will cause your enemies to bring *it*
Into a land you do not know;
For a fire has been kindled in My anger,
It will burn upon you."

*Jeremiah's Prayer and God's Answer*

15¶ Thou who knowest, O LORD,
Remember me, take notice of me,
And take vengeance for me on my persecutors.
Do *not*, in view of Thy patience, take me away;
Know that for Thy sake I endure reproach.
16 Thy words were found and I ate them,
And Thy words became for me a joy and the delight of my heart;
For I have been called by Thy name,
O LORD God of hosts.
17 I did not sit in the circle of merrymakers,
Nor did I exult.
Because of Thy hand *upon me* I sat alone,
For Thou didst fill me with indignation.
18 Why has my pain been perpetual
And my wound incurable, refusing to be healed?
Wilt Thou indeed be to me like a deceptive *stream*
With water that is unreliable?
19¶ Therefore, thus says the LORD,
"If you return, then I will restore you—
Before Me you will stand;
And if you extract the precious from the worthless,
You will become My spokesman.
They for their part may turn to you,
But as for you, you must not turn to them.

## New International

7I will winnow them with a winnowing fork
at the city gates of the land.
I will bring bereavement and destruction on my people,
for they have not changed their ways.
8I will make their widows more numerous
than the sand of the sea.
At midday I will bring a destroyer
against the mothers of their young men;
suddenly I will bring down on them
anguish and terror.
9The mother of seven will grow faint
and breathe her last.
Her sun will set while it is still day;
she will be disgraced and humiliated.
I will put the survivors to the sword
before their enemies,"
declares the LORD.

10Alas, my mother, that you gave me birth,
a man with whom the whole land strives and contends!
I have neither lent nor borrowed,
yet everyone curses me.
11The LORD said,
"Surely I will deliver you for a good purpose;
surely I will make your enemies plead with you
in times of disaster and times of distress.
12"Can a man break iron—
iron from the north—or bronze?
13Your wealth and your treasures
I will give as plunder, without charge,
because of all your sins
throughout your country.
14I will enslave you to your enemies
in[a] a land you do not know,
for my anger will kindle a fire
that will burn against you."

15You understand, O LORD;
remember me and care for me.
Avenge me on my persecutors.
You are long-suffering—do not take me away;
think of how I suffer reproach for your sake.
16When your words came, I ate them;
they were my joy and my heart's delight,
for I bear your name,
O LORD God Almighty.
17I never sat in the company of revelers,
never made merry with them;
I sat alone because your hand was on me
and you had filled me with indignation.
18Why is my pain unending
and my wound grievous and incurable?
Will you be to me like a deceptive brook,
like a spring that fails?

19Therefore this is what the LORD says:
"If you repent, I will restore you
that you may serve me;
if you utter worthy, not worthless, words,
you will be my spokesman.
Let this people turn to you,
but you must not turn to them.

NIV [a] *14* Some Hebrew manuscripts, Septuagint and Syriac (see also Jer. 17:4); most Hebrew manuscripts *I will cause your enemies to bring you / into*

## King James

20And I will make thee unto this people a fenced brasen wall: and they shall fight against thee, but they shall not prevail against thee: for I *am* with thee to save thee and to deliver thee, saith the LORD.

21And I will deliver thee out of the hand of the wicked, and I will redeem thee out of the hand of the terrible.

16 THE WORD of the LORD came also unto me, saying,

2Thou shalt not take thee a wife, neither shalt thou have sons or daughters in this place.

3For thus saith the LORD concerning the sons and concerning the daughters that are born in this place, and concerning their mothers that bare them, and concerning their fathers that begat them in this land;

4They shall die of grievous deaths; they shall not be lamented; neither shall they be buried; *but* they shall be as dung upon the face of the earth: and they shall be consumed by the sword, and by famine; and their carcases shall be meat for the fowls of heaven, and for the beasts of the earth.

5For thus saith the LORD, Enter not into the house of mourning, neither go to lament nor bemoan them: for I have taken away my peace from this people, saith the LORD, *even* lovingkindness and mercies.

6Both the great and the small shall die in this land: they shall not be buried, neither shall *men* lament for them, nor cut themselves, nor make themselves bald for them:

7Neither shall *men* tear *themselves* for them in mourning, to comfort them for the dead; neither shall *men* give them the cup of consolation to drink for their father or for their mother.

8Thou shalt not also go into the house of feasting, to sit with them to eat and to drink.

9For thus saith the LORD of hosts, the God of Israel; Behold, I will cause to cease out of this place in your eyes, and in your days, the voice of mirth, and the voice of gladness, the voice of the bridegroom, and the voice of the bride.

10¶ And it shall come to pass, when thou shalt show this people all these words, and they shall say unto thee, Wherefore hath the LORD pronounced all this great evil against us? or what *is* our iniquity? or what *is* our sin that we have committed against the LORD our God?

11Then shalt thou say unto them, Because your fathers have forsaken me, saith the LORD, and have walked after other gods, and have served them, and have worshipped them, and have forsaken me, and have not kept my law;

12And ye have done worse than your fathers; for, behold, ye walk every one after the imagination of his evil heart, that they may not hearken unto me:

13Therefore will I cast you out of this land into a land that ye know not, *neither* ye nor your fathers; and there shall ye serve other gods day and night; where I will not show you favour.

14¶ Therefore, behold, the days come, saith the LORD, that it shall no more be said, The LORD liveth, that brought up the children of Israel out of the land of Egypt;

15But, The LORD liveth, that brought up the children of Israel from the land of the north, and from all the lands whither he had driven them: and I will bring them again into their land that I gave unto their fathers.

16¶ Behold, I will send for many fishers, saith the LORD, and they shall fish them; and after will I send for many hunters, and they shall hunt them from every mountain, and from every hill, and out of the holes of the rocks.

17For mine eyes *are* upon all their ways: they are not hid from my face, neither is their iniquity hid from mine eyes.

## Amplified

20And I will make you to this people a fortified, brazen wall. They will fight against you, but they shall not prevail over you; for I am with you to save *and* deliver you, says the Lord.

21And I will deliver you out of the hand of the wicked, and I will redeem you out of the palm of the terrible *and* ruthless tyrants.

16 THE WORD of the Lord came also to me, saying,

2You shall not take a wife or have sons and daughters in this place [Jerusalem].

3For thus says the Lord concerning the sons and daughters who are born in this place, and concerning the mothers who bore them and the fathers who begot them in this land:

4They shall die of deadly diseases. They shall not be lamented, nor shall they be buried; but they shall be as dung upon the face of the ground. They shall perish *and* be consumed by the sword and by famine, and their dead bodies shall be food for the fowls of the air and for the beasts of the earth.

5For thus says the Lord, Enter not into the house of mourning, or go to lament or bemoan [the dead], for I have taken away My peace from this people, says the Lord, even My steadfast love *and* loving-kindness and tender mercies.

6Both the great and the small shall die in this land; they shall not be buried, neither shall men lament for them or cut themselves or make themselves bald for them.

7Neither shall men prepare food for the mourners, to comfort them for the dead; nor shall men give them the cup of consolation to drink for their father or for their mother.

8And you [Jeremiah] shall not go into the house of feasting to sit with them, to eat and drink.

9For thus says the Lord of hosts, the God of Israel: Behold, I will cause to cease from this place, before your very eyes and in your days, the voice of mirth and the voice of gladness, the voice of the bridegroom and the voice of the bride.

10And when you tell this people all these words, and they inquire of you, Why has the Lord decreed all this enormous evil against us? Or, What is our iniquity? Or, What is the sin that we have committed against the Lord our God?

11Then you shall say to them, Because your fathers have forsaken Me, says the Lord, and have walked after other gods and have served and worshiped them, and have forsaken Me and have not kept My law.

12And because you have done worse than your fathers; for behold, every one of you walks after the stubbornness of his own evil heart, so that you do not listen *and* obey Me.

13Therefore I will cast you out of this land [of Judah] into the land [of the Babylonians] that neither you nor your fathers have known, and there you will serve other gods day and night, for I will show you no favor there.

14Therefore, behold, the days are coming, says the Lord, when it shall no more be said, As the Lord lives Who brought up the children of Israel out of the land of Egypt,

15But, As the Lord lives Who brought up the children of Israel from the land of the north and from all the countries to which He had driven them. And I will bring them again to their land that I gave to their fathers.

16Behold, I will send for many fishers, says the Lord, and they shall fish them out; and afterward I will send for many hunters, and they shall hunt them from every mountain and from every hill and out of the clefts of the rocks.

17For My eyes are upon all their ways; they are not hid from My face, neither is their iniquity concealed from My eyes.

## New American Standard

20 "Then I will make you to this people
A fortified wall of bronze;
And though they fight against you,
They will not prevail over you;
For I am with you to save you
And deliver you," declares the LORD.
21 "So I will deliver you from the hand of the wicked,
And I will redeem you from the grasp of the violent."

*Distresses Foretold*

16 THE WORD of the LORD also came to me saying,
2"You shall not take a wife for yourself nor have sons
or daughters in this place."
3For thus says the LORD concerning the sons and daughters
born in this place, and concerning their mothers who bear them,
and their fathers who beget them in this land:
4"They will die of deadly diseases, they will not be lamented
or buried; they will be as dung on the surface of the ground and
come to an end by sword and famine, and their carcasses will
become food for the birds of the sky and for the beasts of the
earth."
5¶ For thus says the LORD, "Do not enter a house of mourning,
or go to lament or to console them; for I have withdrawn My peace
from this people," declares the LORD, " *My* lovingkindness and
compassion.
6"Both great men and small will die in this land; they will not
be buried, they will not be lamented, nor will anyone gash himself
or shave his head for them.
7"Neither will men break *bread* in mourning for them, to comfort anyone for the dead, nor give them a cup of consolation to
drink for anyone's father or mother.
8"Moreover you shall not go into a house of feasting to sit with
them to eat and drink."
9For thus says the LORD of hosts, the God of Israel: "Behold,
I am going to eliminate from this place, before your eyes and in
your time, the voice of rejoicing and the voice of gladness, the
voice of the groom and the voice of the bride.
10¶ "Now it will come about when you tell this people all these
words that they will say to you, 'For what reason has the LORD
declared all this great calamity against us? And what is our iniquity, or what is our sin which we have committed against the LORD
our God?'
11"Then you are to say to them, ' *It is* because your forefathers
have forsaken Me,' declares the LORD, 'and have followed other
gods and served them and bowed down to them; but Me they have
forsaken and have not kept My law.
12'You too have done evil, *even* more than your forefathers; for
behold, you are each one walking according to the stubbornness
of his own evil heart, without listening to Me.
13'So I will hurl you out of this land into the land which you
have not known, neither you nor your fathers; and there you will
serve other gods day and night, for I shall grant you no favor.'

*God Will Restore Them*

14¶ "Therefore behold, days are coming," declares the LORD,
"when it will no longer be said, 'As the LORD lives, who brought
up the sons of Israel out of the land of Egypt,'
15but, 'As the LORD lives, who brought up the sons of Israel
from the land of the north and from all the countries where He had
banished them.' For I will restore them to their own land which
I gave to their fathers.
16¶ "Behold, I am going to send for many fishermen," declares
the LORD, "and they will fish for them; and afterwards I shall send
for many hunters, and they will hunt them from every mountain
and every hill, and from the clefts of the rocks.
17"For My eyes are on all their ways; they are not hidden from
My face, nor is their iniquity concealed from My eyes.

## New International

20I will make you a wall to this people,
a fortified wall of bronze;
they will fight against you
but will not overcome you,
for I am with you
to rescue and save you,"
declares the LORD.
21"I will save you from the hands of the wicked
and redeem you from the grasp of the cruel."

*Day of Disaster*

16 THEN THE word of the LORD came to me: 2"You must not
marry and have sons or daughters in this place." 3For this
is what the LORD says about the sons and daughters born in this
land and about the women who are their mothers and the men
who are their fathers: 4"They will die of deadly diseases. They will
not be mourned or buried but will be like refuse lying on the
ground. They will perish by sword and famine, and their dead
bodies will become food for the birds of the air and the beasts of
the earth."
5For this is what the LORD says: "Do not enter a house where
there is a funeral meal; do not go to mourn or show sympathy,
because I have withdrawn my blessing, my love and my pity from
this people," declares the LORD. 6"Both high and low will die in
this land. They will not be buried or mourned, and no one will cut
himself or shave his head for them. 7No one will offer food to
comfort those who mourn for the dead—not even for a father or
a mother—nor will anyone give them a drink to console them.
8"And do not enter a house where there is feasting and sit down
to eat and drink. 9For this is what the LORD Almighty, the God of
Israel, says: Before your eyes and in your days I will bring an end
to the sounds of joy and gladness and to the voices of bride and
bridegroom in this place.
10"When you tell these people all this and they ask you, 'Why
has the LORD decreed such a great disaster against us? What wrong
have we done? What sin have we committed against the LORD our
God?' 11then say to them, 'It is because your fathers forsook me,'
declares the LORD, 'and followed other gods and served and worshiped them. They forsook me and did not keep my law. 12But you
have behaved more wickedly than your fathers. See how each of
you is following the stubbornness of his evil heart instead of obeying me. 13So I will throw you out of this land into a land neither
you nor your fathers have known, and there you will serve other
gods day and night, for I will show you no favor.'
14"However, the days are coming," declares the LORD, "when
men will no longer say, 'As surely as the LORD lives, who brought
the Israelites up out of Egypt,' 15but they will say, 'As surely as the
LORD lives, who brought the Israelites up out of the land of the
north and out of all the countries where he had banished them.'
For I will restore them to the land I gave their forefathers.
16"But now I will send for many fishermen," declares the LORD,
"and they will catch them. After that I will send for many hunters,
and they will hunt them down on every mountain and hill and
from the crevices of the rocks. 17My eyes are on all their ways; they
are not hidden from me, nor is their sin concealed from my eyes.

## King James

18And first I will recompense their iniquity and their sin double; because they have defiled my land, they have filled mine inheritance with the carcases of their detestable and abominable things.

19O LORD, my strength, and my fortress, and my refuge in the day of affliction, the Gentiles shall come unto thee from the ends of the earth, and shall say, Surely our fathers have inherited lies, vanity, and *things* wherein *there is* no profit.

20Shall a man make gods unto himself, and they *are* no gods?

21Therefore, behold, I will this once cause them to know, I will cause them to know mine hand and my might; and they shall know that my name *is* The LORD.

**17** THE SIN of Judah *is* written with a pen of iron, *and* with the point of a diamond: *it is* graven upon the table of their heart, and upon the horns of your altars;

2Whilst their children remember their altars and their groves by the green trees upon the high hills.

3O my mountain in the field, I will give thy substance *and* all thy treasures to the spoil, *and* thy high places for sin, throughout all thy borders.

4And thou, even thyself, shalt discontinue from thine heritage that I gave thee; and I will cause thee to serve thine enemies in the land which thou knowest not: for ye have kindled a fire in mine anger, *which* shall burn for ever.

5¶ Thus saith the LORD; Cursed *be* the man that trusteth in man, and maketh flesh his arm, and whose heart departeth from the LORD.

6For he shall be like the heath in the desert, and shall not see when good cometh; but shall inhabit the parched places in the wilderness, *in* a salt land and not inhabited.

7Blessed *is* the man that trusteth in the LORD, and whose hope the LORD is.

8For he shall be as a tree planted by the waters, and *that* spreadeth out her roots by the river, and shall not see when heat cometh, but her leaf shall be green; and shall not be careful in the year of drought, neither shall cease from yielding fruit.

9¶ The heart *is* deceitful above all *things*, and desperately wicked: who can know it?

10I the LORD search the heart, *I* try the reins, even to give every man according to his ways, *and* according to the fruit of his doings.

## Amplified

18First [before I bring them back to their land], I will doubly recompense *and* punish them for their iniquity and their sin, because they have polluted My land with the carcases of their detestable idols, and with the abominable things offered to false gods with which they have filled My inheritance.

19[Then said Jeremiah] O Lord, my strength and my stronghold, and my refuge in the day of affliction, to You shall the nations come from the ends of the earth and shall say, Surely our fathers have inherited nothing but lies, emptiness *and* futility, worthless things in which there is no profit!

20Can a man make gods for himself? Such are not gods!

21Therefore, [says the Lord,] Behold, I will make them know, *yes*, this once I will make them know My power and My might, and they shall know *and* recognize that My name is the Lord.

**17** THE SIN of Judah is written with a pen *or* stylus of iron, and with the point of a diamond; it is engraved on the tablet of their heart, and on the horns of their altars,

2While their children [earnestly] remember their [heathen] altars and their wooden symbols of the goddess Asherah beside the green trees upon the high hills.

3O [Jerusalem] My mountain in the field, I will give your wealth *and* all your treasures to the spoil, and your high places for sin—as the price of your sin—throughout all your territory.

4And you, through your own fault, shall loosen your hand *and* discontinue from your heritage which I gave you; and I will cause you to serve your enemies in a land which you do not know, for you have kindled a fire in My anger which shall burn age-lasting.

5Thus says the Lord: Cursed [with great evil] is the strong man who trusts *and* relies on frail man, making weak [human] flesh his arm, and whose mind *and* heart turn aside from the Lord.

6For he shall be like a shrub *or* a *person* naked and destitute in the desert, and shall not see any good come; but shall dwell in the parched places in the wilderness, in uninhabited salt land.

7[Most] blessed is the man who believes in, trusts in *and* relies on the Lord, and whose hope *and* confidence the Lord is.

8For he shall be like a tree planted by the waters, that spreads out its roots by the river, and shall not see *and* fear when heat comes, but his leaf shall be green; he shall not be anxious *and* careful in the year of drought, nor shall he cease from yielding fruit.

9The heart is deceitful above all things, and it is exceedingly perverse *and* corrupt and severely, mortally sick! Who can know it [perceive, understand, be acquainted with his own heart and mind]? [Mark 7:21-23; Eph. 4:20-24; Matt. 13:15-17.]

10I, the Lord, search the mind, I try the heart, even to give every man according to his ways, according to the fruit of his doings.

## New American Standard

18"And I will first doubly repay their iniquity and their sin,
because they have polluted My land; they have filled My inheritance with the carcasses of their detestable idols and with their
abominations."

19¶ O LORD, my strength and my stronghold,
And my refuge in the day of distress,
To Thee the nations will come
From the ends of the earth and say,
"Our fathers have inherited nothing but falsehood,
Futility and things of no profit."
20 Can man make gods for himself?
Yet they are not gods!
21¶ "Therefore behold, I am going to make them know—
This time I will make them know
My power and My might;
And they shall know that My name is the LORD."

*The Deceitful Heart*

**17** THE SIN of Judah is written down with an iron stylus;
With a diamond point it is engraved upon the tablet of their heart,
And on the horns of their altars,
2 As they remember their children,
So they *remember* their altars and their Asherim
By green trees on the high hills.
3 O mountain of Mine in the countryside,
I will give over your wealth and all your treasures for booty,
Your high places for sin throughout your borders.
4 And you will, even of yourself, let go of your inheritance
That I gave you;
And I will make you serve your enemies
In the land which you do not know;
For you have kindled a fire in My anger
Which will burn forever.

5¶ Thus says the LORD,
"Cursed is the man who trusts in mankind
And makes flesh his strength,
And whose heart turns away from the LORD.
6 "For he will be like a bush in the desert
And will not see when prosperity comes,
But will live in stony wastes in the wilderness,
A land of salt without inhabitant.
7 "Blessed is the man who trusts in the LORD
And whose trust is the LORD.
8 "For he will be like a tree planted by the water,
That extends its roots by a stream
And will not fear when the heat comes;
But its leaves will be green,
And it will not be anxious in a year of drought
Nor cease to yield fruit.

9¶ "The heart is more deceitful than all else
And is desperately sick;
Who can understand it?
10 "I, the LORD, search the heart,
I test the mind,
Even to give to each man according to his ways,
According to the results of his deeds.

## New International

18I will repay them double for their wickedness and their sin,
because they have defiled my land with the lifeless forms of their
vile images and have filled my inheritance with their detestable
idols."

19O LORD, my strength and my fortress,
my refuge in time of distress,
to you the nations will come
from the ends of the earth and say,
"Our fathers possessed nothing but false gods,
worthless idols that did them no good.
20Do men make their own gods?
Yes, but they are not gods!"

21"Therefore I will teach them—
this time I will teach them
my power and might.
Then they will know
that my name is the LORD.

**17** "JUDAH'S SIN is engraved with an iron tool,
inscribed with a flint point,
on the tablets of their hearts
and on the horns of their altars.
2Even their children remember
their altars and Asherah poles[a]
beside the spreading trees
and on the high hills.
3My mountain in the land
and your[b] wealth and all your treasures
I will give away as plunder,
together with your high places,
because of sin throughout your country.
4Through your own fault you will lose
the inheritance I gave you.
I will enslave you to your enemies
in a land you do not know,
for you have kindled my anger,
and it will burn forever."
5This is what the LORD says:

"Cursed is the one who trusts in man,
who depends on flesh for his strength
and whose heart turns away from the LORD.
6He will be like a bush in the wastelands;
he will not see prosperity when it comes.
He will dwell in the parched places of the desert,
in a salt land where no one lives.
7"But blessed is the man who trusts in the LORD,
whose confidence is in him.
8He will be like a tree planted by the water
that sends out its roots by the stream.
It does not fear when heat comes;
its leaves are always green.
It has no worries in a year of drought
and never fails to bear fruit."

9The heart is deceitful above all things
and beyond cure.
Who can understand it?

10"I the LORD search the heart
and examine the mind,
to reward a man according to his conduct,
according to what his deeds deserve."

NIV [a] 2 That is, symbols of the goddess Asherah [b] 2,3 Or *hills / [3]and the mountains of the land. / Your*

## King James

11 *As* the partridge sitteth *on eggs,* and hatcheth *them* not; *so* he that getteth riches, and not by right, shall leave them in the midst of his days, and at his end shall be a fool.

12¶ A glorious high throne from the beginning *is* the place of our sanctuary.

13O LORD, the hope of Israel, all that forsake thee shall be ashamed, *and* they that depart from me shall be written in the earth, because they have forsaken the LORD, the fountain of living waters.

14Heal me, O LORD, and I shall be healed; save me, and I shall be saved: for thou *art* my praise.

15¶ Behold, they say unto me, Where *is* the word of the LORD? let it come now.

16As for me, I have not hastened from *being* a pastor to follow thee: neither have I desired the woeful day; thou knowest: that which came out of my lips was *right* before thee.

17Be not a terror unto me: thou *art* my hope in the day of evil.

18Let them be confounded that persecute me, but let not me be confounded: let them be dismayed, but let not me be dismayed: bring upon them the day of evil, and destroy them with double destruction.

19¶ Thus said the LORD unto me; Go and stand in the gate of the children of the people, whereby the kings of Judah come in, and by the which they go out, and in all the gates of Jerusalem;

20And say unto them, Hear ye the word of the LORD, ye kings of Judah, and all Judah, and all the inhabitants of Jerusalem, that enter in by these gates:

21Thus saith the LORD; Take heed to yourselves, and bear no burden on the sabbath day, nor bring *it* in by the gates of Jerusalem;

22Neither carry forth a burden out of your houses on the sabbath day, neither do ye any work, but hallow ye the sabbath day, as I commanded your fathers.

23But they obeyed not, neither inclined their ear, but made their neck stiff, that they might not hear, nor receive instruction.

24And it shall come to pass, if ye diligently hearken unto me, saith the LORD, to bring in no burden through the gates of this city on the sabbath day, but hallow the sabbath day, to do no work therein;

25Then shall there enter into the gates of this city kings and princes sitting upon the throne of David, riding in chariots and on horses, they, and their princes, the men of Judah, and the inhabitants of Jerusalem: and this city shall remain for ever.

26And they shall come from the cities of Judah, and from the places about Jerusalem, and from the land of Benjamin, and from the plain, and from the mountains, and from the south, bringing burnt offerings, and sacrifices, and meat offerings, and incense, and bringing sacrifices of praise, unto the house of the LORD.

27But if ye will not hearken unto me to hallow the sabbath day, and not to bear a burden, even entering in at the gates of Jerusalem on the sabbath day; then will I kindle a fire in the gates thereof, and it shall devour the palaces of Jerusalem, and it shall not be quenched.

**18** THE WORD which came to Jeremiah from the LORD, saying,

2Arise, and go down to the potter's house, and there I will cause thee to hear my words.

## Amplified

11As the partridge which gathers a brood that she did not hatch *and* sits on eggs which she has not laid, so is he who gets riches and not by right. He will leave them, *or* they will leave him, in the midst of his days, and at his end he will be a fool.

12A glorious throne set on high from the beginning is the place of our sanctuary [the temple].

13O Lord, the hope of Israel, all who forsake You shall be put to shame. They who depart from *You and* me [Your prophet] shall *disappear like* writing upon the ground, because they have forsaken the Lord, the fountain of living waters.

14Heal me, O Lord, and I shall be healed; save me, and I shall be saved; for You are my praise.

15Behold, they say to me, Where is the word of the Lord [that you said would befall us]? Let it come now!

16But as for me, I have not sought to escape from being a shepherd after You, nor have I desired the woeful day [of judgment]; You know that. Whatever I said was spoken in Your presence *and* was from You.

17Be not a terror to me; You are my refuge *and* my hope in the day of evil.

18Let those be put to shame who persecute me, but let me not be put to shame; let them be dismayed, but let me not be dismayed; bring on them the day of evil, and destroy them with double destruction.

19Thus said the Lord to me: Go and stand in the gate of the sons of the people, by which the kings of Judah enter and by which they go out, and in all the gates of Jerusalem;

20And say, Hear the word of the Lord, you kings of Judah and all Judah, and all the inhabitants of Jerusalem who enter by these gates.

21Thus says the Lord: Take heed to yourselves, *and* for the sake of your lives bear no burden on the sabbath day or bring it in by the gates of Jerusalem.

22And do not carry a burden out of your houses on the sabbath day or do any work, but keep the sabbath day holy [set apart to the worship of God] as I commanded your fathers.

23Yet they would not listen *and* obey or incline their ear, but stiffened their necks, that they might not hear and might not receive instruction.

24But if you diligently listen *and* obey Me, says the Lord, to bring in no burden through the gates of this city on the sabbath day, but keep the sabbath day holy [set apart to the worship of God], to do no work on it,

25Then there shall enter by the gates of this city kings and princes who will sit upon the throne of David, riding in chariots and on horses, the kings and their princes, the men of Judah and the inhabitants of Jerusalem; and this city shall be inhabited *and* be age-lasting.

26And people shall come from the cities of Judah and the places round about Jerusalem, from the land of Benjamin, from the lowland, from the hill country, and from the South, bringing burnt offerings and sacrifices, cereal offerings and frankincense, and bringing sacrifices of thanksgiving to the house of the Lord.

27But if you will not listen to Me to keep the sabbath day holy [set apart to the worship of God], and not to bear a burden and enter in at the gates of Jerusalem *with one* on the sabbath day, then I will kindle a fire in her gates, and it shall devour the palaces of Jerusalem, and it shall not be quenched.

**18** THE WORD which came to Jeremiah from the Lord:

2Arise and go down to the potter's house, and there I will cause you to hear My words.

## New American Standard

11 "As a partridge that hatches eggs which it has not laid,
*So* is he who makes a fortune, but unjustly;
In the midst of his days it will forsake him,
And in the end he will be a fool."

12¶ A glorious throne on high from the beginning
Is the place of our sanctuary.
13 O LORD, the hope of Israel,
All who forsake Thee will be put to shame.
Those who turn away on earth will be written down,
Because they have forsaken the fountain of living water,
even the LORD.
14 Heal me, O LORD, and I will be healed;
Save me and I will be saved,
For Thou art my praise.
15 Look, they keep saying to me,
"Where is the word of the LORD?
Let it come now!"
16 But as for me, I have not hurried away from *being* a
shepherd after Thee,
Nor have I longed for the woeful day;
Thou Thyself knowest the utterance of my lips
Was in Thy presence.
17 Do not be a terror to me;
Thou art my refuge in the day of disaster.
18 Let those who persecute me be put to shame, but as for
me, let me not be put to shame;
Let them be dismayed, but let me not be dismayed.
Bring on them a day of disaster,
And crush them with twofold destruction!

*The Sabbath Must Be Kept*

19¶ Thus the LORD said to me, "Go and stand in the public gate, through which the kings of Judah come in and go out, as well as in all the gates of Jerusalem;

20and say to them, 'Listen to the word of the LORD, kings of Judah, and all Judah, and all inhabitants of Jerusalem, who come in through these gates:

21'Thus says the LORD, "Take heed for yourselves, and do not carry any load on the sabbath day or bring anything in through the gates of Jerusalem.

22"And you shall not bring a load out of your houses on the sabbath day nor do any work, but keep the sabbath day holy, as I commanded your forefathers.

23"Yet they did not listen or incline their ears, but stiffened their necks in order not to listen or take correction.

24¶ "But it will come about, if you listen attentively to Me," declares the LORD, "to bring no load in through the gates of this city on the sabbath day, but to keep the sabbath day holy by doing no work on it,

25then there will come in through the gates of this city kings and princes sitting on the throne of David, riding in chariots and on horses, they and their princes, the men of Judah, and the inhabitants of Jerusalem; and this city will be inhabited forever.

26"They will come in from the cities of Judah and from the environs of Jerusalem, from the land of Benjamin, from the lowland, from the hill country, and from the Negev, bringing burnt offerings, sacrifices, grain offerings and incense, and bringing sacrifices of thanksgiving to the house of the LORD.

27"But if you do not listen to Me to keep the sabbath day holy by not carrying a load and coming in through the gates of Jerusalem on the sabbath day, then I shall kindle a fire in its gates, and it will devour the palaces of Jerusalem and not be quenched."'"

*The Potter and the Clay*

**18** THE WORD which came to Jeremiah from the LORD saying,

2"Arise and go down to the potter's house, and there I shall announce My words to you."

## New International

11Like a partridge that hatches eggs it did not lay
is the man who gains riches by unjust means.
When his life is half gone, they will desert him,
and in the end he will prove to be a fool.

12A glorious throne, exalted from the beginning,
is the place of our sanctuary.
13O LORD, the hope of Israel,
all who forsake you will be put to shame.
Those who turn away from you will be written in the dust
because they have forsaken the LORD,
the spring of living water.
14Heal me, O LORD, and I will be healed;
save me and I will be saved,
for you are the one I praise.
15They keep saying to me,
"Where is the word of the LORD?
Let it now be fulfilled!"
16I have not run away from being your shepherd;
you know I have not desired the day of despair.
What passes my lips is open before you.
17Do not be a terror to me;
you are my refuge in the day of disaster.
18Let my persecutors be put to shame,
but keep me from shame;
let them be terrified,
but keep me from terror.
Bring on them the day of disaster;
destroy them with double destruction.

*Keeping the Sabbath Holy*

19This is what the LORD said to me: "Go and stand at the gate
of the people, through which the kings of Judah go in and out;
stand also at all the other gates of Jerusalem. 20Say to them, 'Hear
the word of the LORD, O kings of Judah and all people of Judah
and everyone living in Jerusalem who come through these gates.
21This is what the LORD says: Be careful not to carry a load on the
Sabbath day or bring it through the gates of Jerusalem. 22Do not
bring a load out of your houses or do any work on the Sabbath,
but keep the Sabbath day holy, as I commanded your forefathers.
23Yet they did not listen or pay attention; they were stiff-necked
and would not listen or respond to discipline. 24But if you are
careful to obey me, declares the LORD, and bring no load through
the gates of this city on the Sabbath, but keep the Sabbath day holy
by not doing any work on it, 25then kings who sit on David's
throne will come through the gates of this city with their officials.
They and their officials will come riding in chariots and on horses,
accompanied by the men of Judah and those living in Jerusalem,
and this city will be inhabited forever. 26People will come from the
towns of Judah and the villages around Jerusalem, from the territory of Benjamin and the western foothills, from the hill country
and the Negev, bringing burnt offerings and sacrifices, grain offerings, incense and thank offerings to the house of the LORD. 27But
if you do not obey me to keep the Sabbath day holy by not carrying
any load as you come through the gates of Jerusalem on the Sabbath day, then I will kindle an unquenchable fire in the gates of
Jerusalem that will consume her fortresses.'"

*At the Potter's House*

**18** THIS IS the word that came to Jeremiah from the LORD:
2"Go down to the potter's house, and there I will give you
my message." 3So I went down to the potter's house, and I saw

## King James

3Then I went down to the potter's house, and, behold, he wrought a work on the wheels.

4And the vessel that he made of clay was marred in the hand of the potter: so he made it again another vessel, as seemed good to the potter to make *it*.

5Then the word of the LORD came to me, saying,

6O house of Israel, cannot I do with you as this potter? saith the LORD. Behold, as the clay *is* in the potter's hand, so *are* ye in mine hand, O house of Israel.

7 *At what* instant I shall speak concerning a nation, and concerning a kingdom, to pluck up, and to pull down, and to destroy *it;*

8If that nation, against whom I have pronounced, turn from their evil, I will repent of the evil that I thought to do unto them.

9And *at what* instant I shall speak concerning a nation, and concerning a kingdom, to build and to plant *it;*

10If it do evil in my sight, that it obey not my voice, then I will repent of the good, wherewith I said I would benefit them.

11¶ Now therefore go to, speak to the men of Judah, and to the inhabitants of Jerusalem, saying, Thus saith the LORD; Behold, I frame evil against you, and devise a device against you: return ye now every one from his evil way, and make your ways and your doings good.

12And they said, There is no hope: but we will walk after our own devices, and we will every one do the imagination of his evil heart.

13Therefore thus saith the LORD; Ask ye now among the heathen, who hath heard such things: the virgin of Israel hath done a very horrible thing.

14Will *a man* leave the snow of Lebanon *which cometh* from the rock of the field? *or* shall the cold flowing waters that come from another place be forsaken?

15Because my people hath forgotten me, they have burned incense to vanity, and they have caused them to stumble in their ways *from* the ancient paths, to walk in paths, *in* a way not cast up;

16To make their land desolate, *and* a perpetual hissing; every one that passeth thereby shall be astonished, and wag his head.

17I will scatter them as with an east wind before the enemy; I will show them the back, and not the face, in the day of their calamity.

18¶ Then said they, Come, and let us devise devices against Jeremiah; for the law shall not perish from the priest, nor counsel from the wise, nor the word from the prophet. Come, and let us smite him with the tongue, and let us not give heed to any of his words.

19Give heed to me, O LORD, and hearken to the voice of them that contend with me.

20Shall evil be recompensed for good? for they have digged a pit for my soul. Remember that I stood before thee to speak good for them, *and* to turn away thy wrath from them.

21Therefore deliver up their children to the famine, and pour out their *blood* by the force of the sword; and let their wives be bereaved of their children, and *be* widows; and let their men be put to death; *let* their young men *be* slain by the sword in battle.

## Amplified

3Then I went down to the potter's house, and behold, he was working at the wheel.

4And the vessel that he was making of clay was spoiled in the hand of the potter; so he made it over, reworking it into another vessel, as it seemed good to the potter to make it.

5Then the word of the Lord came to me:

6O house of Israel, cannot I do with you as this potter? says the Lord. Behold, as the clay is in the potter's hand, so are you in My hand, O house of Israel.

7At one time I shall suddenly speak concerning a nation or kingdom, that I will pluck up and break down and destroy it;

8But if [the people of] that nation, concerning which I have spoken, turn from their evil, I will relent *and* reverse My decision concerning the evil that I thought to do to them.

9At another time I shall suddenly speak concerning a nation or a kingdom that I will build and plant it;

10But if they do evil in My sight, obeying not My voice, then I will regret *and* reverse My decision concerning the good with which I said I would benefit them.

11Now therefore, say to the men of Judah and to the inhabitants of Jerusalem, Thus says the Lord, Behold, I am shaping evil against you and devising a plan against you. Return now every one from his evil way; reform *and* make your [accustomed] ways and your [individual] actions good *and* right.

12But they say, That is in vain, for we will walk after our own devices, and we will every one do as the stubbornness of his own evil heart dictates.

13Therefore thus says the Lord: Ask now among the nations, who has heard such things? The virgin Israel has done a very vile *and* horrible thing.

14Will the snow of Mount Lebanon fail from its rocks [which tower above the land of Israel]? Shall the cold, rushing waters of strange lands that dash down [from afar] be dried up?

15Yet My people have forgotten Me, they burn incense to false gods; they have been caused to stumble in their ways, in the ancient roads, to walk in bypaths, in a way not graded up—not a highway;

16Making their land a desolation *and* a horror, a thing to be hissed at perpetually. Every one who passes by shall be astounded *and* horrified and shake his head.

17I will scatter them as with an east wind before the enemy; I will show them My back and not My face, in the day of their calamity, [says the Lord].

18Then *my enemies* said, Come, and let us devise schemes against Jeremiah, for the law [of Moses] shall not perish from the priest [as this false prophet predicts], or counsel from the wise, or the word from the prophet. Come, let us smite him with the tongue [making a charge against him to the king], and let us not pay any attention to his words.

19Give heed to me, Lord, listen *to what* my adversaries [are plotting to do to me, and intercede].

20Shall evil be recompensed for good? Yet they have dug a pit for my life. [Earnestly] remember that I stood before You to speak good for them, to turn away Your anger from them.

21Therefore deliver up their children to the famine; give them over to the power of the sword, and let their wives become childless and widows. Let their men meet death by pestilence, their young men be slain by the sword in battle.

## New American Standard

3 Then I went down to the potter's house, and there he was,
making something on the wheel.
4 But the vessel that he was making of clay was spoiled in the
hand of the potter; so he remade it into another vessel, as it pleased
the potter to make.
5¶ Then the word of the LORD came to me saying,
6 "Can I not, O house of Israel, deal with you as this potter
*does*?" declares the LORD. "Behold, like the clay in the potter's
hand, so are you in My hand, O house of Israel.
7 "At one moment I might speak concerning a nation or concerning a kingdom to uproot, to pull down, or to destroy *it;*
8 if that nation against which I have spoken turns from its evil,
I will [a]relent concerning the calamity I planned to bring on it.
9 "Or at another moment I might speak concerning a nation or
concerning a kingdom to build up or to plant *it;*
10 if it does evil in My sight by not obeying My voice, then I will
[b]think better of the good with which I had promised to bless it.
11 "So now then, speak to the men of Judah and against the
inhabitants of Jerusalem saying, 'Thus says the LORD, "Behold, I
am fashioning calamity against you and devising a plan against
you. Oh turn back, each of you from his evil way, and reform your
ways and your deeds." '
12 "But they will say, 'It's hopeless! For we are going to follow
our own plans, and each of us will act according to the stubbornness of his evil heart.'
13¶ "Therefore thus says the LORD,
'Ask now among the nations,
Who ever heard the like of this?
The virgin of Israel
Has done a most appalling thing.
14 'Does the snow of Lebanon forsake the rock of the open
country?
Or is the cold flowing water *from* a foreign *land* ever
snatched away?
15 'For My people have forgotten Me,
They burn incense to worthless gods
And they have stumbled from their ways,
From the ancient paths,
To walk in bypaths,
Not on a highway,
16 To make their land a desolation,
*An object of* perpetual hissing;
Everyone who passes by it will be astonished
And shake his head.
17 'Like an east wind I will scatter them
Before the enemy;
I will show them My back and not *My* face
In the day of their calamity.' "
18¶ Then they said, "Come and let us devise plans against
Jeremiah. Surely the law is not going to be lost to the priest, nor
counsel to the sage, nor the *divine* word to the prophet! Come on
and let us strike at him with *our* tongue, and let us give no heed
to any of his words."
19¶ Do give heed to me, O LORD,
And listen to what my opponents are saying!
20 Should good be repaid with evil?
For they have dug a pit for me.
Remember how I stood before Thee
To speak good on their behalf,
So as to turn away Thy wrath from them.
21 Therefore, give their children over to famine,
And deliver them up to the power of the sword;
And let their wives become childless and widowed.
Let their men also be smitten to death,
Their young men struck down by the sword in battle.

NAS [a] Lit., *repent (of)* [b] Lit., *repent (of)*

## New International

him working at the wheel. 4 But the pot he was shaping from the
clay was marred in his hands; so the potter formed it into another
pot, shaping it as seemed best to him.
5 Then the word of the LORD came to me: 6 "O house of Israel,
can I not do with you as this potter does?" declares the LORD. "Like
clay in the hand of the potter, so are you in my hand, O house of
Israel. 7 If at any time I announce that a nation or kingdom is to be
uprooted, torn down and destroyed, 8 and if that nation I warned
repents of its evil, then I will relent and not inflict on it the disaster
I had planned. 9 And if at another time I announce that a nation
or kingdom is to be built up and planted, 10 and if it does evil in
my sight and does not obey me, then I will reconsider the good
I had intended to do for it.
11 "Now therefore say to the people of Judah and those living
in Jerusalem, 'This is what the LORD says: Look! I am preparing a
disaster for you and devising a plan against you. So turn from your
evil ways, each one of you, and reform your ways and your actions.' 12 But they will reply, 'It's no use. We will continue with our
own plans; each of us will follow the stubbornness of his evil
heart.' "

13 Therefore this is what the LORD says:

"Inquire among the nations:
Who has ever heard anything like this?
A most horrible thing has been done
by Virgin Israel.
14 Does the snow of Lebanon
ever vanish from its rocky slopes?
Do its cool waters from distant sources
ever cease to flow?[c]
15 Yet my people have forgotten me;
they burn incense to worthless idols,
which made them stumble in their ways
and in the ancient paths.
They made them walk in bypaths
and on roads not built up.
16 Their land will be laid waste,
an object of lasting scorn;
all who pass by will be appalled
and will shake their heads.
17 Like a wind from the east,
I will scatter them before their enemies;
I will show them my back and not my face
in the day of their disaster."

18 They said, "Come, let's make plans against Jeremiah; for the
teaching of the law by the priest will not be lost, nor will counsel
from the wise, nor the word from the prophets. So come, let's
attack him with our tongues and pay no attention to anything he
says."

19 Listen to me, O LORD;
hear what my accusers are saying!
20 Should good be repaid with evil?
Yet they have dug a pit for me.
Remember that I stood before you
and spoke in their behalf
to turn your wrath away from them.
21 So give their children over to famine;
hand them over to the power of the sword.
Let their wives be made childless and widows;
let their men be put to death,
their young men slain by the sword in battle.

NIV [c] *14* The meaning of the Hebrew for this sentence is uncertain.

## King James

22Let a cry be heard from their houses, when thou shalt bring a troop suddenly upon them: for they have digged a pit to take me, and hid snares for my feet.

23Yet, LORD, thou knowest all their counsel against me to slay *me:* forgive not their iniquity, neither blot out their sin from thy sight, but let them be overthrown before thee; deal *thus* with them in the time of thine anger.

**19** THUS SAITH the LORD, Go and get a potter's earthen bottle, and *take* of the ancients of the people, and of the ancients of the priests;

2And go forth unto the valley of the son of Hinnom, which *is* by the entry of the east gate, and proclaim there the words that I shall tell thee,

3And say, Hear ye the word of the LORD, O kings of Judah, and inhabitants of Jerusalem; Thus saith the LORD of hosts, the God of Israel; Behold, I will bring evil upon this place, the which whosoever heareth, his ears shall tingle.

4Because they have forsaken me, and have estranged this place, and have burned incense in it unto other gods, whom neither they nor their fathers have known, nor the kings of Judah, and have filled this place with the blood of innocents;

5They have built also the high places of Baal, to burn their sons with fire *for* burnt offerings unto Baal, which I commanded not, nor spake *it,* neither came *it* into my mind:

6Therefore, behold, the days come, saith the LORD, that this place shall no more be called Tophet, nor The valley of the son of Hinnom, but The valley of slaughter.

7And I will make void the counsel of Judah and Jerusalem in this place; and I will cause them to fall by the sword before their enemies, and by the hands of them that seek their lives: and their carcases will I give to be meat for the fowls of the heaven, and for the beasts of the earth.

8And I will make this city desolate, and an hissing; every one that passeth thereby shall be astonished and hiss because of all the plagues thereof.

9And I will cause them to eat the flesh of their sons and the flesh of their daughters, and they shall eat every one the flesh of his friend in the siege and straitness, wherewith their enemies, and they that seek their lives, shall straiten them.

10Then shalt thou break the bottle in the sight of the men that go with thee,

11And shalt say unto them, Thus saith the LORD of hosts; Even so will I break this people and this city, as *one* breaketh a potter's vessel, that cannot be made whole again: and they shall bury *them* in Tophet, till *there be* no place to bury.

12Thus will I do unto this place, saith the LORD, and to the inhabitants thereof, and *even* make this city as Tophet:

13And the houses of Jerusalem, and the houses of the kings of Judah, shall be defiled as the place of Tophet, because of all the houses upon whose roofs they have burned incense unto all the host of heaven, and have poured out drink offerings unto other gods.

14Then came Jeremiah from Tophet, whither the LORD had sent him to prophesy; and he stood in the court of the LORD's house; and said to all the people,

15Thus saith the LORD of hosts, the God of Israel; Behold, I will bring upon this city and upon all her towns all the evil that I have pronounced against it, because they have hardened their necks, that they might not hear my words.

## Amplified

22Let a cry be heard from their houses, when You suddenly bring a troop upon them; for they have dug a pit to take me and have hidden snares for my feet.

23Yet, Lord, You know all their plotting against me to slay me. Forgive not their iniquity, nor blot out their sin from Your sight, but let them be overthrown before You; deal with them in the time of Your anger.

**19** THUS SAYS the Lord, Go and get a potter's earthen bottle, and take some of the old people and some of the elderly priests,

2And go out to the Valley of Ben-hinnom, which is by the entrance of the Potsherd Gate, and proclaim there the words that I shall tell you;

3And say, Hear the word of the Lord, O kings of Judah and inhabitants of Jerusalem. Thus says the Lord of hosts, the God of Israel: Behold, I am bringing such evil upon this place that the ears of whoever hears of it will tingle.

4Because the people have forsaken Me, and have estranged *and* profaned this place [Jerusalem], by burning incense in it to other gods that neither they nor their fathers nor the kings of Judah have known; and because they have filled this place with the blood of innocents,

5And have built the high places of Baal to burn their sons in the fire for burnt offerings to Baal, which I commanded not, nor spoke of it, nor did it come into My mind *and* heart;

6Therefore, behold, the days are coming, says the Lord, when this place shall no more be called Topheth, or the Valley of Ben-hinnom, but the Valley of Slaughter.

7And I will pour out *and* make void the counsel *and* the plans of [the men of] Judah and Jerusalem in this place, and I will cause their people to fall by the sword before their enemies, and by the hand of those who seek their life; and their dead bodies I will give to be food for the birds of the air and for the beasts of the earth.

8And I will make the city an astonishment *and* a horror and a hissing; every one who passes by it will be horrified and will hiss [in scorn] because of all its plagues *and* disasters.

9And I will cause them to eat the flesh of their sons and their daughters, and they shall eat every one the flesh of his neighbor *and* friend in the siege and in the distress, with which their enemies and those who seek their life distress them.

10Then you shall break the bottle in the sight of the men who accompany you,

11And you shall say to them, Thus said the Lord of hosts: Even so will I break this people and this city, as one breaks a potter's vessel, so that it cannot be mended. Men shall bury in Topheth because there will be no other place, *and* till there is no more room to bury.

12Thus will I do to this place, says the Lord, and to its inhabitants, and even make this city like Topheth.

13And the houses of Jerusalem and the houses of the kings of Judah, which are defiled, shall be like the place of Topheth, even all the houses upon whose roofs incense has been burned to all the host of the heavens, and drink offerings have been poured out to other gods. [Acts 7:42, 43.]

14Then came Jeremiah from Topheth, where the Lord had sent him to prophesy, and he stood in the court of the Lord's house, and said to all the people,

15Thus says the Lord of hosts, the God of Israel: Behold, I will bring upon this city and upon all its towns all the evil that I have pronounced against it, because they have stiffened their necks, refusing to hear My words.

## New American Standard

22 May an outcry be heard from their houses,
When Thou suddenly bringest raiders upon them;
For they have dug a pit to capture me
And hidden snares for my feet.
23 Yet Thou, O LORD, knowest
All their deadly designs against me;
Do not forgive their iniquity
Or blot out their sin from Thy sight.
But may they be overthrown before Thee;
Deal with them in the time of Thine anger!

*The Broken Jar*

**19** THUS SAYS the LORD, "Go and buy a potter's earthenware jar, and *take* some of the elders of the people and
some of the senior priests.
2"Then go out to the valley of Ben-hinnom, which is by the
entrance of the potsherd gate; and proclaim there the words that
I shall tell you,
3and say, 'Hear the word of the LORD, O kings of Judah and
inhabitants of Jerusalem: thus says the LORD of hosts, the God of
Israel, "Behold I am about to bring a calamity upon this place, at
which the ears of everyone that hears of it will tingle.
4"Because they have forsaken Me and have made this an alien
place and have burned sacrifices in it to other gods that neither
they nor their forefathers nor the kings of Judah had *ever* known,
and *because* they have filled this place with the blood of the innocent
5and have built the high places of Baal to burn their sons in the
fire as burnt offerings to Baal, a thing which I never commanded
or spoke of, nor did it *ever* enter My mind;
6therefore, behold, days are coming," declares the LORD,
"when this place will no longer be called Topheth or the valley of
Ben-hinnom, but rather the valley of Slaughter.
7"And I shall make void the counsel of Judah and Jerusalem
in this place, and I shall cause them to fall by the sword before their
enemies and by the hand of those who seek their life; and I shall
give over their carcasses as food for the birds of the sky and the
beasts of the earth.
8"I shall also make this city a desolation and an *object of* hissing;
everyone who passes by it will be astonished and hiss because of
all its disasters.
9"And I shall make them eat the flesh of their sons and the
flesh of their daughters, and they will eat one another's flesh in the
siege and in the distress with which their enemies and those who
seek their life will distress them."'
**10**¶ "Then you are to break the jar in the sight of the men who
accompany you
11and say to them, 'Thus says the LORD of hosts, "Just so shall
I break this people and this city, even as one breaks a potter's
vessel, which cannot again be repaired; and they will bury in
Topheth because there is no *other* place for burial.
12"This is how I shall treat this place and its inhabitants," declares the LORD, "so as to make this city like Topheth.
13"And the houses of Jerusalem and the houses of the kings of
Judah will be defiled like the place Topheth, because of all the
houses on whose rooftops they burned sacrifices to all the heavenly host and poured out libations to other gods."'"
**14**¶ Then Jeremiah came from Topheth, where the LORD had
sent him to prophesy; and he stood in the court of the LORD's
house and said to all the people:
15"Thus says the LORD of hosts, the God of Israel, 'Behold, I am
about to bring on this city and all its towns the entire calamity that
I have declared against it, because they have stiffened their necks
so as not to heed My words.'"

## New International

22Let a cry be heard from their houses
when you suddenly bring invaders against them,
for they have dug a pit to capture me
and have hidden snares for my feet.
23But you know, O LORD,
all their plots to kill me.
Do not forgive their crimes
or blot out their sins from your sight.
Let them be overthrown before you;
deal with them in the time of your anger.

**19** THIS IS what the LORD says: "Go and buy a clay jar from
a potter. Take along some of the elders of the people and
of the priests 2and go out to the Valley of Ben Hinnom, near the
entrance of the Potsherd Gate. There proclaim the words I tell you,
3and say, 'Hear the word of the LORD, O kings of Judah and people
of Jerusalem. This is what the LORD Almighty, the God of Israel,
says: Listen! I am going to bring a disaster on this place that will
make the ears of everyone who hears of it tingle. 4For they have
forsaken me and made this a place of foreign gods; they have
burned sacrifices in it to gods that neither they nor their fathers nor
the kings of Judah ever knew, and they have filled this place with
the blood of the innocent. 5They have built the high places of Baal
to burn their sons in the fire as offerings to Baal—something I did
not command or mention, nor did it enter my mind. 6So beware,
the days are coming, declares the LORD, when people will no
longer call this place Topheth or the Valley of Ben Hinnom, but the
Valley of Slaughter.
7"'In this place I will ruin[a] the plans of Judah and Jerusalem.
I will make them fall by the sword before their enemies, at the
hands of those who seek their lives, and I will give their carcasses
as food to the birds of the air and the beasts of the earth. 8I will
devastate this city and make it an object of scorn; all who pass by
will be appalled and will scoff because of all its wounds. 9I will
make them eat the flesh of their sons and daughters, and they will
eat one another's flesh during the stress of the siege imposed on
them by the enemies who seek their lives.'
10"Then break the jar while those who go with you are watching, 11and say to them, 'This is what the LORD Almighty says: I will
smash this nation and this city just as this potter's jar is smashed
and cannot be repaired. They will bury the dead in Topheth until
there is no more room. 12This is what I will do to this place and
to those who live here, declares the LORD. I will make this city like
Topheth. 13The houses in Jerusalem and those of the kings of
Judah will be defiled like this place, Topheth—all the houses
where they burned incense on the roofs to all the starry hosts and
poured out drink offerings to other gods.'"
14Jeremiah then returned from Topheth, where the LORD had
sent him to prophesy, and stood in the court of the LORD's temple
and said to all the people, 15"This is what the LORD Almighty, the
God of Israel, says: 'Listen! I am going to bring on this city and the
villages around it every disaster I pronounced against them, because they were stiff-necked and would not listen to my words.'"

**NIV** [a] 7 The Hebrew for *ruin* sounds like the Hebrew for *jar* (see verses 1 and 10).

## King James

**20** NOW PASHUR the son of Immer the priest, who *was* also chief governor in the house of the LORD, heard that Jeremiah prophesied these things.

2Then Pashur smote Jeremiah the prophet, and put him in the stocks that *were* in the high gate of Benjamin, which *was* by the house of the LORD.

3And it came to pass on the morrow, that Pashur brought forth Jeremiah out of the stocks. Then said Jeremiah unto him, The LORD hath not called thy name Pashur, but Magor-missabib.

4For thus saith the LORD, Behold, I will make thee a terror to thyself, and to all thy friends: and they shall fall by the sword of their enemies, and thine eyes shall behold *it:* and I will give all Judah into the hand of the king of Babylon, and he shall carry them captive into Babylon, and shall slay them with the sword.

5Moreover I will deliver all the strength of this city, and all the labours thereof, and all the precious things thereof, and all the treasures of the kings of Judah will I give into the hand of their enemies, which shall spoil them, and take them, and carry them to Babylon.

6And thou, Pashur, and all that dwell in thine house shall go into captivity: and thou shalt come to Babylon, and there thou shalt die, and shalt be buried there, thou, and all thy friends, to whom thou hast prophesied lies.

7¶ O LORD, thou hast deceived me, and I was deceived: thou art stronger than I, and hast prevailed: I am in derision daily, every one mocketh me.

8For since I spake, I cried out, I cried violence and spoil; because the word of the LORD was made a reproach unto me, and a derision, daily.

9Then I said, I will not make mention of him, nor speak any more in his name. But *his word* was in mine heart as a burning fire shut up in my bones, and I was weary with forbearing, and I could not *stay*.

10¶ For I heard the defaming of many, fear on every side. Report, *say they,* and we will report it. All my familiars watched for my halting, *saying,* Peradventure he will be enticed, and we shall prevail against him, and we shall take our revenge on him.

11But the LORD *is* with me as a mighty terrible one: therefore my persecutors shall stumble, and they shall not prevail: they shall be greatly ashamed; for they shall not prosper: *their* everlasting confusion shall never be forgotten.

12But, O LORD of hosts, that triest the righteous, *and* seest the reins and the heart, let me see thy vengeance on them: for unto thee have I opened my cause.

13Sing unto the LORD, praise ye the LORD: for he hath delivered the soul of the poor from the hand of evildoers.

14¶ Cursed *be* the day wherein I was born: let not the day wherein my mother bare me be blessed.

15Cursed *be* the man who brought tidings to my father, saying, A man child is born unto thee; making him very glad.

## Amplified

**20** NOW PASHHUR the son of Immer, the priest, who was *also* chief officer in the house of the Lord, heard Jeremiah prophesying these things.

2Then Pashhur beat Jeremiah the prophet, and put him in the stocks that were in the upper Benjamin Gate of the house of the Lord. [Jer. 1:19.]

3And the next day Pashhur brought Jeremiah out of the stocks. Then Jeremiah said to him, The Lord does not call your name Pashhur, but Magormissa-bib [that is, Terror on every side].

4For thus says the Lord, Behold, I will make you a terror to yourself and to all your friends. They shall fall by the sword of their enemies while you look on. And I will give all Judah into the hand of the king of Babylon; he shall carry them captive to Babylon, and shall slay them with the sword.

5Moreover, I will deliver all the riches of this city, all the results of its labors, all its precious things, and all the treasures of the kings of Judah into the hand of their enemies, who shall make them a prey *and* plunder them, and seize them, and carry them to Babylon.

6And you, Pashhur, and all who dwell in your house shall go into captivity; you shall go to Babylon, and there you shall die and be buried, you and all your friends, to whom you have prophesied falsely.

7[But Jeremiah said] O Lord, You have persuaded *and* deceived me, and I was persuaded *and* deceived; You are stronger than I and have prevailed; I am a laughing stock all the day; every one mocks me.

8For whenever I speak, I must cry out *and* complain; I shout, Violence and destruction! For the word of the Lord has become to me a reproach and a derision all day long.

9If I say, I will not make mention of [the Lord], or speak any more in His name, there is in my mind *and* heart as if it were a burning fire shut up in my bones, and I am weary with enduring *and* holding it in; I cannot *contain it longer*.

10For I have heard many whispering *and* defaming. *There is* terror on every side. Denounce him! Let us denounce him! say all my familiar friends, they who watch for my fall. Perhaps he will be persuaded *and* deceived, then we can prevail against him, and we will get our revenge on him.

11But the Lord is with me as a mighty *and* terrible one; therefore my persecutors will stumble, and they will not overcome *me*. They will be utterly put to shame, for they will not deal wisely *or* prosper [in their schemes]; their eternal dishonor will never be forgotten.

12But, O Lord of hosts, Who tries the righteous, Who sees the heart and the mind, let me see Your vengeance on them, for to You have I revealed *and* committed my cause.

13Sing to the Lord; praise the Lord! For He has delivered the life of the poor *and* needy from the hand of evildoers.

14Cursed be the day on which I was born; let not the day on which my mother bore me be blessed.

15Cursed be the man who brought tidings to my father, saying, A son is born to you, making him very glad.

## New American Standard

*Pashhur Persecutes Jeremiah*

**20** WHEN PASHHUR the priest, the son of Immer, who was chief officer in the house of the LORD, heard Jeremiah prophesying these things,

2Pashhur had Jeremiah the prophet beaten, and put him in the stocks that were at the upper Benjamin Gate, which was by the house of the LORD.

3Then it came about on the next day, when Pashhur released Jeremiah from the stocks, that Jeremiah said to him, "Pashhur is not the name the LORD has called you, but rather [a]Magor-missabib.

4"For thus says the LORD, 'Behold, I am going to make you a terror to yourself and to all your friends; and while your eyes look on, they will fall by the sword of their enemies. So I shall give over all Judah to the hand of the king of Babylon, and he will carry them away as exiles to Babylon and will slay them with the sword.

5'I shall also give over all the wealth of this city, all its produce, and all its costly things; even all the treasures of the kings of Judah I shall give over to the hand of their enemies, and they will plunder them, take them away, and bring them to Babylon.

6'And you, Pashhur, and all who live in your house will go into captivity; and you will enter Babylon, and there you will die, and there you will be buried, you and all your friends to whom you have falsely prophesied.' "

*Jeremiah's Complaint*

7¶ O LORD, Thou hast deceived me and I was deceived;
Thou hast overcome me and prevailed.
I have become a laughingstock all day long;
Everyone mocks me.
8 For each time I speak, I cry aloud;
I proclaim violence and destruction,
Because for me the word of the LORD has resulted
In reproach and derision all day long.
9 But if I say, "I will not remember Him
Or speak anymore in His name,"
Then in my heart it becomes like a burning fire
Shut up in my bones;
And I am weary of holding *it* in,
And I cannot endure *it*.
10 For I have heard the whispering of many,
"Terror on every side!
Denounce *him;* yes, let us denounce him!"
All my trusted friends,
Watching for my fall, say:
"Perhaps he will be deceived, so that we may prevail
against him
And take our revenge on him."
11 But the LORD is with me like a dread champion;
Therefore my persecutors will stumble and not prevail.
They will be utterly ashamed, because they have failed,
With an everlasting disgrace that will not be forgotten.
12 Yet, O LORD of hosts, Thou who dost test the
righteous,
Who seest the mind and the heart;
Let me see Thy vengeance on them;
For to Thee I have set forth my cause.
13 Sing to the LORD, praise the LORD!
For He has delivered the soul of the needy one
From the hand of evildoers.

14¶ Cursed be the day when I was born;
Let the day not be blessed when my mother bore me!
15 Cursed be the man who brought the news
To my father, saying,
"A baby boy has been born to you!"
*And* made him very happy.

**NAS** [a] I.e., terror on every side

## New International

*Jeremiah and Pashhur*

**20** WHEN THE priest Pashhur son of Immer, the chief officer
in the temple of the LORD, heard Jeremiah prophesying
these things, 2he had Jeremiah the prophet beaten and put in the
stocks at the Upper Gate of Benjamin at the LORD's temple. 3The
next day, when Pashhur released him from the stocks, Jeremiah
said to him, "The LORD's name for you is not Pashhur, but Magor-
Missabib.[b] 4For this is what the LORD says: 'I will make you a terror
to yourself and to all your friends; with your own eyes you will see
them fall by the sword of their enemies. I will hand all Judah over
to the king of Babylon, who will carry them away to Babylon or
put them to the sword. 5I will hand over to their enemies all the
wealth of this city—all its products, all its valuables and all the
treasures of the kings of Judah. They will take it away as plunder
and carry it off to Babylon. 6And you, Pashhur, and all who live
in your house will go into exile to Babylon. There you will die and
be buried, you and all your friends to whom you have prophesied
lies.' "

*Jeremiah's Complaint*

7O LORD, you deceived[c] me, and I was deceived[d];
you overpowered me and prevailed.
I am ridiculed all day long;
everyone mocks me.
8Whenever I speak, I cry out
proclaiming violence and destruction.
So the word of the LORD has brought me
insult and reproach all day long.
9But if I say, "I will not mention him
or speak any more in his name,"
his word is in my heart like a fire,
a fire shut up in my bones.
I am weary of holding it in;
indeed, I cannot.
10I hear many whispering,
"Terror on every side!
Report him! Let's report him!"
All my friends
are waiting for me to slip, saying,
"Perhaps he will be deceived;
then we will prevail over him
and take our revenge on him."
11But the LORD is with me like a mighty warrior;
so my persecutors will stumble and not prevail.
They will fail and be thoroughly disgraced;
their dishonor will never be forgotten.
12O LORD Almighty, you who examine the righteous
and probe the heart and mind,
let me see your vengeance upon them,
for to you I have committed my cause.
13Sing to the LORD!
Give praise to the LORD!
He rescues the life of the needy
from the hands of the wicked.
14Cursed be the day I was born!
May the day my mother bore me not be blessed!
15Cursed be the man who brought my father the news,
who made him very glad, saying,
"A child is born to you—a son!"

**NIV** [b] 3 *Magor-Missabib* means *terror on every side.* [c] 7 Or *persuaded* [d] 7 Or *persuaded*

## King James

16 And let that man be as the cities which the LORD overthrew, and repented not: and let him hear the cry in the morning, and the shouting at noontide;

17 Because he slew me not from the womb; or that my mother might have been my grave, and her womb *to be* always great *with me*.

18 Wherefore came I forth out of the womb to see labour and sorrow, that my days should be consumed with shame?

**21** THE WORD which came unto Jeremiah from the LORD, when king Zedekiah sent unto him Pashur the son of Melchiah, and Zephaniah the son of Maaseiah the priest, saying,

2 Inquire, I pray thee, of the LORD for us; for Nebuchadrezzar king of Babylon maketh war against us; if so be that the LORD will deal with us according to all his wondrous works, that he may go up from us.

3 ¶ Then said Jeremiah unto them, Thus shall ye say to Zedekiah:

4 Thus saith the LORD God of Israel; Behold, I will turn back the weapons of war that *are* in your hands, wherewith ye fight against the king of Babylon, and *against* the Chaldeans, which besiege you without the walls, and I will assemble them into the midst of this city.

5 And I myself will fight against you with an outstretched hand and with a strong arm, even in anger, and in fury, and in great wrath.

6 And I will smite the inhabitants of this city, both man and beast: they shall die of a great pestilence.

7 And afterward, saith the LORD, I will deliver Zedekiah king of Judah, and his servants, and the people, and such as are left in this city from the pestilence, from the sword, and from the famine, into the hand of Nebuchadrezzar king of Babylon, and into the hand of their enemies, and into the hand of those that seek their life: and he shall smite them with the edge of the sword; he shall not spare them, neither have pity, nor have mercy.

8 ¶ And unto this people thou shalt say, Thus saith the LORD; Behold, I set before you the way of life, and the way of death.

9 He that abideth in this city shall die by the sword, and by the famine, and by the pestilence: but he that goeth out, and falleth to the Chaldeans that besiege you, he shall live, and his life shall be unto him for a prey.

10 For I have set my face against this city for evil, and not for good, saith the LORD: it shall be given into the hand of the king of Babylon, and he shall burn it with fire.

11 ¶ And touching the house of the king of Judah, *say*, Hear ye the word of the LORD;

12 O house of David, thus saith the LORD; Execute judgment in the morning, and deliver *him that is* spoiled out of the hand of the oppressor, lest my fury go out like fire, and burn that none can quench *it*, because of the evil of your doings.

13 Behold, I *am* against thee, O inhabitant of the valley, *and* rock of the plain, saith the LORD; which say, Who shall come down against us? or who shall enter into our habitations?

14 But I will punish you according to the fruit of your doings, saith the LORD: and I will kindle a fire in the forest thereof, and it shall devour all things round about it.

## Amplified

16 And let that man be as the cities which the Lord overthrew and did not relent. Let him hear the [war] cry in the morning and the shouting of alarm at noon,

17 Because he did not slay me in the womb, so that my mother might have been my grave, and her womb always great.

18 Why did I come out of the womb to see labor and sorrow, that my days should be consumed in shame?

**21** THE WORD which came to Jeremiah from the Lord, when King Zedekiah sent to him Pashhur the son of Malchiah, and Zephaniah the priest, the son of Maaseiah, saying,

2 Inquire, I pray you, of the Lord for us, for Nebuchadrezzar king of Babylon is making war against us; perhaps the Lord will deal with us according to all His wonderful works, forcing him to withdraw from us.

3 Then said Jeremiah to them, Say this to Zedekiah:

4 Thus says the Lord God of Israel: Behold, I will turn back *and* dull the edge of the weapons of war that are in your hands, with which you fight against the king of Babylon and the Chaldeans who are besieging you outside the walls, and I will bring them into the midst of this city [Jerusalem].

5 And I Myself will fight against you with an outstretched hand and with a strong arm, in anger, in fury, and in great indignation *and* wrath.

6 And I will smite the inhabitants of this city, both man and beast; they shall die of a great pestilence.

7 And afterward, says the Lord, I will deliver Zedekiah king of Judah, and his servants, and the people in this city who survive the pestilence, the sword, and the famine, into the hand of Nebuchadrezzar king of Babylon and into the hand of their enemies, into the hand of those who seek their lives. And he shall smite them with the edge of the sword; he shall not spare them, nor have pity or mercy *and* compassion upon them.

8 And to this people you [Jeremiah] shall say, Thus says the Lord: Behold, I set before you the way of life and the way of death.

9 He who remains in this city [Jerusalem] shall die by the sword, and by famine, and by pestilence. But he who goes out and passes over to the Chaldeans who besiege you, he shall live, and his life shall be to him for a prey [as a prize of war].

10 For I have set My face upon this city for evil, and not for good, says the Lord. It shall be given into the hand of the king of Babylon, and he shall burn it with fire.

11 And concerning the royal house of the king of Judah, hear the word of the Lord:

12 O house of David, thus says the Lord: Execute justice in the morning, and deliver from the hand of the oppressor him who has been robbed, lest My wrath go forth like fire, and burn so that none can quench it, because of the evil of your doings.

13 Behold, I am against you, O inhabitant of the valley, O rock of the plain, says the Lord, you who say, Who shall come down against us? Or, Who shall enter into our dwelling places?

14 And I will punish you according to the fruit of your doings, says the Lord; I will kindle a fire in her forest, and it shall devour all that is round about her.

## New American Standard

16 But let that man be like the cities
Which the LORD overthrew without [a]relenting,
And let him hear an outcry in the morning
And a shout of alarm at noon;
17 Because he did not kill me before birth,
So that my mother would have been my grave,
And her womb ever pregnant.
18 Why did I ever come forth from the womb
To look on trouble and sorrow,
So that my days have been spent in shame?

*Jeremiah's Message for Zedekiah*

**21** THE WORD which came to Jeremiah from the LORD when
King Zedekiah sent to him Pashhur the son of Malchijah,
and Zephaniah the priest, the son of Maaseiah, saying,
2"Please inquire of the LORD on our behalf, for Nebuchadnezzar king of Babylon is warring against us; perhaps the LORD will
deal with us according to all His wonderful acts, that *the enemy* may
withdraw from us."
3¶ Then Jeremiah said to them, "You shall say to Zedekiah as
follows:
4'Thus says the LORD God of Israel, "Behold, I am about to turn
back the weapons of war which are in your hands, with which you
are warring against the king of Babylon and the Chaldeans who
are besieging you outside the wall; and I shall gather them into the
center of this city.
5"And I Myself shall war against you with an outstretched
hand and a mighty arm, even in anger and wrath and great indignation.
6"I shall also strike down the inhabitants of this city, both man
and beast; they will die of a great pestilence.
7"Then afterwards," declares the LORD, "I shall give over
Zedekiah king of Judah and his servants and the people, even
those who survive in this city from the pestilence, the sword, and
the famine, into the hand of Nebuchadnezzar king of Babylon, and
into the hand of their foes, and into the hand of those who seek
their lives; and he will strike them down with the edge of the
sword. He will not spare them nor have pity nor compassion."'
8¶ "You shall also say to this people, 'Thus says the LORD,
"Behold, I set before you the way of life and the way of death.
9"He who dwells in this city will die by the sword and by
famine and by pestilence; but he who goes out and falls away to
the Chaldeans who are besieging you will live, and he will have
his own life as booty.
10"For I have set My face against this city for harm and not for
good," declares the LORD. "It will be given into the hand of the
king of Babylon, and he will burn it with fire."'
11¶ "Then *say* to the household of the king of Judah, 'Hear the
word of the LORD,
12O house of David, thus says the LORD:
"Administer justice every morning;
And deliver the *person* who has been robbed from the
power of his oppressor,
That My wrath may not go forth like fire
And burn with none to extinguish *it*,
Because of the evil of their deeds.

13¶ "Behold, I am against you, O valley dweller,
O rocky plain," declares the LORD,
"You men who say, 'Who will come down against us?
Or who will enter into our habitations?'
14 "But I shall punish you according to the results of your
deeds," declares the LORD,
"And I shall kindle a fire in its forest
That it may devour all its environs."'"

NAS [a] Lit., *being sorry*

## New International

16May that man be like the towns
the LORD overthrew without pity.
May he hear wailing in the morning,
a battle cry at noon.
17For he did not kill me in the womb,
with my mother as my grave,
her womb enlarged forever.
18Why did I ever come out of the womb
to see trouble and sorrow
and to end my days in shame?

*God Rejects Zedekiah's Request*

**21** THE WORD came to Jeremiah from the LORD when King
Zedekiah sent to him Pashhur son of Malkijah and the
priest Zephaniah son of Maaseiah. They said: 2"Inquire now of the
LORD for us because Nebuchadnezzar[b] king of Babylon is attacking
us. Perhaps the LORD will perform wonders for us as in times past
so that he will withdraw from us."
3But Jeremiah answered them, "Tell Zedekiah, 4'This is what
the LORD, the God of Israel, says: I am about to turn against you
the weapons of war that are in your hands, which you are using
to fight the king of Babylon and the Babylonians[c] who are outside
the wall besieging you. And I will gather them inside this city. 5I
myself will fight against you with an outstretched hand and a
mighty arm in anger and fury and great wrath. 6I will strike down
those who live in this city—both men and animals—and they will
die of a terrible plague. 7After that, declares the LORD, I will hand
over Zedekiah king of Judah, his officials and the people in this city
who survive the plague, sword and famine, to Nebuchadnezzar
king of Babylon and to their enemies who seek their lives. He will
put them to the sword; he will show them no mercy or pity or
compassion.'
8"Furthermore, tell the people, 'This is what the LORD says: See,
I am setting before you the way of life and the way of death.
9Whoever stays in this city will die by the sword, famine or plague.
But whoever goes out and surrenders to the Babylonians who are
besieging you will live; he will escape with his life. 10I have determined to do this city harm and not good, declares the LORD. It will
be given into the hands of the king of Babylon, and he will destroy
it with fire.'
11"Moreover, say to the royal house of Judah, 'Hear the word
of the LORD; 12O house of David, this is what the LORD says:
"'Administer justice every morning;
rescue from the hand of his oppressor
the one who has been robbed,
or my wrath will break out and burn like fire
because of the evil you have done—
burn with no one to quench it.
13I am against you, Jerusalem,
you who live above this valley
on the rocky plateau,
declares the LORD—
you who say, "Who can come against us?
Who can enter our refuge?"
14I will punish you as your deeds deserve,
declares the LORD.
I will kindle a fire in your forests
that will consume everything around you.'"

NIV [b] 2 Hebrew *Nebuchadrezzar,* of which *Nebuchadnezzar* is a variant; here and often in Jeremiah and Ezekiel [c] 4 Or *Chaldeans;* also in verse 9

## King James

22 THUS SAITH the LORD; Go down to the house of the king
of Judah, and speak there this word,
2And say, Hear the word of the LORD, O king of Judah, that
sittest upon the throne of David, thou, and thy servants, and thy
people that enter in by these gates:
3Thus saith the LORD; Execute ye judgment and righteousness,
and deliver the spoiled out of the hand of the oppressor: and do
no wrong, do no violence to the stranger, the fatherless, nor the
widow, neither shed innocent blood in this place.
4For if ye do this thing indeed, then shall there enter in by the
gates of this house kings sitting upon the throne of David, riding
in chariots and on horses, he, and his servants, and his people.
5But if ye will not hear these words, I swear by myself, saith the
LORD, that this house shall become a desolation.
6For thus saith the LORD unto the king's house of Judah; Thou
*art* Gilead unto me, *and* the head of Lebanon: *yet* surely I will make
thee a wilderness; *and* cities *which* are not inhabited.
7And I will prepare destroyers against thee, every one with his
weapons: and they shall cut down thy choice cedars, and cast *them*
into the fire.
8And many nations shall pass by this city, and they shall say
every man to his neighbour, Wherefore hath the LORD done thus
unto this great city?
9Then they shall answer, Because they have forsaken the covenant of the LORD their God, and worshipped other gods, and
served them.
10¶ Weep ye not for the dead, neither bemoan him: *but* weep
sore for him that goeth away: for he shall return no more, nor see
his native country.
11For thus saith the LORD touching Shallum the son of Josiah
king of Judah, which reigned instead of Josiah his father, which
went forth out of this place; He shall not return thither any more:
12But he shall die in the place whither they have led him captive, and shall see this land no more.
13¶ Woe unto him that buildeth his house by unrighteousness,
and his chambers by wrong; *that* useth his neighbour's service
without wages, and giveth him not for his work;
14That saith, I will build me a wide house and large chambers,
and cutteth him out windows; and *it is* ceiled with cedar, and
painted with vermilion.
15Shalt thou reign, because thou closest *thyself* in cedar? did not
thy father eat and drink, and do judgment and justice, *and* then
*it was* well with him?
16He judged the cause of the poor and needy; then *it was* well
*with him: was* not this to know me? saith the LORD.
17But thine eyes and thine heart *are* not but for thy covetousness, and for to shed innocent blood, and for oppression, and for
violence, to do *it*.

## Amplified

22 THUS SAYS the Lord: Go down to the house of the king
of Judah and speak there this word,
2Hear the word of the Lord, O king of Judah, you who sit upon
the throne of David, you, and your servants, and your people who
enter by these gates.
3Thus says the Lord: Execute justice and righteousness, and
deliver out of the hand of the oppressor him who has been robbed.
And do no wrong; do no violence to the stranger or temporary
resident, the fatherless or the widow, nor shed innocent blood in
this place.
4For if you will obey this word indeed, then shall there enter
in by the gates of this [the king's] house kings sitting [for David]
upon David's throne, riding in chariots and on horses, they, and
their servants, and their people.
5But if you will not hear these words, I swear by Myself, says
the Lord, that this house shall become a desolation.
6For thus says the Lord concerning the house of the king of
Judah: [If you will not listen to Me, though] you are [as valuable]
to Me as [the fat pastures of] Gilead [east of the Jordan], or as the
[plentiful] summit of Lebanon [west of the Jordan], yet surely I will
make you a wilderness and uninhabited cities.
7And I will prepare, solemnly set apart *and* appoint to execute
My judgments against you, destroyers, every one with his weapons; and they shall cut down your [palaces built of] choicest cedars,
and cast them into the fire.
8And many nations will pass by this city, and every man will
say to his neighbor, Why has the Lord done this to this great city?
9Then they will answer, Because [the people] forsook the covenant *or* pledge with the Lord their God, and worshiped other
gods and served them.
10Weep not for him who is dead, nor bemoan him; but weep
bitterly for him who goes away [into captivity], for he shall return
no more, nor see his native country *again*.
11For thus says the Lord concerning Shallum the son of Josiah,
king of Judah, who reigned instead of Josiah his father and who
went forth out of this place: [Shallum] shall not return here any
more;
12But he shall die in the place where they have led him captive,
and he shall see this land no more.
13Woe to him who builds his house by unrighteousness, and his
[upper] chambers by injustice; who uses his neighbor's service
without wages, and does not give him his pay [for his work];
14Who says, I will build me a wide house with large rooms, and
cuts himself out windows, and it is ceiled with cedar and painted
with vermilion.
15Do you think that being a king [merely] means [self-indul-
gent] vying [with Solomon] *and* striving to excel in cedar *palaces*?
Did not your father [Josiah] as he ate and drank, do justice and
righteousness—being upright and in right standing with God?
Then it was well with him.
16He judged the cause of the poor and needy; then it was well.
Was not *all* this to know *and* recognize Me? says the Lord.
17But your eyes and your heart are only for your covetousness
*and* dishonest gain, for shedding innocent blood, for oppression
and doing violence.

## New American Standard

*Warning of Jerusalem's Fall*

**22** THUS SAYS the LORD, "Go down to the house of the king
of Judah, and there speak this word,
2and say, 'Hear the word of the LORD, O king of Judah, who
sits on David's throne, you and your servants and your people
who enter these gates.
3'Thus says the LORD, "Do justice and righteousness, and
deliver the one who has been robbed from the power of *his* oppressor. Also do not mistreat *or* do violence to the stranger, the orphan,
or the widow; and do not shed innocent blood in this place.
4"For if you men will indeed perform this thing, then kings will
enter the gates of this house, sitting in David's place on his throne,
riding in chariots and on horses, *even the king* himself and his
servants and his people.
5"But if you will not obey these words, I swear by Myself,"
declares the LORD, "that this house will become a desolation." ' "
6For thus says the LORD concerning the house of the king of
Judah:

"You are *like* Gilead to Me,
*Like* the summit of Lebanon;
Yet most assuredly I shall make you like a wilderness,
*Like* cities which are not inhabited.
7 "For I shall set apart destroyers against you,
Each with his weapons;
And they will cut down your choicest cedars
And throw *them* on the fire.

8"And many nations will pass by this city; and they will say
to one another, 'Why has the LORD done thus to this great city?'
9"Then they will answer, 'Because they forsook the covenant
of the LORD their God and bowed down to other gods and served
them.' "

10¶ Do not weep for the dead or mourn for him,
*But* weep continually for the one who goes away;
For he will never return
Or see his native land.

11For thus says the LORD in regard to Shallum the son of Josiah,
king of Judah, who became king in the place of Josiah his father,
who went forth from this place, "He will never return there;
12but in the place where they led him captive, there he will die
and not see this land again.

*Messages about the Kings*

13¶ "Woe to him who builds his house without righteousness
And his upper rooms without justice,
Who uses his neighbor's services without pay
And does not give him his wages,
14 Who says, 'I will build myself a roomy house
With spacious upper rooms,
And cut out its windows,
Paneling *it* with cedar and painting *it* bright red.'
15 "Do you become a king because you are competing in
cedar?
Did not your father eat and drink,
And do justice and righteousness?
Then it was well with him.
16 "He pled the cause of the afflicted and needy;
Then it was well.
Is not that what it means to know Me?"
Declares the LORD.
17 "But your eyes and your heart
Are *intent* only upon your own dishonest gain,
And on shedding innocent blood
And on practicing oppression and extortion."

## New International

*Judgment Against Evil Kings*

**22** THIS IS what the LORD says: "Go down to the palace of
the king of Judah and proclaim this message there: 2'Hear
the word of the LORD, O king of Judah, you who sit on David's
throne—you, your officials and your people who come through
these gates. 3This is what the LORD says: Do what is just and right.
Rescue from the hand of his oppressor the one who has been
robbed. Do no wrong or violence to the alien, the fatherless or the
widow, and do not shed innocent blood in this place. 4For if you
are careful to carry out these commands, then kings who sit on
David's throne will come through the gates of this palace, riding
in chariots and on horses, accompanied by their officials and their
people. 5But if you do not obey these commands, declares the
LORD, I swear by myself that this palace will become a ruin.' "
6For this is what the LORD says about the palace of the king of
Judah:

"Though you are like Gilead to me,
like the summit of Lebanon,
I will surely make you like a desert,
like towns not inhabited.
7I will send destroyers against you,
each man with his weapons,
and they will cut up your fine cedar beams
and throw them into the fire.

8"People from many nations will pass by this city and will ask
one another, 'Why has the LORD done such a thing to this great
city?' 9And the answer will be: 'Because they have forsaken the
covenant of the LORD their God and have worshiped and served
other gods.' "

10Do not weep for the dead king or mourn his loss;
rather, weep bitterly for him who is exiled,
because he will never return
nor see his native land again.

11For this is what the LORD says about Shallum[a] son of Josiah, who
succeeded his father as king of Judah but has gone from this place:
"He will never return. 12He will die in the place where they have
led him captive; he will not see this land again."

13"Woe to him who builds his palace by unrighteousness,
his upper rooms by injustice,
making his countrymen work for nothing,
not paying them for their labor.
14He says, 'I will build myself a great palace
with spacious upper rooms.'
So he makes large windows in it,
panels it with cedar
and decorates it in red.

15"Does it make you a king
to have more and more cedar?
Did not your father have food and drink?
He did what was right and just,
so all went well with him.
16He defended the cause of the poor and needy,
and so all went well.
Is that not what it means to know me?"
declares the LORD.
17"But your eyes and your heart
are set only on dishonest gain,
on shedding innocent blood
and on oppression and extortion."

**NIV** [a] *11* Also called *Jehoahaz*

## King James

18 Therefore thus saith the LORD concerning Jehoiakim the son of Josiah king of Judah; They shall not lament for him, *saying*, Ah my brother! or, Ah sister! they shall not lament for him, *saying*, Ah lord! or, Ah his glory!

19 He shall be buried with the burial of an ass, drawn and cast forth beyond the gates of Jerusalem.

20 ¶ Go up to Lebanon, and cry; and lift up thy voice in Bashan, and cry from the passages: for all thy lovers are destroyed.

21 I spake unto thee in thy prosperity; *but* thou saidst, I will not hear. This *hath been* thy manner from thy youth, that thou obeyedst not my voice.

22 The wind shall eat up all thy pastors, and thy lovers shall go into captivity: surely then shalt thou be ashamed and confounded for all thy wickedness.

23 O inhabitant of Lebanon, that makest thy nest in the cedars, how gracious shalt thou be when pangs come upon thee, the pain as of a woman in travail!

24 *As* I live, saith the LORD, though Coniah the son of Jehoiakim king of Judah were the signet upon my right hand, yet would I pluck thee thence;

25 And I will give thee into the hand of them that seek thy life, and into the hand *of them* whose face thou fearest, even into the hand of Nebuchadrezzar king of Babylon, and into the hand of the Chaldeans.

26 And I will cast thee out, and thy mother that bare thee, into another country, where ye were not born; and there shall ye die.

27 But to the land whereunto they desire to return, thither shall they not return.

28 *Is* this man Coniah a despised broken idol? *is he* a vessel wherein *is* no pleasure? wherefore are they cast out, he and his seed, and are cast into a land which they know not?

29 O earth, earth, earth, hear the word of the LORD.

30 Thus saith the LORD, Write ye this man childless, a man *that* shall not prosper in his days: for no man of his seed shall prosper, sitting upon the throne of David, and ruling any more in Judah.

## Amplified

18 Therefore thus says the Lord concerning Jehoiakim the son of Josiah, king of Judah: [Relatives] shall not lament for him, saying, Ah my brother! Or, Ah sister, [how great our loss! Subjects] shall not lament for him saying, Ah lord! or Ah his majesty! *or* Ah [how great was] his glory!

19 [No] he shall be buried with the burial of a donkey, dragged out and cast forth beyond the gates of Jerusalem.

20 Go up [north] to Lebanon and cry out, and raise your voice [in the hills] of Bashan [across the Jordan], and cry from Abarim [a range of mountains southeast of Palestine]; for all your lovers [the king's chosen allies] are destroyed.

21 I spoke to you in your [times of] prosperity, but you said, I will not listen. This has been your attitude from your youth, you have not obeyed My voice.

22 The wind [of adversity] shall pasture upon *and* consume all your shepherds [your princes and statesmen], and your lover [allies] shall go into captivity. Surely then shall you be ashamed and confounded *and* dismayed because of all your wickedness.

23 O inhabitant of Lebanon [Jerusalem, whose palaces are made of Lebanon's trees], who make your nest among the cedars, how you will groan *and* how pitiable you will be when pangs come upon you, pain as of a woman in childbirth!

24 As I live, says the Lord, though Coniah [also called Jeconiah, and Jehoiachin] the son of Jehoiakim, king of Judah, were the signet *ring* upon My right hand, yet would I tear you off;

25 And I will give you into the hand of those who seek your life and into the hand of those of whom you are afraid, even into the hand of Nebuchadrezzar king of Babylon and into the hand of the Chaldeans.

26 And I will hurl you and the mother who bore you into another country, where you were not born, and there you shall die.

27 But to the land to which they will yearn to return, there they shall not return.

28 Is this man [King] Coniah a despised, broken pot? Is he a vessel in which no one takes pleasure? Why are they hurled out, he and his royal offspring, and cast into a land which they do not know, understand *or* recognize?

29 O land, land, land, hear the word of the Lord!

30 Thus says the Lord, Write this man [Coniah] down as childless, a man who shall not prosper in his days; for no man of his offspring shall succeed in sitting upon the throne of David, and ruling any more in Judah.

## King James

**23** WOE BE unto the pastors that destroy and scatter the sheep of my pasture! saith the LORD.

2 Therefore thus saith the LORD God of Israel against the pastors that feed my people; Ye have scattered my flock, and driven them away, and have not visited them: behold, I will visit upon you the evil of your doings, saith the LORD.

3 And I will gather the remnant of my flock out of all countries whither I have driven them, and will bring them again to their folds; and they shall be fruitful and increase.

4 And I will set up shepherds over them which shall feed them: and they shall fear no more, nor be dismayed, neither shall they be lacking, saith the LORD.

## Amplified

**23** WOE TO the shepherds [the civil leaders] who destroy and scatter the sheep of My pasturing! says the Lord.

2 Therefore thus says the Lord, the God of Israel, concerning the shepherds who care for *and* feed My people: You have scattered My flock, and driven them away, and have not visited them; behold, I will visit upon you the evil of your doings, says the Lord.

3 And I will gather the remnant of My flock out of all the countries to which I have driven them, and will bring them again to their folds *and* pastures; and they shall be fruitful and multiply.

4 And I will set up shepherds over them who shall feed them. And they shall fear no more, nor be dismayed, neither shall any be missing *or* lost, says the Lord.

## New American Standard

18Therefore thus says the LORD in regard to Jehoiakim the son of Josiah, king of Judah,
"They will not lament for him:
'Alas, my brother!' or, 'Alas, sister!'
They will not lament for him:
'Alas for the master!' or, 'Alas for his splendor!'
19 "He will be buried with a donkey's burial,
Dragged off and thrown out beyond the gates of Jerusalem.
20 "Go up to Lebanon and cry out,
And lift up your voice in Bashan;
Cry out also from Abarim,
For all your lovers have been crushed.
21 "I spoke to you in your prosperity;
But you said, 'I will not listen!'
This has been your practice from your youth,
That you have not obeyed My voice.
22 "The wind will sweep away all your shepherds,
And your lovers will go into captivity;
Then you will surely be ashamed and humiliated
Because of all your wickedness.
23 "You who dwell in Lebanon,
Nested in the cedars,
How you will groan when pangs come upon you,
Pain like a woman in childbirth!

24¶ "As I live," declares the LORD, "even though [a]Coniah the son of Jehoiakim king of Judah were a signet *ring* on My right hand, yet I would pull you off;

25and I shall give you over into the hand of those who are seeking your life, yes, into the hand of those whom you dread, even into the hand of Nebuchadnezzar king of Babylon, and into the hand of the Chaldeans.

26"I shall hurl you and your mother who bore you into another country where you were not born, and there you will die.

27"But as for the land to which they desire to return, they will not return to it.

28 "Is this man Coniah a despised, shattered jar?
Or is he an undesirable vessel?
Why have he and his descendants been hurled out
And cast into a land that they had not known?
29 "O land, land, land,
Hear the word of the LORD!
30 "Thus says the LORD,
'Write this man down childless,
A man who will not prosper in his days;
For no man of his descendants will prosper
Sitting on the throne of David
Or ruling again in Judah.' "

*The Coming Messiah: the Righteous Branch*

**23** "WOE TO the shepherds who are destroying and scattering the sheep of My pasture!" declares the LORD.

2Therefore thus says the LORD God of Israel concerning the shepherds who are tending My people: "You have scattered My flock and driven them away, and have not attended to them; behold, I am about to attend to you for the evil of your deeds," declares the LORD.

3"Then I Myself shall gather the remnant of My flock out of all the countries where I have driven them and shall bring them back to their pasture; and they will be fruitful and multiply.

4"I shall also raise up shepherds over them and they will tend them; and they will not be afraid any longer, nor be terrified, nor will any be missing," declares the LORD.

NAS [a] I.e., Jehoiachin

## New International

18Therefore this is what the LORD says about Jehoiakim son of Josiah king of Judah:
"They will not mourn for him:
'Alas, my brother! Alas, my sister!'
They will not mourn for him:
'Alas, my master! Alas, his splendor!'
19He will have the burial of a donkey—
dragged away and thrown
outside the gates of Jerusalem."
20"Go up to Lebanon and cry out,
let your voice be heard in Bashan,
cry out from Abarim,
for all your allies are crushed.
21I warned you when you felt secure,
but you said, 'I will not listen!'
This has been your way from your youth;
you have not obeyed me.
22The wind will drive all your shepherds away,
and your allies will go into exile.
Then you will be ashamed and disgraced
because of all your wickedness.
23You who live in 'Lebanon,[b]'
who are nestled in cedar buildings,
how you will groan when pangs come upon you,
pain like that of a woman in labor!

24"As surely as I live," declares the LORD, "even if you, Jehoiachin[c] son of Jehoiakim king of Judah, were a signet ring on my right hand, I would still pull you off. 25I will hand you over to those who seek your life, those you fear—to Nebuchadnezzar king of Babylon and to the Babylonians.[d] 26I will hurl you and the mother who gave you birth into another country, where neither of you was born, and there you both will die. 27You will never come back to the land you long to return to."

28Is this man Jehoiachin a despised, broken pot,
an object no one wants?
Why will he and his children be hurled out,
cast into a land they do not know?
29O land, land, land,
hear the word of the LORD!
30This is what the LORD says:
"Record this man as if childless,
a man who will not prosper in his lifetime,
for none of his offspring will prosper,
none will sit on the throne of David
or rule anymore in Judah."

*The Righteous Branch*

**23** "WOE TO the shepherds who are destroying and scattering the sheep of my pasture!" declares the LORD. 2Therefore this is what the LORD, the God of Israel, says to the shepherds who tend my people: "Because you have scattered my flock and driven them away and have not bestowed care on them, I will bestow punishment on you for the evil you have done," declares the LORD. 3"I myself will gather the remnant of my flock out of all the countries where I have driven them and will bring them back to their pasture, where they will be fruitful and increase in number. 4I will place shepherds over them who will tend them, and they will no longer be afraid or terrified, nor will any be missing," declares the LORD.

NIV [b] 23 That is, the palace in Jerusalem (see 1 Kings 7:2) [c] 24 Hebrew *Coniah,* a variant of *Jehoiachin;* also in verse 28 [d] 25 Or *Chaldeans*

## King James

5¶ Behold, the days come, saith the LORD, that I will raise unto David a righteous Branch, and a King shall reign and prosper, and shall execute judgment and justice in the earth.

6In his days Judah shall be saved, and Israel shall dwell safely: and this *is* his name whereby he shall be called, THE LORD OUR RIGHTEOUSNESS.

7Therefore, behold, the days come, saith the LORD, that they shall no more say, The LORD liveth, which brought up the children of Israel out of the land of Egypt;

8But, The LORD liveth, which brought up and which led the seed of the house of Israel out of the north country, and from all countries whither I had driven them; and they shall dwell in their own land.

9¶ Mine heart within me is broken because of the prophets; all my bones shake; I am like a drunken man, and like a man whom wine hath overcome, because of the LORD, and because of the words of his holiness.

10For the land is full of adulterers; for because of swearing the land mourneth; the pleasant places of the wilderness are dried up, and their course is evil, and their force *is* not right.

11For both prophet and priest are profane; yea, in my house have I found their wickedness, saith the LORD.

12Wherefore their way shall be unto them as slippery *ways* in the darkness: they shall be driven on, and fall therein: for I will bring evil upon them, *even* the year of their visitation, saith the LORD.

13And I have seen folly in the prophets of Samaria; they prophesied in Baal, and caused my people Israel to err.

14I have seen also in the prophets of Jerusalem an horrible thing: they commit adultery, and walk in lies: they strengthen also the hands of evildoers, that none doth return from his wickedness: they are all of them unto me as Sodom, and the inhabitants thereof as Gomorrah.

15Therefore thus saith the LORD of hosts concerning the prophets; Behold, I will feed them with wormwood, and make them drink the water of gall: for from the prophets of Jerusalem is profaneness gone forth into all the land.

16Thus saith the LORD of hosts, Hearken not unto the words of the prophets that prophesy unto you: they make you vain: they speak a vision of their own heart, *and* not out of the mouth of the LORD.

## Amplified

5Behold, the days come, says the Lord, that I will raise to David a righteous Branch [Sprout], and He shall reign as King and do wisely, and shall execute justice and righteousness in the land.

6In His days Judah shall be saved, and Israel shall dwell safely: and this is His name by which He shall be called, The Lord Our Righteousness. [Matt. 1:21-23; Rom. 3:22.]

7Therefore, behold, the days come, says the Lord, that they shall no more say, As the Lord lives Who brought up the children of Israel out of the land of Egypt;

8But, As the Lord lives Who brought up and led the offspring of the house of Israel out of the north country and from all the countries to which I had driven them. And they shall dwell in their own land.

9Concerning the prophets: My heart [says Jeremiah] is broken within me, all my bones shake; I am like a drunken man, a man whom wine has overcome, because of the Lord and because of His holy words [which He has pronounced against unfaithful leaders].

10For the land is full of adulterers [forsakers of God, Israel's true Husband]. Because of the curse [of God upon it] the land mourns, the pastures of the wilderness are dried up. They [both false prophets and people] rush into wickedness, *and* their course is evil, their might is not right.

11For both [false] prophet and priest are ungodly *and* profane; even in My house have I found their wickedness, says the Lord.

12Therefore their way shall be to them like slippery paths in the dark. They shall be driven on and fall into them, for I will bring evil upon them in the year of their punishment, says the Lord.

13And I have seen folly in the prophets of Samaria: they prophesied by Baal and caused My people Israel to err *and* go astray.

14I have seen also in the prophets of Jerusalem a horrible thing: they commit adultery and walk in lies; they encourage *and* strengthen the hands of evildoers, so that none returns from his wickedness. They have all of them become to Me as Sodom, and its inhabitants as Gomorrah.

15Therefore thus says the Lord of hosts concerning the prophets: Behold, I will feed them with [the bitterness of] wormwood, and make them drink the [poisonous] water of gall; for from the [false] prophets of Jerusalem profaneness *and* ungodliness have gone forth into all the land.

16Thus says the Lord of hosts, Do not listen to the words of the [false] prophets who prophesy to you. They teach you vanity—emptiness, falsity and futility— *and* fill you with vain hopes; they speak a vision of their own minds, and not from the mouth of the Lord.

## New American Standard

5¶ "Behold, *the* days are coming," declares the LORD,
"When I shall raise up for David a righteous Branch;
And He will reign as king and act wisely
And do justice and righteousness in the land.
6 "In His days Judah will be saved,
And Israel will dwell securely;
And this is His name by which He will be called,
'The LORD our righteousness.'
7 "Therefore behold, *the* days are coming," declares the LORD,
"when they will no longer say, 'As the LORD lives, who brought
up the sons of Israel from the land of Egypt,'
8 but, 'As the LORD lives, who brought up and led back the
descendants of the household of Israel from *the* north land and
from all the countries where I had driven them.' Then they will live
on their own soil."

*False Prophets Denounced*

9 As for the prophets:
My heart is broken within me,
All my bones tremble;
I have become like a drunken man,
Even like a man overcome with wine,
Because of the LORD
And because of His holy words.
10 For the land is full of adulterers;
For the land mourns because of the curse.
The pastures of the wilderness have dried up.
Their course also is evil,
And their might is not right.
11 "For both prophet and priest are polluted;
Even in My house I have found their wickedness,"
declares the LORD.
12 "Therefore their way will be like slippery paths to them,
They will be driven away into the gloom and fall down in it;
For I shall bring calamity upon them,
The year of their punishment," declares the LORD.

13¶ "Moreover, among the prophets of Samaria I saw an offensive thing:
They prophesied by Baal and led My people Israel astray.
14 "Also among the prophets of Jerusalem I have seen a horrible thing:
The committing of adultery and walking in falsehood;
And they strengthen the hands of evildoers,
So that no one has turned back from his wickedness.
All of them have become to Me like Sodom,
And her inhabitants like Gomorrah.
15 "Therefore thus says the LORD of hosts concerning the prophets,
'Behold, I am going to feed them wormwood
And make them drink poisonous water,
For from the prophets of Jerusalem
Pollution has gone forth into all the land.'"

16¶ Thus says the LORD of hosts,
"Do not listen to the words of the prophets who are prophesying to you.
They are leading you into futility;
They speak a vision of their own imagination,
Not from the mouth of the LORD.

## New International

5 "The days are coming," declares the LORD,
"when I will raise up to David[a] a righteous Branch,
a King who will reign wisely
and do what is just and right in the land.
6 In his days Judah will be saved
and Israel will live in safety.
This is the name by which he will be called:
The LORD Our Righteousness.

7 "So then, the days are coming," declares the LORD, "when people
will no longer say, 'As surely as the LORD lives, who brought the
Israelites up out of Egypt,' 8 but they will say, 'As surely as the
LORD lives, who brought the descendants of Israel up out of the
land of the north and out of all the countries where he had banished them.' Then they will live in their own land."

*Lying Prophets*

9 Concerning the prophets:
My heart is broken within me;
all my bones tremble.
I am like a drunken man,
like a man overcome by wine,
because of the LORD
and his holy words.
10 The land is full of adulterers;
because of the curse[b] the land lies parched[c]
and the pastures in the desert are withered.
The ⌊prophets⌋ follow an evil course
and use their power unjustly.
11 "Both prophet and priest are godless;
even in my temple I find their wickedness,"
declares the LORD.
12 "Therefore their path will become slippery;
they will be banished to darkness
and there they will fall.
I will bring disaster on them
in the year they are punished,"
declares the LORD.

13 "Among the prophets of Samaria
I saw this repulsive thing:
They prophesied by Baal
and led my people Israel astray.
14 And among the prophets of Jerusalem
I have seen something horrible:
They commit adultery and live a lie.
They strengthen the hands of evildoers,
so that no one turns from his wickedness.
They are all like Sodom to me;
the people of Jerusalem are like Gomorrah."

15 Therefore, this is what the LORD Almighty says concerning the prophets:

"I will make them eat bitter food
and drink poisoned water,
because from the prophets of Jerusalem
ungodliness has spread throughout the land."

16 This is what the LORD Almighty says:

"Do not listen to what the prophets are prophesying to you;
they fill you with false hopes.
They speak visions from their own minds,
not from the mouth of the LORD.

**NIV** [a] 5 Or *up from David's line* [b] 10 Or *because of these things* [c] 10 Or *land mourns*

## King James

17They say still unto them that despise me, The LORD hath said, Ye shall have peace; and they say unto every one that walketh after the imagination of his own heart, No evil shall come upon you.

18For who hath stood in the counsel of the LORD, and hath perceived and heard his word? who hath marked his word, and heard *it*?

19Behold, a whirlwind of the LORD is gone forth in fury, even a grievous whirlwind: it shall fall grievously upon the head of the wicked.

20The anger of the LORD shall not return, until he have executed, and till he have performed the thoughts of his heart: in the latter days ye shall consider it perfectly.

21I have not sent these prophets, yet they ran: I have not spoken to them, yet they prophesied.

22But if they had stood in my counsel, and had caused my people to hear my words, then they should have turned them from their evil way, and from the evil of their doings.

23 *Am* I a God at hand, saith the LORD, and not a God afar off?

24Can any hide himself in secret places that I shall not see him? saith the LORD. Do not I fill heaven and earth? saith the LORD.

25I have heard what the prophets said, that prophesy lies in my name, saying, I have dreamed, I have dreamed.

26How long shall *this* be in the heart of the prophets that prophesy lies? yea, *they are* prophets of the deceit of their own heart;

27Which think to cause my people to forget my name by their dreams which they tell every man to his neighbour, as their fathers have forgotten my name for Baal.

28The prophet that hath a dream, let him tell a dream; and he that hath my word, let him speak my word faithfully. What *is* the chaff to the wheat? saith the LORD.

29 *Is* not my word like as a fire? saith the LORD; and like a hammer *that* breaketh the rock in pieces?

30Therefore, behold, I *am* against the prophets, saith the LORD, that steal my words every one from his neighbour.

31Behold, I *am* against the prophets, saith the LORD, that use their tongues, and say, He saith.

32Behold, I *am* against them that prophesy false dreams, saith the LORD, and do tell them, and cause my people to err by their lies, and by their lightness; yet I sent them not, nor commanded them: therefore they shall not profit this people at all, saith the LORD.

33¶ And when this people, or the prophet, or a priest, shall ask thee, saying, What *is* the burden of the LORD? thou shalt then say unto them, What burden? I will even forsake you, saith the LORD.

34And *as for* the prophet, and the priest, and the people, that shall say, The burden of the LORD, I will even punish that man and his house.

35Thus shall ye say every one to his neighbour, and every one to his brother, What hath the LORD answered? and, What hath the LORD spoken?

36And the burden of the LORD shall ye mention no more: for every man's word shall be his burden; for ye have perverted the words of the living God, of the LORD of hosts our God.

37Thus shalt thou say to the prophet, What hath the LORD answered thee? and, What hath the LORD spoken?

## Amplified

17They are continually saying to those who despise Me *and* the word of the Lord, The Lord has said you shall have peace; and they say to every one who walks after the stubbornness of his own mind *and* heart, No evil shall come upon you.

18For who among them has stood in the council of the Lord, that he should perceive and hear His word? Who has marked His word—noticing and observing and giving attention to it—and has *actually* heard it?

19Behold, the tempest of the Lord has gone out in wrath, a whirling tempest; it shall burst [whirling] upon the head of the wicked.

20The anger of the Lord shall not turn back until He has executed *and* accomplished the thoughts *and* intents of His mind *and* heart. In the latter days you shall consider *and* understand it perfectly.

21I did not send these [false] prophets, yet they ran; I did not speak to them, yet they prophesied.

22But if they had stood in My council, then would they have caused My people to hear My words, then they would have turned [My people] from their evil way, and from the evil of their doings.

23And I a God at hand, says the Lord, and not a God afar off?

24Can any hide himself in secret places so that I will not see him? says the Lord. Do not I fill heaven and earth? says the Lord.

25I have heard what the prophets have said who prophesy lies in My name, saying, I have dreamed, I have dreamed [visions on my bed at night].

26How long shall this *state of things continue? How long* still shall it be in the mind of the prophets who prophesy falsehood, even the prophets of the deceit of their own heart,

27To think to cause My people to forget My name by their dreams which every man tells to his neighbor, as their fathers forgot My name because of Baal?

28The prophet who has a dream, let him tell a dream; and he who has My word, let him speak My word faithfully. What has straw in common with wheat [for nourishment]? says the Lord.

29Is not My word like fire [that consumes all that cannot endure the test]? says the Lord, and like a hammer that breaks in pieces the rock [of most stubborn resistance]?

30Therefore, behold I am against the *false* prophets, says the Lord; [I am even now descending upon them with punishment, these prophets] who steal My words from one another [imitating the phrases of the true prophets].

31Behold, I am against the prophets, says the Lord, who use their [own deceitful] tongues and say, Thus says [the Lord].

32Behold, I am against those who prophesy lying dreams, says the Lord, and tell them and cause My people to err *and* go astray by their lies and by their vain boasting *and* recklessness, when I did not send them or command them; nor do they profit this people at all, says the Lord.

33And when this people, or the prophets, or a priest shall ask you, What is the burden of the Lord—the saying to be lifted up *now*? Then you shall say to them, What burden, *indeed*!—You are the burden! And I will disburden Myself of you *and* I will cast you off, says the Lord.

34And as for the prophet, the priest, or *these of* the people, whoever shall [in mockery call the word of the Lord a burden and] say, The burden of the Lord, I will even visit in wrath *and* punish that man and his house.

35[For the future in speaking of the utterances of the Lord] thus shall you say every one to his neighbor and every one to his brother, What has the Lord answered? or, What has the Lord spoken?

36And the burden of the Lord shall you mention no more: for every man's burden is his own response *and* word [for as they mockingly call all prophecies burdens, whether good or bad, so shall it prove to be to them; God will take them at their own word]; for you pervert the words [not of a lifeless idol, but] of the living God, the Lord of hosts, our God!

37Thus shall you [reverently] say to the prophet, What has the Lord answered you? Or, What has the Lord spoken?

## New American Standard

17 "They keep saying to those who despise Me,
'The LORD has said, "You will have peace"';
And as for everyone who walks in the stubbornness of his own heart,
They say, 'Calamity will not come upon you.'
18 "But who has stood in the council of the LORD,
That he should see and hear His word?
Who has given heed to His word and listened?
19 "Behold, the storm of the LORD has gone forth in wrath,
Even a whirling tempest;
It will swirl down on the head of the wicked.
20 "The anger of the LORD will not turn back
Until He has performed and carried out the purposes of His heart;
In the last days you will clearly understand it.
21 "I did not send *these* prophets,
But they ran.
I did not speak to them,
But they prophesied.
22 "But if they had stood in My council,
Then they would have announced My words to My people,
And would have turned them back from their evil way
And from the evil of their deeds.

23¶ "Am I a God who is near," declares the LORD,
"And not a God far off?
24 "Can a man hide himself in hiding places,
So I do not see him?" declares the LORD.
"Do I not fill the heavens and the earth?" declares the LORD.

25¶ "I have heard what the prophets have said who prophesy
falsely in My name, saying, 'I had a dream, I had a dream!'
26"How long? Is there *anything* in the hearts of the prophets
who prophesy falsehood, even *these* prophets of the deception of
their own heart,
27who intend to make My people forget My name by their
dreams which they relate to one another, just as their fathers forgot
My name because of Baal?
28"The prophet who has a dream may relate *his* dream, but let
him who has My word speak My word in truth. What does straw
have *in common* with grain?" declares the LORD.
29"Is not My word like fire?" declares the LORD, "and like a
hammer which shatters a rock?
30"Therefore behold, I am against the prophets," declares the
LORD, "who steal My words from each other.
31"Behold, I am against the prophets," declares the LORD, "who
use their tongues and declare, '*The Lord* declares.'
32"Behold, I am against those who have prophesied false
dreams," declares the LORD, "and related them, and led My
people astray by their falsehoods and reckless boasting; yet I did
not send them or command them, nor do they furnish this people
the slightest benefit," declares the LORD.
33¶ "Now when this people or the prophet or a priest asks you
saying, 'What is the [a]oracle of the LORD?' then you shall say to
them, 'What oracle?' The LORD declares, 'I shall abandon you.'
34"Then as for the prophet or the priest or the people who say,
'The oracle of the LORD,' I shall bring punishment upon that man
and his household.
35"Thus shall each of you say to his neighbor and to his brother,
'What has the LORD answered?' or, 'What has the LORD spoken?'
36"For you will no longer remember the oracle of the LORD,
because every man's own word will become the oracle, and you
have perverted the words of the living God, the LORD of hosts, our
God.
37"Thus you will say to *that* prophet, 'What has the LORD answered you?' and, 'What has the LORD spoken?'

NAS [a] Or, *burden,* and so throughout the ch.

## New International

17They keep saying to those who despise me,
'The LORD says: You will have peace.'
And to all who follow the stubbornness of their hearts
they say, 'No harm will come to you.'
18But which of them has stood in the council of the LORD
to see or to hear his word?
Who has listened and heard his word?
19See, the storm of the LORD
will burst out in wrath,
a whirlwind swirling down
on the heads of the wicked.
20The anger of the LORD will not turn back
until he fully accomplishes
the purposes of his heart.
In days to come
you will understand it clearly.
21I did not send these prophets,
yet they have run with their message;
I did not speak to them,
yet they have prophesied.
22But if they had stood in my council,
they would have proclaimed my words to my people
and would have turned them from their evil ways
and from their evil deeds.

23"Am I only a God nearby,"
declares the LORD,
"and not a God far away?
24Can anyone hide in secret places
so that I cannot see him?"
declares the LORD.
"Do not I fill heaven and earth?"
declares the LORD.

25"I have heard what the prophets say who prophesy lies in my
name. They say, 'I had a dream! I had a dream!' 26How long will
this continue in the hearts of these lying prophets, who prophesy
the delusions of their own minds? 27They think the dreams they
tell one another will make my people forget my name, just as their
fathers forgot my name through Baal worship. 28Let the prophet
who has a dream tell his dream, but let the one who has my word
speak it faithfully. For what has straw to do with grain?" declares
the LORD. 29"Is not my word like fire," declares the LORD, "and
like a hammer that breaks a rock in pieces?
30"Therefore," declares the LORD, "I am against the prophets
who steal from one another words supposedly from me. 31Yes,"
declares the LORD, "I am against the prophets who wag their own
tongues and yet declare, 'The LORD declares.' 32Indeed, I am
against those who prophesy false dreams," declares the LORD.
"They tell them and lead my people astray with their reckless lies,
yet I did not send or appoint them. They do not benefit these
people in the least," declares the LORD.

*False Oracles and False Prophets*

33"When these people, or a prophet or a priest, ask you, 'What
is the oracle[b] of the LORD?' say to them, 'What oracle?[c] I will
forsake you, declares the LORD.' 34If a prophet or a priest or anyone
else claims, 'This is the oracle of the LORD,' I will punish that man
and his household. 35This is what each of you keeps on saying to
his friend or relative: 'What is the LORD's answer?' or 'What has
the LORD spoken?' 36But you must not mention 'the oracle of the
LORD' again, because every man's own word becomes his oracle
and so you distort the words of the living God, the LORD Almighty,
our God. 37This is what you keep saying to a prophet: 'What is the
LORD's answer to you?' or 'What has the LORD spoken?' 38Al-

NIV [b] 33 Or *burden* (see Septuagint and Vulgate) [c] 33 Hebrew; Septuagint and Vulgate *'You are the burden.* (The Hebrew for *oracle* and *burden* is the same.)

## King James

38 But since ye say, The burden of the LORD; therefore thus saith the LORD; Because ye say this word, The burden of the LORD, and I have sent unto you, saying, Ye shall not say, The burden of the LORD;

39 Therefore, behold, I, even I, will utterly forget you, and I will forsake you, and the city that I gave you and your fathers, *and cast you* out of my presence:

40 And I will bring an everlasting reproach upon you, and a perpetual shame, which shall not be forgotten.

**24** THE LORD showed me, and, behold, two baskets of figs *were* set before the temple of the LORD, after that Nebuchadrezzar king of Babylon had carried away captive Jeconiah the son of Jehoiakim king of Judah, and the princes of Judah, with the carpenters and smiths, from Jerusalem, and had brought them to Babylon.

2 One basket *had* very good figs, *even* like the figs *that are* first ripe: and the other basket *had* very naughty figs, which could not be eaten, they were so bad.

3 Then said the LORD unto me, What seest thou, Jeremiah? And I said, Figs; the good figs, very good; and the evil, very evil, that cannot be eaten, they are so evil.

4 ¶ Again the word of the LORD came unto me, saying,

5 Thus saith the LORD, the God of Israel; Like these good figs, so will I acknowledge them that are carried away captive of Judah, whom I have sent out of this place into the land of the Chaldeans for *their* good.

6 For I will set mine eyes upon them for good, and I will bring them again to this land: and I will build them, and not pull *them* down; and I will plant them, and not pluck *them* up.

7 And I will give them an heart to know me, that I *am* the LORD: and they shall be my people, and I will be their God: for they shall return unto me with their whole heart.

8 ¶ And as the evil figs, which cannot be eaten, they are so evil; surely thus saith the LORD, So will I give Zedekiah the king of Judah, and his princes, and the residue of Jerusalem, that remain in this land, and them that dwell in the land of Egypt:

9 And I will deliver them to be removed into all the kingdoms of the earth for *their* hurt, *to be* a reproach and a proverb, a taunt and a curse, in all places whither I shall drive them.

10 And I will send the sword, the famine, and the pestilence, among them, till they be consumed from off the land that I gave unto them and to their fathers.

**25** THE WORD that came to Jeremiah concerning all the people of Judah in the fourth year of Jehoiakim the son of Josiah king of Judah, that *was* the first year of Nebuchadrezzar king of Babylon;

2 The which Jeremiah the prophet spake unto all the people of Judah, and to all the inhabitants of Jerusalem, saying,

3 From the thirteenth year of Josiah the son of Amon king of Judah, even unto this day, that *is* the three and twentieth year, the word of the LORD hath come unto me, and I have spoken unto you, rising early and speaking; but ye have not hearkened.

4 And the LORD hath sent unto you all his servants the prophets, rising early and sending *them;* but ye have not hearkened, nor inclined your ear to hear.

5 They said, Turn ye again now every one from his evil way, and from the evil of your doings, and dwell in the land that the LORD hath given unto you and to your fathers for ever and ever:

6 And go not after other gods to serve them, and to worship them, and provoke me not to anger with the works of your hands; and I will do you no hurt.

## Amplified

38 But if you say, The burden of the Lord, therefore thus says the Lord: Because you say these words, The burden of the Lord, when I sent to you, saying, You shall not say, The burden of the Lord,

39 Therefore, behold, I, even I, will assuredly take you up and cast you away from My presence, you and the city [Jerusalem] which I gave to you and to your fathers.

40 And I will bring an everlasting reproach upon you and a perpetual shame, which shall not be forgotten.

**24** AFTER NEBUCHADREZZAR king of Babylon had taken into exile Jeconiah the son of Jehoiakim, king of Judah, and the princes of Judah, with the craftsmen and smiths, [all] from Jerusalem, and had brought them to Babylon, the Lord showed me [in a vision] two baskets of figs set before the temple of the Lord.

2 One basket had very good figs, like the figs that are first ripe, but the other basket had very bad figs, so bad that they could not be eaten.

3 Then the Lord said to me, What do you see, Jeremiah? And I said, Figs; the good figs very good, and the bad very bad, that cannot be eaten because they are so bad.

4 Again the word of the Lord came to me, saying,

5 Thus says the Lord, the God of Israel: Like these good figs, so will I regard the captives of Judah whom I have sent out of this place into the land of the Chaldeans for their good.

6 For I will set My eyes upon them for good, and I will bring them again to this land; and I will build them and not pull them down, and I will plant them and not pluck them up.

7 And I will give them a heart to recognize, understand *and* be acquainted with Me, that I am the Lord; and they shall be My people and I will be their God, for they shall return to Me with their whole heart.

8 And as for the bad figs, which cannot be eaten because they are so bad, surely thus says the Lord, So will I give up Zedekiah the king of Judah, and his princes, and the residue of Jerusalem, that remain in this land, and those who dwell in the land of Egypt.

9 I will even give them up to be a dismay *and* a horror, *and* to be tossed to and fro among all the kingdoms of the earth for evil, to be a reproach, a byword *or* proverb, a taunt and a curse in all places where I shall drive them.

10 And I will send the sword, famine, and pestilence among them, till they be consumed from off the land that I gave to them and to their fathers.

**25** THE WORD that came to Jeremiah concerning all the people of Judah, in the fourth year of the reign of Jehoiakim the son of Josiah, king of Judah, which was the first year of the reign of Nebuchadrezzar king of Babylon;

2 Which Jeremiah the prophet spoke to all the people of Judah, and to all the inhabitants of Jerusalem:

3 For these twenty-three years, from the thirteenth year of Josiah the son of Amon, king of Judah, even to this day, the word of the Lord has come to me, and I have spoken to you persistently early and late, but you have not listened *and* obeyed.

4 Although the Lord persistently sent you all the prophets, His servants, yet you have not listened and obeyed or [even] inclined your ear to hear.

5 [The prophets came for Me] saying, Turn again now every one from his evil way and wrong doings, [that you may not forfeit the right to] dwell in the land that the Lord gave to you and to your fathers from of old *and* for evermore.

6 Do not go after other gods to serve and worship them, and do not provoke Me to anger with the works of your hands. Then I will do you no harm.

## New American Standard

38"For if you say, 'The oracle of the LORD!' surely thus says the
LORD, 'Because you said this word, "The oracle of the LORD!" I
have also sent to you, saying, "You shall not say, 'The oracle of
the LORD!' " '
39"Therefore behold, I shall surely forget you and cast you away
from My presence, along with the city which I gave you and your
fathers.
40"And I will put an everlasting reproach on you and an everlasting humiliation which will not be forgotten."

*Baskets of Figs and the Returnees*

**24** AFTER NEBUCHADNEZZAR king of Babylon had carried away captive Jeconiah the son of Jehoiakim, king of
Judah, and the officials of Judah with the craftsmen and smiths
from Jerusalem and had brought them to Babylon, the LORD
showed me: behold, two baskets of figs set before the temple of
the LORD!
2One basket had very good figs, like first-ripe figs; and the
other basket had very bad figs, which could not be eaten due to
rottenness.
3Then the LORD said to me, "What do you see, Jeremiah?" And
I said, "Figs, the good figs, very good; and the bad *figs*, very bad,
which cannot be eaten due to rottenness."
4¶ Then the word of the LORD came to me, saying,
5"Thus says the LORD God of Israel, 'Like these good figs, so
I will regard as good the captives of Judah, whom I have sent out
of this place *into* the land of the Chaldeans.
6'For I will set My eyes on them for good, and I will bring them
again to this land; and I will build them up and not overthrow
them, and I will plant them and not pluck *them* up.
7'And I will give them a heart to know Me, for I am the LORD;
and they will be My people, and I will be their God, for they will
return to Me with their whole heart.
8¶ 'But like the bad figs which cannot be eaten due to rottenness—indeed, thus says the LORD—so I will abandon Zedekiah
king of Judah and his officials, and the remnant of Jerusalem who
remain in this land, and the ones who dwell in the land of Egypt.
9'And I will make them a terror *and an* evil for all the kingdoms
of the earth, as a reproach and a proverb, a taunt and a curse in
all places where I shall scatter them.
10'And I will send the sword, the famine, and the pestilence
upon them until they are destroyed from the land which I gave to
them and their forefathers.' "

*Prophecy of the Captivity*

**25** THE WORD that came to Jeremiah concerning all the
people of Judah, in the fourth year of Jehoiakim the son
of Josiah, king of Judah (that was the first year of Nebuchadnezzar
king of Babylon),
2which Jeremiah the prophet spoke to all the people of Judah
and to all the inhabitants of Jerusalem, saying,
3"From the thirteenth year of Josiah the son of Amon, king of
Judah, even to this day, these twenty-three years the word of the
LORD has come to me, and I have spoken to you again and again,
but you have not listened.
4"And the LORD has sent to you all His servants the prophets
again and again, but you have not listened nor inclined your ear
to hear,
5saying, 'Turn now everyone from his evil way and from the
evil of your deeds, and dwell on the land which the LORD has given
to you and your forefathers forever and ever;
6and do not go after other gods to serve them and to worship
them, and do not provoke Me to anger with the work of your
hands, and I will do you no harm.'

## New International

though you claim, 'This is the oracle of the LORD,' this is what the
LORD says: You used the words, 'This is the oracle of the LORD,'
even though I told you that you must not claim, 'This is the oracle
of the LORD.' 39Therefore, I will surely forget you and cast you out
of my presence along with the city I gave to you and your fathers.
40I will bring upon you everlasting disgrace—everlasting shame
that will not be forgotten."

*Two Baskets of Figs*

**24** AFTER JEHOIACHIN[a] son of Jehoiakim king of Judah
and the officials, the craftsmen and the artisans of Judah
were carried into exile from Jerusalem to Babylon by Nebuchadnezzar king of Babylon, the LORD showed me two baskets of
figs placed in front of the temple of the LORD. 2One basket had very
good figs, like those that ripen early; the other basket had very
poor figs, so bad they could not be eaten.
3Then the LORD asked me, "What do you see, Jeremiah?"
"Figs," I answered. "The good ones are very good, but the poor
ones are so bad they cannot be eaten."
4Then the word of the LORD came to me: 5"This is what the
LORD, the God of Israel, says: 'Like these good figs, I regard as
good the exiles from Judah, whom I sent away from this place to
the land of the Babylonians.[b] 6My eyes will watch over them for
their good, and I will bring them back to this land. I will build them
up and not tear them down; I will plant them and not uproot them.
7I will give them a heart to know me, that I am the LORD. They will
be my people, and I will be their God, for they will return to me
with all their heart.
8" 'But like the poor figs, which are so bad they cannot be
eaten,' says the LORD, 'so will I deal with Zedekiah king of Judah,
his officials and the survivors from Jerusalem, whether they remain in this land or live in Egypt. 9I will make them abhorrent and
an offense to all the kingdoms of the earth, a reproach and a
byword, an object of ridicule and cursing, wherever I banish them.
10I will send the sword, famine and plague against them until they
are destroyed from the land I gave to them and their fathers.' "

*Seventy Years of Captivity*

**25** THE WORD came to Jeremiah concerning all the people
of Judah in the fourth year of Jehoiakim son of Josiah king
of Judah, which was the first year of Nebuchadnezzar king of
Babylon. 2So Jeremiah the prophet said to all the people of Judah
and to all those living in Jerusalem: 3For twenty-three years—from
the thirteenth year of Josiah son of Amon king of Judah until this
very day—the word of the LORD has come to me and I have spoken
to you again and again, but you have not listened.
4And though the LORD has sent all his servants the prophets to
you again and again, you have not listened or paid any attention.
5They said, "Turn now, each of you, from your evil ways and your
evil practices, and you can stay in the land the LORD gave to you
and your fathers for ever and ever. 6Do not follow other gods to
serve and worship them; do not provoke me to anger with what
your hands have made. Then I will not harm you."

NIV [a] 1 Hebrew *Jeconiah,* a variant of *Jehoiachin* [b] 5 Or *Chaldeans*

## King James

7Yet ye have not hearkened unto me, saith the LORD; that ye
might provoke me to anger with the works of your hands to your
own hurt.
8¶ Therefore thus saith the LORD of hosts; Because ye have not
heard my words,
9Behold, I will send and take all the families of the north, saith
the LORD, and Nebuchadrezzar the king of Babylon, my servant,
and will bring them against this land, and against the inhabitants
thereof, and against all these nations round about, and will utterly
destroy them, and make them an astonishment, and an hissing,
and perpetual desolations.
10Moreover I will take from them the voice of mirth, and the
voice of gladness, the voice of the bridegroom, and the voice of the
bride, the sound of the millstones, and the light of the candle.
11And this whole land shall be a desolation, *and* an astonishment; and these nations shall serve the king of Babylon seventy
years.
12¶ And it shall come to pass, when seventy years are accomplished, *that* I will punish the king of Babylon, and that nation,
saith the LORD, for their iniquity, and the land of the Chaldeans,
and will make it perpetual desolations.
13And I will bring upon that land all my words which I have
pronounced against it, *even* all that is written in this book, which
Jeremiah hath prophesied against all the nations.
14For many nations and great kings shall serve themselves of
them also: and I will recompense them according to their deeds,
and according to the works of their own hands.
15¶ For thus saith the LORD God of Israel unto me; Take the wine
cup of this fury at my hand, and cause all the nations, to whom
I send thee, to drink it.
16And they shall drink, and be moved, and be mad, because of
the sword that I will send among them.
17Then took I the cup at the LORD's hand, and made all the
nations to drink, unto whom the LORD had sent me:
18 *To wit,* Jerusalem, and the cities of Judah, and the kings
thereof, and the princes thereof, to make them a desolation, an
astonishment, an hissing, and a curse; as *it is* this day;
19Pharaoh king of Egypt, and his servants, and his princes, and
all his people;
20And all the mingled people, and all the kings of the land of
Uz, and all the kings of the land of the Philistines, and Ashkelon,
and Azzah, and Ekron, and the remnant of Ashdod,
21Edom, and Moab, and the children of Ammon,
22And all the kings of Tyrus, and all the kings of Zidon, and the
kings of the isles which *are* beyond the sea,
23Dedan, and Tema, and Buz, and all *that are* in the utmost
corners,
24And all the kings of Arabia, and all the kings of the mingled
people that dwell in the desert,
25And all the kings of Zimri, and all the kings of Elam, and all
the kings of the Medes,
26And all the kings of the north, far and near, one with another,
and all the kingdoms of the world, which *are* upon the face of the
earth: and the king of Sheshach shall drink after them.
27Therefore thou shalt say unto them, Thus saith the LORD of
hosts, the God of Israel; Drink ye, and be drunken, and spew, and
fall, and rise no more, because of the sword which I will send
among you.
28And it shall be, if they refuse to take the cup at thine hand to
drink, then shalt thou say unto them, Thus saith the LORD of hosts;
Ye shall certainly drink.
29For, lo, I begin to bring evil on the city which is called by my
name, and should ye be utterly unpunished? Ye shall not be unpunished: for I will call for a sword upon all the inhabitants of the
earth, saith the LORD of hosts.

**AMP** [a] As both sacred and secular history show, this prophecy was approximately literally fulfilled, whether it refers to the duration of the Babylonian Empire, or to the length of the Jewish captivity in Babylon. For the marvelous literal fulfillment of specific details concerning the destruction and perpetual desolation of Babylon, see the footnotes on Isa. 13:22 and 14:23.

## Amplified

7Yet you have not listened *and* obeyed Me, says the Lord, that
you might provoke Me to anger with [idols] made by your hands
to your own hurt.
8Therefore thus says the Lord of hosts: Because you have not
heard *and* obeyed My words,
9Behold, I will send for all the tribes of the north, says the Lord,
and I will send for Nebuchadrezzar the king of Babylon, My servant [or agent to fulfill My designs], and I will bring them against
this land and its inhabitants, and against all these nations round
about; and I will devote them to destruction, and make them an
amazement, a hissing, and perpetual *and* agelong desolations.
10Moreover, I will take from them the voice of mirth and the
voice of gladness, the voice of the bridegroom and the voice of the
bride, the sound of the millstones [grinding out the meal] and the
light of the candle [which every home burned through the night].
11And this whole land shall be a waste and an astonishment,
and these nations shall serve the king of Babylon [a]seventy years.
[Jer. 4:27; 12:11, 12; Dan. 9:2.]
12Then after seventy years are completed, I will punish the king
of Babylon and that nation, the land of the Chaldeans, says the
Lord, for their iniquity, and will make the land [of the Chaldeans]
a perpetual waste.
13And I will bring upon that land all My words which I have
pronounced against it, even all that is written in this book, which
Jeremiah has prophesied against all the nations.
14For many nations and great kings shall make bondsmen of
them, even of [the Chaldeans who enslaved other nations]; and I
will recompense [all of] them, according to their deeds, and according to the work of their *own* hands.
15For thus says the Lord, the God of Israel, to me: Take this cup
of the wine of wrath from My hand, and cause all the nations to
whom I send you to drink it.
16They shall drink and reel to and fro and be crazed, because
of the sword that I will send among them.
17Then I [Jeremiah] took the cup at the Lord's hand, and made
all the nations drink it to whom the Lord had sent me: *that is,*
18Jerusalem and cities of Judah [being most guilty because their
privileges were greatest], its kings and princes, to make them a
desolation, an astonishment, a hissing and a curse, as it is to this
time; [I Pet. 4:17.]
19Pharaoh king of Egypt, his servants, his princes, all his
people,
20And all the mixed foreign population; all the kings of the land
of Uz, and all the kings of the land of the Philistines and [their cities
of] Ashkelon, Gaza, Ekron, and the remnant of Ashdod;
21Edom, Moab, and the children of Ammon;
22All the kings of Tyre, all the kings of Sidon, and the kings of
the islands *and* the coastland across the [Mediterranean] Sea;
23Dedan, Tema, Buz [neighboring tribes north of Arabia], and
all who cut off the corners of their hair *and* beards; [Lev. 19:27.]
24All the kings of Arabia and all the kings of the mixed tribes
who dwell in the desert;
25All the kings of Zimri, all the kings of Elam [Persia], and all
the kings of Media;
26All the kings of the north, far and near, one after another, and
all the kingdoms of the world, which are on the face of the earth.
And after them the king of Sheshach [Babel or Babylon] shall
drink.
27Then you shall say to them, Thus says the Lord of hosts, the
God of Israel: Drink, be drunk, vomit, and fall to rise no more,
because of the sword which I am sending among you.
28And if they refuse to take the cup at your hand to drink, then
you shall say to them, Thus says the Lord of hosts: You shall surely
drink!
29For, lo, I begin to work evil at the city which is called by My
name, and shall you go unpunished? You shall not go unpunished, for I am calling for a sword against all the inhabitants of the
earth, says the Lord of hosts.

## New American Standard

7"Yet you have not listened to Me," declares the LORD, "in
order that you might provoke Me to anger with the work of your
hands to your own harm.
8"Therefore thus says the LORD of hosts, 'Because you have not
obeyed My words,
9behold, I will send and take all the families of the north,'
declares the LORD, 'and *I will send* to Nebuchadnezzar king of
Babylon, My servant, and will bring them against this land, and
against its inhabitants, and against all these nations round about;
and I will utterly destroy them, and make them a horror, and a
hissing, and an everlasting desolation.
10'Moreover, I will take from them the voice of joy and the voice
of gladness, the voice of the bridegroom and the voice of the bride,
the sound of the millstones and the light of the lamp.
11'And this whole land shall be a desolation and a horror, and
these nations shall serve the king of Babylon seventy years.

*Babylon Will Be Judged*

12¶ 'Then it will be when seventy years are completed I will
punish the king of Babylon and that nation,' declares the LORD, 'for
their iniquity, and the land of the Chaldeans; and I will make it an
everlasting desolation.
13'And I will bring upon that land all My words which I have
pronounced against it, all that is written in this book, which Jeremiah has prophesied against all the nations.
14'(For many nations and great kings shall make slaves of them,
even them; and I will recompense them according to their deeds,
and according to the work of their hands.)' "
15¶ For thus the LORD, the God of Israel, says to me, "Take this
cup of the wine of wrath from My hand, and cause all the nations,
to whom I send you, to drink it.
16"And they shall drink and stagger and go mad because of the
sword that I will send among them."
17Then I took the cup from the LORD's hand, and made all the
nations drink, to whom the LORD sent me:
18Jerusalem and the cities of Judah, and its kings *and* its princes,
to make them a ruin, a horror, a hissing, and a curse, as it is this
day;
19Pharaoh king of Egypt, his servants, his princes, and all his
people;
20and all the foreign people, all the kings of the land of Uz, all
the kings of the land of the Philistines (even Ashkelon, Gaza,
Ekron, and the remnant of Ashdod);
21Edom, Moab, and the sons of Ammon;
22and all the kings of Tyre, all the kings of Sidon, and the kings
of the coastlands which are beyond the sea;
23and Dedan, Tema, Buz, and all who cut the corners *of their
hair;*
24and all the kings of Arabia and all the kings of the foreign
people who dwell in the desert;
25and all the kings of Zimri, all the kings of Elam, and all the
kings of Media;
26and all the kings of the north, near and far, one with another;
and all the kingdoms of the earth which are upon the face of the
ground, and the king of Sheshach shall drink after them.
27¶ "And you shall say to them, 'Thus says the LORD of hosts,
the God of Israel, "Drink, be drunk, vomit, fall, and rise no more
because of the sword which I will send among you." '
28"And it will be, if they refuse to take the cup from your hand
to drink, then you will say to them, 'Thus says the LORD of hosts:
"You shall surely drink!
29"For behold, I am beginning to work calamity in *this* city
which is called by My name, and shall you be completely free from
punishment? You will not be free from punishment; for I am
summoning a sword against all the inhabitants of the earth,"
declares the LORD of hosts.'

## New International

7"But you did not listen to me," declares the LORD, "and you
have provoked me with what your hands have made, and you
have brought harm to yourselves."
8Therefore the LORD Almighty says this: "Because you have not
listened to my words, 9I will summon all the peoples of the north
and my servant Nebuchadnezzar king of Babylon," declares the
LORD, "and I will bring them against this land and its inhabitants
and against all the surrounding nations. I will completely destroy[b]
them and make them an object of horror and scorn, and an everlasting ruin. 10I will banish from them the sounds of joy and
gladness, the voices of bride and bridegroom, the sound of millstones and the light of the lamp. 11This whole country will become
a desolate wasteland, and these nations will serve the king of
Babylon seventy years.
12"But when the seventy years are fulfilled, I will punish the
king of Babylon and his nation, the land of the Babylonians,[c] for
their guilt," declares the LORD, "and will make it desolate forever.
13I will bring upon that land all the things I have spoken against
it, all that are written in this book and prophesied by Jeremiah
against all the nations. 14They themselves will be enslaved by
many nations and great kings; I will repay them according to their
deeds and the work of their hands."

*The Cup of God's Wrath*

15This is what the LORD, the God of Israel, said to me: "Take
from my hand this cup filled with the wine of my wrath and make
all the nations to whom I send you drink it. 16When they drink it,
they will stagger and go mad because of the sword I will send
among them."
17So I took the cup from the LORD's hand and made all the
nations to whom he sent me drink it: 18Jerusalem and the towns
of Judah, its kings and officials, to make them a ruin and an object
of horror and scorn and cursing, as they are today; 19Pharaoh king
of Egypt, his attendants, his officials and all his people, 20and all
the foreign people there; all the kings of Uz; all the kings of the
Philistines (those of Ashkelon, Gaza, Ekron, and the people left at
Ashdod); 21Edom, Moab and Ammon; 22all the kings of Tyre and
Sidon; the kings of the coastlands across the sea; 23Dedan, Tema,
Buz and all who are in distant places[d]; 24all the kings of Arabia and
all the kings of the foreign people who live in the desert; 25all the
kings of Zimri, Elam and Media; 26and all the kings of the north,
near and far, one after the other—all the kingdoms on the face of
the earth. And after all of them, the king of Sheshach[e] will drink
it too.
27"Then tell them, 'This is what the LORD Almighty, the God
of Israel, says: Drink, get drunk and vomit, and fall to rise no more
because of the sword I will send among you.' 28But if they refuse
to take the cup from your hand and drink, tell them, 'This is what
the LORD Almighty says: You must drink it! 29See, I am beginning
to bring disaster on the city that bears my Name, and will you
indeed go unpunished? You will not go unpunished, for I am
calling down a sword upon all who live on the earth, declares the
LORD Almighty.'

**NIV** [b] 9 The Hebrew term refers to the irrevocable giving over of things or persons to the LORD, often by totally destroying them. [c] 12 Or *Chaldeans* [d] 23 Or *who clip the hair by their foreheads* [e] 26 *Sheshach* is a cryptogram for Babylon.

## King James

30 Therefore prophesy thou against them all these words, and say unto them, The LORD shall roar from on high, and utter his voice from his holy habitation; he shall mightily roar upon his habitation; he shall give a shout, as they that tread *the grapes,* against all the inhabitants of the earth.

31 A noise shall come *even* to the ends of the earth; for the LORD hath a controversy with the nations, he will plead with all flesh; he will give them *that are* wicked to the sword, saith the LORD.

32 Thus saith the LORD of hosts, Behold, evil shall go forth from nation to nation, and a great whirlwind shall be raised up from the coasts of the earth.

33 And the slain of the LORD shall be at that day from *one* end of the earth even unto the *other* end of the earth: they shall not be lamented, neither gathered, nor buried; they shall be dung upon the ground.

34 ¶ Howl, ye shepherds, and cry; and wallow yourselves *in the ashes,* ye principal of the flock: for the days of your slaughter and of your dispersions are accomplished; and ye shall fall like a pleasant vessel.

35 And the shepherds shall have no way to flee, nor the principal of the flock to escape.

36 A voice of the cry of the shepherds, and an howling of the principal of the flock, *shall be heard:* for the LORD hath spoiled their pasture.

37 And the peaceable habitations are cut down because of the fierce anger of the LORD.

38 He hath forsaken his covert, as the lion: for their land is desolate because of the fierceness of the oppressor, and because of his fierce anger.

**26** IN THE beginning of the reign of Jehoiakim the son of Josiah king of Judah came this word from the LORD, saying,

2 Thus saith the LORD; Stand in the court of the LORD'S house, and speak unto all the cities of Judah, which come to worship in the LORD'S house, all the words that I command thee to speak unto them; diminish not a word:

3 If so be they will hearken, and turn every man from his evil way, that I may repent me of the evil, which I purpose to do unto them because of the evil of their doings.

4 And thou shalt say unto them, Thus saith the LORD; If ye will not hearken to me, to walk in my law, which I have set before you,

5 To hearken to the words of my servants the prophets, whom I sent unto you, both rising up early, and sending *them,* but ye have not hearkened;

6 Then will I make this house like Shiloh, and will make this city a curse to all the nations of the earth.

7 So the priests and the prophets and all the people heard Jeremiah speaking these words in the house of the LORD.

8 ¶ Now it came to pass, when Jeremiah had made an end of speaking all that the LORD had commanded *him* to speak unto all the people, that the priests and the prophets and all the people took him, saying, Thou shalt surely die.

9 Why hast thou prophesied in the name of the LORD, saying, This house shall be like Shiloh, and this city shall be desolate without an inhabitant? And all the people were gathered against Jeremiah in the house of the LORD.

## Amplified

30 Therefore prophesy against them all these words, and say to them: The Lord shall roar from on high, and utter His voice from His holy habitation; He shall roar mightily against His fold *and* pasture; He shall give a shout, like those *do* who tread grapes [in the winepress, but His shout will be] against all the inhabitants of the earth.

31 A noise shall come even to the ends of the earth; for the Lord has a controversy and an indictment against the nations; He will enter into judgment will all mankind; as for the wicked, He will give them to the sword, says the Lord.

32 Thus says the Lord of hosts, Behold, evil shall go forth from nation to nation, and a great tempest will rise whirling from the uttermost parts of the earth.

33 And the slain of the Lord shall be at that day from one end of the earth even unto the other end of the earth; they shall not be lamented, or gathered, or buried; their *dead bodies* shall be dung upon the ground.

34 Wail, you shepherds, and cry, and roll in ashes, you chief among the flock, for the days of your slaughter and of your dispersions are fully come, and you shall fall *and* be dashed to pieces like a choice vessel.

35 And the shepherds shall have no way to flee, nor the principal ones of the flock any means of escape.

36 A voice! The cry of the shepherds and the wailing of the chief *ones* of the flock! For the Lord is laying waste *and* spoiling their pasture.

37 And the peaceable folds are devastated *and* brought to silence because of the fierce anger of the Lord.

38 He has left His shelter as the lion; for their land has become a waste *and* an astonishment because of the fierceness of the oppressor, and because of [the Lord's] fierce anger.

**26** IN THE beginning of the reign of Jehoiakim the son of Josiah, king of Judah, came this word from the Lord,

2 Thus says the Lord: Stand in the court of the Lord's house [Jeremiah], and speak to all the cities of Judah which come to worship in the Lord's house all the words that I command you to speak to them; diminish not a word.

3 It may be they will listen, and turn every man from his evil way, that I may relent *and* reverse My decision concerning the evil which I purpose to do to them because of their evil doings.

4 And you shall say to them, Thus says the Lord: If you will not listen *and* obey Me, to walk in My law which I have set before you,

5 And to hear *and* obey the words of My servants the prophets whom I sent to you urgently *and* persistently, though you have not listened *and* obeyed;

6 Then will I make this house [the temple] like Shiloh [abandoned home of the tabernacle after the ark was captured by the Philistines], and will make this city subject to the curses of all nations of the earth [so vile in their sight will it be].

7 And the priests and the [false] prophets and all the people heard Jeremiah speaking these words in the house of the Lord.

8 Now when Jeremiah had finished speaking all that the Lord had commanded him to speak to all the people, the priests and the [false] prophets and all the people seized him, saying, You shall surely die!

9 Why have you prophesied in the name of the Lord, saying, This house shall be like Shiloh [after the ark of the Lord had been taken by our enemies], and this city [Jerusalem] shall be desolate without an inhabitant? And all the people were gathered around Jeremiah in the [outer area of the] house of the Lord.

## New American Standard

30¶ "Therefore you shall prophesy against them all these words, and you shall say to them,
'The LORD will roar from on high,
And utter His voice from His holy habitation;
He will roar mightily against His fold.
He will shout like those who tread *the grapes*,
Against all the inhabitants of the earth.
31 'A clamor has come to the end of the earth,
Because the LORD has a controversy with the nations.
He is entering into judgment with all flesh;
As for the wicked, He has given them to the sword,'
declares the LORD."

32¶ Thus says the LORD of hosts,
"Behold, evil is going forth
From nation to nation,
And a great storm is being stirred up
From the remotest parts of the earth.
33"And those slain by the LORD on that day shall be from one end of the earth to the other. They shall not be lamented, gathered, or buried; they shall be like dung on the face of the ground.
34 "Wail, you shepherds, and cry;
And wallow *in ashes*, you masters of the flock;
For the days of your slaughter and your dispersions have come,
And you shall fall like a choice vessel.
35 "Flight shall perish from the shepherds,
And escape from the masters of the flock.
36 "*Hear* the sound of the cry of the shepherds,
And the wailing of the masters of the flock!
For the LORD is destroying their pasture,
37 "And the peaceful folds are made silent
Because of the fierce anger of the LORD.
38 "He has left His hiding place like the lion;
For their land has become a horror
Because of the fierceness of the oppressing *sword*,
And because of His fierce anger."

*Cities of Judah Warned*

**26** IN THE beginning of the reign of Jehoiakim the son of Josiah, king of Judah, this word came from the LORD, saying,
2"Thus says the LORD, 'Stand in the court of the LORD's house,
and speak to all the cities of Judah, who have come to worship *in*
the LORD's house, all the words that I have commanded you to
speak to them. Do not omit a word!
3'Perhaps they will listen and everyone will turn from his evil way, that I may repent of the calamity which I am planning to do to them because of the evil of their deeds.'
4"And you will say to them, 'Thus says the LORD, "If you will not listen to Me, to walk in My law, which I have set before you,
5to listen to the words of My servants the prophets, whom I have been sending to you again and again, but you have not listened;
6then I will make this house like Shiloh, and this city I will make a curse to all the nations of the earth." ' "

*A Plot to Murder Jeremiah*

7¶ And the priests and the prophets and all the people heard Jeremiah speaking these words in the house of the LORD.
8And when Jeremiah finished speaking all that the LORD had commanded *him* to speak to all the people, the priests and the prophets and all the people seized him, saying, "You must die!
9"Why have you prophesied in the name of the LORD saying, 'This house will be like Shiloh, and this city will be desolate, without inhabitant'?" And all the people gathered about Jeremiah in the house of the LORD.

## New International

30"Now prophesy all these words against them and say to them:
" 'The LORD will roar from on high;
he will thunder from his holy dwelling
and roar mightily against his land.
He will shout like those who tread the grapes,
shout against all who live on the earth.
31The tumult will resound to the ends of the earth,
for the LORD will bring charges against the nations;
he will bring judgment on all mankind
and put the wicked to the sword,' "
declares the LORD.

32This is what the LORD Almighty says:

"Look! Disaster is spreading
from nation to nation;
a mighty storm is rising
from the ends of the earth."

33At that time those slain by the LORD will be everywhere—from one end of the earth to the other. They will not be mourned or gathered up or buried, but will be like refuse lying on the ground.

34Weep and wail, you shepherds;
roll in the dust, you leaders of the flock.
For your time to be slaughtered has come;
you will fall and be shattered like fine pottery.
35The shepherds will have nowhere to flee,
the leaders of the flock no place to escape.
36Hear the cry of the shepherds,
the wailing of the leaders of the flock,
for the LORD is destroying their pasture.
37The peaceful meadows will be laid waste
because of the fierce anger of the LORD.
38Like a lion he will leave his lair,
and their land will become desolate
because of the sword[a] of the oppressor
and because of the LORD's fierce anger.

*Jeremiah Threatened With Death*

**26** EARLY IN the reign of Jehoiakim son of Josiah king of Judah, this word came from the LORD: 2"This is what the
LORD says: Stand in the courtyard of the LORD's house and speak to all the people of the towns of Judah who come to worship in the house of the LORD. Tell them everything I command you; do not omit a word.
3Perhaps they will listen and each will turn from his evil way. Then I will relent and not bring on them the disaster I was planning because of the evil they have done.
4Say to them, 'This is what the LORD says: If you do not listen to me and follow my law, which I have set before you,
5and if you do not listen to the words of my servants the prophets, whom I have sent to you again and again (though you have not listened),
6then I will make this house like Shiloh and this city an object of cursing among all the nations of the earth.' "
7The priests, the prophets and all the people heard Jeremiah speak these words in the house of the LORD.
8But as soon as Jeremiah finished telling all the people everything the LORD had commanded him to say, the priests, the prophets and all the people seized him and said, "You must die!
9Why do you prophesy in the LORD's name that this house will be like Shiloh and this city will be desolate and deserted?" And all the people crowded around Jeremiah in the house of the LORD.

NIV [a] *38* Some Hebrew manuscripts and Septuagint (see also Jer. 46:16 and 50:16); most Hebrew manuscripts *anger*

## King James

10¶ When the princes of Judah heard these things, then they came up from the king's house unto the house of the LORD, and sat down in the entry of the new gate of the LORD's *house.*

11Then spake the priests and the prophets unto the princes and to all the people, saying, This man *is* worthy to die; for he hath prophesied against this city, as ye have heard with your ears.

12¶ Then spake Jeremiah unto all the princes and to all the people, saying, The LORD sent me to prophesy against this house and against this city all the words that ye have heard.

13Therefore now amend your ways and your doings, and obey the voice of the LORD your God; and the LORD will repent him of the evil that he hath pronounced against you.

14As for me, behold, I *am* in your hand: do with me as seemeth good and meet unto you.

15But know ye for certain, that if ye put me to death, ye shall surely bring innocent blood upon yourselves, and upon this city, and upon the inhabitants thereof: for of a truth the LORD hath sent me unto you to speak all these words in your ears.

16¶ Then said the princes and all the people unto the priests and to the prophets; This man *is* not worthy to die: for he hath spoken to us in the name of the LORD our God.

17Then rose up certain of the elders of the land, and spake to all the assembly of the people, saying,

18Micah the Morasthite prophesied in the days of Hezekiah king of Judah, and spake to all the people of Judah, saying, Thus saith the LORD of hosts; Zion shall be plowed *like* a field, and Jerusalem shall become heaps, and the mountain of the house as the high places of a forest.

19Did Hezekiah king of Judah and all Judah put him at all to death? did he not fear the LORD, and besought the LORD, and the LORD repented him of the evil which he had pronounced against them? Thus might we procure great evil against our souls.

20And there was also a man that prophesied in the name of the LORD, Urijah the son of Shemaiah of Kirjath-jearim, who prophesied against this city and against this land according to all the words of Jeremiah:

21And when Jehoiakim the king, with all his mighty men, and all the princes, heard his words, the king sought to put him to death: but when Urijah heard it, he was afraid, and fled, and went into Egypt;

22And Jehoiakim the king sent men into Egypt, *namely,* Elnathan the son of Achbor, and *certain* men with him into Egypt.

23And they fetched forth Urijah out of Egypt, and brought him unto Jehoiakim the king; who slew him with the sword, and cast his dead body into the graves of the common people.

24Nevertheless the hand of Ahikam the son of Shaphan was with Jeremiah, that they should not give him into the hand of the people to put him to death.

**27** IN THE beginning of the reign of Jehoiakim the son of Josiah king of Judah came this word unto Jeremiah from the LORD, saying,

## Amplified

10When the princes of Judah heard these things, they came up from the king's house to the house of the Lord and sat down in the entry of the New Gate of the house of the Lord.

11Then the priests and the prophets said to the princes and to all the people, This man is worthy of death, for he has prophesied against this city, as you have heard with your own ears.

12Then Jeremiah said to all the princes and to all the people: The Lord sent me to prophesy against this house and against this city all the words that you have heard.

13Therefore now amend your ways and your doings and obey the voice of the Lord your God, and the Lord will relent of the evil *and* reverse the decision that He has pronounced against you.

14As for me, behold, I am in your hands; do with me as seems good and suitable to you.

15But know for certain that if you put me to death, you will bring innocent blood upon yourselves and upon this city and upon its inhabitants, for in truth the Lord sent me to you to speak all these words in your hearing.

16Then said the princes and all the people to the priests and to the prophets: This man is not deserving of death, for he has spoken to us in the name of the Lord our God.

17Then certain of the elders of the land arose and said to all the assembly of the people,

18Micah of Moresheth prophesied in the days of Hezekiah, king of Judah, and said to all the people of Judah, Thus says the Lord of hosts: Zion shall be [a]plowed like a field, and Jerusalem shall become heaps [of ruins], and the mountain of the house *of the Lord* [Mount Moriah on which stands the temple, shall become covered not with buildings, but] like a densely wooded height.

19Did Hezekiah king of Judah and all Judah put [Micah] to death? Did he not (reverently) fear the Lord, and entreat the Lord, and did not the Lord relent of the evil *and* reverse the decision which He had pronounced against them? But [here] we are thinking of committing what will be a great evil against ourselves.

20And there was also a man who prophesied in the name of the Lord, Uriah the son of Shemaiah of Kiriath-jearim, who prophesied against this city and against this land in words similar to those of Jeremiah.

21And when Jehoiakim the king, with all his mighty men and all the princes, heard his words, the king sought to put [Uriah] to death; but when Uriah heard it, he was afraid and fled and escaped to Egypt.

22And Jehoiakim the king sent men into Egypt, namely, Elnathan the son of Achbor, and certain men *who went* with him into Egypt.

23And they fetched Uriah from Egypt and brought him to Jehoiakim the king, who slew him [God's spokesman] with the sword and cast his dead body in among the graves of the common people.

24But the hand of Ahikam the son of Shaphan was with Jeremiah, that they should not give him into the hand of the people to put him *also* to death.

**27** IN THE beginning of the reign of Zedekiah the son of Josiah, king of Judah, this word came to Jeremiah from the Lord.

**AMP** [a] This prophecy of Micah, made in the days of King Hezekiah, that Mount Zion would become a plowed field, was literally fulfilled. When Nebuchadnezzar and the Chaldeans took Jerusalem, they broke down the walls (II Kings 25:10). That was in B.C. 586. In 1542 A.D. the present walls of Jerusalem were built by the then Sultan of Turkey. By a strange error, the part of the city known as Mount Zion was omitted from the enclosure and remained outside the walls; and for centuries it was literally "plowed like a field." That Mount Zion is the only part of Jerusalem ever known to be plowed, is conclusive evidence of the infinite foreknowledge of the word of the Lord which came to His prophet Micah.

## New American Standard

10¶ And when the princes of Judah heard these things, they
came up from the king's house to the house of the LORD and sat
in the entrance of the New Gate of the LORD's *house.*
11Then the priests and the prophets spoke to the officials and
to all the people, saying, "A death sentence for this man! For he
has prophesied against this city as you have heard in your hearing."
12Then Jeremiah spoke to all the officials and to all the people,
saying, "The LORD sent me to prophesy against this house and
against this city all the words that you have heard.
13"Now therefore amend your ways and your deeds, and obey
the voice of the LORD your God; and the LORD will change His
mind about the misfortune which He has pronounced against you.
14"But as for me, behold, I am in your hands; do with me as is
good and right in your sight.
15"Only know for certain that if you put me to death, you will
bring innocent blood on yourselves, and on this city, and on its
inhabitants; for truly the LORD has sent me to you to speak all these
words in your hearing."

*Jeremiah Is Spared*

16¶ Then the officials and all the people said to the priests and
to the prophets, "No death sentence for this man! For he has
spoken to us in the name of the LORD our God."
17Then some of the elders of the land rose up and spoke to all
the assembly of the people, saying,
18"Micah of Moresheth prophesied in the days of Hezekiah
king of Judah; and he spoke to all the people of Judah, saying,
'Thus the LORD of hosts has said,

"Zion will be plowed *as* a field,
And Jerusalem will become ruins,
And the mountain of the house as the high places of a
forest." '

19"Did Hezekiah king of Judah and all Judah put him to death?
Did he not fear the LORD and entreat the favor of the LORD, and
the LORD changed His mind about the misfortune which He had
pronounced against them? But we are committing a great evil
against ourselves."
20¶ Indeed, there was also a man who prophesied in the name
of the LORD, Uriah the son of Shemaiah from Kiriath-jearim; and
he prophesied against this city and against this land words similar
to all those of Jeremiah.
21When King Jehoiakim and all his mighty men and all the
officials heard his words, then the king sought to put him to death;
but Uriah heard *it,* and he was afraid and fled, and went to Egypt.
22Then King Jehoiakim sent men to Egypt: Elnathan the son of
Achbor and *certain* men with him *went* into Egypt.
23And they brought Uriah from Egypt and led him to King
Jehoiakim, who slew him with a sword, and cast his dead body
into the burial place of the common people.
24¶ But the hand of Ahikam the son of Shaphan was with
Jeremiah, so that he was not given into the hands of the people
to put him to death.

*The Nations to Submit to Nebuchadnezzar*

**27** IN THE beginning of the reign of Zedekiah the son of
Josiah, king of Judah, this word came to Jeremiah from the
LORD, saying—

## New International

10When the officials of Judah heard about these things, they
went up from the royal palace to the house of the LORD and took
their places at the entrance of the New Gate of the LORD's house.
11Then the priests and the prophets said to the officials and all the
people, "This man should be sentenced to death because he has
prophesied against this city. You have heard it with your own
ears!"
12Then Jeremiah said to all the officials and all the people: "The
LORD sent me to prophesy against this house and this city all the
things you have heard. 13Now reform your ways and your actions
and obey the LORD your God. Then the LORD will relent and not
bring the disaster he has pronounced against you. 14As for me, I
am in your hands; do with me whatever you think is good and
right. 15Be assured, however, that if you put me to death, you will
bring the guilt of innocent blood on yourselves and on this city and
on those who live in it, for in truth the LORD has sent me to you
to speak all these words in your hearing."
16Then the officials and all the people said to the priests and the
prophets, "This man should not be sentenced to death! He has
spoken to us in the name of the LORD our God."
17Some of the elders of the land stepped forward and said to the
entire assembly of people, 18"Micah of Moresheth prophesied in
the days of Hezekiah king of Judah. He told all the people of Judah,
'This is what the LORD Almighty says:

" 'Zion will be plowed like a field,
Jerusalem will become a heap of rubble,
the temple hill a mound overgrown with thickets.'[b]

19"Did Hezekiah king of Judah or anyone else in Judah put him
to death? Did not Hezekiah fear the LORD and seek his favor? And
did not the LORD relent, so that he did not bring the disaster he
pronounced against them? We are about to bring a terrible disaster
on ourselves!"
20(Now Uriah son of Shemaiah from Kiriath Jearim was another
man who prophesied in the name of the LORD; he prophesied the
same things against this city and this land as Jeremiah did. 21When
King Jehoiakim and all his officers and officials heard his words,
the king sought to put him to death. But Uriah heard of it and fled
in fear to Egypt. 22King Jehoiakim, however, sent Elnathan son of
Acbor to Egypt, along with some other men. 23They brought Uriah
out of Egypt and took him to King Jehoiakim, who had him struck
down with a sword and his body thrown into the burial place of
the common people.)
24Furthermore, Ahikam son of Shaphan supported Jeremiah,
and so he was not handed over to the people to be put to death.

*Judah to Serve Nebuchadnezzar*

**27** EARLY IN the reign of Zedekiah[c] son of Josiah king of
Judah, this word came to Jeremiah from the LORD: 2This

NIV [b] *18* Micah 3:12 [c] *1* A few Hebrew manuscripts and Syriac (see also Jer. 27:3, 12 and 28:1); most Hebrew manuscripts *Jehoiakim* (Most Septuagint manuscripts do not have this verse.)

## King James

2 Thus saith the LORD to me; Make thee bonds and yokes, and put them upon thy neck,

3 And send them to the king of Edom, and to the king of Moab, and to the king of the Ammonites, and to the king of Tyrus, and to the king of Zidon, by the hand of the messengers which come to Jerusalem unto Zedekiah king of Judah;

4 And command them to say unto their masters, Thus saith the LORD of hosts, the God of Israel; Thus shall ye say unto your masters;

5 I have made the earth, the man and the beast that *are* upon the ground, by my great power and by my outstretched arm, and have given it unto whom it seemed meet unto me.

6 And now have I given all these lands into the hand of Nebuchadnezzar the king of Babylon, my servant; and the beasts of the field have I given him also to serve him.

7 And all nations shall serve him, and his son, and his son's son, until the very time of his land come: and then many nations and great kings shall serve themselves of him.

8 And it shall come to pass, *that* the nation and kingdom which will not serve the same Nebuchadnezzar the king of Babylon, and that will not put their neck under the yoke of the king of Babylon, that nation will I punish, saith the LORD, with the sword, and with the famine, and with the pestilence, until I have consumed them by his hand.

9 Therefore hearken not ye to your prophets, nor to your diviners, nor to your dreamers, nor to your enchanters, nor to your sorcerers, which speak unto you, saying, Ye shall not serve the king of Babylon:

10 For they prophesy a lie unto you, to remove you far from your land; and that I should drive you out, and ye should perish.

11 But the nations that bring their neck under the yoke of the king of Babylon, and serve him, those will I let remain still in their own land, saith the LORD; and they shall till it, and dwell therein.

12 ¶ I spake also to Zedekiah king of Judah according to all these words, saying, Bring your necks under the yoke of the king of Babylon, and serve him and his people, and live.

13 Why will ye die, thou and thy people, by the sword, by the famine, and by the pestilence, as the LORD hath spoken against the nation that will not serve the king of Babylon?

14 Therefore hearken not unto the words of the prophets that speak unto you, saying, Ye shall not serve the king of Babylon: for they prophesy a lie unto you.

15 For I have not sent them, saith the LORD, yet they prophesy a lie in my name; that I might drive you out, and that ye might perish, ye, and the prophets that prophesy unto you.

16 Also I spake to the priests and to all this people, saying, Thus saith the LORD; Hearken not to the words of your prophets that prophesy unto you, saying, Behold, the vessels of the LORD's house shall now shortly be brought again from Babylon: for they prophesy a lie unto you.

17 Hearken not unto them; serve the king of Babylon, and live: wherefore should this city be laid waste?

18 But if they *be* prophets, and if the word of the LORD be with them, let them now make intercession to the LORD of hosts, that the vessels which are left in the house of the LORD, and *in* the house of the king of Judah, and at Jerusalem, go not to Babylon.

19 ¶ For thus saith the LORD of hosts concerning the pillars, and concerning the sea, and concerning the bases, and concerning the residue of the vessels that remain in this city,

20 Which Nebuchadnezzar king of Babylon took not, when he carried away captive Jeconiah the son of Jehoiakim king of Judah from Jerusalem to Babylon, and all the nobles of Judah and Jerusalem;

21 Yea, thus saith the LORD of hosts, the God of Israel, concerning the vessels that remain *in* the house of the LORD, and *in* the house of the king of Judah and of Jerusalem;

## Amplified

2 Thus says the Lord to me: Make yourself thongs and yoke-bars and put them on your neck,

3 And send them to the king of Edom, to the king of Moab, to the king of the Ammonites, to the king of Tyre, and to the king of Sidon by the hand of the messengers who have come to Jerusalem to Zedekiah king of Judah.

4 And command them to say to their masters, Thus says the Lord of hosts, the God of Israel: Thus shall you say to your masters:

5 I have made the earth, the men and the beasts that are upon the face of the earth, by My great power and by My outstretched arm, and I give it to whom it seems right *and* suitable to Me.

6 And now I have given all these lands into the hand of Nebuchadnezzar the king of Babylon, My servant *and* instrument, and the beasts of the field also I have given him to serve him.

7 And all nations shall serve him and his son and his grandson, until the [God-appointed] time [of punishment] of his own land comes. And then many nations and great kings shall make him their slave.

8 But any nation or kingdom that will not serve this same Nebuchadnezzar the king of Babylon, and put its neck under the yoke of the king of Babylon, that nation will I punish, says the Lord, with the sword, with famine, and with pestilence, until I have consumed it by [Nebuchadnezzar's] hand.

9 So do not listen to your [false] prophets, your diviners, your dreams [whether your own or others'], your soothsayers, your sorcerers, who say to you, You shall not serve the king of Babylon.

10 For they prophesy a lie to you, which will cause you to be removed far from your land, and I will drive you out, and you will perish.

11 But any nation that brings its neck under the yoke of the king of Babylon and serves him, I will let remain on its own land, says the Lord, to cultivate it and dwell in it.

12 I spoke also to Zedekiah king of Judah in the same way: Bring your necks under the yoke of the king of Babylon, and serve him and his people, and live.

13 Why will you and your people die by the sword, by the famine, and by the pestilence, as the Lord has spoken concerning any nation that will not serve the king of Babylon?

14 Do not listen to *and* believe the words of the [false] prophets who are saying to you, You shall not serve the king of Babylon, for *it is* a lie *that* they prophesy to you.

15 For I have not sent them, says the Lord, but they are prophesying falsely in My name; [it will only end in] My driving you out to perish together with the [false] prophets who prophesy to you.

16 Also I said to the priests and to all this people, Thus says the Lord: Do not listen to the words of your [false] prophets who are prophesying to you, saying, Behold, the vessels of the Lord's house shall now shortly be brought [a]back from Babylon; for they prophesy a lie to you.

17 Do not listen to them *or* heed them; serve the king of Babylon and live. Why should this city be laid waste?

18 But if they are true prophets and if the word of the Lord is really spoken by them, let them now make intercession to the Lord of hosts, that the vessels which are [still] left in the house of the Lord, in the house of the king of Judah, and in Jerusalem may not go to Babylon.

19 For thus says the Lord of hosts concerning the pillars [of bronze, each twenty-seven feet high], and the *bronze* sea [the laver at which the priests cleansed their hands and feet before ministering at the altar], and the *bronze* bases [of the ten lavers in Solomon's temple for washing animals to be offered as sacrifices], and the remainder of the vessels which are left in this city [Jerusalem], [I Kings 7:23-37; II Chron. 4:6.]

20 Which Nebuchadnezzar king of Babylon did not take, when he carried into exile from Jerusalem to Babylon Jeconiah the son of Jehoiakim, king of Judah, and all the nobles of Judah and Jerusalem;

21 Yes, thus says the Lord of hosts, the God of Israel, concerning the vessels which [still] remain in the house of the Lord, in the house of the king of Judah, and in Jerusalem:

**AMP** [a] Nebuchadnezzar besieged Jerusalem three times. The second time was during the reign of Jeconiah (Jehoiachin) whom he took captive with all the nobles of Jerusalem (verse 20), at which time he carried away some of the sacred vessels of the temple. The third siege was now imminent.

## New American Standard

2thus says the LORD to me—"Make for yourself bonds and
yokes and put them on your neck,
3and send word to the king of Edom, to the king of Moab, to
the king of the sons of Ammon, to the king of Tyre, and to the king
of Sidon by the messengers who come to Jerusalem to Zedekiah
king of Judah.
4"And command them *to go* to their masters, saying, 'Thus
says the LORD of hosts, the God of Israel, thus you shall say to your
masters,
5"I have made the earth, the men and the beasts which are on
the face of the earth by My great power and by My outstretched
arm, and I will give it to the one who is pleasing in My sight.
6"And now I have given all these lands into the hand of Nebuchadnezzar king of Babylon, My servant, and I have given him also
the wild animals of the field to serve him.
7"And all the nations shall serve him, and his son, and his
grandson, until the time of his own land comes; then many nations
and great kings will make him their servant.
8"And it will be, *that* the nation or the kingdom which will not
serve him, Nebuchadnezzar king of Babylon, and which will not
put its neck under the yoke of the king of Babylon, I will punish
that nation with the sword, with famine, and with pestilence,"
declares the LORD, "until I have destroyed it by his hand.
9"But as for you, do not listen to your prophets, your diviners,
your dreamers, your soothsayers, or your sorcerers, who speak to
you, saying, 'You shall not serve the king of Babylon.'
10"For they prophesy a lie to you, in order to remove you far
from your land; and I will drive you out, and you will perish.
11"But the nation which will bring its neck under the yoke of
the king of Babylon and serve him, I will let remain on its land,"
declares the LORD, "and they will till it and dwell in it."'"
12¶ And I spoke words like all these to Zedekiah king of Judah,
saying, "Bring your necks under the yoke of the king of Babylon,
and serve him and his people, and live!
13"Why will you die, you and your people, by the sword,
famine, and pestilence, as the LORD has spoken to that nation
which will not serve the king of Babylon?
14"So do not listen to the words of the prophets who speak to
you, saying, 'You shall not serve the king of Babylon,' for they
prophesy a lie to you;
15for I have not sent them," declares the LORD, "but they
prophesy falsely in My name, in order that I may drive you out,
and that you may perish, you and the prophets who prophesy to
you."
16¶ *Then* I spoke to the priests and to all this people, saying,
"Thus says the LORD: Do not listen to the words of your prophets
who prophesy to you, saying, 'Behold, the vessels of the LORD's
house will now shortly be brought again from Babylon'; for they
are prophesying a lie to you.
17"Do not listen to them; serve the king of Babylon, and live!
Why should this city become a ruin?
18"But if they are prophets, and if the word of the LORD is with
them, let them now entreat the LORD of hosts, that the vessels
which are left in the house of the LORD, in the house of the king
of Judah, and in Jerusalem, may not go to Babylon.
19"For thus says the LORD of hosts concerning the pillars, concerning the sea, concerning the stands, and concerning the rest of
the vessels that are left in this city,
20which Nebuchadnezzar king of Babylon did not take when he
carried into exile Jeconiah the son of Jehoiakim, king of Judah,
from Jerusalem to Babylon, and all the nobles of Judah and Jerusalem.
21"Yes, thus says the LORD of hosts, the God of Israel, concerning the vessels that are left in the house of the LORD, and in the
house of the king of Judah, and in Jerusalem,

## New International

is what the LORD said to me: "Make a yoke out of straps and
crossbars and put it on your neck. 3Then send word to the kings
of Edom, Moab, Ammon, Tyre and Sidon through the envoys who
have come to Jerusalem to Zedekiah king of Judah. 4Give them a
message for their masters and say, 'This is what the LORD Almighty, the God of Israel, says: "Tell this to your masters: 5With
my great power and outstretched arm I made the earth and its
people and the animals that are on it, and I give it to anyone I
please. 6Now I will hand all your countries over to my servant
Nebuchadnezzar king of Babylon; I will make even the wild animals subject to him. 7All nations will serve him and his son and
his grandson until the time for his land comes; then many nations
and great kings will subjugate him.
8" ' "If, however, any nation or kingdom will not serve Nebuchadnezzar king of Babylon or bow its neck under his yoke, I will
punish that nation with the sword, famine and plague, declares
the LORD, until I destroy it by his hand. 9So do not listen to your
prophets, your diviners, your interpreters of dreams, your mediums or your sorcerers who tell you, 'You will not serve the king
of Babylon.' 10They prophesy lies to you that will only serve to
remove you far from your lands; I will banish you and you will
perish. 11But if any nation will bow its neck under the yoke of the
king of Babylon and serve him, I will let that nation remain in its
own land to till it and to live there, declares the LORD." ' "
12I gave the same message to Zedekiah king of Judah. I said,
"Bow your neck under the yoke of the king of Babylon; serve him
and his people, and you will live. 13Why will you and your people
die by the sword, famine and plague with which the LORD has
threatened any nation that will not serve the king of Babylon? 14Do
not listen to the words of the prophets who say to you, 'You will
not serve the king of Babylon,' for they are prophesying lies to you.
15'I have not sent them,' declares the LORD. 'They are prophesying
lies in my name. Therefore, I will banish you and you will perish,
both you and the prophets who prophesy to you.' "
16Then I said to the priests and all these people, "This is what
the LORD says: Do not listen to the prophets who say, 'Very soon
now the articles from the LORD's house will be brought back from
Babylon.' They are prophesying lies to you. 17Do not listen to
them. Serve the king of Babylon, and you will live. Why should
this city become a ruin? 18If they are prophets and have the word
of the LORD, let them plead with the LORD Almighty that the
furnishings remaining in the house of the LORD and in the palace
of the king of Judah and in Jerusalem not be taken to Babylon. 19For
this is what the LORD Almighty says about the pillars, the Sea, the
movable stands and the other furnishings that are left in this city,
20which Nebuchadnezzar king of Babylon did not take away when
he carried Jehoiachin[b] son of Jehoiakim king of Judah into exile
from Jerusalem to Babylon, along with all the nobles of Judah and
Jerusalem— 21yes, this is what the LORD Almighty, the God of
Israel, says about the things that are left in the house of the LORD
and in the palace of the king of Judah and in Jerusalem: 22'They

NIV [b] 20 Hebrew *Jeconiah,* a variant of *Jehoiachin*

## King James

22They shall be carried to Babylon, and there shall they be until the day that I visit them, saith the LORD; then will I bring them up, and restore them to this place.

28 AND IT came to pass the same year, in the beginning of the reign of Zedekiah king of Judah, in the fourth year, *and* in the fifth month, *that* Hananiah the son of Azur the prophet, which *was* of Gibeon, spake unto me in the house of the LORD, in the presence of the priests and of all the people, saying,

2Thus speaketh the LORD of hosts, the God of Israel, saying, I have broken the yoke of the king of Babylon.

3Within two full years will I bring again into this place all the vessels of the LORD's house, that Nebuchadnezzar king of Babylon took away from this place, and carried them to Babylon:

4And I will bring again to this place Jeconiah the son of Jehoiakim king of Judah, with all the captives of Judah, that went into Babylon, saith the LORD: for I will break the yoke of the king of Babylon.

5¶ Then the prophet Jeremiah said unto the prophet Hananiah in the presence of the priests, and in the presence of all the people that stood in the house of the LORD,

6Even the prophet Jeremiah said, Amen: the LORD do so: the LORD perform thy words which thou hast prophesied, to bring again the vessels of the LORD's house, and all that is carried away captive, from Babylon into this place.

7Nevertheless hear thou now this word that I speak in thine ears, and in the ears of all the people;

8The prophets that have been before me and before thee of old prophesied both against many countries, and against great kingdoms, of war, and of evil, and of pestilence.

9The prophet which prophesieth of peace, when the word of the prophet shall come to pass, *then* shall the prophet be known, that the LORD hath truly sent him.

10¶ Then Hananiah the prophet took the yoke from off the prophet Jeremiah's neck, and brake it.

11And Hananiah spake in the presence of all the people, saying, Thus saith the LORD; Even so will I break the yoke of Nebuchadnezzar king of Babylon from the neck of all nations within the space of two full years. And the prophet Jeremiah went his way.

12¶ Then the word of the LORD came unto Jeremiah *the prophet*, after that Hananiah the prophet had broken the yoke from off the neck of the prophet Jeremiah, saying,

13Go and tell Hananiah, saying, Thus saith the LORD; Thou hast broken the yokes of wood; but thou shalt make for them yokes of iron.

14For thus saith the LORD of hosts, the God of Israel; I have put a yoke of iron upon the neck of all these nations, that they may serve Nebuchadnezzar king of Babylon; and they shall serve him: and I have given him the beasts of the field also.

15¶ Then said the prophet Jeremiah unto Hananiah the prophet, Hear now, Hananiah; The LORD hath not sent thee; but thou makest this people to trust in a lie.

16Therefore thus saith the LORD; Behold, I will cast thee from off the face of the earth: this year thou shalt die, because thou hast taught rebellion against the LORD.

17So Hananiah the prophet died the same year in the seventh month.

## Amplified

22They shall be [a]carried to Babylon, and there shall they be until the day that I visit them [with My favor], says the Lord. Then I will bring them back and restore them to this place.

28 IN THAT same year, in the beginning of the reign of Zedekiah king of Judah, in the fourth year and the fifth month, Hananiah the son of Azzur, the [false] prophet, who was of Gibeon [one of the priests' cities], said to me in the house of the Lord, in the presence of the priests and all the people [falsely],

2Thus says the Lord of hosts, the God of Israel: I have broken the yoke of the king of Babylon.

3Within two [full] years will I bring again into this place all the vessels of the Lord's house, that Nebuchadnezzar king of Babylon took away from this place and carried to Babylon.

4And I will also bring again to this place Jeconiah the son of Jehoiakim, king of Judah, with all the exiles from Judah that went to Babylon, says the Lord, for I will break the yoke of the king of Babylon. [Jer. 22:10.]

5Then the prophet Jeremiah spoke to the prophet Hananiah in the presence of the priests and all the people who stood in the house of the Lord.

6The prophet Jeremiah said, Amen! May the Lord do so; may the Lord perform your words which you have prophesied to bring back to this place from Babylon the vessels of the Lord's house, and all who were carried away captive.

7Nevertheless listen now *and* hear this word which I speak in your hearing and in the hearing of all the people:

8The prophets that have been before me and before you of old prophesied against many countries and against great kingdoms, of war, of evil, and of pestilence.

9But as for the prophet who [on the contrary] prophesies of peace, when that prophet's word comes to pass, then [only] will it be known that the Lord has truly sent him.

10Then Hananiah the prophet took the yoke-bar from off the prophet Jeremiah's neck, and smashed it.

11And Hananiah said in the presence of all the people, Thus says the Lord: Even so will I break the yoke-bars of Nebuchadnezzar king of Babylon from the neck of all the nations within the space of two [full] years. But the prophet Jeremiah went his way.

12The word of the Lord came to Jeremiah the prophet [some time] after Hananiah the prophet had broken the yoke-bar from off the neck of the prophet Jeremiah:

13Go, tell Hananiah, Thus says the Lord: You have broken yoke-bars of wood, but you have made in their stead bars of iron.

14For thus says the Lord of hosts, the God of Israel: I have put upon the neck of all these nations an iron yoke of servitude of Nebuchadnezzar king of Babylon, and they shall serve him, for I have given him even the beasts of the field.

15Then said the prophet Jeremiah to Hananiah the prophet, Listen now, Hananiah, The Lord has not sent you, but you have made this people trust in a lie.

16Therefore thus says the Lord: Behold, I will cast you from the face of the earth. This year you shall die, because you have uttered *and* taught rebellion against the Lord.

17So Hananiah the prophet died [two months later], the same year in the seventh month.

**AMP** [a] This prophesy was literally fulfilled. The remaining sacred vessels were carried to Babylon (II Kings 25:13; II Chron. 36:18), where they were kept for seventy years (II Chron. 36:21), the length of the captivity as Jeremiah had foretold (Jer. 29:10), and then brought back to Jerusalem (Ezra 1:7; 7:19).

## New American Standard

22'They shall be carried to Babylon, and they shall be there until
the day I visit them,' declares the LORD. 'Then I will bring them
back and restore them to this place.' "

*Hananiah's False Prophecy*

**28** NOW IT came about in the same year, in the beginning
of the reign of Zedekiah king of Judah, in the fourth year,
in the fifth month, that Hananiah the son of Azzur, the prophet,
who was from Gibeon, spoke to me in the house of the LORD in
the presence of the priests and all the people, saying,
2"Thus says the LORD of hosts, the God of Israel, 'I have broken
the yoke of the king of Babylon.
3'Within two years I am going to bring back to this place all the
vessels of the LORD's house, which Nebuchadnezzar king of Babylon took away from this place and carried to Babylon.
4'I am also going to bring back to this place Jeconiah the son
of Jehoiakim, king of Judah, and all the exiles of Judah who went
to Babylon,' declares the LORD, 'for I will break the yoke of the king
of Babylon.' "
5¶ Then the prophet Jeremiah spoke to the prophet Hananiah
in the presence of the priests and in the presence of all the people
who were standing in the house of the LORD,
6and the prophet Jeremiah said, "Amen! May the LORD do so;
may the LORD confirm your words which you have prophesied to
bring back the vessels of the LORD's house and all the exiles, from
Babylon to this place.
7"Yet hear now this word which I am about to speak in your
hearing and in the hearing of all the people!
8"The prophets who were before me and before you from
ancient times prophesied against many lands and against great
kingdoms, of war and of calamity and of pestilence.
9"The prophet who prophesies of peace, when the word of the
prophet shall come to pass, then that prophet will be known *as* one
whom the LORD has truly sent."
10Then Hananiah the prophet took the yoke from the neck of
Jeremiah the prophet and broke it.
11And Hananiah spoke in the presence of all the people, saying,
"Thus says the LORD, 'Even so will I break within two full years,
the yoke of Nebuchadnezzar king of Babylon from the neck of all
the nations.' " Then the prophet Jeremiah went his way.
12¶ And the word of the LORD came to Jeremiah, after Hananiah
the prophet had broken the yoke from off the neck of the prophet
Jeremiah, saying,
13"Go and speak to Hananiah, saying, 'Thus says the LORD,
"You have broken the yokes of wood, but you have made instead
of them yokes of iron."
14'For thus says the LORD of hosts, the God of Israel, "I have
put a yoke of iron on the neck of all these nations, that they may
serve Nebuchadnezzar king of Babylon; and they shall serve him.
And I have also given him the beasts of the field." ' "
15Then Jeremiah the prophet said to Hananiah the prophet,
"Listen now, Hananiah, the LORD has not sent you, and you have
made this people trust in a lie.
16"Therefore thus says the LORD, 'Behold, I am about to remove
you from the face of the earth. This year you are going to die,
because you have counseled rebellion against the LORD.' "
17So Hananiah the prophet died in the same year in the seventh
month.

## New International

will be taken to Babylon and there they will remain until the day
I come for them,' declares the LORD. 'Then I will bring them back
and restore them to this place.' "

*The False Prophet Hananiah*

**28** IN THE fifth month of that same year, the fourth year,
early in the reign of Zedekiah king of Judah, the prophet
Hananiah son of Azzur, who was from Gibeon, said to me in the
house of the LORD in the presence of the priests and all the people:
2"This is what the LORD Almighty, the God of Israel, says: 'I will
break the yoke of the king of Babylon. 3Within two years I will
bring back to this place all the articles of the LORD's house that
Nebuchadnezzar king of Babylon removed from here and took to
Babylon. 4I will also bring back to this place Jehoiachin[b] son of
Jehoiakim king of Judah and all the other exiles from Judah who
went to Babylon,' declares the LORD, 'for I will break the yoke of
the king of Babylon.' "
5Then the prophet Jeremiah replied to the prophet Hananiah
before the priests and all the people who were standing in the
house of the LORD. 6He said, "Amen! May the LORD do so! May
the LORD fulfill the words you have prophesied by bringing the
articles of the LORD's house and all the exiles back to this place from
Babylon. 7Nevertheless, listen to what I have to say in your hearing and in the hearing of all the people: 8From early times the
prophets who preceded you and me have prophesied war, disaster
and plague against many countries and great kingdoms. 9But the
prophet who prophesies peace will be recognized as one truly sent
by the LORD only if his prediction comes true."
10Then the prophet Hananiah took the yoke off the neck of the
prophet Jeremiah and broke it, 11and he said before all the people,
"This is what the LORD says: 'In the same way will I break the yoke
of Nebuchadnezzar king of Babylon off the neck of all the nations
within two years.' " At this, the prophet Jeremiah went on his
way.
12Shortly after the prophet Hananiah had broken the yoke off
the neck of the prophet Jeremiah, the word of the LORD came to
Jeremiah: 13"Go and tell Hananiah, 'This is what the LORD says:
You have broken a wooden yoke, but in its place you will get a
yoke of iron. 14This is what the LORD Almighty, the God of Israel,
says: I will put an iron yoke on the necks of all these nations to
make them serve Nebuchadnezzar king of Babylon, and they will
serve him. I will even give him control over the wild animals.' "
15Then the prophet Jeremiah said to Hananiah the prophet,
"Listen, Hananiah! The LORD has not sent you, yet you have
persuaded this nation to trust in lies. 16Therefore, this is what the
LORD says: 'I am about to remove you from the face of the earth.
This very year you are going to die, because you have preached
rebellion against the LORD.' "
17In the seventh month of that same year, Hananiah the
prophet died.

NIV [b] 4 Hebrew *Jeconiah,* a variant of *Jehoiachin*

## King James

**29** NOW THESE *are* the words of the letter that Jeremiah the prophet sent from Jerusalem unto the residue of the elders which were carried away captives, and to the priests, and to the prophets, and to all the people whom Nebuchadnezzar had carried away captive from Jerusalem to Babylon;

2 (After that Jeconiah the king, and the queen, and the eunuchs, the princes of Judah and Jerusalem, and the carpenters, and the smiths, were departed from Jerusalem;)

3 By the hand of Elasah the son of Shaphan, and Gemariah the son of Hilkiah, (whom Zedekiah king of Judah sent unto Babylon to Nebuchadnezzar king of Babylon) saying,

4 Thus saith the LORD of hosts, the God of Israel, unto all that are carried away captives, whom I have caused to be carried away from Jerusalem unto Babylon;

5 Build ye houses, and dwell *in them;* and plant gardens, and eat the fruit of them;

6 Take ye wives, and beget sons and daughters; and take wives for your sons, and give your daughters to husbands, that they may bear sons and daughters; that ye may be increased there, and not diminished.

7 And seek the peace of the city whither I have caused you to be carried away captives, and pray unto the LORD for it: for in the peace thereof shall ye have peace.

8 ¶ For thus saith the LORD of hosts, the God of Israel; Let not your prophets and your diviners, that *be* in the midst of you, deceive you, neither hearken to your dreams which ye cause to be dreamed.

9 For they prophesy falsely unto you in my name: I have not sent them, saith the LORD.

10 ¶ For thus saith the LORD, That after seventy years be accomplished at Babylon I will visit you, and perform my good word toward you, in causing you to return to this place.

11 For I know the thoughts that I think toward you, saith the LORD, thoughts of peace, and not of evil, to give you an expected end.

12 Then shall ye call upon me, and ye shall go and pray unto me, and I will hearken unto you.

13 And ye shall seek me, and find *me,* when ye shall search for me with all your heart.

14 And I will be found of you, saith the LORD: and I will turn away your captivity, and I will gather you from all the nations, and from all the places whither I have driven you, saith the LORD; and I will bring you again into the place whence I caused you to be carried away captive.

15 ¶ Because ye have said, The LORD hath raised us up prophets in Babylon;

16 *Know* that thus saith the LORD of the king that sitteth upon the throne of David, and of all the people that dwelleth in this city, *and* of your brethren that are not gone forth with you into captivity;

17 Thus saith the LORD of hosts; Behold, I will send upon them the sword, the famine, and the pestilence, and will make them like vile figs, that cannot be eaten, they are so evil.

18 And I will persecute them with the sword, with the famine, and with the pestilence, and will deliver them to be removed to all the kingdoms of the earth, to be a curse, and an astonishment, and an hissing, and a reproach, among all the nations whither I have driven them:

19 Because they have not hearkened to my words, saith the LORD, which I sent unto them by my servants the prophets, rising up early and sending *them;* but ye would not hear, saith the LORD.

20 ¶ Hear ye therefore the word of the LORD, all ye of the captivity, whom I have sent from Jerusalem to Babylon:

21 Thus saith the LORD of hosts, the God of Israel, of Ahab the son of Kolaiah, and of Zedekiah the son of Maaseiah, which prophesy a lie unto you in my name; Behold, I will deliver them into the hand of Nebuchadrezzar king of Babylon; and he shall slay them before your eyes;

## Amplified

**29** NOW THESE are the words of the letter that Jeremiah the prophet sent from Jerusalem to the rest of the elders in exile, and to the priests, the prophets, and all the people whom Nebuchadnezzar had carried captive from Jerusalem to Babylon.

2 *This was* after King Jeconiah and the queen mother, the eunuchs, the princes of Judah and Jerusalem, the craftsmen and the smiths had departed from Jerusalem.

3 [The letter was sent] by the hand of Elasah the son of Shaphan and Gemariah the son of Hilkiah, whom Zedekiah king of Judah sent to Babylon to Nebuchadnezzar king of Babylon. It said:

4 Thus says the Lord of hosts, the God of Israel, to all the captives whom I have caused to be carried into exile from Jerusalem to Babylon:

5 Build yourselves houses and dwell in them; plant gardens and eat the fruit of them;

6 Take wives and have sons and daughters; take wives for your sons and give your daughters in marriage, that they may bear sons and daughters; multiply there, and do not be diminished.

7 And seek—inquire for, require and request—the peace *and* welfare of the city to which I have caused you to be carried away captive, and pray to the Lord for it; for in the welfare of *the city in which you live* you will have welfare.

8 For thus says the Lord of hosts, the God of Israel: Let not your [false] prophets and your diviners who are in your midst deceive you; pay no attention *and* attach no significance to your dreams which you dream, *or* to theirs,

9 For they prophesy falsely to you in My name; I have not sent them, says the Lord.

10 For thus says the Lord, When seventy years are completed for Babylon, I will visit you and keep My good promise to you, causing you to return to this place.

11 For I know the thoughts *and* plans that I have for you, says the Lord, thoughts *and* plans for welfare *and* peace, and not for evil, to give you hope in your final outcome.

12 Then you will call upon Me, and you will come and pray to Me, and I will hear *and* heed you.

13 Then you will seek Me, inquire for *and* require Me [as a vital necessity] and find Me; when you search for Me with all your heart,

14 I will be found by you, says the Lord, and I will release you from captivity and gather you from all the nations and all the places to which I have driven you, says the Lord, and I will bring you again to the place from which I caused you to be carried away captive.

15 [But as to those still in Jerusalem] because you have said, The Lord has raised up prophets for us in Babylon,—

16 Thus says the Lord concerning the king who sits upon the throne of David, and concerning all the people who dwell in this city, your brethren who are not gone forth with you into captivity,

17 Thus says the Lord of hosts: Behold, I am sending on them the sword, famine, and pestilence, and I will make them like vile figs which are so bad they cannot be eaten.

18 And I will pursue them with sword, famine, and pestilence, and will deliver them to be tossed to and fro *and* to be a horror to all the kingdoms of the earth, to be a curse, an astonishment *and* terror, a hissing and a reproach among all the nations to which I have driven them;

19 Because they did not listen to *and* heed My words, says the Lord, which I sent to you persistently by My servants the prophets; but you would not listen, says the Lord.

20 Hear therefore the word of the Lord, all you exiles whom I have sent from Jerusalem to Babylon;

21 Thus says the Lord of hosts, the God of Israel, of Ahab the son of Kolaiah, and of Zedekiah the son of Maaseiah, who are prophesying a lie to you in My name: Behold, I will deliver them into the hand of Nebuchadrezzar king of Babylon, and he will slay them before your eyes—those [false] prophets [whom you say I have raised up for you in Babylon]! [Verse 15.]

## New American Standard

*Message to the Exiles*

**29** NOW THESE are the words of the letter which Jeremiah the prophet sent from Jerusalem to the rest of the elders of the exile, the priests, the prophets, and all the people whom Nebuchadnezzar had taken into exile from Jerusalem to Babylon.

2(This was after King Jeconiah and the queen mother, the court officials, the princes of Judah and Jerusalem, the craftsmen and the smiths had departed from Jerusalem.)

3 *The letter was sent* by the hand of Elasah the son of Shaphan, and Gemariah the son of Hilkiah, whom Zedekiah king of Judah sent to Babylon to Nebuchadnezzar king of Babylon, saying,

4"Thus says the LORD of hosts, the God of Israel, to all the exiles whom I have sent into exile from Jerusalem to Babylon,

5'Build houses and live *in them;* and plant gardens, and eat their produce.

6'Take wives and become the fathers of sons and daughters, and take wives for your sons and give your daughters to husbands, that they may bear sons and daughters; and multiply there and do not decrease.

7'And seek the welfare of the city where I have sent you into exile, and pray to the LORD on its behalf; for in its welfare you will have welfare.'

8"For thus says the LORD of hosts, the God of Israel, 'Do not let your prophets who are in your midst and your diviners deceive you, and do not listen to the dreams which they dream.

9'For they prophesy falsely to you in My name; I have not sent them,' declares the LORD.

10"For thus says the LORD, 'When seventy years have been completed for Babylon, I will visit you and fulfill My good word to you, to bring you back to this place.

11'For I know the plans that I have for you,' declares the LORD, 'plans for welfare and not for calamity to give you a future and a hope.

12'Then you will call upon Me and come and pray to Me, and I will listen to you.

13'And you will seek Me and find *Me,* when you search for Me with all your heart.

14'And I will be found by you,' declares the LORD, 'and I will restore your fortunes and will gather you from all the nations and from all the places where I have driven you,' declares the LORD, 'and I will bring you back to the place from where I sent you into exile.'

15¶ "Because you have said, 'The LORD has raised up prophets for us in Babylon'—

16for thus says the LORD concerning the king who sits on the throne of David, and concerning all the people who dwell in this city, your brothers who did not go with you into exile—

17thus says the LORD of hosts, 'Behold, I am sending upon them the sword, famine, and pestilence, and I will make them like split-open figs that cannot be eaten due to rottenness.

18'And I will pursue them with the sword, with famine and with pestilence; and I will make them a terror to all the kingdoms of the earth, to be a curse, and a horror, and a hissing, and a reproach among all the nations where I have driven them,

19because they have not listened to My words,' declares the LORD, 'which I sent to them again and again by My servants the prophets; but you did not listen,' declares the LORD.

20"You, therefore, hear the word of the LORD, all you exiles, whom I have sent away from Jerusalem to Babylon.

21¶ "Thus says the LORD of hosts, the God of Israel, concerning Ahab the son of Kolaiah and concerning Zedekiah the son of Maaseiah, who are prophesying to you falsely in My name, 'Behold, I will deliver them into the hand of Nebuchadnezzar king of Babylon, and he shall slay them before your eyes.

## New International

*A Letter to the Exiles*

**29** THIS IS the text of the letter that the prophet Jeremiah sent from Jerusalem to the surviving elders among the exiles and to the priests, the prophets and all the other people Nebuchadnezzar had carried into exile from Jerusalem to Babylon.
2(This was after King Jehoiachin[a] and the queen mother, the court
officials and the leaders of Judah and Jerusalem, the craftsmen and
the artisans had gone into exile from Jerusalem.) 3He entrusted the
letter to Elasah son of Shaphan and to Gemariah son of Hilkiah,
whom Zedekiah king of Judah sent to King Nebuchadnezzar in
Babylon. It said:

4This is what the LORD Almighty, the God of Israel, says
to all those I carried into exile from Jerusalem to Babylon:
5"Build houses and settle down; plant gardens and eat what
they produce. 6Marry and have sons and daughters; find
wives for your sons and give your daughters in marriage, so
that they too may have sons and daughters. Increase in number there; do not decrease. 7Also, seek the peace and prosperity of the city to which I have carried you into exile. Pray to
the LORD for it, because if it prospers, you too will prosper."
8Yes, this is what the LORD Almighty, the God of Israel, says:
"Do not let the prophets and diviners among you deceive
you. Do not listen to the dreams you encourage them to have.
9They are prophesying lies to you in my name. I have not sent
them," declares the LORD.

10This is what the LORD says: "When seventy years are
completed for Babylon, I will come to you and fulfill my
gracious promise to bring you back to this place. 11For I know
the plans I have for you," declares the LORD, "plans to prosper you and not to harm you, plans to give you hope and a
future. 12Then you will call upon me and come and pray to
me, and I will listen to you. 13You will seek me and find me
when you seek me with all your heart. 14I will be found by
you," declares the LORD, "and will bring you back from captivity.[b] I will gather you from all the nations and places where
I have banished you," declares the LORD, "and will bring you
back to the place from which I carried you into exile."

15You may say, "The LORD has raised up prophets for us
in Babylon," 16but this is what the LORD says about the king
who sits on David's throne and all the people who remain in
this city, your countrymen who did not go with you into
exile— 17yes, this is what the LORD Almighty says: "I will send
the sword, famine and plague against them and I will make
them like poor figs that are so bad they cannot be eaten. 18I
will pursue them with the sword, famine and plague and will
make them abhorrent to all the kingdoms of the earth and an
object of cursing and horror, of scorn and reproach, among
all the nations where I drive them. 19For they have not listened to my words," declares the LORD, "words that I sent to
them again and again by my servants the prophets. And you
exiles have not listened either," declares the LORD.

20Therefore, hear the word of the LORD, all you exiles
whom I have sent away from Jerusalem to Babylon. 21This is
what the LORD Almighty, the God of Israel, says about Ahab
son of Kolaiah and Zedekiah son of Maaseiah, who are
prophesying lies to you in my name: "I will hand them over
to Nebuchadnezzar king of Babylon, and he will put them to
death before your very eyes. 22Because of them, all the exiles

**NIV** [a] 2 Hebrew *Jeconiah,* a variant of *Jehoiachin* [b] 14 Or *will restore your fortunes*

## King James

22And of them shall be taken up a curse by all the captivity of Judah which *are* in Babylon, saying, The LORD make thee like Zedekiah and like Ahab, whom the king of Babylon roasted in the fire;

23Because they have committed villainy in Israel, and have committed adultery with their neighbours' wives, and have spoken lying words in my name, which I have not commanded them; even I know, and *am* a witness, saith the LORD.

24¶ *Thus* shalt thou also speak to Shemaiah the Nehelamite, saying,

25Thus speaketh the LORD of hosts, the God of Israel, saying, Because thou hast sent letters in thy name unto all the people that *are* at Jerusalem, and to Zephaniah the son of Maaseiah the priest, and to all the priests, saying,

26The LORD hath made thee priest in the stead of Jehoiada the priest, that ye should be officers in the house of the LORD, for every man *that is* mad, and maketh himself a prophet, that thou shouldest put him in prison, and in the stocks.

27Now therefore why hast thou not reproved Jeremiah of Anathoth, which maketh himself a prophet to you?

28For therefore he sent unto us *in* Babylon, saying, This *captivity is* long: build ye houses, and dwell *in them;* and plant gardens, and eat the fruit of them.

29And Zephaniah the priest read this letter in the ears of Jeremiah the prophet.

30¶ Then came the word of the LORD unto Jeremiah, saying,

31Send to all them of the captivity, saying, Thus saith the LORD concerning Shemaiah the Nehelamite; Because that Shemaiah hath prophesied unto you, and I sent him not, and he caused you to trust in a lie:

32Therefore thus saith the LORD; Behold, I will punish Shemaiah the Nehelamite, and his seed: he shall not have a man to dwell among this people; neither shall he behold the good that I will do for my people, saith the LORD; because he hath taught rebellion against the LORD.

**30** THE WORD that came to Jeremiah from the LORD, saying,

2Thus speaketh the LORD God of Israel, saying, Write thee all the words that I have spoken unto thee in a book.

3For, lo, the days come, saith the LORD, that I will bring again the captivity of my people Israel and Judah, saith the LORD: and I will cause them to return to the land that I gave to their fathers, and they shall possess it.

4¶ And these *are* the words that the LORD spake concerning Israel and concerning Judah.

5For thus saith the LORD; We have heard a voice of trembling, of fear, and not of peace.

6Ask ye now, and see whether a man doth travail with child? wherefore do I see every man with his hands on his loins, as a woman in travail, and all faces are turned into paleness?

7Alas! for that day *is* great, so that none *is* like it: it *is* even the time of Jacob's trouble; but he shall be saved out of it.

8For it shall come to pass in that day, saith the LORD of hosts, *that* I will break his yoke from off thy neck, and will burst thy bonds, and strangers shall no more serve themselves of him:

9But they shall serve the LORD their God, and David their king, whom I will raise up unto them.

## Amplified

22And because of them this curse shall be taken up *and* used by all from Judah who are in captivity in Babylon, The Lord make you like Zedekiah and like Ahab, whom the king of Babylon roasted in the fire;

23Because they have committed folly in Israel, and have committed adultery with their neighbors' wives, and have spoken words in My name falsely, which I had not commanded them. I am the one Who knows, and I am witness, says the Lord.

24Also you shall say this concerning *and* to Shemaiah of Nehelam [among the exiles in Babylonia],

25Thus says the Lord of hosts, the God of Israel: Because you have sent letters in your [own] name to all the people who are in Jerusalem, and to Zephaniah the son of Maaseiah the priest, and to all the priests, saying,

26The Lord has made you [Zephaniah] priest instead of Jehoiada the [deputy] priest, that you should have oversight in the house of the Lord over every madman who makes himself a prophet, that you should put him in the stocks and collar;

27Now therefore, [continued the letter from Shemaiah in Babylon to Zephaniah in Jerusalem] why have you not rebuked Jeremiah of Anathoth, who makes himself a prophet to you?

28For he has sent to us in Babylon, saying, *This captivity of yours* is to be long; build houses and dwell in them; plant gardens and eat the fruit of them.

29And Zephaniah the priest read this letter in the hearing of Jeremiah the prophet.

30Then came the word of the Lord to Jeremiah:

31Send to all them of the captivity, saying, Thus says the Lord concerning Shemaiah of Nehelam: Because Shemaiah has prophesied to you when I did not send him, and has caused you to trust in a lie,

32Therefore thus says the Lord: Behold, I will punish Shemaiah of Nehelam and his offspring: he shall not have any one [born] to dwell among this people, nor shall he see the good that I will do to My people, says the Lord, because he has spoken *and* taught rebellion against the Lord.

**30** THE WORD that came to Jeremiah from the Lord:

2Thus says the Lord, the God of Israel: Write all the words that I have spoken to you in a book.

3For note, the days are coming, says the Lord, that I will release from captivity My people Israel and Judah, says the Lord; and I will cause them to return to the land that I gave to their fathers, and they shall possess it.

4And these are the words that the Lord spoke concerning Israel and Judah:

5Thus says the Lord: We have heard a voice of trembling *and* panic, of terror and no peace.

6Ask now, and see whether a man can give birth to a child? Why then do I see every man with his hands on his loins like a woman in labor? Why are all faces turned pale?

7Alas! for that day is great, so that none is like it; it is the time of Jacob's [unequaled] trouble; but he shall be saved out of it. [Matt. 24:29, 30; Rev. 7:14.]

8For it shall come to pass in that day, says the Lord of hosts, that I will break *the oppressor's* yoke from off your neck, and I will burst your bonds, and strangers shall no more make slaves of [the people of Israel].

9But they shall serve the Lord their God and David's *descendant* their king, whom I will raise up for them.

## New American Standard

22'And because of them a curse shall be used by all the exiles
from Judah who are in Babylon, saying, "May the LORD make you
like Zedekiah and like Ahab, whom the king of Babylon roasted
in the fire,
23because they have acted foolishly in Israel, and have committed adultery with their neighbors' wives, and have spoken words
in My name falsely, which I did not command them; and I am He
who knows, and am a witness," declares the LORD.' "
24¶ And to Shemaiah the Nehelamite you shall speak, saying,
25"Thus says the LORD of hosts, the God of Israel, 'Because you
have sent letters in your own name to all the people who are in
Jerusalem, and to Zephaniah the son of Maaseiah, the priest, and
to all the priests, saying,
26"The LORD has made you priest instead of Jehoiada the priest,
to be the overseer in the house of the LORD over every madman
who prophesies, to put him in the stocks and in the iron collar,
27now then, why have you not rebuked Jeremiah of Anathoth
who prophesies to you?
28"For he has sent to us in Babylon, saying, '*The exile* will be
long; build houses and live *in them* and plant gardens and eat their
produce.' " ' "
29¶ And Zephaniah the priest read this letter to Jeremiah the
prophet.
30Then came the word of the LORD to Jeremiah, saying,
31"Send to all the exiles, saying, 'Thus says the LORD concerning Shemaiah the Nehelamite, "Because Shemaiah has prophesied
to you, although I did not send him, and he has made you trust
in a lie,"
32therefore thus says the LORD, "Behold, I am about to punish
Shemaiah the Nehelamite and his descendants; he shall not have
anyone living among this people, and he shall not see the good
that I am about to do to My people," declares the LORD, "because
he has preached rebellion against the LORD." ' "

*Deliverance from Captivity Promised*

**30** THE WORD which came to Jeremiah from the LORD, saying,
2"Thus says the LORD, the God of Israel, 'Write all the words
which I have spoken to you in a book.
3'For, behold, days are coming,' declares the LORD, 'when I
will restore the fortunes of My people Israel and Judah.' The LORD
says, 'I will also bring them back to the land that I gave to their
forefathers, and they shall possess it.' "
4¶ Now these are the words which the LORD spoke concerning
Israel and concerning Judah,
5"For thus says the LORD,
'I have heard a sound of terror,
Of dread, and there is no peace.
6 'Ask now, and see,
If a male can give birth.
Why do I see every man
*With* his hands on his loins, as a woman in childbirth?
And *why* have all faces turned pale?
7 'Alas! for that day is great,
There is none like it;
And it is the time of Jacob's distress,
But he will be saved from it.
8'And it shall come about on that day,' declares the LORD of
hosts, 'that I will break his yoke from off their neck, and will tear
off their bonds; and strangers shall no longer make them their
slaves.
9'But they shall serve the LORD their God, and David their
king, whom I will raise up for them.

## New International

from Judah who are in Babylon will use this curse: 'The LORD
treat you like Zedekiah and Ahab, whom the king of Babylon
burned in the fire.' 23For they have done outrageous things
in Israel; they have committed adultery with their neighbors'
wives and in my name have spoken lies, which I did not tell
them to do. I know it and am a witness to it," declares the
LORD.

*Message to Shemaiah*

24Tell Shemaiah the Nehelamite, 25"This is what the LORD Almighty, the God of Israel, says: You sent letters in your own name
to all the people in Jerusalem, to Zephaniah son of Maaseiah the
priest, and to all the other priests. You said to Zephaniah, 26'The
LORD has appointed you priest in place of Jehoiada to be in charge
of the house of the LORD; you should put any madman who acts
like a prophet into the stocks and neck-irons. 27So why have you
not reprimanded Jeremiah from Anathoth, who poses as a prophet
among you? 28He has sent this message to us in Babylon: It will
be a long time. Therefore build houses and settle down; plant
gardens and eat what they produce.' "
29Zephaniah the priest, however, read the letter to Jeremiah the
prophet. 30Then the word of the LORD came to Jeremiah: 31"Send
this message to all the exiles: 'This is what the LORD says about
Shemaiah the Nehelamite: Because Shemaiah has prophesied to
you, even though I did not send him, and has led you to believe
a lie, 32this is what the LORD says: I will surely punish Shemaiah
the Nehelamite and his descendants. He will have no one left
among this people, nor will he see the good things I will do for my
people, declares the LORD, because he has preached rebellion
against me.' "

*Restoration of Israel*

**30** THIS IS the word that came to Jeremiah from the LORD:
2"This is what the LORD, the God of Israel, says: 'Write in
a book all the words I have spoken to you. 3The days are coming,'
declares the LORD, 'when I will bring my people Israel and Judah
back from captivity[a] and restore them to the land I gave their
forefathers to possess,' says the LORD."
4These are the words the LORD spoke concerning Israel and
Judah: 5"This is what the LORD says:

" 'Cries of fear are heard—
terror, not peace.
6Ask and see:
Can a man bear children?
Then why do I see every strong man
with his hands on his stomach like a woman in labor,
every face turned deathly pale?
7How awful that day will be!
None will be like it.
It will be a time of trouble for Jacob,
but he will be saved out of it.

8" 'In that day,' declares the LORD Almighty,
'I will break the yoke off their necks
and will tear off their bonds;
no longer will foreigners enslave them.
9Instead, they will serve the LORD their God
and David their king,
whom I will raise up for them.

NIV [a] 3 Or *will restore the fortunes of my people Israel and Judah*

## King James

10¶ Therefore fear thou not, O my servant Jacob, saith the LORD; neither be dismayed, O Israel: for, lo, I will save thee from afar, and thy seed from the land of their captivity; and Jacob shall return, and shall be in rest, and be quiet, and none shall make *him* afraid.

11For I *am* with thee, saith the LORD, to save thee: though I make a full end of all nations whither I have scattered thee, yet will I not make a full end of thee: but I will correct thee in measure, and will not leave thee altogether unpunished.

12For thus saith the LORD, Thy bruise *is* incurable, *and* thy wound *is* grievous.

13 *There is* none to plead thy cause, that thou mayest be bound up: thou hast no healing medicines.

14All thy lovers have forgotten thee; they seek thee not; for I have wounded thee with the wound of an enemy, with the chastisement of a cruel one, for the multitude of thine iniquity; *because* thy sins were increased.

15Why criest thou for thine affliction? thy sorrow *is* incurable for the multitude of thine iniquity: *because* thy sins were increased, I have done these things unto thee.

16Therefore all they that devour thee shall be devoured; and all thine adversaries, every one of them, shall go into captivity; and they that spoil thee shall be a spoil, and all that prey upon thee will I give for a prey.

17For I will restore health unto thee, and I will heal thee of thy wounds, saith the LORD; because they called thee an Outcast, *saying*, This *is* Zion, whom no man seeketh after.

18¶ Thus saith the LORD; Behold, I will bring again the captivity of Jacob's tents, and have mercy on his dwellingplaces; and the city shall be builded upon her own heap, and the palace shall remain after the manner thereof.

19And out of them shall proceed thanksgiving and the voice of them that make merry: and I will multiply them, and they shall not be few; I will also glorify them, and they shall not be small.

20Their children also shall be as aforetime, and their congregation shall be established before me, and I will punish all that oppress them.

21And their nobles shall be of themselves, and their governor shall proceed from the midst of them; and I will cause him to draw near, and he shall approach unto me: for who *is* this that engaged his heart to approach unto me? saith the LORD.

22And ye shall be my people, and I will be your God.

23Behold, the whirlwind of the LORD goeth forth with fury, a continuing whirlwind: it shall fall with pain upon the head of the wicked.

## Amplified

10Therefore fear not, O My servant Jacob, says the Lord, nor be dismayed *or* cast down, O Israel; for lo, I will save you out of the distant land [of exile], and your posterity from the land of their captivity. Jacob shall return and shall be quiet and at ease, and none shall make him afraid *or* cause him to be terrorized *and* to tremble.

11For I am with you, says the Lord, to save you; for I will make a full end of all the nations to which I have scattered you, but I will not make a full end of you; but I will correct you in measure *and* with judgment, and will in no sense hold you guiltless *or* leave you unpunished.

12For thus says the Lord, Your hurt is incurable and your wound is grievous.

13There is none to plead your cause. For [the pressing together of] your wound you have no healing [device], no binding plaster.

14All your lovers [allies] have forgotten you; they neither seek, inquire of *or* require you; for I have hurt you [as though] with the wound of an enemy, [as though] with the chastisement of a cruel *and* merciless foe, because of the greatness of your perversity *and* guilt, because your sins are glaring *and* innumerable.

15Why do you cry out because of your hurt [the natural result of your sins]? Your pain is deadly—incurable. Because of the greatness of your perversity *and* guilt, because your sins are glaring *and* innumerable, I have done these things to you.

16Therefore all who devour you shall be devoured, and all your adversaries, every one of them, shall go into captivity; and they who despoil you shall become a spoil, and all who prey upon you will I give for a prey.

17For I will restore health to you, and I will heal your wounds, says the Lord; because they have called you an outcast, saying, *This* is Zion, whom no one seeks after *and* for whom no one cares!

18Thus says the Lord: Behold, I will release from captivity the tents of Jacob, and have mercy on his dwelling places; the city shall be rebuilt on its own old mound-like site, and the palace shall be dwelt in after its former fashion.

19Out of them [city and palace] shall come songs of thanksgiving and the voices of those who make merry. And I will multiply them, and they shall not be few; I will also glorify them, and they shall not be small.

20Their children too shall be as in former times, and their congregation shall be established before Me, and I will punish all who oppress them.

21And their prince shall be *one* of themselves, and their ruler shall come from the midst of them. I will cause him to draw near, and he shall approach Me, for who is he who would have the boldness *and* would dare [on his own initiative] to approach Me? says the Lord.

22Then you shall be My people, and I will be your God.

23Behold, the tempest of the Lord goes forth with wrath, a sweeping *and* gathering tempest. It shall whirl *and* burst upon the head of the wicked.

## New American Standard

10 'And fear not, O Jacob My servant,' declares the LORD,
'And do not be dismayed, O Israel;
For behold, I will save you from afar,
And your offspring from the land of their captivity.
And Jacob shall return, and shall be quiet and at ease,
And no one shall make him afraid.
11 'For I am with you,' declares the LORD, 'to save you;
For I will destroy completely all the nations where I have scattered you,
Only I will not destroy you completely.
But I will chasten you justly,
And will by no means leave you unpunished.'

12¶ "For thus says the LORD,
'Your wound is incurable,
And your injury is serious.
13 'There is no one to plead your cause;
*No* healing for *your* sore,
No recovery for you.
14 'All your lovers have forgotten you,
They do not seek you;
For I have wounded you with the wound of an enemy,
With the punishment of a cruel one,
Because your iniquity is great
And your sins are numerous.
15 'Why do you cry out over your injury?
Your pain is incurable.
Because your iniquity is great
And your sins are numerous,
I have done these things to you.
16 'Therefore all who devour you shall be devoured;
And all your adversaries, every one of them, shall go into captivity;
And those who plunder you shall be for plunder,
And all who prey upon you I will give for prey.
17 'For I will restore you to health
And I will heal you of your wounds,' declares the LORD,
'Because they have called you an outcast, saying:
"It is Zion; no one cares for her." '

*Restoration of Jacob*

18¶ "Thus says the LORD,
'Behold, I will restore the fortunes of the tents of Jacob
And have compassion on his dwelling places;
And the city shall be rebuilt on its ruin,
And the palace shall stand on its rightful place.
19 'And from them shall proceed thanksgiving
And the voice of those who make merry;
And I will multiply them, and they shall not be diminished;
I will also honor them, and they shall not be insignificant.
20 'Their children also shall be as formerly,
And their congregation shall be established before Me;
And I will punish all their oppressors.
21 'And their leader shall be one of them,
And their ruler shall come forth from their midst;
And I will bring him near, and he shall approach Me;
For who would dare to risk his life to approach Me?'
declares the LORD.
22 'And you shall be My people,
And I will be your God.' "

23¶ Behold, the tempest of the LORD!
Wrath has gone forth,
A sweeping tempest;
It will burst on the head of the wicked.

## New International

10" 'So do not fear, O Jacob my servant;
do not be dismayed, O Israel,'
declares the LORD.
'I will surely save you out of a distant place,
your descendants from the land of their exile.
Jacob will again have peace and security,
and no one will make him afraid.
11I am with you and will save you,'
declares the LORD.
'Though I completely destroy all the nations
among which I scatter you,
I will not completely destroy you.
I will discipline you but only with justice;
I will not let you go entirely unpunished.'

12"This is what the LORD says:

" 'Your wound is incurable,
your injury beyond healing.
13There is no one to plead your cause,
no remedy for your sore,
no healing for you.
14All your allies have forgotten you;
they care nothing for you.
I have struck you as an enemy would
and punished you as would the cruel,
because your guilt is so great
and your sins so many.
15Why do you cry out over your wound,
your pain that has no cure?
Because of your great guilt and many sins
I have done these things to you.

16" 'But all who devour you will be devoured;
all your enemies will go into exile.
Those who plunder you will be plundered;
all who make spoil of you I will despoil.
17But I will restore you to health
and heal your wounds,'
declares the LORD,
'because you are called an outcast,
Zion for whom no one cares.'

18"This is what the LORD says:

" 'I will restore the fortunes of Jacob's tents
and have compassion on his dwellings;
the city will be rebuilt on her ruins,
and the palace will stand in its proper place.
19From them will come songs of thanksgiving
and the sound of rejoicing.
I will add to their numbers,
and they will not be decreased;
I will bring them honor,
and they will not be disdained.
20Their children will be as in days of old,
and their community will be established before me;
I will punish all who oppress them.
21Their leader will be one of their own;
their ruler will arise from among them.
I will bring him near and he will come close to me,
for who is he who will devote himself
to be close to me?'
declares the LORD.

22" 'So you will be my people,
and I will be your God.' "

23See, the storm of the LORD
will burst out in wrath,
a driving wind swirling down
on the heads of the wicked.

## King James

24The fierce anger of the LORD shall not return, until he have done *it*, and until he have performed the intents of his heart: in the latter days ye shall consider it.

31 AT THE same time, saith the LORD, will I be the God of all the families of Israel, and they shall be my people.

2Thus saith the LORD, The people *which were* left of the sword found grace in the wilderness; *even* Israel, when I went to cause him to rest.

3The LORD hath appeared of old unto me, *saying*, Yea, I have loved thee with an everlasting love: therefore with lovingkindness have I drawn thee.

4Again I will build thee, and thou shalt be built, O virgin of Israel: thou shalt again be adorned with thy tabrets, and shalt go forth in the dances of them that make merry.

5Thou shalt yet plant vines upon the mountains of Samaria: the planters shall plant, and shall eat *them* as common things.

6For there shall be a day, *that* the watchmen upon the mount Ephraim shall cry, Arise ye, and let us go up to Zion unto the LORD our God.

7For thus saith the LORD; Sing with gladness for Jacob, and shout among the chief of the nations: publish ye, praise ye, and say, O LORD, save thy people, the remnant of Israel.

8Behold, I will bring them from the north country, and gather them from the coasts of the earth, *and* with them the blind and the lame, the woman with child and her that travaileth with child together: a great company shall return thither.

9They shall come with weeping, and with supplications will I lead them: I will cause them to walk by the rivers of waters in a straight way, wherein they shall not stumble: for I am a father to Israel, and Ephraim *is* my firstborn.

10¶ Hear the word of the LORD, O ye nations, and declare *it* in the isles afar off, and say, He that scattered Israel will gather him, and keep him, as a shepherd *doth* his flock.

11For the LORD hath redeemed Jacob, and ransomed him from the hand of *him that was* stronger than he.

12Therefore they shall come and sing in the height of Zion, and shall flow together to the goodness of the LORD, for wheat, and for wine, and for oil, and for the young of the flock and of the herd: and their soul shall be as a watered garden; and they shall not sorrow any more at all.

13Then shall the virgin rejoice in the dance, both young men and old together: for I will turn their mourning into joy, and will comfort them, and make them rejoice from their sorrow.

## Amplified

24The fierce anger *and* indignation of the Lord shall not turn back until He has executed *and* accomplished the intents of His mind *and* heart. In the latter days you shall understand *this*.

31 AT THAT time, says the Lord, will I be the God of all the families of Israel, and they shall be My people.

2Thus says the Lord: The people who survived the sword found favor in the wilderness [place of exile], when Israel sought to find rest.

3The Lord appeared of old to me [Israel], saying, Yes, I have loved you with an everlasting love; therefore with loving-kindness have I drawn you *and* have continued My faithfulness to you. [Deut. 7:8.]

4Again I will build you, and you shall be built, O virgin of Israel! You shall again be adorned with your timbrels [small one-headed drums], and go forth in the dancing [chorus] of those who make merry.

5Again you shall plant vineyards upon the mountains of Samaria; the planters shall plant, and shall make the fruit common *and* enjoy it [undisturbed].

6For there shall be a day when the watchmen on the hills of Ephraim shall cry, Arise, and let us go up to Zion to the Lord our God.

7For thus says the Lord: Sing aloud with gladness for Jacob, and shout at the head of the nations—on account of the chosen people. Proclaim, praise, and say, The Lord has saved His people, the remnant of Israel!

8Behold, I will bring them from the north country, and gather them from the uttermost parts of the earth, and among them the blind and the lame, the woman with child and her who labors in childbirth together; a great company they shall return here to Jerusalem.

9They shall come with weeping [in penitence and for joy], and pouring out prayers [for the future]; I will lead them back; I will cause them to walk by streams of water, and bring them in a straight way in which they shall not stumble; for I am a father to Israel, and Ephraim is My first-born.

10Hear the word of the Lord, O you nations, and declare it in the isles *and* coastlands far away, and say, He Who scattered Israel will gather him, and will keep him as a shepherd does his flock.

11For the Lord has ransomed Jacob, and has redeemed him from the hand of him who was too strong for him.

12They shall come and sing aloud on the height of Zion, and shall flow together *and* be radiant with joy over the goodness of the Lord, for the corn, for the grape juice, for the oil, and for the young of the flock and the herd. And their life shall be like a watered garden, and they shall not sorrow *or* languish any more at all.

13Then shall the maidens rejoice in the dance, and the young men and old together. For I will turn their mourning into joy, and will comfort them, and make them rejoice after their sorrow.

## New American Standard

24 The fierce anger of the LORD will not turn back,
Until He has performed, and until He has accomplished
The intent of His heart;
In the latter days you will understand this.

*Israel's Mourning Turned to Joy*

31 "AT THAT time," declares the LORD, "I will be the God of all the families of Israel, and they shall be My people."
2 Thus says the LORD,
"The people who survived the sword
Found grace in the wilderness—
Israel, when it went to find its rest."
3 The LORD appeared to him from afar, *saying,*
"I have loved you with an everlasting love;
Therefore I have drawn you with lovingkindness.
4 "Again I will build you, and you shall be rebuilt,
O virgin of Israel!
Again you shall take up your tambourines,
And go forth to the dances of the merrymakers.
5 "Again you shall plant vineyards
On the hills of Samaria;
The planters shall plant
And shall enjoy *them.*
6 "For there shall be a day when watchmen
On the hills of Ephraim shall call out,
'Arise, and let us go up *to* Zion,
To the LORD our God.' "

7¶ For thus says the LORD,
"Sing aloud with gladness for Jacob,
And shout among the chiefs of the nations;
Proclaim, give praise, and say,
'O LORD, save Thy people,
The remnant of Israel.'
8 "Behold, I am bringing them from the north country,
And I will gather them from the remote parts of the earth,
Among them the blind and the lame,
The woman with child and she who is in labor with child, together;
A great company, they shall return here.
9 "With weeping they shall come,
And by supplication I will lead them;
I will make them walk by streams of waters,
On a straight path in which they shall not stumble;
For I am a father to Israel,
And Ephraim is My first-born."

10¶ Hear the word of the LORD, O nations,
And declare in the coastlands afar off,
And say, "He who scattered Israel will gather him,
And keep him as a shepherd keeps his flock."
11 For the LORD has ransomed Jacob,
And redeemed him from the hand of him who was stronger than he.
12 "And they shall come and shout for joy on the height of Zion,
And they shall be radiant over the bounty of the LORD—
Over the grain, and the new wine, and the oil,
And over the young of the flock and the herd;
And their life shall be like a watered garden,
And they shall never languish again.
13 "Then the virgin shall rejoice in the dance,
And the young men and the old, together,
For I will turn their mourning into joy,
And will comfort them, and give them joy for their sorrow.

## New International

24 The fierce anger of the LORD will not turn back
until he fully accomplishes
the purposes of his heart.
In days to come
you will understand this.

31 "AT THAT time," declares the LORD, "I will be the God of all the clans of Israel, and they will be my people."
2 This is what the LORD says:

"The people who survive the sword
will find favor in the desert;
I will come to give rest to Israel."
3 The LORD appeared to us in the past,[a] saying:

"I have loved you with an everlasting love;
I have drawn you with loving-kindness.
4 I will build you up again
and you will be rebuilt, O Virgin Israel.
Again you will take up your tambourines
and go out to dance with the joyful.
5 Again you will plant vineyards
on the hills of Samaria;
the farmers will plant them
and enjoy their fruit.
6 There will be a day when watchmen cry out
on the hills of Ephraim,
'Come, let us go up to Zion,
to the LORD our God.' "
7 This is what the LORD says:

"Sing with joy for Jacob;
shout for the foremost of the nations.
Make your praises heard, and say,
'O LORD, save your people,
the remnant of Israel.'
8 See, I will bring them from the land of the north
and gather them from the ends of the earth.
Among them will be the blind and the lame,
expectant mothers and women in labor;
a great throng will return.
9 They will come with weeping;
they will pray as I bring them back.
I will lead them beside streams of water
on a level path where they will not stumble,
because I am Israel's father,
and Ephraim is my firstborn son.

10 "Hear the word of the LORD, O nations;
proclaim it in distant coastlands:
'He who scattered Israel will gather them
and will watch over his flock like a shepherd.'
11 For the LORD will ransom Jacob
and redeem them from the hand of those stronger than they.
12 They will come and shout for joy on the heights of Zion;
they will rejoice in the bounty of the LORD—
the grain, the new wine and the oil,
the young of the flocks and herds.
They will be like a well-watered garden,
and they will sorrow no more.
13 Then maidens will dance and be glad,
young men and old as well.
I will turn their mourning into gladness;
I will give them comfort and joy instead of sorrow.

NIV [a] 3 Or *LORD has appeared to us from afar*

## King James

14And I will satiate the soul of the priests with fatness, and my people shall be satisfied with my goodness, saith the LORD.

15¶ Thus saith the LORD; A voice was heard in Ramah, lamentation, *and* bitter weeping; Rahel weeping for her children refused to be comforted for her children, because they *were* not.

16Thus saith the LORD; Refrain thy voice from weeping, and thine eyes from tears: for thy work shall be rewarded, saith the LORD; and they shall come again from the land of the enemy.

17And there is hope in thine end, saith the LORD, that thy children shall come again to their own border.

18¶ I have surely heard Ephraim bemoaning himself *thus;* Thou hast chastised me, and I was chastised, as a bullock unaccustomed *to the yoke:* turn thou me, and I shall be turned; for thou *art* the LORD my God.

19Surely after that I was turned, I repented; and after that I was instructed, I smote upon *my* thigh: I was ashamed, yea, even confounded, because I did bear the reproach of my youth.

20 *Is* Ephraim my dear son? *is he* a pleasant child? for since I spake against him, I do earnestly remember him still: therefore my bowels are troubled for him; I will surely have mercy upon him, saith the LORD.

21Set thee up waymarks, make thee high heaps: set thine heart toward the highway, *even* the way *which* thou wentest: turn again, O virgin of Israel, turn again to these thy cities.

22¶ How long wilt thou go about, O thou backsliding daughter? for the LORD hath created a new thing in the earth, A woman shall compass a man.

23Thus saith the LORD of hosts, the God of Israel; As yet they shall use this speech in the land of Judah and in the cities thereof, when I shall bring again their captivity; The LORD bless thee, O habitation of justice, *and* mountain of holiness.

24And there shall dwell in Judah itself, and in all the cities thereof together, husbandmen, and they *that* go forth with flocks.

25For I have satiated the weary soul, and I have replenished every sorrowful soul.

26Upon this I awaked, and beheld; and my sleep was sweet unto me.

27¶ Behold, the days come, saith the LORD, that I will sow the house of Israel and the house of Judah with the seed of man, and with the seed of beast.

28And it shall come to pass, *that* like as I have watched over them, to pluck up, and to break down, and to throw down, and to destroy, and to afflict; so will I watch over them, to build, and to plant, saith the LORD.

29In those days they shall say no more, The fathers have eaten a sour grape, and the children's teeth are set on edge.

## Amplified

14I will satisfy fully the life of the priests with abundance [of offerings shared with them], and My people shall be satisfied with My goodness, says the Lord.

15Thus says the Lord: A [a]voice is heard in Ramah, lamentation and bitter weeping; Rachel is weeping for her children; she refuses to be comforted for her children, because they are not. [Matt. 2:18.]

16Thus says the Lord: Refrain your voice from weeping, and your eyes from tears; for your work shall be rewarded, says the Lord; and [your children] shall return from the enemy's land.

17And there is hope in your future, says the Lord; your children shall come again to their own country.

18I have surely heard Ephraim bemoaning himself thus: You have chastised me, and I was chastised, as a bullock unaccustomed to the yoke; bring me back that I may be restored, for You are the Lord my God.

19Surely after I [Ephraim, which is Israel] was turned [from You], I repented; and after I was instructed, I penitently smote my thigh; I was ashamed, yes, even confounded, because I bore the disgrace of my youth [as a nation].

20Is Ephraim My dear son? Is he a darling child *and* beloved? For as often as I speak against him, I do [earnestly] remember him still. Therefore My affection is stirred *and* my heart yearns for him; I will surely have mercy, pity *and* loving-kindness for him, says the Lord.

21Set you up highway markers [back to Canaan], make yourself guide posts; turn your thoughts *and* attention to the way by which you went [into exile]; retrace your steps, O virgin Israel, return to these your cities.

22How long will you waver *and* hesitate [to return], O you backsliding daughter? For the Lord has created a [b]new thing in the land [of Israel]: a female shall compass [woo, win and protect] a man.

23Thus says the Lord of hosts, the God of Israel: Once more they shall use these words in the land of Judah and in her cities, when I shall have released them from exile: The Lord bless you, O habitation of justice *and* right, O holy mountain!

24And Judah and all its cities shall dwell there together, as [nomad] farmers and those who wander about with their flocks.

25For I will [fully] satisfy the weary soul, and I will replenish every languishing *and* sorrowful person.

26Thereupon I [Jeremiah] awoke and looked, and my [trance-like] sleep was sweet [in the assurance it gave] to me.

27Behold, the days are coming, says the Lord, when I will sow the house of Israel and the house of Judah with the seed [offspring] of man and of beast.

28And it shall be that as I have watched over them to pluck up and to break down, to overthrow, destroy, and afflict [with evil], so will I watch over them to build and to plant [with good], says the Lord.

29In those days they shall say no more, The fathers have eaten sour grapes, and the children's teeth are set on edge.

**AMP** [a] The mourning at Ramah is a forecast of that bitter wailing which would be raised by the mothers of the slaughtered babes of Bethlehem centuries later when Herod would attempt to kill the Christ child (Matt. 2:17, 18). Rachel's name, used in the prophecy, is naturally associated with Bethlehem by the fact that her tomb was in that neighborhood. (Cambridge Bible.) [b] The early Fathers believed this passage had reference to the mystery of Christ's Incarnation, but that interpretation is now generally rejected for various reasons. It is sufficient to say that the word ["female"] here used for "woman" absolutely excludes the idea [that this refers to] the virgin birth [for this was to be a "new thing"]. To "compass" is to woo and win. That the early translators attached that meaning to it is clear from the fact that Shakespeare, their contemporary, so used it. (Based on Ellicott's Commentary.) Probably the implication is that Israel, the erring but deeply penitent wife, instead of going about after other lovers will devote herself to winning back and deserving the love of her divine Husband and Lord, Who had rejected her.

## New American Standard

14 "And I will fill the soul of the priests with abundance,
And My people shall be satisfied with My goodness,"
declares the LORD.

15¶ Thus says the LORD,
"A voice is heard in Ramah,
Lamentation *and* bitter weeping.
Rachel is weeping for her children;
She refuses to be comforted for her children,
Because they are no more."
16 Thus says the LORD,
"Restrain your voice from weeping,
And your eyes from tears;
For your work shall be rewarded," declares the LORD,
"And they shall return from the land of the enemy.
17 "And there is hope for your future," declares the LORD,
"And *your* children shall return to their own territory.
18 "I have surely heard Ephraim grieving,
'Thou hast chastised me, and I was chastised,
Like an untrained calf;
Bring me back that I may be restored,
For Thou art the LORD my God.
19 'For after I turned back, I repented;
And after I was instructed, I smote on *my* thigh;
I was ashamed, and also humiliated,
Because I bore the reproach of my youth.'
20 "Is Ephraim My dear son?
Is he a delightful child?
Indeed, as often as I have spoken against him,
I certainly *still* remember him;
Therefore My heart yearns for him;
I will surely have mercy on him," declares the LORD.
21¶ "Set up for yourself roadmarks,
Place for yourself guideposts;
Direct your mind to the highway,
The way by which you went.
Return, O virgin of Israel,
Return to these your cities.
22 "How long will you go here and there,
O faithless daughter?
For the LORD has created a new thing in the earth—
A woman will encompass a man."
23¶ Thus says the LORD of hosts, the God of Israel, "Once again
they will speak this word in the land of Judah and in its cities,
when I restore their fortunes,
'The LORD bless you, O abode of righteousness,
O holy hill!'
24"And Judah and all its cities will dwell together in it, the
farmer and they who go about with flocks.
25"For I satisfy the weary ones and refresh everyone who languishes."
26At this I awoke and looked, and my sleep was pleasant to me.

*A New Covenant*

27¶ "Behold, days are coming," declares the LORD, "when I will
sow the house of Israel and the house of Judah with the seed of
man and with the seed of beast.
28"And it will come about that as I have watched over them to
pluck up, to break down, to overthrow, to destroy, and to bring
disaster, so I will watch over them to build and to plant," declares
the LORD.
29"In those days they will not say again,
'The fathers have eaten sour grapes,
And the children's teeth are set on edge.'

## New International

14I will satisfy the priests with abundance,
and my people will be filled with my bounty,"
declares the LORD.

15This is what the LORD says:

"A voice is heard in Ramah,
mourning and great weeping,
Rachel weeping for her children
and refusing to be comforted,
because her children are no more."

16This is what the LORD says:

"Restrain your voice from weeping
and your eyes from tears,
for your work will be rewarded,"
declares the LORD.
"They will return from the land of the enemy.
17So there is hope for your future,"
declares the LORD.
"Your children will return to their own land.

18"I have surely heard Ephraim's moaning:
'You disciplined me like an unruly calf,
and I have been disciplined.
Restore me, and I will return,
because you are the LORD my God.
19After I strayed,
I repented;
after I came to understand,
I beat my breast.
I was ashamed and humiliated
because I bore the disgrace of my youth.'
20Is not Ephraim my dear son,
the child in whom I delight?
Though I often speak against him,
I still remember him.
Therefore my heart yearns for him;
I have great compassion for him,"
declares the LORD.

21"Set up road signs;
put up guideposts.
Take note of the highway,
the road that you take.
Return, O Virgin Israel,
return to your towns.
22How long will you wander,
O unfaithful daughter?
The LORD will create a new thing on earth—
a woman will surround[c] a man."

23This is what the LORD Almighty, the God of Israel, says:
"When I bring them back from captivity,[d] the people in the land
of Judah and in its towns will once again use these words: 'The
LORD bless you, O righteous dwelling, O sacred mountain.'
24People will live together in Judah and all its towns—farmers and
those who move about with their flocks. 25I will refresh the weary
and satisfy the faint."
26At this I awoke and looked around. My sleep had been pleasant to me.
27"The days are coming," declares the LORD, "when I will plant
the house of Israel and the house of Judah with the offspring of
men and of animals. 28Just as I watched over them to uproot and
tear down, and to overthrow, destroy and bring disaster, so I will
watch over them to build and to plant," declares the LORD. 29"In
those days people will no longer say,

'The fathers have eaten sour grapes,
and the children's teeth are set on edge.'

NIV [c] 22 Or *will go about* ⌊*seeking*⌋; or *will protect* [d] 23 Or *I restore their fortunes*

## King James

30But every one shall die for his own iniquity: every man that eateth the sour grape, his teeth shall be set on edge.
31¶ Behold, the days come, saith the LORD, that I will make a new covenant with the house of Israel, and with the house of Judah:
32Not according to the covenant that I made with their fathers in the day *that* I took them by the hand to bring them out of the land of Egypt; which my covenant they brake, although I was an husband unto them, saith the LORD:
33But this *shall be* the covenant that I will make with the house of Israel; After those days, saith the LORD, I will put my law in their inward parts, and write it in their hearts; and will be their God, and they shall be my people.
34And they shall teach no more every man his neighbour, and every man his brother, saying, Know the LORD: for they shall all know me, from the least of them unto the greatest of them, saith the LORD: for I will forgive their iniquity, and I will remember their sin no more.
35¶ Thus saith the LORD, which giveth the sun for a light by day, *and* the ordinances of the moon and of the stars for a light by night, which divideth the sea when the waves thereof roar; The LORD of hosts *is* his name:
36If those ordinances depart from before me, saith the LORD, *then* the seed of Israel also shall cease from being a nation before me for ever.
37Thus saith the LORD; If heaven above can be measured, and the foundations of the earth searched out beneath, I will also cast off all the seed of Israel for all that they have done, saith the LORD.
38¶ Behold, the days come, saith the LORD, that the city shall be built to the LORD from the tower of Hananeel unto the gate of the corner.
39And the measuring line shall yet go forth over against it upon the hill Gareb, and shall compass about to Goath.
40And the whole valley of the dead bodies, and of the ashes, and all the fields unto the brook of Kidron, unto the corner of the horse gate toward the east, *shall be* holy unto the LORD; it shall not be plucked up, nor thrown down any more for ever.

## Amplified

30But every one shall die for his own iniquity [only], every man who eats sour grapes, his [own] teeth shall be set on edge.
31Behold, the days are coming, says the Lord, when I will make a new covenant with the house of Israel and with the house of Judah, [Luke 22:20; I Cor. 11:25.]
32Not according to the covenant which I made with their fathers in the day when I took them by the hand to bring them out of the land of Egypt, My covenant which they broke although I was their Husband, says the Lord;
33But this shall be the covenant that I will make with the house of Israel: After those days, says the Lord, I will put My law within them, and on their hearts will I write it; and I will be their God, and they shall be My people.
34And they shall no more teach each man his neighbor and each man his brother, saying, Know the Lord; for they shall all know Me—recognize, understand and be acquainted with Me—from the least of them to the greatest, says the Lord; for I will forgive their iniquity, and I will [seriously] remember their sin no more. [Heb. 8:8-12; 10:16, 17.]
35Thus says the Lord, Who gives the sun for a light by day, and the fixed order of the moon and of the stars for a light by night, Who stirs up the sea's roaring billows *or* stills the waves when they roar; the Lord of hosts is His name.
36If these ordinances [of fixed order] depart from before Me, says the Lord, then the posterity of Israel also shall cease from being a nation before Me throughout the ages.
37Thus says the Lord: If the heavens above can be measured, and the foundations of the earth searched out beneath, then I will cast off all the offspring of Israel for all that they have done, says the Lord.
38Behold, the days are coming, says the Lord, when the city [of Jerusalem] shall be built [again] to the Lord from the [a]tower of Hananel to the Corner Gate.
39And the measuring line shall go out farther, straight onward to the hill Gareb, and shall then turn to Goah [not now certainly identified].
40And the whole valley [Hinnom] of the dead bodies, and [the hill] of the ashes [long dumped there from the temple sacrifices], and all the fields as far as the brook Kidron, to the corner of the Horse Gate toward the east, shall be holy to the Lord. It shall not be plucked up or overthrown any more to the end of the age.

**AMP** [a] Many times after the days of the Old Testament, Jerusalem was destroyed. Travelers in recent centuries reported it as an almost deserted city; its buildings were ruins filled with rubble; its inhabitants were barely enough to populate a village. Yet not only did God's word declare it would be rebuilt, but definitely and in detail drew a word map of the exact outline which the future city would follow—from a well-known tower to the gate at a certain corner, then on over a particular hill, coming now outside the walls of the original city and taking in a large area definitely shown by familiar landmarks. Eight details are unmistakably given here, and Zechariah adds another (Zech. 14:10). Moreover, the city's enlargement was to be in one general direction—to the northwest. Twenty-five hundred years later, in 1935 A.D., the prophecy had been fulfilled to the letter, as if indeed with God's "measuring line" (verse 39). What a God, and what a Book! So unlikely seemed this prophecy's fulfillment that some commentators had said it should be interpreted spiritually!

## New American Standard

30"But everyone will die for his own iniquity; each man who
eats the sour grapes, his teeth will be set on edge.
31"Behold, days are coming," declares the LORD, "when I will
make a new covenant with the house of Israel and with the house
of Judah,
32not like the covenant which I made with their fathers in the
day I took them by the hand to bring them out of the land of Egypt,
My covenant which they broke, although I was a husband to
them," declares the LORD.
33"But this is the covenant which I will make with the house of
Israel after those days," declares the LORD, "I will put My law
within them, and on their heart I will write it; and I will be their
God, and they shall be My people.
34"And they shall not teach again, each man his neighbor and
each man his brother, saying, 'Know the LORD,' for they shall all
know Me, from the least of them to the greatest of them," declares
the LORD, "for I will forgive their iniquity, and their sin I will
remember no more."

35¶ Thus says the LORD,
Who gives the sun for light by day,
And the fixed order of the moon and the stars for light
by night,
Who stirs up the sea so that its waves roar;
The LORD of hosts is His name:
36 "If this fixed order departs
From before Me," declares the LORD,
"Then the offspring of Israel also shall cease
From being a nation before Me forever."
37 Thus says the LORD,
"If the heavens above can be measured,
And the foundations of the earth searched out below,
Then I will also cast off all the offspring of Israel
For all that they have done," declares the LORD.

38¶ "Behold, days are coming," declares the LORD, "when the
city shall be rebuilt for the LORD from the Tower of Hananel to the
Corner Gate.
39"And the measuring line shall go out farther straight ahead
to the hill Gareb; then it will turn to Goah.
40"And the whole valley of the dead bodies and of the ashes,
and all the fields as far as the brook Kidron, to the corner of the
Horse Gate toward the east, shall be holy to the LORD; it shall not
be plucked up, or overthrown anymore forever."

## New International

30Instead, everyone will die for his own sin; whoever eats sour
grapes—his own teeth will be set on edge.

31"The time is coming," declares the LORD,
"when I will make a new covenant
with the house of Israel
and with the house of Judah.
32It will not be like the covenant
I made with their forefathers
when I took them by the hand
to lead them out of Egypt,
because they broke my covenant,
though I was a husband to[b] them,[c]"
declares the LORD.
33"This is the covenant I will make with the house of Israel
after that time," declares the LORD.
"I will put my law in their minds
and write it on their hearts.
I will be their God,
and they will be my people.
34No longer will a man teach his neighbor,
or a man his brother, saying, 'Know the LORD,'
because they will all know me,
from the least of them to the greatest,"
declares the LORD.
"For I will forgive their wickedness
and will remember their sins no more."
35This is what the LORD says,

he who appoints the sun
to shine by day,
who decrees the moon and stars
to shine by night,
who stirs up the sea
so that its waves roar—
the LORD Almighty is his name:
36"Only if these decrees vanish from my sight,"
declares the LORD,
"will the descendants of Israel ever cease
to be a nation before me."
37This is what the LORD says:

"Only if the heavens above can be measured
and the foundations of the earth below be searched out
will I reject all the descendants of Israel
because of all they have done,"
declares the LORD.

38"The days are coming," declares the LORD, "when this city
will be rebuilt for me from the Tower of Hananel to the Corner
Gate. 39The measuring line will stretch from there straight to the
hill of Gareb and then turn to Goah. 40The whole valley where
dead bodies and ashes are thrown, and all the terraces out to the
Kidron Valley on the east as far as the corner of the Horse Gate,
will be holy to the LORD. The city will never again be uprooted or
demolished."

**NIV** [b] 32 Hebrew; Septuagint and Syriac / *and I turned away from* [c] 32 Or *was their master*

## King James

**32** THE WORD that came to Jeremiah from the LORD in the tenth year of Zedekiah king of Judah, which *was* the eighteenth year of Nebuchadrezzar.

2 For then the king of Babylon's army besieged Jerusalem: and Jeremiah the prophet was shut up in the court of the prison, which *was* in the king of Judah's house.

3 For Zedekiah king of Judah had shut him up, saying, Wherefore dost thou prophesy, and say, Thus saith the LORD, Behold, I will give this city into the hand of the king of Babylon, and he shall take it;

4 And Zedekiah king of Judah shall not escape out of the hand of the Chaldeans, but shall surely be delivered into the hand of the king of Babylon, and shall speak with him mouth to mouth, and his eyes shall behold his eyes;

5 And he shall lead Zedekiah to Babylon, and there shall he be until I visit him, saith the LORD: though ye fight with the Chaldeans, ye shall not prosper.

6 ¶ And Jeremiah said, The word of the LORD came unto me, saying,

7 Behold, Hanameel the son of Shallum thine uncle shall come unto thee, saying, Buy thee my field that *is* in Anathoth: for the right of redemption *is* thine to buy *it*.

8 So Hanameel mine uncle's son came to me in the court of the prison according to the word of the LORD, and said unto me, Buy my field, I pray thee, that *is* in Anathoth, which *is* in the country of Benjamin: for the right of inheritance *is* thine, and the redemption *is* thine; buy *it* for thyself. Then I knew that this *was* the word of the LORD.

9 And I bought the field of Hanameel my uncle's son, that *was* in Anathoth, and weighed him the money, *even* seventeen shekels of silver.

10 And I subscribed the evidence, and sealed *it*, and took witnesses, and weighed *him* the money in the balances.

11 So I took the evidence of the purchase, *both* that which was sealed *according* to the law and custom, and that which was open:

12 And I gave the evidence of the purchase unto Baruch the son of Neriah, the son of Maaseiah, in the sight of Hanameel mine uncle's *son*, and in the presence of the witnesses that subscribed the book of the purchase, before all the Jews that sat in the court of the prison.

13 ¶ And I charged Baruch before them, saying,

14 Thus saith the LORD of hosts, the God of Israel; Take these evidences, this evidence of the purchase, both which is sealed, and this evidence which is open; and put them in an earthen vessel, that they may continue many days.

15 For thus saith the LORD of hosts, the God of Israel; Houses and fields and vineyards shall be possessed again in this land.

16 ¶ Now when I had delivered the evidence of the purchase unto Baruch the son of Neriah, I prayed unto the LORD, saying,

17 Ah Lord GOD! behold, thou hast made the heaven and the earth by thy great power and stretched out arm, *and* there is nothing too hard for thee:

18 Thou showest lovingkindness unto thousands, and recompensest the iniquity of the fathers into the bosom of their children after them: the Great, the Mighty God, the LORD of hosts, *is* his name,

19 Great in counsel, and mighty in work: for thine eyes *are* open upon all the ways of the sons of men: to give every one according to his ways, and according to the fruit of his doings:

20 Which hast set signs and wonders in the land of Egypt, *even* unto this day, and in Israel, and among *other* men; and hast made thee a name, as at this day;

21 And hast brought forth thy people Israel out of the land of Egypt with signs, and with wonders, and with a strong hand, and with a stretched out arm, and with great terror;

22 And hast given them this land, which thou didst swear to their fathers to give them, a land flowing with milk and honey;

## Amplified

**32** THE WORD that came to Jeremiah from the Lord in the tenth year of Zedekiah king of Judah, which was the eighteenth year of Nebuchadrezzar.

2 For then the king of Babylon's army besieged Jerusalem, and Jeremiah the prophet was shut up in the court of the guard, which was in the house of the king of Judah.

3 For Zedekiah king of Judah locked him up, saying, Why do you prophesy and say, Thus says the Lord, Behold I am giving this city into the hand of the king of Babylon, and he shall take it;

4 And Zedekiah king of Judah shall not escape out of the hand of the Chaldeans, but shall surely be delivered into the hand of the king of Babylon, and shall speak with him face to face and see him eye to eye;

5 And he shall lead Zedekiah to Babylon, and there shall he be until I visit him [for evil], says the Lord; and though you fight against the Chaldeans, you shall not prosper?

6 And Jeremiah said, The word of the Lord came to me, saying,

7 Behold, Hanamel the son of Shallum your uncle shall come to you and say, Buy my field that is in Anathoth, for the right of redemption is yours to buy it.

8 So Hanamel my uncle's son came to me in the court of the guard in accordance with the word of the Lord, and he said to me, I pray you, buy my field that is in Anathoth, which is in the land of Benjamin; for the right of inheritance is yours and the redemption is yours; buy it for yourself. Then I knew that this was the word of the Lord.

9 And I bought the field that was in Anathoth of Hanamel my uncle's son, and weighed him the money, seventeen shekels of silver.

10 And I signed the deed and sealed it, and called witnesses, and weighed him the money on scales.

11 So I took the deed of the purchase, both that which was sealed, containing the terms and conditions, and the copy which was unsealed,

12 And I gave the purchase deed to Baruch the son of Neriah, the son of Mahseiah, in the sight of Hanamel my uncle's son and the witnesses who signed the purchase deed, in the presence of all the Jews who sat in the court of the guard.

13 And I charged Baruch before them, saying,

14 Thus says the Lord of hosts, the God of Israel: Take these deeds, both this purchase deed which is sealed, and this open deed, and put them in an earthenware vessel, that they may last a long time.

15 For thus says the Lord of hosts, the God of Israel: Houses and fields and vineyards shall be purchased yet again in this land.

16 Now when I had delivered the purchase deed to Baruch the son of Neriah, I prayed to the Lord, saying:

17 Alas, Lord God! Behold, You made the heavens and the earth by Your great power and by Your stretched out arm! There is nothing too hard *or* too wonderful for You,

18 Who shows loving-kindness to thousands, and recompenses the iniquity of the fathers into the bosom of their children after them. The great, the Mighty God, the Lord of hosts is His name,

19 Great in counsel and mighty in deeds; Whose eyes are open upon all the ways of the sons of men, to reward *or* repay to each one according to his ways and according to the fruit of his doings;

20 Who wrought signs and wonders in the land of Egypt, and even to this day [continues to do so], both in Israel and among other men, and made Yourself a name, as at this day.

21 And You brought forth Your people Israel out of the land of Egypt with signs and wonders, with a strong hand and outstretched arm, and with great terror;

22 And You gave them this land which You swore to their fathers to give them, a land flowing with milk and honey;

## New American Standard

*Jeremiah Imprisoned*

**32** THE WORD that came to Jeremiah from the LORD in the tenth year of Zedekiah king of Judah, which was the eighteenth year of Nebuchadnezzar.

2Now at that time the army of the king of Babylon was besieging Jerusalem, and Jeremiah the prophet was shut up in the court of the guard, which was *in* the house of the king of Judah,

3because Zedekiah king of Judah had shut him up, saying, "Why do you prophesy, saying, 'Thus says the LORD, "Behold, I am about to give this city into the hand of the king of Babylon, and he will take it;

4and Zedekiah king of Judah shall not escape out of the hand of the Chaldeans, but he shall surely be given into the hand of the king of Babylon, and he shall speak with him face to face, and see him eye to eye;

5and he shall take Zedekiah to Babylon, and he shall be there until I visit him," declares the LORD. "If you fight against the Chaldeans, you shall not succeed"'?"

6¶ And Jeremiah said, "The word of the LORD came to me, saying,

7'Behold, Hanamel the son of Shallum your uncle is coming to you, saying, "Buy for yourself my field which is at Anathoth, for you have the right of redemption to buy *it*."'

8"Then Hanamel my uncle's son came to me in the court of the guard according to the word of the LORD, and said to me, 'Buy my field, please, that is at Anathoth, which is in the land of Benjamin; for you have the right of possession and the redemption is yours; buy *it* for yourself.' Then I knew that this was the word of the LORD.

9"And I bought the field which was at Anathoth from Hanamel my uncle's son, and I weighed out the silver for him, seventeen shekels of silver.

10"And I signed and sealed the deed, and called in witnesses, and weighed out the silver on the scales.

11"Then I took the deeds of purchase, both the sealed *copy containing* the terms and conditions, and the open *copy;*

12and I gave the deed of purchase to Baruch the son of Neriah, the son of Mahseiah, in the sight of Hanamel my uncle's *son*, and in the sight of the witnesses who signed the deed of purchase, before all the Jews who were sitting in the court of the guard.

13"And I commanded Baruch in their presence, saying,

14'Thus says the LORD of hosts, the God of Israel, "Take these deeds, this sealed deed of purchase, and this open deed, and put them in an earthenware jar, that they may last a long time."

15'For thus says the LORD of hosts, the God of Israel, "Houses and fields and vineyards shall again be bought in this land."'

*Jeremiah Prays and God Explains*

16¶ "After I had given the deed of purchase to Baruch the son of Neriah, then I prayed to the LORD, saying,

17'Ah Lord GOD! Behold, Thou hast made the heavens and the earth by Thy great power and by Thine outstretched arm! Nothing is too difficult for Thee,

18who showest lovingkindness to thousands, but repayest the iniquity of fathers into the bosom of their children after them, O great and mighty God. The LORD of hosts is His name;

19great in counsel and mighty in deed, whose eyes are open to all the ways of the sons of men, giving to everyone according to his ways and according to the fruit of his deeds;

20who hast set signs and wonders in the land of Egypt, *and* even to this day both in Israel and among mankind; and Thou hast made a name for Thyself, as at this day.

21'And Thou didst bring Thy people Israel out of the land of Egypt with signs and with wonders, and with a strong hand and with an outstretched arm, and with great terror;

22and gavest them this land, which Thou didst swear to their forefathers to give them, a land flowing with milk and honey.

## New International

*Jeremiah Buys a Field*

**32** THIS IS the word that came to Jeremiah from the LORD in
the tenth year of Zedekiah king of Judah, which was the
eighteenth year of Nebuchadnezzar. 2The army of the king of
Babylon was then besieging Jerusalem, and Jeremiah the prophet
was confined in the courtyard of the guard in the royal palace of
Judah.

3Now Zedekiah king of Judah had imprisoned him there, saying, "Why do you prophesy as you do? You say, 'This is what the
LORD says: I am about to hand this city over to the king of Babylon,
and he will capture it. 4Zedekiah king of Judah will not escape out
of the hands of the Babylonians[a] but will certainly be handed over
to the king of Babylon, and will speak with him face to face and
see him with his own eyes. 5He will take Zedekiah to Babylon,
where he will remain until I deal with him, declares the LORD. If
you fight against the Babylonians, you will not succeed.'"

6Jeremiah said, "The word of the LORD came to me: 7Hanamel
son of Shallum your uncle is going to come to you and say, 'Buy
my field at Anathoth, because as nearest relative it is your right
and duty to buy it.'

8"Then, just as the LORD had said, my cousin Hanamel came
to me in the courtyard of the guard and said, 'Buy my field at
Anathoth in the territory of Benjamin. Since it is your right to
redeem it and possess it, buy it for yourself.'

"I knew that this was the word of the LORD; 9so I bought the
field at Anathoth from my cousin Hanamel and weighed out for
him seventeen shekels[b] of silver. 10I signed and sealed the deed,
had it witnessed, and weighed out the silver on the scales. 11I took
the deed of purchase—the sealed copy containing the terms and
conditions, as well as the unsealed copy— 12and I gave this deed
to Baruch son of Neriah, the son of Mahseiah, in the presence of
my cousin Hanamel and of the witnesses who had signed the deed
and of all the Jews sitting in the courtyard of the guard.

13"In their presence I gave Baruch these instructions: 14'This is
what the LORD Almighty, the God of Israel, says: Take these documents, both the sealed and unsealed copies of the deed of purchase, and put them in a clay jar so they will last a long time. 15For
this is what the LORD Almighty, the God of Israel, says: Houses,
fields and vineyards will again be bought in this land.'

16"After I had given the deed of purchase to Baruch son of
Neriah, I prayed to the LORD:

17"Ah, Sovereign LORD, you have made the heavens and the
earth by your great power and outstretched arm. Nothing is
too hard for you. 18You show love to thousands but bring the
punishment for the fathers' sins into the laps of their children
after them. O great and powerful God, whose name is the
LORD Almighty, 19great are your purposes and mighty are
your deeds. Your eyes are open to all the ways of men; you
reward everyone according to his conduct and as his deeds
deserve. 20You performed miraculous signs and wonders in
Egypt and have continued them to this day, both in Israel and
among all mankind, and have gained the renown that is still
yours. 21You brought your people Israel out of Egypt with
signs and wonders, by a mighty hand and an outstretched
arm and with great terror. 22You gave them this land you had
sworn to give their forefathers, a land flowing with milk and
honey. 23They came in and took possession of it, but they did

NIV [a] 4 Or *Chaldeans;* also in verses 5, 24, 25, 28, 29 and 43 [b] 9 That is, about 7 ounces (about 200 grams)

## King James

23And they came in, and possessed it; but they obeyed not thy voice, neither walked in thy law; they have done nothing of all that thou commandedst them to do: therefore thou hast caused all this evil to come upon them:

24Behold the mounts, they are come unto the city to take it; and the city is given into the hand of the Chaldeans, that fight against it, because of the sword, and of the famine, and of the pestilence: and what thou hast spoken is come to pass; and, behold, thou seest *it*.

25And thou hast said unto me, O Lord GOD, Buy thee the field for money, and take witnesses; for the city is given into the hand of the Chaldeans.

26¶ Then came the word of the LORD unto Jeremiah, saying,

27Behold, I *am* the LORD, the God of all flesh: is there any thing too hard for me?

28Therefore thus saith the LORD; Behold, I will give this city into the hand of the Chaldeans, and into the hand of Nebuchadrezzar king of Babylon, and he shall take it:

29And the Chaldeans, that fight against this city, shall come and set fire on this city, and burn it with the houses, upon whose roofs they have offered incense unto Baal, and poured out drink offerings unto other gods, to provoke me to anger.

30For the children of Israel and the children of Judah have only done evil before me from their youth: for the children of Israel have only provoked me to anger with the work of their hands, saith the LORD.

31For this city hath been to me *as* a provocation of mine anger and of my fury from the day that they built it even unto this day; that I should remove it from before my face,

32Because of all the evil of the children of Israel and of the children of Judah, which they have done to provoke me to anger, they, their kings, their princes, their priests, and their prophets, and the men of Judah, and the inhabitants of Jerusalem.

33And they have turned unto me the back, and not the face: though I taught them, rising up early and teaching *them*, yet they have not hearkened to receive instruction.

34But they set their abominations in the house, which is called by my name, to defile it.

35And they built the high places of Baal, which *are* in the valley of the son of Hinnom, to cause their sons and their daughters to pass through *the fire* unto Molech; which I commanded them not, neither came it into my mind, that they should do this abomination, to cause Judah to sin.

36¶ And now therefore thus saith the LORD, the God of Israel, concerning this city, whereof ye say, It shall be delivered into the hand of the king of Babylon by the sword, and by the famine, and by the pestilence;

37Behold, I will gather them out of all countries, whither I have driven them in mine anger, and in my fury, and in great wrath; and I will bring them again unto this place, and I will cause them to dwell safely:

38And they shall be my people, and I will be their God:

39And I will give them one heart, and one way, that they may fear me for ever, for the good of them, and of their children after them:

40And I will make an everlasting covenant with them, that I will not turn away from them, to do them good; but I will put my fear in their hearts, that they shall not depart from me.

41Yea, I will rejoice over them to do them good, and I will plant them in this land assuredly with my whole heart and with my whole soul.

42For thus saith the LORD; Like as I have brought all this great evil upon this people, so will I bring upon them all the good that I have promised them.

43And fields shall be bought in this land, whereof ye say, *It is* desolate without man or beast; it is given into the hand of the Chaldeans.

## Amplified

23And they entered and took possession of it; but they obeyed not Your voice, nor walked in Your law; they have done nothing of all that You commanded them to do. Therefore You have caused all this evil to come upon them.

24See the mounds [of earth which the foe has heaped against the walls], they have come up to the city to take it; and the city is given into the hand of the Chaldeans who fight against it, because [the people are overcome] by the sword and the famine and the pestilence. What You have spoken has come to pass, and behold, You see it.

25Yet, O Lord God, You said to me, Buy the field for money and get witnesses, though the city is given into the hand of the Chaldeans.

26Then came the word of the Lord to Jeremiah, saying:

27Behold, I am the Lord, the God of all flesh; is there anything too hard for Me?

28Therefore thus says the Lord: Behold, I am giving this city into the hand of the Chaldeans and into the hand of Nebuchadrezzar king of Babylon, and he shall take it;

29And the Chaldeans who are fighting against this city shall come and set this city on fire, and burn it, with the houses on whose roofs incense has been offered to Baal and drink offerings have been poured out to other gods, to provoke Me to anger.

30For the children of Israel and the children of Judah have done only evil before Me from their youth, for the children of Israel have only provoked Me to anger with [idols] the work of their hands, says the Lord.

31For this city has been to Me a provocation of My anger and My wrath from the day that they *finished* building it [in the time of Solomon, who was the first Jewish king who turned to idolatry] even to this day; so that I will remove it from before My face [I Kings 11:1-13.]

32Because of all the evil of the children of Israel and of the children of Judah which they have done to provoke Me to anger, they, their kings, their princes, their priests, their prophets, the men of Judah, and the inhabitants of Jerusalem.

33And they have turned their back to Me and not their face; though I taught them persistently, yet they have not listened to receive instruction.

34But they set their abominations [of idol-worship] in the house which is called by My name, to defile it.

35And they built the high places [for worship] of Baal in the valley of the son of Hinnom, to cause their sons and their daughters to pass through the fire [in worship also of] Molech; which I did not command them, nor did it come into My mind *or* heart that they should do this abomination, to cause Judah to sin.

36And now therefore thus says the Lord, the God of Israel, concerning this city of which you say, It shall be delivered into the hand of the king of Babylon by sword and by famine and by pestilence:

37Behold, I will gather them out of all countries to which I drove them in My anger and in My wrath and in great indignation; I will bring them again to this place, and I will make them dwell safely;

38And they shall be My people, and I will be their God.

39And I will give them one heart and one way, that they may [reverently] fear Me for ever, for the good of themselves and of their children after them.

40And I will make an everlasting covenant with them, that I will not turn away from following them, to do them good; and I will put My [reverential] fear in their hearts, that they shall not depart from Me. [Jer. 31:31-34.]

41Yes, I will rejoice over them to do them good, and I will plant them in this land assuredly *and* in truth with My whole heart and with My whole being.

42For thus says the Lord: Like as I have brought all this great evil upon this people, so will I bring upon them all the good that I have promised them.

43And fields shall be bought in this land of which you say, It is desolate, without man or beast; it is given into the hands of the Chaldeans.

## New American Standard

23'And they came in and took possession of it, but they did not obey Thy voice or walk in Thy law; they have done nothing of all that Thou commandedst them to do; therefore Thou hast made all this calamity come upon them.

24'Behold, the siege mounds have reached the city to take it; and the city is given into the hand of the Chaldeans who fight against it, because of the sword, the famine, and the pestilence; and what Thou hast spoken has come to pass; and, behold, Thou seest *it.*

25'And Thou hast said to me, O Lord GOD, "Buy for yourself the field with money, and call in witnesses"—although the city is given into the hand of the Chaldeans.' "

26¶ Then the word of the LORD came to Jeremiah, saying,

27"Behold, I am the LORD, the God of all flesh; is anything too difficult for Me?"

28Therefore thus says the LORD, "Behold, I am about to give this city into the hand of the Chaldeans and into the hand of Nebuchadnezzar king of Babylon, and he shall take it.

29"And the Chaldeans who are fighting against this city shall enter and set this city on fire and burn it, with the houses where *people* have offered incense to Baal on their roofs and poured out libations to other gods to provoke Me to anger.

30"Indeed the sons of Israel and the sons of Judah have been doing only evil in My sight from their youth; for the sons of Israel have been only provoking Me to anger by the work of their hands," declares the LORD.

31"Indeed this city has been to Me *a provocation of* My anger and My wrath from the day that they built it, even to this day, that it should be removed from before My face,

32because of all the evil of the sons of Israel and the sons of Judah, which they have done to provoke Me to anger—they, their kings, their leaders, their priests, their prophets, the men of Judah, and the inhabitants of Jerusalem.

33"And they have turned *their* back to Me, and not *their* face; though *I* taught them, teaching again and again, they would not listen and receive instruction.

34"But they put their detestable things in the house which is called by My name, to defile it.

35"And they built the high places of Baal that are in the valley of Ben-hinnom to cause their sons and their daughters to pass through *the fire* to Molech, which I had not commanded them nor had it entered My mind that they should do this abomination, to cause Judah to sin.

36¶ "Now therefore thus says the LORD God of Israel concerning this city of which you say, 'It is given into the hand of the king of Babylon by sword, by famine, and by pestilence.'

37"Behold, I will gather them out of all the lands to which I have driven them in My anger, in My wrath, and in great indignation; and I will bring them back to this place and make them dwell in safety.

38"And they shall be My people, and I will be their God;

39and I will give them one heart and one way, that they may fear Me always, for their own good, and for *the good of* their children after them.

40"And I will make an everlasting covenant with them that I will not turn away from them, to do them good; and I will put the fear of Me in their hearts so that they will not turn away from Me.

41"And I will rejoice over them to do them good, and I will faithfully plant them in this land with all My heart and with all My soul.

42"For thus says the LORD, 'Just as I brought all this great disaster on this people, so I am going to bring on them all the good that I am promising them.

43'And fields shall be bought in this land of which you say, "It is a desolation, without man or beast; it is given into the hand of the Chaldeans."

## New International

not obey you or follow your law; they did not do what you
commanded them to do. So you brought all this disaster upon
them.
24"See how the siege ramps are built up to take the city.
Because of the sword, famine and plague, the city will be
handed over to the Babylonians who are attacking it. What
you said has happened, as you now see. 25And though the
city will be handed over to the Babylonians, you, O Sovereign
LORD, say to me, 'Buy the field with silver and have the
transaction witnessed.' "

26Then the word of the LORD came to Jeremiah: 27"I am the
LORD, the God of all mankind. Is anything too hard for me?
28Therefore, this is what the LORD says: I am about to hand this
city over to the Babylonians and to Nebuchadnezzar king of Babylon, who will capture it. 29The Babylonians who are attacking this
city will come in and set it on fire; they will burn it down, along
with the houses where the people provoked me to anger by burning incense on the roofs to Baal and by pouring out drink offerings
to other gods.
30"The people of Israel and Judah have done nothing but evil
in my sight from their youth; indeed, the people of Israel have
done nothing but provoke me with what their hands have made,
declares the LORD. 31From the day it was built until now, this city
has so aroused my anger and wrath that I must remove it from my
sight. 32The people of Israel and Judah have provoked me by all
the evil they have done—they, their kings and officials, their
priests and prophets, the men of Judah and the people of Jerusalem. 33They turned their backs to me and not their faces; though
I taught them again and again, they would not listen or respond
to discipline. 34They set up their abominable idols in the house that
bears my Name and defiled it. 35They built high places for Baal in
the Valley of Ben Hinnom to sacrifice their sons and daughters[a]
to Molech, though I never commanded, nor did it enter my mind,
that they should do such a detestable thing and so make Judah sin.
36"You are saying about this city, 'By the sword, famine and
plague it will be handed over to the king of Babylon'; but this is
what the LORD, the God of Israel, says: 37I will surely gather them
from all the lands where I banish them in my furious anger and
great wrath; I will bring them back to this place and let them live
in safety. 38They will be my people, and I will be their God. 39I will
give them singleness of heart and action, so that they will always
fear me for their own good and the good of their children after
them. 40I will make an everlasting covenant with them: I will never
stop doing good to them, and I will inspire them to fear me, so that
they will never turn away from me. 41I will rejoice in doing them
good and will assuredly plant them in this land with all my heart
and soul.
42"This is what the LORD says: As I have brought all this great
calamity on this people, so I will give them all the prosperity I have
promised them. 43Once more fields will be bought in this land of
which you say, 'It is a desolate waste, without men or animals, for
it has been handed over to the Babylonians.' 44Fields will be

NIV [a] 35 Or *to make their sons and daughters pass through* ⌊*the fire*⌋

## King James

44 Men shall buy fields for money, and subscribe evidences, and seal *them*, and take witnesses in the land of Benjamin, and in the places about Jerusalem, and in the cities of Judah, and in the cities of the mountains, and in the cities of the valley, and in the cities of the south: for I will cause their captivity to return, saith the LORD.

**33** MOREOVER THE word of the LORD came unto Jeremiah the second time, while he was yet shut up in the court of the prison, saying,

2 Thus saith the LORD the maker thereof, the LORD that formed it, to establish it; the LORD *is* his name;

3 Call unto me, and I will answer thee, and show thee great and mighty things, which thou knowest not.

4 For thus saith the LORD, the God of Israel, concerning the houses of this city, and concerning the houses of the kings of Judah, which are thrown down by the mounts, and by the sword;

5 They come to fight with the Chaldeans, but *it is* to fill them with the dead bodies of men, whom I have slain in mine anger and in my fury, and for all whose wickedness I have hid my face from this city.

6 Behold, I will bring it health and cure, and I will cure them, and will reveal unto them the abundance of peace and truth.

7 And I will cause the captivity of Judah and the captivity of Israel to return, and will build them, as at the first.

8 And I will cleanse them from all their iniquity, whereby they have sinned against me; and I will pardon all their iniquities, whereby they have sinned, and whereby they have transgressed against me.

9 ¶ And it shall be to me a name of joy, a praise and an honour before all the nations of the earth, which shall hear all the good that I do unto them: and they shall fear and tremble for all the goodness and for all the prosperity that I procure unto it.

10 Thus saith the LORD; Again there shall be heard in this place, which ye say *shall be* desolate without man and without beast, *even* in the cities of Judah, and in the streets of Jerusalem, that are desolate, without man, and without inhabitant, and without beast,

11 The voice of joy, and the voice of gladness, the voice of the bridegroom, and the voice of the bride, the voice of them that shall say, Praise the LORD of hosts: for the LORD *is* good; for his mercy *endureth* for ever: *and* of them that shall bring the sacrifice of praise into the house of the LORD. For I will cause to return the captivity of the land, as at the first, saith the LORD.

12 Thus saith the LORD of hosts; Again in this place, which is desolate without man and without beast, and in all the cities thereof, shall be an habitation of shepherds causing *their* flocks to lie down.

13 In the cities of the mountains, in the cities of the vale, and in the cities of the south, and in the land of Benjamin, and in the places about Jerusalem, and in the cities of Judah, shall the flocks pass again under the hands of him that telleth *them*, saith the LORD.

14 Behold, the days come, saith the LORD, that I will perform that good thing which I have promised unto the house of Israel and to the house of Judah.

15 ¶ In those days, and at that time, will I cause the Branch of righteousness to grow up unto David; and he shall execute judgment and righteousness in the land.

16 In those days shall Judah be saved, and Jerusalem shall dwell safely: and this *is the name* wherewith she shall be called, The LORD our righteousness.

## Amplified

44 Men shall buy fields for money and sign deeds, seal them and call witnesses, in the land of Benjamin, in the places about Jerusalem, in the cities of Judah, in the cities of the hill country, in the cities of the lowland, and in the cities of the South; for I will cause them to be released from their exile, says the Lord.

**33** MOREOVER THE word of the Lord came to Jeremiah the second time, while he was still shut up in the court of the guard, saying,

2 Thus says the Lord Who made *the earth,* the Lord Who formed it to establish it; the Lord is His name:

3 Call to Me and I will answer you and show you great and mighty things, fenced in *and* hidden, which you do not know—do not distinguish and recognize, have knowledge of and understand.

4 For thus says the Lord, the God of Israel, concerning the houses of this city and the houses of the kings of Judah which are torn down to make a defense against the [siege] mounds and before the sword:

5 They [the besieged Jews] are coming in to fight against the Chaldeans and to fill [the houses] with the dead bodies of men whom I shall slay in My anger and My wrath, for I have hidden My face [in indignation] from this city because of all their wickedness.

6 Behold, [in the future restored Jerusalem] I will lay upon it health and healing, and I will cure them and will reveal to them the abundance of peace—prosperity, security, stability—and truth.

7 And I will cause the captivity of Judah and the captivity of Israel to be reversed, and will rebuild them as *they were* at first.

8 And I will cleanse them from all the guilt *and* iniquity by which they have sinned against Me, and I will forgive all their guilt *and* iniquities by which they have sinned and rebelled against Me.

9 And [Jerusalem] shall be to Me a name of joy, a praise and a glory before all the nations of the earth who shall hear of all the good I do for them, and they shall fear and tremble because of all the good and all the peace, prosperity, security *and* stability I provide for it.

10 Thus says the Lord: Yet again there shall be heard in this place, of which you say, It is a desolate waste without man and without beast, even in the cities of Judah and in the streets of Jerusalem that are desolate, without man and without inhabitant and without beast,

11 [There shall be heard again] the voice of joy and the voice of gladness, the voice of the bridegroom and the voice of the bride, the voices of those who sing as they bring *sacrifices of* thanksgiving into the house of the Lord, Give praise *and* thanks to the Lord of hosts, for the Lord is good, for His mercy *and* kindness *and* steadfast love endure for ever! For I will cause the captivity of the land to be reversed *and* return to be as it was at first, says the Lord.

12 Thus says the Lord of hosts: In this place, which is desolate, without man and without beast, and in all its cities, there shall again be dwellings *and* pastures of shepherds resting their flocks.

13 In the cities of the hill country, in the cities of the lowlands, in the cities of the South, in the land of Benjamin, in the places about Jerusalem, and in the cities of Judah shall flocks pass again under the hands of him who counts them, says the Lord.

14 Behold, the days are coming, says the Lord, that I will fulfill the good promise I have made to the house of Israel and the house of Judah.

15 In those days, and at that time, will I cause a righteous Branch [the Messiah] to grow up to David; and He shall execute justice and righteousness in the land. [Jer. 23:5; Isa. 4:2; Zech. 3:8; 6:12.]

16 In those days shall Judah be saved and Jerusalem shall dwell safely. And this is the name by which it will be called, The Lord is our righteousness—our rightness, our justice.

## New American Standard

44'Men shall buy fields for money, sign and seal deeds, and call
in witnesses in the land of Benjamin, in the environs of Jerusalem,
in the cities of Judah, in the cities of the hill country, in the cities
of the lowland, and in the cities of the [a]Negev; for I will restore
their fortunes,' declares the LORD."

*Restoration Promised*

**33** THEN THE word of the LORD came to Jeremiah the second
time, while he was still confined in the court of the guard,
saying,
2"Thus says the LORD who made *the earth,* the LORD who
formed it to establish it, the LORD is His name,
3'Call to Me, and I will answer you, and I will tell you great and
mighty things, which you do not know.'
4"For thus says the LORD God of Israel concerning the houses
of this city, and concerning the houses of the kings of Judah, which
are broken down *to make a defense* against the siege mounds and
against the sword,
5'While *they* are coming to fight with the Chaldeans, and to fill
them with the corpses of men whom I have slain in My anger and
in My wrath, and I have hidden My face from this city because of
all their wickedness:
6'Behold, I will bring to it health and healing, and I will heal
them; and I will reveal to them an abundance of peace and truth.
7'And I will restore the fortunes of Judah and the fortunes of
Israel, and I will rebuild them as they were at first.
8'And I will cleanse them from all their iniquity by which they
have sinned against Me, and I will pardon all their iniquities by
which they have sinned against Me, and by which they have
transgressed against Me.
9'And [b]it shall be to Me a name of joy, praise, and glory before
all the nations of the earth, which shall hear of all the good that
I do for them, and they shall fear and tremble because of all the
good and all the peace that I make for it.'
10¶ "Thus says the LORD, 'Yet again there shall be heard in this
place, of which you say, "It is a waste, without man and without
beast," *that is,* in the cities of Judah and in the streets of Jerusalem
that are desolate, without man and without inhabitant and without beast,
11the voice of joy and the voice of gladness, the voice of the
bridegroom and the voice of the bride, the voice of those who say,
"Give thanks to the LORD of hosts,
For the LORD is good,
For His lovingkindness is everlasting";
*and of those* who bring a thank offering into the house of the LORD.
For I will restore the fortunes of the land as they were at first,' says
the LORD.
12¶ "Thus says the LORD of hosts, 'There shall again be in this
place which is waste, without man or beast, and in all its cities, a
habitation of shepherds who rest their flocks.
13'In the cities of the hill country, in the cities of the lowland,
in the cities of the Negev, in the land of Benjamin, in the environs
of Jerusalem, and in the cities of Judah, the flocks shall again pass
under the hands of the one who numbers them,' says the LORD.

*The Davidic Kingdom*

14¶ 'Behold, days are coming,' declares the LORD, 'when I will
fulfill the good word which I have spoken concerning the house
of Israel and the house of Judah.
15'In those days and at that time I will cause a righteous Branch
of David to spring forth; and He shall execute justice and righteousness on the earth.
16'In those days Judah shall be saved, and Jerusalem shall dwell
in safety; and this is *the name* by which she shall be called: the LORD
is our righteousness.'

NAS [a] I.e., South country [b] I.e., this city

## New International

bought for silver, and deeds will be signed, sealed and witnessed
in the territory of Benjamin, in the villages around Jerusalem, in
the towns of Judah and in the towns of the hill country, of the
western foothills and of the Negev, because I will restore their
fortunes,[c] declares the LORD."

*Promise of Restoration*

**33** WHILE JEREMIAH was still confined in the courtyard of
the guard, the word of the LORD came to him a second
time: 2"This is what the LORD says, he who made the earth, the
LORD who formed it and established it—the LORD is his name:
3'Call to me and I will answer you and tell you great and unsearchable things you do not know.' 4For this is what the LORD, the God
of Israel, says about the houses in this city and the royal palaces
of Judah that have been torn down to be used against the siege
ramps and the sword 5in the fight with the Babylonians[d]: 'They
will be filled with the dead bodies of the men I will slay in my anger
and wrath. I will hide my face from this city because of all its
wickedness.
6" 'Nevertheless, I will bring health and healing to it; I will heal
my people and will let them enjoy abundant peace and security.
7I will bring Judah and Israel back from captivity[e] and will rebuild
them as they were before. 8I will cleanse them from all the sin they
have committed against me and will forgive all their sins of rebellion against me. 9Then this city will bring me renown, joy, praise
and honor before all nations on earth that hear of all the good
things I do for it; and they will be in awe and will tremble at the
abundant prosperity and peace I provide for it.'
10"This is what the LORD says: 'You say about this place, "It is
a desolate waste, without men or animals." Yet in the towns of
Judah and the streets of Jerusalem that are deserted, inhabited by
neither men nor animals, there will be heard once more 11the
sounds of joy and gladness, the voices of bride and bridegroom,
and the voices of those who bring thank offerings to the house of
the LORD, saying,

"Give thanks to the LORD Almighty,
for the LORD is good;
his love endures forever."

For I will restore the fortunes of the land as they were before,' says
the LORD.
12"This is what the LORD Almighty says: 'In this place, desolate
and without men or animals—in all its towns there will again be
pastures for shepherds to rest their flocks. 13In the towns of the
hill country, of the western foothills and of the Negev, in the
territory of Benjamin, in the villages around Jerusalem and in the
towns of Judah, flocks will again pass under the hand of the one
who counts them,' says the LORD.
14" 'The days are coming,' declares the LORD, 'when I will fulfill
the gracious promise I made to the house of Israel and to the house
of Judah.

15" 'In those days and at that time
I will make a righteous Branch sprout from David's line;
he will do what is just and right in the land.
16In those days Judah will be saved
and Jerusalem will live in safety.
This is the name by which it[f] will be called:
The LORD Our Righteousness.'

NIV [c] 44 Or *will bring them back from captivity* [d] 5 Or *Chaldeans* [e] 7 Or *will restore the fortunes of Judah and Israel* [f] 16 Or *he*

## King James

17¶ For thus saith the LORD; David shall never want a man to
sit upon the throne of the house of Israel;
18Neither shall the priests the Levites want a man before me to
offer burnt offerings, and to kindle meat offerings, and to do
sacrifice continually.
19¶ And the word of the LORD came unto Jeremiah, saying,
20Thus saith the LORD; if ye can break my covenant of the day,
and my covenant of the night, and that there should not be day
and night in their season;
21 *Then* may also my covenant be broken with David my servant, that he should not have a son to reign upon his throne; and
with the Levites the priests, my ministers.
22As the host of heaven cannot be numbered, neither the sand
of the sea measured: so will I multiply the seed of David my
servant, and the Levites that minister unto me.
23Moreover the word of the LORD came to Jeremiah, saying,
24Considerest thou not what this people have spoken, saying,
The two families which the LORD hath chosen, he hath even cast
them off ? thus they have despised my people, that they should
be no more a nation before them.
25Thus saith the LORD; If my covenant *be* not with day and
night, *and if* I have not appointed the ordinances of heaven and
earth;
26Then will I cast away the seed of Jacob, and David my servant,
*so* that I will not take *any* of his seed *to be* rulers over the seed of
Abraham, Isaac, and Jacob: for I will cause their captivity to return,
and have mercy on them.

**34** THE WORD which came unto Jeremiah from the LORD,
when Nebuchadnezzar king of Babylon, and all his army,
and all the kingdoms of the earth of his dominion, and all the
people, fought against Jerusalem, and against all the cities thereof,
saying,
2Thus saith the LORD, the God of Israel; Go and speak to Zedekiah king of Judah, and tell him, Thus saith the LORD; Behold, I
will give this city into the hand of the king of Babylon, and he shall
burn it with fire:
3And thou shalt not escape out of his hand, but shalt surely be
taken, and delivered into his hand; and thine eyes shall behold the
eyes of the king of Babylon, and he shall speak with thee mouth
to mouth, and thou shalt go to Babylon.
4Yet hear the word of the LORD, O Zedekiah king of Judah; Thus
saith the LORD of thee, Thou shalt not die by the sword:
5 *But* thou shalt die in peace: and with the burnings of thy
fathers, the former kings which were before thee, so shall they
burn *odours* for thee; and they will lament thee, *saying*, Ah lord! for
I have pronounced the word, saith the LORD.
6Then Jeremiah the prophet spake all these words unto Zedekiah king of Judah in Jerusalem,
7When the king of Babylon's army fought against Jerusalem,
and against all the cities of Judah that were left, against Lachish,
and against Azekah: for these defenced cities remained of the cities
of Judah.
8¶ *This is* the word that came unto Jeremiah from the LORD, after
that the king Zedekiah had made a covenant with all the people
which *were* at Jerusalem, to proclaim liberty unto them;
9That every man should let his manservant, and every man his
maidservant, *being* an Hebrew or an Hebrewess, go free; that none
should serve himself of them, *to wit*, of a Jew his brother.
10Now when all the princes, and all the people, which had
entered into the covenant, heard that every one should let his
manservant, and every one his maidservant, go free, that none
should serve themselves of them any more, then they obeyed, and
let *them* go.

## Amplified

17For thus says the Lord: David shall never lack a man [descend-
ant] to sit on the throne of the house of Israel,
18Nor shall the priest of the Levites lack a man [descendant] to
offer burnt offerings before Me and to burn cereal offerings and to
make sacrifices continually—all day long.
19And the word of the Lord came to Jeremiah, saying,
20Thus says the Lord: If you can break My covenant of the day,
and My covenant of the night, so that there should not be day and
night in their season;
21Then may also My covenant be broken with David My servant, so that he shall not have a son to reign upon his throne, and
[My league be broken also] with the Levites the priests, My ministers.
22As the host of [the stars of] the heavens cannot be numbered,
nor the sand of the sea be measured, so will I multiply the offspring
of David My servant, and the Levites who minister to Me.
23Moreover the word of the Lord came to Jeremiah, saying,
24Have you not noticed what these people [the Jews] are saying,
The Lord has cast off the two families [Israel and Judah] which He
had chosen? Thus My people have despised *themselves* [in relation
to God as His covenant people], so that they are no more a nation
in their own sight.
25Thus says the Lord: If My covenant of day and night does not
stand, and if I have not appointed the ordinances of the heavens
and the earth [the whole order of nature],
26Then will I also cast away the descendants of Jacob and David
My servant and will not choose one of his offspring to be ruler over
the descendants of Abraham, Isaac and Jacob. For I will cause their
captivity to be reversed, and I will have mercy, kindness *and*
steadfast love for them. [Gen. 49:10.]

**34** THE WORD which came to Jeremiah from the Lord, when
Nebuchadnezzar king of Babylon and all his army and all
the kingdoms of the earth under his dominion and all the people
were fighting against Jerusalem and all of its cities:
2Thus says the Lord, the God of Israel: Go and speak to Zedekiah king of Judah and tell him, Thus says the Lord: Behold, I am
giving this city into the hand of the king of Babylon, and he will
burn it with fire.
3And you shall not escape out of his hand, but shall surely be
taken and delivered into his hand; you shall see the king of Babylon eye to eye, and he will speak with you face to face, and you
shall go to Babylon.
4Yet hear the word of the Lord, O Zedekiah king of Judah! Thus
says the Lord of you: You shall not die by the sword;
5But you shall die in peace, and with the burnings of [spices and
perfumes on wood that were granted as suitable to] your fathers,
the former kings who were before you, so shall a burning be made
for you; and *people* shall lament for you, saying, Alas, lord! For I
have spoken the word, says the Lord.
6Then Jeremiah the prophet spoke all these words to Zedekiah
king of Judah in Jerusalem,
7When the army of the king of Babylon was fighting against
Jerusalem and against all the cities of Judah that were left, against
Lachish and Azekah; for these were the only fortified cities remaining of the cities of Judah.
8[This is] the word that came to Jeremiah from the Lord, after
King Zedekiah had made a covenant with all the people which
were at Jerusalem to proclaim liberty to them,
9That every man should let his Hebrew slaves, male and female,
go free, so that no one should make a slave of a Jew, his brother.
10And all the princes and all the people obeyed, who had entered into the covenant that every one would let his man servant
and his maid servant go free, so that none should make bondmen
of them any more; they obeyed and let them go.

## New American Standard

17"For thus says the LORD, 'David shall never lack a man to sit
on the throne of the house of Israel;
18and the Levitical priests shall never lack a man before Me to
offer burnt offerings, to burn grain offerings, and to prepare sacrifices continually.' "
19¶ And the word of the LORD came to Jeremiah, saying,
20"Thus says the LORD, 'If you can break My covenant for the
day, and My covenant for the night, so that day and night will not
be at their appointed time,
21then My covenant may also be broken with David My servant
that he shall not have a son to reign on his throne, and with the
Levitical priests, My ministers.
22'As the host of heaven cannot be counted, and the sand of the
sea cannot be measured, so I will multiply the descendants of
David My servant and the Levites who minister to Me.' "
23¶ And the word of the LORD came to Jeremiah, saying,
24"Have you not observed what this people have spoken, saying, 'The two families which the LORD chose, He has rejected
them'? Thus they despise My people, no longer are they as a
nation in their sight.
25"Thus says the LORD, 'If My covenant *for* day and night *stand*
not, *and* the fixed patterns of heaven and earth I have not established,
26then I would reject the descendants of Jacob and David My
servant, not taking from his descendants rulers over the descendants of Abraham, Isaac, and Jacob. But I will restore their fortunes
and will have mercy on them.' "

*A Prophecy against Zedekiah*

**34** THE WORD which came to Jeremiah from the LORD,
when Nebuchadnezzar king of Babylon and all his army,
with all the kingdoms of the earth that were under his dominion
and all the peoples, were fighting against Jerusalem and against
all its cities, saying,
2"Thus says the LORD God of Israel, 'Go and speak to Zedekiah
king of Judah and say to him: "Thus says the LORD, 'Behold, I am
giving this city into the hand of the king of Babylon, and he will
burn it with fire.
3'And you will not escape from his hand, for you will surely
be captured and delivered into his hand; and you will see the king
of Babylon eye to eye, and he will speak with you face to face, and
you will go to Babylon.' " '
4"Yet hear the word of the LORD, O Zedekiah king of Judah!
Thus says the LORD concerning you, 'You will not die by the
sword.
5'You will die in peace; and as spices were burned for your
fathers, the former kings who were before you, so they will burn
spices for you; and they will lament for you, "Alas, lord!" ' For I
have spoken the word," declares the LORD.
6¶ Then Jeremiah the prophet spoke all these words to Zedekiah king of Judah in Jerusalem
7when the army of the king of Babylon was fighting against
Jerusalem and against all the remaining cities of Judah, *that is*,
Lachish and Azekah, for they *alone* remained as fortified cities
among the cities of Judah.
8¶ The word which came to Jeremiah from the LORD, after King
Zedekiah had made a covenant with all the people who were in
Jerusalem to proclaim release to them:
9that each man should set free his male servant and each man
his female servant, a Hebrew man or a Hebrew woman; so that no
one should keep them, a Jew his brother, in bondage.
10And all the officials and all the people obeyed, who had
entered into the covenant that each man should set free his male
servant and each man his female servant, so that no one should
keep them any longer in bondage; they obeyed, and set *them free*.

## New International

17For this is what the LORD says: 'David will never fail to have a
man to sit on the throne of the house of Israel, 18nor will the
priests, who are Levites, ever fail to have a man to stand before
me continually to offer burnt offerings, to burn grain offerings and
to present sacrifices.' "
19The word of the LORD came to Jeremiah: 20"This is what the
LORD says: 'If you can break my covenant with the day and my
covenant with the night, so that day and night no longer come at
their appointed time, 21then my covenant with David my servant—and my covenant with the Levites who are priests ministering before me—can be broken and David will no longer have a
descendant to reign on his throne. 22I will make the descendants
of David my servant and the Levites who minister before me as
countless as the stars of the sky and as measureless as the sand on
the seashore.' "
23The word of the LORD came to Jeremiah: 24"Have you not
noticed that these people are saying, 'The LORD has rejected the
two kingdoms[a] he chose'? So they despise my people and no
longer regard them as a nation. 25This is what the LORD says: 'If
I have not established my covenant with day and night and the
fixed laws of heaven and earth, 26then I will reject the descendants
of Jacob and David my servant and will not choose one of his sons
to rule over the descendants of Abraham, Isaac and Jacob. For I will
restore their fortunes[b] and have compassion on them.' "

*Warning to Zedekiah*

**34** WHILE NEBUCHADNEZZAR king of Babylon and all his
army and all the kingdoms and peoples in the empire he
ruled were fighting against Jerusalem and all its surrounding
towns, this word came to Jeremiah from the LORD: 2"This is what
the LORD, the God of Israel, says: Go to Zedekiah king of Judah
and tell him, 'This is what the LORD says: I am about to hand this
city over to the king of Babylon, and he will burn it down. 3You
will not escape from his grasp but will surely be captured and
handed over to him. You will see the king of Babylon with your
own eyes, and he will speak with you face to face. And you will
go to Babylon.
4" 'Yet hear the promise of the LORD, O Zedekiah king of Judah.
This is what the LORD says concerning you: You will not die by the
sword; 5you will die peacefully. As people made a funeral fire in
honor of your fathers, the former kings who preceded you, so they
will make a fire in your honor and lament, "Alas, O master!" I
myself make this promise, declares the LORD.' "
6Then Jeremiah the prophet told all this to Zedekiah king of
Judah, in Jerusalem, 7while the army of the king of Babylon was
fighting against Jerusalem and the other cities of Judah that were
still holding out—Lachish and Azekah. These were the only fortified cities left in Judah.

*Freedom for Slaves*

8The word came to Jeremiah from the LORD after King Zedekiah
had made a covenant with all the people in Jerusalem to proclaim
freedom for the slaves. 9Everyone was to free his Hebrew slaves,
both male and female; no one was to hold a fellow Jew in bondage.
10So all the officials and people who entered into this covenant
agreed that they would free their male and female slaves and no
longer hold them in bondage. They agreed, and set them free.

NIV [a] 24 Or *families* [b] 26 Or *will bring them back from captivity*

## King James

11 But afterward they turned, and caused the servants and the handmaids, whom they had let go free, to return, and brought them into subjection for servants and for handmaids.

12 ¶ Therefore the word of the LORD came to Jeremiah from the LORD, saying,

13 Thus saith the LORD, the God of Israel; I made a covenant with your fathers in the day that I brought them forth out of the land of Egypt, out of the house of bondmen, saying,

14 At the end of seven years let ye go every man his brother an Hebrew, which hath been sold unto thee; and when he hath served thee six years, thou shalt let him go free from thee: but your fathers hearkened not unto me, neither inclined their ear.

15 And ye were now turned, and had done right in my sight, in proclaiming liberty every man to his neighbour; and ye had made a covenant before me in the house which is called by my name:

16 But ye turned and polluted my name, and caused every man his servant, and every man his handmaid, whom ye had set at liberty at their pleasure, to return, and brought them into subjection, to be unto you for servants and for handmaids.

17 Therefore thus saith the LORD; Ye have not hearkened unto me, in proclaiming liberty, every one to his brother, and every man to his neighbour: behold, I proclaim a liberty for you, saith the LORD, to the sword, to the pestilence, and to the famine; and I will make you to be removed into all the kingdoms of the earth.

18 And I will give the men that have transgressed my covenant, which have not performed the words of the covenant which they had made before me, when they cut the calf in twain, and passed between the parts thereof,

19 The princes of Judah, and the princes of Jerusalem, the eunuchs, and the priests, and all the people of the land, which passed between the parts of the calf;

20 I will even give them into the hand of their enemies, and into the hand of them that seek their life: and their dead bodies shall be for meat unto the fowls of the heaven, and to the beasts of the earth.

21 And Zedekiah king of Judah and his princes will I give into the hand of their enemies, and into the hand of them that seek their life, and into the hand of the king of Babylon's army, which are gone up from you.

22 Behold, I will command, saith the LORD, and cause them to return to this city; and they shall fight against it, and take it, and burn it with fire: and I will make the cities of Judah a desolation without an inhabitant.

**35** THE WORD which came unto Jeremiah from the LORD in the days of Jehoiakim the son of Josiah king of Judah, saying,

2 Go unto the house of the Rechabites, and speak unto them, and bring them into the house of the LORD, into one of the chambers, and give them wine to drink.

3 Then I took Jaazaniah the son of Jeremiah, the son of Habaziniah, and his brethren, and all his sons, and the whole house of the Rechabites;

4 And I brought them into the house of the LORD, into the chamber of the sons of Hanan, the son of Igdaliah, a man of God, which *was* by the chamber of the princes, which *was* above the chamber of Maaseiah the son of Shallum, the keeper of the door:

5 And I set before the sons of the house of the Rechabites pots full of wine, and cups, and I said unto them, Drink ye wine.

6 But they said, We will drink no wine: for Jonadab the son of Rechab our father commanded us, saying, Ye shall drink no wine, *neither* ye, nor your sons for ever:

## Amplified

11 But afterward they turned around and caused the servants and the handmaids, whom they had let go free, to return [to their former masters] and brought them into subjection for servants and for handmaids.

12 Therefore the word of the Lord came to Jeremiah from the Lord, saying,

13 Thus says the Lord, the God of Israel: I made a covenant with your fathers in the day that I brought them forth out of the land of Egypt, out of the house of bondage, saying,

14 At the end of seven years you shall let go free every man his brother who is a Hebrew, who has sold himself *or* been sold to you and has served you six years; but your fathers did not listen to Me *and* obey, nor inclined their ear—submitting and consenting to Me.

15 And you recently turned about *and* repented, doing what was right in My sight by proclaming liberty each man to his neighbor [who was his bondservant], and you made a covenant *or* pledge before Me in the house which is called by My name.

16 But then you turned about and defiled My name; each of you caused to return to him his servants, male and female, whom he had set free as they might desire, and brought them into subjection again to be your slaves.

17 Therefore thus says the Lord, You have not listened to Me *and* obeyed Me in proclaming liberty each one to his brother and neighbor. Behold, I proclaim to you liberty to the sword, to pestilence and to famine, says the Lord, and I will make you to be tossed to and fro *and* be a horror among all the kingdoms of the earth!

18 And the men who transgressed My covenant, who did not keep the terms of the pledge *or* covenant which they had made before Me, I will make them [like] the [sacrificial] calf which they cut in two and then passed between its separated parts [solemnizing their pledge to Me] I will make those men the calf! [Cf. Gen. 15:9, 10, 17.]

19 The princes of Judah, the princes of Jerusalem, the eunuchs, the priests, and all the people of the land, who passed between the parts of the calf;

20 I will give them into the hand of their enemies and into the hand of those who seek their life. And their dead bodies shall be for food for the birds of the heavens and the beasts of the earth.

21 And Zedekiah king of Judah and his princes will I give into the hand of their enemies and into the hand of those who seek their life, and into the hand of the king of Babylon's army which has withdrawn from you.

22 Behold, I will command, says the Lord, and cause [the Chaldeans] to return to this city; and they shall fight against it, and take it, and burn it with fire. I will make the cities of Judah a desolation without inhabitant.

**35** THE WORD which came to Jeremiah from the Lord in the days of Jehoiakim the son of Josiah, king of Judah:

2 Go to the house of the Rechabites, and speak to them and bring them into the house of the Lord, into one of the chambers; then give them [who are pledged to drink no wine] some wine to drink.

3 So I took Jaazaniah the son of Jeremiah, the son of Habazziniah, and his brothers and all his sons, and the whole house of the Rechabites;

4 And I brought them into the house of the Lord, into the chamber of the sons of Hanan the son of Igdaliah, the man of God, which was by the chamber of the princes, above the chamber of Maaseiah the son of Shallum the keeper of the door.

5 And I set before the sons of the house of the Rechabites pitchers full of wine, and cups; and I said to them, Drink wine.

6 But they said, We will drink no wine, for Jonadab the son of Rechab, our father, commanded us, You shall not drink wine, neither you nor your sons for ever.

## New American Standard

11But afterward they turned around and took back the male
servants and the female servants, whom they had set free, and
brought them into subjection for male servants and for female
servants.
12¶ Then the word of the LORD came to Jeremiah from the LORD,
saying,
13"Thus says the LORD God of Israel, 'I made a covenant with
your forefathers in the day that I brought them out of the land of
Egypt, from the house of bondage, saying,
14"At the end of seven years each of you shall set free his
Hebrew brother, who has been sold to you and has served you six
years, you shall send him out free from you; but your forefathers
did not obey Me, or incline their ear to Me.
15"Although recently you *had* turned and done what is right in
My sight, each man proclaiming release to his neighbor, and you
had made a covenant before Me in the house which is called by
My name.
16"Yet you turned and profaned My name, and each man took
back his male servant and each man his female servant, whom you
had set free according to their desire, and you brought them into
subjection to be your male servants and female servants."'
17¶ "Therefore thus says the LORD, 'You have not obeyed Me
in proclaiming release each man to his brother, and each man to
his neighbor. Behold, I am proclaiming a release to you,' declares
the LORD, 'to the sword, to the pestilence, and to the famine; and
I will make you a terror to all the kingdoms of the earth.
18'And I will give the men who have transgressed My covenant,
who have not fulfilled the words of the covenant which they made
before Me, *when* they cut the calf in two and passed between its
parts—
19the officials of Judah, and the officials of Jerusalem, the court
officers, and the priests, and all the people of the land, who passed
between the parts of the calf—
20and I will give them into the hand of their enemies and into
the hand of those who seek their life. And their dead bodies shall
be food for the birds of the sky and the beasts of the earth.
21'And Zedekiah king of Judah and his officials I will give into
the hand of their enemies, and into the hand of those who seek
their life, and into the hand of the army of the king of Babylon
which has gone away from you.
22'Behold, I am going to command,' declares the LORD, 'and I
will bring them back to this city; and they shall fight against it and
take it and burn it with fire; and I will make the cities of Judah a
desolation without inhabitant.'"

*The Rechabites' Obedience*

35 THE WORD which came to Jeremiah from the LORD in the
days of Jehoiakim the son of Josiah, king of Judah, saying,
2"Go to the house of the Rechabites, and speak to them, and
bring them into the house of the LORD, into one of the chambers,
and give them wine to drink."
3Then I took Jaazaniah the son of Jeremiah, son of Habazziniah, and his brothers, and all his sons, and the whole house of
the Rechabites,
4and I brought them into the house of the LORD, into the
chamber of the sons of Hanan the son of Igdaliah, the man of God,
which was near the chamber of the officials, which was above the
chamber of Maaseiah the son of Shallum, the doorkeeper.
5Then I set before the men of the house of the Rechabites
pitchers full of wine, and cups; and I said to them, "Drink wine!"
6But they said, "We will not drink wine, for Jonadab the son
of Rechab, our father, commanded us, saying, 'You shall not drink
wine, you or your sons, forever.

## New International

11But afterward they changed their minds and took back the slaves
they had freed and enslaved them again.
12Then the word of the LORD came to Jeremiah: 13"This is what
the LORD, the God of Israel, says: I made a covenant with your
forefathers when I brought them out of Egypt, out of the land of
slavery. I said, 14'Every seventh year each of you must free any
fellow Hebrew who has sold himself to you. After he has served
you six years, you must let him go free.'[a] Your fathers, however,
did not listen to me or pay attention to me. 15Recently you repented and did what is right in my sight: Each of you proclaimed
freedom to his countrymen. You even made a covenant before me
in the house that bears my Name. 16But now you have turned
around and profaned my name; each of you has taken back the
male and female slaves you had set free to go where they wished.
You have forced them to become your slaves again.
17"Therefore, this is what the LORD says: You have not obeyed
me; you have not proclaimed freedom for your fellow countrymen.
So I now proclaim 'freedom' for you, declares the LORD—'freedom'
to fall by the sword, plague and famine. I will make you abhorrent
to all the kingdoms of the earth. 18The men who have violated my
covenant and have not fulfilled the terms of the covenant they
made before me, I will treat like the calf they cut in two and then
walked between its pieces. 19The leaders of Judah and Jerusalem,
the court officials, the priests and all the people of the land who
walked between the pieces of the calf, 20I will hand over to their
enemies who seek their lives. Their dead bodies will become food
for the birds of the air and the beasts of the earth.
21"I will hand Zedekiah king of Judah and his officials over to
their enemies who seek their lives, to the army of the king of
Babylon, which has withdrawn from you. 22I am going to give the
order, declares the LORD, and I will bring them back to this city.
They will fight against it, take it and burn it down. And I will lay
waste the towns of Judah so no one can live there."

*The Recabites*

35 THIS IS the word that came to Jeremiah from the LORD
during the reign of Jehoiakim son of Josiah king of Judah:
2"Go to the Recabite family and invite them to come to one of the
side rooms of the house of the LORD and give them wine to drink."
3So I went to get Jaazaniah son of Jeremiah, the son of Habazziniah, and his brothers and all his sons—the whole family of the
Recabites. 4I brought them into the house of the LORD, into the
room of the sons of Hanan son of Igdaliah the man of God. It was
next to the room of the officials, which was over that of Maaseiah
son of Shallum the doorkeeper. 5Then I set bowls full of wine and
some cups before the men of the Recabite family and said to them,
"Drink some wine."
6But they replied, "We do not drink wine, because our forefather Jonadab son of Recab gave us this command: 'Neither you
nor your descendants must ever drink wine. 7Also you must never

NIV [a] *14* Deut. 15:12

## King James

7Neither shall ye build house, nor sow seed, nor plant vineyard, nor have *any:* but all your days ye shall dwell in tents; that ye may live many days in the land where ye *be* strangers.

8Thus have we obeyed the voice of Jonadab the son of Rechab our father in all that he hath charged us, to drink no wine all our days, we, our wives, our sons, nor our daughters;

9Nor to build houses for us to dwell in: neither have we vineyard, nor field, nor seed:

10But we have dwelt in tents, and have obeyed, and done according to all that Jonadab our father commanded us.

11But it came to pass, when Nebuchadrezzar king of Babylon came up into the land, that we said, Come, and let us go to Jerusalem for fear of the army of the Chaldeans, and for fear of the army of the Syrians: so we dwell at Jerusalem.

12¶ Then came the word of the LORD unto Jeremiah, saying,

13Thus saith the LORD of hosts, the God of Israel; Go and tell the men of Judah and the inhabitants of Jerusalem, Will ye not receive instruction to hearken to my words? saith the LORD.

14The words of Jonadab the son of Rechab, that he commanded his sons not to drink wine, are performed; for unto this day they drink none, but obey their father's commandment: notwithstanding I have spoken unto you, rising early and speaking; but ye hearkened not unto me.

15I have sent also unto you all my servants the prophets, rising up early and sending *them,* saying, Return ye now every man from his evil way, and amend your doings, and go not after other gods to serve them, and ye shall dwell in the land which I have given to you and to your fathers: but ye have not inclined your ear, nor hearkened unto me.

16Because the sons of Jonadab the son of Rechab have performed the commandment of their father, which he commanded them; but this people hath not hearkened unto me:

17Therefore thus saith the LORD God of hosts, the God of Israel; Behold, I will bring upon Judah and upon all the inhabitants of Jerusalem all the evil that I have pronounced against them: because I have spoken unto them, but they have not heard; and I have called unto them, but they have not answered.

18¶ And Jeremiah said unto the house of the Rechabites, Thus saith the LORD of hosts, the God of Israel; Because ye have obeyed the commandment of Jonadab your father, and kept all his precepts, and done according unto all that he hath commanded you:

19Therefore thus saith the LORD of hosts, the God of Israel; Jonadab the son of Rechab shall not want a man to stand before me for ever.

**36** AND IT came to pass in the fourth year of Jehoiakim the son of Josiah king of Judah, *that* this word came unto Jeremiah from the LORD, saying,

2Take thee a roll of a book, and write therein all the words that I have spoken unto thee against Israel, and against Judah, and against all the nations, from the day I spake unto thee, from the days of Josiah, even unto this day.

3It may be that the house of Judah will hear all the evil which I purpose to do unto them; that they may return every man from his evil way; that I may forgive their iniquity and their sin.

4Then Jeremiah called Baruch the son of Neriah: and Baruch wrote from the mouth of Jeremiah all the words of the LORD, which he had spoken unto him, upon a roll of a book.

5And Jeremiah commanded Baruch, saying, I *am* shut up; I cannot go into the house of the LORD:

## Amplified

7Neither shall you build a house or sow seed or plant a vineyard or have them; but you shall dwell all your days in tents, that you may live many days in the land where you are temporary residents.

8And we have obeyed the voice of Jonadab the son of Rechab, our father, in all that he charged us, to drink no wine all our days, we, our wives, our sons, and our daughters,

9And not to build ourselves houses to live in; nor do we have vineyard or field or seed.

10But we have dwelt in tents, and have obeyed and done according to all that Jonadab our ancestor commanded us.

11But when Nebuchadrezzar king of Babylon came up against the land, we said, Come, and let us go to Jerusalem for fear of the army of the Chaldeans and the army of the Syrians. So we are living in Jerusalem.

12Then came the word of the Lord to Jeremiah:

13Thus says the Lord of hosts, the God of Israel: Go and say to the men of Judah and the inhabitants of Jerusalem, Will you not receive instruction and listen to My words *and* obey them? says the Lord.

14The command which Jonadab the son of Rechab gave to his sons not to drink wine, has been carried out *and* established [as a custom for more than two hundred years]; to this day they drink no *wine,* but have obeyed their father's command. But I, even I, have persistently spoken to you, but you have not listened *and* obeyed Me.

15I have sent also to you all My servants the prophets earnestly *and* persistently, saying, Return now every man from his evil way, and amend your doings, and go not after other gods to serve them, and then you shall dwell in the land which I have given to you and to your fathers. But you did not submit *and* consent to Me or listen *and* obey Me.

16Since the sons of Jonadab the son of Rechab have fulfilled *and* established the command of their father which he commanded them, but this people has not listened and obeyed Me,

17Therefore thus says the Lord God of hosts, the God of Israel: Behold, I am bringing upon Judah and all the inhabitants of Jerusalem all the evil that I have pronounced against them; because I have spoken to them but they have not listened, and I have called to them but they have not answered.

18And Jeremiah said to the house of the Rechabites, Thus says the Lord of hosts, the God of Israel: Because you have obeyed the commandment of Jonadab your father, and kept all his precepts, and done according to all that he commanded you;

19Therefore thus says the Lord of hosts, the God of Israel: Jonadab the son of Rechab shall never lack a man [descendant] to stand before Me.

**36** IN THE fourth year of Jehoiakim the son of Josiah, king of Judah, this word came to Jeremiah from the Lord:

2Take a scroll [of parchment] for a book and write on it all the words that I have spoken to you against Israel and Judah and all the nations, from the day I spoke to you in the days of [King] Josiah until this day.

3It may be that the house of Judah will hear all the evil which I purpose to do to them, so that every one may return from his evil way, that I may forgive their iniquity and their sin.

4Then Jeremiah called Baruch the son of Neriah, and Baruch wrote upon the scroll of the book all the words which Jeremiah dictated that the Lord had spoken to him.

5And Jeremiah commanded Baruch, saying, I am [in hiding, so virtually] restrained *and* shut up; I cannot go into the house of the Lord.

## New American Standard

7'And you shall not build a house, and you shall not sow seed,
and you shall not plant a vineyard or own one; but in tents you
shall dwell all your days, that you may live many days in the land
where you sojourn.'
8"And we have obeyed the voice of Jonadab the son of Rechab,
our father, in all that he commanded us, not to drink wine all our
days, we, our wives, our sons, or our daughters,
9nor to build ourselves houses to dwell in; and we do not have
vineyard or field or seed.
10"We have only dwelt in tents, and have obeyed, and have
done according to all that Jonadab our father commanded us.
11"But it came about, when Nebuchadnezzar king of Babylon
came up against the land, that we said, 'Come and let us go to
Jerusalem before the army of the Chaldeans and before the army
of the Arameans.' So we have dwelt in Jerusalem."

*Judah Rebuked*

12¶ Then the word of the LORD came to Jeremiah, saying,
13"Thus says the LORD of hosts, the God of Israel, 'Go and say
to the men of Judah and the inhabitants of Jerusalem, "Will you
not receive instruction by listening to My words?" declares the
LORD.
14"The words of Jonadab the son of Rechab, which he commanded his sons not to drink wine, are observed. So they do not
drink *wine* to this day, for they have obeyed their father's command. But I have spoken to you again and again; yet you have not
listened to Me.
15"Also I have sent to you all My servants the prophets, sending
*them* again and again, saying: 'Turn now every man from his evil
way, and amend your deeds, and do not go after other gods to
worship them, then you shall dwell in the land which I have given
to you and to your forefathers; but you have not inclined your ear
or listened to Me.
16'Indeed, the sons of Jonadab the son of Rechab have observed
the command of their father which he commanded them, but this
people has not listened to Me.'"'
17"Therefore thus says the LORD, the God of hosts, the God of
Israel, 'Behold, I am bringing on Judah and on all the inhabitants
of Jerusalem all the disaster that I have pronounced against them;
because I spoke to them but they did not listen, and I have called
them but they did not answer.'"
18¶ Then Jeremiah said to the house of the Rechabites, "Thus
says the LORD of hosts, the God of Israel, 'Because you have
obeyed the command of Jonadab your father, kept all his commands, and done according to all that he commanded you;
19therefore thus says the LORD of hosts, the God of Israel,
"Jonadab the son of Rechab shall not lack a man to stand before
Me always."'"

*Jeremiah's Scroll Read in the Temple*

36 AND IT came about in the fourth year of Jehoiakim the son
of Josiah, king of Judah, that this word came to Jeremiah
from the LORD, saying,
2"Take a scroll and write on it all the words which I have
spoken to you concerning Israel, and concerning Judah, and concerning all the nations, from the day I *first* spoke to you, from the
days of Josiah, even to this day.
3"Perhaps the house of Judah will hear all the calamity which
I plan to bring on them, in order that every man will turn from his
evil way; then I will forgive their iniquity and their sin."
4¶ Then Jeremiah called Baruch the son of Neriah, and Baruch
wrote at the dictation of Jeremiah all the words of the LORD, which
He had spoken to him, on a scroll.
5And Jeremiah commanded Baruch, saying, "I am restricted;
I cannot go into the house of the LORD.

## New International

build houses, sow seed or plant vineyards; you must never have
any of these things, but must always live in tents. Then you will
live a long time in the land where you are nomads.' 8We have
obeyed everything our forefather Jonadab son of Recab commanded us. Neither we nor our wives nor our sons and daughters
have ever drunk wine 9or built houses to live in or had vineyards,
fields or crops. 10We have lived in tents and have fully obeyed
everything our forefather Jonadab commanded us. 11But when
Nebuchadnezzar king of Babylon invaded this land, we said,
'Come, we must go to Jerusalem to escape the Babylonian[a] and
Aramean armies.' So we have remained in Jerusalem."
12Then the word of the LORD came to Jeremiah, saying: 13"This
is what the LORD Almighty, the God of Israel, says: Go and tell the
men of Judah and the people of Jerusalem, 'Will you not learn a
lesson and obey my words?' declares the LORD. 14'Jonadab son of
Recab ordered his sons not to drink wine and this command has
been kept. To this day they do not drink wine, because they obey
their forefather's command. But I have spoken to you again and
again, yet you have not obeyed me. 15Again and again I sent all
my servants the prophets to you. They said, "Each of you must
turn from your wicked ways and reform your actions; do not
follow other gods to serve them. Then you will live in the land I
have given to you and your fathers." But you have not paid attention or listened to me. 16The descendants of Jonadab son of Recab
have carried out the command their forefather gave them, but
these people have not obeyed me.'
17"Therefore, this is what the LORD God Almighty, the God of
Israel, says: 'Listen! I am going to bring on Judah and on everyone
living in Jerusalem every disaster I pronounced against them. I
spoke to them, but they did not listen; I called to them, but they
did not answer.'"
18Then Jeremiah said to the family of the Recabites, "This is
what the LORD Almighty, the God of Israel, says: 'You have obeyed
the command of your forefather Jonadab and have followed all his
instructions and have done everything he ordered.' 19Therefore,
this is what the LORD Almighty, the God of Israel, says: 'Jonadab
son of Recab will never fail to have a man to serve me.'"

*Jehoiakim Burns Jeremiah's Scroll*

36 IN THE fourth year of Jehoiakim son of Josiah king of
Judah, this word came to Jeremiah from the LORD: 2"Take
a scroll and write on it all the words I have spoken to you concerning Israel, Judah and all the other nations from the time I began
speaking to you in the reign of Josiah till now. 3Perhaps when the
people of Judah hear about every disaster I plan to inflict on them,
each of them will turn from his wicked way; then I will forgive their
wickedness and their sin."
4So Jeremiah called Baruch son of Neriah, and while Jeremiah
dictated all the words the LORD had spoken to him, Baruch wrote
them on the scroll. 5Then Jeremiah told Baruch, "I am restricted;
I cannot go to the LORD's temple. 6So you go to the house of the

NIV [a] 11 Or *Chaldean*

## King James

6 Therefore go thou, and read in the roll, which thou hast written from my mouth, the words of the LORD in the ears of the people in the LORD's house upon the fasting day: and also thou shalt read them in the ears of all Judah that come out of their cities.

7 It may be they will present their supplication before the LORD, and will return every one from his evil way: for great *is* the anger and the fury that the LORD hath pronounced against this people.

8 And Baruch the son of Neriah did according to all that Jeremiah the prophet commanded him, reading in the book the words of the LORD in the LORD's house.

9 And it came to pass in the fifth year of Jehoiakim the son of Josiah king of Judah, in the ninth month, *that* they proclaimed a fast before the LORD to all the people in Jerusalem, and to all the people that came from the cities of Judah unto Jerusalem.

10 Then read Baruch in the book the words of Jeremiah in the house of the LORD, in the chamber of Gemariah the son of Shaphan the scribe, in the higher court, at the entry of the new gate of the LORD's house, in the ears of all the people.

11 ¶ When Michaiah the son of Gemariah, the son of Shaphan, had heard out of the book all the words of the LORD,

12 Then he went down into the king's house, into the scribe's chamber: and, lo, all the princes sat there, *even* Elishama the scribe, and Delaiah the son of Shemaiah, and Elnathan the son of Achbor, and Gemariah the son of Shaphan, and Zedekiah the son of Hananiah, and all the princes.

13 Then Michaiah declared unto them all the words that he had heard, when Baruch read the book in the ears of the people.

14 Therefore all the princes sent Jehudi the son of Nethaniah, the son of Shelemiah, the son of Cushi, unto Baruch, saying, Take in thine hand the roll wherein thou hast read in the ears of the people, and come. So Baruch the son of Neriah took the roll in his hand, and came unto them.

15 And they said unto him, Sit down now, and read it in our ears. So Baruch read *it* in their ears.

16 Now it came to pass, when they had heard all the words, they were afraid both one and other, and said unto Baruch, We will surely tell the king of all these words.

17 And they asked Baruch, saying, Tell us now, How didst thou write all these words at his mouth?

18 Then Baruch answered them, He pronounced all these words unto me with his mouth, and I wrote *them* with ink in the book.

19 Then said the princes unto Baruch, Go, hide thee, thou and Jeremiah; and let no man know where ye be.

20 ¶ And they went in to the king into the court, but they laid up the roll in the chamber of Elishama the scribe, and told all the words in the ears of the king.

21 So the king sent Jehudi to fetch the roll: and he took it out of Elishama the scribe's chamber. And Jehudi read it in the ears of the king, and in the ears of all the princes which stood beside the king.

22 Now the king sat in the winterhouse in the ninth month: and *there was a fire* on the hearth burning before him.

23 And it came to pass, *that* when Jehudi had read three or four leaves, he cut it with the penknife, and cast *it* into the fire that *was* on the hearth, until all the roll was consumed in the fire that *was* on the hearth.

24 Yet they were not afraid, nor rent their garments, *neither* the king, nor any of his servants that heard all these words.

25 Nevertheless Elnathan and Delaiah and Gemariah had made intercession to the king that he would not burn the roll: but he would not hear them.

26 But the king commanded Jerahmeel the son of Hammelech, and Seraiah the son of Azriel, and Shelemiah the son of Abdeel, to take Baruch the scribe and Jeremiah the prophet: but the LORD hid them.

## Amplified

6 Therefore you go, and on a fast day in the hearing of all the people in the Lord's house you shall read the words of the Lord which you have written on the scroll at my dictation. Also you shall read them in the hearing of all who come out of the cities of Judah.

7 It may be they will make their supplication [for mercy] before the Lord, and each one will turn back from his evil way, for great is the anger and the wrath that the Lord has pronounced against this people.

8 And Baruch the son of Neriah did according to all that Jeremiah the prophet commanded him, reading from [Jeremiah's] book the words of the Lord in the Lord's house.

9 And in the fifth year of Jehoiakim the son of Josiah, king of Judah, in the ninth month, a fast was proclaimed before the Lord for all the people in Jerusalem and all the people who came to Jerusalem from the cities of Judah.

10 Then Baruch read in the hearing of all the people the words of Jeremiah from the scroll of the book, in the house of the Lord, in the chamber of Gemariah the son of Shaphan the scribe, in the upper court, at the entry of the New Gate of the Lord's house.

11 When Micaiah the son of Gemariah, the son of Shaphan, had heard out of the book all the words of the Lord,

12 He went down to the king's house into the scribe's chamber; and lo, all the princes were sitting there: Elishama the scribe, Delaiah the son of Shemaiah, Elnathan the son of Achbor, Gemariah the son of Shaphan, Zedekiah the son of Hananiah, and all the princes.

13 Then Micaiah declared to them all the words that he had heard, when Baruch read the book in the hearing of the people.

14 Therefore all the princes sent Jehudi the son of Nethaniah, son of Shelemiah, son of Cushi, to Baruch, saying, Take in your hand the scroll from which you have read in the hearing of the people and come *to us*. So Baruch the son of Neriah took the scroll in his hand and came to them.

15 And they said to him, Sit down now and read it in our hearing. So Baruch read it in their hearing.

16 Now when they had heard all the words, they turned one to another in fear, and they said to Baruch, We must surely tell the king of all these words.

17 And they asked Baruch, Tell us now, how did you write all these words? At [Jeremiah's] dictation?

18 Then Baruch answered them, He dictated all these words to me, and I wrote them with ink in the book.

19 Then the princes said to Baruch, Go and hide, you and Jeremiah, and let no one know where you are.

20 Then they went into the court to the king, but they [first] put the scroll in the chamber of Elishama the scribe; then they reported all the words to the king.

21 So the king sent Jehudi to bring the scroll, and he took it out of the chamber of Elishama the scribe. And Jehudi read it in the hearing of the king and of all the princes who stood beside the king.

22 Now it was the ninth month, and the king was sitting in the winter house and a fire was burning there before him in the brazier.

23 And [each time] when Jehudi had read three or four columns, [King Jehoiakim] would cut *them* off with a penknife, and cast *them* into the fire that was in the brazier, until the entire scroll was consumed in the fire that was in the brazier.

24 Yet they were not afraid, nor did they rend their garments, neither the king, nor any of his servants who heard all these words.

25 Even when Elnathan and Delaiah and Gemariah tried to persuade the king not to burn the scroll, he would not listen to them.

26 And the king commanded Jerahmeel the king's son and Seraiah the son of Azriel and Shelemiah the son of Abdeel to seize Baruch the scribe and Jeremiah the prophet, but the Lord hid them.

## New American Standard

6"So you go and read from the scroll which you have written at my dictation the words of the LORD to the people in the LORD's house on a fast day. And also you shall read them to all *the people of* Judah who come from their cities.

7"Perhaps their supplication will come before the LORD, and everyone will turn from his evil way, for great is the anger and the wrath that the LORD has pronounced against this people."

8And Baruch the son of Neriah did according to all that Jeremiah the prophet commanded him, reading from the book the words of the LORD in the LORD's house.

9¶ Now it came about in the fifth year of Jehoiakim the son of Josiah, king of Judah, in the ninth month, that all the people in Jerusalem and all the people who came from the cities of Judah to Jerusalem proclaimed a fast before the LORD.

10Then Baruch read from the book the words of Jeremiah in the house of the LORD in the chamber of Gemariah the son of Shaphan the scribe, in the upper court, at the entry of the New Gate of the LORD's house, to all the people.

11¶ Now when Micaiah the son of Gemariah, the son of Shaphan, had heard all the words of the LORD from the book,

12he went down to the king's house, into the scribe's chamber. And, behold, all the officials were sitting there—Elishama the scribe, and Delaiah the son of Shemaiah, and Elnathan the son of Achbor, and Gemariah the son of Shaphan, and Zedekiah the son of Hananiah, and all the *other* officials.

13And Micaiah declared to them all the words that he had heard, when Baruch read from the book to the people.

14Then all the officials sent Jehudi the son of Nethaniah, the son of Shelemiah, the son of Cushi, to Baruch, saying, "Take in your hand the scroll from which you have read to the people and come." So Baruch the son of Neriah took the scroll in his hand and went to them.

15And they said to him, "Sit down please, and read it to us." So Baruch read it to them.

16Now it came about when they had heard all the words, they turned in fear one to another and said to Baruch, "We will surely report all these words to the king."

17And they asked Baruch, saying, "Tell us please, how did you write all these words? *Was it* at his dictation?"

18Then Baruch said to them, "He dictated all these words to me, and I wrote them with ink on the book."

19Then the officials said to Baruch, "Go, hide yourself, you and Jeremiah, and do not let anyone know where you are."

*The Scroll Is Burned*

20¶ So they went to the king in the court, but they had deposited the scroll in the chamber of Elishama the scribe, and they reported all the words to the king.

21Then the king sent Jehudi to get the scroll, and he took it out of the chamber of Elishama the scribe. And Jehudi read it to the king as well as to all the officials who stood beside the king.

22Now the king was sitting in the winter house in the ninth month, with *a fire* burning in the brazier before him.

23And it came about, when Jehudi had read three or four columns, *the king* cut it with a scribe's knife and threw *it* into the fire that was in the brazier, until all the scroll was consumed in the fire that was in the brazier.

24Yet the king and all his servants who heard all these words were not afraid, nor did they rend their garments.

25Even though Elnathan and Delaiah and Gemariah entreated the king not to burn the scroll, he would not listen to them.

26And the king commanded Jerahmeel the king's son, Seraiah the son of Azriel, and Shelemiah the son of Abdeel to seize Baruch the scribe and Jeremiah the prophet, but the LORD hid them.

## New International

LORD on a day of fasting and read to the people from the scroll the words of the LORD that you wrote as I dictated. Read them to all the people of Judah who come in from their towns. 7Perhaps they will bring their petition before the LORD, and each will turn from his wicked ways, for the anger and wrath pronounced against this people by the LORD are great."

8Baruch son of Neriah did everything Jeremiah the prophet told him to do; at the LORD's temple he read the words of the LORD from the scroll. 9In the ninth month of the fifth year of Jehoiakim son of Josiah king of Judah, a time of fasting before the LORD was proclaimed for all the people in Jerusalem and those who had come from the towns of Judah. 10From the room of Gemariah son of Shaphan the secretary, which was in the upper courtyard at the entrance of the New Gate of the temple, Baruch read to all the people at the LORD's temple the words of Jeremiah from the scroll.

11When Micaiah son of Gemariah, the son of Shaphan, heard all the words of the LORD from the scroll, 12he went down to the secretary's room in the royal palace, where all the officials were sitting: Elishama the secretary, Delaiah son of Shemaiah, Elnathan son of Acbor, Gemariah son of Shaphan, Zedekiah son of Hananiah, and all the other officials. 13After Micaiah told them everything he had heard Baruch read to the people from the scroll, 14all the officials sent Jehudi son of Nethaniah, the son of Shelemiah, the son of Cushi, to say to Baruch, "Bring the scroll from which you have read to the people and come." So Baruch son of Neriah went to them with the scroll in his hand. 15They said to him, "Sit down, please, and read it to us."

So Baruch read it to them. 16When they heard all these words, they looked at each other in fear and said to Baruch, "We must report all these words to the king." 17Then they asked Baruch, "Tell us, how did you come to write all this? Did Jeremiah dictate it?"

18"Yes," Baruch replied, "he dictated all these words to me, and I wrote them in ink on the scroll."

19Then the officials said to Baruch, "You and Jeremiah, go and hide. Don't let anyone know where you are."

20After they put the scroll in the room of Elishama the secretary, they went to the king in the courtyard and reported everything to him. 21The king sent Jehudi to get the scroll, and Jehudi brought it from the room of Elishama the secretary and read it to the king and all the officials standing beside him. 22It was the ninth month and the king was sitting in the winter apartment, with a fire burning in the firepot in front of him. 23Whenever Jehudi had read three or four columns of the scroll, the king cut them off with a scribe's knife and threw them into the firepot, until the entire scroll was burned in the fire. 24The king and all his attendants who heard all these words showed no fear, nor did they tear their clothes. 25Even though Elnathan, Delaiah and Gemariah urged the king not to burn the scroll, he would not listen to them. 26Instead, the king commanded Jerahmeel, a son of the king, Seraiah son of Azriel and Shelemiah son of Abdeel to arrest Baruch the scribe and Jeremiah the prophet. But the LORD had hidden them.

## King James

27¶ Then the word of the LORD came to Jeremiah, after that the king had burned the roll, and the words which Baruch wrote at the mouth of Jeremiah, saying,

28Take thee again another roll, and write in it all the former words that were in the first roll, which Jehoiakim the king of Judah hath burned.

29And thou shalt say to Jehoiakim king of Judah, Thus saith the LORD; Thou hast burned this roll, saying, Why hast thou written therein, saying, The king of Babylon shall certainly come and destroy this land, and shall cause to cease from thence man and beast?

30Therefore thus saith the LORD of Jehoiakim king of Judah; He shall have none to sit upon the throne of David: and his dead body shall be cast out in the day to the heat, and in the night to the frost.

31And I will punish him and his seed and his servants for their iniquity; and I will bring upon them, and upon the inhabitants of Jerusalem, and upon the men of Judah, all the evil that I have pronounced against them; but they hearkened not.

32¶ Then took Jeremiah another roll, and gave it to Baruch the scribe, the son of Neriah; who wrote therein from the mouth of Jeremiah all the words of the book which Jehoiakim king of Judah had burned in the fire: and there were added besides unto them many like words.

**37** AND KING Zedekiah the son of Josiah reigned instead of Coniah the son of Jehoiakim, whom Nebuchadrezzar king of Babylon made king in the land of Judah.

2But neither he, nor his servants, nor the people of the land, did hearken unto the words of the LORD, which he spake by the prophet Jeremiah.

3And Zedekiah the king sent Jehucal the son of Shelemiah and Zephaniah the son of Maaseiah the priest to the prophet Jeremiah, saying, Pray now unto the LORD our God for us.

4Now Jeremiah came in and went out among the people: for they had not put him into prison.

5Then Pharaoh's army was come forth out of Egypt: and when the Chaldeans that besieged Jerusalem heard tidings of them, they departed from Jerusalem.

6¶ Then came the word of the LORD unto the prophet Jeremiah, saying,

7Thus saith the LORD, the God of Israel; Thus shall ye say to the king of Judah, that sent you unto me to inquire of me; Behold, Pharaoh's army, which is come forth to help you, shall return to Egypt into their own land.

8And the Chaldeans shall come again, and fight against this city, and take it, and burn it with fire.

9Thus saith the LORD; Deceive not yourselves, saying, The Chaldeans shall surely depart from us: for they shall not depart.

10For though ye had smitten the whole army of the Chaldeans that fight against you, and there remained *but* wounded men among them, *yet* should they rise up every man in his tent, and burn this city with fire.

11¶ And it came to pass, that when the army of the Chaldeans was broken up from Jerusalem for fear of Pharaoh's army,

12Then Jeremiah went forth out of Jerusalem to go into the land of Benjamin, to separate himself thence in the midst of the people.

## Amplified

27Now the word of the Lord came to Jeremiah, after the king had burned the scroll with the words which Baruch wrote at the dictation of Jeremiah, [and the Lord] said:

28Take another scroll and write on it all the former words that were in the first scroll, which Jehoiakim the king of Judah has burned.

29And concerning Jehoiakim king of Judah you shall say, Thus says the Lord: You have burned this scroll saying. Why have you written in it, The king of Babylon shall surely come and destroy this land, and shall cut off man and beast from it?

30Therefore thus says the Lord concerning Jehoiakim king of Judah: [a]He shall have no [heir] to sit upon the throne of David, and his dead body shall be cast out to the heat by day and to the frost by night.

31And I will punish him and his offspring and his servants for their iniquity; and I will bring upon them and the inhabitants of Jerusalem and the men of Judah, all the evil that I have pronounced against them, but they would not hear.

32Then Jeremiah took another scroll and gave it to Baruch the scribe, the son of Neriah, who wrote on it at the dictation of Jeremiah all the words of the book which Jehoiakim king of Judah had burned in the fire; and besides them many similar words were added.

**37** AND ZEDEKIAH the son of Josiah, whom Nebuchadrezzar king of Babylon made king in the land of Judah, reigned instead of Coniah (Jeconiah) the son of Jehoiakim.

2But neither he nor his servants nor the people of the land listened to *and* obeyed the words of the Lord which he spoke through the prophet Jeremiah.

3Zedekiah the king sent Jehucal the son of Shelemiah, and Zephaniah the son of Maaseiah, the priest, to the prophet Jeremiah, saying, Pray now to the Lord our God for us.

4Now Jeremiah was coming in and going out among the people, for they had not [yet] put him in prison.

5And Pharaoh's army had come forth out of Egypt, and when the Chaldeans who were besieging Jerusalem heard news of them, they withdrew from Jerusalem *and* departed.

6Then came the word of the Lord to the prophet Jeremiah:

7Thus says the Lord, God of Israel: Thus shall you say to the king of Judah who sent you to Me to inquire of Me: Behold, Pharaoh's army, which has come forth to help you, will return to Egypt into their own land.

8And the Chaldeans shall come again and fight against this city, and they shall take it and burn it with fire.

9Thus says the Lord: Deceive not yourselves, saying, The Chaldeans will surely stay away from us, for they shall not stay away.

10For though you should defeat the whole army of the Chaldeans who fight against you, and there remained but the wounded *and* men stricken through among them, every man confined to his tent, yet they would rise up and burn this city with fire.

11And when the army of the Chaldeans had departed from Jerusalem for fear of Pharaoh's approaching army,

12Jeremiah went forth out of Jerusalem to go into the land of Benjamin, to slip away *and* receive [the title to] his portion [of land, which the Lord had promised would eventually be valuable] there among the people.

**AMP** [a] This prophecy against King Jehoiakim was literally fulfilled. Several years after these events the king rebelled against Babylon (II Kings 24:1), and was attacked by numerous bands from various nations subject to Babylon (II Kings 24:2). He thus came to a violent death and a disgraceful burial such as Jeremiah had foretold many chapters previous to this one (Jer. 22:13-19). There, after stern censure of the king, the Lord foretells through his prophet that Jehoiakim will "be buried with the burial of a donkey, dragged out and cast forth beyond the gates of Jerusalem." How could Jeremiah possibly have foreseen these events except by divine inspiration?

## New American Standard

*The Scroll Is Replaced*

27¶ Then the word of the LORD came to Jeremiah after the king had burned the scroll and the words which Baruch had written at the dictation of Jeremiah, saying,

28"Take again another scroll and write on it all the former words that were on the first scroll which Jehoiakim the king of Judah burned.

29"And concerning Jehoiakim king of Judah you shall say, 'Thus says the LORD, "You have burned this scroll, saying, 'Why have you written on it that the king of Babylon shall certainly come and destroy this land, and shall make man and beast to cease from it?' "

30'Therefore thus says the LORD concerning Jehoiakim king of Judah, "He shall have no one to sit on the throne of David, and his dead body shall be cast out to the heat of the day and the frost of the night.

31"I shall also punish him and his descendants and his servants for their iniquity, and I shall bring on them and the inhabitants of Jerusalem and the men of Judah all the calamity that I have declared to them—but they did not listen." ' "

32Then Jeremiah took another scroll and gave it to Baruch the son of Neraiah, the scribe, and he wrote on it at the dictation of Jeremiah all the words of the book which Jehoiakim king of Judah had burned in the fire; and many similar words were added to them.

*Jeremiah Warns against Trust in Pharaoh*

**37** NOW ZEDEKIAH the son of Josiah whom Nebuchadnezzar king of Babylon had made king in the land of Judah, reigned as king in place of Coniah the son of Jehoiakim.

2But neither he nor his servants nor the people of the land listened to the words of the LORD which He spoke through Jeremiah the prophet.

3¶ Yet King Zedekiah sent Jehucal the son of Shelemiah, and Zephaniah the son of Maaseiah, the priest, to Jeremiah the prophet, saying, "Please pray to the LORD our God on our behalf."

4Now Jeremiah was *still* coming in and going out among the people, for they had not *yet* put him in the prison.

5Meanwhile, Pharaoh's army had set out from Egypt; and when the Chaldeans who had been besieging Jerusalem heard the report about them, they lifted the *siege* from Jerusalem.

6¶ Then the word of the LORD came to Jeremiah the prophet, saying,

7"Thus says the LORD God of Israel, 'Thus you are to say to the king of Judah, who sent you to Me to inquire of Me: "Behold, Pharaoh's army which has come out for your assistance is going to return to its own land of Egypt.

8"The Chaldeans will also return and fight against this city, and they will capture it and burn it with fire." '

9"Thus says the LORD, 'Do not deceive yourselves, saying, "The Chaldeans will surely go away from us," for they will not go.

10'For even if you had defeated the entire army of Chaldeans who were fighting against you, and there were *only* wounded men left among them, each man in his tent, they would rise up and burn this city with fire.' "

*Jeremiah Imprisoned*

11¶ Now it happened, when the army of the Chaldeans had lifted *the siege* from Jerusalem because of Pharaoh's army,

12that Jeremiah went out from Jerusalem to go to the land of Benjamin in order to take possession of *some* property there among the people.

## New International

27After the king burned the scroll containing the words that Baruch had written at Jeremiah's dictation, the word of the LORD came to Jeremiah: 28"Take another scroll and write on it all the words that were on the first scroll, which Jehoiakim king of Judah burned up. 29Also tell Jehoiakim king of Judah, 'This is what the LORD says: You burned that scroll and said, "Why did you write on it that the king of Babylon would certainly come and destroy this land and cut off both men and animals from it?" 30Therefore, this is what the LORD says about Jehoiakim king of Judah: He will have no one to sit on the throne of David; his body will be thrown out and exposed to the heat by day and the frost by night. 31I will punish him and his children and his attendants for their wickedness; I will bring on them and those living in Jerusalem and the people of Judah every disaster I pronounced against them, because they have not listened.' "

32So Jeremiah took another scroll and gave it to the scribe Baruch son of Neriah, and as Jeremiah dictated, Baruch wrote on it all the words of the scroll that Jehoiakim king of Judah had burned in the fire. And many similar words were added to them.

*Jeremiah in Prison*

**37** ZEDEKIAH SON of Josiah was made king of Judah by Nebuchadnezzar king of Babylon; he reigned in place of Jehoiachin[b] son of Jehoiakim. 2Neither he nor his attendants nor the people of the land paid any attention to the words the LORD had spoken through Jeremiah the prophet.

3King Zedekiah, however, sent Jehucal son of Shelemiah with the priest Zephaniah son of Maaseiah to Jeremiah the prophet with this message: "Please pray to the LORD our God for us."

4Now Jeremiah was free to come and go among the people, for he had not yet been put in prison. 5Pharaoh's army had marched out of Egypt, and when the Babylonians[c] who were besieging Jerusalem heard the report about them, they withdrew from Jerusalem.

6Then the word of the LORD came to Jeremiah the prophet: 7"This is what the LORD, the God of Israel, says: Tell the king of Judah, who sent you to inquire of me, 'Pharaoh's army, which has marched out to support you, will go back to its own land, to Egypt. 8Then the Babylonians will return and attack this city; they will capture it and burn it down.'

9"This is what the LORD says: Do not deceive yourselves, thinking, 'The Babylonians will surely leave us.' They will not! 10Even if you were to defeat the entire Babylonian[d] army that is attacking you and only wounded men were left in their tents, they would come out and burn this city down."

11After the Babylonian army had withdrawn from Jerusalem because of Pharaoh's army, 12Jeremiah started to leave the city to go to the territory of Benjamin to get his share of the property among the people there. 13But when he reached the Benjamin

NIV [b] *1* Hebrew *Coniah,* a variant of *Jehoiachin* [c] *5* Or *Chaldeans;* also in verses 8, 9, 13 and 14 [d] *10* Or *Chaldean;* also in verse 11

## King James

13And when he was in the gate of Benjamin, a captain of the ward *was* there, whose name *was* Irijah, the son of Shelemiah, the son of Hananiah; and he took Jeremiah the prophet, saying, Thou fallest away to the Chaldeans.

14Then said Jeremiah, *It is* false; I fall not away to the Chaldeans. But he hearkened not to him: so Irijah took Jeremiah, and brought him to the princes.

15Wherefore the princes were wroth with Jeremiah, and smote him, and put him in prison in the house of Jonathan the scribe: for they had made that the prison.

16¶ When Jeremiah was entered into the dungeon, and into the cabins, and Jeremiah had remained there many days;

17Then Zedekiah the king sent, and took him out: and the king asked him secretly in his house, and said, Is there *any* word from the LORD? And Jeremiah said, There is: for, said he, thou shalt be delivered into the hand of the king of Babylon.

18Moreover Jeremiah said unto king Zedekiah, What have I offended against thee, or against thy servants, or against this people, that ye have put me in prison?

19Where *are* now your prophets which prophesied unto you, saying, The king of Babylon shall not come against you, nor against this land?

20Therefore hear now, I pray thee, O my lord the king: let my supplication, I pray thee, be accepted before thee; that thou cause me not to return to the house of Jonathan the scribe, lest I die there.

21Then Zedekiah the king commanded that they should commit Jeremiah into the court of the prison, and that they should give him daily a piece of bread out of the bakers' street, until all the bread in the city were spent. Thus Jeremiah remained in the court of the prison.

**38** THEN SHEPHATIAH the son of Mattan, and Gedaliah the son of Pashur, and Jucal the son of Shelemiah, and Pashur the son of Malchiah, heard the words that Jeremiah had spoken unto all the people, saying,

2Thus saith the LORD, He that remaineth in this city shall die by the sword, by the famine, and by the pestilence: but he that goeth forth to the Chaldeans shall live; for he shall have his life for a prey, and shall live.

3Thus saith the LORD, This city shall surely be given into the hand of the king of Babylon's army, which shall take it.

4Therefore the princes said unto the king, We beseech thee, let this man be put to death: for thus he weakeneth the hands of the men of war that remain in this city, and the hands of all the people, in speaking such words unto them: for this man seeketh not the welfare of this people, but the hurt.

5Then Zedekiah the king said, Behold, he *is* in your hand: for the king *is* not *he that* can do *any* thing against you.

6Then took they Jeremiah, and cast him into the dungeon of Malchiah the son of Hammelech, that *was* in the court of the prison: and they let down Jeremiah with cords. And in the dungeon *there was* no water, but mire: so Jeremiah sunk in the mire.

7¶ Now when Ebed-melech the Ethiopian, one of the eunuchs which was in the king's house, heard that they had put Jeremiah in the dungeon; the king then sitting in the gate of Benjamin;

8Ebed-melech went forth out of the king's house, and spake to the king, saying,

9My lord the king, these men have done evil in all that they have done to Jeremiah the prophet, whom they have cast into the dungeon; and he is like to die for hunger in the place where he is: for *there is* no more bread in the city.

## Amplified

13And when he was at the gate of Benjamin, a sentry was [on guard] there, whose name was Irijah the son of Shelemiah, the son of Hananiah, and he seized Jeremiah the prophet, saying, You are deserting to the Chaldeans.

14Then said Jeremiah, It is false; I am not deserting to the Chaldeans. But the sentry would not listen to him. So Irijah took Jeremiah and brought him to the princes.

15Therefore the princes were enraged with Jeremiah, and beat him and put him in prison in the house of Jonathan the scribe, for they had made that the prison.

16When Jeremiah had come into the house of the cistern *and* the dungeon cells and had remained there many days,

17Zedekiah the king sent and brought him out; and the king asked him secretly in his house, Is there any word from the Lord? And Jeremiah said, There is. He said also, You shall be delivered into the hand of the king of Babylon.

18Moreover Jeremiah said to King Zedekiah, In what have I sinned against you or against your servants or against this people, that you have put me in prison?

19Where now are your prophets who prophesied to you, saying, The king of Babylon shall not come against you, nor against this land?

20Therefore hear now, I pray you, O my lord the king. Let my supplication, I pray you, come before you *and* be acceptable, that you will not cause me to return to the house of Jonathan the scribe, lest I die there.

21Then Zedekiah the king commanded and they committed Jeremiah to the court of the guard, and a round loaf of bread from the bakers' street was given to him daily, until all the bread in the city was gone. So Jeremiah remained [imprisoned] in the court of the guard.

**38** NOW SHEPHATIAH the son of Mattan, Gedaliah the son of Pashhur, Jucal the son of Shelemiah, and Pashhur the son of Malchiah heard the words that Jeremiah spoke to all the people, saying,

2Thus says the Lord, He who remains in this city shall die by the sword, by famine, and by pestilence; but he who goes out to the Chaldeans shall live; for he shall have his life for a prize of war, and shall live.

3Thus says the Lord, This city shall surely be given into the hand of the army of the king of Babylon, and he shall take it.

4Therefore the princes said to the king, We beseech you, let this man [Jeremiah] be put to death; for [talking] thus he weakens the hands of the soldiers who remain in this city and the hands of all the people by speaking such words to them. For this man does not seek the welfare of this people, but *to do them* harm.

5Then Zedekiah the king said, Behold, he is in your hand, for the king is in no position to do anything against you.

6So they took Jeremiah and cast him into the dungeon *or* cistern pit [in charge] of Malchiah the king's son, which was in the court of the guard, and they let Jeremiah down [into the pit] with ropes. And in the dungeon *or* cistern pit there was no water, but mire, and Jeremiah sank in the mire.

7Now when Ebedmelech the Ethiopian [a colored man], one of the eunuchs who was in the king's house, heard that they had put Jeremiah in the dungeon *or* cistern pit, and the king was then sitting in the gate of Benjamin,

8Ebedmelech went out of the king's house and spoke to the king, saying,

9My lord the king, these men have done evil in all that they have done to Jeremiah the prophet, whom they have cast into the dungeon *or* cistern pit; and he is liable to die of hunger *and* is [as good as] dead in the place where he is, for there is no more bread left in the city.

## New American Standard

13While he was at the Gate of Benjamin, a captain of the guard whose name was Irijah, the son of Shelemiah the son of Hananiah was there; and he arrested Jeremiah the prophet, saying, "You are going over to the Chaldeans!"

14But Jeremiah said, "A lie! I am not going over to the Chaldeans"; yet he would not listen to him. So Irijah arrested Jeremiah and brought him to the officials.

15Then the officials were angry at Jeremiah and beat him, and they put him in jail in the house of Jonathan the scribe, which they had made into the prison.

16For Jeremiah had come into the dungeon, that is, the vaulted cell; and Jeremiah stayed there many days.

17¶ Now King Zedekiah sent and took him *out;* and in his palace the king secretly asked him and said, "Is there a word from the LORD?" And Jeremiah said, "There is!" Then he said, "You will be given into the hand of the king of Babylon!"

18Moreover Jeremiah said to King Zedekiah, "*In* what *way* have I sinned against you, or against your servants, or against this people, that you have put me in prison?

19"Where then are your prophets who prophesied to you, saying, 'The king of Babylon will not come against you or against this land'?

20"But now, please listen, O my lord the king; please let my petition come before you, and do not make me return to the house of Jonathan the scribe, that I may not die there."

21Then King Zedekiah gave commandment, and they committed Jeremiah to the court of the guardhouse and gave him a loaf of bread daily from the bakers' street, until all the bread in the city was gone. So Jeremiah remained in the court of the guardhouse.

*Jeremiah Thrown into the Cistern*

**38** NOW SHEPHATIAH the son of Mattan, and Gedaliah the son of Pashhur, and Jucal the son of Shelemiah, and Pashhur the son of Malchijah heard the words that Jeremiah was speaking to all the people, saying,

2"Thus says the LORD, 'He who stays in this city will die by the sword and by famine and by pestilence, but he who goes out to the Chaldeans will live and have his *own* life as booty and stay alive.'

3"Thus says the LORD, 'This city will certainly be given into the hand of the army of the king of Babylon, and he will capture it.' "

4Then the officials said to the king, "Now let this man be put to death, inasmuch as he is discouraging the men of war who are left in this city and all the people, by speaking such words to them; for this man is not seeking the well-being of this people, but rather their harm."

5So King Zedekiah said, "Behold, he is in your hands; for the king can *do* nothing against you."

6Then they took Jeremiah and cast him into the cistern *of* Malchijah the king's son, which was in the court of the guardhouse; and they let Jeremiah down with ropes. Now in the cistern there was no water but only mud, and Jeremiah sank into the mud.

7But Ebed-melech the Ethiopian, a eunuch, while he was in the king's palace, heard that they had put Jeremiah into the cistern. Now the king was sitting in the Gate of Benjamin;

8and Ebed-melech went out from the king's palace and spoke to the king, saying,

9"My lord the king, these men have acted wickedly in all that they have done to Jeremiah the prophet whom they have cast into the cistern; and he will die right where he is because of the famine, for there is no more bread in the city."

## New International

Gate, the captain of the guard, whose name was Irijah son of Shelemiah, the son of Hananiah, arrested him and said, "You are deserting to the Babylonians!"

14"That's not true!" Jeremiah said. "I am not deserting to the Babylonians." But Irijah would not listen to him; instead, he arrested Jeremiah and brought him to the officials. 15They were angry with Jeremiah and had him beaten and imprisoned in the house of Jonathan the secretary, which they had made into a prison.

16Jeremiah was put into a vaulted cell in a dungeon, where he remained a long time. 17Then King Zedekiah sent for him and had him brought to the palace, where he asked him privately, "Is there any word from the LORD?"

"Yes," Jeremiah replied, "you will be handed over to the king of Babylon."

18Then Jeremiah said to King Zedekiah, "What crime have I committed against you or your officials or this people, that you have put me in prison? 19Where are your prophets who prophesied to you, 'The king of Babylon will not attack you or this land'? 20But now, my lord the king, please listen. Let me bring my petition before you: Do not send me back to the house of Jonathan the secretary, or I will die there."

21King Zedekiah then gave orders for Jeremiah to be placed in the courtyard of the guard and given bread from the street of the bakers each day until all the bread in the city was gone. So Jeremiah remained in the courtyard of the guard.

*Jeremiah Thrown Into a Cistern*

**38** SHEPHATIAH SON of Mattan, Gedaliah son of Pashhur, Jehucal[a] son of Shelemiah, and Pashhur son of Malkijah heard what Jeremiah was telling all the people when he said, 2"This is what the LORD says: 'Whoever stays in this city will die by the sword, famine or plague, but whoever goes over to the Babylonians[b] will live. He will escape with his life; he will live.' 3And this is what the LORD says: 'This city will certainly be handed over to the army of the king of Babylon, who will capture it.' "

4Then the officials said to the king, "This man should be put to death. He is discouraging the soldiers who are left in this city, as well as all the people, by the things he is saying to them. This man is not seeking the good of these people but their ruin."

5"He is in your hands," King Zedekiah answered. "The king can do nothing to oppose you."

6So they took Jeremiah and put him into the cistern of Malkijah, the king's son, which was in the courtyard of the guard. They lowered Jeremiah by ropes into the cistern; it had no water in it, only mud, and Jeremiah sank down into the mud.

7But Ebed-Melech, a Cushite,[c] an official[d] in the royal palace, heard that they had put Jeremiah into the cistern. While the king was sitting in the Benjamin Gate, 8Ebed-Melech went out of the palace and said to him, 9"My lord the king, these men have acted wickedly in all they have done to Jeremiah the prophet. They have thrown him into a cistern, where he will starve to death when there is no longer any bread in the city."

NIV [a] *1* Hebrew *Jucal,* a variant of *Jehucal* [b] *2* Or *Chaldeans;* also in verses 18, 19 and 23 [c] *7* Probably from the upper Nile region [d] *7* Or *a eunuch*

## King James

10Then the king commanded Ebed-melech the Ethiopian, saying, Take from hence thirty men with thee, and take up Jeremiah the prophet out of the dungeon, before he die.
11So Ebed-melech took the men with him, and went into the house of the king under the treasury, and took thence old cast clouts and old rotten rags, and let them down by cords into the dungeon to Jeremiah.
12And Ebed-melech the Ethiopian said unto Jeremiah, Put now *these* old cast clouts and rotten rags under thine armholes under the cords. And Jeremiah did so.
13So they drew up Jeremiah with cords, and took him up out of the dungeon: and Jeremiah remained in the court of the prison.
14¶ Then Zedekiah the king sent, and took Jeremiah the prophet unto him into the third entry that *is* in the house of the LORD: and the king said unto Jeremiah, I will ask thee a thing; hide nothing from me.
15Then Jeremiah said unto Zedekiah, If I declare *it* unto thee, wilt thou not surely put me to death? and if I give thee counsel, wilt thou not hearken unto me?
16So Zedekiah the king sware secretly unto Jeremiah, saying, *As* the LORD liveth, that made us this soul, I will not put thee to death, neither will I give thee into the hand of these men that seek thy life.
17Then said Jeremiah unto Zedekiah, Thus saith the LORD, the God of hosts, the God of Israel; If thou wilt assuredly go forth unto the king of Babylon's princes, then thy soul shall live, and this city shall not be burned with fire; and thou shalt live, and thine house:
18But if thou wilt not go forth to the king of Babylon's princes, then shall this city be given into the hand of the Chaldeans, and they shall burn it with fire, and thou shalt not escape out of their hand.
19And Zedekiah the king said unto Jeremiah, I am afraid of the Jews that are fallen to the Chaldeans, lest they deliver me into their hand, and they mock me.
20But Jeremiah said, They shall not deliver *thee.* Obey, I beseech thee, the voice of the LORD, which I speak unto thee: so it shall be well unto thee, and thy soul shall live.
21But if thou refuse to go forth, this *is* the word that the LORD hath shown me:
22And, behold, all the women that are left in the king of Judah's house *shall be* brought forth to the king of Babylon's princes, and those *women* shall say, Thy friends have set thee on, and have prevailed against thee: thy feet are sunk in the mire, *and* they are turned away back.
23So they shall bring out all thy wives and thy children to the Chaldeans: and thou shalt not escape out of their hand, but shalt be taken by the hand of the king of Babylon: and thou shalt cause this city to be burned with fire.
24¶ Then said Zedekiah unto Jeremiah, Let no man know of these words, and thou shalt not die.
25But if the princes hear that I have talked with thee, and they come unto thee, and say unto thee, Declare unto us now what thou hast said unto the king, hide it not from us, and we will not put thee to death; also what the king said unto thee:
26Then thou shalt say unto them, I presented my supplication before the king, that he would not cause me to return to Jonathan's house, to die there.
27Then came all the princes unto Jeremiah, and asked him: and he told them according to all these words that the king had commanded. So they left off speaking with him; for the matter was not perceived.
28So Jeremiah abode in the court of the prison until the day that Jerusalem was taken: and he was *there* when Jerusalem was taken.

## Amplified

10Then the king commanded Ebedmelech the Ethiopian, saying, Take from here thirty men with you and raise Jeremiah the prophet out of the dungeon *or* cistern pit before he dies.
11So Ebedmelech took the men with him and went into the house of the king under the treasury, and took along from there old rags and worn-out garments and let them down by ropes into the dungeon *or* cistern pit to Jeremiah.
12And Ebedmelech the Ethiopian said to Jeremiah, Put now these old rags and worn-out garments under your armpits over the ropes. And Jeremiah did so.
13So they drew up Jeremiah with ropes and took him up out of the dungeon *or* cistern pit, and Jeremiah remained in the court of the guard.
14Then Zedekiah the king sent and brought Jeremiah the prophet to him into the third entrance that is in the house of the Lord. And the king said to Jeremiah, I am going to ask you something; hide nothing from me.
15Then Jeremiah said to Zedekiah, If I tell you, will you not surely put me to death? And if I give you counsel, you will not listen to me.
16So Zedekiah the king swore secretly to Jeremiah, As the Lord lives Who made our lives, I will not put you to death or give you into the hand of these men who seek your life.
17Then said Jeremiah to Zedekiah, Thus says the Lord, the God of hosts, the God of Israel: If you will go forth *and* surrender to the princes of the king of Babylon, then you shall live, and this city shall not be burned with fire, and you shall live and your house.
18But if you will not go forth and surrender to the princes of the king of Babylon, then this city shall be given into the hand of the Chaldeans, and they shall burn it with fire, and you shall not escape out of their hand.
19And Zedekiah the king said to Jeremiah, I am afraid of the Jews that have deserted to the Chaldeans, lest the enemy deliver me into [these former subjects'] hand, and they mock me *and* abuse me.
20But Jeremiah said, They will not deliver you [to them]. Obey, I beg of you, the voice of the Lord Who speaks to you through me. Then it will be well with you, and you shall live.
21But if you refuse to go forth *and* surrender to them, this is the word [the vision] that the Lord has shown me:
22Behold, *in it* all the women that were left in the house of the king of Judah were being brought forth to the king of Babylon's princes and were saying [to you, King Zedekiah], Your friends have prevailed against your better judgment *and* have deceived you. Now when your feet are sunk in the mire [of trouble], they have turned their backs.
23All your wives and your children will be brought out to the Chaldeans; and you [yourself] cannot escape out of their hand, but you will be seized by the king of Babylon, and you will be causing this city [Jerusalem] to be burned with fire.
24Then Zedekiah said to Jeremiah, Let no man know of this conversation and you shall not die.
25But if the princes hear that I have talked with you, and they come to you and say, Tell us what you said to the king and what he said to you; hide it not from us and we will not put you to death,
26Then you shall say to them, I presented to the king my humble plea that he would not send me back to Jonathan's house to die there.
27Then came all the princes to Jeremiah, and asked him [just what King Zedekiah had anticipated], and he told them all that the king had commanded. So they left off speaking with him, for what the conversation had been was not discovered.
28So Jeremiah remained in the court of the guard until the day that Jerusalem was taken [by the Chaldeans].

## New American Standard

10Then the king commanded Ebed-melech the Ethiopian, saying, "Take thirty men from here under your authority, and bring
up Jeremiah the prophet from the cistern before he dies."
11So Ebed-melech took the men under his authority and went
into the king's palace to *a place* beneath the storeroom and took
from there worn-out clothes and worn-out rags and let them down
by ropes into the cistern to Jeremiah.
12Then Ebed-melech the Ethiopian said to Jeremiah, "Now put
these worn-out clothes and rags under your armpits under the
ropes"; and Jeremiah did so.
13So they pulled Jeremiah up with the ropes and lifted him out
of the cistern, and Jeremiah stayed in the court of the guardhouse.
14¶ Then King Zedekiah sent and had Jeremiah the prophet
brought to him at the third entrance that is in the house of the
LORD; and the king said to Jeremiah, "I am going to ask you
something; do not hide anything from me."
15Then Jeremiah said to Zedekiah, "If I tell you, will you not
certainly put me to death? Besides, if I give you advice, you will
not listen to me."
16But King Zedekiah swore to Jeremiah in secret saying, "As the
LORD lives, who made this life for us, surely I will not put you to
death nor will I give you over to the hand of these men who are
seeking your life."

*Interview with Zedekiah*

17¶ Then Jeremiah said to Zedekiah, "Thus says the LORD God
of hosts, the God of Israel, 'If you will indeed go out to the officers
of the king of Babylon, then you will live, this city will not be
burned with fire, and you and your household will survive.
18'But if you will not go out to the officers of the king of Babylon,
then this city will be given over to the hand of the Chaldeans; and
they will burn it with fire, and you yourself will not escape from
their hand.' "
19Then King Zedekiah said to Jeremiah, "I dread the Jews who
have gone over to the Chaldeans, lest they give me over into their
hand and they abuse me."
20But Jeremiah said, "They will not give you over. Please obey
the LORD in what I am saying to you, that it may go well with you
and you may live.
21"But if you keep refusing to go out, this is the word which the
LORD has shown me:
22'Then behold, all of the women who have been left in the
palace of the king of Judah are going to be brought out to the
officers of the king of Babylon; and those women will say,

"Your close friends
Have misled and overpowered you;
While your feet were sunk in the mire,
They turned back."

23'They will also bring out all your wives and your sons to the
Chaldeans, and you yourself will not escape from their hand, but
will be seized by the hand of the king of Babylon, and this city will
be burned with fire.' "
24¶ Then Zedekiah said to Jeremiah, "Let no man know about
these words and you will not die.
25"But if the officials hear that I have talked with you and come
to you and say to you, 'Tell us now what you said to the king, and
what the king said to you; do not hide *it* from us, and we will not
put you to death,'
26then you are to say to them, 'I was presenting my petition
before the king, not to make me return to the house of Jonathan
to die there.' "
27Then all the officials came to Jeremiah and questioned him.
So he reported to them in accordance with all these words which
the king had commanded; and they ceased speaking with him,
since the conversation had not been overheard.
28So Jeremiah stayed in the court of the guardhouse until the
day that Jerusalem was captured.

## New International

10Then the king commanded Ebed-Melech the Cushite, "Take
thirty men from here with you and lift Jeremiah the prophet out
of the cistern before he dies."
11So Ebed-Melech took the men with him and went to a room
under the treasury in the palace. He took some old rags and
worn-out clothes from there and let them down with ropes to
Jeremiah in the cistern. 12Ebed-Melech the Cushite said to Jeremiah, "Put these old rags and worn-out clothes under your arms
to pad the ropes." Jeremiah did so, 13and they pulled him up with
the ropes and lifted him out of the cistern. And Jeremiah remained
in the courtyard of the guard.

*Zedekiah Questions Jeremiah Again*

14Then King Zedekiah sent for Jeremiah the prophet and had
him brought to the third entrance to the temple of the LORD. "I am
going to ask you something," the king said to Jeremiah. "Do not
hide anything from me."
15Jeremiah said to Zedekiah, "If I give you an answer, will you
not kill me? Even if I did give you counsel, you would not listen
to me."
16But King Zedekiah swore this oath secretly to Jeremiah: "As
surely as the LORD lives, who has given us breath, I will neither
kill you nor hand you over to those who are seeking your life."
17Then Jeremiah said to Zedekiah, "This is what the LORD God
Almighty, the God of Israel, says: 'If you surrender to the officers
of the king of Babylon, your life will be spared and this city will
not be burned down; you and your family will live. 18But if you
will not surrender to the officers of the king of Babylon, this city
will be handed over to the Babylonians and they will burn it down;
you yourself will not escape from their hands.' "
19King Zedekiah said to Jeremiah, "I am afraid of the Jews who
have gone over to the Babylonians, for the Babylonians may hand
me over to them and they will mistreat me."
20"They will not hand you over," Jeremiah replied. "Obey the
LORD by doing what I tell you. Then it will go well with you, and
your life will be spared. 21But if you refuse to surrender, this is
what the LORD has revealed to me: 22All the women left in the
palace of the king of Judah will be brought out to the officials of
the king of Babylon. Those women will say to you:

" 'They misled you and overcame you—
those trusted friends of yours.
Your feet are sunk in the mud;
your friends have deserted you.'

23"All your wives and children will be brought out to the Babylonians. You yourself will not escape from their hands but will be
captured by the king of Babylon; and this city will[a] be burned
down."
24Then Zedekiah said to Jeremiah, "Do not let anyone know
about this conversation, or you may die. 25If the officials hear that
I talked with you, and they come to you and say, 'Tell us what you
said to the king and what the king said to you; do not hide it from
us or we will kill you,' 26then tell them, 'I was pleading with the
king not to send me back to Jonathan's house to die there.' "
27All the officials did come to Jeremiah and question him, and
he told them everything the king had ordered him to say. So they
said no more to him, for no one had heard his conversation with
the king.
28And Jeremiah remained in the courtyard of the guard until the
day Jerusalem was captured.

NIV [a] 23 Or *and you will cause this city to*

## King James

39 IN THE ninth year of Zedekiah king of Judah, in the tenth month, came Nebuchadrezzar king of Babylon and all his army against Jerusalem, and they besieged it.

2 *And* in the eleventh year of Zedekiah, in the fourth month, the ninth *day* of the month, the city was broken up.

3 And all the princes of the king of Babylon came in, and sat in the middle gate, *even* Nergal-sharezer, Samgar-nebo, Sarsechim, Rabsaris, Nergal-sharezer, Rab-mag, with all the residue of the princes of the king of Babylon.

4 ¶ And it came to pass, *that* when Zedekiah the king of Judah saw them, and all the men of war, then they fled, and went forth out of the city by night, by the way of the king's garden, by the gate betwixt the two walls: and he went out the way of the plain.

5 But the Chaldeans' army pursued after them, and overtook Zedekiah in the plains of Jericho: and when they had taken him, they brought him up to Nebuchadnezzar king of Babylon to Riblah in the land of Hamath, where he gave judgment upon him.

6 Then the king of Babylon slew the sons of Zedekiah in Riblah before his eyes: also the king of Babylon slew all the nobles of Judah.

7 Moreover he put out Zedekiah's eyes, and bound him with chains, to carry him to Babylon.

8 ¶ And the Chaldeans burned the king's house, and the houses of the people, with fire, and brake down the walls of Jerusalem.

9 Then Nebuzar-adan the captain of the guard carried away captive into Babylon the remnant of the people that remained in the city, and those that fell away, that fell to him, with the rest of the people that remained.

10 But Nebuzar-adan the captain of the guard left of the poor of the people, which had nothing, in the land of Judah, and gave them vineyards and fields at the same time.

11 ¶ Now Nebuchadrezzar king of Babylon gave charge concerning Jeremiah to Nebuzar-adan the captain of the guard, saying,

12 Take him, and look well to him, and do him no harm; but do unto him even as he shall say unto thee.

13 So Nebuzar-adan the captain of the guard sent, and Nebushasban, Rabsaris, and Nergal-sharezer, Rab-mag, and all the king of Babylon's princes;

14 Even they sent, and took Jeremiah out of the court of the prison, and committed him unto Gedaliah the son of Ahikam the son of Shaphan, that he should carry him home: so he dwelt among the people.

15 ¶ Now the word of the LORD came unto Jeremiah, while he was shut up in the court of the prison, saying,

16 Go and speak to Ebed-melech the Ethiopian, saying, Thus saith the LORD of hosts, the God of Israel; Behold, I will bring my words upon this city for evil, and not for good; and they shall be *accomplished* in that day before thee.

17 But I will deliver thee in that day, saith the LORD: and thou shalt not be given into the hand of the men of whom thou *art* afraid.

18 For I will surely deliver thee, and thou shalt not fall by the sword, but thy life shall be for a prey unto thee: because thou hast put thy trust in me, saith the LORD.

## Amplified

39 IN THE ninth year of Zedekiah king of Judah, in the tenth month, Nebuchadrezzar king of Babylon and all his army came against Jerusalem and besieged it.

2 And in the eleventh year of Zedekiah, in the fourth month, on the ninth day of the month, they broke into the city.

3 [ [a] When Jerusalem was taken] all the princes of the king of Babylon came in and sat in the middle gate: Nergalsharezer, Samgarnebo, Sarsechim chief of the eunuchs, and Nergalsharezer [II] chief of the magicians, with all the rest of the officers of the king of Babylon.

4 And when Zedekiah the king of Judah and all the men of war saw them, they fled and went forth out of the city by night by the way of the king's garden through the gate between the two walls; and [the king] went out toward the Arabah—the valley of the Jordan.

5 But the Chaldean army pursued after them and overtook Zedekiah in the plains of Jericho. And when they had taken him, they brought him up to Nebuchadrezzar king of Babylon, at Riblah in the [Syrian] land of Hamath, where he pronounced sentence upon him.

6 Then the king of Babylon slew the sons of Zedekiah in Riblah before his eyes; also the king of Babylon slew all the nobles of Judah.

7 Moreover he put out Zedekiah's eyes, and bound him with shackles to take him to Babylon. [Ezek. 12:13.]

8 And the Chaldeans burned the king's house and the houses of the people, and broke down the walls of Jerusalem.

9 Then Nebuzaradan, the [chief executioner and] captain of the guard, carried away captive to Babylon the rest of the people who remained in the city, and those who deserted to him, with the remainder of the [so-called better class of] people who were left.

10 But Nebuzaradan the [Babylonian] captain of the guard left in the land of Judah some of the poor of the people who had nothing, giving them vineyards and fields at the same time.

11 Nebuchadrezzar king of Babylon gave command concerning Jeremiah to Nebuzaradan the captain of the guard, saying,

12 Take him and look after him well; do him no harm, but deal with him as he may ask of you.

13 So Nebuzaradan the captain of the guard, Nebushasban the chief of the eunuchs, Nergalsharezer [II] the chief of the magicians, and all the chief officials of the king of Babylon

14 Sent and took Jeremiah out of the court of the guard and entrusted him to [a prominent man whose father had once saved the prophet's life] Gedaliah the son of Ahikam, son of Shaphan, that he should take him home [with him to Mizpah]. So Jeremiah was freed *and* dwelt among the people. [Jer. 26:24.]

15 Now the word of the Lord came to Jeremiah while he was [still shut up in the court of the guard, saying,

16 Go and say to Ebedmelech the Ethiopian, Thus says the Lord of hosts, the God of Israel: Behold, I will bring to pass My words against this city for evil and not for good, and they shall be accomplished before you on that day.

17 But I will deliver you [Ebedmelech] on that day, says the Lord, and you shall not be given into the hand of the men of whom you are afraid. [Jer. 38:7-13.]

18 For I will surely deliver you, and you shall not fall by the sword, but your life shall be for a reward of battle to you, because you have put your trust in Me, says the Lord.

**AMP** [a] This clause has been supplied from the close of chapter 38, where it seems according to many authorities to have been misplaced.

## New American Standard

*Jerusalem Captured*

**39** NOW IT came about when Jerusalem was captured in the
ninth year of Zedekiah king of Judah, in the tenth month,
Nebuchadnezzar king of Babylon and all his army came to Jerusalem and laid siege to it;
2in the eleventh year of Zedekiah, in the fourth month, in the
ninth *day* of the month, the city *wall* was breached.
3Then all the officials of the king of Babylon came in and sat
down at the Middle Gate: Nergal-sar-ezer, Samgar-nebu, Sarsekim the Rab-saris, Nergal-sar-ezer *the* Rab-mag, and all the rest
of the officials of the king of Babylon.
4And it came about, when Zedekiah the king of Judah and all
the men of war saw them, that they fled and went out of the city
at night by way of the king's garden through the gate between the
two walls; and he went out toward the [b]Arabah.
5But the army of the Chaldeans pursued them and overtook
Zedekiah in the plains of Jericho; and they seized him and brought
him up to Nebuchadnezzar king of Babylon at Riblah in the land
of Hamath, and he passed sentence on him.
6Then the king of Babylon slew the sons of Zedekiah before his
eyes at Riblah; the king of Babylon also slew all the nobles of Judah.
7He then blinded Zedekiah's eyes and bound him in fetters of
bronze to bring him to Babylon.
8The Chaldeans also burned with fire the king's palace and the
houses of the people, and they broke down the walls of Jerusalem.
9And as for the rest of the people who were left in the city, the
deserters who had gone over to him and the rest of the people who
remained, Nebuzaradan the captain of the bodyguard carried *them*
into exile in Babylon.
10But some of the poorest people who had nothing, Nebuzaradan the captain of the bodyguard left behind in the land of Judah,
and gave them vineyards and fields at that time.

*Jeremiah Spared*

11¶ Now Nebuchadnezzar king of Babylon gave orders about
Jeremiah through Nebuzaradan the captain of the bodyguard,
saying,
12"Take him and look after him, and do nothing harmful to him;
but rather deal with him just as he tells you."
13So Nebuzaradan the captain of the bodyguard sent *word,*
along with Nebushazban the Rab-saris, and Nergal-sar-ezer the
Rab-mag, and all the leading officers of the king of Babylon;
14they even sent and took Jeremiah out of the court of the
guardhouse and entrusted him to Gedaliah, the son of Ahikam,
the son of Shaphan, to take him home. So he stayed among the
people.
15¶ Now the word of the LORD had come to Jeremiah while he
was confined in the court of the guardhouse, saying,
16"Go and speak to Ebed-melech the Ethiopian, saying, 'Thus
says the LORD of hosts, the God of Israel, "Behold, I am about to
bring My words on this city for disaster and not for prosperity; and
they will take place before you on that day.
17"But I will deliver you on that day," declares the LORD, "and
you shall not be given into the hand of the men whom you dread.
18"For I will certainly rescue you, and you will not fall by the
sword; but you will have your *own* life as booty, because you have
trusted in Me," declares the LORD.' "

**NAS** [b] I.e., Jordan valley

## New International

*The Fall of Jerusalem*

**39** THIS IS how Jerusalem was taken: 1In the ninth year of
Zedekiah king of Judah, in the tenth month, Nebuchadnezzar king of Babylon marched against Jerusalem with his
whole army and laid siege to it. 2And on the ninth day of the fourth
month of Zedekiah's eleventh year, the city wall was broken
through. 3Then all the officials of the king of Babylon came and
took seats in the Middle Gate: Nergal-Sharezer of Samgar, Nebo-
Sarsekim[c] a chief officer, Nergal-Sharezer a high official and all the
other officials of the king of Babylon. 4When Zedekiah king of
Judah and all the soldiers saw them, they fled; they left the city at
night by way of the king's garden, through the gate between the
two walls, and headed toward the Arabah.[d]
5But the Babylonian[e] army pursued them and overtook Zedekiah in the plains of Jericho. They captured him and took him to
Nebuchadnezzar king of Babylon at Riblah in the land of Hamath,
where he pronounced sentence on him. 6There at Riblah the king
of Babylon slaughtered the sons of Zedekiah before his eyes and
also killed all the nobles of Judah. 7Then he put out Zedekiah's
eyes and bound him with bronze shackles to take him to Babylon.
8The Babylonians[f] set fire to the royal palace and the houses
of the people and broke down the walls of Jerusalem. 9Nebuzar-
adan commander of the imperial guard carried into exile to Babylon the people who remained in the city, along with those who
had gone over to him, and the rest of the people. 10But Nebuzaradan the commander of the guard left behind in the land of Judah
some of the poor people, who owned nothing; and at that time he
gave them vineyards and fields.
11Now Nebuchadnezzar king of Babylon had given these orders
about Jeremiah through Nebuzaradan commander of the imperial
guard: 12"Take him and look after him; don't harm him but do for
him whatever he asks." 13So Nebuzaradan the commander of the
guard, Nebushazban a chief officer, Nergal-Sharezer a high official
and all the other officers of the king of Babylon 14sent and had
Jeremiah taken out of the courtyard of the guard. They turned him
over to Gedaliah son of Ahikam, the son of Shaphan, to take him
back to his home. So he remained among his own people.
15While Jeremiah had been confined in the courtyard of the
guard, the word of the LORD came to him: 16"Go and tell Ebed-
Melech the Cushite, 'This is what the LORD Almighty, the God of
Israel, says: I am about to fulfill my words against this city through
disaster, not prosperity. At that time they will be fulfilled before
your eyes. 17But I will rescue you on that day, declares the LORD;
you will not be handed over to those you fear. 18I will save you;
you will not fall by the sword but will escape with your life,
because you trust in me, declares the LORD.' "

**NIV** [c] 3 Or *Nergal-Sharezer, Samgar-Nebo, Sarsekim* [d] 4 Or *the Jordan Valley*
[e] 5 Or *Chaldean* [f] 8 Or *Chaldeans*

## King James

**40** THE WORD that came to Jeremiah from the LORD, after that Nebuzar-adan the captain of the guard had let him go from Ramah, when he had taken him being bound in chains among all that were carried away captive of Jerusalem and Judah, which were carried away captive unto Babylon.

2 And the captain of the guard took Jeremiah, and said unto him, The LORD thy God hath pronounced this evil upon this place.

3 Now the LORD hath brought *it*, and done according as he hath said: because ye have sinned against the LORD, and have not obeyed his voice, therefore this thing is come upon you.

4 And now, behold, I loose thee this day from the chains which *were* upon thine hand. If it seem good unto thee to come with me into Babylon, come; and I will look well unto thee: but if it seem ill unto thee to come with me into Babylon, forbear: behold, all the land *is* before thee: whither it seemeth good and convenient for thee to go, thither go.

5 Now while he was not yet gone back, *he said*, Go back also to Gedaliah the son of Ahikam the son of Shaphan, whom the king of Babylon hath made governor over the cities of Judah, and dwell with him among the people: or go wheresoever it seemeth convenient unto thee to go. So the captain of the guard gave him victuals and a reward, and let him go.

6 Then went Jeremiah unto Gedaliah the son of Ahikam to Mizpah; and dwelt with him among the people that were left in the land.

7 ¶ Now when all the captains of the forces which *were* in the fields, *even* they and their men, heard that the king of Babylon had made Gedaliah the son of Ahikam governor in the land, and had committed unto him men, and women, and children, and of the poor of the land, of them that were not carried away captive to Babylon;

8 Then they came to Gedaliah to Mizpah, even Ishmael the son of Nethaniah, and Johanan and Jonathan the sons of Kareah, and Seraiah the son of Tanhumeth, and the sons of Ephai the Netophathite, and Jezaniah the son of a Maachathite, they and their men.

9 And Gedaliah the son of Ahikam the son of Shaphan sware unto them and to their men, saying, Fear not to serve the Chaldeans: dwell in the land, and serve the king of Babylon, and it shall be well with you.

10 As for me, behold, I will dwell at Mizpah to serve the Chaldeans, which will come unto us: but ye, gather ye wine, and summer fruits, and oil, and put *them* in your vessels, and dwell in your cities that ye have taken.

11 Likewise when all the Jews that *were* in Moab, and among the Ammonites, and in Edom, and that *were* in all the countries, heard that the king of Babylon had left a remnant of Judah, and that he had set over them Gedaliah the son of Ahikam the son of Shaphan;

12 Even all the Jews returned out of all places whither they were driven, and came to the land of Judah, to Gedaliah, unto Mizpah, and gathered wine and summer fruits very much.

13 ¶ Moreover Johanan the son of Kareah, and all the captains of the forces that *were* in the fields, came to Gedaliah to Mizpah,

14 And said unto him, Dost thou certainly know that Baalis the king of the Ammonites hath sent Ishmael the son of Nethaniah to slay thee? But Gedaliah the son of Ahikam believed them not.

15 Then Johanan the son of Kareah spake to Gedaliah in Mizpah secretly, saying, Let me go, I pray thee, and I will slay Ishmael the son of Nethaniah, and no man shall know *it:* wherefore should he slay thee, that all the Jews which are gathered unto thee should be scattered, and the remnant in Judah perish?

16 But Gedaliah the son of Ahikam said unto Johanan the son of Kareah, Thou shalt not do this thing: for thou speakest falsely of Ishmael.

## Amplified

**40** THE WORD that came to Jeremiah from the Lord, after Nebuzaradan the captain of the guard had let him go from Ramah, where he had taken him bound in chains among all that were carried away captive of Jerusalem and Judah, who were taken as exiles to Babylon.

2 And the captain of the guard took Jeremiah, and said to him, The Lord your God pronounced evil upon this place.

3 Now the Lord has brought it about and has done as He said: [It is] because you [of Judah] have sinned against the Lord, and have not obeyed His voice, therefore this thing is come upon you.

4 Now, see, I am freeing you today [Jeremiah] from the chains upon your hands. If it seems good to you to come with me into Babylon, come, and I will keep an eye on you *and* look well after you. But if it seems bad to you to come with me to Babylon, then do not do it. Behold, all the land is before you. Wherever it seems good, right, *and* convenient for you to go, go there.

5 While [Jeremiah] was hesitating, [the captain of the guard] said, Go back then to Gedaliah the son of Ahikam, son of Shaphan, whom the king of Babylon made governor over the cities of Judah, and dwell with him among the people; or go wherever it seems right to you to go. So the captain of the guard gave him an allowance of food and a present, and let him go.

6 Then Jeremiah went to Gedaliah the son of Ahikam, at Mizpah, and dwelt with him among the people that were left in the land.

7 Now when all the captains of the forces which were in the open country [of Judah] and their men heard that the king of Babylon had made Gedaliah the son of Ahikam governor in the land [of Judah], and had committed to him men, women, and children, those of the poorest of the land who had not been taken into exile to Babylon,

8 They went to Gedaliah at Mizpah: Ishmael the son of Nethaniah, Johanan and Jonathan the sons of Kareah, Seraiah the son of Tanhumeth, the sons of Ephai the Netophathite, and Jezaniah the son of the Maacathite, they and their men.

9 And Gedaliah the son of Ahikam, son of Shaphan, swore to them and their men, saying, Do not be afraid to serve the Chaldeans; dwell in *this* land and serve the king of Babylon, and it shall be well with you.

10 As for me, I will dwell at Mizpah, to stand [for you] before the Chaldeans who will come to us [ministering to them and looking after the king's interests]. But you, gather the grape juice, summer fruits and oil, and store them in your utensils [for such purposes], and dwell in your cities that you have seized.

11 Likewise, when all the Jews who were in Moab and among the people of Ammon and in Edom and who were in all the other countries heard that the king of Babylon had left a remnant in Judah and had set over them [as governor] Gedaliah the son of Ahikam, the son of Shaphan,

12 Then all the Jews returned from all the places to which they had been driven and came to the land of Judah, to Gedaliah at Mizpah, and gathered a great abundance of grape juice and summer fruits.

13 Moreover Johanan the son of Kareah and all the captains of the forces that were in the open country came to Gedaliah at Mizpah

14 And said to him, Do you know that Baalis the king of the Ammonites has sent Ishmael the son of Nethaniah to take your life? But Gedaliah the son of Ahikam did not believe them.

15 Then Johanan the son of Kareah spoke to Gedaliah in Mizpah secretly, saying, Let me go, I pray you, and I will slay Ishmael the son of Nethaniah, and no man shall know it. Why should he slay you, and cause all the Jews who are gathered to you to be scattered, and the remnant in Judah to perish?

16 But Gedaliah the son of Ahikam said to Johanan the son of Kareah, You shall not do this thing for you speak falsely of Ishmael.

## New American Standard

*Jeremiah Remains in Judah*

**40** THE WORD which came to Jeremiah from the LORD after
Nebuzaradan captain of the bodyguard had released him
from Ramah, when he had taken him bound in chains, among all
the exiles of Jerusalem and Judah, who were being exiled to Babylon.
2Now the captain of the bodyguard had taken Jeremiah and
said to him, "The LORD your God promised this calamity against
this place;
3and the LORD has brought *it* on and done just as He promised.
Because you *people* sinned against the LORD and did not listen to
His voice, therefore this thing has happened to you.
4"But now, behold, I am freeing you today from the chains
which are on your hands. If you would prefer to come with me to
Babylon, come *along,* and I will look after you; but if you would
prefer not to come with me to Babylon, never mind. Look, the
whole land is before you; go wherever it seems good and right for
you to go."
5As Jeremiah was still not going back, *he said,* "Go on back then
to Gedaliah the son of Ahikam, the son of Shaphan, whom the
king of Babylon has appointed over the cities of Judah, and stay
with him among the people; or else go anywhere it seems right for
you to go." So the captain of the bodyguard gave him a ration and
a gift and let him go.
6Then Jeremiah went to Mizpah to Gedaliah the son of Ahikam
and stayed with him among the people who were left in the land.
7¶ Now all the commanders of the forces that were in the field,
they and their men, heard that the king of Babylon had appointed
Gedaliah the son of Ahikam over the land and that he had put him
in charge of the men, women and children, those of the poorest
of the land who had not been exiled to Babylon.
8So they came to Gedaliah at Mizpah, along with Ishmael the
son of Nethaniah, and Johanan and Jonathan the sons of Kareah,
and Seraiah the son of Tanhumeth, and the sons of Ephai the
Netophathite, and Jezaniah the son of the Maacathite, *both* they
and their men.
9Then Gedaliah the son of Ahikam, the son of Shaphan, swore
to them and to their men, saying, "Do not be afraid of serving the
Chaldeans; stay in the land and serve the king of Babylon, that it
may go well with you.
10"Now as for me, behold, I am going to stay at Mizpah to stand
*for you* before the Chaldeans who come to us; but as for you, gather
in wine and summer fruit and oil, and put *them* in your *storage*
vessels, and live in your cities that you have taken over."
11Likewise also all the Jews who were in Moab and among the
sons of Ammon and in Edom, and who were in all the *other*
countries, heard that the king of Babylon had left a remnant for
Judah and that he had appointed over them Gedaliah the son of
Ahikam, the son of Shaphan.
12Then all the Jews returned from all the places to which they
had been driven away and came to the land of Judah, to Gedaliah
at Mizpah, and gathered in wine and summer fruit in great abundance.
13¶ Now Johanan the son of Kareah and all the commanders of
the forces that were in the field came to Gedaliah at Mizpah,
14and said to him, "Are you well aware that Baalis the king of
the sons of Ammon has sent Ishmael the son of Nethaniah to take
your life?" But Gedaliah the son of Ahikam did not believe them.
15Then Johanan the son of Kareah spoke secretly to Gedaliah in
Mizpah, saying, "Let me go and kill Ishmael the son of Nethaniah,
and not a man will know! Why should he take your life, so that
all the Jews who are gathered to you should be scattered and the
remnant of Judah perish?"
16But Gedaliah the son of Ahikam said to Johanan the son of
Kareah, "Do not do this thing, for you are telling a lie about
Ishmael."

## New International

*Jeremiah Freed*

**40** THE WORD came to Jeremiah from the LORD after Nebuzaradan commander of the imperial guard had released
him at Ramah. He had found Jeremiah bound in chains among all
the captives from Jerusalem and Judah who were being carried into
exile to Babylon. 2When the commander of the guard found Jeremiah, he said to him, "The LORD your God decreed this disaster
for this place. 3And now the LORD has brought it about; he has
done just as he said he would. All this happened because you
people sinned against the LORD and did not obey him. 4But today
I am freeing you from the chains on your wrists. Come with me
to Babylon, if you like, and I will look after you; but if you do not
want to, then don't come. Look, the whole country lies before you;
go wherever you please." 5However, before Jeremiah turned to
go,[a] Nebuzaradan added, "Go back to Gedaliah son of Ahikam,
the son of Shaphan, whom the king of Babylon has appointed over
the towns of Judah, and live with him among the people, or go
anywhere else you please."
Then the commander gave him provisions and a present and
let him go. 6So Jeremiah went to Gedaliah son of Ahikam at Mizpah and stayed with him among the people who were left behind
in the land.

*Gedaliah Assassinated*

7When all the army officers and their men who were still in the
open country heard that the king of Babylon had appointed Gedaliah son of Ahikam as governor over the land and had put him in
charge of the men, women and children who were the poorest in
the land and who had not been carried into exile to Babylon, 8they
came to Gedaliah at Mizpah—Ishmael son of Nethaniah, Johanan
and Jonathan the sons of Kareah, Seraiah son of Tanhumeth, the
sons of Ephai the Netophathite, and Jaazaniah[b] the son of the
Maacathite, and their men. 9Gedaliah son of Ahikam, the son of
Shaphan, took an oath to reassure them and their men. "Do not
be afraid to serve the Babylonians,[c]" he said. "Settle down in the
land and serve the king of Babylon, and it will go well with you.
10I myself will stay at Mizpah to represent you before the Babylonians who come to us, but you are to harvest the wine, summer
fruit and oil, and put them in your storage jars, and live in the
towns you have taken over."
11When all the Jews in Moab, Ammon, Edom and all the other
countries heard that the king of Babylon had left a remnant in
Judah and had appointed Gedaliah son of Ahikam, the son of
Shaphan, as governor over them, 12they all came back to the land
of Judah, to Gedaliah at Mizpah, from all the countries where they
had been scattered. And they harvested an abundance of wine and
summer fruit.
13Johanan son of Kareah and all the army officers still in the
open country came to Gedaliah at Mizpah 14and said to him,
"Don't you know that Baalis king of the Ammonites has sent
Ishmael son of Nethaniah to take your life?" But Gedaliah son of
Ahikam did not believe them.
15Then Johanan son of Kareah said privately to Gedaliah in
Mizpah, "Let me go and kill Ishmael son of Nethaniah, and no one
will know it. Why should he take your life and cause all the Jews
who are gathered around you to be scattered and the remnant of
Judah to perish?"
16But Gedaliah son of Ahikam said to Johanan son of Kareah,
"Don't do such a thing! What you are saying about Ishmael is not
true."

**NIV** [a] 5 Or *Jeremiah answered* [b] 8 Hebrew *Jezaniah,* a variant of *Jaazaniah*
[c] 9 Or *Chaldeans;* also in verse 10

## King James

**41** NOW IT came to pass in the seventh month, *that* Ishmael the son of Nethaniah the son of Elishama, of the seed royal, and the princes of the king, even ten men with him, came unto Gedaliah the son of Ahikam to Mizpah; and there they did eat bread together in Mizpah.

2 Then arose Ishmael the son of Nethaniah, and the ten men that were with him, and smote Gedaliah the son of Ahikam the son of Shaphan with the sword, and slew him, whom the king of Babylon had made governor over the land.

3 Ishmael also slew all the Jews that were with him, *even* with Gedaliah, at Mizpah, and the Chaldeans that were found there, *and* the men of war.

4 And it came to pass the second day after he had slain Gedaliah, and no man knew *it*,

5 That there came certain from Shechem, from Shiloh, and from Samaria, *even* fourscore men, having their beards shaven, and their clothes rent, and having cut themselves, with offerings and incense in their hand, to bring *them* to the house of the LORD.

6 And Ishmael the son of Nethaniah went forth from Mizpah to meet them, weeping all along as he went: and it came to pass, as he met them, he said unto them, Come to Gedaliah the son of Ahikam.

7 And it was *so*, when they came into the midst of the city, that Ishmael the son of Nethaniah slew them, *and cast them* into the midst of the pit, he, and the men that *were* with him.

8 But ten men were found among them that said unto Ishmael, Slay us not: for we have treasures in the field, of wheat, and of barley, and of oil, and of honey. So he forbare, and slew them not among their brethren.

9 Now the pit wherein Ishmael had cast all the dead bodies of the men, whom he had slain because of Gedaliah, *was* it which Asa the king had made for fear of Baasha king of Israel: *and* Ishmael the son of Nethaniah filled it with *them that were* slain.

10 Then Ishmael carried away captive all the residue of the people that *were* in Mizpah, *even* the king's daughters, and all the people that remained in Mizpah, whom Nebuzar-adan the captain of the guard had committed to Gedaliah the son of Ahikam: and Ishmael the son of Nethaniah carried them away captive, and departed to go over to the Ammonites.

11 ¶ But when Johanan the son of Kareah, and all the captains of the forces that *were* with him, heard of all the evil that Ishmael the son of Nethaniah had done,

12 Then they took all the men, and went to fight with Ishmael the son of Nethaniah, and found him by the great waters that *are* in Gibeon.

13 Now it came to pass, *that* when all the people which *were* with Ishmael saw Johanan the son of Kareah, and all the captains of the forces that *were* with him, then they were glad.

14 So all the people that Ishmael had carried away captive from Mizpah cast about and returned, and went unto Johanan the son of Kareah.

15 But Ishmael the son of Nethaniah escaped from Johanan with eight men, and went to the Ammonites.

16 Then took Johanan the son of Kareah, and all the captains of the forces that *were* with him, all the remnant of the people whom he had recovered from Ishmael the son of Nethaniah, from Mizpah, after *that* he had slain Gedaliah the son of Ahikam, *even* mighty men of war, and the women, and the children, and the eunuchs, whom he had brought again from Gibeon:

17 And they departed, and dwelt in the habitation of Chimham, which is by Bethlehem, to go to enter into Egypt,

18 Because of the Chaldeans: for they were afraid of them, because Ishmael the son of Nethaniah had slain Gedaliah the son of Ahikam, whom the king of Babylon made governor in the land.

## Amplified

**41** NOW IN the seventh month [of that year] Ishmael the son of Nethaniah, the son of Elishama, of the royal descendants, and one of the princes of the king [of the Ammonites], came with ten men to Gedaliah the son of Ahikam, in Mizpah. As they were eating a meal together there in Mizpah,

2 Ishmael the son of Nethaniah and the ten men who were with him arose and struck down Gedaliah the son of Ahikam, the son of Shaphan, with the sword, and killed him, whom the king of Babylon had made governor over the land.

3 Ishmael [the Ammonite] also slew all the Jews who were with Gedaliah at Mizpah, and the Chaldean soldiers who were found there.

4 And the second day after the slaying of Gedaliah, before any one knew about it,

5 There came eighty men from Shechem, from Shiloh, and from Samaria, having their beards shaved and their clothes torn, and having cut themselves, bringing cereal offerings and incense, going up [to Jerusalem] to present them in the house of the Lord.

6 And Ishmael the son of Nethaniah went out from Mizpah to meet them, weeping all the way as he went. As he met them, he said to them, Come to Gedaliah the son of Ahikam.

7 And when they had come into the city, Ishmael the son of Nethaniah slew them, and cast them into the midst of the [city] cistern *or* pit, he and the men with him.

8 But ten men were among them who said to Ishmael, Do not kill us, for we have stores hidden in the field, of wheat and barley and oil and honey. So he refrained and did not slay them with their brethren.

9 Now the cistern pit into which Ishmael had cast all the dead bodies of the men whom he had slain in addition to Gedaliah, was the one which Asa the king [of Judah] had once made for fear of Baasha king of Israel [if he should lay siege to Mizpah]. Ishmael the son of Nethaniah filled it with those who were slain.

10 Then Ishmael [the Ammonite] carried away captive all the rest of the people who were in Mizpah, even the king's daughters and all the people who remained in Mizpah, whom Nebuzaradan the captain of the guard had committed to Gedaliah the son of Ahikam. Ishmael the son of Nethaniah carried them away captive, and departed to cross over [the Jordan] to the Ammonites.

11 But when Johanan the son of Kareah, and all the captains of the forces that were with him, heard of all the evil that Ishmael the son of Nethaniah had done,

12 They took all their men and went to fight with Ishmael the son of Nethaniah, and found him by the great pool that is in Gibeon.

13 Now when all the people who were [captives] with Ishmael saw Johanan the son of Kareah and all the captains of the forces that were with him, they were glad.

14 So all the people whom Ishmael had carried away captive from Mizpah turned around and came back, and went to Johanan the son of Kareah.

15 But Ishmael the son of Nethaniah escaped from Johanan with eight men and went to the Ammonites.

16 Then Johanan the son of Kareah and all the captains of the forces with him took all the remainder of the people whom he had recovered from Ishmael the son of Nethaniah, from Mizpah, after he had slain Gedaliah the son of Ahikam. [They were] the soldiers, the women, the children, and the eunuchs whom [Johanan] had brought back from Gibeon.

17 And they departed and stayed at the lodging place of Chimham, which is near Bethlehem, [intending] to go to Egypt

18 Because of the Chaldeans; for they were afraid of them, because Ishmael the son of Nethaniah had slain Gedaliah the son of Ahikam, whom the king of Babylon had made governor over the land [and whose death the king might avenge without much discrimination].

## New American Standard

*Gedaliah Is Murdered*

41 NOW IT came about in the seventh month that Ishmael the son of Nethaniah, the son of Elishama, of the royal family and *one* of the chief officers of the king, along with ten men, came to Mizpah to Gedaliah the son of Ahikam. While they were eating bread together there in Mizpah,

2Ishmael the son of Nethaniah and the ten men who were with him arose and struck down Gedaliah the son of Ahikam, the son of Shaphan, with the sword and put to death the one whom the king of Babylon had appointed over the land.

3Ishmael also struck down all the Jews who were with him, *that is* with Gedaliah at Mizpah, and the Chaldeans who were found there, the men of war.

4¶ Now it happened on the next day after the killing of Gedaliah, when no one knew about *it,*

5that eighty men came from Shechem, from Shiloh, and from Samaria with their beards shaved off and their clothes torn and their bodies gashed, having grain offerings and incense in their hands to bring to the house of the LORD.

6Then Ishmael the son of Nethaniah went out from Mizpah to meet them, weeping as he went; and it came about as he met them that he said to them, "Come to Gedaliah the son of Ahikam!"

7Yet it turned out that as soon as they came inside the city, Ishmael the son of Nethaniah and the men that were with him slaughtered them, *and cast them* into the cistern.

8But ten men who were found among them said to Ishmael, "Do not put us to death; for we have stores of wheat, barley, oil and honey hidden in the field." So he refrained and did not put them to death along with their companions.

9Now as for the cistern where Ishmael had cast all the corpses of the men whom he had struck down because of Gedaliah, it was the one that King Asa had made on account of Baasha, king of Israel; Ishmael the son of Nethaniah filled it with the slain.

10Then Ishmael took captive all the remnant of the people who were in Mizpah, the king's daughters and all the people who were left in Mizpah, whom Nebuzaradan the captain of the bodyguard had put under the charge of Gedaliah the son of Ahikam; thus Ishmael the son of Nethaniah took them captive and proceeded to cross over to the sons of Ammon.

*Johanan Rescues the People*

11¶ But Johanan the son of Kareah and all the commanders of the forces that were with him heard of all the evil that Ishmael the son of Nethaniah had done.

12So they took all the men and went to fight with Ishmael the son of Nethaniah and they found him by the great pool that is in Gibeon.

13Now it came about, as soon as all the people who were with Ishmael saw Johanan the son of Kareah and the commanders of the forces that were with him, they were glad.

14So all the people whom Ishmael had taken captive from Mizpah turned around and came back, and went to Johanan the son of Kareah.

15But Ishmael the son of Nethaniah escaped from Johanan with eight men and went to the sons of Ammon.

16Then Johanan the son of Kareah and all the commanders of the forces that were with him took from Mizpah all the remnant of the people whom he had recovered from Ishmael the son of Nethaniah, after he had struck down Gedaliah the son of Ahikam, *that is,* the men who were soldiers, *the* women, *the* children, and *the* eunuchs, whom he had brought back from Gibeon.

17And they went and stayed in Geruth Chimham, which is beside Bethlehem, in order to proceed into Egypt

18because of the Chaldeans; for they were afraid of them, since Ishmael the son of Nethaniah had struck down Gedaliah the son of Ahikam, whom the king of Babylon had appointed over the land.

## New International

41 IN THE seventh month Ishmael son of Nethaniah, the son
of Elishama, who was of royal blood and had been one of
the king's officers, came with ten men to Gedaliah son of Ahikam
at Mizpah. While they were eating together there, 2Ishmael son of
Nethaniah and the ten men who were with him got up and struck
down Gedaliah son of Ahikam, the son of Shaphan, with the
sword, killing the one whom the king of Babylon had appointed
as governor over the land. 3Ishmael also killed all the Jews who
were with Gedaliah at Mizpah, as well as the Babylonian[a] soldiers
who were there.

4The day after Gedaliah's assassination, before anyone knew
about it, 5eighty men who had shaved off their beards, torn their
clothes and cut themselves came from Shechem, Shiloh and Samaria, bringing grain offerings and incense with them to the house
of the LORD. 6Ishmael son of Nethaniah went out from Mizpah to
meet them, weeping as he went. When he met them, he said,
"Come to Gedaliah son of Ahikam." 7When they went into the
city, Ishmael son of Nethaniah and the men who were with him
slaughtered them and threw them into a cistern. 8But ten of them
said to Ishmael, "Don't kill us! We have wheat and barley, oil and
honey, hidden in a field." So he let them alone and did not kill
them with the others. 9Now the cistern where he threw all the
bodies of the men he had killed along with Gedaliah was the one
King Asa had made as part of his defense against Baasha king of
Israel. Ishmael son of Nethaniah filled it with the dead.

10Ishmael made captives of all the rest of the people who were
in Mizpah—the king's daughters along with all the others who
were left there, over whom Nebuzaradan commander of the imperial guard had appointed Gedaliah son of Ahikam. Ishmael son
of Nethaniah took them captive and set out to cross over to the
Ammonites.

11When Johanan son of Kareah and all the army officers who
were with him heard about all the crimes Ishmael son of Nethaniah
had committed, 12they took all their men and went to fight Ishmael
son of Nethaniah. They caught up with him near the great pool in
Gibeon. 13When all the people Ishmael had with him saw Johanan
son of Kareah and the army officers who were with him, they were
glad. 14All the people Ishmael had taken captive at Mizpah turned
and went over to Johanan son of Kareah. 15But Ishmael son of
Nethaniah and eight of his men escaped from Johanan and fled to
the Ammonites.

*Flight to Egypt*

16Then Johanan son of Kareah and all the army officers who
were with him led away all the survivors from Mizpah whom he
had recovered from Ishmael son of Nethaniah after he had assassinated Gedaliah son of Ahikam: the soldiers, women, children
and court officials he had brought from Gibeon. 17And they went
on, stopping at Geruth Kimham near Bethlehem on their way to
Egypt 18to escape the Babylonians.[b] They were afraid of them
because Ishmael son of Nethaniah had killed Gedaliah son of
Ahikam, whom the king of Babylon had appointed as governor
over the land.

NIV [a] 3 Or *Chaldean* [b] 18 Or *Chaldeans*

## King James

42 THEN ALL the captains of the forces, and Johanan the son
of Kareah, and Jezaniah the son of Hoshaiah, and all the
people from the least even unto the greatest, came near,
2And said unto Jeremiah the prophet, Let, we beseech thee, our
supplication be accepted before thee, and pray for us unto the
LORD thy God, *even* for all this remnant; (for we are left *but* a few
of many, as thine eyes do behold us:)
3That the LORD thy God may show us the way wherein we may
walk, and the thing that we may do.
4Then Jeremiah the prophet said unto them, I have heard *you;*
behold, I will pray unto the LORD your God according to your
words; and it shall come to pass, *that* whatsoever thing the LORD
shall answer you, I will declare *it* unto you; I will keep nothing back
from you.
5Then they said to Jeremiah, The LORD be a true and faithful
witness between us, if we do not even according to all things for
the which the LORD thy God shall send thee to us.
6Whether *it be* good, or whether *it be* evil, we will obey the voice
of the LORD our God, to whom we send thee; that it may be well
with us, when we obey the voice of the LORD our God.
7¶ And it came to pass after ten days, that the word of the LORD
came unto Jeremiah.
8Then called he Johanan the son of Kareah, and all the captains
of the forces which *were* with him, and all the people from the least
even to the greatest,
9And said unto them, Thus saith the LORD, the God of Israel,
unto whom ye sent me to present your supplication before him;
10If ye will still abide in this land, then will I build you, and not
pull *you* down, and I will plant you, and not pluck *you* up: for I
repent me of the evil that I have done unto you.
11Be not afraid of the king of Babylon, of whom ye are afraid;
be not afraid of him, saith the LORD: for I *am* with you to save you,
and to deliver you from his hand.
12And I will show mercies unto you, that he may have mercy
upon you, and cause you to return to your own land.
13¶ But if ye say, We will not dwell in this land, neither obey
the voice of the LORD your God,
14Saying, No; but we will go into the land of Egypt, where we
shall see no war, nor hear the sound of the trumpet, nor have
hunger of bread; and there will we dwell:
15And now therefore hear the word of the LORD, ye remnant of
Judah; Thus saith the LORD of hosts, the God of Israel; If ye wholly
set your faces to enter into Egypt, and go to sojourn there;
16Then it shall come to pass, *that* the sword, which ye feared,
shall overtake you there in the land of Egypt, and the famine,
whereof ye were afraid, shall follow close after you there in Egypt;
and there ye shall die.
17So shall it be with all the men that set their faces to go into
Egypt to sojourn there; they shall die by the sword, by the famine,
and by the pestilence: and none of them shall remain or escape
from the evil that I will bring upon them.
18For thus saith the LORD of hosts, the God of Israel; As mine
anger and my fury hath been poured forth upon the inhabitants
of Jerusalem; so shall my fury be poured forth upon you, when ye
shall enter into Egypt: and ye shall be an execration, and an astonishment, and a curse, and a reproach; and ye shall see this place
no more.
19¶ The LORD hath said concerning you, O ye remnant of Judah;
Go ye not into Egypt: know certainly that I have admonished you
this day.
20For ye dissembled in your hearts, when ye sent me unto the
LORD your God, saying, Pray for us unto the LORD our God; and
according unto all that the LORD our God shall say, so declare unto
us, and we will do *it.*
21And *now* I have this day declared *it* to you; but ye have not
obeyed the voice of the LORD your God, nor any *thing* for the which
he hath sent me unto you.

## Amplified

42 THEN ALL the captains of the forces, and Johanan the son
of Kareah and Jezaniah [Azariah] the son of Hoshaiah,
and all the people from the least even to the greatest, came near
2And said to Jeremiah the prophet, We beseech you that you
will let our supplication be presented before you and that you will
pray to the Lord your God for us, even for all this remnant [of the
people of Judah]; for of the many, there are but a few of us left,
as you see with your [own] eyes.
3[Pray] that the Lord your God may show us the way in which
we should walk and the thing that we should do.
4Then Jeremiah the prophet said to them, I have heard you;
behold, I will pray to the Lord your God according to your words,
and it shall be that whatever thing the Lord shall answer you, I will
declare it to you; I will keep nothing back from you.
5Then they said to Jeremiah, The Lord be a true and faithful
witness against us if we fail to do according to all the things that
the Lord your God shall send you to tell us.
6Whether it be good or evil, we will obey the voice of the Lord
our God to Whom we send you [to inquire], that it may be well
with us when we obey the voice of the Lord our God.
7And after ten days the word of the Lord came to Jeremiah.
8Then he called Johanan the son of Kareah and all the captains
of the forces who were with him, and all the people from the least
even to the greatest,
9And said to them, Thus says the Lord, the God of Israel, to
Whom you sent me to present your supplication before Him:
10If you will remain in this land, then I will build you up and
not pull you down, and I will plant you and not pull you up; for
I will relent *and* comfort *and* ease Myself concerning the evil that
[in chastisement] I have done to you [and will substitute mercy and
loving-kindness for judgment].
11Be not afraid of the king of Babylon, of whom you are fearful—with the profound and reverent dread inspired by deity; be
not afraid of him, says the Lord, for [he is a mere man, while the
all-wise, all-powerful, and ever-present God] I, [the Lord] am with
you to save you and to deliver you from his hand.
12And I will grant mercy to you, that he may have mercy on you
and permit you to remain in your own land.
13But if you say, We will not dwell in this land, so that you
disobey the voice of the Lord your God,
14Saying, No, but we will go to the land of Egypt, where we
shall not see war, or hear the sound of the trumpet, or be hungry
for bread, and we will dwell there,
15Then hear the word of the Lord, O remnant of Judah. Thus
says the Lord of hosts, the God of Israel: If you are fully determined to go to Egypt and go to dwell there temporarily,
16Then the sword which you fear shall overtake you there in the
land of Egypt, and the famine of which you are afraid shall follow
close after you to Egypt *and* in it, and there you shall die.
17So shall it be with all the men who set their faces to go to Egypt
to sojourn there; they shall die by the sword, by famine, and by
pestilence; none of them shall remain or survive the evil that I will
bring upon them.
18For thus says the Lord of hosts, the God of Israel: As My anger
and My wrath have been poured forth upon the inhabitants of
Jerusalem, so shall My wrath be poured forth upon you when you
enter Egypt. You shall be a detested thing, an astonishment *and*
horror, a curse, a thing lightly esteemed *and* a taunt *and* a reproach.
You shall see this place no more.
19The Lord has said to you, O remnant of Judah, Do not go to
Egypt. Know for a certainty that I [Jeremiah] have warned *and*
testified to you this day
20That you have dealt deceitfully against your own lives. For
you sent me [Jeremiah] to the Lord your God, saying, Pray for us
to the Lord our God, and whatever the Lord our God says, declare
it to us and we will do it.
21And I have this day declared it to you, but you have not
obeyed the voice of the Lord your God in anything that He sent
me to tell you.

## New American Standard

*Warning against Going to Egypt*

**42** THEN ALL the commanders of the forces, Johanan the son of Kareah, Jezaniah the son of Hoshaiah, and all the people both small and great approached

2 and said to Jeremiah the prophet, "Please let our petition come before you, and pray for us to the LORD your God, *that is* for all this remnant; because we are left *but* a few out of many, as your own eyes *now* see us,

3 that the LORD your God may tell us the way in which we should walk and the thing that we should do."

4 Then Jeremiah the prophet said to them, "I have heard *you*. Behold, I am going to pray to the LORD your God in accordance with your words; and it will come about that the whole message which the LORD will answer you I will tell you. I will not keep back a word from you."

5 Then they said to Jeremiah, "May the LORD be a true and faithful witness against us, if we do not act in accordance with the whole message with which the LORD your God will send you to us.

6 "Whether *it* is pleasant or unpleasant, we will listen to the voice of the LORD our God to whom we are sending you, in order that it may go well with us when we listen to the voice of the LORD our God."

7¶ Now it came about at the end of ten days that the word of the LORD came to Jeremiah.

8 Then he called for Johanan the son of Kareah, and all the commanders of the forces that were with him, and for all the people both small and great,

9 and said to them, "Thus says the LORD the God of Israel, to whom you sent me to present your petition before Him:

10 'If you will indeed stay in this land, then I will build you up and not tear you down, and I will plant you and not uproot you; for I shall relent concerning the calamity that I have inflicted on you.

11 'Do not be afraid of the king of Babylon, whom you are *now* fearing; do not be afraid of him,' declares the LORD, 'for I am with you to save you and deliver you from his hand.

12 'I will also show you compassion, so that he will have compassion on you and restore you to your own soil.

13 'But if you are going to say, "We will not stay in this land," so as not to listen to the voice of the LORD your God,

14 saying, "No, but we will go to the land of Egypt, where we shall not see war or hear the sound of a trumpet or hunger for bread, and we will stay there";

15 then in that case listen to the word of the LORD, O remnant of Judah. Thus says the LORD of hosts, the God of Israel, "If you really set your mind to enter Egypt, and go in to reside there,

16 then it will come about that the sword, which you are afraid of will overtake you there in the land of Egypt; and the famine, about which you are anxious, will follow closely after you there *in* Egypt; and you will die there.

17 "So all the men who set their mind to go to Egypt to reside there will die by the sword, by famine, and by pestilence; and they will have no survivors or refugees from the calamity that I am going to bring on them." ' '

18¶ For thus says the LORD of hosts, the God of Israel, "As My anger and wrath have been poured out on the inhabitants of Jerusalem, so My wrath will be poured out on you when you enter Egypt. And you will become a curse, an object of horror, an imprecation, and a reproach; and you will see this place no more."

19 The LORD has spoken to you, O remnant of Judah, "Do not go into Egypt!" You should clearly understand that today I have testified against you.

20 For you have *only* deceived yourselves; for it is you who sent me to the LORD your God, saying, "Pray for us to the LORD our God; and whatever the LORD our God says, tell us so, and we will do it."

21 So, I have told you today, but you have not obeyed the LORD your God, even in whatever He has sent me to *tell* you.

## New International

**42** THEN ALL the army officers, including Johanan son of
Kareah and Jezaniah[a] son of Hoshaiah, and all the people
from the least to the greatest approached 2 Jeremiah the prophet
and said to him, "Please hear our petition and pray to the LORD
your God for this entire remnant. For as you now see, though we
were once many, now only a few are left. 3 Pray that the LORD your
God will tell us where we should go and what we should do."
4 "I have heard you," replied Jeremiah the prophet. "I will
certainly pray to the LORD your God as you have requested; I will
tell you everything the LORD says and will keep nothing back from
you."
5 Then they said to Jeremiah, "May the LORD be a true and
faithful witness against us if we do not act in accordance with
everything the LORD your God sends you to tell us. 6 Whether it
is favorable or unfavorable, we will obey the LORD our God, to
whom we are sending you, so that it will go well with us, for we
will obey the LORD our God."
7 Ten days later the word of the LORD came to Jeremiah. 8 So he
called together Johanan son of Kareah and all the army officers
who were with him and all the people from the least to the greatest. 9 He said to them, "This is what the LORD, the God of Israel,
to whom you sent me to present your petition, says: 10 'If you stay
in this land, I will build you up and not tear you down; I will plant
you and not uproot you, for I am grieved over the disaster I have
inflicted on you. 11 Do not be afraid of the king of Babylon, whom
you now fear. Do not be afraid of him, declares the LORD, for I am
with you and will save you and deliver you from his hands. 12 I will
show you compassion so that he will have compassion on you and
restore you to your land.'
13 "However, if you say, 'We will not stay in this land,' and so
disobey the LORD your God, 14 and if you say, 'No, we will go and
live in Egypt, where we will not see war or hear the trumpet or be
hungry for bread,' 15 then hear the word of the LORD, O remnant
of Judah. This is what the LORD Almighty, the God of Israel, says:
'If you are determined to go to Egypt and you do go to settle there,
16 then the sword you fear will overtake you there, and the famine
you dread will follow you into Egypt, and there you will die.
17 Indeed, all who are determined to go to Egypt to settle there will
die by the sword, famine and plague; not one of them will survive
or escape the disaster I will bring on them.' 18 This is what the LORD
Almighty, the God of Israel, says: 'As my anger and wrath have
been poured out on those who lived in Jerusalem, so will my wrath
be poured out on you when you go to Egypt. You will be an object
of cursing and horror, of condemnation and reproach; you will
never see this place again.'
19 "O remnant of Judah, the LORD has told you, 'Do not go to
Egypt.' Be sure of this: I warn you today 20 that you made a fatal
mistake[b] when you sent me to the LORD your God and said, 'Pray
to the LORD our God for us; tell us everything he says and we will
do it.' 21 I have told you today, but you still have not obeyed the
LORD your God in all he sent me to tell you. 22 So now, be sure of

**NIV** [a] *1* Hebrew; Septuagint (see also 43:2) *Azariah* [b] *20* Or *you erred in your hearts*

## King James

22Now therefore know certainly that ye shall die by the sword, by the famine, and by the pestilence, in the place whither ye desire to go *and* to sojourn.

# 43

AND IT came to pass, *that* when Jeremiah had made an end of speaking unto all the people all the words of the LORD their God, for which the LORD their God had sent him to them, *even* all these words,

2Then spake Azariah the son of Hoshaiah, and Johanan the son of Kareah, and all the proud men, saying unto Jeremiah, Thou speakest falsely: the LORD our God hath not sent thee to say, Go not into Egypt to sojourn there:

3But Baruch the son of Neriah setteth thee on against us, for to deliver us into the hand of the Chaldeans, that they might put us to death, and carry us away captives into Babylon.

4So Johanan the son of Kareah, and all the captains of the forces, and all the people, obeyed not the voice of the LORD, to dwell in the land of Judah.

5But Johanan the son of Kareah, and all the captains of the forces, took all the remnant of Judah, that were returned from all nations, whither they had been driven, to dwell in the land of Judah;

6 *Even* men, and women, and children, and the king's daughters, and every person that Nebuzar-adan the captain of the guard had left with Gedaliah the son of Ahikam the son of Shaphan, and Jeremiah the prophet, and Baruch the son of Neriah.

7So they came into the land of Egypt: for they obeyed not the voice of the LORD: thus came they *even* to Tahpanhes.

8¶ Then came the word of the LORD unto Jeremiah in Tahpanhes, saying,

9Take great stones in thine hand, and hide them in the clay in the brickkiln, which *is* at the entry of Pharaoh's house in Tahpanhes, in the sight of the men of Judah;

10And say unto them, Thus saith the LORD of hosts, the God of Israel; Behold, I will send and take Nebuchadrezzar the king of Babylon, my servant, and will set his throne upon these stones that I have hid; and he shall spread his royal pavilion over them.

11And when he cometh, he shall smite the land of Egypt, *and deliver* such *as are* for death to death; and such *as are* for captivity to captivity; and such *as are* for the sword to the sword.

12And I will kindle a fire in the houses of the gods of Egypt; and he shall burn them, and carry them away captives: and he shall array himself with the land of Egypt, as a shepherd putteth on his garment; and he shall go forth from thence in peace.

13He shall break also the images of Beth-shemesh, that *is* in the land of Egypt; and the houses of the gods of the Egyptians shall he burn with fire.

# 44

THE WORD that came to Jeremiah concerning all the Jews which dwell in the land of Egypt, which dwell at Migdol, and at Tahpanhes, and at Noph, and in the country of Pathros, saying,

2Thus saith the LORD of hosts, the God of Israel; Ye have seen all the evil that I have brought upon Jerusalem, and upon all the cities of Judah; and, behold, this day they *are* a desolation, and no man dwelleth therein,

3Because of their wickedness which they have committed to provoke me to anger, in that they went to burn incense, *and* to serve other gods, whom they knew not, *neither* they, ye, nor your fathers.

## Amplified

22Now therefore know for a certainty that you shall die by the sword, by famine, and by pestilence in [Egypt] the place where you desire to go to sojourn.

# 43

AND WHEN Jeremiah had finished speaking to all the people all these words of the Lord their God, for which the Lord their God had sent him to them,

2Then Azariah the son of Hoshaiah and Johanan the son of Kareah and all the proud *and* insolent men said to Jeremiah, You are not telling the truth! The Lord our God has not sent you to say, Do not go into Egypt to live there temporarily.

3But Baruch the son of Neriah has set you against us, to deliver us into the hand of the Chaldeans, so they may put us to death or carry us away captive to Babylon.

4So Johanan the son of Kareah and all the captains of the forces and all the people did not obey the voice of the Lord, to remain in the land of Judah.

5But Johanan the son of Kareah and all the captains of the forces took all the remnant of Judah who had returned to dwell in the land of Judah from all the nations to which they had been driven,

6Even men, women and children, the king's daughters and every person whom Nebuzaradan the captain of the guard had left with Gedaliah the son of Ahikam, the son of Shaphan; also he took Jeremiah the prophet and Baruch the son of Neriah.

7So they came into the land of Egypt, for they obeyed not the voice of the Lord. And they came to Tahpanhes.

8Then came the word of the Lord to Jeremiah in Tahpanhes, saying,

9Take large stones in your hands and hide them in the mortar in the pavement of brick, which is at the entrance of Pharaoh's house in Tahpanhes, in the sight of the men of Judah,

10And say to them, Thus says the Lord of hosts, the God of Israel: Behold, I will send and take Nebuchadrezzar the king of Babylon, My servant [because he works for Me], and I [through him] will set his throne upon these stones that I have hid; and his [glittering, royal] canopy shall be stretched over them. [Ezek. 29:19, 20.]

11And he shall come and smite the land of Egypt, giving such as are for death to death, and such as are for captivity to captivity, and such as are for the sword to the sword.

12And I [through him] will kindle a fire in the temples of the gods of Egypt; and he shall burn *the houses* and carry [the people] away captives; and he shall array himself with the land of Egypt, as a shepherd puts on his garment [as he wills and when he chooses]; and he shall go away from there in peace.

13[Nebuchadrezzar] shall break also the images *and* obelisks of Heliopolis [called On or Bethshemesh—house of the sun] in the land of Egypt, and the temples of the gods of Egypt shall he burn with fire.

# 44

THE WORD that came to Jeremiah concerning all the Jews that dwell in the land of Egypt, at Migdol, at Tahpanhes, at Memphis, and in the country of Pathros, saying,

2Thus says the Lord of hosts, the God of Israel: You have seen all the evil that I brought upon Jerusalem and upon all the cities of Judah; and see, this day they are a desolation, and no man dwells in them,

3Because of the wickedness which they committed, provoking Me to anger, in that they went to burn incense to serve other gods that they did not know, neither they, nor you, nor your fathers.

## New American Standard

22 Therefore you should now clearly understand that you will
die by the sword, by famine, and by pestilence, in the place where
you wish to go to reside.

*In Egypt Jeremiah Warns of Judgment*

**43** BUT IT came about, as soon as Jeremiah whom the LORD
their God had sent, had finished telling all the people all
the words of the LORD their God—that is, all these words—
2 that Azariah the son of Hoshaiah, and Johanan the son of
Kareah, and all the arrogant men said to Jeremiah, "You are telling
a lie! The LORD our God has not sent you to say, 'You are not to
enter Egypt to reside there';
3 but Baruch the son of Neriah is inciting you against us to give
us over into the hand of the Chaldeans, so they may put us to
death or exile us to Babylon."
4 So Johanan the son of Kareah and all the commanders of the
forces, and all the people, did not obey the voice of the LORD, so
as to stay in the land of Judah.
5 But Johanan the son of Kareah and all the commanders of the
forces took the entire remnant of Judah who had returned from all
the nations to which they had been driven away, in order to reside
in the land of Judah—
6 the men, the women, the children, the king's daughters and
every person that Nebuzaradan the captain of the bodyguard had
left with Gedaliah the son of Ahikam and grandson of Shaphan,
together with Jeremiah the prophet and Baruch the son of Neriah—
7 and they entered the land of Egypt (for they did not obey the
voice of the LORD) and went in as far as Tahpanhes.
8 ¶ Then the word of the LORD came to Jeremiah in Tahpanhes,
saying,
9 "Take *some* large stones in your hands and hide them in the
mortar in the brick *terrace* which is at the entrance of Pharaoh's
palace in Tahpanhes, in the sight of some *of the* Jews;
10 and say to them, 'Thus says the LORD of hosts, the God of
Israel, "Behold, I am going to send and get Nebuchadnezzar the
king of Babylon, My servant, and I am going to set his throne *right*
over these stones that I have hidden; and he will spread his canopy
over them.
11 "He will also come and strike the land of Egypt; those who
are *meant* for death *will be given over* to death, and those for captivity
to captivity, and those for the sword to the sword.
12 "And I shall set fire to the temples of the gods of Egypt, and
he will burn them and take them captive. So he will wrap himself
with the land of Egypt as a shepherd wraps himself with his
garment, and he will depart from there safely.
13 "He will also shatter the obelisks of Heliopolis, which is in the
land of Egypt; and the temples of the gods of Egypt he will burn
with fire." ' "

*Conquest of Egypt Predicted*

**44** THE WORD that came to Jeremiah for all the Jews living
in the land of Egypt, those who were living in Migdol,
Tahpanhes, Memphis, and the land of Pathros, saying,
2 "Thus says the LORD of hosts, the God of Israel, 'You yourselves have seen all the calamity that I have brought on Jerusalem
and all the cities of Judah; and behold, this day they are in ruins
and no one lives in them,
3 because of their wickedness which they committed so as to
provoke Me to anger by continuing to burn sacrifices *and* to serve
other gods whom they had not known, *neither* they, you, nor your
fathers.

## New International

this: You will die by the sword, famine and plague in the place
where you want to go to settle."

**43** WHEN JEREMIAH finished telling the people all the
words of the LORD their God—everything the LORD had
sent him to tell them— 2 Azariah son of Hoshaiah and Johanan son
of Kareah and all the arrogant men said to Jeremiah, "You are
lying! The LORD our God has not sent you to say, 'You must not
go to Egypt to settle there.' 3 But Baruch son of Neriah is inciting
you against us to hand us over to the Babylonians,[a] so they may
kill us or carry us into exile to Babylon."
4 So Johanan son of Kareah and all the army officers and all the
people disobeyed the LORD's command to stay in the land of
Judah. 5 Instead, Johanan son of Kareah and all the army officers
led away all the remnant of Judah who had come back to live in
the land of Judah from all the nations where they had been scattered. 6 They also led away all the men, women and children and
the king's daughters whom Nebuzaradan commander of the imperial guard had left with Gedaliah son of Ahikam, the son of
Shaphan, and Jeremiah the prophet and Baruch son of Neriah. 7 So
they entered Egypt in disobedience to the LORD and went as far
as Tahpanhes.
8 In Tahpanhes the word of the LORD came to Jeremiah: 9 "While
the Jews are watching, take some large stones with you and bury
them in clay in the brick pavement at the entrance to Pharaoh's
palace in Tahpanhes. 10 Then say to them, 'This is what the LORD
Almighty, the God of Israel, says: I will send for my servant
Nebuchadnezzar king of Babylon, and I will set his throne over
these stones I have buried here; he will spread his royal canopy
above them. 11 He will come and attack Egypt, bringing death to
those destined for death, captivity to those destined for captivity,
and the sword to those destined for the sword. 12 He[b] will set fire
to the temples of the gods of Egypt; he will burn their temples and
take their gods captive. As a shepherd wraps his garment around
him, so will he wrap Egypt around himself and depart from there
unscathed. 13 There in the temple of the sun[c] in Egypt he will
demolish the sacred pillars and will burn down the temples of the
gods of Egypt.' "

*Disaster Because of Idolatry*

**44** THIS WORD came to Jeremiah concerning all the Jews
living in Lower Egypt—in Migdol, Tahpanhes and Memphis[d]—and in Upper Egypt[e]: 2 "This is what the LORD Almighty,
the God of Israel, says: You saw the great disaster I brought on
Jerusalem and on all the towns of Judah. Today they lie deserted
and in ruins 3 because of the evil they have done. They provoked
me to anger by burning incense and by worshiping other gods that
neither they nor you nor your fathers ever knew. 4 Again and again

NIV [a] 3 Or *Chaldeans* [b] 12 Or *I* [c] 13 Or *in Heliopolis* [d] 1 Hebrew *Noph*
[e] 1 Hebrew *in Pathros*

## King James

4 Howbeit I sent unto you all my servants the prophets, rising early and sending *them,* saying, Oh, do not this abominable thing that I hate.

5 But they hearkened not, nor inclined their ear to turn from their wickedness, to burn no incense unto other gods.

6 Wherefore my fury and mine anger was poured forth, and was kindled in the cities of Judah and in the streets of Jerusalem; and they are wasted *and* desolate, as at this day.

7 Therefore now thus saith the LORD, the God of hosts, the God of Israel; Wherefore commit ye *this* great evil against your souls, to cut off from you man and woman, child and suckling, out of Judah, to leave you none to remain;

8 In that ye provoke me unto wrath with the works of your hands, burning incense unto other gods in the land of Egypt, whither ye be gone to dwell, that ye might cut yourselves off, and that ye might be a curse and a reproach among all the nations of the earth?

9 Have ye forgotten the wickedness of your fathers, and the wickedness of the kings of Judah, and the wickedness of their wives, and your own wickedness, and the wickedness of your wives, which they have committed in the land of Judah, and in the streets of Jerusalem?

10 They are not humbled *even* unto this day, neither have they feared, nor walked in my law, nor in my statutes, that I set before you and before your fathers.

11 ¶ Therefore thus saith the LORD of hosts, the God of Israel; Behold, I will set my face against you for evil, and to cut off all Judah.

12 And I will take the remnant of Judah, that have set their faces to go into the land of Egypt to sojourn there, and they shall all be consumed, *and* fall in the land of Egypt; they shall *even* be consumed by the sword *and* by the famine: they shall die, from the least even unto the greatest, by the sword and by the famine: and they shall be an execration, *and* an astonishment, and a curse, and a reproach.

13 For I will punish them that dwell in the land of Egypt, as I have punished Jerusalem, by the sword, by the famine, and by the pestilence:

14 So that none of the remnant of Judah, which are gone into the land of Egypt to sojourn there, shall escape or remain, that they should return into the land of Judah, to the which they have a desire to return to dwell there: for none shall return but such as shall escape.

15 ¶ Then all the men which knew that their wives had burned incense unto other gods, and all the women that stood by, a great multitude, even all the people that dwelt in the land of Egypt, in Pathros, answered Jeremiah, saying,

16 *As for* the word that thou hast spoken unto us in the name of the LORD, we will not hearken unto thee.

17 But we will certainly do whatsoever thing goeth forth out of our own mouth, to burn incense unto the queen of heaven, and to pour out drink offerings unto her, as we have done, we, and our fathers, our kings, and our princes, in the cities of Judah, and in the streets of Jerusalem: for *then* had we plenty of victuals, and were well, and saw no evil.

18 But since we left off to burn incense to the queen of heaven, and to pour out drink offerings unto her, we have wanted all *things,* and have been consumed by the sword and by the famine.

19 And when we burned incense to the queen of heaven, and poured out drink offerings unto her, did we make her cakes to worship her, and pour out drink offerings unto her, without our men?

20 ¶ Then Jeremiah said unto all the people, to the men, and to the women, and to all the people which had given him *that* answer, saying,

## Amplified

4 Yet I sent to you all My servants the prophets earnestly *and* persistently, saying, Oh, do not do this loathsome *and* shamefully vile thing that I hate *and* abhor!

5 But they would not listen *and* obey, or submit *and* consent to turn from their wickedness and burn no incense to other gods.

6 Therefore My wrath and My anger were poured out and were kindled in the cities of Judah and in the streets of Jerusalem; and they became wasted and desolate, as at this day.

7 Therefore now thus says the Lord, the God of hosts, the God of Israel: Why do you commit this great evil against yourselves, *that will* cut off from you man and woman, infant and weaned child, out of Judah, to leave you none remaining?

8 Why do you provoke Me to anger with [idols] the works of your own hands, burning incense to other gods in the land of Egypt where you [of your own accord] have come to dwell temporarily, that you may be cut off and become a curse and a reproach—a reviling and a taunt—among all the nations of the earth?

9 Have you forgotten the wickedness of your fathers, the wickedness of the kings of Judah, the wickedness of *their* wives [who clung to their foreign gods], your own wickedness and the wickedness of your wives [who imitated their queens] which they committed in the land of Judah and in the streets of Jerusalem?

10 They are not humbled—contrite, penitent and bruised for their guilt and iniquities—even to this day, neither have they feared *and* revered *Me,* nor walked in My law or My statutes, which I set before you and before your fathers. [Jer. 6:15; 26:4-6; 44:23.]

11 Therefore thus says the Lord of hosts, the God of Israel: Behold, I will set My face against you for evil, even to cut off all Judah [from the land].

12 And I will take the [one] remnant of Judah who have set their faces to come into the land of Egypt to sojourn here [fleeing to Egypt instead of surrendering to the Chaldeans as directed by the Lord through Jeremiah], and they shall all be consumed, and shall fall in the land of Egypt; they shall be consumed by the sword and by famine; from the least even to the greatest they shall die by the sword and by famine; and they shall be a detestable thing, an astonishment, a curse, and a reproach—a horror, a reviling and a taunt.

13 For I will punish all the inhabitants of the land of Egypt as I have punished Jerusalem, by the sword, by famine, and by pestilence,

14 So that none of the remnant of Judah who have come to the land of Egypt to sojourn shall escape or survive or return to the land of Judah, to which they desire *and* lift up their soul to return to dwell there; for none shall return except fugitives.

15 Then all the men who knew that their wives had burned incense to other gods, and all the women who stood by, a great assembly, even all the people who dwelt in Pathros in the land of Egypt, answered Jeremiah:

16 As for the word that you have spoken to us in the name of the Lord, we will not listen to *or* obey you.

17 But we will certainly perform every word of the vows we have made, to burn incense to the queen of heaven [the moon] and to pour out drink offerings to her, as we have done, we and our fathers, our kings and our princes, in the cities of Judah and in the streets of Jerusalem; for then we had plenty of food, and were well *and* prosperous, and saw no evil.

18 But when we stopped burning incense to the queen of heaven and pouring out drink offerings to her, we have lacked everything and have been consumed by the sword and by famine.

19 [And the wives said] When we burned incense to the queen of heaven and poured out drink offerings to her, did we make cakes [with the image of the full moon] to represent *and* honor her and pour out drink offerings to her without [the knowledge and approval of] our husbands?

20 Then Jeremiah said to all the people, to the men and to the women and to all the people who had given him that answer,

## New American Standard

4'Yet I sent you all My servants the prophets, again and again,
saying, "Oh, do not do this abominable thing which I hate."
5'But they did not listen or incline their ears to turn from their
wickedness, so as not to burn sacrifices to other gods.
6'Therefore My wrath and My anger were poured out and
burned in the cities of Judah and in the streets of Jerusalem, so they
have become a ruin and a desolation as it is this day.
7'Now then thus says the LORD God of hosts, the God of Israel,
"Why are you doing great harm to yourselves, so as to cut off from
you man and woman, child and infant, from among Judah, leaving
yourselves without remnant,
8provoking Me to anger with the works of your hands, burning
sacrifices to other gods in the land of Egypt, where you are entering to reside, so that you might be cut off and become a curse and
a reproach among all the nations of the earth?
9"Have you forgotten the wickedness of your fathers, the
wickedness of the kings of Judah, and the wickedness of their
wives, your own wickedness, and the wickedness of your wives,
which they committed in the land of Judah and in the streets of
Jerusalem?
10"But they have not become contrite even to this day, nor have
they feared nor walked in My law or My statutes, which I have set
before you and before your fathers."'
11¶ "Therefore thus says the LORD of hosts, the God of Israel,
'Behold, I am going to set My face against you for woe, even to cut
off all Judah.
12'And I will take away the remnant of Judah who have set their
mind on entering the land of Egypt to reside there, and they will
all meet their end in the land of Egypt; they will fall by the sword
*and* meet their end by famine. Both small and great will die by the
sword and famine; and they will become a curse, an object of
horror, an imprecation and a reproach.
13'And I will punish those who live in the land of Egypt, as I
have punished Jerusalem, with the sword, with famine, and with
pestilence.
14'So there will be no refugees or survivors for the remnant of
Judah who have entered the land of Egypt to reside there and then
to return to the land of Judah, to which they are longing to return
and live; for none will return except *a few* refugees.' "
15¶ Then all the men who were aware that their wives were
burning sacrifices to other gods, along with all the women who
were standing by, *as* a large assembly, including all the people who
were living in Pathros in the land of Egypt, responded to Jeremiah,
saying,
16"As for the message that you have spoken to us in the name
of the LORD, we are not going to listen to you!
17"But rather we will certainly carry out every word that has
proceeded from our mouths, by burning sacrifices to the queen of
heaven and pouring out libations to her, just as we ourselves, our
forefathers, our kings and our princes did in the cities of Judah and
in the streets of Jerusalem; for *then* we had plenty of food, and were
well off, and saw no misfortune.
18"But since we stopped burning sacrifices to the queen of
heaven and pouring out libations to her, we have lacked everything and have met our end by the sword and by famine."
19"And," *said the women,* "when we were burning sacrifices to
the queen of heaven, and were pouring out libations to her, was
it without our husbands that we made for her *sacrificial* cakes in her
image and poured out libations to her?"

*Calamity for the Jews*

20¶ Then Jeremiah said to all the people, to the men and
women—even to all the people who were giving him *such* an
answer—saying,

## New International

I sent my servants the prophets, who said, 'Do not do this detestable thing that I hate!' 5But they did not listen or pay attention; they
did not turn from their wickedness or stop burning incense to
other gods. 6Therefore, my fierce anger was poured out; it raged
against the towns of Judah and the streets of Jerusalem and made
them the desolate ruins they are today.
7"Now this is what the LORD God Almighty, the God of Israel,
says: Why bring such great disaster on yourselves by cutting off
from Judah the men and women, the children and infants, and so
leave yourselves without a remnant? 8Why provoke me to anger
with what your hands have made, burning incense to other gods
in Egypt, where you have come to live? You will destroy yourselves and make yourselves an object of cursing and reproach
among all the nations on earth. 9Have you forgotten the wickedness committed by your fathers and by the kings and queens of
Judah and the wickedness committed by you and your wives in the
land of Judah and the streets of Jerusalem? 10To this day they have
not humbled themselves or shown reverence, nor have they followed my law and the decrees I set before you and your fathers.
11"Therefore, this is what the LORD Almighty, the God of Israel,
says: I am determined to bring disaster on you and to destroy all
Judah. 12I will take away the remnant of Judah who were determined to go to Egypt to settle there. They will all perish in Egypt;
they will fall by the sword or die from famine. From the least to
the greatest, they will die by sword or famine. They will become
an object of cursing and horror, of condemnation and reproach. 13I
will punish those who live in Egypt with the sword, famine and
plague, as I punished Jerusalem. 14None of the remnant of Judah
who have gone to live in Egypt will escape or survive to return to
the land of Judah, to which they long to return and live; none will
return except a few fugitives."
15Then all the men who knew that their wives were burning
incense to other gods, along with all the women who were present—a large assembly—and all the people living in Lower and
Upper Egypt,[a] said to Jeremiah, 16"We will not listen to the message you have spoken to us in the name of the LORD! 17We will
certainly do everything we said we would: We will burn incense
to the Queen of Heaven and will pour out drink offerings to her
just as we and our fathers, our kings and our officials did in the
towns of Judah and in the streets of Jerusalem. At that time we had
plenty of food and were well off and suffered no harm. 18But ever
since we stopped burning incense to the Queen of Heaven and
pouring out drink offerings to her, we have had nothing and have
been perishing by sword and famine."
19The women added, "When we burned incense to the Queen
of Heaven and poured out drink offerings to her, did not our
husbands know that we were making cakes like her image and
pouring out drink offerings to her?"
20Then Jeremiah said to all the people, both men and women,
who were answering him, 21"Did not the LORD remember and

NIV [a] 15 Hebrew *in Egypt and Pathros*

## King James

21The incense that ye burned in the cities of Judah, and in the streets of Jerusalem, ye, and your fathers, your kings, and your princes, and the people of the land, did not the LORD remember them, and came it *not* into his mind?

22So that the LORD could no longer bear, because of the evil of your doings, *and* because of the abominations which ye have committed; therefore is your land a desolation, and an astonishment, and a curse, without an inhabitant, as at this day.

23Because ye have burned incense, and because ye have sinned against the LORD, and have not obeyed the voice of the LORD, nor walked in his law, nor in his statutes, nor in his testimonies; therefore this evil is happened unto you, as at this day.

24Moreover Jeremiah said unto all the people, and to all the women, Hear the word of the LORD, all Judah that *are* in the land of Egypt:

25Thus saith the LORD of hosts, the God of Israel, saying; Ye and your wives have both spoken with your mouths, and fulfilled with your hand, saying, We will surely perform our vows that we have vowed, to burn incense to the queen of heaven, and to pour out drink offerings unto her: ye will surely accomplish your vows, and surely perform your vows.

26Therefore hear ye the word of the LORD, all Judah that dwell in the land of Egypt; Behold, I have sworn by my great name, saith the LORD, that my name shall no more be named in the mouth of any man of Judah in all the land of Egypt, saying, The Lord GOD liveth.

27Behold, I will watch over them for evil, and not for good: and all the men of Judah that *are* in the land of Egypt shall be consumed by the sword and by the famine, until there be an end of them.

28Yet a small number that escape the sword shall return out of the land of Egypt into the land of Judah, and all the remnant of Judah, that are gone into the land of Egypt to sojourn there, shall know whose words shall stand, mine, or theirs.

29¶ And this *shall be* a sign unto you, saith the LORD, that I will punish you in this place, that ye may know that my words shall surely stand against you for evil:

30Thus saith the LORD; Behold, I will give Pharaoh-hophra king of Egypt into the hand of his enemies, and into the hand of them that seek his life; as I gave Zedekiah king of Judah into the hand of Nebuchadrezzar king of Babylon, his enemy, and that sought his life.

**45** THE WORD that Jeremiah the prophet spake unto Baruch the son of Neriah, when he had written these words in a book at the mouth of Jeremiah, in the fourth year of Jehoiakim the son of Josiah king of Judah, saying,

2Thus saith the LORD, the God of Israel, unto thee, O Baruch;

3Thou didst say, Woe is me now! for the LORD hath added grief to my sorrow; I fainted in my sighing, and I find no rest.

4¶ Thus shalt thou say unto him, The LORD saith thus; Behold, *that* which I have built will I break down, and that which I have planted I will pluck up, even this whole land.

## Amplified

21The incense that you burned in the cities of Judah and in the streets of Jerusalem, you and your fathers, your kings and your princes, and the people of the land, did the Lord not [earnestly] remember [your idolatrous wickedness] and did it not come into His mind?

22The Lord could no longer endure the evil of your doings and the abominations which you have committed; because of them therefore has your land become a desolation and an [astonishing] waste and a curse, without inhabitants, as at this day.

23Because you have burned incense [to idols], and because you have sinned against the Lord and have not obeyed the voice of the Lord or walked in His law and in His statutes and in His testimonies, therefore this evil has fallen upon you, as it is this day.

24Moreover Jeremiah said to all the people including all the women, Hear the word of the Lord, all you of Judah who are in the land of Egypt,

25Thus says the Lord of hosts, the God of Israel: You and your wives have both declared with your mouths and fulfilled it with your hands, saying, We will surely perform our vows that we have vowed, to burn incense to the queen of heaven and to pour out drink offerings to her. [If you will defy all My warnings to you, then go ahead by all means!] *Surely* then confirm your vows and *surely* perform your vows!

26Therefore hear the word of the Lord, all [you people of] Judah who dwell in the land of Egypt: Behold, I have sworn by My great name, says the Lord, that My name shall no more be invoked in the mouth of any man of Judah in all the land of Egypt, saying, As the Lord God lives.

27Behold, I am watching over them for evil and not for good; and all the men of Judah that are in the land of Egypt shall be consumed by the sword and by famine, until there is an end of them.

28Yet a small number that escape the sword shall return out of the land of Egypt to the land of Judah; and all the remnant of Judah, who came to the land of Egypt to sojourn, shall know whose words shall stand, Mine or theirs.

29And this shall be the sign to you, says the Lord, that I will punish you in this place, so that you may know that My words shall surely stand against you for evil:

30Thus says the Lord: Behold, I will give Pharaoh Hophra king of Egypt into the hand of his enemies and into the hand of those who seek his life, as I gave Zedekiah king of Judah into the hand of [a]Nebuchadrezzar king of Babylon, who was his enemy and sought his life.

**45** THE WORD that Jeremiah the prophet spoke to Baruch the son of Neriah, when he had written these words in a book at the dictation of Jeremiah, in the fourth year of Jehoiakim the son of Josiah, king of Judah, saying,

2Thus says the Lord, the God of Israel, unto you, O Baruch:

3You said, Woe is me now! For the Lord has added sorrow to my pain; I am weary with my groaning *and* signing and I find no rest.

4Say this to him, The Lord speaks thus: Behold, what I have built I am breaking down, and that which I have planted I am plucking up, and this means the whole land.

**AMP** [a] The reader has probably noticed that the name Nebuchad*n*ezzar is in *Jeremiah* also frequently spelled Nebuchad*r*ezzar. This is also true in *Ezekiel*. "The two forms represent different Hebrew methods of reproducing the name." (Davis Bible Dictionary.)

## New American Standard

21 "As for the smoking sacrifices that you burned in the cities of
Judah and in the streets of Jerusalem, you and your forefathers,
your kings and your princes, and the people of the land, did not
the LORD remember them, and did not *all this* come into His mind?
22 "So the LORD was no longer able to endure *it*, because of the
evil of your deeds, because of the abominations which you have
committed; thus your land has become a ruin, an object of horror
and a curse, without an inhabitant, as *it is* this day.
23 "Because you have burned sacrifices and have sinned against
the LORD and not obeyed the voice of the LORD or walked in His
law, His statutes or His testimonies, therefore this calamity has
befallen you, as *it has* this day."
24 Then Jeremiah said to all the people, including all the women,
"Hear the word of the LORD, all Judah who are in the land of Egypt,
25 thus says the LORD of hosts, the God of Israel, as follows: 'As
for you and your wives, you have spoken with your mouths and
fulfilled *it* with your hands, saying, "We will certainly perform our
vows that we have vowed, to burn sacrifices to the queen of
heaven and pour out libations to her." Go ahead and confirm your
vows, and certainly perform your vows!'
26 "Nevertheless hear the word of the LORD, all Judah who are
living in the land of Egypt, 'Behold, I have sworn by My great
name,' says the LORD, 'never shall My name be invoked again by
the mouth of any man of Judah in all the land of Egypt, saying,
"As the Lord GOD lives."
27 'Behold, I am watching over them for harm and not for good,
and all the men of Judah who are in the land of Egypt will meet
their end by the sword and by famine until they are completely
gone.
28 'And those who escape the sword will return out of the land
of Egypt to the land of Judah few in number. Then all the remnant
of Judah who have gone to the land of Egypt to reside there will
know whose word will stand, Mine or theirs.
29 'And this will be the sign to you,' declares the LORD, 'that I
am going to punish you in this place, so that you may know that
My words will surely stand against you for harm.'
30 "Thus says the LORD, 'Behold, I am going to give over Pharaoh Hophra king of Egypt to the hand of his enemies, to the hand
of those who seek his life, just as I gave over Zedekiah king of
Judah to the hand of Nebuchadnezzar king of Babylon, *who was* his
enemy and was seeking his life.' "

*Message to Baruch*

45 *THIS IS* the message which Jeremiah the prophet spoke
to Baruch the son of Neriah, when he had written down
these words in a book at Jeremiah's dictation, in the fourth year
of Jehoiakim the son of Josiah, king of Judah, saying:
2 "Thus says the LORD the God of Israel to you, O Baruch:
3 'You said, "Ah, woe is me! For the LORD has added sorrow
to my pain; I am weary with my groaning and have found no
rest." '
4 "Thus you are to say to him, 'Thus says the LORD, "Behold,
what I have built I am about to tear down, and what I have planted
I am about to uproot, that is, the whole land."

## New International

think about the incense burned in the towns of Judah and the
streets of Jerusalem by you and your fathers, your kings and your
officials and the people of the land? 22 When the LORD could no
longer endure your wicked actions and the detestable things you
did, your land became an object of cursing and a desolate waste
without inhabitants, as it is today. 23 Because you have burned
incense and have sinned against the LORD and have not obeyed
him or followed his law or his decrees or his stipulations, this
disaster has come upon you, as you now see."
24 Then Jeremiah said to all the people, including the women,
"Hear the word of the LORD, all you people of Judah in Egypt.
25 This is what the LORD Almighty, the God of Israel, says: You and
your wives have shown by your actions what you promised when
you said, 'We will certainly carry out the vows we made to burn
incense and pour out drink offerings to the Queen of Heaven.'
"Go ahead then, do what you promised! Keep your vows! 26 But
hear the word of the LORD, all Jews living in Egypt: 'I swear by my
great name,' says the LORD, 'that no one from Judah living anywhere in Egypt will ever again invoke my name or swear, "As
surely as the Sovereign LORD lives." 27 For I am watching over them
for harm, not for good; the Jews in Egypt will perish by sword and
famine until they are all destroyed. 28 Those who escape the sword
and return to the land of Judah from Egypt will be very few. Then
the whole remnant of Judah who came to live in Egypt will know
whose word will stand—mine or theirs.
29 " 'This will be the sign to you that I will punish you in this
place,' declares the LORD, 'so that you will know that my threats
of harm against you will surely stand.' 30 This is what the LORD
says: 'I am going to hand Pharaoh Hophra king of Egypt over to
his enemies who seek his life, just as I handed Zedekiah king of
Judah over to Nebuchadnezzar king of Babylon, the enemy who
was seeking his life.' "

*A Message to Baruch*

45 THIS IS what Jeremiah the prophet told Baruch son of
Neriah in the fourth year of Jehoiakim son of Josiah king
of Judah, after Baruch had written on a scroll the words Jeremiah
was then dictating: 2 "This is what the LORD, the God of Israel, says
to you, Baruch: 3 You said, 'Woe to me! The LORD has added sorrow
to my pain; I am worn out with groaning and find no rest.' "
4 The LORD said, "Say this to him: 'This is what the LORD says:
I will overthrow what I have built and uproot what I have planted,
throughout the land. 5 Should you then seek great things for your-

## King James

5And seekest thou great things for thyself? seek *them* not: for, behold, I will bring evil upon all flesh, saith the LORD: but thy life will I give unto thee for a prey in all places whither thou goest.

46 THE WORD of the LORD which came to Jeremiah the prophet against the Gentiles;
2Against Egypt, against the army of Pharaoh-necho king of Egypt, which was by the river Euphrates in Carchemish, which Nebuchadrezzar king of Babylon smote in the fourth year of Jehoiakim the son of Josiah king of Judah.
3Order ye the buckler and shield, and draw near to battle.
4Harness the horses; and get up, ye horsemen, and stand forth with *your* helmets; furbish the spears, *and* put on the brigandines.
5Wherefore have I seen them dismayed *and* turned away back? and their mighty ones are beaten down, and are fled apace, and look not back: *for* fear *was* round about, saith the LORD.
6Let not the swift flee away, nor the mighty man escape; they shall stumble, and fall toward the north by the river Euphrates.
7Who *is* this *that* cometh up as a flood, whose waters are moved as the rivers?
8Egypt riseth up like a flood, and *his* waters are moved like the rivers; and he saith, I will go up, *and* will cover the earth; I will destroy the city and the inhabitants thereof.
9Come up, ye horses; and rage, ye chariots; and let the mighty men come forth; the Ethiopians and the Libyans, that handle the shield; and the Lydians, that handle *and* bend the bow.
10For this *is* the day of the Lord GOD of hosts, a day of vengeance, that he may avenge him of his adversaries: and the sword shall devour, and it shall be satiate and made drunk with their blood: for the Lord GOD of hosts hath a sacrifice in the north country by the river Euphrates.
11Go up into Gilead, and take balm, O virgin, the daughter of Egypt: in vain shalt thou use many medicines; *for* thou shalt not be cured.
12The nations have heard of thy shame, and thy cry hath filled the land: for the mighty man hath stumbled against the mighty, *and* they are fallen both together.
13¶ The word that the LORD spake to Jeremiah the prophet, how Nebuchadrezzar king of Babylon should come *and* smite the land of Egypt.

## Amplified

5And do you [a]seek great things for yourself? Seek them not; for behold, I will bring evil upon all flesh, says the Lord; but your life I will give to you as a [snatched up] prize of war wherever you go.

46 THE WORD of the Lord which came to Jeremiah the prophet concerning *and* against the [Gentile] nations.
2Against Egypt: against the army of Pharaoh Necho king of Egypt, which was by the river Euphrates in Carchemish, which Nebuchadrezzar king of Babylon smote *and* defeated in the fourth year of Jehoiakim the son of Josiah, king of Judah: [Isa. 19; Ezek. 29-32; Zech. 14:18, 19.]
3Put in order the buckler and shield, and advance for battle!
4Harness the horses, and mount, you horsemen! Stand forth with your helmets, polish the spears, put on the coats of mail!
5Why have I seen it? They are dismayed and have turned backward, and their mighty warriors are beaten down, and have fled in haste, and look not back; terror is on every side! says the Lord. [Jer. 6:25; 20:3, 10; 49:29; Ps. 31:13.]
6Let not the swift flee away, nor the mighty man escape; in the north by the river Euphrates they have stumbled and fallen.
7Who is this that rises up like the Nile *River*, whose waters surge *and* toss themselves like the branches [of the Nile in the delta of Egypt]?
8Egypt rises up like the Nile, and its waters swell *and* toss themselves like the rivers. He says, I will rise up, I will cover the earth; I will destroy cities and their inhabitants.
9Go up, you horses, and drive furiously, you chariots! Let the warriors go forth: men of Ethiopia and Put who handle the shield, men of Lud who are skilled in handling and stringing the bow.
10But that day is a day of the Lord God of hosts, a day of vengeance, that He may avenge Himself on His adversaries. And the sword shall devour, and it shall be satiated and shall drink its fill of their blood; for the Lord of hosts has a sacrifice [as of a great sin offering] in the north country by the river Euphrates.
11Go up into Gilead, and take [healing] balm, O virgin daughter of Egypt! In vain do you use many medicines; for you there is no healing remedy.
12The nations have heard of your disgrace *and* shame, and your cry has filled the earth. For warrior has stumbled against *and* thrown down warrior, and they are fallen both of them together.
13The word that the Lord spoke to Jeremiah the prophet concerning the coming of Nebuchadrezzar king of Babylon and his smiting of the land of Egypt:

**AMP** [a] Baruch plays a role familiar in normal human life today—that of having to take second place. He was of high birth; his grandfather Maaseiah was governor of Jerusalem in the days of King Josiah (II Chron. 34:8). Considering all that Baruch was doing to make Jeremiah's prophecies permanent, it is not surprising that he seems to have expected to share the prophet's rewards. "To play a prominent part in the impending crisis, to be the hero of a national revival, to gain the favor of the conqueror he announced," seems to have been his dream. When its realization was denied him, "he sank in despair at the seeming fruitlessness of his efforts" (Smith's Bible Dictionary). Yet Baruch is an excellent illustration of how little the gift of prophecy depended on men, and how completely it was for God to grant or deny prominence to His perhaps equally deserving servants. But each man's eternal rewards are proportioned according to his faithfulness, and not to his earthly recognition or the lack of it (Matt. 25:14-30).

## New American Standard

5'But you, are you seeking great things for yourself? Do not seek *them;* for behold, I am going to bring disaster on all flesh,' declares the LORD, 'but I will give your life to you as booty in all the places where you may go.' "

*Defeat of Pharaoh Foretold*

46 THAT WHICH came as the word of the LORD to Jeremiah the prophet concerning the nations.

2To Egypt, concerning the army of Pharaoh Neco king of Egypt, which was by the Euphrates River at Carchemish, which Nebuchadnezzar king of Babylon defeated in the fourth year of Jehoiakim the son of Josiah, king of Judah:

3 "Line up the shield and buckler,
And draw near for the battle!
4 "Harness the horses,
And mount the steeds,
And take your stand with helmets *on!*
Polish the spears,
Put on the scale-armor!
5 "Why have I seen *it?*
They are terrified,
They are drawing back,
And their mighty men are defeated
And have taken refuge in flight,
Without facing back;
Terror is on every side!"
Declares the LORD.
6 Let not the swift man flee,
Nor the mighty man escape;
In the north beside the river Euphrates
They have stumbled and fallen.
7 Who is this that rises like the Nile,
Like the rivers whose waters surge about?
8 Egypt rises like the Nile,
Even like the rivers whose waters surge about;
And He has said, "I will rise and cover *that* land;
I will surely destroy the city and its inhabitants."
9 Go up, you horses, and drive madly, you chariots,
That the mighty men may march forward:
Ethiopia and Put, that handle the shield,
And the Lydians, that handle *and* bend the bow.
10 For that day belongs to the Lord GOD of hosts,
A day of vengeance, so as to avenge Himself on His foes;
And the sword will devour and be satiated
And drink its fill of their blood;
For there will be a slaughter for the Lord GOD of hosts,
In the land of the north by the river Euphrates.
11 Go up to Gilead and obtain balm,
O virgin daughter of Egypt!
In vain have you multiplied remedies;
There is no healing for you.
12 The nations have heard of your shame,
And the earth is full of your cry *of distress;*
For one warrior has stumbled over another,
And both of them have fallen down together.

13¶ *This is* the message which the LORD spoke to Jeremiah the prophet about the coming of Nebuchadnezzar king of Babylon to smite the land of Egypt:

## New International

self? Seek them not. For I will bring disaster on all people, declares the LORD, but wherever you go I will let you escape with your life.' "

*A Message About Egypt*

46 THIS IS the word of the LORD that came to Jeremiah the prophet concerning the nations:

2Concerning Egypt:

This is the message against the army of Pharaoh Neco king of Egypt, which was defeated at Carchemish on the Euphrates River by Nebuchadnezzar king of Babylon in the fourth year of Jehoiakim son of Josiah king of Judah:

3"Prepare your shields, both large and small,
and march out for battle!
4Harness the horses,
mount the steeds!
Take your positions
with helmets on!
Polish your spears,
put on your armor!
5What do I see?
They are terrified,
they are retreating,
their warriors are defeated.
They flee in haste
without looking back,
and there is terror on every side,"
declares the LORD.
6"The swift cannot flee
nor the strong escape.
In the north by the River Euphrates
they stumble and fall.

7"Who is this that rises like the Nile,
like rivers of surging waters?
8Egypt rises like the Nile,
like rivers of surging waters.
She says, 'I will rise and cover the earth;
I will destroy cities and their people.'
9Charge, O horses!
Drive furiously, O charioteers!
March on, O warriors—
men of Cush[b] and Put who carry shields,
men of Lydia who draw the bow.
10But that day belongs to the Lord, the LORD Almighty—
a day of vengeance, for vengeance on his foes.
The sword will devour till it is satisfied,
till it has quenched its thirst with blood.
For the Lord, the LORD Almighty, will offer sacrifice
in the land of the north by the River Euphrates.

11"Go up to Gilead and get balm,
O Virgin Daughter of Egypt.
But you multiply remedies in vain;
there is no healing for you.
12The nations will hear of your shame;
your cries will fill the earth.
One warrior will stumble over another;
both will fall down together."

13This is the message the LORD spoke to Jeremiah the prophet about the coming of Nebuchadnezzar king of Babylon to attack Egypt:

NIV [b] 9 That is, the upper Nile region

## King James

14Declare ye in Egypt, and publish in Migdol, and publish in Noph and in Tahpanhes: say ye, Stand fast, and prepare thee; for the sword shall devour round about thee.

15Why are thy valiant *men* swept away? they stood not, because the LORD did drive them.

16He made many to fall, yea, one fell upon another: and they said, Arise, and let us go again to our own people, and to the land of our nativity, from the oppressing sword.

17They did cry there, Pharaoh king of Egypt *is but* a noise; he hath passed the time appointed.

18 *As* I live, saith the King, whose name *is* the LORD of hosts, Surely as Tabor *is* among the mountains, and as Carmel by the sea, *so* shall he come.

19O thou daughter dwelling in Egypt, furnish thyself to go into captivity: for Noph shall be waste and desolate without an inhabitant.

20Egypt *is like* a very fair heifer, *but* destruction cometh; it cometh out of the north.

21Also her hired men *are* in the midst of her like fatted bullocks; for they also are turned back, *and* are fled away together: they did not stand, because the day of their calamity was come upon them, *and* the time of their visitation.

22The voice thereof shall go like a serpent; for they shall march with an army, and come against her with axes, as hewers of wood.

23They shall cut down her forest, saith the LORD, though it cannot be searched; because they are more than the grasshoppers, and *are* innumerable.

24The daughter of Egypt shall be confounded; she shall be delivered into the hand of the people of the north.

25The LORD of hosts, the God of Israel, saith; Behold, I will punish the multitude of No, and Pharaoh, and Egypt, with their gods, and their kings: even Pharaoh, and *all* them that trust in him:

26And I will deliver them into the hand of those that seek their lives, and into the hand of Nebuchadrezzar king of Babylon, and into the hand of his servants: and afterward it shall be inhabited, as in the days of old, saith the LORD.

27¶ But fear not thou, O my servant Jacob, and be not dismayed, O Israel: for, behold, I will save thee from afar off, and thy seed from the land of their captivity; and Jacob shall return, and be in rest and at ease, and none shall make *him* afraid.

28Fear thou not, O Jacob my servant, saith the LORD: for I *am* with thee; for I will make a full end of all the nations whither I have driven thee: but I will not make a full end of thee, but correct thee in measure; yet will I not leave thee wholly unpunished.

## Amplified

14Declare in Egypt, and proclaim in Migdol, and publish in Memphis and in Tahpanhes; say, Stand forth and get yourself ready, for the sword shall devour round about you.

15Why is your strong one [the sacred bull, Apis] swept *and* dragged away? He stood not, because the Lord drove him *and* thrust him down.

16[The Lord] made many to stumble *and* fall, yes, they fell one upon another; and they said, Arise, and let us go back to our own people and to the land of our birth, away from the sword of the oppressor.

17They cried there, Pharaoh king of Egypt is destroyed *and* but a noise; he has let the appointed time [in which God had him on probation] pass by!

18As I live, says the King, Whose name is the Lord of hosts, surely like Tabor among the mountains, and like Carmel by the sea, so shall he come [the king of Babylon, standing out above other rulers].

19O you daughter who dwells in Egypt *and* you who dwell with her, furnish yourselves [with all you will need] to go into exile; for Memphis shall be waste, desolate *and* burned up, without inhabitant.

20Egypt is a very fair heifer [like Apis the bull-god to which the country is, so to speak, espoused], but destruction [a gadfly] has come, out of the north it has come *upon her*.

21Also her hired *troops* in the midst of her are like fatted calves of the stall, for they also are turned back and are fleeing away together; they do not stand, because the day of their calamity has come upon them, the time of their visitation—of their inspection and punishment.

22The sound [of Egypt fleeing from the enemy] is like the rustling of an escaping serpent, for her foes advance with a mighty army, and come against her with axes, like those who fell trees *and* cut wood.

23They shall cut down her forest, says the Lord, though it is impenetrable, because they are more numerous than locusts and cannot be counted.

24The daughter of Egypt shall be disgraced; she shall be delivered into the hand of the people of the north [the Chaldeans].

25The Lord of hosts, the God of Israel, says, Behold, I will visit punishment upon Amon [the chief god of the sacred city] of No *or* Thebes, and upon Pharaoh and Egypt, with her gods and her kings, even Pharaoh and all those [Jews and others] who put their trust in *Pharaoh* [as a support against Babylon].

26And I will deliver them into the hand of those who seek their lives, and into the hand of Nebuchadrezzar king of Babylon, and into the hand of his servants. Afterward [Egypt] shall be [a]inhabited, as in the days of old, says the Lord.

27But fear not, O My servant Jacob, and be not dismayed, O Israel; for lo, I will save you from afar and your offspring from the land of their exile; and Jacob shall return and be quiet and at ease, and none shall make him afraid.

28Fear not, O Jacob My servant, says the Lord, for I am with you; for I will make a full end of all the nations to which I have driven you. Yet I will not make a full end of you, but I will chasten *and* correct you in just measure, and I will not hold you guiltless by any means, *or* leave you unpunished.

**AMP** [a] It is startling to realize that God through His prophets accurately foretold in detail the future of every one of the prominent nations of Old Testament times, often including particular rulers and chief cities. It will greatly increase the reader's interest if he will look up the literal fulfillment of these prophecies as he comes to them, as indicated in the references or the footnotes. Notice how definite the prophecies are; what was said of Babylon, for instance, would not have been applicable to Egypt or Ammon or Sidon. And secular history proves their fulfillment. If there were no other evidence that there is a God and that the Bible is inspired by Him, this to any person capable of thinking it through should be sufficient proof. Nor are the prophecies against some nations recorded by only one writer, but by a number of them widely separated by time and circumstances. Let us approach these recordings with awe and awakened vision; we are on holy ground.

## New American Standard

14 "Declare in Egypt and proclaim in Migdol,
Proclaim also in Memphis and Tahpanhes;
Say, 'Take your stand and get yourself ready,
For the sword has devoured those around you.'
15 "Why have your mighty ones become prostrate?
They do not stand because the LORD has thrust them down.
16 "They have repeatedly stumbled;
Indeed, they have fallen one against another.
Then they said, 'Get up! And let us go back
To our own people and our native land
Away from the sword of the oppressor.'
17 "They cried there, 'Pharaoh king of Egypt *is but* a big noise;
He has let the appointed time pass by!'
18 "As I live," declares the King
Whose name is the LORD of hosts,
"Surely one shall come *who looms up* like Tabor among the mountains,
Or like Carmel by the sea.
19 "Make your baggage ready for exile,
O daughter dwelling in Egypt,
For Memphis will become a desolation;
It will even be burned down *and* bereft of inhabitants.
20 "Egypt is a pretty heifer,
*But* a horsefly is coming from the north—it is coming!
21 "Also her mercenaries in her midst
Are like fattened calves,
For even they too have turned back *and* have fled away together;
They did not stand *their ground.*
For the day of their calamity has come upon them,
The time of their punishment.
22 "Its sound moves along like a serpent;
For they move on like an army
And come to her as woodcutters with axes.
23 "They have cut down her forest," declares the LORD;
"Surely it will no *more* be found,
Even though they are *now* more numerous than locusts
And are without number.
24 "The daughter of Egypt has been put to shame,
Given over to the power of the people of the north."
25 The LORD of hosts, the God of Israel, says, "Behold, I am going to punish Amon of Thebes, and Pharaoh, and Egypt along with her gods and her kings, even Pharaoh and those who trust in him.
26 "And I shall give them over to the power of those who are seeking their lives, even into the hand of Nebuchadnezzar king of Babylon and into the hand of his officers. Afterwards, however, it will be inhabited as in the days of old," declares the LORD.
27 ¶ "But as for you, O Jacob My servant, do not fear,
Nor be dismayed, O Israel!
For, see, I am going to save you from afar,
And your descendants from the land of their captivity;
And Jacob shall return and be undisturbed
And secure, with no one making *him* tremble.
28 "O Jacob My servant, do not fear," declares the LORD,
"For I am with you.
For I shall make a full end of all the nations
Where I have driven you,
Yet I shall not make a full end of you;
But I shall correct you properly
And by no means leave you unpunished."

## New International

14 "Announce this in Egypt, and proclaim it in Migdol;
proclaim it also in Memphis[b] and Tahpanhes:
'Take your positions and get ready,
for the sword devours those around you.'
15 Why will your warriors be laid low?
They cannot stand, for the LORD will push them down.
16 They will stumble repeatedly;
they will fall over each other.
They will say, 'Get up, let us go back
to our own people and our native lands,
away from the sword of the oppressor.'
17 There they will exclaim,
'Pharaoh king of Egypt is only a loud noise;
he has missed his opportunity.'
18 "As surely as I live," declares the King,
whose name is the LORD Almighty,
"one will come who is like Tabor among the mountains,
like Carmel by the sea.
19 Pack your belongings for exile,
you who live in Egypt,
for Memphis will be laid waste
and lie in ruins without inhabitant.

20 "Egypt is a beautiful heifer,
but a gadfly is coming
against her from the north.
21 The mercenaries in her ranks
are like fattened calves.
They too will turn and flee together,
they will not stand their ground,
for the day of disaster is coming upon them,
the time for them to be punished.
22 Egypt will hiss like a fleeing serpent
as the enemy advances in force;
they will come against her with axes,
like men who cut down trees.
23 They will chop down her forest,"
declares the LORD,
"dense though it be.
They are more numerous than locusts,
they cannot be counted.
24 The Daughter of Egypt will be put to shame,
handed over to the people of the north."

25 The LORD Almighty, the God of Israel, says: "I am about to
bring punishment on Amon god of Thebes,[c] on Pharaoh, on
Egypt and her gods and her kings, and on those who rely on
Pharaoh. 26 I will hand them over to those who seek their lives, to
Nebuchadnezzar king of Babylon and his officers. Later, however,
Egypt will be inhabited as in times past," declares the LORD.

27 "Do not fear, O Jacob my servant;
do not be dismayed, O Israel.
I will surely save you out of a distant place,
your descendants from the land of their exile.
Jacob will again have peace and security,
and no one will make him afraid.
28 Do not fear, O Jacob my servant,
for I am with you," declares the LORD.
"Though I completely destroy all the nations
among which I scatter you,
I will not completely destroy you.
I will discipline you but only with justice;
I will not let you go entirely unpunished."

NIV [b] *14* Hebrew *Noph;* also in verse 19 [c] *25* Hebrew *No*

## King James

**47** THE WORD of the LORD that came to Jeremiah the prophet against the Philistines, before that Pharaoh smote Gaza.

2Thus saith the LORD; Behold, waters rise up out of the north, and shall be an overflowing flood, and shall overflow the land, and all that is therein; the city, and them that dwell therein: then the men shall cry, and all the inhabitants of the land shall howl.

3At the noise of the stamping of the hoofs of his strong *horses*, at the rushing of his chariots, *and at* the rumbling of his wheels, the fathers shall not look back to *their* children for feebleness of hands;

4Because of the day that cometh to spoil all the Philistines, *and* to cut off from Tyrus and Zidon every helper that remaineth: for the LORD will spoil the Philistines, the remnant of the country of Caphtor.

5Baldness is come upon Gaza; Ashkelon is cut off *with* the remnant of their valley: how long wilt thou cut thyself?

6O thou sword of the LORD, how long *will it be* ere thou be quiet? put up thyself into thy scabbard, rest, and be still.

7How can it be quiet, seeing the LORD hath given it a charge against Ashkelon, and against the sea shore? there hath he appointed it.

**48** AGAINST MOAB thus saith the LORD of hosts, the God of Israel; Woe unto Nebo! for it is spoiled: Kiriathaim is confounded *and* taken: Misgab is confounded and dismayed.

2 *There shall be* no more praise of Moab: in Heshbon they have devised evil against it; come, and let us cut it off from *being* a nation. Also thou shalt be cut down, O Madmen; the sword shall pursue thee.

3A voice of crying *shall be* from Horonaim, spoiling and great destruction.

4Moab is destroyed; her little ones have caused a cry to be heard.

5For in the going up of Luhith continual weeping shall go up; for in the going down of Horonaim the enemies have heard a cry of destruction.

6Flee, save your lives, and be like the heath in the wilderness.

7¶ For because thou hast trusted in thy works and in thy treasures, thou shalt also be taken: and Chemosh shall go forth into captivity *with* his priests and his princes together.

## Amplified

**47** THE WORD of the Lord that came to Jeremiah the prophet concerning the Philistines, before Pharaoh smote [the Philistine city] Gaza. [Isa. 14:29-31; Ezek. 25:15-17; Amos 1:6-8; Zeph. 2:4-7; Zech. 9:5-7.]

2Thus says the Lord: Behold, waters rise up out of the north, and shall be an overflowing stream, and shall overflow the land and all that is in it, the city and those who dwell in it. Then the men shall cry, and all the inhabitants of the land [of Philistia] shall wail.

3At the noise of the stamping of the hoofs of [the Chaldean king's] war horses, at the rattling of his chariots, and at the rumbling of his wheels, the fathers do not look back to their children, so feeble are their hands [with terror],

4Because of the day that is coming to destroy all the Philistines, and to cut off from Tyre and Sidon every helper who remains. For the Lord is destroying the Philistines, the remnant [still surviving] of the isle *or* coastland of Caphtor [where the Philistines originated]. [Amos 9:7.]

5Baldness [in token of mourning] is come upon Gaza; Ashkelon is cut off *and* is dumb. O remnant of their valley *and* of the giants, how long will you gash yourselves [in token of mourning]?

6O you sword of the Lord, how long will it be before you are quiet? Put yourself into your scabbard, rest and be still.

7How can it [the sword of the Lord] be quiet when the Lord has given it an assignment to discharge? Against Ashkelon and against the [whole Philistine] seashore He has appointed it.

**48** CONCERNING MOAB, thus says the Lord of hosts, the God of Israel: Woe to [the city of] Nebo, for it is laid waste! Kiriathaim is put to shame and taken; [the high fortress] Misgab is put to shame, broken down *and* crushed. [Isa. 15-16; 25:10-12; Ezek. 25:8-11; Amos 2:1-3; Zeph. 2:8-11.]

2The glory of Moab is no more. In Heshbon [a border town between Reuben and Gad, east of the Jordan River] they planned evil against her, saying, Come, let us cut her off from being a nation. You also, O [town of] Madmen, shall be brought to silence; the sword shall pursue you.

3The sound of a cry from Horonaim, desolation and great destruction!

4Moab is destroyed; her little ones have caused a cry to be heard—as far as Zoar.

5For the ascent of Luhith is being climbed [by successive bands of fugitives] with continual weeping, for on the descent of Horonaim they have heard the distress of the cry of destruction.

6Flee, save your lives! But they shall be like a destitute *and* forsaken *person* in the wilderness.

7For because you have trusted in your [bungling idol image] works and in your treasures [instead of God], you shall also be taken. And [your god] Chemosh shall go into captivity, his priests and his princes together.

## New American Standard

*Prophecy against Philistia*

**47** THAT WHICH came as the word of the LORD to Jeremiah the prophet concerning the Philistines, before Pharaoh conquered Gaza.

2 Thus says the LORD:
"Behold, waters are going to rise from the north
And become an overflowing torrent,
And overflow the land and all its fulness,
The city and those who live in it;
And the men will cry out,
And every inhabitant of the land will wail.
3 "Because of the noise of the galloping hoofs of his stallions,
The tumult of his chariots, *and* the rumbling of his wheels,
The fathers have not turned back for *their* children,
Because of the limpness of *their* hands,
4 On account of the day that is coming
To destroy all the Philistines,
To cut off from Tyre and Sidon
Every ally that is left;
For the LORD is going to destroy the Philistines,
The remnant of the coastland of Caphtor.
5 "Baldness has come upon Gaza;
Ashkelon has been ruined.
O remnant of their valley,
How long will you gash yourself?
6 "Ah, sword of the LORD,
How long will you not be quiet?
Withdraw into your sheath;
Be at rest and stay still.
7 "How can it be quiet,
When the LORD has given it an order?
Against Ashkelon and against the seacoast—
There He has assigned it."

*Prophecy against Moab*

**48** CONCERNING MOAB.
Thus says the LORD of hosts, the God of Israel,
"Woe to Nebo, for it has been destroyed;
Kiriathaim has been put to shame, it has been captured;
The lofty stronghold has been put to shame and shattered.
2 "There is praise for Moab no longer;
In Heshbon they have devised calamity against her:
'Come and let us cut her off from *being* a nation!'
You too, [a]Madmen, will be silenced;
The sword will follow after you.
3 "The sound of an outcry from Horonaim,
'Devastation and great destruction!'
4 "Moab is broken,
Her little ones have sounded out a cry *of distress*.
5 "For by the ascent of Luhith
They will ascend with continual weeping;
For at the descent of Horonaim
They have heard the anguished cry of destruction.
6 "Flee, save your lives,
That you may be like a juniper in the wilderness.
7 "For because of your trust in your own achievements and treasures,
Even you yourself will be captured;
And Chemosh will go off into exile
Together with his priests and his princes.

**NAS** [a] I.e., a city of Moab

## New International

*A Message About the Philistines*

**47** THIS IS the word of the LORD that came to Jeremiah the prophet concerning the Philistines before Pharaoh attacked Gaza:

2This is what the LORD says:

"See how the waters are rising in the north;
they will become an overflowing torrent.
They will overflow the land and everything in it,
the towns and those who live in them.
The people will cry out;
all who dwell in the land will wail
3at the sound of the hoofs of galloping steeds,
at the noise of enemy chariots
and the rumble of their wheels.
Fathers will not turn to help their children;
their hands will hang limp.
4For the day has come
to destroy all the Philistines
and to cut off all survivors
who could help Tyre and Sidon.
The LORD is about to destroy the Philistines,
the remnant from the coasts of Caphtor.[b]
5Gaza will shave her head in mourning;
Ashkelon will be silenced.
O remnant on the plain,
how long will you cut yourselves?

6" 'Ah, sword of the LORD,' you cry,
'how long till you rest?
Return to your scabbard;
cease and be still.'
7But how can it rest
when the LORD has commanded it,
when he has ordered it
to attack Ashkelon and the coast?"

*A Message About Moab*

**48** CONCERNING MOAB:

This is what the LORD Almighty, the God of Israel, says:

"Woe to Nebo, for it will be ruined.
Kiriathaim will be disgraced and captured;
the stronghold[c] will be disgraced and shattered.
2Moab will be praised no more;
in Heshbon[d] men will plot her downfall:
'Come, let us put an end to that nation.'
You too, O Madmen,[e] will be silenced;
the sword will pursue you.
3Listen to the cries from Horonaim,
cries of great havoc and destruction.
4Moab will be broken;
her little ones will cry out.[f]
5They go up the way to Luhith,
weeping bitterly as they go;
on the road down to Horonaim
anguished cries over the destruction are heard.
6Flee! Run for your lives;
become like a bush[g] in the desert.
7Since you trust in your deeds and riches,
you too will be taken captive,
and Chemosh will go into exile,
together with his priests and officials.

**NIV** [b] 4 That is, Crete [c] 1 Or / *Misgab* [d] 2 The Hebrew for *Heshbon* sounds like the Hebrew for *plot*. [e] 2 The name of the Moabite town Madmen sounds like the Hebrew for *be silenced*. [f] 4 Hebrew; Septuagint / *proclaim it to Zoar* [g] 6 Or *like Aroer*

## King James

8And the spoiler shall come upon every city, and no city shall escape: the valley also shall perish, and the plain shall be destroyed, as the LORD hath spoken.
9Give wings unto Moab, that it may flee and get away: for the cities thereof shall be desolate, without any to dwell therein.
10Cursed *be* he that doeth the work of the LORD deceitfully, and cursed *be* he that keepeth back his sword from blood.
11¶ Moab hath been at ease from his youth, and he hath settled on his lees, and hath not been emptied from vessel to vessel, neither hath he gone into captivity: therefore his taste remained in him, and his scent is not changed.
12Therefore, behold, the days come, saith the LORD, that I will send unto him wanderers, that shall cause him to wander, and shall empty his vessels, and break their bottles.
13And Moab shall be ashamed of Chemosh, as the house of Israel was ashamed of Beth-el their confidence.
14¶ How say ye, We *are* mighty and strong men for the war?
15Moab is spoiled, and gone up *out of* her cities, and his chosen young men are gone down to the slaughter, saith the King, whose name *is* the LORD of hosts.
16The calamity of Moab *is* near to come, and his affliction hasteth fast.
17All ye that are about him, bemoan him; and all ye that know his name, say, How is the strong staff broken, *and* the beautiful rod!
18Thou daughter that dost inhabit Dibon, come down from *thy* glory, and sit in thirst; for the spoiler of Moab shall come upon thee, *and* he shall destroy thy strong holds.
19O inhabitant of Aroer, stand by the way, and espy; ask him that fleeth, and her that escapeth, *and* say, What is done?
20Moab is confounded; for it is broken down: howl and cry; tell ye it in Arnon, that Moab is spoiled,
21And judgment is come upon the plain country; upon Holon, and upon Jahazah, and upon Mephaath,
22And upon Dibon, and upon Nebo, and upon Beth-diblathaim,
23And upon Kiriathaim, and upon Beth-gamul, and upon Bethmeon,
24And upon Kerioth, and upon Bozrah, and upon all the cities of the land of Moab, far or near.
25The horn of Moab is cut off, and his arm is broken, saith the LORD.
26¶ Make ye him drunken: for he magnified *himself* against the LORD: Moab also shall wallow in his vomit, and he also shall be in derision.

## Amplified

8And the spoiler shall come upon every city; no city shall escape; the [Jordan] valley also shall perish, and the plain shall be devastated, as the Lord has said.
9Give wings to Moab, [for by that means only] may she flee and get away; her cities shall be desolate, without any to dwell in them.
10Cursed be he who does the work of the Lord negligently—with slackness, deceitfully; and cursed be he who keeps back his sword from blood [in executing judgment pronounced by the Lord].
11Moab has been at ease from his youth, and he has settled on his lees [like wine], and has not been drawn off from one vessel to another, neither has he gone into exile; therefore his taste remains in him and his scent has not changed.
12Therefore, behold, the days are coming, says the Lord, when I shall send to [Moab] tilters who shall tilt him up, and shall empty his vessels and break *his* [earthenware] bottles in pieces.
13And Moab shall be ashamed of [his god] Chemosh, as the house of Israel was ashamed of Bethel, their confidence. [I Kings 12:28, 29.]
14How can you say, We are heroes and mighty men for the war?
15Moab is made desolate and his cities gone up [in smoke and flame], and his chosen young men have gone down to the slaughter, says the King, whose name is the Lord of hosts.
16The destruction of Moab is coming near, and his calamity hastens fast.
17All you [nations] that are around him, bemoan him, and all you [nations more remote] that know his name, say, How is the mighty scepter [of national power] broken and the splendid rod [of glory]!
18Come down from your glory, you inhabitant daughter of [a]Dibon, and sit on the ground among the thirsty! For the destroyer of Moab is advancing against you, he destroys your strongholds.
19O inhabitant of Aroer, stand by the way and watch! Ask him who flees and her who escapes, What has happened?
20Moab is put to shame, for she is broken down. Wail and cry! Tell it on [the banks of] the Arnon, that Moab is laid waste—destroyed.
21Judgment has come upon the land of the plain: upon Holon, and Jahzah, and Mephaath,
22And upon Dibon, and Nebo, and Bethdiblathaim,
23And upon Kiriathaim, and Bethgamul, and Bethmeon,
24And upon Kerioth, and Bozrah, and all the cities of the land of Moab, far and near.
25The horn of Moab's [strength] is cut off, and his arm [of authority] is shattered, says the Lord.
26Make him drunk, for he magnified himself against the Lord [by resisting Reuben's occupation of the land the Lord had assigned him]. Moab also shall splash in his vomit, and he too shall be held in derision. [Num. 22:1-7.]

**AMP** [a] Dibon, later Dhiban, stands on two hills. The "Moabite Stone" was found there. This Aroer (v. 19) stood on the north side of the river Arnon [note name in next verse]. Mesha records on the "Moabite Stone" that he "built (i.e. restored) the city and made the road over the Arnon." (Cambridge Bible.)

## New American Standard

8 "And a destroyer will come to every city,
So that no city will escape;
The valley also will be ruined,
And the plateau will be destroyed,
As the LORD has said.
9 "Give wings to Moab,
For she will flee away;
And her cities will become a desolation,
Without inhabitants in them.
10 "Cursed be the one who does the LORD's work
negligently,
And cursed be the one who restrains his sword from
blood.
11¶ "Moab has been at ease since his youth;
He has also been undisturbed on his lees,
Neither has he been emptied from vessel to vessel,
Nor has he gone into exile.
Therefore he retains his flavor,
And his aroma has not changed.
12"Therefore behold, the days are coming," declares the LORD,
"when I shall send to him those who tip *vessels*, and they will tip
him over, and they will empty his vessels and shatter his jars.
13"And Moab will be ashamed of Chemosh, as the house of
Israel was ashamed of Bethel, their confidence.
14 "How can you say, 'We are mighty warriors,
And men valiant for battle'?
15 "Moab has been destroyed, and men have gone up to
his cities;
His choicest young men have also gone down to the
slaughter,"
Declares the King, whose name is the LORD of hosts.
16 "The disaster of Moab will soon come,
And his calamity has swiftly hastened.
17 "Mourn for him, all you who *live* around him,
Even all of you who know his name;
Say, 'How has the mighty scepter been broken,
A staff of splendor!'
18 "Come down from your glory
And sit on the parched ground,
O daughter dwelling in Dibon,
For the destroyer of Moab has come up against you,
He has ruined your strongholds.
19 "Stand by the road and keep watch,
O inhabitant of Aroer;
Ask him who flees and her who escapes
*And* say, 'What has happened?'
20 "Moab has been put to shame, for it has been shattered.
Wail and cry out;
Declare by the Arnon
That Moab has been destroyed.
21"Judgment has also come upon the plain, upon Holon, Jahzah, and against Mephaath,
22against Dibon, Nebo, and Beth-diblathaim,
23against Kiriathaim, Beth-gamul, and Beth-meon,
24against Kerioth, Bozrah, and all the cities of the land of Moab,
far and near.
25"The horn of Moab has been cut off, and his arm broken,"
declares the LORD.
26"Make him drunk, for he has become arrogant toward the
LORD; so Moab will wallow in his vomit, and he also will become
a laughingstock.

## New International

8The destroyer will come against every town,
and not a town will escape.
The valley will be ruined
and the plateau destroyed,
because the LORD has spoken.
9Put salt on Moab,
for she will be laid waste[b];
her towns will become desolate,
with no one to live in them.

10"A curse on him who is lax in doing the LORD's work!
A curse on him who keeps his sword from bloodshed!

11"Moab has been at rest from youth,
like wine left on its dregs,
not poured from one jar to another—
she has not gone into exile.
So she tastes as she did,
and her aroma is unchanged.
12But days are coming,"
declares the LORD,
"when I will send men who pour from jars,
and they will pour her out;
they will empty her jars
and smash her jugs.
13Then Moab will be ashamed of Chemosh,
as the house of Israel was ashamed
when they trusted in Bethel.

14"How can you say, 'We are warriors,
men valiant in battle'?
15Moab will be destroyed and her towns invaded;
her finest young men will go down in the slaughter,"
declares the King, whose name is the LORD Almighty.
16"The fall of Moab is at hand;
her calamity will come quickly.
17Mourn for her, all who live around her,
all who know her fame;
say, 'How broken is the mighty scepter,
how broken the glorious staff!'

18"Come down from your glory
and sit on the parched ground,
O inhabitants of the Daughter of Dibon,
for he who destroys Moab
will come up against you
and ruin your fortified cities.
19Stand by the road and watch,
you who live in Aroer.
Ask the man fleeing and the woman escaping,
ask them, 'What has happened?'
20Moab is disgraced, for she is shattered.
Wail and cry out!
Announce by the Arnon
that Moab is destroyed.
21Judgment has come to the plateau—
to Holon, Jahzah and Mephaath,
22 to Dibon, Nebo and Beth Diblathaim,
23 to Kiriathaim, Beth Gamul and Beth Meon,
24 to Kerioth and Bozrah—
to all the towns of Moab, far and near.
25Moab's horn[c] is cut off;
her arm is broken,"
declares the LORD.

26"Make her drunk,
for she has defied the LORD.
Let Moab wallow in her vomit;
let her be an object of ridicule.

**NIV** [b] 9 Or *Give wings to Moab, / for she will fly away* [c] 25 *Horn* here symbolizes strength.

## King James

27For was not Israel a derision unto thee? was he found among thieves? for since thou spakest of him, thou skippedst for joy.

28O ye that dwell in Moab, leave the cities, and dwell in the rock, and be like the dove *that* maketh her nest in the sides of the hole's mouth.

29We have heard the pride of Moab, (he is exceeding proud) his loftiness, and his arrogancy, and his pride, and the haughtiness of his heart.

30I know his wrath, saith the LORD; but *it shall* not *be* so; his lies shall not so effect *it*.

31Therefore will I howl for Moab, and I will cry out for all Moab; *mine heart* shall mourn for the men of Kir-heres.

32O vine of Sibmah, I will weep for thee with the weeping of Jazer: thy plants are gone over the sea, they reach *even* to the sea of Jazer: the spoiler is fallen upon thy summer fruits and upon thy vintage.

33And joy and gladness is taken from the plentiful field, and from the land of Moab; and I have caused wine to fail from the winepresses: none shall tread with shouting; *their* shouting *shall be* no shouting.

34From the cry of Heshbon *even* unto Elealeh, *and even* unto Jahaz, have they uttered their voice, from Zoar *even* unto Horonaim, *as* an heifer of three years old: for the waters also of Nimrim shall be desolate.

35Moreover I will cause to cease in Moab, saith the LORD, him that offereth in the high places, and him that burneth incense to his gods.

36Therefore mine heart shall sound for Moab like pipes, and mine heart shall sound like pipes for the men of Kir-heres: because the riches *that* he hath gotten are perished.

37For every head *shall be* bald, and every beard clipped: upon all the hands *shall be* cuttings, and upon the loins sackcloth.

38 *There shall be* lamentation generally upon all the housetops of Moab, and in the streets thereof: for I have broken Moab like a vessel wherein *is* no pleasure, saith the LORD.

39They shall howl, *saying*, How is it broken down! how hath Moab turned the back with shame! so shall Moab be a derision and a dismaying to all them about him.

40For thus saith the LORD; Behold, he shall fly as an eagle. and shall spread his wings over Moab.

41Kerioth is taken, and the strong holds are surprised, and the mighty men's hearts in Moab at that day shall be as the heart of a woman in her pangs.

42And Moab shall be destroyed from *being* a people, because he hath magnified *himself* against the LORD.

**AMP** [a] Nebuchadnezzar (B.C. 605-562) subjugated the Moabites, but they continued to be heard of as a race into the first century A.D., though the national existence of both Moab and Ammon seems to have ended long before the time of Christ. This in itself is a remarkable fulfillment of prophecy, but that Moab's fortunes are to be restored "in the latter days" (verse 47) and have proceeded toward that end before our very eyes is even more startling. Yet Moab is only one of the numerous nations whose fate was accurately pre-written by the ancient prophets of God.

## Amplified

27For was not Israel [an object of] derision to you? Was he found among thieves, since whenever you spoke of him you wagged your head?

28O you inhabitants of Moab, leave the cities and dwell in the rock, and be like the dove that makes her nest in the walls of the yawning ravine.

29We have heard of the [gay] pride of Moab, the extremely proud: his loftiness, his arrogance, his conceit, and the haughtiness of his heart.

30I know his insolent wrath, says the Lord, and the nothingness of his boastings *and* his deeds; they are false *and* have accomplished nothing.

31Therefore I will wail over Moab, and I will cry out over the whole of Moab. Over the men of Kirheres there shall be sighing *and* mourning.

32O vine of Sibmah, I weep for you more than the weeping of Jazer [over its ruins and wasted vineyards]; your tendrils [of influence] have gone over the sea, even to Jazer. The destroyer has fallen upon your summer fruit harvest and your [season's] crop of grapes.

33Joy and gladness are taken from the fruitful orchards *and* fields and from the land of Moab; and I have made the grape juice to fail from what is pressed out in the vats; no one treads with shouting; their shouting is no shouting [of joy, but a battle cry].

34From the cry of Heshbon even to Elealeh, even to Jahaz have they uttered their voice, from Zoar even to Horonaim and Eglath-shelishiyah—like a three-year-old heifer; for even the waters of Nimrim have become desolations.

35Moreover I will cause to cease in Moab, says the Lord, him who ascends *and* offers in the high place, and him who burns incense to his gods.

36Therefore My heart moans *and* sighs for Moab like flutes, and My heart moans *and* sighs like flutes over the men of Kirheres; therefore the remnant of the abundant riches they had gained has perished.

37For every head is shaven bald, and every beard cut off: upon all the hands are cuttings, and upon the loins is sackcloth [all to express mourning].

38On all the housetops of Moab and in its streets there is lamentation everywhere, for I have broken Moab like a vessel in which there is no pleasure, says the Lord.

39How it is broken down! How they do wail! How Moab has turned his back in shame! So Moab has become a derision and a [horrifying] terror to all who are round about him.

40For thus says the Lord: Behold, he [Babylon] shall fly swiftly like an eagle, and shall spread out his wings against Moab.

41Kerioth shall be taken *and* the cities, the strongholds shall be seized; and the heart of the mighty warriors of Moab in that day shall be as the heart of a woman in her pangs [in childbirth].

42And Moab shall be [a]destroyed from being a nation, because he has magnified himself against the Lord.

## New American Standard

27"Now was not Israel a laughingstock to you? Or was he
caught among thieves? For each time you speak about him you
shake *your head in scorn.*
28 "Leave the cities and dwell among the crags,
O inhabitants of Moab,
And be like a dove that nests
Beyond the mouth of the chasm.
29 "We have heard of the pride of Moab—he *is* very
proud—
Of his haughtiness, his pride, his arrogance and his
self-exaltation.
30 "I know his fury," declares the LORD,
"But it is futile;
His idle boasts have accomplished nothing.
31 "Therefore I shall wail for Moab,
Even for all Moab shall I cry out;
I will moan for the men of Kir-heres.
32 "More than the weeping for Jazer
I shall weep for you, O vine of Sibmah!
Your tendrils stretched across the sea,
They reached to the sea of Jazer;
Upon your summer fruits and your grape harvest
The destroyer has fallen.
33 "So gladness and joy are taken away
From the fruitful field, even from the land of Moab.
And I have made the wine to cease from the wine
presses;
No one will tread *them* with shouting,
The shouting will not be shouts *of joy.*
34"From the outcry at Heshbon even to Elealeh, even to Jahaz
they have raised their voice, from Zoar even to Horonaim *and to*
Eglath-shelishiyah; for even the waters of Nimrim will become
desolate.
35"And I shall make an end of Moab," declares the LORD, "the
one who offers *sacrifice* on the high place and the one who burns
incense to his gods.
36¶ "Therefore My heart wails for Moab like flutes; My heart
also wails like flutes for the men of Kir-heres. Therefore they have
lost the abundance it produced.
37"For every head is bald and every beard cut short; there are
gashes on all the hands and sackcloth on the loins.
38"On all the housetops of Moab and in its streets there is
lamentation everywhere; for I have broken Moab like an undesirable vessel," declares the LORD.
39"How shattered it is! *How* they have wailed! How Moab has
turned his back—he is ashamed! So Moab will become a laughingstock and an object of terror to all around him."
40For thus says the LORD,
"Behold, one will fly swiftly like an eagle,
And spread out his wings against Moab.
41 "Kerioth has been captured
And the strongholds have been seized,
So the hearts of the mighty men of Moab in that day
Will be like the heart of a woman in labor.
42 "And Moab will be destroyed from *being* a people
Because he has become arrogant toward the LORD.

## New International

27Was not Israel the object of your ridicule?
Was she caught among thieves,
that you shake your head in scorn
whenever you speak of her?
28Abandon your towns and dwell among the rocks,
you who live in Moab.
Be like a dove that makes its nest
at the mouth of a cave.

29"We have heard of Moab's pride—
her overweening pride and conceit,
her pride and arrogance
and the haughtiness of her heart.
30I know her insolence but it is futile,"
declares the LORD,
"and her boasts accomplish nothing.
31Therefore I wail over Moab,
for all Moab I cry out,
I moan for the men of Kir Hareseth.
32I weep for you, as Jazer weeps,
O vines of Sibmah.
Your branches spread as far as the sea;
they reached as far as the sea of Jazer.
The destroyer has fallen
on your ripened fruit and grapes.
33Joy and gladness are gone
from the orchards and fields of Moab.
I have stopped the flow of wine from the presses;
no one treads them with shouts of joy.
Although there are shouts,
they are not shouts of joy.

34"The sound of their cry rises
from Heshbon to Elealeh and Jahaz,
from Zoar as far as Horonaim and Eglath Shelishiyah,
for even the waters of Nimrim are dried up.
35In Moab I will put an end
to those who make offerings on the high places
and burn incense to their gods,"
declares the LORD.
36"So my heart laments for Moab like a flute;
it laments like a flute for the men of Kir Hareseth.
The wealth they acquired is gone.
37Every head is shaved
and every beard cut off;
every hand is slashed
and every waist is covered with sackcloth.
38On all the roofs in Moab
and in the public squares
there is nothing but mourning,
for I have broken Moab
like a jar that no one wants,"
declares the LORD.
39"How shattered she is! How they wail!
How Moab turns her back in shame!
Moab has become an object of ridicule,
an object of horror to all those around her."

40This is what the LORD says:

"Look! An eagle is swooping down,
spreading its wings over Moab.
41Kerioth[b] will be captured
and the strongholds taken.
In that day the hearts of Moab's warriors
will be like the heart of a woman in labor.
42Moab will be destroyed as a nation
because she defied the LORD.

NIV [b] 41 Or *The cities*

## King James

43Fear, and the pit, and the snare, *shall be* upon thee, O inhabitant of Moab, saith the LORD.
44He that fleeth from the fear shall fall into the pit; and he that
getteth up out of the pit shall be taken in the snare: for I will bring
upon it, *even* upon Moab, the year of their visitation, saith the
LORD.
45They that fled stood under the shadow of Heshbon because
of the force: but a fire shall come forth out of Heshbon, and a flame
from the midst of Sihon, and shall devour the corner of Moab, and
the crown of the head of the tumultuous ones.
46Woe be unto thee, O Moab! the people of Chemosh perisheth:
for thy sons are taken captives, and thy daughters captives.
47¶ Yet will I bring again the captivity of Moab in the latter days,
saith the LORD. Thus far *is* the judgment of Moab.

**49** CONCERNING THE Ammonites, thus saith the LORD;
Hath Israel no sons? hath he no heir? why *then* doth their
king inherit Gad, and his people dwell in his cities?
2Therefore, behold, the days come, saith the LORD, that I will
cause an alarm of war to be heard in Rabbah of the Ammonites;
and it shall be a desolate heap, and her daughters shall be burned
with fire: then shall Israel be heir unto them that were his heirs,
saith the LORD.
3Howl, O Heshbon, for Ai is spoiled: cry, ye daughters of
Rabbah, gird you with sackcloth; lament, and run to and fro by the
hedges; for their king shall go into captivity, *and* his priests and his
princes together.
4Wherefore gloriest thou in the valleys, thy flowing valley, O
backsliding daughter? that trusted in her treasures, *saying*, Who
shall come unto me?
5Behold, I will bring a fear upon thee, saith the Lord GOD of
hosts, from all those that be about thee; and ye shall be driven out
every man right forth; and none shall gather up him that wandereth.
6And afterward I will bring again the captivity of the children
of Ammon, saith the LORD.

## Amplified

43Terror, and the pit, and the snare are before you, O inhabitant
of Moab, says the Lord.
44He who flees from the terror shall fall into the pit, and he who
gets up out of the pit shall be taken in the trap *or* snare; for I will
bring upon it, even upon Moab, the year of their visitation—their
inspection and infliction of punishment—says the Lord.
45In the shadow of Heshbon the fugitives stand powerless—
stopped without strength; for a fire has gone forth from Heshbon,
a flame from the midst of Sihon; it has destroyed the corner of
Moab and the crown of the head of the ones in tumult [the proud
Moabites].
46Woe to you, O Moab! The people of [the god] Chemosh *are*
undone; for your sons are taken captives, and your daughters into
captivity.
47Yet will I reverse the captivity *and* [a]restore the fortunes of
Moab in the latter days, says the Lord. Thus far is the judgment
on Moab.

**49** CONCERNING *AND* against the Ammonites, thus says
the Lord: Has Israel no sons [to return after their captivity
and claim the territory of Gad on the east of Jordan which the
Ammonites have taken over]? Has [Israel's Gad] no heir? Why
then does Milcom—[the god the Ammonites call] their king—dispossess *and* inherit Gad, and his people dwell in Gad's cities?
2Therefore, behold, the days come, says the Lord, that I will
cause an alarm of war to be heard against Rabbah of the Ammonites; and [the high ground on which it stands] shall become a
desolate heap, and its daughter [villages] shall be burned with fire;
then shall Israel dispossess those who had dispossessed him, says
the Lord. [Ezek. 21:28-32; 25:1-7, 11; Amos 1:13-15; Zeph. 2:8-11.]
3Wail, O Heshbon [in Moab just south of Ammon], for Ai *or* Ar
[in Ammon] is laid waste! Cry out, you daughter *villages* of Rabbah!
Gird yourselves with sackcloth, lament, and run to and fro inside
the [sheepfold] enclosures; for Milcom [the god-king] shall go into
exile, with his priests and his princes.
4Why do you boast of your valleys? Your valley flows away, O
[Ammon] rebellious *and* faithless daughter, who trusted in her
treasures, who said, Who can come against me?
5Behold, I will bring terror upon you, says the Lord God of
hosts, from all who are round about you, and you shall be driven
out, each man fleeing straight before him [without thought of his
neighbor], and there will be no one to gather together the fugitives.
6And [b]afterward I will reverse the captivity of the children of
Ammon *and* restore their fortunes, says the Lord.

**AMP** [a] Nebuchadnezzar (B.C. 605-562) subjugated the Moabites, but they continued to be heard of as a race into the first century A.D., though the national existence of both Moab and Ammon seems to have ended long before the time of Christ. This in itself is a remarkable fulfillment of prophecy, but that Moab's fortunes are to be restored "in the latter days" (verse 47) and have proceeded toward that end before our very eyes is even more startling. Yet Moab is only one of the numerous nations whose fate was accurately pre-written by the ancient prophets of God. [b] Complete and continuous as the desolation of Moab and Ammon was for many long centuries, God is keeping His word for their restoration "in the latter days" in a remarkable manner. For instance, Amman, the capital of Trans-Jordan (the ancient Rabbath of Ammon), was a mere village in 1900, but by 1960 it was a city of 200,000 inhabitants. One can only stand in awe and reverent amazement at the precision with which the prophecies of the Word of God are being carried out in the present day and age.

## New American Standard

43 "Terror, pit, and snare are *coming* upon you,
O inhabitant of Moab," declares the LORD.
44 "The one who flees from the terror
Will fall into the pit,
And the one who climbs up out of the pit
Will be caught in the snare;
For I shall bring upon her, *even* upon Moab,
The year of their punishment," declares the LORD.

45¶ "In the shadow of Heshbon
The fugitives stand without strength;
For a fire has gone forth from Heshbon,
And a flame from the midst of Sihon,
And it has devoured the forehead of Moab
And the scalps of the riotous revelers.
46 "Woe to you, Moab!
The people of Chemosh have perished;
For your sons have been taken away captive,
And your daughters into captivity.
47 "Yet I will restore the fortunes of Moab
In the latter days," declares the LORD.
Thus far the judgment on Moab.

*Prophecy against Ammon*

49 CONCERNING THE sons of Ammon.
Thus says the LORD:
"Does Israel have no sons?
Or has he no heirs?
Why then has Malcam taken possession of Gad
And his people settled in its cities?
2 "Therefore behold, the days are coming," declares the LORD,
"That I shall cause a trumpet blast of war to be heard
Against Rabbah of the sons of Ammon;
And it will become a desolate heap,
And her towns will be set on fire.
Then Israel will take possession of his possessors,"
Says the LORD.
3 "Wail, O Heshbon, for Ai has been destroyed!
Cry out, O daughters of Rabbah,
Gird yourselves with sackcloth and lament,
And rush back and forth inside the walls;
For Malcam will go into exile
Together with his priests and his princes.
4 "How boastful you are about the valleys!
Your valley is flowing *away*,
O backsliding daughter
Who trusts in her treasures, *saying*,
'Who will come against me?'
5 "Behold, I am going to bring terror upon you,"
Declares the Lord GOD of hosts,
"From all *directions* around you;
And each of you will be driven out headlong,
With no one to gather the fugitives together.
6 "But afterward I will restore
The fortunes of the sons of Ammon,"
Declares the LORD.

## New International

43Terror and pit and snare await you,
O people of Moab,"
declares the LORD.
44"Whoever flees from the terror
will fall into a pit,
whoever climbs out of the pit
will be caught in a snare;
for I will bring upon Moab
the year of her punishment,"
declares the LORD.

45"In the shadow of Heshbon
the fugitives stand helpless,
for a fire has gone out from Heshbon,
a blaze from the midst of Sihon;
it burns the foreheads of Moab,
the skulls of the noisy boasters.
46Woe to you, O Moab!
The people of Chemosh are destroyed;
your sons are taken into exile
and your daughters into captivity.

47"Yet I will restore the fortunes of Moab
in days to come,"
declares the LORD.

Here ends the judgment on Moab.

*A Message About Ammon*

49 CONCERNING THE Ammonites:

This is what the LORD says:

"Has Israel no sons?
Has she no heirs?
Why then has Molech[c] taken possession of Gad?
Why do his people live in its towns?
2But the days are coming,"
declares the LORD,
"when I will sound the battle cry
against Rabbah of the Ammonites;
it will become a mound of ruins,
and its surrounding villages will be set on fire.
Then Israel will drive out
those who drove her out,"
says the LORD.

3"Wail, O Heshbon, for Ai is destroyed!
Cry out, O inhabitants of Rabbah!
Put on sackcloth and mourn;
rush here and there inside the walls,
for Molech will go into exile,
together with his priests and officials.
4Why do you boast of your valleys,
boast of your valleys so fruitful?
O unfaithful daughter,
you trust in your riches and say,
'Who will attack me?'
5I will bring terror on you
from all those around you,"
declares the Lord, the LORD Almighty.
"Every one of you will be driven away,
and no one will gather the fugitives.

6"Yet afterward, I will restore the fortunes of the Ammonites,"
declares the LORD.

NIV c 1 Or *their king;* Hebrew *malcam;* also in verse 3

# King James

7¶ Concerning Edom, thus saith the LORD of hosts; *Is* wisdom no more in Teman? is counsel perished from the prudent? is their wisdom vanished?

8 Flee ye, turn back, dwell deep, O inhabitants of Dedan; for I will bring the calamity of Esau upon him, the time *that* I will visit him.

9 If grapegatherers come to thee, would they not leave *some* gleaning grapes? if thieves by night, they will destroy till they have enough.

10 But I have made Esau bare, I have uncovered his secret places, and he shall not be able to hide himself: his seed is spoiled, and his brethren, and his neighbours, and he *is* not.

11 Leave thy fatherless children, I will preserve *them* alive; and let thy widows trust in me.

12 For thus saith the LORD; Behold, they whose judgment *was* not to drink of the cup have assuredly drunken; and *art* thou he *that* shall altogether go unpunished? thou shalt not go unpunished, but thou shalt surely drink *of it*.

13 For I have sworn by myself, saith the LORD, that Bozrah shall become a desolation, a reproach, a waste, and a curse; and all the cities thereof shall be perpetual wastes.

14 I have heard a rumour from the LORD, and an ambassador is sent unto the heathen, *saying*, Gather ye together, and come against her, and rise up to the battle.

15 For, lo, I will make thee small among the heathen, *and* despised among men.

16 Thy terribleness hath deceived thee, *and* the pride of thine heart, O thou that dwellest in the clefts of the rock, that holdest the height of the hill: though thou shouldest make thy nest as high as the eagle, I will bring thee down from thence, saith the LORD.

17 Also Edom shall be a desolation: every one that goeth by it shall be astonished, and shall hiss at all the plagues thereof.

18 As in the overthrow of Sodom and Gomorrah and the neighbour *cities* thereof, saith the LORD, no man shall abide there, neither shall a son of man dwell in it.

19 Behold, he shall come up like a lion from the swelling of Jordan against the habitation of the strong: but I will suddenly make him run away from her: and who *is* a chosen *man*, *that* I may appoint over her? for who *is* like me? and who will appoint me the time? and who *is* that shepherd that will stand before me?

20 Therefore hear the counsel of the LORD, that he hath taken against Edom; and his purposes, that he hath purposed against the inhabitants of Teman: Surely the least of the flock shall draw them out: surely he shall make their habitations desolate with them.

21 The earth is moved at the noise of their fall, at the cry the noise thereof was heard in the Red sea.

**AMP** [a] How, except by Divine inspiration, could the prophets have foretold that Edom's desolation would be perpetual? After 2500 years the statement is so literally true, that here where millions once lived, there are only a few people, barely existing, and the land is in ruins. For there was no prophecy that Edom would recover "in the latter days," as would Moab and Ammon, but her desolation was to be lasting. The short book of Obadiah presents an interesting further clarification of God's reason for this exceptional treatment of Edom. It was all the outcome of "only a quarrel" between two brothers, Jacob and Esau, which continued from Genesis to the Gospels. (Gen. 27.) [b] How, except by Divine inspiration, could the prophets have foretold that Edom's desolation would be perpetual? After 2500 years the statement is so literally true, that here where millions once lived, there are only a few people, barely existing, and the land is in ruins. For there was no prophecy that Edom would recover "in the latter days," as would Moab and Ammon, but her desolation was to be lasting. The short book of Obadiah presents an interesting further clarification of God's reason for this exceptional treatment of Edom. It was all the outcome of "only a quarrel" between two brothers, Jacob and Esau, which continued from Genesis to the Gospels. (Gen. 27.) [c] Petra, once an important Roman city in Edom, was lost for many centuries, but rediscovered in 1812. On the height above its ruins is the great high place, and other evidences of idolatry stand on neighboring heights. [d] How, except by Divine inspiration, could the prophets have foretold that Edom's desolation would be perpetual? After 2500 years the statement is so literally true, that here where millions once lived, there are only a few people, barely existing, and the land is in ruins. For there was no prophecy that Edom would recover "in the latter days," as would Moab and Ammon, but her desolation was to be lasting. The short book of Obadiah presents an interesting further clarification of God's reason for this exceptional treatment of Edom. It was all the outcome of "only a quarrel" between two brothers, Jacob and Esau, which continued from Genesis to the Gospels. (Gen. 27.)

# Amplified

7 Concerning *and* against Edom, thus says the Lord of hosts: Is there no longer wisdom in Teman? Is counsel vanished from the intelligent *and* prudent? Is their wisdom all poured out *and* used up? [Isa. 34; 63:1-6; Ezek. 25:12-14; 35; Amos 1:11, 12; Obadiah; Mal. 1:2-5.]

8 Flee, turn back, dwell deep [in the deserts to escape the Chaldeans], O inhabitants of Dedan [neighbor of Edom]! For I will bring the calamity *and* destruction of Esau [Edom] upon Dedan, when I inspect *and* punish him.

9 If grape-gatherers came to you, would they not leave some ungleaned grapes? If thieves came by night, would they not destroy only what is enough [for them]?

10 But I have stripped Esau [Edom] bare, I have uncovered his hiding places, and he cannot hide himself. His offspring are destroyed, and his brethren, and his neighbors; and he is no more.

11 Leave your fatherless children, I will [do what is necessary to] preserve them alive; and let [those made] your widows trust *and* confide in Me.

12 For thus says the Lord: Behold, they [Israel] whose rule was not to drink of the cup [of wrath] shall assuredly drink, and are you to remain unpunished? You shall not go unpunished, but you shall surely drink.

13 For I have sworn by Myself, says the Lord, that Bozrah [in Edom between Petra and the Dead Sea] shall become a horror, a reproach, a waste, and a curse; and all its cities shall be [a]perpetual wastes.

14 I have heard a report from the Lord, and a messenger is sent to the nations, saying, Gather together, and come against her, and rise up to the battle.

15 For, lo, I will make you [Edom] [b]small among the nations, and despised among men. [Ezek. 35:9.]

16 Your object of horror [your idol] deceived you, and the pride of your heart, O you who dwell in the clefts of the rock—Selah or [c]Petra—who hold the height of the hill. Though you should make your nest as high as the eagle's, I will bring you down from there, says the Lord.

17 And Edom shall be an [d]astonishment *and* a horror; every one who goes by it shall be astonished *and* shall hiss with horror at all its plagues *and* disasters.

18 As in the overthrow of Sodom and Gomorrah and their neighboring cities, says the Lord, no man shall dwell there, neither shall a son of man live in it temporarily.

19 See, there comes up one [Nebuchadnezzar] like a lion from [lurking in] the jungles—the pride—of the Jordan against the strong habitation [of Edom] *and* into the permanent pastures; for in a twinkling I will drive him [Edom] from there. And I will appoint over him the one whom I choose. For who is like Me? And who will apoint Me the time *and* prosecute Me for this proceeding? And what [earthly national] shepherd can stand before Me *and* defy Me?

20 Therefore hear the plan of the Lord which He has made against Edom, and His purposes which He has formed against the inhabitants of Teman [a district in Edom]. Surely they shall be dragged away [by Nebuchadnezzar], even the little ones of the flock; surely he shall make their habitation desolate over them *and* their fold shocked at their fate.

21 At the sound of their fall the earth shall tremble; at their crying the sound shall be heard at the Red Sea.

## New American Standard

*Prophecy against Edom*

7¶ Concerning Edom.
Thus says the LORD of hosts,
"Is there no longer any wisdom in Teman?
Has good counsel been lost to the prudent?
Has their wisdom decayed?
8 "Flee away, turn back, dwell in the depths,
O inhabitants of Dedan,
For I will bring the disaster of Esau upon him
At the time I punish him.
9 "If grape gatherers came to you,
Would they not leave gleanings?
If thieves *came* by night,
They would destroy *only* until they had enough.
10 "But I have stripped Esau bare,
I have uncovered his hiding places
So that he will not be able to conceal himself;
His offspring has been destroyed along with his relatives
And his neighbors, and he is no more.
11 "Leave your orphans behind, I will keep *them* alive;
And let your widows trust in Me."

12For thus says the LORD, "Behold, those who were not sentenced to drink the cup will certainly drink *it,* and are you the one
who will be completely acquitted? You will not be acquitted, but
you will certainly drink *it.*
13"For I have sworn by Myself," declares the LORD, "that Bozrah will become an object of horror, a reproach, a ruin and a curse;
and all its cities will become perpetual ruins."

14¶ I have heard a message from the LORD,
And an envoy is sent among the nations, *saying,*
"Gather yourselves together and come against her,
And rise up for battle!"
15 "For behold, I have made you small among the nations,
Despised among men.
16 "As for the terror of you,
The arrogance of your heart has deceived you,
O you who live in the clefts of the rock,
Who occupy the height of the hill.
Though you make your nest as high as an eagle's,
I will bring you down from there," declares the LORD.

17"And Edom will become an object of horror; everyone who
passes by it will be horrified and will hiss at all its wounds.
18"Like the overthrow of Sodom and Gomorrah with its neighbors," says the LORD, "no one will live there, nor will a son of man
reside in it.
19"Behold, one will come up like a lion from the thickets of the
Jordan against a perennially watered pasture; for in an instant I
shall make him run away from it, and whoever is chosen I shall
appoint over it. For who is like Me, and who will summon Me *into
court?* And who then is the shepherd who can stand against Me?"
20¶ Therefore hear the plan of the LORD which He has planned
against Edom, and His purposes which He has purposed against
the inhabitants of Teman: surely they will drag them off, *even* the
little ones of the flock; surely He will make their pasture desolate
because of them.
21The earth has quaked at the noise of their downfall. There is
an outcry! The noise of it has been heard at the Red Sea.

## New International

*A Message About Edom*

7Concerning Edom:

This is what the LORD Almighty says:

"Is there no longer wisdom in Teman?
Has counsel perished from the prudent?
Has their wisdom decayed?
8Turn and flee, hide in deep caves,
you who live in Dedan,
for I will bring disaster on Esau
at the time I punish him.
9If grape pickers came to you,
would they not leave a few grapes?
If thieves came during the night,
would they not steal only as much as they wanted?
10But I will strip Esau bare;
I will uncover his hiding places,
so that he cannot conceal himself.
His children, relatives and neighbors will perish,
and he will be no more.
11Leave your orphans; I will protect their lives.
Your widows too can trust in me."

12This is what the LORD says: "If those who do not deserve to
drink the cup must drink it, why should you go unpunished? You
will not go unpunished, but must drink it. 13I swear by myself,"
declares the LORD, "that Bozrah will become a ruin and an object
of horror, of reproach and of cursing; and all its towns will be in
ruins forever."

14I have heard a message from the LORD:
An envoy was sent to the nations to say,
"Assemble yourselves to attack it!
Rise up for battle!"
15"Now I will make you small among the nations,
despised among men.
16The terror you inspire
and the pride of your heart have deceived you,
you who live in the clefts of the rocks,
who occupy the heights of the hill.
Though you build your nest as high as the eagle's,
from there I will bring you down,"
declares the LORD.
17"Edom will become an object of horror;
all who pass by will be appalled and will scoff
because of all its wounds.
18As Sodom and Gomorrah were overthrown,
along with their neighboring towns,"
says the LORD,
"so no one will live there;
no man will dwell in it.

19"Like a lion coming up from Jordan's thickets
to a rich pastureland,
I will chase Edom from its land in an instant.
Who is the chosen one I will appoint for this?
Who is like me and who can challenge me?
And what shepherd can stand against me?"
20Therefore, hear what the LORD has planned against Edom,
what he has purposed against those who live in Teman:
The young of the flock will be dragged away;
he will completely destroy their pasture because of them.
21At the sound of their fall the earth will tremble;
their cry will resound to the Red Sea.[e]

NIV [e] 21 Hebrew *Yam Suph;* that is, Sea of Reeds

## King James

22Behold, he shall come up and fly as the eagle, and spread his wings over Bozrah: and at that day shall the heart of the mighty men of Edom be as the heart of a woman in her pangs.
23¶ Concerning Damascus. Hamath is confounded, and Arpad: for they have heard evil tidings: they are fainthearted; *there is* sorrow on the sea; it cannot be quiet.
24Damascus is waxed feeble, *and* turneth herself to flee, and fear hath seized on *her:* anguish and sorrows have taken her, as a woman in travail.
25How is the city of praise not left, the city of my joy!
26Therefore her young men shall fall in her streets, and all the men of war shall be cut off in that day, saith the LORD of hosts.
27And I will kindle a fire in the wall of Damascus, and it shall consume the palaces of Ben-hadad.
28¶ Concerning Kedar, and concerning the kingdoms of Hazor, which Nebuchadrezzar king of Babylon shall smite, thus saith the LORD; Arise ye, go up to Kedar, and spoil the men of the east.
29Their tents and their flocks shall they take away: they shall take to themselves their curtains, and all their vessels, and their camels; and they shall cry unto them, Fear *is* on every side.
30¶ Flee, get you far off, dwell deep, O ye inhabitants of Hazor, saith the LORD; for Nebuchadrezzar king of Babylon hath taken counsel against you, and hath conceived a purpose against you.
31Arise, get you up unto the wealthy nation, that dwelleth without care, saith the LORD, which have neither gates nor bars, *which* dwell alone.
32And their camels shall be a booty, and the multitude of their cattle a spoil: and I will scatter into all winds them *that are* in the utmost corners; and I will bring their calamity from all sides thereof, saith the LORD.
33And Hazor shall be a dwelling for dragons, *and* a desolation for ever: there shall no man abide there, nor *any* son of man dwell in it.
34¶ The word of the LORD that came to Jeremiah the prophet against Elam in the beginning of the reign of Zedekiah king of Judah, saying,
35Thus saith the LORD of hosts; Behold, I will break the bow of Elam, the chief of their might.

## Amplified

22Behold, one shall come up and fly swiftly like an eagle, and spread his wings against [the Edomite city of] Bozrah; and in that day the heart of the mighty warriors of Edom will be as the heart of a woman in her pangs [at childbirth].
23Concerning *and* against Damascus [in Syria]. Hamath and Arpad are confounded *and* put to shame, for they have heard bad news; they are faint-hearted *and* waste away; there is trouble *and* anxiety *as* on a [storm-tossed] sea which cannot rest.
24Damascus has become feeble. She turned to flee, and terror *and* panic seized her; anguish and sorrow have taken hold of her, like a woman in childbirth.
25How [remarkable that] the renowned city is not deserted, the city of my joy! [exclaims one from Damascus].
26Therefore her young men shall fall in her streets, and all her soldiers shall be destroyed in that day, says the Lord of hosts. [Isa. 17:1-3; Amos 1:3-5; Zech. 9:1.]
27And I will kindle a fire in the wall of Damascus, and it shall consume the palaces of Benhadad [title of several kings of Syria].
28Concerning Kedar [a tribe of nomad Arabs] and concerning the kingdoms of Hazor [that part of the Arab nation which used fixed dwellings in unwalled towns], which Nebuchadrezzar king of Babylon shall smite, thus says the Lord [to him]: Arise, go up against Kedar and destroy the sons of the east.
29Their tents and their flocks shall [the Chaldeans] take, their tent hangings and all their utensils, and their camels. And men shall cry to them, Terror on every side! [Jer. 6:25; 20:3, 10; 46:5; Ps. 31:13.]
30Flee, wander far off, dwell in the deep places, O you inhabitants of Hazor [in the Arabian Desert] says the Lord, for Nebuchadrezzar king of Babylon has planned a course against you, and has conceived a purpose against you.
31Arise [Nebuchadrezzar], get you up into a nation that is at ease, that dwells without care, says the Lord, which has neither gates nor bars, that dwells apart.
32And their camels shall become a booty, and their herds of cattle a spoil; and I will scatter to all *the four* winds those who [in evidence of their idolatry] have the corners of their hair cut off, and I will bring their calamity from every side of them, says the Lord. [Lev. 19:27.]
33And [a]Hazor shall become a dwelling place for jackals, a desolation for ever; there shall no man remain there, neither shall a son of man dwell there temporarily.
34The word of the Lord that came to Jeremiah the prophet concerning *and* against Elam in the beginning of the reign of Zedekiah king of Judah, saying,
35Thus says the Lord of hosts: Behold, I will break the bow of Elam, the chief [weapon and part] of their strength.

**AMP** [a] This Hazor is not to be confused with three others mentioned elsewhere. It was a region in the Arabian Desert east of Palestine. Jeremiah's prophecy concerning it was literally fulfilled. Nebuchadnezzar conquered Arabia, according to Berosus, and Hazor's exact situation is long since unknown.

## New American Standard

22Behold, He will mount up and swoop like an eagle, and spread out His wings against Bozrah; and the hearts of the mighty men of Edom in that day will be like the heart of a woman in labor.

*Prophecy against Damascus*

23¶ Concerning Damascus.
"Hamath and Arpad are put to shame,
For they have heard bad news;
They are disheartened.
There is anxiety by the sea,
It cannot be calmed.
24 "Damascus has become helpless;
She has turned away to flee,
And panic has gripped her;
Distress and pangs have taken hold of her
Like a woman in childbirth.
25 "How the city of praise has not been deserted,
The town of My joy!
26 "Therefore, her young men will fall in her streets,
And all the men of war will be silenced in that day,"
declares the LORD of hosts.
27 "And I shall set fire to the wall of Damascus,
And it will devour the fortified towers of Ben-hadad."

*Prophecy against Kedar and Hazor*

28¶ Concerning Kedar and the kingdoms of Hazor, which Nebuchadnezzar king of Babylon defeated. Thus says the LORD,
"Arise, go up to Kedar
And devastate the men of the east.
29 "They will take away their tents and their flocks;
They will carry off for themselves
Their tent curtains, all their goods, and their camels,
And they will call out to one another, 'Terror on every side!'
30 "Run away, flee! Dwell in the depths,
O inhabitants of Hazor," declares the LORD;
"For Nebuchadnezzar king of Babylon has formed a plan against you
And devised a scheme against you.
31 "Arise, go up against a nation which is at ease,
Which lives securely," declares the LORD.
"It has no gates or bars;
They dwell alone.
32 "And their camels will become plunder,
And the multitude of their cattle for booty,
And I shall scatter to all the winds those who cut the corners *of their hair;*
And I shall bring their disaster from every side,"
declares the LORD.
33 "And Hazor will become a haunt of jackals,
A desolation forever;
No one will live there,
Nor will a son of man reside in it."

*Prophecy against Elam*

34¶ That which came as the word of the LORD to Jeremiah the prophet concerning Elam, at the beginning of the reign of Zedekiah king of Judah, saying,
35 "Thus says the LORD of hosts,
'Behold, I am going to break the bow of Elam,
The finest of their might.

## New International

22Look! An eagle will soar and swoop down,
spreading its wings over Bozrah.
In that day the hearts of Edom's warriors
will be like the heart of a woman in labor.

*A Message About Damascus*

23Concerning Damascus:

"Hamath and Arpad are dismayed,
for they have heard bad news.
They are disheartened,
troubled like[b] the restless sea.
24Damascus has become feeble,
she has turned to flee
and panic has gripped her;
anguish and pain have seized her,
pain like that of a woman in labor.
25Why has the city of renown not been abandoned,
the town in which I delight?
26Surely, her young men will fall in the streets;
all her soldiers will be silenced in that day,"
declares the LORD Almighty.
27"I will set fire to the walls of Damascus;
it will consume the fortresses of Ben-Hadad."

*A Message About Kedar and Hazor*

28Concerning Kedar and the kingdoms of Hazor, which Nebuchadnezzar king of Babylon attacked:

This is what the LORD says:

"Arise, and attack Kedar
and destroy the people of the East.
29Their tents and their flocks will be taken;
their shelters will be carried off
with all their goods and camels.
Men will shout to them,
'Terror on every side!'

30"Flee quickly away!
Stay in deep caves, you who live in Hazor,"
declares the LORD.
"Nebuchadnezzar king of Babylon has plotted against you;
he has devised a plan against you.

31"Arise and attack a nation at ease,
which lives in confidence,"
declares the LORD,
"a nation that has neither gates nor bars;
its people live alone.
32Their camels will become plunder,
and their large herds will be booty.
I will scatter to the winds those who are in distant places[c]
and will bring disaster on them from every side,"
declares the LORD.

33"Hazor will become a haunt of jackals,
a desolate place forever.
No one will live there;
no man will dwell in it."

*A Message About Elam*

34This is the word of the LORD that came to Jeremiah the prophet concerning Elam, early in the reign of Zedekiah king of Judah:

35This is what the LORD Almighty says:

"See, I will break the bow of Elam,
the mainstay of their might.

NIV [b] 23 Hebrew *on* or *by* [c] 32 Or *who clip the hair by their foreheads*

## King James

36 And upon Elam will I bring the four winds from the four quarters of heaven, and will scatter them toward all those winds; and there shall be no nation whither the outcasts of Elam shall not come.

37 For I will cause Elam to be dismayed before their enemies, and before them that seek their life: and I will bring evil upon them, *even* my fierce anger, saith the LORD; and I will send the sword after them, till I have consumed them:

38 And I will set my throne in Elam, and will destroy from thence the king and the princes, saith the LORD.

39 ¶ But it shall come to pass in the latter days, *that* I will bring again the captivity of Elam, saith the LORD.

**50** THE WORD that the LORD spake against Babylon *and* against the land of the Chaldeans by Jeremiah the prophet.

2 Declare ye among the nations, and publish, and set up a standard; publish, *and* conceal not: say, Babylon is taken, Bel is confounded, Merodach is broken in pieces; her idols are confounded, her images are broken in pieces.

3 For out of the north there cometh up a nation against her, which shall make her land desolate, and none shall dwell therein: they shall remove, they shall depart, both man and beast.

4 ¶ In those days, and in that time, saith the LORD, the children of Israel shall come, they and the children of Judah together, going and weeping: they shall go, and seek the LORD their God.

5 They shall ask the way to Zion with their faces thitherward, *saying,* Come, and let us join ourselves to the LORD in a perpetual covenant *that* shall not be forgotten.

6 My people hath been lost sheep: their shepherds have caused them to go astray, they have turned them away *on* the mountains: they have gone from mountain to hill, they have forgotten their restingplace.

7 All that found them have devoured them: and their adversaries said, We offend not, because they have sinned against the LORD, the habitation of justice, even the LORD, the hope of their fathers.

8 Remove out of the midst of Babylon, and go forth out of the land of the Chaldeans, and be as the he goats before the flocks.

9 ¶ For, lo, I will raise and cause to come up against Babylon an assembly of great nations from the north country: and they shall set themselves in array against her; from thence she shall be taken: their arrows *shall be* as of a mighty expert man; none shall return in vain.

**AMP** [a] Elam was a region beyond the Tigris River. After a long period of subjugation to foreign powers it joined with Media and ultimately captured Babylon. It became a province of the Persian Empire. Elamites were forcibly settled in Palestine when the Jewish Babylonian captives returned; Elamites attempted to prevent the rebuilding of Jerusalem and the temple (Ezra 4:9). Elamites were present on the day of Pentecost (Acts 2:9), but they became extinct in the eleventh century. Elam in modern times is a province of Persia, under the name Khuzistan. Thus (in 1960) this prophecy of that nation's destruction is long since fulfilled, with the restoration of Elam's fortunes an imminent probability for which to watch (verse 39). [b] Elam was a region beyond the Tigris River. After a long period of subjugation to foreign powers it joined with Media and ultimately captured Babylon. It became a province of the Persian Empire. Elamites were forcibly settled in Palestine when the Jewish Babylonian captives returned; Elamites attempted to prevent the rebuilding of Jerusalem and the temple (Ezra 4:9). Elamites were present on the day of Pentecost (Acts 2:9), but they became extinct in the eleventh century. Elam in modern times is a province of Iran, under the name Khuzistan. Thus (in 1960) this prophecy of that nation's destruction is long since fulfilled, with the restoration of Elam's fortunes an imminent probability for which to watch (verse 39).

## Amplified

36 And upon Elam will I bring the four winds from the four corners of heaven, and will scatter them toward all those winds; and there shall be no nation to which the outcasts of Elam shall not come.

37 And I will cause [a]Elam to be dismayed *and* terrified before their enemies, and before them that seek *and* demand their life; and I will bring evil upon them, even My fierce anger, says the Lord; and I will send the sword after them until I have consumed them.

38 And I will set My throne [of judgment] in Elam [whose capital city was Shushan, from which God wrought wonders through Nehemiah, Esther and Daniel]; and I will destroy from their king and princes, says the Lord. [Neh. 1:1; Esth. 1:2; Dan. 8:1, 2.]

39 But it shall be [b]in the latter days—the end of days—that I will turn back the captivity and restore the fortunes of Elam, says the Lord.

**50** THE WORD that the Lord spoke concerning *and* against Babylon and concerning *and* against the land of the Chaldeans by Jeremiah the prophet. [Isa. 13:1-14:23; 47; Hab. 1, 2.]

2 Declare it among the nations and publish it, and set up a signal [to spread the news], publish and conceal it not; say, Babylon is taken, Bel [the patron god] is put to shame, Merodach [Bel] is dismayed *and* broken down; [Babylon's] images are put to shame, her [senseless] idols are thrown down!

3 For out of the north there has come up a nation [Media] against her, which shall make her land desolate, and none shall dwell there. They will have fled, they will be gone, from man even to beast.

4 In those days and at that time, says the Lord, the children of Israel shall come, they and the children of Judah together; they shall come up weeping as they come and seek the Lord their God—inquiring for and of Him, and requiring Him [both by right of necessity and of the promises of God's Word].

5 They shall ask the way to Zion with their faces in that direction, saying, Come, let us join ourselves to the Lord in a perpetual covenant that shall not be forgotten.

6 My people have been lost sheep; their shepherds have led them astray [to favorite places of idolatry] on [seducing] mountains. They have gone from [one sin to another,] mountain to hill; they have forgotten their [own] resting place. [Isa. 53:6; I Pet. 2:25.]

7 All who found them have devoured them, and their adversaries said, We are not guilty, because they have sinned against the Lord [and are no longer holy to Him], their true habitation of righteousness *and* justice, even the Lord, the hope of their fathers.

8 Flee out of the midst of Babylon, and go forth out of the land of the Chaldeans, and be as the he-goats before the flocks [as an example and leaders in the flight]. [Jer. 51:6, 9, 45; II Cor. 6:17; Rev. 18:4.]

9 For lo, I raise and cause to come up against Babylon an assembly of great nations from the north country; they equip *and* set themselves against her; from there she shall be taken. Their arrows shall be like [both] an expert, mighty warrior *and* his arrows, none *of them* shall return in vain.

## New American Standard

36 'And I shall bring upon Elam the four winds
From the four ends of heaven,
And shall scatter them to all these winds;
And there will be no nation
To which the outcasts of Elam will not go.
37 'So I shall shatter Elam before their enemies
And before those who seek their lives;
And I shall bring calamity upon them,
Even My fierce anger,' declares the LORD,
'And I shall send out the sword after them
Until I have consumed them.
38 'Then I shall set My throne in Elam,
And I shall destroy out of it king and princes,'
Declares the LORD.
39 'But it will come about in the last days
That I shall restore the fortunes of Elam,' "
Declares the LORD.

*Prophecy against Babylon*

**50** THE WORD which the LORD spoke concerning Babylon, the land of the Chaldeans, through Jeremiah the prophet:
2 "Declare and proclaim among the nations.
Proclaim it and lift up a standard.
Do not conceal *it but* say,
'Babylon has been captured,
Bel has been put to shame, Marduk has been shattered;
Her images have been put to shame, her idols have been shattered.'
3 "For a nation has come up against her out of the north; it will make her land an object of horror, and there will be no inhabitant in it. Both man and beast have wandered off, they have gone away!
4 "In those days and at that time," declares the LORD, "the sons of Israel will come, *both* they and the sons of Judah as well; they will go along weeping as they go, and it will be the LORD their God they will seek.
5 "They will ask for the way to Zion, *turning* their faces in its direction; they will come that they may join themselves to the LORD *in* an everlasting covenant that will not be forgotten.
6 "My people have become lost sheep;
Their shepherds have led them astray.
They have made them turn aside *on* the mountains;
They have gone along from mountain to hill
And have forgotten their resting place.
7 "All who came upon them have devoured them;
And their adversaries have said, 'We are not guilty,
Inasmuch as they have sinned against the LORD *who is* the habitation of righteousness,
Even the LORD, the hope of their fathers.'
8 "Wander away from the midst of Babylon,
And go forth from the land of the Chaldeans;
Be also like male goats at the head of the flock.
9 "For behold, I am going to arouse and bring up against Babylon
A horde of great nations from the land of the north,
And they will draw up *their* battle lines against her;
From there she will be taken captive.
Their arrows will be like an expert warrior
Who does not return empty-handed.

## New International

36 I will bring against Elam the four winds
from the four quarters of the heavens;
I will scatter them to the four winds,
and there will not be a nation
where Elam's exiles do not go.
37 I will shatter Elam before their foes,
before those who seek their lives;
I will bring disaster upon them,
even my fierce anger,"
declares the LORD.
"I will pursue them with the sword
until I have made an end of them.
38 I will set my throne in Elam
and destroy her king and officials,"
declares the LORD.

39 "Yet I will restore the fortunes of Elam
in days to come,"
declares the LORD.

*A Message About Babylon*

**50** THIS IS the word the LORD spoke through Jeremiah the prophet concerning Babylon and the land of the Babylonians[c]:

2 "Announce and proclaim among the nations,
lift up a banner and proclaim it;
keep nothing back, but say,
'Babylon will be captured;
Bel will be put to shame,
Marduk filled with terror.
Her images will be put to shame
and her idols filled with terror.'
3 A nation from the north will attack her
and lay waste her land.
No one will live in it;
both men and animals will flee away.

4 "In those days, at that time,"
declares the LORD,
"the people of Israel and the people of Judah together
will go in tears to seek the LORD their God.
5 They will ask the way to Zion
and turn their faces toward it.
They will come and bind themselves to the LORD
in an everlasting covenant
that will not be forgotten.

6 "My people have been lost sheep;
their shepherds have led them astray
and caused them to roam on the mountains.
They wandered over mountain and hill
and forgot their own resting place.
7 Whoever found them devoured them;
their enemies said, 'We are not guilty,
for they sinned against the LORD, their true pasture,
the LORD, the hope of their fathers.'

8 "Flee out of Babylon;
leave the land of the Babylonians,
and be like the goats that lead the flock.
9 For I will stir up and bring against Babylon
an alliance of great nations from the land of the north.
They will take up their positions against her,
and from the north she will be captured.
Their arrows will be like skilled warriors
who do not return empty-handed.

NIV [c] *1* Or *Chaldeans;* also in verses 8, 25, 35 and 45

## King James

10And Chaldea shall be a spoil: all that spoil her shall be satisfied, saith the LORD.
11Because ye were glad, because ye rejoiced, O ye destroyers of mine heritage, because ye are grown fat as the heifer at grass, and bellow as bulls;
12Your mother shall be sore confounded; she that bare you shall be ashamed: behold, the hindermost of the nations *shall be* a wilderness, a dry land, and a desert.
13Because of the wrath of the LORD it shall not be inhabited, but it shall be wholly desolate: every one that goeth by Babylon shall be astonished, and hiss at all her plagues.
14Put yourselves in array against Babylon round about: all ye that bend the bow, shoot at her, spare no arrows: for she hath sinned against the LORD.
15Shout against her round about: she hath given her hand: her foundations are fallen, her walls are thrown down: for it *is* the vengeance of the LORD: take vengeance upon her; as she hath done, do unto her.
16Cut off the sower from Babylon, and him that handleth the sickle in the time of harvest: for fear of the oppressing sword they shall turn every one to his people, and they shall flee every one to his own land.
17¶ Israel *is* a scattered sheep; the lions have driven *him* away: first the king of Assyria hath devoured him; and last this Nebuchadrezzar king of Babylon hath broken his bones.
18Therefore thus saith the LORD of hosts, the God of Israel; Behold, I will punish the king of Babylon and his land, as I have punished the king of Assyria.
19And I will bring Israel again to his habitation, and he shall feed on Carmel and Bashan, and his soul shall be satisfied upon mount Ephraim and Gilead.
20In those days, and in that time, saith the LORD, the iniquity of Israel shall be sought for, and *there shall be* none; and the sins of Judah, and they shall not be found: for I will pardon them whom I reserve.
21¶ Go up against the land of Merathaim, *even* against it, and against the inhabitants of Pekod: waste and utterly destroy after them, saith the LORD, and do according to all that I have commanded thee.
22A sound of battle *is* in the land, and of great destruction.
23How is the hammer of the whole earth cut asunder and broken! how is Babylon become a desolation among the nations!

## Amplified

10And Chaldea shall become a prey; all that plunder her shall be satisfied, says the Lord.
11Though you are glad, though you rejoice, O you who plunder My heritage, though you are wanton *and* skip like a heifer at grass and neigh like strong stallions,
12Your mother [Babylon] shall be put to great shame, she who bore you shall blush *and* be disgraced. Behold, she shall be the rear of the nations, a wilderness, waste and desert.
13Because of the wrath of the Lord she shall not be inhabited, but shall be wholly desolate; every one who goes by Babylon shall be appalled, and hiss *and* mock at all her wounds *and* plagues.
14Set yourselves in array against Babylon round about, all you archers; shoot at her, spare not the arrows, for she has sinned against the Lord.
15Raise the battle cry against her round about! She has given her hand [in agreement] *and* surrendered herself; her supports *and* battlements are fallen, her walls are thrown down. For this is the vengeance of the Lord: take vengeance on her; as she has done, do to her.
16Exterminate the sower from Babylon, and the one who handles the sickle in the time of harvest; for fear of the sword of the oppressor they shall every one return to his people, and every one shall flee to his own land.
17Israel is a hunted *and* scattered sheep—driven hither and thither [and preyed upon by savage beasts]. The lions have chased him: first the king of Assyria devoured him, and now at last Nebuchadrezzar king of Babylon has broken *and* gnawed his bones.
18Therefore thus says the Lord of hosts, the God of Israel: Behold, I will visit *and* punish the king of Babylon and his land, as I have visited *and* punished the king of Assyria.
19And I will bring Israel [home] again to his fold *and* pasturage, and he shall feed [on the most fertile districts both west and east] on Carmel and Bashan, and his soul shall be satisfied upon the hills of Ephraim and in Gilead.
20In those days and at that time, says the Lord, the iniquity of Israel shall be sought for, and there shall be none; and the sins of Judah, and none shall be found; for I will pardon those whom I cause to remain as a remnant [the reserved ones, who come forth after the long tribulation]. [Isa. 1:9; 43:25; Jer. 31:34; Rom. 9:27.]
21Go up against [Babylon] the land of Merathaim— *meaning*, of two rebellions and of double or intense defiance; even against it and against the inhabitants of Pekod [in Babylonia]— *meaning*, of visitation and punishment. Slay and utterly destroy after them, says the Lord, and do according to all I have commanded you.
22The cry *and* noise of battle is in the land, and of great destruction.
23How the hammer of the whole earth is crushed and broken! How Babylon has become a horror of desolation among the nations!

## New American Standard

10 "And Chaldea will become plunder;
All who plunder her will have enough," declares the LORD.

11¶ "Because you are glad, because you are jubilant,
O you who pillage My heritage,
Because you skip about like a threshing heifer
And neigh like stallions,
12 Your mother will be greatly ashamed,
She who gave you birth will be humiliated.
Behold, *she will be* the least of the nations,
A wilderness, a parched land, and a desert.
13 "Because of the indignation of the LORD she will not be inhabited,
But she will be completely desolate;
Everyone who passes by Babylon will be horrified
And will hiss because of all her wounds.
14 "Draw up your battle lines against Babylon on every side,
All you who bend the bow;
Shoot at her, do not be sparing with *your* arrows,
For she has sinned against the LORD.
15 "Raise your battle cry against her on every side!
She has given herself up, her pillars have fallen,
Her walls have been torn down.
For this is the vengeance of the LORD:
Take vengeance on her;
As she has done *to others, so* do to her.
16 "Cut off the sower from Babylon,
And the one who wields the sickle at the time of harvest;
From before the sword of the oppressor
They will each turn back to his own people,
And they will each flee to his own land.

17¶ "Israel is a scattered flock, the lions have driven *them* away.
The first one *who* devoured him was the king of Assyria, and this
last one *who* has broken his bones is Nebuchadnezzar king of
Babylon.
18"Therefore thus says the LORD of hosts, the God of Israel:
'Behold, I am going to punish the king of Babylon and his land,
just as I punished the king of Assyria.
19'And I shall bring Israel back to his pasture, and he will graze
on Carmel and Bashan, and his desire will be satisfied in the hill
country of Ephraim and Gilead.
20'In those days and at that time,' declares the LORD, 'search will
be made for the iniquity of Israel, but there will be none; and for
the sins of Judah, but they will not be found; for I shall pardon
those whom I leave as a remnant.'

21¶ "Against the land of [a]Merathaim, go up against it,
And against the inhabitants of [b]Pekod.
Slay and utterly destroy them," declares the LORD,
"And do according to all that I have commanded you.
22 "The noise of battle is in the land,
And great destruction.
23 "How the hammer of the whole earth
Has been cut off and broken!
How Babylon has become
An object of horror among the nations!

NAS [a] Or, *Double Rebellion* [b] Or, *Punishment*

## New International

10So Babylonia[c] will be plundered;
all who plunder her will have their fill,"
declares the LORD.

11"Because you rejoice and are glad,
you who pillage my inheritance,
because you frolic like a heifer threshing grain
and neigh like stallions,
12your mother will be greatly ashamed;
she who gave you birth will be disgraced.
She will be the least of the nations—
a wilderness, a dry land, a desert.
13Because of the LORD's anger she will not be inhabited
but will be completely desolate.
All who pass Babylon will be horrified and scoff
because of all her wounds.

14"Take up your positions around Babylon,
all you who draw the bow.
Shoot at her! Spare no arrows,
for she has sinned against the LORD.
15Shout against her on every side!
She surrenders, her towers fall,
her walls are torn down.
Since this is the vengeance of the LORD,
take vengeance on her;
do to her as she has done to others.
16Cut off from Babylon the sower,
and the reaper with his sickle at harvest.
Because of the sword of the oppressor
let everyone return to his own people,
let everyone flee to his own land.

17"Israel is a scattered flock
that lions have chased away.
The first to devour him
was the king of Assyria;
the last to crush his bones
was Nebuchadnezzar king of Babylon."

18Therefore this is what the LORD Almighty, the God of Israel,
says:

"I will punish the king of Babylon and his land
as I punished the king of Assyria.
19But I will bring Israel back to his own pasture
and he will graze on Carmel and Bashan;
his appetite will be satisfied
on the hills of Ephraim and Gilead.
20In those days, at that time,"
declares the LORD,
"search will be made for Israel's guilt,
but there will be none,
and for the sins of Judah,
but none will be found,
for I will forgive the remnant I spare.

21"Attack the land of Merathaim
and those who live in Pekod.
Pursue, kill and completely destroy[d] them,"
declares the LORD.
"Do everything I have commanded you.
22The noise of battle is in the land,
the noise of great destruction!
23How broken and shattered
is the hammer of the whole earth!
How desolate is Babylon
among the nations!

NIV [c] *10* Or *Chaldea* [d] *21* The Hebrew term refers to the irrevocable giving over of things or persons to the LORD, often by totally destroying them; also in verse 26.

## King James

24I have laid a snare for thee, and thou art also taken, O Babylon, and thou wast not aware: thou art found, and also caught, because thou hast striven against the LORD.

25The LORD hath opened his armoury, and hath brought forth the weapons of his indignation: for this *is* the work of the Lord GOD of hosts in the land of the Chaldeans.

26Come against her from the utmost border, open her storehouses: cast her up as heaps, and destroy her utterly: let nothing of her be left.

27Slay all her bullocks; let them go down to the slaughter: woe unto them! for their day is come, the time of their visitation.

28The voice of them that flee and escape out of the land of Babylon, to declare in Zion the vengeance of the LORD our God, the vengeance of his temple.

29Call together the archers against Babylon: all ye that bend the bow, camp against it round about; let none thereof escape: recompense her according to her work; according to all that she hath done, do unto her: for she hath been proud against the LORD, against the Holy One of Israel.

30Therefore shall her young men fall in the streets, and all her men of war shall be cut off in that day, saith the LORD.

31Behold, I *am* against thee, *O thou* most proud, saith the Lord GOD of hosts: for thy day is come, the time *that* I will visit thee.

32And the most proud shall stumble and fall, and none shall raise him up: and I will kindle a fire in his cities, and it shall devour all round about him.

33¶ Thus saith the LORD of hosts; The children of Israel and the children of Judah *were* oppressed together: and all that took them captives held them fast; they refused to let them go.

34Their Redeemer *is* strong; the LORD of hosts *is* his name: he shall thoroughly plead their cause, that he may give rest to the land, and disquiet the inhabitants of Babylon.

35¶ A sword *is* upon the Chaldeans, saith the LORD, and upon the inhabitants of Babylon, and upon her princes, and upon her wise *men*.

36A sword *is* upon the liars; and they shall dote: a sword *is* upon her mighty men; and they shall be dismayed.

37A sword *is* upon their horses, and upon their chariots, and upon all the mingled people that *are* in the midst of her; and they shall become as women: a sword *is* upon her treasures; and they shall be robbed.

## Amplified

24I have set a trap for you and you also are taken, O Babylon, and you did not know it; you are found and also caught, because you have struggled *and* contended against the Lord.

25The Lord has opened His armory, and has brought forth [the nations who unknowingly are] the weapons of His indignation *and* wrath, for the Lord God of hosts has a work to do in the land of the Chaldeans.

26Come against her from every quarter *and* from the utmost border; open her granaries *and* storehouses; pile up [their contents] as heaps of rubbish, burn *and* destroy her utterly; let nothing be left of her.

27Slay all her bullocks [her choice youths, the strength of her army]; let them go down to the slaughter. Woe to [the Chaldeans]! For their day is come, the time of their visitation—their inspection and punishment.

28Hark! The voice of those [Jews] who flee and escape out of the land of Babylon, to proclaim in Zion the vengeance of the Lord our God, the vengeance [of the Lord upon the Chaldeans] for [the plundering and destruction of] His Temple.

29Call together [many] archers against Babylon, all those who bend the bow; encamp against her round about; let none from there escape. Recompense her according to her deeds; just as she has done, do to her. For against the Lord, against the Holy One of Israel has she been proudly defiant *and* presumptuous.

30Therefore shall her young men fall in her streets *and* squares, and all her soldiers shall be destroyed on that day, says the Lord.

31Behold, I am against you, O Babylon—you who are pride and presumption personified—says the Lord God of hosts; for your day has come, the time when I will visit *and* punish you.

32And Pride shall stumble—totter—and fall, and none shall raise him up. And I will kindle a fire in his cities, and it shall devour all that are round about him.

33Thus says the Lord of hosts: The children of Israel and the children of Judah are oppressed together; all who took them captive have held them fast; they refuse to let them go.

34Their Redeemer is strong; the Lord of hosts is His name. He will surely *and* thoroughly plead their cause, that He may give rest to [the land of Palestine, and to the Babylonian-enslaved nations of] the earth, but unrest to the inhabitants of Babylon.

35A sword upon the Chaldeans, says the Lord, and upon the inhabitants of Babylon, and upon her princes [rulers in civic matters] and upon her wise men [the astrologers, and rulers in religious affairs]!

36A sword upon the babbling liars—the diviners—that they may become fools! A sword upon her mighty warriors that they may be dismayed *and* destroyed!

37A sword upon their horses and upon their chariots, and upon all the mingled troops that are in the midst of her, that they may become [weak and defenseless] as women! A sword upon her treasures, that they may be plundered!

## New American Standard

24 "I set a snare for you, and you were also caught,
O Babylon,
While you yourself were not aware;
You have been found and also seized
Because you have engaged in conflict with the LORD."
25 The LORD has opened His armory
And has brought forth the weapons of His indignation,
For it is a work of the Lord GOD of hosts
In the land of the Chaldeans.
26 Come to her from the farthest border;
Open up her barns,
Pile her up like heaps
And utterly destroy her,
Let nothing be left to her.
27 Put all her young bulls to the sword;
Let them go down to the slaughter!
Woe be upon them, for their day has come,
The time of their punishment.
28 There is a sound of fugitives and refugees from the land
of Babylon,
To declare in Zion the vengeance of the LORD our God,
Vengeance for His temple.

29¶ "Summon [a]many against Babylon,
All those who bend the bow:
Encamp against her on every side,
Let there be no escape.
Repay her according to her work;
According to all that she has done, *so* do to her;
For she has become arrogant against the LORD,
Against the Holy One of Israel.
30 "Therefore her young men will fall in her streets,
And all her men of war will be silenced in that day,"
declares the LORD.
31 "Behold, I am against you, O arrogant one,"
Declares the Lord GOD of hosts,
"For your day has come,
The time when I shall punish you.
32 "And the arrogant one will stumble and fall
With no one to raise him up;
And I shall set fire to his cities,
And it will devour all his environs."

33¶ Thus says the LORD of hosts,
"The sons of Israel are oppressed,
And the sons of Judah as well;
And all who took them captive have held them fast,
They have refused to let them go.
34 "Their Redeemer is strong, the LORD of hosts is His
name;
He will vigorously plead their case,
So that He may bring rest to the earth,
But turmoil to the inhabitants of Babylon.
35 "A sword against the Chaldeans," declares the LORD,
"And against the inhabitants of Babylon,
And against her officials and her wise men!
36 "A sword against the oracle priests, and they will
become fools!
A sword against her mighty men, and they will be
shattered!
37 "A sword against their horses and against their chariots,
And against all the foreigners who are in the midst of
her,
And they will become women!
A sword against her treasures, and they will be
plundered!

NAS [a] Another reading is *archers*

## New International

24I set a trap for you, O Babylon,
and you were caught before you knew it;
you were found and captured
because you opposed the LORD.
25The LORD has opened his arsenal
and brought out the weapons of his wrath,
for the Sovereign LORD Almighty has work to do
in the land of the Babylonians.
26Come against her from afar.
Break open her granaries;
pile her up like heaps of grain.
Completely destroy her
and leave her no remnant.
27Kill all her young bulls;
let them go down to the slaughter!
Woe to them! For their day has come,
the time for them to be punished.
28Listen to the fugitives and refugees from Babylon
declaring in Zion
how the LORD our God has taken vengeance,
vengeance for his temple.

29"Summon archers against Babylon,
all those who draw the bow.
Encamp all around her;
let no one escape.
Repay her for her deeds;
do to her as she has done.
For she has defied the LORD,
the Holy One of Israel.
30Therefore, her young men will fall in the streets;
all her soldiers will be silenced in that day,"
declares the LORD.
31"See, I am against you, O arrogant one,"
declares the Lord, the LORD Almighty,
"for your day has come,
the time for you to be punished.
32The arrogant one will stumble and fall
and no one will help her up;
I will kindle a fire in her towns
that will consume all who are around her."

33This is what the LORD Almighty says:

"The people of Israel are oppressed,
and the people of Judah as well.
All their captors hold them fast,
refusing to let them go.
34Yet their Redeemer is strong;
the LORD Almighty is his name.
He will vigorously defend their cause
so that he may bring rest to their land,
but unrest to those who live in Babylon.

35"A sword against the Babylonians!"
declares the LORD—
"against those who live in Babylon
and against her officials and wise men!
36A sword against her false prophets!
They will become fools.
A sword against her warriors!
They will be filled with terror.
37A sword against her horses and chariots
and all the foreigners in her ranks!
They will become women.
A sword against her treasures!
They will be plundered.

## King James

38 A drought *is* upon her waters; and they shall be dried up: for it *is* the land of graven images, and they are mad upon *their* idols.
39 Therefore the wild beasts of the desert with the wild beasts of the islands shall dwell *there*, and the owls shall dwell therein: and it shall be no more inhabited for ever; neither shall it be dwelt in from generation to generation.
40 As God overthrew Sodom and Gomorrah and the neighbour *cities* thereof, saith the LORD; *so* shall no man abide there, neither shall any son of man dwell therein.
41 Behold, a people shall come from the north, and a great nation, and many kings shall be raised up from the coasts of the earth.
42 They shall hold the bow and the lance: they *are* cruel, and will not show mercy: their voice shall roar like the sea, and they shall ride upon horses, *every one* put in array, like a man to the battle, against thee, O daughter of Babylon.
43 The king of Babylon hath heard the report of them, and his hands waxed feeble: anguish took hold of him, *and* pangs as of a woman in travail.
44 Behold, he shall come up like a lion from the swelling of Jordan unto the habitation of the strong: but I will make them suddenly run away from her: and who *is* a chosen *man*, *that* I may appoint over her? for who *is* like me? and who will appoint me the time? and who *is* that shepherd that will stand before me?
45 Therefore hear ye the counsel of the LORD, that he hath taken against Babylon; and his purposes, that he hath purposed against the land of the Chaldeans: Surely the least of the flock shall draw them out: surely he shall make *their* habitation desolate with them.
46 At the noise of the taking of Babylon the earth is moved, and the cry is heard among the nations.

## Amplified

38 A sword *and* a drought upon her waters, that they may be dried up! For it is a land of images, and they are mad over idols—objects of terror in which they foolishly trust.
39 Therefore [a]wild beasts of the desert shall dwell [in Babylon] with the jackals, and ostriches shall dwell there, and it shall be inhabited with people no more for ever, even from generation to generation.
40 As when God overthrew Sodom and Gomorrah and their neighbor cities, says the Lord, so no man shall dwell there, neither shall any son of man live there temporarily.
41 Behold, a people is coming from the north, and a great nation and many kings are stirring from the uttermost parts of the earth.
42 They lay hold of bow, lance *and* spear; they are cruel *and* have no mercy *or* compassion; they sound like the roaring of the sea; they ride upon horses, every one equipped as a man for the battle, against you, O daughter of Babylon!
43 The king of Babylon has heard the news of them, and his hands fall feeble *and* helpless; anguish has seized him, and pangs as of a woman in childbirth.
44 Look, like a lion coming up from the jungles [the pride] of the Jordan against the strong habitation *and* into the perennial pasturage *and* sheepfold, in a twinkling I will drive [the enemy] away from her. And I will appoint over her him whom I choose. For who is like Me? And who will challenge Me *and* prosecute Me [for this proceeding]? And what [earthly national] shepherd can stand before Me *and* defy Me?
45 Therefore hear the plan of the Lord which He has made against Babylon, and His purposes which He has formed against the land of the Chaldeans: Surely they shall be dragged away, even the little ones of the flock; surely He shall make their habitation desolate *and* their fold amazed *and* appalled at their fate.
46 At the cry, Babylon is taken! the earth shall tremble, and the cry shall be heard among the nations.

## King James

**51** THUS SAITH the LORD; Behold, I will raise up against Babylon, and against them that dwell in the midst of them that rise up against me, a destroying wind;
2 And will send unto Babylon fanners, that shall fan her, and shall empty her land: for in the day of trouble they shall be against her round about.
3 Against *him that* bendeth let the archer bend his bow, and against *him that* lifteth himself up in his brigandine: and spare ye not her young men; destroy ye utterly all her host.
4 Thus the slain shall fall in the land of the Chaldeans, and *they that are* thrust through in her streets.
5 For Israel *hath* not *been* forsaken, nor Judah of his God, of the LORD of hosts; though their land was filled with sin against the Holy One of Israel.

## Amplified

**51** THUS SAYS the Lord: Behold, I will raise up against Babylon, and against them who dwell among those rebelling against Me, a destroying wind;
2 And I will send to Babylon strangers *or* winnowers, who shall winnow her and shall empty her land; for in the day of calamity they shall be against her on every side.
3 Against him who bends let the archer bend his bow, and against him who lifts himself up in his coat of mail. And spare not her young men; devote [to God] and utterly destroy her entire host.
4 Thus slain they shall fall in the land of the Chaldeans and wounded in her streets.
5 For Israel has not been widowed *and* forsaken, nor has Judah by his God, the Lord of hosts; though their land is full of guilt against the Holy One of Israel.

AMP [a] See note on Isaiah 13:22 for this prophecy's fulfillment.

## New American Standard

38 "A drought on her waters, and they will be dried up!
For it is a land of idols,
And they are mad over fearsome idols.
39 "Therefore the desert creatures will live *there* along with
the jackals;
The ostriches also will live in it,
And it will never again be inhabited
Or dwelt in from generation to generation.
40 "As when God overthrew Sodom
And Gomorrah with its neighbors," declares the LORD,
"No man will live there,
Nor will *any* son of man reside in it.

41¶ "Behold, a people is coming from the north,
And a great nation and many kings
Will be aroused from the remote parts of the earth.
42 "They seize *their* bow and javelin;
They are cruel and have no mercy.
Their voice roars like the sea,
And they ride on horses,
Marshalled like a man for the battle
Against you, O daughter of Babylon.
43 "The king of Babylon has heard the report about them,
And his hands hang limp;
Distress has gripped him,
Agony like a woman in childbirth.
44 "Behold, one will come up like a lion from the thicket of the
Jordan to a perennially watered pasture; for in an instant I shall
make them run away from it, and whoever is chosen I shall appoint over it. For who is like Me, and who will summon Me *into
court?* And who then is the shepherd who can stand before Me?"
45 Therefore hear the plan of the LORD which He has planned
against Babylon, and His purposes which He has purposed against
the land of the Chaldeans: surely they will drag them off, *even* the
little ones of the flock; surely He will make their pasture desolate
because of them.
46 At the shout, "Babylon has been seized!" the earth is shaken,
and an outcry is heard among the nations.

*Babylon Judged for Sins against Israel*

51 THUS SAYS the LORD:
"Behold, I am going to arouse against Babylon
And against the inhabitants of [b]Leb-kamai
The spirit of a destroyer.
2 "And I shall dispatch foreigners to Babylon that they
may winnow her
And may devastate her land;
For on every side they will be opposed to her
In the day of *her* calamity.
3 "Let not him who bends his bow bend *it*,
Nor let him rise up in his scale-armor;
So do not spare her young men;
Devote all her army to destruction.
4 "And they will fall down slain in the land of the
Chaldeans,
And pierced through in their streets."

5¶ For neither Israel nor Judah has been forsaken
By his God, the LORD of hosts,
Although their land is full of guilt
Before the Holy One of Israel.

NAS [b] Cryptic name for Chaldea

## New International

38 A drought on[c] her waters!
They will dry up.
For it is a land of idols,
idols that will go mad with terror.

39 "So desert creatures and hyenas will live there,
and there the owl will dwell.
It will never again be inhabited
or lived in from generation to generation.
40 As God overthrew Sodom and Gomorrah
along with their neighboring towns,"
declares the LORD,
"so no one will live there;
no man will dwell in it.

41 "Look! An army is coming from the north;
a great nation and many kings
are being stirred up from the ends of the earth.
42 They are armed with bows and spears;
they are cruel and without mercy.
They sound like the roaring sea
as they ride on their horses;
they come like men in battle formation
to attack you, O Daughter of Babylon.
43 The king of Babylon has heard reports about them,
and his hands hang limp.
Anguish has gripped him,
pain like that of a woman in labor.
44 Like a lion coming up from Jordan's thickets
to a rich pastureland,
I will chase Babylon from its land in an instant.
Who is the chosen one I will appoint for this?
Who is like me and who can challenge me?
And what shepherd can stand against me?"
45 Therefore, hear what the LORD has planned against
Babylon,
what he has purposed against the land of the
Babylonians:
The young of the flock will be dragged away;
he will completely destroy their pasture because of
them.
46 At the sound of Babylon's capture the earth will tremble;
its cry will resound among the nations.

51 THIS IS what the LORD says:
"See, I will stir up the spirit of a destroyer
against Babylon and the people of Leb Kamai.[d]
2 I will send foreigners to Babylon
to winnow her and to devastate her land;
they will oppose her on every side
in the day of her disaster.
3 Let not the archer string his bow,
nor let him put on his armor.
Do not spare her young men;
completely destroy[e] her army.
4 They will fall down slain in Babylon,[f]
fatally wounded in her streets.
5 For Israel and Judah have not been forsaken
by their God, the LORD Almighty,
though their land[g] is full of guilt
before the Holy One of Israel.

NIV [c] 38 Or *A sword against* [d] 1 *Leb Kamai* is a cryptogram for Chaldea, that is, Babylonia. [e] 3 The Hebrew term refers to the irrevocable giving over of things or persons to the LORD, often by totally destroying them. [f] 4 Or *Chaldea* [g] 5 Or / *and the land ⌊of the Babylonians⌋*

## King James

6Flee out of the midst of Babylon, and deliver every man his soul: be not cut off in her iniquity; for this *is* the time of the LORD's vengeance; he will render unto her a recompence.

7Babylon *hath been* a golden cup in the LORD's hand, that made all the earth drunken: the nations have drunken of her wine; therefore the nations are mad.

8Babylon is suddenly fallen and destroyed: howl for her; take balm for her pain, if so be she may be healed.

9We would have healed Babylon, but she is not healed: forsake her, and let us go every one into his own country: for her judgment reacheth unto heaven, and is lifted up *even* to the skies.

10The LORD hath brought forth our righteousness: come, and let us declare in Zion the work of the LORD our God.

11Make bright the arrows; gather the shields: the LORD hath raised up the spirit of the kings of the Medes: for his device *is* against Babylon, to destroy it; because it *is* the vengeance of the LORD, the vengeance of his temple.

12Set up the standard upon the walls of Babylon, make the watch strong, set up the watchmen, prepare the ambushes: for the LORD hath both devised and done that which he spake against the inhabitants of Babylon.

13O thou that dwellest upon many waters, abundant in treasures, thine end is come, *and* the measure of thy covetousness.

14The LORD of hosts hath sworn by himself, *saying*, Surely I will fill thee with men, as with caterpillars; and they shall lift up a shout against thee.

15He hath made the earth by his power, he hath established the world by his wisdom, and hath stretched out the heaven by his understanding.

16When he uttereth *his* voice, *there is* a multitude of waters in the heavens; and he causeth the vapours to ascend from the ends of the earth: he maketh lightnings with rain, and bringeth forth the wind out of his treasures.

17Every man is brutish by *his* knowledge; every founder is confounded by the graven image: for his molten image *is* falsehood, and *there is* no breath in them.

18They *are* vanity, the work of errors: in the time of their visitation they shall perish.

19The portion of Jacob *is* not like them; for he *is* the former of all things: and *Israel is* the rod of his inheritance: the LORD of hosts *is* his name.

20Thou *art* my battle axe *and* weapons of war: for with thee will I break in pieces the nations, and with thee will I destroy kingdoms;

21And with thee will I break in pieces the horse and his rider; and with thee will I break in pieces the chariot and his rider;

22With thee also will I break in pieces man and woman; and with thee will I break in pieces old and young; and with thee will I break in pieces the young man and the maid;

## Amplified

6Flee out of the midst of Babylon, let every man save his life! Let not destruction come upon you through her [punishment for] sin *and* guilt; for it is the time of the Lord's vengeance. He will render to her a recompense. [Jer. 50:28; II Cor. 6:17; Rev. 18:4.]

7Babylon was a golden cup in the Lord's hand, making all the earth drunken; the nations drank of her wine, therefore the nations went mad. [Rev. 17:4; 14:8.]

8Babylon has suddenly fallen and is shattered—destroyed! Wail for her [if you care to!]; take balm for her [incurable] pain, if so be she may [possibly] be healed! [Jer. 25:15; Rev. 14:8-10; 16:19; 18:2, 3.]

9We would have healed Babylon, but she is not healed. Forsake her, and let us go each to his own country; for her guilt *and* the judgment against her reach to heaven, and are lifted even to the skies. [Gen. 18:20, 21.]

10The Lord has brought forth *and* made known the righteousness [of our cause]. Come, and let us declare in Zion the work of the Lord our God.

11Make clean *and* sharp the arrows; take up the shields *or* coats of armor *and* cover your bodies with them; the Lord has stirred up the spirit of the kings of the Medes [who with the Persians will destroy the Babylonian Empire]; for His purpose concerning Babylon is to destroy it; for that is the vengeance of the Lord, the vengeance [upon Babylon for the plundering and the burning] of His temple.

12Set up the standard *or* signal [to spread the news] upon the walls of Babylon, make the watch *and* blockade strong, set the guards, prepare the ambushes! For the Lord has both purposed and done that which He said against the inhabitants of Babylon.

13O [Babylon] you who dwell by many waters, rich in treasures, your end has come, and the line measuring your life is cut. [Cf. Rev. 17:1-6.]

14The Lord of hosts has sworn by Himself, saying, Surely I will fill you with men, as with stripping locusts, and they shall lift up a song *and* shout [of victory] over you.

15He has made the earth by His power, He has established the world by His wisdom, and has stretched out the heavens by His understanding.

16When He utters His voice, there is a tumult of waters in the heavens, and He causes the vapors to ascend from the ends of the earth; He makes lightnings for the rain, and brings forth the wind out of His treasuries.

17Every man has become stupid *and* brute-like, without knowledge; every goldsmith is put to shame by the images he has made, for his molten idols are a lie, and there is no breath [of life] in them.

18They are worthless—emptiness, falsity, futility—the work of delusion and worthy of derision. In the time of their inspection *and* punishment they shall perish.

19Not like these [gods] is He Who is the portion of Jacob, for He is the One Who formed all things, and Israel is the tribe of His inheritance; the Lord of hosts is His name.

20You [Cyrus, later Persian king of conquered Babylon] are My battle-ax *or* maul and weapon of war; for with you I break nations in pieces, and with you will I destroy kingdoms;

21With you I break in pieces the horse and his rider; and with you I break in pieces the chariot and the charioteer;

22With you also I break in pieces man and woman; with you I break in pieces the old man and the youth; with you I break in pieces the young man and the maiden;

## New American Standard

6 Flee from the midst of Babylon,
And each of you save his life!
Do not be destroyed in her punishment,
For this is the LORD's time of vengeance;
He is going to render recompense to her.
7 Babylon has been a golden cup in the hand of the LORD,
Intoxicating all the earth.
The nations have drunk of her wine;
Therefore the nations are going mad.
8 Suddenly Babylon has fallen and been broken;
Wail over her!
Bring balm for her pain;
Perhaps she may be healed.
9 We applied healing to Babylon, but she was not healed;
Forsake her and let us each go to his own country,
For her judgment has reached to heaven
And towers up to the very skies.
10 The LORD has brought about our vindication;
Come and let us recount in Zion
The work of the LORD our God!
11¶ Sharpen the arrows, fill the quivers!
The LORD has aroused the spirit of the kings of the Medes,
Because His purpose is against Babylon to destroy it;
For it is the vengeance of the LORD, vengeance for His temple.
12 Lift up a signal against the walls of Babylon;
Post a strong guard,
Station sentries,
Place men in ambush!
For the LORD has both purposed and performed
What He spoke concerning the inhabitants of Babylon.
13 O you who dwell by many waters,
Abundant in treasures,
Your end has come,
The measure of your end.
14 The LORD of hosts has sworn by Himself:
"Surely I will fill you with a population like locusts,
And they will cry out with shouts of victory over you."
15¶ *It is* He who made the earth by His power,
Who established the world by His wisdom,
And by His understanding He stretched out the heavens.
16 When He utters His voice, *there is* a tumult of waters in the heavens,
And He causes the clouds to ascend from the end of the earth;
He makes lightning for the rain,
And brings forth the wind from His storehouses.
17 All mankind is stupid, devoid of knowledge;
Every goldsmith is put to shame by his idols,
For his molten images are deceitful,
And there is no breath in them.
18 They are worthless, a work of mockery;
In the time of their punishment they will perish.
19 The portion of Jacob is not like these;
For the Maker of all is He,
And of the tribe of His inheritance;
The LORD of hosts is His name.
20 *He says,* "You are My war-club, *My* weapon of war;
And with you I shatter nations,
And with you I destroy kingdoms.
21 "And with you I shatter the horse and his rider,
22 And with you I shatter the chariot and its rider,
And with you I shatter man and woman,
And with you I shatter old man and youth,
And with you I shatter young man and virgin,

## New International

6"Flee from Babylon!
Run for your lives!
Do not be destroyed because of her sins.
It is time for the LORD's vengeance;
he will pay her what she deserves.
7Babylon was a gold cup in the LORD's hand;
she made the whole earth drunk.
The nations drank her wine;
therefore they have now gone mad.
8Babylon will suddenly fall and be broken.
Wail over her!
Get balm for her pain;
perhaps she can be healed.

9" 'We would have healed Babylon,
but she cannot be healed;
let us leave her and each go to his own land,
for her judgment reaches to the skies,
it rises as high as the clouds.'

10" 'The LORD has vindicated us;
come, let us tell in Zion
what the LORD our God has done.'

11"Sharpen the arrows,
take up the shields!
The LORD has stirred up the kings of the Medes,
because his purpose is to destroy Babylon.
The LORD will take vengeance,
vengeance for his temple.
12Lift up a banner against the walls of Babylon!
Reinforce the guard,
station the watchmen,
prepare an ambush!
The LORD will carry out his purpose,
his decree against the people of Babylon.
13You who live by many waters
and are rich in treasures,
your end has come,
the time for you to be cut off.
14The LORD Almighty has sworn by himself:
I will surely fill you with men, as with a swarm of locusts,
and they will shout in triumph over you.

15"He made the earth by his power;
he founded the world by his wisdom
and stretched out the heavens by his understanding.
16When he thunders, the waters in the heavens roar;
he makes clouds rise from the ends of the earth.
He sends lightning with the rain
and brings out the wind from his storehouses.

17"Every man is senseless and without knowledge;
every goldsmith is shamed by his idols.
His images are a fraud;
they have no breath in them.
18They are worthless, the objects of mockery;
when their judgment comes, they will perish.
19He who is the Portion of Jacob is not like these,
for he is the Maker of all things,
including the tribe of his inheritance—
the LORD Almighty is his name.

20"You are my war club,
my weapon for battle—
with you I shatter nations,
with you I destroy kingdoms,
21with you I shatter horse and rider,
with you I shatter chariot and driver,
22with you I shatter man and woman,
with you I shatter old man and youth,
with you I shatter young man and maiden,

## King James

23 I will also break in pieces with thee the shepherd and his flock; and with thee will I break in pieces the husbandman and his yoke of oxen; and with thee will I break in pieces captains and rulers.

24 And I will render unto Babylon and to all the inhabitants of Chaldea all their evil that they have done in Zion in your sight, saith the LORD.

25 Behold, I *am* against thee, O destroying mountain, saith the LORD, which destroyest all the earth: and I will stretch out mine hand upon thee, and roll thee down from the rocks, and will make thee a burnt mountain.

26 And they shall not take of thee a stone for a corner, nor a stone for foundations; but thou shalt be desolate for ever, saith the LORD.

27 Set ye up a standard in the land, blow the trumpet among the nations, prepare the nations against her, call together against her the kingdoms of Ararat, Minni, and Ashchenaz; appoint a captain against her; cause the horses to come up as the rough caterpillars.

28 Prepare against her the nations with the kings of the Medes, the captains thereof, and all the rulers thereof, and all the land of his dominion.

29 And the land shall tremble and sorrow: for every purpose of the LORD shall be performed against Babylon, to make the land of Babylon a desolation without an inhabitant.

30 The mighty men of Babylon have forborne to fight, they have remained in *their* holds: their might hath failed; they became as women: they have burned her dwellingplaces; her bars are broken.

31 One post shall run to meet another, and one messenger to meet another, to show the king of Babylon that his city is taken at *one* end,

32 And that the passages are stopped, and the reeds they have burned with fire, and the men of war are affrighted.

33 For thus saith the LORD of hosts, the God of Israel; The daughter of Babylon *is* like a threshingfloor, *it is* time to thresh her: yet a little while, and the time of her harvest shall come.

34 Nebuchadrezzar the king of Babylon hath devoured me, he hath crushed me, he hath made me an empty vessel, he hath swallowed me up like a dragon, he hath filled his belly with my delicates, he hath cast me out.

35 The violence done to me and to my flesh *be* upon Babylon, shall the inhabitant of Zion say; and my blood upon the inhabitants of Chaldea, shall Jerusalem say.

36 Therefore thus saith the LORD; Behold, I will plead thy cause, and take vengeance for thee; and I will dry up her sea, and make her springs dry.

## Amplified

23 With you I break in pieces the shepherd and his flock; with you I break in pieces the farmer and his yoke of oxen; and with you I break in pieces governors and commanders.

24 And I will completely repay to Babylon and to all the inhabitants of Chaldea all the evil that they have done in Zion, before your very eyes *I will do it*, says the Lord.

25 Behold, I am against you, says the Lord, O destroying *and* burning out mountain, [you who shall be as barren and desolate as an extinct volcano] which *would* destroy the whole earth; I will stretch out My hand over *and* against you, and roll you down from the [burnt] crags, and will make you a burnt out mountain [of combustion fires].

26 And [O Babylon] they shall not take of your cracked stones for a corner stone, or a stone for foundations, but you shall be a waste *and* [a]desolate for ever, says the Lord.

27 Set up a standard *or* signal in the land [to spread the news], blow the trumpet among the nations, prepare *and* dedicate the nations against her, call against her the kingdoms of Ararat, Minni, and Ashkenaz; appoint a marshal against her, cause the horses to come up like locusts [when their wings are not yet released from their horny cases].

28 Prepare *and* dedicate the nations for war against her, the kings of Media, with their governors and deputies, and every land of their dominion. [I foresee this:]

29 The land trembles and writhes in pain *and* sorrow, for the purposes of the Lord against Babylon stand, to make the land of Babylon a desolation without inhabitant.

30 The mighty warriors of Babylon have ceased to fight, they have remained in their holds, their might has failed, they have become [weak and helpless] as women; her dwelling places are burned up, her bars [and defenses generally] are broken.

31 One post shall run to meet another, and one messenger to meet another, to show the king of Babylon that his city is taken on every side *and* to its farthest end;

32 And that the passages [or ferries across the Euphrates] are stopped, and the great [waterworks the Medes] have burned with fire, and the men of war are frightened.

33 For thus the Lord of hosts, the God of Israel: The daughter of Babylon is like a threshing floor at the time when it is *being prepared;* yet a little while and the time of harvest shall come to her.

34 [Say the inhabitants of Zion] Nebuchadrezzar the king of Babylon has devoured us, he has crushed us, he has made us an empty vessel, he like a monster has swallowed us up, he has filled his belly with our delicacies, he has rinsed us out *and* cast us away.

35 The violence done to me and to my flesh *and* blood be upon Babylon, the inhabitant of Zion will say; and, My blood be upon the inhabitants of Chaldea, will Jerusalem say.

36 Therefore thus says the Lord: Behold, I will plead your cause and take vengeance for you. I will dry up her lake *or* great reservoir and make her fountain dry;

**AMP** [a] See note on Isaiah 13:22 for this prophecy's fulfillment.

## New American Standard

23 And with you I shatter the shepherd and his flock,
And with you I shatter the farmer and his team,
And with you I shatter governors and prefects.
24¶ "But I will repay Babylon and all the inhabitants of Chaldea for all their evil that they have done in Zion before your eyes," declares the LORD.
25 "Behold, I am against you, O destroying mountain,
Who destroy the whole earth," declares the LORD,
"And I will stretch out My hand against you,
And roll you down from the crags
And I will make you a burnt out mountain.
26 "And they will not take from you *even* a stone for a corner
Nor a stone for foundations,
But you will be desolate forever," declares the LORD.
27¶ Lift up a signal in the land,
Blow a trumpet among the nations!
Consecrate the nations against her,
Summon against her the kingdoms of Ararat, Minni and Ashkenaz;
Appoint a marshal against her,
Bring up the horses like bristly locusts.
28 Consecrate the nations against her,
The kings of the Medes,
Their governors and all their prefects,
And every land of their dominion.
29 So the land quakes and writhes,
For the purposes of the LORD against Babylon stand,
To make the land of Babylon
A desolation without inhabitants.
30 The mighty men of Babylon have ceased fighting,
They stay in the strongholds;
Their strength is exhausted,
They are becoming *like* women;
Their dwelling places are set on fire,
The bars of her *gates* are broken.
31 One courier runs to meet another,
And one messenger to meet another,
To tell the king of Babylon
That his city has been captured from end *to end;*
32 The fords also have been seized,
And they have burned the marshes with fire,
And the men of war are terrified.
33¶ For thus says the LORD of hosts, the God of Israel:
"The daughter of Babylon is like a threshing floor
At the time it is stamped firm;
Yet in a little while the time of harvest will come for her."
34¶ "Nebuchadnezzar king of Babylon has devoured me *and* crushed me,
He has set me down *like* an empty vessel;
He has swallowed me like a monster,
He has filled his stomach with my delicacies;
He has washed me away.
35 "May the violence *done* to me and to my flesh be upon Babylon,"
The inhabitant of Zion will say;
And, "May my blood be upon the inhabitants of Chaldea,"
Jerusalem will say.
36 Therefore thus says the LORD,
"Behold, I am going to plead your case
And exact full vengeance for you;
And I shall dry up her sea
And make her fountain dry.

## New International

23with you I shatter shepherd and flock,
with you I shatter farmer and oxen,
with you I shatter governors and officials.

24"Before your eyes I will repay Babylon and all who live in Babylonia[b] for all the wrong they have done in Zion," declares the LORD.

25"I am against you, O destroying mountain,
you who destroy the whole earth,"
declares the LORD.
"I will stretch out my hand against you,
roll you off the cliffs,
and make you a burned-out mountain.
26No rock will be taken from you for a cornerstone,
nor any stone for a foundation,
for you will be desolate forever,"
declares the LORD.

27"Lift up a banner in the land!
Blow the trumpet among the nations!
Prepare the nations for battle against her;
summon against her these kingdoms:
Ararat, Minni and Ashkenaz.
Appoint a commander against her;
send up horses like a swarm of locusts.
28Prepare the nations for battle against her—
the kings of the Medes,
their governors and all their officials,
and all the countries they rule.
29The land trembles and writhes,
for the LORD's purposes against Babylon stand—
to lay waste the land of Babylon
so that no one will live there.
30Babylon's warriors have stopped fighting;
they remain in their strongholds.
Their strength is exhausted;
they have become like women.
Her dwellings are set on fire;
the bars of her gates are broken.
31One courier follows another
and messenger follows messenger
to announce to the king of Babylon
that his entire city is captured,
32the river crossings seized,
the marshes set on fire,
and the soldiers terrified."

33This is what the LORD Almighty, the God of Israel, says:

"The Daughter of Babylon is like a threshing floor
at the time it is trampled;
the time to harvest her will soon come."

34"Nebuchadnezzar king of Babylon has devoured us,
he has thrown us into confusion,
he has made us an empty jar.
Like a serpent he has swallowed us
and filled his stomach with our delicacies,
and then has spewed us out.
35May the violence done to our flesh[c] be upon Babylon,"
say the inhabitants of Zion.
"May our blood be on those who live in Babylonia,"
says Jerusalem.

36Therefore, this is what the LORD says:

"See, I will defend your cause
and avenge you;
I will dry up her sea
and make her springs dry.

NIV [b] 24 Or *Chaldea;* also in verse 35 [c] 35 Or *done to us and to our children*

## King James

37And Babylon shall become heaps, a dwellingplace for dragons, an astonishment, and an hissing, without an inhabitant.
38They shall roar together like lions: they shall yell as lions' whelps.
39In their heat I will make their feasts, and I will make them drunken, that they may rejoice, and sleep a perpetual sleep, and not wake, saith the LORD.
40I will bring them down like lambs to the slaughter, like rams with he goats.
41How is Sheshach taken! and how is the praise of the whole earth surprised! how is Babylon become an astonishment among the nations!
42The sea is come up upon Babylon: she is covered with the multitude of the waves thereof.
43Her cities are a desolation, a dry land, and a wilderness, a land wherein no man dwelleth, neither doth *any* son of man pass thereby.
44And I will punish Bel in Babylon, and I will bring forth out of his mouth that which he hath swallowed up: and the nations shall not flow together any more unto him: yea, the wall of Babylon shall fall.
45My people, go ye out of the midst of her, and deliver ye every man his soul from the fierce anger of the LORD.
46And lest your heart faint, and ye fear for the rumour that shall be heard in the land; a rumour shall both come *one* year, and after that in *another* year *shall come* a rumour, and violence in the land, ruler against ruler.
47Therefore, behold, the days come, that I will do judgment upon the graven images of Babylon: and her whole land shall be confounded, and all her slain shall fall in the midst of her.
48Then the heaven and the earth, and all that *is* therein, shall sing for Babylon: for the spoilers shall come unto her from the north, saith the LORD.
49As Babylon *hath caused* the slain of Israel to fall, so at Babylon shall fall the slain of all the earth.
50Ye that have escaped the sword, go away, stand not still: remember the LORD afar off, and let Jerusalem come into your mind.
51We are confounded, because we have heard reproach: shame hath covered our faces: for strangers are come into the sanctuaries of the LORD's house.
52Wherefore, behold, the days come, saith the LORD, that I will do judgment upon her graven images: and through all her land the wounded shall groan.

AMP [a] Here is God's forecast through Jeremiah of what was to happen to great Babylon, of whom Herodotus said she had been "embellished with ornaments more than any city" of his acquaintance. That it happened in all its details is recorded by Daniel (5:1-30), and becomes more and more amazing and awe-inspiring as one considers it all after twenty-five verifying centuries. Truly only a "fool" could say in his heart, "There is no God" (Ps. 14:1).

## Amplified

37And Babylon shall become heaps *of ruins*, a dwelling place for jackals, an astonishing desolation, a horror *and* a hissing [of amazement], without inhabitant.
38They [the Chaldean lords] shall be roaring together [before their sudden capture] like lions *over their prey;* they [the princes] shall be growling like lions' whelps.
39When the revelers are [a]inflamed [with wine and lust at their drinking bouts], I will prepare them a feast [of My wrath] and make them drunk that they may rejoice and fall asleep to a perpetual sleep, and not waken, says the Lord.
40I will bring them down like lambs to the slaughter, like rams with he-goats.
41How Sheshack [Babylon] is taken! And the praise of the whole earth is surprised *and* seized! How is Babylon become an [astonishing] desolation *and* a horror among the nations!
42The sea is come up upon Babylon; she is covered with the tumult *and* multitude of its waves.
43Her cities have become a desolation *and* a horror, a land of drought and a wilderness, a land in which no one lives, nor does any son of man pass through it.
44And I will punish *and* execute judgment upon Bel [the god] in Babylon, and take out of his mouth what he swallowed up [the sacred vessels, the people of Judah and elsewhere which were taken captive]. The nations shall not flow any more to him; yes, the wall of Babylon has fallen!
45My people, go out of the midst of her, and save every man his life from the fierce anger of the Lord! [Jer. 50:8; II Cor. 6:17; Rev. 18:4.]
46And beware lest your heart faint, and you be afraid of the report heard in the land; for in one year shall one rumor come, and in another year another report, and violence shall be in the land, ruler against ruler.
47Therefore, behold, the days will come, when I will execute judgment *and* punishment upon the idols of Babylon; her whole land shall be confounded *and* put to shame, and all her slain shall fall in the midst of her.
48Then heaven and earth and all that is in them shall sing for joy over Babylon; for the *Median* destroyers shall come against her from the north, says the Lord. [Isa. 44:23; Rev. 12:12; 18:20; Jer. 51:11.]
49As Babylon caused the slain of Israel to fall, so at Babylon shall fall the slain of all *her* land.
50You who have escaped the sword, go away, stand not still! [Seriously and earnestly] remember the Lord from afar off [Babylon], and let [desolate] Jerusalem come into your mind.
51We are confounded *and* ashamed, for we have heard reproach; confusion *and* shame have covered our faces; for strangers have come into the most sacred parts of the sanctuary of the Lord [even those forbidden to any but the high priest or the appointed priests].
52Therefore, behold, the days are coming, says the Lord, when I will execute judgment upon [Babylon's] idols *and* images, and through all her land the wounded shall groan.

## New American Standard

37 "And Babylon will become a heap *of ruins,* a haunt of jackals,
An object of horror and hissing, without inhabitants.
38 "They will roar together like young lions,
They will growl like lions' cubs.
39 "When they become heated up, I shall serve *them* their banquet
And make them drunk, that they may become jubilant
And may sleep a perpetual sleep
And not wake up," declares the LORD.
40 "I shall bring them down like lambs to the slaughter,
Like rams together with male goats.

41¶ "How [b]Sheshak has been captured,
And the praise of the whole earth been seized!
How Babylon has become an object of horror among the nations!
42 "The sea has come up over Babylon;
She has been engulfed with its tumultuous waves.
43 "Her cities have become an object of horror,
A parched land and a desert,
A land in which no man lives,
And through which no son of man passes.
44 "And I shall punish Bel in Babylon,
And I shall make what he has swallowed come out of his mouth;
And the nations will no longer stream to him.
Even the wall of Babylon has fallen down!

45¶ "Come forth from her midst, My people,
And each of you save yourselves
From the fierce anger of the LORD.
46 "Now lest your heart grow faint,
And you be afraid at the report that *will be* heard in the land—
For the report will come one year,
And after that another report in another year,
And violence *will be* in the land
With ruler against ruler—
47 Therefore behold, days are coming
When I shall punish the idols of Babylon;
And her whole land will be put to shame,
And all her slain will fall in her midst.
48 "Then heaven and earth and all that is in them
Will shout for joy over Babylon,
For the destroyers will come to her from the north,"
Declares the LORD.

49¶ Indeed Babylon is to fall *for* the slain of Israel,
*As* also for Babylon the slain of all the earth have fallen.
50 You who have escaped the sword,
Depart! Do not stay!
Remember the LORD from afar,
And let Jerusalem come to your mind.
51 We are ashamed because we have heard reproach;
Disgrace has covered our faces,
For aliens have entered
The holy places of the LORD's house.

52¶ "Therefore behold, the days are coming," declares the LORD,
"When I shall punish her idols,
And the mortally wounded will groan throughout her land.

NAS [b] Cryptic name for Babylon

## New International

37Babylon will be a heap of ruins,
a haunt of jackals,
an object of horror and scorn,
a place where no one lives.
38Her people all roar like young lions,
they growl like lion cubs.
39But while they are aroused,
I will set out a feast for them
and make them drunk,
so that they shout with laughter—
then sleep forever and not awake,"
declares the LORD.
40"I will bring them down
like lambs to the slaughter,
like rams and goats.

41"How Sheshach[c] will be captured,
the boast of the whole earth seized!
What a horror Babylon will be
among the nations!
42The sea will rise over Babylon;
its roaring waves will cover her.
43Her towns will be desolate,
a dry and desert land,
a land where no one lives,
through which no man travels.
44I will punish Bel in Babylon
and make him spew out what he has swallowed.
The nations will no longer stream to him.
And the wall of Babylon will fall.

45"Come out of her, my people!
Run for your lives!
Run from the fierce anger of the LORD.
46Do not lose heart or be afraid
when rumors are heard in the land;
one rumor comes this year, another the next,
rumors of violence in the land
and of ruler against ruler.
47For the time will surely come
when I will punish the idols of Babylon;
her whole land will be disgraced
and her slain will all lie fallen within her.
48Then heaven and earth and all that is in them
will shout for joy over Babylon,
for out of the north
destroyers will attack her,"
declares the LORD.

49"Babylon must fall because of Israel's slain,
just as the slain in all the earth
have fallen because of Babylon.
50You who have escaped the sword,
leave and do not linger!
Remember the LORD in a distant land,
and think on Jerusalem."

51"We are disgraced,
for we have been insulted
and shame covers our faces,
because foreigners have entered
the holy places of the LORD's house."

52"But days are coming," declares the LORD,
"when I will punish her idols,
and throughout her land
the wounded will groan.

NIV [c] 41 *Sheshach* is a cryptogram for Babylon.

## King James

53 Though Babylon should mount up to heaven, and though she should fortify the height of her strength, *yet* from me shall spoilers come unto her, saith the LORD.

54 A sound of a cry *cometh* from Babylon, and great destruction from the land of the Chaldeans:

55 Because the LORD hath spoiled Babylon, and destroyed out of her the great voice; when her waves do roar like great waters, a noise of their voice is uttered:

56 Because the spoiler is come upon her, *even* upon Babylon, and her mighty men are taken, every one of their bows is broken: for the LORD God of recompences shall surely requite.

57 And I will make drunk her princes, and her wise *men*, her captains, and her rulers, and her mighty men: and they shall sleep a perpetual sleep, and not wake, saith the King, whose name *is* the LORD of hosts.

58 Thus saith the LORD of hosts; The broad walls of Babylon shall be utterly broken, and her high gates shall be burned with fire; and the people shall labour in vain, and the folk in the fire, and they shall be weary.

59 ¶ The word which Jeremiah the prophet commanded Seraiah the son of Neriah, the son of Maaseiah, when he went with Zedekiah the king of Judah into Babylon in the fourth year of his reign. And *this* Seraiah *was* a quiet prince.

60 So Jeremiah wrote in a book all the evil that should come upon Babylon, *even* all these words that are written against Babylon.

61 And Jeremiah said to Seraiah, When thou comest to Babylon, and shalt see, and shalt read all these words;

62 Then shalt thou say, O LORD, thou hast spoken against this place, to cut it off, that none shall remain in it, neither man nor beast, but that it shall be desolate for ever.

63 And it shall be, when thou hast made an end of reading this book, *that* thou shalt bind a stone to it, and cast it into the midst of Euphrates:

64 And thou shalt say, Thus shall Babylon sink, and shall not rise from the evil that I will bring upon her: and they shall be weary. Thus far *are* the words of Jeremiah.

**52** ZEDEKIAH *WAS* one and twenty years old when he began to reign, and he reigned eleven years in Jerusalem. And his mother's name *was* Hamutal the daughter of Jeremiah of Libnah.

2 And he did *that which was* evil in the eyes of the LORD, according to all that Jehoiakim had done.

3 For through the anger of the LORD it came to pass in Jerusalem and Judah, till he had cast them out from his presence, that Zedekiah rebelled against the king of Babylon.

4 ¶ And it came to pass in the ninth year of his reign, in the tenth month, in the tenth *day* of the month, *that* Nebuchadrezzar king of Babylon came, he and all his army, against Jerusalem, and pitched against it, and built forts against it round about.

5 So the city was besieged unto the eleventh year of king Zedekiah.

6 And in the fourth month, in the ninth *day* of the month, the famine was sore in the city, so that there was no bread for the people of the land.

## Amplified

53 Though Babylon should mount up to heaven, and though she should fortify her strong height, yet destroyers would come upon her from Me, says the Lord.

54 The sound of a cry *comes* from Babylon, and great destruction *and* ruin from the land of the Chaldeans!

55 For the Lord is spoiling Babylon *and* laying her waste, and stilling her great voice [the hum of the city's life]. And the waves [of her conquerors] roar like great waters, the noise of their voice is raised [like the tramping of an army].

56 For the destroyer is come upon her, upon Babylon, and her mighty warriors are taken, their bows are broken in pieces; for the Lord is a God of recompenses, He will surely requite.

57 And I will make drunk her princes and her wise men, her governors and her deputies and her mighty warriors; and they shall sleep a perpetual sleep, and not waken, says the King; the Lord of hosts is His name.

58 Thus says the Lord of hosts: The broad walls of Babylon shall be utterly overthrown *and* [the foundations] made bare, and her high gates shall be burned with fire; the peoples shall labor in vain, and the nations *only* for fire, and they shall be weary. [Hab. 2:13.]

59 The word which Jeremiah the prophet commanded Seraiah the son of Neriah, the son of Mahseiah, when he went with Zedekiah the king of Judah to Babylon in the fourth year of his reign. Now this Seraiah was chief chamberlain *or* quartermaster [and brother of Baruch].

60 So Jeremiah wrote in a book all the evil that should come upon Babylon, even all these words that are written against Babylon.

61 And Jeremiah said to Seraiah, When you come to Babylon, see to it that you read all these words.

62 Then you shall say, O Lord, You have spoken concerning this place that it shall be cut off, so that nothing shall remain and dwell in it, neither man nor beast, but that it shall be desolate for ever.

63 And it shall be, when you have finished reading this book, that you shall bind a stone to it, and cast it into the midst of the Euphrates;

64 And say, Thus shall Babylon sink and shall not rise because of the evil that I will bring upon her; and [the Babylonians] shall be weary [hopelessly exhausted]. Thus far are the words of Jeremiah. [Cf. Rev. 18:21.]

**52** ZEDEKIAH WAS twenty-one years old when he began to reign, and he reigned eleven years in Jerusalem. And his mother's name was Hamutal the daughter of Jeremiah of Libnah.

2 And he did that which was evil in the sight of the Lord, according to all that Jehoiakim had done.

3 For this it came to pass in Jerusalem and Judah, because of the anger of the Lord, that He cast them out from His presence. And Zedekiah rebelled against the king of Babylon.

4 And in the ninth year of his reign, in the tenth month, on the tenth day of the month, Nebuchadrezzar king of Babylon came, he and all his army, against Jerusalem, and pitched against it and built moveable towers *and* siege mounds against it round about.

5 So the city was besieged until the eleventh year of King Zedekiah. [II Chron. 36:11-13.]

6 And in the fourth month, on the ninth day of the month, the famine was so severe in the city, that there was no bread for the people of the land.

## New American Standard

53 "Though Babylon should ascend to the heavens,
And though she should fortify her lofty stronghold,
From Me destroyers will come to her," declares the
LORD.

54¶ The sound of an outcry from Babylon,
And of great destruction from the land of the
Chaldeans!
55 For the LORD is going to destroy Babylon,
And He will make *her* loud noise vanish from her.
And their waves will roar like many waters;
The tumult of their voices sounds forth.
56 For the destroyer is coming against her, against
Babylon,
And her mighty men will be captured,
Their bows are shattered;
For the LORD is a God of recompense,
He will fully repay.
57 "And I shall make her princes and her wise men drunk,
Her governors, her prefects, and her mighty men,
That they may sleep a perpetual sleep and not wake
up,"
Declares the King, whose name is the LORD of hosts.
58 Thus says the LORD of hosts,
"The broad wall of Babylon will be completely razed,
And her high gates will be set on fire;
So the peoples will toil for nothing,
And the nations become exhausted *only* for fire."

59¶ The message which Jeremiah the prophet commanded Seraiah the son of Neriah, the grandson of Mahseiah, when he went
with Zedekiah the king of Judah to Babylon in the fourth year of
his reign. (Now Seraiah was quartermaster.)
60So Jeremiah wrote in a single scroll all the calamity which
would come upon Babylon, *that is,* all these words which have
been written concerning Babylon.
61Then Jeremiah said to Seraiah, "As soon as you come to
Babylon, then see that you read all these words aloud,
62and say, 'Thou, O LORD, hast promised concerning this place
to cut it off, so that there will be nothing dwelling in it, whether
man or beast, but it will be a perpetual desolation.'
63"And it will come about as soon as you finish reading this
scroll, you will tie a stone to it and throw it into the middle of the
Euphrates,
64and say, 'Just so shall Babylon sink down and not rise again,
because of the calamity that I am going to bring upon her; and they
will become exhausted.'" Thus far are the words of Jeremiah.

*Recount the Fall of Jerusalem*

**52** ZEDEKIAH WAS twenty-one years old when he became
king, and he reigned eleven years in Jerusalem; and his
mother's name was Hamutal the daughter of Jeremiah of Libnah.
2And he did evil in the sight of the LORD like all that Jehoiakim
had done.
3For through the anger of the LORD *this* came about in Jerusalem and Judah until He cast them out from His presence. And
Zedekiah rebelled against the king of Babylon.
4Now it came about in the ninth year of his reign, on the tenth
day of the tenth month, that Nebuchadnezzar king of Babylon
came, he and all his army, against Jerusalem, camped against it,
and built a siege wall all around it.
5So the city was under siege until the eleventh year of King
Zedekiah.
6On the ninth day of the fourth month the famine was so
severe in the city that there was no food for the people of the land.

## New International

53Even if Babylon reaches the sky
and fortifies her lofty stronghold,
I will send destroyers against her,"
declares the LORD.

54"The sound of a cry comes from Babylon,
the sound of great destruction
from the land of the Babylonians.[a]
55The LORD will destroy Babylon;
he will silence her noisy din.
Waves ⌊of enemies⌋ will rage like great waters;
the roar of their voices will resound.
56A destroyer will come against Babylon;
her warriors will be captured,
and their bows will be broken.
For the LORD is a God of retribution;
he will repay in full.
57I will make her officials and wise men drunk,
her governors, officers and warriors as well;
they will sleep forever and not awake,"
declares the King, whose name is the LORD Almighty.
58This is what the LORD Almighty says:

"Babylon's thick wall will be leveled
and her high gates set on fire;
the peoples exhaust themselves for nothing,
the nations' labor is only fuel for the flames."

59This is the message Jeremiah gave to the staff officer Seraiah
son of Neriah, the son of Mahseiah, when he went to Babylon with
Zedekiah king of Judah in the fourth year of his reign. 60Jeremiah
had written on a scroll about all the disasters that would come
upon Babylon—all that had been recorded concerning Babylon.
61He said to Seraiah, "When you get to Babylon, see that you read
all these words aloud. 62Then say, 'O LORD, you have said you will
destroy this place, so that neither man nor animal will live in it;
it will be desolate forever.' 63When you finish reading this scroll,
tie a stone to it and throw it into the Euphrates. 64Then say, 'So
will Babylon sink to rise no more because of the disaster I will bring
upon her. And her people will fall.'"

The words of Jeremiah end here.

*The Fall of Jerusalem*

**52** ZEDEKIAH WAS twenty-one years old when he became
king, and he reigned in Jerusalem eleven years. His
mother's name was Hamutal daughter of Jeremiah; she was from
Libnah. 2He did evil in the eyes of the LORD, just as Jehoiakim had
done. 3It was because of the LORD's anger that all this happened
to Jerusalem and Judah, and in the end he thrust them from his
presence.

Now Zedekiah rebelled against the king of Babylon.
4So in the ninth year of Zedekiah's reign, on the tenth day of
the tenth month, Nebuchadnezzar king of Babylon marched
against Jerusalem with his whole army. They camped outside the
city and built siege works all around it. 5The city was kept under
siege until the eleventh year of King Zedekiah.
6By the ninth day of the fourth month the famine in the city had
become so severe that there was no food for the people to eat.

NIV [a] 54 Or *Chaldeans*

## King James

7Then the city was broken up, and all the men of war fled, and went forth out of the city by night by the way of the gate between the two walls, which *was* by the king's garden; (now the Chaldeans *were* by the city round about:) and they went by the way of the plain.

8¶ But the army of the Chaldeans pursued after the king, and overtook Zedekiah in the plains of Jericho; and all his army was scattered from him.

9Then they took the king, and carried him up unto the king of Babylon to Riblah in the land of Hamath; where he gave judgment upon him.

10And the king of Babylon slew the sons of Zedekiah before his eyes: he slew also all the princes of Judah in Riblah.

11Then he put out the eyes of Zedekiah; and the king of Babylon bound him in chains, and carried him to Babylon, and put him in prison till the day of his death.

12¶ Now in the fifth month, in the tenth *day* of the month, which *was* the nineteenth year of Nebuchadrezzar king of Babylon, came Nebuzar-adan, captain of the guard, *which* served the king of Babylon, into Jerusalem,

13And burned the house of the LORD, and the king's house; and all the houses of Jerusalem, and all the houses of the great *men*, burned he with fire:

14And all the army of the Chaldeans, that *were* with the captain of the guard, brake down all the walls of Jerusalem round about.

15Then Nebuzar-adan the captain of the guard carried away captive *certain* of the poor of the people, and the residue of the people that remained in the city, and those that fell away, that fell to the king of Babylon, and the rest of the multitude.

16But Nebuzar-adan the captain of the guard left *certain* of the poor of the land for vinedressers and for husbandmen.

17Also the pillars of brass that *were* in the house of the LORD, and the bases, and the brasen sea that *was* in the house of the LORD, the Chaldeans brake, and carried all the brass of them to Babylon.

18The caldrons also, and the shovels, and the snuffers, and the bowls, and the spoons, and all the vessels of brass wherewith they ministered, took they away.

19And the basins, and the firepans, and the bowls, and the caldrons, and the candlesticks, and the spoons, and the cups; *that* which *was* of gold *in* gold, and *that* which *was* of silver *in* silver, took the captain of the guard away.

20The two pillars, one sea, and twelve brasen bulls that *were* under the bases, which king Solomon had made in the house of the LORD: the brass of all these vessels was without weight.

21And *concerning* the pillars, the height of one pillar *was* eighteen cubits; and a fillet of twelve cubits did compass it; and the thickness thereof *was* four fingers: *it was* hollow.

22And a chapiter of brass *was* upon it; and the height of one chapiter *was* five cubits, with network and pomegranates upon the chapiters round about, all *of* brass. The second pillar also and the pomegranates *were* like unto these.

23And there were ninety and six pomegranates on a side; *and* all the pomegranates upon the network *were* an hundred round about.

24¶ And the captain of the guard took Seraiah the chief priest, and Zephaniah the second priest, and the three keepers of the door:

25He took also out of the city an eunuch, which had the charge of the men of war; and seven men of them that were near the king's person, which were found in the city; and the principal scribe of the host, who mustered the people of the land; and threescore men of the people of the land, that were found in the midst of the city.

## Amplified

7Then the city [wall] was broken through so that all the men of war might flee, and they went forth out of the city by night [as Ezekiel had foretold] by the way of the gate between the two walls, which was by the king's garden. Now the Chaldeans were round about the city, and the [Jewish soldiers fled] by the way to the plain. [Ezek. 12:12.]

8But the army of the Chaldeans pursued after the king and overtook Zedekiah in the plains of Jericho, and all his army was scattered from him.

9Then they seized the king and brought him up to the king of Babylon at Riblah in the land of Hamath [on the northern border of Israel], and he passed sentence upon him.

10And the king of Babylon slew the sons of Zedekiah before his eyes; he slew also all the princes of Judah at Riblah.

11Then he put out the eyes of Zedekiah; and the king of Babylon bound him with a double chain and carried him to Babylon, and put him in the prison [a][mill] till the day of his death. [Ezek. 12:13.]

12Now in the fifth month, on the tenth day of the month, which was the nineteenth year of Nebuchadrezzar king of Babylon, there came to Jerusalem Nebuzaradan, captain of the body-guard who stood *and* served before the king of Babylon.

13And he burned the house of the Lord and the king's house and all the houses of Jerusalem; every great house he consumed with fire.

14And all the army of the Chaldeans, who were with the captain of the guard, broke down all the walls round about Jerusalem.

15Then Nebuzaradan the captain of the guard carried away captive some of the poorest of the people and those who were left in the city [at the time it was captured], and those who went out to the king of Babylon [during the siege], and the remnant of the multitude—the country's working people.

16But Nebuzaradan the captain of the guard left certain of the poorest of the land for vinedressers and for tillers of the soil.

17Also the pillars of bronze that belonged to the house of the Lord, and the bronze bases *or* pedestals [which supported the ten basins] and the bronze sea *or* huge laver which were in the house of the Lord, the Chaldeans broke into pieces, and carried all the bronze of them to Babylon.

18The pots [for carrying away ashes] also, and the shovels, and the snuffers, and the bowls, and the spoons and all the vessels of bronze with which the temple service was ministered, they took away;

19Also the small bowls, and the firepans, and the basins, and the pots, and the lampstands, and the incense cups, and the bowls for the drink offerings; whatever was of gold the captain of the guard took away as gold, and what was of silver, as silver.

20The two pillars, one sea *or* huge laver, and [b]twelve bronze bulls under the sea, which King Solomon had made in the house of the Lord—the bronze of all these things was beyond weighing.

21Concerning the pillars, the height of the one pillar was eighteen cubits *or* twenty-seven feet, and an ornamental molding of twelve cubits *or* eighteen feet went around its circumference; its thickness was four fingers, the pillar being hollow.

22An upper part *or* capital of bronze was upon it. The height of one capital was five cubits *or* seven and one-half feet, and there were around it a network and pomegranates, all of bronze. The second pillar also and the pomegranates were similar to these.

23And there were ninety-six pomegranates on the sides, and all the pomegranates upon the network were a hundred round about.

24And the captain of the guard took Seraiah the chief priest, and Zephaniah the second priest, and the three keepers of the door;

25He took also out of the city a court officer who had been overseer of the soldiers, and seven men of them who were next the king *and* saw his face, who were found in the city; and the scribe of the prince *or* captain of the army, who mustered the people of the land; and sixty men of the people of the land, who were found in the midst of the city.

**AMP** [a] The Septuagint, the Greek version, renders this word "mill." Hence it has been inferred that the Chaldeans ascribed to Zedekiah in his old age the same fate as that to which the Philistines consigned Samson (Judges 16:21). (Cambridge Bible.) [b] King Ahaz had previously removed the twelve bronze bulls from under the big laver and had replaced them with a substructure of stone (II Kings 16:17), but obviously he had not put them beyond the reach of the Chaldeans when they undertook to find them.

## New American Standard

7Then the city was broken into, and all the men of war fled and went forth from the city at night by way of the gate between the two walls which *was* by the king's garden, though the Chaldeans were all around the city. And they went by way of the Arabah.

8But the army of the Chaldeans pursued the king and overtook Zedekiah in the plains of Jericho, and all his army was scattered from him.

9Then they captured the king and brought him up to the king of Babylon at Riblah in the land of Hamath; and he passed sentence on him.

10And the king of Babylon slaughtered the sons of Zedekiah before his eyes, and he also slaughtered all the princes of Judah in Riblah.

11Then he blinded the eyes of Zedekiah; and the king of Babylon bound him with bronze fetters and brought him to Babylon, and put him in prison until the day of his death.

**12**¶ Now on the tenth day of the fifth month, which was the nineteenth year of King Nebuchadnezzar, king of Babylon, Nebuzaradan the captain of the bodyguard, who was in the service of the king of Babylon, came to Jerusalem.

13And he burned the house of the LORD, the king's house, and all the houses of Jerusalem; even every large house he burned with fire.

14So all the army of the Chaldeans who *were* with the captain of the guard broke down all the walls around Jerusalem.

15Then Nebuzaradan the captain of the guard carried away into exile some of the poorest of the people, the rest of the people who were left in the city, the deserters who had deserted to the king of Babylon, and the rest of the artisans.

16But Nebuzaradan the captain of the guard left some of the poorest of the land to be vinedressers and plowmen.

**17**¶ Now the bronze pillars which belonged to the house of the LORD and the stands and the bronze sea, which were in the house of the LORD, the Chaldeans broke in pieces and carried all their bronze to Babylon.

18And they also took away the pots, the shovels, the snuffers, the basins, the pans, and all the bronze vessels which were used in *temple* service.

19The captain of the guard also took away the bowls, the firepans, the basins, the pots, the lampstands, the pans and the libation bowls, what was fine gold and what was fine silver.

20The two pillars, the one sea, and the twelve bronze bulls that were under the sea, *and* the stands, which King Solomon had made for the house of the LORD—the bronze of all these vessels was beyond weight.

21As for the pillars, the height of each pillar was eighteen cubits, and it was twelve cubits in circumference and four fingers in thickness, *and* hollow.

22Now a capital of bronze was on it; and the height of each capital was five cubits, with network and pomegranates upon the capital all around, all of bronze. And the second pillar was like these, including pomegranates.

23And there were ninety-six exposed pomegranates; all the pomegranates *numbered* a hundred on the network all around.

**24**¶ Then the captain of the guard took Seraiah the chief priest and Zephaniah the second priest, with the three officers of the temple.

25He also took from the city one official who was overseer of the men of war, and seven of the king's advisers who were found in the city, and the scribe of the commander of the army who mustered the people of the land, and sixty men of the people of the land who were found in the midst of the city.

## New International

7Then the city wall was broken through, and the whole army fled.
They left the city at night through the gate between the two walls
near the king's garden, though the Babylonians[c] were surrounding the city. They fled toward the Arabah,[d] 8but the Babylonian[e]
army pursued King Zedekiah and overtook him in the plains of
Jericho. All his soldiers were separated from him and scattered,
9and he was captured.
He was taken to the king of Babylon at Riblah in the land of
Hamath, where he pronounced sentence on him. 10There at Riblah
the king of Babylon slaughtered the sons of Zedekiah before his
eyes; he also killed all the officials of Judah. 11Then he put out
Zedekiah's eyes, bound him with bronze shackles and took him
to Babylon, where he put him in prison till the day of his death.
12On the tenth day of the fifth month, in the nineteenth year
of Nebuchadnezzar king of Babylon, Nebuzaradan commander of
the imperial guard, who served the king of Babylon, came to
Jerusalem. 13He set fire to the temple of the LORD, the royal palace
and all the houses of Jerusalem. Every important building he
burned down. 14The whole Babylonian army under the commander of the imperial guard broke down all the walls around
Jerusalem. 15Nebuzaradan the commander of the guard carried
into exile some of the poorest people and those who remained in
the city, along with the rest of the craftsmen[f] and those who had
gone over to the king of Babylon. 16But Nebuzaradan left behind
the rest of the poorest people of the land to work the vineyards and
fields.
17The Babylonians broke up the bronze pillars, the movable
stands and the bronze Sea that were at the temple of the LORD and
they carried all the bronze to Babylon. 18They also took away the
pots, shovels, wick trimmers, sprinkling bowls, dishes and all the
bronze articles used in the temple service. 19The commander of the
imperial guard took away the basins, censers, sprinkling bowls,
pots, lampstands, dishes and bowls used for drink offerings—all
that were made of pure gold or silver.
20The bronze from the two pillars, the Sea and the twelve
bronze bulls under it, and the movable stands, which King Solomon had made for the temple of the LORD, was more than could
be weighed. 21Each of the pillars was eighteen cubits high and
twelve cubits in circumference[g]; each was four fingers thick, and
hollow. 22The bronze capital on top of the one pillar was five
cubits[h] high and was decorated with a network and pomegranates
of bronze all around. The other pillar, with its pomegranates, was
similar. 23There were ninety-six pomegranates on the sides; the
total number of pomegranates above the surrounding network
was a hundred.
24The commander of the guard took as prisoners Seraiah the
chief priest, Zephaniah the priest next in rank and the three doorkeepers. 25Of those still in the city, he took the officer in charge
of the fighting men, and seven royal advisers. He also took the
secretary who was chief officer in charge of conscripting the people
of the land and sixty of his men who were found in the city.

**NIV** [c] *7* Or *Chaldeans;* also in verse 17 [d] *7* Or *the Jordan Valley* [e] *8* Or *Chaldean;* also in verse 14 [f] *15* Or *populace* [g] *21* That is, about 27 feet (about 8.1 meters) high and 18 feet (about 5.4 meters) in circumference [h] *22* That is, about 7 1/2 feet (about 2.3 meters)

## King James

26So Nebuzar-adan the captain of the guard took them, and brought them to the king of Babylon to Riblah.

27And the king of Babylon smote them, and put them to death in Riblah in the land of Hamath. Thus Judah was carried away captive out of his own land.

28This *is* the people whom Nebuchadrezzar carried away captive: in the seventh year three thousand Jews and three and twenty:

29In the eighteenth year of Nebuchadrezzar he carried away captive from Jerusalem eight hundred thirty and two persons:

30In the three and twentieth year of Nebuchadrezzar Nebuzar-adan the captain of the guard carried away captive of the Jews seven hundred forty and five persons: all the persons *were* four thousand and six hundred.

31¶ And it came to pass in the seven and thirtieth year of the captivity of Jehoiachin king of Judah, in the twelfth month, in the five and twentieth *day* of the month, *that* Evil-merodach king of Babylon in the *first* year of his reign lifted up the head of Jehoiachin king of Judah, and brought him forth out of prison,

32And spake kindly unto him, and set his throne above the throne of the kings that *were* with him in Babylon,

33And changed his prison garments: and he did continually eat bread before him all the days of his life.

34And *for* his diet, there was a continual diet given him of the king of Babylon, every day a portion until the day of his death, all the days of his life.

## Amplified

26And Nebuzaradan the captain of the guard took them, and brought them to the king of Babylon at Riblah.

27And the king of Babylon smote them, and put them to death in Riblah in the land of Hamath. Thus Judah was carried away captive out of his own land.

28This is the number of people whom Nebuchadrezzar carried away captive: in the seventh year three thousand and twenty-three Jews;

29In the eighteenth year of Nebuchadrezzar he carried away captive from Jerusalem eight hundred and thirty-two persons;

30In the twenty-third year of Nebuchadrezzar Nebuzaradan the captain of the [Babylonian] guard carried away captive of the Jews seven hundred and forty-five persons; all the persons were four thousand and six hundred.

31And in the thirty-seventh year of the captivity of Jehoiachin king of Judah, in the twelfth month, on the twenty-fifth day of the month, Evil-merodach king of Babylon in the first year of his reign lifted up the head of Jehoiachin king of Judah and brought him out of prison,

32And spoke kindly to him, and gave him a seat above the seats of the kings who were [captives] with him in Babylon,

33And changed his prison garments. And Jehoiachin ate regularly at the king's table all the days of his life.

34As for his allowance, there was a continual allowance given him by the king of Babylon, according to his requirements until the day of his death, [a]all the days of his life.

**AMP** [a] The latter of these clauses is probably an afterthought, in order to prevent ending the book with the word "death." The general object too of the paragraph [the last four verses] seems to have been to leave the reader with a parting ray of comfort and encouragement in the thought that even in exile the Lord remembered His people and softened the heart of the heathen tyrant toward David's seed. (Condensed from Cambridge Bible.)

## New American Standard

26And Nebuzaradan the captain of the guard took them and brought them to the king of Babylon at Riblah.

27Then the king of Babylon struck them down and put them to death at Riblah in the land of Hamath. So Judah was led away into exile from its land.

28¶ These are the people whom Nebuchadnezzar carried away into exile: in the seventh year 3,023 Jews;

29in the eighteenth year of Nebuchadnezzar 832 persons from Jerusalem;

30in the twenty-third year of Nebuchadnezzar, Nebuzaradan the captain of the guard carried into exile 745 Jewish people; there were 4,600 persons in all.

31¶ Now it came about in the thirty-seventh year of the exile of Jehoiachin king of Judah, in the twelfth month, on the twenty-fifth of the month, that Evil-merodach king of Babylon, in the *first* year of his reign, showed favor to Jehoiachin king of Judah and brought him out of prison.

32Then he spoke kindly to him and set his throne above the thrones of the kings who *were* with him in Babylon.

33So Jehoiachin changed his prison clothes, and had his meals in the king's presence regularly all the days of his life.

34And for his allowance, a regular allowance was given him by the king of Babylon, a daily portion all the days of his life until the day of his death.

## New International

26Nebuzaradan the commander took them all and brought them
to the king of Babylon at Riblah. 27There at Riblah, in the land of
Hamath, the king had them executed.

So Judah went into captivity, away from her land. 28This is the
number of the people Nebuchadnezzar carried into exile:

in the seventh year, 3,023 Jews;
29in Nebuchadnezzar's eighteenth year,
832 people from Jerusalem;
30in his twenty-third year,
745 Jews taken into exile by Nebuzaradan
the commander of the imperial guard.
There were 4,600 people in all.

*Jehoiachin Released*

31In the thirty-seventh year of the exile of Jehoiachin king of
Judah, in the year Evil-Merodach[b] became king of Babylon, he
released Jehoiachin king of Judah and freed him from prison on the
twenty-fifth day of the twelfth month. 32He spoke kindly to him
and gave him a seat of honor higher than those of the other kings
who were with him in Babylon. 33So Jehoiachin put aside his
prison clothes and for the rest of his life ate regularly at the king's
table. 34Day by day the king of Babylon gave Jehoiachin a regular
allowance as long as he lived, till the day of his death.

**NIV** [b] *31* Also called *Amel-Marduk*

## King James

THE

# Lamentations

OF JEREMIAH

**1** HOW DOTH the city sit solitary, *that was* full of people! *how* is she become as a widow! she *that was* great among the nations, *and* princess among the provinces, *how* is she become tributary!

2She weepeth sore in the night, and her tears *are* on her cheeks: among all her lovers she hath none to comfort *her:* all her friends have dealt treacherously with her, they are become her enemies.

3Judah is gone into captivity because of affliction, and because of great servitude: she dwelleth among the heathen, she findeth no rest: all her persecutors overtook her between the straits.

4The ways of Zion do mourn, because none come to the solemn feasts: all her gates are desolate: her priests sigh, her virgins are afflicted, and she *is* in bitterness.

5Her adversaries are the chief, her enemies prosper; for the LORD hath afflicted her for the multitude of her transgressions: her children are gone into captivity before the enemy.

6And from the daughter of Zion all her beauty is departed: her princes are become like harts *that* find no pasture, and they are gone without strength before the pursuer.

7Jerusalem remembered in the days of her affliction and of her miseries all her pleasant things that she had in the days of old, when her people fell into the hand of the enemy, and none did help her: the adversaries saw her, *and* did mock at her sabbaths.

## Amplified

THE

# Lamentations

OF JEREMIAH

**1** HOW SOLITARY *and* lonely sits the city [Jerusalem] that was full of people! How like a widow has she become! She who was [a]great among the nations and princess among the provinces has become a tributary—in bond service!

2She weeps bitterly in the night, and her tears are [constantly] on her cheeks; among all her lovers [allies] she has no one to comfort her; all her friends have dealt treacherously with her, they are become her enemies. [Jer. 3:1; 4:30.]

3Judah is gone into exile *to escape* from the affliction and laborious servitude *of the home land.* She dwells among the [heathen] nations, but finds no rest; all her persecutors overtook her amid the straits [of her distress].

4The roads to Zion mourn, because no one comes to the solemn assembly *or* the appointed feasts; all her gates are desolate; her priests sigh *and* groan, her maidens are grieved *and* vexed, and she herself is in bitterness.

5Her adversaries have become the head, her enemies prosper; for the Lord his afflicted her for the multitude of her transgressions; her young children have gone into captivity before the enemy. [Jer. 30:14, 15; 52:28; Dan. 9:7-14.]

6From the daughter of Zion all her beauty *and* majesty *have* departed; her princes are become like harts that find no pasture; they have fled without strength before the pursuer.

7Jerusalem [earnestly] remembers in the days of her affliction, of her [compulsory] wanderings *and* her bitterness, all the pleasant *and* precious things that she had from the days of old. When her people fell into *and* by the hand of the adversary, and there was none to help her, the enemy [gloated as they] looked at her, and they mocked at her desolations *and* downfall.

**AMP** [a] One may read the writings of the prophets only as valuable contributions to Old Testament history. And he may become enriched by familiarity with their forecasts of events which have been startlingly fulfilled, thus proclaiming the divine inspiration of the books and the wisdom and power of the God Who prompted their writings. But to stop there is by no means to grasp their full and outstanding purpose for today. Through the prophets God is speaking definitely to every individual and nation on earth, right now demanding that we see ourselves as He sees us, a world of nations and individuals tobogganing toward disaster; and He declares there is no alternative unless we repent and come to terms with Him.

## New American Standard

# Lamentations

*The Sorrows of Zion*

**1** HOW LONELY sits the city
That was full of people!
She has become like a widow
Who was *once* great among the nations!
She who was a princess among the provinces
Has become a forced laborer!
2 She weeps bitterly in the night,
And her tears are on her cheeks;
She has none to comfort her
Among all her lovers.
All her friends have dealt treacherously with her;
They have become her enemies.
3 Judah has gone into exile under affliction,
And under harsh servitude;
She dwells among the nations,
*But* she has found no rest;
All her pursuers have overtaken her
In the midst of distress.
4 The roads of Zion are in mourning
Because no one comes to the appointed feasts.
All her gates are desolate;
Her priests are groaning,
Her virgins are afflicted,
And she herself is bitter.
5 Her adversaries have become her masters,
Her enemies prosper;
For the LORD has caused her grief
Because of the multitude of her transgressions;
Her little ones have gone away
As captives before the adversary.
6 And all her majesty
Has departed from the daughter of Zion;
Her princes have become like bucks
That have found no pasture;
And they have fled without strength
Before the pursuer.
7 In the days of her affliction and homelessness
Jerusalem remembers all her precious things
That were from the days of old
When her people fell into the hand of the adversary,
And no one helped her.
The adversaries saw her,
They mocked at her ruin.

## New International

# Lamentations

**1**[b] HOW DESERTED lies the city,
once so full of people!
How like a widow is she,
who once was great among the nations!
She who was queen among the provinces
has now become a slave.

2Bitterly she weeps at night,
tears are upon her cheeks.
Among all her lovers
there is none to comfort her.
All her friends have betrayed her;
they have become her enemies.

3After affliction and harsh labor,
Judah has gone into exile.
She dwells among the nations;
she finds no resting place.
All who pursue her have overtaken her
in the midst of her distress.

4The roads to Zion mourn,
for no one comes to her appointed feasts.
All her gateways are desolate,
her priests groan,
her maidens grieve,
and she is in bitter anguish.

5Her foes have become her masters;
her enemies are at ease.
The LORD has brought her grief
because of her many sins.
Her children have gone into exile,
captive before the foe.

6All the splendor has departed
from the Daughter of Zion.
Her princes are like deer
that find no pasture;
in weakness they have fled
before the pursuer.

7In the days of her affliction and wandering
Jerusalem remembers all the treasures
that were hers in days of old.
When her people fell into enemy hands,
there was no one to help her.
Her enemies looked at her
and laughed at her destruction.

**NIV** [b] This chapter is an acrostic poem, the verses of which begin with the successive letters of the Hebrew alphabet.

## King James

8 Jerusalem hath grievously sinned; therefore she is removed: all that honoured her despise her, because they have seen her nakedness: yea, she sigheth, and turneth backward.

9 Her filthiness *is* in her skirts; she remembereth not her last end; therefore she came down wonderfully: she had no comforter. O LORD, behold my affliction: for the enemy hath magnified *himself*.

10 The adversary hath spread out his hand upon all her pleasant things: for she hath seen *that* the heathen entered into her sanctuary, whom thou didst command *that* they should not enter into thy congregation.

11 All her people sigh, they seek bread; they have given their pleasant things for meat to relieve the soul: see, O LORD, and consider; for I am become vile.

12 ¶ *Is it* nothing to you, all ye that pass by? behold, and see if there be any sorrow like unto my sorrow, which is done unto me, wherewith the LORD hath afflicted *me* in the day of his fierce anger.

13 From above hath he sent fire into my bones, and it prevaileth against them: he hath spread a net for my feet, he hath turned me back: he hath made me desolate *and* faint all the day.

14 The yoke of my transgressions is bound by his hand: they are wreathed, *and* come up upon my neck: he hath made my strength to fall, the Lord hath delivered me into *their* hands, *from whom* I am not able to rise up.

15 The Lord hath trodden under foot all my mighty *men* in the midst of me: he hath called an assembly against me to crush my young men: the Lord hath trodden the virgin, the daughter of Judah, *as* in a winepress.

16 For these *things* I weep; mine eye, mine eye runneth down with water, because the comforter that should relieve my soul is far from me: my children are desolate, because the enemy prevailed.

17 Zion spreadeth forth her hands, *and there is* none to comfort her: the LORD hath commanded concerning Jacob, *that* his adversaries *should be* round about him: Jerusalem is as a menstruous woman among them.

## Amplified

8 Jerusalem has grievously sinned; therefore she has become as an unclean thing *and* is removed. All that honored her despise her, because they have seen her nakedness; yes, she herself groans *and* sighs and turns her face away.

9 Her filthiness was in *and* on her skirts; she did not [seriously and earnestly] consider her final end; therefore she has come down [from throne to slavery] singularly *and* astonishingly; she has no comforter. O Lord [cries Jerusalem], behold my affliction, for the enemy magnifies himself *in triumph*!

10 The adversary has spread out his hand upon all her precious *and* desirable things: for she has seen the nations enter into her sanctuary [of the temple], [a]when You commanded that they should not even enter into Your congregation [in the outer courts]. [Jer. 51:51; Deut. 23:3.]

11 All her people groan *and* sigh, seeking for bread; they have given their desirable *and* precious things for food to revive their strength *and* bring back life. See, O Lord, and consider how wretched *and* lightly esteemed, how vile *and* abominable I have become!

12 Is it nothing to you, all you who pass by? Look and see if there is any sorrow like my sorrow, which is being dealt out to me, with which the Lord has afflicted me in the day of His fierce anger!

13 From above He has sent fire into my bones, and it prevails against them; He has spread a net for my feet, He has turned me back; He has made me hopelessly miserable and faint all the day long.

14 The yoke of my transgressions is bound by His hand; they are twined together; they were set upon my neck. He has made my strength to fail *and* [me to] stumble; the Lord has delivered me into the hands of those I am unable to resist *or* withstand. [Deut. 28:48.]

15 The Lord has made of no account all my [Jerusalem's] mighty men in the midst of me; He has proclaimed a set time against me to crush my young men; the Lord has trodden as in a wine press the virgin daughter of Judah.

16 For these things I weep; my eyes flow with tears, because a comforter, one who could refresh *and* restore my soul, is far from me; my children are desolate *and* perishing, for the enemy has prevailed. [Verse 21.]

17 Zion stretches forth her hands, but there is no comforter for her; the Lord has commanded concerning *and* against Jacob that his neighbors should be his adversaries; Jerusalem is as a filthy thing among them—an object of contempt.

**AMP** [a] The Ammonites and Moabites, descendants of Lot and kinsmen of Israel, were forbidden to enter the congregation of the Lord, "even to the tenth generation," because they refused assistance to the Israelites when they were fleeing from Egypt, and because they hired Balaam to curse Israel [Deut. 23:3, 4]. The Israelites themselves never assembled any closer to the sanctuary of the temple than in the court outside its door. No Jew, not even David, or Jesus Himself or any of His apostles, ever ventured into the sanctuary or temple proper, except certain Levites to whom such service was assigned. Two Greek words have customarily been translated "temple" in the New Testament. One, *hieron* always means the temple enclosure (the porches, courts, chambers, etc.); the other word, *naos*, means the sanctuary proper—the Holy Place and the Holy of Holies, into which none but the authorized priests might go, and then only at stated times. / But now, Jeremiah says, the forbidden heathen nations enter the very Holy of Holies [for plunder]! Nothing more humiliating could happen for a Jew than this.

## New American Standard

8 Jerusalem sinned greatly,
Therefore she has become an unclean thing.
All who honored her despise her
Because they have seen her nakedness;
Even she herself groans and turns away.
9 Her uncleanness was in her skirts;
She did not consider her future;
Therefore she has fallen astonishingly;
She has no comforter.
"See, O LORD, my affliction,
For the enemy has magnified himself!"
10 The adversary has stretched out his hand
Over all her precious things,
For she has seen the nations enter her sanctuary,
The ones whom Thou didst command
That they should not enter into Thy congregation.
11 All her people groan seeking bread;
They have given their precious things for food
To restore their lives themselves.
"See, O LORD, and look,
For I am despised."
12 "Is it nothing to all you who pass this way?
Look and see if there is any pain like my pain
Which was severely dealt out to me,
Which the LORD inflicted on the day of His fierce anger.
13 "From on high He sent fire into my bones,
And it prevailed *over them;*
He has spread a net for my feet;
He has turned me back;
He has made me desolate,
Faint all day long.
14 "The yoke of my transgressions is bound;
By His hand they are knit together;
They have come upon my neck;
He has made my strength fail;
The Lord has given me into the hands
Of *those against whom* I am not able to stand.
15 "The Lord has rejected all my strong men
In my midst;
He has called an appointed time against me
To crush my young men;
The Lord has trodden *as in* a wine press
The virgin daughter of Judah.
16 "For these things I weep;
My eyes run down with water;
Because far from me is a comforter,
One who restores my soul;
My children are desolate
Because the enemy has prevailed."
17 Zion stretches out her hands;
There is no one to comfort her;
The LORD has commanded concerning Jacob
That the ones round about him should be his adversaries;
Jerusalem has become an unclean thing among them.

## New International

8Jerusalem has sinned greatly
and so has become unclean.
All who honored her despise her,
for they have seen her nakedness;
she herself groans
and turns away.
9Her filthiness clung to her skirts;
she did not consider her future.
Her fall was astounding;
there was none to comfort her.
"Look, O LORD, on my affliction,
for the enemy has triumphed."
10The enemy laid hands
on all her treasures;
she saw pagan nations
enter her sanctuary—
those you had forbidden
to enter your assembly.

11All her people groan
as they search for bread;
they barter their treasures for food
to keep themselves alive.
"Look, O LORD, and consider,
for I am despised."

12"Is it nothing to you, all you who pass by?
Look around and see.
Is any suffering like my suffering
that was inflicted on me,
that the LORD brought on me
in the day of his fierce anger?

13"From on high he sent fire,
sent it down into my bones.
He spread a net for my feet
and turned me back.
He made me desolate,
faint all the day long.

14"My sins have been bound into a yoke[b];
by his hands they were woven together.
They have come upon my neck
and the Lord has sapped my strength.
He has handed me over
to those I cannot withstand.

15"The Lord has rejected
all the warriors in my midst;
he has summoned an army against me
to[c] crush my young men.
In his winepress the Lord has trampled
the Virgin Daughter of Judah.

16"This is why I weep
and my eyes overflow with tears.
No one is near to comfort me,
no one to restore my spirit.
My children are destitute
because the enemy has prevailed."

17Zion stretches out her hands,
but there is no one to comfort her.
The LORD has decreed for Jacob
that his neighbors become his foes;
Jerusalem has become
an unclean thing among them.

NIV [b] 14 Most Hebrew manuscripts; Septuagint *He kept watch over my sins*
[c] 15 Or *has set a time for me / when he will*

## King James

18¶ The LORD is righteous; for I have rebelled against his commandment: hear, I pray you, all people, and behold my sorrow: my virgins and my young men are gone into captivity.
19I called for my lovers, *but* they deceived me: my priests and mine elders gave up the ghost in the city, while they sought their meat to relieve their souls.
20Behold, O LORD; for I *am* in distress: my bowels are troubled; mine heart is turned within me; for I have grievously rebelled: abroad the sword bereaveth, at home *there is* as death.
21They have heard that I sigh: *there is* none to comfort me: all mine enemies have heard of my trouble; they are glad that thou hast done *it*: thou wilt bring the day *that* thou hast called, and they shall be like unto me.
22Let all their wickedness come before thee; and do unto them, as thou hast done unto me for all my transgressions: for my sighs *are* many, and my heart *is* faint.

2 HOW HATH the Lord covered the daughter of Zion with a cloud in his anger, *and* cast down from heaven unto the earth the beauty of Israel, and remembered not his footstool in the day of his anger!
2The Lord hath swallowed up all the habitations of Jacob, and hath not pitied: he hath thrown down in his wrath the strong holds of the daughter of Judah; he hath brought *them* down to the ground: he hath polluted the kingdom and the princes thereof.
3He hath cut off in *his* fierce anger all the horn of Israel: he hath drawn back his right hand from before the enemy, and he burned against Jacob like a flaming fire, *which* devoureth round about.
4He hath bent his bow like an enemy: he stood with his right hand as an adversary, and slew all *that were* pleasant to the eye in the tabernacle of the daughter of Zion: he poured out his fury like fire.

## Amplified

18The Lord is righteous—just and in the right; for I have rebelled against His commandment—His Word; hear, I pray you, all you peoples, and behold my sorrow *and* suffering; my maidens and my young men have gone into captivity.
19I [Jerusalem] called to my lovers [allies], but they deceived me; my priests and my elders expired in the city, while they sought food to save their lives.
20Behold, O Lord, how distressed I am! My vital parts are in tumult, my heart cannot rest *and* is violently agitated within me; for I have grievously rebelled; outside the house the sword bereaves, at home there is [famine, pestilence] death!
21[My foes] have heard that I [Jerusalem] sigh *and* groan, that I have no comforter *in You;* all my enemies have heard of my trouble. They are glad [O Lord] that You have done it. You will bring the day [of Judah's punishment] that you have foretold *and* proclaimed; [it involves also my foes' punishment] and they shall be as I am. [Isa. 14:5, 6; Jer. 30:16.]
22Let all their wickedness come before You; and deal with them as You have dealt with me because of all my transgressions; for my sighs *and* groans are many and my heart is faint.

2 HOW THE Lord covers the daughter of Zion with a cloud in His anger! He from Heaven has cast down to the earth the beauty *and* splendor of Israel, and has not [earnestly] remembered His footstool in the day of His anger!
2The Lord swallowed up all the country places *and* habitations of Jacob, and spared not *nor* pitied; He has demolished in His wrath the strongholds of the daughter of Judah; He cast down to the ground the kingdom and its rulers, polluting them *and* depriving them of their sanctity.
3He has broken off in His fierce anger every horn [means of defense] of Israel. He has drawn back His right hand from before the enemy, and He has burned amidst Jacob like a flaming fire, consuming all around.
4He has bent His bow like an enemy; He has stood with His right hand set like a foe and has slain all the delights *and* pride of the eye; on *and* in the tent of the daughter of Zion He has poured out His wrath like fire.

## New American Standard

18 "The LORD is righteous;
For I have rebelled against His command;
Hear now, all peoples,
And behold my pain;
My virgins and my young men
Have gone into captivity.
19 "I called to my lovers, *but* they deceived me;
My priests and my elders perished in the city,
While they sought food to restore their strength
themselves.
20 "See, O LORD, for I am in distress;
My spirit is greatly troubled;
My heart is overturned within me,
For I have been very rebellious.
In the street the sword slays;
In the house it is like death.
21 "They have heard that I groan;
There is no one to comfort me;
All my enemies have heard of my calamity;
They are glad that Thou hast done *it*.
Oh, that Thou wouldst bring the day which Thou hast
proclaimed,
That they may become like me.
22 "Let all their wickedness come before Thee;
And deal with them as Thou hast dealt with me
For all my transgressions;
For my groans are many, and my heart is faint."

*God's Anger over Israel*

**2** HOW THE Lord has covered the daughter of Zion
With a cloud in His anger!
He has cast from heaven to earth
The glory of Israel,
And has not remembered His footstool
In the day of His anger.
2 The Lord has swallowed up; He has not spared
All the habitations of Jacob.
In His wrath He has thrown down
The strongholds of the daughter of Judah;
He has brought *them* down to the ground;
He has profaned the kingdom and its princes.
3 In fierce anger He has cut off
All the strength of Israel;
He has drawn back His right hand
From before the enemy.
And He has burned in Jacob like a flaming fire
Consuming round about.
4 He has bent His bow like an enemy,
He has set His right hand like an adversary
And slain all that were pleasant to the eye;
In the tent of the daughter of Zion
He has poured out His wrath like fire.

## New International

18 "The LORD is righteous,
yet I rebelled against his command.
Listen, all you peoples;
look upon my suffering.
My young men and maidens
have gone into exile.

19 "I called to my allies
but they betrayed me.
My priests and my elders
perished in the city
while they searched for food
to keep themselves alive.

20 "See, O LORD, how distressed I am!
I am in torment within,
and in my heart I am disturbed,
for I have been most rebellious.
Outside, the sword bereaves;
inside, there is only death.

21 "People have heard my groaning,
but there is no one to comfort me.
All my enemies have heard of my distress;
they rejoice at what you have done.
May you bring the day you have announced
so they may become like me.

22 "Let all their wickedness come before you;
deal with them
as you have dealt with me
because of all my sins.
My groans are many
and my heart is faint."

**2**[a] HOW THE Lord has covered the Daughter of Zion
with the cloud of his anger[b]!
He has hurled down the splendor of Israel
from heaven to earth;
he has not remembered his footstool
in the day of his anger.

2 Without pity the Lord has swallowed up
all the dwellings of Jacob;
in his wrath he has torn down
the strongholds of the Daughter of Judah.
He has brought her kingdom and its princes
down to the ground in dishonor.

3 In fierce anger he has cut off
every horn[c] of Israel.
He has withdrawn his right hand
at the approach of the enemy.
He has burned in Jacob like a flaming fire
that consumes everything around it.

4 Like an enemy he has strung his bow;
his right hand is ready.
Like a foe he has slain
all who were pleasing to the eye;
he has poured out his wrath like fire
on the tent of the Daughter of Zion.

**NIV** [a] This chapter is an acrostic poem, the verses of which begin with the successive letters of the Hebrew alphabet. [b] 1 Or *How the Lord in his anger / has treated the Daughter of Zion with contempt* [c] 3 Or / *all the strength;* or *every king; horn* here symbolizes strength.

## King James

5 The Lord was as an enemy: he hath swallowed up Israel, he hath swallowed up all her palaces: he hath destroyed his strong holds, and hath increased in the daughter of Judah mourning and lamentation.

6 And he hath violently taken away his tabernacle, as *if it were of* a garden: he hath destroyed his places of the assembly: the LORD hath caused the solemn feasts and sabbaths to be forgotten in Zion, and hath despised in the indignation of his anger the king and the priest.

7 The Lord hath cast off his altar, he hath abhorred his sanctuary, he hath given up into the hand of the enemy the walls of her palaces; they have made a noise in the house of the LORD, as in the day of a solemn feast.

8 The LORD hath purposed to destroy the wall of the daughter of Zion: he hath stretched out a line, he hath not withdrawn his hand from destroying: therefore he made the rampart and the wall to lament; they languished together.

9 Her gates are sunk into the ground; he hath destroyed and broken her bars: her king and her princes *are* among the Gentiles: the law *is no more;* her prophets also find no vision from the LORD.

10 The elders of the daughter of Zion sit upon the ground, *and* keep silence: they have cast up dust upon their heads; they have girded themselves with sackcloth: the virgins of Jerusalem hang down their heads to the ground.

11 Mine eyes do fail with tears, my bowels are troubled, my liver is poured upon the earth, for the destruction of the daughter of my people; because the children and the sucklings swoon in the streets of the city.

12 They say to their mothers, Where *is* corn and wine? when they swooned as the wounded in the streets of the city, when their soul was poured out into their mothers' bosom.

13 What thing shall I take to witness for thee? what thing shall I liken to thee, O daughter of Jerusalem? what shall I equal to thee, that I may comfort thee, O virgin daughter of Zion? for thy breach *is* great like the sea: who can heal thee?

14 Thy prophets have seen vain and foolish things for thee: and they have not discovered thine iniquity, to turn away thy captivity; but have seen for thee false burdens and causes of banishment.

## Amplified

5 The Lord has become like an enemy, He has destroyed Israel; He has destroyed all its palaces, laid in ruins its strongholds, and has multiplied in the daughter of Judah groaning and moaning lamentation.

6 And He has violently broken down His temple like a booth *or* hedge of a garden. He has destroyed the place of His appointed festivals; the Lord has caused the solemn assembly and sabbaths to be forgotten in Zion, and has spurned *and* rejected in the indignation of His anger the king and the priest.

7 The Lord has scorned, rejected *and* cast off His altar, He has abhorred *and* disowned His sanctuary, He has given up into the hand of the enemy the walls of her palaces [and high buildings]; they have raised a clamor in the house of the Lord as on a day of a solemn feast.

8 The Lord purposed to lay in ruins the *city* wall of the daughter of Zion. He marked it off by line; He restrained not His hand from destroying; He made rampart and wall to lament, they languish together.

9 Her gates have sunk into the ground; He has destroyed and broken her bars; her king and her princes are among the nations; the law is no more; her prophets also obtain no vision from the Lord.

10 The elders of the daughter of Zion sit on the ground, keeping silence; they have cast up dust on their heads, they have girded themselves with sackcloth; the maidens of Jerusalem have bowed their heads to the ground [says Jeremiah].

11 My eyes fail from weeping, my emotions are deeply disturbed, my heart is poured upon the ground [in grief] because of the destruction of the daughter of my people, because infants and nurslings faint in the streets of the city.

12 They keep crying to their mothers, Where is corn and wine—food and drink? as they faint like wounded men in the streets of the city, while their life is ebbed away on their mothers' bosom.

13 What [example of suffering in the past] is sufficient for me to remind you for your *comfort*? To what shall I liken you, O daughter of Jerusalem? What shall I compare with you, that I may comfort you, O virgin daughter of Zion? For your ruin is measureless as the sea! Who can heal you? [Lam. 1:12; Dan. 9:12.]

14 Your prophets have predicted for you falsehood and delusion *and* foolish things. And they have not exposed your iniquity *and* guilt, to avert your captivity [by causing you to repent]; but they have divined *and* declared to you false *and* deceptive prophecies, worthless *and* misleading.

## New American Standard

5 The Lord has become like an enemy.
He has swallowed up Israel;
He has swallowed up all its palaces;
He has destroyed its strongholds
And multiplied in the daughter of Judah
Mourning and moaning.
6 And He has violently treated His tabernacle like a garden *booth;*
He has destroyed His appointed meeting place;
The LORD has caused to be forgotten
The appointed feast and sabbath in Zion,
And He has despised king and priest
In the indignation of His anger.
7 The Lord has rejected His altar,
He has abandoned His sanctuary;
He has delivered into the hand of the enemy
The walls of her palaces.
They have made a noise in the house of the LORD
As in the day of an appointed feast.
8 The LORD determined to destroy
The wall of the daughter of Zion.
He has stretched out a line,
He has not restrained His hand from destroying;
And He has caused rampart and wall to lament;
They have languished together.
9 Her gates have sunk into the ground,
He has destroyed and broken her bars.
Her king and her princes are among the nations;
The law is no more;
Also, her prophets find
No vision from the LORD.
10 The elders of the daughter of Zion
Sit on the ground, they are silent.
They have thrown dust on their heads;
They have girded themselves with sackcloth.
The virgins of Jerusalem
Have bowed their heads to the ground.
11 My eyes fail because of tears,
My spirit is greatly troubled;
My heart is poured out on the earth,
Because of the destruction of the daughter of my people,
When little ones and infants faint
In the streets of the city.
12 They say to their mothers,
"Where is grain and wine?"
As they faint like a wounded man
In the streets of the city,
As their life is poured out
On their mothers' bosom.
13 How shall I admonish you?
To what shall I compare you,
O daughter of Jerusalem?
To what shall I liken you as I comfort you,
O virgin daughter of Zion?
For your ruin is as vast as the sea;
Who can heal you?
14 Your prophets have seen for you
False and foolish *visions;*
And they have not exposed your iniquity
So as to restore you from captivity,
But they have seen for you false and misleading oracles.

## New International

5The Lord is like an enemy;
he has swallowed up Israel.
He has swallowed up all her palaces
and destroyed her strongholds.
He has multiplied mourning and lamentation
for the Daughter of Judah.

6He has laid waste his dwelling like a garden;
he has destroyed his place of meeting.
The LORD has made Zion forget
her appointed feasts and her Sabbaths;
in his fierce anger he has spurned
both king and priest.

7The Lord has rejected his altar
and abandoned his sanctuary.
He has handed over to the enemy
the walls of her palaces;
they have raised a shout in the house of the LORD
as on the day of an appointed feast.

8The LORD determined to tear down
the wall around the Daughter of Zion.
He stretched out a measuring line
and did not withhold his hand from destroying.
He made ramparts and walls lament;
together they wasted away.

9Her gates have sunk into the ground;
their bars he has broken and destroyed.
Her king and her princes are exiled among the nations,
the law is no more,
and her prophets no longer find
visions from the LORD.

10The elders of the Daughter of Zion
sit on the ground in silence;
they have sprinkled dust on their heads
and put on sackcloth.
The young women of Jerusalem
have bowed their heads to the ground.

11My eyes fail from weeping,
I am in torment within,
my heart is poured out on the ground
because my people are destroyed,
because children and infants faint
in the streets of the city.

12They say to their mothers,
"Where is bread and wine?"
as they faint like wounded men
in the streets of the city,
as their lives ebb away
in their mothers' arms.

13What can I say for you?
With what can I compare you,
O Daughter of Jerusalem?
To what can I liken you,
that I may comfort you,
O Virgin Daughter of Zion?
Your wound is as deep as the sea.
Who can heal you?

14The visions of your prophets
were false and worthless;
they did not expose your sin
to ward off your captivity.
The oracles they gave you
were false and misleading.

## King James

15 All that pass by clap *their* hands at thee; they hiss and wag their head at the daughter of Jerusalem, *saying, Is* this the city that *men* call The perfection of beauty, The joy of the whole earth?

16 All thine enemies have opened their mouth against thee: they hiss and gnash the teeth: they say, We have swallowed *her* up: certainly this *is* the day that we looked for; we have found, we have seen *it*.

17 The LORD hath done *that* which he had devised; he hath fulfilled his word that he had commanded in the days of old: he hath thrown down, and hath not pitied: and he hath caused *thine* enemy to rejoice over thee, he hath set up the horn of thine adversaries.

18 Their heart cried unto the Lord, O wall of the daughter of Zion, let tears run down like a river day and night: give thyself no rest: let not the apple of thine eye cease.

19 Arise, cry out in the night: in the beginning of the watches pour out thine heart like water before the face of the Lord: lift up thy hands toward him for the life of thy young children, that faint for hunger in the top of every street.

20 ¶ Behold, O LORD, and consider to whom thou hast done this. Shall the women eat their fruit, *and* children of a span long? shall the priest and the prophet be slain in the sanctuary of the Lord?

21 The young and the old lie on the ground in the streets: my virgins and my young men are fallen by the sword; thou hast slain *them* in the day of thine anger; thou hast killed, *and* not pitied.

22 Thou hast called as in a solemn day my terrors round about, so that in the day of the LORD's anger none escaped nor remained: those that I have swaddled and brought up hath mine enemy consumed.

**3** I *AM* the man *that* hath seen affliction by the rod of his wrath.

2 He hath led me, and brought *me into* darkness, but not *into* light.

3 Surely against me is he turned; he turneth his hand *against me* all the day.

## Amplified

15 All who pass by clap their hands at you; they hiss and wag their heads at the daughter of Jerusalem, saying, Is this the city which was called the perfection of beauty, the joy of all the earth?

16 All your enemies have opened wide their mouths against you; they scornfully hiss and gnash their teeth; they cry, We have swallowed her up! Certainly this is the day we have looked for; we have it; we see it!

17 The Lord has done what He planned; He has carried out *and* finished His word that He threatened *and* decreed [a]in the days of old; He has demolished without pity; He has made the enemy rejoice over you, and exalted the might of your foes. [Lev. 26:14-39; Deut. 28:15-68.]

18 The heart [of the inhabitants of Jerusalem] cried to the Lord. [Then to the congregation, I, Jeremiah, cried, addressing the wall as its symbol] O wall of the daughter of Zion, let tears run down like a river day and night, give yourself no rest, let not your eyes stop [shedding tears].

19 Arise *from your bed*, cry out in the night, at the beginning of the watches. Pour out your heart like water before the face of the Lord; lift up your hands toward Him for the life of your young children, who faint with hunger at the corner of every street. [Ps. 62:8.]

20 Behold, O Lord, and consider [carefully] to whom You have done this. Should *and* shall the women eat the fruit of their own bodies, the children whom they have tended *and* swaddled with their hands? Shall priest and prophet be slain in the place set apart [for the worship] of the Lord?

21 The young and the old lie on the ground in the streets; my maidens and my young men have fallen by the sword; You have slain them in the day of Your anger, slaughtering them without pity.

22 You, [Lord,] called together, as on an appointed day of solemn assembly, my terrors [dangers] from every side; and there was not one in the day of God's wrath who escaped or survived. Those I have nursed and brought up my enemy has destroyed.

**3** I AM [Jeremiah], the man who has seen affliction under the rod of His wrath.

2 He has led me, and brought me into darkness, and not light.

3 Surely He has turned away from me; His hand is against me all the day.

**AMP** [a] "This reference to the ancient predictions against Israel for their sins, is of great importance; both as it shows that these prophecies were then extant and well-known among the Jews, and that they were understood by the pious remnant exactly as we now explain them." (Scott, quoted in Lange's Commentary.)

## New American Standard

15 All who pass along the way
Clap their hands *in derision* at you;
They hiss and shake their heads
At the daughter of Jerusalem,
"Is this the city of which they said,
'The perfection of beauty,
A joy to all the earth'?"
16 All your enemies
Have opened their mouths wide against you;
They hiss and gnash *their* teeth.
They say, "We have swallowed *her* up!
Surely this is the day for which we waited;
We have reached *it*, we have seen *it*."
17 The LORD has done what He purposed;
He has accomplished His word
Which He commanded from days of old.
He has thrown down without sparing,
And He has caused the enemy to rejoice over you;
He has exalted the might of your adversaries.
18 Their heart cried out to the Lord,
"O wall of the daughter of Zion,
Let *your* tears run down like a river day and night;
Give yourself no relief;
Let your eyes have no rest.
19 "Arise, cry aloud in the night
At the beginning of the night watches;
Pour out your heart like water
Before the presence of the Lord;
Lift up your hands to Him
For the life of your little ones
Who are faint because of hunger
At the head of every street."
20 See, O LORD, and look!
With whom hast Thou dealt thus?
Should women eat their offspring,
The little ones who were born healthy?
Should priest and prophet be slain
In the sanctuary of the Lord?
21 On the ground in the streets
Lie young and old,
My virgins and my young men
Have fallen by the sword.
Thou hast slain *them* in the day of Thine anger,
Thou hast slaughtered, not sparing.
22 Thou didst call as in the day of an appointed feast
My terrors on every side;
And there was no one who escaped or survived
In the day of the LORD's anger.
Those whom I bore and reared,
My enemy annihilated them.

*Jeremiah Shares Israel's Affliction*

3 I AM the man who has seen affliction
Because of the rod of His wrath.
2 He has driven me and made me walk
In darkness and not in light.
3 Surely against me He has turned His hand
Repeatedly all the day.

## New International

15 All who pass your way
clap their hands at you;
they scoff and shake their heads
at the Daughter of Jerusalem:
"Is this the city that was called
the perfection of beauty,
the joy of the whole earth?"

16 All your enemies open their mouths
wide against you;
they scoff and gnash their teeth
and say, "We have swallowed her up.
This is the day we have waited for;
we have lived to see it."

17 The LORD has done what he planned;
he has fulfilled his word,
which he decreed long ago.
He has overthrown you without pity,
he has let the enemy gloat over you,
he has exalted the horn[b] of your foes.

18 The hearts of the people
cry out to the Lord.
O wall of the Daughter of Zion,
let your tears flow like a river
day and night;
give yourself no relief,
your eyes no rest.
19 Arise, cry out in the night,
as the watches of the night begin;
pour out your heart like water
in the presence of the Lord.
Lift up your hands to him
for the lives of your children,
who faint from hunger
at the head of every street.

20 "Look, O LORD, and consider:
Whom have you ever treated like this?
Should women eat their offspring,
the children they have cared for?
Should priest and prophet be killed
in the sanctuary of the Lord?
21 "Young and old lie together
in the dust of the streets;
my young men and maidens
have fallen by the sword.
You have slain them in the day of your anger;
you have slaughtered them without pity.
22 "As you summon to a feast day,
so you summoned against me terrors on every side.
In the day of the LORD's anger
no one escaped or survived;
those I cared for and reared,
my enemy has destroyed."

3[c] I AM the man who has seen affliction
by the rod of his wrath.
2 He has driven me away and made me walk
in darkness rather than light;
3 indeed, he has turned his hand against me
again and again, all day long.

NIV [b] 17 *Horn* here symbolizes strength. [c] This chapter is an acrostic poem; the verses of each stanza begin with the successive letters of the Hebrew alphabet, and the verses within each stanza begin with the same letter.

## King James

4My flesh and my skin hath he made old; he hath broken my bones.
5He hath builded against me, and compassed *me* with gall and travail.
6He hath set me in dark places, as *they that be* dead of old.
7He hath hedged me about, that I cannot get out: he hath made my chain heavy.
8Also when I cry and shout, he shutteth out my prayer.
9He hath inclosed my ways with hewn stone, he hath made my paths crooked.
10He *was* unto me *as* a bear lying in wait, *and as* a lion in secret places.
11He hath turned aside my ways, and pulled me in pieces: he hath made me desolate.
12He hath bent his bow, and set me as a mark for the arrow.
13He hath caused the arrows of his quiver to enter into my reins.
14I was a derision to all my people; *and* their song all the day.
15He hath filled me with bitterness, he hath made me drunken with wormwood.
16He hath also broken my teeth with gravel stones, he hath covered me with ashes.
17And thou hast removed my soul far off from peace: I forgat prosperity.
18And I said, My strength and my hope is perished from the LORD:
19Remembering mine affliction and my misery, the wormwood and the gall.
20My soul hath *them* still in remembrance, and is humbled in me.
21This I recall to my mind, therefore have I hope.
22¶ *It is of* the LORD's mercies that we are not consumed, because his compassions fail not.
23 *They are* new every morning: great *is* thy faithfulness.
24The LORD *is* my portion, saith my soul; therefore will I hope in him.
25The LORD *is* good unto them that wait for him, to the soul *that* seeketh him.
26 *It is* good that *a man* should both hope and quietly wait for the salvation of the LORD.
27 *It is* good for a man that he bear the yoke in his youth.
28He sitteth alone and keepeth silence, because he hath borne *it* upon him.
29He putteth his mouth in the dust; if so be there may be hope.
30He giveth *his* cheek to him that smiteth him: he is filled full with reproach.
31For the Lord will not cast off for ever:
32But though he cause grief, yet will he have compassion according to the multitude of his mercies.
33For he doth not afflict willingly nor grieve the children of men.
34To crush under his feet all the prisoners of the earth,
35To turn aside the right of a man before the face of the most High,

## Amplified

4My flesh and my skin has He worn out *and* made old; He has shattered my bones.
5He has built up [siege mounds] against me, and surrounded me with bitterness, tribulation *and* anguish.
6He has caused me to dwell in dark places, as those long dead.
7He walled me about, so that I cannot get out; He has weighted down my chain.
8Also when I cry and shout for help, He shuts out my prayer.
9He has enclosed my ways with hewn stone, He has made my paths crooked.
10He is to me like a bear lying in wait, and like a lion *hiding* in secret places.
11He has turned me off my ways, and pulled me in pieces; He has made me desolate.
12He has bent His bow, and set me as a mark for the arrow.
13He has caused the arrows of His quiver to enter into my heart [the seat of my affections and desires].
14I have become a derision to all my people; and [the subject of] their singsong all the day.
15He has filled me with bitterness, He has made me drink to excess *and* until drunken with wormwood—bitterness.
16He has also broken my teeth with gravel stones, He has covered me with ashes.
17And You have bereft my soul *and* cast it off far from peace; I have forgotten what good *and* happiness *are.*
18And I say, Perished is my strength and my expectation from the Lord.
19[O Lord] remember [earnestly] my affliction and my misery, my wandering *and* outcast state, the wormwood and the gall.
20My soul has them continually in remembrance and is bowed down within me.
21But this I recall, therefore have I hope *and* expectation:
22It is of the Lord's mercies *and* loving-kindnesses that we are not consumed, because His (tender) compassions fail not. [Mal. 3:6.]
23They are new every morning; great *and* abundant is Your stability *and* faithfulness. [Isa. 33:2.]
24The Lord is my portion *or* share, says my living being; therefore will I hope in Him *and* expectantly wait for Him. [Num. 18:20.]
25The Lord is good to those who hopefully *and* expectantly wait for Him, to those who seek Him—inquire of and for Him, and require Him [by right of necessity and on the authority of God's Word].
26It is good that one should hope *and* wait quietly for the salvation—the safety and ease—of the Lord.
27It is good for a man that he bear the yoke [of divine disciplinary dealings] in his youth.
28Let him sit alone uncomplaining *and* silent *in hope,* because *God* has laid *the yoke* upon him [for his benefit]. [Rom. 8:28.]
29Let him put his mouth in the dust [in abject recognition of his unworthiness]; there may yet be hope. [Mic. 7:17.]
30Let him give his cheek to the One Who smites him [even through His human agents]; let him be filled full with *men's* reproach [in meekness].
31For the Lord will not cast off for ever! [Ps. 94:14.]
32But, though He causes grief, yet will He be moved to compassion according to the multitude of His loving-kindnesses *and* tender mercies.
33For He does not willingly *and* from His heart afflict or grieve the children of men. [Heb. 12:5-10.]
34To trample *and* crush under foot all the prisoners of the earth,
35To turn aside *and* deprive a man of his rights before the face of the Most High *or* a superior,

## New American Standard

4 He has caused my flesh and my skin to waste away,
He has broken my bones.
5 He has besieged and encompassed me with bitterness
and hardship.
6 In dark places He has made me dwell,
Like those who have long been dead.
7 He has walled *me* in so that I cannot go out;
He has made my chain heavy.
8 Even when I cry out and call for help,
He shuts out my prayer.
9 He has blocked my ways with hewn stone;
He has made my paths crooked.
10 He is to me like a bear lying in wait,
*Like* a lion in secret places.
11 He has turned aside my ways and torn me to pieces;
He has made me desolate.
12 He bent His bow
And set me as a target for the arrow.
13 He made the arrows of His quiver
To enter into my inward parts.
14 I have become a laughingstock to all my people,
Their *mocking* song all the day.
15 He has filled me with bitterness,
He has made me drunk with wormwood.
16 And He has broken my teeth with gravel;
He has made me cower in the dust.
17 And my soul has been rejected from peace;
I have forgotten happiness.
18 So I say, "My strength has perished,
And *so has* my hope from the LORD."

*Hope of Relief in God's Mercy*

19¶ Remember my affliction and my wandering, the
wormwood and bitterness.
20 Surely my soul remembers
And is bowed down within me.
21 This I recall to my mind,
Therefore I have hope.
22 The LORD's lovingkindnesses indeed never cease,
For His compassions never fail.
23 *They* are new every morning;
Great is Thy faithfulness.
24 "The LORD is my portion," says my soul,
"Therefore I have hope in Him."
25 The LORD is good to those who wait for Him,
To the person who seeks Him.
26 *It is* good that he waits silently
For the salvation of the LORD.
27 *It is* good for a man that he should bear
The yoke in his youth.
28 Let him sit alone and be silent
Since He has laid *it* on him.
29 Let him put his mouth in the dust,
Perhaps there is hope.
30 Let him give his cheek to the smiter;
Let him be filled with reproach.
31 For the Lord will not reject forever,
32 For if He causes grief,
Then He will have compassion
According to His abundant lovingkindness.
33 For He does not afflict willingly,
Or grieve the sons of men.
34 To crush under His feet
All the prisoners of the land,
35 To deprive a man of justice
In the presence of the Most High,

## New International

4 He has made my skin and my flesh grow old
and has broken my bones.
5 He has besieged me and surrounded me
with bitterness and hardship.
6 He has made me dwell in darkness
like those long dead.

7 He has walled me in so I cannot escape;
he has weighed me down with chains.
8 Even when I call out or cry for help,
he shuts out my prayer.
9 He has barred my way with blocks of stone;
he has made my paths crooked.
10 Like a bear lying in wait,
like a lion in hiding,
11 he dragged me from the path and mangled me
and left me without help.
12 He drew his bow
and made me the target for his arrows.

13 He pierced my heart
with arrows from his quiver.
14 I became the laughingstock of all my people;
they mock me in song all day long.
15 He has filled me with bitter herbs
and sated me with gall.

16 He has broken my teeth with gravel;
he has trampled me in the dust.
17 I have been deprived of peace;
I have forgotten what prosperity is.
18 So I say, "My splendor is gone
and all that I had hoped from the LORD."
19 I remember my affliction and my wandering,
the bitterness and the gall.
20 I well remember them,
and my soul is downcast within me.
21 Yet this I call to mind
and therefore I have hope:
22 Because of the LORD's great love we are not consumed,
for his compassions never fail.
23 They are new every morning;
great is your faithfulness.
24 I say to myself, "The LORD is my portion;
therefore I will wait for him."

25 The LORD is good to those whose hope is in him,
to the one who seeks him;
26 it is good to wait quietly
for the salvation of the LORD.
27 It is good for a man to bear the yoke
while he is young.

28 Let him sit alone in silence,
for the LORD has laid it on him.
29 Let him bury his face in the dust—
there may yet be hope.
30 Let him offer his cheek to one who would strike him,
and let him be filled with disgrace.

31 For men are not cast off
by the Lord forever.
32 Though he brings grief, he will show compassion,
so great is his unfailing love.
33 For he does not willingly bring affliction
or grief to the children of men.

34 To crush underfoot
all prisoners in the land,
35 to deny a man his rights
before the Most High,

## King James

36 To subvert a man in his cause, the Lord approveth not.

37 ¶ Who *is* he *that* saith, and it cometh to pass, *when* the Lord commandeth *it* not?

38 Out of the mouth of the most High proceedeth not evil and good?

39 Wherefore doth a living man complain, a man for the punishment of his sins?

40 Let us search and try our ways, and turn again to the LORD.

41 Let us lift up our heart with *our* hands unto God in the heavens.

42 We have transgressed and have rebelled: thou hast not pardoned.

43 Thou hast covered with anger, and persecuted us: thou hast slain, thou hast not pitied.

44 Thou hast covered thyself with a cloud, that *our* prayer should not pass through.

45 Thou hast made us *as* the offscouring and refuse in the midst of the people.

46 All our enemies have opened their mouths against us.

47 Fear and a snare is come upon us, desolation and destruction.

48 Mine eye runneth down with rivers of water for the destruction of the daughter of my people.

49 Mine eye trickleth down, and ceaseth not, without any intermission,

50 Till the LORD look down, and behold from heaven.

51 Mine eye affecteth mine heart because of all the daughters of my city.

52 Mine enemies chased me sore, like a bird, without cause.

53 They have cut off my life in the dungeon, and cast a stone upon me.

54 Waters flowed over mine head; *then* I said, I am cut off.

55 ¶ I called upon thy name, O LORD, out of the low dungeon.

56 Thou hast heard my voice: hide not thine ear at my breathing, at my cry.

57 Thou drewest near in the day *that* I called upon thee: thou saidst, Fear not.

58 O Lord, thou hast pleaded the causes of my soul; thou hast redeemed my life.

59 O LORD, thou hast seen my wrong: judge thou my cause.

60 Thou hast seen all their vengeance *and* all their imaginations against me.

61 Thou hast heard their reproach, O LORD, *and* all their imaginations against me;

62 The lips of those that rose up against me, and their device against me all the day.

63 Behold their sitting down, and their rising up; I *am* their music.

64 ¶ Render unto them a recompence, O LORD, according to the work of their hands.

65 Give them sorrow of heart, thy curse unto them.

66 Persecute and destroy them in anger from under the heavens of the LORD.

## Amplified

36 To subvert a man in his cause, the Lord does not approve.

37 Who is he who spoke and it came to pass, when the Lord has not authorized *and* commanded it?

38 Is it not out of the mouth of the Most High that evil and good *both* proceed—adversity and prosperity, physical evil or misfortune and physical good or happiness?

39 Why does a living man sigh [one who is still in this life's school of discipline]? *And why does he* complain, a man for the punishment of his sins?

40 Let us test and examine our ways, and return to the Lord!

41 Let us lift up our hearts to our hands [and then with them mount up in prayer] to God in Heaven:

42 We have transgressed and rebelled, and You have not pardoned.

43 You have covered Yourself with wrath and pursued *and* afflicted us; You have slain without pity.

44 You have covered Yourself with a cloud so that no prayer can pass through.

45 You have made us an offscouring and refuse among the nations.

46 All our enemies gape at us *and* rail against us.

47 Fear and pitfall have come upon us, devastation and destruction.

48 My eyes overflow with streams of tears because of the destruction of the daughter of my people.

49 My eyes overflow continually and will not cease

50 Until the Lord looks down and beholds from Heaven.

51 My eyes cause me grief at the fate of all the maidens *and* the daughter-towns of my city [Jerusalem].

52 I have been hunted down like a bird by those who were my enemies without cause.

53 They [thought they had] destroyed my life in the dungeon (pit), and cast a stone [over it] above me. [Jer. 38.]

54 Water ran down on my head; I said, I am gone.

55 I called upon Your name, O Lord, out of the depths [of the mire] of the dungeon. [Jer. 38:6.]

56 You heard my voice *then;* O hide not Your ear *now* at my prayer *for relief.*

57 You drew near on the day I called to You; You said, Fear not. [James 4:8.]

58 O Lord, You have pleaded the causes of my soul [You have managed my affairs and You have protected my person and my rights]; You have rescued *and* redeemed my life!

59 O Lord, You have seen my wrong; judge *and* maintain my cause.

60 You have seen all their vengeance, all their devices against me.

61 You have heard their reproach *and* revilings, O Lord, and all their devices against me;

62 The lips *and* thoughts of my assailants are against me all day long.

63 Behold their sitting down and their rising up [their movements, doings, and secret counsels]; I am their singsong [the subject of their derision and merriment].

64 Render to them a recompense, O Lord, according to the work of their hands.

65 You will give them hardness *and* blindness of heart, Your curse *will be* upon them.

66 You will pursue *and* afflict them in anger, and destroy them from under Your heavens, O Lord.

## New American Standard

36 To defraud a man in his lawsuit—
Of these things the Lord does not approve.
37 Who is there who speaks and it comes to pass,
Unless the Lord has commanded *it*?
38 *Is it* not from the mouth of the Most High
That both good and ill go forth?
39¶ Why should *any* living mortal, or *any* man,
Offer complaint in view of his sins?
40 Let us examine and probe our ways,
And let us return to the LORD.
41 We lift up our heart and hands
Toward God in heaven;
42 We have transgressed and rebelled,
Thou hast not pardoned.
43 Thou hast covered *Thyself* with anger
And pursued us;
Thou hast slain *and* hast not spared.
44 Thou hast covered Thyself with a cloud
So that no prayer can pass through.
45 *Mere* offscouring and refuse Thou hast made us
In the midst of the peoples.
46 All our enemies have opened their mouths against us.
47 Panic and pitfall have befallen us,
Devastation and destruction;
48 My eyes run down with streams of water
Because of the destruction of the daughter of my people.
49 My eyes pour down unceasingly,
Without stopping,
50 Until the LORD looks down
And sees from heaven.
51 My eyes bring pain to my soul
Because of all the daughters of my city.
52 My enemies without cause
Hunted me down like a bird;
53 They have silenced me in the pit
And have placed a stone on me.
54 Waters flowed over my head;
I said, "I am cut off!"
55 I called on Thy name, O LORD,
Out of the lowest pit.
56 Thou hast heard my voice,
"Do not hide Thine ear from my *prayer for* relief,
From my cry for help."
57 Thou didst draw near when I called on Thee;
Thou didst say, "Do not fear!"
58 O Lord, Thou didst plead my soul's cause;
Thou hast redeemed my life.
59 O LORD, Thou hast seen my oppression;
Judge my case.
60 Thou hast seen all their vengeance,
All their schemes against me.
61 Thou hast heard their reproach, O LORD,
All their schemes against me.
62 The lips of my assailants and their whispering
*Are* against me all day long.
63 Look on their sitting and their rising;
I am their mocking song.
64 Thou wilt recompense them, O LORD,
According to the work of their hands.
65 Thou wilt give them hardness of heart,
Thy curse will be on them.
66 Thou wilt pursue them in anger and destroy them
From under the heavens of the LORD!

## New International

36to deprive a man of justice—
would not the Lord see such things?
37Who can speak and have it happen
if the Lord has not decreed it?
38Is it not from the mouth of the Most High
that both calamities and good things come?
39Why should any living man complain
when punished for his sins?
40Let us examine our ways and test them,
and let us return to the LORD.
41Let us lift up our hearts and our hands
to God in heaven, and say:
42"We have sinned and rebelled
and you have not forgiven.
43"You have covered yourself with anger and pursued us;
you have slain without pity.
44You have covered yourself with a cloud
so that no prayer can get through.
45You have made us scum and refuse
among the nations.
46"All our enemies have opened their mouths
wide against us.
47We have suffered terror and pitfalls,
ruin and destruction."
48Streams of tears flow from my eyes
because my people are destroyed.
49My eyes will flow unceasingly,
without relief,
50until the LORD looks down
from heaven and sees.
51What I see brings grief to my soul
because of all the women of my city.
52Those who were my enemies without cause
hunted me like a bird.
53They tried to end my life in a pit
and threw stones at me;
54the waters closed over my head,
and I thought I was about to be cut off.
55I called on your name, O LORD,
from the depths of the pit.
56You heard my plea: "Do not close your ears
to my cry for relief."
57You came near when I called you,
and you said, "Do not fear."
58O Lord, you took up my case;
you redeemed my life.
59You have seen, O LORD, the wrong done to me.
Uphold my cause!
60You have seen the depth of their vengeance,
all their plots against me.
61O LORD, you have heard their insults,
all their plots against me—
62what my enemies whisper and mutter
against me all day long.
63Look at them! Sitting or standing,
they mock me in their songs.
64Pay them back what they deserve, O LORD,
for what their hands have done.
65Put a veil over their hearts,
and may your curse be on them!
66Pursue them in anger and destroy them
from under the heavens of the LORD.

# King James

**4** HOW IS the gold become dim! *how* is the most fine gold changed! the stones of the sanctuary are poured out in the top of every street.

2 The precious sons of Zion, comparable to fine gold, how are they esteemed as earthen pitchers, the work of the hands of the potter!

3 Even the sea monsters draw out the breast, they give suck to their young ones: the daughter of my people *is become* cruel, like the ostriches in the wilderness.

4 The tongue of the sucking child cleaveth to the roof of his mouth for thirst: the young children ask bread, *and* no man breaketh *it* unto them.

5 They that did feed delicately are desolate in the streets: they that were brought up in scarlet embrace dunghills.

6 For the punishment of the iniquity of the daughter of my people is greater than the punishment of the sin of Sodom, that was overthrown as in a moment, and no hands stayed on her.

7 Her Nazarites were purer than snow, they were whiter than milk, they were more ruddy in body than rubies, their polishing *was* of sapphire:

8 Their visage is blacker than a coal; they are not known in the streets: their skin cleaveth to their bones; it is withered, it is become like a stick.

9 *They that be* slain with the sword are better than *they that be* slain with hunger: for these pine away, stricken through for *want of* the fruits of the field.

10 The hands of the pitiful women have sodden their own children: they were their meat in the destruction of the daughter of my people.

11 The LORD hath accomplished his fury; he hath poured out his fierce anger, and hath kindled a fire in Zion, and it hath devoured the foundations thereof.

12 The kings of the earth, and all the inhabitants of the world, would not have believed that the adversary and the enemy should have entered into the gates of Jerusalem.

13 ¶ For the sins of her prophets, *and* the iniquities of her priests, that have shed the blood of the just in the midst of her,

14 They have wandered *as* blind *men* in the streets, they have polluted themselves with blood, so that men could not touch their garments.

# Amplified

**4** HOW THE gold has become dim! How the most pure gold is changed! The hallowed stones *of the temple* are poured out at the head of every street.

2 The noble *and* precious sons of Zion, worth their weight in fine gold, how they are esteemed [merely] as earthen pots *or* pitchers, the work of the hands of the potter! [Isa. 30:14; Jer. 19:11; II Cor. 4:7.]

3 Even the jackals draw out the breast, they give suck to their young ones, but the daughter of my people has become cruel, like the ostriches in the wilderness [that desert their young].

4 The tongue of the nursing babe cleaves to the roof of its mouth for thirst; the young children beg for food, but no one gives it to them.

5 They who feasted on dainties are perishing in the streets; they who were brought up in purple lie cleaving to refuse *and* ash heaps.

6 For the punishment of the iniquity of the daughter of my people is greater than the punishment of the sin of Sodom, that was overthrown as in a moment, and no hands had come against her *or* been laid on her. [Gen. 19:25.]

7 [In physical appearance] her princes were purer than snow, they were whiter than milk, they were more ruddy in body than rubies *or* corals, their shapely figures [suggested a carefully cut] sapphire.

8 [Prolonged famine has made] them look blacker than darkness; they are not recognized in the streets; their skin clings to their bones; it is withered, it has become *dry* like a stick.

9 They who are slain with the sword are more fortunate than they who are the victims of hunger—slain by the famine; for the latter pine *and* ebb away, stricken through for want of the fruits of the field.

10 The hands of [heretofore] compassionate women have boiled their own children; they were their food in the destruction of the daughter of my people [Judah].

11 The Lord has fulfilled His wrath; He has poured out His fierce anger, and has kindled a fire in Zion that has consumed her foundations.

12 The kings of the earth did not believe, nor did any of the inhabitants of the earth, that oppressor or enemy could enter the gates of Jerusalem.

13 *But this was* for the sins of her [false] prophets and the iniquities of her priests, who had shed the blood of the just *and* righteous in the midst of her.

14 [The false prophets and priests] wandered [staggering] as if blind in the streets; they had so polluted themselves with blood it was not [lawful] for men to touch their garments.

## New American Standard

*Distress of the Siege Described*

4 HOW DARK the gold has become,
How the pure gold has changed!
The sacred stones are poured out
At the corner of every street.
2 The precious sons of Zion,
Weighed against fine gold,
How they are regarded as earthen jars,
The work of a potter's hands!
3 Even jackals offer the breast,
They nurse their young;
*But* the daughter of my people has become cruel
Like ostriches in the wilderness.
4 The tongue of the infant cleaves
To the roof of its mouth because of thirst;
The little ones ask for bread,
*But* no one breaks *it* for them.
5 Those who ate delicacies
Are desolate in the streets;
Those reared in purple
Embrace ash pits.
6 For the iniquity of the daughter of my people
Is greater than the sin of Sodom,
Which was overthrown as in a moment,
And no hands were turned toward her.
7 Her consecrated ones were purer than snow,
They were whiter than milk;
They were more ruddy *in* body than corals,
Their polishing *was* like lapis lazuli.
8 Their appearance is blacker than soot,
They are not recognized in the streets;
Their skin is shriveled on their bones,
It is withered, it has become like wood.
9 Better are those slain with the sword
Than those slain with hunger;
For they pine away, being stricken
For lack of the fruits of the field.
10 The hands of compassionate women
Boiled their own children;
They became food for them
Because of the destruction of the daughter of my people.
11 The LORD has accomplished His wrath,
He has poured out His fierce anger;
And He has kindled a fire in Zion
Which has consumed its foundations.
12 The kings of the earth did not believe,
Nor *did* any of the inhabitants of the world,
That the adversary and the enemy
Could enter the gates of Jerusalem.
13 Because of the sins of her prophets
*And* the iniquities of her priests,
Who have shed in her midst
The blood of the righteous,
14 They wandered, blind, in the streets;
They were defiled with blood
So that no one could touch their garments.

## New International

4[a] HOW THE gold has lost its luster,
the fine gold become dull!
The sacred gems are scattered
at the head of every street.

2 How the precious sons of Zion,
once worth their weight in gold,
are now considered as pots of clay,
the work of a potter's hands!

3 Even jackals offer their breasts
to nurse their young,
but my people have become heartless
like ostriches in the desert.

4 Because of thirst the infant's tongue
sticks to the roof of its mouth;
the children beg for bread,
but no one gives it to them.

5 Those who once ate delicacies
are destitute in the streets.
Those nurtured in purple
now lie on ash heaps.

6 The punishment of my people
is greater than that of Sodom,
which was overthrown in a moment
without a hand turned to help her.

7 Their princes were brighter than snow
and whiter than milk,
their bodies more ruddy than rubies,
their appearance like sapphires.[b]

8 But now they are blacker than soot;
they are not recognized in the streets.
Their skin has shriveled on their bones;
it has become as dry as a stick.

9 Those killed by the sword are better off
than those who die of famine;
racked with hunger, they waste away
for lack of food from the field.

10 With their own hands compassionate women
have cooked their own children,
who became their food
when my people were destroyed.

11 The LORD has given full vent to his wrath;
he has poured out his fierce anger.
He kindled a fire in Zion
that consumed her foundations.

12 The kings of the earth did not believe,
nor did any of the world's people,
that enemies and foes could enter
the gates of Jerusalem.

13 But it happened because of the sins of her prophets
and the iniquities of her priests,
who shed within her
the blood of the righteous.

14 Now they grope through the streets
like men who are blind.
They are so defiled with blood
that no one dares to touch their garments.

**NIV** [a] This chapter is an acrostic poem, the verses of which begin with the successive letters of the Hebrew alphabet. [b] 7 Or *lapis lazuli*

## King James

15 They cried unto them, Depart ye; *It is* unclean; depart, depart, touch not: when they fled away and wandered, they said among the heathen, They shall no more sojourn *there*.

16 The anger of the LORD hath divided them; he will no more regard them: they respected not the persons of the priests, they favoured not the elders.

17 As for us, our eyes as yet failed for our vain help: in our watching we have watched for a nation *that* could not save *us*.

18 They hunt our steps, that we cannot go in our streets: our end is near, our days are fulfilled; for our end is come.

19 Our persecutors are swifter than the eagles of the heaven: they pursued us upon the mountains, they laid wait for us in the wilderness.

20 The breath of our nostrils, the anointed of the LORD, was taken in their pits, of whom we said, Under his shadow we shall live among the heathen.

21 ¶ Rejoice and be glad, O daughter of Edom, that dwellest in the land of Uz; the cup also shall pass through unto thee: thou shalt be drunken, and shalt make thyself naked.

22 ¶ The punishment of thine iniquity is accomplished, O daughter of Zion; he will no more carry thee away into captivity: he will visit thine iniquity, O daughter of Edom; he will discover thy sins.

**5** REMEMBER, O LORD, what is come upon us: consider, and behold our reproach.

2 Our inheritance is turned to strangers, our houses to aliens.

3 We are orphans and fatherless, our mothers *are* as widows.

4 We have drunken our water for money; our wood is sold unto us.

5 Our necks *are* under persecution: we labour, *and* have no rest.

6 We have given the hand *to* the Egyptians, *and to* the Assyrians, to be satisfied with bread.

7 Our fathers have sinned, *and are* not; and we have borne their iniquities.

8 Servants have ruled over us: *there is* none that doth deliver *us* out of their hand.

9 We gat our bread with *the peril of* our lives because of the sword of the wilderness.

10 Our skin was black like an oven because of the terrible famine.

11 They ravished the women in Zion, *and* the maids in the cities of Judah.

12 Princes are hanged up by their hand: the faces of elders were not honoured.

13 They took the young men to grind, and the children fell under the wood.

14 The elders have ceased from the gate, the young men from their music.

## Amplified

15 *People* cried to them, Go away! Unclean! Depart! Depart! Touch not! When they fled away, then they wandered [as fugitives]; men said among the nations, They shall not tarry longer here.

16 The anger of the Lord has scattered *and* divided them [among the nations]; He will no longer regard them; they did not respect the persons of the priests, they did not favor the elders.

17 As for us, our eyes as yet fail *and* waste away in looking for our worthless help. In our watching [on our watchtower] we have expectantly waited for a nation [Egypt or some other to come to our rescue] that could not save *us*.

18 [The missiles of] *the enemy* dog our steps, so that we cannot go into our streets; our end is near, our days are fulfilled, yes, our end is come.

19 Our pursuers were swifter than the eagles of the sky; they pursued us on the mountains, they lay in wait for us in the wilderness.

20 [Our king] the breath of our nostrils, the anointed of the Lord, was taken in their snares, he of whom we said, Under his shadow we shall live among the nations.

21 Rejoice and be glad, O daughter of Edom, who dwells in the land of Uz; but the cup [of the wine of God's wrath] also shall pass through to you; you shall become drunk and make yourself naked. [Jer. 25:17.]

22 The punishment of your iniquity is accomplished, O daughter of Zion; [the Lord] will no more carry you away *or* keep you in exile. But He will inspect *and* punish your iniquity *and* guilt, O daughter of Edom; He will uncover your sins. [Ps. 137:7.]

**5** O LORD, [earnestly] remember what has come upon us! Look down and behold our reproach—our [national] disgrace!

2 Our inheritance is fallen to strangers, our houses to foreigners.

3 We have become orphans, fatherless; our mothers are as widows.

4 We have had to pay money to drink the water that belongs to us; our *own* wood is sold to us.

5 Our pursuers are upon our necks [like a yoke]; we are weary and are allowed no rest.

6 We have given the hand [as a pledge of fidelity] to the Egyptians and to the Assyrians, [merely] to get food to satisfy *our hunger*.

7 Our fathers have sinned and are no more, and [a]we have borne their iniquities. [Jer. 31:29; Ezek. 18:2-4.]

8 Servants *and* slaves rule over us; there is none to deliver us out of their hand. [Neh. 5:15.]

9 We get our bread at the peril of our lives because of the sword of the wilderness [the wild Arabs, if we venture to the fields to reap our harvests].

10 Our skin glows *and* is parched as from an oven, because of the burning heat of [the fever of] famine.

11 They ravished the women in Zion, the virgins in the cities of Judah.

12 They hung princes by their hand; the persons of elders were not respected.

13 The young men have carried millstones, and boys have fallen [staggering] under *burdens of* wood.

14 The elders have ceased from [congregating at] the city's gate, the young men from their music.

**AMP** [a] [But we deserved our punishment.] "Woe to us, that we have sinned! For this our heart has become faint and sick; for these things our eyes have become dim *and* see darkly." (Vss. 16, 17.)

## New American Standard

15 "Depart! Unclean!" they cried of themselves.
"Depart, depart, do not touch!"
So they fled and wandered;
*Men* among the nations said,
"They shall not continue to dwell *with us.*"
16 The presence of the LORD has scattered them;
He will not continue to regard them.
They did not honor the priests,
They did not favor the elders.
17 Yet our eyes failed;
*Looking* for help was useless.
In our watching we have watched
For a nation that could not save.
18 They hunted our steps
So that we could not walk in our streets;
Our end drew near,
Our days were finished
For our end had come.
19 Our pursuers were swifter
Than the eagles of the sky.
They chased us on the mountains;
They waited in ambush for us in the wilderness.
20 The breath of our nostrils, the LORD's anointed,
Was captured in their pits,
Of whom we had said, "Under his shadow
We shall live among the nations."
21 Rejoice and be glad, O daughter of Edom,
Who dwells in the land of Uz;
*But* the cup will come around to you as well,
You will become drunk and make yourself naked.
22 *The punishment* of your iniquity has been completed,
O daughter of Zion;
He will exile you no longer.
*But* He will punish your iniquity, O daughter of Edom;
He will expose your sins!

*A Prayer for Mercy*

5 REMEMBER, O LORD, what has befallen us;
Look, and see our reproach!
2 Our inheritance has been turned over to strangers,
Our houses to aliens.
3 We have become orphans without a father,
Our mothers are like widows.
4 We have to pay for our drinking water,
Our wood comes *to us* at a price.
5 Our pursuers are at our necks;
We are worn out, there is no rest for us.
6 We have submitted to Egypt *and* Assyria to get enough bread.
7 Our fathers sinned, *and* are no more;
It is we who have borne their iniquities.
8 Slaves rule over us;
There is no one to deliver us from their hand.
9 We get our bread at the risk of our lives
Because of the sword in the wilderness.
10 Our skin has become as hot as an oven,
Because of the burning heat of famine.
11 They ravished the women in Zion,
The virgins in the cities of Judah.
12 Princes were hung by their hands;
Elders were not respected.
13 Young men worked at the grinding mill;
And youths stumbled under *loads* of wood.
14 Elders are gone from the gate,
Young men from their music.

## New International

15 "Go away! You are unclean!" men cry to them.
"Away! Away! Don't touch us!"
When they flee and wander about,
people among the nations say,
"They can stay here no longer."

16 The LORD himself has scattered them;
he no longer watches over them.
The priests are shown no honor,
the elders no favor.

17 Moreover, our eyes failed,
looking in vain for help;
from our towers we watched
for a nation that could not save us.

18 Men stalked us at every step,
so we could not walk in our streets.
Our end was near, our days were numbered,
for our end had come.

19 Our pursuers were swifter
than eagles in the sky;
they chased us over the mountains
and lay in wait for us in the desert.

20 The LORD's anointed, our very life breath,
was caught in their traps.
We thought that under his shadow
we would live among the nations.

21 Rejoice and be glad, O Daughter of Edom,
you who live in the land of Uz.
But to you also the cup will be passed;
you will be drunk and stripped naked.

22 O Daughter of Zion, your punishment will end;
he will not prolong your exile.
But, O Daughter of Edom, he will punish your sin
and expose your wickedness.

5 REMEMBER, O LORD, what has happened to us;
look, and see our disgrace.
2 Our inheritance has been turned over to aliens,
our homes to foreigners.
3 We have become orphans and fatherless,
our mothers like widows.
4 We must buy the water we drink;
our wood can be had only at a price.
5 Those who pursue us are at our heels;
we are weary and find no rest.
6 We submitted to Egypt and Assyria
to get enough bread.
7 Our fathers sinned and are no more,
and we bear their punishment.
8 Slaves rule over us,
and there is none to free us from their hands.
9 We get our bread at the risk of our lives
because of the sword in the desert.
10 Our skin is hot as an oven,
feverish from hunger.
11 Women have been ravished in Zion,
and virgins in the towns of Judah.
12 Princes have been hung up by their hands;
elders are shown no respect.
13 Young men toil at the millstones;
boys stagger under loads of wood.
14 The elders are gone from the city gate;
the young men have stopped their music.

## King James

15The joy of our heart is ceased; our dance is turned into mourning.
16The crown is fallen *from* our head: woe unto us, that we have sinned!
17For this our heart is faint; for these *things* our eyes are dim.
18Because of the mountain of Zion, which is desolate, the foxes walk upon it.
19Thou, O LORD, remainest for ever; thy throne from generation to generation.
20Wherefore dost thou forget us for ever, *and* forsake us so long time?
21Turn thou us unto thee, O LORD, and we shall be turned; renew our days as of old.
22But thou hast utterly rejected us; thou art very wroth against us.

## Amplified

15Ceased is the joy of our heart; our dancing has been turned into mourning.
16The crown is fallen from our head [our honor is brought to the dust]! Woe to us, for we have sinned!
17For this our heart has become faint *and* sick; for these things our eyes have become dim *and* see darkly.
18As to Mount Zion which lies desolate, the jackals prowl over it!
19But You, O Lord, remain *and* reign forever; Your throne endures from generation to [all] generations.
20Why do You forget us for ever? Why do You forsake us so long?
21Turn us to Yourself, O Lord, and we shall be turned *and* restored! Renew our days as of old!
22Or have You utterly rejected us? [a]Or are You exceedingly angry with us [still]?

**AMP** [a] "Although the Book of Lamentations, like so many even of the saddest of the Psalms, does in fact close with the language of hope, that is in the present case so little apparent on the first reading that in many Hebrew manuscripts verse twenty-one is repeated at the end, that so its words may rather be the last to fall upon the ear. A similar expedient is used in the case of Ecclesiastes, Isaiah and Malachi. See note on Jeremiah 52:34." (Cambridge Bible.)

## New American Standard

15 The joy of our hearts has ceased;
Our dancing has been turned into mourning.
16 The crown has fallen from our head;
Woe to us, for we have sinned!
17 Because of this our heart is faint;
Because of these things our eyes are dim;
18 Because of Mount Zion which lies desolate,
Foxes prowl in it.

19¶ Thou, O LORD, dost rule forever;
Thy throne is from generation to generation.
20 Why dost Thou forget us forever;
Why dost Thou forsake us so long?
21 Restore us to Thee, O LORD, that we may be restored;
Renew our days as of old,
22 Unless Thou hast utterly rejected us,
*And* art exceedingly angry with us.

## New International

15Joy is gone from our hearts;
our dancing has turned to mourning.
16The crown has fallen from our head.
Woe to us, for we have sinned!
17Because of this our hearts are faint,
because of these things our eyes grow dim
18for Mount Zion, which lies desolate,
with jackals prowling over it.

19You, O LORD, reign forever;
your throne endures from generation to generation.
20Why do you always forget us?
Why do you forsake us so long?
21Restore us to yourself, O LORD, that we may return;
renew our days as of old
22unless you have utterly rejected us
and are angry with us beyond measure.

**King James**

THE BOOK

OF THE PROPHET

# Ezekiel

1 NOW IT came to pass in the thirtieth year, in the fourth *month*, in the fifth *day* of the month, as I *was* among the captives by the river of Chebar, *that* the heavens were opened, and I saw visions of God.

2 In the fifth *day* of the month, which *was* the fifth year of king Jehoiachin's captivity,

3 The word of the LORD came expressly unto Ezekiel the priest, the son of Buzi, in the land of the Chaldeans by the river Chebar; and the hand of the LORD was there upon him.

4 ¶ And I looked, and, behold, a whirlwind came out of the north, a great cloud, and a fire infolding itself, and a brightness *was* about it, and out of the midst thereof as the colour of amber, out of the midst of the fire.

5 Also out of the midst thereof *came* the likeness of four living creatures. And this *was* their appearance; they had the likeness of a man.

6 And every one had four faces, and every one had four wings.

7 And their feet *were* straight feet; and the sole of their feet *was* like the sole of a calf's foot: and they sparkled like the colour of burnished brass.

8 And *they had* the hands of a man under their wings on their four sides; and they four had their faces and their wings.

9 Their wings *were* joined one to another; they turned not when they went; they went every one straight forward.

10 As for the likeness of their faces, they four had the face of a man, and the face of a lion, on the right side: and they four had the face of an ox on the left side; they four also had the face of an eagle.

11 Thus *were* their faces: and their wings *were* stretched upward; two *wings* of every one *were* joined one to another, and two covered their bodies.

12 And they went every one straight forward: whither the spirit was to go, they went; *and* they turned not when they went.

13 As for the likeness of the living creatures, their appearance *was* like burning coals of fire, *and* like the appearance of lamps: it went up and down among the living creatures; and the fire was bright, and out of the fire went forth lightning.

14 And the living creatures ran and returned as the appearance of a flash of lightning.

15 ¶ Now as I beheld the living creatures, behold one wheel upon the earth by the living creatures, with his four faces.

16 The appearance of the wheels and their work *was* like unto the colour of a beryl: and they four had one likeness: and their appearance and their work *was* as it were a wheel in the middle of a wheel.

17 When they went, they went upon their four sides: *and* they turned not when they went.

18 As for their rings, they were so high that they were dreadful; and their rings *were* full of eyes round about them four.

**AMP** [a] It is noteworthy that the four faces of the living creatures as here described are symbolic of "the four portraits of Jesus" as given in the four Gospels. Matthew represents our Lord as the King (the lion); Mark portrays Him as the Servant (the ox); Luke emphasizes His humanity (man), and John proclaims especially His Deity (the eagle).

**Amplified**

THE BOOK OF

# Ezekiel

1 NOW *WHEN I was* in *my* thirtieth year, in the fourth month, in the fifth day of the month, as I was in the midst of captivity beside the river Chebar [in Babylonia], the heavens were opened, and I saw visions of God.

2 On the fifth day of the month, which was in the fifth year of King Jehoiachin's captivity,

3 The word of the Lord came expressly to Ezekiel the priest, the son of Buzi, in the land of the Chaldeans by the river Chebar; and the hand of the Lord was there upon him. [I Kings 18:46; II Kings 3:15.]

4 As I looked, behold, a stormy wind came out of the north, and a great cloud with a fire enveloping it *and* flashing continually, and a brightness was about it, and out of the midst of it as it seemed glowed amber metal, out of the midst of the fire.

5 And out of the midst of it came the likeness of four living creatures [or cherubim]. And this was their appearance: they had the likeness of a man,

6 But each one had four faces, and each one had four wings.

7 And their legs were straight legs, and the sole of their feet was like the sole of a calf's foot, and they sparkled like burnished bronze.

8 And they had the hands of a man under their wings on their four sides. And they four had their faces and their wings thus:

9 Their wings touched one another; they turned not when they went, but went every one straight forward.

10 As for the [a]likeness of their faces, they each had the face of a man *in front*, and they four had the face of a lion on the right side, and they four had the face of an ox on the left side; they four also had the face of an eagle [at the back of their heads].

11 Such were their faces. And their wings were stretched out upward [each creature had four wings]; two wings of each one were touching the *adjacent* wing of the creatures on either side of it, and [the remaining] two wings of each creature covered its body.

12 And they went every one straight forward; wherever the spirit would go, they went, and they turned not when they went.

13 In the midst of the living creatures there was what looked like burning coals of fire, like torches moving to and fro among the living creatures; and the fire was bright, and out of the fire went forth lightning.

14 And the living creatures darted back and forth like a flash of lightning.

15 Now as I was still looking at the living creatures, I saw one wheel upon the ground beside each of the living creatures with its four faces.

16 As to the appearance of the wheels and their construction: in appearance they gleamed like chrysolite; and they four were formed alike; and their construction work was as it were a wheel within a wheel.

17 When they went, they went in one of their four directions, without turning [for they were faced that way].

18 As for their rims, they were so high that they were dreadful; and they four had their rims full of eyes round about.

## New American Standard

# Ezekiel

*The Vision of Four Figures*

**1** NOW IT came about in the thirtieth year, on the fifth *day* of
the fourth month, while I was by the river Chebar among the
exiles, the heavens were opened and I saw visions of God.
2(On the fifth of the month in the fifth year of King Jehoiachin's
exile,
3the word of the LORD came expressly to Ezekiel the priest, son
of Buzi, in the land of the Chaldeans by the river Chebar; and there
the hand of the LORD came upon him.)
4¶ And as I looked, behold, a storm wind was coming from the
north, a great cloud with fire flashing forth continually and a bright
light around it, and in its midst something like glowing metal in
the midst of the fire.
5And within it there were figures resembling four living beings. And this was their appearance: they had human form.
6Each of them had four faces and four wings.
7And their legs were straight and their feet were like a calf's
hoof, and they gleamed like burnished bronze.
8Under their wings on their four sides *were* human hands. As
for the faces and wings of the four of them,
9their wings touched one another; their *faces* did not turn when
they moved, each went straight forward.
10As for the form of their faces, *each* had the face of a man, all
four had the face of a lion on the right and the face of a bull on the
left, and all four had the face of an eagle.
11Such were their faces. Their wings were spread out above;
each had two touching another *being*, and two covering their bodies.
12And each went straight forward; wherever the spirit was
about to go, they would go, without turning as they went.
13In the midst of the living beings there was something that
looked like burning coals of fire, like torches darting back and forth
among the living beings. The fire was bright, and lightning was
flashing from the fire.
14And the living beings ran to and fro like bolts of lightning.
15¶ Now as I looked at the living beings, behold, there was one
wheel on the earth beside the living beings, for *each of* the four of
them.
16The appearance of the wheels and their workmanship *was* like
sparkling beryl, and all four of them had the same form, their
appearance and workmanship *being* as if one wheel were within
another.
17Whenever they moved, they moved in any of their four directions, without turning as they moved.
18As for their rims they were lofty and awesome, and the rims
of all four of them were full of eyes round about.

## New International

# Ezekiel

*The Living Creatures and the Glory of the LORD*

**1** IN THE[b] thirtieth year, in the fourth month on the fifth day,
while I was among the exiles by the Kebar River, the heavens
were opened and I saw visions of God.
2On the fifth of the month—it was the fifth year of the exile of
King Jehoiachin— 3the word of the LORD came to Ezekiel the
priest, the son of Buzi,[c] by the Kebar River in the land of the
Babylonians.[d] There the hand of the LORD was upon him.
4I looked, and I saw a windstorm coming out of the north—an
immense cloud with flashing lightning and surrounded by brilliant
light. The center of the fire looked like glowing metal, 5and in the
fire was what looked like four living creatures. In appearance their
form was that of a man, 6but each of them had four faces and four
wings. 7Their legs were straight; their feet were like those of a calf
and gleamed like burnished bronze. 8Under their wings on their
four sides they had the hands of a man. All four of them had faces
and wings, 9and their wings touched one another. Each one went
straight ahead; they did not turn as they moved.
10Their faces looked like this: Each of the four had the face of
a man, and on the right side each had the face of a lion, and on
the left the face of an ox; each also had the face of an eagle. 11Such
were their faces. Their wings were spread out upward; each had
two wings, one touching the wing of another creature on either
side, and two wings covering its body. 12Each one went straight
ahead. Wherever the spirit would go, they would go, without
turning as they went. 13The appearance of the living creatures was
like burning coals of fire or like torches. Fire moved back and forth
among the creatures; it was bright, and lightning flashed out of it.
14The creatures sped back and forth like flashes of lightning.
15As I looked at the living creatures, I saw a wheel on the
ground beside each creature with its four faces. 16This was the
appearance and structure of the wheels: They sparkled like chrysolite, and all four looked alike. Each appeared to be made like a
wheel intersecting a wheel. 17As they moved, they would go in
any one of the four directions the creatures faced; the wheels did
not turn about[e] as the creatures went. 18Their rims were high and
awesome, and all four rims were full of eyes all around.

**NIV** [b] 1 Or ⌊my⌋ [c] 3 Or *Ezekiel son of Buzi the priest* [d] 3 Or *Chaldeans*
[e] 17 Or *aside*

## King James

19 And when the living creatures went, the wheels went by them: and when the living creatures were lifted up from the earth, the wheels were lifted up.

20 Whithersoever the spirit was to go, they went, thither *was their* spirit to go; and the wheels were lifted up over against them: for the spirit of the living creature *was* in the wheels.

21 When those went, *these* went; and when those stood, *these* stood; and when those were lifted up from the earth, the wheels were lifted up over against them: for the spirit of the living creature *was* in the wheels.

22 And the likeness of the firmament upon the heads of the living creature *was* as the colour of the terrible crystal, stretched forth over their heads above.

23 And under the firmament *were* their wings straight, the one toward the other: every one had two, which covered on this side, and every one had two, which covered on that side, their bodies.

24 And when they went, I heard the noise of their wings, like the noise of great waters, as the voice of the Almighty, the voice of speech, as the noise of an host: when they stood, they let down their wings.

25 And there was a voice from the firmament that *was* over their heads, when they stood, *and* had let down their wings.

26 ¶ And above the firmament that *was* over their heads *was* the likeness of a throne, as the appearance of a sapphire stone: and upon the likeness of the throne *was* the likeness as the appearance of a man above upon it.

27 And I saw as the colour of amber, as the appearance of fire round about within it, from the appearance of his loins even upward, and from the appearance of his loins even downward, I saw as it were the appearance of fire, and it had brightness round about.

28 As the appearance of the bow that is in the cloud in the day of rain, so *was* the appearance of the brightness round about. This *was* the appearance of the likeness of the glory of the Lord. And when I saw *it*, I fell upon my face, and I heard a voice of one that spake.

**2** AND HE said unto me, Son of man, stand upon thy feet, and I will speak unto thee.

2 And the spirit entered into me when he spake unto me, and set me upon my feet, that I heard him that spake unto me.

3 And he said unto me, Son of man, I send thee to the children of Israel, to a rebellious nation that hath rebelled against me: they and their fathers have transgressed against me, *even* unto this very day.

4 For *they are* impudent children and stiffhearted. I do send thee unto them; and thou shalt say unto them, Thus saith the Lord God.

5 And they, whether they will hear, or whether they will forbear, (for they *are* a rebellious house,) yet shall know that there hath been a prophet among them.

6 ¶ And thou, son of man, be not afraid of them, neither be afraid of their words, though briers and thorns *be* with thee, and thou dost dwell among scorpions: be not afraid of their words, nor be dismayed at their looks, though they *be* a rebellious house.

7 And thou shalt speak my words unto them, whether they will hear, or whether they will forbear: for they *are* most rebellious.

8 But thou, son of man, hear what I say unto thee; Be not thou rebellious like that rebellious house: open thy mouth, and eat that I give thee.

9 ¶ And when I looked, behold, an hand *was* sent unto me; and, lo, a roll of a book *was* therein;

10 And he spread it before me; and it *was* written within and without: and *there was* written therein lamentations, and mourning, and woe.

## Amplified

19 And when the living creatures went, the wheels went beside them; and when the living creatures were lifted up from the earth, the wheels were lifted up.

20 Wherever the spirit went, the creatures went; and the wheels rose along with them; for the spirit *or* life of the [four living creatures acting as one] living creature was in the wheels.

21 When those went, these went; and when those stood, these stood; and when those were lifted up from the earth, the wheels were lifted up high beside them; for the spirit *or* life of the [combined] living creature was in the wheels.

22 Over the head of the [combined] living creature there was the likeness of a firmament, to look upon like the terrible *and* awesome *dazzling of shining* crystal *or* ice, stretched across the expanse of sky over their heads.

23 And under the firmament their wings were stretched out straight, one toward another. Every living creature had two wings which covered its body on this side and two which covered it on that side.

24 And when they went, I heard the sound of their wings like the noise of great waters, like the voice of the Almighty, the sound of tumult like the noise of a host. When they stood, they let down their wings.

25 And there was a voice above the firmament that was over their heads; when they stood, they let down their wings.

26 And above the firmament that was over their heads was the likeness of a throne, in appearance like a sapphire stone; and seated above the likeness of a throne was a likeness with the appearance of a Man. [Phil. 2:5-8.]

27 From what had the appearance of His waist upward, I saw a lustre as it were glowing metal, with the appearance of fire enclosed round about within it; and from the appearance of His waist downward, I saw as it were the appearance of fire, and there was brightness [of a halo] round about Him.

28 Like the appearance of the bow that is in the cloud on the day of rain, so was the appearance of the brightness round about. This was the appearance of the likeness of the glory of the Lord. And when I saw it, I fell upon my face, and I heard a voice of One speaking. [Rev. 4:3.]

**2** AND HE said to me [Ezekiel], Son of man, stand upon your feet, and I will speak to you.

2 And the Spirit entered into me when He spoke to me and set me upon my feet, and I heard Him speaking to me.

3 And He said to me, I send you, son of man, to the children of Israel, two rebellious nations that have rebelled against Me. They and their fathers have transgressed against Me, even to this very day.

4 And the children are impudent and hard of heart. I send you to them, and you shall say to them, Thus says the Lord God.

5 And they, whether they will hear or refuse to hear, for they are a rebellious house, yet shall know *and* realize that there has been a prophet among them.

6 And you, son of man, be not afraid of them, neither be afraid of their words; though briers and thorns are all around you and you dwell *and* sit among scorpions, be not afraid of their words, nor be dismayed at their looks, for they are a rebellious house.

7 And you shall speak My words to them, whether they will hear or refuse to hear; for they are most rebellious.

8 As for you, son of man, hear what I say to you; be not rebellious like that rebellious house; open your mouth and eat what I give you.

9 And when I looked, behold, a hand was stretched out to me, and behold, a scroll of a book was in it.

10 And He spread it before me, and it was written within and on the back. And there were written in it words of lamentation and mourning and woe.

## New American Standard

19And whenever the living beings moved, the wheels moved
with them. And whenever the living beings rose from the earth,
the wheels rose *also*.
20Wherever the spirit was about to go, they would go in that
direction. And the wheels rose close beside them; for the spirit of
the living beings *was* in the wheels.
21Whenever those went, these went; and whenever those stood
still, these stood still. And whenever those rose from the earth, the
wheels rose close beside them; for the spirit of the living beings *was*
in the wheels.

*Vision of Divine Glory*

22¶ Now over the heads of the living beings *there was* something
like an expanse, like the awesome gleam of crystal, extended over
their heads.
23And under the expanse their wings *were stretched out* straight,
one toward the other; each one also had two wings covering their
bodies on the one side and on the other.
24I also heard the sound of their wings like the sound of abundant waters as they went, like the voice of the Almighty, a sound
of tumult like the sound of an army camp; whenever they stood
still, they dropped their wings.
25And there came a voice from above the expanse that was over
their heads; whenever they stood still, they dropped their wings.
26¶ Now above the expanse that was over their heads there was
something resembling a throne, like lapis lazuli in appearance; and
on that which resembled a throne, high up, *was* a figure with the
appearance of a man.
27Then I noticed from the appearance of His loins and upward
something like glowing metal that looked like fire all around within it, and from the appearance of His loins and downward I saw
something like fire; and *there was* a radiance around Him.
28As the appearance of the rainbow in the clouds on a rainy day,
so *was* the appearance of the surrounding radiance. Such *was* the
appearance of the likeness of the glory of the LORD. And when I
saw *it*, I fell on my face and heard a voice speaking.

*The Prophet's Call*

2 THEN HE said to me, "Son of man, stand on your feet that
I may speak with you!"
2And as He spoke to me the Spirit entered me and set me on
my feet; and I heard *Him* speaking to me.
3Then He said to me, "Son of man, I am sending you to the
sons of Israel, to a rebellious people who have rebelled against Me;
they and their fathers have transgressed against Me to this very
day.
4"And I am sending you to them who are stubborn and obstinate children; and you shall say to them, 'Thus says the Lord GOD.'
5"As for them, whether they listen or not—for they are a
rebellious house—they will know that a prophet has been among
them.
6"And you, son of man, neither fear them nor fear their words,
though thistles and thorns are with you and you sit on scorpions;
neither fear their words nor be dismayed at their presence, for they
are a rebellious house.
7"But you shall speak My words to them whether they listen
or not, for they are rebellious.
8¶ "Now you, son of man, listen to what I am speaking to you;
do not be rebellious like that rebellious house. Open your mouth
and eat what I am giving you."
9Then I looked, behold, a hand was extended to me; and lo,
a scroll *was* in it.
10When He spread it out before me, it was written on the front
and back; and written on it were lamentations, mourning and woe.

## New International

19When the living creatures moved, the wheels beside them
moved; and when the living creatures rose from the ground, the
wheels also rose. 20Wherever the spirit would go, they would go,
and the wheels would rise along with them, because the spirit of
the living creatures was in the wheels. 21When the creatures
moved, they also moved; when the creatures stood still, they also
stood still; and when the creatures rose from the ground, the
wheels rose along with them, because the spirit of the living creatures was in the wheels.
22Spread out above the heads of the living creatures was what
looked like an expanse, sparkling like ice, and awesome. 23Under
the expanse their wings were stretched out one toward the other,
and each had two wings covering its body. 24When the creatures
moved, I heard the sound of their wings, like the roar of rushing
waters, like the voice of the Almighty,[a] like the tumult of an army.
When they stood still, they lowered their wings.
25Then there came a voice from above the expanse over their
heads as they stood with lowered wings. 26Above the expanse over
their heads was what looked like a throne of sapphire,[b] and high
above on the throne was a figure like that of a man. 27I saw that
from what appeared to be his waist up he looked like glowing
metal, as if full of fire, and that from there down he looked like fire;
and brilliant light surrounded him. 28Like the appearance of a
rainbow in the clouds on a rainy day, so was the radiance around
him.
This was the appearance of the likeness of the glory of the LORD.
When I saw it, I fell facedown, and I heard the voice of one
speaking.

*Ezekiel's Call*

2 HE SAID to me, "Son of man, stand up on your feet and I will
speak to you." 2As he spoke, the Spirit came into me and
raised me to my feet, and I heard him speaking to me.
3He said: "Son of man, I am sending you to the Israelites, to a
rebellious nation that has rebelled against me; they and their fathers have been in revolt against me to this very day. 4The people
to whom I am sending you are obstinate and stubborn. Say to
them, 'This is what the Sovereign LORD says.' 5And whether they
listen or fail to listen—for they are a rebellious house—they will
know that a prophet has been among them. 6And you, son of man,
do not be afraid of them or their words. Do not be afraid, though
briers and thorns are all around you and you live among scorpions.
Do not be afraid of what they say or terrified by them, though they
are a rebellious house. 7You must speak my words to them,
whether they listen or fail to listen, for they are rebellious. 8But
you, son of man, listen to what I say to you. Do not rebel like that
rebellious house; open your mouth and eat what I give you."
9Then I looked, and I saw a hand stretched out to me. In it was
a scroll, 10which he unrolled before me. On both sides of it were
written words of lament and mourning and woe.

NIV [a] 24 Hebrew *Shaddai* [b] 26 Or *lapis lazuli*

## King James

3 MOREOVER HE said unto me, Son of man, eat that thou findest; eat this roll, and go speak unto the house of Israel.

2 So I opened my mouth, and he caused me to eat that roll.

3 And he said unto me, Son of man, cause thy belly to eat, and fill thy bowels with this roll that I give thee. Then did I eat *it;* and it was in my mouth as honey for sweetness.

4 ¶ And he said unto me, Son of man, go, get thee unto the house of Israel, and speak with my words unto them.

5 For thou *art* not sent to a people of a strange speech and of an hard language, *but* to the house of Israel;

6 Not to many people of a strange speech and of an hard language, whose words thou canst not understand. Surely, had I sent thee to them, they would have hearkened unto thee.

7 But the house of Israel will not hearken unto thee; for they will not hearken unto me: for all the house of Israel *are* impudent and hardhearted.

8 Behold, I have made thy face strong against their faces, and thy forehead strong against their foreheads.

9 As an adamant harder than flint have I made thy forehead: fear them not, neither be dismayed at their looks, though they *be* a rebellious house.

10 Moreover he said unto me, Son of man, all my words that I shall speak unto thee receive in thine heart, and hear with thine ears.

11 And go, get thee to them of the captivity, unto the children of thy people, and speak unto them, and tell them, Thus saith the Lord GOD; whether they will hear, or whether they will forbear.

12 Then the spirit took me up, and I heard behind me a voice of a great rushing, *saying,* Blessed *be* the glory of the LORD from his place.

13 *I heard* also the noise of the wings of the living creatures that touched one another, and the noise of the wheels over against them, and a noise of a great rushing.

14 So the spirit lifted me up, and took me away, and I went in bitterness, in the heat of my spirit; but the hand of the LORD was strong upon me.

15 ¶ Then I came to them of the captivity at Tel-abib, that dwelt by the river of Chebar, and I sat where they sat, and remained there astonished among them seven days.

16 And it came to pass at the end of seven days, that the word of the LORD came unto me, saying,

17 Son of man, I have made thee a watchman unto the house of Israel: therefore hear the word at my mouth, and give them warning from me.

18 When I say unto the wicked, Thou shalt surely die; and thou givest him not warning, nor speakest to warn the wicked from his wicked way, to save his life; the same wicked *man* shall die in his iniquity; but his blood will I require at thine hand.

19 Yet if thou warn the wicked, and he turn not from his wickedness, nor from his wicked way, he shall die in his iniquity; but thou hast delivered thy soul.

20 Again, When a righteous *man* doth turn from his righteousness, and commit iniquity, and I lay a stumblingblock before him, he shall die: because thou hast not given him warning, he shall die in his sin, and his righteousness which he hath done shall not be remembered; but his blood will I require at thine hand.

21 Nevertheless if thou warn the righteous *man,* that the righteous sin not, and he doth not sin, he shall surely live, because he is warned; also thou hast delivered thy soul.

22 ¶ And the hand of the LORD was there upon me; and he said unto me, Arise, go forth into the plain, and I will there talk with thee.

23 Then I arose, and went forth into the plain: and, behold, the glory of the LORD stood there, as the glory which I saw by the river of Chebar: and I fell on my face.

## Amplified

3 HE SAID to me, Son of man, eat what you find [in this book]; eat this scroll, then go and speak to the house of Israel.

2 So I opened my mouth, and He caused me to eat the scroll.

3 And He said to me, Son of man, eat this scroll that I give you and fill your stomach with it. Then I ate it, and it was as sweet as honey in my mouth.

4 And He said to me, Son of man, go, get you to the house of Israel, and speak to them with My words.

5 For you are not sent to a people of a foreign speech and of a difficult language, but to the house of Israel;

6 Not to many peoples of foreign speech and of a hard language, whose words you cannot understand. Surely, had I sent you to such people, they would have listened to you *and* heeded My words.

7 But the house of Israel will not listen to you *and* obey you, for they will not listen to Me *and* obey Me; for all the house of Israel are impudent and stubborn of heart.

8 Behold, I have made your face strong *and* hard against their faces, and your forehead strong *and* hard against their foreheads.

9 As an adamant harder than flint *or* a diamond point have I made your forehead; fear them not, neither be dismayed at their looks, for they are a rebellious house. [Isa. 50:7; Jer. 1:18; 15:20; Mic. 3:8.]

10 Moreover He said to me, Son of man, all My words that I shall speak to you receive in your heart and hear with your ears.

11 And go, get you to the [Jewish] captives [in Babylon], to the children of your people, and speak to them, and tell them, Thus says the Lord God; whether they will hear or refuse to hear.

12 Then the Spirit lifted me up, and I heard behind me a voice of a great rushing, saying, Blessed be the glory of the Lord, from His place [above the firmament].

13 I heard the noise of the wings of the living creatures as they touched *and* joined each one the other [its sister wing]; and I heard the noise of the wheels beside them, and the noise of a great rushing.

14 So the Spirit lifted me up, and took me away [in the vision], and I went in bitterness *of* discouragement in the heat of my spirit; and the hand of the Lord was strong upon me.

15 Then I came to them of the captivity at Telabib, who sat *and* dwelt by the river of Chebar, and I sat where they sat, and remained there among them seven days, overwhelmed with astonishment, *and* silent.

16 And at the end of seven days, the word of the Lord came to me:

17 Son of man, I have made you a watchman to the house of Israel; therefore hear the word at My mouth, and give them warning from Me. [Isa. 52:8; 56:10; 62:6; Jer. 6:17.]

18 If I say to the wicked, You shall surely die, and you do not give him warning or speak to warn the wicked from his wicked way, to save his life, the same wicked man shall die in his iniquity; but his blood will I require at your hand.

19 Yet if you warn the wicked, and he turn not from his wickedness or from his wicked way, he shall die in his iniquity; but you have delivered yourself.

20 Again, if a righteous man turns from his righteousness—right doing and right standing with God—and some gift or providence which I lay before him he perverts into an occasion to sin, and he commits iniquity, he shall die; because you have not given him warning, he shall die in his sin, and his righteous deeds which he has done shall not be remembered; but his blood will I require at your hand.

21 Nevertheless if you warn the righteous man not to sin, and he does not sin, he shall surely live, because he is warned; also you have delivered yourself from guilt.

22 And the hand of the Lord was there upon me; and He said to me, Arise, go forth into the plain, and I will talk with you there.

23 Then I arose and went forth into the plain, and behold, the glory of the Lord stood there, like the glory I had seen by the river Chebar; and I fell on my face.

## New American Standard

*Ezekiel's Commission*

**3** THEN HE said to me, "Son of man, eat what you find; eat this
scroll, and go, speak to the house of Israel."
2So I opened my mouth, and He fed me this scroll.
3And He said to me, "Son of man, feed your stomach, and fill
your body with this scroll which I am giving you." Then I ate it,
and it was sweet as honey in my mouth.
4¶ Then He said to me, "Son of man, go to the house of Israel
and speak with My words to them.
5"For you are not being sent to a people of unintelligible
speech or difficult language, *but* to the house of Israel,
6nor to many peoples of unintelligible speech or difficult language, whose words you cannot understand. But I have sent you
to them who should listen to you;
7yet the house of Israel will not be willing to listen to you, since
they are not willing to listen to Me. Surely the whole house of Israel
is stubborn and obstinate.
8"Behold, I have made your face as hard as their faces, and
your forehead as hard as their foreheads.
9"Like emery harder than flint I have made your forehead. Do
not be afraid of them or be dismayed before them, though they are
a rebellious house."
10Moreover, He said to me, "Son of man, take into your heart
all My words which I shall speak to you, and listen closely.
11"And go to the exiles, to the sons of your people, and speak
to them and tell them, whether they listen or not, 'Thus says the
Lord GOD.'"
12¶ Then the Spirit lifted me up, and I heard a great rumbling
sound behind me, "Blessed be the glory of the LORD in His place."
13And I *heard* the sound of the wings of the living beings touching one another, and the sound of the wheels beside them, even
a great rumbling sound.
14So the Spirit lifted me up and took me away; and I went
embittered in the rage of my spirit, and the hand of the LORD was
strong on me.
15Then I came to the exiles who lived beside the river Chebar
at Tel-abib, and I sat there seven days where they were living,
causing consternation among them.
16¶ Now it came about at the end of seven days that the word
of the LORD came to me, saying,
17"Son of man, I have appointed you a watchman to the house
of Israel; whenever you hear a word from My mouth, warn them
from Me.
18"When I say to the wicked, 'You shall surely die'; and you do
not warn him or speak out to warn the wicked from his wicked way
that he may live, that wicked man shall die in his iniquity, but his
blood I will require at your hand.
19"Yet if you have warned the wicked, and he does not turn
from his wickedness or from his wicked way, he shall die in his
iniquity; but you have delivered yourself.
20"Again, when a righteous man turns away from his righteousness and commits iniquity, and I place an obstacle before him,
he shall die; since you have not warned him, he shall die in his sin,
and his righteous deeds which he has done shall not be remembered; but his blood I will require at your hand.
21"However, if you have warned the righteous man that the
righteous should not sin, and he does not sin, he shall surely live
because he took warning; and you have delivered yourself."
22¶ And the hand of the LORD was on me there, and He said to
me, "Get up, go out to the plain, and there I will speak to you."
23So I got up and went out to the plain; and behold, the glory
of the LORD was standing there, like the glory which I saw by the
river Chebar, and I fell on my face.

## New International

**3** AND HE said to me, "Son of man, eat what is before you, eat
this scroll; then go and speak to the house of Israel." 2So I
opened my mouth, and he gave me the scroll to eat.
3Then he said to me, "Son of man, eat this scroll I am giving
you and fill your stomach with it." So I ate it, and it tasted as sweet
as honey in my mouth.
4He then said to me: "Son of man, go now to the house of Israel
and speak my words to them. 5You are not being sent to a people
of obscure speech and difficult language, but to the house of
Israel— 6not to many peoples of obscure speech and difficult language, whose words you cannot understand. Surely if I had sent
you to them, they would have listened to you. 7But the house of
Israel is not willing to listen to you because they are not willing to
listen to me, for the whole house of Israel is hardened and obstinate. 8But I will make you as unyielding and hardened as they are.
9I will make your forehead like the hardest stone, harder than flint.
Do not be afraid of them or terrified by them, though they are a
rebellious house."
10And he said to me, "Son of man, listen carefully and take to
heart all the words I speak to you. 11Go now to your countrymen
in exile and speak to them. Say to them, 'This is what the Sovereign
LORD says,' whether they listen or fail to listen."
12Then the Spirit lifted me up, and I heard behind me a loud
rumbling sound—May the glory of the LORD be praised in his
dwelling place!— 13the sound of the wings of the living creatures
brushing against each other and the sound of the wheels beside
them, a loud rumbling sound. 14The Spirit then lifted me up and
took me away, and I went in bitterness and in the anger of my
spirit, with the strong hand of the LORD upon me. 15I came to the
exiles who lived at Tel Abib near the Kebar River. And there,
where they were living, I sat among them for seven days—overwhelmed.

*Warning to Israel*

16At the end of seven days the word of the LORD came to me:
17"Son of man, I have made you a watchman for the house of
Israel; so hear the word I speak and give them warning from me.
18When I say to a wicked man, 'You will surely die,' and you do
not warn him or speak out to dissuade him from his evil ways in
order to save his life, that wicked man will die for[a] his sin, and
I will hold you accountable for his blood. 19But if you do warn the
wicked man and he does not turn from his wickedness or from his
evil ways, he will die for his sin; but you will have saved yourself.
20"Again, when a righteous man turns from his righteousness
and does evil, and I put a stumbling block before him, he will die.
Since you did not warn him, he will die for his sin. The righteous
things he did will not be remembered, and I will hold you accountable for his blood. 21But if you do warn the righteous man not to
sin and he does not sin, he will surely live because he took warning, and you will have saved yourself."
22The hand of the LORD was upon me there, and he said to me,
"Get up and go out to the plain, and there I will speak to you."
23So I got up and went out to the plain. And the glory of the LORD
was standing there, like the glory I had seen by the Kebar River,
and I fell facedown.

NIV [a] *18* Or *in;* also in verses 19 and 20

## King James

24 Then the spirit entered into me, and set me upon my feet, and spake with me, and said unto me, Go, shut thyself within thine house.

25 But thou, O son of man, behold, they shall put bands upon thee, and shall bind thee with them, and thou shalt not go out among them:

26 And I will make thy tongue cleave to the roof of thy mouth, that thou shalt be dumb, and shalt not be to them a reprover: for they *are* a rebellious house.

27 But when I speak with thee, I will open thy mouth, and thou shalt say unto them, Thus saith the Lord GOD; He that heareth, let him hear; and he that forbeareth, let him forbear: for they *are* a rebellious house.

4 THOU ALSO, son of man, take thee a tile, and lay it before thee, and portray upon it the city, *even* Jerusalem:

2 And lay siege against it, and build a fort against it, and cast a mount against it; set the camp also against it, and set *battering* rams against it round about.

3 Moreover take thou unto thee an iron pan, and set it *for* a wall of iron between thee and the city: and set thy face against it, and it shall be besieged, and thou shalt lay siege against it. This *shall be* a sign to the house of Israel.

4 Lie thou also upon thy left side, and lay the iniquity of the house of Israel upon it: *according* to the number of the days that thou shalt lie upon it thou shalt bear their iniquity.

5 For I have laid upon thee the years of their iniquity, according to the number of the days, three hundred and ninety days: so shalt thou bear the iniquity of the house of Israel.

6 And when thou hast accomplished them, lie again on thy right side, and thou shalt bear the iniquity of the house of Judah forty days: I have appointed thee each day for a year.

7 Therefore thou shalt set thy face toward the siege of Jerusalem, and thine arm *shall be* uncovered, and thou shalt prophesy against it.

8 And, behold, I will lay bands upon thee, and thou shalt not turn thee from one side to another, till thou hast ended the days of thy siege.

9 ¶ Take thou also unto thee wheat, and barley, and beans, and lentils, and millet, and fitches, and put them in one vessel, and make thee bread thereof, *according* to the number of the days that thou shalt lie upon thy side, three hundred and ninety days shalt thou eat thereof.

10 And thy meat which thou shalt eat *shall be* by weight, twenty shekels a day: from time to time shalt thou eat it.

11 Thou shalt drink also water by measure, the sixth part of an hin: from time to time shalt thou drink.

12 And thou shalt eat it *as* barley cakes, and thou shalt bake it with dung that cometh out of man, in their sight.

13 And the LORD said, Even thus shall the children of Israel eat their defiled bread among the Gentiles, whither I will drive them.

14 Then said I, Ah Lord GOD! behold, my soul hath not been polluted: for from my youth up even till now have I not eaten of that which dieth of itself, or is torn in pieces; neither came there abominable flesh into my mouth.

15 Then he said unto me, Lo, I have given thee cow's dung for man's dung, and thou shalt prepare thy bread therewith.

16 Moreover he said unto me, Son of man, behold, I will break the staff of bread in Jerusalem: and they shall eat bread by weight, and with care; and they shall drink water by measure, and with astonishment:

## Amplified

24 Then the Spirit entered into me, and set me on my feet; He spoke and said to me, Go, shut yourself up in your house.

25 But you, O son of man, behold, ropes will be put upon you and you will be bound with them, and you cannot go out among people.

26 And I will make your tongue cleave to the roof of your mouth, so that you cannot talk and be a reprover of the people; for they are a rebellious house.

27 But when I speak with you, I will open your mouth and you shall say to the people, Thus says the Lord God; he who hears, let him hear; and he who refuses to hear, let him refuse; for they are a rebellious house.

4 AND YOU, son of man, take a tile and lay it before you, and make upon it a drawing of a city, even Jerusalem.

2 And put siege-works against it, and build a siege-wall against it, and cast up a mound against it; set camps also against it, and set battering rams against it round about.

3 Moreover take a plate of iron and place it for an iron wall between you and the city; and set your face toward it, and it shall be besieged, and you shall press the siege against it. This is a sign to the house of Israel.

4 Then [bound as you are] lie upon your left [and north] side to bear symbolically the iniquity of the house of the ten tribes of Israel upon that side. According to the number of days that you shall lie upon it you shall bear their iniquity.

5 For I have laid upon you the years of their iniquity, according to the number of the days, three hundred and ninety days [for years]; so you shall bear the iniquity of the house of Israel.

6 And when you have fulfilled the days for Israel, lie again, but on your right [and south] side, and you shall bear the iniquity of the house of Judah forty days. I have appointed you one day for each year.

7 Therefore you shall set your face toward the siege of Jerusalem, and your arm shall be uncovered [ready for battle], and you shall prophesy against *the city.*

8 And, behold, I will lay bands upon you, and you shall not turn yourself from one side to another till you have ended the days of your siege.

9 Also take wheat, barley, beans, lentils, millet and spelt, and put them into one vessel and make bread of them. According to the number of the days that you shall lie upon your side, three hundred and ninety days you shall eat of it.

10 And the food you eat shall be by weight, twenty shekels *or* a full half pound a day, to be eaten at a fixed time each day.

11 You shall drink water by measure also, about one quart *or* the sixth part of a hin; you shall drink at a fixed time each day.

12 And you shall eat your food as barley cakes, and you shall bake it with human dung as fuel in the sight of the people.

13 And the Lord said, Even thus shall the children of Israel eat their defiled bread among the nations to whom I will drive them. [Hos. 9:3.]

14 Then said I, Ah Lord God! Behold, I have never defiled myself. From my youth up even till now have I not eaten of that which dies of itself or is torn in pieces; neither did there ever come abominable flesh into my mouth. [Acts 10:14.]

15 Then He said to me, Lo, I will let you use cow's dung instead of human dung, and you shall prepare your food with it.

16 Moreover He said to me, Son of man, behold, I will break the staff of bread [by which life is supported] in Jerusalem; and they shall eat bread rationed by weight and with fearfulness, and they shall drink water rationed by measure, and with dismay [silent, speechless grief caused by the impending starvation]; [Lev. 26:26; Ps. 105:16; Isa. 3:1.]

## New American Standard

24 The Spirit then entered me and made me stand on my feet,
and He spoke with me and said to me, "Go, shut yourself up in
your house.
25 "As for you, son of man, they will put ropes on you and bind
you with them, so that you cannot go out among them.
26 "Moreover, I will make your tongue stick to the roof of your
mouth so that you will be dumb, and cannot be a man who rebukes
them, for they are a rebellious house.
27 "But when I speak to you, I will open your mouth, and you
will say to them, 'Thus says the Lord GOD.' He who hears, let him
hear; and he who refuses, let him refuse; for they are a rebellious
house.

*Siege of Jerusalem Predicted*

4 "NOW YOU son of man, get yourself a brick, place it before
you, and inscribe a city on it, Jerusalem.
2 "Then lay siege against it, build a siege wall, raise up a ramp,
pitch camps, and place battering rams against it all around.
3 "Then get yourself an iron plate and set it up as an iron wall
between you and the city, and set your face toward it so that it is
under siege, and besiege it. This is a sign to the house of Israel.
4 ¶ "As for you, lie down on your left side, and lay the iniquity
of the house of Israel on it; you shall bear their iniquity for the
number of days that you lie on it.
5 "For I have assigned you a number of days corresponding to
the years of their iniquity, three hundred and ninety days; thus
you shall bear the iniquity of the house of Israel.
6 "When you have completed these, you shall lie down a second time, *but* on your right side, and bear the iniquity of the house
of Judah; I have assigned it to you for forty days, a day for each
year.
7 "Then you shall set your face toward the siege of Jerusalem
with your arm bared, and prophesy against it.
8 "Now behold, I will put ropes on you so that you cannot turn
from one side to the other, until you have completed the days of
your siege.

*Defiled Bread*

9 ¶ "But as for you, take wheat, barley, beans, lentils, millet and
spelt, put them in one vessel and make them into bread for yourself; you shall eat it according to the number of the days that you
lie on your side, three hundred and ninety days.
10 "And your food which you eat *shall be* twenty shekels a day
by weight; you shall eat it from time to time.
11 "And the water you drink will be the sixth part of a hin by
measure; you shall drink it from time to time.
12 "And you shall eat it as a barley cake, having baked *it* in their
sight over human dung."
13 Then the LORD said, "Thus shall the sons of Israel eat their
bread unclean among the nations where I shall banish them."
14 But I said, "Ah, Lord GOD! Behold, I have never been defiled;
for from my youth until now I have never eaten what died of itself
or was torn by beasts, nor has any unclean meat ever entered my
mouth."
15 Then He said to me, "See, I shall give you cow's dung in place
of human dung over which you will prepare your bread."
16 Moreover, He said to me, "Son of man, behold, I am going
to break the staff of bread in Jerusalem, and they will eat bread by
weight and with anxiety, and drink water by measure and in
horror,

## New International

24 Then the Spirit came into me and raised me to my feet. He
spoke to me and said: "Go, shut yourself inside your house. 25 And
you, son of man, they will tie with ropes; you will be bound so that
you cannot go out among the people. 26 I will make your tongue
stick to the roof of your mouth so that you will be silent and unable
to rebuke them, though they are a rebellious house. 27 But when
I speak to you, I will open your mouth and you shall say to them,
'This is what the Sovereign LORD says.' Whoever will listen let him
listen, and whoever will refuse let him refuse; for they are a rebellious house.

*Siege of Jerusalem Symbolized*

4 "NOW, SON of man, take a clay tablet, put it in front of you
and draw the city of Jerusalem on it. 2 Then lay siege to it:
Erect siege works against it, build a ramp up to it, set up camps
against it and put battering rams around it. 3 Then take an iron pan,
place it as an iron wall between you and the city and turn your face
toward it. It will be under siege, and you shall besiege it. This will
be a sign to the house of Israel.
4 "Then lie on your left side and put the sin of the house of Israel
upon yourself.[a] You are to bear their sin for the number of days
you lie on your side. 5 I have assigned you the same number of days
as the years of their sin. So for 390 days you will bear the sin of
the house of Israel.
6 "After you have finished this, lie down again, this time on
your right side, and bear the sin of the house of Judah. I have
assigned you 40 days, a day for each year. 7 Turn your face toward
the siege of Jerusalem and with bared arm prophesy against her.
8 I will tie you up with ropes so that you cannot turn from one side
to the other until you have finished the days of your siege.
9 "Take wheat and barley, beans and lentils, millet and spelt; put
them in a storage jar and use them to make bread for yourself. You
are to eat it during the 390 days you lie on your side. 10 Weigh out
twenty shekels[b] of food to eat each day and eat it at set times.
11 Also measure out a sixth of a hin[c] of water and drink it at set
times. 12 Eat the food as you would a barley cake; bake it in the sight
of the people, using human excrement for fuel." 13 The LORD said,
"In this way the people of Israel will eat defiled food among the
nations where I will drive them."
14 Then I said, "Not so, Sovereign LORD! I have never defiled
myself. From my youth until now I have never eaten anything
found dead or torn by wild animals. No unclean meat has ever
entered my mouth."
15 "Very well," he said, "I will let you bake your bread over cow
manure instead of human excrement."
16 He then said to me: "Son of man, I will cut off the supply of
food in Jerusalem. The people will eat rationed food in anxiety and
drink rationed water in despair, 17 for food and water will be scarce.

NIV [a] *4* Or *your side* [b] *10* That is, about 8 ounces (about 0.2 kilogram)
[c] *11* That is, about 2/3 quart (about 0.6 liter)

## King James

17 That they may want bread and water, and be astonied one with another, and consume away for their iniquity.

5 AND THOU, son of man, take thee a sharp knife, take thee a barber's razor, and cause *it* to pass upon thine head and upon thy beard: then take thee balances to weigh, and divide the *hair.*

2 Thou shalt burn with fire a third part in the midst of the city, when the days of the siege are fulfilled: and thou shalt take a third part, *and* smite about it with a knife: and a third part thou shalt scatter in the wind; and I will draw out a sword after them.

3 Thou shalt also take thereof a few in number, and bind them in thy skirts.

4 Then take of them again, and cast them into the midst of the fire, and burn them in the fire; *for* thereof shall a fire come forth into all the house of Israel.

5 ¶ Thus saith the Lord GOD; This *is* Jerusalem: I have set it in the midst of the nations and countries *that are* round about her.

6 And she hath changed my judgments into wickedness more than the nations, and my statutes more than the countries that *are* round about her: for they have refused my judgments and my statutes, they have not walked in them.

7 Therefore thus saith the Lord GOD; Because ye multiplied more than the nations that *are* round about you, *and* have not walked in my statutes, neither have kept my judgments, neither have done according to the judgments of the nations that *are* round about you;

8 Therefore thus saith the Lord GOD; Behold, I, even I, *am* against thee, and will execute judgments in the midst of thee in the sight of the nations.

9 And I will do in thee that which I have not done, and whereunto I will not do any more the like, because of all thine abominations.

10 Therefore the fathers shall eat the sons in the midst of thee, and the sons shall eat their fathers; and I will execute judgments in thee, and the whole remnant of thee will I scatter into all the winds.

11 Wherefore, *as* I live, saith the Lord GOD; Surely, because thou hast defiled my sanctuary with all thy detestable things, and with all thine abominations, therefore will I also diminish *thee;* neither shall mine eye spare, neither will I have any pity.

12 ¶ A third part of thee shall die with the pestilence, and with famine shall they be consumed in the midst of thee: and a third part shall fall by the sword round about thee; and I will scatter a third part into all the winds, and I will draw out a sword after them.

13 Thus shall mine anger be accomplished, and I will cause my fury to rest upon them, and I will be comforted: and they shall know that I the LORD have spoken *it* in my zeal, when I have accomplished my fury in them.

14 Moreover I will make thee waste, and a reproach among the nations that *are* round about thee, in the sight of all that pass by.

15 So it shall be a reproach and a taunt, an instruction and an astonishment unto the nations that *are* round about thee, when I shall execute judgments in thee in anger and in fury and in furious rebukes. I the LORD have spoken *it.*

16 When I shall send upon them the evil arrows of famine, which shall be for *their* destruction, *and* which I will send to destroy you: and I will increase the famine upon you, and will break your staff of bread:

## Amplified

17 In order that they may lack bread and water, and look at one another in dismay, and waste away [in their punishment] for their iniquity.

5 AND YOU, son of man [Ezekiel], take a sharp sword and use it as a barber's razor and shave your head and your beard. Then take balances for weighing, and divide the hair into three parts.

2 You shall burn one third part with fire in the midst of the city, when the days of the siege are fulfilled; and you shall take a second third part and strike with the sword round about it; and a third part you shall scatter to the wind, and I will draw out a sword after them.

3 You shall also take from these a small number of hairs and bind them in the skirts of your robe.

4 And of these again take some hairs and cast them into the midst of the fire, and burn them in the fire; from there a fire shall come forth into all the house of Israel.

5 Thus says the Lord God: This is Jerusalem, in the center of the nations I have set her, and countries are round about her.

6 And she has changed *and* rebelled against My ordinances more wickedly than the [heathen] nations, and against My statutes more than the countries that are round about her; for [Israel] rejected My ordinances, and as for My statutes, they have not walked in them. [Rom. 2:14, 15.]

7 Therefore thus says the Lord God: Because you were more turbulent *and* raged [against Me] more than the nations that are round about you, and have not walked in My statutes, neither have kept My ordinances, nor have done according to the ordinances [concerning] the nations that are round about you; [Josh. 23:7; Judg. 2:2; Deut. 7:2-6.]

8 Therefore thus says the Lord God: Behold, I, even I, am against you, and I will execute judgments in the midst of you in the sight of the nations.

9 And because of all your abominations I will do in you that which I have not done, and the like of which I will never do again. [Lam. 4:6; Dan. 9:12; Amos 3:2.]

10 Therefore fathers shall eat their sons in your midst, and sons shall eat their fathers; and I will execute judgments on you, and all who are left of you I will scatter to all the winds. [Lev. 26:33; Deut. 28:64; Ezek. 12:14; Zech. 2:6.]

11 Therefore, as I live, says the Lord God, surely because you have defiled My sanctuary with all your detestable things, and with all your abominations, therefore will I also diminish you *and* withdraw My eye that it shall not spare you, and I also will have no pity.

12 And a third part of you shall die of pestilence and be consumed by famine in the midst of you; a third part shall fall by the sword round about you; and I will scatter a third part to all the winds, and I will draw out a sword after them.

13 Thus shall My anger be spent, and I will cause My wrath toward them to rest, and I will be eased *and* comforted. And they shall know, understand *and* realize that I, the Lord, have spoken in My zeal, when I have accomplished My wrath upon them. [Ezek. 36:6; 38:19.]

14 Moreover I will make you a desolation and a reproach among the nations that are round about you and in the sight of all who pass by. [Lev. 26:31, 32; Neh. 2:17.]

15 So it shall be a reproach and a taunt, a warning and a horror *and* an astonishment to the [heathen] nations around you, when I shall execute judgments upon you in anger and in wrath and in furious chastisements *and* rebukes—I, the Lord, have spoken it—[Deut. 28:37; Ps. 79:4; Jer. 24:9.]

16 When I shall loose against them the evil arrows of hunger, that are for destruction, which I will send to destroy you. And I will increase the famine upon you, and will break your staff of bread.

## New American Standard

17because bread and water will be scarce; and they will be
appalled with one another and waste away in their iniquity.

*Jerusalem's Desolation Foretold*

5 "AS FOR you, son of man, take a sharp sword; take and use
it *as* a barber's razor on your head and beard. Then take scales
for weighing and divide the hair.

2"One third you shall burn in the fire at the center of the city,
when the days of the siege are completed. Then you shall take one
third and strike *it* with the sword all around the city, and one third
you shall scatter to the wind; and I will unsheathe a sword behind
them.

3"Take also a few in number from them and bind them in the
edges of your *robes*.

4"And take again some of them and throw them into the fire,
and burn them in the fire; from it a fire will spread to all the house
of Israel.

5"Thus says the Lord GOD, 'This is Jerusalem; I have set her
at the center of the nations, with lands around her.

6'But she has rebelled against My ordinances more wickedly
than the nations and against My statutes more than the lands
which surround her; for they have rejected My ordinances and
have not walked in My statutes.'

7"Therefore, thus says the Lord GOD, 'Because you have more
turmoil than the nations which surround you, and have not
walked in My statutes, nor observed My ordinances, nor observed
the ordinances of the nations which surround you,'

8therefore, thus says the Lord GOD, 'Behold, I, even I, am
against you, and I will execute judgments among you in the sight
of the nations.

9'And because of all your abominations, I will do among you
what I have not done, and the like of which I will never do again.

10'Therefore, fathers will eat *their* sons among you, and sons
will eat their fathers; for I will execute judgments on you, and
scatter all your remnant to every wind.

11'So as I live,' declares the Lord GOD, 'surely, because you have
defiled My sanctuary with all your detestable idols and with all
your abominations, therefore I will also withdraw, and My eye
shall have no pity and I will not spare.

12'One third of you will die by plague or be consumed by famine
among you, one third will fall by the sword around you, and one
third I will scatter to every wind, and I will unsheathe a sword
behind them.

13¶ 'Thus My anger will be spent, and I will satisfy My wrath
on them, and I shall be appeased; then they will know that I, the
LORD, have spoken in My zeal when I have spent My wrath upon
them.

14'Moreover, I will make you a desolation and a reproach
among the nations which surround you, in the sight of all who
pass by.

15'So it will be a reproach, a reviling, a warning and an object
of horror to the nations who surround you, when I execute judgments against you in anger, wrath, and raging rebukes. I, the
LORD, have spoken.

16'When I send against them the deadly arrows of famine which
were for the destruction of those whom I shall send to destroy you,
then I shall also intensify the famine upon you, and break the staff
of bread.

## New International

They will be appalled at the sight of each other and will waste away
because of[a] their sin.

5 "NOW, SON of man, take a sharp sword and use it as a
barber's razor to shave your head and your beard. Then take
a set of scales and divide up the hair. 2When the days of your siege
come to an end, burn a third of the hair with fire inside the city.
Take a third and strike it with the sword all around the city. And
scatter a third to the wind. For I will pursue them with drawn
sword. 3But take a few strands of hair and tuck them away in the
folds of your garment. 4Again, take a few of these and throw them
into the fire and burn them up. A fire will spread from there to the
whole house of Israel.

5"This is what the Sovereign LORD says: This is Jerusalem,
which I have set in the center of the nations, with countries all
around her. 6Yet in her wickedness she has rebelled against my
laws and decrees more than the nations and countries around her.
She has rejected my laws and has not followed my decrees.

7"Therefore this is what the Sovereign LORD says: You have
been more unruly than the nations around you and have not
followed my decrees or kept my laws. You have not even[b] conformed to the standards of the nations around you.

8"Therefore this is what the Sovereign LORD says: I myself am
against you, Jerusalem, and I will inflict punishment on you in the
sight of the nations. 9Because of all your detestable idols, I will do
to you what I have never done before and will never do again.
10Therefore in your midst fathers will eat their children, and children will eat their fathers. I will inflict punishment on you and will
scatter all your survivors to the winds. 11Therefore as surely as I
live, declares the Sovereign LORD, because you have defiled my
sanctuary with all your vile images and detestable practices, I
myself will withdraw my favor; I will not look on you with pity or
spare you. 12A third of your people will die of the plague or perish
by famine inside you; a third will fall by the sword outside your
walls; and a third I will scatter to the winds and pursue with drawn
sword.

13"Then my anger will cease and my wrath against them will
subside, and I will be avenged. And when I have spent my wrath
upon them, they will know that I the LORD have spoken in my zeal.

14"I will make you a ruin and a reproach among the nations
around you, in the sight of all who pass by. 15You will be a
reproach and a taunt, a warning and an object of horror to the
nations around you when I inflict punishment on you in anger and
in wrath and with stinging rebuke. I the LORD have spoken.
16When I shoot at you with my deadly and destructive arrows of
famine, I will shoot to destroy you. I will bring more and more
famine upon you and cut off your supply of food. 17I will send

NIV [a] 17 Or *away in* [b] 7 Most Hebrew manuscripts; some Hebrew manuscripts and Syriac *You have*

## King James

17 So will I send upon you famine and evil beasts, and they shall bereave thee; and pestilence and blood shall pass through thee; and I will bring the sword upon thee. I the LORD have spoken *it*.

**6** AND THE word of the LORD came unto me, saying,

2 Son of man, set thy face toward the mountains of Israel, and prophesy against them,

3 And say, Ye mountains of Israel, hear the word of the Lord GOD; Thus saith the Lord GOD to the mountains, and to the hills, to the rivers, and to the valleys; Behold, I, *even* I, will bring a sword upon you, and I will destroy your high places.

4 And your altars shall be desolate, and your images shall be broken: and I will cast down your slain *men* before your idols.

5 And I will lay the dead carcases of the children of Israel before their idols; and I will scatter your bones round about your altars.

6 In all your dwellingplaces the cities shall be laid waste, and the high places shall be desolate; that your altars may be laid waste and made desolate, and your idols may be broken and cease, and your images may be cut down, and your works may be abolished.

7 And the slain shall fall in the midst of you, and ye shall know that I *am* the LORD.

8 ¶ Yet will I leave a remnant, that ye may have *some* that shall escape the sword among the nations, when ye shall be scattered through the countries.

9 And they that escape of you shall remember me among the nations whither they shall be carried captives, because I am broken with their whorish heart, which hath departed from me, and with their eyes, which go a-whoring after their idols: and they shall loathe themselves for the evils which they have committed in all their abominations.

10 And they shall know that I *am* the LORD, *and that* I have not said in vain that I would do this evil unto them.

11 ¶ Thus saith the Lord GOD; Smite with thine hand, and stamp with thy foot, and say, Alas for all the evil abominations of the house of Israel! for they shall fall by the sword, by the famine, and by the pestilence.

12 He that is far off shall die of the pestilence; and he that is near shall fall by the sword; and he that remaineth and is besieged shall die by the famine: thus will I accomplish my fury upon them.

13 Then shall ye know that I *am* the LORD, when their slain *men* shall be among their idols round about their altars, upon every high hill, in all the tops of the mountains, and under every green tree, and under every thick oak, the place where they did offer sweet savour to all their idols.

14 So will I stretch out my hand upon them, and make the land desolate, yea, more desolate than the wilderness toward Diblath, in all their habitations: and they shall know that I *am* the LORD.

**7** MOREOVER THE word of the LORD came unto me, saying,

2 Also, thou son of man, thus saith the Lord GOD unto the land of Israel; An end, the end is come upon the four corners of the land.

3 Now *is* the end *come* upon thee, and I will send mine anger upon thee, and will judge thee according to thy ways, and will recompense upon thee all thine abominations.

## Amplified

17 And I will send upon you hunger and wild beasts, and they shall bereave you [of your loved ones]; and pestilence and blood shall pass through you, and I will bring the sword upon you. I, the Lord, have spoken it.

**6** AND THE word of the Lord came to me, saying,

2 Son of man, set your face toward the mountains of Israel, and prophesy against them,

3 And say, You mountains of Israel, hear the word of the Lord God! Thus says the Lord God to the mountains and the hills, to the river ravines and the valleys: Behold, I, even I, will bring a sword upon you, and I will destroy your high places [of idolatrous worship],

4 And your altars shall be made desolate, and your sun-pillars shall be broken in pieces, and I will cast down your slain before your idols. [Lev. 26:30.]

5 And I will lay the dead bodies of the children of Israel before their idols, and I will scatter your bones round about your altars.

6 In all your dwelling places the cities shall be laid waste, and the high places shall be made desolate, that your altars may bear their guilt *and* be laid waste and made desolate, and your idols may be broken and destroyed, and your sun images may be hewn down and your handiworks may be wiped away *and* blotted out.

7 And the slain shall fall in the midst of you, and you shall know, understand *and* realize that I am the Lord.

8 Yet will I leave some of you alive. When you have some that shall escape the sword among the nations, when you shall be scattered through the countries,

9 Then those of you who escape shall [earnestly] remember Me among the nations to which they shall be carried captive, how that I have been broken by their lewdness *and* have Myself broken their wanton heart which has departed from Me, and blinded their eyes which turn after their idols wantonly; and they shall be loathsome in their own sight for the evils which they have committed in all their abominations.

10 And they shall know, understand *and* realize that I am the Lord. I have not said in vain that I would bring this evil calamity [in punishment] upon them.

11 Thus says the Lord God: Strike with your fist, stamp with your foot, and say, Alas! over all the vile abominations of the house of Israel, for which [Israel] shall fall by sword, by famine, and by pestilence.

12 He who is far off shall die of the pestilence, and he that is near shall fall by the sword, and he who remains and is preserved shall die by the famine. Thus will I accomplish My wrath upon them.

13 Then shall you know, understand *and* realize that I am the Lord, when their slain shall lie among their idols round about their altars upon every high hill, on all the tops of the mountains, under every green tree, and under every thickly leafed oak, the places where they were accustomed to offer sweet incense to all their idols.

14 And I will stretch out My hand upon them, and make the land desolate and waste, yes, more desolate than the wilderness toward Diblah [a Moabite city], throughout all their dwelling places; and they shall know, understand *and* realize that I am the Lord.

**7** MOREOVER THE word of the Lord came to me, saying,

2 Also, son of man, thus says the Lord God to the land of Israel: An end! The end is come upon the four corners of the land. [Ezek. 11:13; Amos 8:2.]

3 Now is the end upon you, and I will send My anger upon you, and will judge you according to your ways, and will bring upon you retribution for all your abominations.

## New American Standard

17'Moreover, I will send on you famine and wild beasts, and
they will bereave you of children; plague and bloodshed also will
pass through you, and I will bring the sword on you. I, the LORD,
have spoken.' "

*Idolatrous Worship Denounced*

**6** AND THE word of the LORD came to me saying,
2"Son of man, set your face toward the mountains of Israel,
and prophesy against them,
3and say, 'Mountains of Israel, listen to the word of the Lord
GOD! Thus says the Lord GOD to the mountains, the hills, the
ravines and the valleys: "Behold, I Myself am going to bring a
sword on you, and I will destroy your high places.
4"So your altars will become desolate, and your incense altars
will be smashed; and I shall make your slain fall in front of your
idols.
5"I shall also lay the dead bodies of the sons of Israel in front
of their idols; and I shall scatter your bones around your altars.
6"In all your dwellings, cities will become waste and the high
places will be desolate, that your altars may become waste and
desolate, your idols may be broken and brought to an end, your
incense altars may be cut down, and your works may be blotted
out.
7"And the slain will fall among you, and you will know that
I am the LORD.
8¶ "However, I shall leave a remnant, for you will have those
who escaped the sword among the nations when you are scattered
among the countries.
9"Then those of you who escape will remember Me among the
nations to which they will be carried captive, how I have been hurt
by their adulterous hearts which turned away from Me, and by
their eyes, which played the harlot after their idols; and they will
loathe themselves in their own sight for the evils which they have
committed, for all their abominations.
10"Then they will know that I am the LORD; I have not said in
vain that I would inflict this disaster on them." '
11¶ "Thus says the Lord GOD, 'Clap your hand, stamp your foot,
and say, "Alas, because of all the evil abominations of the house
of Israel, which will fall by sword, famine, and plague!
12"He who is far off will die by the plague, and he who is near
will fall by the sword, and he who remains and is besieged will die
by the famine. Thus shall I spend My wrath on them.
13"Then you will know that I am the LORD, when their slain are
among their idols around their altars, on every high hill, on all the
tops of the mountains, under every green tree, and under every
leafy oak—the places where they offered soothing aroma to all
their idols.
14"So throughout all their habitations I shall stretch out My
hand against them and make the land more desolate and waste
than the wilderness toward Diblah; thus they will know that I am
the LORD." ' "

*Punishment for Wickedness Foretold*

**7** MOREOVER, THE word of the LORD came to me saying,
2"And you, son of man, thus says the Lord GOD to the land
of Israel, 'An end! The end is coming on the four corners of the
land.
3'Now the end is upon you, and I shall send My anger against
you; I shall judge you according to your ways, and I shall bring all
your abominations upon you.

## New International

famine and wild beasts against you, and they will leave you childless. Plague and bloodshed will sweep through you, and I will
bring the sword against you. I the LORD have spoken."

*A Prophecy Against the Mountains of Israel*

**6** THE WORD of the LORD came to me: 2"Son of man, set your
face against the mountains of Israel; prophesy against them
3and say: 'O mountains of Israel, hear the word of the Sovereign
LORD. This is what the Sovereign LORD says to the mountains and
hills, to the ravines and valleys: I am about to bring a sword against
you, and I will destroy your high places. 4Your altars will be
demolished and your incense altars will be smashed; and I will slay
your people in front of your idols. 5I will lay the dead bodies of the
Israelites in front of their idols, and I will scatter your bones around
your altars. 6Wherever you live, the towns will be laid waste and
the high places demolished, so that your altars will be laid waste
and devastated, your idols smashed and ruined, your incense
altars broken down, and what you have made wiped out. 7Your
people will fall slain among you, and you will know that I am the
LORD.
8" 'But I will spare some, for some of you will escape the sword
when you are scattered among the lands and nations. 9Then in the
nations where they have been carried captive, those who escape
will remember me—how I have been grieved by their adulterous
hearts, which have turned away from me, and by their eyes, which
have lusted after their idols. They will loathe themselves for the
evil they have done and for all their detestable practices. 10And
they will know that I am the LORD; I did not threaten in vain to
bring this calamity on them.
11" 'This is what the Sovereign LORD says: Strike your hands
together and stamp your feet and cry out "Alas!" because of all the
wicked and detestable practices of the house of Israel, for they will
fall by the sword, famine and plague. 12He that is far away will die
of the plague, and he that is near will fall by the sword, and he that
survives and is spared will die of famine. So will I spend my wrath
upon them. 13And they will know that I am the LORD, when their
people lie slain among their idols around their altars, on every high
hill and on all the mountaintops, under every spreading tree and
every leafy oak—places where they offered fragrant incense to all
their idols. 14And I will stretch out my hand against them and
make the land a desolate waste from the desert to Diblah[a]—wherever they live. Then they will know that I am the
LORD.' "

*The End Has Come*

**7** THE WORD of the LORD came to me: 2"Son of man, this is
what the Sovereign LORD says to the land of Israel: The end!
The end has come upon the four corners of the land. 3The end is
now upon you and I will unleash my anger against you. I will
judge you according to your conduct and repay you for all your
detestable practices. 4I will not look on you with pity or spare you;

NIV [a] 14 Most Hebrew manuscripts; a few Hebrew manuscripts *Riblah*

## King James

4And mine eye shall not spare thee, neither will I have pity: but I will recompense thy ways upon thee, and thine abominations shall be in the midst of thee: and ye shall know that I *am* the LORD.

5Thus saith the Lord GOD; An evil, an only evil, behold, is come.

6An end is come, the end is come: it watcheth for thee; behold, it is come.

7The morning is come unto thee, O thou that dwellest in the land: the time is come, the day of trouble *is* near, and not the sounding again of the mountains.

8Now will I shortly pour out my fury upon thee, and accomplish mine anger upon thee: and I will judge thee according to thy ways, and will recompense thee for all thine abominations.

9And mine eye shall not spare, neither will I have pity: I will recompense thee according to thy ways and thine abominations *that* are in the midst of thee; and ye shall know that I *am* the LORD that smiteth.

10Behold the day, behold, it is come: the morning is gone forth; the rod hath blossomed, pride hath budded.

11Violence is risen up into a rod of wickedness: none of them *shall remain*, nor of their multitude, nor of any of theirs: neither *shall there be* wailing for them.

12The time is come, the day draweth near: let not the buyer rejoice, nor the seller mourn: for wrath *is* upon all the multitude thereof.

13For the seller shall not return to that which is sold, although they were yet alive: for the vision *is* touching the whole multitude thereof, *which* shall not return; neither shall any strengthen himself in the iniquity of his life.

14They have blown the trumpet, even to make all ready; but none goeth to the battle: for my wrath *is* upon all the multitude thereof.

15The sword *is* without, and the pestilence and the famine within: he that *is* in the field shall die with the sword; and he that *is* in the city, famine and pestilence shall devour him.

16¶ But they that escape of them shall escape, and shall be on the mountains like doves of the valleys, all of them mourning, every one for his iniquity.

17All hands shall be feeble, and all knees shall be weak *as* water.

18They shall also gird *themselves* with sackcloth, and horror shall cover them; and shame *shall be* upon all faces, and baldness upon all their heads.

19They shall cast their silver in the streets, and their gold shall be removed: their silver and their gold shall not be able to deliver them in the day of the wrath of the LORD: they shall not satisfy their souls, neither fill their bowels: because it is the stumblingblock of their iniquity.

20¶ As for the beauty of his ornament, he set it in majesty: but they made the images of their abominations *and* of their detestable things therein: therefore have I set it far from them.

21And I will give it into the hands of the strangers for a prey, and to the wicked of the earth for a spoil; and they shall pollute it.

22My face will I turn also from them, and they shall pollute my secret *place:* for the robbers shall enter into it, and defile it.

23¶ Make a chain: for the land is full of bloody crimes, and the city is full of violence.

24Wherefore I will bring the worst of the heathen, and they shall possess their houses: I will also make the pomp of the strong to cease; and their holy places shall be defiled.

## Amplified

4And My eye will not spare you, neither will I have pity; but I will bring recompense for your evil ways upon you, while your abominations are in the midst of you [calling down punishment from a righteous God]; and you shall know—recognize, understand and realize—that I am the Lord.

5Thus says the Lord God: Behold, an evil is come, [an evil so destructive and injurious, so sudden and violent that it stands alone, not as a succession but as] only one evil.

6An end is come! The end is come! *The end* [after sleeping so long] awakes against you. See, it comes!

7Your turn—your doom—has come upon you, O inhabitant of the land, the time has come, the day is near, a day not of joyful shouting, but a day of tumult upon the mountains.

8Now will I shortly pour out My wrath upon you, and finish spending My anger against you; and I will judge you according to your ways, and I will recompense you with punishment for all your abominations.

9And My eye will not spare, nor will I have pity. I will punish you according to your ways while your abominations are right in the midst of you. And you shall know, understand *and* realize that it is I, the Lord, Who smites you.

10Behold, the day! Behold, it comes! Your doom has gone forth, the rod has blossomed, pride has budded.

11Violence has grown up into a rod of wickedness; none of [Israel] shall remain, nor of their abundance, nor of their wealth; neither shall there be preeminence among them *or* wailing for them.

12The time has come, the day draws near. Let not the buyer rejoice, nor the seller mourn, for wrath is upon all their multitude.

13For the seller shall not return to that which is sold, even were they yet alive. For the vision [of punishment] is touching [Israel's] whole multitude; he shall not come back, neither shall any strengthen himself whose life is in his iniquity.

14They have blown the trumpet, and have made all ready; but none goes to the battle, for My wrath is upon all their multitude.

15The sword is without, and pestilence and famine are within. He who is in the field shall die by the sword, and him who is in the city, famine and pestilence shall devour.

16But those of them that escape shall escape, *but* shall be on the mountains like doves of the valleys, all of them moaning, every one in his iniquity's *punishment*.

17All hands shall be feeble, and all knees shall be weak as water. [Isa. 13:7; Jer. 6:24; Ezek. 21:7.]

18They shall also gird themselves with sackcloth; horror *and* dismay shall cover them, and shame shall be upon all faces, and baldness upon all their heads [as evidence of grief].

19They shall cast their silver into the streets, and their gold shall be *discarded* like an unclean thing *or* rubbish; their silver and their gold shall not be able to deliver them in the day of the wrath of the Lord; they shall not satisfy their animal cravings nor fill their stomachs with them, for *wealth* has been the stumbling-block of their iniquity. [Prov. 11:4; Zeph. 1:18.]

20As for the beauty of gold for ornament, they turned it to pride, and they made of it the images of their abominations [idols] and of their detestable things. Therefore I will make it to them as an unclean thing.

21And I will give it for plunder into the hands of strangers, and to the wicked of the earth for a spoil, and they shall profane it.

22Also I will turn My face from them, and they shall profane My secret treasure, *the temple;* and robbers shall enter into it and profane it.

23Prepare the chain [of imprisonment]; for the land is full of blood-guiltiness [murders committed with pretended formalities of justice], and the city is full of violence.

24Therefore I will bring in the worst of the [heathen] nations, who will take possession of the houses [of the people of Judah]; I will also silence their strongholds *and* put an end to their proud might, and their holy places *and* those who sanctify them shall be profaned.

## New American Standard

4'For My eye will have no pity on you, nor shall I spare *you*, but I shall bring your ways upon you, and your abominations will be among you; then you will know that I am the LORD!'

5¶ "Thus says the Lord GOD, 'A disaster, unique disaster, behold it is coming!

6'An end is coming; the end has come! It has awakened against you; behold, it has come!

7'Your doom has come to you, O inhabitant of the land. The time has come, the day is near—tumult rather than joyful shouting on the mountains.

8'Now I will shortly pour out My wrath on you, and spend My anger against you, judge you according to your ways, and bring on you all your abominations.

9'And My eye will show no pity, nor will I spare. I will repay you according to your ways, while your abominations are in your midst; then you will know that I, the LORD, do the smiting.

10¶ 'Behold, the day! Behold, it is coming! *Your* doom has gone forth; the rod has budded, arrogance has blossomed.

11'Violence has grown into a rod of wickedness. None of them *shall remain,* none of their multitude, none of their wealth, nor anything eminent among them.

12'The time has come, the day has arrived. Let not the buyer rejoice nor the seller mourn; for wrath is against all their multitude.

13'Indeed, the seller will not regain what he sold as long as they *both* live; for the vision regarding all their multitude will not be averted, nor will any of them maintain his life by his iniquity.

14¶ 'They have blown the trumpet and made everything ready, but no one is going to the battle; for My wrath is against all their multitude.

15'The sword is outside, and the plague and the famine are within. He who is in the field will die by the sword; famine and the plague will also consume those in the city.

16'Even when their survivors escape, they will be on the mountains like doves of the valleys, all of them mourning, each over his own iniquity.

17'All hands will hang limp, and all knees will become like water.

18'And they will gird themselves with sackcloth, and shuddering will overwhelm them; and shame *will be* on all faces, and baldness on all their heads.

19'They shall fling their silver into the streets, and their gold shall become an abhorrent thing; their silver and their gold shall not be able to deliver them in the day of the wrath of the LORD. They cannot satisfy their appetite, nor can they fill their stomachs, for their iniquity has become an occasion of stumbling.

*The Temple Profaned*

20'And they transformed the beauty of His ornaments into pride, and they made the images of their abominations *and* their detestable things with it; therefore I will make it an abhorrent thing to them.

21'And I shall give it into the hands of the foreigners as plunder and to the wicked of the earth as spoil, and they will profane it.

22'I shall also turn My face from them, and they will profane My secret place; then robbers will enter and profane it.

23¶ 'Make the chain, for the land is full of bloody crimes, and the city is full of violence.

24'Therefore, I shall bring the worst of the nations, and they will possess their houses. I shall also make the pride of the strong ones cease, and their holy places will be profaned.

## New International

I will surely repay you for your conduct and the detestable practices among you. Then you will know that I am the LORD.

5"This is what the Sovereign LORD says: Disaster! An unheard-
of[a] disaster is coming. 6The end has come! The end has come! It
has roused itself against you. It has come! 7Doom has come upon
you—you who dwell in the land. The time has come, the day is
near; there is panic, not joy, upon the mountains. 8I am about to
pour out my wrath on you and spend my anger against you; I will
judge you according to your conduct and repay you for all your
detestable practices. 9I will not look on you with pity or spare you;
I will repay you in accordance with your conduct and the detestable practices among you. Then you will know that it is I the LORD who strikes the blow.

10"The day is here! It has come! Doom has burst forth, the rod
has budded, arrogance has blossomed! 11Violence has grown into[b]
a rod to punish wickedness; none of the people will be left, none
of that crowd—no wealth, nothing of value. 12The time has come,
the day has arrived. Let not the buyer rejoice nor the seller grieve,
for wrath is upon the whole crowd. 13The seller will not recover
the land he has sold as long as both of them live, for the vision
concerning the whole crowd will not be reversed. Because of their
sins, not one of them will preserve his life. 14Though they blow the
trumpet and get everything ready, no one will go into battle, for
my wrath is upon the whole crowd.

15"Outside is the sword, inside are plague and famine; those in
the country will die by the sword, and those in the city will be
devoured by famine and plague. 16All who survive and escape will
be in the mountains, moaning like doves of the valleys, each
because of his sins. 17Every hand will go limp, and every knee will
become as weak as water. 18They will put on sackcloth and be
clothed with terror. Their faces will be covered with shame and
their heads will be shaved. 19They will throw their silver into the
streets, and their gold will be an unclean thing. Their silver and gold will not be able to save them in the day of the LORD's wrath. They will not satisfy their hunger or fill their stomachs with it, for
it has made them stumble into sin. 20They were proud of their
beautiful jewelry and used it to make their detestable idols and vile images. Therefore I will turn these into an unclean thing for them.
21I will hand it all over as plunder to foreigners and as loot to the
wicked of the earth, and they will defile it. 22I will turn my face
away from them, and they will desecrate my treasured place; robbers will enter it and desecrate it.

23"Prepare chains, because the land is full of bloodshed and the
city is full of violence. 24I will bring the most wicked of the nations
to take possession of their houses; I will put an end to the pride
of the mighty, and their sanctuaries will be desecrated. 25When

NIV [a] 5 Most Hebrew manuscripts; some Hebrew manuscripts and Syriac *Disaster after* [b] 11 Or *The violent one has become*

## King James

25 Destruction cometh; and they shall seek peace, and *there shall be* none.

26 Mischief shall come upon mischief, and rumour shall be upon rumour; then shall they seek a vision of the prophet; but the law shall perish from the priest, and counsel from the ancients.

27 The king shall mourn, and the prince shall be clothed with desolation, and the hands of the people of the land shall be troubled: I will do unto them after their way, and according to their deserts will I judge them; and they shall know that I *am* the LORD.

8 AND IT came to pass in the sixth year, in the sixth *month,* in the fifth *day* of the month, *as* I sat in mine house, and the elders of Judah sat before me, that the hand of the Lord GOD fell there upon me.

2 Then I beheld, and lo a likeness as the appearance of fire: from the appearance of his loins even downward, fire; and from his loins even upward, as the appearance of brightness, as the colour of amber.

3 And he put forth the form of an hand, and took me by a lock of mine head; and the spirit lifted me up between the earth and the heaven, and brought me in the visions of God to Jerusalem, to the door of the inner gate that looketh toward the north; where *was* the seat of the image of jealousy, which provoketh to jealousy.

4 And, behold, the glory of the God of Israel *was* there, according to the vision that I saw in the plain.

5 ¶ Then said he unto me, Son of man, lift up thine eyes now the way toward the north. So I lifted up mine eyes the way toward the north, and behold northward at the gate of the altar this image of jealousy in the entry.

6 He said furthermore unto me, Son of man, seest thou what they do? *even* the great abominations that the house of Israel committeth here, that I should go far off from my sanctuary? but turn thee yet again, *and* thou shalt see greater abominations.

7 ¶ And he brought me to the door of the court; and when I looked, behold a hole in the wall.

8 Then said he unto me, Son of man, dig now in the wall: and when I had digged in the wall, behold a door.

9 And he said unto me, Go in, and behold the wicked abominations that they do here.

10 So I went in and saw; and behold every form of creeping things, and abominable beasts, and all the idols of the house of Israel, portrayed upon the wall round about.

11 And there stood before them seventy men of the ancients of the house of Israel, and in the midst of them stood Jaazaniah the son of Shaphan, with every man his censer in his hand; and a thick cloud of incense went up.

12 Then said he unto me, Son of man, hast thou seen what the ancients of the house of Israel do in the dark, every man in the chambers of his imagery? for they say, The LORD seeth us not; the LORD hath forsaken the earth.

13 ¶ He said also unto me, Turn thee yet again, *and* thou shalt see greater abominations that they do.

14 Then he brought me to the door of the gate of the LORD's house which *was* toward the north; and, behold, there sat women weeping for Tammuz.

15 ¶ Then said he unto me, Hast thou seen *this,* O son of man? turn thee yet again, *and* thou shalt see greater abominations than these.

## Amplified

25 Distress, panic *and* destruction shall come, and they [of Judah] shall seek peace, and there shall be none.

26 Calamity shall come upon calamity, and rumor shall be upon rumor; and they shall seek a vision of the prophet; and the law *and* instruction shall cease from the [distracted] priest, and counsel from the [dismayed] elders. [Ps. 74:9; Lam. 2:9.]

27 The king [of Judah] shall wear mourning, and the prince shall clothe himself with garments of despair *and* desolation, while the hands of the people of the land shall tremble—palsied by terror; for I will do to them in accordance with their ways, and according to their deserts will I judge them; and they shall know, recognize *and* realize that I am the Lord.

8 AND IN the sixth year [of the capitivity of King Jehoiachin], in the sixth month, on the fifth day of the month, as I sat in my house [a captive of the Babylonians], with the elders of Judah sitting before me, the hand of Lord God fell there upon me.

2 Then I beheld, and lo, a likeness of a Man with the appearance of fire; from His waist downward was like fire, and from His waist upward had the appearance of brightness like gleaming bronze.

3 And He put forth the form of a hand, and took me by a lock of my head; and the Spirit lifted me up between the earth and the heavens, and brought me in the visions of God to Jerusalem, to the entrance of the door of the inner [court] which faces toward the north, where is the seat of the idol-image of jealousy, which provokes to jealousy. [II Kings 16:10-16; 21:4, 5.]

4 And behold, there was the glory of the God of Israel [Who had loved and chosen them], like the vision I saw in the plain. [Ezek. 1:28; 3:22, 23.]

5 Then He [the Spirit] said to me, Son of man, now lift up your eyes toward the north. So I lifted up my eyes toward the north, and behold, on the north of the altar gate that idol-image of jealousy in the entrance.

6 Furthermore [the Spirit] said to me, Son of man, do you see what they are doing? The great abominations that the house of Israel is committing here to drive Me far from My sanctuary? But you shall again see greater abominations.

7 And He brought me to the door of the court; and when I looked, behold, there was a hole in the wall.

8 Then He said to me, Son of man, dig now in the wall; and when I had dug in the wall, behold, there was a door.

9 And He said to me, Go in, and see the wicked abominations that they do here.

10 So I went in and saw there pictures of every form of creeping things, and loathsome beasts, and all the idols of the house of Israel, painted round about on the wall.

11 And there stood before these [pictures] seventy men of the elders of the house of Israel, and in the midst of them stood Jaazaniah the son of Shaphan [the scribe], with every man his censer in his hand, and a thick cloud of incense was going up [in prayer to these their gods].

12 Then said He to me, Son of man, have you seen what the elders of the house of Israel do in the dark, every man in his *secret* chambers of [idol] pictures? For they say, The Lord does not see us; the Lord has forsaken the land.

13 He said also to me, Yet again you shall see greater abominations which they are committing.

14 Then he brought me to the entrance of the north gate of the Lord's house; and behold, there sat women weeping for Tammuz [a Babylonian god, who was supposed to die annually and subsequently be resurrected].

15 Then said [the Spirit] to me, Have you seen this, O son of man? Yet again you shall see greater abominations that they are committing.

## New American Standard

25'When anguish comes, they will seek peace, but there will be
none.
26'Disaster will come upon disaster, and rumor will be *added* to
rumor; then they will seek a vision from a prophet, but the law will
be lost from the priest and counsel from the elders.
27'The king will mourn, the prince will be clothed with horror,
and the hands of the people of the land will tremble. According
to their conduct I shall deal with them, and by their judgments I
shall judge them. And they will know that I am the LORD.' "

*Vision of Abominations in Jerusalem*

8 AND IT came about in the sixth year, on the fifth *day* of the
sixth month, as I was sitting in my house with the elders of
Judah sitting before me, that the hand of the Lord GOD fell on me
there.
2Then I looked, and behold, a likeness as the appearance of a
man; from His loins and downward *there was* the appearance of
fire, and from His loins and upward the appearance of brightness,
like the appearance of glowing metal.
3And He stretched out the form of a hand and caught me by
a lock of my head; and the Spirit lifted me up between earth and
heaven and brought me in the visions of God to Jerusalem, to the
entrance of the north gate of the inner *court,* where the seat of the
idol of jealousy, which provokes to jealousy, was *located.*
4And behold, the glory of the God of Israel *was* there, like the
appearance which I saw in the plain.
5¶ Then He said to me, "Son of man, raise your eyes, now,
toward the north." So I raised my eyes toward the north, and
behold, to the north of the altar gate *was* this idol of jealousy at the
entrance.
6And He said to me, "Son of man, do you see what they are
doing, the great abominations which the house of Israel are committing here, that I should be far from My sanctuary? But yet you
will see still greater abominations."
7¶ Then He brought me to the entrance of the court, and when
I looked, behold, a hole in the wall.
8And He said to me, "Son of man, now dig through the wall."
So I dug through the wall, and behold, an entrance.
9And He said to me, "Go in and see the wicked abominations
that they are committing here."
10So I entered and looked, and behold, every form of creeping
things and beasts *and* detestable things, with all the idols of the
house of Israel, were carved on the wall all around.
11And standing in front of them were seventy elders of the
house of Israel, with Jaazaniah the son of Shaphan standing
among them, each man with his censer in his hand, and the
fragrance of the cloud of incense rising.
12Then He said to me, "Son of man, do you see what the elders
of the house of Israel are committing in the dark, each man in the
room of his carved images? For they say, 'The LORD does not see
us; the LORD has forsaken the land.' "
13And He said to me, "Yet you will see still greater abominations which they are committing."
14¶ Then He brought me to the entrance of the gate of the LORD's
house which *was* toward the north; and behold, women were
sitting there weeping for Tammuz.
15And He said to me, "Do you see *this,* son of man? Yet you will
see still greater abominations than these."

## New International

terror comes, they will seek peace, but there will be none.
26Calamity upon calamity will come, and rumor upon rumor. They
will try to get a vision from the prophet; the teaching of the law
by the priest will be lost, as will the counsel of the elders. 27The
king will mourn, the prince will be clothed with despair, and the
hands of the people of the land will tremble. I will deal with them
according to their conduct, and by their own standards I will judge
them. Then they will know that I am the LORD."

*Idolatry in the Temple*

8 IN THE sixth year, in the sixth month on the fifth day, while
I was sitting in my house and the elders of Judah were sitting
before me, the hand of the Sovereign LORD came upon me there.
2I looked, and I saw a figure like that of a man.[a] From what
appeared to be his waist down he was like fire, and from there up
his appearance was as bright as glowing metal. 3He stretched out
what looked like a hand and took me by the hair of my head. The
Spirit lifted me up between earth and heaven and in visions of God
he took me to Jerusalem, to the entrance to the north gate of the
inner court, where the idol that provokes to jealousy stood. 4And
there before me was the glory of the God of Israel, as in the vision
I had seen in the plain.
5Then he said to me, "Son of man, look toward the north." So
I looked, and in the entrance north of the gate of the altar I saw
this idol of jealousy.
6And he said to me, "Son of man, do you see what they are
doing—the utterly detestable things the house of Israel is doing
here, things that will drive me far from my sanctuary? But you will
see things that are even more detestable."
7Then he brought me to the entrance to the court. I looked, and
I saw a hole in the wall. 8He said to me, "Son of man, now dig into
the wall." So I dug into the wall and saw a doorway there.
9And he said to me, "Go in and see the wicked and detestable
things they are doing here." 10So I went in and looked, and I saw
portrayed all over the walls all kinds of crawling things and detestable animals and all the idols of the house of Israel. 11In front of
them stood seventy elders of the house of Israel, and Jaazaniah son
of Shaphan was standing among them. Each had a censer in his
hand, and a fragrant cloud of incense was rising.
12He said to me, "Son of man, have you seen what the elders
of the house of Israel are doing in the darkness, each at the shrine
of his own idol? They say, 'The LORD does not see us; the LORD
has forsaken the land.' " 13Again, he said, "You will see them
doing things that are even more detestable."
14Then he brought me to the entrance to the north gate of the
house of the LORD, and I saw women sitting there, mourning for
Tammuz. 15He said to me, "Do you see this, son of man? You will
see things that are even more detestable than this."

NIV [a] 2 Or *saw a fiery figure*

## King James

16And he brought me into the inner court of the LORD's house, and, behold, at the door of the temple of the LORD, between the porch and the altar, *were* about five and twenty men, with their backs toward the temple of the LORD, and their faces toward the east; and they worshipped the sun toward the east.

17¶ Then he said unto me, Hast thou seen *this,* O son of man? Is it a light thing to the house of Judah that they commit the abominations which they commit here? for they have filled the land with violence, and have returned to provoke me to anger: and, lo, they put the branch to their nose.

18Therefore will I also deal in fury: mine eye shall not spare, neither will I have pity: and though they cry in mine ears with a loud voice, *yet* will I not hear them.

9 HE CRIED also in mine ears with a loud voice, saying, Cause them that have charge over the city to draw near, even every man *with* his destroying weapon in his hand.

2And, behold, six men came from the way of the higher gate, which lieth toward the north, and every man a slaughter weapon in his hand; and one man among them *was* clothed with linen, with a writer's inkhorn by his side: and they went in, and stood beside the brasen altar.

3And the glory of the God of Israel was gone up from the cherub, whereupon he was, to the threshold of the house. And he called to the man clothed with linen, which *had* the writer's inkhorn by his side;

4And the LORD said unto him, Go through the midst of the city, through the midst of Jerusalem, and set a mark upon the foreheads of the men that sigh and that cry for all the abominations that be done in the midst thereof.

5¶ And to the others he said in mine hearing, Go ye after him through the city, and smite: let not your eye spare, neither have ye pity:

6Slay utterly old *and* young, both maids, and little children, and women: but come not near any man upon whom *is* the mark; and begin at my sanctuary. Then they began at the ancient men which *were* before the house.

7And he said unto them, Defile the house, and fill the courts with the slain: go ye forth. And they went forth, and slew in the city.

8¶ And it came to pass, while they were slaying them, and I was left, that I fell upon my face, and cried, and said, Ah Lord GOD! wilt thou destroy all the residue of Israel in thy pouring out of thy fury upon Jerusalem?

9Then said he unto me, The iniquity of the house of Israel and Judah *is* exceeding great, and the land is full of blood, and the city full of perverseness: for they say, The LORD hath forsaken the earth, and the LORD seeth not.

10And as for me also, mine eye shall not spare, neither will I have pity, *but* I will recompense their way upon their head.

11And, behold, the man clothed with linen, which *had* the inkhorn by his side, reported the matter, saying, I have done as thou hast commanded me.

## Amplified

16And He brought me to the inner court of the Lord's house, and behold, at the door of the temple of the Lord, between the porch and the bronze altar, were about twenty-five men with their backs to the temple of the Lord and their faces toward the east, and they were bowing themselves toward the east *and* worshiping the sun.

17Then [the Spirit] said to me, Have you seen this, O son of man? Is it too slight a thing to the house of Judah to commit the abominations which they commit here, that they must fill the land with violence, and turn back afresh to provoke Me to anger? And lo, they put the branch to their nose [actually, before their mouths, in superstitious worship]!

18Therefore I will deal in wrath; My eye will not spare, nor will I have pity; and though they cry in My ears with a loud voice, yet will I not hear them. [Prov. 1:28; Isa. 1:15; Jer. 11:11; 14:12; Mic. 3:4; Zech. 7:13.]

9 *THE SPIRIT* cried in my ears [in the vision] with a loud voice, saying, Cause those to draw near who have charge over the city [as executioners], every man with his destroying weapon in his hand.

2And, behold, six men came from the direction of the upper gate, which faces north, every man with his battle-ax in his hand; and one man among them was clothed in linen, with a writer's ink bottle at his side. And they went in and stood beside the bronze altar.

3And the glory of the God of Israel [the Shekinah, cloud] had gone up from the cherubim upon which it had rested to [stand above] the threshold of the [Lord's] house. And [the Lord] called to the man clothed with linen, who had the writer's ink *horn*-bottle at his side.

4And the Lord said to him, Go through the midst of the city, through the midst of Jerusalem, and set a mark upon the foreheads of the men who sigh and groan over all the abominations that are committed in the midst of it.

5And to the others He said in my hearing, Follow [the man with the ink bottle] through the city, and smite; let not your eye spare, neither have any pity.

6Slay outright the elderly, the young man and the virgin, the infant and the women; but do not touch *or* go near any one on whom is the mark. Begin at My sanctuary. So they began with the old men who were in front of the temple [who did not have the Lord's mark on their foreheads]. [I Pet. 4:17.]

7And He said to [the executioners], Defile the temple, and fill its courts with the slain. Go forth! And they went forth, and slew in the city.

8And while they were slaying them, and I was left, I fell upon my face, and cried, Ah Lord God! Will you destroy all that is left of Israel in Your pouring out of Your wrath *and* indignation upon Jerusalem?

9Then said He to me, The iniquity *and* guilt of the house of Israel and Judah *are* exceedingly great; the land is full of blood, and the city full of injustice *and* perverseness; for they say, The Lord has forsaken the land; the Lord does not see [what we are doing].

10And as for Me, My eye will not spare, neither will I have pity, but I will recompense their wicked doings upon their own heads.

11And, behold, the man clothed in linen, who had the ink bottle at his side, reported the matter, saying, I have done as You have commanded me.

## New American Standard

16¶ Then He brought me into the inner court of the LORD's
house. And behold, at the entrance to the temple of the LORD,
between the porch and the altar, *were* about twenty-five men with
their backs to the temple of the LORD and their faces toward the
east; and they were prostrating themselves eastward toward the
sun.
17And He said to me, "Do you see *this,* son of man? Is it too light
a thing for the house of Judah to commit the abominations which
they have committed here, that they have filled the land with
violence and provoked Me repeatedly? For behold, they are putting the twig to their nose.
18"Therefore, I indeed shall deal in wrath. My eye will have no
pity nor shall I spare; and though they cry in My ears with a loud
voice, yet I shall not listen to them."

*The Vision of Slaughter*

9 THEN HE cried out in my hearing with a loud voice saying,
"Draw near, O executioners of the city, each with his destroying weapon in his hand."
2And behold, six men came from the direction of the upper
gate which faces north, each with his shattering weapon in his
hand; and among them was a certain man clothed in linen with a
writing case at his loins. And they went in and stood beside the
bronze altar.
3¶ Then the glory of the God of Israel went up from the cherub
on which it had been, to the threshold of the temple. And He called
to the man clothed in linen at whose loins was the writing case.
4And the LORD said to him, "Go through the midst of the city,
*even* through the midst of Jerusalem, and put a mark on the foreheads of the men who sigh and groan over all the abominations
which are being committed in its midst."
5But to the others He said in my hearing, "Go through the city
after him and strike; do not let your eye have pity, and do not
spare.
6"Utterly slay old men, young men, maidens, little children,
and women, but do not touch any man on whom is the mark; and
you shall start from My sanctuary." So they started with the elders
who *were* before the temple.
7And He said to them, "Defile the temple and fill the courts
with the slain. Go out!" Thus they went out and struck down *the*
*people* in the city.
8Then it came about as they were striking and I *alone* was left,
that I fell on my face and cried out saying, "Alas, Lord GOD! Art
Thou destroying the whole remnant of Israel by pouring out Thy
wrath on Jerusalem?"
9¶ Then He said to me, "The iniquity of the house of Israel and
Judah is very, very great, and the land is filled with blood, and the
city is full of perversion; for they say, 'The LORD has forsaken the
land, and the LORD does not see!'
10"But as for Me, My eye will have no pity nor shall I spare, but
I shall bring their conduct upon their heads."
11¶ Then behold, the man clothed in linen at whose loins was
the writing case reported, saying, "I have done just as Thou hast
commanded me."

## New International

16He then brought me into the inner court of the house of the
LORD, and there at the entrance to the temple, between the portico
and the altar, were about twenty-five men. With their backs
toward the temple of the LORD and their faces toward the east, they
were bowing down to the sun in the east.
17He said to me, "Have you seen this, son of man? Is it a trivial
matter for the house of Judah to do the detestable things they are
doing here? Must they also fill the land with violence and continually provoke me to anger? Look at them putting the branch to their
nose! 18Therefore I will deal with them in anger; I will not look on
them with pity or spare them. Although they shout in my ears, I
will not listen to them."

*Idolaters Killed*

9 THEN I heard him call out in a loud voice, "Bring the guards
of the city here, each with a weapon in his hand." 2And I saw
six men coming from the direction of the upper gate, which faces
north, each with a deadly weapon in his hand. With them was a
man clothed in linen who had a writing kit at his side. They came
in and stood beside the bronze altar.
3Now the glory of the God of Israel went up from above the
cherubim, where it had been, and moved to the threshold of the
temple. Then the LORD called to the man clothed in linen who had
the writing kit at his side 4and said to him, "Go throughout the city
of Jerusalem and put a mark on the foreheads of those who grieve
and lament over all the detestable things that are done in it."
5As I listened, he said to the others, "Follow him through the
city and kill, without showing pity or compassion. 6Slaughter old
men, young men and maidens, women and children, but do not
touch anyone who has the mark. Begin at my sanctuary." So they
began with the elders who were in front of the temple.
7Then he said to them, "Defile the temple and fill the courts
with the slain. Go!" So they went out and began killing throughout
the city. 8While they were killing and I was left alone, I fell facedown, crying out, "Ah, Sovereign LORD! Are you going to destroy
the entire remnant of Israel in this outpouring of your wrath on
Jerusalem?"
9He answered me, "The sin of the house of Israel and Judah is
exceedingly great; the land is full of bloodshed and the city is full
of injustice. They say, 'The LORD has forsaken the land; the LORD
does not see.' 10So I will not look on them with pity or spare them,
but I will bring down on their own heads what they have done."
11Then the man in linen with the writing kit at his side brought
back word, saying, "I have done as you commanded."

## King James

10 THEN I looked, and, behold, in the firmament that was above the head of the cherubims there appeared over them as it were a sapphire stone, as the appearance of the likeness of a throne.

2And he spake unto the man clothed with linen, and said, Go in between the wheels, *even* under the cherub, and fill thine hand with coals of fire from between the cherubims, and scatter *them* over the city. And he went in in my sight.

3Now the cherubims stood on the right side of the house, when the man went in; and the cloud filled the inner court.

4Then the glory of the LORD went up from the cherub, *and stood* over the threshold of the house; and the house was filled with the cloud, and the court was full of the brightness of the LORD's glory.

5And the sound of the cherubims' wings was heard *even* to the outer court, as the voice of the Almighty God when he speaketh.

6And it came to pass, *that* when he had commanded the man clothed with linen, saying, Take fire from between the wheels, from between the cherubims; then he went in, and stood beside the wheels.

7And *one* cherub stretched forth his hand from between the cherubims unto the fire that *was* between the cherubims, and took *thereof*, and put *it* into the hands of *him that was* clothed with linen: who took *it*, and went out.

8¶ And there appeared in the cherubims the form of a man's hand under their wings.

9And when I looked, behold the four wheels by the cherubims, one wheel by one cherub, and another wheel by another cherub: and the appearance of the wheels *was* as the colour of a beryl stone.

10And *as for* their appearances, they four had one likeness, as if a wheel had been in the midst of a wheel.

11When they went, they went upon their four sides; they turned not as they went, but to the place whither the head looked they followed it; they turned not as they went.

12And their whole body, and their backs, and their hands, and their wings, and the wheels, *were* full of eyes round about, *even* the wheels that they four had.

13As for the wheels, it was cried unto them in my hearing, O wheel.

14And every one had four faces: the first face *was* the face of a cherub, and the second face *was* the face of a man, and the third the face of a lion, and the fourth the face of an eagle.

15And the cherubims were lifted up. This *is* the living creature that I saw by the river of Chebar.

16And when the cherubims went, the wheels went by them: and when the cherubims lifted up their wings to mount up from the earth, the same wheels also turned not from beside them.

17When they stood, *these* stood; and when they were lifted up, *these* lifted up themselves *also:* for the spirit of the living creature *was* in them.

18Then the glory of the LORD departed from off the threshold of the house, and stood over the cherubims.

19And the cherubims lifted up their wings, and mounted up from the earth in my sight: when they went out, the wheels also *were* beside them, and *every one* stood at the door of the east gate of the LORD's house; and the glory of the God of Israel *was* over them above.

20This *is* the living creature that I saw under the God of Israel by the river of Chebar; and I knew that they *were* the cherubims.

21Every one had four faces apiece, and every one four wings; and the likeness of the hands of a man *was* under their wings.

22And the likeness of their faces *was* the same faces which I saw by the river of Chebar, their appearances and themselves: they went every one straight forward.

## Amplified

10 THEN I looked, and behold, in the firmament that was over the heads of the cherubim there appeared above them something looking like a sapphire stone, in form resembling a throne.

2And [the Lord] spoke to the man clothed in linen, and said, Go in among the whirling wheels under the cherubim; fill your hands with coals of fire from between the cherubim, and scatter them over the city. And he went in before my eyes. [Rev. 8:5.]

3Now the cherubim stood on the south side of the house, when the man went in; and the [Shekinah] cloud filled the inner court.

4Then the glory of the Lord mounted up from the cherubim to stand over the threshold of the [Lord's] house; and the house was filled with the cloud, and the court was full of the brightness of the Lord's glory. [I Kings 8:10, 11; Ezek. 43:5.]

5And the sound of the wings of the cherubim was heard even to the outer court, as the voice of God Almighty when He speaks. [Ps. 29:3, 4.]

6And when He commanded the man clothed in linen, saying, Take fire from between the whirling wheels, from between the cherubim, [the man] went in and stood beside a wheel.

7And a cherub stretched forth his hand from between the cherubim to the fire that was between the cherubim, and took some of it, and put it into the hands of the man clothed in linen, who took it and went out.

8And the cherubim seemed to have the form of a man's hand under their wings.

9And I looked, and behold, there were four wheels beside the cherubim, one wheel beside one cherub, and another wheel beside another cherub; and the appearance of the wheels was like sparkling chrysolite.

10And as for their appearance, they four looked alike, as if a wheel had been within a wheel.

11When they went, they went in any one of the four directions [in which their four individual faces were turned]; they did not turn as they went, but to the place to which the front wheel faced the others followed; they turned not as they went.

12And their whole body, their backs, their hands, and their wings, and the wheels, were full of eyes round about, even the wheels that they four had.

13As regarding the wheels [attached to them], they were called in my hearing the whirling wheels.

14And every one had four faces: the first face was the face of the cherub, and the second face was the face of a man, and the third the face of a lion, and the fourth the face of an eagle.

15And the cherubim mounted upward. This is the *same* living creature [the four regarded as one] that I saw by the river Chebar [in Babylonia]. [Ezek. 1:5.]

16And when the cherubim went, the wheels went beside them; and when the cherubim lifted up their wings to mount up from the earth, the wheels did not turn from beside them.

17When those stood still, these stood still, and when those mounted up, these [the wheels] mounted up also; for the spirit of life was in these [wheels]. [Ezek. 1:21.]

18Then the glory of the Lord [the Shekinah, cloud] went forth from above the threshold of the temple, and stood over the cherubim.

19And the cherubim lifted up their wings and mounted up from the earth in my sight, and they went forth with the wheels beside them; and they stood at the entrance of the east gate of the house of the Lord, and [the Shekinah, cloud] the glory of the God of Israel was over them.

20This is the living creature [of four combined creatures] that I saw beneath the God of Israel by the river Chebar, and I knew that they were cherubim.

21Each one had four faces and each one had four wings, and what looked like the hands of a man was under their wings.

22And as for the likeness of their faces, they were the same faces which I saw by the river Chebar, as regards their appearances and themselves; they went every one straight forward.

## New American Standard

*Vision of God's Glory Departing from the Temple*

**10** THEN I looked, and behold, in the expanse that was over
the heads of the cherubim something like a sapphire
stone, in appearance resembling a throne, appeared above them.
2And He spoke to the man clothed in linen and said, "Enter
between the whirling wheels under the cherubim, and fill your
hands with coals of fire from between the cherubim, and scatter
*them* over the city." And he entered in my sight.
3¶ Now the cherubim were standing on the right side of the
temple when the man entered, and the cloud filled the inner court.
4Then the glory of the LORD went up from the cherub to the
threshold of the temple, and the temple was filled with the cloud,
and the court was filled with the brightness of the glory of the
LORD.
5Moreover, the sound of the wings of the cherubim was heard
as far as the outer court, like the voice of God Almighty when He
speaks.
6¶ And it came about when He commanded the man clothed
in linen, saying, "Take fire from between the whirling wheels,
from between the cherubim," he entered and stood beside a
wheel.
7Then the cherub stretched out his hand from between the
cherubim to the fire which *was* between the cherubim, took some
and put it into the hands of the one clothed in linen, who took *it*
and went out.
8And the cherubim appeared to have the form of a man's hand
under their wings.
9¶ Then I looked, and behold, four wheels beside the cherubim, one wheel beside each cherub; and the appearance of the
wheels *was* like the gleam of a Tarshish stone.
10And as for their appearance, all four of them had the same
likeness, as if one wheel were within another wheel.
11When they moved, they went in *any of* their four directions
without turning as they went; but they followed in the direction
which they faced, without turning as they went.
12And their whole body, their backs, their hands, their wings,
and the wheels were full of eyes all around, the wheels belonging
to all four of them.
13The wheels were called in my hearing, the whirling wheels.
14And each one had four faces. The first face *was* the face of a
cherub, the second face *was* the face of a man, the third the face
of a lion, and the fourth the face of an eagle.
15¶ Then the cherubim rose up. They are the living beings that
I saw by the river Chebar.
16Now when the cherubim moved, the wheels would go beside
them; also when the cherubim lifted up their wings to rise from the
ground, the wheels would not turn from beside them.
17When the cherubim stood still, the wheels would stand still;
and when they rose up, the wheels would rise with them; for the
spirit of the living beings *was* in them.
18¶ Then the glory of the LORD departed from the threshold of
the temple and stood over the cherubim.
19When the cherubim departed, they lifted their wings and rose
up from the earth in my sight with the wheels beside them; and
they stood still at the entrance of the east gate of the LORD'S house.
And the glory of the God of Israel hovered over them.
20¶ These are the living beings that I saw beneath the God of
Israel by the river Chebar; so I knew that they *were* cherubim.
21Each one had four faces and each one four wings, and beneath
their wings *was* the form of human hands.
22As for the likeness of their faces, they were the same faces
whose appearance I had seen by the river Chebar. Each one went
straight ahead.

## New International

*The Glory Departs From the Temple*

**10** I LOOKED, and I saw the likeness of a throne of sapphire[a]
above the expanse that was over the heads of the cherubim. 2The LORD said to the man clothed in linen, "Go in among
the wheels beneath the cherubim. Fill your hands with burning
coals from among the cherubim and scatter them over the city."
And as I watched, he went in.
3Now the cherubim were standing on the south side of the
temple when the man went in, and a cloud filled the inner court.
4Then the glory of the LORD rose from above the cherubim and
moved to the threshold of the temple. The cloud filled the temple,
and the court was full of the radiance of the glory of the LORD. 5The
sound of the wings of the cherubim could be heard as far away as
the outer court, like the voice of God Almighty[b] when he speaks.
6When the LORD commanded the man in linen, "Take fire from
among the wheels, from among the cherubim," the man went in
and stood beside a wheel. 7Then one of the cherubim reached out
his hand to the fire that was among them. He took up some of it
and put it into the hands of the man in linen, who took it and went
out. 8(Under the wings of the cherubim could be seen what looked
like the hands of a man.)
9I looked, and I saw beside the cherubim four wheels, one
beside each of the cherubim; the wheels sparkled like chrysolite.
10As for their appearance, the four of them looked alike; each was
like a wheel intersecting a wheel. 11As they moved, they would go
in any one of the four directions the cherubim faced; the wheels
did not turn about[c] as the cherubim went. The cherubim went in
whatever direction the head faced, without turning as they went.
12Their entire bodies, including their backs, their hands and their
wings, were completely full of eyes, as were their four wheels. 13I
heard the wheels being called "the whirling wheels." 14Each of the
cherubim had four faces: One face was that of a cherub, the second
the face of a man, the third the face of a lion, and the fourth the
face of an eagle.
15Then the cherubim rose upward. These were the living creatures I had seen by the Kebar River. 16When the cherubim moved,
the wheels beside them moved; and when the cherubim spread
their wings to rise from the ground, the wheels did not leave their
side. 17When the cherubim stood still, they also stood still; and
when the cherubim rose, they rose with them, because the spirit
of the living creatures was in them.
18Then the glory of the LORD departed from over the threshold
of the temple and stopped above the cherubim. 19While I watched,
the cherubim spread their wings and rose from the ground, and
as they went, the wheels went with them. They stopped at the
entrance to the east gate of the LORD'S house, and the glory of the
God of Israel was above them.
20These were the living creatures I had seen beneath the God
of Israel by the Kebar River, and I realized that they were cherubim. 21Each had four faces and four wings, and under their wings
was what looked like the hands of a man. 22Their faces had the
same appearance as those I had seen by the Kebar River. Each one
went straight ahead.

**NIV** [a] *1* Or *lapis lazuli* [b] *5* Hebrew *El-Shaddai* [c] *11* Or *aside*

## King James

11 MOREOVER THE spirit lifted me up, and brought me unto the east gate of the LORD's house, which looketh eastward: and behold at the door of the gate five and twenty men; among whom I saw Jaazaniah the son of Azur, and Pelatiah the son of Benaiah, princes of the people.

2Then said he unto me, Son of man, these *are* the men that devise mischief, and give wicked counsel in this city:

3Which say, *It is* not near; let us build houses: this *city is* the caldron, and we *be* the flesh.

4¶ Therefore prophesy against them, prophesy, O son of man.

5And the spirit of the LORD fell upon me, and said unto me, Speak; Thus saith the LORD; Thus have ye said, O house of Israel: for I know the things that come into your mind, *every one of* them.

6Ye have multiplied your slain in this city, and ye have filled the streets thereof with the slain.

7Therefore thus saith the Lord GOD; Your slain whom ye have laid in the midst of it, they *are* the flesh, and this *city is* the caldron: but I will bring you forth out of the midst of it.

8Ye have feared the sword; and I will bring a sword upon you, saith the Lord GOD.

9And I will bring you out of the midst thereof, and deliver you into the hands of strangers, and will execute judgments among you.

10Ye shall fall by the sword; I will judge you in the border of Israel; and ye shall know that I *am* the LORD.

11This *city* shall not be your caldron, neither shall ye be the flesh in the midst thereof; *but* I will judge you in the border of Israel:

12And ye shall know that I *am* the LORD: for ye have not walked in my statutes, neither executed my judgments, but have done after the manners of the heathen that *are* round about you.

13¶ And it came to pass, when I prophesied, that Pelatiah the son of Benaiah died. Then fell I down upon my face, and cried with a loud voice, and said, Ah Lord GOD! wilt thou make a full end of the remnant of Israel?

14Again the word of the LORD came unto me, saying,

15Son of man, thy brethren, *even* thy brethren, the men of thy kindred, and all the house of Israel wholly, *are* they unto whom the inhabitants of Jerusalem have said, Get you far from the LORD: unto us is this land given in possession.

16Therefore say, Thus saith the Lord GOD; Although I have cast them far off among the heathen, and although I have scattered them among the countries, yet will I be to them as a little sanctuary in the countries where they shall come.

17Therefore say, Thus saith the Lord GOD; I will even gather you from the people, and assemble you out of the countries where ye have been scattered, and I will give you the land of Israel.

18And they shall come thither, and they shall take away all the detestable things thereof and all the abominations thereof from thence.

19And I will give them one heart, and I will put a new spirit within you; and I will take the stony heart out of their flesh, and will give them an heart of flesh:

20That they may walk in my statutes, and keep mine ordinances, and do them: and they shall be my people, and I will be their God.

21But *as for them* whose heart walketh after the heart of their detestable things and their abominations, I will recompense their way upon their own heads, saith the Lord GOD.

22¶ Then did the cherubims lift up their wings, and the wheels beside them; and the glory of the God of Israel *was* over them above.

## Amplified

11 MOREOVER THE Spirit lifted me up, and brought me to the east gate of the Lord's house, which faces east. And behold, at the door of the gateway there were twenty-five men; and I saw in the midst of them Jaazaniah the son of Azzur, and Pelatiah the son of Benaiah, princes of the people.

2Then [the Spirit] said to me, Son of man, these are the men who devise iniquity and give wicked counsel in this city;

3Who say, *The time* is not near to build houses; this *city* is the boiling pot, and we are the flesh.

4Therefore prophesy against them, prophesy, O son of man!

5And the Spirit of the Lord fell upon me, and He said to me, Speak. Say, Thus says the Lord: This is what you thought, O house of Israel; for I know the things that come into your mind.

6You have multiplied your slain in this city, and you have filled its streets with the slain.

7Therefore thus says the Lord God: Your slain whom you have laid in your midst, they are the flesh, and this *city* is the boiling pot; but you shall be brought forth out of the midst of it.

8You have feared the sword, and I will bring a sword upon you, says the Lord God.

9And I will bring you forth out of the midst of it, and deliver you into the hands of foreigners, and will execute judgments among you.

10You shall fall by the sword; I will judge *and* punish you [before your neighbors] at the border *or* outside the land of Israel, and you shall know—understand and realize—that I am the Lord.

11This *city* shall not be your boiling pot, neither shall you be the flesh in the midst of it; I will judge you at the border *or* outside of Israel;

12And you shall know—understand and realize—that I am the Lord; for you have not walked in My statutes nor executed My ordinances, but have acted according to the ordinances of the nations around you.

13And while I was prophesying, Pelatiah the son of Benaiah died. Then I fell down upon my face, and cried with a loud voice, Ah Lord God! will You make a complete end of the remnant of Israel?

14And the word of the Lord came to me, saying,

15Son of man, your brethren, even your kindred, your fellow exiles and all the house of Israel, all of them, are they of whom the [present] inhabitants of Jerusalem have said, They have gone far from the Lord [and from this land], therefore this land is given to us for a possession.

16Therefore say, Thus says the Lord God: Whereas I have removed [Israel] far off among the nations, and whereas I have scattered them among the countries, yet I have been to them a sanctuary for a little while in the countries to which they have come.

17Therefore say, Thus says the Lord God: I will gather you from the peoples, and assemble you out of the countries where you have been scattered, and I will give back to you the land of Israel.

18And when they return there they shall take away from it all traces of its detestable things and all its abominations—sex impurities and heathen religious practices.

19And I will give them one heart—a new heart—and I will put a new spirit within *them;* and I will take the stony [unnaturally hardened] heart out of their flesh, and will give them a heart of flesh [sensitive and responsive to the touch of their God]; [Ezek. 18:31; 36:26; II Cor. 3:3.]

20That they may walk in My statutes, and keep My ordinances, and do them. And they shall be My people, and I will be their God.

21But as for those whose heart yearns for *and* goes after their detestable things and their loathsome abominations [associated with idolatry], I will repay their deeds upon their own heads, says the Lord God.

22Then the cherubim lifted up their wings, with the wheels which were beside them; and the glory of the God of Israel [the Shekinah, cloud] was over them.

## New American Standard

*Evil Rulers to Be Judged*

**11** MOREOVER, THE Spirit lifted me up and brought me to the east gate of the LORD's house which faced eastward. And behold, *there were* twenty-five men at the entrance of the gate, and among them I saw Jaazaniah son of Azzur and Pelatiah son of Benaiah, leaders of the people.

2And He said to me, "Son of man, these are the men who devise iniquity and give evil advice in this city,

3who say, 'Is not *the time* near to build houses? This *city* is the pot and we are the flesh.'

4"Therefore, prophesy against them, son of man, prophesy!"

5¶ Then the Spirit of the LORD fell upon me, and He said to me, "Say, 'Thus says the LORD, "So you think, house of Israel, for I know your thoughts.

6"You have multiplied your slain in this city, filling its streets with them."

7'Therefore, thus says the Lord GOD, "Your slain whom you have laid in the midst of the city are the flesh, and this *city* is the pot; but I shall bring you out of it.

8"You have feared a sword; so I will bring a sword upon you," the Lord GOD declares.

9"And I shall bring you out of the midst of the city, and I shall deliver you into the hands of strangers and execute judgments against you.

10"You will fall by the sword. I shall judge you to the border of Israel; so you shall know that I am the LORD.

11"This *city* will not be a pot for you, nor will you be flesh in the midst of it, *but* I shall judge you to the border of Israel.

12"Thus you will know that I am the LORD; for you have not walked in My statutes nor have you executed My ordinances, but have acted according to the ordinances of the nations around you."'"

13¶ Now it came about as I prophesied, that Pelatiah son of Benaiah died. Then I fell on my face and cried out with a loud voice and said, "Alas, Lord GOD! Wilt Thou bring the remnant of Israel to a complete end?"

*Promise of Restoration*

14¶ Then the word of the LORD came to me, saying,

15"Son of man, your brothers, your relatives, your fellow exiles, and the whole house of Israel, all of them, *are those* to whom the inhabitants of Jerusalem have said, 'Go far from the LORD; this land has been given us as a possession.'

16"Therefore say, 'Thus says the Lord GOD, "Though I had removed them far away among the nations, and though I had scattered them among the countries, yet I was a sanctuary for them a little while in the countries where they had gone."'

17"Therefore say, 'Thus says the Lord GOD, "I shall gather you from the peoples and assemble you out of the countries among which you have been scattered, and I shall give you the land of Israel."'

18"When they come there, they will remove all its detestable things and all its abominations from it.

19"And I shall give them one heart, and shall put a new spirit within them. And I shall take the heart of stone out of their flesh and give them a heart of flesh,

20that they may walk in My statutes and keep My ordinances, and do them. Then they will be My people, and I shall be their God.

21"But as for those whose hearts go after their detestable things and abominations, I shall bring their conduct down on their heads," declares the Lord GOD.

22¶ Then the cherubim lifted up their wings with the wheels beside them, and the glory of the God of Israel hovered over them.

## New International

*Judgment on Israel's Leaders*

**11** THEN THE Spirit lifted me up and brought me to the gate of the house of the LORD that faces east. There at the entrance to the gate were twenty-five men, and I saw among them Jaazaniah son of Azzur and Pelatiah son of Benaiah, leaders of the
people. 2The LORD said to me, "Son of man, these are the men who
are plotting evil and giving wicked advice in this city. 3They say,
'Will it not soon be time to build houses?[a] This city is a cooking
pot, and we are the meat.' 4Therefore prophesy against them;
prophesy, son of man."

5Then the Spirit of the LORD came upon me, and he told me to
say: "This is what the LORD says: That is what you are saying, O
house of Israel, but I know what is going through your mind. 6You
have killed many people in this city and filled its streets with the dead.

7"Therefore this is what the Sovereign LORD says: The bodies you have thrown there are the meat and this city is the pot, but
I will drive you out of it. 8You fear the sword, and the sword is
what I will bring against you, declares the Sovereign LORD. 9I will
drive you out of the city and hand you over to foreigners and inflict
punishment on you. 10You will fall by the sword, and I will execute
judgment on you at the borders of Israel. Then you will know that
I am the LORD. 11This city will not be a pot for you, nor will you
be the meat in it; I will execute judgment on you at the borders of
Israel. 12And you will know that I am the LORD, for you have not
followed my decrees or kept my laws but have conformed to the standards of the nations around you."

13Now as I was prophesying, Pelatiah son of Benaiah died.
Then I fell facedown and cried out in a loud voice, "Ah, Sovereign LORD! Will you completely destroy the remnant of Israel?"

14The word of the LORD came to me: 15"Son of man, your
brothers—your brothers who are your blood relatives[b] and the whole house of Israel—are those of whom the people of Jerusalem have said, 'They are[c] far away from the LORD; this land was given to us as our possession.'

*Promised Return of Israel*

16"Therefore say: 'This is what the Sovereign LORD says: Although I sent them far away among the nations and scattered them among the countries, yet for a little while I have been a sanctuary for them in the countries where they have gone.'

17"Therefore say: 'This is what the Sovereign LORD says: I will gather you from the nations and bring you back from the countries where you have been scattered, and I will give you back the land of Israel again.'

18"They will return to it and remove all its vile images and
detestable idols. 19I will give them an undivided heart and put a
new spirit in them; I will remove from them their heart of stone
and give them a heart of flesh. 20Then they will follow my decrees
and be careful to keep my laws. They will be my people, and I will
be their God. 21But as for those whose hearts are devoted to their vile images and detestable idols, I will bring down on their own heads what they have done, declares the Sovereign LORD."

22Then the cherubim, with the wheels beside them, spread their
wings, and the glory of the God of Israel was above them. 23The

**NIV** [a] 3 Or *This is not the time to build houses.* [b] 15 Or *are in exile with you* (see Septuagint and Syriac) [c] 15 Or *those to whom the people of Jerusalem have said, 'Stay*

## King James

23And the glory of the LORD went up from the midst of the city,
and stood upon the mountain which *is* on the east side of the city.
24¶ Afterwards the spirit took me up, and brought me in a vision
by the spirit of God into Chaldea, to them of the captivity. So the
vision that I had seen went up from me.
25Then I spake unto them of the captivity all the things that the
LORD had shown me.

**12** THE WORD of the LORD also came unto me, saying,
2Son of man, thou dwellest in the midst of a rebellious
house, which have eyes to see, and see not; they have ears to hear,
and hear not: for they *are* a rebellious house.
3Therefore, thou son of man, prepare thee stuff for removing,
and remove by day in their sight; and thou shalt remove from thy
place to another place in their sight: it may be they will consider,
though they *be* a rebellious house.
4Then shalt thou bring forth thy stuff by day in their sight, as
stuff for removing: and thou shalt go forth at even in their sight,
as they that go forth into captivity.
5Dig thou through the wall in their sight, and carry out thereby.
6In their sight shalt thou bear *it* upon *thy* shoulders, *and* carry
*it* forth in the twilight: thou shalt cover thy face, that thou see not
the ground: for I have set thee *for* a sign unto the house of Israel.
7And I did so as I was commanded: I brought forth my stuff by
day, as stuff for captivity, and in the even I digged through the wall
with mine hand; I brought *it* forth in the twilight, *and* I bare *it* upon
*my* shoulder in their sight.
8¶ And in the morning came the word of the LORD unto me,
saying,
9Son of man, hath not the house of Israel, the rebellious house,
said unto thee, What doest thou?
10Say thou unto them, Thus saith the Lord GOD; This burden
*concerneth* the prince in Jerusalem, and all the house of Israel that
*are* among them.
11Say, I *am* your sign: like as I have done, so shall it be done unto
them: they shall remove *and* go into captivity.
12And the prince that *is* among them shall bear upon *his* shoulder in the twilight, and shall go forth: they shall dig through the
wall to carry out thereby: he shall cover his face, that he see not
the ground with *his* eyes.
13My net also will I spread upon him, and he shall be taken in
my snare: and I will bring him to Babylon *to* the land of the
Chaldeans; yet shall he not see it, though he shall die there.
14And I will scatter toward every wind all that *are* about him to
help him, and all his bands; and I will draw out the sword after
them.
15And they shall know that I *am* the LORD, when I shall scatter
them among the nations, and disperse them in the countries.
16But I will leave a few men of them from the sword, from the
famine, and from the pestilence; that they may declare all their
abominations among the heathen whither they come; and they
shall know that I *am* the LORD.
17¶ Moreover the word of the LORD came to me, saying,
18Son of man, eat thy bread with quaking, and drink thy water
with trembling and with carefulness;
19And say unto the people of the land, Thus saith the Lord GOD
of the inhabitants of Jerusalem, *and* of the land of Israel; They shall
eat their bread with carefulness, and drink their water with astonishment, that her land may be desolate from all that is therein,
because of the violence of all them that dwell therein.

**AMP** [a] This prophecy was literally fulfilled as recorded in Jeremiah 52:7-11. King Zedekiah's eyes were put out in Riblah, Palestine, before he was carried to Babylon, where he died. Thus he did "not see it," though he died there.
[b] This prophecy was literally fulfilled as recorded in Jeremiah 52:7-11. King Zedekiah's eyes were put out in Riblah, Palestine, before he was carried to Babylon, where he died. Thus he did "not see it," though he died there.

## Amplified

23Then the glory of the Lord rose up from over the midst of the
city, and stood over the mountain which is on the east side of the
city.
24And the Spirit lifted me up and brought me in a vision by the
Spirit of God into Chaldea, to the exiles. Then the vision that I had
seen went up from me.
25And I told the exiles everything that the Lord had shown me.

**12** THE WORD of the Lord also came to me, saying,
2Son of man, you dwell in the midst of the house of the
rebellious, who have eyes to see and see not, who have ears to hear
and hear not; for they are a rebellious house. [Mark 8:18.]
3Therefore, son of man, prepare your belongings for removing
*and* going into exile, and move out by day in their sight; and you
shall remove from your place to another place in their sight. It may
be they will consider *and* perceive that they are a rebellious house.
4And you shall bring forth your baggage by day in their sight,
as baggage for removing into exile; and you shall go forth yourself
at evening in their sight, as those who go forth into exile.
5Dig through the wall in their sight, and carry the stuff out
through the hole.
6In their sight you shall bear your baggage upon your shoulder,
and carry it forth in the dark; you shall cover your face so that you
cannot see the land; for I have set you as a sign for the house of
Israel.
7And I did as I was commanded. I brought forth my baggage
by day, as baggage for exile, and in the evening I dug through the
wall with my own hands. I brought out my baggage in the dark,
carrying it upon my shoulder in their sight.
8And in the morning came the word of the Lord to me, saying,
9Son of man, has not the house of Israel, the rebellious house,
asked you what you are doing?
10Say to them, Thus says the Lord God: This oracle *or* revelation
concerns the prince in Jerusalem, and all the house of Israel who
are in it.
11Say, I am your sign: as I have done, so shall it be done to them;
into banishment, into captivity they shall go.
12And the prince who is in their midst shall lift up his luggage
to his shoulder in the dark, then shall he go forth. They shall dig
through the wall to carry out through the hole in it. He shall cover
his face because he will [a]not see with his eyes the land.
13My net also will I spread over him, and he shall be taken in
My snare; and I will bring him to Babylon to the land of the
Chaldeans; yet shall he [b]not see it, though he shall die there. [Jer.
52:7-11.]
14And I will scatter toward every wind all that are about him to
help him, and all his bands; and I will draw out the sword after
them.
15And they shall know—recognize, understand and realize—
that I am the Lord, when I shall scatter them among the nations
and disperse them in the countries.
16But I will leave a few survivors who will escape the sword, the
famine and the pestilence, that they may declare *and* confess all
their [idolatrous] abominations among the nations to which they
go, and [thus God's punishment of them will be justified before
everyone and] they shall know—understand and realize—that I
am the Lord.
17Moreover the word of the Lord came to me, saying,
18Son of man, eat your bread with shaking, and drink water
with trembling and with fearfulness;
19And say to the people of the land, Thus says the Lord God
concerning the inhabitants of Jerusalem in the land of Israel: They
shall eat their bread with fearfulness, and drink water with dismay, for their land will be stripped *and* plundered of all its fullness,
because of the violence of all those who dwell in it.

## New American Standard

23And the glory of the LORD went up from the midst of the city,
and stood over the mountain which is east of the city.
24And the Spirit lifted me up and brought me in a vision by the
Spirit of God to the exiles in Chaldea. So the vision that I had seen
left me.
25Then I told the exiles all the things that the LORD had shown
me.

*Ezekiel Prepares for Exile*

**12** THEN THE word of the LORD came to me saying,
2"Son of man, you live in the midst of the rebellious
house, who have eyes to see but do not see, ears to hear but do
not hear; for they are a rebellious house.
3"Therefore, son of man, prepare for yourself baggage for exile
and go into exile by day in their sight; even go into exile from your
place to another place in their sight. Perhaps they will understand
though they are a rebellious house.
4"And bring your baggage out by day in their sight, as baggage
for exile. Then you will go out at evening in their sight, as those
going into exile.
5"Dig a hole through the wall in their sight and go out through
it.
6"Load *the baggage* on *your* shoulder in their sight, *and* carry *it*
out in the dark. You shall cover your face so that you can not see
the land, for I have set you as a sign to the house of Israel."
7¶ And I did so, as I had been commanded. By day I brought
out my baggage like the baggage of an exile. Then in the evening
I dug through the wall with my hands; I went out in the dark *and*
carried *the baggage* on *my* shoulder in their sight.
8¶ And in the morning the word of the LORD came to me,
saying,
9"Son of man, has not the house of Israel, the rebellious house,
said to you, 'What are you doing?'
10"Say to them, 'Thus says the Lord GOD, "This burden *concerns*
the prince in Jerusalem, as well as all the house of Israel who are
in it."'
11"Say, 'I am a sign to you. As I have done, so it will be done
to them; they will go into exile, into captivity.'
12"And the prince who is among them will load *his baggage* on
*his* shoulder in the dark and go out. They will dig a hole through
the wall to bring *it* out. He will cover his face so that he can not
see the land with *his* eyes.
13"I shall also spread My net over him, and he will be caught
in My snare. And I shall bring him to Babylon in the land of the
Chaldeans; yet he will not see it, though he will die there.
14"And I shall scatter to every wind all who are around him, his
helpers and all his troops; and I shall draw out a sword after them.
15"So they will know that I am the LORD when I scatter them
among the nations, and spread them among the countries.
16"But I shall spare a few of them from the sword, the famine,
and the pestilence that they may tell all their abominations among
the nations where they go, and may know that I am the LORD."
17¶ Moreover, the word of the LORD came to me saying,
18"Son of man, eat your bread with trembling, and drink your
water with quivering and anxiety.
19"Then say to the people of the land, 'Thus says the Lord GOD
concerning the inhabitants of Jerusalem in the land of Israel, "They
will eat their bread with anxiety and drink their water with horror,
because their land will be stripped of its fulness on account of the
violence of all who live in it.

## New International

glory of the LORD went up from within the city and stopped above
the mountain east of it. 24The Spirit lifted me up and brought me
to the exiles in Babylonia[c] in the vision given by the Spirit of God.
Then the vision I had seen went up from me, 25and I told the
exiles everything the LORD had shown me.

*The Exile Symbolized*

**12** THE WORD of the LORD came to me: 2"Son of man, you
are living among a rebellious people. They have eyes to
see but do not see and ears to hear but do not hear, for they are
a rebellious people.
3"Therefore, son of man, pack your belongings for exile and in
the daytime, as they watch, set out and go from where you are to
another place. Perhaps they will understand, though they are a
rebellious house. 4During the daytime, while they watch, bring
out your belongings packed for exile. Then in the evening, while
they are watching, go out like those who go into exile. 5While they
watch, dig through the wall and take your belongings out through
it. 6Put them on your shoulder as they are watching and carry them
out at dusk. Cover your face so that you cannot see the land, for
I have made you a sign to the house of Israel."
7So I did as I was commanded. During the day I brought out
my things packed for exile. Then in the evening I dug through the
wall with my hands. I took my belongings out at dusk, carrying
them on my shoulders while they watched.
8In the morning the word of the LORD came to me: 9"Son of
man, did not that rebellious house of Israel ask you, 'What are you
doing?'
10"Say to them, 'This is what the Sovereign LORD says: This
oracle concerns the prince in Jerusalem and the whole house of
Israel who are there.' 11Say to them, 'I am a sign to you.'
"As I have done, so it will be done to them. They will go into
exile as captives.
12"The prince among them will put his things on his shoulder
at dusk and leave, and a hole will be dug in the wall for him to go
through. He will cover his face so that he cannot see the land. 13I
will spread my net for him, and he will be caught in my snare; I
will bring him to Babylonia, the land of the Chaldeans, but he will
not see it, and there he will die. 14I will scatter to the winds all those
around him—his staff and all his troops—and I will pursue them
with drawn sword.
15"They will know that I am the LORD, when I disperse them
among the nations and scatter them through the countries. 16But
I will spare a few of them from the sword, famine and plague, so
that in the nations where they go they may acknowledge all their
detestable practices. Then they will know that I am the LORD."
17The word of the LORD came to me: 18"Son of man, tremble as
you eat your food, and shudder in fear as you drink your water.
19Say to the people of the land: 'This is what the Sovereign LORD
says about those living in Jerusalem and in the land of Israel: They
will eat their food in anxiety and drink their water in despair, for
their land will be stripped of everything in it because of the violence of all who live there. 20The inhabited towns will be laid waste

NIV [c] 24 Or *Chaldea*

## King James

20And the cities that are inhabited shall be laid waste, and the
land shall be desolate; and ye shall know that I *am* the LORD.
21¶ And the word of the LORD came unto me, saying,
22Son of man, what *is* that proverb *that* ye have in the land of
Israel, saying, The days are prolonged, and every vision faileth?
23Tell them therefore, Thus saith the Lord GOD; I will make this
proverb to cease, and they shall no more use it as a proverb in
Israel; but say unto them, The days are at hand, and the effect of
every vision.
24For there shall be no more any vain vision nor flattering
divination within the house of Israel.
25For I *am* the LORD: I will speak, and the word that I shall speak
shall come to pass; it shall be no more prolonged: for in your days,
O rebellious house, will I say the word, and will perform it, saith
the Lord GOD.
26¶ Again the word of the LORD came to me, saying,
27Son of man, behold, *they of* the house of Israel say, The vision
that he seeth *is* for many days *to come*, and he prophesieth of the
times *that are* far off.
28Therefore say unto them, Thus saith the Lord GOD; There
shall none of my words be prolonged any more, but the word
which I have spoken shall be done, saith the Lord GOD.

**13** AND THE word of the LORD came unto me, saying,
2Son of man, prophesy against the prophets of Israel that
prophesy, and say thou unto them that prophesy out of their own
hearts, Hear ye the word of the LORD;
3Thus saith the Lord GOD; Woe unto the foolish prophets, that
follow their own spirit, and have seen nothing!
4O Israel, thy prophets are like the foxes in the deserts.
5Ye have not gone up into the gaps, neither made up the hedge
for the house of Israel to stand in the battle in the day of the LORD.
6They have seen vanity and lying divination, saying, The LORD
saith: and the LORD hath not sent them: and they have made *others*
to hope that they would confirm the word.
7Have ye not seen a vain vision, and have ye not spoken a lying
divination, whereas ye say, The LORD saith *it;* albeit I have not
spoken?
8Therefore thus saith the Lord GOD; Because ye have spoken
vanity, and seen lies, therefore, behold, I *am* against you, saith the
Lord GOD.
9And mine hand shall be upon the prophets that see vanity, and
that divine lies: they shall not be in the assembly of my people,
neither shall they be written in the writing of the house of Israel,
neither shall they enter into the land of Israel; and ye shall know
that I *am* the Lord GOD.
10¶ Because, even because they have seduced my people, saying, Peace; and *there was* no peace; and one built up a wall, and,
lo, others daubed it with untempered *mortar:*
11Say unto them which daub *it* with untempered *mortar*, that it
shall fall: there shall be an overflowing shower; and ye, O great
hailstones, shall fall; and a stormy wind shall rend *it*.
12Lo, when the wall is fallen, shall it not be said unto you,
Where *is* the daubing wherewith ye have daubed *it?*
13Therefore thus saith the Lord GOD; I will even rend *it* with a
stormy wind in my fury; and there shall be an overflowing shower
in mine anger, and great hailstones in *my* fury to consume *it*.

## Amplified

20And the cities that are inhabited shall be laid waste, and the
land shall be deserted *and* become a desolation; and you shall
know—understand and realize—that I am the Lord.
21And the word of the Lord came to me, saying,
22Son of man, what is this proverb that you have in the land of
Israel, saying, The days drag on, and every vision comes to nothing *and* is not fulfilled?
23Tell them therefore, Thus says the Lord God: I will put an end
to this proverb and they shall use it no more as a proverb in Israel.
But say to them, The days are at hand, and the fulfillment of every
vision.
24For there shall be no more any false, empty *and* fruitless vision
or flattering divination in the house of Israel.
25For I am the Lord; I will speak, and the word that I shall speak
shall be performed—come to pass; it shall be no more delayed *or*
prolonged, for in your days, O rebellious house, I will speak the
word and will perform it, says the Lord God.
26Again the word of the Lord came to me, saying,
27Son of man, behold, they of the house of Israel say, The vision
that [Ezekiel] sees is for many days to come, and he prophesies of
the times that are far off.
28Therefore say to them, Thus says the Lord God: There shall
none of My words be deferred any more, but the word which I
have spoken shall be performed, says the Lord God.

**13** AND THE word of the Lord came to me, saying,
2Son of man, prophesy against the prophets of Israel that
prophesy, and say to them that prophesy out of their own mind
*and* heart, Hear the word of the Lord!
3Thus says the Lord God: Woe to the foolish prophets, who
follow their own spirit, and things they have not seen—and have
seen nothing!
4O Israel, your prophets have been like foxes among ruins *and*
in waste places.
5You have not gone up into the gaps *or* breeches, nor built up
the wall for the house of Israel, that it might stand in the battle in
the day of the Lord.
6They have seen falsehood and lying divination, saying, The
Lord says; but the Lord has not sent them. Yet they have hoped
*and* made men to hope for the confirmation of their word.
7Have you not seen a false vision, and have you not spoken a
lying divination when you say, The Lord says, although I have not
spoken?
8Therefore thus says the Lord God: Because you have spoken
empty, false *and* delusive words and have seen lies, therefore
behold, I am against you, says the Lord God.
9And My hand shall be against the prophets who see empty,
false *and* delusive visions, and who give lying prophecies. They
shall not be in the secret council of My people, nor shall they be
recorded in the register of the house of Israel, nor shall they enter
into the land of Israel; and you shall know—understand and realize—that I am the Lord God.
10Because, even because they have seduced My people, saying,
Peace, and there is no peace; and when one builds a [flimsy] wall,
behold, [these prophets] daub it over with whitewash.
11Say to them who daub it with whitewash that it shall fall!
There shall be a downpour of rain, and you, O great hailstones,
shall fall, and a violent wind shall tear apart [the whitewashed,
flimsy wall].
12Lo, when the wall is fallen, will you not be asked, Where is
the coating with which you [prophets] daubed it?
13Therefore thus says the Lord God: I will even rend it with a
stormy wind in My wrath, and there shall be an overwhelming rain
in My anger, and great hailstones in wrath to destroy [that wall].

## New American Standard

20"And the inhabited cities will be laid waste, and the land will
be a desolation. So you will know that I am the LORD."'"
21¶ Then the word of the LORD came to me saying,
22"Son of man, what is this proverb you *people* have concerning
the land of Israel, saying, 'The days are long and every vision
fails'?
23"Therefore say to them, 'Thus says the Lord GOD, "I will
make this proverb cease so that they will no longer use it as a
proverb in Israel." But tell them, "The days draw near as well as
the fulfillment of every vision.
24"For there will no longer be any false vision or flattering
divination within the house of Israel.
25"For I the LORD shall speak, and whatever word I speak will
be performed. It will no longer be delayed, for in your days, O
rebellious house, I shall speak the word and perform it," declares
the Lord GOD.'"
26¶ Furthermore, the word of the LORD came to me saying,
27"Son of man, behold, the house of Israel is saying, 'The vision
that he sees is for many years *from now,* and he prophesies of times
far off.'
28"Therefore say to them, 'Thus says the Lord GOD, "None of
My words will be delayed any longer. Whatever word I speak will
be performed,"'" declares the Lord GOD.

### *False Prophets Condemned*

13 THEN THE word of the LORD came to me saying,
2"Son of man, prophesy against the prophets of Israel
who prophesy, and say to those who prophesy from their own
inspiration, 'Listen to the word of the LORD!
3'Thus says the Lord GOD, "Woe to the foolish prophets who
are following their own spirit and have seen nothing.
4"O Israel, your prophets have been like foxes among ruins.
5"You have not gone up into the breaches, nor did you build
the wall around the house of Israel to stand in the battle on the day
of the LORD.
6"They see falsehood and lying divination who are saying,
'The LORD declares,' when the LORD has not sent them; yet they
hope for the fulfillment of *their* word.
7"Did you not see a false vision and speak a lying divination
when you said, 'The LORD declares,' but it is not I who have
spoken?"'"
8¶ Therefore, thus says the Lord GOD, "Because you have
spoken falsehood and seen a lie, therefore behold, I am against
you," declares the Lord GOD.
9"So My hand will be against the prophets who see false visions
and utter lying divinations. They will have no place in the
council of My people, nor will they be written down in the register
of the house of Israel, nor will they enter the land of Israel, that
you may know that I am the Lord GOD.
10"It is definitely because they have misled My people by saying,
'Peace!' when there is no peace. And when anyone builds a
wall, behold, they plaster it over with whitewash;
11 *so* tell those who plaster it over with whitewash, that it will
fall. A flooding rain will come, and you, O hailstones, will fall; and
a violent wind will break out.
12"Behold, when the wall has fallen, will you not be asked,
'Where is the plaster with which you plastered *it?'*"
13Therefore, thus says the Lord GOD, "I will make a violent
wind break out in My wrath. There will also be in My anger a
flooding rain and hailstones to consume *it* in wrath.

## New International

and the land will be desolate. Then you will know that I am the
LORD.'"
21The word of the LORD came to me: 22"Son of man, what is this
proverb you have in the land of Israel: 'The days go by and every
vision comes to nothing'? 23Say to them, 'This is what the Sovereign
LORD says: I am going to put an end to this proverb, and they
will no longer quote it in Israel.' Say to them, 'The days are near
when every vision will be fulfilled. 24For there will be no more false
visions or flattering divinations among the people of Israel. 25But
I the LORD will speak what I will, and it shall be fulfilled without
delay. For in your days, you rebellious house, I will fulfill whatever
I say, declares the Sovereign LORD.'"
26The word of the LORD came to me: 27"Son of man, the house
of Israel is saying, 'The vision he sees is for many years from now,
and he prophesies about the distant future.'
28"Therefore say to them, 'This is what the Sovereign LORD
says: None of my words will be delayed any longer; whatever I say
will be fulfilled, declares the Sovereign LORD.'"

### *False Prophets Condemned*

13 THE WORD of the LORD came to me: 2"Son of man,
prophesy against the prophets of Israel who are now
prophesying. Say to those who prophesy out of their own imagination:
'Hear the word of the LORD! 3This is what the Sovereign LORD
says: Woe to the foolish[a] prophets who follow their own spirit and
have seen nothing! 4Your prophets, O Israel, are like jackals
among ruins. 5You have not gone up to the breaks in the wall to
repair it for the house of Israel so that it will stand firm in the battle
on the day of the LORD. 6Their visions are false and their divinations
a lie. They say, "The LORD declares," when the LORD has not
sent them; yet they expect their words to be fulfilled. 7Have you
not seen false visions and uttered lying divinations when you say,
"The LORD declares," though I have not spoken?
8" 'Therefore this is what the Sovereign LORD says: Because of
your false words and lying visions, I am against you, declares the
Sovereign LORD. 9My hand will be against the prophets who see
false visions and utter lying divinations. They will not belong to
the council of my people or be listed in the records of the house
of Israel, nor will they enter the land of Israel. Then you will know
that I am the Sovereign LORD.
10" 'Because they lead my people astray, saying, "Peace," when
there is no peace, and because, when a flimsy wall is built, they
cover it with whitewash, 11therefore tell those who cover it with
whitewash that it is going to fall. Rain will come in torrents, and
I will send hailstones hurtling down, and violent winds will burst
forth. 12When the wall collapses, will people not ask you, "Where
is the whitewash you covered it with?"
13" 'Therefore this is what the Sovereign LORD says: In my
wrath I will unleash a violent wind, and in my anger hailstones
and torrents of rain will fall with destructive fury. 14I will tear

NIV [a] 3 Or *wicked*

# King James

14So will I break down the wall that ye have daubed with untempered *mortar*, and bring it down to the ground, so that the foundation thereof shall be discovered, and it shall fall, and ye shall be consumed in the midst thereof: and ye shall know that I *am* the LORD.

15Thus will I accomplish my wrath upon the wall, and upon them that have daubed it with untempered *mortar*, and will say unto you, The wall *is* no *more*, neither they that daubed it;

16 *To wit*, the prophets of Israel which prophesy concerning Jerusalem, and which see visions of peace for her, and *there is* no peace, saith the Lord GOD.

17¶ Likewise, thou son of man, set thy face against the daughters of thy people, which prophesy out of their own heart; and prophesy thou against them,

18And say, Thus saith the Lord GOD; Woe to the *women* that sew pillows to all armholes, and make kerchiefs upon the head of every stature to hunt souls! Will ye hunt the souls of my people, and will ye save the souls alive *that come* unto you?

19And will ye pollute me among my people for handfuls of barley and for pieces of bread, to slay the souls that sould not die, and to save the souls alive that should not live, by your lying to my people that hear *your* lies?

20Wherefore thus saith the Lord GOD; Behold, I *am* against your pillows, wherewith ye there hunt the souls to make *them* fly, and I will tear them from your arms, and will let the souls go, *even* the souls that ye hunt to make *them* fly.

21Your kerchiefs also will I tear, and deliver my people out of your hand, and they shall be no more in your hand to be hunted; and ye shall know that I *am* the LORD.

22Because with lies ye have made the heart of the righteous sad, whom I have not made sad; and strengthened the hands of the wicked, that he should not return from his wicked way, by promising him life:

23Therefore ye shall see no more vanity, nor divine divinations: for I will deliver my people out of your hand: and ye shall know that I *am* the LORD.

**14** THEN CAME certain of the elders of Israel unto me, and sat before me.

2And the word of the LORD came unto me, saying,

3Son of man, these men have set up their idols in their heart, and put the stumblingblock of their iniquity before their face: should I be inquired of at all by them?

4Therefore speak unto them, and say unto them, Thus saith the Lord GOD; Every man of the house of Israel that setteth up his idols in his heart, and putteth the stumblingblock of his iniquity before his face, and cometh to the prophet; I the LORD will answer him that cometh according to the multitude of his idols;

5That I may take the house of Israel in their own heart, because they are all estranged from me through their idols.

6¶ Therefore say unto the house of Israel, Thus saith the Lord GOD; Repent, and turn *yourselves* from your idols; and turn away your faces from all your abominations.

7For every one of the house of Israel, or of the stranger that sojourneth in Israel, which separateth himself from me, and setteth up his idols in his heart, and putteth the stumblingblock of his iniquity before his face, and cometh to a prophet to inquire of him concerning me; I the LORD will answer him by myself:

8And I will set my face against that man, and will make him a sign and a proverb, and I will cut him off from the midst of my people; and ye shall know that I *am* the LORD.

# Amplified

14So will I break down the wall that you have daubed with whitewash, and bring it down to the ground, so that its foundations will be exposed; when it falls, you shall perish *and* be consumed in the midst of it. And you shall know—understand and realize—that I am the Lord.

15Thus will I accomplish My wrath upon the wall, and upon those who have daubed it with whitewash, and I will say to you, The wall is no more, neither are they who daubed it,

16The *false* prophets of Israel who prophesied deceitfully about Jerusalem, seeing visions of peace for her when there is no peace, says the Lord God.

17And you, son of man, set your face against the daughters of your people, who prophesy out of [the wishful thinking of] their own minds *and* hearts; prophesy against them,

18And say, Thus says the Lord God: Woe to the women who sew pillows to all armholes and fasten magic, protective charms to all wrists, and deceptive veils upon the heads of those of every stature to hunt *and* capture human lives! Will you snare the lives of My people to keep your own selves alive?

19You have profaned Me among My people [in payment] for handfuls of barley and for pieces of bread, slaying persons who should not die, and giving [a guaranty of] life to those who should not live, by your lying to My people, who give heed to lies.

20Therefore thus says the Lord God: Behold, I am against your pillows *and* charms *and* veils, with which you snare human lives like birds, and I will tear them from your arms, and I will let the lives you hunt go free, the lives you are snaring like birds.

21Your [deceptive] veils also will I tear, and deliver My people out of your hand, and they shall be no more in your hand to be hunted *and* snared. Then you shall know—understand and realize—that I am the Lord.

22Because with lies you have made the righteous sad *and* disheartened, whom I have not made sad *or* disheartened, and because you have encouraged *and* strengthened the hands of the wicked, that he should not return from his wicked way and be saved—in that you falsely promised him life;

23Therefore you shall no more see false visions or practice divinations, and I will deliver My people out of your hand. Then you shall know—understand and realize—that I am the Lord.

**14** THEN CAME certain of the elders of Israel to me, and sat before me.

2And the word of the Lord came to me:

3Son of man, these men have set up their idols in their hearts, and put the stumblingblock of their iniquity *and* guilt before their faces; should I permit Myself to be inquired of at all by them?

4Therefore speak to them, and say to them, Thus says the Lord God: Every man of the house of Israel who takes his idols [of self-will and unsubmissiveness] into his heart, and puts the stumblingblock of his iniquity [idols of silver and gold] before his face, and yet comes to the prophet *to inquire of him,* I the Lord will answer him, answer him according to the multitude of his idols;

5That I may lay hold of the house of Israel in the thoughts of their own mind *and* heart, because they are all estranged from Me through their idols.

6Therefore say to the house of Israel, Thus says the Lord God: Repent *and* turn away from your idols, and turn away your faces from all your abominations.

7For any one of the house of Israel, or of the strangers who sojourn in Israel, who separates himself from Me, taking his idols into his heart and putting the stumblingblock of his iniquity *and* guilt before his face, and *yet* comes to the prophet to inquire for himself of Me, I the Lord will answer him Myself!

8And I will set My face against that [false worshiper], and will make him a sign and a byword, and I will cut him off from the midst of My people; and you shall know—understand and realize—that I am the Lord.

## New American Standard

14"So I shall tear down the wall which you plastered over with whitewash and bring it down to the ground, so that its foundation is laid bare; and when it falls, you will be consumed in its midst. And you will know that I am the LORD.

15"Thus I shall spend My wrath on the wall and on those who have plastered it over with whitewash; and I shall say to you, 'The wall is gone and its plasterers are gone,

16 *along with* the prophets of Israel who prophesy to Jerusalem, and who see visions of peace for her when there is no peace,' declares the Lord GOD.

17¶ "Now you, son of man, set your face against the daughters of your people who are prophesying from their own inspiration. Prophesy against them,

18and say, 'Thus says the Lord GOD, "Woe to the women who sew *magic* bands on all wrists, and make veils for the heads of *persons* of every stature to hunt down lives! Will you hunt down the lives of My people, but preserve the lives *of others* for yourselves?

19"And for handfuls of barley and fragments of bread, you have profaned Me to My people to put to death some who should not die and to keep others alive who should not live, by your lying to My people who listen to lies."'"

20¶ Therefore, thus says the Lord GOD, "Behold, I am against your *magic* bands by which you hunt lives there as birds, and I will tear them off your arms; and I will let them go, even those lives whom you hunt as birds.

21"I will also tear off your veils and deliver My people from your hands, and they will no longer be in your hands to be hunted; and you will know that I am the LORD.

22"Because you disheartened the righteous with falsehood when I did not cause him grief, but have encouraged the wicked not to turn from his wicked way *and* preserve his life,

23therefore, you women will no longer see false visions or practice divination, and I will deliver My people out of your hand. Thus you will know that I am the LORD."

*Idolatrous Elders Condemned*

**14** THEN SOME elders of Israel came to me and sat down before me.

2And the word of the LORD came to me saying,

3"Son of man, these men have set up their idols in their hearts, and have put right before their faces the stumbling block of their iniquity. Should I be consulted by them at all?

4"Therefore speak to them and tell them, 'Thus says the Lord GOD, "Any man of the house of Israel who sets up his idols in his heart, puts right before his face the stumbling block of his iniquity, and *then* comes to the prophet, I the LORD will be brought to give him an answer in the matter in view of the multitude of his idols,

5in order to lay hold of the hearts of the house of Israel who are estranged from Me through all their idols."'

6¶ "Therefore say to the house of Israel, 'Thus says the Lord GOD, "Repent and turn away from your idols, and turn your faces away from all your abominations.

7"For anyone of the house of Israel or of the immigrants who stay in Israel who separates himself from Me, sets up his idols in his heart, puts right before his face the stumbling block of his iniquity, and *then* comes to the prophet to inquire of Me for himself, I the LORD will be brought to answer him in My own person.

8"And I shall set My face against that man and make him a sign and a proverb, and I shall cut him off from among My people. So you will know that I am the LORD.

## New International

down the wall you have covered with whitewash and will level it
to the ground so that its foundation will be laid bare. When it[a]
falls, you will be destroyed in it; and you will know that I am the
LORD. 15So I will spend my wrath against the wall and against
those who covered it with whitewash. I will say to you, "The wall
is gone and so are those who whitewashed it, 16those prophets of
Israel who prophesied to Jerusalem and saw visions of peace for
her when there was no peace, declares the Sovereign LORD."'

17"Now, son of man, set your face against the daughters of your
people who prophesy out of their own imagination. Prophesy
against them 18and say, 'This is what the Sovereign LORD says:
Woe to the women who sew magic charms on all their wrists and
make veils of various lengths for their heads in order to ensnare
people. Will you ensnare the lives of my people but preserve your
own? 19You have profaned me among my people for a few handfuls of barley and scraps of bread. By lying to my people, who
listen to lies, you have killed those who should not have died and
have spared those who should not live.

20" 'Therefore this is what the Sovereign LORD says: I am
against your magic charms with which you ensnare people like
birds and I will tear them from your arms; I will set free the people
that you ensnare like birds. 21I will tear off your veils and save my
people from your hands, and they will no longer fall prey to your
power. Then you will know that I am the LORD. 22Because you
disheartened the righteous with your lies, when I had brought
them no grief, and because you encouraged the wicked not to turn
from their evil ways and so save their lives, 23therefore you will
no longer see false visions or practice divination. I will save my
people from your hands. And then you will know that I am the
LORD.'"

*Idolaters Condemned*

**14** SOME OF the elders of Israel came to me and sat down
in front of me. 2Then the word of the LORD came to me:
3"Son of man, these men have set up idols in their hearts and put
wicked stumbling blocks before their faces. Should I let them
inquire of me at all? 4Therefore speak to them and tell them, 'This
is what the Sovereign LORD says: When any Israelite sets up idols
in his heart and puts a wicked stumbling block before his face and
then goes to a prophet, I the LORD will answer him myself in
keeping with his great idolatry. 5I will do this to recapture the
hearts of the people of Israel, who have all deserted me for their
idols.'

6"Therefore say to the house of Israel, 'This is what the Sovereign LORD says: Repent! Turn from your idols and renounce all
your detestable practices!

7" 'When any Israelite or any alien living in Israel separates
himself from me and sets up idols in his heart and puts a wicked
stumbling block before his face and then goes to a prophet to
inquire of me, I the LORD will answer him myself. 8I will set my
face against that man and make him an example and a byword. I
will cut him off from my people. Then you will know that I am the
LORD.

NIV [a] 14 Or *the city*

## King James

9 And if the prophet be deceived when he hath spoken a thing, I the LORD have deceived that prophet, and I will stretch out my hand upon him, and will destroy him from the midst of my people Israel.

10 And they shall bear the punishment of their iniquity: the punishment of the prophet shall be even as the punishment of him that seeketh *unto him;*

11 That the house of Israel may go no more astray from me, neither be polluted any more with all their transgressions; but that they may be my people, and I may be their God, saith the Lord GOD.

12 ¶ The word of the LORD came again to me, saying,

13 Son of man, when the land sinneth against me by trespassing grievously, then will I stretch out mine hand upon it, and will break the staff of the bread thereof, and will send famine upon it, and will cut off man and beast from it:

14 Though these three men, Noah, Daniel, and Job, were in it, they should deliver *but* their own souls by their righteousness, saith the Lord GOD.

15 ¶ If I cause noisome beasts to pass through the land, and they spoil it, so that it be desolate, that no man may pass through because of the beasts:

16 *Though* these three men *were* in it, *as* I live, saith the Lord GOD, they shall deliver neither sons nor daughters; they only shall be delivered, but the land shall be desolate.

17 ¶ Or *if* I bring a sword upon that land, and say, Sword, go through the land; so that I cut off man and beast from it:

18 Though these three men *were* in it, *as* I live, saith the Lord GOD, they shall deliver neither sons nor daughters, but they only shall be delivered themselves.

19 ¶ Or *if* I send a pestilence into that land, and pour out my fury upon it in blood, to cut off from it man and beast:

20 Though Noah, Daniel, and Job, *were* in it, *as* I live, saith the Lord GOD, they shall deliver neither son nor daughter; they shall *but* deliver their own souls by their righteousness.

21 For thus saith the Lord GOD; How much more when I send my four sore judgments upon Jerusalem, the sword, and the famine, and the noisome beast, and the pestilence, to cut off from it man and beast?

22 ¶ Yet, behold, therein shall be left a remnant that shall be brought forth, *both* sons and daughters: behold, they shall come forth unto you, and ye shall see their way and their doings: and ye shall be comforted concerning the evil that I have brought upon Jerusalem, *even* concerning all that I have brought upon it.

23 And they shall comfort you, when ye see their ways and their doings: and ye shall know that I have not done without cause all that I have done in it, saith the Lord GOD.

**15** AND THE word of the LORD came unto me, saying,
2 Son of man, What is the vine tree more than any tree, *or than* a branch which is among the trees of the forest?

3 Shall wood be taken thereof to do any work? or will *men* take a pin of it to hang any vessel thereon?

4 Behold, it is cast into the fire for fuel; the fire devoureth both the ends of it, and the midst of it is burned. Is it meet for *any* work?

5 Behold, when it was whole, it was meet for no work: how much less shall it be meet yet for *any* work, when the fire hath devoured it, and it is burned?

## Amplified

9 [The prophet has not been granted permission to give an answer to the hypocritical inquirer] but if the prophet does give the man the answer he desires [thus allowing himself to be a party to the inquirer's sin], I the Lord will see to it that the prophet is deceived in his answer, and I will stretch out My hand against him, and will destroy him from the midst of My people Israel.

10 And they both shall bear the punishment of their iniquity: the iniquity of the [presumptuous] prophet shall be the same as the iniquity of the [hypocritical] inquirer;

11 That the house of Israel may go no more astray from Me, neither defile themselves any more with all their transgressions, but that they may be My people, and I may be their God, says the Lord God.

12 The word of the Lord came *again* to me, saying,

13 Son of man, when a land sins against Me by committing a trespass, and I stretch out My hand against it, and break its staff of bread and send famine upon it, and cut off from it man and beast;

14 Even if these three men, Noah, Daniel, and Job were in it, they would save but their own lives by their righteousness—their uprightness and right standing with Me—says the Lord God.

15 If I cause ferocious *and* evil wild animals to pass through the land, and they ravage *and* bereave it, and it becomes desolate, so that no man may pass through because of the beasts;

16 Though these three men were in it, as I live, says the Lord God, they would deliver neither sons nor daughters; they themselves alone would be delivered, but the land would be desolate—laid waste and deserted.

17 Or if I bring a sword upon that land, and say, Sword, go through the land, so that I cut off man and beast from it;

18 Though these three men were in it, as I live, says the Lord God, they would deliver neither sons nor daughters, but they themselves alone would be delivered.

19 Or if I send a pestilence into that land, and pour out My wrath upon it in blood, to cut off from it man and beast;

20 Though Noah, Daniel, and Job, were in it, as I live, says the Lord God, they would deliver neither son nor daughter; they would but deliver their own lives by their righteousness—their religious and moral rectitude in every area and relation.

21 For thus says the Lord God: How much more when I send My four sore acts of judgment upon Jerusalem, the sword and the famine and the evil wild beasts and the pestilence, to cut off from it man and beast! [Lev. 26:21-33.]

22 And yet, behold, in it shall be left a remnant—an escaped portion, both sons and daughters. They shall be carried forth to you [in Babylon], and when you see their [ungodly] walk and their [wicked] doings, you will be consoled for the evil that I have brought upon Jerusalem, even concerning all that I have brought upon it.

23 And they shall console you, when you see their evil ways and their rebellious actions. Then you shall know—understand and realize—that I have not done without cause all that I have done in Jerusalem, says the Lord God.

**15** AND THE word of the Lord came to me, saying,
2 Son of man, What is the wood of the grapevine [Israel] more than that of any tree, the vine branch which was among the trees of the forest? [Ps. 80:8-13; Jer. 2:21.]

3 Shall wood be taken from it to do any work? Or will men take a peg of it on which to hang any vessel?

4 Behold, it is cast into the fire for fuel; the fire consumes both ends of it, and the middle of it is charred. Is it suitable *or* profitable for any work?

5 Notice, even when it was whole it was good for no work; how much less shall it be useful *and* profitable when the fire has devoured it and it is charred?

## New American Standard

9"But if the prophet is prevailed upon to speak a word, it is I, the LORD, who have prevailed upon that prophet, and I will stretch out My hand against him and destroy him from among My people Israel.

10"And they will bear *the punishment of* their iniquity; as the iniquity of the inquirer is, so the iniquity of the prophet will be,

11in order that the house of Israel may no longer stray from Me and no longer defile themselves with all their transgressions. Thus they will be My people, and I shall be their God," ' declares the Lord GOD."

*The City Will Not Be Spared*

12¶ Then the word of the LORD came to me saying,

13"Son of man, if a country sins against Me by committing unfaithfulness, and I stretch out My hand against it, destroy its supply of bread, send famine against it, and cut off from it both man and beast,

14even *though* these three men, Noah, Daniel, and Job were in its midst, by their *own* righteousness they could *only* deliver themselves," declares the Lord GOD.

15"If I were to cause wild beasts to pass through the land, and they depopulated it, and it became desolate so that no one would pass through it because of the beasts,

16 *though* these three men were in its midst, as I live," declares the Lord GOD, "they could not deliver either *their* sons or *their* daughters. They alone would be delivered, but the country would be desolate.

17"Or *if* I should bring a sword on that country and say, 'Let the sword pass through the country and cut off man and beast from it,'

18even *though* these three men were in its midst, as I live," declares the Lord GOD, "they could not deliver either *their* sons or *their* daughters, but they alone would be delivered.

19"Or *if* I should send a plague against that country and pour out My wrath in blood on it, to cut off man and beast from it,

20even *though* Noah, Daniel, and Job were in its midst, as I live," declares the Lord GOD, "they could not deliver either *their* son or *their* daughter. They would deliver only themselves by their righteousness."

21¶ For thus says the Lord GOD, "How much more when I send My four severe judgments against Jerusalem: sword, famine, wild beasts, and plague to cut off man and beast from it!

22"Yet, behold, survivors will be left in it who will be brought out, *both* sons and daughters. Behold, they are going to come forth to you and you will see their conduct and actions; then you will be comforted for the calamity which I have brought against Jerusalem for everything which I have brought upon it.

23"Then they will comfort you when you see their conduct and actions, for you will know that I have not done in vain whatever I did to it," declares the Lord GOD.

*Jerusalem like a Useless Vine*

**15** THEN THE word of the LORD came to me saying,
2"Son of man, how is the wood of the vine *better* than any wood of a branch which is among the trees of the forest?

3"Can wood be taken from it to make anything, or can *men* take a peg from it on which to hang any vessel?

4"If it has been put into the fire for fuel, *and* the fire has consumed both of its ends, and its middle part has been charred, is it *then* useful for anything?

5"Behold, while it is intact, it is not made into anything. How much less, when the fire has consumed it and it is charred, can it still be made into anything!

## New International

9" 'And if the prophet is enticed to utter a prophecy, I the LORD have enticed that prophet, and I will stretch out my hand against him and destroy him from among my people Israel. 10They will bear their guilt—the prophet will be as guilty as the one who consults him. 11Then the people of Israel will no longer stray from me, nor will they defile themselves anymore with all their sins. They will be my people, and I will be their God, declares the Sovereign LORD.' "

*Judgment Inescapable*

12The word of the LORD came to me: 13"Son of man, if a country sins against me by being unfaithful and I stretch out my hand against it to cut off its food supply and send famine upon it and kill its men and their animals, 14even if these three men—Noah, Daniel[a] and Job—were in it, they could save only themselves by their righteousness, declares the Sovereign LORD.

15"Or if I send wild beasts through that country and they leave it childless and it becomes desolate so that no one can pass through it because of the beasts, 16as surely as I live, declares the Sovereign LORD, even if these three men were in it, they could not save their own sons or daughters. They alone would be saved, but the land would be desolate.

17"Or if I bring a sword against that country and say, 'Let the sword pass throughout the land,' and I kill its men and their animals, 18as surely as I live, declares the Sovereign LORD, even if these three men were in it, they could not save their own sons or daughters. They alone would be saved.

19"Or if I send a plague into that land and pour out my wrath upon it through bloodshed, killing its men and their animals, 20as surely as I live, declares the Sovereign LORD, even if Noah, Daniel and Job were in it, they could save neither son nor daughter. They would save only themselves by their righteousness.

21"For this is what the Sovereign LORD says: How much worse will it be when I send against Jerusalem my four dreadful judgments—sword and famine and wild beasts and plague—to kill its men and their animals! 22Yet there will be some survivors—sons and daughters who will be brought out of it. They will come to you, and when you see their conduct and their actions, you will be consoled regarding the disaster I have brought upon Jerusalem—every disaster I have brought upon it. 23You will be consoled when you see their conduct and their actions, for you will know that I have done nothing in it without cause, declares the Sovereign LORD."

*Jerusalem, A Useless Vine*

**15** THE WORD of the LORD came to me: 2"Son of man, how is the wood of a vine better than that of a branch on any of the trees in the forest? 3Is wood ever taken from it to make anything useful? Do they make pegs from it to hang things on? 4And after it is thrown on the fire as fuel and the fire burns both ends and chars the middle, is it then useful for anything? 5If it was not useful for anything when it was whole, how much less can it be made into something useful when the fire has burned it and it is charred?

**NIV** [a] *14* Or *Danel;* the Hebrew spelling may suggest a person other than the prophet Daniel; also in verse 20.

## King James

6¶ Therefore thus saith the Lord GOD; As the vine tree among the trees of the forest, which I have given to the fire for fuel, so will I give the inhabitants of Jerusalem.

7And I will set my face against them; they shall go out from *one* fire, and *another* fire shall devour them; and ye shall know that I *am* the LORD, when I set my face against them.

8And I will make the land desolate, because they have committed a trespass, saith the Lord GOD.

**16** AGAIN THE word of the LORD came unto me, saying,

2Son of man, cause Jerusalem to know her abominations,

3And say, Thus saith the Lord GOD unto Jerusalem; Thy birth and thy nativity *is* of the land of Canaan; thy father *was* an Amorite, and thy mother an Hittite.

4And *as for* thy nativity, in the day thou wast born thy navel was not cut, neither wast thou washed in water to supple *thee;* thou wast not salted at all, nor swaddled at all.

5None eye pitied thee, to do any of these unto thee, to have compassion upon thee; but thou wast cast out in the open field, to the loathing of thy person, in the day that thou wast born.

6¶ And when I passed by thee, and saw thee polluted in thine own blood, I said unto thee *when thou wast* in thy blood, Live; yea, I said unto thee *when thou wast* in thy blood, Live.

7I have caused thee to multiply as the bud of the field, and thou hast increased and waxen great, and thou art come to excellent ornaments: *thy* breasts are fashioned, and thine hair is grown, whereas thou *wast* naked and bare.

8Now when I passed by thee, and looked upon thee, behold, thy time *was* the time of love; and I spread my skirt over thee, and covered thy nakedness: yea, I sware unto thee, and entered into a covenant with thee, saith the Lord GOD, and thou becamest mine.

9Then washed I thee with water; yea, I thoroughly washed away thy blood from thee, and I anointed thee with oil.

10I clothed thee also with broidered work, and shod thee with badgers' skin, and I girded thee about with fine linen, and I covered thee with silk.

11I decked thee also with ornaments, and I put bracelets upon thy hands, and a chain on thy neck.

12And I put a jewel on thy forehead, and earrings in thine ears, and a beautiful crown upon thine head.

13Thus wast thou decked with gold and silver; and thy raiment *was of* fine linen, and silk, and broidered work; thou didst eat fine flour, and honey, and oil: and thou wast exceeding beautiful, and thou didst prosper into a kingdom.

14And thy renown went forth among the heathen for thy beauty: for it *was* perfect through my comeliness, which I had put upon thee, saith the Lord GOD.

15¶ But thou didst trust in thine own beauty, and playedst the harlot because of thy renown, and pouredst out thy fornications on every one that passed by; his it was.

16And of thy garments thou didst take, and deckedst thy high places with divers colours, and playedst the harlot thereupon: *the like things* shall not come, neither shall it be *so.*

17Thou hast also taken thy fair jewels of my gold and of my silver, which I had given thee, and madest to thyself images of men, and didst commit whoredom with them,

## Amplified

6Therefore thus says the Lord God: Like the wood of the grapevine among the trees of the forest, which I have given to the fire for fuel, so will I give up the inhabitants of Jerusalem.

7And I will set My face against them; they shall go out from one fire, and another fire shall devour them; and you shall know—understand and realize—that I am the Lord, when I set My face against them.

8And I will make the land desolate—laid waste and deserted—because they have acted faithlessly [through their idolatry], says the Lord.

**16** AGAIN THE word of the Lord came to me, saying,

2Son of man, cause Jerusalem to know, understand *and* realize, her [idolatrous] abominations [that they are] disgusting, detestable and shamefully vile.

3And say, Thus says the Lord God to Jerusalem [representing Israel]: Your [spiritual] origin and your birth are thoroughly Canaanitish; your [spiritual] father was an Amorite, and your [spiritual] mother a Hittite. [Ezek. 16:45; John 8:44.]

4And as for your birth, on the day you were born your navel cord was not cut, nor were you washed with water to cleanse you, nor rubbed with salt, nor swaddled with bands at all.

5No eye pitied you, to do any of these things for you, to have compassion on you, but you were cast out in the open field, for your person was abhorrent *and* loathsome on the day that you were born.

6And when I passed by you, and saw you rolling about in your blood, I said to you in your blood, Live! Yes, I said to you still in your natal blood, Live!

7I caused you [Israel] to multiply as the bud which grows in the field, and you increased and became tall and you came to full maidenhood *and* beauty; your breasts were formed and your hair had grown, yet you were naked and bare.

8Now I passed by you again, and looked upon you, behold, you were maturing *and* at the time for love; and I spread My skirt over you and covered your nakedness. Yes, I plighted My troth to you and entered into a covenant with you, says the Lord, and you became Mine.

9Then I washed you with water; yes, I thoroughly washed away your [clinging] blood from you, and I anointed you with oil.

10I clothed you also with embroidered cloth, and shod you with [fine seal] leather, and I girded you about with fine linen, and I covered you with silk.

11I decked you also with ornaments, and I put bracelets on your wrists and a chain on your neck.

12And I put a ring on your nostril and earrings in your ears, and a beautiful crown upon your head!

13Thus you were decked with gold and silver, and your raiment was of fine linen and silk and embroidered cloth; you ate fine flour and honey and oil. And you were exceedingly beautiful, and you prospered into royal estate.

14And your renown went forth among the nations for your beauty; for it was perfect through My majesty *and* splendor which I had put upon you, says the Lord God.

15But you trusted *and* relied on your own beauty, and were unfaithful to God *and* played the harlot [in idolatry] because of your renown, and poured out your fornications upon every one who passed by—worshiping the idols of every nation which prevailed over you; his it was.

16And you took some of your garments and made for yourself gaily decorated high places *or* shrines, and played the harlot on them; things which should not come and that which should not take place.

17You did also take your fair jewels *and* beautiful vessels of My gold and My silver which I had given you, and made for yourself images of men, and you played the harlot with them;

## New American Standard

6"Therefore, thus says the Lord GOD, 'As the wood of the vine
among the trees of the forest, which I have given to the fire for fuel,
so have I given up the inhabitants of Jerusalem;
7and I set My face against them. *Though* they have come out
of the fire, yet the fire will consume them. Then you will know that
I am the LORD, when I set My face against them.
8'Thus I will make the land desolate, because they have acted
unfaithfully,' " declares the Lord GOD.

*God's Grace to Unfaithful Jerusalem*

16 THEN THE word of the LORD came to me saying,
2"Son of man, make known to Jerusalem her abominations,
3and say, 'Thus says the Lord GOD to Jerusalem, "Your origin
and your birth are from the land of the Canaanite, your father was
an Amorite and your mother a Hittite.
4"As for your birth, on the day you were born your navel cord
was not cut, nor were you washed with water for cleansing; you
were not rubbed with salt or even wrapped in cloths.
5"No eye looked with pity on you to do any of these things for
you, to have compassion on you. Rather you were thrown out into
the open field, for you were abhorred on the day you were born.
6¶ "When I passed by you and saw you squirming in your
blood, I said to you *while you were* in your blood, 'Live!' I said to
you while you were in your blood, 'Live!'
7"I made you numerous like plants of the field. Then you grew
up, became tall, and reached the age for fine ornaments; *your*
breasts were formed and your hair had grown. Yet you were naked
and bare.
8"Then I passed by you and saw you, and behold, you were
at the time for love; so I spread My skirt over you and covered your
nakedness. I also swore to you and entered into a covenant with
you so that you became Mine," declares the Lord GOD.
9"Then I bathed you with water, washed off your blood from
you, and anointed you with oil.
10"I also clothed you with embroidered cloth, and put sandals
of porpoise skin on your feet; and I wrapped you with fine linen
and covered you with silk.
11"And I adorned you with ornaments, put bracelets on your
hands, and a necklace around your neck.
12"I also put a ring in your nostril, earrings in your ears, and
a beautiful crown on your head.
13"Thus you were adorned with gold and silver, and your dress
was of fine linen, silk, and embroidered cloth. You ate fine flour,
honey, and oil; so you were exceedingly beautiful and advanced
to royalty.
14"Then your fame went forth among the nations on account of
your beauty, for it was perfect because of My splendor which I
bestowed on you," declares the Lord GOD.
15¶ "But you trusted in your beauty and played the harlot
because of your fame, and you poured out your harlotries on every
passer-by who might be *willing*.
16"And you took some of your clothes, made for yourself high
places of various colors, and played the harlot on them, which
should never come about nor happen.
17"You also took your beautiful jewels *made* of My gold and of
My silver, which I had given you, and made for yourself male
images that you might play the harlot with them.

## New International

6"Therefore this is what the Sovereign LORD says: As I have
given the wood of the vine among the trees of the forest as fuel
for the fire, so will I treat the people living in Jerusalem. 7I will set
my face against them. Although they have come out of the fire, the
fire will yet consume them. And when I set my face against them,
you will know that I am the LORD. 8I will make the land desolate
because they have been unfaithful, declares the Sovereign LORD."

*An Allegory of Unfaithful Jerusalem*

16 THE WORD of the LORD came to me: 2"Son of man,
confront Jerusalem with her detestable practices 3and say,
'This is what the Sovereign LORD says to Jerusalem: Your ancestry
and birth were in the land of the Canaanites; your father was an
Amorite and your mother a Hittite. 4On the day you were born
your cord was not cut, nor were you washed with water to make
you clean, nor were you rubbed with salt or wrapped in cloths.
5No one looked on you with pity or had compassion enough to do
any of these things for you. Rather, you were thrown out into the
open field, for on the day you were born you were despised.
6" 'Then I passed by and saw you kicking about in your blood,
and as you lay there in your blood I said to you, "Live!"[a] 7I made
you grow like a plant of the field. You grew up and developed and
became the most beautiful of jewels.[b] Your breasts were formed
and your hair grew, you who were naked and bare.
8" 'Later I passed by, and when I looked at you and saw that
you were old enough for love, I spread the corner of my garment
over you and covered your nakedness. I gave you my solemn oath
and entered into a covenant with you, declares the Sovereign
LORD, and you became mine.
9" 'I bathed[c] you with water and washed the blood from you
and put ointments on you. 10I clothed you with an embroidered
dress and put leather sandals on you. I dressed you in fine linen
and covered you with costly garments. 11I adorned you with jewelry: I put bracelets on your arms and a necklace around your neck,
12and I put a ring on your nose, earrings on your ears and a
beautiful crown on your head. 13So you were adorned with gold
and silver; your clothes were of fine linen and costly fabric and
embroidered cloth. Your food was fine flour, honey and olive oil.
You became very beautiful and rose to be a queen. 14And your
fame spread among the nations on account of your beauty, because the splendor I had given you made your beauty perfect,
declares the Sovereign LORD.
15" 'But you trusted in your beauty and used your fame to
become a prostitute. You lavished your favors on anyone who
passed by and your beauty became his.[d] 16You took some of your
garments to make gaudy high places, where you carried on your
prostitution. Such things should not happen, nor should they ever
occur. 17You also took the fine jewelry I gave you, the jewelry
made of my gold and silver, and you made for yourself male idols
and engaged in prostitution with them. 18And you took your

**NIV** [a] 6 A few Hebrew manuscripts, Septuagint and Syriac; most Hebrew manuscripts *"Live!" And as you lay there in your blood I said to you, "Live!"* [b] 7 Or *became mature* [c] 9 Or *I had bathed* [d] 15 Most Hebrew manuscripts; one Hebrew manuscript (see some Septuagint manuscripts) *by. Such a thing should not happen*

## King James

18And tookest thy broidered garments, and coveredst them: and thou hast set mine oil and mine incense before them.

19My meat also which I gave thee, fine flour, and oil, and honey, *wherewith* I fed thee, thou hast even set it before them for a sweet savour: and *thus* it was, saith the Lord GOD.

20Moreover thou hast taken thy sons and thy daughters, whom thou hast borne unto me, and these hast thou sacrificed unto them to be devoured. *Is this* of thy whoredoms a small matter,

21That thou hast slain my children, and delivered them to cause them to pass through *the fire* for them?

22And in all thine abominations and thy whoredoms thou hast not remembered the days of thy youth, when thou wast naked and bare, *and* wast polluted in thy blood.

23And it came to pass after all thy wickedness, (woe, woe unto thee! saith the Lord GOD;)

24 *That* thou hast also built unto thee an eminent place, and hast made thee an high place in every street.

25Thou hast built thy high place at every head of the way, and hast made thy beauty to be abhorred, and hast opened thy feet to every one that passed by, and multiplied thy whoredoms.

26Thou hast also committed fornication with the Egyptians thy neighbours, great of flesh; and hast increased thy whoredoms, to provoke me to anger.

27Behold, therefore I have stretched out my hand over thee, and have diminished thine ordinary *food,* and delivered thee unto the will of them that hate thee, the daughters of the Philistines, which are ashamed of thy lewd way.

28Thou hast played the whore also with the Assyrians, because thou wast unsatiable; yea, thou hast played the harlot with them, and yet couldest not be satisfied.

29Thou hast moreover multiplied thy fornication in the land of Canaan unto Chaldea; and yet thou wast not satisfied herewith.

30How weak is thine heart, saith the Lord GOD, seeing thou doest all these *things,* the work of an imperious whorish woman;

31In that thou buildest thine eminent place in the head of every way, and makest thine high place in every street; and hast not been as an harlot, in that thou scornest hire;

32 *But as* a wife that committeth adultery, *which* taketh strangers instead of her husband!

33They give gifts to all whores: but thou givest thy gifts to all thy lovers, and hirest them, that they may come unto thee on every side for thy whoredom.

34And the contrary is in thee from *other* women in thy whoredoms, whereas none followeth thee to commit whoredoms: and in that thou givest a reward, and no reward is given unto thee, therefore thou art contrary.

35¶ Wherefore, O harlot, hear the word of the LORD:

36Thus saith the Lord GOD; Because thy filthiness was poured out, and thy nakedness discovered through thy whoredoms with thy lovers, and with all the idols of thy abominations, and by the blood of thy children, which thou didst give unto them;

37Behold, therefore I will gather all thy lovers, with whom thou hast taken pleasure, and all *them* that thou hast loved, with all *them* that thou hast hated; I will even gather them round about against thee, and will discover thy nakedness unto them, that they may see all thy nakedness.

38And I will judge thee, as women that break wedlock and shed blood are judged; and I will give thee blood in fury and jealousy.

## Amplified

18And you took your embroidered garments and covered them, and set My oil and My incense before them.

19My bread also which I gave you, fine flour and oil and honey with which I fed you, you have even set it before the idols for a sweet odor. Thus it was, says the Lord God.

20Moreover, you have taken your sons and your daughters whom you have borne to Me, and you have sacrificed them [to your idols] to be destroyed. Were your harlotries too little,

21That you have slain My children, and delivered them up, in setting them apart *and* causing them to pass through the fire for [your idols]?

22And in all your abominations and idolatrous whoredoms you have not [earnestly] remembered the days of your youth, when you were naked and bare, rolling about in your natal blood.

23And after all your wickedness (Woe, woe to you! says the Lord God),

24You have built also for yourself a [brothel] vaulted chamber, and have made a high place [of idol worship] in every street.

25At every crossway you built your high place [for idol worship], and have made your beauty an abomination—abhorrent, loathsome, extremely disgusting, and detestable; and you have made your body available to every passerby, and multiplied your [idolatry and spiritual] harlotry.

26You have also played the harlot with the Egyptians, your neighbors, [by adopting their idolatries] whose worship is thoroughly sensuous; and you have multiplied your harlotry to provoke Me to anger.

27Behold, therefore I have stretched out My hand against you, diminished your ordinary allowance of food, and delivered you over to the will of those who hate *and* despise you, the daughters of the Philistines, who turned away in shame from your despicable policy *and* lewd behavior [for they are faithful to their gods]!

28You played the harlot also with the Assyrians, because you were unsatiable; yes, you played the harlot with them, and yet you were not satisfied.

29Moreover you multiplied your harlotry with the land of trade, with Chaldea; and yet even with this you were not satisfied.

30How weak *and* spent with longing *and* lust is your heart *and* mind, says the Lord God, seeing you do all these things, the work of a bold, domineering harlot;

31In that you build your [brothel] vaulted place at the head of every street, and make your high place at every crossing. But you were not like a harlot, because you scorned pay.

32Rather, you were as an adulterous wife, who receives strangers instead of her husband!

33Men give gifts to all harlots; but you give your gifts to all your lovers, and hire them, bribing [the nations] [to ally themselves with you] that they may come to you on every side for your harlotries [your idolatrous unfaithfulnesses to God].

34And you are different [the reverse] from other women in your harlotries, in that nobody follows you to lure you into harlotry, and in your giving hire when no hire is given you; and so you are different.

35Therefore, O harlot [Israel], hear the word of the Lord.

36Thus says the Lord God: Because your brass [coins and gifts] *and* your filthiness were emptied out and your nakedness uncovered through your harlotries with your lovers, and because of all the [filthy] idols of your abominations, and for the blood of your children that you gave to them,

37Therefore, behold, I will gather all your lovers, with whom you have taken pleasure, and all those whom you have loved, with all those whom you have hated; I will even gather them [the allies you have courted] against you on every side, and will uncover your nakedness to them, that they may see all your nakedness [making you, Israel, an object of loathing and of mockery, a spectacle among the nations].

38And I, the Lord, will judge you as women who break wedlock and shed blood are judged, and I will bring upon you the blood of [your divine Husband's] wrath and jealousy. [Num. 5:18.]

## New American Standard

18"Then you took your embroidered cloth and covered them,
and offered My oil and My incense before them.
19"Also My bread which I gave you, fine flour, oil, and honey
with which I fed you, you would offer before them for a soothing
aroma; so it happened," declares the Lord GOD.
20"Moreover, you took your sons and daughters whom you had
borne to Me, and you sacrificed them to idols to be devoured. Were
your harlotries so small a matter?
21"You slaughtered My children, and offered them up to idols
by causing them to pass through *the fire.*
22"And besides all your abominations and harlotries you did
not remember the days of your youth, when you were naked and
bare and squirming in your blood.
23¶ "Then it came about after all your wickedness ('Woe, woe
to you!' declares the Lord GOD),
24that you built yourself a shrine and made yourself a high place
in every square.
25"You built yourself a high place at the top of every street, and
made your beauty abominable; and you spread your legs to every
passer-by to multiply your harlotry.
26"You also played the harlot with the Egyptians, your lustful
neighbors, and multiplied your harlotry to make Me angry.
27"Behold now, I have stretched out My hand against you and
diminished your rations. And I delivered you up to the desire of
those who hate you, the daughters of the Philistines, who are
ashamed of your lewd conduct.
28"Moreover, you played the harlot with the Assyrians because
you were not satisfied; you even played the harlot with them and
still were not satisfied.
29"You also multiplied your harlotry with the land of merchants, Chaldea, yet even with this you were not satisfied." ' "
30¶ "How languishing is your heart," declares the Lord GOD,
"while you do all these things, the actions of a bold-faced harlot.
31"When you built your shrine at the beginning of every street
and made your high place in every square, in disdaining money,
you were not like a harlot.
32"You adulteress wife, who takes strangers instead of her husband!
33"Men give gifts to all harlots, but you give your gifts to all your
lovers to bribe them to come to you from every direction for your
harlotries.
34"Thus you are different from those women in your harlotries,
in that no one plays the harlot as you do, because you give money
and no money is given you; thus you are different."
35¶ Therefore, O harlot, hear the word of the LORD.
36Thus says the Lord GOD, "Because your lewdness was poured
out and your nakedness uncovered through your harlotries with
your lovers and with all your detestable idols, and because of the
blood of your sons which you gave to idols,
37therefore, behold, I shall gather all your lovers with whom
you took pleasure, even all those whom you loved *and* all those
whom you hated. So I shall gather them against you from every
direction and expose your nakedness to them that they may see
all your nakedness.
38"Thus I shall judge you, like women who commit adultery or
shed blood are judged; and I shall bring on you the blood of wrath
and jealousy.

## New International

embroidered clothes to put on them, and you offered my oil and
incense before them. 19Also the food I provided for you—the fine
flour, olive oil and honey I gave you to eat—you offered as fragrant
incense before them. That is what happened, declares the Sovereign LORD.
20" 'And you took your sons and daughters whom you bore to
me and sacrificed them as food to the idols. Was your prostitution
not enough? 21You slaughtered my children and sacrificed them[a]
to the idols. 22In all your detestable practices and your prostitution
you did not remember the days of your youth, when you were
naked and bare, kicking about in your blood.
23" 'Woe! Woe to you, declares the Sovereign LORD. In addition
to all your other wickedness, 24you built a mound for yourself and
made a lofty shrine in every public square. 25At the head of every
street you built your lofty shrines and degraded your beauty,
offering your body with increasing promiscuity to anyone who
passed by. 26You engaged in prostitution with the Egyptians, your
lustful neighbors, and provoked me to anger with your increasing
promiscuity. 27So I stretched out my hand against you and reduced
your territory; I gave you over to the greed of your enemies, the
daughters of the Philistines, who were shocked by your lewd
conduct. 28You engaged in prostitution with the Assyrians too,
because you were insatiable; and even after that, you still were not
satisfied. 29Then you increased your promiscuity to include Babylonia,[b] a land of merchants, but even with this you were not
satisfied.
30" 'How weak-willed you are, declares the Sovereign LORD,
when you do all these things, acting like a brazen prostitute!
31When you built your mounds at the head of every street and
made your lofty shrines in every public square, you were unlike
a prostitute, because you scorned payment.
32" 'You adulterous wife! You prefer strangers to your own
husband! 33Every prostitute receives a fee, but you give gifts to all
your lovers, bribing them to come to you from everywhere for your
illicit favors. 34So in your prostitution you are the opposite of
others; no one runs after you for your favors. You are the very
opposite, for you give payment and none is given to you.
35" 'Therefore, you prostitute, hear the word of the LORD!
36This is what the Sovereign LORD says: Because you poured out
your wealth[c] and exposed your nakedness in your promiscuity
with your lovers, and because of all your detestable idols, and
because you gave them your children's blood, 37therefore I am
going to gather all your lovers, with whom you found pleasure,
those you loved as well as those you hated. I will gather them
against you from all around and will strip you in front of them, and
they will see all your nakedness. 38I will sentence you to the
punishment of women who commit adultery and who shed blood;
I will bring upon you the blood vengeance of my wrath and jealous
anger. 39Then I will hand you over to your lovers, and they will

NIV [a] 21 Or *and made them pass through ⌊the fire⌋* [b] 29 Or *Chaldea* [c] 36 Or *lust*

## King James

39 And I will also give thee into their hand, and they shall throw down thine eminent place, and shall break down thy high places: they shall strip thee also of thy clothes, and shall take thy fair jewels, and leave thee naked and bare.

40 They shall also bring up a company against thee, and they shall stone thee with stones, and thrust thee through with their swords.

41 And they shall burn thine houses with fire, and execute judgments upon thee in the sight of many women: and I will cause thee to cease from playing the harlot, and thou also shalt give no hire any more.

42 So will I make my fury toward thee to rest, and my jealousy shall depart from thee, and I will be quiet, and will be no more angry.

43 Because thou hast not remembered the days of thy youth, but hast fretted me in all these *things;* behold, therefore I also will recompense thy way upon *thine* head, saith the Lord GOD: and thou shalt not commit this lewdness above all thine abominations.

44 ¶ Behold, every one that useth proverbs shall use *this* proverb against thee, saying, As *is* the mother, *so is* her daughter.

45 Thou *art* thy mother's daughter, that loatheth her husband and her children; and thou *art* the sister of thy sisters, which loathed their husbands and their children: your mother *was* an Hittite, and your father an Amorite.

46 And thine elder sister *is* Samaria, she and her daughters that dwell at thy left hand: and thy younger sister, that dwelleth at thy right hand, *is* Sodom and her daughters.

47 Yet hast thou not walked after their ways, nor done after their abominations: but, as *if that were* a very little *thing,* thou wast corrupted more than they in all thy ways.

48 *As* I live, saith the Lord GOD, Sodom thy sister hath not done, she nor her daughters, as thou hast done, thou and thy daughters.

49 Behold, this was the iniquity of thy sister Sodom, pride, fulness of bread, and abundance of idleness was in her and in her daughters, neither did she strengthen the hand of the poor and needy.

50 And they were haughty, and committed abomination before me: therefore I took them away as I saw *good.*

51 Neither hath Samaria committed half of thy sins; but thou hast multiplied thine abominations more than they, and hast justified thy sisters in all thine abominations which thou hast done.

52 Thou also, which hast judged thy sisters, bear thine own shame for thy sins that thou hast committed more abominable than they: they are more righteous than thou: yea, be thou confounded also, and bear thy shame, in that thou hast justified thy sisters.

53 When I shall bring again their captivity, the captivity of Sodom and her daughters, and the captivity of Samaria and her daughters, then *will I bring again* the captivity of thy captives in the midst of them:

54 That thou mayest bear thine own shame, and mayest be confounded in all that thou hast done, in that thou art a comfort unto them.

55 When thy sisters, Sodom and her daughters, shall return to their former estate, and Samaria and her daughters shall return to their former estate, then thou and thy daughters shall return to your former estate.

56 For thy sister Sodom was not mentioned by thy mouth in the day of thy pride,

## Amplified

39 And I will also give you into the hand of those [your enemies] and they shall throw down your [brothel] vaulted place, and shall demolish your high places [of idolatry]; they shall strip you of your clothes and shall take your splendid jewels, and leave you naked and bare.

40 They shall also bring up a company against you, and they shall stone you with stones and hew down *and* thrust you through with their swords.

41 And they shall burn your houses with fire and execute judgments upon you before the eyes of many women spectators [the nations]. And I will cause you to cease playing the harlot, and you also shall give hire no more.

42 So will I make My wrath toward you to rest, and My jealousy shall depart from you [My adulterous wife], and I will be quiet, and will be no more angry.

43 Because you have not [earnestly] remembered the days of your youth, but have enraged Me with all these things, therefore, behold, I also will bring your deeds down on your own head, says the Lord God. Did you not commit this lewdness above *and* in addition to all your other abominations?

44 Behold, every one who uses proverbs will use this proverb against you, As is the mother, so is her daughter.

45 You are your [spiritual] mother's daughter, who loathes her husband and her children; and you are the sister of your sisters, who loathed their husbands and their children. Your mother was a Hittite and your father an Amorite.

46 And your elder sister is Samaria, she and her daughters who dwelt in the north *and* at your left hand; and your younger sister, who dwelt in the south *and* at your right hand, is Sodom and her daughters.

47 Yet you were not satisfied to walk after their ways or to do after their abominations, but very soon you were more corrupt in all your ways than they were [for your sin, as those taught of God, is far blacker than theirs]. [Matt. 11:20-24.]

48 As I live, says the Lord God, Sodom your sister has not done, she nor her daughters, as you have done, you and your daughters.

49 Behold, this was the iniquity of your sister Sodom: pride, over-abundance of food, prosperous ease *and* idleness were hers and her daughters'; neither did she strengthen the hand of the poor and needy.

50 And they were haughty, and committed abominable offenses before Me; therefore I removed them when I saw it *and* I saw fit. [Gen. 13:13; 18:20; 19:5.]

51 Neither has Samaria committed half of your sins, but you have multiplied your [idolatrous] abominations more than they, and have *seemed* to justify your sisters [Samaria and Sodom] in all their wickedness by all the abominable things which you have done—you even make them appear righteous in comparison with you.

52 Take upon you *and* bear your own shame *and* disgrace [in your punishment], you also, who called in question *and* judged your sisters, for you have virtually absolved them by your sins in which you behaved more abominably than they; they are more right than you. Yes, be ashamed *and* confounded and bear your shame *and* disgrace, you also, for you have seemed to justify your sisters *and* make them appear righteous.

53 I will restore them again from their captivity, restore the fortunes of Sodom and her daughters, and the fortunes of Samaria and her daughters, and I will restore your own fortunes in the midst of them [in the day of the Lord], [Isa. 1:9.]

54 That you, [Judah,] amid your shame *and* disgrace may be compelled to recognize your wickedness *and* be thoroughly ashamed *and* confounded at all you have done, becoming [converted and bringing] consolation *and* comfort to *your sisters.*

55 And your sisters, Sodom and her daughters, shall return to their former estate, and Samaria and her daughters shall return to their former estate, then you and your daughters shall return to your former estate.

56 For was your sister Sodom not mentioned by you *except* as a byword in the day of your pride,

## New American Standard

39"I shall also give you into the hands of your lovers, and they will tear down your shrines, demolish your high places, strip you of your clothing, take away your jewels, and will leave you naked and bare.

40"They will incite a crowd against you, and they will stone you and cut you to pieces with their swords.

41"And they will burn your houses with fire and execute judgments on you in the sight of many women. Then I shall stop you from playing the harlot, and you will also no longer pay your lovers.

42"So I shall calm My fury against you, and My jealousy will depart from you, and I shall be pacified and angry no more.
43"Because you have not remembered the days of your youth but have enraged Me by all these things, behold, I in turn will bring your conduct down on your own head," declares the Lord GOD, "so that you will not commit this lewdness on top of all your *other* abominations.

44¶ "Behold, everyone who quotes proverbs will quote *this* proverb concerning you, saying, 'Like mother, like daughter.'

45"You are the daughter of your mother, who loathed her husband and children. You are also the sister of your sisters, who loathed their husbands and children. Your mother was a Hittite and your father an Amorite.

46"Now your older sister is Samaria, who lives north of you with her daughters; and your younger sister, who lives south of you, is Sodom with her daughters.

47"Yet you have not merely walked in their ways or done according to their abominations; but, as if that were too little, you acted more corruptly in all your conduct than they.

48"As I live," declares the Lord GOD, "Sodom, your sister, and her daughters, have not done as you and your daughters have done.

49"Behold, this was the guilt of your sister Sodom: she and her daughters had arrogance, abundant food, and careless ease, but she did not help the poor and needy.

50"Thus they were haughty and committed abominations before Me. Therefore I removed them when I saw *it*.

51"Furthermore, Samaria did not commit half of your sins, for you have multiplied your abominations more than they. Thus you have made your sisters appear righteous by all your abominations which you have committed.

52"Also bear your disgrace in that you have made judgment favorable for your sisters. Because of your sins in which you acted more abominably than they, they are more in the right than you. Yes, be also ashamed and bear your disgrace, in that you made your sisters appear righteous.

53¶ "Nevertheless, I will restore their captivity, the captivity of Sodom and her daughters, the captivity of Samaria and her daughters, and along with them your own captivity,

54in order that you may bear your humiliation, and feel ashamed for all that you have done when you become a consolation to them.

55"And your sisters, Sodom with her daughters and Samaria with her daughters, will return to their former state, and you with your daughters will *also* return to your former state.

56"As *the name of* your sister Sodom was not heard from your lips in your day of pride,

## New International

tear down your mounds and destroy your lofty shrines. They will
strip you of your clothes and take your fine jewelry and leave you
naked and bare. 40They will bring a mob against you, who will
stone you and hack you to pieces with their swords. 41They will
burn down your houses and inflict punishment on you in the sight
of many women. I will put a stop to your prostitution, and you will
no longer pay your lovers. 42Then my wrath against you will
subside and my jealous anger will turn away from you; I will be
calm and no longer angry.
43" 'Because you did not remember the days of your youth but
enraged me with all these things, I will surely bring down on your
head what you have done, declares the Sovereign LORD. Did you
not add lewdness to all your other detestable practices?
44" 'Everyone who quotes proverbs will quote this proverb
about you: "Like mother, like daughter." 45You are a true daughter
of your mother, who despised her husband and her children; and
you are a true sister of your sisters, who despised their husbands
and their children. Your mother was a Hittite and your father an
Amorite. 46Your older sister was Samaria, who lived to the north
of you with her daughters; and your younger sister, who lived to
the south of you with her daughters, was Sodom. 47You not only
walked in their ways and copied their detestable practices, but in
all your ways you soon became more depraved than they. 48As
surely as I live, declares the Sovereign LORD, your sister Sodom
and her daughters never did what you and your daughters have
done.
49" 'Now this was the sin of your sister Sodom: She and her
daughters were arrogant, overfed and unconcerned; they did not
help the poor and needy. 50They were haughty and did detestable
things before me. Therefore I did away with them as you have
seen. 51Samaria did not commit half the sins you did. You have
done more detestable things than they, and have made your sisters
seem righteous by all these things you have done. 52Bear your
disgrace, for you have furnished some justification for your sisters.
Because your sins were more vile than theirs, they appear more
righteous than you. So then, be ashamed and bear your disgrace,
for you have made your sisters appear righteous.
53" 'However, I will restore the fortunes of Sodom and her
daughters and of Samaria and her daughters, and your fortunes
along with them, 54so that you may bear your disgrace and be
ashamed of all you have done in giving them comfort. 55And your
sisters, Sodom with her daughters and Samaria with her daughters, will return to what they were before; and you and your
daughters will return to what you were before. 56You would not
even mention your sister Sodom in the day of your pride, 57before

## King James

57Before thy wickedness was discovered, as at the time of *thy* reproach of the daughters of Syria, and all *that are* round about her, the daughters of the Philistines, which despise thee round about.

58Thou hast borne thy lewdness and thine abominations, saith the LORD.

59For thus saith the Lord GOD; I will even deal with thee as thou hast done, which hast despised the oath in breaking the covenant.

60¶ Nevertheless I will remember my covenant with thee in the days of thy youth, and I will establish unto thee an everlasting covenant.

61Then thou shalt remember thy ways, and be ashamed, when thou shalt receive thy sisters, thine elder and thy younger: and I will give them unto thee for daughters, but not by thy covenant.

62And I will establish my covenant with thee; and thou shalt know that I *am* the LORD:

63That thou mayest remember, and be confounded, and never open thy mouth any more because of thy shame, when I am pacified toward thee for all that thou hast done, saith the Lord GOD.

**17** AND THE word of the LORD came unto me, saying,

2Son of man, put forth a riddle, and speak a parable unto the house of Israel;

3And say, Thus saith the Lord GOD; A great eagle with great wings, longwinged, full of feathers, which had divers colours, came unto Lebanon, and took the highest branch of the cedar:

4He cropped off the top of his young twigs, and carried it into a land of traffic; he set it in a city of merchants.

5He took also of the seed of the land, and planted it in a fruitful field; he placed *it* by great waters, *and* set it *as* a willow tree.

6And it grew, and became a spreading vine of low stature, whose branches turned toward him, and the roots thereof were under him: so it became a vine, and brought forth branches, and shot forth sprigs.

7There was also another great eagle with great wings and many feathers: and, behold, this vine did bend her roots toward him, and shot forth her branches toward him, that he might water it by the furrows of her plantation.

8It was planted in a good soil by great waters, that it might bring forth branches, and that it might bear fruit, that it might be a goodly vine.

9Say thou, Thus saith the Lord GOD; Shall it prosper? shall he not pull up the roots thereof, and cut off the fruit thereof, that it wither? it shall wither in all the leaves of her spring, even without great power or many people to pluck it up by the roots thereof.

10Yea, behold, *being* planted, shall it prosper? shall it not utterly wither, when the east wind toucheth it? it shall wither in the furrows where it grew.

11¶ Moreover the word of the LORD came unto me, saying,

12Say now to the rebellious house, Know ye not what these *things mean?* tell *them,* Behold, the king of Babylon is come to Jerusalem, and hath taken the king thereof, and the princes thereof, and led them with him to Babylon;

## Amplified

57Before your own wickedness was uncovered? Now you have become like her an object of reproach *and* a byword for the daughters of Syria *and* of Edom and for all who are round about them, and for the daughters of the Philistines, those round about who despise you.

58You bear the penalty of your lewdness and your [idolatrous] abominations, says the Lord.

59Yes, thus says the Lord God: I will even deal with you as you have done, who have despised the oath in breaking the covenant;

60Nevertheless I will [earnestly] remember My covenant with you in the days of your youth, and I will establish with you an everlasting covenant. [Ps. 106:45.]

61Then you will [earnestly] remember your ways, and be ashamed *and* confounded, when you shall receive your sisters, both your elder and your younger; I will give them to you for daughters, but not on account of your covenant [with Me]. [John 10:16.]

62And I will establish My covenant with you, and you shall know—understand and realize—that I am the Lord; [Hos. 2:19, 20.]

63That you may [earnestly] remember and be ashamed *and* confounded, and never open your mouth again because of your shame, when I have forgiven you all that you have done, says the Lord God.

**17** AND THE word of the Lord came to me, saying,

2Son of man, put forth a riddle and speak a parable *or* allegory to the house of Israel;

3Say, Thus says the Lord God: A great eagle [Nebuchadnezzar] with great wings and long pinions, rich in feathers of various colors, came to Lebanon [symbolic of Jerusalem] and took the top of the cedar [tree].

4He broke off [the youthful King Jehoiachin] the topmost of its young twigs and carried it into a land of trade [Babylon]; he set it in a city of merchants.

5He took also of the seedlings of the land [Zedekiah, one of the native royal family], and planted it in fertile soil *and* a fruitful field; he placed it beside abundant waters, and set it as a willow tree [to succeed Zedekiah's nephew Jehoiachin in Judah, as vassal king].

6And it grew, and became a spreading vine of low [not Davidic] stature, whose branches turned [in submission] toward him, and its roots remained under *and* subject to him [the king of Babylon]; so it became a vine, and brought forth branches, and shot forth leafy twigs.

7There was also another great eagle [the Egyptian king] with great wings and many feathers; and behold, this vine [Zedekiah] bent its roots [languishingly] toward him, and shot forth its branches toward him, away from the beds of its planting, for him to water.

8Though it was planted in good soil where water was plentiful for it to produce leaves and to bear fruit, that it might become a splendid vine, it was transplanted.

9Thus says the Lord God: Ask, Will it thrive? Will he [the insulted Nebuchadnezzar] not pluck up its roots and strip off its fruit so that all its fresh sprouting leaves will wither? It will not take a strong arm or many people to pluck it up by its roots [totally ending Israel's national existence]. [II Kings 25:1-7.]

10Yes, behold, though transplanted, will it prosper? Will it not utterly wither, when the east wind touches it? It will wither in the furrows *and* beds where it sprouted *and* grew. [Hos. 13:9-12, 15.]

11Moreover the word of the Lord came to me, saying,

12Say now to the rebellious house, Do you not know *and* realize what these things mean? Tell them, Behold, the king of Babylon came to Jerusalem, and took its king [Jehoiachin] and its princes and brought them with him to Babylon. [II Kings 24:11-16.]

## New American Standard

57before your wickedness was uncovered, so now you have
become the reproach of the daughters of Edom, and of all who are
around her, of the daughters of the Philistines—those surrounding
*you* who despise you.
58"You have borne *the penalty of* your lewdness and abominations," the LORD declares.
59For thus says the Lord GOD, "I will also do with you as you
have done, you who have despised the oath by breaking the
covenant.

*The Covenant Remembered*

60¶ "Nevertheless, I will remember My covenant with you in the
days of your youth, and I will establish an everlasting covenant
with you.
61"Then you will remember your ways and be ashamed when
you receive your sisters, *both* your older and your younger; and I
will give them to you as daughters, but not because of your covenant.
62"Thus I will establish My covenant with you, and you shall
know that I am the LORD,
63in order that you may remember and be ashamed, and never
open your mouth anymore because of your humiliation, when I
have forgiven you for all that you have done," the Lord GOD
declares.

*Parable of Two Eagles and a Vine*

**17** NOW THE word of the LORD came to me saying,
2"Son of man, propound a riddle, and speak a parable to
the house of Israel,
3saying, 'Thus says the Lord GOD, "A great eagle with great
wings, long pinions and a full plumage of many colors, came to
Lebanon and took away the top of the cedar.
4"He plucked off the topmost of its young twigs and brought
it to a land of merchants; he set it in a city of traders.
5"He also took some of the seed of the land and planted it in
fertile soil. He placed *it* beside abundant waters; he set it *like* a
willow.
6"Then it sprouted and became a low, spreading vine with its
branches turned toward him, but its roots remained under it. So
it became a vine, and yielded shoots and sent out branches.
7¶ "But there was another great eagle with great wings and
much plumage; and behold, this vine bent its roots toward him
and sent out its branches toward him from the beds where it was
planted, that he might water it.
8"It was planted in good soil beside abundant waters, that it
might yield branches and bear fruit, *and* become a splendid vine."'
9"Say, 'Thus says the Lord GOD, "Will it thrive? Will he not
pull up its roots and cut off its fruit, so that it withers—so that all
its sprouting leaves wither? And neither by great strength nor by
many people can it be raised from its roots *again*.
10"Behold, though it is planted, will it thrive? Will it not completely wither as soon as the east wind strikes it—wither on the
beds where it grew?"'"

*Zedekiah's Rebellion*

11¶ Moreover, the word of the LORD came to me saying,
12"Say now to the rebellious house, 'Do you not know what
these things *mean?*' Say, 'Behold, the king of Babylon came to
Jerusalem, took its king and princes, and brought them to him in
Babylon.

## New International

your wickedness was uncovered. Even so, you are now scorned
by the daughters of Edom[a] and all her neighbors and the daughters of the Philistines—all those around you who despise you.
58You will bear the consequences of your lewdness and your detestable practices, declares the LORD.
59" 'This is what the Sovereign LORD says: I will deal with you
as you deserve, because you have despised my oath by breaking
the covenant. 60Yet I will remember the covenant I made with you
in the days of your youth, and I will establish an everlasting
covenant with you. 61Then you will remember your ways and be
ashamed when you receive your sisters, both those who are older
than you and those who are younger. I will give them to you as
daughters, but not on the basis of my covenant with you. 62So I
will establish my covenant with you, and you will know that I am
the LORD. 63Then, when I make atonement for you for all you have
done, you will remember and be ashamed and never again open
your mouth because of your humiliation, declares the Sovereign
LORD.' "

*Two Eagles and a Vine*

**17** THE WORD of the LORD came to me: 2"Son of man, set
forth an allegory and tell the house of Israel a parable. 3Say
to them, 'This is what the Sovereign LORD says: A great eagle with
powerful wings, long feathers and full plumage of varied colors
came to Lebanon. Taking hold of the top of a cedar, 4he broke off
its topmost shoot and carried it away to a land of merchants, where
he planted it in a city of traders.
5" 'He took some of the seed of your land and put it in fertile
soil. He planted it like a willow by abundant water, 6and it sprouted and became a low, spreading vine. Its branches turned toward
him, but its roots remained under it. So it became a vine and
produced branches and put out leafy boughs.
7" 'But there was another great eagle with powerful wings and
full plumage. The vine now sent out its roots toward him from the
plot where it was planted and stretched out its branches to him for
water. 8It had been planted in good soil by abundant water so that
it would produce branches, bear fruit and become a splendid vine.'
9"Say to them, 'This is what the Sovereign LORD says: Will it
thrive? Will it not be uprooted and stripped of its fruit so that it
withers? All its new growth will wither. It will not take a strong
arm or many people to pull it up by the roots. 10Even if it is
transplanted, will it thrive? Will it not wither completely when the
east wind strikes it—wither away in the plot where it grew?' "
11Then the word of the LORD came to me: 12"Say to this rebellious house, 'Do you not know what these things mean?' Say to
them: 'The king of Babylon went to Jerusalem and carried off her
king and her nobles, bringing them back with him to Babylon.

NIV [a] *57* Many Hebrew manuscripts and Syriac; most Hebrew manuscripts, Septuagint and Vulgate *Aram*

## King James

13And hath taken of the king's seed, and made a covenant with him, and hath taken an oath of him: he hath also taken the mighty of the land:

14That the kingdom might be base, that it might not lift itself up, *but* that by keeping of his covenant it might stand.

15But he rebelled against him in sending his ambassadors into Egypt, that they might give him horses and much people. Shall he prosper? shall he escape that doeth such *things?* or shall he break the covenant, and be delivered?

16 *As* I live, saith the Lord GOD, surely in the place *where* the king *dwelleth* that made him king, whose oath he despised, and whose covenant he brake, *even* with him in the midst of Babylon he shall die.

17Neither shall Pharaoh with *his* mighty army and great company make for him in the war, by casting up mounts, and building forts, to cut off many persons:

18Seeing he despised the oath by breaking the covenant, when, lo, he had given his hand, and hath done all these *things,* he shall not escape.

19Therefore thus saith the Lord GOD; *As* I live, surely mine oath that he hath despised, and my covenant that he hath broken, even it will I recompense upon his own head.

20And I will spread my net upon him, and he shall be taken in my snare, and I will bring him to Babylon, and will plead with him there for his trespass that he hath trespassed against me.

21And all his fugitives with all his bands shall fall by the sword, and they that remain shall be scattered toward all winds: and ye shall know that I the LORD have spoken *it.*

22¶ Thus saith the Lord GOD; I will also take of the highest branch of the high cedar, and will set *it;* I will crop off from the top of his young twigs a tender one, and will plant *it* upon an high mountain and eminent:

23In the mountain of the height of Israel will I plant it: and it shall bring forth boughs, and bear fruit, and be a goodly cedar: and under it shall dwell all fowl of every wing; in the shadow of the branches thereof shall they dwell.

24And all the trees of the field shall know that I the LORD have brought down the high tree, have exalted the low tree, have dried up the green tree, and have made the dry tree to flourish: I the LORD have spoken and have done *it.*

**18** THE WORD of the LORD came unto me again, saying,
2What mean ye, that ye use this proverb concerning the land of Israel, saying, The fathers have eaten sour grapes, and the children's teeth are set on edge?

3 *As* I live, saith the Lord GOD, ye shall not have *occasion* any more to use this proverb in Israel.

4Behold, all souls are mine; as the soul of the father, so also the soul of the son is mine: the soul that sinneth, it shall die.

5¶ But if a man be just, and do that which is lawful and right,

6 *And* hath not eaten upon the mountains, neither hath lifted up his eyes to the idols of the house of Israel, neither hath defiled his neighbour's wife, neither hath come near to a menstruous woman,

## Amplified

13And he took one of the royal family [the king's uncle, Zedekiah] and made a covenant with him, putting him under oath. He also took the mighty *and* chief men of the land, [II Kings 24:17.]

14That the kingdom might become low *and* base, and be unable to lift itself up, but that by keeping his [Nebuchadnezzar's] covenant it might stand.

15But he [Zedekiah] rebelled against him [Nebuchadnezzar] in sending his ambassadors into Egypt, that they might give him horses and much people. Will he prosper? Will he escape who does such things? Can he break the covenant with [Babylon] and yet escape?

16As I live, says the Lord God, surely in the place where the king [Nebuchadnezzar] dwells who made [Zedekiah vassal] king, whose oath [Zedekiah] despised, and whose covenant he broke, even with him in the midst of Babylon shall [Zedekiah] die.

17Neither shall Pharaoh with his mighty army and great company help him in the war, when the [Babylonians] cast up mounds and build forts to destroy many lives.

18For *Zedekiah* despised the oath and broke the covenant, and behold, he had given his hand, and yet has done all these things; he shall not escape.

19Therefore thus says the Lord God: As I live, surely My oath [made for Me by Nebuchadnezzar] that [Zedekiah] has despised and My covenant with him that he has broken, I will even bring down on his own head.

20And I will spread My net over him, and he shall be taken in My snare, and I will bring him to Babylon and will enter into judgment *and* punishment with him there for his trespass *and* treason that he has committed against Me.

21And all his fugitives [from Judah] in all his bands shall fall by the sword, and they that remain shall be scattered toward every wind. And you shall know—understand and realize—that I the Lord have spoken it.

22Thus says the Lord God: I Myself will take a twig from the lofty top of the cedar, and will set it out; I will crop off from the topmost of its young twigs a tender one and will plant it upon a mountain high and exalted. [Isa. 11:1, 10; Jer. 23:5; Zech. 3:8; Isa. 53:2.]

23On the mountain height of Israel will I plant it; that it may bring forth boughs and bear fruit, and be a noble cedar; and under it shall dwell all birds of every feather; in the shade of its branches they shall nestle *and* find rest.

24And all the trees of the field shall know—understand and realize—that I, the Lord, have brought low the high tree, have exalted the low tree, have dried up the green tree, and have made the dry tree flourish. I, the Lord, have spoken, and I will do it.

**18** THE WORD of the Lord came to me again, saying,
2What do you mean by using this proverb concerning the land of Israel, The fathers have eaten sour grapes, and the children's teeth are set on edge?

3As I live, says the Lord God, you shall not have occasion any more to use this proverb in Israel.

4Behold, all souls are mine; as the soul of the father, so also the soul of the son is Mine; the soul that sins, it shall die. [Rom. 6:23.]

5But if a man is [uncompromisingly] righteous—upright and in right standing with God—and does what is lawful and right,

6And has not eaten [at the idol shrines] upon the mountains nor lifted up his eyes to the idols of the house of Israel, has not defiled his neighbor's wife nor come near to a woman in her time of impurity,

## New American Standard

13'And he took one of the royal family and made a covenant
with him, putting him under oath. He also took away the mighty
of the land,
14that the kingdom might be in subjection, not exalting itself,
*but* keeping his covenant, that it might continue.
15'But he rebelled against him by sending his envoys to Egypt
that they might give him horses and many troops. Will he succeed?
Will he who does such things escape? Can he indeed break the
covenant and escape?
16'As I live,' declares the Lord GOD, 'Surely in the country of the
king who put him on the throne, whose oath he despised, and
whose covenant he broke, in Babylon he shall die.
17'And Pharaoh with *his* mighty army and great company will
not help him in the war, when they cast up mounds and build
siege walls to cut off many lives.
18'Now he despised the oath by breaking the covenant, and
behold, he pledged his allegiance, yet did all these things; he shall
not escape.' "
19Therefore, thus says the Lord GOD, "As I live, surely My oath
which he despised and My covenant which he broke, I will inflict
on his head.
20"And I will spread My net over him, and he will be caught
in My snare. Then I will bring him to Babylon and enter into
judgment with him there *regarding* the unfaithful act which he has
committed against Me.
21"And all the choice men in all his troops will fall by the sword,
and the survivors will be scattered to every wind; and you will
know that I, the LORD, have spoken."
22¶ Thus says the Lord GOD, "I shall also take *a sprig* from the
lofty top of the cedar and set *it* out; I shall pluck from the topmost
of its young twigs a tender one, and I shall plant *it* on a high and
lofty mountain.
23"On the high mountain of Israel I shall plant it, that it may
bring forth boughs and bear fruit, and become a stately cedar. And
birds of every kind will nest under it; they will nest in the shade
of its branches.
24"And all the trees of the field will know that I am the LORD;
I bring down the high tree, exalt the low tree, dry up the green tree,
and make the dry tree flourish. I am the LORD; I have spoken, and
I will perform *it*."

### *God Deals Justly with Individuals*

**18** THEN THE word of the LORD came to me saying,
2"What do you mean by using this proverb concerning the
land of Israel saying,

'The fathers eat the sour grapes,
But the children's teeth are set on edge'?

3"As I live," declares the Lord GOD, "you are surely not going
to use this proverb in Israel anymore.
4"Behold, all souls are Mine; the soul of the father as well as
the soul of the son is Mine. The soul who sins will die.
5"But if a man is righteous, and practices justice and righteousness,
6and does not eat at the mountain *shrines* or lift up his eyes to
the idols of the house of Israel, or defile his neighbor's wife, or
approach a woman during her menstrual period—

## New International

13Then he took a member of the royal family and made a treaty
with him, putting him under oath. He also carried away the leading men of the land, 14so that the kingdom would be brought low,
unable to rise again, surviving only by keeping his treaty. 15But the
king rebelled against him by sending his envoys to Egypt to get
horses and a large army. Will he succeed? Will he who does such
things escape? Will he break the treaty and yet escape?
16" 'As surely as I live, declares the Sovereign LORD, he shall die
in Babylon, in the land of the king who put him on the throne,
whose oath he despised and whose treaty he broke. 17Pharaoh
with his mighty army and great horde will be of no help to him
in war, when ramps are built and siege works erected to destroy
many lives. 18He despised the oath by breaking the covenant.
Because he had given his hand in pledge and yet did all these
things, he shall not escape.
19" 'Therefore this is what the Sovereign LORD says: As surely
as I live, I will bring down on his head my oath that he despised
and my covenant that he broke. 20I will spread my net for him, and
he will be caught in my snare. I will bring him to Babylon and
execute judgment upon him there because he was unfaithful to
me. 21All his fleeing troops will fall by the sword, and the survivors
will be scattered to the winds. Then you will know that I the LORD
have spoken.
22" 'This is what the Sovereign LORD says: I myself will take a
shoot from the very top of a cedar and plant it; I will break off a
tender sprig from its topmost shoots and plant it on a high and
lofty mountain. 23On the mountain heights of Israel I will plant it;
it will produce branches and bear fruit and become a splendid
cedar. Birds of every kind will nest in it; they will find shelter in
the shade of its branches. 24All the trees of the field will know that
I the LORD bring down the tall tree and make the low tree grow
tall. I dry up the green tree and make the dry tree flourish.
" 'I the LORD have spoken, and I will do it.' "

### *The Soul Who Sins Will Die*

**18** THE WORD of the LORD came to me: 2"What do you
people mean by quoting this proverb about the land of
Israel:

" 'The fathers eat sour grapes,
and the children's teeth are set on edge'?

3"As surely as I live, declares the Sovereign LORD, you will no
longer quote this proverb in Israel. 4For every living soul belongs
to me, the father as well as the son—both alike belong to me. The
soul who sins is the one who will die.

5"Suppose there is a righteous man
who does what is just and right.
6He does not eat at the mountain shrines
or look to the idols of the house of Israel.
He does not defile his neighbor's wife
or lie with a woman during her period.

## King James

7And hath not oppressed any, *but* hath restored to the debtor his pledge, hath spoiled none by violence, hath given his bread to the hungry, and hath covered the naked with a garment;

8He *that* hath not given forth upon usury, neither hath taken any increase, *that* hath withdrawn his hand from iniquity, hath executed true judgment between man and man,

9Hath walked in my statutes, and hath kept my judgments, to deal truly; he *is* just, he shall surely live, saith the Lord GOD.

10¶ If he beget a son *that is* a robber, a shedder of blood, and *that* doeth the like to *any* one of these *things,*

11And that doeth not any of those *duties,* but even hath eaten upon the mountains, and defiled his neighbour's wife,

12Hath oppressed the poor and needy, hath spoiled by violence, hath not restored the pledge, and hath lifted up his eyes to the idols, hath committed abomination,

13Hath given forth upon usury, and hath taken increase: shall he then live? he shall not live: he hath done all these abominations; he shall surely die; his blood shall be upon him.

14¶ Now, lo, *if* he beget a son, that seeth all his father's sins which he hath done, and considereth, and doeth not such like,

15 *That* hath not eaten upon the mountains, neither hath lifted up his eyes to the idols of the house of Israel, hath not defiled his neighbour's wife,

16Neither hath oppressed any, hath not withholden the pledge, neither hath spoiled by violence, *but* hath given his bread to the hungry, and hath covered the naked with a garment,

17 *That* hath taken off his hand from the poor, *that* hath not received usury nor increase, hath executed my judgments, hath walked in my statutes; he shall not die for the iniquity of his father, he shall surely live.

18 *As for* his father, because he cruelly oppressed, spoiled his brother by violence, and did *that* which *is* not good among his people, lo, even he shall die in his iniquity.

19¶ Yet say ye, Why? doth not the son bear the iniquity of the father? When the son hath done that which is lawful and right, *and* hath kept all my statutes, and hath done them, he shall surely live.

20The soul that sinneth, it shall die. The son shall not bear the iniquity of the father, neither shall the father bear the iniquity of the son: the righteousness of the righteous shall be upon him, and the wickedness of the wicked shall be upon him.

21But if the wicked will turn from all his sins that he hath committed, and keep all my statutes, and do that which is lawful and right, he shall surely live, he shall not die.

22All his transgressions that he hath committed, they shall not be mentioned unto him: in his righteousness that he hath done he shall live.

23Have I any pleasure at all that the wicked should die? saith the Lord GOD: *and* not that he should return from his ways, and live?

24¶ But when the righteous turneth away from his righteousness, and committeth iniquity, *and* doeth according to all the abominations that the wicked *man* doeth, shall he live? All his righteousness that he hath done shall not be mentioned: in his trespass that he hath trespassed, and in his sin that he hath sinned, in them shall he die.

25¶ Yet ye say, The way of the Lord is not equal. Hear now, O house of Israel; Is not my way equal? are not your ways unequal?

## Amplified

7And has not wronged any one, but has restored to the debtor his pledge, has taken nothing by robbery, but has given his bread to the hungry and has covered the naked with a garment,

8Who does not charge interest or percentage of increase on what he lends [in compassion], who withholds his hand from iniquity, who executes true justice between man and man,

9Who has walked in My statutes, and kept My ordinances, to deal justly; *then* he is [truly] righteous; he shall surely live, says the Lord God. [Ezek. 20:11; Amos 5:4.]

10If he begets a son who is a robber, a shedder of blood, who does to a brother either of these sins of violence,

11And leaves undone all of the duties [of a righteous man], but has even eaten [the food set before idols] on the mountains, and defiled his neighbor's wife,

12Has wronged the poor and needy, has taken by robbery, has not restored [to the debtor] his pledge, has lifted up his eyes to the idols, has committed abomination (hateful and exceedingly vile in the eyes of God),

13And has charged interest or percentage of increase on what he has loaned [in supposed compassion]; shall he then live? He shall not live! He has done all these abominations; he shall surely die; his blood shall be upon him.

14But if this wicked man begets a son who sees all the sins which his father has committed, and considers *and* fears [God], and does not do like his father;

15Who has not eaten [food set before idols] upon the mountains, nor has lifted up his eyes to the idols of the house of Israel, has not defiled his neighbor's wife,

16Nor wronged any one, nor has taken anything in pledge, nor has taken by robbery, but has given his bread to the hungry, and has covered the naked with a garment,

17Who has withdrawn his hand from [oppressing] the poor, who has not received interest or increase [from the needy], but has executed My ordinances, and has walked in My statutes; he shall not die for the iniquity of his father; he shall surely live.

18As for his father, because he cruelly oppressed, robbed his brother, and did that which is not good among his people, behold, he shall die for his iniquity *and* guilt.

19Yet do you say, Why does not the son bear the iniquity of the father? When the son has done that which is lawful and right, and has kept all My statutes, and has done them, he shall surely live.

20The soul that sins, it [is the one that] shall die. The son shall not bear *and* be punished for the iniquity of the father, neither shall the father bear *and* be punished for the iniquity of the son; the righteousness of the righteous shall be upon him only, and the wickedness of the wicked shall be upon the wicked only.

21But if the wicked man turns from all his sins that he has committed and keeps all my statutes, and does that which is lawful and right, he shall surely live; he shall not die.

22None of his transgressions which he has committed shall be remembered against him; for his righteousness which he has executed [for his religious and moral rectitude in every area and relation] he shall live.

23Have I any pleasure in the death of the wicked? says the Lord, and not rather that he should turn from his evil way *and* return [to his God] and live?

24But if the righteous turns away from his righteousness, and commits iniquity and does according to all the abominations that the wicked man does, shall he live? None of his righteous deeds which he has done shall be remembered. In his trespass that he has trespassed, and in his sin that he has sinned, in them shall he die.

25Yet you say, The way of the Lord is not fair *and* just. Hear now, O house of Israel: Is not My way fair *and* just? Are not your ways unfair *and* unjust?

## New American Standard

7if a man does not oppress anyone, but restores to the debtor
his pledge, does not commit robbery, *but* gives his bread to the
hungry, and covers the naked with clothing,
8if he does not lend *money* on interest or take increase, *if* he
keeps his hand from iniquity, *and* executes true justice between
man and man,
9 *if* he walks in My statutes and My ordinances so as to deal
faithfully—he is righteous *and* will surely live," declares the Lord
GOD.
10¶ "Then he may have a violent son who sheds blood, and who
does any of these things to a brother
11(though he himself did not do any of these things), that is, he
even eats at the mountain *shrines,* and defiles his neighbor's wife,
12oppresses the poor and needy, commits robbery, does not
restore a pledge, but lifts up his eyes to the idols, *and* commits
abomination,
13he lends *money* on interest and takes increase; will he live? He
will not live! He has committed all these abominations, he will
surely be put to death; his blood will be on his own head.
14¶ "Now behold, he has a son who has observed all his father's
sins which he committed, and observing does not do likewise.
15"He does not eat at the mountain *shrines* or lift up his eyes to
the idols of the house of Israel, or defile his neighbor's wife,
16or oppress anyone, or retain a pledge, or commit robbery, *but*
he gives his bread to the hungry, and covers the naked with
clothing,
17he keeps his hand from the poor, does not take interest or
increase, *but* executes My ordinances, and walks in My statutes;
he will not die for his father's iniquity, he will surely live.
18"As for his father, because he practiced extortion, robbed *his*
brother, and did what was not good among his people, behold, he
will die for his iniquity.
19¶ "Yet you say, 'Why should the son not bear the punishment
for the father's iniquity?' When the son has practiced justice and
righteousness, and has observed all My statutes and done them,
he shall surely live.
20"The person who sins will die. The son will not bear the
punishment for the father's iniquity, nor will the father bear the
punishment for the son's iniquity; the righteousness of the righteous will be upon himself, and the wickedness of the wicked will
be upon himself.
21¶ "But if the wicked man turns from all his sins which he has
committed and observes all My statutes and practices justice and
righteousness, he shall surely live; he shall not die.
22"All his transgressions which he has committed will not be
remembered against him; because of his righteousness which he
has practiced, he will live.
23"Do I have any pleasure in the death of the wicked," declares
the Lord GOD, "rather than that he should turn from his ways and
live?
24¶ "But when a righteous man turns away from his righteousness, commits iniquity, and does according to all the abominations
that a wicked man does, will he live? All his righteous deeds which
he has done will not be remembered for his treachery which he has
committed and his sin which he has committed; for them he will
die.
25"Yet you say, 'The way of the Lord is not right.' Hear now,
O house of Israel! Is My way not right? Is it not your ways that are
not right?

## New International

7He does not oppress anyone,
but returns what he took in pledge for a loan.
He does not commit robbery
but gives his food to the hungry
and provides clothing for the naked.
8He does not lend at usury
or take excessive interest.[a]
He withholds his hand from doing wrong
and judges fairly between man and man.
9He follows my decrees
and faithfully keeps my laws.
That man is righteous;
he will surely live,
declares the Sovereign LORD.

10"Suppose he has a violent son, who sheds blood or does any
of these other things[b] 11(though the father has done none of
them):
"He eats at the mountain shrines.
He defiles his neighbor's wife.
12He oppresses the poor and needy.
He commits robbery.
He does not return what he took in pledge.
He looks to the idols.
He does detestable things.
13He lends at usury and takes excessive interest.

Will such a man live? He will not! Because he has done all these
detestable things, he will surely be put to death and his blood will
be on his own head.
14"But suppose this son has a son who sees all the sins his father
commits, and though he sees them, he does not do such things:
15"He does not eat at the mountain shrines
or look to the idols of the house of Israel.
He does not defile his neighbor's wife.
16He does not oppress anyone
or require a pledge for a loan.
He does not commit robbery
but gives his food to the hungry
and provides clothing for the naked.
17He withholds his hand from sin[c]
and takes no usury or excessive interest.
He keeps my laws and follows my decrees.

He will not die for his father's sin; he will surely live. 18But his
father will die for his own sin, because he practiced extortion,
robbed his brother and did what was wrong among his people.
19"Yet you ask, 'Why does the son not share the guilt of his
father?' Since the son has done what is just and right and has been
careful to keep all my decrees, he will surely live. 20The soul who
sins is the one who will die. The son will not share the guilt of the
father, nor will the father share the guilt of the son. The righteousness of the righteous man will be credited to him, and the wickedness of the wicked will be charged against him.
21"But if a wicked man turns away from all the sins he has
committed and keeps all my decrees and does what is just and
right, he will surely live; he will not die. 22None of the offenses he
has committed will be remembered against him. Because of the
righteous things he has done, he will live. 23Do I take any pleasure
in the death of the wicked? declares the Sovereign LORD. Rather,
am I not pleased when they turn from their ways and live?
24"But if a righteous man turns from his righteousness and
commits sin and does the same detestable things the wicked man
does, will he live? None of the righteous things he has done will
be remembered. Because of the unfaithfulness he is guilty of and
because of the sins he has committed, he will die.
25"Yet you say, 'The way of the Lord is not just.' Hear, O house
of Israel: Is my way unjust? Is it not your ways that are unjust? 26If

NIV [a] 8 Or *take interest;* similarly in verses 13 and 17 [b] 10 Or *things to a brother* [c] 17 Septuagint (see also verse 8); Hebrew *from the poor*

## King James

26When a righteous *man* turneth away from his righteousness, and committeth iniquity, and dieth in them; for his iniquity that he hath done shall he die.

27Again, when the wicked *man* turneth away from his wickedness that he hath committed, and doeth that which is lawful and right, he shall save his soul alive.

28Because he considereth, and turneth away from all his transgressions that he hath committed, he shall surely live, he shall not die.

29Yet saith the house of Israel, The way of the Lord is not equal. O house of Israel, are not my ways equal? are not your ways unequal?

30Therefore I will judge you, O house of Israel, every one according to his ways, saith the Lord GOD. Repent, and turn *yourselves* from all your transgressions; so iniquity shall not be your ruin.

31¶ Cast away from you all your transgressions, whereby ye have transgressed; and make you a new heart and a new spirit: for why will ye die, O house of Israel?

32For I have no pleasure in the death of him that dieth, saith the Lord GOD: wherefore turn *yourselves*, and live ye.

**19** MOREOVER TAKE thou up a lamentation for the princes of Israel,

2And say, What *is* thy mother? A lioness: she lay down among lions, she nourished her whelps among young lions.

3And she brought up one of her whelps: it became a young lion, and it learned to catch the prey; it devoured men.

4The nations also heard of him; he was taken in their pit, and they brought him with chains unto the land of Egypt.

5Now when she saw that she had waited, *and* her hope was lost, then she took another of her whelps, *and* made him a young lion.

6And he went up and down among the lions, he became a young lion, and learned to catch the prey, *and* devoured men.

7And he knew their desolate palaces, and he laid waste their cities; and the land was desolate, and the fulness thereof, by the noise of his roaring.

8Then the nations set against him on every side from the provinces, and spread their net over him: he was taken in their pit.

9And they put him in ward in chains, and brought him to the king of Babylon: they brought him into holds, that his voice should no more be heard upon the mountains of Israel.

10¶ Thy mother *is* like a vine in thy blood, planted by the waters: she was fruitful and full of branches by reason of many waters.

## Amplified

26When a righteous man turns away from his righteousness and committeth iniquity and dies in his sins, for his iniquity that he has done he shall die.

27Again, when the wicked man turns away from his wickedness which he has committed and does that which is lawful and right, he shall save his life.

28Because he considers and turns away from all his transgressions which he has committed, he shall surely live; he shall not die.

29Yet says the house of Israel, The way of the Lord is not fair and just! O house of Israel, are not My ways fair and just? Are not your ways unfair and unjust?

30Therefore I will judge you, O house of Israel, every one according to his ways, says the Lord God. Repent, and turn from all your transgressions, lest iniquity be your ruin; *and* so shall they not be a stumblingblock to you. [Matt. 3:2; Rev. 2:5.]

31Cast away from you all your transgressions, by which you have transgressed against Me, and make you a new mind *and* heart and a new spirit. For why will you die, O house of Israel? [Eph. 4:22, 23.]

32For I have no pleasure in the death of him who dies, says the Lord God. Therefore turn—be converted—and live!

**19** MOREOVER TAKE up a lamentation for the princes of Israel,

2And say, What a lioness was your mother [Jerusalem-Judah]! She couched among lions; in the midst of young lions she nourished her cubs.

3And she [the royal mother-city] brought up one of her cubs [Jehoahaz]; he became a young lion, and he learned to catch the prey; he devoured men. [II Kings 23:30, 32.]

4The nations also heard of him; he was taken in their pit, and they brought him with hooks to the land of Egypt. [II Chron. 36:1, 4.]

5Now when she had waited, she saw her hope was lost. Then she took another of her cubs [Jehoiachin] and made him a young lion. [II Kings 23:34; 24:1, 6.]

6And he [Jehoiachin] went up and down among the lions, he became a young lion, and learned to catch prey, and he devoured men.

7And he knew *and* ravaged their strongholds, and he laid waste their cities; and the land was appalled and all who were in it by the noise of his roaring.

8Then the nations set against [the king] on every side from the provinces, and they spread their net over him [Jehoiachin]; he was taken in their pit. [II Kings 24:8-15.]

9With hooks they put him in a cage, and brought him to the king of Babylon; they brought him into custody *and* put him in strongholds, that his voice should no more be heard upon the mountains of Israel.

10Your mother [the mother-city Jerusalem] was like a vine—like you [Zedekiah], and in your blood—planted by the waters; it was fruitful and full of branches by reason of abundant water. [II Kings 24:17; cf. Ezek. 17:7.]

## New American Standard

26"When a righteous man turns away from his righteousness, commits iniquity, and dies because of it, for his iniquity which he has committed he will die.

27"Again, when a wicked man turns away from his wickedness which he has committed and practices justice and righteousness, he will save his life.

28"Because he considered and turned away from all his transgressions which he had committed, he shall surely live; he shall not die.

29"But the house of Israel says, 'The way of the Lord is not right.' Are My ways not right, O house of Israel? Is it not your ways that are not right?

30¶ "Therefore I will judge you, O house of Israel, each according to his conduct," declares the Lord GOD. "Repent and turn away from all your transgressions, so that iniquity may not become a stumbling block to you.

31"Cast away from you all your transgressions which you have committed, and make yourselves a new heart and a new spirit! For why will you die, O house of Israel?

32"For I have no pleasure in the death of anyone who dies," declares the Lord GOD. "Therefore, repent and live."

*Lament for the Princes of Israel*

**19** "AS FOR you, take up a lamentation for the princes of Israel,
2and say,
'What was your mother?
A lioness among lions!
She lay down among young lions,
She reared her cubs.
3 'When she brought up one of her cubs,
He became a lion,
And he learned to tear *his* prey;
He devoured men.
4 'Then nations heard about him;
He was captured in their pit,
And they brought him with hooks
To the land of Egypt.
5 'When she saw, as she waited,
*That* her hope was lost,
She took another of her cubs
And made him a young lion.
6 'And he walked about among the lions;
He became a young lion,
He learned to tear *his* prey;
He devoured men.
7 'And he destroyed their fortified towers
And laid waste their cities;
And the land and its fulness were appalled
Because of the sound of his roaring.
8 'Then nations set against him
On every side from *their* provinces,
And they spread their net over him;
He was captured in their pit.
9 'And they put him in a cage with hooks
And brought him to the king of Babylon;
They brought him in hunting nets
So that his voice should be heard no more
On the mountains of Israel.
10 'Your mother was like a vine in your vineyard,
Planted by the waters;
It was fruitful and full of branches
Because of abundant waters.

## New International

a righteous man turns from his righteousness and commits sin, he will die for it; because of the sin he has committed he will die. 27But if a wicked man turns away from the wickedness he has committed and does what is just and right, he will save his life. 28Because he considers all the offenses he has committed and turns away from them, he will surely live; he will not die. 29Yet the house of Israel says, 'The way of the Lord is not just.' Are my ways unjust, O house of Israel? Is it not your ways that are unjust?

30"Therefore, O house of Israel, I will judge you, each one according to his ways, declares the Sovereign LORD. Repent! Turn away from all your offenses; then sin will not be your downfall. 31Rid yourselves of all the offenses you have committed, and get a new heart and a new spirit. Why will you die, O house of Israel? 32For I take no pleasure in the death of anyone, declares the Sovereign LORD. Repent and live!

*A Lament for Israel's Princes*

**19** "TAKE UP a lament concerning the princes of Israel 2and say:
" 'What a lioness was your mother
among the lions!
She lay down among the young lions
and reared her cubs.
3She brought up one of her cubs,
and he became a strong lion.
He learned to tear the prey
and he devoured men.
4The nations heard about him,
and he was trapped in their pit.
They led him with hooks
to the land of Egypt.

5" 'When she saw her hope unfulfilled,
her expectation gone,
she took another of her cubs
and made him a strong lion.
6He prowled among the lions,
for he was now a strong lion.
He learned to tear the prey
and he devoured men.
7He broke down[a] their strongholds
and devastated their towns.
The land and all who were in it
were terrified by his roaring.
8Then the nations came against him,
those from regions round about.
They spread their net for him,
and he was trapped in their pit.
9With hooks they pulled him into a cage
and brought him to the king of Babylon.
They put him in prison,
so his roar was heard no longer
on the mountains of Israel.

10" 'Your mother was like a vine in your vineyard[b]
planted by the water;
it was fruitful and full of branches
because of abundant water.

**NIV** [a] 7 Targum (see Septuagint); Hebrew *He knew* [b] *10* Two Hebrew manuscripts; most Hebrew manuscripts *your blood*

## King James

11 And she had strong rods for the sceptres of them that bare rule, and her stature was exalted among the thick branches, and she appeared in her height with the multitude of her branches.

12 But she was plucked up in fury, she was cast down to the ground, and the east wind dried up her fruit: her strong rods were broken and withered; the fire consumed them.

13 And now she *is* planted in the wilderness, in a dry and thirsty ground.

14 And fire is gone out of a rod of her branches, *which* hath devoured her fruit, so that she hath no strong rod *to be* a sceptre to rule. This *is* a lamentation, and shall be for a lamentation.

## Amplified

11 And it had strong rods for the scepters of those who bore rule, and its height was exalted among the thick branches *and* into the clouds, and it was seen in its height among the multitude of its branches *and* was conspicuous.

12 But the vine was plucked up in God's wrath [by His agent the Babylonian king], and it was cast down to the ground; the east wind dried up its fruit, its strong rods were broken off and withered; the fire [of God's judgment] consumed them.

13 And now it is transplanted in the wilderness, in a dry and thirsty land [Babylon].

14 And fire went out of a rod [Zedekiah] of its branches, which has consumed the vine's fruit, so that it has in it no *longer* a strong rod to be a scepter for ruling. This is a lamentation, and shall be for a lamentation *and* a dirge.

## King James

**20** AND IT came to pass in the seventh year, in the fifth *month*, the tenth *day* of the month, *that* certain of the elders of Israel came to inquire of the LORD, and sat before me.

2 Then came the word of the LORD unto me, saying,

3 Son of man, speak unto the elders of Israel, and say unto them, Thus saith the Lord GOD; Are ye come to inquire of me? *As* I live, saith the Lord GOD, I will not be inquired of by you.

4 Wilt thou judge them, son of man, wilt thou judge *them?* cause them to know the abominations of their fathers:

5 ¶ And say unto them, Thus saith the Lord GOD; In the day when I chose Israel, and lifted up mine hand unto the seed of the house of Jacob, and made myself known unto them in the land of Egypt, when I lifted up mine hand unto them, saying, I *am* the LORD your God;

6 In the day *that* I lifted up mine hand unto them, to bring them forth of the land of Egypt into a land that I had espied for them, flowing with milk and honey, which *is* the glory of all lands:

7 Then said I unto them, Cast ye away every man the abominations of his eyes, and defile not yourselves with the idols of Egypt: I *am* the LORD your God.

8 But they rebelled against me, and would not hearken unto me: they did not every man cast away the abominations of their eyes, neither did they forsake the idols of Egypt: then I said, I will pour out my fury upon them, to accomplish my anger against them in the midst of the land of Egypt.

9 But I wrought for my name's sake, that it should not be polluted before the heathen, among whom they *were,* in whose sight I made myself known unto them, in bringing them forth out of the land of Egypt.

10 ¶ Wherefore I caused them to go forth out of the land of Egypt, and brought them into the wilderness.

11 And I gave them my statutes, and showed them my judgments, which *if* a man do, he shall even live in them.

12 Moreover also I gave them my sabbaths, to be a sign between me and them, that they might know that I *am* the LORD that sanctify them.

13 But the house of Israel rebelled against me in the wilderness: they walked not in my statutes, and they despised my judgments, which *if* a man do, he shall even live in them; and my sabbaths they greatly polluted: then I said, I would pour out my fury upon them in the wilderness, to consume them.

## Amplified

**20** IN THE seventh year, in the fifth *month,* on the tenth *day* of the month [after the beginning of the Babylonian captivity which was to last seventy years], certain of the elders of Israel came to inquire of the Lord, and sat down before me [Ezekiel, in Babylonia]. [Jer. 25:11; 29:10.]

2 Then came the word of the Lord to me, saying,

3 Son of man, speak to the elders of Israel, and say to them, Thus says the Lord God: Have you come to inquire of Me? As I live, says the Lord God, I will not be inquired of by you!

4 Will you judge them, [Ezekiel] son of man, will you judge them? Then cause them to know, understand *and* realize the abominations of their fathers. [Matt. 23:29-33; Acts 7:51, 52.]

5 And say to them, Thus says the Lord God: In the day when I chose Israel, and lifted up My hand *and* swore to the offspring of the house of Jacob, and made Myself known to them in the land of Egypt, when I lifted up My hand *and* swore to them, saying, I am the Lord your God,

6 On that day I lifted up My hand *and* swore to them to bring them out of the land of Egypt to a land that I had searched out for them, flowing with milk and honey, *a land* which is an ornament *and* a glory to all lands.

7 Then said I to them, Let every man cast away the abominable things on which he *feasts* his eyes, and defile not yourselves with the idols of Egypt; I am the Lord your God.

8 But they rebelled against Me and would not listen to Me; they did not every man cast away the abominable things on which they *feasted* their eyes, nor did they forsake the idols of Egypt. Then I [thought], I will pour out My wrath upon them and finish My anger against them in the midst of the land of Egypt.

9 But I acted for My name's sake, that it should not be profaned in the sight of the [heathen] nations among whom they dwelt, in whose sight I made Myself known to them, in bringing them out of the land of Egypt.

10 So I caused them to go out from the land of Egypt, and brought them into the wilderness.

11 And I gave them My statutes, and showed *and* made known to them My judgments, which if a man keep, he must live in *and* by them.

12 Moreover also I gave them My sabbaths, to be a sign between Me and them, that they might understand *and* realize that I am the Lord Who sanctifies them—separates and sets them apart.

13 But the house of Israel rebelled against Me in the wilderness: they walked not in My statutes, and they despised *and* cast away My judgments, which if a man keep, he must even live in *and* by them; and they grievously profaned My sabbaths. Then I thought I would pour out My wrath on them in the wilderness and uproot *and* consume them.

## New American Standard

11 'And it had strong branches *fit* for scepters of rulers,
And its height was raised above the clouds
So that it was seen in its height with the mass of its
branches.
12 'But it was plucked up in fury;
It was cast down to the ground;
And the east wind dried up its fruit.
Its strong branch was torn off
So that it withered;
The fire consumed it.
13 'And now it is planted in the wilderness,
In a dry and thirsty land.
14 'And fire has gone out from *its* branch;
It has consumed its shoots *and* fruit,
So that there is not in it a strong branch,
A scepter to rule.' "
This is a lamentation, and has become a lamentation.

*God's Dealings with Israel Rehearsed*

**20** NOW IT came about in the seventh year, in the fifth
*month,* on the tenth of the month, that certain of the elders
of Israel came to inquire of the LORD, and sat before me.
2And the word of the LORD came to me saying,
3"Son of man, speak to the elders of Israel, and say to them,
'Thus says the Lord GOD, "Do you come to inquire of Me? As I
live," declares the Lord GOD, "I will not be inquired of by you." '
4"Will you judge them, will you judge them, son of man? Make
them know the abominations of their fathers;
5and say to them, 'Thus says the Lord GOD, "On the day when
I chose Israel and swore to the descendants of the house of Jacob
and made Myself known to them in the land of Egypt, when I
swore to them, saying, I am the LORD your God,
6on that day I swore to them, to bring them out from the land
of Egypt into a land that I had selected for them, flowing with milk
and honey, which is the glory of all lands.
7"And I said to them, 'Cast away, each of you, the detestable
things of his eyes, and do not defile yourselves with the idols of
Egypt; I am the LORD your God.'
8"But they rebelled against Me and were not willing to listen
to Me; they did not cast away the detestable things of their eyes,
nor did they forsake the idols of Egypt.
¶ Then I resolved to pour out My wrath on them, to accomplish
My anger against them in the midst of the land of Egypt.
9"But I acted for the sake of My name, that it should not be
profaned in the sight of the nations among whom they *lived,* in
whose sight I made Myself known to them by bringing them out
of the land of Egypt.
10"So I took them out of the land of Egypt and brought them
into the wilderness.
11"And I gave them My statutes and informed them of My
ordinances, by which, if a man observes them, he will live.
12"And also I gave them My sabbaths to be a sign between Me
and them, that they might know that I am the LORD who sanctifies
them.
13"But the house of Israel rebelled against Me in the wilderness.
They did not walk in My statutes, and they rejected My ordinances, by which, if a man observes them, he will live; and My
sabbaths they greatly profaned. Then I resolved to pour out My
wrath on them in the wilderness, to annihilate them.

## New International

11Its branches were strong,
fit for a ruler's scepter.
It towered high
above the thick foliage,
conspicuous for its height
and for its many branches.
12But it was uprooted in fury
and thrown to the ground.
The east wind made it shrivel,
it was stripped of its fruit;
its strong branches withered
and fire consumed them.
13Now it is planted in the desert,
in a dry and thirsty land.
14Fire spread from one of its main[a] branches
and consumed its fruit.
No strong branch is left on it
fit for a ruler's scepter.'
This is a lament and is to be used as a lament."

*Rebellious Israel*

**20** IN THE seventh year, in the fifth month on the tenth day,
some of the elders of Israel came to inquire of the LORD,
and they sat down in front of me.
2Then the word of the LORD came to me: 3"Son of man, speak
to the elders of Israel and say to them, 'This is what the Sovereign
LORD says: Have you come to inquire of me? As surely as I live,
I will not let you inquire of me, declares the Sovereign LORD.'
4"Will you judge them? Will you judge them, son of man? Then
confront them with the detestable practices of their fathers 5and
say to them: 'This is what the Sovereign LORD says: On the day I
chose Israel, I swore with uplifted hand to the descendants of the
house of Jacob and revealed myself to them in Egypt. With uplifted
hand I said to them, "I am the LORD your God." 6On that day I
swore to them that I would bring them out of Egypt into a land I
had searched out for them, a land flowing with milk and honey,
the most beautiful of all lands. 7And I said to them, "Each of you,
get rid of the vile images you have set your eyes on, and do not
defile yourselves with the idols of Egypt. I am the LORD your
God."
8" 'But they rebelled against me and would not listen to me;
they did not get rid of the vile images they had set their eyes on,
nor did they forsake the idols of Egypt. So I said I would pour out
my wrath on them and spend my anger against them in Egypt.
9But for the sake of my name I did what would keep it from being
profaned in the eyes of the nations they lived among and in whose
sight I had revealed myself to the Israelites by bringing them out
of Egypt. 10Therefore I led them out of Egypt and brought them
into the desert. 11I gave them my decrees and made known to them
my laws, for the man who obeys them will live by them. 12Also
I gave them my Sabbaths as a sign between us, so they would
know that I the LORD made them holy.
13" 'Yet the people of Israel rebelled against me in the desert.
They did not follow my decrees but rejected my laws—although
the man who obeys them will live by them—and they utterly
desecrated my Sabbaths. So I said I would pour out my wrath on
them and destroy them in the desert. 14But for the sake of my name

NIV [a] 14 Or *from under its*

## King James

14But I wrought for my name's sake, that it should not be polluted before the heathen, in whose sight I brought them out.

15Yet also I lifted up my hand unto them in the wilderness, that I would not bring them into the land which I had given *them,* flowing with milk and honey, which *is* the glory of all lands;

16Because they despised my judgments, and walked not in my statutes, but polluted my sabbaths: for their heart went after their idols.

17Nevertheless mine eye spared them from destroying them, neither did I make an end of them in the wilderness.

18But I said unto their children in the wilderness, Walk ye not in the statutes of your fathers, neither observe their judgments, nor defile yourselves with their idols:

19I *am* the LORD your God; walk in my statutes, and keep my judgments, and do them;

20And hallow my sabbaths; and they shall be a sign between me and you, that ye may know that I *am* the LORD your God.

21Notwithstanding the children rebelled against me: they walked not in my statutes, neither kept my judgments to do them, which *if* a man do, he shall even live in them; they polluted my sabbaths: then I said, I would pour out my fury upon them, to accomplish my anger against them in the wilderness.

22Nevertheless I withdrew mine hand, and wrought for my name's sake, that it should not be polluted in the sight of the heathen, in whose sight I brought them forth.

23I lifted up mine hand unto them also in the wilderness, that I would scatter them among the heathen, and disperse them through the countries;

24Because they had not executed my judgments, but had despised my statutes, and had polluted my sabbaths, and their eyes were after their fathers' idols.

25Wherefore I gave them also statutes *that were* not good, and judgments whereby they should not live;

26And I polluted them in their own gifts, in that they caused to pass through *the fire* all that openeth the womb, that I might make them desolate, to the end that they might know that I *am* the LORD.

27¶ Therefore, son of man, speak unto the house of Israel, and say unto them, Thus saith the Lord GOD; Yet in this your fathers have blasphemed me, in that they have committed a trespass against me.

28 *For* when I had brought them into the land, *for* the which I lifted up mine hand to give it to them, then they saw every high hill, and all the thick trees, and they offered there their sacrifices, and there they presented the provocation of their offering: there also they made their sweet savour, and poured out there their drink offerings.

29Then I said unto them, What *is* the high place whereunto ye go? And the name thereof is called Bamah unto this day.

30Wherefore say unto the house of Israel, Thus saith the Lord GOD; Are ye polluted after the manner of your fathers? and commit ye whoredom after their abominations?

31For when ye offer your gifts, when ye make your sons to pass through the fire, ye pollute yourselves with all your idols, even unto this day: and shall I be inquired of by you, O house of Israel? *As* I live, saith the Lord GOD, I will not be inquired of by you.

32And that which cometh into your mind shall not be at all, that ye say, We will be as the heathen, as the families of the countries, to serve wood and stone.

33¶ *As* I live, saith the Lord GOD, surely with a mighty hand, and with a stretched out arm, and with fury poured out, will I rule over you:

## Amplified

14But I acted for My name's sake, that it should not be profaned before the [heathen] nations in whose sight I brought them out.

15Yet also I lifted up My hand to swear to them in the wilderness, that I would not bring them into the land which I had given them, flowing with milk and honey, which is the ornament *and* glory of all lands;

16Because they despised *and* rejected My ordinances, and walked not in My statutes, and profaned My sabbaths, for their heart went after their idols.

17Yet My eye pitied instead of destroying them, and I did not make a full end of them in the wilderness.

18But I said to their sons in the wilderness, You shall not walk in the statutes of your fathers, neither observe their ordinances, nor defile yourselves with their idols.

19I the Lord am your God; walk in My statutes, and keep My ordinances,

20And hallow—separate and keep holy—My sabbaths, and they shall be a sign between Me and you, that you may know, understand *and* realize that I am the Lord your God.

21Yet the sons rebelled against Me; they walked not in My statutes, neither kept My ordinances, which if a man does, he must live in *and* by them; they profaned My sabbaths. Then I thought I would pour out My wrath on them and finish My anger against them in the wilderness.

22Yet I withheld My hand and acted for My name's sake, that it should not be debased and profaned in the sight of the [heathen] nations, in whose sight I had brought them forth [from bondage].

23Moreover I lifted up My hand *and* swore to them in the wilderness, that I would scatter them among the [heathen] nations and disperse them in the countries;

24Because they had not executed My ordinances, but had despised *and* rejected My statutes, and had profaned My sabbaths, and their eyes were set on their fathers' idols.

25Wherefore also I gave them [over to] statutes that were not good, and ordinances whereby they should not live *and* could not have life; [Ps. 81:12; Isa. 66:4; Rom. 1:21-25, 28.]

26And I [let them] pollute *and* make themselves unclean in their own offerings [to their idols], in that they caused to pass through the fire all the first-born, that I might make them desolate, to the end that they might know, understand *and* realize that I am the Lord. [Lev. 20:2-5.]

27Therefore, son of man, speak to the house of Israel, and say to them, Thus says the Lord God: Again in this your fathers blasphemed Me, in that they dealt faithlessly *and* treacherously with Me and committed a treasonous trespass against Me.

28For when I had brought them into the land, which I lifted up My hand *and* swore to give to them, then they saw every high hill and every dark *and* leafy tree [as a place for idol worship], and they offered there their sacrifices, and there they presented their offering that provoked My anger *and* sadness; there also they made their sweet-smelling savor, and poured out there their drink offerings.

29Then I said to them, What is the high place to which you go? And the name of it is called Bamah *or* High Place to this day.

30Therefore say to the house of Israel, Thus says the Lord God: Do you *exiles* debase *and* defile yourselves after the manner of your fathers? And do you play the harlot after their loathsome *and* detestable things?

31And when you offer your gifts, when you make your sons pass through the fire, do you not debase *and* defile yourselves with all your idols to this day? And shall I be inquired of by you, O house of Israel? As I live, says the Lord God, I will not be inquired of by you!

32And that which has come up in your mind shall never happen, in that you think, We will be as the nations, as the tribes of the countries, to serve idols of wood and stone.

33As I live, says the Lord God, surely with a mighty hand and a stretched out arm, and with wrath poured out, will I be King over you.

## New American Standard

14"But I acted for the sake of My name, that it should not be
profaned in the sight of the nations, before whose sight I had
brought them out.
15"And also I swore to them in the wilderness that I would not
bring them into the land which I had given them, flowing with
milk and honey, which is the glory of all lands,
16because they rejected My ordinances, and as for My statutes,
they did not walk in them; they even profaned My sabbaths, for
their heart continually went after their idols.
17"Yet My eye spared them rather than destroying them, and
I did not cause their annihilation in the wilderness.
18¶ "And I said to their children in the wilderness, 'Do not walk
in the statutes of your fathers, or keep their ordinances, or defile
yourselves with their idols.
19'I am the LORD your God; walk in My statutes, and keep My
ordinances, and observe them.
20'And sanctify My sabbaths; and they shall be a sign between
Me and you, that you may know that I am the LORD your God.'
21"But the children rebelled against Me; they did not walk in My
statutes, nor were they careful to observe My ordinances, by
which, *if* a man observes them, he will live; they profaned My
sabbaths. So I resolved to pour out My wrath on them, to accomplish My anger against them in the wilderness.
22"But I withdrew My hand and acted for the sake of My name,
that it should not be profaned in the sight of the nations in whose
sight I had brought them out.
23"Also I swore to them in the wilderness that I would scatter
them among the nations and disperse them among the lands,
24because they had not observed My ordinances, but had rejected My statutes, and had profaned My sabbaths, and their eyes
were on the idols of their fathers.
25"And I also gave them statutes that were not good and ordinances by which they could not live;
26and I pronounced them unclean because of their gifts, in that
they caused all their first-born to pass through *the fire* so that I
might make them desolate, in order that they might know that I
am the LORD."'
27¶ "Therefore, son of man, speak to the house of Israel, and
say to them, 'Thus says the Lord GOD, "Yet in this your fathers
have blasphemed Me by acting treacherously against Me.
28"When I had brought them into the land which I swore to give
to them, then they saw every high hill and every leafy tree, and
they offered there their sacrifices, and there they presented the
provocation of their offering. There also they made their soothing
aroma, and there they poured out their libations.
29"Then I said to them, 'What is the high place to which you
go?' So its name is called [a]Bamah to this day."'
30"Therefore, say to the house of Israel, 'Thus says the Lord
GOD, "Will you defile yourselves after the manner of your fathers
and play the harlot after their detestable things?
31"And when you offer your gifts, when you cause your sons
to pass through the fire, you are defiling yourselves with all your
idols to this day. And shall I be inquired of by you, O house of
Israel? As I live," declares the Lord GOD, "I will not be inquired
of by you.
32"And what comes into your mind will not come about, when
you say: 'We will be like the nations, like the tribes of the lands,
serving wood and stone.'

*God Will Restore Israel to Her Land*

33"As I live," declares the Lord GOD, "surely with a mighty
hand and with an outstretched arm and with wrath poured out,
I shall be king over you.

NAS [a] Or, *High Place*

## New International

I did what would keep it from being profaned in the eyes of the
nations in whose sight I had brought them out. 15Also with uplifted hand I swore to them in the desert that I would not bring them
into the land I had given them—a land flowing with milk and
honey, most beautiful of all lands— 16because they rejected my
laws and did not follow my decrees and desecrated my Sabbaths.
For their hearts were devoted to their idols. 17Yet I looked on them
with pity and did not destroy them or put an end to them in the
desert. 18I said to their children in the desert, "Do not follow the
statutes of your fathers or keep their laws or defile yourselves with
their idols. 19I am the LORD your God; follow my decrees and be
careful to keep my laws. 20Keep my Sabbaths holy, that they may
be a sign between us. Then you will know that I am the LORD your
God."
21" 'But the children rebelled against me: They did not follow
my decrees, they were not careful to keep my laws—although the
man who obeys them will live by them—and they desecrated my
Sabbaths. So I said I would pour out my wrath on them and spend
my anger against them in the desert. 22But I withheld my hand,
and for the sake of my name I did what would keep it from being
profaned in the eyes of the nations in whose sight I had brought
them out. 23Also with uplifted hand I swore to them in the desert
that I would disperse them among the nations and scatter them
through the countries, 24because they had not obeyed my laws but
had rejected my decrees and desecrated my Sabbaths, and their
eyes ⌊lusted⌋ after their fathers' idols. 25I also gave them over to
statutes that were not good and laws they could not live by; 26I let
them become defiled through their gifts—the sacrifice of every
firstborn[b] —that I might fill them with horror so they would know
that I am the LORD.'
27"Therefore, son of man, speak to the people of Israel and say
to them, 'This is what the Sovereign LORD says: In this also your
fathers blasphemed me by forsaking me: 28When I brought them
into the land I had sworn to give them and they saw any high hill
or any leafy tree, there they offered their sacrifices, made offerings
that provoked me to anger, presented their fragrant incense and
poured out their drink offerings. 29Then I said to them: What is this
high place you go to?' " (It is called Bamah[c] to this day.)

*Judgment and Restoration*

30"Therefore say to the house of Israel: 'This is what the Sovereign LORD says: Will you defile yourselves the way your fathers did
and lust after their vile images? 31When you offer your gifts—the
sacrifice of your sons in[d] the fire—you continue to defile yourselves with all your idols to this day. Am I to let you inquire of me,
O house of Israel? As surely as I live, declares the Sovereign LORD,
I will not let you inquire of me.
32" 'You say, "We want to be like the nations, like the peoples
of the world, who serve wood and stone." But what you have in
mind will never happen. 33As surely as I live, declares the Sovereign LORD, I will rule over you with a mighty hand and an outstretched arm and with outpoured wrath. 34I will bring you from

NIV [b] 26 Or *—making every firstborn pass through ⌊the fire⌋* [c] 29 *Bamah* means *high place.* [d] 31 Or *—making your sons pass through*

## King James

34 And I will bring you out from the people, and will gather you out of the countries wherein ye are scattered, with a mighty hand, and with a stretched out arm, and with fury poured out.

35 And I will bring you into the wilderness of the people, and there will I plead with you face to face.

36 Like as I pleaded with your fathers in the wilderness of the land of Egypt, so will I plead with you, saith the Lord GOD.

37 And I will cause you to pass under the rod, and I will bring you into the bond of the covenant:

38 And I will purge out from among you the rebels, and them that transgress against me: I will bring them forth out of the country where they sojourn, and they shall not enter into the land of Israel: and ye shall know that I *am* the LORD.

39 As for you, O house of Israel, thus saith the Lord GOD; Go ye, serve ye every one his idols, and hereafter *also*, if ye will not hearken unto me: but pollute ye my holy name no more with your gifts, and with your idols.

40 For in mine holy mountain, in the mountain of the height of Israel, saith the Lord GOD, there shall all the house of Israel, all of them in the land, serve me: there will I accept them, and there will I require your offerings, and the firstfruits of your oblations, with all your holy things.

41 I will accept you with your sweet savour, when I bring you out from the people, and gather you out of the countries wherein ye have been scattered; and I will be sanctified in you before the heathen.

42 And ye shall know that I *am* the LORD, when I shall bring you into the land of Israel, into the country *for* the which I lifted up mine hand to give it to your fathers.

43 And there shall ye remember your ways, and all your doings, wherein ye have been defiled; and ye shall loathe yourselves in your own sight for all your evils that ye have committed.

44 And ye shall know that I *am* the LORD, when I have wrought with you for my name's sake, not according to your wicked ways, nor according to your corrupt doings, O ye house of Israel, saith the Lord GOD.

45 ¶ Moreover the word of the LORD came unto me, saying,

46 Son of man, set thy face toward the south, and drop *thy word* toward the south, and prophesy against the forest of the south field;

47 And say to the forest of the south, Hear the word of the LORD; Thus saith the Lord GOD; Behold, I will kindle a fire in thee, and it shall devour every green tree in thee, and every dry tree: the flaming flame shall not be quenched, and all faces from the south to the north shall be burned therein.

48 And all flesh shall see that I the LORD have kindled it: it shall not be quenched.

49 Then said I, Ah Lord GOD! they say of me, Doth he not speak parables?

## Amplified

34 And I will bring you out from the peoples and will gather you out of the countries in which you are scattered, with a mighty hand and a stretched out arm, and with wrath poured out.

35 And I will bring you into the wilderness of the peoples, and there will I enter into judgment with you *and* contend with you face to face.

36 As I entered into judgment *and* contended with your fathers in the wilderness of the land of Egypt, so will I enter into judgment *and* contend with you, says the Lord God. [Num. 11; Ps. 106:15; I Cor. 10:5-10.]

37 And I will cause you to pass under the rod [as the shepherd does his sheep when he counts them, and I will count you as Mine, and I will constrain you] and bring you into the covenant to which you are permanently bound. [Lev. 27:32.]

38 And I will purge out *and* separate from among you the rebels and those who transgress against Me; I will bring them out of the country where they temporarily dwell, but they shall not enter the land of Israel. Then you shall know, understand, *and* realize that I am the Lord [Heb. 4:2, 3.]

39 As for you, O house of Israel, thus says the Lord God: Go, serve every one of you his idols, now and hereafter, if you will not listen to Me! But you shall not profane My holy name any more with your sacrificial gifts and your idols!

40 For on My holy mountain, on the mountain height of Israel, says the Lord God, there all the house of Israel, all of them in the land, shall serve Me. There will I [graciously] accept them, and there will I require your offerings, and the first fruits *and* the choicest of your contributions, with all your sacred things.

41 I will accept you [graciously] as a pleasant odor, when I lead you out from the peoples and gather you out of the countries in which you have been scattered; and I will manifest My holiness among you in the sight of the nations [who will seek Me because of My power displayed in you]. [Eph. 5:2; Phil. 4:18.]

42 And you shall know, understand *and* realize that I am the Lord, when I bring you into the land of Israel, into the country which I lifted up My hand *and* swore to give to your fathers.

43 And there you shall [earnestly] remember your ways, and all your doings, with which you have defiled yourselves, and you shall loathe yourselves in your own sight for all your evil deeds which you have done.

44 And you shall know, understand *and* realize that I am the Lord, when I deal with you for My name's sake, not according to your evil ways, nor according to your corrupt doings, O house of Israel, says the Lord God.

45 Moreover the word of the Lord came to me, saying,

46 Son of man, set your face toward the south, preach against the south, and prophesy against the forest land of the south—the Negeb.

47 And say to the forest of the Negeb, Hear the word of the Lord: Thus says the Lord God, Behold, I will kindle a fire in you, and it shall devour every green tree in you and every dry tree. The blazing flame shall not be quenched, and all faces from the south to the north shall be scorched by it.

48 All flesh shall see that I the Lord have kindled it; it shall not be quenched.

49 Then said I, Ah Lord God! They are saying of me, Does he not speak in parables *and* make allegories?

## King James

**21** AND THE word of the LORD came unto me, saying,

2 Son of man, set thy face toward Jerusalem, and drop *thy word* toward the holy places, and prophesy against the land of Israel,

3 And say to the land of Israel, Thus saith the LORD; Behold, I *am* against thee, and will draw forth my sword out of his sheath, and will cut off from thee the righteous and the wicked.

## Amplified

**21** AND THE word of the Lord came to me:

2 Son of man, set your face toward Jerusalem and direct your [prophetic] word against the holy places; prophesy against the land of Israel

3 And say to the land of Israel, Thus says the Lord: Behold, I am against you, and will draw forth My sword out of its sheath, and will cut off from you *both* the righteous and the wicked.

## New American Standard

34"And I shall bring you out from the peoples and gather you
from the lands where you are scattered, with a mighty hand and
with an outstretched arm and with wrath poured out;
35and I shall bring you into the wilderness of the peoples, and
there I shall enter into judgment with you face to face.
36"As I entered into judgment with your fathers in the wilderness of the land of Egypt, so I will enter into judgment with you,"
declares the Lord GOD.
37"And I shall make you pass under the rod, and I shall bring
you into the bond of the covenant;
38and I shall purge from you the rebels and those who transgress against Me; I shall bring them out of the land where they
sojourn, but they will not enter the land of Israel. Thus you will
know that I am the LORD.
39"As for you, O house of Israel," thus says the Lord GOD, "Go,
serve everyone his idols; but later, you will surely listen to Me, and
My holy name you will profane no longer with your gifts and with
your idols.
40"For on My holy mountain, on the high mountain of Israel,"
declares the Lord GOD, "there the whole house of Israel, all of
them, will serve Me in the land; there I shall accept them, and there
I shall seek your contributions and the choicest of your gifts, with
all your holy things.
41"As a soothing aroma I shall accept you, when I bring you out
from the peoples and gather you from the lands where you are
scattered; and I shall prove Myself holy among you in the sight of
the nations.
42"And you will know that I am the LORD, when I bring you into
the land of Israel, into the land which I swore to give to your
forefathers.
43"And there you will remember your ways and all your deeds,
with which you have defiled yourselves; and you will loathe yourselves in your own sight for all the evil things that you have done.
44"Then you will know that I am the LORD when I have dealt
with you for My name's sake, not according to your evil ways or
according to your corrupt deeds, O house of Israel," declares the
Lord GOD.' "
45Now the word of the LORD came to me saying,
46"Son of man, set your face toward Teman, and speak out
against the south, and prophesy against the forest land of the
Negev,
47and say to the forest of the Negev, 'Hear the word of the LORD:
thus says the Lord GOD, "Behold, I am about to kindle a fire in you,
and it shall consume every green tree in you, as well as every dry
tree; the blazing flame will not be quenched, and the whole surface
from south to north will be burned by it.
48"And all flesh will see that I, the LORD, have kindled it; it shall
not be quenched." ' "
49Then I said, "Ah Lord GOD! They are saying of me, 'Is he not
*just* speaking parables?' "

*Parable of the Sword of the LORD*

**21** AND THE word of the LORD came to me saying,
2"Son of man, set your face toward Jerusalem, and speak
against the sanctuaries, and prophesy against the land of Israel;
3and say to the land of Israel, 'Thus says the LORD, "Behold,
I am against you; and I shall draw My sword out of its sheath and
cut off from you the righteous and the wicked.

## New International

the nations and gather you from the countries where you have
been scattered—with a mighty hand and an outstretched arm and
with outpoured wrath. 35I will bring you into the desert of the
nations and there, face to face, I will execute judgment upon you.
36As I judged your fathers in the desert of the land of Egypt, so
I will judge you, declares the Sovereign LORD. 37I will take note of
you as you pass under my rod, and I will bring you into the bond
of the covenant. 38I will purge you of those who revolt and rebel
against me. Although I will bring them out of the land where they
are living, yet they will not enter the land of Israel. Then you will
know that I am the LORD.
39" 'As for you, O house of Israel, this is what the Sovereign
LORD says: Go and serve your idols, every one of you! But afterward you will surely listen to me and no longer profane my holy
name with your gifts and idols. 40For on my holy mountain, the
high mountain of Israel, declares the Sovereign LORD, there in the
land the entire house of Israel will serve me, and there I will accept
them. There I will require your offerings and your choice gifts,[a]
along with all your holy sacrifices. 41I will accept you as fragrant
incense when I bring you out from the nations and gather you from
the countries where you have been scattered, and I will show
myself holy among you in the sight of the nations. 42Then you will
know that I am the LORD, when I bring you into the land of Israel,
the land I had sworn with uplifted hand to give to your fathers.
43There you will remember your conduct and all the actions by
which you have defiled yourselves, and you will loathe yourselves
for all the evil you have done. 44You will know that I am the LORD,
when I deal with you for my name's sake and not according to your
evil ways and your corrupt practices, O house of Israel, declares
the Sovereign LORD.' "

*Prophecy Against the South*

45The word of the LORD came to me: 46"Son of man, set your
face toward the south; preach against the south and prophesy
against the forest of the southland. 47Say to the southern forest:
'Hear the word of the LORD. This is what the Sovereign LORD says:
I am about to set fire to you, and it will consume all your trees, both
green and dry. The blazing flame will not be quenched, and every
face from south to north will be scorched by it. 48Everyone will see
that I the LORD have kindled it; it will not be quenched.' "
49Then I said, "Ah, Sovereign LORD! They are saying of me,
'Isn't he just telling parables?' "

*Babylon, God's Sword of Judgment*

**21** THE WORD of the LORD came to me: 2"Son of man, set
your face against Jerusalem and preach against the sanctuary. Prophesy against the land of Israel 3and say to her: 'This is
what the LORD says: I am against you. I will draw my sword from
its scabbard and cut off from you both the righteous and the
wicked. 4Because I am going to cut off the righteous and the

NIV [a] 40 Or *and the gifts of your firstfruits*

## King James

4Seeing then that I will cut off from thee the righteous and the wicked, therefore shall my sword go forth out of his sheath against all flesh from the south to the north:

5That all flesh may know that I the LORD have drawn forth my sword out of his sheath: it shall not return any more.

6Sigh therefore, thou son of man, with the breaking of *thy* loins; and with bitterness sigh before their eyes.

7And it shall be, when they say unto thee, Wherefore sighest thou? that thou shalt answer, For the tidings; because it cometh: and every heart shall melt, and all hands shall be feeble, and every spirit shall faint, and all knees shall be weak *as* water: behold, it cometh, and shall be brought to pass, saith the Lord GOD.

8¶ Again the word of the LORD came unto me, saying,

9Son of man, prophesy, and say, Thus saith the LORD; Say, A sword, a sword is sharpened, and also furbished:

10It is sharpened to make a sore slaughter; it is furbished that it may glitter: should we then make mirth? it contemneth the rod of my son, *as* every tree.

11And he hath given it to be furbished, that it may be handled: this sword is sharpened, and it is furbished, to give it into the hand of the slayer.

12Cry and howl, son of man: for it shall be upon my people, it *shall be* upon all the princes of Israel: terrors by reason of the sword shall be upon my people: smite therefore upon *thy* thigh.

13Because *it is* a trial, and what if *the sword* contemn even the rod? it shall be no *more,* saith the Lord GOD.

14Thou therefore, son of man, prophesy, and smite *thine* hands together, and let the sword be doubled the third time, the sword of the slain: it *is* the sword of the great *men that are* slain, which entereth into their privy chambers.

15I have set the point of the sword against all their gates, that *their* heart may faint, and *their* ruins be multiplied: ah! *it is* made bright, *it is* wrapped up for the slaughter.

16Go thee one way or other, *either* on the right hand, *or* on the left, whithersoever thy face *is* set.

17I will also smite mine hands together, and I will cause my fury to rest: I the LORD have said *it.*

18¶ The word of the LORD came unto me again, saying,

19Also, thou son of man, appoint thee two ways, that the sword of the king of Babylon may come: both twain shall come forth out of one land: and choose thou a place, choose *it* at the head of the way to the city.

20Appoint a way, that the sword may come to Rabbath of the Ammonites, and to Judah in Jerusalem the defenced.

21For the king of Babylon stood at the parting of the way, at the head of the two ways, to use divination: he made *his* arrows bright, he consulted with images, he looked in the liver.

22At his right hand was the divination for Jerusalem, to appoint captains, to open the mouth in the slaughter, to lift up the voice with shouting, to appoint *battering* rams against the gates, to cast a mount, *and* to build a fort.

23And it shall be unto them as a false divination in their sight, to them that have sworn oaths: but he will call to remembrance the iniquity, that they may be taken.

## Amplified

4Because I will cut off from you *both* the righteous and the wicked, therefore shall my sword go out of its sheath against all flesh from the south to the north;

5And all living shall know, understand *and* realize that I the Lord have drawn My sword out of its sheath; it shall not be sheathed any more.

6Sigh therefore, son of man, with breaking heart and with bitterness shall you sigh before their eyes.

7And it shall be, when they say to you, Why do you sigh? that you shall answer, Because of the tidings. When it comes, every heart will melt and all hands will be feeble and every spirit will faint and all knees will be weak as water. Behold, it comes, and it shall be fulfilled, says the Lord God.

8Again the word of the Lord came to me:

9Son of man, prophesy and say, Thus says the Lord: Say, A sword, a sword is sharpened and also polished;

10It [the sword of Babylon] is sharpened that it may make a slaughter; polished that it may flash *and* glitter like lightning! Shall we then rejoice *and* make mirth [when such a calamity is impending]? *But* the rod *or* scepter of My son [Judah] rejects *and* views with contempt every tree [that is, since God's promise long ago to Judah is certain, he believes Judah's scepter must remain no matter what power arises against it]! [Gen. 49:9, 10; II Sam. 7:23.]

11And the sword [of Babylon] is given to be polished, that it may be put to use; the sword is sharpened and polished to be given into the hand of the slayer.

12Cry and wail, son of man, for it is against My people; it is against all the princes of Israel; they are thrown to the sword along with My people, *and* terrors by reason of the sword are upon My people. Therefore smite your thigh *in dismay.*

13For this sword has been tested *and* proved [on others], and what if the rejecting *and* despising rod *or* scepter of Judah shall be no more, but completely swept away? says the Lord God.

14Therefore, son of man, prophesy and smite your hands together, and let the sword be doubled, yes, trebled in intensity; the sword for those to be overthrown *and* pierced through; it is the sword of great slaughter which encompasses them [so that none can escape]— *even* entering into their *inner* chambers.

15I have set the threatening *and* glittering sword against all their gates, that their hearts may melt and their stumblings be multiplied. Ah! it is made *to flash* like lightning, it is pointed *and* sharpened for slaughter.

16Turn, [O sword,] and cut right or cut left, whichever way your lust for blood *and* your edge direct you.

17I will also clap My hands, and I will cause My wrath to rest. I the Lord have said it.

18The word of the Lord came to me again, saying,

19Also, son of man, mark out two ways by which the sword of the king of Babylon may come; both shall come forth from the same land. And make a signpost—a hand; make it at the head of the way to a city.

20You shall point out a way for the [Babylonian] sword to come to Rabbah [capital] of the sons of Ammon, and to Judah with Jerusalem, the fortified *and* inaccessible.

21For the king of Babylon stands at the parting of the way, at the fork of the two ways, to use divination. He shakes the arrows to and fro, he consults the teraphim, he looks at the liver.

22In his right hand is the lot marked for Jerusalem, to set battering rams, to open the mouth calling for slaughter, to lift up the voice with a war cry, to set battering rams against the gates, to cast up siege mounds and to build siege towers.

23And it shall seem like a lying divination to them who have sworn oaths [of allegiance to Nebuchadnezzar]. [Will he now fight against their homeland?] But he will remind them of their guilt *and* iniquity [in violating those oaths] that they may be caught. [II Chron. 36:10, 13; Ezek. 17:15, 18, etc.]

## New American Standard

4"Because I shall cut off from you the righteous and the wicked, therefore My sword shall go forth from its sheath against all flesh from south *to* north.

5"Thus all flesh will know that I, the LORD, have drawn My sword out of its sheath. It will not return *to its sheath* again." '

6"As for you, son of man, groan with breaking heart and bitter grief, groan in their sight.

7"And it will come about when they say to you, 'Why do you groan?' that you will say, 'Because of the news that is coming; and every heart will melt, all hands will be feeble, every spirit will faint, and all knees will be weak as water. Behold, it comes and it will happen,' declares the Lord GOD."

8Again the word of the LORD came to me saying,

9"Son of man, prophesy and say, 'Thus says the LORD.' Say,
'A sword, a sword sharpened
And also polished!
10 'Sharpened to make a slaughter,
Polished to flash like lightning!'
Or shall we rejoice, the rod of My son despising every tree?

11"And it is given to be polished, that it may be handled; the sword is sharpened and polished, to give it into the hand of the slayer.

12"Cry out and wail, son of man; for it is against My people, it is against all the officials of Israel. They are delivered over to the sword with My people, therefore strike *your* thigh.

13"For *there is* a testing; and what if even the rod which despises will be no more?" declares the Lord GOD.

14¶ "You therefore, son of man, prophesy, and clap *your* hands together; and let the sword be doubled the third time, the sword for the slain. It is the sword for the great one slain, which surrounds them,

15that *their* hearts may melt, and many fall at all their gates. I have given the glittering sword. Ah! It is made *for striking* like lightning, it is wrapped up *in readiness* for slaughter.

16"Show yourself sharp, go to the right; set yourself; go to the left, wherever your edge is appointed.

17"I shall also clap My hands together, and I shall appease My wrath; I, the LORD, have spoken."

*The Instrument of God's Judgment*

18¶ And the word of the LORD came to me saying,

19"As for you, son of man, make two ways for the sword of the king of Babylon to come; both of them will go out of one land. And make a signpost; make it at the head of the way to the city.

20"You shall mark a way for the sword to come to Rabbah of the sons of Ammon, and to Judah into fortified Jerusalem.

21"For the king of Babylon stands at the parting of the way, at the head of the two ways, to use divination; he shakes the arrows, he consults the household idols, he looks at the liver.

22"Into his right hand came the divination, 'Jerusalem,' to set battering rams, to open the mouth for slaughter, to lift up the voice with a battle cry, to set battering rams against the gates, to cast up mounds, to build a siege wall.

23"And it will be to them like a false divination in their eyes; they have *sworn* solemn oaths. But he brings iniquity to remembrance, that they may be seized.

## ew International

wicked, my swor
south to north. 5The
drawn my sword from unsheathed against everyone from
6"Therefore groan, son le will know that I the LORD have
heart and bitter grief. 7And ard; it will not return again.'
groaning?' you shall say, 'Beca roan before them with broken
Every heart will melt and every ey ask you, 'Why are you
become faint and every knee beco he news that is coming.
coming! It will surely take place, decla limp; every spirit will
8The word of the LORD came to me: 9"So eak as water.' It is
say, 'This is what the Lord says: overeign LORD."
prophesy and

" 'A sword, a sword,
sharpened and polished—
10sharpened for the slaughter,
polished to flash like lightning!

" 'Shall we rejoice in the scepter of my son ⌊Judah⌋? The sv
despises every such stick.

11" 'The sword is appointed to be polished,
to be grasped with the hand;
it is sharpened and polished,
made ready for the hand of the slayer.
12Cry out and wail, son of man,
for it is against my people;
it is against all the princes of Israel.
They are thrown to the sword
along with my people.
Therefore beat your breast.

13" 'Testing will surely come. And what if the scepter ⌊of Judah⌋, which the sword despises, does not continue? declares the Sovereign LORD.'

14"So then, son of man, prophesy
and strike your hands together.
Let the sword strike twice,
even three times.
It is a sword for slaughter—
a sword for great slaughter,
closing in on them from every side.
15So that hearts may melt
and the fallen be many,
I have stationed the sword for slaughter[a]
at all their gates.
Oh! It is made to flash like lightning,
it is grasped for slaughter.
16O sword, slash to the right,
then to the left,
wherever your blade is turned.
17I too will strike my hands together,
and my wrath will subside.
I the LORD have spoken."

18The word of the LORD came to me: 19"Son of man, mark out
two roads for the sword of the king of Babylon to take, both
starting from the same country. Make a signpost where the road
branches off to the city. 20Mark out one road for the sword to come
against Rabbah of the Ammonites and another against Judah and
fortified Jerusalem. 21For the king of Babylon will stop at the fork
in the road, at the junction of the two roads, to seek an omen: He
will cast lots with arrows, he will consult his idols, he will examine
the liver. 22Into his right hand will come the lot for Jerusalem,
where he is to set up battering rams, to give the command to
slaughter, to sound the battle cry, to set battering rams against the
gates, to build a ramp and to erect siege works. 23It will seem like
a false omen to those who have sworn allegiance to him, but he
will remind them of their guilt and take them captive.

**NIV** [a] *15* Septuagint; the meaning of the Hebrew for this word is uncertain.

## King James

ye have made
ransgressions are
24 Therefore thus saith the Lord GOD; do appear; because,
your iniquity to be remembered, in thshall be taken with the
discovered, so that in all your doings
*I say*, that ye are come to remembrance of Israel, whose day is
hand. end,
25 ¶ And thou, profane wremove the diadem, and take off
come, when iniquity *shall* same: exalt *him that is* low, and abase
26 Thus saith the Lor
the crown: this *shall* return, overturn, it: and it shall be no *more*,
*him that is* high. right it is; and I will give it *him*.
27 I will overton of man, prophesy and say, Thus saith the
until he cocerning the Ammonites, and concerning their re-
28 ¶ And say thou, The sword, the sword *is* drawn: for the
Lord G *it is* furbished, to consume because of the glittering:
proailes they see vanity unto thee, whiles they divine a lie unto
s to bring thee upon the necks of *them that are* slain, of the
cked, whose day is come, when their iniquity *shall have* an end.
30 Shall I cause *it* to return into his sheath? I will judge thee in
the place where thou wast created, in the land of thy nativity.
31 And I will pour out mine indignation upon thee, I will blow
against thee in the fire of my wrath, and deliver thee into the hand
of brutish men, *and* skilful to destroy.
32 Thou shalt be for fuel to the fire; thy blood shall be in the midst
of the land; thou shalt be no *more* remembered: for I the LORD have
spoken *it*.

**22** MOREOVER THE word of the LORD came unto me, saying,

2 Now, thou son of man, wilt thou judge, wilt thou judge the bloody city? yea, thou shalt show her all her abominations.

3 Then say thou, Thus saith the Lord GOD, The city sheddeth blood in the midst of it, that her time may come, and maketh idols against herself to defile herself.

4 Thou art become guilty in thy blood that thou hast shed; and hast defiled thyself in thine idols which thou hast made; and thou hast caused thy days to draw near, and art come *even* unto thy years: therefore have I made thee a reproach unto the heathen, and a mocking to all countries.

5 *Those that be* near, and *those that be* far from thee, shall mock thee, *which art* infamous *and* much vexed.

6 Behold, the princes of Israel, every one were in thee to their power to shed blood.

7 In thee have they set light by father and mother: in the midst of thee have they dealt by oppression with the stranger: in thee have they vexed the fatherless and the widow.

8 Thou hast despised mine holy things, and hast profaned my sabbaths.

9 In thee are men that carry tales to shed blood: and in thee they eat upon the mountains: in the midst of thee they commit lewdness.

10 In thee have they discovered their fathers' nakedness: in thee have they humbled her that was set apart for pollution.

## Amplified

24 Therefore thus says the Lord God: Because you have made your guilt *and* iniquity to be remembered, in that your transgressions are uncovered, so that in all your doings your sins appear; because, I say, that you are come to remembrance, you shall be taken with the *enemy's* hand.

25 And you, O dishonored and wicked one [Zedekiah], the prince of Israel, whose day will come at the time of your final reckoning *and* punishment,

26 Thus says the Lord God: Remove the [high priest's] miter *or* headband, and take off the [king's] crown; things shall not remain as they have been; the low is *to be* exalted and the high is *to be* brought low.

27 I will overthrow, overthrow, overthrow it; this also shall be no more until He comes Whose right it is [to reign in judgment and in righteousness], and I will give it to Him. [Gen. 49:10; Isa. 9:6, 7; 11:1-4; Dan. 7:14; Luke 1:31-33.]

28 And you, son of man, prophesy and say, Thus says the Lord God concerning the sons of Ammon, and concerning their reproach: say, A sword, a sword is drawn for the slaughter; it is polished, to cause it to devour to the uttermost *and* to flash like lightning;

29 While they see for you false visions, while they divine lies for you, to lay you [of Ammon] upon the headless trunks of those who are slain, of the wicked whose day is coming at the time of the final reckoning *and* punishment.

30 Return *the sword* to its sheath. In the place where you were created, in the land of your origin *and* of your birth, I will judge you.

31 And I will pour out My indignation upon you [O sons of Ammon], I will blow upon you with the fire of My wrath, and will deliver you into the hand of brutish men, skillful to destroy.

32 You shall be for fuel to the fire; your blood shall be in the midst of the land; you shall be no more remembered; for I the Lord have spoken it. [Ezek. 25:1-7; Jer. 49:1-6; Amos 1:13-15; Zeph. 2:8-11.]

**22** MOREOVER THE word of the Lord came to me, saying,

2 And you [Ezekiel], son of man, will you judge, will you judge the blood-shedding city? Then cause her to know all her abominations.

3 And say, Thus says the Lord God: A city that sheds blood in the midst of her, so that her time [of doom] will come, and makes idols [over those who worship them] to defile her!

4 In your blood which you have shed you have become guilty, and you are defiled by the idols which you have made; and you have caused your time [of judgment and punishment] to draw near, and have arrived at the full measure of your years. Therefore have I made you a reproach to the [heathen] nations, and for a mocking to all countries.

5 Those who are near and those who are far from you will mock you, you infamous one, full of tumult.

6 Behold, the princes of Israel in you, every one according to his power, have been intending to shed blood.

7 In you have they treated father and mother lightly; in the midst of you they have dealt unjustly *and* by oppression in relation to the stranger; in you they have wronged the fatherless and the widow.

8 You have despised *and* scorned My sacred things and have profaned My sabbaths.

9 In you are slanderous men who arouse suspicions to shed blood, and in you are they who have eaten [food offered to idols] upon the mountains; in the midst of you they have committed lewdness.

10 In you men have uncovered the nakedness of mother or stepmother—their fathers' nakedness; in you they have humbled women who are *ceremonially* unclean [during their periods or because of childbirth].

## New American Standard

24"Therefore, thus says the Lord GOD, 'Because you have made
your iniquity to be remembered, in that your transgressions are
uncovered, so that in all your deeds your sins appear—because
you have come to remembrance, you will be seized with the hand.
25'And you, O slain, wicked one, the prince of Israel, whose day
has come, in the time of the punishment of the end,'
26thus says the Lord GOD, 'Remove the turban, and take off the
crown; this will *be* no more the same. Exalt that which is low, and
abase that which is high.
27'A ruin, a ruin, a ruin, I shall make it. This also will be no
more, until He comes whose right it is; and I shall give it *to Him*.'
28¶ "And you, son of man, prophesy and say, 'Thus says the
Lord GOD concerning the sons of Ammon and concerning their
reproach,' and say: 'A sword, a sword is drawn, polished for the
slaughter, to cause it to consume, that it may be like lightning—
29while they see for you false visions, while they divine lies for
you—to place you on the necks of the wicked who are slain, whose
day has come, in the time of the punishment of the end.
30'Return *it* to its sheath. In the place where you were created,
in the land of your origin, I shall judge you.
31'And I shall pour out My indignation on you; I shall blow on
you with the fire of My wrath, and I shall give you into the hand
of brutal men, skilled in destruction.
32'You will be fuel for the fire; your blood will be in the midst
of the land. You will not be remembered, for I, the LORD, have
spoken.'"

*The Sins of Israel*

**22** THEN THE word of the LORD came to me saying,
2"And you, son of man, will you judge, will you judge the
bloody city? Then cause her to know all her abominations.
3"And you shall say, 'Thus says the Lord GOD, "A city shedding blood in her midst, so that her time will come, and that makes
idols, contrary to her *interest*, for defilement!
4"You have become guilty by the blood which you have shed,
and defiled by your idols which you have made. Thus you have
brought your day near and have come to your years; therefore I
have made you a reproach to the nations, and a mocking to all the
lands.
5"Those who are near and those who are far from you will
mock you, you of ill repute, full of turmoil.
6"Behold, the rulers of Israel, each according to his power,
have been in you for the purpose of shedding blood.
7"They have treated father and mother lightly within you. The
alien they have oppressed in your midst; the fatherless and the
widow they have wronged in you.
8"You have despised My holy things and profaned My sabbaths.
9"Slanderous men have been in you for the purpose of shedding blood, and in you they have eaten at the mountain *shrines*.
In your midst they have committed acts of lewdness.
10"In you they have uncovered *their* fathers' nakedness; in you
they have humbled her who was unclean in her menstrual impurity.

## New International

24"Therefore
people have broug what the Sovereign LORD says: 'Because you
revealing your sins in mind your guilt by your open rebellion,
you will be taken captiv you do—because you have done this,
25" 'O profane and wic
come, whose time of punishn rince of Israel, whose day has
what the Sovereign LORD says: s reached its climax, 26this is
crown. It will not be as it was: The ff the turban, remove the
exalted will be brought low. 27A ruin! will be exalted and the
It will not be restored until he comes to wl I will make it a ruin!
to him I will give it.' rightfully belongs;
28"And you, son of man, prophesy and say
Sovereign LORD says about the Ammonites and is what the
" 'A sword, a sword, nsults:
drawn for the slaughter,
polished to consume
and to flash like lightning!
29Despite false visions concerning you
and lying divinations about you,
it will be laid on the necks
of the wicked who are to be slain,
whose day has come,
whose time of punishment has reached its climax.
30Return the sword to its scabbard.
In the place where you were created,
in the land of your ancestry,
I will judge you.
31I will pour out my wrath upon you
and breathe out my fiery anger against you;
I will hand you over to brutal men,
men skilled in destruction.
32You will be fuel for the fire,
your blood will be shed in your land,
you will be remembered no more;
for I the LORD have spoken.' "

*Jerusalem's Sins*

**22** THE WORD of the LORD came to me: 2"Son of man, will
you judge her? Will you judge this city of bloodshed?
Then confront her with all her detestable practices 3and say: 'This
is what the Sovereign LORD says: O city that brings on herself
doom by shedding blood in her midst and defiles herself by making idols, 4you have become guilty because of the blood you have
shed and have become defiled by the idols you have made. You
have brought your days to a close, and the end of your years has
come. Therefore I will make you an object of scorn to the nations
and a laughingstock to all the countries. 5Those who are near and
those who are far away will mock you, O infamous city, full of
turmoil.
6" 'See how each of the princes of Israel who are in you uses his
power to shed blood. 7In you they have treated father and mother
with contempt; in you they have oppressed the alien and mistreated the fatherless and the widow. 8You have despised my holy
things and desecrated my Sabbaths. 9In you are slanderous men
bent on shedding blood; in you are those who eat at the mountain
shrines and commit lewd acts. 10In you are those who dishonor
their fathers' bed; in you are those who violate women during their
period, when they are ceremonially unclean. 11In you one man

## King James

s neighbour's
11And one hath committed abomination wter-in-law; and
wife; and another hath lewdly defiled his father's daughter.
another in thee hath humbled his siste lood; thou hast taken
12In thee have they taken gifts to ily gained of thy neigh-
usury and increase, and thou hast t me, saith the Lord GOD.
bours by extortion, and hast foen mine hand at thy dishonest
13¶ Behold, therefore I have at thy blood which hath been in
gain which thou hast made
the midst of thee. , or can thine hands be strong, in the
14Can thine heart thee? I the LORD have spoken *it*, and will
days that I shall de
do *it*. er thee among the heathen, and disperse thee
15And I w and will consume thy filthiness out of thee.
in the cou shalt take thine inheritance in thyself in the sight
16An ien, and thou shalt know that I *am* the LORD.
of th the word of the LORD came unto me, saying,
on of man, the house of Israel is to me become dross: all they
orass, and tin, and iron, and lead, in the midst of the furnace;
hey are *even* the dross of silver.
19Therefore thus saith the Lord GOD; Because ye are all become
dross, behold, therefore I will gather you into the midst of Jerusalem.
20 *As* they gather silver, and brass, and iron, and lead, and tin,
into the midst of the furnace, to blow the fire upon it, to melt *it*;
so will I gather *you* in mine anger and in my fury, and I will leave
*you there*, and melt you.
21Yea, I will gather you, and blow upon you in the fire of my
wrath, and ye shall be melted in the midst thereof.
22As silver is melted in the midst of the furnace, so shall ye be
melted in the midst thereof; and ye shall know that I the LORD have
poured out my fury upon you.
23¶ And the word of the LORD came unto me, saying,
24Son of man, say unto her, Thou *art* the land that is not
cleansed, nor rained upon in the day of indignation.
25 *There is* a conspiracy of her prophets in the midst thereof, like
a roaring lion ravening the prey; they have devoured souls; they
have taken the treasure and precious things; they have made her
many widows in the midst thereof.
26Her priests have violated my law, and have profaned mine
holy things: they have put no difference between the holy and
profane, neither have they shown *difference* between the unclean
and the clean, and have hid their eyes from my sabbaths, and I am
profaned among them.
27Her princes in the midst thereof *are* like wolves ravening the
prey, to shed blood, *and* to destroy souls, to get dishonest gain.
28And her prophets have daubed them with untempered *mortar*, seeing vanity, and divining lies unto them, saying, Thus saith
the Lord GOD, when the LORD hath not spoken.
29The people of the land have used oppression, and exercised
robbery, and have vexed the poor and needy: yea, they have
oppressed the stranger wrongfully.
30And I sought for a man among them, that should make up the
hedge, and stand in the gap before me for the land, that I should
not destroy it: but I found none.
31Therefore have I poured out mine indignation upon them; I
have consumed them with the fire of my wrath: their own way
have I recompensed upon their heads, saith the Lord GOD.

## Amplified

11And one has committed abomination with his neighbor's
wife, and another has lewdly defiled his daughter-in-law, and
another in you has humbled his sister, his father's daughter.
12In you they have accepted bribes to shed blood; you have
taken [forbidden] interest and [percentage of] increase, and you
have greedily gained from your neighbors by oppression *and* extortion, and have forgotten Me, says the Lord God.
13Behold, therefore, I have struck My hands together at your
dishonest gain which you have made, and at the blood which has
been in the midst of you.
14Can your heart *and* courage endure, or can your hands be
strong, in the days that I shall deal with You? I the Lord have
spoken it, and I will do it.
15And I will scatter you among the nations and disperse you
through the countries, and I will consume your filthiness out of
you.
16And you shall be dishonored *and* profaned yourself in the
sight of the nations, and you shall know—understand and realize—that I am the Lord.
17And the word of the Lord came to me, saying,
18Son of man, the house of Israel has become to Me scum *and*
waste matter. All of them are bronze and tin and iron and lead in
the midst of the furnace; they are the dross of silver.
19Therefore thus says the Lord God: Because you have all
become scum *and* waste matter, behold, therefore I will gather you
[O Israel] into the midst of Jerusalem.
20As they gather silver and bronze and iron and lead and tin
into the midst of the furnace, to blow the fire upon it in order to
melt it; so will I gather you in My anger and in My wrath, and I
will put you in and melt you.
21Yes, I will gather you, and blow upon you with the fire of My
wrath, and you shall be melted in the midst of it.
22As silver is melted in the midst of the furnace, so shall you
be melted in the midst of it, and you shall know, understand *and*
realize that I the Lord have poured out My wrath upon you [O
Israel].
23And the word of the Lord came to me, saying,
24Son of man, say to her, You are a land that is not cleansed,
nor rained upon in the day of indignation.
25There is a conspiracy of [Israel's false] prophets in the midst
of her, like a roaring lion tearing the prey; they have devoured
human lives; they have taken [in their greed] treasure and precious
things; they have made many widows in the midst of her.
26Her priests have done violence to My law and have profaned
My holy things. They have made no distinction between the sacred
and the secular, neither have they taught people the difference
between the unclean and the clean, and have hid their eyes from
My sabbaths, and I am profaned among them.
27Her princes in the midst of her are like wolves rending *and*
devouring the prey, shedding blood and destroying lives to get
dishonest gain.
28And her prophets have daubed for them with whitewash,
seeing false visions and divining lies to them, saying, Thus says
the Lord God, when the Lord has not spoken.
29The people of the land have used oppression *and* extortion
and have committed robbery, yes, they have wronged *and* vexed
the poor and needy; yes, they have oppressed the stranger *and*
temporary resident wrongfully.
30And I sought for a man among them who should build up the
wall, and stand in the gap before Me for the land, that I should not
destroy it; but I found none.
31Therefore have I poured out My indignation upon them; I
have consumed them with the fire of My wrath; their own way
have I repaid *by bringing it* upon their *own* heads, says the Lord
God.

## New American Standard

11"And one has committed abomination with his neighbor's wife, and another has lewdly defiled his daughter-in-law. And another in you has humbled his sister, his father's daughter.

12"In you they have taken bribes to shed blood; you have taken interest and profits, and you have injured your neighbors for gain by oppression, and you have forgotten Me," declares the Lord GOD.

13¶ "Behold, then, I smite My hand at your dishonest gain which you have acquired and at the bloodshed which is among you.

14"Can your heart endure, or can your hands be strong, in the days that I shall deal with you? I, the LORD, have spoken and shall act.

15"And I shall scatter you among the nations, and I shall disperse you through the lands, and I shall consume your uncleanness from you.

16"And you will profane yourself in the sight of the nations, and you will know that I am the LORD."'"

17¶ And the word of the LORD came to me saying,

18"Son of man, the house of Israel has become dross to Me; all of them are bronze and tin and iron and lead in the furnace; they are the dross of silver.

19"Therefore, thus says the Lord GOD, 'Because all of you have become dross, therefore, behold, I am going to gather you into the midst of Jerusalem.

20'As they gather silver and bronze and iron and lead and tin into the furnace to blow fire on it in order to melt *it*, so I shall gather *you* in My anger and in My wrath, and I shall lay you *there* and melt you.

21'And I shall gather you and blow on you with the fire of My wrath, and you will be melted in the midst of it.

22'As silver is melted in the furnace, so you will be melted in the midst of it; and you will know that I, the LORD, have poured out My wrath on you.'"

23¶ And the word of the LORD came to me saying,

24"Son of man, say to her, 'You are a land that is not cleansed or rained on in the day of indignation.'

25"There is a conspiracy of her prophets in her midst, like a roaring lion tearing the prey. They have devoured lives; they have taken treasure and precious things; they have made many widows in the midst of her.

26"Her priests have done violence to My law and have profaned My holy things; they have made no distinction between the holy and the profane, and they have not taught the difference between the unclean and the clean; and they hide their eyes from My sabbaths, and I am profaned among them.

27"Her princes within her are like wolves tearing the prey, by shedding blood *and* destroying lives in order to get dishonest gain.

28"And her prophets have smeared whitewash for them, seeing false visions and divining lies for them, saying, 'Thus says the Lord GOD,' when the LORD has not spoken.

29"The people of the land have practiced oppression and committed robbery, and they have wronged the poor and needy and have oppressed the sojourner without justice.

30"And I searched for a man among them who should build up the wall and stand in the gap before Me for the land, that I should not destroy it; but I found no one.

31"Thus I have poured out My indignation on them; I have consumed them with the fire of My wrath; their way I have brought upon their heads," declares the Lord GOD.

## New International

commits a detestable offense with his neighbor's wife, another
shamefully defiles his daughter-in-law, and another violates his
sister, his own father's daughter. 12In you men accept bribes to
shed blood; you take usury and excessive interest[a] and make
unjust gain from your neighbors by extortion. And you have forgotten me, declares the Sovereign LORD.
13" 'I will surely strike my hands together at the unjust gain you
have made and at the blood you have shed in your midst. 14Will
your courage endure or your hands be strong in the day I deal with
you? I the LORD have spoken, and I will do it. 15I will disperse you
among the nations and scatter you through the countries; and I will
put an end to your uncleanness. 16When you have been defiled[b]
in the eyes of the nations, you will know that I am the LORD.' "
17Then the word of the LORD came to me: 18"Son of man, the
house of Israel has become dross to me; all of them are the copper,
tin, iron and lead left inside a furnace. They are but the dross of
silver. 19Therefore this is what the Sovereign LORD says: 'Because
you have all become dross, I will gather you into Jerusalem. 20As
men gather silver, copper, iron, lead and tin into a furnace to melt
it with a fiery blast, so will I gather you in my anger and my wrath
and put you inside the city and melt you. 21I will gather you and
I will blow on you with my fiery wrath, and you will be melted
inside her. 22As silver is melted in a furnace, so you will be melted
inside her, and you will know that I the LORD have poured out my
wrath upon you.' "
23Again the word of the LORD came to me: 24"Son of man, say
to the land, 'You are a land that has had no rain or showers[c] in
the day of wrath.' 25There is a conspiracy of her princes[d] within
her like a roaring lion tearing its prey; they devour people, take
treasures and precious things and make many widows within her.
26Her priests do violence to my law and profane my holy things;
they do not distinguish between the holy and the common; they
teach that there is no difference between the unclean and the clean;
and they shut their eyes to the keeping of my Sabbaths, so that I
am profaned among them. 27Her officials within her are like
wolves tearing their prey; they shed blood and kill people to make
unjust gain. 28Her prophets whitewash these deeds for them by
false visions and lying divinations. They say, 'This is what the
Sovereign LORD says'—when the LORD has not spoken. 29The
people of the land practice extortion and commit robbery; they
oppress the poor and needy and mistreat the alien, denying them
justice.
30"I looked for a man among them who would build up the wall
and stand before me in the gap on behalf of the land so I would
not have to destroy it, but I found none. 31So I will pour out my
wrath on them and consume them with my fiery anger, bringing
down on their own heads all they have done, declares the Sovereign LORD."

**NIV** [a] 12 Or *usury and interest* [b] 16 Or *When I have allotted you your inheritance* [c] 24 Septuagint; Hebrew *has not been cleansed or rained on* [d] 25 Septuagint; Hebrew *prophets*

## King James

**23** THE WORD of the LORD came again unto me, saying,
2 Son of man, there were two women, the daughters of one mother:

3 And they committed whoredoms in Egypt; they committed whoredoms in their youth: there were their breasts pressed, and there they bruised the teats of their virginity.

4 And the names of them *were* Aholah the elder, and Aholibah her sister: and they were mine, and they bare sons and daughters. Thus *were* their names; Samaria *is* Aholah, and Jerusalem Aholibah.

5 And Aholah played the harlot when she was mine; and she doted on her lovers, on the Assyrians *her* neighbours,

6 *Which were* clothed with blue, captains and rulers, all of them desirable young men, horsemen riding upon horses.

7 Thus she committed her whoredoms with them, with all them *that were* the chosen men of Assyria, and with all on whom she doted: with all their idols she defiled herself.

8 Neither left she her whoredoms *brought* from Egypt: for in her youth they lay with her, and they bruised the breasts of her virginity, and poured their whoredom upon her.

9 Wherefore I have delivered her into the hand of her lovers, into the hand of the Assyrians, upon whom she doted.

10 These discovered her nakedness: they took her sons and her daughters, and slew her with the sword: and she became famous among women; for they had executed judgment upon her.

11 And when her sister Aholibah saw *this*, she was more corrupt in her inordinate love than she, and in her whoredoms more than her sister in *her* whoredoms.

12 She doted upon the Assyrians *her* neighbours, captains and rulers clothed most gorgeously, horsemen riding upon horses, all of them desirable young men.

13 Then I saw that she was defiled, *that* they *took* both one way,

14 And *that* she increased her whoredoms: for when she saw men portrayed upon the wall, the images of the Chaldeans portrayed with vermilion,

15 Girded with girdles upon their loins, exceeding in dyed attire upon their heads, all of them princes to look to, after the manner of the Babylonians of Chaldea, the land of their nativity:

16 And as soon as she saw them with her eyes, she doted upon them, and sent messengers unto them into Chaldea.

17 And the Babylonians came to her into the bed of love, and they defiled her with their whoredom, and she was polluted with them, and her mind was alienated from them.

18 So she discovered her whoredoms, and discovered her nakedness: then my mind was alienated from her, like as my mind was alienated from her sister.

19 Yet she multiplied her whoredoms, in calling to remembrance the days of her youth, wherein she had played the harlot in the land of Egypt.

20 For she doted upon their paramours, whose flesh *is as* the flesh of asses, and whose issue *is like* the issue of horses.

21 Thus thou calledst to remembrance the lewdness of thy youth, in bruising thy teats by the Egyptians for the paps of thy youth.

22 ¶ Therefore, O Aholibah, thus saith the Lord GOD; Behold, I will raise up thy lovers against thee, from whom thy mind is alienated, and I will bring them against thee on every side;

23 The Babylonians, and all the Chaldeans, Pekod, and Shoa, and Koa, *and* all the Assyrians with them: all of them desirable young men, captains and rulers, great lords and renowned, all of them riding upon horses.

## Amplified

**23** THE WORD of the Lord came again to me:
2 Son of man, there were two women, the daughters of one mother;

3 And they played the harlot in Egypt; there they played the harlot in their youth; there their bosoms were pressed, and there their virgin breasts were handled.

4 And the names of them were Aholah the elder and Aholibah her sister; and they became Mine, and they bore sons and daughters. As for the identity of their names, Aholah is Samaria, and Aholibah is Jerusalem.

5 And Aholah played the harlot when she was Mine, and she was foolishly fond of her lovers, *and* doted on the Assyrians her neighbors,

6 Who were clothed with blue, governors and deputies, all of them attractive young men, horsemen riding upon horses.

7 And she bestowed her harlotries upon them, the choicest men of Assyria all of them; and on whomever she doted, with all their idols she defiled herself.

8 Neither has she left her harlotries since the days of Egypt—from which she brought them; for in her youth men there lay with her and handled her girlish bosom, and they poured out their sinful desire upon her.

9 Wherefore I delivered her into the hand of her lovers, into the hand of the Assyrians upon whom she doted.

10 These uncovered her nakedness *and* shame; they took her sons and her daughters, and they slew her with the sword; and her name became notorious *and* a byword among women, when judgments were executed upon her.

11 And her sister Aholibah saw this, yet she was more corrupt in her foolish fondness than she, and in her harlotries she was more wanton than her sister in her harlotries.

12 She doted upon the Assyrians, governors and deputies, her neighbors, clothed most gorgeously; horsemen riding upon horses, all of them desirable young men.

13 And I saw that she was defiled, that both [of the sisters] took one way.

14 But [Aholibah] carried her harlotries further, for she saw men pictured upon the wall, the pictures of the Chaldeans sketched in bright red pigment,

15 Girded with girdles on their loins, with flowing turbans on their heads, all of them looking like officers, a picture of Babylonian men whose native land was Chaldea,

16 Then as soon as she saw [the sketches of] them, she doted on them, and sent messengers to them in Chaldea.

17 And the Babylonians came to her into the bed of love, and they defiled her with their evil desire, and when she was polluted by them, she [Jerusalem] broke the relationship *and* pushed them away from her in disgust.

18 So she flaunted her harlotries and exposed her nakedness, and I was disgusted and turned from her, as I had turned in disgust from her sister.

19 Yet she multiplied her harlotries, remembering the days of her youth in which she had played the harlot in the land of Egypt.

20 For she doted upon her paramours there, whose lust was as sensuous *and* vulgar as that of asses *or* stallions.

21 Thus you yearned for the lewdness of your youth, when those of Egypt handled your bosom on account of your girlish breasts.

22 Therefore, O Aholibah, thus says the Lord God: Behold, I will rouse up your lovers against you, from whom you turned in disgust, and I will bring them against you on every side:

23 The Babylonians and all the Chaldeans, Pekod and Shoa and Koa; and all the Assyrians with them, desirable young men, governors and officers all of them, princes, men of renown *and* counselors, all of them riding on horses.

## New American Standard

*Oholah and Oholibah's Sin and Its Consequences*
**23** THE WORD of the LORD came to me again saying,
2"Son of man, there were two women, the daughters of
one mother;
3and they played the harlot in Egypt. They played the harlot
in their youth; there their breasts were pressed, and there their
virgin bosom was handled.
4"And their names were Oholah the elder and Oholibah her
sister. And they became Mine, and they bore sons and daughters.
And *as for* their names, Samaria is Oholah, and Jerusalem is Oholibah.
5¶ "And Oholah played the harlot while she was Mine; and she
lusted after her lovers, after the Assyrians, *her* neighbors,
6who were clothed in purple, governors and officials, all of
them desirable young men, horsemen riding on horses.
7"And she bestowed her harlotries on them, all of whom *were*
the choicest men of Assyria; and with all whom she lusted after,
with all their idols she defiled herself.
8"And she did not forsake her harlotries from *the time in* Egypt;
for in her youth men had lain with her, and they handled her
virgin bosom and poured out their lust on her.
9"Therefore, I gave her into the hand of her lovers, into the
hand of the Assyrians, after whom she lusted.
10"They uncovered her nakedness; they took her sons and her
daughters, but they slew her with the sword. Thus she became a
byword among women, and they executed judgments on her.
11¶ "Now her sister Oholibah saw *this*, yet she was more corrupt in her lust than she, and her harlotries were more than the
harlotries of her sister.
12"She lusted after the Assyrians, governors and officials, the
ones near, magnificently dressed, horsemen riding on horses, all
of them desirable young men.
13"And I saw that she had defiled herself; they both took the
same way.
14"So she increased her harlotries. And she saw men portrayed
on the wall, images of the Chaldeans portrayed with vermilion,
15girded with belts on their loins, with flowing turbans on their
heads, all of them looking like officers, like the Babylonians *in*
Chaldea, the land of their birth.
16"And when she saw them she lusted after them and sent
messengers to them in Chaldea.
17"And the Babylonians came to her to the bed of love, and they
defiled her with their harlotry. And when she had been defiled by
them, she became disgusted with them.
18"And she uncovered her harlotries and uncovered her nakedness; then I became disgusted with her, as I had become disgusted
with her sister.
19"Yet she multiplied her harlotries, remembering the days of
her youth, when she played the harlot in the land of Egypt.
20"And she lusted after their paramours, whose flesh is *like* the
flesh of donkeys and whose issue is *like* the issue of horses.
21"Thus you longed for the lewdness of your youth, when the
Egyptians handled your bosom because of the breasts of your
youth.
22¶ "Therefore, O Oholibah, thus says the Lord GOD, 'Behold
I will arouse your lovers against you, from whom you were alienated, and I will bring them against you from every side:
23the Babylonians and all the Chaldeans, Pekod and Shoa and
Koa, *and* all the Assyrians with them; desirable young men, governors and officials all of them, officers and men of renown, all of
them riding on horses.

## New International

*Two Adulterous Sisters*
**23** THE WORD of the LORD came to me: 2"Son of man, there
were two women, daughters of the same mother. 3They
became prostitutes in Egypt, engaging in prostitution from their
youth. In that land their breasts were fondled and their virgin
bosoms caressed. 4The older was named Oholah, and her sister
was Oholibah. They were mine and gave birth to sons and daughters. Oholah is Samaria, and Oholibah is Jerusalem.
5"Oholah engaged in prostitution while she was still mine; and
she lusted after her lovers, the Assyrians—warriors 6clothed in
blue, governors and commanders, all of them handsome young
men, and mounted horsemen. 7She gave herself as a prostitute to
all the elite of the Assyrians and defiled herself with all the idols
of everyone she lusted after. 8She did not give up the prostitution
she began in Egypt, when during her youth men slept with her,
caressed her virgin bosom and poured out their lust upon her.
9"Therefore I handed her over to her lovers, the Assyrians, for
whom she lusted. 10They stripped her naked, took away her sons
and daughters and killed her with the sword. She became a byword among women, and punishment was inflicted on her.
11"Her sister Oholibah saw this, yet in her lust and prostitution
she was more depraved than her sister. 12She too lusted after the
Assyrians—governors and commanders, warriors in full dress,
mounted horsemen, all handsome young men. 13I saw that she too
defiled herself; both of them went the same way.
14"But she carried her prostitution still further. She saw men
portrayed on a wall, figures of Chaldeans[a] portrayed in red, 15with
belts around their waists and flowing turbans on their heads; all
of them looked like Babylonian chariot officers, natives of Chaldea.[b] 16As soon as she saw them, she lusted after them and sent
messengers to them in Chaldea. 17Then the Babylonians came to
her, to the bed of love, and in their lust they defiled her. After she
had been defiled by them, she turned away from them in disgust.
18When she carried on her prostitution openly and exposed her
nakedness, I turned away from her in disgust, just as I had turned
away from her sister. 19Yet she became more and more promiscuous as she recalled the days of her youth, when she was a prostitute in Egypt. 20There she lusted after her lovers, whose genitals
were like those of donkeys and whose emission was like that of
horses. 21So you longed for the lewdness of your youth, when in
Egypt your bosom was caressed and your young breasts fondled.[c]
22"Therefore, Oholibah, this is what the Sovereign LORD says:
I will stir up your lovers against you, those you turned away from
in disgust, and I will bring them against you from every side—
23the Babylonians and all the Chaldeans, the men of Pekod and
Shoa and Koa, and all the Assyrians with them, handsome young
men, all of them governors and commanders, chariot officers and
men of high rank, all mounted on horses. 24They will come against

**NIV** [a] *14* Or *Babylonians* [b] *15* Or *Babylonia;* also in verse 16 [c] *21* Syriac (see also verse 3); Hebrew *caressed because of your young breasts*

## King James

24And they shall come against thee with chariots, wagons, and wheels, and with an assembly of people, *which* shall set against thee buckler and shield and helmet round about: and I will set judgment before them, and they shall judge thee according to their judgments.

25And I will set my jealousy against thee, and they shall deal furiously with thee: they shall take away thy nose and thine ears; and thy remnant shall fall by the sword: they shall take thy sons and thy daughters; and thy residue shall be devoured by the fire.

26They shall also strip thee out of thy clothes, and take away thy fair jewels.

27Thus will I make thy lewdness to cease from thee, and thy whoredom *brought* from the land of Egypt: so that thou shalt not lift up thine eyes unto them, nor remember Egypt any more.

28For thus saith the Lord GOD; Behold, I will deliver thee into the hand *of them* whom thou hatest, into the hand *of them* from whom thy mind is alienated:

29And they shall deal with thee hatefully, and shall take away all thy labour, and shall leave thee naked and bare: and the nakedness of thy whoredoms shall be discovered, both thy lewdness and thy whoredoms.

30I will do these *things* unto thee, because thou hast gone awhoring after the heathen, *and* because thou art polluted with their idols.

31Thou hast walked in the way of thy sister; therefore will I give her cup into thine hand.

32Thus saith the Lord GOD; Thou shalt drink of thy sister's cup deep and large: thou shalt be laughed to scorn and had in derision; it containeth much.

33Thou shalt be filled with drunkenness and sorrow, with the cup of astonishment and desolation, with the cup of thy sister Samaria.

34Thou shalt even drink it and suck *it* out, and thou shalt break the sherds thereof, and pluck off thine own breasts: for I have spoken *it*, saith the Lord GOD.

35Therefore thus saith the Lord GOD; Because thou hast forgotten me, and cast me behind thy back, therefore bear thou also thy lewdness and thy whoredoms.

36¶ The LORD said moreover unto me; Son of man, wilt thou judge Aholah and Aholibah? yea, declare unto them their abominations;

37That they have committed adultery, and blood *is* in their hands, and with their idols have they committed adultery, and have also caused their sons, whom they bare unto me, to pass for them through *the fire,* to devour *them.*

38Moreover this they have done unto me: they have defiled my sanctuary in the same day, and have profaned my sabbaths.

39For when they had slain their children to their idols, then they came the same day into my sanctuary to profane it; and, lo, thus have they done in the midst of mine house.

40And furthermore, that ye have sent for men to come from far, unto whom a messenger *was* sent; and, lo, they came: for whom thou didst wash thyself, paintedst thy eyes, and deckedst thyself with ornaments,

41And satest upon a stately bed, and a table prepared before it, whereupon thou hast set mine incense and mine oil.

42And a voice of a multitude being at ease *was* with her: and with the men of the common sort *were* brought Sabeans from the wilderness, which put bracelets upon their hands, and beautiful crowns upon their heads.

43Then said I unto *her that was* old in adulteries, Will they now commit whoredoms with her, and she *with them?*

## Amplified

24And they shall come against you with weapons, chariots, wagons *and* wheels, and with a host of infantry, which shall array themselves against you with buckler and shield and helmet round about; and I will commit the judgment *and* punishment to them, and they shall judge *and* punish you according to their [heathen] customs in such matters.

25And I will set My jealous indignation against you, and they shall deal with you in fury: they shall take away your nose and your ears, and those who are left of you shall fall by the sword; they shall take your sons and your daughters, and the remainder shall be devoured by the fire.

26They shall also strip you of your clothes, and take away your fine jewels, [Judah].

27Thus I will put an end to your lewdness and your harlotry brought from the land of Egypt; so that you will not lift up your eyes to them, nor [earnestly] remember Egypt any more.

28For thus says the Lord God: Behold, I will deliver you into the hand of those whom you hate, into the hand of those from whom you turned away in disgust.

29They shall deal with you in hatred, and shall take away all [the evenings of] your labor, and shall leave you naked and bare, and the nakedness of your harlotry shall be uncovered, both your lewdness and your wanton ways.

30These things shall be done to you because you have played the harlot after the nations, and because you have defiled yourself with their idols.

31You have walked in the way of your sister [Samaria, Israel's capital], therefore I will give her cup into your hand.

32Thus says the Lord God: You shall drink of your sister's cup which is deep and wide *and* brimful; you shall be laughed to scorn and held in derision, for it contains much—too much to endure.

33You shall be filled with drunkenness and sorrow, with the cup of wasting astonishment *and* horror and desolation, with the cup of your sister Samaria.

34You shall drink it and drain it out, and then gnaw the pieces of it [which in your drunkenness you have broken], and shall tear your *own* breasts; for I have spoken it, says the Lord God.

35Therefore thus says the Lord God: Because you have forgotten Me [your divine Husband] and cast Me behind your back, therefore bear also [the consequences of] your lewdness and your harlotry.

36The Lord said moreover to me: Son of man, will you judge Aholah and Aholibah? Then declare *and* show to them their abominations—the detestable, loathsome and shamefully vile things they do;

37That they have committed adultery, and blood is on their hands, even with their idols have they committed adultery [against Me]. And they have also caused their sons, whom they bore to Me, to pass through the fire to their images [as an offering of food] to be devoured [by them].

38Moreover this they have done to Me, they have defiled My sanctuary on the same day [of their idolatries] and have profaned My sabbaths.

39For when they had slain their children [as offerings] to their idols, then they came the same day into My sanctuary to profane it [by daring to offer sacrifice there also]! And lo, thus have they done in the midst of My house!

40And furthermore, you have sent for men to come from far, to whom a messenger was sent; and lo, they came. For whom you washed yourself, painted your eyelids and decked yourself with ornaments;

41And you sat upon a stately couch, with a table spread before it, upon which you set My incense and My oil.

42And the sound of a careless crowd was with her; and with men of the common sort were brought drunkards from the wilderness, who put bracelets upon the hands of both sisters, and beautiful crowns upon their heads.

43Then I said of [Aholah] worn out with adulteries, Will they now play the harlot with her that is old, and she with them?

## New American Standard

24'And they will come against you with weapons, chariots, and
wagons, and with a company of peoples. They will set themselves
against you on every side with buckler and shield and helmet; and
I shall commit the judgment to them, and they will judge you
according to their customs.
25'And I will set My jealousy against you, that they may deal
with you in wrath. They will remove your nose and your ears; and
your survivors will fall by the sword. They will take your sons and
your daughters; and your survivors will be consumed by the fire.
26'They will also strip you of your clothes and take away your
beautiful jewels.
27'Thus I shall make your lewdness and your harlotry *brought*
from the land of Egypt to cease from you, so that you will not lift
up your eyes to them or remember Egypt anymore.'
28"For thus says the Lord GOD, 'Behold, I will give you into the
hand of those whom you hate, into the hand of those from whom
you were alienated.
29'And they will deal with you in hatred, take all your property,
and leave you naked and bare. And the nakedness of your harlotries shall be uncovered, both your lewdness and your harlotries.
30'These things will be done to you because you have played the
harlot with the nations, because you have defiled yourself with
their idols.
31'You have walked in the way of your sister; therefore I will
give her cup into your hand.'
32"Thus says the Lord GOD,

'You will drink your sister's cup,
Which is deep and wide.
You will be laughed at and held in derision;
It contains much.
33 'You will be filled with drunkenness and sorrow,
The cup of horror and desolation,
The cup of your sister Samaria.
34 'And you will drink it and drain it.
Then you will gnaw its fragments
And tear your breasts;
for I have spoken,' declares the Lord GOD.

35"Therefore, thus says the Lord GOD, 'Because you have forgotten Me and cast Me behind your back, bear now the *punishment*
of your lewdness and your harlotries.' "
36¶ Moreover, the LORD said to me, "Son of man, will you judge
Oholah and Oholibah? Then declare to them their abominations.
37"For they have committed adultery, and blood is on their
hands. Thus they have committed adultery with their idols and
even caused their sons, whom they bore to Me, to pass through
*the fire* to them as food.
38"Again, they have done this to Me: they have defiled My
sanctuary on the same day and have profaned My sabbaths.
39"For when they had slaughtered their children for their idols,
they entered My sanctuary on the same day to profane it; and lo,
thus they did within My house.
40"Furthermore, they have even sent for men who come from
afar, to whom a messenger was sent; and lo, they came—for whom
you bathed, painted your eyes, and decorated yourselves with
ornaments;
41and you sat on a splendid couch with a table arranged before
it, on which you had set My incense and My oil.
42"And the sound of a carefree multitude was with her; and
drunkards were brought from the wilderness with men of the
common sort. And they put bracelets on the hands of the women
and beautiful crowns on their heads.
43"Then I said concerning her who was worn out by adulteries,
'Will they now commit adultery with her when she is *thus*?'

## New International

you with weapons,[a] chariots and wagons and with a throng of
people; they will take up positions against you on every side with
large and small shields and with helmets. I will turn you over to
them for punishment, and they will punish you according to their
standards. 25I will direct my jealous anger against you, and they
will deal with you in fury. They will cut off your noses and your
ears, and those of you who are left will fall by the sword. They will
take away your sons and daughters, and those of you who are left
will be consumed by fire. 26They will also strip you of your clothes
and take your fine jewelry. 27So I will put a stop to the lewdness
and prostitution you began in Egypt. You will not look on these
things with longing or remember Egypt anymore.
28"For this is what the Sovereign LORD says: I am about to hand
you over to those you hate, to those you turned away from in
disgust. 29They will deal with you in hatred and take away everything you have worked for. They will leave you naked and bare,
and the shame of your prostitution will be exposed. Your lewdness
and promiscuity 30have brought this upon you, because you lusted
after the nations and defiled yourself with their idols. 31You have
gone the way of your sister; so I will put her cup into your hand.
32"This is what the Sovereign LORD says:

"You will drink your sister's cup,
a cup large and deep;
it will bring scorn and derision,
for it holds so much.
33You will be filled with drunkenness and sorrow,
the cup of ruin and desolation,
the cup of your sister Samaria.
34You will drink it and drain it dry;
you will dash it to pieces
and tear your breasts.

I have spoken, declares the Sovereign LORD.

35"Therefore this is what the Sovereign LORD says: Since you
have forgotten me and thrust me behind your back, you must bear
the consequences of your lewdness and prostitution."
36The LORD said to me: "Son of man, will you judge Oholah and
Oholibah? Then confront them with their detestable practices,
37for they have committed adultery and blood is on their hands.
They committed adultery with their idols; they even sacrificed
their children, whom they bore to me,[b] as food for them. 38They
have also done this to me: At that same time they defiled my
sanctuary and desecrated my Sabbaths. 39On the very day they
sacrificed their children to their idols, they entered my sanctuary
and desecrated it. That is what they did in my house.
40"They even sent messengers for men who came from far
away, and when they arrived you bathed yourself for them, painted your eyes and put on your jewelry. 41You sat on an elegant
couch, with a table spread before it on which you had placed the
incense and oil that belonged to me.
42"The noise of a carefree crowd was around her; Sabeans[c]
were brought from the desert along with men from the rabble, and
they put bracelets on the arms of the woman and her sister and
beautiful crowns on their heads. 43Then I said about the one worn
out by adultery, 'Now let them use her as a prostitute, for that is
all she is.' 44And they slept with her. As men sleep with a prosti-

NIV [a] 24 The meaning of the Hebrew for this word is uncertain. [b] 37 Or *even made the children they bore to me pass through ⌊the fire⌋* [c] 42 Or *drunkards*

## King James

44 Yet they went in unto her, as they go in unto a woman that playeth the harlot: so went they in unto Aholah and unto Aholibah, the lewd women.

45 ¶ And the righteous men, they shall judge them after the manner of adulteresses, and after the manner of women that shed blood; because they *are* adulteresses, and blood *is* in their hands.

46 For thus saith the Lord GOD; I will bring up a company upon them, and will give them to be removed and spoiled.

47 And the company shall stone them with stones, and dispatch them with their swords; they shall slay their sons and their daughters, and burn up their houses with fire.

48 Thus will I cause lewdness to cease out of the land, that all women may be taught not to do after your lewdness.

49 And they shall recompense your lewdness upon you, and ye shall bear the sins of your idols: and ye shall know that I *am* the Lord GOD.

**24** AGAIN IN the ninth year, in the tenth month, in the tenth *day* of the month, the word of the LORD come unto me, saying,

2 Son of man, write thee the name of the day, *even* of this same day: the king of Babylon set himself against Jerusalem this same day.

3 And utter a parable unto the rebellious house, and say unto them, Thus saith the Lord GOD; Set on a pot, set *it* on, and also pour water into it:

4 Gather the pieces thereof into it, *even* every good piece, the thigh, and the shoulder; fill *it* with the choice bones.

5 Take the choice of the flock, and burn also the bones under it, *and* make it boil well, and let them seethe the bones of it therein.

6 ¶ Wherefore thus saith the Lord GOD; Woe to the bloody city, to the pot whose scum *is* therein, and whose scum is not gone out of it! bring it out piece by piece; let no lot fall upon it.

7 For her blood is in the midst of her; she set it upon the top of a rock; she poured it not upon the ground, to cover it with dust;

8 That it might cause fury to come up to take vengeance; I have set her blood upon the top of a rock, that it should not be covered.

9 Therefore thus saith the Lord GOD; Woe to the bloody city! I will even make the pile for fire great.

10 Heap on wood, kindle the fire, consume the flesh, and spice it well, and let the bones be burned.

11 Then set it empty upon the coals thereof, that the brass of it may be hot, and may burn, and *that* the filthiness of it may be molten in it, *that* the scum of it may be consumed.

12 She hath wearied *herself* with lies, and her great scum went not forth out of her: her scum *shall be* in the fire.

13 In thy filthiness *is* lewdness: because I have purged thee, and thou wast not purged, thou shalt not be purged from thy filthiness any more, till I have caused my fury to rest upon thee.

## Amplified

44 Yet they went in to her, as they go in to a woman who plays the harlot; so they went in to Aholah and to Aholibah [Israel and Judah], the lewd women.

45 And the righteous men, they shall judge *and* condemn them to the punishment due to adulteresses, to women who shed blood, for they are adulteresses, and blood is upon their hands.

46 For thus says the Lord God: I will bring up a host upon them, and will give them over to be tossed to and fro and robbed.

47 And the host shall stone them with stones and cut them down with their swords; they shall slay their sons and their daughters, and burn up their houses with fire.

48 Thus will I cause lewdness to cease out of the land, that all women may be taught not to do after your lewdness.

49 Thus your lewdness shall be recompensed upon you, and you shall suffer the penalty for your sinful idolatry; and you shall know—understand and realize—that I am the Lord God.

**24** AGAIN IN the ninth year [of King Jehoiachin's captivity by Nebuchadnezzar of Babylon], in the tenth month, on the tenth day of the month, the word of the Lord came to me:

2 Son of man, record the name of the day, even of this same day; the king of Babylon set himself against *and* assailed Jerusalem this same day.

3 And utter a parable against the rebellious house [of Judah] and say to them, Thus says the Lord God: Set on a pot, set it on, and also pour water into it.

4 Put into it the pieces [of meat], all the good pieces, the thigh and the shoulder; fill it with the choice of the bones.

5 Take the choicest of the flock, and burn also the unused bones under it, and make it boil well, and seethe its bones in [the pot].

6 Therefore thus says the Lord God: Woe to the bloody city, to the pot whose rust *and* scum are in it, and whose rust *and* scum have not gone out of it! Take out of it piece by piece, without making any choice.

7 For the blood she has shed remains in the midst of her; she put it upon the bare rock; she did not pour it on the ground to cover it with dust.

8 That it may cause wrath to come up to take vengeance, I have put her blood [guilt for her children sacrificed to Molech] upon the bare rock, that it should not be covered.

9 Therefore thus says the Lord God: Woe to the blood-guilty city! Also I will make the pile [of fuel] great.

10 Heap on wood, kindle the fire *and* make it hot, boil well the meat *and* mix the spices, pour out the broth when thick, and let the bones be burned up.

11 Then set [the pot Jerusalem] back empty upon the coals, that the bronze of it may be hot and may glow, and the filthiness of it may be melted in it, and the rust *and* scum of it may be consumed.

12 She has wearied herself *and* Me with toil, yet her great rust *and* scum go not forth out of her; for however hotly the fire burns, her thick rust *and* filth will not go out of her by fire.

13 In your filthiness is abomination, *and therefore* because I would have cleansed you and you were not cleansed, you shall not be cleansed from your filthiness any more until I have satisfied My wrath against *and* upon you.

## New American Standard

44"But they went in to her as they would go in to a harlot. Thus
they went in to Oholah and to Oholibah, the lewd women.
45"But they, righteous men, will judge them with the judgment
of adulteresses, and with the judgment of women who shed blood,
because they are adulteresses and blood is on their hands.
46¶ "For thus says the Lord GOD, 'Bring up a company against
them, and give them over to terror and plunder.
47'And the company will stone them with stones and cut them
down with their swords; they will slay their sons and their daughters and burn their houses with fire.
48'Thus I shall make lewdness cease from the land, that all
women may be admonished and not commit lewdness as you have
done.
49'And your lewdness will be requited upon you, and you will
bear the penalty of *worshiping* your idols; thus you will know that
I am the Lord GOD.' "

*Parable of the Boiling Pot*

**24** AND THE word of the LORD came to me in the ninth year,
in the tenth month, on the tenth of the month, saying,
2"Son of man, write the name of the day, this very day. The
king of Babylon has laid siege to Jerusalem this very day.
3"And speak a parable to the rebellious house, and say to
them, 'Thus says the Lord GOD,

"Put on the pot, put *it* on, and also pour water in it;
4 Put in it the pieces,
Every good piece, the thigh, and the shoulder;
Fill *it* with choice bones.
5 "Take the choicest of the flock,
And also pile wood under the pot.
Make it boil vigorously.
Also seethe its bones in it."

6¶ 'Therefore, thus says the Lord GOD,
"Woe to the bloody city,
To the pot in which there is rust
And whose rust has not gone out of it!
Take out of it piece after piece,
Without making a choice.
7 "For her blood is in her midst;
She placed it on the bare rock;
She did not pour it on the ground
To cover it with dust.
8 "That it may cause wrath to come up to take vengeance,
I have put her blood on the bare rock,
That it may not be covered."
9 'Therefore, thus says the Lord GOD,
"Woe to the bloody city!
I also shall make the pile great.
10 "Heap on the wood, kindle the fire,
Boil the flesh well,
And mix in the spices,
And let the bones be burned.
11 "Then set it empty on its coals,
So that it may be hot,
And its bronze may glow,
And its filthiness may be melted in it,
Its rust consumed.
12 "She has wearied *Me* with toil,
Yet her great rust has not gone from her;
*Let* her rust *be* in the fire!
13 "In your filthiness is lewdness.
Because I *would* have cleansed you,
Yet you are not clean,
You will not be cleansed from your filthiness again,
Until I have spent My wrath on you.

## New International

tute, so they slept with those lewd women, Oholah and Oholibah.
45But righteous men will sentence them to the punishment of
women who commit adultery and shed blood, because they are
adulterous and blood is on their hands.
46"This is what the Sovereign LORD says: Bring a mob against
them and give them over to terror and plunder. 47The mob will
stone them and cut them down with their swords; they will kill
their sons and daughters and burn down their houses.
48"So I will put an end to lewdness in the land, that all women
may take warning and not imitate you. 49You will suffer the penalty for your lewdness and bear the consequences of your sins of
idolatry. Then you will know that I am the Sovereign LORD."

*The Cooking Pot*

**24** IN THE ninth year, in the tenth month on the tenth day,
the word of the LORD came to me: 2"Son of man, record
this date, this very date, because the king of Babylon has laid siege
to Jerusalem this very day. 3Tell this rebellious house a parable and
say to them: 'This is what the Sovereign LORD says:

" 'Put on the cooking pot; put it on
and pour water into it.
4Put into it the pieces of meat,
all the choice pieces—the leg and the shoulder.
Fill it with the best of these bones;
5 take the pick of the flock.
Pile wood beneath it for the bones;
bring it to a boil
and cook the bones in it.

6" 'For this is what the Sovereign LORD says:

" 'Woe to the city of bloodshed,
to the pot now encrusted,
whose deposit will not go away!
Empty it piece by piece
without casting lots for them.

7" 'For the blood she shed is in her midst:
She poured it on the bare rock;
she did not pour it on the ground,
where the dust would cover it.
8To stir up wrath and take revenge
I put her blood on the bare rock,
so that it would not be covered.

9" 'Therefore this is what the Sovereign LORD says:

" 'Woe to the city of bloodshed!
I, too, will pile the wood high.
10So heap on the wood
and kindle the fire.
Cook the meat well,
mixing in the spices;
and let the bones be charred.
11Then set the empty pot on the coals
till it becomes hot and its copper glows
so its impurities may be melted
and its deposit burned away.
12It has frustrated all efforts;
its heavy deposit has not been removed,
not even by fire.

13" 'Now your impurity is lewdness. Because I tried to cleanse
you but you would not be cleansed from your impurity, you will
not be clean again until my wrath against you has subsided.

## King James

14I the LORD have spoken *it:* it shall come to pass, and I will do
*it;* I will not go back, neither will I spare, neither will I repent;
according to thy ways, and according to thy doings, shall they
judge thee, saith the Lord GOD.
15¶ Also the word of the LORD came unto me, saying,
16Son of man, behold, I take away from thee the desire of thine
eyes with a stroke: yet neither shalt thou mourn nor weep, neither
shall thy tears run down.
17Forbear to cry, make no mourning for the dead, bind the tire
of thine head upon thee, and put on thy shoes upon thy feet, and
cover not *thy* lips, and eat not the bread of men.
18So I spake unto the people in the morning: and at even my
wife died; and I did in the morning as I was commanded.
19¶ And the people said unto me, Wilt thou not tell us what
these *things are* to us, that thou doest *so?*
20Then I answered them, The word of the LORD came unto me,
saying,
21Speak unto the house of Israel, Thus saith the Lord GOD;
Behold, I will profane my sanctuary, the excellency of your
strength, the desire of your eyes, and that which your soul pitieth;
and your sons and your daughters whom ye have left shall fall by
the sword.
22And ye shall do as I have done: ye shall not cover *your* lips,
nor eat the bread of men.
23And your tires *shall be* upon your heads, and your shoes upon
your feet: ye shall not mourn nor weep; but ye shall pine away for
your iniquities, and mourn one toward another.
24Thus Ezekiel is unto you a sign: according to all that he hath
done shall ye do: and when this cometh, ye shall know that I *am*
the Lord GOD.
25Also, thou son of man, *shall it* not *be* in the day when I take
from them their strength, the joy of their glory, the desire of their
eyes, and that whereupon they set their minds, their sons and
their daughters,
26 *That* he that escapeth in that day shall come unto thee, to
cause *thee* to hear *it* with *thine* ears?
27In that day shall thy mouth be opened to him which is escaped, and thou shalt speak, and be no more dumb: and thou shalt
be a sign unto them; and they shall know that I *am* the LORD.

## Amplified

14I the Lord have spoken it; it shall come to pass, and I will do
it; I will not go back, neither will I spare, neither will I relent;
according to your ways and according to your doings shall they
judge *and* punish you, says the Lord God.
15Also the word of the Lord came to me, saying,
16Son of man [Ezekiel], behold, I take away from you the desire
of your eyes [your wife] at a single stroke. Yet you shall neither
mourn nor weep, neither shall your tears flow.
17Sigh *and* groan, but not aloud—be silent; make no mourning
for the dead, bind your turban upon your head and put your shoes
on your feet, and do not cover your beard or eat the bread of
mourners [furnished by others].
18So I spoke to the people in the morning, and in the evening
my wife died; and I did the next morning as I was commanded.
19And the people said to me, Will you not tell us what these
things are supposed to mean to us, that you are acting as you do?
20Then I answered them, The word of the Lord came to me,
saying,
21Speak to the house of Israel, Thus says the Lord God: Behold,
I will profane My sanctuary, [in which you take] pride as your
strength, the desire of your eyes, and the pity and sympathy of
your soul—that you would spare with your life; and your sons and
your daughters whom you have left behind shall fall by the sword.
22And you shall do as I [Ezekiel] have done; you shall not cover
your beard nor eat the bread of mourning [brought you by others];
23And your turbans shall be upon your heads and your shoes
upon your feet; you shall not mourn or weep, but you shall pine
away for your iniquities—your guilt—and sigh *and* groan to one
another. [Lev. 26:39.]
24Thus Ezekiel is to you a sign; according to all that he has done
you shall do. And when this [destruction of the temple] comes,
you shall know, understand *and* realize that I am the Lord God [the
Sovereign Ruler, calling forth loyalty and obedient service].
25And you, son of man [Ezekiel], on the day when I take from
them [My temple] their strength *and* their stronghold, their joy and
their glory, the delight of their eyes and their hearts' chief desire,
and also *take* their sons and their daughters,
26On that day an escaped fugitive shall come to you to cause
you to hear of it [the destruction of Jerusalem] with your own ears.
27In that day your mouth shall be open to him who has escaped,
and you shall speak and be no more speechless; and you shall be
a sign to them, and they shall [a]know, understand *and* realize, that
I am the Lord.

## King James

**25** THE WORD of the LORD came again unto me, saying,
2Son of man, set thy face against the Ammonites, and
prophesy against them;
3And say unto the Ammonites, Hear the word of the Lord GOD;
Thus saith the Lord GOD; Because thou saidst, Aha, against my
sanctuary, when it was profaned; and against the land of Israel,
when it was desolate; and against the house of Judah, when they
went into captivity;
4Behold, therefore I will deliver thee to the men of the east for
a possession, and they shall set their palaces in thee, and make
their dwellings in thee: they shall eat thy fruit, and they shall drink
thy milk.
5And I will make Rabbah a stable for camels, and the Ammonites a couching place for flocks: and ye shall know that I *am* the
LORD.

## Amplified

**25** THE WORD of the Lord came again to me, saying,
2Son of man, set your face toward the Ammonites and
prophesy against them.
3And say to the Ammonites, Hear the word of the Lord God,
for thus says the Lord God: Because you said, Aha! over My
sanctuary when it was profaned, and over the land of Israel when
it was made desolate, and over the house of Judah when it went
into captivity *and* exile;
4Therefore behold, I am delivering you to the people of the East
for a possession, and they shall set their encampments among you
and make their dwellings in your midst; they shall eat your fruit,
and they shall drink your milk.
5And I will make Rabbah [your chief city] a stable for camels,
and *the cities* of the Ammonites a fold for flocks. And you shall
know, understand *and* realize, that I am the Lord [the Sovereign
Ruler, calling forth loyalty and obedient service].

**AMP** [a] On the basis of the fact that God uses it oftener than any other important word in the Bible, the word "Lord" becomes the most essential term in any language to the welfare of any person. It is not enough that one knows God is God, for only a fool would deny that (Ps. 53:1), but God demands of every person who is to be recognized by Him that he accept Him as Lord of his life, his Sovereign Ruler, to Whom he yields implicit obedience. When Thomas was able to say of Jesus, "My Lord and my God!" (John 20:28) his doubts ceased to exist. Nothing short of that meets God's demands. Watch for the word "Lord" in the Bible; it occurs around 5,000 times by actual count.

## New American Standard

14"I, the LORD, have spoken; it is coming and I shall act. I shall
not relent, and I shall not pity, and I shall not be sorry; according
to your ways and according to your deeds I shall judge you,"
declares the Lord GOD.' "

*Death of Ezekiel's Wife Is a Sign*

15¶ And the word of the LORD came to me saying,
16"Son of man, behold, I am about to take from you the desire
of your eyes with a blow; but you shall not mourn, and you shall
not weep, and your tears shall not come.
17"Groan silently; make no mourning for the dead. Bind on
your turban, and put your shoes on your feet, and do not cover
*your* mustache, and do not eat the bread of men."
18So I spoke to the people in the morning, and in the evening
my wife died. And in the morning I did as I was commanded.
19And the people said to me, "Will you not tell us what these
things that you are doing mean for us?"
20Then I said to them, "The word of the LORD came to me
saying,
21'Speak to the house of Israel, "Thus says the Lord GOD, 'Behold, I am about to profane My sanctuary, the pride of your power,
the desire of your eyes, and the delight of your soul; and your sons
and your daughters whom you have left behind will fall by the
sword.
22'And you will do as I have done; you will not cover *your*
mustache, and you will not eat the bread of men.
23'And your turbans will be on your heads and your shoes on
your feet. You will not mourn, and you will not weep; but you will
rot away in your iniquities, and you will groan to one another.
24'Thus Ezekiel will be a sign to you; according to all that he has
done you will do; when it comes, then you will know that I am the
Lord GOD.' "
25¶ 'As for you, son of man, will *it* not be on the day when I take
from them their stronghold, the joy of their pride, the desire of
their eyes, and their heart's delight, their sons and their daughters,
26that on that day he who escapes will come to you with information for *your* ears?
27'On that day your mouth will be opened to him who escaped,
and you will speak and be dumb no longer. Thus you will be a sign
to them, and they will know that I am the LORD.' "

*Judgment on Gentile Nations—Ammon*

**25** AND THE word of the LORD came to me saying,
2"Son of man, set your face toward the sons of Ammon,
and prophesy against them,
3and say to the sons of Ammon, 'Hear the word of the Lord
GOD! Thus says the Lord GOD, "Because you said, 'Aha!' against
My sanctuary when it was profaned, and against the land of Israel
when it was made desolate, and against the house of Judah when
they went into exile,
4therefore, behold, I am going to give you to the sons of the
east for a possession, and they will set their encampments among
you and make their dwellings among you; they will eat your fruit
and drink your milk.
5"And I shall make Rabbah a pasture for camels and the sons
of Ammon a resting place for flocks. Thus you will know that I am
the LORD."

## New International

14" 'I the LORD have spoken. The time has come for me to act.
I will not hold back; I will not have pity, nor will I relent. You will
be judged according to your conduct and your actions, declares the
Sovereign LORD.' "

*Ezekiel's Wife Dies*

15The word of the LORD came to me: 16"Son of man, with one
blow I am about to take away from you the delight of your eyes.
Yet do not lament or weep or shed any tears. 17Groan quietly; do
not mourn for the dead. Keep your turban fastened and your
sandals on your feet; do not cover the lower part of your face or
eat the customary food ⌊of mourners⌋."
18So I spoke to the people in the morning, and in the evening
my wife died. The next morning I did as I had been commanded.
19Then the people asked me, "Won't you tell us what these
things have to do with us?"
20So I said to them, "The word of the LORD came to me: 21Say
to the house of Israel, 'This is what the Sovereign LORD says: I am
about to desecrate my sanctuary—the stronghold in which you
take pride, the delight of your eyes, the object of your affection.
The sons and daughters you left behind will fall by the sword.
22And you will do as I have done. You will not cover the lower part
of your face or eat the customary food ⌊of mourners⌋. 23You will
keep your turbans on your heads and your sandals on your feet.
You will not mourn or weep but will waste away because of[b] your
sins and groan among yourselves. 24Ezekiel will be a sign to you;
you will do just as he has done. When this happens, you will know
that I am the Sovereign LORD.'
25"And you, son of man, on the day I take away their stronghold, their joy and glory, the delight of their eyes, their heart's
desire, and their sons and daughters as well— 26on that day a
fugitive will come to tell you the news. 27At that time your mouth
will be opened; you will speak with him and will no longer be
silent. So you will be a sign to them, and they will know that I am
the LORD."

*A Prophecy Against Ammon*

**25** THE WORD of the LORD came to me: 2"Son of man, set
your face against the Ammonites and prophesy against
them. 3Say to them, 'Hear the word of the Sovereign LORD. This
is what the Sovereign LORD says: Because you said "Aha!" over my
sanctuary when it was desecrated and over the land of Israel when
it was laid waste and over the people of Judah when they went into
exile, 4therefore I am going to give you to the people of the East
as a possession. They will set up their camps and pitch their tents
among you; they will eat your fruit and drink your milk. 5I will turn
Rabbah into a pasture for camels and Ammon into a resting place
for sheep. Then you will know that I am the LORD. 6For this is what

NIV b 23 Or *away in*

## King James

6For thus saith the Lord GOD; Because thou hast clapped *thine* hands, and stamped with the feet, and rejoiced in heart with all thy despite against the land of Israel;

7Behold, therefore I will stretch out mine hand upon thee, and will deliver thee for a spoil to the heathen; and I will cut thee off from the people, and I will cause thee to perish out of the countries: I will destroy thee; and thou shalt know that I *am* the LORD.

8¶ Thus saith the Lord GOD; Because that Moab and Seir do say, Behold, the house of Judah *is* like unto all the heathen;

9Therefore, behold, I will open the side of Moab from the cities, from his cities *which are* on his frontiers, the glory of the country, Beth-jeshimoth, Baal-meon, and Kiriathaim,

10Unto the men of the east with the Ammonites, and will give them in possession, that the Ammonites may not be remembered among the nations.

11And I will execute judgments upon Moab; and they shall know that I *am* the LORD.

12¶ Thus saith the Lord GOD; Because that Edom hath dealt against the house of Judah by taking vengeance, and hath greatly offended, and revenged himself upon them;

13Therefore thus saith the Lord GOD; I will also stretch out mine hand upon Edom, and will cut off man and beast from it; and I will make it desolate from Teman; and they of Dedan shall fall by the sword.

14And I will lay my vengeance upon Edom by the hand of my people Israel: and they shall do in Edom according to mine anger and according to my fury; and they shall know my vengeance, saith the Lord GOD.

15¶ Thus saith the Lord GOD; Because the Philistines have dealt by revenge, and have taken vengeance with a despiteful heart, to destroy *it* for the old hatred;

16Therefore thus saith the Lord GOD; Behold, I will stretch out mine hand upon the Philistines, and I will cut off the Cherethims, and destroy the remnant of the sea coast.

17And I will execute great vengeance upon them with furious rebukes; and they shall know that I *am* the LORD, when I shall lay my vengeance upon them.

**26** AND IT came to pass in the eleventh year, in the first *day* of the month, *that* the word of the LORD came unto me, saying,

2Son of man, because that Tyrus hath said against Jerusalem, Aha, she is broken *that was* the gates of the people: she is turned unto me: I shall be replenished, *now* she is laid waste:

3Therefore thus saith the Lord GOD; Behold, I *am* against thee, O Tyrus, and will cause many nations to come up against thee, as the sea causeth his waves to come up.

4And they shall destroy the walls of Tyrus, and break down her towers: I will also scrape her dust from her, and make her like the top of a rock.

5It shall be *a place for* the spreading of nets in the midst of the sea: for I have spoken *it*, saith the Lord GOD: and it shall become a spoil to the nations.

**AMP** [a] To prevent Nebuchadnezzar from getting her valuables, Tyre transported herself to an island a half mile out in the sea. The conqueror destroyed the city and left. But more than two centuries later, Alexander the Great took the ruins of the old city, even scraping up the dust, and made a causeway to the island, thus fulfilling the prophecy exactly.

## Amplified

6For thus says the Lord God: Because you have clapped your hands and stamped with the feet and rejoiced *in heart* with all the contempt, malice *and* spite that is in you against the land of Israel,

7Therefore, behold, I have stretched out My hand against you and will hand you over for a prey *and* a spoil to the nations, and I will cut you off from the peoples and will cause you to perish *and* be lost out of the countries; I will destroy you. Then will you know—understand and realize—that I am the Lord [the Sovereign Ruler, calling forth loyalty and obedient service]. [Ezek. 21:28-32; Jer. 49:1-6; Amos 1:13-15; Zeph. 2:8-11.]

8Thus says the Lord God: Because Moab says, as does Seir [Edom], Behold, the house of Judah is like all the [heathen] nations,

9Therefore, behold, I will lay open the flank of Moab from the cities, from its cities on its frontiers *and* in every quarter, the glory of the country, Bethjeshimoth, Baalmeon, and Kiriathaim.

10I will give it along with the children of Ammon to the people of the East for a possession, that it *and* the children of Ammon may not be [any more seriously] remembered among the nations.

11And I will execute judgments *and* punishments upon Moab; and they shall know—understand and realize—that I am the Lord [the Sovereign Ruler, calling forth loyalty and obedient service]. [Isa. 15 and 16; Jer. 48; Amos 2:1-3; Zeph. 2:8-11.]

12Thus says the Lord God: Because Edom has dealt against the house of Judah by taking vengeance and has greatly offended *and* has become doubly guilty by himself taking revenge upon them,

13Therefore thus says the Lord God: I will also stretch out My hand against Edom, and will cut off *and* root out man and beast from it; and I will make it desolate; from Teman even to Dedan they shall fall by the sword.

14And I will lay My vengeance upon Edom by the hand of My people Israel; and they shall do upon Edom according to My anger and according to My wrath; and they shall know My vengeance, says the Lord God. [Ezek. 35; Isa. 34; Amos 1:11, 12; Obad.]

15Thus says the Lord God: Because the Philistines have dealt revengefully and have taken vengeance contemptuously, with malice *and* spite in their hearts, to destroy in perpetual enmity;

16Therefore thus says the Lord God: Behold, I will stretch out My hand against the Philistines, and I will cut off the Cherethites [an immigration in Philistia] and destroy the remainder of the seacoast.

17And I will execute great vengeance upon them with wrathful rebukes *and* chastisements; and they shall know—understand and realize—that I am the Lord, when I lay My vengeance upon them. [Isa. 14:29-31; Jer. 47; Amos 1:6-8; Zeph. 2:4-7; Zech. 9:5-7.]

**26** AND IN the eleventh year, on the first day of the month [after the carrying away of King Jehoiachin], the word of the Lord came to me:

2Son of man, because Tyre has said against Jerusalem, Aha! She is broken that has been the gate of the people; she is open to me [Tyre]; I shall become full, now that she is desolate *and* a waste land,

3Therefore thus says the Lord God: Behold, I am against you, O Tyre, and will cause many nations to come up against you, as the sea mounts up by its waves.

4And they shall destroy the walls of Tyre, and break down her towers; I will also [a]scrape her dust from her, and make her *bare* like the top of a rock.

5Her island in the midst of the sea shall become a place for the spreading of nets, for I have spoken it, says the Lord God; and she shall become a spoil *and* a prey to the nations.

## New American Standard

6'For thus says the Lord GOD, "Because you have clapped your
hands and stamped your feet and rejoiced with all the scorn of
your soul against the land of Israel,
7therefore, behold, I have stretched out My hand against you,
and I shall give you for spoil to the nations. And I shall cut you
off from the peoples and make you perish from the lands; I shall
destroy you. Thus you will know that I am the LORD."

*Moab*

8¶ 'Thus says the Lord GOD, "Because Moab and Seir say,
'Behold, the house of Judah is like all the nations,'
9therefore, behold, I am going to deprive the flank of Moab of
*its* cities, of its cities which are on its frontiers, the glory of the land,
Beth-jeshimoth, Baal-meon, and Kiriathaim,
10and I will give it for a possession, along with the sons of
Ammon, to the sons of the east, that the sons of Ammon may not
be remembered among the nations.
11"Thus I will execute judgments on Moab, and they will know
that I am the LORD."

*Edom*

12¶ 'Thus says the Lord GOD, "Because Edom has acted against
the house of Judah by taking vengeance, and has incurred grievous guilt, and avenged themselves upon them,"
13therefore, thus says the Lord GOD, "I will also stretch out My
hand against Edom and cut off man and beast from it. And I will
lay it waste; from Teman even to Dedan they will fall by the sword.
14"And I will lay My vengeance on Edom by the hand of My
people Israel. Therefore, they will act in Edom according to My
anger and according to My wrath; thus they will know My vengeance," declares the Lord GOD.

*Philistia*

15¶ 'Thus says the Lord GOD, "Because the Philistines have
acted in revenge and have taken vengeance with scorn of soul to
destroy with everlasting enmity,"
16therefore, thus says the Lord GOD, "Behold, I will stretch out
My hand against the Philistines, even cut off the Cherethites and
destroy the remnant of the seacoast.
17"And I will execute great vengeance on them with wrathful
rebukes; and they will know that I am the LORD when I lay My
vengeance on them." ' "

*Judgment on Tyre*

**26** NOW IT came about in the eleventh year, on the first of
the month, that the word of the LORD came to me saying,
2"Son of man, because Tyre has said concerning Jerusalem,
'Aha, the gateway of the peoples is broken; it has opened to me.
I shall be filled, *now that* she is laid waste,'
3therefore, thus says the Lord GOD, 'Behold, I am against you,
O Tyre, and I will bring up many nations against you, as the sea
brings up its waves.
4'And they will destroy the walls of Tyre and break down her
towers; and I will scrape her debris from her and make her a bare
rock.
5'She will be a place for the spreading of nets in the midst of
the sea, for I have spoken,' declares the Lord GOD, 'and she will
become spoil for the nations.

## New International

the Sovereign LORD says: Because you have clapped your hands
and stamped your feet, rejoicing with all the malice of your heart
against the land of Israel, 7therefore I will stretch out my hand
against you and give you as plunder to the nations. I will cut you
off from the nations and exterminate you from the countries. I will
destroy you, and you will know that I am the LORD.' "

*A Prophecy Against Moab*

8"This is what the Sovereign LORD says: 'Because Moab and Seir
said, "Look, the house of Judah has become like all the other
nations," 9therefore I will expose the flank of Moab, beginning at
its frontier towns—Beth Jeshimoth, Baal Meon and Kiriathaim—
the glory of that land. 10I will give Moab along with the Ammonites
to the people of the East as a possession, so that the Ammonites
will not be remembered among the nations; 11and I will inflict
punishment on Moab. Then they will know that I am the LORD.' "

*A Prophecy Against Edom*

12"This is what the Sovereign LORD says: 'Because Edom took
revenge on the house of Judah and became very guilty by doing
so, 13therefore this is what the Sovereign LORD says: I will stretch
out my hand against Edom and kill its men and their animals. I will
lay it waste, and from Teman to Dedan they will fall by the sword.
14I will take vengeance on Edom by the hand of my people Israel,
and they will deal with Edom in accordance with my anger and my
wrath; they will know my vengeance, declares the Sovereign
LORD.' "

*A Prophecy Against Philistia*

15"This is what the Sovereign LORD says: 'Because the Philistines acted in vengeance and took revenge with malice in their
hearts, and with ancient hostility sought to destroy Judah, 16there-
fore this is what the Sovereign LORD says: I am about to stretch out
my hand against the Philistines, and I will cut off the Kerethites
and destroy those remaining along the coast. 17I will carry out
great vengeance on them and punish them in my wrath. Then they
will know that I am the LORD, when I take vengeance on them.' "

*A Prophecy Against Tyre*

**26** IN THE eleventh year, on the first day of the month, the
word of the LORD came to me: 2"Son of man, because Tyre
has said of Jerusalem, 'Aha! The gate to the nations is broken, and
its doors have swung open to me; now that she lies in ruins I will
prosper,' 3therefore this is what the Sovereign LORD says: I am
against you, O Tyre, and I will bring many nations against you,
like the sea casting up its waves. 4They will destroy the walls of
Tyre and pull down her towers; I will scrape away her rubble and
make her a bare rock. 5Out in the sea she will become a place to
spread fishnets, for I have spoken, declares the Sovereign LORD.
She will become plunder for the nations, 6and her settlements on

## King James

6And her daughters which *are* in the field shall be slain by the sword; and they shall know that I *am* the LORD.

7¶ For thus saith the Lord GOD; Behold, I will bring upon Tyrus Nebuchadrezzar king of Babylon, a king of kings, from the north, with horses, and with chariots, and with horsemen, and companies, and much people.

8He shall slay with the sword thy daughters in the field: and he shall make a fort against thee, and cast a mount against thee, and lift up the buckler against thee.

9And he shall set engines of war against thy walls, and with his axes he shall break down thy towers.

10By reason of the abundance of his horses their dust shall cover thee: thy walls shall shake at the noise of the horsemen, and of the wheels, and of the chariots, when he shall enter into thy gates, as men enter into a city wherein is made a breach.

11With the hoofs of his horses shall he tread down all thy streets: he shall slay thy people by the sword, and thy strong garrisons shall go down to the ground.

12And they shall make a spoil of thy riches, and make a prey of thy merchandise: and they shall break down thy walls, and destroy thy pleasant houses: and they shall lay thy stones and thy timber and thy dust in the midst of the water.

13And I will cause the noise of thy songs to cease; and the sound of thy harps shall be no more heard.

14And I will make thee like the top of a rock: thou shalt be *a place* to spread nets upon; thou shalt be built no more: for I the LORD have spoken *it*, saith the Lord GOD.

15¶ Thus saith the Lord GOD to Tyrus; Shall not the isles shake at the sound of thy fall, when the wounded cry, when the slaughter is made in the midst of thee?

16Then all the princes of the sea shall come down from their thrones, and lay away their robes, and put off their broidered garments: they shall clothe themselves with trembling; they shall sit upon the ground, and shall tremble at *every* moment, and be astonished at thee.

17And they shall take up a lamentation for thee, and say to thee, How art thou destroyed, *that wast* inhabited of seafaring men, the renowned city, which wast strong in the sea, she and her inhabitants, which cause their terror *to be* on all that haunt it!

18Now shall the isles tremble in the day of thy fall; yea, the isles that *are* in the sea shall be troubled at thy departure.

19For thus saith the Lord GOD; When I shall make thee a desolate city, like the cities that are not inhabited; when I shall bring up the deep upon thee, and great waters shall cover thee;

20When I shall bring thee down with them that descend into the pit, with the people of old time, and shall set thee in the low parts of the earth, in places desolate of old, with them that go down to the pit, that thou be not inhabited; and I shall set glory in the land of the living;

21I will make thee a terror, and thou *shalt be* no *more:* though thou be sought for, yet shalt thou never be found again, saith the Lord GOD.

## Amplified

6And Tyre's daughters [her towns and villages on the mainland] in the level place shall be slain by the sword, and they shall know—understand and realize—that I am the Lord [the Sovereign Ruler, calling forth loyalty and obedient service].

7For thus says the Lord God: Behold, I will bring from the north upon Tyre Nebuchadrezzar king of Babylon, a king of kings, with horses and chariots, and with horsemen and a host of many people.

8He shall slay with the sword your daughters [the towns and villages] in the level area [on the mainland]; and he shall make a fortified wall against you, and cast up a siege mound against you, and raise up a roof of bucklers *and* shields as a defense against you.

9And he shall set his battering engines in shock against your walls, and with his axes he will break down your towers.

10Because of the great number of [a][Nebuchadrezzar's] horses their dust will cover you; your walls, [O Tyre,] will shake at the noise of the horsemen and of the wagon wheels and of the chariots, when he enters into your gates as men enter into the city in whose walls there has been made a breach.

11With the hoofs of his horses [Nebuchadrezzar] will trample all your streets; he will slay your people with the sword, and your strong pillars *or* obelisks will fall to the ground.

12And [your adversaries] shall make a spoil of your riches, and make booty of your merchandise. And they shall break down your walls, and destroy your pleasant houses; and they shall lay the stones and the timber and the very dust from your demolished city out in the midst of the water [between the island and the mainland city site to make a causeway].

13And I will cause the noise of your songs to cease; and the sound of your lyres shall be no more heard.

14And I will make you, [Tyre,] a [b]bare rock; you shall be a place upon which to spread nets; you shall never be rebuilt; for I the Lord have spoken it, says the Lord God.

15Thus says the Lord God to Tyre: Shall not the isles *and* coastlands shake at the sound of your fall, when the wounded groan, when the slaughter is made in the midst of you?

16Then all the princes of the sea shall come down from their thrones, and lay aside their robes, and strip off their embroidered garments; they shall clothe themselves with tremblings; they shall sit upon the ground, and shall tremble every moment and be astonished at you *and* appalled.

17They shall take up a lamentation over you and say to you, How you are destroyed *and* vanished, you that were won from the seas *and* inhabited by seafaring men, the renowned city, that was mighty on the sea, she and her inhabitants, which caused their terror to fall upon all who dwell there!

18Now the isles *and* coastlands tremble in the day of your fall; yes, the isles that are in the sea are troubled *and* dismayed at your departure.

19For thus says the Lord God: When I make you a desolate city like the cities that are not inhabited, when I bring up the deep over you, and great waters cover you,

20Then I will thrust you down with those who descend into the pit, to the people of olden times, and will make you, [Tyre,] to dwell in the lower world, like the places that were desolate of old, with those who go down to the pit [the place of the dead], that you be not inhabited or shed forth your glory *and* renown in the land of the living.

21I will make you a terror—bring you to a dreadful end—and you shall be no more. Though you be sought for, yet you shall never be found again, says the Lord God.

**AMP** [a] See footnote on Jeremiah 44:30. [b] According to Herodotus, Tyre's history began in B.C. 2750. It was a fortified city in Joshua's time (Josh. 19:29), and later became a great maritime commercial center. Yet Jeremiah (27:2-7; 47:4) and Ezekiel (26:3-21; 28:6-10) foretold utter destruction for Tyre, naming not less than twenty-five separate details, each of which in the following centuries came true literally. Mathematicians have estimated, according to the Law of Compound Probabilities, that if a prophecy concerning a person, place, or event has twenty-five details beyond the possibility of human calculation, collusion, collaboration, comprehension, and coincidence, there is only one chance in more than thirty-three and one-half millions of its accidental fulfillment. Yet Tyre's history at the hands of Nebuchadnezzar, then centuries later at the hands of Alexander the Great, and centuries after that at the hands of the Crusaders, was the striking fulfillment of each detail of the prophets' forecasts. Nor could any other city in the world's history have fulfilled them. The authenticity of God's Word leaves no chance for sane denial.

## New American Standard

6'Also her daughters who are on the mainland will be slain by
the sword, and they will know that I am the LORD.' "
7¶ For thus says the Lord GOD, "Behold, I will bring upon Tyre
from the north Nebuchadnezzar king of Babylon, king of kings,
with horses, chariots, cavalry, and a great army.
8"He will slay your daughters on the mainland with the sword;
and he will make siege walls against you, cast up a mound against
you, and raise up a large shield against you.
9"And the blow of his battering rams he will direct against your
walls, and with his axes he will break down your towers.
10"Because of the multitude of his horses, the dust *raised by*
them will cover you; your walls will shake at the noise of cavalry
and wagons and chariots, when he enters your gates as men enter
a city that is breached.
11"With the hoofs of his horses he will trample all your streets.
He will slay your people with the sword; and your strong pillars
will come down to the ground.
12"Also they will make a spoil of your riches and a prey of your
merchandise, break down your walls and destroy your pleasant
houses, and throw your stones and your timbers and your debris
into the water.
13"So I will silence the sound of your songs, and the sound of
your harps will be heard no more.
14"And I will make you a bare rock; you will be a place for the
spreading of nets. You will be built no more, for I the LORD have
spoken," declares the Lord GOD.
15¶ Thus says the Lord GOD to Tyre, "Shall not the coastlands
shake at the sound of your fall when the wounded groan, when
the slaughter occurs in your midst?
16"Then all the princes of the sea will go down from their
thrones, remove their robes, and strip off their embroidered garments. They will clothe themselves with trembling; they will sit on
the ground, tremble every moment, and be appalled at you.
17"And they will take up a lamentation over you and say to you,

'How you have perished, O inhabited one,
From the seas, O renowned city,
Which was mighty on the sea,
She and her inhabitants,
Who imposed her terror
On all her inhabitants!
18 'Now the coastlands will tremble
On the day of your fall;
Yes, the coastlands which are by the sea
Will be terrified at your passing.' "

19For thus says the Lord GOD, "When I shall make you a desolate city, like the cities which are not inhabited, when I shall bring
up the deep over you, and the great waters will cover you,
20then I shall bring you down with those who go down to the
pit, to the people of old, and I shall make you dwell in the lower
parts of the earth, like the ancient waste places, with those who
go down to the pit, so that you will not be inhabited; but I shall
set glory in the land of the living.
21"I shall bring terrors on you, and you will be no more; though
you will be sought, you will never be found again," declares the
Lord GOD.

## New International

the mainland will be ravaged by the sword. Then they will know
that I am the LORD.
7"For this is what the Sovereign LORD says: From the north I am
going to bring against Tyre Nebuchadnezzar[c] king of Babylon,
king of kings, with horses and chariots, with horsemen and a great
army. 8He will ravage your settlements on the mainland with the
sword; he will set up siege works against you, build a ramp up to
your walls and raise his shields against you. 9He will direct the
blows of his battering rams against your walls and demolish your
towers with his weapons. 10His horses will be so many that they
will cover you with dust. Your walls will tremble at the noise of
the war horses, wagons and chariots when he enters your gates
as men enter a city whose walls have been broken through. 11The
hoofs of his horses will trample all your streets; he will kill your
people with the sword, and your strong pillars will fall to the
ground. 12They will plunder your wealth and loot your merchandise; they will break down your walls and demolish your fine
houses and throw your stones, timber and rubble into the sea. 13I
will put an end to your noisy songs, and the music of your harps
will be heard no more. 14I will make you a bare rock, and you will
become a place to spread fishnets. You will never be rebuilt, for
I the LORD have spoken, declares the Sovereign LORD.
15"This is what the Sovereign LORD says to Tyre: Will not the
coastlands tremble at the sound of your fall, when the wounded
groan and the slaughter takes place in you? 16Then all the princes
of the coast will step down from their thrones and lay aside their
robes and take off their embroidered garments. Clothed with terror, they will sit on the ground, trembling every moment, appalled
at you. 17Then they will take up a lament concerning you and say
to you:

" 'How you are destroyed, O city of renown,
peopled by men of the sea!
You were a power on the seas,
you and your citizens;
you put your terror
on all who lived there.
18Now the coastlands tremble
on the day of your fall;
the islands in the sea
are terrified at your collapse.'

19"This is what the Sovereign LORD says: When I make you a
desolate city, like cities no longer inhabited, and when I bring the
ocean depths over you and its vast waters cover you, 20then I will
bring you down with those who go down to the pit, to the people
of long ago. I will make you dwell in the earth below, as in ancient
ruins, with those who go down to the pit, and you will not return
or take your place[d] in the land of the living. 21I will bring you to
a horrible end and you will be no more. You will be sought, but
you will never again be found, declares the Sovereign LORD."

**NIV** [c] 7 Hebrew *Nebuchadrezzar,* of which *Nebuchadnezzar* is a variant; here and often in Ezekiel and Jeremiah [d] 20 Septuagint; Hebrew *return, and I will give glory*

## King James

**27** THE WORD of the LORD came again unto me, saying,
2Now, thou son of man, take up a lamentation for Tyrus;

3And say unto Tyrus, O thou that art situate at the entry of the sea, *which art* a merchant of the people for many isles, Thus saith the Lord GOD; O Tyrus, thou hast said, I *am* of perfect beauty.

4Thy borders *are* in the midst of the seas, thy builders have perfected thy beauty.

5They have made all thy *ship* boards of fir trees of Senir: they have taken cedars from Lebanon to make masts for thee.

6 *Of* the oaks of Bashan have they made thine oars; the company of the Ashurites have made thy benches *of* ivory, *brought* out of the isles of Chittim.

7Fine linen with broidered work from Egypt was that which thou spreadest forth to be thy sail; blue and purple from the isles of Elishah was that which covered thee.

8The inhabitants of Zidon and Arvad were thy mariners: thy wise *men*, O Tyrus, *that* were in thee, were thy pilots.

9The ancients of Gebal and the wise *men* thereof were in thee thy calkers: all the ships of the sea with their mariners were in thee to occupy thy merchandise.

10They of Persia and of Lud and of Phut were in thine army, thy men of war: they hanged the shield and helmet in thee; they set forth thy comeliness.

11The men of Arvad with thine army *were* upon thy walls round about, and the Gammadims were in thy towers: they hanged their shields upon thy walls round about; they have made thy beauty perfect.

12Tarshish *was* thy merchant by reason of the multitude of all *kind of* riches; with silver, iron, tin, and lead, they traded in thy fairs.

13Javan, Tubal, and Meshech, they *were* thy merchants: they traded the persons of men and vessels of brass in thy market.

14They of the house of Togarmah traded in thy fairs with horses and horsemen and mules.

15The men of Dedan *were* thy merchants; many isles *were* the merchandise of thine hand: they brought thee *for* a present horns of ivory and ebony.

16Syria *was* thy merchant by reason of the multitude of the wares of thy making: they occupied in thy fairs with emeralds, purple, and broidered work, and fine linen, and coral, and agate.

17Judah, and the land of Israel, they *were* thy merchants: they traded in thy market wheat of Minnith, and Pannag, and honey, and oil, and balm.

18Damascus *was* thy merchant in the multitude of the wares of thy making, for the multitude of all riches; in the wine of Helbon, and white wool.

19Dan also and Javan going to and fro occupied in thy fairs: bright iron, cassia, and calamus, were in thy market.

20Dedan *was* thy merchant in precious clothes for chariots.

21Arabia, and all the princes of Kedar, they occupied with thee in lambs, and rams, and goats: in these *were they* thy merchants.

22The merchants of Sheba and Raamah, they *were* thy merchants: they occupied in thy fairs with chief of all spices, and with all precious stones, and gold.

## Amplified

**27** THE WORD of the Lord came again to me:
2Now you, son of man, take up a lamentation over Tyre,

3And say to Tyre, O you who dwell at the entrance to the sea, who are merchant of the peoples of many islands *and* coastlands, thus says the Lord God: O Tyre, you have thought *and* said, I am perfect in beauty.

4Your borders are in the heart of the seas; your builders have perfected your beauty.

5They have made all your planks *and* boards of fir trees from Senir [a peak of Mount Hermon]; they have taken a cedar from Lebanon to make a mast for you.

6Of the oaks of Bashan they have made your oars; they made your deck *and* benches of boxwood from the coasts of Cyprus, inlaid with ivory.

7Of fine linen with embroidered work from Egypt was your sail, that it might be an ensign for you; blue and purple from the coasts of Elishah [of Asia Minor] was the [ship's] awning which covered you.

8The inhabitants of Sidon and [the island] of Arvad were your oarsmen; your skilled *and* wise men, O Tyre, were in you, they were your pilots.

9The old men of Gebal [a city north of Sidon] and its skilled *and* wise men in you were your calkers; all the ships of the sea with their mariners were in you to deal in your merchandise *and* trading.

10Persia and Lud and Put were in your army as your men of war; they hung the shield and helmet in you; they gave you beauty *and* splendor.

11The men of Arvad with your army were upon your walls round about, and valorous men [of Gamad] were in your towers; they hung their shields upon your walls round about; they have perfected your beauty *and* splendor.

12Tarshish [in Spain] carried on traffic with you because of the abundance of your riches of all kinds; with silver, iron, tin, and lead they traded for your wares.

13Javan [Greece], Tubal, and Meshech [in the mountainous region between the Black and Caspian Seas] traded with you. They exchanged the persons of men [taken as slaves], and vessels of bronze for your merchandise.

14They of the house of Togarmah [Armenia] traded for your wares with [chariot] horses, cavalry horses and mules.

15The men of Dedan [in Arabia] traded with you; many islands *and* coastlands were your own markets; they brought you in payment *or* as presents ivory tusks and ebony.

16Aram [Syria or Mesopotamia] *and* Edom traded with you because of the multitude of the wares of your making. They exchanged for your merchandise emeralds, purple, embroidered work, fine linen, coral, and agate *or* rubies.

17Judah and the land of Israel, they were your traders; they exchanged in your market wheat of Minnith [in Ammon], olives *or* early figs, honey, oil, and balm.

18Damascus traded with you because of your abundance of supplies of your handiworks and the immense wealth of every kind, with wine of Helbon [Aleppo], and white wool *of Sachar* [in Syria].

19Vedan also and [Arabic] Javan traded with yarn *from* Uzal [in Arabia] for your wares; wrought iron, cassia, and calamus were exchanged for your merchandise.

20Dedan supplied you with precious [saddle] cloths for riding.

21Arabia and all the princes of Kedar, they were the merchants in lambs, rams, and goats favored by you; in these they traded with you.

22The merchants of Sheba and Raamah [in Arabia] traded with you; they exchanged for your wares the choicest of all kinds of spices and all precious stones, and gold.

## New American Standard

*Lament over Tyre*

27 MOREOVER, THE word of the LORD came to me saying,
2"And you, son of man, take up a lamentation over Tyre;
3and say to Tyre, who dwells at the entrance to the sea, merchant of the peoples to many coastlands, 'Thus says the Lord GOD,
"O Tyre, you have said, 'I am perfect in beauty.'
4 "Your borders are in the heart of the seas;
Your builders have perfected your beauty.
5 "They have made all *your* planks of fir trees from Senir;
They have taken a cedar from Lebanon to make a mast for you.
6 "Of oaks from Bashan they have made your oars;
With ivory they have inlaid your deck of boxwood from the coastlands of Cyprus.
7 "Your sail was of fine embroidered linen from Egypt
So that it became your distinguishing mark;
Your awning was blue and purple from the coastlands of Elishah.
8 "The inhabitants of Sidon and Arvad were your rowers;
Your wise men, O Tyre, were aboard; they were your pilots.
9 "The elders of Gebal and her wise men were with you repairing your seams;
All the ships of the sea and their sailors were with you in order to deal in your merchandise.

10¶ "Persia and Lud and Put were in your army, your men of war. They hung shield and helmet in you; they set forth your splendor.

11"The sons of Arvad and your army were on your walls, *all* around, and the Gammadim were in your towers. They hung their shields on your walls, *all* around; they perfected your beauty.

12¶ "Tarshish was your customer because of the abundance of all *kinds* of wealth; with silver, iron, tin, and lead, they paid for your wares.

13"Javan, Tubal, and Meshech, they were your traders; with the lives of men and vessels of bronze they paid for your merchandise.

14"Those from Beth-togarmah gave horses and war horses and mules for your wares.

15"The sons of Dedan were your traders. Many coastlands were your market; ivory tusks and ebony they brought as your payment.

16"Aram was your customer because of the abundance of your goods; they paid for your wares with emeralds, purple, embroidered work, fine linen, coral, and rubies.

17"Judah and the land of Israel, they were your traders; with the wheat of Minnith, cakes, honey, oil, and balm they paid for your merchandise.

18"Damascus was your customer because of the abundance of your goods, because of the abundance of all *kinds* of wealth, because of the wine of Helbon and white wool.

19"Vedan and Javan paid for your wares from Uzal; wrought iron, cassia, and sweet cane were among your merchandise.

20"Dedan traded with you in saddlecloths for riding.

21"Arabia and all the princes of Kedar, they were your customers for lambs, rams, and goats; for these they were your customers.

22"The traders of Sheba and Raamah, they traded with you; they paid for your wares with the best of all *kinds* of spices, and with all *kinds* of precious stones, and gold.

## New International

*A Lament for Tyre*

27 THE WORD of the LORD came to me: 2"Son of man, take up a lament concerning Tyre. 3Say to Tyre, situated at the gateway to the sea, merchant of peoples on many coasts, 'This is what the Sovereign LORD says:

" 'You say, O Tyre,
"I am perfect in beauty."
4Your domain was on the high seas;
your builders brought your beauty to perfection.
5They made all your timbers
of pine trees from Senir[a];
they took a cedar from Lebanon
to make a mast for you.
6Of oaks from Bashan
they made your oars;
of cypress wood[b] from the coasts of Cyprus[c]
they made your deck, inlaid with ivory.
7Fine embroidered linen from Egypt was your sail
and served as your banner;
your awnings were of blue and purple
from the coasts of Elishah.
8Men of Sidon and Arvad were your oarsmen;
your skilled men, O Tyre, were aboard as your seamen.
9Veteran craftsmen of Gebal[d] were on board
as shipwrights to caulk your seams.
All the ships of the sea and their sailors
came alongside to trade for your wares.
10" 'Men of Persia, Lydia and Put
served as soldiers in your army.
They hung their shields and helmets on your walls,
bringing you splendor.
11Men of Arvad and Helech
manned your walls on every side;
men of Gammad
were in your towers.
They hung their shields around your walls;
they brought your beauty to perfection.

12" 'Tarshish did business with you because of your great wealth of goods; they exchanged silver, iron, tin and lead for your merchandise.

13" 'Greece, Tubal and Meshech traded with you; they exchanged slaves and articles of bronze for your wares.

14" 'Men of Beth Togarmah exchanged work horses, war horses and mules for your merchandise.

15" 'The men of Rhodes[e] traded with you, and many coastlands were your customers; they paid you with ivory tusks and ebony.

16" 'Aram[f] did business with you because of your many products; they exchanged turquoise, purple fabric, embroidered work, fine linen, coral and rubies for your merchandise.

17" 'Judah and Israel traded with you; they exchanged wheat from Minnith and confections,[g] honey, oil and balm for your wares.

18" 'Damascus, because of your many products and great wealth of goods, did business with you in wine from Helbon and wool from Zahar.

19" 'Danites and Greeks from Uzal bought your merchandise; they exchanged wrought iron, cassia and calamus for your wares.

20" 'Dedan traded in saddle blankets with you.

21" 'Arabia and all the princes of Kedar were your customers; they did business with you in lambs, rams and goats.

22" 'The merchants of Sheba and Raamah traded with you; for your merchandise they exchanged the finest of all kinds of spices and precious stones, and gold.

NIV [a] 5 That is, Hermon [b] 6 Targum; the Masoretic Text has a different division of the consonants. [c] 6 Hebrew *Kittim* [d] 9 That is, Byblos [e] *15* Septuagint; Hebrew *Dedan* [f] *16* Most Hebrew manuscripts; some Hebrew manuscripts and Syriac *Edom* [g] *17* The meaning of the Hebrew for this word is uncertain.

## King James

23Haran, and Canneh, and Eden, the merchants of Sheba,
Asshur, *and* Chilmad, *were* thy merchants.
24These *were* thy merchants in all sorts *of things*, in blue clothes,
and broidered work, and in chests of rich apparel, bound with
cords, and made of cedar, among thy merchandise.
25The ships of Tarshish did sing of thee in thy market: and thou
wast replenished, and made very glorious in the midst of the seas.
26¶ Thy rowers have brought thee into great waters: the east
wind hath broken thee in the midst of the seas.
27Thy riches, and thy fairs, thy merchandise, thy mariners, and
thy pilots, thy calkers, and the occupiers of thy merchandise, and
all thy men of war, that *are* in thee, and in all thy company which
*is* in the midst of thee, shall fall into the midst of the seas in the
day of thy ruin.
28The suburbs shall shake at the sound of the cry of thy pilots.
29And all that handle the oar, the mariners, *and* all the pilots of
the sea, shall come down from their ships, they shall stand upon
the land;
30And shall cause their voice to be heard against thee, and shall
cry bitterly, and shall cast up dust upon their heads, they shall
wallow themselves in the ashes:
31And they shall make themselves utterly bald for thee, and
gird them with sackcloth, and they shall weep for thee with bitterness of heart *and* bitter wailing.
32And in their wailing they shall take up a lamentation for thee,
and lament over thee, *saying*, What *city is* like Tyrus, like the
destroyed in the midst of the sea?
33When thy wares went forth out of the seas, thou filledst many
people; thou didst enrich the kings of the earth with the multitude
of thy riches and of thy merchandise.
34In the time *when* thou shalt be broken by the seas in the depths
of the waters thy merchandise and all thy company in the midst
of thee shall fall.
35All the inhabitants of the isles shall be astonished at thee, and
their kings shall be sore afraid, they shall be troubled in *their*
countenance.
36The merchants among the people shall hiss at thee; thou shalt
be a terror, and never *shalt be* any more.

## Amplified

23Haran and Canneh and Eden [in Mesopotamia], the merchants of Sheba [on the Euphrates], Asshur, and Chilmad [near
Bagdad] were your traders.
24These traded with you in choice fabrics, in bales *of* garments
of blue and embroidered work, and in treasures of many colored
rich damask *and* carpets bound with cords and made firm; in these
they traded with you.
25The ships of Tarshish were your caravans for your merchandise, and you were replenished, [Tyre,] and were heavily loaded
*and* made an imposing fleet [in your location] in the heart of the
seas.
26Your rowers have brought you out into great *and* deep waters;
the east wind has broken *and* wrecked you in the heart of the seas.
27Your riches, your wares, your merchandise, your oarsmen
and your pilots, your caulkers, your dealers in merchandise, and
all your men of war who are in you, with all your company which
is in your midst, sink in the heart of the seas on the day of your
ruin!
28The waves *and* the countryside shake at the [piercing] sound
of the [hopeless, wailing] cry of your pilots.
29And down from their ships come all who handle the oar. The
mariners and all the pilots of the sea stand upon the shore,
30And are heard wailing loudly over you, and they cry bitterly.
They cast up dust on their heads, they wallow in ashes;
31And they make themselves [utterly] bald for you and gird
themselves with sackcloth, and they weep over you in bitterness
of heart and with bitter mourning *and* wailing.
32And in their wailing they take up a lamentation for you, and
lament over you, saying, Who was ever like Tyre, the destroyed—
the annihilated, become so still—in the heart of the sea?
33When your wares came forth from the seas, you met the
desire, the demand *and* the necessity of many people; you enriched
the kings of the earth with your abundant wealth and merchandise.
34Now you are shattered by the seas, in the depths of the
waters; your merchandise and all your crew have gone down with
you.
35All the inhabitants of the isles *and* coastlands are astonished
*and* appalled at you; and their kings are horribly frightened *and*
shudder greatly, their faces quiver.
36The merchants among the people hiss over you [with malicious joy]; you have become a horror *and* a source of terrors. You
shall be [a]no more forever.

**AMP** [a] Down to the thirteenth century A.D., the grandeur of the ancient city of Tyre was still visible. But God's Word does not fail. Soon Tyre had become an almost uninhabited pile of ruins. A large part of the western section of "the island" became covered by the sea, and early travelers told of seeing "houses, towers and streets far down in the deep." In modern times the population of Tyre, made up largely of fishermen who spread their nets on its beaches, has increased to around 6,000, but the city as such has never been revived, and the original site has long since become obliterated.

## New American Standard

23"Haran, Canneh, Eden, the traders of Sheba, Asshur, *and* Chilmad traded with you.
24"They traded with you in choice garments, in clothes of blue and embroidered work, and in carpets of many colors, *and* tightly wound cords, *which were* among your merchandise.
25"The ships of Tarshish were the carriers for your merchandise.

And you were filled and were very glorious
In the heart of the seas.

26¶ "Your rowers have brought you
Into great waters;
The east wind has broken you
In the heart of the seas.
27 "Your wealth, your wares, your merchandise,
Your sailors, and your pilots,
Your repairers of seams, your dealers in merchandise,
And all your men of war who are in you,
With all your company that is in your midst,
Will fall into the heart of the seas
On the day of your overthrow.
28 "At the sound of the cry of your pilots
The pasture lands will shake.
29 "And all who handle the oar,
The sailors, *and* all the pilots of the sea
Will come down from their ships;
They will stand on the land,
30 And they will make their voice heard over you
And will cry bitterly.
They will cast dust on their heads,
They will wallow in ashes.
31 "Also they will make themselves bald for you
And gird themselves with sackcloth;
And they will weep for you in bitterness of soul
With bitter mourning.
32 "Moreover, in their wailing they will take up a lamentation for you
And lament over you:
'Who is like Tyre,
Like her who is silent in the midst of the sea?
33 'When your wares went out from the seas,
You satisfied many peoples;
With the abundance of your wealth and your merchandise
You enriched the kings of earth.
34 'Now that you are broken by the seas
In the depths of the waters,
Your merchandise and all your company
Have fallen in the midst of you.
35 'All the inhabitants of the coastlands
Are appalled at you,
And their kings are horribly afraid;
They are troubled in countenance.
36 'The merchants among the peoples hiss at you;
You have become terrified,
And you will be no more.' " ' "

## New International

23" 'Haran, Canneh and Eden and merchants of Sheba, Asshur and Kilmad traded with you. 24In your marketplace they traded with you beautiful garments, blue fabric, embroidered work and multicolored rugs with cords twisted and tightly knotted.

25" 'The ships of Tarshish serve
as carriers for your wares.
You are filled with heavy cargo
in the heart of the sea.
26Your oarsmen take you
out to the high seas.
But the east wind will break you to pieces
in the heart of the sea.
27Your wealth, merchandise and wares,
your mariners, seamen and shipwrights,
your merchants and all your soldiers,
and everyone else on board
will sink into the heart of the sea
on the day of your shipwreck.
28The shorelands will quake
when your seamen cry out.
29All who handle the oars
will abandon their ships;
the mariners and all the seamen
will stand on the shore.
30They will raise their voice
and cry bitterly over you;
they will sprinkle dust on their heads
and roll in ashes.
31They will shave their heads because of you
and will put on sackcloth.
They will weep over you with anguish of soul
and with bitter mourning.
32As they wail and mourn over you,
they will take up a lament concerning you:
"Who was ever silenced like Tyre,
surrounded by the sea?"
33When your merchandise went out on the seas,
you satisfied many nations;
with your great wealth and your wares
you enriched the kings of the earth.
34Now you are shattered by the sea
in the depths of the waters;
your wares and all your company
have gone down with you.
35All who live in the coastlands
are appalled at you;
their kings shudder with horror
and their faces are distorted with fear.
36The merchants among the nations hiss at you;
you have come to a horrible end
and will be no more.' "

## King James

**28** THE WORD of the LORD came again unto me, saying,

2 Son of man, say unto the prince of Tyrus, Thus saith the Lord GOD; Because thine heart *is* lifted up, and thou hast said, I *am* a God, I sit *in* the seat of God, in the midst of the seas; yet thou *art* a man, and not God, though thou set thine heart as the heart of God:

3 Behold, thou *art* wiser than Daniel; there is no secret that they can hide from thee:

4 With thy wisdom and with thine understanding thou hast gotten thee riches, and hast gotten gold and silver into thy treasures:

5 By thy great wisdom *and* by thy traffic hast thou increased thy riches, and thine heart is lifted up because of thy riches:

6 Therefore thus saith the Lord GOD; Because thou hast set thine heart as the heart of God;

7 Behold, therefore I will bring strangers upon thee, the terrible of the nations: and they shall draw their swords against the beauty of thy wisdom, and they shall defile thy brightness.

8 They shall bring thee down to the pit, and thou shalt die the deaths of *them that are* slain in the midst of the seas.

9 Wilt thou yet say before him that slayeth thee, I *am* God? but thou *shalt be* a man, and no God, in the hand of him that slayeth thee.

10 Thou shalt die the deaths of the uncircumcised by the hand of strangers: for I have spoken *it,* saith the Lord GOD.

11 ¶ Moreover the word of the LORD came unto me, saying,

12 Son of man, take up a lamentation upon the king of Tyrus, and say unto him, Thus saith the Lord GOD; Thou sealest up the sum, full of wisdom, and perfect in beauty.

13 Thou hast been in Eden the garden of God; every precious stone *was* thy covering, the sardius, topaz, and the diamond, the beryl, the onyx, and the jasper, the sapphire, the emerald, and the carbuncle, and gold: the workmanship of thy tabrets and of thy pipes was prepared in thee in the day that thou wast created.

14 Thou *art* the anointed cherub that covereth; and I have set thee *so:* thou wast upon the holy mountain of God; thou hast walked up and down in the midst of the stones of fire.

15 Thou *wast* perfect in thy ways from the day that thou wast created, till iniquity was found in thee.

## Amplified

**28** THE WORD of the Lord came again to me:

2 Son of man, say to the prince of Tyre, Thus says the Lord God: Because your heart is lifted up and you have said *and* thought, I am a god, I sit in the seat of the gods, in the heart of the seas, yet you are only man [weak, feeble, made of earth], and not God, though you imagine yourself to be almost more than mortal with your mind as the mind of God;

3 Indeed, you are [imagining yourself] wiser than Daniel; there is no secret [you think] that is hidden from you;

4 With your own wisdom and with your own understanding you have gotten you riches *and* power and have brought gold and silver into your treasuries;

5 By your great wisdom and by your traffic you have increased your riches *and* power, and your heart is proud *and* lifted up because of your wealth;

6 Therefore thus says the Lord God: Because you have imagined your mind as the mind of God—having thoughts and purposes suitable only to God Himself, [Obad. 3.]

7 Behold, therefore I am bringing strangers upon you, the most terrible of the nations; and they shall draw their swords against the beauty of your wisdom, [O Tyre,] and they shall defile your splendor.

8 They shall bring you down to the pit [of destruction], and you shall die the *many* deaths of all the Tyrians that are slain in the heart of the seas.

9 Will you still say, I am a god, before him who slays you? But you are only a man—made of earth—and no god in the hand of him who wounds *and* profanes you.

10 You shall die the death of the uncircumcised by the hand of strangers; for I have spoken it, says the Lord God.

11 Moreover the word of the Lord came to me:

12 Son of man, take up a lamentation over the king of Tyre and say to him, Thus says the Lord God: You are the full measure *and* pattern of exactness—giving the finishing touch to all that constitutes completeness—full of wisdom and perfect in beauty.

13 You were in [a]Eden, the garden of God; every precious stone was your covering, the carnelian, topaz, jasper, chrysolite, beryl, onyx, sapphire, carbuncle, and emerald; and your settings and your sockets *and* engravings were wrought in gold. On the day that you were created they were prepared. [Cf. Gen. 3:14, 15; Matt. 16:23; Isa. 14:12-15.]

14 You were the anointed cherub that covers with over-shadowing [wings], and I set you so. You were upon the holy mountain of God; you walked up and down in the midst of the stones of fire [like the paved work of gleaming sapphire stone upon which the God of Israel walked on Mount Sinai]. [Exod. 24:10.]

15 You were blameless in your ways from the day you were created, until iniquity *and* guilt were found in you.

**AMP** [a] This speech, though not addressed to Satan in his own person, seems to be ironically spoken of his evil genius fulfilling itself in and through the human ruler who appropriates to himself the honors due only to God, as in the case of the king of Babylon (Isa. 14:12-15). Here is to be seen a foreshadowing of "the beast" who is to attribute to himself divine rights in the time of the end (Dan. 7:8-28; II Thess. 2:1-12; Rev. 13; 19:20).

## New American Standard

*Tyre's King Overthrown*

**28** THE WORD of the LORD came again to me saying,
2"Son of man, say to the leader of Tyre, 'Thus says the Lord GOD,
"Because your heart is lifted up
And you have said, 'I am a god,
I sit in the seat of gods,
In the heart of the seas';
Yet you are a man and not God,
Although you make your heart like the heart of God—
3 Behold, you are wiser than Daniel;
There is no secret that is a match for you.
4 "By your wisdom and understanding
You have acquired riches for yourself,
And have acquired gold and silver for your treasuries.
5 "By your great wisdom, by your trade
You have increased your riches,
And your heart is lifted up because of your riches—
6 Therefore, thus says the Lord GOD,
'Because you have made your heart
Like the heart of God,
7 Therefore, behold, I will bring strangers upon you,
The most ruthless of the nations.
And they will draw their swords
Against the beauty of your wisdom
And defile your splendor.
8 They will bring you down to the pit,
And you will die the death of those who are slain
In the heart of the seas.
9 'Will you still say, "I am a god,"
In the presence of your slayer,
Although you are a man and not God,
In the hands of those who wound you?
10 'You will die the death of the uncircumcised
By the hand of strangers,
For I have spoken!' declares the Lord GOD!"'"
11¶ Again the word of the LORD came to me saying,
12"Son of man, take up a lamentation over the king of Tyre, and say to him, 'Thus says the Lord GOD,
"You had the seal of perfection,
Full of wisdom and perfect in beauty.
13 "You were in Eden, the garden of God;
Every precious stone was your covering:
The ruby, the topaz, and the diamond;
The beryl, the onyx, and the jasper;
The lapis lazuli, the turquoise, and the emerald;
And the gold, the workmanship of your settings and sockets,
Was in you.
On the day that you were created
They were prepared.
14 "You were the anointed cherub who covers,
And I placed you *there.*
You were on the holy mountain of God;
You walked in the midst of the stones of fire.
15 "You were blameless in your ways
From the day you were created,
Until unrighteousness was found in you.

## New International

*A Prophecy Against the King of Tyre*

**28** THE WORD of the LORD came to me: 2"Son of man, say to the ruler of Tyre, 'This is what the Sovereign LORD says:

"'In the pride of your heart
you say, "I am a god;
I sit on the throne of a god
in the heart of the seas."
But you are a man and not a god,
though you think you are as wise as a god.
3Are you wiser than Daniel[b]?
Is no secret hidden from you?
4By your wisdom and understanding
you have gained wealth for yourself
and amassed gold and silver
in your treasuries.
5By your great skill in trading
you have increased your wealth,
and because of your wealth
your heart has grown proud.

6"'Therefore this is what the Sovereign LORD says:

"'Because you think you are wise,
as wise as a god,
7I am going to bring foreigners against you,
the most ruthless of nations;
they will draw their swords against your beauty and wisdom
and pierce your shining splendor.
8They will bring you down to the pit,
and you will die a violent death
in the heart of the seas.
9Will you then say, "I am a god,"
in the presence of those who kill you?
You will be but a man, not a god,
in the hands of those who slay you.
10You will die the death of the uncircumcised
at the hands of foreigners.

I have spoken, declares the Sovereign LORD.'"

11The word of the LORD came to me: 12"Son of man, take up a lament concerning the king of Tyre and say to him: 'This is what the Sovereign LORD says:

"'You were the model of perfection,
full of wisdom and perfect in beauty.
13You were in Eden,
the garden of God;
every precious stone adorned you:
ruby, topaz and emerald,
chrysolite, onyx and jasper,
sapphire,[c] turquoise and beryl.[d]
Your settings and mountings[e] were made of gold;
on the day you were created they were prepared.
14You were anointed as a guardian cherub,
for so I ordained you.
You were on the holy mount of God;
you walked among the fiery stones.
15You were blameless in your ways
from the day you were created
till wickedness was found in you.

**NIV** [b] *3* Or *Danel;* the Hebrew spelling may suggest a person other than the prophet Daniel. [c] *13* Or *lapis lazuli* [d] *13* The precise identification of some of these precious stones is uncertain. [e] *13* The meaning of the Hebrew for this phrase is uncertain.

## King James

16 By the multitude of thy merchandise they have filled the midst of thee with violence, and thou hast sinned: therefore I will cast thee as profane out of the mountain of God: and I will destroy thee, O covering cherub, from the midst of the stones of fire.

17 Thine heart was lifted up because of thy beauty, thou hast corrupted thy wisdom by reason of thy brightness: I will cast thee to the ground, I will lay thee before kings, that they may behold thee.

18 Thou hast defiled thy sanctuaries by the multitude of thine iniquities, by the iniquity of thy traffic; therefore will I bring forth a fire from the midst of thee, it shall devour thee, and I will bring thee to ashes upon the earth in the sight of all them that behold thee.

19 All they that know thee among the people shall be astonished at thee: thou shalt be a terror, and never *shalt* thou *be* any more.

20 ¶ Again the word of the LORD came unto me, saying,

21 Son of man, set thy face against Zidon, and prophesy against it,

22 And say, Thus saith the Lord GOD; Behold, I *am* against thee, O Zidon; and I will be glorified in the midst of thee: and they shall know that I *am* the LORD, when I shall have executed judgments in her, and shall be sanctified in her.

23 For I will send into her pestilence, and blood into her streets; and the wounded shall be judged in the midst of her by the sword upon her on every side; and they shall know that I *am* the LORD.

24 ¶ And there shall be no more a pricking brier unto the house of Israel, nor *any* grieving thorn of all *that are* round about them, that despised them; and they shall know that I *am* the Lord GOD.

25 Thus saith the Lord GOD; When I shall have gathered the house of Israel from the people among whom they are scattered, and shall be sanctified in them in the sight of the heathen, then shall they dwell in their land that I have given to my servant Jacob.

26 And they shall dwell safely therein, and shall build houses, and plant vineyards; yea, they shall dwell with confidence, when I have executed judgments upon all those that despise them round about them; and they shall know that I *am* the LORD their God.

**29** IN THE tenth year, in the tenth *month,* in the twelfth *day* of the month, the word of the LORD came unto me, saying,

2 Son of man, set thy face against Pharaoh king of Egypt, and prophesy against him, and against all Egypt:

3 Speak, and say, Thus saith the Lord GOD; Behold, I *am* against thee, Pharaoh king of Egypt, the great dragon that lieth in the midst of his rivers, which hath said, My river *is* mine own, and I have made *it* for myself.

## Amplified

16 Through the abundance of your commerce you were filled with lawlessness *and* violence, and you sinned; therefore I cast you out as a profane thing from the mountain of God, and the guardian cherub drove you out from the midst of the stones of fire.

17 Your heart was proud *and* lifted up because of your beauty; you corrupted your wisdom for the sake of your splendor. I cast you to the ground; I lay you before kings that they might gaze at you.

18 You have profaned your sanctuaries by the multitude of your iniquities *and* the enormity of your guilt, by the unrighteousness of your trade. Therefore I have brought forth a fire from your midst; it has consumed you, and I have reduced you to ashes upon the earth in the sight of all who looked at you.

19 All who know you among the people are astonished and appalled at you; you have come to a horrible end and shall never return to being. [Isa. 23; Joel 3:4-8; Amos 1:9, 10; Zech. 9:3, 4.]

20 Again the word of the Lord came to me:

21 Son of man, set your face toward Sidon and prophesy against her.

22 And say, Thus says the Lord God: Behold, I am against you, O Sidon, and I will show forth My glory *and* be glorified in the midst of you. And they shall know—understand and realize—that I am the Lord, when I execute judgments *and* punishments in her, and am set apart, separated, *and* My holiness is manifested in her.

23 For I will send pestilence into her, and blood into her streets; and the wounded shall be judged *and* fall by the sword in the midst of her on every side; and they shall know—understand and realize—that I am the Lord [the Sovereign Ruler, calling forth loyalty and obedient service].

24 And there shall be no more a brier to prick the house of Israel or a hurting thorn of all those around them, who have treated them with contempt; and they shall know—understand and realize—that I am the Lord God [the Sovereign Ruler, calling forth loyalty and obedient service].

25 Thus says the Lord God: When I gather the house of Israel from the peoples among whom they are scattered, and I shall be set apart, separated, *and* My holiness made apparent in them in the sight of the nations, then shall they dwell in their own land which I gave to My servant Jacob.

26 And they shall dwell safely in it, and shall build houses and plant vineyards; yes, they shall dwell securely *and* with confidence, when I have executed judgments *and* punishments upon all those round about them who have despised *and* trodden upon them *and* pushed them away; and they shall know—understand and realize—that I am the Lord their God [their Sovereign Ruler, calling forth loyalty and obedient service].

**29** IN THE tenth year [of the captivity of King Jehoiachin by the king of Babylon], in the tenth *month,* on the twelfth *day* of the month, the word of the Lord came to me:

2 Son of man, set your face toward Pharaoh king of Egypt, and prophesy against him and against all Egypt.

3 Say, Thus says the Lord God: Behold, I am against you, Pharaoh king of Egypt, the great monster [of sluggish and unwieldy strength] that lies in the midst of his [delta] streams, [boastfully] declaring, My river Nile is my own, and I have made it for myself.

## New American Standard

16 "By the abundance of your trade
You were internally filled with violence,
And you sinned;
Therefore I have cast you as profane
From the mountain of God.
And I have destroyed you, O covering cherub,
From the midst of the stones of fire.
17 "Your heart was lifted up because of your beauty;
You corrupted your wisdom by reason of your
splendor.
I cast you to the ground;
I put you before kings,
That they may see you.
18 "By the multitude of your iniquities,
In the unrighteousness of your trade,
You profaned your sanctuaries.
Therefore I have brought fire from the midst of you;
It has consumed you,
And I have turned you to ashes on the earth
In the eyes of all who see you.
19 "All who know you among the peoples
Are appalled at you;
You have become terrified,
And you will be no more." ' "

*Judgment of Sidon*

20¶ And the word of the LORD came to me saying,
21"Son of man, set your face toward Sidon, prophesy against
her,
22and say, 'Thus says the Lord GOD,
"Behold, I am against you, O Sidon,
And I shall be glorified in your midst.
Then they will know that I am the LORD, when I
execute judgments in her,
And I shall manifest My holiness in her.
23 "For I shall send pestilence to her
And blood to her streets,
And the wounded will fall in her midst
By the sword upon her on every side;
Then they will know that I am the LORD.
24"And there will be no more for the house of Israel a prickling
brier or a painful thorn from any round about them who scorned
them; then they will know that I am the Lord GOD."

*Israel Regathered*

25¶ 'Thus says the Lord GOD, "When I gather the house of Israel
from the peoples among whom they are scattered, and shall manifest My holiness in them in the sight of the nations, then they will
live in their land which I gave to My servant Jacob.
26"And they will live in it securely; and they will build houses,
plant vineyards, and live securely, when I execute judgments
upon all who scorn them round about them. Then they will know
that I am the LORD their God." ' "

*Judgment of Egypt*

29 IN THE tenth year, in the tenth *month*, on the twelfth of
the month, the word of the LORD came to me saying,
2"Son of man, set your face against Pharaoh, king of Egypt,
and prophesy against him and against all Egypt.
3"Speak and say, 'Thus says the Lord GOD,
"Behold, I am against you, Pharaoh, king of Egypt,
The great monster that lies in the midst of his rivers,
That has said, 'My Nile is mine, and I myself have
made it.'

## New International

16Through your widespread trade
you were filled with violence,
and you sinned.
So I drove you in disgrace from the mount of God,
and I expelled you, O guardian cherub,
from among the fiery stones.
17Your heart became proud
on account of your beauty,
and you corrupted your wisdom
because of your splendor.
So I threw you to the earth;
I made a spectacle of you before kings.
18By your many sins and dishonest trade
you have desecrated your sanctuaries.
So I made a fire come out from you,
and it consumed you,
and I reduced you to ashes on the ground
in the sight of all who were watching.
19All the nations who knew you
are appalled at you;
you have come to a horrible end
and will be no more.' "

*A Prophecy Against Sidon*

20The word of the LORD came to me: 21"Son of man, set your
face against Sidon; prophesy against her 22and say: 'This is what
the Sovereign LORD says:

" 'I am against you, O Sidon,
and I will gain glory within you.
They will know that I am the LORD,
when I inflict punishment on her
and show myself holy within her.
23I will send a plague upon her
and make blood flow in her streets.
The slain will fall within her,
with the sword against her on every side.
Then they will know that I am the LORD.

24" 'No longer will the people of Israel have malicious neighbors
who are painful briers and sharp thorns. Then they will know that
I am the Sovereign LORD.
25" 'This is what the Sovereign LORD says: When I gather the
people of Israel from the nations where they have been scattered,
I will show myself holy among them in the sight of the nations.
Then they will live in their own land, which I gave to my servant
Jacob. 26They will live there in safety and will build houses and
plant vineyards; they will live in safety when I inflict punishment
on all their neighbors who maligned them. Then they will know
that I am the LORD their God.' "

*A Prophecy Against Egypt*

29 IN THE tenth year, in the tenth month on the twelfth day,
the word of the LORD came to me: 2"Son of man, set your
face against Pharaoh king of Egypt and prophesy against him and
against all Egypt. 3Speak to him and say: 'This is what the Sovereign LORD says:

" 'I am against you, Pharaoh king of Egypt,
you great monster lying among your streams.
You say, "The Nile is mine;
I made it for myself."

## King James

4But I will put hooks in thy jaws, and I will cause the fish of thy rivers to stick unto thy scales, and I will bring thee up out of the midst of thy rivers, and all the fish of thy rivers shall stick unto thy scales.
5And I will leave thee *thrown* into the wilderness, thee and all the fish of thy rivers: thou shalt fall upon the open fields; thou shalt not be brought together, nor gathered: I have given thee for meat to the beasts of the field and to the fowls of the heaven.
6And all the inhabitants of Egypt shall know that I *am* the LORD, because they have been a staff of reed to the house of Israel.
7When they took hold of thee by thy hand, thou didst break, and rend all their shoulder: and when they leaned upon thee, thou brakest, and madest all their loins to be at a stand.
8¶ Therefore thus saith the Lord GOD; Behold, I will bring a sword upon thee, and cut off man and beast out of thee.
9And the land of Egypt shall be desolate and waste; and they shall know that I *am* the LORD: because he hath said, The river *is* mine, and I have made *it*.
10Behold, therefore I *am* against thee, and against thy rivers, and I will make the land of Egypt utterly waste *and* desolate, from the tower of Syene even unto the border of Ethiopia.
11No foot of man shall pass through it, nor foot of beast shall pass through it, neither shall it be inhabited forty years.
12And I will make the land of Egypt desolate in the midst of the countries *that are* desolate, and her cities among the cities *that are* laid waste shall be desolate forty years: and I will scatter the Egyptians among the nations, and will disperse them through the countries.
13¶ Yet thus saith the Lord GOD; At the end of forty years will I gather the Egyptians from the people whither they were scattered:
14And I will bring again the captivity of Egypt, and will cause them to return *into* the land of Pathros, into the land of their habitation; and they shall be there a base kingdom.
15It shall be the basest of the kingdoms; neither shall it exalt itself any more above the nations: for I will diminish them, that they shall no more rule over the nations.
16And it shall be no more the confidence of the house of Israel, which bringeth *their* iniquity to remembrance, when they shall look after them: but they shall know that I *am* the Lord GOD.
17¶ And it came to pass in the seven and twentieth year, in the first *month*, in the first *day* of the month, the word of the LORD came unto me, saying,
18Son of man, Nebuchadrezzar king of Babylon caused his army to serve a great service against Tyrus: every head *was* made bald, and every shoulder *was* peeled: yet had he no wages, nor his army, for Tyrus, for the service that he had served against it:
19Therefore thus saith the Lord GOD; Behold, I will give the land of Egypt unto Nebuchadrezzar king of Babylon; and he shall take her multitude, and take her spoil, and take her prey; and it shall be the wages for his army.
20I have given him the land of Egypt *for* his labour wherewith he served against it, because they wrought for me, saith the Lord GOD.

## Amplified

4But I will put hooks in your jaws, [O Egyptian dragon,] and I will cause the fish of your rivers to stick to your scales; and I will draw you up out of the midst of your streams, with all the fish of your streams which stick to your scales.
5And I will cast you forth into the wilderness, you and all the fish of your rivers; you shall fall upon the open field, and not be gathered up or buried. I have given you for food to the [wild] beasts of the earth and the birds of the heavens.
6And all the inhabitants of Egypt shall know—understand and realize—that I am the Lord [the Sovereign Ruler, calling forth loyalty and obedient service], because they have been a [deceitful] staff [made of fragile] reeds to the house of Israel.
7When they grasped you with the hand *and* leaned upon you, you broke, and tore their whole shoulder, and [by injuring their muscles made them so stiff and rigid that] they could do no more than stand.
8Therefore thus says the Lord God: Behold, I will bring a sword upon you, and cut off man and beast from you;
9And the land of Egypt shall be a desolation and a waste. And they shall know—understand and realize—that I am the Lord [the Sovereign Ruler, calling forth loyalty and obedient service]. Because you have said, The river is mine, and I have made it,
10Behold, therefore I am against you and against your streams, and I will make the land of Egypt an utter [plundered] waste and desolation [of subjection] from [northern] Migdol to [southern] Syene, even as far as the border of Ethiopia.
11No foot of man shall pass through it [in travel], no foot of beast shall pass through it [in trade with other countries], neither shall [Egypt] be [truly] inhabited *again* for forty years.
12And I will make the land of Egypt a desolation [that is, plundered and reduced to subjection] in the midst of desolated [plundered and reduced to subjection] countries, and her cities among the cities that are laid waste shall be a desolation forty years. I will scatter the Egyptians among the nations and will disperse them through the countries.
13Yet thus says the Lord God: At the end of *their* forty years will I gather the Egyptians from the peoples among whom they were scattered; [Jer. 46:25, 26.]
14And I will reverse the captivity of Egypt [as I will that of Israel], and will cause them to return into the land of Pathros [under Egypt], the land of their origin; and they shall be there a lowly kingdom.
15It shall be the most lowly of the kingdoms; neither shall it [a]exalt itself any more above the nations; I will diminish [the Egyptians], so they shall never again rule over the nations.
16And never again shall Egypt have the confidence *and* be the reliance of the house of Israel; their iniquity will be brought to remembrance whenever *Israel* looks toward them *for help*. They shall know—understand and realize—that I am the Lord God [Who demands loyalty and obedient service].
17In the twenty-seventh year [after King Jehoiachin was taken to Babylon], in the first month, on the first day of the month, the word of the Lord came to me:
18Son of man, Nebuchadrezzar king of Babylon caused his army to render heavy service [at My bidding] against Tyre: every [soldier's] head became bald, and every shoulder was worn *and* peeled [with carrying loads of earth and stones for siege works]. Yet he had no remuneration from Tyre [in proportion to the time and labor expended in the thirteen years' siege], either for himself or his army, for the work that he had done against it [for Me].
19Therefore thus says the Lord God: Behold, I will give the land of Egypt to Nebuchadrezzar king of Babylon; and he shall carry off her great mass of people *and* of things—her riches—and take her spoil and take her prey; and it shall be the wages for his army.
20I have given him the land of Egypt for his labor with which he served [against Tyre], because they did it for Me, says the Lord God.

**AMP** [a] For a little while Egypt struggled against its oppressors, but its power was already broken, and from the time of its conquest by Cambyses, it has never been for any length of time independent. There are few stronger contrasts in any inhabited country than between the ancient glory, dignity, power, and wealth of Egypt, and its later [lack of] significance. (Ellicott's Commentary.)

## New American Standard

4 "And I shall put hooks in your jaws,
And I shall make the fish of your rivers cling to your scales.
And I shall bring you up out of the midst of your rivers,
And all the fish of your rivers will cling to your scales.
5 "And I shall abandon you to the wilderness, you and all the fish of your rivers;
You will fall on the open field; you will not be brought together or gathered.
I have given you for food to the beasts of the earth and to the birds of the sky.
6 "Then all the inhabitants of Egypt will know that I am the LORD,
Because they have been *only* a staff *made* of reed to the house of Israel.
7 "When they took hold of you with the hand,
You broke and tore all their hands;
And when they leaned on you,
You broke and made all their loins quake."

8Therefore, thus says the Lord GOD, "Behold, I shall bring
upon you a sword, and I shall cut off from you man and beast.
9"And the land of Egypt will become a desolation and waste.
Then they will know that I am the LORD.

¶ Because you said, 'The Nile is mine, and I have made *it*,'
10therefore, behold, I am against you and against your rivers,
and I will make the land of Egypt an utter waste and desolation,
from Migdol *to* Syene and even to the border of Ethiopia.

11"A man's foot will not pass through it, and the foot of a beast
will not pass through it, and it will not be inhabited for forty years.

12"So I shall make the land of Egypt a desolation in the midst
of desolated lands. And her cities, in the midst of cities that are laid
waste, will be desolate forty years; and I shall scatter the Egyptians
among the nations and disperse them among the lands."

13¶ 'For thus says the Lord GOD, "At the end of forty years I
shall gather the Egyptians from the peoples among whom they
were scattered.

14"And I shall turn the fortunes of Egypt and shall make them
return to the land of Pathros, to the land of their origin; and there
they will be a lowly kingdom.

15"It will be the lowest of the kingdoms; and it will never again
lift itself up above the nations. And I shall make them so small that
they will not rule over the nations.

16"And it will never again be the confidence of the house of
Israel, bringing to mind the iniquity of their having turned to
Egypt. Then they will know that I am the Lord GOD."'"

17¶ Now in the twenty-seventh year, in the first *month*, on the
first of the month, the word of the LORD came to me saying,
18"Son of man, Nebuchadnezzar king of Babylon made his
army labor hard against Tyre; every head was made bald, and
every shoulder was rubbed bare. But he and his army had no
wages from Tyre for the labor that he had performed against it."
19Therefore, thus says the Lord GOD, "Behold, I shall give the
land of Egypt to Nebuchadnezzar king of Babylon. And he will
carry off her wealth, and capture her spoil and seize her plunder;
and it will be wages for his army.

20"I have given him the land of Egypt *for* his labor which he
performed, because they acted for Me," declares the Lord GOD.

## New International

4But I will put hooks in your jaws
and make the fish of your streams stick to your scales.
I will pull you out from among your streams,
with all the fish sticking to your scales.
5I will leave you in the desert,
you and all the fish of your streams.
You will fall on the open field
and not be gathered or picked up.
I will give you as food
to the beasts of the earth and the birds of the air.

6Then all who live in Egypt will know that I am the LORD.

" 'You have been a staff of reed for the house of Israel. 7When
they grasped you with their hands, you splintered and you tore
open their shoulders; when they leaned on you, you broke and
their backs were wrenched.[b]

8" 'Therefore this is what the Sovereign LORD says: I will bring
a sword against you and kill your men and their animals. 9Egypt
will become a desolate wasteland. Then they will know that I am
the LORD.

" 'Because you said, "The Nile is mine; I made it," 10therefore
I am against you and against your streams, and I will make the land
of Egypt a ruin and a desolate waste from Migdol to Aswan, as far
as the border of Cush.[c] 11No foot of man or animal will pass
through it; no one will live there for forty years. 12I will make the
land of Egypt desolate among devastated lands, and her cities will
lie desolate forty years among ruined cities. And I will disperse the
Egyptians among the nations and scatter them through the countries.

13" 'Yet this is what the Sovereign LORD says: At the end of forty
years I will gather the Egyptians from the nations where they were
scattered. 14I will bring them back from captivity and return them
to Upper Egypt,[d] the land of their ancestry. There they will be a
lowly kingdom. 15It will be the lowliest of kingdoms and will never
again exalt itself above the other nations. I will make it so weak that
it will never again rule over the nations. 16Egypt will no longer be
a source of confidence for the people of Israel but will be a reminder of their sin in turning to her for help. Then they will know that
I am the Sovereign LORD.' "

17In the twenty-seventh year, in the first month on the first day,
the word of the LORD came to me: 18"Son of man, Nebuchadnezzar
king of Babylon drove his army in a hard campaign against Tyre;
every head was rubbed bare and every shoulder made raw. Yet he
and his army got no reward from the campaign he led against Tyre.
19Therefore this is what the Sovereign LORD says: I am going to
give Egypt to Nebuchadnezzar king of Babylon, and he will carry
off its wealth. He will loot and plunder the land as pay for his
army. 20I have given him Egypt as a reward for his efforts because
he and his army did it for me, declares the Sovereign LORD.

NIV [b] 7 Syriac (see also Septuagint and Vulgate); Hebrew *and you caused their backs to stand* [c] 10 That is, the upper Nile region [d] 14 Hebrew *to Pathros*

## King James

21¶ In that day will I cause the horn of the house of Israel to bud
forth, and I will give thee the opening of the mouth in the midst
of them; and they shall know that I *am* the LORD.

**30** THE WORD of the LORD came again unto me, saying,
2Son of man, prophesy and say, Thus saith the Lord GOD;
Howl ye, Woe worth the day!
3For the day *is* near, even the day of the LORD *is* near, a cloudy
day; it shall be the time of the heathen.
4And the sword shall come upon Egypt, and great pain shall be
in Ethiopia, when the slain shall fall in Egypt, and they shall take
away her multitude, and her foundations shall be broken down.
5Ethiopia, and Libya, and Lydia, and all the mingled people,
and Chub, and the men of the land that is in league, shall fall with
them by the sword.
6Thus saith the LORD; They also that uphold Egypt shall fall;
and the pride of her power shall come down: from the tower of
Syene shall they fall in it by the sword, saith the Lord GOD.
7And they shall be desolate in the midst of the countries *that are*
desolate, and her cities shall be in the midst of the cities *that are*
wasted.
8And they shall know that I *am* the LORD, when I have set a fire
in Egypt, and *when* all her helpers shall be destroyed.
9In that day shall messengers go forth from me in ships to make
the careless Ethiopians afraid, and great pain shall come upon
them, as in the day of Egypt: for, lo, it cometh.
10Thus saith the Lord GOD; I will also make the multitude of
Egypt to cease by the hand of Nebuchadrezzar king of Babylon.
11He and his people with him, the terrible of the nations, shall
be brought to destroy the land: and they shall draw their swords
against Egypt, and fill the land with the slain.
12And I will make the rivers dry, and sell the land into the hand
of the wicked: and I will make the land waste, and all that is
therein, by the hand of strangers: I the LORD have spoken *it*.
13Thus saith the Lord GOD; I will also destroy the idols, and I
will cause *their* images to cease out of Noph; and there shall be no
more a prince of the land of Egypt: and I will put a fear in the land
of Egypt.
14And I will make Pathros desolate, and will set fire in Zoan,
and will execute judgments in No.

## Amplified

21In that day will I cause a horn to spring forth to the house of
Israel, and I will open your lips among them; and they shall
know—understand and realize—that I am the Lord [the Sovereign
Ruler, calling forth loyalty and obedient service].

**30** THE WORD of the Lord came again to me:
2Son of man, prophesy and say, Thus says the Lord God:
Wail, Alas for the day!
3For the day is near, even the day of the Lord is near, a cloudy
day; it shall be the time [of doom] for the nations.
4And a sword shall come upon Egypt, and anguish *and* great
sorrow shall be in Ethiopia [Cush], when the slain fall in Egypt,
and they [of Babylon] carry away her great mass of people *and* of
things, and her foundations are broken down.
5Ethiopia [Cush], and Put, and Lud, and all the mingled people
[foreigners living in Egypt], and Cub [Lub, Libya], and the children of the land of the covenant [the Jews who had taken refuge
in Egypt] shall fall with [the Egyptians] by the sword.
6Thus says the Lord: They also who uphold *or* lean upon *and*
are supported by Egypt shall fall, and the pride of her power shall
come down: from Migdol [in the north] to Syene [in the south] they
shall fall within her by the sword, says the Lord God.
7And they shall be desolated in the midst of countries that are
desolated, and her cities shall be in the midst of cities that are
wasted [by plunder and subjection].
8And they shall know—understand and realize—that I am the
Lord [the Sovereign Ruler, calling forth loyalty and obedient ser-
vice], when I have set a fire in Egypt, and all her helpers are broken
*and* destroyed.
9In that day shall [swift] messengers go forth from Me in ships
to terrify the careless *and* unsuspecting Ethiopians, and there shall
be anguish *and* great sorrow upon them as in the day of Egypt's
[doom]; for lo, [their day] comes!
10Thus says the Lord God: I will also make the tumult *and* the
wealth *and* the large population of Egypt to cease by the hand of
Nebuchadrezzar king of Babylon.
11He and his people with him, the [most] terrible of the nations,
shall be brought in to destroy the land; and they shall draw their
swords against Egypt, and fill the land with the slain.
12And I will make the [artificial] streams [of the Nile delta] dry,
and will sell the land into the hand of evil men; and I will make
the land desolate, and all that is in it, by the hand of strangers. I,
the Lord [the Sovereign Ruler, calling forth loyalty and obedient
service], have spoken it.
13Thus says the Lord God: I will also destroy the idols, and I will
put an end to the images in Noph *or* Memphis, and there shall be
no longer a prince of the land of Egypt. And I will put fear in the
land of Egypt.
14And I will make Pathros desolate, and will set fire to Zoan,
and will execute judgments *and* punishments upon No *or* Thebes.

## New American Standard

21¶ "On that day I shall make a horn sprout for the house of
Israel, and I shall open your mouth in their midst. Then they will
know that I am the LORD."

*Lament over Egypt*

**30** THE WORD of the LORD came again to me saying,
2"Son of man, prophesy and say, 'Thus says the Lord
GOD,

"Wail, 'Alas for the day!'
3 "For the day is near,
Even the day of the LORD is near;
It will be a day of clouds,
A time *of doom* for the nations.
4 "And a sword will come upon Egypt,
And anguish will be in Ethiopia,
When the slain fall in Egypt,
They take away her wealth,
And her foundations are torn down.

5"Ethiopia, Put, Lud, all Arabia, Libya, and the people of the
land that is in league will fall with them by the sword."

6¶ Thus says the LORD,
"Indeed, those who support Egypt will fall,
And the pride of her power will come down;
From Migdol *to* Syene
They will fall within her by the sword,"
Declares the Lord GOD.
7 "And they will be desolate
In the midst of the desolated lands;
And her cities will be
In the midst of the devastated cities.
8 "And they will know that I am the LORD,
When I set a fire in Egypt
And all her helpers are broken.

9"On that day messengers will go forth from Me in ships to
frighten secure Ethiopia; and anguish will be on them as on the day
of Egypt; for, behold, it comes!"

10Thus says the Lord GOD,
"I will also make the multitude of Egypt cease
By the hand of Nebuchadnezzar king of Babylon.
11 "He and his people with him,
The most ruthless of the nations,
Will be brought in to destroy the land;
And they will draw their swords against Egypt
And fill the land with the slain.
12 "Moreover, I will make the Nile canals dry
And sell the land into the hands of evil men.
And I will make the land desolate,
And all that is in it,
By the hand of strangers; I, the LORD, have spoken."

13¶ Thus says the Lord GOD,
"I will also destroy the idols
And make the images cease from Memphis.
And there will no longer be a prince in the land of
Egypt;
And I will put fear in the land of Egypt.
14 "And I will make Pathros desolate,
Set a fire in Zoan,
And execute judgments on [a]Thebes.

NAS [a] Or, *No*

## New International

21"On that day I will make a horn[b] grow for the house of Israel,
and I will open your mouth among them. Then they will know that
I am the LORD."

*A Lament for Egypt*

**30** THE WORD of the LORD came to me: 2"Son of man,
prophesy and say: 'This is what the Sovereign LORD says:

"'Wail and say,
"Alas for that day!"
3For the day is near,
the day of the LORD is near—
a day of clouds,
a time of doom for the nations.
4A sword will come against Egypt,
and anguish will come upon Cush.[c]
When the slain fall in Egypt,
her wealth will be carried away
and her foundations torn down.

5Cush and Put, Lydia and all Arabia, Libya[d] and the people of the
covenant land will fall by the sword along with Egypt.

6"'This is what the LORD says:

"'The allies of Egypt will fall
and her proud strength will fail.
From Migdol to Aswan
they will fall by the sword within her,
declares the Sovereign LORD.
7"'They will be desolate
among desolate lands,
and their cities will lie
among ruined cities.
8Then they will know that I am the LORD,
when I set fire to Egypt
and all her helpers are crushed.

9"'On that day messengers will go out from me in ships to
frighten Cush out of her complacency. Anguish will take hold of
them on the day of Egypt's doom, for it is sure to come.

10"'This is what the Sovereign LORD says:

"'I will put an end to the hordes of Egypt
by the hand of Nebuchadnezzar king of Babylon.
11He and his army—the most ruthless of nations—
will be brought in to destroy the land.
They will draw their swords against Egypt
and fill the land with the slain.
12I will dry up the streams of the Nile
and sell the land to evil men;
by the hand of foreigners
I will lay waste the land and everything in it.

I the LORD have spoken.

13"'This is what the Sovereign LORD says:

"'I will destroy the idols
and put an end to the images in Memphis.[e]
No longer will there be a prince in Egypt,
and I will spread fear throughout the land.
14I will lay waste Upper Egypt,[f]
set fire to Zoan
and inflict punishment on Thebes.[g]

NIV [b] *21 Horn* here symbolizes strength. [c] *4* That is, the upper Nile region; also in verses 5 and 9 [d] *5* Hebrew *Cub* [e] *13* Hebrew *Noph;* also in verse 16 [f] *14* Hebrew *waste Pathros* [g] *14* Hebrew *No;* also in verses 15 and 16

## King James

15And I will pour my fury upon Sin, the strength of Egypt; and I will cut off the multitude of No.

16And I will set fire in Egypt: Sin shall have great pain, and No shall be rent asunder, and Noph *shall have* distresses daily.

17The young men of Aven and of Pi-beseth shall fall by the sword: and these *cities* shall go into captivity.

18At Tehaphnehes also the day shall be darkened, when I shall break there the yokes of Egypt: and the pomp of her strength shall cease in her: as for her, a cloud shall cover her, and her daughters shall go into captivity.

19Thus will I execute judgments in Egypt: and they shall know that I *am* the LORD.

20¶ And it came to pass in the eleventh year, in the first *month,* in the seventh *day* of the month, *that* the word of the LORD came unto me, saying,

21Son of man, I have broken the arm of Pharaoh king of Egypt; and, lo, it shall not be bound up to be healed, to put a roller to bind it, to make it strong to hold the sword.

22Therefore thus saith the Lord GOD; Behold, I *am* against Pharaoh king of Egypt, and will break his arms, the strong, and that which was broken; and I will cause the sword to fall out of his hand.

23And I will scatter the Egyptians among the nations, and will disperse them through the countries.

24And I will strengthen the arms of the king of Babylon, and put my sword in his hand: but I will break Pharaoh's arms, and he shall groan before him with the groanings of a deadly wounded *man.*

25But I will strengthen the arms of the king of Babylon, and the arms of Pharaoh shall fall down; and they shall know that I *am* the LORD, when I shall put my sword into the hand of the king of Babylon, and he shall stretch it out upon the land of Egypt.

26And I will scatter the Egyptians among the nations, and disperse them among the countries; and they shall know that I *am* the LORD.

**31** AND IT came to pass in the eleventh year, in the third *month,* in the first *day* of the month, *that* the word of the LORD came unto me, saying,

2Son of man, speak unto Pharaoh king of Egypt, and to his multitude; Whom art thou like in thy greatness?

3¶ Behold, the Assyrian *was* a cedar in Lebanon with fair branches, and with a shadowing shroud, and of an high stature; and his top was among the thick boughs.

4The waters made him great, the deep set him up on high with her rivers running round about his plants, and sent out her little rivers unto all the trees of the field.

5Therefore his height was exalted above all the trees of the field, and his boughs were multiplied, and his branches became long because of the multitude of waters, when he shot forth.

## Amplified

15And I will pour My wrath upon Pelusium, the stronghold of Egypt; and I will cut off the tumult, the prosperity *and* the population of No *or* Thebes.

16And I will set fire to Egypt; Pelusium shall have great anguish, and No *or* Thebes shall be torn open, and Noph *or* Memphis shall have adversaries in the daytime *and* all the day long.

17The young men of Aven *or* On and of Pibeseth shall fall by the sword; and the *women and children* shall go into captivity.

18At Tehaphnehes also the day shall withdraw itself *and* be dark, when I break there the yokes *and* dominion of Egypt; and the pride of her power shall come to an end. As for her, a cloud *of calamities* shall cover her, and her daughters shall go into captivity.

19Thus will I execute judgments *and* punishments upon Egypt. Then shall they know—understand and realize—that I am the Lord [the Sovereign Ruler, calling forth loyalty and obedient service].

20And in the eleventh year [after King Jehoiachin was taken to Babylon], in the first month, on the seventh day of the month, the word of the Lord came to me:

21Son of man, I have broken the arm of Pharaoh king of Egypt; and lo, it has not been bound up, to heal it by binding it with a bandage, to make it strong to hold *and* wield the sword.

22Therefore thus says the Lord God: Behold, I am against Pharaoh king of Egypt, and will break his arms, both the strong one and the one which was broken; and I will cause the sword to fall from his hand.

23And I will scatter the Egyptians among the nations, and will disperse them throughout the countries.

24And I will strengthen the arms of the king of Babylon, and put My sword in his hand; but I will break Pharaoh's arms, and he will groan before *Nebuchadrezzar* with the groanings of a mortally wounded man.

25But I will strengthen *and* hold up the arms of the king of Babylon, and the arms of Pharaoh shall fall down; and they [of Egypt] shall know—understand and realize—that I am the Lord [the Sovereign Ruler, calling forth loyalty and obedient service], when I put My sword into the hand of the king of Babylon, and he shall stretch it out upon the land of Egypt.

26And I will scatter the Egyptians among the nations, and disperse them through the countries; and they shall know—understand and realize—that I am the Lord [the Sovereign Ruler, calling forth loyalty and obedient service].

**31** AND IN the eleventh year [after King Jehoiachin was taken captive to Babylon], in the third month, on the first day of the month, the word of the Lord came to me:

2Son of man, say to Pharaoh king of Egypt and to his multitude: Whom are you like in your greatness?

3Behold, [I will liken you to] Assyria, a cedar in Lebanon, with fair branches and with forest-like shade, and of high stature, and its top among the thick boughs—even the clouds.

4The waters nourished it, the deep made it grow tall; its rivers ran round about its planting, sending out its streams to all the trees of the forest [the other nations].

5Therefore it towered higher than all the trees of the forest; its boughs were multiplied, and its branches became long, because there was much water when they were shot forth.

## New American Standard

15 "And I will pour out My wrath on [a]Sin,
The stronghold of Egypt;
I will also cut off the multitude of Thebes.
16 "And I will set a fire in Egypt;
Sin will writhe in anguish,
Thebes will be breached,
And [b]Memphis *will have* distresses daily.
17 "The young men of [c]On and of Pi-beseth
Will fall by the sword,
And the women will go into captivity.
18 "And in Tehaphnehes the day will be dark
When I break there the yoke bars of Egypt.
Then the pride of her power will cease in her;
A cloud will cover her,
And her daughters will go into captivity.
19 "Thus I will execute judgments on Egypt,
And they will know that I am the LORD." ' "

*Victory for Babylon*

**20**¶ And it came about in the eleventh year, in the first *month*, on the seventh of the month, that the word of the LORD came to me saying,

21 "Son of man, I have broken the arm of Pharaoh king of Egypt; and, behold, it has not been bound up for healing or wrapped with a bandage, that it may be strong to hold the sword.

22 "Therefore, thus says the Lord GOD, 'Behold, I am against Pharaoh king of Egypt and will break his arms, both the strong and the broken; and I will make the sword fall from his hand.

23 'And I will scatter the Egyptians among the nations and disperse them among the lands.

24 'For I will strengthen the arms of the king of Babylon and put My sword in his hand; and I will break the arms of Pharaoh, so that he will groan before him with the groanings of a wounded man.

25 'Thus I will strengthen the arms of the king of Babylon, but the arms of Pharaoh will fall. Then they will know that I am the LORD, when I put My sword into the hand of the king of Babylon and he stretches it out against the land of Egypt.

26 'When I scatter the Egyptians among the nations and disperse them among the lands, then they will know that I am the LORD.' "

*Pharaoh Warned of Assyria's Fate*

**31** AND IT came about in the eleventh year, in the third *month*, on the first of the month, that the word of the LORD came to me saying,

2 "Son of man, say to Pharaoh king of Egypt, and to his multitude,
'Whom are you like in your greatness?
3 'Behold, Assyria *was* a cedar in Lebanon
With beautiful branches and forest shade,
And very high;
And its top was among the clouds.
4 'The waters made it grow, the deep made it high.
With its rivers it continually extended all around its planting place,
And it sent out its channels to all the trees of the field.
5 'Therefore its height was loftier than all the trees of the field
And its boughs became many and its branches long
Because of many waters as it spread them out.

NAS [a] Or, *Pelusium* [b] Or, *Noph* [c] Or, *Aven*

## New International

15 I will pour out my wrath on Pelusium,[d]
the stronghold of Egypt,
and cut off the hordes of Thebes.
16 I will set fire to Egypt;
Pelusium will writhe in agony.
Thebes will be taken by storm;
Memphis will be in constant distress.
17 The young men of Heliopolis[e] and Bubastis[f]
will fall by the sword,
and the cities themselves will go into captivity.
18 Dark will be the day at Tahpanhes
when I break the yoke of Egypt;
there her proud strength will come to an end.
She will be covered with clouds,
and her villages will go into captivity.
19 So I will inflict punishment on Egypt,
and they will know that I am the LORD.' "

20 In the eleventh year, in the first month on the seventh day, the word of the LORD came to me: 21 "Son of man, I have broken the arm of Pharaoh king of Egypt. It has not been bound up for healing or put in a splint so as to become strong enough to hold a sword. 22 Therefore this is what the Sovereign LORD says: I am against Pharaoh king of Egypt. I will break both his arms, the good arm as well as the broken one, and make the sword fall from his hand. 23 I will disperse the Egyptians among the nations and scatter them through the countries. 24 I will strengthen the arms of the king of Babylon and put my sword in his hand, but I will break the arms of Pharaoh, and he will groan before him like a mortally wounded man. 25 I will strengthen the arms of the king of Babylon, but the arms of Pharaoh will fall limp. Then they will know that I am the LORD, when I put my sword into the hand of the king of Babylon and he brandishes it against Egypt. 26 I will disperse the Egyptians among the nations and scatter them through the countries. Then they will know that I am the LORD."

*A Cedar in Lebanon*

**31** IN THE eleventh year, in the third month on the first day, the word of the LORD came to me: 2 "Son of man, say to Pharaoh king of Egypt and to his hordes:

" 'Who can be compared with you in majesty?
3 Consider Assyria, once a cedar in Lebanon,
with beautiful branches overshadowing the forest;
it towered on high,
its top above the thick foliage.
4 The waters nourished it,
deep springs made it grow tall;
their streams flowed
all around its base
and sent their channels
to all the trees of the field.
5 So it towered higher
than all the trees of the field;
its boughs increased
and its branches grew long,
spreading because of abundant waters.

NIV [d] *15* Hebrew *Sin;* also in verse 16 [e] *17* Hebrew *Awen* (or *On*) [f] *17* Hebrew *Pi Beseth*

## King James

6All the fowls of heaven made their nests in his boughs, and
under his branches did all the beasts of the field bring forth their
young, and under his shadow dwelt all great nations.
7Thus was he fair in his greatness, in the length of his branches:
for his root was by great waters.
8The cedars in the garden of God could not hide him: the fir
trees were not like his boughs, and the chestnut trees were not like
his branches; nor any tree in the garden of God was like unto him
in his beauty.
9I have made him fair by the multitude of his branches: so that
all the trees of Eden, that *were* in the garden of God, envied him.
10¶ Therefore thus saith the Lord GOD; Because thou hast lifted
up thyself in height, and he hath shot up his top among the thick
boughs, and his heart is lifted up in his height;
11I have therefore delivered him into the hand of the mighty one
of the heathen; he shall surely deal with him: I have driven him
out for his wickedness.
12And strangers, the terrible of the nations, have cut him off,
and have left him: upon the mountains and in all the valleys his
branches are fallen, and his boughs are broken by all the rivers of
the land; and all the people of the earth are gone down from his
shadow, and have left him.
13Upon his ruin shall all the fowls of the heaven remain, and
all the beasts of the field shall be upon his branches:
14To the end that none of all the trees by the waters exalt
themselves for their height, neither shoot up their top among the
thick boughs, neither their trees stand up in their height, all that
drink water: for they are all delivered unto death, to the nether
parts of the earth, in the midst of the children of men, with them
that go down to the pit.
15Thus saith the Lord GOD; In the day when he went down to
the grave I caused a mourning: I covered the deep for him, and I
restrained the floods thereof, and the great waters were stayed:
and I caused Lebanon to mourn for him, and all the trees of the
field fainted for him.
16I made the nations to shake at the sound of his fall, when I
cast him down to hell with them that descend into the pit: and all
the trees of Eden, the choice and best of Lebanon, all that drink
water, shall be comforted in the nether parts of the earth.
17They also went down into hell with him unto *them that be* slain
with the sword; and *they that were* his arm, *that* dwelt under his
shadow in the midst of the heathen.
18¶ To whom art thou thus like in glory and in greatness among
the trees of Eden? yet shalt thou be brought down with the trees
of Eden unto the nether parts of the earth: thou shalt lie in the
midst of the uncircumcised with *them that be* slain by the sword.
This *is* Pharaoh and all his multitude, saith the Lord GOD.

## Amplified

6All the birds of the heavens made their nests in its boughs, and
under its branches all the wild beasts of the field brought forth
their young, and under its shadow dwelt all of the great nations.
7Thus was it beautiful in its greatness, in the length of its
branches; for its root was by many *and* great waters.
8The cedars in the garden of God could not hide *or* rival it; the
cypress trees did not have boughs like it, and the plane trees did
not have branches like it, nor was any tree in the garden of God
like it in its beauty.
9I made it beautiful with the multitude of its branches, so that
all the trees of [a]Eden, that were in the garden of God, envied it
[Assyria].
10Therefore thus said the Lord God: Because *it is* exalted in
stature, and it has set its top among the thick boughs *and* the
clouds, and its heart is proud of its height; [II Kings 18:31-35.]
11I will even [b]deliver it into the hand of a mighty one of the
nations; he shall surely deal with it. I have driven it out for its
wickedness *and* lawlessness.
12And strangers, the most terrible of the nations, will cut it off
and leave it; upon the mountains and in all the valleys its branches
will fall, and its boughs will lie broken by all the watercourses of
the land; and all the peoples of the earth will go down out of its
shade and leave it.
13Upon its ruins all the birds of the heavens will dwell, and all
the wild beasts of the field will be upon *Assyria's fallen* branches.
14This is all so that none of the trees by the waters may exalt
themselves because of their height, or shoot up their top among
the thick boughs *and* the clouds, and that none of their mighty ones
should stand upon [their own estimate of] themselves for their
height, all that drink water. For they are all delivered over to death,
to the lower world, in the midst of the children of men, with those
who go down to the pit—the grave.
15Thus says the Lord God: When *Assyria* goes down to Sheol
(the place of the dead) I will cause a mourning; I will cover the deep
for it, and I will restrain its floods, and the many waters [that
contributed to its prosperity] will be stayed; and I will cause Lebanon to be in black gloom *and* to mourn for it, and all the trees of
the field, dismayed, will faint because of it.
16I will make the nations quake at the sound of its fall, when
I cast it down to Sheol with those who descend into the pit; and
all the trees of Eden, the choice and best of Lebanon, all *the trees*
that drink water, will be comforted in the nether world [at Assyria's downfall].
17They also shall go down into Sheol with it, to those who were
slain by the sword; yes, they who were its arm, that dwelt under
its shadow in the midst of the nations.
18To whom, *O Egypt*, among the trees of Eden are you thus like
in glory and in greatness? Yet you *also* shall be brought down with
the trees of Eden to the nether world. You shall lie among the
[c]uncircumcised heathen with those who are slain by the sword.
This is [d]how it shall be with Pharaoh and all the multitude of his
strength, his tumult *and* his store [of wealth and glory], says the
Lord God.

**AMP** [a] The traditional site of Eden was within the bounds of the Assyrian Empire. However, this in no sense implies that Assyria was in the garden of God, of Genesis 2:8. [b] The effectiveness of this comparison [of Egypt] with Assyria becomes plain when it is remembered that Assyria had conquered and held Egypt in vassalage, and had then herself been conquered and annihilated only thirty-seven years before the date of this prophecy, and that by the same Chaldean power [then controlled by the father of Nebuchadnezzar, which is] now foretold as about to execute judgment upon Egypt. Egypt could not hope to resist the conqueror of her conqueror. (Ellicott's Commentary.) [c] Though there were other circumcised nations besides the Hebrews, especially the Egyptians, and they as early as 3000 B.C., yet the Philistines, . . . the Moabites, the Ammonites, the Syrians, the Assyrians, the Babylonians, and various other nationalities with whom the Jews were in contact, were uncircumcised; so that the word "uncircumcised" as a term of reproach, meant almost practically (though not etymologically) the same as heathen. (Davis' Bible Dictionary.) [d] The Septuagint (Greek version) so reads at this point.

## New American Standard

6 'All the birds of the heavens nested in its boughs,
And under its branches all the beasts of the field gave birth,
And all great nations lived under its shade.
7 'So it was beautiful in its greatness, in the length of its branches;
For its roots extended to many waters.
8 'The cedars in God's garden could not match it;
The cypresses could not compare with its boughs,
And the plane trees could not match its branches.
No tree in God's garden could compare with it in its beauty.
9 'I made it beautiful with the multitude of its branches,
And all the trees of Eden, which were in the garden of God, were jealous of it.

10¶ 'Therefore, thus says the Lord GOD, "Because it is high in stature, and it has set its top among the clouds, and its heart is haughty in its loftiness,

11therefore, I will give it into the hand of a despot of the nations; he will thoroughly deal with it. According to its wickedness I have driven it away.

12"And alien tyrants of the nations have cut it down and left it; on the mountains and in all the valleys its branches have fallen, and its boughs have been broken in all the ravines of the land. And all the peoples of the earth have gone down from its shade and left it.

13"On its ruin all the birds of the heavens will dwell. And all the beasts of the field will be on its *fallen* branches

14in order that all the trees by the waters may not be exalted in their stature, nor set their top among the clouds, nor their well-watered mighty ones stand *erect* in their height. For they have all been given over to death, to the earth beneath, among the sons of men, with those who go down to the pit."

15¶ 'Thus says the Lord GOD, "On the day when it went down to Sheol I caused lamentations; I closed the deep over it and held back its rivers. And *its* many waters were stopped up, and I made Lebanon mourn for it, and all the trees of the field wilted away on account of it.

16"I made the nations quake at the sound of its fall when I made it go down to Sheol with those who go down to the pit; and all the well-watered trees of Eden, the choicest and best of Lebanon, were comforted in the earth beneath.

17"They also went down with it to Sheol to those who were slain by the sword; and those who were its strength lived under its shade among the nations.

18"To which among the trees of Eden are you thus equal in glory and greatness? Yet you will be brought down with the trees of Eden to the earth beneath; you will lie in the midst of the uncircumcised, with those who were slain by the sword. So is Pharaoh and all his multitude!"' declares the Lord GOD."

## New International

6All the birds of the air
nested in its boughs,
all the beasts of the field
gave birth under its branches;
all the great nations
lived in its shade.
7It was majestic in beauty,
with its spreading boughs,
for its roots went down
to abundant waters.
8The cedars in the garden of God
could not rival it,
nor could the pine trees
equal its boughs,
nor could the plane trees
compare with its branches—
no tree in the garden of God
could match its beauty.
9I made it beautiful
with abundant branches,
the envy of all the trees of Eden
in the garden of God.

10" 'Therefore this is what the Sovereign LORD says: Because it
towered on high, lifting its top above the thick foliage, and because
it was proud of its height, 11I handed it over to the ruler of the
nations, for him to deal with according to its wickedness. I cast it
aside, 12and the most ruthless of foreign nations cut it down and
left it. Its boughs fell on the mountains and in all the valleys; its
branches lay broken in all the ravines of the land. All the nations
of the earth came out from under its shade and left it. 13All the
birds of the air settled on the fallen tree, and all the beasts of the
field were among its branches. 14Therefore no other trees by the
waters are ever to tower proudly on high, lifting their tops above
the thick foliage. No other trees so well-watered are ever to reach
such a height; they are all destined for death, for the earth below,
among mortal men, with those who go down to the pit.

15" 'This is what the Sovereign LORD says: On the day it was
brought down to the grave[e] I covered the deep springs with
mourning for it; I held back its streams, and its abundant waters
were restrained. Because of it I clothed Lebanon with gloom, and
all the trees of the field withered away. 16I made the nations
tremble at the sound of its fall when I brought it down to the grave
with those who go down to the pit. Then all the trees of Eden, the
choicest and best of Lebanon, all the trees that were well-watered,
were consoled in the earth below. 17Those who lived in its shade,
its allies among the nations, had also gone down to the grave with
it, joining those killed by the sword.

18" 'Which of the trees of Eden can be compared with you in
splendor and majesty? Yet you, too, will be brought down with the
trees of Eden to the earth below; you will lie among the uncircumcised, with those killed by the sword.

" 'This is Pharaoh and all his hordes, declares the Sovereign LORD.' "

NIV [e] 15 Hebrew *Sheol;* also in verses 16 and 17

## King James

**32** AND IT came to pass in the twelfth year, in the twelfth
month, in the first *day* of the month, *that* the word of the
LORD came unto me, saying,
2Son of man, take up a lamentation for Pharaoh king of Egypt,
and say unto him, Thou art like a young lion of the nations, and
thou *art* as a whale in the seas: and thou camest forth with thy
rivers, and troubledst the waters with thy feet, and fouledst their
rivers.
3Thus saith the Lord GOD; I will therefore spread out my net
over thee with a company of many people; and they shall bring
thee up in my net.
4Then will I leave thee upon the land, I will cast thee forth upon
the open field, and will cause all the fowls of the heaven to remain
upon thee, and I will fill the beasts of the whole earth with thee.
5And I will lay thy flesh upon the mountains, and fill the valleys
with thy height.
6I will also water with thy blood the land wherein thou swim-
mest, *even* to the mountains; and the rivers shall be full of thee.
7And when I shall put thee out, I will cover the heaven, and
make the stars thereof dark; I will cover the sun with a cloud, and
the moon shall not give her light.
8All the bright lights of heaven will I make dark over thee, and
set darkness upon thy land, saith the Lord GOD.
9I will also vex the hearts of many people, when I shall bring
thy destruction among the nations, into the countries which thou
hast not known.
10Yea, I will make many people amazed at thee, and their kings
shall be horribly afraid for thee, when I shall brandish my sword
before them; and they shall tremble at *every* moment, every man
for his own life, in the day of thy fall.
11¶ For thus saith the Lord GOD; The sword of the king of
Babylon shall come upon thee.
12By the swords of the mighty will I cause thy multitude to fall,
the terrible of the nations, all of them: and they shall spoil the
pomp of Egypt, and all the multitude thereof shall be destroyed.
13I will destroy also all the beasts thereof from beside the great
waters; neither shall the foot of man trouble them any more, nor
the hoofs of beasts trouble them.
14Then will I make their waters deep, and cause their rivers to
run like oil, saith the Lord GOD.
15When I shall make the land of Egypt desolate, and the country
shall be destitute of that whereof it was full, when I shall smite all
them that dwell therein, then shall they know that I *am* the LORD.
16This *is* the lamentation wherewith they shall lament her: the
daughters of the nations shall lament her: they shall lament for her,
*even* for Egypt, and for all her multitude, saith the Lord GOD.
17¶ It came to pass also in the twelfth year, in the fifteenth *day*
of the month, *that* the word of the LORD came unto me, saying,

## Amplified

**32** IN THE twelfth year [after King Jehoiachin of Judah was
taken into exile by the king of Babylon], in the twelfth
month, on the first day of the month, the word of the Lord came
to me:
2Son of man, take up a lamentation over Pharaoh king of Egypt,
and say to him, You have likened *yourself* to a young lion, leader
of the nations, but you are like a [monster] dragon in the seas; you
break forth in your rivers, and trouble the waters with your feet,
and you make foul their rivers [the sources of their prosperity].
3Thus says the Lord God: I will therefore throw out My net over
you with a host of many peoples, and they shall bring you up in
My dragnet.
4Then I will leave you [Egypt] upon the shore, I will cast you
on the open field, and will cause all the birds of the heavens to
settle upon you, and I will fill the beasts of the whole earth with
you.
5And I will scatter your flesh upon the mountains, and fill the
valleys with your high heap of corpses *and their* worms.
6I will also water with your flowing blood the land, even to the
mountains, and the hollows *and* water channels shall be full of you.
7And when I have extinguished you, I will cover the heavens
[of Egypt] and make their stars dark; I will cover the sun with a
cloud, and the moon shall not give her light.
8All the bright lights of the heavens I will make dark over you,
and set darkness upon your land, says the Lord God.
9I will also trouble *and* vex the hearts of many peoples, when
I bring your breaking *and* trembling *and* destruction, *and* carry you
captive among the nations, into the countries which you have not
known.
10I will make many peoples amazed *and* appalled at you [Egypt],
and their kings shall shudder *and* be horribly afraid because of you,
when I brandish My sword before them; they shall tremble every
moment, every man for his own life, in the day of your downfall.
11For thus says the Lord God: The sword of the king of Babylon
shall come upon you.
12I will cause your multitude, your tumult *and* your store [of
wealth, strength and glory] to fall by the swords of the mighty; the
most terrible among the nations are they all. And they shall bring
to nothing the pomp *and* pride of Egypt, and all its multitude—
with its activity, and its wealth in every sphere—shall be destroyed.
13I will destroy also all its beasts from beside many *and* great
waters, and no foot of man shall trouble them any more, nor shall
the hoofs of beasts trouble them.
14Then will I make their waters sink down—subside, be quiet
and clear; their rivers I will cause to run [slowly and smoothly] like
oil, says the Lord God.
15When I make the land of Egypt desolate, and the country is
stripped *and* destitute of all that of which it was full, when I smite
all those who dwell in it, then will they know, understand *and*
realize that I am the Lord [the Sovereign Ruler, requiring and
calling forth loyalty and obedient service].
16This is the lamentation with which they shall intone *or* chant
the lament for her: the daughters of the nations shall chant their
lament with it; over Egypt and over all her multitude, her tumult,
*and* her wealth in every sphere shall they chant it, says the Lord
God.
17In the twelfth year [after King Jehoiachin of Judah was taken
into exile], on the fifteenth day of the month, the word of the Lord
came to me:

## New American Standard

*Lament over Pharaoh and Egypt*

**32** AND IT came about in the twelfth year, in the twelfth *month,* on the first of the month, that the word of the LORD came to me saying,

2"Son of man, take up a lamentation over Pharaoh king of Egypt, and say to him,
'You compared yourself to a young lion of the nations,
Yet you are like the monster in the seas;
And you burst forth in your rivers,
And muddied the waters with your feet,
And fouled their rivers.' "
3Thus says the Lord GOD,
"Now I will spread My net over you
With a company of many peoples,
And they shall lift you up in My net.
4 "And I will leave you on the land;
I will cast you on the open field.
And I will cause all the birds of the heavens to dwell on you,
And I will satisfy the beasts of the whole earth with you.
5 "And I will lay your flesh on the mountains,
And fill the valleys with your refuse.
6 "I will also make the land drink the discharge of your blood,
As far as the mountains,
And the ravines shall be full of you.
7 "And when *I* extinguish you,
I will cover the heavens, and darken their stars;
I will cover the sun with a cloud,
And the moon shall not give its light.
8 "All the shining lights in the heavens
I will darken over you
And will set darkness on your land,"
Declares the Lord GOD.

9"I will also trouble the hearts of many peoples, when I bring your destruction among the nations, into lands which you have not known.

10"And I will make many peoples appalled at you, and their kings shall be horribly afraid of you when I brandish My sword before them; and they shall tremble every moment, every man for his own life, on the day of your fall."

11¶ For thus says the Lord GOD, "The sword of the king of Babylon shall come upon you.

12"By the swords of the mighty ones I will cause your multitude to fall; all of them are tyrants of the nations,
And they shall devastate the pride of Egypt,
And all its multitude shall be destroyed.
13 "I will also destroy all its cattle from beside many waters;
And the foot of man shall not muddy them anymore,
And the hoofs of beasts shall not muddy them.
14 "Then I will make their waters settle,
And will cause their rivers to run like oil,"
Declares the Lord GOD.
15 "When I make the land of Egypt a desolation,
And the land is destitute of that which filled it,
When I smite all those who live in it,
Then they shall know that I am the LORD.

16"This is a lamentation and they shall chant it. The daughters of the nations shall chant it. Over Egypt and over all her multitude they shall chant it," declares the Lord GOD.

17¶ And it came about in the twelfth year, on the fifteenth of the month, that the word of the LORD came to me saying,

## New International

*A Lament for Pharaoh*

**32** IN THE twelfth year, in the twelfth month on the first day, the word of the LORD came to me: 2"Son of man, take up a lament concerning Pharaoh king of Egypt and say to him:

" 'You are like a lion among the nations;
you are like a monster in the seas
thrashing about in your streams,
churning the water with your feet
and muddying the streams.

3" 'This is what the Sovereign LORD says:

" 'With a great throng of people
I will cast my net over you,
and they will haul you up in my net.
4I will throw you on the land
and hurl you on the open field.
I will let all the birds of the air settle on you
and all the beasts of the earth gorge themselves on you.
5I will spread your flesh on the mountains
and fill the valleys with your remains.
6I will drench the land with your flowing blood
all the way to the mountains,
and the ravines will be filled with your flesh.
7When I snuff you out, I will cover the heavens
and darken their stars;
I will cover the sun with a cloud,
and the moon will not give its light.
8All the shining lights in the heavens
I will darken over you;
I will bring darkness over your land,
declares the Sovereign LORD.
9I will trouble the hearts of many peoples
when I bring about your destruction among the nations,
among[a] lands you have not known.
10I will cause many peoples to be appalled at you,
and their kings will shudder with horror because of you
when I brandish my sword before them.
On the day of your downfall
each of them will tremble
every moment for his life.

11" 'For this is what the Sovereign LORD says:

" 'The sword of the king of Babylon
will come against you.
12I will cause your hordes to fall
by the swords of mighty men—
the most ruthless of all nations.
They will shatter the pride of Egypt,
and all her hordes will be overthrown.
13I will destroy all her cattle
from beside abundant waters
no longer to be stirred by the foot of man
or muddied by the hoofs of cattle.
14Then I will let her waters settle
and make her streams flow like oil,
declares the Sovereign LORD.

15When I make Egypt desolate
and strip the land of everything in it,
when I strike down all who live there,
then they will know that I am the LORD.'

16"This is the lament they will chant for her. The daughters of the nations will chant it; for Egypt and all her hordes they will chant it, declares the Sovereign LORD."

17In the twelfth year, on the fifteenth day of the month, the word of the LORD came to me: 18"Son of man, wail for the hordes

NIV [a] 9 Hebrew; Septuagint *bring you into captivity among the nations, / to*

## King James

18 Son of man, wail for the multitude of Egypt, and cast them
down, *even* her, and the daughters of the famous nations, unto the
nether parts of the earth, with them that go down into the pit.
19 Whom dost thou pass in beauty? go down, and be thou laid
with the uncircumcised.
20 They shall fall in the midst of *them that are* slain by the sword:
she is delivered to the sword: draw her and all her multitudes.
21 The strong among the mighty shall speak to him out of the
midst of hell with them that help him: they are gone down, they
lie uncircumcised, slain by the sword.
22 Asshur *is* there and all her company: his graves *are* about him:
all of them slain, fallen by the sword:
23 Whose graves are set in the sides of the pit, and her company
is round about her grave: all of them slain, fallen by the sword,
which caused terror in the land of the living.
24 There *is* Elam and all her multitude round about her grave, all
of them slain, fallen by the sword, which are gone down uncircumcised into the nether parts of the earth, which caused their terror
in the land of the living; yet have they borne their shame with them
that go down to the pit.
25 They have set her a bed in the midst of the slain with all her
multitude: her graves *are* round about him: all of them uncircumcised, slain by the sword: though their terror was caused in the
land of the living, yet have they borne their shame with them that
go down to the pit: he is put in the midst of *them that be* slain.
26 There *is* Meshech, Tubal, and all her multitude: her graves *are*
round about him: all of them uncircumcised, slain by the sword,
though they caused their terror in the land of the living.
27 And they shall not lie with the mighty *that are* fallen of the
uncircumcised, which are gone down to hell with their weapons
of war: and they have laid their swords under their heads, but their
iniquities shall be upon their bones, though *they were* the terror of
the mighty in the land of the living.
28 Yea, thou shalt be broken in the midst of the uncircumcised,
and shalt lie with *them that are* slain with the sword.
29 There *is* Edom, her kings, and all her princes, which with their
might are laid by *them that were* slain by the sword: they shall lie
with the uncircumcised, and with them that go down to the pit.
30 There *be* the princes of the north, all of them, and all the
Zidonians, which are gone down with the slain; with their terror
they are ashamed of their might; and they lie uncircumcised with
*them that be* slain by the sword, and bear their shame with them
that go down to the pit.
31 Pharaoh shall see them, and shall be comforted over all his
multitude, *even* Pharaoh and all his army slain by the sword, saith
the Lord GOD.
32 For I have caused my terror in the land of the living: and he
shall be laid in the midst of the uncircumcised with *them that are*
slain with the sword, *even* Pharaoh and all his multitude, saith the
Lord GOD.

**33** AGAIN THE word of the LORD came unto me, saying,
2 Son of man, speak to the children of thy people, and say
unto them, When I bring the sword upon a land, if the people of
the land take a man of their coasts, and set him for their watchman:
3 If when he seeth the sword come upon the land, he blow the
trumpet, and warn the people;

## Amplified

18 Son of man, wail over the multitude of Egypt, and cast them
down, even her and the daughters of the famous *and* majestic
nations, to the nether world, with those who go down to the pit:
19 Whom [among them] do you surpass in beauty? Go down and
be laid with the uncircumcised—the heathen.
20 They shall fall in the midst of those who are slain by the
sword; she [Egypt] is delivered to the sword; they draw her down
[to her judgment], and all her multitudes with their noise *and*
stores.
21 The strong among the mighty shall speak of [Pharaoh] out of
the midst of Sheol—the nether world—with those who helped
him; they are gone down, they lie still, even the uncircumcised—
the heathen—slain by the sword.
22 Assyria is there and all her company; their graves are round
about her, all of them slain, fallen by the sword;
23 Whose graves are set in the uttermost parts of the pit, and her
company is round about her grave; all of them slain, fallen by the
sword, who caused terror to spread in the land of the living.
24 Elam [an auxiliary of Assyria] is there and all her multitude
round about her grave, all of them slain, fallen by the sword, who
have gone down uncircumcised into the nether world, who caused
their terror to spread in the land of the living, and have borne their
shame with those who go down to the pit.
25 They have set her a bed [a sepulcher] among the slain with
all her multitude; their graves round about her, all of them uncircumcised, slain by the sword; for terror of them was spread in the
land of the living, and they henceforth bear their shame with those
who go down to the pit; they are laid in the midst of the slain.
26 Meshech, Tubal, and all their multitude are there; their graves
are round about [Pharaoh], all of them uncircumcised, slain by the
sword; for they caused their terror to be spread in the land of the
living.
27 And they shall not lie with the mighty that are fallen of the
uncircumcised, who are gone down to Sheol—the nether world—
with their weapons of war, whose swords were laid [with honors]
under their heads, and whose iniquities are upon their bones, for
they caused their terror to spread in the land of the living.
28 But you, [Meshech and Tubal,] shall be broken in the midst
of the uncircumcised and shall lie [without honors] with those who
are slain with the sword.
29 Edom is there, her kings and all her princes, who for all their
might are laid with those who were slain by the sword; they shall
lie with the [a]uncircumcised—the heathen—and with those who
go down to the pit.
30 The princes of the north are there, all of them, and all the
Sidonians, who have gone down with the slain; for all the terror
which they caused by their might they are put to shame; and they
lie uncircumcised with those who are slain by the sword, and
henceforth bear their shame with those who go down to the pit.
31 When Pharaoh sees them, he will comfort himself for all his
multitude; even Pharaoh and all his army, slain by the sword, says
the Lord God.
32 For I have put his *and* My terror in the land of the living; and
he shall be laid in the midst of the uncircumcised—the heathen—
with those slain by the sword, even Pharaoh and all his multitude,
says the Lord God. [Isa. 19; Jer. 46; Zech. 14:18, 19.]

**33** AND THE word of the Lord came to me:
2 Son of man, speak to your people [the Israelite captives
in Babylon] and say to them, When I bring the sword upon a land,
and the people of the land take a man from among them and make
him their watchman;
3 If when he sees the sword coming upon the land, he blows the
trumpet and warns the people;

**AMP** [a] The Edomites observed the rite of circumcision, but were not spared because of that.

## New American Standard

18"Son of man, wail for the multitude of Egypt, and bring it
down, her and the daughters of the powerful nations, to the nether
world, with those who go down to the pit;
19 'Whom do you surpass in beauty?
Go down and make your bed with the uncircumcised.'
20"They shall fall in the midst of those who are slain by the
sword. She is given over to the sword; they have drawn her and
all her multitudes away.
21"The strong among the mighty ones shall speak of him *and* his
helpers from the midst of Sheol, 'They have gone down, they lie
still, the uncircumcised, slain by the sword.'
22¶ "Assyria is there and all her company; her graves are round
about her. All of them are slain, fallen by the sword,
23whose graves are set in the remotest parts of the pit, and her
company is round about her grave. All of them are slain, fallen by
the sword, who spread terror in the land of the living.
24¶ "Elam is there and all her multitude around her grave; all
of them slain, fallen by the sword, who went down uncircumcised
to the lower parts of the earth, who instilled their terror in the land
of the living, and bore their disgrace with those who went down
to the pit.
25"They have made a bed for her among the slain with all her
multitude. Her graves are around it, they are all uncircumcised,
slain by the sword (although their terror was instilled in the land
of the living), and they bore their disgrace with those who go down
to the pit; they were put in the midst of the slain.
26¶ "Meshech, Tubal and all their multitude are there; their
graves surround them. All of them were slain by the sword uncircumcised, though they instilled their terror in the land of the
living.
27"Nor do they lie beside the fallen heroes of the uncircumcised,
who went down to Sheol with their weapons of war, and whose
swords were laid under their heads; but the punishment for their
iniquity rested on their bones, though the terror of *these* heroes *was*
once in the land of the living.
28"But in the midst of the uncircumcised you will be broken and
lie with those slain by the sword.
29¶ "There also is Edom, its kings, and all its princes, who for
*all* their might are laid with those slain by the sword; they will lie
with the uncircumcised, and with those who go down to the pit.
30¶ "There also are the chiefs of the north, all of them, and all
the Sidonians, who in spite of the terror resulting from their might,
in shame went down with the slain. So they lay down uncircumcised with those slain by the sword, and bore their disgrace with
those who go down to the pit.
31¶ "These Pharaoh will see, and he will be comforted for all his
multitude slain by the sword, *even* Pharaoh and all his army,"
declares the Lord GOD.
32"Though I instilled a terror of him in the land of the living,
yet he will be made to lie down among *the* uncircumcised *along*
with those slain by the sword, *even* Pharaoh and all his multitude,"
declares the Lord GOD.

*The Watchman's Duty*

33 AND THE word of the LORD came to me saying,
2"Son of man, speak to the sons of your people, and say
to them, 'If I bring a sword upon a land, and the people of the land
take one man from among them and make him their watchman;
3and he sees the sword coming upon the land, and he blows
on the trumpet and warns the people,

## New International

of Egypt and consign to the earth below both her and the daughters of mighty nations, with those who go down to the pit. 19Say
to them, 'Are you more favored than others? Go down and be laid
among the uncircumcised.' 20They will fall among those killed by
the sword. The sword is drawn; let her be dragged off with all her
hordes. 21From within the grave[b] the mighty leaders will say of
Egypt and her allies, 'They have come down and they lie with the
uncircumcised, with those killed by the sword.'
22"Assyria is there with her whole army; she is surrounded by
the graves of all her slain, all who have fallen by the sword. 23Their
graves are in the depths of the pit and her army lies around her
grave. All who had spread terror in the land of the living are slain,
fallen by the sword.
24"Elam is there, with all her hordes around her grave. All of
them are slain, fallen by the sword. All who had spread terror in
the land of the living went down uncircumcised to the earth below.
They bear their shame with those who go down to the pit. 25A bed
is made for her among the slain, with all her hordes around her
grave. All of them are uncircumcised, killed by the sword. Because
their terror had spread in the land of the living, they bear their
shame with those who go down to the pit; they are laid among the
slain.
26"Meshech and Tubal are there, with all their hordes around
their graves. All of them are uncircumcised, killed by the sword
because they spread their terror in the land of the living. 27Do they
not lie with the other uncircumcised warriors who have fallen,
who went down to the grave with their weapons of war, whose
swords were placed under their heads? The punishment for their
sins rested on their bones, though the terror of these warriors had
stalked through the land of the living.
28"You too, O Pharaoh, will be broken and will lie among the
uncircumcised, with those killed by the sword.
29"Edom is there, her kings and all her princes; despite their
power, they are laid with those killed by the sword. They lie with
the uncircumcised, with those who go down to the pit.
30"All the princes of the north and all the Sidonians are there;
they went down with the slain in disgrace despite the terror caused
by their power. They lie uncircumcised with those killed by the
sword and bear their shame with those who go down to the pit.
31"Pharaoh—he and all his army—will see them and he will be
consoled for all his hordes that were killed by the sword, declares
the Sovereign LORD. 32Although I had him spread terror in the
land of the living, Pharaoh and all his hordes will be laid among
the uncircumcised, with those killed by the sword, declares the
Sovereign LORD."

*Ezekiel a Watchman*

33 THE WORD of the LORD came to me: 2"Son of man, speak
to your countrymen and say to them: 'When I bring the
sword against a land, and the people of the land choose one of
their men and make him their watchman, 3and he sees the sword
coming against the land and blows the trumpet to warn the people,

NIV [b] 21 Hebrew *Sheol;* also in verse 27

## King James

4Then whosoever heareth the sound of the trumpet, and taketh not warning; if the sword come, and take him away, his blood shall be upon his own head.

5He heard the sound of the trumpet, and took not warning; his blood shall be upon him. But he that taketh warning shall deliver his soul.

6But if the watchman see the sword come, and blow not the trumpet, and the people be not warned; if the sword come, and take *any* person from among them, he is taken away in his iniquity; but his blood will I require at the watchman's hand.

7¶ So thou, O son of man, I have set thee a watchman unto the house of Israel; therefore thou shalt hear the word at my mouth, and warn them from me.

8When I say unto the wicked, O wicked *man*, thou shalt surely die; if thou dost not speak to warn the wicked from his way, that wicked *man* shall die in his iniquity; but his blood will I require at thine hand.

9Nevertheless, if thou warn the wicked of his way to turn from it; if he do not turn from his way, he shall die in his iniquity; but thou hast delivered thy soul.

10Therefore, O thou son of man, speak unto the house of Israel; Thus ye speak, saying, If our transgressions and our sins *be* upon us, and we pine away in them, how should we then live?

11Say unto them, *As* I live, saith the Lord GOD, I have no pleasure in the death of the wicked; but that the wicked turn from his way and live: turn ye, turn ye from your evil ways; for why will ye die, O house of Israel?

12Therefore, thou son of man, say unto the children of thy people, The righteousness of the righteous shall not deliver him in the day of his transgression: as for the wickedness of the wicked, he shall not fall thereby in the day that he turneth from his wickedness; neither shall the righteous be able to live for his *righteousness* in the day that he sinneth.

13When I shall say to the righteous, *that* he shall surely live; if he trust to his own righteousness, and commit iniquity, all his righteousnesses shall not be remembered; but for his iniquity that he hath committed, he shall die for it.

14Again, when I say unto the wicked, Thou shalt surely die; if he turn from his sin, and do that which is lawful and right;

15 *If* the wicked restore the pledge, give again that he had robbed, walk in the statutes of life, without committing iniquity; he shall surely live, he shall not die.

16None of his sins that he hath committed shall be mentioned unto him: he hath done that which is lawful and right; he shall surely live.

17¶ Yet the children of thy people say, The way of the Lord is not equal: but as for them, their way is not equal.

18When the righteous turneth from his righteousness, and committeth iniquity, he shall even die thereby.

19But if the wicked turn from his wickedness, and do that which is lawful and right, he shall live thereby.

20¶ Yet ye say, The way of the Lord is not equal. O ye house of Israel, I will judge you every one after his ways.

21¶ And it came to pass in the twelfth year of our captivity, in the tenth *month*, in the fifth *day* of the month, *that* one that had escaped out of Jerusalem came unto me, saying, The city is smitten.

22Now the hand of the LORD was upon me in the evening, afore he that was escaped came; and had opened my mouth, until he came to me in the morning; and my mouth was opened, and I was no more dumb.

23Then the word of the LORD came unto me, saying,

## Amplified

4Then whoever hears the sound of the trumpet, and does not take warning, and the sword comes and takes him away, his blood shall be upon his own head.

5He heard the sound of the trumpet, and did not take warning; his blood shall be upon himself. But he who takes warning shall save his life.

6But if the watchman sees the sword coming and does not blow the trumpet, and the people are not warned, and the sword comes and takes any one of them; he is taken away in *and* for his perversity *and* iniquity, but his blood will I require at the watchman's hand.

7So you, son of man, I have made you a watchman for the house of Israel; therefore hear the word at My mouth and give them warning from Me.

8When I say to the wicked, O wicked man, you shall surely die, and you do not speak to warn the wicked from his way, that wicked man shall die in his perversity *and* iniquity, but his blood will I require at your hand.

9But if you warn the wicked to turn from his evil way, and he does not turn from his evil way, he shall die in his iniquity; but you will have saved your life.

10And you, son of man, say to the house of Israel, Thus you have said: Truly our transgressions and our sins are upon us, and we waste away because of them; how then can we live?

11Say to them, As I live, says the Lord God, I have no pleasure in the death of the wicked, but rather that the wicked turn from his way and live. Turn back, turn back from your evil ways; for why will you die, O house of Israel?

12And you, son of man, say to your people, The uprightness *and* justice of the [uncompromisingly] righteous shall not deliver him in the day of his transgression; and as for the wicked lawlessness of the wicked lawless, he shall not fall because of it in the day that he turns from his wickedness; neither shall the rigidly upright *and* just be able to live because of his past righteousness in the day that he sins *and* misses the mark [in keeping in harmony and right standing with God].

13When I shall say to the [uncompromisingly] righteous, that he shall surely live, and he trusts to his own righteousness [to save him] and commits iniquity—heinous sin—all his righteous deeds shall not be [seriously] remembered; but for his perversity *and* iniquity that he has committed he shall die.

14Again, when I have said to the wicked, You shall surely die, if he turns from his sin, and does that which is lawful and right,

15If the wicked restores [what he took in] pledge, gives back what he had taken in robbery, walks in the statutes of life [right relationship with God], without committing iniquity; he shall surely live, he shall not die.

16None of his sins that he has committed shall be [seriously] remembered against him; he has done that which is lawful and right; he shall surely live.

17Yet your people say, The way of the Lord is not perfect *or* even just; but as for them, it is their own way that is not perfect *or* even just.

18When the righteous turns back from his [uncompromising] righteousness and commits perverseness *and* iniquity, he shall even die in *and* because of it.

19But if the wicked turns back from his wickedness and does what is lawful and right, he shall live because of it.

20Yet you say, The way of the Lord is not perfect *or* even just. O you house of Israel, I will judge you every one according to his own ways!

21In the twelfth year of our captivity [in Babylon], in the tenth *month*, on the fifth *day* of the month, a man who had escaped out of Jerusalem came to me [Ezekiel], saying, The city [Jerusalem] is taken.

22Now the hand of the Lord had been upon me in the evening, before this one who had escaped came, and He had opened my mouth [in readiness for the fugitives] coming to me in the morning; and my mouth was opened, and I was no longer dumb.

23Then the word of the Lord came to me:

## New American Standard

4then he who hears the sound of the trumpet and does not take
warning, and a sword comes and takes him away, his blood will
be on his *own* head.
5'He heard the sound of the trumpet, but did not take warning;
his blood will be on himself. But had he taken warning, he would
have delivered his life.
6'But if the watchman sees the sword coming and does not
blow the trumpet, and the people are not warned, and a sword
comes and takes a person from them, he is taken away in his
iniquity; but his blood I will require from the watchman's hand.'
7¶ "Now as for you, son of man, I have appointed you a
watchman for the house of Israel; so you will hear a message from
My mouth, and give them warning from Me.
8"When I say to the wicked, 'O wicked man, you shall surely
die,' and you do not speak to warn the wicked from his way, that
wicked man shall die in his iniquity, but his blood I will require
from your hand.
9"But if you on your part warn a wicked man to turn from his
way, and he does not turn from his way, he will die in his iniquity;
but you have delivered your life.
10¶ "Now as for you, son of man, say to the house of Israel,
'Thus you have spoken, saying, "Surely our transgressions and
our sins are upon us, and we are rotting away in them; how then
can we survive?"'
11"Say to them, 'As I live!' declares the Lord GOD, 'I take no
pleasure in the death of the wicked, but rather that the wicked turn
from his way and live. Turn back, turn back from your evil ways!
Why then will you die, O house of Israel?'
12"And you, son of man, say to your fellow citizens, 'The righteousness of a righteous man will not deliver him in the day of his
transgression, and as for the wickedness of the wicked, he will not
stumble because of it in the day when he turns from his wickedness; whereas a righteous man will not be able to live by his
righteousness on the day when he commits sin.'
13"When I say to the righteous he will surely live, and he *so*
trusts in his righteousness that he commits iniquity, none of his
righteous deeds will be remembered; but in that same iniquity of
his which he has committed he will die.
14"But when I say to the wicked, 'You will surely die,' and he
turns from his sin and practices justice and righteousness,
15 *if a* wicked man restores a pledge, pays back what he has
taken by robbery, walks by the statutes which ensure life without
committing iniquity, he will surely live; he shall not die.
16"None of his sins that he has committed will be remembered
against him. He has practiced justice and righteousness; he will
surely live.
17¶ "Yet your fellow citizens say, 'The way of the Lord is not
right,' when it is their own way that is not right.
18"When the righteous turns from his righteousness and commits iniquity, then he shall die in it.
19"But when the wicked turns from his wickedness and practices justice and righteousness, he will live by them.
20"Yet you say, 'The way of the Lord is not right.' O house of
Israel, I will judge each of you according to his ways."

*Word of Jerusalem's Capture*

21¶ Now it came about in the twelfth year of our exile, on the
fifth of the tenth month, that the refugees from Jerusalem came to
me, saying, "The city has been taken."
22Now the hand of the LORD had been upon me in the evening,
before the refugees came. And He opened my mouth at the time
*they* came to me in the morning; so my mouth was opened, and
I was no longer speechless.
23¶ Then the word of the LORD came to me saying,

## New International

4then if anyone hears the trumpet but does not take warning and
the sword comes and takes his life, his blood will be on his own
head. 5Since he heard the sound of the trumpet but did not take
warning, his blood will be on his own head. If he had taken
warning, he would have saved himself. 6But if the watchman sees
the sword coming and does not blow the trumpet to warn the
people and the sword comes and takes the life of one of them, that
man will be taken away because of his sin, but I will hold the
watchman accountable for his blood.'
7"Son of man, I have made you a watchman for the house of
Israel; so hear the word I speak and give them warning from me.
8When I say to the wicked, 'O wicked man, you will surely die,'
and you do not speak out to dissuade him from his ways, that
wicked man will die for[a] his sin, and I will hold you accountable
for his blood. 9But if you do warn the wicked man to turn from his
ways and he does not do so, he will die for his sin, but you will
have saved yourself.
10"Son of man, say to the house of Israel, 'This is what you are
saying: "Our offenses and sins weigh us down, and we are wasting away because of[b] them. How then can we live?"' 11Say to
them, 'As surely as I live, declares the Sovereign LORD, I take no
pleasure in the death of the wicked, but rather that they turn from
their ways and live. Turn! Turn from your evil ways! Why will you
die, O house of Israel?'
12"Therefore, son of man, say to your countrymen, 'The righteousness of the righteous man will not save him when he disobeys, and the wickedness of the wicked man will not cause him
to fall when he turns from it. The righteous man, if he sins, will
not be allowed to live because of his former righteousness.' 13If I
tell the righteous man that he will surely live, but then he trusts
in his righteousness and does evil, none of the righteous things he
has done will be remembered; he will die for the evil he has done.
14And if I say to the wicked man, 'You will surely die,' but he then
turns away from his sin and does what is just and right— 15if he
gives back what he took in pledge for a loan, returns what he has
stolen, follows the decrees that give life, and does no evil, he will
surely live; he will not die. 16None of the sins he has committed
will be remembered against him. He has done what is just and
right; he will surely live.
17"Yet your countrymen say, 'The way of the Lord is not just.'
But it is their way that is not just. 18If a righteous man turns from
his righteousness and does evil, he will die for it. 19And if a wicked
man turns away from his wickedness and does what is just and
right, he will live by doing so. 20Yet, O house of Israel, you say,
'The way of the Lord is not just.' But I will judge each of you
according to his own ways."

*Jerusalem's Fall Explained*

21In the twelfth year of our exile, in the tenth month on the fifth
day, a man who had escaped from Jerusalem came to me and said,
"The city has fallen!" 22Now the evening before the man arrived,
the hand of the LORD was upon me, and he opened my mouth
before the man came to me in the morning. So my mouth was
opened and I was no longer silent.
23Then the word of the LORD came to me: 24"Son of man, the

NIV [a] *8* Or *in;* also in verse 9 [b] *10* Or *away in*

## King James

24Son of man, they that inhabit those wastes of the land of Israel speak, saying, Abraham was one, and he inherited the land: but we *are* many; the land is given us for inheritance.

25Wherefore say unto them, Thus saith the Lord GOD; Ye eat with the blood, and lift up your eyes toward your idols, and shed blood: and shall ye possess the land?

26Ye stand upon your sword, ye work abomination, and ye defile every one his neighbour's wife: and shall ye possess the land?

27Say thou thus unto them, Thus saith the Lord GOD; *As* I live, surely they that *are* in the wastes shall fall by the sword, and him that *is* in the open field will I give to the beasts to be devoured, and they that *be* in the forts and in the caves shall die of the pestilence.

28For I will lay the land most desolate, and the pomp of her strength shall cease; and the mountains of Israel shall be desolate, that none shall pass through.

29Then shall they know that I *am* the LORD, when I have laid the land most desolate because of all their abominations which they have committed.

30¶ Also, thou son of man, the children of thy people still are talking against thee by the walls and in the doors of the houses, and speak one to another, every one to his brother, saying, Come, I pray you, and hear what is the word that cometh forth from the LORD.

31And they come unto thee as the people cometh, and they sit before thee *as* my people, and they hear thy words, but they will not do them: for with their mouth they show much love, *but* their heart goeth after their covetousness.

32And, lo, thou *art* unto them as a very lovely song of one that hath a pleasant voice, and can play well on an instrument: for they hear thy words, but they do them not.

33And when this cometh to pass, (lo, it will come,) then shall they know that a prophet hath been among them.

**34** AND THE word of the LORD came unto me, saying,

2Son of man, prophesy against the shepherds of Israel, prophesy, and say unto them, Thus saith the Lord GOD unto the shepherds; Woe *be* to the shepherds of Israel that do feed themselves! should not the shepherds feed the flocks?

3Ye eat the fat, and ye clothe you with the wool, ye kill them that are fed: *but* ye feed not the flock.

4The diseased have ye not strengthened, neither have ye healed that which was sick, neither have ye bound up *that which was* broken, neither have ye brought again that which was driven away, neither have ye sought that which was lost; but with force and with cruelty have ye ruled them.

5And they were scattered, because *there is* no shepherd: and they became meat to all the beasts of the field, when they were scattered.

6My sheep wandered through all the mountains, and upon every high hill: yea, my flock was scattered upon all the face of the earth, and none did search or seek *after them.*

7¶ Therefore, ye shepherds, hear the word of the LORD;

8 *As* I live, saith the Lord GOD, surely because my flock became a prey, and my flock became meat to every beast of the field, because *there was* no shepherd, neither did my shepherds search for my flock, but the shepherds fed themselves, and fed not my flock;

9Therefore, O ye shepherds, hear the word of the LORD;

## Amplified

24Son of man, those [back in Palestine] who inhabit those wastes of the ground of Israel are saying, Abraham was only one man, and he inherited the land; but we are many; the land is surely given to us to possess as our inheritance.

25Therefore say to them, Thus says the Lord God: You eat meat with the blood [as an idolatrous rite], and lift up your eyes to your [filthy] idols, and shed blood; shall you then possess the land? [Gen. 9:4; Lev. 3:17; 7:27; Acts 15:28, 29.]

26You stand upon your sword [as your dependence], you commit abominations, and you each one defile your neighbor's wife; shall you then possess the land?

27Say this to them, Thus says the Lord God: As I live, surely those who are in the waste places shall fall by the sword, and him that is in the open field will I give to the beasts to be devoured, and those who are in strongholds and in caves shall die by pestilence.

28And I will make the land [of Israel] a desolation and a waste, and her proud might shall cease, and the mountains of Israel shall be so desolate that no one will pass through them.

29Then shall they know, understand *and* realize that I am the Lord, when I have made the land a desolation and a waste, because of all their abominations which they have committed.

30As for you, son of man, your people who talk of you by the walls and in the doors of the houses, say one to another, every one to his brother, Come, and hear what the word is that comes forth from the Lord.

31And they come to you as people come, and they sit before you as My people, and they hear the words you say, but they will not do them; for with their mouth they show much love, but their heart goes after *and* is set on their [idolatrous greed for] gain.

32Lo, you are to them as a very lovely [love] song of one who has a pleasant voice and can play well on an instrument, for they hear your words, but do not do them.

33When this comes to pass—for lo, it will come!—then shall they know, understand *and* realize that a prophet has been among them.

**34** AND THE word of the Lord came to me:

2Son of man, prophesy against the shepherds of Israel, prophesy and say to them, even to the [spiritual] shepherds, Thus says the Lord God: Woe to the [spiritual] shepherds of Israel who feed themselves! Should not the shepherds feed the sheep?

3You eat the fat, you clothe yourselves with the wool, you kill the fatlings; but you do not feed the sheep.

4The diseased *and* weak you have not strengthened, the sick you have not healed, the hurt *and* crippled you have not bandaged, those gone astray you have not brought back, the lost you have not sought to find; but with force and hardhearted harshness you have ruled them.

5And they were scattered, because there was no shepherd; and when they were scattered they became food for all the wild beasts of the field.

6My sheep wandered through all the mountains and upon every high hill; yes, My sheep were scattered upon all the face of the earth, and no one searched or sought for them. [Matt. 9:36.]

7Therefore, you [spiritual] shepherds, hear the word of the Lord:

8As I live, says the Lord God, surely because My sheep became a prey, and My sheep became food for every beast of the field, because there was no shepherd; neither did My shepherds search for My sheep, but the shepherds fed themselves, and fed not My sheep;

9Therefore, O you [spiritual] shepherds, hear the word of the Lord:

## New American Standard

24"Son of man, they who live in these waste places in the land
of Israel are saying, 'Abraham was *only* one, yet he possessed the
land; so to us who are many the land has been given as a possession.'

25"Therefore, say to them, 'Thus says the Lord GOD, "You eat
*meat* with the blood *in it,* lift up your eyes to your idols as you shed
blood. Should you then possess the land?

26"You rely on your sword, you commit abominations, and
each of you defiles his neighbor's wife. Should you then possess
the land?" '

27"Thus you shall say to them, 'Thus says the Lord GOD, "As
I live, surely those who are in the waste places will fall by the
sword, and whoever is in the open field I will give to the beasts
to be devoured, and those who are in the strongholds and in the
caves will die of pestilence.

28"And I shall make the land a desolation and a waste, and the
pride of her power will cease; and the mountains of Israel will be
desolate, so that no one will pass through.

29"Then they will know that I am the LORD, when I make the
land a desolation and a waste because of all their abominations
which they have committed." '

30¶ "But as for you, son of man, your fellow citizens who talk
about you by the walls and in the doorways of the houses, speak
to one another, each to his brother, saying, 'Come now, and hear
what the message is which comes forth from the LORD.'

31"And they come to you as people come, and sit before you
*as* My people, and hear your words, but they do not do them, for
they do the lustful desires *expressed* by their mouth, *and* their heart
goes after their gain.

32"And behold, you are to them like a sensual song by one who
has a beautiful voice and plays well on an instrument; for they hear
your words, but they do not practice them.

33"So when it comes to pass—as surely it will—then they will
know that a prophet has been in their midst."

*Prophecy against the Shepherds of Israel*

**34** THEN THE word of the LORD came to me saying,
2"Son of man, prophesy against the shepherds of Israel.
Prophesy and say to those shepherds, 'Thus says the Lord GOD,
"Woe, shepherds of Israel who have been feeding themselves!
Should not the shepherds feed the flock?

3"You eat the fat and clothe yourselves with the wool, you
slaughter the fat *sheep* without feeding the flock.

4"Those who are sickly you have not strengthened, the
diseased you have not healed, the broken you have not bound up,
the scattered you have not brought back, nor have you sought for
the lost; but with force and with severity you have dominated
them.

5"And they were scattered for lack of a shepherd, and they
became food for every beast of the field and were scattered.

6"My flock wandered through all the mountains and on every
high hill, and My flock was scattered over all the surface of the
earth; and there was no one to search or seek *for them.*" ' "

7¶ Therefore, you shepherds, hear the word of the LORD:
8"As I live," declares the Lord GOD, "surely because My flock
has become a prey, My flock has even become food for all the
beasts of the field for lack of a shepherd, and My shepherds did
not search for My flock, but *rather* the shepherds fed themselves
and did not feed My flock;

9therefore, you shepherds, hear the word of the LORD:

## New International

people living in those ruins in the land of Israel are saying, 'Abraham was only one man, yet he possessed the land. But we are
many; surely the land has been given to us as our possession.'
25Therefore say to them, 'This is what the Sovereign LORD says:
Since you eat meat with the blood still in it and look to your idols
and shed blood, should you then possess the land? 26You rely on
your sword, you do detestable things, and each of you defiles his
neighbor's wife. Should you then possess the land?'

27"Say this to them: 'This is what the Sovereign LORD says: As
surely as I live, those who are left in the ruins will fall by the sword,
those out in the country I will give to the wild animals to be
devoured, and those in strongholds and caves will die of a plague.
28I will make the land a desolate waste, and her proud strength will
come to an end, and the mountains of Israel will become desolate
so that no one will cross them. 29Then they will know that I am
the LORD, when I have made the land a desolate waste because of
all the detestable things they have done.'

30"As for you, son of man, your countrymen are talking together about you by the walls and at the doors of the houses,
saying to each other, 'Come and hear the message that has come
from the LORD.' 31My people come to you, as they usually do, and
sit before you to listen to your words, but they do not put them
into practice. With their mouths they express devotion, but their
hearts are greedy for unjust gain. 32Indeed, to them you are nothing more than one who sings love songs with a beautiful voice and
plays an instrument well, for they hear your words but do not put
them into practice.

33"When all this comes true—and it surely will—then they will
know that a prophet has been among them."

*Shepherds and Sheep*

**34** THE WORD of the LORD came to me: 2"Son of man,
prophesy against the shepherds of Israel; prophesy and
say to them: 'This is what the Sovereign LORD says: Woe to the
shepherds of Israel who only take care of themselves! Should not
shepherds take care of the flock? 3You eat the curds, clothe yourselves with the wool and slaughter the choice animals, but you do
not take care of the flock. 4You have not strengthened the weak
or healed the sick or bound up the injured. You have not brought
back the strays or searched for the lost. You have ruled them
harshly and brutally. 5So they were scattered because there was no
shepherd, and when they were scattered they became food for all
the wild animals. 6My sheep wandered over all the mountains and
on every high hill. They were scattered over the whole earth, and
no one searched or looked for them.

7" 'Therefore, you shepherds, hear the word of the LORD: 8As
surely as I live, declares the Sovereign LORD, because my flock
lacks a shepherd and so has been plundered and has become food
for all the wild animals, and because my shepherds did not search
for my flock but cared for themselves rather than for my flock,
9therefore, O shepherds, hear the word of the LORD: 10This is what

## King James

10 Thus saith the Lord GOD; Behold, I *am* against the shepherds; and I will require my flock at their hand, and cause them to cease from feeding the flock; neither shall the shepherds feed themselves any more; for I will deliver my flock from their mouth, that they may not be meat for them.

11 ¶ For thus saith the Lord GOD; Behold, I, *even* I, will both search my sheep, and seek them out.

12 As a shepherd seeketh out his flock in the day that he is among his sheep *that are* scattered; so will I seek out my sheep, and will deliver them out of all places where they have been scattered in the cloudy and dark day.

13 And I will bring them out from the people, and gather them from the countries, and will bring them to their own land, and feed them upon the mountains of Israel by the rivers, and in all the inhabited places of the country.

14 I will feed them in a good pasture, and upon the high mountains of Israel shall their fold be: there shall they lie in a good fold, and *in* a fat pasture shall they feed upon the mountains of Israel.

15 I will feed my flock, and I will cause them to lie down, saith the Lord GOD.

16 I will seek that which was lost, and bring again that which was driven away, and will bind up *that which was* broken, and will strengthen that which was sick: but I will destroy the fat and the strong; I will feed them with judgment.

17 And *as for* you, O my flock, thus saith the Lord GOD; Behold, I judge between cattle and cattle, between the rams and the he goats.

18 *Seemeth it* a small thing unto you to have eaten up the good pasture, but ye must tread down with your feet the residue of your pastures? and to have drunk of the deep waters, but ye must foul the residue with your feet?

19 And *as for* my flock, they eat that which ye have trodden with your feet; and they drink that which ye have fouled with your feet.

20 ¶ Therefore thus saith the Lord GOD unto them; Behold, I, *even* I, will judge between the fat cattle and between the lean cattle.

21 Because ye have thrust with side and with shoulder, and pushed all the diseased with your horns, till ye have scattered them abroad;

22 Therefore will I save my flock, and they shall no more be a prey; and I will judge between cattle and cattle.

23 And I will set up one shepherd over them, and he shall feed them, *even* my servant David; he shall feed them, and he shall be their shepherd.

24 And I the LORD will be their God, and my servant David a prince among them; I the LORD have spoken *it*.

25 And I will make with them a covenant of peace, and will cause the evil beasts to cease out of the land: and they shall dwell safely in the wilderness, and sleep in the woods.

26 And I will make them and the places round about my hill a blessing; and I will cause the shower to come down in his season; there shall be showers of blessing.

27 And the tree of the field shall yield her fruit, and the earth shall yield her increase, and they shall be safe in their land, and shall know that I *am* the LORD, when I have broken the bands of their yoke, and delivered them out of the hand of those that served themselves of them.

## Amplified

10 Thus says the Lord God: Behold, I am against the shepherds; and I will require My sheep at their hand, and cause them to cease feeding the sheep; neither shall the shepherds feed themselves any more. I will rescue My sheep from their mouths, that they may not be food for them.

11 For thus says the Lord God: Behold, I, I Myself will search for My sheep, and will seek them out.

12 As a shepherd seeks out his sheep in the day that he is among his flock that are scattered, so will I seek out My sheep, and I will rescue them out of all places where they have been scattered in the day of clouds and thick darkness.

13 And I will bring them out from the peoples, and gather them from the countries, and will bring them to their own land; and I will feed them upon the mountains of Israel, by the watercourses, and in all the inhabited places of the country.

14 I will feed them with good pasture, and upon the high mountains of Israel shall their fold be; there shall they lie down in a good fold, and in a fat pasture shall they feed upon the mountains of Israel.

15 I will feed My sheep, and I will cause them to lie down, says the Lord God.

16 I will seek that which was lost, and bring back that which has strayed, and I will bandage the hurt *and* the crippled, and will strengthen the weak *and* the sick; but I will destroy the fat and the strong [become hardhearted and perverse]; I will feed them with judgment *and* punishment. [Luke 19:10.]

17 And as for you, O My flock, thus says the Lord God: Behold, I judge between sheep and sheep, between the rams and the great he-goats [the malicious, and the tyrants of the pasture].

18 Is it too little for you that you feed on the best pasture, but you must tread down with your feet the rest of your pasture? And to have drunk of the waters clarified by subsiding, but you must foul the rest of the water with your feet?

19 And My flock, must they feed on what your feet have trodden, and drink what your feet have fouled?

20 Therefore thus says the Lord God to them: Behold, I, I Myself will judge between fat sheep and impoverished sheep, *or* fat goats and lean goats.

21 Because you push with side and with shoulder, and thrust with your horns all those that have become weak *and* diseased, till you have scattered them abroad;

22 Therefore will I rescue My flock, and they shall no more be a prey; and I will judge between sheep and sheep.

23 And I will raise up over them one Shepherd, and He shall feed them, even My servant [a]David; He shall feed them, and He shall be their Shepherd. [Ezek. 37:24; cf. John 10:14-18.]

24 And I the Lord will be their God, and My Servant David a prince among them; I the Lord have spoken it.

25 And I will confirm with them a covenant of peace, and will cause the evil beasts to cease out of the land, and *My people* shall dwell safely in the wilderness, desert, *or* pasture land, and sleep [confidently] in the woods. [Isa. 11:6-9; Ps. 127:2b; John 16:33; 14:27.]

26 And I will make them and the places round about My hill a blessing; and I will cause the showers to come down in their season; there shall be showers of blessing [of good insured by God's favor].

27 And the tree of the field shall yield its fruit, and the earth shall yield its increase, and [My people] shall be secure in their land; and they shall be confident *and* know—understand *and* realize—that I am the Lord, when I have broken the bars of their yoke, and have delivered them out of the hand of those who made slaves of them.

**AMP** [a] The name of David is here put simply, as in verse 24; chapter 37:24, 25; Jer. 30:9; Hos. 3:5, instead of the more usual designations of the Messiah as the Son, the Branch, the Offspring of David; but there can be no possible doubt of the meaning . . . David, as the head of the theocracy and the ancestor of our Lord after the flesh, constantly appears in the Scriptures as the type of the Messiah, and there can be no reasonable doubt that the prophecy must have been so understood, even at the time it was uttered. (Ellicott's Commentary.)

## New American Standard

10"Thus says the Lord GOD, "Behold, I am against the shepherds, and I shall demand My sheep from them and make them
cease from feeding sheep. So the shepherds will not feed themselves anymore, but I shall deliver My flock from their mouth, that
they may not be food for them." ' "

*The Restoration of Israel*

11¶ For thus says the Lord GOD, "Behold, I Myself will search
for My sheep and seek them out.
12"As a shepherd cares for his herd in the day when he is among
his scattered sheep, so I will care for My sheep and will deliver
them from all the places to which they were scattered on a cloudy
and gloomy day.
13"And I will bring them out from the peoples and gather them
from the countries and bring them to their own land; and I will feed
them on the mountains of Israel, by the streams, and in all the
inhabited places of the land.
14"I will feed them in a good pasture, and their grazing ground
will be on the mountain heights of Israel. There they will lie down
in good grazing ground, and they will feed in rich pasture on the
mountains of Israel.
15"I will feed My flock and I will lead them to rest," declares the
Lord GOD.
16"I will seek the lost, bring back the scattered, bind up the
broken, and strengthen the sick; but the fat and the strong I will
destroy. I will feed them with judgment.
17¶ "And as for you, My flock, thus says the Lord GOD, 'Behold,
I will judge between one sheep and another, between the rams and
the male goats.
18'Is it too slight a thing for you that you should feed in the good
pasture, that you must tread down with your feet the rest of your
pastures? Or that you should drink of the clear waters, that you
must foul the rest with your feet?
19'And as for My flock, they must eat what you tread down with
your feet, and they must drink what you foul with your feet!' "
20¶ Therefore, thus says the Lord GOD to them, "Behold, I, even
I, will judge between the fat sheep and the lean sheep.
21"Because you push with side and with shoulder, and thrust
at all the weak with your horns, until you have scattered them
abroad,
22therefore, I will deliver My flock, and they will no longer be
a prey; and I will judge between one sheep and another.
23"Then I will set over them one shepherd, My servant David,
and he will feed them; he will feed them himself and be their
shepherd.
24"And I, the LORD, will be their God, and My servant David
will be prince among them; I, the LORD, have spoken.
25¶ "And I will make a covenant of peace with them and eliminate harmful beasts from the land, so that they may live securely
in the wilderness and sleep in the woods.
26"And I will make them and the places around My hill a
blessing. And I will cause showers to come down in their season;
they will be showers of blessing.
27"Also the tree of the field will yield its fruit, and the earth will
yield its increase, and they will be secure on their land. Then they
will know that I am the LORD, when I have broken the bars of their
yoke and have delivered them from the hand of those who enslaved them.

## New International

the Sovereign LORD says: I am against the shepherds and will hold
them accountable for my flock. I will remove them from tending
the flock so that the shepherds can no longer feed themselves. I
will rescue my flock from their mouths, and it will no longer be
food for them.
11" 'For this is what the Sovereign LORD says: I myself will
search for my sheep and look after them. 12As a shepherd looks
after his scattered flock when he is with them, so will I look after
my sheep. I will rescue them from all the places where they were
scattered on a day of clouds and darkness. 13I will bring them out
from the nations and gather them from the countries, and I will
bring them into their own land. I will pasture them on the mountains of Israel, in the ravines and in all the settlements in the land.
14I will tend them in a good pasture, and the mountain heights of
Israel will be their grazing land. There they will lie down in good
grazing land, and there they will feed in a rich pasture on the
mountains of Israel. 15I myself will tend my sheep and have them
lie down, declares the Sovereign LORD. 16I will search for the lost
and bring back the strays. I will bind up the injured and strengthen
the weak, but the sleek and the strong I will destroy. I will shepherd the flock with justice.
17" 'As for you, my flock, this is what the Sovereign LORD says:
I will judge between one sheep and another, and between rams
and goats. 18Is it not enough for you to feed on the good pasture?
Must you also trample the rest of your pasture with your feet? Is
it not enough for you to drink clear water? Must you also muddy
the rest with your feet? 19Must my flock feed on what you have
trampled and drink what you have muddied with your feet?
20" 'Therefore this is what the Sovereign LORD says to them:
See, I myself will judge between the fat sheep and the lean sheep.
21Because you shove with flank and shoulder, butting all the weak
sheep with your horns until you have driven them away, 22I will
save my flock, and they will no longer be plundered. I will judge
between one sheep and another. 23I will place over them one
shepherd, my servant David, and he will tend them; he will tend
them and be their shepherd. 24I the LORD will be their God, and
my servant David will be prince among them. I the LORD have
spoken.
25" 'I will make a covenant of peace with them and rid the land
of wild beasts so that they may live in the desert and sleep in the
forests in safety. 26I will bless them and the places surrounding my
hill.[b] I will send down showers in season; there will be showers
of blessing. 27The trees of the field will yield their fruit and the
ground will yield its crops; the people will be secure in their land.
They will know that I am the LORD, when I break the bars of their
yoke and rescue them from the hands of those who enslaved them.

NIV [b] 26 Or *I will make them and the places surrounding my hill a blessing*

## King James

28 And they shall no more be a prey to the heathen, neither shall the beast of the land devour them; but they shall dwell safely, and none shall make *them* afraid.

29 And I will raise up for them a plant of renown, and they shall be no more consumed with hunger in the land, neither bear the shame of the heathen any more.

30 Thus shall they know that I the LORD their God *am* with them, and *that* they, *even* the house of Israel, *are* my people, saith the Lord GOD.

31 And ye my flock, the flock of my pasture, *are* men, *and* I *am* your God, saith the Lord GOD.

**35** MOREOVER THE word of the LORD came unto me, saying,

2 Son of man, set thy face against mount Seir, and prophesy against it,

3 And say unto it, Thus saith the Lord GOD; Behold, O mount Seir, I *am* against thee, and I will stretch out mine hand against thee, and I will make thee most desolate.

4 I will lay thy cities waste, and thou shalt be desolate, and thou shalt know that I *am* the LORD.

5 Because thou hast had a perpetual hatred, and hast shed *the blood of* the children of Israel by the force of the sword in the time of their calamity, in the time *that their* iniquity *had* an end:

6 Therefore, *as* I live, saith the Lord GOD, I will prepare thee unto blood, and blood shall pursue thee: since thou hast not hated blood, even blood shall pursue thee.

7 Thus will I make mount Seir most desolate, and cut off from it him that passeth out and him that returneth.

8 And I will fill his mountains with his slain *men:* in thy hills, and in thy valleys, and in all thy rivers, shall they fall that are slain with the sword.

9 I will make thee perpetual desolations, and thy cities shall not return: and ye shall know that I *am* the LORD.

10 Because thou hast said, These two nations and these two countries shall be mine, and we will possess it; whereas the LORD was there:

11 Therefore, *as* I live, saith the Lord GOD, I will even do according to thine anger, and according to thine envy which thou hast used out of thy hatred against them; and I will make myself known among them, when I have judged thee.

## Amplified

28 And they shall no more be a prey to the nations, nor shall the beasts of the earth devour them; but they shall dwell safely, and none shall make them afraid [in the [a]day of the Messiah's reign]. [Isa. 60:21; 61:3.]

29 And I will raise up for them a planting of crops for renown, and they shall be no more consumed with hunger in the land, nor bear the reproach of the nations any longer.

30 Then shall they know [positively] that I, the Lord their God, am with them, and that they, the house of Israel, are My people, says the Lord God;

31 And that you, My sheep, the sheep of My pasture, are *only* men, and I am your God, says the Lord God.

**35** MOREOVER THE word of the Lord came to me, saying,

2 Son of man, set your face against the mountain *range of* Seir [in Edom], and prophesy against it,

3 And say to it, Thus says the Lord God: Behold, O Mount Seir, I am against you, and I will stretch out My hand against you, and I will make you a desolation and an astonishment.

4 I will lay your cities waste, and you shall be desolate, and you shall know, understand *and* realize that I am the Lord [the Sovereign Ruler, calling forth loyalty and obedient service].

5 Because you [of Esau] have had a perpetual enmity [for Jacob], and you gave over the sons of Israel to the power of the sword at the time of their calamity, when they were suffering their final [Babylonian conquest] punishment; [Cf. Ezek. 25:12-14; 36:5.]

6 Therefore, as I live, says the Lord God, I will expose you to slaughter, and slaughter shall pursue you; since you could not bear to live without bloodshed, therefore bloodshed shall pursue you.

7 Thus will I make Mount Seir an astonishment and a desolation, and I will cut off from it him who passes through it and him who returns [that way].

8 And I will fill [Edom's] mountains with his slain men; on your hills and in your valleys and in all your ravines shall those fall who are slain with the sword.

9 I will make you a perpetual desolation, and your [b]cities shall not be inhabited. Then you will know, understand *and* realize that I am the Lord [the Sovereign Ruler, calling forth loyalty and obedient service].

10 Because you, [Edom,] said, These two nations [Israel and Judah] and these two countries shall be mine, and we will take possession of them—although the Lord was there;

11 Therefore, as I live, says the Lord God, I will deal with you according to the anger and envy you showed because of your enmity for them; and I will make Myself known among them—as He Who will judge and punish—when I judge *and* punish you.

**AMP** [a] Once when Jesus visited the synagogue in Nazareth (Luke 4:16-21), He was handed the roll of the book of Isaiah to read aloud. He deliberately turned to Isaiah 61, which tells what His coming to the world would mean, all eleven verses of it. But He read only a few lines of the chapter, stopping in the midst of a sentence, and said, "Today has this scripture been fulfilled in your ears." He had just read of His coming to preach the Gospel, to proclaim release to the captives [of Satan], to give sight to the blind, to set at liberty the bruised, and to proclaim the acceptable year of the Lord. But He had to stop there, for the rest of the chapter could not be fulfilled until His second coming, of which it tells. The chapter before us, Ezekiel 34, verses 24-31 is telling of the same Messianic reign, of which so many Scriptures speak, and for which Jesus definitely promised to return to earth. [Matt. 25:31-34; 24:30; Rev. 1:7, 8. Cf. Luke 1:32, 33; Acts 1:10, 11.] [b] The Edomites gave what help they could to Nebuchadnezzar when he captured Judah. Later these cousins of the Israelites were pushed out of their own country into Southern Judea; Hebron was their chief city. When in 70 A.D. the Romans under Titus besieged Jerusalem, Josephus says the Edomites joined the Jews in rebellion against them, and 20,000 were admitted as defenders of the Holy City. But once in, they pillaged the city, raping and killing, and not even sparing the priests, though the traitors themselves had been previously forced to become circumcised and recognized as Jews. The Roman conqueror slew them, and Edom ceased to be. The forecasts of the prophets regarding Edom are in striking contrast to those of their neighbors, Moab and Ammon. The latter two countries were to suffer great and severe judgments, as was Edom; but restoration and renewed prosperity were promised to them "in the latter days," while Edom was never to be rebuilt. This is all obviously nearing fulfillment in the twentieth century. Truly Edom is the scene of "perpetual desolations," with no hint of restoration.

## New American Standard

28"And they will no longer be a prey to the nations, and the
beasts of the earth will not devour them; but they will live securely,
and no one will make *them* afraid.
29"And I will establish for them a renowned planting place, and
they will not again be victims of famine in the land, and they will
not endure the insults of the nations anymore.
30"Then they will know that I, the LORD their God, am with
them, and that they, the house of Israel, are My people," declares
the Lord GOD.
31"As for you, My sheep, the sheep of My pasture, you are
men, and I am your God," declares the Lord GOD.

*Prophecy against Mount Seir*

**35** MOREOVER, THE word of the LORD came to me saying,
2"Son of man, set your face against Mount Seir, and
prophesy against it,
3and say to it, 'Thus says the Lord GOD,
"Behold, I am against you, Mount Seir,
And I will stretch out My hand against you,
And I will make you a desolation and a waste.
4 "I will lay waste your cities,
And you will become a desolation.
Then you will know that I am the LORD.
5"Because you have had everlasting enmity and have delivered the sons of Israel to the power of the sword at the time of
their calamity, at the time of the punishment of the end,
6therefore, as I live," declares the Lord GOD, "I will give you
over to bloodshed, and bloodshed will pursue you; since you have
not hated bloodshed, therefore bloodshed will pursue you.
7"And I will make Mount Seir a waste and a desolation, and
I will cut off from it the one who passes through and returns.
8"And I will fill its mountains with its slain; on your hills and
in your valleys and in all your ravines those slain by the sword will
fall.
9"I will make you an everlasting desolation, and your cities will
not be inhabited. Then you will know that I am the LORD.
10¶ "Because you have said, 'These two nations and these two
lands will be mine, and we will possess them,' although the LORD
was there,
11therefore, as I live," declares the Lord GOD, "I will deal *with*
*you* according to your anger and according to your envy which you
showed because of your hatred against them; so I will make Myself
known among them when I judge you.

## New International

28They will no longer be plundered by the nations, nor will wild
animals devour them. They will live in safety, and no one will
make them afraid. 29I will provide for them a land renowned for
its crops, and they will no longer be victims of famine in the land
or bear the scorn of the nations. 30Then they will know that I, the
LORD their God, am with them and that they, the house of Israel,
are my people, declares the Sovereign LORD. 31You my sheep, the
sheep of my pasture, are people, and I am your God, declares the
Sovereign LORD.' "

*A Prophecy Against Edom*

**35** THE WORD of the LORD came to me: 2"Son of man, set
your face against Mount Seir; prophesy against it 3and
say: 'This is what the Sovereign LORD says: I am against you,
Mount Seir, and I will stretch out my hand against you and make
you a desolate waste. 4I will turn your towns into ruins and you
will be desolate. Then you will know that I am the LORD.
5" 'Because you harbored an ancient hostility and delivered the
Israelites over to the sword at the time of their calamity, the time
their punishment reached its climax, 6therefore as surely as I live,
declares the Sovereign LORD, I will give you over to bloodshed and
it will pursue you. Since you did not hate bloodshed, bloodshed
will pursue you. 7I will make Mount Seir a desolate waste and cut
off from it all who come and go. 8I will fill your mountains with
the slain; those killed by the sword will fall on your hills and in
your valleys and in all your ravines. 9I will make you desolate
forever; your towns will not be inhabited. Then you will know that
I am the LORD.
10" 'Because you have said, "These two nations and countries
will be ours and we will take possession of them," even though
I the LORD was there, 11therefore as surely as I live, declares the
Sovereign LORD, I will treat you in accordance with the anger and
jealousy you showed in your hatred of them and I will make myself
known among them when I judge you. 12Then you will know that

## King James

12And thou shalt know that I *am* the LORD, *and that* I have heard all thy blasphemies which thou hast spoken against the mountains of Israel, saying, They are laid desolate, they are given us to consume.

13Thus with your mouth ye have boasted against me, and have multiplied your words against me: I have heard *them.*

14Thus saith the Lord GOD; When the whole earth rejoiceth, I will make thee desolate.

15As thou didst rejoice at the inheritance of the house of Israel, because it was desolate, so will I do unto thee: thou shalt be desolate, O mount Seir, and all Idumea, *even* all of it: and they shall know that I *am* the LORD.

**36** ALSO, THOU son of man, prophesy unto the mountains of Israel, and say, Ye mountains of Israel, hear the word of the LORD:

2Thus saith the Lord GOD; Because the enemy hath said against you, Aha, even the ancient high places are ours in possession:

3Therefore prophesy and say, Thus saith the Lord GOD; Because they have made *you* desolate, and swallowed you up on every side, that ye might be a possession unto the residue of the heathen, and ye are taken up in the lips of talkers, and *are* an infamy of the people:

4Therefore, ye mountains of Israel, hear the word of the Lord GOD; Thus saith the Lord GOD to the mountains, and to the hills, to the rivers, and to the valleys, to the desolate wastes, and to the cities that are forsaken, which became a prey and derision to the residue of the heathen that *are* round about;

5Therefore thus saith the Lord GOD; Surely in the fire of my jealousy have I spoken against the residue of the heathen, and against all Idumea, which have appointed my land into their possession with the joy of all *their* heart, with despiteful minds, to cast it out for a prey.

6Prophesy therefore concerning the land of Israel, and say unto the mountains, and to the hills, to the rivers, and to the valleys, Thus saith the Lord GOD; Behold, I have spoken in my jealousy and in my fury, because ye have borne the shame of the heathen:

7Therefore thus saith the Lord GOD; I have lifted up mine hand, Surely the heathen that *are* about you, they shall bear their shame.

8¶ But ye, O mountains of Israel, ye shall shoot forth your branches, and yield your fruit to my people of Israel; for they are at hand to come.

9For, behold, I *am* for you, and I will turn unto you, and ye shall be tilled and sown:

10And I will multiply men upon you, all the house of Israel, *even* all of it: and the cities shall be inhabited, and the wastes shall be builded:

11And I will multiply upon you man and beast; and they shall increase and bring fruit: and I will settle you after your old estates, and will do better *unto you* than at your beginnings: and ye shall know that I *am* the LORD.

12Yea, I will cause men to walk upon you, *even* my people Israel; and they shall possess thee, and thou shalt be their inheritance, and thou shalt no more henceforth bereave them *of men.*

13Thus saith the Lord GOD; Because they say unto you, Thou *land* devourest up men, and hast bereaved thy nations;

14Therefore thou shalt devour men no more, neither bereave thy nations any more, saith the Lord GOD.

## Amplified

12And you shall know, understand *and* realize that I am the Lord [the Sovereign Ruler, calling forth loyalty and obedient service], and that I have heard all your revilings *and* scornful speeches that you have uttered against the mountains of Israel, saying, They are laid waste *and* desolate; they are given us to devour.

13Thus you have boasted *and* magnified yourselves against Me with your mouth, multiplying your words against Me; I have heard it.

14Thus says the Lord God: While the whole earth rejoices, I will make you a waste *and* desolation.

15As you rejoiced over the inheritance of the house of Israel, because it was desolate, so will I deal with you; you shall be a waste *and* desolation, O Mount Seir, and all Edom, all of it. Then they shall know, understand *and* realize that I am the Lord [the Sovereign Ruler, calling forth loyalty and obedient service].

**36** ALSO YOU, son of man, prophesy to the mountains of Israel, and say, You mountains of Israel, hear the word of the Lord.

2Thus says the Lord God: Because the enemy has said over you, Aha! and, the ancient heights have become our possession,

3Therefore prophesy and say, Thus says the Lord God: Because, yes, because they made you a desolation, and they snap after *and* crush you from every side, so that you may become the possession of the rest of the nations, and you become the talk and evil gossip of the people;

4Therefore, O mountains of Israel, hear the word of the Lord God: Thus says the Lord God to the mountains and hills, to the ravines and valleys, to the desolate wastes and the cities that are forsaken, which have become a prey and derision to the rest of the nations that are round about;

5Therefore thus says the Lord God: Surely in the fire of My hot jealousy have I spoken against the rest of the nations, and against all Edom, who have given to themselves My land with wholehearted joy and with uttermost contempt, that they might empty it out *and* possess it for a prey *and* a spoil.

6Prophesy therefore concerning the land of Israel, and say to the mountains and hills, to the ravines and valleys, Thus says the Lord God: Behold, I have spoken in My jealousy and in My wrath, because you have suffered the shame *and* reproach of the nations;

7Therefore thus says the Lord God: I have lifted up My hand *and* sworn, Surely the nations that are round about you shall themselves suffer shame and reproach.

8But you, O mountains of Israel, shall shoot forth your branches and yield your fruit to My people Israel; for they are soon to come *home.*

9For, behold, I am for you, and I will turn to you, and you shall be tilled and sown;

10And I will multiply men upon you, the whole house of Israel, even all of it; the cities shall be inhabited, and the waste places shall be rebuilt;

11And I will multiply upon you man and beast; and they shall increase and be fruitful. And I will cause you to be inhabited according to your former estate, and I will do better for you than at your beginnings; and you shall know, understand *and* realize that I am the Lord [the Sovereign Ruler, calling forth loyalty and obedient service].

12Yes, [O Mountains of Israel,] I will cause men to walk upon you, even My people Israel; and they shall possess you, and you shall be their inheritance, and you shall no more after this bereave them of children [for idol sacrifices].

13Thus says the Lord God: Because they say to you, You, [O Land,] are a devourer of men, and have bereaved your nation of children [offered to idols];

14Therefore you shall devour men no more, neither bereave your nation *or* cause it to stumble any more, says the Lord God.

## New American Standard

12"Then you will know that I, the LORD, have heard all your
revilings which you have spoken against the mountains of Israel
saying, 'They are laid desolate; they are given to us for food.'
13"And you have spoken arrogantly against Me and have multiplied your words against Me; I have heard."
14'Thus says the Lord GOD, "As all the earth rejoices, I will make
you a desolation.
15"As you rejoiced over the inheritance of the house of Israel
because it was desolate, so I will do to you. You will be a desolation, O Mount Seir, and all Edom, all of it. Then they will know
that I am the LORD."'

*The Mountains of Israel to Be Blessed*

36 "AND YOU, son of man, prophesy to the mountains of
Israel and say, 'O mountains of Israel, hear the word of
the LORD.
2'Thus says the Lord GOD, "Because the enemy has spoken
against you, 'Aha!' and, 'The everlasting heights have become our
possession,'
3therefore, prophesy and say, 'Thus says the Lord GOD, "For
good cause they have made you desolate and crushed you from
every side, that you should become a possession of the rest of the
nations, and you have been taken up in the talk and the whispering of the people."'"
4'Therefore, O mountains of Israel, hear the word of the Lord
GOD. Thus says the Lord GOD to the mountains and to the hills,
to the ravines and to the valleys, to the desolate wastes and to the
forsaken cities, which have become a prey and a derision to the rest
of the nations which are round about,
5therefore, thus says the Lord GOD, "Surely in the fire of My
jealousy I have spoken against the rest of the nations, and against
all Edom, who appropriated My land for themselves as a possession with wholehearted joy *and* with scorn of soul, to drive it out
for a prey."
6'Therefore, prophesy concerning the land of Israel, and say to
the mountains and to the hills, to the ravines and to the valleys,
"Thus says the Lord GOD, 'Behold, I have spoken in My jealousy
and in My wrath because you have endured the insults of the
nations.'
7"Therefore, thus says the Lord GOD, 'I have sworn that surely
the nations which are around you will themselves endure their
insults.
8'But you, O mountains of Israel, you will put forth your
branches and bear your fruit for My people Israel; for they will
soon come.
9'For, behold, I am for you, and I will turn to you, and you shall
be cultivated and sown.
10'And I will multiply men on you, all the house of Israel, all
of it; and the cities will be inhabited, and the waste places will be
rebuilt.
11'And I will multiply on you man and beast; and they will
increase and be fruitful; and I will cause you to be inhabited as you
were formerly and will treat you better than at the first. Thus you
will know that I am the LORD.
12'Yes, I will cause men—My people Israel—to walk on you and
possess you, so that you will become their inheritance and never
again bereave them of children.'
13"Thus says the Lord GOD, 'Because they say to you, "You are
a devourer of men and have bereaved your nation of children,"
14therefore, you will no longer devour men, and no longer
bereave your nation of children,' declares the Lord GOD.

## New International

I the LORD have heard all the contemptible things you have said
against the mountains of Israel. You said, "They have been laid
waste and have been given over to us to devour." 13You boasted
against me and spoke against me without restraint, and I heard it.
14This is what the Sovereign LORD says: While the whole earth
rejoices, I will make you desolate. 15Because you rejoiced when the
inheritance of the house of Israel became desolate, that is how I
will treat you. You will be desolate, O Mount Seir, you and all of
Edom. Then they will know that I am the LORD.'"

*A Prophecy to the Mountains of Israel*

36 "SON OF man, prophesy to the mountains of Israel and
say, 'O mountains of Israel, hear the word of the LORD.
2This is what the Sovereign LORD says: The enemy said of you,
"Aha! The ancient heights have become our possession."' 3There-
fore prophesy and say, 'This is what the Sovereign LORD says:
Because they ravaged and hounded you from every side so that
you became the possession of the rest of the nations and the object
of people's malicious talk and slander, 4therefore, O mountains of
Israel, hear the word of the Sovereign LORD: This is what the
Sovereign LORD says to the mountains and hills, to the ravines and
valleys, to the desolate ruins and the deserted towns that have
been plundered and ridiculed by the rest of the nations around
you— 5this is what the Sovereign LORD says: In my burning zeal
I have spoken against the rest of the nations, and against all Edom,
for with glee and with malice in their hearts they made my land
their own possession so that they might plunder its pastureland.'
6Therefore prophesy concerning the land of Israel and say to the
mountains and hills, to the ravines and valleys: 'This is what the
Sovereign LORD says: I speak in my jealous wrath because you
have suffered the scorn of the nations. 7Therefore this is what the
Sovereign LORD says: I swear with uplifted hand that the nations
around you will also suffer scorn.
8"'But you, O mountains of Israel, will produce branches and
fruit for my people Israel, for they will soon come home. 9I am
concerned for you and will look on you with favor; you will be
plowed and sown, 10and I will multiply the number of people
upon you, even the whole house of Israel. The towns will be
inhabited and the ruins rebuilt. 11I will increase the number of men
and animals upon you, and they will be fruitful and become numerous. I will settle people on you as in the past and will make
you prosper more than before. Then you will know that I am the
LORD. 12I will cause people, my people Israel, to walk upon you.
They will possess you, and you will be their inheritance; you will
never again deprive them of their children.
13"'This is what the Sovereign LORD says: Because people say
to you, "You devour men and deprive your nation of its children,"
14therefore you will no longer devour men or make your nation
childless, declares the Sovereign LORD. 15No longer will I make

## King James

15 Neither will I cause *men* to hear in thee the shame of the heathen any more, neither shalt thou bear the reproach of the people any more, neither shalt thou cause thy nations to fall any more, saith the Lord GOD.

16 ¶ Moreover the word of the LORD came unto me, saying,

17 Son of man, when the house of Israel dwelt in their own land, they defiled it by their own way and by their doings: their way was before me as the uncleanness of a removed woman.

18 Wherefore I poured my fury upon them for the blood that they had shed upon the land, and for their idols *wherewith* they had polluted it:

19 And I scattered them among the heathen, and they were dispersed through the countries: according to their way and according to their doings I judged them.

20 And when they entered unto the heathen, whither they went, they profaned my holy name, when they said to them, These *are* the people of the LORD, and are gone forth out of his land.

21 ¶ But I had pity for mine holy name, which the house of Israel had profaned among the heathen, whither they went.

22 Therefore say unto the house of Israel, Thus saith the Lord GOD; I do not *this* for your sakes, O house of Israel, but for mine holy name's sake, which ye have profaned among the heathen, whither ye went.

23 And I will sanctify my great name, which was profaned among the heathen, which ye have profaned in the midst of them; and the heathen shall know that I *am* the LORD, saith the Lord GOD, when I shall be sanctified in you before their eyes.

24 For I will take you from among the heathen, and gather you out of all countries, and will bring you into your own land.

25 ¶ Then will I sprinkle clean water upon you, and ye shall be clean: from all your filthiness, and from all your idols, will I cleanse you.

26 A new heart also will I give you, and a new spirit will I put within you: and I will take away the stony heart out of your flesh, and I will give you an heart of flesh.

27 And I will put my spirit within you, and cause you to walk in my statutes, and ye shall keep my judgments, and do *them*.

28 And ye shall dwell in the land that I gave to your fathers; and ye shall be my people, and I will be your God.

29 I will also save you from all your uncleannesses: and I will call for the corn, and will increase it, and lay no famine upon you.

30 And I will multiply the fruit of the tree, and the increase of the field, that ye shall receive no more reproach of famine among the heathen.

31 Then shall ye remember your own evil ways, and your doings that *were* not good, and shall loathe yourselves in your own sight for your iniquities and for your abominations.

32 Not for your sakes do I *this*, saith the Lord GOD, be it known unto you: be ashamed and confounded for your own ways, O house of Israel.

33 Thus saith the Lord GOD; In the day that I shall have cleansed you from all your iniquities I will also cause *you* to dwell in the cities, and the wastes shall be builded.

34 And the desolate land shall be tilled, whereas it lay desolate in the sight of all that passed by.

35 And they shall say, This land that was desolate is become like the garden of Eden; and the waste and desolate and ruined cities *are become* fenced, *and* are inhabited.

36 Then the heathen that are left round about you shall know that I the LORD build the ruined *places*, *and* plant that that was desolate: I the LORD have spoken *it*, and I will do *it*.

37 Thus saith the Lord GOD; I will yet *for* this be inquired of by the house of Israel, to do *it* for them; I will increase them with men like a flock.

## Amplified

15 Neither will I let you hear any more the reproach of the nations, nor shall you suffer the dishonor of the peoples any more, nor shall you cause your nation to stumble *and* fall any more [through idolatry], says the Lord God.

16 Moreover the word of the Lord came to me, saying,

17 Son of man, when the house of Israel dwelt in their own land, they defiled it by *doing* their *own* way and by their [idolatrous] doings. Their conduct before Me was as the uncleanness of a woman during her [physical] impurity.

18 So I poured out My wrath upon them for the blood that they had shed upon the land, and for their idols with which they had defiled it.

19 And I scattered them among the nations, and they were dispersed through the countries; according to their conduct and their [idolatrous] deeds I judged *and* punished them.

20 And when they came to the nations to which they went, they profaned My holy name, in that men said of them, These are the people of the Lord, and yet they had to go forth out of His land.

21 But I had regard, concern *and* compassion for My holy name, which the house of Israel had profaned among the nations to which they went.

22 Therefore say to the house of Israel, Thus says the Lord God: I do not do this for your sakes, O house of Israel, but for My holy name's sake, which you have profaned among the nations to which you went.

23 And I will vindicate the holiness of My great name *and* separate it for its holy purpose from all that defiles; My name, which has been profaned among the nations, which you have profaned among them; and the nations will know, understand *and* realize that I am the Lord [the Sovereign Ruler, calling forth loyalty and obedient service], when I shall be set apart by you *and* My holiness vindicated in you before their eyes *and* yours.

24 For I will [a]take you from among the nations, and gather you out of all countries, and bring you into your own land.

25 Then will I sprinkle clean water upon you, and you shall be clean from all your uncleanness, and from all your idols will I cleanse you.

26 A new heart will I give you, and a new spirit will I put within you: and I will take away the stony heart out of your flesh and give you a heart of flesh.

27 And I will put my Spirit within you and cause you to walk in My statutes, and you shall heed My ordinances, and do them.

28 And you shall dwell in the land that I gave to your fathers, and you shall be My people, and I will be your God.

29 I will also save you from all your uncleannesses, and I will call forth the grain and make it abundant and lay no famine on you.

30 And I will multiply the fruit of the tree and the increase of the field, that you may no more suffer the reproach *and* disgrace of famine among the nations.

31 Then you shall [earnestly] remember your own evil ways and your doings that were not good, and shall loathe yourselves in your own sight for your iniquities and for your abominable deeds.

32 Not for your sake do I do this, says the Lord God; let that be known to you. Be ashamed and confounded for your *own* wicked ways, O house of Israel!

33 Thus says the Lord God: In the day that I cleanse you from all your iniquities I will *also* cause [Israel's] cities to be inhabited, and the waste places shall be rebuilt.

34 And the desolate land shall be tilled, that which had lain desolate in the sight of all who passed by.

35 And they shall say, This land that was desolate has become like the garden of Eden, and the waste and desolate and ruined cities are fortified and inhabited.

36 Then the nations that are left round about you shall know that I, the Lord, have rebuilt the ruined places, and replanted that which was desolate. I, the Lord, have spoken it, and I will do it.

37 Thus says the Lord God: For this also I will let the house of Israel inquire of Me to do it for them; I will increase their men like a flock.

**AMP** [a] See footnote on Ezekiel 37:21.

## New American Standard

15"And I will not let you hear insults from the nations anymore,
nor will you bear disgrace from the peoples any longer, nor will
you cause your nation to stumble any longer," declares the Lord
GOD.'"
16¶ Then the word of the LORD came to me saying,
17"Son of man, when the house of Israel was living in their own
land, they defiled it by their ways and their deeds; their way before
Me was like the uncleanness of a woman in her impurity.
18"Therefore, I poured out My wrath on them for the blood
which they had shed on the land, because they had defiled it with
their idols.
19"Also I scattered them among the nations, and they were
dispersed throughout the lands. According to their ways and their
deeds I judged them.
20"When they came to the nations where they went, they profaned My holy name, because it was said of them, 'These are the
people of the LORD; yet they have come out of His land.'
21"But I had concern for My holy name, which the house of
Israel had profaned among the nations where they went.

*Israel to Be Renewed for His Name's Sake*

22¶ "Therefore, say to the house of Israel, 'Thus says the Lord
GOD, "It is not for your sake, O house of Israel, that I am about
to act, but for My holy name, which you have profaned among the
nations where you went.
23"And I will vindicate the holiness of My great name which has
been profaned among the nations, which you have profaned in
their midst. Then the nations will know that I am the LORD,"
declares the Lord GOD, "when I prove Myself holy among you in
their sight.
24"For I will take you from the nations, gather you from all the
lands, and bring you into your own land.
25"Then I will sprinkle clean water on you, and you will be
clean; I will cleanse you from all your filthiness and from all your
idols.
26"Moreover, I will give you a new heart and put a new spirit
within you; and I will remove the heart of stone from your flesh
and give you a heart of flesh.
27"And I will put My Spirit within you and cause you to walk
in My statutes, and you will be careful to observe My ordinances.
28"And you will live in the land that I gave to your forefathers;
so you will be My people, and I will be your God.
29"Moreover, I will save you from all your uncleanness; and I
will call for the grain and multiply it, and I will not bring a famine
on you.
30"And I will multiply the fruit of the tree and the produce of
the field, that you may not receive again the disgrace of famine
among the nations.
31"Then you will remember your evil ways and your deeds that
were not good, and you will loathe yourselves in your own sight
for your iniquities and your abominations.
32"I am not doing *this* for your sake," declares the Lord GOD,
"let it be known to you. Be ashamed and confounded for your
ways, O house of Israel!"
33¶ 'Thus says the Lord GOD, "On the day that I cleanse you
from all your iniquities, I will cause the cities to be inhabited, and
the waste places will be rebuilt.
34"And the desolate land will be cultivated instead of being a
desolation in the sight of everyone who passed by.
35"And they will say, 'This desolate land has become like the
garden of Eden; and the waste, desolate, and ruined cities are
fortified *and* inhabited.'
36"Then the nations that are left round about you will know that
I, the LORD, have rebuilt the ruined places *and* planted that which
was desolate; I, the LORD, have spoken and will do it."
37¶ 'Thus says the Lord GOD, "This also I will let the house of
Israel ask Me to do for them: I will increase their men like a flock.

## New International

you hear the taunts of the nations, and no longer will you suffer
the scorn of the peoples or cause your nation to fall, declares the
Sovereign LORD.' "
16Again the word of the LORD came to me: 17"Son of man, when
the people of Israel were living in their own land, they defiled it
by their conduct and their actions. Their conduct was like a
woman's monthly uncleanness in my sight. 18So I poured out my
wrath on them because they had shed blood in the land and
because they had defiled it with their idols. 19I dispersed them
among the nations, and they were scattered through the countries;
I judged them according to their conduct and their actions. 20And
wherever they went among the nations they profaned my holy
name, for it was said of them, 'These are the LORD's people, and
yet they had to leave his land.' 21I had concern for my holy name,
which the house of Israel profaned among the nations where they
had gone.
22"Therefore say to the house of Israel, 'This is what the Sovereign LORD says: It is not for your sake, O house of Israel, that I am
going to do these things, but for the sake of my holy name, which
you have profaned among the nations where you have gone. 23I
will show the holiness of my great name, which has been profaned
among the nations, the name you have profaned among them.
Then the nations will know that I am the LORD, declares the
Sovereign LORD, when I show myself holy through you before
their eyes.
24" 'For I will take you out of the nations; I will gather you from
all the countries and bring you back into your own land. 25I will
sprinkle clean water on you, and you will be clean; I will cleanse
you from all your impurities and from all your idols. 26I will give
you a new heart and put a new spirit in you; I will remove from
you your heart of stone and give you a heart of flesh. 27And I will
put my Spirit in you and move you to follow my decrees and be
careful to keep my laws. 28You will live in the land I gave your
forefathers; you will be my people, and I will be your God. 29I will
save you from all your uncleanness. I will call for the grain and
make it plentiful and will not bring famine upon you. 30I will
increase the fruit of the trees and the crops of the field, so that you
will no longer suffer disgrace among the nations because of famine. 31Then you will remember your evil ways and wicked deeds,
and you will loathe yourselves for your sins and detestable practices. 32I want you to know that I am not doing this for your sake,
declares the Sovereign LORD. Be ashamed and disgraced for your
conduct, O house of Israel!
33" 'This is what the Sovereign LORD says: On the day I cleanse
you from all your sins, I will resettle your towns, and the ruins will
be rebuilt. 34The desolate land will be cultivated instead of lying
desolate in the sight of all who pass through it. 35They will say,
"This land that was laid waste has become like the garden of Eden;
the cities that were lying in ruins, desolate and destroyed, are now
fortified and inhabited." 36Then the nations around you that remain will know that I the LORD have rebuilt what was destroyed
and have replanted what was desolate. I the LORD have spoken,
and I will do it.'
37"This is what the Sovereign LORD says: Once again I will yield
to the plea of the house of Israel and do this for them: I will make
their people as numerous as sheep, 38as numerous as the flocks for

## King James

38As the holy flock, as the flock of Jerusalem in her solemn feasts; so shall the waste cities be filled with flocks of men: and they shall know that I *am* the LORD.

37 THE HAND of the LORD was upon me, and carried me out in the spirit of the LORD, and set me down in the midst of the valley which *was* full of bones,

2And caused me to pass by them round about: and, behold, *there were* very many in the open valley; and, lo, *they were* very dry.
3And he said unto me, Son of man, can these bones live? And I answered, O Lord GOD, thou knowest.
4Again he said unto me, Prophesy upon these bones, and say unto them, O ye dry bones, hear the word of the LORD.
5Thus saith the Lord GOD unto these bones; Behold, I will cause breath to enter into you, and ye shall live:
6And I will lay sinews upon you, and will bring up flesh upon you, and cover you with skin, and put breath in you, and ye shall live; and ye shall know that I *am* the LORD.
7So I prophesied as I was commanded: and as I prophesied, there was a noise, and behold a shaking, and the bones came together, bone to his bone.
8And when I beheld, lo, the sinews and the flesh came up upon them, and the skin covered them above: but *there was* no breath in them.
9Then said he unto me, Prophesy unto the wind, prophesy, son of man, and say to the wind, Thus saith the Lord GOD; Come from the four winds, O breath, and breathe upon these slain, that they may live.
10So I prophesied as he commanded me, and the breath came into them, and they lived, and stood up upon their feet, an exceeding great army.
11¶ Then he said unto me, Son of man, these bones are the whole house of Israel: behold, they say, Our bones are dried, and our hope is lost: we are cut off for our parts.
12Therefore prophesy and say unto them, Thus saith the Lord GOD; Behold, O my people, I will open your graves, and cause you to come up out of your graves, and bring you into the land of Israel.
13And ye shall know that I *am* the LORD, when I have opened your graves, O my people, and brought you up out of your graves,
14And shall put my spirit in you, and ye shall live, and I shall place you in your own land: then shall ye know that I the LORD have spoken *it*, and performed *it*, saith the LORD.
15¶ The word of the LORD came again unto me, saying,
16Moreover, thou son of man, take thee one stick, and write upon it, For Judah, and for the children of Israel his companions: then take another stick, and write upon it, For Joseph, the stick of Ephraim, and *for* all the house of Israel his companions:
17And join them one to another into one stick; and they shall become one in thine hand.
18¶ And when the children of thy people shall speak unto thee, saying, Wilt thou not show us what thou *meanest* by these?
19Say unto them, Thus saith the Lord GOD; Behold, I will take the stick of Joseph, which *is* in the hand of Ephraim, and the tribes of Israel his fellows, and will put them with him, *even* with the stick of Judah, and make them one stick, and they shall be one in mine hand.

## Amplified

38Like the flock of holy things for sacrifice, like the flock of Jerusalem in her *solemn* appointed feasts, so shall the waste cities be filled with flocks of men, and they shall know, understand *and* realize, that I am the Lord [the Sovereign Ruler, calling forth loyalty and obedient service].

37 THE HAND of the Lord was upon me, and He brought me out in the Spirit of the Lord, and set me down in the midst of the valley, and it was full of bones.

2And He caused me to pass round about among them; and behold, there were very many [human bones] in the open valley *or* plain, and lo, they were very dry.
3And He said to me, Son of man, can these bones live? And I answered, O Lord God, You know! [I Cor. 15:35.]
4Again He said to me, Prophesy to these bones, and say to them, O you dry bones, hear the word of the Lord. [John 5:28.]
5Thus says the Lord God to these bones: Behold, I will cause breath *and* spirit to enter you, and you shall live;
6And I will lay sinews upon you, and will bring up flesh upon you, and cover you with skin, and put breath *and* spirit in you, and you [dry bones] shall live; and you shall know, understand *and* realize, that I am the Lord [the Sovereign Ruler, calling forth loyalty and obedient service].
7So I prophesied as I was commanded; and as I prophesied, there was a [thundering] noise, and behold, a shaking *and* trembling *and* a rattling, and the bones came together, bone to its bone.
8And I beheld, and lo, there were sinews upon [the bones], and flesh came upon them, and skin covered them over; but there was no breath *or* spirit in them.
9Then said He to me, Prophesy to the breath *and* spirit, son of man, and say to the breath *and* spirit, Thus says the Lord God: Come from the four winds, O breath *and* spirit, and breathe upon these slain, that they may live.
10So I prophesied as He commanded me, and the breath *and* spirit came into [the bones], and they lived and stood up upon their feet, an exceedingly great host. [Rev. 11:11.]
11Then He said to me, Son of man, these bones are the whole house of Israel. Behold, they say, Our bones are dried up, and our hope is lost; we are completely cut off.
12Therefore prophesy and say to them, Thus says the Lord God: Behold, I will open your graves, and cause you to come up out of your graves, O My people; and I will bring you [back home] to the land of Israel. [Hos. 13:14.]
13And you shall know that I am the Lord [your Sovereign Ruler] when I have opened your graves, and caused you to come up out of your graves, O My people.
14And I shall put My Spirit in you, and you shall live, and I shall place you in your own land. Then you shall know, understand *and* realize that I the Lord have spoken it, and performed it, says the Lord.
15The word of the Lord came again to me:
16Son of man, take a stick and write on it, For Judah and the children of Israel his companions; then take another stick and write upon it, For Joseph, the stick of Ephraim, and all the house of Israel his companions;
17And join them together into one stick, that they may become one in your hand.
18And when your people say to you, Will you not show us what you mean by these?
19Say to them, Thus says the Lord God: Behold, I will take the stick of Joseph, which is in the hand of Ephraim, and the tribes of Israel his associates, and will join with it the stick of Judah, and make them one stick, and they shall be one in My hand.

## New American Standard

38"Like the flock for sacrifices, like the flock at Jerusalem during
her appointed feasts, so will the waste cities be filled with flocks
of men. Then they will know that I am the LORD."' "

*Vision of the Valley of Dry Bones*

**37** THE HAND of the LORD was upon me, and He brought
me out by the Spirit of the LORD and set me down in the
middle of the valley; and it was full of bones.

2And He caused me to pass among them round about, and
behold, *there were* very many on the surface of the valley; and lo,
*they were* very dry.

3And He said to me, "Son of man, can these bones live?" And
I answered, "O Lord GOD, Thou knowest."

4Again He said to me, "Prophesy over these bones, and say to
them, 'O dry bones, hear the word of the LORD.'

5"Thus says the Lord GOD to these bones, 'Behold, I will cause
[a]breath to enter you that you may come to life.

6'And I will put sinews on you, make flesh grow back on you,
cover you with skin, and put breath in you that you may come
alive; and you will know that I am the LORD.' "

7¶ So I prophesied as I was commanded; and as I prophesied,
there was a noise, and behold, a rattling; and the bones came
together, bone to its bone.

8And I looked, and behold, sinews were on them, and flesh
grew, and skin covered them; but there was no breath in them.

9Then He said to me, "Prophesy to the breath, prophesy, son
of man, and say to the breath, 'Thus says the Lord GOD, "Come
from the four winds, O breath, and breathe on these slain, that
they come to life." ' "

10So I prophesied as He commanded me, and the breath came
into them, and they came to life, and stood on their feet, an
exceedingly great army.

*The Vision Explained*

11¶ Then He said to me, "Son of man, these bones are the whole
house of Israel; behold, they say, 'Our bones are dried up, and our
hope has perished. We are completely cut off.'

12"Therefore prophesy, and say to them, 'Thus says the Lord
GOD, "Behold, I will open your graves and cause you to come up
out of your graves, My people; and I will bring you into the land
of Israel.

13"Then you will know that I am the LORD, when I have opened
your graves and caused you to come up out of your graves, My
people.

14"And I will put My [b]Spirit within you, and you will come to
life, and I will place you on your own land. Then you will know
that I, the LORD, have spoken and done it," declares the LORD.' "

*Reunion of Judah and Israel*

15¶ The word of the LORD came again to me saying,

16"And you, son of man, take for yourself one stick and write
on it, 'For Judah and for the sons of Israel, his companions'; then
take another stick and write on it, 'For Joseph, the stick of Ephraim
and all the house of Israel, his companions.'

17"Then join them for yourself one to another into one stick,
that they may become one in your hand.

18"And when the sons of your people speak to you saying, 'Will
you not declare to us what you mean by these?'

19say to them, 'Thus says the Lord GOD, "Behold, I will take the
stick of Joseph, which is in the hand of Ephraim, and the tribes of
Israel, his companions; and I will put them with it, with the stick
of Judah, and make them one stick, and they will be one in My
hand." '

NAS [a] Or, *spirit*, and so throughout this context [b] Or, *breath*

## New International

offerings at Jerusalem during her appointed feasts. So will the
ruined cities be filled with flocks of people. Then they will know
that I am the LORD."

*The Valley of Dry Bones*

**37** THE HAND of the LORD was upon me, and he brought
me out by the Spirit of the LORD and set me in the middle
of a valley; it was full of bones.
2He led me back and forth among
them, and I saw a great many bones on the floor of the valley,
bones that were very dry.
3He asked me, "Son of man, can these
bones live?"

I said, "O Sovereign LORD, you alone know."

4Then he said to me, "Prophesy to these bones and say to them,
'Dry bones, hear the word of the LORD!
5This is what the Sovereign
LORD says to these bones: I will make breath[c] enter you, and you
will come to life.
6I will attach tendons to you and make flesh come
upon you and cover you with skin; I will put breath in you, and
you will come to life. Then you will know that I am the LORD.' "

7So I prophesied as I was commanded. And as I was prophesying, there was a noise, a rattling sound, and the bones came
together, bone to bone.
8I looked, and tendons and flesh appeared
on them and skin covered them, but there was no breath in them.

9Then he said to me, "Prophesy to the breath; prophesy, son
of man, and say to it, 'This is what the Sovereign LORD says: Come
from the four winds, O breath, and breathe into these slain, that
they may live.' "
10So I prophesied as he commanded me, and
breath entered them; they came to life and stood up on their
feet—a vast army.

11Then he said to me: "Son of man, these bones are the whole
house of Israel. They say, 'Our bones are dried up and our hope
is gone; we are cut off.'
12Therefore prophesy and say to them:
'This is what the Sovereign LORD says: O my people, I am going
to open your graves and bring you up from them; I will bring you
back to the land of Israel.
13Then you, my people, will know that
I am the LORD, when I open your graves and bring you up from
them.
14I will put my Spirit in you and you will live, and I will settle
you in your own land. Then you will know that I the LORD have
spoken, and I have done it, declares the LORD.' "

*One Nation Under One King*

15The word of the LORD came to me:
16"Son of man, take a stick
of wood and write on it, 'Belonging to Judah and the Israelites
associated with him.' Then take another stick of wood, and write
on it, 'Ephraim's stick, belonging to Joseph and all the house of
Israel associated with him.'
17Join them together into one stick so
that they will become one in your hand.

18"When your countrymen ask you, 'Won't you tell us what
you mean by this?'
19say to them, 'This is what the Sovereign LORD
says: I am going to take the stick of Joseph—which is in Ephraim's
hand—and of the Israelite tribes associated with him, and join it
to Judah's stick, making them a single stick of wood, and they will
become one in my hand.'
20Hold before their eyes the sticks you

NIV [c] 5 The Hebrew for this word can also mean *wind* or *spirit* (see verses 6-14).

## King James

20¶ And the sticks whereon thou writest shall be in thine hand
before their eyes.
21 And say unto them, Thus saith the Lord God; Behold, I will
take the children of Israel from among the heathen, whither they
be gone, and will gather them on every side, and bring them into
their own land:
22 And I will make them one nation in the land upon the mountains of Israel; and one king shall be king to them all: and they shall
be no more two nations, neither shall they be divided into two
kingdoms any more at all:
23 Neither shall they defile themselves any more with their idols,
nor with their detestable things, nor with any of their transgressions: but I will save them out of all their dwellingplaces, wherein
they have sinned, and will cleanse them: so shall they be my
people, and I will be their God.
24 And David my servant *shall be* king over them; and they all
shall have one shepherd: they shall also walk in my judgments,
and observe my statutes, and do them.
25 And they shall dwell in the land that I have given unto Jacob
my servant, wherein your fathers have dwelt; and they shall dwell
therein, *even* they, and their children, and their children's children
for ever: and my servant David *shall be* their prince for ever.
26 Moreover I will make a covenant of peace with them; it shall
be an everlasting covenant with them: and I will place them, and
multiply them, and will set my sanctuary in the midst of them for
evermore.
27 My tabernacle also shall be with them: yea, I will be their God,
and they shall be my people.
28 And the heathen shall know that I the LORD do sanctify Israel,
when my sanctuary shall be in the midst of them for evermore.

**38** AND THE word of the LORD came unto me, saying,
2 Son of man, set thy face against Gog, the land of Magog,
the chief prince of Meshech and Tubal, and prophesy against him,
3 And say, Thus saith the Lord God; Behold, I *am* against thee,
O Gog, the chief prince of Meshech and Tubal:
4 And I will turn thee back, and put hooks into thy jaws, and
I will bring thee forth, and all thine army, horses and horsemen,
all of them clothed with all sorts *of armour, even* a great company
*with* bucklers and shields, all of them handling swords:
5 Persia, Ethiopia, and Libya with them; all of them with shield
and helmet:
6 Gomer, and all his bands; the house of Togarmah of the north
quarters, and all his bands: *and* many people with thee.
7 Be thou prepared, and prepare for thyself, thou, and all thy
company that are assembled unto thee, and be thou a guard unto
them.

## Amplified

20 When the sticks on which you write shall be in your hand
before their eyes,
21 Then say to them, Thus says the Lord God: Behold, I will take
the children of Israel from among the nations to which they have
gone, and will [a]gather them from every side and bring them into
their own land.
22 And I will make them one nation in the land, upon the mountains of Israel; and one King shall be King over them all; and they
shall be no longer two nations, neither be divided into two kingdoms any more. [Jer. 50:4.]
23 They shall not defile themselves any more with their idols and
their detestable things, or with any of their transgressions; but I
will save them out of all their dwelling places, *and* from all their
backslidings in which they have sinned, and I will cleanse them.
So shall they be My people, and I will be their God.
24 And [b]David My Servant shall be King over them, and they
all shall have one Shepherd. They shall also walk in My ordinances
and heed My statutes and do them.
25 They shall dwell in the land in which your fathers dwelt, that
I gave to My servant Jacob; and they shall dwell there, they and
their children and their children's children, for ever; and My Servant David shall be their Prince for ever. [Isa. 60:21; Joel 3:20; Amos
9:15.]
26 I will make a covenant of peace with them; it shall be an
everlasting covenant with them; and I will give blessings to them
and multiply them, and will set My sanctuary in the midst of them
for evermore.
27 My tabernacle *or* dwelling place also shall be with them; and
I will be their God, and they shall be My people.
28 Then the nations shall know, understand *and* realize that I the
Lord do set apart *and* consecrate Israel for holy use, when My
sanctuary shall be in their midst for evermore.

**38** AND THE word of the Lord came to me:
2 Son of man, set your face against Gog, of the land of
[c]Magog, the prince of Rosh, of Meshech, and Tubal, and prophesy
against him,
3 And say, Thus says the Lord God: Behold, I am against you,
O Gog, chief prince (or ruler) of Rosh, of Meshech and Tubal.
4 And I will turn you back, and put hooks into your jaws, and
I will bring you forth and all your army, horses and horsemen, all
of them clothed in full armor, a great company with buckler and
shield, all of them handling swords;
5 Persia, Cush, and Put *or* Libya with them; all of them with
shield and helmet;
6 Gomer and all his hordes; the house of Togarmah in the uttermost parts of the north, and all his hordes; many people are with
you.
7 You, [Gog,] be prepared; yes, prepare yourself, you and all
your companies that are assembled about you, and you be a guard
*and* a commander for them.

AMP [a] No person needs to be reminded of the startling way in which this prophecy has been in process of fulfillment since World War II. The Jews have for centuries been dispersed among all the nations with only a few left in the homeland which lay waste and desolate. It was said that travelers in Palestine had no difficulty in recognizing the appropriateness of Ezekiel's labeling the country as he saw it, the "valley of dry bones" (verse 11). But by 1960 A.D. one-sixth of the Jewish population of the world was in Palestine. Already they had been made "one nation" (verse 22a) and that between sunrise of one day and sunset of the next, "a nation in a day" (Isa. 66:8)! But the greatest event of all is yet to come (Ezek. 37:22b-25). This prophecy will be fulfilled in its entirety. [b] See footnote on Ezekiel 34:23. [c] Gog is a symbolic name, standing for the leader of the world powers antagonistic to God./ Meshech and Tubal are understood to have been the same as the Moschi and Tibareni of the Greeks—tribes that inhabited regions in the Caucasus. Rosh, which some would identify with Russia, must have designated a land and people somewhere in the same quarter. And therefore the Gog of Ezekiel must be viewed as in some sense the head of the high regions in the northwest of Asia. (Fairbairn's Imperial Standard Bible Encyclopedia.)

## New American Standard

20"And the sticks on which you write will be in your hand
before their eyes.
21"And say to them, 'Thus says the Lord GOD, "Behold, I will
take the sons of Israel from among the nations where they have
gone, and I will gather them from every side and bring them into
their own land;
22and I will make them one nation in the land, on the mountains
of Israel; and one king will be king for all of them; and they will
no longer be two nations, and they will no longer be divided into
two kingdoms.
23"And they will no longer defile themselves with their idols,
or with their detestable things, or with any of their transgressions;
but I will deliver them from all their [d]dwelling places in which they
have sinned, and will cleanse them. And they will be My people,
and I will be their God.

*The Davidic Kingdom*

24¶ "And My servant David will be king over them, and they
will all have one shepherd; and they will walk in My ordinances,
and keep My statutes, and observe them.
25"And they shall live on the land that I gave to Jacob My
servant, in which your fathers lived; and they will live on it, they,
and their sons, and their sons' sons, forever; and David My servant
shall be their prince forever.
26"And I will make a covenant of peace with them; it will be an
everlasting covenant with them. And I will place them and multiply them, and will set My sanctuary in their midst forever.
27"My dwelling place also will be with them; and I will be their
God, and they will be My people.
28"And the nations will know that I am the LORD who sanctifies
Israel, when My sanctuary is in their midst forever." ' "

*Prophecy about Gog and Future Invasion of Israel*

38 AND THE word of the LORD came to me saying,
2"Son of man, set your face toward Gog of the land of
Magog, the prince of Rosh, Meshech, and Tubal, and prophesy
against him,
3and say, 'Thus says the Lord GOD, "Behold, I am against you,
O Gog, prince of Rosh, Meshech, and Tubal.
4"And I will turn you about, and put hooks into your jaws, and
I will bring you out, and all your army, horses and horsemen, all
of them splendidly attired, a great company *with* buckler and
shield, all of them wielding swords;
5Persia, Ethiopia, and Put with them, all of them *with* shield
and helmet;
6Gomer with all its troops; Beth-togarmah *from* the remote
parts of the north with all its troops—many peoples with you.
7¶ "Be prepared, and prepare yourself, you and all your companies that are assembled about you, and be a guard for them.

NAS [d] Another reading is *backslidings*

## New International

have written on 21and say to them, 'This is what the Sovereign
LORD says: I will take the Israelites out of the nations where they
have gone. I will gather them from all around and bring them back
into their own land. 22I will make them one nation in the land, on
the mountains of Israel. There will be one king over all of them and
they will never again be two nations or be divided into two kingdoms. 23They will no longer defile themselves with their idols and
vile images or with any of their offenses, for I will save them from
all their sinful backsliding,[e] and I will cleanse them. They will be
my people, and I will be their God.
24" 'My servant David will be king over them, and they will all
have one shepherd. They will follow my laws and be careful to
keep my decrees. 25They will live in the land I gave to my servant
Jacob, the land where your fathers lived. They and their children
and their children's children will live there forever, and David my
servant will be their prince forever. 26I will make a covenant of
peace with them; it will be an everlasting covenant. I will establish
them and increase their numbers, and I will put my sanctuary
among them forever. 27My dwelling place will be with them; I will
be their God, and they will be my people. 28Then the nations will
know that I the LORD make Israel holy, when my sanctuary is
among them forever.' "

*A Prophecy Against Gog*

38 THE WORD of the LORD came to me: 2"Son of man, set
your face against Gog, of the land of Magog, the chief
prince of[f] Meshech and Tubal; prophesy against him 3and say:
'This is what the Sovereign LORD says: I am against you, O Gog,
chief prince of[g] Meshech and Tubal. 4I will turn you around, put
hooks in your jaws and bring you out with your whole army—your
horses, your horsemen fully armed, and a great horde with large
and small shields, all of them brandishing their swords. 5Persia,
Cush[h] and Put will be with them, all with shields and helmets,
6also Gomer with all its troops, and Beth Togarmah from the far
north with all its troops—the many nations with you.
7" 'Get ready; be prepared, you and all the hordes gathered
about you, and take command of them. 8After many days you will

NIV [e] 23 Many Hebrew manuscripts (see also Septuagint); most Hebrew manuscripts *all their dwelling places where they sinned* [f] 2 Or *the prince of Rosh,* [g] 3 Or *Gog, prince of Rosh,* [h] 5 That is, the upper Nile region

## King James

8¶ After many days thou shalt be visited: in the latter years thou shalt come into the land *that is* brought back from the sword, *and is* gathered out of many people, against the mountains of Israel, which have been always waste: but it is brought forth out of the nations, and they shall dwell safely all of them.

9Thou shalt ascend and come like a storm, thou shalt be like a cloud to cover the land, thou, and all thy bands, and many people with thee.

10Thus saith the Lord GOD; It shall also come to pass, *that* at the same time shall things come into thy mind, and thou shalt think an evil thought:

11And thou shalt say, I will go up to the land of unwalled villages; I will go to them that are at rest, that dwell safely, all of them dwelling without walls, and having neither bars nor gates,

12To take a spoil, and to take a prey; to turn thine hand upon the desolate places *that are now* inhabited, and upon the people *that are* gathered out of the nations, which have gotten cattle and goods, that dwell in the midst of the land.

13Sheba, and Dedan, and the merchants of Tarshish, with all the young lions thereof, shall say unto thee, Art thou come to take a spoil? hast thou gathered thy company to take a prey? to carry away silver and gold, to take away cattle and goods, to take a great spoil?

14¶ Therefore, son of man, prophesy and say unto Gog, Thus saith the Lord GOD; In that day when my people of Israel dwelleth safely, shalt thou not know *it?*

15And thou shalt come from thy place out of the north parts, thou, and many people with thee, all of them riding upon horses, a great company, and a mighty army:

16And thou shalt come up against my people of Israel, as a cloud to cover the land; it shall be in the latter days, and I will bring thee against my land, that the heathen may know me, when I shall be sanctified in thee, O Gog, before their eyes.

17Thus saith the Lord GOD; *Art* thou he of whom I have spoken in old time by my servants the prophets of Israel, which prophesied in those days *many* years that I would bring thee against them?

18And it shall come to pass at the same time when Gog shall come against the land of Israel, saith the Lord GOD, *that* my fury shall come up in my face.

19For in my jealousy *and* in the fire of my wrath have I spoken, Surely in that day there shall be a great shaking in the land of Israel;

20So that the fishes of the sea, and the fowls of the heaven, and the beasts of the field, and all creeping things that creep upon the earth, and all the men that *are* upon the face of the earth, shall shake at my presence, and the mountains shall be thrown down, and the steep places shall fall, and every wall shall fall to the ground.

21And I will call for a sword against him throughout all my mountains, saith the Lord GOD: every man's sword shall be against his brother.

22And I will plead against him with pestilence and with blood; and I will rain upon him, and upon his bands, and upon the many people that *are* with him, an overflowing rain, and great hailstones, fire, and brimstone.

23Thus will I magnify myself, and sanctify myself; and I will be known in the eyes of many nations, and they shall know that I *am* the LORD.

## Amplified

8After many days you shall be visited *and* mustered [for service]; in the latter years you shall go against the land that is restored from the ravages of the sword, where people are gathered out of many nations upon the mountains of Israel, which had been a continual waste; but its [people] are brought forth out of the nations, and they shall dwell securely, all of them. [Isa. 24:22.]

9You shall ascend and come like a storm, you shall be like a cloud to cover the land, you and all your hosts, and many people with you.

10Thus says the Lord God: At the same time thoughts shall come into your mind, and you will devise an evil plan.

11And you will say, I will go up against an open country—the land of unwalled villages; I will fall upon those who are at rest, who dwell securely, all of them dwelling without walls and having neither bars nor gates,

12To take spoil and prey; to turn your hand upon the desolate places now inhabited, and assail the people gathered out of the nations, who have obtained livestock and goods, who dwell at the center of the earth [Palestine].

13Sheba and Dedan and the merchants of Tarshish, with all their lion-like cubs [or satellite areas], shall say to you, Have you come to take spoil? Have you gathered your hosts to take the prey? To carry away silver and gold, to take away livestock and goods, to take a great spoil?

14Therefore, son of man, prophesy and say to Gog, Thus says the Lord God: In that day when My people Israel dwell securely, will you not know it *and* be aroused?

15And you will come from your place out of the uttermost parts of the north, you and many peoples with you, all of them riding on horses, a great host, a mighty army.

16And you shall come up against My people Israel like a cloud to cover the land. In the latter days I will bring you against My land, that the nations may know, understand *and* realize Me, when My holiness shall be vindicated through you—vindicated and honored [in your overwhelming destruction]—O Gog, before their eyes.

17Thus says the Lord God: Are you he of whom I have spoken in olden times by My servants the prophets of Israel, who prophesied in those days for years that I would bring you, [Gog], against them?

18But in that day when Gog shall come against the land of Israel, says the Lord God, My wrath shall come up into My nostrils.

19For in My jealousy and in the fire of My wrath have I said, Surely in that day there shall be a great shaking [or cosmic catastrophe] in the land of Israel;

20So that the fishes of the sea, and the birds of the heavens, and the beasts of the field, and all creeping things that creep upon the earth, and all the men that are upon the face of the earth, shall tremble *and* shake at My presence, and the mountains shall be thrown down, and the steep places shall fall, and every wall [natural or artificial] shall fall to the ground.

21And I will call for a sword against [Gog] throughout all My mountains, says the Lord God, every man's sword shall be against his brother [over the dividing of booty].

22And with pestilence and with bloodshed will I enter into judgment with [Gog], and I will rain upon him and upon his hordes and upon the many peoples that are with him, torrents of rain and great hailstones, fire and brimstone. [Ps. 11:6.]

23Thus will I demonstrate My greatness and My holiness, and I will be recognized, understood *and* known in the eyes of many nations; yes, they shall know that I am the Lord [the Sovereign Ruler, calling forth loyalty and obedient service].

## New American Standard

8"After many days you will be summoned; in the latter years
you will come into the land that is restored from the sword, *whose
inhabitants* have been gathered from many nations to the mountains of Israel which had been a continual waste; but its people
were brought out from the nations, and they are living securely,
all of them.
9"And you will go up, you will come like a storm; you will be
like a cloud covering the land, you and all your troops, and many
peoples with you."
10¶ 'Thus says the Lord God, "It will come about on that day,
that thoughts will come into your mind, and you will devise an evil
plan,
11and you will say, 'I will go up against the land of [a]unwalled
villages. I will go against those who are at rest, that live securely,
all of them living without walls, and having no bars or gates,
12to capture spoil and to seize plunder, to turn your hand
against the waste places which are *now* inhabited, and against the
people who are gathered from the nations, who have acquired
cattle and goods, who live at the center of the world.'
13"Sheba, and Dedan, and the merchants of Tarshish, with all
its villages, will say to you, 'Have you come to capture spoil? Have
you assembled your company to seize plunder, to carry away
silver and gold, to take away cattle and goods, to capture great
spoil?' " '
14¶ "Therefore, prophesy, son of man, and say to Gog, 'Thus
says the Lord God, "On that day when My people Israel are living
securely, will you not know *it*?
15"And you will come from your place out of the remote parts
of the north, you and many peoples with you, all of them riding
on horses, a great assembly and a mighty army;
16and you will come up against My people Israel like a cloud to
cover the land. It will come about in the last days that I shall bring
you against My land, in order that the nations may know Me when
I shall be sanctified through you before their eyes, O Gog."
17¶ 'Thus says the Lord God, "Are you the one of whom I spoke
in former days through My servants the prophets of Israel, who
prophesied in those days for *many* years that I would bring you
against them?
18"And it will come about on that day, when Gog comes against
the land of Israel," declares the Lord God, "that My fury will
mount up in My anger.
19"And in My zeal and in My blazing wrath I declare *that* on that
day there will surely be a great earthquake in the land of Israel.
20"And the fish of the sea, the birds of the heavens, the beasts
of the field, all the creeping things that creep on the earth, and all
the men who are on the face of the earth will shake at My presence;
the mountains also will be thrown down, the steep pathways will
collapse, and every wall will fall to the ground.
21"And I shall call for a sword against him on all My mountains," declares the Lord God. "Every man's sword will be against
his brother.
22"And with pestilence and with blood I shall enter into judgment with him; and I shall rain on him, and on his troops, and on
the many peoples who are with him, a torrential rain, with hailstones, fire, and brimstone.
23"And I shall magnify Myself, sanctify Myself, and make Myself known in the sight of many nations; and they will know that
I am the Lord." '

NAS [a] Or, *open country*

## New International

be called to arms. In future years you will invade a land that has
recovered from war, whose people were gathered from many
nations to the mountains of Israel, which had long been desolate.
They had been brought out from the nations, and now all of them
live in safety. 9You and all your troops and the many nations with
you will go up, advancing like a storm; you will be like a cloud
covering the land.
10" 'This is what the Sovereign Lord says: On that day thoughts
will come into your mind and you will devise an evil scheme.
11You will say, "I will invade a land of unwalled villages; I will
attack a peaceful and unsuspecting people—all of them living
without walls and without gates and bars. 12I will plunder and loot
and turn my hand against the resettled ruins and the people gathered from the nations, rich in livestock and goods, living at the
center of the land." 13Sheba and Dedan and the merchants of
Tarshish and all her villages[b] will say to you, "Have you come to
plunder? Have you gathered your hordes to loot, to carry off silver
and gold, to take away livestock and goods and to seize much
plunder?" '
14"Therefore, son of man, prophesy and say to Gog: 'This is
what the Sovereign Lord says: In that day, when my people Israel
are living in safety, will you not take notice of it? 15You will come
from your place in the far north, you and many nations with you,
all of them riding on horses, a great horde, a mighty army. 16You
will advance against my people Israel like a cloud that covers the
land. In days to come, O Gog, I will bring you against my land,
so that the nations may know me when I show myself holy
through you before their eyes.
17" 'This is what the Sovereign Lord says: Are you not the one
I spoke of in former days by my servants the prophets of Israel?
At that time they prophesied for years that I would bring you
against them. 18This is what will happen in that day: When Gog
attacks the land of Israel, my hot anger will be aroused, declares
the Sovereign Lord. 19In my zeal and fiery wrath I declare that at
that time there shall be a great earthquake in the land of Israel.
20The fish of the sea, the birds of the air, the beasts of the field,
every creature that moves along the ground, and all the people on
the face of the earth will tremble at my presence. The mountains
will be overturned, the cliffs will crumble and every wall will fall
to the ground. 21I will summon a sword against Gog on all my
mountains, declares the Sovereign Lord. Every man's sword will
be against his brother. 22I will execute judgment upon him with
plague and bloodshed; I will pour down torrents of rain, hailstones
and burning sulfur on him and on his troops and on the many
nations with him. 23And so I will show my greatness and my
holiness, and I will make myself known in the sight of many
nations. Then they will know that I am the Lord.'

NIV [b] 13 Or *her strong lions*

## King James

39 THEREFORE, THOU son of man, prophesy against Gog, and say, Thus saith the Lord GOD; Behold, I *am* against thee, O Gog, the chief prince of Meshech and Tubal:

2And I will turn thee back, and leave but the sixth part of thee, and will cause thee to come up from the north parts, and will bring thee upon the mountains of Israel:

3And I will smite thy bow out of thy left hand, and will cause thine arrows to fall out of thy right hand.

4Thou shalt fall upon the mountains of Israel, thou, and all thy bands, and the people that *is* with thee: I will give thee unto the ravenous birds of every sort, and *to* the beasts of the field to be devoured.

5Thou shalt fall upon the open field: for I have spoken *it*, saith the Lord GOD.

6And I will send a fire on Magog, and among them that dwell carelessly in the isles: and they shall know that I *am* the LORD.

7So will I make my holy name known in the midst of my people Israel; and I will not *let them* pollute my holy name any more: and the heathen shall know that I *am* the LORD, the Holy One in Israel.

8¶ Behold, it is come, and it is done, saith the Lord GOD; this *is* the day whereof I have spoken.

9And they that dwell in the cities of Israel shall go forth, and shall set on fire and burn the weapons, both the shields and the bucklers, the bows and the arrows, and the handstaves, and the spears, and they shall burn them with fire seven years:

10So that they shall take no wood out of the field, neither cut down *any* out of the forests; for they shall burn the weapons with fire: and they shall spoil those that spoiled them, and rob those that robbed them, saith the Lord GOD.

11¶ And it shall come to pass in that day, *that* I will give unto Gog a place there of graves in Israel, the valley of the passengers on the east of the sea: and it shall stop the *noses* of the passengers: and there shall they bury Gog and all his multitude: and they shall call *it* The valley of Hamon-gog.

12And seven months shall the house of Israel be burying of them, that they may cleanse the land.

13Yea, all the people of the land shall bury *them;* and it shall be to them a renown the day that I shall be glorified, saith the Lord GOD.

14And they shall sever out men of continual employment, passing through the land to bury with the passengers those that remain upon the face of the earth, to cleanse it: after the end of seven months shall they search.

15And the passengers *that* pass through the land, when *any* seeth a man's bone, then shall he set up a sign by it, till the buriers have buried it in the valley of Hamon-gog.

16And also the name of the city *shall be* Hamonah. Thus shall they cleanse the land.

17¶ And, thou son of man, thus saith the Lord GOD; Speak unto every feathered fowl, and to every beast of the field, Assemble yourselves, and come; gather yourselves on every side to my sacrifice that I do sacrifice for you, *even* a great sacrifice upon the mountains of Israel, that ye may eat flesh, and drink blood.

18Ye shall eat the flesh of the mighty, and drink the blood of the princes of the earth, of rams, of lambs, and of goats, of bullocks, all of them fatlings of Bashan.

19And ye shall eat fat till ye be full, and drink blood till ye be drunken, of my sacrifice which I have sacrificed for you.

20Thus ye shall be filled at my table with horses and chariots, with mighty men, and with all men of war, saith the Lord GOD.

## Amplified

39 AND YOU, son of man, prophesy against Gog, Thus says the Lord God: Behold, I am against you, O Gog, chief prince (or ruler) of Rosh, of Meshech and Tubal.

2And I will turn you about, and will lead you on, and will cause you to come up from the uttermost parts of the north, and will lead you against the mountains of Israel;

3And I will smite your bow from your left hand, and will cause your arrows to fall out of your right hand.

4You shall fall [dead] upon the mountains of Israel, you and all your hosts and the peoples who are with you. I will give you to the ravenous birds of every sort and to the beasts of the field to be devoured.

5You shall fall in the open field; for I have spoken *it*, says the Lord God.

6I will send fire on Magog and upon those who dwell securely in the coastlands; and they shall know, understand *and* realize that I am the Lord [the Sovereign Ruler, calling forth loyalty and obedient service].

7And I will make My holy name known in the midst of My people Israel; and I will not let them profane My holy name any more; and the nations shall know, understand *and* realize that I am the Lord, the Holy One of Israel.

8Behold, it is coming and it will be done, says the Lord God; that is the day of which I have spoken.

9And [when you, Gog, are no longer] they who dwell in the cities of Israel shall go forth, and shall set on fire and burn the battle gear, the shields and the bucklers, the bows and the arrows, the handspikes *or* riding whips and the spears, and they shall burn them as fuel for seven years.

10So that My people shall take no firewood out of the field or cut down any out of the forests, for they shall make their fires of the weapons. And they shall despoil those who despoiled them, and plunder those who plundered them, says the Lord God.

11And in that day, I will give to Gog a place for burial there in Israel, the valley of those who pass through on the east side in front of the *Dead* Sea [the highway between Syria, Petra and Egypt], and it will delay *and* stop those who pass through. And there shall they [a]bury Gog and all his multitude, and they shall call it the Valley of Hamon-gog [that is, the multitude of Gog].

12For seven months the house of Israel will be burying them, that they may cleanse the land.

13Yes, all the people of the land will bury them; and it shall bring them renown in the day that I shall be glorified, says the Lord God.

14And they shall set apart men to work continually, who shall pass through the land commissioned to bury, with the help of those who are passing by, those bodies that lie unburied on the face of the ground, in order to cleanse the land. After the end of seven months they shall make their search.

15And when these pass through the land and any one sees a human bone, he shall set up a marker by it as a sign to the buriers, until they have buried it in the Valley of Hamon-gog *or* of Gog's Multitude.

16And Hamonah *or* Multitude shall also be the name of the city [of the dead]. Thus shall they cleanse the land.

17And you, son of man, thus says the Lord God: Say to the birds of prey of every sort and to every beast of the field, Assemble yourselves and come, gather from every side to the sacrificial feast that I am preparing for you, even a great sacrificial feast on the mountains of Israel, at which you may eat flesh and drink blood.

18You shall eat the flesh of the mighty, and drink the blood of the princes of the earth, of rams, of lambs, and of goats, of bullocks, all of them fatlings of Bashan [east of Jordan].

19And you shall eat fat till you are filled, and drink blood till you are drunk, at the sacrificial feast which I am preparing for you.

20And you shall be filled at My table with horses and riders, with mighty men and with soldiers of every kind, says the Lord God.

**AMP** [a] The number of dead bodies left, after the great catastrophe which God will send upon Gog and his hosts, as here described, would necessarily amount to several millions. Their graves would naturally interfere with traffic on the interstate highway. The dead will not be slain in battle. God will slay them by a great cosmic catastrophe (38:18-23). And not some, but "all" of Gog's multitude will die then (39:4, 11); before they have had a chance to use their weapons they will be struck from their hands (39:3). That one-sixth of the horde from the north will be left alive, as the King James Version says (39:2), is without noted exception conceded to be a mistaken translation by all authorities of modern times.

## New American Standard

*Prophecy against Gog—Invaders Destroyed*

39 "AND YOU, son of man, prophesy against Gog, and say,
'Thus says the Lord GOD, "Behold, I am against you, O
Gog, prince of Rosh, Meshech, and Tubal;

2and I shall turn you around, drive you on, take you up from
the remotest parts of the north, and bring you against the mountains of Israel.

3"And I shall strike your bow from your left hand, and dash
down your arrows from your right hand.

4"You shall fall on the mountains of Israel, you and all your
troops, and the peoples who are with you; I shall give you as food
to every kind of predatory bird and beast of the field.

5"You will fall on the open field; for it is I who have spoken,"
declares the Lord GOD.

6"And I shall send fire upon Magog and those who inhabit the
coastlands in safety; and they will know that I am the LORD.

7¶ "And My holy name I shall make known in the midst of My
people Israel; and I shall not let My holy name be profaned anymore. And the nations will know that I am the LORD, the Holy One
in Israel.

8"Behold, it is coming and it shall be done," declares the Lord
GOD. "That is the day of which I have spoken.

9¶ "Then those who inhabit the cities of Israel will go out, and
make fires with the weapons and burn *them*, both shields and
bucklers, bows and arrows, war clubs and spears and for seven
years they will make fires of them.

10"And they will not take wood from the field or gather firewood from the forests, for they will make fires with the weapons;
and they will take the spoil of those who despoiled them, and seize
the plunder of those who plundered them," declares the Lord
GOD.

11¶ "And it will come about on that day that I shall give Gog a
burial ground there in Israel, the valley of those who pass by east
of the sea, and it will block off the passers-by. So they will bury
Gog there with all his multitude, and they will call *it* the valley of
Hamon-gog.

12"For seven months the house of Israel will be burying them
in order to cleanse the land.

13"Even all the people of the land will bury *them;* and it will be
to their renown *on* the day that I glorify Myself," declares the Lord
GOD.

14"And they will set apart men who will constantly pass
through the land, burying those who were passing through, even
those left on the surface of the ground, in order to cleanse it. At
the end of seven months they will make a search.

15"And as those who pass through the land pass through and
anyone sees a man's bone, then he will set up a marker by it until
the buriers have buried it in the valley of Hamon-gog.

16"And even *the* name of *the* city will be Hamonah. So they will
cleanse the land." '

17¶ "And as for you, son of man, thus says the Lord GOD, 'Speak
to every kind of bird and to every beast of the field, "Assemble and
come, gather from every side to My sacrifice which I am going to
sacrifice for you, as a great sacrifice on the mountains of Israel, that
you may eat flesh and drink blood.

18"You shall eat the flesh of mighty men, and drink the blood
of the princes of the earth, as *though they were* rams, lambs, goats,
and bulls, all of them fatlings of Bashan.

19"So you will eat fat until you are glutted, and drink blood until
you are drunk, from My sacrifice which I have sacrificed for you.

20"And you will be glutted at My table with horses and charioteers, with mighty men and all the men of war," declares the Lord
GOD.

## New International

39 "SON OF man, prophesy against Gog and say: 'This is
what the Sovereign LORD says: I am against you, O Gog,
chief prince of[b] Meshech and Tubal. 2I will turn you around and
drag you along. I will bring you from the far north and send you
against the mountains of Israel. 3Then I will strike your bow from
your left hand and make your arrows drop from your right hand.
4On the mountains of Israel you will fall, you and all your troops
and the nations with you. I will give you as food to all kinds of
carrion birds and to the wild animals. 5You will fall in the open
field, for I have spoken, declares the Sovereign LORD. 6I will send
fire on Magog and on those who live in safety in the coastlands,
and they will know that I am the LORD.

7" 'I will make known my holy name among my people Israel.
I will no longer let my holy name be profaned, and the nations will
know that I the LORD am the Holy One in Israel. 8It is coming! It
will surely take place, declares the Sovereign LORD. This is the day
I have spoken of.

9" 'Then those who live in the towns of Israel will go out and
use the weapons for fuel and burn them up—the small and large
shields, the bows and arrows, the war clubs and spears. For seven
years they will use them for fuel. 10They will not need to gather
wood from the fields or cut it from the forests, because they will
use the weapons for fuel. And they will plunder those who plundered them and loot those who looted them, declares the Sovereign LORD.

11" 'On that day I will give Gog a burial place in Israel, in the
valley of those who travel east toward[c] the Sea.[d] It will block the
way of travelers, because Gog and all his hordes will be buried
there. So it will be called the Valley of Hamon Gog.[e]

12" 'For seven months the house of Israel will be burying them
in order to cleanse the land. 13All the people of the land will bury
them, and the day I am glorified will be a memorable day for them,
declares the Sovereign LORD.

14" 'Men will be regularly employed to cleanse the land. Some
will go throughout the land and, in addition to them, others will
bury those that remain on the ground. At the end of the seven
months they will begin their search. 15As they go through the land
and one of them sees a human bone, he will set up a marker beside
it until the gravediggers have buried it in the Valley of Hamon
Gog. 16(Also a town called Hamonah[f] will be there.) And so they
will cleanse the land.'

17"Son of man, this is what the Sovereign LORD says: Call out
to every kind of bird and all the wild animals: 'Assemble and come
together from all around to the sacrifice I am preparing for you, the
great sacrifice on the mountains of Israel. There you will eat flesh
and drink blood. 18You will eat the flesh of mighty men and drink
the blood of the princes of the earth as if they were rams and lambs,
goats and bulls—all of them fattened animals from Bashan. 19At
the sacrifice I am preparing for you, you will eat fat till you are
glutted and drink blood till you are drunk. 20At my table you will
eat your fill of horses and riders, mighty men and soldiers of every
kind,' declares the Sovereign LORD.

NIV [b] *1* Or *Gog, prince of Rosh,* [c] *11* Or *of* [d] *11* That is, the Dead Sea
[e] *11 Hamon Gog* means *hordes of Gog.* [f] *16 Hamonah* means *horde.*

## King James

21And I will set my glory among the heathen, and all the heathen shall see my judgment that I have executed, and my hand that I have laid upon them.
22So the house of Israel shall know that I *am* the LORD their God from that day and forward.
23¶ And the heathen shall know that the house of Israel went into captivity for their iniquity: because they trespassed against me, therefore hid I my face from them, and gave them into the hand of their enemies: so fell they all by the sword.
24According to their uncleanness and according to their transgressions have I done unto them, and hid my face from them.
25Therefore thus saith the Lord GOD; Now will I bring again the captivity of Jacob, and have mercy upon the whole house of Israel, and will be jealous for my holy name;
26After that they have borne their shame, and all their trespasses whereby they have trespassed against me, when they dwelt safely in their land, and none made *them* afraid.
27When I have brought them again from the people, and gathered them out of their enemies' lands, and am sanctified in them in the sight of many nations;
28Then shall they know that I *am* the LORD their God, which caused them to be led into captivity among the heathen: but I have gathered them unto their own land, and have left none of them any more there.
29Neither will I hide my face any more from them: for I have poured out my spirit upon the house of Israel, saith the Lord GOD.

**40** IN THE five and twentieth year of our captivity, in the beginning of the year, in the tenth *day* of the month, in the fourteenth year after that the city was smitten, in the selfsame day the hand of the LORD was upon me, and brought me thither.
2In the visions of God brought he me into the land of Israel, and set me upon a very high mountain, by which *was* as the frame of a city on the south.
3And he brought me thither, and, behold, *there was* a man, whose appearance *was* like the appearance of brass, with a line of flax in his hand, and a measuring reed; and he stood in the gate.
4And the man said unto me, Son of man, behold with thine eyes, and hear with thine ears, and set thine heart upon all that I shall show thee; for to the intent that I might show *them* unto thee *art* thou brought hither: declare all that thou seest to the house of Israel.
5And behold a wall on the outside of the house round about, and in the man's hand a measuring reed of six cubits *long* by the cubit and an handbreadth: so he measured the breadth of the building, one reed; and the height, one reed.
6¶ Then came he unto the gate which looketh toward the east, and went up the stairs thereof, and measured the threshold of the gate, *which was* one reed broad; and the other threshold *of the gate, which was* one reed broad.
7And *every* little chamber *was* one reed long, and one reed broad; and between the little chambers *were* five cubits; and the threshold of the gate by the porch of the gate within *was* one reed.
8He measured also the porch of the gate within, one reed.

## Amplified

21And I will manifest My honor *and* glory among the nations, and all the nations shall see My judgment *and* justice [in the punishment] which I have executed and My hand which I have laid on them.
22So the house of Israel shall know, understand *and* realize beyond all question that I am the Lord their God from that day forward.
23And the nations shall know, understand *and* realize positively that the house of Israel went into captivity for their iniquity, because they trespassed against Me; and I hid My face from them. So I gave them into the hand of their enemies, and they all fell [into captivity or were slain] by the power of the sword. [Deut. 31:17.]
24According to their uncleanness and according to their transgressions I dealt with them, and hid My face from them.
25Therefore thus says the Lord God: Now will I reverse the captivity of Jacob, and have mercy upon the whole house of Israel, and will be jealous for My holy name.
26They shall forget their shame *and* self-reproach, and all their treachery *and* unfaithfulness in which they have transgressed against Me, when they dwell securely in their land and there is none who makes them afraid.
27When I have brought them again from the peoples and gathered them out of their enemies' lands, and My justice *and* holiness are set apart *and* vindicated through them in the sight of many nations;
28Then shall they know, understand *and* realize positively that I am the Lord their God, because I sent them into captivity *and* exile among the nations, and then gathered them to their own land. I will leave none of them remaining among the nations any more [in the latter days].
29Neither will I hide My face any more then from them, when I have poured out My Spirit upon the house of Israel, says the Lord God.

**40** IN THE twenty-fifth year of our captivity [by Babylon], in the beginning of the year, on the tenth day of the month, in the fourteenth year after the city [of Jerusalem] was taken, on the very same day the hand of the Lord was upon me, and He brought me to that place.
2In the visions of God He brought me into the land of Israel and set me down upon a very high mountain, on the south side of which there was what seemed to be the structure of a city.
3He brought me there, and behold, there was a man [an angel] whose appearance was like bronze, with a line of flax and a measuring reed in his hand, and he stood in the gateway.
4And the man said to me, Son of man, look with your eyes and hear with your ears and set your heart *and* mind on all that I will show you, for you are brought here that I may show them to you. Declare all that you see to the house of Israel.
5And behold, there was a wall all around the outside area of the house [of the Lord], and in the man's hand a measuring reed six cubits long in length, each cubit being longer [than the usual one] by a hand's breadth; so he measured the thickness of the wall, one reed, and the height, one reed.
6Then he came to the gate which faced the east and went up its [seven] steps, and measured the threshold of the gateway which was one reed broad, and the other threshold of the gateway [inside the thick wall], which was one reed broad.
7And every room for the guards was one reed long and one reed broad, and the space between the guard rooms *or* lodges was five cubits, and the threshold of the gate by the porch *or* vestibule of the gateway within was one reed.
8He measured also the porch *or* vestibule of the gate toward the house [of the Lord], one reed.

## New American Standard

21¶ "And I shall set My glory among the nations; and all the nations will see My judgment which I have executed, and My hand which I have laid on them.

22"And the house of Israel will know that I am the LORD their God from that day onward.

23"And the nations will know that the house of Israel went into exile for their iniquity because they acted treacherously against Me, and I hid My face from them; so I gave them into the hand of their adversaries, and all of them fell by the sword.

24"According to their uncleanness and according to their transgressions I dealt with them, and I hid My face from them." ' "

*Israel Restored*

25¶ Therefore thus says the Lord GOD, "Now I shall restore the fortunes of Jacob, and have mercy on the whole house of Israel; and I shall be jealous for My holy name.

26"And they shall [a]forget their disgrace and all their treachery which they [b]perpetrated against Me, when they live securely on their *own* land with no one to make them afraid.

27"When I bring them back from the peoples and gather them from the lands of their enemies, then I shall be sanctified through them in the sight of the many nations.

28"Then they will know that I am the LORD their God because I made them go into exile among the nations, and then gathered them *again* to their own land; and I will leave none of them there any longer.

29"And I will not hide My face from them any longer, for I shall have poured out My Spirit on the house of Israel," declares the Lord GOD.

*Vision of the Man with a Measuring Rod*

40 IN THE twenty-fifth year of our exile, at the beginning of the year, on the tenth of the month, in the fourteenth year after the city was taken, on that same day the hand of the LORD was upon me and He brought me there.

2In the visions of God He brought me into the land of Israel, and set me on a very high mountain; and on it to the south *there was* a structure like a city.

3So He brought me there; and behold, there was a man whose appearance was like the appearance of bronze, with a line of flax and a measuring rod in his hand; and he was standing in the gateway.

4And the man said to me, "Son of man, see with your eyes, hear with your ears, and give attention to all that I am going to show you; for you have been brought here in order to show *it* to you. Declare to the house of Israel all that you see."

*Measurements Relating to the Temple*

5¶ And behold, there was a wall on the outside of the temple all around, and in the man's hand was a measuring rod of six cubits, *each of which was* a cubit and a handbreadth. So he measured the thickness of the wall, one rod; and the height, one rod.

6Then he went to the gate which faced east, went up its steps, and measured the threshold of the gate, one rod in width; and the other threshold *was* one rod in width.

7And the guardroom *was* one rod long and one rod wide; and *there were* five cubits between the guardrooms. And the threshold of the gate by the porch of the gate facing inward *was* one rod.

8Then he measured the porch of the gate facing inward, one rod.

NAS [a] Another reading is *bear* [b] Lit., *did treacherously*

## New International

21"I will display my glory among the nations, and all the nations
will see the punishment I inflict and the hand I lay upon them.
22From that day forward the house of Israel will know that I am
the LORD their God. 23And the nations will know that the people
of Israel went into exile for their sin, because they were unfaithful
to me. So I hid my face from them and handed them over to their
enemies, and they all fell by the sword. 24I dealt with them according to their uncleanness and their offenses, and I hid my face from
them.

25"Therefore this is what the Sovereign LORD says: I will now
bring Jacob back from captivity[c] and will have compassion on all
the people of Israel, and I will be zealous for my holy name. 26They
will forget their shame and all the unfaithfulness they showed
toward me when they lived in safety in their land with no one to
make them afraid. 27When I have brought them back from the
nations and have gathered them from the countries of their enemies, I will show myself holy through them in the sight of many
nations. 28Then they will know that I am the LORD their God, for
though I sent them into exile among the nations, I will gather them
to their own land, not leaving any behind. 29I will no longer hide
my face from them, for I will pour out my Spirit on the house of
Israel, declares the Sovereign LORD."

*The New Temple Area*

40 IN THE twenty-fifth year of our exile, at the beginning of
the year, on the tenth of the month, in the fourteenth year
after the fall of the city—on that very day the hand of the LORD was
upon me and he took me there. 2In visions of God he took me to
the land of Israel and set me on a very high mountain, on whose
south side were some buildings that looked like a city. 3He took
me there, and I saw a man whose appearance was like bronze; he
was standing in the gateway with a linen cord and a measuring rod
in his hand. 4The man said to me, "Son of man, look with your
eyes and hear with your ears and pay attention to everything I am
going to show you, for that is why you have been brought here.
Tell the house of Israel everything you see."

*The East Gate to the Outer Court*

5I saw a wall completely surrounding the temple area. The
length of the measuring rod in the man's hand was six long cubits,
each of which was a cubit[d] and a handbreadth.[e] He measured the
wall; it was one measuring rod thick and one rod high.

6Then he went to the gate facing east. He climbed its steps and
measured the threshold of the gate; it was one rod deep.[f] 7The
alcoves for the guards were one rod long and one rod wide, and
the projecting walls between the alcoves were five cubits thick.
And the threshold of the gate next to the portico facing the temple
was one rod deep.

8Then he measured the portico of the gateway; 9its[g] was eight

NIV [c] 25 Or *now restore the fortunes of Jacob* [d] 5 The common cubit was about 1 1/2 feet (about 0.5 meter). [e] 5 That is, about 3 inches (about 8 centimeters) [f] 6 Septuagint; Hebrew *deep, the first threshold, one rod deep* [g] 8,9 Many Hebrew manuscripts, Septuagint, Vulgate and Syriac; most Hebrew manuscripts *gateway facing the temple; it was one rod deep. 9Then he measured the portico of the gateway; it*

## King James

9 Then measured he the porch of the gate, eight cubits; and the posts thereof, two cubits; and the porch of the gate *was* inward.

10 And the little chambers of the gate eastward *were* three on this side, and three on that side; they three *were* of one measure: and the posts had one measure on this side and on that side.

11 And he measured the breadth of the entry of the gate, ten cubits; *and* the length of the gate, thirteen cubits.

12 The space also before the little chambers *was* one cubit *on this side,* and the space *was* one cubit on that side: and the little chambers *were* six cubits on this side, and six cubits on that side.

13 He measured then the gate from the roof of *one* little chamber to the roof of another: the breadth *was* five and twenty cubits, door against door.

14 He made also posts of threescore cubits, even unto the post of the court round about the gate.

15 And from the face of the gate of the entrance unto the face of the porch of the inner gate *were* fifty cubits.

16 And *there were* narrow windows to the little chambers, and to their posts within the gate round about, and likewise to the arches: and windows *were* round about inward: and upon *each* post *were* palm trees.

17 Then brought he me into the outward court, and, lo, *there were* chambers, and a pavement made for the court round about: thirty chambers *were* upon the pavement.

18 And the pavement by the side of the gates over against the length of the gates *was* the lower pavement.

19 Then he measured the breadth from the forefront of the lower gate unto the forefront of the inner court without, an hundred cubits eastward and northward.

20 ¶ And the gate of the outward court that looked toward the north, he measured the length thereof, and the breadth thereof.

21 And the little chambers thereof *were* three on this side and three on that side; and the posts thereof and the arches thereof were after the measure of the first gate: the length thereof *was* fifty cubits, and the breadth five and twenty cubits.

22 And their windows, and their arches, and their palm trees, *were* after the measure of the gate that looketh toward the east; and they went up unto it by seven steps; and the arches thereof *were* before them.

23 And the gate of the inner court *was* over against the gate toward the north, and toward the east; and he measured from gate to gate an hundred cubits.

24 ¶ After that he brought me toward the south, and behold a gate toward the south: and he measured the posts thereof and the arches thereof according to these measures.

25 And *there were* windows in it and in the arches thereof round about, like those windows: the length *was* fifty cubits, and the breadth five and twenty cubits.

26 And *there were* seven steps to go up to it, and the arches thereof *were* before them: and it had palm trees, one on this side, and another on that side, upon the posts thereof.

27 And *there was* a gate in the inner court toward the south: and he measured from gate to gate toward the south an hundred cubits.

28 And he brought me to the inner court by the south gate: and he measured the south gate according to these measures;

29 And the little chambers thereof, and the posts thereof, and the arches thereof, according to these measures: and *there were* windows in it and in the arches thereof round about: *it was* fifty cubits long, and five and twenty cubits broad.

30 And the arches round about *were* five and twenty cubits long, and five cubits broad.

31 And the arches thereof *were* toward the utter court; and palm trees *were* upon the posts thereof: and the going up to it *had* eight steps.

**AMP** [a] As the Septuagint (Greek) Version gives these verses. The Hebrew is obscure. [b] As the Septuagint (Greek) Version gives these verses. The Hebrew is obscure.

## Amplified

9 Then he measured the porch *or* vestibule of the gateway, eight cubits, and its posts *or* jambs, two cubits, and the porch *or* vestibule of the gate was inside—toward the house [of the Lord].

10 And the guard rooms *or* lodges of the east gateway were three on this side and three on that side; the three were the same size, and the posts *or* jambs were the same size on either side.

11 And he measured the breadth of the opening of the gateway, ten cubits, and the length of the gateway, thirteen cubits.

12 And a border *or* barrier before the guard rooms was one cubit on this side and a border *or* barrier, one cubit on that side. And the guard rooms *or* lodges were six cubits on this side, and six cubits on that side.

13 And [a] *the man* [an angel] measured the gate from the outer wall of one chamber *or* guard room to the outer wall of another; a breadth of twenty-five cubits, from door to door.

14 And [b]the open part of the porch *or* vestibule of the gateway on the outside was twenty cubits, the chambers *or* guard rooms of the gate being round about.

15 And including this porch *or* vestibule of the gate on the outside and the porch *or* vestibule on the inside the extent was fifty cubits.

16 And there were closed windows to the guard rooms *or* chambers, and to their posts *or* pillars within the gate round about, and likewise to the arches *or* colonnade; and windows were round about facing into the court, and upon each post *or* column were palm tree [decorations].

17 Then he brought me into the outward court, and, lo, there were chambers and a pavement round about the court; thirty chambers fronted on the pavement.

18 And the pavement was along by the side of the gates, answerable to the length of the gateways; this was the lower pavement.

19 Then [the man] measured the distance from the inner front before the lower gate to the outer front of the inner court, a hundred cubits, both on the east and on the north.

20 And the gate of the outward court which faced the north, of it he measured both the length and the breadth.

21 And its guard rooms *or* lodges, three on this side and three on that side, and its pillars *or* posts and arches *or* vestibule were the same size as those of the first gate: their length was fifty cubits and the breadth twenty-five cubits.

22 And its windows and its arches *or* vestibule and its palm trees were of the same size as those of the gate that faces toward the east. It was reached by going up seven steps, and the arches of its vestibule were on the inner side.

23 Opposite the gate on the north and on the east, was a gate to the inner court; and [the man with the measuring rod of reed] measured from gate to gate, a hundred cubits.

24 After that *the man* brought me toward the south, and behold, there was a gate on the south, and he measured its pillars *or* posts and its arches *or* vestibule; they measured as the others did.

25 And there were windows round about in it and in its arches *or* vestibule, like those windows in the other gateways; its length was fifty cubits and the breadth twenty-five cubits.

26 And there were seven steps going up to the gate, and its arches *or* vestibule were on the inside. And it had palm trees, one on this side and another on that side, carved on its pillars *or* posts.

27 And there was a gate to the inner court on the south; and he measured from gate to gate toward the south, a hundred cubits.

28 And [the man, an angel] brought me into the inner court by the south gate, and he measured the south gate; its measurements were the same as those of the other gateways.

29 And its guard rooms *or* chambers and its pillars *or* posts and its arches *or* vestibule measured as did the others. And there were windows in the gateway and in its arches *or* vestibule round about; its length was fifty cubits and its breadth twenty-five cubits.

30 And there were arches *or* a vestibule round about, twenty-five cubits long [the long way of the vestibule] and five cubits wide.

31 And its [arched] vestibule faced the outer court, and palm trees were carved upon its posts *or* pillars, and the steps going up to it were eight.

## New American Standard

9And he measured the porch of the gate, eight cubits; and its
side pillars, two cubits. And the porch of the gate was faced
inward.
10And the guardrooms of the gate toward the east *numbered*
three on each side; the three of them had the same measurement.
The side pillars also had the same measurement on each side.
11And he measured the width of the gateway, ten cubits, and
the length of the gate, thirteen cubits.
12And *there was* a barrier *wall* one cubit *wide* in front of the
guardrooms on each side; and the guardrooms *were* six cubits
*square* on each side.
13And he measured the gate from the roof of the one guardroom
to the roof of the other, a width of twenty-five cubits from *one* door
to *the* door opposite.
14And he made the side pillars sixty cubits *high;* the gate *extended* round about to the side pillar of the courtyard.
15And *from* the front of the entrance gate to the front of the inner
porch of the gate *was* fifty cubits.
16And *there were* shuttered windows *looking* toward the guardrooms, and toward their side pillars within the gate all around, and
likewise for the porches. And *there were* windows all around inside;
and on *each* side pillar *were* palm tree ornaments.
17¶ Then he brought me into the outer court, and behold, *there
were* chambers and a pavement, made for the court all around;
thirty chambers faced the pavement.
18And the pavement ( *that is,* the lower pavement) *was* by the
side of the gates, corresponding to the length of the gates.
19Then he measured the width from the front of the lower gate
to the front of the exterior of the inner court, a hundred cubits on
the east and on the north.
20¶ And *as for* the gate of the outer court which faced the north,
he measured its length and its width.
21And it had three guardrooms on each side; and its side pillars
and its porches had the same measurement as the first gate. Its
length *was* fifty cubits, and the width twenty-five cubits.
22And its windows, and its porches, and its palm tree ornaments *had* the same measurements as the gate which faced toward
the east; and it was reached by seven steps, and its porch *was* in
front of them.
23And the inner court had a gate opposite the gate on the north
as well as *the gate* on the east; and he measured a hundred cubits
from gate to gate.
24¶ Then he led me toward the south, and behold, there was a
gate toward the south; and he measured its side pillars and its
porches according to those same measurements.
25And the gate and its porches had windows all around like
those other windows; the length *was* fifty cubits and the width
twenty-five cubits.
26And *there were* seven steps going up to it, and its porches *were*
in front of them; and it had palm tree ornaments on its side pillars,
one on each side.
27And the inner court had a gate toward the south; and he
measured from gate to gate toward the south, a hundred cubits.
28¶ Then he brought me to the inner court by the south gate;
and he measured the south gate according to those same measurements.
29Its guardrooms also, its side pillars, and its porches *were* according to those same measurements. And the gate and its porches
had windows all around; it *was* fifty cubits long and twenty-five
cubits wide.
30And *there were* porches all around, twenty-five cubits long and
five cubits wide.
31And its porches *were* toward the outer court; and palm tree
ornaments *were* on its side pillars, and its stairway had eight steps.

## New International

cubits deep and its jambs were two cubits thick. The portico of the
gateway faced the temple.
10Inside the east gate were three alcoves on each side; the three
had the same measurements, and the faces of the projecting walls
on each side had the same measurements. 11Then he measured the
width of the entrance to the gateway; it was ten cubits and its
length was thirteen cubits. 12In front of each alcove was a wall one
cubit high, and the alcoves were six cubits square. 13Then he
measured the gateway from the top of the rear wall of one alcove
to the top of the opposite one; the distance was twenty-five cubits
from one parapet opening to the opposite one. 14He measured
along the faces of the projecting walls all around the inside of the
gateway—sixty cubits. The measurement was up to the portico[c]
facing the courtyard.[d] 15The distance from the entrance of the
gateway to the far end of its portico was fifty cubits. 16The alcoves
and the projecting walls inside the gateway were surmounted by
narrow parapet openings all around, as was the portico; the openings all around faced inward. The faces of the projecting walls were
decorated with palm trees.

### *The Outer Court*

17Then he brought me into the outer court. There I saw some
rooms and a pavement that had been constructed all around the
court; there were thirty rooms along the pavement. 18It abutted the
sides of the gateways and was as wide as they were long; this was
the lower pavement. 19Then he measured the distance from the
inside of the lower gateway to the outside of the inner court; it was
a hundred cubits on the east side as well as on the north.

### *The North Gate*

20Then he measured the length and width of the gate facing
north, leading into the outer court. 21Its alcoves—three on each
side—its projecting walls and its portico had the same measurements as those of the first gateway. It was fifty cubits long and
twenty-five cubits wide. 22Its openings, its portico and its palm
tree decorations had the same measurements as those of the gate
facing east. Seven steps led up to it, with its portico opposite them.
23There was a gate to the inner court facing the north gate, just as
there was on the east. He measured from one gate to the opposite
one; it was a hundred cubits.

### *The South Gate*

24Then he led me to the south side and I saw a gate facing south.
He measured its jambs and its portico, and they had the same
measurements as the others. 25The gateway and its portico had
narrow openings all around, like the openings of the others. It was
fifty cubits long and twenty-five cubits wide. 26Seven steps led up
to it, with its portico opposite them; it had palm tree decorations
on the faces of the projecting walls on each side. 27The inner court
also had a gate facing south, and he measured from this gate to
the outer gate on the south side; it was a hundred cubits.

### *Gates to the Inner Court*

28Then he brought me into the inner court through the south
gate, and he measured the south gate; it had the same measurements as the others. 29Its alcoves, its projecting walls and its
portico had the same measurements as the others. The gateway
and its portico had openings all around. It was fifty cubits long and
twenty-five cubits wide. 30(The porticoes of the gateways around
the inner court were twenty-five cubits wide and five cubits deep.)
31Its portico faced the outer court; palm trees decorated its jambs,
and eight steps led up to it.

**NIV** [c] *14* Septuagint; Hebrew *projecting wall* [d] *14* The meaning of the Hebrew for this verse is uncertain.

## King James

32¶ And he brought me into the inner court toward the east: and he measured the gate according to these measures.

33And the little chambers thereof, and the posts thereof, and the arches thereof, *were* according to these measures: and *there were* windows therein and in the arches thereof round about: *it was* fifty cubits long, and five and twenty cubits broad.

34And the arches thereof *were* toward the outward court; and palm trees *were* upon the posts thereof, on this side, and on that side: and the going up to it *had* eight steps.

35¶ And he brought me to the north gate, and measured *it* according to these measures;

36The little chambers thereof, the posts thereof, and the arches thereof, and the windows to it round about: the length *was* fifty cubits, and the breadth five and twenty cubits.

37And the posts thereof *were* toward the utter court; and palm trees *were* upon the posts thereof, on this side, and on that side: and the going up to it *had* eight steps.

38And the chambers and the entries thereof *were* by the posts of the gates, where they washed the burnt offering.

39¶ And in the porch of the gate *were* two tables on this side, and two tables on that side, to slay thereon the burnt offering and the sin offering and the trespass offering.

40And at the side without, as one goeth up to the entry of the north gate, *were* two tables; and on the other side, which *was* at the porch of the gate, *were* two tables.

41Four tables *were* on this side, and four tables on that side, by the side of the gate; eight tables, whereupon they slew *their sacrifices*.

42And the four tables *were* of hewn stone for the burnt offering, of a cubit and an half long, and a cubit and an half broad, and one cubit high: whereupon also they laid the instruments wherewith they slew the burnt offering and the sacrifice.

43And within *were* hooks, an hand broad, fastened round about: and upon the tables *was* the flesh of the offering.

44¶ And without the inner gate *were* the chambers of the singers in the inner court, which *was* at the side of the north gate; and their prospect *was* toward the south: one at the side of the east gate *having* the prospect toward the north.

45And he said unto me, This chamber, whose prospect *is* toward the south, *is* for the priests, the keepers of the charge of the house.

46And the chamber whose prospect *is* toward the north *is* for the priests, the keepers of the charge of the altar: these *are* the sons of Zadok among the sons of Levi, which come near to the LORD to minister unto him.

47So he measured the court, an hundred cubits long, and an hundred cubits broad, foursquare; and the altar *that was* before the house.

48¶ And he brought me to the porch of the house, and measured *each* post of the porch, five cubits on this side, and five cubits on that side: and the breadth of the gate *was* three cubits on this side, and three cubits on that side.

49The length of the porch *was* twenty cubits, and the breadth eleven cubits; and *he brought me* by the steps whereby they went up to it: and *there were* pillars by the posts, one on this side, and another on that side.

## Amplified

32And he brought me into the inner court toward the east, and he measured the gate; it measured the same as the others.

33And its guard rooms *or* chambers and its posts *or* pillars and its arches *or* vestibule measured as did the others. And there were windows in it and in its [arched] vestibule round about; the gateway was fifty cubits long and twenty-five cubits wide.

34And its [arched] vestibule faced the outer court, and palm trees were carved upon its posts *or* pillars on either side, and the steps leading to it were eight.

35And [the man, an angel] brought me to the north gate and measured it; the measurements were the same as those of the other gates.

36Its guard rooms *or* chambers, its posts *or* pillars and its [arched] vestibule, and the windows to it round about [were of the same size as the others]. The length of the gateway was fifty cubits and the width was twenty-five cubits.

37And its posts *or* pillars were toward the outer court, and palm trees were carved upon them on either side. And the approach to it had eight steps.

38There was an attached chamber with its door beside the posts of the gates, where the burnt offering was to be washed.

39And in the porch *or* vestibule of the gate were two tables on this side and two tables on that side, on which to slay the burnt offering and the sin offering and the trespass *or* guilt offering.

40And on the one side without, as one goes up to the entrance of the gate to the north, were two tables; and on the other side at the vestibule of the gate were two tables.

41Four tables were on the inside and four tables on the outside of the side of the gate, eight tables upon which the sacrifices were to be slain.

42Moreover, there were four tables of hewn stone for the burnt offering, a cubit and a half long, and a cubit and a half broad, and one cubit high. Upon them were to be laid the instruments with which were slain the burnt offering and the sacrifice.

43And slabs *or* hooks a hand-breadth long were fastened within [the room] round about. Upon the tables was to be placed the flesh of the offering.

44 [a]Then [the man, an angel] led me [from without] into the inner court, and behold, there were two chambers in the inner court: one beside the north gate, but facing the south, and one beside the south gate, but looking toward the north.

45And [the man, an angel who was guiding me] said, This chamber with its view to the south is for the priests who have charge of the house [of the Lord].

46And the chamber with its view to the north is for the priests who have charge of the altar. These are the sons of Zadok, who alone among the sons of Levi may come near to the Lord to minister to Him.

47And he measured the court, a hundred cubits long and a hundred cubits broad, foursquare; and the altar was in front of the house [of the Lord].

48Then he brought me to the vestibule *or* porch of the temple proper, and he measured each post *or* pillar of the porch, five cubits on either side. And the width of the gate was three cubits for this *leaf* and three cubits for that one.

49And the length of the vestibule *or* porch was twenty cubits, and the breadth eleven cubits, and he brought me by the steps by which it was reached; and there were two pillars standing on the posts [as bases], *or* beside them, one on either side of the entrance.

**AMP** [a] Taken from the Septuagint (Greek) Version for clearer description.

## New American Standard

32¶ And he brought me into the inner court toward the east. And he measured the gate according to those same measurements.
33Its guardrooms also, its side pillars, and its porches *were* according to those same measurements. And the gate and its porches had windows all around; it *was* fifty cubits long and twenty-five cubits wide.
34And its porches *were* toward the outer court; and palm tree ornaments *were* on its side pillars, on each side, and its stairway had eight steps.
35¶ Then he brought me to the north gate; and he measured *it* according to those same measurements,
36 *with* its guardrooms, its side pillars, and its porches. And the gate had windows all around; the length *was* fifty cubits and the width twenty-five cubits.
37And its side pillars *were* toward the outer court; and palm tree ornaments *were* on its side pillars on each side, and its stairway had eight steps.
38¶ And a chamber with its doorway was by the side pillars at the gates; there they rinse the burnt offering.
39And in the porch of the gate *were* two tables on each side, on which to slaughter the burnt offering, the sin offering, and the guilt offering.
40And on the outer side, as one went up to the gateway toward the north, were two tables; and on the other side of the porch of the gate *were* two tables.
41Four tables *were* on each side next to the gate; *or,* eight tables on which they slaughter *sacrifices.*
42And for the burnt offering *there were* four tables of hewn stone, a cubit and a half long, a cubit and a half wide, and one cubit high, on which they lay the instruments with which they slaughter the burnt offering and the sacrifice.
43And the double hooks, one handbreadth in length, were installed in the house all around; and on the tables *was* the flesh of the offering.
44¶ And from the outside to the inner gate were chambers for the singers in the inner court, *one of* which was at the side of the north gate, with its front toward the south, and one at the side of the east gate facing toward the north.
45And he said to me, "This is the chamber which faces toward the south, *intended* for the priests who keep charge of the temple;
46but the chamber which faces toward the north is for the priests who keep charge of the altar. These are the sons of Zadok, who from the sons of Levi come near to the LORD to minister to Him."
47And he measured the court, a *perfect* square, a hundred cubits long and a hundred cubits wide; and the altar was in front of the temple.
48¶ Then he brought me to the porch of the temple and measured *each* side pillar of the porch, five cubits on each side; and the width of the gate was three cubits on each side.
49The length of the porch was twenty cubits, and the width eleven cubits; and at the stairway by which it was ascended *were* columns belonging to the side pillars, one on each side.

## New International

32Then he brought me to the inner court on the east side, and he measured the gateway; it had the same measurements as the others. 33Its alcoves, its projecting walls and its portico had the same measurements as the others. The gateway and its portico had openings all around. It was fifty cubits long and twenty-five cubits wide. 34Its portico faced the outer court; palm trees decorated the jambs on either side, and eight steps led up to it.

35Then he brought me to the north gate and measured it. It had the same measurements as the others, 36as did its alcoves, its projecting walls and its portico, and it had openings all around. It was fifty cubits long and twenty-five cubits wide. 37Its portico[b] faced the outer court; palm trees decorated the jambs on either side, and eight steps led up to it.

*The Rooms for Preparing Sacrifices*

38A room with a doorway was by the portico in each of the inner gateways, where the burnt offerings were washed. 39In the portico of the gateway were two tables on each side, on which the burnt offerings, sin offerings and guilt offerings were slaughtered. 40By the outside wall of the portico of the gateway, near the steps at the entrance to the north gateway were two tables, and on the other side of the steps were two tables. 41So there were four tables on one side of the gateway and four on the other—eight tables in all—on which the sacrifices were slaughtered. 42There were also four tables of dressed stone for the burnt offerings, each a cubit and a half long, a cubit and a half wide and a cubit high. On them were placed the utensils for slaughtering the burnt offerings and the other sacrifices. 43And double-pronged hooks, each a handbreadth long, were attached to the wall all around. The tables were for the flesh of the offerings.

*Rooms for the Priests*

44Outside the inner gate, within the inner court, were two rooms, one[c] at the side of the north gate and facing south, and another at the side of the south[d] gate and facing north. 45He said to me, "The room facing south is for the priests who have charge of the temple, 46and the room facing north is for the priests who have charge of the altar. These are the sons of Zadok, who are the only Levites who may draw near to the LORD to minister before him."

47Then he measured the court: It was square—a hundred cubits long and a hundred cubits wide. And the altar was in front of the temple.

*The Temple*

48He brought me to the portico of the temple and measured the jambs of the portico; they were five cubits wide on either side. The width of the entrance was fourteen cubits and its projecting walls were[e] three cubits wide on either side. 49The portico was twenty cubits wide, and twelve[f] cubits from front to back. It was reached by a flight of stairs,[g] and there were pillars on each side of the jambs.

NIV [b] *37* Septuagint (see also verses 31 and 34); Hebrew *jambs* [c] *44* Septuagint; Hebrew *were rooms for singers, which were* [d] *44* Septuagint; Hebrew *east* [e] *48* Septuagint; Hebrew *entrance was* [f] *49* Septuagint; Hebrew *eleven* [g] *49* Hebrew; Septuagint *Ten steps led up to it*

## King James

**41** AFTERWARD HE brought me to the temple, and measured the posts, six cubits broad on the one side, and six cubits broad on the other side, *which was* the breadth of the tabernacle.

2 And the breadth of the door *was* ten cubits; and the sides of the door *were* five cubits on the one side, and five cubits on the other side: and he measured the length thereof, forty cubits: and the breadth, twenty cubits.

3 Then went he inward, and measured the post of the door, two cubits; and the door, six cubits; and the breadth of the door, seven cubits.

4 So he measured the length thereof, twenty cubits; and the breadth, twenty cubits, before the temple: and he said unto me, This *is* the most holy *place*.

5 After he measured the wall of the house, six cubits; and the breadth of *every* side chamber, four cubits, round about the house on every side.

6 And the side chambers *were* three, one over another, and thirty in order; and they entered into the wall which *was* of the house for the side chambers round about, that they might have hold, but they had not hold in the wall of the house.

7 And *there was* an enlarging, and a winding about still upward to the side chambers: for the winding about of the house went still upward round about the house: therefore the breadth of the house *was still* upward, and so increased *from* the lowest *chamber* to the highest by the midst.

8 I saw also the height of the house round about: the foundations of the side chambers *were* a full reed of six great cubits.

9 The thickness of the wall, which *was* for the side chamber without, *was* five cubits: and *that* which *was* left *was* the place of the side chambers that *were* within.

10 And between the chambers *was* the wideness of twenty cubits round about the house on every side.

11 And the doors of the side chambers *were* toward *the place that was* left, one door toward the north, and another door toward the south: and the breadth of the place that was left *was* five cubits round about.

12 Now the building that *was* before the separate place at the end toward the west *was* seventy cubits broad; and the wall of the building *was* five cubits thick round about, and the length thereof ninety cubits.

13 So he measured the house, an hundred cubits long; and the separate place, and the building, with the walls thereof, an hundred cubits long;

14 Also the breadth of the face of the house, and of the separate place toward the east, an hundred cubits.

15 And he measured the length of the building over against the separate place which *was* behind it, and the galleries thereof on the one side and on the other side, an hundred cubits, with the inner temple, and the porches of the court;

16 The door posts, and the narrow windows, and the galleries round about on their three stories, over against the door, ceiled with wood round about, and from the ground up to the windows, and the windows *were* covered;

17 To that above the door, even unto the inner house, and without, and by all the wall round about within and without, by measure.

18 And *it was* made with cherubims and palm trees, so that a palm tree *was* between a cherub and a cherub; and *every* cherub had two faces;

19 So that the face of a man *was* toward the palm tree on the one side, and the face of a young lion toward the palm tree on the other side: *it was* made through all the house round about.

## Amplified

**41** AND [THE man, an angel] brought me to [the holy place of] the temple, and measured the wall pillars, six cubits broad on one side [of the ten-cubit door], and six cubits broad on the other side, which was the breadth of the tabernacle *or* tent [later called the temple].

2 And the breadth of the entrance was ten cubits, and the leaves of the door were five cubits on the one side and five cubits on the other side; and he measured its length, forty cubits and the breadth, twenty cubits.

3 Then [the man, being an angel and unrestricted] went inside [the inner room, but went alone], and measured each post of the door, two cubits, and the doorway, six cubits, and the breadth of the entrance, seven cubits. [Heb. 9:6, 7; 10:19-25.]

4 And he measured the length [of the interior of the second room] in the temple proper, twenty cubits, and the breadth, twenty cubits; and he said to me, This is the most holy place—the holy of holies.

5 Then he measured the wall of the temple, six cubits thick [to accommodate side chambers]; and the breadth of every side chamber, four cubits, round about the temple proper on every side.

6 These side chambers were three stories high, one over another, and thirty in each story; and they entered into the wall which belonged to the house for the side chambers round about, that they might have hold of that wall, but they did not have hold of the wall of the temple.

7 And the side rooms became broader as they encompassed the temple higher and higher, for the encircling of the house went higher and higher round about the temple; therefore the breadth of the house continued upward, and so one went up from the lowest story to the highest one by way of the middle story [on a winding stairway].

8 I saw also that the temple had an elevation *or* foundation platform round about it. The foundations of the side chambers measured a full reed measure of six long cubits.

9 The thickness of the outer wall of the side chamber was five cubits, and so was the width of that part of the foundation that was left free of the side chambers that belonged to the house.

10 And between [the free space of the foundation platform and] the chambers was a breadth of twenty cubits round about the temple on every side.

11 And the doors of the attached side chambers opened on the free space that was left, one door toward the north and another door toward the south; and the breadth of the space on the foundation platform that was left free was five cubits round about.

12 And the building that faced the temple yard on the west side was seventy cubits broad, and the wall of the building was five cubits thick round about, and its length ninety cubits.

13 And [the man, an angel in my vision] measured the temple, a hundred cubits long, and the yard and the building with its walls, a hundred cubits long;

14 Also the breadth of the east front of the temple and the yard, a hundred cubits.

15 Then [the man, an angel] measured the length of the building on the west side of the yard with its walls on either side, a hundred cubits. The holy place of the temple, the inner holy of holies, and the outer vestibule

16 Were roofed over, and all three had latticed windows all around. The inside walls of the temple were paneled with wood round about from the floor up to the windows and from the windows to the roof,

17 Including the space above the door leading to the inner room inside and out. And on the walls round about in the inner room and the holy place were carvings,

18 With figures of cherubim and palm trees, so that a palm tree was between a cherub and a cherub; and every cherub had two faces,

19 So that the face of a man was toward the palm tree on the one side, and the face of a young lion toward the palm tree on the other side. It was made this way through all the house round about.

## New American Standard

*The Inner Temple*

**41** THEN HE brought me to the nave and measured the side
pillars; six cubits wide on each side *was* the width of the
side pillar.
2And the width of the entrance *was* ten cubits, and the sides
of the entrance were five cubits on each side. And he measured the
length of the nave, forty cubits, and the width, twenty cubits.
3Then he went inside and measured each side pillar of the
doorway, two cubits, and the doorway, six cubits *high;* and the
width of the doorway, seven cubits.
4And he measured its length, twenty cubits, and the width,
twenty cubits, before the nave; and he said to me, "This is the most
holy *place.*"
5¶ Then he measured the wall of the temple, six cubits; and the
width of the side chambers, four cubits, all around about the house
on every side.
6And the side chambers were in three stories, one above another, and thirty in each story; and the side chambers extended to
the wall which *stood* on their inward side all around, that they
might be fastened, and not be fastened into the wall of the temple
*itself.*
7And the side chambers surrounding the temple were wider
at each successive story. Because the structure surrounding the
temple went upward by stages on all sides of the temple, therefore
the width of the temple *increased* as it went higher; and thus one
went up from the lowest *story* to the highest by way of the second
*story.*
8I saw also that the house had a raised platform all around; the
foundations of the side chambers were a full rod of six long cubits
*in height.*
9The thickness of the outer wall of the side chambers was five
cubits. But the free space between the side chambers belonging to
the temple
10and the *outer* chambers *was* twenty cubits in width all around
the temple on every side.
11And the doorways of the side chambers toward the free space
*consisted of* one doorway toward the north and another doorway
toward the south; and the width of the free space was five cubits
all around.
12¶ And the building that *was* in front of the separate area at the
side toward the west *was* seventy cubits wide; and the wall of the
building was five cubits thick all around, and its length *was* ninety
cubits.
13Then he measured the temple, a hundred cubits long; the
separate area with the building and its walls *were* also a hundred
cubits long.
14Also the width of the front of the temple and *that of* the
separate areas along the east *side totaled* a hundred cubits.
15¶ And he measured the length of the building along the front
of the separate area behind it, with a gallery on each side, a
hundred cubits; *he* also *measured* the inner nave and the porches
of the court.
16The thresholds, the latticed windows, and the galleries round
about their three stories, opposite the threshold, were paneled
with wood all around, and *from* the ground to the windows (but
the windows were covered),
17over the entrance, and to the inner house, and on the outside,
and on all the wall all around inside and outside, by measurement.
18And it was carved with cherubim and palm trees; and a palm
tree was between cherub and cherub, and every cherub had two
faces,
19a man's face toward the palm tree on one side, and a young
lion's face toward the palm tree on the other side; they were carved
on all the house all around.

## New International

**41** THEN THE man brought me to the outer sanctuary and
measured the jambs; the width of the jambs was six cubits[a] on each side.[b] 2The entrance was ten cubits wide, and the
projecting walls on each side of it were five cubits wide. He also
measured the outer sanctuary; it was forty cubits long and twenty
cubits wide.
3Then he went into the inner sanctuary and measured the jambs
of the entrance; each was two cubits wide. The entrance was six
cubits wide, and the projecting walls on each side of it were seven
cubits wide. 4And he measured the length of the inner sanctuary;
it was twenty cubits, and its width was twenty cubits across the
end of the outer sanctuary. He said to me, "This is the Most Holy
Place."
5Then he measured the wall of the temple; it was six cubits
thick, and each side room around the temple was four cubits wide.
6The side rooms were on three levels, one above another, thirty on
each level. There were ledges all around the wall of the temple to
serve as supports for the side rooms, so that the supports were not
inserted into the wall of the temple. 7The side rooms all around the
temple were wider at each successive level. The structure surrounding the temple was built in ascending stages, so that the
rooms widened as one went upward. A stairway went up from the
lowest floor to the top floor through the middle floor.
8I saw that the temple had a raised base all around it, forming
the foundation of the side rooms. It was the length of the rod, six
long cubits. 9The outer wall of the side rooms was five cubits thick.
The open area between the side rooms of the temple 10and the
⌞priests'⌟ rooms was twenty cubits wide all around the temple.
11There were entrances to the side rooms from the open area, one
on the north and another on the south; and the base adjoining the
open area was five cubits wide all around.
12The building facing the temple courtyard on the west side was
seventy cubits wide. The wall of the building was five cubits thick
all around, and its length was ninety cubits.
13Then he measured the temple; it was a hundred cubits long,
and the temple courtyard and the building with its walls were also
a hundred cubits long. 14The width of the temple courtyard on the
east, including the front of the temple, was a hundred cubits.
15Then he measured the length of the building facing the courtyard at the rear of the temple, including its galleries on each side;
it was a hundred cubits.
The outer sanctuary, the inner sanctuary and the portico facing
the court, 16as well as the thresholds and the narrow windows and
galleries around the three of them—everything beyond and including the threshold was covered with wood. The floor, the wall
up to the windows, and the windows were covered. 17In the space
above the outside of the entrance to the inner sanctuary and on the
walls at regular intervals all around the inner and outer sanctuary
18were carved cherubim and palm trees. Palm trees alternated with
cherubim. Each cherub had two faces: 19the face of a man toward
the palm tree on one side and the face of a lion toward the palm
tree on the other. They were carved all around the whole temple.

**NIV** [a] *1* The common cubit was about 1 1/2 feet (about 0.5 meter). [b] *1* One Hebrew manuscript and Septuagint; most Hebrew manuscripts *side, the width of the tent*

## King James

20From the ground unto above the door *were* cherubims and
palm trees made, and *on* the wall of the temple.
21The posts of the temple *were* squared, *and* the face of the
sanctuary; the appearance *of the one* as the appearance *of the other*.
22The altar of wood *was* three cubits high, and the length thereof
two cubits; and the corners thereof, and the length thereof, and the
walls thereof, *were* of wood: and he said unto me, This *is* the table
that *is* before the LORD.
23And the temple and the sanctuary had two doors.
24And the doors had two leaves *apiece*, two turning leaves; two
*leaves* for the one door, and two leaves for the other *door*.
25And *there were* made on them, on the doors of the temple,
cherubims and palm trees, like as *were* made upon the walls; and
*there were* thick planks upon the face of the porch without.
26And *there were* narrow windows and palm trees on the one
side and on the other side, on the sides of the porch, and *upon* the
side chambers of the house, and thick planks.

**42** THEN HE brought me forth into the utter court, the way
toward the north: and he brought me into the chamber
that *was* over against the separate place, and which *was* before the
building toward the north.
2Before the length of an hundred cubits *was* the north door, and
the breadth *was* fifty cubits.
3Over against the twenty *cubits* which *were* for the inner court,
and over against the pavement which *was* for the utter court, *was*
gallery against gallery in three *stories*.
4And before the chambers *was* a walk of ten cubits breadth
inward, a way of one cubit; and their doors toward the north.
5Now the upper chambers *were* shorter: for the galleries were
higher than these, than the lower, and than the middlemost of the
building.
6For they *were* in three *stories*, but had not pillars as the pillars
of the courts: therefore *the building* was straitened more than the
lowest and the middlemost from the ground.
7And the wall that *was* without over against the chambers,
toward the utter court on the forepart of the chambers, the length
thereof *was* fifty cubits.
8For the length of the chambers that *were* in the utter court *was*
fifty cubits: and, lo, before the temple *were* an hundred cubits.
9And from under these chambers *was* the entry on the east side,
as one goeth into them from the utter court.
10The chambers *were* in the thickness of the wall of the court
toward the east, over against the separate place, and over against
the building.
11And the way before them *was* like the appearance of the
chambers which *were* toward the north, as long as they, *and* as
broad as they: and all their goings out *were* both according to their
fashions, and according to their doors.
12And according to the doors of the chambers that *were* toward
the south *was* a door in the head of the way, *even* the way directly
before the wall toward the east, as one entereth into them.
13¶ Then said he unto me, The north chambers *and* the south
chambers, which *are* before the separate place, they *be* holy chambers, where the priests that approach unto the LORD shall eat the
most holy things: there shall they lay the most holy things, and the
meat offering, and the sin offering, and the trespass offering; for
the place *is* holy.
14When the priests enter therein, then shall they not go out of
the holy *place* into the utter court, but there they shall lay their
garments wherein they minister; for they *are* holy; and shall put
on other garments, and shall approach to *those things* which *are* for
the people.
15Now when he had made an end of measuring the inner
house, he brought me forth toward the gate whose prospect *is*
toward the east, and measured it round about.

## Amplified

20From the floor to above the entrance were cherubim and palm
trees made, and so on the wall of the temple [the holy place].
21The door frames of the temple were squared, and in front
[outside of the sanctuary *or* holy of holies] was what appeared to
be
22An altar of wood, three cubits high and two cubits long [and
wide], and its corners, its base and its sides were of wood. And
the man said to me, This is the table that is before the Lord.
23And the temple *or* holy place and the sanctuary *or* holy of
holies, had two doors [one for each of them].
24And the doors had two leaves apiece, two folding leaves; two
leaves for the one door and two leaves for the other door.
25And there were carved on them, on the doors of the temple,
cherubim and palm trees, like those carved upon the walls; and
there was also a canopy of wood in front of the porch outside.
26And there were recessed windows and palm trees on the one
side and on the other side of the porch. Thus were the side chambers of the house, and the canopies.

**42** THEN [THE man, an angel] brought me forth into the
outer court northward, and he brought me to the attached
chambers that were opposite the temple yard and were opposite
the building on the north.
2Before the long side of one hundred cubits was the door
toward the north, and the breadth was fifty cubits.
3Adjoining the twenty cubits which belonged to the inner court,
and opposite the pavement which belonged to the outer court, was
balcony facing balcony in three stories.
4And before the attached chambers was a walk inward of ten
cubits breadth and a hundred cubits long, and their doors were on
the north.
5Now the upper chambers were shorter, for the balconies took
off from these more than from the lower and middle chambers of
the building.
6For they were in three stories, but did not have pillars as the
pillars of the [outer] court; therefore the upper chambers were set
back more than the lower and the middle ones from the ground.
7And the wall *or* fence that was outside, opposite *and* parallel
to the chambers, toward the outer court before the chambers, was
fifty cubits long.
8For the length of the [combined] chambers that were on the
outer court was fifty cubits, while *the length* of those opposite the
temple was a hundred cubits.
9And under these chambers was the entrance on the east side,
as one approached them from the outer court.
10In the breadth of the wall of the court going toward the east,
before the yard and before the building, were the chambers
11With a passage before them that gave the appearance of the
attached chambers on the north, of the same length and breadth,
with similar exits and arrangements and doors.
12And like the doors of the chambers that were toward the
south there was an entrance at the head of the way, the way before
the dividing wall toward the east, as one enters them.
13Then said [the man, an angel] to me, The north chambers and
the south chambers, which are opposite the yard, are the holy
chambers where the priests who approach the Lord shall eat the
most holy offerings; there shall they lay the most holy things, the
meal offering, the sin offering, and the trespass *or* guilt offering,
for the place is holy.
14When the priests enter the holy place they shall not go out of
it into the outer court unless they lay aside there the garments in
which they minister, for these are holy, separate *and* set apart.
They shall put on other garments before they approach that which
is for the people.
15Now when he had finished measuring the inner temple area,
he brought me forth toward the gate which faces east and measured it [the outer area] round about.

# New American Standard

20From the ground to above the entrance cherubim and palm trees were carved, as well as *on* the wall of the nave.

21¶ The doorposts of the nave were square; as for the front of the sanctuary, the appearance of one doorpost was like that of the other.

22The altar *was* of wood, three cubits high, and its length two cubits; its corners, its base, and its sides *were* of wood. And he said to me, "This is the table that is before the LORD."

23And the nave and the sanctuary each had a double door.

24And each of the doors had two leaves, two swinging leaves; two *leaves* for one door and two leaves for the other.

25Also there were carved on them, on the doors of the nave, cherubim and palm trees like those carved on the walls; and *there was* a threshold of wood on the front of the porch outside.

26And *there were* latticed windows and palm trees on one side and on the other, on the sides of the porch; thus *were* the side chambers of the house and the thresholds.

*Chambers of the Temple*

**42** THEN HE brought me out into the outer court, the way toward the north; and he brought me to the chamber which *was* opposite the separate area and opposite the building toward the north.

2Along the length, *which was* a hundred cubits, *was* the north door; the width *was* fifty cubits.

3Opposite the twenty *cubits* which belonged to the inner court, and opposite the pavement which belonged to the outer court, *was* gallery corresponding to gallery in three stories.

4And before the chambers *was* an inner walk ten cubits wide, a way of one *hundred* cubits; and their openings *were* on the north.

5Now the upper chambers *were* smaller because the galleries took more *space* away from them than from the lower and middle ones in the building.

6For they *were* in three stories and had no pillars like the pillars of the courts; therefore *the upper chambers* were set back from the ground upward, more than the lower and middle ones.

7As for the outer wall by the side of the chambers, toward the outer court facing the chambers, its length *was* fifty cubits.

8For the length of the chambers which *were* in the outer court *was* fifty cubits; and behold, *the length of those* facing the temple *was* a hundred cubits.

9And below these chambers *was* the entrance on the east side, as one enters them from the outer court.

10¶ In the thickness of the wall of the court toward the east, facing the separate area and facing the building, *there were* chambers.

11And the way in front of them *was* like the appearance of the chambers which *were* on the north, according to their length so was their width; and all their exits *were* both according to their arrangements and openings.

12And corresponding to the openings of the chambers which were toward the south was an opening at the head of the way, the way in front of the wall toward the east, as one enters them.

13¶ Then he said to me, "The north chambers *and* the south chambers, which are opposite the separate area, they are the holy chambers where the priests who are near to the LORD shall eat the most holy things. There they shall lay the most holy things, the grain offering, the sin offering, and the guilt offering; for the place is holy.

14"When the priests enter, then they shall not go out into the outer court from the sanctuary without laying there their garments in which they minister, for they are holy. They shall put on other garments; then they shall approach that which is for the people."

15¶ Now when he had finished measuring the inner house, he brought me out by the way of the gate which faced toward the east, and measured it all around.

# New International

20From the floor to the area above the entrance, cherubim and palm trees were carved on the wall of the outer sanctuary.

21The outer sanctuary had a rectangular doorframe, and the one at the front of the Most Holy Place was similar. 22There was a wooden altar three cubits high and two cubits square[a] ; its corners, its base[b] and its sides were of wood. The man said to me, "This is the table that is before the LORD." 23Both the outer sanctuary and the Most Holy Place had double doors. 24Each door had two leaves—two hinged leaves for each door. 25And on the doors of the outer sanctuary were carved cherubim and palm trees like those carved on the walls, and there was a wooden overhang on the front of the portico. 26On the sidewalls of the portico were narrow windows with palm trees carved on each side. The side rooms of the temple also had overhangs.

*Rooms for the Priests*

**42** THEN THE man led me northward into the outer court and brought me to the rooms opposite the temple courtyard and opposite the outer wall on the north side. 2The building whose door faced north was a hundred cubits[c] long and fifty cubits wide. 3Both in the section twenty cubits from the inner court and in the section opposite the pavement of the outer court, gallery faced gallery at the three levels. 4In front of the rooms was an inner passageway ten cubits wide and a hundred cubits[d] long. Their doors were on the north. 5Now the upper rooms were narrower, for the galleries took more space from them than from the rooms on the lower and middle floors of the building. 6The rooms on the third floor had no pillars, as the courts had; so they were smaller in floor space than those on the lower and middle floors. 7There was an outer wall parallel to the rooms and the outer court; it extended in front of the rooms for fifty cubits. 8While the row of rooms on the side next to the outer court was fifty cubits long, the row on the side nearest the sanctuary was a hundred cubits long. 9The lower rooms had an entrance on the east side as one enters them from the outer court.

10On the south side[e] along the length of the wall of the outer court, adjoining the temple courtyard and opposite the outer wall, were rooms 11with a passageway in front of them. These were like the rooms on the north; they had the same length and width, with similar exits and dimensions. Similar to the doorways on the north 12were the doorways of the rooms on the south. There was a doorway at the beginning of the passageway that was parallel to the corresponding wall extending eastward, by which one enters the rooms.

13Then he said to me, "The north and south rooms facing the temple courtyard are the priests' rooms, where the priests who approach the LORD will eat the most holy offerings. There they will put the most holy offerings—the grain offerings, the sin offerings and the guilt offerings—for the place is holy. 14Once the priests enter the holy precincts, they are not to go into the outer court until they leave behind the garments in which they minister, for these are holy. They are to put on other clothes before they go near the places that are for the people."

15When he had finished measuring what was inside the temple area, he led me out by the east gate and measured the area all around: 16He measured the east side with the measuring rod; it

**NIV** [a] 22 Septuagint; Hebrew *long* [b] 22 Septuagint; Hebrew *length* [c] 2 The common cubit was about 1 1/2 feet (about 0.5 meter). [d] 4 Septuagint and Syriac; Hebrew *and one cubit* [e] 10 Septuagint; Hebrew *Eastward*

## King James

16He measured the east side with the measuring reed, five hundred reeds, with the measuring reed round about.
17He measured the north side, five hundred reeds, with the measuring reed round about.
18He measured the south side, five hundred reeds, with the measuring reed.
19¶ He turned about to the west side, *and* measured five hundred reeds with the measuring reed.
20He measured it by the four sides: it had a wall round about, five hundred *reeds* long, and five hundred broad, to make a separation between the sanctuary and the profane place.

**43** AFTERWARD HE brought me to the gate, *even* the gate that looketh toward the east:
2And, behold, the glory of the God of Israel came from the way of the east: and his voice *was* like a noise of many waters: and the earth shined with his glory.
3And *it was* according to the appearance of the vision which I saw, *even* according to the vision that I saw when I came to destroy the city: and the visions *were* like the vision that I saw by the river Chebar; and I fell upon my face.
4And the glory of the LORD came into the house by the way of the gate whose prospect *is* toward the east.
5So the spirit took me up, and brought me into the inner court; and, behold, the glory of the LORD filled the house.
6And I heard *him* speaking unto me out of the house; and the man stood by me.
7¶ And he said unto me, Son of man, the place of my throne, and the place of the soles of my feet, where I will dwell in the midst of the children of Israel for ever, and my holy name, shall the house of Israel no more defile, *neither* they, nor their kings, by their whoredom, nor by the carcases of their kings in their high places.
8In their setting of their threshold by my thresholds, and their post by my posts, and the wall between me and them, they have even defiled my holy name by their abominations that they have committed: wherefore I have consumed them in mine anger.
9Now let them put away their whoredom, and the carcases of their kings, far from me, and I will dwell in the midst of them for ever.
10¶ Thou son of man, show the house to the house of Israel, that they may be ashamed of their iniquities: and let them measure the pattern.
11And if they be ashamed of all that they have done, show them the form of the house, and the fashion thereof, and the goings out thereof, and the comings in thereof, and all the forms thereof, and all the ordinances thereof, and all the forms thereof, and all the laws thereof: and write *it* in their sight, that they may keep the whole form thereof, and all the ordinances thereof, and do them.
12This *is* the law of the house; Upon the top of the mountain the whole limit thereof round about *shall be* most holy. Behold, this *is* the law of the house.
13¶ And these *are* the measures of the altar after the cubits: The cubit *is* a cubit and an handbreadth; even the bottom *shall be* a cubit, and the breadth a cubit, and the border thereof by the edge thereof round about *shall be* a span: and this *shall be* the higher place of the altar.
14And from the bottom *upon* the ground *even* to the lower settle *shall be* two cubits, and the breadth one cubit; and from the lesser settle *even* to the greater settle *shall be* four cubits, and the breadth *one* cubit.
15So the altar *shall be* four cubits; and from the altar and upward *shall be* four horns.

## Amplified

16He measured the east side with the measuring reed, five hundred reeds, with the measuring reed round about.
17He measured the north side, five hundred reeds, with the measuring reed round about.
18He measured the south side, five hundred reeds, with the measuring reed.
19He turned about to the west side and measured five hundred reeds with the measuring reed.
20He measured it on the four sides: it had a wall round about, the length five hundred reeds and the breadth five hundred, to make a separation between that which was holy [the temple proper] and that which was common [the outer area].

**43** AFTERWARD [THE man, an angel] brought me to the gate, the gate that faces east.
2And behold, the glory of the God of Israel came from the east, and His voice was like the sound of many waters, and the earth shone with His glory. [Rev. 1:15; 14:2.]
3And the vision which I saw was like the vision I had seen when I came to foretell the destruction of the city, and like the vision I had seen beside the river Chebar [near Babylon]; and I fell on my face. [Ezek. 1:4; 3:23; 10:15, 22.]
4And the glory of the Lord entered the temple by the gate facing east.
5Then the Spirit caught me up and brought me into the inner court, and behold, the glory of the Lord filled the temple.
6And I heard One speaking to me out of the temple, and a Man stood by me.
7And He, [the Lord,] said to me, Son of man, *this is* the place of My throne, and the place of the soles of My feet, where I will dwell in the midst of the children of Israel for ever, and My holy name the house of Israel shall no more profane, neither they nor their kings, by their [idolatrous] harlotry, nor by the dead bodies *and* monuments of their kings;
8By setting their threshold by My thresholds and their doorposts by My doorposts, with a mere wall between Me and them. They have profaned My holy name by their abominations which they have committed; therefore I have consumed them in My anger.
9Now let them put away their [idolatrous] harlotry and the dead bodies *and* monuments of their kings far from Me, and I will dwell in their midst for ever.
10You, son of man, show the temple *by* your description of it to the house of Israel, that they may be ashamed of their iniquities, and let them measure accurately its appearance and plan.
11And if they are ashamed of all that they have done, make known to them the form of the temple and the arrangement of it, its exits and its entrances and the whole form of it, and all its ordinances and all their forms, and all its laws. And write it down in their sight so that they may keep the whole form of it and all the ordinances of it, and do them.
12This is the law of the house *of the Lord:* The whole area round about on the top of the mountain [Mount Moriah] shall be most holy, separated *and* set apart. Behold, this is the law of the house *of the Lord.*
13And these are the measurements of the altar [of burnt offering] in cubits. The cubit is a royal cubit—the length of a forearm—and a palm of the hand; the bottom *or* gutter shall be a cubit deep and a cubit wide, with a rim or lip round about it of a span's breadth. And this shall be the height of the altar:
14From the bottom *or* gutter on the ground to the lower ledge *or* brim shall be two cubits, and the breadth one cubit; and from the lesser ledge to the greater ledge shall be four cubits, and the breadth one cubit.
15And the altar hearth shall be four cubits high, and from the altar hearth reaching upward there shall be four horns one cubit high.

## New American Standard

16He measured on the east side with the measuring reed five
hundred reeds, by the measuring reed.
17He measured on the north side five hundred reeds by the
measuring reed.
18On the south side he measured five hundred reeds with the
measuring reed.
19He turned to the west side, *and* measured five hundred reeds
with the measuring reed.
20He measured it on the four sides; it had a wall all around, the
length five hundred and the width five hundred, to divide between the holy and the profane.

*Vision of the Glory of God Filling the Temple*

**43** THEN HE led me to the gate, the gate facing toward the
east;
2and behold, the glory of the God of Israel was coming from
the way of the east. And His voice was like the sound of many
waters; and the earth shone with His glory.
3And *it was* like the appearance of the vision which I saw, like
the vision which I saw when He came to destroy the city. And the
visions *were* like the vision which I saw by the river Chebar; and
I fell on my face.
4And the glory of the LORD came into the house by the way of
the gate facing toward the east.
5And the Spirit lifted me up and brought me into the inner
court; and behold, the glory of the LORD filled the house.
6¶ Then I heard one speaking to me from the house, while a
man was standing beside me.
7And He said to me, "Son of man, *this is* the place of My throne
and the place of the soles of My feet, where I will dwell among the
sons of Israel forever. And the house of Israel will not again defile
My holy name, neither they nor their kings, by their harlotry and
by the [a]corpses of their kings [b]when they die,
8by setting their threshold by My threshold, and their door
post beside My door post, with *only* the wall between Me and
them. And they have defiled My holy name by their abominations
which they have committed. So I have consumed them in My
anger.
9"Now let them put away their harlotry and the [c]corpses of
their kings far from Me; and I will dwell among them forever.
10¶ "As for you, son of man, describe the temple to the house
of Israel, that they may be ashamed of their iniquities; and let them
measure the plan.
11"And if they are ashamed of all that they have done, make
known to them the design of the house, its structure, its exits, its
entrances, all its designs, all its statutes, and all its laws. And write
*it* in their sight, so that they may observe its whole design and all
its statutes, and do them.
12"This is the law of the house: its entire area on the top of the
mountain all around *shall be* most holy. Behold, this is the law of
the house.

*The Altar of Sacrifice*

13¶ "And these are the measurements of the altar by cubits (the
cubit being a cubit and a handbreadth): the base *shall be* a cubit,
and the width a cubit, and its border on its edge round about one
span; and this *shall be* the *height of the* base of the altar.
14"And from the base on the ground to the lower ledge *shall be*
two cubits, and the width one cubit; and from the smaller ledge
to the larger ledge *shall be* four cubits, and the width one cubit.
15"And the altar hearth *shall be* four cubits; and from the altar
hearth shall extend upwards four horns.

NAS [a] Or, *monuments* [b] Or, *in their high places* [c] Or, *monuments*

## New International

was five hundred cubits.[d] 17He measured the north side; it was
five hundred cubits[e] by the measuring rod. 18He measured the
south side; it was five hundred cubits by the measuring rod.
19Then he turned to the west side and measured; it was five hundred cubits by the measuring rod. 20So he measured the area on
all four sides. It had a wall around it, five hundred cubits long and
five hundred cubits wide, to separate the holy from the common.

*The Glory Returns to the Temple*

**43** THEN THE man brought me to the gate facing east, 2and
I saw the glory of the God of Israel coming from the east.
His voice was like the roar of rushing waters, and the land was
radiant with his glory. 3The vision I saw was like the vision I had
seen when he[f] came to destroy the city and like the visions I had
seen by the Kebar River, and I fell facedown. 4The glory of the
LORD entered the temple through the gate facing east. 5Then the
Spirit lifted me up and brought me into the inner court, and the
glory of the LORD filled the temple.
6While the man was standing beside me, I heard someone
speaking to me from inside the temple. 7He said: "Son of man, this
is the place of my throne and the place for the soles of my feet. This
is where I will live among the Israelites forever. The house of Israel
will never again defile my holy name—neither they nor their
kings—by their prostitution[g] and the lifeless idols[h] of their kings
at their high places. 8When they placed their threshold next to my
threshold and their doorposts beside my doorposts, with only a
wall between me and them, they defiled my holy name by their
detestable practices. So I destroyed them in my anger. 9Now let
them put away from me their prostitution and the lifeless idols of
their kings, and I will live among them forever.
10"Son of man, describe the temple to the people of Israel, that
they may be ashamed of their sins. Let them consider the plan,
11and if they are ashamed of all they have done, make known to
them the design of the temple—its arrangement, its exits and
entrances—its whole design and all its regulations[i] and laws.
Write these down before them so that they may be faithful to its
design and follow all its regulations.
12"This is the law of the temple: All the surrounding area on top
of the mountain will be most holy. Such is the law of the temple.

*The Altar*

13"These are the measurements of the altar in long cubits, that
cubit being a cubit[j] and a handbreadth[k]: Its gutter is a cubit deep
and a cubit wide, with a rim of one span[l] around the edge. And
this is the height of the altar: 14From the gutter on the ground up
to the lower ledge it is two cubits high and a cubit wide, and from
the smaller ledge up to the larger ledge it is four cubits high and
a cubit wide. 15The altar hearth is four cubits high, and four horns
project upward from the hearth. 16The altar hearth is square,

NIV [d] *16* See Septuagint of verse 17; Hebrew *rods;* also in verses 18 and 19. [e] *17* Septuagint; Hebrew *rods* [f] *3* Some Hebrew manuscripts and Vulgate; most Hebrew manuscripts *I* [g] *7* Or *their spiritual adultery;* also in verse 9 [h] *7* Or *the corpses;* also in verse 9 [i] *11* Some Hebrew manuscripts and Septuagint; most Hebrew manuscripts *regulations and its whole design* [j] *13* The common cubit was about 1 1/2 feet (about 0.5 meter). [k] *13* That is, about 3 inches (about 8 centimeters) [l] *13* That is, about 9 inches (about 22 centimeters)

## King James

16 And the altar *shall be* twelve *cubits* long, twelve broad, square in the four squares thereof.

17 And the settle *shall be* fourteen *cubits* long and fourteen broad in the four squares thereof; and the border about it *shall be* half a cubit; and the bottom thereof *shall be* a cubit about; and his stairs shall look toward the east.

18 ¶ And he said unto me, Son of man, thus saith the Lord GOD; These *are* the ordinances of the altar in the day when they shall make it, to offer burnt offerings thereon, and to sprinkle blood thereon.

19 And thou shalt give to the priests the Levites that be of the seed of Zadok, which approach unto me, to minister unto me, saith the Lord GOD, a young bullock for a sin offering.

20 And thou shalt take of the blood thereof, and put *it* on the four horns of it, and on the four corners of the settle, and upon the border round about: thus shalt thou cleanse and purge it.

21 Thou shalt take the bullock also of the sin offering, and he shall burn it in the appointed place of the house, without the sanctuary.

22 And on the second day thou shalt offer a kid of the goats without blemish for a sin offering; and they shall cleanse the altar, as they did cleanse *it* with the bullock.

23 When thou hast made an end of cleansing *it*, thou shalt offer a young bullock without blemish, and a ram out of the flock without blemish.

24 And thou shalt offer them before the LORD, and the priests shall cast salt upon them, and they shall offer them up *for* a burnt offering unto the LORD.

25 Seven days shalt thou prepare every day a goat *for* a sin offering: they shall also prepare a young bullock, and a ram out of the flock, without blemish.

26 Seven days shall they purge the altar and purify it; and they shall consecrate themselves.

27 And when these days are expired, it shall be, *that* upon the eighth day, and *so* forward, the priests shall make your burnt offerings upon the altar, and your peace offerings; and I will accept you, saith the Lord GOD.

**44** THEN HE brought me back the way of the gate of the outward sanctuary which looketh toward the east; and it *was* shut.

2 Then said the LORD unto me; This gate shall be shut, it shall not be opened, and no man shall enter in by it; because the LORD, the God of Israel, hath entered in by it, therefore it shall be shut.

3 *It is* for the prince; the prince, he shall sit in it to eat bread before the LORD; he shall enter by the way of the porch of *that* gate, and shall go out by the way of the same.

4 ¶ Then brought he me the way of the north gate before the house: and I looked, and, behold, the glory of the LORD filled the house of the LORD: and I fell upon my face.

5 And the LORD said unto me, Son of man, mark well, and behold with thine eyes, and hear with thine ears all that I say unto thee concerning all the ordinances of the house of the LORD, and all the laws thereof; and mark well the entering in of the house, with every going forth of the sanctuary.

6 And thou shalt say to the rebellious, *even* to the house of Israel, Thus saith the Lord GOD; O ye house of Israel, let it suffice you of all your abominations,

## Amplified

16 And the altar hearth shall be twelve cubits long, twelve broad, square, and on its four sides squares.

17 And the ledge shall be fourteen cubits long and fourteen cubits broad on its four sides, and the border about it shall be half a cubit; and its bottom *or* gutter shall be a cubit deep and wide; and its ascent [not steps] shall face the east. [Cf. Exod. 20:26.]

18 And [the Lord] said to me, Son of man, thus says the Lord God: These are the regulations for the use of the altar in the day that it is erected, upon which to offer burnt offerings and to sprinkle blood against it:

19 You shall give to the priests, the Levites who are of the offspring of Zadok, who are near to Me to minister to Me, says the Lord God, a young bull for a sin offering.

20 And you shall take of its blood and put it on the four horns of [the altar of burnt offering], and on the four corners of the ledge, and upon the rim *or* border round about. Thus shall you cleanse *and* make atonement for [the altar].

21 You shall also take the bullock of the sin offering, and it shall be burned in the appointed place of the temple, outside the sacred enclosure. [Heb. 13:11.]

22 And on the second day you shall offer a male goat without blemish for a sin offering. Thus the altar shall be cleansed, as it was cleansed with the bullock.

23 When you have finished cleansing it, you shall offer a young bull without blemish and a ram out of the flock without blemish.

24 And you shall bring them near before the Lord, and the priests shall cast salt upon them, and they shall offer them up for a burnt offering to the Lord.

25 Seven days you shall prepare every day a goat for a sin offering; also a young bull and a ram out of the flock, without blemish, shall be prepared.

26 Seven days shall they make atonement for the altar and purify it; so the priests shall consecrate, separate *and* set it apart to receive offerings. [Exod. 29:37.]

27 And when these days have been accomplished, on the eighth day and from then on, the priests shall offer your burnt offerings upon the altar and your peace offerings; and I will accept you, says the Lord God. [Rom. 12:1; I Pet. 2:5.]

**44** THEN [THE man] brought me back the way of the outer gate of the sanctuary which faces the east, and it was shut.

2 Then the Lord said to me, This gate shall be [a]shut; it shall not be opened, and no man shall enter in by it; for the Lord, the God of Israel, has entered in by it; therefore it shall remain shut.

3 As for the prince, being the prince, he shall sit in it to eat bread before the Lord; he shall enter by way of the porch *or* vestibule of the gate and shall go out the same way.

4 Then He brought me by way of the north gate to the front of the temple; I looked, and behold, the glory of the Lord filled the house of the Lord, and I fell upon my face. [Rev. 15:8.]

5 And the Lord said to me, Son of man, mark well, *and* set your heart to see with your eyes and hear with your ears all that I say to you concerning all the ordinances of the house of the Lord and all its laws, and mark well *and* set your heart to know who are allowed to enter the temple and all those who are excluded from the sanctuary.

6 And you shall say to the rebellious, even to the house of Israel, Thus says the Lord God: O you house of Israel, let all your previous abominations be enough for you—do not repeat them.

**AMP** [a] In Christ's time the Golden Gate was the principal eastside thoroughfare. Through it the Prince of Peace would naturally make His triumphal entry. But by 1542-3 A.D. when Sultan Suleiman the Magnificent rebuilt the wall of Jerusalem, tradition says the road that once led to this gate had fallen into disuse, and what is now St. Stephen's Gate was the accepted entrance. So the Sultan walled up the Golden Gate with its double entrance and it has remained so ever since.

## New American Standard

16"Now the altar hearth *shall be* twelve *cubits* long by twelve
wide, square in its four sides.
17"And the ledge *shall be* fourteen *cubits* long by fourteen wide
in its four sides, the border around it *shall be* half a cubit, and its
base *shall be* a cubit round about; and its steps shall face the east."

*The Offerings*

18¶ And He said to me, "Son of man, thus says the Lord GOD,
'These are the statutes for the altar on the day it is built, to offer
burnt offerings on it and to sprinkle blood on it.
19'And you shall give to the Levitical priests who are from the
offspring of Zadok, who draw near to Me to minister to Me,'
declares the Lord GOD, 'a young bull for a sin offering.
20'And you shall take some of its blood, and put it on its four
horns, and on the four corners of the ledge, and on the border
round about; thus you shall cleanse it and make atonement for it.
21'You shall also take the bull for the sin offering; and it *shall be*
burned in the appointed place of the house, outside the sanctuary.
22'And on the second day you shall offer a male goat without
blemish for a sin offering; and they shall cleanse the altar, as they
cleansed *it* with the bull.
23'When you have finished cleansing *it*, you shall present a
young bull without blemish and a ram without blemish from the
flock.
24'And you shall present them before the LORD, and the priests
shall throw salt on them, and they shall offer them up as a burnt
offering to the LORD.
25'For seven days you shall prepare daily a goat for a sin offering; also a young bull and a ram from the flock, without blemish,
shall be prepared.
26'For seven days they shall make atonement for the altar and
purify it; so shall they consecrate it.
27'And when they have completed the days, it shall be that on
the eighth day and onward, the priests shall offer your burnt
offerings on the altar, and your peace offerings; and I will accept
you,' declares the Lord GOD."

*Gate for the Prince*

44 THEN HE brought me back by the way of the outer gate
of the sanctuary, which faces the east; and it was shut.
2And the LORD said to me, "This gate shall be shut; it shall not
be opened, and no one shall enter by it, for the LORD God of Israel
has entered by it; therefore it shall be shut.
3"As for the prince, he shall sit in it as prince to eat bread before
the LORD; he shall enter by way of the porch of the gate, and shall
go out by the same way."
4¶ Then He brought me by way of the north gate to the front
of the house; and I looked, and behold, the glory of the LORD filled
the house of the LORD, and I fell on my face.
5And the LORD said to me, "Son of man, mark well, see with
your eyes, and hear with your ears all that I say to you concerning
all the statutes of the house of the LORD and concerning all its laws;
and mark well the entrance of the house, with all exits of the
sanctuary.
6"And you shall say to the rebellious ones, to the house of
Israel, 'Thus says the Lord GOD, "Enough of all your abominations, O house of Israel,

## New International

twelve cubits long and twelve cubits wide. 17The upper ledge also
is square, fourteen cubits long and fourteen cubits wide, with a rim
of half a cubit and a gutter of a cubit all around. The steps of the
altar face east."
18Then he said to me, "Son of man, this is what the Sovereign
LORD says: These will be the regulations for sacrificing burnt offerings and sprinkling blood upon the altar when it is built: 19You are
to give a young bull as a sin offering to the priests, who are Levites,
of the family of Zadok, who come near to minister before me,
declares the Sovereign LORD. 20You are to take some of its blood
and put it on the four horns of the altar and on the four corners
of the upper ledge and all around the rim, and so purify the altar
and make atonement for it. 21You are to take the bull for the sin
offering and burn it in the designated part of the temple area
outside the sanctuary.
22"On the second day you are to offer a male goat without
defect for a sin offering, and the altar is to be purified as it was
purified with the bull. 23When you have finished purifying it, you
are to offer a young bull and a ram from the flock, both without
defect. 24You are to offer them before the LORD, and the priests are
to sprinkle salt on them and sacrifice them as a burnt offering to
the LORD.
25"For seven days you are to provide a male goat daily for a sin
offering; you are also to provide a young bull and a ram from the
flock, both without defect. 26For seven days they are to make
atonement for the altar and cleanse it; thus they will dedicate it.
27At the end of these days, from the eighth day on, the priests are
to present your burnt offerings and fellowship offerings[b] on the
altar. Then I will accept you, declares the Sovereign LORD."

*The Prince, the Levites, the Priests*

44 THEN THE man brought me back to the outer gate of the
sanctuary, the one facing east, and it was shut. 2The LORD
said to me, "This gate is to remain shut. It must not be opened;
no one may enter through it. It is to remain shut because the LORD,
the God of Israel, has entered through it. 3The prince himself is the
only one who may sit inside the gateway to eat in the presence of
the LORD. He is to enter by way of the portico of the gateway and
go out the same way."
4Then the man brought me by way of the north gate to the front
of the temple. I looked and saw the glory of the LORD filling the
temple of the LORD, and I fell facedown.
5The LORD said to me, "Son of man, look carefully, listen closely
and give attention to everything I tell you concerning all the regulations regarding the temple of the LORD. Give attention to the
entrance of the temple and all the exits of the sanctuary. 6Say to
the rebellious house of Israel, 'This is what the Sovereign LORD
says: Enough of your detestable practices, O house of Israel! 7In

NIV [b] 27 Traditionally *peace offerings*

## King James

7 In that ye have brought *into my sanctuary* strangers, uncircumcised in heart, and uncircumcised in flesh, to be in my sanctuary,
to pollute it, *even* my house, when ye offer my bread, the fat and
the blood, and they have broken my covenant because of all your
abominations.
8 And ye have not kept the charge of mine holy things: but ye
have set keepers of my charge in my sanctuary for yourselves.
9 ¶ Thus saith the Lord GOD; No stranger, uncircumcised in
heart, nor uncircumcised in flesh, shall enter into my sanctuary,
of any stranger that *is* among the children of Israel.
10 And the Levites that are gone away far from me, when Israel
went astray, which went astray away from me after their idols;
they shall even bear their iniquity.
11 Yet they shall be ministers in my sanctuary, *having* charge at
the gates of the house, and ministering to the house: they shall slay
the burnt offering and the sacrifice for the people, and they shall
stand before them to minister unto them.
12 Because they ministered unto them before their idols, and
caused the house of Israel to fall into iniquity; therefore have I
lifted up mine hand against them, saith the Lord GOD, and they
shall bear their iniquity.
13 And they shall not come near unto me, to do the office of a
priest unto me, nor to come near to any of my holy things, in the
most holy *place:* but they shall bear their shame, and their abominations which they have committed.
14 But I will make them keepers of the charge of the house, for
all the service thereof, and for all that shall be done therein.
15 ¶ But the priests the Levites, the sons of Zadok, that kept the
charge of my sanctuary when the children of Israel went astray
from me, they shall come near to me to minister unto me, and they
shall stand before me to offer unto me the fat and the blood, saith
the Lord GOD:
16 They shall enter into my sanctuary, and they shall come near
to my table, to minister unto me, and they shall keep my charge.
17 ¶ And it shall come to pass, *that* when they enter in at the
gates of the inner court, they shall be clothed with linen garments;
and no wool shall come upon them, whiles they minister in the
gates of the inner court, and within.
18 They shall have linen bonnets upon their heads, and shall
have linen breeches upon their loins; they shall not gird *themselves*
with any thing that causeth sweat.
19 And when they go forth into the utter court, *even* into the utter
court to the people, they shall put off their garments wherein they
ministered, and lay them in the holy chambers, and they shall put
on other garments; and they shall not sanctify the people with their
garments.
20 Neither shall they shave their heads, nor suffer their locks to
grow long; they shall only poll their heads.
21 Neither shall any priest drink wine, when they enter into the
inner court.
22 Neither shall they take for their wives a widow, nor her that
is put away: but they shall take maidens of the seed of the house
of Israel, or a widow that had a priest before.
23 And they shall teach my people *the difference* between the holy
and profane, and cause them to discern between the unclean and
the clean.
24 And in controversy they shall stand in judgment; *and* they
shall judge it according to my judgments: and they shall keep my
laws and my statutes in all mine assemblies; and they shall hallow
my sabbaths.
25 And they shall come at no dead person to defile themselves:
but for father, or for mother, or for son, or for daughter, for
brother, or for sister that hath had no husband, they may defile
themselves.

## Amplified

7 You have brought into My sanctuary aliens, uncircumcised in
heart and uncircumcised in flesh, to be in My sanctuary, to pollute
*and* profane it, even My house, when you offer My bread, the fat
and the blood, and in it all *and* in addition to all your abominations,
they *and* you have broken My covenant.
8 And you have not kept charge of My holy things, but you have
chosen foreign keepers to please yourselves and have set them in
charge of My sanctuary.
9 Therefore thus says the Lord God: No foreigner, uncircumcised in heart and flesh, shall enter into My sanctuary [where no
one but the priests might enter], of any foreigners that are among
the children of Israel.
10 But the Levites who went far away from Me, when Israel went
astray, who went astray from Me after their idols, they shall bear
[the punishment for] their iniquity *and* guilt.
11 They shall minister in My sanctuary having oversight as
guards at the gates of the temple and ministering in the temple.
They shall slay the burnt offering and the sacrifice for the people,
and they shall attend the people to serve them.
12 Because [the priests] ministered to [the people] before their
idols, and became a stumblingblock of iniquity *and* guilt to the
house of Israel, therefore I have lifted up My hand *and* have sworn
against them, says the Lord God, that they shall bear the punishment for their iniquity *and* guilt.
13 And they shall not come near to Me to do the office of a priest
to Me, nor come near to any of My holy things that are most sacred;
but they shall bear their shame *and* their punishment for the abominations which they have committed.
14 Yet I will appoint them as caretakers to have charge of the
temple, for all the service of the temple and for all that will be done
in it.
15 But the priests of the Levites, the sons of Zadok, who kept the
charge of My sanctuary when the children of Israel went astray
from Me, shall come near to Me to minister to Me, and they shall
attend Me to offer to Me the fat and the blood, says the Lord God.
16 They shall enter into My sanctuary, and they shall come near
to My table to minister to Me, and they shall keep My charge.
17 When they enter the gates of the inner court, they shall be
clothed in linen garments; no wool shall be on them while they
minister at the gates of the inner court and within the temple.
18 They shall have linen turbans on their heads and linen
breeches upon their loins; they shall not gird themselves with
anything that causes sweat.
19 And when they go out into the outer court to the people, they
shall put off the garments in which they ministered and lay them
in the holy chambers, and they shall put on other garments, lest
by contact of their garments with the people they should consecrate—separate and set apart for holy use—such persons [uninten-
tionally and unfittingly].
20 Neither shall they shave their heads or allow their locks to
grow long; they shall only cut short *or* trim the hair of their heads.
21 Neither shall any priest drink wine, when he enters the inner
court.
22 Neither shall they take for their wives a widow, or a woman
separated *or* divorced from her husband; but they shall marry
maidens [who are virgins] of the offspring of the house of Israel,
or a widow previously married to a priest.
23 The priests shall teach My people the difference between the
holy and the common *or* profane, and cause them to distinguish
between the unclean and the clean.
24 And in a controversy they shall act as judges, and they shall
judge according to My judgments; and they shall keep My laws
and My statutes in all My appointed feasts, and they shall keep My
sabbaths holy.
25 And they shall go near to no dead person to defile themselves,
except for father or for mother, for son or for daughter, for brother
or for sister who has had no husband; for them they may defile
themselves. [Lev. 21:1, 2.]

## New American Standard

7when you brought in foreigners, uncircumcised in heart and uncircumcised in flesh, to be in My sanctuary to profane it, *even* My house, when you offered My food, the fat and the blood; for they made My covenant void— *this* in addition to all your abominations.

8"And you have not kept charge of My holy things yourselves, but you have set *foreigners* to keep charge of My sanctuary."

9¶ 'Thus says the Lord GOD, "No foreigner, uncircumcised in heart and uncircumcised in flesh, of all the foreigners who are among the sons of Israel, shall enter My sanctuary.

10"But the Levites who went far from Me, when Israel went astray, who went astray from Me after their idols, shall bear the punishment for their iniquity.

11"Yet they shall be ministers in My sanctuary, having oversight at the gates of the house and ministering in the house; they shall slaughter the burnt offering and the sacrifice for the people, and they shall stand before them to minister to them.

12"Because they ministered to them before their idols and became a stumbling block of iniquity to the house of Israel, therefore I have sworn against them," declares the Lord GOD, "that they shall bear the punishment for their iniquity.

13"And they shall not come near to Me to serve as a priest to Me, nor come near to any of My holy things, to the things that are most holy; but they shall bear their shame and their abominations which they have committed.

14"Yet I will appoint them to keep charge of the house, of all its service, and of all that shall be done in it.

*Ordinances for the Levites*

15¶ "But the Levitical priests, the sons of Zadok, who kept charge of My sanctuary when the sons of Israel went astray from Me, shall come near to Me to minister to Me; and they shall stand before Me to offer Me the fat and the blood," declares the Lord GOD.

16"They shall enter My sanctuary; they shall come near to My table to minister to Me and keep My charge.

17"And it shall be that when they enter at the gates of the inner court, they shall be clothed with linen garments; and wool shall not be on them while they are ministering in the gates of the inner court and in the house.

18"Linen turbans shall be on their heads, and linen undergarments shall be on their loins; they shall not gird themselves with *anything which makes them* sweat.

19"And when they go out into the outer court, into the outer court to the people, they shall put off their garments in which they have been ministering and lay them in the holy chambers; then they shall put on other garments that they may not transmit holiness to the people with their garments.

20"Also they shall not shave their heads, yet they shall not let their locks grow long; they shall only trim *the hair of* their heads.

21"Nor shall any of the priests drink wine when they enter the inner court.

22"And they shall not marry a widow or a divorced woman but shall take virgins from the offspring of the house of Israel, or a widow who is the widow of a priest.

23"Moreover, they shall teach My people *the difference* between the holy and the profane, and cause them to discern between the unclean and the clean.

24"And in a dispute they shall take their stand to judge; they shall judge it according to My ordinances. They shall also keep My laws and My statutes in all My appointed feasts, and sanctify My sabbaths.

25"And they shall not go to a dead person to defile *themselves;* however, for father, for mother, for son, for daughter, for brother, or for a sister who has not had a husband, they may defile themselves.

## New International

addition to all your other detestable practices, you brought foreigners uncircumcised in heart and flesh into my sanctuary, desecrating my temple while you offered me food, fat and blood, and
you broke my covenant. 8Instead of carrying out your duty in
regard to my holy things, you put others in charge of my sanctuary. 9This is what the Sovereign LORD says: No foreigner uncircumcised in heart and flesh is to enter my sanctuary, not even the foreigners who live among the Israelites.
10" 'The Levites who went far from me when Israel went astray and who wandered from me after their idols must bear the consequences of their sin. 11They may serve in my sanctuary, having
charge of the gates of the temple and serving in it; they may slaughter the burnt offerings and sacrifices for the people and stand before the people and serve them. 12But because they served
them in the presence of their idols and made the house of Israel fall into sin, therefore I have sworn with uplifted hand that they must bear the consequences of their sin, declares the Sovereign
LORD. 13They are not to come near to serve me as priests or come
near any of my holy things or my most holy offerings; they must
bear the shame of their detestable practices. 14Yet I will put them
in charge of the duties of the temple and all the work that is to be done in it.
15" 'But the priests, who are Levites and descendants of Zadok and who faithfully carried out the duties of my sanctuary when the Israelites went astray from me, are to come near to minister before me; they are to stand before me to offer sacrifices of fat and blood,
declares the Sovereign LORD. 16They alone are to enter my sanctuary; they alone are to come near my table to minister before me and perform my service.
17" 'When they enter the gates of the inner court, they are to wear linen clothes; they must not wear any woolen garment while ministering at the gates of the inner court or inside the temple.
18They are to wear linen turbans on their heads and linen undergarments around their waists. They must not wear anything that
makes them perspire. 19When they go out into the outer court
where the people are, they are to take off the clothes they have been ministering in and are to leave them in the sacred rooms, and put on other clothes, so that they do not consecrate the people by means of their garments.
20" 'They must not shave their heads or let their hair grow long,
but they are to keep the hair of their heads trimmed. 21No priest
is to drink wine when he enters the inner court. 22They must not
marry widows or divorced women; they may marry only virgins
of Israelite descent or widows of priests. 23They are to teach my
people the difference between the holy and the common and show them how to distinguish between the unclean and the clean.
24" 'In any dispute, the priests are to serve as judges and decide it according to my ordinances. They are to keep my laws and my decrees for all my appointed feasts, and they are to keep my Sabbaths holy.
25" 'A priest must not defile himself by going near a dead person; however, if the dead person was his father or mother, son or daughter, brother or unmarried sister, then he may defile himself.

## King James

26And after he is cleansed, they shall reckon unto him seven days.

27And in the day that he goeth into the sanctuary, unto the inner court, to minister in the sanctuary, he shall offer his sin offering, saith the Lord GOD.

28And it shall be unto them for an inheritance: I *am* their inheritance: and ye shall give them no possession in Israel: I *am* their possession.

29They shall eat the meat offering, and the sin offering, and the trespass offering; and every dedicated thing in Israel shall be theirs.

30And the first of all the firstfruits of all *things*, and every oblation of all, of every *sort* of your oblations, shall be the priest's: ye shall also give unto the priest the first of your dough, that he may cause the blessing to rest in thine house.

31The priests shall not eat of any thing that is dead of itself, or torn, whether it be fowl or beast.

**45** MOREOVER, WHEN ye shall divide by lot the land for inheritance, ye shall offer an oblation unto the LORD, an holy portion of the land: the length *shall be* the length of five and twenty thousand *reeds,* and the breadth *shall be* ten thousand. This *shall be* holy in all the borders thereof round about.

2Of this there shall be for the sanctuary five hundred *in length,* with five hundred *in breadth,* square round about; and fifty cubits round about for the suburbs thereof.

3And of this measure shalt thou measure the length of five and twenty thousand, and the breadth of ten thousand: and in it shall be the sanctuary *and* the most holy *place.*

4The holy *portion* of the land shall be for the priests the ministers of the sanctuary, which shall come near to minister unto the LORD: and it shall be a place for their houses, and an holy place for the sanctuary.

5And the five and twenty thousand of length, and the ten thousand of breadth, shall also the Levites, the ministers of the house, have for themselves, for a possession for twenty chambers.

6¶ And ye shall appoint the possession of the city five thousand broad, and five and twenty thousand long, over against the oblation of the holy *portion:* it shall be for the whole house of Israel.

7¶ And *a portion shall be* for the prince on the one side and on the other side of the oblation of the holy *portion,* and of the possession of the city, before the oblation of the holy *portion,* and before the possession of the city, from the west side westward, and from the east side eastward: and the length *shall be* over against one of the portions, from the west border unto the east border.

8In the land shall be his possession in Israel: and my princes shall no more oppress my people; and *the rest of* the land shall they give to the house of Israel according to their tribes.

9¶ Thus saith the Lord GOD; Let it suffice you, O princes of Israel: remove violence and spoil, and execute judgment and justice, take away your exactions from my people, saith the Lord GOD.

10Ye shall have just balances, and a just ephah, and a just bath.

11The ephah and the bath shall be of one measure, that the bath may contain the tenth part of an homer, and the ephah the tenth part of an homer: the measure thereof shall be after the homer.

12And the shekel *shall be* twenty gerahs: twenty shekels, five and twenty shekels, fifteen shekels, shall be your maneh.

## Amplified

26And after he is cleansed [from the defilement of a dead body] they shall reckon to him seven days more before returning to the temple.

27And on the day that he goes into the sanctuary, into the inner court to minister in the sanctuary, he shall offer his sin offering, says the Lord God.

28This [their ministry to Me] shall be to them as an inheritance, for I am their inheritance; and you shall give them no possession in Israel, for I am their possession. [Josh. 13:14, 33.]

29They shall eat the meal offering and the sin offering, and the trespass offering; and every offering in Israel dedicated by a solemn vow to God shall be theirs.

30And the first of all the first fruits of all kinds, and every offering of all kinds from all your offerings, shall belong to the priests. You shall also give to the priest the first of your coarse meal *and* bread dough, that a blessing may rest on your house.

31The priests shall not eat of anything that has died of itself or is torn, whether it be bird or beast.

**45** MOREOVER, WHEN you shall divide the land by apportioned *and* assigned lots for inheritance, you shall set apart as an offering to the Lord a portion of the land to be used for holy purposes. The length shall be twenty-five thousand [a] *cubits,* and the breadth twenty thousand. It shall be holy—set apart and consecrated to sacred use—in its every area. [Cf. Ezek. 48:9, 12, 13.]

2Of this there shall belong to the sanctuary a square plot five hundred by five hundred, and fifty *cubits* for the open space around it.

3And in this sacred section you shall measure off a portion twenty-five thousand [b] *cubits* in length and ten thousand *cubits* in breadth. And in it shall be the sanctuary which is most holy.

4It is a holy portion of the land; it shall be for the priests, the ministers of the sanctuary, who come near to minister to the Lord; and it shall be a place for their houses and a holy place—set apart as sacred—for the sanctuary.

5And another portion of land, twenty-five thousand *cubits* long and ten thousand *cubits* wide, shall also be for the Levites, the ministers of the temple, and they shall possess it as a place in which to live.

6And you shall appoint for the possession of the city an area of five thousand *cubits* wide and twenty-five thousand *cubits* long, along beside the portion set aside as a holy section. It shall belong to the whole house of Israel.

7And to the prince shall belong the land on the one side and on the other side of the portion set aside as a holy section and the property of the city, in front of the holy section and the property of the city, from the west side westward and from the east side eastward, and the length shall be answerable to that of one of the tribal portions *and* parallel to it from the western boundary to the eastern boundary of the land.

8It shall be for the prince, his possession in Israel. And My princes shall no more oppress My people; but they shall give the rest of the land to the house of Israel according to their tribes.

9Thus says the Lord God: That is enough for you, O princes of Israel! Stop the violence and plundering *and* oppression [that you did when you were given no property], and do justice and righteousness, and take away your exactions *and* cease your evictions of My people, says the Lord God.

10You shall have just weights on your scales, and just measures—both a just ephah measure and a just bath measure.

11The ephah and the bath measures shall both be the same size, the bath containing one tenth of a homer and the ephah one tenth of a homer; the standard measure shall be the homer.

12And the shekel shall be twenty gerahs; twenty shekels, twenty-five shekels, fifteen shekels [according to the metal used?] shall be your maneh.

**AMP** [a] The Septuagint (Greek) Version so reads. The term "cubits," rather than "reeds," is supplied throughout this chapter only as the more probable. Neither is definitely designated. [b] The Septuagint (Greek) Version so reads. The term "cubits," rather than "reeds," is supplied throughout this chapter only as the more probable. Neither is definitely designated.

## New American Standard

26"And after he is cleansed, seven days shall [c]elapse for him.
27"And on the day that he goes into the sanctuary, into the
inner court to minister in the sanctuary, he shall offer his sin
offering," declares the Lord GOD.
28¶ "And it shall be with regard to an inheritance for them, *that*
I am their inheritance; and you shall give them no possession in
Israel—I am their possession.
29"They shall eat the grain offering, the sin offering, and the
guilt offering; and every devoted thing in Israel shall be theirs.
30"And the first of all the first fruits of every kind and every
contribution of every kind, from all your contributions, shall be for
the priests; you shall also give to the priest the first of your dough
to cause a blessing to rest on your house.
31"The priests shall not eat any bird or beast that has died a
natural death or has been torn to pieces.

*The LORD's Portion of the Land*

45 "AND WHEN you shall divide by lot the land for inheritance, you shall offer an allotment to the LORD, a holy
portion of the land; the length shall be the length of 25,000 *cubits*,
and the width shall be 10,000. It shall be holy within all its boundary round about.
2"Out of this there shall be for the holy place a square round
about five hundred by five hundred *cubits*, and fifty cubits for its
open space round about.
3"And from this area you shall measure a length of 25,000
*cubits*, and a width of 10,000 *cubits*; and in it shall be the sanctuary,
the most holy place.
4"It shall be the holy portion of the land; it shall be for the
priests, the ministers of the sanctuary, who come near to minister
to the LORD, and it shall be a place for their houses and a holy place
for the sanctuary.
5"And *an area* 25,000 *cubits* in length and 10,000 in width shall
be for the Levites, the ministers of the house, *and* for their possession cities to dwell in.
6"And you shall give the city possession of *an area* 5,000 *cubits*
wide and 25,000 *cubits* long, alongside the [d]allotment of the holy
portion; it shall be for the whole house of Israel.

*Portion for the Prince*

7"And the prince shall have *land* on either side of the holy
[e]allotment and the property of the city, adjacent to the holy
[f]allotment and the property of the city, on the west side toward
the west and on the east side toward the east, and in length
comparable to one of the portions, from the west border to the east
border.
8"This shall be his land for a possession in Israel; so My princes
shall no longer oppress My people, but they shall give *the rest of*
the land to the house of Israel according to their tribes."
9¶ 'Thus says the Lord GOD, "Enough, you princes of Israel;
put away violence and destruction, and practice justice and righteousness. Stop your expropriations from My people," declares the
Lord GOD.
10"You shall have just balances, a just ephah, and a just bath.
11"The ephah and the bath shall be the same quantity, so that
the bath may contain a tenth of a homer, and the ephah a tenth
of a homer; their standard shall be according to the homer.
12"And the shekel shall be twenty gerahs; twenty shekels,
twenty-five shekels, *and* fifteen shekels shall be your maneh.

**NAS** [c] Lit., *be counted* [d] Or, *contribution* [e] Or, *contribution* [f] Or, *contribution*

## New International

26After he is cleansed, he must wait seven days. 27On the day he
goes into the inner court of the sanctuary to minister in the sanctuary, he is to offer a sin offering for himself, declares the Sovereign
LORD.
28" 'I am to be the only inheritance the priests have. You are to
give them no possession in Israel; I will be their possession. 29They
will eat the grain offerings, the sin offerings and the guilt offerings;
and everything in Israel devoted[g] to the LORD will belong to them.
30The best of all the firstfruits and of all your special gifts will
belong to the priests. You are to give them the first portion of your
ground meal so that a blessing may rest on your household. 31The
priests must not eat anything, bird or animal, found dead or torn
by wild animals.

*Division of the Land*

45 " 'WHEN YOU allot the land as an inheritance, you are to
present to the LORD a portion of the land as a sacred
district, 25,000 cubits long and 20,000[h] cubits wide; the entire area
will be holy. 2Of this, a section 500 cubits square is to be for the
sanctuary, with 50 cubits around it for open land. 3In the sacred
district, measure off a section 25,000 cubits[i] long and 10,000 cubits[j] wide. In it will be the sanctuary, the Most Holy Place. 4It will
be the sacred portion of the land for the priests, who minister in
the sanctuary and who draw near to minister before the LORD. It
will be a place for their houses as well as a holy place for the
sanctuary. 5An area 25,000 cubits long and 10,000 cubits wide will
belong to the Levites, who serve in the temple, as their possession
for towns to live in.[k]
6" 'You are to give the city as its property an area 5,000 cubits
wide and 25,000 cubits long, adjoining the sacred portion; it will
belong to the whole house of Israel.
7" 'The prince will have the land bordering each side of the area
formed by the sacred district and the property of the city. It will
extend westward from the west side and eastward from the east
side, running lengthwise from the western to the eastern border
parallel to one of the tribal portions. 8This land will be his possession in Israel. And my princes will no longer oppress my people
but will allow the house of Israel to possess the land according to
their tribes.
9" 'This is what the Sovereign LORD says: You have gone far
enough, O princes of Israel! Give up your violence and oppression
and do what is just and right. Stop dispossessing my people,
declares the Sovereign LORD. 10You are to use accurate scales, an
accurate ephah[l] and an accurate bath.[m] 11The ephah and the bath
are to be the same size, the bath containing a tenth of a homer[n]
and the ephah a tenth of a homer; the homer is to be the standard
measure for both. 12The shekel[o] is to consist of twenty gerahs.
Twenty shekels plus twenty-five shekels plus fifteen shekels equal
one mina.[p]

**NIV** [g] *29* The Hebrew term refers to the irrevocable giving over of things or persons to the LORD. [h] *1* Septuagint (see also verses 3 and 5 and 48:9); Hebrew *10,000* [i] *3* That is, about 7 miles (about 12 kilometers) [j] *3* That is, about 3 miles (about 5 kilometers) [k] *5* Septuagint; Hebrew *temple; they will have as their possession 20 rooms* [l] *10* An ephah was a dry measure. [m] *10* A bath was a liquid measure. [n] *11* A homer was a dry measure. [o] *12* A shekel weighed about 2/5 ounce (about 11.5 grams). [p] *12* That is, 60 shekels; the common mina was 50 shekels.

## King James

13This *is* the oblation that ye shall offer; the sixth part of an ephah of an homer of wheat, and ye shall give the sixth part of an ephah of an homer of barley:

14Concerning the ordinance of oil, the bath of oil, *ye shall offer* the tenth part of a bath out of the cor, *which is* an homer of ten baths; for ten baths *are* an homer:

15And one lamb out of the flock, out of two hundred, out of the fat pastures of Israel; for a meat offering, and for a burnt offering, and for peace offerings, to make reconciliation for them, saith the Lord GOD.

16All the people of the land shall give this oblation for the prince in Israel.

17And it shall be the prince's part *to give* burnt offerings, and meat offerings, and drink offerings, in the feasts, and in the new moons, and in the sabbaths, in all solemnities of the house of Israel: he shall prepare the sin offering, and the meat offering, and the burnt offering, and the peace offerings, to make reconciliation for the house of Israel.

18Thus saith the Lord GOD; In the first *month,* in the first *day* of the month, thou shalt take a young bullock without blemish, and cleanse the sanctuary:

19And the priest shall take of the blood of the sin offering, and put *it* upon the posts of the house, and upon the four corners of the settle of the altar, and upon the posts of the gate of the inner court.

20And so thou shalt do the seventh *day* of the month for every one that erreth, and for *him that is* simple: so shall ye reconcile the house.

21In the first *month,* in the fourteenth day of the month, ye shall have the passover, a feast of seven days; unleavened bread shall be eaten.

22And upon that day shall the prince prepare for himself and for all the people of the land a bullock *for* a sin offering.

23And seven days of the feast he shall prepare a burnt offering to the LORD, seven bullocks and seven rams without blemish daily the seven days; and a kid of the goats daily *for* a sin offering.

24And he shall prepare a meat offering of an ephah for a bullock, and an ephah for a ram, and an hin of oil for an ephah.

25In the seventh *month,* in the fifteenth day of the month, shall he do the like in the feast of the seven days, according to the sin offering, according to the burnt offering, and according to the meat offering, and according to the oil.

**46** THUS SAITH the Lord GOD; The gate of the inner court that looketh toward the east shall be shut the six working days; but on the sabbath it shall be opened, and in the day of the new moon it shall be opened.

2And the prince shall enter by the way of the porch of *that* gate without, and shall stand by the post of the gate, and the priests shall prepare his burnt offering and his peace offerings, and he shall worship at the threshold of the gate: then he shall go forth; but the gate shall not be shut until the evening.

3Likewise the people of the land shall worship at the door of this gate before the LORD in the sabbaths and in the new moons.

4And the burnt offering that the prince shall offer unto the LORD in the sabbath day *shall be* six lambs without blemish, and a ram without blemish.

5And the meat offering *shall be* an ephah for a ram, and the meat offering for the lambs as he shall be able to give, and an hin of oil to an ephah.

6And in the day of the new moon *it shall be* a young bullock without blemish, and six lambs, and a ram: they shall be without blemish.

## Amplified

13This is the offering which you shall make: one sixth of an ephah from each homer of wheat and one sixth of an ephah from each homer of barley.

14And as to the set portion of oil, you shall offer the tenth part of a bath of oil out of each cor, which is a homer of ten baths, for ten baths make [both a cor and] a homer.

15And one lamb out of every flock of two hundred, out of the well-watered pastures of Israel *and* from all the families of Israel, to provide for a meal offering and for a burnt offering and for peace offerings, to make atonement for those who brought them, says the Lord God.

16All the people of the land shall give this offering for the prince in Israel.

17And it shall be the prince's part to furnish [from the contributions of the people] the burnt offerings and meal offerings and drink offerings, at the feasts and on the new moons and on the sabbaths, at all the appointed feasts of the house of Israel. He shall prepare *and* make the sin offering and the meal offering and the burnt offering and the peace offerings, to make atonement, bringing forgiveness *and* reconciliation for the house of Israel.

18Thus says the Lord God: In the first *month,* on the first *day* of the month, you shall take a young bull without blemish, and you shall cleanse the sanctuary.

19And the priest shall take some of the blood of the sin offering and put it upon the doorposts of the temple and upon the four corners of the ledge of the altar and upon the posts of the gate of the inner court.

20You shall do this on the seventh day of the month for every one who has sinned through error *or* ignorance and for him who is simple-minded. So shall you make atonement for the temple.

21In the first month, on the fourteenth day of the *month,* you shall have the passover, a feast of seven days; unleavened bread shall be eaten.

22Upon that day the prince shall prepare for himself and for all the people of the land a bullock for a sin offering.

23And for the seven days of the feast he shall prepare a burnt offering to the Lord, seven bullocks and seven rams without blemish daily for the seven days, and a he-goat daily for a sin offering.

24And he shall prepare as a meal offering to be offered with each bullock an ephah of meal, an ephah for each ram, and a hin of oil for each ephah of meal.

25In the seventh *month,* on the fifteenth day of the month, he shall make the same provision *and* preparation for the seven days of the feast, for sin offerings, burnt offerings, bloodless *or* meal offerings, and for the oil.

**46** THUS SAYS the Lord God: The gate of the inner court that faces east shall be shut during the six working days, but on the sabbath it shall be opened, and also on the day of the new moon it shall be opened.

2And the prince shall enter by the porch *or* vestibule of the gate from without and shall stand by the sidepost of the gate. The priests shall prepare *and* offer his burnt offering and his peace offerings, and he shall worship at the threshold of the gate. Then he shall go out, but the gate shall not be shut until evening.

3The people of the land shall worship at the entrance of that gate before the Lord on the sabbaths and on the new moons.

4And the burnt offering that the prince shall offer to the Lord on the sabbath day shall be six lambs without blemish and a ram without blemish.

5And the bloodless *or* meal offering with the ram shall be an ephah, and the meal offering with the lambs shall be as much as he is able [willing] to give, and a hin of oil with each ephah.

6And on the day of the new moon the offering shall be a young bull without blemish, and six lambs and a ram without blemish.

## New American Standard

13¶ "This is the offering that you shall offer: a sixth of an ephah from a homer of wheat; a sixth of an ephah from a homer of barley;

14and the prescribed portion of oil ( *namely,* the bath of oil), a tenth of a bath from *each* kor ( *which is* ten baths *or* a homer, for ten baths are a homer);

15and one sheep from *each* flock of two hundred from the watering places of Israel—for a grain offering, for a burnt offering, and for peace offerings, to make atonement for them," declares the Lord GOD.

16"All the people of the land shall give to this offering for the prince in Israel.

17"And it shall be the prince's part *to provide* the burnt offerings, the grain offerings, and the libations, at the feasts, on the new moons, and on the sabbaths, at all the appointed feasts of the house of Israel; he shall provide the sin offering, the grain offering, the burnt offering, and the peace offerings, to make atonement for the house of Israel."

18¶ 'Thus says the Lord GOD, "In the first *month,* on the first of the month, you shall take a young bull without blemish and cleanse the sanctuary.

19"And the priest shall take some of the blood from the sin offering and put *it* on the door posts of the house, on the four corners of the ledge of the altar, and on the posts of the gate of the inner court.

20"And thus you shall do on the seventh *day* of the month for everyone who goes astray or is naive; so you shall make atonement for the house.

21¶ "In the first *month,* on the fourteenth day of the month, you shall have the Passover, a feast of seven days; unleavened bread shall be eaten.

22"And on that day the prince shall provide for himself and all the people of the land a bull for a sin offering.

23"And *during* the seven days of the feast he shall provide as a burnt offering to the LORD seven bulls and seven rams without blemish on every day of the seven days, and a male goat daily for a sin offering.

24"And he shall provide as a grain offering an ephah with a bull, an ephah with a ram, and a hin of oil with an ephah.

25"In the seventh *month,* on the fifteenth day of the month, at the feast, he shall provide like this, seven days for the sin offering, the burnt offering, the grain offering, and the oil."

*The Prince's Offerings*

**46** 'THUS SAYS the Lord GOD, "The gate of the inner court facing east shall be shut the six working days; but it shall be opened on the sabbath day, and opened on the day of the new moon.

2"And the prince shall enter by way of the porch of the gate from outside and stand by the post of the gate. Then the priests shall provide his burnt offering and his peace offerings, and he shall worship at the threshold of the gate and then go out; but the gate shall not be shut until the evening.

3"The people of the land shall also worship at the doorway of that gate before the LORD on the sabbaths and on the new moons.

4"And the burnt offering which the prince shall offer to the LORD on the sabbath day shall be six lambs without blemish and a ram without blemish;

5and the grain offering shall be an ephah with the ram, and the grain offering with the lambs as much as he is able to give, and a hin of oil with an ephah.

6"And on the day of the new moon *he shall offer* a young bull without blemish, also six lambs and a ram, *which* shall be without blemish.

## New International

*Offerings and Holy Days*

13" 'This is the special gift you are to offer: a sixth of an ephah
from each homer of wheat and a sixth of an ephah from each
homer of barley. 14The prescribed portion of oil, measured by the
bath, is a tenth of a bath from each cor (which consists of ten baths
or one homer, for ten baths are equivalent to a homer). 15Also one
sheep is to be taken from every flock of two hundred from the
well-watered pastures of Israel. These will be used for the grain
offerings, burnt offerings and fellowship offerings[a] to make atonement for the people, declares the Sovereign LORD. 16All the people
of the land will participate in this special gift for the use of the
prince in Israel. 17It will be the duty of the prince to provide the
burnt offerings, grain offerings and drink offerings at the festivals,
the New Moons and the Sabbaths—at all the appointed feasts of
the house of Israel. He will provide the sin offerings, grain offerings, burnt offerings and fellowship offerings to make atonement
for the house of Israel.

18" 'This is what the Sovereign LORD says: In the first month on
the first day you are to take a young bull without defect and purify
the sanctuary. 19The priest is to take some of the blood of the sin
offering and put it on the doorposts of the temple, on the four
corners of the upper ledge of the altar and on the gateposts of the
inner court. 20You are to do the same on the seventh day of the
month for anyone who sins unintentionally or through ignorance;
so you are to make atonement for the temple.

21" 'In the first month on the fourteenth day you are to observe
the Passover, a feast lasting seven days, during which you shall
eat bread made without yeast. 22On that day the prince is to
provide a bull as a sin offering for himself and for all the people
of the land. 23Every day during the seven days of the Feast he is
to provide seven bulls and seven rams without defect as a burnt
offering to the LORD, and a male goat for a sin offering. 24He is to
provide as a grain offering an ephah for each bull and an ephah
for each ram, along with a hin[b] of oil for each ephah.

25" 'During the seven days of the Feast, which begins in the
seventh month on the fifteenth day, he is to make the same provision for sin offerings, burnt offerings, grain offerings and oil.

**46** " 'THIS IS what the Sovereign LORD says: The gate of the
inner court facing east is to be shut on the six working
days, but on the Sabbath day and on the day of the New Moon it
is to be opened. 2The prince is to enter from the outside through
the portico of the gateway and stand by the gatepost. The priests
are to sacrifice his burnt offering and his fellowship offerings.[c] He
is to worship at the threshold of the gateway and then go out, but
the gate will not be shut until evening. 3On the Sabbaths and New
Moons the people of the land are to worship in the presence of the
LORD at the entrance to that gateway. 4The burnt offering the
prince brings to the LORD on the Sabbath day is to be six male lambs
and a ram, all without defect. 5The grain offering given with the
ram is to be an ephah,[d] and the grain offering with the lambs is
to be as much as he pleases, along with a hin[e] of oil for each ephah.
6On the day of the New Moon he is to offer a young bull, six lambs
and a ram, all without defect. 7He is to provide as a grain offering

**NIV** [a] *15* Traditionally *peace offerings;* also in verse 17 [b] *24* That is, probably about 4 quarts (about 4 liters) [c] *2* Traditionally *peace offerings;* also in verse 12 [d] *5* That is, probably about 3/5 bushel (about 22 liters) [e] *5* That is, probably about 4 quarts (about 4 liters)

## King James

7 And he shall prepare a meat offering, an ephah for a bullock, and an ephah for a ram, and for the lambs according as his hand shall attain unto, and an hin of oil to an ephah.

8 And when the prince shall enter, he shall go in by the way of the porch of *that* gate, and he shall go forth by the way thereof.

9 ¶ But when the people of the land shall come before the LORD in the solemn feasts, he that entereth in by the way of the north gate to worship shall go out by the way of the south gate; and he that entereth by the way of the south gate shall go forth by the way of the north gate: he shall not return by the way of the gate whereby he came in, but shall go forth over against it.

10 And the prince in the midst of them, when they go in, shall go in; and when they go forth, shall go forth.

11 And in the feasts and in the solemnities the meat offering shall be an ephah to a bullock, and an ephah to a ram, and to the lambs as he is able to give, and an hin of oil to an ephah.

12 Now when the prince shall prepare a voluntary burnt offering or peace offerings voluntarily unto the LORD, *one* shall then open him the gate that looketh toward the east, and he shall prepare his burnt offering and his peace offerings, as he did on the sabbath day: then he shall go forth; and after his going forth *one* shall shut the gate.

13 Thou shalt daily prepare a burnt offering unto the LORD *of* a lamb of the first year without blemish: thou shalt prepare it every morning.

14 And thou shalt prepare a meat offering for it every morning, the sixth part of an ephah, and the third part of an hin of oil, to temper with the fine flour; a meat offering continually by a perpetual ordinance unto the LORD.

15 Thus shall they prepare the lamb, and the meat offering, and the oil, every morning *for* a continual burnt offering.

16 ¶ Thus saith the Lord GOD; If the prince give a gift unto any of his sons, the inheritance thereof shall be his sons'; it *shall be* their possession by inheritance.

17 But if he give a gift of his inheritance to one of his servants, then it shall be his to the year of liberty; after it shall return to the prince: but his inheritance shall be his sons' for them.

18 Moreover the prince shall not take of the people's inheritance by oppression, to thrust them out of their possession; *but* he shall give his sons inheritance out of his own possession: that my people be not scattered every man from his possession.

19 ¶ After he brought me through the entry, which *was* at the side of the gate, into the holy chambers of the priests, which looked toward the north: and, behold, there *was* a place on the two sides westward.

20 Then said he unto me, This *is* the place where the priests shall boil the trespass offering and the sin offering, where they shall bake the meat offering; that they bear *them* not out into the utter court, to sanctify the people.

21 Then he brought me forth into the utter court, and caused me to pass by the four corners of the court; and, behold, in every corner of the court *there was* a court.

22 In the four corners of the court *there were* courts joined of forty *cubits* long and thirty broad: these four corners *were* of one measure.

23 And *there was* a row *of building* round about in them, round about them four, and *it was* made with boiling places under the rows round about.

24 Then said he unto me, These *are* the places of them that boil, where the ministers of the house shall boil the sacrifice of the people.

## Amplified

7 And the prince shall provide *and* make a meal *or* bloodless offering, an ephah for the bullock and an ephah for the ram, and for the lambs as he is able *and* willing according to what has been made available to his hand, and a hin of oil to each ephah.

8 And when the prince shall enter, he shall go in by the porch *or* vestibule of that gate, and he shall go out by way of it.

9 But when the people of the land shall come before the Lord at the appointed solemn feasts, he who enters the north gate to worship shall go out by the south gate; and he who enters by the south gate shall go out by the north gate; he shall not return by the gate by which he came in, but shall go out by the opposite gate—straight ahead. [Phil. 3:13.]

10 And the prince, when they go in, shall go in with them, and when they go out, he shall go out.

11 And in the appointed and solemn feasts the meal *or* bloodless offering shall be with a bullock an ephah, and with a ram an ephah, and with the lambs as much as the prince is willing *and* able to give [from what has been made available to him], and a hin of oil with each ephah.

12 When the prince shall prepare *and* make a freewill burnt offering or peace offerings voluntarily to the Lord, the gate that faces east shall be opened for him, and he shall offer his burnt offering and his peace offerings, as he does on the sabbath day. Then he shall go out, and after he has gone out the gate shall be shut.

13 And a lamb a year old without blemish shall you [the priests, for the congregation] offer daily to the Lord; you shall prepare *and* offer it every morning.

14 And you [the priests] shall prepare a meal offering to go with it every morning, one-sixth of an ephah, and one-third of a hin of oil to moisten the fine flour. This is a perpetual ordinance for a continual meal offering to the Lord.

15 Thus shall they prepare *and* offer the lamb and the meal offering and the oil every morning for a continual burnt offering.

16 Thus says the Lord God: If the prince gives a gift to any of his sons out of his inheritance, it shall belong to his sons; it is their property by inheritance.

17 But if he gives a gift out of his inheritance to one of his servants, then it shall be his until the year of liberty—the year of jubilee; after that it shall be returned to the prince; only his sons may keep a gift from his inheritance [permanently].

18 Moreover the prince shall not take of the people's inheritance by oppression, thrusting them out of their property; what he gives to his sons he shall take out of his own possession, so that none of My people shall be separated from his [inherited] possession.

19 Then [my guide] led me through the entrance which was at the side of the gate, into the holy chambers for the priests, which faced the north; and behold, there was a place at the extreme western end of them.

20 And he said to me, This is the place where the priests shall boil the guilt offering and the sin offering, and where they shall bake the [bloodless] meal offering; to prevent their having to bring them into the outer court, lest they should thereby wrongfully sanctify—separate and consecrate for holy service—the people who are there.

21 And he brought me out into the outer court and caused me to pass by the four corners of the court; and behold, in every corner of the court there was a court.

22 In the four corners of the court there were courts joined on *and* enclosed, forty cubits long and thirty broad; these four in the corners were the same size.

23 And there was a row of masonry inside them, round about *each of* the four courts, and it was made with hearths for boiling at the bottom of the rows round about.

24 Then said he to me, These are the kitchens of those who do the boiling, where the ministers [the mere Levites] of the temple shall boil the sacrifices of the people.

## New American Standard

7"And he shall provide a grain offering, an ephah with the bull, and an ephah with the ram, and with the lambs as much as he is able, and a hin of oil with an ephah.

8"And when the prince enters, he shall go in by way of the porch of the gate and go out by the same way.

9"But when the people of the land come before the LORD at the appointed feasts, he who enters by way of the north gate to worship shall go out by way of the south gate. And he who enters by way of the south gate shall go out by way of the north gate. No one shall return by way of the gate by which he entered but shall go straight out.

10"And when they go in, the prince shall go in among them; and when they go out, he shall go out.

11"And at the festivals and the appointed feasts the grain offering shall be an ephah with a bull and an ephah with a ram, and with the lambs as much as one is able to give, and a hin of oil with an ephah.

12"And when the prince provides a freewill offering, a burnt offering, or peace offerings *as* a freewill offering to the LORD, the gate facing east shall be opened for him. And he shall provide his burnt offering and his peace offerings as he does on the sabbath day. Then he shall go out, and the gate shall be shut after he goes out.

13¶ "And you shall provide a lamb a year old without blemish for a burnt offering to the LORD daily; morning by morning you shall provide it.

14"Also you shall provide a grain offering with it morning by morning, a sixth of an ephah, and a third of a hin of oil to moisten the fine flour, a grain offering to the LORD continually by a perpetual ordinance.

15"Thus they shall provide the lamb, the grain offering, and the oil, morning by morning, for a continual burnt offering."

16¶ 'Thus says the Lord GOD, "If the prince gives a gift *out of* his inheritance to any of his sons, it shall belong to his sons; it is their possession by inheritance.

17"But if he gives a gift from his inheritance to one of his servants, it shall be his until the year of liberty; then it shall return to the prince. His inheritance *shall be* only his sons'; it shall belong to them.

18"And the prince shall not take from the people's inheritance, thrusting them out of their possession; he shall give his sons inheritance from his own possession so that My people shall not be scattered, anyone from his possession." ' "

*The Boiling Places*

19¶ Then he brought me through the entrance, which *was* at the side of the gate, into the holy chambers for the priests, which faced north; and behold, there *was* a place at the extreme rear toward the west.

20And he said to me, "This is the place where the priests shall boil the guilt offering and the sin offering, *and* where they shall bake the grain offering, in order that they may not bring *them* out into the outer court to transmit holiness to the people."

21Then he brought me out into the outer court and led me across to the four corners of the court; and behold, in every corner of the court *there was* a *small* court.

22In the four corners of the court *there were* enclosed courts, forty *cubits* long and thirty wide; these four in the corners *were* the same size.

23And *there was* a row *of masonry* round about in them, around the four of them, and boiling places were made under the rows round about.

24Then he said to me, "These are the boiling places where the ministers of the house shall boil the sacrifices of the people."

## New International

one ephah with the bull, one ephah with the ram, and with the
lambs as much as he wants to give, along with a hin of oil with each
ephah. 8When the prince enters, he is to go in through the portico
of the gateway, and he is to come out the same way.
9" 'When the people of the land come before the LORD at the
appointed feasts, whoever enters by the north gate to worship is
to go out the south gate; and whoever enters by the south gate is
to go out the north gate. No one is to return through the gate by
which he entered, but each is to go out the opposite gate. 10The
prince is to be among them, going in when they go in and going
out when they go out.
11" 'At the festivals and the appointed feasts, the grain offering
is to be an ephah with a bull, an ephah with a ram, and with the
lambs as much as one pleases, along with a hin of oil for each
ephah. 12When the prince provides a freewill offering to the
LORD—whether a burnt offering or fellowship offerings—the gate
facing east is to be opened for him. He shall offer his burnt offering
or his fellowship offerings as he does on the Sabbath day. Then he
shall go out, and after he has gone out, the gate will be shut.
13" 'Every day you are to provide a year-old lamb without defect
for a burnt offering to the LORD; morning by morning you shall
provide it. 14You are also to provide with it morning by morning
a grain offering, consisting of a sixth of an ephah with a third of
a hin of oil to moisten the flour. The presenting of this grain
offering to the LORD is a lasting ordinance. 15So the lamb and the
grain offering and the oil shall be provided morning by morning
for a regular burnt offering.
16" 'This is what the Sovereign LORD says: If the prince makes
a gift from his inheritance to one of his sons, it will also belong to
his descendants; it is to be their property by inheritance. 17If,
however, he makes a gift from his inheritance to one of his servants, the servant may keep it until the year of freedom; then it
will revert to the prince. His inheritance belongs to his sons only;
it is theirs. 18The prince must not take any of the inheritance of the
people, driving them off their property. He is to give his sons their
inheritance out of his own property, so that none of my people will
be separated from his property.' "
19Then the man brought me through the entrance at the side of
the gate to the sacred rooms facing north, which belonged to the
priests, and showed me a place at the western end. 20He said to
me, "This is the place where the priests will cook the guilt offering
and the sin offering and bake the grain offering, to avoid bringing
them into the outer court and consecrating the people."
21He then brought me to the outer court and led me around to
its four corners, and I saw in each corner another court. 22In the
four corners of the outer court were enclosed[a] courts, forty cubits
long and thirty cubits wide; each of the courts in the four corners
was the same size. 23Around the inside of each of the four courts
was a ledge of stone, with places for fire built all around under the
ledge. 24He said to me, "These are the kitchens where those who
minister at the temple will cook the sacrifices of the people."

NIV [a] 22 The meaning of the Hebrew for this word is uncertain.

## King James

47 AFTERWARD HE brought me again unto the door of the
house; and, behold, waters issued out from under the
threshold of the house eastward: for the forefront of the house
*stood toward* the east, and the waters came down from under from
the right side of the house, at the south *side* of the altar.
2Then brought he me out of the way of the gate northward, and
led me about the way without unto the utter gate by the way that
looketh eastward; and, behold, there ran out waters on the right
side.
3And when the man that had the line in his hand went forth
eastward, he measured a thousand cubits, and he brought me
through the waters; the waters *were* to the ankles.
4Again he measured a thousand, and brought me through the
waters; the waters *were* to the knees. Again he measured a thousand, and brought me through; the waters *were* to the loins.
5Afterward he measured a thousand; *and it was* a river that I
could not pass over: for the waters were risen, waters to swim in,
a river that could not be passed over.
6¶ And he said unto me, Son of man, hast thou seen *this?* Then
he brought me, and caused me to return to the brink of the river.
7Now when I had returned, behold, at the bank of the river *were*
very many trees on the one side and on the other.
8Then said he unto me, These waters issue out toward the east
country, and go down into the desert, and go into the sea: *which
being* brought forth into the sea, the waters shall be healed.
9And it shall come to pass, *that* every thing that liveth, which
moveth, whithersoever the rivers shall come, shall live: and there
shall be a very great multitude of fish, because these waters shall
come thither: for they shall be healed; and every thing shall live
whither the river cometh.
10And it shall come to pass, *that* the fishers shall stand upon it
from En-gedi even unto En-eglaim; they shall be a *place* to spread
forth nets; their fish shall be according to their kinds, as the fish
of the great sea, exceeding many.
11But the miry places thereof and the marshes thereof shall not
be healed; they shall be given to salt.
12And by the river upon the bank thereof, on this side and on
that side, shall grow all trees for meat, whose leaf shall not fade,
neither shall the fruit thereof be consumed: it shall bring forth new
fruit according to his months, because their waters they issued out
of the sanctuary: and the fruit thereof shall be for meat, and the
leaf thereof for medicine.
13¶ Thus saith the Lord GOD; This *shall be* the border, whereby
ye shall inherit the land according to the twelve tribes of Israel:
Joseph *shall have two* portions.
14And ye shall inherit it, one as well as another: *concerning* the
which I lifted up mine hand to give it unto your fathers: and this
land shall fall unto you for inheritance.
15And this *shall be* the border of the land toward the north side,
from the great sea, the way of Hethlon, as men go to Zedad;
16Hamath, Berothah, Sibraim, which *is* between the border of
Damascus and the border of Hamath; Hazar-hatticon, which *is* by
the coast of Hauran.
17And the border from the sea shall be Hazar-enan, the border
of Damascus, and the north northward, and the border of Hamath.
And *this is* the north side.
18And the east side ye shall measure from Hauran, and from
Damascus, and from Gilead, and from the land of Israel *by* Jordan,
from the border unto the east sea. And *this is* the east side.

## Amplified

47 THEN [MY guide] brought me again to the door of the
house [of the Lord]—the temple; and behold, waters issued out from under the threshold of the temple toward the east,
for the front of the temple was toward the east; and the waters
came down from under, from the right side of the temple, on the
south side of the altar.
2Then he brought me out by way of the north gate and led me
around outside to the outer gate by the way that faces east; and
behold, waters were running out [in a trickle] on the right side.
[Zech. 14:8; cf. Rev. 22:1, 2.]
3And when the man went on eastward with the line in his hand,
he measured a thousand cubits, and he caused me to pass through
the waters, waters that were ankle deep.
4Again he measured a thousand cubits and caused me to pass
through the waters, waters that reached to the knees. Again he
measured a thousand cubits and caused me to pass through the
waters, waters that reached to the loins.
5Afterward he measured a thousand; and it was a river that I
could not pass through, for the waters had risen, waters to swim
in, a river that could not be passed over *or* through.
6And he said to me, Son of man, have you seen this? Then he
led me and caused me to return to the bank of the river.
7Now when I had returned, behold, on the bank of the river
were very many trees on the one side and on the other.
8Then he said to me, These waters pour out toward the eastern
region and go down into the Arabah [the valley of the Jordan] and
on into the Dead Sea. And when they shall enter into the sea [the
sea of putrid waters] the waters shall be healed *and* made fresh.
9And wherever the double river shall go, every living creature
which swarms shall live, and there shall be a very great number
of fish; because these waters go there that [the waters of the sea]
may be healed *and* made fresh, and every thing shall live wherever
the river goes.
10The fishermen shall stand on [the banks of the Dead Sea];
from Engedi even to Eneglaim shall be a place to spread nets; their
fish shall be of very many kinds, as the fish of the Great *or* Mediterranean Sea.
11But its swamps and marshes will not become wholesome for
animal life; they shall [as the river subsides] be left encrusted with
salt *and* given over to it.
12And on the banks of the river on both its sides, there shall
grow all kinds of trees for food; their leaf shall not fade, nor shall
their fruit fail [to meet the demand]. Each tree shall bring forth new
first fruits every month, [these supernatural qualities being] because their waters came from out of the sanctuary. And their fruit
shall be for food, and their leaf for healing.
13Thus says the Lord God: These shall be the boundaries by
which you shall divide the land among the twelve tribes of Israel:
Joseph shall have two portions.
14And you shall divide it equally. I lifted up My hand *and* swore
to give it to your fathers, and this land shall fall to you as your
inheritance.
15And this shall be the boundary of the land on the north side:
from the Great *or* Mediterranean Sea by way of Hethlon to the
entrance of Zedad,
16Hamath, Berothah, Sibraim, which is on the border between
Damascus and Hamath; as far as Hazerhatticon on the border of
Hauran.
17So the boundary shall extend from the [Mediterranean] Sea to
Hazarenon, at the boundary of Damascus on the north, together
with the boundary of Hamath to the north. This is the north side.
18And on the east side you shall measure the boundary from
between Hauran and Damascus, and Gilead on one side, and the
land of Israel on the other, with the Jordan forming the border
down to the East *or* Dead Sea. And this [from Damascus to the
Dead Sea and including it] is the east side.

## New American Standard

### *Water from the Temple*

47 THEN HE brought me back to the door of the house; and
behold, water was flowing from under the threshold of
the house toward the east, for the house faced east. And the water
was flowing down from under, from the right side of the house,
from south of the altar.

2 And he brought me out by way of the north gate and led me
around on the outside to the outer gate by way of *the gate* that faces
east. And behold, water was trickling from the south side.

3 ¶ When the man went out toward the east with a line in his
hand, he measured a thousand cubits, and he led me through the
water, water *reaching* the ankles.

4 Again he measured a thousand and led me through the water,
water *reaching* the knees. Again he measured a thousand and led
me through *the water,* water *reaching* the loins.

5 Again he measured a thousand; *and it was* a river that I could
not ford, for the water had risen, *enough* water to swim in, a river
that could not be forded.

6 And he said to me, "Son of man, have you seen *this?*" Then
he brought me back to the bank of the river.

7 Now when I had returned, behold, on the bank of the river
there *were* very many trees on the one side and on the other.

8 Then he said to me, "These waters go out toward the eastern
region and go down into the Arabah; then they go toward the sea,
being made to flow into the sea, and the waters *of the sea* become
fresh.

9 "And it will come about that every living creature which
swarms in every place where the river goes, will live. And there
will be very many fish, for these waters go there, and *the others*
become fresh; so everything will live where the river goes.

10 "And it will come about that fishermen will stand beside it;
from Engedi to Eneglaim there will be a place for the spreading of
nets. Their fish will be according to their kinds, like the fish of the
Great Sea, very many.

11 "But its swamps and marshes will not become fresh; they will
be left for salt.

12 "And by the river on its bank, on one side and on the other,
will grow all *kinds of* trees for food. Their leaves will not wither,
and their fruit will not fail. They will bear every month because
their water flows from the sanctuary, and their fruit will be for food
and their leaves for healing."

### *Boundaries and Division of the Land*

13 ¶ Thus says the Lord GOD, "This *shall be* the boundary by
which you shall divide the land for an inheritance among the
twelve tribes of Israel; Joseph *shall have two* portions.

14 "And you shall divide it for an inheritance, each one equally
with the other; for I swore to give it to your forefathers, and this
land shall fall to you as an inheritance.

15 ¶ "And this *shall be* the boundary of the land: on the north
side, from the Great Sea *by* the way of Hethlon, to the entrance of
Zedad;

16 Hamath, Berothah, Sibraim, which is between the border of
Damascus and the border of Hamath; Hazer-hatticon, which is by
the border of Hauran.

17 "And the boundary shall extend from the sea *to* Hazar-enan
*at* the border of Damascus, and on the north toward the north is
the border of Hamath. This is the north side.

18 "And the east side, from between Hauran, Damascus, Gilead,
and the land of Israel, *shall be* the Jordan; from the *north* border to
the eastern sea you shall measure. This is the east side.

## New International

### *The River From the Temple*

47 THE MAN brought me back to the entrance of the temple,
and I saw water coming out from under the threshold of
the temple toward the east (for the temple faced east). The water
was coming down from under the south side of the temple, south
of the altar.
2 He then brought me out through the north gate and
led me around the outside to the outer gate facing east, and the
water was flowing from the south side.

3 As the man went eastward with a measuring line in his hand,
he measured off a thousand cubits[a] and then led me through
water that was ankle-deep.
4 He measured off another thousand
cubits and led me through water that was knee-deep. He measured off another thousand and led me through water that was up
to the waist.
5 He measured off another thousand, but now it was
a river that I could not cross, because the water had risen and was
deep enough to swim in—a river that no one could cross.
6 He
asked me, "Son of man, do you see this?"

Then he led me back to the bank of the river.
7 When I arrived
there, I saw a great number of trees on each side of the river.
8 He
said to me, "This water flows toward the eastern region and goes
down into the Arabah,[b] where it enters the Sea.[c] When it empties
into the Sea,[d] the water there becomes fresh.
9 Swarms of living
creatures will live wherever the river flows. There will be large
numbers of fish, because this water flows there and makes the salt
water fresh; so where the river flows everything will live.
10 Fish-
ermen will stand along the shore; from En Gedi to En Eglaim there
will be places for spreading nets. The fish will be of many kinds—
like the fish of the Great Sea.[e]
11 But the swamps and marshes will
not become fresh; they will be left for salt.
12 Fruit trees of all kinds
will grow on both banks of the river. Their leaves will not wither,
nor will their fruit fail. Every month they will bear, because the
water from the sanctuary flows to them. Their fruit will serve for
food and their leaves for healing."

### *The Boundaries of the Land*

13 This is what the Sovereign LORD says: "These are the boundaries by which you are to divide the land for an inheritance among
the twelve tribes of Israel, with two portions for Joseph.
14 You are
to divide it equally among them. Because I swore with uplifted
hand to give it to your forefathers, this land will become your
inheritance.

15 "This is to be the boundary of the land:

"On the north side it will run from the Great Sea by the Hethlon
road past Lebo[f] Hamath to Zedad,
16 Berothah[g] and
Sibraim (which lies on the border between Damascus and
Hamath), as far as Hazer Hatticon, which is on the border
of Hauran.
17 The boundary will extend from the sea to
Hazar Enan,[h] along the northern border of Damascus, with
the border of Hamath to the north. This will be the north
boundary.

18 "On the east side the boundary will run between Hauran and
Damascus, along the Jordan between Gilead and the land of
Israel, to the eastern sea and as far as Tamar.[i] This will be
the east boundary.

NIV [a] 3 That is, about 1,500 feet (about 450 meters) [b] *8* Or *the Jordan Valley*
[c] *8* That is, the Dead Sea [d] *8* That is, the Dead Sea [e] *10* That is, the
Mediterranean; also in verses 15, 19 and 20 [f] *15* Or *past the entrance to*
[g] *15,16* See Septuagint and Ezekiel 48:1; Hebrew *road to go into Zedad, 16Hamath,
Berothah* [h] *17* Hebrew *Enon,* a variant of *Enan* [i] *18* Septuagint and Syriac;
Hebrew *Israel. You will measure to the eastern sea*

## King James

19 And the south side southward, from Tamar *even* to the waters of strife *in* Kadesh, the river to the great sea. And *this is* the south side southward.

20 The west side also *shall be* the great sea from the border, till a man come over against Hamath. This *is* the west side.

21 So shall ye divide this land unto you according to the tribes of Israel.

22 ¶ And it shall come to pass, *that* ye shall divide it by lot for an inheritance unto you, and to the strangers that sojourn among you, which shall beget children among you: and they shall be unto you as born in the country among the children of Israel; they shall have inheritance with you among the tribes of Israel.

23 And it shall come to pass, *that* in what tribe the stranger sojourneth, there shall ye give *him* his inheritance, saith the Lord God.

**48** NOW THESE *are* the names of the tribes. From the north end to the coast of the way of Hethlon, as one goeth to Hamath, Hazar-enan, the border of Damascus northward, to the coast of Hamath; for these are his sides east *and* west; a *portion for* Dan.

2 And by the border of Dan, from the east side unto the west side, a *portion for* Asher.

3 And by the border of Asher, from the east side even unto the west side, a *portion for* Naphtali.

4 And by the border of Naphtali, from the east side unto the west side, a *portion for* Manasseh.

5 And by the border of Manasseh, from the east side unto the west side, a *portion for* Ephraim.

6 And by the border of Ephraim, from the east side even unto the west side, a *portion for* Reuben.

7 And by the border of Reuben, from the east side unto the west side, a *portion for* Judah.

8 ¶ And by the border of Judah, from the east side unto the west side, shall be the offering which ye shall offer of five and twenty thousand *reeds in* breadth, and *in* length as one of the *other* parts, from the east side unto the west side: and the sanctuary shall be in the midst of it.

9 The oblation that ye shall offer unto the Lord *shall be* of five and twenty thousand in length, and of ten thousand in breadth.

10 And for them, *even* for the priests, shall be *this* holy oblation; toward the north five and twenty thousand *in length,* and toward the west ten thousand in breadth, and toward the east ten thousand in breadth, and toward the south five and twenty thousand in length: and the sanctuary of the Lord shall be in the midst thereof.

11 *It shall be* for the priests that are sanctified of the sons of Zadok; which have kept my charge, which went not astray when the children of Israel went astray, as the Levites went astray.

12 And *this* oblation of the land that is offered shall be unto them a thing most holy by the border of the Levites.

13 And over against the border of the priests the Levites *shall have* five and twenty thousand in length, and ten thousand in breadth: all the length *shall be* five and twenty thousand, and the breadth ten thousand.

14 And they shall not sell of it, neither exchange, nor alienate the firstfruits of the land: for *it is* holy unto the Lord.

15 ¶ And the five thousand, that are left in the breadth over against the five and twenty thousand, shall be a profane *place* for the city, for dwelling, and for suburbs: and the city shall be in the midst thereof.

## Amplified

19 And the south side [border] southward, from Tamar [near the Dead Sea] shall run as far as the waters of Meriboth-kadesh, then along the Brook of Egypt to the Great *or* Mediterranean Sea. And this is the south side.

20 On the west side [the boundary] shall be the Great *or* Mediterranean Sea to a point opposite the entrance of Hamath [north of Mount Hermon]. This is the west side.

21 So you shall divide this land among you according to the tribes of Israel.

22 You shall divide it by allotment as an inheritance for yourselves and for the foreigners who reside among you and shall have children born among you. They shall be to you as those born in the country among the children of Israel; they shall inherit with you among the tribes of Israel.

23 In whatever tribe the foreigner resides, there shall you give him his inheritance, says the Lord God.

**48** NOW THESE are the names of the tribes: From the north end, beside the way of Hethlon to the entrance of Hamath, as far as Hazarenon, which is on the northern border of Damascus opposite Hamath, and reaching from the east border to the west, Dan, one *portion.*

2 And beside the border of Dan, from the east side to the west side, Asher, one *portion.*

3 And beside the border of Asher, from the east side even to the west side, Naphtali, one *portion.*

4 And beside the border of Naphtali, from the east side to the west side, Manasseh, one *portion.*

5 And beside the border of Manasseh, from the east side to the west side, Ephraim, one *portion.*

6 And beside the border of Ephraim, from the east side even to the west side, Reuben, one *portion.*

7 And beside the border of Reuben, from the east side to the west side, Judah, one *portion.*

8 And beside the border of Judah, from the east side to the west side, shall be the offering of land which you shall offer of twenty-five thousand reeds in breadth, and in length as one of the tribal portions, from the east side to the west side, and the sanctuary shall be in the midst of it.

9 The portion of land that you shall set apart and offer to the Lord shall be twenty-five thousand *measures* in length, and ten thousand in breadth [for each of the two districts].

10 And for these, even for the priests, shall be this holy offering of land; toward the north twenty-five thousand *measures* in length, and toward the west ten thousand in breadth, and toward the east ten thousand in breadth, and toward the south twenty-five thousand in length; and the sanctuary of the Lord shall be in the midst of it.

11 The set apart *and* sacred portion shall be for the consecrated priests of the sons of Zadok, who have kept My charge and who did not go astray when the children of Israel went astray, as the other Levites did.

12 And this land offering shall be for the priests as a thing most holy beside the boundary of the *other* Levites.

13 And opposite the boundary of the priests the *other* Levites shall have twenty-five thousand *measures* in length and ten thousand in breadth. The whole length shall be twenty-five thousand and the breadth ten thousand.

14 And they shall not sell any of it or exchange it; they shall not convey *or* transfer this the first fruits of the land, for it has been offered to the Lord and is holy to Him.

15 And the remaining strip of five thousand *measures* in breadth and twenty-five thousand in length, shall be for the city's secular use, for a place in which to dwell and for open country *or* suburbs. The city shall be in the midst of the plot.

## New American Standard

19"And the south side toward the south *shall extend* from Tamar
as far as the waters of Meribath-kadesh, to the brook *of Egypt, and*
to the Great Sea. This is the south side toward the south.
20"And the west side *shall be* the Great Sea, from the *south*
border to a point opposite Lebo-hamath. This is the west side.
21¶ "So you shall divide this land among yourselves according
to the tribes of Israel.
22"And it will come about that you shall divide it by lot for an
inheritance among yourselves and among the aliens who stay in
your midst, who bring forth sons in your midst. And they shall be
to you as the native-born among the sons of Israel; they shall be
allotted an inheritance with you among the tribes of Israel.
23"And it will come about that in the tribe with which the alien
stays, there you shall give *him* his inheritance," declares the Lord
GOD.

*Division of the Land*

48 "NOW THESE are the names of the tribes: from the northern extremity, beside the way of Hethlon to Lebo-hamath,
*as far as* Hazar-enan *at* the border of Damascus, toward the north
beside Hamath, running from east to west, Dan, one *portion*.
2"And beside the border of Dan, from the east side to the west
side, Asher, one *portion*.
3"And beside the border of Asher, from the east side to the
west side, Naphtali, one *portion*.
4"And beside the border of Naphtali, from the east side to the
west side, Manasseh, one *portion*.
5"And beside the border of Manasseh, from the east side to the
west side, Ephraim, one *portion*.
6"And beside the border of Ephraim, from the east side to the
west side, Reuben, one *portion*.
7"And beside the border of Reuben, from the east side to the
west side, Judah, one *portion*.
8¶ "And beside the border of Judah, from the east side to the
west side, shall be the [a]allotment which you shall set apart, 25,000
*cubits* in width, and in length like one of the portions, from the east
side to the west side; and the sanctuary shall be in the middle
of it.
9"The allotment that you shall set apart to the LORD *shall be*
25,000 *cubits* in length, and 10,000 in width.

*Portion for the Priests*

10"And the holy allotment shall be for these, *namely* for the
priests, toward the north 25,000 *cubits in length*, toward the west
10,000 in width, toward the east 10,000 in width, and toward the
south 25,000 in length; and the sanctuary of the LORD shall be in
its midst.
11" *It shall be* for the priests who are sanctified of the sons of
Zadok, who have kept My charge, who did not go astray when the
sons of Israel went astray, as the Levites went astray.
12"And it shall be an allotment to them from the allotment of
the land, a most holy place, by the border of the Levites.
13"And alongside the border of the priests the Levites *shall have*
25,000 *cubits* in length and 10,000 in width. The whole length *shall
be* 25,000 *cubits* and the width 10,000.
14"Moreover, they shall not sell or exchange any of it, or alienate this choice *portion* of land; for it is holy to the LORD.
15¶ "And the remainder, 5,000 *cubits* in width and 25,000 in
length, shall be for common use for the city, for dwellings and for
open spaces; and the city shall be in its midst.

NAS [a] Or, *contribution*, and so throughout this context

## New International

19"On the south side it will run from Tamar as far as the waters
of Meribah Kadesh, then along the Wadi ⌊of Egypt⌋ to the
Great Sea. This will be the south boundary.
20"On the west side, the Great Sea will be the boundary to a point
opposite Lebo[b] Hamath. This will be the west boundary.
21"You are to distribute this land among yourselves according
to the tribes of Israel. 22You are to allot it as an inheritance for
yourselves and for the aliens who have settled among you and
who have children. You are to consider them as native-born Israelites; along with you they are to be allotted an inheritance among
the tribes of Israel. 23In whatever tribe the alien settles, there you
are to give him his inheritance," declares the Sovereign LORD.

*The Division of the Land*

48 "THESE ARE the tribes, listed by name: At the northern
frontier, Dan will have one portion; it will follow the Hethlon road to Lebo[c] Hamath; Hazar Enan and the northern border
of Damascus next to Hamath will be part of its border from the east
side to the west side.
2"Asher will have one portion; it will border the territory of Dan
from east to west.
3"Naphtali will have one portion; it will border the territory of
Asher from east to west.
4"Manasseh will have one portion; it will border the territory of
Naphtali from east to west.
5"Ephraim will have one portion; it will border the territory of
Manasseh from east to west.
6"Reuben will have one portion; it will border the territory of
Ephraim from east to west.
7"Judah will have one portion; it will border the territory of
Reuben from east to west.
8"Bordering the territory of Judah from east to west will be the
portion you are to present as a special gift. It will be 25,000 cubits[d]
wide, and its length from east to west will equal one of the tribal
portions; the sanctuary will be in the center of it.
9"The special portion you are to offer to the LORD will be 25,000
cubits long and 10,000 cubits[e] wide. 10This will be the sacred
portion for the priests. It will be 25,000 cubits long on the north
side, 10,000 cubits wide on the west side, 10,000 cubits wide on the
east side and 25,000 cubits long on the south side. In the center of
it will be the sanctuary of the LORD. 11This will be for the consecrated priests, the Zadokites, who were faithful in serving me and
did not go astray as the Levites did when the Israelites went astray.
12It will be a special gift to them from the sacred portion of the land,
a most holy portion, bordering the territory of the Levites.
13"Alongside the territory of the priests, the Levites will have
an allotment 25,000 cubits long and 10,000 cubits wide. Its total
length will be 25,000 cubits and its width 10,000 cubits. 14They
must not sell or exchange any of it. This is the best of the land and
must not pass into other hands, because it is holy to the LORD.
15"The remaining area, 5,000 cubits wide and 25,000 cubits
long, will be for the common use of the city, for houses and for
pastureland. The city will be in the center of it 16and will have these

NIV [b] 20 Or *opposite the entrance to* [c] 1 Or *to the entrance to* [d] 8 That is, about 7 miles (about 12 kilometers) [e] 9 That is, about 3 miles (about 5 kilometers)

## King James

16And these *shall be* the measures thereof; the north side four thousand and five hundred, and the south side four thousand and five hundred, and on the east side four thousand and five hundred, and the west side four thousand and five hundred.
17And the suburbs of the city shall be toward the north two hundred and fifty, and toward the south two hundred and fifty, and toward the east two hundred and fifty, and toward the west two hundred and fifty.
18And the residue in length over against the oblation of the holy *portion shall be* ten thousand eastward, and ten thousand westward: and it shall be over against the oblation of the holy *portion;* and the increase thereof shall be for food unto them that serve the city.
19And they that serve the city shall serve it out of all the tribes of Israel.
20All the oblation *shall be* five and twenty thousand by five and twenty thousand: ye shall offer the holy oblation foursquare, with the possession of the city.
21¶ And the residue *shall be* for the prince, on the one side and on the other of the holy oblation, and of the possession of the city, over against the five and twenty thousand of the oblation toward the east border, and westward over against the five and twenty thousand toward the west border, over against the portions for the prince: and it shall be the holy oblation; and the sanctuary of the house *shall be* in the midst thereof.
22Moreover from the possession of the Levites, and from the possession of the city, *being* in the midst *of that* which is the prince's, between the border of Judah and the border of Benjamin, shall be for the prince.
23As for the rest of the tribes, from the east side unto the west side, Benjamin *shall have* a *portion.*
24And by the border of Benjamin, from the east side unto the west side, Simeon *shall have* a *portion.*
25And by the border of Simeon, from the east side unto the west side, Issachar a *portion.*
26And by the border of Issachar, from the east side unto the west side, Zebulun a *portion.*
27And by the border of Zebulun, from the east side unto the west side, Gad a *portion.*
28And by the border of Gad, at the south side southward, the border shall be even from Tamar *unto* the waters of strife *in* Kadesh, *and* to the river toward the great sea.
29This *is* the land which ye shall divide by lot unto the tribes of Israel for inheritance, and these *are* their portions, saith the Lord GOD.
30¶ And these *are* the goings out of the city on the north side, four thousand and five hundred measures.
31And the gates of the city *shall be* after the names of the tribes of Israel: three gates northward; one gate of Reuben, one gate of Judah, one gate of Levi.
32And at the east side four thousand and five hundred: and three gates; and one gate of Joseph, one gate of Benjamin, one gate of Dan.
33And at the south side four thousand and five hundred measures: and three gates; one gate of Simeon, one gate of Issachar, one gate of Zebulun.
34At the west side four thousand and five hundred, *with* their three gates; one gate of Gad, one gate of Asher, one gate of Naphtali.
35 *It was* round about eighteen thousand *measures:* and the name of the city from *that* day *shall be,* The LORD *is* there.

## Amplified

16And these shall be the dimensions of it: the north side four thousand five hundred *measures,* and the south side four thousand five hundred, and on the east side four thousand five hundred, and the west side four thousand five hundred. [Cf. Rev. 21:16.]
17And the city shall have suburbs *or* open country: toward the north two hundred and fifty *measures,* and toward the south two hundred and fifty, and toward the east two hundred and fifty, and toward the west two hundred and fifty.
18The remainder of the length along beside the holy portion shall be ten thousand *measures* to the east, and ten thousand to the west, and it shall be along beside the holy portion. The produce from it shall be for food for those who work in the city.
19And the workers of the city from all the tribes of Israel shall till the open land.
20The whole portion that you shall set apart as an offering to God shall be twenty-five thousand *measures* by twenty-five thousand; you shall set apart the holy portion foursquare, together with the property of the city.
21And what is left unallotted, on both sides of the holy portion and of that possessed by the city, shall belong to the prince. Reaching from the twenty-five thousand *measures* of the holy portion to the east boundary, and west from the twenty-five thousand *measures* to the west boundary, parallel to the tribal allotments, it belongs to the prince. The holy portion with the sanctuary of the temple in its midst,
22And the possession of the Levites and the property of the city [of Jerusalem], shall be in the midst of that which belongs to the prince. What lies between the border of Judah and the border of Benjamin shall be for the prince.
23As for the rest of the tribes, from the east side to the west side, Benjamin, one *portion.*
24And beside the border of Benjamin, from the east side to the west side, Simeon, one *portion.*
25And beside the border of Simeon, from the east side to the west side, Issachar, one *portion.*
26And beside the border of Issachar, from the east side to the west side Zebulun, one *portion.*
27And beside the border of Zebulun, from the east side to the west side, Gad, one *portion.*
28And beside the border of Gad, at the south side southward, the border shall extend from Tamar to the waters of Meribath-kadesh and on along the Brook *of Egypt* to the Great *or* Mediterranean Sea.
29This is the land which you shall divide by allotment among the tribes of Israel as their inheritance, and these are their several portions, says the Lord God.
30And these shall be the exits of the city: On the north side, which is to extend four thousand five hundred measures,
31Three gates: one gate of Reuben, one gate of Judah, one gate of Levi, the gates of the city being called after the names of the tribes of Israel.
32And on the east side's four thousand and five hundred measures, three gates: one gate of Joseph, one gate of Benjamin, one gate of Dan.
33And on the south side's four thousand and five hundred measures, three gates: one gate of Simeon, one gate of Issachar, one gate of Zebulun.
34On the west side's four thousand and five hundred measures, three gates: one gate of Gad, one gate of Asher, one gate of Naphtali.
35The distance around the city shall be [four times four and one-half thousands or] eighteen thousand measures; and the name of the city from that day *and* ever after shall be, THE LORD IS THERE. [Cf. Rev. 21:12, 13, 16.]

## New American Standard

16"And these *shall be* its measurements: the north side 4,500 *cubits*, the south side 4,500 *cubits*, the east side 4,500 *cubits*, and the west side 4,500 *cubits*.

17"And the city shall have open spaces: on the north 250 *cubits*, on the south 250 *cubits*, on the east 250 *cubits*, and on the west 250 *cubits*.

18"And the remainder of the length alongside the holy allotment shall be 10,000 *cubits* toward the east, and 10,000 toward the west; and it shall be alongside the holy allotment. And its produce shall be food for the workers of the city.

19"And the workers of the city, out of all the tribes of Israel, shall cultivate it.

20"The whole allotment *shall be* 25,000 by 25,000 *cubits*; you shall set apart the holy allotment, a square, with the property of the city.

*Portion for the Prince*

**21**¶ "And the remainder *shall be* for the prince, on the one side and on the other of the holy allotment and of the property of the city; in front of the 25,000 *cubits* of the allotment toward the east border and westward in front of the 25,000 toward the west border, alongside the portions, *it shall be* for the prince. And the holy allotment and the sanctuary of the house shall be in the middle of it.

22"And exclusive of the property of the Levites and the property of the city, *which* are in the middle of that which belongs to the prince, *everything* between the border of Judah and the border of Benjamin shall be for the prince.

*Portion for Other Tribes*

**23**¶ "As for the rest of the tribes: from the east side to the west side, Benjamin, one *portion*.

24"And beside the border of Benjamin, from the east side to the west side, Simeon, one *portion*.

25"And beside the border of Simeon, from the east side to the west side, Issachar, one *portion*.

26"And beside the border of Issachar, from the east side to the west side, Zebulun, one *portion*.

27"And beside the border of Zebulun, from the east side to the west side, Gad, one *portion*.

28"And beside the border of Gad, at the south side toward the south, the border shall be from Tamar to the waters of Meribath-kadesh, to the brook *of Egypt*, to the Great Sea.

29"This is the land which you shall divide by lot to the tribes of Israel for an inheritance, and these are their *several* portions," declares the Lord God.

*The City Gates*

**30**¶ "And these are the exits of the city: on the north side, 4,500 *cubits* by measurement,

31shall be the gates of the city, named for the tribes of Israel, three gates toward the north: the gate of Reuben, one; the gate of Judah, one; the gate of Levi, one.

32"And on the east side, 4,500 *cubits*, shall be three gates: the gate of Joseph, one; the gate of Benjamin, one; the gate of Dan, one.

33"And on the south side, 4,500 *cubits* by measurement, shall be three gates: the gate of Simeon, one; the gate of Issachar, one; the gate of Zebulun, one.

34"On the west side, 4,500 *cubits*, *shall be* three gates: the gate of Gad, one; the gate of Asher, one; the gate of Naphtali, one.

35" *The city shall be* 18,000 *cubits* round about; and the name of the city from *that* day *shall be*, 'The LORD is there.' "

## New International

measurements: the north side 4,500 cubits, the south side 4,500
cubits, the east side 4,500 cubits, and the west side 4,500 cubits.
17The pastureland for the city will be 250 cubits on the north, 250
cubits on the south, 250 cubits on the east, and 250 cubits on the
west. 18What remains of the area, bordering on the sacred portion
and running the length of it, will be 10,000 cubits on the east side
and 10,000 cubits on the west side. Its produce will supply food
for the workers of the city. 19The workers from the city who farm
it will come from all the tribes of Israel. 20The entire portion will
be a square, 25,000 cubits on each side. As a special gift you will
set aside the sacred portion, along with the property of the city.

21"What remains on both sides of the area formed by the sacred
portion and the city property will belong to the prince. It will
extend eastward from the 25,000 cubits of the sacred portion to the
eastern border, and westward from the 25,000 cubits to the western border. Both these areas running the length of the tribal portions will belong to the prince, and the sacred portion with the
temple sanctuary will be in the center of them. 22So the property
of the Levites and the property of the city will lie in the center of
the area that belongs to the prince. The area belonging to the
prince will lie between the border of Judah and the border of
Benjamin.

23"As for the rest of the tribes: Benjamin will have one portion; it will extend from the east side to the west side.

24"Simeon will have one portion; it will border the territory of Benjamin from east to west.

25"Issachar will have one portion; it will border the territory of Simeon from east to west.

26"Zebulun will have one portion; it will border the territory of Issachar from east to west.

27"Gad will have one portion; it will border the territory of Zebulun from east to west.

28"The southern boundary of Gad will run south from Tamar to the waters of Meribah Kadesh, then along the Wadi ⌞of Egypt⌟ to the Great Sea.[a]

29"This is the land you are to allot as an inheritance to the tribes of Israel, and these will be their portions," declares the Sovereign LORD.

*The Gates of the City*

30"These will be the exits of the city: Beginning on the north
side, which is 4,500 cubits long, 31the gates of the city will be
named after the tribes of Israel. The three gates on the north side
will be the gate of Reuben, the gate of Judah and the gate of Levi.

32"On the east side, which is 4,500 cubits long, will be three gates: the gate of Joseph, the gate of Benjamin and the gate of Dan.

33"On the south side, which measures 4,500 cubits, will be three gates: the gate of Simeon, the gate of Issachar and the gate of Zebulun.

34"On the west side, which is 4,500 cubits long, will be three gates: the gate of Gad, the gate of Asher and the gate of Naphtali.

35"The distance all around will be 18,000 cubits.

"And the name of the city from that time on will be:

THE LORD IS THERE."

NIV [a] *28* That is, the Mediterranean

## King James

THE BOOK OF

# Daniel

1 IN THE third year of the reign of Jehoiakim king of Judah came Nebuchadnezzar king of Babylon unto Jerusalem, and besieged it.

2 And the Lord gave Jehoiakim king of Judah into his hand, with part of the vessels of the house of God: which he carried into the land of Shinar to the house of his god; and he brought the vessels into the treasure house of his god.

3 ¶ And the king spake unto Ashpenaz the master of his eunuchs, that he should bring *certain* of the children of Israel, and of the king's seed, and of the princes;

4 Children in whom *was* no blemish, but wellfavoured, and skilful in all wisdom, and cunning in knowledge, and understanding science, and such as *had* ability in them to stand in the king's palace, and whom they might teach the learning and the tongue of the Chaldeans.

5 And the king appointed them a daily provision of the king's meat, and of the wine which he drank: so nourishing them three years, that at the end thereof they might stand before the king.

6 Now among these were of the children of Judah, Daniel, Hananiah, Mishael, and Azariah:

7 Unto whom the prince of the eunuchs gave names: for he gave unto Daniel *the name* of Belteshazzar; and to Hananiah, of Shadrach; and to Mishael, of Meshach; and to Azariah, of Abed-nego.

8 ¶ But Daniel purposed in his heart that he would not defile himself with the portion of the king's meat, nor with the wine which he drank: therefore he requested of the prince of the eunuchs that he might not defile himself.

9 Now God had brought Daniel into favour and tender love with the prince of the eunuchs.

10 And the prince of the eunuchs said unto Daniel, I fear my lord the king, who hath appointed your meat and your drink: for why should he see your faces worse liking than the children which *are* of your sort? then shall ye make *me* endanger my head to the king.

11 Then said Daniel to Melzar, whom the prince of the eunuchs had set over Daniel, Hananiah, Mishael, and Azariah,

12 Prove thy servants, I beseech thee, ten days; and let them give us pulse to eat, and water to drink.

13 Then let our countenances be looked upon before thee, and the countenance of the children that eat of the portion of the king's meat: and as thou seest, deal with thy servants.

14 So he consented to them in this matter, and proved them ten days.

15 And at the end of ten days their countenances appeared fairer and fatter in flesh than all the children which did eat the portion of the king's meat.

## Amplified

THE BOOK OF

# Daniel

1 IN THE third year of the reign of Jehoiakim king of Judah, Nebuchadnezzar king of Babylon came to Jerusalem and besieged it.

2 And the Lord gave Jehoiakim king of Judah into his hand, with a part of the vessels of the house of God; and he carried them into the land of Shinar [Babylonia] to the house of his god, and placed the vessels in the treasury of his god. [II Chron. 36:5-7; Jer. 27:19, 20; Dan. 5:1-3.]

3 And the [Babylonian] king told Ashpenaz, the master of his eunuchs, to bring in some of the children of Israel, both of the royal family and of the nobility, [II Kings 20:17, 18.]

4 Youths without blemish, well-favored in appearance and skillful in all wisdom, discernment *and* understanding, apt in learning knowledge, competent to stand *and* serve in the king's palace, and to teach them the literature and language of the Chaldeans.

5 And the king assigned for them a daily portion of his own rich *and* dainty food and of the wine which he drank. They were to be so educated *and* so nourished for three years, that at the end of that time they might stand before the king.

6 Among these were of the children of Judah, Daniel, Hananiah, Mishael, and Azariah.

7 The chief of the eunuchs gave them names: Daniel he called Belteshazzar [the king's attendant], Hananiah he called Shadrach, Mishael he called Meshach, and Azariah he called Abednego.

8 But Daniel determined in his heart that he would not defile himself by [eating his portion of] the king's rich *and* dainty food or with the wine which he drank; therefore he requested of the chief of the eunuchs that he might *be allowed* not to defile himself. [See Num. 6:1-4; I Cor. 10:21.]

9 Now God made Daniel to find favor, compassion *and* lovingkindness with the chief of the eunuchs.

10 And the chief of the eunuchs said to Daniel, I fear lest my lord the king, who has appointed your food and your drink, should see your faces worse looking *or* more sad than the other youths of your age. Then you would endanger my head with the king.

11 Then said Daniel to the steward whom the chief of the eunuchs had set over Daniel, Hananiah, Mishael and Azariah,

12 Prove your servants, I beseech you, for ten days and let us be given a vegetable diet and water to drink.

13 Then let our appearance and the appearance of the youths who eat of the king's *rich* dainties be observed *and* compared by you, and deal with us your servants according to what you see.

14 So [the man] consented to them in this matter and proved them ten days.

15 And at the end of ten days it was seen that they were looking better and had taken on more flesh than all the youths who ate of the king's rich dainties.

## New American Standard

# Daniel

*The Choice Young Men*

**1** IN THE third year of the reign of Jehoiakim king of Judah, Nebuchadnezzar king of Babylon came to Jerusalem and besieged it.

2And the Lord gave Jehoiakim king of Judah into his hand, along with some of the vessels of the house of God; and he brought them to the land of Shinar, to the house of his [a]god, and he brought the vessels into the treasury of his [b]god.

3Then the king ordered Ashpenaz, the chief of his [c]officials, to bring in some of the sons of Israel, including some of the royal family and of the nobles,

4youths in whom was no defect, who were good-looking, showing intelligence in every *branch of* wisdom, endowed with understanding, and discerning knowledge, and who had ability for serving in the king's court; and *he ordered him* to teach them the [d]literature and language of the Chaldeans.

5And the king appointed for them a daily ration from the king's choice food and from the wine which he drank, and *appointed* that they should be educated three years, at the end of which they were to enter the king's personal service.

6Now among them from the sons of Judah were Daniel, Hananiah, Mishael and Azariah.

7Then the commander of the officials assigned *new* names to them; and to Daniel he assigned *the name* Belteshazzar, to Hananiah Shadrach, to Mishael Meshach, and to Azariah Abed-nego.

*Daniel's Resolve*

8¶ But Daniel made up his mind that he would not defile himself with the king's choice food or with the wine which he drank; so he sought *permission* from the commander of the officials that he might not defile himself.

9Now God granted Daniel favor and compassion in the sight of the commander of the officials,

10and the commander of the officials said to Daniel, "I am afraid of my lord the king, who has appointed your food and your drink; for why should he see your faces looking more haggard than the youths who are your own age? Then you would make me forfeit my head to the king."

11But Daniel said to the overseer whom the commander of the officials had appointed over Daniel, Hananiah, Mishael and Azariah,

12"Please test your servants for ten days, and let us be given some vegetables to eat and water to drink.

13"Then let our appearance be observed in your presence, and the appearance of the youths who are eating the king's choice food; and deal with your servants according to what you see."

14¶ So he listened to them in this matter and tested them for ten days.

15And at the end of ten days their appearance seemed better and they were fatter than all the youths who had been eating the king's choice food.

**NAS** [a]Or, *gods* [b]Or, *gods* [c]Or, *eunuchs,* and so throughout the ch. [d]Or, *writing*

## New International

# Daniel

*Daniel's Training in Babylon*

**1** IN THE third year of the reign of Jehoiakim king of Judah, Nebuchadnezzar king of Babylon came to Jerusalem and besieged it. 2And the Lord delivered Jehoiakim king of Judah into his hand, along with some of the articles from the temple of God. These he carried off to the temple of his god in Babylonia[e] and put in the treasure house of his god.

3Then the king ordered Ashpenaz, chief of his court officials, to bring in some of the Israelites from the royal family and the nobility— 4young men without any physical defect, handsome, showing aptitude for every kind of learning, well informed, quick to understand, and qualified to serve in the king's palace. He was to teach them the language and literature of the Babylonians.[f] 5The king assigned them a daily amount of food and wine from the king's table. They were to be trained for three years, and after that they were to enter the king's service.

6Among these were some from Judah: Daniel, Hananiah, Mishael and Azariah. 7The chief official gave them new names: to Daniel, the name Belteshazzar; to Hananiah, Shadrach; to Mishael, Meshach; and to Azariah, Abednego.

8But Daniel resolved not to defile himself with the royal food and wine, and he asked the chief official for permission not to defile himself this way. 9Now God had caused the official to show favor and sympathy to Daniel, 10but the official told Daniel, "I am afraid of my lord the king, who has assigned your[g] food and drink. Why should he see you looking worse than the other young men your age? The king would then have my head because of you."

11Daniel then said to the guard whom the chief official had appointed over Daniel, Hananiah, Mishael and Azariah, 12"Please test your servants for ten days: Give us nothing but vegetables to eat and water to drink. 13Then compare our appearance with that of the young men who eat the royal food, and treat your servants in accordance with what you see." 14So he agreed to this and tested them for ten days.

15At the end of the ten days they looked healthier and better nourished than any of the young men who ate the royal food. 16So

**NIV** [e] 2 Hebrew *Shinar* [f] 4 Or *Chaldeans* [g] 10 The Hebrew for *your* and *you* in this verse is plural.

## King James

16 Thus Melzar took away the portion of their meat, and the wine that they should drink; and gave them pulse.

17¶ As for these four children, God gave them knowledge and skill in all learning and wisdom: and Daniel had understanding in all visions and dreams.

18 Now at the end of the days that the king had said he should bring them in, then the prince of the eunuchs brought them in before Nebuchadnezzar.

19 And the king communed with them; and among them all was found none like Daniel, Hananiah, Mishael, and Azariah: therefore stood they before the king.

20 And in all matters of wisdom *and* understanding, that the king inquired of them, he found them ten times better than all the magicians *and* astrologers that *were* in all his realm.

21 And Daniel continued *even* unto the first year of king Cyrus.

**2** AND IN the second year of the reign of Nebuchadnezzar, Nebuchadnezzar dreamed dreams, wherewith his spirit was troubled, and his sleep brake from him.

2 Then the king commanded to call the magicians, and the astrologers, and the sorcerers, and the Chaldeans, for to show the king his dreams. So they came and stood before the king.

3 And the king said unto them, I have dreamed a dream, and my spirit was troubled to know the dream.

4 Then spake the Chaldeans to the king in Syriac, O king, live for ever: tell thy servants the dream, and we will show the interpretation.

5 The king answered and said to the Chaldeans, The thing is gone from me: if ye will not make known unto me the dream, with the interpretation thereof, ye shall be cut in pieces, and your houses shall be made a dunghill.

6 But if ye show the dream, and the interpretation thereof, ye shall receive of me gifts and rewards and great honour: therefore show me the dream, and the interpretation thereof.

7 They answered again and said, Let the king tell his servants the dream, and we will show the interpretation of it.

8 The king answered and said, I know of certainty that ye would gain the time, because ye see the thing is gone from me.

9 But if ye will not make known unto me the dream, *there is but* one decree for you: for ye have prepared lying and corrupt words to speak before me, till the time be changed: therefore tell me the dream, and I shall know that ye can show me the interpretation thereof.

10¶ The Chaldeans answered before the king, and said, There is not a man upon the earth that can show the king's matter: therefore *there is* no king, lord, nor ruler, *that* asked such things at any magician, or astrologer, or Chaldean.

11 And *it is* a rare thing that the king requireth, and there is none other that can show it before the king, except the gods, whose dwelling is not with flesh.

12 For this cause the king was angry and very furious, and commanded to destroy all the wise *men* of Babylon.

13 And the decree went forth that the wise *men* should be slain; and they sought Daniel and his fellows to be slain.

14¶ Then Daniel answered with counsel and wisdom to Arioch the captain of the king's guard, which was gone forth to slay the wise *men* of Babylon:

15 He answered and said to Arioch the king's captain, Why *is* the decree *so* hasty from the king? Then Arioch made the thing known to Daniel.

## Amplified

16 So the steward took away their *rich* dainties, and the wine they were to drink, and gave them vegetables.

17 As for these four youths, God gave them knowledge and skill in all learning and wisdom; and Daniel had understanding in all visions and dreams. [Luke 21:15; James 1:5-7.]

18 Now at the end of the time which the king had set for bringing [all the young men in], the chief of the eunuchs brought them before Nebuchadnezzar.

19 And the king conversed with them, and among them all none was found like Daniel, Hananiah, Mishael, and Azariah; therefore they were assigned to stand before the king.

20 And in all matters of wisdom and understanding concerning which the king asked them, he found them ten times better than all the [learned] magicians and enchanters that were in his whole realm.

21 And Daniel continued there even to the first year of King Cyrus [at the close of the seventy years' exile of Judah in Babylonia, which Jeremiah had foretold]. [Jer. 25:11, 12; 29:10; Ezra 1:1-3.]

**2** IN THE second year of the reign of Nebuchadnezzar, Nebuchadnezzar had dreams, by which his spirit was troubled *and* agitated and his sleep went from him.

2 Then the king commanded to call the magicians and the enchanters *or* soothsayers, and the sorcerers and Chaldean [diviners] to tell the king his dreams. So they came and stood before the king.

3 And the king said to them, I had a dream, and my spirit is troubled to know the dream.

4 Then said the Chaldean [diviners] to the king in Aramaic [the Syrian language], O king, live for ever! Tell your servants the dream, and we will show the interpretation.

5 The king answered the Chaldeans, The thing is gone from me! And the decree goes forth from me *and* I say it with all emphasis, that if you do not make known to me the dream with its interpretation, you shall be cut in pieces, and your houses shall be made a dunghill!

6 But if you show the dream and its interpretation, you shall receive from me gifts and rewards and great honor. So show me the dream and the interpretation of it.

7 They answered again, Let the king tell his servants the dream, and we will show the interpretation of it.

8 The king answered, I know with certainty that you are trying to gain time, because you see the thing is gone from me *and* because you see that my word [against you] is sure

9 That if you will not make known to me the dream, there is but one sentence for you; for you have prepared lying and corrupt words to speak before me, [hoping to delay your execution] until the time be changed. Therefore tell me the dream, and I shall know that you can tell me the interpretation of it.

10 The Chaldean [diviners] answered before the king, and said, There is not a man on earth who can show the king this matter; for no king, lord, or ruler has *ever* asked such a thing of any magician or enchanter or Chaldean.

11 A rare *and* weighty thing indeed the king requires! None except the gods can reveal it to the king, and their dwelling is not with [human] flesh.

12 For this cause the king was angry and very furious, and commanded that all the wise men of Babylon be destroyed.

13 So the decree went forth that the wise men were to be killed, and [the officers] sought Daniel and his companions to be slain.

14 Then Daniel returned an answer which was full of prudence and wisdom to Arioch the captain *or* executioner of the king's guard, who had gone forth to slay the wise men of Babylon.

15 He said to Arioch, the king's captain, Why is the decree so urgent *and* hasty from the king? Then Arioch explained the matter to Daniel.

## New American Standard

16So the overseer continued to withhold their choice food and the wine they were to drink, and kept giving them vegetables.

17¶ And as for these four youths, God gave them knowledge and intelligence in every *branch of* literature and wisdom; Daniel even understood all *kinds of* visions and dreams.

18Then at the end of the days which the king had specified for presenting them, the commander of the officials presented them before Nebuchadnezzar.

19And the king talked with them, and out of them all not one was found like Daniel, Hananiah, Mishael and Azariah; so they entered the king's personal service.

20And as for every matter of wisdom and understanding about which the king consulted them, he found them ten times better than all the magicians *and* conjurers who *were* in all his realm.

21And Daniel continued until the first year of Cyrus the king.

*The King's Forgotten Dream*

**2** NOW IN the second year of the reign of Nebuchadnezzar, Nebuchadnezzar had dreams; and his spirit was troubled and his sleep left him.

2Then the king gave orders to call in the [a]magicians, the conjurers, the sorcerers and the [b]Chaldeans, to tell the king his dreams. So they came in and stood before the king.

3And the king said to them, "I had a dream, and my spirit is anxious to understand the dream."

4¶ Then the Chaldeans spoke to the king in Aramaic: "O king, live forever! Tell the dream to your servants, and we will declare the interpretation."

5The king answered and said to the Chaldeans, "The command from me is firm: if you do not make known to me the dream and its interpretation, you will be torn limb from limb, and your houses will be made a rubbish heap.

6"But if you declare the dream and its interpretation, you will receive from me gifts and a reward and great honor; therefore declare to me the dream and its interpretation."

7They answered a second time and said, "Let the king tell the dream to his servants, and we will declare the interpretation."

8The king answered and said, "I know for certain that you are bargaining for time, inasmuch as you have seen that the command from me is firm,

9that if you do not make the dream known to me, there is only one decree for you. For you have agreed together to speak lying and corrupt words before me until the situation is changed; therefore tell me the dream, that I may know that you can declare to me its interpretation."

10The Chaldeans answered the king and said, "There is not a man on earth who could declare the matter for the king, inasmuch as no great king or ruler has *ever* asked anything like this of any magician, conjurer or Chaldean.

11"Moreover, the thing which the king demands is difficult, and there is no one else who could declare it to the king except gods, whose dwelling place is not with *mortal* flesh."

12Because of this the king became indignant and very furious, and gave orders to destroy all the wise men of Babylon.

13So the decree went forth that the wise men should be slain; and they looked for Daniel and his friends to kill *them*.

14¶ Then Daniel replied with discretion and discernment to Arioch, the captain of the king's bodyguard, who had gone forth to slay the wise men of Babylon;

15he answered and said to Arioch, the king's commander, "For what reason is the decree from the king *so* urgent?" Then Arioch informed Daniel about the matter.

**NAS** [a] Or, *soothsayer priests* [b] Or, *master astrologers,* and so throughout this context

## New International

the guard took away their choice food and the wine they were to drink and gave them vegetables instead.

17To these four young men God gave knowledge and understanding of all kinds of literature and learning. And Daniel could understand visions and dreams of all kinds.

18At the end of the time set by the king to bring them in, the chief official presented them to Nebuchadnezzar. 19The king talked with them, and he found none equal to Daniel, Hananiah, Mishael and Azariah; so they entered the king's service. 20In every matter of wisdom and understanding about which the king questioned them, he found them ten times better than all the magicians and enchanters in his whole kingdom.

21And Daniel remained there until the first year of King Cyrus.

*Nebuchadnezzar's Dream*

**2** IN THE second year of his reign, Nebuchadnezzar had dreams; his mind was troubled and he could not sleep. 2So the king summoned the magicians, enchanters, sorcerers and astrologers[c] to tell him what he had dreamed. When they came in and stood before the king, 3he said to them, "I have had a dream that troubles me and I want to know what it means.[d]"

4Then the astrologers answered the king in Aramaic,[e] "O king, live forever! Tell your servants the dream, and we will interpret it."

5The king replied to the astrologers, "This is what I have firmly decided: If you do not tell me what my dream was and interpret it, I will have you cut into pieces and your houses turned into piles of rubble. 6But if you tell me the dream and explain it, you will receive from me gifts and rewards and great honor. So tell me the dream and interpret it for me."

7Once more they replied, "Let the king tell his servants the dream, and we will interpret it."

8Then the king answered, "I am certain that you are trying to gain time, because you realize that this is what I have firmly decided: 9If you do not tell me the dream, there is just one penalty for you. You have conspired to tell me misleading and wicked things, hoping the situation will change. So then, tell me the dream, and I will know that you can interpret it for me."

10The astrologers answered the king, "There is not a man on earth who can do what the king asks! No king, however great and mighty, has ever asked such a thing of any magician or enchanter or astrologer. 11What the king asks is too difficult. No one can reveal it to the king except the gods, and they do not live among men."

12This made the king so angry and furious that he ordered the execution of all the wise men of Babylon. 13So the decree was issued to put the wise men to death, and men were sent to look for Daniel and his friends to put them to death.

14When Arioch, the commander of the king's guard, had gone out to put to death the wise men of Babylon, Daniel spoke to him with wisdom and tact. 15He asked the king's officer, "Why did the king issue such a harsh decree?" Arioch then explained the matter

**NIV** [c] 2 Or *Chaldeans;* also in verses 4, 5 and 10 [d] 3 Or *was* [e] 4 The text from here through chapter 7 is in Aramaic.

## King James

16 Then Daniel went in, and desired of the king that he would give him time, and that he would show the king the interpretation.

17 Then Daniel went to his house, and made the thing known to Hananiah, Mishael, and Azariah, his companions:

18 That they would desire mercies of the God of heaven concerning this secret; that Daniel and his fellows should not perish with the rest of the wise *men* of Babylon.

19 ¶ Then was the secret revealed unto Daniel in a night vision. Then Daniel blessed the God of heaven.

20 Daniel answered and said, Blessed be the name of God for ever and ever: for wisdom and might are his:

21 And he changeth the times and the seasons: he removeth kings, and setteth up kings: he giveth wisdom unto the wise, and knowledge to them that know understanding:

22 He revealeth the deep and secret things: he knoweth what *is* in the darkness, and the light dwelleth with him.

23 I thank thee, and praise thee, O thou God of my fathers, who hast given me wisdom and might, and hast made known unto me now what we desired of thee: for thou hast *now* made known unto us the king's matter.

24 ¶ Therefore Daniel went in unto Arioch, whom the king had ordained to destroy the wise *men* of Babylon: he went and said thus unto him; Destroy not the wise *men* of Babylon: bring me in before the king, and I will show unto the king the interpretation.

25 Then Arioch brought in Daniel before the king in haste, and said thus unto him, I have found a man of the captives of Judah, that will make known unto the king the interpretation.

26 The king answered and said to Daniel, whose name *was* Belteshazzar, Art thou able to make known unto me the dream which I have seen, and the interpretation thereof?

27 Daniel answered in the presence of the king, and said, The secret which the king hath demanded cannot the wise *men*, the astrologers, the magicians, the soothsayers, show unto the king;

28 But there is a God in heaven that revealeth secrets, and maketh known to the king Nebuchadnezzar what shall be in the latter days. Thy dream, and the visions of thy head upon thy bed, are these;

29 As for thee, O king, thy thoughts came *into thy mind* upon thy bed, what should come to pass hereafter: and he that revealeth secrets maketh known to thee what shall come to pass.

30 But as for me, this secret is not revealed to me for *any* wisdom that I have more than any living, but for *their* sakes that shall make known the interpretation to the king, and that thou mightest know the thoughts of thy heart.

31 ¶ Thou, O king, sawest, and behold a great image. This great image, whose brightness *was* excellent, stood before thee; and the form thereof *was* terrible.

32 This image's head *was* of fine gold, his breast and his arms of silver, his belly and his thighs of brass,

33 His legs of iron, his feet part of iron and part of clay.

34 Thou sawest till that a stone was cut out without hands, which smote the image upon his feet *that were* of iron and clay, and brake them to pieces.

## Amplified

16 And Daniel went in, and desired of the king that he would set a date *and* give him time, and he would show the king the interpretation.

17 Then Daniel went to his house and made the thing known to Hananiah, Mishael, and Azariah, his companions,

18 So that they would desire *and* request mercies of the God of heaven concerning this secret, that Daniel and his companions with the rest of the wise men of Babylon should not perish.

19 Then the secret was revealed to Daniel in a vision of the night. And Daniel blessed the God of heaven.

20 Daniel answered, Blessed be the name of God for ever and ever! For wisdom and might are His!

21 He changes the times and the seasons, He removes kings and sets up kings, He gives wisdom to the wise and knowledge to those who have understanding! [Dan. 4:35.]

22 He reveals the deep and secret things; He knows what is in the darkness, and the light dwells with Him! [Job 15:8; Ps. 25:14; Matt. 6:6.]

23 I thank You and praise You, O God of my fathers, Who has given me wisdom and might, and has made known to me now what we desired of You; for You have made known to us the solution to the king's problem.

24 Therefore Daniel went to Arioch, whom the king had appointed to destroy the wise men of Babylon; he went and said thus to him, Do not destroy the wise men of Babylon! Bring me in before the king, and I will show to the king the interpretation.

25 Then Arioch brought in Daniel before the king in haste, and said thus to him, I have found a man of the captives of Judah who will make known to the king the interpretation *of his dream.*

26 The king said to Daniel, whose name was Belteshazzar, Are you able to make known to me the dream which I have seen and the interpretation of it?

27 Daniel answered the king, The [mysterious] secret which the king has demanded neither the wise men, enchanters, magicians, nor astrologers can show the king;

28 But there is a God in Heaven Who reveals secrets, and He has made known to King Nebuchadnezzar what it is that shall be in the latter days—at the end of days. Your dream and the visions of your head upon your bed are these:

29 As for you, O king, as you lay upon your bed thoughts came into your mind about what should come to pass hereafter; and He Who reveals secrets was making known to you what shall come to pass.

30 But as for me, this secret is not revealed to me for any wisdom that I have more than any one living, but in order that the interpretation may be made known to the king, and that you may know the thoughts of your heart *and* mind.

31 You, O king, saw, and behold, a great image. This image which was mighty and of exceedingly great brightness, stood before you, and the appearance of it was frightening *and* terrible.

32 As for this [a]image, its head was of fine gold, its breast and its arms of silver, its belly and its thighs of bronze,

33 Its legs of iron, its feet part of iron and part of [burned potter's] clay.

34 As you looked a Stone was cut out without human hands, which smote the image on its feet that were of iron and clay—the burned clay of the potter—and broke them to pieces. [I Pet. 2:3-8.]

**AMP** [a] Daniel's interpretation of Nebuchadnezzar's dream outlines the further history of Gentile world power. The four metals of which the image was made represented four successive empires, each of which would have the power to possess the whole inhabited earth, though each stopped short of that. They were: (1) Babylon, (2) Media-Persia, (3) Greece under Alexander, and (4) Rome. The latter power was divided first into the two legs, corresponding to the Eastern and Western Roman empires, and then (after a very long time apparently) into the ten toes, a confederacy largely of European nations, in the latter days (Dan. 7:24-27).

## New American Standard

16So Daniel went in and requested of the king that he would
give him time, in order that he might declare the interpretation to
the king.
17¶ Then Daniel went to his house and informed his friends,
Hananiah, Mishael and Azariah, about the matter,
18in order that they might request compassion from the God of
heaven concerning this mystery, so that Daniel and his friends
might not be destroyed with the rest of the wise men of Babylon.

*The Secret Is Revealed to Daniel*

19Then the mystery was revealed to Daniel in a night vision.
Then Daniel blessed the God of heaven;
20Daniel answered and said,
"Let the name of God be blessed forever and ever,
For wisdom and power belong to Him.
21 "And it is He who changes the times and the epochs;
He removes kings and establishes kings;
He gives wisdom to wise men,
And knowledge to men of understanding.
22 "It is He who reveals the profound and hidden things;
He knows what is in the darkness,
And the light dwells with Him.
23 "To Thee, O God of my fathers, I give thanks and
praise,
For Thou hast given me wisdom and power;
Even now Thou hast made known to me what we
requested of Thee,
For Thou hast made known to us the king's matter."
24Therefore, Daniel went in to Arioch, whom the king had
appointed to destroy the wise men of Babylon; he went and spoke
to him as follows: "Do not destroy the wise men of Babylon! Take
me into the king's presence, and I will declare the interpretation
to the king."
25¶ Then Arioch hurriedly brought Daniel into the king's presence and spoke to him as follows: "I have found a man among the
exiles from Judah who can make the interpretation known to the
king!"
26The king answered and said to Daniel, whose name was
Belteshazzar, "Are you able to make known to me the dream
which I have seen and its interpretation?"
27Daniel answered before the king and said, "As for the mystery about which the king has inquired, neither wise men, conjurers, magicians, *nor* diviners are able to declare *it* to the king.
28"However, there is a God in heaven who reveals mysteries,
and He has made known to King Nebuchadnezzar what will take
place in the latter days. This was your dream and the visions in
your mind *while* on your bed.
29"As for you, O king, *while* on your bed your thoughts turned
to what would take place in the future; and He who reveals mysteries has made known to you what will take place.
30"But as for me, this mystery has not been revealed to me for
any wisdom residing in me more than *in* any *other* living man, but
for the purpose of making the interpretation known to the king,
and that you may understand the thoughts of your mind.

*The King's Dream*

31¶ "You, O king, were looking and behold, there was a single
great statue; that statue, which was large and of extraordinary
splendor, was standing in front of you, and its appearance was
awesome.
32"The head of that statue *was made* of fine gold, its breast and
its arms of silver, its belly and its thighs of bronze,
33its legs of iron, its feet partly of iron and partly of clay.
34"You continued looking until a stone was cut out without
hands, and it struck the statue on its feet of iron and clay, and
crushed them.

## New International

to Daniel. 16At this, Daniel went in to the king and asked for time,
so that he might interpret the dream for him.
17Then Daniel returned to his house and explained the matter
to his friends Hananiah, Mishael and Azariah. 18He urged them
to plead for mercy from the God of heaven concerning this mystery, so that he and his friends might not be executed with the rest
of the wise men of Babylon. 19During the night the mystery was
revealed to Daniel in a vision. Then Daniel praised the God of
heaven 20and said:

"Praise be to the name of God for ever and ever;
wisdom and power are his.
21He changes times and seasons;
he sets up kings and deposes them.
He gives wisdom to the wise
and knowledge to the discerning.
22He reveals deep and hidden things;
he knows what lies in darkness,
and light dwells with him.
23I thank and praise you, O God of my fathers:
You have given me wisdom and power,
you have made known to me what we asked of you,
you have made known to us the dream of the king."

*Daniel Interprets the Dream*

24Then Daniel went to Arioch, whom the king had appointed
to execute the wise men of Babylon, and said to him, "Do not
execute the wise men of Babylon. Take me to the king, and I will
interpret his dream for him."
25Arioch took Daniel to the king at once and said, "I have found
a man among the exiles from Judah who can tell the king what his
dream means."
26The king asked Daniel (also called Belteshazzar), "Are you
able to tell me what I saw in my dream and interpret it?"
27Daniel replied, "No wise man, enchanter, magician or diviner
can explain to the king the mystery he has asked about, 28but there
is a God in heaven who reveals mysteries. He has shown King
Nebuchadnezzar what will happen in days to come. Your dream
and the visions that passed through your mind as you lay on your
bed are these:
29"As you were lying there, O king, your mind turned to things
to come, and the revealer of mysteries showed you what is going
to happen. 30As for me, this mystery has been revealed to me, not
because I have greater wisdom than other living men, but so that
you, O king, may know the interpretation and that you may understand what went through your mind.
31"You looked, O king, and there before you stood a large
statue—an enormous, dazzling statue, awesome in appearance.
32The head of the statue was made of pure gold, its chest and arms
of silver, its belly and thighs of bronze, 33its legs of iron, its feet
partly of iron and partly of baked clay. 34While you were watching,
a rock was cut out, but not by human hands. It struck the statue
on its feet of iron and clay and smashed them. 35Then the iron, the

# King James

35 Then was the iron, the clay, the brass, the silver, and the gold, broken to pieces together, and became like the chaff of the summer threshingfloors; and the wind carried them away, that no place was found for them: and the stone that smote the image became a great mountain, and filled the whole earth.

36 ¶ This *is* the dream; and we will tell the interpretation thereof before the king.

37 Thou, O king, *art* a king of kings: for the God of heaven hath given thee a kingdom, power, and strength, and glory.

38 And wheresoever the children of men dwell, the beasts of the field and the fowls of the heaven hath he given into thine hand, and hath made thee ruler over them all. Thou *art* this head of gold.

39 And after thee shall arise another kingdom inferior to thee, and another third kingdom of brass, which shall bear rule over all the earth.

40 And the fourth kingdom shall be strong as iron: forasmuch as iron breaketh in pieces and subdueth all *things:* and as iron that breaketh all these, shall it break in pieces and bruise.

41 And whereas thou sawest the feet and toes, part of potters' clay, and part of iron, the kingdom shall be divided; but there shall be in it of the strength of the iron, forasmuch as thou sawest the iron mixed with miry clay.

42 And *as* the toes of the feet *were* part of iron, and part of clay, *so* the kingdom shall be partly strong, and partly broken.

43 And whereas thou sawest iron mixed with miry clay, they shall mingle themselves with the seed of men: but they shall not cleave one to another, even as iron is not mixed with clay.

44 And in the days of these kings shall the God of heaven set up a kingdom, which shall never be destroyed: and the kingdom shall not be left to other people, *but* it shall break in pieces and consume all these kingdoms, and it shall stand for ever.

45 Forasmuch as thou sawest that the stone was cut out of the mountain without hands, and that it brake in pieces the iron, the brass, the clay, the silver, and the gold; the great God hath made known to the king what shall come to pass hereafter: and the dream *is* certain, and the interpretation thereof sure.

46 ¶ Then the king Nebuchadnezzar fell upon his face, and worshipped Daniel, and commanded that they should offer an oblation and sweet odours unto him.

47 The king answered unto Daniel, and said, Of a truth *it is*, that your God *is* a God of gods, and a Lord of kings, and a revealer of secrets, seeing thou couldest reveal this secret.

48 Then the king made Daniel a great man, and gave him many great gifts, and made him ruler over the whole province of Babylon, and chief of the governors over all the wise *men* of Babylon.

49 Then Daniel requested of the king, and he set Shadrach, Meshach, and Abed-nego, over the affairs of the province of Babylon: but Daniel *sat* in the gate of the king.

# Amplified

35 Then was the iron, the [burned potter's] clay, the bronze, the silver, and the gold, broken *and* crushed together and became like the chaff of the summer threshing-floors, and the wind carried them away, so that not a trace of them could be found. And the Stone that smote the image became a great mountain *or* rock and filled the whole earth.

36 This was the dream, and we will tell the interpretation of it to the king.

37 You, O king, are king of the [earthly] kings, to whom the God of heaven has given the kingdom, the power, and the might, and the glory. [Jer. 25:9; 27:6; 28:14.]

38 And wherever the children of men dwell, the beasts of the field and the birds of the heavens He has given into your hand and has made you to rule over them all. You [king of Babylon] are the head of gold.

39 And after you shall arise another kingdom [the Medo-Persian], inferior to *and* earthward from you, and still a third kingdom of bronze [Greece under Alexander the Great], which shall bear rule over all the earth.

40 And the fourth kingdom [Rome] shall be strong as iron, since iron breaks to pieces and subdues all things; and like iron which crushes, it shall break and crush all these. [Dan. 7:7, 23.]

41 And as you saw the feet and toes, part of potters' [burned] clay and part of iron, it shall be a divided kingdom; but there shall be in it some of the firmness *and* strength of iron, just as you saw the iron mixed with miry [earthenware] clay.

42 And as the toes of the feet were part of iron and part of [burned, potter's] clay, so the kingdom shall be partly strong and partly brittle *and* broken.

43 And as you saw the iron mixed with miry *and* earthenware clay, so they shall mingle themselves in the seed of men [in marriage bonds]; but they will not hold together [for two such elements or ideologies can never harmonize], even as iron does not mingle itself with clay.

44 And in the days of these [final ten] kings shall the God of heaven set up a kingdom which shall never be destroyed, nor shall its sovereignty be left to another people, but it shall break *and* crush and consume all these kingdoms, and it shall stand for ever. [Luke 1:31-33; Dan. 7:14-17; Rev. 11:15.]

45 Just as you saw that the Stone was cut out of the mountain without hands, and that it broke in pieces the iron, the bronze, the clay, the silver, and the gold, the great God has made known to the king what shall come to pass hereafter. The dream is certain, and the interpretation of it is sure.

46 Then King Nebuchadnezzar fell on his face, and paid homage to Daniel [as a great prophet of the highest God], and ordered that an offering and incense should be offered up to him [in honor of his God].

47 The king answered Daniel, Of a truth your God is God of gods and Lord of kings, and a revealer of secret mysteries, seeing that you could reveal this secret mystery! [Rev. 19:16; Prov. 3:32.]

48 Then the king made Daniel great, and gave him many great gifts, and made him to rule over the whole province of Babylon, and to be chief governor over all the wise men of Babylon.

49 And Daniel requested of the king, and he appointed Shadrach, Meshach and Abednego over the affairs of the province of Babylon. But Daniel remained in the gate of the king—at the king's court.

## New American Standard

35"Then the iron, the clay, the bronze, the silver and the gold were crushed all at the same time, and became like chaff from the summer threshing floors; and the wind carried them away so that not a trace of them was found. But the stone that struck the statue became a great mountain and filled the whole earth.

*The Interpretation—Babylon the First Kingdom*

36¶ "This *was* the dream; now we shall tell its interpretation before the king.

37"You, O king, are the king of kings, to whom the God of heaven has given the kingdom, the power, the strength, and the glory;

38and wherever the sons of men dwell, *or* the beasts of the field, or the birds of the sky, He has given *them* into your hand and has caused you to rule over them all. You are the head of gold.

*Medo-Persia and Greece*

39"And after you there will arise another kingdom inferior to you, then another third kingdom of bronze, which will rule over all the earth.

*Rome*

40"Then there will be a fourth kingdom as strong as iron; inasmuch as iron crushes and shatters all things, so, like iron that breaks in pieces, it will crush and break all these in pieces.

41"And in that you saw the feet and toes, partly of potter's clay and partly of iron, it will be a divided kingdom; but it will have in it the toughness of iron, inasmuch as you saw the iron mixed with common clay.

42"And *as* the toes of the feet *were* partly of iron and partly of pottery, *so* some of the kingdom will be strong and part of it will be brittle.

43"And in that you saw the iron mixed with common clay, they will combine with one another in the seed of men; but they will not adhere to one another, even as iron does not combine with pottery.

*The Divine Kingdom*

44"And in the days of those kings the God of heaven will set up a kingdom which will never be destroyed, and *that* kingdom will not be left for another people; it will crush and put an end to all these kingdoms, but it will itself endure forever.

45"Inasmuch as you saw that a stone was cut out of the mountain without hands and that it crushed the iron, the bronze, the clay, the silver, and the gold, the great God has made known to the king what will take place in the future; so the dream is true, and its interpretation is trustworthy."

*Daniel Promoted*

46¶ Then King Nebuchadnezzar fell on his face and did homage to Daniel, and gave orders to present to him an offering and fragrant incense.

47The king answered Daniel and said, "Surely your God is a God of gods and a Lord of kings and a revealer of mysteries, since you have been able to reveal this mystery."

48Then the king promoted Daniel and gave him many great gifts, and he made him ruler over the whole province of Babylon and chief prefect over all the wise men of Babylon.

49And Daniel made request of the king, and he appointed Shadrach, Meshach and Abed-nego over the administration of the province of Babylon, while Daniel *was* at the king's court.

## New International

clay, the bronze, the silver and the gold were broken to pieces at the same time and became like chaff on a threshing floor in the summer. The wind swept them away without leaving a trace. But the rock that struck the statue became a huge mountain and filled the whole earth.

36"This was the dream, and now we will interpret it to the king.
37You, O king, are the king of kings. The God of heaven has given you dominion and power and might and glory;
38in your hands he has placed mankind and the beasts of the field and the birds of the air. Wherever they live, he has made you ruler over them all. You are that head of gold.

39"After you, another kingdom will rise, inferior to yours. Next, a third kingdom, one of bronze, will rule over the whole earth.
40Finally, there will be a fourth kingdom, strong as iron—for iron breaks and smashes everything—and as iron breaks things to pieces, so it will crush and break all the others.
41Just as you saw that the feet and toes were partly of baked clay and partly of iron, so this will be a divided kingdom; yet it will have some of the strength of iron in it, even as you saw iron mixed with clay.
42As the toes were partly iron and partly clay, so this kingdom will be partly strong and partly brittle.
43And just as you saw the iron mixed with baked clay, so the people will be a mixture and will not remain united, any more than iron mixes with clay.

44"In the time of those kings, the God of heaven will set up a kingdom that will never be destroyed, nor will it be left to another people. It will crush all those kingdoms and bring them to an end, but it will itself endure forever.
45This is the meaning of the vision of the rock cut out of a mountain, but not by human hands—a rock that broke the iron, the bronze, the clay, the silver and the gold to pieces.

"The great God has shown the king what will take place in the future. The dream is true and the interpretation is trustworthy."

46Then King Nebuchadnezzar fell prostrate before Daniel and paid him honor and ordered that an offering and incense be presented to him.
47The king said to Daniel, "Surely your God is the God of gods and the Lord of kings and a revealer of mysteries, for you were able to reveal this mystery."

48Then the king placed Daniel in a high position and lavished many gifts on him. He made him ruler over the entire province of Babylon and placed him in charge of all its wise men.
49Moreover, at Daniel's request the king appointed Shadrach, Meshach and Abednego administrators over the province of Babylon, while Daniel himself remained at the royal court.

# King James

**3** NEBUCHADNEZZAR THE king made an image of gold, whose height *was* threescore cubits, *and* the breadth thereof six cubits: he set it up in the plain of Dura, in the province of Babylon.

2 Then Nebuchadnezzar the king sent to gather together the princes, the governors, and the captains, the judges, the treasurers, the counsellors, the sheriffs, and all the rulers of the provinces, to come to the dedication of the image which Nebuchadnezzar the king had set up.

3 Then the princes, the governors, and captains, the judges, the treasurers, the counsellors, the sheriffs, and all the rulers of the provinces, were gathered together unto the dedication of the image that Nebuchadnezzar the king had set up; and they stood before the image that Nebuchadnezzar had set up.

4 Then an herald cried aloud, To you it is commanded, O people, nations, and languages,

5 *That* at what time ye hear the sound of the cornet, flute, harp, sackbut, psaltery, dulcimer, and all kinds of music, ye fall down and worship the golden image that Nebuchadnezzar the king hath set up:

6 And whoso falleth not down and worshippeth shall the same hour be cast into the midst of a burning fiery furnace.

7 Therefore at that time, when all the people heard the sound of the cornet, flute, harp, sackbut, psaltery, and all kinds of music, all the people, the nations, and the languages, fell down *and* worshipped the golden image that Nebuchadnezzar the king had set up.

8 ¶ Wherefore at that time certain Chaldeans came near, and accused the Jews.

9 They spake and said to the king Nebuchadnezzar, O king, live for ever.

10 Thou, O king, hast made a decree, that every man that shall hear the sound of the cornet, flute, harp, sackbut, psaltery, and dulcimer, and all kinds of music, shall fall down and worship the golden image:

11 And whoso falleth not down and worshippeth, *that* he should be cast into the midst of a burning fiery furnace.

12 There are certain Jews whom thou hast set over the affairs of the province of Babylon, Shadrach, Meshach, and Abed-nego; these men, O king, have not regarded thee: they serve not thy gods, nor worship the golden image which thou hast set up.

13 ¶ Then Nebuchadnezzar in *his* rage and fury commanded to bring Shadrach, Meshach, and Abed-nego. Then they brought these men before the king.

14 Nebuchadnezzar spake and said unto them, *Is it* true, O Shadrach, Meshach, and Abed-nego, do not ye serve my gods, nor worship the golden image which I have set up?

15 Now if ye be ready that at what time ye hear the sound of the cornet, flute, harp, sackbut, psaltery, and dulcimer, and all kinds of music, ye fall down and worship the image which I have made; *well:* but if ye worship not, ye shall be cast the same hour into the midst of a burning fiery furnace; and who *is* that God that shall deliver you out of my hands?

16 Shadrach, Meshach, and Abed-nego, answered and said to the king, O Nebuchadnezzar, we *are* not careful to answer thee in this matter.

17 If it be *so,* our God whom we serve is able to deliver us from the burning fiery furnace, and he will deliver *us* out of thine hand, O king.

18 But if not, be it known unto thee, O king, that we will not serve thy gods, nor worship the golden image which thou hast set up.

# Amplified

**3** NEBUCHADNEZZAR THE king [caused to be] made an image of gold, whose height was sixty cubits *or* ninety feet and its breadth six cubits *or* nine feet. He set it up on the plain of Dura in the province of Babylon.

2 Then Nebuchadnezzar the king sent to gather together the satraps, the deputies, the governors, the judges *and* chief star-gazers, the treasurers, the counselors, the sheriffs *and* lawyers, and all the chief officials of the provinces to come to the dedication of the image which King Nebuchadnezzar had [caused to be] set up.

3 Then the satraps, the deputies, the governors, the judges *and* chief star-gazers, the treasurers, the counselors, the sheriffs *and* lawyers, and all the chief officials of the provinces were gathered together for the dedication of the image that King Nebuchadnezzar had set up; and they stood before the image that Nebuchadnezzar had set up.

4 Then the herald cried aloud, You are commanded, O peoples, nations, and languages,

5 That when you hear the sound of the horn, pipe, lyre, trigon, harp, dulcimer *or* bagpipe, and every kind of music, you are to fall down and worship the golden image that King Nebuchadnezzar has set up.

6 And whoever does not fall down and worship shall that very hour be cast into the midst of a burning fiery furnace.

7 Therefore, when all the peoples heard the sound of the horn, pipe, lyre, trigon, dulcimer *or* bagpipe, and every kind of music, all the peoples, nations, and languages fell down and worshiped the golden image that King Nebuchadnezzar had set up.

8 Therefore at that time certain *men of* Chaldean *descent* came near, and brought [malicious] accusations against the Jews.

9 They said to King Nebuchadnezzar, O king, live for ever!

10 You, O king, have made a decree that every man who hears the sound of the horn, pipe, lyre, trigon, harp, dulcimer *or* bagpipe, and every kind of music, shall fall down and worship the golden image;

11 And whoever does not fall down and worship shall be cast into the midst of a burning fiery furnace.

12 There are certain Jews whom you have appointed *and* set over the affairs of the province of Babylon, Shadrach, Meshach and Abednego; these men, O king, pay no attention to you; they do not serve your gods or worship the golden image which you have set up.

13 Then Nebuchadnezzar in rage and fury commanded to bring Shadrach, Meshach, and Abednego. And these men were brought before the king.

14 *Then* Nebuchadnezzar said to them, Is it true, O Shadrach, Meshach, and Abednego, that you do not serve my gods, or worship the golden image which I have [caused to be] set up?

15 Now if you are ready when you hear the sound of the horn, pipe, lyre, trigon, harp, dulcimer *or* bagpipe, and every kind of music, to fall down and worship the image which I have made, good. But if you do not worship, you shall be cast at once into the midst of a burning fiery furnace, and who is that god who can deliver you out of my hands?

16 Shadrach, Meshach and Abednego answered the king, O Nebuchadnezzar, it is not necessary for us to answer you on this point.

17 If our God Whom we serve is able to deliver us from the burning fiery furnace, He will deliver us out of your hand, O king.

18 But if not, be it known to you, O king, that we will not serve your gods, or worship the golden image which you have set up! [Job 13:15; Acts 4:19, 20.]

# New American Standard

*The King's Golden Image*

3 NEBUCHADNEZZAR THE king made an image of gold, the
height of which *was* sixty cubits *and* its width six cubits; he set
it up on the plain of Dura in the province of Babylon.
2Then Nebuchadnezzar the king sent *word* to assemble the
satraps, the prefects and the governors, the counselors, the treasurers, the judges, the magistrates and all the rulers of the provinces to come to the dedication of the image that Nebuchadnezzar
the king had set up.
3Then the satraps, the prefects and the governors, the counselors, the treasurers, the judges, the magistrates and all the rulers
of the provinces were assembled for the dedication of the image
that Nebuchadnezzar the king had set up; and they stood before
the image that Nebuchadnezzar had set up.
4Then the herald loudly proclaimed: "To you the command is
given, O peoples, nations and *men of every* language,
5that at the moment you hear the sound of the horn, flute, lyre,
trigon, psaltery, bagpipe, and all kinds of music, you are to fall
down and worship the golden image that Nebuchadnezzar the
king has set up.
6"But whoever does not fall down and worship shall immediately be cast into the midst of a furnace of blazing fire."
7Therefore at that time, when all the peoples heard the sound
of the horn, flute, lyre, trigon, psaltery, bagpipe, and all kinds of
music, all the peoples, nations and *men of every* language fell down
*and* worshiped the golden image that Nebuchadnezzar the king
had set up.

*Worship of the Image Refused*

8¶ For this reason at that time certain Chaldeans came forward
and brought charges against the Jews.
9They responded and said to Nebuchadnezzar the king: "O
king, live forever!
10"You yourself, O king, have made a decree that every man
who hears the sound of the horn, flute, lyre, trigon, psaltery, and
bagpipe, and all kinds of music, is to fall down and worship the
golden image.
11"But whoever does not fall down and worship shall be cast
into the midst of a furnace of blazing fire.
12"There are certain Jews whom you have appointed over the
administration of the province of Babylon, *namely* Shadrach, Meshach and Abed-nego. These men, O king, have disregarded you;
they do not serve your gods or worship the golden image which
you have set up."
13¶ Then Nebuchadnezzar in rage and anger gave orders to
bring Shadrach, Meshach and Abed-nego; then these men were
brought before the king.
14Nebuchadnezzar responded and said to them, "Is it true,
Shadrach, Meshach and Abed-nego, that you do not serve my
gods or worship the golden image that I have set up?
15"Now if you are ready, at the moment you hear the sound of
the horn, flute, lyre, trigon, psaltery, and bagpipe, and all kinds
of music, to fall down and worship the image that I have made,
*very well*. But if you will not worship, you will immediately be cast
into the midst of a furnace of blazing fire; and what god is there
who can deliver you out of my hands?"
16Shadrach, Meshach and Abed-nego answered and said to the
king, "O Nebuchadnezzar, we do not need to give you an answer
concerning this matter.
17"If it be *so*, our God whom we serve is able to deliver us from
the furnace of blazing fire; and He will deliver us out of your hand,
O king.
18"But *even* if *He does* not, let it be known to you, O king, that
we are not going to serve your gods or worship the golden image
that you have set up."

# New International

*The Image of Gold and the Fiery Furnace*

3 KING NEBUCHADNEZZAR made an image of gold, ninety
feet high and nine feet[a] wide, and set it up on the plain of
Dura in the province of Babylon. 2He then summoned the satraps,
prefects, governors, advisers, treasurers, judges, magistrates and
all the other provincial officials to come to the dedication of the
image he had set up. 3So the satraps, prefects, governors, advisers,
treasurers, judges, magistrates and all the other provincial officials
assembled for the dedication of the image that King Nebuchadnezzar had set up, and they stood before it.
4Then the herald loudly proclaimed, "This is what you are
commanded to do, O peoples, nations and men of every language:
5As soon as you hear the sound of the horn, flute, zither, lyre,
harp, pipes and all kinds of music, you must fall down and worship the image of gold that King Nebuchadnezzar has set up.
6Whoever does not fall down and worship will immediately be
thrown into a blazing furnace."
7Therefore, as soon as they heard the sound of the horn, flute,
zither, lyre, harp and all kinds of music, all the peoples, nations
and men of every language fell down and worshiped the image of
gold that King Nebuchadnezzar had set up.
8At this time some astrologers[b] came forward and denounced
the Jews. 9They said to King Nebuchadnezzar, "O king, live forever! 10You have issued a decree, O king, that everyone who hears
the sound of the horn, flute, zither, lyre, harp, pipes and all kinds
of music must fall down and worship the image of gold, 11and that
whoever does not fall down and worship will be thrown into a
blazing furnace. 12But there are some Jews whom you have set
over the affairs of the province of Babylon—Shadrach, Meshach
and Abednego—who pay no attention to you, O king. They
neither serve your gods nor worship the image of gold you have
set up."
13Furious with rage, Nebuchadnezzar summoned Shadrach,
Meshach and Abednego. So these men were brought before the
king, 14and Nebuchadnezzar said to them, "Is it true, Shadrach,
Meshach and Abednego, that you do not serve my gods or worship the image of gold I have set up? 15Now when you hear the
sound of the horn, flute, zither, lyre, harp, pipes and all kinds of
music, if you are ready to fall down and worship the image I made,
very good. But if you do not worship it, you will be thrown
immediately into a blazing furnace. Then what god will be able to
rescue you from my hand?"
16Shadrach, Meshach and Abednego replied to the king, "O
Nebuchadnezzar, we do not need to defend ourselves before you
in this matter. 17If we are thrown into the blazing furnace, the God
we serve is able to save us from it, and he will rescue us from your
hand, O king. 18But even if he does not, we want you to know,
O king, that we will not serve your gods or worship the image of
gold you have set up."

**NIV** [a] *1* Aramaic *sixty cubits high and six cubits wide* (about 27 meters high and 2.7 meters wide) [b] *8* Or *Chaldeans*

## King James

19¶ Then was Nebuchadnezzar full of fury, and the form of his visage was changed against Shadrach, Meshach, and Abed-nego: *therefore* he spake, and commanded that they should heat the furnace one seven times more than it was wont to be heated.

20And he commanded the most mighty men that *were* in his army to bind Shadrach, Meshach, and Abed-nego, *and* to cast *them* into the burning fiery furnace.

21Then these men were bound in their coats, their hosen, and their hats, and their *other* garments, and were cast into the midst of the burning fiery furnace.

22Therefore because the king's commandment was urgent, and the furnace exceeding hot, the flame of the fire slew those men that took up Shadrach, Meshach, and Abed-nego.

23And these three men, Shadrach, Meshach, and Abed-nego, fell down bound into the midst of the burning fiery furnace.

24Then Nebuchadnezzar the king was astonied, and rose up in haste, *and* spake, and said unto his counsellors, Did not we cast three men bound into the midst of the fire? They answered and said unto the king, True, O king.

25He answered and said, Lo, I see four men loose, walking in the midst of the fire, and they have no hurt; and the form of the fourth is like the Son of God.

26¶ Then Nebuchadnezzar came near to the mouth of the burning fiery furnace, *and* spake, and said, Shadrach, Meshach, and Abed-nego, ye servants of the most high God, come forth, and come *hither*. Then Shadrach, Meshach, and Abed-nego, came forth of the midst of the fire.

27And the princes, governors, and captains, and the king's counsellors, being gathered together, saw these men, upon whose bodies the fire had no power, nor was an hair of their head singed, neither were their coats changed, nor the smell of fire had passed on them.

28 *Then* Nebuchadnezzar spake, and said, Blessed *be* the God of Shadrach, Meshach, and Abed-nego, who hath sent his angel, and delivered his servants that trusted in him, and have changed the king's word, and yielded their bodies, that they might not serve nor worship any god, except their own God.

29Therefore I make a decree, That every people, nation, and language, which speak any thing amiss against the God of Shadrach, Meshach, and Abed-nego, shall be cut in pieces, and their houses shall be made a dunghill: because there is no other God that can deliver after this sort.

30Then the king promoted Shadrach, Meshach, and Abed-nego, in the province of Babylon.

4 NEBUCHADNEZZAR THE king, unto all people, nations, and languages, that dwell in all the earth; Peace be multiplied unto you.

2I thought it good to show the signs and wonders that the high God hath wrought toward me.

3How great *are* his signs! and how mighty *are* his wonders! his kingdom *is* an everlasting kingdom, and his dominion *is* from generation to generation.

4¶ I Nebuchadnezzar was at rest in mine house, and flourishing in my palace:

5I saw a dream which made me afraid, and the thoughts upon my bed and the visions of my head troubled me.

6Therefore made I a decree to bring in all the wise *men* of Babylon before me, that they might make known unto me the interpretation of the dream.

## Amplified

19Then Nebuchadnezzar was full of fury, and his facial expression was changed [to antagonism] against Shadrach, Meshach and Abednego. Therefore he commanded that the furnace should be heated seven times hotter than it was usually heated.

20And he commanded the strongest men in his army to bind Shadrach, Meshach and Abednego and to cast them into the burning fiery furnace.

21Then these *three* men were bound in their cloaks, their tunics *or* undergarments, their turbans, and their other clothing, and they were cast into the midst of the burning fiery furnace.

22Therefore because the king's commandment was urgent, and the furnace exceedingly hot, the flame *and* sparks from the fire killed those men who handled Shadrach, Meshach and Abednego.

23And these three men, Shadrach, Meshach and Abednego, fell down bound into the burning fiery furnace.

24Then Nebuchadnezzar the king [saw and was] astounded, and he jumped up and said to his counselors, Did we not cast three men bound into the midst of the fire? They answered, True, O king.

25He answered, Lo, I see four men loose, walking in the midst of the fire, and they are not hurt! And the form of the fourth is like a son of the gods! [Phil. 2:5-8.]

26Then Nebuchadnezzar came near to the mouth of the burning fiery furnace, and said, Shadrach, Meshach and Abednego, you servants of the Most High God, come out and come here. Then Shadrach, Meshach and Abednego came out from the midst of the fire.

27And the satraps, the deputies, the governors, and the king's counselors being gathered together saw these men, that the fire had no power upon their bodies, nor was the hair of their head singed, neither were their garments scorched *or* changed in color *or* condition, nor had even the smell of smoke clung to them.

28Then Nebuchadnezzar said, Blessed be the God of Shadrach, Meshach and Abednego, Who has sent His angel and delivered His servants who believed, trusted in *and* relied on Him! And they set aside the king's command and yielded their bodies, rather than serve or worship any god except their own God.

29Therefore I make a decree that any people, nation, and language that speaks anything amiss against the God of Shadrach, Meshach and Abednego shall be cut in pieces, and their houses shall be made a dunghill; for there is no other God that can deliver in this way!

30Then the king promoted Shadrach, Meshach and Abednego in the province of Babylon.

4 NEBUCHADNEZZAR THE king, to all people, nations, and languages that dwell on all the earth: Peace be multiplied to you!

2It seemed good to me to show the signs and wonders that the Most High God has performed toward me.

3How great are His signs! And how mighty His wonders! His kingdom is an everlasting kingdom, and His dominion is from generation to generation. [Daniel 7:13, 14; Luke 1:31-33.]

4I, Nebuchadnezzar, was at rest in my house and prospering in my palace.

5I had a dream which made me afraid, and the thoughts *and* imaginations and the visions of my head as I lay upon my bed troubled *and* agitated me.

6Therefore I made a decree to bring in all the wise men of Babylon before me, that they might make known to me the interpretation of the dream.

## New American Standard

*Daniel's Friends Protected*

19¶ Then Nebuchadnezzar was filled with wrath, and his facial
expression was altered toward Shadrach, Meshach and Abed-
nego. He answered by giving orders to heat the furnace seven
times more than it was usually heated.
20And he commanded certain valiant warriors who *were* in his
army to tie up Shadrach, Meshach and Abed-nego, in order to cast
*them* into the furnace of blazing fire.
21Then these men were tied up in their trousers, their coats,
their caps and their *other* clothes, and were cast into the midst of
the furnace of blazing fire.
22For this reason, because the king's command *was* urgent and
the furnace had been made extremely hot, the flame of the fire slew
those men who carried up Shadrach, Meshach and Abed-nego.
23But these three men, Shadrach, Meshach and Abed-nego, fell
into the midst of the furnace of blazing fire *still* tied up.
24¶ Then Nebuchadnezzar the king was astounded and stood
up in haste; he responded and said to his high officials, "Was it
not three men we cast bound into the midst of the fire?" They
answered and said to the king, "Certainly, O king."
25He answered and said, "Look! I see four men loosed *and*
walking *about* in the midst of the fire without harm, and the appearance of the fourth is like a son of *the* gods!"
26Then Nebuchadnezzar came near to the door of the furnace
of blazing fire; he responded and said, "Shadrach, Meshach and
Abed-nego, come out, you servants of the Most High God, and
come here!" Then Shadrach, Meshach and Abed-nego came out of
the midst of the fire.
27And the satraps, the prefects, the governors and the king's
high officials gathered around *and* saw in regard to these men that
the fire had no effect on the bodies of these men nor was the hair
of their head singed, nor were their trousers damaged, nor had the
smell of fire *even* come upon them.
28¶ Nebuchadnezzar responded and said, "Blessed be the God
of Shadrach, Meshach and Abed-nego, who has sent His angel and
delivered His servants who put their trust in Him, violating the
king's command, and yielded up their bodies so as not to serve or
worship any god except their own God.
29"Therefore, I make a decree that any people, nation or tongue
that speaks anything offensive against the God of Shadrach, Meshach and Abed-nego shall be torn limb from limb and their houses
reduced to a rubbish heap, inasmuch as there is no other god who
is able to deliver in this way."
30Then the king caused Shadrach, Meshach and Abed-nego to
prosper in the province of Babylon.

*The King Acknowledges God*

**4** NEBUCHADNEZZAR THE king to all the peoples, nations,
and *men of every* language that live in all the earth: "May your
peace abound!
2"It has seemed good to me to declare the signs and wonders
which the Most High God has done for me.

3 "How great are His signs,
And how mighty are His wonders!
His kingdom is an everlasting kingdom,
And His dominion is from generation to generation.

*The Vision of a Great Tree*

4¶ "I, Nebuchadnezzar, was at ease in my house and flourishing in my palace.
5"I saw a dream and it made me fearful; and *these* fantasies *as
I lay* on my bed and the visions in my mind kept alarming me.
6"So I gave orders to bring into my presence all the wise men
of Babylon, that they might make known to me the interpretation
of the dream.

## New International

19Then Nebuchadnezzar was furious with Shadrach, Meshach
and Abednego, and his attitude toward them changed. He ordered
the furnace heated seven times hotter than usual 20and commanded some of the strongest soldiers in his army to tie up Shadrach, Meshach and Abednego and throw them into the blazing
furnace. 21So these men, wearing their robes, trousers, turbans
and other clothes, were bound and thrown into the blazing furnace. 22The king's command was so urgent and the furnace so hot
that the flames of the fire killed the soldiers who took up Shadrach,
Meshach and Abednego, 23and these three men, firmly tied, fell
into the blazing furnace.
24Then King Nebuchadnezzar leaped to his feet in amazement
and asked his advisers, "Weren't there three men that we tied up
and threw into the fire?"
They replied, "Certainly, O king."
25He said, "Look! I see four men walking around in the fire,
unbound and unharmed, and the fourth looks like a son of the
gods."
26Nebuchadnezzar then approached the opening of the blazing
furnace and shouted, "Shadrach, Meshach and Abednego, servants of the Most High God, come out! Come here!"
So Shadrach, Meshach and Abednego came out of the fire,
27and the satraps, prefects, governors and royal advisers crowded
around them. They saw that the fire had not harmed their bodies,
nor was a hair of their heads singed; their robes were not scorched,
and there was no smell of fire on them.
28Then Nebuchadnezzar said, "Praise be to the God of Shadrach, Meshach and Abednego, who has sent his angel and rescued his servants! They trusted in him and defied the king's command and were willing to give up their lives rather than serve or
worship any god except their own God. 29Therefore I decree that
the people of any nation or language who say anything against the
God of Shadrach, Meshach and Abednego be cut into pieces and
their houses be turned into piles of rubble, for no other god can
save in this way."
30Then the king promoted Shadrach, Meshach and Abednego
in the province of Babylon.

*Nebuchadnezzar's Dream of a Tree*

**4** KING NEBUCHADNEZZAR,
To the peoples, nations and men of every language, who
live in all the world:

May you prosper greatly!

2It is my pleasure to tell you about the miraculous signs
and wonders that the Most High God has performed for me.

3How great are his signs,
how mighty his wonders!
His kingdom is an eternal kingdom;
his dominion endures from generation to generation.

4I, Nebuchadnezzar, was at home in my palace, contented
and prosperous. 5I had a dream that made me afraid. As I was
lying in my bed, the images and visions that passed through
my mind terrified me. 6So I commanded that all the wise men
of Babylon be brought before me to interpret the dream for
me. 7When the magicians, enchanters, astrologers[a] and di-

NIV [a] 7 Or *Chaldeans*

## King James

7 Then came in the magicians, the astrologers, the Chaldeans, and the soothsayers: and I told the dream before them; but they did not make known unto me the interpretation thereof.

8 ¶ But at the last Daniel came in before me, whose name *was* Belteshazzar, according to the name of my god, and in whom *is* the spirit of the holy gods: and before him I told the dream, *saying*,

9 O Belteshazzar, master of the magicians, because I know that the spirit of the holy gods *is* in thee, and no secret troubleth thee, tell me the visions of my dream that I have seen, and the interpretation thereof.

10 Thus *were* the visions of mine head in my bed; I saw, and behold a tree in the midst of the earth, and the height thereof *was* great.

11 The tree grew, and was strong, and the height thereof reached unto heaven, and the sight thereof to the end of all the earth:

12 The leaves thereof *were* fair, and the fruit thereof much, and in it *was* meat for all: the beasts of the field had shadow under it, and the fowls of the heaven dwelt in the boughs thereof, and all flesh was fed of it.

13 I saw in the visions of my head upon my bed, and, behold, a watcher and an holy one came down from heaven;

14 He cried aloud, and said thus, Hew down the tree, and cut off his branches, shake off his leaves, and scatter his fruit: let the beasts get away from under it, and the fowls from his branches:

15 Nevertheless leave the stump of his roots in the earth, even with a band of iron and brass, in the tender grass of the field; and let it be wet with the dew of heaven, and *let* his portion *be* with the beasts in the grass of the earth:

16 Let his heart be changed from man's, and let a beast's heart be given unto him; and let seven times pass over him.

17 This matter *is* by the decree of the watchers, and the demand by the word of the holy ones: to the intent that the living may know that the most High ruleth in the kingdom of men, and giveth it to whomsoever he will, and setteth up over it the basest of men.

18 This dream I king Nebuchadnezzar have seen. Now thou, O Belteshazzar, declare the interpretation thereof, forasmuch as all the wise *men* of my kingdom are not able to make known unto me the interpretation: but thou *art* able; for the spirit of the holy gods *is* in thee.

19 ¶ Then Daniel, whose name *was* Belteshazzar, was astonied for one hour, and his thoughts troubled him. The king spake, and said, Belteshazzar, let not the dream, or the interpretation thereof, trouble thee. Belteshazzar answered and said, My lord, the dream *be* to them that hate thee, and the interpretation thereof to thine enemies.

20 The tree that thou sawest, which grew, and was strong, whose height reached unto the heaven, and the sight thereof to all the earth;

21 Whose leaves *were* fair, and the fruit thereof much, and in it *was* meat for all; under which the beasts of the field dwelt, and upon whose branches the fowls of the heaven had their habitation:

22 It *is* thou, O king, that art grown and become strong: for thy greatness is grown, and reacheth unto heaven, and thy dominion to the end of the earth.

## Amplified

7 Then the magicians, the enchanters, the Chaldeans, and the astrologers came in; and I told them the dream, but they could not make known to me the interpretation of it.

8 But at last Daniel came in before me, he who was named Belteshazzar after the name of my god, and in whom is the Spirit of the Holy God, and I told the dream before him, saying,

9 O Belteshazzar, chief of the magicians, because I know that the Spirit of the Holy God is in you, and no secret mystery is a burden *or* troubles you, tell me the visions of my dream that I have seen, and the interpretation of it.

10 The visions of my head [as I lay] on my bed were *these:* I saw, and behold, a tree in the midst of the earth, and its height was great.

11 The tree grew and was strong, and its height reached to the heavens, and the sight of it reached to the end of the whole earth.

12 Its leaves were fair and its fruit abundant, and in it was food for all. The living creatures of the field found shade under it, and the birds of the sky dwelt in its branches, and all flesh was fed from it.

13 I saw in the visions of my head [as I lay] on my bed, and behold, a watcher, a holy one, came down from Heaven.

14 He cried aloud [with might] and said, Hew down the tree and cut off its branches, shake off its leaves and scatter its fruit; let the living creatures flee from under it and the fowls from its branches.

15 Nevertheless leave the stump of its roots in the earth, bound with a band of iron and bronze, in the midst of the tender grass of the field. Let him be wet with the dew of the heavens, and let him share the lot of the living creatures in the grass of the earth;

16 Let his nature *and* understanding be changed from a man's, and let a beast's nature *and* understanding be given him, and let seven times [or years] pass over him.

17 This sentence is by the decree of the [heavenly] watchers, and the decision is by the word of the holy ones, to the intent that the living may know that the Most High [God] rules the kingdom of mankind, and gives it to whomever He will, and sets over it the humblest *and* lowliest of men. [Dan. 2:21; 5:21.]

18 This dream I, King Nebuchadnezzar, have seen. And you, O Belteshazzar [Daniel], declare now its interpretation, since all the wise men of my kingdom are not able to make known to me the interpretation, but you are able, for the Spirit of the Holy God is in you.

19 Then Daniel, whose name was Belteshazzar, was astonished *and* dismayed *and* stricken dumb for a while [concerned about the king's destiny], and his thoughts troubled, agitated *and* alarmed him. The king said, Belteshazzar, let not the dream or its interpretation trouble *or* alarm you. Belteshazzar answered, My lord, may the dream be for those who hate you and its message for your enemies.

20 The tree that you saw, which grew [great] and was strong, whose height reached to the heavens and which was visible to all the earth,

21 Whose foliage was beautiful and its fruit abundant, and on it was food for all; under which the living creatures of the field dwelt, and on whose branches the birds of the sky had their nests—

22 It is you, O king, who have grown and become strong: your greatness has increased and reaches to the heavens, and your dominion to the ends of the earth.

## New American Standard

7"Then the magicians, the conjurers, the Chaldeans, and the
diviners came in, and I related the dream to them; but they could
not make its interpretation known to me.
8"But finally Daniel came in before me, whose name is Belteshazzar according to the name of my god, and in whom is [a]a spirit
of the holy gods; and I related the dream to him, *saying,*
9'O Belteshazzar, chief of the magicians, since I know that a
spirit of the holy gods is in you and no mystery baffles you, tell
*me* the visions of my dream which I have seen, along with its
interpretation.
10'Now *these were* the visions in my mind *as I lay* on my bed: I
was looking, and behold, *there was* a tree in the midst of the earth,
and its height *was* great.

11 'The tree grew large and became strong,
And its height reached to the sky,
And it *was* visible to the end of the whole earth.
12 'Its foliage *was* beautiful and its fruit abundant,
And in it *was* food for all.
The beasts of the field found shade under it,
And the birds of the sky dwelt in its branches,
And all living creatures fed themselves from it.

13¶ 'I was looking in the visions in my mind *as I lay* on my bed,
and behold, an *angelic* watcher, a holy one, descended from
heaven.
14'He shouted out and spoke as follows:
"Chop down the tree and cut off its branches,
Strip off its foliage and scatter its fruit;
Let the beasts flee from under it,
And the birds from its branches.
15 "Yet leave the stump with its roots in the ground,
But with a band of iron and bronze *around it*
In the new grass of the field;
And let him be drenched with the dew of heaven,
And let him share with the beasts in the grass of the
earth.
16 "Let his mind be changed from *that of* a man,
And let a beast's mind be given to him,
And let seven periods of time pass over him.
17 "This sentence is by the decree of the *angelic* watchers,
And the decision is a command of the holy ones,
In order that the living may know
That the Most High is ruler over the realm of mankind,
And bestows it on whom He wishes,
And sets over it the lowliest of men."

18'This is the dream *which* I, King Nebuchadnezzar, have seen.
Now you, Belteshazzar, tell *me* its interpretation, inasmuch as
none of the wise men of my kingdom is able to make known to me
the interpretation; but you are able, for a spirit of the holy gods is
in you.'

*Daniel Interprets the Vision*

19¶ "Then Daniel, whose name is Belteshazzar, was appalled for
a while as his thoughts alarmed him. The king responded and said,
'Belteshazzar, do not let the dream or its interpretation alarm you.'
Belteshazzar answered and said, 'My lord, *if only* the dream applied to those who hate you, and its interpretation to your adversaries!
20'The tree that you saw, which became large and grew strong,
whose height reached to the sky and was visible to all the earth,
21and whose foliage *was* beautiful and its fruit abundant, and
in which *was* food for all, under which the beasts of the field dwelt
and in whose branches the birds of the sky lodged—
22it is you, O king; for you have become great and grown
strong, and your majesty has become great and reached to the sky
and your dominion to the end of the earth.

## New International

viners came, I told them the dream, but they could not interpret it for me. 8Finally, Daniel came into my presence and I
told him the dream. (He is called Belteshazzar, after the name
of my god, and the spirit of the holy gods is in him.)
9I said, "Belteshazzar, chief of the magicians, I know that
the spirit of the holy gods is in you, and no mystery is too
difficult for you. Here is my dream; interpret it for me. 10These
are the visions I saw while lying in my bed: I looked, and there
before me stood a tree in the middle of the land. Its height was
enormous. 11The tree grew large and strong and its top
touched the sky; it was visible to the ends of the earth. 12Its
leaves were beautiful, its fruit abundant, and on it was food
for all. Under it the beasts of the field found shelter, and the
birds of the air lived in its branches; from it every creature was
fed.
13"In the visions I saw while lying in my bed, I looked, and
there before me was a messenger,[b] a holy one, coming down
from heaven. 14He called in a loud voice: 'Cut down the tree
and trim off its branches; strip off its leaves and scatter its
fruit. Let the animals flee from under it and the birds from its
branches. 15But let the stump and its roots, bound with iron
and bronze, remain in the ground, in the grass of the field.
" 'Let him be drenched with the dew of heaven, and let
him live with the animals among the plants of the earth. 16Let
his mind be changed from that of a man and let him be given
the mind of an animal, till seven times[c] pass by for him.
17" 'The decision is announced by messengers, the holy
ones declare the verdict, so that the living may know that the
Most High is sovereign over the kingdoms of men and gives
them to anyone he wishes and sets over them the lowliest of
men.'
18"This is the dream that I, King Nebuchadnezzar, had.
Now, Belteshazzar, tell me what it means, for none of the
wise men in my kingdom can interpret it for me. But you can,
because the spirit of the holy gods is in you."

*Daniel Interprets the Dream*

19Then Daniel (also called Belteshazzar) was greatly perplexed for a time, and his thoughts terrified him. So the king
said, "Belteshazzar, do not let the dream or its meaning alarm
you."
Belteshazzar answered, "My lord, if only the dream applied to your enemies and its meaning to your adversaries!
20The tree you saw, which grew large and strong, with its top
touching the sky, visible to the whole earth, 21with beautiful
leaves and abundant fruit, providing food for all, giving shelter to the beasts of the field, and having nesting places in its
branches for the birds of the air— 22you, O king, are that tree!
You have become great and strong; your greatness has grown
until it reaches the sky, and your dominion extends to distant
parts of the earth.

NAS [a] Or possibly, *the Spirit of the holy God,* and so throughout this context

NIV [b] 13 Or *watchman;* also in verses 17 and 23 [c] 16 Or *years;* also in verses 23, 25 and 32

## King James

23 And whereas the king saw a watcher and an holy one coming
down from heaven, and saying, Hew the tree down, and destroy
it; yet leave the stump of the roots thereof in the earth, even with
a band of iron and brass, in the tender grass of the field; and let
it be wet with the dew of heaven, and *let* his portion *be* with the
beasts of the field, till seven times pass over him;
24 This *is* the interpretation, O king, and this *is* the decree of the
most High, which is come upon my lord the king:
25 That they shall drive thee from men, and thy dwelling shall
be with the beasts of the field, and they shall make thee to eat grass
as oxen, and they shall wet thee with the dew of heaven, and seven
times shall pass over thee, till thou know that the most High ruleth
in the kingdom of men, and giveth it to whomsoever he will.
26 And whereas they commanded to leave the stump of the tree
roots; thy kingdom shall be sure unto thee, after that thou shalt
have known that the heavens do rule.
27 Wherefore, O king, let my counsel be acceptable unto thee,
and break off thy sins by righteousness, and thine iniquities by
showing mercy to the poor; if it may be a lengthening of thy
tranquillity.
28 ¶ All this came upon the king Nebuchadnezzar.
29 At the end of twelve months he walked in the palace of the
kingdom of Babylon.
30 The king spake, and said, Is not this great Babylon, that I have
built for the house of the kingdom by the might of my power, and
for the honour of my majesty?
31 While the word *was* in the king's mouth, there fell a voice from
heaven, *saying*, O king Nebuchadnezzar, to thee it is spoken; The
kingdom is departed from thee.
32 And they shall drive thee from men, and thy dwelling *shall*
*be* with the beasts of the field: they shall make thee to eat grass as
oxen, and seven times shall pass over thee, until thou know that
the most High ruleth in the kingdom of men, and giveth it to
whomsoever he will.
33 The same hour was the thing fulfilled upon Nebuchadnezzar:
and he was driven from men, and did eat grass as oxen, and his
body was wet with the dew of heaven, till his hairs were grown
like eagles' *feathers*, and his nails like birds' *claws*.
34 And at the end of the days I Nebuchadnezzar lifted up mine
eyes unto heaven, and mine understanding returned unto me, and
I blessed the most High, and I praised and honoured him that
liveth for ever, whose dominion *is* an everlasting dominion, and
his kingdom *is* from generation to generation:
35 And all the inhabitants of the earth *are* reputed as nothing:
and he doeth according to his will in the army of heaven, and
*among* the inhabitants of the earth: and none can stay his hand, or
say unto him, What doest thou?
36 At the same time my reason returned unto me; and for the
glory of my kingdom, mine honour and brightness returned unto
me; and my counsellors and my lords sought unto me; and I was
established in my kingdom, and excellent majesty was added unto
me.
37 Now I Nebuchadnezzar praise and extol and honour the King
of heaven, all whose works *are* truth, and his ways judgment: and
those that walk in pride he is able to abase.

**5** BELSHAZZAR THE king made a great feast to a thousand of
his lords, and drank wine before the thousand.

## Amplified

23 And whereas the king saw a watcher, a holy one, coming
down from Heaven, and saying, Cut the tree down and destroy
it, but leave the stump of its roots in the earth with a band of iron
and bronze around it, in the tender grass of the field; and let him
be wet with the dew of the heavens and let his portion be with the
living creatures of the field, until seven times [or years] pass over
him;
24 This is the interpretation, O king: It is the decree of the Most
High [God], which has come upon my lord the king,
25 That you shall be driven from among men, and your dwelling
shall be with the beasts of the field; you shall be made to eat grass
as do the oxen, and you shall be wet with the dew of the heavens,
and seven times [or years] shall pass over you; until you know that
the Most High [God] rules the kingdom of mankind, and gives it
to whomever He will.
26 And as it was commanded to leave the stump of the roots of
the tree, your kingdom shall be sure to you after you have learned
*and* know that [the God of] heaven rules.
27 Therefore, O king, let my counsel be acceptable to you; break
off your sins *and* show the reality of your repentance by righteousness [right standing with God and rightness in every area and
relation], *and* liberate yourself from your iniquities by showing
mercy *and* loving-kindness to the poor *and* oppressed, that [if the
king will repent] there may be possibly a continuance *and* lengthening of your peace *and* tranquility *and* a healing of your error.
28 All this was fulfilled *and* came upon King Nebuchadnezzar.
29 At the end of twelve months he was walking in the royal
palace of Babylon.
30 The king said, Is not this great Babylon, that I have built as
the royal residence *and* seat of government by the might of my
power and for the honor *and* glory of my majesty?
31 While the words *were still* in the king's mouth, there fell a
voice from heaven, saying, O King Nebuchadnezzar, to you it is
spoken: The kingdom has departed from you,
32 And you shall be driven from among men, and your dwelling
will be with the living creatures of the field. You will be made to
eat grass like the oxen, and seven times [or years] shall pass over
you, until you have learned *and* know that the Most High [God]
rules in the kingdom of men and gives it to whomever He will.
33 That very hour the thing was [in process of] being fulfilled
upon Nebuchadnezzar. He was driven from among men, and did
eat grass as oxen [as Daniel had said], and his body was wet with
the dew of the heavens, until his hair grew like eagles' *feathers* and
his nails were like birds' *claws*.
34 And at the end of the days [seven years], I, Nebuchadnezzar,
lifted up my eyes to heaven, and my understanding *and* the right
use of my mind returned to me, and I blessed the Most High [God],
and I praised and honored *and* glorified Him Who lives for ever,
Whose dominion is an everlasting dominion, and His kingdom
endures from generation to generation.
35 And all the inhabitants of the earth are accounted as nothing,
and He does according to His will in the host of heaven and among
the inhabitants of the earth; and none can stay His hand or say to
Him, What are You doing?
36 *Now* at the same time my reason *and* understanding returned
to me; and for the glory of my kingdom, my majesty and splendor
returned to me; and my counselors and my lords sought me, I was
re-established in my kingdom, and still more greatness was added
to me [than before].
37 Now I, Nebuchadnezzar, praise and extol and honor the King
of heaven, all of Whose works are faithful *and* right, and His ways
are just; and those who walk in pride He is able to abase *and*
humble.

**5** BELSHAZZAR THE king [descendant of Nebuchadnezzar]
made a great feast for a thousand of his lords, and he drank
his wine in the presence of the thousand.

## New American Standard

23'And in that the king saw an *angelic* watcher, a holy one,
descending from heaven and saying, "Chop down the tree and
destroy it; yet leave the stump with its roots in the ground, but
with a band of iron and bronze *around it* in the new grass of the
field, and let him be drenched with the dew of heaven, and let him
share with the beasts of the field until seven periods of time pass
over him";
24this is the interpretation, O king, and this is the decree of the
Most High, which has come upon my lord the king:
25that you be driven away from mankind, and your dwelling
place be with the beasts of the field, and you be given grass to eat
like cattle and be drenched with the dew of heaven; and seven
periods of time will pass over you, until you recognize that the
Most High is ruler over the realm of mankind, and bestows it on
whomever He wishes.
26'And in that it was commanded to leave the stump with the
roots of the tree, your kingdom will be assured to you after you
recognize that *it is* Heaven *that* rules.
27'Therefore, O king, may my advice be pleasing to you: break
away now from your sins by *doing* righteousness, and from your
iniquities by showing mercy to *the* poor, in case there may be a
prolonging of your prosperity.'

*The Vision Fulfilled*

**28¶** "All *this* happened to Nebuchadnezzar the king.
29"Twelve months later he was walking on the *roof of* the royal
palace of Babylon.
30"The king reflected and said, 'Is this not Babylon the great,
which I myself have built as a royal residence by the might of my
power and for the glory of my majesty?'
31"While the word *was* in the king's mouth, a voice came from
heaven, *saying*, 'King Nebuchadnezzar, to you it is declared: sovereignty has been removed from you,
32and you will be driven away from mankind, and your dwelling place *will be* with the beasts of the field. You will be given grass
to eat like cattle, and seven periods of time will pass over you, until
you recognize that the Most High is ruler over the realm of mankind, and bestows it on whomever He wishes.'
33"Immediately the word concerning Nebuchadnezzar was fulfilled; and he was driven away from mankind and began eating
grass like cattle, and his body was drenched with the dew of
heaven, until his hair had grown like eagles' *feathers* and his nails
like birds' *claws*.
**34¶** "But at the end of that period I, Nebuchadnezzar, raised my
eyes toward heaven, and my reason returned to me, and I blessed
the Most High and praised and honored Him who lives forever;
For His dominion is an everlasting dominion,
And His kingdom *endures* from generation to
generation.
35 "And all the inhabitants of the earth are accounted as
nothing,
But He does according to His will in the host of heaven
And *among* the inhabitants of earth;
And no one can ward off His hand
Or say to Him, 'What hast Thou done?'
36"At that time my reason returned to me. And my majesty and
splendor were restored to me for the glory of my kingdom, and my
counselors and my nobles began seeking me out; so I was reestablished in my sovereignty, and surpassing greatness was added to
me.
37"Now I Nebuchadnezzar praise, exalt, and honor the King of
heaven, for all His works are true and His ways just, and He is able
to humble those who walk in pride."

*Belshazzar's Feast*

**5** BELSHAZZAR THE king held a great feast for a thousand of
his nobles, and he was drinking wine in the presence of the
thousand.

## New International

23"You, O king, saw a messenger, a holy one, coming
down from heaven and saying, 'Cut down the tree and destroy it, but leave the stump, bound with iron and bronze, in
the grass of the field, while its roots remain in the ground. Let
him be drenched with the dew of heaven; let him live like the
wild animals, until seven times pass by for him.'
24"This is the interpretation, O king, and this is the decree
the Most High has issued against my lord the king: 25You will
be driven away from people and will live with the wild animals; you will eat grass like cattle and be drenched with the
dew of heaven. Seven times will pass by for you until you
acknowledge that the Most High is sovereign over the kingdoms of men and gives them to anyone he wishes. 26The
command to leave the stump of the tree with its roots means
that your kingdom will be restored to you when you acknowledge that Heaven rules. 27Therefore, O king, be pleased to
accept my advice: Renounce your sins by doing what is right,
and your wickedness by being kind to the oppressed. It may
be that then your prosperity will continue."

*The Dream Is Fulfilled*

28All this happened to King Nebuchadnezzar. 29Twelve
months later, as the king was walking on the roof of the royal
palace of Babylon, 30he said, "Is not this the great Babylon I
have built as the royal residence, by my mighty power and for
the glory of my majesty?"
31The words were still on his lips when a voice came from
heaven, "This is what is decreed for you, King Nebuchadnezzar: Your royal authority has been taken from you. 32You will
be driven away from people and will live with the wild animals; you will eat grass like cattle. Seven times will pass by
for you until you acknowledge that the Most High is sovereign over the kingdoms of men and gives them to anyone he
wishes."
33Immediately what had been said about Nebuchadnezzar
was fulfilled. He was driven away from people and ate grass
like cattle. His body was drenched with the dew of heaven
until his hair grew like the feathers of an eagle and his nails
like the claws of a bird.
34At the end of that time, I, Nebuchadnezzar, raised my
eyes toward heaven, and my sanity was restored. Then I
praised the Most High; I honored and glorified him who lives
forever.
His dominion is an eternal dominion;
his kingdom endures from generation to generation.
35All the peoples of the earth
are regarded as nothing.
He does as he pleases
with the powers of heaven
and the peoples of the earth.
No one can hold back his hand
or say to him: "What have you done?"
36At the same time that my sanity was restored, my honor
and splendor were returned to me for the glory of my kingdom. My advisers and nobles sought me out, and I was restored to my throne and became even greater than before.
37Now I, Nebuchadnezzar, praise and exalt and glorify the
King of heaven, because everything he does is right and all
his ways are just. And those who walk in pride he is able to
humble.

*The Writing on the Wall*

**5** KING BELSHAZZAR gave a great banquet for a thousand of
his nobles and drank wine with them. 2While Belshazzar was

## King James

2 Belshazzar, whiles he tasted the wine, commanded to bring the golden and silver vessels which his father Nebuchadnezzar had taken out of the temple which *was* in Jerusalem; that the king, and his princes, his wives, and his concubines, might drink therein.

3 Then they brought the golden vessels that were taken out of the temple of the house of God which *was* at Jerusalem; and the king, and his princes, his wives, and his concubines, drank in them.

4 They drank wine, and praised the gods of gold, and of silver, of brass, of iron, of wood, and of stone.

5 ¶ In the same hour came forth fingers of a man's hand, and wrote over against the candlestick upon the plaster of the wall of the king's palace: and the king saw the part of the hand that wrote.

6 Then the king's countenance was changed, and his thoughts troubled him, so that the joints of his loins were loosed, and his knees smote one against another.

7 The king cried aloud to bring in the astrologers, the Chaldeans, and the soothsayers. *And* the king spake, and said to the wise *men* of Babylon, Whosoever shall read this writing, and show me the interpretation thereof, shall be clothed with scarlet, and *have* a chain of gold about his neck, and shall be the third ruler in the kingdom.

8 Then came in all the king's wise *men:* but they could not read the writing, nor make known to the king the interpretation thereof.

9 Then was king Belshazzar greatly troubled, and his countenance was changed in him, and his lords were astonied.

10 ¶ *Now* the queen, by reason of the words of the king and his lords, came into the banquet house: *and* the queen spake and said, O king, live for ever: let not thy thoughts trouble thee, nor let thy countenance be changed:

11 There is a man in thy kingdom, in whom *is* the spirit of the holy gods; and in the days of thy father light and understanding and wisdom, like the wisdom of the gods, was found in him; whom the king Nebuchadnezzar thy father, the king, *I say*, thy father, made master of the magicians, astrologers, Chaldeans, *and* soothsayers;

12 Forasmuch as an excellent spirit, and knowledge, and understanding, interpreting of dreams, and showing of hard sentences, and dissolving of doubts, were found in the same Daniel, whom the king named Belteshazzar: now let Daniel be called, and he will show the interpretation.

13 Then was Daniel brought in before the king. *And* the king spake and said unto Daniel, *Art* thou that Daniel, which *art* of the children of the captivity of Judah, whom the king my father brought out of Jewry?

14 I have even heard of thee, that the spirit of the gods *is* in thee, and *that* light and understanding and excellent wisdom is found in thee.

15 And now the wise *men,* the astrologers, have been brought in before me, that they should read this writing, and make known unto me the interpretation thereof: but they could not show the interpretation of the thing:

16 And I have heard of thee, that thou canst make interpretations, and dissolve doubts: now if thou canst read the writing, and make known to me the interpretation thereof, thou shalt be clothed with scarlet, and *have* a chain of gold about thy neck, and shalt be the third ruler in the kingdom.

17 ¶ Then Daniel answered and said before the king, Let thy gifts be to thyself, and give thy rewards to another; yet I will read the writing unto the king, and make known to him the interpretation.

18 O thou king, the most high God gave Nebuchadnezzar thy father a kingdom, and majesty, and glory, and honour:

## Amplified

2 Belshazzar, while he was tasting the wine, commanded that the golden and silver vessels which his father Nebuchadnezzar had taken out of the temple which was in Jerusalem be brought, that the king and his lords, his wives and his concubines might drink from them.

3 Then they brought in the gold *and* silver vessels which had been taken out [of the sacred area, the holy place and the holy of holies] of the temple, the house of God which was in Jerusalem; and the king and his lords, his wives and his concubines drank from them.

4 They drank wine, and praised the gods of gold and silver, of bronze, iron, wood, and stone.

5 Immediately *and* suddenly there appeared the fingers of a man's hand and wrote on the plaster of the wall opposite the candlestick [so exposed especially to the light] in the king's palace, and the king saw the part of the hand that wrote.

6 Then the color *and* the [drunken] hilarious brightness of the king's face was changed, and his [terrifying] thoughts troubled *and* alarmed him; the joints *and* muscles of his hips *and* back gave way and his knees smote together.

7 The king cried aloud [mightily] to bring in the enchanters *or* soothsayers, the Chaldean [diviners], and the astrologers. The king said to the wise men of Babylon, Whoever will read this writing and show me the interpretation of it, shall be clothed with purple, and have a chain of gold put about his neck, and shall be the third ruler in the kingdom.

8 And all the king's wise men came in, but they could not read the writing or make known to the king the interpretation of it.

9 Then King Belshazzar was greatly perplexed *and* alarmed, and the color faded from his face, and his lords were puzzled *and* astounded.

10 *Now* the queen [mother] because of overhearing the exciting words of the king and his lords came into the banquet house. The queen [mother] said, O king, live for ever! Do not be alarmed at your thoughts or let your cheerful expression *and* the color of your face be changed.

11 There is a man in your kingdom, in whom is the Spirit of the holy God [or gods], and in the days of your father light and understanding and wisdom, like the wisdom of the gods, were found in him; and King Nebuchadnezzar, your father—the king, I say, your father—appointed him master of the magicians, enchanters *or* soothsayers, Chaldeans, and astrologers;

12 Because an excellent spirit, knowledge, and understanding to interpret dreams, clarify riddles, and solve knotty problems were found in this same Daniel, whom the king named Belteshazzar. Now let Daniel be called, and he will show the interpretation.

13 Then Daniel was brought in before the king. And the king said to Daniel, Are you that Daniel of the children of the captivity of Judah, whom the king my father brought out of Judah?

14 I have heard of you, that the Spirit of the holy God [or gods] is in you, and that light and understanding and superior wisdom are found in you.

15 Now the wise men, the enchanters, have been brought in before me that they might read this writing and make known to me the interpretation of it; but they could not show the interpretation of the matter.

16 But I have heard of you, that you can make interpretations and solve knotty problems. Now if you can read the writing and make known to me its interpretation, you shall be clothed with purple, and have a chain of gold put around your neck, and shall be the third ruler in the kingdom.

17 Then Daniel answered before the king, Let your gifts be for yourself, and give your rewards to another. However, I will read the writing to the king and make known to him the interpretation.

18 O king, the Most High God gave Nebuchadnezzar your father a kingdom and greatness and glory and majesty;

## New American Standard

2When Belshazzar tasted the wine, he gave orders to bring the gold and silver vessels which Nebuchadnezzar his father had taken out of the temple which *was* in Jerusalem, in order that the king and his nobles, his wives, and his concubines might drink from them.

3Then they brought the gold vessels that had been taken out of the temple, the house of God which *was* in Jerusalem; and the king and his nobles, his wives, and his concubines drank from them.

4They drank the wine and praised the gods of gold and silver, of bronze, iron, wood, and stone.

**5**¶ Suddenly the fingers of a man's hand emerged and began writing opposite the lampstand on the plaster of the wall of the king's palace, and the king saw the back of the hand that did the writing.

6Then the king's face grew pale, and his thoughts alarmed him; and his hip joints went slack, and his knees began knocking together.

7The king called aloud to bring in the conjurers, the Chaldeans and the diviners. The king spoke and said to the wise men of Babylon, "Any man who can read this inscription and explain its interpretation to me will be clothed with purple, and *have* a necklace of gold around his neck, and have authority as third *ruler* in the kingdom."

8Then all the king's wise men came in, but they could not read the inscription or make known its interpretation to the king.

9Then King Belshazzar was greatly alarmed, his face grew *even* paler, and his nobles were perplexed.

**10**¶ The queen entered the banquet hall because of the words of the king and his nobles; the queen spoke and said, "O king, live forever! Do not let your thoughts alarm you or your face be pale.

11"There is a man in your kingdom in whom is a spirit of the holy gods; and in the days of your father, illumination, insight, and wisdom like the wisdom of the gods were found in him. And King Nebuchadnezzar, your father, your father the king, appointed him chief of the magicians, conjurers, Chaldeans, *and* diviners.

12" *This was* because an extraordinary spirit, knowledge and insight, interpretation of dreams, explanation of enigmas, and solving of difficult problems were found in this Daniel, whom the king named Belteshazzar. Let Daniel now be summoned, and he will declare the interpretation."

*Daniel Interprets Handwriting on the Wall*

**13**¶ Then Daniel was brought in before the king. The king spoke and said to Daniel, "Are you that Daniel who is one of the exiles from Judah, whom my father the king brought from Judah?

14"Now I have heard about you that a spirit of the gods is in you, and that illumination, insight, and extraordinary wisdom have been found in you.

15"Just now the wise men *and* the conjurers were brought in before me that they might read this inscription and make its interpretation known to me, but they could not declare the interpretation of the message.

16"But I personally have heard about you, that you are able to give interpretations and solve difficult problems. Now if you are able to read the inscription and make its interpretation known to me, you will be clothed with purple and *wear* a necklace of gold around your neck, and you will have authority as the third *ruler* in the kingdom."

**17**¶ Then Daniel answered and said before the king, "Keep your gifts for yourself, or give your rewards to someone else; however, I will read the inscription to the king and make the interpretation known to him.

18"O king, the Most High God granted sovereignty, grandeur, glory, and majesty to Nebuchadnezzar your father.

## New International

drinking his wine, he gave orders to bring in the gold and silver
goblets that Nebuchadnezzar his father[a] had taken from the temple in Jerusalem, so that the king and his nobles, his wives and his
concubines might drink from them. 3So they brought in the gold
goblets that had been taken from the temple of God in Jerusalem,
and the king and his nobles, his wives and his concubines drank
from them. 4As they drank the wine, they praised the gods of gold
and silver, of bronze, iron, wood and stone.

5Suddenly the fingers of a human hand appeared and wrote on
the plaster of the wall, near the lampstand in the royal palace. The
king watched the hand as it wrote. 6His face turned pale and he
was so frightened that his knees knocked together and his legs
gave way.

7The king called out for the enchanters, astrologers[b] and diviners to be brought and said to these wise men of Babylon, "Whoever
reads this writing and tells me what it means will be clothed in
purple and have a gold chain placed around his neck, and he will
be made the third highest ruler in the kingdom."

8Then all the king's wise men came in, but they could not read
the writing or tell the king what it meant. 9So King Belshazzar
became even more terrified and his face grew more pale. His
nobles were baffled.

10The queen,[c] hearing the voices of the king and his nobles,
came into the banquet hall. "O king, live forever!" she said. "Don't
be alarmed! Don't look so pale! 11There is a man in your kingdom
who has the spirit of the holy gods in him. In the time of your
father he was found to have insight and intelligence and wisdom
like that of the gods. King Nebuchadnezzar your father—your
father the king, I say—appointed him chief of the magicians, enchanters, astrologers and diviners. 12This man Daniel, whom the
king called Belteshazzar, was found to have a keen mind and
knowledge and understanding, and also the ability to interpret
dreams, explain riddles and solve difficult problems. Call for Daniel, and he will tell you what the writing means."

13So Daniel was brought before the king, and the king said to
him, "Are you Daniel, one of the exiles my father the king brought
from Judah? 14I have heard that the spirit of the gods is in you and
that you have insight, intelligence and outstanding wisdom. 15The
wise men and enchanters were brought before me to read this
writing and tell me what it means, but they could not explain it.
16Now I have heard that you are able to give interpretations and
to solve difficult problems. If you can read this writing and tell me
what it means, you will be clothed in purple and have a gold chain
placed around your neck, and you will be made the third highest
ruler in the kingdom."

17Then Daniel answered the king, "You may keep your gifts for
yourself and give your rewards to someone else. Nevertheless, I
will read the writing for the king and tell him what it means.

18"O king, the Most High God gave your father Nebuchadnezzar sovereignty and greatness and glory and splendor. 19Because

**NIV** [a] 2 Or *ancestor;* or *predecessor;* also in verses 11, 13 and 18 [b] 7 Or *Chaldeans;* also in verse 11 [c] 10 Or *queen mother*

## King James

19And for the majesty that he gave him, all people, nations, and
languages, trembled and feared before him: whom he would he
slew; and whom he would he kept alive; and whom he would he
set up; and whom he would he put down.
20But when his heart was lifted up, and his mind hardened in
pride, he was deposed from his kingly throne, and they took his
glory from him:
21And he was driven from the sons of men; and his heart was
made like the beasts, and his dwelling *was* with the wild asses: they
fed him with grass like oxen, and his body was wet with the dew
of heaven; till he knew that the most high God ruled in the kingdom of men, and *that* he appointeth over it whomsoever he will.
22And thou his son, O Belshazzar, hast not humbled thine
heart, though thou knewest all this;
23But hast lifted up thyself against the Lord of heaven; and they
have brought the vessels of his house before thee, and thou, and
thy lords, thy wives, and thy concubines, have drunk wine in
them; and thou hast praised the gods of silver, and gold, of brass,
iron, wood, and stone, which see not, nor hear, nor know: and the
God in whose hand thy breath *is,* and whose *are* all thy ways, hast
thou not glorified:
24Then was the part of the hand sent from him; and this writing
was written.
25¶ And this *is* the writing that was written, MENE, MENE,
TEKEL, UPHARSIN.
26This *is* the interpretation of the thing: MENE; God hath numbered thy kingdom, and finished it.
27TEKEL; Thou art weighed in the balances, and art found
wanting.
28PERES; Thy kingdom is divided, and given to the Medes and
Persians.
29Then commanded Belshazzar, and they clothed Daniel with
scarlet, and *put* a chain of gold about his neck, and made a proclamation concerning him, that he should be the third ruler in the
kingdom.
30¶ In that night was Belshazzar the king of the Chaldeans slain.
31And Darius the Median took the kingdom, *being* about threescore and two years old.

**6** IT PLEASED Darius to set over the kingdom an hundred and
twenty princes, which should be over the whole kingdom;
2And over these three presidents; of whom Daniel *was* first: that
the princes might give accounts unto them, and the king should
have no damage.
3Then this Daniel was preferred above the presidents and
princes, because an excellent spirit *was* in him; and the king
thought to set him over the whole realm.
4¶ Then the presidents and princes sought to find occasion
against Daniel concerning the kingdom; but they could find none
occasion nor fault; forasmuch as he *was* faithful, neither was there
any error or fault found in him.
5Then said these men, We shall not find any occasion against
this Daniel, except we find *it* against him concerning the law of his
God.

**AMP** [a] For many people it may be difficult to understand why all the wise men, the soothsayers, the Chaldeans, and the astrologers were unable to translate a few simple words, especially when Daniel's prescribed education in languages was the same as their own, and he had no difficulty. The answer is that any wise man present probably could recognize the four inscribed words, but only the uncompromising man of God—who knew God by daily fellowship and communion with Him, who was so dedicated to Him that God could speak to him and through him—only such a man could tell what the words really meant. Blessed—happy, fortunate, prosperous and enviable—are those who dare to be a Daniel!

## Amplified

19And because of the greatness that He gave him, all peoples,
nations, and languages trembled and feared before him. Whom he
would he slew, and whom he would he kept alive; and whom he
would he set up, and whom he would he put down.
20But when his heart was lifted up, and his mind *and* spirit were
hardened so that he dealt proudly, he was deposed from his kingly
throne, and his glory was taken from him;
21He was driven from among men, and his heart *or* mind was
made like the beasts', and his dwelling was with the wild asses.
He was fed with grass like oxen, and his body was wet with the
dew of the heavens, until he learned *and* knew that the Most High
God rules in the kingdom of men, and that He appoints *and* sets
over it whomever He will.
22And you his son, O Belshazzar, have not humbled your heart
*and* mind, though you knew all this [knew it and were defiant].
23And you have lifted yourself up against the Lord of heaven,
and the vessels of His house have been brought before you, and
you and your lords, your wives and your concubines have drunk
wine from them; and you have praised the gods of silver and gold,
of bronze, iron, wood and stone, which do not see or hear or know;
and the God in Whose hand your breath is, and Whose are all your
ways, you have not honored *and* glorified [but have dishonored
and disgraced].
24Then was the part of the hand sent from the presence of [the
Most High God], and this writing was inscribed.
25And this is the inscription that was written, MENE, MENE,
TEKEL, UPHARSIN—numbered, numbered, weighed, divisions.
26This is the interpretation of the matter: MENE, God has numbered the days of your kingship and brought them to an end;
27TEKEL, You are weighed in the balances and are found wanting.
28 [a]PERES [singular form, same root as upharsin], Your kingdom
*and* your kingship *are* divided and given to the Medes and Persians. [Foretold, Isa. 21:2, 5, 9.]
29Then Belshazzar commanded, and Daniel was clothed with
purple, and a chain of gold put about his neck, and a proclamation
was made concerning him, that he should be the third ruler in the
kingdom.
30During that night Belshazzar the king of the Chaldeans was
slain,
31And Darius the Mede took the kingdom; he was about sixty-
two years old.

**6** IT PLEASED [King] Darius [successor to Belshazzar] to set
over the kingdom a hundred and twenty satraps, who should
be throughout all the kingdom,
2And over them three presidents, of whom Daniel was one; that
these satraps might give account to them, so that the king should
have no loss *or* damage.
3Then this Daniel was distinguished above the presidents and
the satraps, because an excellent spirit was in him, and the king
thought to set him over the whole realm.
4Then the presidents and satraps sought to find occasion [to
bring accusation] against Daniel concerning the kingdom; but they
could find no occasion or fault, for he was faithful, nor was there
any error or fault found in him.
5Then said these men, We shall not find any occasion [to bring
accusation] against this Daniel, except we find it against him concerning the law of his God. [Acts 24:13-21; I Pet. 4:12-16.]

## New American Standard

19"And because of the grandeur which He bestowed on him, all the peoples, nations, and *men of every* language feared and trembled before him; whomever he wished he killed, and whomever he wished he spared alive; and whomever he wished he elevated, and whomever he wished he humbled.

20"But when his heart was lifted up and his spirit became so proud that he behaved arrogantly, he was deposed from his royal throne, and *his* glory was taken away from him.

21"He was also driven away from mankind, and his heart was made like *that of* beasts, and his dwelling place *was* with the wild donkeys. He was given grass to eat like cattle, and his body was drenched with the dew of heaven, until he recognized that the Most High God is ruler over the realm of mankind, and *that* He sets over it whomever He wishes.

22"Yet you, his son, Belshazzar, have not humbled your heart, even though you knew all this,

23but you have exalted yourself against the Lord of heaven; and they have brought the vessels of His house before you, and you and your nobles, your wives and your concubines have been drinking wine from them; and you have praised the gods of silver and gold, of bronze, iron, wood and stone, which do not see, hear or understand. But the God in whose hand are your life-breath and your ways, you have not glorified.

24"Then the hand was sent from Him, and this inscription was written out.

25¶ "Now this is the inscription that was written out: 'MENĒ, MENĒ, TEKĒL, UPHARSIN.'

26"This is the interpretation of the message: 'MENĒ,'—God has numbered your kingdom and put an end to it.

27" 'TEKĒL'—you have been weighed on the scales and found deficient.

28" 'PERĒS'—your kingdom has been divided and given over to the Medes and Persians."

29¶ Then Belshazzar gave orders, and they clothed Daniel with purple and *put* a necklace of gold around his neck, and issued a proclamation concerning him that he *now* had authority as the third *ruler* in the kingdom.

30¶ That same night Belshazzar the Chaldean king was slain.

31So Darius the Mede received the kingdom at about the age of sixty-two.

*Daniel Serves Darius*

**6** IT SEEMED good to Darius to appoint 120 satraps over the kingdom, that they should be in charge of the whole kingdom,

2and over them three commissioners (of whom Daniel was one), that these satraps might be accountable to them, and that the king might not suffer loss.

3Then this Daniel began distinguishing himself among the commissioners and satraps because he possessed an extraordinary spirit, and the king planned to appoint him over the entire kingdom.

4Then the commissioners and satraps began trying to find a ground of accusation against Daniel in regard to government affairs; but they could find no ground of accusation or *evidence of* corruption, inasmuch as he was faithful, and no negligence or corruption was *to be* found in him.

5Then these men said, "We shall not find any ground of accusation against this Daniel unless we find *it* against him with regard to the law of his God."

## New International

of the high position he gave him, all the peoples and nations and
men of every language dreaded and feared him. Those the king
wanted to put to death, he put to death; those he wanted to spare,
he spared; those he wanted to promote, he promoted; and those
he wanted to humble, he humbled. 20But when his heart became
arrogant and hardened with pride, he was deposed from his royal
throne and stripped of his glory. 21He was driven away from
people and given the mind of an animal; he lived with the wild
donkeys and ate grass like cattle; and his body was drenched with
the dew of heaven, until he acknowledged that the Most High God
is sovereign over the kingdoms of men and sets over them anyone
he wishes.

22"But you his son,[b] O Belshazzar, have not humbled yourself,
though you knew all this. 23Instead, you have set yourself up
against the Lord of heaven. You had the goblets from his temple
brought to you, and you and your nobles, your wives and your
concubines drank wine from them. You praised the gods of silver
and gold, of bronze, iron, wood and stone, which cannot see or
hear or understand. But you did not honor the God who holds in
his hand your life and all your ways. 24Therefore he sent the hand
that wrote the inscription.

25"This is the inscription that was written:

MENE, MENE, TEKEL, PARSIN[c]

26"This is what these words mean:

*Mene*[d] : God has numbered the days of your reign and brought it to an end.

27 *Tekel*[e] : You have been weighed on the scales and found wanting.

28 *Peres*[f] : Your kingdom is divided and given to the Medes and Persians."

29Then at Belshazzar's command, Daniel was clothed in purple,
a gold chain was placed around his neck, and he was proclaimed
the third highest ruler in the kingdom.

30That very night Belshazzar, king of the Babylonians,[g] was
slain, 31and Darius the Mede took over the kingdom, at the age of
sixty-two.

*Daniel in the Den of Lions*

**6** IT PLEASED Darius to appoint 120 satraps to rule throughout
the kingdom, 2with three administrators over them, one of
whom was Daniel. The satraps were made accountable to them so
that the king might not suffer loss. 3Now Daniel so distinguished
himself among the administrators and the satraps by his exceptional qualities that the king planned to set him over the whole
kingdom. 4At this, the administrators and the satraps tried to find
grounds for charges against Daniel in his conduct of government
affairs, but they were unable to do so. They could find no corruption in him, because he was trustworthy and neither corrupt nor
negligent. 5Finally these men said, "We will never find any basis
for charges against this man Daniel unless it has something to do
with the law of his God."

**NIV** [b] 22 Or *descendant;* or *successor* [c] 25 Aramaic *UPARSIN* (that is, *AND PARSIN*) [d] 26 *Mene* can mean *numbered* or *mina* (a unit of money). [e] 27 *Tekel* can mean *weighed* or *shekel.* [f] 28 *Peres* (the singular of *Parsin*) can mean *divided* or *Persia* or *a half mina* or *a half shekel.* [g] 30 Or *Chaldeans*

## King James

6Then these presidents and princes assembled together to the king, and said thus unto him, King Darius, live for ever.

7All the presidents of the kingdom, the governors, and the princes, the counsellors, and the captains, have consulted together to establish a royal statute, and to make a firm decree, that whosoever shall ask a petition of any God or man for thirty days, save of thee, O king, he shall be cast into the den of lions.

8Now, O king, establish the decree, and sign the writing, that it be not changed, according to the law of the Medes and Persians, which altereth not.

9Wherefore king Darius signed the writing and the decree.

10¶ Now when Daniel knew that the writing was signed, he went into his house; and his windows being open in his chamber toward Jerusalem, he kneeled upon his knees three times a day, and prayed, and gave thanks before his God, as he did aforetime.

11Then these men assembled, and found Daniel praying and making supplication before his God.

12Then they came near, and spake before the king concerning the king's decree; Hast thou not signed a decree, that every man that shall ask *a petition* of any God or man within thirty days, save of thee, O king, shall be cast into the den of lions? The king answered and said, The thing *is* true, according to the law of the Medes and Persians, which altereth not.

13Then answered they and said before the king, That Daniel, which *is* of the children of the captivity of Judah, regardeth not thee, O king, nor the decree that thou hast signed, but maketh his petition three times a day.

14Then the king, when he heard *these* words, was sore displeased with himself, and set *his* heart on Daniel to deliver him: and he laboured till the going down of the sun to deliver him.

15Then these men assembled unto the king, and said unto the king, Know, O king, that the law of the Medes and Persians *is*, That no decree nor statute which the king establisheth may be changed.

16Then the king commanded, and they brought Daniel, and cast *him* into the den of lions. *Now* the king spake and said unto Daniel, Thy God whom thou servest continually, he will deliver thee.

17And a stone was brought, and laid upon the mouth of the den; and the king sealed it with his own signet, and with the signet of his lords; that the purpose might not be changed concerning Daniel.

18¶ Then the king went to his palace, and passed the night fasting: neither were instruments of music brought before him: and his sleep went from him.

19Then the king arose very early in the morning, and went in haste unto the den of lions.

20And when he came to the den, he cried with a lamentable voice unto Daniel: *and* the king spake and said to Daniel, O Daniel, servant of the living God, is thy God, whom thou servest continually, able to deliver thee from the lions?

21Then said Daniel unto the king, O king, live for ever.

22My God hath sent his angel, and hath shut the lions' mouths, that they have not hurt me: forasmuch as before him innocency was found in me; and also before thee, O king, have I done no hurt.

23Then was the king exceeding glad for him, and commanded that they should take Daniel up out of the den. So Daniel was taken up out of the den, and no manner of hurt was found upon him, because he believed in his God.

24¶ And the king commanded, and they brought those men which had accused Daniel, and they cast *them* into the den of lions, them, their children, and their wives; and the lions had the mastery of them, and brake all their bones in pieces or ever they came at the bottom of the den.

## Amplified

6Then these presidents and satraps came tumultuously together to the king, and said to him, King Darius, live for ever!

7All the presidents of the kingdom, the deputies and the satraps, the counselors and the governors, have consulted *and* agreed that the king should establish a royal statute and make a firm decree, that whoever shall ask a petition of any god or man for thirty days, except of you, O king, shall be cast into the den of lions.

8Now, O king, establish the decree and sign the writing, that it be not changed, according to the law of the Medes and Persians, which cannot be altered.

9So King Darius signed the writing and the decree.

10Now when Daniel knew that the writing was signed, he went into his house, and his windows being open in his chamber toward Jerusalem, he got down upon his knees three times a day and prayed and gave thanks before his God, as he had done previously. [Ps. 5:7.]

11Then these men came thronging [by agreement] and found Daniel praying and making supplication before his God.

12Then they came near and said before the king concerning his prohibitory decree, Have you not signed an edict that any man who shall make a petition to any god or man within thirty days save of you, O king, shall be cast into the den of lions? The king answered and said, The thing is true, according to the law of the Medes and Persians, which cannot be changed *or* repealed.

13Then they said before the king, That Daniel, who is one of the exiles from Judah, does not regard *or* pay any attention to you, O king, or to the decree that you have signed, but makes his petition three times a day.

14Then the king, when he heard these words, was much distressed [over what he had done] and set his mind on Daniel to deliver him; and he labored until the sun went down to rescue him.

15Then these same men came thronging [by agreement] to the king and said, Know, O king, that it is a law of the Medes and Persians that no decree or statute which the king establishes may be changed *or* repealed.

16Then the king commanded, and Daniel was brought and cast into the den of lions. The king said to Daniel, May your God, Whom you are serving continually, deliver you! [Pss. 34:7, 19; 37:39, 40; 50:15.]

17And a stone was brought and laid upon the mouth of the den, and the king sealed it with his own signet and with the signet of his lords, that there might be no change of purpose concerning Daniel.

18Then the king went to his palace and passed the night fasting; neither were instruments of music or dancing girls brought before him, and his sleep fled from him.

19Then the king arose very early in the morning and went in haste to the den of lions.

20And when he came to the den and to Daniel, he cried out in a voice of anguish. The king said to Daniel, O Daniel, servant of the living God, is your God Whom you serve continually able to deliver you from the lions?

21Then Daniel said to the king, O king, live for ever!

22My God has sent His angel and has shut the lions' mouths so that they have not hurt me, because I was found innocent *and* blameless before Him; and also before you, O king, [as you very well know] I have done no harm *or* wrong. [II Tim. 4:17.]

23Then the king was exceedingly glad, and commanded that Daniel should be taken up out of the den. So Daniel was taken up out of the den, and no hurt of any kind was found on him, because he believed—relied on, adhered to and trusted—in his God.

24And the king commanded, and those men who had accused Daniel were brought and cast into the den of lions, they, their children, and their wives; and before ever they reached the bottom of the den the lions had overpowered them and had broken their bones in pieces.

## New American Standard

6 Then these commissioners and satraps came by agreement to the king and spoke to him as follows: "King Darius, live forever!

7 "All the commissioners of the kingdom, the prefects and the satraps, the high officials and the governors have consulted together that the king should establish a statute and enforce an injunction that anyone who makes a petition to any god or man besides you, O king, for thirty days, shall be cast into the lions' den.

8 "Now, O king, establish the injunction and sign the document so that it may not be changed, according to the law of the Medes and Persians, which may not be revoked."

9 Therefore King Darius signed the document, that is, the injunction.

10 ¶ Now when Daniel knew that the document was signed, he entered his house (now in his roof chamber he had windows open toward Jerusalem); and he continued kneeling on his knees three times a day, praying and giving thanks before his God, as he had been doing previously.

11 Then these men came by agreement and found Daniel making petition and supplication before his God.

12 Then they approached and spoke before the king about the king's injunction, "Did you not sign an injunction that any man who makes a petition to any god or man besides you, O king, for thirty days, is to be cast into the lions' den?" The king answered and said, "The statement is true, according to the law of the Medes and Persians, which may not be revoked."

13 Then they answered and spoke before the king, "Daniel, who is one of the exiles from Judah, pays no attention to you, O king, or to the injunction which you signed, but keeps making his petition three times a day."

14 Then, as soon as the king heard this statement, he was deeply distressed and set *his* mind on delivering Daniel; and even until sunset he kept exerting himself to rescue him.

15 Then these men came by agreement to the king and said to the king, "Recognize, O king, that it is a law of the Medes and Persians that no injunction or statute which the king establishes may be changed."

*Daniel in the Lions' Den*

16 ¶ Then the king gave orders, and Daniel was brought in and cast into the lions' den. The king spoke and said to Daniel, "Your God whom you constantly serve will Himself deliver you."

17 And a stone was brought and laid over the mouth of the den; and the king sealed it with his own signet ring and with the signet rings of his nobles, so that nothing might be changed in regard to Daniel.

18 Then the king went off to his palace and spent the night fasting, and no entertainment was brought before him; and his sleep fled from him.

19 ¶ Then the king arose with the dawn, at the break of day, and went in haste to the lions' den.

20 And when he had come near the den to Daniel, he cried out with a troubled voice. The king spoke and said to Daniel, "Daniel, servant of the living God, has your God, whom you constantly serve, been able to deliver you from the lions?"

21 Then Daniel spoke to the king, "O king, live forever!

22 "My God sent His angel and shut the lions' mouths, and they have not harmed me, inasmuch as I was found innocent before Him; and also toward you, O king, I have committed no crime."

23 Then the king was very pleased and gave orders for Daniel to be taken up out of the den. So Daniel was taken up out of the den, and no injury whatever was found on him, because he had trusted in his God.

24 The king then gave orders, and they brought those men who had maliciously accused Daniel, and they cast them, their children, and their wives into the lions' den; and they had not reached the bottom of the den before the lions overpowered them and crushed all their bones.

## New International

6 So the administrators and the satraps went as a group to the
king and said: "O King Darius, live forever! 7 The royal administrators, prefects, satraps, advisers and governors have all agreed that
the king should issue an edict and enforce the decree that anyone
who prays to any god or man during the next thirty days, except
to you, O king, shall be thrown into the lions' den. 8 Now, O king,
issue the decree and put it in writing so that it cannot be altered—
in accordance with the laws of the Medes and Persians, which
cannot be repealed." 9 So King Darius put the decree in writing.
10 Now when Daniel learned that the decree had been published, he went home to his upstairs room where the windows
opened toward Jerusalem. Three times a day he got down on his
knees and prayed, giving thanks to his God, just as he had done
before. 11 Then these men went as a group and found Daniel praying and asking God for help. 12 So they went to the king and spoke
to him about his royal decree: "Did you not publish a decree that
during the next thirty days anyone who prays to any god or man
except to you, O king, would be thrown into the lions' den?"
The king answered, "The decree stands—in accordance with
the laws of the Medes and Persians, which cannot be repealed."
13 Then they said to the king, "Daniel, who is one of the exiles
from Judah, pays no attention to you, O king, or to the decree you
put in writing. He still prays three times a day." 14 When the king
heard this, he was greatly distressed; he was determined to rescue
Daniel and made every effort until sundown to save him.
15 Then the men went as a group to the king and said to him,
"Remember, O king, that according to the law of the Medes and
Persians no decree or edict that the king issues can be changed."
16 So the king gave the order, and they brought Daniel and
threw him into the lions' den. The king said to Daniel, "May your
God, whom you serve continually, rescue you!"
17 A stone was brought and placed over the mouth of the den,
and the king sealed it with his own signet ring and with the rings
of his nobles, so that Daniel's situation might not be changed.
18 Then the king returned to his palace and spent the night without
eating and without any entertainment being brought to him. And
he could not sleep.
19 At the first light of dawn, the king got up and hurried to the
lions' den. 20 When he came near the den, he called to Daniel in
an anguished voice, "Daniel, servant of the living God, has your
God, whom you serve continually, been able to rescue you from
the lions?"
21 Daniel answered, "O king, live forever! 22 My God sent his
angel, and he shut the mouths of the lions. They have not hurt me,
because I was found innocent in his sight. Nor have I ever done
any wrong before you, O king."
23 The king was overjoyed and gave orders to lift Daniel out of
the den. And when Daniel was lifted from the den, no wound was
found on him, because he had trusted in his God.
24 At the king's command, the men who had falsely accused
Daniel were brought in and thrown into the lions' den, along with
their wives and children. And before they reached the floor of the
den, the lions overpowered them and crushed all their bones.

## King James

25¶ Then king Darius wrote unto all people, nations, and languages, that dwell in all the earth; Peace be multiplied unto you.

26I make a decree, That in every dominion of my kingdom men tremble and fear before the God of Daniel: for he *is* the living God, and stedfast for ever, and his kingdom *that* which shall not be destroyed, and his dominion *shall be even* unto the end.

27He delivereth and rescueth, and he worketh signs and wonders in heaven and in earth, who hath delivered Daniel from the power of the lions.

28So this Daniel prospered in the reign of Darius, and in the reign of Cyrus the Persian.

**7** IN THE first year of Belshazzar king of Babylon Daniel had a dream and visions of his head upon his bed: then he wrote the dream, *and* told the sum of the matters.

2Daniel spake and said, I saw in my vision by night, and, behold, the four winds of the heaven strove upon the great sea.

3And four great beasts came up from the sea, diverse one from another.

4The first *was* like a lion, and had eagle's wings: I beheld till the wings thereof were plucked, and it was lifted up from the earth, and made stand upon the feet as a man, and a man's heart was given to it.

5And behold another beast, a second, like to a bear, and it raised up itself on one side, and *it had* three ribs in the mouth of it between the teeth of it: and they said thus unto it, Arise, devour much flesh.

6After this I beheld, and lo another, like a leopard, which had upon the back of it four wings of a fowl; the beast had also four heads; and dominion was given to it.

7After this I saw in the night visions, and behold a fourth beast, dreadful and terrible, and strong exceedingly; and it had great iron teeth: it devoured and brake in pieces, and stamped the residue with the feet of it: and it *was* diverse from all the beasts that *were* before it; and it had ten horns.

8I considered the horns, and, behold, there came up among them another little horn, before whom there were three of the first horns plucked up by the roots: and, behold, in this horn *were* eyes like the eyes of man, and a mouth speaking great things.

9¶ I beheld till the thrones were cast down, and the Ancient of days did sit, whose garment *was* white as snow, and the hair of his head like the pure wool: his throne *was like* the fiery flame, *and* his wheels *as* burning fire.

10A fiery stream issued and came forth from before him: thousand thousands ministered unto him, and ten thousand times ten thousand stood before him: the judgment was set, and the books were opened.

11I beheld then because of the voice of the great words which the horn spake: I beheld *even* till the beast was slain, and his body destroyed, and given to the burning flame.

## Amplified

25Then King Darius wrote to all peoples, nations, and languages [in his realm] that dwell in all the earth: Peace be multiplied to you!

26I make a decree, That in all my royal dominion men tremble and fear before the God of Daniel, for He is the living God, enduring *and* steadfast for ever, and His kingdom shall not be destroyed, and His dominion shall be even to the end [of the world].

27He is a savior and deliverer, and He works signs and wonders in the heavens and on the earth, Who has delivered Daniel from the power of the lions.

28So this *man* Daniel prospered in the reign of Darius and in the reign of Cyrus the Persian.

**7** IN THE first year of Belshazzar king of Babylon [a]Daniel had a dream and visions of his head as he lay upon his bed. Then he wrote down the dream, and told the gist of the matter.

2Daniel said, I saw in my vision by night, and behold, the four winds of the heavens [political and social agitations] were stirring up the great sea [the nations of the world].

3And four great beasts came up out of the sea in succession and different from one another.

4The first [the Babylonian empire under Nebuchadnezzar] was like a lion, and had eagle's wings. I beheld till the wings of it were plucked, and it was lifted up from the earth, and made to stand upon two feet as a man, and a man's heart was given to it. [Dan. 2:37, 38.]

5And behold another beast, a second one [the Media-Persia empire], was like a bear, and it raised up itself on one side [or one dominion], and three ribs were in its mouth between its teeth, and it was told, Arise, devour much flesh.

6After this I beheld, and lo, another [the Grecian Empire of Alexander the Great], like a leopard, which had four wings of a bird on its back. The beast had also four heads [Alexander's generals, his successors], and dominion was given to it. [Cf. Dan. 2:39; 8:20-22.]

7After this I saw in the night visions, and behold, a fourth beast, terrible, powerful *and* dreadful, and exceedingly strong; and it had great iron teeth; it devoured and crushed, and trampled what was left with its feet. And it was different from all the beasts that came before it, and it had ten horns [symbolizing ten kings]. [Dan. 2:40-43; 7:23.]

8I considered the horns, and behold, there came up among them another horn, a little one, before which three of the first horns were plucked up by the roots; and behold, in this horn were eyes like the eyes of a man, and a mouth speaking great things.

9I kept looking until thrones were placed [for the assessors with the Judge], and the Ancient of days [God, the eternal Father] took His seat, Whose garment was white as snow, and the hair of His head like pure wool; His throne was like the fiery flame, its wheels were burning fire. [Rev. 20:4; cf. Matt. 19:28; I Kings 22:19; Dan. 7:13, 22; cf. Ps. 90:2; Ezek. 1:26-28.]

10A stream of fire came forth from before Him; a thousand thousands ministered to Him, and ten thousand times ten thousand rose up *and* stood before Him; the Judge was seated—the court was in session—and the books were opened.

11I looked then because of the sound of the great words which the horn was speaking. I watched until the beast was slain and its body destroyed and given over to be burned with fire.

**AMP** [a] This chapter, in its matter as well as its position in the central part of the book, is to the book of Daniel what the eighth chapter of Romans is to that epistle. Next to the fifty-third chapter of Isaiah and perhaps the ninth chapter also, we have here the most precious and prominent portion of the sure word of prophecy concerning the coming of the Messiah. The chapter is worthy of the most careful prayer and study. It is referred to directly or indirectly by Christ and His apostles perhaps more than other portions of the Old Testament of similar extent. It appears to have been regarded by the Old Testament saints, in the centuries preceding the Messiah's first advent, as pre-eminently the "word of prophecy." (Homiletic Commentary, adapted.)

## New American Standard

[25]¶ Then Darius the king wrote to all the peoples, nations, and *men of every* language who were living in all the land: "May your peace abound!
[26]"I make a decree that in all the dominion of my kingdom men are to fear and tremble before the God of Daniel;
For He is the living God and enduring forever,
And His kingdom is one which will not be destroyed,
And His dominion *will be* forever.
27 "He delivers and rescues and performs signs and wonders
In heaven and on earth,
Who has *also* delivered Daniel from the power of the lions."
[28]¶ So this Daniel enjoyed success in the reign of Darius and in the reign of Cyrus the Persian.

*Vision of the Four Beasts*

7 IN THE first year of Belshazzar king of Babylon Daniel saw a dream and visions in his mind *as he lay* on his bed; then he wrote the dream down *and* related the *following* summary of it.
[2]Daniel said, "I was looking in my vision by night, and behold, the four winds of heaven were stirring up the great sea.
[3]"And four great beasts were coming up from the sea, different from one another.
[4]"The first *was* like a lion and had *the* wings of an eagle. I kept looking until its wings were plucked, and it was lifted up from the ground and made to stand on two feet like a man; a human mind also was given to it.
[5]"And behold, another beast, a second one, resembling a bear. And it was raised up on one side, and three ribs *were* in its mouth between its teeth; and thus they said to it, 'Arise, devour much meat!'
[6]"After this I kept looking, and behold, another one, like a leopard, which had on its back four wings of a bird; the beast also had four heads, and dominion was given to it.
[7]"After this I kept looking in the night visions, and behold, a fourth beast, dreadful and terrifying and extremely strong; and it had large iron teeth. It devoured and crushed, and trampled down the remainder with its feet; and it was different from all the beasts that were before it, and it had ten horns.
[8]"While I was contemplating the horns, behold, another horn, a little one, came up among them, and three of the first horns were pulled out by the roots before it; and behold, this horn possessed eyes like the eyes of a man, and a mouth uttering great *boasts*.

*The Ancient of Days Reigns*

9 "I kept looking
Until thrones were set up,
And the Ancient of Days took *His* seat;
His vesture *was* like white snow,
And the hair of His head like pure wool.
His throne *was* ablaze with flames,
Its wheels *were* a burning fire.
10 "A river of fire was flowing
And coming out from before Him;
Thousands upon thousands were attending Him,
And myriads upon myriads were standing before Him;
The court sat,
And the books were opened.
[11]"Then I kept looking because of the sound of the boastful words which the horn was speaking; I kept looking until the beast was slain, and its body was destroyed and given to the burning fire.

## New International

[25]Then King Darius wrote to all the peoples, nations and men of every language throughout the land:
"May you prosper greatly!
[26]"I issue a decree that in every part of my kingdom people must fear and reverence the God of Daniel.
"For he is the living God
and he endures forever;
his kingdom will not be destroyed,
his dominion will never end.
[27]He rescues and he saves;
he performs signs and wonders
in the heavens and on the earth.
He has rescued Daniel
from the power of the lions."
[28]So Daniel prospered during the reign of Darius and the reign of Cyrus[b] the Persian.

*Daniel's Dream of Four Beasts*

7 IN THE first year of Belshazzar king of Babylon, Daniel had a dream, and visions passed through his mind as he was lying on his bed. He wrote down the substance of his dream.
[2]Daniel said: "In my vision at night I looked, and there before me were the four winds of heaven churning up the great sea. [3]Four great beasts, each different from the others, came up out of the sea.
[4]"The first was like a lion, and it had the wings of an eagle. I watched until its wings were torn off and it was lifted from the ground so that it stood on two feet like a man, and the heart of a man was given to it.
[5]"And there before me was a second beast, which looked like a bear. It was raised up on one of its sides, and it had three ribs in its mouth between its teeth. It was told, 'Get up and eat your fill of flesh!'
[6]"After that, I looked, and there before me was another beast, one that looked like a leopard. And on its back it had four wings like those of a bird. This beast had four heads, and it was given authority to rule.
[7]"After that, in my vision at night I looked, and there before me was a fourth beast—terrifying and frightening and very powerful. It had large iron teeth; it crushed and devoured its victims and trampled underfoot whatever was left. It was different from all the former beasts, and it had ten horns.
[8]"While I was thinking about the horns, there before me was another horn, a little one, which came up among them; and three of the first horns were uprooted before it. This horn had eyes like the eyes of a man and a mouth that spoke boastfully.
[9]"As I looked,
"thrones were set in place,
and the Ancient of Days took his seat.
His clothing was as white as snow;
the hair of his head was white like wool.
His throne was flaming with fire,
and its wheels were all ablaze.
[10]A river of fire was flowing,
coming out from before him.
Thousands upon thousands attended him;
ten thousand times ten thousand stood before him.
The court was seated,
and the books were opened.
[11]"Then I continued to watch because of the boastful words the horn was speaking. I kept looking until the beast was slain and its body destroyed and thrown into the blazing fire. [12](The other

NIV [b] 28 *Or Darius, that is, the reign of Cyrus*

## King James

12 As concerning the rest of the beasts, they had their dominion taken away: yet their lives were prolonged for a season and time.

13 I saw in the night visions, and, behold, *one* like the Son of man came with the clouds of heaven, and came to the Ancient of days, and they brought him near before him.

14 And there was given him dominion, and glory, and a kingdom, that all people, nations, and languages, should serve him: his dominion *is* an everlasting dominion, which shall not pass away, and his kingdom *that* which shall not be destroyed.

15 ¶ I Daniel was grieved in my spirit in the midst of *my* body, and the visions of my head troubled me.

16 I came near unto one of them that stood by, and asked him the truth of all this. So he told me, and made me know the interpretation of the things.

17 These great beasts, which are four, *are* four kings, *which* shall arise out of the earth.

18 But the saints of the most High shall take the kingdom, and possess the kingdom for ever, even for ever and ever.

19 Then I would know the truth of the fourth beast, which was diverse from all the others, exceeding dreadful, whose teeth *were of* iron, and his nails *of* brass; *which* devoured, brake in pieces, and stamped the residue with his feet;

20 And of the ten horns that *were* in his head, and *of* the other which came up, and before whom three fell; even *of* that horn that had eyes, and a mouth that spake very great things, whose look *was* more stout than his fellows.

21 I beheld, and the same horn made war with the saints, and prevailed against them;

22 Until the Ancient of days came, and judgment was given to the saints of the most High; and the time came that the saints possessed the kingdom.

23 Thus he said, The fourth beast shall be the fourth kingdom upon earth, which shall be diverse from all kingdoms, and shall devour the whole earth, and shall tread it down, and break it in pieces.

24 And the ten horns out of this kingdom *are* ten kings *that* shall arise: and another shall rise after them; and he shall be diverse from the first, and he shall subdue three kings.

25 And he shall speak *great* words against the most High, and shall wear out the saints of the most High, and think to change times and laws: and they shall be given into his hand until a time and times and the dividing of time.

26 But the judgment shall sit, and they shall take away his dominion, to consume and to destroy *it* unto the end.

27 And the kingdom and dominion, and the greatness of the kingdom under the whole heaven, shall be given to the people of the saints of the most High, whose kingdom *is* an everlasting kingdom, and all dominions shall serve and obey him.

28 Hitherto *is* the end of the matter. As for me Daniel, my cogitations much troubled me, and my countenance changed in me: but I kept the matter in my heart.

## Amplified

12 And as for the rest of the beasts, their power of dominion was taken away, yet their lives were prolonged [for the duration of their lives was fixed] for a season and a time.

13 I saw in the night visions, and behold, [a]on the clouds of the heavens came One like a Son of man, and He came to the Ancient of days and was presented before Him.

14 And there was given Him, [the Messiah,] dominion and glory and kingdom, that all peoples, nations and languages should serve Him. His dominion is an everlasting dominion, which shall not pass away, and his kingdom one which shall not be destroyed. [Rev. 5:1-10.]

15 As for me, Daniel, my spirit was grieved *and* anxious within me, and the visions of my head alarmed *and* agitated me.

16 I came near to one of those who stood there and asked him the truth of all this. So he told me, and made known to me the interpretation of the things.

17 These four great beasts are four kings who shall arise out of the earth.

18 But the saints of the Most High [God] shall receive the kingdom, and possess the kingdom for ever, even for ever and ever. [Rom. 8:17; I Pet. 2:9; Rev. 3:21.]

19 Then I wished to know the truth about the fourth beast, which was different from all the others, exceedingly terrible *and* shocking, whose teeth were of iron and its nails of bronze; which devoured, broke *and* crushed, and trampled what was left with its feet;

20 And concerning the ten horns [representing kings] that were on its head, and the other horn which came up later and before which three of *the horns* fell, the horn which had eyes and a mouth that spoke great things, and which looked greater than the others.

21 As I looked, this horn made war with the saints and prevailed over them, [Rev. 13:7-9.]

22 Until the Ancient of days came, and judgment was given to the saints of the Most High [God], and the time came when the saints possessed the kingdom.

23 Thus [the angel] said, The fourth beast shall be a fourth kingdom on earth, which shall be different from all other kingdoms, and shall devour the whole earth, tread it down and break it in pieces *and* crush it.

24 And as for the ten horns, out of this kingdom ten kings shall arise; and another shall arise after them, and he shall be different from the former ones, and he shall subdue *and* put down three kings.

25 And he shall speak words against the Most High [God], and shall wear out the saints of the Most High, and think to change the time [of sacred feasts and holy days] and the law; and the saints shall be given into his hand for a time, two times and half a time [three and one-half years]. [Rev. 13:1-6.]

26 But the judgment shall be set [by the court of the Most High], and they shall take away his dominion, to consume it [gradually] and to destroy it [suddenly] in the end.

27 And the kingdom and the dominion and the greatness of the kingdom under the whole heavens shall be given to the people of the saints of the Most High; His kingdom is an everlasting kingdom, and all the dominions shall serve and obey Him.

28 Here is the end of the matter. As for me, Daniel, my *waking* thoughts troubled and alarmed me much, and my cheerfulness of countenance was changed in me; but I kept the matter [of the interpreting angel's information] in my heart *and* mind.

**AMP** [a] Notice that the four beasts of this seventh chapter of Daniel symbolize the same world kingdoms that were pictured by the image in chapter two, and the ten horns of the last beast answer to the ten toes of the image. Most of both prophecies have been fulfilled, and at this writing "the blessed hope" of the ages is also showing every evidence of nearing realization. Both visions show the end of Gentile world power. View today's events in the light of these disclosures and they fall into focus and make sense. The individual child of God is challenged as never before in the world's history to let go of the trivial and the transient, and yield himself unreservedly to Him Who is coming to fulfill the longings of every true believer—for ever and ever!

## New American Standard

12"As for the rest of the beasts, their dominion was taken away, but an extension of life was granted to them for an appointed period of time.

*The Son of Man Presented*

13¶ "I kept looking in the night visions,
And behold, with the clouds of heaven
One like a Son of Man was coming,
And He came up to the Ancient of Days
And was presented before Him.
14 "And to Him was given dominion,
Glory and a kingdom,
That all the peoples, nations, and *men of every* language
Might serve Him.
His dominion is an everlasting dominion
Which will not pass away;
And His kingdom is one
Which will not be destroyed.

*The Vision Interpreted*

15"As for me, Daniel, my spirit was distressed within me, and the visions in my mind kept alarming me.

16"I approached one of those who were standing by and began asking him the exact meaning of all this. So he told me and made known to me the interpretation of these things:

17'These great beasts, which are four *in number,* are four kings *who* will arise from the earth.

18'But the saints of the Highest One will receive the kingdom and possess the kingdom forever, for all ages to come.'

19"Then I desired to know the exact meaning of the fourth beast, which was different from all the others, exceedingly dreadful, with its teeth of iron and its claws of bronze, *and which* devoured, crushed, and trampled down the remainder with its feet,

20and *the meaning* of the ten horns that *were* on its head, and the other *horn* which came up, and before which three *of them* fell, namely, that horn which had eyes and a mouth uttering great *boasts,* and which was larger in appearance than its associates.

21"I kept looking, and that horn was waging war with the saints and overpowering them

22until the Ancient of Days came, and judgment was passed in favor of the saints of the Highest One, and the time arrived when the saints took possession of the kingdom.

23¶ "Thus he said: 'The fourth beast will be a fourth kingdom on the earth, which will be different from all the *other* kingdoms, and it will devour the whole earth and tread it down and crush it.

24'As for the ten horns, out of this kingdom ten kings will arise; and another will arise after them, and he will be different from the previous ones and will subdue three kings.

25'And he will speak out against the Most High and wear down the saints of the Highest One, and he will intend to make alterations in times and in law; and they will be given into his hand for a time, times, and half a time.

26'But the court will sit *for judgment,* and his dominion will be taken away, annihilated and destroyed forever.

27'Then the sovereignty, the dominion, and the greatness of *all* the kingdoms under the whole heaven will be given to the people of the saints of the Highest One; His kingdom *will be* an everlasting kingdom, and all the dominions will serve and obey Him.'

28"At this point the revelation ended. As for me, Daniel, my thoughts were greatly alarming me and my face grew pale, but I kept the matter to myself."

## New International

beasts had been stripped of their authority, but were allowed to
live for a period of time.)
13"In my vision at night I looked, and there before me was one
like a son of man, coming with the clouds of heaven. He approached the Ancient of Days and was led into his presence. 14He
was given authority, glory and sovereign power; all peoples, nations and men of every language worshiped him. His dominion is
an everlasting dominion that will not pass away, and his kingdom
is one that will never be destroyed.

*The Interpretation of the Dream*

15"I, Daniel, was troubled in spirit, and the visions that passed
through my mind disturbed me. 16I approached one of those
standing there and asked him the true meaning of all this.
"So he told me and gave me the interpretation of these things:
17'The four great beasts are four kingdoms that will rise from the
earth. 18But the saints of the Most High will receive the kingdom
and will possess it forever—yes, for ever and ever.'
19"Then I wanted to know the true meaning of the fourth beast,
which was different from all the others and most terrifying, with
its iron teeth and bronze claws—the beast that crushed and devoured its victims and trampled underfoot whatever was left. 20I
also wanted to know about the ten horns on its head and about
the other horn that came up, before which three of them fell—the
horn that looked more imposing than the others and that had eyes
and a mouth that spoke boastfully. 21As I watched, this horn was
waging war against the saints and defeating them, 22until the
Ancient of Days came and pronounced judgment in favor of the
saints of the Most High, and the time came when they possessed
the kingdom.
23"He gave me this explanation: 'The fourth beast is a fourth
kingdom that will appear on earth. It will be different from all the
other kingdoms and will devour the whole earth, trampling it
down and crushing it. 24The ten horns are ten kings who will come
from this kingdom. After them another king will arise, different
from the earlier ones; he will subdue three kings. 25He will speak
against the Most High and oppress his saints and try to change the
set times and the laws. The saints will be handed over to him for
a time, times and half a time.[b]
26" 'But the court will sit, and his power will be taken away and
completely destroyed forever. 27Then the sovereignty, power and
greatness of the kingdoms under the whole heaven will be handed
over to the saints, the people of the Most High. His kingdom will
be an everlasting kingdom, and all rulers will worship and obey
him.'
28"This is the end of the matter. I, Daniel, was deeply troubled
by my thoughts, and my face turned pale, but I kept the matter
to myself."

NIV [b] 25 Or *for a year, two years and half a year*

## King James

8 IN THE third year of the reign of king Belshazzar a vision appeared unto me, *even unto* me Daniel, after that which appeared unto me at the first.

2 And I saw in a vision; and it came to pass, when I saw, that I *was* at Shushan *in* the palace, which *is* in the province of Elam; and I saw in a vision, and I was by the river of Ulai.

3 Then I lifted up mine eyes, and saw, and, behold, there stood before the river a ram which had *two* horns: and the *two* horns *were* high; but one *was* higher than the other, and the higher came up last.

4 I saw the ram pushing westward, and northward, and southward; so that no beasts might stand before him, neither *was there any* that could deliver out of his hand; but he did according to his will, and became great.

5 And as I was considering, behold, an he goat came from the west on the face of the whole earth, and touched not the ground: and the goat *had* a notable horn between his eyes.

6 And he came to the ram that had *two* horns, which I had seen standing before the river, and ran unto him in the fury of his power.

7 And I saw him come close unto the ram, and he was moved with choler against him, and smote the ram, and brake his two horns: and there was no power in the ram to stand before him, but he cast him down to the ground, and stamped upon him: and there was none that could deliver the ram out of his hand.

8 Therefore the he goat waxed very great: and when he was strong, the great horn was broken; and for it came up four notable ones toward the four winds of heaven.

9 And out of one of them came forth a little horn, which waxed exceeding great, toward the south, and toward the east, and toward the pleasant *land.*

10 And it waxed great, *even* to the host of heaven; and it cast down *some* of the host and of the stars to the ground, and stamped upon them.

11 Yea, he magnified *himself* even to the prince of the host, and by him the daily *sacrifice* was taken away, and the place of his sanctuary was cast down.

12 And an host was given *him* against the daily *sacrifice* by reason of transgression, and it cast down the truth to the ground; and it practised, and prospered.

13 ¶ Then I heard one saint speaking, and another saint said unto that certain *saint* which spake, How long *shall be* the vision *concerning* the daily *sacrifice,* and the transgression of desolation, to give both the sanctuary and the host to be trodden under foot?

14 And he said unto me, Unto two thousand and three hundred days; then shall the sanctuary be cleansed.

15 ¶ And it came to pass, when I, *even* I Daniel, had seen the vision, and sought for the meaning, then, behold, there stood before me as the appearance of a man.

16 And I heard a man's voice between *the banks of* Ulai, which called, and said, Gabriel, make this *man* to understand the vision.

## Amplified

8 IN THE third year of the reign of King Belshazzar a vision appeared to me, to me Daniel, after the one that appeared to me at the first.

2 And I saw in the vision, and it seemed that I was at Shushan the palace *or* fortress [in Susa, the capital of Persia], which is in the province of Elam, and I saw in the vision and I was by the river of Ulai.

3 And I lifted up my eyes and saw, and behold, there stood before the river a *single* ram which had two horns [representing two kings of Media-Persia, Darius the Mede, then Cyrus]; and the two horns were high, but one [Persia] was higher than the other, and the higher one came up last.

4 I looked *and* saw the ram [Medo-Persia] pushing *and* charging westward and northward and southward; no beast could stand before him, neither could any one rescue from his power, but he did according to his *own* will *and* pleasure, and magnified himself. [Verse 20.]

5 As I was considering, behold, a he-goat [the king of Greece] came from the west across the face of the whole earth, without touching the ground, and the goat had a conspicuous *and* remarkable horn between his eyes [symbolizing Alexander the Great]. [Verse 21.]

6 And he came to the ram that had the two horns, which I had seen standing on the bank of the river, and ran at him in the heat of his power.

7 [In my vision] I saw him come close to the ram [the Medo-Persian Empire], and he was moved with anger against him, and he [Alexander] struck the ram and broke his two horns; and there was no power in the ram to stand before him, but the goat threw him to the ground and trampled on him. And there was no one who could rescue the ram [Medo-Persia] from his power.

8 And the he-goat [Alexander the Great] magnified himself exceedingly, and when he was [young and] strong *he,* the [a]great horn, was [suddenly] broken, and instead of *him* there came up four notable horns [to whom the kingdom was divided, one] toward *each* of the four winds of the heavens.

9 Out from littleness *and* small beginnings one of them came forth [Antiochus Epiphanes], a [b]horn whose [impious presumption and pride] grew exceedingly great toward the south and toward the east and toward the ornament—the precious, blessed land *of Israel.* [Verse 23.]

10 And [in my vision] *this horn* grew great, even against the host of heaven [God's true people, the saints], and some of the host and of the stars [priests] it cast down to the ground and trampled on them,

11 Yes, [this horn] magnified itself, even [matching itself] against the Prince of the host [of heaven]; and from Him the continual *burnt offering* was taken away, and the place of *God's* sanctuary was cast down *and* profaned.

12 And the host [the chosen people] *and* strength were given to [the wicked horn] together with the continual burnt offering, because of the transgression [of God's people]—their abounding irreverence, ungodliness and lack of piety. And righteousness *and* truth *were* cast down to the ground, and [the wicked horn] accomplished this [by divine permission] and prospered.

13 Then I heard a holy one speaking, and another holy one said to the one that spoke, For how long is the vision concerning the continual offering, the transgression that makes desolate, and the giving over of both the sanctuary and the host [of the people] to be trampled under foot? [Luke 21:24.]

14 And he said to him *and* to me, For two thousand and three hundred evenings and mornings; then the sanctuary shall be cleansed *and* restored.

15 When I, even I, Daniel, had seen the vision, I sought to understand it; then behold, there stood before me one [Gabriel] with the appearance of a man.

16 And I heard a man's voice between the banks of the *river* Ulai, which called and said, Gabriel, make this man [Daniel] understand the vision. [Dan. 9:21; Luke 1:19, 26.]

**AMP** [a] Alexander the Great suddenly died, and his empire was divided into four parts, east, west, north and south, ruled over by his four generals. [b] This horn (verses 9 to 12) is not to be confused with the "little horn" of Dan. 7. This one is a prophetic forecast of Antiochus Epiphanes, who came out of Syria, one of the four dynasties into which Alexander's empire was divided, and became a great conqueror. Hating God, he profaned the temple and terribly persecuted the Jews. However, he foreshadows the "little horn" of Dan. 7, "the beast" of Daniel's final time of the end (Rev. 13:4-9).

## New American Standard

*Vision of the Ram and Goat*

**8** IN THE third year of the reign of Belshazzar the king a vision appeared to me, Daniel, subsequent to the one which appeared to me previously.

2And I looked in the vision, and it came about while I was looking, that I was in the citadel of Susa, which is in the province of Elam; and I looked in the vision, and I myself was beside the Ulai Canal.

3Then I lifted my gaze and looked, and behold, a ram which had two horns was standing in front of the canal. Now the two horns *were* long, but one *was* longer than the other, with the longer one coming up last.

4I saw the ram butting westward, northward, and southward, and no *other* beasts could stand before him, nor was there anyone to rescue from his power; but he did as he pleased and magnified *himself*.

5¶ While I was observing, behold, a male goat was coming from the west over the surface of the whole earth without touching the ground; and the goat *had* a conspicuous horn between his eyes.

6And he came up to the ram that had the two horns, which I had seen standing in front of the canal, and rushed at him in his mighty wrath.

7And I saw him come beside the ram, and he was enraged at him; and he struck the ram and shattered his two horns, and the ram had no strength to withstand him. So he hurled him to the ground and trampled on him, and there was none to rescue the ram from his power.

8Then the male goat magnified *himself* exceedingly. But as soon as he was mighty, the large horn was broken; and in its place there came up four conspicuous *horns* toward the four winds of heaven.

*The Little Horn*

9¶ And out of one of them came forth a rather small horn which grew exceedingly great toward the south, toward the east, and toward the [c]Beautiful *Land*.

10And it grew up to the host of heaven and caused some of the host and some of the stars to fall to the earth, and it trampled them down.

11It even magnified *itself* to be equal with the Commander of the host; and it removed the regular sacrifice from Him, and the place of His sanctuary was thrown down.

12And on account of transgression the host will be given over *to the horn* along with the regular sacrifice; and it will fling truth to the ground and perform *its will* and prosper.

13Then I heard a holy one speaking, and another holy one said to that particular one who was speaking, "How long will the vision *about* the regular sacrifice apply, while the transgression causes horror, so as to allow both the holy place and the host to be trampled?"

14And he said to me, "For 2,300 evenings *and* mornings; then the holy place will be properly restored."

*Interpretation of the Vision*

15¶ And it came about when I, Daniel, had seen the vision, that I sought to understand it; and behold, standing before me was one who looked like a man.

16And I heard the voice of a man between *the banks of* Ulai, and he called out and said, "Gabriel, give this *man* an understanding of the vision."

NAS [c] I.e., Palestine

## New International

*Daniel's Vision of a Ram and a Goat*

**8** IN THE third year of King Belshazzar's reign, I, Daniel, had
a vision, after the one that had already appeared to me. 2In
my vision I saw myself in the citadel of Susa in the province of
Elam; in the vision I was beside the Ulai Canal. 3I looked up, and
there before me was a ram with two horns, standing beside the
canal, and the horns were long. One of the horns was longer than
the other but grew up later. 4I watched the ram as he charged
toward the west and the north and the south. No animal could
stand against him, and none could rescue from his power. He did
as he pleased and became great.

5As I was thinking about this, suddenly a goat with a prominent
horn between his eyes came from the west, crossing the whole
earth without touching the ground. 6He came toward the two-
horned ram I had seen standing beside the canal and charged at
him in great rage. 7I saw him attack the ram furiously, striking the
ram and shattering his two horns. The ram was powerless to stand
against him; the goat knocked him to the ground and trampled on
him, and none could rescue the ram from his power. 8The goat
became very great, but at the height of his power his large horn
was broken off, and in its place four prominent horns grew up
toward the four winds of heaven.

9Out of one of them came another horn, which started small but
grew in power to the south and to the east and toward the Beautiful Land. 10It grew until it reached the host of the heavens, and
it threw some of the starry host down to the earth and trampled
on them. 11It set itself up to be as great as the Prince of the host;
it took away the daily sacrifice from him, and the place of his
sanctuary was brought low. 12Because of rebellion, the host ⌊of the
saints⌋[d] and the daily sacrifice were given over to it. It prospered
in everything it did, and truth was thrown to the ground.

13Then I heard a holy one speaking, and another holy one said
to him, "How long will it take for the vision to be fulfilled—the
vision concerning the daily sacrifice, the rebellion that causes desolation, and the surrender of the sanctuary and of the host that will
be trampled underfoot?"

14He said to me, "It will take 2,300 evenings and mornings; then
the sanctuary will be reconsecrated."

*The Interpretation of the Vision*

15While I, Daniel, was watching the vision and trying to understand it, there before me stood one who looked like a man. 16And
I heard a man's voice from the Ulai calling, "Gabriel, tell this man
the meaning of the vision."

NIV [d] 12 Or *rebellion, the armies*

## King James

17So he came near where I stood: and when he came, I was afraid, and fell upon my face: but he said unto me, Understand, O son of man: for at the time of the end *shall be* the vision.

18Now as he was speaking with me, I was in a deep sleep on my face toward the ground: but he touched me, and set me upright.

19And he said, Behold, I will make thee know what shall be in the last end of the indignation: for at the time appointed the end *shall be*.

20The ram which thou sawest having *two* horns *are* the kings of Media and Persia.

21And the rough goat *is* the king of Grecia: and the great horn that *is* between his eyes *is* the first king.

22Now that being broken, whereas four stood up for it, four kingdoms shall stand up out of the nation, but not in his power.

23And in the latter time of their kingdom, when the transgressors are come to the full, a king of fierce countenance, and understanding dark sentences, shall stand up.

24And his power shall be mighty, but not by his own power: and he shall destroy wonderfully, and shall prosper, and practise, and shall destroy the mighty and the holy people.

25And through his policy also he shall cause craft to prosper in his hand; and he shall magnify *himself* in his heart, and by peace shall destroy many: he shall also stand up against the Prince of princes; but he shall be broken without hand.

26And the vision of the evening and the morning which was told *is* true: wherefore shut thou up the vision; for it *shall be* for many days.

27And I Daniel fainted, and was sick *certain* days; afterward I rose up, and did the king's business; and I was astonished at the vision, but none understood *it*.

**9** IN THE first year of Darius the son of Ahasuerus, of the seed of the Medes, which was made king over the realm of the Chaldeans;

2In the first year of his reign I Daniel understood by books the number of the years, whereof the word of the LORD came to Jeremiah the prophet, that he would accomplish seventy years in the desolations of Jerusalem.

3¶ And I set my face unto the Lord God, to seek by prayer and supplications, with fasting, and sackcloth, and ashes:

4And I prayed unto the LORD my God, and made my confession, and said, O Lord, the great and dreadful God, keeping the covenant and mercy to them that love him, and to them that keep his commandments;

5We have sinned, and have committed iniquity, and have done wickedly, and have rebelled, even by departing from thy precepts and from thy judgments:

6Neither have we hearkened unto thy servants the prophets, which spake in thy name to our kings, our princes, and our fathers, and to all the people of the land.

## Amplified

17So he came near where I stood, and when he came, I was frightened and fell on my face. But he said to me, Understand, O son of man; for the [fulfillment of the] vision belongs to [events that shall occur in] the time of the end.

18Now as he [Gabriel] was speaking with me, I fell stunned *and* in deep unconsciousness with my face to the ground; but he touched me and set me upright—where I had stood.

19And he said, Behold, I will make you know what shall be in the latter time of the indignation [of God upon the ungodly]; for it has to do with the time of the end.

20The ram you saw having two horns, they are the kings of Media and Persia.

21And the shaggy *and* rough he-goat is the king of Grecia; and the great horn between his eyes is the first king [who consolidated the whole realm, Alexander the Great].

22And as for the horn which was shattered, in whose place four others arose, four kingdoms shall arise out of *his* nation, but not having his [Alexander's] power.

23And at the latter end of their kingdom, when the transgressors [the apostate Jews] have reached the fullness [of their wickedness, exceeding the limits of God's mercy], a king of fierce countenance and understanding dark trickery *and* craftiness, shall stand up.

24And his power shall be mighty, but not by his own power; and he shall corrupt *and* destroy astonishingly, and shall prosper, and do his own pleasure, and he shall corrupt *and* destroy the mighty men and the holy people—the people of the saints. [Rev. 13:4-10; Dan. 8:9-12; II Thess. 2:3-10.]

25And through his policy he shall cause trickery to prosper in his hand; he shall magnify himself in his heart *and* mind, and in their security he will corrupt *and* destroy many. He shall also stand up against the Prince of princes, but he shall be broken *and that* by no [human] hand. [Rev. 19:19, 20.]

26The vision of the evenings and the mornings which has been told *you* is true. But seal up the vision, for it has to do with *and* belongs to the *now* distant future.

27And I, Daniel, fainted and was sick certain days; afterward I rose up and did the king's business; and I wondered at the vision, but there was no one who understood it *or* could make it understood.

**9** IN THE first year of Darius the son of Ahasuerus, of the offspring of the Medes, who was made king over the realm of the Chaldeans,

2In the first year of his reign, I, Daniel, understood from the books the number of years, which according to the word of the Lord to Jeremiah the prophet must pass by before the desolations *which had been* pronounced on Jerusalem should end, and *it was* seventy years. [Jer. 25:11, 12; 29:10.]

3And I, *Daniel*, set my face to the Lord God to seek Him by prayer and supplications, with fasting and sackcloth and ashes;

4And I prayed to the Lord my God and made confession, and said, O Lord, the great and dreadful God, Who keeps covenant, mercy *and* loving-kindness with those who love Him and keep His commandments,

5We have sinned and dealt perversely and done wickedly and have rebelled, turning aside from Your commandments and ordinances.

6Neither have we listened to *and* heeded Your servants the prophets, who spoke in Your name to our kings, our princes, and our fathers, and to all the people of the land.

## New American Standard

17 So he came near to where I was standing, and when he came
I was frightened and fell on my face; but he said to me, "Son of
man, understand that the vision pertains to the time of the end."
18 Now while he was talking with me, I sank into a deep sleep
with my face to the ground; but he touched me and made me stand
upright.
19 And he said, "Behold, I am going to let you know what will
occur at the final period of the indignation, for *it* pertains to the
appointed time of the end.

*The Ram's Identity*

20 "The ram which you saw with the two horns represents the
kings of Media and Persia.

*The Goat*

21 "And the shaggy goat *represents* the kingdom of Greece, and
the large horn that is between his eyes is the first king.
22 "And the broken *horn* and the four *horns that* arose in its place
*represent* four kingdoms *which* will arise from *his* nation, although
not with his power.

23 "And in the latter period of their rule,
When the transgressors have run *their course,*
A king will arise
Insolent and skilled in intrigue.
24 "And his power will be mighty, but not by his *own*
power,
And he will destroy to an extraordinary degree
And prosper and perform *his will;*
He will destroy mighty men and the holy people.
25 "And through his shrewdness
He will cause deceit to succeed by his influence;
And he will magnify *himself* in his heart,
And he will destroy many while *they are* at ease.
He will even oppose the Prince of princes,
But he will be broken without human agency.
26 "And the vision of the evenings and mornings
Which has been told is true;
But keep the vision secret,
For *it* pertains to many days *in the future.*"

27 Then I, Daniel, was exhausted and sick for days. Then I got
up *again* and carried on the king's business; but I was astounded
at the vision, and there was none to explain *it.*

*Daniel's Prayer for His People*

9 IN THE first year of Darius the son of Ahasuerus, of Median
descent, who was made king over the kingdom of the Chaldeans—
2 in the first year of his reign I, Daniel, observed in the books
the number of the years which was *revealed as* the word of the LORD
to Jeremiah the prophet for the completion of the desolations of
Jerusalem, *namely,* seventy years.
3 So I gave my attention to the Lord God to seek *Him by* prayer
and supplications, with fasting, sackcloth, and ashes.
4 And I prayed to the LORD my God and confessed and said,
"Alas, O Lord, the great and awesome God, who keeps His covenant and lovingkindness for those who love Him and keep His
commandments,
5 we have sinned, committed iniquity, acted wickedly, and
rebelled, even turning aside from Thy commandments and ordinances.
6 "Moreover, we have not listened to Thy servants the prophets, who spoke in Thy name to our kings, our princes, our fathers,
and all the people of the land.

## New International

17 As he came near the place where I was standing, I was terrified and fell prostrate. "Son of man," he said to me, "understand
that the vision concerns the time of the end."
18 While he was speaking to me, I was in a deep sleep, with my
face to the ground. Then he touched me and raised me to my feet.
19 He said: "I am going to tell you what will happen later in the
time of wrath, because the vision concerns the appointed time of
the end.[a] 20 The two-horned ram that you saw represents the kings
of Media and Persia. 21 The shaggy goat is the king of Greece, and
the large horn between his eyes is the first king. 22 The four horns
that replaced the one that was broken off represent four kingdoms
that will emerge from his nation but will not have the same power.
23 "In the latter part of their reign, when rebels have become
completely wicked, a stern-faced king, a master of intrigue, will
arise. 24 He will become very strong, but not by his own power. He
will cause astounding devastation and will succeed in whatever he
does. He will destroy the mighty men and the holy people. 25 He
will cause deceit to prosper, and he will consider himself superior.
When they feel secure, he will destroy many and take his stand
against the Prince of princes. Yet he will be destroyed, but not by
human power.
26 "The vision of the evenings and mornings that has been given
you is true, but seal up the vision, for it concerns the distant
future."
27 I, Daniel, was exhausted and lay ill for several days. Then I
got up and went about the king's business. I was appalled by the
vision; it was beyond understanding.

*Daniel's Prayer*

9 IN THE first year of Darius son of Xerxes[b] (a Mede by descent), who was made ruler over the Babylonian[c] kingdom—
2 in the first year of his reign, I, Daniel, understood from the
Scriptures, according to the word of the LORD given to Jeremiah
the prophet, that the desolation of Jerusalem would last seventy
years. 3 So I turned to the Lord God and pleaded with him in prayer
and petition, in fasting, and in sackcloth and ashes.
4 I prayed to the LORD my God and confessed:

"O Lord, the great and awesome God, who keeps his
covenant of love with all who love him and obey his commands, 5 we have sinned and done wrong. We have been
wicked and have rebelled; we have turned away from your
commands and laws. 6 We have not listened to your servants
the prophets, who spoke in your name to our kings, our
princes and our fathers, and to all the people of the land.

NIV [a] 19 Or *because the end will be at the appointed time* [b] 1 Hebrew *Ahasuerus*
[c] 1 Or *Chaldean*

## King James

7O Lord, righteousness *belongeth* unto thee, but unto us confusion of faces, as at this day; to the men of Judah, and to the inhabitants of Jerusalem, and unto all Israel, *that are* near, and *that are* far off, through all the countries whither thou hast driven them, because of their trespass that they have trespassed against thee.

8O Lord, to us *belongeth* confusion of face, to our kings, to our princes, and to our fathers, because we have sinned against thee.

9To the Lord our God *belong* mercies and forgivenesses, though we have rebelled against him;

10Neither have we obeyed the voice of the LORD our God, to walk in his laws, which he set before us by his servants the prophets.

11Yea, all Israel have transgressed thy law, even by departing, that they might not obey thy voice; therefore the curse is poured upon us, and the oath that *is* written in the law of Moses the servant of God, because we have sinned against him.

12And he hath confirmed his words, which he spake against us, and against our judges that judged us, by bringing upon us a great evil: for under the whole heaven hath not been done as hath been done upon Jerusalem.

13As *it is* written in the law of Moses, all this evil is come upon us: yet made we not our prayer before the LORD our God, that we might turn from our iniquities, and understand thy truth.

14Therefore hath the LORD watched upon the evil, and brought it upon us: for the LORD our God *is* righteous in all his works which he doeth: for we obeyed not his voice.

15And now, O Lord our God, that hast brought thy people forth out of the land of Egypt with a mighty hand, and hast gotten thee renown, as at this day; we have sinned, we have done wickedly.

16¶ O Lord, according to all thy righteousness, I beseech thee, let thine anger and thy fury be turned away from thy city Jerusalem, thy holy mountain: because for our sins, and for the iniquities of our fathers, Jerusalem and thy people *are become* a reproach to all *that are* about us.

17Now therefore, O our God, hear the prayer of thy servant, and his supplications, and cause thy face to shine upon thy sanctuary that is desolate, for the Lord's sake.

18O my God, incline thine ear, and hear; open thine eyes, and behold our desolations, and the city which is called by thy name: for we do not present our supplications before thee for our righteousnesses, but for thy great mercies.

19O Lord, hear; O Lord, forgive; O Lord, hearken and do; defer not, for thine own sake, O my God: for thy city and thy people are called by thy name.

20¶ And whiles I *was* speaking, and praying, and confessing my sin and the sin of my people Israel, and presenting my supplication before the LORD my God for the holy mountain of my God;

21Yea, whiles I *was* speaking in prayer, even the man Gabriel, whom I had seen in the vision at the beginning, being caused to fly swiftly, touched me about the time of the evening oblation.

22And he informed *me,* and talked with me, and said, O Daniel, I am now come forth to give thee skill and understanding.

23At the beginning of thy supplications the commandment came forth, and I am come to show *thee;* for thou *art* greatly beloved: therefore understand the matter, and consider the vision.

## Amplified

7O Lord, righteousness belongs to You, but to us confusion *and* shame of face, as at this day; to the men of Judah, to the inhabitants of Jerusalem, and to all Israel, those who are near and those who are far off, through all the countries to which You have driven them because of the (treacherous) trespass which they have committed against You.

8O Lord, to us belong confusion *and* shame of face, to our kings, to our princes, and to our fathers, because we have sinned against You.

9To the Lord our God belong mercies *and* loving-kindnesses and forgiveness; for we have rebelled against Him,

10And we have not obeyed the voice of the Lord our God by walking in His laws, which He set before us by His servants the prophets.

11Yea, all Israel have transgressed Your law, even turning aside that they might not obey Your voice. Therefore the curse has been poured out on us, and the oath that is written in the law of Moses the servant of God, because we have sinned against Him. [Lev. 26:14-45; Deut. 28:15-68.]

12And He has carried out intact His *threatening* words, which He threatened against us and against our judges—the kings, princes and rulers generally—who ruled us, and *He* has brought upon us a great evil; for under the whole heavens there has not been done before [anything so dreadful] as *He has caused to be* done against Jerusalem.

13 *Just* as it is written in the law of Moses as to all this evil [that would surely come upon transgressors], so it has come upon us. Yet we have not earnestly begged for *forgiveness and* entreated the favor of the Lord our God, that we might turn from our iniquities, and have understanding *and* become wise in Your truth.

14Therefore the Lord has kept ready the (evil) calamity and has brought it upon us, for the Lord our God is [uncompromisingly] righteous *and* rigidly just in all His works which He does [keeping His word], and we have not obeyed His voice.

15And now, O Lord our God, Who brought Your people forth out of the land of Egypt with a mighty hand, and have secured Yourself renown *and* a name as at this day, we have sinned, we have done wickedly!

16O Lord, according to all Your rightness *and* justice, I beseech You, let Your anger and Your wrath be turned away from Your city Jerusalem, Your holy mountain. Because for our sins, and for the iniquities of our fathers, Jerusalem and Your people have become a reproach *and* a byword to all who are around about us.

17Now therefore, O our God, listen to *and* heed the prayer of Your servant *Daniel* and his supplications, and for Your own sake cause Your face to shine upon Your sanctuary, which is desolate. [But see Ezek. 14:12-20.]

18O my God, incline Your ear and hear; open Your eyes and look at our desolations, and the city which is called by Your name; for we do not present our supplications before You for our own righteousness *and* justice, but for Your great mercies *and* loving-kindnesses.

19O Lord, hear! O Lord, forgive! O Lord, give heed and act! Do not delay, for Your own sake, O my God, because Your city and Your people are called by Your name.

20While I was speaking and praying, confessing my sin and the sin of my people Israel, and presenting my supplication before the Lord my God for the holy hill of my God;

21Yes, while I was speaking in prayer, the man Gabriel, whom I had seen in the former vision, being caused to fly swiftly, came near to me *and* touched me about the time of the evening sacrifice. [Dan. 8:16.]

22He instructed me *and* made me understand; he talked with me and said, O Daniel, I am now come forth to give you skill *and* wisdom and understanding.

23At the beginning of your prayers the word went forth, and I have come to tell you, for you are greatly beloved. Therefore consider the matter and understand the vision.

## New American Standard

7"Righteousness belongs to Thee, O Lord, but to us open shame, as it is this day—to the men of Judah, the inhabitants of Jerusalem, and all Israel, those who are nearby and those who are far away in all the countries to which Thou hast driven them, because of their unfaithful deeds which they have committed against Thee.

8"Open shame belongs to us, O Lord, to our kings, our princes, and our fathers, because we have sinned against Thee.

9"To the Lord our God belong compassion and forgiveness, for we have rebelled against Him;

10nor have we obeyed the voice of the LORD our God, to walk in His teachings which He set before us through His servants the prophets.

11"Indeed all Israel has transgressed Thy law and turned aside, not obeying Thy voice; so the curse has been poured out on us, along with the oath which is written in the law of Moses the servant of God, for we have sinned against Him.

12"Thus He has confirmed His words which He had spoken against us and against our rulers who ruled us, to bring on us great calamity; for under the whole heaven there has not been done *anything* like what was done to Jerusalem.

13"As it is written in the law of Moses, all this calamity has come on us; yet we have not sought the favor of the LORD our God by turning from our iniquity and giving attention to Thy truth.

14"Therefore, the LORD has kept the calamity in store and brought it on us; for the LORD our God is righteous with respect to all His deeds which He has done, but we have not obeyed His voice.

15"And now, O Lord our God, who hast brought Thy people out of the land of Egypt with a mighty hand and hast made a name for Thyself, as it is this day—we have sinned, we have been wicked.

16"O Lord, in accordance with all Thy righteous acts, let now Thine anger and Thy wrath turn away from Thy city Jerusalem, Thy holy mountain; for because of our sins and the iniquities of our fathers, Jerusalem and Thy people *have become* a reproach to all those around us.

17"So now, our God, listen to the prayer of Thy servant and to his supplications, and for Thy sake, O Lord, let Thy face shine on Thy desolate sanctuary.

18"O my God, incline Thine ear and hear! Open Thine eyes and see our desolations and the city which is called by Thy name; for we are not presenting our supplications before Thee on account of any merits of our own, but on account of Thy great compassion.

19"O Lord, hear! O Lord, forgive! O Lord, listen and take action! For Thine own sake, O my God, do not delay, because Thy city and Thy people are called by Thy name."

*Gabriel Brings an Answer*

20¶ Now while I was speaking and praying, and confessing my sin and the sin of my people Israel, and presenting my supplication before the LORD my God in behalf of the holy mountain of my God,

21while I was still speaking in prayer, then the man Gabriel, whom I had seen in the vision previously, came to me in *my* extreme weariness about the time of the evening offering.

22And he gave *me* instruction and talked with me, and said, "O Daniel, I have now come forth to give you insight with understanding.

23"At the beginning of your supplications the command was issued, and I have come to tell *you*, for you are highly esteemed; so give heed to the message and gain understanding of the vision.

## New International

7"Lord, you are righteous, but this day we are covered
with shame—the men of Judah and people of Jerusalem and
all Israel, both near and far, in all the countries where you
have scattered us because of our unfaithfulness to you. 8O
LORD, we and our kings, our princes and our fathers are
covered with shame because we have sinned against you.
9The Lord our God is merciful and forgiving, even though we
have rebelled against him; 10we have not obeyed the LORD our
God or kept the laws he gave us through his servants the
prophets. 11All Israel has transgressed your law and turned
away, refusing to obey you.
"Therefore the curses and sworn judgments written in the
Law of Moses, the servant of God, have been poured out on
us, because we have sinned against you. 12You have fulfilled
the words spoken against us and against our rulers by bringing upon us great disaster. Under the whole heaven nothing
has ever been done like what has been done to Jerusalem.
13Just as it is written in the Law of Moses, all this disaster has
come upon us, yet we have not sought the favor of the LORD
our God by turning from our sins and giving attention to your
truth. 14The LORD did not hesitate to bring the disaster upon
us, for the LORD our God is righteous in everything he does;
yet we have not obeyed him.

15"Now, O Lord our God, who brought your people out
of Egypt with a mighty hand and who made for yourself a
name that endures to this day, we have sinned, we have done
wrong. 16O Lord, in keeping with all your righteous acts, turn
away your anger and your wrath from Jerusalem, your city,
your holy hill. Our sins and the iniquities of our fathers have
made Jerusalem and your people an object of scorn to all those
around us.

17"Now, our God, hear the prayers and petitions of your
servant. For your sake, O Lord, look with favor on your
desolate sanctuary. 18Give ear, O God, and hear; open your
eyes and see the desolation of the city that bears your Name.
We do not make requests of you because we are righteous, but
because of your great mercy. 19O Lord, listen! O Lord, forgive!
O Lord, hear and act! For your sake, O my God, do not delay,
because your city and your people bear your Name."

*The Seventy "Sevens"*

20While I was speaking and praying, confessing my sin and the
sin of my people Israel and making my request to the LORD my God
for his holy hill— 21while I was still in prayer, Gabriel, the man I
had seen in the earlier vision, came to me in swift flight about the
time of the evening sacrifice. 22He instructed me and said to me,
"Daniel, I have now come to give you insight and understanding.
23As soon as you began to pray, an answer was given, which I have
come to tell you, for you are highly esteemed. Therefore, consider
the message and understand the vision:

## King James

24 Seventy weeks are determined upon thy people and upon thy holy city, to finish the transgression, and to make an end of sins, and to make reconciliation for iniquity, and to bring in everlasting righteousness, and to seal up the vision and prophecy, and to anoint the most Holy.

25 Know therefore and understand, *that* from the going forth of the commandment to restore and to build Jerusalem unto the Messiah the Prince *shall be* seven weeks, and threescore and two weeks: the street shall be built again, and the wall, even in troublous times.

26 And after threescore and two weeks shall Messiah be cut off, but not for himself: and the people of the prince that shall come shall destroy the city and the sanctuary; and the end thereof *shall be* with a flood, and unto the end of the war desolations are determined.

27 And he shall confirm the covenant with many for one week: and in the midst of the week he shall cause the sacrifice and the oblation to cease, and for the overspreading of abominations he shall make *it* desolate, even until the consummation, and that determined shall be poured upon the desolate.

**10** IN THE third year of Cyrus king of Persia a thing was revealed unto Daniel, whose name was called Belteshazzar; and the thing *was* true, but the time appointed *was* long: and he understood the thing, and had understanding of the vision.

2 In those days I Daniel was mourning three full weeks.

3 I ate no pleasant bread, neither came flesh nor wine in my mouth, neither did I anoint myself at all, till three whole weeks were fulfilled.

4 And in the four and twentieth day of the first month, as I was by the side of the great river, which *is* Hiddekel;

5 Then I lifted up mine eyes, and looked, and behold a certain man clothed in linen, whose loins *were* girded with fine gold of Uphaz:

6 His body also *was* like the beryl, and his face as the appearance of lightning, and his eyes as lamps of fire, and his arms and his feet like in colour to polished brass, and the voice of his words like the voice of a multitude.

7 And I Daniel alone saw the vision: for the men that were with me saw not the vision; but a great quaking fell upon them, so that they fled to hide themselves.

8 Therefore I was left alone, and saw this great vision, and there remained no strength in me: for my comeliness was turned in me into corruption, and I retained no strength.

9 Yet heard I the voice of his words: and when I heard the voice of his words, then was I in a deep sleep on my face, and my face toward the ground.

10 ¶ And, behold, an hand touched me, which set me upon my knees and *upon* the palms of my hands.

11 And he said unto me, O Daniel, a man greatly beloved, understand the words that I speak unto thee, and stand upright: for unto thee am I now sent. And when he had spoken this word unto me, I stood trembling.

12 Then said he unto me, Fear not, Daniel: for from the first day that thou didst set thine heart to understand, and to chasten thyself before thy God, thy words were heard, and I am come for thy words.

## Amplified

24 Seventy weeks [of years, or four hundred and ninety years] are decreed upon your people and upon your holy city *Jerusalem,* to finish *and* put an end to transgression, to seal up *and* make full the measure of sin, to purge away *and* make expiation *and* reconciliation for sin, and to bring in everlasting righteousness [permanent spiritual and moral rectitude in every area and relation] and to seal up vision and prophecy *and* prophet, and to anoint a holy of holies.

25 Know therefore and understand that from the going forth of the commandment to restore and to build Jerusalem until [the coming of] the anointed one, a prince, shall be seven weeks [of years], and sixty-two weeks [of years]; it shall be built again with *city* square and moat, but in troublous times.

26 And after the sixty-two weeks [of years] shall the anointed one be cut off *or* killed, and shall have nothing [and no one belonging] to [and defending] him. And the people of the *other* prince who shall come will destroy the city and the sanctuary. Its end shall come with a flood, and even to the end there shall be war, and desolations are decreed. [Isa. 53:7-9; Nah. 1:8; Matt. 24:6-14.]

27 And he shall enter into a strong *and* firm covenant with the many for one week [seven years]; and in the midst of the week he shall cause *the* sacrifice and offering to cease [for the remaining three and one-half years]; and upon the wing *or* pinnacle of abominations (shall come) one who makes desolate; until the full determined end is poured out on the desolator.

**10** IN THE third year of Cyrus king of Persia a word was revealed to Daniel, who was called Belteshazzar. And the word was true and it *referred to* great tribulation, conflict [and wretchedness]. And he understood the word and had understanding of the vision. [Dan. 8:26; Rev. 19:9.]

2 In those days I, Daniel, was mourning for three *whole* weeks.

3 I ate no pleasant *or* desirable food, nor did any meat or wine come into my mouth, and I did not anoint myself at all, for the full three weeks.

4 On the twenty-fourth day of the first month, as I was on the bank of the great river *Hiddekel,* which is the Tigris,

5 I lifted up my eyes and looked, and behold, a man clothed in linen, whose loins were girded with pure gold of Uphaz.

6 His body also was [a golden lustre] like beryl, his face had the appearance of lightning, his eyes were like flaming torches, his arms and his feet like glowing burnished bronze, and the sound of his words was like the roaring *of the sea or* the noise of a multitude *of people.*

7 And I, Daniel, alone saw the vision [of this heavenly being], for the men that were with me did not see the vision, but a great trembling fell upon them, so that they fled to hide themselves.

8 So I was left alone and saw this great vision, and no strength was left in me; for my fresh appearance was turned to pallor; I grew weak *and* faint *with fright.*

9 Then I heard the sound of his words; and when I heard the sound of his words I fell on my face in a deep sleep, with my face *sunk* to the ground.

10 And behold, a hand touched me, which set me (unsteadily) upon my knees and upon the palms of my hands.

11 And *the angel* said to me, O Daniel, you greatly beloved man, understand the words that I speak to you, and stand upright, for to you I am now sent. And while he was saying this word to me, I stood up trembling.

12 Then he said to me, Fear not, Daniel, for from the first day that you set your mind *and* heart to understand and to humble yourself before your God, your words were heard, and I have come in consequence of your words.

## New American Standard

*Seventy Weeks and the Messiah*

24¶ "Seventy weeks have been decreed for your people and
your holy city, to finish the transgression, to make an end of sin,
to make atonement for iniquity, to bring in everlasting righteousness, to seal up vision and prophecy, and to anoint the most holy
*place*.
25"So you are to know and discern *that* from the issuing of a
decree to restore and rebuild Jerusalem until Messiah the Prince
*there will be* seven weeks and sixty-two weeks; it will be built again,
with plaza and moat, even in times of distress.
26"Then after the sixty-two weeks the Messiah will be cut off
and have nothing, and the people of the prince who is to come will
destroy the city and the sanctuary. And its end *will come* with a
flood; even to the end there will be war; desolations are determined.
27"And he will make a firm covenant with the many for one
week, but in the middle of the week he will put a stop to sacrifice
and grain offering; and on the wing of abominations *will come* one
who makes desolate, even until a complete destruction, one that
is decreed, is poured out on the one who makes desolate."

*Daniel Is Terrified by a Vision*

10 IN THE third year of Cyrus king of Persia a message was
revealed to Daniel, who was named Belteshazzar; and the
message was true and *one of* great conflict, but he understood the
message and had an understanding of the vision.
2In those days I, Daniel, had been mourning for three entire
weeks.
3I did not eat any tasty food, nor did meat or wine enter my
mouth, nor did I use any ointment at all, until the entire three
weeks were completed.
4And on the twenty-fourth day of the first month, while I was
by the bank of the great river, that is, the Tigris,
5I lifted my eyes and looked, and behold, there was a certain
man dressed in linen, whose waist was girded with *a belt of* pure
gold of Uphaz.
6His body also was like beryl, his face had the appearance of
lightning, his eyes were like flaming torches, his arms and feet like
the gleam of polished bronze, and the sound of his words like the
sound of a tumult.
7Now I, Daniel, alone saw the vision, while the men who were
with me did not see the vision; nevertheless, a great dread fell on
them, and they ran away to hide themselves.
8So I was left alone and saw this great vision; yet no strength
was left in me, for my natural color turned to a deathly pallor, and
I retained no strength.
9But I heard the sound of his words; and as soon as I heard the
sound of his words, I fell into a deep sleep on my face, with my
face to the ground.

*Daniel Comforted*

10¶ Then behold, a hand touched me and set me trembling on
my hands and knees.
11And he said to me, "O Daniel, man of high esteem, understand the words that I am about to tell you and stand upright, for
I have now been sent to you." And when he had spoken this word
to me, I stood up trembling.
12Then he said to me, "Do not be afraid, Daniel, for from the
first day that you set your heart on understanding *this* and on
humbling yourself before your God, your words were heard, and
I have come in response to your words.

## New International

24"Seventy 'sevens'[a] are decreed for your people and your holy
city to finish[b] transgression, to put an end to sin, to atone for
wickedness, to bring in everlasting righteousness, to seal up vision
and prophecy and to anoint the most holy.[c]
25"Know and understand this: From the issuing of the decree[d]
to restore and rebuild Jerusalem until the Anointed One,[e] the
ruler, comes, there will be seven 'sevens,' and sixty-two 'sevens.'
It will be rebuilt with streets and a trench, but in times of trouble.
26After the sixty-two 'sevens,' the Anointed One will be cut off and
will have nothing.[f] The people of the ruler who will come will
destroy the city and the sanctuary. The end will come like a flood:
War will continue until the end, and desolations have been decreed. 27He will confirm a covenant with many for one 'seven.'[g]
In the middle of the 'seven'[h] he will put an end to sacrifice and
offering. And on a wing ⌊of the temple⌋ he will set up an abomination that causes desolation, until the end that is decreed is poured
out on him.[i] "[j]

*Daniel's Vision of a Man*

10 IN THE third year of Cyrus king of Persia, a revelation was
given to Daniel (who was called Belteshazzar). Its message
was true and it concerned a great war.[k] The understanding of the
message came to him in a vision.
2At that time I, Daniel, mourned for three weeks. 3I ate no
choice food; no meat or wine touched my lips; and I used no lotions
at all until the three weeks were over.
4On the twenty-fourth day of the first month, as I was standing
on the bank of the great river, the Tigris, 5I looked up and there
before me was a man dressed in linen, with a belt of the finest gold
around his waist. 6His body was like chrysolite, his face like lightning, his eyes like flaming torches, his arms and legs like the gleam
of burnished bronze, and his voice like the sound of a multitude.
7I, Daniel, was the only one who saw the vision; the men with
me did not see it, but such terror overwhelmed them that they fled
and hid themselves. 8So I was left alone, gazing at this great vision;
I had no strength left, my face turned deathly pale and I was
helpless. 9Then I heard him speaking, and as I listened to him, I
fell into a deep sleep, my face to the ground.
10A hand touched me and set me trembling on my hands and
knees. 11He said, "Daniel, you who are highly esteemed, consider
carefully the words I am about to speak to you, and stand up, for
I have now been sent to you." And when he said this to me, I stood
up trembling.
12Then he continued, "Do not be afraid, Daniel. Since the first
day that you set your mind to gain understanding and to humble
yourself before your God, your words were heard, and I have
come in response to them. 13But the prince of the Persian kingdom

NIV [a] 24 Or *'weeks'*; also in verses 25 and 26 [b] 24 Or *restrain* [c] 24 Or *Most Holy Place*; or *most holy One* [d] 25 Or *word* [e] 25 Or *an anointed one*; also in verse 26 [f] 26 Or *off and will have no one*; or *off, but not for himself* [g] 27 Or *'week'* [h] 27 Or *'week'* [i] 27 Or *it* [j] 27 Or *And one who causes desolation will come upon the pinnacle of the abominable ⌊temple⌋, until the end that is decreed is poured out on the desolated ⌊city⌋* [k] 1 Or *true and burdensome*

## King James

13But the prince of the kingdom of Persia withstood me one and
twenty days: but, lo, Michael, one of the chief princes, came to
help me; and I remained there with the kings of Persia.
14Now I am come to make thee understand what shall befall thy
people in the latter days: for yet the vision *is* for *many* days.
15And when he had spoken such words unto me, I set my face
toward the ground, and I became dumb.
16And, behold, *one* like the similitude of the sons of men
touched my lips: then I opened my mouth, and spake, and said
unto him that stood before me, O my lord, by the vision my
sorrows are turned upon me, and I have retained no strength.
17For how can the servant of this my lord talk with this my lord?
for as for me, straightway there remained no strength in me,
neither is there breath left in me.
18Then there came again and touched me *one* like the appearance of a man, and he strengthened me,
19And said, O man greatly beloved, fear not: peace *be* unto thee,
be strong, yea, be strong. And when he had spoken unto me, I was
strengthened, and said, Let my lord speak; for thou hast strengthened me.
20Then said he, Knowest thou wherefore I come unto thee? and
now will I return to fight with the prince of Persia: and when I am
gone forth, lo, the prince of Grecia shall come.
21But I will show thee that which is noted in the scripture of
truth: and *there is* none that holdeth with me in these things, but
Michael your prince.

**11** ALSO I in the first year of Darius the Mede, *even* I, stood
to confirm and to strengthen him.
2And now will I show thee the truth. Behold, there shall stand
up yet three kings in Persia; and the fourth shall be far richer than
*they* all: and by his strength through his riches he shall stir up all
against the realm of Grecia.
3And a mighty king shall stand up, that shall rule with great
dominion, and do according to his will.
4And when he shall stand up, his kingdom shall be broken, and
shall be divided toward the four winds of heaven; and not to his
posterity, nor according to his dominion which he ruled: for his
kingdom shall be plucked up, even for others beside those.
5¶ And the king of the south shall be strong, and *one* of his
princes; and he shall be strong above him, and have dominion; his
dominion *shall be* a great dominion.
6And in the end of years they shall join themselves together; for
the king's daughter of the south shall come to the king of the north
to make an agreement: but she shall not retain the power of the
arm; neither shall he stand, nor his arm: but she shall be given up,
and they that brought her, and he that begat her, and he that
strengthened her in *these* times.

**AMP** [a] There are numerous reasons for identifying this mighty king as Alexander the Great, and the other characters according to their relationship to the events of those times. "But the mere similarity which exists between certain things predicted here and what actually occurred in the times of the Ptolemies of Egypt is not sufficient to limit the fulfillment of the prophecy to those times—certainly [we find here what] was characteristic of Alexander, but there was nothing in the context which makes it necessary to limit the passage to him. Some autocrat may arise 'in the latter days' to whom it will apply with greater force than it did to Alexander."—Ellicott's Commentary on the Whole Bible.
[b] There are numerous reasons for identifying this mighty king as Alexander the Great, and the other characters according to their relationship to the events of those times. "But the mere similarity which exists between certain things predicted here and what actually occurred in the times of the Ptolemies of Egypt is not sufficient to limit the fulfillment of the prophecy to those times—certainly [we find here what] was characteristic of Alexander, but there was nothing in the context which makes it necessary to limit the passage to him. Some autocrat may arise 'in the latter days' to whom it will apply with greater force than it did to Alexander."—Ellicott's Commentary on the Whole Bible.

## Amplified

13But the prince of the kingdom of Persia withstood me for
twenty-one days. But Michael, one of the chief *of the celestial*
princes, came to help me; and I remained [was not needed] *there*
with the kings of Persia.
14Now I have come to make you understand what is to befall
your people in the latter days. For the vision is for *many* days yet
*to come.*
15When he had spoken to me according to these words, I turned
my face toward the ground and was dumb.
16And, behold, one in the likeness of the sons of men touched
my lips. Then I opened my mouth and spoke. I said to him who
stood before me, O my lord, by reason of the vision sorrows *and*
pains have come upon me, and I retain no strength.
17For how can my lord's servant [who am so feeble] talk with
this my lord? For now no strength remains in me, nor is there any
breath left in me.
18Then there touched me again one whose appearance was like
that of a man, and he strengthened me.
19And he said, O man greatly beloved, fear not; peace be to you,
be strong, yes, be strong. And when he had spoken to me, I was
strengthened and said, Let my lord speak, for you have strengthened me.
20Then he said, Do you know why I have come to you? And
now I will return to fight with the [hostile] prince of Persia, and
when I have gone, notice, the [hostile] prince of Greece will come.
21But I will tell you what is inscribed in the writing *or* book of
truth. There is no one who holds with me *and* strengthens himself
against these [hostile spirit forces], except Michael, your [national
guardian angel] prince.

**11** ALSO I [the angel], in the first year of Darius the Mede,
even I, stood up to confirm and to strengthen him [Mi-
chael, the angel].
2And now I will show you the truth. Behold, there shall arise
three more kings in Persia, and a fourth shall be far richer than they
all. And when he has become strong through his riches he shall
stir up *and stake* all against the realm of Greece.
3Then a [a]mighty [warlike, threatening] king shall arise, who
shall rule with great dominion and do according to his *own* will.
4And *as soon as* he has fully arisen, his [ [b]Alexander's] kingdom
shall be broken *by his death* and divided toward [the east, west,
north, and south] the four winds of the heavens, but not to his
posterity, nor according to the [Grecian] dominion which he ruled,
for his kingdom shall be torn out *and* uprooted and go to others
[that is, to his four generals] to the exclusion of these.
5Then the king of the south [Egypt] shall be strong, but one of
his princes shall be stronger than he is and have dominion; his
dominion shall be a great dominion.
6At the end of some years they [the king of the north, Syria, and
the king of the south, Egypt] shall make an alliance; the daughter
of the king of the south shall come to the king of the north to make
[a just and peaceful marriage] agreement; but she shall not retain
the power of her might, neither shall he and his might endure. She
shall be surrendered with her attendants, her child, and him who
strengthened her in those times.

## New American Standard

13"But the prince of the kingdom of Persia was withstanding me for twenty-one days; then behold, Michael, one of the chief princes, came to help me, for I had been left there with the kings of Persia.

14"Now I have come to give you an understanding of what will happen to your people in the latter days, for the vision pertains to the days yet *future*."

15And when he had spoken to me according to these words, I turned my face toward the ground and became speechless.

16And behold, one who resembled a human being was touching my lips; then I opened my mouth and spoke, and said to him who was standing before me, "O my lord, as a result of the vision anguish has come upon me, and I have retained no strength.

17"For how can such a servant of my lord talk with such as my lord? As for me, there remains just now no strength in me, nor has any breath been left in me."

18¶ Then *this* one with human appearance touched me again and strengthened me.

19And he said, "O man of high esteem, do not be afraid. Peace be with you; take courage and be courageous!" Now as soon as he spoke to me, I received strength and said, "May my lord speak, for you have strengthened me."

20Then he said, "Do you understand why I came to you? But I shall now return to fight against the prince of Persia; so I am going forth, and behold, the prince of Greece is about to come.

21"However, I will tell you what is inscribed in the writing of truth. Yet there is no one who stands firmly with me against these *forces* except Michael your prince.

*Conflicts to Come*

**11** "AND IN the first year of Darius the Mede, I arose to be an encouragement and a protection for him.

2"And now I will tell you the truth. Behold, three more kings are going to arise in Persia. Then a fourth will gain far more riches than all *of them;* as soon as he becomes strong through his riches, he will arouse the whole *empire* against the realm of Greece.

3"And a mighty king will arise, and he will rule with great authority and do as he pleases.

4"But as soon as he has arisen, his kingdom will be broken up and parceled out toward the four points of the compass, though not to his *own* descendants, nor according to his authority which he wielded; for his sovereignty will be uprooted and *given* to others besides them.

5¶ "Then the king of the South will grow strong, along with *one* of his princes who will gain ascendancy over him and obtain dominion; his domain *will be* a great dominion *indeed*.

6"And after some years they will form an alliance, and the daughter of the king of the South will come to the king of the North to carry out a peaceful arrangement. But she will not retain her position of power, nor will he remain with his power, but she will be given up, along with those who brought her in, and the one who sired her, as well as he who supported her in *those* times.

## New International

resisted me twenty-one days. Then Michael, one of the chief princes, came to help me, because I was detained there with the king of Persia. 14Now I have come to explain to you what will happen to your people in the future, for the vision concerns a time yet to come."

15While he was saying this to me, I bowed with my face toward the ground and was speechless. 16Then one who looked like a man[c] touched my lips, and I opened my mouth and began to speak. I said to the one standing before me, "I am overcome with anguish because of the vision, my lord, and I am helpless. 17How can I, your servant, talk with you, my lord? My strength is gone and I can hardly breathe."

18Again the one who looked like a man touched me and gave me strength. 19"Do not be afraid, O man highly esteemed," he said. "Peace! Be strong now; be strong."

When he spoke to me, I was strengthened and said, "Speak, my lord, since you have given me strength."

20So he said, "Do you know why I have come to you? Soon I will return to fight against the prince of Persia, and when I go, the prince of Greece will come; 21but first I will tell you what is written in the Book of Truth. (No one supports me against them except Michael, your prince.

**11** AND IN the first year of Darius the Mede, I took my stand to support and protect him.)

*The Kings of the South and the North*

2"Now then, I tell you the truth: Three more kings will appear in Persia, and then a fourth, who will be far richer than all the others. When he has gained power by his wealth, he will stir up everyone against the kingdom of Greece. 3Then a mighty king will appear, who will rule with great power and do as he pleases. 4After he has appeared, his empire will be broken up and parceled out toward the four winds of heaven. It will not go to his descendants, nor will it have the power he exercised, because his empire will be uprooted and given to others.

5"The king of the South will become strong, but one of his commanders will become even stronger than he and will rule his own kingdom with great power. 6After some years, they will become allies. The daughter of the king of the South will go to the king of the North to make an alliance, but she will not retain her power, and he and his power[d] will not last. In those days she will be handed over, together with her royal escort and her father[e] and the one who supported her.

**NIV** [c] *16* Most manuscripts of the Masoretic Text; one manuscript of the Masoretic Text, Dead Sea Scrolls and Septuagint *Then something that looked like a man's hand* [d] *6* Or *offspring* [e] *6* Or *child* (see Vulgate and Syriac)

## King James

7But out of a branch of her roots shall *one* stand up in his estate, which shall come with an army, and shall enter into the fortress of the king of the north, and shall deal against them, and shall prevail:

8And shall also carry captives into Egypt their gods, with their princes, *and* with their precious vessels of silver and of gold; and he shall continue *more* years than the king of the north.

9So the king of the south shall come into *his* kingdom, and shall return into his own land.

10But his sons shall be stirred up, and shall assemble a multitude of great forces: and *one* shall certainly come, and overflow, and pass through: then shall he return, and be stirred up, *even* to his fortress.

11And the king of the south shall be moved with choler, and shall come forth and fight with him, *even* with the king of the north: and he shall set forth a great multitude; but the multitude shall be given into his hand.

12 *And* when he hath taken away the multitude, his heart shall be lifted up; and he shall cast down *many* ten thousands: but he shall not be strengthened *by it.*

13For the king of the north shall return, and shall set forth a multitude greater than the former, and shall certainly come after certain years with a great army and with much riches.

14And in those times there shall many stand up against the king of the south: also the robbers of thy people shall exalt themselves to establish the vision; but they shall fall.

15So the king of the north shall come, and cast up a mount, and take the most fenced cities: and the arms of the south shall not withstand, neither his chosen people, neither *shall there be any* strength to withstand.

16But he that cometh against him shall do according to his own will, and none shall stand before him: and he shall stand in the glorious land, which by his hand shall be consumed.

17He shall also set his face to enter with the strength of his whole kingdom, and upright ones with him; thus shall he do: and he shall give him the daughter of women, corrupting her: but she shall not stand *on his side,* neither be for him.

18After this shall he turn his face unto the isles, and shall take many: but a prince for his own behalf shall cause the reproach offered by him to cease; without his own reproach he shall cause *it* to turn upon him.

19Then he shall turn his face toward the fort of his own land: but he shall stumble and fall, and not be found.

20Then shall stand up in his estate a raiser of taxes *in* the glory of the kingdom: but within few days he shall be destroyed, neither in anger, nor in battle.

21And in his estate shall stand up a vile person, to whom they shall not give the honour of the kingdom: but he shall come in peaceably, and obtain the kingdom by flatteries.

22And with the arms of a flood shall they be overflown from before him, and shall be broken; yea, also the prince of the covenant.

23And after the league *made* with him he shall work deceitfully: for he shall come up, and shall become strong with a small people.

## Amplified

7But out of a branch of the [same ancestral] roots *as* hers, shall one [her brother] stand up in his place *or* office, who shall come against the [Syrian] army and shall enter into the fortress of the king of the north, and shall deal against them and shall prevail.

8And also he shall carry off to Egypt [Syria's] gods with their molten images and with their precious vessels of silver and of gold; and he shall refrain for some years from [waging war against] the king of the north.

9And he [the king of Syria] shall come into the kingdom of the king of the south, but shall return to his own land.

10But his sons shall be stirred up *and* shall prepare for war, and shall assemble a multitude of great forces, which shall come on and overflow and pass through, and again shall make war even to the fortress [of the southern king].

11And the king of the south [Eygpt] shall be moved with anger, and shall come forth and fight with the king of the north [Syria]; and he, [the Syrian,] shall set forth a great multitude, but the multitude shall be given into his, [the Egyptian's,] hand.

12When the multitude is taken *and* carried away, the heart *and* mind [of the Egyptian] shall be exalted, and he shall cast down tens of thousands, but he shall not prevail.

13For the king of the north shall raise a multitude greater than [he had] before, and after some years shall certainly return, coming with a great army and much substance *and* equipment.

14In those times many shall rise up against the king of the south [Egypt]; also the men of violence among your own people shall lift themselves up in order to fulfill the visions [of chapters eight and nine] but they shall fail *and* fall.

15Then the king of the north shall come, and cast up siegeworks and take a well-fortified city, and the forces of the south shall not stand, or even his chosen troops, for there shall be no strength to stand [against the Syrian].

16But he [Antiochus the Great] who comes against him [from Syria] shall do according to his own will, and none shall stand before him; he shall stand in the glorious land [of Israel], and in his hand shall be destruction *and* all the land shall be in his power.

17He [Antiochus the Great] shall set his face to come with the strength of his whole kingdom, and with him upright conditions *and* terms of peace, and he shall perform them [by making an agreement with the southern king]. He shall give him *his* daughter to corrupt *and* destroy it [his league with Egypt] *and* the kingdom; but it shall not succeed or be to his advantage.

18After this he shall turn his attention to the islands *and* coastlands and shall take over many *of them.* But a prince *or* commander shall teach him [Antiochus] to put an end to the insults offered by him; in fact he shall turn his insolence *and* reproaches back upon him.

19Then he shall turn his face back toward the fortresses of his own land [of Syria]; but he shall stumble and fall, and not be found.

20Then shall [a]stand up in his place *or* office one who shall send an exactor of tribute to pass through the glory of the kingdom; but within a few days he shall be destroyed, neither in anger nor in battle.

21And in his place *or* office [in Syria] shall arise a [b]contemptuous *and* contemptible person, to whom royal majesty *and* honor of the kingdom *have* not been given. But he shall come in without warning in time of security and shall obtain the kingdom by flatteries, intrigues *and* cunning hypocritical conduct.

22Before him the overwhelming forces of invading armies shall be broken *and* utterly swept away; yes, and a prince of the covenant [with those who were at peace with him] also [shall be broken and] swept away.

23And from the time that an alliance is made with him he shall work deceitfully, and he shall come up unexpectedly and shall become strong with a small people.

**AMP** [a] The reference here is undoubtedly to Seleucus Philopator [a king of Syria], the eldest son of Antiochus the Great, and his immediate successor. (Barnes' Notes on the Old Testament.) [b] This contemptible conqueror is generally identified as Antiochus Epiphanes, the younger son of Antiochus the Great, king of Syria, and is symbolic of the final Antichrist referred to in I John 4:3; II John 7; II Thess. 2:3-12; and Matt. 24:23-27. "He stirred up the Jews by robbing the temple and setting up a statue of Jupiter in the holy of holies. He also pulled down the walls of Jerusalem, commanded the sacrifice of [forbidden] swine, forbade circumcision, and destroyed all the sacred books that could be found." *(Davis Dictionary of the Bible.)* See also Daniel 8:8-12, 23, 24.

## New American Standard

7"But one of the descendants of her line will arise in his place,
and he will come against *their* army and enter the fortress of the
king of the North, and he will deal with them and display *great*
strength.
8"And also their gods with their metal images *and* their precious vessels of silver and gold he will take into captivity to Egypt,
and he on his part will refrain from *attacking* the king of the North
for *some* years.
9"Then the latter will enter the realm of the king of the South,
but will return to his *own* land.
10¶ "And his sons will mobilize and assemble a multitude of
great forces; and one of them will keep on coming and overflow
and pass through, that he may again wage war up to his *very*
fortress.
11"And the king of the South will be enraged and go forth and
fight with the king of the North. Then the latter will raise a great
multitude, but *that* multitude will be given into the hand of the
*former*.
12"When the multitude is carried away, his heart will be lifted
up, and he will cause tens of thousands to fall; yet he will not
prevail.
13"For the king of the North will again raise a greater multitude
than the former, and after an interval of some years he will press
on with a great army and much equipment.
14¶ "Now in those times many will rise up against the king of
the South; the violent ones among your people will also lift themselves up in order to fulfill the vision, but they will fall down.
15"Then the king of the North will come, cast up a siege mound,
and capture a well-fortified city; and the forces of the South will
not stand *their ground*, not even their choicest troops, for there will
be no strength to make a stand.
16"But he who comes against him will do as he pleases, and no
one will *be able to* withstand him; he will also stay *for a time* in the
Beautiful Land, with destruction in his hand.
17"And he will set his face to come with the power of his whole
kingdom, bringing with him a proposal of peace which he will put
into effect; he will also give him the daughter of women to ruin it.
But she will not take a stand *for him* or be on his side.
18"Then he will turn his face to the coastlands and capture
many. But a commander will put a stop to his scorn against him;
moreover, he will repay him for his scorn.
19"So he will turn his face toward the fortresses of his own land,
but he will stumble and fall and be found no more.
20¶ "Then in his place one will arise who will send an oppressor
through the [c]Jewel of *his* kingdom; yet within a few days he will
be shattered, though neither in anger nor in battle.
21"And in his place a despicable person will arise, on whom the
honor of kingship has not been conferred, but he will come in a
time of tranquility and seize the kingdom by intrigue.
22"And the overflowing forces will be flooded away before him
and shattered, and also the prince of the covenant.
23"And after an alliance is made with him he will practice
deception, and he will go up and gain power with a small *force of*
people.

NAS [c] Lit., *adornment;* i.e., probably Jerusalem and its temple

## New International

7"One from her family line will arise to take her place. He will
attack the forces of the king of the North and enter his fortress; he
will fight against them and be victorious.
8He will also seize their
gods, their metal images and their valuable articles of silver and
gold and carry them off to Egypt. For some years he will leave the
king of the North alone.
9Then the king of the North will invade
the realm of the king of the South but will retreat to his own
country.
10His sons will prepare for war and assemble a great
army, which will sweep on like an irresistible flood and carry the
battle as far as his fortress.
11"Then the king of the South will march out in a rage and fight
against the king of the North, who will raise a large army, but it
will be defeated.
12When the army is carried off, the king of the
South will be filled with pride and will slaughter many thousands,
yet he will not remain triumphant.
13For the king of the North will
muster another army, larger than the first; and after several years,
he will advance with a huge army fully equipped.
14"In those times many will rise against the king of the South.
The violent men among your own people will rebel in fulfillment
of the vision, but without success.
15Then the king of the North
will come and build up siege ramps and will capture a fortified city.
The forces of the South will be powerless to resist; even their best
troops will not have the strength to stand.
16The invader will do
as he pleases; no one will be able to stand against him. He will
establish himself in the Beautiful Land and will have the power to
destroy it.
17He will determine to come with the might of his entire
kingdom and will make an alliance with the king of the South. And
he will give him a daughter in marriage in order to overthrow the
kingdom, but his plans[d] will not succeed or help him.
18Then he
will turn his attention to the coastlands and will take many of
them, but a commander will put an end to his insolence and will
turn his insolence back upon him.
19After this, he will turn back
toward the fortresses of his own country but will stumble and fall,
to be seen no more.
20"His successor will send out a tax collector to maintain the
royal splendor. In a few years, however, he will be destroyed, yet
not in anger or in battle.
21"He will be succeeded by a contemptible person who has not
been given the honor of royalty. He will invade the kingdom when
its people feel secure, and he will seize it through intrigue.
22Then
an overwhelming army will be swept away before him; both it and
a prince of the covenant will be destroyed.
23After coming to an
agreement with him, he will act deceitfully, and with only a few
people he will rise to power.
24When the richest provinces feel

NIV [d] 17 Or *but she*

## King James

24He shall enter peaceably even upon the fattest places of the province; and he shall do *that* which his fathers have not done, nor his fathers' fathers; he shall scatter among them the prey, and spoil, and riches: *yea,* and he shall forecast his devices against the strong holds, even for a time.
25And he shall stir up his power and his courage against the king of the south with a great army; and the king of the south shall be stirred up to battle with a very great and mighty army; but he shall not stand: for they shall forecast devices against him.
26Yea, they that feed of the portion of his meat shall destroy him, and his army shall overflow: and many shall fall down slain.
27And both these kings' hearts *shall be* to do mischief, and they shall speak lies at one table; but it shall not prosper: for yet the end *shall be* at the time appointed.
28Then shall he return into his land with great riches; and his heart *shall be* against the holy covenant; and he shall do *exploits,* and return to his own land.
29At the time appointed he shall return, and come toward the south; but it shall not be as the former, or as the latter.
30¶ For the ships of Chittim shall come against him: therefore he shall be grieved, and return, and have indignation against the holy covenant: so shall he do; he shall even return, and have intelligence with them that forsake the holy covenant.
31And arms shall stand on his part, and they shall pollute the sanctuary of strength, and shall take away the daily *sacrifice,* and they shall place the abomination that maketh desolate.
32And such as do wickedly against the covenant shall he corrupt by flatteries: but the people that do know their God shall be strong, and do *exploits.*
33And they that understand among the people shall instruct many: yet they shall fall by the sword, and by flame, by captivity, and by spoil, *many* days.
34Now when they shall fall, they shall be helped with a little help: but many shall cleave to them with flatteries.
35And *some* of them of understanding shall fall, to try them, and to purge, and to make *them* white, *even* to the time of the end: because *it is* yet for a time appointed.
36And the king shall do according to his will; and he shall exalt himself, and magnify himself above every god, and shall speak marvellous things against the God of gods, and shall prosper till the indignation be accomplished: for that that is determined shall be done.
37Neither shall he regard the God of his fathers, nor the desire of women, nor regard any god: for he shall magnify himself above all.
38But in his estate shall he honour the God of forces: and a god whom his fathers knew not shall he honour with gold, and silver, and with precious stones, and pleasant things.
39Thus shall he do in the most strong holds with a strange god, whom he shall acknowledge *and* increase with glory: and he shall cause them to rule over many, and shall divide the land for gain.

## Amplified

24Without warning *and* stealthily he shall come into the most productive places of a province *or* among the richest men of a province [of Egypt], and he shall do that which his fathers have not done nor his fathers' fathers; he shall distribute among them plunder, spoil, and goods. He shall devise plans against strongholds, *but only* for a time [the period decreed by God].
25And he shall stir up his power and his courage against the king of the south [Egypt] with a great army; and the king of the south shall wage war with an exceedingly great and mighty army; but he shall not stand, for schemes shall be devised against [the king of the south].
26Yes, those who eat of his rich *and* dainty food shall break *and* destroy him, and his army shall drift *or* turn away to flee, and many shall fall down slain.
27And as for both of these kings, their hearts *and* minds shall be set on doing mischief; they shall speak lies over the same table, but it will not succeed; for the end is yet to be at the time appointed.
28Then shall [the vile northern conqueror] return into his land with much booty, and his heart *and* purpose shall be set against [God's] holy covenant [with His people], and he shall accomplish [his malicious intention] and return to his own land [Syria].
29At the time appointed [God's own time] he shall return, and come into the south; but it shall not be successful as were the former invasions of Egypt.
30For the ships of Kittim [or Cyprus, in Roman hands] shall come against him; therefore he shall be grieved *and* discouraged and turn back [to Palestine] and carry out his rage *and* indignation against the holy covenant *and* God's people; and he shall do his own pleasure; he shall even turn back and make common cause with those *Jews* who abandon the holy covenant [with God].
31And armed forces of his shall appear [in the holy land], and they shall pollute the sanctuary, the [spiritual] stronghold, and shall take away the continual [daily] *burnt offering,* and they shall set up [in the sanctuary] the abomination that astonishes *and* makes desolate [probably an idol-altar].
32And such as violate the covenant he shall pervert *and* seduce with flatteries; but the people who know their God shall prove themselves strong *and* shall stand firm, and do exploits [for God].
33And they who are wise *and* understand among the people shall instruct many *and* make them understand, though some [of them and their followers] shall fall by the sword and by flame, by captivity and plunder, for many days.
34Now when they fall, they shall receive a little help. Many shall join themselves to them with flatteries *and* hypocrisies.
35And some of those who are wise, prudent *and* understanding shall be weakened *and* fall; [thus then the insincere among the people will lose courage and become deserters. It will be a test] to refine, to purify and make those among [God's people] white, even to the time of the end; because it is yet for the time [God] appointed.
36And the king shall do according to his will; he shall exalt himself and magnify himself above every god, and shall speak astonishing things against the God of gods, and shall prosper till the indignation be accomplished; for that which is determined [by God] shall be done.
37He shall not regard the gods of his fathers, or Him [to Whom] women desire [to give birth], or any other god, for he shall magnify himself above all.
38But in their place he shall honor the god of fortresses; a god whom his fathers knew not shall he honor with gold and silver, and with precious stones and pleasant *and* expensive things.
39And he shall deal with the strongest fortresses by the help of a foreign god. Those who acknowledge him he shall magnify with glory *and* honor, and he shall cause them to rule over many, and shall divide the land for a price.

## New American Standard

24"In a time of tranquility he will enter the richest *parts* of the realm, and he will accomplish what his fathers never did, nor his ancestors; he will distribute plunder, booty, and possessions among them, and he will devise his schemes against strongholds, but *only* for a time.

25"And he will stir up his strength and courage against the king of the South with a large army; so the king of the South will mobilize an extremely large and mighty army for war; but he will not stand, for schemes will be devised against him.

26"And those who eat his choice food will destroy him, and his army will overflow, but many will fall down slain.

27"As for both kings, their hearts will be *intent* on evil, and they will speak lies *to each other* at the same table; but it will not succeed, for the end is still *to come* at the appointed time.

28"Then he will return to his land with much plunder; but his heart will be *set* against the holy covenant, and he will take action and *then* return to his *own* land.

29¶ "At the appointed time he will return and come into the South, but this last time it will not turn out the way it did before.

30"For ships of Kittim will come against him; therefore he will be disheartened, and will return and become enraged at the holy covenant and take action; so he will come back and show regard for those who forsake the holy covenant.

31"And forces from him will arise, desecrate the sanctuary fortress, and do away with the regular sacrifice. And they will set up the abomination of desolation.

32"And by smooth *words* he will turn to godlessness those who act wickedly toward the covenant, but the people who know their God will display strength and take action.

33"And those who have insight among the people will give understanding to the many; yet they will fall by sword and by flame, by captivity and by plunder, for *many* days.

34"Now when they fall they will be granted a little help, and many will join with them in hypocrisy.

35"And some of those who have insight will fall, in order to refine, purge, and make them pure, until the end time; because *it is* still *to come* at the appointed time.

36¶ "Then the king will do as he pleases, and he will exalt and magnify himself above every god, and will speak monstrous things against the God of gods; and he will prosper until the indignation is finished, for that which is decreed will be done.

37"And he will show no regard for the gods of his fathers or for the desire of women, nor will he show regard for any *other* god; for he will magnify himself above *them* all.

38"But instead he will honor a god of fortresses, a god whom his fathers did not know; he will honor *him* with gold, silver, costly stones, and treasures.

39"And he will take action against the strongest of fortresses with *the help of* a foreign god; he will give great honor to those who acknowledge *him*, and he will cause them to rule over the many, and will parcel out land for a price.

## New International

secure, he will invade them and will achieve what neither his fathers nor his forefathers did. He will distribute plunder, loot and wealth among his followers. He will plot the overthrow of fortresses—but only for a time.

25"With a large army he will stir up his strength and courage
against the king of the South. The king of the South will wage war
with a large and very powerful army, but he will not be able to
stand because of the plots devised against him. 26Those who eat
from the king's provisions will try to destroy him; his army will be
swept away, and many will fall in battle. 27The two kings, with
their hearts bent on evil, will sit at the same table and lie to each
other, but to no avail, because an end will still come at the appointed time. 28The king of the North will return to his own
country with great wealth, but his heart will be set against the holy
covenant. He will take action against it and then return to his own
country.

29"At the appointed time he will invade the South again, but
this time the outcome will be different from what it was before.
30Ships of the western coastlands[a] will oppose him, and he will
lose heart. Then he will turn back and vent his fury against the holy
covenant. He will return and show favor to those who forsake the
holy covenant.

31"His armed forces will rise up to desecrate the temple fortress
and will abolish the daily sacrifice. Then they will set up the
abomination that causes desolation. 32With flattery he will corrupt
those who have violated the covenant, but the people who know
their God will firmly resist him.

33"Those who are wise will instruct many, though for a time
they will fall by the sword or be burned or captured or plundered.
34When they fall, they will receive a little help, and many who are
not sincere will join them. 35Some of the wise will stumble, so that
they may be refined, purified and made spotless until the time of
the end, for it will still come at the appointed time.

*The King Who Exalts Himself*

36"The king will do as he pleases. He will exalt and magnify
himself above every god and will say unheard-of things against the
God of gods. He will be successful until the time of wrath is
completed, for what has been determined must take place. 37He
will show no regard for the gods of his fathers or for the one
desired by women, nor will he regard any god, but will exalt
himself above them all. 38Instead of them, he will honor a god of
fortresses; a god unknown to his fathers he will honor with gold
and silver, with precious stones and costly gifts. 39He will attack
the mightiest fortresses with the help of a foreign god and will
greatly honor those who acknowledge him. He will make them
rulers over many people and will distribute the land at a price.[b]

NIV [a] 30 Hebrew *of Kittim* [b] 39 Or *land for a reward*

## King James

40And at the time of the end shall the king of the south push at him: and the king of the north shall come against him like a whirlwind, with chariots, and with horsemen, and with many ships; and he shall enter into the countries, and shall overflow and pass over.

41He shall enter also into the glorious land, and many *countries* shall be overthrown: but these shall escape out of his hand, *even* Edom, and Moab, and the chief of the children of Ammon.

42He shall stretch forth his hand also upon the countries: and the land of Egypt shall not escape.

43But he shall have power over the treasures of gold and of silver, and over all the precious things of Egypt: and the Libyans and the Ethiopians *shall be* at his steps.

44But tidings out of the east and out of the north shall trouble him: therefore he shall go forth with great fury to destroy, and utterly to make away many.

45And he shall plant the tabernacles of his palace between the seas in the glorious holy mountain; yet he shall come to his end, and none shall help him.

**12** AND AT that time shall Michael stand up, the great prince which standeth for the children of thy people: and there shall be a time of trouble, such as never was since there was a nation *even* to that same time: and at that time thy people shall be delivered, every one that shall be found written in the book.

2And many of them that sleep in the dust of the earth shall awake, some to everlasting life, and some to shame *and* everlasting contempt.

3And they that be wise shall shine as the brightness of the firmament; and they that turn many to righteousness as the stars for ever and ever.

4But thou, O Daniel, shut up the words, and seal the book, *even* to the time of the end: many shall run to and fro, and knowledge shall be increased.

5¶ Then I Daniel looked, and, behold, there stood other two, the one on this side of the bank of the river, and the other on that side of the bank of the river.

6And *one* said to the man clothed in linen, which *was* upon the waters of the river, How long *shall it be to* the end of these wonders?

7And I heard the man clothed in linen, which *was* upon the waters of the river, when he held up his right hand and his left hand unto heaven, and sware by him that liveth for ever that *it shall be* for a time, times, and an half; and when he shall have accomplished to scatter the power of the holy people, all these *things* shall be finished.

8And I heard, but I understood not: then said I, O my Lord, what *shall be* the end of these *things?*

9And he said, Go thy way, Daniel: for the words *are* closed up and sealed till the time of the end.

10Many shall be purified, and made white, and tried; but the wicked shall do wickedly: and none of the wicked shall understand; but the wise shall understand.

11And from the time *that* the daily *sacrifice* shall be taken away, and the abomination that maketh desolate set up, *there shall be* a thousand two hundred and ninety days.

## Amplified

40And at the time of the end the king of the south shall push at *and* attack him, and the king of the north shall come against him like a whirlwind, with chariots and horsemen, and with many ships; and he shall enter into the countries and shall overflow and pass through.

41He shall enter into the glorious land [Palestine], and many shall be overthrown; but these shall be delivered out of his hand: Edom, and Moab, and the main [kernel] of the people of Ammon.

42He shall stretch out his hand also against the *other* countries, but the land of Egypt shall not be among the escaped ones.

43But he shall have power over the treasures of gold and of silver and over all the precious things of Egypt, and the Libyans and the Ethiopians shall accompany him [compelled to follow his steps].

44But rumors from the east and from the north shall alarm *and* hasten him. And he shall go forth with great fury to destroy and utterly to sweep away many.

45And he shall pitch his palatial tents between the seas and the glorious holy mount [Zion]; yet he shall come to his end with none to help him.

**12** AND AT that time [of the end] Michael shall arise, the great [angelic] prince who defends *and* has charge of your [Daniel's] people. And there shall be a time of trouble, straitness *and* distress, such as never was since there was a nation till that time. But at that time your people shall be delivered, every one whose name shall be found written in the book [of God's plan for His own].

2And many of those who sleep in the dust of the earth shall awake, some to everlasting life and some to shame and everlasting contempt *and* abhorrence.

3And the teachers *and* those who are wise shall shine like the brightness of the firmament; and those who turn many to righteousness—to uprightness and right standing with God [shall give forth light] like the stars for ever and ever. [Matt. 13:43.]

4But you, O Daniel, shut up the words and seal the book until the time of the end. [Then] many shall run to and fro *and* search anxiously [through the Book], and knowledge [of God's purposes as revealed by His prophets] shall be increased *and* become great. [Cf. Amos 8:12.]

5Then I, Daniel, looked, and behold, there stood two others, the one on the brink of the river on this side, and the other on the brink of the river on that side.

6And one said to the man clothed in linen, who was above the waters of the river, How long shall it be to the end of these wonders?

7And I heard the man clothed in linen, who was above the waters of the river, when he held up his right and his left hand toward the heavens and swore by Him Who lives for ever that it shall be for a time, times, and a half [or three and one-half years]; and when they have made an end of shattering *and* crushing the power of the holy people, all these things shall be finished.

8And I heard, but I did not understand. Then I said, O my lord, what shall be the issue *and* final end of these things?

9And he, [the angel,] said, Go your way, Daniel; for the words are shut up and sealed till the time of the end.

10Many shall purify themselves, and make themselves white, and be tried, smelted *and* refined; but the wicked shall do wickedly. And none of the wicked shall understand, but the teachers *and* those who are wise shall understand. [Dan. 11:33-35.]

11And from the time that the continual burnt offering is taken away, and the abomination that makes desolate is set up, there shall be a thousand two hundred and ninety days. [Dan. 11:31.]

## New American Standard

40¶ "And at the end time the king of the South will collide with
him, and the king of the North will storm against him with chariots, with horsemen, and with many ships; and he will enter countries, overflow *them,* and pass through.
41"He will also enter the Beautiful Land, and many *countries* will
fall; but these will be rescued out of his hand: Edom, Moab and
the foremost of the sons of Ammon.
42"Then he will stretch out his hand against *other* countries, and
the land of Egypt will not escape.
43"But he will gain control over the hidden treasures of gold and
silver, and over all the precious things of Egypt; and Libyans and
Ethiopians *will follow* at his heels.
44"But rumors from the East and from the North will disturb
him, and he will go forth with great wrath to destroy and annihilate many.
45"And he will pitch the tents of his royal pavilion between the
seas and the beautiful Holy Mountain; yet he will come to his end,
and no one will help him.

*The Time of the End*

12 "NOW AT that time Michael, the great prince who stands
*guard* over the sons of your people, will arise. And there
will be a time of distress such as never occurred since there was
a nation until that time; and at that time your people, everyone
who is found written in the book, will be rescued.
2"And many of those who sleep in the dust of the ground will
awake, these to everlasting life, but the others to disgrace *and*
everlasting contempt.
3"And those who have insight will shine brightly like the
brightness of the expanse of heaven, and those who lead the many
to righteousness, like the stars forever and ever.
4"But as for you, Daniel, conceal these words and seal up the
book until the end of time; many will go back and forth, and
knowledge will increase."
5¶ Then I, Daniel, looked and behold, two others were standing, one on this bank of the river, and the other on that bank of
the river.
6And one said to the man dressed in linen, who was above the
waters of the river, "How long *will it be* until the end of *these*
wonders?"
7And I heard the man dressed in linen, who was above the
waters of the river, as he raised his right hand and his left toward
heaven, and swore by Him who lives forever that it would be for
a time, times, and half *a time;* and as soon as they finish shattering
the power of the holy people, all these *events* will be completed.
8As for me, I heard but could not understand; so I said, "My
lord, what *will be* the outcome of these *events?*"
9And he said, "Go *your way,* Daniel, for *these* words are concealed and sealed up until the end time.
10"Many will be purged, purified and refined; but the wicked
will act wickedly, and none of the wicked will understand, but
those who have insight will understand.
11"And from the time that the regular sacrifice is abolished, and
the abomination of desolation is set up, *there will be* 1,290 days.

## New International

40"At the time of the end the king of the South will engage him
in battle, and the king of the North will storm out against him with
chariots and cavalry and a great fleet of ships. He will invade many
countries and sweep through them like a flood. 41He will also
invade the Beautiful Land. Many countries will fall, but Edom,
Moab and the leaders of Ammon will be delivered from his hand.
42He will extend his power over many countries; Egypt will not
escape. 43He will gain control of the treasures of gold and silver
and all the riches of Egypt, with the Libyans and Nubians in
submission. 44But reports from the east and the north will alarm
him, and he will set out in a great rage to destroy and annihilate
many. 45He will pitch his royal tents between the seas at[a] the
beautiful holy mountain. Yet he will come to his end, and no one
will help him.

*The End Times*

12 "AT THAT time Michael, the great prince who protects
your people, will arise. There will be a time of distress
such as has not happened from the beginning of nations until then.
But at that time your people—everyone whose name is found
written in the book—will be delivered. 2Multitudes who sleep in
the dust of the earth will awake: some to everlasting life, others to
shame and everlasting contempt. 3Those who are wise[b] will shine
like the brightness of the heavens, and those who lead many to
righteousness, like the stars for ever and ever. 4But you, Daniel,
close up and seal the words of the scroll until the time of the end.
Many will go here and there to increase knowledge."

5Then I, Daniel, looked, and there before me stood two others,
one on this bank of the river and one on the opposite bank. 6One
of them said to the man clothed in linen, who was above the waters
of the river, "How long will it be before these astonishing things
are fulfilled?"
7The man clothed in linen, who was above the waters of the
river, lifted his right hand and his left hand toward heaven, and
I heard him swear by him who lives forever, saying, "It will be for
a time, times and half a time.[c] When the power of the holy people
has been finally broken, all these things will be completed."
8I heard, but I did not understand. So I asked, "My lord, what
will the outcome of all this be?"
9He replied, "Go your way, Daniel, because the words are
closed up and sealed until the time of the end. 10Many will be
purified, made spotless and refined, but the wicked will continue
to be wicked. None of the wicked will understand, but those who
are wise will understand.
11"From the time that the daily sacrifice is abolished and the
abomination that causes desolation is set up, there will be 1,290

NIV [a] 45 Or *the sea and* [b] 3 Or *who impart wisdom* [c] 7 Or *a year, two years and half a year*

## King James

12Blessed *is* he that waiteth, and cometh to the thousand three hundred and five and thirty days.

13But go thou thy way till the end *be:* for thou shalt rest, and stand in thy lot at the end of the days.

## Amplified

12Blessed, happy, fortunate, spiritually prosperous *and* to be envied is he who waits expectantly *and* earnestly—who endures without wavering beyond the period of tribulation—and comes to the thousand three hundred and thirty-five days!

13But you, [Daniel who was now over ninety years of age], go your way until the end, for you shall rest, and shall stand [fast] in your allotted place at the end of the days. [Heb. 11:32-40.]

## New American Standard

12"How blessed is he who keeps waiting and attains to the 1,335 days!
13"But as for you, go *your way* to the end; then you will enter into rest and rise *again* for your allotted portion at the end of the age."

## New International

days. 12Blessed is the one who waits for and reaches the end of the 1,335 days.
13"As for you, go your way till the end. You will rest, and then at the end of the days you will rise to receive your allotted inheritance."

## King James

# Hosea

1 THE WORD of the LORD that came unto Hosea, the son of
Beeri, in the days of Uzziah, Jotham, Ahaz, *and* Hezekiah,
kings of Judah, and in the days of Jeroboam the son of Joash, king
of Israel.
2The beginning of the word of the LORD by Hosea. And the
LORD said to Hosea, Go, take unto thee a wife of whoredoms and
children of whoredoms: for the land hath committed great whoredom, *departing* from the LORD.
3So he went and took Gomer the daughter of Diblaim; which
conceived, and bare him a son.
4And the LORD said unto him, Call his name Jezreel; for yet a
little *while,* and I will avenge the blood of Jezreel upon the house
of Jehu, and will cause to cease the kingdom of the house of Israel.
5And it shall come to pass at that day, that I will break the bow
of Israel in the valley of Jezreel.
6¶ And she conceived again, and bare a daughter. And *God* said
unto him, Call her name Lo-ruhamah: for I will no more have
mercy upon the house of Israel; but I will utterly take them away.
7But I will have mercy upon the house of Judah, and will save
them by the LORD their God, and will not save them by bow, nor
by sword, nor by battle, by horses, nor by horsemen.
8¶ Now when she had weaned Lo-ruhamah, she conceived, and
bare a son.
9Then said *God,* Call his name Lo-ammi: for ye *are* not my
people, and I will not be your *God.*
10¶ Yet the number of the children of Israel shall be as the sand
of the sea, which cannot be measured nor numbered; and it shall
come to pass, *that* in the place where it was said unto them, Ye *are*
not my people, *there* it shall be said unto them, *Ye are* the sons of
the living God.
11Then shall the children of Judah and the children of Israel be
gathered together, and appoint themselves one head, and they
shall come up out of the land: for great *shall be* the day of Jezreel.

2 SAY YE unto your brethren, Ammi; and to your sisters, Ruhamah.

## Amplified

THE BOOK OF

# Hosea

1 THE WORD of the Lord that came to Hosea the son of Beeri,
in the days of Uzziah, Jotham, Ahaz and Hezekiah, kings of
Judah, and in the days of Jeroboam the son of Joash, king of Israel.
2When the Lord first spoke with *and* through Hosea, the Lord
said to him, Go, take to yourself a wife of harlotry and have
children of [her] harlotry, for the land commits great whoredom
by departing from the Lord.
3So he went and took Gomer the daughter of Diblaim, and she
became pregnant and bore him a son.
4And the Lord said to him, Call his name Jezreel *or* God-sows-it,
for yet a little while, and I will avenge the blood of Jezreel *and* visit
the punishment for it upon the house of Jehu, and will put to an
end the kingdom of the house of Israel. [II Kings 10:11.]
5And on that day I will break the bow of Israel in the valley of
Jezreel.
6And [Gomer] conceived again and bore a daughter. And the
Lord said to Hosea, Call her name Loruhamah *or* Not-pitied, for
I will no more have loving-kindness, pity *and* mercy *for* the house
of Israel, that I should in any way pardon them.
7But I will have love, pity *and* mercy on the house of Judah, and
will deliver them by the Lord their God, and will [a]not save them
by bow, nor by sword, nor by equipment of war, nor by horses,
nor by horsemen. [Isa. 31:8; 37:33-35.]
8Now when [Gomer] had weaned Loruhamah [Not-pitied], she
became pregnant [again] and bore a son.
9And the Lord said, Call his name Loammi or [Not-my-people],
for you are not My people, and I am not yours.
10Yet the number of the children of Israel shall be as the sand
of the sea, which cannot be measured or numbered; and instead
of its being said to them, You are not My people, it shall be said
to them, Sons of the Living God! [Rom. 9:26.]
11Then shall the children of Judah and the children of Israel be
gathered together and appoint themselves one head; and they
shall go up out of the land, for great shall be the day of Jezreel [for
the spiritually reborn Israel, a divine offspring, the people whom
the Lord has blessed.] [Heb. 12:22; Eph. 2:6, 7.]

2 *HOSEA,* SAY to your brethren, Ammi [or You-are-my-peo-
ple], and to your sisters, Ruhamah [or Who-has- been- pitied-
and- obtained- mercy].

**AMP** [a] Isaiah also made this prophecy, and both he and Hosea lived to see its remarkable literal fulfillment [Isa. 37:36].

## New American Standard

# Hosea

*Hosea's Wife and Children*

**1** THE WORD of the LORD which came to Hosea the son of
Beeri, during the days of Uzziah, Jotham, Ahaz, *and* Hezekiah, kings of Judah, and during the days of Jeroboam the son of
Joash, king of Israel.
2¶ When the LORD first spoke through Hosea, the LORD said
to Hosea, "Go, take to yourself a wife of harlotry, and *have* children
of harlotry; for the land commits flagrant harlotry, forsaking the
LORD."
3So he went and took Gomer the daughter of Diblaim, and she
conceived and bore him a son.
4And the LORD said to him, "Name him Jezreel; for yet a little
while, and I will punish the house of Jehu for the bloodshed of
Jezreel, and I will put an end to the kingdom of the house of Israel.
5"And it will come about on that day, that I will break the bow
of Israel in the valley of Jezreel."
6Then she conceived again and gave birth to a daughter. And
the LORD said to him, "Name her [b]Lo-ruhamah, for I will no longer
have compassion on the house of Israel, that I should ever forgive
them.
7"But I will have compassion on the house of Judah and deliver
them by the LORD their God, and will not deliver them by bow,
sword, battle, horses, or horsemen."
8When she had weaned Lo-ruhamah, she conceived and gave
birth to a son.
9And the LORD said, "Name him [c]Lo-ammi, for you are not
My people and I am not your God."

10¶ Yet the number of the sons of Israel
Will be like the sand of the sea,
Which cannot be measured or numbered;
And it will come about that, in the place
Where it is said to them,
"You are not My people,"
It will be said to them,
"*You are* the sons of the living God."
11 And the sons of Judah and the sons of Israel will be
gathered together,
And they will appoint for themselves one leader,
And they will go up from the land,
For great will be the day of Jezreel.

*Israel's Unfaithfulness Condemned*

**2** SAY TO your brothers, "[d]Ammi," and to your sisters,
"[e]Ruhamah."

NAS [b] I.e., she has not obtained compassion [c] I.e., not my people [d] I.e., my people [e] I.e., she has obtained compassion

## New International

# Hosea

**1** THE WORD of the LORD that came to Hosea son of Beeri
during the reigns of Uzziah, Jotham, Ahaz and Hezekiah,
kings of Judah, and during the reign of Jeroboam son of Jehoash[f]
king of Israel:

*Hosea's Wife and Children*

2When the LORD began to speak through Hosea, the LORD said
to him, "Go, take to yourself an adulterous wife and children of
unfaithfulness, because the land is guilty of the vilest adultery in
departing from the LORD." 3So he married Gomer daughter of
Diblaim, and she conceived and bore him a son.
4Then the LORD said to Hosea, "Call him Jezreel, because I will
soon punish the house of Jehu for the massacre at Jezreel, and I
will put an end to the kingdom of Israel. 5In that day I will break
Israel's bow in the Valley of Jezreel."
6Gomer conceived again and gave birth to a daughter. Then the
LORD said to Hosea, "Call her Lo-Ruhamah,[g] for I will no longer
show love to the house of Israel, that I should at all forgive them.
7Yet I will show love to the house of Judah; and I will save them—
not by bow, sword or battle, or by horses and horsemen, but by
the LORD their God."
8After she had weaned Lo-Ruhamah, Gomer had another son.
9Then the LORD said, "Call him Lo-Ammi,[h] for you are not my
people, and I am not your God.
10"Yet the Israelites will be like the sand on the seashore, which
cannot be measured or counted. In the place where it was said to
them, 'You are not my people,' they will be called 'sons of the
living God.' 11The people of Judah and the people of Israel will be
reunited, and they will appoint one leader and will come up out
of the land, for great will be the day of Jezreel.

**2** "SAY OF your brothers, 'My people,' and of your sisters, 'My
loved one.'

NIV [f] *1* Hebrew *Joash,* a variant of *Jehoash* [g] *6 Lo-Ruhamah* means *not loved.* [h] *9 Lo-Ammi* means *not my people.*

## King James

2 Plead with your mother, plead: for she *is* not my wife, neither *am* I her husband: let her therefore put away her whoredoms out of her sight, and her adulteries from between her breasts;

3 Lest I strip her naked, and set her as in the day that she was born, and make her as a wilderness, and set her like a dry land, and slay her with thirst.

4 And I will not have mercy upon her children; for they *be* the children of whoredoms.

5 For their mother hath played the harlot: she that conceived them hath done shamefully: for she said, I will go after my lovers, that give *me* my bread and my water, my wool and my flax, mine oil and my drink.

6 ¶ Therefore, behold, I will hedge up thy way with thorns, and make a wall, that she shall not find her paths.

7 And she shall follow after her lovers, but she shall not overtake them; and she shall seek them, but shall not find *them:* then shall she say, I will go and return to my first husband; for then *was it* better with me than now.

8 For she did not know that I gave her corn, and wine, and oil, and multiplied her silver and gold, *which* they prepared for Baal.

9 Therefore will I return, and take away my corn in the time thereof, and my wine in the season thereof, and will recover my wool and my flax *given* to cover her nakedness.

10 And now will I discover her lewdness in the sight of her lovers, and none shall deliver her out of mine hand.

11 I will also cause all her mirth to cease, her feast days, her new moons, and her sabbaths, and all her solemn feasts.

12 And I will destroy her vines and her fig trees, whereof she hath said, These *are* my rewards that my lovers have given me: and I will make them a forest, and the beasts of the field shall eat them.

13 And I will visit upon her the days of Baalim, wherein she burned incense to them, and she decked herself with her earrings and her jewels, and she went after her lovers, and forgat me, saith the LORD.

14 ¶ Therefore, behold, I will allure her, and bring her into the wilderness, and speak comfortably unto her.

15 And I will give her her vineyards from thence, and the valley of Achor for a door of hope: and she shall sing there, as in the days of her youth, and as in the day when she came up out of the land of Egypt.

16 And it shall be at that day, saith the LORD, *that* thou shalt call me Ishi; and shalt call me no more Baali.

17 For I will take away the names of Baalim out of her mouth, and they shall no more be remembered by their name.

## Amplified

2 Plead with your mother [your nation]; plead, for she is not My wife, and I am not her husband; *plead* that she put away her [marks of] harlotry from her face and her adulteries from between her breasts; [Isa. 50:1.]

3 Lest I strip her naked and make her as in the day she was born, and make her as a wilderness, and set her like a parched land, and slay her with thirst.

4 Yes, for her children I will have no love *nor* mercy *nor* pity, for they are the children of harlotry.

5 For their mother has played the harlot; she who conceived them has done shamefully, for she said, I will go after my lovers that give me my food and my water, my wool and my flax, my oil and my refreshing drinks.

6 Therefore, behold, I, [the Lord God,] will hedge up *her* way, *even* yours, [O Israel,] with thorns; and I will build a wall against her, that she shall not find her paths.

7 And she shall follow after her lovers, but she shall not overtake them; and she shall seek them, inquiring for *and* requiring them, but shall not find them. Then shall she say, Let me go and return to my first husband, for then was it better with me than now.

8 For she has not taken notice, understood *or* realized it was I [the Lord God], Who gave her the grain and the new wine and the fresh oil, and Who lavished upon her silver and gold, which they used for Baal *and* made into his image.

9 Therefore will I return *and* take back My grain in the time for it and My new wine in the season for it, and will pluck away *and* recover My wool and My flax which were to cover her [Israel's] nakedness.

10 And now will I uncover her lewdness *and* her shame in the sight of her lovers, and no one shall rescue her out of My hand.

11 I will also cause to cease all her mirth, her feastmaking, her new moons, her sabbaths, and all her solemn feasts *and* appointed festive assemblies.

12 And I will lay waste *and* destroy her vines and her fig trees, of which she has said, These are my reward *or* loose woman's hire that my lovers have given me; and I will make [her plantations an inaccessible] forest, and the wild beasts of the open country shall eat them.

13 And I will visit [punishment] upon her for the feast days of the Baals, when she burned incense to them and decked herself with her ear *and* nose-rings and her jewelry, and went after her lovers, and forgot Me, says the Lord.

14 Therefore, behold, I will allure her [Israel] and bring her into the wilderness, and I will speak tenderly *and* to her heart.

15 There I will give her her vineyards, and make the Valley of Achor *or* Troubling to be for her a door of hope *and* expectation. And she shall sing there *and* respond as in the days of her youth, and as at the time when she came up out of the land of Egypt. [Josh. 7:24-26; Exod. 15:2.]

16 And it shall be in that day, says the Lord, that you will call Me Ishi *or* My Husband, and you shall call Me no more Baali *or* My Baal.

17 For I will take away the names of Baalim [the Baals] out of her mouth, and they shall no more be mentioned *or* seriously remembered by their name.

## New American Standard

2 "Contend with your mother, contend,
For she is not my wife, and I am not her husband;
And let her put away her harlotry from her face,
And her adultery from between her breasts,
3 Lest I strip her naked
And expose her as on the day when she was born.
I will also make her like a wilderness,
Make her like desert land,
And slay her with thirst.
4 "Also, I will have no compassion on her children,
Because they are children of harlotry.
5 "For their mother has played the harlot;
She who conceived them has acted shamefully.
For she said, 'I will go after my lovers,
Who give *me* my bread and my water,
My wool and my flax, my oil and my drink.'
6 "Therefore, behold, I will hedge up her way with thorns,
And I will build a wall against her so that she cannot find her paths.
7 "And she will pursue her lovers, but she will not overtake them;
And she will seek them, but will not find *them*.
Then she will say, 'I will go back to my first husband,
For it was better for me then than now!'

8¶ "For she does not know that it was I who gave her the grain, the new wine, and the oil,
And lavished on her silver and gold,
*Which* they used for Baal.
9 "Therefore, I will take back My grain at harvest time
And My new wine in its season.
I will also take away My wool and My flax
*Given* to cover her nakedness.
10 "And then I will uncover her lewdness
In the sight of her lovers,
And no one will rescue her out of My hand.
11 "I will also put an end to all her gaiety,
Her feasts, her new moons, her sabbaths,
And all her festal assemblies.
12 "And I will destroy her vines and fig trees,
Of which she said, 'These are my wages
Which my lovers have given me.'
And I will make them a forest,
And the beasts of the field will devour them.
13 "And I will punish her for the days of the Baals
When she used to offer sacrifices to them
And adorn herself with her earrings and jewelry,
And follow her lovers, so that she forgot Me," declares the LORD.

*Restoration of Israel*

14¶ "Therefore, behold, I will allure her,
Bring her into the wilderness,
And speak kindly to her.
15 "Then I will give her her vineyards from there,
And the valley of Achor as a door of hope.
And she will sing there as in the days of her youth,
As in the day when she came up from the land of Egypt.
16 "And it will come about in that day," declares the LORD,
"That you will call Me [a]Ishi
And will no longer call Me [b]Baali.
17 "For I will remove the names of the Baals from her mouth,
So that they will be mentioned by their names no more.

NAS [a] I.e., my Husband [b] I.e., my Master, or, my Baal

## New International

*Israel Punished and Restored*

2 "Rebuke your mother, rebuke her,
for she is not my wife,
and I am not her husband.
Let her remove the adulterous look from her face
and the unfaithfulness from between her breasts.
3 Otherwise I will strip her naked
and make her as bare as on the day she was born;
I will make her like a desert,
turn her into a parched land,
and slay her with thirst.
4 I will not show my love to her children,
because they are the children of adultery.
5 Their mother has been unfaithful
and has conceived them in disgrace.
She said, 'I will go after my lovers,
who give me my food and my water,
my wool and my linen, my oil and my drink.'
6 Therefore I will block her path with thornbushes;
I will wall her in so that she cannot find her way.
7 She will chase after her lovers but not catch them;
she will look for them but not find them.
Then she will say,
'I will go back to my husband as at first,
for then I was better off than now.'
8 She has not acknowledged that I was the one
who gave her the grain, the new wine and oil,
who lavished on her the silver and gold—
which they used for Baal.

9 "Therefore I will take away my grain when it ripens,
and my new wine when it is ready.
I will take back my wool and my linen,
intended to cover her nakedness.
10 So now I will expose her lewdness
before the eyes of her lovers;
no one will take her out of my hands.
11 I will stop all her celebrations:
her yearly festivals, her New Moons,
her Sabbath days—all her appointed feasts.
12 I will ruin her vines and her fig trees,
which she said were her pay from her lovers;
I will make them a thicket,
and wild animals will devour them.
13 I will punish her for the days
she burned incense to the Baals;
she decked herself with rings and jewelry,
and went after her lovers,
but me she forgot,"
declares the LORD.

14 "Therefore I am now going to allure her;
I will lead her into the desert
and speak tenderly to her.
15 There I will give her back her vineyards,
and will make the Valley of Achor[c] a door of hope.
There she will sing[d] as in the days of her youth,
as in the day she came up out of Egypt.

16 "In that day," declares the LORD,
"you will call me 'my husband';
you will no longer call me 'my master.[e]'
17 I will remove the names of the Baals from her lips;
no longer will their names be invoked.

NIV [c] 15 *Achor* means *trouble.* [d] 15 Or *respond* [e] 16 Hebrew *baal*

## King James

18And in that day will I make a covenant for them with the beasts of the field, and with the fowls of heaven, and *with* the creeping things of the ground: and I will break the bow and the sword and the battle out of the earth, and will make them to lie down safely.

19And I will betroth thee unto me for ever; yea, I will betroth thee unto me in righteousness, and in judgment, and in lovingkindness, and in mercies.

20I will even betroth thee unto me in faithfulness: and thou shalt know the LORD.

21And it shall come to pass in that day, I will hear, saith the LORD, I will hear the heavens, and they shall hear the earth;

22And the earth shall hear the corn, and the wine, and the oil; and they shall hear Jezreel.

23And I will sow her unto me in the earth; and I will have mercy upon her that had not obtained mercy; and I will say to *them which were* not my people, Thou *art* my people; and they shall say, *Thou art* my God.

3 THEN SAID the LORD unto me, Go yet, love a woman beloved of *her* friend, yet an adulteress, according to the love of the LORD toward the children of Israel, who look to other gods, and love flagons of wine.

2So I bought her to me for fifteen *pieces* of silver, and *for* an homer of barley, and an half homer of barley:

3And I said unto her, Thou shalt abide for me many days; thou shalt not play the harlot, and thou shalt not be for *another* man: so *will* I also *be* for thee.

4For the children of Israel shall abide many days without a king, and without a prince, and without a sacrifice, and without an image, and without an ephod, and *without* teraphim:

5Afterward shall the children of Israel return, and seek the LORD their God, and David their king; and shall fear the LORD and his goodness in the latter days.

4 HEAR THE word of the LORD, ye children of Israel: for the LORD hath a controversy with the inhabitants of the land, because *there is* no truth, nor mercy, nor knowledge of God in the land.

2By swearing, and lying, and killing, and stealing, and committing adultery, they break out, and blood toucheth blood.

## Amplified

18And in that day will I make a covenant for [Israel] with the living creatures of the open country, and with the birds of the heavens, and with the creeping things of the ground. And I will break the bow and the sword and [abolish battle equipment and] conflict out of the land, and will make you lie down safely.

19And I will betroth you to Me for ever; yes, I will betroth you to Me in righteousness and justice, and in steadfast love, and in mercies.

20I will even betroth you to Me in stability *and* in faithfulness, and you shall know—recognize, be acquainted with, appreciate, give heed to and cherish—the Lord.

21And in that day, I will respond, says the Lord; I will respond to the heavens [which ask for rain to pour on the earth], and they shall respond to the earth [which begs for the rain it needs];

22And the earth shall respond to the grain and the wine and the oil [which beseech it to bring them forth], and these shall respond to Jezreel [restored Israel, who prays for a supply of them].

23And I will sow her for Myself anew in the land, and I will have pity, mercy *and* love for her who had not obtained pity, mercy *and* love, and I will say to those who were not My people, You are My people, and they shall say, You are my God! [I Pet. 2:9, 10.]

3 THEN SAID the Lord to me, Go again, love [the same] woman [Gomer] who is beloved of a paramour and is an adulteress, even as the Lord loves the children of Israel, though they turn to other gods and love cakes of raisins [used in the sacrificial feasts in idol worship].

2So I bought her for fifteen pieces of silver and a homer and a half of barley [the price of a slave].

3And I said to her, You shall be [betrothed] to me for many days; you shall not play the harlot and you shall not belong to another man. So will I also be to you [until you have proved your loyalty to me and our marital relations may be resumed].

4For the children of Israel shall dwell *and* sit deprived many days, without king or prince, without sacrifice or [idolatrous] pillar, and without ephod [a garment worn by priests when seeking divine counsel] or teraphim [household gods].

5Afterward shall the children of Israel return, and seek the Lord their God, inquiring of *and* requiring Him, and [from the line of] David, their King [of Kings]; and they shall come in [anxious] fear to the Lord and to His goodness *and* His good things in the latter days.

4 HEAR THE word of the Lord, you children of Israel; for the Lord has a controversy—a pleading contention—with the inhabitants of the land, because there is no faithfulness, lovingkindness, pity *and* mercy, or knowledge of God [from personal experience with Him] in the land.

2There is nothing but [false] swearing and breaking faith, and killing, and stealing and committing adultery; they break out [into violence], one [deed of] bloodshed following close on another.

## New American Standard

18 "In that day I will also make a covenant for them
With the beasts of the field,
The birds of the sky,
And the creeping things of the ground.
And I will abolish the bow, the sword, and war from the land,
And will make them lie down in safety.
19 "And I will betroth you to Me forever;
Yes, I will betroth you to Me in righteousness and in justice,
In lovingkindness and in compassion,
20 And I will betroth you to Me in faithfulness.
Then you will know the LORD.

21¶ "And it will come about in that day that I will respond," declares the LORD.
"I will respond to the heavens, and they will respond to the earth,
22 And the earth will respond to the grain, to the new wine, and to the oil,
And they will respond to [a]Jezreel.
23 "And I will sow her for Myself in the land.
I will also have compassion on her who had not obtained compassion,
And I will say to those who were not My people,
'You are My people!'
And they will say, '*Thou art* my God!'"

*Hosea's Second Symbolic Marriage*

3 THEN THE LORD said to me, "Go again, love a woman *who* is loved by *her* husband, yet an adulteress, even as the LORD loves the sons of Israel, though they turn to other gods and love raisin cakes."

2So I bought her for myself for fifteen *shekels* of silver and a homer and a half of barley.

3Then I said to her, "You shall stay with me for many days. You shall not play the harlot, nor shall you have a man; so I will also be toward you."

4For the sons of Israel will remain for many days without king or prince, without sacrifice or *sacred* pillar, and without ephod or household idols.

5Afterward the sons of Israel will return and seek the LORD their God and David their king; and they will come trembling to the LORD and to His goodness in the last days.

*God's Controversy with Israel*

4 LISTEN TO the word of the LORD, O sons of Israel,
For the LORD has a case against the inhabitants of the land,
Because there is no faithfulness or kindness
Or knowledge of God in the land.
2 *There is* swearing, deception, murder, stealing, and adultery.
They employ violence, so that bloodshed follows bloodshed.

NAS [a] I.e., God sows

## New International

18In that day I will make a covenant for them
with the beasts of the field and the birds of the air
and the creatures that move along the ground.
Bow and sword and battle
I will abolish from the land,
so that all may lie down in safety.
19I will betroth you to me forever;
I will betroth you in[b] righteousness and justice,
in[c] love and compassion.
20I will betroth you in faithfulness,
and you will acknowledge the LORD.

21"In that day I will respond,"
declares the LORD—
"I will respond to the skies,
and they will respond to the earth;
22and the earth will respond to the grain,
the new wine and oil,
and they will respond to Jezreel.[d]
23I will plant her for myself in the land;
I will show my love to the one I called 'Not my loved one.[e]'
I will say to those called 'Not my people,[f]' 'You are my people';
and they will say, 'You are my God.'"

*Hosea's Reconciliation With His Wife*

3 THE LORD said to me, "Go, show your love to your wife again, though she is loved by another and is an adulteress. Love her as the LORD loves the Israelites, though they turn to other gods and love the sacred raisin cakes."

2So I bought her for fifteen shekels[g] of silver and about a homer and a lethek[h] of barley. 3Then I told her, "You are to live with[i] me many days; you must not be a prostitute or be intimate with any man, and I will live with[j] you."

4For the Israelites will live many days without king or prince, without sacrifice or sacred stones, without ephod or idol. 5Afterward the Israelites will return and seek the LORD their God and David their king. They will come trembling to the LORD and to his blessings in the last days.

*The Charge Against Israel*

4 HEAR THE word of the LORD, you Israelites,
because the LORD has a charge to bring
against you who live in the land:
"There is no faithfulness, no love,
no acknowledgment of God in the land.
2There is only cursing,[k] lying and murder,
stealing and adultery;
they break all bounds,
and bloodshed follows bloodshed.

NIV [b] 19 Or *with;* also in verse 20 [c] 19 Or *with* [d] 22 *Jezreel* means *God plants.* [e] 23 Hebrew *Lo-Ruhamah* [f] 23 Hebrew *Lo-Ammi* [g] 2 That is, about 6 ounces (about 170 grams) [h] 2 That is, probably about 10 bushels (about 330 liters) [i] 3 Or *wait for* [j] 3 Or *wait for* [k] 2 That is, to pronounce a curse upon

## King James

3 Therefore shall the land mourn, and every one that dwelleth therein shall languish, with the beasts of the field, and with the fowls of heaven; yea, the fishes of the sea also shall be taken away.

4 Yet let no man strive, nor reprove another: for thy people *are* as they that strive with the priest.

5 Therefore shalt thou fall in the day, and the prophet also shall fall with thee in the night, and I will destroy thy mother.

6 ¶ My people are destroyed for lack of knowledge: because thou hast rejected knowledge, I will also reject thee, that thou shalt be no priest to me: seeing thou hast forgotten the law of thy God, I will also forget thy children.

7 As they were increased, so they sinned against me: *therefore* will I change their glory into shame.

8 They eat up the sin of my people, and they set their heart on their iniquity.

9 And there shall be, like people, like priest: and I will punish them for their ways, and reward them their doings.

10 For they shall eat, and not have enough: they shall commit whoredom, and shall not increase: because they have left off to take heed to the LORD.

11 Whoredom and wine and new wine take away the heart.

12 ¶ My people ask counsel at their stocks, and their staff declareth unto them: for the spirit of whoredoms hath caused *them* to err, and they have gone a-whoring from under their God.

13 They sacrifice upon the tops of the mountains, and burn incense upon the hills, under oaks and poplars and elms, because the shadow thereof *is* good: therefore your daughters shall commit whoredom, and your spouses shall commit adultery.

14 I will not punish your daughters when they commit whoredom, nor your spouses when they commit adultery: for themselves are separated with whores, and they sacrifice with harlots: therefore the people *that* doth not understand shall fall.

15 ¶ Though thou, Israel, play the harlot, *yet* let not Judah offend; and come not ye unto Gilgal, neither go ye up to Beth-aven, nor swear, The LORD liveth.

16 For Israel slideth back as a backsliding heifer: now the LORD will feed them as a lamb in a large place.

17 Ephraim *is* joined to idols: let him alone.

18 Their drink is sour: they have committed whoredom continually: her rulers *with* shame do love, Give ye.

## Amplified

3 Therefore shall the land [continually] mourn, and all who dwell in it shall languish, together with the wild beasts of the open country and the birds of the heavens; yes, the fishes of the sea also shall [perish because of the drought] be collected *and* taken away.

4 Yet let no man strive, neither let any man reprove [another]—do not waste your time in mutual recriminations—for with you is *My* contention, O priest.

5 And you shall stumble in the daytime, and the [false] prophet also shall stumble with you in the night; and I will destroy your mother [the priestly nation]. [Exod. 19:6.]

6 My people are destroyed for lack of knowledge; because you, [the priestly nation,] have rejected knowledge, I will also reject you, that you shall be no priest to Me; seeing you have forgotten the law of your God, I will also forget your children.

7 The more they increased *and* multiplied [in prosperity and power], the more they sinned against Me; I will change their glory into shame.

8 They feed on the sin of My people and set their heart on their iniquity.

9 And it shall be, like people, like priest; I will punish them for their ways and repay them for their doings.

10 For they shall eat and not have enough; they shall play the harlot and beget no increase; because they have forsaken the Lord for harlotry;

11 [Harlotry] and wine and new wine take away the heart *and* the mind [and spiritual] understanding.

12 My people [habitually] ask counsel of their [senseless] wood [idols], and their staff [of wood] gives them oracles *and* instructs them. For the spirit of harlotry has led them astray, and they have played the harlot, withdrawing themselves from subjection to their God.

13 They sacrifice on the tops of the mountains, and they burn incense upon the hills, and under oaks, poplars, and terebinths, because there the shade is good. Therefore your daughters play the harlot, and your sons' wives commit adultery.

14 I will not punish your daughters when they play the harlot, nor your daughters-in-law when they commit adultery, for [the fathers and husbands] themselves go aside in order to be alone with women who prostitute themselves for gain, and they sacrifice at the altar with dedicated harlots [who surrender their chastity in honor of the goddess]. Therefore the people without understanding shall stumble *and* fall *and* come to ruin.

15 Though you, Israel, play the harlot *and* worship idols, let not Judah offend *and* become guilty; come not to Gilgal, neither go up to Bethaven [contemptuous reference to Bethel, then noted for idolatry], nor swear [in idolatrous service], *saying,* As the Lord lives.

16 For Israel has behaved stubbornly, like a stubborn heifer. *How then* should he expect to be fed *and* treated by the Lord like a lamb in a large pasture?

17 Ephraim is joined *fast* to idols, *so* let him alone [to take the consequences].

18 Their drinking carousal over, they go habitually to play the harlot; [Ephraim's] rulers [continue to] love shame more than her glory [which is the Lord, Israel's God].

## New American Standard

3 Therefore the land mourns,
And everyone who lives in it languishes
Along with the beasts of the field and the birds of the sky;
And also the fish of the sea disappear.

4¶ Yet let no one find fault, and let none offer reproof;
For your people are like those who contend with the priest.
5 So you will stumble by day,
And the prophet also will stumble with you by night;
And I will destroy your mother.
6 My people are destroyed for lack of knowledge.
Because you have rejected knowledge,
I also will reject you from being My priest.
Since you have forgotten the law of your God,
I also will forget your children.
7¶ The more they multiplied, the more they sinned against Me;
I will change their glory into shame.
8 They feed on the sin of My people,
And direct their desire toward their iniquity.
9 And it will be, like people, like priest;
So I will punish them for their ways,
And repay them for their deeds.
10 And they will eat, but not have enough;
They will play the harlot, but not increase,
Because they have stopped giving heed to the LORD.
11¶ Harlotry, wine, and new wine take away the understanding.
12 My people consult their wooden idol, and their *diviner's* wand informs them;
For a spirit of harlotry has led *them* astray,
And they have played the harlot, *departing* from their God.
13 They offer sacrifices on the tops of the mountains
And burn incense on the hills,
Under oak, poplar, and terebinth,
Because their shade is pleasant.
Therefore your daughters play the harlot,
And your brides commit adultery.
14 I will not punish your daughters when they play the harlot
Or your brides when they commit adultery,
For *the men* themselves go apart with harlots
And offer sacrifices with temple prostitutes;
So the people without understanding are ruined.
15¶ Though you, Israel, play the harlot,
Do not let Judah become guilty;
Also do not go to Gilgal,
Or go up to Beth-aven,
And take the oath:
"As the LORD lives!"
16 Since Israel is stubborn
Like a stubborn heifer,
Can the LORD now pasture them
Like a lamb in a large field?
17 Ephraim is joined to idols;
Let him alone.
18 Their liquor gone,
They play the harlot continually;
Their rulers dearly love shame.

## New International

3Because of this the land mourns,[a]
and all who live in it waste away;
the beasts of the field and the birds of the air
and the fish of the sea are dying.

4"But let no man bring a charge,
let no man accuse another,
for your people are like those
who bring charges against a priest.
5You stumble day and night,
and the prophets stumble with you.
So I will destroy your mother—
6 my people are destroyed from lack of knowledge.
"Because you have rejected knowledge,
I also reject you as my priests;
because you have ignored the law of your God,
I also will ignore your children.
7The more the priests increased,
the more they sinned against me;
they exchanged[b] their[c] Glory for something disgraceful.
8They feed on the sins of my people
and relish their wickedness.
9And it will be: Like people, like priests.
I will punish both of them for their ways
and repay them for their deeds.

10"They will eat but not have enough;
they will engage in prostitution but not increase,
because they have deserted the LORD
to give themselves 11to prostitution,
to old wine and new,
which take away the understanding 12of my people.
They consult a wooden idol
and are answered by a stick of wood.
A spirit of prostitution leads them astray;
they are unfaithful to their God.
13They sacrifice on the mountaintops
and burn offerings on the hills,
under oak, poplar and terebinth,
where the shade is pleasant.
Therefore your daughters turn to prostitution
and your daughters-in-law to adultery.

14"I will not punish your daughters
when they turn to prostitution,
nor your daughters-in-law
when they commit adultery,
because the men themselves consort with harlots
and sacrifice with shrine prostitutes—
a people without understanding will come to ruin!

15"Though you commit adultery, O Israel,
let not Judah become guilty.

"Do not go to Gilgal;
do not go up to Beth Aven.[d]
And do not swear, 'As surely as the LORD lives!'
16The Israelites are stubborn,
like a stubborn heifer.
How then can the LORD pasture them
like lambs in a meadow?
17Ephraim is joined to idols;
leave him alone!
18Even when their drinks are gone,
they continue their prostitution;
their rulers dearly love shameful ways.

NIV [a] 3 Or *dries up* [b] 7 Syriac and an ancient Hebrew scribal tradition; Masoretic Text *I will exchange* [c] 7 Masoretic Text; an ancient Hebrew scribal tradition *my* [d] 15 *Beth Aven* means *house of wickedness* (a name for Bethel, which means *house of God*).

## King James

19The wind hath bound her up in her wings, and they shall be ashamed because of their sacrifices.

5 HEAR YE this, O priests; and hearken, ye house of Israel; and give ye ear, O house of the king; for judgment *is* toward you, because ye have been a snare on Mizpah, and a net spread upon Tabor.

2And the revolters are profound to make slaughter, though I *have been* a rebuker of them all.

3I know Ephraim, and Israel is not hid from me: for now, O Ephraim, thou committest whoredom, *and* Israel is defiled.

4They will not frame their doings to turn unto their God: for the spirit of whoredoms *is* in the midst of them, and they have not known the LORD.

5And the pride of Israel doth testify to his face: therefore shall Israel and Ephraim fall in their iniquity; Judah also shall fall with them.

6They shall go with their flocks and with their herds to seek the LORD; but they shall not find *him;* he hath withdrawn himself from them.

7They have dealt treacherously against the LORD: for they have begotten strange children: now shall a month devour them with their portions.

8Blow ye the cornet in Gibeah, *and* the trumpet in Ramah: cry aloud *at* Beth-aven, after thee, O Benjamin.

9Ephraim shall be desolate in the day of rebuke: among the tribes of Israel have I made known that which shall surely be.

10The princes of Judah were like them that remove the bound: *therefore* I will pour out my wrath upon them like water.

11Ephraim *is* oppressed *and* broken in judgment, because he willingly walked after the commandment.

12Therefore *will* I *be* unto Ephraim as a moth, and to the house of Judah as rottenness.

13When Ephraim saw his sickness, and Judah *saw* his wound, then went Ephraim to the Assyrian, and sent to king Jareb: yet could he not heal you, nor cure you of your wound.

14For I *will be* unto Ephraim as a lion, and as a young lion to the house of Judah: I, *even* I, will tear and go away; I will take away, and none shall rescue *him.*

15¶ I will go *and* return to my place, till they acknowledge their offence, and seek my face: in their affliction they will seek me early.

## Amplified

19The resistless wind [of God's wrath] has bound up [Israel] in its wings *or* skirts, and [in captivity] they *and* their altars shall be put to shame because of their sacrifices [to calves, to sun, moon and stars, and to heathen gods].

5 HEAR THIS, O you priests! And listen, O house of Israel! And give ear, O house of the king! For the judgment pronounced pertains to you *and* is meant for you, because you have been a snare at Mizpah and a net spread upon Tabor [military strongholds on either side of the Jordan River].

2The revolters are deeply sunk in corruption *and* slaughter, but I, [the Lord God,] am a rebuke *and* a chastisement for them all.

3I know Ephraim, and Israel is not hid from Me; for now, O Ephraim, you have played the harlot *and* idolator; Israel is defiled.

4Their doings will not permit them to return to their God, for the spirit of harlotry is within them, and they know not the Lord—they do not recognize, appreciate, give heed to, or cherish the Lord.

5But the pride *and* self-reliance of Israel testifies before his *own* face. Therefore shall *all* Israel, and *especially* Ephraim [the northern ten tribes], totter *and* fall in their iniquity *and* guilt, and Judah shall stumble *and* fall with them.

6They shall go with their flocks and with their herds to seek the Lord—inquiring for and requiring Him; but they will not find Him; He has withdrawn Himself from them.

7They have dealt faithlessly *and* treacherously with the Lord [their espoused Husband], for they have borne alien children. Now shall a [single] new moon—one month—devour them with their fields.

8Blow the horn in Gibeah and the trumpet in Ramah [both lofty hills on Benjamin's northern border]. Sound the alarm at Beth-aven, [The enemy is] behind you *and* after you, O Benjamin [be on your guard]!

9Ephraim shall become a desolation in the day of rebuke *and* punishment. Among the tribes of Israel I declare what shall surely be.

10The princes of Judah are like those who remove the landmark [the barrier between right and wrong]; I will pour out My wrath upon them like water.

11Ephraim is oppressed, he is broken *and* crushed by [divine] judgment, because he was content to walk after idol-images and man's [evil] command [a][vanities and filth].

12Therefore I am like a moth to Ephraim, and like dry rot to the house of Judah [in My judgment against them].

13When Ephraim saw his sickness, and Judah saw his wound, then Ephraim went to Assyria, and sent to *her* great King Jareb, a contender. Yet he cannot heal you nor will he cure you of your wound [received in divine judgment].

14For I will be to Ephraim like a lion, and like a young lion to the house of Judah. I, even I, will rend and go on [rending]; I will carry off, and there will be no one to deliver.

15I will return to My place [on high], until they acknowledge their offense *and* feel their guilt and seek My face; in their affliction *and* distress they will seek, inquire for *and* require Me earnestly, saying,

**AMP** [a] "Vanities" is the rendering of the Septuagint (Greek) Version; "filth," of the Dead Sea Scrolls.

## New American Standard

19 The wind wraps them in its wings,
And they will be ashamed because of their sacrifices.

*The People's Apostasy Rebuked*

5 HEAR THIS, O priests! Give heed, O house of Israel!
Listen, O house of the king!
For the judgment applies to you,
For you have been a snare at Mizpah,
And a net spread out on Tabor.
2 And the revolters have gone deep in depravity,
But I will chastise all of them.
3 I know Ephraim, and Israel is not hidden from Me;
For now, O Ephraim, you have played the harlot,
Israel has defiled itself.
4 Their deeds will not allow them
To return to their God.
For a spirit of harlotry is within them,
And they do not know the LORD.
5 Moreover, the pride of Israel testifies against him,
And Israel and Ephraim stumble in their iniquity;
Judah also has stumbled with them.
6 They will go with their flocks and herds
To seek the LORD, but they will not find *Him*;
He has withdrawn from them.
7 They have dealt treacherously against the LORD,
For they have borne illegitimate children.
Now the new moon will devour them with their land.
8¶ Blow the horn in Gibeah,
The trumpet in Ramah.
Sound an alarm at Beth-aven:
"Behind you, Benjamin!"
9 Ephraim will become a desolation in the day of rebuke;
Among the tribes of Israel I declare what is sure.
10 The princes of Judah have become like those who move a boundary;
On them I will pour out My wrath like water.
11 Ephraim is oppressed, crushed in judgment,
Because he was determined to follow *man's* command.
12 Therefore I am like a moth to Ephraim,
And like rottenness to the house of Judah.
13 When Ephraim saw his sickness,
And Judah his wound,
Then Ephraim went to Assyria
And sent to King Jareb.
But he is unable to heal you,
Or to cure you of your wound.
14 For I *will be* like a lion to Ephraim,
And like a young lion to the house of Judah.
I, even I, will tear to pieces and go away,
I will carry away, and there will be none to deliver.
15 I will go away *and* return to My place
Until they acknowledge their guilt and seek My face;
In their affliction they will earnestly seek Me.

## New International

19 A whirlwind will sweep them away,
and their sacrifices will bring them shame.

*Judgment Against Israel*

5 "HEAR THIS, you priests!
Pay attention, you Israelites!
Listen, O royal house!
This judgment is against you:
You have been a snare at Mizpah,
a net spread out on Tabor.
2 The rebels are deep in slaughter.
I will discipline all of them.
3 I know all about Ephraim;
Israel is not hidden from me.
Ephraim, you have now turned to prostitution;
Israel is corrupt.

4 "Their deeds do not permit them
to return to their God.
A spirit of prostitution is in their heart;
they do not acknowledge the LORD.
5 Israel's arrogance testifies against them;
the Israelites, even Ephraim, stumble in their sin;
Judah also stumbles with them.
6 When they go with their flocks and herds
to seek the LORD,
they will not find him;
he has withdrawn himself from them.
7 They are unfaithful to the LORD;
they give birth to illegitimate children.
Now their New Moon festivals
will devour them and their fields.

8 "Sound the trumpet in Gibeah,
the horn in Ramah.
Raise the battle cry in Beth Aven[b];
lead on, O Benjamin.
9 Ephraim will be laid waste
on the day of reckoning.
Among the tribes of Israel
I proclaim what is certain.
10 Judah's leaders are like those
who move boundary stones.
I will pour out my wrath on them
like a flood of water.
11 Ephraim is oppressed,
trampled in judgment,
intent on pursuing idols.[c]
12 I am like a moth to Ephraim,
like rot to the people of Judah.

13 "When Ephraim saw his sickness,
and Judah his sores,
then Ephraim turned to Assyria,
and sent to the great king for help.
But he is not able to cure you,
not able to heal your sores.
14 For I will be like a lion to Ephraim,
like a great lion to Judah.
I will tear them to pieces and go away;
I will carry them off, with no one to rescue them.
15 Then I will go back to my place
until they admit their guilt.
And they will seek my face;
in their misery they will earnestly seek me."

NIV [b] *8 Beth Aven* means *house of wickedness* (a name for Bethel, which means *house of God*). [c] *11* The meaning of the Hebrew for this word is uncertain.

## King James

6 COME, AND let us return unto the LORD: for he hath torn, and he will heal us; he hath smitten, and he will bind us up.

2 After two days will he revive us: in the third day he will raise us up, and we shall live in his sight.

3 Then shall we know, *if* we follow on to know the LORD: his going forth is prepared as the morning; and he shall come unto us as the rain, as the latter *and* former rain unto the earth.

4 ¶ O Ephraim, what shall I do unto thee? O Judah, what shall I do unto thee? for your goodness *is* as a morning cloud, and as the early dew it goeth away.

5 Therefore have I hewed *them* by the prophets; I have slain them by the words of my mouth: and thy judgments *are as* the light *that* goeth forth.

6 For I desired mercy, and not sacrifice; and the knowledge of God more than burnt offerings.

7 But they like men have transgressed the covenant: there have they dealt treacherously against me.

8 Gilead *is* a city of them that work iniquity, *and is* polluted with blood.

9 And as troops of robbers wait for a man, *so* the company of priests murder in the way by consent: for they commit lewdness.

10 I have seen an horrible thing in the house of Israel: there *is* the whoredom of Ephraim, Israel is defiled.

11 Also, O Judah, he hath set an harvest for thee, when I returned the captivity of my people.

7 WHEN I would have healed Israel, then the iniquity of Ephraim was discovered, and the wickedness of Samaria: for they commit falsehood; and the thief cometh in, *and* the troop of robbers spoileth without.

2 And they consider not in their hearts *that* I remember all their wickedness: now their own doings have beset them about; they are before my face.

3 They make the king glad with their wickedness, and the princes with their lies.

4 They *are* all adulterers, as an oven heated by the baker, *who* ceaseth from raising after he hath kneaded the dough, until it be leavened.

5 In the day of our king the princes have made *him* sick with bottles of wine; he stretched out his hand with scorners.

## Amplified

6 COME, AND let us return to the Lord; for He has torn so that He may heal us; He has stricken so that He may bind us up.

2 After two days He will revive us—quicken us, give us life; on the third day He will raise us up, that we may live before Him. [Isa. 26:19; Ezek. 37:1-10.]

3 Yes, let us know—recognize, be acquainted with and understand Him; let us be zealous to know the Lord—to appreciate, give heed to and cherish Him. His going forth is prepared *and* certain as the dawn, and He will come to us as the [heavy] rain, as the latter rain that waters the earth.

4 O Ephraim, what shall I do with you? [says the Lord] O Judah, what shall I do with you? For your [wavering] love *and* kindness are as the night mist *or* as the dew that goes early away.

5 Therefore have I hewn down *and* smitten them by means of the prophets; I have slain them by the words of My mouth; My judgments [pronounced upon them by you prophets] are like the light that goes forth.

6 For I desire *and* delight in dutiful, steadfast love *and* goodness, not sacrifice, and the knowledge of *and* acquaintance with God more than burnt offerings. [Matt. 9:13; 12:7.]

7 But they, like [less privileged] men *and* like Adam, have transgressed the covenant; there have they dealt faithlessly *and* treacherously with Me.

8 Gilead is a city of evildoers; it is tracked with bloody [footprints].

9 And as troops of robbers lie in wait for a man, so the company of priests murder on the road toward Shechem; yes, they commit villainy *and* outrages.

10 I have seen a horrible thing in the house of Israel! There harlotry *and* idolatry *are* found in Ephraim, Israel is defiled.

11 Also, O Judah, there is a harvest [of divine judgment] appointed for you, when I would return My people from their captivity [in which they are slaves to the misery brought on by their own sins],

7 WHEN I would heal Israel, then Ephraim's guilt is uncovered, and the wickedness of Samaria; how they practice falsehood, and the thief enters, and the troop of bandits ravage *and* raid without.

2 But they do not consider *and* say to their minds *and* hearts that I [earnestly] remember all their wickedness. Now their own doings surround and entangle them; they are before My face.

3 They make the king glad with their wickedness, and the princes with their lies.

4 They are all [idolatrous] adulterers; their passion smolders like heat of an oven, when the baker ceases to stir the fire from the kneading of the dough until it is leavened.

5 On the [special] day of our king the princes made themselves *and* him sick with the heat of wine; [the king] stretched out his hand with scoffers *and* lawless men.

## New American Standard

*The Response to God's Rebuke*

6 "COME, LET us return to the LORD.
For He has torn *us*, but He will heal us;
He has wounded *us*, but He will bandage us.
2 "He will revive us after two days;
He will raise us up on the third day
That we may live before Him.
3 "So let us know, let us press on to know the LORD.
His going forth is as certain as the dawn;
And He will come to us like the rain,
Like the spring rain watering the earth."

4¶ What shall I do with you, O Ephraim?
What shall I do with you, O Judah?
For your loyalty is like a morning cloud,
And like the dew which goes away early.
5 Therefore I have hewn *them* in pieces by the prophets;
I have slain them by the words of My mouth;
And the judgments on you are *like* the light that goes forth.
6 For I delight in loyalty rather than sacrifice,
And in the knowledge of God rather than burnt offerings.
7 But like Adam they have transgressed the covenant;
There they have dealt treacherously against Me.
8 Gilead is a city of wrongdoers,
Tracked with bloody *footprints*.
9 And as raiders wait for a man,
*So* a band of priests murder on the way to Shechem;
Surely they have committed crime.
10 In the house of Israel I have seen a horrible thing;
Ephraim's harlotry is there, Israel has defiled itself.
11 Also, O Judah, there is a harvest appointed for you,
When I restore the fortunes of My people.

*Ephraim's Iniquity*

7 WHEN I would heal Israel,
The iniquity of Ephraim is uncovered,
And the evil deeds of Samaria,
For they deal falsely;
The thief enters in,
Bandits raid outside,
2 And they do not consider in their hearts
That I remember all their wickedness.
Now their deeds are all around them;
They are before My face.
3 With their wickedness they make the king glad,
And the princes with their lies.
4 They are all adulterers
Like an oven heated by the baker,
Who ceases to stir up *the fire*
From the kneading of the dough until it is leavened.
5 On the day of our king, the princes became sick with the heat of wine;
He stretched out his hand with scoffers,

## New International

*Israel Unrepentant*

6 "COME, LET us return to the LORD.
He has torn us to pieces
but he will heal us;
he has injured us
but he will bind up our wounds.
2 After two days he will revive us;
on the third day he will restore us,
that we may live in his presence.
3 Let us acknowledge the LORD;
let us press on to acknowledge him.
As surely as the sun rises,
he will appear;
he will come to us like the winter rains,
like the spring rains that water the earth."
4 "What can I do with you, Ephraim?
What can I do with you, Judah?
Your love is like the morning mist,
like the early dew that disappears.
5 Therefore I cut you in pieces with my prophets,
I killed you with the words of my mouth;
my judgments flashed like lightning upon you.
6 For I desire mercy, not sacrifice,
and acknowledgment of God rather than burnt offerings.
7 Like Adam,[a] they have broken the covenant—
they were unfaithful to me there.
8 Gilead is a city of wicked men,
stained with footprints of blood.
9 As marauders lie in ambush for a man,
so do bands of priests;
they murder on the road to Shechem,
committing shameful crimes.
10 I have seen a horrible thing
in the house of Israel.
There Ephraim is given to prostitution
and Israel is defiled.

11 "Also for you, Judah,
a harvest is appointed.

7 "WHENEVER I would restore the fortunes of my people,
whenever I would heal Israel,
the sins of Ephraim are exposed
and the crimes of Samaria revealed.
They practice deceit,
thieves break into houses,
bandits rob in the streets;
2 but they do not realize
that I remember all their evil deeds.
Their sins engulf them;
they are always before me.
3 "They delight the king with their wickedness,
the princes with their lies.
4 They are all adulterers,
burning like an oven
whose fire the baker need not stir
from the kneading of the dough till it rises.
5 On the day of the festival of our king
the princes become inflamed with wine,
and he joins hands with the mockers.

**NIV** [a] 7 Or *As at Adam;* or *Like men*

## King James

6 For they have made ready their heart like an oven, whiles they lie in wait: their baker sleepeth all the night; in the morning it burneth as a flaming fire.

7 They are all hot as an oven, and have devoured their judges; all their kings are fallen: *there is* none among them that calleth unto me.

8 Ephraim, he hath mixed himself among the people; Ephraim is a cake not turned.

9 Strangers have devoured his strength, and he knoweth *it* not: yea, gray hairs are here and there upon him, yet he knoweth not.

10 And the pride of Israel testifieth to his face: and they do not return to the LORD their God, nor seek him for all this.

11 ¶ Ephraim also is like a silly dove without heart: they call to Egypt, they go to Assyria.

12 When they shall go, I will spread my net upon them; I will bring them down as the fowls of the heaven; I will chastise them, as their congregation hath heard.

13 Woe unto them! for they have fled from me: destruction unto them! because they have transgressed against me: though I have redeemed them, yet they have spoken lies against me.

14 And they have not cried unto me with their heart, when they howled upon their beds: they assemble themselves for corn and wine, *and* they rebel against me.

15 Though I have bound *and* strengthened their arms, yet do they imagine mischief against me.

16 They return, *but* not to the most High: they are like a deceitful bow: their princes shall fall by the sword for the rage of their tongue: this *shall be* their derision in the land of Egypt.

## Amplified

6 For they have made ready their heart, *and* their mind burns [with intrigue] like an oven, while they lie in wait. Their anger smolders all night; in the morning it blazes forth as a flaming fire.

7 They are all hot as an oven, and devour their judges; all their kings are fallen; there is none among them who calls to Me.

8 Ephraim mixes himself among the peoples [courting the favor of first one country, then another]; Ephraim is a cake not turned.

9 Strangers have devoured his strength, and he knows it not; yes, gray hairs are sprinkled here and there upon him, and he does not know it.

10 And the pride of Israel testifies against him *and* to his face. But they do not return to the Lord their God, nor seek *nor* inquire of *nor* require Him, in spite of all this.

11 Ephraim also is like a silly dove without heart *or* understanding; they call to Egypt, they go to Assyria.

12 As they go, I will spread My net over them; I will bring them down like birds of the heavens. I will chastise them, according to the announcement [or prediction made] to their congregation [in the Scriptures]. [Lev. 26:14-39.]

13 Woe to them, for they have wandered from Me! Destruction to them, because they have rebelled *and* trespassed against Me! Though I would redeem them, yet they have spoken lies against Me.

14 They do not cry to Me from their heart, but they wail upon their beds; they gash *and* distress *and* assemble themselves [in mourning] for grain and new wine; they rebel against Me.

15 Although I have chastened them *and* trained and strengthened their arms, yet they think *and* devise evil against Me.

16 They turn back, shift *or* change, but not upwards—to the Most High. They are like a deceitful bow, their princes shall fall by the sword for the insolence *and* rage of their tongue. This shall be [cause for] their derision *and* scorning in the land of Egypt.

## King James

**8** *SET* THE trumpet to thy mouth. *He shall come* as an eagle against the house of the LORD, because they have transgressed my covenant, and trespassed against my law.

2 Israel shall cry unto me, My God, we know thee.

3 Israel hath cast off *the thing that is* good: the enemy shall pursue him.

4 They have set up kings, but not by me: they have made princes, and I knew *it* not: of their silver and their gold have they made them idols, that they may be cut off.

5 ¶ Thy calf, O Samaria, hath cast *thee* off; mine anger is kindled against them: how long *will it be* ere they attain to innocency?

## Amplified

**8** SET THE trumpet to your lips! [The enemy] comes as a [great] vulture against the house of the Lord, because they have broken My covenant, and transgressed against My law.

2 Then they will cry to Me, My God, we know You, we, Israel!

3 Israel has rejected the good with [loathing]; the enemy shall pursue him.

4 They set up kings, but not from Me [therefore without My blessing]; they have made princes or removed them [without consulting Me, therefore], I knew *and* recognized *them* not. With their silver and their gold they made idols for themselves, that they [the silver and the gold], may be destroyed.

5 Your calf [idol], O Samaria, is loathsome, *and* I have spurned it. My wrath burns against them. How long will it be before they attain purity?

## New American Standard

6 For their hearts are like an oven
*As* they approach their plotting;
Their anger smolders all night,
In the morning it burns like a flaming fire.
7 All of them are hot like an oven,
And they consume their rulers;
All their kings have fallen.
None of them calls on Me.

8¶ Ephraim mixes himself with the nations;
Ephraim has become a cake not turned.
9 Strangers devour his strength,
Yet he does not know *it;*
Gray hairs also are sprinkled on him,
Yet he does not know *it.*
10 Though the pride of Israel testifies against him,
Yet they have neither returned to the LORD their God,
Nor have they sought Him, for all this.
11 So Ephraim has become like a silly dove, without sense;
They call to Egypt, they go to Assyria.
12 When they go, I will spread My net over them;
I will bring them down like the birds of the sky.
I will chastise them in accordance with the proclamation
to their assembly.
13 Woe to them, for they have strayed from Me!
Destruction is theirs, for they have rebelled against Me!
I would redeem them, but they speak lies against Me.
14 And they do not cry to Me from their heart
When they wail on their beds;
For the sake of grain and new wine they assemble
themselves,
They turn away from Me.
15 Although I trained *and* strengthened their arms,
Yet they devise evil against Me.
16 They turn, *but* not upward,
They are like a deceitful bow;
Their princes will fall by the sword
Because of the insolence of their tongue.
This *will be* their derision in the land of Egypt.

*Israel Reaps the Whirlwind*

**8** *PUT* THE trumpet to your lips!
Like an eagle *the enemy comes* against the house of the
LORD,
Because they have transgressed My covenant,
And rebelled against My law.
2 They cry out to Me,
"My God, we of Israel know Thee!"
3 Israel has rejected the good;
The enemy will pursue him.
4 They have set up kings, but not by Me;
They have appointed princes, but I did not know *it.*
With their silver and gold they have made idols for
themselves,
That they might be cut off.
5 He has rejected your calf, O Samaria, saying,
"My anger burns against them!"
How long will they be incapable of innocence?

## New International

6Their hearts are like an oven;
they approach him with intrigue.
Their passion smolders all night;
in the morning it blazes like a flaming fire.
7All of them are hot as an oven;
they devour their rulers.
All their kings fall,
and none of them calls on me.

8"Ephraim mixes with the nations;
Ephraim is a flat cake not turned over.
9Foreigners sap his strength,
but he does not realize it.
His hair is sprinkled with gray,
but he does not notice.
10Israel's arrogance testifies against him,
but despite all this
he does not return to the LORD his God
or search for him.
11"Ephraim is like a dove,
easily deceived and senseless—
now calling to Egypt,
now turning to Assyria.
12When they go, I will throw my net over them;
I will pull them down like birds of the air.
When I hear them flocking together,
I will catch them.
13Woe to them,
because they have strayed from me!
Destruction to them,
because they have rebelled against me!
I long to redeem them
but they speak lies against me.
14They do not cry out to me from their hearts
but wail upon their beds.
They gather together[a] for grain and new wine
but turn away from me.
15I trained them and strengthened them,
but they plot evil against me.
16They do not turn to the Most High;
they are like a faulty bow.
Their leaders will fall by the sword
because of their insolent words.
For this they will be ridiculed
in the land of Egypt.

*Israel to Reap the Whirlwind*

**8** "PUT THE trumpet to your lips!
An eagle is over the house of the LORD
because the people have broken my covenant
and rebelled against my law.
2Israel cries out to me,
'O our God, we acknowledge you!'
3But Israel has rejected what is good;
an enemy will pursue him.
4They set up kings without my consent;
they choose princes without my approval.
With their silver and gold
they make idols for themselves
to their own destruction.
5Throw out your calf-idol, O Samaria!
My anger burns against them.
How long will they be incapable of purity?

NIV [a] *14* Most Hebrew manuscripts; some Hebrew manuscripts and Septuagint *They slash themselves*

## King James

6For from Israel *was* it also: the workman made it; therefore it *is* not God: but the calf of Samaria shall be broken in pieces.

7For they have sown the wind, and they shall reap the whirlwind: it hath no stalk: the bud shall yield no meal: if so be it yield, the strangers shall swallow it up.

8Israel is swallowed up: now shall they be among the Gentiles as a vessel wherein *is* no pleasure.

9For they are gone up to Assyria, a wild ass alone by himself: Ephraim hath hired lovers.

10Yea, though they have hired among the nations, now will I gather them, and they shall sorrow a little for the burden of the king of princes.

11Because Ephraim hath made many altars to sin, altars shall be unto him to sin.

12I have written to him the great things of my law, *but* they were counted as a strange thing.

13They sacrifice flesh *for* the sacrifices of mine offerings, and eat *it; but* the LORD accepteth them not; now will he remember their iniquity, and visit their sins: they shall return to Egypt.

14For Israel hath forgotten his Maker, and buildeth temples; and Judah hath multiplied fenced cities: but I will send a fire upon his cities, and it shall devour the palaces thereof.

**9** REJOICE NOT, O Israel, for joy, as *other* people: for thou hast gone a-whoring from thy God, thou hast loved a reward upon every cornfloor.

2The floor and the winepress shall not feed them, and the new wine shall fail in her.

3They shall not dwell in the LORD's land; but Ephraim shall return to Egypt, and they shall eat unclean *things* in Assyria.

4They shall not offer wine *offerings* to the LORD, neither shall they be pleasing unto him: their sacrifices *shall be* unto them as the bread of mourners; all that eat thereof shall be polluted: for their bread for their soul shall not come into the house of the LORD.

5What will ye do in the solemn day, and in the day of the feast of the LORD?

6For, lo, they are gone because of destruction: Egypt shall gather them up, Memphis shall bury them: the pleasant *places* for their silver, nettles shall possess them: thorns *shall be* in their tabernacles.

## Amplified

6For this [calf] too is from Israel; a craftsman made it, therefore it is no God. The calf of Samaria shall be broken to shivers *and* go up in flames.

7For they sow the wind, and they shall reap the whirlwind. The standing grain has no heads, it shall yield no meal; if it were to yield, strangers *and* aliens would eat it up.

8Israel is [the same as] swallowed up. Already they have become among the nations as a vessel [of cheap, coarse pottery] that is useless.

9For they are gone up to Assyria, a wild ass taking her own way by herself; Ephraim has hired lovers.

10Yes, though with presents they hire [allies] among the nations, now will I gather them up, and in a little while they will sorrow *and* begin to diminish [their gifts] because of the [tribute] burden imposed by [the king of Assyria] the king of princes.

11For Ephraim has multiplied altars for sinning; yes, to him altars are intended for sinning.

12I wrote for him the ten thousand things of My law, but they are counted as a strange thing [as something which does not concern him].

13My sacrificial gifts they sacrifice [as a mere form]; yes, they sacrifice flesh and eat it; but the Lord does not accept them. Now He will [earnestly] remember their guilt *and* iniquity and will punish their sins. They shall return to [another] Egypt [Assyria]. [Deut. 28:68.]

14For Israel has forgotten his Maker and built palaces *and idol* temples, and Judah has multiplied fortified cities; but I will send a fire upon his cities, and it shall devour his palaces *and* fortified buildings. [Amos 1:4, 7, 10, 12, 14; 2:2, 5.]

**9** REJOICE NOT, O Israel, *with* exultation as do the peoples; for you have played the harlot, forsaking your God. You have loved [a harlot's] hire upon every threshing floor [ascribing the harvest to the Baals instead of to God].

2The threshing floor and the winevat shall not feed them, and the new wine shall fail *them.*

3They shall not remain in the Lord's land, but Ephraim shall return to [another] Egypt, and they shall eat unclean food in Assyria. [Cf. Ezek. 4:13.]

4They shall not pour out wine offerings to the Lord, neither shall they be pleasing to Him. Their sacrifices shall be to them as the bread of mourners; all who eat of them shall be defiled; for their bread shall be *only* for their appetite; it shall not come into the house of the Lord [to be offered first to Him].

5What will you do on the day of appointed solemn assembly *or* festival, and on the day of the feast of the Lord [when you are in exile]?

6For lo, they are gone away from devastation *and* destruction; Egypt shall gather them in, Memphis shall bury them. Their precious things of silver shall be in the possession of nettles; thorns shall be [growing] in their tents.

## New American Standard

6 For from Israel is even this!
A craftsman made it, so it is not God;
Surely the calf of Samaria will be broken to pieces.
7 For they sow the wind,
And they reap the whirlwind.
The standing grain has no heads;
It yields no grain.
Should it yield, strangers would swallow it up.

8¶ Israel is swallowed up;
They are now among the nations
Like a vessel in which no one delights.
9 For they have gone up to Assyria,
*Like* a wild donkey all alone;
Ephraim has hired lovers.
10 Even though they hire *allies* among the nations,
Now I will gather them up;
And they will begin to diminish
Because of the burden of the king of princes.
11¶ Since Ephraim has multiplied altars for sin,
They have become altars of sinning for him.
12 Though I wrote for him ten thousand *precepts* of My law,
They are regarded as a strange thing.
13 As for My sacrificial gifts,
They sacrifice the flesh and eat *it*,
*But* the LORD has taken no delight in them.
Now He will remember their iniquity,
And punish *them* for their sins;
They will return to Egypt.
14 For Israel has forgotten his Maker and built palaces;
And Judah has multiplied fortified cities,
But I will send a fire on its cities that it may consume its palatial dwellings.

*Ephraim Punished*

**9** DO NOT rejoice, O Israel, with exultation like the nations!
For you have played the harlot, forsaking your God.
You have loved *harlots'* earnings on every threshing floor.
2 Threshing floor and wine press will not feed them,
And the new wine will fail them.
3 They will not remain in the LORD's land,
But Ephraim will return to Egypt,
And in Assyria they will eat unclean *food*.
4 They will not pour out libations of wine to the LORD,
Their sacrifices will not please Him.
*Their bread will be* like mourners' bread;
All who eat of it will be defiled,
For their bread will be for themselves *alone*;
It will not enter the house of the LORD.
5 What will you do on the day of the appointed festival
And on the day of the feast of the LORD?
6 For behold, they will go because of destruction;
Egypt will gather them up, Memphis will bury them.
Weeds will take over their treasures of silver;
Thorns *will be* in their tents.

## New International

6 They are from Israel!
This calf—a craftsman has made it;
it is not God.
It will be broken in pieces,
that calf of Samaria.

7 "They sow the wind
and reap the whirlwind.
The stalk has no head;
it will produce no flour.
Were it to yield grain,
foreigners would swallow it up.
8 Israel is swallowed up;
now she is among the nations
like a worthless thing.
9 For they have gone up to Assyria
like a wild donkey wandering alone.
Ephraim has sold herself to lovers.
10 Although they have sold themselves among the nations,
I will now gather them together.
They will begin to waste away
under the oppression of the mighty king.
11 "Though Ephraim built many altars for sin offerings,
these have become altars for sinning.
12 I wrote for them the many things of my law,
but they regarded them as something alien.
13 They offer sacrifices given to me
and they eat the meat,
but the LORD is not pleased with them.
Now he will remember their wickedness
and punish their sins:
They will return to Egypt.
14 Israel has forgotten his Maker
and built palaces;
Judah has fortified many towns.
But I will send fire upon their cities
that will consume their fortresses."

*Punishment for Israel*

**9** DO NOT rejoice, O Israel;
do not be jubilant like the other nations.
For you have been unfaithful to your God;
you love the wages of a prostitute
at every threshing floor.
2 Threshing floors and winepresses will not feed the people;
the new wine will fail them.
3 They will not remain in the LORD's land;
Ephraim will return to Egypt
and eat unclean[a] food in Assyria.
4 They will not pour out wine offerings to the LORD,
nor will their sacrifices please him.
Such sacrifices will be to them like the bread of mourners;
all who eat them will be unclean.
This food will be for themselves;
it will not come into the temple of the LORD.
5 What will you do on the day of your appointed feasts,
on the festival days of the LORD?
6 Even if they escape from destruction,
Egypt will gather them,
and Memphis will bury them.
Their treasures of silver will be taken over by briers,
and thorns will overrun their tents.

NIV [a] 3 That is, ceremonially unclean

## King James

7 The days of visitation are come, the days of recompence are come; Israel shall know *it:* the prophet *is* a fool, the spiritual man *is* mad, for the multitude of thine iniquity, and the great hatred.

8 The watchman of Ephraim *was* with my God: *but* the prophet *is* a snare of a fowler in all his ways, *and* hatred in the house of his God.

9 They have deeply corrupted *themselves,* as in the days of Gibeah: *therefore* he will remember their iniquity, he will visit their sins.

10 I found Israel like grapes in the wilderness; I saw your fathers as the firstripe in the fig tree at her first time: *but* they went to Baal-peor, and separated themselves unto *that* shame; and *their* abominations were according as they loved.

11 *As for* Ephraim, their glory shall fly away like a bird, from the birth, and from the womb, and from the conception.

12 Though they bring up their children, yet will I bereave them, *that there shall* not *be* a man *left:* yea, woe also to them when I depart from them!

13 Ephraim, as I saw Tyrus, *is* planted in a pleasant place: but Ephraim shall bring forth his children to the murderer.

14 Give them, O LORD: what wilt thou give? give them a miscarrying womb and dry breasts.

15 All their wickedness *is* in Gilgal: for there I hated them: for the wickedness of their doings I will drive them out of mine house, I will love them no more: all their princes *are* revolters.

16 Ephraim is smitten, their root is dried up, they shall bear no fruit: yea, though they bring forth, yet will I slay *even* the beloved *fruit* of their womb.

17 My God will cast them away, because they did not hearken unto him: and they shall be wanderers among the nations.

**10** ISRAEL *IS* an empty vine, he bringeth forth fruit unto himself: according to the multitude of his fruit he hath increased the altars; according to the goodness of his land they have made goodly images.

2 Their heart is divided; now shall they be found faulty: he shall break down their altars, he shall spoil their images.

## Amplified

7 The days of visitation *and* punishment have come, the days of recompense have come; Israel shall know it. The prophet is [considered] a crazed fool, and the man who is inspired is [treated as if] mad *or* a fanatic, because of the abundance of your iniquity and because the enmity, hostility *and* persecution are great. [Luke 21:22.]

8 Ephraim was [intended to be] a watchman with my God [and a prophet to the surrounding nations]; but he, that prophet, has become a fowler's snare in all his ways. There is enmity, hostility *and* persecution in the house of his God.

9 They have deeply corrupted themselves, as in the days of Gibeah. The Lord will [earnestly] remember their iniquity, He will punish their sins. [Judg. 20:46-48.]

10 I found Israel like grapes in the wilderness; I saw your fathers as the first ripe fruit on the fig tree in its first season; but they went to Baalpeor, and consecrated themselves to [Baal] that shameful thing, and they became detestable *and* loathsome like that which they loved.

11 As for Ephraim, their glory shall fly away like a bird; there shall be no birth, no being with child, and [because of their impurity] no becoming pregnant.

12 Though they bring up their children, yet will I bereave them, so that not a man shall be left; yes, woe also to them when I look away *and* depart from them!

13 Ephraim, like as I have seen Tyre, is planted in a pleasant place; but Ephraim shall bring out his children to the slayer.

14 Give them [their due], O Lord! *But* what will You give? Give them a miscarrying womb and dry breasts.

15 All their wickedness, [says the Lord,] is focused in Gilgal for there I hated them: for the wickedness of their [idolatrous] doings I will drive them out of My house [the Holy Land]; I will love them no more; all their princes are rebels. [Hos. 4:15; 12:11.]

16 Ephraim is smitten, their root is dried up, they shall bear no fruit. Yes, though they bring forth, yet will I slay even their beloved children.

17 My God will cast them away, because they did not listen to *and* obey Him, and they shall be wanderers *and* fugitives among the nations.

**10** ISRAEL IS a luxuriant vine that puts forth its [material] fruit. According to the abundance of his fruit he has multiplied his altars [to idols]; according to the goodness *and* prosperity of their land they have made goodly pillars *or* obelisks [to false gods].

2 Their heart is divided *and* deceitful; now shall they be found guilty *and* suffer punishment. The Lord will smite *and* break down [the horns of] their altars, He will destroy their [idolatrous] pillars.

## New American Standard

7¶ The days of punishment have come,
The days of retribution have come;
Let Israel know *this*!
The prophet is a fool,
The inspired man is demented,
Because of the grossness of your iniquity,
And *because* your hostility is *so* great.
8 Ephraim *was* a watchman with my God, a prophet;
*Yet* the snare of a bird catcher is in all his ways,
*And* there is *only* hostility in the house of his God.
9 They have gone deep in depravity
As in the days of Gibeah;
He will remember their iniquity,
He will punish their sins.

10¶ I found Israel like grapes in the wilderness;
I saw your forefathers as the earliest fruit on the fig tree
in its first *season*.
*But* they came to Baal-peor and devoted themselves to [a]shame,
And they became as detestable as that which they loved.
11 As for Ephraim, their glory will fly away like a bird—
No birth, no pregnancy, and no conception!
12 Though they bring up their children,
Yet I will bereave them until not a man is left.
Yes, woe to them indeed when I depart from them!
13 Ephraim, as I have seen,
Is planted in a pleasant meadow like Tyre;
But Ephraim will bring out his children for slaughter.
14 Give them, O LORD—what wilt Thou give?
Give them a miscarrying womb and dry breasts.

15¶ All their evil is at Gilgal;
Indeed, I came to hate them there!
Because of the wickedness of their deeds
I will drive them out of My house!
I will love them no more;
All their princes are rebels.
16 Ephraim is stricken, their root is dried up,
They will bear no fruit.
Even though they bear children,
I will slay the precious ones of their womb.
17 My God will cast them away
Because they have not listened to Him;
And they will be wanderers among the nations.

*Retribution for Israel's Sin*

**10** ISRAEL IS a luxuriant vine;
He produces fruit for himself.
The more his fruit,
The more altars he made;
The richer his land,
The better he made the *sacred* pillars.
2 Their heart is faithless;
Now they must bear their guilt.
The LORD will break down their altars
*And* destroy their *sacred* pillars.

NAS [a] I.e., Baal

## New International

7The days of punishment are coming,
the days of reckoning are at hand.
Let Israel know this.
Because your sins are so many
and your hostility so great,
the prophet is considered a fool,
the inspired man a maniac.
8The prophet, along with my God,
is the watchman over Ephraim,[b]
yet snares await him on all his paths,
and hostility in the house of his God.
9They have sunk deep into corruption,
as in the days of Gibeah.
God will remember their wickedness
and punish them for their sins.

10"When I found Israel,
it was like finding grapes in the desert;
when I saw your fathers,
it was like seeing the early fruit on the fig tree.
But when they came to Baal Peor,
they consecrated themselves to that shameful idol
and became as vile as the thing they loved.
11Ephraim's glory will fly away like a bird—
no birth, no pregnancy, no conception.
12Even if they rear children,
I will bereave them of every one.
Woe to them
when I turn away from them!
13I have seen Ephraim, like Tyre,
planted in a pleasant place.
But Ephraim will bring out
their children to the slayer."
14Give them, O LORD—
what will you give them?
Give them wombs that miscarry
and breasts that are dry.

15"Because of all their wickedness in Gilgal,
I hated them there.
Because of their sinful deeds,
I will drive them out of my house.
I will no longer love them;
all their leaders are rebellious.
16Ephraim is blighted,
their root is withered,
they yield no fruit.
Even if they bear children,
I will slay their cherished offspring."

17My God will reject them
because they have not obeyed him;
they will be wanderers among the nations.

**10** ISRAEL WAS a spreading vine;
he brought forth fruit for himself.
As his fruit increased,
he built more altars;
as his land prospered,
he adorned his sacred stones.
2Their heart is deceitful,
and now they must bear their guilt.
The LORD will demolish their altars
and destroy their sacred stones.

NIV [b] 8 Or *The prophet is the watchman over Ephraim, / the people of my God*

# King James

3For now they shall say, We have no king, because we feared not the LORD; what then should a king do to us?

4They have spoken words, swearing falsely in making a covenant: thus judgment springeth up as hemlock in the furrows of the field.

5The inhabitants of Samaria shall fear because of the calves of Beth-aven: for the people thereof shall mourn over it, and the priests thereof *that* rejoiced on it, for the glory thereof, because it is departed from it.

6It shall be also carried unto Assyria *for* a present to king Jareb: Ephraim shall receive shame, and Israel shall be ashamed of his own counsel.

7 *As for* Samaria, her king is cut off as the foam upon the water.

8The high places also of Aven, the sin of Israel, shall be destroyed: the thorn and the thistle shall come up on their altars; and they shall say to the mountains, Cover us; and to the hills, Fall on us.

9O Israel, thou hast sinned from the days of Gibeah: there they stood: the battle in Gibeah against the children of iniquity did not overtake them.

10 *It is* in my desire that I should chastise them; and the people shall be gathered against them, when they shall bind themselves in their two furrows.

11And Ephraim *is as* an heifer *that is* taught, *and* loveth to tread out *the corn;* but I passed over upon her fair neck: I will make Ephraim to ride; Judah shall plow, *and* Jacob shall break his clods.

12Sow to yourselves in righteousness, reap in mercy; break up your fallow ground: for *it is* time to seek the LORD, till he come and rain righteousness upon you.

13Ye have plowed wickedness, ye have reaped iniquity; ye have eaten the fruit of lies: because thou didst trust in thy way, in the multitude of thy mighty men.

14Therefore shall a tumult arise among thy people, and all thy fortresses shall be spoiled, as Shalman spoiled Beth-arbel in the day of battle: the mother was dashed in pieces upon *her* children.

15So shall Beth-el do unto you because of your great wickedness: in a morning shall the king of Israel utterly be cut off.

# Amplified

3Surely now they shall say, We have no [actual] king, because we fear not the Lord; and as for the king, what can he do for us?

4They have spoken mere words of the lips, swearing falsely in making covenants; therefore judgment springs up like hemlock [or other] poisonous plant in the furrows of the field.

5The inhabitants of Samaria shall be in terror for the calf-idols of Bethaven [the house of idolatry, contemptuously meaning Bethel]; for its people shall mourn over it, and its [idolatrous] priests who rejoiced over it [shall tremble] for the glory of [their calf-god], because it is departed from it.

6[The golden calf] shall also be carried into Assyria as a tribute-gift to the fighting King Jareb; Ephraim shall be put to shame, and Israel shall be ashamed of his own counsel [to set up calf-worship and detach Israel from Judah].

7As for Samaria, her king *and* her whole monarchy are cut off like twigs *or* foam upon the water.

8The high places also of Aven [once Beth(el), house of God, now (Beth)aven, house of idols], the sin of Israel, shall be destroyed; the thorn and the thistle shall come up on their [idol] altars, and they shall say to the mountains, Cover us! And to the hills, Fall on us! [Luke 23:30; Rev. 6:16; 9:6.]

9O Israel, you have [willfully] sinned from the days of Gibeah [when you all but wiped out the tribe of Benjamin]! There [Israel] stood *then, only* that the battle against the sons of unrighteousness might not overtake *and* turn against them at Gibeah [but now the kingdom of the ten tribes and the name of Ephraim shall be utterly blotted out]. [Judg. 20:46-48.]

10When I please I will chastise them, and hostile peoples shall be gathered against them, when I shall bind *and* yoke them for their two transgressions [revolt from the Lord their God and the worship of idols]. [Jer. 2:13; Lam. 3:31-33.]

11Ephraim indeed is a heifer broken in *and* loving to tread out the grain, but I have [heretofore] spared the beauty of her fair neck. I will now set a rider upon Ephraim *and* make him to draw; Judah shall plow, and Jacob shall break his clods.

12Sow for yourselves according to righteousness—uprightness and right standing with God; reap according to mercy *and* loving-kindness. Break up your uncultivated ground, for it is time to seek the Lord, to inquire for *and* of Him *and* to require [His favor], till He comes and teaches you righteousness *and* rains His righteous gift of salvation upon you. [II Cor. 9:10.]

13You have plowed *and* plotted wickedness, you have reaped the [willful] injustice [of oppressors]; you have eaten the fruit of lies. Because you have trusted in your *own* way *and* your chariots, in the multitude of your mighty men.

14Therefore shall a tumult arise against your people, and all your fortresses shall be wasted *and* destroyed, as Shalmanezer wasted *and* destroyed Betharbel on the day of battle; the mother was dashed in pieces with her children. [II Kings 17:3.]

15So shall it be done to you at [idolatrous] Bethel because of your great wickedness; at daybreak shall the king of Israel be utterly cut off.

## New American Standard

3¶ Surely now they will say, "We have no king,
For we do not revere the LORD.
As for the king, what can he do for us?"
4 They speak *mere* words,
With worthless oaths they make covenants;
And judgment sprouts like poisonous weeds in the furrows of the field.
5 The inhabitants of Samaria will fear
For the calf of Beth-aven.
Indeed, its people will mourn for it,
And its idolatrous priests will cry out over it,
Over its glory, since it has departed from it.
6 The thing itself will be carried to Assyria
As tribute to King Jareb;
Ephraim will be seized with shame,
And Israel will be ashamed of its own counsel.
7 Samaria will be cut off *with* her king,
Like a stick on the surface of the water.
8 Also the high places of Aven, the sin of Israel, will be destroyed;
Thorn and thistle will grow on their altars,
Then they will say to the mountains,
"Cover us!" And to the hills, "Fall on us!"
9 From the days of Gibeah you have sinned, O Israel;
There they stand!
Will not the battle against the sons of iniquity overtake them in Gibeah?
10 When it is My desire, I will chastise them;
And the peoples will be gathered against them
When they are bound for their double guilt.

11¶ And Ephraim is a trained heifer that loves to thresh,
But I will come over her fair neck *with a yoke;*
I will harness Ephraim,
Judah will plow, Jacob will harrow for himself.
12 Sow with a view to righteousness,
Reap in accordance with kindness;
Break up your fallow ground,
For it is time to seek the LORD
Until He comes to rain righteousness on you.
13 You have plowed wickedness, you have reaped injustice,
You have eaten the fruit of lies.
Because you have trusted in your way, in your numerous warriors,
14 Therefore, a tumult will arise among your people,
And all your fortresses will be destroyed,
As Shalman destroyed Beth-arbel on the day of battle,
*When* mothers were dashed in pieces with *their* children.
15 Thus it will be done to you at Bethel because of your great wickedness.
At dawn the king of Israel will be completely cut off.

## New International

3Then they will say, "We have no king
because we did not revere the LORD.
But even if we had a king,
what could he do for us?"
4They make many promises,
take false oaths
and make agreements;
therefore lawsuits spring up
like poisonous weeds in a plowed field.
5The people who live in Samaria fear
for the calf-idol of Beth Aven.[a]
Its people will mourn over it,
and so will its idolatrous priests,
those who had rejoiced over its splendor,
because it is taken from them into exile.
6It will be carried to Assyria
as tribute for the great king.
Ephraim will be disgraced;
Israel will be ashamed of its wooden idols.[b]
7Samaria and its king will float away
like a twig on the surface of the waters.
8The high places of wickedness[c] will be destroyed—
it is the sin of Israel.
Thorns and thistles will grow up
and cover their altars.
Then they will say to the mountains, "Cover us!"
and to the hills, "Fall on us!"
9"Since the days of Gibeah, you have sinned, O Israel,
and there you have remained.[d]
Did not war overtake
the evildoers in Gibeah?
10When I please, I will punish them;
nations will be gathered against them
to put them in bonds for their double sin.
11Ephraim is a trained heifer
that loves to thresh;
so I will put a yoke
on her fair neck.
I will drive Ephraim,
Judah must plow,
and Jacob must break up the ground.
12Sow for yourselves righteousness,
reap the fruit of unfailing love,
and break up your unplowed ground;
for it is time to seek the LORD,
until he comes
and showers righteousness on you.
13But you have planted wickedness,
you have reaped evil,
you have eaten the fruit of deception.
Because you have depended on your own strength
and on your many warriors,
14the roar of battle will rise against your people,
so that all your fortresses will be devastated—
as Shalman devastated Beth Arbel on the day of battle,
when mothers were dashed to the ground with their children.
15Thus will it happen to you, O Bethel,
because your wickedness is great.
When that day dawns,
the king of Israel will be completely destroyed.

**NIV** [a] 5 *Beth Aven* means *house of wickedness* (a name for Bethel, which means *house of God*). [b] 6 *Or its counsel* [c] 8 Hebrew *aven,* a reference to Beth Aven (a derogatory name for Bethel) [d] 9 *Or there a stand was taken*

## King James

11 WHEN ISRAEL *was* a child, then I loved him, and called
my son out of Egypt.
2 *As* they called them, so they went from them: they sacrificed
unto Baalim, and burned incense to graven images.
3 I taught Ephraim also to go, taking them by their arms; but
they knew not that I healed them.
4 I drew them with cords of a man, with bands of love: and I was
to them as they that take off the yoke on their jaws, and I laid meat
unto them.
5 ¶ He shall not return into the land of Egypt, but the Assyrian
shall be his king, because they refused to return.
6 And the sword shall abide on his cities, and shall consume his
branches, and devour *them,* because of their own counsels.
7 And my people are bent to backsliding from me: though they
called them to the most High, none at all would exalt *him.*
8 How shall I give thee up, Ephraim? *how* shall I deliver thee,
Israel? how shall I make thee as Admah? *how* shall I set thee as
Zeboim? mine heart is turned within me, my repentings are kindled together.
9 I will not execute the fierceness of mine anger, I will not return
to destroy Ephraim: for I *am* God, and not man; the Holy One in
the midst of thee: and I will not enter into the city.
10 They shall walk after the LORD: he shall roar like a lion: when
he shall roar, then the children shall tremble from the west.
11 They shall tremble as a bird out of Egypt, and as a dove out
of the land of Assyria: and I will place them in their houses, saith
the LORD.
12 Ephraim compasseth me about with lies, and the house of
Israel with deceit: but Judah yet ruleth with God, and is faithful
with the saints.

## Amplified

11 WHEN ISRAEL was a child, then I loved him, and called
My son out of Egypt. [Matt. 2:15.]
2 The more [the prophets] called to them, the more they went
from them; they kept sacrificing to the Baals, and burning incense
to the graven images.
3 Yet I taught Ephraim to walk, taking them by their arms *or*
taking them up in *My* arms, but they did not know that I healed
them.
4 I drew them with cords of a man, with bands of love, and I was
to them as *one* who lifts up *and* eases the yoke over their cheeks,
and I bent down to them *and* gently laid food before them.
5 They shall not [literally] return into [another bondage in] the
land of Egypt, but the Assyrian shall be their king, because they
refused to return to Me.
6 And the sword shall rage against *and* fall upon their cities, and
shall consume the bars *of* their *gates,* and shall make an end [of their
defenses], because of their own counsels *and* devices.
7 My people are bent on backsliding from Me; though [the
prophets] call them to Him Who is on high, none at all will exalt
Him *or* lift himself up [to come].
8 How can I give you up, O Ephraim! How can I surrender you
*and* cast you off, O Israel! How can I make you as Admah, *or* how
can I treat you as Zeboiim [both destroyed with Sodom]! My heart
recoils within Me, My compassions are kindled together.
9 I will not execute the fierceness of My anger, I will not bring
back Ephraim to nothing *or* again destroy him; for I am God and
not man, the Holy One in the midst of you, and I will not come
in wrath *or* enter into the city.
10 They shall walk after the Lord, Who will roar like a lion; He
Himself will roar and [His] sons shall come trembling *and* eagerly
from the west.
11 They shall come trembling *but* hurriedly as a bird out of Egypt,
and as a dove out of the land of Assyria; and I will cause them to
dwell in their houses, says the Lord.
12 Ephraim surrounds Me with lies, and the house of Israel with
deceit, and Judah is not yet steadfast with God, with the faithful
Holy One.

## King James

12 EPHRAIM FEEDETH on wind, and followeth after the
east wind: he daily increaseth lies and desolation; and
they do make a covenant with the Assyrians, and oil is carried into
Egypt.
2 The LORD hath also a controversy with Judah, and will punish
Jacob according to his ways; according to his doings will he recompense him.
3 ¶ He took his brother by the heel in the womb, and by his
strength he had power with God:

## Amplified

12 EPHRAIM HERDS *and* feeds on the wind and pursues the
[parching] east wind; every day he increases lies and violence; and a covenant is made with Assyria, and oil is carried to
Egypt. [Isa. 30:6, 7.]
2 The Lord has also a controversy—a pleading contention—with
Judah, and will punish Jacob by visiting upon him according to his
ways; according to his doings will He recompense him.
3 He took his brother by the heel in [their mother's] womb, and
in the strength *of* his manhood he contended *and* had power with
God. [Gen. 25:26.]

## New American Standard

*God Yearns over His People*

11 WHEN ISRAEL *was* a youth I loved him,
And out of Egypt I called My son.
2 The more they called them,
The more they went from them;
They kept sacrificing to the Baals
And burning incense to idols.
3 Yet it is I who taught Ephraim to walk,
I took them in My arms;
But they did not know that I healed them.
4 I led them with cords of a man, with bonds of love,
And I became to them as one who lifts the yoke from their jaws;
And I bent down *and* fed them.

5¶ They will not return to the land of Egypt;
But Assyria—he will be their king,
Because they refused to return *to Me.*
6 And the sword will whirl against their cities,
And will demolish their gate bars
And consume *them* because of their counsels.
7 So My people are bent on turning from Me.
Though they call them to *the One* on high,
None at all exalts *Him.*

8¶ How can I give you up, O Ephraim?
How can I surrender you, O Israel?
How can I make you like Admah?
How can I treat you like Zeboiim?
My heart is turned over within Me,
All my compassions are kindled.
9 I will not execute My fierce anger;
I will not destroy Ephraim again.
For I am God and not man, the Holy One in your midst,
And I will not come in wrath.
10 They will walk after the LORD,
He will roar like a lion;
Indeed He will roar,
And *His* sons will come trembling from the west.
11 They will come trembling like birds from Egypt,
And like doves from the land of Assyria;
And I will settle them in their houses, declares the LORD.

12¶ Ephraim surrounds Me with lies,
And the house of Israel with deceit;
Judah is also unruly against God,
Even against the Holy One who is faithful.

*Ephraim Reminded*

12 EPHRAIM FEEDS on wind,
And pursues the east wind continually;
He multiplies lies and violence.
Moreover, he makes a covenant with Assyria,
And oil is carried to Egypt.
2 The LORD also has a dispute with Judah,
And will punish Jacob according to his ways;
He will repay him according to his deeds.
3 In the womb he took his brother by the heel,
And in his maturity he contended with God.

## New International

*God's Love for Israel*

11 "WHEN ISRAEL was a child, I loved him,
and out of Egypt I called my son.
2But the more I[a] called Israel,
the further they went from me.[b]
They sacrificed to the Baals
and they burned incense to images.
3It was I who taught Ephraim to walk,
taking them by the arms;
but they did not realize
it was I who healed them.
4I led them with cords of human kindness,
with ties of love;
I lifted the yoke from their neck
and bent down to feed them.

5"Will they not return to Egypt
and will not Assyria rule over them
because they refuse to repent?
6Swords will flash in their cities,
will destroy the bars of their gates
and put an end to their plans.
7My people are determined to turn from me.
Even if they call to the Most High,
he will by no means exalt them.

8"How can I give you up, Ephraim?
How can I hand you over, Israel?
How can I treat you like Admah?
How can I make you like Zeboiim?
My heart is changed within me;
all my compassion is aroused.
9I will not carry out my fierce anger,
nor will I turn and devastate Ephraim.
For I am God, and not man—
the Holy One among you.
I will not come in wrath.[c]
10They will follow the LORD;
he will roar like a lion.
When he roars,
his children will come trembling from the west.
11They will come trembling
like birds from Egypt,
like doves from Assyria.
I will settle them in their homes,"
declares the LORD.

*Israel's Sin*

12Ephraim has surrounded me with lies,
the house of Israel with deceit.
And Judah is unruly against God,
even against the faithful Holy One.

12 EPHRAIM FEEDS on the wind;
he pursues the east wind all day
and multiplies lies and violence.
He makes a treaty with Assyria
and sends olive oil to Egypt.
2The LORD has a charge to bring against Judah;
he will punish Jacob[d] according to his ways
and repay him according to his deeds.
3In the womb he grasped his brother's heel;
as a man he struggled with God.

**NIV** [a] 2 Some Septuagint manuscripts; Hebrew *they* [b] 2 Septuagint; Hebrew *them* [c] 9 Or *come against any city* [d] 2 *Jacob* means *he grasps the heel* (figuratively, *he deceives*).

## King James

4 Yea, he had power over the angel, and prevailed: he wept, and made supplication unto him: he found him *in* Beth-el, and there he spake with us;

5 Even the LORD God of hosts; the LORD *is* his memorial.

6 Therefore turn thou to thy God: keep mercy and judgment, and wait on thy God continually.

7 ¶ *He is* a merchant, the balances of deceit *are* in his hand: he loveth to oppress.

8 And Ephraim said, Yet I am become rich, I have found me out substance: *in* all my labours they shall find none iniquity in me that *were* sin.

9 And I *that am* the LORD thy God from the land of Egypt will yet make thee to dwell in tabernacles, as in the days of the solemn feast.

10 I have also spoken by the prophets, and I have multiplied visions, and used similitudes, by the ministry of the prophets.

11 *Is there* iniquity *in* Gilead? surely they are vanity: they sacrifice bullocks in Gilgal; yea, their altars *are* as heaps in the furrows of the fields.

12 And Jacob fled into the country of Syria, and Israel served for a wife, and for a wife he kept *sheep.*

13 And by a prophet the LORD brought Israel out of Egypt, and by a prophet was he preserved.

14 Ephraim provoked *him* to anger most bitterly: therefore shall he leave his blood upon him, and his reproach shall his Lord return unto him.

**13** WHEN EPHRAIM spake trembling, he exalted himself in Israel; but when he offended in Baal, he died.

2 And now they sin more and more, and have made them molten images of their silver, *and* idols according to their own understanding, all of it the work of the craftsmen: they say of them, Let the men that sacrifice kiss the calves.

3 Therefore they shall be as the morning cloud, and as the early dew that passeth away, as the chaff *that* is driven with the whirlwind out of the floor, and as the smoke out of the chimney.

4 Yet I *am* the LORD thy God from the land of Egypt, and thou shalt know no god but me: for *there is* no saviour beside me.

5 ¶ I did know thee in the wilderness, in the land of great drought.

6 According to their pasture, so were they filled; they were filled, and their heart was exalted; therefore have they forgotten me.

7 Therefore I will be unto them as a lion: as a leopard by the way will I observe *them:*

## Amplified

4 Yes, he had power over the Angel [of the Lord] and prevailed; he wept and sought His favor. He met Him in Bethel, and there [God] spoke with him [and through him] with us, [Gen. 32:28.]

5 Even the Lord the God of hosts, the name of Him [Who spoke with Jacob] is the Lord.

6 Therefore return to your God! Hold fast to love *and* mercy, and righteousness *and* justice, and wait [expectantly] for your God continually!

7 *Like* Canaan, [Israel whose ideals have sunk to those of Canaan] is a trader, the balances of deceit are in his hand; he loves to oppress *and* defraud.

8 Ephraim has said, Ah, but I have become rich, I have gained for myself wealth; all my profits shall bring on me no iniquity that would be sin. *But* all his profits will never offset nor suffice to expiate the guilt which he has incurred. [Rev. 3:17.]

9 But I *Who* am the Lord your God from [when you became a nation in] the land of Egypt, will yet make you to dwell in tents, as in the days of the appointed *and* solemn feast [of tabernacles]. [Lev. 23:39-43.]

10 I have also spoken to *you by* the prophets, and I have multiplied visions [for you], and [have appealed to you] through parables acted out by the prophets.

11 If Gilead is given over to idolatry, they shall come to nought *and* be mere waste; if they [insult God by] sacrificing bullocks in Gilgal [on heathen altars], their altars shall be as heaps in the furrows of the fields.

12 Jacob fled into the open country of Aram *or* Paddan-aram, and *there* Israel served for a wife, and for a wife he herded sheep. [Gen. 29:18-20; 30:31; 31:38-41.]

13 And by a prophet the Lord brought Israel out of Egypt, and by a prophet was [Israel] preserved.

14 Ephraim has provoked most bitter anger; therefore shall his blood [guilt] be left upon him, and his disgrace *and* reproach shall his Lord return upon him.

**13** WHEN EPHRAIM spoke with trembling, he exalted himself in Israel; but when he offended *and* became guilty in Baal worship, he died [spiritually, and then outward ruin came also, sealing Israel's doom as a nation].

2 And now they sin more and more, and have made them molten images of their silver, even idols according to their own understanding, [as they pleased], all of them the work of the craftsmen. To these [very works of their hands] they speak *or* pray who sacrifice to them, they kiss the calves [as if they were alive]!

3 Therefore they shall be like the morning mist or like the dew that passes early away, like the chaff that swirls with the whirlwind from the threshing floor, and as the smoke out of the chimney *or* through the window.

4 Yet I am the Lord your God from [the time you became a nation in] the land of Egypt, and you shall know *or* recognize no God but Me, for there is no Savior besides Me.

5 I knew—recognized, understood and had regard for—you in the wilderness, in the land of great drought.

6 According to their pasture, so were they filled [when they fed, they grew full], and their heart was lifted up; therefore have they forgotten Me.

7 Therefore I have become to them like a lion; like a leopard I will lurk by the way [to Assyria] *and* watch them.

## New American Standard

4 Yes, he wrestled with the angel and prevailed;
He wept and sought His favor.
He found Him at Bethel,
And there He spoke with us,
5 Even the LORD, the God of hosts;
The LORD is His name.
6 Therefore, return to your God,
Observe kindness and justice,
And wait for your God continually.
7 A merchant, in whose hands are false balances,
He loves to oppress.
8 And Ephraim said, "Surely I have become rich,
I have found wealth for myself;
In all my labors they will find in me
No iniquity, which *would be* sin."
9 But I *have been* the LORD your God since the land of
Egypt;
I will make you live in tents again,
As in the days of the appointed festival.
10 I have also spoken to the prophets,
And I gave numerous visions;
And through the prophets I gave parables.
11 Is there iniquity *in* Gilead?
Surely they are worthless.
In Gilgal they sacrifice bulls,
Yes, their altars are like the stone heaps
Beside the furrows of the field.

12¶ Now Jacob fled to the land of Aram,
And Israel worked for a wife,
And for a wife he kept *sheep.*
13 But by a prophet the LORD brought Israel from Egypt,
And by a prophet he was kept.
14 Ephraim has provoked to bitter anger;
So his Lord will leave his bloodguilt on him,
And bring back his reproach to him.

*Ephraim's Idolatry*

# 13

WHEN EPHRAIM spoke, *there was* trembling.
He exalted himself in Israel,
But through Baal he did wrong and died.
2 And now they sin more and more,
And make for themselves molten images,
Idols skillfully made from their silver,
All of them the work of craftsmen.
They say of them, "Let the men who sacrifice kiss the
calves!"
3 Therefore, they will be like the morning cloud,
And like dew which soon disappears,
Like chaff which is blown away from the threshing
floor,
And like smoke from a chimney.

4¶ Yet I *have been* the LORD your God
Since the land of Egypt;
And you were not to know any god except Me,
For there is no savior besides Me.
5 I cared for you in the wilderness,
In the land of drought.
6 As *they had* their pasture, they became satisfied,
And being satisfied, their heart became proud;
Therefore, they forgot Me.
7 So I will be like a lion to them;
Like a leopard I will lie in wait by the wayside.

## New International

4 He struggled with the angel and overcame him;
he wept and begged for his favor.
He found him at Bethel
and talked with him there—
5 the LORD God Almighty,
the LORD is his name of renown!
6 But you must return to your God;
maintain love and justice,
and wait for your God always.

7 The merchant uses dishonest scales;
he loves to defraud.
8 Ephraim boasts,
"I am very rich; I have become wealthy.
With all my wealth they will not find in me
any iniquity or sin."

9 "I am the LORD your God,
who brought you⌟ out of[a] Egypt;
I will make you live in tents again,
as in the days of your appointed feasts.
10 I spoke to the prophets,
gave them many visions
and told parables through them."

11 Is Gilead wicked?
Its people are worthless!
Do they sacrifice bulls in Gilgal?
Their altars will be like piles of stones
on a plowed field.
12 Jacob fled to the country of Aram[b];
Israel served to get a wife,
and to pay for her he tended sheep.
13 The LORD used a prophet to bring Israel up from Egypt,
by a prophet he cared for him.
14 But Ephraim has bitterly provoked him to anger;
his Lord will leave upon him the guilt of his bloodshed
and will repay him for his contempt.

*The LORD's Anger Against Israel*

# 13

WHEN EPHRAIM spoke, men trembled;
he was exalted in Israel.
But he became guilty of Baal worship and died.
2 Now they sin more and more;
they make idols for themselves from their silver,
cleverly fashioned images,
all of them the work of craftsmen.
It is said of these people,
"They offer human sacrifice
and kiss[c] the calf-idols."
3 Therefore they will be like the morning mist,
like the early dew that disappears,
like chaff swirling from a threshing floor,
like smoke escaping through a window.

4 "But I am the LORD your God,
⌞who brought you⌟ out of[d] Egypt.
You shall acknowledge no God but me,
no Savior except me.
5 I cared for you in the desert,
in the land of burning heat.
6 When I fed them, they were satisfied;
when they were satisfied, they became proud;
then they forgot me.
7 So I will come upon them like a lion,
like a leopard I will lurk by the path.

NIV [a] 9 Or *God / ever since you were in* [b] 12 That is, Northwest Mesopotamia
[c] 2 Or *"Men who sacrifice / kiss* [d] 4 Or *God / ever since you were in*

## King James

8I will meet them as a bear *that is* bereaved *of her whelps,* and will rend the caul of their heart, and there will I devour them like a lion: the wild beast shall tear them.
9¶ O Israel, thou hast destroyed thyself; but in me *is* thine help.
10I will be thy king: where *is any other* that may save thee in all thy cities? and thy judges of whom thou saidst, Give me a king and princes?
11I gave thee a king in mine anger, and took *him* away in my wrath.
12The iniquity of Ephraim *is* bound up; his sin *is* hid.
13The sorrows of a travailing woman shall come upon him: he *is* an unwise son; for he should not stay long in *the place of* the breaking forth of children.
14I will ransom them from the power of the grave; I will redeem them from death: O death, I will be thy plagues; O grave, I will be thy destruction: repentance shall be hid from mine eyes.
15¶ Though he be fruitful among *his* brethren, an east wind shall come, the wind of the LORD shall come up from the wilderness, and his spring shall become dry, and his fountain shall be dried up: he shall spoil the treasure of all pleasant vessels.
16Samaria shall become desolate; for she hath rebelled against her God: they shall fall by the sword: their infants shall be dashed in pieces, and their women with child shall be ripped up.

**14** O ISRAEL, return unto the LORD thy God; for thou hast fallen by thine iniquity.
2Take with you words, and turn to the LORD: say unto him, Take away all iniquity, and receive *us* graciously: so will we render the calves of our lips.
3Asshur shall not save us; we will not ride upon horses: neither will we say any more to the work of our hands, *Ye are* our gods: for in thee the fatherless findeth mercy.
4¶ I will heal their backsliding, I will love them freely: for mine anger is turned away from him.
5I will be as the dew unto Israel: he shall grow as the lily, and cast forth his roots as Lebanon.
6His branches shall spread, and his beauty shall be as the olive tree, and his smell as Lebanon.

## Amplified

8I will meet them as a bear that is robbed of her cubs, and I will rend the covering of their heart, and there will I devour them like a lioness, as a wild beast would tear them.
9It is your destruction, O Israel, that you have been against Me, for in Me is your help.
10Where now is your king, that he may save you in all your cities? And your judges of whom you said, Give me a king and princes?
11I have given you a king in My anger, and I have taken him away in My wrath.
12The iniquity of Ephraim [not fully punished yet] is bound up—as in a bag; his sin is laid up in store [for judgment and destruction].
13The pains of a woman in childbirth are coming on for him [to be born]; but he is an unwise son, for now, when it is time [to be born], he comes not to the place where *unborn* children break forth—he needs new birth, but makes no effort to acquire it.
14Should I ransom them from the power of Sheol [the place of the dead]? Should I redeem them from death? [a]O Death, where are your plagues? O Sheol, where is your destruction? Relenting *and* compassion *are* hid from My eyes. [I Cor. 15:55.]
15For though among his brethren [his fellow tribes] he may be fruitful, an east wind [Assyria] will come, the breath of the Lord rising from the desert, and Ephraim's spring shall become dry, and his fountain be dried up. [Assyria] shall plunder his treasury of every precious vessel.
16Samaria shall bear her guilt *and* become desolate, for she rebelled against her God; they shall fall by the sword, their infants shall be dashed in pieces, and their pregnant women shall be ripped up.

**14** O ISRAEL, return to the Lord your God, for you have stumbled *and* fallen, [visited by calamity] due to your iniquity.
2Take with you words, and return to the Lord. Say to Him, Take away all *our* iniquity, accept what is good *and* receive us graciously: so will we render [our thanks] as bullocks [to be sacrificed] *and* pay the confession of our lips. [Heb. 13:15.]
3Assyria shall not save us; we will not ride upon horses, neither will we say any more to [idols] the work of our hands, You are our gods. For in You, [O Lord,] the fatherless find love, pity *and* mercy.
4I will heal their faithlessness, I will love them freely, for My anger is turned away from [Israel].
5I will be as the dew *and* the night mist to Israel; he shall grow *and* blossom as the lily, and cast forth his roots as [the sturdy evergreens of] Lebanon.
6His suckers *and* shoots shall spread, and his beauty shall be as the olive tree, and his fragrance like [the cedars and aromatic shrubs of] Lebanon.

**AMP** [a] The Apostle Paul in I Cor. 15:55 brings to mind this passage, but with a triumphant reversed meaning, made possible by our Lord's resurrection.

## New American Standard

8 I will encounter them like a bear robbed of her cubs,
And I will tear open their chests;
There I will also devour them like a lioness,
*As* a wild beast would tear them.

9¶ *It is* your destruction, O Israel,
That *you are* against Me, against your help.
10 Where now is your king
That he may save you in all your cities,
And your judges of whom you requested,
"Give me a king and princes"?
11 I gave you a king in My anger,
And took him away in My wrath.

12¶ The iniquity of Ephraim is bound up;
His sin is stored up.
13 The pains of childbirth come upon him;
He is not a wise son,
For it is not the time that he should delay at the opening of the womb.
14 Shall I ransom them from the power of Sheol?
Shall I redeem them from death?
O Death, where are your thorns?
O Sheol, where is your sting?
Compassion will be hidden from My sight.

15¶ Though he flourishes among the reeds,
An east wind will come,
The wind of the LORD coming up from the wilderness;
And his fountain will become dry,
And his spring will be dried up;
It will plunder *his* treasury of every precious article.
16 Samaria will be held guilty,
For she has rebelled against her God.
They will fall by the sword,
Their little ones will be dashed in pieces,
And their pregnant women will be ripped open.

*Israel's Future Blessing*

14 RETURN, O Israel, to the LORD your God,
For you have stumbled because of your iniquity.
2 Take words with you and return to the LORD.
Say to Him, "Take away all iniquity,
And receive *us* graciously,
That we may present the fruit of our lips.
3 "Assyria will not save us,
We will not ride on horses;
Nor will we say again, 'Our god,'
To the work of our hands;
For in Thee the orphan finds mercy."

4¶ I will heal their apostasy,
I will love them freely,
For My anger has turned away from them.
5 I will be like the dew to Israel;
He will blossom like the lily,
And he will take root like *the cedars of* Lebanon.
6 His shoots will sprout,
And his beauty will be like the olive tree,
And his fragrance like *the cedars of* Lebanon.

## New International

8 Like a bear robbed of her cubs,
I will attack them and rip them open.
Like a lion I will devour them;
a wild animal will tear them apart.

9 "You are destroyed, O Israel,
because you are against me, against your helper.
10 Where is your king, that he may save you?
Where are your rulers in all your towns,
of whom you said,
'Give me a king and princes'?
11 So in my anger I gave you a king,
and in my wrath I took him away.
12 The guilt of Ephraim is stored up,
his sins are kept on record.
13 Pains as of a woman in childbirth come to him,
but he is a child without wisdom;
when the time arrives,
he does not come to the opening of the womb.

14 "I will ransom them from the power of the grave[b];
I will redeem them from death.
Where, O death, are your plagues?
Where, O grave,[c] is your destruction?

"I will have no compassion,
15 even though he thrives among his brothers.
An east wind from the LORD will come,
blowing in from the desert;
his spring will fail
and his well dry up.
His storehouse will be plundered
of all its treasures.
16 The people of Samaria must bear their guilt,
because they have rebelled against their God.
They will fall by the sword;
their little ones will be dashed to the ground,
their pregnant women ripped open."

*Repentance to Bring Blessing*

14 RETURN, O Israel, to the LORD your God.
Your sins have been your downfall!
2 Take words with you
and return to the LORD.
Say to him:
"Forgive all our sins
and receive us graciously,
that we may offer the fruit of our lips.[d]
3 Assyria cannot save us;
we will not mount war-horses.
We will never again say 'Our gods'
to what our own hands have made,
for in you the fatherless find compassion."

4 "I will heal their waywardness
and love them freely,
for my anger has turned away from them.
5 I will be like the dew to Israel;
he will blossom like a lily.
Like a cedar of Lebanon
he will send down his roots;
6 his young shoots will grow.
His splendor will be like an olive tree,
his fragrance like a cedar of Lebanon.

NIV [b] 14 Hebrew *Sheol* [c] 14 Hebrew *Sheol* [d] 2 Or *offer our lips as sacrifices of bulls*

## King James

7They that dwell under his shadow shall return; they shall revive *as* the corn, and grow as the vine: the scent thereof *shall be* as the wine of Lebanon.

8Ephraim *shall say,* What have I to do any more with idols? I have heard *him,* and observed him: I *am* like a green fir tree. From me is thy fruit found.

9Who *is* wise, and he shall understand these *things?* prudent, and he shall know them? for the ways of the LORD *are* right, and the just shall walk in them: but the transgressors shall fall therein.

## Amplified

7They that dwell under his shade shall return; they shall revive as the grain and blossom as the vine; the scent of it shall be as the wine of Lebanon.

8Ephraim shall say, What have I to do any more with idols? I have answered [him], and will regard *and* watch over him; I am like a green fir *or* cypress tree. With Me is the fruit found [which is to nourish you].

9Who is wise, that he may understand these things? Prudent, that he may know them? For the ways of the Lord are right, and the [uncompromisingly] just shall walk in them; but transgressors shall stumble *and* fall in them. [Dan. 12:10; Ps. 107:43; Jer. 9:12; Isa. 26:7.]

## New American Standard

7 Those who live in his shadow
Will again raise grain,
And they will blossom like the vine.
His renown *will be* like the wine of Lebanon.

8¶ O Ephraim, what more have I to do with idols?
It is I who answer and look after you.
I am like a luxuriant cypress;
From Me comes your fruit.

9¶ Whoever is wise, let him understand these things;
*Whoever* is discerning, let him know them.
For the ways of the LORD are right,
And the righteous will walk in them,
But transgressors will stumble in them.

## New International

7Men will dwell again in his shade.
He will flourish like the grain.
He will blossom like a vine,
and his fame will be like the wine from Lebanon.
8O Ephraim, what more have I[a] to do with idols?
I will answer him and care for him.
I am like a green pine tree;
your fruitfulness comes from me."

9Who is wise? He will realize these things.
Who is discerning? He will understand them.
The ways of the LORD are right;
the righteous walk in them,
but the rebellious stumble in them.

NIV [a] 8 Or *What more has Ephraim*

## King James

# Joel

**1** THE WORD of the LORD that came to Joel the son of Pethuel.

2Hear this, ye old men, and give ear, all ye inhabitants of the land. Hath this been in your days, or even in the days of your fathers?

3Tell ye your children of it, and *let* your children *tell* their children, and their children another generation.

4That which the palmerworm hath left hath the locust eaten; and that which the locust hath left hath the cankerworm eaten; and that which the cankerworm hath left hath the caterpillar eaten.

5Awake, ye drunkards, and weep; and howl, all ye drinkers of wine, because of the new wine; for it is cut off from your mouth.

6For a nation is come up upon my land, strong, and without number, whose teeth *are* the teeth of a lion, and he hath the cheek teeth of a great lion.

7He hath laid my vine waste, and barked my fig tree: he hath made it clean bare, and cast *it* away; the branches thereof are made white.

8¶ Lament like a virgin girded with sackcloth for the husband of her youth.

9The meat offering and the drink offering is cut off from the house of the LORD; the priests, the LORD's ministers, mourn.

10The field is wasted, the land mourneth; for the corn is wasted: the new wine is dried up, the oil languisheth.

11Be ye ashamed, O ye husbandmen; howl, O ye vinedressers, for the wheat and for the barley; because the harvest of the field is perished.

## Amplified

THE BOOK OF

# Joel

**1** THE WORD of the Lord that came to [a]Joel the son of Pethuel.

2Hear this, you aged men, and give ear, all you inhabitants of the land! Has such a thing as this occurred in your days, or even in the days of your fathers?

3Tell your children of it, and let your children tell their children, and their children another generation.

4What the crawling locust left, the swarming locust has eaten; and what the swarming locust left, the hopping locust has eaten; and what the hopping locust left, the stripping locust has eaten.

5Awake, you drunkards, and weep; wail, all you drinkers of wine, because of the [fresh] sweet fruit juice, for it is cut off *and* removed from your mouth.

6For a [heathen and hostile] nation [of locusts, illustrative of a human foe] has invaded My land, mighty and without number; whose teeth are the teeth of a lion, and it has the jaw teeth of a lioness. [Rev. 9:7, 8.]

7It has laid waste My vine [symbol of God's people], and barked *and* broken My fig tree; it has made them completely bare and thrown them down; their branches are made white. [Isa. 5:5, 6.]

8Lament like a virgin [bride] girded with sackcloth for the husband of her youth [who has died].

9The meal *or* cereal offering and the drink offering are cut off from the house of the Lord; the priests, the Lord's ministers, mourn.

10The field is laid waste; the ground mourns, for the grain is destroyed, the new grape juice is dried up, the oil fails.

11Be ashamed, O you tillers of the soil; wail, O you vinedressers, for the wheat and for the barley, because the harvest of the field has perished.

**AMP** [a] Joel was a prophet of Judah and possibly a contemporary of Elisha.

## New American Standard

# Joel

*The Devastation of Locusts*

**1** THE WORD of the LORD that came to Joel, the son of Pethuel.
2 Hear this, O elders,
And listen, all inhabitants of the land.
Has *anything like* this happened in your days
Or in your fathers' days?
3 Tell your sons about it,
And *let* your sons *tell* their sons,
And their sons the next generation.

4¶ What the gnawing locust has left, the swarming locust has eaten;
And what the swarming locust has left, the creeping locust has eaten;
And what the creeping locust has left, the stripping locust has eaten.
5 Awake, drunkards, and weep;
And wail, all you wine drinkers,
On account of the sweet wine
That is cut off from your mouth.
6 For a nation has invaded my land,
Mighty and without number;
Its teeth are the teeth of a lion,
And it has the fangs of a lioness.
7 It has made my vine a waste,
And my fig tree splinters.
It has stripped them bare and cast *them* away;
Their branches have become white.

8¶ Wail like a virgin girded with sackcloth
For the bridegroom of her youth.
9 The grain offering and the libation are cut off
From the house of the LORD.
The priests mourn,
The ministers of the LORD.
10 The field is ruined,
The land mourns,
For the grain is ruined,
The new wine dries up,
Fresh oil fails.
11 Be ashamed, O farmers,
Wail, O vinedressers,
For the wheat and the barley;
Because the harvest of the field is destroyed.

## New International

# Joel

**1** THE WORD of the LORD that came to Joel son of Pethuel.

*An Invasion of Locusts*

2 Hear this, you elders;
listen, all who live in the land.
Has anything like this ever happened in your days
or in the days of your forefathers?
3 Tell it to your children,
and let your children tell it to their children,
and their children to the next generation.
4 What the locust swarm has left
the great locusts have eaten;
what the great locusts have left
the young locusts have eaten;
what the young locusts have left
other locusts[b] have eaten.

5 Wake up, you drunkards, and weep!
Wail, all you drinkers of wine;
wail because of the new wine,
for it has been snatched from your lips.
6 A nation has invaded my land,
powerful and without number;
it has the teeth of a lion,
the fangs of a lioness.
7 It has laid waste my vines
and ruined my fig trees.
It has stripped off their bark
and thrown it away,
leaving their branches white.

8 Mourn like a virgin[c] in sackcloth
grieving for the husband[d] of her youth.
9 Grain offerings and drink offerings
are cut off from the house of the LORD.
The priests are in mourning,
those who minister before the LORD.
10 The fields are ruined,
the ground is dried up[e];
the grain is destroyed,
the new wine is dried up,
the oil fails.
11 Despair, you farmers,
wail, you vine growers;
grieve for the wheat and the barley,
because the harvest of the field is destroyed.

NIV [b] 4 The precise meaning of the four Hebrew words used here for locusts is uncertain. [c] 8 Or *young woman* [d] 8 Or *betrothed* [e] 10 Or *ground mourns*

## King James

12 The vine is dried up, and the fig tree languisheth; the pomegranate tree, the palm tree also, and the apple tree, *even* all the
trees of the field, are withered: because joy is withered away from
the sons of men.
13 Gird yourselves, and lament, ye priests: howl, ye ministers of
the altar: come, lie all night in sackcloth, ye ministers of my God:
for the meat offering and the drink offering is withholden from the
house of your God.
14 ¶ Sanctify ye a fast, call a solemn assembly, gather the elders
*and* all the inhabitants of the land *into* the house of the LORD your
God, and cry unto the LORD.
15 Alas for the day! for the day of the LORD *is* at hand, and as
a destruction from the Almighty shall it come.
16 Is not the meat cut off before our eyes, *yea,* joy and gladness
from the house of our God?
17 The seed is rotten under their clods, the garners are laid
desolate, the barns are broken down; for the corn is withered.
18 How do the beasts groan! the herds of cattle are perplexed,
because they have no pasture; yea, the flocks of sheep are made
desolate.
19 O LORD, to thee will I cry: for the fire hath devoured the
pastures of the wilderness, and the flame hath burned all the trees
of the field.
20 The beasts of the field cry also unto thee: for the rivers of
waters are dried up, and the fire hath devoured the pastures of the
wilderness.

**2** BLOW YE the trumpet in Zion, and sound an alarm in my
holy mountain: let all the inhabitants of the land tremble: for
the day of the LORD cometh, for *it is* nigh at hand;
2 A day of darkness and of gloominess, a day of clouds and of
thick darkness, as the morning spread upon the mountains: a great
people and a strong; there hath not been ever the like, neither shall
be any more after it, *even* to the years of many generations.
3 A fire devoureth before them; and behind them a flame
burneth: the land *is* as the garden of Eden before them, and behind
them a desolate wilderness; yea, and nothing shall escape them.
4 The appearance of them *is* as the appearance of horses; and as
horsemen, so shall they run.

## Amplified

12 The vine is dried up, and the fig tree fails; the pomegranate
tree, the palm tree also, and the apple *or* quince tree, even all the
trees of the field are withered; so that joy has withered *and* fled
away from the sons of men.
13 Gird yourselves and lament, you priests; wail, you ministers
of the altar; come, lie all night in sackcloth, you ministers of my
[Joel's] God, for the cereal *or* meal offering and the drink offering
are withheld from the house of your God.
14 Sanctify a fast, call a solemn assembly, gather the elders and
all the inhabitants of the land in the house of the Lord your God,
and cry to the Lord [in penitent pleadings].
15 Alas for the day! For the day of [the judgment of] the Lord is
at hand, and as a destructive tempest from the Almighty will it
come. [Zeph. 1:14-18.]
16 Is not the food cut off before our eyes, joy and gladness from
the house of our God?
17 The seed *grain* rots *and* shrivels under the clods, the garners
are desolate *and* empty, the barns are in ruins because the grain has
failed.
18 How the beasts groan! The herds of cattle are perplexed *and*
huddle together because they have no pasture; even the flocks of
sheep suffer punishment—are forsaken and made wretched.
19 O Lord, to You will I cry, for the fire has devoured the pastures *and* folds of the plain *and* the wilderness, and flame has
burned all the trees of the field.
20 Even the wild beasts of the field pant *and* cry to You, for the
water brooks are dried up, and fire has consumed the pastures *and*
folds of the wilderness *and* the plain.

**2** BLOW THE trumpet in Zion, sound an alarm on My holy
Mount [Zion]. Let all the inhabitants of the land tremble, for
the day of [the judgment of] the Lord is coming, it is close at hand.
[Amos 5:16-20; Ezek. 7:2-4.]
2 A day of darkness and gloom, a day of clouds and of thick
mists *and* darkness, like the morning dawn spread upon the mountains; *so there* comes a [heathen, hostile] people numerous and
mighty, the like of which has never been before and shall not be
again even to the years of many generations.
3 A fire devours before them, and behind them a flame burns;
the land is as the garden of Eden before them, and behind them
a desolate wilderness; yes, and none has escaped [the ravages of
the devouring hordes].
4 Their appearance is like the appearance of horses, and as war
horses *and* horsemen, so do they run.

## New American Standard

12 The vine dries up,
And the fig tree fails;
The pomegranate, the palm also, and the apple tree,
All the trees of the field dry up.
Indeed, rejoicing dries up
From the sons of men.

13¶ Gird yourselves *with sackcloth,*
And lament, O priests;
Wail, O ministers of the altar!
Come, spend the night in sackcloth,
O ministers of my God,
For the grain offering and the libation
Are withheld from the house of your God.

*Starvation and Drought*

14 Consecrate a fast,
Proclaim a solemn assembly;
Gather the elders
*And* all the inhabitants of the land
To the house of the LORD your God,
And cry out to the LORD.
15 Alas for the day!
For the day of the LORD is near,
And it will come as destruction from the Almighty.
16 Has not food been cut off before our eyes,
Gladness and joy from the house of our God?
17 The seeds shrivel under their clods;
The storehouses are desolate,
The barns are torn down,
For the grain is dried up.
18 How the beasts groan!
The herds of cattle wander aimlessly
Because there is no pasture for them;
Even the flocks of sheep suffer.
19 To Thee, O LORD, I cry;
For fire has devoured the pastures of the wilderness,
And the flame has burned up all the trees of the field.
20 Even the beasts of the field pant for Thee;
For the water brooks are dried up,
And fire has devoured the pastures of the wilderness.

*The Terrible Visitation*

**2** BLOW A trumpet in Zion,
And sound an alarm on My holy mountain!
Let all the inhabitants of the land tremble,
For the day of the LORD is coming;
Surely it is near,
2 A day of darkness and gloom,
A day of clouds and thick darkness.
As the dawn is spread over the mountains,
*So* there is a great and mighty people;
There has never been *anything* like it,
Nor will there be again after it
To the years of many generations.
3 A fire consumes before them,
And behind them a flame burns.
The land is like the garden of Eden before them,
But a desolate wilderness behind them,
And nothing at all escapes them.
4 Their appearance is like the appearance of horses;
And like war horses, so they run.

## New International

12The vine is dried up
and the fig tree is withered;
the pomegranate, the palm and the apple tree—
all the trees of the field—are dried up.
Surely the joy of mankind
is withered away.

*A Call to Repentance*

13Put on sackcloth, O priests, and mourn;
wail, you who minister before the altar.
Come, spend the night in sackcloth,
you who minister before my God;
for the grain offerings and drink offerings
are withheld from the house of your God.
14Declare a holy fast;
call a sacred assembly.
Summon the elders
and all who live in the land
to the house of the LORD your God,
and cry out to the LORD.
15Alas for that day!
For the day of the LORD is near;
it will come like destruction from the Almighty.[a]
16Has not the food been cut off
before our very eyes—
joy and gladness
from the house of our God?
17The seeds are shriveled
beneath the clods.[b]
The storehouses are in ruins,
the granaries have been broken down,
for the grain has dried up.
18How the cattle moan!
The herds mill about
because they have no pasture;
even the flocks of sheep are suffering.
19To you, O LORD, I call,
for fire has devoured the open pastures
and flames have burned up all the trees of the field.
20Even the wild animals pant for you;
the streams of water have dried up
and fire has devoured the open pastures.

*An Army of Locusts*

**2** BLOW THE trumpet in Zion;
sound the alarm on my holy hill.
Let all who live in the land tremble,
for the day of the LORD is coming.
It is close at hand—
2 a day of darkness and gloom,
a day of clouds and blackness.
Like dawn spreading across the mountains
a large and mighty army comes,
such as never was of old
nor ever will be in ages to come.

3Before them fire devours,
behind them a flame blazes.
Before them the land is like the garden of Eden,
behind them, a desert waste—
nothing escapes them.
4They have the appearance of horses;
they gallop along like cavalry.

**NIV** [a] 15 Hebrew *Shaddai* [b] 17 The meaning of the Hebrew for this word is uncertain.

## King James

5Like the noise of chariots on the tops of mountains shall they leap, like the noise of a flame of fire that devoureth the stubble, as a strong people set in battle array.

6Before their face the people shall be much pained: all faces shall gather blackness.

7They shall run like mighty men; they shall climb the wall like men of war; and they shall march every one on his ways, and they shall not break their ranks:

8Neither shall one thrust another; they shall walk every one in his path: and *when* they fall upon the sword, they shall not be wounded.

9They shall run to and fro in the city; they shall run upon the wall, they shall climb up upon the houses; they shall enter in at the windows like a thief.

10The earth shall quake before them; the heavens shall tremble: the sun and the moon shall be dark, and the stars shall withdraw their shining:

11And the LORD shall utter his voice before his army: for his camp *is* very great: for *he is* strong that executeth his word: for the day of the LORD *is* great and very terrible; and who can abide it?

12¶ Therefore also now, saith the LORD, turn ye *even* to me with all your heart, and with fasting, and with weeping, and with mourning:

13And rend your heart, and not your garments, and turn unto the LORD your God: for he *is* gracious and merciful, slow to anger, and of great kindness, and repenteth him of the evil.

14Who knoweth *if* he will return and repent, and leave a blessing behind him; *even* a meat offering and a drink offering unto the LORD your God?

15¶ Blow the trumpet in Zion, sanctify a fast, call a solemn assembly:

16Gather the people, sanctify the congregation, assemble the elders, gather the children, and those that suck the breasts: let the bridegroom go forth of his chamber, and the bride out of her closet.

17Let the priests, the ministers of the LORD, weep between the porch and the altar, and let them say, Spare thy people, O LORD, and give not thine heritage to reproach, that the heathen should rule over them: wherefore should they say among the people, Where *is* their God?

18¶ Then will the LORD be jealous for his land, and pity his people.

## Amplified

5Like the noise of chariots on the tops of the mountains they leap, like the noise of a flame of fire devouring the stubble, like a mighty people set in battle array. [Rev. 9:7, 9.]

6Before them the peoples are in anguish, all faces become pale.

7They run like mighty men, they climb the wall like men of war, they march every one [straight ahead] on his ways, and they do not break their ranks.

8Neither does one thrust another, they walk every one in his path; and they burst through *and* upon the weapons, yet they are not wounded *and* do not change their course.

9They leap upon the city, they run upon the wall, they climb up on *and* into the houses, they enter in at the windows like a thief.

10The earth quakes before them, the heavens tremble. The sun and the moon are darkened, and the stars withdraw their shining. [Rev. 16:14; 9:2-4.]

11And the Lord utters His voice before His army, for His host is very great, for [they are] strong *and* powerful who executes *God's* word. For the day of the Lord is great and very terrible, and who can endure it? [Rev. 6:16, 17; Isa. 26:20, 21; 34:1-4, 8.]

12Therefore also now, says the Lord, turn *and* keep on coming to Me with all your heart, with fasting, with weeping, and with mourning [until every hindrance is removed and the broken fellowship is restored].

13Rend your hearts and not your garments, and return to the Lord your God, for He is gracious and merciful, slow to anger, and abounding in loving-kindness, and He revokes His sentence of evil [when His conditions are met].

14Who knows but what He will turn, revoke your sentence [of evil], and leave a blessing behind Him [giving you the means with which to serve Him], even a cereal *or* meal offering and a drink offering for the Lord, your God?

15Blow the trumpet in Zion; set apart a fast—a day of restraint and humility; call a solemn assembly.

16Gather the people, sanctify the congregation, assemble the elderly people, gather the children and the nursing infants; let the bridegroom [who is legally exempt from attending] go forth from his chamber, and the bride out of her closet. [None is exempt from the humiliation.]

17Let the priests, the ministers of the Lord, weep between the porch and the altar, and let them say, Have pity *and* spare Your people, O Lord, and give not Your heritage to reproach, that the [heathen] nations should rule over them *or* use a byword against them. Why should they say among the peoples, Where is their God?

18Then was the Lord jealous for His land, and had pity on His people.

## New American Standard

5 With a noise as of chariots
They leap on the tops of the mountains,
Like the crackling of a flame of fire consuming the stubble,
Like a mighty people arranged for battle.
6 Before them the people are in anguish;
All faces turn pale.
7 They run like mighty men;
They climb the wall like soldiers;
And they each march in line,
Nor do they deviate from their paths.
8 They do not crowd each other;
They march everyone in his path.
When they burst through the defenses,
They do not break ranks.
9 They rush on the city,
They run on the wall;
They climb into the houses,
They enter through the windows like a thief.
10 Before them the earth quakes,
The heavens tremble,
The sun and the moon grow dark,
And the stars lose their brightness.
11 And the LORD utters His voice before His army;
Surely His camp is very great,
For strong is he who carries out His word.
The day of the LORD is indeed great and very awesome,
And who can endure it?
12 "Yet even now," declares the LORD,
"Return to Me with all your heart,
And with fasting, weeping, and mourning;
13 And rend your heart and not your garments."
Now return to the LORD your God,
For He is gracious and compassionate,
Slow to anger, abounding in lovingkindness,
And relenting of evil.
14 Who knows whether He will *not* turn and relent,
And leave a blessing behind Him,
*Even* a grain offering and a libation
For the LORD your God?
15 Blow a trumpet in Zion,
Consecrate a fast, proclaim a solemn assembly,
16 Gather the people, sanctify the congregation,
Assemble the elders,
Gather the children and the nursing infants.
Let the bridegroom come out of his room
And the bride out of her *bridal* chamber.
17 Let the priests, the LORD's ministers,
Weep between the porch and the altar,
And let them say, "Spare Thy people, O LORD,
And do not make Thine inheritance a reproach,
A byword among the nations.
Why should they among the peoples say,
'Where is their God?' "

*Deliverance Promised*

**18**¶ Then the LORD will be zealous for His land,
And will have pity on His people.

## New International

5 With a noise like that of chariots
they leap over the mountaintops,
like a crackling fire consuming stubble,
like a mighty army drawn up for battle.

6 At the sight of them, nations are in anguish;
every face turns pale.
7 They charge like warriors;
they scale walls like soldiers.
They all march in line,
not swerving from their course.
8 They do not jostle each other;
each marches straight ahead.
They plunge through defenses
without breaking ranks.
9 They rush upon the city;
they run along the wall.
They climb into the houses;
like thieves they enter through the windows.
10 Before them the earth shakes,
the sky trembles,
the sun and moon are darkened,
and the stars no longer shine.
11 The LORD thunders
at the head of his army;
his forces are beyond number,
and mighty are those who obey his command.
The day of the LORD is great;
it is dreadful.
Who can endure it?

*Rend Your Heart*

12 "Even now," declares the LORD,
"return to me with all your heart,
with fasting and weeping and mourning."

13 Rend your heart
and not your garments.
Return to the LORD your God,
for he is gracious and compassionate,
slow to anger and abounding in love,
and he relents from sending calamity.
14 Who knows? He may turn and have pity
and leave behind a blessing—
grain offerings and drink offerings
for the LORD your God.

15 Blow the trumpet in Zion,
declare a holy fast,
call a sacred assembly.
16 Gather the people,
consecrate the assembly;
bring together the elders,
gather the children,
those nursing at the breast.
Let the bridegroom leave his room
and the bride her chamber.
17 Let the priests, who minister before the LORD,
weep between the temple porch and the altar.
Let them say, "Spare your people, O LORD.
Do not make your inheritance an object of scorn,
a byword among the nations.
Why should they say among the peoples,
'Where is their God?' "

*The LORD's Answer*

18 Then the LORD will be jealous for his land
and take pity on his people.

## King James

19 Yea, the LORD will answer and say unto his people, Behold, I will send you corn, and wine, and oil, and ye shall be satisfied therewith: and I will no more make you a reproach among the heathen:

20 But I will remove far off from you the northern *army*, and will drive him into a land barren and desolate, with his face toward the east sea, and his hinder part toward the utmost sea, and his stink shall come up, and his ill savour shall come up, because he hath done great things.

21 ¶ Fear not, O land; be glad and rejoice: for the LORD will do great things.

22 Be not afraid, ye beasts of the field: for the pastures of the wilderness do spring, for the tree beareth her fruit, the fig tree and the vine do yield their strength.

23 Be glad then, ye children of Zion, and rejoice in the LORD your God: for he hath given you the former rain moderately, and he will cause to come down for you the rain, the former rain, and the latter rain in the first *month*.

24 And the floors shall be full of wheat, and the vats shall overflow with wine and oil.

25 And I will restore to you the years that the locust hath eaten, the cankerworm, and the caterpillar, and the palmerworm, my great army which I sent among you.

26 And ye shall eat in plenty, and be satisfied, and praise the name of the LORD your God, that hath dealt wondrously with you: and my people shall never be ashamed.

27 And ye shall know that I *am* in the midst of Israel, and *that* I *am* the LORD your God, and none else: and my people shall never be ashamed.

28 ¶ And it shall come to pass afterward, *that* I will pour out my spirit upon all flesh; and your sons and your daughters shall prophesy, your old men shall dream dreams, your young men shall see visions:

29 And also upon the servants and upon the handmaids in those days will I pour out my spirit.

30 And I will show wonders in the heavens and in the earth, blood, and fire, and pillars of smoke.

31 The sun shall be turned into darkness, and the moon into blood, before the great and the terrible day of the LORD come.

32 And it shall come to pass, *that* whosoever shall call on the name of the LORD shall be delivered: for in mount Zion and in Jerusalem shall be deliverance, as the LORD hath said, and in the remnant whom the LORD shall call.

## Amplified

19 Yes, the Lord answered and said to His people, Behold, I am sending you grain, and grape juice, and oil, and you shall be satisfied with them; and I will no more make you a reproach among the [heathen] nations.

20 But I will remove far off from you the northern [destroyer's] army, and will drive it into a land barren and desolate, with its front toward the eastern [Dead] Sea and with its rear toward the western [Mediterranean] Sea. And its stench shall come up [as had that of the decaying mass of locusts, symbolic and a forecast of the fate of the Northern army in the final day of the Lord], and its foul odor shall come up, because [the Lord will have destroyed the invaders] [a]He has done great things! [Isa. 34:1-4, 8; Jer. 25:31-35; Joel 2:11.]

21 Fear not, O land, be glad and rejoice, for the Lord has done great things! [Zech. 12:8-10.]

22 Be not afraid, you wild beasts of the field, for the pastures of the wilderness have sprung up *and* are green, for the tree bears its fruit, the fig tree and the vine yield their [full] strength.

23 Be glad then, you children of Zion, and rejoice in the Lord, your God; for He gives you the former *or* early rain in just measure *and* in righteousness, and He causes to come down for you the rain, the former rain and the latter rain, as before.

24 And the [threshing] floors shall be full of grain, and the vats shall overflow with grape juice and oil.

25 And I will restore *or* replace for you the years that the locust has eaten, the hopping locust, the stripping locust, and the crawling locust, My great army which I sent among you.

26 And you shall eat in plenty and be satisfied, and praise the name of the Lord, your God, Who has dealt wondrously with you. And My people shall never be put to shame.

27 And you shall know that I am in the midst of Israel and that I, the Lord, am your God, and there is none else. My people shall never be put to shame.

28 And afterward I will pour out My Spirit upon all flesh, and your sons and your daughters shall prophesy, your old men shall dream dreams, your young men shall see visions.

29 Even upon the menservants and upon the maidservants in those days will I pour out My Spirit.

30 And I will show signs *and* wonders in the heavens and on the earth, blood and fire and columns of smoke.

31 The sun shall be turned to darkness, and the moon to blood, before the great and terrible day of the Lord comes. [Isa. 13:6, 9-11; 24:21-23; Ezek. 32:7-10; Matt. 24:29, 30; Rev. 6:12-17.]

32 And whoever shall call on the name of the Lord shall be delivered *and* saved, for in Mount Zion and in Jerusalem there shall be those who escape, as the Lord has said, and among the remnant [of survivors] shall be those whom the Lord calls. [Acts 2:17-21; Rom. 10:13.]

**AMP** [a] The capitalization here is suppositional. Interpreters are divided as to whether it is the northern destroyer who has "done great things" or the Lord; either, in different senses, is true. However, the latter view is strongly supported by the statement to the same effect in verse twenty-one which immediately follows.

## New American Standard

19 And the LORD will answer and say to His people,
"Behold, I am going to send you grain, new wine, and oil,
And you will be satisfied *in full* with them;
And I will never again make you a reproach among the nations.
20 "But I will remove the northern *army* far from you,
And I will drive it into a parched and desolate land,
And its vanguard into the eastern sea,
And its rear guard into the western sea.
And its stench will arise and its foul smell will come up,
For it has done great things."

21¶ Do not fear, O land, rejoice and be glad,
For the LORD has done great things.
22 Do not fear, beasts of the field,
For the pastures of the wilderness have turned green,
For the tree has borne its fruit,
The fig tree and the vine have yielded in full.
23 So rejoice, O sons of Zion,
And be glad in the LORD your God;
For He has given you the [b]early rain for *your* vindication.
And He has poured down for you the rain,
The [c]early and [d]latter rain as before.
24 And the threshing floors will be full of grain,
And the vats will overflow with the new wine and oil.
25 "Then I will make up to you for the years
That the swarming locust has eaten,
The creeping locust, the stripping locust, and the gnawing locust,
My great army which I sent among you.
26 "And you shall have plenty to eat and be satisfied,
And praise the name of the LORD your God,
Who has dealt wondrously with you;
Then My people will never be put to shame.
27 "Thus you will know that I am in the midst of Israel,
And that I am the LORD your God
And there is no other;
And My people will never be put to shame.

*The Promise of the Spirit*

28¶ "And it will come about after this
That I will pour out My Spirit on all mankind;
And your sons and daughters will prophesy,
Your old men will dream dreams,
Your young men will see visions.
29 "And even on the male and female servants
I will pour out My Spirit in those days.

*The Day of the LORD*

30 "And I will display wonders in the sky and on the earth,
Blood, fire, and columns of smoke.
31 "The sun will be turned into darkness,
And the moon into blood,
Before the great and awesome day of the LORD comes.
32 "And it will come about that whoever calls on the name of the LORD
Will be delivered;
For on Mount Zion and in Jerusalem
There will be those who escape,
As the LORD has said,
Even among the survivors whom the LORD calls.

NAS [b] I.e., autumn [c] I.e., autumn [d] I.e., spring

## New International

19 The LORD will reply[e] to them:
"I am sending you grain, new wine and oil,
enough to satisfy you fully;
never again will I make you
an object of scorn to the nations.

20 "I will drive the northern army far from you,
pushing it into a parched and barren land,
with its front columns going into the eastern sea[f]
and those in the rear into the western sea.[g]
And its stench will go up;
its smell will rise."

Surely he has done great things.[h]
21 Be not afraid, O land;
be glad and rejoice.
Surely the LORD has done great things.
22 Be not afraid, O wild animals,
for the open pastures are becoming green.
The trees are bearing their fruit;
the fig tree and the vine yield their riches.
23 Be glad, O people of Zion,
rejoice in the LORD your God,
for he has given you
the autumn rains in righteousness.[i]
He sends you abundant showers,
both autumn and spring rains, as before.
24 The threshing floors will be filled with grain;
the vats will overflow with new wine and oil.

25 "I will repay you for the years the locusts have eaten—
the great locust and the young locust,
the other locusts and the locust swarm[j] —
my great army that I sent among you.
26 You will have plenty to eat, until you are full,
and you will praise the name of the LORD your God,
who has worked wonders for you;
never again will my people be shamed.
27 Then you will know that I am in Israel,
that I am the LORD your God,
and that there is no other;
never again will my people be shamed.

*The Day of the LORD*

28 "And afterward,
I will pour out my Spirit on all people.
Your sons and daughters will prophesy,
your old men will dream dreams,
your young men will see visions.
29 Even on my servants, both men and women,
I will pour out my Spirit in those days.
30 I will show wonders in the heavens
and on the earth,
blood and fire and billows of smoke.
31 The sun will be turned to darkness
and the moon to blood
before the coming of the great and dreadful day of the LORD.
32 And everyone who calls
on the name of the LORD will be saved;
for on Mount Zion and in Jerusalem
there will be deliverance,
as the LORD has said,
among the survivors
whom the LORD calls.

NIV [e] 18,19 Or *LORD was jealous . . . / and took pity . . . / 19The LORD replied* [f] 20 That is, the Dead Sea [g] 20 That is, the Mediterranean [h] 20 Or *rise. / Surely it has done great things."* [i] 23 Or / *the teacher for righteousness:* [j] 25 The precise meaning of the four Hebrew words used here for locusts is uncertain.

## King James

**3** FOR, BEHOLD, in those days, and in that time, when I shall bring again the captivity of Judah and Jerusalem,

2 I will also gather all nations, and will bring them down into the valley of Jehoshaphat, and will plead with them there for my people and *for* my heritage Israel, whom they have scattered among the nations, and parted my land.

3 And they have cast lots for my people; and have given a boy for an harlot, and sold a girl for wine, that they might drink.

4 Yea, and what have ye to do with me, O Tyre, and Zidon, and all the coasts of Palestine? will ye render me a recompense? and if ye recompense me, swiftly *and* speedily will I return your recompense upon your own head;

5 Because ye have taken my silver and my gold, and have carried into your temples my goodly pleasant things:

6 The children also of Judah and the children of Jerusalem have ye sold unto the Grecians, that ye might remove them far from their border.

7 Behold, I will raise them out of the place whither ye have sold them, and will return your recompense upon your own head:

8 And I will sell your sons and your daughters into the hand of the children of Judah, and they shall sell them to the Sabeans, to a people far off: for the LORD hath spoken *it*.

9 ¶ Proclaim ye this among the Gentiles; Prepare war, wake up the mighty men, let all the men of war draw near; let them come up:

10 Beat your plowshares into swords, and your pruning hooks into spears: let the weak say, I *am* strong.

11 Assemble yourselves, and come, all ye heathen, and gather yourselves together round about: thither cause thy mighty ones to come down, O LORD.

12 Let the heathen be wakened, and come up to the valley of Jehoshaphat: for there will I sit to judge all the heathen round about.

13 Put ye in the sickle, for the harvest is ripe: come, get you down; for the press is full, the vats overflow; for their wickedness *is* great.

14 Multitudes, multitudes in the valley of decision: for the day of the LORD *is* near in the valley of decision.

15 The sun and the moon shall be darkened, and the stars shall withdraw their shining.

16 The LORD also shall roar out of Zion, and utter his voice from Jerusalem; and the heavens and the earth shall shake: but the LORD *will be* the hope of his people, and the strength of the children of Israel.

17 So shall ye know that I *am* the LORD your God dwelling in Zion, my holy mountain: then shall Jerusalem be holy, and there shall no strangers pass through her any more.

## Amplified

**3** FOR, BEHOLD, in those days and at that time, when I shall reverse the captivity *and* restore the fortunes of Judah and Jerusalem,

2 I will gather all nations, and will bring them down into the valley of Jehoshaphat, and there will I deal with *and* execute judgment upon them for [their treatment of] My people and of My heritage Israel, whom they have scattered among the nations, and [because] they have divided My land.

3 And they have cast lots for My people, and have given a boy for a harlot, and have sold a girl for wine, and have drunk it.

4 Yes, and what are you to me, O Tyre and Sidon, and all the [five small] divisions of Philistia? Will you pay Me back for something? Even if you pay Me back, swiftly and speedily I will return your deed [of retaliation] upon your own head; [Isa. 23; Zech. 9:2-7; Ezek. 26:1-18; Amos 1:6-10; Zeph. 2:4-7.]

5 Because you have taken My silver and My gold and have carried into your temples *and* palaces My precious treasures,

6 And have sold the children of Judah and the children of Jerusalem to the sons of the Grecians, that you may remove them far from their border.

7 Behold, I will stir them up out of the place to which you have sold them, and will return your deed [of retaliation] upon your own head.

8 I will sell your sons and your daughters into the hand of the children of Judah, and they will sell them to the Sabeans, to a nation far off; for the Lord has spoken it. [Isa. 14:2; 60:14.]

9 Proclaim this among the nations: Prepare war, stir up the mighty men, let all the men of war draw near, let them come up.

10 Beat your plowshares into swords, and your pruning hooks into spears; let the weak say, I am strong—a warrior! [Isa. 2:4; Mic. 4:3.]

11 Hasten and come, all you nations round about, and assemble yourselves; there You, O Lord, will bring down Your mighty ones—Your warriors.

12 Let the nations bestir themselves and come up to the valley of Jehoshaphat, for there will I sit to judge all the nations round about.

13 Put in the sickle, for the [vintage] harvest is ripe; come, get down *and* tread the grapes, for the wine press is full, the vats overflow; for the wickedness [of the peoples] is great. [Mark 4:29; Rev. 14:15, 18-20.]

14 Multitudes, multitudes in the valley of decision! For the day of the Lord is near in the valley of decision. [Zech. 14:1-9.]

15 The sun and the moon are darkened, and the stars withdraw their shining.

16 The Lord will thunder *and* roar from Zion and utter His voice from Jerusalem, and the heavens and the earth shall shake; but the Lord will be a refuge for His people and a stronghold to the children of Israel. [Amos 9:11-15; Mic. 4:1-3; 5:2; Zeph. 3:13-20; Zech. 6:12, 13; 12:8, 9.]

17 So shall you know that I am the Lord your God, dwelling in Zion, My holy mountain. Then shall Jerusalem be holy, and strangers *and* foreigners [not born into the family of God] shall no more pass through it.

## New American Standard

*The Nations Will Be Judged*

3 "FOR BEHOLD, in those days and at that time,
When I restore the fortunes of Judah and Jerusalem,
2 I will gather all the nations,
And bring them down to the valley of Jehoshaphat.
Then I will enter into judgment with them there
On behalf of My people and My inheritance, Israel,
Whom they have scattered among the nations;
And they have divided up My land.
3 "They have also cast lots for My people,
Traded a boy for a harlot,
And sold a girl for wine that they may drink.

4 "Moreover, what are you to Me, O Tyre, Sidon, and all the
regions of Philistia? Are you rendering Me a recompense? But if
you do recompense Me, swiftly and speedily I will return your
recompense on your head.
5 "Since you have taken My silver and My gold, brought My
precious treasures to your temples,
6 and sold the sons of Judah and Jerusalem to the Greeks in
order to remove them far from their territory,
7 behold, I am going to arouse them from the place where you
have sold them, and return your recompense on your head.
8 "Also I will sell your sons and your daughters into the hand
of the sons of Judah, and they will sell them to the Sabeans, to a
distant nation," for the LORD has spoken.

9 ¶ Proclaim this among the nations:
Prepare a war; rouse the mighty men!
Let all the soldiers draw near, let them come up!
10 Beat your plowshares into swords,
And your pruning hooks into spears;
Let the weak say, "I am a mighty man."
11 Hasten and come, all you surrounding nations,
And gather yourselves there.
Bring down, O LORD, Thy mighty ones.
12 Let the nations be aroused
And come up to the valley of Jehoshaphat,
For there I will sit to judge
All the surrounding nations.
13 Put in the sickle, for the harvest is ripe.
Come, tread, for the wine press is full;
The vats overflow, for their wickedness is great.
14 Multitudes, multitudes in the valley of decision!
For the day of the LORD is near in the valley of
decision.
15 The sun and moon grow dark,
And the stars lose their brightness.
16 And the LORD roars from Zion
And utters His voice from Jerusalem,
And the heavens and the earth tremble.
But the LORD is a refuge for His people
And a stronghold to the sons of Israel.
17 Then you will know that I am the LORD your God,
Dwelling in Zion My holy mountain.
So Jerusalem will be holy,
And strangers will pass through it no more.

## New International

*The Nations Judged*

3 "IN THOSE days and at that time,
when I restore the fortunes of Judah and Jerusalem,
2 I will gather all nations
and bring them down to the Valley of Jehoshaphat.[a]
There I will enter into judgment against them
concerning my inheritance, my people Israel,
for they scattered my people among the nations
and divided up my land.
3 They cast lots for my people
and traded boys for prostitutes;
they sold girls for wine
that they might drink.

4 "Now what have you against me, O Tyre and Sidon and all you
regions of Philistia? Are you repaying me for something I have
done? If you are paying me back, I will swiftly and speedily return
on your own heads what you have done. 5 For you took my silver
and my gold and carried off my finest treasures to your temples.
6 You sold the people of Judah and Jerusalem to the Greeks, that
you might send them far from their homeland.
7 "See, I am going to rouse them out of the places to which you
sold them, and I will return on your own heads what you have
done. 8 I will sell your sons and daughters to the people of Judah,
and they will sell them to the Sabeans, a nation far away." The
LORD has spoken.

9 Proclaim this among the nations:
Prepare for war!
Rouse the warriors!
Let all the fighting men draw near and attack.
10 Beat your plowshares into swords
and your pruning hooks into spears.
Let the weakling say,
"I am strong!"
11 Come quickly, all you nations from every side,
and assemble there.

Bring down your warriors, O LORD!

12 "Let the nations be roused;
let them advance into the Valley of Jehoshaphat,
for there I will sit
to judge all the nations on every side.
13 Swing the sickle,
for the harvest is ripe.
Come, trample the grapes,
for the winepress is full
and the vats overflow—
so great is their wickedness!"

14 Multitudes, multitudes
in the valley of decision!
For the day of the LORD is near
in the valley of decision.
15 The sun and moon will be darkened,
and the stars no longer shine.
16 The LORD will roar from Zion
and thunder from Jerusalem;
the earth and the sky will tremble.
But the LORD will be a refuge for his people,
a stronghold for the people of Israel.

*Blessings for God's People*

17 "Then you will know that I, the LORD your God,
dwell in Zion, my holy hill.
Jerusalem will be holy;
never again will foreigners invade her.

**NIV** [a] 2 *Jehoshaphat* means *the LORD judges;* also in verse 12.

## King James

18¶ And it shall come to pass in that day, *that* the mountains shall drop down new wine, and the hills shall flow with milk, and all the rivers of Judah shall flow with waters, and a fountain shall come forth of the house of the LORD, and shall water the valley of Shittim.

19Egypt shall be a desolation, and Edom shall be a desolate wilderness, for the violence *against* the children of Judah, because they have shed innocent blood in their land.

20But Judah shall dwell for ever, and Jerusalem from generation to generation.

21For I will cleanse their blood *that* I have not cleansed: for the LORD dwelleth in Zion.

## Amplified

18And in that day, the mountains shall drip with fresh fruit juice, and the hills shall flow with milk, and all the brooks *and* river beds of Judah shall flow with water; and a fountain shall come forth from the house of the Lord and shall water the valley of Shittim. [Ezek. 47:1-12; Amos 9:13; Zech. 14:8.]

19Egypt shall be a desolation, and Edom shall be a desolate wilderness, for their violence against the children of Judah, because they have shed innocent blood in their land.

20But Judah shall remain *and* be inhabited for ever, and Jerusalem from generation to generation.

21And I will cleanse *and* hold as innocent their blood *and* avenge it, which I have not cleansed, held innocent *and* avenged, for the Lord dwells in Zion.

## New American Standard

*Judah Will Be Blessed*

18¶ And it will come about in that day
That the mountains will drip with sweet wine,
And the hills will flow with milk,
And all the brooks of Judah will flow with water;
And a spring will go out from the house of the LORD,
To water the valley of Shittim.
19 Egypt will become a waste,
And Edom will become a desolate wilderness,
Because of the violence done to the sons of Judah,
In whose land they have shed innocent blood.
20 But Judah will be inhabited forever,
And Jerusalem for all generations.
21 And I will avenge their blood which I have not
avenged,
For the LORD dwells in Zion.

## New International

18"In that day the mountains will drip new wine,
and the hills will flow with milk;
all the ravines of Judah will run with water.
A fountain will flow out of the LORD's house
and will water the valley of acacias.[a]
19But Egypt will be desolate,
Edom a desert waste,
because of violence done to the people of Judah,
in whose land they shed innocent blood.
20Judah will be inhabited forever
and Jerusalem through all generations.
21Their bloodguilt, which I have not pardoned,
I will pardon."

The LORD dwells in Zion!

NIV [a] 18 Or *Valley of Shittim*

## King James

# Amos

1 THE WORDS of Amos, who was among the herdmen of Tekoa, which he saw concerning Israel in the days of Uzziah king of Judah, and in the days of Jeroboam the son of Joash king of Israel, two years before the earthquake.

2 And he said, the LORD will roar from Zion, and utter his voice from Jerusalem; and the habitations of the shepherds shall mourn, and the top of Carmel shall wither.

3 Thus saith the LORD; For three transgressions of Damascus, and for four, I will not turn away *the punishment* thereof; because they have threshed Gilead with threshing instruments of iron:

4 But I will send a fire into the house of Hazael, which shall devour the palaces of Ben-hadad.

5 I will break also the bar of Damascus, and cut off the inhabitant from the plain of Aven, and him that holdeth the sceptre from the house of Eden: and the people of Syria shall go into captivity unto Kir, saith the LORD.

6 ¶ Thus saith the LORD; For three transgressions of Gaza, and for four, I will not turn away *the punishment* thereof; because they carried away captive the whole captivity, to deliver *them* up to Edom:

7 But I will send a fire on the wall of Gaza, which shall devour the palaces thereof:

8 And I will cut off the inhabitant from Ashdod, and him that holdeth the sceptre from Ashkelon, and I will turn mine hand against Ekron: and the remnant of the Philistines shall perish, saith the Lord GOD.

9 ¶ Thus saith the LORD; For three transgressions of Tyrus, and for four, I will not turn away *the punishment* thereof; because they delivered up the whole captivity to Edom, and remembered not the brotherly covenant:

10 But I will send a fire on the wall of Tyrus, which shall devour the palaces thereof.

## Amplified

THE BOOK OF

# Amos

1 THE WORDS of Amos, who was among the herdsmen *and* sheep masters of Tekoa, which he saw [in divine revelation] concerning Israel in the days of Uzziah king of Judah and in the days of Jeroboam the son of Joash, king of Israel, two years before the earthquake. [Zech. 14:5.]

2 And he said, The Lord roars out of Zion and utters His voice from Jerusalem, then the pastures of the shepherds mourn, and the top of *Mount* Carmel dries up. [Isa. 42:13; Jer. 25:30; Joel 3:16.]

3 Thus says the Lord: For three transgressions of Damascus [the capital of Syria], and for four— *that is,* for multiplied delinquencies—I will not reverse the punishment of it *or* revoke My word concerning it; because they have threshed Gilead [east of the Jordan River] with iron sledges. [II Kings 10:32, 33.]

4 So I will send a fire [of war, conquest and destruction] upon the house of Hazael [who killed and succeeded King Benhadad], which shall devour the palaces *and* strongholds of Benhadad.

5 I will break also the bar *of the gate* of Damascus, and cut off the inhabitant from the plain of Aven *or* On, and him who holds the scepter from Beth-eden; and the people of Syria [conquered by the Assyrians] shall go into exile to Kir, says the Lord.

6 Thus says the Lord: For three transgressions of *Philistine* Gaza, and for four— *that is,* for multiplied delinquencies—I will not reverse the punishment of it *or* revoke My word concerning it; because [as slave traders] they carried away captive the whole *Jewish* population [of defenseless Judean border villages]—of which none was spared, none left behind—and delivered them up to Edom's [slave trade]. [Joel 3:6.]

7 So I will send a fire on the wall of Gaza, which shall devour its strongholds.

8 And I will cut off the inhabitants from Ashdod, and him who holds the scepter from Ashkelon, and I will turn My hand against Ekron; and the rest of the Philistines [Gath, and the towns dependent on these four cities] shall perish, says the Lord God.

9 Thus says the Lord: For three transgressions of Tyre, and for four— *that is,* for multiplied delinquencies—I will not reverse the punishment of it *or* revoke My word concerning it; because they [as middlemen] delivered up a whole [Jewish] population to Edom, and did not [seriously] remember *their* brotherly covenant. [I Kings 5:1, 12; 9:12, 13.]

10 So I will send a fire on the wall of Tyre, which shall devour its strongholds.

## New American Standard

# Amos

*Judgment on Neighbor Nations*

**1** THE WORDS of Amos, who was among the sheepherders
from Tekoa, which he envisioned in visions concerning Israel
in the days of Uzziah king of Judah, and in the days of Jeroboam
son of Joash, king of Israel, two years before the earthquake.
2And he said,

"The LORD roars from Zion,
And from Jerusalem He utters His voice;
And the shepherds' pasture grounds mourn,
And the summit of Carmel dries up."

3¶ Thus says the LORD,
"For three transgressions of Damascus and for four
I will not revoke its *punishment*,
Because they threshed Gilead with *implements* of sharp
iron.
4 "So I will send fire upon the house of Hazael,
And it will consume the citadels of Ben-hadad.
5 "I will also break the *gate* bar of Damascus,
And cut off the inhabitant from the valley of Aven,
And him who holds the scepter, from Beth-eden;
So the people of Aram will go exiled to Kir,"
Says the LORD.

6¶ Thus says the LORD,
"For three transgressions of Gaza and for four
I will not revoke its *punishment*,
Because they deported an entire population
To deliver *it* up to Edom.
7 "So I will send fire upon the wall of Gaza,
And it will consume her citadels.
8 "I will also cut off the inhabitant from Ashdod,
And him who holds the scepter, from Ashkelon;
I will even unleash My power upon Ekron,
And the remnant of the Philistines will perish,"
Says the Lord GOD.

9¶ Thus says the LORD,
"For three transgressions of Tyre and for four
I will not revoke its *punishment*,
Because they delivered up an entire population to Edom
And did not remember *the* covenant of brotherhood.
10 "So I will send fire upon the wall of Tyre,
And it will consume her citadels."

## New International

# Amos

**1** THE WORDS of Amos, one of the shepherds of Tekoa—what
he saw concerning Israel two years before the earthquake,
when Uzziah was king of Judah and Jeroboam son of Jehoash[a] was
king of Israel.
2He said:

"The LORD roars from Zion
and thunders from Jerusalem;
the pastures of the shepherds dry up,[b]
and the top of Carmel withers."

*Judgment on Israel's Neighbors*

3This is what the LORD says:

"For three sins of Damascus,
even for four, I will not turn back ⌊my wrath⌋.
Because she threshed Gilead
with sledges having iron teeth,
4I will send fire upon the house of Hazael
that will consume the fortresses of Ben-Hadad.
5I will break down the gate of Damascus;
I will destroy the king who is in[c] the Valley of Aven[d]
and the one who holds the scepter in Beth Eden.
The people of Aram will go into exile to Kir,"
says the LORD.

6This is what the LORD says:

"For three sins of Gaza,
even for four, I will not turn back ⌊my wrath⌋.
Because she took captive whole communities
and sold them to Edom,
7I will send fire upon the walls of Gaza
that will consume her fortresses.
8I will destroy the king[e] of Ashdod
and the one who holds the scepter in Ashkelon.
I will turn my hand against Ekron,
till the last of the Philistines is dead,"
says the Sovereign LORD.

9This is what the LORD says:

"For three sins of Tyre,
even for four, I will not turn back ⌊my wrath⌋.
Because she sold whole communities of captives to Edom,
disregarding a treaty of brotherhood,
10I will send fire upon the walls of Tyre
that will consume her fortresses."

**NIV** [a] 1 Hebrew *Joash*, a variant of *Jehoash* [b] 2 Or *shepherds mourn* [c] 5 Or *the inhabitants of* [d] 5 *Aven* means *wickedness.* [e] 8 Or *inhabitants*

# King James

11¶ Thus saith the LORD; For three transgressions of Edom, and for four, I will not turn away *the punishment* thereof; because he did pursue his brother with the sword, and did cast off all pity, and his anger did tear perpetually, and he kept his wrath for ever:

12But I will send a fire upon Teman, which shall devour the palaces of Bozrah.

13¶ Thus saith the LORD; For three transgressions of the children of Ammon, and for four, I will not turn away *the punishment* thereof; because they have ripped up the women with child of Gilead, that they might enlarge their border:

14But I will kindle a fire in the wall of Rabbah, and it shall devour the palaces thereof, with shouting in the day of battle, with a tempest in the day of the whirlwind:

15And their king shall go into captivity, he and his princes together, saith the LORD.

**2** THUS SAITH the LORD; For three transgressions of Moab, and for four, I will not turn away *the punishment* thereof; because he burned the bones of the king of Edom into lime:

2But I will send a fire upon Moab, and it shall devour the palaces of Kirioth: and Moab shall die with tumult, with shouting, *and* with the sound of the trumpet:

3And I will cut off the judge from the midst thereof, and will slay all the princes thereof with him, saith the LORD.

4¶ Thus saith the LORD; For three transgressions of Judah, and for four, I will not turn away *the punishment* thereof; because they have despised the law of the LORD, and have not kept his commandments, and their lies caused them to err, after the which their fathers have walked:

5But I will send a fire upon Judah, and it shall devour the palaces of Jerusalem.

6¶ Thus saith the LORD; For three transgressions of Israel, and for four, I will not turn away *the punishment* thereof; because they sold the righteous for silver, and the poor for a pair of shoes;

7That pant after the dust of the earth on the head of the poor, and turn aside the way of the meek: and a man and his father will go in unto the *same* maid, to profane my holy name:

8And they lay *themselves* down upon clothes laid to pledge by every altar, and they drink the wine of the condemned *in* the house of their god.

# Amplified

11Thus says the Lord: For three transgressions of Edom [descendants of Esau], and for four— *that is,* for multiplied delinquencies—I will not reverse the punishment of it *or* revoke My word concerning it; because he pursued his brother Jacob (Israel) with the sword, corrupting his compassions *and* casting off all pity, and his anger tore perpetually, and his wrath he kept *and* heeded for ever.

12So I will send a fire upon Teman, which shall devour the strongholds of Bozrah [in Edom].

13Thus says the Lord: For three transgressions of the children of Ammon [descendants of Lot], and for four— *that is,* for multiplied delinquencies—I will not reverse the punishment of it *or* revoke My word concerning it; because *the Ammonites* have ripped up women with child in Gilead, that they might enlarge their border.

14So I will kindle a fire in the wall of Rabbah [in Ammon], and it shall devour the strongholds of it, with shouting in the day of battle, with a tempest in the day of the whirlwind;

15And their king shall go into exile, he and his princes together, says the Lord.

**2** THUS SAYS the Lord: For three transgressions of Moab [descendants of Lot], and for four— *that is,* for multiplied delinquencies—I will not reverse the punishment of it *or* revoke My word concerning it; because he burned the bones of the king of Edom [Esau's descendant] into lime.

2So I will send a fire upon Moab, and it shall devour the strongholds of Kerioth; and Moab shall die amid uproar, shouting and the sound of the trumpet.

3And I will cut off the ruler from its midst, and will slay all its princes with him, says the Lord.

4Thus says the Lord: For three transgressions of Judah, and for four— *that is,* for multiplied delinquencies—I will not reverse the punishment of it *or* revoke My word concerning it; because they have despised *and* rejected the law of the Lord, and have not kept His commandments, but their lies, after which their fathers have walked, caused them to err *and* go astray.

5So I will send a fire upon Judah, and it shall devour the strongholds of Jerusalem.

6Thus says the Lord: For three transgressions of Israel, and for four— *that is,* for multiplied delinquencies—I will not reverse the punishment of it *or* revoke My word concerning it; because they have sold the strictly just *and* uncompromisingly righteous for silver, and the needy for a pair of sandals;

7They pant after the *sight* of the poor [reduced to such misery that they will be] *throwing* dust of the earth on their heads [in token of their grief]; they defraud *and* turn aside the humble [who are too meek to defend themselves]; and a man and his father will have sexual relations with the same maiden, so that My holy name is profaned.

8And they lay themselves down beside every [pagan] altar upon clothes they have taken in pledge [for indebtedness]; and in the house of their God [in daring contempt of Him] they frivolously drink the wine which has been *exacted* from those *unjustly* fined.

## New American Standard

11¶ Thus says the LORD,
"For three transgressions of Edom and for four
I will not revoke its *punishment*,
Because he pursued his brother with the sword,
While he stifled his compassion;
His anger also tore continually,
And he maintained his fury forever.
12 "So I will send fire upon Teman,
And it will consume the citadels of Bozrah."

13¶ Thus says the LORD,
"For three transgressions of the sons of Ammon and for four
I will not revoke its *punishment*,
Because they ripped open the pregnant women of Gilead
In order to enlarge their borders.
14 "So I will kindle a fire on the wall of Rabbah,
And it will consume her citadels
Amid war cries on the day of battle
And a storm on the day of tempest.
15 "Their king will go into exile,
He and his princes together," says the LORD.

### *Judgment on Judah and Israel*

2 THUS SAYS the LORD,
"For three transgressions of Moab and for four
I will not revoke its *punishment*,
Because he burned the bones of the king of Edom to lime.
2 "So I will send fire upon Moab,
And it will consume the citadels of Kerioth;
And Moab will die amid tumult,
With war cries and the sound of a trumpet.
3 "I will also cut off the judge from her midst,
And slay all her princes with him," says the LORD.

4¶ Thus says the LORD,
"For three transgressions of Judah and for four
I will not revoke its *punishment*,
Because they rejected the law of the LORD
And have not kept His statutes;
Their lies also have led them astray,
Those after which their fathers walked.
5 "So I will send fire upon Judah,
And it will consume the citadels of Jerusalem."

6¶ Thus says the LORD,
"For three transgressions of Israel and for four
I will not revoke its *punishment*,
Because they sell the righteous for money
And the needy for a pair of sandals.
7 "These who pant after the *very* dust of the earth on the head of the helpless
Also turn aside the way of the humble;
And a man and his father resort to the same girl
In order to profane My holy name.
8 "And on garments taken as pledges they stretch out beside every altar,
And in the house of their God they drink the wine of those who have been fined.

## New International

11 This is what the LORD says:

"For three sins of Edom,
even for four, I will not turn back ⌊my wrath⌋.
Because he pursued his brother with a sword,
stifling all compassion,[a]
because his anger raged continually
and his fury flamed unchecked,
12 I will send fire upon Teman
that will consume the fortresses of Bozrah."

13 This is what the LORD says:

"For three sins of Ammon,
even for four, I will not turn back ⌊my wrath⌋.
Because he ripped open the pregnant women of Gilead
in order to extend his borders,
14 I will set fire to the walls of Rabbah
that will consume her fortresses
amid war cries on the day of battle,
amid violent winds on a stormy day.
15 Her king[b] will go into exile,
he and his officials together,"
says the LORD.

2 THIS IS what the LORD says:

"For three sins of Moab,
even for four, I will not turn back ⌊my wrath⌋.
Because he burned, as if to lime,
the bones of Edom's king,
2 I will send fire upon Moab
that will consume the fortresses of Kerioth.[c]
Moab will go down in great tumult
amid war cries and the blast of the trumpet.
3 I will destroy her ruler
and kill all her officials with him,"
says the LORD.

4 This is what the LORD says:

"For three sins of Judah,
even for four, I will not turn back ⌊my wrath⌋.
Because they have rejected the law of the LORD
and have not kept his decrees,
because they have been led astray by false gods,[d]
the gods[e] their ancestors followed,
5 I will send fire upon Judah
that will consume the fortresses of Jerusalem."

### *Judgment on Israel*

6 This is what the LORD says:

"For three sins of Israel,
even for four, I will not turn back ⌊my wrath⌋.
They sell the righteous for silver,
and the needy for a pair of sandals.
7 They trample on the heads of the poor
as upon the dust of the ground
and deny justice to the oppressed.
Father and son use the same girl
and so profane my holy name.
8 They lie down beside every altar
on garments taken in pledge.
In the house of their god
they drink wine taken as fines.

**NIV** [a] 11 Or *sword / and destroyed his allies* [b] 15 Or / *Molech;* Hebrew *malcam*
[c] 2 Or *of her cities* [d] 4 Or *by lies* [e] 4 Or *lies*

## King James

9¶ Yet destroyed I the Amorite before them, whose height *was*
like the height of the cedars, and he *was* strong as the oaks; yet I
destroyed his fruit from above, and his roots from beneath.
10Also I brought you up from the land of Egypt, and led you
forty years through the wilderness, to possess the land of the
Amorite.
11And I raised up of your sons for prophets, and of your young
men for Nazarites. *Is it* not even thus, O ye children of Israel? saith
the LORD.
12But ye gave the Nazarites wine to drink; and commanded the
prophets, saying, Prophesy not.
13Behold, I am pressed under you, as a cart is pressed *that is* full
of sheaves.
14Therefore the flight shall perish from the swift, and the strong
shall not strengthen his force, neither shall the mighty deliver
himself:
15Neither shall he stand that handleth the bow; and *he that is*
swift of foot shall not deliver *himself:* neither shall he that rideth
the horse deliver himself.
16And *he that is* courageous among the mighty shall flee away
naked in that day, saith the LORD.

**3** HEAR THIS word that the LORD hath spoken against you, O
children of Israel, against the whole family which I brought
up from the land of Egypt, saying,
2You only have I known of all the families of the earth: therefore
I will punish you for all your iniquities.
3Can two walk together, except they be agreed?
4Will a lion roar in the forest, when he hath no prey? will a
young lion cry out of his den, if he have taken nothing?
5Can a bird fall in a snare upon the earth, where no gin *is* for
him? shall *one* take up a snare from the earth, and have taken
nothing at all?
6Shall a trumpet be blown in the city, and the people not be
afraid? shall there be evil in a city, and the LORD hath not done *it?*
7Surely the Lord GOD will do nothing, but he revealeth his
secret unto his servants the prophets.
8The lion hath roared, who will not fear? the Lord GOD hath
spoken, who can but prophesy?
9¶ Publish in the palaces at Ashdod, and in the palaces in the
land of Egypt, and say, Assemble yourselves upon the mountains
of Samaria, and behold the great tumults in the midst thereof, and
the oppressed in the midst thereof.
10For they know not to do right, saith the LORD, who store up
violence and robbery in their palaces.

## Amplified

9Yet I destroyed the Amorite before them, whose height was
like the height of the cedars, and he was strong as the oaks; yet
I destroyed his fruit from above, and his roots from beneath.
10Also I brought you up out of the land of Egypt and led you
forty years through the wilderness, to possess the land of the
Amorite.
11And I raised up *some* of your sons for prophets, and of your
young men for dedicated ones—Nazirites. Is not this true, O you
children of Israel? says the Lord. [Num. 6:1-8.]
12But you gave the dedicated ones—the Nazirites—wine to
drink and commanded the prophets, saying, Prophesy not.
13Behold, I am pressed under you, *and* I will press you down
in your place, as a cart presses that is full of sheaves.
14And flight shall be lost to the swift *and* refuge shall fail him;
the strong shall not retain *and* confirm his strength, neither shall
the mighty deliver himself.
15Neither shall he stand who handles the bow, and he who is
swift of foot shall not deliver himself; neither shall he who rides
the horse deliver his life.
16And he who is courageous among the mighty shall flee away
naked on that day, says the Lord.

**3** HEAR THIS word that the Lord has spoken against you, O
children of Israel, against the whole family which I brought
up from the land of Egypt:
2You only have I known [chosen, sympathized with and loved]
of all the families of the earth; therefore I will visit upon you all
your wickedness *and* punish you for all your iniquities.
3Do two walk together, except they make an appointment *and*
have agreed?
4Will a lion roar in the forest, when he has no prey? Will a young
lion cry out of his den, if he has taken nothing?
5Can a bird fall in a snare upon the earth, where there is no trap
for him? Does a trap spring up from the ground, when nothing at
all has sprung it?
6Shall a trumpet be blown in the city, and the people not be
alarmed *and* afraid? Shall misfortune occur *or* evil [that is for pun-
ishment], and the Lord has not caused it?
7Surely the Lord God will do nothing [a]without revealing His
secret to His servants the prophets. [Rev. 10:7.]
8The lion has roared; who will not fear? The Lord God has
spoken; who can but prophesy? [Acts 4:20; 5:20, 29; I Cor. 9:16.]
9Publish to the strongholds in Ashdod [Philistia], and to the
strongholds in the land of Egypt, and say, Assemble yourselves
upon the mountains of Samaria, and behold what great tumults—
confusion and disorder—are in her, and what oppressions are in
the midst of her.
10For they know not how to do right, says the Lord, they who
store up violence and robbery in their strongholds.

**AMP** [a] God has always warned the world of coming judgments, in order that it may not bring them upon itself. He warned Noah of the coming flood, Abraham and Lot of the future destruction of Sodom, told Joseph of the seven years' famine, Moses of the ten plagues on Egypt, Jonah of the destruction of Nineveh, Amos of the downfall of Syria, Philistia, Tyre, Edom, Ammon, Moab, Judah and Israel. Various prophets were told in detail of the final events in connection with the captivities of the chosen people, and in every case the warnings were startlingly executed. At first in the case of Nineveh the judgment was postponed after Jonah's preaching, but when later generations of Ninevites backslid, the warning of Nahum was carried out completely against them. Christ's coming was foretold from Genesis to Malachi. Equally plain and inevitable of fulfillment are the warnings of Jesus and the prophets concerning the future that daily comes nearer to every nation on earth.

## New American Standard

9¶ "Yet it was I who destroyed the Amorite before them,
Though his height *was* like the height of cedars
And he *was* strong as the oaks;
I even destroyed his fruit above and his root below.
10 "And it was I who brought you up from the land of Egypt,
And I led you in the wilderness forty years
That you might take possession of the land of the Amorite.
11 "Then I raised up some of your sons to be prophets
And some of your young men to be Nazirites.
Is this not so, O sons of Israel?" declares the LORD.
12 "But you made the Nazirites drink wine,
And you commanded the prophets saying, 'You shall not prophesy!'
13 "Behold, I am weighted down beneath you
As a wagon is weighted down when filled with sheaves.
14 "Flight will perish from the swift,
And the stalwart will not strengthen his power,
Nor the mighty man save his life.
15 "He who grasps the bow will not stand *his ground*,
The swift of foot will not escape,
Nor will he who rides the horse save his life.
16 "Even the bravest among the warriors will flee naked in that day," declares the LORD.

*All the Tribes Are Guilty*

**3** HEAR THIS word which the LORD has spoken against you, sons of Israel, against the entire family which He brought up from the land of Egypt,
2 "You only have I chosen among all the families of the earth;
Therefore, I will punish you for all your iniquities."
3 Do two men walk together unless they have made an appointment?
4 Does a lion roar in the forest when he has no prey?
Does a young lion growl from his den unless he has captured *something*?
5 Does a bird fall into a trap on the ground when there is no bait in it?
Does a trap spring up from the earth when it captures nothing at all?
6 If a trumpet is blown in a city will not the people tremble?
If a calamity occurs in a city has not the LORD done it?
7 Surely the Lord GOD does nothing
Unless He reveals His secret counsel
To His servants the prophets.
8 A lion has roared! Who will not fear?
The Lord GOD has spoken! Who can but prophesy?
9¶ Proclaim on the citadels in Ashdod and on the citadels in the land of Egypt and say, "Assemble yourselves on the mountains of Samaria and see *the* great tumults within her and *the* oppressions in her midst.
10 "But they do not know how to do what is right," declares the LORD, "these who hoard up violence and devastation in their citadels."

## New International

9 "I destroyed the Amorite before them,
though he was tall as the cedars
and strong as the oaks.
I destroyed his fruit above
and his roots below.
10 "I brought you up out of Egypt,
and I led you forty years in the desert
to give you the land of the Amorites.
11 I also raised up prophets from among your sons
and Nazirites from among your young men.
Is this not true, people of Israel?"
declares the LORD.
12 "But you made the Nazirites drink wine
and commanded the prophets not to prophesy.

13 "Now then, I will crush you
as a cart crushes when loaded with grain.
14 The swift will not escape,
the strong will not muster their strength,
and the warrior will not save his life.
15 The archer will not stand his ground,
the fleet-footed soldier will not get away,
and the horseman will not save his life.
16 Even the bravest warriors
will flee naked on that day,"
declares the LORD.

*Witnesses Summoned Against Israel*

**3** HEAR THIS word the LORD has spoken against you, O people of Israel—against the whole family I brought up out of Egypt:
2 "You only have I chosen
of all the families of the earth;
therefore I will punish you
for all your sins."

3 Do two walk together
unless they have agreed to do so?
4 Does a lion roar in the thicket
when he has no prey?
Does he growl in his den
when he has caught nothing?
5 Does a bird fall into a trap on the ground
where no snare has been set?
Does a trap spring up from the earth
when there is nothing to catch?
6 When a trumpet sounds in a city,
do not the people tremble?
When disaster comes to a city,
has not the LORD caused it?
7 Surely the Sovereign LORD does nothing
without revealing his plan
to his servants the prophets.

8 The lion has roared—
who will not fear?
The Sovereign LORD has spoken—
who can but prophesy?

9 Proclaim to the fortresses of Ashdod
and to the fortresses of Egypt:
"Assemble yourselves on the mountains of Samaria;
see the great unrest within her
and the oppression among her people."

10 "They do not know how to do right," declares the LORD,
"who hoard plunder and loot in their fortresses."

## King James

11 Therefore thus saith the Lord GOD; An adversary *there shall be* even round about the land; and he shall bring down thy strength from thee, and thy palaces shall be spoiled.

12 Thus saith the LORD; As the shepherd taketh out of the mouth of the lion two legs, or a piece of an ear; so shall the children of Israel be taken out that dwell in Samaria in the corner of a bed, and in Damascus *in* a couch.

13 Hear ye, and testify in the house of Jacob, saith the Lord GOD, the God of hosts,

14 That in the day that I shall visit the transgressions of Israel upon him I will also visit the altars of Beth-el: and the horns of the altar shall be cut off, and fall to ground.

15 And I will smite the winter house with the summer house; and the houses of ivory shall perish, and the great houses shall have an end, saith the LORD.

**4** HEAR THIS word, ye kine of Bashan, that *are* in the mountain of Samaria, which oppress the poor, which crush the needy, which say to their masters, Bring, and let us drink.

2 The Lord GOD hath sworn by his holiness, that, lo, the days shall come upon you, that he will take you away with hooks, and your posterity with fishhooks.

3 And ye shall go out at the breaches, every *cow at that which is* before her; and ye shall cast *them* into the palace, saith the LORD.

4 ¶ Come to Beth-el, and transgress; at Gilgal multiply transgression; and bring your sacrifices every morning, *and* your tithes after three years:

5 And offer a sacrifice of thanksgiving with leaven, and proclaim *and* publish the free offerings: for this liketh you, O ye children of Israel, saith the Lord GOD.

6 ¶ And I also have given you cleanness of teeth in all your cities, and want of bread in all your places: yet have ye not returned unto me, saith the LORD.

7 And also I have withholden the rain from you, when *there were* yet three months to the harvest: and I caused it to rain upon one city, and caused it not to rain upon another city: one piece was rained upon, and the piece whereupon it rained not withered.

8 So two *or* three cities wandered unto one city, to drink water; but they were not satisfied: yet have ye not returned unto me, saith the LORD.

## Amplified

11 Therefore thus says the Lord God: An adversary shall surround the land, and he shall bring down your defenses from you, and your strongholds shall be plundered.

12 Thus says the Lord: As the shepherd rescues out of the mouth of the lion two legs, or a piece of an ear, so shall the children of Israel who dwell in Samaria be rescued, with the corner of a couch and *part of* the damask covering of a bed.

13 Hear, and bear witness in the house of Jacob, says the Lord God, the God of hosts,

14 That in the day when I visit Israel's transgressions upon him I will also visit [with punishment] the altars of Bethel [with its golden calf], and the horns of the altar shall be cut off and fall to the ground.

15 And I will smite the winter house with the summer house; and the houses of ivory shall perish, and the many *and* great houses shall come to an end, says the Lord.

**4** HEAR THIS word, you cows [women] of Bashan, who are in the mountain of Samaria, who oppress the poor, who crush the needy, who say to their husbands, Bring, and let us drink! [Ps. 22:12; Ezek. 39:18.]

2 The Lord God has sworn by His holiness, that behold, the days shall come upon you, when they shall take you away with hooks, and the last of you with fishhooks. [Ps. 89:35.]

3 And you shall go out through the breaches [made in the city's wall], every *woman* straight before her, and you shall be cast forth into Harmon [an unknown place of exile], says the Lord.

4 Come to Bethel [where the golden calf is] and transgress; at Gilgal [another idol worship center] multiply transgression; and bring your sacrifices every morning, and your tithes every three days;

5 And offer [by burning] a sacrifice of thanksgiving of that which is leavened, and proclaim and publish freewill offerings; for this you like to do, O children of Israel! says the Lord God.

6 I also gave you cleanness of teeth in all your cities and want of bread in all your places, yet you did not return to Me, says the Lord.

7 And also I withheld the rain from you when there were yet three months to the harvest. I caused it to rain upon one city, and caused it not to rain upon another city; one piece of ground was rained upon, and the piece upon which it did not rain withered.

8 So [the people of] two or three cities wandered *and* staggered into one city to drink water, but they were not satisfied; yet you did not return to Me, says the Lord.

## New American Standard

11¶ Therefore, thus says the Lord GOD,
"An enemy, even one surrounding the land,
Will pull down your strength from you
And your citadels will be looted."
12 Thus says the LORD,
"Just as the shepherd snatches from the lion's mouth a couple of legs or a piece of an ear,
So will the sons of Israel dwelling in Samaria be snatched away—
With *the* corner of a bed and *the* cover of a couch!
13 "Hear and testify against the house of Jacob,"
Declares the Lord GOD, the God of hosts.
14 "For on the day that I punish Israel's transgressions,
I will also punish the altars of Bethel;
The horns of the altar will be cut off,
And they will fall to the ground.
15 "I will also smite the winter house together with the summer house;
The houses of ivory will also perish
And the great houses will come to an end,"
Declares the LORD.

*"Yet You Have Not Returned to Me"*

**4** HEAR THIS word, you cows of Bashan who are on the mountain of Samaria,
Who oppress the poor, who crush the needy,
Who say to your husbands, "Bring now, that we may drink!"
2 The Lord GOD has sworn by His holiness,
"Behold, the days are coming upon you
When they will take you away with meat hooks,
And the last of you with fish hooks.
3 "You will go out *through* breaches *in the walls,*
Each one straight before her,
And you will be cast to Harmon," declares the LORD.
4¶ "Enter Bethel and transgress;
In Gilgal multiply transgression!
Bring your sacrifices every morning,
Your tithes every three days.
5 "Offer a thank offering also from that which is leavened,
And proclaim freewill offerings, make them known.
For so you love *to do,* you sons of Israel,"
Declares the Lord GOD.
6¶ "But I gave you also cleanness of teeth in all your cities
And lack of bread in all your places,
Yet you have not returned to Me," declares the LORD.
7 "And furthermore, I withheld the rain from you
While *there were* still three months until harvest.
Then I would send rain on one city
And on another city I would not send rain;
One part would be rained on,
While the part not rained on would dry up.
8 "So two or three cities would stagger to another city to drink water,
But would not be satisfied;
Yet you have not returned to Me," declares the LORD.

## New International

11 Therefore this is what the Sovereign LORD says:
"An enemy will overrun the land;
he will pull down your strongholds
and plunder your fortresses."
12 This is what the LORD says:
"As a shepherd saves from the lion's mouth
only two leg bones or a piece of an ear,
so will the Israelites be saved,
those who sit in Samaria
on the edge of their beds
and in Damascus on their couches.[a]"
13 "Hear this and testify against the house of Jacob," declares the Lord, the LORD God Almighty.
14 "On the day I punish Israel for her sins,
I will destroy the altars of Bethel;
the horns of the altar will be cut off
and fall to the ground.
15 I will tear down the winter house
along with the summer house;
the houses adorned with ivory will be destroyed
and the mansions will be demolished,"
declares the LORD.

*Israel Has Not Returned to God*

**4** HEAR THIS word, you cows of Bashan on Mount Samaria,
you women who oppress the poor and crush the needy
and say to your husbands, "Bring us some drinks!"
2 The Sovereign LORD has sworn by his holiness:
"The time will surely come
when you will be taken away with hooks,
the last of you with fishhooks.
3 You will each go straight out
through breaks in the wall,
and you will be cast out toward Harmon,[b]"
declares the LORD.
4 "Go to Bethel and sin;
go to Gilgal and sin yet more.
Bring your sacrifices every morning,
your tithes every three years.[c]
5 Burn leavened bread as a thank offering
and brag about your freewill offerings—
boast about them, you Israelites,
for this is what you love to do,"
declares the Sovereign LORD.
6 "I gave you empty stomachs[d] in every city
and lack of bread in every town,
yet you have not returned to me,"
declares the LORD.
7 "I also withheld rain from you
when the harvest was still three months away.
I sent rain on one town,
but withheld it from another.
One field had rain;
another had none and dried up.
8 People staggered from town to town for water
but did not get enough to drink,
yet you have not returned to me,"
declares the LORD.

**NIV** [a] *12* The meaning of the Hebrew for this line is uncertain. [b] *3* Masoretic Text; with a different word division of the Hebrew (see Septuagint) *out, O mountain of oppression* [c] *4* Or *tithes on the third day* [d] *6* Hebrew *you cleanness of teeth*

## King James

9I have smitten you with blasting and mildew: when your gardens and your vineyards and your fig trees and your olive trees
increased, the palmerworm devoured *them:* yet have ye not returned unto me, saith the LORD.
10I have sent among you the pestilence after the manner of
Egypt: your young men have I slain with the sword, and have
taken away your horses; and I have made the stink of your camps
to come up unto your nostrils: yet have ye not returned unto me,
saith the LORD.
11I have overthrown *some* of you, as God overthrew Sodom and
Gomorrah, and ye were as a firebrand plucked out of the burning:
yet have ye not returned unto me, saith the LORD.
12Therefore thus will I do unto thee, O Israel: *and* because I will
do this unto thee, prepare to meet thy God, O Israel.
13For, lo, he that formeth the mountains, and createth the wind,
and declareth unto man what *is* his thought, that maketh the
morning darkness, and treadeth upon the high places of the earth,
The LORD, The God of hosts, *is* his name.

5 HEAR YE this word which I take up against you, *even* a
lamentation, O house of Israel.
2The virgin of Israel is fallen; she shall no more rise: she is
forsaken upon her land; *there is* none to raise her up.
3For thus saith the Lord GOD; The city that went out *by* a
thousand shall leave an hundred, and that which went forth *by* an
hundred shall leave ten, to the house of Israel.
4¶ For thus saith the LORD unto the house of Israel, Seek ye me,
and ye shall live:
5But seek not Beth-el, nor enter into Gilgal, and pass not to
Beer-sheba: for Gilgal shall surely go into captivity, and Beth-el
shall come to nought.
6Seek the LORD, and ye shall live; lest he break out like fire in
the house of Joseph, and devour *it,* and *there be* none to quench
*it* in Beth-el.
7Ye who turn judgment to wormwood, and leave off righteousness in the earth,
8 *Seek him* that maketh the seven stars and Orion, and turneth
the shadow of death into the morning, and maketh the day dark
with night: that calleth for the waters of the sea, and poureth them
out upon the face of the earth: The LORD *is* his name:

## Amplified

9I smote you with blight [from the poisonous east wind] and
with mildew; I laid waste the multitude of your gardens and your
vineyards; your fig trees and your olive trees the palmerworm [a
form of locust] devoured. Yet you did not return to Me, says the
Lord.
10I have sent among you the pestilence [which I made] epidemic
in Egypt; your young men I slew with the sword, and I took into
exile your horses; and I made the stench of your camp come up
into your nostrils; yet you did not return to Me, says the Lord.
[II Kings 8:12; 13:3, 7.]
11I have overthrown *some* among you, as when God overthrew
Sodom and Gomorrah, and you were as a brand plucked out of the
burning. Yet you did not return to Me, says the Lord. [Gen. 19:24,
25; Isa. 13:19; Jer. 49:18.]
12Therefore thus will I do to you, O Israel; and because I will
do this to you, prepare to meet your God, O Israel!
13For, lo, He Who forms the mountains, and creates the wind,
and declares to man what is his thought; Who makes the morning
darkness, and treads on the heights of the earth—the Lord, the
God of hosts, is His name! [Ps. 139:2; Dan. 2:28.]

5 HEAR THIS word which I take up concerning you in lamentation, O house of Israel:
2The virgin of Israel has fallen; she shall no more rise; she lies
cast down *and* forsaken on her land; there is no one to raise her
up.
3For thus says the Lord God: The city that went forth a thousand shall have a hundred left, and that which went forth a hundred shall have ten left to the house of Israel.
4For thus says the Lord to the house of Israel, Seek Me—inquire
for and of Me, and require Me [as you require food]—and you shall
live! [II Chron. 15:2; Jer. 29:13.]
5But seek not [the golden calf at] Bethel, nor enter into [idola-
trous] Gilgal, and pass not over to [the idols of] Beersheba; for
Gilgal shall surely go into captivity *and* exile, and Bethel [house of
God] shall become Bethaven [house of vanity, emptiness, falsity
and futility] and come to nothing.
6Seek the Lord—inquire for and of Him and require Him—and
you shall live; lest He rush down like fire upon the house of Joseph
[representing the ten tribes] and devour it, and there be none to
quench it in Bethel [the center of their idol hopes].
7You who turn justice into [the bitterness of] wormwood, and
cast righteousness—uprightness and right standing with God—
down to the ground,
8Seek Him Who made the [cluster of stars called] Pleiades and
[the constellation] Orion, and turns the shadow of death *or* deep
darkness into the morning, and darkens the day into night, Who
calls for the waters of the sea, and pours them out upon the face
of the earth, the Lord is His name,

## New American Standard

9 "I smote you with scorching *wind* and mildew;
And the caterpillar was devouring
Your many gardens and vineyards, fig trees and olive trees;
Yet you have not returned to Me," declares the LORD.
10 "I sent a plague among you after the manner of Egypt;
I slew your young men by the sword along with your captured horses,
And I made the stench of your camp rise up in your nostrils;
Yet you have not returned to Me," declares the LORD.
11 "I overthrew you as God overthrew Sodom and Gomorrah,
And you were like a firebrand snatched from a blaze;
Yet you have not returned to Me," declares the LORD.
12 "Therefore, thus I will do to you, O Israel;
Because I shall do this to you,
Prepare to meet your God, O Israel."
13 For behold, He who forms mountains and creates the wind
And declares to man what are His thoughts,
He who makes dawn into darkness
And treads on the high places of the earth,
The LORD God of hosts is His name.

*"Seek Me that You May Live"*

5 HEAR THIS word which I take up for you as a dirge, O house of Israel.
2 She has fallen, she will not rise again—
The virgin Israel.
She *lies* neglected on her land;
There is none to raise her up.
3 For thus says the Lord GOD,
"The city which goes forth a thousand *strong*
Will have a hundred left,
And the one which goes forth a hundred *strong*
Will have ten left to the house of Israel."

4¶ For thus says the LORD to the house of Israel,
"Seek Me that you may live.
5 "But do not resort to Bethel,
And do not come to Gilgal,
Nor cross over to Beersheba;
For Gilgal will certainly go into captivity,
And Bethel will come to trouble.
6 "Seek the LORD that you may live,
Lest He break forth like a fire, O house of Joseph,
And it consume with none to quench *it* for Bethel,
7 *For* those who turn justice into wormwood
And cast righteousness down to the earth."

8¶ He who made the Pleiades and Orion
And changes deep darkness into morning,
Who also darkens day *into* night,
Who calls for the waters of the sea
And pours them out on the surface of the earth,
The LORD is His name.

## New International

9"Many times I struck your gardens and vineyards,
I struck them with blight and mildew.
Locusts devoured your fig and olive trees,
yet you have not returned to me,"
declares the LORD.

10"I sent plagues among you
as I did to Egypt.
I killed your young men with the sword,
along with your captured horses.
I filled your nostrils with the stench of your camps,
yet you have not returned to me,"
declares the LORD.

11"I overthrew some of you
as I[a] overthrew Sodom and Gomorrah.
You were like a burning stick snatched from the fire,
yet you have not returned to me,"
declares the LORD.

12"Therefore this is what I will do to you, Israel,
and because I will do this to you,
prepare to meet your God, O Israel."

13He who forms the mountains,
creates the wind,
and reveals his thoughts to man,
he who turns dawn to darkness,
and treads the high places of the earth—
the LORD God Almighty is his name.

*A Lament and Call to Repentance*

5 HEAR THIS word, O house of Israel, this lament I take up concerning you:

2"Fallen is Virgin Israel,
never to rise again,
deserted in her own land,
with no one to lift her up."

3This is what the Sovereign LORD says:

"The city that marches out a thousand strong for Israel
will have only a hundred left;
the town that marches out a hundred strong
will have only ten left."

4This is what the LORD says to the house of Israel:

"Seek me and live;
5 do not seek Bethel,
do not go to Gilgal,
do not journey to Beersheba.
For Gilgal will surely go into exile,
and Bethel will be reduced to nothing.[b]"
6Seek the LORD and live,
or he will sweep through the house of Joseph like a fire;
it will devour,
and Bethel will have no one to quench it.

7You who turn justice into bitterness
and cast righteousness to the ground
8(he who made the Pleiades and Orion,
who turns blackness into dawn
and darkens day into night,
who calls for the waters of the sea
and pours them out over the face of the land—
the LORD is his name—

NIV [a] *11* Hebrew *God* [b] *5* Or *grief;* or *wickedness;* Hebrew *aven,* a reference to Beth Aven (a derogatory name for Bethel)

## King James

9That strengtheneth the spoiled against the strong, so that the
spoiled shall come against the fortress.
10They hate him that rebuketh in the gate, and they abhor him
that speaketh uprightly.
11Forasmuch therefore as your treading *is* upon the poor, and
ye take from him burdens of wheat: ye have built houses of hewn
stone, but ye shall not dwell in them; ye have planted pleasant
vineyards, but ye shall not drink wine of them.
12For I know your manifold transgressions and your mighty
sins: they afflict the just, they take a bribe, and they turn aside the
poor in the gate *from their right.*
13Therefore the prudent shall keep silence in that time; for it *is*
an evil time.
14Seek good, and not evil, that ye may live: and so the LORD,
the God of hosts, shall be with you, as ye have spoken.
15Hate the evil, and love the good, and establish judgment in
the gate: it may be that the LORD God of hosts will be gracious unto
the remnant of Joseph.
16Therefore the LORD, the God of hosts, the Lord, saith thus;
Wailing *shall be* in all streets; and they shall say in all the highways,
Alas! alas! and they shall call the husbandman to mourning, and
such as are skilful of lamentation to Wailing.
17And in all vineyards *shall be* wailing: for I will pass through
thee, saith the LORD.
18Woe unto you that desire the day of the LORD! to what end
*is* it for you? the day of the LORD *is* darkness, and not light.
19As if a man did flee from a lion, and a bear met him; or went
into the house, and leaned his hand on the wall, and a serpent bit
him.
20 *Shall* not the day of the LORD *be* darkness, and not light? even
very dark, and no brightness in it?
21¶ I hate, I despise your feast days, and I will not smell in your
solemn assemblies.
22Though ye offer me burnt offerings and your meat offerings,
I will not accept *them:* neither will I regard the peace offerings of
your fat beasts.
23Take thou away from me the noise of thy songs; for I will not
hear the melody of thy viols.
24But let judgment run down as waters, and righteousness as
a mighty stream.
25Have ye offered unto me sacrifices and offerings in the wilderness forty years, O house of Israel?
26But ye have borne the tabernacle of your Moloch and Chiun
your images, the star of your god, which ye made to yourselves.

## Amplified

9Who causes sudden destruction to flash forth upon the strong,
so that destruction comes upon the fortress.
10They hate him who reproves in the [city] gate—holding him
as an abomination and rejecting his rebuke—and they abhor him
who speaks uprightly.
11Therefore because you tread upon the poor and take from him
exactions of wheat, you have built houses of hewn stone, but you
shall not dwell in them; you have planted pleasant vineyards, but
you shall not drink their grape juice.
12For I know how manifold are your transgressions, and how
mighty are your sins; you who afflict the [uncompromisingly]
righteous, who take a bribe, and who turn aside the needy in the
[court of the city] gate from their right.
13Therefore he who is prudent will keep silence in such a time,
for it is an evil time.
14Seek—inquire for and require—good and not evil, that you
may live; and so the Lord, the God of hosts, will be with you, as
you have said.
15Hate the evil, and love the good, and establish justice in the
[court of the city's] gate. It may be that the Lord, the God of hosts,
will be gracious to the remnant of Joseph [the northern kingdom].
16Therefore thus says the Lord, the God of hosts, the Lord:
There shall be wailing in all the broad ways, and in all the streets
they shall say, Alas! Alas! And they shall call the farmers to mourning and such as are skilled in lamentation to wailing.
17And in all vineyards there shall be wailing, for I will pass
through the midst of you, says the Lord.
18Woe to you who desire the day of the Lord! Why would you
want the day of the Lord? It is darkness, and not light;
19As if a man should flee from a lion, and a bear met him; or
went into the house and leaned with his hand against the wall, and
a serpent bit him.
20Shall not the day of the Lord be darkness, and not light? Even
very dark with no brightness in it?
21I hate, I despise your feasts, and I will not smell a savor *or* take
delight in your solemn assemblies.
22Though you offer Me burnt offerings and your cereal offerings, I will not accept them; neither will I look upon the peace *or*
thank offerings of your fatted beasts.
23Take away from Me the noise of your songs; for I will not
listen to the melody of your harps.
24But let justice run down like waters, and righteousness as a
mighty *and* everflowing stream.
25Did you bring to Me sacrifices and cereal offerings during
those forty years in the wilderness, O house of Israel?
26[No,] but [instead of bringing Me the appointed sacrifices]
you carried about the tent of your king Sakkuth and Kaiwan
[names for the planet Saturn], your images *of* your star-god, which
you made for yourselves [and you will do so again].

## New American Standard

9 It is He who flashes forth *with* destruction upon the strong,
So that destruction comes upon the fortress.

10¶ They hate him who reproves in the gate,
And they abhor him who speaks *with* integrity.
11 Therefore, because you impose heavy rent on the poor
And exact a tribute of grain from them,
*Though* you have built houses of well-hewn stone,
Yet you will not live in them;
You have planted pleasant vineyards, yet you will not drink their wine.
12 For I know your transgressions are many and your sins are great,
*You* who distress the righteous *and* accept bribes,
And turn aside the poor in the gate.
13 Therefore, at such a time the prudent person keeps silent, for it is an evil time.

14¶ Seek good and not evil, that you may live;
And thus may the LORD God of hosts be with you,
Just as you have said!
15 Hate evil, love good,
And establish justice in the gate!
Perhaps the LORD God of hosts
May be gracious to the remnant of Joseph.

16¶ Therefore, thus says the LORD God of hosts, the Lord,
"There is wailing in all the plazas,
And in all the streets they say, 'Alas! Alas!'
They also call the farmer to mourning
And professional mourners to lamentation.
17 "And in all the vineyards *there is* wailing,
Because I shall pass through the midst of you," says the LORD.

18¶ Alas, you who are longing for the day of the LORD,
For what purpose *will* the day of the LORD *be* to you?
It *will be* darkness and not light;
19 As when a man flees from a lion,
And a bear meets him,
Or goes home, leans his hand against the wall,
And a snake bites him.
20 *Will* not the day of the LORD *be* darkness instead of light,
Even gloom with no brightness in it?

21¶ "I hate, I reject your festivals,
Nor do I delight in your solemn assemblies.
22 "Even though you offer up to Me burnt offerings and your grain offerings,
I will not accept *them;*
And I will not *even* look at the peace offerings of your fatlings.
23 "Take away from Me the noise of your songs;
I will not even listen to the sound of your harps.
24 "But let justice roll down like waters
And righteousness like an ever-flowing stream.

25¶ "Did you present Me with sacrifices and grain offerings in the wilderness for forty years, O house of Israel?
26 "You also carried along Sikkuth your king and Kiyyun, your images, the star of your gods which you made for yourselves.

## New International

9 he flashes destruction on the stronghold
and brings the fortified city to ruin),
10 you hate the one who reproves in court
and despise him who tells the truth.

11 You trample on the poor
and force him to give you grain.
Therefore, though you have built stone mansions,
you will not live in them;
though you have planted lush vineyards,
you will not drink their wine.
12 For I know how many are your offenses
and how great your sins.

You oppress the righteous and take bribes
and you deprive the poor of justice in the courts.
13 Therefore the prudent man keeps quiet in such times,
for the times are evil.

14 Seek good, not evil,
that you may live.
Then the LORD God Almighty will be with you,
just as you say he is.
15 Hate evil, love good;
maintain justice in the courts.
Perhaps the LORD God Almighty will have mercy
on the remnant of Joseph.

16 Therefore this is what the Lord, the LORD God Almighty, says:
"There will be wailing in all the streets
and cries of anguish in every public square.
The farmers will be summoned to weep
and the mourners to wail.
17 There will be wailing in all the vineyards,
for I will pass through your midst,"
says the LORD.

### *The Day of the LORD*

18 Woe to you who long
for the day of the LORD!
Why do you long for the day of the LORD?
That day will be darkness, not light.
19 It will be as though a man fled from a lion
only to meet a bear,
as though he entered his house
and rested his hand on the wall
only to have a snake bite him.
20 Will not the day of the LORD be darkness, not light—
pitch-dark, without a ray of brightness?

21 "I hate, I despise your religious feasts;
I cannot stand your assemblies.
22 Even though you bring me burnt offerings and grain offerings,
I will not accept them.
Though you bring choice fellowship offerings,[a]
I will have no regard for them.
23 Away with the noise of your songs!
I will not listen to the music of your harps.
24 But let justice roll on like a river,
righteousness like a never-failing stream!

25 "Did you bring me sacrifices and offerings
forty years in the desert, O house of Israel?
26 You have lifted up the shrine of your king,
the pedestal of your idols,
the star of your god[b]—
which you made for yourselves.

**NIV** [a] 22 Traditionally *peace offerings* [b] 26 Or *lifted up Sakkuth your king / and Kaiwan your idols, / your star-gods;* Septuagint *lifted up the shrine of Molech / and the star of your god Rephan, / their idols*

## King James

27 Therefore will I cause you to go into captivity beyond Damascus, saith the LORD, whose name *is* The God of hosts.

**6** WOE TO them *that are* at ease in Zion, and trust in the
mountain of Samaria, *which are* named chief of the nations,
to whom the house of Israel came!
2 Pass ye unto Calneh, and see; and from thence go ye to
Hamath the great: then go down to Gath of the Philistines: *be they*
better than these kingdoms? or their border greater than your
border?
3 Ye that put far away the evil day, and cause the seat of violence
to come near;
4 That lie upon beds of ivory, and stretch themselves upon their
couches, and eat the lambs out of the flock, and the calves out of
the midst of the stall;
5 That chant to the sound of the viol, *and* invent to themselves
instruments of music, like David;
6 That drink wine in bowls, and anoint themselves with the chief
ointments: but they are not grieved for the affliction of Joseph.
7 ¶ Therefore now shall they go captive with the first that go
captive, and the banquet of them that stretched themselves shall
be removed.
8 The Lord GOD hath sworn by himself, saith the LORD the God
of hosts, I abhor the excellency of Jacob, and hate his palaces:
therefore will I deliver up the city with all that is therein.
9 And it shall come to pass, if there remain ten men in one
house, that they shall die.
10 And a man's uncle shall take him up, and he that burneth
him, to bring out the bones out of the house, and shall say unto
him that *is* by the sides of the house, *Is there* yet *any* with thee? and
he shall say, No. Then shall he say, Hold thy tongue: for we may
not make mention of the name of the LORD.
11 For, behold, the LORD commandeth, and he will smite the
great house with breaches, and the little house with clefts.
12 ¶ Shall horses run upon the rock? will *one* plow *there* with
oxen? for ye have turned judgment into gall, and the fruit of
righteousness into hemlock:
13 Ye which rejoice in a thing of nought, which say, Have we not
taken to us horns by our own strength?
14 But, behold, I will raise up against you a nation, O house of
Israel, saith the LORD the God of hosts; and they shall afflict you
from the entering in of Hemath unto the river of the wilderness.

**7** THUS HATH the Lord GOD shown unto me; and, behold, he
formed grasshoppers in the beginning of the shooting up of
the latter growth; and, lo, *it was* the latter growth after the king's
mowings.

## Amplified

27 Therefore I will cause you to go into exile beyond Damascus,
says the Lord, whose name is the God of hosts. [Acts 7:42, 43.]

**6** WOE TO those who are at ease in Zion, and to those on the
mountain of Samaria who are careless *and* feel secure, the
notable men of the chief [because chosen by God] of the nations,
to whom the house of Israel come! [Luke 6:24, 25.]
2 Pass over to Calneh and see, and from there go to Hamath the
great *city* [north of Damascus]; then go down to Gath of the Philistines. Are they better than these [your] kingdoms? Or are their
boundaries greater than your boundaries,
3 O you who put far away the evil day [of punishment], yet
cause the sitting of violence [upon you] to come near?
4 Woe to those who lie upon beds of ivory and stretch themselves upon their couches, and eat the lambs out of the flock, and
the calves out of the midst of the stall;
5 Who sing idle songs to the sound of the harp, and invent for
themselves instruments of music, like David's; [I Chron. 23:5.]
6 Who drink wine in bowls, and anoint themselves with the
finest oils, but are not grieved *and* sick at heart over the affliction
*and* ruin of Joseph [Israel]! [Gen. 49:22, 23.]
7 Therefore now shall they go captive with the first who go into
exile, and the revelry *and* banqueting of those who stretch themselves shall be ended.
8 The Lord God has sworn by Himself, says the Lord, the God
of hosts: I abhor, reject *and* despise the pride *and* false, futile glory
of Jacob [Israel], and I hate his palaces *and* strongholds; and I will
deliver up the city [idol-worshiping Samaria] with all that is in it.
9 And it shall come to pass, if there remain ten men in one
house, that they shall die [by the pestilence that comes with war].
10 And when a man's uncle *or* kinsman, he who is to make a
burning to cremate *and* dispose [of his pestilence-infected body]
comes in to bring the bones out of the house, and shall say to
another still alive in the farthest parts of the house, Is there anyone
else with you? and he shall say, No; then shall the newcomer say,
Hush! Hold your [cursing] tongue! We dare not so mention the
name of the Lord [lest we invoke more punishment]. [I Sam.
31:12.]
11 For behold, the Lord commands, and He will smite the great
house into ruins and the little house into fragments.
12 Do horses run upon rocks? Do men plow the ocean with
oxen? But you have turned justice into the poison *of* gall and the
fruit of righteousness into [the bitterness of] wormwood—
13 You who rejoice in Lodebar *or* a thing of nought, who say,
Have we not by our own strength taken Kar-naim *or* horns [of
resistance] for ourselves?
14 For behold, I will raise up against you a nation, O house of
Israel, says the Lord, the God of hosts; and they shall afflict *and*
oppress you [to the entire limits of Israel] from the entrance of
Hamath to the brook of the Arabah.

**7** THUS THE Lord God showed me [Amos]: behold, He formed
locusts in the beginning of the shooting up of the second crop;
and lo, it was the second crop after the king's mowings.

## New American Standard

27"Therefore, I will make you go into exile beyond Damascus,"
says the LORD, whose name is the God of hosts.

*"Those at Ease in Zion"*

6 WOE TO those who are at ease in Zion,
And to those who *feel* secure in the mountain of Samaria,
The distinguished men of the foremost of nations,
To whom the house of Israel comes.
2 Go over to Calneh and look,
And go from there to Hamath the great,
Then go down to Gath of the Philistines.
Are they better than these kingdoms,
Or is their territory greater than yours?
3 Do you put off the day of calamity,
And would you bring near the seat of violence?
4¶ Those who recline on beds of ivory
And sprawl on their couches,
And eat lambs from the flock
And calves from the midst of the stall,
5 Who improvise to the sound of the harp,
*And* like David have composed songs for themselves,
6 Who drink wine from sacrificial bowls
While they anoint themselves with the finest of oils,
Yet they have not grieved over the ruin of Joseph.
7 Therefore, they will now go into exile at the head of the exiles,
And the sprawlers' banqueting will pass away.
8¶ The Lord GOD has sworn by Himself, the LORD God of hosts has declared:
"I loathe the arrogance of Jacob,
And I detest his citadels;
Therefore, I will deliver up *the* city and all it contains."
9And it will be, if ten men are left in one house, they will die.
10Then one's uncle, or his undertaker, will lift him up to carry
out *his* bones from the house, and he will say to the one who is
in the innermost part of the house, "Is anyone else with you?" And
that one will say, "No one." Then he will answer, "Keep quiet. For
the name of the LORD is not to be mentioned."
11For behold, the LORD is going to command that the great
house be smashed to pieces and the small house to fragments.
12¶ Do horses run on rocks?
Or does one plow them with oxen?
Yet you have turned justice into poison,
And the fruit of righteousness into [a]wormwood,
13 You who rejoice in [b]Lo-debar,
And say, "Have we not by our *own* strength taken [c]Karnaim for ourselves?"
14 "For behold, I am going to raise up a nation against you,
O house of Israel," declares the LORD God of hosts,
"And they will afflict you from the entrance of Hamath
To the brook of the Arabah.

*Warning Through Visions*

7 THUS THE Lord GOD showed me, and behold, He was forming a locust-swarm when the spring crop began to sprout. And behold, the spring crop *was* after the king's mowing.

NAS [a] I.e., bitterness [b] Lit., *a thing of nothing* [c] Lit., *a pair of horns*

## New International

27Therefore I will send you into exile beyond Damascus,"
says the LORD, whose name is God Almighty.

*Woe to the Complacent*

6 WOE TO you who are complacent in Zion,
and to you who feel secure on Mount Samaria,
you notable men of the foremost nation,
to whom the people of Israel come!
2Go to Calneh and look at it;
go from there to great Hamath,
and then go down to Gath in Philistia.
Are they better off than your two kingdoms?
Is their land larger than yours?
3You put off the evil day
and bring near a reign of terror.
4You lie on beds inlaid with ivory
and lounge on your couches.
You dine on choice lambs
and fattened calves.
5You strum away on your harps like David
and improvise on musical instruments.
6You drink wine by the bowlful
and use the finest lotions,
but you do not grieve over the ruin of Joseph.
7Therefore you will be among the first to go into exile;
your feasting and lounging will end.

*The LORD Abhors the Pride of Israel*

8The Sovereign LORD has sworn by himself—the LORD God Almighty declares:

"I abhor the pride of Jacob
and detest his fortresses;
I will deliver up the city
and everything in it."

9If ten men are left in one house, they too will die. 10And if a
relative who is to burn the bodies comes to carry them out of the
house and asks anyone still hiding there, "Is anyone with you?"
and he says, "No," then he will say, "Hush! We must not mention
the name of the LORD."

11For the LORD has given the command,
and he will smash the great house into pieces
and the small house into bits.

12Do horses run on the rocky crags?
Does one plow there with oxen?
But you have turned justice into poison
and the fruit of righteousness into bitterness—
13you who rejoice in the conquest of Lo Debar[d]
and say, "Did we not take Karnaim[e] by our own strength?"

14For the LORD God Almighty declares,
"I will stir up a nation against you, O house of Israel,
that will oppress you all the way
from Lebo[f] Hamath to the valley of the Arabah."

*Locusts, Fire and a Plumb Line*

7 THIS IS what the Sovereign LORD showed me: He was preparing swarms of locusts after the king's share had been
harvested and just as the second crop was coming up. 2When they

NIV [d] *13 Lo Debar* means *nothing.* [e] *13 Karnaim* means *horns; horn* here symbolizes strength. [f] *14* Or *from the entrance to*

## King James

2And it came to pass, *that* when they had made an end of eating the grass of the land, then I said, O Lord GOD, forgive, I beseech thee: by whom shall Jacob arise? for he *is* small.

3The LORD repented for this: It shall not be, saith the LORD.

4¶ Thus hath the Lord GOD shown unto me: and, behold, the Lord GOD called to contend by fire, and it devoured the great deep, and did eat up a part.

5Then said I, O Lord GOD, cease, I beseech thee: by whom shall Jacob arise? for he *is* small.

6The LORD repented for this: This also shall not be, saith the Lord GOD.

7¶ Thus he showed me: and, behold, the Lord stood upon a wall *made* by a plumbline, with a plumbline in his hand.

8And the LORD said unto me, Amos, what seest thou? And I said, A plumbline. Then said the Lord, Behold, I will set a plumbline in the midst of my people Israel: I will not again pass by them any more:

9And the high places of Isaac shall be desolate, and the sanctuaries of Israel shall be laid waste; and I will rise against the house of Jeroboam with the sword.

10¶ Then Amaziah the priest of Beth-el sent to Jeroboam king of Israel, saying, Amos hath conspired against thee in the midst of the house of Israel: the land is not able to bear all his words.

11For thus Amos saith, Jeroboam shall die by the sword, and Israel shall surely be led away captive out of their own land.

12Also Amaziah said unto Amos, O thou seer, go, flee thee away into the land of Judah, and there eat bread, and prophesy there:

13But prophesy not again any more at Beth-el: for it *is* the king's chapel, and it *is* the king's court.

14¶ Then answered Amos, and said to Amaziah, I *was* no prophet, neither *was* I a prophet's son; but I *was* an herdman, and a gatherer of sycamore fruit:

15And the LORD took me as I followed the flock, and the LORD said unto me, Go, prophesy unto my people Israel.

16¶ Now therefore hear thou the word of the LORD: Thou sayest, Prophesy not against Israel, and drop not *thy word* against the house of Isaac.

17Therefore thus saith the LORD; Thy wife shall be an harlot in the city, and thy sons and thy daughters shall fall by the sword, and thy land shall be divided by line; and thou shalt die in a polluted land: and Israel shall surely go into captivity forth of his land.

**8** THUS HATH the Lord GOD shown unto me: and behold a basket of summer fruit.

2And he said, Amos, what seest thou? And I said, A basket of summer fruit. Then said the LORD unto me, The end is come upon my people of Israel; I will not again pass by them any more.

3And the songs of the temple shall be howlings in that day, saith the Lord GOD: *there shall be* many dead bodies in every place; they shall cast *them* forth with silence.

4¶ Hear this, O ye that swallow up the needy, even to make the poor of the land to fail,

## Amplified

2And when [the locusts] had finished eating the plants of the land, then I said, O Lord God, forgive, I pray You. How can Jacob stand? For he is so small!

3The Lord relented *and* revoked this sentence: It shall not take place, said the Lord, *and* He was eased *and* comforted concerning it.

4Thus the Lord God showed me: behold, the Lord God called for punishment with fire, and it devoured the great deep, and would have eaten up the land.

5Then said I, O Lord God, cease, I pray You! How can Jacob stand? He is so little!

6The Lord relented *and* revoked this sentence: This also shall not be, said the Lord, *and* He was eased *and* comforted concerning it.

7Thus He showed me: behold, the Lord stood upon a wall with a plumb line, with a plumb line in His hand. [II Kings 21:13; Isa. 34:11.]

8And the Lord said to me, Amos, what do you see? And I said, A plumb line. Then said the Lord, Behold, I am setting a plumb line as a standard in the midst of My people Israel. I will not pass by *and* spare them any more [the door of mercy is shut].

9And the [idolatrous] high places of Isaac [Israel] shall be desolate, and the sanctuaries of Israel shall be laid waste; and I will rise with the sword against the house of King Jeroboam [who set up the golden calf shrines].

10Then Amaziah the priest of [the golden calf shrine at] Bethel sent to Jeroboam king of Israel, saying, Amos has conspired against you in the midst of the house of Israel; the land is not able to bear all his words. [I Kings 12:31, 32.]

11For thus Amos has said, Jeroboam shall die by the sword, and Israel shall surely be led away captive out of his land.

12Also Amaziah said to Amos, O you seer, go, flee back to [your own country] the land of Judah, and you may eat your bread and live from your profession as a prophet there [as I do here].

13But do not prophesy any more at Bethel, for it is the king's sanctuary and a seat of his kingdom. [Cf. Luke 10:10-12.]

14Then Amos said to Amaziah, I was no prophet [by profession]! Neither was I a prophet's son [and so a scholar; but I had my occupation]; I was a herdsman and a dresser of sycamore trees and a gatherer of sycamore figs.

15And the Lord took me as I followed the flock, and the Lord said to me, Go, prophesy to My people Israel.

16Now therefore listen to the word of the Lord: You say, Do not prophesy against Israel, and drop no statements not complimentary to the house of Isaac.

17Therefore thus says the Lord: Your wife shall be a harlot in the city, and your sons and your daughters shall fall by the sword, and your land shall be divided up by line; you yourself shall die in an unclean *and* defiled land; and Israel shall surely go forth out of his land into exile.

**8** THUS THE Lord God showed to me: behold, a basket of [ripe and therefore soon-to-perish] summer fruit.

2And He said, Amos, what do you see? And I said, A basket of summer fruit. Then said the Lord to me, The end has come upon My people Israel; I will not pass by *and* spare them any more.

3And the songs of the temple shall become wailings in that day, says the Lord God; the dead bodies shall be many; in every place they shall be cast forth in silence.

4Hear this, O you who would swallow up *and* trample down the needy, even to make the poor of the land to fail *and* come to an end,

## New American Standard

2And it came about, when it had finished eating the vegetation
of the land, that I said,
"Lord GOD, please pardon!
How can Jacob stand,
For he is small?"
3 The LORD changed His mind about this.
"It shall not be," said the LORD.
4¶ Thus the Lord GOD showed me, and behold, the Lord GOD
was calling to contend *with them* by fire, and it consumed the great
deep and began to consume the farm land.
5Then I said,
"Lord GOD, please stop!
How can Jacob stand, for he is small?"
6 The LORD changed His mind about this.
"This too shall not be," said the Lord GOD.
7¶ Thus He showed me, and behold, the Lord was standing by
a vertical wall, with a plumb line in His hand.
8And the LORD said to me, "What do you see, Amos?" And
I said, "A plumb line." Then the Lord said,
"Behold I am about to put a plumb line
In the midst of My people Israel.
I will spare them no longer.
9 "The high places of Isaac will be desolated
And the sanctuaries of Israel laid waste.
Then shall I rise up against the house of Jeroboam with
the sword."

*Amos Accused, Answers*

10¶ Then Amaziah, the priest of Bethel, sent *word* to Jeroboam,
king of Israel, saying, "Amos has conspired against you in the
midst of the house of Israel; the land is unable to endure all his
words.
11"For thus Amos says, 'Jeroboam will die by the sword and
Israel will certainly go from its land into exile.' "
12Then Amaziah said to Amos, "Go, you seer, flee away to the
land of Judah, and there eat bread and there do your prophesying!
13"But no longer prophesy at Bethel, for it is a sanctuary of the
king and a royal residence."
14¶ Then Amos answered and said to Amaziah, "I am not a
prophet, nor am I the son of a prophet; for I am a herdsman and
a grower of sycamore figs.
15"But the LORD took me from following the flock and the LORD
said to me, 'Go prophesy to My people Israel.'
16"And now hear the word of the LORD: you are saying, 'You
shall not prophesy against Israel nor shall you speak against the
house of Isaac.'
17"Therefore, thus says the LORD, 'Your wife will become a
harlot in the city, your sons and your daughters will fall by the
sword, your land will be parceled up by a *measuring* line, and you
yourself will die upon unclean soil. Moreover, Israel will certainly
go from its land into exile.' "

*Basket of Fruit and Israel's Captivity*

**8** THUS THE Lord GOD showed me, and behold, *there was* a
basket of summer fruit.
2And He said, "What do you see, Amos?" And I said, "A
basket of summer fruit." Then the LORD said to me, "The end has
come for My people Israel. I will spare them no longer.
3"The songs of the palace will turn to wailing in that day,"
declares the Lord GOD. "Many *will be* the corpses; in every place
they will cast them forth in silence."
4¶ Hear this, you who trample the needy, to do away with the
humble of the land,

## New International

had stripped the land clean, I cried out, "Sovereign LORD, forgive!
How can Jacob survive? He is so small!"
3So the LORD relented.
"This will not happen," the LORD said.
4This is what the Sovereign LORD showed me: The Sovereign
LORD was calling for judgment by fire; it dried up the great deep
and devoured the land. 5Then I cried out, "Sovereign LORD, I beg
you, stop! How can Jacob survive? He is so small!"
6So the LORD relented.
"This will not happen either," the Sovereign LORD said.

7This is what he showed me: The Lord was standing by a wall
that had been built true to plumb, with a plumb line in his hand.
8And the LORD asked me, "What do you see, Amos?"
"A plumb line," I replied.
Then the Lord said, "Look, I am setting a plumb line among my
people Israel; I will spare them no longer.

9"The high places of Isaac will be destroyed
and the sanctuaries of Israel will be ruined;
with my sword I will rise against the house of
Jeroboam."

*Amos and Amaziah*

10Then Amaziah the priest of Bethel sent a message to Jeroboam
king of Israel: "Amos is raising a conspiracy against you in the very
heart of Israel. The land cannot bear all his words. 11For this is
what Amos is saying:

" 'Jeroboam will die by the sword,
and Israel will surely go into exile,
away from their native land.' "

12Then Amaziah said to Amos, "Get out, you seer! Go back to
the land of Judah. Earn your bread there and do your prophesying
there. 13Don't prophesy anymore at Bethel, because this is the
king's sanctuary and the temple of the kingdom."
14Amos answered Amaziah, "I was neither a prophet nor a
prophet's son, but I was a shepherd, and I also took care of sycamore-fig trees. 15But the LORD took me from tending the flock and
said to me, 'Go, prophesy to my people Israel.' 16Now then, hear
the word of the LORD. You say,

" 'Do not prophesy against Israel,
and stop preaching against the house of Isaac.'

17"Therefore this is what the LORD says:

" 'Your wife will become a prostitute in the city,
and your sons and daughters will fall by the sword.
Your land will be measured and divided up,
and you yourself will die in a pagan[a] country.
And Israel will certainly go into exile,
away from their native land.' "

*A Basket of Ripe Fruit*

**8** THIS IS what the Sovereign LORD showed me: a basket of ripe
fruit. 2"What do you see, Amos?" he asked.
"A basket of ripe fruit," I answered.
Then the LORD said to me, "The time is ripe for my people
Israel; I will spare them no longer.
3"In that day," declares the Sovereign LORD, "the songs in the
temple will turn to wailing.[b] Many, many bodies—flung everywhere! Silence!"

4Hear this, you who trample the needy
and do away with the poor of the land,

NIV [a] 17 Hebrew *an unclean* [b] 3 Or *"the temple singers will wail*

## King James

5Saying, When will the new moon be gone, that we may sell corn? and the sabbath, that we may set forth wheat, making the ephah small, and the shekel great, and falsifying the balances by deceit?
6That we may buy the poor for silver, and the needy for a pair of shoes; *yea,* and sell the refuse of the wheat?
7The LORD hath sworn by the excellency of Jacob, Surely I will never forget any of their works.
8Shall not the land tremble for this, and every one mourn that dwelleth therein? and it shall rise up wholly as a flood; and it shall be cast out and drowned, as *by* the flood of Egypt.
9And it shall come to pass in that day, saith the Lord GOD, that I will cause the sun to go down at noon, and I will darken the earth in the clear day:
10And I will turn your feasts into mourning, and all your songs into lamentation; and I will bring up sackcloth upon all loins, and baldness upon every head; and I will make it as the mourning of an only *son,* and the end thereof as a bitter day.
11¶ Behold, the days come, saith the Lord GOD, that I will send a famine in the land, not a famine of bread, nor a thirst for water, but of hearing the words of the LORD:
12And they shall wander from sea to sea, and from the north even to the east, they shall run to and fro to seek the word of the LORD, and shall not find *it.*
13In that day shall the fair virgins and young men faint for thirst.
14They that swear by the sin of Samaria, and say, Thy god, O Dan, liveth; and, The manner of Beer-sheba liveth; even they shall fall, and never rise up again.

**9** I SAW the Lord standing upon the altar: and he said, Smite the lintel of the door, that the posts may shake: and cut them in the head, all of them; and I will slay the last of them with the sword: he that fleeth of them shall not flee away, and he that escapeth of them shall not be delivered.
2Though they dig into hell, thence shall mine hand take them; though they climb up to heaven, thence will I bring them down:
3And though they hide themselves in the top of Carmel, I will search and take them out thence; and though they be hid from my sight in the bottom of the sea, thence will I command the serpent, and he shall bite them:

## Amplified

5Saying, When will the new moon festival be past, that we may sell grain? And the sabbath, that we may offer wheat for sale, making the ephah *measure* small, and the shekel *measure* great, and falsifying the scales by deceit,
6That we may buy [into slavery] the poor for silver and the needy for a pair of sandals; yes, and sell the refuse of the wheat [as if it were good grade]?
7The Lord has sworn by [Himself Who is] the glory *and* pride of Jacob, Surely I will never forget any of their [rebellious] deeds.
8Shall not the land tremble on this account, and every one mourn who dwells in it? Yes, it shall all of it rise like the river [Nile], and it shall be tossed about and sink back again to normal level, as does the Nile of Egypt.
9And in that day, says the Lord God, I will cause the sun to go down at noon, and I will darken the earth in the broad daylight time. [Ezek. 32:7-10.]
10And I will turn your feasts into mourning, and all your songs into lamentation; and I will cause sackcloth to be put upon all loins, and baldness [for mourning] shall come on every head; and I will make it as the mourning for an only son, and the end of it as a bitter day.
11Behold, the days come, says the Lord God, that I will send a famine in the land, not a famine of bread, nor a thirst for water, but *a famine* for hearing the words of the Lord.
12And *the people* shall wander from sea to sea, and from the north even to the east, they shall run to and fro to seek the word of the Lord—inquiring for and requiring it [as one requires food]—but shall not find it.
13In that day shall the fair virgins and young men faint for thirst.
14Those who swear by Ashimah *or* the sin of Samaria, and say, By the life of your god [the golden calf], O Dan! and *swear,* By the life of the way of [idolatrous] Beersheba, they shall fall and rise no more.

**9** I SAW the Lord standing at the altar, and He said, Smite the tops of the pillars until the thresholds tremble, and shatter them on the heads of all of the people, and the remainder of them I will slay with the sword. He who flees of them shall not get away, and he who escapes of them shall not be delivered.
2Though they dig into Sheol [Hades, the dark abode of the gathered dead], from there shall My hand take them; though they climb up to Heaven [the abode of light] from there will I bring them down;
3And though they hide themselves on the top of *Mount* Carmel, from there I will search out and take them; and though they [try to] hide from My sight at the bottom of the sea, there I will command the serpent, and it shall bite them.

## New American Standard

5 saying,
"When will the new moon be over,
So that we may sell grain,
And the sabbath, that we may open the wheat *market*,
To make the bushel smaller and the shekel bigger,
And to cheat with dishonest scales,
6 So as to buy the helpless for money
And the needy for a pair of sandals,
And *that* we may sell the refuse of the wheat?"

7 The LORD has sworn by the pride of Jacob,
"Indeed, I will never forget any of their deeds.
8 "Because of this will not the land quake
And everyone who dwells in it mourn?
Indeed, all of it will rise up like the Nile,
And it will be tossed about,
And subside like the Nile of Egypt.
9 "And it will come about in that day," declares the Lord GOD,
"That I shall make the sun go down at noon
And make the earth dark in broad daylight.
10 "Then I shall turn your festivals into mourning
And all your songs into lamentation;
And I will bring sackcloth on everyone's loins
And baldness on every head.
And I will make it like *a time of* mourning for an only son,
And the end of it will be like a bitter day.

11 ¶ "Behold, days are coming," declares the Lord GOD,
"When I will send a famine on the land,
Not a famine for bread or a thirst for water,
But rather for hearing the words of the LORD.
12 "And people will stagger from sea to sea,
And from the north even to the east;
They will go to and fro to seek the word of the LORD,
But they will not find *it*.
13 "In that day the beautiful virgins
And the young men will faint from thirst.
14 "*As for* those who swear by the guilt of Samaria,
Who say, 'As your god lives, O Dan,'
And, 'As the way of Beersheba lives,'
They will fall and not rise again."

*God's Judgment Unavoidable*

9 I SAW the Lord standing beside the altar, and He said,
"Smite the capitals so that the thresholds will shake,
And break them on the heads of them all!
Then I will slay the rest of them with the sword;
They will not have a fugitive who will flee,
Or a refugee who will escape.
2 "Though they dig into Sheol,
From there shall My hand take them;
And though they ascend to heaven,
From there will I bring them down.
3 "And though they hide on the summit of Carmel,
I will search them out and take them from there;
And though they conceal themselves from My sight on the floor of the sea,
From there I will command the serpent and it will bite them.

## New International

5 saying,
"When will the New Moon be over
that we may sell grain,
and the Sabbath be ended
that we may market wheat?"—
skimping the measure,
boosting the price
and cheating with dishonest scales,
6 buying the poor with silver
and the needy for a pair of sandals,
selling even the sweepings with the wheat.

7 The LORD has sworn by the Pride of Jacob: "I will never forget
anything they have done.

8 "Will not the land tremble for this,
and all who live in it mourn?
The whole land will rise like the Nile;
it will be stirred up and then sink
like the river of Egypt.
9 "In that day," declares the Sovereign LORD,

"I will make the sun go down at noon
and darken the earth in broad daylight.
10 I will turn your religious feasts into mourning
and all your singing into weeping.
I will make all of you wear sackcloth
and shave your heads.
I will make that time like mourning for an only son
and the end of it like a bitter day.
11 "The days are coming," declares the Sovereign LORD,
"when I will send a famine through the land—
not a famine of food or a thirst for water,
but a famine of hearing the words of the LORD.
12 Men will stagger from sea to sea
and wander from north to east,
searching for the word of the LORD,
but they will not find it.
13 "In that day

"the lovely young women and strong young men
will faint because of thirst.
14 They who swear by the shame[a] of Samaria,
or say, 'As surely as your god lives, O Dan,'
or, 'As surely as the god[b] of Beersheba lives'—
they will fall,
never to rise again."

*Israel to Be Destroyed*

9 I SAW the Lord standing by the altar, and he said:

"Strike the tops of the pillars
so that the thresholds shake.
Bring them down on the heads of all the people;
those who are left I will kill with the sword.
Not one will get away,
none will escape.
2 Though they dig down to the depths of the grave,[c]
from there my hand will take them.
Though they climb up to the heavens,
from there I will bring them down.
3 Though they hide themselves on the top of Carmel,
there I will hunt them down and seize them.
Though they hide from me at the bottom of the sea,
there I will command the serpent to bite them.

NIV [a] 14 Or *by Ashima;* or *by the idol* [b] 14 Or *power* [c] 2 Hebrew *to Sheol*

## King James

4And though they go into captivity before their enemies, thence will I command the sword, and it shall slay them: and I will set mine eyes upon them for evil, and not for good.

5And the Lord GOD of hosts *is* he that toucheth the land, and it shall melt, and all that dwell therein shall mourn: and it shall rise up wholly like a flood; and shall be drowned, as *by* the flood of Egypt.

6 *It is* he that buildeth his stories in the heaven, and hath founded his troop in the earth; he that calleth for the waters of the sea, and poureth them out upon the face of the earth: The LORD *is* his name.

7 *Are* ye not as children of the Ethiopians unto me, O children of Israel? saith the LORD. Have not I brought up Israel out of the land of Egypt? and the Philistines from Caphtor, and the Syrians from Kir?

8Behold, the eyes of the Lord GOD *are* upon the sinful kingdom, and I will destroy it from off the face of the earth; saving that I will not utterly destroy the house of Jacob, saith the LORD.

9For, lo, I will command, and I will sift the house of Israel among all nations, like as *corn* is sifted in a sieve, yet shall not the least grain fall upon the earth.

10All the sinners of my people shall die by the sword, which say, The evil shall not overtake nor prevent us.

11¶ In that day will I raise up the tabernacle of David that is fallen, and close up the breaches thereof; and I will raise up his ruins, and I will build it as in the days of old:

12That they may possess the remnant of Edom, and of all the heathen, which are called by my name, saith the LORD that doeth this.

13Behold, the days come, saith the LORD, that the plowman shall overtake the reaper, and the treader of grapes him that soweth seed; and the mountains shall drop sweet wine, and all the hills shall melt.

14And I will bring again the captivity of my people of Israel, and they shall build the waste cities, and inhabit *them;* and they shall plant vineyards, and drink the wine thereof; they shall also make gardens, and eat the fruit of them.

15And I will plant them upon their land, and they shall no more be pulled up out of their land which I have given them, saith the LORD thy God.

## Amplified

4And though they go into captivity before their enemies, there will I command the sword, and it shall slay them, and I will set My eyes upon them for evil and not for good.

5The Lord God of hosts, it is He Who touches the earth and it melts, and all who dwell in it mourn; it shall rise like the *river* Nile, all of it, and it shall sink again like the Nile of Egypt.

6It is He Who builds His upper chambers in the heavens, and Who founds His vault over the earth; Who calls to the waters of the sea and pours them out on the face of the earth. The Lord is His name.

7You, [O degenerate children of Israel,] are *no more* to Me than these [despised] Cushites, says the Lord. I brought up Israel out of the land of Egypt, but have I not *also* brought the Philistines out of Caphtor and the Syrians from Kir?

8Behold, the eyes of the Lord God are upon the sinful kingdom [of Israel's ten tribes], and I will destroy it from the surface of the ground, except that I will not utterly destroy the house of Jacob, says the Lord.

9For, lo, I will command, and I will sift the house of Israel among all nations *and* cause it to move to and fro, like as grain is sifted in a sieve, yet shall not the least kernel fall upon the earth *and* be lost [from My sight]. [Lev. 26:33; Deut. 28:64; Hos. 9:17.]

10All the sinners of My people shall die by the sword, who say, The evil shall not overtake or meet [and assail] us.

11In that day will I raise up the tabernacle of David, the fallen hut *or* booth and close up its breaches, and I will raise up its ruins, and I will build it as in the days of old;

12That they may possess the remnant of Edom and of all the nations that are called by My name, says the Lord Who does this. [Acts 15:15-17.]

13Behold, the days are coming, says the Lord, that the plowman shall overtake the reaper, and the treader of grapes him who sows the seed; and the mountains shall drop sweet wine, and all the hills shall melt [that is, everything heretofore barren and unfruitful shall overflow with spiritual blessing]. [Lev. 26:5; Joel 3:18.]

14And I will bring back the exiles of My people, Israel, and they shall build the waste cities, and inhabit them; and they shall plant vineyards, and drink the grape juice from them; they shall also make gardens, and eat the fruit of them.

15And I will plant them upon their land, and they shall no more be torn up out of their land which I gave them, says the Lord your God.

## New American Standard

4 "And though they go into captivity before their enemies,
From there I will command the sword that it slay them,
And I will set My eyes against them for evil and not for good."

5¶ And the Lord GOD of hosts,
The One who touches the land so that it melts,
And all those who dwell in it mourn,
And all of it rises up like the Nile
And subsides like the Nile of Egypt;
6 The One who builds His upper chambers in the heavens,
And has founded His vaulted dome over the earth,
He who calls for the waters of the sea
And pours them out on the face of the earth,
The LORD is His name.

7 "Are you not as the sons of Ethiopia to Me,
O sons of Israel?" declares the LORD.
"Have I not brought up Israel from the land of Egypt,
And the Philistines from Caphtor and the Arameans from Kir?
8 "Behold, the eyes of the Lord GOD are on the sinful kingdom,
And I will destroy it from the face of the earth;
Nevertheless, I will not totally destroy the house of Jacob,"
Declares the LORD.
9 "For behold, I am commanding,
And I will shake the house of Israel among all nations
As *grain* is shaken in a sieve,
But not a kernel will fall to the ground.
10 "All the sinners of My people will die by the sword,
Those who say, 'The calamity will not overtake or confront us.'

*The Restoration of Israel*

11 "In that day I will raise up the fallen booth of David,
And wall up its breaches;
I will also raise up its ruins,
And rebuild it as in the days of old;
12 That they may possess the remnant of Edom
And all the nations who are called by My name,"
Declares the LORD who does this.

13¶ "Behold, days are coming," declares the LORD,
"When the plowman will overtake the reaper
And the treader of grapes him who sows seed;
When the mountains will drip sweet wine,
And all the hills will be dissolved.
14 "Also I will restore the captivity of My people Israel,
And they will rebuild the ruined cities and live *in them,*
They will also plant vineyards and drink their wine,
And make gardens and eat their fruit.
15 "I will also plant them on their land,
And they will not again be rooted out from their land
Which I have given them,"
Says the LORD your God.

## New International

4 Though they are driven into exile by their enemies,
there I will command the sword to slay them.
I will fix my eyes upon them
for evil and not for good."

5 The Lord, the LORD Almighty,
he who touches the earth and it melts,
and all who live in it mourn—
the whole land rises like the Nile,
then sinks like the river of Egypt—
6 he who builds his lofty palace[a] in the heavens
and sets its foundation[b] on the earth,
who calls for the waters of the sea
and pours them out over the face of the land—
the LORD is his name.

7 "Are not you Israelites
the same to me as the Cushites[c]?"
declares the LORD.
"Did I not bring Israel up from Egypt,
the Philistines from Caphtor[d]
and the Arameans from Kir?

8 "Surely the eyes of the Sovereign LORD
are on the sinful kingdom.
I will destroy it
from the face of the earth—
yet I will not totally destroy
the house of Jacob,"
declares the LORD.
9 "For I will give the command,
and I will shake the house of Israel
among all the nations
as grain is shaken in a sieve,
and not a pebble will reach the ground.
10 All the sinners among my people
will die by the sword,
all those who say,
'Disaster will not overtake or meet us.'

*Israel's Restoration*

11 "In that day I will restore
David's fallen tent.
I will repair its broken places,
restore its ruins,
and build it as it used to be,
12 so that they may possess the remnant of Edom
and all the nations that bear my name,[e]"
declares the LORD, who will do these things.

13 "The days are coming," declares the LORD,
"when the reaper will be overtaken by the plowman
and the planter by the one treading grapes.
New wine will drip from the mountains
and flow from all the hills.
14 I will bring back my exiled[f] people Israel;
they will rebuild the ruined cities and live in them.
They will plant vineyards and drink their wine;
they will make gardens and eat their fruit.
15 I will plant Israel in their own land,
never again to be uprooted
from the land I have given them,"
says the LORD your God.

**NIV** [a] 6 The meaning of the Hebrew for this phrase is uncertain. [b] 6 The meaning of the Hebrew for this word is uncertain. [c] 7 That is, people from the upper Nile region [d] 7 That is, Crete [e] 12 Hebrew; Septuagint *so that the remnant of men / and all the nations that bear my name may seek ⌊the Lord⌋* [f] 14 Or *will restore the fortunes of my*

## King James

# Obadiah

1 THE VISION of Obadiah. Thus saith the Lord GOD concerning
Edom; We have heard a rumour from the LORD, and an ambassador is sent among the heathen, Arise ye, and let us rise up against
her in battle.
2 Behold, I have made thee small among the heathen: thou art
greatly despised.
3 ¶ The pride of thine heart hath deceived thee, thou that dwellest in the clefts of the rock, whose habitation *is* high; that saith in
his heart, Who shall bring me down to the ground?
4 Though thou exalt *thyself* as the eagle, and though thou set thy
nest among the stars, thence will I bring thee down, saith the
LORD.
5 If thieves came to thee, if robbers by night, (how art thou cut
off!) would they not have stolen till they had enough? if the
grapegatherers came to thee, would they not leave *some* grapes?
6 How are *the things* of Esau searched out! *how* are his hidden
things sought up!
7 All the men of thy confederacy have brought thee *even* to the
border: the men that were at peace with thee have deceived thee,
*and* prevailed against thee; *they that eat* thy bread have laid a
wound under thee: *there is* none understanding in him.
8 Shall I not in that day, saith the LORD, even destroy the wise
*men* out of Edom, and understanding out of the mount of Esau?
9 And thy mighty *men*, O Teman, shall be dismayed, to the end
that every one of the mount of Esau may be cut off by slaughter.
10 ¶ For *thy* violence against thy brother Jacob shame shall cover
thee, and thou shalt be cut off for ever.
11 In the day that thou stoodest on the other side, in the day that
the strangers carried away captive his forces, and foreigners entered into his gates, and cast lots upon Jerusalem, even thou *wast*
as one of them.
12 But thou shouldest not have looked on the day of thy brother
in the day that he became a stranger; neither shouldest thou have
rejoiced over the children of Judah in the day of their destruction;
neither shouldest thou have spoken proudly in the day of distress.

## Amplified

THE BOOK OF

# Obadiah

1 THE VISION of Obadiah. Thus says the Lord God concerning
[a]Edom: We have heard tidings from the Lord, and an ambassador
is sent forth among the nations, *saying*, Arise, and let us rise up
against *Edom* to battle! [Ps. 137:7; Isa. 34:1-15; 63:1-6; Jer. 49:7-22.]
2 Behold, I will make you small among the nations, *Edom;* you
shall be despised exceedingly. [Ezek. 35.]
3 The pride of your heart has deceived you, you dweller in the
refuges of the rock [Petra, Edom's capital], whose habitation is
high, who says in his heart, Who can bring me down to the
ground?
4 Though you mount on high as the eagle, and though you set
your nest among the stars, I will bring you down from there, says
the Lord.
5 If thieves came to you, if robbers by night—how you are
brought to nothing!—would they not steal only enough for themselves? If grape gatherers came to you, would they not leave some
grapes for gleaning? [But this was done by God, not men.]
6 How are the things of Esau [Edom] searched out! How are his
hidden treasures sought out!
7 All the men of your confederacy—your allies—have brought
you on your way, even to the border; the men who were at peace
with you have deceived you and prevailed against you; they who
eat your bread have laid a snare under you. There is no understanding [in Edom, or] of it.
8 Will not I in that day, says the Lord, destroy the wise men out
of Edom, and understanding out of Mount Esau [Idumea, a mountainous region]?
9 And your mighty men, O Teman, shall be dismayed, to the
end that every one from Mount Esau will be cut off by slaughter.
10 For the violence you did against your brother Jacob, shame
shall cover you, and you shall be cut off for ever.
11 On the day that you stood aloof [from your brother Jacob], on
the day that strangers took captive his forces *and* carried off his
wealth, and foreigners entered into his gates and cast lots for
Jerusalem, you were even as one of them. [Amos 1:11, 12; Num.
20:18-20.]
12 But you should not have gloated over your brother's day, the
day when his misfortune came *and* he was made a stranger; you
should not have rejoiced over the sons of Judah in the day of their
ruin; you should not have spoken arrogantly in the day of *their*
distress.

**AMP** [a] Edom or Seir was the country southeast of Judah extending from the Dead Sea to the eastern arm of the Red Sea. It included the city of Petra. It was bounded on the north by Moab, and was populated by the descendants of Esau. Edom and Moab have a remarkably prominent place in prophecy as "the scene of the final destruction of Gentile world-power in the day of the Lord," as revealed in the accompanying Scripture references which are important to the full vivid picture of what lies ahead for the nations of the world.

## New American Standard

# Obadiah

*Edom Will Be Humbled*

1 THE VISION of Obadiah.
Thus says the Lord GOD concerning Edom—
We have heard a report from the LORD,
And an envoy has been sent among the nations saying,
"Arise and let us go against her for battle"—
2 "Behold, I will make you small among the nations;
You are greatly despised.
3 "The arrogance of your heart has deceived you,
You who live in the clefts of the rock,
In the loftiness of your dwelling place,
Who say in your heart,
'Who will bring me down to earth?'
4 "Though you build high like the eagle,
Though you set your nest among the stars,
From there I will bring you down," declares the LORD.
5 "If thieves came to you,
If robbers by night—
O how you will be ruined!—
Would they not steal *only* until they had enough?
If grape gatherers came to you,
Would they not leave *some* gleanings?
6 "O how Esau will be ransacked,
And his hidden treasures searched out!
7 "All the men allied with you
Will send you forth to the border,
And the men at peace with you
Will deceive you and overpower you.
*They who eat* your bread
Will set an ambush for you.
(There is no understanding in him.)
8 "Will I not on that day," declares the LORD,
"Destroy wise men from Edom
And understanding from the mountain of Esau?
9 "Then your mighty men will be dismayed, O Teman,
In order that everyone may be cut off from the
mountain of Esau by slaughter.

**10**¶ "Because of violence to your brother Jacob,
You will be covered *with* shame,
And you will be cut off forever.
11 "On the day that you stood aloof,
On the day that strangers carried off his wealth,
And foreigners entered his gate
And cast lots for Jerusalem—
You too were as one of them.
12 "Do not gloat over your brother's day,
The day of his misfortune.
And do not rejoice over the sons of Judah
In the day of their destruction;
Yes, do not boast
In the day of *their* distress.

## New International

# Obadiah

1 THE VISION of Obadiah.

This is what the Sovereign LORD says about Edom—
We have heard a message from the LORD:
An envoy was sent to the nations to say,
"Rise, and let us go against her for battle"—
2 "See, I will make you small among the nations;
you will be utterly despised.
3 The pride of your heart has deceived you,
you who live in the clefts of the rocks[b]
and make your home on the heights,
you who say to yourself,
'Who can bring me down to the ground?'
4 Though you soar like the eagle
and make your nest among the stars,
from there I will bring you down,"
declares the LORD.

5 "If thieves came to you,
if robbers in the night—
Oh, what a disaster awaits you—
would they not steal only as much as they wanted?
If grape pickers came to you,
would they not leave a few grapes?
6 But how Esau will be ransacked,
his hidden treasures pillaged!
7 All your allies will force you to the border;
your friends will deceive and overpower you;
those who eat your bread will set a trap for you,[c]
but you will not detect it.

8 "In that day," declares the LORD,
"will I not destroy the wise men of Edom,
men of understanding in the mountains of Esau?
9 Your warriors, O Teman, will be terrified,
and everyone in Esau's mountains
will be cut down in the slaughter.
10 Because of the violence against your brother Jacob,
you will be covered with shame;
you will be destroyed forever.
11 On the day you stood aloof
while strangers carried off his wealth
and foreigners entered his gates
and cast lots for Jerusalem,
you were like one of them.
12 You should not look down on your brother
in the day of his misfortune,
nor rejoice over the people of Judah
in the day of their destruction,
nor boast so much
in the day of their trouble.

**NIV** [b] 3 Or *of Sela* [c] 7 The meaning of the Hebrew for this clause is uncertain.

## King James

13 Thou shouldest not have entered into the gate of my people in the day of their calamity; yea, thou shouldest not have looked on their affliction in the day of their calamity, nor have laid *hands* on their substance in the day of their calamity;

14 Neither shouldest thou have stood in the crossway, to cut off those of his that did escape; neither shouldest thou have delivered up those of his that did remain in the day of distress.

15 For the day of the LORD *is* near upon all the heathen: as thou hast done, it shall be done unto thee: thy reward shall return upon thine own head.

16 For as ye have drunk upon my holy mountain, *so* shall all the heathen drink continually, yea, they shall drink, and they shall swallow down, and they shall be as though they had not been.

17 ¶ But upon mount Zion shall be deliverance, and there shall be holiness; and the house of Jacob shall possess their possessions.

18 And the house of Jacob shall be a fire, and the house of Joseph a flame, and the house of Esau for stubble, and they shall kindle in them, and devour them; and there shall not be *any* remaining of the house of Esau; for the LORD hath spoken *it*.

19 And *they of* the south shall possess the mount of Esau; and *they of* the plain the Philistines: and they shall possess the fields of Ephraim, and the fields of Samaria: and Benjamin *shall possess* Gilead.

20 And the captivity of this host of the children of Israel *shall possess* that of the Canaanites, *even* unto Zarephath; and the captivity of Jerusalem, which *is* in Sepharad, shall possess the cities of the south.

21 And saviours shall come up on mount Zion to judge the mount of Esau; and the kingdom shall be the LORD'S.

## Amplified

13 You should not have entered the gate of My people in the day of their calamity *and* ruin; yes, you should not have looked *with delight* on their misery in the day of their calamity *and* ruin; and not have reached after their army *and* their possessions in the day of their calamity *and* ruin.

14 And you should not have stood at the crossway to cut off those of Judah who escaped, neither have delivered up those [of Judah] who remained in the day of distress.

15 For the day of the Lord is near upon all the nations. As you have done, it shall be done to you, your dealing will return upon your own head. [Isa. 2:10-22; Zeph. 3:8-20; Zech. 12:1-14; Rev. 19:11-21.]

16 For as you, [Edom,] have drunk upon the mountain of My holiness [desecrating it in the wild revelry of the destroyers], so shall all the nations drink continually [in turn, of My wrath]; yes, they shall drink, talk foolishly *and* swallow down [the full measure of punishment], and they shall be [destroyed] as though they had not been. [Rev. 16:14-16.]

17 But on Mount Zion [in Jerusalem] there shall be deliverance, *for* those who escape, and it shall be holy; and the house of Jacob shall possess their *own* [former] possessions. [Joel 2:32; Ezek. 36.]

18 The house of Jacob shall be a fire and the house of Joseph a flame, but the house of Esau shall be stubble; they shall kindle *and* burn them and consume them, and there shall be no survivor of the house of Esau, for the Lord has spoken it. [Ezek. 25:12-14.]

19 They of the South—the Negeb—shall possess Mount Esau, and they of the lowland the land of the Philistines; they shall possess the land of Ephraim and the fields of Samaria, and Benjamin shall possess Gilead [across the Jordan River]. [Amos 9:12; Zeph. 2:7.]

20 And the exiles of this host of the children of Israel who *are among the* Canaanites shall possess [Phoenicia] as far as Zarephath, and the exiles of Jerusalem who are in Sepharad shall possess the cities of the South—the Negev.

21 And deliverers shall go up on Mount Zion to rule *and* judge Mount Esau, and the kingdom *and* the kingship shall be the Lord's. [Mal. 1:2-5; Zech. 12:8, 9; Matt. 24:27-30; Luke 1:31-33; Acts 15:14-17.]

## New American Standard

13 "Do not enter the gate of My people
In the day of their disaster.
Yes, you, do not gloat over their calamity
In the day of their disaster.
And do not loot their wealth
In the day of their disaster.
14 "And do not stand at the fork of the road
To cut down their fugitives;
And do not imprison their survivors
In the day of their distress.

*The Day of the* LORD *and the Future*

**15**¶ "For the day of the LORD draws near on all the nations.
As you have done, it will be done to you.
Your dealings will return on your own head.
16 "Because just as you drank on My holy mountain,
All the nations will drink continually.
They will drink and swallow,
And become as if they had never existed.
17 "But on Mount Zion there will be those who escape,
And it will be holy.
And the house of Jacob will possess their possessions.
18 "Then the house of Jacob will be a fire
And the house of Joseph a flame;
But the house of Esau *will be* as stubble.
And they will set them on fire and consume them,
So that there will be no survivor of the house of Esau,"
For the LORD has spoken.
19 Then *those of* the [a]Negev will possess the mountain of Esau,
And *those of* the [b]Shephelah the Philistine *plain;*
Also, they will possess the territory of Ephraim and the territory of Samaria,
And Benjamin *will possess* Gilead.
20 And the exiles of this host of the sons of Israel,
Who are *among* the Canaanites as far as Zarephath,
And the exiles of Jerusalem who are in Sepharad
Will possess the cities of the Negev.
21 The deliverers will ascend Mount Zion
To judge the mountain of Esau,
And the kingdom will be the LORD's.

NAS [a] I.e., South country [b] I.e., the foothills

## New International

13 You should not march through the gates of my people
in the day of their disaster,
nor look down on them in their calamity
in the day of their disaster,
nor seize their wealth
in the day of their disaster.
14 You should not wait at the crossroads
to cut down their fugitives,
nor hand over their survivors
in the day of their trouble.

15 "The day of the LORD is near
for all nations.
As you have done, it will be done to you;
your deeds will return upon your own head.
16 Just as you drank on my holy hill,
so all the nations will drink continually;
they will drink and drink
and be as if they had never been.
17 But on Mount Zion will be deliverance;
it will be holy,
and the house of Jacob
will possess its inheritance.
18 The house of Jacob will be a fire
and the house of Joseph a flame;
the house of Esau will be stubble,
and they will set it on fire and consume it.
There will be no survivors
from the house of Esau."

The LORD has spoken.

19 People from the Negev will occupy
the mountains of Esau,
and people from the foothills will possess
the land of the Philistines.
They will occupy the fields of Ephraim and Samaria,
and Benjamin will possess Gilead.
20 This company of Israelite exiles who are in Canaan
will possess ⌊the land⌋ as far as Zarephath;
the exiles from Jerusalem who are in Sepharad
will possess the towns of the Negev.
21 Deliverers will go up on[c] Mount Zion
to govern the mountains of Esau.
And the kingdom will be the LORD's.

NIV [c] *21* Or *from*

## King James

# Jonah

**1** NOW THE word of the LORD came unto Jonah the son of Amittai, saying,

2 Arise, go to Nineveh, that great city, and cry against it; for their wickedness is come up before me.

3 But Jonah rose up to flee unto Tarshish from the presence of the LORD, and went down to Joppa; and he found a ship going to Tarshish: so he paid the fare thereof, and went down into it, to go with them unto Tarshish from the presence of the LORD.

4 ¶ But the LORD sent out a great wind into the sea, and there was a mighty tempest in the sea, so that the ship was like to be broken.

5 Then the mariners were afraid, and cried every man unto his god, and cast forth the wares that *were* in the ship into the sea, to lighten *it* of them. But Jonah was gone down into the sides of the ship; and he lay, and was fast asleep.

6 So the shipmaster came to him, and said unto him, What meanest thou, O sleeper? arise, call upon thy God, if so be that God will think upon us, that we perish not.

7 And they said every one to his fellow, Come, and let us cast lots, that we may know for whose cause this evil *is* upon us. So they cast lots, and the lot fell upon Jonah.

8 Then said they unto him, Tell us, we pray thee, for whose cause this evil *is* upon us; What *is* thine occupation? and whence comest thou? what *is* thy country? and of what people *art* thou?

9 And he said unto them, I *am* an Hebrew; and I fear the LORD, the God of heaven, which hath made the sea and the dry *land*.

10 Then were the men exceedingly afraid, and said unto him, Why hast thou done this? For the men knew that he fled from the presence of the LORD, because he had told them.

11 ¶ Then said they unto him, What shall we do unto thee, that the sea may be calm unto us? for the sea wrought, and was tempestuous.

12 And he said unto them, Take me up, and cast me forth into the sea; so shall the sea be calm unto you: for I know that for my sake this great tempest *is* upon you.

13 Nevertheless the men rowed hard to bring *it* to the land; but they could not: for the sea wrought, and was tempestuous against them.

## Amplified

THE BOOK OF

# Jonah

**1** NOW THE word of the Lord came to [a]Jonah the son of Amittai, saying,

2 Arise, go to [b]Nineveh, that great city, and proclaim against it; for their wickedness has come up before Me. [Gen. 10:11, 12.]

3 But Jonah rose up to flee to Tarshish from being in the presence of the Lord [as His prophet], and went down to Joppa, and found a ship going to Tarshish [the most remote of the Phoenician trading places then known]. So he paid the appointed fare and went down into the ship, to go with them to Tarshish from being in the presence of the Lord [as His servant and minister]. [Gen. 4:16; Job 1:12; 2:7.]

4 But the Lord sent out a great wind upon the sea, and there was a violent tempest on the sea, so that the ship was about to be broken. [Ps. 104:4.]

5 Then the mariners were afraid, and each man cried to his god; and they cast the goods that were in the ship into the sea, to lighten it for them. But Jonah had gone down into the inner part of the ship and had lain down and was fast asleep.

6 So the captain came and said to him, What do you mean, you sleeper? Arise, call upon your God! Perhaps the God will give a thought to us, so that we shall not perish.

7 And they each said to one another, Come, let us cast lots, that we may know on whose account this evil has come upon us. So they cast lots, and the lot fell on Jonah.

8 Then they said to him, Tell us, we pray you, on whose account this evil has come upon us. What is your occupation? Where did you come from? And what is your country and nationality?

9 And he said to them, I am a Hebrew, and I reverently fear *and* worship the Lord, the God of heaven, Who made the sea and the dry land.

10 Then the men were exceedingly afraid and said to him, What is this that you have done? For the men knew that he fled from being in the presence of the Lord [as His prophet and servant], because he had told them.

11 Then they said to him, What shall we do to you, that the sea may subside *and* be calm for us? For the sea became more and more [violently] tempestuous.

12 And [Jonah] said to them, Take me up and cast me into the sea; so shall the sea become calm for you, for I know that it is because of me that this great tempest has come upon you.

13 Nevertheless the men rowed hard to bring the ship to the land, but they could not, for the sea became more and more violent against them.

**AMP** [a] That Jonah was a historical character and not fictional, is evidenced beyond question by the reference to him in II Kings 14:25: "[Jeroboam] restored the border of Israel . . . according to the word of the Lord . . . which He spoke by His servant Jonah the son of Amittai, the prophet, who was from Gath-hepher." [b] In spite of the fact that three times in the Old Testament (Gen. 10:11, 12; Jonah 1:2; 3:3) and once in the Apocrypha (Judith 1:1) Nineveh is called a "great city," skeptical Bible critics long believed the statement to be greatly exaggerated. When the walled city was excavated it was found to be less than nine miles in circumference. There were claims that the author, Jonah, did not know what he was talking about; but the real author, the Holy Spirit, was being overlooked. Later excavations have proved that Nineveh had many suburbs, three of which are mentioned in connection with it in Genesis 10:11, 12. One first century writer (Diodorus Siculus) justifiably says Nineveh was a quadrangle measuring about sixty miles in circuit. A "great city" indeed.

## New American Standard

# Jonah

*Jonah's Disobedience*

1 THE WORD of the LORD came to Jonah the son of Amittai
saying,
2"Arise, go to Nineveh the great city, and cry against it, for
their wickedness has come up before Me."
3But Jonah rose up to flee to Tarshish from the presence of the
LORD. So he went down to Joppa, found a ship which was going
to Tarshish, paid the fare, and went down into it to go with them
to Tarshish from the presence of the LORD.
4¶ And the LORD hurled a great wind on the sea and there was
a great storm on the sea so that the ship was about to break up.
5Then the sailors became afraid, and every man cried to his
god, and they threw the cargo which was in the ship into the sea
to lighten *it* for them. But Jonah had gone below into the hold of
the ship, lain down, and fallen sound asleep.
6So the captain approached him and said, "How is it that you
are sleeping? Get up, call on your god. Perhaps *your* god will be
concerned about us so that we will not perish."
7And each man said to his mate, "Come, let us cast lots so we
may learn on whose account this calamity *has struck* us." So they
cast lots and the lot fell on Jonah.
8Then they said to him, "Tell us, now! On whose account *has*
this calamity *struck* us? What is your occupation? And where do
you come from? What is your country? From what people are
you?"
9And he said to them, "I am a Hebrew, and I fear the LORD God
of heaven who made the sea and the dry land."
10¶ Then the men became extremely frightened and they said
to him, "How could you do this?" For the men knew that he was
fleeing from the presence of the LORD, because he had told them.
11So they said to him, "What should we do to you that the sea
may become calm for us?"—for the sea was becoming increasingly
stormy.
12And he said to them, "Pick me up and throw me into the sea.
Then the sea will become calm for you, for I know that on account
of me this great storm *has come* upon you."
13However, the men rowed *desperately* to return to land but they
could not, for the sea was becoming *even* stormier against them.

## New International

# Jonah

*Jonah Flees From the LORD*

1 THE WORD of the LORD came to Jonah son of Amittai: 2"Go
to the great city of Nineveh and preach against it, because its
wickedness has come up before me."
3But Jonah ran away from the LORD and headed for Tarshish.
He went down to Joppa, where he found a ship bound for that
port. After paying the fare, he went aboard and sailed for Tarshish
to flee from the LORD.
4Then the LORD sent a great wind on the sea, and such a violent
storm arose that the ship threatened to break up. 5All the sailors
were afraid and each cried out to his own god. And they threw the
cargo into the sea to lighten the ship.
But Jonah had gone below deck, where he lay down and fell
into a deep sleep. 6The captain went to him and said, "How can
you sleep? Get up and call on your god! Maybe he will take notice
of us, and we will not perish."
7Then the sailors said to each other, "Come, let us cast lots to
find out who is responsible for this calamity." They cast lots and
the lot fell on Jonah.
8So they asked him, "Tell us, who is responsible for making all
this trouble for us? What do you do? Where do you come from?
What is your country? From what people are you?"
9He answered, "I am a Hebrew and I worship the LORD, the
God of heaven, who made the sea and the land."
10This terrified them and they asked, "What have you done?"
(They knew he was running away from the LORD, because he had
already told them so.)
11The sea was getting rougher and rougher. So they asked him,
"What should we do to you to make the sea calm down for us?"
12"Pick me up and throw me into the sea," he replied, "and it
will become calm. I know that it is my fault that this great storm
has come upon you."
13Instead, the men did their best to row back to land. But they
could not, for the sea grew even wilder than before. 14Then they

## King James

14Wherefore they cried unto the LORD, and said, We beseech thee, O LORD, we beseech thee, let us not perish for this man's life, and lay not upon us innocent blood: for thou, O LORD, hast done as it pleased thee.
15So they took up Jonah, and cast him forth into the sea: and the sea ceased from her raging.
16Then the men feared the LORD exceedingly, and offered a sacrifice unto the LORD, and made vows.
17¶ Now the LORD had prepared a great fish to swallow up Jonah. And Jonah was in the belly of the fish three days and three nights.

**2** THEN JONAH prayed unto the LORD his God out of the fish's belly,
2And said, I cried by reason of mine affliction unto the LORD, and he heard me; out of the belly of hell cried I, *and* thou heardest my voice.
3For thou hadst cast me into the deep, in the midst of the seas; and the floods compassed me about: all thy billows and thy waves passed over me.
4Then I said, I am cast out of thy sight; yet I will look again toward thy holy temple.
5The waters compassed me about, *even* to the soul: the depth closed me round about, the weeds were wrapped about my head.
6I went down to the bottoms of the mountains; the earth with her bars *was* about me for ever: yet hast thou brought up my life from corruption, O LORD my God.
7When my soul fainted within me I remembered the LORD: and my prayer came in unto thee, into thine holy temple.
8They that observe lying vanities forsake their own mercy.
9But I will sacrifice unto thee with the voice of thanksgiving; I will pay *that* that I have vowed. Salvation *is* of the LORD.
10¶ And the LORD spake unto the fish, and it vomited out Jonah upon the dry *land*.

**3** AND THE word of the LORD came unto Jonah the second time, saying,
2Arise, go unto Nineveh, that great city, and preach unto it the preaching that I bid thee.
3So Jonah arose, and went unto Nineveh, according to the word of the LORD. Now Nineveh was an exceeding great city of three days' journey.
4And Jonah began to enter into the city a day's journey, and he cried, and said, Yet forty days, and Nineveh shall be overthrown.
5¶ So the people of Nineveh believed God, and proclaimed a fast, and put on sackcloth, from the greatest of them even to the least of them.

## Amplified

14Therefore they cried to the Lord, We beseech You, O Lord, we beseech You, let us not perish for this man's life, and lay not upon us innocent blood; for You, O Lord, have done as it pleased You.
15So they took up Jonah and cast him into the sea, and the sea ceased from its raging.
16Then the men reverently *and* worshipfully feared the Lord exceedingly, and they offered a sacrifice to the Lord and made vows.
17Now the Lord had prepared *and* appointed a great fish to swallow up Jonah. And Jonah was in the belly of the fish three days and three nights. [Matt. 12:40.]

**2** THEN JONAH prayed to the Lord his God from the fish's belly,
2And said, I cried out of my distress to the Lord, and He heard me; out of the belly of Sheol cried I, and You heard my voice. [Pss. 120:1; 130:1; 142:1; Lam. 3:55-58.]
3For You cast me into the deep, into the heart of the seas, and the floods surrounded me; all Your waves and Your billows passed over me. [Ps. 42:7.]
4Then I said, I am cast out of Your presence *and* Your sight; yet I will look again toward Your holy temple. [Ps. 31:22.]
5The waters compassed me about, even to [the extinction of] life; the abyss surrounded me, the sea-weeds were wrapped about my head. [Ps. 69:1; Lam. 3:54.]
6I went down to the bottoms *and* the very roots of the mountains; the earth with its bars closed behind me for ever. Yet You have brought up my life from the pit *and* corruption, O Lord my God.
7When my soul fainted upon me [crushing me] I earnestly *and* seriously remembered the Lord; and my prayer came to You, into Your holy temple.
8Those who pay regard to false, useless *and* worthless idols forsake their own [Source of] mercy *and* loving-kindness.
9But as for me, I will sacrifice to You with the voice of thanksgiving; I will pay that which I have vowed. Salvation *and* deliverance belong to the Lord!
10And the Lord spoke to the fish, and it vomited out Jonah upon the dry land.

**3** AND THE word of the Lord came to Jonah the second time, saying,
2Arise, go to Nineveh, that great city, and preach *and* cry out to it the preaching that I tell you.
3So Jonah arose and went to Nineveh, according to the word of the Lord. Now Nineveh was an exceedingly great city of three days' journey [sixty miles in circumference].
4And Jonah began to enter into the city a day's journey, and he cried, Yet forty days and Nineveh shall be overthrown!
5So the people of Nineveh believed in God, and proclaimed a fast, and put on sackcloth [in penitent mourning], from the greatest of them even to the least of them.

## New American Standard

14Then they called on the LORD and said, "We earnestly pray, O LORD, do not let us perish on account of this man's life and do not put innocent blood on us; for Thou, O LORD, hast done as Thou hast pleased."

15¶ So they picked up Jonah, threw him into the sea, and the sea stopped its raging.

16Then the men feared the LORD greatly, and they offered a sacrifice to the LORD and made vows.

17¶ And the LORD appointed a great fish to swallow Jonah, and Jonah was in the stomach of the fish three days and three nights.

*Jonah's Prayer*

**2** THEN JONAH prayed to the LORD his God from the stomach of the fish,
2and he said,
"I called out of my distress to the LORD,
And He answered me.
I cried for help from the depth of Sheol;
Thou didst hear my voice.
3 "For Thou hadst cast me into the deep,
Into the heart of the seas,
And the current engulfed me.
All Thy breakers and billows passed over me.
4 "So I said, 'I have been expelled from Thy sight.
Nevertheless I will look again toward Thy holy temple.'
5 "Water encompassed me to the point of death.
The great deep engulfed me,
Weeds were wrapped around my head.
6 "I descended to the roots of the mountains.
The earth with its bars *was* around me forever,
But Thou hast brought up my life from the pit, O LORD my God.
7 "While I was fainting away,
I remembered the LORD;
And my prayer came to Thee,
Into Thy holy temple.
8 "Those who regard vain idols
Forsake their faithfulness,
9 But I will sacrifice to Thee
With the voice of thanksgiving.
That which I have vowed I will pay.
Salvation is from the LORD."

10¶ Then the LORD commanded the fish, and it vomited Jonah up onto the dry land.

*Nineveh Repents*

**3** NOW THE word of the LORD came to Jonah the second time, saying,

2"Arise, go to Nineveh the great city and proclaim to it the proclamation which I am going to tell you."

3So Jonah arose and went to Nineveh according to the word of the LORD. Now Nineveh was [a]an exceedingly great city, a three days' walk.

4Then Jonah began to go through the city one day's walk; and he cried out and said, "Yet forty days and Nineveh will be overthrown."

5¶ Then the people of Nineveh believed in God; and they called a fast and put on sackcloth from the greatest to the least of them.

NAS [a] Lit., *a great city to God*

## New International

cried to the LORD, "O LORD, please do not let us die for taking this man's life. Do not hold us accountable for killing an innocent man, for you, O LORD, have done as you pleased." 15Then they took Jonah and threw him overboard, and the raging sea grew calm. 16At this the men greatly feared the LORD, and they offered a sacrifice to the LORD and made vows to him.

17But the LORD provided a great fish to swallow Jonah, and Jonah was inside the fish three days and three nights.

*Jonah's Prayer*

**2** FROM INSIDE the fish Jonah prayed to the LORD his God.
2He said:

"In my distress I called to the LORD,
and he answered me.
From the depths of the grave[b] I called for help,
and you listened to my cry.
3You hurled me into the deep,
into the very heart of the seas,
and the currents swirled about me;
all your waves and breakers
swept over me.
4I said, 'I have been banished
from your sight;
yet I will look again
toward your holy temple.'
5The engulfing waters threatened me,[c]
the deep surrounded me;
seaweed was wrapped around my head.
6To the roots of the mountains I sank down;
the earth beneath barred me in forever.
But you brought my life up from the pit,
O LORD my God.

7"When my life was ebbing away,
I remembered you, LORD,
and my prayer rose to you,
to your holy temple.

8"Those who cling to worthless idols
forfeit the grace that could be theirs.
9But I, with a song of thanksgiving,
will sacrifice to you.
What I have vowed I will make good.
Salvation comes from the LORD."

10And the LORD commanded the fish, and it vomited Jonah onto dry land.

*Jonah Goes to Nineveh*

**3** THEN THE word of the LORD came to Jonah a second time: 2"Go to the great city of Nineveh and proclaim to it the message I give you."

3Jonah obeyed the word of the LORD and went to Nineveh. Now Nineveh was a very important city—a visit required three days. 4On the first day, Jonah started into the city. He proclaimed: "Forty more days and Nineveh will be overturned." 5The Ninevites believed God. They declared a fast, and all of them, from the greatest to the least, put on sackcloth.

NIV [b] 2 Hebrew *Sheol* [c] 5 Or *waters were at my throat*

## King James

6For word came unto the king of Nineveh, and he arose from
his throne, and he laid his robe from him, and covered *him* with
sackcloth, and sat in ashes.
7And he caused *it* to be proclaimed and published through
Nineveh by the decree of the king and his nobles, saying, Let
neither man nor beast, herd nor flock, taste any thing: let them not
feed, nor drink water:
8But let man and beast be covered with sackcloth, and cry
mightily unto God: yea, let them turn every one from his evil way,
and from the violence that *is* in their hands.
9Who can tell *if* God will turn and repent, and turn away from
his fierce anger, that we perish not?
10¶ And God saw their works, that they turned from their evil
way; and God repented of the evil, that he had said that he would
do unto them; and he did *it* not.

4 BUT IT displeased Jonah exceedingly, and he was very angry.
2And he prayed unto the LORD, and said, I pray thee, O LORD,
*was* not this my saying, when I was yet in my country? Therefore
I fled before unto Tarshish: for I knew that thou *art* a gracious God,
and merciful, slow to anger, and of great kindness, and repentest
thee of the evil.
3Therefore now, O LORD, take, I beseech thee, my life from me;
for *it is* better for me to die than to live.
4¶ Then said the LORD, Doest thou well to be angry?
5So Jonah went out of the city, and sat on the east side of the
city, and there made him a booth, and sat under it in the shadow,
till he might see what would become of the city.
6And the LORD God prepared a gourd, and made *it* to come up
over Jonah, that it might be a shadow over his head, to deliver him
from his grief. So Jonah was exceeding glad of the gourd.
7But God prepared a worm when the morning rose the next
day, and it smote the gourd that it withered.
8And it came to pass, when the sun did arise, that God prepared
a vehement east wind; and the sun beat upon the head of Jonah,
that he fainted, and wished in himself to die, and said, *It is* better
for me to die than to live.
9And God said to Jonah, Doest thou well to be angry for the
gourd? And he said, I do well to be angry, *even* unto death.
10Then said the LORD, Thou hast had pity on the gourd, for the
which thou hast not laboured, neither madest it grow; which came
up in a night, and perished in a night:
11And should not I spare Nineveh, that great city, wherein are
more than sixscore thousand persons that cannot discern between
their right hand and their left hand; and *also* much cattle?

## Amplified

6For word came to the king of Nineveh [of all that had happened to Jonah, and his terrifying message from God], and he
arose from his throne, and he laid his robe aside, covered himself
with sackcloth, and sat in ashes.
7And he made proclamation and published through Nineveh,
By the decree of the king and his nobles: Let neither man nor beast,
herd nor flock, taste anything; let them not feed nor drink water.
8But let man and beast be covered with sackcloth, and let them
cry mightily to God. Yes, let every one turn from his evil way and
from the violence that is in his hands.
9Who can tell, God may turn and revoke His sentence against
us [when we have met His terms], and turn away from His fierce
anger, so that we perish not. [Joel 2:13, 14.]
10And God saw their works, that they turned from their evil
way; and God revoked His *sentence* of evil that He had said that
He would do to them, and He did not do it—for He was comforted
and eased concerning them.

4 BUT IT displeased Jonah exceedingly, and he was very angry.
2And he prayed to the Lord, and said, I pray You, O Lord,
is not this just what I said when I was still in my country? That is
why I fled to Tarshish; for I knew that You are a gracious God and
merciful, slow to anger and of great kindness, and [when sinners
turn to You and meet Your conditions] You revoke the [sentence
of] evil against them. [Exod. 34:6.]
3Therefore now, O Lord, I beseech You, take my life from me,
for it is better for me to die than to live.
4Then said the Lord, Do you do well to be angry?
5So Jonah went out of the city and sat to the east of the city, and
he made a booth there for himself. He sat there under it in the
shade till he might see what would become of the city.
6And the Lord God prepared a gourd, and made it to come up
over Jonah, that it might be a shade over his head, to deliver him
from his evil situation. So Jonah was exceedingly glad [to have the
protection] of the gourd.
7But God prepared a cutworm when the morning dawned the
next day, and it smote the gourd so that it withered.
8And when the sun arose, God prepared a sultry east wind, and
the sun beat upon the head of Jonah so that he fainted, and wished
in himself to die and said, It is better for me to die than to live.
9And God said to Jonah, Do you do well to be angry for the loss
of the gourd? And he said, I do well to be angry, angry enough
to die!
10Then said the Lord, You have had pity on the gourd, for
which you have not labored nor made it grow, which came up in
a night and perished in a night.
11And should not I spare Nineveh, that great city, in which
there are more than one hundred and twenty thousand persons
not [yet old enough to] know their right hand from their left, and
also many cattle [not accountable for sin]?

## New American Standard

6When the word reached the king of Nineveh, he arose from
his throne, laid aside his robe from him, covered *himself* with
sackcloth, and sat on the ashes.
7And he issued a proclamation and it said, "In Nineveh by the
decree of the king and his nobles: Do not let man, beast, herd, or
flock taste a thing. Do not let them eat or drink water.
8"But both man and beast must be covered with sackcloth; and
let men call on God earnestly that each may turn from his wicked
way and from the violence which is in his hands.
9"Who knows, God may turn and relent, and withdraw His
burning anger so that we shall not perish?"
10¶ When God saw their deeds, that they turned from their
wicked way, then God relented concerning the calamity which He
had declared He would bring upon them. And He did not do *it*.

*Jonah's Displeasure Rebuked*

4 BUT IT greatly displeased Jonah, and he became angry.
2And he prayed to the LORD and said, "Please LORD, was not
this what I said while I was still in my *own* country? Therefore, in
order to forestall this I fled to Tarshish, for I knew that Thou art
a gracious and compassionate God, slow to anger and abundant
in lovingkindness, and one who relents concerning calamity.
3"Therefore now, O LORD, please take my life from me, for
death is better to me than life."
4And the LORD said, "Do you have good reason to be angry?"
5¶ Then Jonah went out from the city and sat east of it. There
he made a shelter for himself and sat under it in the shade until
he could see what would happen in the city.
6So the LORD God appointed a plant and it grew up over Jonah
to be a shade over his head to deliver him from his discomfort. And
Jonah was extremely happy about the plant.
7But God appointed a worm when dawn came the next day,
and it attacked the plant and it withered.
8And it came about when the sun came up that God appointed
a scorching east wind, and the sun beat down on Jonah's head so
that he became faint and begged with *all* his soul to die, saying,
"Death is better to me than life."
9¶ Then God said to Jonah, "Do you have good reason to be
angry about the plant?" And he said, "I have good reason to be
angry, even to death."
10Then the LORD said, "You had compassion on the plant for
which you did not work, and *which* you did not cause to grow,
which came up overnight and perished overnight.
11"And should I not have compassion on Nineveh, the great
city in which there are more than 120,000 persons who do not
know *the difference* between their right and left hand, as well as
many animals?"

## New International

6When the news reached the king of Nineveh, he rose from his
throne, took off his royal robes, covered himself with sackcloth
and sat down in the dust. 7Then he issued a proclamation in
Nineveh:

"By the decree of the king and his nobles:

Do not let any man or beast, herd or flock, taste anything;
do not let them eat or drink. 8But let man and beast be covered
with sackcloth. Let everyone call urgently on God. Let them
give up their evil ways and their violence. 9Who knows? God
may yet relent and with compassion turn from his fierce anger
so that we will not perish."

10When God saw what they did and how they turned from their
evil ways, he had compassion and did not bring upon them the
destruction he had threatened.

*Jonah's Anger at the LORD's Compassion*

4 BUT JONAH was greatly displeased and became angry. 2He
prayed to the LORD, "O LORD, is this not what I said when
I was still at home? That is why I was so quick to flee to Tarshish.
I knew that you are a gracious and compassionate God, slow to
anger and abounding in love, a God who relents from sending
calamity. 3Now, O LORD, take away my life, for it is better for me
to die than to live."
4But the LORD replied, "Have you any right to be angry?"
5Jonah went out and sat down at a place east of the city. There
he made himself a shelter, sat in its shade and waited to see what
would happen to the city. 6Then the LORD God provided a vine
and made it grow up over Jonah to give shade for his head to ease
his discomfort, and Jonah was very happy about the vine. 7But at
dawn the next day God provided a worm, which chewed the vine
so that it withered. 8When the sun rose, God provided a scorching
east wind, and the sun blazed on Jonah's head so that he grew
faint. He wanted to die, and said, "It would be better for me to die
than to live."
9But God said to Jonah, "Do you have a right to be angry about
the vine?"
"I do," he said. "I am angry enough to die."
10But the LORD said, "You have been concerned about this vine,
though you did not tend it or make it grow. It sprang up overnight
and died overnight. 11But Nineveh has more than a hundred and
twenty thousand people who cannot tell their right hand from
their left, and many cattle as well. Should I not be concerned about
that great city?"

## King James

# Micah

1 THE WORD of the LORD that came to Micah the Morasthite
in the days of Jotham, Ahaz, *and* Hezekiah, kings of Judah,
which he saw concerning Samaria and Jerusalem.
2Hear, all ye people; hearken, O earth, and all that therein is:
and let the Lord GOD be witness against you, the Lord from his
holy temple.
3For, behold, the LORD cometh forth out of his place, and will
come down, and tread upon the high places of the earth.
4And the mountains shall be molten under him, and the valleys
shall be cleft, as wax before the fire, *and* as the waters *that are*
poured down a steep place.
5For the transgression of Jacob *is* all this, and for the sins of the
house of Israel. What *is* the transgression of Jacob? *is it* not Samaria? and what *are* the high places of Judah? *are they* not Jerusalem?
6Therefore I will make Samaria as an heap of the field, *and* as
plantings of a vineyard: and I will pour down the stones thereof
into the valley, and I will discover the foundations thereof.
7And all the graven images thereof shall be beaten to pieces,
and all the hires thereof shall be burned with the fire, and all the
idols thereof will I lay desolate: for she gathered *it* of the hire of
an harlot, and they shall return to the hire of an harlot.
8Therefore I will wail and howl, I will go stripped and naked:
I will make a wailing like the dragons, and mourning as the owls.
9For her wound *is* incurable; for it is come unto Judah; he is
come unto the gate of my people, *even* to Jerusalem.
10¶ Declare ye *it* not at Gath, weep ye not at all: in the house
of Aphrah roll thyself in the dust.

**AMP** [a] In his book *Syria and Palestine,* written in the Nineteenth Century, Van de Velde after visiting Sebaste or Samaria wrote: "Samaria, a heap of stones! Her foundations discovered, her streets plowed up and covered with corn fields and olive gardens. Samaria has been destroyed; her rubbish has been thrown down into the valley; her foundation stones lie scattered about on the slope of the hill." Yet through the inspiration of the omniscient and omnipotent God, Micah was able to foretell all this more than 2,000 years before as if he had seen it occur.

## Amplified

THE BOOK OF

# Micah

1 THE WORD of the Lord that came to Micah of Moresheth in
the days of Jotham, Ahaz, and Hezekiah, kings of Judah,
which he saw [through divine revelation] concerning Samaria and
Jerusalem.
2Hear, all you people; listen closely, O earth, and all that is in
it, and let the Lord God be witness among you *and* against you,
the Lord from His holy temple. [I Kings 22:28.]
3For, behold, the Lord comes forth out of His place, and will
come down and tread upon the high places of the earth. [Zech.
14:3, 4; Mal. 4:2, 3; Matt. 24:27-30; Rev. 1:7; 19:11-16.]
4And the mountains shall melt under Him and the valleys shall
be cleft like wax before the fire, like waters poured down a steep
place.
5All this is because of the transgression of Jacob and the sins of
the house of Israel. What is the transgression of Jacob? Is it not *the*
*idol worship of* Samaria? And what are the high places *of idolatry* in
Judah? Are they not Jerusalem?
6Therefore I will make Samaria a [a]heap in the open country, a
place for planting vineyards; and I will pour down into the ravine
her stones and lay bare her foundations. [Ezek. 13:14; II Kings
19:25.]
7And all her carved images shall be broken in pieces, and all her
hires [all that man would gain from desertion of God] shall be
burned with fire, and all her idols will be laid waste; for from the
hire of *one* harlot she gathered them, and to the hire of *another*
harlot they shall return.
8Therefore I [Micah] will lament and wail; I will go stripped and
[virtually] naked; I will make a wailing like the jackals, and a
lamentation like the ostriches.
9For *Samaria's* wounds are incurable, and they come even to
Judah; [He, the Lord,] has reached to the gate of my people, to
Jerusalem.
10In *Philistine* Gath announce it not; in Acco weep not at all,
[betraying your grief to foreigners; but among your own people]
in Beth-le-aphrah [dusthouse] roll yourself in the dust.

## New American Standard

# Micah

*Destruction in Israel and Judah*

**1** THE WORD of the LORD which came *to* Micah of Moresheth
in the days of Jotham, Ahaz, *and* Hezekiah, kings of Judah,
which he saw concerning Samaria and Jerusalem.

2 Hear, O peoples, all of you;
Listen, O earth and all it contains,
And let the Lord GOD be a witness against you,
The Lord from His holy temple.
3 For behold, the LORD is coming forth from His place.
He will come down and tread on the high places of the earth.
4 The mountains will melt under Him,
And the valleys will be split,
Like wax before the fire,
Like water poured down a steep place.
5 All this is for the rebellion of Jacob
And for the sins of the house of Israel.
What is the rebellion of Jacob?
Is it not Samaria?
What is the high place of Judah?
Is it not Jerusalem?
6 For I will make Samaria a heap of ruins in the open country,
Planting places for a vineyard.
I will pour her stones down into the valley,
And will lay bare her foundations.
7 All of her idols will be smashed,
All of her earnings will be burned with fire,
And all of her images I will make desolate,
For she collected *them* from a harlot's earnings,
And to the earnings of a harlot they will return.

8¶ Because of this I must lament and wail,
I must go barefoot and naked;
I must make a lament like the jackals
And a mourning like the ostriches.
9 For her wound is incurable,
For it has come to Judah;
It has reached the gate of my people,
*Even* to Jerusalem.
10 Tell it not in Gath,
Weep not at all.
At [b]Bethleaphrah roll yourself in the dust.

**NAS** [b] I.e., house of dust

## New International

# Micah

**1** THE WORD of the LORD that came to Micah of Moresheth
during the reigns of Jotham, Ahaz and Hezekiah, kings of
Judah—the vision he saw concerning Samaria and Jerusalem.

2 Hear, O peoples, all of you,
listen, O earth and all who are in it,
that the Sovereign LORD may witness against you,
the Lord from his holy temple.

*Judgment Against Samaria and Jerusalem*

3 Look! The LORD is coming from his dwelling place;
he comes down and treads the high places of the earth.
4 The mountains melt beneath him
and the valleys split apart,
like wax before the fire,
like water rushing down a slope.
5 All this is because of Jacob's transgression,
because of the sins of the house of Israel.
What is Jacob's transgression?
Is it not Samaria?
What is Judah's high place?
Is it not Jerusalem?

6 "Therefore I will make Samaria a heap of rubble,
a place for planting vineyards.
I will pour her stones into the valley
and lay bare her foundations.
7 All her idols will be broken to pieces;
all her temple gifts will be burned with fire;
I will destroy all her images.
Since she gathered her gifts from the wages of prostitutes,
as the wages of prostitutes they will again be used."

*Weeping and Mourning*

8 Because of this I will weep and wail;
I will go about barefoot and naked.
I will howl like a jackal
and moan like an owl.
9 For her wound is incurable;
it has come to Judah.
It[c] has reached the very gate of my people,
even to Jerusalem itself.
10 Tell it not in Gath[d];
weep not at all.[e]
In Beth Ophrah[f]
roll in the dust.

**NIV** [c] 9 Or *He* [d] 10 *Gath* sounds like the Hebrew for *tell.* [e] 10 Hebrew; Septuagint may suggest *not in Acco.* The Hebrew for *in Acco* sounds like the Hebrew for *weep.* [f] 10 *Beth Ophrah* means *house of dust.*

## King James

11Pass ye away, thou inhabitant of Saphir, having thy shame
naked: the inhabitant of Zaanan came not forth in the mourning
of Beth-ezel; he shall receive of you his standing.
12For the inhabitant of Maroth waited carefully for good: but
evil came down from the LORD unto the gate of Jerusalem.
13O thou inhabitant of Lachish, bind the chariot to the swift
beast: she *is* the beginning of the sin to the daughter of Zion: for
the transgressions of Israel were found in thee.
14Therefore shalt thou give presents to Moresheth-gath: the
houses of Achzib *shall be* a lie to the kings of Israel.
15Yet will I bring an heir unto thee, O inhabitant of Mareshah:
he shall come unto Adullam the glory of Israel.
16Make thee bald, and poll thee for thy delicate children; enlarge thy baldness as the eagle; for they are gone into captivity
from thee.

**2** WOE TO them that devise iniquity, and work evil upon their
beds! when the morning is light, they practice it, because it
is in the power of their hand.
2And they covet fields, and take *them* by violence; and houses,
and take *them* away: so they oppress a man and his house, even
a man and his heritage.
3Therefore thus saith the LORD; Behold, against this family do
I devise an evil, from which ye shall not remove your necks;
neither shall ye go haughtily: for this time *is* evil.
4¶ In that day shall *one* take up a parable against you, and lament
with a doleful lamentation, *and* say, We be utterly spoiled: he hath
changed the portion of my people: how hath he removed *it* from
me! turning away he hath divided our fields.
5Therefore thou shalt have none that shall cast a cord by lot in
the congregation of the LORD.
6 Prophesy ye not, *say they to them that* prophesy: they shall not
prophesy to them, *that* they shall not take shame.

## Amplified

11Pass on your way *into exile,* dwellers of Shaphir, in shameful
nakedness. The dwellers of Zaanan dare not come forth; the wailing of Bethezel takes away from you the place *on which it* stands.
12For the inhabitant of Maroth [bitterness] writhes in pain *at its
losses and* waits anxiously for good, because evil comes down from
the Lord to the gate of Jerusalem.
13Bind the chariot to the swift steed, O lady inhabitant of Lachish; *you were* the beginning of sin to the daughter of Zion, for the
transgressions of Israel were found in you.
14Therefore you must give parting gifts to Moresheth-gath
[Micah's home town]; the houses of Achzib [place of deceit] shall
be a deception to the kings of Israel.
15Yet will I bring a conqueror upon you, O lady inhabitant of
Mareshah, who shall possess you; the glory *and* nobility of Israel
shall come to Adullam [to hide in the caves, as did David]. [I Sam.
22:1.]
16Make yourself bald in mourning, and cut off your hair for the
children of your delight; enlarge your baldness as the eagle, for
*your children* shall be carried from you into exile.

**2** WOE TO those who devise iniquity and work out evil upon
their beds! When the morning is light, they perform *and*
practice it, because it is in their power.
2They covet fields and seize them, and houses, and take them
away; they oppress *and* crush a man and his house, a man and his
inheritance. [Isa. 5:8.]
3Therefore thus says the Lord: Behold, against this family I am
planning a disaster from which you cannot remove your necks; nor
will you be able to walk erect, for it will be an evil time.
4In that day shall they take up a (taunting) parable against you,
and wail with a doleful *and* bitter lamentation, and say, We are
utterly ruined *and* laid waste! *God* changes the portion of my
people. How He removes it from me! He divides our fields [to the
rebellious—our captors].
5Therefore you shall have no one to cast a line by lot upon a plot
[of ground] in the assembly of the Lord. [Rev. 21:27.]
6Do not preach, say the prophesying false prophets; one should
not babble *and* harp on such things; disgrace will not overtake us
[the reviling has no end].

## New American Standard

11 Go on your way, inhabitant of [a]Shaphir, in shameful nakedness.
The inhabitant of [b]Zaanan does not escape.
The lamentation of [c]Bethezel: "He will take from you its support."
12 For the inhabitant of [d]Maroth
Becomes weak waiting for good,
Because a calamity has come down from the LORD
To the gate of Jerusalem.
13 Harness the chariot to the team of horses,
O inhabitant of Lachish—
She was the beginning of sin
To the daughter of Zion—
Because in you were found
The rebellious acts of Israel.
14 Therefore, you will give parting gifts
On behalf of Moreshethgath;
The houses of Achzib *will* become a deception
To the kings of Israel.
15 Moreover, I will bring on you
The one who takes possession,
O inhabitant of [e]Mareshah.
The glory of Israel will enter Adullam.
16 Make yourself bald and cut off your hair,
Because of the children of your delight;
Extend your baldness like the eagle,
For they will go from you into exile.

*Woe to Oppressors*

2 WOE TO those who scheme iniquity,
Who work out evil on their beds!
When morning comes, they do it,
For it is in the power of their hands.
2 They covet fields and then seize *them*,
And houses, and take *them* away.
They rob a man and his house,
A man and his inheritance.
3 Therefore, thus says the LORD,
"Behold, I am planning against this family a calamity
From which you cannot remove your necks;
And you will not walk haughtily,
For it will be an evil time.
4 "On that day they will take up against you a taunt
And utter a bitter lamentation *and* say,
'We are completely destroyed!
He exchanges the portion of my people;
How He removes it from me!
To the apostate He apportions our fields.'
5 "Therefore, you will have no one stretching a measuring line
For you by lot in the assembly of the LORD.

6¶ 'Do not speak out,' *so* they speak out.
*But if* they do not speak out concerning these things,
Reproaches will not be turned back.

NAS [a] I.e., pleasantness [b] I.e., going out [c] I.e., house of removal [d] I.e., bitterness [e] I.e., possession

## New International

11 Pass on in nakedness and shame,
you who live in Shaphir.[f]
Those who live in Zaanan[g]
will not come out.
Beth Ezel is in mourning;
its protection is taken from you.
12 Those who live in Maroth[h] writhe in pain,
waiting for relief,
because disaster has come from the LORD,
even to the gate of Jerusalem.
13 You who live in Lachish,[i]
harness the team to the chariot.
You were the beginning of sin
to the Daughter of Zion,
for the transgressions of Israel
were found in you.
14 Therefore you will give parting gifts
to Moresheth Gath.
The town of Aczib[j] will prove deceptive
to the kings of Israel.
15 I will bring a conqueror against you
who live in Mareshah.[k]
He who is the glory of Israel
will come to Adullam.
16 Shave your heads in mourning
for the children in whom you delight;
make yourselves as bald as the vulture,
for they will go from you into exile.

*Man's Plans and God's*

2 WOE TO those who plan iniquity,
to those who plot evil on their beds!
At morning's light they carry it out
because it is in their power to do it.
2 They covet fields and seize them,
and houses, and take them.
They defraud a man of his home,
a fellowman of his inheritance.

3 Therefore, the LORD says:
"I am planning disaster against this people,
from which you cannot save yourselves.
You will no longer walk proudly,
for it will be a time of calamity.
4 In that day men will ridicule you;
they will taunt you with this mournful song:
'We are utterly ruined;
my people's possession is divided up.
He takes it from me!
He assigns our fields to traitors.'"
5 Therefore you will have no one in the assembly of the LORD
to divide the land by lot.

*False Prophets*

6 "Do not prophesy," their prophets say.
"Do not prophesy about these things;
disgrace will not overtake us."

NIV [f] 11 *Shaphir* means *pleasant*. [g] 11 *Zaanan* sounds like the Hebrew for *come out*. [h] 12 *Maroth* sounds like the Hebrew for *bitter*. [i] 13 *Lachish* sounds like the Hebrew for *team*. [j] 14 *Aczib* means *deception*. [k] 15 *Mareshah* sounds like the Hebrew for *conqueror*.

# King James

7¶ O *thou that art* named the house of Jacob, is the spirit of the LORD straitened? *are* these his doings? do not my words do good to him that walketh uprightly?

8Even of late my people is risen up as an enemy: ye pull off the robe with the garment from them that pass by securely as men averse from war.

9The women of my people have ye cast out from their pleasant houses; from their children have ye taken away my glory for ever.

10Arise ye, and depart; for this *is* not *your* rest: because it is polluted, it shall destroy *you*, even with a sore destruction.

11If a man walking in the spirit and falsehood do lie, *saying*, I will prophesy unto thee of wine and of strong drink; he shall even be the prophet of this people.

12¶ I will surely assemble, O Jacob, all of thee; I will surely gather the remnant of Israel; I will put them together as the sheep of Bozrah, as the flock in the midst of their fold: they shall make great noise by reason of *the multitude of* men.

13The breaker is come up before them: they have broken up, and have passed through the gate, and are gone out by it: and their king shall pass before them, and the LORD on the head of them.

**3** AND I said, Hear, I pray you, O heads of Jacob, and ye princes of the house of Israel; *Is it* not for you to know judgment?

2Who hate the good, and love the evil; who pluck off their skin from off them, and their flesh from off their bones;

3Who also eat the flesh of my people, and flay their skin from off them; and they break their bones, and chop them in pieces, as for the pot, and as flesh within the caldron.

4Then shall they cry unto the LORD, but he will not hear them: he will even hide his face from them at that time, as they have behaved themselves ill in their doings.

5¶ Thus saith the LORD concerning the prophets that make my people err, that bite with their teeth, and cry, Peace; and he that putteth not into their mouths, they even prepare war against him.

6Therefore night *shall be* unto you, that ye shall not have a vision; and it shall be dark unto you, that ye shall not divine; and the sun shall go down over the prophets, and the day shall be dark over them.

7Then shall the seers be ashamed, and the diviners confounded: yea, they shall all cover their lips; for *there is* no answer of God.

# Amplified

7O house of Jacob, shall it be said, Is the Spirit of the Lord straitened, impatient *and* shortened? Or are these [prophesied plagues] His doings? Do not My words do good to him who walks uprightly?

8But lately—yesterday—My people *have* stood up as an enemy [and have made Me their antagonist]. Off from the garment you strip the cloak of those who pass by in secure confidence of safety, *and* averse to war.

9The women of My people you cast out from their pleasant houses; from their young children you take away My glory for ever.

10Arise and depart, for this is not the rest [which was promised to the righteous in Canaan]; because of uncleanness that works destruction, and that a sharp *and* grievous destruction.

11If a man walking in a spirit [of vanity] and falsehood should lie and say, I will prophesy to you of wine and strong drink, O Israel, he would even be the acceptable prophet of this people! [Jer. 5:31.]

12I will surely gather all of you, O Jacob; I will surely collect the remnant of Israel; I will bring them [Israel] together as sheep in a fold, as a flock in the midst of their pasture. They [the fold and the pasture] shall swarm with men *and* hum with their much noise.

13The Breaker [the Messiah] will go up before them. They will break through, pass in through the gate and go out through it. And their King will pass on before them, the Lord at their head. [Amos 9:11; Hos. 3:5; Exod. 23:20, 21; 33:14; Isa. 63:8, 9.]

**3** AND I [Micah] said, Hear, I pray you, you heads of Jacob and rulers of the house of Israel! Is it not for you to know justice?

2You who hate the good and love the evil, who pluck *and* steal the skin from off *my people,* and their flesh from off their bones;

3Yes, those who eat the flesh of my people, and strip their skin from off them, and break their bones, and chop them in pieces as for the pot, like meat in a big kettle.

4Then will they cry to the Lord, but He will not answer them; He will even hide His face from them at that time, because they have made their deeds evil. [Isa. 1:15.]

5Thus says the Lord: Concerning the false prophets who make My people err, who when they have anything good to bite with their teeth cry, Peace; and whoever gives them nothing to chew, against him they declare a sanctified war.

6Therefore it shall be night to you, that you shall have no vision; yes, it shall be dark to you without divination; and the sun shall go down over the false prophets, and the day shall be black over them.

7And the seers shall be put to shame, and the diviners shall blush *and* be confounded; yes, they shall all cover their lips, for there is no answer from God.

## New American Standard

7 "Is it being said, O house of Jacob:
'Is the Spirit of the LORD impatient?
Are these His doings?'
Do not My words do good
To the one walking uprightly?
8 "Recently My people have arisen as an enemy—
You strip the robe off the garment,
From unsuspecting passers-by,
*From* those returned from war.
9 "The women of My people you evict,
Each *one* from her pleasant house.
From her children you take My splendor forever.
10 "Arise and go,
For this is no place of rest
Because of the uncleanness that brings on destruction,
A painful destruction.
11 "If a man walking after wind and falsehood
Had told lies *and said,*
'I will speak out to you concerning wine and liquor,'
He would be spokesman to this people.

12¶ "I will surely assemble all of you, Jacob,
I will surely gather the remnant of Israel.
I will put them together like sheep in the fold;
Like a flock in the midst of its pasture
They will be noisy with men.
13 "The breaker goes up before them;
They break out, pass through the gate, and go out by it.
So their king goes on before them,
And the LORD at their head."

*Rulers Denounced*

3 AND I said,
"Hear now, heads of Jacob
And rulers of the house of Israel.
Is it not for you to know justice?
2 "You who hate good and love evil,
Who tear off their skin from them
And their flesh from their bones,
3 And who eat the flesh of my people,
Strip off their skin from them,
Break their bones,
And chop *them* up as for the pot
And as meat in a kettle."
4 Then they will cry out to the LORD,
But He will not answer them.
Instead, He will hide His face from them at that time,
Because they have practiced evil deeds.

5¶ Thus says the LORD concerning the prophets
Who lead my people astray;
When they have *something* to bite with their teeth,
They cry, "Peace,"
But against him who puts nothing in their mouths,
They declare holy war.
6 Therefore *it will be* night for you—without vision,
And darkness for you—without divination.
The sun will go down on the prophets,
And the day will become dark over them.
7 The seers will be ashamed
And the diviners will be embarrassed.
Indeed, they will all cover *their* mouths
Because there is no answer from God.

## New International

7 Should it be said, O house of Jacob:
"Is the Spirit of the LORD angry?
Does he do such things?"

"Do not my words do good
to him whose ways are upright?
8 Lately my people have risen up
like an enemy.
You strip off the rich robe
from those who pass by without a care,
like men returning from battle.
9 You drive the women of my people
from their pleasant homes.
You take away my blessing
from their children forever.
10 Get up, go away!
For this is not your resting place,
because it is defiled,
it is ruined, beyond all remedy.
11 If a liar and deceiver comes and says,
'I will prophesy for you plenty of wine and beer,'
he would be just the prophet for this people!

*Deliverance Promised*

12 "I will surely gather all of you, O Jacob;
I will surely bring together the remnant of Israel.
I will bring them together like sheep in a pen,
like a flock in its pasture;
the place will throng with people.
13 One who breaks open the way will go up before them;
they will break through the gate and go out.
Their king will pass through before them,
the LORD at their head."

*Leaders and Prophets Rebuked*

3 THEN I said,
"Listen, you leaders of Jacob,
you rulers of the house of Israel.
Should you not know justice,
2 you who hate good and love evil;
who tear the skin from my people
and the flesh from their bones;
3 who eat my people's flesh,
strip off their skin
and break their bones in pieces;
who chop them up like meat for the pan,
like flesh for the pot?"
4 Then they will cry out to the LORD,
but he will not answer them.
At that time he will hide his face from them
because of the evil they have done.

5 This is what the LORD says:

"As for the prophets
who lead my people astray,
if one feeds them,
they proclaim 'peace';
if he does not,
they prepare to wage war against him.
6 Therefore night will come over you, without visions,
and darkness, without divination.
The sun will set for the prophets,
and the day will go dark for them.
7 The seers will be ashamed
and the diviners disgraced.
They will all cover their faces
because there is no answer from God."

## King James

8¶ But truly I am full of power by the spirit of the LORD, and of
judgment, and of might, to declare unto Jacob his transgression,
and to Israel his sin.
9Hear this, I pray you, ye heads of the house of Jacob, and
princes of the house of Israel, that abhor judgment, and pervert
all equity.
10They build up Zion with blood, and Jerusalem with iniquity.
11The heads thereof judge for reward, and the priests thereof
teach for hire, and the prophets thereof divine for money: yet will
they lean upon the LORD, and say, *Is* not the LORD among us? none
evil can come upon us.
12Therefore shall Zion for your sake be plowed *as* a field, and
Jerusalem shall become heaps, and the mountain of the house as
the high places of the forest.

4 BUT IN the last days it shall come to pass, *that* the mountain
of the house of the LORD shall be established in the top of the
mountains, and it shall be exalted above the hills; and people shall
flow unto it.
2And many nations shall come, and say, Come, and let us go
up to the mountain of the LORD, and to the house of the God of
Jacob; and he will teach us of his ways, and we will walk in his
paths: for the law shall go forth of Zion, and the word of the LORD
from Jerusalem.
3¶ And he shall judge among many people, and rebuke strong
nations afar off; and they shall beat their swords into plowshares,
and their spears into pruninghooks: nation shall not lift up a sword
against nation, neither shall they learn war any more.
4But they shall sit every man under his vine and under his fig
tree; and none shall make *them* afraid: for the mouth of the LORD
of hosts hath spoken *it*.
5For all people will walk every one in the name of his god, and
we will walk in the name of the LORD our God for ever and ever.
6In that day, saith the LORD, will I assemble her that halteth,
and I will gather her that is driven out, and her that I have afflicted;
7And I will make her that halted a remnant, and her that was
cast far off a strong nation: and the LORD shall reign over them in
mount Zion from henceforth, even for ever.
8¶ And thou, O tower of the flock, the strong hold of the
daughter of Zion, unto thee shall it come, even the first dominion;
the kingdom shall come to the daughter of Jerusalem.

## Amplified

8But truly I [Micah] am full of power, of the Spirit of the Lord,
and with justice and might, to declare to Jacob his transgression
and to Israel his sin.
9Hear this, I pray you, you heads of the house of Jacob and
rulers of the house of Israel, who abhor *and* reject justice and
pervert all equity,
10Who build up Zion with blood, and Jerusalem with iniquity.
11Its heads judge for reward *and* a bribe, and its priests teach
for hire, and its prophets divine for money; yet they lean on the
Lord, and say, Is not the Lord among us? No evil can come upon
us. [Isa. 1:10-15.]
12Therefore shall Zion on your account be [a]plowed as a field,
and Jerusalem shall become heaps *of ruins*, and the mountain of the
house [of the Lord] as the high places of a forest. [Jer. 26:17-19.]

4 BUT IN the latter days it shall come to pass, that the mountain
of the house of the Lord shall be established as the highest
of the mountains, and it shall be exalted above the hills, and
peoples shall flow to it.
2And many nations shall come, and say, Come, let us go up to
the mountain of the Lord, to the house of the God of Jacob; that
He may teach us His ways and we may walk in His paths. For the
law shall go forth out of Zion, and the word of the Lord from
Jerusalem.
3And He shall judge between many peoples, and shall decide
for strong nations afar off; and they shall beat their swords into
plowshares, and their spears into pruning hooks; nation shall not
lift up sword against nation, neither shall they learn war any more.
[Isa. 2:2-4; Joel 3:10.]
4But they shall sit every man under his vine and under his fig
tree, and none shall make them afraid; for the mouth of the Lord
of hosts has spoken it. [Zech. 3:10.]
5For all the peoples [now] walk every one in the name of his
god, but we will walk in the name of the Lord our God for ever
and ever.
6In that day, says the Lord, I will assemble the lame, and I will
gather those who have been driven away, and those whom I have
afflicted.
7And I will make the lame a remnant, and those who were cast
off, a strong nation; and the Lord shall reign over them in Mount
Zion from this time forth and for ever.
8And you, O tower of the flock, the hill *and* stronghold of the
daughter of Zion, unto you the former dominion shall come, the
kingdom of the daughter of Jerusalem.

**AMP** [a] In his book *The Land and the Book*, Dr. William Thomson wrote, "Mount Zion is now [Eighteenth Century] for the most part a rough field. From the tomb of David I passed on through the fields of ripe grain. It is the only part of Jerusalem that is now or ever has been plowed." When Sultan Suleiman the Magnificent rebuilt the walls of Jerusalem in 1542, the architect omitted Mount Zion, the city of David, from the area he enclosed, and strangely enough it was only partly built up again. How, except by divine inspiration, could Micah have foretold that this particular part of Jerusalem would be "plowed as a field"?

## New American Standard

8 On the other hand I am filled with power—
With the Spirit of the LORD—
And with justice and courage
To make known to Jacob his rebellious act,
Even to Israel his sin.
9 Now hear this, heads of the house of Jacob
And rulers of the house of Israel,
Who abhor justice
And twist everything that is straight,
10 Who build Zion with bloodshed
And Jerusalem with violent injustice.
11 Her leaders pronounce judgment for a bribe,
Her priests instruct for a price,
And her prophets divine for money.
Yet they lean on the LORD saying,
"Is not the LORD in our midst?
Calamity will not come upon us."
12 Therefore, on account of you,
Zion will be plowed as a field,
Jerusalem will become a heap of ruins,
And the mountain of the temple *will become* high places of a forest.

*Peaceful Latter Days*

4 AND IT will come about in the last days
That the mountain of the house of the LORD
Will be established as the chief of the mountains.
It will be raised above the hills,
And the peoples will stream to it.
2 And many nations will come and say,
"Come and let us go up to the mountain of the LORD
And to the house of the God of Jacob,
That He may teach us about His ways
And that we may walk in His paths."
For from Zion will go forth the law,
Even the word of the LORD from Jerusalem.
3 And He will judge between many peoples
And render decisions for mighty, distant nations.
Then they will hammer their swords into plowshares
And their spears into pruning hooks;
Nation will not lift up sword against nation,
And never again will they train for war.
4 And each of them will sit under his vine
And under his fig tree,
With no one to make *them* afraid,
For the mouth of the LORD of hosts has spoken.
5 Though all the peoples walk
Each in the name of his god,
As for us, we will walk
In the name of the LORD our God forever and ever.
6¶ "In that day," declares the LORD,
"I will assemble the lame,
And gather the outcasts,
Even those whom I have afflicted.
7 "I will make the lame a remnant,
And the outcasts a strong nation,
And the LORD will reign over them in Mount Zion
From now on and forever.
8 "And as for you, tower of the flock,
Hill of the daughter of Zion,
To you it will come—
Even the former dominion will come,
The kingdom of the daughter of Jerusalem.

## New International

8 But as for me, I am filled with power,
with the Spirit of the LORD,
and with justice and might,
to declare to Jacob his transgression,
to Israel his sin.
9 Hear this, you leaders of the house of Jacob,
you rulers of the house of Israel,
who despise justice
and distort all that is right;
10 who build Zion with bloodshed,
and Jerusalem with wickedness.
11 Her leaders judge for a bribe,
her priests teach for a price,
and her prophets tell fortunes for money.
Yet they lean upon the LORD and say,
"Is not the LORD among us?
No disaster will come upon us."
12 Therefore because of you,
Zion will be plowed like a field,
Jerusalem will become a heap of rubble,
the temple hill a mound overgrown with thickets.

*The Mountain of the LORD*

4 IN THE last days
the mountain of the LORD's temple will be established
as chief among the mountains;
it will be raised above the hills,
and peoples will stream to it.

2 Many nations will come and say,
"Come, let us go up to the mountain of the LORD,
to the house of the God of Jacob.
He will teach us his ways,
so that we may walk in his paths."
The law will go out from Zion,
the word of the LORD from Jerusalem.
3 He will judge between many peoples
and will settle disputes for strong nations far and wide.
They will beat their swords into plowshares
and their spears into pruning hooks.
Nation will not take up sword against nation,
nor will they train for war anymore.
4 Every man will sit under his own vine
and under his own fig tree,
and no one will make them afraid,
for the LORD Almighty has spoken.
5 All the nations may walk
in the name of their gods;
we will walk in the name of the LORD
our God for ever and ever.

*The LORD's Plan*

6 "In that day," declares the LORD,

"I will gather the lame;
I will assemble the exiles
and those I have brought to grief.
7 I will make the lame a remnant,
those driven away a strong nation.
The LORD will rule over them in Mount Zion
from that day and forever.
8 As for you, O watchtower of the flock,
O stronghold[b] of the Daughter of Zion,
the former dominion will be restored to you;
kingship will come to the Daughter of Jerusalem."

NIV [b] 8 Or *hill*

## King James

9 Now why dost thou cry out aloud? *is there* no king in thee? is thy counsellor perished? for pangs have taken thee as a woman in travail.

10 Be in pain, and labour to bring forth, O daughter of Zion, like a woman in travail: for now shalt thou go forth out of the city, and thou shalt dwell in the field, and thou shalt go *even* to Babylon; there shalt thou be delivered; there the LORD shall redeem thee from the hand of thine enemies.

11 ¶ Now also many nations are gathered against thee, that say, Let her be defiled, and let our eye look upon Zion.

12 But they know not the thoughts of the LORD, neither understand they his counsel: for he shall gather them as the sheaves into the floor.

13 Arise and thresh, O daughter of Zion: for I will make thine horn iron, and I will make thy hoofs brass: and thou shalt beat in pieces many people: and I will consecrate their gain unto the LORD, and their substance unto the Lord of the whole earth.

5 NOW GATHER thyself in troops, O daughter of troops: he hath laid siege against us: they shall smite the judge of Israel with a rod upon the cheek.

2 But thou, Bethlehem Ephratah, *though* thou be little among the thousands of Judah, *yet* out of thee shall he come forth unto me *that is* to be ruler in Israel; whose goings forth *have been* from of old, from everlasting.

3 Therefore will he give them up, until the time *that* she which travaileth hath brought forth: then the remnant of his brethren shall return unto the children of Israel.

4 ¶ And he shall stand and feed in the strength of the LORD, in the majesty of the name of the LORD his God; and they shall abide: for now shall he be great unto the ends of the earth.

5 And this *man* shall be the peace, when the Assyrian shall come into our land: and when he shall tread in our palaces, then shall we raise against him seven shepherds, and eight principal men.

6 And they shall waste the land of Assyria with the sword, and the land of Nimrod in the entrances thereof: thus shall he deliver *us* from the Assyrian, when he cometh into our land, and when he treadeth within our borders.

## Amplified

9 Now why do you cry aloud? Is there no king among you? Has your counselor perished, that pains have taken you like a woman in labor?

10 Writhe in pain, and labor to bring forth, O daughter of Zion, like a woman in childbirth; for now you shall go forth out of the city, and you shall live in the open country; you shall go to Babylon. There you shall be rescued; there the Lord shall redeem you from the hand of your enemies.

11 Now many nations are assembled against you, saying, Let her be profaned, and let our eye gaze upon Zion.

12 But they know not the thoughts of the Lord, neither do they understand His plan; for He shall gather them as the sheaves to the threshing floor.

13 Arise and thresh, O daughter of Zion! For I will make your horn iron, and I will make your hoofs bronze; you shall beat in pieces many peoples, and I will devote their gain to the Lord, and their treasure to the Lord of all the earth. [Zech. 12:1-8; 14:14.]

5 NOW GATHER yourself in troops, O daughter of troops; a state of siege has been placed against us; they shall smite the ruler of Israel with a rod—a scepter—on the cheek.

2 But you, Bethlehem Ephratah, you are little to be among the clans of Judah, *yet* out of you shall One come forth for Me Who is to be Ruler in Israel; Whose goings forth have been from of old, from ancient days—eternity. [Gen. 49:10; Matt. 2:5-12; John 7:42.]

3 Therefore shall He give them up, until the time that she who travails has brought forth; then what is left of His brethren shall return to the children of Israel.

4 And He shall stand and feed His flock in the strength of the Lord, in the majesty of the name of the Lord His God, and they shall dwell *secure,* for then shall He be great *even* to the ends of the earth. [Ps. 72:8; Isa. 52:13; Zech. 9:10; Luke 1:32, 33.]

5 And this shall be peace. When the Assyrian comes into our land and treads upon our soil *and* in our palaces, then will we raise against him seven shepherds and eight princes among men.

6 And they shall rule *and* waste the land of Assyria with the sword, and the land of Nimrod within her [Assyria's own] gates. Thus shall He, *the Messiah,* deliver us from Asshur [representing the opposing powers] when he [in His day] comes into our land and when he treads on our borders.

## New American Standard

9¶ "Now, why do you cry out loudly?
Is there no king among you,
Or has your counselor perished,
That agony has gripped you like a woman in childbirth?
10 "Writhe and labor to give birth,
Daughter of Zion,
Like a woman in childbirth,
For now you will go out of the city,
Dwell in the field,
And go to Babylon.
There you will be rescued;
There the LORD will redeem you
From the hand of your enemies.
11 "And now many nations have been assembled against you
Who say, 'Let her be polluted,
And let our eyes gloat over Zion.'
12 "But they do not know the thoughts of the LORD,
And they do not understand His purpose;
For He has gathered them like sheaves to the threshing floor.
13 "Arise and thresh, daughter of Zion,
For your horn I will make iron
And your hoofs I will make bronze,
That you may pulverize many peoples,
That you may devote to the LORD their unjust gain
And their wealth to the Lord of all the earth.

*Birth of the King in Bethlehem*

5 "NOW MUSTER yourselves in troops, daughter of troops;
They have laid siege against us;
With a rod they will smite the judge of Israel on the cheek.
2 "But as for you, Bethlehem Ephrathah,
*Too* little to be among the clans of Judah,
From you One will go forth for Me to be ruler in Israel.
His goings forth are from long ago,
From the days of eternity."
3 Therefore, He will give them *up* until the time
When she who is in labor has borne a child.
Then the remainder of His brethren
Will return to the sons of Israel.
4 And He will arise and shepherd *His flock*
In the strength of the LORD,
In the majesty of the name of the LORD His God.
And they will remain,
Because at that time He will be great
To the ends of the earth.
5 And this One will be *our* peace.
¶ When the Assyrian invades our land,
When he tramples on our citadels,
Then we will raise against him
Seven shepherds and eight leaders of men.
6 And they will shepherd the land of Assyria with the sword,
The land of Nimrod at its entrances;
And He will deliver *us* from the Assyrian
When he attacks our land
And when he tramples our territory.

## New International

9Why do you now cry aloud—
have you no king?
Has your counselor perished,
that pain seizes you like that of a woman in labor?
10Writhe in agony, O Daughter of Zion,
like a woman in labor,
for now you must leave the city
to camp in the open field.
You will go to Babylon;
there you will be rescued.
There the LORD will redeem you
out of the hand of your enemies.
11But now many nations
are gathered against you.
They say, "Let her be defiled,
let our eyes gloat over Zion!"
12But they do not know
the thoughts of the LORD;
they do not understand his plan,
he who gathers them like sheaves to the threshing floor.
13"Rise and thresh, O Daughter of Zion,
for I will give you horns of iron;
I will give you hoofs of bronze
and you will break to pieces many nations."

You will devote their ill-gotten gains to the LORD,
their wealth to the Lord of all the earth.

*A Promised Ruler From Bethlehem*

5 MARSHAL YOUR troops, O city of troops,[a]
for a siege is laid against us.
They will strike Israel's ruler
on the cheek with a rod.
2"But you, Bethlehem Ephrathah,
though you are small among the clans[b] of Judah,
out of you will come for me
one who will be ruler over Israel,
whose origins[c] are from of old,
from ancient times.[d]"
3Therefore Israel will be abandoned
until the time when she who is in labor gives birth
and the rest of his brothers return
to join the Israelites.
4He will stand and shepherd his flock
in the strength of the LORD,
in the majesty of the name of the LORD his God.
And they will live securely, for then his greatness
will reach to the ends of the earth.
5 And he will be their peace.

*Deliverance and Destruction*

When the Assyrian invades our land
and marches through our fortresses,
we will raise against him seven shepherds,
even eight leaders of men.
6They will rule[e] the land of Assyria with the sword,
the land of Nimrod with drawn sword.[f]
He will deliver us from the Assyrian
when he invades our land
and marches into our borders.

**NIV** [a] 1 Or *Strengthen your walls, O walled city* [b] 2 Or *rulers* [c] 2 Hebrew *goings out* [d] 2 Or *from days of eternity* [e] 6 Or *crush* [f] 6 Or *Nimrod in its gates*

# King James

7And the remnant of Jacob shall be in the midst of many people as a dew from the LORD, as the showers upon the grass, that tarrieth not for man, nor waiteth for the sons of men.

8¶ And the remnant of Jacob shall be among the Gentiles in the midst of many people as a lion among the beasts of the forest, as a young lion among the flocks of sheep: who, if he go through, both treadeth down, and teareth for pieces, and none can deliver.

9Thine hand shall be lifted up upon thine adversaries, and all thine enemies shall be cut off.

10And it shall come to pass in that day, saith the LORD, that I will cut off thy horses out of the midst of thee, and I will destroy thy chariots:

11And I will cut off the cities of thy land, and throw down all thy strong holds:

12And I will cut off witchcrafts out of thine hand; and thou shalt have no *more* soothsayers:

13Thy graven images also will I cut off, and thy standing images out of the midst of thee; and thou shalt no more worship the work of thine hands.

14And I will pluck up thy groves out of the midst of thee: so will I destroy thy cities.

15And I will execute vengeance in anger and fury upon the heathen, such as they have not heard.

**6** HEAR YE now what the LORD saith; Arise, contend thou before the mountains, and let the hills hear thy voice.

2Hear ye, O mountains, the LORD's controversy, and ye strong foundations of the earth: for the LORD hath a controversy with his people, and he will plead with Israel.

3O my people, what have I done unto thee? and wherein have I wearied thee? testify against me.

4For I brought thee up out of the land of Egypt, and redeemed thee out of the house of servants; and I sent before thee Moses, Aaron, and Miriam.

5O my people, remember now what Balak king of Moab consulted, and what Balaam the son of Beor answered him from Shittim unto Gilgal; that ye may know the righteousness of the LORD.

6¶ Wherewith shall I come before the LORD, *and* bow myself before the high God? shall I come before him with burnt offerings, with calves of a year old?

7Will the LORD be pleased with thousands of rams, *or* with ten thousands of rivers of oil? shall I give my firstborn *for* my transgression, the fruit of my body *for* the sin of my soul?

8He hath shown thee, O man, what *is* good; and what doth the LORD require of thee, but to do justly, and to love mercy, and to walk humbly with thy God?

# Amplified

7Then the remnant of Jacob shall be in the midst of many peoples like dew from the Lord, [suddenly] like showers upon the grass, which tarry not for man nor wait for the sons of men. [Ps. 72:6; 110:3.]

8And the remnant of Jacob shall be among the nations in the midst of many peoples like a lion among the beasts of the forest, like a young lion [suddenly] among the flocks of sheep, which, when it goes through, treads down and tears in pieces, and there is no deliverer.

9Your hand will be lifted up above your adversaries, and all your enemies shall be cut off.

10And in that day, says the Lord, I will cut off your horses [on which you depend] from among you and will destroy your chariots; [Ps. 20:7, 8; Zech. 9:10.]

11And I will cut off the cities of your land and throw down all your strongholds;

12And I will cut off witchcrafts *and* sorceries from your hand, and you shall have no more soothsayers;

13Your carved images also I will cut off and your statues *or* pillars out of your midst, and you shall no more worship the work of your hands;

14And I will root out your Asherim [symbols of a goddess Asherah], and I will destroy your cities [the seats of false worship]. [Deut. 16:21.]

15And in anger and wrath I will execute vengeance upon the nations which would not obey—vengeance such as they have not heard of before.

**6** HEAR NOW what the Lord says: Arise, contend *and* plead your case before the mountains, and let the hills hear your voice.

2Hear, O mountains, the Lord's controversy, and you strong *and* enduring foundations of the earth; for the Lord has a controversy—a pleading contention—with His people, and He will [pleadingly] contend with Israel.

3O My people, what have I done to you? And in what have I wearied you? Testify against Me—answer Me!

4For I brought you up out of the land of Egypt, and redeemed you out of the house *where you were* bondservants; and I sent before you Moses, Aaron, and Miriam.

5O My people, [earnestly] remember now what Balak king of Moab devised, and what Balaam the son of Beor answered him; *remember all they did* from Shittim to Gilgal, that you may know the righteous *and* saving acts of the Lord. [Num. 23:7-24; 24:3-24.]

6With what shall I come before the Lord, and bow myself before God on high? Shall I come before Him with burnt offerings, with calves a year old?

7Will the Lord be pleased with thousands of rams, or with ten thousands of rivers of oil? Shall I give my first-born for my transgression, the fruit of my body for the sin of my soul?

8He has showed you, O man, what is good; and what does the Lord require of you, but to do justly, and to love kindness *and* mercy, and to humble yourself *and* walk humbly with your God? [Deut. 10:12, 13.]

## New American Standard

7¶ Then the remnant of Jacob
Will be among many peoples
Like dew from the LORD,
Like showers on vegetation
Which do not wait for man
Or delay for the sons of men.
8 And the remnant of Jacob
Will be among the nations,
Among many peoples
Like a lion among the beasts of the forest,
Like a young lion among flocks of sheep,
Which, if he passes through,
Tramples down and tears,
And there is none to rescue.
9 Your hand will be lifted up against your adversaries,
And all your enemies will be cut off.

10¶ "And it will be in that day," declares the LORD,
"That I will cut off your horses from among you
And destroy your chariots.
11 "I will also cut off the cities of your land
And tear down all your fortifications.
12 "I will cut off sorceries from your hand,
And you will have fortunetellers no more.
13 "I will cut off your carved images
And your *sacred* pillars from among you,
So that you will no longer bow down
To the work of your hands.
14 "I will root out your Asherim from among you
And destroy your cities.
15 "And I will execute vengeance in anger and wrath
On the nations which have not obeyed."

*God's Indictment of His People*

6 HEAR NOW what the LORD is saying,
"Arise, plead your case before the mountains,
And let the hills hear your voice.
2 "Listen, you mountains, to the indictment of the LORD,
And you enduring foundations of the earth,
Because the LORD has a case against His people;
Even with Israel He will dispute.
3 "My people, what have I done to you,
And how have I wearied you? Answer Me.
4 "Indeed, I brought you up from the land of Egypt
And ransomed you from the house of slavery,
And I sent before you Moses, Aaron, and Miriam.
5 "My people, remember now
What Balak king of Moab counseled
And what Balaam son of Beor answered him,
*And* from Shittim to Gilgal,
In order that you might know the righteous acts of the LORD."

*What God Requires of Man*

6¶ With what shall I come to the LORD
And bow myself before the God on high?
Shall I come to Him with burnt offerings,
With yearling calves?
7 Does the LORD take delight in thousands of rams,
In ten thousand rivers of oil?
Shall I present my first-born *for* my rebellious acts,
The fruit of my body for the sin of my soul?
8 He has told you, O man, what is good;
And what does the LORD require of you
But to do justice, to love kindness,
And to walk humbly with your God?

## New International

7The remnant of Jacob will be
in the midst of many peoples
like dew from the LORD,
like showers on the grass,
which do not wait for man
or linger for mankind.
8The remnant of Jacob will be among the nations,
in the midst of many peoples,
like a lion among the beasts of the forest,
like a young lion among flocks of sheep,
which mauls and mangles as it goes,
and no one can rescue.
9Your hand will be lifted up in triumph over your enemies,
and all your foes will be destroyed.

10"In that day," declares the LORD,
"I will destroy your horses from among you
and demolish your chariots.
11I will destroy the cities of your land
and tear down all your strongholds.
12I will destroy your witchcraft
and you will no longer cast spells.
13I will destroy your carved images
and your sacred stones from among you;
you will no longer bow down
to the work of your hands.
14I will uproot from among you your Asherah poles[a]
and demolish your cities.
15I will take vengeance in anger and wrath
upon the nations that have not obeyed me."

*The LORD's Case Against Israel*

6 LISTEN TO what the LORD says:
"Stand up, plead your case before the mountains;
let the hills hear what you have to say.
2Hear, O mountains, the LORD's accusation;
listen, you everlasting foundations of the earth.
For the LORD has a case against his people;
he is lodging a charge against Israel.

3"My people, what have I done to you?
How have I burdened you? Answer me.
4I brought you up out of Egypt
and redeemed you from the land of slavery.
I sent Moses to lead you,
also Aaron and Miriam.
5My people, remember
what Balak king of Moab counseled
and what Balaam son of Beor answered.
Remember ⌞your journey⌟ from Shittim to Gilgal,
that you may know the righteous acts of the LORD."

6With what shall I come before the LORD
and bow down before the exalted God?
Shall I come before him with burnt offerings,
with calves a year old?
7Will the LORD be pleased with thousands of rams,
with ten thousand rivers of oil?
Shall I offer my firstborn for my transgression,
the fruit of my body for the sin of my soul?
8He has showed you, O man, what is good.
And what does the LORD require of you?
To act justly and to love mercy
and to walk humbly with your God.

NIV [a] *14* That is, symbols of the goddess Asherah

## King James

9The LORD'S voice crieth unto the city, and *the man of* wisdom shall see thy name: hear ye the rod, and who hath appointed it.

10¶ Are there yet the treasures of wickedness in the house of the wicked, and the scant measure *that is* abominable?

11Shall I count *them* pure with the wicked balances, and with the bag of deceitful weights?

12For the rich men thereof are full of violence, and the inhabitants thereof have spoken lies, and their tongue *is* deceitful in their mouth.

13Therefore also will I make *thee* sick in smiting thee, in making *thee* desolate because of thy sins.

14Thou shalt eat, but not be satisfied; and thy casting down *shall be* in the midst of thee; and thou shalt take hold, but shalt not deliver; and *that* which thou deliverest will I give up to the sword.

15Thou shalt sow, but thou shalt not reap; thou shalt tread the olives, but thou shalt not anoint thee with oil; and sweet wine, but shalt not drink wine.

16¶ For the statutes of Omri are kept, and all the works of the house of Ahab, and ye walk in their counsels; that I should make thee a desolation, and the inhabitants thereof an hissing: therefore ye shall bear the reproach of my people.

7 WOE IS me! for I am as when they have gathered the summer fruits, as the grapegleanings of the vintage: *there is* no cluster to eat: my soul desired the firstripe fruit.

2The good *man* is perished out of the earth: and *there is* none upright among men: they all lie in wait for blood; they hunt every man his brother with a net.

3¶ That they may do evil with both hands earnestly, the prince asketh, and the judge *asketh* for a reward; and the great *man*, he uttereth his mischievous desire: so they wrap it up.

4The best of them *is* as a brier: the most upright *is sharper* than a thorn hedge: the day of thy watchmen *and* thy visitation cometh; now shall be their perplexity.

5¶ Trust ye not in a friend, put ye not confidence in a guide: keep the doors of thy mouth from her that lieth in thy bosom.

6For the son dishonoureth the father, the daughter riseth up against her mother, the daughter-in-law against her mother-in-law; a man's enemies *are* the men of his own house.

7Therefore I will look unto the LORD; I will wait for the God of my salvation: my God will hear me.

## Amplified

9The voice of the Lord calls to [Jerusalem] the city, and *it is* sound wisdom to hear *and* fear Your name. Hear the rod and *Him* Who has appointed it.

10Are there not still treasures *gained by* wickedness in the house of the wicked, and [a false measure for grain] a scant measure that is abominable *and* accursed?

11Can I be pure *Myself* [and acquit the man] with wicked scales and with a bag of deceitful weights? [I Thess. 4:6.]

12For *the city's* rich men are full of violence, and her inhabitants have spoken lies, and their tongue is deceitful in their mouth.

13Therefore I have also smitten you with a deadly wound *and* made you sick, laying you desolate, waste *and* deserted because of your sins.

14You shall eat, but not be satisfied, and your emptiness *and* hunger shall remain in you; you shall carry away [goods and those you love], but fail to save them, and those you do deliver I will give to the sword.

15You shall sow, but not reap; you shall tread olives, but not anoint yourselves with oil; and you shall [extract the] grape juice, but not drink the wine.

16For the statutes of [idolatrous] Omri *you* have kept, and all the works of the house of [wicked] Ahab; and you walk in their counsels; that I may make you a desolation *and* an astonishment, and your *city's* inhabitants a hissing, and you shall bear the reproach *and* scorn of My people.

7 WOE IS me! For I am as when the summer fruits have been gathered, as when the vintage grapes have been gleaned, and there is no cluster to eat, no first-ripe fig for which my appetite craves.

2The godly man has perished from the earth, and there is none upright among men; they all lie in wait for blood; each hunts his brother with a net.

3Both their hands are put forth *and* are upon what is evil to do it diligently; the prince and the judge ask for a bribe, and the great man utters his evil desire. Thus they twist between them [the course of justice].

4The best of them is like a brier; the most upright *or* the straightest is as a thorn hedge. The day of your watchmen, even of *God's* judgment *and* your punishment is come; now shall be their perplexity *and* confusion.

5Trust not in a neighbor, put not confidence in a friend; keep the doors of your mouth from her who lies in your bosom. [Cf. Luke 12:51-53.]

6For the son dishonors the father, the daughter rises up against her mother, the daughter-in-law against her mother-in-law; a man's enemies are the men of his own house. [Matt. 10:21, 35, 36; Mark 13:12, 13.]

7But as for me, I will look to the Lord *and* [confident] in Him I will keep watch; I will wait with hope *and* expectancy for the God of my salvation; my God will hear me.

## New American Standard

9¶ The voice of the LORD will call to the city—
And it is sound wisdom to fear Thy name:
"Hear, O tribe. Who has appointed its time?
10 "Is there yet a man in the wicked house,
*Along with* treasures of wickedness,
And a short measure *that is* cursed?
11 "Can I justify wicked scales
And a bag of deceptive weights?
12 "For the rich men of *the* city are full of violence,
Her residents speak lies,
And their tongue is deceitful in their mouth.
13 "So also I will make *you* sick, striking you down,
Desolating *you* because of your sins.
14 "You will eat, but you will not be satisfied,
And your [a]vileness will be in your midst.
You will *try to* remove *for safekeeping*,
But you will not preserve *anything*,
And what you do preserve I will give to the sword.
15 "You will sow but you will not reap.
You will tread the olive but will not anoint yourself
with oil;
And the grapes, but you will not drink wine.
16 "The statutes of Omri
And all the works of the house of Ahab are observed;
And in their devices you walk.
Therefore, I will give you up for destruction
And your inhabitants for derision,
And you will bear the reproach of My people."

*The Prophet Acknowledges*

7 WOE IS me! For I am
Like the fruit pickers and the grape gatherers.
There is not a cluster of grapes to eat,
*Or* a first-ripe fig *which* I crave.
2 The godly person has perished from the land,
And there is no upright *person* among men.
All of them lie in wait for bloodshed;
Each of them hunts the other with a net.
3 Concerning evil, both hands do it well.
The prince asks, also the judge, for a bribe,
And a great man speaks the desire of his soul;
So they weave it together.
4 The best of them is like a briar,
The most upright like a thorn hedge.
The day when you post a watchman,
Your punishment will come.
Then their confusion will occur.
5 Do not trust in a neighbor;
Do not have confidence in a friend.
From her who lies in your bosom
Guard your lips.
6 For son treats father contemptuously,
Daughter rises up against her mother,
Daughter-in-law against her mother-in-law;
A man's enemies are the men of his own household.

*God Is the Source of Salvation and Light*

7¶ But as for me, I will watch expectantly for the LORD;
I will wait for the God of my salvation.
My God will hear me.

NAS [a] Or possibly, *garbage* or *excreta*

## New International

*Israel's Guilt and Punishment*

9 Listen! The LORD is calling to the city—
and to fear your name is wisdom—
"Heed the rod and the One who appointed it.[b]
10 Am I still to forget, O wicked house,
your ill-gotten treasures
and the short ephah,[c] which is accursed?
11 Shall I acquit a man with dishonest scales,
with a bag of false weights?
12 Her rich men are violent;
her people are liars
and their tongues speak deceitfully.
13 Therefore, I have begun to destroy you,
to ruin you because of your sins.
14 You will eat but not be satisfied;
your stomach will still be empty.[d]
You will store up but save nothing,
because what you save I will give to the sword.
15 You will plant but not harvest;
you will press olives but not use the oil on yourselves,
you will crush grapes but not drink the wine.
16 You have observed the statutes of Omri
and all the practices of Ahab's house,
and you have followed their traditions.
Therefore I will give you over to ruin
and your people to derision;
you will bear the scorn of the nations.[e]"

*Israel's Misery*

7 WHAT MISERY is mine!
I am like one who gathers summer fruit
at the gleaning of the vineyard;
there is no cluster of grapes to eat,
none of the early figs that I crave.
2 The godly have been swept from the land;
not one upright man remains.
All men lie in wait to shed blood;
each hunts his brother with a net.
3 Both hands are skilled in doing evil;
the ruler demands gifts,
the judge accepts bribes,
the powerful dictate what they desire—
they all conspire together.
4 The best of them is like a brier,
the most upright worse than a thorn hedge.
The day of your watchmen has come,
the day God visits you.
Now is the time of their confusion.
5 Do not trust a neighbor;
put no confidence in a friend.
Even with her who lies in your embrace
be careful of your words.
6 For a son dishonors his father,
a daughter rises up against her mother,
a daughter-in-law against her mother-in-law—
a man's enemies are the members of his own
household.

7 But as for me, I watch in hope for the LORD,
I wait for God my Savior;
my God will hear me.

NIV [b] *9* The meaning of the Hebrew for this line is uncertain. [c] *10* An ephah was a dry measure. [d] *14* The meaning of the Hebrew for this word is uncertain. [e] *16* Septuagint; Hebrew *scorn due my people*

## King James

8¶ Rejoice not against me, O mine enemy: when I fall, I shall
arise; when I sit in darkness, the LORD *shall be* a light unto me.
9I will bear the indignation of the LORD, because I have sinned
against him, until he plead my cause, and execute judgment for
me: he will bring me forth to the light, *and* I shall behold his
righteousness.
10Then *she that is* mine enemy shall see *it*, and shame shall cover
her which said unto me, Where is the LORD thy God? mine eyes
shall behold her: now shall she be trodden down as the mire of the
streets.
11 *In* the day that thy walls are to be built, *in* that day shall the
decree be far removed.
12 *In* that day *also* he shall come even to thee from Assyria, and
*from* the fortified cities, and from the fortress even to the river, and
from sea to sea, and *from* mountain to mountain.
13Notwithstanding the land shall be desolate because of them
that dwell therein, for the fruit of their doings.
14¶ Feed thy people with thy rod, the flock of thine heritage,
which dwell solitarily *in* the wood, in the midst of Carmel: let them
feed *in* Bashan and Gilead, as in the days of old.
15According to the days of thy coming out of the land of Egypt
will I show unto him marvellous *things*.
16¶ The nations shall see and be confounded at all their might:
they shall lay *their* hand upon *their* mouth, their ears shall be deaf.
17They shall lick the dust like a serpent, they shall move out of
their holes like worms of the earth: they shall be afraid of the LORD
our God, and shall fear because of thee.
18Who *is* a God like unto thee, that pardoneth iniquity, and
passeth by the transgression of the remnant of his heritage? he
retaineth not his anger for ever, because he delighteth *in* mercy.
19He will turn again, he will have compassion upon us; he will
subdue our iniquities; and thou wilt cast all their sins into the
depths of the sea.
20Thou wilt perform the truth to Jacob, *and* the mercy to Abraham, which thou hast sworn unto our fathers from the days of old.

## Amplified

8Rejoice not against me, O my enemy; when I fall, I shall arise;
when I sit in darkness, the Lord shall be a light to me.
9I will bear the indignation of the Lord, because I have sinned
against Him, until He pleads my cause and executes judgment for
me. He will bring me forth to the light, and I shall behold His
righteous deliverance. [Rom. 10:1-4; 11:23-27.]
10Then my enemy will see it, and shame will cover her who said
to me, Where is the Lord your God? My eyes will see my desire
upon her; now she will be trodden down as the mire of the streets.
11In the day that your walls are to be built—a day for building—
in that day shall the boundary *of Israel* be far extended *and* the
decree [against her] be far removed. [Amos 9:11; Isa. 33:17.]
12In that day they will come to you from Assyria, and from the
cities of Matzor [Egypt], and from Egypt even to the river [Euphra-
tes], and from sea to sea, and from mountain to mountain.
13Yet shall the earth be desolate because of those who dwell in
it, for the fruit of their doings.
14Rule *and* feed Your people with Your rod *and* scepter, the flock
of Your inheritance, who dwell alone in a forest in the midst of
Carmel—a garden land; they shall feed in Bashan and Gilead, as
in the days of old.
15As in the days of your coming forth from the land of Egypt
I will show them marvelous things.
16The nations shall see [God's deliverance] and be ashamed of
all their might [which cannot be compared to His]. They shall lay
their hands upon their mouths in consternation; their ears shall be
deaf.
17They shall lick the dust like a serpent, like crawling things of
the earth they shall come trembling out of their strongholds *and*
close places; they shall turn *and* come with fear *and* dread to the
Lord our God, and shall be afraid *and* stand in awe because of You,
*O Lord.* [Jer. 33:9.]
18Who is a God like You, Who forgives iniquity and passes over
the transgression of the remnant of His heritage? He retains not
His anger for ever, because He delights in mercy *and* loving-kindness.
19He will again have compassion on us, He will subdue *and*
tread under foot our iniquities. You will cast all *our* sins into the
depths of the sea. [Ps. 103:12.]
20You will show Your faithfulness *and* perform the sure promise
to Jacob, and loving-kindness *and* mercy to Abraham, as You have
sworn to our fathers from the days of old. [Luke 1:54, 55.]

## New American Standard

8 Do not rejoice over me, O my enemy.
Though I fall I will rise;
Though I dwell in darkness, the LORD is a light for me.

9¶ I will bear the indignation of the LORD
Because I have sinned against Him,
Until He pleads my case and executes justice for me.
He will bring me out to the light,
*And* I will see His righteousness.
10 Then my enemy will see,
And shame will cover her who said to me,
"Where is the LORD your God?"
My eyes will look on her;
At that time she will be trampled down,
Like mire of the streets.
11 *It will be* a day for building your walls.
On that day will your boundary be extended.
12 It *will be* a day when they will come to you
From Assyria and the cities of Egypt,
From Egypt even to the Euphrates,
Even from sea to sea and mountain to mountain.
13 And the earth will become desolate because of her inhabitants,
On account of the fruit of their deeds.

14¶ Shepherd Thy people with Thy scepter,
The flock of Thy possession
Which dwells by itself in the woodland,
In the midst of a fruitful field.
Let them feed in Bashan and Gilead
As in the days of old.
15 "As in the days when you came out from the land of Egypt,
I will show you miracles."
16 Nations will see and be ashamed
Of all their might.
They will put *their* hand on *their* mouth,
Their ears will be deaf.
17 They will lick the dust like a serpent,
Like reptiles of the earth.
They will come trembling out of their fortresses;
To the LORD our God they will come in dread,
And they will be afraid before Thee.
18 Who is a God like Thee, who pardons iniquity
And passes over the rebellious act of the remnant of His possession?
He does not retain His anger forever,
Because He delights in unchanging love.
19 He will again have compassion on us;
He will tread our iniquities under foot.
Yes, Thou wilt cast all their sins
Into the depths of the sea.
20 Thou wilt give truth to Jacob
*And* unchanging love to Abraham,
Which Thou didst swear to our forefathers
From the days of old.

## New International

*Israel Will Rise*

8Do not gloat over me, my enemy!
Though I have fallen, I will rise.
Though I sit in darkness,
the LORD will be my light.
9Because I have sinned against him,
I will bear the LORD's wrath,
until he pleads my case
and establishes my right.
He will bring me out into the light;
I will see his righteousness.
10Then my enemy will see it
and will be covered with shame,
she who said to me,
"Where is the LORD your God?"
My eyes will see her downfall;
even now she will be trampled underfoot
like mire in the streets.

11The day for building your walls will come,
the day for extending your boundaries.
12In that day people will come to you
from Assyria and the cities of Egypt,
even from Egypt to the Euphrates
and from sea to sea
and from mountain to mountain.
13The earth will become desolate because of its inhabitants,
as the result of their deeds.

*Prayer and Praise*

14Shepherd your people with your staff,
the flock of your inheritance,
which lives by itself in a forest,
in fertile pasturelands.[a]
Let them feed in Bashan and Gilead
as in days long ago.

15"As in the days when you came out of Egypt,
I will show them my wonders."

16Nations will see and be ashamed,
deprived of all their power.
They will lay their hands on their mouths
and their ears will become deaf.
17They will lick dust like a snake,
like creatures that crawl on the ground.
They will come trembling out of their dens;
they will turn in fear to the LORD our God
and will be afraid of you.
18Who is a God like you,
who pardons sin and forgives the transgression
of the remnant of his inheritance?
You do not stay angry forever
but delight to show mercy.
19You will again have compassion on us;
you will tread our sins underfoot
and hurl all our iniquities into the depths of the sea.
20You will be true to Jacob,
and show mercy to Abraham,
as you pledged on oath to our fathers
in days long ago.

**NIV** [a] 14 Or *in the middle of Carmel*

## King James

THE BOOK OF

# Nahum

**1** THE BURDEN of Nineveh. The book of the vision of Nahum the Elkoshite.

2God *is* jealous, and the LORD revengeth; the LORD revengeth, and *is* furious; the LORD will take vengeance on his adversaries, and he reserveth *wrath* for his enemies.

3The LORD *is* slow to anger, and great in power, and will not at all acquit *the wicked:* the LORD *hath* his way in the whirlwind and in the storm, and the clouds *are* the dust of his feet.

4He rebuketh the sea, and maketh it dry, and drieth up all the rivers: Bashan languisheth, and Carmel, and the flower of Lebanon languisheth.

5The mountains quake at him, and the hills melt, and the earth is burned at his presence, yea, the world, and all that dwell therein.

6Who can stand before his indignation? and who can abide in the fierceness of his anger? his fury is poured out like fire, and the rocks are thrown down by him.

7The LORD *is* good, a strong hold in the day of trouble; and he knoweth them that trust in him.

8But with an overrunning flood he will make an utter end of the place thereof, and darkness shall pursue his enemies.

9What do ye imagine against the LORD? he will make an utter end: affliction shall not rise up the second time.

10For while *they be* folden together *as* thorns, and while they are drunken *as* drunkards, they shall be devoured as stubble fully dry.

11There is *one* come out of thee, that imagineth evil against the LORD, a wicked counsellor.

12Thus saith the LORD; Though *they be* quiet, and likewise many, yet thus shall they be cut down, when he shall pass through. Though I have afflicted thee, I will afflict thee no more.

13For now will I break his yoke from off thee, and will burst thy bonds in sunder.

## Amplified

THE BOOK OF

# Nahum

**1** THE BURDEN *or* oracle—the thing to be lifted up—concerning [a]Nineveh [the capital of Assyria]. The book of the vision of Nahum of Elkosh.

2The Lord is a jealous God and avenging, the Lord avenges and He is full of wrath; the Lord takes vengeance on His adversaries and reserves wrath for His enemies. [Exod. 20:5.]

3The Lord is slow to anger and great in power, and will by no means clear the guilty. The Lord has His way in the whirlwind and in the storm, and the clouds are the dust of His feet. [Exod. 34:6, 7.]

4He rebukes *and* threatens the sea and makes it dry, and dries up all the rivers. Bashan [on the east] and Mount Carmel [on the west] wither, and [in the north] the blossom of Lebanon fades.

5The mountains tremble *and* quake before Him and the hills melt away, and the earth is upheaved at His presence, yes, the world and all that dwell in it.

6Who can stand before His indignation? And who can stand up *and* endure the fierceness of His anger? His wrath is poured out like fire, and the rocks are broken asunder by Him.

7The Lord is good, a strength *and* stronghold in the day of trouble; He knows—recognizes, has knowledge of and understands—those who take refuge *and* trust in Him. [Ps. 1:6; John 10:14, 27; Hos. 13:5.]

8But with an [b]overrunning flood He will make a full end of [Nineveh's very] site and pursue His enemies into darkness.

9What do you devise *and* [how mad is your attempt to] plot against the Lord? He will make a full end *of Nineveh;* affliction [which My people shall suffer from Assyria] shall not rise up the second time.

10For [the Ninevites] are as bundles of thorn branches [for fuel], and even while drowned in their drunken [carousing] they shall be consumed like stubble fully dry [in the day of the Lord's wrath]. [Mal. 4:1.]

11There is one gone forth out of you [O Nineveh] who plots evil against the Lord, a villainous counselor [Sennacherib?]—who counsels for wickedness and worthlessness. [II Kings 19:20-23; Isa. 10:5-7; 36:15-20.]

12Thus says the Lord: Though they be in full strength and likewise many, even so shall [the Assyrians] be cut down when [their evil counselor] shall pass away. Though I have afflicted you [Jerusalem], I will not cause you to be afflicted [for your past sins] any more. [John 5:14; II Kings 19:35-37.]

13For now will I break his yoke from off you, and will burst your bonds asunder. [Isa. 14:25.]

**AMP** [a] Under the preaching of Jonah, the king of Nineveh and all its people repented. They not only heard his startling report of the terrible experience which running away from obedience to God had cost him, but they were terrified at the evidence of the truth of his having been in the belly of the great fish. So the whole city turned to God. But when Nahum came to Nineveh some 150 years later, all that was forgotten, and the later generations had become hopelessly godless. God's wrath was not to be turned away this time. Jonah had been sent to preach "Repent!" But Nahum's one "burden—the thing to be lifted up" is that Nineveh is to be destroyed—utterly. [b] Countless authorities confirm the literal accuracy of this reference. Diodorus Siculus refers to a legend that Nineveh could never be taken until the river became its enemy. Arbaces the Scythian had besieged the city in vain for two years, but in the third year the river Khosr during a flood season carried away a considerable section of the very great wall, and through this opening the besiegers gained entrance. Nah. 2:6 refers to the devastating flood, and 3:13, 15 probably to the destruction of Nineveh by fire. The vivid descriptions of chapter 3 "are true to their records and their sculptures."

## New American Standard

# Nahum

*God Is Awesome*

1 THE [c]ORACLE of Nineveh. The book of the vision of Nahum the Elkoshite.

2 A jealous and avenging God is the LORD;
The LORD is avenging and wrathful.
The LORD takes vengeance on His adversaries,
And He reserves wrath for His enemies.
3 The LORD is slow to anger and great in power,
And the LORD will by no means leave *the guilty* unpunished.
In whirlwind and storm is His way,
And clouds are the dust beneath His feet.
4 He rebukes the sea and makes it dry;
He dries up all the rivers.
Bashan and Carmel wither;
The blossoms of Lebanon wither.
5 Mountains quake because of Him,
And the hills dissolve;
Indeed the earth is upheaved by His presence,
The world and all the inhabitants in it.
6 Who can stand before His indignation?
Who can endure the burning of His anger?
His wrath is poured out like fire,
And the rocks are broken up by Him.
7 The LORD is good,
A stronghold in the day of trouble,
And He knows those who take refuge in Him.
8 But with an overflowing flood
He will make a complete end of its site,
And will pursue His enemies into darkness.

9¶ Whatever you devise against the LORD,
He will make a complete end of it.
Distress will not rise up twice.
10 Like tangled thorns,
And like those who are drunken with their drink,
They are consumed
As stubble completely withered.
11 From you has gone forth
One who plotted evil against the LORD,
A wicked counselor.
12 Thus says the LORD,
"Though they are at full *strength* and likewise many,
Even so, they will be cut off and pass away.
Though I have afflicted you,
I will afflict you no longer.
13 "So now, I will break his yoke bar from upon you,
And I will tear off your shackles."

NAS [c] Or, *burden*

## New International

# Nahum

1 AN ORACLE concerning Nineveh. The book of the vision of Nahum the Elkoshite.

*The LORD's Anger Against Nineveh*

2 The LORD is a jealous and avenging God;
the LORD takes vengeance and is filled with wrath.
The LORD takes vengeance on his foes
and maintains his wrath against his enemies.
3 The LORD is slow to anger and great in power;
the LORD will not leave the guilty unpunished.
His way is in the whirlwind and the storm,
and clouds are the dust of his feet.
4 He rebukes the sea and dries it up;
he makes all the rivers run dry.
Bashan and Carmel wither
and the blossoms of Lebanon fade.
5 The mountains quake before him
and the hills melt away.
The earth trembles at his presence,
the world and all who live in it.
6 Who can withstand his indignation?
Who can endure his fierce anger?
His wrath is poured out like fire;
the rocks are shattered before him.

7 The LORD is good,
a refuge in times of trouble.
He cares for those who trust in him,
8 but with an overwhelming flood
he will make an end of ⌊Nineveh⌋;
he will pursue his foes into darkness.
9 Whatever they plot against the LORD
he[d] will bring to an end;
trouble will not come a second time.
10 They will be entangled among thorns
and drunk from their wine;
they will be consumed like dry stubble.[e]
11 From you, ⌊O Nineveh⌋, has one come forth
who plots evil against the LORD
and counsels wickedness.

12 This is what the LORD says:

"Although they have allies and are numerous,
they will be cut off and pass away.
Although I have afflicted you, ⌊O Judah⌋,
I will afflict you no more.
13 Now I will break their yoke from your neck
and tear your shackles away."

NIV [d] 9 Or *What do you foes plot against the LORD? / He* [e] 10 The meaning of the Hebrew for this verse is uncertain.

## King James

14And the LORD hath given a commandment concerning thee,
*that* no more of thy name be sown: out of the house of thy gods
will I cut off the graven image and the molten image: I will make
thy grave; for thou art vile.
15Behold upon the mountains the feet of him that bringeth good
tidings, that publisheth peace! O Judah, keep thy solemn feasts,
perform thy vows: for the wicked shall no more pass through thee;
he is utterly cut off.

## Amplified

14And the Lord has given a commandment concerning you,
[evil Assyrian counselor,] that no more of your name shall be born
*or* your name be perpetuated. Out of the house of your gods I will
cut off the graven and molten images; I will make [their temple]
your tomb, for you are vile *and* despised. [See Isa. 37:38.]
15Behold upon the mountains the feet of him [who comes telling
of the Assyrian's death] who brings good tidings, who publishes
peace! Celebrate your feasts, O Judah, perform your vows, for the
wicked counselor, [the king of Assyria,] shall no more come
against you *or* pass through your land; he is utterly cut off. [Then
the prophet Nahum sarcastically addresses his message to Nineveh:]

## King James

**2** HE THAT dasheth in pieces is come up before thy face: keep
the munition, watch the way, make *thy* loins strong, fortify
*thy* power mightily.
2For the LORD hath turned away the excellency of Jacob, as the
excellency of Israel: for the emptiers have emptied them out, and
marred their vine branches.
3The shield of his mighty men is made red, the valiant men *are*
in scarlet: the chariots *shall be* with flaming torches in the day of
his preparation, and the fir trees shall be terribly shaken.
4The chariots shall rage in the streets, they shall justle one
against another in the broad ways: they shall seem like torches,
they shall run like the lightnings.
5He shall recount his worthies: they shall stumble in their walk;
they shall make haste to the wall thereof, and the defence shall be
prepared.
6The gates of the rivers shall be opened, and the palace shall be
dissolved.
7And Huzzab shall be led away captive, she shall be brought
up, and her maids shall lead *her* as with the voice of doves, taber-
ing upon their breasts.
8But Nineveh *is* of old like a pool of water: yet they shall flee
away. Stand, stand, *shall they cry;* but none shall look back.
9Take ye the spoil of silver, take the spoil of gold: for *there is*
none end of the store *and* glory out of all the pleasant furniture.
10She is empty, and void, and waste: and the heart melteth, and
the knees smite together, and much pain *is* in all loins, and the
faces of them all gather blackness.
11Where *is* the dwelling of the lions, and the feedingplace of the
young lions, where the lion, *even* the old lion, walked, *and* the
lion's whelp, and none made *them* afraid?
12The lion did tear in pieces enough for his whelps, and strangled for his lionesses, and filled his holes with prey, and his dens
with ravin.

## Amplified

**2** HE WHO dashes in pieces [that is, the king of Medo-Babylon]
is come up before your face [Nineveh]. Keep the fortress *and*
ramparts manned; watch the road; gird your loins; collect *and*
fortify all your strength *and* power mightily.
2For the Lord restores the excellency of Jacob as the excellency
of [ancient] Israel; for plunderers have plundered them *and* emptied them out, and [outrageously] destroyed their vine branches.
[Isa. 10:12.]
3The shield of the mighty men [of Media and Babylon] is *dyed*
red; the valiant men are [clothed] in dyed scarlet; the chariots blaze
with fire of steel on the day of his preparation [for battle], and the
officers' horses prance like a cypress forest [reeling in the wind].
4The chariots rage in confusion in the streets, they run to and
fro [in wild terror] in the broad ways; they flash with steel—making them appear like torches; they rush [in various directions] like
forked lightnings.
5[The Assyrian leader] remembers *and* summons his bravest
men; they stumble in their march; they hasten to the city's wall,
and their movable defense shelter is prepared *and* set up.
6The gates *or* dams of the rivers [surrounding and guarding
Nineveh] are opened, and the *imperial* palace [of sun-dried brick]
is dissolved [by the torrents] *and* is in dismay.
7It is decreed. [Its mistress] is stripped and removed, and her
maids are lamenting *and* moaning like doves [softly for fear], beating upon their breasts—and hearts.
8And Nineveh, like a standing pool are her waters, and [her
inhabitants] are fleeing away! Stand! Stand *firm! a few cry;* but no
one looks back *or* causes them to return.
9Take the spoil of silver, take the spoil of gold! For there is no
end of the treasure, the glory *and* wealth of all the precious furnishings.
10Emptiness! Desolation! Utter waste! Hearts faint and knees
smite together, and anguish is in all loins, and the faces of all grow
pale! [Isa. 13:7, 8.]
11Where is the den of the lions, which was the feeding place of
the young lions, where the lion and the lioness walked, and the
lion's whelp, and none made them afraid?
12The lion tore in pieces enough for his whelps and strangled
[prey] for his lionesses; he filled his caves with prey and his dens
with what he had seized *and* carried off.

## New American Standard

14¶ The LORD has issued a command concerning you:
"Your name will no longer be perpetuated.
I will cut off idol and image
From the house of your gods.
I will prepare your grave,
For you are contemptible."

15¶ Behold, on the mountains the feet of him who brings
good news,
Who announces peace!
Celebrate your feasts, O Judah;
Pay your vows.
For never again will the wicked one pass through you;
He is cut off completely.

*The Overthrow of Nineveh*

**2** THE ONE who scatters has come up against you.
Man the fortress, watch the road;
Strengthen your back, summon all *your* strength.
2 For the LORD will restore the splendor of Jacob
Like the splendor of Israel,
Even though devastators have devastated them
And destroyed their vine branches.
3¶ The shields of his mighty men are *colored* red,
The warriors are dressed in scarlet,
The chariots are *enveloped* in flashing steel
When he is prepared *to march*,
And the cypress *spears* are brandished.
4 The chariots race madly in the streets,
They rush wildly in the squares,
Their appearance is like torches,
They dash to and fro like lightning flashes.
5 He remembers his nobles;
They stumble in their march,
They hurry to her wall,
And the mantelet is set up.
6 The gates of the rivers are opened,
And the palace is dissolved.
7 And it is fixed:
She is stripped, she is carried away,
And her handmaids are moaning like the sound of
doves,
Beating on their breasts.
8¶ Though Nineveh *was* like a pool of water throughout
her days,
Now they are fleeing;
"Stop, stop,"
But no one turns back.
9 Plunder the silver!
Plunder the gold!
For there is no limit to the treasure—
Wealth from every kind of desirable object.
10 She is emptied! Yes, she is desolate and waste!
Hearts are melting and knees knocking!
Also anguish is in the whole body,
And all their faces are grown pale!
11 Where is the den of the lions
And the feeding place of the young lions,
Where the lion, lioness, and lion's cub prowled,
With nothing to disturb *them*?
12 The lion tore enough for his cubs,
Killed *enough* for his lionesses,
And filled his lairs with prey
And his dens with torn flesh.

## New International

14The LORD has given a command concerning you,
⌞Nineveh⌟:
"You will have no descendants to bear your name.
I will destroy the carved images and cast idols
that are in the temple of your gods.
I will prepare your grave,
for you are vile."

15Look, there on the mountains,
the feet of one who brings good news,
who proclaims peace!
Celebrate your festivals, O Judah,
and fulfill your vows.
No more will the wicked invade you;
they will be completely destroyed.

*Nineveh to Fall*

**2** AN ATTACKER advances against you, ⌞Nineveh⌟.
Guard the fortress,
watch the road,
brace yourselves,
marshal all your strength!
2The LORD will restore the splendor of Jacob
like the splendor of Israel,
though destroyers have laid them waste
and have ruined their vines.
3The shields of his soldiers are red;
the warriors are clad in scarlet.
The metal on the chariots flashes
on the day they are made ready;
the spears of pine are brandished.[a]
4The chariots storm through the streets,
rushing back and forth through the squares.
They look like flaming torches;
they dart about like lightning.
5He summons his picked troops,
yet they stumble on their way.
They dash to the city wall;
the protective shield is put in place.
6The river gates are thrown open
and the palace collapses.
7It is decreed[b] that ⌞the city⌟
be exiled and carried away.
Its slave girls moan like doves
and beat upon their breasts.
8Nineveh is like a pool,
and its water is draining away.
"Stop! Stop!" they cry,
but no one turns back.
9Plunder the silver!
Plunder the gold!
The supply is endless,
the wealth from all its treasures!
10She is pillaged, plundered, stripped!
Hearts melt, knees give way,
bodies tremble, every face grows pale.

11Where now is the lions' den,
the place where they fed their young,
where the lion and lioness went,
and the cubs, with nothing to fear?
12The lion killed enough for his cubs
and strangled the prey for his mate,
filling his lairs with the kill
and his dens with the prey.

**NIV** [a] 3 Hebrew; Septuagint and Syriac / *the horsemen rush to and fro* [b] 7 The meaning of the Hebrew for this word is uncertain.

## King James

13Behold, I *am* against thee, saith the LORD of hosts, and I will burn her chariots in the smoke, and the sword shall devour thy young lions: and I will cut off thy prey from the earth, and the voice of thy messengers shall no more be heard.

3 WOE TO the bloody city! it *is* all full of lies *and* robbery; the prey departeth not;

2The noise of a whip, and the noise of the rattling of the wheels, and of the prancing horses, and of the jumping chariots.

3The horseman lifteth up both the bright sword and the glittering spear: and *there is* a multitude of slain, and a great number of carcases; and *there is* none end of *their* corpses; they stumble upon their corpses:

4Because of the multitude of the whoredoms of the well-favoured harlot, the mistress of witchcrafts, that selleth nations through her whoredoms, and families through her witchcrafts.

5Behold, I *am* against thee, saith the LORD of hosts; and I will discover thy skirts upon thy face, and I will show the nations thy nakedness, and the kingdoms thy shame.

6And I will cast abominable filth upon thee, and make thee vile, and will set thee as a gazingstock.

7And it shall come to pass, *that* all they that look upon thee shall flee from thee, and say, Nineveh is laid waste: who will bemoan her? whence shall I seek comforters for thee?

8Art thou better than populous No, that was situate among the rivers, *that had* the waters round about it, whose rampart *was* the sea, *and* her wall *was* from the sea?

9Ethiopia and Egypt *were* her strength, and *it was* infinite; Put and Lubim were thy helpers.

10Yet *was* she carried away, she went into captivity: her young children also were dashed in pieces at the top of all the streets: and they cast lots for her honourable men, and all her great men were bound in chains.

11Thou also shalt be drunken: thou shalt be hid, thou also shalt seek strength because of the enemy.

12All thy strong holds *shall be like* fig trees with the firstripe figs: if they be shaken, they shall even fall into the mouth of the eater.

13Behold, thy people in the midst of thee *are* women: the gates of thy land shall be set wide open unto thine enemies: the fire shall devour thy bars.

## Amplified

13Behold, I am against you, [Nineveh,] says the Lord of hosts, and I will burn *your* chariots in the smoke, and the sword shall devour your young lions; and I will cut off your prey from the earth, and the voice of your messengers shall no more be heard.

3 WOE TO the bloody city! It is full of lies and booty, and *there is* no end to the plunder! [Ezek. 24:6, 9, 10; Hab. 2:12.]

2The cracking of the whip, and the noise of the rattling of wheels, and prancing horses and chariots rumbling *and* bounding,

3Horsemen mounting *and* charging, the flashing sword, the gleaming spear, a multitude of slain and a great number of corpses, no end of corpses! [The horsemen] stumble over the corpses!

4All because of the multitude of the harlotries *of* [Nineveh,] the well-favored harlot, the mistress of deadly charms, who betrays *and* sells nations through her whoredoms [idolatry] and peoples through her enchantments.

5Behold I am against you, says the Lord of hosts, and I will lift up your skirts over your face; and I will let the nations look on your nakedness, [O Nineveh,] and the kingdoms on your shame.

6I will cast abominable things at you *and* make you filthy, treat you with contempt, and make you a gazing-stock.

7And all who look on you will shrink *and* flee from you, and say, Nineveh is laid waste; who will pity *and* bemoan her? Where *then* shall I seek comforters for you?

8Are you better than No-amon [Thebes, capital of Upper Egypt], that dwelt by the rivers *or* canals, that had the waters round about her, whose rampart was a sea— *that is,* the Nile—and water her wall?

9Ethiopia and Egypt were her strength, and that without limit. Put and the Libyans were *her* helpers.

10Yet she was carried away, she went into captivity. Her young children also were dashed in pieces at all the street corners, lots were cast [by the Assyrian officers] for her nobles, and all her great men were bound with chains.

11You will be drunk [Nineveh, with the cup of God's wrath], you will be dazed, you will seek *and* require a refuge because of the enemy.

12All your fortresses are fig trees with early figs; if they are shaken they will fall into the mouth of the eater.

13Behold, your troops in the midst of you are [weak and helpless as] women; the gates of your land [without effort] are set wide open to your enemies; fire consumes your bars.

## New American Standard

13"Behold, I am against you," declares the LORD of hosts. "I will
burn up her chariots in smoke, a sword will devour your young
lions, I will cut off your prey from the land, and no longer will the
voice of your messengers be heard."

*Nineveh's Complete Ruin*

3 WOE TO the bloody city, completely full of lies *and* pillage;
*Her* prey never departs.
2 The noise of the whip,
The noise of the rattling of the wheel,
Galloping horses,
And bounding chariots!
3 Horsemen charging,
Swords flashing, spears gleaming,
Many slain, a mass of corpses,
And countless dead bodies—
They stumble over the dead bodies!
4 *All* because of the many harlotries of the harlot,
The charming one, the mistress of sorceries,
Who sells nations by her harlotries
And families by her sorceries.
5 "Behold, I am against you," declares the LORD of hosts;
"And I will lift up your skirts over your face,
And show to the nations your nakedness
And to the kingdoms your disgrace.
6 "I will throw filth on you
And make you vile,
And set you up as a spectacle.
7 "And it will come about that all who see you
Will shrink from you and say,
'Nineveh is devastated!
Who will grieve for her?'
Where will I seek comforters for you?"

8¶ Are you better than [a]Noamon,
Which was situated by the waters of the Nile,
With water surrounding her,
Whose rampart *was* the sea,
Whose wall *consisted* of the sea?
9 Ethiopia was *her* might,
And Egypt too, without limits.
Put and Lubim were among her helpers.
10 Yet she became an exile,
She went into captivity;
Also her small children were dashed to pieces
At the head of every street;
They cast lots for her honorable men,
And all her great men were bound with fetters.
11 You too will become drunk,
You will be hidden.
You too will search for a refuge from the enemy.
12 All your fortifications are fig trees with ripe fruit—
When shaken, they fall into the eater's mouth.
13 Behold, your people are women in your midst!
The gates of your land are opened wide to your enemies;
Fire consumes your gate bars.

NAS [a] I.e., the city of Amon: Thebes

## New International

13"I am against you,"
declares the LORD Almighty.
"I will burn up your chariots in smoke,
and the sword will devour your young lions.
I will leave you no prey on the earth.
The voices of your messengers
will no longer be heard."

*Woe to Nineveh*

3 WOE TO the city of blood,
full of lies,
full of plunder,
never without victims!
2The crack of whips,
the clatter of wheels,
galloping horses
and jolting chariots!
3Charging cavalry,
flashing swords
and glittering spears!
Many casualties,
piles of dead,
bodies without number,
people stumbling over the corpses—
4all because of the wanton lust of a harlot,
alluring, the mistress of sorceries,
who enslaved nations by her prostitution
and peoples by her witchcraft.

5"I am against you," declares the LORD Almighty.
"I will lift your skirts over your face.
I will show the nations your nakedness
and the kingdoms your shame.
6I will pelt you with filth,
I will treat you with contempt
and make you a spectacle.
7All who see you will flee from you and say,
'Nineveh is in ruins—who will mourn for her?'
Where can I find anyone to comfort you?"

8Are you better than Thebes,[b]
situated on the Nile,
with water around her?
The river was her defense,
the waters her wall.
9Cush[c] and Egypt were her boundless strength;
Put and Libya were among her allies.
10Yet she was taken captive
and went into exile.
Her infants were dashed to pieces
at the head of every street.
Lots were cast for her nobles,
and all her great men were put in chains.
11You too will become drunk;
you will go into hiding
and seek refuge from the enemy.

12All your fortresses are like fig trees
with their first ripe fruit;
when they are shaken,
the figs fall into the mouth of the eater.
13Look at your troops—
they are all women!
The gates of your land
are wide open to your enemies;
fire has consumed their bars.

NIV [b] *8* Hebrew *No Amon* [c] *9* That is, the upper Nile region

## King James

14Draw thee waters for the siege, fortify thy strong holds: go into clay, and tread the mortar, make strong the brickkiln.
15There shall the fire devour thee; the sword shall cut thee off, it shall eat thee up like the cankerworm: make thyself many as the cankerworm, make thyself many as the locusts.
16Thou hast multiplied thy merchants above the stars of heaven: the cankerworm spoileth, and flieth away.
17Thy crowned *are* as the locusts, and thy captains as the great grasshoppers, which camp in the hedges in the cold day, *but* when the sun ariseth they flee away, and their place is not known where they *are*.
18Thy shepherds slumber, O king of Assyria: thy nobles shall dwell *in the dust:* thy people is scattered upon the mountains, and no man gathereth *them*.
19 *There is* no healing of thy bruise; thy wound is grievous: all that hear the bruit of thee shall clap the hands over thee: for upon whom hath not thy wickedness passed continually?

## Amplified

14Draw for yourself the water [necessary] for a [long continued] siege; make strong your fortresses; go down into the clay pits and trample the mortar; make ready the brickkiln [to burn bricks for the bulwarks]!
15 *But* there [in the very midst of these preparations] will the fire devour you; the sword will cut you off, it will destroy you as the locusts *destroy*. Multiply yourselves like the licking locusts, make yourselves many like the swarming locusts!
16You increased your merchants more than the [visible] stars of the heavens. The swarming locust spreads itself *and* destroys, then flies away.
17Your princes are like the grasshoppers, and your marshals like the swarms of locusts, which encamp in the hedges on a cold day, but when the sun rises they fly away, and no one knows where they are.
18Your shepherds are asleep, O king of Assyria; your nobles are lying still [in death]; your people are scattered on the mountains, and there is no one to gather them.
19There is no healing of your hurt, your wound is grievous. All who hear the news about you clap their hands over [what has happened to] you. For upon whom has not your [unceasing] evil come continually?

## New American Standard

14 Draw for yourself water for the siege!
Strengthen your fortifications!
Go into the clay and tread the mortar!
Take hold of the brick mold!
15 There fire will consume you,
The sword will cut you down;
It will consume you as the locust *does*.

¶ Multiply yourself like the creeping locust,
Multiply yourself like the swarming locust.
16 You have increased your traders more than the stars of heaven—
The creeping locust strips and flies away.
17 Your guardsmen are like the swarming locust.
Your marshals are like hordes of grasshoppers
Settling in the stone walls on a cold day.
The sun rises and they flee,
And the place where they are is not known.
18 Your shepherds are sleeping, O king of Assyria;
Your nobles are lying down.
Your people are scattered on the mountains,
And there is no one to regather *them*.
19 There is no relief for your breakdown,
Your wound is incurable.
All who hear about you
Will clap *their* hands over you,
For on whom has not your evil passed continually?

## New International

14 Draw water for the siege,
strengthen your defenses!
Work the clay,
tread the mortar,
repair the brickwork!
15 There the fire will devour you;
the sword will cut you down
and, like grasshoppers, consume you.
Multiply like grasshoppers,
multiply like locusts!
16 You have increased the number of your merchants
till they are more than the stars of the sky,
but like locusts they strip the land
and then fly away.
17 Your guards are like locusts,
your officials like swarms of locusts
that settle in the walls on a cold day—
but when the sun appears they fly away,
and no one knows where.

18 O king of Assyria, your shepherds[a] slumber;
your nobles lie down to rest.
Your people are scattered on the mountains
with no one to gather them.
19 Nothing can heal your wound;
your injury is fatal.
Everyone who hears the news about you
claps his hands at your fall,
for who has not felt
your endless cruelty?

**NIV** [a] *18* Or *rulers*

## King James

THE BOOK OF (Amplified)

# Habakkuk

1 THE BURDEN which Habakkuk the prophet did see.

2O LORD, how long shall I cry, and thou wilt not hear! *even* cry out unto thee *of* violence, and thou wilt not save!

3Why dost thou show me iniquity, and cause *me* to behold grievance? for spoiling and violence *are* before me: and there are *that* raise up strife and contention.

4Therefore the law is slacked, and judgment doth never go forth: for the wicked doth compass about the righteous; therefore wrong judgment proceedeth.

5¶ Behold ye among the heathen, and regard, and wonder marvellously: for *I* will work a work in your days, *which* ye will not believe, though it be told *you*.

6For, lo, I raise up the Chaldeans, *that* bitter and hasty nation, which shall march through the breadth of the land, to possess the dwellingplaces *that are* not theirs.

7They *are* terrible and dreadful: their judgment and their dignity shall proceed of themselves.

8Their horses also are swifter than the leopards, and are more fierce than the evening wolves: and their horsemen shall spread themselves, and their horsemen shall come from far; they shall fly as the eagle *that* hasteth to eat.

9They shall come all for violence: their faces shall sup up *as* the east wind, and they shall gather the captivity as the sand.

10And they shall scoff at the kings, and the princes shall be a scorn unto them: they shall deride every strong hold; for they shall heap dust, and take it.

11Then shall *his* mind change, and he shall pass over, and offend, *imputing* this his power unto his god.

12¶ *Art* thou not from everlasting, O LORD my God, mine Holy One? we shall not die. O LORD, thou hast ordained them for judgment; and, O mighty God, thou hast established them for correction.

## Amplified

THE BOOK OF

# Habakkuk

1 THE BURDEN *or* oracle, *or* that which is to be lifted up, which Habakkuk the prophet saw.

2O Lord, how long shall I cry for help and You will not hear? Or cry out to You of violence, and You will not save?

3Why do You show me iniquity *and* wrong, and Yourself look upon *or* cause me to see perverseness *and* trouble? For destruction and violence are before me, and there is strife, and contention arises.

4Therefore the law is slackened, and justice *and* a righteous sentence never go forth; for the [hostility of the] wicked surrounds the [uncompromisingly] righteous, therefore justice goes forth perverted.

5Look around [you, Habakkuk, replied the Lord] among the nations and see! And be astonished! Astounded! For I am putting into effect a work in your days that you would not believe it if it were told you. [Acts 13:40, 41.]

6For behold! I am rousing up the Chaldeans, that bitter and impetuous nation, who march through the breadth of the earth, to take possession of dwelling places that do not belong to them. [II Kings 24:2.]

7[The Chaldeans] are terrible and dreadful; their justice and dignity proceed *only* from themselves.

8Their horses also are swifter than leopards and are more fierce than the evening wolves, and their horsemen spread themselves *and* press on proudly; yes, their horsemen come from afar; they fly like an eagle that hastens to devour.

9They all come for violence; their faces turn eagerly forward, and they gather prisoners together like sand.

10They scoff at kings, and rulers are a derision to them; they ridicule every stronghold, for they heap up dust [for earth mounds] and take it.

11Then they sweep by like a wind and pass on, and they load themselves with guilt, [as do all men] whose own power is their god.

12Are not You from everlasting, O Lord my God, my Holy One? We shall not die. O Lord, You have appointed [the Chaldean] to execute [Your] judgment, and You, O Rock, have established him for chastisement *and* correction. [Deut. 32:4.]

## New American Standard

# Habakkuk

*Chaldeans Used to Punish Judah*

1 THE [a]ORACLE which Habakkuk the prophet saw.
2 How long, O LORD, will I call for help,
And Thou wilt not hear?
I cry out to Thee, "Violence!"
Yet Thou dost not save.
3 Why dost Thou make me see iniquity,
And cause *me* to look on wickedness?
Yes, destruction and violence are before me;
Strife exists and contention arises.
4 Therefore, the law is ignored
And justice is never upheld.
For the wicked surround the righteous;
Therefore, justice comes out perverted.

5¶ "Look among the nations! Observe!
Be astonished! Wonder!
Because *I* am doing something in your days—
You would not believe if you were told.
6 "For behold, I am raising up the Chaldeans,
That fierce and impetuous people
Who march throughout the earth
To seize dwelling places which are not theirs.
7 "They are dreaded and feared.
Their justice and authority originate with themselves.
8 "Their horses are swifter than leopards
And keener than wolves in the evening.
Their horsemen come galloping,
Their horsemen come from afar;
They fly like an eagle swooping *down* to devour.
9 "All of them come for violence.
Their horde of faces *moves* forward.
They collect captives like sand.
10 "They mock at kings,
And rulers are a laughing matter to them.
They laugh at every fortress,
And heap up rubble to capture it.
11 "Then they will sweep through *like* the wind and pass on.
But they will be held guilty,
They whose strength is their god."

12¶ Art Thou not from everlasting,
O LORD, my God, my Holy One?
We will not die.
Thou, O LORD, hast appointed them to judge;
And Thou, O Rock, hast established them to correct.

**NAS** [a] Or, *burden*

## New International

# Habakkuk

1 THE ORACLE that Habakkuk the prophet received.

*Habakkuk's Complaint*

2 How long, O LORD, must I call for help,
but you do not listen?
Or cry out to you, "Violence!"
but you do not save?
3 Why do you make me look at injustice?
Why do you tolerate wrong?
Destruction and violence are before me;
there is strife, and conflict abounds.
4 Therefore the law is paralyzed,
and justice never prevails.
The wicked hem in the righteous,
so that justice is perverted.

*The LORD's Answer*

5 "Look at the nations and watch—
and be utterly amazed.
For I am going to do something in your days
that you would not believe,
even if you were told.
6 I am raising up the Babylonians,[b]
that ruthless and impetuous people,
who sweep across the whole earth
to seize dwelling places not their own.
7 They are a feared and dreaded people;
they are a law to themselves
and promote their own honor.
8 Their horses are swifter than leopards,
fiercer than wolves at dusk.
Their cavalry gallops headlong;
their horsemen come from afar.
They fly like a vulture swooping to devour;
9 they all come bent on violence.
Their hordes[c] advance like a desert wind
and gather prisoners like sand.
10 They deride kings
and scoff at rulers.
They laugh at all fortified cities;
they build earthen ramps and capture them.
11 Then they sweep past like the wind and go on—
guilty men, whose own strength is their god."

*Habakkuk's Second Complaint*

12 O LORD, are you not from everlasting?
My God, my Holy One, we will not die.
O LORD, you have appointed them to execute judgment;
O Rock, you have ordained them to punish.

**NIV** [b] 6 Or *Chaldeans* [c] 9 The meaning of the Hebrew for this word is uncertain.

## King James

13 *Thou art* of purer eyes than to behold evil, and canst not look on iniquity: wherefore lookest thou upon them that deal treacherously, *and* holdest thy tongue when the wicked devoureth *the man that is* more righteous than he?

14And makest men as the fishes of the sea, as the creeping things, *that have* no ruler over them?

15They take up all of them with the angle, they catch them in their net, and gather them in their drag: therefore they rejoice and are glad.

16Therefore they sacrifice unto their net, and burn incense unto their drag; because by them their portion *is* fat, and their meat plenteous.

17Shall they therefore empty their net, and not spare continually to slay the nations?

**2** I WILL stand upon my watch, and set me upon the tower, and will watch to see what he will say unto me, and what I shall answer when I am reproved.

2And the LORD answered me, and said, Write the vision, and make *it* plain upon tables, that he may run that readeth it.

3For the vision *is* yet for an appointed time, but at the end it shall speak, and not lie: though it tarry, wait for it; because it will surely come, it will not tarry.

4Behold, his soul *which* is lifted up is not upright in him: but the just shall live by his faith.

5¶ Yea also, because he transgresseth by wine, *he is* a proud man, neither keepeth at home, who enlargeth his desire as hell, and *is* as death, and cannot be satisfied, but gathereth unto him all nations, and heapeth unto him all people:

6Shall not all these take up a parable against him, and a taunting proverb against him, and say, Woe to him that increaseth *that which is* not his! how long? and to him that ladeth himself with thick clay!

7Shall they not rise up suddenly that shall bite thee, and awake that shall vex thee, and thou shalt be for booties unto them?

8Because thou hast spoiled many nations, all the remnant of the people shall spoil thee; because of men's blood, and *for* the violence of the land, of the city, and of all that dwell therein.

9¶ Woe to him that coveteth an evil covetousness to his house, that he may set his nest on high, that he may be delivered from the power of evil!

10Thou hast consulted shame to thy house by cutting off many people, and hast sinned *against* thy soul.

## Amplified

13You are of purer eyes than to behold evil, and can not look [inactively] upon injustice. Why then do You look upon the plunderer? Why are you silent when the wicked *one* destroys him who is more righteous than he [the Chaldean oppressor] is?

14Why do You make men like the fishes of the sea, like reptiles *and* creeping things that have no ruler [and are defenseless against their foes]?

15He [the Chaldean] brings all of them up with his hook, he catches and drags them out with his net, he gathers them in his dragnet: so he rejoices and is in high spirits.

16Therefore he sacrifices [offerings] to his net and burns incense to his dragnet, because from them he lives luxuriously and his food is plentiful *and* rich.

17Shall he therefore continue to empty his net, and mercilessly go on slaying the nations for ever?

**2** [OH, I know, I have been rash to talk out plainly this way to God!] I will [in my thinking] stand upon my post of observation, and station myself on the tower *or* fortress, and will watch to see what He will say within me, and what answer I will make [as His mouthpiece] to the perplexities of my complaint against Him.

2And the Lord answered me, and said, Write the vision, and engrave it *so* plainly upon tablets that *every one who* passes may *be able to* read [it easily and quickly] *as he* hastens by.

3For the vision is yet for an appointed time, and it hastens to the end [fulfillment]; it will not deceive *or* disappoint. Though it tarry, wait [earnestly] for it; because it will surely come, it will not be behindhand on its appointed day. [Heb. 10:37, 38.]

4Behold the proud; his soul is not straight *or* right within him; but the rigidly just *and* the uncompromisingly righteous *man* shall [a]live by his faith *and* in his faithfulness. [Rom. 1:17; Gal. 3:11.]

5Moreover, wine *and* [b] *wealth are* treacherous; the proud man [the Chaldean invader] is restless *and* cannot stay at home. His appetite is large like that of Sheol and [his greed] is like death and cannot be satisfied; he gathers to himself all nations, and collects all people as if he owned them.

6Shall not all these [victims of his greed] take up a taunt against him, and in scoffing derision of him say, Woe to him who piles up that which is not his!—how long [will he possess it]? And [woe to him] who loads himself with promissory notes for usury!

7Shall [your debtors] not rise up suddenly who shall bite you, exacting usury of you, and those awake who will vex you—toss you to and fro and make you tremble violently? Then you will be booty for them.

8Because you [king of Babylon] have plundered many nations, all who are left of the people shall plunder you, because of men's blood, and for the violence done to the earth, to the city and all the people who live in each city.

9Woe to him who obtains wicked gain for his house, [who thinks by so doing] to set his nest on high, that he may be preserved from calamity *and* delivered from the power of evil!

10You have devised shame to your house by cutting off *and* putting an end to many peoples, and you have sinned against *and* forfeited your own life.

**AMP** [a] There is a curious passage in the Talmud [the body of Jewish civil and religious law], which says that in the Law Moses gave six hundred injunctions to the Israelites. As these might prove too numerous to commit to memory, David brought them down to eleven in Psalm 15. Isaiah reduced these eleven to six in [his] chapter 33:15. Micah (6:8) further reduced them to three; and Isaiah (56:1) once more brought them down, to two. These two Amos (5:4) reduced to one. But lest it might be supposed from this that God could be found in the fulfillment of the law only, Habakkuk (2:4) said, "The just shall live by his faith."—William H. Saulez in *The Romance of the Hebrew Language* (1913). [b] The Dead Sea Scrolls read "wealth."

## New American Standard

13 *Thine* eyes are too pure to approve evil,
And Thou canst not look on wickedness *with favor.*
Why dost Thou look with favor
On those who deal treacherously?
Why art Thou silent when the wicked swallow up
Those more righteous than they?
14 *Why* hast Thou made men like the fish of the sea,
Like creeping things without a ruler over them?
15 *The Chaldeans* bring all of them up with a hook,
Drag them away with their net,
And gather them together in their fishing net.
Therefore, they rejoice and are glad.
16 Therefore, they offer a sacrifice to their net.
And burn incense to their fishing net;
Because through these things their catch is large,
And their food is plentiful.
17 Will they therefore empty their net
And continually slay nations without sparing?

*God Answers the Prophet*

**2** I WILL stand on my guard post
And station myself on the rampart;
And I will keep watch to see what He will speak to me,
And how I may reply when I am reproved.
2 Then the LORD answered me and said,
"Record the vision
And inscribe *it* on tablets,
That the one who reads it may run.
3 "For the vision is yet for the appointed time;
It hastens toward the goal, and it will not fail.
Though it tarries, wait for it;
For it will certainly come, it will not delay.

4¶ "Behold, as for the proud one,
His soul is not right within him;
But the righteous will live by his faith.
5 "Furthermore, wine betrays the haughty man,
So that he does not stay at home.
He enlarges his appetite like Sheol,
And he is like death, never satisfied.
He also gathers to himself all nations
And collects to himself all peoples.
6¶ "Will not all of these take up a taunt-song against him,
Even mockery *and* insinuations against him,
And say, 'Woe to him who increases what is not his—
For how long—
And makes himself rich with loans?'
7 "Will not your creditors rise up suddenly,
And those who collect from you awaken?
Indeed, you will become plunder for them.
8 "Because you have looted many nations,
All the remainder of the peoples will loot you—
Because of human bloodshed and violence done to the land,
To the town and all its inhabitants.

9¶ "Woe to him who gets evil gain for his house
To put his nest on high
To be delivered from the hand of calamity!
10 "You have devised a shameful thing for your house
By cutting off many peoples;
So you are sinning against yourself.

## New International

13 Your eyes are too pure to look on evil;
you cannot tolerate wrong.
Why then do you tolerate the treacherous?
Why are you silent while the wicked
swallow up those more righteous than themselves?
14 You have made men like fish in the sea,
like sea creatures that have no ruler.
15 The wicked foe pulls all of them up with hooks,
he catches them in his net,
he gathers them up in his dragnet;
and so he rejoices and is glad.
16 Therefore he sacrifices to his net
and burns incense to his dragnet,
for by his net he lives in luxury
and enjoys the choicest food.
17 Is he to keep on emptying his net,
destroying nations without mercy?

**2** I WILL stand at my watch
and station myself on the ramparts;
I will look to see what he will say to me,
and what answer I am to give to this complaint.[c]

*The LORD's Answer*

2 Then the LORD replied:

"Write down the revelation
and make it plain on tablets
so that a herald[d] may run with it.
3 For the revelation awaits an appointed time;
it speaks of the end
and will not prove false.
Though it linger, wait for it;
it[e] will certainly come and will not delay.

4 "See, he is puffed up;
his desires are not upright—
but the righteous will live by his faith[f] —
5 indeed, wine betrays him;
he is arrogant and never at rest.
Because he is as greedy as the grave[g]
and like death is never satisfied,
he gathers to himself all the nations
and takes captive all the peoples.

6 "Will not all of them taunt him with ridicule and scorn, saying,
" 'Woe to him who piles up stolen goods
and makes himself wealthy by extortion!
How long must this go on?'
7 Will not your debtors[h] suddenly arise?
Will they not wake up and make you tremble?
Then you will become their victim.
8 Because you have plundered many nations,
the peoples who are left will plunder you.
For you have shed man's blood;
you have destroyed lands and cities and everyone in them.

9 "Woe to him who builds his realm by unjust gain
to set his nest on high,
to escape the clutches of ruin!
10 You have plotted the ruin of many peoples,
shaming your own house and forfeiting your life.

NIV [c] 1 Or *and what to answer when I am rebuked* [d] 2 Or *so that whoever reads it* [e] 3 Or *Though he linger, wait for him; / he* [f] 4 Or *faithfulness* [g] 5 Hebrew *Sheol* [h] 7 Or *creditors*

## King James

11For the stone shall cry out of the wall, and the beam out of
the timber shall answer it.
12¶ Woe to him that buildeth a town with blood, and stablisheth
a city by iniquity!
13Behold, *is it* not of the LORD of hosts that the people shall
labour in the very fire, and the people shall weary themselves for
very vanity?
14For the earth shall be filled with the knowledge of the glory
of the LORD, as the waters cover the sea.
15¶ Woe unto him that giveth his neighbour drink, that puttest
thy bottle to *him*, and makest *him* drunken also, that thou mayest
look on their nakedness!
16Thou art filled with shame for glory: drink thou also, and let
thy foreskin be uncovered: the cup of the LORD's right hand shall
be turned unto thee, and shameful spewing *shall be* on thy glory.
17For the violence of Lebanon shall cover thee, and the spoil of
beasts, *which* made them afraid, because of men's blood, and for
the violence of the land, of the city, and of all that dwell therein.
18¶ What profiteth the graven image that the maker thereof hath
graven it; the molten image, and a teacher of lies, that the maker
of his work trusteth therein, to make dumb idols?
19Woe unto him that saith to the wood, Awake; to the dumb
stone, Arise, it shall teach! Behold, it *is* laid over with gold and
silver, and *there is* no breath at all in the midst of it.
20But the LORD *is* in his holy temple: let all the earth keep silence
before him.

**3** A PRAYER of Habakkuk the prophet upon Shigionoth.
2O LORD, I have heard thy speech, *and* was afraid: O LORD,
revive thy work in the midst of the years, in the midst of the years
make known; in wrath remember mercy.
3God came from Teman, and the Holy One from mount Paran.
Selah. His glory covered the heavens, and the earth was full of his
praise.
4And *his* brightness was as the light; he had horns *coming* out
of his hand: and there *was* the hiding of his power.
5Before him went the pestilence, and burning coals went forth
at his feet.
6He stood, and measured the earth: he beheld, and drove asunder the nations; and the everlasting mountains were scattered, the
perpetual hills did bow: his ways *are* everlasting.
7I saw the tents of Cushan in affliction: *and* the curtains of the
land of Midian did tremble.

## Amplified

11For the stone shall cry out of the wall [built in sin, to accuse
you], and the beam out of the woodwork will answer it [agreeing
with its charge against you].
12Woe to him who builds a town with blood, and establishes a
city by iniquity!
13Behold, is it not by appointment of the Lord of hosts that the
nations toil only to satisfy the fire [that will consume their work],
and the peoples weary themselves only for emptiness, falseness
*and* futility?
14But [the time is coming when] the earth shall be filled with the
knowledge of the glory of the Lord, as the waters cover the sea.
[Isa. 11:9.]
15Woe to him [who delays that day!] who gives his neighbors
drink, who pours out your bottle to them *and* adds to it your
poisonous *and* blighting wrath, and also makes them drunk, that
you may look on their stripped condition *and pour out foul* shame
[on their glory]!
16You [yourself] will be filled with shame *and* contempt instead
of glory. Drink also, and be as *an* uncircumcised [heathen]! The cup
[of wrath] in the Lord's right hand will come around to you, *O
destroyer,* and foul shame shall be upon your *own* glory! [Rev.
16:19.]
17For the violence done to Lebanon will cover *and* overwhelm
you; the destruction of the animals [which the violence frightened
away] will terrify *you,* on account of men's blood and the violence
done to the land, to the city and all its inhabitants.
18What profit is the graven image when its maker has formed
it? It is only a molten image and a teacher of lies. For the maker
trusts in his own creations [as his gods] when he makes dumb
idols.
19Woe to him who says to the wooden image, Awake! and to
the dumb stone, Arise, it shall teach! Behold, it is laid over with
gold and silver, and there is no breath at all inside it!
20But the Lord is in His holy temple; let all the earth hush *and*
keep silence before Him. [Zeph. 1:7; Zech. 2:13.]

**3** A PRAYER of Habakkuk the prophet, set to wild, enthusiastic
*and* triumphal music.
2O Lord, I have heard the report of You, and was afraid. O
Lord, revive Your work in the midst of the years, in the midst of
the years make *Yourself* known! In wrath [earnestly] remember
love, pity *and* mercy.
3God [approaching from Sinai] came from Teman, [which
represents Edom,] and the Holy One from Mount Paran [in the
Sinai region]. Selah [stop and think calmly of that]! His glory
covered the heavens, and the earth was full of His praise.
4And His brightness was like the sunlight; rays streamed from
His hand; and there [in the sun-like splendor] was the hiding place
of His power.
5Before Him went the pestilence [as in Egypt], and burning
plague followed His feet [as in Sennacherib's army]. [Exod. 7:2-4;
II Kings 19:32-35.]
6He stood and measured the earth; He looked and shook the
nations; and the eternal mountains were scattered, the perpetual
hills bowed low; His ways are everlasting *and* His goings are of old.
7I [Habakkuk, in vision] saw the tents of Cushan [probably
Ethiopia] in affliction; the [tent] curtains of the land of Midian
trembled.

## New American Standard

11 "Surely the stone will cry out from the wall,
And the rafter will answer it from the framework.

12¶ "Woe to him who builds a city with bloodshed
And founds a town with violence!
13 "Is it not indeed from the LORD of hosts
That peoples toil for fire,
And nations grow weary for nothing?
14 "For the earth will be filled
With the knowledge of the glory of the LORD,
As the waters cover the sea.

15¶ "Woe to you who make your neighbors drink,
Who mix in your venom even to make *them* drunk
So as to look on their nakedness!
16 "You will be filled with disgrace rather than honor.
Now you yourself drink and expose your *own* nakedness.
The cup in the LORD's right hand will come around to you,
And utter disgrace *will come* upon your glory.
17 "For the violence done to Lebanon will overwhelm you,
And the devastation of *its* beasts by which you terrified them,
Because of human bloodshed and violence done to the land,
To the town and all its inhabitants.

18¶ "What profit is the idol when its maker has carved it,
*Or* an image, a teacher of falsehood?
For *its* maker trusts in his *own* handiwork
When he fashions speechless idols.
19 "Woe to him who says to a *piece of* wood, 'Awake!'
To a dumb stone, 'Arise!'
*And* that is *your* teacher?
Behold, it is overlaid with gold and silver,
And there is no breath at all inside it.
20 "But the LORD is in His holy temple.
Let all the earth be silent before Him."

*God's Deliverance of His People*

3 A PRAYER of Habakkuk the prophet, according to [a]Shigionoth.
2¶ LORD, I have heard the report about Thee *and* I fear.
O LORD, revive Thy work in the midst of the years,
In the midst of the years make it known;
In wrath remember mercy.

3¶ God comes from Teman,
And the Holy One from Mount Paran. Selah.
His splendor covers the heavens,
And the earth is full of His praise.
4 *His* radiance is like the sunlight;
He has rays *flashing* from His hand,
And there is the hiding of His power.
5 Before Him goes pestilence,
And plague comes after Him.
6 He stood and surveyed the earth;
He looked and startled the nations.
Yes, the perpetual mountains were shattered,
The ancient hills collapsed.
His ways are everlasting.
7 I saw the tents of Cushan under distress,
The tent curtains of the land of Midian were trembling.

NAS [a] I.e., A highly emotional poetic form

## New International

11 The stones of the wall will cry out,
and the beams of the woodwork will echo it.

12 "Woe to him who builds a city with bloodshed
and establishes a town by crime!
13 Has not the LORD Almighty determined
that the people's labor is only fuel for the fire,
that the nations exhaust themselves for nothing?
14 For the earth will be filled with the knowledge of the glory of the LORD,
as the waters cover the sea.

15 "Woe to him who gives drink to his neighbors,
pouring it from the wineskin till they are drunk,
so that he can gaze on their naked bodies.
16 You will be filled with shame instead of glory.
Now it is your turn! Drink and be exposed[b]!
The cup from the LORD's right hand is coming around to you,
and disgrace will cover your glory.
17 The violence you have done to Lebanon will overwhelm you,
and your destruction of animals will terrify you.
For you have shed man's blood;
you have destroyed lands and cities and everyone in them.

18 "Of what value is an idol, since a man has carved it?
Or an image that teaches lies?
For he who makes it trusts in his own creation;
he makes idols that cannot speak.
19 Woe to him who says to wood, 'Come to life!'
Or to lifeless stone, 'Wake up!'
Can it give guidance?
It is covered with gold and silver;
there is no breath in it.
20 But the LORD is in his holy temple;
let all the earth be silent before him."

*Habakkuk's Prayer*

3 A PRAYER of Habakkuk the prophet. On *shigionoth*.[c]
2 LORD, I have heard of your fame;
I stand in awe of your deeds, O LORD.
Renew them in our day,
in our time make them known;
in wrath remember mercy.

3 God came from Teman,
the Holy One from Mount Paran. *Selah*[d]
His glory covered the heavens
and his praise filled the earth.
4 His splendor was like the sunrise;
rays flashed from his hand,
where his power was hidden.
5 Plague went before him;
pestilence followed his steps.
6 He stood, and shook the earth;
he looked, and made the nations tremble.
The ancient mountains crumbled
and the age-old hills collapsed.
His ways are eternal.
7 I saw the tents of Cushan in distress,
the dwellings of Midian in anguish.

NIV [b] *16* Masoretic Text; Dead Sea Scrolls, Aquila, Vulgate and Syriac (see also Septuagint) *and stagger* [c] *1* Probably a literary or musical term [d] *3* A word of uncertain meaning; possibly a musical term; also in verses 9 and 13

# King James

8 Was the LORD displeased against the rivers? *was* thine anger against the rivers? *was* thy wrath against the sea, that thou didst ride upon thine horses *and* thy chariots of salvation?

9 Thy bow was made quite naked, *according* to the oaths of the tribes, *even thy* word. Selah. Thou didst cleave the earth with rivers.

10 The mountains saw thee, *and* they trembled: the overflowing of the water passed by: the deep uttered his voice, *and* lifted up his hands on high.

11 The sun *and* moon stood still in their habitation: at the light of thine arrows they went, *and* at the shining of thy glittering spear.

12 Thou didst march through the land in indignation, thou didst thresh the heathen in anger.

13 Thou wentest forth for the salvation of thy people, *even* for salvation with thine anointed; thou woundedst the head out of the house of the wicked, by discovering the foundation unto the neck. Selah.

14 Thou didst strike through with his staves the head of his villages: they came out as a whirlwind to scatter me: their rejoicing *was* as to devour the poor secretly.

15 Thou didst walk through the sea with thine horses, *through* the heap of great waters.

16 When I heard, my belly trembled; my lips quivered at the voice: rottenness entered into my bones, and I trembled in myself, that I might rest in the day of trouble: when he cometh up unto the people, he will invade them with his troops.

17 ¶ Although the fig tree shall not blossom, neither *shall* fruit *be* in the vines; the labour of the olive shall fail, and the fields shall yield no meat; the flock shall be cut off from the fold, and *there shall be* no herd in the stalls:

18 Yet I will rejoice in the LORD, I will joy in the God of my salvation.

19 The LORD God *is* my strength, and he will make my feet like hinds' *feet*, and he will make me to walk upon mine high places. To the chief singer on my stringed instruments.

# Amplified

8 Were *You* displeased with the rivers, O Lord? Or was Your anger against the rivers [You divided]? Was Your wrath against the *Red* Sea, that You rode *before* upon Your horses and Your chariots of victory *and* deliverance?

9 Your bow was made quite bare; sworn to the tribes [of Israel] by Your sure word were the rods of chastisement, scourges *and* calamities. Selah [stop and think calmly of that]! With rivers You cleaved the earth [bringing forth waters in dry places]. [Cf. Exod. 17:6; Num. 20:11.]

10 The mountains saw You, they trembled *and* writhed *as* in pain; the overflowing of the water passed by [as at the deluge]; the deep uttered its voice and lifted its hands on high.

11 The sun and moon stood back [as before Joshua] in their habitation at the light of Your arrows as they sped, at the flash of Your glittering spear. [Josh. 10:12, 13.]

12 You marched through the land in indignation, You trampled *and* threshed the nations in anger.

13 You went forth *and* have come for the salvation of Your people, for the deliverance *and* victory of Your anointed [people Israel]; You smote the head of the house of the wicked, laying bare the foundation even to the neck. Selah [stop and calmly think of that]!

14 You pierced with his own arrows the head of [the enemy's] hordes; they came out as a whirlwind to scatter me [the people], rejoicing as if to devour the poor [Israel] secretly.

15 You have trodden the sea with Your horses, [beside] the heap of great *and* surging waters. [Exod. 15:8.]

16 I heard, and my [whole inner self] trembled, my lips quivered at the sound. Rottenness enters into my bones and under me—down *to my feet*—I tremble. I will wait quietly for the day of trouble and distress, when there shall come up against [my] people him who is about to invade *and* oppress them.

17 Though the fig tree does not blossom, and there be no fruit on the vines; [though] the product of the olive fail, and the fields yield no food; though the flock be cut off from the fold, and there be no cattle in the stalls;

18 Yet I will rejoice in the Lord, I will exult in the [victorious] God of my salvation! [Rom. 8:37.]

19 The Lord God is my strength, my personal bravery *and* my invincible army; He makes my feet like hinds' feet, and will make me to walk [not to stand still in terror, but to walk] *and* make [spiritual] progress upon my high places [of trouble, suffering or responsibility]!

For the Chief Musician,
with my stringed instruments.

## New American Standard

8¶ Did the LORD rage against the rivers,
Or *was* Thine anger against the rivers,
Or *was* Thy wrath against the sea,
That Thou didst ride on Thy horses,
On Thy chariots of salvation?
9 Thy bow was made bare,
The rods of chastisement were sworn. Selah.
Thou didst cleave the earth with rivers.
10 The mountains saw Thee *and* quaked;
The downpour of waters swept by.
The deep uttered forth its voice,
It lifted high its hands.
11 Sun *and* moon stood in their places;
They went away at the light of Thine arrows,
At the radiance of Thy gleaming spear.
12 In indignation Thou didst march through the earth;
In anger Thou didst trample the nations.
13 Thou didst go forth for the salvation of Thy people,
For the salvation of Thine anointed.
Thou didst strike the head of the house of the evil
To lay him open from thigh to neck. Selah.
14 Thou didst pierce with his own spears
The head of his throngs.
They stormed in to scatter us;
Their exultation *was* like those
Who devour the oppressed in secret.
15 Thou didst tread on the sea with Thy horses,
On the surge of many waters.

16¶ I heard and my inward parts trembled,
At the sound my lips quivered.
Decay enters my bones,
And in my place I tremble.
Because I must wait quietly for the day of distress,
For the people to arise *who* will invade us.
17 Though the fig tree should not blossom,
And there be no fruit on the vines,
*Though* the yield of the olive should fail,
And the fields produce no food,
Though the flock should be cut off from the fold,
And there be no cattle in the stalls,
18 Yet I will exult in the LORD,
I will rejoice in the God of my salvation.
19 The Lord GOD is my strength,
And He has made my feet like hinds' *feet*,
And makes me walk on my high places.
For the choir director, on my stringed instruments.

## New International

8Were you angry with the rivers, O LORD?
Was your wrath against the streams?
Did you rage against the sea
when you rode with your horses
and your victorious chariots?
9You uncovered your bow,
you called for many arrows. *Selah*
You split the earth with rivers;
10 the mountains saw you and writhed.
Torrents of water swept by;
the deep roared
and lifted its waves on high.

11Sun and moon stood still in the heavens
at the glint of your flying arrows,
at the lightning of your flashing spear.
12In wrath you strode through the earth
and in anger you threshed the nations.
13You came out to deliver your people,
to save your anointed one.
You crushed the leader of the land of wickedness,
you stripped him from head to foot. *Selah*
14With his own spear you pierced his head
when his warriors stormed out to scatter us,
gloating as though about to devour
the wretched who were in hiding.
15You trampled the sea with your horses,
churning the great waters.

16I heard and my heart pounded,
my lips quivered at the sound;
decay crept into my bones,
and my legs trembled.
Yet I will wait patiently for the day of calamity
to come on the nation invading us.
17Though the fig tree does not bud
and there are no grapes on the vines,
though the olive crop fails
and the fields produce no food,
though there are no sheep in the pen
and no cattle in the stalls,
18yet I will rejoice in the LORD,
I will be joyful in God my Savior.
19The Sovereign LORD is my strength;
he makes my feet like the feet of a deer,
he enables me to go on the heights.
For the director of music. On my stringed instruments.

## King James

# Zephaniah

**1** THE WORD of the LORD which came unto Zephaniah the son of Cushi, the son of Gedaliah, the son of Amariah, the son of Hizkiah, in the days of Josiah the son of Amon, king of Judah.

2 I will utterly consume all *things* from off the land, saith the LORD.

3 I will consume man and beast; I will consume the fowls of the heaven, and the fishes of the sea, and the stumblingblocks with the wicked; and I will cut off man from off the land, saith the LORD.

4 I will also stretch out mine hand upon Judah, and upon all the inhabitants of Jerusalem; and I will cut off the remnant of Baal from this place, *and* the name of the Chemarims with the priests;

5 And them that worship the host of heaven upon the housetops; and them that worship *and* that swear by the LORD, and that swear by Malcham;

6 And them that are turned back from the LORD; and *those* that have not sought the LORD, nor inquired for him.

7 Hold thy peace at the presence of the Lord GOD: for the day of the LORD *is* at hand: for the LORD hath prepared a sacrifice, he hath bid his guests.

8 And it shall come to pass in the day of the LORD's sacrifice, that I will punish the princes, and the king's children, and all such as are clothed with strange apparel.

9 In the same day also will I punish all those that leap on the threshold, which fill their masters' houses with violence and deceit.

10 And it shall come to pass in that day, saith the LORD, *that there shall be* the noise of a cry from the fish gate, and an howling from the second, and a great crashing from the hills.

11 Howl, ye inhabitants of Maktesh, for all the merchant people are cut down; all they that bear silver are cut off.

## Amplified

For the Chief Musician, with my stringed instruments.

THE BOOK OF

# Zephaniah

**1** THE WORD of the Lord which came to Zephaniah the son of Cushi, son of Gedaliah, son of Amariah, son of Hezekiah, in the days of Josiah, king of Judah and son of Amon.

2 By taking away I will make an end *and* I will utterly consume *and* sweep away all things from the face of the earth, says the Lord.

3 I will consume *and* sweep away man and beast; I will consume *and* sweep away the birds of the air and the fish of the sea. I will overthrow the stumbling blocks—the idols—with the wicked [worshipers], and I will cut off mankind from the face of the earth, says the Lord.

4 I will also stretch out My hand over Judah, and over all the inhabitants of Jerusalem; and I will cut off the remnant of Baal from this place and the name of the idol-priests with the [false] priests,

5 And those who worship the starry host of the heavens upon their housetops, and those who [pretend to] worship the Lord and swear by *and* to Him and yet swear by *and* to [the heathen god Molech or] Malcam [their idol king],

6 And those who have drawn back from following the Lord, and those who have not sought the Lord nor inquired for, inquired of *and* required the Lord [as their first necessity].

7 [Hush!] Be silent before the Lord God, for the day [of the vengeance] of the Lord is near; for the Lord has prepared a sacrifice and He has set apart [for His use] those who have accepted His invitation. [Hab. 2:20.]

8 And on the day of the Lord's sacrifice, I will punish the officials and the king's sons and all who are clothed with [lavish] foreign apparel [instead of the Jewish dress with its reminders to obey God's commandments]. [Num. 15:38, 39.]

9 In the same day also will I punish all those who leap swiftly on *or* over the threshold [on entering houses to steal], who fill their master's house with violence and deceit *and* fraud.

10 And in that day, says the Lord, there shall be heard the voice of crying from the Fish Gate [in the wall of Jerusalem], and a wailing from the Second Quarter *or* Lower City, and a great crashing *and* sound of destruction from the hills.

11 Wail, you inhabitants of the Mortar [those located in the hollow part of the city]! For all the merchant people, like the people of Canaan, will be silent [entirely destroyed]; all those who weighed out silver *and* were loaded with it will be cut off.

## New American Standard

# Zephaniah

*Day of Judgment on Judah*

1 THE WORD of the LORD which came to Zephaniah son of
Cushi, son of Gedaliah, son of Amariah, son of Hezekiah, in
the days of Josiah son of Amon, king of Judah,
2¶ "I will completely remove all *things*
From the face of the earth," declares the LORD.
3 "I will remove man and beast;
I will remove the birds of the sky
And the fish of the sea,
And the ruins along with the wicked;
And I will cut off man from the face of the earth,"
declares the LORD.
4 "So I will stretch out My hand against Judah
And against all the inhabitants of Jerusalem.
And I will cut off the remnant of Baal from this place,
*And* the names of the idolatrous priests along with the
priests.
5 "And those who bow down on the housetops to the host
of heaven,
And those who bow down *and* swear to the LORD and
*yet* swear by Milcom,
6 And those who have turned back from following the
LORD,
And those who have not sought the LORD or inquired
of Him."

7¶ Be silent before the Lord GOD!
For the day of the LORD is near,
For the LORD has prepared a sacrifice,
He has consecrated His guests.
8 "Then it will come about on the day of the LORD's
sacrifice,
That I will punish the princes, the king's sons,
And all who clothe themselves with foreign garments.
9 "And I will punish on that day all who leap on the
*temple* threshold,
Who fill the house of their lord with violence and
deceit.
10 "And on that day," declares the LORD,
"There will be the sound of a cry from the Fish Gate,
A wail from the [a]Second Quarter,
And a loud crash from the hills.
11 "Wail, O inhabitants of the [b]Mortar,
For all the people of Canaan will be silenced;
All who weigh out silver will be cut off.

NAS [a] I.e., a district of Jerusalem [b] I.e., a district of Jerusalem

## New International

# Zephaniah

1 THE WORD of the LORD that came to Zephaniah son of
Cushi, the son of Gedaliah, the son of Amariah, the son of
Hezekiah, during the reign of Josiah son of Amon king of Judah:

*Warning of Coming Destruction*

2 "I will sweep away everything
from the face of the earth,"
declares the LORD.
3 "I will sweep away both men and animals;
I will sweep away the birds of the air
and the fish of the sea.
The wicked will have only heaps of rubble[c]
when I cut off man from the face of the earth,"
declares the LORD.

*Against Judah*

4 "I will stretch out my hand against Judah
and against all who live in Jerusalem.
I will cut off from this place every remnant of Baal,
the names of the pagan and the idolatrous priests—
5 those who bow down on the roofs
to worship the starry host,
those who bow down and swear by the LORD
and who also swear by Molech,[d]
6 those who turn back from following the LORD
and neither seek the LORD nor inquire of him.
7 Be silent before the Sovereign LORD,
for the day of the LORD is near.
The LORD has prepared a sacrifice;
he has consecrated those he has invited.
8 On the day of the LORD's sacrifice
I will punish the princes
and the king's sons
and all those clad
in foreign clothes.
9 On that day I will punish
all who avoid stepping on the threshold,[e]
who fill the temple of their gods
with violence and deceit.

10 "On that day," declares the LORD,
"a cry will go up from the Fish Gate,
wailing from the New Quarter,
and a loud crash from the hills.
11 Wail, you who live in the market district[f];
all your merchants will be wiped out,
all who trade with[g] silver will be ruined.

NIV [c] 3 The meaning of the Hebrew for this line is uncertain. [d] 5 Hebrew *Malcam*, that is, Milcom [e] 9 See 1 Samuel 5:5. [f] *11* Or *the Mortar* [g] *11* Or *in*

## King James

12And it shall come to pass at that time, *that* I will search Jerusalem with candles, and punish the men that are settled on their lees: that say in their heart, The LORD will not do good, neither will he do evil.

13Therefore their goods shall become a booty, and their houses a desolation: they shall also build houses, but not inhabit *them;* and they shall plant vineyards, but not drink the wine thereof.

14The great day of the LORD *is* near, *it is* near, and hasteth greatly, *even* the voice of the day of the LORD: the mighty man shall cry there bitterly.

15That day *is* a day of wrath, a day of trouble and distress, a day of wasteness and desolation, a day of darkness and gloominess, a day of clouds and thick darkness,

16A day of the trumpet and alarm against the fenced cities, and against the high towers.

17And I will bring distress upon men, that they shall walk like blind men, because they have sinned against the LORD: and their blood shall be poured out as dust, and their flesh as the dung.

18Neither their silver nor their gold shall be able to deliver them in the day of the LORD'S wrath; but the whole land shall be devoured by the fire of his jealousy: for he shall make even a speedy riddance of all them that dwell in the land.

**2** GATHER YOURSELVES together, yea, gather together, O nation not desired;

2Before the decree bring forth, *before* the day pass as the chaff, before the fierce anger of the LORD come upon you, before the day of the LORD's anger come upon you.

3Seek ye the LORD, all ye meek of the earth, which have wrought his judgment; seek righteousness, seek meekness: it may be ye shall be hid in the day of the LORD's anger.

4¶ For Gaza shall be forsaken, and Ashkelon a desolation: they shall drive out Ashdod at the noon day, and Ekron shall be rooted up.

5Woe unto the inhabitants of the sea coast, the nation of the Cherethites! the word of the LORD *is* against you; O Canaan, the land of the Philistines, I will even destroy thee, that there shall be no inhabitant.

6And the sea coast shall be dwellings *and* cottages for shepherds, and folds for flocks.

## Amplified

12And at that time I will search Jerusalem with lamps, and punish the men who [like old wine] are thickening *and* settling on their lees, who say in their heart, The Lord will not do good, nor will He do evil.

13And their wealth shall become plunder, and their houses a desolation. Though they build houses, they shall not inhabit them; though they plant vineyards, they shall not drink the wine from them. [Deut. 28:30, 39; Amos 5:11, 12.]

14The great day of the Lord is near, near and hastening fast. Hark! the voice of the day of the Lord! The mighty man [unable to fight or to flee] will cry then bitterly.

15That day is a day of wrath, a day of distress and anguish, a day of ruin and devastation, a day of darkness and gloom, a day of clouds and thick darkness, [Jer. 30:7; Joel 2:11; Amos 5:18.]

16A day of the blast of trumpet and battle cry against the fortified cities and against the high towers *and* battlements.

17And I will bring distress upon men, so that they shall walk like blind men, because they have sinned against the Lord; their blood shall be poured out like dust, and their flesh like dung.

18Neither their silver nor their gold shall be able to deliver them in the day of the Lord's indignation *and* wrath. But the whole earth shall be consumed in the fire of His jealous wrath; for a full, yes, a sudden end will He make of all the inhabitants of the earth. [Cf. Luke 21:35, 36; I Thess. 4:15-17; John 14:3; Matt. 24:31.]

**2** COLLECT YOUR thoughts, yes, unbend yourselves [in submission, and see if there is no sense of shame and no consciousness of sin left in you], O shameless nation—not desirous or desired!

2[The time for repentance is speeding by like chaff whirled before the wind!] Therefore consider, before God's decree brings forth [the curse upon you], before the time [to repent] is gone like the drifting chaff, before the fierce anger of the Lord comes upon you, yes, before the day of the wrath of the Lord comes upon you!

3Seek the Lord—inquire for Him, inquire of Him, and require Him [as the foremost necessity of your life]—all you humble of the land, who have acted in compliance with His revealed will *and* have kept His commandments; seek righteousness, seek humility—inquire for them, require them [as vital]. It may be you will be hidden in the day of the Lord's anger.

4For [hear the fate of the Philistines:] Gaza shall be forsaken, and Ashkelon shall become a desolation; the people of Ashdod shall be driven out at noonday, and Ekron shall be uprooted.

5Woe to the inhabitants of the seacoast, the nation of the Cherethites [in Philistia]! The word of the Lord is against you, O Canaan, land of the Philistines; I will destroy you until no inhabitant is left.

6And the seacoast shall be pastures, with [deserted] dwelling places *and* caves for shepherds and folds for flocks.

## New American Standard

12 "And it will come about at that time
That I will search Jerusalem with lamps,
And I will punish the men
Who are stagnant in spirit,
Who say in their hearts,
'The LORD will not do good or evil!'
13 "Moreover, their wealth will become plunder,
And their houses desolate;
Yes, they will build houses but not inhabit *them*,
And plant vineyards but not drink their wine."

14¶ Near is the great day of the LORD,
Near and coming very quickly;
Listen, the day of the LORD!
In it the warrior cries out bitterly.
15 A day of wrath is that day,
A day of trouble and distress,
A day of destruction and desolation,
A day of darkness and gloom,
A day of clouds and thick darkness,
16 A day of trumpet and battle cry,
Against the fortified cities
And the high corner towers.
17 And I will bring distress on men,
So that they will walk like the blind,
Because they have sinned against the LORD;
And their blood will be poured out like dust,
And their flesh like dung.
18 Neither their silver nor their gold
Will be able to deliver them
On the day of the LORD's wrath;
And all the earth will be devoured
In the fire of His jealousy,
For He will make a complete end,
Indeed a terrifying one,
Of all the inhabitants of the earth.

*Judgments on Judah's Enemies*

2 GATHER YOURSELVES together, yes, gather,
O nation without shame,
2 Before the decree takes effect—
The day passes like the chaff—
Before the burning anger of the LORD comes upon you,
Before the day of the LORD's anger comes upon you.
3 Seek the LORD,
All you humble of the earth
Who have carried out His ordinances;
Seek righteousness, seek humility.
Perhaps you will be hidden
In the day of the LORD's anger.

4¶ For Gaza will be abandoned,
And Ashkelon a desolation;
Ashdod will be driven out at noon,
And Ekron will be uprooted.
5 Woe to the inhabitants of the seacoast,
The nation of the [a]Cherethites!
The word of the LORD is against you,
O Canaan, land of the Philistines;
And I will destroy you,
So that there will be no inhabitant.
6 So the seacoast will be pastures,
*With* caves for shepherds and folds for flocks.

NAS [a] I.e., a segment of the Philistines with roots in Crete

## New International

12At that time I will search Jerusalem with lamps
and punish those who are complacent,
who are like wine left on its dregs,
who think, 'The LORD will do nothing,
either good or bad.'
13Their wealth will be plundered,
their houses demolished.
They will build houses
but not live in them;
they will plant vineyards
but not drink the wine.

*The Great Day of the LORD*

14"The great day of the LORD is near—
near and coming quickly.
Listen! The cry on the day of the LORD will be bitter,
the shouting of the warrior there.
15That day will be a day of wrath,
a day of distress and anguish,
a day of trouble and ruin,
a day of darkness and gloom,
a day of clouds and blackness,
16a day of trumpet and battle cry
against the fortified cities
and against the corner towers.
17I will bring distress on the people
and they will walk like blind men,
because they have sinned against the LORD.
Their blood will be poured out like dust
and their entrails like filth.
18Neither their silver nor their gold
will be able to save them
on the day of the LORD's wrath.
In the fire of his jealousy
the whole world will be consumed,
for he will make a sudden end
of all who live in the earth."

2 GATHER TOGETHER, gather together,
O shameful nation,
2before the appointed time arrives
and that day sweeps on like chaff,
before the fierce anger of the LORD comes upon you,
before the day of the LORD's wrath comes upon you.
3Seek the LORD, all you humble of the land,
you who do what he commands.
Seek righteousness, seek humility;
perhaps you will be sheltered
on the day of the LORD's anger.

*Against Philistia*

4Gaza will be abandoned
and Ashkelon left in ruins.
At midday Ashdod will be emptied
and Ekron uprooted.
5Woe to you who live by the sea,
O Kerethite people;
the word of the LORD is against you,
O Canaan, land of the Philistines.

"I will destroy you,
and none will be left."

6The land by the sea, where the Kerethites[b] dwell,
will be a place for shepherds and sheep pens.

NIV [b] 6 The meaning of the Hebrew for this word is uncertain.

## King James

7And the coast shall be for the remnant of the house of Judah; they shall feed thereupon: in the houses of Ashkelon shall they lie down in the evening: for the LORD their God shall visit them, and turn away their captivity.

8¶ I have heard the reproach of Moab, and the revilings of the children of Ammon, whereby they have reproached my people, and magnified *themselves* against their border.

9Therefore *as* I live, saith the LORD of hosts, the God of Israel, Surely Moab shall be as Sodom, and the children of Ammon as Gomorrah, *even* the breeding of nettles, and saltpits, and a perpetual desolation: the residue of my people shall spoil them, and the remnant of my people shall possess them.

10This shall they have for their pride, because they have reproached and magnified *themselves* against the people of the LORD of hosts.

11The LORD *will be* terrible unto them: for he will famish all the gods of the earth; and *men* shall worship him, every one from his place, *even* all the isles of the heathen.

12¶ Ye Ethiopians also, ye *shall be* slain by my sword.

13And he will stretch out his hand against the north, and destroy Assyria; and will make Nineveh a desolation, *and* dry like a wilderness.

14And flocks shall lie down in the midst of her, all the beasts of the nations: both the cormorant and the bittern shall lodge in the upper lintels of it; *their* voice shall sing in the windows; desolation *shall be* in the thresholds: for he shall uncover the cedar work.

15This *is* the rejoicing city that dwelt carelessly, that said in her heart, I *am*, and *there is* none beside me: how is she become a desolation, a place for beasts to lie down in! every one that passeth by her shall hiss, *and* wag his hand.

## Amplified

7The [a]seacoast shall belong to the remnant of the house of Judah; they shall pasture their flocks upon it; in the houses of [deserted Philistine] Ashkelon shall they of Judah lie down in the evening. For the Lord their [Judah's] God shall visit them [for their relief], and restore them from their captivity. [Isa. 14:29-31; Amos 1:6-8.]

8I have heard the taunts of Moab and the revilings of the Ammonites by which they have reproached My people, and magnified themselves *and* made boasts against their territory.

9Therefore, as I live, says the Lord of hosts, the God of Israel, Moab shall become like Sodom, and the Ammonites like Gomorrah, a land possessed by nettles *and* wild vetches and saltpits, and a perpetual desolation. The remnant of My people shall make a prey of them, and what is left of My nation shall possess them.

10This shall they have for their pride, because they have taunted and boasted against the people of the Lord of hosts.

11The Lord will be terrible to them, for He will make lean *and* famish all the gods of the earth; and men shall worship Him, every one from his place, even all the isles *and* coastlands of the nations. [Joel 2:11; Zeph. 1:4; 3:9.]

12You Ethiopians also, you shall be slain by My sword. [Isa. 18.]

13And [the Lord] will stretch out His hand against the north and destroy Assyria, and will make Nineveh [b]a desolation, dry as the desert.

14Herds shall lie down in the midst of [Nineveh], all the [wild] beasts of the nations *and* of every kind; both the pelican and the hedgehog shall lodge on the upper part of her [fallen] pillars; the voice [of the nesting bird] shall sing in the windows, desolation *and* drought shall be on the thresholds; for her cedar paneling will He lay bare.

15This is the joyous *and* exultant city that dwelt carelessly—feeling so secure; that said in her heart, I am and there is none beside me. What a desolation she has become, a lair for *wild* beasts! Every one who passes by her shall hiss and wave his hand [indicating his gratification]. [Isa. 10:5-34; 47:8.]

**AMP** [a] This is one of the more than twenty-five details of Bible prophecy concerning the land of Palestine that have been literally fulfilled. Probability computers estimate that *if a prophecy concerning a person, place or event has twenty-five details, there is one chance in more than thirty-three millions of its accidental fulfillment.* And such prophecy must be (1) above possibility of human collusion; (2) beyond the ability of human calculation; (3) proof against human coincidence, and (4) above all possibility of human comprehension. What inconceivable omniscience was behind the writing of the Bible! Twenty-five details also concerning the betrayal, trial, death and burial of our Lord were fulfilled, fulfilled within twenty-four hours! And the fulfillment of the most remarkable prophecies of all time is scheduled in the Bible for the rapidly approaching future! [b] This is one of the more than twenty-five details of Bible prophecy concerning the land of Palestine that have been literally fulfilled. Probability computers estimate that *if a prophecy concerning a person, place or event has twenty-five details, there is one chance in more than thirty-three millions of its accidental fulfillment.* And such prophecy must be (1) above possibility of human collusion; (2) beyond the ability of human calculation; (3) proof against human coincidence, and (4) above all possibility of human comprehension. What inconceivable omniscience was behind the writing of the Bible! Twenty-five details also concerning the betrayal, trial, death and burial of our Lord were fulfilled, fulfilled within twenty-four hours! And the fulfillment of the most remarkable prophecies of all time is scheduled in the Bible for the rapidly approaching future!

## New American Standard

7 And the coast will be
For the remnant of the house of Judah,
They will pasture on it.
In the houses of Ashkelon they will lie down at
evening;
For the LORD their God will care for them
And restore their fortune.
8¶ "I have heard the taunting of Moab
And the revilings of the sons of Ammon,
With which they have taunted My people
And become arrogant against their territory.
9 "Therefore, as I live," declares the LORD of hosts,
The God of Israel,
"Surely Moab will be like Sodom,
And the sons of Ammon like Gomorrah—
A place possessed by nettles and salt pits,
And a perpetual desolation.
The remnant of My people will plunder them,
And the remainder of My nation will inherit them."
10 This they will have in return for their pride, because they have taunted and become arrogant against the people of the LORD of hosts.
11 The LORD will be terrifying to them, for He will starve all the gods of the earth; and all the coastlands of the nations will bow down to Him, everyone from his *own* place.
12¶ "You also, O Ethiopians, will be slain by My sword."
13 And He will stretch out His hand against the north
And destroy Assyria,
And He will make Nineveh a desolation,
Parched like the wilderness.
14 And flocks will lie down in her midst,
All beasts which range in herds;
Both the pelican and the hedgehog
Will lodge in the tops of her pillars;
Birds will sing in the window,
Desolation *will be* on the threshold;
For He has laid bare the cedar work.
15 This is the exultant city
Which dwells securely,
Who says in her heart,
"I am, and there is no one besides me."
How she has become a desolation,
A resting place for beasts!
Everyone who passes by her will hiss
*And* wave his hand *in contempt*.

## New International

7 It will belong to the remnant of the house of Judah;
there they will find pasture.
In the evening they will lie down
in the houses of Ashkelon.
The LORD their God will care for them;
he will restore their fortunes.[c]

*Against Moab and Ammon*

8 "I have heard the insults of Moab
and the taunts of the Ammonites,
who insulted my people
and made threats against their land.
9 Therefore, as surely as I live,"
declares the LORD Almighty, the God of Israel,
"surely Moab will become like Sodom,
the Ammonites like Gomorrah—
a place of weeds and salt pits,
a wasteland forever.
The remnant of my people will plunder them;
the survivors of my nation will inherit their land."
10 This is what they will get in return for their pride,
for insulting and mocking the people of the LORD
Almighty.
11 The LORD will be awesome to them
when he destroys all the gods of the land.
The nations on every shore will worship him,
every one in its own land.

*Against Cush*

12 "You too, O Cushites,[d]
will be slain by my sword."

*Against Assyria*

13 He will stretch out his hand against the north
and destroy Assyria,
leaving Nineveh utterly desolate
and dry as the desert.
14 Flocks and herds will lie down there,
creatures of every kind.
The desert owl and the screech owl
will roost on her columns.
Their calls will echo through the windows,
rubble will be in the doorways,
the beams of cedar will be exposed.
15 This is the carefree city
that lived in safety.
She said to herself,
"I am, and there is none besides me."
What a ruin she has become,
a lair for wild beasts!
All who pass by her scoff
and shake their fists.

**NIV** [c] 7 Or *will bring back their captives* [d] 12 That is, people from the upper Nile region

## King James

**3** WOE TO her that is filthy and polluted, to the oppressing city!

2She obeyed not the voice; she received not correction; she trusted not in the LORD; she drew not near to her God.

3Her princes within her *are* roaring lions; her judges *are* evening wolves; they gnaw not the bones till the morrow.

4Her prophets *are* light *and* treacherous persons: her priests have polluted the sanctuary, they have done violence to the law.

5The just LORD *is* in the midst thereof; he will not do iniquity: every morning doth he bring his judgment to light, he faileth not; but the unjust knoweth no shame.

6I have cut off the nations: their towers are desolate; I made their streets waste, that none passeth by: their cities are destroyed, so that there is no man, that there is none inhabitant.

7I said, Surely thou wilt fear me, thou wilt receive instruction; so their dwelling should not be cut off, howsoever I punished them: but they rose early, *and* corrupted all their doings.

8¶ Therefore wait ye upon me, saith the LORD, until the day that I rise up to the prey: for my determination *is* to gather the nations, that I may assemble the kingdoms, to pour upon them mine indignation, *even* all my fierce anger: for all the earth shall be devoured with the fire of my jealousy.

9For then will I turn to the people a pure language, that they may all call upon the name of the LORD, to serve him with one consent.

10From beyond the rivers of Ethiopia my suppliants, *even* the daughter of my dispersed, shall bring mine offering.

11In that day shalt thou not be ashamed for all thy doings, wherein thou hast transgressed against me: for then I will take away out of the midst of thee them that rejoice in thy pride, and thou shalt no more be haughty because of my holy mountain.

12I will also leave in the midst of thee an afflicted and poor people, and they shall trust in the name of the LORD.

13The remnant of Israel shall not do iniquity, nor speak lies; neither shall a deceitful tongue be found in their mouth: for they shall feed and lie down, and none shall make *them* afraid.

14¶ Sing, O daughter of Zion; shout, O Israel; be glad and rejoice with all the heart, O daughter of Jerusalem.

## Amplified

**3** WOE TO her that is rebellious and polluted, the oppressing city—Jerusalem!

2She did not listen *and* heed the voice *of God;* she accepted no correction *or* instruction; she trusted not in the Lord—nor leaned on or was confident in Him [but in her own wealth]; she drew not near to her God [but to the god of Baal or Molech].

3Her officials in the midst of her are roaring lions; her judges are evening wolves; they gnaw not the bones on the morrow, *for* nothing is left by morning.

4Her prophets are light—lacking truth, gravity and steadiness—and men of treachery; her priests have profaned the sanctuary; [defrauding God and man by pretending their own word is God's word] they have done violence to the law. [Jer. 23:11; Hos. 9:7; Ezek. 22:26.]

5The Lord in the midst of her is [uncompromisingly] righteous; He will not do iniquity; every morning He brings His justice to light, He fails not; but the unjust *person* knows no shame.

6I, [the Lord,] have cut off nations; their battlements *and* corner towers are desolate *and* in ruins; I laid their streets waste so that none passes over *them;* their cities are destroyed, so that there is no man, there is no inhabitant.

7I said, Only let her [reverently *and* worshipfully] fear Me, receive correction and instruction, and *Jerusalem's* dwelling shall not be cut off. However I have punished her—according to all that I have appointed concerning her in the way of punishment—but all the more they are eager to make all their doings corrupt *and* infamous.

8Therefore [earnestly] wait for Me, says the Lord, *waiting* for the day when I rise up to the attack—as a witness [accuser, judge] and a testimony. For My decision *and* determination *and* right it is to gather the nations together, to assemble the kingdoms, to pour upon them My indignation, even all [the heat of] My fierce anger; for [in that day] all the earth shall be consumed with the fire of My zeal *and* jealousy.

9For then [changing their impure language] I will give to the people a clear *and* pure speech from pure lips, that they may all call upon the name of the Lord, to serve Him with one unanimous consent *and* one united shoulder [bearing the yoke of the Lord].

10From beyond the rivers of Cush *or* Ethiopia those who pray to Me, the daughter of My dispersed people, will bring *and* present My offering.

11In that day you [the congregation of Israel] shall not be put to shame for all your deeds by which you have rebelled *and* transgressed against Me; for then I will take away out of your midst those who exult in your majesty *and* pride, and you shall no more be haughty [and carry yourselves arrogantly on or] because of My holy mountain.

12For I will leave in the midst of you a people afflicted and poor, and they shall [trust,] seek refuge [and be confident] in the name of the Lord.

13What is left of Israel shall not do iniquity or speak lies, neither shall a deceitful tongue be found in their mouth; for they shall feed and lie down, and none shall make them afraid.

14Sing, O daughter of Zion; shout, O Israel! Rejoice, be in high spirits *and* glory with all your heart, O daughter of Jerusalem [in that day].

## New American Standard

*Woe to Jerusalem and the Nations*

3 WOE TO her who is rebellious and defiled,
The tyrannical city!
2 She heeded no voice;
She accepted no instruction.
She did not trust in the LORD;
She did not draw near to her God.
3 Her princes within her are roaring lions,
Her judges are wolves at evening;
They leave nothing for the morning.
4 Her prophets are reckless, treacherous men;
Her priests have profaned the sanctuary.
They have done violence to the law.
5 The LORD is righteous within her;
He will do no injustice.
Every morning He brings His justice to light;
He does not fail.
But the unjust knows no shame.
6 "I have cut off nations;
Their corner towers are in ruins.
I have made their streets desolate,
With no one passing by;
Their cities are laid waste,
Without a man, without an inhabitant.
7 "I said, 'Surely you will revere Me,
Accept instruction.'
So her dwelling will not be cut off
*According to* all that I have appointed concerning her.
But they were eager to corrupt all their deeds.

8¶ "Therefore, wait for Me," declares the LORD,
"For the day when I rise up to the prey.
Indeed, My decision is to gather nations,
To assemble kingdoms,
To pour out on them My indignation,
All My burning anger;
For all the earth will be devoured
By the fire of My zeal.
9 "For then I will give to the peoples purified lips,
That all of them may call on the name of the LORD,
To serve Him shoulder to shoulder.
10 "From beyond the rivers of Ethiopia
My worshipers, My dispersed ones,
Will bring My offerings.
11 "In that day you will feel no shame
Because of all your deeds
By which you have rebelled against Me;
For then I will remove from your midst
Your proud, exulting ones,
And you will never again be haughty
On My holy mountain.

*A Remnant of Israel*

12 "But I will leave among you
A humble and lowly people,
And they will take refuge in the name of the LORD.
13 "The remnant of Israel will do no wrong
And tell no lies,
Nor will a deceitful tongue
Be found in their mouths;
For they shall feed and lie down
With no one to make them tremble."

14¶ Shout for joy, O daughter of Zion!
Shout *in triumph*, O Israel!
Rejoice and exult with all *your* heart,
O daughter of Jerusalem!

## New International

*The Future of Jerusalem*

3 WOE TO the city of oppressors,
rebellious and defiled!
2She obeys no one,
she accepts no correction.
She does not trust in the LORD,
she does not draw near to her God.
3Her officials are roaring lions,
her rulers are evening wolves,
who leave nothing for the morning.
4Her prophets are arrogant;
they are treacherous men.
Her priests profane the sanctuary
and do violence to the law.
5The LORD within her is righteous;
he does no wrong.
Morning by morning he dispenses his justice,
and every new day he does not fail,
yet the unrighteous know no shame.

6"I have cut off nations;
their strongholds are demolished.
I have left their streets deserted,
with no one passing through.
Their cities are destroyed;
no one will be left—no one at all.
7I said to the city,
'Surely you will fear me
and accept correction!'
Then her dwelling would not be cut off,
nor all my punishments come upon her.
But they were still eager
to act corruptly in all they did.
8Therefore wait for me," declares the LORD,
"for the day I will stand up to testify.[a]
I have decided to assemble the nations,
to gather the kingdoms
and to pour out my wrath on them—
all my fierce anger.
The whole world will be consumed
by the fire of my jealous anger.

9"Then will I purify the lips of the peoples,
that all of them may call on the name of the LORD
and serve him shoulder to shoulder.
10From beyond the rivers of Cush[b]
my worshipers, my scattered people,
will bring me offerings.
11On that day you will not be put to shame
for all the wrongs you have done to me,
because I will remove from this city
those who rejoice in their pride.
Never again will you be haughty
on my holy hill.
12But I will leave within you
the meek and humble,
who trust in the name of the LORD.
13The remnant of Israel will do no wrong;
they will speak no lies,
nor will deceit be found in their mouths.
They will eat and lie down
and no one will make them afraid."

14Sing, O Daughter of Zion;
shout aloud, O Israel!
Be glad and rejoice with all your heart,
O Daughter of Jerusalem!

**NIV** [a] *8* Septuagint and Syriac; Hebrew *will rise up to plunder* [b] *10* That is, the upper Nile region

## King James

15 The LORD hath taken away thy judgments, he hath cast out
thine enemy: the king of Israel, *even* the LORD, *is* in the midst of
thee: thou shalt not see evil any more.
16 In that day it shall be said to Jerusalem, Fear thou not: *and to*
Zion, Let not thine hands be slack.
17 The LORD thy God in the midst of thee *is* mighty; he will save,
he will rejoice over thee with joy; he will rest in his love, he will
joy over thee with singing.
18 I will gather *them that are* sorrowful for the solemn assembly,
*who* are of thee, *to whom* the reproach of it *was* a burden.
19 Behold, at that time I will undo all that afflict thee: and I will
save her that halteth, and gather her that was driven out; and I will
get them praise and fame in every land where they have been put
to shame.
20 At that time will I bring you *again*, even in the time that I
gather you: for I will make you a name and a praise among all
people of the earth, when I turn back your captivity before your
eyes, saith the LORD.

## Amplified

15 [For then it will be that] the Lord has taken away the judgments against you, He has cast out your enemy; the King of Israel,
even the Lord [Himself], is in the midst of you; [and after He has
come to you] you shall not experience *or* fear evil any more.
16 In that day it shall be said to Jerusalem, Fear not, O Zion. Let
not your hands sink down *or* be slow *and* listless.
17 The Lord your God is in the midst of you, a mighty One, a
Savior—Who saves! He will rejoice over you with joy; He will rest
[in silent satisfaction] *and* in His love He will be silent *and* make no
mention [of past sins, or even recall them]; He will exult over you
with singing.
18 I will gather those belonging to you [those Israelites in captivi-
ty] who yearn *and* grieve for the solemn assembly [and the festi-
vals], on whom [their exile and inability to attend services at
Jerusalem have brought derision and] the reproach of it is a burden.
19 Behold, at that time I will deal with all those who afflict you;
I will save the limping and gather the outcasts, and will make them
a praise and a name in every land of their shame. [Mic. 4:6, 7.]
20 At that time I will bring you in; yes, at that time I will gather
you: for I will make you a name and a praise among all the nations
of the earth, when I reverse your captivity before your eyes, says
the Lord.

## New American Standard

15 The LORD has taken away *His* judgments against you,
He has cleared away your enemies.
The King of Israel, the LORD, is in your midst;
You will fear disaster no more.
16 In that day it will be said to Jerusalem:
"Do not be afraid, O Zion;
Do not let your hands fall limp.
17 "The LORD your God is in your midst,
A victorious warrior.
He will exult over you with joy,
He will be quiet in His love,
He will rejoice over you with shouts of joy.
18 "I will gather those who grieve about the appointed feasts—
They came from you, *O Zion;*
*The* reproach *of exile* is a burden on them.
19 "Behold, I am going to deal at that time
With all your oppressors,
I will save the lame
And gather the outcast,
And I will turn their shame into praise and renown
In all the earth.
20 "At that time I will bring you in,
Even at the time when I gather you together;
Indeed, I will give you renown and praise
Among all the peoples of the earth,
When I restore your fortunes before your eyes,"
Says the LORD.

## New International

15The LORD has taken away your punishment,
he has turned back your enemy.
The LORD, the King of Israel, is with you;
never again will you fear any harm.
16On that day they will say to Jerusalem,
"Do not fear, O Zion;
do not let your hands hang limp.
17The LORD your God is with you,
he is mighty to save.
He will take great delight in you,
he will quiet you with his love,
he will rejoice over you with singing."

18"The sorrows for the appointed feasts
I will remove from you;
they are a burden and a reproach to you.[a]
19At that time I will deal
with all who oppressed you;
I will rescue the lame
and gather those who have been scattered.
I will give them praise and honor
in every land where they were put to shame.
20At that time I will gather you;
at that time I will bring you home.
I will give you honor and praise
among all the peoples of the earth
when I restore your fortunes[b]
before your very eyes,"
says the LORD.

**NIV** [a] *18* Or *"I will gather you who mourn for the appointed feasts; / your reproach is a burden to you* [b] *20* Or *I bring back your captives*

## King James

THE BOOK OF

# Haggai

**1** IN THE second year of Darius the king, in the sixth month, in the first day of the month, came the word of the LORD by Haggai the prophet unto Zerubbabel the son of Shealtiel, governor of Judah, and to Joshua the son of Josedech, the high priest, saying,

2 Thus speaketh the LORD of hosts, saying, This people say, The time is not come, the time that the LORD's house should be built.

3 Then came the word of the LORD by Haggai the prophet, saying,

4 *Is it* time for you, O ye, to dwell in your ceiled houses, and this house *lie* waste?

5 Now therefore thus saith the LORD of hosts; Consider your ways.

6 Ye have sown much, and bring in little; ye eat, but ye have not enough; ye drink, but ye are not filled with drink; ye clothe you, but there is none warm; and he that earneth wages earneth wages *to put it* into a bag with holes.

7 ¶ Thus saith the LORD of hosts; Consider your ways.

8 Go up to the mountain, and bring wood, and build the house; and I will take pleasure in it, and I will be glorified, saith the LORD.

9 Ye looked for much, and, lo, *it came* to little; and when ye brought *it* home, I did blow upon it. Why? saith the LORD of hosts. Because of mine house that *is* waste, and ye run every man unto his own house.

10 Therefore the heaven over you is stayed from dew, and the earth is stayed *from* her fruit.

11 And I called for a drought upon the land, and upon the mountains, and upon the corn, and upon the new wine, and upon the oil, and upon *that* which the ground bringeth forth, and upon men, and upon cattle, and upon all the labour of the hands.

12 ¶ Then Zerubbabel the son of Shealtiel, and Joshua the son of Josedech, the high priest, with all the remnant of the people, obeyed the voice of the LORD their God, and the words of Haggai the prophet, as the LORD their God had sent him, and the people did fear before the LORD.

13 Then spake Haggai the LORD's messenger in the LORD's message unto the people, saying, I *am* with you, saith the LORD.

14 And the LORD stirred up the spirit of Zerubbabel the son of Shealtiel, governor of Judah, and the spirit of Joshua the son of Josedech, the high priest, and the spirit of all the remnant of the people; and they came and did work in the house of the LORD of hosts, their God,

15 In the four and twentieth day of the sixth month, in the second year of Darius the king.

## Amplified

THE BOOK OF

# Haggai

**1** IN THE second year of Darius the king [of Persia, successor to King Cyrus], in the sixth month, on the first day of the month, the word of the Lord came by means of Haggai the prophet [in Jerusalem after the Babylonian captivity] to Zerubbabel the son of Shealtiel, governor of Judah, and to Joshua the son of Jehozadak, the high priest, saying,

2 Thus says the Lord of hosts: This people say, The time is not yet come that the Lord's house should be rebuilt [although Cyrus had ordered it done sixteen years before; rebuilding of Jerusalem's walls had later been forbidden, but not so of the temple].

3 Then came the word of the Lord by Haggai the prophet, saying,

4 Is it time for you yourselves to dwell in your paneled houses, while this house [of the Lord] lies in ruins?

5 Now therefore thus says the Lord of hosts: Consider your ways [and set your mind on what has come to you].

6 You have sown much, but you have reaped little; you eat, but you do not have enough; you drink, but you do not have your fill; you clothe yourselves, but no one is warm; and he who earns wages has earned them to put them in a bag with holes in it.

7 Thus says the Lord of hosts: Consider your ways [your previous and present conduct] *and* how you have fared.

8 Go up to the hill country and bring lumber and rebuild *My* house, and I will take pleasure in it and I will be glorified, says the Lord [by accepting it as done for My glory, and by displaying My glory in it].

9 You looked for much [harvest], and lo, it came to little; and even when you brought that home, I blew it away. Why? says the Lord of hosts. Because of My house which lies waste, while you yourselves run each man to his own house [eager to build and adorn it].

10 Therefore the heavens above you [for your sake] withhold the dew, and the earth withholds its produce.

11 And I have called for a drought upon the land and the hill country, upon the grain, the fresh fruit juice, the oil, upon what the ground brings forth, upon men and cattle, and upon all the [wearisome] toil of *men's* hands.

12 Then Zerubbabel the son of Shealtiel, and Joshua the son of Jehozadak, the high priest, with all the remnant of the people [returned from captivity], listened to [and obeyed] the voice of the Lord their God [not vaguely or partly, but completely] *according to* the words of Haggai the prophet, since the Lord their God had sent him, and the people reverently feared *and* worshipfully turned to the Lord.

13 Then Haggai, the Lord's messenger, spoke the Lord's message to the people saying, I am with you, says the Lord.

14 And the Lord aroused the spirit of Zerubbabel the son of Shealtiel, governor of Judah, and the spirit of Joshua the son of Jehozadak, the high priest, and the spirit of all the remnant of the people, so that they came and labored on the house of the Lord of hosts, their God,

15 On the twenty-fourth day of the sixth month.

## New American Standard

# Haggai

*Haggai Begins Temple Building*

**1** IN THE second year of Darius the king, on the first day of the
sixth month, the word of the LORD came by the prophet
Haggai to Zerubbabel the son of Shealtiel, governor of Judah, and
to Joshua the son of Jehozadak, the high priest saying,
2"Thus says the LORD of hosts, 'This people says, "The time
has not come, *even* the time for the house of the LORD to be
rebuilt." ' "
3Then the word of the LORD came by Haggai the prophet
saying,
4"Is it time for you yourselves to dwell in your paneled houses
while this house *lies* desolate?"
5Now therefore, thus says the LORD of hosts, "Consider your
ways!
6"You have sown much, but harvest little; *you* eat, but *there is*
not *enough* to be satisfied; *you* drink, but *there is* not *enough* to
become drunk; *you* put on clothing, but no one is warm *enough*;
and he who earns, earns wages *to put* into a purse with holes."
7¶ Thus says the LORD of hosts, "Consider your ways!
8"Go up to the mountains, bring wood and rebuild the temple,
that I may be pleased with it and be glorified," says the LORD.
9" *You* look for much, but behold, *it comes* to little; when you
bring *it* home, I blow it *away*. Why?" declares the LORD of hosts,
"Because of My house which *lies* desolate, while each of you runs
to his own house.
10"Therefore, because of you the sky has withheld its dew, and
the earth has withheld its produce.
11"And I called for a drought on the land, on the mountains,
on the grain, on the new wine, on the oil, on what the ground
produces, on men, on cattle, and on all the labor of your hands."
12¶ Then Zerubbabel the son of Shealtiel, and Joshua the son of
Jehozadak, the high priest, with all the remnant of the people,
obeyed the voice of the LORD their God and the words of Haggai
the prophet, as the LORD their God had sent him. And the people
showed reverence for the LORD.
13Then Haggai, the messenger of the LORD, spoke by the commission of the LORD to the people saying, " 'I am with you,' declares the LORD."
14So the LORD stirred up the spirit of Zerubbabel the son of
Shealtiel, governor of Judah, and the spirit of Joshua the son of
Jehozadak, the high priest, and the spirit of all the remnant of the
people; and they came and worked on the house of the LORD of
hosts, their God,
15on the twenty-fourth day of the sixth month in the second
year of Darius the king.

## New International

# Haggai

*A Call to Build the House of the LORD*

**1** IN THE second year of King Darius, on the first day of the
sixth month, the word of the LORD came through the prophet
Haggai to Zerubbabel son of Shealtiel, governor of Judah, and to
Joshua[a] son of Jehozadak, the high priest:
2This is what the LORD Almighty says: "These people say, 'The
time has not yet come for the LORD's house to be built.' "
3Then the word of the LORD came through the prophet Haggai:
4"Is it a time for you yourselves to be living in your paneled
houses, while this house remains a ruin?"
5Now this is what the LORD Almighty says: "Give careful
thought to your ways. 6You have planted much, but have harvested little. You eat, but never have enough. You drink, but never
have your fill. You put on clothes, but are not warm. You earn
wages, only to put them in a purse with holes in it."
7This is what the LORD Almighty says: "Give careful thought to
your ways. 8Go up into the mountains and bring down timber and
build the house, so that I may take pleasure in it and be honored,"
says the LORD. 9"You expected much, but see, it turned out to be
little. What you brought home, I blew away. Why?" declares the
LORD Almighty. "Because of my house, which remains a ruin,
while each of you is busy with his own house. 10Therefore, because of you the heavens have withheld their dew and the earth
its crops. 11I called for a drought on the fields and the mountains,
on the grain, the new wine, the oil and whatever the ground
produces, on men and cattle, and on the labor of your hands."

12Then Zerubbabel son of Shealtiel, Joshua son of Jehozadak,
the high priest, and the whole remnant of the people obeyed the
voice of the LORD their God and the message of the prophet Haggai, because the LORD their God had sent him. And the people
feared the LORD.
13Then Haggai, the LORD's messenger, gave this message of the
LORD to the people: "I am with you," declares the LORD. 14So the
LORD stirred up the spirit of Zerubbabel son of Shealtiel, governor
of Judah, and the spirit of Joshua son of Jehozadak, the high priest,
and the spirit of the whole remnant of the people. They came and
began to work on the house of the LORD Almighty, their God, 15on
the twenty-fourth day of the sixth month in the second year of
King Darius.

NIV [a] 1 A variant of *Jeshua*; here and elsewhere in Haggai

## King James

**2** IN THE seventh *month,* in the one and twentieth *day* of the
month, came the word of the LORD by the prophet Haggai,
saying,
2 Speak now to Zerubbabel the son of Shealtiel, governor of
Judah, and to Joshua the son of Josedech, the high priest, and to
the residue of the people, saying,
3 Who *is* left among you that saw this house in her first glory?
and how do ye see it now? *is it* not in your eyes in comparison of
it as nothing?
4 Yet now be strong, O Zerubbabel, saith the LORD; and be
strong, O Joshua, son of Josedech, the high priest; and be strong,
all ye people of the land, saith the LORD, and work: for I *am* with
you, saith the LORD of hosts:
5 *According to* the word that I covenanted with you when ye
came out of Egypt, so my spirit remaineth among you: fear ye not.
6 For thus saith the LORD of hosts; Yet once, it *is* a little while,
and I will shake the heavens, and the earth, and the sea, and the
dry *land;*
7 And I will shake all nations, and the desire of all nations shall
come: and I will fill this house with glory, saith the LORD of hosts.
8 The silver *is* mine, and the gold *is* mine, saith the LORD of
hosts.
9 The glory of this latter house shall be greater than of the
former, saith the LORD of hosts: and in this place will I give peace,
saith the LORD of hosts.
10 ¶ In the four and twentieth *day* of the ninth *month,* in the
second year of Darius, came the word of the LORD by Haggai the
prophet, saying,
11 Thus saith the LORD of hosts; Ask now the priests *concerning*
the law, saying,
12 If one bear holy flesh in the skirt of his garment, and with his
skirt do touch bread, or pottage, or wine, or oil, or any meat, shall
it be holy? And the priests answered and said, No.
13 Then said Haggai, If *one that is* unclean by a dead body touch
any of these, shall it be unclean? And the priests answered and
said, It shall be unclean.
14 Then answered Haggai, and said, So *is* this people, and so *is*
this nation before me, saith the LORD; and so *is* every work of their
hands; and that which they offer there *is* unclean.
15 And now, I pray you, consider from this day and upward,
from before a stone was laid upon a stone in the temple of the
LORD:
16 Since those *days* were, when *one* came to an heap of twenty
*measures,* there were *but* ten: when *one* came to the pressvat for to
draw out fifty *vessels* out of the press, there were *but* twenty.
17 I smote you with blasting and with mildew and with hail in
all the labours of your hands; yet ye *turned* not to me, saith the
LORD.
18 Consider now from this day and upward, from the four and
twentieth day of the ninth *month, even* from the day that the
foundation of the LORD's temple was laid, consider *it.*
19 Is the seed yet in the barn? yea, as yet the vine, and the fig
tree, and the pomegranate, and the olive tree, hath not brought
forth: from this day will I bless *you.*
20 ¶ And again the word of the LORD came unto Haggai in the
four and twentieth *day* of the month, saying,
21 Speak to Zerubbabel, governor of Judah, saying, I will shake
the heavens and the earth;

## Amplified

**2** IN THE seventh month, on the twenty-first day of the month,
in the second year of Darius the king [of Persia, including the
Chaldeans], came the word of the Lord by the prophet Haggai,
saying,
2 Speak now to Zerubbabel the son of Shealtiel, governor of
Judah, and to Joshua the son of Jehozadak, the high priest, and to
the remainder of the people, saying,
3 Who is left among you who saw this house in its former glory?
And how do you see it now? Is not this in your sight as nothing
in comparison to that?
4 Yet now be strong, alert *and* courageous, O Zerubbabel, says
the Lord; be strong, alert *and* courageous, O Joshua, son of Jehozadak, the high priest; and be strong, alert *and* courageous, all you
people of the land, says the Lord, and work! For I am with you,
says the Lord of hosts.
5 According to the promise that I covenanted with you when
you came out of Egypt, so My Spirit stands *and* abides in the midst
of you; fear not.
6 For thus says the Lord of hosts: Yet once more, in a little while,
I will shake *and* make tremble the [starry] heavens, the earth, the
sea, and the dry land; [Heb. 12:26.]
7 And I will shake all nations, and the [a]desire *and* the precious
things of all nations shall come in, and I will fill this house with
splendor, says the Lord of hosts.
8 The silver is Mine, and the gold is Mine, says the Lord of hosts.
9 The latter glory of this house [with its successor, to which Jesus
came] shall be greater than the former, says the Lord of hosts; and
in this place will I give peace *and* prosperity, says the Lord of hosts.
10 On the twenty-fourth day of the ninth month, in the second
year of Darius, came the word of the Lord by Haggai the prophet,
11 Thus says the Lord of hosts: Ask now the priests to decide this
question of law:
12 If one carries in the skirt of his garment flesh that is holy
[because it has been offered in sacrifice to God], and with his skirt
*or* the flaps of his garment he touches bread, or pottage, or wine,
or oil, or any kind of food, does what he touches become holy—
dedicated to God's service exclusively? And the priests answered,
No! [Holiness is not infectious.]
13 Then said Haggai, If one who is [ceremonially] unclean, because he has come in contact with a dead body, should touch any
of these articles of food, shall it be [ceremonially] unclean? And the
priests answered, It shall be unclean. [Unholiness is infectious.]
14 Then answered Haggai, So is this people, and so is this nation
before Me, says the Lord; and so is every work of their hands; and
what they offer there [on the altar] is unclean [because they who
offer it are themselves unclean].
15 And now I pray you, consider what will happen from this day
onward. Since the time before a stone was laid upon a stone in the
temple of the Lord, how have you fared?
16 Through all that time [these things being so, the harvests have
not fulfilled expectations, for] when one has gone expecting to find
a heap [of sheaves] of twenty measures, there were but ten; when
he has gone to the wine vat to draw out fifty bucketfuls from the
press, there were only twenty.
17 I smote you with blight and with mildew and with hail in all
[the products of] the labors of your hands; yet you returned not
*nor* were converted to Me, says the Lord.
18 Consider, I pray you, from this day onward, from the twenty-
fourth day of the ninth month, even from the day that the foundation of the Lord's temple was *re*laid, consider this:
19 Is the harvested grain any longer in the barn? As to the grapevine, the fig tree, the pomegranate, and the olive tree, they have
not yet borne. From this day on I will bless you.
20 And again the word of the Lord came to Haggai on the
twenty-fourth *day* of the month, saying,
21 Speak to Zerubbabel [the representative of the Davidic monarchy and covenant, and in direct line of the ancestry of Jesus
Christ], governor of Judah, saying, I will shake the heavens and
the earth; [Hag. 1:1; Ezra 5:1-5; Zech. 4:6-10; Matt. 1:12, 13.]

AMP [a] It is with great reluctance that we refrain from capitalizing the word "desire" here and making the phrase point directly to the Messiah, as has been the accepted interpretation through many centuries until modern times. But the verb "shall come" is plural, and, as many commentators agree, refers to the most desired treasures that all nations will bring as gifts to adorn the temple to which the Messiah will one day have come. Thus the Messianic reference of the prophecy is neither questioned nor obscured, but the picture presented is like that of the coming of the Magi to find the Babe of Bethlehem, the Desire of all of them; and when they found Him they fell down and worshiped Him, bringing Him their most desirable treasures, gold, frankincense and myrrh.

## New American Standard

*The Builders Encouraged*

**2** ON THE twenty-first of the seventh month, the word of the LORD came by Haggai the prophet saying,

2 "Speak now to Zerubbabel the son of Shealtiel, governor of Judah, and to Joshua the son of Jehozadak, the high priest, and to the remnant of the people saying,

3 'Who is left among you who saw this temple in its former glory? And how do you see it now? Does it not seem to you like nothing in comparison?

4 'But now take courage, Zerubbabel,' declares the LORD, 'take courage also, Joshua son of Jehozadak, the high priest, and all you people of the land take courage,' declares the LORD, 'and work; for I am with you,' says the LORD of hosts.

5 'As for the promise which I made you when you came out of Egypt, My Spirit is abiding in your midst; do not fear!'

6 "For thus says the LORD of hosts, 'Once more in a little while, I am going to shake the heavens and the earth, the sea also and the dry land.

7 'And I will shake all the nations; and they will come with the wealth of all nations; and I will fill this house with glory,' says the LORD of hosts.

8 'The silver is Mine, and the gold is Mine,' declares the LORD of hosts.

9 'The latter glory of this house will be greater than the former,' says the LORD of hosts, 'and in this place I shall give peace,' declares the LORD of hosts."

**10**¶ On the twenty-fourth of the ninth *month,* in the second year of Darius, the word of the LORD came to Haggai the prophet saying,

11 "Thus says the LORD of hosts, 'Ask now the priests *for* a ruling:

12 'If a man carries holy meat in the fold of his garment, and touches bread with this fold, or cooked food, wine, oil, or any *other* food, will it become holy?' " And the priests answered and said, "No."

13 Then Haggai said, "If one who is unclean from a corpse touches any of these, will *the latter* become unclean?" And the priests answered and said, "It will become unclean."

14 Then Haggai answered and said, " 'So is this people. And so is this nation before Me,' declares the LORD, 'and so is every work of their hands; and what they offer there is unclean.

15 'But now, do consider from this day onward: before one stone was placed on another in the temple of the LORD,

16 from that time *when* one came to a *grain* heap of twenty *measures,* there would be only ten; and *when* one came to the wine vat to draw fifty measures, there would be *only* twenty.

17 'I smote you *and* every work of your hands with blasting wind, mildew, and hail; yet you *did* not *come back* to Me,' declares the LORD.

18 'Do consider from this day onward, from the twenty-fourth day of the ninth *month;* from the day when the temple of the LORD was founded, consider:

19 'Is the seed still in the barn? Even including the vine, the fig tree, the pomegranate, and the olive tree, it has not borne *fruit.* Yet from this day on I will bless *you.*' "

**20**¶ Then the word of the LORD came a second time to Haggai on the twenty-fourth *day* of the month saying,

21 "Speak to Zerubbabel governor of Judah saying, 'I am going to shake the heavens and the earth.

## New International

*The Promised Glory of the New House*

**2** ON THE twenty-first day of the seventh month, the word of
the LORD came through the prophet Haggai: 2 "Speak to
Zerubbabel son of Shealtiel, governor of Judah, to Joshua son of
Jehozadak, the high priest, and to the remnant of the people. Ask
them, 3 'Who of you is left who saw this house in its former glory?
How does it look to you now? Does it not seem to you like nothing?
4 But now be strong, O Zerubbabel,' declares the LORD. 'Be strong,
O Joshua son of Jehozadak, the high priest. Be strong, all you
people of the land,' declares the LORD, 'and work. For I am with
you,' declares the LORD Almighty. 5 'This is what I covenanted with
you when you came out of Egypt. And my Spirit remains among
you. Do not fear.'
6 "This is what the LORD Almighty says: 'In a little while I will
once more shake the heavens and the earth, the sea and the dry
land. 7 I will shake all nations, and the desired of all nations will
come, and I will fill this house with glory,' says the LORD Almighty. 8 'The silver is mine and the gold is mine,' declares the
LORD Almighty. 9 'The glory of this present house will be greater
than the glory of the former house,' says the LORD Almighty. 'And
in this place I will grant peace,' declares the LORD Almighty."

*Blessings for a Defiled People*

10 On the twenty-fourth day of the ninth month, in the second
year of Darius, the word of the LORD came to the prophet Haggai:
11 "This is what the LORD Almighty says: 'Ask the priests what the
law says: 12 If a person carries consecrated meat in the fold of his
garment, and that fold touches some bread or stew, some wine,
oil or other food, does it become consecrated?' "
The priests answered, "No."
13 Then Haggai said, "If a person defiled by contact with a dead
body touches one of these things, does it become defiled?"
"Yes," the priests replied, "it becomes defiled."
14 Then Haggai said, " 'So it is with this people and this nation
in my sight,' declares the LORD. 'Whatever they do and whatever
they offer there is defiled.
15 " 'Now give careful thought to this from this day
on[b]—consider how things were before one stone was laid on
another in the LORD's temple. 16 When anyone came to a heap of
twenty measures, there were only ten. When anyone went to a
wine vat to draw fifty measures, there were only twenty. 17 I struck
all the work of your hands with blight, mildew and hail, yet you
did not turn to me,' declares the LORD. 18 'From this day on, from
this twenty-fourth day of the ninth month, give careful thought to
the day when the foundation of the LORD's temple was laid. Give
careful thought: 19 Is there yet any seed left in the barn? Until now,
the vine and the fig tree, the pomegranate and the olive tree have
not borne fruit.
" 'From this day on I will bless you.' "

*Zerubbabel the LORD's Signet Ring*

20 The word of the LORD came to Haggai a second time on the
twenty-fourth day of the month: 21 "Tell Zerubbabel governor of
Judah that I will shake the heavens and the earth. 22 I will overturn

**NIV** [b] 15 Or *to the days past*

## King James

22And I will overthrow the throne of kingdoms, and I will destroy the strength of the kingdoms of the heathen; and I will overthrow the chariots, and those that ride in them; and the horses and their riders shall come down, every one by the sword of his brother.

23In that day, saith the LORD of hosts, will I take thee, O Zerubbabel, my servant, the son of Shealtiel, saith the LORD, and will make thee as a signet: for I have chosen thee, saith the LORD of hosts.

## Amplified

22And I will [in the distant future] overthrow the throne of kingdoms, and I will destroy the strength of the kingdoms of the [ungodly] nations, and I will overthrow the chariots and those who ride in them, and the horses and their riders shall go down, every one by the sword of his brother. [Dan. 2:34, 35, 44, 45; Rev. 19:11-21.]

23In that day, says the Lord of hosts, will I take you, O Zerubbabel, My servant, the son of Shealtiel, says the Lord, and will make you [through the Messiah, your descendant] *My* signet ring; for I have chosen you [with whom to renew My covenant to David's line], says the Lord of hosts. [II Sam. 7:12, 16.]

## New American Standard

22'And I will overthrow the thrones of kingdoms and destroy the power of the kingdoms of the nations; and I will overthrow the chariots and their riders, and the horses and their riders will go down, everyone by the sword of another.'
23'On that day,' declares the LORD of hosts, 'I will take you, Zerubbabel, son of Shealtiel, my servant,' declares the LORD, 'and I will make you like a signet *ring*, for I have chosen you,' " declares the LORD of hosts.

## New International

royal thrones and shatter the power of the foreign kingdoms. I will overthrow chariots and their drivers; horses and their riders will fall, each by the sword of his brother.
23" 'On that day,' declares the LORD Almighty, 'I will take you, my servant Zerubbabel son of Shealtiel,' declares the LORD, 'and I will make you like my signet ring, for I have chosen you,' declares the LORD Almighty."

## King James

THE BOOK OF

# Zechariah

**1** IN THE eighth month, in the second year of Darius, came the word of the LORD unto Zechariah, the son of Berechiah, the son of Iddo the prophet, saying,

2 The LORD hath been sore displeased with your fathers.

3 Therefore say thou unto them, Thus saith the LORD of hosts; Turn ye unto me, saith the LORD of hosts, and I will turn unto you, saith the LORD of hosts.

4 Be ye not as your fathers, unto whom the former prophets have cried, saying, Thus saith the LORD of hosts; Turn ye now from your evil ways, and *from* your evil doings: but they did not hear, nor hearken unto me, saith the LORD.

5 Your fathers, where *are* they? and the prophets, do they live for ever?

6 But my words and my statutes, which I commanded my servants the prophets, did they not take hold of your fathers? and they returned and said, Like as the LORD of hosts thought to do unto us, according to our ways, and according to our doings, so hath he dealt with us.

7 ¶ Upon the four and twentieth day of the eleventh month, which *is* the month Sebat, in the second year of Darius, came the word of the LORD unto Zechariah, the son of Berechiah, the son of Iddo the prophet, saying,

8 I saw by night, and behold a man riding upon a red horse, and he stood among the myrtle trees that *were* in the bottom; and behind him *were there* red horses, speckled, and white.

9 Then said I, O my lord, what *are* these? And the angel that talked with me said unto me, I will show thee what these *be*.

10 And the man that stood among the myrtle trees answered and said, These *are they* whom the LORD hath sent to walk to and fro through the earth.

11 And they answered the angel of the LORD that stood among the myrtle trees, and said, We have walked to and fro through the earth, and, behold, all the earth sitteth still, and is at rest.

12 ¶ Then the angel of the LORD answered and said, O LORD of hosts, how long wilt thou not have mercy on Jerusalem and on the cities of Judah, against which thou hast had indignation these threescore and ten years?

13 And the LORD answered the angel that talked with me *with* good words *and* comfortable words.

14 So the angel that communed with me said unto me, Cry thou, saying, Thus saith the LORD of hosts; I am jealous for Jerusalem and for Zion with a great jealousy.

15 And I am very sore displeased with the heathen *that are* at ease: for I was but a little displeased, and they helped forward the affliction.

## Amplified

THE BOOK OF

# Zechariah

**1** IN THE eighth month, in the second year *of the reign* of Darius, came the word of the Lord to Zechariah the son of Berechiah, the son of Iddo, the prophet, saying,

2 The Lord was very angry with your fathers.

3 Therefore say to them [the Jews of this day], Thus says the Lord of hosts: Return to Me, says the Lord of hosts, and I will return to you; it is the utterance of the Lord of hosts.

4 Be not as your fathers, to whom the former prophets cried, Thus says the Lord of hosts: Return now from your evil ways and your evil doings; but they would not hear or listen to Me, says the Lord.

5 Your fathers, where are they? And the prophets, do they live for ever?

6 But My words and My statutes, which I commanded My servants the prophets, did they not overtake *and* take hold of your fathers? So they repented and said, As the Lord of hosts planned *and* purposed to do to us, according to our ways and according to our doings, so has He dealt with us.

7 Upon the twenty-fourth day of the eleventh month, which is the month of Shebat, in the second year of the reign of Darius, the word of the Lord came to Zechariah the son of Berechiah, the son of Iddo, the prophet. Zechariah said,

8 I saw in the night [vision], and behold a man riding upon a red horse, and he stood among the myrtle trees that were in a low valley *or* bottom, and behind him there were horses, red, bay or flame-colored, and white.

9 Then said I, O my lord, what are these? And the angel who talked with me said, I will show you what these are.

10 And the man who stood among the myrtle trees answered and said, These are they whom the Lord has sent to walk to and fro through the earth *and* patrol it.

11 And the men on the horses answered [a]the Angel of the Lord Who stood among the myrtle trees, and said, We have walked to and fro through the earth (patrolling it), and behold, all the earth sits at rest—in peaceful security.

12 Then the Angel of the Lord said, O Lord of hosts, how long will You not have mercy *and* loving-kindness for Jerusalem and the cities of Judah, against which You have had indignation these seventy years [of the Babylonian captivity]?

13 And the Lord answered the angel who talked with me with gracious and comforting words.

14 So the angel who talked with me said to me, Cry out, Thus says the Lord of hosts: I am jealous for Jerusalem and for Zion with a great jealousy.

15 And I am very angry with the nations that are at ease; for while I was but a little displeased they helped forward the affliction *and* disaster.

**AMP** [a] That the Angel of the Lord is an uncreated angel, distinguished from other angels, and in many places identified with the Lord God is undeniable (Gen. 16:7-10; 31:11-13; 32:25-31 compared with Hos. 12:3-5; Exod. 3:2-4; Judg. 6:11-22; Zech. 3:1, 2). On the other hand there are passages in which He seems to be distinguished from God the Father (Exod. 23:20-22; 32:34). The simplest way of reconciling these two classes is to adopt the old view that this Angel is Christ, the second person of the Godhead, even at that early period appearing as the revealer of the Father.—Lange's Commentary, adapted.

## New American Standard

# Zechariah

*A Call to Repentance*

**1** IN THE eighth month of the second year of Darius, the word of the LORD came to Zechariah the prophet, the son of Berechiah, the son of Iddo saying,

2"The LORD was very angry with your fathers.

3"Therefore say to them, 'Thus says the LORD of hosts, "Return to Me," declares the LORD of hosts, "that I may return to you," says the LORD of hosts.

4"Do not be like your fathers, to whom the former prophets proclaimed, saying, 'Thus says the LORD of hosts, "Return now from your evil ways and from your evil deeds." ' But they did not listen or give heed to Me," declares the LORD.

5"Your fathers, where are they? And the prophets, do they live forever?

6"But did not My words and My statutes, which I commanded My servants the prophets, overtake your fathers? Then they repented and said, 'As the LORD of hosts purposed to do to us in accordance with our ways and our deeds, so He has dealt with us.' " ' "

*Patrol of the Earth*

7¶ On the twenty-fourth day of the eleventh month, which is the month Shebat, in the second year of Darius, the word of the LORD came to Zechariah the prophet, the son of Berechiah, the son of Iddo, as follows:

8I saw at night, and behold, a man was riding on a red horse, and he was standing among the myrtle trees which were in the ravine, with red, sorrel, and white horses behind him.

9Then I said, "My lord, what are these?" And the angel who was speaking with me said to me, "I will show you what these are."

10And the man who was standing among the myrtle trees answered and said, "These are those whom the LORD has sent to patrol the earth."

11So they answered the angel of the LORD who was standing among the myrtle trees, and said, "We have patrolled the earth, and behold, all the earth is peaceful and quiet."

12¶ Then the angel of the LORD answered and said, "O LORD of hosts, how long wilt Thou have no compassion for Jerusalem and the cities of Judah, with which Thou hast been indignant these seventy years?"

13And the LORD answered the angel who was speaking with me with gracious words, comforting words.

14So the angel who was speaking with me said to me, "Proclaim, saying, 'Thus says the LORD of hosts, "I am exceedingly jealous for Jerusalem and Zion.

15"But I am very angry with the nations who are at ease; for while I was only a little angry, they furthered the disaster."

## New International

# Zechariah

*A Call to Return to the LORD*

**1** IN THE eighth month of the second year of Darius, the word of the LORD came to the prophet Zechariah son of Berekiah, the son of Iddo:

2"The LORD was very angry with your forefathers. 3Therefore tell the people: This is what the LORD Almighty says: 'Return to me,' declares the LORD Almighty, 'and I will return to you,' says the LORD Almighty. 4Do not be like your forefathers, to whom the earlier prophets proclaimed: This is what the LORD Almighty says: 'Turn from your evil ways and your evil practices.' But they would not listen or pay attention to me, declares the LORD. 5Where are your forefathers now? And the prophets, do they live forever? 6But did not my words and my decrees, which I commanded my servants the prophets, overtake your forefathers?

"Then they repented and said, 'The LORD Almighty has done to us what our ways and practices deserve, just as he determined to do.' "

*The Man Among the Myrtle Trees*

7On the twenty-fourth day of the eleventh month, the month of Shebat, in the second year of Darius, the word of the LORD came to the prophet Zechariah son of Berekiah, the son of Iddo.

8During the night I had a vision—and there before me was a man riding a red horse! He was standing among the myrtle trees in a ravine. Behind him were red, brown and white horses.

9I asked, "What are these, my lord?"

The angel who was talking with me answered, "I will show you what they are."

10Then the man standing among the myrtle trees explained, "They are the ones the LORD has sent to go throughout the earth."

11And they reported to the angel of the LORD, who was standing among the myrtle trees, "We have gone throughout the earth and found the whole world at rest and in peace."

12Then the angel of the LORD said, "LORD Almighty, how long will you withhold mercy from Jerusalem and from the towns of Judah, which you have been angry with these seventy years?" 13So the LORD spoke kind and comforting words to the angel who talked with me.

14Then the angel who was speaking to me said, "Proclaim this word: This is what the LORD Almighty says: 'I am very jealous for Jerusalem and Zion, 15but I am very angry with the nations that feel secure. I was only a little angry, but they added to the calamity.'

## King James

16Therefore thus saith the LORD; I am returned to Jerusalem with mercies: my house shall be built in it, saith the LORD of hosts, and a line shall be stretched forth upon Jerusalem.

17Cry yet, saying, Thus saith the LORD of hosts; My cities through prosperity shall yet be spread abroad; and the LORD shall yet comfort Zion, and shall yet choose Jerusalem.

18¶ Then lifted I up mine eyes, and saw, and behold four horns.

19And I said unto the angel that talked with me, What *be* these? And he answered me, These *are* the horns which have scattered Judah, Israel, and Jerusalem.

20And the LORD showed me four carpenters.

21Then said I, What come these to do? And he spake, saying, These *are* the horns which have scattered Judah, so that no man did lift up his head: but these are come to fray them, to cast out the horns of the Gentiles, which lifted up *their* horn over the land of Judah to scatter it.

**2** I LIFTED up mine eyes again, and looked, and behold a man with a measuring line in his hand.

2Then said I, Whither goest thou? And he said unto me, To measure Jerusalem, to see what *is* the breadth thereof, and what *is* the length thereof.

3And, behold, the angel that talked with me went forth, and another angel went out to meet him,

4And said unto him, Run, speak to this young man, saying, Jerusalem shall be inhabited *as* towns without walls for the multitude of men and cattle therein:

5For I, saith the LORD, will be unto her a wall of fire round about, and will be the glory in the midst of her.

6¶ Ho, ho, *come forth,* and flee from the land of the north, saith the LORD: for I have spread you abroad as the four winds of the heaven, saith the LORD.

7Deliver thyself, O Zion, that dwellest *with* the daughter of Babylon.

8For thus saith the LORD of hosts; After the glory hath he sent me unto the nations which spoiled you: for he that toucheth you toucheth the apple of his eye.

9For, behold, I will shake mine hand upon them, and they shall be a spoil to their servants: and ye shall know that the LORD of hosts hath sent me.

10¶ Sing and rejoice, O daughter of Zion: for, lo, I come, and I will dwell in the midst of thee, saith the LORD.

11And many nations shall be joined to the LORD in that day, and shall be my people: and I will dwell in the midst of thee, and thou shalt know that the LORD of hosts hath sent me unto thee.

12And the LORD shall inherit Judah his portion in the holy land, and shall choose Jerusalem again.

13Be silent, O all flesh, before the LORD: for he is raised up out of his holy habitation.

**3** AND HE showed me Joshua the high priest standing before the angel of the LORD, and Satan standing at his right hand to resist him.

2And the LORD said unto Satan, The LORD rebuke thee, O Satan; even the LORD that hath chosen Jerusalem rebuke thee: *is* not this a brand plucked out of the fire?

## Amplified

16Therefore, thus says the Lord: I have returned to Jerusalem with compassion (loving-kindness and mercies). My house shall be built in it, says the Lord of hosts, and a *measuring* line shall be stretched out over Jerusalem [with a view to rebuilding its walls].

17Cry yet again saying, Thus says the Lord of hosts: My cities shall yet again overflow with prosperity, and the Lord shall yet comfort Zion, and shall yet choose Jerusalem.

18Then I lifted up my eyes, and saw, and behold four horns [symbols of strength].

19And I said to the angel who talked with me, What are these? And he answered me, These are the horns [powers] which have scattered Judah, Israel, and Jerusalem.

20Then the Lord showed me four smiths *or* workmen [one for each enemy horn, to beat it down].

21Then said I, What are these *horns and smiths* coming to do? And he said, These are the horns *or* powers that scattered Judah, so that no man lifted up his head. But these smiths *or* workmen have come to terrorize them *and* cause them to be panic-stricken, to cast out the horns *or* powers of the nations who lifted up their horn against the land of Judah to scatter it.

**2** AND I lifted up my eyes and saw, and behold, a man with a measuring line in his hand.

2Then said I, Where are you going? And he said to me, To measure Jerusalem, to see what is its breadth and what is its length.

3And behold, the angel who talked with me went forth, and another angel went out to meet him,

4And he said to the second angel, Run, speak to this young man, saying, Jerusalem shall be inhabited *and* dwell as villages without walls, because of the multitude of people and livestock in it.

5For I, says the Lord, will be to her a wall of fire round about, and I will be the glory in the midst of her.

6Ho! ho! *Hear and* flee from the land of the north, says the Lord, and from the four winds of the heavens, for to them have I scattered you, says the Lord.

7Ho! Escape to Zion, you who dwell with the daughter of Babylon!

8For thus said the Lord of hosts, after *His* glory had sent me [His messenger] to the nations who plundered you, for he who touches you touches the apple *or* pupil of His eye:

9Behold, I will swing my hand over them and they shall become plunder for those who served them. Then you shall recognize *and* know that the Lord of hosts has sent me [His messenger].

10Sing and rejoice, O daughter of Zion; for lo, I come, and I will dwell in the midst of you, says the Lord.

11And many nations shall join themselves to the Lord in that day, and shall be My people. And I will dwell in the midst of you, and you shall know—recognize and understand—that the Lord of hosts has sent me [His messenger] to you. [Isa. 2:3; Mic. 4:2.]

12And the Lord shall inherit Judah as His portion in the holy land, and shall again choose Jerusalem.

13Be still, all flesh, before the Lord; for He is aroused *and* risen from His holy habitation. [Hab. 2:20; Zeph. 1:7.]

**3** THEN *THE guiding angel* showed me Joshua the high priest standing before [a]the Angel of the Lord, and Satan standing at Joshua's right hand to be his adversary *and* to accuse him.

2And the Lord said to Satan, The Lord rebuke you, O Satan! Even the Lord Who now *and* habitually chooses Jerusalem, rebuke you! Is not this [returned captive Joshua] a brand plucked out of the fire? [Jude 9.]

**AMP** [a] See footnote on chapter 1:11.

## New American Standard

16"Therefore, thus says the LORD, "I will return to Jerusalem
with compassion; My house will be built in it," declares the LORD
of hosts, "and a measuring line will be stretched over Jerusalem." '
17"Again, proclaim, saying, 'Thus says the LORD of hosts, "My
cities will again overflow with prosperity, and the LORD will again
comfort Zion and again choose Jerusalem." ' "
18¶ Then I lifted up my eyes and looked, and behold, *there were*
four horns.
19So I said to the angel who was speaking with me, "What are
these?" And he answered me, "These are the horns which have
scattered Judah, Israel, and Jerusalem."
20Then the LORD showed me four craftsmen.
21And I said, "What are these coming to do?" And he said,
"These are the horns which have scattered Judah, so that no man
lifts up his head; but these *craftsmen* have come to terrify them, to
throw down the horns of the nations who have lifted up *their* horns
against the land of Judah in order to scatter it."

*God's Favor to Zion*

**2** THEN I lifted up my eyes and looked, and behold, *there was*
a man with a measuring line in his hand.
2So I said, "Where are you going?" And he said to me, "To
measure Jerusalem, to see how wide it is and how long it is."
3And behold, the angel who was speaking with me was going
out, and another angel was coming out to meet him,
4and said to him, "Run, speak to that young man, saying,
'Jerusalem will be inhabited without walls, because of the multitude of men and cattle within it.
5'For I,' declares the LORD, 'will be a wall of fire around her,
and I will be the glory in her midst.' "
6¶ "Ho there! Flee from the land of the north," declares the
LORD, "for I have dispersed you as the four winds of the heavens,"
declares the LORD.
7"Ho, Zion! Escape, you who are living with the daughter of
Babylon."
8For thus says the LORD of hosts, "After glory He has sent me
against the nations which plunder you, for he who touches you,
touches the apple of His eye.
9"For behold, I will wave My hand over them, so that they will
be plunder for their slaves. Then you will know that the LORD of
hosts has sent Me.
10"Sing for joy and be glad, O daughter of Zion; for behold I am
coming and I will dwell in your midst," declares the LORD.
11"And many nations will join themselves to the LORD in that
day and will become My people. Then I will dwell in your midst,
and you will know that the LORD of hosts has sent Me to you.
12"And the LORD will possess Judah as His portion in the holy
land, and will again choose Jerusalem.
13"Be silent, all flesh, before the LORD; for He is aroused from
His holy habitation."

*Joshua, the High Priest*

**3** THEN HE showed me Joshua the high priest standing before
the angel of the LORD, and Satan standing at his right hand
to accuse him.
2And the LORD said to Satan, "The LORD rebuke you, Satan!
Indeed, the LORD who has chosen Jerusalem rebuke you! Is this not
a brand plucked from the fire?"

## New International

16"Therefore, this is what the LORD says: 'I will return to Jerusalem with mercy, and there my house will be rebuilt. And the
measuring line will be stretched out over Jerusalem,' declares the
LORD Almighty.
17"Proclaim further: This is what the LORD Almighty says: 'My
towns will again overflow with prosperity, and the LORD will again
comfort Zion and choose Jerusalem.' "

*Four Horns and Four Craftsmen*

18Then I looked up—and there before me were four horns! 19I
asked the angel who was speaking to me, "What are these?"
He answered me, "These are the horns that scattered Judah,
Israel and Jerusalem."
20Then the LORD showed me four craftsmen. 21I asked, "What
are these coming to do?"
He answered, "These are the horns that scattered Judah so that
no one could raise his head, but the craftsmen have come to terrify
them and throw down these horns of the nations who lifted up
their horns against the land of Judah to scatter its people."

*A Man With a Measuring Line*

**2** THEN I looked up—and there before me was a man with a
measuring line in his hand! 2I asked, "Where are you going?"
He answered me, "To measure Jerusalem, to find out how wide
and how long it is."
3Then the angel who was speaking to me left, and another angel
came to meet him 4and said to him: "Run, tell that young man,
'Jerusalem will be a city without walls because of the great number
of men and livestock in it. 5And I myself will be a wall of fire
around it,' declares the LORD, 'and I will be its glory within.'
6"Come! Come! Flee from the land of the north," declares the
LORD, "for I have scattered you to the four winds of heaven,"
declares the LORD.
7"Come, O Zion! Escape, you who live in the Daughter of
Babylon!" 8For this is what the LORD Almighty says: "After he has
honored me and has sent me against the nations that have plundered you—for whoever touches you touches the apple of his
eye— 9I will surely raise my hand against them so that their slaves
will plunder them.[b] Then you will know that the LORD Almighty
has sent me.
10"Shout and be glad, O Daughter of Zion. For I am coming,
and I will live among you," declares the LORD. 11"Many nations
will be joined with the LORD in that day and will become my
people. I will live among you and you will know that the LORD
Almighty has sent me to you. 12The LORD will inherit Judah as his
portion in the holy land and will again choose Jerusalem. 13Be still
before the LORD, all mankind, because he has roused himself from
his holy dwelling."

*Clean Garments for the High Priest*

**3** THEN HE showed me Joshua[c] the high priest standing before the angel of the LORD, and Satan[d] standing at his right
side to accuse him. 2The LORD said to Satan, "The LORD rebuke
you, Satan! The LORD, who has chosen Jerusalem, rebuke you! Is
not this man a burning stick snatched from the fire?"

NIV [b] *8,9* Or *says after . . . eye:* [9]*"I . . . plunder them."* [c] *1* A variant of *Jeshua;*
here and elsewhere in Zechariah [d] *1* Satan means *accuser.*

## King James

3 Now Joshua was clothed with filthy garments, and stood before the angel.

4 And he answered and spake unto those that stood before him, saying, Take away the filthy garments from him. And unto him he said, Behold, I have caused thine iniquity to pass from thee, and I will clothe thee with change of raiment.

5 And I said, Let them set a fair mitre upon his head. So they set a fair mitre upon his head, and clothed him with garments. And the angel of the LORD stood by.

6 And the angel of the LORD protested unto Joshua, saying,

7 Thus saith the LORD of hosts; If thou wilt walk in my ways, and if thou wilt keep my charge, then thou shalt also judge my house, and shalt also keep my courts, and I will give thee places to walk among these that stand by.

8 Hear now, O Joshua the high priest, thou, and thy fellows that sit before thee: for they *are* men wondered at: for, behold, I will bring forth my servant the BRANCH.

9 For behold the stone that I have laid before Joshua; upon one stone *shall be* seven eyes: behold, I will engrave the graving thereof, saith the LORD of hosts, and I will remove the iniquity of that land in one day.

10 In that day, saith the LORD of hosts, shall ye call every man his neighbour under the vine and under the fig tree.

**4** AND THE angel that talked with me came again, and waked me, as a man that is wakened out of his sleep,

2 And said unto me, What seest thou? And I said, I have looked, and behold a candlestick all *of* gold, with a bowl upon the top of it, and his seven lamps thereon, and seven pipes to the seven lamps, which *are* upon the top thereof:

3 And two olive trees by it, one upon the right *side* of the bowl, and the other upon the left *side* thereof.

4 So I answered and spake to the angel that talked with me, saying, What *are* these, my lord?

5 Then the angel that talked with me answered and said unto me, Knowest thou not what these be? And I said, No, my lord.

6 Then he answered and spake unto me, saying, This *is* the word of the LORD unto Zerubbabel, saying, Not by might, nor by power, but by my spirit, saith the LORD of hosts.

7 Who *art* thou, O great mountain? before Zerubbabel *thou shalt become* a plain: and he shall bring forth the headstone *thereof with* shoutings, *crying*, Grace, grace unto it.

8 Moreover the word of the LORD came unto me, saying,

9 The hands of Zerubbabel have laid the foundation of this house; his hands shall also finish it; and thou shalt know that the LORD of hosts hath sent me unto you.

10 For who hath despised the day of small things? for they shall rejoice, and shall see the plummet in the hand of Zerubbabel *with* those seven; they *are* the eyes of the LORD, which run to and fro through the whole earth.

11 ¶ Then answered I, and said unto him, What *are* these two olive trees upon the right *side* of the candlestick and upon the left *side* thereof?

12 And I answered again, and said unto him, What *be these* two olive branches which through the two golden pipes empty the golden *oil* out of themselves?

## Amplified

3 Now Joshua was clothed with filthy garments, and was standing before the Angel *of the Lord.*

4 And He spoke to those who stood before Him, saying, Take away the filthy garments from him. And He said to *Joshua,* Behold, I have caused your iniquity to pass from you, and I will clothe you with rich apparel.

5 And I [Zechariah] said, Let them put a clean turban on his head. So they put a clean turban on his head, and clothed him with *rich* garments. And the Angel of the Lord stood by.

6 And the Angel of the Lord solemnly *and* earnestly protested *and* affirmed to Joshua, saying,

7 Thus says the Lord of hosts: If you will walk in My ways and keep My charge, then also you shall rule My house and have charge of My courts, and I will give you access [to My presence] *and* places to walk among these who stand here.

8 Hear now, O Joshua the high priest, you and your colleagues who [usually] sit before you; for they are men who are a sign *or* omen [types of what is to come]; for behold, I will bring forth My servant the Branch. [Isa. 4:2; Jer. 23:5; 33:15; Zech. 6:12.]

9 For behold, upon the stone which I have set before Joshua, upon *that* one stone are seven eyes *or* facets [the all-embracing providence of God and the sevenfold radiations of the Spirit of God]. Behold, I will carve *upon it* its inscription, says the Lord of hosts, and I will remove the iniquity *and* guilt of this land in a single day. [Zech. 4:10; II Chron. 16:9; Jer. 50:20.]

10 In that day, says the Lord of hosts, you shall invite each man his neighbor under his own vine and his own fig tree. [Mic. 4:1-4.]

**4** AND THE angel who talked with me came again, and awakened me, like a man who is wakened out of his sleep.

2 And said to me, What do you see? I said, I see, and behold, a lampstand all of gold, with its bowl [for oil] on the top of it, and its seven lamps on it, and *there are* seven pipes to each of the seven lamps which are upon the top of it. [Rev. 1:20; Matt. 5:14, 16; Luke 12:35; Phil. 2:15.]

3 And *there are* two olive trees by it, one upon the right side of the bowl, and the other upon the left side of it [feeding it continuously with oil]. [Rev. 11:4-13.]

4 So I asked the angel who talked with me, What are these, my lord?

5 Then the angel who talked with me answered me, Do you not know what these are? And I said, No, my lord.

6 Then he said to me, This [addition of the bowl to the candlestick, causing it to yield a ceaseless supply of oil from the olive trees] is the word of the Lord to Zerubbabel, saying, Not by might, nor by power, but by My Spirit [of Whom the oil is a symbol], says the Lord of hosts.

7 *For* who are you, O great mountain [of human obstacles]? Before Zerubbabel [who with Joshua had led the return of the exiles from Babylon and was undertaking the rebuilding of the temple, before him] you shall become a plain [a mere mole hill]! And he shall bring forth the finishing gable stone [of the new temple] with loud shoutings of the people, crying, Grace, grace to it!

8 Moreover the word of the Lord came to me, saying,

9 The hands of Zerubbabel have laid the foundations of this house; his hands shall also finish it. Then you shall know that the Lord of hosts has sent me [His messenger] to you.

10 Who [with reason] despises the day of small things? For these seven shall rejoice when they see the plummet in the hand of Zerubbabel. [These seven] are the eyes of the Lord which run to and fro throughout the whole earth. [Rev. 5:6.]

11 Then I said to him, What are these two olive trees on the right side of the lampstand and on the left side of it?

12 And a second time I said to him, What are these two olive branches which are beside the two golden tubes *or* spouts by which the golden oil is emptied out?

## New American Standard

3Now Joshua was clothed with filthy garments and standing
before the angel.
4And he spoke and said to those who were standing before
him saying, "Remove the filthy garments from him." Again he
said to him, "See, I have taken your iniquity away from you and
will clothe you with festal robes."
5Then I said, "Let them put a clean turban on his head." So
they put a clean turban on his head and clothed him with garments, while the angel of the LORD was standing by.
6¶ And the angel of the LORD admonished Joshua saying,
7"Thus says the LORD of hosts, 'If you will walk in My ways,
and if you will perform My service, then you will also govern My
house and also have charge of My courts, and I will grant you free
access among these who are standing *here.*

*The Branch*

8'Now listen, Joshua the high priest, you and your friends who
are sitting in front of you—indeed they are men who are a symbol,
for behold, I am going to bring in My servant the Branch.
9'For behold, the stone that I have set before Joshua; on one
stone are seven eyes. Behold, I will engrave an inscription on it,'
declares the LORD of hosts, 'and I will remove the iniquity of that
land in one day.
10'In that day,' declares the LORD of hosts, 'every one of you will
invite his neighbor to *sit* under *his* vine and under *his* fig tree.' "

*The Golden Lampstand and Olive Trees*

4 THEN THE angel who was speaking with me returned, and
roused me as a man who is awakened from his sleep.
2And he said to me, "What do you see?" And I said, "I see,
and behold, a lampstand all of gold with its bowl on the top of it,
and its seven lamps on it with seven spouts belonging to each of
the lamps which are on the top of it;
3also two olive trees by it, one on the right side of the bowl and
the other on its left side."
4Then I answered and said to the angel who was speaking with
me saying, "What are these, my lord?"
5So the angel who was speaking with me answered and said
to me, "Do you not know what these are?" And I said, "No, my
lord."
6Then he answered and said to me, "This is the word of the
LORD to Zerubbabel saying, 'Not by might nor by power, but by
My Spirit,' says the LORD of hosts.
7'What are you, O great mountain? Before Zerubbabel *you will
become* a plain; and he will bring forth the top stone with shouts
of "Grace, grace to it!" '"
8Also the word of the LORD came to me saying,
9"The hands of Zerubbabel have laid the foundation of this
house, and his hands will finish *it.* Then you will know that the
LORD of hosts has sent me to you.
10"For who has despised the day of small things? But these
seven will be glad when they see the plumb line in the hand of
Zerubbabel— *these are* the eyes of the LORD which range to and fro
throughout the earth."
11¶ Then I answered and said to him, "What are these two olive
trees on the right of the lampstand and on its left?"
12And I answered the second time and said to him, "What are
the two olive branches which are beside the two golden pipes,
which empty the golden *oil* from themselves?"

## New International

3Now Joshua was dressed in filthy clothes as he stood before
the angel. 4The angel said to those who were standing before him,
"Take off his filthy clothes."
Then he said to Joshua, "See, I have taken away your sin, and
I will put rich garments on you."
5Then I said, "Put a clean turban on his head." So they put a
clean turban on his head and clothed him, while the angel of the
LORD stood by.
6The angel of the LORD gave this charge to Joshua: 7"This is
what the LORD Almighty says: 'If you will walk in my ways and
keep my requirements, then you will govern my house and have
charge of my courts, and I will give you a place among these
standing here.
8" 'Listen, O high priest Joshua and your associates seated before you, who are men symbolic of things to come: I am going to
bring my servant, the Branch. 9See, the stone I have set in front
of Joshua! There are seven eyes[a] on that one stone, and I will
engrave an inscription on it,' says the LORD Almighty, 'and I will
remove the sin of this land in a single day.
10" 'In that day each of you will invite his neighbor to sit under
his vine and fig tree,' declares the LORD Almighty."

*The Gold Lampstand and the Two Olive Trees*

4 THEN THE angel who talked with me returned and wakened
me, as a man is wakened from his sleep. 2He asked me,
"What do you see?"
I answered, "I see a solid gold lampstand with a bowl at the top
and seven lights on it, with seven channels to the lights. 3Also
there are two olive trees by it, one on the right of the bowl and the
other on its left."
4I asked the angel who talked with me, "What are these, my
lord?"
5He answered, "Do you not know what these are?"
"No, my lord," I replied.
6So he said to me, "This is the word of the LORD to Zerubbabel:
'Not by might nor by power, but by my Spirit,' says the LORD
Almighty.
7"What[b] are you, O mighty mountain? Before Zerubbabel you
will become level ground. Then he will bring out the capstone to
shouts of 'God bless it! God bless it!' "
8Then the word of the LORD came to me: 9"The hands of Zerubbabel have laid the foundation of this temple; his hands will also
complete it. Then you will know that the LORD Almighty has sent
me to you.
10"Who despises the day of small things? Men will rejoice when
they see the plumb line in the hand of Zerubbabel.
"(These seven are the eyes of the LORD, which range throughout the earth.)"
11Then I asked the angel, "What are these two olive trees on the
right and the left of the lampstand?"
12Again I asked him, "What are these two olive branches beside
the two gold pipes that pour out golden oil?"

NIV [a] 9 Or *facets* [b] 7 Or *Who*

## King James

13And he answered me and said, Knowest thou not what these *be?* And I said, No, my lord.

14Then said he, These *are* the two anointed ones, that stand by the Lord of the whole earth.

**5** THEN I turned, and lifted up mine eyes, and looked, and behold a flying roll.

2And he said unto me, What seest thou? And I answered, I see a flying roll; the length thereof *is* twenty cubits, and the breadth thereof ten cubits.

3Then said he unto me, This *is* the curse that goeth forth over the face of the whole earth: for every one that stealeth shall be cut off *as* on this side according to it; and every one that sweareth shall be cut off *as* on that side according to it.

4I will bring it forth, saith the LORD of hosts, and it shall enter into the house of the thief, and into the house of him that sweareth falsely by my name: and it shall remain in the midst of his house, and shall consume it with the timber thereof and the stones thereof.

5¶ Then the angel that talked with me went forth, and said unto me, Lift up now thine eyes, and see what *is* this that goeth forth.

6And I said, What *is* it? And he said, This *is* an ephah that goeth forth. He said moreover, This *is* their resemblance through all the earth.

7And, behold, there was lifted up a talent of lead: and this *is* a woman that sitteth in the midst of the ephah.

8And he said, This *is* wickedness. And he cast it into the midst of the ephah; and he cast the weight of lead upon the mouth thereof.

9Then lifted I up mine eyes, and looked, and, behold, there came out two women, and the wind *was* in their wings; for they had wings like the wings of a stork: and they lifted up the ephah between the earth and the heaven.

10Then said I to the angel that talked with me, Whither do these bear the ephah?

11And he said unto me, To build it an house in the land of Shinar: and it shall be established, and set there upon her own base.

**6** AND I turned, and lifted up mine eyes, and looked, and, behold, there came four chariots out from between two mountains; and the mountains *were* mountains of brass.

2In the first chariot *were* red horses; and in the second chariot black horses;

3And in the third chariot white horses; and in the fourth chariot grisled and bay horses.

4Then I answered and said unto the angel that talked with me, What *are* these, my lord?

5And the angel answered and said unto me, These *are* the four spirits of the heavens, which go forth from standing before the Lord of all the earth.

6The black horses which *are* therein go forth into the north country; and the white go forth after them; and the grisled go forth toward the south country.

7And the bay went forth, and sought to go that they might walk to and fro through the earth: and he said, Get you hence, walk to and fro through the earth. So they walked to and fro through the earth.

## Amplified

13And he answered me, Do you not know what these are? And I said, No, my lord.

14Then said he, These are the two sons of oil [Joshua the high priest and Zerubbabel the prince of Judah]—the two anointed ones—who stand before the Lord of the whole earth [as His anointed instruments]. [Rev. 11:4.]

**5** AGAIN I lifted up my eyes and behold, I saw a scroll flying *or* floating in the air!

2And the angel said to me, What do you see? And I answered, I see a flying scroll; its length is twenty cubits *or* thirty feet, and its breadth is ten cubits *or* fifteen feet.

3Then he said to me, This is the curse that goes out over the face of the whole land; for every one who steals shall be cut off from henceforth according to it [the curse written on this subject on the scroll]; and every one who swears falsely shall be cut off from henceforth according to it. [Isa. 24:6; Zech. 5:4; Mal. 3:8, 9.]

4I will bring [the curse] forth, says the Lord of hosts, and it shall enter into the house of the thief, and into the house of him who swears falsely by My name; and it shall abide in the midst of his house and shall consume it, both its timber and its stones.

5Then the angel who talked with me came forward and said to me, Lift up now your eyes and see what this is that goes forth.

6And I said, What is it?—What does it symbolize?—And he said, This that goes forth is an ephah[-like vessel for separate grains all collected together]. This, he continued, is the symbol of the sinners mentioned above *and* is the resemblance of their iniquity throughout the whole land. [Amos 8:5.]

7And behold, a round, flat weight of lead was lifted and there sat a woman in the midst of the ephah-like vessel.

8And he said, This is lawlessness—wickedness! And he thrust her back into the ephah, and he cast the weight of lead upon the mouth of it!

9Then lifted I up my eyes, and looked, and behold, there were two women coming forward! The wind was in their wings, for they had wings like the wings of a stork, and they lifted up the ephah[-like vessel] between the earth and the heavens.

10Then said I to the angel who talked with me, Where are they taking the ephah?

11And he said to me, To the land of Shinar [Babylonia] to build it a house, and when it is finished, to set up the ephah [the symbol of such sinners and their guilt] there upon its own base.

**6** AND AGAIN I lifted up my eyes and saw, and behold, four chariots came out from between two mountains; and the mountains were mountains of firm, immovable bronze.

2The first chariot had red *or* bay horses, the second chariot had black horses,

3The third chariot had white horses, and the fourth chariot had dappled, active *and* strong horses.

4Then I said to the angel who talked with me, What are these, my lord?

5And the angel answered me, These are the four winds *or* spirits of the heavens, which go forth from presenting themselves before the Lord of all the earth. [Ps. 104:4; Matt. 24:31.]

6The chariot with the black horses is going forth into the north country, and the white ones are going forth after them [because there are two northern powers to overcome], and the dappled ones are going forth toward the south country.

7And [the chariot with] the strong, [red or bay horses] went forth and sought to go that they might patrol the earth. And [the Lord] said to them, Go, walk to and fro through the earth *and* patrol it. So they walked about through the earth, watching *and* protecting it.

## New American Standard

13So he answered me saying, "Do you not know what these are?" And I said, "No, my lord."
14Then he said, "These are the two anointed ones, who are standing by the Lord of the whole earth."

*The Flying Scroll*

5 THEN I lifted up my eyes again and looked, and behold, *there was* a flying scroll.
2And he said to me, "What do you see?" And I answered, "I see a flying scroll; its length is twenty cubits and its width ten cubits."
3Then he said to me, "This is the curse that is going forth over the face of the whole land; surely everyone who steals will be purged away according to the writing on one side, and everyone who swears will be purged away according to the writing on the other side.
4"I will make it go forth," declares the LORD of hosts, "and it will enter the house of the thief and the house of the one who swears falsely by My name; and it will spend the night within that house and consume it with its timber and stones."
5¶ Then the angel who was speaking with me went out, and said to me, "Lift up now your eyes, and see what this is, going forth."
6And I said, "What is it?" And he said, "This is the ephah going forth." Again he said, "This is their appearance in all the land
7(and behold, a lead cover was lifted up); and this is a woman sitting inside the ephah."
8Then he said, "This is Wickedness!" And he threw her down into the middle of the ephah and cast the lead weight on its opening.
9Then I lifted up my eyes and looked, and there two women were coming out with the wind in their wings; and they had wings like the wings of a stork, and they lifted up the ephah between the earth and the heavens.
10And I said to the angel who was speaking with me, "Where are they taking the ephah?"
11Then he said to me, "To build a temple for her in the land of Shinar; and when it is prepared, she will be set there on her own pedestal."

*The Four Chariots*

6 NOW I lifted up my eyes again and looked, and behold, four chariots were coming forth from between the two mountains; and the mountains *were* bronze mountains.
2With the first chariot *were* red horses, with the second chariot black horses,
3with the third chariot white horses, and with the fourth chariot strong dappled horses.
4Then I spoke and said to the angel who was speaking with me, "What are these, my lord?"
5And the angel answered and said to me, "These are the four spirits of heaven, going forth after standing before the Lord of all the earth,
6with one of which the black horses are going forth to the north country; and the white ones go forth after them, while the dappled ones go forth to the south country.
7"When the strong ones went out, they were eager to go to patrol the earth." And He said, "Go, patrol the earth." So they patrolled the earth.

## New International

13He replied, "Do you not know what these are?"
"No, my lord," I said.
14So he said, "These are the two who are anointed to[a] serve the Lord of all the earth."

*The Flying Scroll*

5 I LOOKED again—and there before me was a flying scroll!
2He asked me, "What do you see?"
I answered, "I see a flying scroll, thirty feet long and fifteen feet wide.[b]"
3And he said to me, "This is the curse that is going out over the whole land; for according to what it says on one side, every thief will be banished, and according to what it says on the other, everyone who swears falsely will be banished. 4The LORD Almighty declares, 'I will send it out, and it will enter the house of the thief and the house of him who swears falsely by my name. It will remain in his house and destroy it, both its timbers and its stones.'"

*The Woman in a Basket*

5Then the angel who was speaking to me came forward and said to me, "Look up and see what this is that is appearing."
6I asked, "What is it?"
He replied, "It is a measuring basket.[c]" And he added, "This is the iniquity[d] of the people throughout the land."
7Then the cover of lead was raised, and there in the basket sat a woman! 8He said, "This is wickedness," and he pushed her back into the basket and pushed the lead cover down over its mouth.
9Then I looked up—and there before me were two women, with the wind in their wings! They had wings like those of a stork, and they lifted up the basket between heaven and earth.
10"Where are they taking the basket?" I asked the angel who was speaking to me.
11He replied, "To the country of Babylonia[e] to build a house for it. When it is ready, the basket will be set there in its place."

*Four Chariots*

6 I LOOKED up again—and there before me were four chariots coming out from between two mountains—mountains of bronze! 2The first chariot had red horses, the second black, 3the third white, and the fourth dappled—all of them powerful. 4I asked the angel who was speaking to me, "What are these, my lord?"
5The angel answered me, "These are the four spirits[f] of heaven, going out from standing in the presence of the Lord of the whole world. 6The one with the black horses is going toward the north country, the one with the white horses toward the west,[g] and the one with the dappled horses toward the south."
7When the powerful horses went out, they were straining to go throughout the earth. And he said, "Go throughout the earth!" So they went throughout the earth.

**NIV** [a] 14 Or *two who bring oil and* [b] 2 Hebrew *twenty cubits long and ten cubits wide* (about 9 meters long and 4.5 meters wide) [c] 6 Hebrew *an ephah;* also in verses 7-11 [d] 6 Or *appearance* [e] 11 Hebrew *Shinar* [f] 5 Or *winds* [g] 6 Or *horses after them*

## King James

8Then cried he upon me, and spake unto me, saying, Behold, these that go toward the north country have quieted my spirit in the north country.

9¶ And the word of the LORD came unto me, saying,

10Take of *them of* the captivity, *even* of Heldai, of Tobijah, and of Jedaiah, which are come from Babylon, and come thou the same day, and go into the house of Josiah the son of Zephaniah;

11Then take silver and gold, and make crowns, and set *them* upon the head of Joshua the son of Josedech, the high priest;

12And speak unto him, saying, Thus speaketh the LORD of hosts, saying, Behold the man whose name *is* The BRANCH; and he shall grow up out of his place, and he shall build the temple of the LORD:

13Even he shall build the temple of the LORD; and he shall bear the glory, and shall sit and rule upon his throne; and he shall be a priest upon his throne: and the counsel of peace shall be between them both.

14And the crowns shall be to Helem, and to Tobijah, and to Jedaiah, and to Hen the son of Zephaniah, for a memorial in the temple of the LORD.

15And they *that are* far off shall come and build in the temple of the LORD, and ye shall know that the LORD of hosts hath sent me unto you. And *this* shall come to pass, if ye will diligently obey the voice of the LORD your God.

**7** AND IT came to pass in the fourth year of king Darius, *that* the word of the LORD came unto Zechariah in the fourth *day* of the ninth month, *even* in Chisleu;

2When they had sent unto the house of God Sherezer and Regem-melech, and their men, to pray before the LORD,

3 *And* to speak unto the priests which *were* in the house of the LORD of hosts, and to the prophets, saying, Should I weep in the fifth month, separating myself, as I have done these so many years?

4¶ Then came the word of the LORD of hosts unto me, saying,

5Speak unto all the people of the land, and to the priests, saying, When ye fasted and mourned in the fifth and seventh *month*, even those seventy years, did ye at all fast unto me, *even* to me?

6And when ye did eat, and when ye did drink, did not ye eat *for yourselves*, and drink *for yourselves*?

7 *Should ye* not *hear* the words which the LORD hath cried by the former prophets, when Jerusalem was inhabited and in prosperity, and the cities thereof round about her, when *men* inhabited the south and the plain?

8¶ And the word of the LORD came unto Zechariah, saying,

9Thus speaketh the LORD of hosts, saying, Execute true judgment, and show mercy and compassions every man to his brother:

10And oppress not the widow, nor the fatherless, the stranger, nor the poor; and let none of you imagine evil against his brother in your heart.

11But they refused to hearken, and pulled away the shoulder, and stopped their ears, that they should not hear.

12Yea, they made their hearts *as* an adamant stone, lest they should hear the law, and the words which the LORD of hosts hath sent in his spirit by the former prophets: therefore came a great wrath from the LORD of hosts.

## Amplified

8Then He summoned me, and said to me, Behold, these that go toward the north country have quieted My Spirit [of wrath] *and* have caused it to rest in the north country.

9And the word of the Lord came to me, saying,

10Accept donations *and* offerings from these [as representatives of the] exiles, from Heldai, from Tobijah, and from Jedaiah; and you come the same day and go to the house of Josiah the son of Zephaniah, where they have come from Babylon.

11Yes, take from them silver and gold, and make crowns and set *one* upon the head of Joshua the son of Jehozadak, the high priest;

12And say to him, Thus says the Lord of hosts: [You, Joshua] behold—look at, keep in sight, watch—the Man [the Messiah] whose name is the Branch; for He shall grow up in His place, and He shall build the [true] temple of the Lord. [Isa. 4:2; Jer. 23:5; 33:15; Zech. 3:8.]

13Yes, [you are building a temple of the Lord, but] it is He Who shall build the [true] temple of the Lord, and He shall bear the honor *and* glory [as of the only begotten of the Father], and shall sit and rule upon His throne. And He shall be a priest upon His throne, and the counsel of peace shall be between the two [offices] [Priest and King]. [John 1:14; 17:5; Heb. 2:9.]

14And the *other* crown shall be [credited] to Helem (Heldai), and to Tobijah, and to Jedaiah, and to the kindness *and* favor of Josiah the son of Zephaniah, and shall be in the temple of the Lord for a reminder *and* memorial. [Cf. verse 10; Matt. 10:41.]

15And those who are far off shall come and help build the temple of the Lord, and you shall know that the Lord sent me [Zechariah] to you. And [your part in this] shall come to pass, if you will diligently obey the voice of the Lord your God.

**7** AND IN the fourth year of the reign of King Darius, the word of the Lord came to Zechariah on the fourth day of the ninth month, Chislev.

2Now the people of Bethel had sent Sharezer and Regemmelech and their men, to pray *and* entreat the favor of the Lord,

3And to speak to the priests of the house of the Lord of hosts, and to the prophets, saying, [Now that I am returned from exile] should I weep in the fifth month, separating myself, as I have done these so many years [in Babylonia]?

4Then came the word of the Lord of hosts to me [Zechariah], saying,

5Speak to all the people of the land and to the priests, saying, When you fasted and mourned in the fifth and seventh months, even those seventy years you were in exile, was it for Me that you fasted, for Me?

6And when you eat and when you drink, do you not eat for yourselves and drink for yourselves?

7Should you not hear the words which the Lord cried by the former prophets, when Jerusalem was inhabited and in prosperity, with her cities round about her, and the South and the lowlands were inhabited?

8And the word of the Lord came to Zechariah, saying,

9Thus has the Lord of hosts spoken: Execute true judgment, and show mercy *and* kindness and tender compassion every man to his brother;

10And oppress not the widow, or the fatherless, the temporary resident, or the poor; and let none of you devise *or* imagine *or* think evil against his brother in your heart.

11But they refused to listen, and turned a rebellious *and* stubborn shoulder, and made heavy *and* dull their ears that they might not hear.

12Yes, they made their hearts as an adamant stone *or* diamond point, lest they should hear the law and the words which the Lord of hosts had sent by His Spirit through the former prophets. Therefore there came great wrath from the Lord of hosts.

## New American Standard

8Then He cried out to me and spoke to me saying, "See, those
who are going to the land of the north have appeased My wrath
in the land of the north."

9¶ The word of the LORD also came to me saying,

10"Take *an offering* from the exiles, from Heldai, Tobijah, and
Jedaiah; and you go the same day and enter the house of Josiah
the son of Zephaniah, where they have arrived from Babylon.

*The Symbolic Crowns*

11"And take silver and gold, make an *ornate* crown, and set *it*
on the head of Joshua the son of Jehozadak, the high priest.

12"Then say to him, 'Thus says the LORD of hosts, "Behold, a
man whose name is Branch, for He will branch out from where He
is; and He will build the temple of the LORD.

13"Yes, it is He who will build the temple of the LORD, and He
who will bear the honor and sit and rule on His throne. Thus, He
will be a priest on His throne, and the counsel of peace will be
between the two offices." '

14"Now the crown will become a reminder in the temple of the
LORD to Helem, Tobijah, Jedaiah, and Hen the son of Zephaniah.

15"And those who are far off will come and build the temple of
the LORD." Then you will know that the LORD of hosts has sent me
to you. And it will take place, if you completely obey the LORD your
God.

*Hearts like Flint*

7 THEN IT came about in the fourth year of King Darius, that
the word of the LORD came to Zechariah on the fourth *day* of
the ninth month, *which is* Chislev.

2Now *the town of* Bethel had sent Sharezer and Regemmelech
and their men to seek the favor of the LORD,

3speaking to the priests who belong to the house of the LORD
of hosts, and to the prophets saying, "Shall I weep in the fifth
month and abstain, as I have done these many years?"

4Then the word of the LORD of hosts came to me saying,

5"Say to all the people of the land and to the priests, 'When
you fasted and mourned in the fifth and seventh months these
seventy years, was it actually for Me that you fasted?

6'And when you eat and drink, do you not eat for yourselves
and do you not drink for yourselves?

7'Are not *these* the words which the LORD proclaimed by the
former prophets, when Jerusalem was inhabited and prosperous
with its cities around it, and the Negev and the foothills were
inhabited?' "

8¶ Then the word of the LORD came to Zechariah saying,

9"Thus has the LORD of hosts said, 'Dispense true justice, and
practice kindness and compassion each to his brother;

10and do not oppress the widow or the orphan, the stranger or
the poor; and do not devise evil in your hearts against one another.'

11"But they refused to pay attention, and turned a stubborn
shoulder and stopped their ears from hearing.

12"And they made their hearts *like* flint so that they could not
hear the law and the words which the LORD of hosts had sent by
His Spirit through the former prophets; therefore great wrath came
from the LORD of hosts.

## New International

8Then he called to me, "Look, those going toward the north
country have given my Spirit[a] rest in the land of the north."

*A Crown for Joshua*

9The word of the LORD came to me: 10"Take silver and gold
from the exiles Heldai, Tobijah and Jedaiah, who have arrived
from Babylon. Go the same day to the house of Josiah son of
Zephaniah. 11Take the silver and gold and make a crown, and set
it on the head of the high priest, Joshua son of Jehozadak. 12Tell
him this is what the LORD Almighty says: 'Here is the man whose
name is the Branch, and he will branch out from his place and build
the temple of the LORD. 13It is he who will build the temple of the
LORD, and he will be clothed with majesty and will sit and rule on
his throne. And he will be a priest on his throne. And there will
be harmony between the two.' 14The crown will be given to Heldai,[b] Tobijah, Jedaiah and Hen[c] son of Zephaniah as a memorial
in the temple of the LORD. 15Those who are far away will come and
help to build the temple of the LORD, and you will know that the
LORD Almighty has sent me to you. This will happen if you diligently obey the LORD your God."

*Justice and Mercy, Not Fasting*

7 IN THE fourth year of King Darius, the word of the LORD
came to Zechariah on the fourth day of the ninth month, the
month of Kislev. 2The people of Bethel had sent Sharezer and
Regem-Melech, together with their men, to entreat the LORD 3by
asking the priests of the house of the LORD Almighty and the
prophets, "Should I mourn and fast in the fifth month, as I have
done for so many years?"

4Then the word of the LORD Almighty came to me: 5"Ask all the
people of the land and the priests, 'When you fasted and mourned
in the fifth and seventh months for the past seventy years, was it
really for me that you fasted? 6And when you were eating and
drinking, were you not just feasting for yourselves? 7Are these not
the words the LORD proclaimed through the earlier prophets when
Jerusalem and its surrounding towns were at rest and prosperous,
and the Negev and the western foothills were settled?' "

8And the word of the LORD came again to Zechariah: 9"This is
what the LORD Almighty says: 'Administer true justice; show
mercy and compassion to one another. 10Do not oppress the
widow or the fatherless, the alien or the poor. In your hearts do
not think evil of each other.'

11"But they refused to pay attention; stubbornly they turned
their backs and stopped up their ears. 12They made their hearts as
hard as flint and would not listen to the law or to the words that
the LORD Almighty had sent by his Spirit through the earlier
prophets. So the LORD Almighty was very angry.

**NIV** [a] 8 Or *spirit* [b] 14 Syriac; Hebrew *Helem* [c] 14 Or *and the gracious one, the*

## King James

13Therefore it is come to pass, *that* as he cried, and they would not hear; so they cried, and I would not hear, saith the LORD of hosts:

14But I scattered them with a whirlwind among all the nations whom they knew not. Thus the land was desolate after them, that no man passed through nor returned: for they laid the pleasant land desolate.

8 AGAIN THE word of the LORD of hosts came *to me*, saying,

2Thus saith the LORD of hosts; I was jealous for Zion with great jealousy, and I was jealous for her with great fury.

3Thus saith the LORD; I am returned unto Zion, and will dwell in the midst of Jerusalem: and Jerusalem shall be called a city of truth; and the mountain of the LORD of hosts the holy mountain.

4Thus saith the LORD of hosts; There shall yet old men and old women dwell in the streets of Jerusalem, and every man with his staff in his hand for very age.

5And the streets of the city shall be full of boys and girls playing in the streets thereof.

6Thus saith the LORD of hosts; If it be marvellous in the eyes of the remnant of this people in these days, should it also be marvellous in mine eyes? saith the LORD of hosts.

7Thus saith the LORD of hosts; Behold, I will save my people from the east country, and from the west country;

8And I will bring them, and they shall dwell in the midst of Jerusalem: and they shall be my people, and I will be their God, in truth and in righteousness.

9¶ Thus saith the LORD of hosts; Let your hands be strong, ye that hear in these days these words by the mouth of the prophets, which *were* in the day *that* the foundation of the house of the LORD of hosts was laid, that the temple might be built.

10For before these days there was no hire for man, nor any hire for beast; neither *was there any* peace to him that went out or came in because of the affliction: for I set all men every one against his neighbour.

11But now I *will* not *be* unto the residue of this people as in the former days, saith the LORD of hosts.

12For the seed *shall be* prosperous; the vine shall give her fruit, and the ground shall give her increase, and the heavens shall give their dew; and I will cause the remnant of this people to possess all these *things*.

13And it shall come to pass, *that* as ye were a curse among the heathen, O house of Judah, and house of Israel; so will I save you, and ye shall be a blessing: fear not, *but* let your hands be strong.

14For thus saith the LORD of hosts; As I thought to punish you, when your fathers provoked me to wrath, saith the LORD of hosts, and I repented not:

15So again have I thought in these days to do well unto Jerusalem and to the house of Judah: fear ye not.

16¶ These *are* the things that ye shall do; Speak ye every man the truth to his neighbour; execute the judgment of truth and peace in your gates:

17And let none of you imagine evil in your hearts against his neighbour; and love no false oath: for all these *are things* that I hate, saith the LORD.

18¶ And the word of the LORD of hosts came unto me, saying,

## Amplified

13So it came to pass that as He cried and they would not hear, *He said,* So they shall cry and I will not answer, says the Lord of hosts,

14But I will scatter them with a whirlwind among all the nations whom they know not *and* who know not them. Thus the land was desolate after they had gone, so that no man passed through or returned; for they [the Jews by their sins] had *caused to be* laid waste *and* forsaken the pleasant land—the land of desire.

8 AND THE word of the Lord of hosts came to me, saying,

2Thus says the Lord of hosts: I am jealous for Zion with great jealousy, and I am jealous for her with great wrath [against her enemies].

3Thus says the Lord: I shall return to Zion, and will dwell in the midst of Jerusalem; and Jerusalem shall be called the (faithful) city of truth, and the mountain of the Lord of hosts, the holy mountain.

4Thus says the Lord of hosts: Old men and old women shall again dwell in Jerusalem *and* sit out in the streets, every man with his staff in his hand for very *advanced* age.

5And the streets of the city shall be full of boys and girls playing in its streets.

6Thus says the Lord of hosts: Because it will be marvelous in the eyes of the remnant of this people in those days [in which it comes to pass], should it also be marvelous in My eyes? says the Lord of hosts. [Luke 18:27.]

7Thus says the Lord of hosts: Behold, I will save My people from the east country, and from the west—the country of the going down of the sun. [Cf. Isa. 43:5, 6.]

8And I will bring them [home], and they shall dwell in the midst of Jerusalem; and they shall be My people, and I will be their God, in truth *and* faithfulness and in righteousness.

9Thus says the Lord of hosts: Let your hands be strong *and* hardened, you who in these days hear these words from the mouth of the prophets, who on the day that the foundation of the house of the Lord of hosts was laid, foretold that the temple should be rebuilt.

10For before those days there was no hire for man, nor any hire for beast, neither was there any peace *or* success to him who went out or came in, because of the adversary *and* oppressor; for I set—let loose—all men every one against his neighbor.

11But now [in this period since you began to build] I am not to the remnant of this people as in the former days, says the Lord of hosts.

12For there shall be the seed sowing of peace *and* prosperity; the vine shall yield her fruit, and the ground shall give its increase, and the heavens shall give their dew; and I will cause the remnant of this people to inherit *and* possess all these things.

13And as you have been a curse *and* a byword among the nations, O house of Judah and house of Israel, so will I save you and you shall be a blessing. Fear not, but let your hands be strong *and* hardened. [Jer. 22:8, 9.]

14For thus says the Lord of hosts: As I thought to bring calamity upon you, when your fathers provoked Me to wrath, says the Lord of hosts, and I did not relent *or* revoke your sentence,

15So again have I purposed in these days to do good to Jerusalem and to the house of Judah. Fear not!

16These are the things that you shall do: speak every man the truth with his neighbor; render the truth, and pronounce the judgment *or* verdict that makes for peace in [the courts at] your gates. [Eph. 4:25.]

17And let none of you think *or* imagine *or* devise evil *or* injury in your hearts against his neighbor, and love no false oath, for all these things I hate, says the Lord.

18And the word of the Lord of hosts came to me [Zechariah], saying,

## New American Standard

13"And it came about that just as He called and they would not
listen, so they called and I would not listen," says the LORD of
hosts;
14"but I scattered them with a storm wind among all the nations
whom they have not known. Thus the land is desolated behind
them, so that no one went back and forth, for they made the
pleasant land desolate."

*The Coming Peace and Prosperity of Zion*

8 THEN THE word of the LORD of hosts came saying,
2"Thus says the LORD of hosts, 'I am exceedingly jealous for
Zion, yes, with great wrath I am jealous for her.'
3"Thus says the LORD, 'I will return to Zion and will dwell in
the midst of Jerusalem. Then Jerusalem will be called the City of
Truth, and the mountain of the LORD of hosts *will be called* the Holy
Mountain.'
4"Thus says the LORD of hosts, 'Old men and old women will
again sit in the [a]streets of Jerusalem, each man with his staff in his
hand because of age.
5'And the [b]streets of the city will be filled with boys and girls
playing in its [c]streets.'
6"Thus says the LORD of hosts, 'If it is too difficult in the sight
of the remnant of this people in those days, will it also be too
difficult in My sight?' declares the LORD of hosts.
7"Thus says the LORD of hosts, 'Behold, I am going to save My
people from the land of the east and from the land of the west;
8and I will bring them *back*, and they will live in the midst of
Jerusalem, and they will be My people and I will be their God in
truth and righteousness.'
9¶ "Thus says the LORD of hosts, 'Let your hands be strong,
you who are listening in these days to these words from the mouth
of the prophets, *those* who *spoke* in the day that the foundation of
the house of the LORD of hosts was laid, to the end that the temple
might be built.
10'For before those days there was no wage for man or any wage
for animal; and for him who went out or came in there was no
peace because of his enemies, and I set all men one against another.
11'But now I will not treat the remnant of this people as in the
former days,' declares the LORD of hosts.
12'For *there will be* peace for the seed: the vine will yield its fruit,
the land will yield its produce, and the heavens will give their dew;
and I will cause the remnant of this people to inherit all these
*things*.
13'And it will come about that just as you were a curse among
the nations, O house of Judah and house of Israel, so I will save
you that you may become a blessing. Do not fear; let your hands
be strong.'
14¶ "For thus says the LORD of hosts, 'Just as I purposed to do
harm to you when your fathers provoked Me to wrath,' says the
LORD of hosts, 'and I have not relented,
15so I have again purposed in these days to do good to Jerusalem and to the house of Judah. Do not fear!
16'These are the things which you should do: speak the truth
to one another; judge with truth and judgment for peace in your
[d]gates.
17'Also let none of you devise evil in your heart against another,
and do not love perjury; for all these are what I hate,' declares the
LORD."
18¶ Then the word of the LORD of hosts came to me saying,

NAS [a] Or, *squares* [b] Or, *squares* [c] Or, *squares* [d] I.e., the place where court was held

## New International

13" 'When I called, they did not listen; so when they called, I
would not listen,' says the LORD Almighty. 14'I scattered them with
a whirlwind among all the nations, where they were strangers.
The land was left so desolate behind them that no one could come
or go. This is how they made the pleasant land desolate.' "

*The LORD Promises to Bless Jerusalem*

8 AGAIN THE word of the LORD Almighty came to me. 2This
is what the LORD Almighty says: "I am very jealous for Zion;
I am burning with jealousy for her."
3This is what the LORD says: "I will return to Zion and dwell in
Jerusalem. Then Jerusalem will be called the City of Truth, and the
mountain of the LORD Almighty will be called the Holy Mountain."
4This is what the LORD Almighty says: "Once again men and
women of ripe old age will sit in the streets of Jerusalem, each with
cane in hand because of his age. 5The city streets will be filled with
boys and girls playing there."
6This is what the LORD Almighty says: "It may seem marvelous
to the remnant of this people at that time, but will it seem marvelous to me?" declares the LORD Almighty.
7This is what the LORD Almighty says: "I will save my people
from the countries of the east and the west. 8I will bring them back
to live in Jerusalem; they will be my people, and I will be faithful
and righteous to them as their God."
9This is what the LORD Almighty says: "You who now hear
these words spoken by the prophets who were there when the
foundation was laid for the house of the LORD Almighty, let your
hands be strong so that the temple may be built. 10Before that time
there were no wages for man or beast. No one could go about his
business safely because of his enemy, for I had turned every man
against his neighbor. 11But now I will not deal with the remnant
of this people as I did in the past," declares the LORD Almighty.
12"The seed will grow well, the vine will yield its fruit, the
ground will produce its crops, and the heavens will drop their
dew. I will give all these things as an inheritance to the remnant
of this people. 13As you have been an object of cursing among the
nations, O Judah and Israel, so will I save you, and you will be a
blessing. Do not be afraid, but let your hands be strong."
14This is what the LORD Almighty says: "Just as I had determined to bring disaster upon you and showed no pity when your
fathers angered me," says the LORD Almighty, 15"so now I have
determined to do good again to Jerusalem and Judah. Do not be
afraid. 16These are the things you are to do: Speak the truth to each
other, and render true and sound judgment in your courts; 17do
not plot evil against your neighbor, and do not love to swear
falsely. I hate all this," declares the LORD.
18Again the word of the LORD Almighty came to me. 19This is

## King James

19Thus saith the LORD of hosts; The fast of the fourth *month,* and the fast of the fifth, and the fast of the seventh, and the fast of the tenth, shall be to the house of Judah joy and gladness, and cheerful feasts; therefore love the truth and peace.

20Thus saith the LORD of hosts; *It shall* yet *come to pass,* that there shall come people, and the inhabitants of many cities:

21And the inhabitants of one *city* shall go to another, saying, Let us go speedily to pray before the LORD, and to seek the LORD of hosts: I will go also.

22Yea, many people and strong nations shall come to seek the LORD of hosts in Jerusalem, and to pray before the LORD.

23Thus saith the LORD of hosts; In those days *it shall come to pass,* that ten men shall take hold out of all languages of the nations, even shall take hold of the skirt of him that is a Jew, saying, We will go with you: for we have heard *that* God *is* with you.

9 THE BURDEN of the word of the LORD in the land of Hadrach, and Damascus *shall be* the rest thereof: when the eyes of man, as of all the tribes of Israel, *shall be* toward the LORD.

2And Hamath also shall border thereby; Tyrus, and Zidon, though it be very wise.

3And Tyrus did build herself a strong hold, and heaped up silver as the dust, and fine gold as the mire of the streets.

4Behold, the Lord will cast her out, and he will smite her power in the sea; and she shall be devoured with fire.

5Ashkelon shall see *it,* and fear; Gaza also *shall see it,* and be very sorrowful, and Ekron; for her expectation shall be ashamed; and the king shall perish from Gaza, and Ashkelon shall not be inhabited.

6And a bastard shall dwell in Ashdod, and I will cut off the pride of the Philistines.

7And I will take away his blood out of his mouth, and his abominations from between his teeth: but he that remaineth, even he, *shall be* for our God, and he shall be as a governor in Judah, and Ekron as a Jebusite.

8And I will encamp about mine house because of the army, because of him that passeth by, and because of him that returneth: and no oppressor shall pass through them any more: for now have I seen with mine eyes.

9¶ Rejoice greatly, O daughter of Zion; shout, O daughter of Jerusalem: behold, thy King cometh unto thee: he *is* just, and having salvation; lowly, and riding upon an ass, and upon a colt the foal of an ass.

10And I will cut off the chariot from Ephraim, and the horse from Jerusalem, and the battle bow shall be cut off: and he shall speak peace unto the heathen: and his dominion *shall be* from sea *even* to sea, and from the river *even* to the ends of the earth.

## Amplified

19Thus says the Lord of hosts: The fast of the fourth month, and the fast of the fifth, and the fast of the seventh, and the fast of the tenth, shall be to the house of Judah times of joy and gladness, and cheerful appointed seasons; therefore [in order that this may happen to you, as the condition of fulfilling the promise] love truth and peace.

20Thus says the Lord of hosts: It shall yet come to pass, that there shall come [to Jerusalem] peoples and the inhabitants of many *and* great cities;

21And the inhabitants of one city shall go to them of another, saying, Let us go speedily to pray *and* entreat the favor of the Lord, and to seek, inquire of *and* require [to meet our own most essential need] the Lord of hosts. I will go also.

22Yes, many people and strong nations shall come to Jerusalem to seek, inquire of *and* require [to fill their own urgent need] the Lord of hosts, and to pray to the Lord for His favor.

23Thus says the Lord of hosts: In those days ten men, out of all languages of the nations, shall take hold of the robe of him who is a Jew, saying, Let us go with you, for we have heard that God is with you.

9 THE BURDEN *or* oracle—the thing to be lifted up—of the word of the Lord is against the land of Hadrach [in Syria], and Damascus shall be its resting place, for the Lord has an eye upon mankind as upon all the tribes of Israel;

2And Hamath also which borders on [Damascus], Tyre with Sidon, though they are very wise.

3And Tyre has built herself a stronghold [on an island, a half mile from the shore, which seems impregnable], and heaped up silver like dust, and fine gold like the mire of the streets.

4Behold, the Lord will [a]cast her out *and* dispossess her; He will smite her power in the sea *and* into it, and [Tyre] shall be devoured by fire.

5[The strong cities of Philistia] shall see it, and fear; [b]Ashkelon, Gaza also, and be sorely pained; and Ekron, for her confidence *and* expectation shall be put to shame; and a king [monarchial government] shall perish from Gaza, and Ashkelon shall not be inhabited.

6And a mongrel people shall dwell in Ashdod, and I will put an end to the pride of the Philistines.

7And I will take out of [the Philistine's] mouth and from between his teeth the abominable idolatrous sacrifices eaten with the blood. And he too shall remain *and* be a remnant for our God, and he shall be as a chieftain—the head over a thousand—in Judah, and Ekron shall be like one of the Jebusites [who at last were merged and had lost their identity in Israel].

8Then I will encamp about My house as a guard *or* a garrison, so that none shall march back and forth; and no oppressor *or* demanding collector shall again over-run them, for now My eyes are upon *them.*

9Rejoice greatly, O daughter of Zion! Shout aloud, O daughter of Jerusalem! Lo, your King comes to you; He is [uncompromisingly] just, and having salvation—triumphant and victorious; patient, meek, lowly and riding on a donkey, upon a colt, the foal of a donkey. [John 12:14, 15.]

10And I will cut off *and* exterminate the war chariot from Ephraim, and the *war* horse from Jerusalem, and the battle-bow shall be cut off; and He shall speak the word and peace shall come to the nations, and His dominion shall be from the *Mediterranean* Sea to *any other* sea, and from the River *Euphrates* to the ends of the earth! [Ps. 72:8.]

**AMP** [a] Tyre was utterly destroyed by Alexander the Great and has never been rebuilt. History records that after he had slain everyone except those who had fled to the temples, Alexander ordered the houses to be set afire. Yet Sidon, Tyre's sister city (verse 2), though meeting with many adversities, has survived and kept her identity (modern Saida) for an estimated 4000 years (cf. Gen. 10:15, 19). How did Zechariah know that it was Tyre, not Sidon, that was to be permanently destroyed? Ezekiel wrote of Tyre, after telling the details of her destruction, "You shall be built no more; for I the Lord have spoken it, says the Lord God" (Ezek. 26:3-14). [b] Ashkelon was one of the five strong, leading Philistine cities, Gath and Ashdod being the ones not named here. It was the birthplace of Herod the Great, and his sister Salome lived there, centuries after this period. It was not until 1270 A.D. that Zechariah's prophecy of its total destruction was fulfilled, when the Sultan Bibars reduced it to ruins and filled the harbor with stones. Nearly 700 years later the city is still uninhabited, and the seacoast has been and continues to be the site of "dwellings and cottages for shepherds, and folds for flocks" (Zeph. 2:6).

## New American Standard

19"Thus says the LORD of hosts, 'The fast of the fourth, the fast
of the fifth, the fast of the seventh, and the fast of the tenth *months*
will become joy, gladness, and cheerful feasts for the house of
Judah; so love truth and peace.'
20"Thus says the LORD of hosts, '*It will* yet *be* that peoples will
come, even the inhabitants of many cities.
21'And the inhabitants of one will go to another saying, "Let us
go at once to entreat the favor of the LORD, and to seek the LORD
of hosts; I will also go."
22'So many peoples and mighty nations will come to seek the
LORD of hosts in Jerusalem and to entreat the favor of the LORD.'
23"Thus says the LORD of hosts, 'In those days ten men from
all the nations will grasp the garment of a Jew saying, "Let us go
with you, for we have heard that God is with you." ' "

*Prophecies against Neighboring Nations*

9 THE BURDEN of the word of the LORD is against the land of
Hadrach, with Damascus as its resting place (for the eyes of
men, especially of all the tribes of Israel, are toward the LORD),
2 And Hamath also, which borders on it;
Tyre and Sidon, though they are very wise.
3 For Tyre built herself a fortress
And piled up silver like dust,
And gold like the mire of the streets.
4 Behold, the Lord will dispossess her
And cast her wealth into the sea;
And she will be consumed with fire.
5 Ashkelon will see *it* and be afraid.
Gaza too will writhe in great pain;
Also Ekron, for her expectation has been confounded.
Moreover, the king will perish from Gaza,
And Ashkelon will not be inhabited.
6 And a mongrel race will dwell in Ashdod,
And I will cut off the pride of the Philistines.
7 And I will remove their blood from their mouth,
And their detestable things from between their teeth.
Then they also will be a remnant for our God,
And be like a clan in Judah,
And Ekron like a Jebusite.
8 But I will camp around My house because of an army,
Because of him who passes by and returns;
And no oppressor will pass over them anymore,
For now I have seen with My eyes.
9 Rejoice greatly, O daughter of Zion!
Shout *in triumph,* O daughter of Jerusalem!
Behold, your king is coming to you;
He is just and endowed with salvation,
Humble, and mounted on a donkey,
Even on a colt, the foal of a donkey.
10 And I will cut off the chariot from Ephraim,
And the horse from Jerusalem;
And the bow of war will be cut off.
And He will speak peace to the nations;
And His dominion will be from sea to sea,
And from the [c]River to the ends of the earth.

NAS [c] I.e., Euphrates

## New International

what the LORD Almighty says: "The fasts of the fourth, fifth,
seventh and tenth months will become joyful and glad occasions
and happy festivals for Judah. Therefore love truth and peace."
20This is what the LORD Almighty says: "Many peoples and the
inhabitants of many cities will yet come, 21and the inhabitants of
one city will go to another and say, 'Let us go at once to entreat
the LORD and seek the LORD Almighty. I myself am going.' 22And
many peoples and powerful nations will come to Jerusalem to seek
the LORD Almighty and to entreat him."
23This is what the LORD Almighty says: "In those days ten men
from all languages and nations will take firm hold of one Jew by
the hem of his robe and say, 'Let us go with you, because we have
heard that God is with you.' "

*Judgment on Israel's Enemies*

An Oracle

9 THE WORD of the LORD is against the land of Hadrach
and will rest upon Damascus—
for the eyes of men and all the tribes of Israel
are on the LORD—[d]
2and upon Hamath too, which borders on it,
and upon Tyre and Sidon, though they are very skillful.
3Tyre has built herself a stronghold;
she has heaped up silver like dust,
and gold like the dirt of the streets.
4But the Lord will take away her possessions
and destroy her power on the sea,
and she will be consumed by fire.
5Ashkelon will see it and fear;
Gaza will writhe in agony,
and Ekron too, for her hope will wither.
Gaza will lose her king
and Ashkelon will be deserted.
6Foreigners will occupy Ashdod,
and I will cut off the pride of the Philistines.
7I will take the blood from their mouths,
the forbidden food from between their teeth.
Those who are left will belong to our God
and become leaders in Judah,
and Ekron will be like the Jebusites.
8But I will defend my house
against marauding forces.
Never again will an oppressor overrun my people,
for now I am keeping watch.

*The Coming of Zion's King*

9Rejoice greatly, O Daughter of Zion!
Shout, Daughter of Jerusalem!
See, your king[e] comes to you,
righteous and having salvation,
gentle and riding on a donkey,
on a colt, the foal of a donkey.
10I will take away the chariots from Ephraim
and the war-horses from Jerusalem,
and the battle bow will be broken.
He will proclaim peace to the nations.
His rule will extend from sea to sea
and from the River[f] to the ends of the earth.[g]

NIV [d] 1 Or *Damascus. / For the eye of the LORD is on all mankind, / as well as on the tribes of Israel,* [e] 9 Or *King* [f] 10 That is, the Euphrates [g] 10 Or *the end of the land*

## King James

11As for thee also, by the blood of thy covenant I have sent forth thy prisoners out of the pit wherein *is* no water.

12¶ Turn you to the strong hold, ye prisoners of hope: even today do I declare *that* I will render double unto thee;

13When I have bent Judah for me, filled the bow with Ephraim, and raised up thy sons, O Zion, against thy sons, O Greece, and made thee as the sword of a mighty man.

14And the LORD shall be seen over them, and his arrow shall go forth as the lightning: and the Lord GOD shall blow the trumpet, and shall go with whirlwinds of the south.

15The LORD of hosts shall defend them; and they shall devour, and subdue with sling stones; and they shall drink, *and* make a noise as through wine; and they shall be filled like bowls, *and* as the corners of the altar.

16And the LORD their God shall save them in that day as the flock of his people: for *they shall be as* the stones of a crown, lifted up as an ensign upon his land.

17For how great *is* his goodness, and how great *is* his beauty! corn shall make the young men cheerful, and new wine the maids.

**10** ASK YE of the LORD rain in the time of the latter rain; *so* the LORD shall make bright clouds, and give them showers of rain, to every one grass in the field.

2For the idols have spoken vanity, and the diviners have seen a lie, and have told false dreams; they comfort in vain: therefore they went their way as a flock, they were troubled, because *there was* no shepherd.

3Mine anger was kindled against the shepherds, and I punished the goats: for the LORD of hosts hath visited his flock the house of Judah, and hath made them as his goodly horse in the battle.

4Out of him came forth the corner, out of him the nail, out of him the battle bow, out of him every oppressor together.

5¶ And they shall be as mighty *men*, which tread down *their enemies* in the mire of the streets in the battle: and they shall fight, because the LORD *is* with them, and the riders on horses shall be confounded.

6And I will strengthen the house of Judah, and I will save the house of Joseph, and I will bring them again to place them; for I have mercy upon them: and they shall be as though I had not cast them off: for I *am* the LORD their God, and will hear them.

## Amplified

11As for you also, because of *and* for the sake of the [covenant of the Lord with His people which was sealed with sprinkled] covenant blood, I have released *and* sent forth your imprisoned people out of the waterless pit. [Exod. 24:4-8; Gen. 37:24; Heb. 9:16.]

12Turn you to the stronghold [of security and prosperity], you prisoners of hope; even today do I declare that I will restore double your former prosperity to you. [Ps. 40:2; Isa. 40:2.]

13For I have bent Judah for me as My bow, filled the bow with Ephraim as My arrow, and will stir up your sons, O Zion, against your sons, O Greece, and will make you [Israel] as the sword of a mighty man.

14And the Lord shall be seen over them, and His arrow shall go forth as the lightning; and the Lord God will blow the trumpet, and will go forth in the windstorms of the south.

15The Lord of hosts shall defend *and* protect them; and they shall devour and they shall tread on *their fallen enemies* as on sling stones [that have missed their aim], and they shall drink [of victory] and be noisy *and* turbulent as from wine, and become full like bowls [used to catch the sacrificial blood], like the corners of the [sacrificial] altar.

16And the Lord their God will save them on that day as the flock of His people, for they shall be as the [precious] jewels of a crown, lifted high over *and* shining glitteringly upon His land.

17For how great is God's goodness and how great is His beauty! *And* how great [He will make] *Israel's* goodliness and *Israel's* beauty! Grain shall make the young men thrive, and fresh wine the maidens.

**10** ASK OF the Lord rain in the time of the latter *or* spring rain. It is the Lord Who makes lightnings, which usher in the rain *and* give men showers of it, to every one grass in the field.

2For the teraphim [household idols] have spoken vanity—emptiness, falsity and futility—and the diviners have seen a lie and the dreamers have told false dreams; they comfort in vain. Therefore the people go their way like sheep, they are afflicted *and* hurt because there is no shepherd.

3My anger is kindled against the shepherds [who are not true shepherds], and I will punish the goat-leaders; for the Lord of hosts has visited His flock, the house of Judah, and will make them as His beautiful *and* majestic horse in the battle.

4Out of him [Judah] shall come forth the cornerstone, out of him the tent peg, out of him the battle bow; every ruler shall proceed from him. [Jer. 30:21.]

5And they shall be as mighty men, treading down their enemies in the mire of the streets in the battle; and they shall fight, because the Lord is with them, and the [oppressor's] riders on horses shall be confounded *and* put to shame.

6And I will strengthen the house of Judah, and I will save the house of Joseph [Ephraim]. I will bring them back *and* cause them to dwell securely; for I have mercy, loving-kindness *and* compassion for them. They shall be as though I had not cast them off, for I am the Lord their God, and I will hear them.

## New American Standard

*Deliverance of Judah and Ephraim*

11¶ As for you also, because of the blood of *My* covenant with you,
I have set your prisoners free from the waterless pit.
12 Return to the stronghold, O prisoners who have the hope;
This very day I am declaring that I will restore double to you.
13 For I will bend Judah as My bow,
I will fill the bow with Ephraim.
And I will stir up your sons, O Zion, against your sons, O Greece;
And I will make you like a warrior's sword.
14 Then the LORD will appear over them,
And His arrow will go forth like lightning;
And the Lord GOD will blow the trumpet,
And will march in the storm winds of the south.
15 The LORD of hosts will defend them.
And they will devour, and trample on the sling stones;
And they will drink, *and* be boisterous as with wine;
And they will be filled like a *sacrificial* basin,
*Drenched* like the corners of the altar.
16 And the LORD their God will save them in that day
As the flock of His people;
For *they are as* the stones of a crown,
Sparkling in His land.
17 For what comeliness and beauty *will be* theirs!
Grain will make the young men flourish, and new wine the virgins.

*God Will Bless Judah and Ephraim*

**10** ASK RAIN from the LORD at the time of the spring rain—
The LORD who makes the storm clouds;
And He will give them showers of rain, vegetation in the field to *each* man.
2 For the teraphim speak iniquity,
And the diviners see lying visions,
And tell false dreams;
They comfort in vain.
Therefore *the people* wander like sheep,
They are afflicted, because there is no shepherd.
3 "My anger is kindled against the shepherds,
And I will punish the male goats;
For the LORD of hosts has visited His flock, the house of Judah,
And will make them like His majestic horse in battle.
4 "From them will come the cornerstone,
From them the tent peg,
From them the bow of battle,
From them every ruler, *all* of them together.
5 "And they will be as mighty men,
Treading down *the enemy* in the mire of the streets in battle;
And they will fight, for the LORD *will be* with them;
And the riders on horses will be put to shame.
6 "And I shall strengthen the house of Judah,
And I shall save the house of Joseph,
And I shall bring them back,
Because I have had compassion on them;
And they will be as though I had not rejected them,
For I am the LORD their God, and I will answer them.

## New International

11As for you, because of the blood of my covenant with you,
I will free your prisoners from the waterless pit.
12Return to your fortress, O prisoners of hope;
even now I announce that I will restore twice as much to you.
13I will bend Judah as I bend my bow
and fill it with Ephraim.
I will rouse your sons, O Zion,
against your sons, O Greece,
and make you like a warrior's sword.

*The LORD Will Appear*

14Then the LORD will appear over them;
his arrow will flash like lightning.
The Sovereign LORD will sound the trumpet;
he will march in the storms of the south,
15 and the LORD Almighty will shield them.
They will destroy
and overcome with slingstones.
They will drink and roar as with wine;
they will be full like a bowl
used for sprinkling[a] the corners of the altar.
16The LORD their God will save them on that day
as the flock of his people.
They will sparkle in his land
like jewels in a crown.
17How attractive and beautiful they will be!
Grain will make the young men thrive,
and new wine the young women.

*The LORD Will Care for Judah*

**10** ASK THE LORD for rain in the springtime;
it is the LORD who makes the storm clouds.
He gives showers of rain to men,
and plants of the field to everyone.
2The idols speak deceit,
diviners see visions that lie;
they tell dreams that are false,
they give comfort in vain.
Therefore the people wander like sheep
oppressed for lack of a shepherd.
3"My anger burns against the shepherds,
and I will punish the leaders;
for the LORD Almighty will care
for his flock, the house of Judah,
and make them like a proud horse in battle.
4From Judah will come the cornerstone,
from him the tent peg,
from him the battle bow,
from him every ruler.
5Together they[b] will be like mighty men
trampling the muddy streets in battle.
Because the LORD is with them,
they will fight and overthrow the horsemen.

6"I will strengthen the house of Judah
and save the house of Joseph.
I will restore them
because I have compassion on them.
They will be as though
I had not rejected them,
for I am the LORD their God
and I will answer them.

NIV [a] 15 Or *bowl, / like* [b] 4,5 Or *ruler, all of them together. / [5]They*

## King James

7And *they of* Ephraim shall be like a mighty *man*, and their heart shall rejoice as through wine: yea, their children shall see *it*, and be glad; their heart shall rejoice in the LORD.

8I will hiss for them, and gather them; for I have redeemed them: and they shall increase as they have increased.

9And I will sow them among the people: and they shall remember me in far countries; and they shall live with their children, and turn again.

10I will bring them again also out of the land of Egypt, and gather them out of Assyria; and I will bring them into the land of Gilead and Lebanon; and *place* shall not be found for them.

11And he shall pass through the sea with affliction, and shall smite the waves in the sea, and all the deeps of the river shall dry up: and the pride of Assyria shall be brought down, and the sceptre of Egypt shall depart away.

12And I will strengthen them in the LORD; and they shall walk up and down in his name, saith the LORD.

**11** OPEN THY doors, O Lebanon, that the fire may devour thy cedars.

2Howl, fir tree; for the cedar is fallen; because the mighty are spoiled: howl, O ye oaks of Bashan; for the forest of the vintage is come down.

3¶ *There is* a voice of the howling of the shepherds; for their glory is spoiled: a voice of the roaring of young lions; for the pride of Jordan is spoiled.

4Thus saith the LORD my God; Feed the flock of the slaughter;

5Whose possessors slay them, and hold themselves not guilty: and they that sell them say, Blessed *be* the LORD; for I am rich: and their own shepherds pity them not.

6For I will no more pity the inhabitants of the land, saith the LORD: but, lo, I will deliver the men every one into his neighbour's hand, and into the hand of his king: and they shall smite the land, and out of their hand I will not deliver *them*.

7And I will feed the flock of slaughter, *even* you, O poor of the flock. And I took unto me two staves; the one I called Beauty, and the other I called Bands; and I fed the flock.

8Three shepherds also I cut off in one month; and my soul loathed them, and their soul also abhorred me.

9Then said I, I will not feed you: that that dieth, let it die; and that that is to be cut off, let it be cut off; and let the rest eat every one the flesh of another.

10¶ And I took my staff, *even* Beauty, and cut it asunder, that I might break my covenant which I had made with all the people.

11And it was broken in that day: and so the poor of the flock that waited upon me knew that it *was* the word of the LORD.

12And I said unto them, If ye think good, give *me* my price; and if not, forbear. So they weighed for my price thirty *pieces* of silver.

## Amplified

7Then Ephraim [the ten tribes] shall become like a mighty warrior, and their hearts shall rejoice as through wine; yes, their children shall see it and rejoice; their hearts shall feel great delight *and* glory triumphantly in the Lord!

8I will hiss for them [as the keeper does for his bees] and gather them in, for I have redeemed them, and they shall increase *again* as they have increased *before* [in Egypt]. [Ezek. 36:10, 11.]

9And though I sow them among the nations, yet they shall [earnestly] remember Me in far countries, and with their children they shall live and shall return [to God and the land He gave them].

10I will bring them [all Israel] home again from the land of Egypt, and gather them out of Assyria; and I will bring them into the land [on the east and on the west of Jordan, into] Gilead and Lebanon; and room enough shall not be found for them.

11And *the Lord* will pass through the sea of distress *and* affliction [at the head of His people, as He did at the Red Sea] and He will smite down the waves of the sea, and all the depths of the *river* Nile shall be dried up *and* put to shame; and the pride of Assyria shall be brought down, and the scepter *or* rod [of the taskmasters of Egypt] shall pass away.

12And I will strengthen *Israel* in the Lord, and they shall walk up and down *and* glory in His name, says the Lord.

**11** OPEN YOUR doors, O Lebanon, that the fire may devour your cedars!

2Wail, O fir tree *and* cypress, for the cedar has fallen; because the glorious *and* lofty trees are laid waste! Wail, O you oaks of Bashan, for the thick *and* inaccessible forest [on the steep mountain side] has in flames been felled.

3A voice of the wailing of the shepherds! For their glory, the broad pasturage, is laid waste! A voice of the roaring of young lions! For the pride of the Jordan [the jungle or thickets] is ruined!

4Thus says the Lord my God: Shepherd the flock *destined* for slaughter,

5Whose buyers *or* possessors slay them and hold themselves not guilty; and they who sell them say, Blessed be the Lord, for I have become rich! And their own shepherds neither pity *nor* spare them [from the wolves].

6For I will no more pity *or* spare the inhabitants of the land, says the Lord; but lo, I will deliver every man into his neighbor's hand, and into the hand of his *foreign* king. And *the enemy* shall lay waste the land, and I will not deliver *the people* out of the hand [of the foreign oppressor].

7So I [Zechariah] shepherded the flock of slaughter, truly [as the name implies] the most miserable of sheep. And I took two *shepherd's* staffs, the one I called Beauty *or* Grace, and the other I called Bands *or* Union; and I fed *and* shepherded the flock.

8And I cut off the three shepherds [the civil authorities, the priests and the prophets] in one month, for I was weary *and* impatient with them, and they also loathed me. [Jer. 2:8, 26; 18:18.]

9So I [Zechariah] said, I will not be your shepherd. What is to die, let it die, and what is to be destroyed, let it be destroyed; and let the survivors devour one another's flesh.

10And I took my staff Beauty *or* Grace, and broke it in pieces, to show that I was annulling the covenant *or* agreement which I had made with all the peoples [not to molest them].

11So the covenant was annulled on that day, and thus the most wretched of the flock *and* the traffickers in the sheep, who were watching me, knew—recognized and understood—that it was truly the word of the Lord.

12And I said to them, If it seems just *and* right to you, give me my wages; but if not, withhold *them*. So they weighed out for my price thirty *pieces* of silver.

## New American Standard

7 "And Ephraim will be like a mighty man,
And their heart will be glad as if *from* wine;
Indeed, their children will see *it* and be glad,
Their heart will rejoice in the LORD.
8 "I will whistle for them to gather them together,
For I have redeemed them;
And they will be as numerous as they were before.
9 "When I scatter them among the peoples,
They will remember Me in far countries,
And they with their children will live and come back.
10 "I will bring them back from the land of Egypt,
And gather them from Assyria;
And I will bring them into the land of Gilead and Lebanon,
Until no *room* can be found for them.
11 "And He will pass through the sea *of* distress,
And strike the waves in the sea,
So that all the depths of the Nile will dry up;
And the pride of Assyria will be brought down,
And the scepter of Egypt will depart.
12 "And I shall strengthen them in the LORD,
And in His name they will walk," declares the LORD.

*The Doomed Flock*

11 OPEN YOUR doors, O Lebanon,
That a fire may feed on your cedars.
2 Wail, O cypress, for the cedar has fallen,
Because the glorious *trees* have been destroyed;
Wail, O oaks of Bashan,
For the impenetrable forest has come down.
3 There is a sound of the shepherds' wail,
For their glory is ruined;
There is a sound of the young lions' roar,
For the pride of the Jordan is ruined.

4¶ Thus says the LORD my God, "Pasture the flock *doomed* to
slaughter.
5"Those who buy them slay them and go unpunished, and *each*
*of* those who sell them says, 'Blessed be the LORD, for I have
become rich!' And their own shepherds have no pity on them.
6"For I shall no longer have pity on the inhabitants of the
land," declares the LORD; "but behold, I shall cause the men to fall,
each into another's power and into the power of his king; and they
will strike the land, and I shall not deliver *them* from their power."
7So I pastured the flock *doomed* to slaughter, hence the afflicted
of the flock. And I took for myself two staffs: the one I called Favor,
and the other I called Union; so I pastured the flock.
8Then I annihilated the three shepherds in one month, for my
soul was impatient with them, and their soul also was weary of
me.
9Then I said, "I will not pasture you. What is to die, let it die,
and what is to be annihilated, let it be annihilated; and let those
who are left eat one another's flesh."
10And I took my staff, Favor, and cut it in pieces, to break my
covenant which I had made with all the peoples.
11So it was broken on that day, and [a]thus the afflicted of the
flock who were watching me realized that it was the word of the
LORD.
12And I said to them, "If it is good in your sight, give *me* my
wages; but if not, never mind!" So they weighed out thirty *shekels*
of silver as my wages.

NAS [a] Another reading is *the sheep dealers who*

## New International

7The Ephraimites will become like mighty men,
and their hearts will be glad as with wine.
Their children will see it and be joyful;
their hearts will rejoice in the LORD.
8I will signal for them
and gather them in.
Surely I will redeem them;
they will be as numerous as before.
9Though I scatter them among the peoples,
yet in distant lands they will remember me.
They and their children will survive,
and they will return.
10I will bring them back from Egypt
and gather them from Assyria.
I will bring them to Gilead and Lebanon,
and there will not be room enough for them.
11They will pass through the sea of trouble;
the surging sea will be subdued
and all the depths of the Nile will dry up.
Assyria's pride will be brought down
and Egypt's scepter will pass away.
12I will strengthen them in the LORD
and in his name they will walk,"
declares the LORD.

11 OPEN YOUR doors, O Lebanon,
so that fire may devour your cedars!
2Wail, O pine tree, for the cedar has fallen;
the stately trees are ruined!
Wail, oaks of Bashan;
the dense forest has been cut down!
3Listen to the wail of the shepherds;
their rich pastures are destroyed!
Listen to the roar of the lions;
the lush thicket of the Jordan is ruined!

*Two Shepherds*

4This is what the LORD my God says: "Pasture the flock marked
for slaughter. 5Their buyers slaughter them and go unpunished.
Those who sell them say, 'Praise the LORD, I am rich!' Their own
shepherds do not spare them. 6For I will no longer have pity on
the people of the land," declares the LORD. "I will hand everyone
over to his neighbor and his king. They will oppress the land, and
I will not rescue them from their hands."
7So I pastured the flock marked for slaughter, particularly the
oppressed of the flock. Then I took two staffs and called one Favor
and the other Union, and I pastured the flock. 8In one month I got
rid of the three shepherds.
The flock detested me, and I grew weary of them 9and said, "I
will not be your shepherd. Let the dying die, and the perishing
perish. Let those who are left eat one another's flesh."
10Then I took my staff called Favor and broke it, revoking the
covenant I had made with all the nations. 11It was revoked on that
day, and so the afflicted of the flock who were watching me knew
it was the word of the LORD.
12I told them, "If you think it best, give me my pay; but if not,
keep it." So they paid me thirty pieces of silver.

## King James

13And the LORD said unto me, Cast it unto the potter: a goodly price that I was prised at of them. And I took the thirty *pieces* of silver, and cast them to the potter in the house of the LORD.

14Then I cut asunder mine other staff, *even* Bands, that I might break the brotherhood between Judah and Israel.

15¶ And the LORD said unto me, Take unto thee yet the instruments of a foolish shepherd.

16For, lo, I will raise up a shepherd in the land, *which* shall not visit those that be cut off, neither shall seek the young one, nor heal that that is broken, nor feed that that standeth still: but he shall eat the flesh of the fat, and tear their claws in pieces.

17Woe to the idol shepherd that leaveth the flock! the sword *shall be* upon his arm, and upon his right eye: his arm shall be clean dried up, and his right eye shall be utterly darkened.

**12** THE BURDEN of the word of the LORD for Israel, saith the LORD, which stretcheth forth the heavens, and layeth the foundation of the earth, and formeth the spirit of man within him.

2Behold, I will make Jerusalem a cup of trembling unto all the people round about, when they shall be in the siege both against Judah *and* against Jerusalem.

3¶ And in that day will I make Jerusalem a burdensome stone for all people: all that burden themselves with it shall be cut in pieces, though all the people of the earth be gathered together against it.

4In that day, saith the LORD, I will smite every horse with astonishment, and his rider with madness: and I will open mine eyes upon the house of Judah, and will smite every horse of the people with blindness.

5And the governors of Judah shall say in their heart, The inhabitants of Jerusalem *shall be* my strength in the LORD of hosts their God.

6¶ In that day will I make the governors of Judah like an hearth of fire among the wood, and like a torch of fire in a sheaf; and they shall devour all the people round about, on the right hand and on the left: and Jerusalem shall be inhabited again in her own place, *even* in Jerusalem.

7The LORD also shall save the tents of Judah first, that the glory of the house of David and the glory of the inhabitants of Jerusalem do not magnify *themselves* against Judah.

8In that day shall the LORD defend the inhabitants of Jerusalem; and he that is feeble among them at that day shall be as David; and the house of David *shall be* as God, as the angel of the LORD before them.

9¶ And it shall come to pass in that day, *that* I will seek to destroy all the nations that come against Jerusalem.

10And I will pour upon the house of David, and upon the inhabitants of Jerusalem, the spirit of grace and of supplications: and they shall look upon me whom they have pierced, and they shall mourn for him, as one mourneth for *his* only *son,* and shall be in bitterness for him, as one that is in bitterness for *his* firstborn.

## Amplified

13And the Lord said to me, Cast it to the potter [as if He said, To the dogs!], the munificently *miserable* sum at which I [and My shepherd] am priced by them! And I [Zechariah] took the thirty *pieces* of silver, and cast them to the potter in the house of the Lord. [Matt. 26:14, 15; 27:3-10.]

14Then I broke into pieces my other staff, Bands *or* Union, indicating that I was annulling the brotherhood between Judah and Israel.

15And the Lord said to me, Take up once more the implements [the staff and rod of a shepherd, but this time] of a worthless *and* wicked shepherd. [Ezek. 34:2-6.]

16For lo, I raise up a false shepherd in the land; the lost *and* perishing he will not miss *or* visit, the young *and* scattered he will not go to seek, the wounded *and* broken he will not heal, nor will he feed those that are sound *and* strong; but he will eat the flesh of the fat ones and break off their hoofs [to consume all the flesh].

17Woe to the worthless *and* foolish shepherd who deserts the flock! The sword shall smite his arm and his right eye; his arm shall be utterly withered and his right eye utterly blinded. [Jer. 23:1; John 10:12, 13.]

**12** THE BURDEN *or* oracle—the thing to be lifted up—of the word of the Lord concerning Israel. Thus says the Lord, Who stretches out the heavens and lays the foundation of the earth and forms the spirit of man within him:

2Behold, I am about to make Jerusalem a cup *or* bowl of reeling to all the peoples round about, and against *and* upon Judah also it will be in the siege against Jerusalem.

3And in that day I will make Jerusalem a burdensome stone for all peoples; all who lift it *or* burden themselves with it shall be sorely wounded. And all the nations of the earth shall come *and* gather together against it.

4In that day, says the Lord, I will smite every horse [of the armies that contend against Jerusalem] with terror *and* panic, and his rider with madness; and I will open My eyes *and* regard with favor the house of Judah, and will smite every horse of the opposing nations with blindness.

5And the chiefs of Judah shall say in their heart, The inhabitants of Jerusalem are my strength in the Lord of hosts their God.

6In that day will I make the chiefs of Judah like a big, blazing pot among *sticks of* wood and like a flaming torch among sheaves *of grain;* and they shall devour all the peoples round about, on the right hand and on the left; and they of Jerusalem shall yet again dwell *and* sit securely in their own place, in Jerusalem.

7And the Lord shall save *and* give victory to the tents of Judah first, that the glory of the house of David and the glory of the inhabitants of Jerusalem may not be magnified *and* exalted above Judah.

8In that day will the Lord guard *and* defend the inhabitants of Jerusalem; and he who is [spiritually] feeble *and* stumbles among them in that day [of persecution] shall become [strong and noble] like David; and the house of David [shall maintain its supremacy] like God, like the [a]Angel of the Lord Who is before them.

9And it shall be in that day, that I will make it My aim to destroy all the nations that come against Jerusalem.

10And I will pour out upon the house of David and upon the inhabitants of Jerusalem the Spirit of grace *or* unmerited favor, and supplication. And they shall look [earnestly] upon Me Whom they have pierced, and they shall mourn for Him as one mourns for his only son, and shall be in bitterness for Him as one who is in bitterness for his first-born. [John 19:37; Rev. 1:7.]

**AMP** [a] See footnote on Zech. 1:11.

## New American Standard

13Then the LORD said to me, "Throw it to the potter, *that* magnificent price at which I was valued by them." So I took the thirty *shekels* of silver and threw them to the potter in the house of the LORD.

14Then I cut my second staff, Union, in pieces, to break the brotherhood between Judah and Israel.

15¶ And the LORD said to me, "Take again for yourself the equipment of a foolish shepherd.

16"For behold, I am going to raise up a shepherd in the land who will not care for the perishing, seek the scattered, heal the broken, or sustain the one standing, but will devour the flesh of the fat *sheep* and tear off their hoofs.

17 "Woe to the worthless shepherd
Who leaves the flock!
A sword will be on his arm
And on his right eye!
His arm will be totally withered,
And his right eye will be blind."

*Jerusalem to Be Attacked*

**12** THE [b]BURDEN of the word of the LORD concerning Israel. ¶*Thus* declares the LORD who stretches out the heavens, lays the foundation of the earth, and forms the spirit of man within him,

2"Behold, I am going to make Jerusalem a cup that causes reeling to all the peoples around; and when the siege is against Jerusalem, it will also be against Judah.

3"And it will come about in that day that I will make Jerusalem a heavy stone for all the peoples; all who lift it will be severely injured. And all the nations of the earth will be gathered against it.

4"In that day," declares the LORD, "I will strike every horse with bewilderment, and his rider with madness. But I will watch over the house of Judah, while I strike every horse of the peoples with blindness.

5"Then the clans of Judah will say in their hearts, 'A strong support for us are the inhabitants of Jerusalem through the LORD of hosts, their God.'

6"In that day I will make the clans of Judah like a firepot among pieces of wood and a flaming torch among sheaves, so they will consume on the right hand and on the left all the surrounding peoples, while the inhabitants of Jerusalem again dwell on their own sites in Jerusalem.

7"The LORD also will save the tents of Judah first in order that the glory of the house of David and the glory of the inhabitants of Jerusalem may not be magnified above Judah.

8"In that day the LORD will defend the inhabitants of Jerusalem, and the one who is feeble among them in that day will be like David, and the house of David *will be* like God, like the angel of the LORD before them.

9"And it will come about in that day that I will set about to destroy all the nations that come against Jerusalem.

10¶ "And I will pour out on the house of David and on the inhabitants of Jerusalem, the Spirit of grace and of supplication, so that they will look on Me whom they have pierced; and they will mourn for Him, as one mourns for an only son, and they will weep bitterly over Him, like the bitter weeping over a first-born.

NAS [b] Or, *oracle*

## New International

13And the LORD said to me, "Throw it to the potter"—the handsome price at which they priced me! So I took the thirty pieces of silver and threw them into the house of the LORD to the potter.

14Then I broke my second staff called Union, breaking the brotherhood between Judah and Israel.

15Then the LORD said to me, "Take again the equipment of a foolish shepherd. 16For I am going to raise up a shepherd over the land who will not care for the lost, or seek the young, or heal the injured, or feed the healthy, but will eat the meat of the choice sheep, tearing off their hoofs.

17"Woe to the worthless shepherd,
who deserts the flock!
May the sword strike his arm and his right eye!
May his arm be completely withered,
his right eye totally blinded!"

*Jerusalem's Enemies to Be Destroyed*

An Oracle

**12** THIS IS the word of the LORD concerning Israel. The LORD, who stretches out the heavens, who lays the foundation of the earth, and who forms the spirit of man within him, declares: 2"I am going to make Jerusalem a cup that sends all the surrounding peoples reeling. Judah will be besieged as well as Jerusalem. 3On that day, when all the nations of the earth are gathered against her, I will make Jerusalem an immovable rock for all the nations. All who try to move it will injure themselves. 4On that day I will strike every horse with panic and its rider with madness," declares the LORD. "I will keep a watchful eye over the house of Judah, but I will blind all the horses of the nations. 5Then the leaders of Judah will say in their hearts, 'The people of Jerusalem are strong, because the LORD Almighty is their God.'

6"On that day I will make the leaders of Judah like a firepot in a woodpile, like a flaming torch among sheaves. They will consume right and left all the surrounding peoples, but Jerusalem will remain intact in her place.

7"The LORD will save the dwellings of Judah first, so that the honor of the house of David and of Jerusalem's inhabitants may not be greater than that of Judah. 8On that day the LORD will shield those who live in Jerusalem, so that the feeblest among them will be like David, and the house of David will be like God, like the Angel of the LORD going before them. 9On that day I will set out to destroy all the nations that attack Jerusalem.

*Mourning for the One They Pierced*

10"And I will pour out on the house of David and the inhabitants of Jerusalem a spirit[c] of grace and supplication. They will look on[d] me, the one they have pierced, and they will mourn for him as one mourns for an only child, and grieve bitterly for him as one grieves for a firstborn son. 11On that day the weeping in Jerusalem

NIV [c] 10 Or *the Spirit* [d] 10 Or *to*

## King James

11 In that day shall there be a great mourning in Jerusalem, as the mourning of Hadadrimmon in the valley of Megiddon.

12 And the land shall mourn, every family apart; the family of the house of David apart, and their wives apart; the family of the house of Nathan apart, and their wives apart;

13 The family of the house of Levi apart, and their wives apart; the family of Shimei apart, and their wives apart;

14 All the families that remain, every family apart, and their wives apart.

## Amplified

11 In that day shall there be a great mourning in Jerusalem, as the mourning of *the city of* Hadadrimmon in the valley of Megiddo [over beloved King Josiah, who was mortally wounded at thirty-nine, and for whom the people's grief was extraordinarily deep. Like that will be the mourning of Israel, when they recognize as their once crucified Messiah Him Who has come to reign]. [II Chron. 35:22-25.]

12 And the land shall mourn, every family apart; the [kingly] family of the house of David apart, and their wives apart; the family of the house of Nathan [David's son] apart, and their wives apart;

13 The [priestly] family of the house of Levi apart, and their wives apart; the family of Shimei [grandson of Levi] apart, and their wives apart;

14 All the families that are left, each by itself, and their wives by themselves [each with an overwhelming individual sorrow over having blindly rejected their unrecognized Messiah].

## King James

**13** IN THAT day there shall be a fountain opened to the house of David and to the inhabitants of Jerusalem for sin and for uncleanness.

2 ¶ And it shall come to pass in that day, saith the LORD of hosts, *that* I will cut off the names of the idols out of the land, and they shall no more be remembered: and also I will cause the prophets and the unclean spirit to pass out of the land.

3 And it shall come to pass, *that* when any shall yet prophesy, then his father and his mother that begat him shall say unto him, Thou shalt not live; for thou speakest lies in the name of the LORD: and his father and his mother that begat him shall thrust him through when he prophesieth.

4 And it shall come to pass in that day, *that* the prophets shall be ashamed every one of his vision, when he hath prophesied; neither shall they wear a rough garment to deceive:

5 But he shall say, I *am* no prophet, I *am* an husbandman; for man taught me to keep cattle from my youth.

6 And *one* shall say unto him, What *are* these wounds in thine hands? Then he shall answer, *Those* with which I was wounded *in* the house of my friends.

7 ¶ Awake, O sword, against my shepherd, and against the man *that is* my fellow, saith the LORD of hosts: smite the shepherd, and the sheep shall be scattered: and I will turn mine hand upon the little ones.

8 And it shall come to pass, *that* in all the land, saith the LORD, two parts therein shall be cut off *and* die; but the third shall be left therein.

9 And I will bring the third part through the fire, and will refine them as silver is refined, and will try them as gold is tried: they shall call on my name, and I will hear them: I will say, It *is* my people: and they shall say, The LORD *is* my God.

## Amplified

**13** IN THAT day there shall be a fountain opened for the house of David and for the inhabitants of Jerusalem *to cleanse them from* sin and uncleanness.

2 And in that day, says the Lord of hosts, I will cut off the names of the idols from the land, and they shall no more be remembered; and also I will remove from the land the *false* prophets and the unclean spirit.

3 And if any one again appears *falsely* as a prophet, then his father and his mother who bore him shall say to him, You shall not live, for you speak lies in the name of the Lord; and his father and his mother who bore him shall thrust him through when he prophesies.

4 And in that day the *false* prophets shall every one be ashamed of his vision when he prophesies. Nor will *he* wear a hairy *or* rough garment to deceive,

5 But he will [deny his identity and] say, I am no prophet, I am a tiller of the ground, for I have been made a bond servant from my youth.

6 And one shall say to him, What are these wounds on your breast—between your hands? Then he will answer, Those with which I was wounded [when disciplined] in the house of my (loving) friends.

7 Awake, O sword, against My shepherd, and against the man who is My associate, says the Lord of hosts; smite the shepherd, and the sheep *of the flock* shall be scattered; and I will turn back My hand *and* stretch it out again upon the little ones *of the flock.* [Matt. 26:31, 32.]

8 And in all the land, says the Lord, two thirds shall be cut off and perish, but one third shall be left alive. [Hos. 2:23; Rom. 11:5.]

9 And I will bring the third part through the fire, and will refine them as silver is refined, and will test them as gold is tested. They will call on My name, and I will hear *and* answer them. I will say, It is My people; and they will say, The Lord is my God.

## King James

**14** BEHOLD, THE day of the LORD cometh, and thy spoil shall be divided in the midst of thee.

2 For I will gather all nations against Jerusalem to battle; and the city shall be taken, and the houses rifled, and the women ravished; and half of the city shall go forth into captivity, and the residue of the people shall not be cut off from the city.

## Amplified

**14** BEHOLD, A day of the Lord is coming, when the spoil [taken from you] shall be divided [among the victors] in the midst of you.

2 For I will gather all nations against Jerusalem to battle, and the city shall be taken and the houses rifled and the women ravished, and half of the city shall go into exile, but the rest of the people shall not be cut off from the city.

## New American Standard

11"In that day there will be great mourning in Jerusalem, like
the mourning of Hadadrimmon in the plain of Megiddo.
12"And the land will mourn, every family by itself; the family of the house of David by itself, and their wives by themselves; the family of the house of Nathan by itself, and their wives by themselves;
13the family of the house of Levi by itself, and their wives by themselves; the family of the Shimeites by itself, and their wives by themselves;
14all the families that remain, every family by itself, and their wives by themselves.

*False Prophets Ashamed*

**13** "IN THAT day a fountain will be opened for the house of David and for the inhabitants of Jerusalem, for sin and for impurity.
2¶ "And it will come about in that day," declares the LORD of hosts, "that I will cut off the names of the idols from the land, and they will no longer be remembered; and I will also remove the prophets and the unclean spirit from the land.
3"And it will come about that if anyone still prophesies, then his father and mother who gave birth to him will say to him, 'You shall not live, for you have spoken falsely in the name of the LORD'; and his father and mother who gave birth to him will pierce him through when he prophesies.
4"Also it will come about in that day that the prophets will each be ashamed of his vision when he prophesies, and they will not put on a hairy robe in order to deceive;
5but he will say, 'I am not a prophet; I am a tiller of the ground, for a man sold me as a slave in my youth.'
6"And one will say to him, 'What are these wounds between your arms?' Then he will say, '*Those* with which I was wounded in the house of my friends.'
7¶ "Awake, O sword, against My Shepherd,
And against the man, My Associate,"
Declares the LORD of hosts.
"Strike the Shepherd that the sheep may be scattered;
And I will turn My hand against the little ones.
8 "And it will come about in all the land,"
Declares the LORD,
"That two parts in it will be cut off *and* perish;
But the third will be left in it.
9 "And I will bring the third part through the fire,
Refine them as silver is refined,
And test them as gold is tested.
They will call on My name,
And I will answer them;
I will say, 'They are My people,'
And they will say, 'The LORD is my God.'"

*God Will Battle Jerusalem's Foes*

**14** BEHOLD, A day is coming for the LORD when the spoil taken from you will be divided among you.
2For I will gather all the nations against Jerusalem to battle, and the city will be captured, the houses plundered, the women ravished, and half of the city exiled, but the rest of the people will not be cut off from the city.

## New International

will be great, like the weeping of Hadad Rimmon in the plain of
Megiddo. 12The land will mourn, each clan by itself, with their
wives by themselves: the clan of the house of David and their
wives, the clan of the house of Nathan and their wives, 13the clan
of the house of Levi and their wives, the clan of Shimei and their
wives, 14and all the rest of the clans and their wives.

*Cleansing From Sin*

**13** "ON THAT day a fountain will be opened to the house of
David and the inhabitants of Jerusalem, to cleanse them
from sin and impurity.
2"On that day, I will banish the names of the idols from the
land, and they will be remembered no more," declares the LORD
Almighty. "I will remove both the prophets and the spirit of impurity from the land. 3And if anyone still prophesies, his father
and mother, to whom he was born, will say to him, 'You must die,
because you have told lies in the LORD's name.' When he prophesies, his own parents will stab him.
4"On that day every prophet will be ashamed of his prophetic
vision. He will not put on a prophet's garment of hair in order to
deceive. 5He will say, 'I am not a prophet. I am a farmer; the land
has been my livelihood since my youth.[a]' 6If someone asks him,
'What are these wounds on your body[b]?' he will answer, 'The
wounds I was given at the house of my friends.'

*The Shepherd Struck, the Sheep Scattered*

7"Awake, O sword, against my shepherd,
against the man who is close to me!"
declares the LORD Almighty.
"Strike the shepherd,
and the sheep will be scattered,
and I will turn my hand against the little ones.
8In the whole land," declares the LORD,
"two-thirds will be struck down and perish;
yet one-third will be left in it.
9This third I will bring into the fire;
I will refine them like silver
and test them like gold.
They will call on my name
and I will answer them;
I will say, 'They are my people,'
and they will say, 'The LORD is our God.'"

*The LORD Comes and Reigns*

**14** A DAY of the LORD is coming when your plunder will be
divided among you.
2I will gather all the nations to Jerusalem to fight against it; the
city will be captured, the houses ransacked, and the women raped.
Half of the city will go into exile, but the rest of the people will not
be taken from the city.

NIV [a] 5 Or *farmer; a man sold me in my youth* [b] 6 Or *wounds between your hands*

## King James

3Then shall the LORD go forth, and fight against those nations,
as when he fought in the day of battle.
4¶ And his feet shall stand in that day upon the mount of Olives,
which *is* before Jerusalem on the east, and the mount of Olives
shall cleave in the midst thereof toward the east and toward the
west, *and there shall be* a very great valley; and half of the mountain
shall remove toward the north, and half of it toward the south.
5And ye shall flee *to* the valley of the mountains; for the valley
of the mountains shall reach unto Azal: yea, ye shall flee, like as
ye fled from before the earthquake in the days of Uzziah king of
Judah: and the LORD my God shall come, *and* all the saints with
thee.
6And it shall come to pass in that day, *that* the light shall not
be clear, *nor* dark:
7But it shall be one day which shall be known to the LORD, not
day, nor night: but it shall come to pass, *that* at evening time it shall
be light.
8And it shall be in that day, *that* living waters shall go out from
Jerusalem; half of them toward the former sea, and half of them
toward the hinder sea: in summer and in winter shall it be.
9And the LORD shall be king over all the earth: in that day shall
there be one LORD, and his name one.
10All the land shall be turned as a plain from Geba to Rimmon
south of Jerusalem: and it shall be lifted up, and inhabited in her
place, from Benjamin's gate unto the place of the first gate, unto
the corner gate, and *from* the tower of Hananeel unto the king's
winepresses.
11And *men* shall dwell in it, and there shall be no more utter
destruction; but Jerusalem shall be safely inhabited.
12¶ And this shall be the plague wherewith the LORD will smite
all the people that have fought against Jerusalem; Their flesh shall
consume away while they stand upon their feet, and their eyes
shall consume away in their holes, and their tongue shall consume
away in their mouth.
13And it shall come to pass in that day, *that* a great tumult from
the LORD shall be among them; and they shall lay hold every one
on the hand of his neighbour, and his hand shall rise up against
the hand of his neighbour.
14And Judah also shall fight at Jerusalem; and the wealth of all
the heathen round about shall be gathered together, gold, and
silver, and apparel, in great abundance.
15And so shall be the plague of the horse, of the mule, of the
camel, and of the ass, and of all the beasts that shall be in these
tents, as this plague.
16¶ And it shall come to pass, *that* every one that is left of all
the nations which came against Jerusalem shall even go up from
year to year to worship the King, the LORD of hosts, and to keep
the feast of tabernacles.
17And it shall be, *that* whoso will not come up of *all* the families
of the earth unto Jerusalem to worship the King, the LORD of hosts,
even upon them shall be no rain.
18And if the family of Egypt go not up, and come not, that *have*
no *rain;* there shall be the plague, wherewith the LORD will smite
the heathen that come not up to keep the feast of tabernacles.
19This shall be the punishment of Egypt, and the punishment
of all nations that come not up to keep the feast of tabernacles.
20¶ In that day shall there be upon the bells of the horses,
HOLINESS UNTO THE LORD; and the pots in the LORD's house
shall be like the bowls before the altar.

**AMP** [a] The second advent of Christ is the coming of GOD to earth, hence the emphasis placed upon it in the Scriptures. It is heralded not just once, but many times, plainly, without opportunity for misinterpretation; such as in Deut. 30:3; Zech. 14:3, 4; Matt. 16:27; 24:3-14, 27, 36-39; 25:31, 32; 26:64; Luke 21:25-28; Acts 1:9-11; I Cor. 1:7, 8; 4:5; I Tim. 6:14; II Tim. 4:1; Titus 2:13; Heb. 9:28; I John 2:28; Rev. 3:11; 16:15; 22:7, 20.

## Amplified

3Then shall the Lord go forth and fight against those nations,
as when He fought in the day of battle.
4And His feet shall stand in that day upon the Mount of Olives,
which lies before Jerusalem on the east, and the Mount of Olives
shall be split in two from the east to the west by a very great valley;
and half of the mountain shall remove toward the north, and half
of it toward the south. [Isa. 64:1, 2.]
5And you shall flee by the valley of My mountains, for the valley
of the mountains shall reach to Azal, and you shall flee as you fled
from before the earthquake in the days of Uzziah king of Judah:
and the Lord my [Zechariah's] [a]God shall come, and all the holy
ones [saints and angels] with *Him.* [Amos 1:1; Jude 14, 15; Col. 3:4;
I Thess. 4:14; Matt. 25:31.]
6And it shall come to pass in that day that there shall not be
light; the glorious *and* bright ones [the heavenly bodies] shall be
darkened.
7But it shall be one continuous day, known to the Lord, not day
and not night, but at evening time there shall be light.
8And it shall be in that day, that living waters shall go out from
Jerusalem, half of them to the eastern [Dead] Sea, and half of them
to the western [Mediterranean] Sea; in summer and in winter shall
it be.
9And the Lord shall be King over all the earth; in that day the
Lord shall be one [in the recognition and worship of men] and His
name one.
10All the land shall be turned into a plain from Geba to Rimmon,
[the Rimmon that is] south of Jerusalem. But Jerusalem shall remain lifted up on its site and dwell in its place, from Benjamin's
gate to the place of the former gate, to the Corner Gate, and from
the Tower of Hananeel to the king's wine presses.
11And it shall be inhabited, for there shall be no more curse *or*
ban of utter destruction; but Jerusalem shall dwell securely. [Rev.
22:3.]
12And this shall be the plague wherewith the Lord will smite all
the peoples that have warred against Jerusalem: their flesh shall
rot away while they stand upon their feet, and their eyes shall
corrode away in their sockets, and their tongue shall decay away
in their mouth.
13And in that day there shall be a great confusion, discomfiture
*and* panic among them from the Lord, and they shall seize each his
neighbor's hand, and the hand of the one shall be raised against
the hand of the other.
14And Judah also shall fight at Jerusalem; and the wealth of all
the nations round about shall be gathered together, gold, and
silver, and apparel, in great abundance.
15And as that plague on men, so shall be the plague on the
horse, on the mule, on the camel, on the donkey, and on all the
livestock *and* beasts that may be in those camps.
16And every one that is left of all the nations which came against
Jerusalem shall even go up from year to year to worship the King,
the Lord of hosts, and to keep the feast of tabernacles *or* booths.
17And it shall be, that whoso of the families of the earth shall
not go up to Jerusalem to worship the King, the Lord of hosts,
upon them there shall be no rain.
18And if the family of Egypt do not go up to Jerusalem and
present themselves, upon them there shall be no *rain,* but there
shall be the plague with which the Lord will smite the nations that
go not up to keep the feast of tabernacles.
19This shall be the consequent punishment of the sin of Egypt,
and the consequent punishment of the sin of all the nations that
do not go up to keep the feast of tabernacles.
20In that day there shall be [written] upon the [little] bells on the
horses, HOLINESS UNTO THE LORD; and the pots in the Lord's
house shall be holy to the Lord like the bowls before the altar.

## New American Standard

3 Then the LORD will go forth and fight against those nations, as when He fights on a day of battle.

4 And in that day His feet will stand on the Mount of Olives, which is in front of Jerusalem on the east; and the Mount of Olives will be split in its middle from east to west by a very large valley, so that half of the mountain will move toward the north and the other half toward the south.

5 And you will flee by the valley of My mountains, for the valley of the mountains will reach to Azel; yes, you will flee just as you fled before the earthquake in the days of Uzziah king of Judah. Then the LORD, my God, will come, *and* all the holy ones with Him!

6 And it will come about in that day that there will be no light; the luminaries will dwindle.

7 For it will be a unique day which is known to the LORD, neither day nor night, but it will come about that at evening time there will be light.

8 And it will come about in that day that living waters will flow out of Jerusalem, half of them toward the eastern sea and the other half toward the western sea; it will be in summer as well as in winter.

*God Will Be King over All*

9 ¶ And the LORD will be king over all the earth; in that day the LORD will be *the only* one, and His name *the only* one.

10 All the land will be changed into a plain from Geba to Rimmon south of Jerusalem; but Jerusalem will rise and remain on its site from Benjamin's Gate as far as the place of the First Gate to the Corner Gate, and from the Tower of Hananel to the king's wine presses.

11 And people will live in it, and there will be no more curse, for Jerusalem will dwell in security.

12 ¶ Now this will be the plague with which the LORD will strike all the peoples who have gone to war against Jerusalem; their flesh will rot while they stand on their feet, and their eyes will rot in their sockets, and their tongue will rot in their mouth.

13 And it will come about in that day that a great panic from the LORD will fall on them; and they will seize one another's hand, and the hand of one will be lifted against the hand of another.

14 And Judah also will fight at Jerusalem; and the wealth of all the surrounding nations will be gathered, gold and silver and garments in great abundance.

15 So also like this plague, will be the plague on the horse, the mule, the camel, the donkey, and all the cattle that will be in those camps.

16 ¶ Then it will come about that any who are left of all the nations that went against Jerusalem will go up from year to year to worship the King, the LORD of hosts, and to celebrate the Feast of Booths.

17 And it will be that whichever of the families of the earth does not go up to Jerusalem to worship the King, the LORD of hosts, there will be no rain on them.

18 And if the family of Egypt does not go up or enter, then no *rain will fall* on them; it will be the plague with which the LORD smites the nations who do not go up to celebrate the Feast of Booths.

19 This will be the punishment of Egypt, and the punishment of all the nations who do not go up to celebrate the Feast of Booths.

20 In that day there will *be inscribed* on the bells of the horses, "HOLY TO THE LORD." And the cooking pots in the LORD's house will be like the bowls before the altar.

## New International

3 Then the LORD will go out and fight against those nations, as
he fights in the day of battle. 4 On that day his feet will stand on
the Mount of Olives, east of Jerusalem, and the Mount of Olives
will be split in two from east to west, forming a great valley, with
half of the mountain moving north and half moving south. 5 You
will flee by my mountain valley, for it will extend to Azel. You will
flee as you fled from the earthquake[b] in the days of Uzziah king
of Judah. Then the LORD my God will come, and all the holy ones
with him.

6 On that day there will be no light, no cold or frost. 7 It will be
a unique day, without daytime or nighttime—a day known to the
LORD. When evening comes, there will be light.

8 On that day living water will flow out from Jerusalem, half to
the eastern sea[c] and half to the western sea,[d] in summer and in
winter.

9 The LORD will be king over the whole earth. On that day there
will be one LORD, and his name the only name.

10 The whole land, from Geba to Rimmon, south of Jerusalem,
will become like the Arabah. But Jerusalem will be raised up and
remain in its place, from the Benjamin Gate to the site of the First
Gate, to the Corner Gate, and from the Tower of Hananel to the
royal winepresses. 11 It will be inhabited; never again will it be
destroyed. Jerusalem will be secure.

12 This is the plague with which the LORD will strike all the
nations that fought against Jerusalem: Their flesh will rot while
they are still standing on their feet, their eyes will rot in their
sockets, and their tongues will rot in their mouths. 13 On that day
men will be stricken by the LORD with great panic. Each man will
seize the hand of another, and they will attack each other. 14 Judah
too will fight at Jerusalem. The wealth of all the surrounding
nations will be collected—great quantities of gold and silver and
clothing. 15 A similar plague will strike the horses and mules, the
camels and donkeys, and all the animals in those camps.

16 Then the survivors from all the nations that have attacked
Jerusalem will go up year after year to worship the King, the LORD
Almighty, and to celebrate the Feast of Tabernacles. 17 If any of the
peoples of the earth do not go up to Jerusalem to worship the King,
the LORD Almighty, they will have no rain. 18 If the Egyptian
people do not go up and take part, they will have no rain. The
LORD[e] will bring on them the plague he inflicts on the nations that
do not go up to celebrate the Feast of Tabernacles. 19 This will be
the punishment of Egypt and the punishment of all the nations
that do not go up to celebrate the Feast of Tabernacles.

20 On that day HOLY TO THE LORD will be inscribed on the bells
of the horses, and the cooking pots in the LORD's house will be like
the sacred bowls in front of the altar. 21 Every pot in Jerusalem and

**NIV** [b] *5* Or *5My mountain valley will be blocked and will extend to Azel. It will be blocked as it was blocked because of the earthquake* [c] *8* That is, the Dead Sea [d] *8* That is, the Mediterranean [e] *18* Or *part, then the* LORD

## King James

[21]Yea, every pot in Jerusalem and in Judah shall be holiness unto the LORD of hosts: and all they that sacrifice shall come and take of them, and seethe therein: and in that day there shall be no more the Canaanite in the house of the LORD of hosts.

## Amplified

[21]Yes, every pot in all the houses of Jerusalem and in Judah shall be dedicated *and* holy to the Lord of hosts; and all who sacrifice may come and take of them and boil their sacrifices in them [and traders in such wares will no longer be seen at the temple]. *And* in that day, there shall be no more a Canaanite [that is, any godless or unclean person, whether Jew or Gentile] in the house of the Lord of hosts. [Eph. 2:19-22.]

## New American Standard

21And every cooking pot in Jerusalem and in Judah will be holy to the LORD of hosts; and all who sacrifice will come and take of them and boil in them. And there will no longer be a Canaanite in the house of the LORD of hosts in that day.

## New International

Judah will be holy to the LORD Almighty, and all who come to sacrifice will take some of the pots and cook in them. And on that day there will no longer be a Canaanite[a] in the house of the LORD Almighty.

NIV a 21 Or *merchant*

## King James

# Malachi

**1** THE BURDEN of the word of the LORD to Israel by Malachi.
2 I have loved you, saith the LORD. Yet ye say, Wherein hast
thou loved us? *Was* not Esau Jacob's brother? saith the LORD: yet
I loved Jacob,
3 And I hated Esau, and laid his mountains and his heritage
waste for the dragons of the wilderness.
4 Whereas Edom saith, We are impoverished, but we will return
and build the desolate places; thus saith the LORD of hosts, They
shall build, but I will throw down; and they shall call them, The
border of wickedness, and, The people against whom the LORD
hath indignation for ever.
5 And your eyes shall see, and ye shall say, The LORD will be
magnified from the border of Israel.
6 ¶ A son honoureth *his* father, and a servant his master: if then
I *be* a father, where *is* mine honour? and if I *be* a master, where *is*
my fear? saith the LORD of hosts unto you, O priests, that despise
my name. And ye say, Wherein have we despised thy name?
7 Ye offer polluted bread upon mine altar; and ye say, Wherein
have we polluted thee? In that ye say, The table of the LORD *is*
contemptible.
8 And if ye offer the blind for sacrifice, *is it* not evil? and if ye
offer the lame and sick, *is it* not evil? offer it now unto thy governor; will he be pleased with thee, or accept thy person? saith the
LORD of hosts.
9 And now, I pray you, beseech God that he will be gracious
unto us: this hath been by your means: will he regard your persons? saith the LORD of hosts.
10 Who *is there* even among you that would shut the doors *for
nought?* neither do ye kindle *fire* on mine altar for nought. I have
no pleasure in you, saith the LORD of hosts, neither will I accept
an offering at your hand.
11 For from the rising of the sun even unto the going down of
the same my name *shall be* great among the Gentiles; and in every
place incense *shall be* offered unto my name, and a pure offering:
for my name *shall be* great among the heathen, saith the LORD of
hosts.
12 ¶ But ye have profaned it, in that ye say, The table of the LORD
*is* polluted; and the fruit thereof, *even* his meat, *is* contemptible.
13 Ye said also, Behold, what a weariness *is it!* and ye have
snuffed at it, saith the LORD of hosts; and ye brought *that which was*
torn, and the lame, and the sick; thus ye brought an offering:
should I accept this of your hand? saith the LORD.

**AMP** [a] Exod. 22:31, "You shall not eat any flesh that is torn by beasts in the field; you shall cast it to the dogs."

## Amplified

THE BOOK OF

# Malachi

**1** THE BURDEN *or* oracle *or* the thing to be lifted up of the word
of the Lord to Israel by Malachi—My messenger.
2 I have loved you, says the Lord. Yet you say, In what *and* how
have You loved us? Was not Esau Jacob's brother? says the Lord;
yet I loved Jacob (Israel),
3 But [in comparison with the degree of love I have for Jacob] I
have hated Esau [Edom], and have laid waste his mountains, and
his heritage I have given to the jackals of the wilderness. [Rom.
9:13, 16.]
4 Though [impoverished] Edom should say, We are beaten
down, but we will return and build the waste places, says the Lord
of hosts. They may build, but I will tear *and* throw down, and men
will call them the wicked country, the people against whom the
Lord has indignation for ever.
5 Your own eyes shall see this, and you shall say, The Lord is
great *and* will be magnified over *and* beyond the border of Israel!
[Isa. 34; 63:1-6; Jer. 49:7-22; Ezek. 25:12-14; Obad. 1.]
6 A son honors his father, and a servant his master. If then I am
a father, where is My honor? And if I am a master, where is the
[reverent] fear due Me? says the Lord of hosts to you, O priests,
who despise My name. You say, How *and* in what have we despised Your name?
7 By offering polluted food upon My altar. And you ask, How
have we polluted it *and* profaned You? By thinking that the table
of the Lord is contemptible *and* may be despised.
8 When you *priests* offer blind [animals] for sacrifice, is it no evil?
And when you offer the lame and the sick, is it no evil? Present
such a thing—a blind or lame or sick animal—now to your governor [in payment of your taxes, and see what will happen]. Will he
be pleased with you? Or will he receive you graciously? says the
Lord of hosts.
9 Now then, I [Malachi] beg of you priests, entreat God earnestly
that He will be gracious to us. With such a gift from your hand [as
a defective animal for sacrifice], will He accept it *or* show favor to
any of you? says the Lord of hosts.
10 Oh, that there were one among even you [whose duty it is to
minister to Me] who would shut the doors, that you might not
kindle fire on My altar to no purpose [an empty, futile, fruitless
pretense]! I have no pleasure in you, says the Lord of hosts, nor
will I accept an offering from your hand.
11 For from the rising of the sun to its setting My name shall be
great among the nations, and in every place incense shall be offered to My name, and indeed a pure offering; for My name shall
be great among the nations, says the Lord of hosts.
12 But you *priests* profane it, when [by your actions] you say, The
table of the Lord is polluted, and the fruit of it, its food, is contemptible *and* may be despised.
13 You say also, Behold, what a drudgery *and* weariness this is!
And you have sniffed at it, says the Lord of hosts. And you have
brought that which was [a]taken by violence, or the lame, or the
sick. This you bring as an offering! Shall I accept this from your
hand? says the Lord.

## New American Standard

# Malachi

*God's Love for Jacob*

**1** THE ORACLE of the word of the LORD to Israel through
Malachi.
2¶ "I have loved you," says the LORD. But you say, "How hast
Thou loved us?" "*Was* not Esau Jacob's brother?" declares the
LORD. "Yet I have loved Jacob;
3but I have hated Esau, and I have made his mountains a
desolation, and *appointed* his inheritance for the jackals of the
wilderness."
4Though Edom says, "We have been beaten down, but we will
return and build up the ruins"; thus says the LORD of hosts, "They
may build, but I will tear down; and *men* will call them the wicked
territory, and the people toward whom the LORD is indignant
forever."
5And your eyes will see this and you will say, "The LORD be
magnified beyond the border of Israel!"

*Sin of the Priests*

6¶ " 'A son honors *his* father, and a servant his master. Then if
I am a father, where is My honor? And if I am a master, where is
My respect?' says the LORD of hosts to you, O priests who despise
My name. But you say, 'How have we despised Thy name?'
7"*You* are presenting defiled food upon My altar. But you say,
'How have we defiled Thee?' In that you say, 'The table of the
LORD is to be despised.'
8"But when you present the blind for sacrifice, is it not evil?
And when you present the lame and sick, is it not evil? Why not
offer it to your governor? Would he be pleased with you? Or would
he receive you kindly?" says the LORD of hosts.
9"But now will you not entreat God's favor, that He may be
gracious to us? With such an offering on your part, will He receive
any of you kindly?" says the LORD of hosts.
10"Oh that there were one among you who would shut the
gates, that you might not uselessly kindle *fire on* My altar! I am not
pleased with you," says the LORD of hosts, "nor will I accept an
offering from you.
11"For from the rising of the sun, even to its setting, My name
*will be* great among the nations, and in every place incense is going
to be offered to My name, and a grain offering *that is* pure; for My
name *will be* great among the nations," says the LORD of hosts.
12"But you are profaning it, in that you say, 'The table of the
Lord is defiled, and as for its fruit, its food is to be despised.'
13"You also say, 'My, how tiresome it is!' And you disdainfully
sniff at it," says the LORD of hosts, "and you bring what was taken
by robbery, and *what is* lame or sick; so you bring the offering!
Should I receive that from your hand?" says the LORD.

## New International

# Malachi

**1** AN ORACLE: The word of the LORD to Israel through
Malachi.[b]

*Jacob Loved, Esau Hated*

2"I have loved you," says the LORD.
"But you ask, 'How have you loved us?'
"Was not Esau Jacob's brother?" the LORD says. "Yet I have
loved Jacob, 3but Esau I have hated, and I have turned his mountains into a wasteland and left his inheritance to the desert jackals."
4Edom may say, "Though we have been crushed, we will rebuild the ruins."
But this is what the LORD Almighty says: "They may build, but
I will demolish. They will be called the Wicked Land, a people
always under the wrath of the LORD. 5You will see it with your own
eyes and say, 'Great is the LORD—even beyond the borders of
Israel!'

*Blemished Sacrifices*

6"A son honors his father, and a servant his master. If I am a
father, where is the honor due me? If I am a master, where is the
respect due me?" says the LORD Almighty. "It is you, O priests,
who show contempt for my name.
"But you ask, 'How have we shown contempt for your name?'
7"You place defiled food on my altar.
"But you ask, 'How have we defiled you?'
"By saying that the LORD's table is contemptible. 8When you
bring blind animals for sacrifice, is that not wrong? When you
sacrifice crippled or diseased animals, is that not wrong? Try offering them to your governor! Would he be pleased with you? Would
he accept you?" says the LORD Almighty.
9"Now implore God to be gracious to us. With such offerings
from your hands, will he accept you?"—says the LORD Almighty.
10"Oh, that one of you would shut the temple doors, so that you
would not light useless fires on my altar! I am not pleased with
you," says the LORD Almighty, "and I will accept no offering from
your hands. 11My name will be great among the nations, from the
rising to the setting of the sun. In every place incense and pure
offerings will be brought to my name, because my name will be
great among the nations," says the LORD Almighty.
12"But you profane it by saying of the Lord's table, 'It is defiled,'
and of its food, 'It is contemptible.' 13And you say, 'What a burden!' and you sniff at it contemptuously," says the LORD Almighty.
"When you bring injured, crippled or diseased animals and
offer them as sacrifices, should I accept them from your hands?"
says the LORD. 14"Cursed is the cheat who has an acceptable male

NIV [b] *1 Malachi* means *my messenger.*

## King James

14 But cursed *be* the deceiver, which hath in his flock a male, and voweth, and sacrificeth unto the Lord a corrupt thing: for I *am* a great King, saith the LORD of hosts, and my name *is* dreadful among the heathen.

**2** AND NOW, O ye priests, this commandment *is* for you.

2 If ye will not hear, and if ye will not lay *it* to heart, to give glory unto my name, saith the LORD of hosts, I will even send a curse upon you, and I will curse your blessings: yea, I have cursed them already, because ye do not lay *it* to heart.

3 Behold, I will corrupt your seed, and spread dung upon your faces, *even* the dung of your solemn feasts; and *one* shall take you away with it.

4 And ye shall know that I have sent this commandment unto you, that my covenant might be with Levi, saith the LORD of hosts.

5 My covenant was with him of life and peace; and I gave them to him *for* the fear wherewith he feared me, and was afraid before my name.

6 The law of truth was in his mouth, and iniquity was not found in his lips: he walked with me in peace and equity, and did turn many away from iniquity.

7 For the priest's lips should keep knowledge, and they should seek the law at his mouth: for he *is* the messenger of the LORD of hosts.

8 But ye are departed out of the way; ye have caused many to stumble at the law; ye have corrupted the covenant of Levi, saith the LORD of hosts.

9 Therefore have I also made you contemptible and base before all the people, according as ye have not kept my ways, but have been partial in the law.

10 Have we not all one father? hath not one God created us? why do we deal treacherously every man against his brother, by profaning the covenant of our fathers?

11 ¶ Judah hath dealt treacherously, and an abomination is committed in Israel and in Jerusalem; for Judah hath profaned the holiness of the LORD which he loved, and hath married the daughter of a strange god.

12 The LORD will cut off the man that doeth this, the master and the scholar, out of the tabernacles of Jacob, and him that offereth an offering unto the LORD of hosts.

13 And this have ye done again, covering the altar of the LORD with tears, with weeping, and with crying out, insomuch that he regardeth not the offering any more, or receiveth *it* with good will at your hand.

14 ¶ Yet ye say, Wherefore? Because the LORD hath been witness between thee and the wife of thy youth, against whom thou hast dealt treacherously: yet *is* she thy companion, and the wife of thy covenant.

15 And did not he make one? Yet had he the residue of the spirit. And wherefore one? That he might seek a godly seed. Therefore take heed to your spirit, and let none deal treacherously against the wife of his youth.

16 For the LORD, the God of Israel, saith that he hateth putting away: for *one* covereth violence with his garment, saith the LORD of hosts: therefore take heed to your spirit, that ye deal not treacherously.

AMP [a] The edible portions of the sacrificed animals were the pay for the work of the priests (Deut. 18:3).

## Amplified

14 But cursed be the [cheating] deceiver who has a male in his flock, and vows to offer it, yet sacrifices to the [sovereign] Lord a blemished *or* diseased thing! For I am a great King, says the Lord of hosts, and My name is terrible *and* to be [reverently] feared among the nations.

**2** AND NOW, O you priests, this commandment is for you.

2 If you will not hear, and if you will not lay it to heart to give glory to My name, says the Lord of hosts, then I will send the curse upon you, and I will curse your blessings; yes, I have already turned them to curses, because you do not lay it to heart.

3 Behold, I will rebuke your seed [grain to prevent due harvest, and instead of [a]shoulder, cheeks and stomach from the festival offerings], I will give you the dung, spread upon your faces, and you shall be taken away with it.

4 And you shall recognize *and* understand that I have sent this [new] decree to you priests, to be My [new] covenant with Levi [the priestly tribe], says the Lord of hosts.

5 My covenant [on My part] *with Levi* was to give him life and peace; because [on his part] of the reverent *and* worshipful fear with which *the priests* would revere Me and stand in awe of My name.

6 The law of truth was in *Levi's* mouth, and unrighteousness was not found in his lips; he walked with Me in peace and uprightness, and turned many away from iniquity.

7 For the priest's lips should guard *and* keep pure the knowledge [of My law], and the people should seek—inquire for and require—instruction at his mouth; for he is the messenger of the Lord of hosts.

8 But you have turned aside out of the way; you have caused many to stumble by your instruction [in the law]; you have corrupted the covenant of Levi [with Me], says the Lord of hosts.

9 Therefore have I also made you despised and abased before all the people, inasmuch as you have not kept My ways, but have shown favoritism to persons in your administration of the law [of God].

10 Have we not all one Father? Has not one God created us? Why then do we deal faithlessly and treacherously each against his brother, profaning the covenant of *God with* our fathers?

11 Judah has been faithless *and* dealt treacherously, and an abomination has been committed in Israel and in Jerusalem; for Judah [that is, Jewish men] has profaned the holy sanctuary of the Lord, which He loves, and has married the daughter of a foreign god [having divorced his Jewish wife]. [Ezra 9:2; Jer. 2:3.]

12 The Lord will cast out of the tents of Jacob to the last man those who do this [evil thing, the master] and [the pupil or] servant alike, and him who brings an offering to the Lord of hosts.

13 And this you do with double guilt; you cover the altar of the Lord with tears [shed by your unoffending wives, divorced by you that you might take heathen wives], and with *your own* weeping and crying out because the Lord does not regard your offering any more or accept it with favor at your hand.

14 Yet you ask, Why does He reject it? Because the Lord was witness [to the covenant made at your marriage] between you and the wife of your youth, against whom you have dealt treacherously *and* to whom you were faithless. Yet she is your companion and the wife of your covenant [made by your marriage vows].

15 And did not God make [you and your wife] one [flesh]? Did not One make you and preserve your spirit alive? And why *did God make you two* one? Because He sought a godly offspring [from your union]. Therefore take heed to yourselves, and let no one deal treacherously *and* be faithless to the wife of his youth.

16 For the Lord, the God of Israel, says: I hate divorce *and* marital separation, and him who covers his garment [his wife] with violence. Therefore keep a watch upon your spirit [that it may be controlled by My Spirit], that you deal not treacherously *and* faithlessly [with your marriage mate].

## New American Standard

14 "But cursed be the swindler who has a male in his flock, and
vows it, but sacrifices a blemished animal to the Lord, for I am a
great King," says the LORD of hosts, "and My name is feared
among the nations."

*Priests to Be Disciplined*

2 "AND NOW, this commandment is for you, O priests.
2 "If you do not listen, and if you do not take it to heart to give
honor to My name," says the LORD of hosts, "then I will send the
curse upon you, and I will curse your blessings; and indeed, I have
cursed them *already*, because you are not taking *it* to heart.
3 "Behold, I am going to rebuke your offspring, and I will
spread refuse on your faces, the refuse of your feasts; and you will
be taken away with it.
4 "Then you will know that I have sent this commandment to
you, that My covenant may continue with Levi," says the LORD of
hosts.
5 "My covenant with him was *one of* life and peace, and I gave
them to him *as an object of* reverence; so he revered Me, and stood
in awe of My name.
6 "True instruction was in his mouth, and unrighteousness was
not found on his lips; he walked with Me in peace and uprightness, and he turned many back from iniquity.
7 "For the lips of a priest should preserve knowledge, and men
should seek instruction from his mouth; for he is the messenger
of the LORD of hosts.
8 "But as for you, you have turned aside from the way; you
have caused many to stumble by the instruction; you have corrupted the covenant of Levi," says the LORD of hosts.
9 "So I also have made you despised and abased before all the
people, just as you are not keeping My ways, but are showing
partiality in the instruction.

*Sin in the Family*

10 ¶ "Do we not all have one father? Has not one God created
us? Why do we deal treacherously each against his brother so as
to profane the covenant of our fathers?
11 "Judah has dealt treacherously, and an abomination has been
committed in Israel and in Jerusalem; for Judah has profaned the
sanctuary of the LORD which He loves, and has married the daughter of a foreign god.
12 "*As* for the man who does this, may the LORD cut off from
the tents of Jacob *everyone* who awakes and answers, or who
presents an offering to the LORD of hosts.
13 "And this is another thing you do: you cover the altar of the
LORD with tears, with weeping and with groaning, because He no
longer regards the offering or accepts *it with* favor from your hand.
14 "Yet you say, 'For what reason?' Because the LORD has been
a witness between you and the wife of your youth, against whom
you have dealt treacherously, though she is your companion and
your wife by covenant.
15 "But not one has done *so* who has a remnant of the Spirit. And
what did *that* one *do* while he was seeking a godly offspring? Take
heed then, to your spirit, and let no one deal treacherously against
the wife of your youth.
16 "For I hate divorce," says the LORD, the God of Israel, "and
him who covers his garment with wrong," says the LORD of hosts.
"So take heed to your spirit, that you do not deal treacherously."

## New International

in his flock and vows to give it, but then sacrifices a blemished
animal to the Lord. For I am a great king," says the LORD Almighty,
"and my name is to be feared among the nations.

*Admonition for the Priests*

2 "AND NOW this admonition is for you, O priests. 2 If you do
not listen, and if you do not set your heart to honor my
name," says the LORD Almighty, "I will send a curse upon you,
and I will curse your blessings. Yes, I have already cursed them,
because you have not set your heart to honor me.
3 "Because of you I will rebuke[b] your descendants[c]; I will
spread on your faces the offal from your festival sacrifices, and you
will be carried off with it. 4 And you will know that I have sent you
this admonition so that my covenant with Levi may continue,"
says the LORD Almighty. 5 "My covenant was with him, a covenant
of life and peace, and I gave them to him; this called for reverence
and he revered me and stood in awe of my name. 6 True instruction
was in his mouth and nothing false was found on his lips. He
walked with me in peace and uprightness, and turned many from
sin.
7 "For the lips of a priest ought to preserve knowledge, and from
his mouth men should seek instruction—because he is the messenger of the LORD Almighty. 8 But you have turned from the way and
by your teaching have caused many to stumble; you have violated
the covenant with Levi," says the LORD Almighty. 9 "So I have
caused you to be despised and humiliated before all the people,
because you have not followed my ways but have shown partiality
in matters of the law."

*Judah Unfaithful*

10 Have we not all one Father[d]? Did not one God create us? Why
do we profane the covenant of our fathers by breaking faith with
one another?
11 Judah has broken faith. A detestable thing has been committed in Israel and in Jerusalem: Judah has desecrated the sanctuary
the LORD loves, by marrying the daughter of a foreign god. 12 As
for the man who does this, whoever he may be, may the LORD cut
him off from the tents of Jacob[e]—even though he brings offerings
to the LORD Almighty.
13 Another thing you do: You flood the LORD's altar with tears.
You weep and wail because he no longer pays attention to your
offerings or accepts them with pleasure from your hands. 14 You
ask, "Why?" It is because the LORD is acting as the witness between you and the wife of your youth, because you have broken
faith with her, though she is your partner, the wife of your marriage covenant.
15 Has not ⌞the LORD⌟ made them one? In flesh and spirit they are
his. And why one? Because he was seeking godly offspring.[f] So
guard yourself in your spirit, and do not break faith with the wife
of your youth.
16 "I hate divorce," says the LORD God of Israel, "and I hate a
man's covering himself[g] with violence as well as with his garment," says the LORD Almighty.
So guard yourself in your spirit, and do not break faith.

**NIV** [b] 3 Or *cut off* (see Septuagint) [c] 3 Or *will blight your grain* [d] 10 Or *father* [e] 12 Or 12 *May the LORD cut off from the tents of Jacob anyone who gives testimony in behalf of the man who does this* [f] 15 Or 15 *But the one ⌞who is our father⌟ did not do this, not as long as life remained in him. And what was he seeking? An offspring from God* [g] 16 Or *his wife*

## King James

17¶ Ye have wearied the LORD with your words. Yet ye say, Wherein have we wearied *him?* When ye say, Every one that doeth evil *is* good in the sight of the LORD, and he delighteth in them; or, Where *is* the God of judgment?

**3** BEHOLD, I will send my messenger, and he shall prepare the way before me: and the Lord, whom ye seek, shall suddenly come to his temple, even the messenger of the covenant, whom ye delight in: behold, he shall come, saith the LORD of hosts.

2But who may abide the day of his coming? and who shall stand when he appeareth? for he *is* like a refiner's fire, and like fullers' soap:

3And he shall sit *as* a refiner and purifier of silver: and he shall purify the sons of Levi, and purge them as gold and silver, that they may offer unto the LORD an offering in righteousness.

4Then shall the offering of Judah and Jerusalem be pleasant unto the LORD, as in the days of old, and as in former years.

5And I will come near to you to judgment; and I will be a swift witness against the sorcerers, and against the adulterers, and against false swearers, and against those that oppress the hireling in *his* wages, the widow, and the fatherless, and that turn aside the stranger *from his right,* and fear not me, saith the LORD of hosts.

6For I *am* the LORD, I change not; therefore ye sons of Jacob are not consumed.

7¶ Even from the days of your fathers ye are gone away from mine ordinances, and have not kept *them.* Return unto me, and I will return unto you, saith the LORD of hosts. But ye said, Wherein shall we return?

8¶ Will a man rob God? Yet ye have robbed me. But ye say, Wherein have we robbed thee? In tithes and offerings.

9Ye *are* cursed with a curse: for ye have robbed me, *even* this whole nation.

10Bring ye all the tithes into the storehouse, that there may be meat in mine house, and prove me now herewith, saith the LORD of hosts, if I will not open you the windows of heaven, and pour you out a blessing, that *there shall* not *be room* enough *to receive it.*

11And I will rebuke the devourer for your sakes, and he shall not destroy the fruits of your ground; neither shall your vine cast her fruit before the time in the field, saith the LORD of hosts.

12And all nations shall call you blessed: for ye shall be a delightsome land, saith the LORD of hosts.

13¶ Your words have been stout against me, saith the LORD. Yet ye say, What have we spoken *so much* against thee?

14Ye have said, It *is* vain to serve God: and what profit *is it* that we have kept his ordinance, and that we have walked mournfully before the LORD of hosts?

15And now we call the proud happy; yea, they that work wickedness are set up; yea, *they that* tempt God are even delivered.

16¶ Then they that feared the LORD spake often one to another: and the LORD hearkened, and heard *it,* and a book of remembrance was written before him for them that feared the LORD, and that thought upon his name.

17And they shall be mine, saith the LORD of hosts, in that day when I make up my jewels; and I will spare them, as a man spareth his own son that serveth him.

## Amplified

17You have wearied the Lord with your words. Yet you say, In what way have we wearied Him? [You do it when by your actions] you say, Every one who does evil is good in the sight of the Lord, and He delights in them. Or [by asking], Where is the God of justice?

**3** BEHOLD, I send My messenger, and he shall prepare the way before Me. And the Lord, *the Messiah,* Whom you seek will suddenly come to His temple; the Messenger *or* Angel of the covenant Whom you desire, behold, He shall come, says the Lord of hosts. [Matt. 11:10; Luke 1:13-17, 76.]

2But who can endure the day of His coming? And who can stand when He appears? For He is like a refiner's fire and like fullers' soap; [Rev. 6:12-17.]

3He will sit as a refiner and purifier of silver; and He will purify the priests, the sons of Levi, and refine them like gold and silver, that they may offer to the Lord offerings in righteousness.

4Then will the offering of Judah and Jerusalem be pleasing to the Lord as in the days of old and as in ancient years.

5Then I will draw near to you for judgment; I will be a swift witness against the sorcerers, against the adulterers, against the false swearers, and against those who oppress the hireling in his wages, the widow and the fatherless, and who turn aside the temporary resident from his right, and fear not Me, says the Lord of hosts.

6For I am the Lord, I do not change; that is why you, O sons of Jacob, are not consumed.

7Even from the days of your fathers you have turned aside from My ordinances and have not kept them. Return to me, and I will return to you, says the Lord of hosts. But you say, How shall we return?

8Will a man rob *or* defraud God? Yet you rob *and* defraud Me. But you say, In what way do we rob *or* defraud You? *You have withheld your* tithes and offerings.

9You are cursed with the curse; for you are robbing Me, even this whole nation. [Lev. 26:14-17.]

10Bring all the tithes—the whole tenth of your income—into the storehouse, that there may be food in My house, and prove Me now by it, says the Lord of hosts, if I will not open the windows of Heaven for you and pour you out a blessing, that there shall not be room enough to receive it. [Mal. 2:2.]

11And I will rebuke the devourer [insects and plagues] for your sakes, and he shall not destroy the fruits of your ground; neither shall your vine drop its fruit before the time in the field, says the Lord of hosts.

12And all nations shall call you happy *and* blessed; for you shall be a land of delight, says the Lord of hosts.

13Your words have been strong *and* hard against Me, says the Lord. Yet you say, What have we spoken against You?

14You have said, It is useless to serve God; and what profit is it if we keep His ordinances and walk gloomily *and as if* in mourning apparel before the Lord of hosts?

15And now we consider the proud *and* arrogant happy *and* favored; evildoers are exalted *and* prosper; yes, and when they test God they escape *unpunished.*

16Then those who feared the Lord talked often one to another; and the Lord listened and heard it, and a book of remembrance was written before Him of those who reverenced *and* worshipfully feared the Lord, and who thought on His name.

17And they shall be Mine, says the Lord of hosts, in that day when I publicly recognize *and* openly declare them to be My jewels—My special possession, My peculiar treasure. And I will spare them, as a man spares his own son who serves him.

## New American Standard

17¶ You have wearied the LORD with your words. Yet you say,
"How have we wearied *Him*?" In that you say, "Everyone who
does evil is good in the sight of the LORD, and He delights in
them," or, "Where is the God of justice?"

*The Purifier*

3 "BEHOLD, I am going to send My messenger, and he will
clear the way before Me. And the Lord, whom you seek, will
suddenly come to His temple; and the messenger of the covenant,
in whom you delight, behold, He is coming," says the LORD of
hosts.
2"But who can endure the day of His coming? And who can
stand when He appears? For He is like a refiner's fire and like
fullers' soap.
3"And He will sit as a smelter and purifier of silver, and He will
purify the sons of Levi and refine them like gold and silver, so that
they may present to the LORD offerings in righteousness.
4"Then the offering of Judah and Jerusalem will be pleasing to
the LORD, as in the days of old and as in former years.
5"Then I will draw near to you for judgment; and I will be a
swift witness against the sorcerers and against the adulterers and
against those who swear falsely, and against those who oppress
the wage earner in his wages, the widow and the orphan, and
those who turn aside the alien, and do not fear Me," says the LORD
of hosts.
6"For I, the LORD, do not change; therefore you, O sons of
Jacob, are not consumed.
7¶ "From the days of your fathers you have turned aside from
My statutes, and have not kept *them*. Return to Me, and I will
return to you," says the LORD of hosts. "But you say, 'How shall
we return?'

*You Have Robbed God*

8"Will a man [a]rob God? Yet you are robbing Me! But you say,
'How have we robbed Thee?' In tithes and offerings.
9"You are cursed with a curse, for you are [b]robbing Me, the
whole nation *of you*!
10"Bring the whole tithe into the storehouse, so that there may
be food in My house, and test Me now in this," says the LORD of
hosts, "if I will not open for you the windows of heaven, and pour
out for you a blessing until [c]it overflows.
11"Then I will rebuke the devourer for you, so that it may not
destroy the fruits of the ground; nor will your vine in the field cast
*its grapes*," says the LORD of hosts.
12"And all the nations will call you blessed, for you shall be a
delightful land," says the LORD of hosts.
13¶ "Your words have been arrogant against Me," says the
LORD. "Yet you say, 'What have we spoken against Thee?'
14"You have said, 'It is vain to serve God; and what profit is it
that we have kept His charge, and that we have walked in mourning before the LORD of hosts?
15'So now we call the arrogant blessed; not only are the doers
of wickedness built up, but they also test God and escape.' "

*The Book of Remembrance*

16¶ Then those who [d]feared the LORD spoke to one another, and
the LORD gave attention and heard *it*, and a book of remembrance
was written before Him for those who [e]fear the LORD and who
esteem His name.
17"And they will be Mine," says the LORD of hosts, "on the day
that I prepare *My* own possession, and I will spare them as a man
spares his own son who serves him."

NAS [a] Or, *defraud(ing)* [b] Or, *defraud(ing)* [c] Or, *there is not room enough* [d] *Or, revere(d)* [e] Or, *revere(d)*

## New International

*The Day of Judgment*

17You have wearied the LORD with your words.
"How have we wearied him?" you ask.
By saying, "All who do evil are good in the eyes of the LORD,
and he is pleased with them" or "Where is the God of justice?"

3 "SEE, I will send my messenger, who will prepare the way
before me. Then suddenly the Lord you are seeking will come
to his temple; the messenger of the covenant, whom you desire,
will come," says the LORD Almighty.
2But who can endure the day of his coming? Who can stand
when he appears? For he will be like a refiner's fire or a launderer's
soap. 3He will sit as a refiner and purifier of silver; he will purify
the Levites and refine them like gold and silver. Then the LORD will
have men who will bring offerings in righteousness, 4and the
offerings of Judah and Jerusalem will be acceptable to the LORD,
as in days gone by, as in former years.
5"So I will come near to you for judgment. I will be quick to
testify against sorcerers, adulterers and perjurers, against those
who defraud laborers of their wages, who oppress the widows and
the fatherless, and deprive aliens of justice, but do not fear me,"
says the LORD Almighty.

*Robbing God*

6"I the LORD do not change. So you, O descendants of Jacob,
are not destroyed. 7Ever since the time of your forefathers you
have turned away from my decrees and have not kept them.
Return to me, and I will return to you," says the LORD Almighty.
"But you ask, 'How are we to return?'
8"Will a man rob God? Yet you rob me.
"But you ask, 'How do we rob you?'
"In tithes and offerings. 9You are under a curse—the whole
nation of you—because you are robbing me. 10Bring the whole
tithe into the storehouse, that there may be food in my house. Test
me in this," says the LORD Almighty, "and see if I will not throw
open the floodgates of heaven and pour out so much blessing that
you will not have room enough for it. 11I will prevent pests from
devouring your crops, and the vines in your fields will not cast
their fruit," says the LORD Almighty. 12"Then all the nations will
call you blessed, for yours will be a delightful land," says the LORD
Almighty.
13"You have said harsh things against me," says the LORD.
"Yet you ask, 'What have we said against you?'
14"You have said, 'It is futile to serve God. What did we gain
by carrying out his requirements and going about like mourners
before the LORD Almighty? 15But now we call the arrogant blessed.
Certainly the evildoers prosper, and even those who challenge
God escape.' "
16Then those who feared the LORD talked with each other, and
the LORD listened and heard. A scroll of remembrance was written
in his presence concerning those who feared the LORD and honored his name.
17"They will be mine," says the LORD Almighty, "in the day
when I make up my treasured possession.[f] I will spare them, just
as in compassion a man spares his son who serves him. 18And you

NIV [f] 17 Or *Almighty, "my treasured possession, in the day when I act*

## King James

18Then shall ye return, and discern between the righteous and the wicked, between him that serveth God and him that serveth him not.

**4** FOR, BEHOLD, the day cometh, that shall burn as an oven; and all the proud, yea, and all that do wickedly, shall be stubble: and the day that cometh shall burn them up, saith the LORD of hosts, that it shall leave them neither root nor branch.

2¶ But unto you that fear my name shall the Sun of righteousness arise with healing in his wings; and ye shall go forth, and grow up as calves of the stall.

3And ye shall tread down the wicked; for they shall be ashes under the soles of your feet in the day that I shall do *this*, saith the LORD of hosts.

4¶ Remember ye the law of Moses my servant, which I commanded unto him in Horeb for all Israel, *with* the statutes and judgments.

5¶ Behold, I will send you Elijah the prophet before the coming of the great and dreadful day of the LORD:

6And he shall turn the heart of the fathers to the children, and the heart of the children to their fathers, lest I come and smite the earth with a curse.

## Amplified

18Then shall you return, and discern between the righteous and the wicked, between him who serves God and him who does not serve Him.

**4** FOR BEHOLD, the day comes that shall burn as an oven; and all the proud *and* arrogant, yes, and all that do wickedly *and* are lawless shall be stubble; the day that comes shall burn them up, says the Lord of hosts, so that it will leave them neither root nor branch. [Isa. 5:21-25; Matt. 3:12.]

2But unto you who revere *and* worshipfully fear My name shall the Sun of righteousness arise with healing in His wings *and* His beams, and you shall go forth and gambol like calves *released from* the stall *and* leap for joy.

3And you shall tread down the lawless *and* wicked, for they shall be ashes under the soles of your feet in the day that I shall do this, says the Lord of hosts.

4[Earnestly] remember the law of Moses My servant, which I commanded him on *Mount* Horeb *to give* to all Israel, the statutes and the ordinances.

5Behold, I will send you Elijah the prophet before the great and terrible day of the Lord comes. [Matt. 11:14; 17:10-13.]

6And he shall turn [and reconcile] the hearts of the [estranged] fathers to the [ungodly] children, and the hearts of the [rebellious] children to [the piety of] their fathers [a reconciliation produced by repentance of the ungodly]; lest I come and smite the land with a curse [and a ban of utter destruction]. [Luke 1:17.]

## New American Standard

18So you will again distinguish between the righteous and the wicked, between one who serves God and one who does not serve Him.

*Final Admonition*

4 "FOR BEHOLD, the day is coming, burning like a furnace; and all the arrogant and every evildoer will be chaff; and the day that is coming will set them ablaze," says the LORD of hosts, "so that it will leave them neither root nor branch."

2"But for you who [a]fear My name the sun of righteousness will rise with healing in its wings; and you will go forth and skip about like calves from the stall.

3"And you will tread down the wicked, for they shall be ashes under the soles of your feet on the day which I am preparing," says the LORD of hosts.

4¶ "Remember the law of Moses My servant, *even the* statutes and ordinances which I commanded him in Horeb for all Israel.

5"Behold, I am going to send you Elijah the prophet before the coming of the great and terrible day of the LORD.

6"And he will restore the hearts of the fathers to *their* children, and the hearts of the children to their fathers, lest I come and smite the land with a curse."

NAS [a] Or, *revere(d)*

## New International

will again see the distinction between the righteous and the wicked, between those who serve God and those who do not.

*The Day of the LORD*

4 "SURELY THE day is coming; it will burn like a furnace. All the arrogant and every evildoer will be stubble, and that day that is coming will set them on fire," says the LORD Almighty. "Not a root or a branch will be left to them. 2But for you who revere my name, the sun of righteousness will rise with healing in its wings. And you will go out and leap like calves released from the stall. 3Then you will trample down the wicked; they will be ashes under the soles of your feet on the day when I do these things," says the LORD Almighty.

4"Remember the law of my servant Moses, the decrees and laws I gave him at Horeb for all Israel.

5"See, I will send you the prophet Elijah before that great and dreadful day of the LORD comes. 6He will turn the hearts of the fathers to their children, and the hearts of the children to their fathers; or else I will come and strike the land with a curse."

# The New Testament

## King James

THE GOSPEL

ACCORDING TO

# St. Matthew

1 THE BOOK of the generation of Jesus Christ, the son of
David, the son of Abraham.
2 Abraham begat Isaac; and Isaac begat Jacob; and Jacob begat
Judas and his brethren;
3 And Judas begat Phares and Zara of Thamar; and Phares begat
Esrom; and Esrom begat Aram;
4 And Aram begat Aminadab; and Aminadab begat Naasson;
and Naasson begat Salmon;
5 And Salmon begat Booz of Rachab; and Booz begat Obed of
Ruth; and Obed begat Jesse;
6 And Jesse begat David the king; and David the king begat
Solomon of her *that had been the wife* of Urias;
7 And Solomon begat Roboam; and Roboam begat Abia; and
Abia begat Asa;
8 And Asa begat Josaphat; and Josaphat begat Joram; and Joram
begat Ozias;
9 And Ozias begat Joatham; and Joatham begat Achaz; and
Achaz begat Ezekias;
10 And Ezekias begat Manasses; and Manasses begat Amon; and
Amon begat Josias;
11 And Josias begat Jechonias and his brethren, about the time
they were carried away to Babylon:
12 And after they were brought to Babylon, Jechonias begat
Salathiel; and Salathiel begat Zorobabel;
13 And Zorobabel begat Abiud; and Abiud begat Eliakim; and
Eliakim begat Azor;
14 And Azor begat Sadoc; and Sadoc begat Achim; and Achim
begat Eliud;
15 And Eliud begat Eleazar; and Eleazar begat Matthan; and
Matthan begat Jacob;
16 And Jacob begat Joseph the husband of Mary, of whom was
born Jesus, who is called Christ.

## Amplified

THE GOSPEL

ACCORDING TO

# Matthew

1 THE BOOK of the ancestry (genealogy) of Jesus Christ, the
Messiah, the Anointed, the son (descendant) of David, the
son (descendant) of Abraham. [Ps. 132:11; Isa. 11:1.]
2 Abraham was the father of Isaac, Isaac the father of Jacob,
Jacob the father of Judah and his brothers,
3 Judah the father of Perez and Zerah, whose mother was Tamar; Perez the father of Hezron, Hezron the father of Aram,
4 Aram the father of Aminadab, Aminadab the father of Nashon, Nashon the father of Salmon,
5 Salmon the father of Boaz, whose mother was Rahab; Boaz the
father of Obed, whose mother was Ruth; Obed the father of Jesse,
6 Jesse the father of King David, King David the father of Solomon, whose mother had been the wife of Uriah; [Ruth 4:18-22;
I Chron. 2:13-15.]
7 Solomon the father of Rehoboam, Rehoboam the father of
Abijah, Abijah the father of Asa,
8 Asa the father of Jehoshaphat, Jehoshaphat the father of
Joram, Joram the father of Uzziah,
9 Uzziah the father of Jotham, Jotham the father of Ahaz, Ahaz
the father of Hezekiah,
10 Hezekiah the father of Manasseh, Manasseh the father of
Amon, Amon the father of Josiah,
11 And Josiah became the father of Jechoniah and his brothers,
about the time of the removal (deportation) to Babylon. [II Kings
24:14; I Chron. 3:15, 16.]
12 After the exile to Babylon, Jechoniah became the father of
Shealtiel (Salathiel), Shealtiel the father of Zerubbabel,
13 Zerubbabel the father of Abiud, Abiud the father of Eliakim,
Eliakim the father of Azor,
14 Azor the father of Sadoc, Sadoc the father of Achim, Achim
the father of Elihud,
15 Elihud the father of Eliazar, Eliazar the father of Matthan,
Matthan the father of Jacob,
16 Jacob the father of Joseph, the husband of Mary of whom was
born Jesus Who is called the Christ.

## New American Standard

# Matthew

*Genealogy of Jesus Christ*

**1** THE BOOK of the genealogy of Jesus Christ, the son of David, the son of Abraham.
2¶ To Abraham was born Isaac; and to Isaac, Jacob; and to Jacob, [a]Judah and his brothers;
3and to Judah were born Perez and Zerah by Tamar; and to Perez was born Hezron; and to Hezron, Ram;
4and to Ram was born Amminadab; and to Amminadab, Nahshon; and to Nahshon, Salmon;
5and to Salmon was born Boaz by Rahab; and to Boaz was born Obed by Ruth; and to Obed, Jesse;
6and to Jesse was born David the king.
¶ And to David was born Solomon by her *who had been the wife* of Uriah;
7and to Solomon was born Rehoboam; and to Rehoboam, Abijah; and to Abijah, Asa;
8and to Asa was born Jehoshaphat; and to Jehoshaphat, Joram; and to Joram, Uzziah;
9and to Uzziah was born Jotham; and to Jotham, Ahaz; and to Ahaz, Hezekiah;
10and to Hezekiah was born Manasseh; and to Manasseh, Amon; and to Amon, Josiah;
11and to Josiah were born Jeconiah and his brothers, at the time of the deportation to Babylon.
12¶ And after the deportation to Babylon, to Jeconiah was born Shealtiel; and to Shealtiel, Zerubbabel;
13and to Zerubbabel was born Abiud; and to Abiud, Eliakim; and to Eliakim, Azor;
14and to Azor was born Zadok; and to Zadok, Achim; and to Achim, Eliud;
15and to Eliud was born Eleazar; and to Eleazar, Matthan; and to Matthan, Jacob;
16and to Jacob was born Joseph the husband of Mary, by whom was born Jesus, who is called Christ.

**NAS** [a] Gr., *Judas.* Names of Old Testament characters will be given in their Old Testament form.

## New International

# Matthew

*The Genealogy of Jesus*

**1** A RECORD of the genealogy of Jesus Christ the son of David, the son of Abraham:

2Abraham was the father of Isaac,
Isaac the father of Jacob,
Jacob the father of Judah and his brothers,
3Judah the father of Perez and Zerah, whose mother was Tamar,
Perez the father of Hezron,
Hezron the father of Ram,
4Ram the father of Amminadab,
Amminadab the father of Nahshon,
Nahshon the father of Salmon,
5Salmon the father of Boaz, whose mother was Rahab,
Boaz the father of Obed, whose mother was Ruth,
Obed the father of Jesse,
6and Jesse the father of King David.

David was the father of Solomon, whose mother had been Uriah's wife,
7Solomon the father of Rehoboam,
Rehoboam the father of Abijah,
Abijah the father of Asa,
8Asa the father of Jehoshaphat,
Jehoshaphat the father of Jehoram,
Jehoram the father of Uzziah,
9Uzziah the father of Jotham,
Jotham the father of Ahaz,
Ahaz the father of Hezekiah,
10Hezekiah the father of Manasseh,
Manasseh the father of Amon,
Amon the father of Josiah,
11and Josiah the father of Jeconiah[b] and his brothers at the time of the exile to Babylon.

12After the exile to Babylon:
Jeconiah was the father of Shealtiel,
Shealtiel the father of Zerubbabel,
13Zerubbabel the father of Abiud,
Abiud the father of Eliakim,
Eliakim the father of Azor,
14Azor the father of Zadok,
Zadok the father of Akim,
Akim the father of Eliud,
15Eliud the father of Eleazar,
Eleazar the father of Matthan,
Matthan the father of Jacob,
16and Jacob the father of Joseph, the husband of Mary, of whom was born Jesus, who is called Christ.

**NIV** [b] *11* That is, Jehoiachin; also in verse 12

## King James

17So all the generations from Abraham to David *are* fourteen generations; and from David until the carrying away into Babylon *are* fourteen generations; and from the carrying away into Babylon unto Christ *are* fourteen generations.

18¶ Now the birth of Jesus Christ was on this wise: When as his mother Mary was espoused to Joseph, before they came together, she was found with child of the Holy Ghost.

19Then Joseph her husband, being a just *man,* and not willing to make her a public example, was minded to put her away privily.

20But while he thought on these things, behold, the angel of the Lord appeared unto him in a dream, saying, Joseph, thou son of David, fear not to take unto thee Mary thy wife: for that which is conceived in her is of the Holy Ghost.

21And she shall bring forth a son, and thou shalt call his name JESUS: for he shall save his people from their sins.

22Now all this was done, that it might be fulfilled which was spoken of the Lord by the prophet, saying,

23Behold, a virgin shall be with child, and shall bring forth a son, and they shall call his name Emmanuel, which being interpreted is, God with us.

24Then Joseph being raised from sleep did as the angel of the Lord had bidden him, and took unto him his wife:

25And knew her not till she had brought forth her firstborn son: and he called his name JESUS.

**2** NOW WHEN Jesus was born in Bethlehem of Judaea in the days of Herod the king, behold, there came wise men from the east to Jerusalem,

2Saying, Where is he that is born King of the Jews? for we have seen his star in the east, and are come to worship him.

3When Herod the king had heard *these things,* he was troubled, and all Jerusalem with him.

4And when he had gathered all the chief priests and scribes of the people together, he demanded of them where Christ should be born.

5And they said unto him, In Bethlehem of Judaea: for thus it is written by the prophet,

6And thou Bethlehem, *in* the land of Judah, art not the least among the princes of Judah: for out of thee shall come a Governor, that shall rule my people Israel.

7Then Herod, when he had privily called the wise men, inquired of them diligently what time the star appeared.

8And he sent them to Bethlehem, and said, Go and search diligently for the young child; and when ye have found *him,* bring me word again, that I may come and worship him also.

9When they had heard the king, they departed; and, lo, the star, which they saw in the east, went before them, till it came and stood over where the young child was.

10When they saw the star, they rejoiced with exceeding great joy.

11¶ And when they were come into the house, they saw the young child with Mary his mother, and fell down, and worshipped him: and when they had opened their treasures, they presented unto him gifts; gold, and frankincense, and myrrh.

**AMP** [a] Vincent's "Word Studies in the New Testament." [b] Alternate reading. [c] Williams' "The New Testament in the Language of the People." [d] Thayer's "Greek-English Lexicon of the New Testament—Grimm." [e] Moulton and Milligan's "The Vocabulary of the Greek Testament." [f] Vincent. [g] Vincent. [h] Vincent. [i] Capitalized because of what He is, the spotless Son of God, not what the speaker may have thought He was. [j] Alternate reading.

## Amplified

17So all the generations from Abraham to David are fourteen, from David to the Babylonian Exile (deportation) fourteen, from the Babylonian Exile to the Christ fourteen generations.

18Now the birth of Jesus Christ took place under these circumstances: When His mother Mary had been promised in marriage to Joseph, before they came together she was found to be pregnant [through the power] of the Holy Spirit.

19And her [promised] husband Joseph, being a just *and* upright man and not willing to expose her publicly *and* shame *and* disgrace her, decided to repudiate *and* dismiss (divorce) her quietly *and* secretly.

20But as he was thinking this over, behold, an angel of the Lord appeared to him in a dream, saying, Joseph, descendant of David, do not be afraid to take Mary [as] your wife, for that which is conceived in her is of (from, out of) the Holy Spirit.

21She will bear a Son, and you shall call His name Jesus [in Hebrew means Savior], for He will save His people from their sins [that is, prevent their [a]failing and missing the true end and scope of life, which is God].

22All this took place that it might be fulfilled which the Lord had spoken through the prophet,

23Behold, the virgin shall become pregnant and give birth to a Son, and they shall call His name Emmanuel, which when translated means, God with us. [Isa. 7:14.]

24Then Joseph being aroused from his sleep, did as the angel of the Lord had commanded him; he took [her to his side as] his wife,

25But he had no union with her as her husband until she had borne *her first-born* Son, and he called His name Jesus.

**2** NOW WHEN Jesus was born in Bethlehem of Judea in the days of Herod the king, behold, wise men [astrologers] from the East came to Jerusalem, asking,

2Where is He Who has been born King of the Jews? For we have seen His star in the East [b]at its rising, and have come to worship Him. [Jer. 23:5; Zech. 9:9; Num. 24:17.]

3When Herod the king heard this, he was disturbed *and* troubled, and the whole of Jerusalem with him;

4So he called together all the chief priests and learned men (scribes) of the people, and [c]anxiously asked them where the Christ was to be born.

5They replied to him, In Bethlehem of Judea; for so it is written by the prophet:

6And you Bethlehem, in the land of Judah, you are not in any way least *or* insignificant among the [d]chief cities of Judah; for from you shall come a Ruler ([e]Leader) Who will govern *and* [f]shepherd My people Israel. [Mic. 5:2.]

7Then Herod sent for the wise men [astrologers] secretly, and [g]accurately to the last point ascertained from them the time of the appearing of the star—that is, [h]how long the star had made itself visible since its rising in the East.

8Then he sent them to Bethlehem, saying, Go and search out the Child carefully *and* diligently, and when you have found [i]Him bring me word, that I too may come and worship Him.

9When they had listened to the king they went their way, and lo, the star which had been seen in the East [j]in its rising went before them, until it came and stood over the place where the young Child was.

10When they saw the star, they were thrilled with ecstatic joy.

11And going into the house they saw the Child with Mary His mother, and they fell down and worshipped Him. Then opening their treasure bags, they presented to Him gifts, gold and frankincense and myrrh.

## New American Standard

17¶ Therefore all the generations from Abraham to David are
fourteen generations; and from David to the deportation to Babylon fourteen generations; and from the deportation to Babylon to
*the time of* Christ fourteen generations.

*Conception and Birth of Jesus*

18¶ Now the birth of Jesus Christ was as follows. When His
mother Mary had been betrothed to Joseph, before they came
together she was found to be with child by the Holy Spirit.
19And Joseph her husband, being a righteous man, and not
wanting to disgrace her, desired [k]to put her away secretly.
20But when he had considered this, behold, an angel of the Lord
appeared to him in a dream, saying, "Joseph, son of David, do not
be afraid to take Mary as your wife; for that which has been
[l]conceived in her is of the Holy Spirit.
21"And she will bear a Son; and you shall call His name Jesus,
for it is He who will save His people from their sins."
22Now all this took place that what was spoken by the Lord
through the prophet might be fulfilled, saying,
23"BEHOLD, THE VIRGIN SHALL BE WITH CHILD, AND SHALL BEAR
A SON, AND THEY SHALL CALL HIS NAME IMMANUEL," which translated means, "GOD WITH US."
24And Joseph arose from his sleep, and did as the angel of the
Lord commanded him, and took *her* as his wife,
25and [m]kept her a virgin until she gave birth to a Son; and he
called His name Jesus.

*Visit of the Wise Men*

**2** NOW AFTER Jesus was born in Bethlehem of Judea in the
days of Herod the king, behold, [n]magi from the east arrived
in Jerusalem, saying,
2"Where is He who has been born King of the Jews? For we
saw His star in the east, and have come to worship Him."
3And when Herod the king heard it, he was troubled, and all
Jerusalem with him.
4And gathering together all the chief priests and scribes of the
people, he *began* to inquire of them where the Christ was to be
born.
5And they said to him, "In Bethlehem of Judea, for so it has
been written by the prophet,
6 'AND YOU, BETHLEHEM, LAND OF JUDAH,
ARE BY NO MEANS LEAST AMONG THE LEADERS OF JUDAH;
FOR OUT OF YOU SHALL COME FORTH A RULER,
WHO WILL SHEPHERD MY PEOPLE ISRAEL.' "
7¶ Then Herod secretly called the magi, and ascertained from
them the time the star appeared.
8And he sent them to Bethlehem, and said, "Go and make
careful search for the Child; and when you have found *Him*, report
to me, that I too may come and worship Him."
9And having heard the king, they went their way; and lo, the
star, which they had seen in the east, went on before them, until
it came and stood over where the Child was.
10And when they saw the star, they rejoiced exceedingly with
great joy.
11And they came into the house and saw the Child with Mary
His mother; and they fell down and worshiped Him; and opening
their treasures they presented to Him gifts of gold and frankincense and myrrh.

**NAS** [k] Or, *to divorce her* [l] Lit., *begotten* [m] Lit., *was not knowing her*
[n] Pronounced may-ji, a caste of wise men specializing in astrology, medicine
and natural science

## New International

17Thus there were fourteen generations in all from Abraham to
David, fourteen from David to the exile to Babylon, and fourteen
from the exile to the Christ.[o]

*The Birth of Jesus Christ*

18This is how the birth of Jesus Christ came about: His mother
Mary was pledged to be married to Joseph, but before they came
together, she was found to be with child through the Holy Spirit.
19Because Joseph her husband was a righteous man and did not
want to expose her to public disgrace, he had in mind to divorce
her quietly.
20But after he had considered this, an angel of the Lord appeared to him in a dream and said, "Joseph son of David, do not
be afraid to take Mary home as your wife, because what is conceived in her is from the Holy Spirit. 21She will give birth to a son,
and you are to give him the name Jesus,[p] because he will save his
people from their sins."
22All this took place to fulfill what the Lord had said through
the prophet: 23"The virgin will be with child and will give birth to
a son, and they will call him Immanuel"[q]—which means, "God
with us."
24When Joseph woke up, he did what the angel of the Lord had
commanded him and took Mary home as his wife. 25But he had
no union with her until she gave birth to a son. And he gave him
the name Jesus.

*The Visit of the Magi*

**2** AFTER JESUS was born in Bethlehem in Judea, during the
time of King Herod, Magi[r] from the east came to Jerusalem
2and asked, "Where is the one who has been born king of the Jews?
We saw his star in the east[s] and have come to worship him."
3When King Herod heard this he was disturbed, and all Jerusalem with him. 4When he had called together all the people's chief
priests and teachers of the law, he asked them where the Christ[t]
was to be born. 5"In Bethlehem in Judea," they replied, "for this
is what the prophet has written:

6" 'But you, Bethlehem, in the land of Judah,
are by no means least among the rulers of Judah;
for out of you will come a ruler
who will be the shepherd of my people Israel.'[u]"

7Then Herod called the Magi secretly and found out from them
the exact time the star had appeared. 8He sent them to Bethlehem
and said, "Go and make a careful search for the child. As soon as
you find him, report to me, so that I too may go and worship him."
9After they had heard the king, they went on their way, and the
star they had seen in the east[v] went ahead of them until it stopped
over the place where the child was. 10When they saw the star, they
were overjoyed. 11On coming to the house, they saw the child with
his mother Mary, and they bowed down and worshiped him. Then
they opened their treasures and presented him with gifts of gold
and of incense and of myrrh. 12And having been warned in a

**NIV** [o] 17 Or *Messiah.* "The Christ" (Greek) and "the Messiah" (Hebrew) both
mean "the Anointed One." [p] 21 *Jesus* is the Greek form of *Joshua*, which
means *the LORD saves.* [q] 23 Isaiah 7:14 [r] 1 Traditionally *Wise Men* [s] 2 Or
*star when it rose* [t] 4 Or *Messiah* [u] 6 Micah 5:2 [v] 9 Or *seen when it rose*

## King James

12And being warned of God in a dream that they should not return to Herod, they departed into their own country another way.

13And when they were departed, behold, the angel of the Lord appeareth to Joseph in a dream, saying, Arise, and take the young child and his mother, and flee into Egypt, and be thou there until I bring thee word: for Herod will seek the young child to destroy him.

14When he arose, he took the young child and his mother by night, and departed into Egypt:

15And was there until the death of Herod: that it might be fulfilled which was spoken of the Lord by the prophet, saying, Out of Egypt have I called my son.

16¶ Then Herod, when he saw that he was mocked of the wise men, was exceeding wroth, and sent forth, and slew all the children that were in Bethlehem, and in all the coasts thereof, from two years old and under, according to the time which he had diligently inquired of the wise men.

17Then was fulfilled that which was spoken by Jeremy the prophet, saying,

18In Rama was there a voice heard, lamentation, and weeping, and great mourning, Rachel weeping *for* her children, and would not be comforted, because they are not.

19¶ But when Herod was dead, behold, an angel of the Lord appeareth in a dream to Joseph in Egypt,

20Saying, Arise, and take the young child and his mother, and go into the land of Israel: for they are dead which sought the young child's life.

21And he arose, and took the young child and his mother, and came into the land of Israel.

22But when he heard that Archelaus did reign in Judaea in the room of his father Herod, he was afraid to go thither: notwithstanding, being warned of God in a dream, he turned aside into the parts of Galilee:

23And he came and dwelt in a city called Nazareth: that it might be fulfilled which was spoken by the prophets, He shall be called a Nazarene.

3 IN THOSE days came John the Baptist, preaching in the wilderness of Judaea,

2And saying, Repent ye: for the kingdom of heaven is at hand.

3For this is he that was spoken of by the prophet Esaias, saying, The voice of one crying in the wilderness, Prepare ye the way of the Lord, make his paths straight.

4And the same John had his raiment of camel's hair, and a leathern girdle about his loins; and his meat was locusts and wild honey.

5Then went out to him Jerusalem, and all Judaea, and all the region round about Jordan,

6And were baptized of him in Jordan, confessing their sins.

7¶ But when he saw many of the Pharisees and Sadducees come to his baptism, he said unto them, O generation of vipers, who hath warned you to flee from the wrath to come?

8Bring forth therefore fruits meet for repentance:

9And think not to say within yourselves, We have Abraham to *our* father: for I say unto you, that God is able of these stones to raise up children unto Abraham.

## Amplified

12And [a]receiving an answer to their asking, they were divinely instructed *and* warned in a dream not to go back to Herod; so they departed to their own country by a different way.

13Now after they had gone, behold, an angel of the Lord appeared to Joseph in a dream and said, Get up! [ [b]Tenderly] take unto you the young Child and His mother and flee to Egypt, and remain there till I tell you [otherwise]; for Herod intends to search for the Child in order to destroy Him.

14And having risen, he took the Child and His mother by night and withdrew to Eygpt,

15And remained there until Herod's death. This was to fulfill what the Lord had spoken by the prophet, Out of Egypt have I called My Son. [Hos. 11:1.]

16Then Herod, when he realized that he had been misled by the wise men, was furiously enraged, and he sent and put to death all the male children in Bethlehem and in all that territory who were two years old or under, reckoning according to the date which he had investigated diligently *and* learned exactly from the wise men.

17Then was fulfilled what was spoken by the prophet Jeremiah:

18A voice was heard in Ramah, wailing and loud lamentation, Rachel weeping for her children; she refused to be comforted, because they were no more. [Jer. 31:15.]

19But when Herod died, behold, an angel of the Lord appeared in a dream to Joseph in Egypt, and said,

20Rise, [ [c]tenderly] take unto you the Child and His mother, and go to the land of Israel, for those who sought the Child's life are dead.

21Then he awoke and arose and [ [d]tenderly] took the Child and His mother, and came into the land of Israel.

22But because he heard that Archelaus was ruling over Judea in the place of his father Herod, he was afraid to go there; and being divinely warned in a dream he withdrew to the region of Galilee.

23He went and dwelt in a town called Nazareth, so that what was spoken through the prophets might be fulfilled, He shall be called a Nazarene (meaning Branch, Separated One). [Isa. 11:1.]

3 IN THOSE days there appeared John the Baptist, preaching in the wilderness (desert) of Judea, and saying,

2Repent—that is, [e]think differently; change your mind, regretting your sins and changing your conduct—for the kingdom of heaven is at hand.

3This is he who was mentioned by the prophet Isaiah when he said, The voice of one crying in the wilderness—shouting in the desert: Prepare the road for the Lord; make His highways straight (level, [f]direct). [Isa. 40:3.]

4This John's garments were made of camel's hair, and he wore a leather girdle about his waist, and his food was locusts and wild honey. [II Kings 1:8; Zech. 13:4; Lev. 11:22.]

5Then Jerusalem and all Judea and all the country round about the Jordan went out to him,

6And they were baptized in the Jordan by him, confessing their sins.

7But when he saw many of the Pharisees and Sadducees coming for baptism, he said to them, You brood of vipers, who warned you to flee *and* escape from the wrath *and* indignation [of God against disobedience,] that is coming?

8Bring forth fruit that is consistent with repentance—let your lives prove your change of heart;

9And do not presume to say to yourselves, We have Abraham for our forefather; for I tell you God is able to raise up descendants for Abraham from these stones!

AMP [a] Vincent. [b] Williams. [c] Williams. [d] Williams. [e] Vincent.
[f] Abbott-Smith's "Manual Greek Lexicon of the New Testament."

## New American Standard

12And having been warned *by God* in a dream not to return to
Herod, they departed for their own country by another way.

*The Flight to Egypt*

13¶ Now when they had departed, behold, an angel of the Lord
*appeared to Joseph in a dream, saying, "Arise and take the Child
and His mother, and flee to Egypt, and remain there until I tell you;
for Herod is going to search for the Child to destroy Him."
14And he arose and took the Child and His mother by night,
and departed for Egypt;
15and was there until the death of Herod, that what was spoken
by the Lord through the prophet might be fulfilled, saying, "OUT
OF EGYPT DID I CALL MY SON."

*Herod Slaughters Babies*

16¶ Then when Herod saw that he had been tricked by the magi,
he became very enraged, and sent and slew all the male children
who were in Bethlehem and in all its environs, from two years old
and under, according to the time which he had ascertained from
the magi.
17Then that which was spoken through Jeremiah the prophet
was fulfilled, saying,

18 "A VOICE WAS HEARD IN RAMAH,
WEEPING AND GREAT MOURNING,
RACHEL WEEPING FOR HER CHILDREN;
AND SHE REFUSED TO BE COMFORTED,
BECAUSE THEY WERE NO MORE."

19¶ But when Herod was dead, behold, an angel of the Lord
*appeared in a dream to Joseph in Egypt, saying,
20"Arise and take the Child and His mother, and go into the
land of Israel; for those who sought the Child's life are dead."
21And he arose and took the Child and His mother, and came
into the land of Israel.
22But when he heard that Archelaus was reigning over Judea in
place of his father Herod, he was afraid to go there. And being
warned *by God* in a dream, he departed for the regions of Galilee,
23and came and resided in a city called Nazareth, that what was
spoken through the prophets might be fulfilled, "He shall be called
a Nazarene."

*John the Baptist Preaches*

3 NOW IN those days John the Baptist *came, preaching in the
wilderness of Judea, saying,
2"Repent, for the kingdom of heaven is at hand."
3For this is the one referred to by Isaiah the prophet, saying,

"THE VOICE OF ONE CRYING IN THE WILDERNESS,
'MAKE READY THE WAY OF THE LORD,
MAKE HIS PATHS STRAIGHT!' "

4Now John himself had a garment of camel's hair, and a leather
belt about his waist; and his food was locusts and wild honey.
5Then Jerusalem was going out to him, and all Judea, and all
the district around the Jordan;
6and they were being baptized by him in the Jordan River, as
they confessed their sins.
7But when he saw many of the Pharisees and Sadducees coming for baptism, he said to them, "You brood of vipers, who
warned you to flee from the wrath to come?
8"Therefore bring forth fruit in keeping with repentance;
9and do not suppose that you can say to yourselves, 'We have
Abraham for our father'; for I say to you, that God is able from
these stones to raise up children to Abraham.

## New International

dream not to go back to Herod, they returned to their country by
another route.

*The Escape to Egypt*

13When they had gone, an angel of the Lord appeared to Joseph
in a dream. "Get up," he said, "take the child and his mother and
escape to Egypt. Stay there until I tell you, for Herod is going to
search for the child to kill him."
14So he got up, took the child and his mother during the night
and left for Egypt, 15where he stayed until the death of Herod. And
so was fulfilled what the Lord had said through the prophet: "Out
of Egypt I called my son."[g]
16When Herod realized that he had been outwitted by the Magi,
he was furious, and he gave orders to kill all the boys in Bethlehem
and its vicinity who were two years old and under, in accordance
with the time he had learned from the Magi. 17Then what was said
through the prophet Jeremiah was fulfilled:

18"A voice is heard in Ramah,
weeping and great mourning,
Rachel weeping for her children
and refusing to be comforted,
because they are no more."[h]

*The Return to Nazareth*

19After Herod died, an angel of the Lord appeared in a dream
to Joseph in Egypt 20and said, "Get up, take the child and his
mother and go to the land of Israel, for those who were trying to
take the child's life are dead."
21So he got up, took the child and his mother and went to the
land of Israel. 22But when he heard that Archelaus was reigning
in Judea in place of his father Herod, he was afraid to go there.
Having been warned in a dream, he withdrew to the district of
Galilee, 23and he went and lived in a town called Nazareth. So was
fulfilled what was said through the prophets: "He will be called a
Nazarene."

*John the Baptist Prepares the Way*

3 IN THOSE days John the Baptist came, preaching in the
Desert of Judea 2and saying, "Repent, for the kingdom of
heaven is near." 3This is he who was spoken of through the
prophet Isaiah:

"A voice of one calling in the desert,
'Prepare the way for the Lord,
make straight paths for him.' "[i]

4John's clothes were made of camel's hair, and he had a leather
belt around his waist. His food was locusts and wild honey.
5People went out to him from Jerusalem and all Judea and the
whole region of the Jordan. 6Confessing their sins, they were
baptized by him in the Jordan River.
7But when he saw many of the Pharisees and Sadducees coming
to where he was baptizing, he said to them: "You brood of vipers!
Who warned you to flee from the coming wrath? 8Produce fruit in
keeping with repentance. 9And do not think you can say to yourselves, 'We have Abraham as our father.' I tell you that out of these
stones God can raise up children for Abraham. 10The ax is already

NIV [g] *15* Hosea 11:1 [h] *18* Jer. 31:15 [i] 3 Isaiah 40:3

## King James

10 And now also the axe is laid unto the root of the trees: therefore every tree which bringeth not forth good fruit is hewn down, and cast into the fire.

11 I indeed baptize you with water unto repentance: but he that cometh after me is mightier than I, whose shoes I am not worthy to bear: he shall baptize you with the Holy Ghost, and *with* fire:

12 Whose fan *is* in his hand, and he will thoroughly purge his floor, and gather his wheat into the garner; but he will burn up the chaff with unquenchable fire.

13 ¶ Then cometh Jesus from Galilee to Jordan unto John, to be baptized of him.

14 But John forbad him, saying, I have need to be baptized of thee, and comest thou to me?

15 And Jesus answering said unto him, Suffer *it to be so* now: for thus it becometh us to fulfil all righteousness. Then he suffered him.

16 And Jesus, when he was baptized, went up straightway out of the water: and, lo, the heavens were opened unto him, and he saw the Spirit of God descending like a dove, and lighting upon him:

17 And lo a voice from heaven, saying, This is my beloved Son, in whom I am well pleased.

**4** THEN WAS Jesus led up of the Spirit into the wilderness to be tempted of the devil.

2 And when he had fasted forty days and forty nights, he was afterward an hungered.

3 And when the tempter came to him, he said, If thou be the Son of God, command that these stones be made bread.

4 But he answered and said, It is written, Man shall not live by bread alone, but by every word that proceedeth out of the mouth of God.

5 Then the devil taketh him up into the holy city, and setteth him on a pinnacle of the temple,

6 And saith unto him, If thou be the Son of God, cast thyself down: for it is written, He shall give his angels charge concerning thee: and in *their* hands they shall bear thee up, lest at any time thou dash thy foot against a stone.

7 Jesus said unto him, It is written again, Thou shalt not tempt the Lord thy God.

8 Again, the devil taketh him up into an exceeding high mountain, and showeth him all the kingdoms of the world, and the glory of them;

9 And saith unto him, All these things will I give thee, if thou wilt fall down and worship me.

10 Then saith Jesus unto him, Get thee hence, Satan: for it is written, Thou shalt worship the Lord thy God, and him only shalt thou serve.

11 Then the devil leaveth him, and, behold, angels came and ministered unto him.

12 ¶ Now when Jesus had heard that John was cast into prison, he departed into Galilee;

## Amplified

10 And already the ax is lying at the root of the trees; every tree therefore that does not bear good fruit is cut down and thrown into the fire.

11 I indeed baptize you [a]in (with) water [b]because of repentance—that is, because of your [c]changing your minds for the better, heartily amending your ways with abhorrence of your past sins; but He Who is coming after me is mightier than I, Whose sandals I am not worthy *or* fit to take off *or* carry; He will baptize you with the Holy Spirit and with fire.

12 His winnowing fan (shovel, fork) is in His hand, and He will thoroughly clear out *and* clean His threshing floor, and gather *and* store His wheat in His barn; but the chaff He will burn up with fire that cannot be put out.

13 Then Jesus came from Galilee to the Jordan to John to be baptized by him.

14 But John [d]protested strenuously, having in mind to prevent Him, saying, It is I who have need to be baptized by You, and do You come to me?

15 But Jesus replied to him, [e]Permit it just now, for this is the fitting way for [both of] us to fulfill all righteousness—that is, to [f]perform completely whatever is right.

16 And when Jesus was baptized, He went up at once out of the water, and behold, the heavens were opened, and he [John] saw the Spirit of God descending like a dove and alighting on Him;

17 And lo, a voice out from heaven said, This is My Son, My Beloved, in Whom I delight! [Ps. 2:7; Isa. 42:1.]

**4** THEN JESUS was led (guided) by the (Holy) Spirit into the wilderness (desert) to be tempted—that is, tested and tried—by the devil.

2 And He went without food for forty days and forty nights, and later He was hungry. [Exod. 34:28; I Kings 19:8.]

3 And the tempter came and said to Him, If You are God's Son, command these stones to be made [ [g]loaves of] bread.

4 But He replied, It has been written, Man shall not live *and* be upheld *and* sustained by bread alone, but by every word that comes forth from the mouth of God. [Deut. 8:3.]

5 Then the devil took Him into the holy city, and placed Him on [h]a turret (pinnacle, [i]gable) of the temple [j]sanctuary, [Neh. 11:1; Dan. 9:24.]

6 And he said to Him, If You are the Son of God, throw Yourself down; for it is written, He will give His angels charge over you, and they will bear you up on their hands, lest you strike your foot against a stone. [Ps. 91:11, 12.]

7 Jesus said to him, [k]On the other hand it is written also, You shall not tempt, [l]test thoroughly *or* [m]try exceedingly the Lord your God. [Deut. 6:16.]

8 Again the devil took Him up on a very high mountain, and showed Him all the kingdoms of the world and the glory—the splendor, magnificence, pre-eminence and excellence—of them;

9 And he said to Him, These things all taken together I will give You, if You will prostrate Yourself before me and do homage *and* worship me.

10 Then Jesus said to him, Begone, Satan! for it has been written, You shall worship the Lord your God and Him alone shall you serve. [Deut. 6:13.]

11 Then the devil departed from Him, and behold, angels came and ministered to Him.

12 Now when Jesus heard that John had been arrested *and* put in prison, He withdrew into Galilee.

**AMP** [a] "En", the preposition used here, is translated both "in" and "with" in the Greek lexicons and concordances generally. The *Authorized Version* gives preference to "with", putting "in" in the margin; the *American "Revised" Version* gives preference to "in", putting "with" in the margin; the many modern versions choose one or the other about equally. [b] Williams. [c] Thayer. [d] Vincent. [e] Thayer. [f] Thayer. [g] Wycliffe's "Version of the New Testament." [h] Abbott-Smith. [i] Moulton and Milligan. [j] Trench. [k] Vincent. [l] Thayer. [m] Young's "Analytical Concordance."

## New American Standard

10"And the axe is already laid at the root of the trees; every tree
therefore that does not bear good fruit is cut down and thrown into
the fire.

11"As for me, I baptize you [n]with water for repentance, but He
who is coming after me is mightier than I, and I am not fit to
remove His sandals; He will baptize you with the Holy Spirit and
fire.

12"And His winnowing fork is in His hand, and He will
thoroughly clear His threshing floor; and He will gather His wheat
into the barn, but He will burn up the chaff with unquenchable
fire."

*The Baptism of Jesus*

13¶ Then Jesus *arrived from Galilee at the Jordan *coming* to
John, to be baptized by him.

14But John tried to prevent Him, saying, "I have need to be
baptized by You, and do You come to me?"

15But Jesus answering said to him, "Permit *it* at this time; for
in this way it is fitting for us to fulfill all righteousness." Then he
*permitted Him.

16And after being baptized, Jesus went up immediately from
the water; and behold, the heavens were opened, and he saw the
Spirit of God descending as a dove, *and* coming upon Him,

17and behold, a voice out of the heavens, saying, "This is [o]My
beloved Son, in whom I am well-pleased."

*Temptation of Jesus*

4 THEN JESUS was led up by the Spirit into the wilderness to
be tempted by the devil.

2And after He had fasted forty days and forty nights, He [p]then
became hungry.

3And the tempter came and said to Him, "If You are the Son
of God, command that these stones become bread."

4But He answered and said, "It is written, 'MAN SHALL NOT
LIVE ON BREAD ALONE, BUT ON EVERY WORD THAT PROCEEDS OUT OF
THE MOUTH OF GOD.' "

5Then the devil *took Him into the holy city; and he had Him
stand on the pinnacle of the temple,

6and *said to Him, "If You are the Son of God throw Yourself
down; for it is written,

'HE WILL GIVE HIS ANGELS CHARGE CONCERNING YOU';
and
'ON *their* HANDS THEY WILL BEAR YOU UP,
LEST YOU STRIKE YOUR FOOT AGAINST A STONE.' "

7Jesus said to him, "On the other hand, it is written, 'YOU
SHALL NOT [q]PUT THE LORD YOUR GOD TO THE TEST.' "

8Again, the devil *took Him to a very high mountain, and
*showed Him all the kingdoms of the world, and their glory;

9and he said to Him, "All these things will I give You, if You
fall down and worship me."

10Then Jesus *said to him, "Begone, Satan! For it is written,
'YOU SHALL WORSHIP THE LORD YOUR GOD, AND SERVE HIM ONLY.' "

11Then the devil *left Him; and behold, angels came and *began*
to minister to Him.

*Jesus Begins His Ministry*

12¶ Now when He heard that John had been taken into custody,
He withdrew into Galilee;

NAS [n] The Gr. here can be translated *in, with* or *by* [o] Lit., *My Son, the Beloved* [p] Lit., *later, afterward* [q] Or, *tempt . . . God*

## New International

at the root of the trees, and every tree that does not produce good
fruit will be cut down and thrown into the fire.

11"I baptize you with[r] water for repentance. But after me will
come one who is more powerful than I, whose sandals I am not
fit to carry. He will baptize you with the Holy Spirit and with fire.
12His winnowing fork is in his hand, and he will clear his threshing
floor, gathering his wheat into the barn and burning up the chaff
with unquenchable fire."

*The Baptism of Jesus*

13Then Jesus came from Galilee to the Jordan to be baptized by
John. 14But John tried to deter him, saying, "I need to be baptized
by you, and do you come to me?"

15Jesus replied, "Let it be so now; it is proper for us to do this
to fulfill all righteousness." Then John consented.

16As soon as Jesus was baptized, he went up out of the water.
At that moment heaven was opened, and he saw the Spirit of God
descending like a dove and lighting on him. 17And a voice from
heaven said, "This is my Son, whom I love; with him I am well
pleased."

*The Temptation of Jesus*

4 THEN JESUS was led by the Spirit into the desert to be
tempted by the devil. 2After fasting forty days and forty
nights, he was hungry. 3The tempter came to him and said, "If you
are the Son of God, tell these stones to become bread."

4Jesus answered, "It is written: 'Man does not live on bread
alone, but on every word that comes from the mouth of God.'[s] "

5Then the devil took him to the holy city and had him stand on
the highest point of the temple. 6"If you are the Son of God," he
said, "throw yourself down. For it is written:

" 'He will command his angels concerning you,
and they will lift you up in their hands,
so that you will not strike your foot against a stone.'[t] "

7Jesus answered him, "It is also written: 'Do not put the Lord
your God to the test.'[u] "

8Again, the devil took him to a very high mountain and showed
him all the kingdoms of the world and their splendor. 9"All this
I will give you," he said, "if you will bow down and worship me."

10Jesus said to him, "Away from me, Satan! For it is written:
'Worship the Lord your God, and serve him only.'[v] "

11Then the devil left him, and angels came and attended him.

*Jesus Begins to Preach*

12When Jesus heard that John had been put in prison, he returned to Galilee. 13Leaving Nazareth, he went and lived in Caper-

NIV [r] *11* Or *in* [s] *4* Deut. 8:3 [t] *6* Psalm 91:11,12 [u] *7* Deut. 6:16 [v] *10* Deut. 6:13

## King James

13And leaving Nazareth, he came and dwelt in Capernaum, which is upon the sea coast, in the borders of Zabulon and Nephthalim:

14That it might be fulfilled which was spoken by Esaias the prophet, saying,

15The land of Zabulon, and the land of Nephthalim, *by* the way of the sea, beyond Jordan, Galilee of the Gentiles;

16The people which sat in darkness saw great light; and to them which sat in the region and shadow of death light is sprung up.

17¶ From that time Jesus began to preach, and to say, Repent: for the kingdom of heaven is at hand.

18¶ And Jesus, walking by the sea of Galilee, saw two brethren, Simon called Peter, and Andrew his brother, casting a net into the sea: for they were fishers.

19And he saith unto them, Follow me, and I will make you fishers of men.

20And they straightway left *their* nets, and followed him.

21And going on from thence, he saw other two brethren, James *the son* of Zebedee, and John his brother, in a ship with Zebedee their father, mending their nets; and he called them.

22And they immediately left the ship and their father, and followed him.

23¶ And Jesus went about all Galilee, teaching in their synagogues, and preaching the gospel of the kingdom, and healing all manner of sickness and all manner of disease among the people.

24And his fame went throughout all Syria: and they brought unto him all sick people that were taken with divers diseases and torments, and those which were possessed with devils, and those which were lunatic, and those that had the palsy; and he healed them.

25And there followed him great multitudes of people from Galilee, and *from* Decapolis, and *from* Jerusalem, and *from* Judaea, and *from* beyond Jordan.

5 AND SEEING the multitudes, he went up into a mountain: and when he was set, his disciples came unto him:

2And he opened his mouth, and taught them, saying,

3Blessed *are* the poor in spirit: for theirs is the kingdom of heaven.

4Blessed *are* they that mourn: for they shall be comforted.

5Blessed *are* the meek: for they shall inherit the earth.

6Blessed *are* they which do hunger and thirst after righteousness: for they shall be filled.

7Blessed *are* the merciful: for they shall obtain mercy.

## Amplified

13And leaving Nazareth He went *and* dwelt in Capernaum by the sea, in the country of Zebulun and Naphtali,

14That what was spoken by the prophet Isaiah might be brought to pass:

15The land of Zebulun and the land of Naphtali in the [a]way to the sea beyond the Jordan, Galilee of the Gentiles [that is, of the [b]peoples who are not of Israel]; [Isa. 9:1-2.]

16The people who sat [c](dwelt enveloped) in darkness have seen a great Light, and for those who sat in the land and shadow of death Light has dawned.

17From that time Jesus began to preach, [d]crying out, Repent—that is, [e]change your mind for the better, heartily amend your ways, with abhorrence of your past sins—for the kingdom of heaven is at hand.

18As He was walking by the sea of Galilee, He noticed two brothers, Simon who is called Peter and Andrew his brother, throwing a dragnet into the sea, for they were fishermen.

19And He said to them, Come [f]after Me [as disciples]—letting Me be your Guide, follow Me—and I will make you fishers of men!

20At once they left their nets and [g]became His disciples—sided with His party and followed Him.

21And going on further from there He noticed two other brothers, James the son of Zebedee and John his brother, in the boat with their father Zebedee, mending their nets *and* putting them to rights, and He called them.

22At once they left the boat and their father and [h]joined Jesus as disciples—sided with His party and followed Him.

23And He went about all Galilee, teaching in their synagogues and preaching the good news (Gospel) of the kingdom and healing every disease and every weakness *and* infirmity among the people.

24So the report of Him spread throughout all Syria, and they brought Him all that were sick, those afflicted with various diseases and torments, those under the power of demons, and epileptics, and paralyzed people; and He healed them.

25And great crowds joined *and* accompanied Him about, coming from Galilee and Decapolis [the district of the ten cities east of the Sea of Galilee] and Jerusalem and Judea and from the other [the east] side of the Jordan.

5 SEEING THE crowds, He went up on the mountain, and when He was seated His disciples came to Him.

2Then He opened His mouth and taught them saying:

3Blessed—happy, [i]to be envied, and [j]spiritually prosperous [that is, [k]with life-joy and satisfaction in God's favor and salvation, regardless of their outward conditions]—are the poor in spirit (the humble, rating themselves insignificant), for theirs is the kingdom of heaven!

4Blessed *and* enviably happy, [with a [l]happiness produced by experience of God's favor and especially conditioned by the revelation of His matchless grace] are those who mourn, for they shall be comforted! [Isa. 61:2.]

5Blessed—happy, blithesome, joyous, [m]spiritually prosperous [that is, [n]with life-joy and satisfaction in God's favor and salvation, regardless of their outward conditions]—are the meek (the mild, patient, long-suffering), for they shall inherit the earth! [Ps. 37:11.]

6Blessed *and* fortunate *and* happy *and* [o]spiritually prosperous [that is, in that state in which the born-again child of God [p]enjoys His favor and salvation] are those who hunger and thirst for righteousness (uprightness and right standing with God), for they shall be [q]completely satisfied! [Isa. 55:1, 2.]

7Blessed—happy, [r]to be envied, and [s]spiritually prosperous [that is, [t]with life-joy and satisfaction in God's favor and salvation, regardless of their outward conditions]—are the merciful, for they shall obtain mercy!

**AMP** [a] Cremer's "Biblico-Theological Lexicon of New Testament Greek." [b] Cremer's "Biblico-Theological Lexicon of New Testament Greek." [c] Wycliffe. [d] Vincent. [e] Thayer. [f] Thayer. [g] Thayer. [h] Thayer. [i] Souter's "A Pocket Lexicon to the Greek New Testament." [j] Wuest's "Mark in the Greek New Testament." [k] Cremer. [l] Cremer. [m] Vincent. [n] Cremer. [o] Vincent. [p] Cremer. [q] Vincent. [r] Souter's "Pocket Lexicon to the Greek New Testament." [s] Vincent. [t] Cremer.

## New American Standard

13and leaving Nazareth, He came and settled in Capernaum,
which is by the sea, in the region of Zebulun and Naphtali.
14 *This was* to fulfill what was spoken through Isaiah the
prophet, saying,
15 "THE LAND OF ZEBULUN AND THE LAND OF NAPHTALI,
BY THE WAY OF THE SEA, BEYOND THE JORDAN, GALILEE
OF THE [u]GENTILES—
16 "THE PEOPLE WHO WERE SITTING IN DARKNESS SAW A
GREAT LIGHT,
AND TO THOSE WHO WERE SITTING IN THE LAND AND
SHADOW OF DEATH,
UPON THEM A LIGHT DAWNED."
17¶ From that time Jesus began to preach and say, "Repent, for
the kingdom of heaven is at hand."

*The First Disciples*

18¶ And walking by the Sea of Galilee, He saw two brothers,
Simon who was called Peter, and Andrew his brother, casting a net
into the sea; for they were fishermen.
19And He *said to them, "Follow Me, and I will make you
fishers of men."
20And they immediately left the nets, and followed Him.
21And going on from there He saw two other brothers, James
the *son* of Zebedee, and John his brother, in the boat with Zebedee
their father, mending their nets; and He called them.
22And they immediately left the boat and their father, and
followed Him.

*Ministry in Galilee*

23¶ And *Jesus* was going about in all Galilee, teaching in their
synagogues, and proclaiming the gospel of the kingdom, and
healing every kind of disease and every kind of sickness among the
people.
24And the news about Him went out into all Syria; and they
brought to Him all who were ill, taken with various diseases and
pains, demoniacs, epileptics, paralytics; and He healed them.
25And great multitudes followed Him from Galilee and Decapolis and Jerusalem and Judea and *from* beyond the Jordan.

*The Sermon on the Mount*
*The Beatitudes*

5 AND WHEN He saw the multitudes, He went up on the
mountain; and after He sat down, His disciples came to Him.
2And opening His mouth He *began* to teach them, saying,
3¶ "Blessed are the poor in spirit, for theirs is the kingdom of
heaven.
4¶ "Blessed are those who mourn, for they shall be comforted.
5¶ "Blessed are the [v]gentle, for they shall inherit the earth.
6¶ "Blessed are those who hunger and thirst for righteousness,
for they shall be satisfied.
7¶ "Blessed are the merciful, for they shall receive mercy.

NAS [u] Or, *nations* [v] Or, *humble, meek*

## New International

naum, which was by the lake in the area of Zebulun and Naphtali— 14to fulfill what was said through the prophet Isaiah:

15"Land of Zebulun and land of Naphtali,
the way to the sea, along the Jordan,
Galilee of the Gentiles—
16the people living in darkness
have seen a great light;
on those living in the land of the shadow of death
a light has dawned."[w]

17From that time on Jesus began to preach, "Repent, for the
kingdom of heaven is near."

*The Calling of the First Disciples*

18As Jesus was walking beside the Sea of Galilee, he saw two
brothers, Simon called Peter and his brother Andrew. They were
casting a net into the lake, for they were fishermen. 19"Come,
follow me," Jesus said, "and I will make you fishers of men." 20At
once they left their nets and followed him.
21Going on from there, he saw two other brothers, James son
of Zebedee and his brother John. They were in a boat with their
father Zebedee, preparing their nets. Jesus called them, 22and
immediately they left the boat and their father and followed him.

*Jesus Heals the Sick*

23Jesus went throughout Galilee, teaching in their synagogues,
preaching the good news of the kingdom, and healing every disease and sickness among the people. 24News about him spread all
over Syria, and people brought to him all who were ill with various
diseases, those suffering severe pain, the demon-possessed, those
having seizures, and the paralyzed, and he healed them. 25Large
crowds from Galilee, the Decapolis,[x] Jerusalem, Judea and the
region across the Jordan followed him.

*The Beatitudes*

5 NOW WHEN he saw the crowds, he went up on a mountainside and sat down. His disciples came to him, 2and he began
to teach them, saying:

3"Blessed are the poor in spirit,
for theirs is the kingdom of heaven.
4Blessed are those who mourn,
for they will be comforted.
5Blessed are the meek,
for they will inherit the earth.
6Blessed are those who hunger and thirst for
righteousness,
for they will be filled.
7Blessed are the merciful,
for they will be shown mercy.

NIV [w] *16* Isaiah 9:1,2 [x] *25* That is, the Ten Cities

## King James

8 Blessed *are* the pure in heart: for they shall see God.

9 Blessed *are* the peacemakers: for they shall be called the children of God.

10 Blessed *are* they which are persecuted for righteousness' sake: for theirs is the kingdom of heaven.

11 Blessed are ye, when *men* shall revile you, and persecute *you*, and shall say all manner of evil against you falsely, for my sake.

12 Rejoice, and be exceeding glad: for great *is* your reward in heaven: for so persecuted they the prophets which were before you.

13 ¶ Ye are the salt of the earth: but if the salt have lost his savour, wherewith shall it be salted? it is thenceforth good for nothing, but to be cast out, and to be trodden under foot of men.

14 Ye are the light of the world. A city that is set on an hill cannot be hid.

15 Neither do men light a candle, and put it under a bushel, but on a candlestick; and it giveth light unto all that are in the house.

16 Let your light so shine before men, that they may see your good works, and glorify your Father which is in heaven.

17 ¶ Think not that I am come to destroy the law, or the prophets: I am not come to destroy, but to fulfil.

18 For verily I say unto you, Till heaven and earth pass, one jot or one tittle shall in no wise pass from the law, till all be fulfilled.

19 Whosoever therefore shall break one of these least commandments, and shall teach men so, he shall be called the least in the kingdom of heaven: but whosoever shall do and teach *them*, the same shall be called great in the kingdom of heaven.

20 For I say unto you, That except your righteousness shall exceed *the righteousness* of the scribes and Pharisees, ye shall in no case enter into the kingdom of heaven.

21 ¶ Ye have heard that it was said by them of old time, Thou shalt not kill; and whosoever shall kill shall be in danger of the judgment:

22 But I say unto you, That whosoever is angry with his brother without a cause shall be in danger of the judgment: and whosoever shall say to his brother, Raca, shall be in danger of the council: but whosoever shall say, Thou fool, shall be in danger of hell fire.

23 Therefore if thou bring thy gift to the altar, and there rememberest that thy brother hath aught against thee;

24 Leave there thy gift before the altar, and go thy way; first be reconciled to thy brother, and then come and offer thy gift.

25 Agree with thine adversary quickly, whiles thou art in the way with him; lest at any time the adversary deliver thee to the judge, and the judge deliver thee to the officer, and thou be cast into prison.

26 Verily I say unto thee, Thou shalt by no means come out thence, till thou hast paid the uttermost farthing.

AMP [a] Souter's "Pocket Lexicon to the Greek New Testament." [b] Vincent. [c] Cremer. [d] Souter's "Pocket Lexicon to the Greek New Testament." [e] Vincent. [f] Cremer. [g] Tyndale's "Version of the New Testament." [h] Souter's "Pocket Lexicon to the Greek New Testament." [i] Wuest. [j] Cremer. [k] Souter's "Pocket Lexicon to the Greek New Testament." [l] Wuest. [m] Cremer. [n] Cremer. [o] Cremer. [p] Wycliffe. [q] Thayer. [r] Many ancient authorities insert "without cause." [s] Thayer. [t] Thayer. [u] Williams. [v] Thayer.

## Amplified

8 Blessed—happy, [a]enviably fortunate, and [b]spiritually prosperous [that is, possessing the [c]happiness produced by experience of God's favor and especially conditioned by the revelation of His grace, regardless of their outward conditions]—are the pure in heart, for they shall see God! [Ps. 24:3, 4.]

9 Blessed—enjoying [d]enviable happiness, [e]spiritually prosperous [that is, [f]with life-joy and satisfaction in God's favor and salvation, regardless of their outward conditions]—are the makers *and* [g]maintainers of peace, for they shall be called the sons of God!

10 Blessed *and* happy *and* [h]enviably fortunate *and* [i]spiritually prosperous [that is, [j]in the state in which one enjoys and finds satisfaction in God's favor and salvation, regardless of his outward conditions], are those who are persecuted for righteousness' sake (for being and doing right), for theirs is the kingdom of heaven!

11 Blessed—happy, [k]to be envied, and [l]spiritually prosperous [that is, [m]with life-joy and satisfaction in God's favor and salvation, regardless of your outward conditions]—are you when people revile you and persecute you and say all kinds of evil things against you falsely on My account.

12 Be glad *and* supremely joyful, for your reward in heaven is great (strong and intense), for in this same way people persecuted the prophets who were before you. [II Chron. 36:16.]

13 You are the salt of the earth, but if salt has lost its taste—its strength, its quality—how can its saltness be restored? It is not good for anything any longer but to be thrown out and trodden under foot by men.

14 You are the light of the world. A city set on a hill cannot be hid.

15 Nor do men light a lamp and put it under a peck-measure but on a lamp stand, and it gives light to all in the house.

16 Let your light so shine before men that they may see your [n]moral excellence *and* your praiseworthy, noble *and* good deeds, and [o]recognize *and* honor *and* praise *and* glorify your Father Who is in heaven.

17 Do not think that I have come to do away with *or* [p]undo the Law and the prophets; I have come not to do away with *or* undo, but to complete *and* fulfill them.

18 For truly, I tell you, until the sky and earth pass away *and* perish not one smallest letter nor one little hook [identifying certain Hebrew letters] will pass from the Law until all things [it foreshadows] have been accomplished.

19 Whoever then breaks *or* does away with *or* relaxes one of the least important of these commandments and teaches men so, shall be called least important in the kingdom of heaven; but he who practices them and teaches others to do so shall be called great in the kingdom of heaven.

20 For I tell you, unless your righteousness (your uprightness and your right standing with God) is more than that of the scribes and Pharisees, you will never enter the kingdom of heaven.

21 You have heard that it was said to the men of old, You shall not kill; and whoever kills shall be [q]liable *so* that he cannot escape the punishment imposed by the court. [Exod. 20:13; Deut. 5:17; 16:18.]

22 But I say to you that every one who continues to be [r]angry with his brother *or* harbors malice [enmity of heart] against him shall be [s]liable to *and* unable to escape the punishment imposed by the court; and whoever speaks contemptuously *and* insultingly to his brother shall be [t]liable to *and* unable to escape the punishment imposed by the Sanhedrin, and whoever says, You [u]cursed fool!—You empty-headed idiot! shall be [v]liable to *and* unable to escape the hell (Gehenna) of fire.

23 So if, when you are offering your gift at the altar you there remember that your brother has any [grievance] against you,

24 Leave your gift at the altar and go; first make peace with your brother, and then come back *and* present your gift.

25 Come to terms quickly with your accuser while you are on the way traveling with him, lest your accuser hand you over to the judge, and the judge to the guard, and you be put in prison;

26 Truly, I say to you, you will never be released until you have paid the last fraction of a penny.

## New American Standard

8¶ "Blessed are the pure in heart, for they shall see God.
9¶ "Blessed are the peacemakers, for they shall be called sons of God.
10¶ "Blessed are those who have been persecuted for the sake of righteousness, for theirs is the kingdom of heaven.
11"Blessed are you when *men* cast insults at you, and persecute you, and say all kinds of evil against you falsely, on account of Me.
12"Rejoice, and be glad, for your reward in heaven is great, for so they persecuted the prophets who were before you.

*Disciples and the World*

13"You are the salt of the earth; but if the salt has become tasteless, how will it be made salty *again*? It is good for nothing anymore, except to be thrown out and trampled under foot by men.
14"You are the light of the world. A city set on a hill cannot be hidden.
15"Nor do *men* light a lamp, and put it under the peck-measure, but on the lampstand; and it gives light to all who are in the house.
16"Let your light shine before men in such a way that they may see your good works, and glorify your Father who is in heaven.
17¶ "Do not think that I came to abolish the Law or the Prophets; I did not come to abolish, but to fulfill.
18"For truly I say to you, until heaven and earth pass away, not the smallest letter or stroke shall pass away from the Law, until all is accomplished.
19"Whoever then annuls one of the least of these commandments, and so teaches others, shall be called least in the kingdom of heaven; but whoever keeps and teaches *them*, he shall be called great in the kingdom of heaven.
20"For I say to you, that unless your righteousness surpasses *that* of the scribes and Pharisees, you shall not enter the kingdom of heaven.

*Personal Relationships*

21¶ "You have heard that the ancients were told, 'YOU SHALL NOT COMMIT MURDER' and 'Whoever commits murder shall be [w]liable to the court.'
22"But I say to you that everyone who is angry with his brother [x] shall be guilty before the court; and whoever shall say to his brother, '[y]Raca,' shall be guilty before [z]the supreme court; and whoever shall say, 'You fool,' shall be guilty *enough to go* into the [a]fiery hell.
23"If therefore you are presenting your offering at the altar, and there remember that your brother has something against you,
24leave your offering there before the altar, and go your way; first be reconciled to your brother, and then come and present your offering.
25"Make friends quickly with your opponent at law while you are with him on the way, in order that your opponent may not deliver you to the judge, and the judge to the officer, and you be thrown into prison.
26"Truly I say to you, you shall not come out of there, until you have paid up the last [b]cent.

**NAS** [w]Or, *guilty before* [x]Some mss. insert here: *without cause* [y]Aramaic for *empty-head* or, *good for nothing* [z]Lit., *the Sanhedrin* [a]Lit., *Gehenna of fire* [b]Lit., *quadrans* (equaling two lepta or mites), i.e., 1/64 of a denarius

## New International

8Blessed are the pure in heart,
for they will see God.
9Blessed are the peacemakers,
for they will be called sons of God.
10Blessed are those who are persecuted because of righteousness,
for theirs is the kingdom of heaven.

11"Blessed are you when people insult you, persecute you and
falsely say all kinds of evil against you because of me. 12Rejoice and
be glad, because great is your reward in heaven, for in the same
way they persecuted the prophets who were before you.

*Salt and Light*

13"You are the salt of the earth. But if the salt loses its saltiness,
how can it be made salty again? It is no longer good for anything,
except to be thrown out and trampled by men.
14"You are the light of the world. A city on a hill cannot be
hidden. 15Neither do people light a lamp and put it under a bowl.
Instead they put it on its stand, and it gives light to everyone in
the house. 16In the same way, let your light shine before men, that
they may see your good deeds and praise your Father in heaven.

*The Fulfillment of the Law*

17"Do not think that I have come to abolish the Law or the
Prophets; I have not come to abolish them but to fulfill them. 18I
tell you the truth, until heaven and earth disappear, not the smallest letter, not the least stroke of a pen, will by any means disappear
from the Law until everything is accomplished. 19Anyone who
breaks one of the least of these commandments and teaches others
to do the same will be called least in the kingdom of heaven, but
whoever practices and teaches these commands will be called great
in the kingdom of heaven. 20For I tell you that unless your righteousness surpasses that of the Pharisees and the teachers of the
law, you will certainly not enter the kingdom of heaven.

*Murder*

21"You have heard that it was said to the people long ago, 'Do
not murder,[c] and anyone who murders will be subject to judgment.' 22But I tell you that anyone who is angry with his brother[d]
will be subject to judgment. Again, anyone who says to his brother, 'Raca,[e]' is answerable to the Sanhedrin. But anyone who says,
'You fool!' will be in danger of the fire of hell.
23"Therefore, if you are offering your gift at the altar and there
remember that your brother has something against you, 24leave
your gift there in front of the altar. First go and be reconciled to
your brother; then come and offer your gift.
25"Settle matters quickly with your adversary who is taking you
to court. Do it while you are still with him on the way, or he may
hand you over to the judge, and the judge may hand you over to
the officer, and you may be thrown into prison. 26I tell you the
truth, you will not get out until you have paid the last penny.[f]

**NIV** [c]*21* Exodus 20:13 [d]22 Some manuscripts *brother without cause* [e]22 An Aramaic term of contempt [f]26 Greek *kodrantes*

## King James

27¶ Ye have heard that it was said by them of old time, Thou shalt not commit adultery:

28 But I say unto you, That whosoever looketh on a woman to lust after her hath committed adultery with her already in his heart.

29 And if thy right eye offend thee, pluck it out, and cast *it* from thee: for it is profitable for thee that one of thy members should perish, and not *that* thy whole body should be cast into hell.

30 And if thy right hand offend thee, cut it off, and cast *it* from thee: for it is profitable for thee that one of thy members should perish, and not *that* thy whole body should be cast into hell.

31 It hath been said, Whosoever shall put away his wife, let him give her a writing of divorcement:

32 But I say unto you, That whosoever shall put away his wife, saving for the cause of fornication, causeth her to commit adultery: and whosoever shall marry her that is divorced committeth adultery.

33¶ Again, ye have heard that it hath been said by them of old time, Thou shalt not forswear thyself, but shalt perform unto the Lord thine oaths:

34 But I say unto you, Swear not at all; neither by heaven; for it is God's throne:

35 Nor by the earth; for it is his footstool: neither by Jerusalem; for it is the city of the great King.

36 Neither shalt thou swear by thy head, because thou canst not make one hair white or black.

37 But let your communication be, Yea, yea; Nay, nay: for whatsoever is more than these cometh of evil.

38¶ Ye have heard that it hath been said, An eye for an eye, and a tooth for a tooth:

39 But I say unto you, That ye resist not evil: but whosoever shall smite thee on thy right cheek, turn to him the other also.

40 And if any man will sue thee at the law, and take away thy coat, let him have *thy* cloak also.

41 And whosoever shall compel thee to go a mile, go with him twain.

42 Give to him that asketh thee, and from him that would borrow of thee turn not thou away.

43¶ Ye have heard that it hath been said, Thou shalt love thy neighbour, and hate thine enemy.

44 But I say unto you, Love your enemies, bless them that curse you, do good to them that hate you, and pray for them which despitefully use you, and persecute you;

45 That ye may be the children of your Father which is in heaven: for he maketh his sun to rise on the evil and on the good, and sendeth rain on the just and on the unjust.

46 For if ye love them which love you, what reward have ye? do not even the publicans the same?

47 And if ye salute your brethren only, what do ye more *than others?* do not even the publicans so?

48 Be ye therefore perfect, even as your Father which is in heaven is perfect.

6 TAKE HEED that ye do not your alms before men, to be seen of them: otherwise ye have no reward of your Father which is in heaven.

## Amplified

27 You have heard that it was said, You shall not commit adultery, [Exod. 20:14; Deut. 5:18.]

28 But I say to you that every one who so much as looks at a woman with evil desire for her has already committed adultery with her in his heart.

29 If your right eye serves as a trap to ensnare you *or* is an occasion for you to stumble *and* sin, pluck it out and throw it away. It is better that you lose one of your members than that your whole body be cast into hell (Gehenna).

30 And if your right hand serves as a trap to ensnare you *or* is an occasion for you to stumble *and* sin, cut it off and cast it from you. It is better that you lose one of your members than that your entire body should be cast into hell (Gehenna).

31 It was also said, Whoever divorces his wife must give her a certificate of divorcement.

32 But I tell you, Whoever dismisses *and* repudiates *and* divorces his wife, except on the grounds of unfaithfulness (sexual immorality), causes her to commit adultery; and whoever marries a woman who has been divorced commits adultery. [Deut. 24:1-4.]

33 Again, you have heard that it was said to the men of old, You shall not swear falsely, but you shall perform your oaths to the Lord—as a religious duty.

34 But I tell you, Do not bind yourselves by an oath at all, either by heaven, for it is the throne of God,

35 Or by the earth, for it is the footstool of His feet, or by Jerusalem, for it is the city of the great King. [Isa. 66:1; Ps. 48:2.]

36 And do not swear by your head, for you are not able to make a single hair white or black.

37 Let your Yes be simply Yes, and your No be simply No; anything more than that comes from the evil one. [Lev. 19:12; Num. 30:2; Deut. 23:21.]

38 You have heard that it was said, An eye for an eye and a tooth for a tooth, [Exod. 21:24; Lev. 24:20; Deut. 19:21.]

39 But I say to you, Do not resist the evil man [who injures you]; but if any one strikes you on the right jaw *or* cheek, turn to him the other one too;

40 And if any one wants to sue you and take your undershirt (tunic), let him have your coat also;

41 And if any one forces you to go one mile, go with him two [miles].

42 Give to him who keeps on begging from you, and do not turn away from him who would borrow ([a]at interest) from you, [Deut. 15:8; Prov. 24:29.]

43 You have heard that it was said, You shall love your neighbor and hate your enemy;

44 But I tell you, Love your enemies and pray for those who persecute you, [Prov. 25:21, 22.]

45 [b]To show that you are the children of your Father Who is in heaven; for He makes His sun rise on the wicked and on the good, and makes the rain fall upon the upright and the wrongdoers [alike].

46 For if you love those who love you, what reward can you have? Do not even the tax collectors do that?

47 And if you greet only your brethren, what more than others are you doing? Do not even the Gentiles (the heathen) do that?

48 You, therefore, must be perfect, as your heavenly Father is perfect [that is, grow into complete [c]maturity of godliness in mind and character, [d]having reached the proper height of virtue and integrity]. [Lev. 19:2, 18.]

6 TAKE CARE not to do your good deeds publicly *or* before men in order to be seen by them; otherwise you will have no reward [ [e]reserved for and awaiting you] with *and* from your Father Who is in heaven.

AMP [a] Vincent. [b] Thayer. [c] Wuest. [d] Thayer. [e] Vincent.

## New American Standard

27¶ "You have heard that it was said, 'YOU SHALL NOT COMMIT ADULTERY';
28but I say to you, that everyone who looks on a woman to lust for her has committed adultery with her already in his heart.
29"And if your right eye makes you stumble, tear it out, and throw it from you; for it is better for you that one of the parts of your body perish, than for your whole body to be thrown into hell.
30"And if your right hand makes you stumble, cut it off, and throw it from you; for it is better for you that one of the parts of your body perish, than for your whole body to go into hell.
31"And it was said, 'WHOEVER SENDS HIS WIFE AWAY, LET HIM GIVE HER A CERTIFICATE OF DIVORCE';
32but I say to you that everyone who divorces his wife, except for *the* cause of unchastity, makes her commit adultery; and whoever marries a divorced woman commits adultery.
33¶ "Again, you have heard that the ancients were told, 'YOU SHALL NOT MAKE FALSE VOWS, BUT SHALL FULFILL YOUR VOWS TO THE LORD.'
34"But I say to you, make no oath at all, either by heaven, for it is the throne of God,
35or by the earth, for it is the footstool of His feet, or by Jerusalem, for it is THE CITY OF THE GREAT KING.
36"Nor shall you make an oath by your head, for you cannot make one hair white or black.
37"But let your statement be, 'Yes, yes' *or* 'No, no'; and anything beyond these is of evil.
38¶ "You have heard that it was said, 'AN EYE FOR AN EYE, AND A TOOTH FOR A TOOTH.'
39"But I say to you, do not resist him who is evil; but whoever slaps you on your right cheek, turn to him the other also.
40"And if anyone wants to sue you, and take your [f]shirt, let him have your [g]coat also.
41"And whoever shall force you to go one mile, go with him two.
42"Give to him who asks of you, and do not turn away from him who wants to borrow from you.
43¶ "You have heard that it was said, 'YOU SHALL LOVE YOUR NEIGHBOR, and hate your enemy.'
44"But I say to you, love your enemies, and pray for those who persecute you
45in order that you may be sons of your Father who is in heaven; for He causes His sun to rise on *the* evil and *the* good, and sends rain on *the* righteous and *the* unrighteous.
46"For if you love those who love you, what reward have you? Do not even the tax-gatherers do the same?
47"And if you greet your brothers only, what do you do more *than others*? Do not even the Gentiles do the same?
48"Therefore you are to be perfect, as your heavenly Father is perfect.

*Concerning Alms and Prayer*

6 "BEWARE OF practicing your righteousness before men to be noticed by them; otherwise you have no reward with your Father who is in heaven.

NAS [f] Or, *tunic;* i.e., garment worn next to the body [g] Or, *cloak;* i.e., outer garment

## New International

*Adultery*

27"You have heard that it was said, 'Do not commit adultery.'[h]
28But I tell you that anyone who looks at a woman lustfully has
already committed adultery with her in his heart. 29If your right
eye causes you to sin, gouge it out and throw it away. It is better
for you to lose one part of your body than for your whole body to
be thrown into hell. 30And if your right hand causes you to sin,
cut it off and throw it away. It is better for you to lose one part of
your body than for your whole body to go into hell.

*Divorce*

31"It has been said, 'Anyone who divorces his wife must give
her a certificate of divorce.'[i] 32But I tell you that anyone who
divorces his wife, except for marital unfaithfulness, causes her to
become an adulteress, and anyone who marries the divorced
woman commits adultery.

*Oaths*

33"Again, you have heard that it was said to the people long
ago, 'Do not break your oath, but keep the oaths you have made
to the Lord.' 34But I tell you, Do not swear at all: either by heaven,
for it is God's throne; 35or by the earth, for it is his footstool; or by
Jerusalem, for it is the city of the Great King. 36And do not swear
by your head, for you cannot make even one hair white or black.
37Simply let your 'Yes' be 'Yes,' and your 'No,' 'No'; anything
beyond this comes from the evil one.

*An Eye for an Eye*

38"You have heard that it was said, 'Eye for eye, and tooth for
tooth.'[j] 39But I tell you, Do not resist an evil person. If someone
strikes you on the right cheek, turn to him the other also. 40And
if someone wants to sue you and take your tunic, let him have your
cloak as well. 41If someone forces you to go one mile, go with him
two miles. 42Give to the one who asks you, and do not turn away
from the one who wants to borrow from you.

*Love for Enemies*

43"You have heard that it was said, 'Love your neighbor[k] and
hate your enemy.' 44But I tell you: Love your enemies[l] and pray
for those who persecute you, 45that you may be sons of your Father
in heaven. He causes his sun to rise on the evil and the good, and
sends rain on the righteous and the unrighteous. 46If you love
those who love you, what reward will you get? Are not even the
tax collectors doing that? 47And if you greet only your brothers,
what are you doing more than others? Do not even pagans do that?
48Be perfect, therefore, as your heavenly Father is perfect.

*Giving to the Needy*

6 "BE CAREFUL not to do your 'acts of righteousness' before men, to be seen by them. If you do, you will have no reward from your Father in heaven.

NIV [h] *27* Exodus 20:14 [i] *31* Deut. 24:1 [j] *38* Exodus 21:24; Lev. 24:20; Deut. 19:21 [k] *43* Lev. 19:18 [l] *44* Some late manuscripts *enemies, bless those who curse you, do good to those who hate you*

## King James

2 Therefore when thou doest *thine* alms, do not sound a trumpet before thee, as the hypocrites do in the synagogues and in the streets, that they may have glory of men. Verily I say unto you, They have their reward.

3 But when thou doest alms, let not thy left hand know what thy right hand doeth:

4 That thine alms may be in secret: and thy Father which seeth in secret himself shall reward thee openly.

5 ¶ And when thou prayest, thou shalt not be as the hypocrites *are:* for they love to pray standing in the synagogues and in the corners of the streets, that they may be seen of men. Verily I say unto you, They have their reward.

6 But thou, when thou prayest, enter into thy closet, and when thou hast shut thy door, pray to thy Father which is in secret; and thy Father which seeth in secret shall reward thee openly.

7 But when ye pray, use not vain repetitions, as the heathen *do:* for they think that they shall be heard for their much speaking.

8 Be not ye therefore like unto them: for your Father knoweth what things ye have need of, before ye ask him.

9 After this manner therefore pray ye: Our Father which art in heaven, Hallowed be thy name.

10 Thy kingdom come. Thy will be done in earth, as *it is* in heaven.

11 Give us this day our daily bread.

12 And forgive us our debts, as we forgive our debtors.

13 And lead us not into temptation, but deliver us from evil: For thine is the kingdom, and the power, and the glory, for ever. Amen.

14 For if ye forgive men their trespasses, your heavenly Father will also forgive you:

15 But if ye forgive not men their trespasses, neither will your Father forgive your trespasses.

16 ¶ Moreover when ye fast, be not, as the hypocrites, of a sad countenance: for they disfigure their faces, that they may appear unto men to fast. Verily I say unto you, They have their reward.

17 But thou, when thou fastest, anoint thine head, and wash thy face;

18 That thou appear not unto men to fast, but unto thy Father which is in secret: and thy Father, which seeth in secret, shall reward thee openly.

19 ¶ Lay not up for yourselves treasures upon earth, where moth and rust doth corrupt, and where thieves break through and steal:

20 But lay up for yourselves treasures in heaven, where neither moth nor rust doth corrupt, and where thieves do not break through nor steal:

21 For where your treasure is, there will your heart be also.

22 The light of the body is the eye: if therefore thine eye be single, thy whole body shall be full of light.

23 But if thine eye be evil, thy whole body shall be full of darkness. If therefore the light that is in thee be darkness, how great *is* that darkness!

24 ¶ No man can serve two masters: for either he will hate the one, and love the other; or else he will hold to the one, and despise the other. Ye cannot serve God and mammon.

25 Therefore I say unto you, Take no thought for your life, what ye shall eat, or what ye shall drink; nor yet for your body, what ye shall put on. Is not the life more than meat, and the body than raiment?

## Amplified

2 Thus, whenever you give to the poor, do not blow a trumpet before you, as the hypocrites in the synagogues and in the streets like to do, that they may be [a]recognized *and* honored *and* praised by men. Truly, I tell you, they have their reward— [b]in full already.

3 But when you give to charity, do not let your left hand know what your right hand is doing,

4 So that your deeds of charity may be in secret; and your Father Who sees in secret will reward you *openly.*

5 Also when you pray you must not be like the hypocrites, for they love to pray standing in the synagogues and on the corners of the streets, that they may be seen by people. Truly, I tell you, they have their reward— [c]in full already.

6 But when you pray, go into your most private room, and closing the door, pray to your Father Who is in secret; and your Father Who sees in secret will reward you *in the open.*

7 And when you pray do not (multiply words, repeating the same ones over and over, and) heap up phrases as the Gentiles do, for they think they will be heard for their much speaking. [I Kings 18:25-29.]

8 Do not be like them, for your Father knows what you need before you ask Him.

9 Pray therefore like this: Our Father Who is in heaven, hallowed (kept holy) be Your name.

10 Your kingdom come, Your will be done, on earth as it is in heaven.

11 Give us this day our daily bread,

12 And forgive us our debts, as we also have forgiven ([d]left, remitted and let go the debts, and [e]given up resentment against) our debtors.

13 And lead (bring) us not into temptation, but deliver us from the evil one. *For Yours is the kingdom and the power and the glory forever. Amen.*

14 For if you forgive people their trespasses—that is, their reckless and wilful sins, [f]leaving them, letting them go and [g]giving up resentment—your heavenly Father will also forgive you.

15 But if you do not forgive others their trespasses—their [h]reckless and wilful sins, [i]leaving them, letting them go and [j]giving up resentment—neither will your Father forgive you your trespasses.

16 And whenever you are fasting, do not look gloomy *and* [k]sour *and* [l]dreary like the hypocrites, for they put on a dismal countenance that their fasting may be apparent *and* seen by men. Truly, I say to you, they have their reward—[m]in full already. [Isa. 58:5.]

17 But when you fast, perfume your head and wash your face,

18 So that your fasting may not be noticed by men but by your Father Who sees in secret; and your Father Who sees in secret will reward you *in the open.*

19 Do not [n]gather *and* heap up *and* store for yourselves treasures on earth, where moth and rust *and* [o]worm consume *and* destroy, and where thieves break through and steal;

20 But [p]gather *and* heap up *and* store for yourselves treasures in heaven, where neither moth nor rust *nor* [q]worm consume *and* destroy, and where thieves do not break through and steal;

21 For where your treasure is, there will your heart be also.

22 The eye is the lamp of the body. So, if your eye is sound, your entire body will be full of light;

23 But if your eye is unsound, your whole body will be full of darkness. If then the very light in you [your [r]conscience] is darkened, how dense is that darkness!

24 No one can serve two masters; for either he will hate the one and love the other, or he will stand by *and* be devoted to the one and despise and be [s]against the other. You cannot serve God and mammon [that is, [t]deceitful riches, money, possessions or [u]what is trusted in].

25 Therefore I tell you, stop being [v]perpetually uneasy (anxious and worried) about your life, what you shall eat *or what you shall drink,* and about your body, what you shall put on. Is not life greater [in quality] than food, and the body [far above and more excellent] than clothing?

**AMP** [a] Cremer. [b] Vincent. [c] Vincent. [d] Moulton and Milligan. [e] Webster for "forgive." [f] Moulton and Milligan. [g] Webster for "forgive." [h] Vincent. [i] Moulton and Milligan. [j] Webster for "forgive." [k] Luther. [l] Trench. [m] Vincent. [n] Thayer. [o] Alternate reading. [p] Thayer. [q] Alternate reading. [r] Cremer. [s] Vincent. [t] Cremer. [u] Thayer. [v] Wuest.

## New American Standard

2¶ "When therefore you give alms, do not sound a trumpet before you, as the hypocrites do in the synagogues and in the streets, that they may be honored by men. Truly I say to you, they have their reward in full.

3"But when you give alms, do not let your left hand know what your right hand is doing

4that your alms may be in secret; and your Father who sees in secret will repay you.

5¶ "And when you pray, you are not to be as the hypocrites; for they love to stand and pray in the synagogues and on the street corners, in order to be seen by men. Truly I say to you, they have their reward in full.

6"But you, when you pray, go into your inner room, and when you have shut your door, pray to your Father who is in secret, and your Father who sees in secret will repay you.

7"And when you are praying, do not use meaningless repetition, as the Gentiles do, for they suppose that they will be heard for their many words.

8"Therefore do not be like them; for your Father knows what you need, before you ask Him.

9"Pray, then, in this way:
'Our Father who art in heaven,
Hallowed be Thy name.
10 'Thy kingdom come.
Thy will be done,
On earth as it is in heaven.
11 'Give us this day our daily bread.
12 'And forgive us our debts, as we also have forgiven our debtors.
13 'And do not lead us into temptation, but deliver us from evil. [For Thine is the kingdom, and the power, and the glory, forever. Amen.]'

14"For if you forgive men for their transgressions, your heavenly Father will also forgive you.

15"But if you do not forgive men, then your Father will not forgive your transgressions.

*Concerning Fasting*

*True Treasure*

*Mammon*

16¶ "And whenever you fast, do not put on a gloomy face as the hypocrites *do*, for they neglect their appearance in order to be seen fasting by men. Truly I say to you, they have their reward in full.

17"But you, when you fast, anoint your head, and wash your face

18so that you may not be seen fasting by men, but by your Father who is in secret; and your Father who sees in secret will repay you.

19¶ "Do not lay up for yourselves treasures upon earth, where moth and rust destroy, and where thieves break in and steal.

20"But lay up for yourselves treasures in heaven, where neither moth nor rust destroys, and where thieves do not break in or steal;

21for where your treasure is, there will your heart be also.

22"The lamp of the body is the eye; if therefore your eye is clear, your whole body will be full of light.

23"But if your eye is bad, your whole body will be full of darkness. If therefore the light that is in you is darkness, how great is the darkness!

24"No one can serve two masters; for either he will hate the one and love the other, or he will hold to one and despise the other. You cannot serve God and [w]mammon.

*The Cure for Anxiety*

25"For this reason I say to you, do not be anxious for your life, *as to* what you shall eat, or what you shall drink; nor for your body, *as to* what you shall put on. Is not life more than food, and the body than clothing?

NAS [w]Or, *riches*

## New International

2"So when you give to the needy, do not announce it with
trumpets, as the hypocrites do in the synagogues and on the
streets, to be honored by men. I tell you the truth, they have
received their reward in full. 3But when you give to the needy, do
not let your left hand know what your right hand is doing, 4so that
your giving may be in secret. Then your Father, who sees what is
done in secret, will reward you.

*Prayer*

5"And when you pray, do not be like the hypocrites, for they
love to pray standing in the synagogues and on the street corners
to be seen by men. I tell you the truth, they have received their
reward in full. 6But when you pray, go into your room, close the
door and pray to your Father, who is unseen. Then your Father,
who sees what is done in secret, will reward you. 7And when you
pray, do not keep on babbling like pagans, for they think they will
be heard because of their many words. 8Do not be like them, for
your Father knows what you need before you ask him.

9"This, then, is how you should pray:
" 'Our Father in heaven,
hallowed be your name,
10your kingdom come,
your will be done
on earth as it is in heaven.
11Give us today our daily bread.
12Forgive us our debts,
as we also have forgiven our debtors.
13And lead us not into temptation,
but deliver us from the evil one.[x] '

14For if you forgive men when they sin against you, your heavenly
Father will also forgive you. 15But if you do not forgive men their
sins, your Father will not forgive your sins.

*Fasting*

16"When you fast, do not look somber as the hypocrites do, for
they disfigure their faces to show men they are fasting. I tell you
the truth, they have received their reward in full. 17But when you
fast, put oil on your head and wash your face, 18so that it will not
be obvious to men that you are fasting, but only to your Father,
who is unseen; and your Father, who sees what is done in secret,
will reward you.

*Treasures in Heaven*

19"Do not store up for yourselves treasures on earth, where
moth and rust destroy, and where thieves break in and steal. 20But
store up for yourselves treasures in heaven, where moth and rust
do not destroy, and where thieves do not break in and steal. 21For
where your treasure is, there your heart will be also.

22"The eye is the lamp of the body. If your eyes are good, your
whole body will be full of light. 23But if your eyes are bad, your
whole body will be full of darkness. If then the light within you
is darkness, how great is that darkness!

24"No one can serve two masters. Either he will hate the one
and love the other, or he will be devoted to the one and despise
the other. You cannot serve both God and Money.

*Do Not Worry*

25"Therefore I tell you, do not worry about your life, what you
will eat or drink; or about your body, what you will wear. Is not
life more important than food, and the body more important than
clothes? 26Look at the birds of the air; they do not sow or reap or

NIV [x] 13 Or *from evil; some late manuscripts one, / for yours is the kingdom and the power and the glory forever. Amen.*

## King James

26Behold the fowls of the air: for they sow not, neither do they reap, nor gather into barns; yet your heavenly Father feedeth them. Are ye not much better than they?

27Which of you by taking thought can add one cubit unto his stature?

28And why take ye thought for raiment? Consider the lilies of the field, how they grow; they toil not, neither do they spin:

29And yet I say unto you, That even Solomon in all his glory was not arrayed like one of these.

30Wherefore, if God so clothe the grass of the field, which today is, and tomorrow is cast into the oven, *shall he* not much more *clothe* you, O ye of little faith?

31Therefore take no thought, saying, What shall we eat? or, What shall we drink? or, Wherewithal shall we be clothed?

32(For after all these things do the Gentiles seek:) for your heavenly Father knoweth that ye have need of all these things.

33But seek ye first the kingdom of God, and his righteousness; and all these things shall be added unto you.

34Take therefore no thought for the morrow: for the morrow shall take thought for the things of itself. Sufficient unto the day *is* the evil thereof.

7 JUDGE NOT, that ye be not judged.

2For with what judgment ye judge, ye shall be judged: and with what measure ye mete, it shall be measured to you again.

3And why beholdest thou the mote that is in thy brother's eye, but considerest not the beam that is in thine own eye?

4Or how wilt thou say to thy brother, Let me pull out the mote out of thine eye; and, behold, a beam *is* in thine own eye?

5Thou hypocrite, first cast out the beam out of thine own eye; and then shalt thou see clearly to cast out the mote out of thy brother's eye.

6¶ Give not that which is holy unto the dogs, neither cast ye your pearls before swine, lest they trample them under their feet, and turn again and rend you.

7¶ Ask, and it shall be given you; seek, and ye shall find; knock, and it shall be opened unto you:

8For every one that asketh receiveth; and he that seeketh findeth; and to him that knocketh it shall be opened.

9Or what man is there of you, whom if his son ask bread, will he give him a stone?

10Or if he ask a fish, will he give him a serpent?

11If ye then, being evil, know how to give good gifts unto your children, how much more shall your Father which is in heaven give good things to them that ask him?

12Therefore all things whatsoever ye would that men should do to you, do ye even so to them: for this is the law and the prophets.

13¶ Enter ye in at the strait gate: for wide *is* the gate, and broad *is* the way, that leadeth to destruction, and many there be which go in thereat:

14Because strait *is* the gate, and narrow *is* the way, which leadeth unto life, and few there be that find it.

**AMP** [a] Souter: [cubit] used as a measurement of time. [b] Thayer. [c] Thayer. [d] Thayer. [e] Williams. [f] Thayer. [g] Vincent. [h] Moulton and Milligan. [i] Abbott-Smith. [j] Abbott-Smith. [k] Wuest's "Golden Nuggets from the Greek New Testament." [l] Wuest's "Golden Nuggets from the Greek New Testament." [m] Wuest's "Golden Nuggets from the Greek New Testament." [n] Cremer. [o] Cremer. [p] Wuest's "Golden Nuggets from the Greek New Testament." [q] Souter.

## Amplified

26Look at the birds of the air; they neither sow nor reap nor gather into barns, and yet your heavenly Father keeps feeding them. Are you not worth more than they?

27And which of you by worrying *and* being anxious can add one unit of measure [cubit] to his stature *or* to the [a]span of his life? [Ps. 39:5-7.]

28And why should you be anxious about clothes? Consider the lilies of the field *and* [b]learn thoroughly how they grow; they neither toil nor spin;

29Yet I tell you, even Solomon in all his [c]magnificence (excellence, dignity and grace) was not arrayed like one of these. [I Kings 10:4-7.]

30But if God so clothes the grass of the field, which today is alive *and* green and tomorrow is tossed into the furnace, will He not much more surely clothe you, O you men with little faith?

31Therefore do not worry *and* be anxious, saying, What are we going to have to eat? or, What are we going to have to drink? or, What are we going to have to wear?

32For the Gentiles (heathen) wish for *and* crave *and* diligently seek after all these things; and your heavenly Father well knows that you need them all.

33But seek for ([d]aim at and strive after) first of all His kingdom, and His righteousness [[e]His way of doing and being right], and then all these things [f]taken together will be given you besides.

34So do not worry *or* be anxious about tomorrow, for tomorrow will have worries *and* anxieties of its own. Sufficient for each day is its own trouble.

7 DO NOT judge *and* criticize *and* condemn others, so that you may not be judged *and* criticized *and* condemned yourselves.

2For just as you judge *and* criticize *and* condemn others you will be judged *and* criticized *and* condemned, and in accordance with the measure you deal out to others it will be dealt out again to you.

3Why do you [g]stare from without at the [h]very small particle that is in your brother's eye, but do not become aware of *and* consider the beam [i]of timber that is in your own eye?

4Or how can you say to your brother, Let me get the tiny particle out of your eye, when there is the beam [j]of timber in your own eye?

5You hypocrite, first get the beam of timber out of your own eye, and then you will see clearly to take the tiny particle out of your brother's eye.

6Do not give that which is holy—the sacred thing—to the dogs; and do not throw your pearls before hogs, lest they trample upon them with their feet and turn *and* tear you in pieces.

7 [k]Keep on asking and it will be given you; [l]keep on seeking and you will find; [m]keep on knocking [reverently] and the door will be opened to you.

8For every one who keeps on asking receives, and he who keeps on seeking finds, and to him who keeps on knocking it will be opened.

9Or what man is there of you, if his son asks him for a loaf of bread, will hand him a stone?

10Or if he asks for a fish, will hand him a serpent?

11If you then, evil as you are, know how to give good *and* [n]advantageous gifts to your children, how much more will your Father Who is in heaven [perfect as He is] give good *and* [o]advantageous things to those who [p]keep on asking Him!

12So then whatever you desire that others would do to *and* for you, even so do you also to *and* for them, for this is [sums up] the Law and the prophets.

13Enter through the narrow gate, for wide is the gate and spacious *and* broad is the way that leads away to destruction, and many are those who are entering it.

14But the gate is narrow—contracted [q]by pressure—and the way is straitened *and* compressed that leads away to life, and few are they who find it. [Jer. 21:8; Deut. 30:19.]

## New American Standard

26"Look at the birds of the air, that they do not sow, neither do
they reap, nor gather into barns, and *yet* your heavenly Father
feeds them. Are you not worth much more than they?
27"And which of you by being anxious can add a *single* cubit to
his life's span?
28"And why are you anxious about clothing? Observe how the
lilies of the field grow; they do not toil nor do they spin,
29yet I say to you that even Solomon in all his glory did not
clothe himself like one of these.
30"But if God so arrays the grass of the field, which is *alive* today
and tomorrow is thrown into the furnace, *will He* not much more
*do so for* you, O men of little faith?
31"Do not be anxious then, saying, 'What shall we eat?' or
'What shall we drink?' or 'With what shall we clothe ourselves?'
32"For all these things the Gentiles eagerly seek; for your heavenly Father knows that you need all these things.
33"But seek first His kingdom and His righteousness; and all
these things shall be added to you.
34"Therefore do not be anxious for tomorrow; for tomorrow will
care for itself. *Each* day has enough trouble of its own.

*Concerning Judging Others*

**7** "DO NOT judge lest you be judged.
2"For in the way you judge, you will be judged; and by your
standard of measure, it will be measured to you.
3"And why do you look at the speck that is in your brother's
eye, but do not notice the log that is in your own eye?
4"Or how can you say to your brother, 'Let me take the speck
out of your eye,' and behold, the log is in your own eye?
5"You hypocrite, first take the log out of your own eye, and
then you will see clearly to take the speck out of your brother's eye.
6¶ "Do not give what is holy to dogs, and do not throw your
pearls before swine, lest they trample them under their feet, and
turn and tear you to pieces.

*Encouragement to Pray*

7¶ "Ask, and it shall be given to you; seek, and you shall find;
knock, and it shall be opened to you.
8"For everyone who asks receives, and he who seeks finds,
and to him who knocks it shall be opened.
9"Or what man is there among you, when his son shall ask him
for a loaf, will give him a stone?
10"Or if he shall ask for a fish, he will not give him a snake, will
he?
11"If you then, being evil, know how to give good gifts to your
children, how much more shall your Father who is in heaven give
what is good to those who ask Him!
12"Therefore, however you want people to treat you, so treat
them, for this is the Law and the Prophets.

*Ways Contrasted*

*Fruits Contrasted*

13¶ "Enter by the narrow gate; for the gate is wide, and the way
is broad that leads to destruction, and many are those who enter
by it.
14"For the gate is small, and the way is narrow that leads to life,
and few are those who find it.

## New International

store away in barns, and yet your heavenly Father feeds them. Are
you not much more valuable than they? 27Who of you by worrying
can add a single hour to his life[r] ?
28"And why do you worry about clothes? See how the lilies of
the field grow. They do not labor or spin. 29Yet I tell you that not
even Solomon in all his splendor was dressed like one of these. 30If
that is how God clothes the grass of the field, which is here today
and tomorrow is thrown into the fire, will he not much more clothe
you, O you of little faith? 31So do not worry, saying, 'What shall
we eat?' or 'What shall we drink?' or 'What shall we wear?' 32For
the pagans run after all these things, and your heavenly Father
knows that you need them. 33But seek first his kingdom and his
righteousness, and all these things will be given to you as well.
34Therefore do not worry about tomorrow, for tomorrow will worry about itself. Each day has enough trouble of its own.

*Judging Others*

**7** "DO NOT judge, or you too will be judged. 2For in the same
way you judge others, you will be judged, and with the
measure you use, it will be measured to you.
3"Why do you look at the speck of sawdust in your brother's
eye and pay no attention to the plank in your own eye? 4How can
you say to your brother, 'Let me take the speck out of your eye,'
when all the time there is a plank in your own eye? 5You hypocrite,
first take the plank out of your own eye, and then you will see
clearly to remove the speck from your brother's eye.
6"Do not give dogs what is sacred; do not throw your pearls to
pigs. If you do, they may trample them under their feet, and then
turn and tear you to pieces.

*Ask, Seek, Knock*

7"Ask and it will be given to you; seek and you will find; knock
and the door will be opened to you. 8For everyone who asks
receives; he who seeks finds; and to him who knocks, the door will
be opened.
9"Which of you, if his son asks for bread, will give him a stone?
10Or if he asks for a fish, will give him a snake? 11If you, then,
though you are evil, know how to give good gifts to your children,
how much more will your Father in heaven give good gifts to those
who ask him! 12So in everything, do to others what you would
have them do to you, for this sums up the Law and the Prophets.

*The Narrow and Wide Gates*

13"Enter through the narrow gate. For wide is the gate and
broad is the road that leads to destruction, and many enter through
it. 14But small is the gate and narrow the road that leads to life, and
only a few find it.

NIV [r] 27 Or *single cubit to his height*

## King James

15¶ Beware of false prophets, which come to you in sheep's clothing, but inwardly they are ravening wolves.

16Ye shall know them by their fruits. Do men gather grapes of thorns, or figs of thistles?

17Even so every good tree bringeth forth good fruit; but a corrupt tree bringeth forth evil fruit.

18A good tree cannot bring forth evil fruit, neither *can* a corrupt tree bring forth good fruit.

19Every tree that bringeth not forth good fruit is hewn down, and cast into the fire.

20Wherefore by their fruits ye shall know them.

21¶ Not every one that saith unto me, Lord, Lord, shall enter into the kingdom of heaven; but he that doeth the will of my Father which is in heaven.

22Many will say to me in that day, Lord, Lord, have we not prophesied in thy name? and in thy name have cast out devils? and in thy name done many wonderful works?

23And then will I profess unto them, I never knew you: depart from me, ye that work iniquity.

24¶ Therefore whosoever heareth these sayings of mine, and doeth them, I will liken him unto a wise man, which built his house upon a rock:

25And the rain descended, and the floods came, and the winds blew, and beat upon that house; and it fell not: for it was founded upon a rock.

26And every one that heareth these sayings of mine, and doeth them not, shall be likened unto a foolish man, which built his house upon the sand:

27And the rain descended, and the floods came, and the winds blew, and beat upon that house; and it fell: and great was the fall of it.

28And it came to pass, when Jesus had ended these sayings, the people were astonished at his doctrine:

29For he taught them as *one* having authority, and not as the scribes.

## Amplified

15Beware of false prophets, who come to you dressed as sheep, but inside they are devouring wolves. [Ezek. 22:27.]

16You will [a]fully recognize them by their fruits. Do people pick grapes from thorns, or figs from thistles?

17Even so every healthy (sound) tree bears good fruit— [b]worthy of admiration; but the sickly (decaying, worthless) tree bears bad *and* worthless fruit.

18A good (healthy) tree cannot bear bad (worthless) fruit; nor can a bad (diseased) tree bear [c]excellent fruit—worthy of admiration.

19Every tree that does not bear good fruit is cut down and cast into the fire.

20Therefore you will [d]fully know them by their fruits.

21Not every one who says to Me, Lord, Lord, will enter the kingdom of heaven, but he who does the will of My Father Who is in heaven.

22Many will say to Me on that day, Lord, Lord, have we not prophesied in Your name, and driven out demons in Your name, and done many mighty works in Your name?

23And then I will say to them openly (publicly), I never knew you; depart from Me, you who act wickedly—disregarding My commands. [Ps. 6:8.]

24So every one who hears these words of Mine and acts upon them—obeying them—will be like a [e]sensible (prudent, practical, wise) man who built his house upon the rock;

25And the rain fell and the floods came, and the winds blew and beat against that house, but it did not fall, because it had been founded on the rock.

26And every one who hears these words of Mine and does not do them will be like a stupid (foolish) man who built his house upon the sand;

27And the rain fell, and the floods came, and the winds blew and beat against that house, and it fell; and great *and* complete was the fall of it.

28When Jesus had finished these sayings [the Sermon on the Mount], the crowds were astonished *and* overwhelmed with bewildered wonder at His teaching,

29For He was teaching as [One] Who had [and was] authority, and not as did the scribes.

## King James

8 WHEN HE was come down from the mountain, great multitudes followed him.

2And, behold, there came a leper and worshipped him, saying, Lord, if thou wilt, thou canst make me clean.

3And Jesus put forth *his* hand, and touched him, saying, I will; be thou clean. And immediately his leprosy was cleansed.

4And Jesus saith unto him, See thou tell no man; but go thy way, show thyself to the priest, and offer the gift that Moses commanded, for a testimony unto them.

5¶ And when Jesus was entered into Capernaum, there came unto him a centurion, beseeching him,

6And saying, Lord, my servant lieth at home sick of the palsy, grievously tormented.

7And Jesus saith unto him, I will come and heal him.

8The centurion answered and said, Lord, I am not worthy that thou shouldest come under my roof: but speak the word only, and my servant shall be healed.

9For I am a man under authority, having soldiers under me: and I say to this *man*, Go, and he goeth; and to another, Come, and he cometh; and to my servant, Do this, and he doeth *it*.

## Amplified

8 WHEN JESUS came down from the mountain, great throngs followed Him.

2And behold, a leper came up to Him and prostrating himself, worshipped Him, saying, Lord, if You will, You are able to [f]cleanse me by curing me.

3And He reached out His hand and touched him, saying, I will; be cleansed [g]by being cured. And instantly his leprosy was cured *and* cleansed.

4And Jesus said to him, See that you tell nothing about this to any one; but go, show yourself to the priest, and present the offering that Moses commanded, for a testimony [to your healing] *and* as an evidence to the people. [Lev. 14:2.]

5As Jesus went into Capernaum, a centurion came up to Him, begging Him

6And saying, Lord, my servant boy is lying at the house paralyzed *and* [h]distressed with intense pains.

7And Jesus said to him, I will come and restore him.

8But the centurion replied to Him, Lord, I am not worthy *or* fit to have You come under my roof; but only speak the word, and my servant boy will be cured.

9For I also am a man subject to authority, with soldiers subject to me; and I say to one, Go, and he goes; and to another, Come, and he comes; and to my slave, Do this, and he does it.

**AMP** [a] Vincent. [b] Cremer. [c] Cremer. [d] Vincent. [e] Abbott-Smith. [f] Thayer. [g] Thayer. [h] Thayer.

## New American Standard

15¶ "Beware of the false prophets, who come to you in sheep's clothing, but inwardly are ravenous wolves.

16"You will know them by their fruits. Grapes are not gathered from thorn *bushes,* nor figs from thistles, are they?

17"Even so, every good tree bears good fruit; but the bad tree bears bad fruit.

18"A good tree cannot produce bad fruit, nor can a bad tree produce good fruit.

19"Every tree that does not bear good fruit is cut down and thrown into the fire.

20"So then, you will know them by their fruits.

21"Not everyone who says to Me, 'Lord, Lord,' will enter the kingdom of heaven; but he who does the will of My Father who is in heaven.

22"Many will say to Me on that day, 'Lord, Lord, did we not prophesy in Your name, and in Your name cast out demons, and in Your name perform many miracles?'

23"And then I will declare to them, 'I never knew you; DEPART FROM ME, YOU WHO PRACTICE LAWLESSNESS.'

*The Two Foundations*

24¶ "Therefore everyone who hears these words of Mine, and acts upon them, may be compared to a wise man, who built his house upon the rock.

25"And the rain descended, and the floods came, and the winds blew, and burst against that house; and *yet* it did not fall, for it had been founded upon the rock.

26"And everyone who hears these words of Mine, and does not act upon them, will be like a foolish man, who built his house upon the sand.

27"And the rain descended, and the floods came, and the winds blew, and burst against that house; and it fell, and great was its fall."

28¶ The result was that when Jesus had finished these words, the multitudes were amazed at His teaching;

29for He was teaching them as *one* having authority, and not as their scribes.

*Jesus Cleanses a Leper*
*The Centurion's Faith*

**8** AND WHEN He had come down from the mountain, great multitudes followed Him.

2And behold, a leper came to Him, and bowed down to Him, saying, "Lord, if You are willing, You can make me clean."

3And He stretched out His hand and touched him, saying, "I am willing; be cleansed." And immediately his leprosy was cleansed.

4And Jesus *said to him, "See that you tell no one; but go, show yourself to the priest, and present the offering that Moses commanded, for a testimony to them."

5¶ And when He had entered Capernaum, a centurion came to Him, entreating Him,

6and saying, "Lord, my servant is lying paralyzed at home, suffering great pain."

7And He *said to him, "I will come and heal him."

8But the centurion answered and said, "Lord, I am not worthy for You to come under my roof, but just say the word, and my servant will be healed.

9"For I, too, am a man under authority, with soldiers under me; and I say to this one, 'Go!' and he goes, and to another, 'Come!' and he comes, and to my slave, 'Do this!' and he does *it.*"

## New International

*A Tree and Its Fruit*

15"Watch out for false prophets. They come to you in sheep's
clothing, but inwardly they are ferocious wolves. 16By their fruit
you will recognize them. Do people pick grapes from thornbushes,
or figs from thistles? 17Likewise every good tree bears good fruit,
but a bad tree bears bad fruit. 18A good tree cannot bear bad fruit,
and a bad tree cannot bear good fruit. 19Every tree that does not
bear good fruit is cut down and thrown into the fire. 20Thus, by
their fruit you will recognize them.

21"Not everyone who says to me, 'Lord, Lord,' will enter the
kingdom of heaven, but only he who does the will of my Father
who is in heaven. 22Many will say to me on that day, 'Lord, Lord,
did we not prophesy in your name, and in your name drive out
demons and perform many miracles?' 23Then I will tell them plainly, 'I never knew you. Away from me, you evildoers!'

*The Wise and Foolish Builders*

24"Therefore everyone who hears these words of mine and puts
them into practice is like a wise man who built his house on the
rock. 25The rain came down, the streams rose, and the winds blew
and beat against that house; yet it did not fall, because it had its
foundation on the rock. 26But everyone who hears these words of
mine and does not put them into practice is like a foolish man who
built his house on sand. 27The rain came down, the streams rose,
and the winds blew and beat against that house, and it fell with
a great crash."

28When Jesus had finished saying these things, the crowds
were amazed at his teaching, 29because he taught as one who had
authority, and not as their teachers of the law.

*The Man With Leprosy*

**8** WHEN HE came down from the mountainside, large crowds
followed him. 2A man with leprosy[i] came and knelt before
him and said, "Lord, if you are willing, you can make me clean."
3Jesus reached out his hand and touched the man. "I am willing," he said. "Be clean!" Immediately he was cured[j] of his leprosy. 4Then Jesus said to him, "See that you don't tell anyone. But
go, show yourself to the priest and offer the gift Moses commanded, as a testimony to them."

*The Faith of the Centurion*

5When Jesus had entered Capernaum, a centurion came to him,
asking for help. 6"Lord," he said, "my servant lies at home paralyzed and in terrible suffering."

7Jesus said to him, "I will go and heal him."

8The centurion replied, "Lord, I do not deserve to have you
come under my roof. But just say the word, and my servant will
be healed. 9For I myself am a man under authority, with soldiers
under me. I tell this one, 'Go,' and he goes; and that one, 'Come,'
and he comes. I say to my servant, 'Do this,' and he does it."

NIV [i] 2 The Greek word was used for various diseases affecting the skin—not necessarily leprosy. [j] 3 Greek *made clean*

## King James

10When Jesus heard *it,* he marvelled, and said to them that followed, Verily I say unto you, I have not found so great faith, no, not in Israel.

11And I say unto you, That many shall come from the east and west, and shall sit down with Abraham, and Isaac, and Jacob, in the kingdom of heaven.

12But the children of the kingdom shall be cast out into outer darkness: there shall be weeping and gnashing of teeth.

13And Jesus said unto the centurion, Go thy way; and as thou hast believed, *so* be it done unto thee. And his servant was healed in the selfsame hour.

14¶ And when Jesus was come into Peter's house, he saw his wife's mother laid, and sick of a fever.

15And he touched her hand, and the fever left her: and she arose, and ministered unto them.

16¶ When the even was come, they brought unto him many that were possessed with devils: and he cast out the spirits with *his* word, and healed all that were sick:

17That it might be fulfilled which was spoken by Esaias the prophet, saying, Himself took our infirmities, and bare *our* sicknesses.

18¶ Now when Jesus saw great multitudes about him, he gave commandment to depart unto the other side.

19And a certain scribe came, and said unto him, Master, I will follow thee whithersoever thou goest.

20And Jesus saith unto him, The foxes have holes, and the birds of the air *have* nests; but the Son of man hath not where to lay *his* head.

21And another of his disciples said unto him, Lord, suffer me first to go and bury my father.

22But Jesus said unto him, Follow me; and let the dead bury their dead.

23¶ And when he was entered into a ship, his disciples followed him.

24And, behold, there arose a great tempest in the sea, insomuch that the ship was covered with the waves: but he was asleep.

25And his disciples came to *him,* and awoke him, saying, Lord, save us: we perish.

26And he saith unto them, Why are ye fearful, O ye of little faith? Then he arose, and rebuked the winds and the sea; and there was a great calm.

27But the men marvelled, saying, What manner of man is this, that even the winds and the sea obey him!

28¶ And when he was come to the other side into the country of the Gergesenes, there met him two possessed with devils, coming out of the tombs, exceeding fierce, so that no man might pass by that way.

29And, behold, they cried out, saying, What have we to do with thee, Jesus, thou Son of God? art thou come hither to torment us before the time?

30And there was a good way off from them an herd of many swine feeding.

31So the devils besought him, saying, If thou cast us out, suffer us to go away into the herd of swine.

32And he said unto them, Go. And when they were come out, they went into the herd of swine: and, behold, the whole herd of swine ran violently down a steep place into the sea, and perished in the waters.

33And they that kept them fled, and went their ways into the city, and told every thing, and what was befallen to the possessed of the devils.

34And, behold, the whole city came out to meet Jesus: and when they saw him, they besought *him* that he would depart out of their coasts.

## Amplified

10When Jesus heard him, He marveled, and said to those who followed Him [that is, [a]who adhered steadfastly to Him, conforming to His example in living and if need be in dying also], I tell you, truly I have not found so much faith as this [b]with any one, even in Israel.

11I tell you, many will come from east and west and sit at table with Abraham, Isaac, and Jacob in the kingdom of heaven,

12While the sons *and* heirs of the kingdom will be driven out into the darkness outside, where there will be weeping and grinding of teeth. [Isa. 49:12; 59:19; Mal. 1:11; Ps. 107:2, 3.]

13Then to the centurion Jesus said, Go; it shall be done for you as you have believed. And the servant boy was restored to health at that very [c]moment.

14And when Jesus went into Peter's house, He saw his mother-in-law lying ill with a fever;

15He touched her hand and the fever left her, and she got up and began waiting on Him.

16When evening came they brought to Him many who were [d]under the power of demons, and He drove out the spirits with a word, and restored to health all who were sick;

17And thus He fulfilled what was spoken by the prophet Isaiah, He Himself took ( [e]in order to carry away) our weaknesses *and* infirmities and bore [f]away our diseases. [Isa. 53:4.]

18Now Jesus, when He saw great throngs around Him, gave orders to cross to the other side [of the lake].

19And a scribe came up and said to Him, Master, I will accompany You wherever You go.

20And Jesus replied to him, Foxes have holes, and the birds of the air have lodging places; but the Son of man has nowhere to lay His head.

21Another of the disciples said to Him, Lord, let me first go and bury [ [g]care for till death] my father.

22But Jesus said to him, Follow Me, and leave the dead [ [h]in sin] to bury their own dead.

23And after He got into the boat, His disciples followed Him.

24And [i]suddenly, behold, there arose a violent storm on the sea, so that the boat was being covered up by the waves; but He was sleeping.

25And they went and awakened Him, saying, Lord, rescue *and* preserve us! We are perishing!

26And He said to them, Why are you timid *and* afraid, O you of little faith? Then He got up and rebuked the winds and the sea, and there was a great *and* wonderful calm ( [j]a perfect peaceableness).

27And the men were stunned with bewildered wonder *and* marveled, saying, What kind of Man is this, that even the winds and the sea obey Him!

28And when He arrived at the other side, at the country of the Gadarenes, two men under the control of demons went to meet Him, coming out of the tombs, so fierce *and* savage that no one was able to pass that way.

29And behold, they shrieked *and* screamed, What have You to do with us, *Jesus,* Son of God? Have You come to torment us before the appointed time? [Judg. 11:12; II Sam. 16:10.]

30Now at some distance from there a drove of many hogs was grazing.

31And the demons begged Him, If You drive us out, send us into the drove of hogs.

32And He said to them, Begone! So they came out and went into the hogs; and behold, the whole drove rushed down the steep bank into the sea, and died in the water.

33The herdsmen fled, and went into the town and reported everything, including what had happened to the men under the power of demons.

34And behold, the whole town went out to meet Jesus, and as soon as they saw Him, they begged Him to depart from their locality.

**AMP** [a] Thayer. [b] Alternate reading. [c] Moulton and Milligan. [d] Thayer. [e] Thayer. [f] Abbott-Smith. Berry. Souter. Thayer. Hickie. (Greek-English lexicons to the New Testament.) [g] Most commentators. [h] Barnes. [i] Vincent. [j] Wycliffe.

## New American Standard

10 Now when Jesus heard *this,* He marveled, and said to those who were following, "Truly I say to you, I have not found such great faith with anyone in Israel.

11 "And I say to you, that many shall come from east and west, and [k]recline *at the table* with Abraham, and Isaac, and Jacob, in the kingdom of heaven;

12 but the sons of the kingdom shall be cast out into the outer darkness; in that place there shall be weeping and gnashing of teeth."

13 And Jesus said to the centurion, "Go your way; let it be done to you as you have believed." And the servant was healed that *very* hour.

*Peter's Mother-in-law Healed*
*Many Healed*

14¶ And when Jesus had come to Peter's home, He saw his mother-in-law lying sick in bed with a fever.

15 And He touched her hand, and the fever left her; and she arose, and waited on Him.

16 And when evening had come, they brought to Him many who were demon-possessed; and He cast out the spirits with a word, and healed all who were ill

17 in order that what was spoken through Isaiah the prophet might be fulfilled, saying, "HE HIMSELF TOOK OUR INFIRMITIES, AND CARRIED AWAY OUR DISEASES."

*Discipleship Tested*

18¶ Now when Jesus saw a crowd around Him, He gave orders to depart to the other side.

19 And a certain scribe came and said to Him, "Teacher, I will follow You wherever You go."

20 And Jesus *said to him, "The foxes have holes, and the birds of the air *have* nests; but the Son of Man has nowhere to lay His head."

21 And another of the disciples said to Him, "Lord, permit me first to go and bury my father."

22 But Jesus *said to him, "Follow Me; and allow the dead to bury their own dead."

23¶ And when He got into the boat, His disciples followed Him.

24 And behold, there arose a great storm in the sea, so that the boat was covered with the waves; but He Himself was asleep.

25 And they came to *Him,* and awoke Him, saying, "Save *us,* Lord; we are perishing!"

26 And He *said to them, "Why are you timid, you men of little faith?" Then He arose, and rebuked the winds and the sea; and it became perfectly calm.

27 And the men marveled, saying, "What kind of a man is this, that even the winds and the sea obey Him?"

*Jesus Casts Out Demons*

28¶ And when He had come to the other side into the country of the Gadarenes, two men who were demon-possessed met Him as they were coming out of the tombs; *they were* so exceedingly violent that no one could pass by that road.

29 And behold, they cried out, saying, "What do we have to do with You, Son of God? Have You come here to torment us before the time?"

30 Now there was at a distance from them a herd of many swine feeding.

31 And the demons *began* to entreat Him, saying, "If You are *going to* cast us out, send us into the herd of swine."

32 And He said to them, "Begone!" And they came out, and went into the swine, and behold, the whole herd rushed down the steep bank into the sea and perished in the waters.

33 And the herdsmen ran away, and went to the city, and reported everything, including the *incident* of the demoniacs.

34 And behold, the whole city came out to meet Jesus; and when they saw Him, they entreated *Him* to depart from their region.

NAS [k] Or, *dine*

## New International

10 When Jesus heard this, he was astonished and said to those
following him, "I tell you the truth, I have not found anyone in
Israel with such great faith. 11 I say to you that many will come from
the east and the west, and will take their places at the feast with
Abraham, Isaac and Jacob in the kingdom of heaven. 12 But the
subjects of the kingdom will be thrown outside, into the darkness,
where there will be weeping and gnashing of teeth."
13 Then Jesus said to the centurion, "Go! It will be done just as
you believed it would." And his servant was healed at that very
hour.

*Jesus Heals Many*

14 When Jesus came into Peter's house, he saw Peter's mother-
in-law lying in bed with a fever. 15 He touched her hand and the
fever left her, and she got up and began to wait on him.
16 When evening came, many who were demon-possessed were
brought to him, and he drove out the spirits with a word and
healed all the sick. 17 This was to fulfill what was spoken through
the prophet Isaiah:

"He took up our infirmities
and carried our diseases."[l]

*The Cost of Following Jesus*

18 When Jesus saw the crowd around him, he gave orders to
cross to the other side of the lake. 19 Then a teacher of the law came
to him and said, "Teacher, I will follow you wherever you go."
20 Jesus replied, "Foxes have holes and birds of the air have
nests, but the Son of Man has no place to lay his head."
21 Another disciple said to him, "Lord, first let me go and bury
my father."
22 But Jesus told him, "Follow me, and let the dead bury their
own dead."

*Jesus Calms the Storm*

23 Then he got into the boat and his disciples followed him.
24 Without warning, a furious storm came up on the lake, so that
the waves swept over the boat. But Jesus was sleeping. 25 The
disciples went and woke him, saying, "Lord, save us! We're going
to drown!"
26 He replied, "You of little faith, why are you so afraid?" Then
he got up and rebuked the winds and the waves, and it was
completely calm.
27 The men were amazed and asked, "What kind of man is this?
Even the winds and the waves obey him!"

*The Healing of Two Demon-possessed Men*

28 When he arrived at the other side in the region of the Gadarenes,[m] two demon-possessed men coming from the tombs met
him. They were so violent that no one could pass that way.
29 "What do you want with us, Son of God?" they shouted. "Have
you come here to torture us before the appointed time?"
30 Some distance from them a large herd of pigs was feeding.
31 The demons begged Jesus, "If you drive us out, send us into the
herd of pigs."
32 He said to them, "Go!" So they came out and went into the
pigs, and the whole herd rushed down the steep bank into the lake
and died in the water. 33 Those tending the pigs ran off, went into
the town and reported all this, including what had happened to
the demon-possessed men. 34 Then the whole town went out to
meet Jesus. And when they saw him, they pleaded with him to
leave their region.

NIV [l] *17* Isaiah 53:4 [m] *28* Some manuscripts *Gergesenes;* others *Gerasenes*

## King James

9 AND HE entered into a ship, and passed over, and came into his own city.

2And, behold, they brought to him a man sick of the palsy, lying on a bed: and Jesus seeing their faith said unto the sick of the palsy; Son, be of good cheer; thy sins be forgiven thee.

3And, behold, certain of the scribes said within themselves, This *man* blasphemeth.

4And Jesus knowing their thoughts said, Wherefore think ye evil in your hearts?

5For whether is easier, to say, *Thy* sins be forgiven thee; or to say, Arise, and walk?

6But that ye may know that the Son of man hath power on earth to forgive sins, (then saith he to the sick of the palsy,) Arise, take up thy bed, and go unto thine house.

7And he arose, and departed to his house.

8But when the multitudes saw *it*, they marvelled, and glorified God, which had given such power unto men.

9¶ And as Jesus passed forth from thence, he saw a man, named Matthew, sitting at the receipt of custom: and he saith unto him, Follow me. And he arose, and followed him.

10¶ And it came to pass, as Jesus sat at meat in the house, behold, many publicans and sinners came and sat down with him and his disciples.

11And when the Pharisees saw *it*, they said unto his disciples, Why eateth your Master with publicans and sinners?

12But when Jesus heard *that*, he said unto them, They that be whole need not a physician, but they that are sick.

13But go ye and learn what *that* meaneth, I will have mercy, and not sacrifice: for I am not come to call the righteous, but sinners to repentance.

14¶ Then came to him the disciples of John, saying, Why do we and the Pharisees fast oft, but thy disciples fast not?

15And Jesus said unto them, Can the children of the bridechamber mourn, as long as the bridegroom is with them? but the days will come, when the bridegroom shall be taken from them, and then shall they fast.

16No man putteth a piece of new cloth unto an old garment, for that which is put in to fill it up taketh from the garment, and the rent is made worse.

17Neither do men put new wine into old bottles: else the bottles break, and the wine runneth out, and the bottles perish: but they put new wine into new bottles, and both are preserved.

18¶ While he spake these things unto them, behold, there came a certain ruler, and worshipped him, saying, My daughter is even now dead: but come and lay thy hand upon her, and she shall live.

19And Jesus arose, and followed him, and *so did* his disciples.

20¶ And, behold, a woman, which was diseased with an issue of blood twelve years, came behind *him*, and touched the hem of his garment:

21For she said within herself, If I may but touch his garment, I shall be whole.

22But Jesus turned him about, and when he saw her, he said, Daughter, be of good comfort; thy faith hath made thee whole. And the woman was made whole from that hour.

23And when Jesus came into the ruler's house, and saw the minstrels and the people making a noise,

24He said unto them, Give place: for the maid is not dead, but sleepeth. And they laughed him to scorn.

## Amplified

9 AND JESUS getting into a boat crossed to the other side and came to His own town [Capernaum].

2And behold, they brought to Him a man paralyzed *and* prostrated by illness, lying on a sleeping pad, and when Jesus saw their faith He said to the paralyzed man, Take courage, son; your sins are forgiven *and* the [a]penalty remitted.

3And behold, some of the scribes said to themselves, This man blasphemes—He claims the rights and prerogatives of God!

4But Jesus, knowing ( [b]seeing) their thoughts, said, Why do you think evil *and* harbor [c]malice in your hearts?

5For which is easier, to say, Your sins are forgiven *and* the [d]penalty remitted, or say, Get up and walk?

6And in order that you may know that the Son of man has authority on earth to forgive sins *and* [e]remit the penalty, He then said to the paralyzed man, Get up! Pick up your sleeping pad and go to your own house.

7And he got up and went away to his own house.

8When the crowds saw it, they were struck with fear *and* awe, and they [f]recognized God *and* praised *and* thanked Him, Who had given such power *and* authority to men.

9As Jesus passed on from there, He saw a man named Matthew sitting at the tax collector's office; and He said to him, [g]Be My disciple—side with My party and follow Me. And he rose and followed Him.

10And as Jesus reclined at table in the house, behold, many tax collectors and especially wicked sinners came and sat (reclined) with Him and His disciples.

11And when the Pharisees saw this, they said to His disciples, Why does your Master eat with tax collectors and those pre-eminently sinful?

12But when Jesus heard it, He replied, Those who are strong *and* well have no need of a physician, but those who are weak *and* sick.

13Go and learn what this means, I desire mercy [that is, [h]readiness to help those in trouble] and not sacrifice *and* sacrificial victims. For I came not to call *and* invite [to repentance] the righteous—those who are upright and in right standing with God; but sinners—the erring ones *and* all those not free from sin. [Hos. 6:6.]

14Then the disciples of John came to Jesus, inquiring, Why is it that we and the Pharisees fast [i] *often*, [that is, abstain from food and drink, as a religious exercise], but Your disciples do not fast?

15And Jesus replied to them, Can the wedding guests mourn while the bridegroom is still with them? The days will come when the bridegroom is taken away from them, and then they will fast.

16And no one puts a piece of cloth that has not been shrunk on an old garment, for such a patch tears away from the garment and a worse rent is made.

17Neither is new wine put in old wineskins, for if it is, the skins burst and are [j]torn in pieces, and the wine is spilled and the skins ruined; but new wine is put into fresh wineskins, and so both are preserved.

18While He was talking this way to them, behold, a ruler entered and kneeling down, worshipped Him, saying, My daughter has just [k]now died; but come and lay Your hand on her and she will come to life.

19And Jesus got up and accompanied him, with His disciples.

20And behold, a woman who had suffered from a flow of blood for twelve years came up behind Him and touched the fringe of His garment; [Num. 15:38; Deut. 22:12.]

21For she kept saying to herself, If I only touch His garment, I shall be restored to health.

22Jesus turned around and seeing her He said, Take courage, daughter! Your faith has made you well. And at once the woman was restored to health.

23And when Jesus came to the ruler's house and saw the flute players, and the crowd making an uproar *and* din,

24He said, Go away; for the girl is not dead but sleeping. And they laughed *and* jeered at Him.

**AMP** [a] Thayer. [b] Many ancient authorities so read. [c] Thayer. [d] Thayer. [e] Thayer. [f] Cremer. [g] Thayer. [h] Thayer. [i] Many ancient authorities so read. [j] Thayer. [k] Vincent.

## New American Standard

*A Paralytic Cured*

9 AND GETTING into a boat, He crossed over, and came to His
own city.
2And behold, they were bringing to Him a paralytic, lying on
a bed; and Jesus seeing their faith said to the paralytic, "Take
courage, My son, your sins are forgiven."
3And behold, some of the scribes said to themselves, "This
*fellow* blasphemes."
4And Jesus knowing their thoughts said, "Why are you thinking evil in your hearts?
5"For which is easier, to say, 'Your sins are forgiven,' or to say,
'Rise, and walk'?
6"But in order that you may know that the Son of Man has
authority on earth to forgive sins"—then He *said to the paralytic—"Rise, take up your bed, and go home."
7And he rose, and went home.
8But when the multitudes saw *this,* they were filled with awe,
and glorified God, who had given such authority to men.

*Matthew Called*

9¶ And as Jesus passed on from there, He saw a man, called
Matthew, sitting in the tax office; and He *said to him, "Follow
Me!" And he rose, and followed Him.
10¶ And it happened that as He was reclining *at the table* in the
house, behold many tax-gatherers and sinners came and were
dining with Jesus and His disciples.
11And when the Pharisees saw *this,* they said to His disciples,
"Why is your Teacher eating with the tax-gatherers and sinners?"
12But when He heard this, He said, "*It is* not those who are
healthy who need a physician, but those who are sick.
13"But go and learn what *this* means, 'I DESIRE COMPASSION,
[1]AND NOT SACRIFICE,' for I did not come to call the righteous, but
sinners."
14¶ Then the disciples of John *came to Him, saying, "Why do
we and the Pharisees fast, but Your disciples do not fast?"
15And Jesus said to them, "The attendants of the bridegroom
cannot mourn as long as the bridegroom is with them, can they?
But the days will come when the bridegroom is taken away from
them, and then they will fast.
16"But no one puts a patch of unshrunk cloth on an old garment; for the patch pulls away from the garment, and a worse tear
results.
17"Nor do *men* put new wine into old wineskins; otherwise the
wineskins burst, and the wine pours out, and the wineskins are
ruined; but they put new wine into fresh wineskins, and both are
preserved."

*Miracles of Healing*

18¶ While He was saying these things to them, behold, there
came a *synagogue* official, and bowed down before Him, saying,
"My daughter has just died; but come and lay Your hand on her,
and she will live."
19And Jesus rose and *began* to follow him, and *so did* His disciples.
20And behold, a woman who had been suffering from a hemorrhage for twelve years, came up behind Him and touched the
fringe of His cloak;
21for she was saying to herself, "If I only touch His garment,
I shall get well."
22But Jesus turning and seeing her said, "Daughter, take courage; your faith has made you well." And at once the woman was
made well.
23And when Jesus came into the official's house, and saw the
flute-players, and the crowd in noisy disorder,
24He *began* to say, "Depart; for the girl has not died, but is
asleep." And they *began* laughing at Him.

NAS [1] I.e., more than

## New International

*Jesus Heals a Paralytic*

9 JESUS STEPPED into a boat, crossed over and came to his
own town. 2Some men brought to him a paralytic, lying on
a mat. When Jesus saw their faith, he said to the paralytic, "Take
heart, son; your sins are forgiven."
3At this, some of the teachers of the law said to themselves,
"This fellow is blaspheming!"
4Knowing their thoughts, Jesus said, "Why do you entertain
evil thoughts in your hearts? 5Which is easier: to say, 'Your sins
are forgiven,' or to say, 'Get up and walk'? 6But so that you may
know that the Son of Man has authority on earth to forgive sins. . .
." Then he said to the paralytic, "Get up, take your mat and go
home." 7And the man got up and went home. 8When the crowd
saw this, they were filled with awe; and they praised God, who
had given such authority to men.

*The Calling of Matthew*

9As Jesus went on from there, he saw a man named Matthew
sitting at the tax collector's booth. "Follow me," he told him, and
Matthew got up and followed him.
10While Jesus was having dinner at Matthew's house, many tax
collectors and "sinners" came and ate with him and his disciples.
11When the Pharisees saw this, they asked his disciples, "Why
does your teacher eat with tax collectors and 'sinners'?"
12On hearing this, Jesus said, "It is not the healthy who need
a doctor, but the sick. 13But go and learn what this means: 'I desire
mercy, not sacrifice.'[m] For I have not come to call the righteous,
but sinners."

*Jesus Questioned About Fasting*

14Then John's disciples came and asked him, "How is it that we
and the Pharisees fast, but your disciples do not fast?"
15Jesus answered, "How can the guests of the bridegroom
mourn while he is with them? The time will come when the bridegroom will be taken from them; then they will fast.
16"No one sews a patch of unshrunk cloth on an old garment,
for the patch will pull away from the garment, making the tear
worse. 17Neither do men pour new wine into old wineskins. If
they do, the skins will burst, the wine will run out and the wineskins will be ruined. No, they pour new wine into new wineskins,
and both are preserved."

*A Dead Girl and a Sick Woman*

18While he was saying this, a ruler came and knelt before him
and said, "My daughter has just died. But come and put your hand
on her, and she will live." 19Jesus got up and went with him, and
so did his disciples.
20Just then a woman who had been subject to bleeding for
twelve years came up behind him and touched the edge of his
cloak. 21She said to herself, "If I only touch his cloak, I will be
healed."
22Jesus turned and saw her. "Take heart, daughter," he said,
"your faith has healed you." And the woman was healed from that
moment.
23When Jesus entered the ruler's house and saw the flute players and the noisy crowd, 24he said, "Go away. The girl is not dead
but asleep." But they laughed at him. 25After the crowd had been

NIV [m]*13* Hosea 6:6

## King James

25But when the people were put forth, he went in, and took her by the hand, and the maid arose.
26And the fame hereof went abroad into all that land.
27¶ And when Jesus departed thence, two blind men followed him, crying, and saying, *Thou* Son of David, have mercy on us.
28And when he was come into the house, the blind men came to him: and Jesus saith unto them, Believe ye that I am able to do this? They said unto him, Yea, Lord.
29Then touched he their eyes, saying, According to your faith be it unto you.
30And their eyes were opened; and Jesus straitly charged them, saying, See *that* no man know *it*.
31But they, when they were departed, spread abroad his fame in all that country.
32¶ As they went out, behold, they brought to him a dumb man possessed with a devil.
33And when the devil was cast out, the dumb spake: and the multitudes marvelled, saying, It was never so seen in Israel.
34But the Pharisees said, He casteth out devils through the prince of the devils.
35And Jesus went about all the cities and villages, teaching in their synagogues, and preaching the gospel of the kingdom, and healing every sickness and every disease among the people.
36¶ But when he saw the multitudes, he was moved with compassion on them, because they fainted, and were scattered abroad, as sheep having no shepherd.
37Then saith he unto his disciples, The harvest truly *is* plenteous, but the labourers *are* few;
38Pray ye therefore the Lord of the harvest, that he will send forth labourers into his harvest.

**10** AND WHEN he had called unto *him* his twelve disciples, he gave them power *against* unclean spirits, to cast them out, and to heal all manner of sickness and all manner of disease.
2Now the names of the twelve apostles are these; The first, Simon, who is called Peter, and Andrew his brother; James *the son* of Zebedee, and John his brother;
3Philip, and Bartholomew; Thomas, and Matthew the publican; James *the son* of Alphaeus, and Lebbaeus, whose surname was Thaddaeus;
4Simon the Canaanite, and Judas Iscariot, who also betrayed him.
5These twelve Jesus sent forth, and commanded them, saying, Go not into the way of the Gentiles, and into *any* city of the Samaritans enter ye not:
6But go rather to the lost sheep of the house of Israel.
7And as ye go, preach, saying, The kingdom of heaven is at hand.
8Heal the sick, cleanse the lepers, raise the dead, cast out devils: freely ye have received, freely give.
9Provide neither gold, nor silver, nor brass in your purses,
10Nor scrip for *your* journey, neither two coats, neither shoes, nor yet staves: for the workman is worthy of his meat.
11And into whatsoever city or town ye shall enter, inquire who in it is worthy; and there abide till ye go thence.
12And when ye come into an house, salute it.

## Amplified

25But when the crowd had been ordered to go outside, He went in and took her by the hand, and the girl arose.
26And the news about this spread through all that district.
27As Jesus was passing on from there, two blind men followed Him, shouting loudly, Have pity *and* mercy on us, Son of David!
28When He reached the house and went in, the blind men came to Him. And Jesus said to them, Do you believe that I am able to do this? They said to Him, Yes, Lord.
29Then He touched their eyes, saying, According to your faith *and* trust *and* reliance [on the power invested in Me] be it done to you.
30And their eyes were opened. And Jesus earnestly *and* sternly charged them, See that you let no one know about this.
31But they went off and blazed *and* spread His fame abroad throughout that whole district.
32And while they were going away, behold, a dumb man under the power of a demon was brought to Jesus.
33And when the demon had been driven out, the dumb man spoke; and the crowds were stunned with bewildered wonder, saying, Never before has anything like this been seen in Israel.
34But the Pharisees said, He drives out demons through *and* with the help of the prince of demons.
35And Jesus went about all the cities and villages, teaching in their synagogues and proclaiming the good news (the Gospel) of the kingdom, and curing all kinds of disease and every weakness *and* infirmity.
36When He saw the throngs, He was moved with pity *and* sympathy for them, because they were bewildered—harassed and distressed and dejected and helpless—like sheep without a shepherd. [Zech. 10:2.]
37Then He said to His disciples, The harvest is indeed plentiful, but the laborers are few.
38So pray the Lord of the harvest to [a]force out *and* thrust laborers into His harvest.

**10** AND JESUS summoned to Him His twelve disciples and gave them power *and* authority over unclean spirits, to drive them out, and to cure all kinds of disease and all kinds of weakness *and* infirmity.
2Now these are the names of the twelve apostles: first, Simon, who is called Peter, and Andrew his brother; James the son of Zebedee, and John his brother;
3Philip and Bartholomew [Nathaniel]; Thomas and Matthew the tax collector; James the son of Alphaeus, and Thaddaeus [Judas, not Iscariot];
4Simon the Cananaean, and Judas Iscariot, who also betrayed Him.
5Jesus sent out these twelve, charging them, Go nowhere among the Gentiles, and do not go into any town of the Samaritans,
6But go rather to the lost sheep of the house of Israel.
7And as you go, preach saying, The kingdom of heaven is at hand!
8Cure the sick; raise the dead; cleanse the lepers; drive out demons. Freely (without pay) you have received; freely (without charge) give.
9Take no gold, nor silver, nor [even] copper money in your purses (belts),
10And do not take a provision-bag *or* a [b]wallet for a collection-bag for your journey, nor two undergarments, nor sandals, nor a staff, for the workman deserves his support—his living, his food.
11And into whatever town or village you go, inquire who in it is deserving, and stay there [at his house] until you leave [that vicinity].
12As you go into the house, give your greetings *and* wish it well.

AMP [a] Vincent. [b] Moulton and Milligan.

## New American Standard

25But when the crowd had been put out, He entered and took
her by the hand; and the girl arose.
26And this news went out into all that land.
27¶ And as Jesus passed on from there, two blind men followed
Him, crying out, and saying, "Have mercy on us, Son of David!"
28And after He had come into the house, the blind men came
up to Him, and Jesus *said to them, "Do you believe that I am able
to do this?" They *said to Him, "Yes, Lord."
29Then He touched their eyes, saying, "Be it done to you according to your faith."
30And their eyes were opened. And Jesus sternly warned them,
saying, "See *here*, let no one know *about this*!"
31But they went out, and spread the news about Him in all that
land.
32¶ And as they were going out, behold, a dumb man, demon-
possessed, was brought to Him.
33And after the demon was cast out, the dumb man spoke; and
the multitudes marveled, saying, "Nothing like this was ever seen
in Israel."
34But the Pharisees were saying, "He casts out the demons by
the ruler of the demons."
35¶ And Jesus was going about all the cities and the villages,
teaching in their synagogues, and proclaiming the gospel of the
kingdom, and healing every kind of disease and every kind of
sickness.
36And seeing the multitudes, He felt compassion for them,
because they were distressed and downcast like sheep without a
shepherd.
37Then He *said to His disciples, "The harvest is plentiful, but
the workers are few.
38"Therefore beseech the Lord of the harvest to send out workers into His harvest."

*The Twelve Disciples*
*Instructions for Service*

10 AND HAVING summoned His twelve disciples, He gave
them authority over unclean spirits, to cast them out, and
to heal every kind of disease and every kind of sickness.
2¶ Now the names of the twelve apostles are these: The first,
Simon, who is called Peter, and Andrew his brother; and James the
*son* of Zebedee, and John his brother;
3Philip and Bartholomew; Thomas and Matthew the tax-gatherer; James the *son* of Alphaeus, and Thaddaeus;
4Simon the Zealot, and Judas Iscariot, the one who betrayed
Him.
5¶ These twelve Jesus sent out after instructing them, saying,
"Do not go in *the* way of *the* Gentiles, and do not enter *any* city of
the Samaritans;
6but rather go to the lost sheep of the house of Israel.
7"And as you go, preach, saying, 'The kingdom of heaven is
at hand.'
8"Heal *the* sick, raise *the* dead, cleanse *the* lepers, cast out
demons; freely you received, freely give.
9"Do not acquire gold, or silver, or copper for your money
belts,
10or a bag for *your* journey, or even two tunics, or sandals, or
a staff; for the worker is worthy of his support.
11"And into whatever city or village you enter, inquire who is
worthy in it; and abide there until you go away.
12"And as you enter the house, give it your greeting.

## New International

put outside, he went in and took the girl by the hand, and she got
up. 26News of this spread through all that region.

*Jesus Heals the Blind and Mute*

27As Jesus went on from there, two blind men followed him,
calling out, "Have mercy on us, Son of David!"
28When he had gone indoors, the blind men came to him, and
he asked them, "Do you believe that I am able to do this?"
"Yes, Lord," they replied.
29Then he touched their eyes and said, "According to your faith
will it be done to you"; 30and their sight was restored. Jesus
warned them sternly, "See that no one knows about this." 31But
they went out and spread the news about him all over that region.
32While they were going out, a man who was demon-possessed
and could not talk was brought to Jesus. 33And when the demon
was driven out, the man who had been mute spoke. The crowd
was amazed and said, "Nothing like this has ever been seen in
Israel."
34But the Pharisees said, "It is by the prince of demons that he
drives out demons."

*The Workers Are Few*

35Jesus went through all the towns and villages, teaching in
their synagogues, preaching the good news of the kingdom and
healing every disease and sickness. 36When he saw the crowds, he
had compassion on them, because they were harassed and helpless, like sheep without a shepherd. 37Then he said to his disciples,
"The harvest is plentiful but the workers are few. 38Ask the Lord
of the harvest, therefore, to send out workers into his harvest
field."

*Jesus Sends Out the Twelve*

10 HE CALLED his twelve disciples to him and gave them
authority to drive out evil[c] spirits and to heal every disease and sickness.
2These are the names of the twelve apostles: first, Simon (who
is called Peter) and his brother Andrew; James son of Zebedee, and
his brother John; 3Philip and Bartholomew; Thomas and Matthew
the tax collector; James son of Alphaeus, and Thaddaeus; 4Simon
the Zealot and Judas Iscariot, who betrayed him.
5These twelve Jesus sent out with the following instructions:
"Do not go among the Gentiles or enter any town of the Samaritans. 6Go rather to the lost sheep of Israel. 7As you go, preach this
message: 'The kingdom of heaven is near.' 8Heal the sick, raise the
dead, cleanse those who have leprosy,[d] drive out demons. Freely
you have received, freely give. 9Do not take along any gold or
silver or copper in your belts; 10take no bag for the journey, or extra
tunic, or sandals or a staff; for the worker is worth his keep.
11"Whatever town or village you enter, search for some worthy
person there and stay at his house until you leave. 12As you enter
the home, give it your greeting. 13If the home is deserving, let your

NIV [c] *1* Greek *unclean* [d] *8* The Greek word was used for various diseases
affecting the skin—not necessarily leprosy.

## King James

13And if the house be worthy, let your peace come upon it: but
if it be not worthy, let your peace return to you.
14And whosoever shall not receive you, nor hear your words,
when ye depart out of that house or city, shake off the dust of your
feet.
15Verily I say unto you, It shall be more tolerable for the land
of Sodom and Gomorrha in the day of judgment, than for that city.
16¶ Behold, I send you forth as sheep in the midst of wolves:
be ye therefore wise as serpents, and harmless as doves.
17But beware of men: for they will deliver you up to the councils, and they will scourge you in their synagogues;
18And ye shall be brought before governors and kings for my
sake, for a testimony against them and the Gentiles.
19But when they deliver you up, take no thought how or what
ye shall speak: for it shall be given you in that same hour what ye
shall speak.
20For it is not ye that speak, but the Spirit of your Father which
speaketh in you.
21And the brother shall deliver up the brother to death, and the
father the child: and the children shall rise up against *their* parents,
and cause them to be put to death.
22And ye shall be hated of all *men* for my name's sake: but he
that endureth to the end shall be saved.
23But when they persecute you in this city, flee ye into another:
for verily I say unto you, Ye shall not have gone over the cities of
Israel, till the Son of man be come.
24The disciple is not above *his* master, nor the servant above his
lord.
25It is enough for the disciple that he be as his master, and the
servant as his lord. If they have called the master of the house
Beelzebub, how much more *shall they call* them of his household?
26Fear them not therefore: for there is nothing covered, that
shall not be revealed; and hid, that shall not be known.
27What I tell you in darkness, *that* speak ye in light: and what
ye hear in the ear, *that* preach ye upon the housetops.
28And fear not them which kill the body, but are not able to kill
the soul: but rather fear him which is able to destroy both soul and
body in hell.
29Are not two sparrows sold for a farthing? and one of them
shall not fall on the ground without your Father.
30But the very hairs of your head are all numbered.
31Fear ye not therefore, ye are of more value than many sparrows.
32Whosoever therefore shall confess me before men, him will
I confess also before my Father which is in heaven.
33But whosoever shall deny me before men, him will I also deny
before my Father which is in heaven.
34Think not that I am come to send peace on earth: I came not
to send peace, but a sword.
35For I am come to set a man at variance against his father, and
the daughter against her mother, and the daughter-in-law against
her mother-in-law.
36And a man's foes *shall be* they of his own household.
37He that loveth father or mother more than me is not worthy
of me: and he that loveth son or daughter more than me is not
worthy of me.

## Amplified

13Then if indeed that house is deserving, let come upon it your
peace [that is, [a]freedom from all the distresses that are experienced as the result of sin]. But if it is not deserving, let your peace
return to you.
14And whoever will not receive *and* accept *and* welcome you nor
listen to your message, as you leave that house or town shake the
dust of it from your feet.
15Truly, I tell you, it shall be more tolerable on the day of
judgment for the land of Sodom and Gomorrah than for that town.
16Lo, I am sending you out as sheep in the midst of wolves; be
[b]wary *and* wise as serpents, and be innocent—harmless, guileless
and [c]without falsity—as doves. [Gen. 3:1.]
17Be on guard against the men [whose [d]way or nature is to act
in opposition to God]; for they will deliver you up to councils and
flog you in their synagogues,
18And you will be brought before governors and kings for My
sake, for a witness to bear testimony before them and to the
Gentiles (the nations).
19But when they deliver you up, do not be anxious about how
*or* what you are to speak; for what you are to say will be given you
in that very hour *and* [e]moment.
20For it is not you who are speaking, but the Spirit of your
Father speaking through you.
21Brother will deliver up brother to death, and the father his
child, and children will take a stand against their parents, and will
have them put to death;
22And you will be hated by all for My name's sake. But he who
perseveres *and* endures to the end will be saved [ [f]from spiritual
disease and death in the world to come].
23When they persecute you in one town [that is, pursue you in
a manner to injure you and cause you to suffer because of your
belief], flee to another town; for truly, I tell you, you will not have
gone through all the towns of Israel before [g]the Son of man comes.
24A disciple is not above his teacher, nor is a servant *or* slave
above his master.
25It is sufficient for the disciple to be like his teacher, and the
servant *or* slave like his master. If they have called the Master of
the house Beelzebub [ [h]meaning master of the dwelling], how
much more will they speak evil of those of His household. [II Kings
1:2.]
26So have no fear of them; for nothing is concealed that will not
be revealed, *or* kept secret that will not become known.
27What I say to you in the dark, tell in the light; and what you
hear whispered in the ear, proclaim upon the housetops.
28And do not be afraid of those who kill the body but cannot
kill the soul, but rather be afraid of him who can destroy both soul
and body in hell (Gehenna).
29Are not two [i]little sparrows sold for a penny? And yet not one
of them will fall to the ground without your Father's leave *and*
notice.
30But even the very hairs of your head are all numbered.
31Fear not, then; you are of more value than many sparrows.
32Therefore, every one who acknowledges Me before men *and*
confesses Me [ [j]out of a state of oneness with Me], I will also
acknowledge before My Father Who is in heaven, *and* [k]confess
[abiding] in him.
33But whoever denies *and* disowns Me before men, I also will
deny *and* disown before My Father Who is in heaven.
34Do not think that I have come to bring peace upon the earth;
I have not come to bring peace but a sword.
35For I have come to part asunder a man from his father, and
a daughter from her mother, and a [l]newly married wife from her
mother-in-law;
36And a man's foes will be they of his own household. [Mic.
7:6.]
37He who loves *and* [m]takes more pleasure in father or mother
than in Me is not worthy of Me; and he who loves *and* takes more
pleasure in son or daughter than in Me is not worthy of Me;

**AMP** [a] Cremer. [b] Wycliffe. [c] Luther (-Vincent). [d] Cremer. [e] Moulton and Milligan. [f] Abbott-Smith. [g] Believed by many to mean the coming of the Holy Spirit at Pentecost. [h] Davis' "Dictionary of the Bible." [i] Vincent. [j] Vincent. [k] Vincent. [l] Vincent. [m] Wuest.

## New American Standard

13"And if the house is worthy, let your *greeting of* peace come upon it; but if it is not worthy, let your *greeting of* peace return to you.

14"And whoever does not receive you, nor heed your words, as you go out of that house or that city, shake off the dust of your feet.

15"Truly I say to you, it will be more tolerable for *the* land of Sodom and Gomorrah in the day of judgment, than for that city.

*A Hard Road before Them*

16¶ "Behold, I send you out as sheep in the midst of wolves; therefore be shrewd as serpents, and innocent as doves.

17"But beware of men; for they will deliver you up to *the* courts, and scourge you in their synagogues;

18and you shall even be brought before governors and kings for My sake, as a testimony to them and to the Gentiles.

19"But when they deliver you up, do not become anxious about how or what you will speak; for it shall be given you in that hour what you are to speak.

20"For it is not you who speak, but *it is* the Spirit of your Father who speaks in you.

21"And brother will deliver up brother to death, and a father *his* child; and children will rise up against parents, and cause them to be put to death.

22"And you will be hated by all on account of My name, but it is the one who has endured to the end who will be saved.

23"But whenever they persecute you in this city, flee to the next; for truly I say to you, you shall not finish *going through* the cities of Israel, until the Son of Man comes.

*The Meaning of Discipleship*

24¶ "A disciple is not above his teacher, nor a slave above his master.

25"It is enough for the disciple that he become as his teacher, and the slave as his master. If they have called the head of the house Beelzebul, how much more the members of his household!

26"Therefore do not fear them, for there is nothing covered that will not be revealed, and hidden that will not be known.

27"What I tell you in the darkness, speak in the light; and what you hear *whispered* in *your* ear, proclaim upon the housetops.

28"And do not fear those who kill the body, but are unable to kill the soul; but rather fear Him who is able to destroy both soul and body in hell.

29"Are not two sparrows sold for a [n]cent? And *yet* not one of them will fall to the ground apart from your Father.

30"But the very hairs of your head are all numbered.

31"Therefore do not fear; you are of more value than many sparrows.

32"Everyone therefore who shall confess Me before men, I will also confess him before My Father who is in heaven.

33"But whoever shall deny Me before men, I will also deny him before My Father who is in heaven.

34¶ "Do not think that I came to bring peace on the earth; I did not come to bring peace, but a sword.

35"For I came to SET A MAN AGAINST HIS FATHER, AND A DAUGHTER AGAINST HER MOTHER, AND A DAUGHTER-IN-LAW AGAINST HER MOTHER-IN-LAW;

36and A MAN'S ENEMIES WILL BE THE MEMBERS OF HIS HOUSEHOLD.

37"He who loves father or mother more than Me is not worthy of Me; and he who loves son or daughter more than Me is not worthy of Me.

NAS [n] Gr., *assarion,* the smallest copper coin

## New International

peace rest on it; if it is not, let your peace return to you. 14If anyone will not welcome you or listen to your words, shake the dust off your feet when you leave that home or town. 15I tell you the truth, it will be more bearable for Sodom and Gomorrah on the day of judgment than for that town. 16I am sending you out like sheep among wolves. Therefore be as shrewd as snakes and as innocent as doves.

17"Be on your guard against men; they will hand you over to the local councils and flog you in their synagogues. 18On my account you will be brought before governors and kings as witnesses to them and to the Gentiles. 19But when they arrest you, do not worry about what to say or how to say it. At that time you will be given what to say, 20for it will not be you speaking, but the Spirit of your Father speaking through you.

21"Brother will betray brother to death, and a father his child; children will rebel against their parents and have them put to death. 22All men will hate you because of me, but he who stands firm to the end will be saved. 23When you are persecuted in one place, flee to another. I tell you the truth, you will not finish going through the cities of Israel before the Son of Man comes.

24"A student is not above his teacher, nor a servant above his master. 25It is enough for the student to be like his teacher, and the servant like his master. If the head of the house has been called Beelzebub,[o] how much more the members of his household!

26"So do not be afraid of them. There is nothing concealed that will not be disclosed, or hidden that will not be made known. 27What I tell you in the dark, speak in the daylight; what is whispered in your ear, proclaim from the roofs. 28Do not be afraid of those who kill the body but cannot kill the soul. Rather, be afraid of the One who can destroy both soul and body in hell. 29Are not two sparrows sold for a penny[p]? Yet not one of them will fall to the ground apart from the will of your Father. 30And even the very hairs of your head are all numbered. 31So don't be afraid; you are worth more than many sparrows.

32"Whoever acknowledges me before men, I will also acknowledge him before my Father in heaven. 33But whoever disowns me before men, I will disown him before my Father in heaven.

34"Do not suppose that I have come to bring peace to the earth. I did not come to bring peace, but a sword. 35For I have come to turn

> " 'a man against his father,
> a daughter against her mother,
> a daughter-in-law against her mother-in-law—
> 36 a man's enemies will be the members of his own
> household.'[q]

37"Anyone who loves his father or mother more than me is not worthy of me; anyone who loves his son or daughter more than me is not worthy of me; 38and anyone who does not take his cross

NIV [o] 25 Greek *Beezeboul* or *Beelzeboul* [p] 29 Greek *an assarion* [q] 36 Micah 7:6

## King James

38And he that taketh not his cross, and followeth after me, is not worthy of me.

39He that findeth his life shall lose it: and he that loseth his life for my sake shall find it.

40¶ He that receiveth you receiveth me, and he that receiveth me receiveth him that sent me.

41He that receiveth a prophet in the name of a prophet shall receive a prophet's reward; and he that receiveth a righteous man in the name of a righteous man shall receive a righteous man's reward.

42And whosoever shall give to drink unto one of these little ones a cup of cold *water* only in the name of a disciple, verily I say unto you, he shall in no wise lose his reward.

**11** AND IT came to pass, when Jesus had made an end of commanding his twelve disciples, he departed thence to teach and to preach in their cities.

2Now when John had heard in the prison the works of Christ, he sent two of his disciples,

3And said unto him, Art thou he that should come, or do we look for another?

4Jesus answered and said unto them, Go and show John again those things which ye do hear and see:

5The blind receive their sight, and the lame walk, the lepers are cleansed, and the deaf hear, the dead are raised up, and the poor have the gospel preached to them.

6And blessed is *he,* whosoever shall not be offended in me.

7¶ And as they departed, Jesus began to say unto the multitudes concerning John, What went ye out into the wilderness to see? A reed shaken with the wind?

8But what went ye out for to see? A man clothed in soft raiment? behold, they that wear soft *clothing* are in kings' houses.

9But what went ye out for to see? A prophet? yea, I say unto you, and more than a prophet.

10For this is *he,* of whom it is written, Behold, I send my messenger before thy face, which shall prepare thy way before thee.

11Verily I say unto you, Among them that are born of women there hath not risen a greater than John the Baptist: notwithstanding he that is least in the kingdom of heaven is greater than he.

12And from the days of John the Baptist until now the kingdom of heaven suffereth violence, and the violent take it by force.

13For all the prophets and the law prophesied until John.

14And if ye will receive *it,* this is Elias, which was for to come.

15He that hath ears to hear, let him hear.

16¶ But whereunto shall I liken this generation? It is like unto children sitting in the markets, and calling unto their fellows,

17And saying, We have piped unto you, and ye have not danced; we have mourned unto you, and ye have not lamented.

18For John came neither eating nor drinking, and they say, He hath a devil.

## Amplified

38And he who does not take up his cross and follow Me [that is, [a]cleave steadfastly to Me, conforming wholly to My example in living and if need be in dying also] is not worthy of Me.

39Whoever finds his [ [b]lower] life will lose [the higher life], and whoever loses his [lower] life on My account will find [the higher life].

40He who receives *and* welcomes *and* accepts you, receives *and* welcomes *and* accepts Me; and he who receives *and* welcomes *and* accepts Me, receives *and* welcomes *and* accepts Him Who sent Me.

41He who receives *and* welcomes *and* accepts a prophet because he is a prophet shall receive a prophet's reward, and he who receives *and* welcomes *and* accepts a righteous man because he is a righteous man shall receive a righteous man's reward.

42And whoever gives to one of these little ones [in rank or influence] even a cup of cold water because he is My disciple, surely, I declare to you, he shall not lose his reward.

**11** WHEN JESUS had finished His charge to His twelve disciples, He left there to teach and to preach in their [Galilean] cities.

2Now when John in prison heard about the activities of Christ, he sent a message by his disciples,

3And asked Him, Are You He Who was to come, or should we keep on expecting a different one? [Gen. 49:10; Num. 24:17.]

4And Jesus replied to them, Go and report to John what you hear and see:

5The blind receive their sight, and the lame walk, lepers are cleansed (by healing), and the deaf hear, and the dead are raised up, and the poor have good news (the Gospel) preached to them. [Isa. 35:5, 6; 61:1.]

6And blessed—happy, fortunate and [c]to be envied—is he who takes no offense at Me, *and* finds no cause for stumbling in *or* through Me, *and* is not hindered from seeing the Truth.

7Then as these men went their way, Jesus began to speak to the crowds about John: What did you go out in the wilderness (desert) to see? A reed swayed by the wind?

8What did you go out to see then? A man clothed in soft garments? Behold, those who wear soft clothing are in the houses of kings.

9But what did you go out to see? A prophet? Yes, I tell you, and one ( [d]out of the common, more eminent, more remarkable and) [e]superior to a prophet.

10This is the one of whom it is written, Behold I send My messenger on ahead of You, who shall make ready Your way before You. [Mal. 3:1.]

11Truly, I tell you, among those born of women there has not risen one greater than John the Baptist; yet he who is least in the kingdom of heaven is greater than he.

12And from the days of John the Baptist until the present time the kingdom of heaven has endured violent assault, and violent men seize it by force [as a precious prize]—a [f]share in the heavenly kingdom is sought for with most ardent zeal and intense exertion.

13For all the Law and the prophets prophesied up until John,

14And if you are willing to receive *and* accept it, John himself is Elijah who was to come [before the kingdom]. [Mal. 4:5.]

15He who has ears to hear, let him be listening, *and* consider *and* [g]perceive *and* comprehend by hearing.

16But to what shall I liken this generation? It is like little children sitting in the market places who call to their playmates,

17We piped to you [playing wedding], and you did not dance; we wailed dirges [playing funeral], and you did not mourn *and* beat your breasts *and* weep aloud.

18For John came neither eating nor drinking with others, and they say, He has a demon!

**AMP** [a] Thayer. [b] Wuest. [c] Souter. [d] Abbott-Smith. [e] Abbott-Smith. [f] Thayer. [g] Abbott-Smith.

## New American Standard

38"And he who does not take his cross and follow after Me is not worthy of Me.

39"He who has found his life shall lose it, and he who has lost his life for My sake shall find it.

40¶ "He who receives you receives Me, and he who receives Me receives Him who sent Me.

41"He who receives a prophet in *the* name of a prophet shall receive a prophet's reward; and he who receives a righteous man in the name of a righteous man shall receive a righteous man's reward.

42"And whoever in the name of a disciple gives to one of these little ones even a cup of cold water to drink, truly I say to you he shall not lose his reward."

*John's Questions*

11 AND IT came about that when Jesus had finished giving instructions to His twelve disciples, He departed from there to teach and preach in their cities.

2¶ Now when John in prison heard of the works of Christ, he sent *word* by his disciples,

3and said to Him, "Are You the Expected One, or shall we look for someone else?"

4And Jesus answered and said to them, "Go and report to John what you hear and see:

5 *the* BLIND RECEIVE SIGHT and *the* lame walk, *the* lepers are cleansed and *the* deaf hear, and *the* dead are raised up, and *the* POOR HAVE THE GOSPEL PREACHED TO THEM.

6"And blessed is he who keeps from stumbling over Me."

*Jesus' Tribute to John*

7¶ And as these were going *away,* Jesus began to speak to the multitudes about John, "What did you go out into the wilderness to look at? A reed shaken by the wind?

8"But what did you go out to see? A man dressed in soft *clothing*? Behold, those who wear soft *clothing* are in kings' palaces.

9"But why did you go out? To see a prophet? Yes, I say to you, and one who is more than a prophet.

10"This is the one about whom it is written,

'BEHOLD, I SEND MY MESSENGER BEFORE YOUR FACE,
WHO WILL PREPARE YOUR WAY BEFORE YOU.'

11"Truly, I say to you, among those born of women there has not arisen *anyone* greater than John the Baptist; yet he who is least in the kingdom of heaven is greater than he.

12"And from the days of John the Baptist until now the kingdom of heaven suffers violence, and violent men take it by force.

13"For all the prophets and the Law prophesied until John.

14"And if you care to accept *it,* he himself is Elijah, who was to come.

15"He who has ears to hear, let him hear.

16"But to what shall I compare this generation? It is like children sitting in the market places, who call out to the other *children,*

17and say, 'We played the flute for you, and you did not dance; we sang a dirge, and you did not mourn.'

18"For John came neither eating nor drinking, and they say, 'He has a demon!'

## New International

and follow me is not worthy of me. 39Whoever finds his life will
lose it, and whoever loses his life for my sake will find it.
40"He who receives you receives me, and he who receives me
receives the one who sent me. 41Anyone who receives a prophet
because he is a prophet will receive a prophet's reward, and anyone who receives a righteous man because he is a righteous man
will receive a righteous man's reward. 42And if anyone gives even
a cup of cold water to one of these little ones because he is my
disciple, I tell you the truth, he will certainly not lose his reward."

*Jesus and John the Baptist*

11 AFTER JESUS had finished instructing his twelve disciples, he went on from there to teach and preach in the towns of Galilee.[h]
2When John heard in prison what Christ was doing, he sent his
disciples 3to ask him, "Are you the one who was to come, or
should we expect someone else?"
4Jesus replied, "Go back and report to John what you hear and
see: 5The blind receive sight, the lame walk, those who have
leprosy[i] are cured, the deaf hear, the dead are raised, and the
good news is preached to the poor. 6Blessed is the man who does
not fall away on account of me."
7As John's disciples were leaving, Jesus began to speak to the
crowd about John: "What did you go out into the desert to see?
A reed swayed by the wind? 8If not, what did you go out to see?
A man dressed in fine clothes? No, those who wear fine clothes
are in kings' palaces. 9Then what did you go out to see? A prophet?
Yes, I tell you, and more than a prophet. 10This is the one about
whom it is written:

" 'I will send my messenger ahead of you,
who will prepare your way before you.'[j]

11I tell you the truth: Among those born of women there has not
risen anyone greater than John the Baptist; yet he who is least in
the kingdom of heaven is greater than he. 12From the days of John
the Baptist until now, the kingdom of heaven has been forcefully
advancing, and forceful men lay hold of it. 13For all the Prophets
and the Law prophesied until John. 14And if you are willing to
accept it, he is the Elijah who was to come. 15He who has ears, let
him hear.
16"To what can I compare this generation? They are like children sitting in the marketplaces and calling out to others:

17" 'We played the flute for you,
and you did not dance;
we sang a dirge,
and you did not mourn.'

18For John came neither eating nor drinking, and they say, 'He has
a demon.' 19The Son of Man came eating and drinking, and they

NIV [h] *1* Greek *in their towns* [i] *5* The Greek word was used for various diseases affecting the skin—not necessarily leprosy. [j] *10* Mal. 3:1

## King James

19 The Son of man came eating and drinking, and they say, Behold a man gluttonous, and a winebibber, a friend of publicans and sinners. But wisdom is justified of her children.

20 ¶ Then began he to upbraid the cities wherein most of his mighty works were done, because they repented not:

21 Woe unto thee, Chorazin! woe unto thee, Bethsaida! for if the mighty works, which were done in you, had been done in Tyre and Sidon, they would have repented long ago in sackcloth and ashes.

22 But I say unto you, It shall be more tolerable for Tyre and Sidon at the day of judgment, than for you.

23 And thou, Capernaum, which art exalted unto heaven, shalt be brought down to hell: for if the mighty works, which have been done in thee, had been done in Sodom, it would have remained until this day.

24 But I say unto you, That it shall be more tolerable for the land of Sodom in the day of judgment, than for thee.

25 ¶ At that time Jesus answered and said, I thank thee, O Father, Lord of heaven and earth, because thou hast hid these things from the wise and prudent, and hast revealed them unto babes.

26 Even so, Father: for so it seemed good in thy sight.

27 All things are delivered unto me of my Father: and no man knoweth the Son, but the Father; neither knoweth any man the Father, save the Son, and *he* to whomsoever the Son will reveal *him.*

28 ¶ Come unto me, all *ye* that labour and are heavy laden, and I will give you rest.

29 Take my yoke upon you, and learn of me; for I am meek and lowly in heart: and ye shall find rest unto your souls.

30 For my yoke *is* easy, and my burden is light.

**12** AT THAT time Jesus went on the sabbath day through the corn; and his disciples were an hungered, and began to pluck the ears of corn, and to eat.

2 But when the Pharisees saw *it,* they said unto him, Behold, thy disciples do that which is not lawful to do upon the sabbath day.

3 But he said unto them, Have ye not read what David did, when he was an hungered, and they that were with him;

4 How he entered into the house of God, and did eat the showbread, which was not lawful for him to eat, neither for them which were with him, but only for the priests?

5 Or have ye not read in the law, how that on the sabbath days the priests in the temple profane the sabbath, and are blameless?
6 But I say unto you, That in this place is *one* greater than the temple.

7 But if ye had known what *this* meaneth, I will have mercy, and not sacrifice, ye would not have condemned the guiltless.

8 For the Son of man is Lord even of the sabbath day.

9 And when he was departed thence, he went into their synagogue:

## Amplified

19 The Son of man came eating and drinking with others and they say, Behold, a glutton and a wine drinker, a friend of tax collectors *and* [a]especially wicked sinners! Yet wisdom is justified *and* vindicated by what she does (her deeds) *and* by [b] *her children.*

20 Then He began to censure *and* reproach the cities in which most of His mighty works had been performed, because they did not repent—their hearts were not changed.

21 Woe to you, Chorazin! Woe to you, Bethsaida! for if the mighty works done in you had been done in Tyre and Sidon, they would long ago have repented in sackcloth and ashes—and their hearts have been changed.

22 I tell you [further], it shall be more endurable for Tyre and Sidon on the day of judgment than for you.

23 And you, Capernaum, are you to be lifted up to heaven? You shall be brought down to Hades [the region of the dead]! For if the mighty works done in you had been done in Sodom, it would have continued until today.

24 But I tell you, it shall be more endurable for the land of Sodom on the day of judgment than for you.

25 At that time Jesus began to say, I thank You, Father, Lord of heaven and earth, *and* [c]acknowledge openly *and* joyfully to Your honor that you have hidden these things from the wise *and* clever and learned, and revealed them to babies—to the [d]childish, untaught and unskilled.

26 Yes, Father, [I praise You that] such was Your gracious will *and* good pleasure.

27 All things were entrusted *and* delivered to Me by My Father; and no one [e]fully knows *and* [f]accurately understands the Son except the Father; and no one [g]fully knows *and* [h]accurately understands the Father except the Son and any one to whom the Son [i]deliberately wills to make Him known.

28 Come to Me, all you who labor and are heavy-laden *and* over burdened, and I will cause you to rest—I will [j]ease *and* relieve *and* [k]refresh [l]your souls.

29 Take My yoke upon you, and learn of Me; for I am gentle (meek) *and* humble (lowly) in heart, and you will find rest—[m]relief, ease and refreshment and [n]recreation and blessed quiet—for your souls. [Jer. 6:16.]

30 For My yoke is wholesome (useful, [o]good)—not harsh, hard, sharp or pressing, but comfortable, gracious and pleasant; and My burden is light *and* easy to be borne.

**12** AT THAT [p]particular time Jesus went through the fields of standing grain on the Sabbath, and His disciples were hungry, and they began to pick off the spikes of grain and to eat. [Deut. 23:25.]

2 And when the Pharisees saw it, they said to Him, See there! Your disciples are doing what is unlawful *and* not permitted on the Sabbath.

3 He said to them, Have you not even read what David did when he was hungry, and those who accompanied him? [I Sam. 21:1-6; Lev. 24:9.]

4 How he went into the house of God and ate the loaves of the showbread, which it was not lawful for him to eat, nor for the men who accompanied him, but for the priests only?

5 Or have you never read in the Law how on the Sabbath the priests in the temple violate the sanctity of the Sabbath, breaking it, and yet are guiltless? [Num. 28:9, 10.]

6 But I tell you, Something greater *and* [q]more exalted *and* more majestic than the temple is here!

7 And if you had only known what this saying means, I want mercy [readiness to help, to spare, to forgive] rather than sacrifice *and* sacrificial victims, you would not have condemned the guiltless. [Hos. 6:6.]

8 For the Son of man is Lord [even] of the Sabbath.

9 And going on from there, He went into their synagogue.

**AMP** [a] Abbott-Smith. [b] Many ancient authorities read *children,* as in Luke 7:35. [c] Thayer. [d] Thayer. [e] Vincent. [f] Thayer. [g] Vincent. [h] Thayer. [i] Thayer. [j] Tyndale. [k] Wycliffe. [l] Thayer. [m] Souter. [n] Thayer. [o] Moulton and Milligan. [p] Vincent. [q] Thayer.

## New American Standard

19"The Son of Man came eating and drinking, and they say, 'Behold, a gluttonous man and a drunkard, a friend of tax-gatherers and sinners!' Yet wisdom is vindicated by her deeds."

*The Unrepenting Cities*

20¶ Then He began to reproach the cities in which most of His miracles were done, because they did not repent.

21"Woe to you, Chorazin! Woe to you, Bethsaida! For if the miracles had occurred in Tyre and Sidon which occurred in you, they would have repented long ago in sackcloth and ashes.

22"Nevertheless I say to you, it shall be more tolerable for Tyre and Sidon in *the* day of judgment, than for you.

23"And you, Capernaum, will not be exalted to heaven, will you? You shall descend to Hades; for if the miracles had occurred in Sodom which occurred in you, it would have remained to this day.

24"Nevertheless I say to you that it shall be more tolerable for the land of Sodom in *the* day of judgment, than for you."

*Come to Me*

25¶ At that time Jesus answered and said, "I praise Thee, O Father, Lord of heaven and earth, that Thou didst hide these things from *the* wise and intelligent and didst reveal them to babes.

26"Yes, Father, for thus it was well-pleasing in Thy sight.

27"All things have been handed over to Me by My Father; and no one knows the Son, except the Father; nor does anyone know the Father, except the Son, and anyone to whom the Son wills to reveal *Him.*

28"Come to Me, all who are weary and heavy-laden, and I will give you rest.

29"Take My yoke upon you, and learn from Me, for I am gentle and humble in heart; and YOU SHALL FIND REST FOR YOUR SOULS.

30"For My yoke is easy, and My load is light."

*Sabbath Questions*

**12** AT THAT time Jesus went on the Sabbath through the grainfields, and His disciples became hungry and began to pick the heads *of grain* and eat.

2But when the Pharisees saw it, they said to Him, "Behold, Your disciples do what is not lawful to do on a Sabbath."

3But He said to them, "Have you not read what David did, when he became hungry, he and his companions;

4how he entered the house of God, and they ate the consecrated bread, which was not lawful for him to eat, nor for those with him, but for the priests alone?

5"Or have you not read in the Law, that on the Sabbath the priests in the temple break the Sabbath, and are innocent?

6"But I say to you, that something greater than the temple is here.

7"But if you had known what this means, 'I DESIRE COMPASSION, AND NOT A SACRIFICE,' you would not have condemned the innocent.

*Lord of the Sabbath*

8"For the Son of Man is Lord of the Sabbath."

9¶ And departing from there, He went into their synagogue.

## New International

say, 'Here is a glutton and a drunkard, a friend of tax collectors and
"sinners." ' But wisdom is proved right by her actions."

*Woe on Unrepentant Cities*

20Then Jesus began to denounce the cities in which most of his
miracles had been performed, because they did not repent.
21"Woe to you, Korazin! Woe to you, Bethsaida! If the miracles that
were performed in you had been performed in Tyre and Sidon,
they would have repented long ago in sackcloth and ashes. 22But
I tell you, it will be more bearable for Tyre and Sidon on the day
of judgment than for you. 23And you, Capernaum, will you be
lifted up to the skies? No, you will go down to the depths.[r] If the
miracles that were performed in you had been performed in
Sodom, it would have remained to this day. 24But I tell you that
it will be more bearable for Sodom on the day of judgment than
for you."

*Rest for the Weary*

25At that time Jesus said, "I praise you, Father, Lord of heaven
and earth, because you have hidden these things from the wise
and learned, and revealed them to little children. 26Yes, Father, for
this was your good pleasure.
27"All things have been committed to me by my Father. No one
knows the Son except the Father, and no one knows the Father
except the Son and those to whom the Son chooses to reveal him.
28"Come to me, all you who are weary and burdened, and I will
give you rest. 29Take my yoke upon you and learn from me, for
I am gentle and humble in heart, and you will find rest for your
souls. 30For my yoke is easy and my burden is light."

*Lord of the Sabbath*

**12** AT THAT time Jesus went through the grainfields on the
Sabbath. His disciples were hungry and began to pick
some heads of grain and eat them. 2When the Pharisees saw this,
they said to him, "Look! Your disciples are doing what is unlawful
on the Sabbath."
3He answered, "Haven't you read what David did when he and
his companions were hungry? 4He entered the house of God, and
he and his companions ate the consecrated bread—which was not
lawful for them to do, but only for the priests. 5Or haven't you read
in the Law that on the Sabbath the priests in the temple desecrate
the day and yet are innocent? 6I tell you that one[s] greater than the
temple is here. 7If you had known what these words mean, 'I
desire mercy, not sacrifice,'[t] you would not have condemned the
innocent. 8For the Son of Man is Lord of the Sabbath."
9Going on from that place, he went into their synagogue, 10and

NIV [r] 23 Greek *Hades* [s] 6 Or *something;* also in verses 41 and 42 [t] 7 Hosea 6:6

## King James

10¶ And, behold, there was a man which had *his* hand withered. And they asked him, saying, Is it lawful to heal on the sabbath days? that they might accuse him.

11And he said unto them, What man shall there be among you, that shall have one sheep, and if it fall into a pit on the sabbath day, will he not lay hold on it, and lift *it* out?

12How much then is a man better than a sheep? Wherefore it is lawful to do well on the sabbath days.

13Then saith he to the man, Stretch forth thine hand. And he stretched *it* forth; and it was restored whole, like as the other.

14¶ Then the Pharisees went out, and held a council against him, how they might destroy him.

15But when Jesus knew *it*, he withdrew himself from thence: and great multitudes followed him, and he healed them all;

16And charged them that they should not make him known:

17That it might be fulfilled which was spoken by Esaias the prophet, saying,

18Behold my servant, whom I have chosen; my beloved, in whom my soul is well pleased: I will put my spirit upon him, and he shall show judgment to the Gentiles.

19He shall not strive, nor cry; neither shall any man hear his voice in the streets.

20A bruised reed shall he not break, and smoking flax shall he not quench, till he send forth judgment unto victory.

21And in his name shall the Gentiles trust.

22¶ Then was brought unto him one possessed with a devil, blind, and dumb: and he healed him, insomuch that the blind and dumb both spake and saw.

23And all the people were amazed, and said, Is not this the son of David?

24But when the Pharisees heard *it*, they said, This *fellow* doth not cast out devils, but by Beelzebub the prince of the devils.

25And Jesus knew their thoughts, and said unto them, Every kingdom divided against itself is brought to desolation; and every city or house divided against itself shall not stand:

26And if Satan cast out Satan, he is divided against himself; how shall then his kingdom stand?

27And if I by Beelzebub cast out devils, by whom do your children cast *them* out? therefore they shall be your judges.

28But if I cast out devils by the Spirit of God, then the kingdom of God is come unto you.

29Or else how can one enter into a strong man's house, and spoil his goods, except he first bind the strong man? and then he will spoil his house.

30He that is not with me is against me; and he that gathereth not with me scattereth abroad.

31¶ Wherefore I say unto you, All manner of sin and blasphemy shall be forgiven unto men: but the blasphemy *against* the *Holy* Ghost shall not be forgiven unto men.

32And whosoever speaketh a word against the Son of man, it shall be forgiven him: but whosoever speaketh against the Holy Ghost, it shall not be forgiven him, neither in this world, neither in the *world* to come.

33Either make the tree good, and his fruit good; or else make the tree corrupt, and his fruit corrupt: for the tree is known by *his* fruit.

## Amplified

10And behold, a man was there with one withered hand. And they said to Him, Is it lawful *or* allowable to cure people on the Sabbath days? that they might accuse him.

11But He said to them, What man is there among you, if he has only one sheep, and it falls into a pit *or* ditch on the Sabbath, will not take hold of it and lift it out?

12How much better *and* of more value is a man than a sheep! So it is lawful *and* allowable to do good on the Sabbath days.

13Then He said to the man, Reach out your hand. And the man reached it out, and it was restored, sound as the other one.

14But the Pharisees went out and held a consultation against Him, how they might do away with Him.

15But being aware of this, Jesus went away from there. And many people [a]joined *and* accompanied Him, and He cured all of them,

16And strictly charged them *and* sharply warned [them] not to make Him [b]publicly known.

17This was in fulfillment of what was spoken by the prophet Isaiah,

18Behold, My Servant Whom I have chosen, My Beloved in *and* with Whom My soul is well pleased *and* [c]has found its delight. I will put My Spirit upon Him, and He shall proclaim *and* [d]show forth judgment to the nations.

19He will not strive *or* wrangle or cry out loudly, nor will any one hear His voice in the streets;

20A bruised reed He will not break, and a smoldering (dimly burning) wick He will not quench till He brings [e]justice *and* a just cause to victory.

21And in *and* on His name will the Gentiles—the [f]peoples outside of Israel—set their hopes. [Isa. 42:1-4.]

22Then a blind and dumb man, under the power of a demon, was brought to Jesus, and He cured him, so that the blind and dumb man both spoke and saw.

23And all the [crowds of] people were stunned with bewildered wonder, and said, This cannot be the Son of David, can it?

24But the Pharisees hearing it said, This [g]Man drives out demons only by *and* with the help of Beelzebub, the prince of demons.

25And knowing their thoughts, He said to them, Any kingdom that is divided against itself is being brought to desolation *and* laid waste, and no city *or* house divided against itself will last *or* continue to stand.

26And if Satan drives out Satan, he has become divided against himself *and* disunited; how then will his kingdom last *or* continue to stand?

27And if I drive out the demons by [help of] Beelzebub, by whose [help] do your sons drive them out? [h]For this reason they shall be your judges.

28But if it is by the Spirit of God that I drive out the demons, then the kingdom of God has come upon you [ [i]before you expected it].

29Or how can a person go into a strong man's house and carry off his goods—the entire equipment of his house—without first binding the strong man? Then indeed he may plunder his house.

30He who is not with Me (definitely [j]on My side), is against Me, and he who does not (definitely) gather with Me *and* for [k]My side, scatters.

31Therefore I tell you, every sin and blasphemy—that is, every evil, abusive, [l]injurious speaking or indignity against sacred things—can be forgiven men, but blasphemy against the (Holy) Spirit shall not *and* [m]cannot be forgiven.

32And whoever speaks a word against the Son of man will be forgiven, but whoever speaks against the Spirit, the Holy One, will not be forgiven, either in this world *and* age or in the world *and* age to come.

33Either make the tree sound (healthy and good), and its fruit sound (healthy and good), or make the tree rotten (diseased and bad) and its fruit rotten (diseased and bad); for the tree is known *and* recognized *and* judged by its fruit.

**AMP** [a] Thayer. [b] Darby's "The New Testament, a New Translation." [c] Darby's "The New Testament, a New Translation." [d] Darby's "The New Testament, a New Translation." [e] Thayer. [f] Cremer. [g] Capitalized because of what He is, the spotless Son of God, not what the speakers may have thought He was. [h] Darby's "The New Testament, a New Translation." [i] Vincent. [j] Thayer. [k] Thayer. [l] Williams. [m] Williams.

## New American Standard

10And behold, *there was* a man with a withered hand. And they questioned Him, saying, "Is it lawful to heal on the Sabbath?"—in order that they might accuse Him.

11And He said to them, "What man shall there be among you, who shall have one sheep, and if it falls into a pit on the Sabbath, will he not take hold of it, and lift it out?

12"Of how much more value then is a man than a sheep! So then, it is lawful to do good on the Sabbath."

13Then He *said to the man, "Stretch out your hand!" And he stretched it out, and it was restored to normal, like the other.

14But the Pharisees went out, and counseled together against Him, *as to* how they might destroy Him.

15¶ But Jesus, aware of *this*, withdrew from there. And many followed Him, and He healed them all,

16and warned them not to make Him known,

17in order that what was spoken through Isaiah the prophet, might be fulfilled, saying,

18 "BEHOLD, MY SERVANT WHOM I HAVE CHOSEN;
MY BELOVED IN WHOM MY SOUL IS WELL-PLEASED;
I WILL PUT MY SPIRIT UPON HIM,
AND HE SHALL PROCLAIM JUSTICE TO THE GENTILES.
19 "HE WILL NOT QUARREL, NOR CRY OUT;
NOR WILL ANYONE HEAR HIS VOICE IN THE STREETS.
20 "A BATTERED REED HE WILL NOT BREAK OFF,
AND A SMOLDERING WICK HE WILL NOT PUT OUT,
UNTIL HE LEADS JUSTICE TO VICTORY.
21 "AND IN HIS NAME THE GENTILES WILL HOPE."

*The Pharisees Rebuked*

22¶ Then there was brought to Him a demon-possessed man *who was* blind and dumb, and He healed him, so that the dumb man spoke and saw.

23And all the multitudes were amazed, and *began* to say, "This *man* cannot be the Son of David, can he?"

24But when the Pharisees heard it, they said, "This man casts out demons only by Beelzebul the ruler of the demons."

25And knowing their thoughts He said to them, "Any kingdom divided against itself is laid waste; and any city or house divided against itself shall not stand.

26"And if Satan casts out Satan, he is divided against himself; how then shall his kingdom stand?

27"And if I by Beelzebul cast out demons, by whom do your sons cast them out? Consequently they shall be your judges.

28"But if I cast out demons by the Spirit of God, then the kingdom of God has come upon you.

29"Or how can anyone enter the strong man's house and carry off his property, unless he first binds the strong *man*? And then he will plunder his house.

*The Unpardonable Sin*

30"He who is not with Me is against Me; and he who does not gather with Me scatters.

31"Therefore I say to you, any sin and blasphemy shall be forgiven men, but blasphemy against the Spirit shall not be forgiven.

32"And whoever shall speak a word against the Son of Man, it shall be forgiven him; but whoever shall speak against the Holy Spirit, it shall not be forgiven him, either in this age, or in the *age* to come.

*Words Reveal Character*

33"Either make the tree good, and its fruit good; or make the tree bad, and its fruit bad; for the tree is known by its fruit.

## New International

a man with a shriveled hand was there. Looking for a reason to accuse Jesus, they asked him, "Is it lawful to heal on the Sabbath?"
11He said to them, "If any of you has a sheep and it falls into a pit on the Sabbath, will you not take hold of it and lift it out?
12How much more valuable is a man than a sheep! Therefore it is lawful to do good on the Sabbath."
13Then he said to the man, "Stretch out your hand." So he stretched it out and it was completely restored, just as sound as the other. 14But the Pharisees went out and plotted how they might kill Jesus.

*God's Chosen Servant*

15Aware of this, Jesus withdrew from that place. Many followed him, and he healed all their sick, 16warning them not to tell who he was. 17This was to fulfill what was spoken through the prophet Isaiah:

18"Here is my servant whom I have chosen,
the one I love, in whom I delight;
I will put my Spirit on him,
and he will proclaim justice to the nations.
19He will not quarrel or cry out;
no one will hear his voice in the streets.
20A bruised reed he will not break,
and a smoldering wick he will not snuff out,
till he leads justice to victory.
21 In his name the nations will put their hope."[n]

*Jesus and Beelzebub*

22Then they brought him a demon-possessed man who was blind and mute, and Jesus healed him, so that he could both talk and see. 23All the people were astonished and said, "Could this be the Son of David?"
24But when the Pharisees heard this, they said, "It is only by Beelzebub,[o] the prince of demons, that this fellow drives out demons."
25Jesus knew their thoughts and said to them, "Every kingdom divided against itself will be ruined, and every city or household divided against itself will not stand. 26If Satan drives out Satan, he is divided against himself. How then can his kingdom stand?
27And if I drive out demons by Beelzebub, by whom do your people drive them out? So then, they will be your judges. 28But if I drive out demons by the Spirit of God, then the kingdom of God has come upon you.
29"Or again, how can anyone enter a strong man's house and carry off his possessions unless he first ties up the strong man? Then he can rob his house.
30"He who is not with me is against me, and he who does not gather with me scatters. 31And so I tell you, every sin and blasphemy will be forgiven men, but the blasphemy against the Spirit will not be forgiven. 32Anyone who speaks a word against the Son of Man will be forgiven, but anyone who speaks against the Holy Spirit will not be forgiven, either in this age or in the age to come.
33"Make a tree good and its fruit will be good, or make a tree bad and its fruit will be bad, for a tree is recognized by its fruit.

NIV [n] 21 Isaiah 42:1-4 [o] 24 Greek *Beezeboul* or *Beelzeboul;* also in verse 27

## King James

34 O generation of vipers, how can ye, being evil, speak good things? for out of the abundance of the heart the mouth speaketh.
35 A good man out of the good treasure of the heart bringeth forth good things: and an evil man out of the evil treasure bringeth forth evil things.
36 But I say unto you, That every idle word that men shall speak, they shall give account thereof in the day of judgment.
37 For by thy words thou shalt be justified, and by thy words thou shalt be condemned.
38 ¶ Then certain of the scribes and of the Pharisees answered, saying, Master, we would see a sign from thee.
39 But he answered and said unto them, An evil and adulterous generation seeketh after a sign; and there shall no sign be given to it, but the sign of the prophet Jonas:
40 For as Jonas was three days and three nights in the whale's belly; so shall the Son of man be three days and three nights in the heart of the earth.
41 The men of Nineveh shall rise in judgment with this generation, and shall condemn it: because they repented at the preaching of Jonas; and, behold, a greater than Jonas *is* here.
42 The queen of the south shall rise up in the judgment with this generation, and shall condemn it: for she came from the uttermost parts of the earth to hear the wisdom of Solomon; and, behold, a greater than Solomon *is* here.
43 When the unclean spirit is gone out of a man, he walketh through dry places, seeking rest, and findeth none.
44 Then he saith, I will return into my house from whence I came out; and when he is come, he findeth *it* empty, swept, and garnished.
45 Then goeth he, and taketh with himself seven other spirits more wicked than himself, and they enter in and dwell there: and the last *state* of that man is worse than the first. Even so shall it be also unto this wicked generation.
46 ¶ While he yet talked to the people, behold, *his* mother and his brethren stood without, desiring to speak with him.
47 Then one said unto him, Behold, thy mother and thy brethren stand without, desiring to speak with thee.
48 But he answered and said unto him that told him, Who is my mother? and who are my brethren?
49 And he stretched forth his hand toward his disciples, and said, Behold my mother and my brethren!
50 For whosoever shall do the will of my Father which is in heaven, the same is my brother, and sister, and mother.

**13** THE SAME day went Jesus out of the house, and sat by the sea side.
2 And great multitudes were gathered together unto him, so that he went into a ship, and sat; and the whole multitude stood on the shore.
3 And he spake many things unto them in parables, saying, Behold, a sower went forth to sow;
4 And when he sowed, some *seeds* fell by the way side, and the fowls came and devoured them up:
5 Some fell upon stony places, where they had not much earth: and forthwith they sprung up, because they had no deepness of earth:
6 And when the sun was up, they were scorched; and because they had no root, they withered away.

## Amplified

34 You offspring of vipers! How can you speak good things when you are evil—wicked? For out of the fullness—the overflow, the [a]superabundance—of the heart the mouth speaks.
35 The good man from his inner good treasure [b]flings forth good things, and the evil man out of his inner evil storehouse [c]flings forth evil things.
36 But I tell you, on the day of judgment men will have to give account for every [d]idle (inoperative, non-working) word they speak.
37 For by your words you will be justified *and* acquitted, and by your words you will be condemned *and* sentenced.
38 Then some of the scribes and Pharisees said to Him, Teacher, we desire to see a sign *or* miracle from You [proving that You are what You claim to be].
39 But He replied to them, An evil and adulterous generation [that is, a generation [e]morally unfaithful to God] seeks *and* demands a sign; but no sign shall be given to it except the sign of the prophet Jonah.
40 For even as Jonah was three days and three nights in the belly of the sea monster, so will the Son of man be three days and three nights in the heart of the earth. [Jonah 1:17.]
41 The men of Nineveh will stand up at the judgment with this generation and condemn it; for they repented at the preaching of Jonah, and behold, Someone more *and* greater than Jonah is here! [Jonah 3:5.]
42 The queen of the South will stand up at the judgment with this generation and condemn it; for she came from the ends of the earth to listen to the wisdom of Solomon, and behold, Someone more *and* greater than Solomon is here. [I Kings 10:1; II Chron. 9:1.]
43 But when the unclean spirit has gone out of a man, he roams through dry places in search of rest, but he does not find any.
44 Then he says, I will go back to my house from which I came out. And when he arrives he finds the place unoccupied, swept, put in order *and* decorated.
45 Then he goes and brings with him seven other spirits more wicked than himself, and they go in and make their home there. And the last condition of that man becomes worse than the first. So also shall it be with this wicked generation.
46 Jesus was still speaking to the people when behold, His mother and brothers stood outside, seeking to speak to Him.
47 *Some one said to Him, Listen! Your mother and Your brothers are standing outside, seeking to speak to You.*
48 But He replied to the man who told Him, Who is My mother, and who are My brothers?
49 And stretching out His hand toward [not only the twelve disciples but all] [f]His adherents, He said, Here are My mother and My brothers.
50 For whoever does the will of My Father in heaven is My brother and sister and mother!

**13** THAT SAME day Jesus went out of the house and was sitting beside the sea.
2 But such great crowds gathered about Him that He got into a boat and remained sitting there, while all the throng stood on the shore.
3 And He told them many things in parables—that is, stories by way of illustration; saying, A sower went out to sow,
4 And as he sowed, some seeds fell by the roadside, and the birds came and ate them up.
5 Other seeds fell on rocky ground, where they had not much soil, and at once they sprang up, because they had no depth of soil;
6 But when the sun rose they were scorched, and because they had no root they dried up *and* withered away.

AMP [a] Souter. [b] Vincent. [c] Vincent. [d] Vincent. [e] Vincent. [f] Cremer.

## New American Standard

34 "You brood of vipers, how can you, being evil, speak what
is good? For the mouth speaks out of that which fills the heart.
35 "The good man out of *his* good treasure brings forth what is
good; and the evil man out of *his* evil treasure brings forth what
is evil.
36 "And I say to you, that every careless word that men shall
speak, they shall render account for it in the day of judgment.
37 "For by your words you shall be justified, and by your words
you shall be condemned."

*The Desire for Signs*

38 ¶ Then some of the scribes and Pharisees answered Him,
saying, "Teacher, we want to see a sign from You."
39 But He answered and said to them, "An evil and adulterous
generation craves for a sign; and *yet* no sign shall be given to it but
the sign of Jonah the prophet;
40 for just as JONAH WAS THREE DAYS AND THREE NIGHTS IN THE
BELLY OF THE SEA MONSTER, so shall the Son of Man be three days
and three nights in the heart of the earth.
41 "The men of Nineveh shall stand up with this generation at
the judgment, and shall condemn it because they repented at the
preaching of Jonah; and behold, something greater than Jonah is
here.
42 " *The* Queen of *the* South shall rise up with this generation at
the judgment and shall condemn it, because she came from the
ends of the earth to hear the wisdom of Solomon; and behold,
something greater than Solomon is here.
43 "Now when the unclean spirit goes out of a man, it passes
through waterless places, seeking rest, and does not find *it.*
44 "Then it says, 'I will return to my house from which I came';
and when it comes, it finds it unoccupied, swept, and put in order.
45 "Then it goes, and takes along with it seven other spirits more
wicked than itself, and they go in and live there; and the last state
of that man becomes worse than the first. That is the way it will
also be with this evil generation."

*Changed Relationships*

46 ¶ While He was still speaking to the multitudes, behold, His
mother and brothers were standing outside, seeking to speak to
Him.
47 And someone said to Him, "Behold, Your mother and Your
brothers are standing outside seeking to speak to You."
48 But He answered the one who was telling Him and said,
"Who is My mother and who are My brothers?"
49 And stretching out His hand toward His disciples, He said,
"Behold, My mother and My brothers!
50 "For whoever does the will of My Father who is in heaven,
he is My brother and sister and mother."

*Jesus Teaches in Parables*

**13** ON THAT day Jesus went out of the house, and was
sitting by the sea.
2 And great multitudes gathered to Him, so that He got into a
boat and sat down, and the whole multitude was standing on the
beach.
3 And He spoke many things to them in parables, saying, "Behold, the sower went out to sow;
4 and as he sowed, some *seeds* fell beside the road, and the birds
came and ate them up.
5 "And others fell upon the rocky places, where they did not
have much soil; and immediately they sprang up, because they
had no depth of soil.
6 "But when the sun had risen, they were scorched; and because they had no root, they withered away.

## New International

34 You brood of vipers, how can you who are evil say anything
good? For out of the overflow of the heart the mouth speaks. 35 The
good man brings good things out of the good stored up in him,
and the evil man brings evil things out of the evil stored up in him.
36 But I tell you that men will have to give account on the day of
judgment for every careless word they have spoken. 37 For by your
words you will be acquitted, and by your words you will be condemned."

*The Sign of Jonah*

38 Then some of the Pharisees and teachers of the law said to
him, "Teacher, we want to see a miraculous sign from you."
39 He answered, "A wicked and adulterous generation asks for
a miraculous sign! But none will be given it except the sign of the
prophet Jonah. 40 For as Jonah was three days and three nights in
the belly of a huge fish, so the Son of Man will be three days and
three nights in the heart of the earth. 41 The men of Nineveh will
stand up at the judgment with this generation and condemn it; for
they repented at the preaching of Jonah, and now one[g] greater
than Jonah is here. 42 The Queen of the South will rise at the
judgment with this generation and condemn it; for she came from
the ends of the earth to listen to Solomon's wisdom, and now one
greater than Solomon is here.
43 "When an evil[h] spirit comes out of a man, it goes through arid
places seeking rest and does not find it. 44 Then it says, 'I will return
to the house I left.' When it arrives, it finds the house unoccupied,
swept clean and put in order. 45 Then it goes and takes with it seven
other spirits more wicked than itself, and they go in and live there.
And the final condition of that man is worse than the first. That
is how it will be with this wicked generation."

*Jesus' Mother and Brothers*

46 While Jesus was still talking to the crowd, his mother and
brothers stood outside, wanting to speak to him. 47 Someone told
him, "Your mother and brothers are standing outside, wanting to
speak to you."[i]
48 He replied to him, "Who is my mother, and who are my
brothers?" 49 Pointing to his disciples, he said, "Here are my
mother and my brothers. 50 For whoever does the will of my Father
in heaven is my brother and sister and mother."

*The Parable of the Sower*

**13** THAT SAME day Jesus went out of the house and sat by
the lake. 2 Such large crowds gathered around him that he
got into a boat and sat in it, while all the people stood on the shore.
3 Then he told them many things in parables, saying: "A farmer
went out to sow his seed. 4 As he was scattering the seed, some fell
along the path, and the birds came and ate it up. 5 Some fell on
rocky places, where it did not have much soil. It sprang up quickly,
because the soil was shallow. 6 But when the sun came up, the
plants were scorched, and they withered because they had no root.

NIV [g] *41* Or *something;* also in verse 42 [h] *43* Greek *unclean* [i] *47* Some
manuscripts do not have verse 47.

## King James

7And some fell among thorns; and the thorns sprung up, and choked them:

8But other fell into good ground, and brought forth fruit, some an hundredfold, some sixtyfold, some thirtyfold.

9Who hath ears to hear, let him hear.

10And the disciples came, and said unto him, Why speakest thou unto them in parables?

11He answered and said unto them, Because it is given unto you to know the mysteries of the kingdom of heaven, but to them it is not given.

12For whosoever hath, to him shall be given, and he shall have more abundance: but whosoever hath not, from him shall be taken away even that he hath.

13Therefore speak I to them in parables: because they seeing see not; and hearing they hear not, neither do they understand.

14And in them is fulfilled the prophecy of Esaias, which saith, By hearing ye shall hear, and shall not understand; and seeing ye shall see, and shall not perceive:

15For this people's heart is waxed gross, and *their* ears are dull of hearing, and their eyes they have closed; lest at any time they should see with *their* eyes, and hear with *their* ears, and should understand with *their* heart, and should be converted, and I should heal them.

16But blessed *are* your eyes, for they see: and your ears, for they hear.

17For verily I say unto you, That many prophets and righteous *men* have desired to see *those things* which ye see, and have not seen *them;* and to hear *those things* which ye hear, and have not heard *them.*

18¶ Hear ye therefore the parable of the sower.

19When any one heareth the word of the kingdom, and understandeth *it* not, then cometh the wicked *one,* and catcheth away that which was sown in his heart. This is he which received seed by the way side.

20But he that received the seed into stony places, the same is he that heareth the word, and anon with joy receiveth it;

21Yet hath he not root in himself, but dureth for a while: for when tribulation or persecution ariseth because of the word, by and by he is offended.

22He also that received seed among the thorns is he that heareth the word; and the care of this world, and the deceitfulness of riches, choke the word, and he becometh unfruitful.

23But he that received seed into the good ground is he that heareth the word, and understandeth *it;* which also beareth fruit, and bringeth forth, some an hundredfold, some sixty, some thirty.

24¶ Another parable put he forth unto them, saying, The kingdom of heaven is likened unto a man which sowed good seed in his field:

25But while men slept, his enemy came and sowed tares among the wheat, and went his way.

26But when the blade was sprung up, and brought forth fruit, then appeared the tares also.

27So the servants of the householder came and said unto him, Sir, didst not thou sow good seed in thy field? from whence then hath it tares?

## Amplified

7Other seeds fell among thorns, and the thorns grew up and choked them out.

8Other seeds fell on good soil and yielded grain, some a hundred times as much as was sown, some sixty times as much, and some thirty.

9He who has ears [to hear], let him be listening *and* [a]consider *and* [b]perceive *and* comprehend by hearing.

10Then the disciples came to Him and said, Why do You speak to them in parables?

11And He replied to them, To you it has been given to know the secrets *and* mysteries of the kingdom of heaven, but to them it has not been given.

12For whoever has [spiritual knowledge], to him will more be given *and* he will [c]be furnished richly, *so that* he will have abundance; but from him who has not, even what he has will be taken away.

13This is the reason that I speak to them in parables, because [d]having the power of seeing they do not see, and [e]having the power of hearing they do not hear, nor do they grasp *and* understand.

14In them indeed is [f]the process of fulfillment of the prophecy of Isaiah which says: You shall indeed hear *and* hear, but never grasp *and* understand; and you shall indeed look *and* look, but never see *and* perceive.

15For this nation's heart has grown gross—fat and dull; and their ears heavy *and* difficult of hearing, and their eyes they have tightly closed, lest they see *and* perceive with their eyes, and hear *and* comprehend the sense with their ears, and grasp *and* understand with their heart, and turn *and* I should heal them. [Isa. 6:9, 10.]

16But blessed—happy, fortunate and [g]to be envied—are your eyes, because they do see, and your ears, because they do hear.

17Truly, I tell you, many prophets and righteous men—men who were upright and in right standing with God—yearned to see what you see, and did not see it, and to hear what you hear, and did not hear it.

18Listen then to the parable of the sower.

19 [h]While any one is hearing the Word of the kingdom and does not grasp *and* comprehend it, the evil one comes and snatches away what is sown in his heart. This is what was sown along the roadside.

20As for what was sown on thin (rocky) soil, this is he who hears the Word and at once welcomes *and* accepts it with joy;

21Yet it has no real root in himself, but is temporary—inconstant, [i]lasts but a little while and when affliction *or* trouble *or* persecution comes on account of the Word, at once he is caused to stumble—he is repelled and [j]begins to distrust and desert Him Whom he ought to trust and obey, and he falls away.

22As for what was sown among thorns, this is he who hears the Word, but the cares of the world and the pleasure *and* delight *and* glamour *and* deceitfulness of riches choke *and* suffocate the Word, and it yields no fruit.

23As for what was sown on good soil, this is he who hears the Word and grasps *and* comprehends it; he indeed bears fruit, and yields in one case a hundred times as much as was sown, in another sixty times as much, and in another thirty.

24Another parable He set forth before them, saying, The kingdom of heaven is like a man who sowed good seed in his field;

25But while he was sleeping, his enemy came and sowed also darnel [black, wild wheat] among the wheat, and went his way.

26So when the plants sprouted and formed grain, the darnel [weeds resembling wheat] appeared also.

27And the servants of the owner came to him and said, Sir, did you not sow good seed in your field? Then how does it have darnel shoots in it?

**AMP** [a] Thayer. [b] Abbott-Smith. [c] Thayer. [d] Thayer. [e] Thayer. [f] Vincent. [g] Souter. [h] Vincent. [i] Wycliffe. [j] Thayer.

## New American Standard

7"And others fell among the thorns, and the thorns came up and choked them out.

8"And others fell on the good soil, and *yielded a crop, some a hundredfold, some sixty, and some thirty.

9"He who has ears, let him hear."

*An Explanation*

10¶ And the disciples came and said to Him, "Why do You speak to them in parables?"

11And He answered and said to them, "To you it has been granted to know the mysteries of the kingdom of heaven, but to them it has not been granted.

12"For whoever has, to him shall *more* be given, and he shall have an abundance; but whoever does not have, even what he has shall be taken away from him.

13"Therefore I speak to them in parables; because while seeing they do not see, and while hearing they do not hear, nor do they understand.

14"And in their case the prophecy of Isaiah is being fulfilled, which says,

'YOU WILL KEEP ON HEARING, BUT WILL NOT UNDERSTAND;
AND YOU WILL KEEP ON SEEING, BUT WILL NOT PERCEIVE;
15 FOR THE HEART OF THIS PEOPLE HAS BECOME DULL,
AND WITH THEIR EARS THEY SCARCELY HEAR,
AND THEY HAVE CLOSED THEIR EYES
LEST THEY SHOULD SEE WITH THEIR EYES,
AND HEAR WITH THEIR EARS,
AND UNDERSTAND WITH THEIR HEART AND RETURN,
AND I SHOULD HEAL THEM.'

16"But blessed are your eyes, because they see; and your ears, because they hear.

17"For truly I say to you, that many prophets and righteous men desired to see what you see, and did not see *it*; and to hear what you hear, and did not hear *it*.

*The Sower Explained*

18"Hear then the parable of the sower.

19"When anyone hears the word of the kingdom, and does not understand it, the evil *one* comes and snatches away what has been sown in his heart. This is the one on whom seed was sown beside the road.

20"And the one on whom seed was sown on the rocky places, this is the man who hears the word, and immediately receives it with joy;

21yet he has no *firm* root in himself, but is *only* temporary, and when affliction or persecution arises because of the word, immediately he falls away.

22"And the one on whom seed was sown among the thorns, this is the man who hears the word, and the worry of the world, and the deceitfulness of riches choke the word, and it becomes unfruitful.

23"And the one on whom seed was sown on the good soil, this is the man who hears the word and understands it; who indeed bears fruit, and brings forth, some a hundredfold, some sixty, and some thirty."

*Tares among Wheat*

24¶ He presented another parable to them, saying, "The kingdom of heaven may be compared to a man who sowed good seed in his field.

25"But while men were sleeping, his enemy came and sowed [k]tares also among the wheat, and went away.

26"But when the wheat sprang up and bore grain, then the tares became evident also.

27"And the slaves of the landowner came and said to him, 'Sir, did you not sow good seed in your field? How then does it have tares?'

NAS [k] Or, *darnel*, a weed resembling wheat

## New International

7Other seed fell among thorns, which grew up and choked the
plants. 8Still other seed fell on good soil, where it produced a
crop—a hundred, sixty or thirty times what was sown. 9He who
has ears, let him hear."

10The disciples came to him and asked, "Why do you speak to
the people in parables?"

11He replied, "The knowledge of the secrets of the kingdom of
heaven has been given to you, but not to them. 12Whoever has will
be given more, and he will have an abundance. Whoever does not
have, even what he has will be taken from him. 13This is why I
speak to them in parables:

"Though seeing, they do not see;
though hearing, they do not hear or understand.

14In them is fulfilled the prophecy of Isaiah:

"You will be ever hearing but never understanding;
you will be ever seeing but never perceiving.
15For this people's heart has become calloused;
they hardly hear with their ears,
and they have closed their eyes.
Otherwise they might see with their eyes,
hear with their ears,
understand with their hearts
and turn, and I would heal them.'[1]

16But blessed are your eyes because they see, and your ears because they hear. 17For I tell you the truth, many prophets and
righteous men longed to see what you see but did not see it, and
to hear what you hear but did not hear it.

18"Listen then to what the parable of the sower means: 19When
anyone hears the message about the kingdom and does not understand it, the evil one comes and snatches away what was sown in
his heart. This is the seed sown along the path. 20The one who
received the seed that fell on rocky places is the man who hears
the word and at once receives it with joy. 21But since he has no
root, he lasts only a short time. When trouble or persecution comes
because of the word, he quickly falls away. 22The one who received
the seed that fell among the thorns is the man who hears the word,
but the worries of this life and the deceitfulness of wealth choke
it, making it unfruitful. 23But the one who received the seed that
fell on good soil is the man who hears the word and understands
it. He produces a crop, yielding a hundred, sixty or thirty times
what was sown."

*The Parable of the Weeds*

24Jesus told them another parable: "The kingdom of heaven is
like a man who sowed good seed in his field. 25But while everyone
was sleeping, his enemy came and sowed weeds among the
wheat, and went away. 26When the wheat sprouted and formed
heads, then the weeds also appeared.

27"The owner's servants came to him and said, 'Sir, didn't you
sow good seed in your field? Where then did the weeds come
from?'

NIV [1] *15* Isaiah 6:9,10

## King James

28He said unto them, An enemy hath done this. The servants said unto him, Wilt thou then that we go and gather them up?

29But he said, Nay; lest while ye gather up the tares, ye root up also the wheat with them.

30Let both grow together until the harvest: and in the time of harvest I will say to the reapers, Gather ye together first the tares, and bind them in bundles to burn them: but gather the wheat into my barn.

31¶ Another parable put he forth unto them, saying, The kingdom of heaven is like to a grain of mustard seed, which a man took, and sowed in his field:

32Which indeed is the least of all seeds: but when it is grown, it is the greatest among herbs, and becometh a tree, so that the birds of the air come and lodge in the branches thereof.

33¶ Another parable spake he unto them; The kingdom of heaven is like unto leaven, which a woman took, and hid in three measures of meal, till the whole was leavened.

34All these things spake Jesus unto the multitude in parables; and without a parable spake he not unto them:

35That it might be fulfilled which was spoken by the prophet, saying, I will open my mouth in parables; I will utter things which have been kept secret from the foundation of the world.

36Then Jesus sent the multitude away, and went into the house: and his disciples came unto him, saying, Declare unto us the parable of the tares of the field.

37He answered and said unto them, He that soweth the good seed is the Son of man;

38The field is the world; the good seed are the children of the kingdom; but the tares are the children of the wicked *one;*

39The enemy that sowed them is the devil; the harvest is the end of the world; and the reapers are the angels.

40As therefore the tares are gathered and burned in the fire; so shall it be in the end of this world.

41The Son of man shall send forth his angels, and they shall gather out of his kingdom all things that offend, and them which do iniquity;

42And shall cast them into a furnace of fire: there shall be wailing and gnashing of teeth.

43Then shall the righteous shine forth as the sun in the kingdom of their Father. Who hath ears to hear, let him hear.

44¶ Again, the kingdom of heaven is like unto treasure hid in a field; the which when a man hath found, he hideth, and for joy thereof goeth and selleth all that he hath, and buyeth that field.

45¶ Again, the kingdom of heaven is like unto a merchant man, seeking goodly pearls:

46Who, when he had found one pearl of great price, went and sold all that he had, and bought it.

47¶ Again, the kingdom of heaven is like unto a net, that was cast into the sea, and gathered of every kind:

48Which, when it was full, they drew to shore, and sat down, and gathered the good into vessels, but cast the bad away.

49So shall it be at the end of the world: the angels shall come forth, and sever the wicked from among the just,

## Amplified

28He replied to them, An enemy has done this. The servants said to him, Then do you want us to go and weed them out?

29But he said, No, lest in gathering the wild wheat you root up the [true] wheat along with it.

30Let them grow together until the harvest; and at harvest time I will say to the reapers, Gather the darnel first and bind it in bundles to be burned, but gather the wheat into my granary.

31Another story by way of comparison He set forth before them, saying, The kingdom of heaven is like a grain of mustard seed which a man took and sowed in his field.

32Of all the seeds it is the smallest, but when it has grown it is the largest of the garden herbs and becomes a tree, so that the birds of the air come and find shelter in its branches.

33He told them another parable: The kingdom of heaven is like leaven ([a]sour dough) which a woman took and covered over in three measures of meal *or* flour, till all of it was leavened. [Gen. 18:6.]

34These things [b]all taken together Jesus said to the crowds in parables; indeed without a parable He said nothing to them.

35This was in fulfillment of what was spoken by the prophet: I will open My mouth in parables; I will utter things that have been hidden since the foundation of the world. [Ps. 78:2.]

36Then He left the throngs and went into the house. And His disciples came to Him saying, Explain to us the parable of the darnel in the field.

37He answered, He Who sows the good seed is the Son of man;

38The field is the world, and the good seed means the children of the kingdom; the darnel is the children of the evil one,

39And the enemy who sowed it is the devil; the harvest is the close *and* consummation of the age, and the reapers are angels.

40Just as the darnel (wild wheat) is gathered and burned with fire, so it will be at the close of the age.

41The Son of man will send forth His angels, and they will gather out of His kingdom all causes of offense—[c]persons by whom others are drawn into error *or* sin—and all who do iniquity *and* act wickedly,

42And cast them into the furnace of fire; there will be weeping *and* wailing and grinding of teeth.

43Then will the righteous—those who are upright and in right standing with God—shine forth as the sun in the kingdom of their Father. Let him who has ears be listening, *and* [d]consider *and* perceive *and* understand by listening.

44The kingdom of heaven is like [e]something precious buried in a field, which a man found and hid again; then in his joy he goes and sells all he has and buys that field.

45Again the kingdom of heaven is like a man who is a dealer in search of fine *and* [f]precious pearls,

46Who, on finding a single pearl of great price, went and sold all he had and bought it.

47Again, the kingdom of heaven is like a [g]dragnet which was cast into the sea and gathered in fish of every sort;

48When it was full, men dragged it up on the beach and sat down and sorted out the good fish into vessels, but the worthless ones they threw away.

49So it will be at the close *and* consummation of the age. The angels will go forth and separate the wicked from the righteous—those who are upright and in right standing with God—

**AMP** [a] Wycliffe. [b] Thayer. [c] Thayer. [d] Thayer. [e] Thayer. [f] Thayer. [g] Vincent.

## New American Standard

28"And he said to them, 'An enemy has done this!' And the
slaves *said to him, 'Do you want us, then, to go and gather them
up?'
29"But he *said, 'No; lest while you are gathering up the tares,
you may root up the wheat with them.
30'Allow both to grow together until the harvest; and in the time
of the harvest I will say to the reapers, "First gather up the tares
and bind them in bundles to burn them up; but gather the wheat
into my barn." ' "

*The Mustard Seed*

31¶ He presented another parable to them, saying, "The kingdom of heaven is like a mustard seed, which a man took and sowed
in his field;
32and this is smaller than all *other* seeds; but when it is full
grown, it is larger than the garden plants, and becomes a tree, so
that THE BIRDS OF THE AIR come and NEST IN ITS BRANCHES."

*The Leaven*

33¶ He spoke another parable to them, "The kingdom of heaven
is like leaven, which a woman took, and hid in three pecks of meal,
until it was all leavened."
34¶ All these things Jesus spoke to the multitudes in parables,
and He did not speak to them without a parable,
35so that what was spoken through the prophet might be fulfilled, saying,

"I WILL OPEN MY MOUTH IN PARABLES;
I WILL UTTER THINGS HIDDEN SINCE THE FOUNDATION OF
THE WORLD."

*The Tares Explained*

36¶ Then He left the multitudes, and went into the house. And
His disciples came to Him, saying, "Explain to us the parable of
the tares of the field."
37And He answered and said, "The one who sows the good
seed is the Son of Man,
38and the field is the world; and *as for* the good seed, these are
the sons of the kingdom; and the tares are the sons of the evil *one;*
39and the enemy who sowed them is the devil, and the harvest
is the end of the age; and the reapers are angels.
40"Therefore just as the tares are gathered up and burned with
fire, so shall it be at the end of the age.
41"The Son of Man will send forth His angels, and they will
gather out of His kingdom all stumbling blocks, and those who
commit lawlessness,
42and will cast them into the furnace of fire; in that place there
shall be weeping and gnashing of teeth.
43"Then THE RIGHTEOUS WILL SHINE FORTH AS THE SUN in the
kingdom of their Father. He who has ears, let him hear.

*Hidden Treasure*

44¶ "The kingdom of heaven is like a treasure hidden in the
field, which a man found and hid; and from joy over it he goes and
sells all that he has, and buys that field.

*A Costly Pearl*

45¶ "Again, the kingdom of heaven is like a merchant seeking
fine pearls,
46and upon finding one pearl of great value, he went and sold
all that he had, and bought it.

*A Dragnet*

47¶ "Again, the kingdom of heaven is like a dragnet cast into
the sea, and gathering *fish* of every kind;
48and when it was filled, they drew it up on the beach; and they
sat down, and gathered the good *fish* into containers, but the bad
they threw away.
49"So it will be at the end of the age; the angels shall come forth,
and take out the wicked from among the righteous,

## New International

28" 'An enemy did this,' he replied.
"The servants asked him, 'Do you want us to go and pull them
up?'
29" 'No,' he answered, 'because while you are pulling the
weeds, you may root up the wheat with them. 30Let both grow
together until the harvest. At that time I will tell the harvesters:
First collect the weeds and tie them in bundles to be burned; then
gather the wheat and bring it into my barn.' "

*The Parables of the Mustard Seed and the Yeast*

31He told them another parable: "The kingdom of heaven is like
a mustard seed, which a man took and planted in his field.
32Though it is the smallest of all your seeds, yet when it grows, it
is the largest of garden plants and becomes a tree, so that the birds
of the air come and perch in its branches."
33He told them still another parable: "The kingdom of heaven
is like yeast that a woman took and mixed into a large amount[h]
of flour until it worked all through the dough."
34Jesus spoke all these things to the crowd in parables; he did
not say anything to them without using a parable. 35So was fulfilled what was spoken through the prophet:

"I will open my mouth in parables,
I will utter things hidden since the creation of the
world."[i]

*The Parable of the Weeds Explained*

36Then he left the crowd and went into the house. His disciples
came to him and said, "Explain to us the parable of the weeds in
the field."
37He answered, "The one who sowed the good seed is the Son
of Man. 38The field is the world, and the good seed stands for the
sons of the kingdom. The weeds are the sons of the evil one, 39and
the enemy who sows them is the devil. The harvest is the end of
the age, and the harvesters are angels.
40"As the weeds are pulled up and burned in the fire, so it will
be at the end of the age. 41The Son of Man will send out his angels,
and they will weed out of his kingdom everything that causes sin
and all who do evil. 42They will throw them into the fiery furnace,
where there will be weeping and gnashing of teeth. 43Then the
righteous will shine like the sun in the kingdom of their Father. He
who has ears, let him hear.

*The Parables of the Hidden Treasure and the Pearl*

44"The kingdom of heaven is like treasure hidden in a field.
When a man found it, he hid it again, and then in his joy went and
sold all he had and bought that field.
45"Again, the kingdom of heaven is like a merchant looking for
fine pearls. 46When he found one of great value, he went away and
sold everything he had and bought it.

*The Parable of the Net*

47"Once again, the kingdom of heaven is like a net that was let
down into the lake and caught all kinds of fish. 48When it was full,
the fishermen pulled it up on the shore. Then they sat down and
collected the good fish in baskets, but threw the bad away. 49This
is how it will be at the end of the age. The angels will come and
separate the wicked from the righteous 50and throw them into the

NIV [h] 33 Greek *three satas* (probably about 1/2 bushel or 22 liters) [i] 35 Psalm 78:2

## King James

50And shall cast them into the furnace of fire: there shall be wailing and gnashing of teeth.

51Jesus saith unto them, Have ye understood all these things? They say unto him, Yea, Lord.

52Then said he unto them, Therefore every scribe *which is* instructed unto the kingdom of heaven is like unto a man *that is* an householder, which bringeth forth out of his treasure *things* new and old.

53¶ And it came to pass, *that* when Jesus had finished these parables, he departed thence.

54And when he was come into his own country, he taught them in their synagogue, insomuch that they were astonished, and said, Whence hath this *man* this wisdom, and *these* mighty works?

55Is not this the carpenter's son? is not his mother called Mary? and his brethren, James, and Joses, and Simon, and Judas?

56And his sisters, are they not all with us? Whence then hath this *man* all these things?

57And they were offended in him. But Jesus said unto them, A prophet is not without honour, save in his own country, and in his own house.

58And he did not many mighty works there because of their unbelief.

**14** AT THAT time Herod the tetrarch heard of the fame of Jesus,

2And said unto his servants, This is John the Baptist; he is risen from the dead; and therefore mighty works do show forth themselves in him.

3¶ For Herod had laid hold on John, and bound him, and put *him* in prison for Herodias' sake, his brother Philip's wife.

4For John said unto him, It is not lawful for thee to have her.

5And when he would have put him to death, he feared the multitude, because they counted him as a prophet.

6But when Herod's birthday was kept, the daughter of Herodias danced before them, and pleased Herod.

7Whereupon he promised with an oath to give her whatsoever she would ask.

8And she, being before instructed of her mother, said, Give me here John Baptist's head in a charger.

9And the king was sorry: nevertheless for the oath's sake, and them which sat with him at meat, he commanded *it* to be given *her*.

10And he sent, and beheaded John in the prison.

11And his head was brought in a charger, and given to the damsel: and she brought *it* to her mother.

12And his disciples came, and took up the body, and buried it, and went and told Jesus.

13¶ When Jesus heard *of it,* he departed thence by ship into a desert place apart: and when the people had heard *thereof,* they followed him on foot out of the cities.

14And Jesus went forth, and saw a great multitude, and was moved with compassion toward them, and he healed their sick.

15¶ And when it was evening, his disciples came to him, saying, This is a desert place, and the time is now past; send the multitude away, that they may go into the villages, and buy themselves victuals.

16But Jesus said unto them, They need not depart; give ye them to eat.

17And they say unto him, We have here but five loaves, and two fishes.

18He said, Bring them hither to me.

## Amplified

50And cast [the wicked] into the furnace of fire; there will be weeping *and* wailing and grinding of teeth.

51Have you understood [a]all these [parables] taken together? They said to Him, Yes, *Lord.*

52He said to them, Therefore every [b]teacher *and* interpreter of the Sacred Writings who has been instructed *and* trained for the kingdom of heaven and [c]become a disciple, is like a householder who brings forth out of his storehouse treasure that is new and [treasure that is] old—the fresh [as well as] the familiar.

53When Jesus had finished these parables—these comparisons—He left there.

54And coming to His own country [Capernaum] He taught in their synagogue so that they were amazed with bewildered wonder, and said, Where did this Man get this wisdom and these miraculous powers?

55Is not this the carpenter's Son? Is not His mother called Mary? And are not His brothers James and Joseph and Simon and Judas?

56And do not all His sisters live here among us? Where then did this Man get all this?

57And they took offense at Him—[that is], they were repelled and hindered from acknowledging His authority and caused to stumble. But Jesus said to them, A prophet is not without honor except in his own country and in his own house.

58And He did not do many works of power there, because of their unbelief—their lack of faith [ [d]in the divine mission of Jesus].

**14** AT THAT time Herod the governor heard the reports about Jesus.

2And he said to his attendants, This is John the Baptist; He has been raised from the dead, and that is why the powers [e]of performing miracles are at work in Him.

3For Herod had arrested John and bound him and (to [f]stow him out of the way) put him in prison, on account *and* for the sake of Herodias, his brother Philip's wife; for John had said to him,

4It is not lawful *or* right for you to have her. [Lev. 18:16; 20:21.]

5Although he wished to have him put to death, he was afraid of the people, for they regarded John as a prophet.

6But when Herod's birthday came, the daughter of Herodias danced in the midst [before the company], and pleased *and* fascinated Herod,

7And so he promised with an oath to give her whatever she might ask.

8And she, being put forward *and* prompted by her mother, said, Give me the head of John the Baptist right here on a [g]platter.

9And the king was distressed *and* sorry; but because of his oaths and his guests he ordered it to be given her;

10He sent and had John beheaded in the prison.

11And his head was brought in on a [h]platter and given [i]to the little maid, and she brought it to her mother.

12And John's disciples came and took up the body and buried it. Then they went and told Jesus.

13When Jesus heard it, He withdrew from there privately in a boat to a solitary place. But when the crowds heard of it, they followed Him by land on foot from the towns.

14When He went ashore and saw a great throng of people, He had compassion (pity and deep sympathy) for them and cured their sick.

15When evening came, the disciples came to Him and said, This is a remote *and* barren place, and the day is now over; send the throngs away into the villages to buy food for themselves.

16Jesus said, They do not need to go away; you give them something to eat.

17They said to Him, We have nothing here but five loaves and two fish.

18He said, Bring them here to Me.

AMP [a] Thayer. [b] Thayer. [c] Vincent. [d] Vincent. [e] Vincent. [f] Abbott-Smith. [g] Tyndale. [h] Tyndale. [i] Luther (-Vincent).

## New American Standard

50and will cast them into the furnace of fire; there shall be
weeping and gnashing of teeth.
51¶ "Have you understood all these things?" They *said to Him,
"Yes."
52And He said to them, "Therefore every scribe who has
become a disciple of the kingdom of heaven is like a head of a
household, who brings forth out of his treasure things new and
old."

*Jesus Revisits Nazareth*

53¶ And it came about that when Jesus had finished these parables, He departed from there.
54And coming to His home town He *began* teaching them in
their synagogue, so that they became astonished, and said,
"Where *did* this man *get* this wisdom, and *these* miraculous powers?
55"Is not this the carpenter's son? Is not His mother called
Mary, and His brothers, James and Joseph and Simon and Judas?
56"And His sisters, are they not all with us? Where then *did* this
man *get* all these things?"
57And they took offense at Him. But Jesus said to them, "A
prophet is not without honor except in his home town, and in his
*own* household."
58And He did not do many miracles there because of their
unbelief.

*John the Baptist Beheaded*

14 AT THAT time Herod the tetrarch heard the news about
Jesus,
2and said to his servants, "This is John the Baptist; he has risen
from the dead; and that is why miraculous powers are at work in
him."
3For when Herod had John arrested, he bound him, and put
him in prison on account of Herodias, the wife of his brother
Philip.
4For John had been saying to him, "It is not lawful for you to
have her."
5And although he wanted to put him to death, he feared the
multitude, because they regarded him as a prophet.
6But when Herod's birthday came, the daughter of Herodias
danced before *them* and pleased Herod.
7Thereupon he promised with an oath to give her whatever she
asked.
8And having been prompted by her mother, she *said, "Give
me here on a platter the head of John the Baptist."
9And although he was grieved, the king commanded *it* to be
given because of his oaths, and because of his dinner guests.
10And he sent and had John beheaded in the prison.
11And his head was brought on a platter and given to the girl;
and she brought *it* to her mother.
12And his disciples came and took away the body and buried
it; and they went and reported to Jesus.

*Five Thousand Fed*

13¶ Now when Jesus heard *it*, He withdrew from there in a boat,
to a lonely place by Himself; and when the multitudes heard *of this*,
they followed Him on foot from the cities.
14And when He went ashore, He saw a great multitude, and felt
compassion for them, and healed their sick.
15And when it was evening, the disciples came to Him, saying,
"The place is desolate, and the time is already past; so send the
multitudes away, that they may go into the villages and buy food
for themselves."
16But Jesus said to them, "They do not need to go away; you
give them *something* to eat!"
17And they *said to Him, "We have here only five loaves and
two fish."
18And He said, "Bring them here to Me."

## New International

fiery furnace, where there will be weeping and gnashing of teeth.
51"Have you understood all these things?" Jesus asked.
"Yes," they replied.
52He said to them, "Therefore every teacher of the law who has
been instructed about the kingdom of heaven is like the owner of
a house who brings out of his storeroom new treasures as well as
old."

*A Prophet Without Honor*

53When Jesus had finished these parables, he moved on from
there. 54Coming to his hometown, he began teaching the people
in their synagogue, and they were amazed. "Where did this man
get this wisdom and these miraculous powers?" they asked.
55"Isn't this the carpenter's son? Isn't his mother's name Mary,
and aren't his brothers James, Joseph, Simon and Judas? 56Aren't
all his sisters with us? Where then did this man get all these
things?" 57And they took offense at him.
But Jesus said to them, "Only in his hometown and in his own
house is a prophet without honor."
58And he did not do many miracles there because of their lack
of faith.

*John the Baptist Beheaded*

14 AT THAT time Herod the tetrarch heard the reports about
Jesus, 2and he said to his attendants, "This is John the
Baptist; he has risen from the dead! That is why miraculous powers
are at work in him."
3Now Herod had arrested John and bound him and put him in
prison because of Herodias, his brother Philip's wife, 4for John had
been saying to him: "It is not lawful for you to have her." 5Herod
wanted to kill John, but he was afraid of the people, because they
considered him a prophet.
6On Herod's birthday the daughter of Herodias danced for
them and pleased Herod so much 7that he promised with an oath
to give her whatever she asked. 8Prompted by her mother, she
said, "Give me here on a platter the head of John the Baptist." 9The
king was distressed, but because of his oaths and his dinner
guests, he ordered that her request be granted 10and had John
beheaded in the prison. 11His head was brought in on a platter and
given to the girl, who carried it to her mother. 12John's disciples
came and took his body and buried it. Then they went and told
Jesus.

*Jesus Feeds the Five Thousand*

13When Jesus heard what had happened, he withdrew by boat
privately to a solitary place. Hearing of this, the crowds followed
him on foot from the towns. 14When Jesus landed and saw a large
crowd, he had compassion on them and healed their sick.
15As evening approached, the disciples came to him and said,
"This is a remote place, and it's already getting late. Send the
crowds away, so they can go to the villages and buy themselves
some food."
16Jesus replied, "They do not need to go away. You give them
something to eat."
17"We have here only five loaves of bread and two fish," they
answered.
18"Bring them here to me," he said. 19And he directed the

## King James

19 And he commanded the multitude to sit down on the grass, and took the five loaves, and the two fishes, and looking up to heaven, he blessed, and brake, and gave the loaves to *his* disciples, and the disciples to the multitude.

20 And they did all eat, and were filled: and they took up of the fragments that remained twelve baskets full.

21 And they that had eaten were about five thousand men, beside women and children.

22 ¶ And straightway Jesus constrained his disciples to get into a ship, and to go before him unto the other side, while he sent the multitudes away.

23 And when he had sent the multitudes away, he went up into a mountain apart to pray: and when the evening was come, he was there alone.

24 But the ship was now in the midst of the sea, tossed with waves: for the wind was contrary.

25 And in the fourth watch of the night Jesus went unto them, walking on the sea.

26 And when the disciples saw him walking on the sea, they were troubled, saying, It is a spirit; and they cried out for fear.

27 But straightway Jesus spake unto them, saying, Be of good cheer; it is I; be not afraid.

28 And Peter answered him and said, Lord, if it be thou, bid me come unto thee on the water.

29 And he said, Come. And when Peter was come down out of the ship, he walked on the water, to go to Jesus.

30 But when he saw the wind boisterous, he was afraid; and beginning to sink, he cried, saying, Lord, save me.

31 And immediately Jesus stretched forth *his* hand, and caught him, and said unto him, O thou of little faith, wherefore didst thou doubt?

32 And when they were come into the ship, the wind ceased.

33 Then they that were in the ship came and worshipped him, saying, Of a truth thou art the Son of God.

34 ¶ And when they were gone over, they came into the land of Gennesaret.

35 And when the men of that place had knowledge of him, they sent out into all that country round about, and brought unto him all that were diseased;

36 And besought him that they might only touch the hem of his garment: and as many as touched were made perfectly whole.

**15** THEN CAME to Jesus scribes and Pharisees, which were of Jerusalem, saying,

2 Why do thy disciples transgress the tradition of the elders? for they wash not their hands when they eat bread.

3 But he answered and said unto them, Why do ye also transgress the commandment of God by your tradition?

4 For God commanded, saying, Honour thy father and mother: and, He that curseth father or mother, let him die the death.

5 But ye say, Whosoever shall say to *his* father or *his* mother, *It is* a gift, by whatsoever thou mightest be profited by me;

6 And honour not his father or his mother, *he shall be free*. Thus have ye made the commandment of God of none effect by your tradition.

7 *Ye* hypocrites, well did Esaias prophesy of you, saying,

AMP [a] Vincent. But Moulton and Milligan: Term *"refers to material, not size."*

## Amplified

19 Then He ordered the crowds to recline on the grass; and He took the five loaves and two fish, and looking up to heaven He gave thanks, and blessed and broke the loaves and handed the pieces to the disciples, and the disciples gave them to the people.

20 And they all ate and were satisfied. And they picked up twelve [[a]small hand] baskets full of the broken pieces left over.

21 And those who ate were about five thousand men, not including women and children.

22 Then He directed the disciples to get into the boat and go before Him to the other side, while He sent away the crowds.

23 And after He had dismissed the multitude, He went up into the hills by Himself to pray. When it was evening He was still there alone.

24 But the boat was by this time out on the sea, *many furlongs* [one-eighth miles] *distant from the land,* beaten and tossed by the waves, for the wind was against them.

25 And in the fourth watch [between three and six o'clock] of the night, Jesus came to them, walking on the sea.

26 And when the disciples saw Him walking on the sea, they were terrified, and said, It is a ghost! And they screamed out with fright.

27 But instantly He spoke to them, saying, Take courage! I AM; stop being afraid! [Exod. 3:14.]

28 And Peter answered Him, Lord, if it is You, command me to come to You on the water.

29 He said, Come! So Peter got out of the boat and walked on the water, and he came to Jesus;

30 But when he perceived *and* felt the strong wind, he was frightened, and as he began to sink, he cried out, Lord, save me [from death]!

31 Instantly Jesus reached out His hand and caught *and* held him, saying to him, O you of little faith, why did you doubt?

32 And when they got into the boat, the wind ceased.

33 And those in the boat knelt and worshipped Him, saying, Truly, You are the Son of God!

34 And when they had crossed over to the other side, they went ashore at Gennesaret.

35 And when the men of that place recognized Him, they sent around into all the surrounding country and brought to Him all that were sick,

36 And begged Him to let them merely touch the fringe of His garment; and as many as touched it were perfectly restored. [Num. 15:38.]

**15** THEN FROM Jerusalem there came scribes and Pharisees and said,

2 Why do Your disciples transgress *and* violate the rules handed down by the elders of the past? For they do not practice [ceremonially] washing their hands before they eat.

3 He replied to them, And why also do you transgress *and* violate the commandment of God for the sake of the rules handed down to you by your forefathers—the elders?

4 For God commanded, Honor your father and your mother, and, He who curses *or* reviles *or* speaks evil of *or* abuses *or* treats improperly his father or mother, let him surely come to his end by death. [Exod. 20:12; Deut. 5:16; Exod. 21:17; Lev. 20:9.]

5 But you say, If any one tells his father or mother, What you would have gained from me [that is, the money and whatever I have that might be used for helping you] is already dedicated as a gift to God, then he is exempt *and* no longer under obligation to honor *and* help his father *and his mother.*

6 So for the sake of your tradition (the rules handed down by your forefathers), you have set aside the Word of God—depriving it of force and authority and making it of no effect.

7 You pretenders—hypocrites! Admirably *and* truly did Isaiah prophesy of you when he said:

## New American Standard

19 And ordering the multitudes to recline on the grass, He took
the five loaves and the two fish, and looking up toward heaven,
He blessed *the food,* and breaking the loaves He gave them to the
disciples, and the disciples *gave* to the multitudes,
20 and they all ate, and were satisfied. And they picked up what
was left over of the broken pieces, twelve full baskets.
21 And there were about five thousand men who ate, aside from
women and children.

*Jesus Walks on the Water*

22 ¶ And immediately He made the disciples get into the boat,
and go ahead of Him to the other side, while He sent the multitudes away.
23 And after He had sent the multitudes away, He went up to
the mountain by Himself to pray; and when it was evening, He
was there alone.
24 But the boat was already many [b]stadia away from the land,
battered by the waves; for the wind was contrary.
25 And in the [c]fourth watch of the night He came to them,
walking on the sea.
26 And when the disciples saw Him walking on the sea, they
were frightened, saying, "It is a ghost!" And they cried out for
fear.
27 But immediately Jesus spoke to them, saying, "Take courage,
it is I; do not be afraid."
28 And Peter answered Him and said, "Lord, if it is You, command me to come to You on the water."
29 And He said, "Come!" And Peter got out of the boat, and
walked on the water and came toward Jesus.
30 But seeing the wind, he became afraid, and beginning to sink,
he cried out, saying, "Lord, save me!"
31 And immediately Jesus stretched out His hand and took hold
of him, and *said to him, "O you of little faith, why did you
doubt?"
32 And when they got into the boat, the wind stopped.
33 And those who were in the boat worshiped Him, saying,
"You are certainly God's Son!"
34 ¶ And when they had crossed over, they came to land at
Gennesaret.
35 And when the men of that place recognized Him, they sent
into all that surrounding district and brought to Him all who were
sick;
36 and they *began* to entreat Him that they might just touch the
fringe of His cloak; and as many as touched *it* were cured.

*Tradition and Commandment*

15 THEN SOME Pharisees and scribes *came to Jesus from
Jerusalem, saying,
2 "Why do Your disciples transgress the tradition of the elders?
For they do not wash their hands when they eat bread."
3 And He answered and said to them, "And why do you yourselves transgress the commandment of God for the sake of your
tradition?
4 "For God said, 'HONOR YOUR FATHER AND MOTHER,' and, 'HE
WHO SPEAKS EVIL OF FATHER OR MOTHER, LET HIM BE PUT TO DEATH.'
5 "But you say, 'Whoever shall say to *his* father or mother,
"Anything of mine you might have been helped by has been given
*to God,*"
6 he is not to honor his father [d]or his mother [e].' And *thus* you
invalidated the word of God for the sake of your tradition.
7 "You hypocrites, rightly did Isaiah prophesy of you, saying,

NAS [b] A stadion was about 600 feet [c] I.e., 3–6 a.m. [d] Many mss. do not contain *or his mother* [e] I.e., by supporting them with it

## New International

people to sit down on the grass. Taking the five loaves and the two
fish and looking up to heaven, he gave thanks and broke the
loaves. Then he gave them to the disciples, and the disciples gave
them to the people. 20 They all ate and were satisfied, and the
disciples picked up twelve basketfuls of broken pieces that were
left over. 21 The number of those who ate was about five thousand
men, besides women and children.

*Jesus Walks on the Water*

22 Immediately Jesus made the disciples get into the boat and go
on ahead of him to the other side, while he dismissed the crowd.
23 After he had dismissed them, he went up on a mountainside by
himself to pray. When evening came, he was there alone, 24 but the
boat was already a considerable distance[f] from land, buffeted by
the waves because the wind was against it.
25 During the fourth watch of the night Jesus went out to them,
walking on the lake. 26 When the disciples saw him walking on the
lake, they were terrified. "It's a ghost," they said, and cried out
in fear.
27 But Jesus immediately said to them: "Take courage! It is I.
Don't be afraid."
28 "Lord, if it's you," Peter replied, "tell me to come to you on
the water."
29 "Come," he said.
Then Peter got down out of the boat, walked on the water and
came toward Jesus. 30 But when he saw the wind, he was afraid
and, beginning to sink, cried out, "Lord, save me!"
31 Immediately Jesus reached out his hand and caught him.
"You of little faith," he said, "why did you doubt?"
32 And when they climbed into the boat, the wind died down.
33 Then those who were in the boat worshiped him, saying, "Truly
you are the Son of God."
34 When they had crossed over, they landed at Gennesaret.
35 And when the men of that place recognized Jesus, they sent
word to all the surrounding country. People brought all their sick
to him 36 and begged him to let the sick just touch the edge of his
cloak, and all who touched him were healed.

*Clean and Unclean*

15 THEN SOME Pharisees and teachers of the law came to
Jesus from Jerusalem and asked, 2 "Why do your disciples
break the tradition of the elders? They don't wash their hands
before they eat!"
3 Jesus replied, "And why do you break the command of God
for the sake of your tradition? 4 For God said, 'Honor your father
and mother'[g] and 'Anyone who curses his father or mother must
be put to death.'[h] 5 But you say that if a man says to his father or
mother, 'Whatever help you might otherwise have received from
me is a gift devoted to God,' 6 he is not to 'honor his father[i]' with
it. Thus you nullify the word of God for the sake of your tradition.
7 You hypocrites! Isaiah was right when he prophesied about you:

NIV [f] 24 Greek *many stadia* [g] 4 Exodus 20:12; Deut. 5:16 [h] 4 Exodus 21:17; Lev. 20:9 [i] 6 Some manuscripts *father or his mother*

## King James

8 This people draweth nigh unto me with their mouth, and honoureth me with *their* lips; but their heart is far from me.

9 But in vain they do worship me, teaching *for* doctrines the commandments of men.

10 ¶ And he called the multitude, and said unto them, Hear, and understand:

11 Not that which goeth into the mouth defileth a man; but that which cometh out of the mouth, this defileth a man.

12 Then came his disciples, and said unto him, Knowest thou that the Pharisees were offended, after they heard this saying?

13 But he answered and said, Every plant, which my heavenly Father hath not planted, shall be rooted up.

14 Let them alone: they be blind leaders of the blind. And if the blind lead the blind, both shall fall into the ditch.

15 Then answered Peter and said unto him, Declare unto us this parable.

16 And Jesus said, Are ye also yet without understanding?

17 Do not ye yet understand, that whatsoever entereth in at the mouth goeth into the belly, and is cast out into the draught?

18 But those things which proceed out of the mouth come forth from the heart; and they defile the man.

19 For out of the heart proceed evil thoughts, murders, adulteries, fornications, thefts, false witness, blasphemies:

20 These are *the things* which defile a man: but to eat with unwashen hands defileth not a man.

21 ¶ Then Jesus went thence, and departed into the coasts of Tyre and Sidon.

22 And, behold, a woman of Canaan came out of the same coasts, and cried unto him, saying, Have mercy on me, O Lord, *thou* Son of David; my daughter is grievously vexed with a devil.

23 But he answered her not a word. And his disciples came and besought him, saying, Send her away; for she crieth after us.

24 But he answered and said, I am not sent but unto the lost sheep of the house of Israel.

25 Then came she and worshipped him, saying, Lord, help me.

26 But he answered and said, It is not meet to take the children's bread, and to cast *it* to dogs.

27 And she said, Truth, Lord: yet the dogs eat of the crumbs which fall from their masters' table.

28 Then Jesus answered and said unto her, O woman, great *is* thy faith: be it unto thee even as thou wilt. And her daughter was made whole from that very hour.

29 And Jesus departed from thence, and came nigh unto the sea of Galilee; and went up into a mountain, and sat down there.

30 And great multitudes came unto him, having with them *those that were* lame, blind, dumb, maimed, and many others, and cast them down at Jesus' feet; and he healed them:

31 Insomuch that the multitude wondered, when they saw the dumb to speak, the maimed to be whole, the lame to walk, and the blind to see: and they glorified the God of Israel.

32 ¶ Then Jesus called his disciples *unto him,* and said, I have compassion on the multitude, because they continue with me now three days, and have nothing to eat: and I will not send them away fasting, lest they faint in the way.

33 And his disciples say unto him, Whence should we have so much bread in the wilderness, as to fill so great a multitude?

## Amplified

8 This people *draw near Me with their mouth and* honor Me with their lips, but their heart holds off *and* is far away from Me;

9 Uselessly do they worship Me, for they teach as doctrines the commands of men. [Isa. 29:13.]

10 And Jesus called the people to Him and said to them, Listen, and grasp *and* comprehend this:

11 It is not what goes into the mouth of a man that makes him unclean *and* defiled, but what comes out of the mouth; this makes a man unclean *and* defiles [him].

12 Then the disciples came and said to Him, Do You know that the Pharisees were displeased *and* offended *and* indignant when they heard this saying?

13 He answered, Every plant which My heavenly Father has not planted will be torn up by the roots. [Isa. 60:21.]

14 Let them alone *and* disregard them; they are blind guides *and* teachers. And if a blind man leads a blind man, both will fall into a ditch.

15 But Peter said to Him, Explain this [a]proverb—this [b]maxim—to us.

16 And He said, Are you also even yet dull *and* ignorant—without understanding and [c]unable to put things together?

17 Do you not see *and* understand that whatever goes into the mouth passes into the [d]abdomen, and so passes on into the place where discharges are deposited?

18 But what comes out of the mouth comes from the heart, and this is what makes a man unclean *and* defiles [him].

19 For out of the heart come evil thoughts (reasonings and disputings and designs) such as murder, adultery, sexual vice, theft, false witnessing, slander *and* irreverent speech.

20 These are what make a man unclean *and* defile [him]; but eating with hands unwashed does not make him unclean *or* defile [him].

21 And going away from there, Jesus withdrew to the district of Tyre and Sidon.

22 And behold, a woman who was a Canaanite of that district came out and with a (loud, troublesomely urgent) cry begged, Have mercy on me, O Lord, Son of David! My daughter is miserably *and* distressingly *and* cruelly possessed by a demon!

23 But He did not answer her a word. And His disciples came and implored Him, saying, Send her away, for she is crying after us.

24 He answered, I was sent only to the lost sheep of the house of Israel.

25 But she came and kneeling, worshipped Him, and kept praying, Lord, help me!

26 And He answered, It is not right—proper, becoming or fair—to take the children's bread and throw it to the [e]little dogs.

27 She said, Yes, Lord, yet even the [f]little pups eat the crumbs that fall from their (young) masters' table.

28 Then Jesus answered her, O woman, great is your faith! Be it done for you as you wish. And her daughter was cured from that [g]moment.

29 And Jesus went on from there and passed along the shore of the sea of Galilee. Then He went up into the hills and kept sitting there.

30 And a great multitude came to Him, bringing with them the lame, the maimed, the blind, the dumb, and many others, and they put them down at His feet and He cured them.

31 So that the crowd was amazed when they saw the dumb speaking, the maimed whole, the lame walking, and the blind seeing, and they [h]recognized *and* praised *and* thanked *and* glorified the God of Israel.

32 Then Jesus called His disciples to Him and said, I have pity *and* sympathy *and* am deeply moved for the crowd, because they have been with Me now three days, and they have nothing [at all left] to eat, and I am not willing to send them away hungry lest they faint *or* become exhausted on the way.

33 And the disciples said to Him, Where are we to get bread sufficient to feed so great a crowd in this isolated *and* desert place?

**AMP** [a] Abbott-Smith. [b] Thayer. [c] Cremer. [d] Moulton and Milligan. [e] Vincent. [f] Wycliffe: "little whelps." [g] Moulton and Milligan. [h] Cremer.

## New American Standard

8 'This people honors Me with their lips,
But their heart is far away from Me.
9 'But in vain do they worship Me,
Teaching as doctrines the precepts of men.' "
10And after He called the multitude to Him, He said to them,
"Hear, and understand.
11"Not what enters into the mouth defiles the man, but what
proceeds out of the mouth, this defiles the man."
12Then the disciples *came and *said to Him, "Do You know
that the Pharisees were offended when they heard this
statement?"
13But He answered and said, "Every plant which My heavenly
Father did not plant shall be rooted up.
14"Let them alone; they are blind guides [i]of the blind. And if
a blind man guides a blind man, both will fall into a pit."

*The Heart of Man*

15And Peter answered and said to Him, "Explain the parable to
us."
16And He said, "Are you still lacking in understanding also?
17"Do you not understand that everything that goes into the
mouth passes into the stomach, and is eliminated?
18"But the things that proceed out of the mouth come from the
heart, and those defile the man.
19"For out of the heart come evil thoughts, murders, adulteries,
fornications, thefts, false witness, slanders.
20"These are the things which defile the man; but to eat with
unwashed hands does not defile the man."

*The Syrophoenician Woman*

**21**¶ And Jesus went away from there, and withdrew into the
district of Tyre and Sidon.
22And behold, a Canaanite woman came out from that region,
and *began* to cry out, saying, "Have mercy on me, O Lord, Son of
David; my daughter is cruelly demon-possessed."
23But He did not answer her a word. And His disciples came
to *Him* and kept asking Him, saying, "Send her away, for she is
shouting out after us."
24But He answered and said, "I was sent only to the lost sheep
of the house of Israel."
25But she came and *began* to bow down before Him, saying,
"Lord, help me!"
26And He answered and said, "It is not good to take the children's bread and throw it to the dogs."
27But she said, "Yes, Lord; but even the dogs feed on the
crumbs which fall from their masters' table."
28Then Jesus answered and said to her, "O woman, your faith
is great; be it done for you as you wish." And her daughter was
healed at once.

*Healing Multitudes*

**29**¶ And departing from there, Jesus went along by the Sea of
Galilee, and having gone up to the mountain, He was sitting there.
30And great multitudes came to Him, bringing with them *those
who were* lame, crippled, blind, dumb, and many others, and they
laid them down at His feet; and He healed them,
31so that the multitude marveled as they saw the dumb speaking, the crippled restored, and the lame walking, and the blind
seeing; and they glorified the God of Israel.

*Four Thousand Fed*

**32**¶ And Jesus called His disciples to Him, and said, "I feel
compassion for the multitude, because they have remained with
Me now three days and have nothing to eat; and I do not wish to
send them away hungry, lest they faint on the way."
33And the disciples *said to Him, "Where would we get so
many loaves in a desolate place to satisfy such a great multitude?"

NAS [i] Some mss. do not contain *of the blind*

## New International

8" 'These people honor me with their lips,
but their hearts are far from me.
9They worship me in vain;
their teachings are but rules taught by men.'[j] "
10Jesus called the crowd to him and said, "Listen and understand. 11What goes into a man's mouth does not make him 'unclean,' but what comes out of his mouth, that is what makes him
'unclean.' "
12Then the disciples came to him and asked, "Do you know that
the Pharisees were offended when they heard this?"
13He replied, "Every plant that my heavenly Father has not
planted will be pulled up by the roots. 14Leave them; they are blind
guides.[k] If a blind man leads a blind man, both will fall into a pit."
15Peter said, "Explain the parable to us."
16"Are you still so dull?" Jesus asked them. 17"Don't you see
that whatever enters the mouth goes into the stomach and then out
of the body? 18But the things that come out of the mouth come
from the heart, and these make a man 'unclean.' 19For out of the
heart come evil thoughts, murder, adultery, sexual immorality,
theft, false testimony, slander. 20These are what make a man 'unclean'; but eating with unwashed hands does not make him 'unclean.' "

*The Faith of the Canaanite Woman*

21Leaving that place, Jesus withdrew to the region of Tyre and
Sidon. 22A Canaanite woman from that vicinity came to him, crying out, "Lord, Son of David, have mercy on me! My daughter is
suffering terribly from demon-possession."
23Jesus did not answer a word. So his disciples came to him and
urged him, "Send her away, for she keeps crying out after us."
24He answered, "I was sent only to the lost sheep of Israel."
25The woman came and knelt before him. "Lord, help me!" she
said.
26He replied, "It is not right to take the children's bread and toss
it to their dogs."
27"Yes, Lord," she said, "but even the dogs eat the crumbs that
fall from their masters' table."
28Then Jesus answered, "Woman, you have great faith! Your
request is granted." And her daughter was healed from that very
hour.

*Jesus Feeds the Four Thousand*

29Jesus left there and went along the Sea of Galilee. Then he
went up on a mountainside and sat down. 30Great crowds came
to him, bringing the lame, the blind, the crippled, the mute and
many others, and laid them at his feet; and he healed them. 31The
people were amazed when they saw the mute speaking, the crippled made well, the lame walking and the blind seeing. And they
praised the God of Israel.
32Jesus called his disciples to him and said, "I have compassion
for these people; they have already been with me three days and
have nothing to eat. I do not want to send them away hungry, or
they may collapse on the way."
33His disciples answered, "Where could we get enough bread
in this remote place to feed such a crowd?"

NIV [j] *9* Isaiah 29:13 [k] *14* Some manuscripts *guides of the blind*

## King James

34And Jesus saith unto them, How many loaves have ye? And they said, Seven, and a few little fishes.
35And he commanded the multitude to sit down on the ground.
36And he took the seven loaves and the fishes, and gave thanks, and brake *them,* and gave to his disciples, and the disciples to the multitude.
37And they did all eat, and were filled: and they took up of the broken *meat* that was left seven baskets full.
38And they that did eat were four thousand men, beside women and children.
39And he sent away the multitude, and took ship, and came into the coasts of Magdala.

**16** THE PHARISEES also with the Sadducees came, and tempting desired him that he would show them a sign from heaven.
2He answered and said unto them, When it is evening, ye say, *It will be* fair weather: for the sky is red.
3And in the morning, *It will be* foul weather today: for the sky is red and lowering. O *ye* hypocrites, ye can discern the face of the sky; but can ye not *discern* the signs of the times?
4A wicked and adulterous generation seeketh after a sign; and there shall no sign be given unto it, but the sign of the prophet Jonas. And he left them, and departed.
5And when his disciples were come to the other side, they had forgotten to take bread.
6¶ Then Jesus said unto them, Take heed and beware of the leaven of the Pharisees and of the Sadducees.
7And they reasoned among themselves, saying, *It is* because we have taken no bread.
8 *Which* when Jesus perceived, he said unto them, O ye of little faith, why reason ye among yourselves, because ye have brought no bread?
9Do ye not yet understand, neither remember the five loaves of the five thousand, and how many baskets ye took up?
10Neither the seven loaves of the four thousand, and how many baskets ye took up?
11How is it that ye do not understand that I spake *it* not to you concerning bread, that ye should beware of the leaven of the Pharisees and of the Sadducees?
12Then understood they how that he bade *them* not beware of the leaven of bread, but of the doctrine of the Pharisees and of the Sadducees.
13¶ When Jesus came into the coasts of Caesarea Philippi, he asked his disciples, saying, Whom do men say that I the Son of man am?
14And they said, Some *say that thou art* John the Baptist: some, Elias; and others, Jeremias, or one of the prophets.
15He saith unto them, But whom say ye that I am?
16And Simon Peter answered and said, Thou art the Christ, the Son of the living God.
17And Jesus answered and said unto him, Blessed art thou, Simon Bar-jona: for flesh and blood hath not revealed *it* unto thee, but my Father which is in heaven.
18And I say also unto thee, That thou art Peter, and upon this rock I will build my church; and the gates of hell shall not prevail against it.

## Amplified

34And Jesus asked them, How many loaves of bread do you have? They replied, Seven and a few small fish.
35And ordering the crowd to recline on the ground,
36He took the seven loaves and the fish, and when He had given thanks He broke them and gave them to the disciples, and the disciples gave them to the people.
37And they all ate and were satisfied; and they gathered up seven [ [a]large provision] baskets full of the broken pieces that were left.
38Those who ate were four thousand men, not including the women and the children.
39Then He dismissed the crowds, got into the boat, and went to the district of Magadan.

**16** NOW THE Pharisees and Sadducees came up to Jesus and they asked Him to show them a sign (spectacular miracle) from heaven—attesting His divine authority.
2He replied to them, *When it is evening you say, It will be fair weather, for the sky is red.*
3 *And in the morning, It will be stormy today, for the sky is red and has a gloomy* and *threatening look. You know how to interpret the appearance of the sky, but you cannot interpret the signs of the times.*
4A wicked and morally unfaithful generation craves for a sign, but no sign shall be given to it except the sign of *the prophet* Jonah. Then He left them and went away. [Jonah 3:4, 5.]
5When the disciples reached the other side of the sea, they found they had forgotten to bring any bread.
6Jesus said to them, Be careful *and* on your guard against the leaven (ferment) of the Pharisees and Sadducees.
7And they reasoned among themselves about it, saying, [It is] because we did not bring any bread.
8But Jesus, aware of this asked, Why are you discussing among yourselves the fact that you have no bread? O [men, how] little trust [you have in Me, how]—little faith!
9Do you not yet discern—perceive *and* understand? Do you not remember the five loaves of the five thousand, and how many [ [b]small hand] baskets you gathered?
10Nor the seven loaves for the four thousand, and how many [ [c]large] provision baskets you took up?
11How is it that you fail to understand that I was not talking to you about bread? But beware of the leaven (ferment) of the Pharisees and Sadducees.
12Then they discerned that He did not tell them to beware of the leaven of bread, but of the teaching of the Pharisees and Sadducees.
13Now when Jesus went into the region of Caesarea Philippi, He asked His disciples, Who do people say that the Son of man is?
14And they answered, Some say John the Baptist, others say Elijah, and others Jeremiah or one of the prophets.
15He said to them, But who do you [yourselves] say that I am?
16Simon Peter replied, You are the Christ, the Son of the living God.
17Then Jesus answered him, Blessed—happy, fortunate and [d]to be envied—are you, Simon Bar-Jonah. For flesh and blood [men] have not revealed this to you, but My Father Who is in heaven.
18And I tell you, you are Peter [Petr *os,* masculine, a large piece of rock], and on this rock [petr *a,* feminine, a [e]huge rock like Gibraltar] I will build My church, and the gates of Hades (the powers of the [f]infernal region) shall [g]not overpower it—or be strong to its detriment, or hold out against it.

**AMP** [a] Vincent. But Moulton and Milligan think size not indicated. [b] Vincent. (Moulton and Milligan think size not indicated, but material.) [c] Vincent. But Moulton and Milligan do not agree. [d] Souter. [e] Wuest. [f] Wuest. [g] Thayer.

## New American Standard

34And Jesus *said to them, "How many loaves do you have?"
And they said, "Seven, and a few small fish."
35And He directed the multitude to sit down on the ground;
36and He took the seven loaves and the fish; and giving thanks,
He broke them and started giving them to the disciples, and the
disciples *in turn,* to the multitudes.
37And they all ate, and were satisfied, and they picked up what
was left over of the broken pieces, seven large baskets full.
38And those who ate were four thousand men, besides women
and children.
39And sending away the multitudes, He got into the boat, and
came to the region of Magadan.

*Pharisees Test Jesus*

16 AND THE Pharisees and Sadducees came up, and testing
Him asked Him to show them a sign from heaven.
2But He answered and said to them, "When it is evening, you
say, '*It will be* fair weather, for the sky is red.'
3"And in the morning, '*There will be* a storm today, for the sky
is red and threatening.' Do you know how to discern the appearance of the sky, but cannot *discern* the signs of the times?
4"An evil and adulterous generation seeks after a sign; and a
sign will not be given it, except the sign of Jonah." And He left
them, and went away.
5¶ And the disciples came to the other side and had forgotten
to take bread.
6And Jesus said to them, "Watch out and beware of the leaven
of the Pharisees and Sadducees."
7And they began to discuss among themselves, saying, "*It is*
because we took no bread."
8But Jesus, aware of this, said, "You men of little faith, why
do you discuss among yourselves that you have no bread?
9"Do you not yet understand or remember the five loaves of
the five thousand, and how many baskets you took up?
10"Or the seven loaves of the four thousand, and how many
large baskets you took up?
11"How is it that you do not understand that I did not speak to
you concerning bread? But beware of the leaven of the Pharisees
and Sadducees."
12Then they understood that He did not say to beware of the
leaven of bread, but of the teaching of the Pharisees and Sadducees.

*Peter's Confession of Christ*

13¶ Now when Jesus came into the district of Caesarea Philippi,
He *began* asking His disciples, saying, "Who do people say that the
Son of Man is?"
14And they said, "Some *say* John the Baptist; and others, Elijah;
but still others, Jeremiah, or one of the prophets."
15He *said to them, "But who do you say that I am?"
16And Simon Peter answered and said, "Thou art the Christ,
the Son of the living God."
17And Jesus answered and said to him, "Blessed are you, Simon
Barjona, because flesh and blood did not reveal *this* to you, but My
Father who is in heaven.
18"And I also say to you that you are Peter, and upon this rock
I will build My church; and the gates of Hades shall not overpower
it.

## New International

34"How many loaves do you have?" Jesus asked.
"Seven," they replied, "and a few small fish."
35He told the crowd to sit down on the ground. 36Then he took
the seven loaves and the fish, and when he had given thanks, he
broke them and gave them to the disciples, and they in turn to the
people. 37They all ate and were satisfied. Afterward the disciples
picked up seven basketfuls of broken pieces that were left over.
38The number of those who ate was four thousand, besides women
and children. 39After Jesus had sent the crowd away, he got into
the boat and went to the vicinity of Magadan.

*The Demand for a Sign*

16 THE PHARISEES and Sadducees came to Jesus and tested
him by asking him to show them a sign from heaven.
2He replied,[h] "When evening comes, you say, 'It will be fair
weather, for the sky is red,' 3and in the morning, 'Today it will be
stormy, for the sky is red and overcast.' You know how to interpret
the appearance of the sky, but you cannot interpret the signs of the
times. 4A wicked and adulterous generation looks for a miraculous
sign, but none will be given it except the sign of Jonah." Jesus then
left them and went away.

*The Yeast of the Pharisees and Sadducees*

5When they went across the lake, the disciples forgot to take
bread. 6"Be careful," Jesus said to them. "Be on your guard against
the yeast of the Pharisees and Sadducees."
7They discussed this among themselves and said, "It is because
we didn't bring any bread."
8Aware of their discussion, Jesus asked, "You of little faith, why
are you talking among yourselves about having no bread? 9Do you
still not understand? Don't you remember the five loaves for the
five thousand, and how many basketfuls you gathered? 10Or the
seven loaves for the four thousand, and how many basketfuls you
gathered? 11How is it you don't understand that I was not talking
to you about bread? But be on your guard against the yeast of the
Pharisees and Sadducees." 12Then they understood that he was
not telling them to guard against the yeast used in bread, but
against the teaching of the Pharisees and Sadducees.

*Peter's Confession of Christ*

13When Jesus came to the region of Caesarea Philippi, he asked
his disciples, "Who do people say the Son of Man is?"
14They replied, "Some say John the Baptist; others say Elijah;
and still others, Jeremiah or one of the prophets."
15"But what about you?" he asked. "Who do you say I am?"
16Simon Peter answered, "You are the Christ,[i] the Son of the
living God."
17Jesus replied, "Blessed are you, Simon son of Jonah, for this
was not revealed to you by man, but by my Father in heaven.
18And I tell you that you are Peter,[j] and on this rock I will build
my church, and the gates of Hades[k] will not overcome it.[l] 19I will

**NIV** [h] 2 Some early manuscripts do not have the rest of verse 2 and all of verse 3. [i] *16* Or *Messiah;* also in verse 20 [j] *18 Peter* means *rock.* [k] *18* Or *hell* [l] *18* Or *not prove stronger than it*

## King James

19And I will give unto thee the keys of the kingdom of heaven: and whatsoever thou shalt bind on earth shall be bound in heaven: and whatsoever thou shalt loose on earth shall be loosed in heaven.

20Then charged he his disciples that they should tell no man that he was Jesus the Christ.

21¶ From that time forth began Jesus to show unto his disciples, how that he must go unto Jerusalem, and suffer many things of the elders and chief priests and scribes, and be killed, and be raised again the third day.

22Then Peter took him, and began to rebuke him, saying, Be it far from thee, Lord: this shall not be unto thee.

23But he turned, and said unto Peter, Get thee behind me, Satan: thou art an offence unto me: for thou savourest not the things that be of God, but those that be of men.

24¶ Then said Jesus unto his disciples, If any *man* will come after me, let him deny himself, and take up his cross, and follow me.

25For whosoever will save his life shall lose it: and whosoever will lose his life for my sake shall find it.

26For what is a man profited, if he shall gain the whole world, and lose his own soul? or what shall a man give in exchange for his soul?

27For the Son of man shall come in the glory of his Father with his angels; and then he shall reward every man according to his works.

28Verily I say unto you, There be some standing here, which shall not taste of death, till they see the Son of man coming in his kingdom.

**17** AND AFTER six days Jesus taketh Peter, James, and John his brother, and bringeth them up into an high mountain apart,

2And was transfigured before them: and his face did shine as the sun, and his raiment was white as the light.

3And, behold, there appeared unto them Moses and Elias talking with him.

4Then answered Peter, and said unto Jesus, Lord, it is good for us to be here: if thou wilt, let us make here three tabernacles; one for thee, and one for Moses, and one for Elias.

5While he yet spake, behold, a bright cloud overshadowed them: and behold a voice out of the cloud, which said, This is my beloved Son, in whom I am well pleased; hear ye him.

6And when the disciples heard *it*, they fell on their face, and were sore afraid.

7And Jesus came and touched them, and said, Arise, and be not afraid.

8And when they had lifted up their eyes, they saw no man, save Jesus only.

9And as they came down from the mountain, Jesus charged them, saying, Tell the vision to no man, until the Son of man be risen again from the dead.

## Amplified

19I will give you the keys of the kingdom of heaven, and whatever you bind—that is, declare to be improper and unlawful—on earth [a]must be already bound in heaven; and whatever you loose on earth—declare lawful—[b]must be what is already loosed in heaven. [Isa. 22:22.]

20Then He sternly *and* strictly charged *and* warned the disciples to tell no one that He was *Jesus* the Christ.

21From that time forth Jesus began [clearly] to show His disciples that He must go to Jerusalem and suffer many things at the hands of the elders and the high priests and scribes, and be killed, and on the third day be raised [c]from death.

22Then Peter took Him aside [d]to speak to Him privately, and began to reprove and [e]charge Him sharply, saying, God forbid, Lord! This must never happen to You!

23But Jesus turned [f]away from Peter and said to him, Get behind Me, Satan! You are in My way—an offense and a hindrance and a snare to Me; for you are [g]minding what partakes not of the nature *and* quality of God, but of men.

24Then Jesus said to His disciples, If any one desires to be My disciple, let him deny himself—that is, disregard, lose sight of and forget himself and his own interests—and take up his cross and follow Me [[h]cleave steadily to Me, conform wholly to My example in living and if need be in dying, also].

25For whoever is bent on saving his [temporal] life [his comfort and security here], shall lose [eternal life]; and whoever loses his life [his comfort and security here] for My sake, shall find [life everlasting].

26For what will it profit a man if he gains the whole world and forfeits his life—his [blessed] [i]life in the kingdom of God? Or what would a man give as an exchange for his [blessed] [j]life—in the kingdom of God?

27For the Son of man is going to come in the glory (majesty, splendor) of His Father, with His angels, and then He will render account *and* reward every man in accordance with what he has done.

28Truly, I tell you, there are some standing here who will not taste of death before they see the Son of man coming in (into) His kingdom.

**17** AND SIX days after this Jesus took with Him Peter and James and John his brother, and led them up on a high mountain by themselves.

2And His appearance underwent a change in their presence, and His face shone [k]clear and bright like the sun, and His clothing became white as light.

3And behold, there appeared to them Moses and Elijah, who kept talking with Him.

4Then Peter began to speak and said to Jesus, Lord, it is good *and* delightful that we are here; if You approve, I will put up three booths here, one for You and one for Moses and one for Elijah.

5While he was still speaking, lo, a shining cloud ([l]composed of light) overshadowed them, and a voice from the cloud said, This is My Son, My Beloved, with Whom I am [and [m]have always been] delighted. Listen to Him! [Isa. 42:1; Ps. 2:7.]

6When the disciples heard it, they fell on their faces and were [n]seized with alarm *and* struck with fear.

7But Jesus came and touched them, and said, Get up, and do not be afraid.

8And when they raised their eyes they saw no one but Jesus only.

9And as they were going down the mountain, Jesus cautioned *and* commanded them, Do not mention to any one what you have seen, until the Son of man is raised from the dead.

**AMP** [a] Williams: "Perfect passive participle, so things in a state of having been already forbidden [or permitted]." [b] Williams: "Perfect passive participle, so things in a state of having been already forbidden [or permitted]." [c] Cremer. [d] Vincent. [e] Thayer. [f] Vincent. [g] Vincent. [h] Thayer. [i] Thayer. [j] Thayer. [k] Cremer. [l] Thayer. [m] Williams: "suggested by the aorist." [n] Thayer.

## New American Standard

19"I will give you the keys of the kingdom of heaven; and
whatever you shall bind on earth shall be bound in heaven, and
whatever you shall loose on earth shall be loosed in heaven."
20Then He warned the disciples that they should tell no one that
He was the Christ.

*Jesus Foretells His Death*

21¶ From that time Jesus Christ began to show His disciples that
He must go to Jerusalem, and suffer many things from the elders
and chief priests and scribes, and be killed, and be raised up on
the third day.
22And Peter took Him aside and began to rebuke Him, saying,
"God forbid *it,* Lord! This shall never happen to You."
23But He turned and said to Peter, "Get behind Me, Satan! You
are a stumbling block to Me; for you are not setting your mind on
God's interests, but man's."

*Discipleship Is Costly*

24Then Jesus said to His disciples, "If anyone wishes to come
after Me, let him deny himself, and take up his cross, and follow
Me.
25"For whoever wishes to save his life shall lose it; but whoever
loses his life for My sake shall find it.
26"For what will a man be profited, if he gains the whole world,
and forfeits his soul? Or what will a man give in exchange for his
soul?
27"For the Son of Man is going to come in the glory of His Father
with His angels; and WILL THEN RECOMPENSE EVERY MAN ACCORD-
ING TO HIS DEEDS.
28"Truly I say to you, there are some of those who are standing
here who shall not taste death until they see the Son of Man
coming in His kingdom."

*The Transfiguration*

**17** AND SIX days later Jesus *took with Him Peter and James
and John his brother, and *brought them up to a high
mountain by themselves.
2And He was transfigured before them; and His face shone like
the sun, and His garments became as white as light.
3And behold, Moses and Elijah appeared to them, talking with
Him.
4And Peter answered and said to Jesus, "Lord, it is good for
us to be here; if You wish, I will make three tabernacles here, one
for You, and one for Moses, and one for Elijah."
5While he was still speaking, behold, a bright cloud overshadowed them; and behold, a voice out of the cloud, saying, "This is
My beloved Son, with whom I am well-pleased; listen to Him!"
6And when the disciples heard *this,* they fell on their faces and
were much afraid.
7And Jesus came to *them* and touched them and said, "Arise,
and do not be afraid."
8And lifting up their eyes, they saw no one, except Jesus
Himself alone.
9¶ And as they were coming down from the mountain, Jesus
commanded them, saying, "Tell the vision to no one until the Son
of Man has risen from the dead."

## New International

give you the keys of the kingdom of heaven; whatever you bind
on earth will be[o] bound in heaven, and whatever you loose on
earth will be[p] loosed in heaven." 20Then he warned his disciples
not to tell anyone that he was the Christ.

*Jesus Predicts His Death*

21From that time on Jesus began to explain to his disciples that
he must go to Jerusalem and suffer many things at the hands of
the elders, chief priests and teachers of the law, and that he must
be killed and on the third day be raised to life.
22Peter took him aside and began to rebuke him. "Never,
Lord!" he said. "This shall never happen to you!"
23Jesus turned and said to Peter, "Get behind me, Satan! You
are a stumbling block to me; you do not have in mind the things
of God, but the things of men."
24Then Jesus said to his disciples, "If anyone would come after
me, he must deny himself and take up his cross and follow me.
25For whoever wants to save his life[q] will lose it, but whoever loses
his life for me will find it. 26What good will it be for a man if he
gains the whole world, yet forfeits his soul? Or what can a man
give in exchange for his soul? 27For the Son of Man is going to come
in his Father's glory with his angels, and then he will reward each
person according to what he has done. 28I tell you the truth, some
who are standing here will not taste death before they see the Son
of Man coming in his kingdom."

*The Transfiguration*

**17** AFTER SIX days Jesus took with him Peter, James and
John the brother of James, and led them up a high mountain by themselves. 2There he was transfigured before them. His
face shone like the sun, and his clothes became as white as the
light. 3Just then there appeared before them Moses and Elijah,
talking with Jesus.
4Peter said to Jesus, "Lord, it is good for us to be here. If you
wish, I will put up three shelters—one for you, one for Moses and
one for Elijah."
5While he was still speaking, a bright cloud enveloped them,
and a voice from the cloud said, "This is my Son, whom I love; with
him I am well pleased. Listen to him!"
6When the disciples heard this, they fell facedown to the
ground, terrified. 7But Jesus came and touched them. "Get up,"
he said. "Don't be afraid." 8When they looked up, they saw no one
except Jesus.
9As they were coming down the mountain, Jesus instructed
them, "Don't tell anyone what you have seen, until the Son of Man
has been raised from the dead."

NIV [o] 19 Or *have been* [p] 19 Or *have been* [q] 25 The Greek word means either *life* or *soul;* also in verse 26.

## King James

10 And his disciples asked him, saying, Why then say the scribes that Elias must first come?
11 And Jesus answered and said unto them, Elias truly shall first come, and restore all things.
12 But I say unto you, That Elias is come already, and they knew him not, but have done unto him whatsoever they listed. Likewise shall also the Son of man suffer of them.
13 Then the disciples understood that he spake unto them of John the Baptist.
14 ¶ And when they were come to the multitude, there came to him a *certain* man, kneeling down to him, and saying,
15 Lord, have mercy on my son: for he is lunatic, and sore vexed: for ofttimes he falleth into the fire, and oft into the water.
16 And I brought him to thy disciples, and they could not cure him.
17 Then Jesus answered and said, O faithless and perverse generation, how long shall I be with you? how long shall I suffer you? bring him hither to me.
18 And Jesus rebuked the devil; and he departed out of him: and the child was cured from that very hour.
19 Then came the disciples to Jesus apart, and said, Why could not we cast him out?
20 And Jesus said unto them, Because of your unbelief: for verily I say unto you, If ye have faith as a grain of mustard seed, ye shall say unto this mountain, Remove hence to yonder place; and it shall remove; and nothing shall be impossible unto you.
21 Howbeit this kind goeth not out but by prayer and fasting.
22 ¶ And while they abode in Galilee, Jesus said unto them, The Son of man shall be betrayed into the hands of men:
23 And they shall kill him, and the third day he shall be raised again. And they were exceeding sorry.
24 ¶ And when they were come to Capernaum, they that received tribute *money* came to Peter, and said, Doth not your master pay tribute?
25 He saith, Yes. And when he was come into the house, Jesus prevented him, saying, What thinkest thou, Simon? of whom do the kings of the earth take custom or tribute? of their own children, or of strangers?
26 Peter saith unto him, Of strangers. Jesus saith unto him, Then are the children free.
27 Notwithstanding, lest we should offend them, go thou to the sea, and cast an hook, and take up the fish that first cometh up; and when thou hast opened his mouth, thou shalt find a piece of money: that take, and give unto them for me and thee.

**18** AT THE same time came the disciples unto Jesus, saying, Who is the greatest in the kingdom of heaven?
2 And Jesus called a little child unto him, and set him in the midst of them,
3 And said, Verily I say unto you, Except ye be converted, and become as little children, ye shall not enter into the kingdom of heaven.
4 Whosoever therefore shall humble himself as this little child, the same is greatest in the kingdom of heaven.
5 And whoso shall receive one such little child in my name receiveth me.

## Amplified

10 The disciples asked Him, Then why do the scribes say that first Elijah must come?
11 He replied, Elijah does come and will get everything restored *and* ready;
12 But I tell you that Elijah has come already, and they did not know *or* recognize him, but did to him as they liked. So also the Son of man is going to be treated *and* suffer at their hands.
13 Then the disciples understood that He spoke to them about John the Baptist. [Mal. 4:5.]
14 And when they approached the multitude, a man came up to Him, kneeling before Him and saying,
15 Lord, do pity *and* have mercy on my son, for he has epilepsy (is [a]moonstruck) and he suffers terribly, for frequently he falls into the fire, and many times into the water.
16 And I brought him to Your disciples, and they were not able to cure him.
17 And Jesus answered, O you unbelieving ([b]warped, wayward, rebellious) and [c]thoroughly perverse generation! How long am I to remain with you? How long am I to bear with you? Bring him here to Me.
18 And Jesus rebuked the demon, and it came out of him; and the boy was cured instantly.
19 Then the disciples came to Jesus and asked privately, Why could we not drive it out?
20 He said to them, Because of the littleness of your faith—that is, your lack of [d]firmly relying trust. For truly, I say to you, if you have faith [[e]that is living] like a grain of mustard seed, you can say to this mountain, Move from here to yonder place, and it will move, and nothing will be impossible to you.
21 *But this kind does not go out except by prayer and fasting.*
22 When they were going about here and there in Galilee, Jesus said to them, The Son of man is going to be turned over to the hands of men.
23 And they will kill Him, and He will rise [to life] again on the third day. And they were deeply *and* exceedingly grieved *and* distressed.
24 When they arrived in Capernaum, the collectors of the half-shekel [the temple tax] went up to Peter and said, Does not your Teacher pay the half-shekel? [Exod. 30:13; 38:26.]
25 He answered, Yes. And when he came home, Jesus spoke to him [about it] first, saying, What do you think, Simon? From whom do earthly rulers collect duties *or* tribute? from their own sons or from others [f]not of their own family?
26 And when Peter said, From other people—[g]not of their own family—Jesus said to him, Then the sons are exempt.
27 However, in order not to give offense *and* cause them to stumble—that is, [h]to judge unfavorably and unjustly—go down to the sea and throw in a hook; take the first fish that comes up, and when you open its mouth you will find there a shekel. Take it and give it to them to pay the temple tax for Me and for yourself.

**18** AT THAT time the disciples came up and asked Jesus, Who then is [really] the greatest in the kingdom of heaven?
2 And He called a little child to Him and put him in the midst of them,
3 And said, Truly, I say to you, unless you repent (change, turn about) and become like little children [trusting, lowly, loving, forgiving] you can never enter the kingdom of heaven at all.
4 Whoever will humble himself therefore, and becomes [trusting, lowly, loving, forgiving] as this little child, is greatest in the kingdom of heaven;
5 And whoever receives *and* accepts *and* welcomes one little child like this for My sake and in My name receives *and* accepts *and* welcomes Me.

AMP [a] Thayer: "Epilepsy being supposed to return and increase with the increase of the moon." [b] Vincent. [c] Literally, "throughout" *(dia)*. [d] Cremer. [e] Williams. [f] Thayer. [g] Thayer. [h] Thayer.

## New American Standard

10And His disciples asked Him, saying, "Why then do the scribes say that Elijah must come first?"
11And He answered and said, "Elijah is coming and will restore all things;
12but I say to you, that Elijah already came, and they did not recognize him, but did to him whatever they wished. So also the Son of Man is going to suffer at their hands."
13Then the disciples understood that He had spoken to them about John the Baptist.

*The Demoniac*

14¶ And when they came to the multitude, a man came up to Him, falling on his knees before Him, and saying,
15"Lord, have mercy on my son, for he is a lunatic, and is very ill; for he often falls into the fire, and often into the water.
16"And I brought him to Your disciples, and they could not cure him."
17And Jesus answered and said, "O unbelieving and perverted generation, how long shall I be with you? How long shall I put up with you? Bring him here to Me."
18And Jesus rebuked him, and the demon came out of him, and the boy was cured at once.
19¶ Then the disciples came to Jesus privately and said, "Why could we not cast it out?"
20And He *said to them, "Because of the littleness of your faith; for truly I say to you, if you have faith as a mustard seed, you shall say to this mountain, 'Move from here to there,' and it shall move; and nothing shall be impossible to you.
21[" [i]But this kind does not go out except by prayer and fasting."]
22¶ And while they were gathering together in Galilee, Jesus said to them, "The Son of Man is going to be delivered into the hands of men;
23and they will kill Him, and He will be raised on the third day." And they were deeply grieved.

*The Tribute Money*

24¶ And when they had come to Capernaum, those who collected the [j]two-drachma *tax* came to Peter, and said, "Does your teacher not pay the [k]two-drachma *tax*?"
25He *said, "Yes." And when he came into the house, Jesus spoke to him first, saying, "What do you think, Simon? From whom do the kings of the earth collect customs or poll-tax, from their sons or from strangers?"
26And upon his saying, "From strangers," Jesus said to him, "Consequently the sons are exempt.
27"But, lest we give them offense, go to the sea, and throw in a hook, and take the first fish that comes up; and when you open its mouth, you will find a [l]stater. Take that and give it to them for you and Me."

*Rank in the Kingdom*

18 AT THAT time the disciples came to Jesus, saying, "Who then is greatest in the kingdom of heaven?"
2And He called a child to Himself and set him before them,
3and said, "Truly I say to you, unless you are converted and become like children, you shall not enter the kingdom of heaven.
4"Whoever then humbles himself as this child, he is the greatest in the kingdom of heaven.
5"And whoever receives one such child in My name receives Me;

NAS [i] Many mss. do not contain this verse [j] Equivalent to two denarii or two days' wages paid as a temple tax [k] Equivalent to two denarii or two days' wages paid as a temple tax [l] Or, *shekel*, worth four drachmas

## New International

10The disciples asked him, "Why then do the teachers of the law say that Elijah must come first?"
11Jesus replied, "To be sure, Elijah comes and will restore all
things. 12But I tell you, Elijah has already come, and they did not recognize him, but have done to him everything they wished. In the same way the Son of Man is going to suffer at their hands."
13Then the disciples understood that he was talking to them about John the Baptist.

*The Healing of a Boy With a Demon*

14When they came to the crowd, a man approached Jesus and
knelt before him. 15"Lord, have mercy on my son," he said. "He has seizures and is suffering greatly. He often falls into the fire or
into the water. 16I brought him to your disciples, but they could not heal him."
17"O unbelieving and perverse generation," Jesus replied, "how long shall I stay with you? How long shall I put up with you?
Bring the boy here to me." 18Jesus rebuked the demon, and it came out of the boy, and he was healed from that moment.
19Then the disciples came to Jesus in private and asked, "Why couldn't we drive it out?"
20He replied, "Because you have so little faith. I tell you the truth, if you have faith as small as a mustard seed, you can say to this mountain, 'Move from here to there' and it will move. Nothing will be impossible for you.[m]"
22When they came together in Galilee, he said to them, "The
Son of Man is going to be betrayed into the hands of men. 23They
will kill him, and on the third day he will be raised to life." And the disciples were filled with grief.

*The Temple Tax*

24After Jesus and his disciples arrived in Capernaum, the collectors of the two-drachma tax came to Peter and asked, "Doesn't your teacher pay the temple tax[n]?"
25"Yes, he does," he replied.
When Peter came into the house, Jesus was the first to speak. "What do you think, Simon?" he asked. "From whom do the kings of the earth collect duty and taxes—from their own sons or from others?"
26"From others," Peter answered.
"Then the sons are exempt," Jesus said to him. 27"But so that
we may not offend them, go to the lake and throw out your line. Take the first fish you catch; open its mouth and you will find a four-drachma coin. Take it and give it to them for my tax and yours."

*The Greatest in the Kingdom of Heaven*

18 AT THAT time the disciples came to Jesus and asked, "Who is the greatest in the kingdom of heaven?"
2He called a little child and had him stand among them. 3And
he said: "I tell you the truth, unless you change and become like little children, you will never enter the kingdom of heaven. 4Therefore, whoever humbles himself like this child is the greatest in the kingdom of heaven.
5"And whoever welcomes a little child like this in my name
welcomes me. 6But if anyone causes one of these little ones who

NIV [m]20 Some manuscripts *you.* *21But this kind does not go out except by prayer and fasting.* [n]24 Greek *the two drachmas*

## King James

6 But whoso shall offend one of these little ones which believe in me, it were better for him that a millstone were hanged about his neck, and *that* he were drowned in the depth of the sea.

7 ¶ Woe unto the world because of offences! for it must needs be that offences come; but woe to that man by whom the offence cometh!

8 Wherefore if thy hand or thy foot offend thee, cut them off, and cast *them* from thee: it is better for thee to enter into life halt or maimed, rather than having two hands or two feet to be cast into everlasting fire.

9 And if thine eye offend thee, pluck it out, and cast *it* from thee: it is better for thee to enter into life with one eye, rather than having two eyes to be cast into hell fire.

10 Take heed that ye despise not one of these little ones; for I say unto you, That in heaven their angels do always behold the face of my Father which is in heaven.

11 For the Son of man is come to save that which was lost.

12 How think ye? if a man have an hundred sheep, and one of them be gone astray, doth he not leave the ninety and nine, and goeth into the mountains, and seeketh that which is gone astray?

13 And if so be that he find it, verily I say unto you, he rejoiceth more of that *sheep,* than of the ninety and nine which went not astray.

14 Even so it is not the will of your Father which is in heaven, that one of these little ones should perish.

15 ¶ Moreover if thy brother shall trespass against thee, go and tell him his fault between thee and him alone: if he shall hear thee, thou hast gained thy brother.

16 But if he will not hear *thee, then* take with thee one or two more, that in the mouth of two or three witnesses every word may be established.

17 And if he shall neglect to hear them, tell *it* unto the church: but if he neglect to hear the church, let him be unto thee as an heathen man and a publican.

18 Verily I say unto you, Whatsoever ye shall bind on earth shall be bound in heaven: and whatsoever ye shall loose on earth shall be loosed in heaven.

19 Again I say unto you, That if two of you shall agree on earth as touching any thing that they shall ask, it shall be done for them of my Father which is in heaven.

20 For where two or three are gathered together in my name, there am I in the midst of them.

21 ¶ Then came Peter to him, and said, Lord, how oft shall my brother sin against me, and I forgive him? till seven times?

22 Jesus saith unto him, I say not unto thee, Until seven times: but, Until seventy times seven.

23 ¶ Therefore is the kingdom of heaven likened unto a certain king, which would take account of his servants.

24 And when he had begun to reckon, one was brought unto him, which owed him ten thousand talents.

25 But forasmuch as he had not to pay, his lord commanded him to be sold, and his wife, and children, and all that he had, and payment to be made.

26 The servant therefore fell down, and worshipped him, saying, Lord, have patience with me, and I will pay thee all.

27 Then the lord of that servant was moved with compassion, and loosed him, and forgave him the debt.

## Amplified

6 But whoever causes one of these little ones who believe in *and* [a]acknowledge *and* cleave to Me to stumble and sin—that is, who entices him, or hinders him in right conduct or thought—it would be better ( [b]more expedient and profitable or advantageous) for him to have a great millstone fastened around his neck and to be sunk in the depth of the sea.

7 Woe to the world for such temptations to sin *and* influences to do wrong! It is necessary that temptations come, but woe to the person on whose account *or* by whom the temptation comes!

8 And if your hand or your foot causes you to stumble *and* sin, cut it off and throw it away from you; it is better (more profitable and wholesome) for you to enter life maimed or lame than with two hands or two feet to be thrown into everlasting fire.

9 And if your eye causes you to stumble *and* sin, pluck it out and throw it away from you; it is better, (more profitable and wholesome) for you to enter life with only one eye than with two eyes to be thrown into the hell (Gehenna) of fire.

10 Beware that you do not despise *or* feel scornful toward *or* think little of one of these little ones, for I tell you that in heaven their angels always are in the presence of *and* look upon the face of My Father Who is in heaven.

11 *For the Son of man came to save ( [c]from the penalty of eternal death) that which was lost.*

12 What do you think? If a man has a hundred sheep, and one of them has gone astray *and* gets lost, will he not leave the ninety-nine on the mountain and go in search of the one that is lost?

13 And if it should be that he finds it, truly I say to you, he rejoices more over it than over the ninety-nine that did not get lost.

14 Just so it is not the will of My Father Who is in heaven that one of these little ones should be lost *and* perish.

15 If your brother wrongs you, go and show him his fault, between you and him privately. If he listens to you, you have won back your brother.

16 But if he does not listen, take along with you one or two others, so that every word may be confirmed *and* upheld by the testimony of two or three witnesses.

17 If he pays no attention to them—refusing to listen and obey—tell it to the church; and if he refuses to listen even to the church, let him be to you as a pagan and a tax collector. [Lev. 19:17; Deut. 19:15.]

18 Truly, I tell you, whatever you forbid *and* declare to be improper *and* unlawful on earth must be [d]what is already forbidden in heaven, and whatever you permit and declare proper and lawful on earth must be [e]already permitted in heaven.

19 Again I tell you, if two of you on earth agree (harmonize together, together make a symphony) about—anything and [f]everything—whatever they shall ask, it will come to pass *and* be done for them by My Father in heaven.

20 For wherever two or three are gathered (drawn together as My followers) in (into) My name, there I AM in the midst of them. [Exod. 3:14.]

21 Then Peter came up to Him and said, Lord, how many times may my brother sin against me, and I forgive him *and* [g]let it go? As many as up to seven times?

22 Jesus answered him, I tell you, not up to seven times, but seventy times seven! [Gen. 4:24.]

23 Therefore the kingdom of heaven is like a human king who wished to settle accounts with his attendants.

24 When he began the accounting, one was brought to him who owed him ten thousand talents [probably about $10,000,000],

25 And because he could not pay, his master ordered him to be sold, with his wife and his children and everything that he possessed, and payment to be made.

26 So the attendant fell on his knees, begging him, Have patience with me and I will pay you everything.

27 And his master's heart was moved with compassion, and he released him and forgave him (cancelling) the debt.

**AMP** [a] Cremer. [b] Abbott-Smith. [c] Cremer. [d] Williams: See footnote on Mt. 16:19. [e] Williams: See footnote on Mt. 16:19. [f] Wycliffe. [g] Thayer.

## New American Standard

6but whoever causes one of these little ones who believe in Me to stumble, it is better for him that a heavy millstone be hung around his neck, and that he be drowned in the depth of the sea.

*Stumbling Blocks*

7¶ "Woe to the world because of *its* stumbling blocks! For it is inevitable that stumbling blocks come; but woe to that man through whom the stumbling block comes!

8"And if your hand or your foot causes you to stumble, cut it off and throw it from you; it is better for you to enter life crippled or lame, than having two hands or two feet, to be cast into the eternal fire.

9"And if your eye causes you to stumble, pluck it out, and throw it from you. It is better for you to enter life with one eye, than having two eyes, to be cast into the fiery hell.

10"See that you do not despise one of these little ones, for I say to you, that their angels in heaven continually behold the face of My Father who is in heaven.

11[" [h]For the Son of Man has come to save that which was lost.]

*Ninety-nine Plus One*

12"What do you think? If any man has a hundred sheep, and one of them has gone astray, does he not leave the ninety-nine on the mountains and go and search for the one that is straying?

13"And if it turns out that he finds it, truly I say to you, he rejoices over it more than over the ninety-nine which have not gone astray.

14"Thus it is not *the* will of your Father who is in heaven that one of these little ones perish.

*Discipline and Prayer*

15¶ "And if your brother sins [i], go and reprove him in private; if he listens to you, you have won your brother.

16"But if he does not listen *to you,* take one or two more with you, so that BY THE MOUTH OF TWO OR THREE WITNESSES EVERY FACT MAY BE CONFIRMED.

17"And if he refuses to listen to them, tell it to the church; and if he refuses to listen even to the church, let him be to you as a Gentile and a tax-gatherer.

18"Truly I say to you, whatever you shall bind on earth shall be bound in heaven; and whatever you loose on earth shall be loosed in heaven.

19"Again I say to you, that if two of you agree on earth about anything that they may ask, it shall be done for them by My Father who is in heaven.

20"For where two or three have gathered together in My name, there I am in their midst."

*Forgiveness*

21¶ Then Peter came and said to Him, "Lord, how often shall my brother sin against me and I forgive him? Up to seven times?"

22Jesus *said to him, "I do not say to you, up to seven times, but up to seventy times seven.

23"For this reason the kingdom of heaven may be compared to a certain king who wished to settle accounts with his slaves.

24"And when he had begun to settle *them,* there was brought to him one who owed him [j]ten thousand talents.

25"But since he did not have *the means* to repay, his lord commanded him to be sold, along with his wife and children and all that he had, and repayment to be made.

26"The slave therefore falling down, prostrated himself before him, saying, 'Have patience with me, and I will repay you everything.'

27"And the lord of that slave felt compassion and released him and forgave him the debt.

NAS [h] Most ancient mss. do not contain this verse [i] Many mss. add here: *against you* [j] About $10,000,000 in silver content but worth much more in buying power

## New International

believe in me to sin, it would be better for him to have a large millstone hung around his neck and to be drowned in the depths of the sea.

7"Woe to the world because of the things that cause people to sin! Such things must come, but woe to the man through whom they come! 8If your hand or your foot causes you to sin, cut it off and throw it away. It is better for you to enter life maimed or crippled than to have two hands or two feet and be thrown into eternal fire. 9And if your eye causes you to sin, gouge it out and throw it away. It is better for you to enter life with one eye than to have two eyes and be thrown into the fire of hell.

*The Parable of the Lost Sheep*

10"See that you do not look down on one of these little ones. For I tell you that their angels in heaven always see the face of my Father in heaven.[k]

12"What do you think? If a man owns a hundred sheep, and one of them wanders away, will he not leave the ninety-nine on the hills and go to look for the one that wandered off? 13And if he finds it, I tell you the truth, he is happier about that one sheep than about the ninety-nine that did not wander off. 14In the same way your Father in heaven is not willing that any of these little ones should be lost.

*A Brother Who Sins Against You*

15"If your brother sins against you,[l] go and show him his fault, just between the two of you. If he listens to you, you have won your brother over. 16But if he will not listen, take one or two others along, so that 'every matter may be established by the testimony of two or three witnesses.'[m] 17If he refuses to listen to them, tell it to the church; and if he refuses to listen even to the church, treat him as you would a pagan or a tax collector.

18"I tell you the truth, whatever you bind on earth will be[n] bound in heaven, and whatever you loose on earth will be[o] loosed in heaven.

19"Again, I tell you that if two of you on earth agree about anything you ask for, it will be done for you by my Father in heaven. 20For where two or three come together in my name, there am I with them."

*The Parable of the Unmerciful Servant*

21Then Peter came to Jesus and asked, "Lord, how many times shall I forgive my brother when he sins against me? Up to seven times?"

22Jesus answered, "I tell you, not seven times, but seventy-seven times.[p]

23"Therefore, the kingdom of heaven is like a king who wanted to settle accounts with his servants. 24As he began the settlement, a man who owed him ten thousand talents[q] was brought to him. 25Since he was not able to pay, the master ordered that he and his wife and his children and all that he had be sold to repay the debt.

26"The servant fell on his knees before him. 'Be patient with me,' he begged, 'and I will pay back everything.' 27The servant's master took pity on him, canceled the debt and let him go.

NIV [k] 10 Some manuscripts *heaven.* 11*The Son of Man came to save what was lost.* [l] 15 Some manuscripts do not have *against you.* [m] 16 Deut. 19:15 [n] 18 Or *have been* [o] 18 Or *have been* [p] 22 Or *seventy times seven* [q] 24 That is, millions of dollars

## King James

28But the same servant went out, and found one of his fellowservants, which owed him an hundred pence: and he laid hands on him, and took *him* by the throat, saying, Pay me that thou owest.

29And his fellowservant fell down at his feet, and besought him, saying, Have patience with me, and I will pay thee all.

30And he would not: but went and cast him into prison, till he should pay the debt.

31So when his fellowservants saw what was done, they were very sorry, and came and told unto their lord all that was done.

32Then his lord, after that he had called him, said unto him, O thou wicked servant, I forgave thee all that debt, because thou desiredst me:

33Shouldest not thou also have had compassion on thy fellowservant, even as I had pity on thee?

34And his lord was wroth, and delivered him to the tormentors, till he should pay all that was due unto him.

35So likewise shall my heavenly Father do also unto you, if ye from your hearts forgive not every one his brother their trespasses.

**19** AND IT came to pass, *that* when Jesus had finished these sayings, he departed from Galilee, and came into the coasts of Judaea beyond Jordan;

2And great multitudes followed him; and he healed them there.

3¶ The Pharisees also came unto him, tempting him, and saying unto him, Is it lawful for a man to put away his wife for every cause?

4And he answered and said unto them, Have ye not read, that he which made *them* at the beginning made them male and female,

5And said, For this cause shall a man leave father and mother, and shall cleave to his wife: and they twain shall be one flesh?

6Wherefore they are no more twain, but one flesh. What therefore God hath joined together, let not man put asunder.

7They say unto him, Why did Moses then command to give a writing of divorcement, and to put her away?

8He saith unto them, Moses because of the hardness of your hearts suffered you to put away your wives: but from the beginning it was not so.

9And I say unto you, Whosoever shall put away his wife, except *it be* for fornication, and shall marry another, committeth adultery: and whoso marrieth her which is put away doth commit adultery.

10¶ His disciples say unto him, If the case of the man be so with *his* wife, it is not good to marry.

11But he said unto them, All *men* cannot receive this saying, save *they* to whom it is given.

12For there are some eunuchs, which were so born from *their* mother's womb: and there are some eunuchs, which were made eunuchs of men: and there be eunuchs, which have made themselves eunuchs for the kingdom of heaven's sake. He that is able to receive *it*, let him receive *it*.

13¶ Then were there brought unto him little children, that he should put *his* hands on them, and pray: and the disciples rebuked them.

14But Jesus said, Suffer little children, and forbid them not, to come unto me: for of such is the kingdom of heaven.

15And he laid *his* hands on them, and departed thence.

16¶ And, behold, one came and said unto him, Good Master, what good thing shall I do, that I may have eternal life?

## Amplified

28But that same attendant, as he went out, found one of his fellow attendants who owed him a hundred denarii [about twenty dollars]; and he caught him by the throat and said, Pay what you owe!

29So his fellow attendant fell down and begged him earnestly, Give me time, and I will pay you *all*!

30But he was unwilling and went out and had him put in prison till he should pay the debt.

31When his fellow attendants saw what had happened, they were greatly distressed, and they went and told everything that had taken place to their master.

32Then his master called him and said to him, You contemptible *and* wicked attendant! I forgave *and* cancelled all that [great] debt of yours because you begged me;

33And should you not have had pity *and* mercy on your fellow attendant, as I had pity *and* mercy on you?

34And in wrath his master turned him over to the torturers (the jailers), till he should pay all that he owed.

35So also My heavenly Father will deal with every one of you, if you do not freely forgive your brother from your heart *his offenses*.

**19** NOW WHEN Jesus had finished saying these things, He left Galilee and went into the part of Judea that is beyond the Jordan;

2And great throngs accompanied Him, and He cured them there.

3And Pharisees came to Him and put Him to the test by asking, Is it lawful *and* right to dismiss *and* repudiate *and* divorce one's wife for any *and* [a]every cause?

4He replied, Have you never read that He Who made them from the beginning made them male and female,

5And said, For this reason a man shall leave his father and mother and shall be united firmly (joined inseparably) to his wife, and the two shall become one flesh? [Gen. 1:27; 2:24.]

6So they are no longer two but one flesh. What therefore God has joined together, let not man put asunder (separate).

7They said to Him, Why then did Moses command [us] to give a certificate of divorce, and thus to dismiss *and* repudiate a wife? [Deut. 24:1-4.]

8He said to them, Because of the hardness (stubbornness and perversity) of your hearts Moses permitted you to dismiss *and* repudiate *and* divorce your wives; but from the beginning it has not been [b]so [ordained].

9I say to you: whoever dismisses (repudiates, divorces) his wife, except for unchastity, and marries another, commits adultery, *and he who marries a divorced woman commits adultery*.

10The disciples said to Him, If the case of a man with his wife is like that, it is neither profitable *nor* advisable to marry.

11But He said to them, Not all men can accept this saying, but it is for those to whom [the capacity to receive] it has been given.

12For there are eunuchs who have been born incapable of marriage, and there are eunuchs who have been made so by men, and there are eunuchs who have made themselves incapable of marriage for the sake of the kingdom of heaven. Let him who is able to accept this, accept it.

13Then little children were brought to Jesus that He might put His hands on them and pray, but the disciples rebuked those who brought them.

14But He said, Leave the children alone! Allow the little ones to come to Me, and do not forbid *or* restrain *or* hinder them, for of such [as these] the kingdom of heaven is composed.

15And He put His hands upon them, and then went His way.

16And behold, there came a man up to Him, saying, Teacher, what excellent, *and* perfectly *and* essentially good deed must I do to possess eternal life? [Lev. 18:5.]

**AMP** [a] Vincent. [b] Thayer.

## New American Standard

28"But that slave went out and found one of his fellow slaves
who owed him a hundred [c]denarii; and he seized him and *began*
to choke *him*, saying, 'Pay back what you owe.'
29"So his fellow slave fell down and *began* to entreat him, saying, 'Have patience with me and I will repay you.'
30"He was unwilling however, but went and threw him in
prison until he should pay back what was owed.
31"So when his fellow slaves saw what had happened, they
were deeply grieved and came and reported to their lord all that
had happened.
32"Then summoning him, his lord *said to him, 'You wicked
slave, I forgave you all that debt because you entreated me.
33'Should you not also have had mercy on your fellow slave,
even as I had mercy on you?'
34"And his lord, moved with anger, handed him over to the
torturers until he should repay all that was owed him.
35"So shall My heavenly Father also do to you, if each of you
does not forgive his brother from your heart."

*Concerning Divorce*

**19** AND IT came about that when Jesus had finished these
words, He departed from Galilee, and came into the region of Judea beyond the Jordan;
2and great multitudes followed Him, and He healed them
there.
3¶ And *some* Pharisees came to Him, testing Him, and saying,
"Is it lawful *for a man* to divorce his wife for any cause at all?"
4And He answered and said, "Have you not read, that He who
created *them* from the beginning MADE THEM MALE AND FEMALE,
5and said, 'FOR THIS CAUSE A MAN SHALL LEAVE HIS FATHER AND
MOTHER, AND SHALL CLEAVE TO HIS WIFE; AND THE TWO SHALL
BECOME ONE FLESH'?
6"Consequently they are no longer two, but one flesh. What
therefore God has joined together, let no man separate."
7They *said to Him, "Why then did Moses command to GIVE
HER A CERTIFICATE OF DIVORCE AND SEND *her* AWAY?"
8He *said to them, "Because of your hardness of heart, Moses
permitted you to divorce your wives; but from the beginning it has
not been this way.
9"And I say to you, whoever divorces his wife, except for
immorality, and marries another woman commits adultery."
10The disciples *said to Him, "If the relationship of the man
with his wife is like this, it is better not to marry."
11But He said to them, "Not all men *can* accept this statement,
but *only* those to whom it has been given.
12"For there are eunuchs who were born that way from their
mother's womb; and there are eunuchs who were made eunuchs
by men; and there are *also* eunuchs who made themselves eunuchs
for the sake of the kingdom of heaven. He who is able to accept
*this*, let him accept *it*."

*Jesus Blesses Little Children*

13¶ Then *some* children were brought to Him so that He might
lay His hands on them and pray; and the disciples rebuked them.
14But Jesus said, "Let the children alone, and do not hinder
them from coming to Me; for the kingdom of heaven belongs to
such as these."
15And after laying His hands on them, He departed from there.

*The Rich Young Ruler*

16¶ And behold, one came to Him and said, "Teacher, what
good thing shall I do that I may obtain eternal life?"

**NAS** [c] The denarius was equivalent to one day's wage

## New International

28"But when that servant went out, he found one of his fellow
servants who owed him a hundred denarii.[d] He grabbed him and
began to choke him. 'Pay back what you owe me!' he demanded.
29"His fellow servant fell to his knees and begged him, 'Be
patient with me, and I will pay you back.'
30"But he refused. Instead, he went off and had the man
thrown into prison until he could pay the debt. 31When the other
servants saw what had happened, they were greatly distressed
and went and told their master everything that had happened.
32"Then the master called the servant in. 'You wicked servant,'
he said, 'I canceled all that debt of yours because you begged me
to. 33Shouldn't you have had mercy on your fellow servant just as
I had on you?' 34In anger his master turned him over to the jailers
to be tortured, until he should pay back all he owed.
35"This is how my heavenly Father will treat each of you unless
you forgive your brother from your heart."

*Divorce*

**19** WHEN JESUS had finished saying these things, he left
Galilee and went into the region of Judea to the other side
of the Jordan. 2Large crowds followed him, and he healed them
there.
3Some Pharisees came to him to test him. They asked, "Is it
lawful for a man to divorce his wife for any and every reason?"
4"Haven't you read," he replied, "that at the beginning the
Creator 'made them male and female,'[e] 5and said, 'For this reason
a man will leave his father and mother and be united to his wife,
and the two will become one flesh'[f]? 6So they are no longer two,
but one. Therefore what God has joined together, let man not
separate."
7"Why then," they asked, "did Moses command that a man
give his wife a certificate of divorce and send her away?"
8Jesus replied, "Moses permitted you to divorce your wives
because your hearts were hard. But it was not this way from the
beginning. 9I tell you that anyone who divorces his wife, except
for marital unfaithfulness, and marries another woman commits
adultery."
10The disciples said to him, "If this is the situation between a
husband and wife, it is better not to marry."
11Jesus replied, "Not everyone can accept this word, but only
those to whom it has been given. 12For some are eunuchs because
they were born that way; others were made that way by men; and
others have renounced marriage[g] because of the kingdom of
heaven. The one who can accept this should accept it."

*The Little Children and Jesus*

13Then little children were brought to Jesus for him to place his
hands on them and pray for them. But the disciples rebuked those
who brought them.
14Jesus said, "Let the little children come to me, and do not
hinder them, for the kingdom of heaven belongs to such as these."
15When he had placed his hands on them, he went on from there.

*The Rich Young Man*

16Now a man came up to Jesus and asked, "Teacher, what good
thing must I do to get eternal life?"

**NIV** [d] *28* That is, a few dollars [e] *4* Gen. 1:27 [f] *5* Gen. 2:24 [g] *12* Or *have made themselves eunuchs*

# King James

17And he said unto him, Why callest thou me good? *there is* none good but one, *that is,* God: but if thou wilt enter into life, keep the commandments.

18He saith unto him, Which? Jesus said, Thou shalt do no murder, Thou shalt not commit adultery, Thou shalt not steal, Thou shalt not bear false witness,

19Honour thy father and *thy* mother: and, Thou shalt love thy neighbour as thyself.

20The young man saith unto him, All these things have I kept from my youth up: what lack I yet?

21Jesus said unto him, If thou wilt be perfect, go *and* sell that thou hast, and give to the poor, and thou shalt have treasure in heaven: and come *and* follow me.

22But when the young man heard that saying, he went away sorrowful: for he had great possessions.

23¶ Then said Jesus unto his disciples, Verily I say unto you, That a rich man shall hardly enter into the kingdom of heaven.

24And again I say unto you, It is easier for a camel to go through the eye of a needle, than for a rich man to enter into the kingdom of God.

25When his disciples heard *it,* they were exceedingly amazed, saying, Who then can be saved?

26But Jesus beheld *them,* and said unto them, With men this is impossible; but with God all things are possible.

27¶ Then answered Peter and said unto him, Behold, we have forsaken all, and followed thee; what shall we have therefore?

28And Jesus said unto them, Verily I say unto you, That ye which have followed me, in the regeneration when the Son of man shall sit in the throne of his glory, ye also shall sit upon twelve thrones, judging the twelve tribes of Israel.

29And every one that hath forsaken houses, or brethren, or sisters, or father, or mother, or wife, or children, or lands, for my name's sake, shall receive an hundredfold, and shall inherit everlasting life.

30But many *that are* first shall be last; and the last *shall be* first.

20 FOR THE kingdom of heaven is like unto a man *that is* an householder, which went out early in the morning to hire labourers into his vineyard.

2And when he had agreed with the labourers for a penny a day, he sent them into his vineyard.

3And he went out about the third hour, and saw others standing idle in the marketplace,

4And said unto them; Go ye also into the vineyard, and whatsoever is right I will give you. And they went their way.

5Again he went out about the sixth and ninth hour, and did likewise.

6And about the eleventh hour he went out, and found others standing idle, and saith unto them, Why stand ye here all the day idle?

7They say unto him, Because no man hath hired us. He saith unto them, Go ye also into the vineyard; and whatsoever is right, *that* shall ye receive.

8So when even was come, the lord of the vineyard saith unto his steward, Call the labourers, and give them *their* hire, beginning from the last unto the first.

# Amplified

17And He said to him, Why do you ask Me about the perfectly *and* essentially good? One only there is who is good—perfectly and essentially; God. If you would enter into the Life, you must continually keep the commandments.

18He said to Him, What [a]sort of commandments?— *Or,* which ones? And Jesus answered, You shall not kill, You shall not commit adultery, You shall not steal, You shall not bear false witness, [Exod. 20:12-16; Deut. 5:16-20.]

19Honor your father and your mother, and, You shall love your neighbor as yourself. [Lev. 19:18.]

20The young man said, I have observed all these *from my youth;* what still do I lack?

21Jesus answered him, If you would be perfect [that is, [b]have that spiritual maturity which accompanies self-sacrificing character], go and sell what you have and give to the poor, and you will have riches in heaven; and come, [c]be My disciple—side with My party and follow Me.

22But when the young man heard this, he went away sad (grieved and in much distress), for he had great possessions.

23And Jesus said to His disciples, Truly, I say to you, it will be difficult for a rich man to get into the kingdom of heaven.

24Again I tell you, it is easier for a camel to go through the eye of a needle than for a rich man to go into the kingdom of heaven.

25When the disciples heard this, they were utterly puzzled (astonished, bewildered), saying, Who then can be saved [ [d]from eternal death]?

26But Jesus looked at them and said, With men this is impossible, but all things are possible with God. [Gen. 18:14; Job 42:2.]

27Then Peter answered Him saying, Lo, we have left [our] all and have become [e]Your disciples—sided with Your party and followed You. What then shall we receive?

28Jesus said to them, Truly, I say to you, in the new age—the [f]Messianic rebirth of the world—when the Son of man shall sit down on the throne of His glory, you who have [become My disciples, sided with My party and] followed Me will also sit on twelve thrones and judge the twelve tribes of Israel.

29And any one *and* every one who has left houses or brothers or sisters or father or mother or children or lands for My name's sake, will receive [g]many—even a hundred—times more, and inherit eternal life.

30But many that [now] are first will be last [then], and many who [now] are last will be first [then].

20 FOR THE kingdom of heaven is like the owner of an estate who went out in the morning [h]along with the dawn to hire workmen for his vineyard.

2After agreeing with the laborers for a denarius a day, he sent them into his vineyard.

3And going out about the third hour (nine o'clock) he saw others standing idle in the market place;

4And he said to them, You go also into the vineyard, and whatever is right I will pay you. And they went.

5He went out again about the sixth hour (noon), and the ninth hour (three o'clock) he did the same.

6And about the eleventh hour (five o'clock) he went out and found still others standing around, and said to them, Why do you stand here idle all day?

7They answered him, Because nobody has hired us. He told them, You go out into the vineyard also *and you will get whatever is just and fair.*

8When evening came, the owner of the vineyard said to his manager, Call the workmen and pay them their wages, beginning with the last and ending with the first. [Lev. 19:13; Deut. 24:15.]

**AMP** a Williams: "Interrogative of quality." b Wuest. c Thayer. d Cremer. e Thayer. f Moulton and Milligan. g Some ancient authorities read "manifold." h Vincent.

## New American Standard

17And He said to him, "Why are you asking Me about what is
good? There is *only* One who is good; but if you wish to enter into
life, keep the commandments."
18He *said to Him, "Which ones?" And Jesus said, "YOU SHALL
NOT COMMIT MURDER; YOU SHALL NOT COMMIT ADULTERY; YOU
SHALL NOT STEAL; YOU SHALL NOT BEAR FALSE WITNESS;
19HONOR YOUR FATHER AND MOTHER; and YOU SHALL LOVE YOUR
NEIGHBOR AS YOURSELF."
20The young man *said to Him, "All these things I have kept;
what am I still lacking?"
21Jesus said to him, "If you wish to be complete, go *and* sell your
possessions and give to *the* poor, and you shall have treasure in
heaven; and come, follow Me."
22But when the young man heard this statement, he went away
grieved; for he was one who owned much property.
23¶ And Jesus said to His disciples, "Truly I say to you, it is hard
for a rich man to enter the kingdom of heaven.
24"And again I say to you, it is easier for a camel to go through
the eye of a needle, than for a rich man to enter the kingdom of
God."
25And when the disciples heard *this,* they were very astonished
and said, "Then who can be saved?"
26And looking upon *them* Jesus said to them, "With men this
is impossible, but with God all things are possible."

*The Disciples' Reward*

27Then Peter answered and said to Him, "Behold, we have left
everything and followed You; what then will there be for us?"
28And Jesus said to them, "Truly I say to you, that you who
have followed Me, in the regeneration when the Son of Man will
sit on His glorious throne, you also shall sit upon twelve thrones,
judging the twelve tribes of Israel.
29"And everyone who has left houses or brothers or sisters or
father or mother [i] or children or farms for My name's sake, shall
receive many times as much, and shall inherit eternal life.
30"But many *who are* first will be last; and *the* last, first.

*Laborers in the Vineyard*

20 "FOR THE kingdom of heaven is like a landowner who
went out early in the morning to hire laborers for his
vineyard.
2"And when he had agreed with the laborers for a [j]denarius
for the day, he sent them into his vineyard.
3"And he went out about the [k]third hour and saw others
standing idle in the market place;
4and to those he said, 'You too go into the vineyard, and
whatever is right I will give you.' And *so* they went.
5"Again he went out about the [l]sixth and the ninth hour, and
did the same thing.
6"And about the [m]eleventh *hour* he went out, and found others
standing; and he *said to them, 'Why have you been standing here
idle all day long?'
7"They *said to him, 'Because no one hired us.' He *said to
them, 'You too go into the vineyard.'
8"And when evening had come, the owner of the vineyard
*said to his foreman, 'Call the laborers and pay them their wages,
beginning with the last *group* to the first.'

NAS [i] Many mss. add here, *or wife* [j] The denarius was equivalent to one day's wage [k] I.e., 9 a.m. [l] I.e., Noon and 3 p.m. [m] I.e., 5 p.m.

## New International

17"Why do you ask me about what is good?" Jesus replied.
"There is only One who is good. If you want to enter life, obey the
commandments."
18"Which ones?" the man inquired.
Jesus replied, " 'Do not murder, do not commit adultery, do not
steal, do not give false testimony, 19honor your father and
mother,'[n] and 'love your neighbor as yourself.'[o] "
20"All these I have kept," the young man said. "What do I still
lack?"
21Jesus answered, "If you want to be perfect, go, sell your
possessions and give to the poor, and you will have treasure in
heaven. Then come, follow me."
22When the young man heard this, he went away sad, because
he had great wealth.
23Then Jesus said to his disciples, "I tell you the truth, it is hard
for a rich man to enter the kingdom of heaven. 24Again I tell you,
it is easier for a camel to go through the eye of a needle than for
a rich man to enter the kingdom of God."
25When the disciples heard this, they were greatly astonished
and asked, "Who then can be saved?"
26Jesus looked at them and said, "With man this is impossible,
but with God all things are possible."
27Peter answered him, "We have left everything to follow you!
What then will there be for us?"
28Jesus said to them, "I tell you the truth, at the renewal of all
things, when the Son of Man sits on his glorious throne, you who
have followed me will also sit on twelve thrones, judging the
twelve tribes of Israel. 29And everyone who has left houses or
brothers or sisters or father or mother[p] or children or fields for my
sake will receive a hundred times as much and will inherit eternal
life. 30But many who are first will be last, and many who are last
will be first.

*The Parable of the Workers in the Vineyard*

20 "FOR THE kingdom of heaven is like a landowner who
went out early in the morning to hire men to work in his
vineyard. 2He agreed to pay them a denarius for the day and sent
them into his vineyard.
3"About the third hour he went out and saw others standing
in the marketplace doing nothing. 4He told them, 'You also go and
work in my vineyard, and I will pay you whatever is right.' 5So
they went.
"He went out again about the sixth hour and the ninth hour and
did the same thing. 6About the eleventh hour he went out and
found still others standing around. He asked them, 'Why have you
been standing here all day long doing nothing?'
7" 'Because no one has hired us,' they answered.
"He said to them, 'You also go and work in my vineyard.'
8"When evening came, the owner of the vineyard said to his
foreman, 'Call the workers and pay them their wages, beginning
with the last ones hired and going on to the first.'

NIV [n] *19* Exodus 20:12-16; Deut. 5:16-20 [o] *19* Lev. 19:18 [p] *29* Some manuscripts *mother or wife*

## King James

9 And when they came that *were hired* about the eleventh hour, they received every man a penny.

10 But when the first came, they supposed that they should have received more; and they likewise received every man a penny.

11 And when they had received *it*, they murmured against the goodman of the house,

12 Saying, These last have wrought *but* one hour, and thou hast made them equal unto us, which have borne the burden and heat of the day.

13 But he answered one of them, and said, Friend, I do thee no wrong: didst not thou agree with me for a penny?

14 Take *that* thine *is*, and go thy way: I will give unto this last, even as unto thee.

15 Is it not lawful for me to do what I will with mine own? Is thine eye evil, because I am good?

16 So the last shall be first, and the first last: for many be called, but few chosen.

17 ¶ And Jesus going up to Jerusalem took the twelve disciples apart in the way, and said unto them,

18 Behold, we go up to Jerusalem; and the Son of man shall be betrayed unto the chief priests and unto the scribes, and they shall condemn him to death,

19 And shall deliver him to the Gentiles to mock, and to scourge, and to crucify *him*: and the third day he shall rise again.

20 ¶ Then came to him the mother of Zebedee's children with her sons, worshipping *him*, and desiring a certain thing of him.

21 And he said unto her, What wilt thou? She saith unto him, Grant that these my two sons may sit, the one on thy right hand, and the other on the left, in thy kingdom.

22 But Jesus answered and said, Ye know not what ye ask. Are ye able to drink of the cup that I shall drink of, and to be baptized with the baptism that I am baptized with? They say unto him, We are able.

23 And he saith unto them, Ye shall drink indeed of my cup, and be baptized with the baptism that I am baptized with: but to sit on my right hand, and on my left, is not mine to give, but *it shall be given to them* for whom it is prepared of my Father.

24 And when the ten heard *it*, they were moved with indignation against the two brethren.

25 But Jesus called them *unto him*, and said, Ye know that the princes of the Gentiles exercise dominion over them, and they that are great exercise authority upon them.

26 But it shall not be so among you: but whosoever will be great among you, let him be your minister;

27 And whosoever will be chief among you, let him be your servant:

28 Even as the Son of man came not to be ministered unto, but to minister, and to give his life a ransom for many.

29 And as they departed from Jericho, a great multitude followed him.

30 ¶ And, behold, two blind men sitting by the way side, when they heard that Jesus passed by, cried out, saying, Have mercy on us, O Lord, *thou* Son of David.

31 And the multitude rebuked them, because they should hold their peace: but they cried the more, saying, Have mercy on us, O Lord, *thou* Son of David.

32 And Jesus stood still, and called them, and said, What will ye that I shall do unto you?

33 They say unto him, Lord, that our eyes may be opened.

34 So Jesus had compassion *on them*, and touched their eyes: and immediately their eyes received sight, and they followed him.

## Amplified

9 And they who had been hired at the eleventh hour (five o'clock) came, and received a denarius each.

10 Now when the first came, they supposed they would get more, but each of them also received a denarius.

11 And when they received it they grumbled at the owner of the estate,

12 Saying, These who came last worked no more than an hour, and yet you have made them rank with us who have borne the burden and the [a]scorching heat of the day.

13 But he answered one of them, Friend, I am doing you no injustice. Did you not agree with me for a denarius?

14 Take what belongs to you and go. I choose to give to this man hired last the same as I give to you.

15 Am I not permitted to do what I choose with what is mine? Or do you begrudge my being generous? Is your eye evil because I am good?

16 So those who [now] are last will be first [then], and those who [now] are first will be last [then]. *For many are called, but few chosen.*

17 And as Jesus was going up to Jerusalem, He took the twelve disciples aside along the way, and said to them,

18 Behold, we are going up to Jerusalem; and the Son of man will be handed over to the chief priests and scribes and they will sentence Him to death,

19 And deliver Him over to the Gentiles to be mocked and whipped and crucified, and He will be raised [to life] on the third day.

20 Then the mother of Zebedee's children came up to Him with her sons, and kneeling, worshipped Him and asked a favor of Him.

21 And He asked her, What do you wish? She answered Him, Give orders that these two sons of mine may sit, one at Your right hand and one at Your left in Your kingdom.

22 But Jesus replied, You do not realize what you are asking. Are you able to drink the cup that I am about to drink *and to be baptized with the baptism with which I am baptized*? They answered, We are able.

23 He said to them, You will drink My cup, but seats at My right hand and at My left are not Mine to give, but they are for those for whom they have been [b]ordained *and* prepared by My Father.

24 But when the ten [other disciples] heard this, they were indignant at the two brothers.

25 And Jesus called them to Him and said, You know that the rulers of the Gentiles lord it over them, and their great men hold them in subjection, tyrannizing over them.

26 Not so shall it be among you; but whoever wishes to be great among you must be your servant,

27 And whoever desires to be first among you must be your slave;

28 Just as the Son of man came not to be waited on but to serve, and to give His life as a ransom for many—the price paid to set them free.

29 And as they were going out of Jericho, a great throng accompanied Him.

30 And behold, two blind men were sitting by the roadside, and when they heard that Jesus was passing by, they cried out, Lord, have pity *and* mercy on us, [You] Son of David!

31 The crowds reproved them and told them to keep still; but they cried out the more, Lord, have pity *and* mercy on us, [You] Son of David!

32 And Jesus stopped and called them, and asked, What do you want Me to do for you?

33 They answered Him, Lord, we want our eyes to be opened!

34 And Jesus in pity touched their eyes, and instantly they received their sight and followed Him.

**AMP** [a] Vincent. [b] Thayer.

## New American Standard

9"And when those *hired* about the eleventh hour came, each
one received a [c]denarius.
10"And when those *hired* first came, they thought that they
would receive more; and they also received each one a [d]denarius.
11"And when they received it, they grumbled at the landowner,
12saying, 'These last men have worked *only* one hour, and you
have made them equal to us who have borne the burden and the
scorching heat of the day.'
13"But he answered and said to one of them, 'Friend, I am doing
you no wrong; did you not agree with me for a [e]denarius?
14'Take what is yours and go your way, but I wish to give to this
last man the same as to you.
15'Is it not lawful for me to do what I wish with what is my own?
Or is your eye envious because I am generous?'
16"Thus the last shall be first, and the first last."

*Death, Resurrection Foretold*

17¶ And as Jesus was about to go up to Jerusalem, He took the
twelve *disciples* aside by themselves, and on the way He said to
them,
18"Behold, we are going up to Jerusalem; and the Son of Man
will be delivered to the chief priests and scribes, and they will
condemn Him to death,
19and will deliver Him to the Gentiles to mock and scourge and
crucify *Him*, and on the third day He will be raised up."

*Preferment Asked*

20¶ Then the mother of the sons of Zebedee came to Him with
her sons, bowing down, and making a request of Him.
21And He said to her, "What do you wish?" She *said to Him,
"Command that in Your kingdom these two sons of mine may sit,
one on Your right and one on Your left."
22But Jesus answered and said, "You do not know what you are
asking for. Are you able to drink the cup that I am about to drink?"
They *said to Him, "We are able."
23He *said to them, "My cup you shall drink; but to sit on My
right and on *My* left, this is not Mine to give, but it is for those for
whom it has been prepared by My Father."
24And hearing *this*, the ten became indignant with the two
brothers.
25But Jesus called them to Himself, and said, "You know that
the rulers of the Gentiles lord it over them, and *their* great men
exercise authority over them.
26"It is not so among you, but whoever wishes to become great
among you shall be your servant,
27and whoever wishes to be first among you shall be your slave;
28just as the Son of Man did not come to be served, but to serve,
and to give His life a ransom for many."

*Sight for the Blind*

29¶ And as they were going out from Jericho, a great multitude
followed Him.
30And behold, two blind men sitting by the road, hearing that
Jesus was passing by, cried out, saying, "Lord, have mercy on us,
Son of David!"
31And the multitude sternly told them to be quiet; but they cried
out all the more, saying, "Lord, have mercy on us, Son of David!"
32And Jesus stopped and called them, and said, "What do you
want Me to do for you?"
33They *said to Him, "Lord, *we want* our eyes to be opened."
34And moved with compassion, Jesus touched their eyes; and
immediately they regained their sight and followed Him.

**NAS** [c] The denarius was equivalent to one day's wage [d] The denarius was equivalent to one day's wage [e] The denarius was equivalent to one day's wage

## New International

9"The workers who were hired about the eleventh hour came
and each received a denarius. 10So when those came who were
hired first, they expected to receive more. But each one of them
also received a denarius. 11When they received it, they began to
grumble against the landowner. 12'These men who were hired last
worked only one hour,' they said, 'and you have made them equal
to us who have borne the burden of the work and the heat of the
day.'
13"But he answered one of them, 'Friend, I am not being unfair
to you. Didn't you agree to work for a denarius? 14Take your pay
and go. I want to give the man who was hired last the same as I
gave you. 15Don't I have the right to do what I want with my own
money? Or are you envious because I am generous?'
16"So the last will be first, and the first will be last."

*Jesus Again Predicts His Death*

17Now as Jesus was going up to Jerusalem, he took the twelve
disciples aside and said to them, 18"We are going up to Jerusalem,
and the Son of Man will be betrayed to the chief priests and the
teachers of the law. They will condemn him to death 19and will
turn him over to the Gentiles to be mocked and flogged and
crucified. On the third day he will be raised to life!"

*A Mother's Request*

20Then the mother of Zebedee's sons came to Jesus with her
sons and, kneeling down, asked a favor of him.
21"What is it you want?" he asked.
She said, "Grant that one of these two sons of mine may sit at
your right and the other at your left in your kingdom."
22"You don't know what you are asking," Jesus said to them.
"Can you drink the cup I am going to drink?"
"We can," they answered.
23Jesus said to them, "You will indeed drink from my cup, but
to sit at my right or left is not for me to grant. These places belong
to those for whom they have been prepared by my Father."
24When the ten heard about this, they were indignant with the
two brothers. 25Jesus called them together and said, "You know
that the rulers of the Gentiles lord it over them, and their high
officials exercise authority over them. 26Not so with you. Instead,
whoever wants to become great among you must be your servant,
27and whoever wants to be first must be your slave— 28just as the
Son of Man did not come to be served, but to serve, and to give
his life as a ransom for for many."

*Two Blind Men Receive Sight*

29As Jesus and his disciples were leaving Jericho, a large crowd
followed him. 30Two blind men were sitting by the roadside, and
when they heard that Jesus was going by, they shouted, "Lord,
Son of David, have mercy on us!"
31The crowd rebuked them and told them to be quiet, but they
shouted all the louder, "Lord, Son of David, have mercy on us!"
32Jesus stopped and called them. "What do you want me to do
for you?" he asked.
33"Lord," they answered, "we want our sight."
34Jesus had compassion on them and touched their eyes.
Immediately they received their sight and followed him.

## King James

21 AND WHEN they drew nigh unto Jerusalem, and were
come to Bethphage, unto the mount of Olives, then sent
Jesus two disciples,
2Saying unto them, Go into the village over against you, and
straightway ye shall find an ass tied, and a colt with her: loose
*them,* and bring *them* unto me.
3And if any *man* say aught unto you, ye shall say, The Lord hath
need of them; and straightway he will send them.
4All this was done, that it might be fulfilled which was spoken
by the prophet, saying,
5Tell ye the daughter of Sion, Behold, thy King cometh unto
thee, meek, and sitting upon an ass, and a colt the foal of an ass.
6And the disciples went, and did as Jesus commanded them,
7And brought the ass, and the colt, and put on them their
clothes, and they set *him* thereon.
8And a very great multitude spread their garments in the way;
others cut down branches from the trees, and strawed *them* in the
way.
9And the multitudes that went before, and that followed, cried,
saying, Hosanna to the son of David: Blessed *is* he that cometh in
the name of the Lord; Hosanna in the highest.
10And when he was come into Jerusalem, all the city was
moved, saying, Who is this?
11And the multitude said, This is Jesus the prophet of Nazareth
of Galilee.
12¶ And Jesus went into the temple of God, and cast out all them
that sold and bought in the temple, and overthrew the tables of the
moneychangers, and the seats of them that sold doves,
13And said unto them, It is written, My house shall be called
the house of prayer; but ye have made it a den of thieves.
14And the blind and the lame came to him in the temple; and
he healed them.
15And when the chief priests and scribes saw the wonderful
things that he did, and the children crying in the temple, and
saying, Hosanna to the son of David; they were sore displeased,
16And said unto him, Hearest thou what these say? And Jesus
saith unto them, Yea; have ye never read, Out of the mouth of
babes and sucklings thou hast perfected praise?
17¶ And he left them, and went out of the city into Bethany; and
he lodged there.
18Now in the morning as he returned into the city, he hungered.
19And when he saw a fig tree in the way, he came to it, and
found nothing thereon, but leaves only, and said unto it, Let no
fruit grow on thee henceforward for ever. And presently the fig
tree withered away.
20And when the disciples saw *it,* they marvelled, saying, How
soon is the fig tree withered away!
21Jesus answered and said unto them, Verily I say unto you, If
ye have faith, and doubt not, ye shall not only do this *which is done*
to the fig tree, but also if ye shall say unto this mountain, Be thou
removed, and be thou cast into the sea; it shall be done.
22And all things, whatsoever ye shall ask in prayer, believing,
ye shall receive.

**AMP** [a] Thayer. [b] Thayer. [c] Literal meaning. [d] Capitalized because of what He is, the spotless Son of God, not what the speakers may have thought Him to be. [e] Trench's "Synonyms of the New Testament." [f] Thayer. [g] Moulton and Milligan. [h] Trench's "Synonyms of the New Testament." [i] Abbott-Smith. [j] Trench's "Synonyms of the New Testament." [k] Literal meaning. [l] Thayer. [m] International Standard Bible Encyclopedia. [n] Cremer.

## Amplified

21 AND WHEN they came near Jerusalem and had reached
Bethphage, at the Mount of Olives, Jesus sent two disciples on ahead,
2Saying to them, Go into the village that is opposite you, and
at once you will find a donkey tied, and a colt with her; untie her
and bring them to Me.
3If any one says anything to you, you shall reply, The Lord
needs them, and he will let them go without delay.
4This happened that what was spoken by the prophet might be
fulfilled, saying,
5Say to the daughter of Zion [inhabitants of Jerusalem], Behold
your King is coming to you, lowly and riding on a donkey, and on
a colt, the foal of a donkey [a beast of burden]. [Isa. 62:11; Zech.
9:9.]
6Then the disciples went and did as Jesus had directed them.
7They brought the donkey and the colt and laid their coats upon
them, and He seated Himself on [the clothing].
8And most of the crowd kept spreading their garments on the
road, and others kept cutting branches from the trees and scattering them on the road.
9And the crowds that went ahead of Him and those that followed Him kept shouting, Hosanna ([a]O be propitious, graciously
inclined) to the Son of David, [b]the Messiah! Blessed (praised,
glorified) be He Who comes in the name of the Lord! Hosanna (O
be favorably disposed) in the highest (heaven)! [Ps. 118:26.]
10And when He entered Jerusalem, all the city became agitated,
and [c]trembling with excitement said, Who is [d]This?
11And the crowds replied, This is the prophet Jesus from Nazareth of Galilee.
12And Jesus went into the temple ([e]whole temple enclosure)
and drove out all who bought and sold in the [f]sacred place, and
He turned over the [g]four-footed tables of the money-changers and
the chairs of those who sold pigeons.
13He said to them, The Scripture says, My house shall be called
a house of prayer, but you have made it a den of robbers. [Isa. 56:7;
Jer. 7:11.]
14And the blind and the lame came to Him in the [h]porches *and*
courts of the temple, and He cured them.
15But when the chief priests and the scribes saw the wonderful
things that He did, and the boys *and* the girls *and* the [i]youths *and*
the maidens crying out in the [j]porches *and* courts of the temple,
Hosanna (O be propitious, graciously inclined) to the Son of David! they were indignant.
16And they said to Him, Do You hear what these are saying?
And Jesus replied to them, Yes; have you never read, Out of the
mouths of children and infants You have made (provided) perfect
praise? [Ps. 8:2.]
17And leaving them, He departed from the city and went out
to Bethany and lodged there.
18In the early dawn next morning, as He was coming back to
the city He was hungry.
19And as He saw [k]one single leafy fig tree [l]above the roadside
He went to it [[m]seeing that in the fig tree the fruit appears at the
same time as the leaves], but He found nothing but leaves on it.
And He said to it, Never again shall fruit grow on you! And the
fig tree withered up at once.
20When the disciples saw it they marveled greatly and asked,
How is it that the fig tree has withered away all at once?
21And Jesus answered them, Truly, I say to you, if you have
faith—a [n]firm relying trust—and do not doubt, you will not only
do what has been done to the fig tree, but even if you say to this
mountain, Be taken up and cast into the sea, it will be done.
22And whatever you ask for in prayer, having faith *and* [really]
believing, you will receive.

## New American Standard

*The Triumphal Entry*

**21** AND WHEN they had approached Jerusalem and had come to Bethphage, to the Mount of Olives, then Jesus sent two disciples,

2saying to them, "Go into the village opposite you, and immediately you will find a donkey tied *there* and a colt with her; untie *them,* and bring *them* to Me.

3"And if anyone says something to you, you shall say, 'The Lord has need of them,' and immediately he will send them."

4Now this took place that what was spoken through the prophet might be fulfilled, saying,

5 "SAY TO THE DAUGHTER OF ZION,
'BEHOLD YOUR KING IS COMING TO YOU,
GENTLE, AND MOUNTED ON A DONKEY,
EVEN ON A COLT, THE FOAL OF A BEAST OF BURDEN.' "

6And the disciples went and did just as Jesus had directed them,

7and brought the donkey and the colt, and laid on them their garments, on which He sat.

8And most of the multitude spread their garments in the road, and others were cutting branches from the trees, and spreading them in the road.

9And the multitudes going before Him, and those who followed after were crying out, saying,
"Hosanna to the Son of David;
BLESSED IS HE WHO COMES IN THE NAME OF THE LORD;
Hosanna in the highest!"

10And when He had entered Jerusalem, all the city was stirred, saying, "Who is this?"

11And the multitudes were saying, "This is the prophet Jesus, from Nazareth in Galilee."

*Cleansing the Temple*

12¶ And Jesus entered the temple and cast out all those who were buying and selling in the temple, and overturned the tables of the moneychangers and the seats of those who were selling doves.

13And He *said to them, "It is written, 'MY HOUSE SHALL BE CALLED A HOUSE OF PRAYER'; but you are making it a ROBBERS' DEN."

14And *the* blind and *the* lame came to Him in the temple, and He healed them.

15But when the chief priests and the scribes saw the wonderful things that He had done, and the children who were crying out in the temple and saying, "Hosanna to the Son of David," they became indignant,

16and said to Him, "Do You hear what these are saying?" And Jesus *said to them, "Yes; have you never read, 'OUT OF THE MOUTH OF INFANTS AND NURSING BABES THOU HAST PREPARED PRAISE FOR THYSELF'?"

17And He left them and went out of the city to Bethany, and lodged there.

*The Barren Fig Tree*

18¶ Now in the morning, when He returned to the city, He became hungry.

19And seeing a lone fig tree by the road, He came to it, and found nothing on it except leaves only; and He *said to it, "No longer shall there ever be *any* fruit from you." And at once the fig tree withered.

20And seeing *this,* the disciples marveled, saying, "How did the fig tree wither at once?"

21And Jesus answered and said to them, "Truly I say to you, if you have faith, and do not doubt, you shall not only do what was done to the fig tree, but even if you say to this mountain, 'Be taken up and cast into the sea,' it shall happen.

22"And all things you ask in prayer, believing, you shall receive."

## New International

*The Triumphal Entry*

**21** AS THEY approached Jerusalem and came to Bethphage
on the Mount of Olives, Jesus sent two disciples, 2saying
to them, "Go to the village ahead of you, and at once you will find
a donkey tied there, with her colt by her. Untie them and bring
them to me. 3If anyone says anything to you, tell him that the Lord
needs them, and he will send them right away."
4This took place to fulfill what was spoken through the prophet:
5"Say to the Daughter of Zion,
'See, your king comes to you,
gentle and riding on a donkey,
on a colt, the foal of a donkey.' "[o]
6The disciples went and did as Jesus had instructed them. 7They
brought the donkey and the colt, placed their cloaks on them, and
Jesus sat on them. 8A very large crowd spread their cloaks on the
road, while others cut branches from the trees and spread them on
the road. 9The crowds that went ahead of him and those that
followed shouted,

"Hosanna[p] to the Son of David!"

"Blessed is he who comes in the name of the Lord!"[q]

"Hosanna[r] in the highest!"

10When Jesus entered Jerusalem, the whole city was stirred and
asked, "Who is this?"
11The crowds answered, "This is Jesus, the prophet from Nazareth in Galilee."

*Jesus at the Temple*

12Jesus entered the temple area and drove out all who were
buying and selling there. He overturned the tables of the money
changers and the benches of those selling doves. 13"It is written,"
he said to them, " 'My house will be called a house of prayer,'[s]
but you are making it a 'den of robbers.'[t] "
14The blind and the lame came to him at the temple, and he
healed them. 15But when the chief priests and the teachers of the
law saw the wonderful things he did and the children shouting in
the temple area, "Hosanna to the Son of David," they were indignant.
16"Do you hear what these children are saying?" they asked
him.
"Yes," replied Jesus, "have you never read,

" 'From the lips of children and infants
you have ordained praise'[u] ?"

17And he left them and went out of the city to Bethany, where
he spent the night.

*The Fig Tree Withers*

18Early in the morning, as he was on his way back to the city,
he was hungry. 19Seeing a fig tree by the road, he went up to it
but found nothing on it except leaves. Then he said to it, "May you
never bear fruit again!" Immediately the tree withered.
20When the disciples saw this, they were amazed. "How did the
fig tree wither so quickly?" they asked.
21Jesus replied, "I tell you the truth, if you have faith and do
not doubt, not only can you do what was done to the fig tree, but
also you can say to this mountain, 'Go, throw yourself into the
sea,' and it will be done. 22If you believe, you will receive whatever
you ask for in prayer."

**NIV** [o] *5* Zech. 9:9 [p] *9* A Hebrew expression meaning "Save!" which became an exclamation of praise; also in verse 15 [q] *9* Psalm 118:26 [r] *9* A Hebrew expression meaning "Save!" which became an exclamation of praise; also in verse 15 [s] *13* Isaiah 56:7 [t] *13* Jer. 7:11 [u] *16* Psalm 8:2

## King James

23¶ And when he was come into the temple, the chief priests and the elders of the people came unto him as he was teaching, and said, By what authority doest thou these things? and who gave thee this authority?

24And Jesus answered and said unto them, I also will ask you one thing, which if ye tell me, I in like wise will tell you by what authority I do these things.

25The baptism of John, whence was it? from heaven, or of men? And they reasoned with themselves, saying, If we shall say, From heaven; he will say unto us, Why did ye not then believe him?

26But if we shall say, Of men; we fear the people; for all hold John as a prophet.

27And they answered Jesus, and said, We cannot tell. And he said unto them, Neither tell I you by what authority I do these things.

28¶ But what think ye? A *certain* man had two sons; and he came to the first, and said, Son, go work today in my vineyard.

29He answered and said, I will not: but afterward he repented, and went.

30And he came to the second, and said likewise. And he answered and said, I *go,* sir: and went not.

31Whether of them twain did the will of *his* father? They say unto him, The first. Jesus saith unto them, Verily I say unto you, That the publicans and the harlots go into the kingdom of God before you.

32For John came unto you in the way of righteousness, and ye believed him not: but the publicans and the harlots believed him: and ye, when ye had seen *it,* repented not afterward, that ye might believe him.

33¶ Hear another parable: There was a certain householder, which planted a vineyard, and hedged it round about, and digged a winepress in it, and built a tower, and let it out to husbandmen, and went into a far country:

34And when the time of the fruit drew near, he sent his servants to the husbandmen, that they might receive the fruits of it.

35And the husbandmen took his servants, and beat one, and killed another, and stoned another.

36Again, he sent other servants more than the first: and they did unto them likewise.

37But last of all he sent unto them his son, saying, They will reverence my son.

38But when the husbandmen saw the son, they said among themselves, This is the heir; come, let us kill him, and let us seize on his inheritance.

39And they caught him, and cast *him* out of the vineyard, and slew *him.*

40When the lord therefore of the vineyard cometh, what will he do unto those husbandmen?

41They say unto him, He will miserably destroy those wicked men, and will let out *his* vineyard unto other husbandmen, which shall render him the fruits in their seasons.

42Jesus saith unto them, Did ye never read in the scriptures, The stone which the builders rejected, the same is become the head of the corner: this is the Lord's doing, and it is marvellous in our eyes?

43Therefore say I unto you, The kingdom of God shall be taken from you, and given to a nation bringing forth the fruits thereof.

44And whosoever shall fall on this stone shall be broken: but on whomsoever it shall fall, it will grind him to powder.

45And when the chief priests and Pharisees had heard his parables, they perceived that he spake of them.

46But when they sought to lay hands on him, they feared the multitude, because they took him for a prophet.

## Amplified

23And when He entered the sacred [a]enclosure of the temple, the chief priests and elders of the people came up to Him as He was teaching and said, By what [b]power of authority are You doing these things, and who gave You this power of authority?

24Jesus answered them, I also will ask you a question, and if you give Me the answer, then I also will tell you by what [c]power of authority I do these things.

25The baptism of John, from whence was it? From heaven or from men? And they reasoned *and* argued with one another, If we say, From heaven, [d]He will ask us, Why then did you not believe him?

26But if we say, From men, we are afraid of *and* must reckon with the multitude; for they all regard John as a prophet.

27So they answered Jesus, We do not know. And He said to them, Nor will I tell you by what [e]power of authority I do these things.

28What do you think? There was a man who had two sons. He came to the first and said, Son, go and work today in the vineyard.

29And he answered, I will not; but afterward he changed his mind and went.

30Then the man came to the second and said the same [thing], and he replied, I will [go], sir; but he did not go.

31Which of the two did the will of the father? They replied, The first one. Jesus said to them, Truly, I tell you, the tax collectors and the harlots will get into the kingdom of heaven before you.

32For John came to you walking in the way of an upright man in right standing with God, and you did not believe him, but the tax collectors and the harlots did believe him; and you, even when you saw that, did not afterward change your minds and believe him—adhere to, trust in and rely on what he told you.

33Listen to another parable. There was a master of a house who planted a vineyard, and put a hedge around it, and dug a wine vat in it, and built a watchtower. Then he let it out to tenants, and went into another country.

34When the fruit season drew near, he sent his servants to the tenants, to get his [share of the] fruit;

35But the tenants took his servants and beat one, killed another, and stoned another.

36Again he sent other servants, more than the first time, and they treated them the same way.

37Finally he sent his own son to them, saying, They will respect *and* give heed to my son.

38But when the tenants saw the son, they said to themselves, This is the heir; come on, let us kill him, and have his inheritance.

39And they took him, and threw him out of the vineyard, and killed him.

40Now when the owner of the vineyard comes back, what will he do to those tenants?

41They said to Him, He will put those wretches to a miserable death, and rent the vineyard to other tenants [f]of such a character that they will give him the fruits promptly in their season. [Isa. 5:1-7.]

42Jesus asked them, Have you never read in the Scriptures, The very Stone which the builders rejected *and* threw away has become the Cornerstone; this was the Lord's doings, and it is marvelous in our eyes? [Ps. 118:22, 23.]

43I tell you, for this reason the kingdom of God will be taken away from you and given to a people who will produce the fruits of it.

44 *And whoever falls on this Stone will be broken to pieces, but he on whom it falls will be crushed to powder, and it will [g]winnow him, [h]scattering him as dust.* [Isa. 8:14; Dan. 2:34, 35.]

45And when the chief priests and the Pharisees heard His parables (comparisons, stories used to illustrate and explain), they perceived that He was talking about them;

46And although they were trying to arrest Him, they feared the throngs, because they regarded Him as a prophet.

**AMP** [a] Trench. [b] Thayer. [c] Thayer. [d] Capitalized because of what He is, the spotless Son of God, not what the speakers may have thought He was. [e] Thayer. [f] Vincent. [g] Thayer. [h] Vincent.

## New American Standard

*Authority Challenged*

23¶ And when He had come into the temple, the chief priests
and the elders of the people came to Him as He was teaching, and
said, "By what authority are You doing these things, and who gave
You this authority?"
24And Jesus answered and said to them, "I will ask you one
thing too, which if you tell Me, I will also tell you by what authority
I do these things.
25"The baptism of John was from what *source,* from heaven or
from men?" And they *began* reasoning among themselves, saying,
"If we say, 'From heaven,' He will say to us, 'Then why did you
not believe him?'
26"But if we say, 'From men,' we fear the multitude; for they
all hold John to be a prophet."
27And answering Jesus, they said, "We do not know." He also
said to them, "Neither will I tell you by what authority I do these
things.

*Parable of Two Sons*

28"But what do you think? A man had two sons, and he came
to the first and said, 'Son, go work today in the vineyard.'
29"And he answered and said, 'I will, sir'; and he did not go.
30"And he came to the second and said the same thing. But he
answered and said, 'I will not'; *yet* he afterward regretted *it* and
went.
31"Which of the two did the will of his father?" They *said, "The
latter." Jesus *said to them, "Truly I say to you that the tax-gatherers and harlots will get into the kingdom of God before you.
32"For John came to you in the way of righteousness and you
did not believe him; but the tax-gatherers and harlots did believe
him; and you, seeing this, did not even feel remorse afterward so
as to believe him.

*Parable of the Landowner*

33¶ "Listen to another parable. There was a landowner who
PLANTED A VINEYARD AND PUT A WALL AROUND IT AND DUG A WINE
PRESS IN IT, AND BUILT A TOWER, and rented it out to vine-growers,
and went on a journey.
34"And when the harvest time approached, he sent his slaves
to the vine-growers to receive his produce.
35"And the vine-growers took his slaves and beat one, and
killed another, and stoned a third.
36"Again he sent another group of slaves larger than the first;
and they did the same thing to them.
37"But afterward he sent his son to them, saying, 'They will
respect my son.'
38"But when the vine-growers saw the son, they said among
themselves, 'This is the heir; come, let us kill him, and seize his
inheritance.'
39"And they took him, and threw him out of the vineyard, and
killed him.
40"Therefore when the owner of the vineyard comes, what will
he do to those vine-growers?"
41They *said to Him, "He will bring those wretches to a
wretched end, and will rent out the vineyard to other vine-growers, who will pay him the proceeds at the *proper* seasons."
42Jesus *said to them, "Did you never read in the Scriptures,
'THE STONE WHICH THE BUILDERS REJECTED,
THIS BECAME THE CHIEF CORNER *stone;*
THIS CAME ABOUT FROM THE LORD,
AND IT IS MARVELOUS IN OUR EYES'?
43"Therefore I say to you, the kingdom of God will be taken
away from you, and be given to a nation producing the fruit of it.
44"And he who falls on this stone will be broken to pieces; but
on whomever it falls, it will scatter him like dust."
45And when the chief priests and the Pharisees heard His parables, they understood that He was speaking about them.
46And when they sought to seize Him, they feared the multitudes, because they held Him to be a prophet.

## New International

*The Authority of Jesus Questioned*

23Jesus entered the temple courts, and, while he was teaching,
the chief priests and the elders of the people came to him. "By
what authority are you doing these things?" they asked. "And
who gave you this authority?"
24Jesus replied, "I will also ask you one question. If you answer
me, I will tell you by what authority I am doing these things.
25John's baptism—where did it come from? Was it from heaven,
or from men?"
They discussed it among themselves and said, "If we say, 'From
heaven,' he will ask, 'Then why didn't you believe him?' 26But if
we say, 'From men'—we are afraid of the people, for they all hold
that John was a prophet."
27So they answered Jesus, "We don't know."
Then he said, "Neither will I tell you by what authority I am
doing these things.

*The Parable of the Two Sons*

28"What do you think? There was a man who had two sons. He
went to the first and said, 'Son, go and work today in the vineyard.'
29" 'I will not,' he answered, but later he changed his mind and
went.
30"Then the father went to the other son and said the same
thing. He answered, 'I will, sir,' but he did not go.
31"Which of the two did what his father wanted?"
"The first," they answered.
Jesus said to them, "I tell you the truth, the tax collectors and
the prostitutes are entering the kingdom of God ahead of you.
32For John came to you to show you the way of righteousness, and
you did not believe him, but the tax collectors and the prostitutes
did. And even after you saw this, you did not repent and believe
him.

*The Parable of the Tenants*

33"Listen to another parable: There was a landowner who
planted a vineyard. He put a wall around it, dug a winepress in
it and built a watchtower. Then he rented the vineyard to some
farmers and went away on a journey. 34When the harvest time
approached, he sent his servants to the tenants to collect his fruit.
35"The tenants seized his servants; they beat one, killed another, and stoned a third. 36Then he sent other servants to them,
more than the first time, and the tenants treated them the same
way. 37Last of all, he sent his son to them. 'They will respect my
son,' he said.
38"But when the tenants saw the son, they said to each other,
'This is the heir. Come, let's kill him and take his inheritance.' 39So
they took him and threw him out of the vineyard and killed him.
40"Therefore, when the owner of the vineyard comes, what will
he do to those tenants?"
41"He will bring those wretches to a wretched end," they replied, "and he will rent the vineyard to other tenants, who will
give him his share of the crop at harvest time."
42Jesus said to them, "Have you never read in the Scriptures:
" 'The stone the builders rejected
has become the capstone[i];
the Lord has done this,
and it is marvelous in our eyes'[j]?
43"Therefore I tell you that the kingdom of God will be taken
away from you and given to a people who will produce its fruit.
44He who falls on this stone will be broken to pieces, but he on
whom it falls will be crushed."[k]
45When the chief priests and the Pharisees heard Jesus' parables, they knew he was talking about them. 46They looked for a
way to arrest him, but they were afraid of the crowd because the
people held that he was a prophet.

NIV [i] 42 Or *cornerstone* [j] 42 Psalm 118:22,23 [k] 44 Some manuscripts do not have verse 44.

## King James

**22** AND JESUS answered and spake unto them again by parables, and said,

2 The kingdom of heaven is like unto a certain king, which made a marriage for his son,

3 And sent forth his servants to call them that were bidden to the wedding: and they would not come.

4 Again, he sent forth other servants, saying, Tell them which are bidden, Behold, I have prepared my dinner: my oxen and *my* fatlings *are* killed, and all things *are* ready: come unto the marriage.

5 But they made light of *it*, and went their ways, one to his farm, another to his merchandise:

6 And the remnant took his servants, and entreated *them* spitefully, and slew *them*.

7 But when the king heard *thereof*, he was wroth: and he sent forth his armies, and destroyed those murderers, and burned up their city.

8 Then saith he to his servants, The wedding is ready, but they which were bidden were not worthy.

9 Go ye therefore into the highways, and as many as ye shall find, bid to the marriage.

10 So those servants went out into the highways, and gathered together all as many as they found, both bad and good: and the wedding was furnished with guests.

11 ¶ And when the king came in to see the guests, he saw there a man which had not on a wedding garment:

12 And he saith unto him, Friend, how camest thou in hither not having a wedding garment? And he was speechless.

13 Then said the king to the servants, Bind him hand and foot, and take him away, and cast *him* into outer darkness; there shall be weeping and gnashing of teeth.

14 For many are called, but few *are* chosen.

15 ¶ Then went the Pharisees, and took counsel how they might entangle him in *his* talk.

16 And they sent out unto him their disciples with the Herodians, saying, Master, we know that thou art true, and teachest the way of God in truth, neither carest thou for any *man:* for thou regardest not the person of men.

17 Tell us therefore, What thinkest thou? Is it lawful to give tribute unto Caesar, or not?

18 But Jesus perceived their wickedness, and said, Why tempt ye me, *ye* hypocrites?

19 Show me the tribute money. And they brought unto him a penny.

20 And he saith unto them, Whose *is* this image and superscription?

21 They say unto him, Caesar's. Then saith he unto them, Render therefore unto Caesar the things which are Caesar's; and unto God the things that are God's.

22 When they had heard *these words*, they marvelled, and left him, and went their way.

23 ¶ The same day came to him the Sadducees, which say that there is no resurrection, and asked him,

24 Saying, Master, Moses said, If a man die, having no children, his brother shall marry his wife, and raise up seed unto his brother.

25 Now there were with us seven brethren: and the first, when he had married a wife, deceased, and having no issue, left his wife unto his brother:

26 Likewise the second also, and the third, unto the seventh.

27 And last of all the woman died also.

28 Therefore in the resurrection whose wife shall she be of the seven? for they all had her.

## Amplified

**22** AND AGAIN Jesus spoke to them in parables (comparisons, stories used to illustrate and explain), saying,

2 The kingdom of heaven is like a king who gave a wedding banquet for his son,

3 And sent his servants to summon those who had been invited to the wedding banquet, but they refused to come.

4 Again he sent other servants, saying, Tell those who are invited, Behold, I have prepared my banquet; my bullocks and my fat calves are killed, and everything is prepared; come to the wedding feast.

5 But they were not concerned *and* paid no attention—they ignored and made light of the summons, treating it with contempt—and they went away, one to his farm, another to his business,

6 While the others seized his servants, treated them shamefully and put them to death.

7 [Hearing this] the king was infuriated, and he sent his soldiers and put those murderers to death and burned their city.

8 Then he said to his servants, the wedding [feast] is prepared, but those invited were not worthy.

9 So go to the thoroughfares where they leave the city—where the main roads and those from the country end—and invite to the wedding feast as many as you find.

10 And those servants went out on the crossroads and got together as many as they found, both bad and good, so [the room in which] the wedding feast [was held] was filled with guests.

11 But when the king came in to view the guests, he looked intently at a man there who had on no wedding garment;

12 And he said, Friend, how did you come in here without putting on the [appropriate] wedding garment? And he was speechless ([a]muzzled, gagged).

13 Then the king said to the attendants, Tie him hand and foot, and throw him into the darkness outside; there will be weeping and the grinding of teeth.

14 For many are called (invited and summoned), but few chosen.

15 Then the Pharisees went and consulted *and* plotted together how they might entangle Jesus in His talk.

16 And they sent their disciples to Him, along with the Herodians, saying, Teacher, we know that You are [b]sincere *and* what You profess to be, and that You teach the way of God truthfully, regardless of consequences *and* being afraid of no man; for You are impartial *and* do not regard either the person *or* the position of any one.

17 Tell us, then, what You think about this: Is it lawful to pay tribute [levied on individuals and to be paid yearly] to Caesar, or not?

18 But Jesus, aware of their malicious plot, asked, Why do you put Me to the test *and* try to entrap Me, you pretenders—hypocrites?

19 Show me the money for the tribute. And they brought Him a denarius.

20 And Jesus said to them, Whose likeness and title are these?

21 They said, Caesar's. Then He said to them, Pay therefore to Caesar the things that are due to Caesar, and pay to God the things that are due to God.

22 When they heard it they were amazed *and* marveled, and they left Him and departed.

23 The same day some Sadducees came to Him, who say that there is no resurrection [of the dead], and they asked Him a question,

24 Saying, Teacher, Moses said, If a man dies, leaving no children, his brother shall marry the widow and raise up a family for his brother. [Deut. 25:5.]

25 Now there were seven brothers among us; the first married and died, and having no children left his wife to his brother.

26 The second also died childless, and the third, down to the seventh.

27 Last of all, the woman died also.

28 Now in the resurrection to which of the seven will she be wife? For they all had her.

AMP [a] Literal translation. [b] Cremer.

## New American Standard

*Parable of the Marriage Feast*

**22** AND JESUS answered and spoke to them again in parables, saying,

2"The kingdom of heaven may be compared to a king, who gave a wedding feast for his son.

3"And he sent out his slaves to call those who had been invited to the wedding feast, and they were unwilling to come.

4"Again he sent out other slaves saying, 'Tell those who have been invited, "Behold, I have prepared my dinner; my oxen and my fattened livestock are *all* butchered and everything is ready; come to the wedding feast." '

5"But they paid no attention and went their way, one to his own farm, another to his business,

6and the rest seized his slaves and mistreated them and killed them.

7"But the king was enraged and sent his armies, and destroyed those murderers, and set their city on fire.

8"Then he *said to his slaves, 'The wedding is ready, but those who were invited were not worthy.

9'Go therefore to the main highways, and as many as you find *there,* invite to the wedding feast.'

10"And those slaves went out into the streets, and gathered together all they found, both evil and good; and the wedding hall was filled with dinner guests.

11"But when the king came in to look over the dinner guests, he saw there a man not dressed in wedding clothes,

12and he *said to him, 'Friend, how did you come in here without wedding clothes?' And he was speechless.

13"Then the king said to the servants, 'Bind him hand and foot, and cast him into the outer darkness; in that place there shall be weeping and gnashing of teeth.'

14"For many are called, but few *are* chosen."

*Tribute to Caesar*

15¶ Then the Pharisees went and counseled together how they might trap Him in what He said.

16And they *sent their disciples to Him, along with the Herodians, saying, "Teacher, we know that You are truthful and teach the way of God in truth, and defer to no one; for You are not partial to any.

17"Tell us therefore, what do You think? Is it lawful to give a poll-tax to Caesar, or not?"

18But Jesus perceived their malice, and said, "Why are you testing Me, you hypocrites?

19"Show Me the coin *used* for the poll-tax." And they brought Him a denarius.

20And He *said to them, "Whose likeness and inscription is this?"

21They *said to Him, "Caesar's." Then He *said to them, "Then render to Caesar the things that are Caesar's; and to God the things that are God's."

22And hearing *this,* they marveled, and leaving Him, they went away.

*Jesus Answers the Saddusees*

23¶ On that day *some* Sadducees (who say there is no resurrection) came to Him and questioned Him,

24saying, "Teacher, Moses said, 'IF A MAN DIES, HAVING NO CHILDREN, HIS BROTHER AS NEXT OF KIN SHALL MARRY HIS WIFE, AND RAISE UP AN OFFSPRING TO HIS BROTHER.'

25"Now there were seven brothers with us; and the first married and died, and having no offspring left his wife to his brother;

26so also the second, and the third, down to the seventh.

27"And last of all, the woman died.

28"In the resurrection therefore whose wife of the seven shall she be? For they all had her."

## New International

*The Parable of the Wedding Banquet*

**22** JESUS SPOKE to them again in parables, saying: 2"The
kingdom of heaven is like a king who prepared a wedding
banquet for his son. 3He sent his servants to those who had been
invited to the banquet to tell them to come, but they refused to
come.

4"Then he sent some more servants and said, 'Tell those who have been invited that I have prepared my dinner: My oxen and fattened cattle have been butchered, and everything is ready. Come to the wedding banquet.'

5"But they paid no attention and went off—one to his field,
another to his business. 6The rest seized his servants, mistreated
them and killed them. 7The king was enraged. He sent his army
and destroyed those murderers and burned their city.

8"Then he said to his servants, 'The wedding banquet is ready,
but those I invited did not deserve to come. 9Go to the street
corners and invite to the banquet anyone you find.' 10So the servants went out into the streets and gathered all the people they
could find, both good and bad, and the wedding hall was filled
with guests.

11"But when the king came in to see the guests, he noticed a
man there who was not wearing wedding clothes. 12'Friend,' he
asked, 'how did you get in here without wedding clothes?' The
man was speechless.

13"Then the king told the attendants, 'Tie him hand and foot, and throw him outside, into the darkness, where there will be weeping and gnashing of teeth.'

14"For many are invited, but few are chosen."

*Paying Taxes to Caesar*

15Then the Pharisees went out and laid plans to trap him in his
words. 16They sent their disciples to him along with the Herodians. "Teacher," they said, "we know you are a man of integrity
and that you teach the way of God in accordance with the truth.
You aren't swayed by men, because you pay no attention to who
they are. 17Tell us then, what is your opinion? Is it right to pay
taxes to Caesar or not?"

18But Jesus, knowing their evil intent, said, "You hypocrites,
why are you trying to trap me? 19Show me the coin used for paying
the tax." They brought him a denarius, 20and he asked them,
"Whose portrait is this? And whose inscription?"

21"Caesar's," they replied.

Then he said to them, "Give to Caesar what is Caesar's, and to God what is God's."

22When they heard this, they were amazed. So they left him and went away.

*Marriage at the Resurrection*

23That same day the Sadducees, who say there is no resurrection, came to him with a question. 24"Teacher," they said, "Moses
told us that if a man dies without having children, his brother must
marry the widow and have children for him. 25Now there were
seven brothers among us. The first one married and died, and
since he had no children, he left his wife to his brother. 26The same
thing happened to the second and third brother, right on down to
the seventh. 27Finally, the woman died. 28Now then, at the resurrection, whose wife will she be of the seven, since all of them were
married to her?"

## King James

29Jesus answered and said unto them, Ye do err, not knowing the scriptures, nor the power of God.
30For in the resurrection they neither marry, nor are given in marriage, but are as the angels of God in heaven.
31But as touching the resurrection of the dead, have ye not read that which was spoken unto you by God, saying,
32I am the God of Abraham, and the God of Isaac, and the God of Jacob? God is not the God of the dead, but of the living.
33And when the multitude heard *this*, they were astonished at his doctrine.
34¶ But when the Pharisees had heard that he had put the Sadducees to silence, they were gathered together.
35Then one of them, *which was* a lawyer, asked *him a question*, tempting him, and saying,
36Master, which *is* the great commandment in the law?
37Jesus said unto him, Thou shalt love the Lord thy God with all thy heart, and with all thy soul, and with all thy mind.
38This is the first and great commandment.
39And the second *is* like unto it, Thou shalt love thy neighbour as thyself.
40On these two commandments hang all the law and the prophets.
41¶ While the Pharisees were gathered together, Jesus asked them,
42Saying, What think ye of Christ? whose son is he? They say unto him, *The son* of David.
43He saith unto them, How then doth David in spirit call him Lord, saying,
44The LORD said unto my Lord, Sit thou on my right hand, till I make thine enemies thy footstool?
45If David then call him Lord, how is he his son?
46And no man was able to answer him a word, neither durst any *man* from that day forth ask him any more *questions*.

**23** THEN SPAKE Jesus to the multitude, and to his disciples,
2Saying, The scribes and the Pharisees sit in Moses' seat:
3All therefore whatsoever they bid you observe, *that* observe and do; but do not ye after their works: for they say, and do not.
4For they bind heavy burdens and grievous to be borne, and lay *them* on men's shoulders; but they *themselves* will not move them with one of their fingers.
5But all their works they do for to be seen of men: they make broad their phylacteries, and enlarge the borders of their garments,
6And love the uppermost rooms at feasts, and the chief seats in the synagogues,
7And greetings in the markets, and to be called of men, Rabbi, Rabbi.
8But be not ye called Rabbi: for one is your Master, *even* Christ; and all ye are brethren.
9And call no *man* your father upon the earth: for one is your Father, which is in heaven.
10Neither be ye called masters: for one is your Master, *even* Christ.
11But he that is greatest among you shall be your servant.
12And whosoever shall exalt himself shall be abased; and he that shall humble himself shall be exalted.

## Amplified

29But Jesus replied to them, You are wrong, because you know neither the Scriptures nor God's power.
30For in the resurrected state neither do [men] marry nor are [women] given in marriage, but they are as the angels in heaven.
31But as to the resurrection of the dead, have you never read what was said to you by God,
32I am the God of Abraham, and the God of Isaac, and the God of Jacob? He is not the God of the dead, but of the living! [Exod. 3:6.]
33And when the throng heard it, they were astonished *and* filled with [ [a]glad] amazement at His teaching.
34Now when the Pharisees heard that He had silenced ( [b]muzzled) the Sadducees, they gathered together;
35And one of their number, a lawyer, asked Him a question to test Him.
36Teacher, which [c]kind of commandment is great and important—the principal kind—in the Law? [Some are light; which are heavy?]
37And He replied to him, You shall love the Lord your God with all your heart, and with all your soul, and with all your mind (intellect). [Deut. 6:5.]
38This is the great (most important, principal) and first commandment.
39And a second is like it, You shall love your neighbor as [you do] yourself. [Lev. 19:18.]
40These two commandments [d]sum up *and* upon them depends all the Law and the prophets.
41Now while the Pharisees were still assembled there, Jesus asked them a question,
42Saying, What do you think of the Christ? Whose Son is He? They said to Him, The Son of David.
43He said to them, How is it then that David, under the influence of the (Holy) Spirit, calls Him Lord, saying,
44The Lord said to My Lord, Sit at My right hand until I put Your enemies under Your feet? [Ps. 110:1.]
45If then David thus calls Him Lord, how is He his son?
46And no one was able to answer Him a word, nor from that day did any one venture *or* dare to question Him.

**23** THEN JESUS said to the multitudes and to His disciples,
2The scribes and Pharisees sit on Moses' seat [of authority],
3So observe and practice all they tell you; but do not do what they do, for they preach, but do not practice.
4They tie up heavy loads, *hard to bear*, and place them on men's shoulders, but they themselves will not lift a finger to help bear them.
5They do all their works to be seen of men; for they make wide their phylacteries [ [e]small cases enclosing certain Scripture passages, worn during prayer on left arm and forehead], and make long their fringes [worn by all male Israelites, according to the command]. [Num. 15:38; Exod. 13:9; Deut. 6:8.]
6And they [f]take pleasure in *and* [thus] love the place of honor at feasts and the best seats in the synagogues,
7And to be greeted with honor in the market places, and to have people call them rabbi.
8But you are not to be called rabbi (teacher), for One is your Teacher, and you are all brothers.
9And do not call any one [in the church] on earth father, for you have one Father, Who is in heaven.
10And you must not be called masters (leaders), for you have one Master (Leader), the Christ.
11He who is greatest among you shall be your servant.
12Whoever exalts himself [ [g]with haughtiness and empty pride] shall be humbled (brought low); and whoever humbles himself—who has a modest opinion of himself and behaves accordingly—shall be [h]raised to honor.

**AMP** [a] Thayer. [b] Literal translation. [c] Vincent. [d] Thayer. [e] Condensed from "Davis Dictionary of the Bible." [f] Wuest. [g] Thayer. [h] Thayer.

## New American Standard

29But Jesus answered and said to them, "You are mistaken, not
understanding the Scriptures, or the power of God.
30"For in the resurrection they neither marry, nor are given in
marriage, but are like angels in heaven.
31"But regarding the resurrection of the dead, have you not
read that which was spoken to you by God, saying,
32'I AM THE GOD OF ABRAHAM, AND THE GOD OF ISAAC, AND THE
GOD OF JACOB'? He is not the God of the dead but of the living."
33And when the multitudes heard *this,* they were astonished at
His teaching.
34¶ But when the Pharisees heard that He had put the Sadducees to silence, they gathered themselves together.
35And one of them, [i]a lawyer, asked Him *a question,* testing
Him,
36"Teacher, which is the great commandment in the Law?"
37And He said to him, " 'YOU SHALL LOVE THE LORD YOUR GOD
WITH ALL YOUR HEART, AND WITH ALL YOUR SOUL, AND WITH ALL
YOUR MIND.'
38"This is the great and foremost commandment.
39"The second is like it, 'YOU SHALL LOVE YOUR NEIGHBOR AS
YOURSELF.'
40"On these two commandments depend the whole Law and
the Prophets."
41¶ Now while the Pharisees were gathered together, Jesus
asked them a question,
42saying, "What do you think about the Christ, whose son is
He?" They *said to Him, "*The son* of David."
43He *said to them, "Then how does David in the Spirit call Him
'Lord,' saying,
44 'THE LORD SAID TO MY LORD,
"SIT AT MY RIGHT HAND,
UNTIL I PUT THINE ENEMIES BENEATH THY FEET" '?
45"If David then calls Him 'Lord,' how is He his son?"
46And no one was able to answer Him a word, nor did anyone
dare from that day on to ask Him another question.

*Pharisaism Exposed*

23 THEN JESUS spoke to the multitudes and to His disciples,
2saying, "The scribes and the Pharisees have seated themselves in the chair of Moses;
3therefore all that they tell you, do and observe, but do not do
according to their deeds; for they say *things,* and do not do *them.*
4"And they tie up heavy loads, and lay them on men's shoulders; but they themselves are unwilling to move them with *so much
as* a finger.
5"But they do all their deeds to be noticed by men; for they
broaden their [j]phylacteries, and lengthen the tassels *of their garments.*
6"And they love the place of honor at banquets, and the chief
seats in the synagogues,
7and respectful greetings in the market places, and being called
by men, Rabbi.
8"But do not be called Rabbi; for One is your Teacher, and you
are all brothers.
9"And do not call *anyone* on earth your father; for One is your
Father, He who is in heaven.
10"And do not be called leaders; for One is your Leader, *that is,*
Christ.
11"But the greatest among you shall be your servant.
12"And whoever exalts himself shall be humbled; and whoever
humbles himself shall be exalted.

**NAS** [i] I.e., an expert in the Mosaic law [j] I.e., small boxes containing
Scripture texts worn for religious purposes

## New International

29Jesus replied, "You are in error because you do not know the
Scriptures or the power of God. 30At the resurrection people will
neither marry nor be given in marriage; they will be like the angels
in heaven. 31But about the resurrection of the dead—have you not
read what God said to you, 32'I am the God of Abraham, the God
of Isaac, and the God of Jacob'[k]? He is not the God of the dead but
of the living."
33When the crowds heard this, they were astonished at his
teaching.

*The Greatest Commandment*

34Hearing that Jesus had silenced the Sadducees, the Pharisees
got together. 35One of them, an expert in the law, tested him with
this question: 36"Teacher, which is the greatest commandment in
the Law?"
37Jesus replied: " 'Love the Lord your God with all your heart
and with all your soul and with all your mind.'[l] 38This is the first
and greatest commandment. 39And the second is like it: 'Love your
neighbor as yourself.'[m] 40All the Law and the Prophets hang on
these two commandments."

*Whose Son Is the Christ?*

41While the Pharisees were gathered together, Jesus asked
them, 42"What do you think about the Christ[n]? Whose son is he?"
"The son of David," they replied.
43He said to them, "How is it then that David, speaking by the
Spirit, calls him 'Lord'? For he says,

44" 'The Lord said to my Lord:
"Sit at my right hand
until I put your enemies
under your feet." '[o]

45If then David calls him 'Lord,' how can he be his son?" 46No one
could say a word in reply, and from that day on no one dared to
ask him any more questions.

*Seven Woes*

23 THEN JESUS said to the crowds and to his disciples: 2"The
teachers of the law and the Pharisees sit in Moses' seat.
3So you must obey them and do everything they tell you. But do
not do what they do, for they do not practice what they preach.
4They tie up heavy loads and put them on men's shoulders, but
they themselves are not willing to lift a finger to move them.
5"Everything they do is done for men to see: They make their
phylacteries[p] wide and the tassels on their garments long; 6they
love the place of honor at banquets and the most important seats
in the synagogues; 7they love to be greeted in the marketplaces
and to have men call them 'Rabbi.'
8"But you are not to be called 'Rabbi,' for you have only one
Master and you are all brothers. 9And do not call anyone on earth
'father,' for you have one Father, and he is in heaven. 10Nor are
you to be called 'teacher,' for you have one Teacher, the Christ.[q]
11The greatest among you will be your servant. 12For whoever
exalts himself will be humbled, and whoever humbles himself will
be exalted.

**NIV** [k] 32 Exodus 3:6 [l] 37 Deut. 6:5 [m] 39 Lev. 19:18 [n] 42 Or *Messiah*
[o] 44 Psalm 110:1 [p] 5 That is, boxes containing Scripture verses, worn on
forehead and arm [q] 10 Or *Messiah*

## King James

13¶ But woe unto you, scribes and Pharisees, hypocrites! for ye
shut up the kingdom of heaven against men: for ye neither go in
*yourselves,* neither suffer ye them that are entering to go in.
14Woe unto you, scribes and Pharisees, hypocrites! for ye devour widows' houses, and for a pretence make long prayer: therefore ye shall receive the greater damnation.
15Woe unto you, scribes and Pharisees, hypocrites! for ye compass sea and land to make one proselyte, and when he is made,
ye make him twofold more the child of hell than yourselves.
16Woe unto you, *ye* blind guides, which say, Whosoever shall
swear by the temple, it is nothing; but whosoever shall swear by
the gold of the temple, he is a debtor!
17 *Ye* fools and blind: for whether is greater, the gold, or the
temple that sanctifieth the gold?
18And, Whosoever shall swear by the altar, it is nothing; but
whosoever sweareth by the gift that is upon it, he is guilty.
19 *Ye* fools and blind: for whether *is* greater, the gift, or the altar
that sanctifieth the gift?
20Whoso therefore shall swear by the altar, sweareth by it, and
by all things thereon.
21And whoso shall swear by the temple, sweareth by it, and by
him that dwelleth therein.
22And he that shall swear by heaven, sweareth by the throne
of God, and by him that sitteth thereon.
23Woe unto you, scribes and Pharisees, hypocrites! for ye pay
tithe of mint and anise and cummin, and have omitted the weightier *matters* of the law, judgment, mercy, and faith: these ought ye
to have done, and not to leave the other undone.
24 *Ye* blind guides, which strain at a gnat, and swallow a camel.
25Woe unto you, scribes and Pharisees, hypocrites! for ye make
clean the outside of the cup and of the platter, but within they are
full of extortion and excess.
26 *Thou* blind Pharisee, cleanse first that *which is* within the cup
and platter, that the outside of them may be clean also.
27Woe unto you, scribes and Pharisees, hypocrites! for ye are
like unto whited sepulchres, which indeed appear beautiful outward, but are within full of dead *men's* bones, and of all uncleanness.
28Even so ye also outwardly appear righteous unto men, but
within ye are full of hypocrisy and iniquity.
29Woe unto you, scribes and Pharisees, hypocrites! because ye
build the tombs of the prophets, and garnish the sepulchres of the
righteous,
30And say, If we had been in the days of our fathers, we would
not have been partakers with them in the blood of the prophets.
31Wherefore ye be witnesses unto yourselves, that ye are the
children of them which killed the prophets.
32Fill ye up then the measure of your fathers.
33 *Ye* serpents, *ye* generation of vipers, how can ye escape the
damnation of hell?
34¶ Wherefore, behold, I send unto you prophets, and wise
men, and scribes: and *some* of them ye shall kill and crucify; and
*some* of them shall ye scourge in your synagogues, and persecute
*them* from city to city:

## Amplified

13But woe to you, scribes and Pharisees, pretenders—hypocrites! because you shut the kingdom of heaven in men's faces; for
you neither enter yourselves, nor do you allow those who are
about to go in to do so.
14 *Woe to you, scribes and Pharisees, pretenders—hypocrites! for you
swallow up widows' houses, and for a pretense to cover it up make long
prayers; therefore you will receive the greater condemnation and the
heavier sentence.*
15Woe to you scribes and Pharisees, pretenders—hypocrites!
for you travel over sea and land to make a single proselyte, and
when he becomes [a proselyte], you make him doubly as much a
child of hell (Gehenna) as you are.
16Woe to you, blind guides, who say, If any one swears by the
[a]sanctuary of the temple, it is nothing; but if any one swears by
the gold of the [b]sanctuary, he is a debtor—bound by his oath.
17You blind fools! For which is greater, the gold or the
[c]sanctuary of the temple that has made the gold sacred? [Exod.
30:29.]
18You say too, Whoever swears by the altar is not duty bound,
but whoever swears by the offering on the altar, his oath is binding.
19You blind men! Which is greater, the gift or the altar which
makes the gift sacred?
20So whoever swears by the altar, swears by it and by everything on it;
21And he who swears by the [d]sanctuary of the temple, swears
by it and by Him Who dwells in it; [I Kings 8:13; Ps. 26:8.]
22And whoever swears by heaven, swears by the throne of God
and by Him Who sits upon it.
23Woe to you, scribes and Pharisees, pretenders—hypocrites!
for you give a tenth of your mint and dill and cummin, and have
neglected *and* omitted the weightier (more important) matters of
the Law, right *and* justice and mercy and fidelity. These you ought
[particularly] to have done, without neglecting the others.
24You blind guides, filtering out a gnat and gulping down a
[e]camel! [Lev. 27:30; Mic. 6:8.]
25Woe to you, scribes and Pharisees, pretenders—hypocrites!
for you clean the outside of the cup and of the platter, but within
they are full of extortion—prey, spoil, plunder—and grasping self-
indulgence.
26You blind Pharisee! First clean the inside of the cup and of the
plate, so that the outside may be clean also.
27Woe to you, scribes and Pharisees, pretenders—hypocrites!
for you are like tombs that have been white-washed, which look
beautiful on the outside, but inside are full of dead men's bones
and everything impure.
28Just so, you also outwardly seem to people to be just *and*
upright, but inside you are full of pretense and lawlessness *and*
iniquity. [Ps. 5:9.]
29Woe to you, scribes and Pharisees, pretenders—hypocrites!
for you build tombs for the prophets and decorate the monuments
of the righteous,
30Saying, If we had lived in the days of our forefathers, we
would not have aided them in shedding the blood of the prophets.
31Thus you are testifying [against] yourselves that you are the
descendants of those who murdered the prophets.
32Fill up then the measure of your fathers' sins to the brim [so
[f]that nothing may be wanting to a full measure].
33You serpents! You spawn of vipers! How can you escape the
[g]penalty to be suffered in hell (Gehenna)?
34Because of this, take notice, I am sending you prophets and
wise men (interpreters and teachers) and scribes (men learned in
the Mosaic Law and the prophets); some of them you will kill, even
crucify, and some you will flog in your synagogues, and pursue
*and* persecute from town to town,

**AMP** [a] Trench. [b] Trench. [c] Trench. [d] Trench. [e] The camel was also unclean (Lev. 11:4). [f] Thayer. [g] Thayer.

## New American Standard

*Seven Woes*

13¶ "But woe to you, scribes and Pharisees, hypocrites, because you shut off the kingdom of heaven from men; for you do not enter in yourselves, nor do you allow those who are entering to go in.

14[" [h]Woe to you, scribes and Pharisees, hypocrites, because you devour widows' houses, even while for a pretense you make long prayers; therefore you shall receive greater condemnation.]

15¶ "Woe to you, scribes and Pharisees, hypocrites, because you travel about on sea and land to make one proselyte; and when he becomes one, you make him twice as much a son of hell as yourselves.

16¶ "Woe to you, blind guides, who say, 'Whoever swears by the temple, that is nothing; but whoever swears by the gold of the temple, he is obligated.'

17"You fools and blind men; which is more important, the gold, or the temple that sanctified the gold?

18"And, 'Whoever swears by the altar, *that* is nothing, but whoever swears by the offering upon it, he is obligated.'

19"You blind men, which is more important, the offering or the altar that sanctifies the offering?

20"Therefore he who swears, swears *both* by the altar and by everything on it.

21"And he who swears by the temple, swears *both* by the temple and by Him who dwells within it.

22"And he who swears by heaven, swears *both* by the throne of God and by Him who sits upon it.

23¶ "Woe to you, scribes and Pharisees, hypocrites! For you tithe the mint and dill and cummin, and have neglected the weightier provisions of the law: justice and mercy and faithfulness; but these are the things you should have done without neglecting the others.

24"You blind guides, who strain out a gnat and swallow a camel!

25¶ "Woe to you, scribes and Pharisees, hypocrites! For you clean the outside of the cup and of the dish, but inside they are full of robbery and self-indulgence.

26"You blind Pharisee, first clean the inside of the cup and of the dish, so that the outside of it may become clean also.

27¶ "Woe to you, scribes and Pharisees, hypocrites! For you are like whitewashed tombs which on the outside appear beautiful, but inside they are full of dead men's bones and all uncleanness.

28"Even so you too outwardly appear righteous to men, but inwardly you are full of hypocrisy and lawlessness.

29¶ "Woe to you, scribes and Pharisees, hypocrites! For you build the tombs of the prophets and adorn the monuments of the righteous,

30and say, 'If we had been *living* in the days of our fathers, we would not have been partners with them in *shedding* the blood of the prophets.'

31"Consequently you bear witness against yourselves, that you are sons of those who murdered the prophets.

32"Fill up then the measure *of the guilt* of your fathers.

33"You serpents, you brood of vipers, how shall you escape the sentence of hell?

34"Therefore, behold, I am sending you prophets and wise men and scribes; some of them you will kill and crucify, and some of them you will scourge in your synagogues, and persecute from city to city,

NAS [h] This verse not found in the earliest mss.

## New International

13"Woe to you, teachers of the law and Pharisees, you hypocrites! You shut the kingdom of heaven in men's faces. You yourselves do not enter, nor will you let those enter who are trying to.[i]
15"Woe to you, teachers of the law and Pharisees, you hypocrites! You travel over land and sea to win a single convert, and
when he becomes one, you make him twice as much a son of hell
as you are.
16"Woe to you, blind guides! You say, 'If anyone swears by the
temple, it means nothing; but if anyone swears by the gold of the
temple, he is bound by his oath.'
17You blind fools! Which is
greater: the gold, or the temple that makes the gold sacred?
18You
also say, 'If anyone swears by the altar, it means nothing; but if
anyone swears by the gift on it, he is bound by his oath.'
19You
blind men! Which is greater: the gift, or the altar that makes the
gift sacred?
20Therefore, he who swears by the altar swears by it
and by everything on it.
21And he who swears by the temple
swears by it and by the one who dwells in it.
22And he who swears
by heaven swears by God's throne and by the one who sits on it.
23"Woe to you, teachers of the law and Pharisees, you hypocrites! You give a tenth of your spices—mint, dill and cummin. But
you have neglected the more important matters of the law—justice, mercy and faithfulness. You should have practiced the latter,
without neglecting the former.
24You blind guides! You strain out
a gnat but swallow a camel.
25"Woe to you, teachers of the law and Pharisees, you hypocrites! You clean the outside of the cup and dish, but inside they
are full of greed and self-indulgence.
26Blind Pharisee! First clean
the inside of the cup and dish, and then the outside also will be
clean.
27"Woe to you, teachers of the law and Pharisees, you hypocrites! You are like whitewashed tombs, which look beautiful on
the outside but on the inside are full of dead men's bones and
everything unclean.
28In the same way, on the outside you appear
to people as righteous but on the inside you are full of hypocrisy
and wickedness.
29"Woe to you, teachers of the law and Pharisees, you hypocrites! You build tombs for the prophets and decorate the graves
of the righteous.
30And you say, 'If we had lived in the days of our
forefathers, we would not have taken part with them in shedding
the blood of the prophets.'
31So you testify against yourselves that
you are the descendants of those who murdered the prophets.
32Fill up, then, the measure of the sin of your forefathers!
33"You snakes! You brood of vipers! How will you escape being
condemned to hell?
34Therefore I am sending you prophets and
wise men and teachers. Some of them you will kill and crucify;
others you will flog in your synagogues and pursue from town to
town.
35And so upon you will come all the righteous blood that

**NIV** [i] 13 Some manuscripts *to.* 14*Woe to you, teachers of the law and Pharisees, you hypocrites! You devour widows' houses and for a show make lengthy prayers. Therefore you will be punished more severely.*

## King James

35That upon you may come all the righteous blood shed upon
the earth, from the blood of righteous Abel unto the blood of
Zacharias son of Barachias, whom ye slew between the temple and
the altar.
36Verily I say unto you, All these things shall come upon this
generation.
37O Jerusalem, Jerusalem, *thou* that killest the prophets, and
stonest them which are sent unto thee, how often would I have
gathered thy children together, even as a hen gathereth her chick-
ens under *her* wings, and ye would not!
38Behold, your house is left unto you desolate.
39For I say unto you, Ye shall not see me henceforth, till ye shall
say, Blessed *is* he that cometh in the name of the Lord.

**24** AND JESUS went out, and departed from the temple: and
his disciples came to *him* for to show him the buildings of
the temple.
2And Jesus said unto them, See ye not all these things? verily
I say unto you, There shall not be left here one stone upon another,
that shall not be thrown down.
3¶ And as he sat upon the mount of Olives, the disciples came
unto him privately, saying, Tell us, when shall these things be?
and what *shall be* the sign of thy coming, and of the end of the
world?
4And Jesus answered and said unto them, Take heed that no
man deceive you.
5For many shall come in my name, saying, I am Christ; and shall
deceive many.
6And ye shall hear of wars and rumours of wars: see that ye be
not troubled: for all *these things* must come to pass, but the end is
not yet.
7For nation shall rise against nation, and kingdom against kingdom: and there shall be famines, and pestilences, and earthquakes, in divers places.
8All these *are* the beginning of sorrows.
9Then shall they deliver you up to be afflicted, and shall kill you:
and ye shall be hated of all nations for my name's sake.
10And then shall many be offended, and shall betray one another, and shall hate one another.
11And many false prophets shall rise, and shall deceive many.
12And because iniquity shall abound, the love of many shall
wax cold.
13But he that shall endure unto the end, the same shall be
saved.
14And this gospel of the kingdom shall be preached in all the
world for a witness unto all nations; and then shall the end come.
15When ye therefore shall see the abomination of desolation,
spoken of by Daniel the prophet, stand in the holy place, (whoso
readeth, let him understand:)
16Then let them which be in Judaea flee into the mountains:
17Let him which is on the housetop not come down to take any
thing out of his house:
18Neither let him which is in the field return back to take his
clothes.
19And woe unto them that are with child, and to them that give
suck in those days!

**AMP** [a] Abbott-Smith. [b] Thayer. [c] Trench's "Synonyms of the New Testament." [d] Thayer. [e] Literal translation. [f] Thayer. [g] Thayer. [h] Vincent. [i] Thayer.

## Amplified

35So that upon your heads may come all the blood of the righteous [ [a]those who correspond to the divine standard of right] shed
on earth from the blood of the righteous Abel to the blood of
Zechariah son of Barachiah, whom you murdered between the
sanctuary and the altar [of burnt offering]. [Gen. 4:8; II Chron.
24:21.]
36Truly, I declare to you, all these [ [b]evil, calamitous times] will
come upon this generation. [II Chron. 36:15, 16.]
37O Jerusalem, Jerusalem, murdering the prophets and stoning
those who are sent to you! How often would I have gathered your
children together as a mother fowl gathers her brood under her
wings, and you refused!
38Behold, your house is forsaken and desolate—abandoned and
left destitute [of God's help]. [I Kings 9:7; Jer. 22:5.]
39For I declare to you, you will not see Me again until you say,
Blessed—magnified in worship, adored and exalted—be He Who
comes in the name of the Lord! [Ps. 118:26.]

**24** JESUS DEPARTED from the temple [c]area and was going
on His way, when His disciples came up to Him to call His
attention to the buildings of the temple *and* point them out to Him.
2But He answered them, Do you see all these? Truly, I tell you,
there will not be left here one stone upon another that will not be
thrown down.
3While He was seated on the Mount of Olives, the disciples
came to Him privately and said, Tell us, when will this take place,
and what will be the sign of Your coming and of the end—that is,
the completion, the consummation—of the age?
4Jesus answered them, Be careful that no one midleads you—
deceiving you and leading you into error.
5For many will come in (on the strength of) My name—
[d]appropriating the name which belongs to Me—saying, I am the
Messiah, the Christ; and they will lead many astray.
6And you will hear of wars and rumors of wars; see that you
are not frightened *or* troubled, for this must take place, but the end
is not yet.
7For nation will rise against nation, and kingdom against kingdom, and there will be famines and earthquakes in place after
place;
8All this is but the beginning—the early pains of the [e]birth
pangs—of the [f]intolerable anguish.
9Then they will hand you over to suffer affliction *and* tribulation, and put you to death; and you will be hated by all nations
for My name's sake.
10And then many will be offended *and* repelled *and* [g]begin to
distrust *and* desert [Him Whom they ought to trust and obey] *and*
will stumble and fall away, and betray one another *and* pursue one
another with hatred.
11And many false prophets will rise up and deceive *and* lead
many into error.
12And the love of [h]the great body of people will grow cold,
because of the multiplied lawlessness *and* iniquity.
13But he who endures to the end will be saved.
14And this good news of the kingdom (the Gospel) will be
preached throughout the whole world as a testimony to all the
nations, and then will come the end.
15So when you see the appalling sacrilege spoken of by the
prophet Daniel, standing in the Holy Place, [and] let the reader
take notice *and* [i]ponder *and* consider *and* heed [this], [Dan. 9:27;
11:31; 12:11.]
16Then let those who are in Judea flee to the mountains;
17Let him who is on the housetop not come down *and* go into
the house to take anything;
18And let him who is in the field not turn back to get his
overcoat.
19And alas for the women who are pregnant and for those who
have nursing babies in those days!

## New American Standard

35that upon you may fall *the guilt of* all the righteous blood shed
on earth, from the blood of righteous Abel to the blood of Zechariah, the son of Berechiah, whom you murdered between the
temple and the altar.
36"Truly I say to you, all these things shall come upon this
generation.

*Lament over Jerusalem*

37¶ "O Jerusalem, Jerusalem, who kills the prophets and stones
those who are sent to her! How often I wanted to gather your
children together, the way a hen gathers her chicks under her
wings, and you were unwilling.
38"Behold, your house is being left to you desolate!
39"For I say to you, from now on you shall not see Me until you
say, 'BLESSED IS HE WHO COMES IN THE NAME OF THE LORD!' "

*Signs of Christ's Return*

**24** AND JESUS came out from the temple and was going
away when His disciples came up to point out the temple
buildings to Him.
2And He answered and said to them, "Do you not see all these
things? Truly I say to you, not one stone here shall be left upon
another, which will not be torn down."
3¶ And as He was sitting on the Mount of Olives, the disciples
came to Him privately, saying, "Tell us, when will these things be,
and what *will be* the sign of Your coming, and of the end of the
age?"
4And Jesus answered and said to them, "See to it that no one
misleads you.
5"For many will come in My name, saying, 'I am the Christ,'
and will mislead many.
6"And you will be hearing of wars and rumors of wars; see that
you are not frightened, for *those things* must take place, but *that* is
not yet the end.
7"For nation will rise against nation, and kingdom against
kingdom, and in various places there will be famines and earthquakes.
8"But all these things are *merely* the beginning of birth pangs.
9"Then they will deliver you to tribulation, and will kill you,
and you will be hated by all nations on account of My name.
10"And at that time many will fall away and will deliver up one
another and hate one another.
11"And many false prophets will arise, and will mislead many.
12"And because lawlessness is increased, most people's love
will grow cold.
13"But the one who endures to the end, he shall be saved.
14"And this gospel of the kingdom shall be preached in the
whole world for a witness to all the nations, and then the end shall
come.

*Perilous Times*

15¶ "Therefore when you see the ABOMINATION OF DESOLATION
which was spoken of through Daniel the prophet, standing in the
holy place (let the reader understand),
16then let those who are in Judea flee to the mountains;
17let him who is on the housetop not go down to get the things
out that are in his house;
18and let him who is in the field not turn back to get his cloak.
19"But woe to those who are with child and to those who nurse
babes in those days!

## New International

has been shed on earth, from the blood of righteous Abel to the
blood of Zechariah son of Berekiah, whom you murdered between
the temple and the altar. 36I tell you the truth, all this will come
upon this generation.
37"O Jerusalem, Jerusalem, you who kill the prophets and stone
those sent to you, how often I have longed to gather your children
together, as a hen gathers her chicks under her wings, but you
were not willing. 38Look, your house is left to you desolate. 39For
I tell you, you will not see me again until you say, 'Blessed is he
who comes in the name of the Lord.'[j] "

*Signs of the End of the Age*

**24** JESUS LEFT the temple and was walking away when his
disciples came up to him to call his attention to its buildings. 2"Do you see all these things?" he asked. "I tell you the truth,
not one stone here will be left on another; every one will be thrown
down."
3As Jesus was sitting on the Mount of Olives, the disciples came
to him privately. "Tell us," they said, "when will this happen, and
what will be the sign of your coming and of the end of the age?"
4Jesus answered: "Watch out that no one deceives you. 5For
many will come in my name, claiming, 'I am the Christ,[k]' and will
deceive many. 6You will hear of wars and rumors of wars, but see
to it that you are not alarmed. Such things must happen, but the
end is still to come. 7Nation will rise against nation, and kingdom
against kingdom. There will be famines and earthquakes in various places. 8All these are the beginning of birth pains.
9"Then you will be handed over to be persecuted and put to
death, and you will be hated by all nations because of me. 10At that
time many will turn away from the faith and will betray and hate
each other, 11and many false prophets will appear and deceive
many people. 12Because of the increase of wickedness, the love of
most will grow cold, 13but he who stands firm to the end will be
saved. 14And this gospel of the kingdom will be preached in the
whole world as a testimony to all nations, and then the end will
come.
15"So when you see standing in the holy place 'the abomination
that causes desolation,'[l] spoken of through the prophet Daniel—
let the reader understand— 16then let those who are in Judea flee
to the mountains. 17Let no one on the roof of his house go down
to take anything out of the house. 18Let no one in the field go back
to get his cloak. 19How dreadful it will be in those days for pregnant women and nursing mothers! 20Pray that your flight will not

NIV [j] 39 Psalm 118:26 [k] 5 Or *Messiah;* also in verse 23 [l] 15 Daniel 9:27; 11:31; 12:11

## King James

20But pray ye that your flight be not in the winter, neither on the sabbath day:

21For then shall be great tribulation, such as was not since the beginning of the world to this time, no, nor ever shall be.

22And except those days should be shortened, there should no flesh be saved: but for the elect's sake those days shall be shortened.

23Then if any man shall say unto you, Lo, here *is* Christ, or there; believe *it* not.

24For there shall arise false Christs, and false prophets, and shall show great signs and wonders; insomuch that, if *it were* possible, they shall deceive the very elect.

25Behold, I have told you before.

26Wherefore if they shall say unto you, Behold, he is in the desert; go not forth: behold, *he is* in the secret chambers; believe *it* not.

27For as the lightning cometh out of the east, and shineth even unto the west; so shall also the coming of the Son of man be.

28For wheresoever the carcase is, there will the eagles be gathered together.

29¶ Immediately after the tribulation of those days shall the sun be darkened, and the moon shall not give her light, and the stars shall fall from heaven, and the powers of the heavens shall be shaken:

30And then shall appear the sign of the Son of man in heaven: and then shall all the tribes of the earth mourn, and they shall see the Son of man coming in the clouds of heaven with power and great glory.

31And he shall send his angels with a great sound of a trumpet, and they shall gather together his elect from the four winds, from one end of heaven to the other.

32Now learn a parable of the fig tree; When his branch is yet tender, and putteth forth leaves, ye know that summer *is* nigh:

33So likewise ye, when ye shall see all these things, know that it is near, *even* at the doors.

34Verily I say unto you, This generation shall not pass, till all these things be fulfilled.

35Heaven and earth shall pass away, but my words shall not pass away.

36¶ But of that day and hour knoweth no *man*, no, not the angels of heaven, but my Father only.

37But as the days of Noe *were*, so shall also the coming of the Son of man be.

38For as in the days that were before the flood they were eating and drinking, marrying and giving in marriage, until the day that Noe entered into the ark,

39And knew not until the flood came, and took them all away; so shall also the coming of the Son of man be.

40Then shall two be in the field; the one shall be taken, and the other left.

41Two *women shall be* grinding at the mill; the one shall be taken, and the other left.

42¶ Watch therefore: for ye know not what hour your Lord doth come.

43But know this, that if the goodman of the house had known in what watch the thief would come, he would have watched, and would not have suffered his house to be broken up.

44Therefore be ye also ready: for in such an hour as ye think not the Son of man cometh.

## Amplified

20Pray that your flight may not be in winter or on a Sabbath,

21For then there will be great tribulation—affliction, distress and oppression—such as has not been from the beginning of the world until now; no, and never will be [again]. [Dan. 12:1; Joel 2:2.]

22And if those days had not been shortened, no human being would endure *and* survive; but for the sake of the elect (God's chosen ones) those days will be shortened.

23If any one says to you then, Lo, here is Christ, the Messiah! or, There He is! do not believe it.

24For false Christs and false prophets will arise, and they will show great signs and wonders, so as to deceive *and* lead astray, if possible, even the elect (God's chosen ones).

25See, I have warned you beforehand.

26So if they say to you, Lo, He is in the wilderness (desert), do not go out there; if they tell you, Lo, He is in the secret places *or* inner rooms, do not believe it.

27For just as the lightning flashes from the east and shines *and* [a]is seen as far as the west, so will the coming of the Son of man be.

28Wherever there is a fallen body (a corpse), there the vultures (or eagles) will flock together. [Job 39:30.]

29Immediately after the tribulation of those days the sun will be darkened, and the moon will not shed her light, and the stars will fall from the sky, and the powers of the heavens will be shaken. [Isa. 13:10; 34:4; Joel 2:10, 11; Zeph. 1:15.]

30Then the sign of the Son of man will appear in the sky, and then all the tribes of the earth will mourn *and* [b]beat their breasts *and* lament in anguish, and they will see the Son of man coming on the clouds of heaven with power and great glory—in brilliancy and splendor. [Dan. 7:13.]

31And He will send out His angels with a loud trumpet call, and they will gather His elect [His chosen ones] from the four winds, [even] from one end of the [c]universe to the other. [Isa. 27:13; Zech. 9:14.]

32From the fig tree learn its lesson: as soon as its [d]young shoots become soft and tender and it puts out its leaves, you know [e]of a surety that summer is near.

33So also when you see these signs [f]all taken together coming to pass, you may know [g]of a surety that He is near, at the very doors.

34Truly, I tell you, this generation—that is, [h]the whole multitude of people living at the same time, [i]in a definite, [j]given period—will not pass away till all these things [k]taken together take place.

35 [l]Sky and earth will pass away, but My words will not pass away.

36But of that [exact] day and hour no one knows, not even the angels of heaven, nor the Son, but only the Father.

37As were the days of Noah, so will be the coming of the Son of man.

38For just as in those days before the flood they were eating and drinking, [men] marrying and [women] being given in marriage, until the [very] day when Noah went into the ark,

39And they did not know *or* understand until the flood came and swept them all away, so will be the coming of the Son of man. [Gen. 6:5-8; 7:6-24.]

40At that time two men will be in the field; one will be taken and one will be left.

41Two women will be grinding at the hand mill; one will be taken and one will be left.

42Watch, therefore—[m]give strict attention, be cautious and active—for you do not know in what kind of a day [ [n]whether a near or remote one] your Lord is coming.

43But understand this: that had the householder known in what [part of the night, whether in a [o]night or a morning] watch the thief was coming, he would have watched and would not have allowed his house to be [p]undermined *and* broken through.

44You also must be ready therefore; for the Son of man is coming at an hour when you do not expect Him.

**AMP** [a] Vincent. [b] Vincnet. [c] Abbott-Smith. [d] Vincent. [e] Thayer. [f] Thayer. [g] Thayer. [h] Thayer. [i] Cremer. [j] Abbott-Smith. [k] Thayer. [l] Moulton and Milligan. [m] Thayer. [n] Vincent. [o] Vincent. [p] Wycliffe.

## New American Standard

20"But pray that your flight may not be in the winter, or on a Sabbath;

21for then there will be a great tribulation, such as has not occurred since the beginning of the world until now, nor ever shall.

22"And unless those days had been cut short, no life would have been saved; but for the sake of the elect those days shall be cut short.

23"Then if anyone says to you, 'Behold, here is the Christ,' or 'There *He is*,' do not believe *him*.

24"For false Christs and false prophets will arise and will show great signs and wonders, so as to mislead, if possible, even the elect.

25"Behold, I have told you in advance.

26"If therefore they say to you, 'Behold, He is in the wilderness,' do not go forth, *or*, 'Behold, He is in the inner rooms,' do not believe *them*.

27"For just as the lightning comes from the east, and flashes even to the west, so shall the coming of the Son of Man be.

28"Wherever the corpse is, there the vultures will gather.

*The Glorious Return*

29¶ "But immediately after the tribulation of those days THE SUN WILL BE DARKENED, AND THE MOON WILL NOT GIVE ITS LIGHT, AND THE STARS WILL FALL from the sky, and the powers of the heavens will be shaken,

30and then the sign of the Son of Man will appear in the sky, and then all the tribes of the earth will mourn, and they will see the SON OF MAN COMING ON THE CLOUDS OF THE SKY with power and great glory.

31"And He will send forth His angels with A GREAT TRUMPET and THEY WILL GATHER TOGETHER His elect from the four winds, from one end of the sky to the other.

*Parable of the Fig Tree*

32¶ "Now learn the parable from the fig tree: when its branch has already become tender, and puts forth its leaves, you know that summer is near;

33even so you too, when you see all these things, recognize that He is near, *right* at the door.

34"Truly I say to you, this generation will not pass away until all these things take place.

35"Heaven and earth will pass away, but My words shall not pass away.

36"But of that day and hour no one knows, not even the angels of heaven, nor the Son, but the Father alone.

37"For the coming of the Son of Man will be just like the days of Noah.

38"For as in those days which were before the flood they were eating and drinking, they were marrying and giving in marriage, until the day that Noah entered the ark,

39and they did not understand until the flood came and took them all away; so shall the coming of the Son of Man be.

40"Then there shall be two men in the field; one will be taken, and one will be left.

41"Two women *will be* grinding at the mill; one will be taken, and one will be left.

*Be Ready for His Coming*

42"Therefore be on the alert, for you do not know which day your Lord is coming.

43"But be sure of this, that if the head of the house had known at what time of the night the thief was coming, he would have been on the alert and would not have allowed his house to be broken into.

44"For this reason you be ready too; for the Son of Man is coming at an hour when you do not think *He will*.

## New International

take place in winter or on the Sabbath. 21For then there will be great distress, unequaled from the beginning of the world until now—and never to be equaled again. 22If those days had not been cut short, no one would survive, but for the sake of the elect those days will be shortened. 23At that time if anyone says to you, 'Look, here is the Christ!' or, 'There he is!' do not believe it. 24For false Christs and false prophets will appear and perform great signs and miracles to deceive even the elect—if that were possible. 25See, I have told you ahead of time.

26"So if anyone tells you, 'There he is, out in the desert,' do not go out; or, 'Here he is, in the inner rooms,' do not believe it. 27For as lightning that comes from the east is visible even in the west, so will be the coming of the Son of Man. 28Wherever there is a carcass, there the vultures will gather.

29"Immediately after the distress of those days

" 'the sun will be darkened,
and the moon will not give its light;
the stars will fall from the sky,
and the heavenly bodies will be shaken.'[q]

30"At that time the sign of the Son of Man will appear in the sky, and all the nations of the earth will mourn. They will see the Son of Man coming on the clouds of the sky, with power and great glory. 31And he will send his angels with a loud trumpet call, and they will gather his elect from the four winds, from one end of the heavens to the other.

32"Now learn this lesson from the fig tree: As soon as its twigs get tender and its leaves come out, you know that summer is near. 33Even so, when you see all these things, you know that it[r] is near, right at the door. 34I tell you the truth, this generation[s] will certainly not pass away until all these things have happened. 35Heaven and earth will pass away, but my words will never pass away.

*The Day and Hour Unknown*

36"No one knows about that day or hour, not even the angels in heaven, nor the Son,[t] but only the Father. 37As it was in the days of Noah, so it will be at the coming of the Son of Man. 38For in the days before the flood, people were eating and drinking, marrying and giving in marriage, up to the day Noah entered the ark; 39and they knew nothing about what would happen until the flood came and took them all away. That is how it will be at the coming of the Son of Man. 40Two men will be in the field; one will be taken and the other left. 41Two women will be grinding with a hand mill; one will be taken and the other left.

42"Therefore keep watch, because you do not know on what day your Lord will come. 43But understand this: If the owner of the house had known at what time of night the thief was coming, he would have kept watch and would not have let his house be broken into. 44So you also must be ready, because the Son of Man will come at an hour when you do not expect him.

NIV [q] 29 Isaiah 13:10; 34:4 [r] 33 Or *he* [s] 34 Or *race* [t] 36 Some manuscripts do not have *nor the Son.*

## King James

45Who then is a faithful and wise servant, whom his lord hath made ruler over his household, to give them meat in due season?
46Blessed *is* that servant, whom his lord when he cometh shall find so doing.
47Verily I say unto you, That he shall make him ruler over all his goods.
48But and if that evil servant shall say in his heart, My lord delayeth his coming;
49And shall begin to smite *his* fellowservants, and to eat and drink with the drunken;
50The lord of that servant shall come in a day when he looketh not for *him*, and in an hour that he is not aware of,
51And shall cut him asunder, and appoint *him* his portion with the hypocrites: there shall be weeping and gnashing of teeth.

**25** THEN SHALL the kingdom of heaven be likened unto ten virgins, which took their lamps, and went forth to meet the bridegroom.
2And five of them were wise, and five *were* foolish.
3They that *were* foolish took their lamps, and took no oil with them:
4But the wise took oil in their vessels with their lamps.
5While the bridegroom tarried, they all slumbered and slept.
6And at midnight there was a cry made, Behold, the bridegroom cometh; go ye out to meet him.
7Then all those virgins arose, and trimmed their lamps.
8And the foolish said unto the wise, Give us of your oil; for our lamps are gone out.
9But the wise answered, saying, *Not so;* lest there be not enough for us and you: but go ye rather to them that sell, and buy for yourselves.
10And while they went to buy, the bridegroom came; and they that were ready went in with him to the marriage: and the door was shut.
11Afterward came also the other virgins, saying, Lord, Lord, open to us.
12But he answered and said, Verily I say unto you, I know you not.
13Watch therefore, for ye know neither the day nor the hour wherein the Son of man cometh.
14¶ For *the kingdom of heaven is* as a man travelling into a far country, *who* called his own servants, and delivered unto them his goods.
15And unto one he gave five talents, to another two, and to another one; to every man according to his several ability; and straightway took his journey.
16Then he that had received the five talents went and traded with the same, and made *them* other five talents.
17And likewise he that *had received* two, he also gained other two.
18But he that had received one went and digged in the earth, and hid his lord's money.
19After a long time the lord of those servants cometh, and reckoneth with them.
20And so he that had received five talents came and brought other five talents, saying, Lord, thou deliveredst unto me five talents: behold, I have gained beside them five talents more.
21His lord said unto him, Well done, *thou* good and faithful servant: thou hast been faithful over a few things, I will make thee ruler over many things: enter thou into the joy of thy lord.

## Amplified

45Who then is the faithful, thoughtful *and* wise servant, whom his master has put in charge of his household, to give to the others the food *and* supplies at the proper time?
46Blessed—happy, fortunate and [a]to be envied—is that servant whom when his master comes he will find so doing.
47I solemnly declare to you, he will set him over all his possessions.
48But if that servant is wicked and says to himself, My master is delayed *and* is going to be gone a long time,
49And begins to beat his fellow servants, and to eat and drink with the drunken,
50The master of that servant will come on a day when he does not expect him and at and hour of which he is not aware,
51And will punish him— [b]cut him up [by scourging]—and put him with the pretenders (hypocrites); there will be weeping and grinding of teeth.

**25** THEN THE kingdom of heaven shall be likened to ten virgins who took their lamps and went to meet the bridegroom.
2Five of them were foolish—thoughtless, without forethought; and five were wise—sensible, intelligent and prudent.
3For when the foolish took their lamps, they did not take any [extra] oil with them;
4But the wise took flasks of oil along with them [also] with their lamps.
5While the bridegroom lingered *and* was slow in coming, they all began nodding their heads and fell asleep.
6But at midnight there was a shout, Behold, the bridegroom! Go out to meet him!
7Then all those virgins got up and put their own lamps in order.
8And the foolish said to the wise, Give us some of your oil, for our lamps are going out.
9But the wise replied, There will not be enough for us and for you; go instead to the dealers and buy for yourselves.
10But while they were gone away to buy, the bridegroom came, and those who were prepared went in with him to the marriage feast; and the door was shut.
11Later the other virgins also came, and said, Lord, Lord, open [the door] to us!
12But He replied, I solemnly declare to you, I do not know you—I am not acquainted with you.
13Watch therefore—give strict attention and be cautious and active—for you know neither the day nor the hour *when the Son of man will come.*
14For it is as a man who was about to take a long journey, and he called his servants together and entrusted them with his property.
15To one he gave five talents [probably about $5,000], to another two, to another one; to each in proportion to his own [c]personal ability. Then he departed *and* left the country.
16He who had received the five talents went at once and traded with them, and he gained five talents more.
17And likewise he who had received the two talents; he also gained two talents more.
18But he who had received the one talent went and dug a hole in the ground and hid his master's money.
19Now after a long time the master of those servants returned and settled accounts with them.
20And he who had received the five talents came and brought him five more, saying, Master, you entrusted to me five talents; see, here I have gained five talents more.
21His master said to him, Well done, you upright (honorable, [d]admirable) and faithful servant! You have been faithful *and* trustworthy over a little; I will put you in charge of much. Enter into *and* share the joy—the delight, the [e]blessedness—which your master [enjoys].

**AMP** [a] Souter. [b] Thayer. [c] Vincent. [d] Cremer. [e] Thayer.

## New American Standard

45¶ "Who then is the faithful and sensible slave whom his
master put in charge of his household to give them their food at
the proper time?
46"Blessed is that slave whom his master finds so doing when
he comes.
47"Truly I say to you, that he will put him in charge of all his
possessions.
48"But if that evil slave says in his heart, 'My master is not
coming for a long time,'
49and shall begin to beat his fellow slaves and eat and drink with
drunkards;
50the master of that slave will come on a day when he does not
expect *him* and at an hour which he does not know,
51and shall cut him in pieces and assign him a place with the
hypocrites; weeping shall be there and the gnashing of teeth.

*Parable of Ten Virgins*

25 "THEN THE kingdom of heaven will be comparable to ten
virgins, who took their lamps, and went out to meet the
bridegroom.
2"And five of them were foolish, and five were prudent.
3"For when the foolish took their lamps, they took no oil with
them,
4but the prudent took oil in flasks along with their lamps.
5"Now while the bridegroom was delaying, they all got
drowsy and *began* to sleep.
6"But at midnight there was a shout, 'Behold, the bridegroom!
Come out to meet *him*.'
7"Then all those virgins rose, and trimmed their lamps.
8"And the foolish said to the prudent, 'Give us some of your
oil, for our lamps are going out.'
9"But the prudent answered, saying, 'No, there will not be
enough for us and you *too*; go instead to the dealers and buy *some*
for yourselves.'
10"And while they were going away to make the purchase, the
bridegroom came, and those who were ready went in with him to
the wedding feast; and the door was shut.
11"And later the other virgins also came, saying, 'Lord, lord,
open up for us.'
12"But he answered and said, 'Truly I say to you, I do not know
you.'
13"Be on the alert then, for you do not know the day nor the
hour.

*Parable of the Talents*

14¶ "For *it is* just like a man *about* to go on a journey, who called
his own slaves, and entrusted his possessions to them.
15"And to one he gave five talents, to another, two, and to
another, one, each according to his own ability; and he went on
his journey.
16"Immediately the one who had received the five talents went
and traded with them, and gained five more talents.
17"In the same manner the one who *had received* the two *talents*
gained two more.
18"But he who received the one *talent* went away and dug in the
ground, and hid his master's money.
19"Now after a long time the master of those slaves *came and
*settled accounts with them.
20"And the one who had received the five talents came up and
brought five more talents, saying, 'Master, you entrusted five
talents to me; see, I have gained five more talents.'
21"His master said to him, 'Well done, good and faithful slave;
you were faithful with a few things, I will put you in charge of
many things, enter into the joy of your master.'

## New International

45"Who then is the faithful and wise servant, whom the master
has put in charge of the servants in his household to give them
their food at the proper time? 46It will be good for that servant
whose master finds him doing so when he returns. 47I tell you the
truth, he will put him in charge of all his possessions. 48But suppose that servant is wicked and says to himself, 'My master is
staying away a long time,' 49and he then begins to beat his fellow
servants and to eat and drink with drunkards. 50The master of that
servant will come on a day when he does not expect him and at
an hour he is not aware of. 51He will cut him to pieces and assign
him a place with the hypocrites, where there will be weeping and
gnashing of teeth.

*The Parable of the Ten Virgins*

25 "AT THAT time the kingdom of heaven will be like ten
virgins who took their lamps and went out to meet the
bridegroom. 2Five of them were foolish and five were wise. 3The
foolish ones took their lamps but did not take any oil with them.
4The wise, however, took oil in jars along with their lamps. 5The
bridegroom was a long time in coming, and they all became
drowsy and fell asleep.
6"At midnight the cry rang out: 'Here's the bridegroom! Come
out to meet him!'
7"Then all the virgins woke up and trimmed their lamps. 8The
foolish ones said to the wise, 'Give us some of your oil; our lamps
are going out.'
9" 'No,' they replied, 'there may not be enough for both us and
you. Instead, go to those who sell oil and buy some for yourselves.'
10"But while they were on their way to buy the oil, the bridegroom arrived. The virgins who were ready went in with him to
the wedding banquet. And the door was shut.
11"Later the others also came. 'Sir! Sir!' they said. 'Open the
door for us!'
12"But he replied, 'I tell you the truth, I don't know you.'
13"Therefore keep watch, because you do not know the day or
the hour.

*The Parable of the Talents*

14"Again, it will be like a man going on a journey, who called
his servants and entrusted his property to them. 15To one he gave
five talents[f] of money, to another two talents, and to another one
talent, each according to his ability. Then he went on his journey.
16The man who had received the five talents went at once and put
his money to work and gained five more. 17So also, the one with
the two talents gained two more. 18But the man who had received
the one talent went off, dug a hole in the ground and hid his
master's money.
19"After a long time the master of those servants returned and
settled accounts with them. 20The man who had received the five
talents brought the other five. 'Master,' he said, 'you entrusted me
with five talents. See, I have gained five more.'
21"His master replied, 'Well done, good and faithful servant!
You have been faithful with a few things; I will put you in charge
of many things. Come and share your master's happiness!'

NIV f 15 A talent was worth more than a thousand dollars.

## King James

22 He also that had received two talents came and said, Lord, thou deliveredst unto me two talents: behold, I have gained two other talents beside them.

23 His lord said unto him, Well done, good and faithful servant; thou hast been faithful over a few things, I will make thee ruler over many things: enter thou into the joy of thy lord.

24 Then he which had received the one talent came and said, Lord, I knew thee that thou art an hard man, reaping where thou hast not sown, and gathering where thou hast not strawed:

25 And I was afraid, and went and hid thy talent in the earth: lo, *there* thou hast *that is* thine.

26 His lord answered and said unto him, *Thou* wicked and slothful servant, thou knewest that I reap where I sowed not, and gather where I have not strawed:

27 Thou oughtest therefore to have put my money to the exchangers, and *then* at my coming I should have received mine own with usury.

28 Take therefore the talent from him, and give *it* unto him which hath ten talents.

29 For unto every one that hath shall be given, and he shall have abundance: but from him that hath not shall be taken away even that which he hath.

30 And cast ye the unprofitable servant into outer darkness: there shall be weeping and gnashing of teeth.

31 ¶ When the Son of man shall come in his glory, and all the holy angels with him, then shall he sit upon the throne of his glory:

32 And before him shall be gathered all nations: and he shall separate them one from another, as a shepherd divideth *his* sheep from the goats:

33 And he shall set the sheep on his right hand, but the goats on the left.

34 Then shall the King say unto them on his right hand, Come, ye blessed of my Father, inherit the kingdom prepared for you from the foundation of the world:

35 For I was an hungered, and ye gave me meat: I was thirsty, and ye gave me drink: I was a stranger, and ye took me in:

36 Naked, and ye clothed me: I was sick, and ye visited me: I was in prison, and ye came unto me.

37 Then shall the righteous answer him, saying, Lord, when saw we thee an hungered, and fed *thee?* or thirsty, and gave *thee* drink?

38 When saw we thee a stranger, and took *thee* in? or naked, and clothed *thee?*

39 Or when saw we thee sick, or in prison, and came unto thee?

40 And the King shall answer and say unto them, Verily I say unto you, Inasmuch as ye have done *it* unto one of the least of these my brethren, ye have done *it* unto me.

41 Then shall he say also unto them on the left hand, Depart from me, ye cursed, into everlasting fire, prepared for the devil and his angels:

42 For I was an hungered, and ye gave me no meat; I was thirsty, and ye gave me no drink:

43 I was a stranger, and ye took me not in: naked, and ye clothed me not: sick, and in prison, and ye visited me not.

44 Then shall they also answer him, saying, Lord, when saw we thee an hungered, or athirst, or a stranger, or naked, or sick, or in prison, and did not minister unto thee?

45 Then shall he answer them, saying, Verily I say unto you, Inasmuch as ye did *it* not to one of the least of these, ye did *it* not to me.

## Amplified

22 And he also who had the two talents came forward, saying, Master, you entrusted two talents to me; here I have gained two talents more.

23 His master said to him, Well done, you upright (honorable, [a]admirable) and faithful servant! You have been faithful *and* trustworthy over a little; I will put you in charge of much. Enter into *and* share the joy—the delight, the [b]blessedness—which your master [enjoys].

24 He who had received one talent also came forward, saying, Master, I knew you to be a harsh *and* hard man, reaping where you did not sow, and gathering where you had not winnowed [the grain];

25 So I was afraid, and I went and hid your talent in the ground. Here you have what is your own.

26 But his master answered him, You wicked *and* lazy *and* idle servant! Did you indeed know that I reap where I have not sowed, and gather grain where I have not winnowed?

27 Then you should have invested my money with the bankers, and at my coming I could have received what was my own with interest.

28 So take the talent away from him, and give it to the one who has the ten talents.

29 For to every one who has will more be given, and he will be [c]furnished richly so that he will have abundance, but from the one who does not have, even what he does have shall be taken away.

30 And throw the good-for-nothing servant into the outer darkness; there will be weeping and grinding of teeth.

31 When the Son of man comes in His glory (His majesty and splendor) and all the *holy* angels with Him, then He will sit on the throne of His glory.

32 All nations shall be gathered before Him, and He will separate them [the people] from one another as a shepherd separates his sheep from the goats, [Ezek. 34:17.]

33 And He will cause the sheep to stand at His right hand, but the goats at His left.

34 Then the King will say to those at His right hand, Come, you blessed of My Father [that is, you [d]favored of God and appointed to eternal salvation], inherit—receive as your own—the kingdom prepared for you from the foundation of the world.

35 For I was hungry and you gave Me food; I was thirsty and you gave Me something to drink; I was a stranger and you [e]brought Me together with yourselves *and* welcomed *and* entertained *and* [f]lodged Me;

36 I was naked and you clothed Me; I was sick and you visited Me [g]with help *and* ministering care; I was in prison and you came to see Me. [Isa. 58:7.]

37 Then the just *and* upright will answer Him, Lord, when did we see You hungry and gave You food, or thirsty and gave You something to drink?

38 And when did we see You a stranger and welcomed *and* entertained You, or naked and clothed You?

39 And when did we see You sick or in prison and came to visit You?

40 And the King will reply to them, Truly, I tell you, in as far as you did it to one of the least [ [h]in the estimation of men] of these My brethren, you did it to Me. [Prov. 19:17.]

41 Then He will say to those at His left hand, Be gone from Me, you cursed, into the eternal fire prepared for the devil and his angels!

42 For I was hungry and you gave Me no food; I was thirsty and you gave Me nothing to drink;

43 I was a stranger and you did not welcome Me *and* entertain Me; I was naked and you did not clothe Me; I was sick and in prison and you did not visit Me [i]with help *and* ministering care.

44 Then they also [in their turn] will answer, Lord, when did we see You hungry or thirsty or a stranger or naked or sick or in prison, and did not minister to You?

45 And He will reply to them, Solemnly I declare to you, in so far as you failed to do it for the least of these [ [j]in the estimation of men] you failed to do it for Me.

**AMP** [a] Cremer. [b] Thayer. [c] Thayer. [d] Thayer. [e] Literal meaning. [f] Tyndale. [g] Wuest's "Treasures from the Greek New Testament." [h] Thayer. [i] Wuest's "Treasures from the Greek New Testament." [j] Thayer.

## New American Standard

22"The one also who *had received* the two talents came up and
said, 'Master, you entrusted to me two talents; see, I have gained
two more talents.'
23"His master said to him, 'Well done, good and faithful slave;
you were faithful with a few things, I will put you in charge of
many things; enter into the joy of your master.'
24"And the one also who had received the one talent came up
and said, 'Master, I knew you to be a hard man, reaping where you
did not sow, and gathering where you scattered no *seed.*
25'And I was afraid, and went away and hid your talent in the
ground; see, you have what is yours.'
26"But his master answered and said to him, 'You wicked, lazy
slave, you knew that I reap where I did not sow, and gather where
I scattered no *seed.*
27'Then you ought to have put my money in the bank, and on
my arrival I would have received my *money* back with interest.
28'Therefore take away the talent from him, and give it to the
one who has the ten talents.'
29"For to everyone who has shall *more* be given, and he shall
have an abundance; but from the one who does not have, even
what he does have shall be taken away.
30"And cast out the worthless slave into the outer darkness; in
that place there shall be weeping and gnashing of teeth.

*The Judgment*

31¶ "But when the Son of Man comes in His glory, and all the
angels with Him, then He will sit on His glorious throne.
32"And all the nations will be gathered before Him; and He will
separate them from one another, as the shepherd separates the
sheep from the goats;
33and He will put the sheep on His right, and the goats on the
left.
34"Then the King will say to those on His right, 'Come, you who
are blessed of My Father, inherit the kingdom prepared for you
from the foundation of the world.
35'For I was hungry, and you gave Me *something* to eat; I was
thirsty, and you gave Me drink; I was a stranger, and you invited
Me in;
36naked, and you clothed Me; I was sick, and you visited Me;
I was in prison, and you came to Me.'
37"Then the righteous will answer Him, saying, 'Lord, when
did we see You hungry, and feed You, or thirsty, and give You
drink?
38'And when did we see You a stranger, and invite You in, or
naked, and clothe You?
39'And when did we see You sick, or in prison, and come to
You?'
40"And the King will answer and say to them, 'Truly I say to
you, to the extent that you did it to one of these brothers of Mine,
*even* the least *of them,* you did it to Me.'
41"Then He will also say to those on His left, 'Depart from Me,
accursed ones, into the eternal fire which has been prepared for
the devil and his angels;
42for I was hungry, and you gave Me *nothing* to eat; I was
thirsty, and you gave Me nothing to drink;
43I was a stranger, and you did not invite Me in; naked, and you
did not clothe Me; sick, and in prison, and you did not visit Me.'
44"Then they themselves also will answer, saying, 'Lord, when
did we see You hungry, or thirsty, or a stranger, or naked, or sick,
or in prison, and did not take care of You?'
45"Then He will answer them, saying, 'Truly I say to you, to the
extent that you did not do it to one of the least of these, you did
not do it to Me.'

## New International

22"The man with the two talents also came. 'Master,' he said,
'you entrusted me with two talents; see, I have gained two more.'
23"His master replied, 'Well done, good and faithful servant!
You have been faithful with a few things; I will put you in charge
of many things. Come and share your master's happiness!'
24"Then the man who had received the one talent came. 'Master,' he said, 'I knew that you are a hard man, harvesting where
you have not sown and gathering where you have not scattered
seed. 25So I was afraid and went out and hid your talent in the
ground. See, here is what belongs to you.'
26"His master replied, 'You wicked, lazy servant! So you knew
that I harvest where I have not sown and gather where I have not
scattered seed? 27Well then, you should have put my money on
deposit with the bankers, so that when I returned I would have
received it back with interest.
28" 'Take the talent from him and give it to the one who has the
ten talents. 29For everyone who has will be given more, and he will
have an abundance. Whoever does not have, even what he has will
be taken from him. 30And throw that worthless servant outside,
into the darkness, where there will be weeping and gnashing of
teeth.'

*The Sheep and the Goats*

31"When the Son of Man comes in his glory, and all the angels
with him, he will sit on his throne in heavenly glory. 32All the
nations will be gathered before him, and he will separate the
people one from another as a shepherd separates the sheep from
the goats. 33He will put the sheep on his right and the goats on his
left.
34"Then the King will say to those on his right, 'Come, you who
are blessed by my Father; take your inheritance, the kingdom
prepared for you since the creation of the world. 35For I was
hungry and you gave me something to eat, I was thirsty and you
gave me something to drink, I was a stranger and you invited me
in, 36I needed clothes and you clothed me, I was sick and you
looked after me, I was in prison and you came to visit me.'
37"Then the righteous will answer him, 'Lord, when did we see
you hungry and feed you, or thirsty and give you something to
drink? 38When did we see you a stranger and invite you in, or
needing clothes and clothe you? 39When did we see you sick or in
prison and go to visit you?'
40"The King will reply, 'I tell you the truth, whatever you did
for one of the least of these brothers of mine, you did for me.'
41"Then he will say to those on his left, 'Depart from me, you
who are cursed, into the eternal fire prepared for the devil and his
angels. 42For I was hungry and you gave me nothing to eat, I was
thirsty and you gave me nothing to drink, 43I was a stranger and
you did not invite me in, I needed clothes and you did not clothe
me, I was sick and in prison and you did not look after me.'
44"They also will answer, 'Lord, when did we see you hungry
or thirsty or a stranger or needing clothes or sick or in prison, and
did not help you?'
45"He will reply, 'I tell you the truth, whatever you did not do
for one of the least of these, you did not do for me.'

## King James

46And these shall go away into everlasting punishment: but the righteous into life eternal.

# 26

AND IT came to pass, when Jesus had finished all these sayings, he said unto his disciples,

2Ye know that after two days is *the feast of* the passover, and the Son of man is betrayed to be crucified.

3Then assembled together the chief priests, and the scribes, and the elders of the people, unto the palace of the high priest, who was called Caiaphas,

4And consulted that they might take Jesus by subtlety, and kill *him*.

5But they said, Not on the feast *day*, lest there be an uproar among the people.

6¶ Now when Jesus was in Bethany, in the house of Simon the leper,

7There came unto him a woman having an alabaster box of very precious ointment, and poured it on his head, as he sat *at meat*.

8But when his disciples saw *it*, they had indignation, saying, To what purpose *is* this waste?

9For this ointment might have been sold for much, and given to the poor.

10When Jesus understood *it*, he said unto them, Why trouble ye the woman? for she hath wrought a good work upon me.

11For ye have the poor always with you; but me ye have not always.

12For in that she hath poured this ointment on my body, she did *it* for my burial.

13Verily I say unto you, Wheresoever this gospel shall be preached in the whole world, *there* shall also this, that this woman hath done, be told for a memorial of her.

14¶ Then one of the twelve, called Judas Iscariot, went unto the chief priests,

15And said *unto them*, What will ye give me, and I will deliver him unto you? And they covenanted with him for thirty pieces of silver.

16And from that time he sought opportunity to betray him.

17¶ Now the first *day* of the *feast of* unleavened bread the disciples came to Jesus, saying unto him, Where wilt thou that we prepare for thee to eat the passover?

18And he said, Go into the city to such a man, and say unto him, The Master saith, My time is at hand; I will keep the passover at thy house with my disciples.

19And the disciples did as Jesus had appointed them; and they made ready the passover.

20Now when the even was come, he sat down with the twelve.

21And as they did eat, he said, Verily I say unto you, that one of you shall betray me.

22And they were exceeding sorrowful, and began every one of them to say unto him, Lord, is it I?

23And he answered and said, He that dippeth *his* hand with me in the dish, the same shall betray me.

24The Son of man goeth as it is written of him: but woe unto that man by whom the Son of man is betrayed! it had been good for that man if he had not been born.

25Then Judas, which betrayed him, answered and said, Master, is it I? He said unto him, Thou hast said.

## Amplified

46Then they will go away into eternal punishment, but those who are just *and* upright *and* in right standing with God into eternal life. [Dan. 12:2.]

# 26

WHEN JESUS had ended this discourse, He said to His disciples,

2You know that the Passover is in two days, and the Son of man will be delivered up [a]treacherously to be crucified.

3Then the chief priests and the elders of the people gathered in the [ [b]open] court of the palace of the high priest, whose name was Caiaphas,

4And consulted together in order to arrest Jesus by stratagem secretly, and put Him to death.

5But they said, It must not be during the feast, for fear there will be a riot among the people.

6Now when Jesus came back to Bethany and was in the house of Simon the leper,

7A woman came up to Him with an alabaster flask of very precious perfume, and she poured it on His head as He reclined at table.

8And when the disciples saw it, they were indignant, saying, For what purpose is all this waste?

9For this perfume might have been sold for a large sum, and the money given to the poor.

10But Jesus, fully aware of this, said to them, Why do you bother the woman? She has done a noble (praiseworthy and beautiful) thing to Me.

11For you always have the poor among you, but you will not always have Me. [Deut. 15:11.]

12In pouring this perfume on My body she has done something to prepare Me for My burial.

13Truly, I tell you, wherever this good news (the Gospel) is preached in the whole world, what this woman has done will be told also in memory of her.

14Then one of the twelve [apostles], who was called Judas Iscariot, went to the chief priests

15And said, What are you willing to give me if I hand Him over to you? And they weighed out *and* paid him thirty pieces of silver [about twenty-one dollars and sixty cents]. [Exod. 21:32; Zech. 11:12.]

16And from that moment he sought for a fitting opportunity to betray Him.

17Now on the first day of Unleavened Bread [Passover week], the disciples came to Jesus and said *to Him*, Where do You wish us to prepare for You to eat the passover supper?

18He said, Go into the city to a certain man, and say to him, The Master says, My time is near; I will keep the passover at your house with My disciples.

19And accordingly the disciples did as Jesus had directed them, and they made ready the passover supper. [Deut. 16:5-8.]

20When it was evening, He was reclining at table with the twelve disciples;

21And as they were eating He said, Solemnly I say to you, one of you will betray Me!

22They were exceedingly pained *and* distressed *and* deeply hurt *and* sorrowful, and began to say to Him one after another, [c]Surely, it cannot be I, Lord, can it?

23He replied, He who has [just] dipped his hand in the same dish with Me will betray Me!

24The Son of man is going as it is written of Him, but woe to that man by whom the Son of man is betrayed! It would have been better (more profitable and wholesome) for that man if he had never been born! [Ps. 41:9.]

25Judas, the betrayer, said, [d]Surely, it is not I, is it, Master? He said to him, You have stated [the fact].

**AMP** [a] Thayer. [b] Vincent. [c] Vincent. [d] Vincent.

## New American Standard

46"And these will go away into eternal punishment, but the
righteous into eternal life."

*The Plot to Kill Jesus*

**26** AND IT came about that when Jesus had finished all these
words, He said to His disciples,
2"You know that after two days the Passover is coming, and
the Son of Man is *to be* delivered up for crucifixion."
3Then the chief priests and the elders of the people were gathered together in the court of the high priest, named Caiaphas;
4and they plotted together to seize Jesus by stealth, and kill
*Him.*
5But they were saying, "Not during the festival, lest a riot
occur among the people."

*The Precious Ointment*

6¶ Now when Jesus was in Bethany, at the home of Simon the
leper,
7a woman came to Him with an alabaster vial of very costly
perfume, and she poured it upon His head as He reclined *at the
table.*
8But the disciples were indignant when they saw *this,* and said,
"Why this waste?
9"For this *perfume* might have been sold for a high price and
*the money* given to the poor."
10But Jesus, aware of this, said to them, "Why do you bother
the woman? For she has done a good deed to Me.
11"For the poor you have with you always; but you do not
always have Me.
12"For when she poured this perfume upon My body, she did
it to prepare Me for burial.
13"Truly I say to you, wherever this gospel is preached in the
whole world, what this woman has done shall also be spoken of
in memory of her."

*Judas' Bargain*

14¶ Then one of the twelve, named Judas Iscariot, went to the
chief priests,
15and said, "What are you willing to give me to deliver Him up
to you?" And they weighed out to him thirty pieces of silver.
16And from then on he *began* looking for a good opportunity to
betray Him.
17¶ Now on the first *day* of Unleavened Bread the disciples came
to Jesus, saying, "Where do You want us to prepare for You to eat
the Passover?"
18And He said, "Go into the city to a certain man, and say to
him, 'The Teacher says, "My time is at hand; I *am to* keep the
Passover at your house with My disciples." ' "
19And the disciples did as Jesus had directed them; and they
prepared the Passover.

*The Last Passover*

20¶ Now when evening had come, He was reclining *at the table*
with the twelve disciples.
21And as they were eating, He said, "Truly I say to you that one
of you will betray Me."
22And being deeply grieved, they each one began to say to Him,
"Surely not I, Lord?"
23And He answered and said, "He who dipped his hand with
Me in the bowl is the one who will betray Me.
24"The Son of Man *is to* go, just as it is written of Him; but woe
to that man by whom the Son of Man is betrayed! It would have
been good for that man if he had not been born."
25And Judas, who was betraying Him, answered and said,
"Surely it is not I, Rabbi?" He *said to him, "You have said *it*
yourself."

## New International

46"Then they will go away to eternal punishment, but the righteous to eternal life."

*The Plot Against Jesus*

**26** WHEN JESUS had finished saying all these things, he said
to his disciples, 2"As you know, the Passover is two days
away—and the Son of Man will be handed over to be crucified."
3Then the chief priests and the elders of the people assembled
in the palace of the high priest, whose name was Caiaphas, 4and
they plotted to arrest Jesus in some sly way and kill him. 5"But not
during the Feast," they said, "or there may be a riot among the
people."

*Jesus Anointed at Bethany*

6While Jesus was in Bethany in the home of a man known as
Simon the Leper, 7a woman came to him with an alabaster jar of
very expensive perfume, which she poured on his head as he was
reclining at the table.
8When the disciples saw this, they were indignant. "Why this
waste?" they asked. 9"This perfume could have been sold at a high
price and the money given to the poor."
10Aware of this, Jesus said to them, "Why are you bothering
this woman? She has done a beautiful thing to me. 11The poor you
will always have with you, but you will not always have me.
12When she poured this perfume on my body, she did it to prepare
me for burial. 13I tell you the truth, wherever this gospel is
preached throughout the world, what she has done will also be
told, in memory of her."

*Judas Agrees to Betray Jesus*

14Then one of the Twelve—the one called Judas Iscariot—went
to the chief priests 15and asked, "What are you willing to give me
if I hand him over to you?" So they counted out for him thirty silver
coins. 16From then on Judas watched for an opportunity to hand
him over.

*The Lord's Supper*

17On the first day of the Feast of Unleavened Bread, the disciples came to Jesus and asked, "Where do you want us to make
preparations for you to eat the Passover?"
18He replied, "Go into the city to a certain man and tell him,
'The Teacher says: My appointed time is near. I am going to
celebrate the Passover with my disciples at your house.' " 19So the
disciples did as Jesus had directed them and prepared the Passover.
20When evening came, Jesus was reclining at the table with the
Twelve. 21And while they were eating, he said, "I tell you the
truth, one of you will betray me."
22They were very sad and began to say to him one after the
other, "Surely not I, Lord?"
23Jesus replied, "The one who has dipped his hand into the
bowl with me will betray me. 24The Son of Man will go just as it
is written about him. But woe to that man who betrays the Son of
Man! It would be better for him if he had not been born."
25Then Judas, the one who would betray him, said, "Surely not
I, Rabbi?"
Jesus answered, "Yes, it is you."[e]

NIV [e] 25 Or *"You yourself have said it"*

## King James

26¶ And as they were eating, Jesus took bread, and blessed *it*,
and brake *it*, and gave *it* to the disciples, and said, Take, eat; this
is my body.
27And he took the cup, and gave thanks, and gave *it* to them,
saying, Drink ye all of it;
28For this is my blood of the new testament, which is shed for
many for the remission of sins.
29But I say unto you, I will not drink henceforth of this fruit of
the vine, until that day when I drink it new with you in my Father's
kingdom.
30And when they had sung an hymn, they went out into the
mount of Olives.
31Then saith Jesus unto them, All ye shall be offended because
of me this night: for it is written, I will smite the shepherd, and
the sheep of the flock shall be scattered abroad.
32But after I am risen again, I will go before you into Galilee.
33Peter answered and said unto him, Though all *men* shall be
offended because of thee, *yet* will I never be offended.
34Jesus said unto him, Verily I say unto thee, That this night,
before the cock crow, thou shalt deny me thrice.
35Peter said unto him, Though I should die with thee, yet will
I not deny thee. Likewise also said all the disciples.
36¶ Then cometh Jesus with them unto a place called Gethsemane, and saith unto the disciples, Sit ye here, while I go and pray
yonder.
37And he took with him Peter and the two sons of Zebedee, and
began to be sorrowful and very heavy.
38Then saith he unto them, My soul is exceeding sorrowful,
even unto death: tarry ye here, and watch with me.
39And he went a little farther, and fell on his face, and prayed,
saying, O my Father, if it be possible, let this cup pass from me:
nevertheless not as I will, but as thou *wilt*.
40And he cometh unto the disciples, and findeth them asleep,
and saith unto Peter, What, could ye not watch with me one hour?
41Watch and pray, that ye enter not into temptation: the spirit
indeed *is* willing, but the flesh *is* weak.
42He went away again the second time, and prayed, saying, O
my Father, if this cup may not pass away from me, except I drink
it, thy will be done.
43And he came and found them asleep again: for their eyes were
heavy.
44And he left them, and went away again, and prayed the third
time, saying the same words.
45Then cometh he to his disciples, and saith unto them, Sleep
on now, and take *your* rest: behold, the hour is at hand, and the
Son of man is betrayed into the hands of sinners.
46Rise, let us be going: behold, he is at hand that doth betray
me.
47¶ And while he yet spake, lo, Judas, one of the twelve, came,
and with him a great multitude with swords and staves, from the
chief priests and elders of the people.
48Now he that betrayed him gave them a sign, saying, Whomsoever I shall kiss, that same is he: hold him fast.
49And forthwith he came to Jesus, and said, Hail, master; and
kissed him.
50And Jesus said unto him, Friend, wherefore art thou come?
Then came they, and laid hands on Jesus, and took him.

## Amplified

26Now as they were eating, Jesus took bread, and [a]praising
God gave thanks *and* asked Him to bless it to their use, and when
He had broken it He gave it to the disciples and said, Take, eat;
this is My body.
27And He took a cup, and when He had given thanks He gave
it to them, saying, Drink of it, all of you;
28For this is My blood of the *new* covenant, which [ [b]ratifies the
agreement and] is [c]being poured out for many for the forgiveness
of sins. [Exod. 24:6-8.]
29I say to you, I shall not drink again of this fruit of the vine until
that day when I drink it with you new *and* [d]of superior quality in
My Father's kingdom.
30And when they had sung a hymn, they went out to the Mount
of Olives.
31Then Jesus said to them, You will all be offended *and* stumble
*and* fall away because of Me this night—distrusting and deserting
Me; for it is written, I will strike the Shepherd, and the sheep of
the flock will be scattered. [Zech. 13:7.]
32But after I am raised up [to life again], I will go ahead of you
to Galilee.
33Peter declared to Him, Though they all are offended *and* stumble *and* fall away because of You *and* distrust *and* desert You, I will
never do so.
34Jesus said to him, Solemnly I declare to you, this very night
before a [e]single rooster crows you will deny *and* disown Me three
times.
35Peter said to Him, Even if I must die with You, I will not deny
*or* disown You! And all the disciples said the same thing.
36Then Jesus went with them to a place called Gethsemane, and
He told His disciples, Sit down here, while I go over yonder and
pray.
37And taking with Him Peter and the two sons of Zebedee, He
began to [f]show grief *and* distress of mind and was [g]deeply depressed.
38Then He said to them, My soul is very sad *and* deeply grieved,
so that [h]I am almost dying of sorrow. Stay here and keep awake
*and* watch with Me.
39And going a little farther, He threw Himself upon the ground
on His face and prayed saying, My Father, if it is possible, let this
cup pass away from Me; nevertheless, not what I will—not what
I desire—but as You will *and* desire.
40And He came to the disciples and found them sleeping, and
He said to Peter, What! Are you so utterly unable to stay awake
*and* watch with Me for one hour?
41All of you must keep awake (give strict attention, be cautious)
*and* watch and pray that you may not come into temptation. The
spirit indeed is willing, but the flesh is weak.
42Again, a second time, He went away and prayed, My Father,
if this cannot pass by unless I drink it, Your will be done.
43And again He came and found them sleeping, for their eyes
were weighed down with sleep.
44So, leaving them again, He went away and prayed for the
third time, using the same words.
45Then He returned to the disciples and said to them, Are you
still sleeping and taking your rest? Behold, the hour is at hand, and
the Son of man is betrayed into the hands of [i]especially wicked
sinners— [j]whose way or nature it is to act in opposition to God.
46Get up, let us be going! See, My betrayer is at hand!
47As He was still speaking, Judas, one of the twelve [apostles],
came up and with him a great crowd with swords and clubs, from
the chief priests and elders of the people.
48Now the betrayer had given them a sign, saying, The One I
shall kiss is the Man. Seize Him.
49And he came up to Jesus at once and said, Hail (greeting,
good health to You, long life to You), Master! And he [k]embraced
Him and kissed Him [l]with [pretended] warmth and devotion.
50Jesus said to him, Friend, for what are you here? Then they
came up and laid hands on Jesus and arrested Him.

**AMP** [a] Thayer. [b] Thayer. [c] Vincent. [d] Thayer. [e] Vincent. [f] Vincent. [g] Berry's "Greek-English New Testament Lexicon." [h] Thayer. [i] Abbott-Smith. [j] Cremer. [k] Meyer's "Commentary on Matthew." [l] Wuest.

## New American Standard

*The Lord's Supper Instituted*
26¶ And while they were eating, Jesus took *some* bread, and after
a blessing, He broke *it* and gave *it* to the disciples, and said, "Take,
eat; this is My body."
27And when He had taken a cup and given thanks, He gave *it*
to them, saying, "Drink from it, all of you;
28for this is My blood of the covenant, which is poured out for
many for forgiveness of sins.
29"But I say to you, I will not drink of this fruit of the vine from
now on until that day when I drink it new with you in My Father's
kingdom."
30¶ And after singing a hymn, they went out to the Mount of
Olives.
31¶ Then Jesus *said to them, "You will all fall away because of
Me this night, for it is written, 'I WILL STRIKE DOWN THE SHEPHERD,
AND THE SHEEP OF THE FLOCK SHALL BE SCATTERED.'
32"But after I have been raised, I will go before you to Galilee."
33But Peter answered and said to Him, "*Even* though all may fall
away because of You, I will never fall away."
34Jesus said to him, "Truly I say to you that this *very* night,
before a cock crows, you shall deny Me three times."
35Peter *said to Him, "Even if I have to die with You, I will not
deny You." All the disciples said the same thing too.

*The Garden of Gethsemane*
36¶ Then Jesus *came with them to a place called Gethsemane,
and *said to His disciples, "Sit here while I go over there and
pray."
37And He took with Him Peter and the two sons of Zebedee,
and began to be grieved and distressed.
38Then He *said to them, "My soul is deeply grieved, to the
point of death; remain here and keep watch with Me."
39And He went a little beyond *them,* and fell on His face and
prayed, saying, "My Father, if it is possible, let this cup pass from
Me; yet not as I will, but as Thou wilt."
40And He *came to the disciples and *found them sleeping, and
*said to Peter, "So, you *men* could not keep watch with Me for one
hour?
41"Keep watching and praying, that you may not enter into
temptation; the spirit is willing, but the flesh is weak."
42He went away again a second time and prayed, saying, "My
Father, if this cannot pass away unless I drink it, Thy will be
done."
43And again He came and found them sleeping, for their eyes
were heavy.
44And He left them again, and went away and prayed a third
time, saying the same thing once more.
45Then He *came to the disciples, and *said to them, "Are you
still sleeping and taking your rest? Behold, the hour is at hand and
the Son of Man is being betrayed into the hands of sinners.
46"Arise, let us be going; behold, the one who betrays Me is at
hand!"

*Jesus' Betrayal and Arrest*
47¶ And while He was still speaking, behold, Judas, one of the
twelve, came up, accompanied by a great multitude with swords
and clubs, from the chief priests and elders of the people.
48Now he who was betraying Him gave them a sign, saying,
"Whomever I shall kiss, He is the one; seize Him."
49And immediately he went to Jesus and said, "Hail, Rabbi!"
and kissed Him.
50And Jesus said to him, "Friend, *do* what you have come for."
Then they came and laid hands on Jesus and seized Him.

## New International

26While they were eating, Jesus took bread, gave thanks and
broke it, and gave it to his disciples, saying, "Take and eat; this
is my body."
27Then he took the cup, gave thanks and offered it to them,
saying, "Drink from it, all of you. 28This is my blood of the[m]
covenant, which is poured out for many for the forgiveness of sins.
29I tell you, I will not drink of this fruit of the vine from now on
until that day when I drink it anew with you in my Father's
kingdom."
30When they had sung a hymn, they went out to the Mount of
Olives.

*Jesus Predicts Peter's Denial*
31Then Jesus told them, "This very night you will all fall away
on account of me, for it is written:

"'I will strike the shepherd,
and the sheep of the flock will be scattered.'[n]

32But after I have risen, I will go ahead of you into Galilee."
33Peter replied, "Even if all fall away on account of you, I never
will."
34"I tell you the truth," Jesus answered, "this very night, before
the rooster crows, you will disown me three times."
35But Peter declared, "Even if I have to die with you, I will never
disown you." And all the other disciples said the same.

*Gethsemane*
36Then Jesus went with his disciples to a place called Gethsemane, and he said to them, "Sit here while I go over there and pray."
37He took Peter and the two sons of Zebedee along with him, and
he began to be sorrowful and troubled. 38Then he said to them,
"My soul is overwhelmed with sorrow to the point of death. Stay
here and keep watch with me."
39Going a little farther, he fell with his face to the ground and
prayed, "My Father, if it is possible, may this cup be taken from
me. Yet not as I will, but as you will."
40Then he returned to his disciples and found them sleeping.
"Could you men not keep watch with me for one hour?" he asked
Peter. 41"Watch and pray so that you will not fall into temptation.
The spirit is willing, but the body is weak."
42He went away a second time and prayed, "My Father, if it is
not possible for this cup to be taken away unless I drink it, may
your will be done."
43When he came back, he again found them sleeping, because
their eyes were heavy. 44So he left them and went away once more
and prayed the third time, saying the same thing.
45Then he returned to the disciples and said to them, "Are you
still sleeping and resting? Look, the hour is near, and the Son of
Man is betrayed into the hands of sinners. 46Rise, let us go! Here
comes my betrayer!"

*Jesus Arrested*
47While he was still speaking, Judas, one of the Twelve, arrived.
With him was a large crowd armed with swords and clubs, sent
from the chief priests and the elders of the people. 48Now the
betrayer had arranged a signal with them: "The one I kiss is the
man; arrest him." 49Going at once to Jesus, Judas said, "Greetings,
Rabbi!" and kissed him.
50Jesus replied, "Friend, do what you came for."[o]
Then the men stepped forward, seized Jesus and arrested him.

**NIV** [m] 28 Some manuscripts *the new* [n] 31 Zech. 13:7 [o] 50 Or *"Friend, why have you come?"*

## King James

51And, behold, one of them which were with Jesus stretched
out *his* hand, and drew his sword, and struck a servant of the high
priest's, and smote off his ear.
52Then said Jesus unto him, Put up again thy sword into his
place: for all they that take the sword shall perish with the sword.
53Thinkest thou that I cannot now pray to my Father, and he
shall presently give me more than twelve legions of angels?
54But how then shall the scriptures be fulfilled, that thus it must
be?
55In that same hour said Jesus to the multitudes, Are ye come
out as against a thief with swords and staves for to take me? I sat
daily with you teaching in the temple, and ye laid no hold on me.
56But all this was done, that the scriptures of the prophets might
be fulfilled. Then all the disciples forsook him, and fled.
57¶ And they that had laid hold on Jesus led *him* away to
Caiaphas the high priest, where the scribes and the elders were
assembled.
58But Peter followed him afar off unto the high priest's palace,
and went in, and sat with the servants, to see the end.
59Now the chief priests, and elders, and all the council, sought
false witness against Jesus, to put him to death;
60But found none: yea, though many false witnesses came, *yet*
found they none. At the last came two false witnesses,
61And said, This *fellow* said, I am able to destroy the temple of
God, and to build it in three days.
62And the high priest arose, and said unto him, Answerest thou
nothing? what *is it which* these witness against thee?
63But Jesus held his peace. And the high priest answered and
said unto him, I adjure thee by the living God, that thou tell us
whether thou be the Christ, the Son of God.
64Jesus saith unto him, Thou hast said: nevertheless I say unto
you, Hereafter shall ye see the Son of man sitting on the right hand
of power, and coming in the clouds of heaven.
65Then the high priest rent his clothes, saying, He hath spoken
blasphemy; what further need have we of witnesses? behold, now
ye have heard his blasphemy.
66What think ye? They answered and said, He is guilty of death.
67Then did they spit in his face, and buffeted him; and others
smote *him* with the palms of their hands,
68Saying, Prophesy unto us, thou Christ, Who is he that smote
thee?
69¶ Now Peter sat without in the palace: and a damsel came unto
him, saying, Thou also wast with Jesus of Galilee.
70But he denied before *them* all, saying, I know not what thou
sayest.
71And when he was gone out into the porch, another *maid* saw
him, and said unto them that were there, This *fellow* was also with
Jesus of Nazareth.
72And again he denied with an oath, I do not know the man.
73And after a while came unto *him* they that stood by, and said
to Peter, Surely thou also art *one* of them; for thy speech betrayeth
thee.
74Then began he to curse and to swear, *saying*, I know not the
man. And immediately the cock crew.
75And Peter remembered the word of Jesus, which said unto
him, Before the cock crow, thou shalt deny me thrice. And he went
out, and wept bitterly.

## Amplified

51And behold, one of those who were with Jesus reached out
his hand and drew his sword, and striking the body servant of the
high priest, cut off his ear.
52Then Jesus said to him, Put your sword back into its place, for
all who draw the sword will die by the sword. [Gen. 9:6.]
53Do you suppose that I cannot appeal to My Father, and He
will immediately provide Me with more than twelve legions
[ [a]more than 80,000] of angels?
54But how then should the Scripture be fulfilled that it must
come about this way?
55At that moment Jesus said to the crowds, Have you come out
as against a robber with swords and clubs to capture Me? Day after
day I was [b]accustomed to sit in the [c]porches *and* courts of the
temple teaching, and you did not arrest Me.
56But all this has taken place in order that the Scriptures of the
prophets might be fulfilled. Then all the disciples deserted Him
and fleeing escaped.
57But those who had seized Jesus took Him away to Caiaphas
the high priest, where the scribes and the elders had assembled.
58But Peter followed Him at a distance as far as the courtyard
of the high priest's home; he even went inside and sat with the
guards to see the end.
59Now the chief priests and the whole council [the Sanhedrin]
sought to get false witnesses to testify against Jesus, so that they
might put Him to death;
60But they found none, though many witnesses came forward
[to testify]. At last two men came forward
61And testified, This [d]Fellow said, I am able to tear down the
[e]sanctuary of the temple of God and to build it up again in three
days.
62And the high priest stood up and said, Have You no answer
to make? What about this that these men testify against You?
63But Jesus kept silent. And the high priest said to Him, [f]I call
upon you to swear by the living God, and tell us whether you are
the Christ, the Son of God.
64Jesus said to him, [g]You have stated [the fact]. More than that,
I tell you, You will in the future see the Son of man seated at the
right hand of [h]the Almighty, and coming on the clouds of the sky.
[Dan. 7:13; Ps. 110:1.]
65Then the high priest tore his clothes and exclaimed, He has
uttered blasphemy! What need have we of further evidence? You
have now heard His blasphemy. [Num. 14:6; Lev. 24:16.]
66What do you think now? They answered, He deserves to be
put to death.
67Then they spat in His face, and struck Him with their fists;
and some [i]slapped Him in the face, [Isa. 50:6.]
68Saying, Prophesy to us, You Christ, the Messiah! Who was it
that struck You?
69Now Peter was sitting outside in the courtyard and [j]one maid
came up to him and said, You were also with Jesus the Galilean!
70But he denied it [k]falsely before them all, saying, I do not
know what you mean.
71And when he had gone out to the porch, another maid saw
him, and she said to the bystanders, This [fellow] was with Jesus
the Nazarene!
72And again he denied it and [l]disowned Him with an oath,
saying, I do not know the Man!
73After a little while the bystanders came up and said to Peter,
You certainly are one of them too, for even your accent betrays
you.
74Then Peter began to invoke a curse on himself and to swear,
I do not even know the Man! And at that moment a rooster
crowed.
75And Peter remembered Jesus' words when He said, Before a
[m]single rooster crows, you will deny *and* disown Me three times.
And he went outside and wept bitterly.

**AMP** [a] Thayer. [b] Vincent. [c] Trench. [d] Capitalized because of what He is, the spotless Son of God, not what the speakers may have thought He was. [e] Trench. [f] Vincent. [g] Vincent. [h] Thayer. [i] Thayer. [j] Vincent. [k] Cremer. [l] Cremer. [m] Vincent.

## New American Standard

51And behold, one of those who were with Jesus reached and
drew out his sword, and struck the slave of the high priest, and
cut off his ear.
52Then Jesus *said to him, "Put your sword back into its place;
for all those who take up the sword shall perish by the sword.
53"Or do you think that I cannot appeal to My Father, and He
will at once put at My disposal more than twelve [n]legions of
angels?
54"How then shall the Scriptures be fulfilled, that it must happen this way?"
55At that time Jesus said to the multitudes, "Have you come out
with swords and clubs to arrest Me as against a robber? Every day
I used to sit in the temple teaching and you did not seize Me.
56"But all this has taken place that the Scriptures of the prophets
may be fulfilled." Then all the disciples left Him and fled.

*Jesus before Caiaphas*

57¶ And those who had seized Jesus led Him away to Caiaphas,
the high priest, where the scribes and the elders were gathered
together.
58But Peter also was following Him at a distance as far as the
courtyard of the high priest, and entered in, and sat down with the
officers to see the outcome.
59Now the chief priests and the whole Council kept trying to
obtain false testimony against Jesus, in order that they might put
Him to death;
60and they did not find *any*, even though many false witnesses
came forward. But later on two came forward,
61and said, "This man stated, 'I am able to destroy the temple
of God and to rebuild it in three days.'"
62And the high priest stood up and said to Him, "Do You make
no answer? What is it that these men are testifying against You?"
63But Jesus kept silent. And the high priest said to Him, "I
adjure You by the living God, that You tell us whether You are the
Christ, the Son of God."
64Jesus *said to him, "You have said it *yourself*; nevertheless I
tell you, hereafter you shall see THE SON OF MAN SITTING AT THE
RIGHT HAND OF POWER, and COMING ON THE CLOUDS OF HEAVEN."
65Then the high priest tore his robes, saying, "He has blasphemed! What further need do we have of witnesses? Behold, you
have now heard the blasphemy;
66what do you think?" They answered and said, "He is deserving of death!"
67Then they spat in His face and beat Him with their fists; and
others slapped Him,
68and said, "Prophesy to us, You Christ; who is the one who
hit You?"

*Peter's Denials*

69¶ Now Peter was sitting outside in the courtyard, and a certain
servant-girl came to him and said, "You too were with Jesus the
Galilean."
70But he denied *it* before them all, saying, "I do not know what
you are talking about."
71And when he had gone out to the gateway, another *servant-
girl* saw him and *said to those who were there, "This man was
with Jesus of Nazareth."
72And again he denied *it* with an oath, "I do not know the
man."
73And a little later the bystanders came up and said to Peter,
"Surely you too are *one* of them; for the way you talk gives you
away."
74Then he began to curse and swear, "I do not know the man!"
And immediately a cock crowed.
75And Peter remembered the word which Jesus had said, "Before a cock crows, you will deny Me three times." And he went
out and wept bitterly.

NAS [n] A legion equaled 6,000 troops

## New International

51With that, one of Jesus' companions reached for his sword, drew
it out and struck the servant of the high priest, cutting off his ear.
52"Put your sword back in its place," Jesus said to him, "for all
who draw the sword will die by the sword. 53Do you think I cannot
call on my Father, and he will at once put at my disposal more than
twelve legions of angels? 54But how then would the Scriptures be
fulfilled that say it must happen in this way?"
55At that time Jesus said to the crowd, "Am I leading a rebellion, that you have come out with swords and clubs to capture me?
Every day I sat in the temple courts teaching, and you did not
arrest me. 56But this has all taken place that the writings of the
prophets might be fulfilled." Then all the disciples deserted him
and fled.

*Before the Sanhedrin*

57Those who had arrested Jesus took him to Caiaphas, the high
priest, where the teachers of the law and the elders had assembled.
58But Peter followed him at a distance, right up to the courtyard
of the high priest. He entered and sat down with the guards to see
the outcome.
59The chief priests and the whole Sanhedrin were looking for
false evidence against Jesus so that they could put him to death.
60But they did not find any, though many false witnesses came
forward.
Finally two came forward 61and declared, "This fellow said, 'I
am able to destroy the temple of God and rebuild it in three days.'"
62Then the high priest stood up and said to Jesus, "Are you not
going to answer? What is this testimony that these men are bringing against you?" 63But Jesus remained silent.
The high priest said to him, "I charge you under oath by the
living God: Tell us if you are the Christ,[o] the Son of God."
64"Yes, it is as you say," Jesus replied. "But I say to all of you:
In the future you will see the Son of Man sitting at the right hand
of the Mighty One and coming on the clouds of heaven."
65Then the high priest tore his clothes and said, "He has spoken
blasphemy! Why do we need any more witnesses? Look, now you
have heard the blasphemy. 66What do you think?"
"He is worthy of death," they answered.
67Then they spit in his face and struck him with their fists.
Others slapped him 68and said, "Prophesy to us, Christ. Who hit
you?"

*Peter Disowns Jesus*

69Now Peter was sitting out in the courtyard, and a servant girl
came to him. "You also were with Jesus of Galilee," she said.
70But he denied it before them all. "I don't know what you're
talking about," he said.
71Then he went out to the gateway, where another girl saw him
and said to the people there, "This fellow was with Jesus of Nazareth."
72He denied it again, with an oath: "I don't know the man!"
73After a little while, those standing there went up to Peter and
said, "Surely you are one of them, for your accent gives you
away."
74Then he began to call down curses on himself and he swore
to them, "I don't know the man!"
Immediately a rooster crowed. 75Then Peter remembered the
word Jesus had spoken: "Before the rooster crows, you will disown me three times." And he went outside and wept bitterly.

NIV [o] 63 Or *Messiah*; also in verse 68

## King James

**27** WHEN THE morning was come, all the chief priests and elders of the people took counsel against Jesus to put him to death:

2 And when they had bound him, they led *him* away, and delivered him to Pontius Pilate the governor.

3 ¶ Then Judas, which had betrayed him, when he saw that he was condemned, repented himself, and brought again the thirty pieces of silver to the chief priests and elders,

4 Saying, I have sinned in that I have betrayed the innocent blood. And they said, What *is that* to us? see thou *to that*.

5 And he cast down the pieces of silver in the temple, and departed, and went and hanged himself.

6 And the chief priests took the silver pieces, and said, It is not lawful for to put them into the treasury, because it is the price of blood.

7 And they took counsel, and bought with them the potter's field, to bury strangers in.

8 Wherefore that field was called, The field of blood, unto this day.

9 Then was fulfilled that which was spoken by Jeremy the prophet, saying, And they took the thirty pieces of silver, the price of him that was valued, whom they of the children of Israel did value;

10 And gave them for the potter's field, as the Lord appointed me.

11 And Jesus stood before the governor: and the governor asked him, saying, Art thou the King of the Jews? And Jesus said unto him, Thou sayest.

12 And when he was accused of the chief priests and elders, he answered nothing.

13 Then said Pilate unto him, Hearest thou not how many things they witness against thee?

14 And he answered him to never a word; insomuch that the governor marvelled greatly.

15 Now at *that* feast the governor was wont to release unto the people a prisoner, whom they would.

16 And they had then a notable prisoner, called Barabbas.

17 Therefore when they were gathered together, Pilate said unto them, Whom will ye that I release unto you? Barabbas, or Jesus which is called Christ?

18 For he knew that for envy they had delivered him.

19 ¶ When he was set down on the judgment seat, his wife sent unto him, saying, Have thou nothing to do with that just man: for I have suffered many things this day in a dream because of him.

20 But the chief priests and elders persuaded the multitude that they should ask Barabbas, and destroy Jesus.

21 The governor answered and said unto them, Whether of the twain will ye that I release unto you? They said, Barabbas.

22 Pilate saith unto them, What shall I do then with Jesus which is called Christ? *They* all say unto him, Let him be crucified.

23 And the governor said, Why, what evil hath he done? But they cried out the more, saying, Let him be crucified.

24 ¶ When Pilate saw that he could prevail nothing, but *that* rather a tumult was made, he took water, and washed *his* hands before the multitude, saying, I am innocent of the blood of this just person: see ye *to it*.

25 Then answered all the people, and said, His blood *be* on us, and on our children.

26 ¶ Then released he Barabbas unto them: and when he had scourged Jesus, he delivered *him* to be crucified.

## Amplified

**27** WHEN IT was morning, all the chief priests and the elders of the people held a consultation against Jesus to put Him to death;

2 And they bound Him, and led Him away and handed Him over to Pilate the governor.

3 When Judas, His betrayer, saw that [Jesus] was condemned, (he was [a]afflicted in mind and troubled for his former folly; and) with remorse [that is, [b]an after care and little more than a selfish dread of the consequences] he brought back the thirty pieces of silver to the chief priests and the elders, [Exod. 21:32.]

4 Saying, I have sinned in betraying innocent blood. They replied, What is that to us? See to that yourself.

5 And casting the pieces of silver [forward] into the Holy Place *of* the [c]sanctuary of the temple, he departed, and he went off and hanged himself.

6 But the chief priests, picking up the pieces of silver, said, It is not legal to put these in the [consecrated] treasury, for it is the price of blood. [Deut. 23:18.]

7 So after consultation they bought with them the potter's field in which to bury strangers.

8 Therefore that piece of ground has been called the Field of Blood to the present day.

9 Then were fulfilled the words spoken by Jeremiah the prophet when he said, And they took the thirty pieces of silver, the price of Him on Whom a price had been set by some of the sons of Israel, [Zech. 11:12, 13.]

10 And they gave them for the potter's field, as the Lord directed me.

11 Now Jesus stood before the governor [Pilate]; and the governor asked Him, Are you the King of the Jews? Jesus said to him, You have stated [the fact].

12 But when the charges were made against Him by the chief priests and elders, He made no answer. [Isa. 53:7.]

13 Then Pilate said to Him, Do You not hear how many *and* how serious are the things they are testifying against You?

14 But He made no reply to him, not even to a single accusation, so that the governor marveled greatly.

15 Now at the feast (of the Passover) the governor was in the habit of setting free for the people any one prisoner whom they chose.

16 And at that time they had a notorious prisoner whose name was Barabbas.

17 So when they had assembled for this purpose, Pilate said to them, Whom do you want me to set free for you, Barabbas, or Jesus Who is called Christ?

18 For he knew that it was because of envy that they had handed Him over to him.

19 Also, while he was seated on the judgment bench, his wife sent him a message, saying, Have nothing to do with that just *and* upright Man, for I have had a painful experience because of Him today in a dream.

20 But the chief priests and the elders prevailed on the people to ask for Barabbas and put Jesus to death.

21 Again the governor said to them, Which of the two do you wish me to release for you? And they said, Barabbas!

22 Pilate said to them, Then what shall I do with Jesus Who is called Christ?

23 They all replied, Let Him be crucified! And he said, Why, what has He done that is evil? But they shouted all the louder, Let Him be crucified!

24 So when Pilate saw that he was getting nowhere, but rather that a riot was about to break out, he took water and washed his hands in the presence of the crowd, saying, I am not guilty of *nor* responsible for this [d] *righteous* Man's blood; see to it yourselves. [Deut. 21:6-9; Ps. 26:6.]

25 And all the people answered, His blood be on us and on our children! [Josh. 2:19.]

26 So he set free for them Barabbas, and [had] Jesus whipped, and delivered Him up to be crucified.

**AMP** [a] Jeremy Taylor, and, Aristotle; both quoted in Trench's "Synonyms of the New Testament." [b] Aristotle. [c] Trench. [d] Some authorities so read.

## New American Standard

*Judas' Remorse*

**27** NOW WHEN morning had come, all the chief priests and
the elders of the people took counsel against Jesus to put
Him to death;

2and they bound Him, and led Him away, and delivered Him
up to Pilate the governor.

3¶ Then when Judas, who had betrayed Him, saw that He had
been condemned, he felt remorse and returned the thirty pieces
of silver to the chief priests and elders,

4saying, "I have sinned by betraying innocent blood." But they
said, "What is that to us? See *to that* yourself!"

5And he threw the pieces of silver into the sanctuary and
departed; and he went away and hanged himself.

6And the chief priests took the pieces of silver and said, "It is
not lawful to put them into the temple treasury, since it is the price
of blood."

7And they counseled together and with the money bought the
Potter's Field as a burial place for strangers.

8For this reason that field has been called the Field of Blood to
this day.

9Then that which was spoken through Jeremiah the prophet
was fulfilled, saying, "AND THEY TOOK THE THIRTY PIECES OF SIL-
VER, THE PRICE OF THE ONE WHOSE PRICE HAD BEEN SET by the sons
of Israel;

10AND THEY GAVE THEM FOR THE POTTER'S FIELD, AS THE LORD
DIRECTED ME."

*Jesus before Pilate*

11¶ Now Jesus stood before the governor, and the governor
questioned Him, saying, "Are You the King of the Jews?" And
Jesus said to him, "*It is as* you say."

12And while He was being accused by the chief priests and
elders, He made no answer.

13Then Pilate *said to Him, "Do You not hear how many things
they testify against You?"

14And He did not answer him with regard to even a *single*
charge, so that the governor was quite amazed.

15Now at *the* feast the governor was accustomed to release for
the multitude *any* one prisoner whom they wanted.

16And they were holding at that time a notorious prisoner,
called Barabbas.

17When therefore they were gathered together, Pilate said to
them, "Whom do you want me to release for you? Barabbas, or
Jesus who is called Christ?"

18For he knew that because of envy they had delivered Him up.

19And while he was sitting on the judgment seat, his wife sent
to him, saying, "Have nothing to do with that righteous Man; for
last night I suffered greatly in a dream because of Him."

20But the chief priests and the elders persuaded the multitudes
to ask for Barabbas, and to put Jesus to death.

21But the governor answered and said to them, "Which of the
two do you want me to release for you?" And they said, "Barabbas."

22Pilate *said to them, "Then what shall I do with Jesus who is
called Christ?" They all *said, "Let Him be crucified!"

23And he said, "Why, what evil has He done?" But they kept
shouting all the more, saying, "Let Him be crucified!"

24And when Pilate saw that he was accomplishing nothing, but
rather that a riot was starting, he took water and washed his hands
in front of the multitude, saying, "I am innocent of this Man's
blood; see *to that* yourselves."

25And all the people answered and said, "His blood *be* on us
and on our children!"

26Then he released Barabbas for them; but after having Jesus
scourged, he delivered Him to be crucified.

## New International

*Judas Hangs Himself*

**27** EARLY IN the morning, all the chief priests and the elders
of the people came to the decision to put Jesus to death.
2They bound him, led him away and handed him over to Pilate,
the governor.

3When Judas, who had betrayed him, saw that Jesus was condemned, he was seized with remorse and returned the thirty silver
coins to the chief priests and the elders. 4"I have sinned," he said,
"for I have betrayed innocent blood."

"What is that to us?" they replied. "That's your responsibility."

5So Judas threw the money into the temple and left. Then he
went away and hanged himself.

6The chief priests picked up the coins and said, "It is against the
law to put this into the treasury, since it is blood money." 7So they
decided to use the money to buy the potter's field as a burial place
for foreigners. 8That is why it has been called the Field of Blood
to this day. 9Then what was spoken by Jeremiah the prophet was
fulfilled: "They took the thirty silver coins, the price set on him by
the people of Israel, 10and they used them to buy the potter's field,
as the Lord commanded me."[e]

*Jesus Before Pilate*

11Meanwhile Jesus stood before the governor, and the governor
asked him, "Are you the king of the Jews?"

"Yes, it is as you say," Jesus replied.

12When he was accused by the chief priests and the elders, he
gave no answer. 13Then Pilate asked him, "Don't you hear the
testimony they are bringing against you?" 14But Jesus made no
reply, not even to a single charge—to the great amazement of the
governor.

15Now it was the governor's custom at the Feast to release a
prisoner chosen by the crowd. 16At that time they had a notorious
prisoner, called Barabbas. 17So when the crowd had gathered,
Pilate asked them, "Which one do you want me to release to you:
Barabbas, or Jesus who is called Christ?" 18For he knew it was out
of envy that they had handed Jesus over to him.

19While Pilate was sitting on the judge's seat, his wife sent him
this message: "Don't have anything to do with that innocent man,
for I have suffered a great deal today in a dream because of him."

20But the chief priests and the elders persuaded the crowd to
ask for Barabbas and to have Jesus executed.

21"Which of the two do you want me to release to you?" asked
the governor.

"Barabbas," they answered.

22"What shall I do, then, with Jesus who is called Christ?" Pilate
asked.

They all answered, "Crucify him!"

23"Why? What crime has he committed?" asked Pilate.

But they shouted all the louder, "Crucify him!"

24When Pilate saw that he was getting nowhere, but that instead an uproar was starting, he took water and washed his hands
in front of the crowd. "I am innocent of this man's blood," he said.
"It is your responsibility!"

25All the people answered, "Let his blood be on us and on our
children!"

26Then he released Barabbas to them. But he had Jesus flogged,
and handed him over to be crucified.

NIV [e] *10* See Zech. 11:12,13; Jer. 19:1-13; 32:6-9.

## King James

27 Then the soldiers of the governor took Jesus into the common hall, and gathered unto him the whole band *of soldiers*.

28 And they stripped him, and put on him a scarlet robe.

29 ¶ And when they had plaited a crown of thorns, they put *it* upon his head, and a reed in his right hand: and they bowed the knee before him, and mocked him, saying, Hail, King of the Jews!

30 And they spit upon him, and took the reed, and smote him on the head.

31 And after that they had mocked him, they took the robe off from him, and put his own raiment on him, and led him away to crucify *him*.

32 And as they came out, they found a man of Cyrene, Simon by name: him they compelled to bear his cross.

33 And when they were come unto a place called Golgotha, that is to say, a place of a skull,

34 ¶ They gave him vinegar to drink mingled with gall: and when he had tasted *thereof*, he would not drink.

35 And they crucified him, and parted his garments, casting lots: that it might be fulfilled which was spoken by the prophet, They parted my garments among them, and upon my vesture did they cast lots.

36 And sitting down they watched him there;

37 And set up over his head his accusation written, THIS IS JESUS THE KING OF THE JEWS.

38 Then were there two thieves crucified with him, one on the right hand, and another on the left.

39 ¶ And they that passed by reviled him, wagging their heads,

40 And saying, Thou that destroyest the temple, and buildest *it* in three days, save thyself. If thou be the Son of God, come down from the cross.

41 Likewise also the chief priests mocking *him*, with the scribes and elders, said,

42 He saved others; himself he cannot save. If he be the King of Israel, let him now come down from the cross, and we will believe him.

43 He trusted in God; let him deliver him now, if he will have him: for he said, I am the Son of God.

44 The thieves also, which were crucified with him, cast the same in his teeth.

45 Now from the sixth hour there was darkness over all the land unto the ninth hour.

46 And about the ninth hour Jesus cried with a loud voice, saying, Eli, Eli, lama sabachthani? that is to say, My God, my God, why hast thou forsaken me?

47 Some of them that stood there, when they heard *that*, said, This *man* calleth for Elias.

48 And straightway one of them ran, and took a sponge, and filled *it* with vinegar, and put *it* on a reed, and gave him to drink.

49 The rest said, Let be, let us see whether Elias will come to save him.

50 ¶ Jesus, when he had cried again with a loud voice, yielded up the ghost.

51 And, behold, the veil of the temple was rent in twain from the top to the bottom; and the earth did quake, and the rocks rent;

52 And the graves were opened; and many bodies of the saints which slept arose,

53 And came out of the graves after his resurrection, and went into the holy city, and appeared unto many.

54 Now when the centurion, and they that were with him, watching Jesus, saw the earthquake, and those things that were done, they feared greatly, saying, Truly this was the Son of God.

## Amplified

27 Then the governor's soldiers took Jesus into the palace, and they gathered the whole battalion about Him.

28 And they stripped off His clothes and put a scarlet robe [ [a]garment of dignity and office, worn by Roman officers of rank] upon Him,

29 And weaving a crown of thorns they put it on His head, and put a reed-staff in His right hand. And kneeling before Him they made sport of Him, saying, Hail (greeting, good health to you, long life to you), King of the Jews!

30 And they spat on Him, and took the reed-staff and struck Him on the head.

31 And when they finished making sport of Him, they stripped Him of the robe and put His own garments on Him, and led Him away to be crucified.

32 As they were marching forth, they came upon a man of Cyrene named Simon; this man they forced to carry the cross of Jesus.

33 And when they came to a place called Golgotha [Calvary, in Latin], which means the place of a skull,

34 They offered Him wine mingled with gall to drink, but when He tasted it, He refused to drink it.

35 And when they had crucified Him, they divided *and* distributed His garments [among them] by casting lots *so that the prophet's saying was fulfilled, They parted My garments among them and over My apparel they cast lots.* [Ps. 22:18.]

36 Then they sat down there and kept watch over Him.

37 And over His head they put the accusation against Him ( [b]the cause of His death), which read, This is Jesus the King of the Jews.

38 At the same time two robbers were crucified with Him, one on the right hand and one on the left.

39 And those who passed by spoke reproachfully *and* abusively *and* jeered at Him, wagging their heads, [Ps. 22:7, 8; 109:25.]

40 And they said, You Who would tear down the [c]sanctuary of the temple and rebuild it in three days, rescue Yourself [d]from death. If You are the Son of God, come down from the cross.

41 In the same way the chief priests with the scribes and elders made sport of Him, saying,

42 He rescued others [e]from death; Himself He cannot rescue [f]from death. He is the King of Israel? Let Him come down from the cross now, and we will believe *and* [g]acknowledge *and* cleave to Him.

43 He trusts in God; let God deliver Him now, if He cares for Him *and* will [have] Him, for He said, I am the Son of God.

44 And the robbers who were crucified with Him also abused *and* reproached *and* made sport of Him in the same way.

45 Now from the sixth hour [noon] there was darkness over all the land until the ninth hour [three o'clock].

46 And about the ninth hour [three o'clock] Jesus cried with a loud voice, Eli, Eli, lama sabachthani? that is, My God, My God, why have You abandoned Me—leaving Me [h]helpless, forsaking and failing Me in My need? [Ps. 22:1.]

47 And some of the bystanders when they heard it said, This Man is calling for Elijah!

48 And one of them immediately ran and took a sponge, soaked it with vinegar [a sour wine], and put it on a reed-staff and was [i]about to give it to Him to drink. [Ps. 69:21.]

49 But the others said, Wait! Let us see whether Elijah will come to save Him [j]from death.

50 And Jesus cried again with a loud voice, and gave up His spirit.

51 And at once the curtain of the [k]sanctuary of the temple was torn in two from top to bottom; the earth shook, and the rocks were split; [Exod. 26:31-35.]

52 The tombs were opened, and many bodies of the saints who had fallen asleep [l]in death were raised,

53 And coming out of the tombs after His resurrection, they went into the holy city and appeared to many people.

54 When the centurion and those that were with him keeping watch over Jesus, observed the earthquake and all that was happening, they were terribly frightened *and* filled with awe, and said, Truly this was God's Son!

**AMP** [a] Trench. [b] Tyndale. [c] Trench. [d] Cremer. [e] Cremer. [f] Cremer. [g] Cremer. [h] Wuest. [i] Vincent. [j] Vincent. [k] Trench. [l] Cremer.

## New American Standard

*Jesus Is Mocked*

27¶ Then the soldiers of the governor took Jesus into the Praetorium and gathered the whole *Roman* cohort around Him.

28And they stripped Him, and put a scarlet robe on Him.

29And after weaving a crown of thorns, they put it on His head, and a reed in His right hand; and they kneeled down before Him and mocked Him, saying, "Hail, King of the Jews!"

30And they spat on Him, and took the reed and *began* to beat Him on the head.

31And after they had mocked Him, they took His robe off and put His garments on Him, and led Him away to crucify *Him*.

32¶ And as they were coming out, they found a man of Cyrene named Simon, whom they pressed into service to bear His cross.

*The Crucifixion*

33¶ And when they had come to a place called Golgotha, which means Place of a Skull,

34they gave Him wine to drink mingled with gall; and after tasting *it*, He was unwilling to drink.

35And when they had crucified Him, they divided up His garments among themselves, casting lots;

36and sitting down, they *began* to keep watch over Him there.

37And they put up above His head the charge against Him which read, "THIS IS JESUS THE KING OF THE JEWS."

38At that time two robbers *were crucified with Him, one on the right and one on the left.

39And those passing by were hurling abuse at Him, wagging their heads,

40and saying, "You who *are going to* destroy the temple and rebuild it in three days, save Yourself! If You are the Son of God, come down from the cross."

41In the same way the chief priests also, along with the scribes and elders, were mocking *Him*, and saying,

42"He saved others; He cannot save Himself. He is the King of Israel; let Him now come down from the cross, and we shall believe in Him.

43"HE TRUSTS IN GOD; LET HIM DELIVER *Him* now, IF HE TAKES PLEASURE IN HIM; for He said, 'I am the Son of God.'"

44And the robbers also who had been crucified with Him were casting the same insult at Him.

45¶ Now from the [m]sixth hour darkness fell upon all the land until the [n]ninth hour.

46And about the ninth hour Jesus cried out with a loud voice, saying, "ELI, ELI, LAMA SABACHTHANI?" that is, "MY GOD, MY GOD, WHY HAST THOU FORSAKEN ME?"

47And some of those who were standing there, when they heard it, *began* saying, "This man is calling for Elijah."

48And immediately one of them ran, and taking a sponge, he filled it with sour wine, and put it on a reed, and gave Him a drink.

49But the rest *of them* said, "Let us see whether Elijah will come to save Him." [o]

50And Jesus cried out again with a loud voice, and yielded up *His* spirit.

51And behold, the veil of the temple was torn in two from top to bottom, and the earth shook; and the rocks were split,

52and the tombs were opened; and many bodies of the saints who had fallen asleep were raised;

53and coming out of the tombs after His resurrection they entered the holy city and appeared to many.

54Now the centurion, and those who were with him keeping guard over Jesus, when they saw the earthquake and the things that were happening, became very frightened and said, "Truly this was the Son of God!"

**NAS** [m]I.e., noon [n]I.e., 3 p.m. [o]Some early mss. add: *And another took a spear and pierced His side, and there came out water and blood.* (cf. John 19:34)

## New International

*The Soldiers Mock Jesus*

27Then the governor's soldiers took Jesus into the Praetorium
and gathered the whole company of soldiers around him. 28They
stripped him and put a scarlet robe on him, 29and then twisted
together a crown of thorns and set it on his head. They put a staff
in his right hand and knelt in front of him and mocked him. "Hail,
king of the Jews!" they said. 30They spit on him, and took the staff
and struck him on the head again and again. 31After they had
mocked him, they took off the robe and put his own clothes on
him. Then they led him away to crucify him.

*The Crucifixion*

32As they were going out, they met a man from Cyrene, named
Simon, and they forced him to carry the cross. 33They came to a
place called Golgotha (which means The Place of the Skull).
34There they offered Jesus wine to drink, mixed with gall; but after
tasting it, he refused to drink it. 35When they had crucified him,
they divided up his clothes by casting lots.[p] 36And sitting down,
they kept watch over him there. 37Above his head they placed the
written charge against him: THIS IS JESUS, THE KING OF THE JEWS.
38Two robbers were crucified with him, one on his right and one
on his left. 39Those who passed by hurled insults at him, shaking
their heads 40and saying, "You who are going to destroy the
temple and build it in three days, save yourself! Come down from
the cross, if you are the Son of God!"

41In the same way the chief priests, the teachers of the law and
the elders mocked him. 42"He saved others," they said, "but he
can't save himself! He's the King of Israel! Let him come down now
from the cross, and we will believe in him. 43He trusts in God. Let
God rescue him now if he wants him, for he said, 'I am the Son
of God.'" 44In the same way the robbers who were crucified with
him also heaped insults on him.

*The Death of Jesus*

45From the sixth hour until the ninth hour darkness came over
all the land. 46About the ninth hour Jesus cried out in a loud voice,
*"Eloi, Eloi,*[q] *lama sabachthani?"*—which means, "My God, my God,
why have you forsaken me?"[r]

47When some of those standing there heard this, they said,
"He's calling Elijah."

48Immediately one of them ran and got a sponge. He filled it
with wine vinegar, put it on a stick, and offered it to Jesus to drink.
49The rest said, "Now leave him alone. Let's see if Elijah comes to
save him."

50And when Jesus had cried out again in a loud voice, he gave
up his spirit.

51At that moment the curtain of the temple was torn in two from
top to bottom. The earth shook and the rocks split. 52The tombs
broke open and the bodies of many holy people who had died
were raised to life. 53They came out of the tombs, and after Jesus'
resurrection they went into the holy city and appeared to many
people.

54When the centurion and those with him who were guarding
Jesus saw the earthquake and all that had happened, they were
terrified, and exclaimed, "Surely he was the Son[s] of God!"

**NIV** [p]35 A few late manuscripts *lots that the word spoken by the prophet might be fulfilled: "They divided my garments among themselves and cast lots for my clothing"* (Psalm 22:18) [q]46 Some manuscripts *Eli, Eli* [r]46 Psalm 22:1 [s]54 Or *a son*

## King James

55And many women were there beholding afar off, which followed Jesus from Galilee, ministering unto him:
56Among which was Mary Magdalene, and Mary the mother of James and Joses, and the mother of Zebedee's children.
57When the even was come, there came a rich man of Arimathaea, named Joseph, who also himself was Jesus' disciple:
58He went to Pilate, and begged the body of Jesus. Then Pilate commanded the body to be delivered.
59And when Joseph had taken the body, he wrapped it in a clean linen cloth,
60And laid it in his own new tomb, which he had hewn out in the rock: and he rolled a great stone to the door of the sepulchre, and departed.
61And there was Mary Magdalene, and the other Mary, sitting over against the sepulchre.
62¶ Now the next day, that followed the day of the preparation, the chief priests and Pharisees came together unto Pilate,
63Saying, Sir, we remember that that deceiver said, while he was yet alive, After three days I will rise again.
64Command therefore that the sepulchre be made sure until the third day, lest his disciples come by night, and steal him away, and say unto the people, He is risen from the dead: so the last error shall be worse than the first.
65Pilate said unto them, Ye have a watch: go your way, make *it* as sure as ye can.
66So they went, and made the sepulchre sure, sealing the stone, and setting a watch.

**28** IN THE end of the sabbath, as it began to dawn toward the first *day* of the week, came Mary Magdalene and the other Mary to see the sepulchre.
2And, behold, there was a great earthquake: for the angel of the Lord descended from heaven, and came and rolled back the stone from the door, and sat upon it.
3His countenance was like lightning, and his raiment white as snow:
4And for fear of him the keepers did shake, and became as dead *men*.
5And the angel answered and said unto the women, Fear not ye: for I know that ye seek Jesus, which was crucified.
6He is not here: for he is risen, as he said. Come, see the place where the Lord lay.
7And go quickly, and tell his disciples that he is risen from the dead; and, behold, he goeth before you into Galilee; there shall ye see him: lo, I have told you.
8And they departed quickly from the sepulchre with fear and great joy; and did run to bring his disciples word.
9¶ And as they went to tell his disciples, behold, Jesus met them, saying, All hail. And they came and held him by the feet, and worshipped him.
10Then said Jesus unto them, Be not afraid: go tell my brethren that they go into Galilee, and there shall they see me.
11¶ Now when they were going, behold, some of the watch came into the city, and showed unto the chief priests all the things that were done.
12And when they were assembled with the elders, and had taken counsel, they gave large money unto the soldiers,
13Saying, Say ye, His disciples came by night, and stole him *away* while we slept.

## Amplified

55There were also numerous women there looking on from a distance, who were of those who had accompanied Jesus from Galilee, ministering to Him;
56Among them were Mary of Magdala, and Mary the mother of James and Joseph, and the mother of Zebedee's sons.
57When it was evening, there came a rich man from Arimathea, named Joseph, who also was a disciple of Jesus.
58He went to Pilate and asked for the body of Jesus, and Pilate ordered that it be given him.
59And Joseph took the body and [a]rolled it up in a clean linen cloth [b]used for swathing dead bodies,
60And laid it in his own fresh [ [c]undefiled] tomb, which he had hewn in the rock; and he rolled a big boulder over the door of the tomb and went away.
61And Mary of Magdala and the other Mary kept sitting there opposite the tomb.
62The next day, that is, the day after the day of preparation [for the Sabbath], the chief priests and the Pharisees assembled before Pilate
63And said, Sir, we have just remembered how that [d]vagabond Imposter said, while He was still alive, After three days I will rise again.
64Therefore give an order to have the tomb made secure *and* safeguarded until the third day, for fear His disciples go and steal Him away, and tell the people that He has risen from the dead, and the last deception *and* fraud will be worse than the first.
65Pilate said to them, You have a guard of soldiers; [take them and] go, make it as secure as you can.
66So they went off and made the tomb secure by sealing the boulder, a guard of soldiers being with them *and* remaining to watch.

**28** NOW AFTER the Sabbath, near dawn of the first day of the week, Mary of Magdala and the other Mary went to take a look at the tomb.
2And behold, there was a great earthquake, for an angel of the Lord descended from heaven and came and rolled the boulder back and sat upon it.
3His appearance was like lightning, and his garments as white as snow.
4And those keeping guard were so frightened at sight of him that they were agitated *and* trembled, and became like dead men.
5But the angel said to the women, Do not be alarmed *and* frightened, for I know that you are looking for Jesus Who was crucified.
6He is not here; He has risen, as He said [He would do]. Come, see the place where He lay.
7Then go quickly and tell His disciples, He has risen from the dead, and behold, He is going before you to Galilee; there you will see Him. Lo, I have told you.
8So they left the tomb hastily with fear and great joy, and ran to tell the disciples.
9And *as they went,* behold, Jesus met them and said, Hail (greeting)! And they went up to Him and clasped His feet and worshipped Him.
10Then Jesus said to them, Do not be alarmed *and* afraid; go and tell My brethren to go into Galilee, and there they will see Me.
11While they were on their way, behold, some of the guard went into the city and reported to the chief priests everything that had occurred.
12And when they had gathered with the elders and had consulted together, they gave a sufficient sum of money to the soldiers,
13And said, Tell people, His disciples came at night and stole Him away while we were sleeping.

**AMP** [a] Young's Concordance. [b] Moulton and Milligan. [c] Vincent. [d] Vincent.

## New American Standard

55And many women were there looking on from a distance,
who had followed Jesus from Galilee, ministering to Him,
56among whom was Mary Magdalene, *along with* Mary the
mother of James and Joseph, and the mother of the sons of Zebedee.

*Jesus Is Buried*

57¶ And when it was evening, there came a rich man from
Arimathea, named Joseph, who himself had also become a disciple
of Jesus.
58This man went to Pilate and asked for the body of Jesus. Then
Pilate ordered *it* to be given over *to him.*
59And Joseph took the body and wrapped it in a clean linen
cloth,
60and laid it in his own new tomb, which he had hewn out in
the rock; and he rolled a large stone against the entrance of the
tomb and went away.
61And Mary Magdalene was there, and the other Mary, sitting
opposite the grave.
62¶ Now on the next day, which is *the one* after the preparation,
the chief priests and the Pharisees gathered together with Pilate,
63and said, "Sir, we remember that when He was still alive that
deceiver said, 'After three days I *am to* rise again.'
64"Therefore, give orders for the grave to be made secure until
the third day, lest the disciples come and steal Him away and say
to the people, 'He has risen from the dead,' and the last deception
will be worse than the first."
65Pilate said to them, "You have a guard; go, make it *as* secure
as you know how."
66And they went and made the grave secure, and along with the
guard they set a seal on the stone.

## New International

55Many women were there, watching from a distance. They had
followed Jesus from Galilee to care for his needs. 56Among them
were Mary Magdalene, Mary the mother of James and Joses, and
the mother of Zebedee's sons.

*The Burial of Jesus*

57As evening approached, there came a rich man from Arimathea, named Joseph, who had himself become a disciple of Jesus.
58Going to Pilate, he asked for Jesus' body, and Pilate ordered that
it be given to him. 59Joseph took the body, wrapped it in a clean
linen cloth, 60and placed it in his own new tomb that he had cut
out of the rock. He rolled a big stone in front of the entrance to the
tomb and went away. 61Mary Magdalene and the other Mary were
sitting there opposite the tomb.

*The Guard at the Tomb*

62The next day, the one after Preparation Day, the chief priests
and the Pharisees went to Pilate. 63"Sir," they said, "we remember
that while he was still alive that deceiver said, 'After three days I
will rise again.' 64So give the order for the tomb to be made secure
until the third day. Otherwise, his disciples may come and steal
the body and tell the people that he has been raised from the dead.
This last deception will be worse than the first."
65"Take a guard," Pilate answered. "Go, make the tomb as
secure as you know how." 66So they went and made the tomb
secure by putting a seal on the stone and posting the guard.

*Jesus Is Risen!*

28 NOW AFTER the Sabbath, as it began to dawn toward the
first *day* of the week, Mary Magdalene and the other Mary
came to look at the grave.
2And behold, a severe earthquake had occurred, for an angel
of the Lord descended from heaven and came and rolled away the
stone and sat upon it.
3And his appearance was like lightning, and his garment as
white as snow;
4and the guards shook for fear of him, and became like dead
men.
5And the angel answered and said to the women, "Do not be
afraid; for I know that you are looking for Jesus who has been
crucified.
6"He is not here, for He has risen, just as He said. Come, see
the place where He was lying.
7"And go quickly and tell His disciples that He has risen from
the dead; and behold, He is going before you into Galilee, there
you will see Him; behold, I have told you."
8And they departed quickly from the tomb with fear and great
joy and ran to report it to His disciples.
9And behold, Jesus met them and greeted them. And they
came up and took hold of His feet and worshiped Him.
10Then Jesus *said to them, "Do not be afraid; go and take word
to My brethren to leave for Galilee, and there they shall see Me."
11¶ Now while they were on their way, behold, some of the
guard came into the city and reported to the chief priests all that
had happened.
12And when they had assembled with the elders and counseled
together, they gave a large sum of money to the soldiers,
13and said, "You are to say, 'His disciples came by night and
stole Him away while we were asleep.'

*The Resurrection*

28 AFTER THE Sabbath, at dawn on the first day of the week,
Mary Magdalene and the other Mary went to look at the
tomb.
2There was a violent earthquake, for an angel of the Lord came
down from heaven and, going to the tomb, rolled back the stone
and sat on it. 3His appearance was like lightning, and his clothes
were white as snow. 4The guards were so afraid of him that they
shook and became like dead men.
5The angel said to the women, "Do not be afraid, for I know that
you are looking for Jesus, who was crucified. 6He is not here; he
has risen, just as he said. Come and see the place where he lay.
7Then go quickly and tell his disciples: 'He has risen from the dead
and is going ahead of you into Galilee. There you will see him.'
Now I have told you."
8So the women hurried away from the tomb, afraid yet filled
with joy, and ran to tell his disciples. 9Suddenly Jesus met them.
"Greetings," he said. They came to him, clasped his feet and
worshiped him. 10Then Jesus said to them, "Do not be afraid. Go
and tell my brothers to go to Galilee; there they will see me."

*The Guards' Report*

11While the women were on their way, some of the guards went
into the city and reported to the chief priests everything that had
happened. 12When the chief priests had met with the elders and
devised a plan, they gave the soldiers a large sum of money,
13telling them, "You are to say, 'His disciples came during the
night and stole him away while we were asleep.' 14If this report

## King James

14And if this come to the governor's ears, we will persuade him, and secure you.
15So they took the money, and did as they were taught: and this saying is commonly reported among the Jews until this day.
16¶ Then the eleven disciples went away into Galilee, into a mountain where Jesus had appointed them.
17And when they saw him, they worshipped him: but some doubted.
18And Jesus came and spake unto them, saying, All power is given unto me in heaven and in earth.
19¶ Go ye therefore, and teach all nations, baptizing them in the name of the Father, and of the Son, and of the Holy Ghost:
20Teaching them to observe all things whatsoever I have commanded you: and, lo, I am with you always, *even* unto the end of the world. Amen.

## Amplified

14And if the governor hears of it, we will appease him and make you safe *and* free from trouble *and* care.
15So they took the money and did as they were instructed, and this story has been current among the Jews to the present day.
16Now the eleven disciples went to Galilee, to the mountain to which Jesus had directed *and* made appointment with them.
17And when they saw Him they fell down and worshipped Him, but some doubted.
18Jesus approached and [a]breaking the silence said to them, All authority—all power of rule—in heaven and on earth has been given to Me.
19Go then and make disciples of all the nations, baptizing them [b]into the name of the Father and of the Son and of the Holy Spirit;
20Teaching them to observe everything that I have commanded you, and lo, I am with you [c]all the days,—[d]perpetually, uniformly and on every occasion—to the [very] close *and* consummation of the age. *Amen—so let it be.*

AMP [a] Vincent. [b] Vincent. [c] Wycliffe. [d] Webster's definition of "alway."

## New American Standard

14"And if this should come to the governor's ears, we will win him over and keep you out of trouble."

15And they took the money and did as they had been instructed; and this story was widely spread among the Jews, *and is* to this day.

*The Great Commission*

16¶ But the eleven disciples proceeded to Galilee, to the mountain which Jesus had designated.

17And when they saw Him, they worshiped *Him;* but some were doubtful.

18And Jesus came up and spoke to them, saying, "All authority has been given to Me in heaven and on earth.

19"Go therefore and make disciples of all the nations, baptizing them in the name of the Father and the Son and the Holy Spirit,

20teaching them to observe all that I commanded you; and lo, I am with you always, even to the end of the age."

## New International

gets to the governor, we will satisfy him and keep you out of
trouble." 15So the soldiers took the money and did as they were
instructed. And this story has been widely circulated among the
Jews to this very day.

*The Great Commission*

16Then the eleven disciples went to Galilee, to the mountain
where Jesus had told them to go. 17When they saw him, they
worshiped him; but some doubted. 18Then Jesus came to them and
said, "All authority in heaven and on earth has been given to me.
19Therefore go and make disciples of all nations, baptizing them
in[e] the name of the Father and of the Son and of the Holy Spirit,
20and teaching them to obey everything I have commanded you.
And surely I am with you always, to the very end of the age."

**NIV** [e] *19* Or *into;* see Acts 8:16; 19:5; Romans 6:3; 1 Cor. 1:13; 10:2 and Gal. 3:27.

## King James

THE GOSPEL

ACCORDING TO

# St. Mark

1 THE BEGINNING of the gospel of Jesus Christ, the Son of God;

2 As it is written in the prophets, Behold, I send my messenger before thy face, which shall prepare thy way before thee.

3 The voice of one crying in the wilderness, Prepare ye the way of the Lord, make his paths straight.

4 John did baptize in the wilderness, and preach the baptism of repentance for the remission of sins.

5 And there went out unto him all the land of Judaea, and they of Jerusalem, and were all baptized of him in the river of Jordan, confessing their sins.

6 And John was clothed with camel's hair, and with a girdle of a skin about his loins; and he did eat locusts and wild honey;

7 And preached, saying, There cometh one mightier than I after me, the latchet of whose shoes I am not worthy to stoop down and unloose.

8 I indeed have baptized you with water: but he shall baptize you with the Holy Ghost.

9 And it came to pass in those days, that Jesus came from Nazareth of Galilee, and was baptized of John in Jordan.

10 And straightway coming up out of the water, he saw the heavens opened, and the Spirit like a dove descending upon him:

11 And there came a voice from heaven, *saying*, Thou art my beloved Son, in whom I am well pleased.

12 And immediately the Spirit driveth him into the wilderness.

13 And he was there in the wilderness forty days, tempted of Satan; and was with the wild beasts; and the angels ministered unto him.

14 Now after that John was put in prison, Jesus came into Galilee, preaching the gospel of the kingdom of God,

15 And saying, The time is fulfilled, and the kingdom of God is at hand: repent ye, and believe the gospel.

16 Now as he walked by the sea of Galilee, he saw Simon and Andrew his brother casting a net into the sea: for they were fishers.

17 And Jesus said unto them, Come ye after me, and I will make you to become fishers of men.

18 And straightway they forsook their nets, and followed him.

## Amplified

THE GOSPEL

ACCORDING TO

# Mark

1 THE BEGINNING [of the facts] of the good news (the Gospel) of Jesus Christ, *the Son of God*.

2 [a]Just as it is written in the prophet Isaiah: Behold, I send My messenger before Your face, who will make ready Your way; [Mal. 3:1.]

3 A voice of one crying in the wilderness—shouting in the desert—Prepare the way of the Lord, make His [b]beaten-tracks straight (level and passable)! [Isa. 40:3.]

4 John the Baptist appeared in the wilderness (desert), preaching a baptism [[c]obligating] repentance—[that is] [d]a change of one's mind for the better and heartily to amend one's ways with abhorrence of his past sins—in order [e]to obtain forgiveness of *and* release from sins.

5 And there kept going out to him (continuously) all the country of Judea, and all the inhabitants of Jerusalem; and they were baptized by him in the river Jordan, [f]as they were confessing their sins.

6 And John wore clothing woven of camel's hair, and had a leather girdle around his loins, and ate locusts and wild honey.

7 And he preached, saying, After me comes He Who is stronger—more powerful and more valiant—than I, the strap of Whose sandals I am not worthy *or* fit to stoop down and unloose.

8 I have baptized you with water, but He will baptize you with the Holy Spirit.

9 In those days Jesus came from Nazareth of Galilee and was baptized by John in the Jordan.

10 And when He came up out of the water, at once [g]he saw the heavens torn open and the [Holy] Spirit like a dove, coming down [[h]to enter] [i]into Him;

11 And there came a voice [j]out from within heaven, You are My Beloved Son; in You I am well pleased. [Ps. 2:7; Isa. 42:1.]

12 Immediately the [Holy] Spirit [from within] drove Him out into the wilderness (desert).

13 And He stayed in the wilderness (desert) forty days, being tempted [the while] by Satan; and He was with the wild beasts, and the angels ministered to Him (continually).

14 Now after John was arrested *and* put in prison, Jesus came into Galilee, preaching the good news (the Gospel) *of the kingdom* of God,

15 And saying, The [appointed period of] time is (completed) fulfilled, and the kingdom of God is at hand; repent ([k]have a change of mind which issues in regret for past sins and in change of conduct for the better) and believe—trust in, rely on and adhere to the good news—the Gospel.

16 And passing along the shore of the sea of Galilee, He saw Simon [Peter] and Andrew the brother of Simon casting a net (to and fro) in the sea, for they were fishermen.

17 And Jesus said to them, Come after Me *and* [l]be My disciples, and I will make you to become fishers of men.

18 And at once they left their nets *and* [m]yielding up all claim to them followed [with] Him—[n]joining Him as disciples and siding with His party.

**AMP** [a] Wuest's "Mark in the Greek Testament." [b] Moulton and Milligan's "The Vocabulary of the Greek Testament." [c] Wuest's "Mark in the Greek Testament." [d] Thayer's "Greek-English Lexicon of the New Testament—Grimm." [e] Williams' "The New Testament in the Language of the People." [f] Wuest's "Mark in the Greek Testament." [g] John 1:32. [h] Wuest's "Mark in the Greek Testament." [i] Literal translation of "eis." [j] Wuest's "Mark in the Greek Testament." [k] Vincent. [l] Thayer. [m] Thayer. [n] Thayer.

## New American Standard

# Mark

*Preaching of John the Baptist*

1 THE BEGINNING of the gospel of Jesus Christ, [o]the Son of
God.

2¶ As it is written in Isaiah the prophet,
"Behold, I send My messenger before Your face,
Who will prepare Your way;
3 The voice of one crying in the wilderness,
'Make ready the way of the Lord,
Make His paths straight.'"

4John the Baptist appeared in the wilderness [p]preaching a
baptism of repentance for the forgiveness of sins.
5And all the country of Judea was going out to him, and all the
people of Jerusalem; and they were being baptized by him in the
Jordan River, confessing their sins.
6And John was clothed with camel's hair and *wore* a leather belt
around his waist, and his diet was locusts and wild honey.
7And he was preaching, and saying, "After me One is coming
who is mightier than I, and I am not fit to stoop down and untie
the thong of His sandals.
8"I baptized you [q]with water; but He will baptize you [r]with
the Holy Spirit."

*The Baptism of Jesus*

9¶ And it came about in those days that Jesus came from
Nazareth in Galilee, and was baptized by John in the Jordan.
10And immediately coming up out of the water, He saw the
heavens opening, and the Spirit like a dove descending upon Him;
11and a voice came out of the heavens: "Thou art My beloved
Son, in Thee I am well-pleased."
12¶ And immediately the Spirit *impelled Him *to go* out into the
wilderness.
13And He was in the wilderness forty days being tempted by
Satan; and He was with the wild beasts, and the angels were
ministering to Him.

*Jesus Preaches in Galilee*

14¶ And after John had been taken into custody, Jesus came into
Galilee, preaching the gospel of God,
15and saying, "The time is fulfilled, and the kingdom of God is
at hand; repent and believe in the gospel."
16¶ And as He was going along by the Sea of Galilee, He saw
Simon and Andrew, the brother of Simon, casting a net in the sea;
for they were fishermen.
17And Jesus said to them, "Follow Me, and I will make you
become fishers of men."
18And they immediately left the nets and followed Him.

**NAS** [o] Many mss. do not contain *the Son of God* [p] Or, *proclaiming* [q] The Gr. here can be translated *in, with* or *by* [r] The Gr. here can be translated *in, with* or *by*

## New International

# Mark

*John the Baptist Prepares the Way*

1 THE BEGINNING of the gospel about Jesus Christ, the Son
of God.[s]

2It is written in Isaiah the prophet:
"I will send my messenger ahead of you,
who will prepare your way"[t] —
3"a voice of one calling in the desert,
'Prepare the way for the Lord,
make straight paths for him.'"[u]

4And so John came, baptizing in the desert region and preaching
a baptism of repentance for the forgiveness of sins. 5The whole
Judean countryside and all the people of Jerusalem went out to
him. Confessing their sins, they were baptized by him in the
Jordan River. 6John wore clothing made of camel's hair, with a
leather belt around his waist, and he ate locusts and wild honey.
7And this was his message: "After me will come one more powerful than I, the thongs of whose sandals I am not worthy to stoop
down and untie. 8I baptize you with[v] water, but he will baptize
you with the Holy Spirit."

*The Baptism and Temptation of Jesus*

9At that time Jesus came from Nazareth in Galilee and was
baptized by John in the Jordan. 10As Jesus was coming up out of
the water, he saw heaven being torn open and the Spirit descending on him like a dove. 11And a voice came from heaven: "You are
my Son, whom I love; with you I am well pleased."
12At once the Spirit sent him out into the desert, 13and he was
in the desert forty days, being tempted by Satan. He was with the
wild animals, and angels attended him.

*The Calling of the First Disciples*

14After John was put in prison, Jesus went into Galilee, proclaiming the good news of God. 15"The time has come," he said.
"The kingdom of God is near. Repent and believe the good news!"
16As Jesus walked beside the Sea of Galilee, he saw Simon and
his brother Andrew casting a net into the lake, for they were
fishermen. 17"Come, follow me," Jesus said, "and I will make you
fishers of men." 18At once they left their nets and followed him.

**NIV** [s] *1* Some manuscripts do not have *the Son of God.* [t] 2 Mal. 3:1 [u] 3 Isaiah 40:3 [v] *8* Or *in*

## King James

19 And when he had gone a little farther thence, he saw James the *son* of Zebedee, and John his brother, who also were in the ship mending their nets.

20 And straightway he called them: and they left their father Zebedee in the ship with the hired servants, and went after him.

21 And they went into Capernaum; and straightway on the sabbath day he entered into the synagogue, and taught.

22 And they were astonished at his doctrine: for he taught them as one that had authority, and not as the scribes.

23 And there was in their synagogue a man with an unclean spirit; and he cried out,

24 Saying, Let *us* alone; what have we to do with thee, thou Jesus of Nazareth? art thou come to destroy us? I know thee who thou art, the Holy One of God.

25 And Jesus rebuked him, saying, Hold thy peace, and come out of him.

26 And when the unclean spirit had torn him, and cried with a loud voice, he came out of him.

27 And they were all amazed, insomuch that they questioned among themselves, saying, What thing is this? what new doctrine *is* this? for with authority commandeth he even the unclean spirits, and they do obey him.

28 And immediately his fame spread abroad throughout all the region round about Galilee.

29 And forthwith, when they were come out of the synagogue, they entered into the house of Simon and Andrew, with James and John.

30 But Simon's wife's mother lay sick of a fever, and anon they tell him of her.

31 And he came and took her by the hand, and lifted her up; and immediately the fever left her, and she ministered unto them.

32 And at even, when the sun did set, they brought unto him all that were diseased, and them that were possessed with devils.

33 And all the city was gathered together at the door.

34 And he healed many that were sick of divers diseases, and cast out many devils; and suffered not the devils to speak, because they knew him.

35 And in the morning, rising up a great while before day, he went out, and departed into a solitary place, and there prayed.

36 And Simon and they that were with him followed after him.

37 And when they had found him, they said unto him, All *men* seek for thee.

38 And he said unto them, Let us go into the next towns, that I may preach there also: for therefore came I forth.

39 And he preached in their synagogues throughout all Galilee, and cast out devils.

40 And there came a leper to him, beseeching him, and kneeling down to him, and saying unto him, If thou wilt, thou canst make me clean.

41 And Jesus, moved with compassion, put forth *his* hand, and touched him, and saith unto him, I will; be thou clean.

42 And as soon as he had spoken, immediately the leprosy departed from him, and he was cleansed.

43 And he straitly charged him, and forthwith sent him away;

44 And saith unto him, See thou say nothing to any man: but go thy way, show thyself to the priest, and offer for thy cleansing those things which Moses commanded, for a testimony unto them.

45 But he went out, and began to publish *it* much, and to blaze abroad the matter, insomuch that Jesus could no more openly enter into the city, but was without in desert places: and they came to him from every quarter.

## Amplified

19 He went on a little farther and saw James the [son] of Zebedee and John his brother, who were in [their] boat putting their nets in order.

20 And immediately He called out to them, and [ [a]abandoning all mutual claims] they left their father Zebedee in the boat with the hired men, and went off after Him— [b]to be His disciples, side with His party and follow Him.

21 And they entered into Capernaum, and immediately on the Sabbath He went into the synagogue and began to teach.

22 And they were completely astonished at His teaching, for He was teaching as one who possessed authority, and not as the scribes.

23 Just at that time there was in their synagogue a man [who was in the power] of an unclean spirit; and now immediately he raised a deep *and* terrible cry from the depths of his throat, saying,

24 What have You to do with us, Jesus of Nazareth? Have You come to destroy us? I know who You are, the Holy [One] of God!

25 And Jesus rebuked him, saying, Hush up (be muzzled, gagged), and come out of him!

26 And the unclean spirit, throwing the man into convulsions and [c]screeching with a loud voice, came out of him.

27 And they were all so amazed *and* [d]almost terrified that they kept questioning *and* demanding one of another, saying, What is this? What new (fresh) teaching! With authority He gives orders even to the unclean spirits and they obey Him!

28 And immediately rumors concerning Him spread [everywhere] throughout all the region surrounding Galilee.

29 And at once He left the synagogue and went into the house of Simon [Peter] and Andrew, accompained by James and John.

30 Now Simon's mother-in-law [e]had for some time been lying sick with a fever, and at once they told Him about her.

31 And He went up to her, and took her by the hand, and raised her up; and the fever left her, and she began to wait on them.

32 Now when it was evening, after the sun had set, they brought to Him all who were sick and those under the power of demons,

33 Until the whole town was gathered together about the door.

34 And He cured many who were afflicted with various diseases, and He drove out many demons; and would not allow the demons to talk, because they knew Him [ [f]intuitively].

35 And in the morning, long before daylight, He got up and went out to a [g]deserted place, and there He prayed.

36 And Simon [Peter] and those who were with him followed Him— [h]pursuing Him eagerly and hunting Him out;

37 And they found Him, and said to Him, Everybody is looking for You.

38 And He said to them, Let us be going on into the neighboring country towns, that I may preach there also, for that is why I came out.

39 [So] He went throughout the whole of Galilee, preaching in their synagogues and driving out demons.

40 And a leper came to Him, begging Him on his knees and saying to Him, If You will, You are able to make me clean.

41 And being moved with pity *and* sympathy, Jesus reached out His hand and touched him, and said to him, I will; be made clean!

42 And at once the leprosy [completely] left him, and he was made clean (by being healed).

43 And Jesus charged him sternly (sharply and threateningly, and with earnest admonition), and (acting with deep feeling thrust him forth and) sent him away at once;

44 And said to him, See that you tell nothing [of this] to any one; but begone, show yourself to the priest, and offer for your purification what Moses commanded, as a proof (an evidence and witness) to the people [that you are really healed]. [Lev. 13:49; 14:2-32.]

45 But he went out and began to talk so freely about it and blaze abroad the news (spreading it everywhere), that [Jesus] could no longer openly go into a town, but was outside in (lonely) desert places. But the people kept on coming to Him from [i]all sides *and* every quarter.

**AMP** [a] Thayer. [b] Thayer. [c] Robertson's "Word Pictures in the New Testament." [d] Souter's "Pocket Lexicon to the Greek New Testament." [e] Wuest. [f] Williams. [g] Moulton and Milligan. [h] Vincent. [i] Moulton and Milligan.

## New American Standard

19And going on a little farther, He saw James the *son* of Zebedee, and John his brother, who were also in the boat mending the nets.
20And immediately He called them; and they left their father Zebedee in the boat with the hired servants, and went away to follow Him.
21¶ And they *went into Capernaum; and immediately on the Sabbath He entered the synagogue and *began* to teach.
22And they were amazed at His teaching; for He was teaching them as *one* having authority, and not as the scribes.
23And just then there was in their synagogue a man with an unclean spirit; and he cried out,
24saying, "What do we have to do with You, Jesus [j]of Nazareth? Have You come to destroy us? I know who You are—the Holy One of God!"
25And Jesus rebuked him, saying, "Be quiet, and come out of him!"
26And throwing him into convulsions, the unclean spirit cried out with a loud voice, and came out of him.
27And they were all amazed, so that they debated among themselves, saying, "What is this? A new teaching with authority! He commands even the unclean spirits, and they obey Him."
28And immediately the news about Him went out everywhere into all the surrounding district of Galilee.

*Multitudes Healed*

29¶ And immediately after they had come out of the synagogue, they came into the house of Simon and Andrew, with James and John.
30Now Simon's mother-in-law was lying sick with a fever; and immediately they *spoke to Him about her.
31And He came to her and raised her up, taking her by the hand, and the fever left her, and she [k]waited on them.
32¶ And when evening had come, after the sun had set, they *began* bringing to Him all who were ill and those who were demon-possessed.
33And the whole city had gathered at the door.
34And He healed many who were ill with various diseases, and cast out many demons; and He was not permitting the demons to speak, because they [l]knew who He was.
35¶ And in the early morning, while it was still dark, He arose and went out and departed to a lonely place, and was praying there.
36And Simon and his companions hunted for Him;
37and they found Him, and *said to Him, "Everyone is looking for You."
38And He *said to them, "Let us go somewhere else to the towns nearby, in order that I may preach there also; for that is what I came out for."
39And He went into their synagogues throughout all Galilee, preaching and casting out the demons.
40¶ And a leper *came to Him, beseeching Him and falling on his knees before Him, and saying to Him, "If You are willing, You can make me clean."
41And moved with compassion, He stretched out His hand, and touched him, and *said to him, "I am willing; be cleansed."
42And immediately the leprosy left him and he was cleansed.
43And He sternly warned him and immediately sent him away,
44and He *said to him, "See that you say nothing to anyone; but go, show yourself to the priest and offer for your cleansing what Moses commanded, for a testimony to them."
45But he went out and began to proclaim it freely and to spread the news about, to such an extent that Jesus could no longer publicly enter a city, but [m]stayed out in unpopulated areas; and they were coming to Him from everywhere.

NAS [j] Lit., *the Nazarene* [k] Or, *served* [l] Some mss. read: *knew Him to be Christ* [m] Lit., *was*

## New International

19When he had gone a little farther, he saw James son of Zebedee and his brother John in a boat, preparing their nets. 20Without
delay he called them, and they left their father Zebedee in the boat
with the hired men and followed him.

*Jesus Drives Out an Evil Spirit*

21They went to Capernaum, and when the Sabbath came, Jesus
went into the synagogue and began to teach. 22The people were
amazed at his teaching, because he taught them as one who had
authority, not as the teachers of the law. 23Just then a man in their
synagogue who was possessed by an evil[n] spirit cried out,
24"What do you want with us, Jesus of Nazareth? Have you come
to destroy us? I know who you are—the Holy One of God!"
25"Be quiet!" said Jesus sternly. "Come out of him!" 26The evil
spirit shook the man violently and came out of him with a shriek.
27The people were all so amazed that they asked each other,
"What is this? A new teaching—and with authority! He even gives
orders to evil spirits and they obey him." 28News about him spread
quickly over the whole region of Galilee.

*Jesus Heals Many*

29As soon as they left the synagogue, they went with James and
John to the home of Simon and Andrew. 30Simon's mother-in-law
was in bed with a fever, and they told Jesus about her. 31So he
went to her, took her hand and helped her up. The fever left her
and she began to wait on them.
32That evening after sunset the people brought to Jesus all the
sick and demon-possessed. 33The whole town gathered at the
door, 34and Jesus healed many who had various diseases. He also
drove out many demons, but he would not let the demons speak
because they knew who he was.

*Jesus Prays in a Solitary Place*

35Very early in the morning, while it was still dark, Jesus got
up, left the house and went off to a solitary place, where he
prayed. 36Simon and his companions went to look for him, 37and
when they found him, they exclaimed: "Everyone is looking for
you!"
38Jesus replied, "Let us go somewhere else—to the nearby villages—so I can preach there also. That is why I have come." 39So
he traveled throughout Galilee, preaching in their synagogues and
driving out demons.

*A Man With Leprosy*

40A man with leprosy[o] came to him and begged him on his
knees, "If you are willing, you can make me clean."
41Filled with compassion, Jesus reached out his hand and
touched the man. "I am willing," he said. "Be clean!" 42Immedi-
ately the leprosy left him and he was cured.
43Jesus sent him away at once with a strong warning: 44"See
that you don't tell this to anyone. But go, show yourself to the
priest and offer the sacrifices that Moses commanded for your
cleansing, as a testimony to them." 45Instead he went out and
began to talk freely, spreading the news. As a result, Jesus could
no longer enter a town openly but stayed outside in lonely places.
Yet the people still came to him from everywhere.

NIV [n] 23 Greek *unclean;* also in verses 26 and 27 [o] 40 The Greek word was used for various diseases affecting the skin—not necessarily leprosy.

## King James

**2** AND AGAIN he entered into Capernaum after *some* days; and it was noised that he was in the house.

2And straightway many were gathered together, insomuch that there was no room to receive *them*, no, not so much as about the door: and he preached the word unto them.

3And they come unto him, bringing one sick of the palsy, which was borne of four.

4And when they could not come nigh unto him for the press, they uncovered the roof where he was: and when they had broken *it* up, they let down the bed wherein the sick of the palsy lay.

5When Jesus saw their faith, he said unto the sick of the palsy, Son, thy sins be forgiven thee.

6But there were certain of the scribes sitting there, and reasoning in their hearts,

7Why doth this *man* thus speak blasphemies? who can forgive sins but God only?

8And immediately when Jesus perceived in his spirit that they so reasoned within themselves, he said unto them, Why reason ye these things in your hearts?

9Whether is it easier to say to the sick of the palsy, *Thy* sins be forgiven thee; or to say, Arise, and take up thy bed, and walk?

10But that ye may know that the Son of man hath power on earth to forgive sins, (he saith to the sick of the palsy,)

11I say unto thee, Arise, and take up thy bed, and go thy way into thine house.

12And immediately he arose, took up the bed, and went forth before them all; insomuch that they were all amazed, and glorified God, saying, We never saw it on this fashion.

13And he went forth again by the sea side; and all the multitude resorted unto him, and he taught them.

14And as he passed by, he saw Levi the *son* of Alphaeus sitting at the receipt of custom, and said unto him, Follow me. And he arose and followed him.

15And it came to pass, that, as Jesus sat at meat in his house, many publicans and sinners sat also together with Jesus and his disciples: for there were many, and they followed him.

16And when the scribes and Pharisees saw him eat with publicans and sinners, they said unto his disciples, How is it that he eateth and drinketh with publicans and sinners?

17When Jesus heard *it*, he saith unto them, They that are whole have no need of the physician, but they that are sick: I came not to call the righteous, but sinners to repentance.

18And the disciples of John and of the Pharisees used to fast: and they come and say unto him, Why do the disciples of John and of the Pharisees fast, but thy disciples fast not?

19And Jesus said unto them, Can the children of the bridechamber fast, while the bridegroom is with them? as long as they have the bridegroom with them, they cannot fast.

20But the days will come, when the bridegroom shall be taken away from them, and then shall they fast in those days.

## Amplified

**2** AND JESUS having returned to Capernaum, after some days it was rumored about that He was in the house [Peter's, probably].

2And so many people gathered together there that there was no longer room [for them], not even around the door; and He was discussing the Word.

3Then they came bringing a paralytic to Him, who had been picked up *and* was being carried by four men.

4And when they could not get him to a place in front of Jesus because of the throng, they dug through the roof above Him; and when they had [a]scooped out an opening, they let down the ([b]thickly padded) quilt *or* mat upon which the paralyzed man lay.

5And when Jesus saw their faith [that is, their confidence in God through Him], He said to the paralyzed man, Son, your sins are forgiven [you] *and* put away—[that is,] the [c]penalty is remitted, the sense of guilt removed, and you are made upright and in right standing with God.

6Now some of the scribes were sitting there, holding a dialogue with themselves as they questioned in their hearts,

7Why does this [d]Man talk like this? He is blaspheming! Who can forgive sins—[that is] [e]remove guilt, remit the penalty and bestow righteousness instead—except God alone?

8And at once Jesus, becoming fully aware in His spirit that they thus debated within themselves, said to them, Why do you argue (debate, reason) about all this in your hearts?

9Which is easier, to say to the paralyzed man, Your sins are forgiven *and* [f]put away, or to say, Rise, take up your sleeping pad and start walking about—and [g]keep on walking?

10But that you may know positively *and* beyond a doubt that the Son of man has right *and* authority *and* power on earth to forgive sins, He said to the paralyzed man,

11I say to you, arise, pick up *and* carry your sleeping pad and be going on home.

12And he arose at once and picked up the pallet and went out before them all; so that they were all amazed and [h]recognized *and* praised *and* thanked God, saying, We have never seen anything like this before!

13[Jesus] went out again along the seashore, and all the multitude kept gathering about Him, and He kept teaching them.

14And as He was passing by, He saw Levi [Matthew] the son of Alphaeus sitting at the tax office, and He said to him, (Be [i]joined to Me as a disciple, side with My party and) follow Me! And he arose and joined Him as His disciple *and* sided with His party *and* accompanied Him.

15And as Jesus together with His disciples sat at table in his [Levi's] house, many tax collectors and persons ([j]definitely stained) with sin were dining with Him, for there were many who walked the same road (followed) with Him.

16And the scribes (belonging to the party) of the Pharisees, when they saw that He was eating with (those [k]definitely known to be especially wicked) sinners and tax collectors, said to His disciples, Why does He eat *and drink* with tax collectors and (notorious) sinners?

17And when Jesus heard it, He said to them, Those who are strong *and* well have no need of a physician, but those who are weak *and* sick; I came not to call the righteous ones *to repentance*, but sinners—the [l]erring ones and [m]all those not free from sin.

18Now John's disciples and the Pharisees were observing a fast, and [some people] came and asked Jesus, Why are John's disciples and the disciples of the Pharisees fasting, but Your disciples are not doing so?

19Jesus answered them, Can the wedding guests fast (abstain from food and drink) while the bridegroom is with them? As long as they have the bridegroom with them they cannot fast.

20But the days will come when the bridegroom is taken away from them, and they will fast in that day.

**AMP** [a] Vincent. [b] Vincent. [c] Wuest. [d] Capitalized because of what He is, the spotless Son of God, not for what the speakers may have thought He was. [e] Wuest. [f] Wuest. [g] Wuest. [h] Cremer's "Biblico—Theological Lexicon of New Testament Greek." [i] Thayer. [j] Thayer. [k] Thayer. [l] Young's Concordance. [m] Thayer.

## New American Standard

*The Paralytic Healed*

**2** AND WHEN He had come back to Capernaum several days
afterward, it was heard that He was at home.
2And many were gathered together, so that there was no
longer room, even near the door; and He was speaking the word
to them.
3And they *came, bringing to Him a paralytic, carried by four
men.
4And being unable to get to Him because of the crowd, they
removed the roof above Him; and when they had dug an opening,
they let down the pallet on which the paralytic was lying.
5And Jesus seeing their faith *said to the paralytic, "My [n]son,
your sins are forgiven."
6But there were some of the scribes sitting there and reasoning
in their hearts,
7"Why does this man speak that way? He is blaspheming; who
can forgive sins but God alone?"
8And immediately Jesus, aware in His spirit that they were
reasoning that way within themselves, *said to them, "Why are
you reasoning about these things in your hearts?
9"Which is easier, to say to the paralytic, 'Your sins are forgiven'; or to say, 'Arise, and take up your pallet and walk'?
10"But in order that you may know that the Son of Man has
authority on earth to forgive sins"—He *said to the paralytic—
11"I say to you, rise, take up your pallet and go home."
12And he rose and immediately took up the pallet and went out
in the sight of all; so that they were all amazed and were glorifying
God, saying, "We have never seen anything like this."
**13**¶ And He went out again by the seashore; and all the multitude were coming to Him, and He was teaching them.

*Levi (Matthew) Called*

14And as He passed by, He saw Levi the *son* of Alphaeus sitting
in the tax office, and He *said to him, "Follow Me!" And he rose
and followed Him.
**15**¶ And it came about that He was reclining *at the table* in his
house, and many tax-gatherers and sinners were dining with Jesus
and His disciples; for there were many of them, and they were
following Him.
16And when the scribes of the Pharisees saw that He was eating
with the sinners and tax-gatherers, they *began* saying to His disciples, "Why is He eating and drinking with tax-gatherers and sinners?"
17And hearing this, Jesus *said to them, "*It is* not those who
are healthy who need a physician, but those who are sick; I did not
come to call the righteous, but sinners."
**18**¶ And John's disciples and the Pharisees were fasting; and
they *came and *said to Him, "Why do John's disciples and the
disciples of the Pharisees fast, but Your disciples do not fast?"
19And Jesus said to them, "While the bridegroom is with them,
the attendants of the bridegroom do not fast, do they? So long as
they have the bridegroom with them, they cannot fast.
20"But the days will come when the bridegroom is taken away
from them, and then they will fast in that day.

NAS [n] Lit., *child*

## New International

*Jesus Heals a Paralytic*

**2** A FEW days later, when Jesus again entered Capernaum, the
people heard that he had come home. 2So many gathered that
there was no room left, not even outside the door, and he preached
the word to them. 3Some men came, bringing to him a paralytic,
carried by four of them. 4Since they could not get him to Jesus
because of the crowd, they made an opening in the roof above
Jesus and, after digging through it, lowered the mat the paralyzed
man was lying on. 5When Jesus saw their faith, he said to the
paralytic, "Son, your sins are forgiven."
6Now some teachers of the law were sitting there, thinking to
themselves, 7"Why does this fellow talk like that? He's blaspheming! Who can forgive sins but God alone?"
8Immediately Jesus knew in his spirit that this was what they
were thinking in their hearts, and he said to them, "Why are you
thinking these things? 9Which is easier: to say to the paralytic,
'Your sins are forgiven,' or to say, 'Get up, take your mat and
walk'? 10But that you may know that the Son of Man has authority
on earth to forgive sins . . . ." He said to the paralytic, 11"I tell you,
get up, take your mat and go home." 12He got up, took his mat
and walked out in full view of them all. This amazed everyone and
they praised God, saying, "We have never seen anything like
this!"

*The Calling of Levi*

13Once again Jesus went out beside the lake. A large crowd
came to him, and he began to teach them. 14As he walked along,
he saw Levi son of Alphaeus sitting at the tax collector's booth.
"Follow me," Jesus told him, and Levi got up and followed him.
15While Jesus was having dinner at Levi's house, many tax
collectors and "sinners" were eating with him and his disciples,
for there were many who followed him. 16When the teachers of the
law who were Pharisees saw him eating with the "sinners" and tax
collectors, they asked his disciples: "Why does he eat with tax
collectors and 'sinners'?"
17On hearing this, Jesus said to them, "It is not the healthy who
need a doctor, but the sick. I have not come to call the righteous,
but sinners."

*Jesus Questioned About Fasting*

18Now John's disciples and the Pharisees were fasting. Some
people came and asked Jesus, "How is it that John's disciples and
the disciples of the Pharisees are fasting, but yours are not?"
19Jesus answered, "How can the guests of the bridegroom fast
while he is with them? They cannot, so long as they have him with
them. 20But the time will come when the bridegroom will be taken
from them, and on that day they will fast.

## King James

21No man also seweth a piece of new cloth on an old garment: else the new piece that filled it up taketh away from the old, and the rent is made worse.

22And no man putteth new wine into old bottles: else the new wine doth burst the bottles, and the wine is spilled, and the bottles will be marred: but new wine must be put into new bottles.

23And it came to pass, that he went through the corn fields on the sabbath day; and his disciples began, as they went, to pluck the ears of corn.

24And the Pharisees said unto him, Behold, why do they on the sabbath day that which is not lawful?

25And he said unto them, Have ye never read what David did, when he had need, and was an hungered, he, and they that were with him?

26How he went into the house of God in the days of Abiathar the high priest, and did eat the showbread, which is not lawful to eat but for the priests, and gave also to them which were with him?

27And he said unto them, The sabbath was made for man, and not man for the sabbath:

28Therefore the Son of man is Lord also of the sabbath.

**3** AND HE entered again into the synagogue; and there was a man there which had a withered hand.

2And they watched him, whether he would heal him on the sabbath day; that they might accuse him.

3And he saith unto the man which had the withered hand, Stand forth.

4And he saith unto them, Is it lawful to do good on the sabbath days, or to do evil? to save life, or to kill? But they held their peace.

5And when he had looked round about on them with anger, being grieved for the hardness of their hearts, he saith unto the man, Stretch forth thine hand. And he stretched *it* out: and his hand was restored whole as the other.

6And the Pharisees went forth, and straightway took counsel with the Herodians against him, how they might destroy him.

7But Jesus withdrew himself with his disciples to the sea: and a great multitude from Galilee followed him, and from Judaea,

8And from Jerusalem, and from Idumaea, and *from* beyond Jordan; and they about Tyre and Sidon, a great multitude, when they had heard what great things he did, came unto him.

9And he spake to his disciples, that a small ship should wait on him because of the multitude, lest they should throng him.

10For he had healed many; insomuch that they pressed upon him for to touch him, as many as had plagues.

11And unclean spirits, when they saw him, fell down before him, and cried, saying, Thou art the Son of God.

12And he straitly charged them that they should not make him known.

13And he goeth up into a mountain, and calleth *unto him* whom he would: and they came unto him.

14And he ordained twelve, that they should be with him, and that he might send them forth to preach,

15And to have power to heal sicknesses, and to cast out devils:

16And Simon he surnamed Peter;

## Amplified

21No one sews a patch of (new) unshrunken goods on an old garment; if he does, the patch tears away from it, the new from the old, and the rent becomes bigger *and* worse [than it was before].

22And no one puts new wine into old wineskins; if he does, the wine will burst the skins, and the wine is lost and the bottles destroyed; *but new wine is to be put in new (fresh) wineskins.*

23One Sabbath He was going along beside the fields of standing grain; and as they made their way, His disciples began to [a]pick off the grains. [Deut. 23:25.]

24And the Pharisees said to Him, Look! Why are they doing what is not permitted *or* lawful on the Sabbath?

25And He said to them, Have you never [even] read what David did, when he was in need and was hungry, he and those who were accompanying him?

26How he went into the house of God, when Abiathar was the high priest, and ate the sacred loaves set forth [before God], which it is not permitted *or* lawful for any but the priests to eat, and [how he] also gave [them] to those who were with him? [I Sam. 21:1-6; II Sam. 8:17.]

27And Jesus said to them, The Sabbath was made on account *and* for the sake of man, not man for the Sabbath; [Exod. 23:12; Deut. 5:14.]

28So the Son of man is Lord even of the Sabbath.

**3** AGAIN JESUS went into a synagogue, and a man was there who had one withered hand ([b]as the result of accident or disease).

2And [the Pharisees] kept watching Jesus (closely), to see whether He would cure on the Sabbath, so that they might get a charge to bring against Him ([c]formally).

3And He said to the man that had the withered hand, Get up [and stand here] in the midst.

4And He said to them, Is it lawful *and* right on the Sabbath to do good or to do evil, to save life or to take it? But they kept silence.

5And He glanced around at them with vexation *and* anger, grieved at the hardening of their hearts, and said to the man, Hold out your hand. He held it out, and his hand was (completely) restored.

6Then the Pharisees went out and immediately held a consultation with the Herodians against Him, how they might (devise some means to) put Him to death.

7And Jesus retired with His disciples to the lake, and a great throng from Galilee followed Him. Also from Judea

8And from Jerusalem and Idumea and from beyond the Jordan and from about Tyre and Sidon a vast multitude, hearing all the many things that He was doing, came to Him.

9And He told His disciples to have a little boat in [constant] readiness for Him because of the crowd, lest they press hard upon Him *and* crush Him;

10For He had healed so many that all who had distressing bodily diseases kept falling upon Him *and* pressing upon Him in order that they might touch Him.

11And the spirits, the unclean ones, [d]as often as they might see Him, fell down before Him and kept screaming out, You are the Son of God!

12And He charged them strictly *and* severely under penalty again *and* again that they should not make Him known.

13And He went up on the hillside, and called to Him ([e]for Himself those) whom He wanted *and* chose, and they came to Him.

14And He appointed twelve to [f]continue to be with Him, and that He might send them out to preach (as apostles),

15And to have authority *and* power to *heal the sick and to* drive out demons.

16[They were] Simon, and He surnamed [him] Peter;

**AMP** [a] Wuest. [b] Vincent. [c] Wuest. [d] Vincent. [e] Wuest. [f] Wuest.

## New American Standard

21"No one sews a patch of unshrunk cloth on an old garment;
otherwise the patch pulls away from it, the new from the old, and
a worse tear results.
22"And no one puts new wine into old wineskins; otherwise the
wine will burst the skins, and the wine is lost, and the skins *as well;*
but *one puts* new wine into fresh wineskins."

*Question of the Sabbath*

23¶ And it came about that He was passing through the grainfields on the Sabbath, and His disciples began to make their way
along while picking the heads *of grain.*
24And the Pharisees were saying to Him, "See here, why are
they doing what is not lawful on the Sabbath?"
25And He *said to them, "Have you never read what David did
when he was in need and became hungry, he and his companions:
26how he entered the house of God in the time of Abiathar *the*
high priest, and ate the consecrated bread, which is not lawful for
*anyone* to eat except the priests, and he gave *it* also to those who
were with him?"
27And He was saying to them, "The Sabbath was made for man,
and not man for the Sabbath.
28"Consequently, the Son of Man is Lord even of the Sabbath."

*Jesus Heals on the Sabbath*

3 AND HE entered again into a synagogue; and a man was
there with a withered hand.
2And they were watching Him *to see* if He would heal him on
the Sabbath, in order that they might accuse Him.
3And He *said to the man with the withered hand, "Rise and
*come* forward!"
4And He *said to them, "Is it lawful on the Sabbath to do good
or to do harm, to save a life or to kill?" But they kept silent.
5And after looking around at them with anger, grieved at their
hardness of heart, He *said to the man, "Stretch out your hand."
And he stretched it out, and his hand was restored.
6And the Pharisees went out and immediately *began* taking
counsel with the Herodians against Him, *as to* how they might
destroy Him.
7¶ And Jesus withdrew to the sea with His disciples; and a
great multitude from Galilee followed; and *also* from Judea,
8and from Jerusalem, and from Idumea, and beyond the Jordan, and the vicinity of Tyre and Sidon, a great multitude heard
of all that He was doing and came to Him.
9And He told His disciples that a boat should stand ready for
Him because of the multitude, in order that they might not crowd
Him;
10for He had healed many, with the result that all those who
had afflictions pressed about Him in order to touch Him.
11And whenever the unclean spirits beheld Him, they would
fall down before Him and cry out, saying, "You are the Son of
God!"
12And He earnestly warned them not to make Him known.

*The Twelve Are Chosen*

13¶ And He *went up to the mountain and *summoned those
whom He Himself wanted, and they came to Him.
14And He appointed twelve [g], that they might be with Him, and
that He might send them out to preach,
15and to have authority to cast out the demons.
16And He appointed the twelve: Simon (to whom He gave the
name Peter),

NAS [g] Some early mss. add: *whom He named apostles*

## New International

21"No one sews a patch of unshrunk cloth on an old garment.
If he does, the new piece will pull away from the old, making the
tear worse. 22And no one pours new wine into old wineskins. If
he does, the wine will burst the skins, and both the wine and the
wineskins will be ruined. No, he pours new wine into new wineskins."

*Lord of the Sabbath*

23One Sabbath Jesus was going through the grainfields, and as
his disciples walked along, they began to pick some heads of grain.
24The Pharisees said to him, "Look, why are they doing what is
unlawful on the Sabbath?"
25He answered, "Have you never read what David did when
he and his companions were hungry and in need? 26In the days
of Abiathar the high priest, he entered the house of God and ate
the consecrated bread, which is lawful only for priests to eat. And
he also gave some to his companions."
27Then he said to them, "The Sabbath was made for man, not
man for the Sabbath. 28So the Son of Man is Lord even of the
Sabbath."

3 ANOTHER TIME he went into the synagogue, and a man
with a shriveled hand was there. 2Some of them were looking
for a reason to accuse Jesus, so they watched him closely to see if
he would heal him on the Sabbath. 3Jesus said to the man with the
shriveled hand, "Stand up in front of everyone."
4Then Jesus asked them, "Which is lawful on the Sabbath: to
do good or to do evil, to save life or to kill?" But they remained
silent.
5He looked around at them in anger and, deeply distressed at
their stubborn hearts, said to the man, "Stretch out your hand."
He stretched it out, and his hand was completely restored. 6Then
the Pharisees went out and began to plot with the Herodians how
they might kill Jesus.

*Crowds Follow Jesus*

7Jesus withdrew with his disciples to the lake, and a large crowd
from Galilee followed. 8When they heard all he was doing, many
people came to him from Judea, Jerusalem, Idumea, and the regions across the Jordan and around Tyre and Sidon. 9Because of
the crowd he told his disciples to have a small boat ready for him,
to keep the people from crowding him. 10For he had healed many,
so that those with diseases were pushing forward to touch him.
11Whenever the evil[h] spirits saw him, they fell down before him
and cried out, "You are the Son of God." 12But he gave them strict
orders not to tell who he was.

*The Appointing of the Twelve Apostles*

13Jesus went up on a mountainside and called to him those he
wanted, and they came to him. 14He appointed twelve—designating them apostles[i] —that they might be with him and that he
might send them out to preach 15and to have authority to drive out
demons. 16These are the twelve he appointed: Simon (to whom he
gave the name Peter); 17James son of Zebedee and his brother John

NIV [h] 11 Greek *unclean;* also in verse 30 [i] 14 Some manuscripts do not have *designating them apostles.*

## King James

17And James the *son* of Zebedee, and John the brother of James;
and he surnamed them Boanerges, which is, The sons of thunder:
18And Andrew, and Philip, and Bartholomew, and Matthew,
and Thomas, and James the *son* of Alphaeus, and Thaddaeus, and
Simon the Canaanite,
19And Judas Iscariot, which also betrayed him: and they went
into an house.
20And the multitude cometh together again, so that they could
not so much as eat bread.
21And when his friends heard *of it*, they went out to lay hold
on him: for they said, He is beside himself.
22¶ And the scribes which came down from Jerusalem said, He
hath Beelzebub, and by the prince of the devils casteth he out
devils.
23And he called them *unto him*, and said unto them in parables,
How can Satan cast out Satan?
24And if a kingdom be divided against itself, that kingdom
cannot stand.
25And if a house be divided against itself, that house cannot
stand.
26And if Satan rise up against himself, and be divided, he
cannot stand, but hath an end.
27No man can enter into a strong man's house, and spoil his
goods, except he will first bind the strong man; and then he will
spoil his house.
28Verily I say unto you, All sins shall be forgiven unto the sons
of men, and blasphemies wherewith soever they shall blaspheme:
29But he that shall blaspheme against the Holy Ghost hath
never forgiveness, but is in danger of eternal damnation:
30Because they said, He hath an unclean spirit.
31¶ There came then his brethren and his mother, and, standing
without, sent unto him, calling him.
32And the multitude sat about him, and they said unto him,
Behold, thy mother and thy brethren without seek for thee.
33And he answered them, saying, Who is my mother, or my
brethren?
34And he looked round about on them which sat about him,
and said, Behold my mother and my brethren!
35For whosoever shall do the will of God, the same is my brother, and my sister, and mother.

4 AND HE began again to teach by the sea side: and there was
gathered unto him a great multitude, so that he entered into
a ship, and sat in the sea; and the whole multitude was by the sea
on the land.
2And he taught them many things by parables, and said unto
them in his doctrine,
3Hearken; Behold, there went out a sower to sow:
4And it came to pass, as he sowed, some fell by the way side,
and the fowls of the air came and devoured it up.
5And some fell on stony ground, where it had not much earth;
and immediately it sprang up, because it had no depth of earth:
6But when the sun was up, it was scorched; and because it had
no root, it withered away.
7And some fell among thorns, and the thorns grew up, and
choked it, and it yielded no fruit.

## Amplified

17James the son of Zebedee and John the brother of James, and
He surnamed them Boanerges, that is, Sons of Thunder; and
18Andrew, and Philip, and Bartholomew [Nathaniel], and Matthew, and Thomas, and James the son of Alphaeus, and Thaddaeus [Judas, not Iscariot], and Simon the Cananaean [also called
Zelotes],
19And Judas Iscariot, he who betrayed Him. Then He went to
a house [probably Peter's].
20But a throng came together again, so that Jesus and His disciples could not even take food.
21And when those [a]who belonged to Him ([b]His kinsmen)
heard it, they went out to take Him by force, for they kept saying,
He is out of [c]His mind—beside Himself, deranged!
22And the scribes who came down from Jerusalem said, He is
possessed by Beelzebub, and by [the help of] the prince of demons
He is casting out demons.
23And He summoned them to Him, and said to them in parables, How can Satan drive out Satan?
24And if a kingdom is divided *and* rebelling against itself, that
kingdom cannot stand.
25And if a house is divided—split into factions and rebelling—
against itself that house will not be able to last.
26And if Satan has raised an insurrection against himself and is
divided, he cannot stand, but is [surely] coming to an end.
27But no one can go into a strong man's house and ransack his
household goods right and left *and* seize them as plunder, unless
he first binds the strong man; then indeed he may [thoroughly]
plunder his house. [Isa. 49:24, 25.]
28Truly *and* solemnly I say to you, all sins will be forgiven the
sons of men, and whatever abusive *and* blasphemous things they
utter;
29But whoever speaks abusively against *or* maliciously mis-
represents the Holy Spirit can never get forgiveness, but is guilty
of *and* is in the grasp of [d]an everlasting trespass.
30For they [e]persisted in saying, [f]He has an unclean spirit.
31Then His mother and His brothers came, and standing outside they sent word to Him, calling [for] Him.
32And a crowd was sitting around Him, and they said to Him,
Your mother and Your brothers *and Your sisters* are outside, asking
for You.
33And He replied, Who are My mother and My brothers?
34And looking around on those who sat in a circle about Him,
He said, See! Here are My mother and My brothers,
35For whoever does the things God wills is My brother, and
sister, and mother!

4 AGAIN JESUS began to teach beside the lake. And a very
great crowd gathered about Him, so that He got into a ship
in order to sit in it on the sea; and the whole crowd was at the
lakeside on the shore.
2And He taught them many things in parables [concrete illustrations put beside truths to explain them], and in His teaching He
said to them:
3Give attention to this. Behold, a sower went out to sow.
4And as he was sowing, some seed fell along the path, and the
birds came and ate it up.
5Other seed [of the same kind] fell on ground full of rocks,
where it had not much soil, and at once it sprang up, because it
had no depth of soil;
6And when the sun came up, it was scorched, and because it
had not taken root withered away.
7Other seed [of the same kind] fell among thorn-plants, and the
thistles grew *and* pressed together *and* utterly choked *and* suffocated it, and it yielded no grain.

**AMP** [a] Tyndale. [b] Wycliffe. [c] Capitalized for what He is, the spotless Son of God, not what the speakers may have thought He was. [d] Wycliffe. [e] Vincent. [f] Capitalized for what He is, the spotless Son of God, not what the speakers may have thought He was.

## New American Standard

17and James, the *son* of Zebedee, and John the brother of James
(to them He gave the name Boanerges, which means, "Sons of
Thunder");
18and Andrew, and Philip, and Bartholomew, and Matthew,
and Thomas, and James the *son* of Alphaeus, and Thaddaeus, and
Simon the Zealot;
19and Judas Iscariot, who also betrayed Him.
20¶ And He *came [g]home, and the multitude *gathered again,
to such an extent that they could not even eat a meal.
21And when His own [h]people heard *of this*, they went out to
take custody of Him; for they were saying, "He has lost His
senses."
22And the scribes who came down from Jerusalem were saying,
"He is possessed by Beelzebul," and "He casts out the demons by
the ruler of the demons."
23And He called them to Himself and began speaking to them
in parables, "How can Satan cast out Satan?
24"And if a kingdom is divided against itself, that kingdom
cannot stand.
25"And if a house is divided against itself, that house will not
be able to stand.
26"And if Satan has risen up against himself and is divided, he
cannot stand, but he is finished!
27"But no one can enter the strong man's house and plunder his
property unless he first binds the strong man, and then he will
plunder his house.
28"Truly I say to you, all sins shall be forgiven the sons of men,
and whatever blasphemies they utter;
29but whoever blasphemes against the Holy Spirit never has
forgiveness, but is guilty of an eternal sin"—
30because they were saying, "He has an unclean spirit."
31¶ And His mother and His brothers *arrived, and standing
outside they sent *word* to Him, and called Him.
32And a multitude was sitting around Him, and they *said to
Him, "Behold, Your mother and Your brothers [i] are outside looking for You."
33And answering them, He *said, "Who are My mother and My
brothers?"
34And looking about on those who were sitting around Him, He
*said, "Behold, My mother and My brothers!
35"For whoever does the will of God, he is My brother and sister
and mother."

*Parable of the Sower and Soils*

4 AND HE began to teach again by the sea. And such a very
great multitude gathered to Him that He got into a boat in the
sea and sat down; and the whole multitude was by the sea on the
land.
2And He was teaching them many things in parables, and was
saying to them in His teaching,
3"Listen *to this*! Behold, the sower went out to sow;
4and it came about that as he was sowing, some *seed* fell beside
the road, and the birds came and ate it up.
5"And other *seed* fell on the rocky *ground* where it did not have
much soil; and immediately it sprang up because it had no depth
of soil.
6"And after the sun had risen, it was scorched; and because it
had no root, it withered away.
7"And other *seed* fell among the thorns, and the thorns came
up and choked it, and it yielded no crop.

NAS [g] Lit., *into a house* [h] Or, *kinsmen* [i] Later mss. add: *and Your sisters*

## New International

(to them he gave the name Boanerges, which means Sons of Thunder); 18Andrew, Philip, Bartholomew, Matthew, Thomas, James
son of Alphaeus, Thaddaeus, Simon the Zealot 19and Judas Iscariot, who betrayed him.

*Jesus and Beelzebub*

20Then Jesus entered a house, and again a crowd gathered, so
that he and his disciples were not even able to eat. 21When his
family heard about this, they went to take charge of him, for they
said, "He is out of his mind."
22And the teachers of the law who came down from Jerusalem
said, "He is possessed by Beelzebub[j] ! By the prince of demons he
is driving out demons."
23So Jesus called them and spoke to them in parables: "How can
Satan drive out Satan? 24If a kingdom is divided against itself, that
kingdom cannot stand. 25If a house is divided against itself, that
house cannot stand. 26And if Satan opposes himself and is divided, he cannot stand; his end has come. 27In fact, no one can
enter a strong man's house and carry off his possessions unless he
first ties up the strong man. Then he can rob his house. 28I tell you
the truth, all the sins and blasphemies of men will be forgiven
them. 29But whoever blasphemes against the Holy Spirit will never
be forgiven; he is guilty of an eternal sin."
30He said this because they were saying, "He has an evil spirit."

*Jesus' Mother and Brothers*

31Then Jesus' mother and brothers arrived. Standing outside,
they sent someone in to call him. 32A crowd was sitting around
him, and they told him, "Your mother and brothers are outside
looking for you."
33"Who are my mother and my brothers?" he asked.
34Then he looked at those seated in a circle around him and
said, "Here are my mother and my brothers! 35Whoever does
God's will is my brother and sister and mother."

*The Parable of the Sower*

4 AGAIN JESUS began to teach by the lake. The crowd that
gathered around him was so large that he got into a boat and
sat in it out on the lake, while all the people were along the shore
at the water's edge. 2He taught them many things by parables, and
in his teaching said: 3"Listen! A farmer went out to sow his seed.
4As he was scattering the seed, some fell along the path, and the
birds came and ate it up. 5Some fell on rocky places, where it did
not have much soil. It sprang up quickly, because the soil was
shallow. 6But when the sun came up, the plants were scorched,
and they withered because they had no root. 7Other seed fell
among thorns, which grew up and choked the plants, so that they
did not bear grain. 8Still other seed fell on good soil. It came up,

NIV [j] 22 Greek *Beezeboul* or *Beelzeboul*

## King James

8And other fell on good ground, and did yield fruit that sprang up and increased; and brought forth, some thirty, and some sixty, and some an hundred.

9And he said unto them, He that hath ears to hear, let him hear.

10And when he was alone, they that were about him with the twelve asked of him the parable.

11And he said unto them, Unto you it is given to know the mystery of the kingdom of God: but unto them that are without, all *these* things are done in parables:

12That seeing they may see, and not perceive; and hearing they may hear, and not understand; lest at any time they should be converted, and *their* sins should be forgiven them.

13And he said unto them, Know ye not this parable? and how then will ye know all parables?

14¶ The sower soweth the word.

15And these are they by the way side, where the word is sown; but when they have heard, Satan cometh immediately, and taketh away the word that was sown in their hearts.

16And these are they likewise which are sown on stony ground; who, when they have heard the word, immediately receive it with gladness;

17And have no root in themselves, and so endure but for a time: afterward, when affliction or persecution ariseth for the word's sake, immediately they are offended.

18And these are they which are sown among thorns; such as hear the word,

19And the cares of this world, and the deceitfulness of riches, and the lusts of other things entering in, choke the word, and it becometh unfruitful.

20And these are they which are sown on good ground; such as hear the word, and receive *it*, and bring forth fruit, some thirtyfold, some sixty, and some an hundred.

21¶ And he said unto them, Is a candle brought to be put under a bushel, or under a bed? and not to be set on a candlestick?

22For there is nothing hid, which shall not be manifested; neither was any thing kept secret, but that it should come abroad.

23If any man have ears to hear, let him hear.

24And he said unto them, Take heed what ye hear: with what measure ye mete, it shall be measured to you: and unto you that hear shall more be given.

25For he that hath, to him shall be given: and he that hath not, from him shall be taken even that which he hath.

26¶ And he said, So is the kingdom of God, as if a man should cast seed into the ground;

27And should sleep, and rise night and day, and the seed should spring and grow up, he knoweth not how.

28For the earth bringeth forth fruit of herself; first the blade, then the ear, after that the full corn in the ear.

29But when the fruit is brought forth, immediately he putteth in the sickle, because the harvest is come.

30¶ And he said, Whereunto shall we liken the kingdom of God? or with what comparison shall we compare it?

31 *It is* like a grain of mustard seed, which, when it is sown in the earth, is less than all the seeds that be in the earth:

## Amplified

8And other seed [of the same kind] fell into good (well adapted) soil, and brought forth grain, growing up and increasing, and yielded up to thirty times as much, and sixty times as much, and even a hundred times as much as had been sown.

9And He said, He who has ears to hear, let him be hearing—and [a]consider, and comprehend.

10And as soon as He was alone, those who were around Him with the twelve [apostles] began to ask Him about the parables.

11And He said to them, To you has been entrusted the mystery of the kingdom of God, [that is, [b]the secret counsels of God which are hidden from the ungodly;] but for those outside [ [c]of our circle] everything becomes a parable,

12In order that they may [indeed] look *and* look but not perceive, and may hear *and* hear but not grasp *and* comprehend; [d]lest haply they should turn again, and it [ [e]their wilful rejection of the truth] should be forgiven them. [Isa. 6:9, 10.]

13And He said to them, Do you not discern *and* understand this parable? How then [is it possible for] you to discern *and* understand all the parables?

14The sower sows the Word.

15The ones along the path are those who have the Word sown [in their hearts], but when they hear, Satan comes at once and (by force) takes away the message which is sown in them.

16And in the same way the ones sown upon stony ground are those who, when they hear the Word, at once receive *and* accept *and* welcome it with joy;

17And they have no real root in themselves, and so they endure for a little while, then when trouble or persecution arises on account of the Word, they immediately are offended—become displeased, indignant, resentful; *and* they stumble *and* fall away.

18And the ones sown among the thorns are others who hear the Word,

19Then the cares *and* anxieties of the world, *and* distractions of the age, and the pleasure *and* delight *and* false glamour *and* deceitfulness of riches, and the craving *and* passionate desire for other things creep in and choke *and* suffocate the Word, and it becomes fruitless.

20And those that were sown on the good (well-adapted) soil are the ones who hear the Word, and receive *and* accept *and* welcome it and bear fruit, some thirty times as much as was sown, some sixty times as much, and some [even] a hundred times as much.

21And He said to them, Is the lamp brought in to be put under a [f]peck-measure, or under a bed, and not on the [lamp] stand?

22—[g]Things are hidden [temporarily] only as a means to revelation. For there is nothing hidden except to be revealed, nor is anything [temporarily] kept secret except in order that it may be made known.

23If any man has ears to hear, let him be listening, *and* perceive *and* comprehend.

24And He said to them, Be careful what you are hearing. The measure [h][of thought and study] you give [to [i]the truth you hear] will be the measure [j][of virtue and knowledge] that comes back to you, and more [besides] will be given to you *who hear*.

25For to him who has will more be given, and from him who has nothing, even what he has will be taken away ( [k]by force),

26And He said, The kingdom of God is like a man who scatters seed upon the ground,

27Then continues sleeping and rising night and day while the seed sprouts and grows *and* [l]increases, he knows not how.

28The earth produces [acting] by itself, first the blade, then the ear, then the full grain in the ear.

29But when the grain is ripe *and* permits, immediately he [m]sends forth [the reapers] *and* puts in the sickle, because the harvest stands ready.

30And He said, With what can we compare the kingdom of God, or what parable shall we use to illustrate *and* explain it?

31It is like a grain of mustard seed, which when sown upon the ground is the smallest of all seeds upon the earth;

**AMP** [a] Thayer. [b] Wuest. [c] Vincent. [d] Robertson. [e] Wuest. [f] Moulton and Milligan. [g] After Swete, Robertson, Vincent, etc. [h] After "Expositor's Greek Testament." [i] After Gray and Adams' "Bible Commentary," Euthy, Wuest, Barnes, etc. [j] After "Expositor's Greek Testament," etc. [k] Thayer. [l] Thayer. [m] Vincent.

## New American Standard

8"And other *seeds* fell into the good soil and as they grew up
and increased, they yielded a crop and produced thirty, sixty, and
a hundredfold."
9And He was saying, "He who has ears to hear, let him hear."
10¶ And as soon as He was alone, His followers, along with the
twelve, *began* asking Him *about* the parables.
11And He was saying to them, "To you has been given the
mystery of the kingdom of God; but those who are outside get
everything in parables,
12in order that WHILE SEEING, THEY MAY SEE AND NOT PERCEIVE;
AND WHILE HEARING, THEY MAY HEAR AND NOT UNDERSTAND LEST
THEY RETURN AND BE FORGIVEN."

*Explanation*

13And He *said to them, "Do you not understand this parable?
And how will you understand all the parables?
14"The sower sows the word.
15"And these are the ones who are beside the road where the
word is sown; and when they hear, immediately Satan comes and
takes away the word which has been sown in them.
16"And in a similar way these are the ones on whom seed was
sown on the rocky *places*, who, when they hear the word, immediately receive it with joy;
17and they have no *firm* root in themselves, but are *only* temporary; then, when affliction or persecution arises because of the
word, immediately they fall away.
18"And others are the ones on whom seed was sown among the
thorns; these are the ones who have heard the word,
19and the worries of the [n]world, and the deceitfulness of riches,
and the desires for other things enter in and choke the word, and
it becomes unfruitful.
20"And those are the ones on whom seed was sown on the good
soil; and they hear the word and accept it, and bear fruit, thirty,
sixty, and a hundredfold."
21¶ And He was saying to them, "A lamp is not brought to be
put under a peck-measure, is it, or under a bed? Is it not *brought*
to be put on the lampstand?
22"For nothing is hidden, except to be revealed; nor has *anything* been secret, but that it should come to light.
23"If any man has ears to hear, let him hear."
24And He was saying to them, "Take care what you listen to.
By your standard of measure it shall be measured to you; and more
shall be given you besides.
25"For whoever has, to him shall *more* be given; and whoever
does not have, even what he has shall be taken away from him."

*Parable of the Seed*

26¶ And He was saying, "The kingdom of God is like a man who
casts seed upon the soil;
27and goes to bed at night and gets up by day, and the seed
sprouts up and grows—how, he himself does not know.
28"The soil produces crops by itself; first the blade, then the
head, then the mature grain in the head.
29"But when the crop permits, he immediately puts in the sickle, because the harvest has come."

*Parable of the Mustard Seed*

30¶ And He said, "How shall we [o]picture the kingdom of God,
or by what parable shall we present it?
31" *It is* like a mustard seed, which, when sown upon the soil,
though it is smaller than all the seeds that are upon the soil,

NAS [n] Or, *age* [o] Lit., *compare*

## New International

grew and produced a crop, multiplying thirty, sixty, or even a
hundred times."
9Then Jesus said, "He who has ears to hear, let him hear."
10When he was alone, the Twelve and the others around him
asked him about the parables. 11He told them, "The secret of the
kingdom of God has been given to you. But to those on the outside
everything is said in parables 12so that,

" 'they may be ever seeing but never perceiving,
and ever hearing but never understanding;
otherwise they might turn and be forgiven!'[p]"

13Then Jesus said to them, "Don't you understand this parable?
How then will you understand any parable? 14The farmer sows the
word. 15Some people are like seed along the path, where the word
is sown. As soon as they hear it, Satan comes and takes away the
word that was sown in them. 16Others, like seed sown on rocky
places, hear the word and at once receive it with joy. 17But since
they have no root, they last only a short time. When trouble or
persecution comes because of the word, they quickly fall away.
18Still others, like seed sown among thorns, hear the word; 19but
the worries of this life, the deceitfulness of wealth and the desires
for other things come in and choke the word, making it unfruitful.
20Others, like seed sown on good soil, hear the word, accept it, and
produce a crop—thirty, sixty or even a hundred times what was
sown."

*A Lamp on a Stand*

21He said to them, "Do you bring in a lamp to put it under a
bowl or a bed? Instead, don't you put it on its stand? 22For whatever is hidden is meant to be disclosed, and whatever is concealed
is meant to be brought out into the open. 23If anyone has ears to
hear, let him hear."
24"Consider carefully what you hear," he continued. "With the
measure you use, it will be measured to you—and even more.
25Whoever has will be given more; whoever does not have, even
what he has will be taken from him."

*The Parable of the Growing Seed*

26He also said, "This is what the kingdom of God is like. A man
scatters seed on the ground. 27Night and day, whether he sleeps
or gets up, the seed sprouts and grows, though he does not know
how. 28All by itself the soil produces grain—first the stalk, then the
head, then the full kernel in the head. 29As soon as the grain is
ripe, he puts the sickle to it, because the harvest has come."

*The Parable of the Mustard Seed*

30Again he said, "What shall we say the kingdom of God is like,
or what parable shall we use to describe it? 31It is like a mustard
seed, which is the smallest seed you plant in the ground. 32Yet

NIV [p] 12 Isaiah 6:9,10

## King James

32But when it is sown, it groweth up, and becometh greater than all herbs, and shooteth out great branches; so that the fowls of the air may lodge under the shadow of it.

33And with many such parables spake he the word unto them, as they were able to hear *it*.

34But without a parable spake he not unto them: and when they were alone, he expounded all things to his disciples.

35And the same day, when the even was come, he saith unto them, Let us pass over unto the other side.

36And when they had sent away the multitude, they took him even as he was in the ship. And there were also with him other little ships.

37And there arose a great storm of wind, and the waves beat into the ship, so that it was now full.

38And he was in the hinder part of the ship, asleep on a pillow: and they awake him, and say unto him, Master, carest thou not that we perish?

39And he arose, and rebuked the wind, and said unto the sea, Peace, be still. And the wind ceased, and there was a great calm.

40And he said unto them, Why are ye so fearful? how is it that ye have no faith?

41And they feared exceedingly, and said one to another, What manner of man is this, that even the wind and the sea obey him?

5 AND THEY came over unto the other side of the sea, into the country of the Gadarenes.

2And when he was come out of the ship, immediately there met him out of the tombs a man with an unclean spirit,

3Who had *his* dwelling among the tombs; and no man could bind him, no, not with chains:

4Because that he had been often bound with fetters and chains, and the chains had been plucked asunder by him, and the fetters broken in pieces: neither could any *man* tame him.

5And always, night and day, he was in the mountains, and in the tombs, crying, and cutting himself with stones.

6But when he saw Jesus afar off, he ran and worshipped him,

7And cried with a loud voice, and said, What have I to do with thee, Jesus, *thou* Son of the most high God? I adjure thee by God, that thou torment me not.

8For he said unto him, Come out of the man, *thou* unclean spirit.

9And he asked him, What *is* thy name? And he answered, saying, My name *is* Legion: for we are many.

10And he besought him much that he would not send them away out of the country.

11Now there was there nigh unto the mountains a great herd of swine feeding.

12And all the devils besought him, saying, Send us into the swine, that we may enter into them.

13And forthwith Jesus gave them leave. And the unclean spirits went out, and entered into the swine: and the herd ran violently down a steep place into the sea, (they were about two thousand;) and were choked in the sea.

14And they that fed the swine fled, and told *it* in the city, and in the country. And they went out to see what it was that was done.

## Amplified

32Yet after it is sown it grows up and becomes the greatest of all garden herbs, and puts out large branches, so that the birds of the air are able to make nests *and* dwell in its shade.

33With many such parables [Jesus] spoke the Word to them, as they were able to hear *and* [a]to comprehend *and* understand.

34He did not tell them anything without a parable, but privately to His disciples [ [b]those who were peculiarly His own] He explained everything [fully].

35On that same day [when] evening had come, He said to them, Let us go over to the other side [of the lake].

36And leaving the throng, they took Him with them, [just] as He was, in the boat [in which He was sitting]. And other boats were with Him.

37And a furious storm of wind ( [c]of hurricane proportions) arose, and the waves kept beating into the boat, so that it was already becoming filled.

38But He [Himself] was in the stern [of the boat] asleep on the [leather] cushion; and they awoke Him and said to Him, Master, do You not care that we are perishing?

39And He arose and rebuked the wind, and said to the sea, Hush now! Be still (muzzled)! And the wind ceased, [that is, [d]sank to rest as if exhausted by its beating] and there was (immediately) a great calm— [e]a perfect peacefulness.

40He said to them, Why are you so timid *and* fearful? How is it that you have no faith—no [f]firmly relying trust?

41And they were filled with great awe *and* [g]feared exceedingly, and said one to another, Who then is this, that even wind and sea obey Him?

5 THEY CAME to the other side of the sea, to the region of the Gerasenes.

2And as soon as He got out of the boat, there met Him a man out of the tombs [under the power of] an unclean spirit.

3This man [h]continually lived among the tombs, and no one could subdue him any more, even with a chain;

4For he had been bound often with shackles for the feet, and [i]handcuffs, but the handcuffs [of light] chains he wrenched apart, and the shackles he rubbed *and* ground together *and* broke in pieces; and no one had strength enough to restrain *or* tame him.

5Night and day among the tombs and on the mountains he was always [j]shrieking *and* screaming, and [k]beating *and* bruising *and* [l]cutting himself with stones.

6And when from a distance he saw Jesus, he ran and fell on his knees before Him in homage,

7And crying out with a loud voice, he said, What have You to do with me, Jesus, Son of the Most High God? What is there in common between us? I [m]solemnly implore you by God, do not begin to torment me!

8For Jesus was commanding, Come out of the man, you unclean spirit!

9And He asked him, What is your name? He replied, My name is Legion, for we are many.

10And he kept begging Him urgently not to send them [himself and the other demons] away out of that region.

11Now a great herd of hogs was grazing there on the hillside;

12And *the demons* begged Him, saying, Send us to the hogs that we may go into them!

13So He gave them permission. And the unclean spirits came out [of the man] and entered into the hogs, and the herd, numbering about two thousand, rushed headlong down the steep slope into the lake, and were drowned in the sea.

14The hog-feeders ran away, and told [it] in the town and in the country. And [the people] came to see what it was that had taken place.

**AMP** [a] Thayer. [b] Wuest. [c] Wuest. [d] Vincent. [e] After Wycliffe. [f] Cremer. [g] Vincent. [h] Wuest. [i] Thayer. [j] Thayer. [k] Moulton and Milligan. [l] Abbott-Smith. [m] Wuest.

## New American Standard

32 yet when it is sown, grows up and becomes larger than all the garden plants and forms large branches; so that THE BIRDS OF THE [n]AIR can NEST UNDER ITS SHADE."

33¶ And with many such parables He was speaking the word to them as they were able to hear it;

34 and He did not speak to them without a parable; but He was explaining everything privately to His own disciples.

*Jesus Stills the Sea*

35¶ And on that day, when evening had come, He *said to them, "Let us go over to the other side."

36 And leaving the multitude, they *took Him along with them, just as He was, in the boat; and other boats were with Him.

37 And there *arose a fierce gale of wind, and the waves were breaking over the boat so much that the boat was already filling up.

38 And He Himself was in the stern, asleep on the cushion; and they *awoke Him and *said to Him, "Teacher, do You not care that we are perishing?"

39 And being aroused, He rebuked the wind and said to the sea, "Hush, be still." And the wind died down and it became perfectly calm.

40 And He said to them, "Why are you so timid? How is it that you have no faith?"

41 And they became very much afraid and said to one another, "Who then is this, that even the wind and the sea obey Him?"

*The Gerasene Demoniac*

5 AND THEY came to the other side of the sea, into the country of the Gerasenes.

2 And when He had come out of the boat, immediately a man from the tombs with an unclean spirit met Him,

3 and he had his dwelling among the tombs. And no one was able to bind him anymore, even with a chain;

4 because he had often been bound with shackles and chains, and the chains had been torn apart by him, and the shackles broken in pieces, and no one was strong enough to subdue him.

5 And constantly night and day, among the tombs and in the mountains, he was crying out and gashing himself with stones.

6 And seeing Jesus from a distance, he ran up and bowed down before Him;

7 and crying out with a loud voice, he *said, "What do I have to do with You, Jesus, Son of the Most High God? I implore You by God, do not torment me!"

8 For He had been saying to him, "Come out of the man, you unclean spirit!"

9 And He was asking him, "What is your name?" And he *said to Him, "My name is Legion; for we are many."

10 And he *began* to entreat Him earnestly not to send them out of the country.

11 Now there was a big herd of swine feeding there on the mountain.

12 And *the demons* entreated Him, saying, "Send us into the swine so that we may enter them."

13 And He gave them permission. And coming out, the unclean spirits entered the swine; and the herd rushed down the steep bank into the sea, about two thousand *of them;* and they were drowned in the sea.

14 And their herdsmen ran away and reported it in the city and *out* in the country. And *the people* came to see what it was that had happened.

NAS [n] Or, *sky*

## New International

when planted, it grows and becomes the largest of all garden plants, with such big branches that the birds of the air can perch in its shade."

33 With many similar parables Jesus spoke the word to them, as much as they could understand. 34 He did not say anything to them without using a parable. But when he was alone with his own disciples, he explained everything.

*Jesus Calms the Storm*

35 That day when evening came, he said to his disciples, "Let us go over to the other side." 36 Leaving the crowd behind, they took him along, just as he was, in the boat. There were also other boats with him. 37 A furious squall came up, and the waves broke over the boat, so that it was nearly swamped. 38 Jesus was in the stern, sleeping on a cushion. The disciples woke him and said to him, "Teacher, don't you care if we drown?"

39 He got up, rebuked the wind and said to the waves, "Quiet! Be still!" Then the wind died down and it was completely calm.

40 He said to his disciples, "Why are you so afraid? Do you still have no faith?"

41 They were terrified and asked each other, "Who is this? Even the wind and the waves obey him!"

*The Healing of a Demon-possessed Man*

5 THEY WENT across the lake to the region of the Gerasenes.[o] 2 When Jesus got out of the boat, a man with an evil[p] spirit came from the tombs to meet him. 3 This man lived in the tombs, and no one could bind him any more, not even with a chain. 4 For he had often been chained hand and foot, but he tore the chains apart and broke the irons on his feet. No one was strong enough to subdue him. 5 Night and day among the tombs and in the hills he would cry out and cut himself with stones.

6 When he saw Jesus from a distance, he ran and fell on his knees in front of him. 7 He shouted at the top of his voice, "What do you want with me, Jesus, Son of the Most High God? Swear to God that you won't torture me!" 8 For Jesus had said to him, "Come out of this man, you evil spirit!"

9 Then Jesus asked him, "What is your name?"

"My name is Legion," he replied, "for we are many." 10 And he begged Jesus again and again not to send them out of the area.

11 A large herd of pigs was feeding on the nearby hillside. 12 The demons begged Jesus, "Send us among the pigs; allow us to go into them." 13 He gave them permission, and the evil spirits came out and went into the pigs. The herd, about two thousand in number, rushed down the steep bank into the lake and were drowned.

14 Those tending the pigs ran off and reported this in the town and countryside, and the people went out to see what had happened. 15 When they came to Jesus, they saw the man who had

NIV [o] 1 Some manuscripts *Gadarenes;* other manuscripts *Gergesenes*
[p] 2 Greek *unclean;* also in verses 8 and 13

## King James

15And they come to Jesus, and see him that was possessed with the devil, and had the legion, sitting, and clothed, and in his right mind: and they were afraid.

16And they that saw *it* told them how it befell to him that was possessed with the devil, and *also* concerning the swine.

17And they began to pray him to depart out of their coasts.

18And when he was come into the ship, he that had been possessed with the devil prayed him that he might be with him.

19Howbeit Jesus suffered him not, but saith unto him, Go home to thy friends, and tell them how great things the Lord hath done for thee, and hath had compassion on thee.

20And he departed, and began to publish in Decapolis how great things Jesus had done for him: and all *men* did marvel.

21And when Jesus was passed over again by ship unto the other side, much people gathered unto him: and he was nigh unto the sea.

22And, behold, there cometh one of the rulers of the synagogue, Jairus by name; and when he saw him, he fell at his feet,

23And besought him greatly, saying, My little daughter lieth at the point of death: *I pray thee,* come and lay thy hands on her, that she may be healed; and she shall live.

24And *Jesus* went with him; and much people followed him, and thronged him.

25And a certain woman, which had an issue of blood twelve years,

26And had suffered many things of many physicians, and had spent all that she had, and was nothing bettered, but rather grew worse,

27When she had heard of Jesus, came in the press behind, and touched his garment.

28For she said, If I may touch but his clothes, I shall be whole.

29And straightway the fountain of her blood was dried up; and she felt in *her* body that she was healed of that plague.

30And Jesus, immediately knowing in himself that virtue had gone out of him, turned him about in the press, and said, Who touched my clothes?

31And his disciples said unto him, Thou seest the multitude thronging thee, and sayest thou, Who touched me?

32And he looked round about to see her that had done this thing.

33But the woman fearing and trembling, knowing what was done in her, came and fell down before him, and told him all the truth.

34And he said unto her, Daughter, thy faith hath made thee whole; go in peace, and be whole of thy plague.

35While he yet spake, there came from the ruler of the synagogue's *house certain* which said, Thy daughter is dead: why troublest thou the Master any further?

36As soon as Jesus heard the word that was spoken, he saith unto the ruler of the synagogue, Be not afraid, only believe.

37And he suffered no man to follow him, save Peter, and James, and John the brother of James.

38And he cometh to the house of the ruler of the synagogue, and seeth the tumult, and them that wept and wailed greatly.

39And when he was come in, he saith unto them, Why make ye this ado, and weep? the damsel is not dead, but sleepeth.

40And they laughed him to scorn. But when he had put them all out, he taketh the father and the mother of the damsel, and them that were with him, and entereth in where the damsel was lying.

## Amplified

15And they came to Jesus, and looked intently *and* searchingly at the man who had been a demoniac, sitting there clothed and in his right mind, [the same man] who had had the legion [of demons]; and they were [a]seized with alarm *and* struck with fear.

16And those who had seen it related in full what had happened to the man possessed by demons and to the hogs.

17And they began to beg [Jesus] to leave their neighborhood.

18And when He had stepped into the boat, the man who had been controlled by the unclean spirits kept begging Him that he might be with Him.

19But Jesus refused to permit him, but said to him, Go home to your own [family and relatives and friends], and bring back word to them of how much the Lord has done for you, and [how He has] had sympathy for you *and* mercy on you.

20And he departed and began to publicly proclaim in Decapolis [the region of the ten cities] how much Jesus had done for him, and all the people were astonished *and* marveled.

21And when Jesus had recrossed in the boat to the other side, a great throng gathered about Him, and He was at the lakeshore.

22Then one of the rulers of the synagogue came up, Jairus by name; and seeing Him, he prostrated himself at His feet,

23And begged Him earnestly, saying, My little daughter is at the point of death. Come and lay Your hands on her, so that she may be healed *and* live.

24And Jesus went with him, and a great crowd kept following Him, and pressed Him [b]from all sides—so as almost to suffocate Him.

25And there was a woman who had had a flow of blood for twelve years,

26And who had endured much [c]suffering under [the hands of] many physicians, and had spent all that she had; and was no better but instead grew worse.

27She had heard the reports concerning Jesus, and she came up behind Him in the throng and touched His garment,

28For she kept saying, If I only touch His garments, I shall be restored to health.

29And immediately her (flow of) blood was dried up at the source, and ([d]suddenly) she felt in her body that she was healed of her ([e]distressing) ailment.

30And Jesus, recognizing in Himself that the power proceeding from Him had gone forth, turned around immediately in the crowd, and said, Who touched My clothes?

31And the disciples kept saying to Him, You see the crowd pressing hard around You (from all sides), and You ask, Who touched Me?

32Still He kept looking around to see her who had done it.

33But the woman, knowing what had been done for her, though alarmed *and* frightened and trembling, fell down before Him, and told Him the whole truth.

34And He said to her, Daughter, your faith [that is, your [f]trust and confidence in Me, springing from faith in God] has restored you to health. Go [g]in (to) peace, and be continually healed *and* free from your ([h]distressing bodily) disease.

35While He was still speaking, there came some from the ruler's house who said [to Jairus], Your daughter has died. Why bother *and* distress the Teacher any further?

36([i]Overhearing) but ignoring what they said, Jesus said to the ruler of the synagogue, Do not be seized with alarm *and* have no fear, only keep on believing.

37And He permitted no one to accompany Him except Peter and James and John the brother of James.

38When they arrived at the house of the ruler of the synagogue, He [j]looked (carefully and with understanding) at [the] tumult and [the people] weeping and wailing loudly.

39And when He had gone in, He said to them, Why do you make an uproar and weep? The little girl is not dead, but is sleeping.

40And they laughed *and* [k]jeered at Him. But He put them all out, and taking the child's father and mother and those who were with Him, He went in where the little girl was *lying*.

**AMP** [a] Thayer. [b] Thayer. [c] Vincent. [d] Wuest. [e] Thayer. [f] Thayer. [g] Wuest. [h] Thayer. [i] Alternate reading. [j] Wuest. [k] Abbott-Smith.

## New American Standard

15And they *came to Jesus and *observed the man who had been demon-possessed sitting down, clothed and in his right mind, the very man who had had the "legion"; and they became frightened.

16And those who had seen it described to them how it had happened to the demon-possessed man, and *all* about the swine.

17And they began to entreat Him to depart from their region.

18And as He was getting into the boat, the man who had been demon-possessed was entreating Him that he might accompany Him.

19And He did not let him, but He *said to him, "Go home to your people and report to them [l]what great things the Lord has done for you, and *how* He had mercy on you."

20And he went away and began to proclaim in Decapolis what great things Jesus had done for him; and everyone marveled.

*Miracles and Healing*

21¶ And when Jesus had crossed over again in the boat to the other side, a great multitude gathered about Him; and He stayed by the seashore.

22And one of the synagogue officials named Jairus *came up, and upon seeing Him, *fell at His feet,

23and *entreated Him earnestly, saying, "My little daughter is at the point of death; *please* come and lay Your hands on her, that she may get well and live."

24And He went off with him; and a great multitude was following Him and pressing in on Him.

25¶ And a woman who had had a hemorrhage for twelve years,

26and had endured much at the hands of many physicians, and had spent all that she had and was not helped at all, but rather had grown worse,

27after hearing about Jesus, came up in the crowd behind *Him*, and touched His cloak.

28For she thought, "If I just touch His garments, I shall get well."

29And immediately the flow of her blood was dried up; and she felt in her body that she was healed of her affliction.

30And immediately Jesus, perceiving in Himself that the power *proceeding* from Him had gone forth, turned around in the crowd and said, "Who touched My garments?"

31And His disciples said to Him, "You see the multitude pressing in on You, and You say, 'Who touched Me?' "

32And He looked around to see the woman who had done this.

33But the woman fearing and trembling, aware of what had happened to her, came and fell down before Him, and told Him the whole truth.

34And He said to her, "Daughter, your faith has made you well; go in peace, and be healed of your affliction."

35¶ While He was still speaking, they *came from the *house of* the synagogue official, saying, "Your daughter has died; why trouble the Teacher anymore?"

36But Jesus, overhearing what was being spoken, *said to the synagogue official, "Do not be afraid *any longer*, only believe."

37And He allowed no one to follow with Him, except Peter and James and John the brother of James.

38And they *came to the house of the synagogue official; and He *beheld a commotion, and *people* loudly weeping and wailing.

39And entering in, He *said to them, "Why make a commotion and weep? The child has not died, but is asleep."

40And they *began* laughing at Him. But putting them all out, He *took along the child's father and mother and His own companions, and *entered *the room* where the child was.

## New International

been possessed by the legion of demons, sitting there, dressed and
in his right mind; and they were afraid. 16Those who had seen it
told the people what had happened to the demon-possessed
man—and told about the pigs as well. 17Then the people began to
plead with Jesus to leave their region.
18As Jesus was getting into the boat, the man who had been
demon-possessed begged to go with him. 19Jesus did not let him,
but said, "Go home to your family and tell them how much the
Lord has done for you, and how he has had mercy on you." 20So
the man went away and began to tell in the Decapolis[m] how much
Jesus had done for him. And all the people were amazed.

*A Dead Girl and a Sick Woman*

21When Jesus had again crossed over by boat to the other side
of the lake, a large crowd gathered around him while he was by
the lake. 22Then one of the synagogue rulers, named Jairus, came
there. Seeing Jesus, he fell at his feet 23and pleaded earnestly with
him, "My little daughter is dying. Please come and put your hands
on her so that she will be healed and live." 24So Jesus went with
him.
A large crowd followed and pressed around him. 25And a
woman was there who had been subject to bleeding for twelve
years. 26She had suffered a great deal under the care of many
doctors and had spent all she had, yet instead of getting better she
grew worse. 27When she heard about Jesus, she came up behind
him in the crowd and touched his cloak, 28because she thought,
"If I just touch his clothes, I will be healed." 29Immediately her
bleeding stopped and she felt in her body that she was freed from
her suffering.
30At once Jesus realized that power had gone out from him. He
turned around in the crowd and asked, "Who touched my
clothes?"
31"You see the people crowding against you," his disciples
answered, "and yet you can ask, 'Who touched me?' "
32But Jesus kept looking around to see who had done it. 33Then
the woman, knowing what had happened to her, came and fell at
his feet and, trembling with fear, told him the whole truth. 34He
said to her, "Daughter, your faith has healed you. Go in peace and
be freed from your suffering."
35While Jesus was still speaking, some men came from the
house of Jairus, the synagogue ruler. "Your daughter is dead,"
they said. "Why bother the teacher any more?"
36Ignoring what they said, Jesus told the synagogue ruler,
"Don't be afraid; just believe."
37He did not let anyone follow him except Peter, James and
John the brother of James. 38When they came to the home of the
synagogue ruler, Jesus saw a commotion, with people crying and
wailing loudly. 39He went in and said to them, "Why all this
commotion and wailing? The child is not dead but asleep." 40But
they laughed at him.
After he put them all out, he took the child's father and mother
and the disciples who were with him, and went in where the child
was. 41He took her by the hand and said to her, *"Talitha koum!"*

NAS [l] Or, *everything that*

NIV [m]20 That is, the Ten Cities

## King James

41And he took the damsel by the hand, and said unto her, Talitha cumi; which is, being interpreted, Damsel, I say unto thee, arise.

42And straightway the damsel arose, and walked; for she was *of the age* of twelve years. And they were astonished with a great astonishment.

43And he charged them straitly that no man should know it; and commanded that something should be given her to eat.

6 AND HE went out from thence, and came into his own country; and his disciples follow him.

2And when the sabbath day was come, he began to teach in the synagogue: and many hearing *him* were astonished, saying, From whence hath this *man* these things? and what wisdom *is* this which is given unto him, that even such mighty works are wrought by his hands?

3Is not this the carpenter, the son of Mary, the brother of James, and Joses, and of Judah, and Simon? and are not his sisters here with us? And they were offended at him.

4But Jesus said unto them, A prophet is not without honour, but in his own country, and among his own kin, and in his own house.

5And he could there do no mighty work, save that he laid his hands upon a few sick folk, and healed *them*.

6And he marvelled because of their unbelief. And he went round about the villages, teaching.

7¶ And he called *unto him* the twelve, and began to send them forth by two and two; and gave them power over unclean spirits;

8And commanded them that they should take nothing for *their* journey, save a staff only; no scrip, no bread, no money in *their* purse:

9But *be* shod with sandals; and not put on two coats.

10And he said unto them, In what place soever ye enter into an house, there abide till ye depart from that place.

11And whosoever shall not receive you, nor hear you, when ye depart thence, shake off the dust under your feet for a testimony against them. Verily I say unto you, It shall be more tolerable for Sodom and Gomorrha in the day of judgment, than for that city.

12And they went out, and preached that men should repent.

13And they cast out many devils, and anointed with oil many that were sick, and healed *them*.

14And king Herod heard *of him;* (for his name was spread abroad:) and he said, That John the Baptist was risen from the dead, and therefore mighty works do show forth themselves in him.

15Others said, That it is Elias. And others said, That it is a prophet, or as one of the prophets.

16But when Herod heard *thereof*, he said, It is John, whom I beheaded: he is risen from the dead.

17For Herod himself had sent forth and laid hold upon John, and bound him in prison for Herodias' sake, his brother Philip's wife: for he had married her.

18For John had said unto Herod, It is not lawful for thee to have thy brother's wife.

19Therefore Herodias had a quarrel against him, and would have killed him; but she could not:

**AMP** [a] Thayer. [b] Thayer. [c] Capitalized because of what He is, the spotless Son of God, not what the speakers may have thought He was. [d] Tyndale. [e] Wuest. [f] Wuest. [g] Moulton and Milligan. [h] Thayer. [i] Some ancient authorities read "he." [j] Abbott-Smith. [k] Vincent.

## Amplified

41Gripping her (firmly) by the hand, He said to her, Talitha cumi, which translated is, Little girl, I say to you, arise ( [a]from the sleep of death)!

42And instantly the girl got up and started walking around, for she was twelve years [old]. And they were utterly astonished *and* overcome with amazement.

43And He strictly commanded *and* warned them that no one should know this, and He ( [b]expressly) told them to give her [something] to eat.

6 JESUS WENT away from there and came to His [own] country *and* home town [Nazareth], and His disciples followed (with) Him.

2And on the Sabbath He began to teach in the synagogue; and many who listened to Him were utterly astonished, saying, Where did this [Man] acquire all this? What is the wisdom—the broad and full intelligence—[which has been] given to [c]Him? What mighty works *and* exhibitions of power are wrought by His hands!

3Is not this the Carpenter, the son of Mary and the brother of James and Joses and Judas and Simon, and are not His sisters here among us? And they took offense at Him *and* [d]were hurt [that is, they [e]disapproved of Him and it hindered them from acknowledging His authority]; *and* they were caused to stumble *and* fall.

4But Jesus said to them, A prophet is not without honor (deference, reverence), except in his [own] country and among [his] relatives and in his [own] house.

5And He was not able to do [f]even one work of power there, except that He laid His hands on a few sickly people [and] cured them.

6And He marveled because of their unbelief—their lack of faith in Him. And He went about among the surrounding villages [and] continued teaching.

7And He called to Him the twelve [apostles], and began to send them out [as His ambassadors] two by two, and gave them authority *and* power over the unclean spirits.

8He charged them to take nothing for their journey except a walking stick; no bread, [g]no wallet for a collection bag, no money in their belts (girdles, purses);

9But to go with sandals on their feet and not put on two tunics (undergarments).

10And He told them, Where you go into a house, stay there until you leave that place.

11And if any [community] will not receive *and* accept *and* welcome you, and they refuse to listen to you, when you depart shake off the dust that is on your feet for a testimony against them. *Truly, I tell you, it will be more tolerable for Sodom and Gomorrah in the judgment day than for that town.*

12So they went out and preached that men should repent [that is [h]that they should change their minds for the better, and heartily amend their ways with abhorrence for their past sins].

13And they drove out many unclean spirits, and anointed with oil many who were sick, and cured them.

14King Herod heard of it, for [Jesus'] name had become well known. [i]He *and* they [of his court] said, John the Baptist has been raised from the dead; that is why these mighty powers ( [j]of performing miracles) are at work in Him.

15[But] others kept saying, It is Elijah! And others said, It is a prophet, like one of the prophets [of old].

16But when Herod heard [of it], he said, ( [k]This very) John, whom I beheaded, has been raised [from the dead].

17For this Herod himself had sent and seized John, and bound him in prison for the sake of Herodias, his brother Philip's wife, because he [Herod] had married her.

18For John had told Herod, It is not lawful *and* you have no right to have your brother's wife.

19And Herodias was angry (enraged) with him, *and* held a grudge against him, and wanted to kill him, but she could not.

## New American Standard

41And taking the child by the hand, He *said to her, "Talitha
kum!" (which translated means, "Little girl, I say to you, arise!").
42And immediately the girl rose and *began* to walk; for she was
twelve years old. And immediately they were completely astounded.
43And He gave them strict orders that no one should know
about this; and He said that *something* should be given her to eat.

*Teaching at Nazareth*

6 AND HE went out from there, and He *came into His home
town; and His disciples *followed Him.
2And when the Sabbath had come, He began to teach in the
synagogue; and the many listeners were astonished, saying,
"Where did this man *get* these things, and what is *this* wisdom
given to Him, and such miracles as these performed by His hands?
3"Is not this the carpenter, the son of Mary, and brother of
James, and Joses, and Judas, and Simon? Are not His sisters here
with us?" And they took offense at Him.
4And Jesus said to them, "A prophet is not without honor
except in his home town and among his *own* relatives and in his
*own* household."
5And He could do no miracle there except that He laid His
hands upon a few sick people and healed them.
6And He wondered at their unbelief.
¶ **And He was going around the villages teaching.**

*The Twelve Sent Out*

7¶ And He *summoned the twelve and began to send them out
in pairs; and He was giving them authority over the unclean
spirits;
8and He instructed them that they should take nothing for *their*
journey, except a mere staff; no bread, no bag, no money in their
belt;
9but *to* wear sandals; and *He added,* "Do not put on two
[l]tunics."
10And He said to them, "Wherever you enter a house, stay
there until you leave town.
11"And any place that does not receive you or listen to you, as
you go out from there, shake off the dust from the soles of your
feet for a testimony against them."
12And they went out and preached that *men* should repent.
13And they were casting out many demons and were anointing
with oil many sick people and healing them.

*John's Fate Recalled*

14¶ And King Herod heard *of it,* for His name had become well
known; and *people* were saying, "John the Baptist has risen from
the dead, and that is why these miraculous powers are at work in
Him."
15But others were saying, "He is Elijah." And others were
saying, "He is a prophet, like one of the prophets *of old.*"
16But when Herod heard *of it,* he kept saying, "John, whom I
beheaded, has risen!"
17For Herod himself had sent and had John arrested and bound
in prison on account of Herodias, the wife of his brother Philip,
because he had married her.
18For John had been saying to Herod, "It is not lawful for you
to have your brother's wife."
19And Herodias had a grudge against him and wanted to put
him to death and could not *do so;*

NAS [l] Or, *inner garments*

## New International

(which means, "Little girl, I say to you, get up!"). 42Immediately
the girl stood up and walked around (she was twelve years old).
At this they were completely astonished. 43He gave strict orders
not to let anyone know about this, and told them to give her
something to eat.

*A Prophet Without Honor*

6 JESUS LEFT there and went to his hometown, accompanied
by his disciples. 2When the Sabbath came, he began to teach
in the synagogue, and many who heard him were amazed.
"Where did this man get these things?" they asked. "What's
this wisdom that has been given him, that he even does miracles!
3Isn't this the carpenter? Isn't this Mary's son and the brother of
James, Joseph,[m] Judas and Simon? Aren't his sisters here with us?"
And they took offense at him.
4Jesus said to them, "Only in his hometown, among his relatives and in his own house is a prophet without honor." 5He could
not do any miracles there, except lay his hands on a few sick people
and heal them. 6And he was amazed at their lack of faith.

*Jesus Sends Out the Twelve*

Then Jesus went around teaching from village to village. 7Call-
ing the Twelve to him, he sent them out two by two and gave them
authority over evil[n] spirits.
8These were his instructions: "Take nothing for the journey
except a staff—no bread, no bag, no money in your belts. 9Wear
sandals but not an extra tunic. 10Whenever you enter a house, stay
there until you leave that town. 11And if any place will not welcome you or listen to you, shake the dust off your feet when you
leave, as a testimony against them."
12They went out and preached that people should repent.
13They drove out many demons and anointed many sick people
with oil and healed them.

*John the Baptist Beheaded*

14King Herod heard about this, for Jesus' name had become
well known. Some were saying,[o] "John the Baptist has been raised
from the dead, and that is why miraculous powers are at work in
him."
15Others said, "He is Elijah."
And still others claimed, "He is a prophet, like one of the
prophets of long ago."
16But when Herod heard this, he said, "John, the man I beheaded, has been raised from the dead!"
17For Herod himself had given orders to have John arrested,
and he had him bound and put in prison. He did this because of
Herodias, his brother Philip's wife, whom he had married. 18For
John had been saying to Herod, "It is not lawful for you to have
your brother's wife." 19So Herodias nursed a grudge against John
and wanted to kill him. But she was not able to, 20because Herod

NIV [m]3 Greek *Joses,* a variant of *Joseph* [n]7 Greek *unclean* [o]14 Some early manuscripts *He was saying*

## King James

20For Herod feared John, knowing that he was a just man and an holy, and observed him; and when he heard him, he did many things, and heard him gladly.

21And when a convenient day was come, that Herod on his birthday made a supper to his lords, high captains, and chief *estates* of Galilee;

22And when the daughter of the said Herodias came in, and danced, and pleased Herod and them that sat with him, the king said unto the damsel, Ask of me whatsoever thou wilt, and I will give *it* thee.

23And he sware unto her, Whatsoever thou shalt ask of me, I will give *it* thee, unto the half of my kingdom.

24And she went forth, and said unto her mother, What shall I ask? And she said, The head of John the Baptist.

25And she came in straightway with haste unto the king, and asked, saying, I will that thou give me by and by in a charger the head of John the Baptist.

26And the king was exceeding sorry; *yet* for his oath's sake, and for their sakes which sat with him, he would not reject her.

27And immediately the king sent an executioner, and commanded his head to be brought: and he went and beheaded him in the prison,

28And brought his head in a charger, and gave it to the damsel: and the damsel gave it to her mother.

29And when his disciples heard *of it*, they came and took up his corpse, and laid it in a tomb.

30And the apostles gathered themselves together unto Jesus, and told him all things, both what they had done, and what they had taught.

31And he said unto them, Come ye yourselves apart into a desert place, and rest a while: for there were many coming and going, and they had no leisure so much as to eat.

32And they departed into a desert place by ship privately.

33And the people saw them departing, and many knew him, and ran afoot thither out of all cities, and outwent them, and came together unto him.

34And Jesus, when he came out, saw much people, and was moved with compassion toward them, because they were as sheep not having a shepherd: and he began to teach them many things.

35And when the day was now far spent, his disciples came unto him, and said, This is a desert place, and now the time *is* far passed:

36Send them away, that they may go into the country round about, and into the villages, and buy themselves bread: for they have nothing to eat.

37He answered and said unto them, Give ye them to eat. And they say unto him, Shall we go and buy two hundred pennyworth of bread, and give them to eat?

38He saith unto them, How many loaves have ye? go and see. And when they knew, they say, Five, and two fishes.

39And he commanded them to make all sit down by companies upon the green grass.

40And they sat down in ranks, by hundreds, and by fifties.

41And when he had taken the five loaves and the two fishes, he looked up to heaven, and blessed, and brake the loaves, and gave *them* to his disciples to set before them; and the two fishes divided he among them all.

42And they did all eat, and were filled.

43And they took up twelve baskets full of the fragments, and of the fishes.

44And they that did eat of the loaves were about five thousand men.

45And straightway he constrained his disciples to get into the ship, and to go to the other side before unto Bethsaida, while he sent away the people.

**AMP** [a] Abbott-Smith. [b] Vincent. [c] Wuest. [d] Wuest. [e] Wuest. [f] Wuest. [g] Moulton and Milligan. [h] Trench's "Notes on the Miracles of our Lord." [i] Vincent. But Moulton and Milligan do not think size is meant.

## Amplified

20For Herod had ([a]a reverential) fear of John, knowing that he was a righteous and holy man, and (continually) kept him safe [[b]under guard]. When he heard [John speak] he was much perplexed. And [yet] he heard him gladly.

21But an opportune time came [for Herodias] when Herod on his birthday gave a banquet for his nobles and the high military and chief men of Galilee.

22For when the daughter [c]of Herodias herself came in and danced, she pleased *and* [d]fascinated Herod and his guests; and the king said to the girl, Ask me for whatever you desire, and I will give it to you.

23And he put himself under oath to her, Whatever you ask me, I will give it to you, even to the half of my kingdom. [Esth. 5:3, 6.]

24Then she left the room and said to her mother, What shall I ask [for myself]? And she replied, The head of John the Baptist!

25And she rushed back instantly to the king, and requested, saying, I wish you to give me right now the head of John the Baptist on a platter.

26And the king was deeply pained *and* grieved *and* exceedingly sorry; but because of his oaths and his guests he did not want to slight her [by breaking faith with her].

27And immediately the king sent off one [of the soldiers] of his bodyguard, and gave him orders to bring [John's] head. He went and beheaded him in the prison,

28And brought his head on a platter, and handed it to the girl, and the girl gave it to her mother.

29When his disciples learned of it, they came and took [John's] body and laid it in a tomb.

30The apostles [sent out as missionaries] came back *and* gathered together to Jesus, and told Him all that they had done and taught.

31And He said to them, [[e]As for you] come away by yourselves to a deserted place, and rest a while. For many were (continually) coming and going, and they had not even leisure enough to eat.

32And they went away in a boat to a solitary place by themselves.

33Now many [people] saw them going and recognized them, and they ran there on foot from all the surrounding towns, and they got there ahead [of those in the boat].

34As Jesus landed He saw a great crowd waiting, and He was moved with compassion for them, because they were like sheep without a shepherd; and He began to teach them many things.

35And when [f]the day was already far gone, His disciples came to Him and said, This is a desolate *and* isolated place, and the hour is now late;

36Send the crowds away to go into the country and villages round about and buy themselves something to eat.

37But He replied to them, Give them something to eat yourselves. And they said to Him, Shall we go and buy two hundred denarii [about forty dollars] worth of bread, and give it to them to eat? [II Kings 4:42-44.]

38And He said to them, How many loaves do you have? Go and see. And when they [had looked and] knew, they said, Five [loaves] and two fish.

39Then He commanded the people all to recline on the green grass by companies.

40So they threw themselves down in ranks in hundreds and fifties—with the [g]regularity of arrangement of beds of herbs, looking [h]like so many garden plots.

41And taking the five loaves and two fish, He looked up to heaven, and praising God gave thanks, and broke the loaves, and kept on giving them to the disciples to set before the people; and He [also] divided the two fish among [them] all.

42And they all ate and were satisfied.

43And they took up twelve [[i]small hand] baskets full of broken pieces [from the loaves] and of the fish.

44And those who ate the loaves were five thousand men.

45And at once He insisted that the disciples get into the boat and go ahead of Him to the other side, to Bethsaida, while He was sending the throng away.

## New American Standard

20for Herod was afraid of John, knowing that he was a righteous
and holy man, and kept him safe. And when he heard him, he was
very perplexed; but he used to enjoy listening to him.
21And a strategic day came when Herod on his birthday gave
a banquet for his lords and military commanders and the leading
men of Galilee;
22and when the daughter of Herodias herself came in and
danced, she pleased Herod and his dinner guests; and the king
said to the girl, "Ask me for whatever you want and I will give it
to you."
23And he swore to her, "Whatever you ask of me, I will give it
to you; up to half of my kingdom."
24And she went out and said to her mother, "What shall I ask
for?" And she said, "The head of John the Baptist."
25And immediately she came in haste before the king and
asked, saying, "I want you to give me right away the head of John
the Baptist on a platter."
26And although the king was very sorry, *yet* because of his oaths
and because of his dinner guests, he was unwilling to refuse her.
27And immediately the king sent an executioner and commanded *him* to bring *back* his head. And he went and had him
beheaded in the prison,
28and brought his head on a platter, and gave it to the girl; and
the girl gave it to her mother.
29And when his disciples heard *about this*, they came and took
away his body and laid it in a tomb.
**30**¶ And the apostles *gathered together with Jesus; and they
reported to Him all that they had done and taught.
31And He *said to them, "Come away by yourselves to a lonely
place and rest a while." (For there were many *people* coming and
going, and they did not even have time to eat.)
32And they went away in the boat to a lonely place by themselves.

*Five Thousand Fed*

33And *the people* saw them going, and many recognized *them*,
and they ran there together on foot from all the cities, and got there
ahead of them.
34And when He went ashore, He saw a great multitude, and He
felt compassion for them because they were like sheep without a
shepherd; and He began to teach them many things.
35And when it was already quite late, His disciples came up to
Him and *began* saying, "The place is desolate and it is already quite
late;
36send them away so that they may go into the surrounding
countryside and villages and buy themselves something to eat."
37But He answered and said to them, "You give them *something*
to eat!" And they *said to Him, "Shall we go and spend two
hundred [j]denarii on bread and give them *something* to eat?"
38And He *said to them, "How many loaves do you have? Go
look!" And when they found out, they *said, "Five and two fish."
39And He commanded them all to recline by groups on the
green grass.
40And they reclined in companies of hundreds and of fifties.
41And He took the five loaves and the two fish, and looking up
toward heaven, He blessed *the food* and broke the loaves and He
kept giving *them* to the disciples to set before them; and He divided
up the two fish among them all.
42And they all ate and were satisfied.
43And they picked up twelve full baskets of the broken pieces,
and also of the fish.
44And there were five thousand men who ate the loaves.

*Jesus Walks on the Water*

**45**¶ And immediately He made His disciples get into the boat
and go ahead of *Him* to the other side to Bethsaida, while He
Himself was sending the multitude away.

**NAS** [j] The denarius was equivalent to one day's wage

## New International

feared John and protected him, knowing him to be a righteous and
holy man. When Herod heard John, he was greatly puzzled[k]; yet
he liked to listen to him.
21Finally the opportune time came. On his birthday Herod gave
a banquet for his high officials and military commanders and the
leading men of Galilee. 22When the daughter of Herodias came in
and danced, she pleased Herod and his dinner guests.
The king said to the girl, "Ask me for anything you want, and
I'll give it to you." 23And he promised her with an oath, "Whatever
you ask I will give you, up to half my kingdom."
24She went out and said to her mother, "What shall I ask for?"
"The head of John the Baptist," she answered.
25At once the girl hurried in to the king with the request: "I want
you to give me right now the head of John the Baptist on a platter."
26The king was greatly distressed, but because of his oaths and
his dinner guests, he did not want to refuse her. 27So he immediately sent an executioner with orders to bring John's head. The
man went, beheaded John in the prison, 28and brought back his
head on a platter. He presented it to the girl, and she gave it to her
mother. 29On hearing of this, John's disciples came and took his
body and laid it in a tomb.

*Jesus Feeds the Five Thousand*

30The apostles gathered around Jesus and reported to him all
they had done and taught. 31Then, because so many people were
coming and going that they did not even have a chance to eat, he
said to them, "Come with me by yourselves to a quiet place and
get some rest."
32So they went away by themselves in a boat to a solitary place.
33But many who saw them leaving recognized them and ran on
foot from all the towns and got there ahead of them. 34When Jesus
landed and saw a large crowd, he had compassion on them, because they were like sheep without a shepherd. So he began
teaching them many things.
35By this time it was late in the day, so his disciples came to him.
"This is a remote place," they said, "and it's already very late.
36Send the people away so they can go to the surrounding countryside and villages and buy themselves something to eat."
37But he answered, "You give them something to eat."
They said to him, "That would take eight months of a man's
wages[l]! Are we to go and spend that much on bread and give it
to them to eat?"
38"How many loaves do you have?" he asked. "Go and see."
When they found out, they said, "Five—and two fish."
39Then Jesus directed them to have all the people sit down in
groups on the green grass. 40So they sat down in groups of hundreds and fifties. 41Taking the five loaves and the two fish and
looking up to heaven, he gave thanks and broke the loaves. Then
he gave them to his disciples to set before the people. He also
divided the two fish among them all. 42They all ate and were
satisfied, 43and the disciples picked up twelve basketfuls of broken
pieces of bread and fish. 44The number of the men who had eaten
was five thousand.

*Jesus Walks on the Water*

45Immediately Jesus made his disciples get into the boat and go
on ahead of him to Bethsaida, while he dismissed the crowd.

**NIV** [k] 20 Some early manuscripts *he did many things* [l] 37 Greek *take two hundred denarii*

## King James

46And when he had sent them away, he departed into a mountain to pray.
47And when even was come, the ship was in the midst of the sea, and he alone on the land.
48And he saw them toiling in rowing; for the wind was contrary unto them: and about the fourth watch of the night he cometh unto them, walking upon the sea, and would have passed by them.
49But when they saw him walking upon the sea, they supposed it had been a spirit, and cried out:
50For they all saw him, and were troubled. And immediately he talked with them, and saith unto them, Be of good cheer: it is I; be not afraid.
51And he went up unto them into the ship; and the wind ceased: and they were sore amazed in themselves beyond measure, and wondered.
52For they considered not *the miracle* of the loaves: for their heart was hardened.
53And when they had passed over, they came into the land of Gennesaret, and drew to the shore.
54And when they were come out of the ship, straightway they knew him,
55And ran through that whole region round about, and began to carry about in beds those that were sick, where they heard he was.
56And whithersoever he entered, into villages, or cities, or country, they laid the sick in the streets, and besought him that they might touch if it were but the border of his garment: and as many as touched him were made whole.

7 THEN CAME together unto him the Pharisees, and certain of the scribes, which came from Jerusalem.
2And when they saw some of his disciples eat bread with defiled, that is to say, with unwashen, hands, they found fault.
3For the Pharisees, and all the Jews, except they wash *their* hands oft, eat not, holding the tradition of the elders.
4And *when they come* from the market, except they wash, they eat not. And many other things there be, which they have received to hold, *as* the washing of cups, and pots, brasen vessels, and of tables.
5Then the Pharisees and scribes asked him, Why walk not thy disciples according to the tradition of the elders, but eat bread with unwashen hands?
6He answered and said unto them, Well hath Esaias prophesied of you hypocrites, as it is written, This people honoureth me with *their* lips, but their heart is far from me.
7Howbeit in vain do they worship me, teaching *for* doctrines the commandments of men.
8For laying aside the commandment of God, ye hold the tradition of men, *as* the washing of pots and cups: and many other such like things ye do.
9And he said unto them, Full well ye reject the commandment of God, that ye may keep your own tradition.

## Amplified

46And after He had taken leave of them, He went off into the hills to pray.
47Now when evening had come, the boat was out in the middle of the lake, and He was by Himself on the land.
48And having seen that they were troubled *and* tormented in rowing, for the wind was against them, about the fourth watch of the night [3:00 o'clock] He came to them, walking (directly) on the sea. And He acted as if He meant to pass by them,
49But when they saw Him walking on the sea they thought [it] was a ghost, and [a]raised a (deep, throaty) shriek of terror.
50For they all saw Him, and were agitated—troubled and filled with fear and dread. But immediately He talked with them and said, Take heart! I AM! Stop being alarmed *and* afraid. [Exod. 3:14.]
51And He went up into the boat with them and the wind ceased, [[b]sank to rest as if exhausted by its own beating]. And they were astonished exceedingly—beyond measure.
52For they failed to consider *or* understand [the teaching and meaning of the miracle of] the loaves; [in fact] their hearts had [c]grown callous—had become dull and had [d]lost the power of understanding.
53And when they had crossed over they reached the land of Gennesaret, and [e]came to (anchor at) the shore.
54As soon as they got out of the boat [the people] recognized Him,
55And they ran about the whole countryside, and began to carry around sick people on their pallets (sleeping pads) to any place where they heard that He was.
56And wherever He came into villages or cities or the country, they would lay the sick in the market places, and beg Him that they might touch even the fringe of His outer garment; and as many as touched Him were restored to health.

7 NOW THERE gathered together to [Jesus] the Pharisees and some of the scribes who had come from Jerusalem,
2For they had seen that some of His disciples ate with [f]common hands, that is, [with hands defiled and unhallowed, because] they had not [given them a [g]ceremonial] washing.
3For the Pharisees and all of the Jews do not eat unless [merely for ceremonial reasons] they wash their hands (diligently [h]up to the elbow) with clenched fist, adhering (carefully and faithfully) to the tradition of (practices and customs handed down to them by) their forefathers—to be observed.
4And [when they come] from the market place, they do not eat unless they purify themselves; and there are many other traditions—[that is] oral, man-made laws handed down to them, which they observe faithfully and diligently—washing of cups and wooden pitchers and widemouthed jugs and utensils of copper and [i]beds.
5And the Pharisees and scribes kept asking [Jesus], Why do Your disciples not order their way of living according to the tradition handed down by the forefathers to be observed, but eat with hands unwashed *and* ceremonially not purified?
6But He said to them, Excellently *and* truly— [j]so that there will be no room for blame—did Isaiah prophesy of you, the pretenders *and* hypocrites, as it stands written: This people (constantly) honor Me with their lips, but their heart holds itself off *and* is far distant from Me.
7In vain—fruitlessly and without profit—do they worship Me, ordering *and* teaching to be obeyed as doctrines the commandments *and* precepts of men. [Isa. 29:13.]
8You disregard *and* give up *and* bid depart from you the commandment of God, and cling to the tradition of men—keeping it carefully and faithfully.
9And He said to them, You have a fine way of rejecting (thus thwarting and nullifying and doing away with) the commandment of God, in order to keep your tradition—your own human regulations!

**AMP** [a] Thayer. [b] Vincent. [c] Thayer. [d] Thayer. [e] Thayer. [f] Tyndale. [g] Williams. [h] Abbott-Smith. [i] Rendered "beds" in most lexicons, and by Moulton and Milligan, and Young; mistranslated "tables" by the Authorized Version; omitted by Nestle. [j] Thayer.

## New American Standard

46 And after bidding them farewell, He departed to the mountain to pray.

47 And when it was evening, the boat was in the midst of the sea, and He *was* alone on the land.

48 And seeing them straining at the oars, for the wind was against them, at about the fourth watch of the night, He *came to them, walking on the sea; and He intended to pass by them.

49 But when they saw Him walking on the sea, they supposed that it was a ghost, and cried out;

50 for they all saw Him and were frightened. But immediately He spoke with them and *said to them, "Take courage; it is I, do not be afraid."

51 And He got into the boat with them, and the wind stopped; and they were greatly astonished,

52 for they had not gained any insight from the *incident of* the loaves, but their heart was hardened.

*Healing at Gennesaret*

53 ¶ And when they had crossed over they came to land at Gennesaret, and moored to the shore.

54 And when they had come out of the boat, immediately *the people* recognized Him,

55 and ran about that whole country and began to carry about on their pallets those who were sick, to the place they heard He was.

56 And wherever He entered villages, or cities, or countryside, they were laying the sick in the market places, and entreating Him that they might just touch the fringe of His cloak; and as many as touched it were being cured.

*Followers of Tradition*

7 AND THE Pharisees and some of the scribes gathered together around Him when they had come from Jerusalem,

2 and had seen that some of His disciples were eating their bread with impure hands, that is, unwashed.

3 (For the Pharisees and all the Jews do not eat unless they carefully wash their hands, *thus* observing the traditions of the elders;

4 and *when they come* from the market place, they do not eat unless they cleanse themselves; and there are many other things which they have received in order to observe, such as the washing of cups and pitchers and copper pots.)

5 And the Pharisees and the scribes *asked Him, "Why do Your disciples not walk according to the tradition of the elders, but eat their bread with impure hands?"

6 And He said to them, "Rightly did Isaiah prophesy of you hypocrites, as it is written,

'THIS PEOPLE HONORS ME WITH THEIR LIPS,
BUT THEIR HEART IS FAR AWAY FROM ME.
7 'BUT IN VAIN DO THEY WORSHIP ME,
TEACHING AS DOCTRINES THE PRECEPTS OF MEN.'

8 "Neglecting the commandment of God, you hold to the tradition of men."

9 He was also saying to them, "You nicely set aside the commandment of God in order to keep your tradition.

## New International

46 After leaving them, he went up on a mountainside to pray.
47 When evening came, the boat was in the middle of the lake,
and he was alone on land. 48 He saw the disciples straining at the
oars, because the wind was against them. About the fourth watch
of the night he went out to them, walking on the lake. He was
about to pass by them, 49 but when they saw him walking on the
lake, they thought he was a ghost. They cried out, 50 because they
all saw him and were terrified.
Immediately he spoke to them and said, "Take courage! It is I.
Don't be afraid." 51 Then he climbed into the boat with them, and
the wind died down. They were completely amazed, 52 for they
had not understood about the loaves; their hearts were hardened.
53 When they had crossed over, they landed at Gennesaret and
anchored there. 54 As soon as they got out of the boat, people
recognized Jesus. 55 They ran throughout that whole region and
carried the sick on mats to wherever they heard he was. 56 And
wherever he went—into villages, towns or countryside—they
placed the sick in the marketplaces. They begged him to let them
touch even the edge of his cloak, and all who touched him were
healed.

*Clean and Unclean*

7 THE PHARISEES and some of the teachers of the law who
had come from Jerusalem gathered around Jesus and 2 saw
some of his disciples eating food with hands that were "unclean,"
that is, unwashed. 3 (The Pharisees and all the Jews do not eat
unless they give their hands a ceremonial washing, holding to the
tradition of the elders. 4 When they come from the marketplace
they do not eat unless they wash. And they observe many other
traditions, such as the washing of cups, pitchers and kettles.[k])
5 So the Pharisees and teachers of the law asked Jesus, "Why
don't your disciples live according to the tradition of the elders
instead of eating their food with 'unclean' hands?"
6 He replied, "Isaiah was right when he prophesied about you
hypocrites; as it is written:

" 'These people honor me with their lips,
but their hearts are far from me.
7 They worship me in vain;
their teachings are but rules taught by men.'[l]

8 You have let go of the commands of God and are holding on to
the traditions of men."
9 And he said to them: "You have a fine way of setting aside the
commands of God in order to observe[m] your own traditions! 10 For

NIV [k] 4 Some early manuscripts *pitchers, kettles and dining couches*
[l] 6,7 Isaiah 29:13 [m] 9 Some manuscripts *set up*

## King James

10For Moses said, Honour thy father and thy mother; and, Whoso curseth father or mother, let him die the death:

11But ye say, If a man shall say to his father or mother, *It is* Corban, that is to say, a gift, by whatsoever thou mightest be profited by me; *he shall be free.*

12And ye suffer him no more to do aught for his father or his mother;

13Making the word of God of none effect through your tradition, which ye have delivered: and many such like things do ye.

14¶ And when he had called all the people *unto him,* he said unto them, Hearken unto me every one *of you,* and understand:

15There is nothing from without a man, that entering into him can defile him: but the things which come out of him, those are they that defile the man.

16If any man have ears to hear, let him hear.

17And when he was entered into the house from the people, his disciples asked him concerning the parable.

18And he saith unto them, Are ye so without understanding also? Do ye not perceive, that whatsoever thing from without entereth into the man, *it* cannot defile him;

19Because it entereth not into his heart, but into the belly, and goeth out into the draught, purging all meats?

20And he said, That which cometh out of the man, that defileth the man.

21For from within, out of the heart of men, proceed evil thoughts, adulteries, fornications, murders,

22Thefts, covetousness, wickedness, deceit, lasciviousness, an evil eye, blasphemy, pride, foolishness:

23All these evil things come from within, and defile the man.

24¶ And from thence he arose, and went into the borders of Tyre and Sidon, and entered into an house, and would have no man know *it:* but he could not be hid.

25For a *certain* woman, whose young daughter had an unclean spirit, heard of him, and came and fell at his feet:

26The woman was a Greek, a Syrophenician by nation; and she besought him that he would cast forth the devil out of her daughter.

27But Jesus said unto her, Let the children first be filled: for it is not meet to take the children's bread, and to cast *it* unto the dogs.

28And she answered and said unto him, Yes, Lord: yet the dogs under the table eat of the children's crumbs.

29And he said unto her, For this saying go thy way; the devil is gone out of thy daughter.

30And when she was come to her house, she found the devil gone out, and her daughter laid upon the bed.

31¶ And again, departing from the coasts of Tyre and Sidon, he came unto the sea of Galilee, through the midst of the coasts of Decapolis.

32And they bring unto him one that was deaf, and had an impediment in his speech; and they beseech him to put his hand upon him.

**AMP** [a] Abbott-Smith. [b] "Expositor's Greek Testament." [c] Souter. [d] Vincent.

## Amplified

10For Moses said, Honor (revere with tenderness of feeling and deference) your father and your mother; and, He who speaks ill of, *or* reviles *or* abuses *or* treats improperly father or mother, let him (surely) die. [Exod. 20:12; Deut. 5:16; Exod. 21:17; Lev. 20:9.]

11But [as for you] you say, A man is exempt if he tells [his] father or [his] mother, What you would otherwise have gained from me (everything I have that would have been of use to you) is Corban, that is, is a gift—already given as an offering to God.

12Then you no longer are permitting him to do anything for [his] father or mother—but are letting him off from doing for them.

13Thus you are nullifying *and* making void *and* of no effect [the authority of] the Word of God through your tradition, which you [in turn] hand on. And many [things] of this kind you are doing.

14And He called the people to [Him] again, and said to them, Listen to Me, all of you, and understand [what I say].

15There is not [even] one thing outside a man which by going into him can pollute *and* defile him, but the things which come out of a man are what defile him *and* make him unhallowed *and* unclean.

16 *If any man has ears to hear, let him be listening—and* [a]*perceive, comprehend by hearing.*

17And when He had left the crowd and had gone into the house, His disciples began asking Him about the parable.

18And He said to them, Then are you also unintelligent *and* dull *and* without understanding? Do you not discern *and* see that whatever goes into a man from the outside cannot make him unhallowed *or* unclean,

19Since it does not reach *and* enter his heart but [only his] digestive tract, and so passes on (into the place designed to receive waste)? Thus He was making *and* declaring all foods (ceremonially) clean [that is, [b]abolishing the ceremonial distinctions of the Levitical Law].

20And He said, What comes out of a man is what makes a man unclean *and* renders [him] unhallowed.

21For from within, [that is] out of the heart of men, come base *and* wicked thoughts: sexual immorality, stealing, murder, adultery,

22Coveting (a greedy desire to have more wealth), dangerous *and* destructive wickedness, deceit; [c]unrestrained (indecent) conduct; an evil eye (envy), slander (evil speaking, malicious misrepresentation, abusiveness); pride—[that is] [d]the sin of an uplifted heart against God and man; foolishness (folly, lack of sense, recklessness, thoughtlessness).

23All these evil [purposes and desires] come from within, and they make the man unclean *and* render him unhallowed.

24And Jesus arose and went away from there to the region of Tyre *and Sidon.* And He went into a house and did not want any one to know [that He was there], but it was not possible for Him to be hidden [from public notice].

25Instead, at once a woman whose little daughter (was under the control of) an unclean spirit, heard about Him, and came and flung herself down at His feet.

26Now the woman was a Greek [Gentile in religion], a Syrophoenician by race. And she kept begging Him to drive the demon out of her little daughter.

27And He said to her, First let the children be fed, for it is not becoming *or* proper *or* right to take the children's bread and throw it to the (little house) dogs.

28But she answered Him, Yes, Lord; yet even the small pups under the table eat the little children's scraps of food.

29And He said to her, Because of this saying you may go your way; the demon has gone out of your daughter [permanently].

30And she went home, and found the child thrown on the couch, and the demon departed.

31Soon after this Jesus coming back from the region of Tyre, passed through Sidon on to the Sea of Galilee through the region of Decapolis [the ten cities].

32And they brought to Him a man who was deaf and had difficulty in speaking, and they begged Jesus to place His hand upon him.

## New American Standard

10 "For Moses said, 'HONOR YOUR FATHER AND YOUR MOTHER'; and, 'HE WHO SPEAKS EVIL OF FATHER OR MOTHER, LET HIM BE PUT TO DEATH';

11 but you say, 'If a man says to *his* father or *his* mother, anything of mine you might have been helped by is Corban (that is to say, [e]given *to God* ),'

12 you no longer permit him to do anything for *his* father or *his* mother;

13 *thus* invalidating the word of God by your tradition which you have handed down; and you do many things such as that."

*The Heart of Man*

14 And after He called the multitude to Him again, He *began* saying to them, "Listen to Me, all of you, and understand:

15 there is nothing outside the man which going into him can defile him; but the things which proceed out of the man are what defile the man.

16 [" [f]If any man has ears to hear, let him hear."]

17 And when leaving the multitude, He had entered the house, His disciples questioned Him about the parable.

18 And He *said to them, "Are you so lacking in understanding also? Do you not understand that whatever goes into the man from outside cannot defile him;

19 because it does not go into his heart, but into his stomach, and is eliminated?" ( *Thus He* declared all foods clean.)

20 And He was saying, "That which proceeds out of the man, that is what defiles the man.

21 "For from within, out of the heart of men, proceed the evil thoughts, fornications, thefts, murders, adulteries,

22 deeds of coveting *and* wickedness, *as well as* deceit, sensuality, envy, slander, pride *and* foolishness.

23 "All these evil things proceed from within and defile the man."

*The Syrophoenician Woman*

24 ¶ And from there He arose and went away to the region of Tyre [g]. And when He had entered a house, He wanted no one to know *of it;* yet He could not escape notice.

25 But after hearing of Him, a woman whose little daughter had an unclean spirit, immediately came and fell at His feet.

26 Now the woman was a [h]Gentile, of the Syrophoenician race. And she kept asking Him to cast the demon out of her daughter.

27 And He was saying to her, "Let the children be satisfied first, for it is not good to take the children's bread and throw it to the dogs."

28 But she answered and *said to Him, "Yes, Lord, *but* even the dogs under the table feed on the children's crumbs."

29 And He said to her, "Because of this answer go your way; the demon has gone out of your daughter."

30 And going back to her home, she found the child lying on the bed, the demon having departed.

31 ¶ And again He went out from the region of Tyre, and came through Sidon to the Sea of Galilee, within the region of Decapolis.

32 And they *brought to Him one who was deaf and spoke with difficulty, and they *entreated Him to lay His hand upon him.

NAS [e] Or, *a gift, an offering* [f] Many mss. do not contain this verse [g] Some early mss. add: *and Sidon* [h] Lit., *Greek*

## New International

Moses said, 'Honor your father and your mother,'[i] and, 'Anyone
who curses his father or mother must be put to death.'[j] 11 But you
say that if a man says to his father or mother: 'Whatever help you
might otherwise have received from me is Corban' (that is, a gift
devoted to God), 12 then you no longer let him do anything for his
father or mother. 13 Thus you nullify the word of God by your
tradition that you have handed down. And you do many things
like that."

14 Again Jesus called the crowd to him and said, "Listen to me,
everyone, and understand this. 15 Nothing outside a man can make
him 'unclean' by going into him. Rather, it is what comes out of
a man that makes him 'unclean.'[k]"

17 After he had left the crowd and entered the house, his disciples asked him about this parable. 18 "Are you so dull?" he asked.
"Don't you see that nothing that enters a man from the outside can
make him 'unclean'? 19 For it doesn't go into his heart but into his
stomach, and then out of his body." (In saying this, Jesus declared
all foods "clean.")

20 He went on: "What comes out of a man is what makes him
'unclean.' 21 For from within, out of men's hearts, come evil
thoughts, sexual immorality, theft, murder, adultery, 22 greed,
malice, deceit, lewdness, envy, slander, arrogance and folly. 23 All
these evils come from inside and make a man 'unclean.' "

*The Faith of a Syrophoenician Woman*

24 Jesus left that place and went to the vicinity of Tyre.[l] He
entered a house and did not want anyone to know it; yet he could
not keep his presence secret. 25 In fact, as soon as she heard about
him, a woman whose little daughter was possessed by an evil[m]
spirit came and fell at his feet. 26 The woman was a Greek, born in
Syrian Phoenicia. She begged Jesus to drive the demon out of her
daughter.

27 "First let the children eat all they want," he told her, "for it
is not right to take the children's bread and toss it to their dogs."

28 "Yes, Lord," she replied, "but even the dogs under the table
eat the children's crumbs."

29 Then he told her, "For such a reply, you may go; the demon
has left your daughter."

30 She went home and found her child lying on the bed, and the
demon gone.

*The Healing of a Deaf and Mute Man*

31 Then Jesus left the vicinity of Tyre and went through Sidon,
down to the Sea of Galilee and into the region of the Decapolis.[n]
32 There some people brought to him a man who was deaf and
could hardly talk, and they begged him to place his hand on the
man.

NIV [i] *10* Exodus 20:12; Deut. 5:16 [j] *10* Exodus 21:17; Lev. 20:9 [k] *15* Some early manuscripts *'unclean.' 16If anyone has ears to hear, let him hear.* [l] *24* Many early manuscripts *Tyre and Sidon* [m] *25* Greek *unclean* [n] *31* That is, the Ten Cities

## King James

33And he took him aside from the multitude, and put his fingers
into his ears, and he spit, and touched his tongue;
34And looking up to heaven, he sighed, and saith unto him,
Ephphatha, that is, Be opened.
35And straightway his ears were opened, and the string of his
tongue was loosed, and he spake plain.
36And he charged them that they should tell no man: but the
more he charged them, so much the more a great deal they published *it;*
37And were beyond measure astonished, saying, He hath done
all things well: he maketh both the deaf to hear, and the dumb to
speak.

**8** IN THOSE days the multitude being very great, and having
nothing to eat, Jesus called his disciples *unto him,* and saith
unto them,
2I have compassion on the multitude, because they have now
been with me three days, and have nothing to eat:
3And if I send them away fasting to their own houses, they will
faint by the way: for divers of them came from far.
4And his disciples answered him, From whence can a man
satisfy these *men* with bread here in the wilderness?
5And he asked them, How many loaves have ye? And they
said, Seven.
6And he commanded the people to sit down on the ground: and
he took the seven loaves, and gave thanks, and brake, and gave
to his disciples to set before *them;* and they did set *them* before the
people.
7And they had a few small fishes: and he blessed, and commanded to set them also before *them.*
8So they did eat, and were filled: and they took up of the broken
*meat* that was left seven baskets.
9And they that had eaten were about four thousand: and he
sent them away.
10¶ And straightway he entered into a ship with his disciples,
and came into the parts of Dalmanutha.
11And the Pharisees came forth, and began to question with
him, seeking of him a sign from heaven, tempting him.
12And he sighed deeply in his spirit, and saith, Why doth this
generation seek after a sign? verily I say unto you, There shall no
sign be given unto this generation.
13And he left them, and entering into the ship again departed
to the other side.
14¶ Now *the disciples* had forgotten to take bread, neither had
they in the ship with them more than one loaf.
15And he charged them, saying, Take heed, beware of the
leaven of the Pharisees, and *of* the leaven of Herod.
16And they reasoned among themselves, saying, *It is* because
we have no bread.
17And when Jesus knew *it,* he saith unto them, Why reason ye,
because ye have no bread? perceive ye not yet, neither understand? have ye your heart yet hardened?
18Having eyes, see ye not? and having ears, hear ye not? and
do ye not remember?
19When I brake the five loaves among five thousand, how many
baskets full of fragments took ye up? They say unto him, Twelve.

## Amplified

33And taking him aside from the crowd privately, He thrust His
fingers into the man's ears, and spat and touched his tongue;
34And looking up to heaven, He sighed as He said, Ephphatha,
which means, Be opened.
35And his ears were opened, his tongue was loosed, and he
began to speak distinctly *and* as he should.
36And Jesus [ [a]in His own interest] admonished *and* ordered
them sternly *and* expressly to tell no one, but the more He commanded them, the more zealously they proclaimed it.
37And they were overwhelmingly astonished, saying, He has
done everything excellently—commendably and nobly! He even
makes the deaf to hear and the dumb to speak!

**8** IN THOSE days when [again] an immense crowd had gathered, and they had nothing to eat, Jesus called His disciples
to Him, and told them,
2I have pity *and* sympathy for the people *and* My heart goes out
to them, for they have been with Me now three days, and have
nothing [left] to eat;
3And if I send them away to their homes hungry, they will be
feeble through exhaustion *and* faint along the road; and some of
them have come a long way.
4And His disciples replied to Him, How can any one fill *and*
satisfy [these people] with loaves of bread here in [this] desolate
*and* uninhabited region?
5And He asked them, How many loaves have you? They said,
Seven.
6And He commanded the multitude to recline upon the
ground, and He [then] took the seven loaves [of bread], and having given thanks, He broke them and kept on giving them to His
disciples to put before [the people]; and they placed them before
the crowd.
7And they had a few small fish; and when He had [b]praised God
*and* given thanks *and* asked Him to bless them [to their use], He
ordered that these also should be set before [them].
8And they ate and were satisfied, and they took up seven
[ [c]large provision] baskets full of the broken pieces left over.
9And there were about four thousand people. And He dismissed them,
10And at once He got into the boat with His disciples, and went
to the district of Dalmanutha (or Magdala).
11The Pharisees came and began to argue with *and* question
Him, demanding from Him a sign—an attesting miracle from
heaven—[maliciously] to test Him.
12And He groaned *and* sighed deeply in His spirit, and said,
Why does this generation seek for a sign? Positively I say to you,
no sign shall be given this generation.
13And He went away *and* left them, and getting into the boat
again He departed to the other side.
14Now they had [ [d]completely] forgotten to bring bread, and
they had only one loaf with them in the boat.
15And Jesus (repeatedly expressly) charged *and* admonished
them saying, Look out; keep on your guard *and* beware of the
leaven of the Pharisees and the leaven of Herod [ [e]and the Herodi-
ans].
16And they discussed it *and* reasoned with one another, [It is]
because we have no bread.
17And being aware [of it], Jesus said to them, Why are you
reasoning *and* saying [it is] because you have no bread? Do you not
yet discern or understand? Are your hearts in (a settled state of)
hardness? [Jer. 5:21; Isa. 6:9, 10.]
18Having eyes do you not see [with them], and having ears do
you not hear *and* perceive *and* understand the sense of what is said?
And do you not remember?
19When I broke the five loaves for the five thousand, how many
[ [f]small hand] baskets full of broken pieces did you take up? They
said to Him, Twelve.

**AMP** [a] Wuest: In the middle voice showing charge given with speaker's personal interest in view. [b] Thayer. [c] Vincent. But Moulton and Milligan: *Size not meant.* [d] Wuest. [e] Some ancient authorities so read. [f] Vincent.

## New American Standard

33And He took him aside from the multitude by himself, and
put His fingers into his ears, and after spitting, He touched his
tongue *with the saliva;*
34and looking up to heaven with a deep sigh, He *said to him,
"Ephphatha!" that is, "Be opened!"
35And his ears were opened, and the impediment of his tongue
was removed, and he *began* speaking plainly.
36And He gave them orders not to tell anyone; but the more He
ordered them, the more widely they continued to proclaim it.
37And they were utterly astonished, saying, "He has done all
things well; He makes even the deaf to hear, and the dumb to
speak."

*Four Thousand Fed*

8 IN THOSE days again, when there was a great multitude and
they had nothing to eat, He called His disciples and *said to
them,
2"I feel compassion for the multitude because they have remained with Me now three days, and have nothing to eat;
3and if I send them away hungry to their home, they will faint
on the way; and some of them have come from a distance."
4And His disciples answered Him, "Where will anyone be able
to *find enough to* satisfy these men with bread here in a desolate
place?"
5And He was asking them, "How many loaves do you have?"
And they said, "Seven."
6And He *directed the multitude to sit down on the ground;
and taking the seven loaves, He gave thanks and broke them, and
started giving them to His disciples to serve to them, and they
served them to the multitude.
7They also had a few small fish; and after He had blessed them,
He ordered these to be served as well.
8And they ate and were satisfied; and they picked up seven
large baskets full of what was left over of the broken pieces.
9And about four thousand were *there;* and He sent them away.
10And immediately He entered the boat with His disciples, and
came to the district of Dalmanutha.
11¶ And the Pharisees came out and began to argue with Him,
seeking from Him a sign from heaven, to test Him.
12And sighing deeply in His spirit, He *said, "Why does this
generation seek for a sign? Truly I say to you, no sign shall be given
to this generation."
13And leaving them, He again embarked and went away to the
other side.
14¶ And they had forgotten to take bread; and did not have more
than one loaf in the boat with them.
15And He was giving orders to them, saying, "Watch out!
Beware of the leaven of the Pharisees and the leaven of Herod."
16And they *began* to discuss with one another *the fact* that they
had no bread.
17And Jesus, aware of this, *said to them, "Why do you discuss
*the fact* that you have no bread? Do you not yet see or understand?
Do you have a hardened heart?
18"HAVING EYES, DO YOU NOT SEE? AND HAVING EARS, DO YOU
NOT HEAR? And do you not remember,
19when I broke the five loaves for the five thousand, how many
baskets full of broken pieces you picked up?" They *said to Him,
"Twelve."

## New International

33After he took him aside, away from the crowd, Jesus put his
fingers into the man's ears. Then he spit and touched the man's
tongue. 34He looked up to heaven and with a deep sigh said to
him, *"Ephphatha!"* (which means, "Be opened!"). 35At this, the
man's ears were opened, his tongue was loosened and he began
to speak plainly.
36Jesus commanded them not to tell anyone. But the more he
did so, the more they kept talking about it. 37People were overwhelmed with amazement. "He has done everything well," they
said. "He even makes the deaf hear and the mute speak."

*Jesus Feeds the Four Thousand*

8 DURING THOSE days another large crowd gathered. Since
they had nothing to eat, Jesus called his disciples to him and
said, 2"I have compassion for these people; they have already been
with me three days and have nothing to eat. 3If I send them home
hungry, they will collapse on the way, because some of them have
come a long distance."
4His disciples answered, "But where in this remote place can
anyone get enough bread to feed them?"
5"How many loaves do you have?" Jesus asked.
"Seven," they replied.
6He told the crowd to sit down on the ground. When he had
taken the seven loaves and given thanks, he broke them and gave
them to his disciples to set before the people, and they did so.
7They had a few small fish as well; he gave thanks for them also
and told the disciples to distribute them. 8The people ate and were
satisfied. Afterward the disciples picked up seven basketfuls of
broken pieces that were left over. 9About four thousand men were
present. And having sent them away, 10he got into the boat with
his disciples and went to the region of Dalmanutha.
11The Pharisees came and began to question Jesus. To test him,
they asked him for a sign from heaven. 12He sighed deeply and
said, "Why does this generation ask for a miraculous sign? I tell
you the truth, no sign will be given to it." 13Then he left them, got
back into the boat and crossed to the other side.

*The Yeast of the Pharisees and Herod*

14The disciples had forgotten to bring bread, except for one loaf
they had with them in the boat. 15"Be careful," Jesus warned
them. "Watch out for the yeast of the Pharisees and that of Herod."
16They discussed this with one another and said, "It is because
we have no bread."
17Aware of their discussion, Jesus asked them: "Why are you
talking about having no bread? Do you still not see or understand?
Are your hearts hardened? 18Do you have eyes but fail to see, and
ears but fail to hear? And don't you remember? 19When I broke the
five loaves for the five thousand, how many basketfuls of pieces
did you pick up?"
"Twelve," they replied.

## King James

20 And when the seven among four thousand, how many baskets full of fragments took ye up? And they said, Seven.

21 And he said unto them, How is it that ye do not understand?

22 ¶ And he cometh to Bethsaida; and they bring a blind man unto him, and besought him to touch him.

23 And he took the blind man by the hand, and led him out of the town; and when he had spit on his eyes, and put his hands upon him, he asked him if he saw aught.

24 And he looked up, and said, I see men as trees, walking.

25 After that he put *his* hands again upon his eyes, and made him look up: and he was restored, and saw every man clearly.

26 And he sent him away to his house, saying, Neither go into the town, nor tell *it* to any in the town.

27 ¶ And Jesus went out, and his disciples, into the towns of Caesarea Philippi: and by the way he asked his disciples, saying unto them, Whom do men say that I am?

28 And they answered, John the Baptist: but some *say,* Elias; and others, One of the prophets.

29 And he saith unto them, But whom say ye that I am? And Peter answereth and saith unto him, Thou art the Christ.

30 And he charged them that they should tell no man of him.

31 And he began to teach them, that the Son of man must suffer many things, and be rejected of the elders, and *of* the chief priests, and scribes, and be killed, and after three days rise again.

32 And he spake that saying openly. And Peter took him, and began to rebuke him.

33 But when he had turned about and looked on his disciples, he rebuked Peter, saying, Get thee behind me, Satan: for thou savourest not the things that be of God, but the things that be of men.

34 ¶ And when he had called the people *unto him* with his disciples also, he said unto them, Whosoever will come after me, let him deny himself, and take up his cross, and follow me.

35 For whosoever will save his life shall lose it; but whosoever shall lose his life for my sake and the gospel's, the same shall save it.

36 For what shall it profit a man, if he shall gain the whole world, and lose his own soul?

37 Or what shall a man give in exchange for his soul?

38 Whosoever therefore shall be ashamed of me and of my words in this adulterous and sinful generation; of him also shall the Son of man be ashamed, when he cometh in the glory of his Father with the holy angels.

## Amplified

20 And the seven loaves for the four thousand, how many [[a]large provision] baskets full of broken pieces did you take up? And they said to Him, Seven.

21 And He ([b]kept repeating), Do you not yet understand?

22 And they came to Bethsaida. And [people] brought to Him a blind man, and begged Him to touch him.

23 And He [c]caught the blind man by the hand, and led him out of the village; and when He had spit on his eyes and put His hands upon him, He asked him, Do you ([d]possibly) see anything?

24 And he looked up and said, I see people, but [they look] like trees, walking.

25 Then He put His hands on his eyes again, and the man looked intently [that is, fixed his eyes on definite objects], and he was restored, and saw everything distinctly—even what was [e]at a distance.

26 And He sent him away to his house, telling [him], Do not [even] enter the village *or tell any one there.*

27 And Jesus went on with His disciples to the villages of Caesarea Philippi, and on the way He asked His disciples, Who do people say that I am?

28 And they answered [Him], John the Baptist; and others, Elijah, but others, One of the prophets.

29 And He asked them, But who do you yourselves say that I am? Peter replied to Him, You are the Christ, the Messiah, the Anointed One.

30 And He charged them sharply to tell no one about Him.

31 And He began to teach them that the Son of man must of necessity suffer many things, and be tested *and* disapproved *and* rejected by the elders and the chief priests and the scribes, and be put to death, and after three days rise [again [f]from death].

32 And He said this freely—frankly, plainly and explicitly, making it unmistakable. And Peter took Him [g]by the hand *and* led Him aside, then [facing Him] began to rebuke Him.

33 But turning around [His back to Peter], and seeing His disciples, He rebuked Peter, saying, Get behind Me, Satan! For you do not have a mind [h]intent on promoting what God wills, but what pleases men—you are not on God's side, but that of men.

34 And Jesus called to [Him] the throng with His disciples, and said to them, If any one intends to come after Me, let him deny himself—forget, ignore, disown, [i]lose sight of himself and his own interests—and take up his cross, and ([j]joining Me as a disciple and siding with My party) follow [k]with Me—continually, [that is,] cleave steadfastly to Me.

35 For whoever wants to save his [[l]higher, spiritual, eternal] life, will lose [the [m]lower, natural, temporal life [n]which is lived (only) on earth]; and whoever gives up his life [which is lived (only) on earth], for My sake and the Gospel's, will save [his [o]higher, spiritual life [p]in the eternal kingdom of God].

36 For what does it profit a man to gain the whole world, and forfeit his life [[q]in the eternal kingdom of God]?

37 For what can a man give as an exchange—[r]a compensation, a ransom, in return—for his [blessed] life [[s]in the eternal kingdom of God]?

38 For whoever [t]is ashamed [here and now] of Me and My words in this adulterous (unfaithful) and (pre-eminently) sinful generation, of him will the Son of man also be ashamed, when He comes in the glory (splendor and majesty) of His Father with the holy angels.

**9** AND HE said unto them, Verily I say unto you, That there be some of them that stand here, which shall not taste of death, till they have seen the kingdom of God come with power.

**9** AND JESUS said to them, Truly *and* solemnly, I say to you, there are some standing here who will in no way taste death before they see the kingdom of God come in [its] power.

**AMP** [a] Vincent. [b] "Expositor's Greek Testament." [c] Tyndale. [d] "Expositor's Greek Testament." [e] Thayer. [f] Cremer. [g] Thayer. [h] Thayer. [i] Thayer. [j] Thayer. [k] Wuest. [l] Jamieson, Fausett and Brown. [m] Jamieson, Fausett and Brown. [n] Thayer. [o] Jamieson, Fausett and Brown. [p] Thayer. [q] Thayer. [r] Cremer. [s] Thayer. [t] Robertson.

## New American Standard

20"And when *I broke* the seven for the four thousand, how many
large baskets full of broken pieces did you pick up?" And they
*said to Him, "Seven."
21And He was saying to them, "Do you not yet understand?"
22¶ And they *came to Bethsaida. And they *brought a blind
man to Him, and *entreated Him to touch him.
23And taking the blind man by the hand, He brought him out
of the village; and after spitting on his eyes, and laying His hands
upon him, He asked him, "Do you see anything?"
24And he looked up and said, "I see men, for I am seeing *them*
like trees, walking about."
25Then again He laid His hands upon his eyes; and he looked
intently and was restored, and *began* to see everything clearly.
26And He sent him to his home, saying, "Do not even enter the
village."

*Peter's Confession of Christ*

27¶ And Jesus went out, along with His disciples, to the villages
of Caesarea Philippi; and on the way He questioned His disciples,
saying to them, "Who do people say that I am?"
28And they told Him, saying, "John the Baptist; and others *say*
Elijah; but others, one of the prophets."
29And He *continued* by questioning them, "But who do you say
that I am?" Peter *answered and *said to Him, "Thou art the
Christ."
30And He warned them to tell no one about Him.
31¶ And He began to teach them that the Son of Man must suffer
many things and be rejected by the elders and the chief priests and
the scribes, and be killed, and after three days rise again.
32And He was stating the matter plainly. And Peter took Him
aside and began to rebuke Him.
33But turning around and seeing His disciples, He rebuked
Peter, and *said, "Get behind Me, Satan; for you are not setting
your mind on [u]God's interests, but man's."
34And He summoned the multitude with His disciples, and said
to them, "If anyone wishes to come after Me, let him deny himself,
and take up his cross, and follow Me.
35"For whoever wishes to save his life shall lose it; but whoever
loses his life for My sake and the gospel's shall save it.
36"For what does it profit a man to gain the whole world, and
forfeit his soul?
37"For what shall a man give in exchange for his soul?
38"For whoever is ashamed of Me and My words in this adulterous and sinful generation, the Son of Man will also be ashamed of
him when He comes in the glory of His Father with the holy
angels."

*The Transfiguration*

9 AND HE was saying to them, "Truly I say to you, there are
some of those who are standing here who shall not taste
death until they see the kingdom of God after it has come with
power."

NAS [u] Lit., *the things of God*

## New International

20"And when I broke the seven loaves for the four thousand,
how many basketfuls of pieces did you pick up?"
They answered, "Seven."
21He said to them, "Do you still not understand?"

*The Healing of a Blind Man at Bethsaida*

22They came to Bethsaida, and some people brought a blind
man and begged Jesus to touch him. 23He took the blind man by
the hand and led him outside the village. When he had spit on the
man's eyes and put his hands on him, Jesus asked, "Do you see
anything?"
24He looked up and said, "I see people; they look like trees
walking around."
25Once more Jesus put his hands on the man's eyes. Then his
eyes were opened, his sight was restored, and he saw everything
clearly. 26Jesus sent him home, saying, "Don't go into the village.[v]"

*Peter's Confession of Christ*

27Jesus and his disciples went on to the villages around Caesarea Philippi. On the way he asked them, "Who do people say I
am?"
28They replied, "Some say John the Baptist; others say Elijah;
and still others, one of the prophets."
29"But what about you?" he asked. "Who do you say I am?"
Peter answered, "You are the Christ.[w]"
30Jesus warned them not to tell anyone about him.

*Jesus Predicts His Death*

31He then began to teach them that the Son of Man must suffer
many things and be rejected by the elders, chief priests and teachers of the law, and that he must be killed and after three days rise
again. 32He spoke plainly about this, and Peter took him aside and
began to rebuke him.
33But when Jesus turned and looked at his disciples, he rebuked
Peter. "Get behind me, Satan!" he said. "You do not have in mind
the things of God, but the things of men."
34Then he called the crowd to him along with his disciples and
said: "If anyone would come after me, he must deny himself and
take up his cross and follow me. 35For whoever wants to save his
life[x] will lose it, but whoever loses his life for me and for the gospel
will save it. 36What good is it for a man to gain the whole world,
yet forfeit his soul? 37Or what can a man give in exchange for his
soul? 38If anyone is ashamed of me and my words in this adulterous and sinful generation, the Son of Man will be ashamed of him
when he comes in his Father's glory with the holy angels."

9 AND HE said to them, "I tell you the truth, some who are
standing here will not taste death before they see the kingdom of God come with power."

NIV [v] 26 Some manuscripts *Don't go and tell anyone in the village* [w] 29 Or *Messiah.* "The Christ" (Greek) and "the Messiah" (Hebrew) both mean "the Anointed One." [x] 35 The Greek word means either *life* or *soul;* also in verse 36.

## King James

2¶ And after six days Jesus taketh *with him* Peter, and James, and John, and leadeth them up into an high mountain apart by themselves: and he was transfigured before them.

3And his raiment became shining, exceeding white as snow; so as no fuller on earth can white them.

4And there appeared unto them Elias with Moses: and they were talking with Jesus.

5And Peter answered and said to Jesus, Master, it is good for us to be here: and let us make three tabernacles; one for thee, and one for Moses, and one for Elias.

6For he wist not what to say; for they were sore afraid.

7And there was a cloud that overshadowed them: and a voice came out of the cloud, saying, This is my beloved Son: hear him.

8And suddenly, when they had looked round about, they saw no man any more, save Jesus only with themselves.

9And as they came down from the mountain, he charged them that they should tell no man what things they had seen, till the Son of man were risen from the dead.

10And they kept that saying with themselves, questioning one with another what the rising from the dead should mean.

11¶ And they asked him, saying, Why say the scribes that Elias must first come?

12And he answered and told them, Elias verily cometh first, and restoreth all things; and how it is written of the Son of man, that he must suffer many things, and be set at nought.

13But I say unto you, That Elias is indeed come, and they have done unto him whatsoever they listed, as it is written of him.

14¶ And when he came to *his* disciples, he saw a great multitude about them, and the scribes questioning with them.

15And straightway all the people, when they beheld him, were greatly amazed, and running to *him* saluted him.

16And he asked the scribes, What question ye with them?

17And one of the multitude answered and said, Master, I have brought unto thee my son, which hath a dumb spirit;

18And wheresoever he taketh him, he teareth him: and he foameth, and gnasheth with his teeth, and pineth away: and I spake to thy disciples that they should cast him out; and they could not.

19He answereth him, and saith, O faithless generation, how long shall I be with you? how long shall I suffer you? bring him unto me.

20And they brought him unto him: and when he saw him, straightway the spirit tare him; and he fell on the ground, and wallowed foaming.

21And he asked his father, How long is it ago since this came unto him? And he said, Of a child.

22And ofttimes it hath cast him into the fire, and into the waters, to destroy him: but if thou canst do any thing, have compassion on us, and help us.

23Jesus said unto him, If thou canst believe, all things *are* possible to him that believeth.

24And straightway the father of the child cried out, and said with tears, Lord, I believe; help thou mine unbelief.

25When Jesus saw that the people came running together, he rebuked the foul spirit, saying unto him, *Thou* dumb and deaf spirit, I charge thee, come out of him, and enter no more into him.

## Amplified

2Six days after this Jesus took with Him Peter and James and John, and led them up on a high mountain, apart by themselves. And He was transfigured before them *and* became resplendent with divine brightness.

3And His garments became glistening, intensely white, as no fuller (cloth dresser) on earth could bleach them.

4And Elijah appeared [there] to them, accompanied by Moses, and they were [a]holding (a protracted) conversation with Jesus.

5And [b]Peter took up the conversation saying, Master, it is good *and* suitable *and* beautiful for us to be here. Let us make three booths (tents), one for You and one for Moses and one for Elijah.

6For he did not [really] know what to say, for they were in a violent fright— [c]aghast [with] dread.

7And a cloud threw a shadow upon them, and a voice came out of the cloud, saying, This is My Son, the ([d]most dearworthy) Beloved One; be [e]constantly listening to *and* obeying Him.

8And looking around they suddenly no longer saw any one with them except Jesus only.

9And as they were coming back down the mountain, He admonished *and* [f]expressly ordered them to tell no one what they had seen, until the Son of man should rise from among the dead.

10So they carefully *and* faithfully kept the matter to themselves, questioning *and* disputing with one another about what rising from among the dead [meant].

11And they asked Him, Why do the scribes say that it is necessary for Elijah first to come? [Mal. 4:5, 6.]

12And He said to them, Elijah, it is true, does come first to restore all things *and* [g]set them to right; and how is it written of the Son of man that He will suffer many things *and* be utterly despised *and* be treated with contempt *and* rejected? [Isa. 53:3.]

13But I tell you that Elijah has already come, and [people] did to him whatever they desired, as it is written of him.

14And when they came to the [nine] disciples, they saw a great crowd around them, and scribes questioning *and* disputing with them.

15And immediately all the crowd, when they saw Jesus [ [h]returning from the holy mount, His face and person yet glistening] were greatly amazed, and ran up to Him [and] greeted Him.

16And He asked them, About what are you questioning *and* discussing with them?

17And one of the throng replied to Him, Teacher, I brought my son to You, for he has a dumb spirit.

18And wherever it lays hold of him (so as to make him its own), it dashes him down *and* convulses him, and he foams (at the mouth) and grinds his teeth, *and* he [ [i]falls into a motionless stupor] and is wasting away; and I asked Your disciples to drive it out, and they were not able [to do it].

19And He answered them, O unbelieving generation—without any faith! How long [j]shall I (have to do) with you? How long am I to bear with you? Bring him to Me.

20So they brought [the boy] to Him, and when the spirit saw Him, at once it completely convulsed the boy, and he fell to the ground and kept rolling about, foaming [at the mouth].

21And [Jesus] asked his father, How long has he had this? And he answered, From the time he was a little boy.

22And it has often thrown him both into fire and into water, intending to kill him; but if You can do anything, do have pity on us and help us.

23And Jesus said, [You say to Me], If You can do anything? [Why,] all things can be—are possible—to him who believes!

24At once the father of the boy gave (an [k]eager, [l]piercing, inarticulate) cry *with tears,* and he said, Lord, I believe! Constantly help my [m]weakness of faith!

25But when Jesus noticed that a crowd [of people] came running together, He rebuked the unclean spirit, saying to it, You dumb and deaf spirit, I charge you to come out of him and never go into him again.

**AMP** [a] Wuest. [b] Kennedy's "Sources of New Testament Greek." [c] Wycliffe. [d] Wycliffe. [e] Wuest. [f] Abbott-Smith. [g] Henry's "Commentary." [h] Trench's "Notes on the Miracles of Our Lord." [i] Wuest. [j] Wuest. [k] "Expositor's Greek Testament." [l] Swete in "Mark." [m] Thayer.

## New American Standard

2¶ And six days later, Jesus *took with Him Peter and James and John, and *brought them up to a high mountain by themselves. And He was transfigured before them;

3 and His garments became radiant and exceedingly white, as no launderer on earth can whiten them.

4 And Elijah appeared to them along with Moses; and they were talking with Jesus.

5 And Peter answered and *said to Jesus, "Rabbi, it is good for us to be here; and let us make three tabernacles, one for You, and one for Moses, and one for Elijah."

6 For he did not know what to answer; for they became terrified.

7 Then a cloud formed, overshadowing them, and a voice came out of the cloud, "This is My beloved Son, listen to Him!"

8 And all at once they looked around and saw no one with them anymore, except Jesus alone.

9¶ And as they were coming down from the mountain, He gave them orders not to relate to anyone what they had seen, until the Son of Man should rise from the dead.

10 And they seized upon that statement, discussing with one another what rising from the dead might mean.

11 And they asked Him, saying, "*Why is it* that the scribes say that Elijah must come first?"

12 And He said to them, "Elijah does first come and restore all things. And *yet* how is it written of the Son of Man that He should suffer many things and be treated with contempt?

13 "But I say to you, that Elijah has indeed come, and they did to him whatever they wished, just as it is written of him."

*All Things Possible*

14¶ And when they came *back* to the disciples, they saw a large crowd around them, and *some* scribes arguing with them.

15 And immediately, when the entire crowd saw Him, they were amazed, and *began* running up to greet Him.

16 And He asked them, "What are you discussing with them?"

17 And one of the crowd answered Him, "Teacher, I brought You my son, possessed with a spirit which makes him mute;

18 and whenever it seizes him, it dashes him *to the ground* and he foams *at the mouth*, and grinds his teeth, and stiffens out. And I told Your disciples to cast it out, and they could not *do it*."

19 And He *answered them and *said, "O unbelieving generation, how long shall I be with you? How long shall I put up with you? Bring him to Me!"

20 And they brought the boy to Him. And when he saw Him, immediately the spirit threw him into a convulsion, and falling to the ground, he *began* rolling about and foaming *at the mouth*.

21 And He asked his father, "How long has this been happening to him?" And he said, "From childhood.

22 "And it has often thrown him both into the fire and into the water to destroy him. But if You can do anything, take pity on us and help us!"

23 And Jesus said to him, " 'If You can!' All things are possible to him who believes."

24 Immediately the boy's father cried out and *began* saying, "I do believe; help my unbelief."

25 And when Jesus saw that a crowd was rapidly gathering, He rebuked the unclean spirit, saying to it, "You deaf and dumb spirit, I command you, come out of him and do not enter him again."

## New International

*The Transfiguration*

2 After six days Jesus took Peter, James and John with him and
led them up a high mountain, where they were all alone. There he
was transfigured before them. 3 His clothes became dazzling white,
whiter than anyone in the world could bleach them. 4 And there
appeared before them Elijah and Moses, who were talking with
Jesus.

5 Peter said to Jesus, "Rabbi, it is good for us to be here. Let us
put up three shelters—one for you, one for Moses and one for
Elijah." 6 (He did not know what to say, they were so frightened.)

7 Then a cloud appeared and enveloped them, and a voice came
from the cloud: "This is my Son, whom I love. Listen to him!"

8 Suddenly, when they looked around, they no longer saw anyone with them except Jesus.

9 As they were coming down the mountain, Jesus gave them
orders not to tell anyone what they had seen until the Son of Man
had risen from the dead. 10 They kept the matter to themselves,
discussing what "rising from the dead" meant.

11 And they asked him, "Why do the teachers of the law say that Elijah must come first?"

12 Jesus replied, "To be sure, Elijah does come first, and restores
all things. Why then is it written that the Son of Man must suffer
much and be rejected? 13 But I tell you, Elijah has come, and they
have done to him everything they wished, just as it is written
about him."

*The Healing of a Boy With an Evil Spirit*

14 When they came to the other disciples, they saw a large crowd
around them and the teachers of the law arguing with them. 15 As
soon as all the people saw Jesus, they were overwhelmed with
wonder and ran to greet him.

16 "What are you arguing with them about?" he asked.

17 A man in the crowd answered, "Teacher, I brought you my
son, who is possessed by a spirit that has robbed him of speech.
18 Whenever it seizes him, it throws him to the ground. He foams
at the mouth, gnashes his teeth and becomes rigid. I asked your
disciples to drive out the spirit, but they could not."

19 "O unbelieving generation," Jesus replied, "how long shall I stay with you? How long shall I put up with you? Bring the boy to me."

20 So they brought him. When the spirit saw Jesus, it immediately threw the boy into a convulsion. He fell to the ground and rolled around, foaming at the mouth.

21 Jesus asked the boy's father, "How long has he been like
this?"

"From childhood," he answered. 22 "It has often thrown him
into fire or water to kill him. But if you can do anything, take pity
on us and help us."

23 " 'If you can'?" said Jesus. "Everything is possible for him who believes."

24 Immediately the boy's father exclaimed, "I do believe; help me overcome my unbelief!"

25 When Jesus saw that a crowd was running to the scene, he rebuked the evil[n] spirit. "You deaf and mute spirit," he said, "I command you, come out of him and never enter him again."

NIV [n] 25 Greek *unclean*

## King James

26And *the spirit* cried, and rent him sore, and came out of him:
and he was as one dead; insomuch that many said, He is dead.
27But Jesus took him by the hand, and lifted him up; and he
arose.
28And when he was come into the house, his disciples asked
him privately, Why could not we cast him out?
29And he said unto them, This kind can come forth by nothing,
but by prayer and fasting.
30¶ And they departed thence, and passed through Galilee; and
he would not that any man should know *it*.
31For he taught his disciples, and said unto them, The Son of
man is delivered into the hands of men, and they shall kill him;
and after that he is killed, he shall rise the third day.
32But they understood not that saying, and were afraid to ask
him.
33¶ And he came to Capernaum: and being in the house he
asked them, What was it that ye disputed among yourselves by the
way?
34But they held their peace: for by the way they had disputed
among themselves, who *should be* the greatest.
35And he sat down, and called the twelve, and saith unto them,
If any man desire to be first, *the same* shall be last of all, and servant
of all.
36And he took a child, and set him in the midst of them: and
when he had taken him in his arms, he said unto them,
37Whosoever shall receive one of such children in my name,
receiveth me: and whosoever shall receive me, receiveth not me,
but him that sent me.
38¶ And John answered him, saying, Master, we saw one casting out devils in thy name, and he followeth not us: and we forbad
him, because he followeth not us.
39But Jesus said, Forbid him not: for there is no man which shall
do a miracle in my name, that can lightly speak evil of me.
40For he that is not against us is on our part.
41For whosoever shall give you a cup of water to drink in my
name, because ye belong to Christ, verily I say unto you, he shall
not lose his reward.
42And whosoever shall offend one of *these* little ones that believe in me, it is better for him that a millstone were hanged about
his neck, and he were cast into the sea.
43And if thy hand offend thee, cut it off: it is better for thee to
enter into life maimed, than having two hands to go into hell, into
the fire that never shall be quenched:
44Where their worm dieth not, and the fire is not quenched.
45And if thy foot offend thee, cut it off: it is better for thee to
enter halt into life, than having two feet to be cast into hell, into
the fire that never shall be quenched:
46Where their worm dieth not, and the fire is not quenched.
47And if thine eye offend thee, pluck it out: it is better for thee
to enter into the kingdom of God with one eye, than having two
eyes to be cast into hell fire:
48Where their worm dieth not, and the fire is not quenched.
49For every one shall be salted with fire, and every sacrifice shall
be salted with salt.
50Salt *is* good: but if the salt have lost his saltness, wherewith
will ye season it? Have salt in yourselves, and have peace one with
another.

## Amplified

26And after giving a (hoarse, clamoring, fear-stricken) shriek of
anguish and convulsing him terribly, it came out; and the boy lay
(pale and motionless) like a corpse, so that many of them said, He
is dead.
27But Jesus took ( [a]a strong grip of) his hand and began lifting
him up, and he stood.
28And when He had gone indoors His disciples asked Him
privately, Why could not we drive it out?
29And He replied to them, This kind cannot be driven out by
anything but prayer *and fasting*.
30They went on from there, and passed along through Galilee.
And He did not wish to have any one know it,
31For He was [engaged for the time in] teaching His disciples.
He said to them, The Son of man is being delivered into the hands
of men, and they will put Him to death; and when He is killed,
after three days He will rise [ [b]from death].
32But they did not comprehend what He was saying, and they
were afraid to ask Him [what this statement meant].
33And they arrived at Capernaum; and when [they were] in the
house He asked them, What were you discussing *and* arguing
about on the road?
34But they kept still, for on the road they had discussed *and*
disputed with one another as to who [was the] greatest.
35And He sat down and called the twelve [apostles], and He
said to them, If any one desires to be first, he must be last of all
and servant of all.
36And He took a little child, and put him in the center of their
group; and taking him in [His] arms, He said to them,
37Whoever in My name *and* for My sake accepts *and* receives *and*
welcomes one such child, also accepts *and* receives *and* welcomes
Me; and whoever so receives Me, receives not only Me, but Him
Who sent Me.
38John said to Him, Teacher, we saw a man driving out demons
in Your name who does not follow along with us, and we forbade
him to do it, because he [c]is not of our band [of Your disciples].
39But Jesus said, Do not restrain *or* hinder *or* forbid him; for no
one who does a mighty work in My name will soon afterward be
able to speak evil of Me.
40For he who is not against us is for us. [Num. 11:27-29.]
41For I tell you truly, whoever gives you a cup of water to drink
because you belong to *and* bear the name of Christ, will by no
means fail to get his reward.
42And whoever causes one of (these believers,) these little ones
who [d]acknowledge *and* cleave to Me, to stumble *and* sin, it would
be better—more profitable and wholesome—for him if a (huge)
millstone were hung about his neck, and he were thrown into the
sea.
43And if your hand puts a stumbling block before you *and*
causes you to sin, cut it off; it is more profitable *and* wholesome
for you to go into the life [ [e]that is really worthwhile] maimed, than
with two hands to go to hell (Gehenna), into the fire that cannot
be put out. [f]
45And if your foot is a cause of stumbling *and* sin to you, cut it
off! It is more profitable *and* wholesome for you to enter into the
life [that is really worthwhile] crippled, than having two feet to be
cast into hell (Gehenna) [g].
47And if your eye causes you to stumble *and* sin, pluck it out!
It is more profitable *and* wholesome for you to enter the kingdom
of God with one eye, than with two eyes to be thrown into hell
(Gehenna),
48Where their worm [ [h]which preys on the inhabitants, (and is
a symbol of) the wounds inflicted on the man himself by his sins]
does not die, and the fire is not put out. [Isa. 66:24.]
49For everyone shall be salted with fire.
50Salt is good (beneficial); but if salt has lost its saltness, how
will you restore [the saltness to] it? Have salt within yourselves,
and be at peace *and* live in harmony with one another.

**AMP** [a] Wuest. [b] Cremer. [c] Thayer. [d] Cremer. [e] Wuest. [f] See footnote, verse 45. [g] Verses 44 and 46 (identical with verse 48) are omitted by the best ancient authorities. [h] Gould, quoted by Robertson, and by Swete.

## New American Standard

26And after crying out and throwing him into terrible convulsions, it came out; and *the boy* became so much like a corpse that
most *of them* said, "He is dead!"
27But Jesus took him by the hand and raised him; and he got
up.
28And when He had come into *the* house, His disciples *began*
questioning Him privately, "Why could we not cast it out?"
29And He said to them, "This kind cannot come out by anything
but prayer [i]."

*Death and Resurrection Foretold*

30¶ And from there they went out and *began* to go through
Galilee, and He was unwilling for anyone to know *about it.*
31For He was teaching His disciples and telling them, "The Son
of Man is to be [j]delivered into the hands of men, and they will
kill Him; and when He has been killed, He will rise three days
later."
32But they did not understand *this* statement, and they were
afraid to ask Him.
33¶ And they came to Capernaum; and when He was in the
house, He *began* to question them, "What were you discussing on
the way?"
34But they kept silent, for on the way they had discussed with
one another which *of them was* the greatest.
35And sitting down, He called the twelve and *said to them, "If
anyone wants to be first, he shall be last of all, and servant of all."
36And taking a child, He set him before them, and taking him
in His arms, He said to them,
37"Whoever receives one child like this in My name receives
Me; and whoever receives Me does not receive Me, but Him who
sent Me."

*Dire Warnings*

38¶ John said to Him, "Teacher, we saw someone casting out
demons in Your name, and we tried to hinder him because he was
not following us."
39But Jesus said, "Do not hinder him, for there is no one who
shall perform a miracle in My name, and be able soon afterward
to speak evil of Me.
40"For he who is not against us is [k]for us.
41"For whoever gives you a cup of water to drink because of
your name as *followers* of Christ, truly I say to you, he shall not lose
his reward.
42"And whoever causes one of these little ones who believe to
stumble, it would be better for him if, with a heavy millstone hung
around his neck, he had been cast into the sea.
43"And if your hand causes you to stumble, cut it off; it is better
for you to enter life crippled, than having your two hands, to go
into hell, into the unquenchable fire,
44[ [l]where THEIR WORM DOES NOT DIE, AND THE FIRE IS NOT
QUENCHED.]
45"And if your foot causes you to stumble, cut it off; it is better
for you to enter life lame, than having your two feet, to be cast into
hell,
46[[m]where THEIR WORM DOES NOT DIE, AND THE FIRE IS NOT
QUENCHED.]
47"And if your eye causes you to stumble, cast it out; it is better
for you to enter the kingdom of God with one eye, than having two
eyes, to be cast into hell,
48where THEIR WORM DOES NOT DIE, AND THE FIRE IS NOT
QUENCHED.
49"For everyone will be salted with fire.
50"Salt is good; but if the salt becomes unsalty, with what will
you make it salty *again*? Have salt in yourselves, and be at peace
with one another."

NAS [i] Many mss. add: *and fasting* [j] Or, *betrayed* [k] Or, *on our side* [l] Vv. 44 and 46, which are identical with v. 48, are not found in the best ancient mss. [m]Vv. 44 and 46, which are identical with v. 48, are not found in the best ancient mss.

## New International

26The spirit shrieked, convulsed him violently and came out.
The boy looked so much like a corpse that many said, "He's dead."
27But Jesus took him by the hand and lifted him to his feet, and
he stood up.
28After Jesus had gone indoors, his disciples asked him privately, "Why couldn't we drive it out?"
29He replied, "This kind can come out only by prayer.[n]"
30They left that place and passed through Galilee. Jesus did not
want anyone to know where they were, 31because he was teaching
his disciples. He said to them, "The Son of Man is going to be
betrayed into the hands of men. They will kill him, and after three
days he will rise." 32But they did not understand what he meant
and were afraid to ask him about it.

*Who Is the Greatest?*

33They came to Capernaum. When he was in the house, he
asked them, "What were you arguing about on the road?" 34But
they kept quiet because on the way they had argued about who
was the greatest.
35Sitting down, Jesus called the Twelve and said, "If anyone
wants to be first, he must be the very last, and the servant of all."
36He took a little child and had him stand among them. Taking
him in his arms, he said to them, 37"Whoever welcomes one of
these little children in my name welcomes me; and whoever welcomes me does not welcome me but the one who sent me."

*Whoever Is Not Against Us Is for Us*

38"Teacher," said John, "we saw a man driving out demons in
your name and we told him to stop, because he was not one of us."
39"Do not stop him," Jesus said. "No one who does a miracle
in my name can in the next moment say anything bad about me,
40for whoever is not against us is for us. 41I tell you the truth,
anyone who gives you a cup of water in my name because you
belong to Christ will certainly not lose his reward.

*Causing to Sin*

42"And if anyone causes one of these little ones who believe in
me to sin, it would be better for him to be thrown into the sea with
a large millstone tied around his neck. 43If your hand causes you
to sin, cut it off. It is better for you to enter life maimed than with
two hands to go into hell, where the fire never goes out.[o] 45And
if your foot causes you to sin, cut it off. It is better for you to enter
life crippled than to have two feet and be thrown into hell.[p] 47And
if your eye causes you to sin, pluck it out. It is better for you to
enter the kingdom of God with one eye than to have two eyes and
be thrown into hell, 48where

" 'their worm does not die,
and the fire is not quenched.'[q]

49Everyone will be salted with fire.
50"Salt is good, but if it loses its saltiness, how can you make
it salty again? Have salt in yourselves, and be at peace with each
other."

NIV [n] 29 Some manuscripts *prayer and fasting* [o] 43 Some manuscripts *out, 44where / " 'their worm does not die, / and the fire is not quenched.'* [p] 45 Some manuscripts *hell, 46where / " 'their worm does not die, / and the fire is not quenched.'* [q] *48* Isaiah 66:24

## King James

**10** AND HE arose from thence, and cometh into the coasts of Judaea by the farther side of Jordan: and the people resort unto him again; and, as he was wont, he taught them again.

2¶ And the Pharisees came to him, and asked him, Is it lawful for a man to put away *his* wife? tempting him.

3And he answered and said unto them, What did Moses command you?

4And they said, Moses suffered to write a bill of divorcement, and to put *her* away.

5And Jesus answered and said unto them, For the hardness of your heart he wrote you this precept.

6But from the beginning of the creation God made them male and female.

7For this cause shall a man leave his father and mother, and cleave to his wife;

8And they twain shall be one flesh: so then they are no more twain, but one flesh.

9What therefore God hath joined together, let not man put asunder.

10And in the house his disciples asked him again of the same *matter*.

11And he saith unto them, Whosoever shall put away his wife, and marry another, committeth adultery against her.

12And if a woman shall put away her husband, and be married to another, she committeth adultery.

13¶ And they brought young children to him, that he should touch them: and *his* disciples rebuked those that brought *them*.

14But when Jesus saw *it*, he was much displeased, and said unto them, Suffer the little children to come unto me, and forbid them not: for of such is the kingdom of God.

15Verily I say unto you, Whosoever shall not receive the kingdom of God as a little child, he shall not enter therein.

16And he took them up in his arms, put *his* hands upon them, and blessed them.

17¶ And when he was gone forth into the way, there came one running, and kneeled to him, and asked him, Good Master, what shall I do that I may inherit eternal life?

18And Jesus said unto him, Why callest thou me good? *there is* none good but one, *that is*, God.

19Thou knowest the commandments, Do not commit adultery, Do not kill, Do not steal, Do not bear false witness, Defraud not, Honour thy father and mother.

20And he answered and said unto him, Master, all these have I observed from my youth.

21Then Jesus beholding him loved him, and said unto him, One thing thou lackest: go thy way, sell whatsoever thou hast, and give to the poor, and thou shalt have treasure in heaven: and come, take up the cross, and follow me.

22And he was sad at that saying, and went away grieved: for he had great possessions.

23¶ And Jesus looked round about, and saith unto his disciples, How hardly shall they that have riches enter into the kingdom of God!

24And the disciples were astonished at his words. But Jesus answereth again, and saith unto them, Children, how hard is it for them that trust in riches to enter into the kingdom of God!

25It is easier for a camel to go through the eye of a needle, than for a rich man to enter into the kingdom of God.

## Amplified

**10** AND [JESUS] left there [Capernaum] and went to the region of Judea and beyond [east of] the Jordan, and crowds (constantly) gathered around Him again; and again, as was His custom, He began to teach them.

2And some Pharisees came up, and in order to test Him *and* try to find a weakness in Him asked, Is it lawful for a man to [a]dismiss *and* repudiate *and* divorce his wife?

3He answered them, What did Moses command you?

4They replied, Moses allowed a man to write a bill of divorce, and to put her away. [Deut. 24:1-4.]

5But Jesus said to them, Because of your hardness of heart [that is, of [b]your condition of insensibility to the call of God] he wrote you this [c]precept in your Law.

6But from the beginning of creation God made them male and female. [Gen. 1:27; 5:2.]

7For this reason a man shall leave (behind) his father and his mother *and be* [d] *joined to his wife, and cleave closely to her (permanently).*

8And the two shall become one flesh, so that they are no longer two, but one flesh. [Gen. 2:24.]

9What therefore God has united—joined together—let not man separate *or* divide.

10And indoors the disciples questioned Him again about this subject.

11And He said to them, Whoever [e]dismisses (repudiates and divorces) his wife and marries another, commits adultery against her;

12And if a woman dismisses (repudiates and divorces) her husband and marries another, she commits adultery.

13And they kept bringing young children to Him that He might touch them; and the disciples were reproving them [for it].

14But when Jesus saw [it], He was indignant *and* [f]pained, and said to them, Allow the children to come to Me—do not forbid or prevent or hinder them—for to such belongs the kingdom of God.

15Truly I tell you, whoever does not receive *and* accept *and* welcome the kingdom of God as a little child [does], positively shall not enter it at all.

16And He took [the children up [g]one by one] in His arms and ([h]fervently invoked a) blessing, placing His hands upon them.

17And as He was setting out on His journey, a man ran up and knelt before Him, and asked Him, Teacher, (You are [i]essentially and perfectly [j]morally) good, what must I do to inherit eternal life (that is, [k]to partake of eternal salvation in the Messiah's kingdom)?

18And Jesus said to him, Why do you call Me ( [l]essentially and perfectly [m]morally) good? There is no one ( [n]essentially and perfectly [o]morally) good except God alone.

19You know the commandments: Do not kill; do not commit adultery; do not steal; do not bear false witness; do not defraud; honor your father and mother. [Exod. 20:12-16; Deut. 5:16-20.]

20And he replied to Him, Teacher, I have carefully guarded *and* observed all these *and* taken care not to violate them from my boyhood.

21And Jesus looking upon him loved him, and He said to him, You lack one thing; go and sell all you have, and give [the money] to the poor, and you will have treasure in heaven; and come [and] accompany Me— [p]walking the same road that I walk.

22At that saying the man's countenance fell *and* was gloomy, and he went away grieved *and* sorrowing, for he was holding great possessions.

23And Jesus looked around and said to His disciples, With what difficulty will those who possess wealth *and* [q]keep on holding it enter the kingdom of God!

24And the disciples were amazed *and* bewildered *and* perplexed at His words. But Jesus said to them again, Children, how hard it is *for those who trust (place their confidence, their sense of safety) in riches* to enter the kingdom of God!

25It is easier for a camel to go through the eye of a needle than [for] a rich man to enter the kingdom of God.

**AMP** [a] Thayer. [b] Swete in "Mark." [c] Thayer. [d] Moulton and Milligan. [e] Swete in "Mark." [f] Robertson. [g] "Expositor's Greek Testament." [h] Alford's Greek Testament. [i] Thayer. [j] Cremer. [k] Thayer. [l] Thayer. [m] Cremer. [n] Thayer. [o] Cremer. [p] Literal translation. [q] Wuest.

## New American Standard

*Jesus' Teaching about Divorce*

**10** AND RISING up, He *went from there to the region of
Judea, and beyond the Jordan; and crowds *gathered
around Him again, and, according to His custom, He once more
*began* to teach them.
2¶ And *some* Pharisees came up to Him, testing Him, and *began*
to question Him whether it was lawful for a man to divorce a wife.
3And He answered and said to them, "What did Moses command you?"
4And they said, "Moses permitted *a man* TO WRITE A CERTIFI-
CATE OF DIVORCE AND SEND *her* AWAY."
5But Jesus said to them, "Because of your hardness of heart he
wrote you this commandment.
6"But from the beginning of creation, *God* MADE THEM MALE
AND FEMALE.
7"FOR THIS CAUSE A MAN SHALL LEAVE HIS FATHER AND
MOTHER, [r]
8AND THE TWO SHALL BECOME ONE FLESH; consequently they are
no longer two, but one flesh.
9"What therefore God has joined together, let no man separate."
10And in the house the disciples *began* questioning Him about
this again.
11And He *said to them, "Whoever divorces his wife and marries another woman commits adultery against her;
12and if she herself divorces her husband and marries another
man, she is committing adultery."

*Jesus Blesses Little Children*

13¶ And they were bringing children to Him so that He might
touch them; and the disciples rebuked them.
14But when Jesus saw this, He was indignant and said to them,
"Permit the children to come to Me; do not hinder them; for the
kingdom of God belongs to such as these.
15"Truly I say to you, whoever does not receive the kingdom
of God like a child shall not enter it *at all.*"
16And He took them in His arms and *began* blessing them,
laying His hands upon them.

*The Rich Young Ruler*

17¶ And as He was setting out on a journey, a man ran up to
Him and knelt before Him, and *began* asking Him, "Good Teacher,
what shall I do to inherit eternal life?"
18And Jesus said to him, "Why do you call Me good? No one
is good except God alone.
19"You know the commandments, 'DO NOT MURDER, DO NOT
COMMIT ADULTERY, DO NOT STEAL, DO NOT BEAR FALSE WITNESS, Do
not defraud, HONOR YOUR FATHER AND MOTHER.'"
20And he said to Him, "Teacher, I have kept all these things
from my youth up."
21And looking at him, Jesus felt a love for him, and said to him,
"One thing you lack: go and sell all you possess, and give to the
poor, and you shall have treasure in heaven; and come, follow
Me."
22But at these words his face fell, and he went away grieved,
for he was one who owned much property.
23¶ And Jesus, looking around, *said to His disciples, "How
hard it will be for those who are wealthy to enter the kingdom of
God!"
24And the disciples were amazed at His words. But Jesus *answered again and *said to them, "Children, how hard it is [s]to enter
the kingdom of God!
25"It is easier for a camel to go through the eye of a needle than
for a rich man to enter the kingdom of God."

**NAS** [r] Some mss. add: *and shall cleave to his wife* [s] Later mss. insert: *for those who trust in wealth*

## New International

*Divorce*

**10** JESUS THEN left that place and went into the region of
Judea and across the Jordan. Again crowds of people came
to him, and as was his custom, he taught them.
2Some Pharisees came and tested him by asking, "Is it lawful
for a man to divorce his wife?"
3"What did Moses command you?" he replied.
4They said, "Moses permitted a man to write a certificate of
divorce and send her away."
5"It was because your hearts were hard that Moses wrote you
this law," Jesus replied. 6"But at the beginning of creation God
'made them male and female.'[t] 7'For this reason a man will leave
his father and mother and be united to his wife,[u] 8and the two will
become one flesh.'[v] So they are no longer two, but one. 9Therefore
what God has joined together, let man not separate."
10When they were in the house again, the disciples asked Jesus
about this. 11He answered, "Anyone who divorces his wife and
marries another woman commits adultery against her. 12And if she
divorces her husband and marries another man, she commits adultery."

*The Little Children and Jesus*

13People were bringing little children to Jesus to have him touch
them, but the disciples rebuked them. 14When Jesus saw this, he
was indignant. He said to them, "Let the little children come to
me, and do not hinder them, for the kingdom of God belongs to
such as these. 15I tell you the truth, anyone who will not receive
the kingdom of God like a little child will never enter it." 16And
he took the children in his arms, put his hands on them and
blessed them.

*The Rich Young Man*

17As Jesus started on his way, a man ran up to him and fell on
his knees before him. "Good teacher," he asked, "what must I do
to inherit eternal life?"
18"Why do you call me good?" Jesus answered. "No one is
good—except God alone. 19You know the commandments: 'Do
not murder, do not commit adultery, do not steal, do not give false
testimony, do not defraud, honor your father and mother.'[w]"
20"Teacher," he declared, "all these I have kept since I was a
boy."
21Jesus looked at him and loved him. "One thing you lack," he
said. "Go, sell everything you have and give to the poor, and you
will have treasure in heaven. Then come, follow me."
22At this the man's face fell. He went away sad, because he had
great wealth.
23Jesus looked around and said to his disciples, "How hard it
is for the rich to enter the kingdom of God!"
24The disciples were amazed at his words. But Jesus said again,
"Children, how hard it is[x] to enter the kingdom of God! 25It is
easier for a camel to go through the eye of a needle than for a rich
man to enter the kingdom of God."

**NIV** [t] 6 Gen. 1:27 [u] 7 Some early manuscripts do not have *and be united to his wife.* [v] 8 Gen. 2:24 [w] 19 Exodus 20:12-16; Deut. 5:16-20 [x] 24 Some manuscripts *is for those who trust in riches*

## King James

26 And they were astonished out of measure, saying among themselves, Who then can be saved?

27 And Jesus looking upon them saith, With men *it is* impossible, but not with God: for with God all things are possible.

28 ¶ Then Peter began to say unto him, Lo, we have left all, and have followed thee.

29 And Jesus answered and said, Verily I say unto you, There is no man that hath left house, or brethren, or sisters, or father, or mother, or wife, or children, or lands, for my sake, and the gospel's,

30 But he shall receive an hundredfold now in this time, houses, and brethren, and sisters, and mothers, and children, and lands, with persecutions; and in the world to come eternal life.

31 But many *that are* first shall be last; and the last first.

32 ¶ And they were in the way going up to Jerusalem; and Jesus went before them: and they were amazed; and as they followed, they were afraid. And he took again the twelve, and began to tell them what things should happen unto him,

33 *Saying*, Behold, we go up to Jerusalem; and the Son of man shall be delivered unto the chief priests, and unto the scribes; and they shall condemn him to death, and shall deliver him to the Gentiles:

34 And they shall mock him, and shall scourge him, and shall spit upon him, and shall kill him: and the third day he shall rise again.

35 ¶ And James and John, the sons of Zebedee, come unto him, saying, Master, we would that thou shouldest do for us whatsoever we shall desire.

36 And he said unto them, What would ye that I should do for you?

37 They said unto him, Grant unto us that we may sit, one on thy right hand, and the other on thy left hand, in thy glory.

38 But Jesus said unto them, Ye know not what ye ask: can ye drink of the cup that I drink of? and be baptized with the baptism that I am baptized with?

39 And they said unto him, We can. And Jesus said unto them, Ye shall indeed drink of the cup that I drink of; and with the baptism that I am baptized withal shall ye be baptized:

40 But to sit on my right hand and on my left hand is not mine to give; but *it shall be given to them* for whom it is prepared.

41 And when the ten heard *it*, they began to be much displeased with James and John.

42 But Jesus called them *to him*, and saith unto them, Ye know that they which are accounted to rule over the Gentiles exercise lordship over them; and their great ones exercise authority upon them.

43 But so shall it not be among you: but whosoever will be great among you, shall be your minister:

44 And whosoever of you will be the chiefest, shall be servant of all.

45 For even the Son of man came not to be ministered unto, but to minister, and to give his life a ransom for many.

46 ¶ And they came to Jericho: and as he went out of Jericho with his disciples and a great number of people, blind Bartimaeus, the son of Timaeus, sat by the highway side begging.

47 And when he heard that it was Jesus of Nazareth, he began to cry out, and say, Jesus, *thou* son of David, have mercy on me.

48 And many charged him that he should hold his peace: but he cried the more a great deal, *Thou* son of David, have mercy on me.

49 And Jesus stood still, and commanded him to be called. And they call the blind man, saying unto him, Be of good comfort, rise; he calleth thee.

## Amplified

26 And they were shocked *and* exceedingly astonished, and said to Him *and* [a]to one another, Then who can be saved?

27 Jesus glanced around at them and said, With men [it is] impossible, but not with God; for all things are possible with God.

28 Peter started to say to Him, Lo, we have [b]yielded up *and* abandoned everything (once and for all and [c]joined You as Your disciples, sided with Your party) and accompanied You—[d]walking the same road that You walk.

29 Jesus said, Truly, I tell you, there is no one who has given up *and* left house or brothers or sisters or mother or father or children or lands, for My sake and for the Gospel,

30 Who will not receive a hundred times as much now in this time, houses and brothers and sisters and mothers and children and lands, with persecutions, and in the age to come eternal life.

31 But many [that are now] first will be last [then], and many [who are now] last will be first [then].

32 They were on the way going up to Jerusalem, and Jesus was walking on in front of them; and they were bewildered *and* perplexed *and* greatly astonished, and [those who were still] following were seized with alarm *and* were afraid. And He took the twelve [apostles] again, and began to tell them what was about to happen to Him.

33 [Saying], Behold, we are going up to Jerusalem; and the Son of man will be turned over to the chief priests and the scribes, and they will condemn *and* sentence Him to death and turn Him over to the Gentiles.

34 And they will mock Him, and spit on Him, and whip Him, and put Him to death; but after three days He will rise again [ [e]from death].

35 And James and John, the sons of Zebedee, approached Him, and said to Him, Teacher, we desire You to do for us whatever we ask of You.

36 And He replied to them, What do you desire Me to do for you?

37 And they said to Him, Grant that we may sit one at Your right hand and one at [Your] left hand, in Your glory—Your majesty and splendor.

38 But Jesus said to them, You do not know what you are asking. Are you able to drink the cup that I drink, or be baptized with the baptism [of affliction] with which I am baptized?

39 And they replied to Him, We are able. And Jesus told them, The cup that I drink you will drink, and you will be baptized with the baptism with which I am baptized;

40 But to sit at My right hand or at My left hand is not Mine to give; but [will be given those] for whom it is ordained *and* prepared.

41 And when the other ten [apostles] heard it, they began to be indignant with James and John.

42 But Jesus called them to [Him], and said to them, You know that those who are recognized as governing *and* are supposed to rule the Gentiles (the nations) lord it over them—ruling with absolute power, holding them in subjection—and their great men exercise authority *and* dominion over them.

43 But this is not to be so among you; instead, whoever desires to be great among you must be your servant,

44 And whoever wishes to be most important *and* first in rank among you must be the slave of all.

45 For even the Son of man came not to have service rendered to Him, but to serve, and to give His life as a ransom for ( [f]instead of) many.

46 Then they came to Jericho; and as He was leaving Jericho with His disciples and a great crowd, Bartimaeus, a blind beggar, a son of Timaeus, was sitting by the roadside.

47 And when he heard that it was Jesus of Nazareth, he began to shout saying, Jesus, Son of David, have pity *and* mercy on me ( [g]now)!

48 And many [h]severely censured *and* reproved him, telling him to keep still; but he kept on shouting out all the more, You Son of David, have pity *and* mercy on me (now)!

49 And Jesus stopped and said, Call him. And they called the blind man, telling him, Take courage; get up, He is calling you.

**AMP** [a] Many ancient authorities read "to one another." [b] Wuest. [c] Thayer. [d] Literal translation. [e] Cremer. [f] Vincent. [g] In the aorist imperative. (Wuest.) [h] Thayer.

## New American Standard

26And they were even more astonished and said to Him, "Then
who can be saved?"
27Looking upon them, Jesus *said, "With men it is impossible,
but not with God; for all things are possible with God."
28Peter began to say to Him, "Behold, we have left everything
and followed You."
29Jesus said, "Truly I say to you, there is no one who has left
house or brothers or sisters or mother or father or children or
farms, for My sake and for the gospel's sake,
30but that he shall receive a hundred times as much now in the
present age, houses and brothers and sisters and mothers and
children and farms, along with persecutions; and in the age to
come, eternal life.
31"But many *who are* first, will be last; and the last, first."

*Jesus' Sufferings Foretold*

32¶ And they were on the road, going up to Jerusalem, and Jesus
was walking on ahead of them; and they were amazed, and those
who followed were fearful. And again He took the twelve aside
and began to tell them what was going to happen to Him,
33 *saying*, "Behold, we are going up to Jerusalem, and the Son
of Man will be [i]delivered to the chief priests and the scribes; and
they will condemn Him to death, and will deliver Him to the
Gentiles.
34"And they will mock Him and spit upon Him, and scourge
Him, and kill *Him*, and three days later He will rise again."
35¶ And James and John, the two sons of Zebedee, *came up to
Him, saying to Him, "Teacher, we want You to do for us whatever
we ask of You."
36And He said to them, "What do you want Me to do for you?"
37And they said to Him, "Grant that we may sit in Your glory,
one on Your right, and one on *Your* left."
38But Jesus said to them, "You do not know what you are asking
for. Are you able to drink the cup that I drink, or to be baptized
with the baptism with which I am baptized?"
39And they said to Him, "We are able." And Jesus said to them,
"The cup that I drink you shall drink; and you shall be baptized
with the baptism with which I am baptized.
40"But to sit on My right or on *My* left, this is not Mine to give;
but it is for those for whom it has been prepared."
41And hearing this, the ten began to feel indignant with James
and John.
42And calling them to Himself, Jesus *said to them, "You know
that those who are recognized as rulers of the Gentiles lord it over
them; and their great men exercise authority over them.
43"But it is not so among you, but whoever wishes to become
great among you shall be your servant;
44and whoever wishes to be first among you shall be slave of
all.
45"For even the Son of Man did not come to be served, but to
serve, and to give His life a ransom for many."

*Bartimaeus Receives His Sight*

46¶ And they *came to Jericho. And as He was going out from
Jericho with His disciples and a great multitude, a blind beggar
*named* Bartimaeus, the son of Timaeus, was sitting by the road.
47And when he heard that it was Jesus the Nazarene, he began
to cry out and say, "Jesus, Son of David, have mercy on me!"
48And many were sternly telling him to be quiet, but he kept
crying out all the more, "Son of David, have mercy on me!"
49And Jesus stopped and said, "Call him *here*." And they *called
the blind man, saying to him, "Take courage, arise! He is calling
for you."

NAS [i] Or, *betrayed*

## New International

26The disciples were even more amazed, and said to each other,
"Who then can be saved?"
27Jesus looked at them and said, "With man this is impossible,
but not with God; all things are possible with God."
28Peter said to him, "We have left everything to follow you!"
29"I tell you the truth," Jesus replied, "no one who has left
home or brothers or sisters or mother or father or children or fields
for me and the gospel 30will fail to receive a hundred times as much
in this present age (homes, brothers, sisters, mothers, children
and fields—and with them, persecutions) and in the age to come,
eternal life. 31But many who are first will be last, and the last first."

*Jesus Again Predicts His Death*

32They were on their way up to Jerusalem, with Jesus leading
the way, and the disciples were astonished, while those who
followed were afraid. Again he took the Twelve aside and told
them what was going to happen to him. 33"We are going up to
Jerusalem," he said, "and the Son of Man will be betrayed to the
chief priests and teachers of the law. They will condemn him to
death and will hand him over to the Gentiles, 34who will mock him
and spit on him, flog him and kill him. Three days later he will
rise."

*The Request of James and John*

35Then James and John, the sons of Zebedee, came to him.
"Teacher," they said, "we want you to do for us whatever we
ask."
36"What do you want me to do for you?" he asked.
37They replied, "Let one of us sit at your right and the other at
your left in your glory."
38"You don't know what you are asking," Jesus said. "Can you
drink the cup I drink or be baptized with the baptism I am baptized
with?"
39"We can," they answered.
Jesus said to them, "You will drink the cup I drink and be
baptized with the baptism I am baptized with, 40but to sit at my
right or left is not for me to grant. These places belong to those for
whom they have been prepared."
41When the ten heard about this, they became indignant with
James and John. 42Jesus called them together and said, "You know
that those who are regarded as rulers of the Gentiles lord it over
them, and their high officials exercise authority over them. 43Not
so with you. Instead, whoever wants to become great among you
must be your servant, 44and whoever wants to be first must be
slave of all. 45For even the Son of Man did not come to be served,
but to serve, and to give his life as a ransom for many."

*Blind Bartimaeus Receives His Sight*

46Then they came to Jericho. As Jesus and his disciples, together
with a large crowd, were leaving the city, a blind man, Bartimaeus
(that is, the Son of Timaeus), was sitting by the roadside begging.
47When he heard that it was Jesus of Nazareth, he began to shout,
"Jesus, Son of David, have mercy on me!"
48Many rebuked him and told him to be quiet, but he shouted
all the more, "Son of David, have mercy on me!"
49Jesus stopped and said, "Call him."
So they called to the blind man, "Cheer up! On your feet! He's

## King James

50 And he, casting away his garment, rose, and came to Jesus.

51 And Jesus answered and said unto him, What wilt thou that I should do unto thee? The blind man said unto him, Lord, that I might receive my sight.

52 And Jesus said unto him, Go thy way; thy faith hath made thee whole. And immediately he received his sight, and followed Jesus in the way.

**11** AND WHEN they came nigh to Jerusalem, unto Bethphage and Bethany, at the mount of Olives, he sendeth forth two of his disciples,

2 And saith unto them, Go your way into the village over against you: and as soon as ye be entered into it, ye shall find a colt tied, whereon never man sat; loose him, and bring *him*.

3 And if any man say unto you, Why do ye this? say ye that the Lord hath need of him; and straightway he will send him hither.

4 And they went their way, and found the colt tied by the door without in a place where two ways met; and they loose him.

5 And certain of them that stood there said unto them, What do ye, loosing the colt?

6 And they said unto them even as Jesus had commanded: and they let them go.

7 And they brought the colt to Jesus, and cast their garments on him; and he sat upon him.

8 And many spread their garments in the way: and others cut down branches off the trees, and strawed *them* in the way.

9 And they that went before, and they that followed, cried, saying, Hosanna; Blessed *is* he that cometh in the name of the Lord:

10 Blessed *be* the kingdom of our father David, that cometh in the name of the Lord: Hosanna in the highest.

11 And Jesus entered into Jerusalem, and into the temple: and when he had looked round about upon all things, and now the eventide was come, he went out unto Bethany with the twelve.

12 ¶ And on the morrow, when they were come from Bethany, he was hungry:

13 And seeing a fig tree afar off having leaves, he came, if haply he might find any thing thereon: and when he came to it, he found nothing but leaves; for the time of figs was not *yet*.

14 And Jesus answered and said unto it, No man eat fruit of thee hereafter for ever. And his disciples heard *it*.

15 ¶ And they come to Jerusalem: and Jesus went into the temple, and began to cast out them that sold and bought in the temple, and overthrew the tables of the moneychangers, and the seats of them that sold doves;

16 And would not suffer that any man should carry *any* vessel through the temple.

17 And he taught, saying unto them, Is it not written, My house shall be called of all nations the house of prayer? but ye have made it a den of thieves.

18 And the scribes and chief priests heard *it*, and sought how they might destroy him: for they feared him, because all the people was astonished at his doctrine.

19 And when even was come, he went out of the city.

20 ¶ And in the morning, as they passed by, they saw the fig tree dried up from the roots.

21 And Peter calling to remembrance saith unto him, Master, behold, the fig tree which thou cursedst is withered away.

## Amplified

50 And throwing off his outer garment, he leaped up and came to Jesus.

51 And Jesus said to him, What do you want Me to do for you? And the blind man said to Him, Master, let me receive my sight.

52 And Jesus said to him, Go your way; your faith has healed you. And at once he received his sight and accompanied Jesus on the road. [Isa. 42:6, 7.]

**11** WHEN THEY were getting near to Jerusalem, to Bethphage and Bethany at the Mount of Olives, He sent ahead two of His disciples,

2 And instructed them, Go into the village in front of you, and as soon as you enter it you will find a colt tied which has never been ridden by any one; unfasten it and bring it [here].

3 If any one asks you, Why are you doing this? answer, The Lord needs it, and He will send it back here presently.

4 So they went away and found a colt tied at the door out in the (winding) open street, and they loosed it.

5 And some who were standing there said to them, What are you doing, untying the colt?

6 And they replied as Jesus had directed them, and they allowed them to go.

7 And they brought the colt to Jesus, and threw their outer garments upon it, and He sat on it.

8 And many [of the people] spread their garments on the road, and others *scattered* (a layer of) leafy branches which they had cut from the fields.

9 And those who went before and those who followed cried out, [a]Hosanna! (Be graciously inclined and propitious [to Him]!) Praised *and* blessed be He Who comes in the name of the Lord! [Ps. 118:26.]

10 Praised *and* blessed *in the name of the Lord* be the coming kingdom of our father David! Hosanna (O save us) in the highest (heaven)!

11 And Jesus went into Jerusalem, and entered the temple ([b]enclosure); and when He had looked around, surveying *and* observing everything, as it was already late He went out to Bethany together with the twelve [apostles].

12 On the day following, when they had come away from Bethany, He was hungry.

13 And seeing in the distance a fig tree [covered] with leaves, He went to see if He could find any [fruit] on it [ [c]for in the fig tree the fruit appears at the same time as the leaves]. But when He came up to it, He found nothing but leaves, for the fig season had not yet come.

14 And He said to it, No one ever again shall eat fruit from you. And His disciples were listening [to what He said].

15 And they came to Jerusalem. And He went into the temple (area, [d]porches and courts) and began to drive out those who sold and bought in the temple area, and He overturned the ( [e]four-footed) tables of the money-changers and the seats of those who dealt in doves;

16 And He would not permit any one to carry any household equipment through the temple enclosure [thus making the temple area a short-cut traffic lane].

17 And He taught, and said to them, Is it not written, My house shall be called a house of prayer for all the nations? But you have turned it into a den of robbers. [Isa. 56:7; Jer. 7:11.]

18 And the chief priests and the scribes heard [of this] and kept seeking some way to destroy Him, for they feared Him, because the entire multitude was struck with astonishment at His teaching.

19 And when evening came on, He *and* [ [f]His disciples] as accustomed went out of the city.

20 In the morning when they were passing along, they noticed that the fig tree was withered (completely) away to its roots.

21 And Peter remembered and said to Him, Master, look! The fig tree which You doomed has withered away!

**AMP** [a] A cry of happiness (—Souter). [b] Trench's "Synonyms of the New Testament." [c] International Standard Bible Encyclopedia. [d] Trench's "Synonyms of the New Testament." [e] Moulton and Milligan. [f] Some authorities read "they."

## New American Standard

50And casting aside his cloak, he jumped up, and came to Jesus.
51And answering him, Jesus said, "What do you want Me to do
for you?" And the blind man said to Him, "[g]Rabboni, *I want* to
regain my sight!"
52And Jesus said to him, "Go your way; your faith has made
you well." And immediately he regained his sight and *began* following Him on the road.

*The Triumphal Entry*

11 AND AS they *approached Jerusalem, at Bethphage and
Bethany, near the Mount of Olives, He *sent two of His
disciples,
2and *said to them, "Go into the village opposite you, and
immediately as you enter it, you will find a colt tied *there*, on which
no one yet has ever sat; untie it and bring it *here*.
3"And if anyone says to you, 'Why are you doing this?' you
say, 'The Lord has need of it'; and immediately he will send it back
here."
4And they went away and found a colt tied at the door outside
in the street; and they *untied it.
5And some of the bystanders were saying to them, "What are
you doing, untying the colt?"
6And they spoke to them just as Jesus had told *them*, and they
gave them permission.
7And they *brought the colt to Jesus and put their garments on
it; and He sat upon it.
8And many spread their garments in the road, and others
*spread* leafy branches which they had cut from the fields.
9And those who went before, and those who followed after,
were crying out,

"Hosanna!
BLESSED IS HE WHO COMES IN THE NAME OF THE LORD;
10 Blessed *is* the coming kingdom of our father David;
Hosanna in the highest!"

11¶ And He entered Jerusalem *and came* into the temple; and
after looking all around, He departed for Bethany with the twelve,
since it was already late.
12¶ And on the next day, when they had departed from Bethany, He became hungry.
13And seeing at a distance a fig tree in leaf, He went *to see* if
perhaps He would find anything on it; and when He came to it,
He found nothing but leaves, for it was not the season for figs.
14And He answered and said to it, "May no one ever eat fruit
from you again!" And His disciples were listening.

*Jesus Drives Moneychangers from the Temple*

15¶ And they *came to Jerusalem. And He entered the temple
and began to cast out those who were buying and selling in the
temple, and overturned the tables of the moneychangers and the
seats of those who were selling doves;
16and He would not permit anyone to carry goods through the
temple.
17And He *began* to teach and say to them, "Is it not written, 'MY
HOUSE SHALL BE CALLED A HOUSE OF PRAYER FOR ALL THE NATIONS'?
But you have made it a ROBBERS' DEN."
18And the chief priests and the scribes heard *this*, and *began*
seeking how to destroy Him; for they were afraid of Him, for all
the multitude was astonished at His teaching.
19¶ And whenever evening came, they would go out of the city.
20¶ And as they were passing by in the morning, they saw the
fig tree withered from the roots *up*.
21And being reminded, Peter *said to Him, "Rabbi, behold, the
fig tree which You cursed has withered."

**NAS** [g] I.e., My Master

## New International

calling you." 50Throwing his cloak aside, he jumped to his feet and
came to Jesus.
51"What do you want me to do for you?" Jesus asked him.
The blind man said, "Rabbi, I want to see."
52"Go," said Jesus, "your faith has healed you." Immediately
he received his sight and followed Jesus along the road.

*The Triumphal Entry*

11 AS THEY approached Jerusalem and came to Bethphage
and Bethany at the Mount of Olives, Jesus sent two of his
disciples, 2saying to them, "Go to the village ahead of you, and just
as you enter it, you will find a colt tied there, which no one has
ever ridden. Untie it and bring it here. 3If anyone asks you, 'Why
are you doing this?' tell him, 'The Lord needs it and will send it
back here shortly.' "
4They went and found a colt outside in the street, tied at a
doorway. As they untied it, 5some people standing there asked,
"What are you doing, untying that colt?" 6They answered as Jesus
had told them to, and the people let them go. 7When they brought
the colt to Jesus and threw their cloaks over it, he sat on it. 8Many
people spread their cloaks on the road, while others spread
branches they had cut in the fields. 9Those who went ahead and
those who followed shouted,

"Hosanna![h]"

"Blessed is he who comes in the name of the Lord!"[i]

10"Blessed is the coming kingdom of our father David!"

"Hosanna in the highest!"

11Jesus entered Jerusalem and went to the temple. He looked
around at everything, but since it was already late, he went out to
Bethany with the Twelve.

*Jesus Clears the Temple*

12The next day as they were leaving Bethany, Jesus was hungry.
13Seeing in the distance a fig tree in leaf, he went to find out if it
had any fruit. When he reached it, he found nothing but leaves,
because it was not the season for figs. 14Then he said to the tree,
"May no one ever eat fruit from you again." And his disciples
heard him say it.
15On reaching Jerusalem, Jesus entered the temple area and
began driving out those who were buying and selling there. He
overturned the tables of the money changers and the benches of
those selling doves, 16and would not allow anyone to carry merchandise through the temple courts. 17And as he taught them, he
said, "Is it not written:

" 'My house will be called
a house of prayer for all nations'[j]?

But you have made it 'a den of robbers.'[k]"
18The chief priests and the teachers of the law heard this and
began looking for a way to kill him, for they feared him, because
the whole crowd was amazed at his teaching.
19When evening came, they[l] went out of the city.

*The Withered Fig Tree*

20In the morning, as they went along, they saw the fig tree
withered from the roots. 21Peter remembered and said to Jesus,
"Rabbi, look! The fig tree you cursed has withered!"

**NIV** [h] *9* A Hebrew expression meaning "Save!" which became an exclamation of praise; also in verse 10 [i] *9* Psalm 118:25,26 [j] *17* Isaiah 56:7 [k] *17* Jer. 7:11 [l] *19* Some early manuscripts *he*

## King James

22And Jesus answering saith unto them, Have faith in God.
23For verily I say unto you, That whosoever shall say unto this
mountain, Be thou removed, and be thou cast into the sea; and
shall not doubt in his heart, but shall believe that those things
which he saith shall come to pass; he shall have whatsoever he
saith.
24Therefore I say unto you, What things soever ye desire, when
ye pray, believe that ye receive *them,* and ye shall have *them.*
25And when ye stand praying, forgive, if ye have aught against
any: that your Father also which is in heaven may forgive you your
trespasses.
26But if ye do not forgive, neither will your Father which is in
heaven forgive your trespasses.
27¶ And they come again to Jerusalem: and as he was walking
in the temple, there come to him the chief priests, and the scribes,
and the elders,
28And say unto him, By what authority doest thou these things?
and who gave thee this authority to do these things?
29And Jesus answered and said unto them, I will also ask of you
one question, and answer me, and I will tell you by what authority
I do these things.
30The baptism of John, was *it* from heaven, or of men? answer
me.
31And they reasoned with themselves, saying, If we shall say,
From heaven; he will say, Why then did ye not believe him?
32But if we shall say, Of men; they feared the people: for all *men*
counted John, that he was a prophet indeed.
33And they answered and said unto Jesus, We cannot tell. And
Jesus answering saith unto them, Neither do I tell you by what
authority I do these things.

**12** AND HE began to speak unto them by parables. A *certain*
man planted a vineyard, and set an hedge about *it,* and
digged *a place for* the winevat, and built a tower, and let it out to
husbandmen, and went into a far country.
2And at the season he sent to the husbandmen a servant, that
he might receive from the husbandmen of the fruit of the vineyard.
3And they caught *him,* and beat him, and sent *him* away empty.
4And again he sent unto them another servant; and at him they
cast stones, and wounded *him* in the head, and sent *him* away
shamefully handled.
5And again he sent another; and him they killed, and many
others; beating some, and killing some.
6Having yet therefore one son, his wellbeloved, he sent him
also last unto them, saying, They will reverence my son.
7But those husbandmen said among themselves, This is the
heir; come, let us kill him, and the inheritance shall be ours.
8And they took him, and killed *him,* and cast *him* out of the
vineyard.
9What shall therefore the lord of the vineyard do? he will come
and destroy the husbandmen, and will give the vineyard unto
others.
10And have ye not read this scripture; The stone which the
builders rejected is become the head of the corner:
11This was the Lord's doing, and it is marvellous in our eyes?
12And they sought to lay hold on him, but feared the people:
for they knew that he had spoken the parable against them: and
they left him, and went their way.

## Amplified

22And Jesus replying said to them, Have faith in God (constantly).
23Truly, I tell you, whoever says to this mountain, Be lifted up
and thrown into the sea! and does not doubt at all in his heart, but
believes that what he says will take place, it will be done for him.
24For this reason I am telling you, whatever you ask for in
prayer, believe—trust and be confident—that it is granted to you,
and you will [get it].
25And whenever you stand praying, if you have anything
against any one, forgive him *and* [a]let it drop—leave it, let it go—in
order that your Father Who is in heaven may also forgive you your
[own] failings *and* shortcomings *and* let them drop.
*26 But if you do not forgive, neither will your Father in heaven forgive
your failings and shortcomings.*
27And they came again to Jerusalem. And when Jesus was
walking about in the ( [b]courts and porches of the) temple, the chief
priests and the scribes and the elders came to Him,
28And they kept saying to Him, By what (sort of) authority are
You doing these things, or who gave You this authority to do
them?
29Jesus told them, I will ask you a question. Answer Me, and
then I will tell you by what (sort of) authority I do these things.
30Was the baptism of John from heaven or from men? Answer
Me.
31And they reasoned *and* argued with one another, If we say,
From heaven, He will say, Why then did you not believe him?
32But [on the other hand] can we say, from men? For they were
afraid of the people, because everybody considered *and* held John
actually to be a prophet.
33So they replied to Jesus, We do not know. And Jesus said to
them, Neither am I going to tell you what (sort of) authority I have
for doing these things.

**12** AND [JESUS] started to speak to them in parables—[that
is,] with comparisons and illustrations. A man planted a
vineyard, and put a hedge about it, and dug a pit for the wine
press, and built a tower, and let it out [for rent] to vinedressers,
and went into another country.
2When the season came, he sent a bond servant to the tenants,
to collect from them some of the fruit of the vineyard.
3But they took him and beat him, and sent him away without
anything.
4Again he sent to them another bond servant, and they *stoned
him and* wounded him in the head and treated him shamefully—
sending him away with insults.
5And he sent another, and that one they killed; then many
others, some they beat and some they put to death.
6He had still one left, a beloved son; last of all he sent him to
them, saying, They will respect my son.
7But those tenants said to one another, Here is the heir; come
on, let us put him to death, and [then] the inheritance will be ours.
8And they took him and killed him, and threw [his body] outside the vineyard.
9Now what will the owner of the vineyard do? He will come and
destroy the tenants, and give the vineyard to others.
10Have you not even read this [passage of] Scripture: The very
Stone which [ [c]after putting It to the test] the builders rejected, has
become the Head of the corner;
11This is from the Lord *and* is His doing, and it is marvelous in
our eyes? [Ps. 118:22, 23.]
12And they were trying to get hold of Him, but they were afraid
of the people, for they knew that He spoke this parable with
reference to *and* against them. So they left Him and departed. [Isa.
5:1-7.]

**AMP** [a] Moulton and Milligan. [b] Trench. [c] Wuest.

## New American Standard

22And Jesus *answered saying to them, "Have faith in God.
23"Truly I say to you, whoever says to this mountain, 'Be taken
up and cast into the sea,' and does not doubt in his heart, but
believes that what he says is going to happen, it shall be *granted*
him.
24"Therefore I say to you, all things for which you pray and ask,
believe that you have received them, and they shall be *granted* you.
25"And whenever you stand praying, forgive, if you have anything against anyone; so that your Father also who is in heaven
may forgive you your transgressions.
26[" [d]But if you do not forgive, neither will your Father who is
in heaven forgive your transgressions."]

*Jesus' Authority Questioned*

27¶ And they *came again to Jerusalem. And as He was walking
in the temple, the chief priests, and scribes, and elders *came to
Him,
28and *began* saying to Him, "By what authority are You doing
these things, or who gave You this authority to do these things?"
29And Jesus said to them, "I will ask you one question, and you
answer Me, and *then* I will tell you by what authority I do these
things.
30"Was the baptism of John from heaven, or from men? Answer
Me."
31And they *began* reasoning among themselves, saying, "If we
say, 'From heaven,' He will say, 'Then why did you not believe
him?'
32"But shall we say, 'From men'?"—they were afraid of the
multitude, for all considered John to have been a prophet indeed.
33And answering Jesus, they *said, "We do not know." And
Jesus *said to them, "Neither will I tell you by what authority I do
these things."

*Parable of the Vine-growers*

**12** AND HE began to speak to them in parables: "A man
PLANTED A VINEYARD, AND PUT A WALL AROUND IT, AND
DUG A VAT UNDER THE WINE PRESS, AND BUILT A TOWER, and rented
it out to [e]vine-growers and went on a journey.
2"And at the *harvest* time he sent a slave to the vine-growers,
in order to receive *some* of the produce of the vineyard from the
vine-growers.
3"And they took him, and beat him, and sent him away empty-
handed.
4"And again he sent them another slave, and they wounded
him in the head, and treated him shamefully.
5"And he sent another, and that one they killed; and *so with*
many others, beating some, and killing others.
6"He had one more *to send,* a beloved son; he sent him last *of
all* to them, saying, 'They will respect my son.'
7"But those vine-growers said to one another, 'This is the heir;
come, let us kill him, and the inheritance will be ours!'
8"And they took him, and killed him, and threw him out of the
vineyard.
9"What will the owner of the vineyard do? He will come and
destroy the vine-growers, and will give the vineyard to others.
10"Have you not even read this Scripture:
'THE STONE WHICH THE BUILDERS REJECTED,
THIS BECAME THE CHIEF CORNER *stone;*
11 THIS CAME ABOUT FROM THE LORD,
AND IT IS MARVELOUS IN OUR EYES'?"
12And they were seeking to seize Him; and *yet* they feared the
multitude; for they understood that He spoke the parable against
them. And *so* they left Him, and went away.

**NAS** [d] Many mss. do not contain this verse [e] Or, *tenant farmers,* also vv. 2, 7, 9

## New International

22"Have[f] faith in God," Jesus answered. 23"I tell you the truth,
if anyone says to this mountain, 'Go, throw yourself into the sea,'
and does not doubt in his heart but believes that what he says will
happen, it will be done for him. 24Therefore I tell you, whatever
you ask for in prayer, believe that you have received it, and it will
be yours. 25And when you stand praying, if you hold anything
against anyone, forgive him, so that your Father in heaven may
forgive you your sins.[g]"

*The Authority of Jesus Questioned*

27They arrived again in Jerusalem, and while Jesus was walking
in the temple courts, the chief priests, the teachers of the law and
the elders came to him. 28"By what authority are you doing these
things?" they asked. "And who gave you authority to do this?"
29Jesus replied, "I will ask you one question. Answer me, and
I will tell you by what authority I am doing these things. 30John's
baptism—was it from heaven, or from men? Tell me!"
31They discussed it among themselves and said, "If we say,
'From heaven,' he will ask, 'Then why didn't you believe him?'
32But if we say, 'From men'. . . ." (They feared the people, for
everyone held that John really was a prophet.)
33So they answered Jesus, "We don't know."
Jesus said, "Neither will I tell you by what authority I am doing
these things."

*The Parable of the Tenants*

**12** HE THEN began to speak to them in parables: "A man
planted a vineyard. He put a wall around it, dug a pit for
the winepress and built a watchtower. Then he rented the vineyard to some farmers and went away on a journey. 2At harvest
time he sent a servant to the tenants to collect from them some of
the fruit of the vineyard. 3But they seized him, beat him and sent
him away empty-handed. 4Then he sent another servant to them;
they struck this man on the head and treated him shamefully. 5He
sent still another, and that one they killed. He sent many others;
some of them they beat, others they killed.
6"He had one left to send, a son, whom he loved. He sent him
last of all, saying, 'They will respect my son.'
7"But the tenants said to one another, 'This is the heir. Come,
let's kill him, and the inheritance will be ours.' 8So they took him
and killed him, and threw him out of the vineyard.
9"What then will the owner of the vineyard do? He will come
and kill those tenants and give the vineyard to others. 10Haven't
you read this scripture:

" 'The stone the builders rejected
has become the capstone[h];
11the Lord has done this,
and it is marvelous in our eyes'[i]?"

12Then they looked for a way to arrest him because they knew
he had spoken the parable against them. But they were afraid of
the crowd; so they left him and went away.

**NIV** [f] 22 Some early manuscripts *If you have* [g] 25 Some manuscripts *sins. 26But if you do not forgive, neither will your Father who is in heaven forgive your sins.* [h] *10* Or *cornerstone* [i] *11* Psalm 118:22,23

## King James

13¶ And they send unto him certain of the Pharisees and of the Herodians, to catch him in *his* words.

14And when they were come, they say unto him, Master, we know that thou art true, and carest for no man: for thou regardest not the person of men, but teachest the way of God in truth: Is it lawful to give tribute to Caesar, or not?

15Shall we give, or shall we not give? But he, knowing their hypocrisy, said unto them, Why tempt ye me? bring me a penny, that I may see *it*.

16And they brought *it*. And he saith unto them, Whose *is* this image and superscription? And they said unto him, Caesar's.

17And Jesus answering said unto them, Render to Caesar the things that are Caesar's, and to God the things that are God's. And they marvelled at him.

18¶ Then come unto him the Sadducees, which say there is no resurrection; and they asked him, saying,

19Master, Moses wrote unto us, If a man's brother die, and leave *his* wife *behind him*, and leave no children, that his brother should take his wife, and raise up seed unto his brother.

20Now there were seven brethren: and the first took a wife, and dying left no seed.

21And the second took her, and died, neither left he any seed: and the third likewise.

22And the seven had her, and left no seed: last of all the woman died also.

23In the resurrection therefore, when they shall rise, whose wife shall she be of them? for the seven had her to wife.

24And Jesus answering said unto them, Do ye not therefore err, because ye know not the scriptures, neither the power of God?

25For when they shall rise from the dead, they neither marry, nor are given in marriage; but are as the angels which are in heaven.

26And as touching the dead, that they rise: have ye not read in the book of Moses, how in the bush God spake unto him, saying, I *am* the God of Abraham, and the God of Isaac, and the God of Jacob?

27He is not the God of the dead, but the God of the living: ye therefore do greatly err.

28¶ And one of the scribes came, and having heard them reasoning together, and perceiving that he had answered them well, asked him, Which is the first commandment of all?

29And Jesus answered him, The first of all the commandments *is*, Hear, O Israel; The Lord our God is one Lord:

30And thou shalt love the Lord thy God with all thy heart, and with all thy soul, and with all thy mind, and with all thy strength: this *is* the first commandment.

31And the second *is* like, *namely* this, Thou shalt love thy neighbour as thyself. There is none other commandment greater than these.

32And the scribe said unto him, Well, Master, thou hast said the truth: for there is one God; and there is none other but he:

33And to love him with all the heart, and with all the understanding, and with all the soul, and with all the strength, and to love *his* neighbour as himself, is more than all whole burnt offerings and sacrifices.

34And when Jesus saw that he answered discreetly, he said unto him, Thou art not far from the kingdom of God. And no man after that durst ask him *any question*.

## Amplified

13But they sent some of the Pharisees and of the Herodians to Him, for the purpose of entrapping Him in His speech.

14And they came up and said to Him, Teacher, we know that You are [a]sincere *and* what You profess to be; that You cannot lie *and* that You have no personal bias for any one; for You are not influenced by partiality *and* have no [b]regard for any one's external condition *or* position, but [on the basis of] truth You teach the way of God. Is it lawful (permissible and right) to give tribute ([c]poll taxes) to Caesar, or not?

15Should we pay [them], or should we not pay [them]? But knowing their hypocrisy, He asked them, Why do you put Me to the test? Bring Me a coin (a denarius), so I may see it.

16And they brought [Him one]. Then He asked them, Whose image (picture) is this, and whose superscription ([d]title)? They said to Him, Caesar's.

17Jesus said to them, Pay to Caesar the things that are Caesar's and to [e]God the things that are God's. And they [f]stood marveling *and* greatly amazed at Him.

18And [some] Sadducees came to Him, [of that party] that say there is no resurrection; and they asked Him a question, saying,

19Teacher, Moses gave us [a law] that if a man's brother died leaving a wife but no child, the man must marry the widow, and raise up offspring for his brother. [Deut. 25:5.]

20Now there were seven brothers; the first one took a wife and died leaving no children;

21And the second [brother] married her, and died, leaving no children; and the third did the same,

22And all seven, leaving no children. Last of all the woman died also.

23Now in the resurrection, whose wife will she be? For the seven were married to her.

24Jesus said to them, Is not this where you wander out of the way *and* go wrong, because you know neither the Scriptures nor the power of God?

25For when they arise from among the dead, [men] do not marry nor are [women] given in marriage, but are like the angels in heaven.

26But concerning the dead being raised, have you not read in the book of Moses, [in the passage] about the [burning] bush, how God said to him, I am the God of Abraham, and the God of Isaac, and the God of Jacob? [Exod. 3:2-6.]

27He is not the God of [the] dead, but of [the] living! You are very wrong.

28Then one of the scribes came up and listened to them disputing with one another, and noticing that Jesus answered them fitly *and* admirably, he asked Him, Which commandment is first *and* most important of all ([g]in its nature)?

29Jesus answered, The first *and* principal *one of all commands* is, Hear, O Israel: The Lord our God is one Lord;

30And you shall love the Lord your God [h]out of *and* with your whole heart, and out of *and* with all your soul (your [i]life) and out of *and* with all your mind—[that is] with [j]your faculty of thought and your moral understanding—and out of *and* with all your strength. *This is the first and principal commandment.* [Deut. 6:4, 5.]

31The second *is like it and* is this, You shall love your neighbor as yourself. There is no other commandment greater than these. [Lev. 19:18.]

32And the scribe said to Him, Excellently *and* fitly *and* admirably answered, Teacher! You have said truly that He is One, and there is no other but He;

33And to love Him out of all the heart, and with all the understanding—[that is,] with the [k]faculty of quick apprehension and intelligence and keenness of discernment—and with all the strength, and to love one's neighbor as oneself, is much more than all the whole burnt offerings and sacrifices. [I Sam. 15:22; Hos. 6:6; Mic. 6:6-8.]

34And when Jesus saw that he answered intelligently—discreetly and [l]having his wits about him—He said to him, You are not far from the kingdom of God. And after that no one ventured *or* dared to ask Him any further question.

**AMP** [a] Cremer. [b] Thayer. [c] Thayer. [d] Wuest. [e] A rebuke of Emperor worship. [f] Wuest. [g] Vincent. [h] Vincent. [i] Cremer. [j] Vincent. [k] Vincent. [l] Vincent.

## New American Standard

*Jesus Answers the Pharisees, Sadducees and Scribes*

13¶ And they *sent some of the Pharisees and Herodians to Him, in order to trap Him in a statement.

14And they *came and *said to Him, "Teacher, we know that You are truthful, and defer to no one; for You are not partial to any, but teach the way of God in truth. Is it lawful to pay a poll-tax to Caesar, or not?

15"Shall we pay, or shall we not pay?" But He, knowing their hypocrisy, said to them, "Why are you testing Me? Bring Me a [m]denarius to look at."

16And they brought *one.* And He *said to them, "Whose likeness and inscription is this?" And they said to Him, "Caesar's."

17And Jesus said to them, "Render to Caesar the things that are Caesar's, and to God the things that are God's." And they were amazed at Him.

18¶ And *some* Sadducees (who say that there is no resurrection) *came to Him, and *began* questioning Him, saying,

19"Teacher, Moses wrote for us that IF A MAN'S BROTHER DIES, and leaves behind a wife, AND LEAVES NO CHILD, HIS BROTHER SHOULD TAKE THE WIFE, AND RAISE UP OFFSPRING TO HIS BROTHER.

20"There were seven brothers; and the first took a wife, and died, leaving no offspring.

21"And the second one took her, and died, leaving behind no offspring; and the third likewise;

22and *so* all seven left no offspring. Last of all the woman died also.

23"In the resurrection, [n]when they rise again, which one's wife will she be? For all seven had her as wife."

24Jesus said to them, "Is this not the reason you are mistaken, that you do not understand the Scriptures, or the power of God?

25"For when they rise from the dead, they neither marry, nor are given in marriage, but are like angels in heaven.

26"But regarding the fact that the dead rise again, have you not read in the book of Moses, in the *passage about the burning* bush, how God spoke to him, saying, 'I AM THE GOD OF ABRAHAM, AND THE GOD OF ISAAC, AND THE GOD OF JACOB'?

27"He is not the God of the dead, but of the living; you are greatly mistaken."

28¶ And one of the scribes came and heard them arguing, and recognizing that He had answered them well, asked Him, "What commandment is the foremost of all?"

29Jesus answered, "The foremost is, 'HEAR, O ISRAEL! THE LORD OUR GOD IS ONE LORD;

30AND YOU SHALL LOVE THE LORD YOUR GOD WITH ALL YOUR HEART, AND WITH ALL YOUR SOUL, AND WITH ALL YOUR MIND, AND WITH ALL YOUR STRENGTH.'

31"The second is this, 'YOU SHALL LOVE YOUR NEIGHBOR AS YOURSELF.' There is no other commandment greater than these."

32And the scribe said to Him, "Right, Teacher, You have truly stated that HE IS ONE; AND THERE IS NO ONE ELSE BESIDES HIM;

33AND TO LOVE HIM WITH ALL THE HEART AND WITH ALL THE UNDERSTANDING AND WITH ALL THE STRENGTH, AND TO LOVE ONE'S NEIGHBOR AS HIMSELF, is much more than all burnt offerings and sacrifices."

34And when Jesus saw that he had answered intelligently, He said to him, "You are not far from the kingdom of God." And after that, no one would venture to ask Him any more questions.

NAS [m]The denarius was equivalent to one day's wage [n]Most ancient mss. do not contain *when they rise again*

## New International

*Paying Taxes to Caesar*

13Later they sent some of the Pharisees and Herodians to Jesus
to catch him in his words. 14They came to him and said, "Teacher,
we know you are a man of integrity. You aren't swayed by men,
because you pay no attention to who they are; but you teach the
way of God in accordance with the truth. Is it right to pay taxes
to Caesar or not? 15Should we pay or shouldn't we?"

But Jesus knew their hypocrisy. "Why are you trying to trap
me?" he asked. "Bring me a denarius and let me look at it." 16They
brought the coin, and he asked them, "Whose portrait is this? And
whose inscription?"

"Caesar's," they replied.

17Then Jesus said to them, "Give to Caesar what is Caesar's and
to God what is God's."

And they were amazed at him.

*Marriage at the Resurrection*

18Then the Sadducees, who say there is no resurrection, came
to him with a question. 19"Teacher," they said, "Moses wrote for
us that if a man's brother dies and leaves a wife but no children,
the man must marry the widow and have children for his brother.
20Now there were seven brothers. The first one married and died
without leaving any children. 21The second one married the
widow, but he also died, leaving no child. It was the same with
the third. 22In fact, none of the seven left any children. Last of all,
the woman died too. 23At the resurrection[o] whose wife will she
be, since the seven were married to her?"

24Jesus replied, "Are you not in error because you do not know
the Scriptures or the power of God? 25When the dead rise, they will
neither marry nor be given in marriage; they will be like the angels
in heaven. 26Now about the dead rising—have you not read in the
book of Moses, in the account of the bush, how God said to him,
'I am the God of Abraham, the God of Isaac, and the God of
Jacob'[p]? 27He is not the God of the dead, but of the living. You are
badly mistaken!"

*The Greatest Commandment*

28One of the teachers of the law came and heard them debating.
Noticing that Jesus had given them a good answer, he asked him,
"Of all the commandments, which is the most important?"

29"The most important one," answered Jesus, "is this: 'Hear,
O Israel, the Lord our God, the Lord is one.[q] 30Love the Lord your
God with all your heart and with all your soul and with all your
mind and with all your strength.'[r] 31The second is this: 'Love your
neighbor as yourself.'[s] There is no commandment greater than
these."

32"Well said, teacher," the man replied. "You are right in saying that God is one and there is no other but him. 33To love him
with all your heart, with all your understanding and with all your
strength, and to love your neighbor as yourself is more important
than all burnt offerings and sacrifices."

34When Jesus saw that he had answered wisely, he said to him,
"You are not far from the kingdom of God." And from then on no
one dared ask him any more questions.

NIV [o]23 Some manuscripts *resurrection, when men rise from the dead,* [p]26 Exodus 3:6 [q]29 Or *the Lord our God is one Lord* [r]30 Deut. 6:4,5 [s]31 Lev. 19:18

## King James

35¶ And Jesus answered and said, while he taught in the temple, How say the scribes that Christ is the son of David?

36For David himself said by the Holy Ghost, The LORD said to my Lord, Sit thou on my right hand, till I make thine enemies thy footstool.

37David therefore himself calleth him Lord; and whence is he *then* his son? And the common people heard him gladly.

38¶ And he said unto them in his doctrine, Beware of the scribes, which love to go in long clothing, and *love* salutations in the marketplaces,

39And the chief seats in the synagogues, and the uppermost rooms at feasts:

40Which devour widows' houses, and for a pretence make long prayers: these shall receive greater damnation.

41¶ And Jesus sat over against the treasury, and beheld how the people cast money into the treasury: and many that were rich cast in much.

42And there came a certain poor widow, and she threw in two mites, which make a farthing.

43And he called *unto him* his disciples, and saith unto them, Verily I say unto you, That this poor widow hath cast more in, than all they which have cast into the treasury:

44For all *they* did cast in of their abundance; but she of her want did cast in all that she had, *even* all her living.

**13** AND AS he went out of the temple, one of his disciples saith unto him, Master, see what manner of stones and what buildings *are here!*

2And Jesus answering said unto him, Seest thou these great buildings? there shall not be left one stone upon another, that shall not be thrown down.

3And as he sat upon the mount of Olives over against the temple, Peter and James and John and Andrew asked him privately,

4Tell us, when shall these things be? and what *shall be* the sign when all these things shall be fulfilled?

5And Jesus answering them began to say, Take heed lest any *man* deceive you:

6For many shall come in my name, saying, I am *Christ;* and shall deceive many.

7And when ye shall hear of wars and rumours of wars, be ye not troubled: for *such things* must needs be; but the end *shall* not *be* yet.

8For nation shall rise against nation, and kingdom against kingdom: and there shall be earthquakes in divers places, and there shall be famines and troubles: these *are* the beginnings of sorrows.

9¶ But take heed to yourselves: for they shall deliver you up to councils; and in the synagogues ye shall be beaten: and ye shall be brought before rulers and kings for my sake, for a testimony against them.

10And the gospel must first be published among all nations.

11But when they shall lead *you,* and deliver you up, take no thought beforehand what ye shall speak, neither do ye premeditate: but whatsoever shall be given you in that hour, that speak ye: for it is not ye that speak, but the Holy Ghost.

12Now the brother shall betray the brother to death, and the father the son; and children shall rise up against *their* parents, and shall cause them to be put to death.

## Amplified

35And as Jesus taught in (a [a]porch or court of) the temple, He said, How can the scribes say that the Christ is David's Son?

36David, himself (inspired), in the Holy Spirit declared, The Lord said to my Lord, Sit at My right hand until I make Your enemies (a footstool) under Your feet. [Ps. 110:1.]

37David himself calls Him Lord, so how can it be that He is his Son? Now the great mass of the people heard [Jesus] gladly—listening to Him with delight.

38And in [the course of] His teaching He said, Beware of the scribes, who like to go around in long robes, and [to get] greetings in the market places [public forums],

39And the front seats in the synagogues and the [b]chief couches (places of honor) at feasts,

40Who devour widows' houses and to cover it up make long prayers. They will receive the heavier (sentence of) condemnation.

41And He sat down opposite the treasury and saw how the crowd was casting money into the treasury. Many rich [people] were throwing in large sums.

42And a widow who was poverty-stricken came and put in two copper mites [the smallest of coins], which together make [c]half of a cent.

43And He called His disciples to [Him] and said to them, Truly *and* surely I tell you, this widow, (and she) poverty-stricken, has put in more than all those contributing to the treasury.

44For they all threw in out of their abundance, but she out of her deep poverty has put in everything that she had, [even] all she had on which to live.

**13** AND AS [Jesus] was coming out of the temple ([d]area), one of His disciples said to Him, Look, Teacher! Notice the sort *and* quality of these stones and buildings!

2And Jesus replied to him, You see these great buildings? There will not be left here one stone upon another that will not be loosened *and* torn down.

3And as He sat on the Mount of Olives opposite the temple ([e]enclosure), Peter and James and John and Andrew asked Him privately,

4Tell us when is this to take place and what will be the sign when these things, all [of them], are about to be accomplished?

5And Jesus began to tell them, Be careful *and* watchful that no one misleads you [about it].

6Many will come ([f]appropriating to themselves) the name (of Messiah) which belongs to Me—[g]basing their claims on the use of My name—saying I am [He]! and they will mislead many.

7And when you hear of wars and rumors of wars, do not get alarmed—troubled and frightened; it is necessary [that these things] take place, but the end is not yet.

8For nation will rise against nation, and kingdom against kingdom; there will be earthquakes in various places; there will be famines *and calamities;* this is but a beginning of the [h]intolerable anguish *and* sufferings—only the first of the [i]birth pangs.

9But look to yourselves, for they will turn you over to councils, and you will be beaten in the synagogues, and you will stand before governors and kings for My sake, for a testimony to them.

10And the good news (the Gospel) must first be preached to all nations.

11Now when they take you [to court] and put you under arrest, do not be anxious beforehand about what you are to say *nor* [*even*] *meditate about it;* but say whatever is given you in that hour *and* at [j]the moment, for it is not you who will be speaking but the Holy Spirit.

12And brother will hand over brother to death, and the father his child, and children will take a stand against their parents and [have] them put to death,

**AMP** [a] Trench. [b] Trench. [c] Davis' "Dictionary of the Bible." [d] Trench. [e] Trench. [f] Thayer. [g] Vincent. [h] Thayer. [i] Literal meaning. [j] Moulton and Milligan.

## New American Standard

35¶ And Jesus answering *began* to say, as He taught in the
temple, "How *is it that* the scribes say that the Christ is the son of
David?
36"David himself said in the Holy Spirit,
'THE LORD SAID TO MY LORD,
"SIT AT MY RIGHT HAND,
UNTIL I PUT THINE ENEMIES BENEATH THY FEET." '
37"David himself calls Him 'Lord'; and *so* in what sense is He
his son?" And the great crowd enjoyed listening to Him.
38¶ And in His teaching He was saying: "Beware of the scribes
who like to walk around in long robes, and *like* respectful greetings
in the market places,
39and chief seats in the synagogues, and places of honor at
banquets,
40who devour widows' houses, and for appearance's sake offer
long prayers; these will receive greater condemnation."

*The Widow's Mite*

41¶ And He sat down opposite the treasury, and *began* observing
how the multitude were putting money into the treasury; and
many rich people were putting in large sums.
42And a poor widow came and put in two small copper coins,
which amount to a cent.
43And calling His disciples to Him, He said to them, "Truly I
say to you, this poor widow put in more than all the contributors
to the treasury;
44for they all put in out of their surplus, but she, out of her
poverty, put in all she owned, all she had to live on."

*Things to Come*

13 AND AS He was going out of the temple, one of His
disciples *said to Him, "Teacher, behold [k]what wonderful
stones and what wonderful buildings!"
2And Jesus said to him, "Do you see these great buildings? Not
one stone shall be left upon another which will not be torn down."
3¶ And as He was sitting on the Mount of Olives opposite the
temple, Peter and James and John and Andrew were questioning
Him privately,
4"Tell us, when will these things be, and what *will be* the sign
when all these things are going to be fulfilled?"
5And Jesus began to say to them, "See to it that no one misleads you.
6"Many will come in My name, saying, 'I am *He!*' and will
mislead many.
7"And when you hear of wars and rumors of wars, do not be
frightened; *those things* must take place; but *that is* not yet the end.
8"For nation will arise against nation, and kingdom against
kingdom; there will be earthquakes in various places; there will *also*
be famines. These things are *merely* the beginning of birth pangs.
9¶ "But be on your guard; for they will deliver you to *the* courts,
and you will be flogged in *the* synagogues, and you will stand
before governors and kings for My sake, as a testimony to them.
10"And the gospel must first be preached to all the nations.
11"And when they arrest you and deliver you up, do not be
anxious beforehand about what you are to say, but say whatever
is given you in that hour; for it is not you who speak, but *it is* the
Holy Spirit.
12"And brother will deliver brother to death, and a father *his*
child; and children will rise up against parents and have them put
to death.

NAS [k] Lit., *how great*

## New International

*Whose Son Is the Christ?*

35While Jesus was teaching in the temple courts, he asked,
"How is it that the teachers of the law say that the Christ[l] is the
son of David? 36David himself, speaking by the Holy Spirit, declared:

" 'The Lord said to my Lord:
"Sit at my right hand
until I put your enemies
under your feet." '[m]

37David himself calls him 'Lord.' How then can he be his son?"
The large crowd listened to him with delight.
38As he taught, Jesus said, "Watch out for the teachers of the
law. They like to walk around in flowing robes and be greeted in
the marketplaces, 39and have the most important seats in the
synagogues and the places of honor at banquets. 40They devour
widows' houses and for a show make lengthy prayers. Such men
will be punished most severely."

*The Widow's Offering*

41Jesus sat down opposite the place where the offerings were
put and watched the crowd putting their money into the temple
treasury. Many rich people threw in large amounts. 42But a poor
widow came and put in two very small copper coins,[n] worth only
a fraction of a penny.[o]
43Calling his disciples to him, Jesus said, "I tell you the truth,
this poor widow has put more into the treasury than all the others.
44They all gave out of their wealth; but she, out of her poverty, put
in everything—all she had to live on."

*Signs of the End of the Age*

13 AS HE was leaving the temple, one of his disciples said
to him, "Look, Teacher! What massive stones! What magnificent buildings!"
2"Do you see all these great buildings?" replied Jesus. "Not one
stone here will be left on another; every one will be thrown down."
3As Jesus was sitting on the Mount of Olives opposite the
temple, Peter, James, John and Andrew asked him privately,
4"Tell us, when will these things happen? And what will be the
sign that they are all about to be fulfilled?"
5Jesus said to them: "Watch out that no one deceives you.
6Many will come in my name, claiming, 'I am he,' and will deceive
many. 7When you hear of wars and rumors of wars, do not be
alarmed. Such things must happen, but the end is still to come.
8Nation will rise against nation, and kingdom against kingdom.
There will be earthquakes in various places, and famines. These
are the beginning of birth pains.
9"You must be on your guard. You will be handed over to the
local councils and flogged in the synagogues. On account of me
you will stand before governors and kings as witnesses to them.
10And the gospel must first be preached to all nations. 11Whenever
you are arrested and brought to trial, do not worry beforehand
about what to say. Just say whatever is given you at the time, for
it is not you speaking, but the Holy Spirit.
12"Brother will betray brother to death, and a father his child.
Children will rebel against their parents and have them put to

NIV [l] 35 Or *Messiah* [m] 36 Psalm 110:1 [n] 42 Greek *two lepta* [o] 42 Greek *kodrantes*

## King James

13 And ye shall be hated of all *men* for my name's sake: but he that shall endure unto the end, the same shall be saved.

14 ¶ But when ye shall see the abomination of desolation, spoken of by Daniel the prophet, standing where it ought not, (let him that readeth understand,) then let them that be in Judaea flee to the mountains:

15 And let him that is on the housetop not go down into the house, neither enter *therein,* to take any thing out of his house:

16 And let him that is in the field not turn back again for to take up his garment.

17 But woe to them that are with child, and to them that give suck in those days!

18 And pray ye that your flight be not in the winter.

19 For *in* those days shall be affliction, such as was not from the beginning of the creation which God created unto this time, neither shall be.

20 And except that the Lord had shortened those days, no flesh should be saved: but for the elect's sake, whom he hath chosen, he hath shortened the days.

21 And then if any man shall say to you, Lo, here *is* Christ; or, lo, *he is* there; believe *him* not:

22 For false Christs and false prophets shall rise, and shall show signs and wonders, to seduce, if *it were* possible, even the elect.

23 But take ye heed: behold, I have foretold you all things.

24 ¶ But in those days, after that tribulation, the sun shall be darkened, and the moon shall not give her light,

25 And the stars of heaven shall fall, and the powers that are in heaven shall be shaken.

26 And then shall they see the Son of man coming in the clouds with great power and glory.

27 And then shall he send his angels, and shall gather together his elect from the four winds, from the uttermost part of the earth to the uttermost part of heaven.

28 Now learn a parable of the fig tree; When her branch is yet tender, and putteth forth leaves, ye know that summer is near:

29 So ye in like manner, when ye shall see these things come to pass, know that it is nigh, *even* at the doors.

30 Verily I say unto you, that this generation shall not pass, till all these things be done.

31 Heaven and earth shall pass away: but my words shall not pass away.

32 ¶ But of that day and *that* hour knoweth no man, no, not the angels which are in heaven, neither the Son, but the Father.

33 Take ye heed, watch and pray: for ye know not when the time is.

34 *For the Son of man is* as a man taking a far journey, who left his house, and gave authority to his servants, and to every man his work, and commanded the porter to watch.

35 Watch ye therefore: for ye know not when the master of the house cometh, at even, or at midnight, or at the cockcrowing, or in the morning:

36 Lest coming suddenly he find you sleeping.

37 And what I say unto you I say unto all, Watch.

## Amplified

13 And you will be hated *and* detested by everybody for My name's sake. But he who patiently perseveres *and* endures to the end will be saved [that is, [a]made a partaker of the salvation by Christ, and delivered [b]from spiritual death].

14 But when you see the abomination of desolation *mentioned by Daniel the prophet* standing where it ought not to be, [and] let the one who reads take notice *and* consider *and* understand *and* heed [this], then let those who are in Judea flee to the mountains. [Dan. 11:31; 12:11.]

15 Let him who is on the housetop not go down *into the house,* nor go inside to take anything out of his house;

16 And let him who is in the field not turn back again to get his mantle (cloak).

17 And alas for those who are pregnant and for those who have nursing babies in those days!

18 Pray that it may not occur in winter,

19 For at that time there will be such affliction—oppression and tribulation—as has not been from the beginning of the creation which God created until this particular time, and [c]positively never will be [again].

20 And unless the Lord had shortened the days, no human being would be saved (rescued); but for the sake of the elect, His chosen ones—those whom He [d]picked out for Himself—He has shortened the days. [Dan. 12:1.]

21 And then if any one says to you, See, here is the Christ! or, Look, there He is! do not believe it.

22 False Christs (Messiahs) and false prophets will arise and show signs and (work) miracles to deceive *and* lead astray, if possible, even the elect—those God has chosen out for Himself.

23 But look to yourselves *and* be on your guard; I have told you everything beforehand.

24 But in those days, after (the affliction and oppression and distress of) that tribulation, the sun will be darkened, and the moon will not give its light. [Isa. 13:10.]

25 And the stars will be falling from the sky, and the powers in the heavens will be shaken. [Isa. 34:4.]

26 And then they will see the Son of man coming in clouds with great (kingly) power and glory (majesty and splendor). [Dan. 7:13, 14.]

27 And then He will send out the angels and will gather together His elect—those He has [e]picked out for Himself—from the four winds, from the farthest bounds of the earth to the farthest bounds of heaven.

28 Now learn a lesson from the fig tree; as soon as its branch becomes tender, and it puts forth its leaves, you recognize *and* know that summer is near.

29 So also, when you see these things happening, you will recognize *and* know that He is near, at [the very] door.

30 Surely, I say to you, this generation [ [f]the whole mulitude of people living at that one time] positively will not perish *or* pass away before all these things take place.

31 Heaven and earth will perish *and* pass away, but My words will not perish *or* pass away.

32 But of that day or that hour not a [single] person knows, not even the angels in heaven, nor the Son, but only the Father.

33 Be on your guard (constantly alert) and watch *and pray,* for you do not know when the time will come.

34 It is like a man ( [g]already) going on a journey; when he leaves home he puts his servants in charge, each with his particular task, and he gives orders to the doorkeeper to be constantly alert *and* on the watch.

35 Therefore watch—give strict attention, be cautious and alert—for you do not know when the Master of the house is coming, in the evening, or at midnight, or at cockcrowing, or in the morning.

36 [Watch, I say] lest He come suddenly *and* unexpectedly and find you asleep.

37 And what I say to you I say to everybody: (Give strict attention, be cautious, active, alert, and) watch!

**AMP** [a] Thayer. [b] Thayer. [c] Wuest. [d] Abbott-Smith. [e] Abbott-Smith. [f] Cremer; Thayer, and Abbott-Smith. [g] Wycliffe; Tyndale.

## New American Standard

13"And you will be hated by all on account of My name, but the one who endures to the end, he shall be saved.
14¶ "But when you see the ABOMINATION OF DESOLATION standing where it should not be (let the reader understand), then let those who are in Judea flee to the mountains.
15"And let him who is on the housetop not go down, or enter in, to get anything out of his house;
16and let him who is in the field not turn back to get his cloak.
17"But woe to those who are with child and to those who nurse babes in those days!
18"But pray that it may not happen in the winter.
19"For those days will be a *time of* tribulation such as has not occurred since the beginning of the creation which God created, until now, and never shall.
20"And unless the Lord had shortened *those* days, no life would have been saved; but for the sake of the elect whom He chose, He shortened the days.
21"And then if anyone says to you, 'Behold, here is the Christ'; or, 'Behold, *He is* there'; do not believe *him;*
22for false Christs and false prophets will arise, and will show signs and wonders, in order, if possible, to lead the elect astray.
23"But take heed; behold, I have told you everything in advance.

*The Return of Christ*

24¶ "But in those days, after that tribulation, THE SUN WILL BE DARKENED, AND THE MOON WILL NOT GIVE ITS LIGHT,
25AND THE STARS WILL BE FALLING from heaven, and the powers that are in the heavens will be shaken.
26"And then they will see THE SON OF MAN COMING IN CLOUDS with great power and glory.
27"And then He will send forth the angels, and will gather together His elect from the four winds, from the farthest end of the earth, to the farthest end of heaven.
28¶ "Now learn the parable from the fig tree: when its branch has already become tender, and puts forth its leaves, you know that summer is near.
29"Even so, you too, when you see these things happening, recognize that He is near, *right* at the door.
30"Truly I say to you, this [h]generation will not pass away until all these things take place.
31"Heaven and earth will pass away, but My words will not pass away.
32"But of that day or hour no one knows, not even the angels in heaven, nor the Son, but the Father *alone.*
33¶ "Take heed, keep on the alert; for you do not know when the *appointed* time is.
34 " *It is* like a man, away on a journey, *who* upon leaving his house and putting his slaves in charge, *assigning* to each one his task, also commanded the doorkeeper to stay on the alert.
35"Therefore, be on the alert—for you do not know when the master of the house is coming, whether in the evening, at midnight, at cockcrowing, or in the morning—
36lest he come suddenly and find you asleep.
37"And what I say to you I say to all, 'Be on the alert!' "

NAS [h] Or, *race*

## New International

death. 13All men will hate you because of me, but he who stands
firm to the end will be saved.
14"When you see 'the abomination that causes desolation'[i]
standing where it[j] does not belong—let the reader understand—
then let those who are in Judea flee to the mountains. 15Let no one
on the roof of his house go down or enter the house to take
anything out. 16Let no one in the field go back to get his cloak.
17How dreadful it will be in those days for pregnant women and
nursing mothers! 18Pray that this will not take place in winter,
19because those will be days of distress unequaled from the beginning,
when God created the world, until now—and never to be
equaled again. 20If the Lord had not cut short those days, no one
would survive. But for the sake of the elect, whom he has chosen,
he has shortened them. 21At that time if anyone says to you, 'Look,
here is the Christ[k]!' or, 'Look, there he is!' do not believe it. 22For
false Christs and false prophets will appear and perform signs and
miracles to deceive the elect—if that were possible. 23So be on your
guard; I have told you everything ahead of time.
24"But in those days, following that distress,

" 'the sun will be darkened,
and the moon will not give its light;
25the stars will fall from the sky,
and the heavenly bodies will be shaken.'[l]

26"At that time men will see the Son of Man coming in clouds
with great power and glory. 27And he will send his angels and
gather his elect from the four winds, from the ends of the earth to
the ends of the heavens.
28"Now learn this lesson from the fig tree: As soon as its twigs
get tender and its leaves come out, you know that summer is near.
29Even so, when you see these things happening, you know that
it is near, right at the door. 30I tell you the truth, this generation[m]
will certainly not pass away until all these things have happened.
31Heaven and earth will pass away, but my words will never pass
away.

*The Day and Hour Unknown*

32"No one knows about that day or hour, not even the angels
in heaven, nor the Son, but only the Father. 33Be on guard! Be
alert[n]! You do not know when that time will come. 34It's like a man
going away: He leaves his house and puts his servants in charge,
each with his assigned task, and tells the one at the door to keep
watch.
35"Therefore keep watch because you do not know when the
owner of the house will come back—whether in the evening, or at
midnight, or when the rooster crows, or at dawn. 36If he comes
suddenly, do not let him find you sleeping. 37What I say to you,
I say to everyone: 'Watch!' "

NIV [i] *14* Daniel 9:27; 11:31; 12:11 [j] *14* Or *he;* also in verse 29 [k] *21* Or *Messiah* [l] *25* Isaiah 13:10; 34:4 [m] *30* Or *race* [n] *33* Some manuscripts *alert and pray*

## King James

**14** AFTER TWO days was *the feast of* the passover, and of unleavened bread: and the chief priests and the scribes sought how they might take him by craft, and put *him* to death.

2But they said, Not on the feast *day*, lest there be an uproar of the people.

3¶ And being in Bethany in the house of Simon the leper, as he sat at meat, there came a woman having an alabaster box of ointment of spikenard very precious; and she brake the box, and poured *it* on his head.

4And there were some that had indignation within themselves, and said, Why was this waste of the ointment made?

5For it might have been sold for more than three hundred pence, and have been given to the poor. And they murmured against her.

6And Jesus said, Let her alone; why trouble ye her? she hath wrought a good work on me.

7For ye have the poor with you always, and whensoever ye will ye may do them good: but me ye have not always.

8She hath done what she could: she is come aforehand to anoint my body to the burying.

9Verily I say unto you, Wheresoever this gospel shall be preached throughout the whole world, *this* also that she hath done shall be spoken of for a memorial of her.

10¶ And Judas Iscariot, one of the twelve, went unto the chief priests, to betray him unto them.

11And when they heard *it*, they were glad, and promised to give him money. And he sought how he might conveniently betray him.

12¶ And the first day of unleavened bread, when they killed the passover, his disciples said unto him, Where wilt thou that we go and prepare that thou mayest eat the passover?

13And he sendeth forth two of his disciples, and saith unto them, Go ye into the city, and there shall meet you a man bearing a pitcher of water: follow him.

14And wheresoever he shall go in, say ye to the goodman of the house, The Master saith, Where is the guestchamber, where I shall eat the passover with my disciples?

15And he will show you a large upper room furnished *and* prepared: there make ready for us.

16And his disciples went forth, and came into the city, and found as he had said unto them: and they made ready the passover.

17And in the evening he cometh with the twelve.

18And as they sat and did eat, Jesus said, Verily I say unto you, One of you which eateth with me shall betray me.

19And they began to be sorrowful, and to say unto him one by one, *Is* it I? and another *said, Is* it I?

20And he answered and said unto them, *It is* one of the twelve, that dippeth with me in the dish.

21The Son of man indeed goeth, as it is written of him: but woe to that man by whom the Son of man is betrayed! good were it for that man if he had never been born.

22¶ And as they did eat, Jesus took bread, and blessed, and brake *it*, and gave to them, and said, Take, eat: this is my body.

23And he took the cup, and when he had given thanks, he gave *it* to them: and they all drank of it.

## Amplified

**14** IT WAS now two days before the Passover and the feast of Unleavened Bread. And the chief priests and the scribes were all the while seeking to arrest [Jesus] by secrecy *and* deceit, and put [Him] to death,

2For they kept saying, It must not be during the feast, for fear there might be a riot of the people.

3And while He was in Bethany, [a guest] in the house of Simon the leper, as He was reclining [at table], a woman came with an alabaster jar of ointment ( [a]perfume) of pure nard, very costly *and* precious, and she broke the jar and poured [the perfume] over His head.

4But there were some who were moved with indignation and said to themselves, To what purpose was the ointment ( [b]perfume) thus wasted?

5For it was possible to have sold this [perfume] for more than three hundred denarii [a laboring man's wages for a year], and to have given [them] to the poor. And they censured *and* reproved her.

6But Jesus said, Let her alone; why are you troubling her? She has done a good *and* beautiful thing to Me—praiseworthy and noble.

7For you always have the poor with you, and whenever you wish you can do good to them; but you will not always have Me. [Deut. 15:11.]

8She has done what she could; she came beforehand to anoint My body for the burial.

9And surely, I tell you, wherever the good news (the Gospel) is proclaimed in the entire world, what she has done will be told for a memorial of her.

10Then Judas Iscariot, who was one of the twelve [apostles], went off to the chief priests in order to betray *and* hand Him over to them.

11And when they heard it they rejoiced *and* were delighted, and they promised to give him money. And he (busying himself continually) sought an opportunity to betray Him.

12On the first day [of the feast] of Unleavened Bread, when [as was customary] they killed the passover lamb, [Jesus'] disciples said to Him, Where do You wish us to go [and] prepare the passover [supper] for You to eat?

13And He sent two of His disciples, and said to them, Go into the city, and a man carrying an (earthenware) jar *or* pitcher of water will meet you; follow him.

14And whatever [house] he enters, say to the master of the house, The Teacher says, Where is My guest room, where I may eat the passover [supper] with My disciples?

15And he will [himself] show you a large upper room furnished [that is, with carpets and with dining couches properly spread] and ready; there prepare for us.

16Then the disciples set out and came to the city, and found [everything] as He had told them; and they prepared the passover.

17And when it was evening He came with the twelve [apostles].

18And while they were at the table eating, Jesus said, Surely, I say to you, one of you will betray Me, [one] who is eating [here] with Me. [Ps. 41:9.]

19And they began to show that they were sad *and* hurt, and to say to Him one after another, Is it I? *or,* It is not I, is it?

20He replied to them, It is one of the twelve [apostles], one who is dipping [bread] into the (same deep) dish with Me.

21For the Son of man goes as it stands written concerning Him, but woe to that man by whom the Son of man is betrayed! It would have been good (profitable and wholesome) for that man if he had never been born. [Ps. 41:9.]

22And while they were eating, He took a loaf [of bread], praised God *and* gave thanks *and* asked Him to bless it to their use. [Then] He broke [it], and gave to them, and said, Take. *Eat*. This is My body.

23He also took a cup [of juice of grapes], and when He had given thanks He gave [it] to them, and they all drank of it.

**AMP** [a] Moulton and Milligan. [b] Moulton and Milligan.

## New American Standard

*Death Plot and Anointing*

**14** NOW THE Passover and Unleavened Bread was two days off; and the chief priests and the scribes were seeking how to seize Him by stealth, and kill *Him;*

2for they were saying, "Not during the festival, lest there be a riot of the people."

**3**¶ And while He was in Bethany at the home of Simon the leper, and reclining *at the table,* there came a woman with an alabaster vial of very costly perfume of pure nard; *and* she broke the vial and poured it over His head.

4But some were indignantly *remarking* to one another, "Why has this perfume been wasted?

5"For this perfume might have been sold for over three hundred [c]denarii, and *the money* given to the poor." And they were scolding her.

6But Jesus said, "Let her alone; why do you bother her? She has done a good deed to Me.

7"For the poor you always have with you, and whenever you wish, you can do them good; but you do not always have Me.

8"She has done what she could; she has anointed My body beforehand for the burial.

9"And truly I say to you, wherever the gospel is preached in the whole world, that also which this woman has done shall be spoken of in memory of her."

**10**¶ And Judas Iscariot, who was one of the twelve, went off to the chief priests, in order to betray Him to them.

11And they were glad when they heard *this,* and promised to give him money. And he *began* seeking how to betray Him at an opportune time.

*The Last Passover*

**12**¶ And on the first day of Unleavened Bread, when the Passover *lamb* was being sacrificed, His disciples *said to Him, "Where do You want us to go and prepare for You to eat the Passover?"

13And He *sent two of His disciples, and *said to them, "Go into the city, and a man will meet you carrying a pitcher of water; follow him;

14and wherever he enters, say to the owner of the house, 'The Teacher says, "Where is My guest room in which I may eat the Passover with My disciples?"'

15"And he himself will show you a large upper room furnished *and* ready; and prepare for us there."

16And the disciples went out, and came to the city, and found *it* just as He had told them; and they prepared the Passover.

**17**¶ And when it was evening He *came with the twelve.

18And as they were reclining *at the table* and eating, Jesus said, "Truly I say to you that one of you will betray Me—one who is eating with Me."

19They began to be grieved and to say to Him one by one, "Surely not I?"

20And He said to them, *"It is* one of the twelve, one who dips with Me in the bowl.

21"For the Son of Man *is to* go, just as it is written of Him; but woe to that man by whom the Son of Man is betrayed! *It would have been* good for that man if he had not been born."

*The Lord's Supper*

**22**¶ And while they were eating, He took *some* bread, and after a blessing He broke *it;* and gave *it* to them, and said, "Take *it;* this is My body."

23And when He had taken a cup, *and* given thanks, He gave *it* to them; and they all drank from it.

NAS [c] The denarius was equivalent to one day's wage

## New International

*Jesus Anointed at Bethany*

**14** NOW THE Passover and the Feast of Unleavened Bread
were only two days away, and the chief priests and the
teachers of the law were looking for some sly way to arrest Jesus
and kill him. 2"But not during the Feast," they said, "or the people
may riot."

3While he was in Bethany, reclining at the table in the home of
a man known as Simon the Leper, a woman came with an alabaster
jar of very expensive perfume, made of pure nard. She broke the
jar and poured the perfume on his head.

4Some of those present were saying indignantly to one another,
"Why this waste of perfume? 5It could have been sold for more
than a year's wages[d] and the money given to the poor." And they
rebuked her harshly.

6"Leave her alone," said Jesus. "Why are you bothering her?
She has done a beautiful thing to me. 7The poor you will always
have with you, and you can help them any time you want. But you
will not always have me. 8She did what she could. She poured
perfume on my body beforehand to prepare for my burial. 9I tell
you the truth, wherever the gospel is preached throughout the
world, what she has done will also be told, in memory of her."

10Then Judas Iscariot, one of the Twelve, went to the chief
priests to betray Jesus to them. 11They were delighted to hear this
and promised to give him money. So he watched for an opportunity to hand him over.

*The Lord's Supper*

12On the first day of the Feast of Unleavened Bread, when it was
customary to sacrifice the Passover lamb, Jesus' disciples asked
him, "Where do you want us to go and make preparations for you
to eat the Passover?"

13So he sent two of his disciples, telling them, "Go into the city,
and a man carrying a jar of water will meet you. Follow him. 14Say
to the owner of the house he enters, 'The Teacher asks: Where is
my guest room, where I may eat the Passover with my disciples?'
15He will show you a large upper room, furnished and ready.
Make preparations for us there."

16The disciples left, went into the city and found things just as
Jesus had told them. So they prepared the Passover.

17When evening came, Jesus arrived with the Twelve. 18While
they were reclining at the table eating, he said, "I tell you the truth,
one of you will betray me—one who is eating with me."

19They were saddened, and one by one they said to him, "Surely not I?"

20"It is one of the Twelve," he replied, "one who dips bread into
the bowl with me. 21The Son of Man will go just as it is written
about him. But woe to that man who betrays the Son of Man! It
would be better for him if he had not been born."

22While they were eating, Jesus took bread, gave thanks and
broke it, and gave it to his disciples, saying, "Take it; this is my
body."

23Then he took the cup, gave thanks and offered it to them, and
they all drank from it.

NIV [d] 5 Greek *than three hundred denarii*

## King James

24And he said unto them, This is my blood of the new testament, which is shed for many.

25Verily I say unto you, I will drink no more of the fruit of the vine, until that day that I drink it new in the kingdom of God.

26¶ And when they had sung an hymn, they went out into the mount of Olives.

27And Jesus saith unto them, All ye shall be offended because of me this night: for it is written, I will smite the shepherd, and the sheep shall be scattered.

28But after that I am risen, I will go before you into Galilee.

29But Peter said unto him, Although all shall be offended, yet *will* not I.

30And Jesus saith unto him, Verily I say unto thee, That this day, *even* in this night, before the cock crow twice, thou shalt deny me thrice.

31But he spake the more vehemently, If I should die with thee, I will not deny thee in any wise. Likewise also said they all.

32And they came to a place which was named Gethsemane: and he saith to his disciples, Sit ye here, while I shall pray.

33And he taketh with him Peter and James and John, and began to be sore amazed, and to be very heavy;

34And saith unto them, My soul is exceeding sorrowful unto death: tarry ye here, and watch.

35And he went forward a little, and fell on the ground, and prayed that, if it were possible, the hour might pass from him.

36And he said, Abba, Father, all things *are* possible unto thee; take away this cup from me: nevertheless not what I will, but what thou wilt.

37And he cometh, and findeth them sleeping, and saith unto Peter, Simon, sleepest thou? couldest not thou watch one hour?

38Watch ye and pray, lest ye enter into temptation. The spirit truly *is* ready, but the flesh *is* weak.

39And again he went away, and prayed, and spake the same words.

40And when he returned, he found them asleep again, (for their eyes were heavy,) neither wist they what to answer him.

41And he cometh the third time, and saith unto them, Sleep on now, and take *your* rest: it is enough, the hour is come; behold, the Son of man is betrayed into the hands of sinners.

42Rise up, let us go; lo, he that betrayeth me is at hand.

43¶ And immediately, while he yet spake, cometh Judas, one of the twelve, and with him a great multitude with swords and staves, from the chief priests and the scribes and the elders.

44And he that betrayed him had given them a token, saying, Whomsoever I shall kiss, that same is he; take him, and lead *him* away safely.

45And as soon as he was come, he goeth straightway to him, and saith, Master, master; and kissed him.

46¶ And they laid their hands on him, and took him.

47And one of them that stood by drew a sword, and smote a servant of the high priest, and cut off his ear.

48And Jesus answered and said unto them, Are ye come out, as against a thief, with swords and *with* staves to take me?

49I was daily with you in the temple teaching, and ye took me not: but the scriptures must be fulfilled.

50And they all forsook him, and fled.

## Amplified

24And He said to them, This is My blood [which ratifies] the *new* covenant, [the blood] which is being poured out for (on account of) many. [Exod. 24:8.]

25Solemnly *and* surely, I tell you, I shall not again drink of the fruit of the vine till that day when I drink it [a]of a new *and* a higher quality in God's kingdom.

26And when they had sung a hymn, they went out to the Mount of Olives.

27And Jesus said to them, You will all fall away *this night*—[that is,] you will be caused to stumble and will begin to distrust and desert Me; for it stands written, I will strike the shepherd, and the sheep will be scattered. [Zech. 13:7.]

28But after I am raised [to life], I will go before you into Galilee.

29But Peter said to Him, Even if they all fall away *and* are caused to stumble *and* distrust *and* desert You, yet I will not [do so]!

30And Jesus said to him, Truly, I tell you, this very night, before a cock crows twice, you will utterly deny Me—disclaiming all connection with Me—three times.

31But [Peter] said more vehemently *and* repeatedly, [Even] if it should be necessary for me to die with You, I will not deny *or* disown You! And they all kept saying the same thing.

32Then they went to a place called Gethsemane, and He said to His disciples, Sit down here while I pray.

33And He took with Him Peter and James and John, and began to be [b]struck with terror *and* amazement and deeply troubled *and* depressed.

34And He said to them, My soul is exceedingly sad—overwhelmed with grief—so that it almost kills Me! Remain here, and [c]keep awake *and* be watching.

35And going a little farther, He fell on the ground and kept praying that, if it were possible, the [ [d]fatal] hour might pass from Him.

36And He was saying, Abba, [which means] Father, everything is possible for You; take away this cup from Me; yet not what I will, but what You [will].

37And He came back and found them sleeping, and He said to Peter, Simon, are you asleep? Have you not the strength to [e]keep awake *and* watch [with Me] one hour?

38 [f]Keep awake *and* watch and pray (constantly) that you may not enter into temptation; the spirit indeed is willing, but the flesh is weak.

39He went away again and prayed, saying the same words.

40And again He came back and found them sleeping, for their eyes were very heavy; and they did not know what answer to give Him.

41And He came back a third time, and said to them, Are you still sleeping and resting? It is enough [of that]. The hour has come. The Son of man is betrayed into the hands of sinful men—[that is,] of men [g]whose way or nature is to act in opposition to God.

42Get up; let us be going. See, My betrayer is at hand.

43And at once, while He was still speaking, Judas came, one of the twelve [apostles], and with him a crowd of men with swords and clubs, [who came] from the chief priests and the scribes and the elders [of the Sanhedrin].

44Now the betrayer had given them a signal, saying, The one I shall kiss is [the Man]; seize Him and lead [Him] away safely—so as to prevent His escape.

45And when he came he went up to Jesus immediately, and said, Master! *Master!* and he [h]embraced Him *and* kissed Him fervently.

46And they threw their hands on Him and arrested Him.

47But one of the bystanders drew his sword, and struck the bond servant of the high priest and cut off his ear.

48And Jesus said to them, Have you come out as against a robber, to capture Me with swords and clubs?

49I was with you daily in the temple ( [i]porches and courts) teaching, and you did not seize Me; but that the Scriptures be fulfilled.

50Then [His disciples], forsaking Him, fled, all [of them].

**AMP** [a] Vincent. [b] Thayer. [c] Alternate reading. [d] Thayer. [e] Alternate reading. [f] Alternate reading. [g] Cremer. [h] Meyer's "Commentary on Mark." [i] Trench.

## New American Standard

24 And He said to them, "This is My blood of the covenant,
which is poured out for many.
25 "Truly I say to you, I shall never again drink of the fruit of the
vine until that day when I drink it new in the kingdom of God."
26 ¶ And after singing a hymn, they went out to the Mount of
Olives.
27 ¶ And Jesus *said to them, "You will all fall away, because it
is written, 'I WILL STRIKE DOWN THE SHEPHERD, AND THE SHEEP
SHALL BE SCATTERED.'
28 "But after I have been raised, I will go before you to Galilee."
29 But Peter said to Him, "*Even* though all may fall away, yet
I will not."
30 And Jesus *said to him, "Truly I say to you, that you yourself
this very night, before a cock crows twice, shall three times deny
Me."
31 But *Peter* kept saying insistently, "*Even* if I have to die with
You, I will not deny You!" And they all were saying the same
thing, too.

*Jesus in Gethsemane*

32 ¶ And they *came to a place named Gethsemane; and He *said
to His disciples, "Sit here until I have prayed."
33 And He *took with Him Peter and James and John, and began
to be very distressed and troubled.
34 And He *said to them, "My soul is deeply grieved to the point
of death; remain here and keep watch."
35 And He went a little beyond *them,* and fell to the ground, and
*began* to pray that if it were possible, the hour might pass Him by.
36 And He was saying, "Abba! Father! All things are possible for
Thee; remove this cup from Me; yet not what I will, but what Thou
wilt."
37 And He *came and *found them sleeping, and *said to Peter,
"Simon, are you asleep? Could you not keep watch for one hour?
38 "Keep watching and praying, that you may not come into
temptation; the spirit is willing, but the flesh is weak."
39 And again He went away and prayed, saying the same words.
40 And again He came and found them sleeping, for their eyes
were very heavy; and they did not know what to answer Him.
41 And He *came the third time, and *said to them, "Are you still
sleeping and taking your rest? It is enough; the hour has come;
behold, the Son of Man is being betrayed into the hands of sinners.
42 "Arise, let us be going; behold, the one who betrays Me is at
hand!"

*Betrayal and Arrest*

43 ¶ And immediately while He was still speaking, Judas, one of
the twelve, *came up, accompanied by a multitude with swords
and clubs, from the chief priests and the scribes and the elders.
44 Now he who was betraying Him had given them a signal,
saying, "Whomever I shall kiss, He is the one; seize Him, and lead
Him away under guard."
45 And after coming, he immediately went to Him, saying,
"Rabbi!" and kissed Him.
46 And they laid hands on Him, and seized Him.
47 But a certain one of those who stood by drew his sword, and
struck the slave of the high priest, and cut off his ear.
48 And Jesus answered and said to them, "Have you come out
with swords and clubs to arrest Me, as against a robber?
49 "Every day I was with you in the temple teaching, and you
did not seize Me; but *this has happened* that the Scriptures might be
fulfilled."
50 And they all left Him and fled.

## New International

24 "This is my blood of the[j] covenant, which is poured out for
many," he said to them. 25 "I tell you the truth, I will not drink
again of the fruit of the vine until that day when I drink it anew
in the kingdom of God."
26 When they had sung a hymn, they went out to the Mount of
Olives.

*Jesus Predicts Peter's Denial*

27 "You will all fall away," Jesus told them, "for it is written:

"'I will strike the shepherd,
and the sheep will be scattered.'[k]

28 But after I have risen, I will go ahead of you into Galilee."
29 Peter declared, "Even if all fall away, I will not."
30 "I tell you the truth," Jesus answered, "today—yes, tonight—
before the rooster crows twice[l] you yourself will disown me three
times."
31 But Peter insisted emphatically, "Even if I have to die with
you, I will never disown you." And all the others said the same.

*Gethsemane*

32 They went to a place called Gethsemane, and Jesus said to his
disciples, "Sit here while I pray." 33 He took Peter, James and John
along with him, and he began to be deeply distressed and troubled. 34 "My soul is overwhelmed with sorrow to the point of
death," he said to them. "Stay here and keep watch."
35 Going a little farther, he fell to the ground and prayed that if
possible the hour might pass from him. 36 "*Abba,*[m] Father," he
said, "everything is possible for you. Take this cup from me. Yet
not what I will, but what you will."
37 Then he returned to his disciples and found them sleeping.
"Simon," he said to Peter, "are you asleep? Could you not keep
watch for one hour? 38 Watch and pray so that you will not fall into
temptation. The spirit is willing, but the body is weak."
39 Once more he went away and prayed the same thing. 40 When
he came back, he again found them sleeping, because their eyes
were heavy. They did not know what to say to him.
41 Returning the third time, he said to them, "Are you still
sleeping and resting? Enough! The hour has come. Look, the Son
of Man is betrayed into the hands of sinners. 42 Rise! Let us go! Here
comes my betrayer!"

*Jesus Arrested*

43 Just as he was speaking, Judas, one of the Twelve, appeared.
With him was a crowd armed with swords and clubs, sent from
the chief priests, the teachers of the law, and the elders.
44 Now the betrayer had arranged a signal with them: "The one
I kiss is the man; arrest him and lead him away under guard."
45 Going at once to Jesus, Judas said, "Rabbi!" and kissed him.
46 The men seized Jesus and arrested him. 47 Then one of those
standing near drew his sword and struck the servant of the high
priest, cutting off his ear.
48 "Am I leading a rebellion," said Jesus, "that you have come
out with swords and clubs to capture me? 49 Every day I was with
you, teaching in the temple courts, and you did not arrest me. But
the Scriptures must be fulfilled." 50 Then everyone deserted him
and fled.

**NIV** [j] 24 Some manuscripts *the new* [k] 27 Zech. 13:7 [l] 30 Some early manuscripts do not have *twice.* [m] 36 Aramaic for *Father*

## King James

51And there followed him a certain young man, having a linen cloth cast about *his* naked *body;* and the young men laid hold on him:
52And he left the linen cloth, and fled from them naked.
53¶ And they led Jesus away to the high priest: and with him were assembled all the chief priests and the elders and the scribes.
54And Peter followed him afar off, even into the palace of the high priest: and he sat with the servants, and warmed himself at the fire.
55And the chief priests and all the council sought for witness against Jesus to put him to death; and found none.
56For many bare false witness against him, but their witness agreed not together.
57And there arose certain, and bare false witness against him, saying,
58We heard him say, I will destroy this temple that is made with hands, and within three days I will build another made without hands.
59But neither so did their witness agree together.
60And the high priest stood up in the midst, and asked Jesus, saying, Answerest thou nothing? what *is it which* these witness against thee?
61But he held his peace, and answered nothing. Again the high priest asked him, and said unto him, Art thou the Christ, the Son of the Blessed?
62And Jesus said, I am: and ye shall see the Son of man sitting on the right hand of power, and coming in the clouds of heaven.
63Then the high priest rent his clothes, and saith, What need we any further witnesses?
64Ye have heard the blasphemy: what think ye? And they all condemned him to be guilty of death.
65And some began to spit on him, and to cover his face, and to buffet him, and to say unto him, Prophesy: and the servants did strike him with the palms of their hands.
66¶ And as Peter was beneath in the palace, there cometh one of the maids of the high priest:
67And when she saw Peter warming himself, she looked upon him, and said, And thou also wast with Jesus of Nazareth.
68But he denied, saying, I know not, neither understand I what thou sayest. And he went out into the porch; and the cock crew.
69And a maid saw him again, and began to say to them that stood by, This is *one* of them.
70And he denied it again. And a little after, they that stood by said again to Peter, Surely thou art *one* of them: for thou art a Galilaean, and thy speech agreeth *thereto*.
71But he began to curse and to swear, *saying*, I know not this man of whom ye speak.
72And the second time the cock crew. And Peter called to mind the word that Jesus said unto him, Before the cock crow twice, thou shalt deny me thrice. And when he thought thereon, he wept.

## Amplified

51And a young man was following Him, with nothing but a linen cloth ( [a]sheet) thrown about [his] naked [body]; and they laid hold of him,
52But leaving behind the linen cloth ( [b]sheet), he fled from them naked.
53And they led Jesus away to the high priest, and all the chief priests and the elders and the scribes were gathered together.
54And Peter followed Him at a distance, even right into the courtyard of the high priest. And he was sitting ( [c]in the firelight) with the guards, and warming himself at the fire.
55Now the chief priests and the entire council (the Sanhedrin) were constantly seeking [to get] testimony against Jesus with a view to condemning Him *and* putting Him to death, but they did not find any.
56For many were repeatedly bearing false witness against Him, but their testimonies did not agree.
57And some stood up and were bearing false witness against Him, saying,
58We heard Him say, I will destroy this temple (sanctuary) which is made with hands, and in three days I will build another, made without hands.
59Still not even [in this] did their testimony agree.
60And the high priest stood up in the midst, and asked Jesus, Have You not even one answer to make? What [about this which] these [men] are testifying against You?
61But He kept still and did not answer at all. Again the high priest asked Him, Are You the Christ—the Messiah, the Anointed One—the Son of the Blessed?
62And Jesus said, I AM; and you will (all) see the Son of man seated at the right hand of Power ( [d]the Almighty), and coming with the clouds of heaven. [Ps. 110:1; Dan. 7:13.]
63Then the high priest tore his garments, and said, What need have we for more witnesses? [Num. 14:6.]
64You have heard His blasphemy. What is your decision? And they all condemned Him as being guilty *and* deserving death. [Lev. 24:16.]
65And some of them began to spit on Him, and to blindfold Him, and to strike Him with their fists, saying to Him, Prophesy! And the guards received Him with blows *and* by slapping Him.
66While Peter was down below in the courtyard, one of the (serving) maids of the high priest came;
67And when she saw Peter warming himself, she gazed intently at him, and said, You were with Jesus of Nazareth too.
68But he denied it [e]falsely *and* disowned Him, saying, I neither know nor understand what you say. Then he went outside [the courtyard and was] in the [f]vestibule to it. *And a cock crowed.*
69And the maid servant saw him, and began again to say to the bystanders, This [man] is [one] of them.
70But again he denied it [g]falsely *and* disowned Him. And after a short while again the bystanders said to Peter, [h]Really you are one of them, for you are a Galilean, *and your dialect shows it.*
71Then he commenced invoking a curse on himself [if he were not telling the truth] and to swear, I do not know the Man about Whom you are talking!
72And at once for the second time a cock crowed. And Peter remembered how Jesus said to him, Before a cock crows twice, you will ( [i]utterly deny Me—disclaiming all connection with Me—three times. And [j]having put his thought upon it, he broke down *and* wept aloud *and* [k]lamented.

**AMP** [a] Souter. [b] Souter. [c] Vincent. [d] Thayer. [e] Cremer. [f] Vincent. [g] Cremer. [h] Cremer. [i] Vincent. [j] Wuest. [k] Thayer.

## New American Standard

[51]¶ And a certain young man was following Him, wearing *nothing but* a linen sheet over *his* naked *body;* and they *seized him.
[52]But he left the linen sheet behind, and escaped naked.

*Jesus before His Accusers*

[53]¶ And they led Jesus away to the high priest; and all the chief priests and the elders and the scribes *gathered together.
[54]And Peter had followed Him at a distance, right into the courtyard of the high priest; and he was sitting with the officers, and warming himself at the fire.
[55]Now the chief priests and the whole [l]Council kept trying to obtain testimony against Jesus to put Him to death; and they were not finding any.
[56]For many were giving false testimony against Him, and *yet* their testimony was not consistent.
[57]And some stood up and *began* to give false testimony against Him, saying,
[58]"We heard Him say, 'I will destroy this temple made with hands, and in three days I will build another made without hands.' "
[59]And not even in this respect was their testimony consistent.
[60]And the high priest stood up *and came* forward and questioned Jesus, saying, "Do You make no answer? What is it that these men are testifying against You?"
[61]But He kept silent, and made no answer. Again the high priest was questioning Him, and saying to Him, "Are You the Christ, the Son of the Blessed *One?*"
[62]And Jesus said, "I am; and you shall see THE SON OF MAN SITTING AT THE RIGHT HAND OF POWER, and COMING WITH THE CLOUDS OF HEAVEN."
[63]And tearing his clothes, the high priest *said, "What further need do we have of witnesses?
[64]"You have heard the blasphemy; how does it seem to you?" And they all condemned Him to be deserving of death.
[65]And some began to spit at Him, and to blindfold Him, and to beat Him with their fists, and to say to Him, "Prophesy!" And the officers received Him with slaps *in the face.*

*Peter's Denials*

[66]¶ And as Peter was below in the courtyard, one of the servant-girls of the high priest *came,
[67]and seeing Peter warming himself, she looked at him, and *said, "You, too, were with Jesus the Nazarene."
[68]But he denied *it,* saying, "I neither know nor understand what you are talking about." And he went out onto the porch.[m]
[69]And the maid saw him, and began once more to say to the bystanders, "This is *one* of them!"
[70]But again he was denying it. And after a little while the bystanders were again saying to Peter, "Surely you are *one* of them, for you are a Galilean too."
[71]But he began to curse and swear, "I do not know this man you are talking about!"
[72]And immediately a cock crowed a second time. And Peter remembered how Jesus had made the remark to him, "Before a cock crows twice, you will deny Me three times." And he began to weep.

NAS [l] Or, *Sanhedrin* [m]Later mss. add: *and a cock crowed*

## New International

[51]A young man, wearing nothing but a linen garment, was following Jesus. When they seized him, [52]he fled naked, leaving his garment behind.

*Before the Sanhedrin*

[53]They took Jesus to the high priest, and all the chief priests, elders and teachers of the law came together. [54]Peter followed him at a distance, right into the courtyard of the high priest. There he sat with the guards and warmed himself at the fire.
[55]The chief priests and the whole Sanhedrin were looking for evidence against Jesus so that they could put him to death, but they did not find any. [56]Many testified falsely against him, but their statements did not agree.
[57]Then some stood up and gave this false testimony against him: [58]"We heard him say, 'I will destroy this man-made temple and in three days will build another, not made by man.' " [59]Yet even then their testimony did not agree.
[60]Then the high priest stood up before them and asked Jesus, "Are you not going to answer? What is this testimony that these men are bringing against you?" [61]But Jesus remained silent and gave no answer.
Again the high priest asked him, "Are you the Christ,[n] the Son of the Blessed One?"
[62]"I am," said Jesus. "And you will see the Son of Man sitting at the right hand of the Mighty One and coming on the clouds of heaven."
[63]The high priest tore his clothes. "Why do we need any more witnesses?" he asked. [64]"You have heard the blasphemy. What do you think?"
They all condemned him as worthy of death. [65]Then some began to spit at him; they blindfolded him, struck him with their fists, and said, "Prophesy!" And the guards took him and beat him.

*Peter Disowns Jesus*

[66]While Peter was below in the courtyard, one of the servant girls of the high priest came by. [67]When she saw Peter warming himself, she looked closely at him.
"You also were with that Nazarene, Jesus," she said.
[68]But he denied it. "I don't know or understand what you're talking about," he said, and went out into the entryway.[o]
[69]When the servant girl saw him there, she said again to those standing around, "This fellow is one of them." [70]Again he denied it.
After a little while, those standing near said to Peter, "Surely you are one of them, for you are a Galilean."
[71]He began to call down curses on himself, and he swore to them, "I don't know this man you're talking about."
[72]Immediately the rooster crowed the second time.[p] Then Peter remembered the word Jesus had spoken to him: "Before the rooster crows twice[q] you will disown me three times." And he broke down and wept.

NIV [n] 61 Or *Messiah* [o] 68 Some early manuscripts *entryway and the rooster crowed* [p] 72 Some early manuscripts do not have *the second time.* [q] 72 Some early manuscripts do not have *twice.*

## King James

15 AND STRAIGHTWAY in the morning the chief priests held a consultation with the elders and scribes and the whole council, and bound Jesus, and carried *him* away, and delivered *him* to Pilate.

2And Pilate asked him, Art thou the King of the Jews? And he answering said unto him, Thou sayest *it*.

3And the chief priests accused him of many things: but he answered nothing.

4And Pilate asked him again, saying, Answerest thou nothing? behold how many things they witness against thee.

5But Jesus yet answered nothing; so that Pilate marvelled.

6Now at *that* feast he released unto them one prisoner, whomsoever they desired.

7And there was *one* named Barabbas, *which lay* bound with them that had made insurrection with him, who had committed murder in the insurrection.

8And the multitude crying aloud began to desire *him to do* as he had ever done unto them.

9But Pilate answered them, saying, Will ye that I release unto you the King of the Jews?

10For he knew that the chief priests had delivered him for envy.

11But the chief priests moved the people, that he should rather release Barabbas unto them.

12And Pilate answered and said again unto them, What will ye then that I shall do *unto him* whom ye call the King of the Jews?

13And they cried out again, Crucify him.

14Then Pilate said unto them, Why, what evil hath he done? And they cried out the more exceedingly, Crucify him.

15¶ And *so* Pilate, willing to content the people, released Barabbas unto them, and delivered Jesus, when he had scourged *him*, to be crucified.

16And the soldiers led him away into the hall, called Praetorium; and they call together the whole band.

17And they clothed him with purple, and plaited a crown of thorns, and put it about his *head*,

18And began to salute him, Hail, King of the Jews!

19And they smote him on the head with a reed, and did spit upon him, and bowing *their* knees worshipped him.

20And when they had mocked him, they took off the purple from him, and put his own clothes on him, and led him out to crucify him.

21And they compel one Simon a Cyrenian, who passed by, coming out of the country, the father of Alexander and Rufus, to bear his cross.

22And they bring him unto the place Golgotha, which is, being interpreted, The place of a skull.

23And they gave him to drink wine mingled with myrrh: but he received *it* not.

24And when they had crucified him, they parted his garments, casting lots upon them, what every man should take.

25And it was the third hour, and they crucified him.

26And the superscription of his accusation was written over, THE KING OF THE JEWS.

27And with him they crucify two thieves; the one on his right hand, and the other on his left.

28And the scripture was fulfilled, which saith, And he was numbered with the transgressors.

29And they that passed by railed on him, wagging their heads, and saying, Ah, thou that destroyest the temple, and buildest *it* in three days,

30Save thyself, and come down from the cross.

**AMP** [a] Thayer. [b] Capitalized because of what He is, the spotless Son of God, not what the speaker may have thought He was. [c] Thayer. [d] Wuest. [e] Capitalized because of what He is, the spotless Son of God, not what the speakers may have thought He was. [f] Cremer.

## Amplified

15 AND IMMEDIATELY when it was morning the chief priests, with the elders and scribes and the whole council, held a consultation; and when they had bound Jesus they took Him away [ [a]violently] and handed Him over to Pilate. [Isa. 53:8.]

2And Pilate inquired of Him, Are You the King of the Jews? And He replied, It is as you say.

3And the chief priests kept accusing Him of many things.

4And Pilate again asked Him, Have [b]You no answer to make? See how many charges they are bringing against You!

5But Jesus made no further answer at all, so that Pilate wondered *and* marveled. [Isa. 53:7.]

6Now at the feast he [was accustomed] to set free for them any one prisoner whom they requested.

7And among the rioters in the prison who had committed murder in the insurrection there was a man named Barabbas.

8And the throng came up and began asking Pilate to do as he usually did for them.

9And he replied to them, Do you wish me to set free for you the King of the Jews?

10For he was aware that it was ( [c]because they were prompted) by envy that the chief priests had delivered Him up.

11But the chief priests stirred up the crowd [to get] him to release for them Barabbas instead.

12And again Pilate said to them, Then what shall I do [with the Man] Whom you call the King of the Jews?

13And they shouted back again, Crucify Him!

14But Pilate said to them, (Why?) What has He done that is evil? But they shouted with all their might the more, Crucify Him [ [d]at once]!

15So Pilate, wishing to satisfy the crowd, set Barabbas free for them; and after having whipped Jesus, he handed [Him] over to be crucified. [Isa. 53:5.]

16Then the soldiers led Him away to the courtyard inside the palace which is the praetorium, and they called the entire detachment of soldiers together.

17And they dressed Him in a purple [robe], and weaving together a crown of thorns they placed it on Him.

18And they began to salute Him, Hail (greeting, good health to You, long life to You), King of the Jews!

19And they struck His head with a staff made of a [bamboo-like] reed, and spat on Him, and kept bowing their knees in homage to Him. [Isa. 50:6.]

20And when they had [finished] making sport of Him, they took the purple [robe] off of Him, and put His own clothes on Him. And they led Him out [of the city] to crucify Him.

21And they forced a passerby, Simon of Cyrene, the father of Alexander and Rufus, who was coming in from the field (country), to carry His cross.

22And they led Him to Golgotha [in Latin, Calvary], meaning the place of a skull.

23And they (attempted to) give Him wine mingled with myrrh, but He would not take it.

24And they crucified Him, and divided His garments *and* distributed them among them, throwing lots for them, to decide who should take each. [Ps. 22:18.]

25And it was the third hour (about nine o'clock in the morning) when they crucified Him. [Ps. 22:14-16.]

26And the inscription of the accusation against Him was written above, The King of the Jews.

27And with Him they crucified two robbers, one on [His] right hand and one on His left.

28 *And the Scripture was fulfilled which says, He was counted among the transgressors.* [Isa. 53:12.]

29And those who passed by kept reviling Him *and* reproaching Him abusively in harsh *and* insolent language, wagging their heads and saying, Aha! You Who would destroy the temple and build it in three days,

30Now rescue [e]Yourself ( [f]from death), coming down from the cross!

## New American Standard

*Jesus before Pilate*

15 AND EARLY in the morning the chief priests with the
elders and scribes, and the whole [g]Council, immediately
held a consultation; and binding Jesus, they led Him away, and
delivered Him up to Pilate.
2And Pilate questioned Him, "Are You the King of the Jews?"
And answering He *said to him, " *It is as* you say."
3And the chief priests *began* to accuse Him harshly.
4And Pilate was questioning Him again, saying, "Do You
make no answer? See how many charges they bring against You!"
5But Jesus made no further answer; so that Pilate was amazed.
6¶ Now at *the* feast he used to release for them *any* one prisoner
whom they requested.
7And the man named Barabbas had been imprisoned with the
insurrectionists who had committed murder in the insurrection.
8And the multitude went up and began asking him *to do* as he
had been accustomed to do for them.
9And Pilate answered them, saying, "Do you want me to
release for you the King of the Jews?"
10For he was aware that the chief priests had delivered Him up
because of envy.
11But the chief priests stirred up the multitude *to ask* him to
release Barabbas for them instead.
12And answering again, Pilate was saying to them, "Then what
shall I do with Him whom you call the King of the Jews?"
13And they shouted back, "Crucify Him!"
14But Pilate was saying to them, "Why, what evil has He
done?" But they shouted all the more, "Crucify Him!"
15And wishing to satisfy the multitude, Pilate released Barabbas
for them, and after having Jesus scourged, he delivered *Him* to be
crucified.

*Jesus Is Mocked*

16¶ And the soldiers took Him away into the palace (that is, the
Praetorium), and they *called together the whole *Roman* [h]cohort.
17And they *dressed Him up in purple, and after weaving a
crown of thorns, they put it on Him;
18and they began to acclaim Him, "Hail, King of the Jews!"
19And they kept beating His head with a [i]reed, and spitting at
Him, and kneeling and bowing before Him.
20And after they had mocked Him, they took the purple off
Him, and put His garments on Him. And they *led Him out to
crucify Him.
21¶ And they *pressed into service a passer-by coming from the
country, Simon of Cyrene (the father of Alexander and Rufus), to
bear His cross.

*The Crucifixion*

22¶ And they *brought Him to the place Golgotha, which is
translated, Place of a Skull.
23And they tried to give Him wine mixed with myrrh; but He
did not take it.
24And they *crucified Him, and *divided up His garments
among themselves, casting lots for them, *to decide* what each
should take.
25And it was the [j]third hour when they crucified Him.
26And the inscription of the charge against Him read, "THE
KING OF THE JEWS."
27And they *crucified two robbers with Him, one on His right
and one on His left.
28[ [k]And the Scripture was fulfilled which says, "And He was
numbered with transgressors."]
29And those passing by were hurling abuse at Him, wagging
their heads, and saying, "Ha! You who *are going to* destroy the
temple and rebuild it in three days,
30save Yourself, and come down from the cross!"

NAS [g] Or, *Sanhedrin* [h] Or, *battalion* [i] Or, *staff* (made of a reed) [j] I.e., 9 a.m. [k] Many mss. do not contain this verse

## New International

*Jesus Before Pilate*

15 VERY EARLY in the morning, the chief priests, with the
elders, the teachers of the law and the whole Sanhedrin,
reached a decision. They bound Jesus, led him away and handed
him over to Pilate.
2"Are you the king of the Jews?" asked Pilate.
"Yes, it is as you say," Jesus replied.
3The chief priests accused him of many things. 4So again Pilate
asked him, "Aren't you going to answer? See how many things
they are accusing you of."
5But Jesus still made no reply, and Pilate was amazed.
6Now it was the custom at the Feast to release a prisoner whom
the people requested. 7A man called Barabbas was in prison with
the insurrectionists who had committed murder in the uprising.
8The crowd came up and asked Pilate to do for them what he
usually did.
9"Do you want me to release to you the king of the Jews?" asked
Pilate, 10knowing it was out of envy that the chief priests had
handed Jesus over to him. 11But the chief priests stirred up the
crowd to have Pilate release Barabbas instead.
12"What shall I do, then, with the one you call the king of the
Jews?" Pilate asked them.
13"Crucify him!" they shouted.
14"Why? What crime has he committed?" asked Pilate.
But they shouted all the louder, "Crucify him!"
15Wanting to satisfy the crowd, Pilate released Barabbas to
them. He had Jesus flogged, and handed him over to be crucified.

*The Soldiers Mock Jesus*

16The soldiers led Jesus away into the palace (that is, the Praetorium) and called together the whole company of soldiers. 17They
put a purple robe on him, then twisted together a crown of thorns
and set it on him. 18And they began to call out to him, "Hail, king
of the Jews!" 19Again and again they struck him on the head with
a staff and spit on him. Falling on their knees, they paid homage
to him. 20And when they had mocked him, they took off the
purple robe and put his own clothes on him. Then they led him
out to crucify him.

*The Crucifixion*

21A certain man from Cyrene, Simon, the father of Alexander
and Rufus, was passing by on his way in from the country, and
they forced him to carry the cross. 22They brought Jesus to the
place called Golgotha (which means The Place of the Skull). 23Then
they offered him wine mixed with myrrh, but he did not take it.
24And they crucified him. Dividing up his clothes, they cast lots
to see what each would get.
25It was the third hour when they crucified him. 26The written
notice of the charge against him read: THE KING OF THE JEWS. 27They
crucified two robbers with him, one on his right and one on his
left.[1] 29Those who passed by hurled insults at him, shaking their
heads and saying, "So! You who are going to destroy the temple
and build it in three days, 30come down from the cross and save
yourself!"

NIV [1] 27 Some manuscripts *left*, *28and the scripture was fulfilled which says, "He was counted with the lawless ones"* (Isaiah 53:12)

## King James

31Likewise also the chief priests mocking said among themselves with the scribes, He saved others; himself he cannot save.

32Let Christ the King of Israel descend now from the cross, that we may see and believe. And they that were crucified with him reviled him.

33And when the sixth hour was come, there was darkness over the whole land until the ninth hour.

34And at the ninth hour Jesus cried with a loud voice, saying, Eloi, Eloi, lama sabachthani? which is, being interpreted, My God, my God, why hast thou forsaken me?

35And some of them that stood by, when they heard *it,* said, Behold, he calleth Elias.

36And one ran and filled a sponge full of vinegar, and put *it* on a reed, and gave him to drink, saying, Let alone; let us see whether Elias will come to take him down.

37And Jesus cried with a loud voice, and gave up the ghost.

38And the veil of the temple was rent in twain from the top to the bottom.

39¶ And when the centurion, which stood over against him, saw that he so cried out, and gave up the ghost, he said, Truly this man was the Son of God.

40There were also women looking on afar off: among whom was Mary Magdalene, and Mary the mother of James the less and of Joses, and Salome;

41(Who also, when he was in Galilee, followed him, and ministered unto him;) and many other women which came up with him unto Jerusalem.

42¶ And now when the even was come, because it was the preparation, that is, the day before the sabbath,

43Joseph of Arimathaea, an honourable counsellor, which also waited for the kingdom of God, came, and went in boldly unto Pilate, and craved the body of Jesus.

44And Pilate marvelled if he were already dead: and calling *unto him* the centurion, he asked him whether he had been any while dead.

45And when he knew *it* of the centurion, he gave the body to Joseph.

46And he bought fine linen, and took him down, and wrapped him in the linen, and laid him in a sepulchre which was hewn out of a rock, and rolled a stone unto the door of the sepulchre.

47And Mary Magdalene and Mary *the mother* of Joses beheld where he was laid.

**16** AND WHEN the sabbath was past, Mary Magdalene, and Mary the *mother* of James, and Salome, had bought sweet spices, that they might come and anoint him.

2And very early in the morning the first *day* of the week, they came unto the sepulchre at the rising of the sun.

3And they said among themselves, Who shall roll us away the stone from the door of the sepulchre?

4And when they looked, they saw that the stone was rolled away: for it was very great.

## Amplified

31So also the chief priests with the scribes made sport of Him to one another, saying, He rescued others ( [a]from death); Himself He is unable to rescue. [Ps. 22:7, 8.]

32Let the Christ, the Messiah, the King of Israel, come down now from the cross, that we may see [it] and trust in *and* rely on Him *and* adhere to Him! Those who were crucified with Him also reviled *and* reproached Him—speaking abusively, harshly and insolently.

33And when the sixth hour had come (about mid-day), there was darkness over the whole land until the ninth hour (about three o'clock).

34And at the ninth hour Jesus cried with a loud voice, Eloi, Eloi, lama sabachthani? which means, My God, My God, why have You forsaken Me— [b]deserting Me and leaving Me helpless and abandoned? [Ps. 22:1.]

35And some of those standing by [and] hearing it said, See! He is calling Elijah!

36And one man ran, and, filling a sponge with vinegar [a [c]mixture of sour wine and water], put it on a staff made of a [bamboo-like] reed, and gave it to Him to drink, saying, Hold off! Let us see whether Elijah [does] come to take Him down. [Ps. 69:21.]

37And Jesus uttered a loud cry, and breathed out His life.

38And the curtain [of the Holy of Holies] of the temple was torn in two from top to bottom.

39And when the centurion who stood facing Him saw Him expire this way, he said, [d]Really this Man was God's Son!

40Now some women were there also, looking on from a distance, among whom were Mary Magdalene, and Mary the mother of James the younger and of Joses, and Salome,

41Who, when [Jesus] was in Galilee, were in the habit of accompanying and ministering to Him; and also many other [women] who came up with Him to Jerusalem.

42As evening had already come, since it was the day of Preparation, that is, [the day] before the Sabbath, [Deut. 21:22, 23.]

43Joseph, he of Arimathea, noble *and* honorable in rank *and* a respected member of the council (Sanhedrin), who was himself waiting for the kingdom of God, daring the consequences, took courage *and* ventured to go to Pilate, and asked for the body of Jesus.

44But Pilate wondered whether He was dead so soon, and having called the centurion, he asked him whether [Jesus] was already dead.

45And when he learned from the centurion [that He was indeed dead], he gave the body to Joseph.

46And Joseph bought a (fine) linen cloth [ [e]for swathing dead bodies], and taking Him down from the cross, he [f]rolled Him up in the (fine) linen cloth; and placed Him in a tomb which had been hewn out of a rock. Then he rolled a [ [g]very large] stone against the door of the tomb. [Isa. 53:9.]

47And Mary Magdalene and Mary [the mother] of Joses were [ [h]attentively] observing where He was laid.

**16** AND WHEN the Sabbath was past [that is, after the sun had set], Mary Magdalene, and Mary [the mother] of James, and Salome purchased sweet-smelling spices, so that they might go and anoint [Jesus' body].

2And very early on the first day of the week they came to the tomb; [by then] the sun had risen.

3And they said to one another, Who will roll back the stone for us out of [the groove across the floor at] the door of the tomb?

4And when they looked up, they [distinctly] saw that the stone was already rolled back, for it was very large.

**AMP** [a] Cremer. [b] Thayer. [c] Thayer. [d] Cremer. [e] Moulton and Milligan. [f] Young. [g] Chap. 16:4. [h] Vincent.

## New American Standard

31In the same way the chief priests also, along with the scribes,
were mocking *Him* among themselves and saying, "He saved
others; He cannot save Himself.
32"Let *this* Christ, the King of Israel, now come down from the
cross, so that we may see and believe!" And those who were
crucified with Him were casting the same insult at Him.
33¶ And when the [i]sixth hour had come, darkness fell over the
whole land until the [j]ninth hour.
34And at the ninth hour Jesus cried out with a loud voice, "ELOI,
ELOI, LAMA SABACHTHANI?" which is translated, "MY GOD, MY
GOD, WHY HAST THOU FORSAKEN ME?"
35And when some of the bystanders heard it, they *began* saying,
"Behold, He is calling for Elijah."
36And someone ran and filled a sponge with sour wine, put it
on a reed, and gave Him a drink, saying, "Let us see whether
Elijah will come to take Him down."
37And Jesus uttered a loud cry, and breathed His last.
38And the veil of the temple was torn in two from top to bottom.
39And when the centurion, who was standing right in front of
Him, saw the way He breathed His last, he said, "Truly this man
was the Son of God!"
40And there were also *some* women looking on from a distance,
among whom *were* Mary Magdalene, and Mary the mother of
James the Less and Joses, and Salome.
41And when He was in Galilee, they used to follow Him and
minister to Him; and *there were* many other women who had come
up with Him to Jerusalem.

*Jesus Is Buried*

42¶ And when evening had already come, because it was the
preparation day, that is, the day before the Sabbath,
43Joseph of Arimathea came, a prominent member of the Council, who himself was waiting for the kingdom of God; and he
gathered up courage and went in before Pilate, and asked for the
body of Jesus.
44And Pilate wondered if He was dead by this time, and summoning the centurion, he questioned him as to whether He was
already dead.
45And ascertaining this from the centurion, he granted the body
to Joseph.
46And *Joseph* bought a linen cloth, took Him down, wrapped
Him in the linen cloth, and laid Him in a tomb which had been
hewn out in the rock; and he rolled a stone against the entrance
of the tomb.
47And Mary Magdalene and Mary the *mother* of Joses were
looking on *to see* where He was laid.

*The Resurrection*

**16** AND WHEN the Sabbath was over, Mary Magdalene, and
Mary the *mother* of James, and Salome, bought spices, that
they might come and anoint Him.
2And very early on the first day of the week, they *came to the
tomb when the sun had risen.
3And they were saying to one another, "Who will roll away the
stone for us from the entrance of the tomb?"
4And looking up, they *saw that the stone had been rolled
away, although it was extremely large.

NAS [i] I.e., noon [j] I.e., 3 p.m.

## New International

31In the same way the chief priests and the teachers of the law
mocked him among themselves. "He saved others," they said,
"but he can't save himself! 32Let this Christ,[k] this King of Israel,
come down now from the cross, that we may see and believe."
Those crucified with him also heaped insults on him.

*The Death of Jesus*

33At the sixth hour darkness came over the whole land until the
ninth hour. 34And at the ninth hour Jesus cried out in a loud voice,
*"Eloi, Eloi, lama sabachthani?"*—which means, "My God, my God,
why have you forsaken me?"[l]
35When some of those standing near heard this, they said,
"Listen, he's calling Elijah."
36One man ran, filled a sponge with wine vinegar, put it on a
stick, and offered it to Jesus to drink. "Now leave him alone. Let's
see if Elijah comes to take him down," he said.
37With a loud cry, Jesus breathed his last.
38The curtain of the temple was torn in two from top to bottom.
39And when the centurion, who stood there in front of Jesus,
heard his cry and[m] saw how he died, he said, "Surely this man was
the Son[n] of God!"
40Some women were watching from a distance. Among them
were Mary Magdalene, Mary the mother of James the younger and
of Joses, and Salome. 41In Galilee these women had followed him
and cared for his needs. Many other women who had come up
with him to Jerusalem were also there.

*The Burial of Jesus*

42It was Preparation Day (that is, the day before the Sabbath).
So as evening approached, 43Joseph of Arimathea, a prominent
member of the Council, who was himself waiting for the kingdom
of God, went boldly to Pilate and asked for Jesus' body. 44Pilate
was surprised to hear that he was already dead. Summoning the
centurion, he asked him if Jesus had already died. 45When he
learned from the centurion that it was so, he gave the body to
Joseph. 46So Joseph bought some linen cloth, took down the body,
wrapped it in the linen, and placed it in a tomb cut out of rock.
Then he rolled a stone against the entrance of the tomb. 47Mary
Magdalene and Mary the mother of Joses saw where he was laid.

*The Resurrection*

**16** WHEN THE Sabbath was over, Mary Magdalene, Mary
the mother of James, and Salome bought spices so that
they might go to anoint Jesus' body. 2Very early on the first day
of the week, just after sunrise, they were on their way to the tomb
3and they asked each other, "Who will roll the stone away from
the entrance of the tomb?"
4But when they looked up, they saw that the stone, which was
very large, had been rolled away. 5As they entered the tomb, they

NIV [k] 32 Or *Messiah* [l] 34 Psalm 22:1 [m] 39 Some manuscripts do not have *heard his cry and.* [n] 39 Or *a son*

## King James

5And entering into the sepulchre, they saw a young man sitting on the right side, clothed in a long white garment; and they were affrighted.

6And he saith unto them, Be not affrighted: Ye seek Jesus of Nazareth, which was crucified: he is risen; he is not here: behold the place where they laid him.

7But go your way, tell his disciples and Peter that he goeth before you into Galilee: there shall ye see him, as he said unto you.

8And they went out quickly, and fled from the sepulchre; for they trembled and were amazed: neither said they any thing to any *man;* for they were afraid.

9¶ Now when *Jesus* was risen early the first *day* of the week, he appeared first to Mary Magdalene, out of whom he had cast seven devils.

10 *And* she went and told them that had been with him, as they mourned and wept.

11And they, when they had heard that he was alive, and had been seen of her, believed not.

12¶ After that he appeared in another form unto two of them, as they walked, and went into the country.

13And they went and told *it* unto the residue: neither believed they them.

14¶ Afterward he appeared unto the eleven as they sat at meat, and upbraided them with their unbelief and hardness of heart, because they believed not them which had seen him after he was risen.

15And he said unto them, Go ye into all the world, and preach the gospel to every creature.

16He that believeth and is baptized shall be saved; but he that believeth not shall be damned.

17And these signs shall follow them that believe; In my name shall they cast out devils; they shall speak with new tongues;
18They shall take up serpents; and if they drink any deadly thing, it shall not hurt them; they shall lay hands on the sick, and they shall recover.

19¶ So then after the Lord had spoken unto them, he was received up into heaven, and sat on the right hand of God.

20And they went forth, and preached every where, the Lord working with *them,* and confirming the word with signs following. Amen.

## Amplified

5And going into the tomb, they saw a young man sitting [there] on the right [side], clothed in a ([a]long, stately, sweeping) robe of white, and they were utterly amazed *and* struck with terror.

6And he said to them, Do not be amazed *and* terrified; you are looking for Jesus of Nazareth Who was crucified. He is risen; He is not here. See the place where they laid Him. [Ps. 16:10.]

7But be going; tell the disciples and Peter, He goes before you into Galilee; you will see Him there, [just] as He told you.

8Then they went out [and] fled from the tomb, for trembling and bewilderment *and* consternation had seized them. And they said nothing about it to any one, for they were held by alarm *and* fear.

9 [b]Now Jesus, having risen ([c]from death) early on the first day of the week, appeared first to Mary Magdalene, from whom He had driven out seven demons.

10She went and reported it to those who had been with Him, as they grieved and wept.

11And when they heard that He was alive and that she had seen Him, they did not believe it.

12After this He appeared in a different form to two of them, as they were walking [along the way] into the country.

13And they returned [to Jerusalem] and told the others, but they did not believe them either.

14Afterward He appeared to the eleven [apostles, themselves] as they reclined at table; and He reproved *and* reproached them for their unbelief (their lack of faith) and their hardness of heart, because they had refused to believe those who had seen Him *and* looked at Him attentively after He was risen ([d]from death).

15And He said to them, Go into all the world and preach *and* publish openly the good news (the Gospel) to every creature (of the whole [e]human race).

16He who believes—[that is,] who adheres to and trusts in and relies on the Gospel and Him Whom it sets forth—and is baptized will be saved [[f]from the penalty of eternal death]; but he who does not believe—who does not adhere to and trust in and rely on the Gospel and Him Whom it sets forth—will be condemned.

17And these attesting signs will accompany those who believe: in My name they will drive out demons; they will speak in new languages;

18They will pick up serpents, and [even] if they drink anything deadly, it will not hurt them; they will lay their hands on the sick, and they will get well.

19So then the Lord Jesus, after He had spoken to them, was taken up into heaven and He sat down at the right hand of God. [Ps. 110:1.]

20And they went out and preached everywhere, while the Lord kept working with them and confirming the message by the attesting signs *and* miracles that closely accompanied [it]. Amen—so be it.

**AMP** [a] Trench. [b] Verses 9 to 20 not in the two earliest manuscripts. [c] Cremer. [d] Cremer. [e] Thayer. [f] Cremer.

## New American Standard

5 And entering the tomb, they saw a young man sitting at the right, wearing a white robe; and they were amazed.

6 And he *said to them, "Do not be amazed; you are looking for Jesus the Nazarene, who has been crucified. He has risen; He is not here; behold, *here is* the place where they laid Him.

7 "But go, tell His disciples and Peter, 'He is going before you into Galilee; there you will see Him, just as He said to you.' "

8 And they went out and fled from the tomb, for trembling and astonishment had gripped them; and they said nothing to anyone, for they were afraid.

9 ¶ [ [g]Now after He had risen early on the first day of the week, He first appeared to Mary Magdalene, from whom He had cast out seven demons.

10 She went and reported to those who had been with Him, while they were mourning and weeping.

11 And when they heard that He was alive, and had been seen by her, they refused to believe it.

12 ¶ And after that, He appeared in a different form to two of them, while they were walking along on their way to the country.

13 And they went away and reported it to the others, but they did not believe them either.

*The Disciples Commissioned*

14 ¶ And afterward He appeared to the eleven themselves as they were reclining *at the table;* and He reproached them for their unbelief and hardness of heart, because they had not believed those who had seen Him after He had risen.

15 And He said to them, "Go into all the world and preach the gospel to all creation.

16 "He who has believed and has been baptized shall be saved; but he who has disbelieved shall be condemned.

17 "And these signs will accompany those who have believed: in My name they will cast out demons, they will speak with new tongues;

18 they will pick up serpents, and if they drink any deadly *poison,* it shall not hurt them; they will lay hands on the sick, and they will recover."

19 ¶ So then, when the Lord Jesus had spoken to them, He was received up into heaven, and sat down at the right hand of God.

20 And they went out and preached everywhere, while the Lord worked with them, and confirmed the word by the signs that followed.][ [h] *And they promptly reported all these instructions to Peter and his companions. And after that, Jesus Himself sent out through them from east to west the sacred and imperishable proclamation of eternal salvation.*]

NAS [g] Some of the oldest mss. do not contain vv. 9–20 [h] A few later mss. and versions contain this paragraph, usually after verse 8; a few have it at the end of chapter.

## New International

saw a young man dressed in a white robe sitting on the right side, and they were alarmed.

6 "Don't be alarmed," he said. "You are looking for Jesus the
Nazarene, who was crucified. He has risen! He is not here. See the
place where they laid him. 7 But go, tell his disciples and Peter, 'He
is going ahead of you into Galilee. There you will see him, just as
he told you.' "

8 Trembling and bewildered, the women went out and fled from the tomb. They said nothing to anyone, because they were afraid.

---

[The most reliable early manuscripts and other ancient witnesses do not have Mark 16:9-20.]

9 When Jesus rose early on the first day of the week, he appeared
first to Mary Magdalene, out of whom he had driven seven demons. 10 She went and told those who had been with him and who
were mourning and weeping. 11 When they heard that Jesus was
alive and that she had seen him, they did not believe it.

12 Afterward Jesus appeared in a different form to two of them
while they were walking in the country. 13 These returned and
reported it to the rest; but they did not believe them either.

14 Later Jesus appeared to the Eleven as they were eating; he
rebuked them for their lack of faith and their stubborn refusal to
believe those who had seen him after he had risen.

15 He said to them, "Go into all the world and preach the good
news to all creation. 16 Whoever believes and is baptized will be
saved, but whoever does not believe will be condemned. 17 And
these signs will accompany those who believe: In my name they
will drive out demons; they will speak in new tongues; 18 they will
pick up snakes with their hands; and when they drink deadly
poison, it will not hurt them at all; they will place their hands on
sick people, and they will get well."

19 After the Lord Jesus had spoken to them, he was taken up into
heaven and he sat at the right hand of God. 20 Then the disciples
went out and preached everywhere, and the Lord worked with
them and confirmed his word by the signs that accompanied it.

## King James

THE GOSPEL
ACCORDING TO

# St. Luke

1 FORASMUCH AS many have taken in hand to set forth in order a declaration of those things which are most surely believed among us,

2 Even as they delivered them unto us, which from the beginning were eyewitnesses, and ministers of the word;

3 It seemed good to me also, having had perfect understanding of all things from the very first, to write unto thee in order, most excellent Theophilus,

4 That thou mightest know the certainty of those things, wherein thou hast been instructed.

5 ¶ There was in the days of Herod, the king of Judaea, a certain priest named Zacharias, of the course of Abia: and his wife *was* of the daughters of Aaron, and her name *was* Elisabeth.

6 And they were both righteous before God, walking in all the commandments and ordinances of the Lord blameless.

7 And they had no child, because that Elisabeth was barren, and they both were *now* well stricken in years.

8 And it came to pass, that while he executed the priest's office before God in the order of his course,

9 According to the custom of the priest's office, his lot was to burn incense when he went into the temple of the Lord.

10 And the whole multitude of the people were praying without at the time of incense.

11 And there appeared unto him an angel of the Lord standing on the right side of the altar of incense.

12 And when Zacharias saw *him*, he was troubled, and fear fell upon him.

13 But the angel said unto him, Fear not, Zacharias: for thy prayer is heard; and thy wife Elisabeth shall bear thee a son, and thou shalt call his name John.

14 And thou shalt have joy and gladness; and many shall rejoice at his birth.

15 For he shall be great in the sight of the Lord, and shall drink neither wine nor strong drink; and he shall be filled with the Holy Ghost, even from his mother's womb.

16 And many of the children of Israel shall he turn to the Lord their God.

## Amplified

THE GOSPEL ACCORDING TO

# Luke

1 SINCE ( [a]AS is well known) many have undertaken to put in order *and* draw up a ( [b]thorough) narrative of the surely established deeds which have been accomplished *and* fulfilled [c]in *and* among us,

2 Exactly as they were handed down to us by those who from the ( [d]official) beginning [of Jesus' ministry] were eye-witnesses and ministers of the Word [that is, of [e]the doctrine concerning the attainment through Christ of salvation in the kingdom of God],

3 It seeming good *and* desirable to me, [I have determined] also after [f]having searched out diligently *and* followed all things closely *and* traced accurately the course from the highest to the minutest detail from the very first, to write an orderly account for you, most excellent Theophilus,

4 [My purpose is] that you may know the full truth, *and* understand with certainty *and* security against error the accounts (histories) *and* doctrines of the faith of which you have been informed *and* in which you have been [g]orally instructed.

5 In the days when Herod was king of Judea, there was a certain priest whose name was Zachariah, [h]of the daily service (the division) of Abia; and his wife was also a descendant of Aaron, and her name was Elizabeth.

6 And they both were righteous in the sight of God, walking blamelessly in all the commandments and requirements of the Lord.

7 But they had no child, for Elizabeth was barren, and both were [i]far advanced in years.

8 Now while on duty, serving as priest before God in the order of his division,

9 As was the custom of the priesthood, it fell to him by lot to enter (the [j]sanctuary of) the temple of the Lord and burn incense. [Exod. 30:7.]

10 And all the throng of people were praying outside [in the court] at the hour of incense [burning].

11 And there appeared to him an angel of the Lord, standing at [the] right side of the altar of incense.

12 And when Zachariah saw him he was troubled, and fear took possession of him.

13 But the angel said to him, Do not be afraid, Zachariah, because your petition [k]was heard, and your wife Elizabeth will bear you a son, and you must call his name John [meaning God is favorable].

14 And you shall have joy and exultant delight, and many will rejoice over his birth,

15 For he will be great *and* distinguished in the sight of the Lord. And he must drink no wine nor strong drink, and he will be filled with *and* controlled by the Holy Spirit, even [l]in *and* from his mother's womb. [Num. 6:3.]

16 And he will turn *and* cause to return many of the sons of Israel to the Lord their God,

**AMP** [a] Vincent's "Word Studies in the New Testament." [b] Vincent's "Word Studies in the New Testament." [c] Wycliffe's Version of the New Testament. [d] Vincent's "Word Studies in the New Testament." [e] Thayer's "Greek-English Lexicon of the New Testament—Grimm." [f] Tyndale's Version of the New Testament. [g] Vincent's "Word Studies in the New Testament." [h] Vincent's "Word Studies in the New Testament." [i] Wycliffe. [j] Trench's "Synonyms of the New Testament." [k] Tyndale. [l] Tyndale.

## New American Standard

# Luke

*Introduction*

**1** INASMUCH AS many have undertaken to compile an account of the things accomplished among us,

2just as those who from the beginning were eyewitnesses and servants of the [m]word have handed them down to us,

3it seemed fitting for me as well, having investigated everything carefully from the beginning, to write *it* out for you in consecutive order, most excellent Theophilus;

4so that you might know the exact truth about the things you have been taught.

*Birth of John the Baptist Foretold*

5¶ In the days of Herod, king of Judea, there was a certain priest named Zacharias, of the division of [n]Abijah; and he had a wife [o]from the daughters of Aaron, and her name was Elizabeth.

6And they were both righteous in the sight of God, walking blamelessly in all the commandments and requirements of the Lord.

7And they had no child, because Elizabeth was barren, and they were both advanced in years.

8¶ Now it came about, while he was performing his priestly service before God in the *appointed* order of his division,

9according to the custom of the priestly office, he was chosen by lot to enter the temple of the Lord and burn incense.

10And the whole multitude of the people were in prayer outside at the hour of the incense offering.

11And an angel of the Lord appeared to him, standing to the right of the altar of incense.

12And Zacharias was troubled when he saw *him,* and fear gripped him.

13But the angel said to him, "Do not be afraid, Zacharias, for your petition has been heard, and your wife Elizabeth will bear you a son, and you will give him the name John.

14"And you will have joy and gladness, and many will rejoice at his birth.

15"For he will be great in the sight of the Lord, and he will drink no wine or liquor; and he will be filled with the Holy Spirit, while yet in his mother's womb.

16"And he will turn back many of the sons of Israel to the Lord their God.

NAS [m]I.e., gospel [n]Gr., *Abia* [o]I.e., of priestly descent

## New International

# Luke

*Introduction*

**1** MANY HAVE undertaken to draw up an account of the
things that have been fulfilled[p] among us, 2just as they were
handed down to us by those who from the first were eyewitnesses
and servants of the word. 3Therefore, since I myself have carefully
investigated everything from the beginning, it seemed good also
to me to write an orderly account for you, most excellent Theophilus, 4so that you may know the certainty of the things you have
been taught.

*The Birth of John the Baptist Foretold*

5In the time of Herod king of Judea there was a priest named
Zechariah, who belonged to the priestly division of Abijah; his
wife Elizabeth was also a descendant of Aaron. 6Both of them were
upright in the sight of God, observing all the Lord's commandments and regulations blamelessly. 7But they had no children,
because Elizabeth was barren; and they were both well along in
years.

8Once when Zechariah's division was on duty and he was
serving as priest before God, 9he was chosen by lot, according to
the custom of the priesthood, to go into the temple of the Lord and
burn incense. 10And when the time for the burning of incense
came, all the assembled worshipers were praying outside.

11Then an angel of the Lord appeared to him, standing at the
right side of the altar of incense. 12When Zechariah saw him, he
was startled and was gripped with fear. 13But the angel said to him:
"Do not be afraid, Zechariah; your prayer has been heard. Your
wife Elizabeth will bear you a son, and you are to give him the
name John. 14He will be a joy and delight to you, and many will
rejoice because of his birth, 15for he will be great in the sight of the
Lord. He is never to take wine or other fermented drink, and he
will be filled with the Holy Spirit even from birth.[q] 16Many of the
people of Israel will he bring back to the Lord their God. 17And he

NIV [p]1 Or *been surely believed* [q]15 Or *from his mother's womb*

## King James

17 And he shall go before him in the spirit and power of Elias, to turn the hearts of the fathers to the children, and the disobedient to the wisdom of the just; to make ready a people prepared for the Lord.

18 And Zacharias said unto the angel, Whereby shall I know this? for I am an old man, and my wife well stricken in years.

19 And the angel answering said unto him, I am Gabriel, that stand in the presence of God; and am sent to speak unto thee, and to show thee these glad tidings.

20 And, behold, thou shalt be dumb, and not able to speak, until the day that these things shall be performed, because thou believest not my words, which shall be fulfilled in their season.

21 And the people waited for Zacharias, and marvelled that he tarried so long in the temple.

22 And when he came out, he could not speak unto them: and they perceived that he had seen a vision in the temple: for he beckoned unto them, and remained speechless.

23 And it came to pass, that as soon as the days of his ministration were accomplished, he departed to his own house.

24 And after those days his wife Elisabeth conceived, and hid herself five months, saying,

25 Thus hath the Lord dealt with me in the days wherein he looked on *me*, to take away my reproach among men.

26 And in the sixth month the angel Gabriel was sent from God unto a city of Galilee, named Nazareth,

27 To a virgin espoused to a man whose name was Joseph, of the house of David; and the virgin's name *was* Mary.

28 And the angel came in unto her, and said, Hail, *thou that art* highly favoured, the Lord *is* with thee: blessed *art* thou among women.

29 And when she saw *him*, she was troubled at his saying, and cast in her mind what manner of salutation this should be.

30 And the angel said unto her, Fear not, Mary: for thou hast found favour with God.

31 And, behold, thou shalt conceive in thy womb, and bring forth a son, and shalt call his name JESUS.

32 He shall be great, and shall be called the Son of the Highest: and the Lord God shall give unto him the throne of his father David:

33 And he shall reign over the house of Jacob for ever; and of his kingdom there shall be no end.

34 Then said Mary unto the angel, How shall this be, seeing I know not a man?

35 And the angel answered and said unto her, The Holy Ghost shall come upon thee, and the power of the Highest shall overshadow thee: therefore also that holy thing which shall be born of thee shall be called the Son of God.

36 And, behold, thy cousin Elisabeth, she hath also conceived a son in her old age: and this is the sixth month with her, who was called barren.

37 For with God nothing shall be impossible.

38 And Mary said, Behold the handmaid of the Lord; be it unto me according to thy word. And the angel departed from her.

39 And Mary arose in those days, and went into the hill country with haste, into a city of Judah;

40 And entered into the house of Zacharias, and saluted Elisabeth.

## Amplified

17 And he will [himself] go before Him in the spirit and power of Elijah, to turn back the hearts of the fathers to the children, and the disobedient *and* incredulous *and* unpersuadable to the wisdom of the upright [which is [a]the knowledge and holy love of the will of God], in order to make ready for the Lord a people [perfectly] prepared—in spirit, [b]adjusted and disposed and placed in the right moral state. [Mal. 4:5, 6; Isa. 40:3.]

18 And Zachariah said to the angel, By what shall I know *and* be sure of this? For I am an old man, and my wife is well advanced in years.

19 And the angel replied to him, I am Gabriel; I stand in the [very] presence of God, and I was sent to talk to you, and to bring you this good news. [Dan. 8:16; 9:21.]

20 And lo, you will be *and* [c]will continue to be silent, and not able to speak till the day when these things take place, because you have not believed what I told you; but my words are [d]of a kind which will be fulfilled in the appointed *and* proper time.

21 Now the people kept waiting for Zachariah, and they wondered at his delaying [so long] in the [e]sanctuary.

22 But when he did come out, he was unable to speak to them, and they ([f]clearly) perceived that he had seen a vision in the [g]sanctuary; and he kept making signs to them, still he remained dumb.

23 And when his time of performing priestly functions was ended, he returned to his [own] house.

24 Now after this his wife Elizabeth became pregnant, and for five months she secluded herself [h]entirely, saying, [I have hid myself]

25 [i]Because thus the Lord has dealt with me in the days when He deigned to look on me, to take away my reproach among men. [Gen. 30:23; Isa. 4:1.]

26 Now in the sixth month [after that], the angel Gabriel was sent from God to a town of Galilee named Nazareth,

27 To a girl never having been married *and* a [j]virgin, engaged to be married to a man whose name was Joseph, a descendant of the house of David; and the virgin's name was Mary.

28 And he came to her and said, Hail, O favored one ([k]endued with grace), the Lord is with you! *Blessed—favored of God—are you before all other women!*

29 But *when she saw him*, she was greatly troubled *and* disturbed *and* confused at what he said, and kept revolving in her mind what such a greeting might mean.

30 And the angel said to her, Do not be afraid, Mary, for you have found grace—[l]free, spontaneous, absolute favor and loving kindness—with God.

31 And listen! You will become pregnant and will give birth to a Son, and you shall call His name Jesus.

32 He will be great (eminent) and will be called the Son of the Most High; and the Lord God will give to Him the throne of His forefather David,

33 And He will reign over the house of Jacob throughout the ages, and of His reign there will be no end. [Isa. 9:6, 7; Dan. 2:44.]

34 And Mary said to the angel, How can this be, since I have no [intimacy with any man as a] husband?

35 Then the angel said to her, The Holy Spirit will come upon you, and the power of the Most High will overshadow you (as a shining cloud); and so the holy (pure, sinless) Thing which shall be born *of you*, will be called the Son of God. [Exod. 40:34; Isa. 7:14.]

36 And listen! Your relative Elizabeth in her old age has also conceived a son, and this is now the sixth month with her who was called barren;

37 For with God nothing is ever impossible, *and* no word from God shall be without power *or* impossible of fulfillment.

38 Then Mary said, Behold I am the handmaiden of the Lord; let it be done to me according to what you have said. And the angel left her.

39 And at that time Mary arose and went with haste into the hill country, to a town of Judah,

40 And she went to the house of Zachariah and entering it saluted Elizabeth.

**AMP** [a] Thayer. [b] Vincent. [c] Vincent. [d] Vincent. [e] Trench. [f] Vincent. [g] Trench. [h] Trench. [i] Vincent. [j] This Greek word, *parthenos* (virgin) is used in Isa. 7:14 in the Septuagint, the Greek O.T. translation Jesus read and quoted. [k] Literal translation. [l] Vincent.

## New American Standard

17"And it is he who will go *as a forerunner* before Him in the spirit and power of Elijah, TO TURN THE HEARTS OF THE FATHERS BACK TO THE CHILDREN, and the disobedient to the attitude of the righteous; so as to make ready a people prepared for the Lord."

18¶ And Zacharias said to the angel, "How shall I know this *for certain*? For I am an old man, and my wife is advanced in years."

19And the angel answered and said to him, "I am Gabriel, who stands in the presence of God; and I have been sent to speak to you, and to bring you this good news.

20"And behold, you shall be silent and unable to speak until the day when these things take place, because you did not believe my words, which shall be fulfilled in their proper time."

21And the people were waiting for Zacharias, and were wondering at his delay in the temple.

22But when he came out, he was unable to speak to them; and they realized that he had seen a vision in the temple; and he kept making signs to them, and remained mute.

23And it came about, when the days of his priestly service were ended, that he went back home.

24¶ And after these days Elizabeth his wife became pregnant; and she kept herself in seclusion for five months, saying,

25"This is the way the Lord has dealt with me in the days when He looked *with favor* upon *me*, to take away my disgrace among men."

*Jesus' Birth Foretold*

26¶ Now in the sixth month the angel Gabriel was sent from God to a city in Galilee, called Nazareth,

27to a virgin engaged to a man whose name was Joseph, of the descendants of David; and the virgin's name was Mary.

28And coming in, he said to her, "Hail, favored one! The Lord *is* with you."[m]

29But she was greatly troubled at *this* statement, and kept pondering what kind of salutation this might be.

30And the angel said to her, "Do not be afraid, Mary; for you have found favor with God.

31"And behold, you will conceive in your womb, and bear a son, and you shall name Him Jesus.

32"He will be great, and will be called the Son of the Most High; and the Lord God will give Him the throne of His father David;

33and He will reign over the house of Jacob forever; and His kingdom will have no end."

34And Mary said to the angel, "How can this be, since I am a virgin?"

35And the angel answered and said to her, "The Holy Spirit will come upon you, and the power of the Most High will overshadow you; and for that reason the holy offspring shall be called the Son of God.

36"And behold, even your relative Elizabeth has also conceived a son in her old age; and she who was called barren is now in her sixth month.

37"For nothing will be impossible with God."

38And Mary said, "Behold, the [n]bondslave of the Lord; be it done to me according to your word." And the angel departed from her.

*Mary Visits Elizabeth*

39¶ Now at this time Mary arose and went with haste to the hill country, to a city of Judah,

40and entered the house of Zacharias and greeted Elizabeth.

NAS [m]Later mss. add: *you are blessed among women* [n]I.e., female slave

## New International

will go on before the Lord, in the spirit and power of Elijah, to turn the hearts of the fathers to their children and the disobedient to the wisdom of the righteous—to make ready a people prepared for the Lord."

18Zechariah asked the angel, "How can I be sure of this? I am an old man and my wife is well along in years."

19The angel answered, "I am Gabriel. I stand in the presence of God, and I have been sent to speak to you and to tell you this good
news. 20And now you will be silent and not able to speak until the day this happens, because you did not believe my words, which will come true at their proper time."

21Meanwhile, the people were waiting for Zechariah and wondering why he stayed so long in the temple.
22When he came out, he could not speak to them. They realized he had seen a vision in the temple, for he kept making signs to them but remained unable to speak.

23When his time of service was completed, he returned home.
24After this his wife Elizabeth became pregnant and for five months remained in seclusion.
25"The Lord has done this for me," she said. "In these days he has shown his favor and taken away my disgrace among the people."

*The Birth of Jesus Foretold*

26In the sixth month, God sent the angel Gabriel to Nazareth, a town in Galilee,
27to a virgin pledged to be married to a man named Joseph, a descendant of David. The virgin's name was Mary.
28The angel went to her and said, "Greetings, you who are highly favored! The Lord is with you."

29Mary was greatly troubled at his words and wondered what kind of greeting this might be.
30But the angel said to her, "Do not be afraid, Mary, you have found favor with God.
31You will be with child and give birth to a son, and you are to give him the name Jesus.
32He will be great and will be called the Son of the Most High. The Lord God will give him the throne of his father David,
33and he will reign over the house of Jacob forever; his kingdom will never end."

34"How will this be," Mary asked the angel, "since I am a virgin?"

35The angel answered, "The Holy Spirit will come upon you, and the power of the Most High will overshadow you. So the holy one to be born will be called[o] the Son of God.
36Even Elizabeth your relative is going to have a child in her old age, and she who was said to be barren is in her sixth month.
37For nothing is impossible with God."

38"I am the Lord's servant," Mary answered. "May it be to me as you have said." Then the angel left her.

*Mary Visits Elizabeth*

39At that time Mary got ready and hurried to a town in the hill country of Judea,
40where she entered Zechariah's home and greeted Elizabeth.
41When Elizabeth heard Mary's greeting, the

NIV [o]35 Or *So the child to be born will be called holy,*

## King James

41And it came to pass, that, when Elisabeth heard the salutation of Mary, the babe leaped in her womb; and Elisabeth was filled with the Holy Ghost:

42And she spake out with a loud voice, and said, Blessed *art* thou among women, and blessed *is* the fruit of thy womb.

43And whence *is* this to me, that the mother of my Lord should come to me?

44For, lo, as soon as the voice of thy salutation sounded in mine ears, the babe leaped in my womb for joy.

45And blessed *is* she that believed: for there shall be a performance of those things which were told her from the Lord.

46And Mary said, My soul doth magnify the Lord,

47And my spirit hath rejoiced in God my Saviour.

48For he hath regarded the low estate of his handmaiden: for, behold, from henceforth all generations shall call me blessed.

49For he that is mighty hath done to me great things; and holy *is* his name.

50And his mercy *is* on them that fear him from generation to generation.

51He hath shown strength with his arm; he hath scattered the proud in the imagination of their hearts.

52He hath put down the mighty from *their* seats, and exalted them of low degree.

53He hath filled the hungry with good things; and the rich he hath sent empty away.

54He hath helped his servant Israel, in remembrance of *his* mercy;

55As he spake to our fathers, to Abraham, and to his seed for ever.

56And Mary abode with her about three months, and returned to her own house.

57Now Elisabeth's full time came that she should be delivered; and she brought forth a son.

58And her neighbours and her cousins heard how the Lord had shown great mercy upon her; and they rejoiced with her.

59And it came to pass, that on the eighth day they came to circumcise the child; and they called him Zacharias, after the name of his father.

60And his mother answered and said, Not *so;* but he shall be called John.

61And they said unto her, There is none of thy kindred that is called by this name.

62And they made signs to his father, how he would have him called.

63And he asked for a writing table, and wrote, saying, His name is John. And they marvelled all.

64And his mouth was opened immediately, and his tongue *loosed,* and he spake, and praised God.

65And fear came on all that dwelt round about them: and all these sayings were noised abroad throughout all the hill country of Judaea.

66And all they that heard *them* laid *them* up in their hearts, saying, What manner of child shall this be! And the hand of the Lord was with him.

67And his father Zacharias was filled with the Holy Ghost, and prophesied, saying,

68Blessed *be* the Lord God of Israel; for he hath visited and redeemed his people,

## Amplified

41And it occurred that when Elizabeth heard Mary's greeting, the baby leaped in her womb; and Elizabeth was filled with *and* controlled by the Holy Spirit,

42And she cried out with a loud cry, then exclaimed, Blessed—favored of God—above all other women are you! And blessed—favored of God—is the Fruit of your womb!

43And how [have I deserved that this honor should] be granted to me, that the mother of my Lord should come to me?

44For lo, the instant the sound of your salutation reached my ears, the baby in my womb leaped for joy.

45And blessed—happy, [a]to be envied—is she who believed that there would be a fulfillment of the things that were spoken to her from the Lord.

46And Mary said, My soul magnifies *and* extols the Lord,

47And my spirit rejoices in God my Savior;

48For He has looked upon the low station *and* humiliation of His handmaiden. For behold, from now on all generations (of all ages) will call me blessed *and* declare me happy *and* [b]to be envied!

49For He Who is almighty has done great things for me, and holy is His name—to be venerated in His purity, majesty and glory!

50And His mercy—His compassion and kindness toward the miserable and afflicted—is on those who fear Him with godly reverence, from generation to generation *and* age to age.

51He has shown strength *and* [c]made might with His arm; He has scattered the proud *and* haughty in *and* by the imagination *and* purpose *and* designs of their hearts;

52He has put down the mighty from their thrones, and exalted those of low degree.

53He has filled *and* satisfied the hungry with good things, and the rich He has sent away empty-handed—without a gift.

54He has laid hold on His servant Israel (to help him, to espouse his cause), in remembrance of His mercy,

55Even as He promised to our forefathers, to Abraham and to his descendants forever. [I Sam. 2:1-10; Mic. 7:20; Gen. 17:7; 18:18; 22:17.]

56And Mary remained with [Elizabeth] for about three months, and [then] returned to her [own] home.

57Now the time that Elizabeth should be delivered came, and she gave birth to a son.

58And her neighbors and relatives heard that the Lord had shown great mercy on her, and they rejoiced with her.

59And it occurred that on the eighth day when they came to circumcise the child, they were intending to call him Zachariah after his father; [Lev. 12:3; Gen. 17:12.]

60But his mother answered, Not so, but he shall be called John.

61And they said to her, None of your relatives is called by that name.

62And they inquired with signs of his father what he wanted to have him called.

63Then Zachariah asked for a writing tablet and wrote, His name is John. And they were all astonished.

64And at once his mouth was opened and his tongue [loosed], and he began to speak, blessing *and* praising *and* thanking God.

65And awe *and* reverential fear came on all their neighbors. And all these things were discussed throughout the hill country of Judea;

66And all who heard them laid them up in their hearts, saying, Whatever will this little boy be then? For the hand of the Lord was [ [d]so evidently] with him—protecting and aiding him.

67Now Zachariah his father was filled with *and* controlled by the Holy Spirit, and prophesied saying,

68Blessed—praised and extolled and thanked—be the Lord God of Israel, because He has come and brought deliverance *and* redemption to His people!

**AMP** [a] Souter's "Pocket Lexicon to the Greek New Testament." [b] Souter. [c] Wycliffe. [d] Some translators, quoted in Barnes' "Notes on Luke and John."

## New American Standard

41And it came about that when Elizabeth heard Mary's greeting,
the baby leaped in her womb; and Elizabeth was filled with the
Holy Spirit.
42And she cried out with a loud voice, and said, "Blessed
among women *are* you, and blessed *is* the fruit of your womb!
43"And how has it *happened* to me, that the mother of my Lord
should come to me?
44"For behold, when the sound of your greeting reached my
ears, the baby leaped in my womb for joy.
45"And blessed *is* she who believed that there would be a fulfillment of what had been spoken to her by the Lord."

*The Magnificat*

46And Mary said:
"My soul exalts the Lord,
47 "And my spirit has rejoiced in God my Savior.
48 "For He has had regard for the humble state of His
bondslave;
For behold, from this time on all generations will count
me blessed.
49 "For the Mighty One has done great things for me;
And holy is His name.
50 "AND HIS MERCY IS UPON GENERATION AFTER GENERATION
TOWARD THOSE WHO FEAR HIM.
51 "He has done mighty deeds with His arm;
He has scattered *those who were* proud in the thoughts
of their heart.
52 "He has brought down rulers from *their* thrones,
And has exalted those who were humble.
53 "HE HAS FILLED THE HUNGRY WITH GOOD THINGS;
And sent away the rich empty-handed.
54 "He has given help to Israel His servant,
In remembrance of His mercy,
55 As He spoke to our fathers,
To Abraham and his offspring forever."
56¶ And Mary stayed with her about three months, and *then*
returned to her home.

*John Is Born*

57¶ Now the time had come for Elizabeth to give birth, and she
brought forth a son.
58And her neighbors and her relatives heard that the Lord had
displayed His great mercy toward her; and they were rejoicing
with her.
59And it came about that on the eighth day they came to circumcise the child, and they were going to call him Zacharias, after his
father.
60And his mother answered and said, "No indeed; but he shall
be called John."
61And they said to her, "There is no one among your relatives
who is called by that name."
62And they made signs to his father, as to what he wanted him
called.
63And he asked for a tablet, and wrote as follows, "His name
is John." And they were all astonished.
64And at once his mouth was opened and his tongue *loosed,* and
he *began* to speak in praise of God.
65And fear came on all those living around them; and all these
matters were being talked about in all the hill country of Judea.
66And all who heard them kept them in mind, saying, "What
then will this child *turn out to* be?" For the hand of the Lord was
certainly with him.

*Zacharias' Prophecy*

67¶ And his father Zacharias was filled with the Holy Spirit, and
prophesied, saying:
68 "Blessed *be* the Lord God of Israel,
For He has visited us and accomplished redemption for
His people,

## New International

baby leaped in her womb, and Elizabeth was filled with the Holy
Spirit. 42In a loud voice she exclaimed: "Blessed are you among
women, and blessed is the child you will bear! 43But why am I so
favored, that the mother of my Lord should come to me? 44As soon
as the sound of your greeting reached my ears, the baby in my
womb leaped for joy. 45Blessed is she who has believed that what
the Lord has said to her will be accomplished!"

*Mary's Song*

46And Mary said:

"My soul glorifies the Lord
47 and my spirit rejoices in God my Savior,
48for he has been mindful
of the humble state of his servant.
From now on all generations will call me blessed,
49 for the Mighty One has done great things for me—
holy is his name.
50His mercy extends to those who fear him,
from generation to generation.
51He has performed mighty deeds with his arm;
he has scattered those who are proud in their inmost
thoughts.
52He has brought down rulers from their thrones
but has lifted up the humble.
53He has filled the hungry with good things
but has sent the rich away empty.
54He has helped his servant Israel,
remembering to be merciful
55to Abraham and his descendants forever,
even as he said to our fathers."

56Mary stayed with Elizabeth for about three months and then
returned home.

*The Birth of John the Baptist*

57When it was time for Elizabeth to have her baby, she gave
birth to a son. 58Her neighbors and relatives heard that the Lord
had shown her great mercy, and they shared her joy.
59On the eighth day they came to circumcise the child, and they
were going to name him after his father Zechariah, 60but his
mother spoke up and said, "No! He is to be called John."
61They said to her, "There is no one among your relatives who
has that name."
62Then they made signs to his father, to find out what he would
like to name the child. 63He asked for a writing tablet, and to
everyone's astonishment he wrote, "His name is John." 64Immedi-
ately his mouth was opened and his tongue was loosed, and he
began to speak, praising God. 65The neighbors were all filled with
awe, and throughout the hill country of Judea people were talking
about all these things. 66Everyone who heard this wondered about
it, asking, "What then is this child going to be?" For the Lord's
hand was with him.

*Zechariah's Song*

67His father Zechariah was filled with the Holy Spirit and
prophesied:

68"Praise be to the Lord, the God of Israel,
because he has come and has redeemed his people.

## King James

69 And hath raised up an horn of salvation for us in the house of his servant David;

70 As he spake by the mouth of his holy prophets, which have been since the world began:

71 That we should be saved from our enemies, and from the hand of all that hate us;

72 To perform the mercy *promised* to our fathers, and to remember his holy covenant;

73 The oath which he sware to our father Abraham,

74 That he would grant unto us, that we being delivered out of the hand of our enemies might serve him without fear,

75 In holiness and righteousness before him, all the days of our life.

76 And thou, child, shalt be called the prophet of the Highest: for thou shalt go before the face of the Lord to prepare his ways;

77 To give knowledge of salvation unto his people by the remission of their sins,

78 Through the tender mercy of our God; whereby the dayspring from on high hath visited us,

79 To give light to them that sit in darkness and *in* the shadow of death, to guide our feet into the way of peace.

80 And the child grew, and waxed strong in spirit, and was in the deserts till the day of his showing unto Israel.

**2** AND IT came to pass in those days, that there went out a decree from Caesar Augustus, that all the world should be taxed.

2 ( *And* this taxing was first made when Cyrenius was governor of Syria.)

3 And all went to be taxed, every one into his own city.

4 And Joseph also went up from Galilee, out of the city of Nazareth, into Judaea, unto the city of David, which is called Bethlehem; (because he was of the house and lineage of David:)

5 To be taxed with Mary his espoused wife, being great with child.

6 And so it was, that, while they were there, the days were accomplished that she should be delivered.

7 And she brought forth her firstborn son, and wrapped him in swaddling clothes, and laid him in a manger; because there was no room for them in the inn.

8 And there were in the same country shepherds abiding in the field, keeping watch over their flock by night.

9 And, lo, the angel of the Lord came upon them, and the glory of the Lord shone round about them: and they were sore afraid.

10 And the angel said unto them, Fear not: for, behold, I bring you good tidings of great joy, which shall be to all people.

11 For unto you is born this day in the city of David a Saviour, which is Christ the Lord.

12 And this *shall be* a sign unto you; Ye shall find the babe wrapped in swaddling clothes, lying in a manger.

13 And suddenly there was with the angel a multitude of the heavenly host praising God, and saying,

## Amplified

69 And He has raised up a Horn of salvation [that is, a mighty and valiant Helper, the Author of salvation] for us in the house of David His servant.

70 This is as He promised by the mouth of His holy prophets from the most ancient times (in the memory of man),

71 That we should have deliverance *and* be saved from our enemies, and from the hand of all who detest *and* pursue us with hatred;

72 To make true *and* show the mercy *and* compassion *and* kindness [promised] to our forefathers, and to remember *and* carry out His Holy covenant [to bless, which is [a]the more sacred because made by God Himself].

73 That covenant He sealed by oath to our forefather Abraham,

74 To grant us that we, being delivered from the hand of our foes, might serve Him fearlessly,

75 In holiness (divine consecration) and righteousness (that is, in accordance with the everlasting principles of right) within His presence all the days of our life.

76 And you, little one, shall be called prophet of the Most High; for you shall go before the face of the Lord to make ready His ways, [Isa. 40:3; Mal. 4:5.]

77 To bring *and* give the knowledge of salvation to His people in the forgiveness *and* remission of their sins.

78 Because of *and* through the heart of tender mercy *and* loving kindness of our God, a Light from on high will dawn upon us *and* visit [us], [Mal. 4:2.]

79 To shine upon *and* give light to those who sit in darkness and in the shadow of death, to direct *and* guide our feet in a straight line into [the] way of peace. [Isa. 9:2.]

80 And the little boy grew and became strong in spirit, and he was in the deserts (wildernesses) until the day of his appearing to Israel [the commencement of his public ministry].

**2** IN THOSE days it occurred that a decree went out from Caesar Augustus that the whole [b]Roman Empire should be registered.

2 This was the first enrollment and it was made when Quirinius was governor of Syria.

3 And all the people were going to be registered, each to his own city *or* town.

4 And Joseph also went up from Galilee from the town of Nazareth to Judea, to the town of David which is called Bethlehem, because he was of the house and family of David,

5 To be enrolled with Mary, his espoused ( [c]married) wife, who was about to become a mother.

6 And while they were there, the time came for her delivery.

7 And she gave birth to her Son, her first-born, and she wrapped Him in swaddling clothes, and laid Him in a manger, because there was no room *or* place for them in the inn.

8 And in that vicinity there were shepherds living (out under the open sky) in the field, watching (in shifts) over their flock by night.

9 And *behold*, an angel of the Lord stood by them, and the glory of the Lord flashed *and* shone all about them, and they were terribly frightened.

10 But the angel said to them, Do not be afraid, for behold, I bring you good news of a great joy which will come to all the people.

11 For to you is born this day in the town of David a Savior, Who is Christ, the Messiah, the Lord! [Mic. 5:2.]

12 And this will be a sign for you [by which you will recognize Him]: you will find [d]after searching, a Baby wrapped in swaddling clothes and lying in a manger. [I Sam. 2:34; II Kings 19:29; Isa. 7:14.]

13 Then suddenly there appeared with the angel an army of the troops of heaven— [e]a heavenly knighthood—praising God and saying,

**AMP** [a] Thayer. [b] Berry's "Greek-English New Testament Lexicon." [c] Vincent. Compare Matthew 1:20, 24, 25. Also Matthew 1:18, 19. [d] Thayer. [e] Wycliffe.

## New American Standard

69 And has raised up a horn of salvation for us
In the house of David His servant—
70 As He spoke by the mouth of His holy prophets from
of old—
71 Salvation FROM OUR ENEMIES,
And FROM THE HAND OF ALL WHO HATE US;
72 To show mercy toward our fathers,
And to remember His holy covenant,
73 The oath which He swore to Abraham our father,
74 To grant us that we, being delivered from the hand of
our enemies,
Might serve Him without fear,
75 In holiness and righteousness before Him all our days.
76 "And you, child, will be called the prophet of the Most
High;
For you will go on BEFORE THE LORD TO PREPARE HIS
WAYS;
77 To give to His people *the* knowledge of salvation
By the forgiveness of their sins,
78 Because of the tender mercy of our God,
With which the Sunrise from on high shall visit us,
79 TO SHINE UPON THOSE WHO SIT IN DARKNESS AND THE
SHADOW OF DEATH,
To guide our feet into the way of peace."

80¶ And the child continued to grow, and to become strong in spirit, and he lived in the deserts until the day of his public appearance to Israel.

*Jesus' Birth in Bethlehem*

2 NOW IT came about in those days that a decree went out
from Caesar Augustus, that a census be taken of all [f]the
inhabited earth.
2This was the first census taken while [g]Quirinius was governor of Syria.
3And all were proceeding to register for the census, everyone
to his own city.
4And Joseph also went up from Galilee, from the city of Nazareth, to Judea, to the city of David, which is called Bethlehem,
because he was of the house and family of David,
5in order to register, along with Mary, who was engaged to
him, and was with child.
6And it came about that while they were there, the days were
completed for her to give birth.
7And she gave birth to her first-born son; and she wrapped
Him in cloths, and laid Him in a manger, because there was no
room for them in the inn.
8¶ And in the same region there were *some* shepherds staying
out in the fields, and keeping watch over their flock by night.
9And an angel of the Lord suddenly stood before them, and
the glory of the Lord shone around them; and they were terribly
frightened.
10And the angel said to them, "Do not be afraid; for behold, I
bring you good news of a great joy which shall be for all the people;
11for today in the city of David there has been born for you a
Savior, who is [h]Christ the Lord.
12"And this *will be* a sign for you: you will find a baby wrapped
in cloths, and lying in a manger."
13And suddenly there appeared with the angel a multitude of
the heavenly host praising God, and saying,

NAS [f] I.e., the Roman empire [g] Gr., *Kyrenios* [h] I.e., Messiah

## New International

69He has raised up a horn[i] of salvation for us
in the house of his servant David
70(as he said through his holy prophets of long ago),
71salvation from our enemies
and from the hand of all who hate us—
72to show mercy to our fathers
and to remember his holy covenant,
73 the oath he swore to our father Abraham:
74to rescue us from the hand of our enemies,
and to enable us to serve him without fear
75 in holiness and righteousness before him all our days.

76And you, my child, will be called a prophet of the Most
High;
for you will go on before the Lord to prepare the way
for him,
77to give his people the knowledge of salvation
through the forgiveness of their sins,
78because of the tender mercy of our God,
by which the rising sun will come to us from heaven
79to shine on those living in darkness
and in the shadow of death,
to guide our feet into the path of peace."

80And the child grew and became strong in spirit; and he lived
in the desert until he appeared publicly to Israel.

*The Birth of Jesus*

2 IN THOSE days Caesar Augustus issued a decree that a census should be taken of the entire Roman world. 2(This was the
first census that took place while Quirinius was governor of Syria.)
3And everyone went to his own town to register.
4So Joseph also went up from the town of Nazareth in Galilee
to Judea, to Bethlehem the town of David, because he belonged to
the house and line of David. 5He went there to register with Mary,
who was pledged to be married to him and was expecting a child.
6While they were there, the time came for the baby to be born, 7and
she gave birth to her firstborn, a son. She wrapped him in cloths
and placed him in a manger, because there was no room for them
in the inn.

*The Shepherds and the Angels*

8And there were shepherds living out in the fields nearby,
keeping watch over their flocks at night. 9An angel of the Lord
appeared to them, and the glory of the Lord shone around them,
and they were terrified. 10But the angel said to them, "Do not be
afraid. I bring you good news of great joy that will be for all the
people. 11Today in the town of David a Savior has been born
to you; he is Christ[j] the Lord. 12This will be a sign to you: You will
find a baby wrapped in cloths and lying in a manger."
13Suddenly a great company of the heavenly host appeared
with the angel, praising God and saying,

NIV [i] 69 *Horn* here symbolizes strength. [j] 11 Or *Messiah*. "The Christ" (Greek) and "the Messiah" (Hebrew) both mean "the Anointed One"; also in verse 26.

## King James

14 Glory to God in the highest, and on earth peace, good will toward men.

15 And it came to pass, as the angels were gone away from them into heaven, the shepherds said one to another, Let us now go even unto Bethlehem, and see this thing which is come to pass, which the Lord hath made known unto us.

16 And they came with haste, and found Mary, and Joseph, and the babe lying in a manger.

17 And when they had seen *it*, they made known abroad the saying which was told them concerning this child.

18 And all they that heard *it* wondered at those things which were told them by the shepherds.

19 But Mary kept all these things, and pondered *them* in her heart.

20 And the shepherds returned, glorifying and praising God for all the things that they had heard and seen, as it was told unto them.

21 And when eight days were accomplished for the circumcising of the child, his name was called JESUS, which was so named of the angel before he was conceived in the womb.

22 And when the days of her purification according to the law of Moses were accomplished, they brought him to Jerusalem, to present *him* to the Lord;

23 (As it is written in the law of the Lord, Every male that openeth the womb shall be called holy to the Lord;)

24 And to offer a sacrifice according to that which is said in the law of the Lord, A pair of turtledoves, or two young pigeons.

25 And, behold, there was a man in Jerusalem, whose name *was* Simeon; and the same man *was* just and devout, waiting for the consolation of Israel: and the Holy Ghost was upon him.

26 And it was revealed unto him by the Holy Ghost, that he should not see death, before he had seen the Lord's Christ.

27 And he came by the Spirit into the temple: and when the parents brought in the child Jesus, to do for him after the custom of the law,

28 Then took he him up in his arms, and blessed God, and said,

29 Lord, now lettest thou thy servant depart in peace, according to thy word:

30 For mine eyes have seen thy salvation,

31 Which thou hast prepared before the face of all people;

32 A light to lighten the Gentiles, and the glory of thy people Israel.

33 And Joseph and his mother marvelled at those things which were spoken of him.

34 And Simeon blessed them, and said unto Mary his mother, Behold, this *child* is set for the fall and rising again of many in Israel; and for a sign which shall be spoken against;

35 (Yea, a sword shall pierce through thy own soul also,) that the thoughts of many hearts may be revealed.

36 And there was one Anna, a prophetess, the daughter of Phanuel, of the tribe of Aser: she was of a great age, and had lived with an husband seven years from her virginity;

37 And she *was* a widow of about fourscore and four years, which departed not from the temple, but served *God* with fastings and prayers night and day.

38 And she coming in that instant gave thanks likewise unto the Lord, and spake of him to all them that looked for redemption in Jerusalem.

**AMP** [a] Wycliffe. [b] Vincent. [c] Thayer. [d] Vincent. [e] Vincent. [f] Trench. [g] Vincent. [h] Trench.

## Amplified

14 Glory to God in the highest [heaven], and on earth peace among men with whom He is well-pleased— [a] men of good will, of His favor.

15 When the angels went away from them into heaven, the shepherds said one to another, Let us go over to Bethlehem and see this thing ( [b]saying) that has come to pass, which the Lord has made known to us.

16 So they went with haste, and ( [c]by searching) found Mary and Joseph, and the Baby lying in a manger.

17 And when they saw it, they made known what had been told them concerning this Child;

18 And all who heard it were astounded *and* marvelled at what the shepherds told them.

19 But Mary was keeping [d]within herself all these things ( [e]sayings), weighing *and* pondering them in her heart.

20 And the shepherds returned, glorifying and praising God for all things they had heard and seen, just as it had been told them.

21 And at the end of eight days, when [the Baby] was to be circumcised, He was called Jesus, the name given by the angel before He was conceived in the womb.

22 And when the time for their purification [the mother's purification and the Baby's dedication] came according to the Law of Moses, they brought Him up to Jerusalem to present Him to the Lord, [Lev. 12:1-4.]

23 As it is written in the Law of the Lord, Every [first-born] male that opens the womb shall be set apart *and* dedicated *and* called holy to the Lord. [Exod. 13:1, 2, 12; Num. 8:17.]

24 And [they came also] to offer a sacrifice according to what is said in the Law of the Lord, a pair of turtledoves or two young pigeons. [Lev. 12:6-8.]

25 Now there was a man in Jerusalem whose name was Simeon, and this man was righteous and devout—cautiously and carefully observing the divine Law—and looking for the Consolation of Israel.

26 And the Holy Spirit was upon him and it had been divinely revealed (communicated) to him by the Holy Spirit that he should not see death before he had seen the Lord's Christ, the Messiah, the Anointed One.

27 And prompted by the (Holy) Spirit he came into the temple [f]enclosure; and when the parents brought in the little child Jesus, to do for Him what was customary according to the Law,

28 [Simeon] took Him up in his arms and praised *and* thanked God and said,

29 And now, Lord, You are releasing Your servant to depart (leave this world) in peace, according to Your word.

30 For with my [own] eyes I have seen Your Salvation [Isa. 52:10.]

31 Which You have ordained *and* prepared before (in the presence of) all peoples,

32 A Light for [g]revelation to the Gentiles—to disclose what was before unknown—and [to bring] praise *and* honor *and* glory to Your people Israel. [Isa. 42:6; 49:6.]

33 And His [legal] father and [His] mother were marvelling at what was said about Him;

34 And Simeon blessed them and said to Mary His mother, Behold, this Child is appointed *and* destined for the fall and rising of many in Israel, and for a sign that is spoken against, [Isa. 8:14, 15.]

35 And a sword will pierce through your own soul also, that the secret thoughts *and* purposes of many hearts may be brought out *and* disclosed.

36 And there was also a prophetess, Anna, the daughter of Phanuel of the tribe of Asher. She was very old, having lived with her husband seven years from her maidenhood, [Josh. 19:24.]

37 And as a widow even for eighty-four years. She did not go out from the temple [h]enclosure, but was worshiping night and day with fasting and prayer.

38 And she too came up that same hour and she returned thanks to God, and talked of [Jesus] to all who were looking for the redemption (deliverance) of Jerusalem.

## New American Standard

14 "Glory to God in the highest,
And on earth peace among men [i]with whom He is
pleased."
15 And it came about when the angels had gone away from them
into heaven, that the shepherds *began* saying to one another, "Let
us go straight to Bethlehem then, and see this thing that has
happened which the Lord has made known to us."
16 And they came in haste and found their way to Mary and
Joseph, and the baby as He lay in the manger.
17 And when they had seen this, they made known the
statement which had been told them about this Child.
18 And all who heard it wondered at the things which were told
them by the shepherds.
19 But Mary treasured up all these things, pondering them in her
heart.
20 And the shepherds went back, glorifying and praising God
for all that they had heard and seen, just as had been told them.

*Jesus Presented at the Temple*

**21**¶ And when eight days were completed before His circumcision, His name was *then* called Jesus, the name given by the angel
before He was conceived in the womb.
**22**¶ And when the days for their purification according to the
law of Moses were completed, they brought Him up to Jerusalem
to present Him to the Lord
23 (as it is written in the Law of the Lord, "EVERY *first-born* MALE
THAT OPENS THE WOMB SHALL BE CALLED HOLY TO THE LORD"),
24 and to offer a sacrifice according to what was said in the Law
of the Lord, "A PAIR OF TURTLEDOVES, OR TWO YOUNG PIGEONS."
25 And behold, there was a man in Jerusalem whose name was
Simeon; and this man was righteous and devout, looking for the
consolation of Israel; and the Holy Spirit was upon him.
26 And it had been revealed to him by the Holy Spirit that he
would not see death before he had seen the Lord's Christ.
27 And he came in the Spirit into the temple; and when the
parents brought in the child Jesus, to carry out for Him the custom
of the Law,
28 then he took Him into his arms, and blessed God, and said,
29 "Now Lord, Thou dost let Thy bond-servant depart
In peace, according to Thy word;
30 For my eyes have seen Thy salvation,
31 Which Thou hast prepared in the presence of all
peoples,
32 A LIGHT OF REVELATION TO THE GENTILES,
And the glory of Thy people Israel."
33 And His father and mother were amazed at the things which
were being said about Him.
34 And Simeon blessed them, and said to Mary His mother,
"Behold, this *Child* is appointed for the fall and rise of many in
Israel, and for a sign to be opposed—
35 and a sword will pierce even your own soul—to the end that
thoughts from many hearts may be revealed."
36 And there was a prophetess, Anna the daughter of Phanuel,
of the tribe of Asher. She was advanced in years, having lived with
a husband seven years after her marriage,
37 and then as a widow to the age of eighty-four. And she never
left the temple, serving night and day with fastings and prayers.
38 And at that very moment she came up and *began* giving
thanks to God, and continued to speak of Him to all those who
were looking for the redemption of Jerusalem.

NAS [i] Lit., *of good pleasure;* or possibly, *of good will*

## New International

14 "Glory to God in the highest,
and on earth peace to men on whom his favor rests."
15 When the angels had left them and gone into heaven, the
shepherds said to one another, "Let's go to Bethlehem and see this
thing that has happened, which the Lord has told us about."
16 So they hurried off and found Mary and Joseph, and the baby,
who was lying in the manger. 17 When they had seen him, they
spread the word concerning what had been told them about this
child, 18 and all who heard it were amazed at what the shepherds
said to them. 19 But Mary treasured up all these things and pondered them in her heart. 20 The shepherds returned, glorifying and
praising God for all the things they had heard and seen, which
were just as they had been told.

*Jesus Presented in the Temple*

21 On the eighth day, when it was time to circumcise him, he
was named Jesus, the name the angel had given him before he had
been conceived.
22 When the time of their purification according to the Law of
Moses had been completed, Joseph and Mary took him to Jerusalem to present him to the Lord 23 (as it is written in the Law of the
Lord, "Every firstborn male is to be consecrated to the Lord"[j] ),
24 and to offer a sacrifice in keeping with what is said in the Law
of the Lord: "a pair of doves or two young pigeons."[k]
25 Now there was a man in Jerusalem called Simeon, who was
righteous and devout. He was waiting for the consolation of Israel,
and the Holy Spirit was upon him. 26 It had been revealed to him
by the Holy Spirit that he would not die before he had seen the
Lord's Christ. 27 Moved by the Spirit, he went into the temple
courts. When the parents brought in the child Jesus to do for him
what the custom of the Law required, 28 Simeon took him in his
arms and praised God, saying:

29 "Sovereign Lord, as you have promised,
you now dismiss[l] your servant in peace.
30 For my eyes have seen your salvation,
31 which you have prepared in the sight of all people,
32 a light for revelation to the Gentiles
and for glory to your people Israel."

33 The child's father and mother marveled at what was said
about him. 34 Then Simeon blessed them and said to Mary, his
mother: "This child is destined to cause the falling and rising of
many in Israel, and to be a sign that will be spoken against, 35 so
that the thoughts of many hearts will be revealed. And a sword
will pierce your own soul too."
36 There was also a prophetess, Anna, the daughter of Phanuel,
of the tribe of Asher. She was very old; she had lived with her
husband seven years after her marriage, 37 and then was a widow
until she was eighty-four.[m] She never left the temple but worshiped night and day, fasting and praying. 38 Coming up to them
at that very moment, she gave thanks to God and spoke about the
child to all who were looking forward to the redemption of Jerusalem.

NIV [j] 23 Exodus 13:2,12 [k] 24 Lev. 12:8 [l] 29 Or *promised, / now dismiss*
[m] 37 Or *widow for eighty-four years*

## King James

39 And when they had performed all things according to the law of the Lord, they returned into Galilee, to their own city Nazareth.

40 And the child grew, and waxed strong in spirit, filled with wisdom: and the grace of God was upon him.

41 Now his parents went to Jerusalem every year at the feast of the passover.

42 And when he was twelve years old, they went up to Jerusalem after the custom of the feast.

43 And when they had fulfilled the days, as they returned, the child Jesus tarried behind in Jerusalem; and Joseph and his mother knew not *of it*.

44 But they, supposing him to have been in the company, went a day's journey; and they sought him among *their* kinsfolk and acquaintance.

45 And when they found him not, they turned back again to Jerusalem, seeking him.

46 And it came to pass, that after three days they found him in the temple, sitting in the midst of the doctors, both hearing them, and asking them questions.

47 And all that heard him were astonished at his understanding and answers.

48 And when they saw him, they were amazed: and his mother said unto him, Son, why hast thou thus dealt with us? behold, thy father and I have sought thee sorrowing.

49 And he said unto them, How is it that ye sought me? wist ye not that I must be about my Father's business?

50 And they understood not the saying which he spake unto them.

51 And he went down with them, and came to Nazareth, and was subject unto them: but his mother kept all these sayings in her heart.

52 And Jesus increased in wisdom and stature, and in favour with God and man.

3 NOW IN the fifteenth year of the reign of Tiberius Caesar, Pontius Pilate being governor of Judaea, and Herod being tetrarch of Galilee, and his brother Philip tetrarch of Ituraea and of the region of Trachonitis, and Lysanias the tetrarch of Abilene,

2 Annas and Caiaphas being the high priests, the word of God came unto John the son of Zacharias in the wilderness.

3 And he came into all the country about Jordan, preaching the baptism of repentance for the remission of sins;

4 As it is written in the book of the words of Esaias the prophet, saying, The voice of one crying in the wilderness, Prepare ye the way of the Lord, make his paths straight.

5 Every valley shall be filled, and every mountain and hill shall be brought low; and the crooked shall be made straight, and the rough ways *shall be* made smooth;

6 And all flesh shall see the salvation of God.

7 Then said he to the multitude that came forth to be baptized of him, O generation of vipers, who hath warned you to flee from the wrath to come?

8 Bring forth therefore fruits worthy of repentance, and begin not to say within yourselves, We have Abraham to *our* father: for I say unto you, That God is able of these stones to raise up children unto Abraham.

## Amplified

39 And when they had done everything according to the Law of the Lord, they went back into Galilee to their own town, Nazareth.

40 And the Child grew and became strong *in spirit*, filled with wisdom, and the grace (favor and spiritual blessing) of God was upon Him. [Judg. 13:24; I Sam. 2:26.]

41 Now His parents went to Jerusalem every year to the Passover feast. [Deut. 16:1-8; Exod. 23:15.]

42 And when He was twelve years [old], they went up as was their custom.

43 And when the feast was ended, as they were returning, the boy Jesus remained behind in Jerusalem. Now His parents did not know this,

44 But supposing Him to be in the caravan they travelled on a day's journey, and [then] they sought Him (diligently, looking up and down for Him) among their kinsfolk and acquaintances.

45 And when they failed to find Him, they went back to Jerusalem, looking for Him (up and down) all the way.

46 After three days they found Him; [came upon Him] in the [a](court of the) temple, sitting among the teachers, listening to them and asking them questions.

47 And all who heard Him were astonished *and* overwhelmed with bewildered wonder at His intelligence *and* understanding and His replies.

48 And when they [Joseph and Mary] saw Him they were amazed, and His mother said to Him, Child, why have You treated us like this? Here Your father and I have been anxiously looking for You—distressed *and* tormented.

49 And He said to them, How is it that you had to look for Me? Did you not see *and* know that it is necessary (as a duty) for Me [b]to be in My Father's house, *and* [occupied] about My Father's business?

50 But they did not comprehend what He was saying to them.

51 And He went down with them and came to Nazareth, and was (habitually) obedient to them; and his mother kept *and* closely *and* persistently guarded all these things in her heart.

52 And Jesus increased in wisdom (in broad and full understanding), and in stature *and* [c]years, and in favor with God and man.

3 IN THE fifteenth year of Tiberius Caesar's reign, when Pontius Pilate was governor of Judea, and Herod was tetrarch of Galilee, and his brother Philip tetrarch of the region of Iturea and Trachonitis, and Lysanias tetrarch of Abilene,

2 In the high priesthood of Annas and Caiaphas, the Word of God [ [d]concerning the attainment through Christ of salvation in the kingdom of God], came to John the son of Zachariah in the wilderness (desert).

3 And he went into all the country round about the Jordan, preaching a baptism of repentance (that is, [e]of hearty amending of their ways with abhorrence for past wrongdoing) unto the forgiveness of sin.

4 As it is written in the book of the words of Isaiah the prophet, The voice of one crying in the wilderness (shouting in the desert): Prepare the way of the Lord; make His beaten paths straight.

5 Every valley *and* ravine shall be filled up, and every mountain and hill shall be leveled down, and the crooked places shall be made straight, and the rough roads shall be made smooth;

6 And all mankind shall see (behold and [f]understand [and at last acknowledge]) the salvation of God—the deliverance from eternal death [g]decreed by God. [Isa. 40:3-5.]

7 So he said to the crowds that came out to be baptized by him, You offspring of vipers! Who [h]secretly warned you to flee from the coming wrath?

8 Bear fruits that are deserving *and* consistent with [i]your repentance—[that is,] [j]conduct worthy of a heart changed and abhorring sin. And do not begin to say to yourselves, We have Abraham as our father; for I tell you God is able from these stones to raise up descendants for Abraham.

**AMP** [a] Trench. [b] Literally, "in the things of My Father." [c] Alternate reading. [d] Thayer. [e] Thayer. [f] Gray and Adams Bible Commentary. [g] Thayer. [h] Literal meaning. [i] Alternate reading (ASV). [j] Thayer.

## New American Standard

*Return to Nazareth*

39¶ And when they had performed everything according to the Law of the Lord, they returned to Galilee, to their own city of Nazareth.

40And the Child continued to grow and become strong, increasing in wisdom; and the grace of God was upon Him.

*Visit to Jerusalem*

41¶ And His parents used to go to Jerusalem every year at the Feast of the Passover.

42And when He became twelve, they went up *there* according to the custom of the Feast;

43and as they were returning, after spending the full number of days, the boy Jesus stayed behind in Jerusalem. And His parents were unaware of it,

44but supposed Him to be in the caravan, and went a day's journey; and they *began* looking for Him among their relatives and acquaintances.

45And when they did not find Him, they returned to Jerusalem, looking for Him.

46And it came about that after three days they found Him in the temple, sitting in the midst of the teachers, both listening to them, and asking them questions.

47And all who heard Him were amazed at His understanding and His answers.

48And when they saw Him, they were astonished; and His mother said to Him, "Son, why have You treated us this way? Behold, Your father and I have been anxiously looking for You."

49And He said to them, "Why is it that you were looking for Me? Did you not know that I had to be in My Father's *house?*"

50And they did not understand the statement which He had made to them.

51And He went down with them, and came to Nazareth; and He continued in subjection to them; and His mother treasured all *these* things in her heart.

52¶ And Jesus kept increasing in wisdom and stature, and in favor with God and men.

*John the Baptist Preaches*

**3** NOW IN the fifteenth year of the reign of Tiberius Caesar, when Pontius Pilate was governor of Judea, and Herod was tetrarch of Galilee, and his brother Philip was tetrarch of the region of Ituraea and Trachonitis, and Lysanias was tetrarch of Abilene,

2in the high priesthood of Annas and Caiaphas, the word of God came to John, the son of Zacharias, in the wilderness.

3And he came into all the district around the Jordan, preaching a baptism of repentance for the forgiveness of sins;

4as it is written in the book of the words of Isaiah the prophet,
"THE VOICE OF ONE CRYING IN THE WILDERNESS,
'MAKE READY THE WAY OF THE LORD,
MAKE HIS PATHS STRAIGHT.
5 'EVERY RAVINE SHALL BE FILLED UP,
AND EVERY MOUNTAIN AND HILL SHALL BE BROUGHT LOW;
AND THE CROOKED SHALL BECOME STRAIGHT,
AND THE ROUGH ROADS SMOOTH;
6 AND ALL FLESH SHALL SEE THE SALVATION OF GOD.' "

7¶ He therefore *began* saying to the multitudes who were going out to be baptized by him, "You brood of vipers, who warned you to flee from the wrath to come?

8"Therefore bring forth fruits in keeping with repentance, and do not begin to say to yourselves, 'We have Abraham for our father,' for I say to you that God is able from these stones to raise up children to Abraham.

## New International

39When Joseph and Mary had done everything required by the
Law of the Lord, they returned to Galilee to their own town of
Nazareth. 40And the child grew and became strong; he was filled
with wisdom, and the grace of God was upon him.

*The Boy Jesus at the Temple*

41Every year his parents went to Jerusalem for the Feast of the
Passover. 42When he was twelve years old, they went up to the
Feast, according to the custom. 43After the Feast was over, while
his parents were returning home, the boy Jesus stayed behind in
Jerusalem, but they were unaware of it. 44Thinking he was in their
company, they traveled on for a day. Then they began looking for
him among their relatives and friends. 45When they did not find
him, they went back to Jerusalem to look for him. 46After three
days they found him in the temple courts, sitting among the teachers, listening to them and asking them questions. 47Everyone who
heard him was amazed at his understanding and his answers.
48When his parents saw him, they were astonished. His mother
said to him, "Son, why have you treated us like this? Your father
and I have been anxiously searching for you."
49"Why were you searching for me?" he asked. "Didn't you
know I had to be in my Father's house?" 50But they did not understand what he was saying to them.
51Then he went down to Nazareth with them and was obedient
to them. But his mother treasured all these things in her heart.
52And Jesus grew in wisdom and stature, and in favor with God
and men.

*John the Baptist Prepares the Way*

**3** IN THE fifteenth year of the reign of Tiberius Caesar—when
Pontius Pilate was governor of Judea, Herod tetrarch of Galilee, his brother Philip tetrarch of Iturea and Traconitis, and Lysanias tetrarch of Abilene— 2during the high priesthood of Annas
and Caiaphas, the word of God came to John son of Zechariah in
the desert. 3He went into all the country around the Jordan,
preaching a baptism of repentance for the forgiveness of sins. 4As
is written in the book of the words of Isaiah the prophet:
"A voice of one calling in the desert,
'Prepare the way for the Lord,
make straight paths for him.
5Every valley shall be filled in,
every mountain and hill made low.
The crooked roads shall become straight,
the rough ways smooth.
6And all mankind will see God's salvation.' "[k]

7John said to the crowds coming out to be baptized by him,
"You brood of vipers! Who warned you to flee from the coming
wrath? 8Produce fruit in keeping with repentance. And do not
begin to say to yourselves, 'We have Abraham as our father.' For
I tell you that out of these stones God can raise up children for
Abraham. 9The ax is already at the root of the trees, and every tree

NIV [k] 6 Isaiah 40:3-5

## King James

9And now also the axe is laid unto the root of the trees: every tree therefore which bringeth not forth good fruit is hewn down, and cast into the fire.

10And the people asked him, saying, What shall we do then?

11He answereth and saith unto them, He that hath two coats, let him impart to him that hath none; and he that hath meat, let him do likewise.

12Then came also publicans to be baptized, and said unto him, Master, what shall we do?

13And he said unto them, Exact no more than that which is appointed you.

14And the soldiers likewise demanded of him, saying, And what shall we do? And he said unto them, Do violence to no man, neither accuse *any* falsely; and be content with your wages.

15And as the people were in expectation, and all men mused in their hearts of John, whether he were the Christ, or not;

16John answered, saying unto *them* all, I indeed baptize you with water; but one mightier than I cometh, the latchet of whose shoes I am not worthy to unloose: he shall baptize you with the Holy Ghost and with fire:

17Whose fan *is* in his hand, and he will thoroughly purge his floor, and will gather the wheat into his garner; but the chaff he will burn with fire unquenchable.

18And many other things in his exhortation preached he unto the people.

19But Herod the tetrarch, being reproved by him for Herodias his brother Philip's wife, and for all the evils which Herod had done,

20Added yet this above all, that he shut up John in prison.

21Now when all the people were baptized, it came to pass, that Jesus also being baptized, and praying, the heaven was opened,

22And the Holy Ghost descended in a bodily shape like a dove upon him, and a voice came from heaven, which said, Thou art my beloved Son; in thee I am well pleased.

23And Jesus himself began to be about thirty years of age, being (as was supposed) the son of Joseph, which was *the son* of Heli,

24Which was *the son* of Matthat, which was *the son* of Levi, which was *the son* of Melchi, which was *the son* of Janna, which was *the son* of Joseph,

25Which was *the son* of Mattathias, which was *the son* of Amos, which was *the son* of Naum, which was *the son* of Esli, which was *the son* of Nagge,

26Which was *the son* of Maath, which was *the son* of Mattathias, which was *the son* of Semei, which was *the son* of Joseph, which was *the son* of Judah,

27Which was *the son* of Joanna, which was *the son* of Rhesa, which was *the son* of Zorobabel, which was *the son* of Salathiel, which was *the son* of Neri,

28Which was *the son* of Melchi, which was *the son* of Addi, which was *the son* of Cosam, which was *the son* of Elmodam, which was *the son* of Er,

29Which was *the son* of Jose, which was *the son* of Eliezer, which was *the son* of Jorim, which was *the son* of Matthat, which was *the son* of Levi,

30Which was *the son* of Simeon, which was *the son* of Judah, which was *the son* of Joseph, which was *the son* of Jonan, which was *the son* of Eliakim,

31Which was *the son* of Melea, which was *the son* of Menan, which was *the son* of Mattatha, which was *the son* of Nathan, which was *the son* of David,

32Which was *the son* of Jesse, which was *the son* of Obed, which was *the son* of Booz, which was *the son* of Salmon, which was *the son* of Naasson,

33Which was *the son* of Aminadab, which was *the son* of Aram, which was *the son* of Esrom, which was *the son* of Phares, which was *the son* of Judah,

## Amplified

9Even now the ax is laid to the root of the trees, so that every tree that does not bear good fruit is cut down and cast into the fire.

10And the multitudes asked him, Then what shall we do?

11And he replied to them, He who has two tunics (undergarments), let him share with him who has none; and he who has food, let him do the same way.

12Even tax collectors came to be baptized, and they said to him, Teacher, what shall we do?

13And he said to them, Exact *and* collect no more than the fixed amount appointed you.

14Those serving as soldiers also asked him, And we, what shall we do? And he replied to them, Never demand *or* enforce [a]by terrifying people or by accusing wrongfully, and always be satisfied with your rations (supplies) *and* with your allowance (wages).

15As the people were in suspense *and* waiting expectantly, and everybody reasoned *and* questioned in their hearts concerning John whether he perhaps might be the Christ, the Messiah, the Anointed One,

16John answered them all by saying, I baptize you with water, but He Who is mightier than I is coming, the strap of Whose sandals I am not fit to unfasten; He will baptize you with the Holy Spirit and with fire.

17His winnowing shovel (fork) is in His hand, to thoroughly clear *and* cleanse His [threshing] floor, and to gather the wheat *and* store it in His granary, but the chaff He will burn with fire that cannot be extinguished.

18So, with many other (various) appeals and admonitions, he preached the good news (the Gospel) to the people.

19But Herod the tetrarch, who had been (repeatedly) told his fault *and* reproved *with* rebuke [b]producing conviction, by *John* for [having] Herodias, his brother's wife, and for all the wicked things that Herod had done,

20Added this to them all, that he shut up John in prison.

21Now when all the people were baptized, and when Jesus also had been baptized, and [while He was still] praying, the (visible) heaven was opened,

22And the Holy Spirit descended upon Him in bodily form, like a dove, and a voice came from heaven, *saying*, You are My Son, the Beloved! In You I am well pleased *and* find delight! [Ps. 2:7; Isa. 42:1.]

23Jesus Himself, when He began [His ministry], was about thirty years of age, being the Son, as was supposed, of Joseph, the son of Heli,

24The son of Matthat, the son of Levi, the son of Melchi, the son of Jannai, the son of Joseph,

25The son of Mattathias, the son of Amos, the son of Nahum, the son of Esli, the son of Naggai,

26The son of Maath, the son of Mattathias, the son of Semein, the son of Josech, the son of Joda,

27The son of Joanan, the son of Rhesa, the son of Zerubbabel, the son of Shealtiel, the son of Neri,

28The son of Melchi, the son of Addi, the son of Cosam, the son of Elmadam, the son of Er,

29The son of Jesus, the son of Eliezer, the son of Jorim, the son of Matthat, the son of Levi,

30The son of Symeon, the son of Judas, the son of Joseph, the son of Jonam, the son of Eliakim,

31The son of Melea, the son of Menna, the son of Mattatha, the son of Nathan, the son of David,

32The son of Jesse, the son of Obed, the son of Boaz, the son of Salmon (Sala), the son of Nahshon,

33The son of Adminadab, (the son of Admin), the son of Arni, the son of Hezron, the son of Perez, the son of Judah,

**AMP** [a] Vincent. [b] Vincent.

## New American Standard

9"And also the axe is already laid at the root of the trees; every
tree therefore that does not bear good fruit is cut down and thrown
into the fire."
10And the multitudes were questioning him, saying, "Then
what shall we do?"
11And he would answer and say to them, "Let the man who has
two tunics share with him who has none; and let him who has food
do likewise."
12And *some* [c]tax-gatherers also came to be baptized, and they
said to him, "Teacher, what shall we do?"
13And he said to them, "Collect no more than what you have
been ordered to."
14And *some* [d]soldiers were questioning him, saying, "And *what
about* us, what shall we do?" And he said to them, "Do not take
money from anyone by force, or accuse *anyone* falsely, and be
content with your wages."
**15**¶ Now while the people were in a state of expectation and all
were wondering in their hearts about John, as to whether he might
be the Christ,
16John answered and said to them all, "As for me, I baptize you
with water; but One is coming who is mightier than I, and I am
not fit to untie the thong of His sandals; He will baptize you with
the Holy Spirit and fire.
17"And His winnowing fork is in His hand to thoroughly clear
His threshing floor, and to gather the wheat into His barn; but He
will burn up the chaff with unquenchable fire."
**18**¶ So with many other exhortations also he preached the gospel to the people.
19But when Herod the tetrarch was reproved by him on account
of Herodias, his brother's wife, and on account of all the wicked
things which Herod had done,
20he added this also to them all, that he locked John up in
prison.

*Jesus Is Baptized*

**21**¶ Now it came about when all the people were baptized, that
Jesus also was baptized, and while He was praying, heaven was
opened,
22and the Holy Spirit descended upon Him in bodily form like
a dove, and a voice came out of heaven, "Thou art My beloved
Son, in Thee I am well-pleased."

*Genealogy of Jesus*

**23**¶ And when He began His ministry, Jesus Himself was about
thirty years of age, being supposedly *the* son of Joseph, the *son* of
Eli,
24the *son* of Matthat, the *son* of Levi, the *son* of Melchi, the *son*
of Jannai, the *son* of Joseph,
25the *son* of Mattathias, the *son* of Amos, the *son* of Nahum, the
*son* of Hesli, the *son* of Naggai,
26the *son* of Maath, the *son* of Mattathias, the *son* of Semein, the
*son* of Josech, the *son* of Joda,
27the *son* of Joanan, the *son* of Rhesa, the *son* of Zerubbabel, the
*son* of Shealtiel, the *son* of Neri,
28the *son* of Melchi, the *son* of Addi, the *son* of Cosam, the *son*
of Elmadam, the *son* of Er,
29the *son* of Joshua, the *son* of Eliezer, the *son* of Jorim, the *son*
of Matthat, the *son* of Levi,
30the *son* of Simeon, the *son* of Judah, the *son* of Joseph, the *son*
of Jonam, the *son* of Eliakim,
31the *son* of Melea, the *son* of Menna, the *son* of Mattatha, the
*son* of Nathan, the *son* of David,
32the *son* of Jesse, the *son* of Obed, the *son* of Boaz, the *son* of
Salmon, the *son* of Nahshon,
33the *son* of Amminadab, the *son* of Admin, the *son* of Ram, the
*son* of Hezron, the *son* of Perez, the *son* of Judah,

NAS [c] I.e., Collectors of Roman taxes for profit [d] I.e., men in active military service

## New International

that does not produce good fruit will be cut down and thrown into
the fire."
10"What should we do then?" the crowd asked.
11John answered, "The man with two tunics should share with
him who has none, and the one who has food should do the
same."
12Tax collectors also came to be baptized. "Teacher," they
asked, "what should we do?"
13"Don't collect any more than you are required to," he told
them.
14Then some soldiers asked him, "And what should we do?"
He replied, "Don't extort money and don't accuse people falsely—be content with your pay."
15The people were waiting expectantly and were all wondering
in their hearts if John might possibly be the Christ.[e] 16John answered them all, "I baptize you with[f] water. But one more powerful than I will come, the thongs of whose sandals I am not worthy
to untie. He will baptize you with the Holy Spirit and with fire.
17His winnowing fork is in his hand to clear his threshing floor and
to gather the wheat into his barn, but he will burn up the chaff with
unquenchable fire." 18And with many other words John exhorted
the people and preached the good news to them.
19But when John rebuked Herod the tetrarch because of Herodias, his brother's wife, and all the other evil things he had done,
20Herod added this to them all: He locked John up in prison.

*The Baptism and Genealogy of Jesus*

21When all the people were being baptized, Jesus was baptized
too. And as he was praying, heaven was opened 22and the Holy
Spirit descended on him in bodily form like a dove. And a voice
came from heaven: "You are my Son, whom I love; with you I am
well pleased."
23Now Jesus himself was about thirty years old when he began
his ministry. He was the son, so it was thought, of Joseph,
the son of Heli, 24the son of Matthat,
the son of Levi, the son of Melki,
the son of Jannai, the son of Joseph,
25the son of Mattathias, the son of Amos,
the son of Nahum, the son of Esli,
the son of Naggai, 26the son of Maath,
the son of Mattathias, the son of Semein,
the son of Josech, the son of Joda,
27the son of Joanan, the son of Rhesa,
the son of Zerubbabel, the son of Shealtiel,
the son of Neri, 28the son of Melki,
the son of Addi, the son of Cosam,
the son of Elmadam, the son of Er,
29the son of Joshua, the son of Eliezer,
the son of Jorim, the son of Matthat,
the son of Levi, 30the son of Simeon,
the son of Judah, the son of Joseph,
the son of Jonam, the son of Eliakim,
31the son of Melea, the son of Menna,
the son of Mattatha, the son of Nathan,
the son of David, 32the son of Jesse,
the son of Obed, the son of Boaz,
the son of Salmon,[g] the son of Nahshon,
33the son of Amminadab, the son of Ram,[h]
the son of Hezron, the son of Perez,
the son of Judah, 34the son of Jacob,

NIV [e] 15 Or *Messiah* [f] 16 Or *in* [g] 32 Some early manuscripts *Sala*
[h] 33 Some manuscripts *Amminadab, the son of Admin, the son of Arni;* other manuscripts vary widely.

## King James

34Which was *the son* of Jacob, which was *the son* of Isaac, which was *the son* of Abraham, which was *the son* of Thara, which was *the son* of Nachor,

35Which was *the son* of Saruch, which was *the son* of Ragau, which was *the son* of Phalec, which was *the son* of Heber, which was *the son* of Sala,

36Which was *the son* of Cainan, which was *the son* of Arphaxad, which was *the son* of Sem, which was *the son* of Noe, which was *the son* of Lamech,

37Which was *the son* of Mathusala, which was *the son* of Enoch, which was *the son* of Jared, which was *the son* of Maleleel, which was *the son* of Cainan,

38Which was *the son* of Enos, which was *the son* of Seth, which was *the son* of Adam, which was *the son* of God.

**4** AND JESUS being full of the Holy Ghost returned from Jordan, and was led by the Spirit into the wilderness,

2Being forty days tempted of the devil. And in those days he did eat nothing: and when they were ended, he afterward hungered.

3And the devil said unto him, If thou be the Son of God, command this stone that it be made bread.

4And Jesus answered him, saying, It is written, That man shall not live by bread alone, but by every word of God.

5And the devil, taking him up into an high mountain, showed unto him all the kingdoms of the world in a moment of time.

6And the devil said unto him, All this power will I give thee, and the glory of them: for that is delivered unto me; and to whomsoever I will I give it.

7If thou therefore wilt worship me, all shall be thine.

8And Jesus answered and said unto him, Get thee behind me, Satan: for it is written, Thou shalt worship the Lord thy God, and him only shalt thou serve.

9And he brought him to Jerusalem, and set him on a pinnacle of the temple, and said unto him, If thou be the Son of God, cast thyself down from hence:

10For it is written, He shall give his angels charge over thee, to keep thee:

11And in *their* hands they shall bear thee up, lest at any time thou dash thy foot against a stone.

12And Jesus answering said unto him, It is said, Thou shalt not tempt the Lord thy God.

13And when the devil had ended all the temptation, he departed from him for a season.

14¶ And Jesus returned in the power of the Spirit into Galilee: and there went out a fame of him through all the region round about.

15And he taught in their synagogues, being glorified of all.

16¶ And he came to Nazareth, where he had been brought up: and, as his custom was, he went into the synagogue on the sabbath day, and stood up for to read.

17And there was delivered unto him the book of the prophet Esaias. And when he had opened the book, he found the place where it was written,

18The Spirit of the Lord *is* upon me, because he hath anointed me to preach the gospel to the poor; he hath sent me to heal the brokenhearted, to preach deliverance to the captives, and recovering of sight to the blind, to set at liberty them that are bruised,

## Amplified

34The son of Jacob, the son of Isaac, the son of Abraham, the son of Terah, the son of Nahor,

35The son of Serug, the son of Reu, the son of Peleg, the son of Eber, the son of Shelah,

36The son of Cainan, the son of Arphaxad, the son of Shem, the son of Noah, the son of Lamech,

37The son of Methuselah, the son of Enoch, the son of Jared, the son of Mahalaleel, the son of Cainan,

38The son of Enos, the son of Seth, the son of Adam, the son of God. [Gen. 5:3-32; 11:10-26; Ruth 4:18-22; I Chron. 1:1-4, 24-28; 2:1-15.]

**4** THEN JESUS, full of *and* controlled by the Holy Spirit, returned from the Jordan, and was led in (by) the (Holy) Spirit

2For (during) forty days in the wilderness (desert), where He was tempted ([a]tried, tested exceedingly) by the devil. And He ate nothing during those days, and when they were completed, He was hungry. [Deut. 9:9; I Kings 19:8.]

3Then the devil said to Him, If You are the Son of God, order this stone to turn into a loaf [of bread].

4And Jesus replied to him, It is written, Man shall not live *and* be sustained by (on) bread alone *but by every word* and *expression of God.* [Deut. 8:3.]

5Then the devil took Him up *to a high mountain,* and showed Him all the kingdoms of the habitable world in a moment of time—[b]in the twinkling of an eye;

6And he said to Him, To You I will give all this power *and* authority and their glory, (that is, all their magnificence, excellence, pre-eminence, dignity and grace,) for it has been turned over to me, and I give it to whom I will;

7Therefore if You will do homage to *and* worship me ([c]just once), it shall all be Yours.

8And Jesus replied to him, *Get behind Me, Satan!* It is written, You shall do homage to *and* worship the Lord your God; and Him only shall you serve. [Deut. 6:13; 10:20.]

9Then he took Him to Jerusalem, and set Him on [d]a gable of the temple, and said to Him, If You are the Son of God, cast Yourself down from here;

10For it is written, He will give His angels charge of you, to guard *and* watch over you closely *and* carefully;

11And on their hands they will bear you up, lest you strike your foot against a stone. [Ps. 91:11, 12.]

12And Jesus replied to him, [The Scripture] says, You shall not tempt (try, [e]test exceedingly) the Lord your God. [Deut. 6:16.]

13And when the devil had ended every [the complete cycle of] temptation, he left Him—temporarily, that is, [f]stood off from Him until another more opportune *and* favorable time.

14Then Jesus went back full of *and* under the power of the (Holy) Spirit into Galilee, and the fame of Him spread through the whole region round about.

15And He Himself conducted ([g]a course of) teaching in their synagogues, being [h]recognized *and* honored *and* praised by all.

16So He came to Nazareth, [[i]that Nazareth] where He had been brought up; and He entered the synagogue, as was His custom on the Sabbath day. And He stood up to read.

17And there was handed to Him [the roll of] the book of the prophet Isaiah. He opened (unrolled) the book, and found the place where it was written, [Isa. 61:1, 2.]

18The Spirit of the Lord [is] upon Me, because He has anointed Me [the Anointed One, the Messiah] to preach the good news (the Gospel) to the poor; He has sent Me to announce release to the captives, and recovery of sight to the blind; to send forth delivered those who are oppressed—who are downtrodden, bruised, crushed and broken down by calamity;

**AMP** [a] Young's Analytical Concordance. [b] Tyndale. [c] Williams' New Testament, "expressed by the aorist." [d] Moulton and Milligan's "Vocabulary of the Greek Testament." [e] Young's Analytical Concordance. [f] Wuest's "Golden Nuggets from the Greek New Testament." [g] Vincent: in imperfect tense. [h] Cremer's "Biblico-Theological Lexicon of New Testament Greek." [i] Moulton and Milligan's "Vocabulary of the Greek Testament."

## New American Standard

34the *son* of Jacob, the *son* of Isaac, the *son* of Abraham, the *son*
of Terah, the *son* of Nahor,
35the *son* of Serug, the *son* of Reu, the *son* of Peleg, the *son* of
Heber, the *son* of Shelah,
36the *son* of Cainan, the *son* of Arphaxad, the *son* of Shem, the
*son* of Noah, the *son* of Lamech,
37the *son* of Methuselah, the *son* of Enoch, the *son* of Jared, the
*son* of Mahalaleel, the *son* of Cainan,
38the *son* of Enosh, the *son* of Seth, the *son* of Adam, the *son* of
God.

*The Temptation of Jesus*

4 AND JESUS, full of the Holy Spirit, returned from the Jordan
and was led about by the Spirit in the wilderness
2for forty days, being tempted by the devil. And He ate nothing during those days; and when they had ended, He became
hungry.
3And the devil said to Him, "If You are the Son of God, tell this
stone to become bread."
4And Jesus answered him, "It is written, 'MAN SHALL NOT LIVE
ON BREAD ALONE.' "
5And he led Him up and showed Him all the kingdoms of the
world in a moment of time.
6And the devil said to Him, "I will give You all this domain and
its glory; for it has been handed over to me, and I give it to
whomever I wish.
7"Therefore if You worship before me, it shall all be Yours."
8And Jesus answered and said to him, "It is written, 'YOU
SHALL WORSHIP THE LORD YOUR GOD AND SERVE HIM ONLY.' "
9And he led Him to Jerusalem and had Him stand on the
pinnacle of the temple, and said to Him, "If You are the Son of
God, throw Yourself down from here;
10for it is written,

'HE WILL GIVE HIS ANGELS CHARGE CONCERNING YOU TO
GUARD YOU,'

11 and,

'ON *their* HANDS THEY WILL BEAR YOU UP,
LEST YOU STRIKE YOUR FOOT AGAINST A STONE.' "

12And Jesus answered and said to him, "It is said, 'YOU SHALL
NOT [j]PUT THE LORD YOUR GOD TO THE TEST.' "
13¶ And when the devil had finished every temptation, he
departed from Him until an opportune time.

*Jesus' Public Ministry*

14¶ And Jesus returned to Galilee in the power of the Spirit; and
news about Him spread through all the surrounding district.
15And He *began* teaching in their synagogues and was praised
by all.
16¶ And He came to Nazareth, where He had been brought up;
and as was His custom, He entered the synagogue on the Sabbath,
and stood up to read.
17And the book of the prophet Isaiah was handed to Him. And
He opened the book, and found the place where it was written,

18 "THE SPIRIT OF THE LORD IS UPON ME,
BECAUSE HE ANOINTED ME TO PREACH THE GOSPEL TO
THE POOR.
HE HAS SENT ME TO PROCLAIM RELEASE TO THE CAPTIVES,
AND RECOVERY OF SIGHT TO THE BLIND,
TO SET FREE THOSE WHO ARE DOWNTRODDEN,

NAS [j] Or, *tempt . . . God*

## New International

the son of Isaac, the son of Abraham,
the son of Terah, the son of Nahor,
35the son of Serug, the son of Reu,
the son of Peleg, the son of Eber,
the son of Shelah, 36the son of Cainan,
the son of Arphaxad, the son of Shem,
the son of Noah, the son of Lamech,
37the son of Methuselah, the son of Enoch,
the son of Jared, the son of Mahalalel,
the son of Kenan, 38the son of Enosh,
the son of Seth, the son of Adam,
the son of God.

*The Temptation of Jesus*

4 JESUS, FULL of the Holy Spirit, returned from the Jordan and
was led by the Spirit in the desert, 2where for forty days he
was tempted by the devil. He ate nothing during those days, and
at the end of them he was hungry.
3The devil said to him, "If you are the Son of God, tell this stone
to become bread."
4Jesus answered, "It is written: 'Man does not live on bread
alone.'[k] "
5The devil led him up to a high place and showed him in an
instant all the kingdoms of the world. 6And he said to him, "I will
give you all their authority and splendor, for it has been given to
me, and I can give it to anyone I want to. 7So if you worship me,
it will all be yours."
8Jesus answered, "It is written: 'Worship the Lord your God
and serve him only.'[l] "
9The devil led him to Jerusalem and had him stand on the
highest point of the temple. "If you are the Son of God," he said,
"throw yourself down from here. 10For it is written:

" 'He will command his angels concerning you
to guard you carefully;
11they will lift you up in their hands,
so that you will not strike your foot against a stone.'[m]"

12Jesus answered, "It says: 'Do not put the Lord your God to
the test.'[n] "
13When the devil had finished all this tempting, he left him until
an opportune time.

*Jesus Rejected at Nazareth*

14Jesus returned to Galilee in the power of the Spirit, and news
about him spread through the whole countryside. 15He taught in
their synagogues, and everyone praised him.
16He went to Nazareth, where he had been brought up, and on
the Sabbath day he went into the synagogue, as was his custom.
And he stood up to read. 17The scroll of the prophet Isaiah was
handed to him. Unrolling it, he found the place where it is written:

18"The Spirit of the Lord is on me,
because he has anointed me
to preach good news to the poor.
He has sent me to proclaim freedom for the prisoners
and recovery of sight for the blind,
to release the oppressed,

NIV [k] *4* Deut. 8:3 [l] *8* Deut. 6:13 [m] *11* Psalm 91:11,12 [n] *12* Deut. 6:16

## King James

19To preach the acceptable year of the Lord.
20And he closed the book, and he gave *it* again to the minister,
and sat down. And the eyes of all them that were in the synagogue
were fastened on him.
21And he began to say unto them, This day is this scripture
fulfilled in your ears.
22And all bare him witness, and wondered at the gracious
words which proceeded out of his mouth. And they said, Is not
this Joseph's son?
23And he said unto them, Ye will surely say unto me this
proverb, Physician, heal thyself: whatsoever we have heard done
in Capernaum, do also here in thy country.
24And he said, Verily I say unto you, No prophet is accepted
in his own country.
25But I tell you of a truth, many widows were in Israel in the
days of Elias, when the heaven was shut up three years and six
months, when great famine was throughout all the land;
26But unto none of them was Elias sent, save unto Sarepta, *a city*
of Sidon, unto a woman *that was* a widow.
27And many lepers were in Israel in the time of Eliseus the
prophet; and none of them was cleansed, saving Naaman the
Syrian.
28And all they in the synagogue, when they heard these things,
were filled with wrath,
29And rose up, and thrust him out of the city, and led him unto
the brow of the hill whereon their city was built, that they might
cast him down headlong.
30But he passing through the midst of them went his way,
31And came down to Capernaum, a city of Galilee, and taught
them on the sabbath days.
32And they were astonished at his doctrine: for his word was
with power.
33¶ And in the synagogue there was a man, which had a spirit
of an unclean devil, and cried out with a loud voice,
34Saying, Let *us* alone; what have we to do with thee, *thou* Jesus
of Nazareth? art thou come to destroy us? I know thee who thou
art; the Holy One of God.
35And Jesus rebuked him, saying, Hold thy peace, and come
out of him. And when the devil had thrown him in the midst, he
came out of him, and hurt him not.
36And they were all amazed, and spake among themselves,
saying, What a word *is* this! for with authority and power he
commandeth the unclean spirits, and they come out.
37And the fame of him went out into every place of the country
round about.
38¶ And he arose out of the synagogue, and entered into Simon's house. And Simon's wife's mother was taken with a great
fever; and they besought him for her.
39And he stood over her, and rebuked the fever; and it left her:
and immediately she arose and ministered unto them.
40¶ Now when the sun was setting, all they that had any sick
with divers diseases brought them unto him; and he laid his hands
on every one of them, and healed them.
41And devils also came out of many, crying out, and saying,
Thou art Christ the Son of God. And he rebuking *them* suffered
them not to speak: for they knew that he was Christ.
42And when it was day, he departed and went into a desert
place: and the people sought him, and came unto him, and stayed
him, that he should not depart from them.
43And he said unto them, I must preach the kingdom of God
to other cities also: for therefore am I sent.

## Amplified

19To proclaim the accepted *and* acceptable year of the Lord—the
day [a]when salvation and the free favors of God profusely abound.
[Isa. 61:1, 2.]
20Then He rolled up the book, and gave it back to the attendant
and sat down; and the eyes of all in the synagogue were gazing
(attentively) at Him.
21And He began to speak to them: Today this Scripture has been
fulfilled [b]while you are present *and* hearing.
22And all spoke well of Him, and marveled at the words of grace
that came forth from His mouth; and they said, Is not this Joseph's
[c]Son?
23So He said to them, You will doubtless quote to Me this
proverb, Physician, heal Yourself! What we have learned by hearsay that You did in Capernaum, do here also in Your [own] town.
24Then He said, Solemnly I say to you, no prophet is acceptable
*and* welcome in his [own] town (country).
25But in truth I tell you, there were many widows in Israel in
the days of Elijah, when the heavens were closed up for three years
and six months, so that there came a great famine over all the land;
26And yet Elijah was not sent to a single one of them, but only
to Zarephath in the country of Sidon, to a woman who was a
widow. [I Kings 17:1, 8-16; 18:1.]
27And there were many lepers in Israel in the time of Elisha the
prophet, and yet not one of them was cleansed (by being healed),
but only Naaman the Syrian. [II Kings 5:1-14.]
28When they heard these things, all the people in the synagogue were filled with rage.
29And rising up they pushed *and* drove Him out of the town,
and (laying hold of Him) they led Him to the (projecting) upper
part of the hill on which their town was built, that they might hurl
Him headlong down [over the cliff].
30But passing through their midst, He went on His way.
31And He descended to Capernaum, a town of Galilee, and
there He continued to teach the people on the Sabbath days.
32And they were amazed at His teaching, for His word was with
authority *and* ability *and* weight *and* power.
33Now in the synagogue there was a man who was possessed
by the foul spirit of a demon; and he cried out with a loud (deep,
terrible) cry,
34Ah, [d]let us alone! What have You to do with us?—What have
[e]we in common—Jesus of Nazareth? Have You come to destroy
us? I know Who You are, the Holy One of God!
35But Jesus rebuked him, saying, Be silent (muzzled, gagged),
and come out of him! And when the demon had thrown the man
down in their midst, he came out of him, without injuring him in
any [f]possible way.
36And they were all amazed and said to one another, What kind
of talk is this? For with authority and power He commands the foul
spirits, and they come out!
37And a rumor about Him spread into every place in the surrounding country.
38Then He arose and left the synagogue, and went into Simon's
(Peter's) house. Now Simon's mother-in-law was suffering in the
grip of a burning fever, and they pleaded with Him for her.
39And standing over her, He rebuked the fever, and it left her;
and immediately she got up and began waiting on them.
40Now at the setting of the sun [indicating the end of the Sabbath], all those who had [any that were] sick with various diseases
brought them to Him, and He laid His hands upon every one of
them and cured them.
41And demons even came out of many people, screaming *and*
crying out, You are the Son of God! But He rebuked them, and
would not permit them to speak, because they knew that He was
the Christ, the Messiah.
42And when daybreak came He left [Peter's house] and went
into an isolated (desert) place. And the people looked for Him until
they came up to Him, and tried to prevent Him from leaving them.
43But He said to them, I must preach the good news (the Gospel) of the kingdom of God to the other cities and towns also; for
I was sent for this [purpose].

**AMP** [a] Thayer. [b] Thayer. [c] Capitalized because of what He is, the spotless Son of God, not what the speakers may have thought He was. [d] Alternate reading. [e] After Wycliffe's translation. [f] Literal meaning.

## New American Standard

19 To PROCLAIM THE FAVORABLE YEAR OF THE LORD."

20And He closed the book, and gave it back to the attendant, and sat down; and the eyes of all in the synagogue were fixed upon Him.

21And He began to say to them, "Today this Scripture has been fulfilled in your hearing."

22And all were speaking well of Him, and wondering at the gracious words which were falling from His lips; and they were saying, "Is this not Joseph's son?"

23And He said to them, "No doubt you will quote this proverb to Me, 'Physician, heal yourself! Whatever we heard was done at Capernaum, do here in your home town as well.' "

24And He said, "Truly I say to you, no prophet is welcome in his home town.

25"But I say to you in truth, there were many widows in Israel in the days of Elijah, when the sky was shut up for three years and six months, when a great famine came over all the land;

26and yet Elijah was sent to none of them, but only to Zarephath, *in the land* of Sidon, to a woman who was a widow.

27"And there were many lepers in Israel in the time of Elisha the prophet; and none of them was cleansed, but only Naaman the Syrian."

28And all in the synagogue were filled with rage as they heard these things;

29and they rose up and cast Him out of the city, and led Him to the brow of the hill on which their city had been built, in order to throw Him down the cliff.

30But passing through their midst, He went His way.

**31**¶ And He came down to Capernaum, a city of Galilee. And He was teaching them on the Sabbath;

32and they were amazed at His teaching, for His message was with authority.

33And there was a man in the synagogue possessed by the spirit of an unclean demon, and he cried out with a loud voice,

34"Ha! What do we have to do with You, Jesus of Nazareth? Have You come to destroy us? I know who You are—the Holy One of God!"

35And Jesus rebuked him, saying, "Be quiet and come out of him!" And when the demon had thrown him down in *their* midst, he came out of him without doing him any harm.

36And amazement came upon them all, and they *began* discussing with one another saying, "What is this message? For with authority and power He commands the unclean spirits, and they come out."

37And the report about Him was getting out into every locality in the surrounding district.

*Many Are Healed*

**38**¶ And He arose and *left* the synagogue, and entered Simon's home. Now Simon's mother-in-law was suffering from a high fever; and they made request of Him on her behalf.

39And standing over her, He rebuked the fever, and it left her; and she immediately arose and waited on them.

**40**¶ And while the sun was setting, all who had any sick with various diseases brought them to Him; and laying His hands on every one of them, He was healing them.

41And demons also were coming out of many, crying out and saying, "You are the Son of God!" And rebuking them, He would not allow them to speak, because they knew Him to be the Christ.

**42**¶ And when day came, He departed and went to a lonely place; and the multitudes were searching for Him, and came to Him, and tried to keep Him from going away from them.

43But He said to them, "I must preach the kingdom of God to the other cities also, for I was sent for this purpose."

## New International

19 to proclaim the year of the Lord's favor."[g]

20Then he rolled up the scroll, gave it back to the attendant and
sat down. The eyes of everyone in the synagogue were fastened
on him, 21and he began by saying to them, "Today this scripture
is fulfilled in your hearing."

22All spoke well of him and were amazed at the gracious words
that came from his lips. "Isn't this Joseph's son?" they asked.

23Jesus said to them, "Surely you will quote this proverb to me:
'Physician, heal yourself! Do here in your hometown what we
have heard that you did in Capernaum.' "

24"I tell you the truth," he continued, "no prophet is accepted
in his hometown. 25I assure you that there were many widows in
Israel in Elijah's time, when the sky was shut for three and a half
years and there was a severe famine throughout the land. 26Yet
Elijah was not sent to any of them, but to a widow in Zarephath
in the region of Sidon. 27And there were many in Israel with
leprosy[h] in the time of Elisha the prophet, yet not one of them was
cleansed—only Naaman the Syrian."

28All the people in the synagogue were furious when they
heard this. 29They got up, drove him out of the town, and took him
to the brow of the hill on which the town was built, in order to
throw him down the cliff. 30But he walked right through the crowd
and went on his way.

*Jesus Drives Out an Evil Spirit*

31Then he went down to Capernaum, a town in Galilee, and on
the Sabbath began to teach the people. 32They were amazed at his
teaching, because his message had authority.

33In the synagogue there was a man possessed by a demon, an
evil[i] spirit. He cried out at the top of his voice, 34"Ha! What do
you want with us, Jesus of Nazareth? Have you come to destroy
us? I know who you are—the Holy One of God!"

35"Be quiet!" Jesus said sternly. "Come out of him!" Then the
demon threw the man down before them all and came out without
injuring him.

36All the people were amazed and said to each other, "What is
this teaching? With authority and power he gives orders to evil
spirits and they come out!" 37And the news about him spread
throughout the surrounding area.

*Jesus Heals Many*

38Jesus left the synagogue and went to the home of Simon. Now
Simon's mother-in-law was suffering from a high fever, and they
asked Jesus to help her. 39So he bent over her and rebuked the
fever, and it left her. She got up at once and began to wait on them.

40When the sun was setting, the people brought to Jesus all who
had various kinds of sickness, and laying his hands on each one,
he healed them. 41Moreover, demons came out of many people,
shouting, "You are the Son of God!" But he rebuked them and
would not allow them to speak, because they knew he was the
Christ.[j]

42At daybreak Jesus went out to a solitary place. The people
were looking for him and when they came to where he was, they
tried to keep him from leaving them. 43But he said, "I must preach
the good news of the kingdom of God to the other towns also,

**NIV** [g] *19* Isaiah 61:1,2 [h] *27* The Greek word was used for various diseases affecting the skin—not necessarily leprosy. [i] *33* Greek *unclean;* also in verse 36 [j] *41* Or *Messiah*

## King James

44 And he preached in the synagogues of Galilee.

# 5

AND IT came to pass, that, as the people pressed upon him to hear the word of God, he stood by the lake of Gennesaret,

2 And saw two ships standing by the lake: but the fishermen were gone out of them, and were washing *their* nets.

3 And he entered into one of the ships, which was Simon's, and prayed him that he would thrust out a little from the land. And he sat down, and taught the people out of the ship.

4 Now when he had left speaking, he said unto Simon, Launch out into the deep, and let down your nets for a draught.

5 And Simon answering said unto him, Master, we have toiled all the night, and have taken nothing: nevertheless at thy word I will let down the net.

6 And when they had this done, they inclosed a great multitude of fishes: and their net brake.

7 And they beckoned unto *their* partners, which were in the other ship, that they should come and help them. And they came, and filled both the ships, so that they began to sink.

8 When Simon Peter saw *it,* he fell down at Jesus' knees, saying, Depart from me; for I am a sinful man, O Lord.

9 For he was astonished, and all that were with him, at the draught of the fishes which they had taken:

10 And so *was* also James, and John, the sons of Zebedee, which were partners with Simon. And Jesus said unto Simon, Fear not; from henceforth thou shalt catch men.

11 And when they had brought their ships to land, they forsook all, and followed him.

12 ¶ And it came to pass, when he was in a certain city, behold a man full of leprosy: who seeing Jesus fell on *his* face, and besought him, saying, Lord, if thou wilt, thou canst make me clean.

13 And he put forth *his* hand, and touched him, saying, I will: be thou clean. And immediately the leprosy departed from him.

14 And he charged him to tell no man: but go, and show thyself to the priest, and offer for thy cleansing, according as Moses commanded, for a testimony unto them.

15 But so much the more went there a fame abroad of him: and great multitudes came together to hear, and to be healed by him of their infirmities.

16 ¶ And he withdrew himself into the wilderness, and prayed.

17 And it came to pass on a certain day, as he was teaching, that there were Pharisees and doctors of the law sitting by, which were come out of every town of Galilee, and Judaea, and Jerusalem: and the power of the Lord was *present* to heal them.

18 ¶ And, behold, men brought in a bed a man which was taken with a palsy: and they sought *means* to bring him in, and to lay *him* before him.

19 And when they could not find by what *way* they might bring him in because of the multitude, they went upon the housetop, and let him down through the tiling with *his* couch into the midst before Jesus.

20 And when he saw their faith, he said unto him, Man, thy sins are forgiven thee.

21 And the scribes and the Pharisees began to reason, saying, Who is this which speaketh blasphemies? Who can forgive sins, but God alone?

22 But when Jesus perceived their thoughts, he answering said unto them, What reason ye in your hearts?

23 Whether is easier, to say, Thy sins be forgiven thee; or to say, Rise up and walk?

## Amplified

44 And He continued to preach in the synagogues of Galilee.

# 5

NOW IT occurred that while the people pressed upon Jesus to hear the message of God, He was standing by the lake of Gennesaret [Sea of Galilee].

2 And He saw two boats drawn up by the lake, but the fishermen had gone down from them and were washing their nets.

3 And getting into one of the boats, [the one] that belonged to Simon (Peter), He requested him to draw away a little from the shore. Then He sat down and continued to teach the crowd (of people) from the boat.

4 When He had stopped speaking, He said to Simon (Peter), Put out into the deep [water], and lower your nets for a haul.

5 And Simon (Peter) answered, Master, we toiled all night ( [a]exhaustingly) and caught nothing [in our nets]. But [b]on the ground of Your word, I will lower the nets [again].

6 And when they had done this, they caught a great number of fish; and as their nets were ( [c]at the point of) breaking,

7 They signaled to their partners in the other boat to come and take hold with them. And they came and filled both the boats, so that they began to sink.

8 But when Simon Peter saw this, he fell down at Jesus' knees, saying, Depart from me, for I am a sinful man, O Lord.

9 For he was gripped with bewildering amazement—allied to terror—and all that were with him, at the haul of fish which they had made;

10 And so also were James and John, sons of Zebedee, who were partners with Simon (Peter). And Jesus said to Simon, Have no fear; from now on you will be catching men!

11 And after they had run their boats on shore, they left everything and joined Him as His disciples *and* sided with His party *and* accompanied Him.

12 While He was in one of the towns, there came a man full of (covered with) leprosy; and when he saw Jesus, he fell on his face and implored Him, saying, Lord, if You will, You are able to cure me *and* make me clean.

13 And [Jesus] reached out His hand and touched him, saying, I will; be cleansed! And immediately the leprosy left him.

14 And [Jesus] charged him to tell no one ( [d]that he might chance to meet), [e]Until, *He said,* you go and show yourself to the priest, and make an offering for your purification, as Moses commanded, for a testimony *and* proof to the people, that they may have evidence [of your healing]. [Lev. 13:49; 14:2-32.]

15 But so much the more the news spread abroad concerning Him and great crowds kept coming together to hear and to be healed by Him of their infirmities.

16 But He Himself withdrew [in retirement] to the wilderness (desert) and prayed.

17 One of those days, as He was teaching, there were Pharisees and teachers of the Law sitting by, who had come from every village *and* town of Galilee and Judea and from Jerusalem. And the power of the Lord was with Him ( [f]present) to heal (them).

18 And behold, some men were bringing on a stretcher a man who was paralyzed, and they tried to carry him in and lay him before [Jesus].

19 But finding no way to bring him in, because of the crowd, they went up on the roof, and lowered him with his stretcher down through the tiles into the midst in front of Jesus.

20 And when He saw [their confidence in Him, springing from] their faith, He said, Man, your sins are forgiven you!

21 And the scribes and the Pharisees began to reason *and* question *and* argue, saying, Who is this [Man] Who speaks blasphemies? Who can forgive sins but God alone?

22 But Jesus, knowing their thoughts *and* questionings, answered them, Why do you question in your hearts?

23 Which is easier, to say, Your sins are forgiven you, or to say, Arise and walk (about)?

**AMP** [a] Vincent. [b] Vincent. [c] Trench. [d] Vincent. [e] Trench. [f] Some ancient authorities so read.

## New American Standard

44¶ And He kept on preaching in the synagogues of [g]Judea.

*The First Disciples*

5 NOW IT came about that while the multitude were pressing
around Him and listening to the word of God, He was standing by the lake of Gennesaret;
2and He saw two boats lying at the edge of the lake; but the
fishermen had gotten out of them, and were washing their nets.
3And He got into one of the boats, which was Simon's, and
asked him to put out a little way from the land. And He sat down
and *began* teaching the multitudes from the boat.
4And when He had finished speaking, He said to Simon, "Put
out into the deep water and let down your nets for a catch."
5And Simon answered and said, "Master, we worked hard all
night and caught nothing, but at Your bidding I will let down the
nets."
6And when they had done this, they enclosed a great quantity
of fish; and their nets *began* to break;
7and they signaled to their partners in the other boat, for them
to come and help them. And they came, and filled both of the
boats, so that they began to sink.
8But when Simon Peter saw *that,* he fell down at Jesus' feet,
saying, "Depart from me, for I am a sinful man, O Lord!"
9For amazement had seized him and all his companions because of the catch of fish which they had taken;
10and so also James and John, sons of Zebedee, who were
partners with Simon. And Jesus said to Simon, "Do not fear, from
now on you will be catching men."
11And when they had brought their boats to land, they left
everything and followed Him.

*The Leper and the Paralytic*

12¶ And it came about that while He was in one of the cities,
behold, *there was* a man full of leprosy; and when he saw Jesus,
he fell on his face and implored Him, saying, "Lord, if You are
willing, You can make me clean."
13And He stretched out His hand, and touched him, saying, "I
am willing; be cleansed." And immediately the leprosy left him.
14And He ordered him to tell no one, "But go and show yourself
to the priest, and make an offering for your cleansing, just as
Moses commanded, for a testimony to them."
15But the news about Him was spreading even farther, and
great multitudes were gathering to hear *Him* and to be healed of
their sicknesses.
16But He Himself would *often* slip away to the wilderness and
pray.
17¶ And it came about one day that He was teaching; and there
were *some* Pharisees and teachers of the law sitting *there,* who had
come from every village of Galilee and Judea and *from* Jerusalem;
and the power of the Lord was *present* for Him to perform healing.
18And behold, *some* men *were* carrying on a bed a man who was
paralyzed; and they were trying to bring him in, and to set him
down in front of Him.
19And not finding any *way* to bring him in because of the crowd,
they went up on the roof and let him down through the tiles with
his stretcher, right in the center, in front of Jesus.
20And seeing their faith, He said, "Friend, your sins are forgiven you."
21And the scribes and the Pharisees began to reason, saying,
"Who is this *man* who speaks blasphemies? Who can forgive sins,
but God alone?"
22But Jesus, aware of their reasonings, answered and said to
them, "Why are you reasoning in your hearts?
23"Which is easier, to say, 'Your sins have been forgiven you,'
or to say, 'Rise and walk'?

NAS [g] I.e., the country of the Jews (including Galilee); some mss. read *Galilee*

## New International

because that is why I was sent." 44And he kept on preaching in
the synagogues of Judea.[h]

*The Calling of the First Disciples*

5 ONE DAY as Jesus was standing by the Lake of Gennesaret,[i]
with the people crowding around him and listening to the
word of God, 2he saw at the water's edge two boats, left there by
the fishermen, who were washing their nets. 3He got into one of
the boats, the one belonging to Simon, and asked him to put out
a little from shore. Then he sat down and taught the people from
the boat.
4When he had finished speaking, he said to Simon, "Put out
into deep water, and let down[j] the nets for a catch."
5Simon answered, "Master, we've worked hard all night and
haven't caught anything. But because you say so, I will let down
the nets."
6When they had done so, they caught such a large number of
fish that their nets began to break. 7So they signaled their partners
in the other boat to come and help them, and they came and filled
both boats so full that they began to sink.
8When Simon Peter saw this, he fell at Jesus' knees and said,
"Go away from me, Lord; I am a sinful man!" 9For he and all his
companions were astonished at the catch of fish they had taken,
10and so were James and John, the sons of Zebedee, Simon's
partners.
Then Jesus said to Simon, "Don't be afraid; from now on you
will catch men." 11So they pulled their boats up on shore, left
everything and followed him.

*The Man With Leprosy*

12While Jesus was in one of the towns, a man came along who
was covered with leprosy.[k] When he saw Jesus, he fell with his
face to the ground and begged him, "Lord, if you are willing, you
can make me clean."
13Jesus reached out his hand and touched the man. "I am
willing," he said. "Be clean!" And immediately the leprosy left
him.
14Then Jesus ordered him, "Don't tell anyone, but go, show
yourself to the priest and offer the sacrifices that Moses commanded for your cleansing, as a testimony to them."
15Yet the news about him spread all the more, so that crowds
of people came to hear him and to be healed of their sicknesses.
16But Jesus often withdrew to lonely places and prayed.

*Jesus Heals a Paralytic*

17One day as he was teaching, Pharisees and teachers of the
law, who had come from every village of Galilee and from Judea
and Jerusalem, were sitting there. And the power of the Lord was
present for him to heal the sick. 18Some men came carrying a
paralytic on a mat and tried to take him into the house to lay him
before Jesus. 19When they could not find a way to do this because
of the crowd, they went up on the roof and lowered him on his
mat through the tiles into the middle of the crowd, right in front
of Jesus.
20When Jesus saw their faith, he said, "Friend, your sins are
forgiven."
21The Pharisees and the teachers of the law began thinking to
themselves, "Who is this fellow who speaks blasphemy? Who can
forgive sins but God alone?"
22Jesus knew what they were thinking and asked, "Why are
you thinking these things in your hearts? 23Which is easier: to say,
'Your sins are forgiven,' or to say, 'Get up and walk'? 24But that

NIV [h] 44 Or *the land of the Jews;* some manuscripts *Galilee* [i] 1 That is, Sea of Galilee [j] 4 The Greek verb is plural. [k] 12 The Greek word was used for various diseases affecting the skin—not necessarily leprosy.

## King James

24But that ye may know that the Son of man hath power upon earth to forgive sins, (he said unto the sick of the palsy,) I say unto thee, Arise, and take up thy couch, and go into thine house.

25And immediately he rose up before them, and took up that whereon he lay, and departed to his own house, glorifying God.

26And they were all amazed, and they glorified God, and were filled with fear, saying, We have seen strange things today.

27¶ And after these things he went forth, and saw a publican, named Levi, sitting at the receipt of custom: and he said unto him, Follow me.

28And he left all, rose up, and followed him.

29And Levi made him a great feast in his own house: and there was a great company of publicans and of others that sat down with them.

30But their scribes and Pharisees murmured against his disciples, saying, Why do ye eat and drink with publicans and sinners?

31And Jesus answering said unto them, They that are whole need not a physician; but they that are sick.

32I came not to call the righteous, but sinners to repentance.

33¶ And they said unto him, Why do the disciples of John fast often, and make prayers, and likewise *the disciples* of the Pharisees; but thine eat and drink?

34And he said unto them, Can ye make the children of the bridechamber fast, while the bridegroom is with them?

35But the days will come, when the bridegroom shall be taken away from them, and then shall they fast in those days.

36¶ And he spake also a parable unto them; No man putteth a piece of a new garment upon an old; if otherwise, then both the new maketh a rent, and the piece that was *taken* out of the new agreeth not with the old.

37And no man putteth new wine into old bottles; else the new wine will burst the bottles, and be spilled, and the bottles shall perish.

38But new wine must be put into new bottles; and both are preserved.

39No man also having drunk old *wine* straightway desireth new: for he saith, The old is better.

6 AND IT came to pass on the second sabbath after the first, that he went through the corn fields; and his disciples plucked the ears of corn, and did eat, rubbing *them* in *their* hands.

2And certain of the Pharisees said unto them, Why do ye that which is not lawful to do on the sabbath days?

3And Jesus answering them said, Have ye not read so much as this, what David did, when himself was an hungered, and they which were with him.

4How he went into the house of God, and did take and eat the showbread, and gave also to them that were with him; which it is not lawful to eat but for the priests alone?

5And he said unto them, That the Son of man is Lord also of the sabbath.

6And it came to pass also on another sabbath, that he entered into the synagogue and taught: and there was a man whose right hand was withered.

**AMP** [a] Thayer. [b] Cremer. [c] Cremer. [d] Young. [e] Thayer. [f] Thayer. [g] Abbott-Smith's "Manual Greek Lexicon of the New Testament." [h] Many ancient authorities read "better."

## Amplified

24But that you may know that the Son of man has the ( [a]power of) authority *and* right on earth to forgive sins, He said to the paralyzed man, I say to you, arise, pick up your litter (little bed), and go to your own house!

25And instantly *the man* stood up before them, and picked up what he had been lying on, and went away to his house, [b]recognizing *and* praising *and* thanking God.

26And overwhelming astonishment *and* ecstasy seized them all, and they [c]recognized *and* praised *and* thanked God, and they were filled with *and* controlled by reverential fear, and kept saying, We have seen wonderful *and* strange *and* incredible *and* unthinkable things today!

27And after this Jesus went out and looked attentively at a tax collector named Levi, sitting at the tax office; and He said to him, Join Me as a disciple *and* side with My party *and* accompany Me.

28And he forsook everything, and got up [and] followed Him—becoming His disciple and siding with His party.

29And Levi [Matthew] made a great banquet for Him in his own house, and there was a large company of tax collectors and others who were reclining [at the table] with them.

30Now the Pharisees and their scribes were grumbling against Jesus' disciples, saying, Why are you eating and drinking with tax collectors and pre-eminently sinful people?

31And Jesus replied to them, It is not those who are healthy who need a physician, but those who are sick.

32I have not come to arouse *and* invite *and* call the righteous, but [d]the erring ones ( [e]those not free from sin) to repentance—[that is,] [f]to change their minds for the better and heartily to amend their ways, with abhorrence of their past sins.

33Then they said to Him, The disciples of John practice fasting often and offer up prayers of [special] petition, and so do [the disciples] of the Pharisees also, but Yours eat and drink.

34And Jesus said to them, Can you make the wedding guests fast as long as the bridegroom is with them?

35But the days will come when the bridegroom is taken from them, and then they will fast in those days.

36He told them a [g]proverb also: No one puts a patch from a new garment on an old garment; if he does, he will both tear the new one, and the patch from the new [one] will not match the old [garment].

37And no one pours new wine into old wineskins; if he does, the fresh wine will burst the skins and it will be spilled, and the skins will be ruined (destroyed).

38But new wine must be put in fresh wineskins;

39And no one after drinking old wine immediately desires new wine, for he says, The old is good *or* [h]better.

6 ONE SABBATH while Jesus was passing through the fields of standing grain, it occurred that His disciples picked some of the spikes and ate [of the grain], rubbing it out in their hands. [Deut. 23:25.]

2But some of the Pharisees asked them, Why are you doing what is not permitted to be done on the Sabbath days? [Exod. 20:10; 23:12; Deut. 5:14.]

3And Jesus replied to them saying, Have you never so much as read what David did when he was hungry, he and those who were with him? [I Sam. 21:1-6.]

4How he went into the house of God, and took and ate the [sacred] loaves of the showbread, which it is not permitted for any except only the priests to eat, and also gave to those [who were] with him? [Lev. 24:9.]

5And He said to them, The Son of man is Lord even over the Sabbath.

6And it occurred on another Sabbath that when He went into the synagogue and taught, a man was present whose right hand was withered.

## New American Standard

24"But in order that you may know that the Son of Man has authority on earth to forgive sins,"—He said to the paralytic—"I say to you, rise, and take up your stretcher and go home."

25And at once he rose up before them, and took up what he had been lying on, and went home, glorifying God.

26And they were all seized with astonishment and *began* glorifying God; and they were filled with fear, saying, "We have seen remarkable things today."

*Call of Levi (Matthew)*

27¶ And after that He went out, and noticed a [i]tax-gatherer named Levi, sitting in the tax office, and He said to him, "Follow Me."

28And he left everything behind, and rose and *began* to follow Him.

29¶ And Levi gave a big reception for Him in his house; and there was a great crowd of tax-gatherers and other *people* who were reclining *at the table* with them.

30And the Pharisees and their scribes *began* grumbling at His disciples, saying, "Why do you eat and drink with the tax-gatherers and sinners?"

31And Jesus answered and said to them, "*It is* not those who are well who need a physician, but those who are sick.

32"I have not come to call the righteous but sinners to repentance."

33¶ And they said to Him, "The disciples of John often fast and offer prayers; the *disciples* of the Pharisees also do the same; but Yours eat and drink."

34And Jesus said to them, "You cannot make the attendants of the bridegroom fast while the bridegroom is with them, can you?

35"But *the* days will come; and when the bridegroom is taken away from them, then they will fast in those days."

36And He was also telling them a parable: "No one tears a piece from a new garment and puts it on an old garment; otherwise he will both tear the new, and the piece from the new will not match the old.

37"And no one puts new wine into old wineskins; otherwise the new wine will burst the skins, and it will be spilled out, and the skins will be ruined.

38"But new wine must be put into fresh wineskins.

39"And no one, after drinking old *wine* wishes for new; for he says, 'The old is good *enough*.' "

*Jesus Is Lord of the Sabbath*

6 NOW IT came about that on a *certain* Sabbath He was passing through *some* grainfields; and His disciples were picking and eating the heads *of grain*, rubbing them in their hands.

2But some of the Pharisees said, "Why do you do what is not lawful on the Sabbath?"

3And Jesus answering them said, "Have you not even read what David did when he was hungry, he and those who were with him,

4how he entered the house of God, and took and ate the [j]consecrated bread which is not lawful for any to eat except the priests alone, and gave it to his companions?"

5And He was saying to them, "The Son of Man is Lord of the Sabbath."

6¶ And it came about on another Sabbath, that He entered the synagogue and was teaching; and there was a man there whose right hand was withered.

NAS [i] I.e., Collector of Roman taxes for profit [j] Or, *showbread*, lit., *loaves of presentation*

## New International

you may know that the Son of Man has authority on earth to
forgive sins. . . ." He said to the paralyzed man, "I tell you, get up,
take your mat and go home." 25Immediately he stood up in front
of them, took what he had been lying on and went home praising
God. 26Everyone was amazed and gave praise to God. They were
filled with awe and said, "We have seen remarkable things today."

*The Calling of Levi*

27After this, Jesus went out and saw a tax collector by the name
of Levi sitting at his tax booth. "Follow me," Jesus said to him,
28and Levi got up, left everything and followed him.
29Then Levi held a great banquet for Jesus at his house, and a
large crowd of tax collectors and others were eating with them.
30But the Pharisees and the teachers of the law who belonged to
their sect complained to his disciples, "Why do you eat and drink
with tax collectors and 'sinners'?"
31Jesus answered them, "It is not the healthy who need a doctor, but the sick. 32I have not come to call the righteous, but sinners
to repentance."

*Jesus Questioned About Fasting*

33They said to him, "John's disciples often fast and pray, and
so do the disciples of the Pharisees, but yours go on eating and
drinking."
34Jesus answered, "Can you make the guests of the bridegroom
fast while he is with them? 35But the time will come when the
bridegroom will be taken from them; in those days they will fast."
36He told them this parable: "No one tears a patch from a new
garment and sews it on an old one. If he does, he will have torn
the new garment, and the patch from the new will not match the
old. 37And no one pours new wine into old wineskins. If he does,
the new wine will burst the skins, the wine will run out and the
wineskins will be ruined. 38No, new wine must be poured into
new wineskins. 39And no one after drinking old wine wants the
new, for he says, 'The old is better.' "

*Lord of the Sabbath*

6 ONE SABBATH Jesus was going through the grainfields, and
his disciples began to pick some heads of grain, rub them in
their hands and eat the kernels. 2Some of the Pharisees asked,
"Why are you doing what is unlawful on the Sabbath?"
3Jesus answered them, "Have you never read what David did
when he and his companions were hungry? 4He entered the house
of God, and taking the consecrated bread, he ate what is lawful
only for priests to eat. And he also gave some to his companions."
5Then Jesus said to them, "The Son of Man is Lord of the Sabbath."
6On another Sabbath he went into the synagogue and was
teaching, and a man was there whose right hand was shriveled.

## King James

7 And the scribes and Pharisees watched him, whether he would heal on the sabbath day; that they might find an accusation against him.

8 But he knew their thoughts, and said to the man which had the withered hand, Rise up, and stand forth in the midst. And he arose and stood forth.

9 Then said Jesus unto them, I will ask you one thing; Is it lawful on the sabbath days to do good, or to do evil? to save life, or to destroy *it?*

10 And looking round about upon them all, he said unto the man, Stretch forth thy hand. And he did so: and his hand was restored whole as the other.

11 And they were filled with madness; and communed one with another what they might do to Jesus.

12 And it came to pass in those days, that he went out into a mountain to pray, and continued all night in prayer to God.

13 ¶ And when it was day, he called *unto him* his disciples: and of them he chose twelve, whom also he named apostles;

14 Simon, (whom he also named Peter,) and Andrew his brother, James and John, Philip and Bartholomew,

15 Matthew and Thomas, James the *son* of Alphaeus, and Simon called Zelotes,

16 And Judas *the brother* of James, and Judas Iscariot, which also was the traitor.

17 ¶ And he came down with them, and stood in the plain, and the company of his disciples, and a great multitude of people out of all Judaea and Jerusalem, and from the sea coast of Tyre and Sidon, which came to hear him, and to be healed of their diseases;

18 And they that were vexed with unclean spirits: and they were healed.

19 And the whole multitude sought to touch him: for there went virtue out of him, and healed *them* all.

20 ¶ And he lifted up his eyes on his disciples, and said, Blessed *be ye* poor: for yours is the kingdom of God.

21 Blessed *are ye* that hunger now: for ye shall be filled. Blessed *are ye* that weep now: for ye shall laugh.

22 Blessed are ye, when men shall hate you, and when they shall separate you *from their company,* and shall reproach *you,* and cast out your name as evil, for the Son of man's sake.

23 Rejoice ye in that day, and leap for joy: for, behold, your reward *is* great in heaven: for in the like manner did their fathers unto the prophets.

24 But woe unto you that are rich! for ye have received your consolation.

25 Woe unto you that are full! for ye shall hunger. Woe unto you that laugh now! for ye shall mourn and weep.

## Amplified

7 And the scribes and the Pharisees kept watching Jesus to see whether He would [actually] heal on the Sabbath, in order that they might get [some ground for] accusation against Him.

8 But He was aware all along of their thoughts, and He said to the man with the withered hand, Come and stand here in the midst. And he arose and stood there.

9 Then Jesus said to them, I ask you, is it lawful *and* right on the Sabbath to do good ([a]so that someone derives advantage from it), or to do evil? to save a life (and [b]make a soul safe) or to destroy it?

10 Then He glanced around at them all, and said to the man, Stretch out your hand! And he did so, and his hand was fully restored *like the other one.*

11 But they were filled with lack of understanding *and* senseless rage, and discussed (consulted) with one another what they might do to Jesus.

12 Now in those days it occurred that He went up into a mountain to pray, and spent the whole night in prayer to God.

13 And when it was day, He summoned His disciples, and selected from them twelve, whom He named apostles (special messengers).

14 They were Simon, whom He named Peter, and his brother Andrew, and James and John, and Philip and Bartholomew,

15 And Matthew and Thomas, and James the son of Alphaeus, and Simon who was called the Zealot,

16 And Judas the son of James, and Judas Iscariot, who became a traitor—a treacherous, basely faithless person.

17 And Jesus came down with them and took His stand on a level spot, with a great crowd of His disciples and a vast throng of people from all over Judea and Jerusalem and the seacoast of Tyre and Sidon, who came to listen to Him and to be cured of their diseases;

18 Even those who were disturbed *and* troubled with unclean spirits, and they were being healed [also].

19 And all the multitude were seeking to touch Him, for healing power was all the while going forth from Him and cured them all [that is, [c]saving them from severe illnesses or calamities].

20 And solemnly lifting up His eyes on His disciples He said: Blessed—happy [[d]with life-joy and satisfaction in God's favor and salvation, apart from your outward condition] and [e]to be envied—are you poor *and* [f]lowly *and* afflicted (destitute of wealth, influence, position and honors), for the kingdom of God is yours!

21 Blessed—happy [[g]with life-joy and satisfaction in God's favor and salvation, apart from your outward condition] and [h]to be envied—are you that hunger *and* seek with eager desire now, for you shall be filled *and* completely satisfied! Blessed—happy [[i]with life-joy and satisfaction in God's favor and salvation, apart from your outward condition] and [j]to be envied—are you who weep *and* sob now, for you shall laugh!

22 Blessed—happy [[k]with life-joy and satisfaction in God's favor and salvation, apart from your outward condition] and [l]to be envied—are you when people despise (hate) you, and when they exclude *and* excommunicate you (as disreputable), and revile *and* denounce you, and defame *and* cast out *and* spurn your name as evil (wicked) on account of the Son of man.

23 Rejoice *and* be glad at such a time, and exult *and* leap for joy, for behold, your reward is rich *and* great *and* strong *and* intense *and* abundant in heaven; for even so their forefathers treated the prophets.

24 But woe to (alas for) you rich—[m]abounding in material resources—for you already are receiving your consolation [the solace and sense of strengthening and cheer that come from prosperity]; and have taken *and* enjoyed your comfort in full [having nothing left to be awarded you].

25 Woe to (alas for) you who are full now—completely filled, luxuriously gorged and satiated; for you shall hunger *and* suffer want! Woe to (alas for) you that laugh now, for you shall mourn and weep *and* wail!

**AMP** [a] Cremer. [b] Wycliffe. [c] Vincent. [d] Cremer. [e] Souter. [f] Thayer. [g] Cremer. [h] Souter. [i] Cremer. [j] Souter. [k] Cremer. [l] Souter. [m] Thayer.

## New American Standard

7And the scribes and the Pharisees were watching Him closely,
*to see* if He healed on the Sabbath, in order that they might find
*reason* to accuse Him.
8But He knew what they were thinking, and He said to the
man with the withered hand, "Rise and come forward!" And he
rose and came forward.
9And Jesus said to them, "I ask you, is it lawful on the Sabbath
to do good, or to do harm, to save a life, or to destroy it?"
10And after looking around at them all, He said to him, "Stretch
out your hand!" And he did *so;* and his hand was restored.
11But they themselves were filled with rage, and discussed
together what they might do to Jesus.

*Choosing the Twelve*

12¶ And it was at this time that He went off to the mountain to
pray, and He spent the whole night in prayer to God.
13And when day came, He called His disciples to Him; and
chose twelve of them, whom He also named as apostles:
14Simon, whom He also named Peter, and Andrew his brother;
and James and John; and Philip and Bartholomew;
15and Matthew and Thomas; James *the son* of Alphaeus, and
Simon who was called the Zealot;
16Judas *the son* of James, and Judas Iscariot, who became a
traitor.
17And He descended with them, and stood on a level place; and
*there was* a great multitude of His disciples, and a great throng of
people from all Judea and Jerusalem and the coastal region of Tyre
and Sidon,
18who had come to hear Him, and to be healed of their diseases;
and those who were troubled with unclean spirits were being
cured.
19And all the multitude were trying to touch Him, for power
was coming from Him and healing *them* all.

*The Beatitudes*

20¶ And turning His gaze on His disciples, He *began* to say,
"Blessed *are* you *who are* poor, for yours is the kingdom of God.
21"Blessed *are* you who hunger now, for you shall be satisfied.
Blessed *are* you who weep now, for you shall laugh.
22"Blessed are you when men hate you, and ostracize you, and
cast insults at you, and spurn your name as evil, for the sake of
the Son of Man.
23"Be glad in that day, and leap *for joy,* for behold, your reward
is great in heaven; for in the same way their fathers used to treat
the prophets.
24"But woe to you who are rich, for you are receiving your
comfort in full.
25"Woe to you who are well-fed now, for you shall be hungry.
Woe *to you* who laugh now, for you shall mourn and weep.

## New International

7The Pharisees and the teachers of the law were looking for a
reason to accuse Jesus, so they watched him closely to see if he
would heal on the Sabbath. 
8But Jesus knew what they were
thinking and said to the man with the shriveled hand, "Get up and
stand in front of everyone." So he got up and stood there.
9Then Jesus said to them, "I ask you, which is lawful on the
Sabbath: to do good or to do evil, to save life or to destroy it?"
10He looked around at them all, and then said to the man,
"Stretch out your hand." He did so, and his hand was completely
restored. 
11But they were furious and began to discuss with one
another what they might do to Jesus.

*The Twelve Apostles*

12One of those days Jesus went out to a mountainside to pray,
and spent the night praying to God. 
13When morning came, he
called his disciples to him and chose twelve of them, whom he also
designated apostles: 
14Simon (whom he named Peter), his brother
Andrew, James, John, Philip, Bartholomew, 
15Matthew, Thomas,
James son of Alphaeus, Simon who was called the Zealot, 
16Judas
son of James, and Judas Iscariot, who became a traitor.

*Blessings and Woes*

17He went down with them and stood on a level place. A large
crowd of his disciples was there and a great number of people from
all over Judea, from Jerusalem, and from the coast of Tyre and
Sidon, 
18who had come to hear him and to be healed of their
diseases. Those troubled by evil[n] spirits were cured, 
19and the
people all tried to touch him, because power was coming from him
and healing them all.
20Looking at his disciples, he said:

"Blessed are you who are poor,
for yours is the kingdom of God.
21Blessed are you who hunger now,
for you will be satisfied.
Blessed are you who weep now,
for you will laugh.
22Blessed are you when men hate you,
when they exclude you and insult you
and reject your name as evil,
because of the Son of Man.

23"Rejoice in that day and leap for joy, because great is your
reward in heaven. For that is how their fathers treated the prophets.

24"But woe to you who are rich,
for you have already received your comfort.
25Woe to you who are well fed now,
for you will go hungry.
Woe to you who laugh now,
for you will mourn and weep.

NIV [n] 18 Greek *unclean*

## King James

26 Woe unto you, when all men shall speak well of you! for so did their fathers to the false prophets.

27 ¶ But I say unto you which hear, Love your enemies, do good to them which hate you,

28 Bless them that curse you, and pray for them which despitefully use you.

29 And unto him that smiteth thee on the *one* cheek offer also the other; and him that taketh away thy cloak forbid not *to take thy* coat also.

30 Give to every man that asketh of thee; and of him that taketh away thy goods ask *them* not again.

31 And as ye would that men should do to you, do ye also to them likewise.

32 For if ye love them which love you, what thank have ye? for sinners also love those that love them.

33 And if ye do good to them which do good to you, what thank have ye? for sinners also do even the same.

34 And if ye lend *to them* of whom ye hope to receive, what thank have ye? for sinners also lend to sinners, to receive as much again.

35 But love ye your enemies, and do good, and lend, hoping for nothing again; and your reward shall be great, and ye shall be the children of the Highest: for he is kind unto the unthankful and *to* the evil.

36 Be ye therefore merciful, as your Father also is merciful.

37 Judge not, and ye shall not be judged: condemn not, and ye shall not be condemned: forgive, and ye shall be forgiven:

38 Give, and it shall be given unto you; good measure, pressed down, and shaken together, and running over, shall men give into your bosom. For with the same measure that ye mete withal it shall be measured to you again.

39 And he spake a parable unto them, Can the blind lead the blind? shall they not both fall into the ditch?

40 The disciple is not above his master: but every one that is perfect shall be as his master.

41 And why beholdest thou the mote that is in thy brother's eye, but perceivest not the beam that is in thine own eye?

42 Either how canst thou say to thy brother, Brother, let me pull out the mote that is in thine eye, when thou thyself beholdest not the beam that is in thine own eye? Thou hypocrite, cast out first the beam out of thine own eye, and then shalt thou see clearly to pull out the mote that is in thy brother's eye.

43 For a good tree bringeth not forth corrupt fruit; neither doth a corrupt tree bring forth good fruit.

44 For every tree is known by his own fruit. For of thorns men do not gather figs, nor of a bramble bush gather they grapes.

## Amplified

26 Woe to (alas for) you when everyone speaks fairly *and* handsomely of you *and* praises you, for even so their forefathers did to the false prophets.

27 But I say to you who are listening now to Me ([a]in order to heed, make it a practice to) love your enemies; treat well (do good to, act nobly toward) those who detest you *and* pursue you with hatred.

28 Invoke blessings upon *and* pray for the happiness of those who curse you; implore God's blessing (favor) upon those who abuse you—who revile, reproach, disparage and high-handedly misuse you.

29 To the one who strikes you on the [b]jaw *or* cheek, offer the other [c]jaw *or* cheek also; and from him who takes away your outer garment, do not withhold your undergarment as well.

30 Give away to every one who begs of you [who is [d]in want of necessities]; and of him who takes away from you your goods, do not demand *or* require them back again.

31 And as you would like *and* desire that men would do to you, do exactly so to them.

32 If you [merely] love those who love you, what [e]quality of credit *and* thanks is that to you? For even [f]the [very] sinners love their lovers—those who love them.

33 And if you are kind *and* good *and* do favors to *and* benefit those who are kind *and* good *and* do favors to *and* benefit you, what [g]quality of credit *and* thanks is that to you? For even [h]the pre-eminently sinful do the same.

34 And if you lend money [i]at interest to those from whom you hope to receive, what [j]quality of credit *and* thanks is that to you? Even notorious sinners lend money [k]at interest to sinners, so as to recover as much again.

35 But love your enemies, and be kind *and* do good—doing favors [l]so that someone derives benefit from them; and lend expecting *and* hoping for nothing in return, *but* [m]considering nothing as lost *and* [n]despairing of no one; and then your recompense (your reward) will be great—rich, strong, intense and abundant—and you will be sons of the Most High; for He is kind *and* charitable *and* good to the ungrateful *and* the selfish and wicked.

36 So be merciful—sympathetic, tender, responsive and compassionate—even as your Father is [all these].

37 Judge not—neither pronouncing judgment nor subjecting to censure—and you will not be judged; do not condemn *and* pronounce guilty, and you will not be condemned *and* pronounced guilty; acquit *and* forgive *and* [o]release (give up resentment, let it drop), and you will be acquitted *and* forgiven *and* [p]released.

38 Give, and [gifts] will be given you, good measure, pressed down, shaken together and running over will they pour [q]into [the pouch formed by] the bosom [of your robe and used as a bag]. For with the measure you deal out—that is, with the measure you use when you confer benefits on others—it will be measured back to you.

39 He further told them [r]a proverb: Can a blind [man] guide *and* direct a blind [man]? Will they not both stumble into a ditch *or* a [s]hole in the ground?

40 A pupil is not superior to his teacher, but every one [when he is] completely trained—readjusted, restored, set to rights and perfected—will be like his teacher.

41 Why do you see the speck that is in your brother's eye, but do not notice *or* consider the beam [of timber] that is in your own eye?

42 Or how can you say to your brother, Brother, allow me to take out the speck that is in your eye, when you yourself do not see the beam that is in your own eye? You actor—pretender, hypocrite! First take the beam out of your own eye, and then you will see clearly to take out the speck that is in your brother's eye.

43 For there is no good (healthy) tree that bears decayed (worthless, stale) fruit; nor on the other hand does a decayed (worthless, sickly) tree bear good fruit;

44 For each tree is known *and* identified by its own fruit; for figs are not gathered from thornbushes, nor is a cluster of grapes picked from a bramblebush.

**AMP** [a] Vincent. [b] Thayer. [c] Thayer. [d] Thayer. [e] Vincent. [f] Tyndale. [g] Vincent. [h] Thayer. [i] Vincent. [j] Vincent. [k] Vincent. [l] Cremer [m] Vincent. [n] Some ancient authorities so read. [o] Literal meaning. [p] Literal meaning. [q] Vincent. [r] Abbott-Smith. [s] Souter.

## New American Standard

26"Woe *to you* when all men speak well of you, for in the same
way their fathers used to treat the false prophets.
27¶ "But I say to you who hear, love your enemies, do good to
those who hate you,
28bless those who curse you, pray for those who mistreat you.
29"Whoever hits you on the cheek, offer him the other also; and
whoever takes away your coat, do not withhold your shirt from
him either.
30"Give to everyone who asks of you, and whoever takes away
what is yours, do not demand it back.
31"And just as you want people to treat you, treat them in the
same way.
32"And if you love those who love you, what credit is *that* to
you? For even sinners love those who love them.
33"And if you do good to those who do good to you, what credit
is *that* to you? For even sinners do the same.
34"And if you lend to those from whom you expect to receive,
what credit is *that* to you? Even sinners lend to sinners, in order
to receive back the same *amount*.
35"But love your enemies, and do good, and lend, expecting
nothing in return; and your reward will be great, and you will be
sons of the Most High; for He Himself is kind to ungrateful and
evil *men*.
36"Be merciful, just as your Father is merciful.
37"And do not judge and you will not be judged; and do not
condemn, and you will not be condemned; pardon, and you will
be pardoned.
38"Give, and it will be given to you; good measure, pressed
down, shaken together, running over, they will pour into your lap.
For by your standard of measure it will be measured to you in
return."
39¶ And He also spoke a parable to them: "A blind man cannot
guide a blind man, can he? Will they not both fall into a pit?
40"A pupil is not above his teacher; but everyone, after he has
been fully trained, will be like his teacher.
41"And why do you look at the speck that is in your brother's
eye, but do not notice the log that is in your own eye?
42"Or how can you say to your brother, 'Brother, let me take
out the speck that is in your eye,' when you yourself do not see
the log that is in your own eye? You hypocrite, first take the log
out of your own eye, and then you will see clearly to take out the
speck that is in your brother's eye.
43"For there is no good tree which produces bad fruit; nor, on
the other hand, a bad tree which produces good fruit.
44"For each tree is known by its own fruit. For men do not
gather figs from thorns, nor do they pick grapes from a briar bush.

## New International

26Woe to you when all men speak well of you,
for that is how their fathers treated the false prophets.

*Love for Enemies*

27"But I tell you who hear me: Love your enemies, do good to
those who hate you, 28bless those who curse you, pray for those
who mistreat you. 29If someone strikes you on one cheek, turn to
him the other also. If someone takes your cloak, do not stop him
from taking your tunic. 30Give to everyone who asks you, and if
anyone takes what belongs to you, do not demand it back. 31Do
to others as you would have them do to you.
32"If you love those who love you, what credit is that to you?
Even 'sinners' love those who love them. 33And if you do good to
those who are good to you, what credit is that to you? Even
'sinners' do that. 34And if you lend to those from whom you expect
repayment, what credit is that to you? Even 'sinners' lend to
'sinners,' expecting to be repaid in full. 35But love your enemies,
do good to them, and lend to them without expecting to get
anything back. Then your reward will be great, and you will be
sons of the Most High, because he is kind to the ungrateful and
wicked. 36Be merciful, just as your Father is merciful.

*Judging Others*

37"Do not judge, and you will not be judged. Do not condemn,
and you will not be condemned. Forgive, and you will be forgiven.
38Give, and it will be given to you. A good measure, pressed
down, shaken together and running over, will be poured into your
lap. For with the measure you use, it will be measured to you."
39He also told them this parable: "Can a blind man lead a blind
man? Will they not both fall into a pit? 40A student is not above
his teacher, but everyone who is fully trained will be like his
teacher.
41"Why do you look at the speck of sawdust in your brother's
eye and pay no attention to the plank in your own eye? 42How can
you say to your brother, 'Brother, let me take the speck out of your
eye,' when you yourself fail to see the plank in your own eye? You
hypocrite, first take the plank out of your eye, and then you will
see clearly to remove the speck from your brother's eye.

*A Tree and Its Fruit*

43"No good tree bears bad fruit, nor does a bad tree bear good
fruit. 44Each tree is recognized by its own fruit. People do not pick
figs from thornbushes, or grapes from briers. 45The good man

## King James

45A good man out of the good treasure of his heart bringeth forth that which is good; and an evil man out of the evil treasure of his heart bringeth forth that which is evil: for of the abundance of the heart his mouth speaketh.

46¶ And why call ye me, Lord, Lord, and do not the things which I say?

47Whosoever cometh to me, and heareth my sayings, and doeth them, I will show you to whom he is like:

48He is like a man which built an house, and digged deep, and laid the foundation on a rock: and when the flood arose, the stream beat vehemently upon that house, and could not shake it: for it was founded upon a rock.

49But he that heareth, and doeth not, is like a man that without a foundation built an house upon the earth; against which the stream did beat vehemently, and immediately it fell; and the ruin of that house was great.

**7** NOW WHEN he had ended all his sayings in the audience of the people, he entered into Capernaum.

2And a certain centurion's servant, who was dear unto him, was sick, and ready to die.

3And when he heard of Jesus, he sent unto him the elders of the Jews, beseeching him that he would come and heal his servant.

4And when they came to Jesus, they besought him instantly, saying, That he was worthy for whom he should do this:

5For he loveth our nation, and he hath built us a synagogue.

6Then Jesus went with them. And when he was now not far from the house, the centurion sent friends to him, saying unto him, Lord, trouble not thyself: for I am not worthy that thou shouldest enter under my roof:

7Wherefore neither thought I myself worthy to come unto thee: but say in a word, and my servant shall be healed.

8For I also am a man set under authority, having under me soldiers, and I say unto one, Go, and he goeth; and to another, Come, and he cometh; and to my servant, Do this, and he doeth *it*.

9When Jesus heard these things, he marvelled at him, and turned him about, and said unto the people that followed him, I say unto you, I have not found so great faith, no, not in Israel.

10And they that were sent, returning to the house, found the servant whole that had been sick.

11¶ And it came to pass the day after, that he went into a city called Nain; and many of his disciples went with him, and much people.

12Now when he came nigh to the gate of the city, behold, there was a dead man carried out, the only son of his mother, and she was a widow: and much people of the city was with her.

13And when the Lord saw her, he had compassion on her, and said unto her, Weep not.

14And he came and touched the bier: and they that bare *him* stood still. And he said, Young man, I say unto thee, Arise.

15And he that was dead sat up, and began to speak. And he delivered him to his mother.

16And there came a fear on all: and they glorified God, saying, That a great prophet is risen up among us; and, That God hath visited his people.

**AMP** [a] Alternate reading. [b] Literal reading, "sufficient." [c] Many ancient authorities read "the next day." [d] Cremer. [e] Thayer.

## Amplified

45The upright (honorable, intrinsically good) man out of the good treasure [stored] in his heart produces what is upright (honorable and intrinsically good); and the evil man out of the evil storehouse brings forth that which is depraved (wicked and intrinsically evil), for out of the abundance (overflow) of the heart his mouth speaks.

46Why do you call Me, Lord, Lord, and do not [practice] what I tell you?

47For every one who comes to Me and listens to My words (in order to heed their teaching) and does them, I will show you what he is like:

48He is like a man building a house, who dug and went down deep, and laid a foundation upon the rock; and when a flood arose, the torrent broke against that house and could not shake *or* move it, because it had been securely built— [a]founded on a rock.

49But he who merely hears, and does not practice doing My words, is like a man who built a house on the ground, without a foundation; against which the torrent burst and immediately it collapsed *and* fell, and the breaking *and* ruin of that house was great.

**7** AFTER JESUS had finished all that He had to say in the hearing of the people [on the mountain], He entered Capernaum.

2Now a centurion had a bond servant who was held in honor *and* highly valued by him, who was sick and at the point of death.

3And when the centurion heard of Jesus, he sent some Jewish elders to Him, requesting Him to come and make his bond servant well.

4And when they reached Jesus, they begged Him earnestly, saying, He is worthy that You should do this for him,

5For he loves our nation, and he built us our synagogue [at his own expense].

6And Jesus went with them. But when He was not far from the house, the centurion sent [some] friends to Him, saying, Lord, do not trouble [Yourself], for I am not [b]sufficiently worthy to have You come under my roof;

7Neither did I consider myself worthy to come to You. But [just] speak a word, and my servant boy will be healed.

8For I also am a man daily subject to authority, with soldiers under me; and I say to one, Go, and he goes; and to another, Come, and he comes; and to my bond servant, Do this, and he does it.

9Now when Jesus heard this He marveled at him, and He turned and said to the crowd that followed Him, I tell you, not even in [all] Israel have I found such great faith [as this].

10And when the messengers who had been sent returned to the house, they found the bond servant *who had been ill* quite well again.

11 [c]Soon afterward Jesus went to a town called Nain, and His disciples and a great throng accompanied Him.

12[Just] as He drew near the gate of the town, behold, a man who had died was being carried out, the only son of his mother, and she was a widow; and a large gathering from the town was accompanying her.

13And when the Lord saw her, He had compassion on her and said to her, Do not weep.

14And He went forward and touched the funeral couch, and the pallbearers stood still. And He said, Young man, I say to you, arise [ [d]from death]!

15And the man [who was] dead sat up, and began to speak. And [Jesus] gave him [back] to his mother.

16Profound *and* reverent fear seized them all; and they began [e]to recognize God *and* praise *and* give thanks, saying, A great prophet has appeared among us! And God has visited His people (in order to help and care for and provide for them)!

## New American Standard

45"The good man out of the good treasure of his heart brings
forth what is good; and the evil *man* out of the evil *treasure* brings
forth what is evil; for his mouth speaks from that which fills his
heart.

*Builders and Foundations*

46¶ "And why do you call Me, 'Lord, Lord,' and do not do what
I say?
47"Everyone who comes to Me, and hears My words, and acts
upon them, I will show you whom he is like:
48he is like a man building a house, who dug deep and laid a
foundation upon the rock; and when a flood rose, the torrent burst
against that house and could not shake it, because it had been well
built.
49"But the one who has heard, and has not acted *accordingly*, is
like a man who built a house upon the ground without any foundation; and the torrent burst against it and immediately it collapsed,
and the ruin of that house was great."

*Jesus Heals a Centurion's Servant*

7 WHEN HE had completed all His discourse in the hearing of
the people, He went to Capernaum.
2¶ And a certain centurion's slave, who was highly regarded
by him, was sick and about to die.
3And when he heard about Jesus, he sent some Jewish elders
asking Him to come and save the life of his slave.
4And when they had come to Jesus, they earnestly entreated
Him, saying, "He is worthy for You to grant this to him;
5for he loves our nation, and it was he who built us our synagogue."
6Now Jesus *started* on His way with them; and when He was
already not far from the house, the centurion sent friends, saying
to Him, "Lord, do not trouble Yourself further, for I am not worthy
for You to come under my roof;
7for this reason I did not even consider myself worthy to come
to You, but *just* say the word, and my servant will be healed.
8"For I, too, am a man under authority, with soldiers under
me; and I say to this one, 'Go!' and he goes; and to another,
'Come!' and he comes; and to my slave, 'Do this!' and he does it."
9Now when Jesus heard this, He marveled at him, and turned
and said to the multitude that was following Him, "I say to you,
not even in Israel have I found such great faith."
10And when those who had been sent returned to the house,
they found the slave in good health.
11¶ And it came about soon afterwards, that He went to a city
called Nain; and His disciples were going along with Him, accompanied by a large multitude.
12Now as He approached the gate of the city, behold, a dead
man was being carried out, the only son of his mother, and she
was a widow; and a sizeable crowd from the city was with her.
13And when the Lord saw her, He felt compassion for her, and
said to her, "Do not weep."
14And He came up and touched the coffin; and the bearers came
to a halt. And He said, "Young man, I say to you, arise!"
15And the dead man sat up, and began to speak. And *Jesus* gave
him back to his mother.
16And fear gripped them all, and they *began* glorifying God,
saying, "A great prophet has arisen among us!" and, "God has
visited His people!"

## New International

brings good things out of the good stored up in his heart, and the
evil man brings evil things out of the evil stored up in his heart.
For out of the overflow of his heart his mouth speaks.

*The Wise and Foolish Builders*

46"Why do you call me, 'Lord, Lord,' and do not do what I say?
47I will show you what he is like who comes to me and hears my
words and puts them into practice. 48He is like a man building a
house, who dug down deep and laid the foundation on rock.
When a flood came, the torrent struck that house but could not
shake it, because it was well built. 49But the one who hears my
words and does not put them into practice is like a man who built
a house on the ground without a foundation. The moment the
torrent struck that house, it collapsed and its destruction was
complete."

*The Faith of the Centurion*

7 WHEN JESUS had finished saying all this in the hearing of
the people, he entered Capernaum. 2There a centurion's servant, whom his master valued highly, was sick and about to die.
3The centurion heard of Jesus and sent some elders of the Jews to
him, asking him to come and heal his servant. 4When they came
to Jesus, they pleaded earnestly with him, "This man deserves to
have you do this, 5because he loves our nation and has built our
synagogue." 6So Jesus went with them.
He was not far from the house when the centurion sent friends
to say to him: "Lord, don't trouble yourself, for I do not deserve
to have you come under my roof. 7That is why I did not even
consider myself worthy to come to you. But say the word, and my
servant will be healed. 8For I myself am a man under authority,
with soldiers under me. I tell this one, 'Go,' and he goes; and that
one, 'Come,' and he comes. I say to my servant, 'Do this,' and he
does it."
9When Jesus heard this, he was amazed at him, and turning to
the crowd following him, he said, "I tell you, I have not found such
great faith even in Israel." 10Then the men who had been sent
returned to the house and found the servant well.

*Jesus Raises a Widow's Son*

11Soon afterward, Jesus went to a town called Nain, and his
disciples and a large crowd went along with him. 12As he approached the town gate, a dead person was being carried out—the
only son of his mother, and she was a widow. And a large crowd
from the town was with her. 13When the Lord saw her, his heart
went out to her and he said, "Don't cry."
14Then he went up and touched the coffin, and those carrying
it stood still. He said, "Young man, I say to you, get up!" 15The
dead man sat up and began to talk, and Jesus gave him back to his
mother.
16They were all filled with awe and praised God. "A great
prophet has appeared among us," they said. "God has come to

## King James

17 And this rumour of him went forth throughout all Judaea, and throughout all the region round about.

18 And the disciples of John showed him of all these things.

19 ¶ And John calling *unto him* two of his disciples sent *them* to Jesus, saying, Art thou he that should come? or look we for another?

20 When the men were come unto him, they said, John Baptist hath sent us unto thee, saying, Art thou he that should come? or look we for another?

21 And in that same hour he cured many of *their* infirmities and plagues, and of evil spirits; and unto many *that were* blind he gave sight.

22 Then Jesus answering said unto them, Go your way, and tell John what things ye have seen and heard; how that the blind see, the lame walk, the lepers are cleansed, the deaf hear, the dead are raised, to the poor the gospel is preached.

23 And blessed is *he,* whosoever shall not be offended in me.

24 ¶ And when the messengers of John were departed, he began to speak unto the people concerning John, What went ye out into the wilderness for to see? A reed shaken with the wind?

25 But what went ye out for to see? A man clothed in soft raiment? Behold, they which are gorgeously apparelled, and live delicately, are in kings' courts.

26 But what went ye out for to see? A prophet? Yea, I say unto you, and much more than a prophet.

27 This is *he,* of whom it is written, Behold, I send my messenger before thy face, which shall prepare thy way before thee.

28 For I say unto you, Among those that are born of women there is not a greater prophet than John the Baptist: but he that is least in the kingdom of God is greater than he.

29 And all the people that heard *him,* and the publicans, justified God, being baptized with the baptism of John.

30 But the Pharisees and lawyers rejected the counsel of God against themselves, being not baptized of him.

31 ¶ And the Lord said, Whereunto then shall I liken the men of this generation? and to what are they like?

32 They are like unto children sitting in the marketplace, and calling one to another, and saying, We have piped unto you, and ye have not danced; we have mourned to you, and ye have not wept.

33 For John the Baptist came neither eating bread nor drinking wine; and ye say, He hath a devil.

34 The Son of man is come eating and drinking; and ye say, Behold a gluttonous man, and a winebibber, a friend of publicans and sinners!

35 But wisdom is justified of all her children.

36 ¶ And one of the Pharisees desired him that he would eat with him. And he went into the Pharisee's house, and sat down to meat.

37 And, behold, a woman in the city, which was a sinner, when she knew that *Jesus* sat at meat in the Pharisee's house, brought an alabaster box of ointment,

38 And stood at his feet behind *him* weeping, and began to wash his feet with tears, and did wipe *them* with the hairs of her head, and kissed his feet, and anointed *them* with the ointment.

## Amplified

17 And this report concerning [Jesus] spread through the whole of Judea and all the country round about. [I Kings 17:17-24; II Kings 4:32-37.]

18 And John's disciples brought him [now in prison] word of all these things.

19 And John summoned to him a certain two of his disciples and sent them to the Lord saying, Are You He Who is to come, or shall we (continue to) look for another?

20 So the men came to Jesus and said, John the Baptist sent us to You to ask, Are You the One Who is to come, or shall we (continue to) look for another?

21 In that very hour Jesus was healing many of sicknesses and distressing bodily plagues and evil spirits, and to many who were blind He gave ([a]a free, gracious, joy-giving gift of) sight.

22 So He replied to them, Go and tell John what you have seen and heard: the blind are receiving their sight; the lame are walking; the lepers are cleansed; the deaf are hearing; the dead are raised up, and the poor have the good news (the Gospel) preached to them. [Isa. 29:18, 19; 35:5, 6; 61:1.]

23 And blessed—happy [[b]with life-joy and satisfaction in God's favor and salvation apart from outward conditions] and [c]to be envied—is he who takes no offense in Me *and* who is not hurt *or* resentful *or* annoyed *or* repelled *or* made to stumble, [[d]whatever may occur].

24 And the messengers of John having departed, Jesus began to speak to the crowds about John: What did you go out into the desert to gaze on? A reed shaken *and* swayed by the wind?

25 Then what did you go out to see? A man dressed up in soft garments? Behold, those who wear fine apparel and live in luxury are in the courts *or* palaces of kings.

26 What then did you go out to see? A prophet—a forth-teller? Yes, I tell you, and far more than a prophet.

27 This is he concerning whom it is written, Behold, I send My messenger before Your face, who shall make ready Your way before You. [Mal. 3:1.]

28 I tell you, among those born of women there is not a greater than John; but [e]he that is inferior [to the other citizens] in the kingdom of God is greater [in incomparable privilege] than he.

29 And all the people who heard Him, even the tax collectors, acknowledged the justice of God [in [f]calling them to repentance, and in pronouncing future wrath on the impenitent], being baptized with the baptism of John;

30 But the Pharisees and the lawyers [of the Mosaic Law] annulled *and* rejected *and* brought to nothing God's purpose concerning themselves, by [refusing and] not being baptized by [John].

31 So to what shall I compare the men of this generation, and what are they like?

32 They are like little children sitting in the market place, calling to one another and saying, We piped [playing wedding] to you, and you did not dance; we sang dirges *and* wailed [playing funeral], and you did not weep.

33 For John the Baptist has come neither eating bread nor drinking wine, and you say, He has a demon.

34 The Son of man has come eating and drinking, and you say, Behold, a Man Who is a glutton and a wine-drinker, a friend of tax collectors and notorious sinners.

35 Yet wisdom is vindicated [[g]shown to be true and divine] by all her children [that is, [h]by their life, character and deeds].

36 One of the Pharisees asked Jesus to dine with him, and He went into the Pharisee's house and reclined at table.

37 And behold, a woman of the town, who was [i]an especially wicked sinner, when she learned that He was reclining at table in the Pharisee's house, brought an alabaster flask of ointment (perfume).

38 And standing behind Him at His feet weeping, she began to wet His feet with [her] tears, and she wiped them with the hair of her head; and kissed His feet affectionately, and anointed them with the ointment (perfume).

**AMP** [a] Vincent. [b] Cremer. [c] Souter. [d] Vincent. [e] Thayer. [f] Thayer. [g] Barnes' "Notes on the New Testament." [h] Barnes' "Notes on the New Testament." [i] Thayer.

## New American Standard

17And this report concerning Him went out all over Judea, and in all the surrounding district.

*A Deputation from John*

18¶ And the disciples of John reported to him about all these things.

19And summoning two of his disciples, John sent them to the Lord, saying, "Are You the Expected One, or do we look for someone else?"

20And when the men had come to Him, they said, "John the Baptist has sent us to You, saying, 'Are You the Expected One, or do we look for someone else?' "

21At that very time He cured many *people* of diseases and afflictions and evil spirits; and He granted sight to many *who were* blind.

22And He answered and said to them, "Go and report to John what you have seen and heard: *the* BLIND RECEIVE SIGHT, *the* lame walk, *the* lepers are cleansed, and *the* deaf hear, *the* dead are raised up, *the* POOR HAVE THE GOSPEL PREACHED TO THEM.

23"And blessed is he who keeps from stumbling over Me."

24¶ And when the messengers of John had left, He began to speak to the multitudes about John, "What did you go out into the wilderness to look at? A reed shaken by the wind?

25"But what did you go out to see? A man dressed in soft clothing? Behold, those who are splendidly clothed and live in luxury are *found* in royal palaces.

26"But what did you go out to see? A prophet? Yes, I say to you, and one who is more than a prophet.

27"This is the one about whom it is written,

'BEHOLD, I SEND MY MESSENGER BEFORE YOUR FACE,
WHO WILL PREPARE YOUR WAY BEFORE YOU.'

28"I say to you, among those born of women, there is no one greater than John; yet he who is least in the kingdom of God is greater than he."

29And when all the people and the [j]tax-gatherers heard *this*, they acknowledged God's justice, having been baptized with the baptism of John.

30But the Pharisees and the [k]lawyers rejected God's purpose for themselves, not having been baptized by John.

31"To what then shall I compare the men of this generation, and what are they like?

32"They are like children who sit in the market place and call to one another; and they say, 'We played the flute for you, and you did not dance; we sang a dirge, and you did not weep.'

33"For John the Baptist has come eating no bread and drinking no wine; and you say, 'He has a demon!'

34"The Son of Man has come eating and drinking; and you say, 'Behold, a gluttonous man, and a drunkard, a friend of tax-gatherers and sinners!'

35"Yet wisdom is vindicated by all her children."

36¶ Now one of the Pharisees was requesting Him to dine with him. And He entered the Pharisee's house, and reclined *at the table*.

37And behold, there was a woman in the city who was a sinner; and when she learned that He was reclining *at the table* in the Pharisee's house, she brought an alabaster vial of perfume,

38and standing behind *Him* at His feet, weeping, she began to wet His feet with her tears, and kept wiping them with the hair of her head, and kissing His feet, and anointing them with the perfume.

NAS [j] I.e., Collectors of Roman taxes for profit [k] I.e., experts in the Mosaic law

## New International

help his people." 17This news about Jesus spread throughout
Judea[l] and the surrounding country.

*Jesus and John the Baptist*

18John's disciples told him about all these things. Calling two
of them, 19he sent them to the Lord to ask, "Are you the one who
was to come, or should we expect someone else?"
20When the men came to Jesus, they said, "John the Baptist sent
us to you to ask, 'Are you the one who was to come, or should we
expect someone else?' "
21At that very time Jesus cured many who had diseases, sicknesses and evil spirits, and gave sight to many who were blind.
22So he replied to the messengers, "Go back and report to John
what you have seen and heard: The blind receive sight, the lame
walk, those who have leprosy[m] are cured, the deaf hear, the dead
are raised, and the good news is preached to the poor. 23Blessed
is the man who does not fall away on account of me."
24After John's messengers left, Jesus began to speak to the
crowd about John: "What did you go out into the desert to see?
A reed swayed by the wind? 25If not, what did you go out to see?
A man dressed in fine clothes? No, those who wear expensive
clothes and indulge in luxury are in palaces. 26But what did you
go out to see? A prophet? Yes, I tell you, and more than a prophet.
27This is the one about whom it is written:

" 'I will send my messenger ahead of you,
who will prepare your way before you.'[n]

28I tell you, among those born of women there is no one greater than John; yet the one who is least in the kingdom of God is greater than he."

29(All the people, even the tax collectors, when they heard
Jesus' words, acknowledged that God's way was right, because
they had been baptized by John. 30But the Pharisees and experts
in the law rejected God's purpose for themselves, because they had not been baptized by John.)

31"To what, then, can I compare the people of this generation?
What are they like? 32They are like children sitting in the marketplace and calling out to each other:

" 'We played the flute for you,
and you did not dance;
we sang a dirge,
and you did not cry.'

33For John the Baptist came neither eating bread nor drinking
wine, and you say, 'He has a demon.' 34The Son of Man came
eating and drinking, and you say, 'Here is a glutton and a drunkard, a friend of tax collectors and "sinners." ' 35But wisdom is
proved right by all her children."

*Jesus Anointed by a Sinful Woman*

36Now one of the Pharisees invited Jesus to have dinner with
him, so he went to the Pharisee's house and reclined at the table.
37When a woman who had lived a sinful life in that town learned
that Jesus was eating at the Pharisee's house, she brought an
alabaster jar of perfume, 38and as she stood behind him at his feet
weeping, she began to wet his feet with her tears. Then she wiped
them with her hair, kissed them and poured perfume on them.

NIV [l] 17 *Or the land of the Jews* [m] 22 The Greek word was used for various diseases affecting the skin—not necessarily leprosy. [n] 27 Mal. 3:1

## King James

39Now when the Pharisee which had bidden him saw *it*, he spake within himself, saying, This man, if he were a prophet, would have known who and what manner of woman *this is* that toucheth him: for she is a sinner.

40And Jesus answering said unto him, Simon, I have somewhat to say unto thee. And he saith, Master, say on.

41There was a certain creditor which had two debtors: the one owed five hundred pence, and the other fifty.

42And when they had nothing to pay, he frankly forgave them both. Tell me therefore, which of them will love him most?

43Simon answered and said, I suppose that *he*, to whom he forgave most. And he said unto him, Thou hast rightly judged.

44And he turned to the woman, and said unto Simon, Seest thou this woman? I entered into thine house, thou gavest me no water for my feet: but she hath washed my feet with tears, and wiped *them* with the hairs of her head.

45Thou gavest me no kiss: but this woman since the time I came in hath not ceased to kiss my feet.

46My head with oil thou didst not anoint: but this woman hath anointed my feet with ointment.

47Wherefore I say unto thee, Her sins, which are many, are forgiven; for she loved much: but to whom little is forgiven, *the same* loveth little.

48And he said unto her, Thy sins are forgiven.

49And they that sat at meat with him began to say within themselves, Who is this that forgiveth sins also?

50And he said to the woman, Thy faith hath saved thee; go in peace.

8 AND IT came to pass afterward, that he went throughout every city and village, preaching and showing the glad tidings of the kingdom of God: and the twelve *were* with him,

2And certain women, which had been healed of evil spirits and infirmities, Mary called Magdalene, out of whom went seven devils,

3And Joanna the wife of Chuza Herod's steward, and Susanna, and many others, which ministered unto him of their substance.

4¶ And when much people were gathered together, and were come to him out of every city, he spake by a parable:

5A sower went out to sow his seed: and as he sowed, some fell by the way side; and it was trodden down, and the fowls of the air devoured it.

6And some fell upon a rock; and as soon as it was sprung up, it withered away, because it lacked moisture.

7And some fell among thorns; and the thorns sprang up with it, and choked it.

8And other fell on good ground, and sprang up, and bare fruit an hundredfold. And when he had said these things, he cried, He that hath ears to hear, let him hear.

9And his disciples asked him, saying, What might this parable be?

10And he said, Unto you it is given to know the mysteries of the kingdom of God: but to others in parables; that seeing they might not see, and hearing they might not understand.

11Now the parable is this: The seed is the word of God.

## Amplified

39Now when the Pharisee who had invited Him saw it, he said to himself, If this Man were a prophet, He would surely know who and what sort of woman this is who is touching Him, for she is a notorious sinner—a social outcast, devoted to sin.

40And Jesus replying said to him, Simon, I have something to say to you. And he answered, Teacher, say it.

41A certain lender of money at interest had two debtors; one owed him five hundred denarii, and the other fifty.

42When they had no means of paying, he freely forgave them both. Now which of them will love him more?

43Simon answered, The one, I take it, for whom he forgave *and* canceled more. And Jesus said to him, You have decided correctly.

44Then turning toward the woman, He said to Simon, Do you see this woman? When I came into your house, you gave Me no water for My feet, but she has wet My feet with her tears and wiped them with her hair.

45You gave Me no kiss, but she from the moment I came in has not ceased ([a]intermittently) to kiss My feet tenderly *and* caressingly.

46You did not anoint My head with [b][cheap, ordinary] oil, but she has anointed My feet with [c][costly, rare] perfume.

47Therefore I tell you, her sins, many [as they are], are forgiven her, because she has loved much; but he who is forgiven little, loves little.

48And He said to her, Your sins are forgiven!

49Then those who were at table with Him began to say among themselves, Who is this, Who even forgives sins?

50But Jesus said to the woman, Your faith has saved you; go (enter) [d]into peace—[e]in freedom from all the distresses that are experienced as the result of sin.

8 SOON AFTERWARD [Jesus] went on through towns and villages, preaching and bringing the good news (the Gospel) of the kingdom of God. And the twelve [apostles] were with Him,

2And also some women who had been cured of evil spirits and diseases: Mary, called Magdalene, from whom seven demons had been expelled;

3And Joanna, the wife of Chuza, Herod's household manager, and Susanna, and many others, who ministered to *and* provided for [f]Him *and* them out of their property *and* personal belongings.

4And when a very great throng was gathering together, and people from town after town kept coming to Jesus, He said in a parable:

5A sower went out to sow seed, and as he sowed, some fell along the traveled path, and was trodden under foot; and the birds of the air ate it up.

6And some [seed] fell on the rock, and as soon as it sprouted, it withered away, because it had no moisture.

7And other [seed] fell in the midst of the thorns, and the thorns grew up with it and choked it (off).

8And some seed fell into good soil, and grew up and yielded a crop a hundred times [as great]. As He said these things, He called out, He who has ears to hear, let him be listening *and* [g]consider *and* understand by hearing!

9And when His disciples asked Him the meaning of this parable,

10He said to them, To you it has been given to (come progressively to) know—that is, to recognize and understand more strongly and clearly—the mysteries *and* secrets of the kingdom of God; but for others they are in parables, so that looking they may not see, and hearing they may not comprehend. [Isa. 6:9, 10; Jer. 5:21; Ezek. 12:2.]

11Now the meaning of the parable is this: The seed is the Word of God.

**AMP** [a] Vincent. [b] Cremer. [c] Cremer. [d] Vincent. [e] Cremer. [f] Some ancient authorities read "Him" instead of "them." [g] Thayer.

## New American Standard

39 Now when the Pharisee who had invited Him saw this, he
said to himself, "If this man were a prophet He would know who
and what sort of person this woman is who is touching Him, that
she is a sinner."

*Parable of Two Debtors*

40 And Jesus answered and said to him, "Simon, I have something to say to you." And he replied, "Say it, Teacher."
41 "A certain moneylender had two debtors: one owed five hundred [h]denarii, and the other fifty.
42 "When they were unable to repay, he graciously forgave them
both. Which of them therefore will love him more?"
43 Simon answered and said, "I suppose the one whom he forgave more." And He said to him, "You have judged correctly."
44 And turning toward the woman, He said to Simon, "Do you
see this woman? I entered your house; you gave Me no water for
My feet, but she has wet My feet with her tears, and wiped them
with her hair.
45 "You gave Me no kiss; but she, since the time I came in, has
not ceased to kiss My feet.
46 "You did not anoint My head with oil, but she anointed My
feet with perfume.
47 "For this reason I say to you, her sins, which are many, have
been forgiven, for she loved much; but he who is forgiven little,
loves little."
48 And He said to her, "Your sins have been forgiven."
49 And those who were reclining *at the table* with Him began to
say to themselves, "Who is this *man* who even forgives sins?"
50 And He said to the woman, "Your faith has saved you; go in
peace."

*Ministering Women*

8 AND IT came about soon afterwards, that He *began* going
about from one city and village to another, proclaiming and
preaching the kingdom of God; and the twelve were with Him,
2 and *also* some women who had been healed of evil spirits and
sicknesses: Mary who was called Magdalene, from whom seven
demons had gone out,
3 and Joanna the wife of Chuza, Herod's steward, and Susanna, and many others who were contributing to their support out
of their private means.

*Parable of the Sower*

4 ¶ And when a great multitude were coming together, and
those from the various cities were journeying to Him, He spoke by
way of a parable:
5 "The sower went out to sow his seed; and as he sowed, some
fell beside the road; and it was trampled under foot, and the birds
of the air ate it up.
6 "And other *seed* fell on rocky *soil*, and as soon as it grew up,
it withered away, because it had no moisture.
7 "And other *seed* fell among the thorns; and the thorns grew
up with it, and choked it out.
8 "And other *seed* fell into the good soil, and grew up, and
produced a crop a hundred times as great." As He said these
things, He would call out, "He who has ears to hear, let him hear."
9 ¶ And His disciples *began* questioning Him as to what this
parable might be.
10 And He said, "To you it has been granted to know the mysteries of the kingdom of God, but to the rest *it is* in parables, in order
that SEEING THEY MAY NOT SEE, AND HEARING THEY MAY NOT UNDER-
STAND.
11 "Now the parable is this: the seed is the word of God.

NAS [h] The denarius was equivalent to one day's wage

## New International

39 When the Pharisee who had invited him saw this, he said to
himself, "If this man were a prophet, he would know who is
touching him and what kind of woman she is—that she is a sinner."
40 Jesus answered him, "Simon, I have something to tell you."
"Tell me, teacher," he said.
41 "Two men owed money to a certain moneylender. One owed
him five hundred denarii,[i] and the other fifty. 42 Neither of them
had the money to pay him back, so he canceled the debts of both.
Now which of them will love him more?"
43 Simon replied, "I suppose the one who had the bigger debt
canceled."
"You have judged correctly," Jesus said.
44 Then he turned toward the woman and said to Simon, "Do
you see this woman? I came into your house. You did not give me
any water for my feet, but she wet my feet with her tears and
wiped them with her hair. 45 You did not give me a kiss, but this
woman, from the time I entered, has not stopped kissing my feet.
46 You did not put oil on my head, but she has poured perfume on
my feet. 47 Therefore, I tell you, her many sins have been forgiv-
en—for she loved much. But he who has been forgiven little loves
little."
48 Then Jesus said to her, "Your sins are forgiven."
49 The other guests began to say among themselves, "Who is
this who even forgives sins?"
50 Jesus said to the woman, "Your faith has saved you; go in
peace."

*The Parable of the Sower*

8 AFTER THIS, Jesus traveled about from one town and village
to another, proclaiming the good news of the kingdom of
God. The Twelve were with him, 2 and also some women who had
been cured of evil spirits and diseases: Mary (called Magdalene)
from whom seven demons had come out; 3 Joanna the wife of
Cuza, the manager of Herod's household; Susanna; and many
others. These women were helping to support them out of their
own means.
4 While a large crowd was gathering and people were coming to
Jesus from town after town, he told this parable: 5 "A farmer went
out to sow his seed. As he was scattering the seed, some fell along
the path; it was trampled on, and the birds of the air ate it up.
6 Some fell on rock, and when it came up, the plants withered
because they had no moisture. 7 Other seed fell among thorns,
which grew up with it and choked the plants. 8 Still other seed fell
on good soil. It came up and yielded a crop, a hundred times more
than was sown."
When he said this, he called out, "He who has ears to hear, let
him hear."
9 His disciples asked him what this parable meant. 10 He said,
"The knowledge of the secrets of the kingdom of God has been
given to you, but to others I speak in parables, so that,

" 'though seeing, they may not see;
though hearing, they may not understand.'[j]

11 "This is the meaning of the parable: The seed is the word of
God. 12 Those along the path are the ones who hear, and then the

NIV [i] *41* A denarius was a coin worth about a day's wages. [j] *10* Isaiah 6:9

## King James

12 Those by the way side are they that hear; then cometh the devil, and taketh away the word out of their hearts, lest they should believe and be saved.

13 They on the rock *are they,* which, when they hear, receive the word with joy; and these have no root, which for a while believe, and in time of temptation fall away.

14 And that which fell among thorns are they, which, when they have heard, go forth, and are choked with cares and riches and pleasures of *this* life, and bring no fruit to perfection.

15 But that on the good ground are they, which in an honest and good heart, having heard the word, keep *it,* and bring forth fruit with patience.

16 ¶ No man, when he hath lighted a candle, covereth it with a vessel, or putteth *it* under a bed; but setteth *it* on a candlestick, that they which enter in may see the light.

17 For nothing is secret, that shall not be made manifest; neither *any thing* hid, that shall not be known and come abroad.

18 Take heed therefore how ye hear: for whosoever hath, to him shall be given; and whosoever hath not, from him shall be taken even that which he seemeth to have.

19 ¶ Then came to him *his* mother and his brethren, and could not come at him for the press.

20 And it was told him *by certain* which said, Thy mother and thy brethren stand without, desiring to see thee.

21 And he answered and said unto them, My mother and my brethren are these which hear the word of God, and do it.

22 ¶ Now it came to pass on a certain day, that he went into a ship with his disciples: and he said unto them, Let us go over unto the other side of the lake. And they launched forth.

23 But as they sailed he fell asleep: and there came down a storm of wind on the lake; and they were filled *with water,* and were in jeopardy.

24 And they came to him, and awoke him, saying, Master, master, we perish. Then he arose, and rebuked the wind and the raging of the water: and they ceased, and there was a calm.

25 And he said unto them, Where is your faith? And they being afraid wondered, saying one to another, What manner of man is this! for he commandeth even the winds and water, and they obey him.

26 ¶ And they arrived at the country of the Gadarenes, which is over against Galilee.

27 And when he went forth to land, there met him out of the city a certain man, which had devils long time, and ware no clothes, neither abode in *any* house, but in the tombs.

28 When he saw Jesus, he cried out, and fell down before him, and with a loud voice said, What have I to do with thee, Jesus, *thou* Son of God most high? I beseech thee, torment me not.

29 (For he had commanded the unclean spirit to come out of the man. For oftentimes it had caught him: and he was kept bound with chains and in fetters; and he brake the bands, and was driven of the devil into the wilderness.)

30 And Jesus asked him, saying, What is thy name? And he said, Legion: because many devils were entered into him.

31 And they besought him that he would not command them to go out into the deep.

32 And there was there an herd of many swine feeding on the mountain: and they besought him that he would suffer them to enter into them. And he suffered them.

## Amplified

12 Those along the traveled road are the people who have heard; then the devil comes and carries away the message out of their hearts, that they may not believe [ [a]acknowledge Me as their Savior and devote themselves to Me], and be saved [here and hereafter].

13 And those upon the rock [are the people] who, when they hear [the Word], receive *and* welcome it with joy; but these have no root; they believe for a while, and in time of trial *and* temptation fall away—withdraw and stand aloof.

14 And as for what fell among the thorns, these are [the people] who hear, but as they go on their way they are choked *and* suffocated with the anxieties *and* cares and riches and pleasures of life, and their fruit does not ripen—come to maturity and perfection.

15 But as for that in the good soil, these are [the people] who hearing the Word, hold it fast in a just— [b]noble, virtuous—and worthy heart, and steadily bring forth fruit with patience.

16 No one after he has lighted a lamp covers it with a vessel, or puts it under a [dining table-]couch; but he puts it on a [lamp]stand, that those who come in may see the light.

17 For there is nothing hid that shall not be disclosed, nor anything secret that shall not be known and come out into the open.

18 Be careful therefore how you listen, for to him who has [spiritual knowledge] will more be given, and from him who does not have [spiritual knowledge] even what he thinks *and* [c]guesses *and* [d]supposes that he has will be taken away.

19 Then Jesus' mother and His brothers came along toward Him, but they could not get to Him for the crowd.

20 And it was told Him, Your mother and Your brothers are standing outside, desiring to have an interview with You.

21 But He answered them, My mother and My brothers are those who listen to the Word of God and do it!

22 One of those days He and His disciples got into a boat, and He said to them, Let us go across to the other side of the lake. So they put off to sea.

23 But as they were sailing, He fell off to sleep. And a [e]whirlwind revolving from below upwards swept down on the lake, and the boat was filling with water, and they were in great danger.

24 And the disciples came and woke Him, saying, Master, Master, we are perishing! And He, being thoroughly awakened, [f]censured *and* [g]blamed *and* rebuked the wind and the raging waves; and they ceased, and there came a calm.

25 And He said to them, (Why are you so fearful?) Where is your faith—your trust, your confidence in Me, [in My veracity and My integrity]? And they were seized with alarm *and* profound *and* reverent dread, and they marveled, saying to one another, Who then is this, that He commands even wind and sea, and they obey Him?

26 Then they came to the country of the Gerasenes, which is opposite Galilee.

27 Now when Jesus stepped out on land, there met Him a certain man out of the town who had [was possessed by] demons. For a long time he had worn no clothes, and he lived not in a house but in the tombs.

28 And when he saw Jesus, he raised a deep (terrible) cry (from the depths of his throat), and fell down before Him [in terror], and shouted loudly, What have You [to do] with me, Jesus, Son of the Most High God?—What have we in common? I beg You, do not torment me!

29 For Jesus was already commanding the unclean spirit to come out of the man. For many times it snatched *and* held him; he was kept under guard and bound with chains and fetters, but he would break the bonds and be driven by the demon into the wilderness (desert).

30 Jesus then asked him, What is your name? And he answered, Legion; for many demons had entered him.

31 And they begged [Jesus] not to command them to depart into the bottomless pit (abyss).

32 Now a great herd of swine was there feeding on the hillside, and [the demons] begged Him to give them leave to enter these. And He allowed them [to do so].

**AMP** [a] Thayer. [b] Vincent. [c] Wycliffe. [d] Tyndale. [e] Schmidt's "Synonymik der Griechischen Sprache." (-Thayer). [f] Moulton and Milligan. [g] Wycliffe.

## New American Standard

12"And those beside the road are those who have heard; then
the devil comes and takes away the word from their heart, so that
they may not believe and be saved.
13"And those on the rocky *soil are* those who, when they hear,
receive the word with joy; and these have no *firm* root; they believe
for a while, and in time of temptation fall away.
14"And the *seed* which fell among the thorns, these are the ones
who have heard, and as they go on their way they are choked with
worries and riches and pleasures of *this* life, and bring no fruit to
maturity.
15"And the *seed* in the good soil, these are the ones who have
heard the word in an honest and good heart, and hold it fast, and
bear fruit with perseverance.

*Parable of the Lamp*

**16**¶ "Now no one after lighting a lamp covers it over with a
container, or puts it under a bed; but he puts it on a lampstand,
in order that those who come in may see the light.
17"For nothing is hidden that shall not become evident, nor
*anything* secret that shall not be known and come to light.
18"Therefore take care how you listen; for whoever has, to him
shall *more* be given; and whoever does not have, even what he
thinks he has shall be taken away from him."
**19**¶ And His mother and brothers came to Him, and they were
unable to get to Him because of the crowd.
20And it was reported to Him, "Your mother and Your brothers
are standing outside, wishing to see You."
21But He answered and said to them, "My mother and My
brothers are these who hear the word of God and do it."

*Jesus Stills the Sea*

**22**¶ Now it came about on one of *those* days, that He and His
disciples got into a boat, and He said to them, "Let us go over to
the other side of the lake." And they launched out.
23But as they were sailing along He fell asleep; and a fierce gale
of wind descended upon the lake, and they *began* to be swamped
and to be in danger.
24And they came to Him and woke Him up, saying, "Master,
Master, we are perishing!" And being aroused, He rebuked the
wind and the surging waves, and they stopped, and it became
calm.
25And He said to them, "Where is your faith?" And they were
fearful and amazed, saying to one another, "Who then is this, that
He commands even the winds and the water, and they obey
Him?"

*The Demoniac Cured*

**26**¶ And they sailed to the country of the Gerasenes, which is
opposite Galilee.
27And when He had come out onto the land, He was met by
a certain man from the city who was possessed with demons; and
who had not put on any clothing for a long time, and was not living
in a house, but in the tombs.
28And seeing Jesus, he cried out and fell before Him, and said
in a loud voice, "What do I have to do with You, Jesus, Son of the
Most High God? I beg You, do not torment me."
29For He had been commanding the unclean spirit to come out
of the man. For it had seized him many times; and he was bound
with chains and shackles and kept under guard; and *yet* he would
burst his fetters and be driven by the demon into the desert.
30And Jesus asked him, "What is your name?" And he said,
"Legion"; for many demons had entered him.
31And they were entreating Him not to command them to depart into the abyss.
32Now there was a herd of many swine feeding there on the
mountain; and *the demons* entreated Him to permit them to enter
the swine. And He gave them permission.

## New International

devil comes and takes away the word from their hearts, so that
they may not believe and be saved. 13Those on the rock are the
ones who receive the word with joy when they hear it, but they
have no root. They believe for a while, but in the time of testing
they fall away. 14The seed that fell among thorns stands for those
who hear, but as they go on their way they are choked by life's
worries, riches and pleasures, and they do not mature. 15But the
seed on good soil stands for those with a noble and good heart,
who hear the word, retain it, and by persevering produce a crop.

*A Lamp on a Stand*

16"No one lights a lamp and hides it in a jar or puts it under a
bed. Instead, he puts it on a stand, so that those who come in can
see the light. 17For there is nothing hidden that will not be disclosed, and nothing concealed that will not be known or brought
out into the open. 18Therefore consider carefully how you listen.
Whoever has will be given more; whoever does not have, even
what he thinks he has will be taken from him."

*Jesus' Mother and Brothers*

19Now Jesus' mother and brothers came to see him, but they
were not able to get near him because of the crowd. 20Someone
told him, "Your mother and brothers are standing outside, wanting to see you."
21He replied, "My mother and brothers are those who hear
God's word and put it into practice."

*Jesus Calms the Storm*

22One day Jesus said to his disciples, "Let's go over to the other
side of the lake." So they got into a boat and set out. 23As they
sailed, he fell asleep. A squall came down on the lake, so that the
boat was being swamped, and they were in great danger.
24The disciples went and woke him, saying, "Master, Master,
we're going to drown!"
He got up and rebuked the wind and the raging waters; the
storm subsided, and all was calm. 25"Where is your faith?" he
asked his disciples.
In fear and amazement they asked one another, "Who is this?
He commands even the winds and the water, and they obey him."

*The Healing of a Demon-possessed Man*

26They sailed to the region of the Gerasenes,[h] which is across
the lake from Galilee. 27When Jesus stepped ashore, he was met
by a demon-possessed man from the town. For a long time this
man had not worn clothes or lived in a house, but had lived in the
tombs. 28When he saw Jesus, he cried out and fell at his feet,
shouting at the top of his voice, "What do you want with me,
Jesus, Son of the Most High God? I beg you, don't torture me!"
29For Jesus had commanded the evil[i] spirit to come out of the
man. Many times it had seized him, and though he was chained
hand and foot and kept under guard, he had broken his chains and
had been driven by the demon into solitary places.
30Jesus asked him, "What is your name?"
"Legion," he replied, because many demons had gone into
him. 31And they begged him repeatedly not to order them to go
into the Abyss.
32A large herd of pigs was feeding there on the hillside. The
demons begged Jesus to let them go into them, and he gave them
permission. 33When the demons came out of the man, they went

**NIV** [h] 26 Some manuscripts *Gadarenes;* other manuscripts *Gergesenes;* also in verse 37 [i] 29 Greek *unclean*

## King James

33Then went the devils out of the man, and entered into the swine: and the herd ran violently down a steep place into the lake, and were choked.

34When they that fed *them* saw what was done, they fled, and went and told *it* in the city and in the country.

35Then they went out to see what was done; and came to Jesus, and found the man, out of whom the devils were departed, sitting at the feet of Jesus, clothed, and in his right mind: and they were afraid.

36They also which saw *it* told them by what means he that was possessed of the devils was healed.

37¶ Then the whole multitude of the country of the Gadarenes round about besought him to depart from them; for they were taken with great fear: and he went up into the ship, and returned back again.

38Now the man out of whom the devils were departed besought him that he might be with him: but Jesus sent him away, saying,

39Return to thine own house, and show how great things God hath done unto thee. And he went his way, and published throughout the whole city how great things Jesus had done unto him.

40And it came to pass, that, when Jesus was returned, the people *gladly* received him: for they were all waiting for him.

41¶ And, behold, there came a man named Jairus, and he was a ruler of the synagogue: and he fell down at Jesus' feet, and besought him that he would come into his house:

42For he had one only daughter, about twelve years of age, and she lay a dying. But as he went the people thronged him.

43¶ And a woman having an issue of blood twelve years, which had spent all her living upon physicians, neither could be healed of any,

44Came behind *him*, and touched the border of his garment: and immediately her issue of blood stanched.

45And Jesus said, Who touched me? When all denied, Peter and they that were with him said, Master, the multitude throng thee and press *thee*, and sayest thou, Who touched me?

46And Jesus said, Somebody hath touched me: for I perceive that virtue is gone out of me.

47And when the woman saw that she was not hid, she came trembling, and falling down before him, she declared unto him before all the people for what cause she had touched him, and how she was healed immediately.

48And he said unto her, Daughter, be of good comfort: thy faith hath made thee whole; go in peace.

49¶ While he yet spake, there cometh one from the ruler of the synagogue's *house*, saying to him, Thy daughter is dead; trouble not the Master.

50But when Jesus heard *it*, he answered him, saying, Fear not: believe only, and she shall be made whole.

51And when he came into the house, he suffered no man to go in, save Peter, and James, and John, and the father and the mother of the maiden.

52And all wept, and bewailed her: but he said, Weep not; she is not dead, but sleepeth.

53And they laughed him to scorn, knowing that she was dead.

54And he put them all out, and took her by the hand, and called, saying, Maid, arise.

55And her spirit came again, and she arose straightway: and he commanded to give her meat.

56And her parents were astonished: but he charged them that they should tell no man what was done.

## Amplified

33Then the demons came out of the man and entered into the swine, and the herd rushed down the steep cliff into the lake and were drowned.

34When the herdsmen saw what had happened, they ran away, and told it in the town and in the country.

35And [people] went out to see what had occurred, and they came to Jesus and found the man from whom the demons had gone, sitting at the feet of Jesus, clothed and in his right (sound) mind, and they were seized with alarm *and* fear.

36And those *also* who had seen it, told them how he who had been possessed with demons was restored (to health).

37Then all the people of the country surrounding the Gerasenes' district asked [Jesus] to depart from them, for they were possessed *and* suffering with dread *and* terror; so He entered a boat and returned [to the west side of the sea of Galilee].

38But the man from whom the demons had gone kept begging *and* [a]praying that he might accompany Him *and* be with Him, but [Jesus] sent him away, saying,

39Return to your home, and recount [the story] throughout of how many *and* great things God has done for you. And [the man] departed, proclaiming throughout the whole city how much Jesus had done for him.

40Now when Jesus came back [to Galilee], the crowd received *and* welcomed Him gladly, for they were all waiting *and* looking for Him.

41And there came a man named Jairus, who had (for a [b]long time) been a director of the synagogue; and falling at the feet of Jesus he begged Him to come to his house,

42For he had an only daughter, about twelve years of age, and she was dying. As [Jesus] went, the people pressed together around Him—almost suffocating Him;

43And a woman who had suffered from a flow of blood for twelve years *and had spent all her living upon physicians* and could not be healed by any one,

44Came up behind Him and touched the tassel of His garment; and immediately her flow of blood ceased.

45And Jesus said, Who is it that touched Me? When all were denying it, Peter *and those who were with him* said, Master, the multitudes surround You *and* press You on every side!

46But Jesus said, Some one did touch Me; for I perceived that [healing] power has gone forth from Me.

47And when the woman saw that she had not escaped notice, she came up trembling, and falling down before Him she declared in the presence of all the people for what reason she had touched Him, and how she had been instantly cured.

48And He said to her, Daughter, your faith—that is, your confidence and trust in Me—has made you well! Go (enter) [c]into peace—[d]untroubled, undisturbed well-being.

49While He was still speaking, a man from the house of the director of the synagogue came and said [to Jairus], Your daughter is dead; do not [e]weary *and* trouble the Teacher any further.

50But Jesus on hearing this answered him, Do not be seized with alarm *or* struck with fear; simply believe [ [f]in Me as able to do this], and she shall be well.

51And when He came to the house, He permitted no one to enter with Him, except Peter and John and James, and the girl's father and mother.

52And all were weeping and bewailing her; but He said, Do not weep, for she is not dead but sleeping.

53And they laughed Him to scorn, knowing well that she was dead.

54And grasping her hand He called, saying, Child, arise [ [g]from the sleep of death]!

55And her spirit returned [ [h]from death], and she arose immediately; and He directed that she should be given something to eat.

56And her parents were amazed, but He charged them to tell no one what had occurred.

**AMP** [a] Vincent. [b] Williams: "Imperfect expresses this idea of duration." [c] Trench. [d] Cremer. [e] Trench. [f] Thayer. [g] Thayer. [h] Cremer.

## New American Standard

33And the demons came out from the man and entered the
swine; and the herd rushed down the steep bank into the lake, and
were drowned.
34And when the herdsmen saw what had happened, they ran
away and reported it in the city and *out* in the country.
35And *the people* went out to see what had happened; and they
came to Jesus, and found the man from whom the demons had
gone out, sitting down at the feet of Jesus, clothed and in his right
mind; and they became frightened.
36And those who had seen it reported to them how the man
who was demon-possessed had been made well.
37And all the people of the country of the Gerasenes and the
surrounding district asked Him to depart from them; for they were
gripped with great fear; and He got into a boat, and returned.
38But the man from whom the demons had gone out was begging Him that he might accompany Him; but He sent him away,
saying,
39"Return to your house and describe what great things God
has done for you." And he went away, proclaiming throughout
the whole city what great things Jesus had done for him.

*Miracles of Healing*

40¶ And as Jesus returned, the multitude welcomed Him, for
they had all been waiting for Him.
41And behold, there came a man named Jairus, and he was an
official of the synagogue; and he fell at Jesus' feet, and *began* to
entreat Him to come to his house;
42for he had an only daughter, about twelve years old, and she
was dying. But as He went, the multitudes were pressing against
Him.
43¶ And a woman who had a hemorrhage for twelve years,
[i]and could not be healed by anyone,
44came up behind Him, and touched the fringe of His cloak; and
immediately her hemorrhage stopped.
45And Jesus said, "Who is the one who touched Me?" And
while they were all denying it, Peter said, "Master, the multitudes
are crowding and pressing upon You."
46But Jesus said, "Someone did touch Me, for I was aware that
power had gone out of Me."
47And when the woman saw that she had not escaped notice,
she came trembling and fell down before Him, and declared in the
presence of all the people the reason why she had touched Him,
and how she had been immediately healed.
48And He said to her, "Daughter, your faith has made you well;
go in peace."
49¶ While He was still speaking, someone *came from *the house
of* the synagogue official, saying, "Your daughter has died; do not
trouble the Teacher anymore."
50But when Jesus heard *this,* He answered him, "Do not be
afraid *any longer;* only believe, and she shall be made well."
51And when He had come to the house, He did not allow
anyone to enter with Him, except Peter and John and James, and
the girl's father and mother.
52Now they were all weeping and lamenting for her; but He
said, "Stop weeping, for she has not died, but is asleep."
53And they *began* laughing at Him, knowing that she had died.
54He, however, took her by the hand and called, saying,
"Child, arise!"
55And her spirit returned, and she rose immediately; and He
gave orders for *something* to be given her to eat.
56And her parents were amazed; but He instructed them to tell
no one what had happened.

NAS [i] Some mss. add *who had spent all her living upon physicians*

## New International

into the pigs, and the herd rushed down the steep bank into the
lake and was drowned.
34When those tending the pigs saw what had happened, they
ran off and reported this in the town and countryside,
35and the
people went out to see what had happened. When they came to
Jesus, they found the man from whom the demons had gone out,
sitting at Jesus' feet, dressed and in his right mind; and they were
afraid.
36Those who had seen it told the people how the demon-
possessed man had been cured.
37Then all the people of the region
of the Gerasenes asked Jesus to leave them, because they were
overcome with fear. So he got into the boat and left.
38The man from whom the demons had gone out begged to go
with him, but Jesus sent him away, saying,
39"Return home and
tell how much God has done for you." So the man went away and
told all over town how much Jesus had done for him.

*A Dead Girl and a Sick Woman*

40Now when Jesus returned, a crowd welcomed him, for they
were all expecting him.
41Then a man named Jairus, a ruler of the
synagogue, came and fell at Jesus' feet, pleading with him to come
to his house
42because his only daughter, a girl of about twelve,
was dying.
As Jesus was on his way, the crowds almost crushed him.
43And a woman was there who had been subject to bleeding for
twelve years,[j] but no one could heal her.
44She came up behind
him and touched the edge of his cloak, and immediately her bleeding stopped.
45"Who touched me?" Jesus asked.
When they all denied it, Peter said, "Master, the people are
crowding and pressing against you."
46But Jesus said, "Someone touched me; I know that power has
gone out from me."
47Then the woman, seeing that she could not go unnoticed,
came trembling and fell at his feet. In the presence of all the people,
she told why she had touched him and how she had been instantly
healed.
48Then he said to her, "Daughter, your faith has healed
you. Go in peace."
49While Jesus was still speaking, someone came from the house
of Jairus, the synagogue ruler. "Your daughter is dead," he said.
"Don't bother the teacher any more."
50Hearing this, Jesus said to Jairus, "Don't be afraid; just believe, and she will be healed."
51When he arrived at the house of Jairus, he did not let anyone
go in with him except Peter, John and James, and the child's father
and mother.
52Meanwhile, all the people were wailing and mourning for her. "Stop wailing," Jesus said. "She is not dead but
asleep."
53They laughed at him, knowing that she was dead.
54But he
took her by the hand and said, "My child, get up!"
55Her spirit
returned, and at once she stood up. Then Jesus told them to give
her something to eat.
56Her parents were astonished, but he ordered them not to tell anyone what had happened.

NIV [j] 43 Many manuscripts *years, and she had spent all she had on doctors*

## King James

9 THEN HE called his twelve disciples together, and gave them power and authority over all devils, and to cure diseases.
2And he sent them to preach the kingdom of God, and to heal the sick.
3And he said unto them, Take nothing for *your* journey, neither staves, nor scrip, neither bread, neither money; neither have two coats apiece.
4And whatsoever house ye enter into, there abide, and thence depart.
5And whosoever will not receive you, when ye go out of that city, shake off the very dust from your feet for a testimony against them.
6And they departed, and went through the towns, preaching the gospel, and healing every where.
7¶ Now Herod the tetrarch heard of all that was done by him: and he was perplexed, because that it was said of some, that John was risen from the dead;
8And of some, that Elias had appeared; and of others, that one of the old prophets was risen again.
9And Herod said, John have I beheaded: but who is this, of whom I hear such things? And he desired to see him.
10¶ And the apostles, when they were returned, told him all that they had done. And he took them, and went aside privately into a desert place belonging to the city called Bethsaida.
11And the people, when they knew *it*, followed him: and he received them, and spake unto them of the kingdom of God, and healed them that had need of healing.
12And when the day began to wear away, then came the twelve, and said unto him, Send the multitude away, that they may go into the towns and country round about, and lodge, and get victuals: for we are here in a desert place.
13But he said unto them, Give ye them to eat. And they said, We have no more but five loaves and two fishes; except we should go and buy meat for all this people.
14For they were about five thousand men. And he said to his disciples, Make them sit down by fifties in a company.
15And they did so, and made them all sit down.
16Then he took the five loaves and the two fishes, and looking up to heaven, he blessed them, and brake, and gave to the disciples to set before the multitude.
17And they did eat, and were all filled: and there was taken up of fragments that remained to them twelve baskets.
18¶ And it came to pass, as he was alone praying, his disciples were with him: and he asked them, saying, Whom say the people that I am?
19They answering said, John the Baptist; but some *say*, Elias; and others *say*, that one of the old prophets is risen again.
20He said unto them, But whom say ye that I am? Peter answering said, The Christ of God.
21And he straitly charged them, and commanded *them* to tell no man that thing;
22Saying, The Son of man must suffer many things, and be rejected of the elders and chief priests and scribes, and be slain, and be raised the third day.

## Amplified

9 THEN JESUS called together the twelve *apostles*, and gave them power and authority over all demons and to cure diseases,
2And He sent them out to announce *and* preach the kingdom of God and to bring healing.
3And He said to them, Do not take anything for your journey, neither walking stick, nor [a]wallet [for a collection-bag], nor food of any kind, nor money, and do not have two undergarments (tunics).
4And whatever house you enter, stay there until you go away [from that place].
5And wherever they do not receive *and* accept *and* welcome you, when you leave that town shake off *even* the dust from your feet as a testimony against them.
6And departing they went about from village to village, preaching the Gospel and restoring the afflicted to health everywhere.
7Now Herod the tetrarch heard of all that was being done by [Jesus], and he was (thoroughly) perplexed *and* troubled, because it was said by some that John [the Baptist] had been raised from the dead;
8And by others that Elijah had appeared; and by others, that one of the prophets of old had come back to life.
9But Herod said, John I beheaded; but Who is this about Whom I [learn] such things by hearsay? And he sought to see Him.
10On their return the apostles reported to Jesus all that they had done. And He took them [along with Him] and withdrew into privacy near a town called Bethsaida.
11But when the crowds learned of it, [they] followed Him; and He welcomed them [and] talked to them about the kingdom of God, and healed those who needed restoration to health.
12Now the day began to decline, and the twelve came and said to Him, Dismiss the crowds *and* send them away, so that they may go to the neighboring hamlets *and* villages and the surrounding country and find lodging, and get a [b]supply of provisions; for we are here in an uninhabited (barren, solitary) place.
13But He said to them, You [yourselves] give them [food] to eat. They said, We have not more than five loaves and two fishes, unless we are to go and buy food for all this crowd, [II Kings 4:42-44.]
14For there were about five thousand men. And [Jesus] said to His disciples, Have them [sit down] reclining in table-groups (companies), of about fifty each.
15And they did so, and made them all recline.
16And taking the five loaves and the two fishes, He looked up to heaven, and (praising God) gave thanks *and* asked Him to bless them [to their use]. Then He broke them and gave them to the disciples to place before the multitude.
17And all the people ate and were satisfied. And they gathered up what remained over, twelve [ [c]small hand] baskets of broken pieces.
18Now it occurred that as Jesus was praying privately the disciples were with Him, and He asked them, Who do men say that I am?
19And they answered, John the Baptist; but some say, Elijah, and others, that one of the ancient prophets has come back to life.
20And He said to them, But who do you [yourselves] say that I am? And Peter replied, The Christ of God!
21But He strictly charged and sharply commanded them ( [d]under penalty) to tell this to no one—no one, [e]whoever he might be,
22Saying, The Son of man must suffer many things, and be ( [f]deliberately) disapproved *and* repudiated *and* rejected on the part of the elders and chief priests and scribes, and be put to death, and on the third day be raised [again].

**AMP** [a] Moulton and Milligan. [b] Vincent. [c] Vincent. But Moulton and Milligan think size not meant. [d] Vincent. [e] Vincent. [f] Vincent.

## New American Standard

*Ministry of the Twelve*

9 AND HE called the twelve together, and gave them power
and authority over all the demons, and to heal diseases.
2And He sent them out to proclaim the kingdom of God, and
to perform healing.
3And He said to them, "Take nothing for *your* journey, neither
a staff, nor a bag, nor bread, nor money; and do not *even* have two
tunics apiece.
4"And whatever house you enter, stay there, and take your
leave from there.
5"And as for those who do not receive you, as you go out from
that city, shake off the dust from your feet as a testimony against
them."
6And departing, they *began* going about among the villages,
preaching the gospel, and healing everywhere.
7¶ Now Herod the tetrarch heard of all that was happening;
and he was greatly perplexed, because it was said by some that
John had risen from the dead,
8and by some that Elijah had appeared, and by others, that one
of the prophets of old had risen again.
9And Herod said, "I myself had John beheaded; but who is this
man about whom I hear such things?" And he kept trying to see
Him.
10¶ And when the apostles returned, they gave an account to
Him of all that they had done. And taking them with Him, He
withdrew by Himself to a city called Bethsaida.
11But the multitudes were aware of this and followed Him; and
welcoming them, He *began* speaking to them about the kingdom
of God and curing those who had need of healing.

*Five Thousand Fed*

12And the day began to decline, and the twelve came and said
to Him, "Send the multitude away, that they may go into the
surrounding villages and countryside and find lodging and get
something to eat; for here we are in a desolate place."
13But He said to them, "You give them *something* to eat!" And
they said, "We have no more than five loaves and two fish, unless
perhaps we go and buy food for all these people."
14(For there were about five thousand men.) And He said to His
disciples, "Have them recline *to eat* in groups of about fifty each."
15And they did so, and had them all recline.
16And He took the five loaves and the two fish, and looking up
to heaven, He blessed them, and broke *them*, and kept giving *them*
to the disciples to set before the multitude.
17And they all ate and were satisfied; and the broken pieces
which they had left over were picked up, twelve baskets *full*.
18¶ And it came about that while He was praying alone, the
disciples were with Him, and He questioned them, saying, "Who
do the multitudes say that I am?"
19And they answered and said, "John the Baptist, and others
*say* Elijah; but others, that one of the prophets of old has risen
again."
20And He said to them, "But who do you say that I am?" And
Peter answered and said, "The Christ of God."
21But He warned them, and instructed *them* not to tell this to
anyone,
22saying, "The Son of Man must suffer many things, and be
rejected by the elders and chief priests and scribes, and be killed,
and be raised up on the third day."

## New International

*Jesus Sends Out the Twelve*

9 WHEN JESUS had called the Twelve together, he gave them
power and authority to drive out all demons and to cure
diseases, 2and he sent them out to preach the kingdom of God and
to heal the sick. 3He told them: "Take nothing for the journey—no
staff, no bag, no bread, no money, no extra tunic. 4Whatever
house you enter, stay there until you leave that town. 5If people
do not welcome you, shake the dust off your feet when you leave
their town, as a testimony against them." 6So they set out and
went from village to village, preaching the gospel and healing
people everywhere.
7Now Herod the tetrarch heard about all that was going on.
And he was perplexed, because some were saying that John had
been raised from the dead, 8others that Elijah had appeared, and
still others that one of the prophets of long ago had come back to
life. 9But Herod said, "I beheaded John. Who, then, is this I hear
such things about?" And he tried to see him.

*Jesus Feeds the Five Thousand*

10When the apostles returned, they reported to Jesus what they
had done. Then he took them with him and they withdrew by
themselves to a town called Bethsaida, 11but the crowds learned
about it and followed him. He welcomed them and spoke to them
about the kingdom of God, and healed those who needed healing.
12Late in the afternoon the Twelve came to him and said, "Send
the crowd away so they can go to the surrounding villages and
countryside and find food and lodging, because we are in a remote
place here."
13He replied, "You give them something to eat."
They answered, "We have only five loaves of bread and two
fish—unless we go and buy food for all this crowd." 14(About five
thousand men were there.)
But he said to his disciples, "Have them sit down in groups of
about fifty each." 15The disciples did so, and everybody sat down.
16Taking the five loaves and the two fish and looking up to heaven,
he gave thanks and broke them. Then he gave them to the disciples
to set before the people. 17They all ate and were satisfied, and the
disciples picked up twelve basketfuls of broken pieces that were
left over.

*Peter's Confession of Christ*

18Once when Jesus was praying in private and his disciples
were with him, he asked them, "Who do the crowds say I am?"
19They replied, "Some say John the Baptist; others say Elijah;
and still others, that one of the prophets of long ago has come back
to life."
20"But what about you?" he asked. "Who do you say I am?"
Peter answered, "The Christ[g] of God."
21Jesus strictly warned them not to tell this to anyone. 22And
he said, "The Son of Man must suffer many things and be rejected
by the elders, chief priests and teachers of the law, and he must
be killed and on the third day be raised to life."

**NIV** [g] 20 Or *Messiah*

## King James

23¶ And he said to *them* all, If any *man* will come after me, let him deny himself, and take up his cross daily, and follow me.

24For whosoever will save his life shall lose it: but whosoever will lose his life for my sake, the same shall save it.

25For what is a man advantaged, if he gain the whole world, and lose himself, or be cast away?

26For whosoever shall be ashamed of me and of my words, of him shall the Son of man be ashamed, when he shall come in his own glory, and *in his* Father's, and of the holy angels.

27But I tell you of a truth, there be some standing here, which shall not taste of death, till they see the kingdom of God.

28¶ And it came to pass about an eight days after these sayings, he took Peter and John and James, and went up into a mountain to pray.

29And as he prayed, the fashion of his countenance was altered, and his raiment *was* white *and* glistering.

30And, behold, there talked with him two men, which were Moses and Elias:

31Who appeared in glory, and spake of his decease which he should accomplish at Jerusalem.

32But Peter and they that were with him were heavy with sleep: and when they were awake, they saw his glory, and the two men that stood with him.

33And it came to pass, as they departed from him, Peter said unto Jesus, Master, it is good for us to be here: and let us make three tabernacles; one for thee, and one for Moses, and one for Elias: not knowing what he said.

34While he thus spake, there came a cloud, and overshadowed them: and they feared as they entered into the cloud.

35And there came a voice out of the cloud, saying, This is my beloved Son: hear him.

36And when the voice was past, Jesus was found alone. And they kept *it* close, and told no man in those days any of those things which they had seen.

37¶ And it came to pass, that on the next day, when they were come down from the hill, much people met him.

38And, behold, a man of the company cried out, saying, Master, I beseech thee, look upon my son: for he is mine only child.

39And, lo, a spirit taketh him, and he suddenly crieth out; and it teareth him that he foameth again, and bruising him hardly departeth from him.

40And I besought thy disciples to cast him out; and they could not.

41And Jesus answering said, O faithless and perverse generation, how long shall I be with you, and suffer you? Bring thy son hither.

42And as he was yet a-coming, the devil threw him down, and tare *him*. And Jesus rebuked the unclean spirit, and healed the child, and delivered him again to his father.

43¶ And they were all amazed at the mighty power of God. But while they wondered every one at all things which Jesus did, he said unto his disciples,

44Let these sayings sink down into your ears: for the Son of man shall be delivered into the hands of men.

## Amplified

23And He said to all, If any person wills to come after Me, let him deny himself—that is, [a]disown himself, [b]forget, lose sight of himself and his own interests, [c]refuse and give up himself—and take up his cross daily, and follow Me [that is, [d]cleave steadfastly to Me, conform wholly to My example, in living and if need be in dying also].

24For whoever would preserve his life *and* save it, will lose *and* destroy it; but whoever loses his life for My sake, he will preserve *and* save it [ [e]from the penalty of eternal death].

25For what does it profit a man, if he gains the whole world and ruins or forfeits (loses) himself?

26Because whoever is ashamed of Me and of My teachings, of him will the Son of man be ashamed when He comes in the [ [f]threefold] glory (that is, the splendor and majesty) of Himself and of the Father and of the holy angels.

27However I tell you truly, there are some of those standing here who will not taste of death before they see the kingdom of God.

28Now about eight days after these teachings, Jesus took with Him Peter and John and James, and went up on the mountain to pray.

29And as He was praying, the appearance of His countenance became altered (different), and His raiment became dazzling white— [g]flashing with the brilliance of lightning.

30And behold, two men were conversing with Him, Moses and Elijah,

31Who appeared in splendor *and* majesty *and* brightness and were speaking of His exit [from life], which He was about to bring to realization at Jerusalem.

32Now Peter and those with him were weighed down with sleep. But when they fully awoke they saw His glory (splendor and majesty and brightness) and the two men who stood with Him.

33And it occurred as the men were parting from Him, that Peter said to Jesus, Master, it is delightful *and* good that we are here; and let us construct three booths *or* huts, one for You and one for Moses and one for Elijah! not noticing *or* knowing what he was saying.

34But even as he was saying this, a cloud came and began to overshadow them; and they were seized with alarm *and* struck with fear as they entered into the cloud.

35Then there came a voice out of the cloud, saying, This is My Son, My Chosen One— [h]My Beloved; listen to *and* yield to *and* obey Him!

36And when the voice had died away, Jesus was found there alone. And they kept still and told no one at that time any of these things that they had seen.

37Now it occurred the next day, when they had come down from the mountain, that a great multitude met Him.

38And behold, a man from the crowd shouted out, Master, I implore You to look at my son, for he is my only child;

39And behold, a spirit seizes him and suddenly he cries out; it convulses him so that he foams at the mouth, and he is sorely shattered, and it will scarcely leave him.

40And I implored Your disciples to drive it out, but they could not.

41Jesus answered, O (faithless ones,) unbelieving *and* without trust in God, a perverse ( [i]wayward, [j]crooked and [k]warped) generation! Until when am I to be with you and bear with you? Bring your son here [to Me].

42And even while he was coming the demon threw him down, and (completely) convulsed him. But Jesus censured *and* severely rebuked the unclean spirit and healed the child, and restored him to his father.

43And all were astounded at the evidence of God's mighty power *and* His majesty *and* magnificence. But [while] they were all marveling at everything Jesus was doing, He said to His disciples,

44Let these words sink into your ears: the Son of man is about to be delivered into the hands of men [ [l]whose conduct is opposed to God].

**AMP** [a] Moulton and Milligan. [b] Thayer. [c] Cremer. [d] Thayer. [e] Cremer. [f] Vincent. [g] Vincent. [h] Many ancient authorities so read. [i] Wycliffe. [j] Tyndale. [k] Vincent. [l] Cremer.

## New American Standard

23And He was saying to *them* all, "If anyone wishes to come after Me, let him deny himself, and take up his cross daily, and follow Me.

24"For whoever wishes to save his life shall lose it, but whoever loses his life for My sake, he is the one who will save it.

25"For what is a man profited if he gains the whole world, and loses or forfeits himself?

26"For whoever is ashamed of Me and My words, of him will the Son of Man be ashamed when He comes in His glory, and *the glory* of the Father and of the holy angels.

27"But I say to you truthfully, there are some of those standing here who shall not taste death until they see the kingdom of God."

*The Transfiguration*

28¶ And some eight days after these sayings, it came about that He took along Peter and John and James, and went up to the mountain to pray.

29And while He was praying, the appearance of His face became different, and His clothing *became* white *and* gleaming.

30And behold, two men were talking with Him; and they were Moses and Elijah,

31who, appearing in glory, were speaking of His departure which He was about to accomplish at Jerusalem.

32Now Peter and his companions had been overcome with sleep; but when they were fully awake, they saw His glory and the two men standing with Him.

33And it came about, as these were parting from Him, Peter said to Jesus, "Master, it is good for us to be here; and let us make three tabernacles: one for You, and one for Moses, and one for Elijah"—not realizing what he was saying.

34And while he was saying this, a cloud formed and *began* to overshadow them; and they were afraid as they entered the cloud.

35And a voice came out of the cloud, saying, "This is My Son, *My* Chosen One; listen to Him!"

36And when the voice had spoken, Jesus was found alone. And they kept silent, and reported to no one in those days any of the things which they had seen.

37¶ And it came about on the next day, that when they had come down from the mountain, a great multitude met Him.

38And behold, a man from the multitude shouted out, saying, "Teacher, I beg You to look at my son, for he is my only *boy*,

39and behold, a spirit seizes him, and he suddenly screams, and it throws him into a convulsion with foaming *at the mouth*, and as it mauls him, it scarcely leaves him.

40"And I begged Your disciples to cast it out, and they could not."

41And Jesus answered and said, "O unbelieving and perverted generation, how long shall I be with you, and put up with you? Bring your son here."

42And while he was still approaching, the demon dashed him *to the ground*, and threw him into a convulsion. But Jesus rebuked the unclean spirit, and healed the boy, and gave him back to his father.

43And they were all amazed at the greatness of God.

¶ But while everyone was marveling at all that He was doing, He said to His disciples,

44"Let these words sink into your ears; for the Son of Man is going to be delivered into the hands of men."

## New International

23Then he said to them all: "If anyone would come after me, he
must deny himself and take up his cross daily and follow me. 24For
whoever wants to save his life will lose it, but whoever loses his
life for me will save it. 25What good is it for a man to gain the whole
world, and yet lose or forfeit his very self? 26If anyone is ashamed
of me and my words, the Son of Man will be ashamed of him when
he comes in his glory and in the glory of the Father and of the holy
angels. 27I tell you the truth, some who are standing here will not
taste death before they see the kingdom of God."

*The Transfiguration*

28About eight days after Jesus said this, he took Peter, John and
James with him and went up onto a mountain to pray. 29As he was
praying, the appearance of his face changed, and his clothes
became as bright as a flash of lightning. 30Two men, Moses and
Elijah, 31appeared in glorious splendor, talking with Jesus. They
spoke about his departure, which he was about to bring to fulfillment at Jerusalem. 32Peter and his companions were very sleepy,
but when they became fully awake, they saw his glory and the two
men standing with him. 33As the men were leaving Jesus, Peter
said to him, "Master, it is good for us to be here. Let us put up
three shelters—one for you, one for Moses and one for Elijah." (He
did not know what he was saying.)

34While he was speaking, a cloud appeared and enveloped
them, and they were afraid as they entered the cloud. 35A voice
came from the cloud, saying, "This is my Son, whom I have
chosen; listen to him." 36When the voice had spoken, they found
that Jesus was alone. The disciples kept this to themselves, and
told no one at that time what they had seen.

*The Healing of a Boy With an Evil Spirit*

37The next day, when they came down from the mountain, a
large crowd met him. 38A man in the crowd called out, "Teacher,
I beg you to look at my son, for he is my only child. 39A spirit seizes
him and he suddenly screams; it throws him into convulsions so
that he foams at the mouth. It scarcely ever leaves him and is
destroying him. 40I begged your disciples to drive it out, but they
could not."

41"O unbelieving and perverse generation," Jesus replied,
"how long shall I stay with you and put up with you? Bring your
son here."

42Even while the boy was coming, the demon threw him to the
ground in a convulsion. But Jesus rebuked the evil[m] spirit, healed
the boy and gave him back to his father. 43And they were all
amazed at the greatness of God.

While everyone was marveling at all that Jesus did, he said to
his disciples, 44"Listen carefully to what I am about to tell you: The
Son of Man is going to be betrayed into the hands of men." 45But

NIV m42 Greek *unclean*

## King James

45But they understood not this saying, and it was hid from them, that they perceived it not: and they feared to ask him of that saying.

46¶ Then there arose a reasoning among them, which of them should be greatest.

47And Jesus, perceiving the thought of their heart, took a child, and set him by him,

48And said unto them, Whosoever shall receive this child in my name receiveth me: and whosoever shall receive me receiveth him that sent me: for he that is least among you all, the same shall be great.

49¶ And John answered and said, Master, we saw one casting out devils in thy name; and we forbad him, because he followeth not with us.

50And Jesus said unto him, Forbid *him* not: for he that is not against us is for us.

51¶ And it came to pass, when the time was come that he should be received up, he stedfastly set his face to go to Jerusalem,

52And sent messengers before his face: and they went, and entered into a village of the Samaritans, to make ready for him.

53And they did not receive him, because his face was as though he would go to Jerusalem.

54And when his disciples James and John saw *this*, they said, Lord, wilt thou that we command fire to come down from heaven, and consume them, even as Elias did?

55But he turned, and rebuked them, and said, Ye know not what manner of spirit ye are of.

56For the Son of man is not come to destroy men's lives, but to save *them*. And they went to another village.

57¶ And it came to pass, that, as they went in the way, a certain *man* said unto him, Lord, I will follow thee whithersoever thou goest.

58And Jesus said unto him, Foxes have holes, and birds of the air *have* nests; but the Son of man hath not where to lay *his* head.

59And he said unto another, Follow me. But he said, Lord, suffer me first to go and bury my father.

60Jesus said unto him, Let the dead bury their dead: but go thou and preach the kingdom of God.

61And another also said, Lord, I will follow thee; but let me first go bid them farewell, which are at home at my house.

62And Jesus said unto him, No man, having put his hand to the plough, and looking back, is fit for the kingdom of God.

**10** AFTER THESE things the Lord appointed other seventy also, and sent them two and two before his face into every city and place, whither he himself would come.

2Therefore said he unto them, The harvest truly *is* great, but the labourers *are* few: pray ye therefore the Lord of the harvest, that he would send forth labourers into his harvest.

3Go your ways: behold, I send you forth as lambs among wolves.

4Carry neither purse, nor scrip, nor shoes: and salute no man by the way.

5And into whatsoever house ye enter, first say, Peace *be* to this house.

6And if the son of peace be there, your peace shall rest upon it: if not, it shall turn to you again.

## Amplified

45However, they did not comprehend this saying, and it was kept hidden from them so that they should not grasp it *and* understand, and they were afraid to ask Him about the statement.

46But a controversy arose among them as to which of them might be the greatest—that is, be surpassing the others in excellence, worth and authority.

47But Jesus, as He perceived the thought of their heart, took a little child and put him at His side,

48And told them, Whoever receives *and* accepts *and* welcomes this child in My name *and* for My sake receives *and* accepts *and* welcomes Me; and whoever so receives Me so also receives Him Who sent Me; for he who is least *and* lowliest among you all, he is [the one who is truly] great.

49John said, Master, we saw a man driving out demons in Your name, and we commanded him to stop it, for he does not follow along with us.

50But Jesus told him, Do not forbid [people]; for whoever is not against you is for you.

51Now when the time was almost come for Jesus to be received up, He steadfastly *and* determinedly set His face to go to Jerusalem. And He sent messengers before Him.

52And they reached and entered a Samaritan village to make ready for Him;

53But [the people] would not welcome *or* receive *or* accept Him, because His face was [set as if He were] going to Jerusalem.

54And when His disciples James and John observed this, they said, Lord, do You wish us to command fire to come down from heaven and consume them, *even as Elijah did*? [II Kings 1:9-16.]

55But He turned and rebuked *and* severely censured them. *He said, You do not know of what sort of spirit you are,*

56 *For the Son of man did not come to destroy men's lives, but to save (them* [a] *from the penalty of eternal death)*. And they journeyed on to another village.

57And it occurred that, as they were going along the road, a man said to Him, *Lord*, I will follow You wherever You go.

58And Jesus told him, Foxes have lurking-holes, and the birds of the air have roosts *and* nests; but the Son of man has no place to lay His head.

59And He said to another, [b]Become My disciple, side with My party, and accompany Me! But he replied, *Lord*, permit me first to go and bury [ [c]await the death of] my father.

60But Jesus said to him, Allow the dead to bury their own dead; but as for you, go *and* publish abroad [d]throughout all regions the kingdom of God.

61Another also said, I will follow You, Lord, *and* become Your disciple, *and* side with Your party; but let me first say goodbye to those at my home.

62Jesus said to him, No one who puts his hand to the plow and looks back [to the things behind] is fit for the kingdom of God.

**10** NOW AFTER this the Lord chose *and* appointed seventy others, and sent them out ahead of Him, two by two, into every town and place where He Himself was about to come (visit).

2And He said to them, [e](There is much ripe *grain*,) the harvest indeed is abundant, but the farm hands are few. Pray therefore the Lord of the harvest to send out laborers into His harvest.

3Go your way; behold, I send you out as lambs into the midst of wolves.

4Carry no purse, no provisions bag, no [change of] sandals; refrain from [retarding your journey by] saluting *and* wishing well any one along the way.

5Whatever house you enter, first say, Peace be to this household!—[that is,] [f]freedom from all the distresses that result from sin be with this family.

6And if any one [worthy] of peace *and* blessedness is there, the peace *and* blessedness you wish shall come upon him; but if not, it shall come back to you.

**AMP** [a] Cremer. [b] Thayer. [c] Many commentators. [d] Vincent. [e] Wycliffe. [f] Cremer.

## New American Standard

45 But they did not understand this statement, and it was concealed from them so that they might not perceive it; and they were afraid to ask Him about this statement.

*The Test of Greatness*

46¶ And an argument arose among them as to which of them might be the greatest.

47 But Jesus, knowing what they were thinking in their heart, took a child and stood him by His side,

48 and said to them, "Whoever receives this child in My name receives Me; and whoever receives Me receives Him who sent Me; for he who is least among you, this is the one who is great."

49¶ And John answered and said, "Master, we saw someone casting out demons in Your name; and we tried to hinder him because he does not follow along with us."

50 But Jesus said to him, "Do not hinder *him;* for he who is not against you is for you."

51¶ And it came about, when the days were approaching for His ascension, that He resolutely set His face to go to Jerusalem;

52 and He sent messengers on ahead of Him. And they went, and entered a village of the Samaritans, to make arrangements for Him.

53 And they did not receive Him, because He was journeying with His face toward Jerusalem.

54 And when His disciples James and John saw *this,* they said, "Lord, do You want us to command fire to come down from heaven and consume them?"

55 But He turned and rebuked them, [and said, "You do not know what kind of spirit you are of;

56 for the Son of Man did not come to destroy men's lives, but to save them."] And they went on to another village.

*Exacting Discipleship*

57¶ And as they were going along the road, someone said to Him, "I will follow You wherever You go."

58 And Jesus said to him, "The foxes have holes, and the birds of the air *have* nests, but the Son of Man has nowhere to lay His head."

59 And He said to another, "Follow Me." But he said, "[g]Permit me first to go and bury my father."

60 But He said to him, "Allow the dead to bury their own dead; but as for you, go and proclaim everywhere the kingdom of God."

61 And another also said, "I will follow You, Lord; but first permit me to say good-bye to those at home."

62 But Jesus said to him, "No one, after putting his hand to the plow and looking back, is fit for the kingdom of God."

*The Seventy Sent Out*

**10** NOW AFTER this the Lord appointed seventy others, and sent them two and two ahead of Him to every city and place where He Himself was going to come.

2 And He was saying to them, "The harvest is plentiful, but the laborers are few; therefore beseech the Lord of the harvest to send out laborers into His harvest.

3 "Go your ways; behold, I send you out as lambs in the midst of wolves.

4 "Carry no purse, no bag, no shoes; and greet no one on the way.

5 "And whatever house you enter, first say, 'Peace *be* to this house.'

6 "And if a man of peace is there, your peace will rest upon him; but if not, it will return to you.

NAS [g] Some mss. add *Lord*

## New International

they did not understand what this meant. It was hidden from them, so that they did not grasp it, and they were afraid to ask him about it.

*Who Will Be the Greatest?*

46 An argument started among the disciples as to which of them
would be the greatest. 47 Jesus, knowing their thoughts, took a little
child and had him stand beside him. 48 Then he said to them,
"Whoever welcomes this little child in my name welcomes me; and whoever welcomes me welcomes the one who sent me. For he who is least among you all—he is the greatest."

49 "Master," said John, "we saw a man driving out demons in your name and we tried to stop him, because he is not one of us."

50 "Do not stop him," Jesus said, "for whoever is not against you is for you."

*Samaritan Opposition*

51 As the time approached for him to be taken up to heaven,
Jesus resolutely set out for Jerusalem. 52 And he sent messengers
on ahead, who went into a Samaritan village to get things ready
for him; 53 but the people there did not welcome him, because he
was heading for Jerusalem. 54 When the disciples James and John
saw this, they asked, "Lord, do you want us to call fire down from
heaven to destroy them[h]?" 55 But Jesus turned and rebuked them,
56 and[i] they went to another village.

*The Cost of Following Jesus*

57 As they were walking along the road, a man said to him, "I will follow you wherever you go."

58 Jesus replied, "Foxes have holes and birds of the air have nests, but the Son of Man has no place to lay his head."

59 He said to another man, "Follow me."

But the man replied, "Lord, first let me go and bury my father."

60 Jesus said to him, "Let the dead bury their own dead, but you go and proclaim the kingdom of God."

61 Still another said, "I will follow you, Lord; but first let me go back and say good-by to my family."

62 Jesus replied, "No one who puts his hand to the plow and looks back is fit for service in the kingdom of God."

*Jesus Sends Out the Seventy-two*

**10** AFTER THIS the Lord appointed seventy-two[j] others and sent them two by two ahead of him to every town and
place where he was about to go. 2 He told them, "The harvest is
plentiful, but the workers are few. Ask the Lord of the harvest,
therefore, to send out workers into his harvest field. 3 Go! I am
sending you out like lambs among wolves. 4 Do not take a purse
or bag or sandals; and do not greet anyone on the road.

5 "When you enter a house, first say, 'Peace to this house.' 6 If
a man of peace is there, your peace will rest on him; if not, it will
return to you. 7 Stay in that house, eating and drinking whatever

NIV [h] 54 Some manuscripts *them, even as Elijah did* [i] 55,56 Some manuscripts *them. And he said, "You do not know what kind of spirit you are of, for the Son of Man did not come to destroy men's lives, but to save them."* 56 *And* [j] 1 Some manuscripts *seventy;* also in verse 17

## King James

7 And in the same house remain, eating and drinking such things as they give: for the labourer is worthy of his hire. Go not from house to house.

8 And into whatsoever city ye enter, and they receive you, eat such things as are set before you:

9 And heal the sick that are therein, and say unto them, The kingdom of God is come nigh unto you.

10 But into whatsoever city ye enter, and they receive you not, go your ways out into the streets of the same, and say,

11 Even the very dust of your city, which cleaveth on us, we do wipe off against you: notwithstanding be ye sure of this, that the kingdom of God is come nigh unto you.

12 But I say unto you, that it shall be more tolerable in that day for Sodom, than for that city.

13 Woe unto thee, Chorazin! woe unto thee, Bethsaida! for if the mighty works had been done in Tyre and Sidon, which have been done in you, they had a great while ago repented, sitting in sackcloth and ashes.

14 But it shall be more tolerable for Tyre and Sidon at the judgment, than for you.

15 And thou, Capernaum, which art exalted to heaven, shalt be thrust down to hell.

16 He that heareth you heareth me; and he that despiseth you despiseth me; and he that despiseth me despiseth him that sent me.

17 ¶ And the seventy returned again with joy, saying, Lord, even the devils are subject unto us through thy name.

18 And he said unto them, I beheld Satan as lightning fall from heaven.

19 Behold, I give unto you power to tread on serpents and scorpions, and over all the power of the enemy: and nothing shall by any means hurt you.

20 Notwithstanding in this rejoice not, that the spirits are subject unto you; but rather rejoice, because your names are written in heaven.

21 ¶ In that hour Jesus rejoiced in spirit, and said, I thank thee, O Father, Lord of heaven and earth, that thou hast hid these things from the wise and prudent, and hast revealed them unto babes: even so, Father; for so it seemed good in thy sight.

22 All things are delivered to me of my Father: and no man knoweth who the Son is, but the Father; and who the Father is, but the Son, and *he* to whom the Son will reveal *him.*

23 ¶ And he turned him unto *his* disciples, and said privately, Blessed *are* the eyes which see the things that ye see:

24 For I tell you, that many prophets and kings have desired to see those things which ye see, and have not seen *them;* and to hear those things which ye hear, and have not heard *them.*

25 ¶ And, behold, a certain lawyer stood up, and tempted him, saying, Master, what shall I do to inherit eternal life?

26 He said unto him, What is written in the law? how readest thou?

27 And he answering said, Thou shalt love the Lord thy God with all thy heart, and with all thy soul, and with all thy strength, and with all thy mind; and thy neighbour as thyself.

28 And he said unto him, Thou hast answered right: this do, and thou shalt live.

29 But he, willing to justify himself, said unto Jesus, And who is my neighbour?

30 And Jesus answering said, A certain *man* went down from Jerusalem to Jericho, and fell among thieves, which stripped him of his raiment, and wounded *him,* and departed, leaving *him* half dead.

## Amplified

7 And stay on in the same house, eating and drinking what they provide, for the laborer is worthy of his wages; do not keep moving from house to house. [Deut. 24:15.]

8 Whenever you go into a town and they receive *and* accept *and* welcome you, eat what is set before you;

9 And heal the sick in it and say to them, The kingdom of God has come close to you.

10 But whenever you go into a town and they do not receive *and* accept *and* welcome you, go out into its streets and say,

11 Even the dust of your town that clings to our feet we are wiping off against you; yet know *and* understand this, that the kingdom of God has come near you.

12 I tell you, it shall be more tolerable in that day for Sodom than for that town. [Gen. 19:24-28.]

13 Woe to you, Chorazin! Woe to you, Bethsaida! For if the mighty miracles performed in you had been performed in Tyre and Sidon, they would have repented long ago, sitting in sackcloth and ashes.

14 However it shall be more tolerable in the judgment for Tyre and Sidon than for you.

15 And you, Capernaum, will you be exalted unto heaven? You shall be brought down to Hades (the regions of the dead).

16 He who hears *and* heeds you [disciples] hears *and* heeds Me; and he who slights *and* rejects you, slights *and* rejects Me; *and* he who slights *and* rejects Me, slights *and* rejects Him who sent Me.

17 The seventy returned with joy, saying, Lord, even the demons are subject to us in Your name!

18 And He said to them, I saw Satan falling like a lightning [flash] from heaven.

19 Behold! I have given you authority *and* power to trample upon serpents and scorpions, and (physical and mental strength and ability) over all the power that the enemy [possesses], and nothing shall in any way harm you.

20 Nevertheless do not rejoice at this, that the spirits are subject to you, but rejoice that your names are enrolled in heaven. [Exod. 32:32; Ps. 69:28; Dan. 12:1.]

21 In that same hour He rejoiced *and* gloried in the Holy Spirit and said, I thank You, Father, Lord of heaven and earth, that You have concealed these things [relating to salvation] from the wise and understanding *and* learned, and revealed them to babes—the childish, unskilled and untaught. Yes, Father, for such was Your gracious [a]will *and* choice *and* good pleasure.

22 All things have been given over into My power by My Father, and no one knows Who the Son is except the Father, or Who the Father is except the Son and any one to whom the Son may choose to reveal *and* make Him known.

23 Then turning to His disciples He said privately, Blessed—happy, [b]to be envied—are those whose eyes see what you see!

24 For I tell you that many prophets and kings longed to see what you see, and they did not see it, and to hear what you hear, and they did not hear it.

25 And then a certain lawyer arose to try (test, tempt) Him, saying, Teacher, what am I to do to inherit everlasting life—[that is,] to partake of eternal salvation in the Messiah's kingdom?

26 Jesus said to him, What is written in the Law? How do you read it?

27 And he replied, You must love the Lord your God with all your heart, and with all your soul, and with all your strength, and with all your mind; and your neighbor as yourself. [Deut. 6:5; Lev. 19:18.]

28 And Jesus said to him, You have answered correctly; do this, and you will live—enjoy active, blessed, endless life in the kingdom of God.

29 And he, [c]determined to acquit himself of reproach, said to Jesus, And who is my neighbor?

30 Jesus [d]taking him up replied, A certain man was going from Jerusalem down to Jericho and he fell among robbers, who stripped him of his clothes and belongings, and beat him, and went their way [ [e]unconcernedly] leaving him half dead, as it happened.

**AMP** [a] Thayer. [b] Souter. [c] Vincent. [d] Vincent. [e] Vincent.

## New American Standard

7"And stay in that house, eating and drinking what they give
you; for the laborer is worthy of his wages. Do not keep moving
from house to house.
8"And whatever city you enter, and they receive you, eat what
is set before you;
9and heal those in it who are sick, and say to them, 'The
kingdom of God has come near to you.'
10"But whatever city you enter and they do not receive you, go
out into its streets and say,
11'Even the dust of your city which clings to our feet, we wipe
off *in protest* against you; yet be sure of this, that the kingdom of
God has come near.'
12"I say to you, it will be more tolerable in that day for Sodom,
than for that city.
13"Woe to you, Chorazin! Woe to you, Bethsaida! For if the
miracles had been performed in Tyre and Sidon which occurred in
you, they would have repented long ago, sitting in sackcloth and
ashes.
14"But it will be more tolerable for Tyre and Sidon in the judgment, than for you.
15"And you, Capernaum, will not be exalted to heaven, will
you? You will be brought down to Hades!
16"The one who listens to you listens to Me, and the one who
rejects you rejects Me; and he who rejects Me rejects the One who
sent Me."

*The Happy Results*

17¶ And the seventy returned with joy, saying, "Lord, even the
demons are subject to us in Your name."
18And He said to them, "I was watching Satan fall from heaven
like lightning.
19"Behold, I have given you authority to tread upon serpents
and scorpions, and over all the power of the enemy, and nothing
shall injure you.
20"Nevertheless do not rejoice in this, that the spirits are subject
to you, but rejoice that your names are recorded in heaven."
21¶ At that very time He rejoiced greatly in the Holy Spirit, and
said, "I praise Thee, O Father, Lord of heaven and earth, that Thou
didst hide these things from *the* wise and intelligent and didst
reveal them to babes. Yes, Father, for thus it was well-pleasing in
Thy sight.
22"All things have been handed over to Me by My Father, and
no one knows who the Son is except the Father, and who the
Father is except the Son, and anyone to whom the Son wills to
reveal *Him.*"
23And turning to the disciples, He said privately, "Blessed *are*
the eyes which see the things you see,
24for I say to you, that many prophets and kings wished to see
the things which you see, and did not see *them,* and to hear the
things which you hear, and did not hear *them.*"
25¶ And behold, a certain lawyer stood up and put Him to the
test, saying, "Teacher, what shall I do to inherit eternal life?"
26And He said to him, "What is written in the Law? How does
it read to you?"
27And he answered and said, "YOU SHALL LOVE THE LORD YOUR
GOD WITH ALL YOUR HEART, AND WITH ALL YOUR SOUL, AND WITH
ALL YOUR STRENGTH, AND WITH ALL YOUR MIND; AND YOUR NEIGH-
BOR AS YOURSELF."
28And He said to him, "You have answered correctly; DO THIS,
AND YOU WILL LIVE."
29But wishing to justify himself, he said to Jesus, "And who is
my neighbor?"

*The Good Samaritan*

30Jesus replied and said, "A certain man was going down from
Jerusalem to Jericho; and he fell among robbers, and they stripped
him and beat him, and went off leaving him half dead.

## New International

they give you, for the worker deserves his wages. Do not move
around from house to house.
8"When you enter a town and are welcomed, eat what is set
before you. 9Heal the sick who are there and tell them, 'The kingdom of God is near you.' 10But when you enter a town and are not
welcomed, go into its streets and say, 11'Even the dust of your
town that sticks to our feet we wipe off against you. Yet be sure
of this: The kingdom of God is near.' 12I tell you, it will be more
bearable on that day for Sodom than for that town.
13"Woe to you, Korazin! Woe to you, Bethsaida! For if the
miracles that were performed in you had been performed in Tyre
and Sidon, they would have repented long ago, sitting in sackcloth
and ashes. 14But it will be more bearable for Tyre and Sidon at the
judgment than for you. 15And you, Capernaum, will you be lifted
up to the skies? No, you will go down to the depths.[f]
16"He who listens to you listens to me; he who rejects you
rejects me; but he who rejects me rejects him who sent me."
17The seventy-two returned with joy and said, "Lord, even the
demons submit to us in your name."
18He replied, "I saw Satan fall like lightning from heaven. 19I
have given you authority to trample on snakes and scorpions and
to overcome all the power of the enemy; nothing will harm you.
20However, do not rejoice that the spirits submit to you, but rejoice
that your names are written in heaven."
21At that time Jesus, full of joy through the Holy Spirit, said,
"I praise you, Father, Lord of heaven and earth, because you have
hidden these things from the wise and learned, and revealed them
to little children. Yes, Father, for this was your good pleasure.
22"All things have been committed to me by my Father. No one
knows who the Son is except the Father, and no one knows who
the Father is except the Son and those to whom the Son chooses
to reveal him."
23Then he turned to his disciples and said privately, "Blessed
are the eyes that see what you see. 24For I tell you that many
prophets and kings wanted to see what you see but did not see it,
and to hear what you hear but did not hear it."

*The Parable of the Good Samaritan*

25On one occasion an expert in the law stood up to test Jesus.
"Teacher," he asked, "what must I do to inherit eternal life?"
26"What is written in the Law?" he replied. "How do you read
it?"
27He answered: " 'Love the Lord your God with all your heart
and with all your soul and with all your strength and with all your
mind'[g]; and, 'Love your neighbor as yourself.'[h]"
28"You have answered correctly," Jesus replied. "Do this and
you will live."
29But he wanted to justify himself, so he asked Jesus, "And who
is my neighbor?"
30In reply Jesus said: "A man was going down from Jerusalem
to Jericho, when he fell into the hands of robbers. They stripped
him of his clothes, beat him and went away, leaving him half dead.

NIV [f] 15 Greek *Hades* [g] 27 Deut. 6:5 [h] 27 Lev. 19:18

## King James

31 And by chance there came down a certain priest that way: and when he saw him, he passed by on the other side.

32 And likewise a Levite, when he was at the place, came and looked *on him,* and passed by on the other side.

33 But a certain Samaritan, as he journeyed, came where he was: and when he saw him, he had compassion *on him,*

34 And went to *him,* and bound up his wounds, pouring in oil and wine, and set him on his own beast, and brought him to an inn, and took care of him.

35 And on the morrow when he departed, he took out two pence, and gave *them* to the host, and said unto him, Take care of him; and whatsoever thou spendest more, when I come again, I will repay thee.

36 Which now of these three, thinkest thou, was neighbour unto him that fell among the thieves?

37 And he said, He that showed mercy on him. Then said Jesus unto him, Go, and do thou likewise.

38 ¶ Now it came to pass, as they went, that he entered into a certain village: and a certain woman named Martha received him into her house.

39 And she had a sister called Mary, which also sat at Jesus' feet, and heard his word.

40 But Martha was cumbered about much serving, and came to him, and said, Lord, dost thou not care that my sister hath left me to serve alone? bid her therefore that she help me.

41 And Jesus answered and said unto her, Martha, Martha, thou art careful and troubled about many things:

42 But one thing is needful: and Mary hath chosen that good part, which shall not be taken away from her.

11 AND IT came to pass, that, as he was praying in a certain place, when he ceased, one of his disciples said unto him, Lord, teach us to pray, as John also taught his disciples.

2 And he said unto them, When ye pray, say, Our Father which art in heaven, Hallowed be thy name. Thy kingdom come. Thy will be done, as in heaven, so in earth.

3 Give us day by day our daily bread.

4 And forgive us our sins; for we also forgive every one that is indebted to us. And lead us not into temptation; but deliver us from evil.

5 And he said unto them, Which of you shall have a friend, and shall go unto him at midnight, and say unto him, Friend, lend me three loaves;

6 For a friend of mine in his journey is come to me, and I have nothing to set before him?

7 And he from within shall answer and say, Trouble me not: the door is now shut, and my children are with me in bed; I cannot rise and give thee.

8 I say unto you, Though he will not rise and give him, because he is his friend, yet because of his importunity he will rise and give him as many as he needeth.

9 And I say unto you, Ask, and it shall be given you; seek, and ye shall find; knock, and it shall be opened unto you.

10 For every one that asketh receiveth; and he that seeketh findeth; and to him that knocketh it shall be opened.

## Amplified

31 Now by [a]coincidence a certain priest was going down along that road; and when he saw him he passed by on the other side.

32 A Levite likewise came down to the place and saw him, and passed by on the other side [of the road].

33 But a certain Samaritan, as he traveled along came down to where he was, and when he saw him was moved with pity *and* sympathy [for him],

34 And went to him and dressed his wounds, pouring on [them] oil and wine. Then he set him on his own beast, and brought him to an inn, and took care of him.

35 And the next day he took out two denarii [two day's wages], and gave [them] to the innkeeper, saying, Take care of him; and whatever more you spend, I [myself] will repay you when I return.

36 Which of these three, do you think, proved himself neighbor to him who fell among the robbers?

37 He answered, The one who showed pity *and* mercy to him. And Jesus said to him, Go and do likewise.

38 Now while they were on their way, it occurred that Jesus entered a certain village, and a woman named Martha received *and* welcomed Him into her house.

39 And she had a sister named Mary, who seated herself at the Lord's feet and was listening to His teaching.

40 But Martha (overoccupied and too busy) was distracted about much serving; and she came up to Him and said, Lord, is it nothing to You that my sister has left me to serve alone? Tell her then to help me—to lend a hand and do her part along with me.

41 But the Lord replied to her by saying, Martha, Martha, you are anxious and troubled about many things;

42 There is need of (but [b]a few things, or) [c]only one. Mary has chosen the good portion—[d]that which is to advantage—which shall not be taken away from her.

11 THEN HE was praying in a certain place, and when He stopped, one of His disciples said to Him, Lord, teach us to pray, as John taught his disciples.

2 And He said to them, When you pray, say, [Our] Father, [Who is in heaven,] hallowed be Your name. Your kingdom come. *Your will be done—held holy and revered—on earth as it is in heaven.*

3 Give us daily our bread ( [e]food for the morrow),

4 And forgive us our sins, for we ourselves also forgive every one who is indebted to us—who has offended us or done us wrong; and bring us not into temptation, *but rescue us from evil.*

5 And He said to them, Which of you who has a friend will go to him at midnight and will say to him, Friend, lend me three loaves [of bread],

6 For a friend of mine who is on a journey has just come, and I have nothing to put before him;

7 And he from within will answer, Do not disturb me; the door is now closed, and my children are with me in bed; I cannot get up and supply you [with anything]?

8 I tell you, although he will not get up and supply him anything because he is his friend, yet because of his shameless persistence *and* insistence, he will get up and give him as much as he needs.

9 So I say to you, Ask *and* [f]keep on asking, and it shall be given you; seek *and* [g]keep on seeking, and you shall find; knock *and* [h]keep on knocking, and the door shall be opened to you.

10 For every one who asks *and* [i]keeps on asking receives, and he who seeks *and* [j]keeps on seeking finds, and to him who knocks *and* [k]keeps on knocking the door shall be opened.

**AMP** [a] Vincent. [b] Many ancient authorities read "few things" or "only one." [c] Many ancient authorities read "few things" or "only one." [d] Cremer. [e] Moulton and Milligan. [f] Williams: "This continuance is in the present imperative and present participles often repeated." [g] Williams: "This continuance is in the present imperative and present participles often repeated." [h] Williams: "This continuance is in the present imperative and present participles often repeated." [i] Williams: "This continuance is in the present imperative and present participles often repeated." [j] Williams: "This continuance is in the present imperative and present participles often repeated." [k] Williams: "This continuance is in the present imperative and present participles often repeated."

## New American Standard

31"And by chance a certain priest was going down on that road, and when he saw him, he passed by on the other side.
32"And likewise a Levite also, when he came to the place and saw him, passed by on the other side.
33"But a certain Samaritan, who was on a journey, came upon him; and when he saw him, he felt compassion,
34and came to him, and bandaged up his wounds, pouring oil and wine on *them;* and he put him on his own beast, and brought him to an inn, and took care of him.
35"And on the next day he took out two [l]denarii and gave them to the innkeeper and said, 'Take care of him; and whatever more you spend, when I return, I will repay you.'
36"Which of these three do you think proved to be a neighbor to the man who fell into the robbers' *hands?"*
37And he said, "The one who showed mercy toward him." And Jesus said to him, "Go and do the same."

*Martha and Mary*

38¶ Now as they were traveling along, He entered a certain village; and a woman named Martha welcomed Him into her home.
39And she had a sister called Mary, who moreover was listening to the Lord's word, seated at His feet.
40But Martha was distracted with all her preparations; and she came up *to Him,* and said, "Lord, do You not care that my sister has left me to do all the serving alone? Then tell her to help me."
41But the Lord answered and said to her, "Martha, Martha, you are worried and bothered about so many things;
42but *only* a few things are necessary, really *only* one, for Mary has chosen the good part, which shall not be taken away from her."

*Instruction about Prayer*

**11** AND IT came about that while He was praying in a certain place, after He had finished, one of His disciples said to Him, "Lord, teach us to pray just as John also taught his disciples."
2And He said to them, "When you pray, say:
'[m]Father, hallowed be Thy name.
Thy kingdom come.
3 'Give us each day our daily bread.
4 'And forgive us our sins,
For we ourselves also forgive everyone who is indebted to us.
And lead us not into temptation.' "
5¶ And He said to them, "Suppose one of you shall have a friend, and shall go to him at midnight, and say to him, 'Friend, lend me three loaves;
6for a friend of mine has come to me from a journey, and I have nothing to set before him';
7and from inside he shall answer and say, 'Do not bother me; the door has already been shut and my children and I are in bed; I cannot get up and give you *anything.*'
8"I tell you, even though he will not get up and give him *anything* because he is his friend, yet because of his persistence he will get up and give him as much as he needs.
9"And I say to you, ask, and it shall be given to you; seek, and you shall find; knock, and it shall be opened to you.
10"For everyone who asks, receives; and he who seeks, finds; and to him who knocks, it shall be opened.

**NAS** [l] The denarius was equivalent to one day's wage [m]Some mss. insert phrases from Matt. 6:9–13 to make the two passages closely similar

## New International

31A priest happened to be going down the same road, and when
he saw the man, he passed by on the other side. 32So too, a Levite,
when he came to the place and saw him, passed by on the other
side. 33But a Samaritan, as he traveled, came where the man was;
and when he saw him, he took pity on him. 34He went to him and
bandaged his wounds, pouring on oil and wine. Then he put the
man on his own donkey, took him to an inn and took care of him.
35The next day he took out two silver coins[n] and gave them to the
innkeeper. 'Look after him,' he said, 'and when I return, I will
reimburse you for any extra expense you may have.'
36"Which of these three do you think was a neighbor to the man
who fell into the hands of robbers?"
37The expert in the law replied, "The one who had mercy on
him."
Jesus told him, "Go and do likewise."

*At the Home of Martha and Mary*

38As Jesus and his disciples were on their way, he came to a
village where a woman named Martha opened her home to him.
39She had a sister called Mary, who sat at the Lord's feet listening
to what he said. 40But Martha was distracted by all the preparations that had to be made. She came to him and asked, "Lord,
don't you care that my sister has left me to do the work by myself?
Tell her to help me!"
41"Martha, Martha," the Lord answered, "you are worried and
upset about many things, 42but only one thing is needed.[o] Mary
has chosen what is better, and it will not be taken away from her."

*Jesus' Teaching on Prayer*

**11** ONE DAY Jesus was praying in a certain place. When he finished, one of his disciples said to him, "Lord, teach us to pray, just as John taught his disciples."
2He said to them, "When you pray, say:

" 'Father,[p]
hallowed be your name,
your kingdom come.[q]
3Give us each day our daily bread.
4Forgive us our sins,
for we also forgive everyone who sins against us.[r]
And lead us not into temptation.[s] ' "

5Then he said to them, "Suppose one of you has a friend, and
he goes to him at midnight and says, 'Friend, lend me three loaves
of bread, 6because a friend of mine on a journey has come to me,
and I have nothing to set before him.'
7"Then the one inside answers, 'Don't bother me. The door is
already locked, and my children are with me in bed. I can't get up
and give you anything.' 8I tell you, though he will not get up and
give him the bread because he is his friend, yet because of the
man's boldness[t] he will get up and give him as much as he needs.
9"So I say to you: Ask and it will be given to you; seek and you
will find; knock and the door will be opened to you. 10For everyone
who asks receives; he who seeks finds; and to him who knocks,
the door will be opened.

**NIV** [n] 35 Greek *two denarii* [o] 42 Some manuscripts *but few things are needed—or only one* [p] 2 Some manuscripts *Our Father in heaven* [q] 2 Some manuscripts *come. May your will be done on earth as it is in heaven.* [r] 4 Greek *everyone who is indebted to us* [s] 4 Some manuscripts *temptation but deliver us from the evil one* [t] 8 Or *persistence*

## King James

11 If a son shall ask bread of any of you that is a father, will he
give him a stone? or if *he ask* a fish, will he for a fish give him a
serpent?
12 Or if he shall ask an egg, will he offer him a scorpion?
13 If ye then, being evil, know how to give good gifts unto your
children: how much more shall *your* heavenly Father give the Holy
Spirit to them that ask him?
14 ¶ And he was casting out a devil, and it was dumb. And it
came to pass, when the devil was gone out, the dumb spake; and
the people wondered.
15 But some of them said, He casteth out devils through Beelzebub the chief of the devils.
16 And others, tempting *him*, sought of him a sign from heaven.
17 But he, knowing their thoughts, said unto them, Every kingdom divided against itself is brought to desolation; and a house
*divided* against a house falleth.
18 If Satan also be divided against himself, how shall his kingdom stand? because ye say that I cast out devils through Beelzebub.
19 And if I by Beelzebub cast out devils, by whom do your sons
cast *them* out? therefore shall they be your judges.
20 But if I with the finger of God cast out devils, no doubt the
kingdom of God is come upon you.
21 When a strong man armed keepeth his palace, his goods are
in peace:
22 But when a stronger than he shall come upon him, and overcome him, he taketh from him all his armour wherein he trusted,
and divideth his spoils.
23 He that is not with me is against me: and he that gathereth
not with me scattereth.
24 When the unclean spirit is gone out of a man, he walketh
through dry places, seeking rest; and finding none, he saith, I will
return unto my house whence I came out.
25 And when he cometh, he findeth *it* swept and garnished.
26 Then goeth he, and taketh *to him* seven other spirits more
wicked than himself; and they enter in, and dwell there: and the
last *state* of that man is worse than the first.
27 ¶ And it came to pass, as he spake these things, a certain
woman of the company lifted up her voice, and said unto him,
Blessed *is* the womb that bare thee, and the paps which thou hast
sucked.
28 But he said, Yea rather, blessed *are* they that hear the word
of God, and keep it.
29 ¶ And when the people were gathered thick together, he
began to say, This is an evil generation: they seek a sign; and there
shall no sign be given it, but the sign of Jonas the prophet.
30 For as Jonas was a sign unto the Ninevites, so shall also the
Son of man be to this generation.
31 The queen of the south shall rise up in the judgment with the
men of this generation, and condemn them: for she came from the
utmost parts of the earth to hear the wisdom of Solomon; and,
behold, a greater than Solomon *is* here.
32 The men of Nineve shall rise up in the judgment with this
generation, and shall condemn it: for they repented at the preaching of Jonas; and, behold, a greater than Jonas *is* here.
33 No man, when he hath lighted a candle, putteth *it* in a secret
place, neither under a bushel, but on a candlestick, that they which
come in may see the light.

## Amplified

11 What father among you, if his son asks for *a loaf of bread, will
give him a stone; or if he asks for* a fish, will instead of a fish give him
a serpent;
12 Or if he asks for an egg, will give him a scorpion?
13 If you then, evil-minded as you are, know how to give good
gifts—gifts [a]that are to advantage—to your children, how much
more will your heavenly Father give the Holy Spirit to those who
ask *and* [b]continue to ask Him!
14 Now Jesus was driving out a demon that was dumb, and it
occurred that when the demon had gone out, the dumb man
spoke. And the crowds marveled.
15 But some of them said, He drives out demons [because He is
in league with, and] by Beelzebub, the prince of demons;
16 While others, to try *and* test *and* tempt Him, demanded a sign
of Him from heaven.
17 But He, [well] aware of their intent *and* purpose, said to them,
Every kingdom split up against itself is doomed *and* brought to
desolation, and so house falls upon house.—The disunited household will collapse.
18 And if Satan also is divided against himself, how will his
kingdom last? For you say that I expel demons with the help of *and*
by Beelzebub.
19 Now if I expel demons with the help of *and* by Beelzebub, with
whose help *and* by whom do your sons drive them out? Therefore
they shall be your judges.
20 But if I drive out the demons by the finger of God, then the
kingdom of God has (already) come upon you.
21 When the strong man, fully armed, ( [c]from his courtyard)
guards his own dwelling, his belongings are undisturbed—his
property is at peace (secure).
22 But when one stronger than he attacks him and conquers him,
he robs him of his whole armor on which he had relied, and
divides up *and* distributes all his goods as plunder (spoil).
23 He who is not with Me—siding and believing with Me—is
against Me, and he who does not gather with Me (engage in My
interest), scatters.
24 When the unclean spirit has gone out of a person, he roams
through waterless places in search [of a place] of rest (release,
refreshing, ease); and finding none he says, I will go back to my
house from which I came.
25 And when he arrives, he finds [the place] swept *and* put in
order and furnished *and* decorated.
26 And he goes and brings other spirits, seven [of them], more
evil than himself, and they enter in, settle down *and* dwell there;
and the last state of that person is worse than the first.
27 Now it occurred that as He was saying these things, a certain
woman in the crowd raised her voice and said to Him, Blessed—
happy and [d]to be envied—is the womb that bore You, and the
breasts that You sucked!
28 But He said, Blessed—happy and [e]to be envied—rather are
they who hear the Word of God and obey *and* practice it!
29 Now as the crowds were (increasingly) thronging Him, He
began to say, This present generation is a wicked one; it seeks *and*
demands a sign (miracle), but no sign shall be given to it except
the sign of Jonah [the prophet]. [Jonah 1:17 with Matt. 12:40.]
30 For [just] as Jonah became a sign to the people of Nineveh,
so will also the Son of man be [a sign] to this age *and* generation.
[Jonah 3:4-10.]
31 The queen of the South will arise in the judgment with the
people of this age *and* generation and condemn them; for she came
from the ends of the (inhabited) earth to listen to the wisdom of
Solomon, and notice, [f]here is more than Solomon. [I Kings
10:1-13; II Chron. 9:1-12.]
32 The men of Nineveh will appear as witnesses at the judgment
with this generation and will condemn it; for they repented at the
preaching of Jonah, and behold, [g]here is more than Jonah. [Jonah
3:4-10.]
33 No one after lighting a lamp puts it in a cellar *or* crypt or under
a bushel measure, but on a [lamp]stand, that those who are coming
in may see the light.

**AMP** [a] Cremer. [b] Williams: "This continuance is in the present imperative and present participles often repeated." [c] Vincent. [d] Souter. [e] Souter. [f] Wycliffe. [g] Wycliffe.

## New American Standard

11"Now suppose one of you fathers is asked by his son for a fish;
he will not give him a snake instead of a fish, will he?
12"Or *if* he is asked for an egg, he will not give him a scorpion,
will he?
13"If you then, being evil, know how to give good gifts to your
children, how much more shall *your* heavenly Father give the Holy
Spirit to those who ask Him?"

*Pharisees' Blasphemy*

**14**¶ And He was casting out a demon, and it was dumb; and it
came about that when the demon had gone out, the dumb man
spoke; and the multitudes marveled.
15But some of them said, "He casts out demons by Beelzebul,
the ruler of the demons."
16And others, to test *Him*, were demanding of Him a sign from
heaven.
17But He knew their thoughts, and said to them, "Any kingdom
divided against itself is laid waste; and a house *divided* against itself
falls.
18"And if Satan also is divided against himself, how shall his
kingdom stand? For you say that I cast out demons by Beelzebul.
19"And if I by Beelzebul cast out demons, by whom do your
sons cast them out? Consequently they shall be your judges.
20"But if I cast out demons by the finger of God, then the
kingdom of God has come upon you.
21"When a strong *man*, fully armed, guards his own homestead,
his possessions are undisturbed;
22but when someone stronger than he attacks him and overpowers him, he takes away from him all his armor on which he
had relied, and distributes his plunder.
23"He who is not with Me is against Me; and he who does not
gather with Me, scatters.
24"When the unclean spirit goes out of a man, it passes through
waterless places seeking rest, and not finding any, it says, 'I will
return to my house from which I came.'
25"And when it comes, it finds it swept and put in order.
26"Then it goes and takes *along* seven other spirits more evil
than itself, and they go in and live there; and the last state of that
man becomes worse than the first."
**27**¶ And it came about while He said these things, one of the
women in the crowd raised her voice, and said to Him, "Blessed
is the womb that bore You, and the breasts at which You nursed."
28But He said, "On the contrary, blessed are those who hear the
word of God, and observe it."

*The Sign of Jonah*

**29**¶ And as the crowds were increasing, He began to say, "This
generation is a wicked generation; it seeks for a sign, and *yet* no
sign shall be given to it but the sign of Jonah.
30"For just as Jonah became a sign to the Ninevites, so shall the
Son of Man be to this generation.
31"The Queen of the South shall rise up with the men of this
generation at the judgment and condemn them, because she came
from the ends of the earth to hear the wisdom of Solomon; and
behold, something greater than Solomon is here.
32"The men of Nineveh shall stand up with this generation at
the judgment and condemn it, because they repented at the
preaching of Jonah; and behold, something greater than Jonah is
here.
**33**¶ "No one, after lighting a lamp, puts it away in a cellar, nor
under a peck-measure, but on the lampstand, in order that those
who enter may see the light.

## New International

11"Which of you fathers, if your son asks for[h] a fish, will give
him a snake instead? 12Or if he asks for an egg, will give him a
scorpion? 13If you then, though you are evil, know how to give
good gifts to your children, how much more will your Father in
heaven give the Holy Spirit to those who ask him!"

*Jesus and Beelzebub*

14Jesus was driving out a demon that was mute. When the
demon left, the man who had been mute spoke, and the crowd
was amazed. 15But some of them said, "By Beelzebub,[i] the prince
of demons, he is driving out demons." 16Others tested him by
asking for a sign from heaven.
17Jesus knew their thoughts and said to them: "Any kingdom
divided against itself will be ruined, and a house divided against
itself will fall. 18If Satan is divided against himself, how can his
kingdom stand? I say this because you claim that I drive out
demons by Beelzebub. 19Now if I drive out demons by Beelzebub,
by whom do your followers drive them out? So then, they will be
your judges. 20But if I drive out demons by the finger of God, then
the kingdom of God has come to you.
21"When a strong man, fully armed, guards his own house, his
possessions are safe. 22But when someone stronger attacks and
overpowers him, he takes away the armor in which the man
trusted and divides up the spoils.
23"He who is not with me is against me, and he who does not
gather with me, scatters.
24"When an evil[j] spirit comes out of a man, it goes through arid
places seeking rest and does not find it. Then it says, 'I will return
to the house I left.' 25When it arrives, it finds the house swept clean
and put in order. 26Then it goes and takes seven other spirits more
wicked than itself, and they go in and live there. And the final
condition of that man is worse than the first."
27As Jesus was saying these things, a woman in the crowd
called out, "Blessed is the mother who gave you birth and nursed
you."
28He replied, "Blessed rather are those who hear the word of
God and obey it."

*The Sign of Jonah*

29As the crowds increased, Jesus said, "This is a wicked generation. It asks for a miraculous sign, but none will be given it except
the sign of Jonah. 30For as Jonah was a sign to the Ninevites, so
also will the Son of Man be to this generation. 31The Queen of the
South will rise at the judgment with the men of this generation and
condemn them; for she came from the ends of the earth to listen
to Solomon's wisdom, and now one[k] greater than Solomon is
here. 32The men of Nineveh will stand up at the judgment with
this generation and condemn it; for they repented at the preaching
of Jonah, and now one greater than Jonah is here.

*The Lamp of the Body*

33"No one lights a lamp and puts it in a place where it will be
hidden, or under a bowl. Instead he puts it on its stand, so that
those who come in may see the light. 34Your eye is the lamp of your

NIV [h] *11* Some manuscripts *for bread, will give him a stone; or if he asks for*
[i] *15* Greek *Beezeboul* or *Beelzeboul;* also in verses 18 and 19 [j] *24* Greek *unclean*
[k] *31* Or *something;* also in verse 32

## King James

34The light of the body is the eye: therefore when thine eye is
single, thy whole body also is full of light; but when *thine eye* is evil,
thy body also *is* full of darkness.
35Take heed therefore that the light which is in thee be not
darkness.
36If thy whole body therefore *be* full of light, having no part
dark, the whole shall be full of light, as when the bright shining
of a candle doth give thee light.
37¶ And as he spake, a certain Pharisee besought him to dine
with him: and he went in, and sat down to meat.
38And when the Pharisee saw *it,* he marvelled that he had not
first washed before dinner.
39And the Lord said unto him, Now do ye Pharisees make clean
the outside of the cup and the platter; but your inward part is full
of ravening and wickedness.
40 *Ye* fools, did not he that made that which is without make that
which is within also?
41But rather give alms of such things as ye have; and, behold,
all things are clean unto you.
42But woe unto you, Pharisees! for ye tithe mint and rue and
all manner of herbs, and pass over judgment and the love of God:
these ought ye to have done, and not to leave the other undone.
43Woe unto you, Pharisees! for ye love the uppermost seats in
the synagogues, and greetings in the markets.
44Woe unto you, scribes and Pharisees, hypocrites! for ye are
as graves which appear not, and the men that walk over *them* are
not aware *of them.*
45¶ Then answered one of the lawyers, and said unto him,
Master, thus saying thou reproachest us also.
46And he said, Woe unto you also, *ye* lawyers! for ye lade men
with burdens grievous to be borne, and ye yourselves touch not
the burdens with one of your fingers.
47Woe unto you! for ye build the sepulchres of the prophets,
and your fathers killed them.
48Truly ye bear witness that ye allow the deeds of your fathers:
for they indeed killed them, and ye build their sepulchres.
49Therefore also said the wisdom of God, I will send them
prophets and apostles, and *some* of them they shall slay and persecute:
50That the blood of all the prophets, which was shed from the
foundation of the world, may be required of this generation;
51From the blood of Abel unto the blood of Zacharias, which
perished between the altar and the temple: verily I say unto you,
It shall be required of this generation.
52Woe unto you, lawyers! for ye have taken away the key of
knowledge: ye entered not in yourselves, and them that were
entering in ye hindered.
53And as he said these things unto them, the scribes and the
Pharisees began to urge *him* vehemently, and to provoke him to
speak of many things:
54Laying wait for him, and seeking to catch something out of
his mouth, that they might accuse him.

## Amplified

34Your eye is the lamp of your body; when your eye [ [a]your
conscience] is sound *and* fulfilling its office, your whole body is full
of light; but when it is not sound *and* is not fulfilling its office, your
body is full of darkness.
35Be careful therefore that the light that is in you be not darkness.
36If then your entire body is illuminated, having no part dark,
it will be wholly bright [with light], as when a lamp with its bright
rays gives you light.
37Now while Jesus was speaking, a Pharisee invited Him to take
dinner with him, so He entered and reclined at table.
38The Pharisee noticed and was astonished [to see] that Jesus
did not first wash before dinner.
39But the Lord said to him, Now you Pharisees cleanse the
outside of the cup and of the plate, but inside you yourselves are
full of greed *and* robbery *and* extortion and malice *and* wickedness.
40You senseless (foolish, stupid) ones—acting without reflection *or* intelligence! Did not He Who made the outside make the
inside also?
41But [dedicate your inner self and] give for donations to the
poor of those things which are within [of inward righteousness]
and behold, everything is purified *and* clean for you.
42But woe to you, Pharisees! Because you tithe the mint and rue and
every (little) herb, and disregard *and* neglect justice and the love
of God. These you ought to have done without leaving the others
undone. [Lev. 27:30; Mic. 6:8.]
43Woe to you, Pharisees! For you love the best seats in the
synagogues and to be greeted *and* bowed down to in the market
(public) places.
44Woe to you! For you are like graves which are not marked *or*
seen, and men walk over them without being aware of it [and are
ceremonially defiled].
45One of the experts of the [Mosaic] Law answered Him,
Teacher, in saying this You reproach *and* outrage *and* affront even
us!
46But He said, Woe to you, the lawyers, also! For you load men
with oppressive burdens hard to bear, and you do not personally
[even [b]gently] touch the burdens with one of your fingers.
47Woe to you! For you are [c]rebuilding *and* repairing the tombs
of the prophets whom your fathers killed (destroyed).
48So you bear witness, and give your full approval *and* consent
to the deeds of your fathers; for they actually killed them, and you
rebuild *and* repair monuments to them.
49For this reason also the Wisdom of God said, I will send them
prophets and apostles, [some] of whom they will put to death and
persecute,
50So that the blood of all the prophets shed from the foundation
of the world may be charged against *and* required of this age *and*
generation,
51From the blood of Abel to the blood of Zechariah, who was
slain between the altar and the sanctuary. Yes, I tell you, it shall
be charged against *and* required of this age *and* generation. [Gen.
4:8; II Chron. 24:20, 21; Zech. 1:1.]
52Woe to you, lawyers—experts in the [Mosaic] Law! For you
have taken away the key to knowledge; you did not go in yourselves, and you hindered *and* prevented those who were entering.
53As He left there, the scribes and the Pharisees [followed Him
closely, and they] began [d]to be enraged with *and* set themselves
violently against Him, and to draw Him out *and* provoke Him to
speak of many things,
54Secretly watching *and* plotting *and* lying in wait for Him, to
seize upon something He might say [that they might accuse Him].

AMP [a] Cremer. [b] Vincent. [c] Thayer. [d] Thayer.

## New American Standard

34"The lamp of your body is your eye; when your eye is clear,
your whole body also is full of light; but when it is bad, your body
also is full of darkness.
35"Then watch out that the light in you may not be darkness.
36"If therefore your whole body is full of light, with no dark part
in it, it shall be wholly illumined, as when the lamp illumines you
with its rays."

*Woes upon the Pharisees*

**37**¶ Now when He had spoken, a Pharisee *asked Him to have
lunch with him; and He went in, and reclined *at the table*.
38And when the Pharisee saw it, he was surprised that He had
not first ceremonially washed before the meal.
39But the Lord said to him, "Now you Pharisees clean the
outside of the cup and of the platter; but inside of you, you are full
of robbery and wickedness.
40"You foolish ones, did not He who made the outside make the
inside also?
41"But give that which is within as charity, and then all things
are clean for you.
**42**¶ "But woe to you Pharisees! For you pay tithe of mint and
rue and every *kind of* garden herb, and *yet* disregard justice and the
love of God; but these are the things you should have done without neglecting the others.
43"Woe to you Pharisees! For you love the front seats in the
synagogues, and the respectful greetings in the market places.
44"Woe to you! For you are like concealed tombs, and the
people who walk over *them* are unaware *of it*."
**45**¶ And one of the [e]lawyers *said to Him in reply, "Teacher,
when You say this, You insult us too."
46But He said, "Woe to you lawyers as well! For you weigh men
down with burdens hard to bear, while you yourselves will not
even touch the burdens with one of your fingers.
47"Woe to you! For you build the tombs of the prophets, and
*it was* your fathers *who* killed them.
48"Consequently, you are witnesses and approve the deeds of
your fathers; because it was they who killed them, and you build
*their tombs*.
49"For this reason also the wisdom of God said, 'I will send to
them prophets and apostles, and *some* of them they will kill and
*some* they will persecute,
50in order that the blood of all the prophets, shed since the
foundation of the world, may be charged against this generation,
51from the blood of Abel to the blood of Zechariah, who perished between the altar and the house *of God;* yes, I tell you, it shall
be charged against this generation.'
52"Woe to you lawyers! For you have taken away the key of
knowledge; you did not enter in yourselves, and those who were
entering in you hindered."
**53**¶ And when He left there, the scribes and the Pharisees began
to be very hostile and to question Him closely on many subjects,
54plotting against Him, to catch *Him* in something He might
say.

NAS [e] I.e., experts in the Mosaic law

## New International

body. When your eyes are good, your whole body also is full of
light. But when they are bad, your body also is full of darkness.
35See to it, then, that the light within you is not darkness. 36There-
fore, if your whole body is full of light, and no part of it dark, it
will be completely lighted, as when the light of a lamp shines on
you."

*Six Woes*

37When Jesus had finished speaking, a Pharisee invited him to
eat with him; so he went in and reclined at the table. 38But the
Pharisee, noticing that Jesus did not first wash before the meal,
was surprised.
39Then the Lord said to him, "Now then, you Pharisees clean
the outside of the cup and dish, but inside you are full of greed
and wickedness. 40You foolish people! Did not the one who made
the outside make the inside also? 41But give what is inside ⌊the
dish⌋[f] to the poor, and everything will be clean for you.
42"Woe to you Pharisees, because you give God a tenth of your
mint, rue and all other kinds of garden herbs, but you neglect
justice and the love of God. You should have practiced the latter
without leaving the former undone.
43"Woe to you Pharisees, because you love the most important
seats in the synagogues and greetings in the marketplaces.
44"Woe to you, because you are like unmarked graves, which
men walk over without knowing it."
45One of the experts in the law answered him, "Teacher, when
you say these things, you insult us also."
46Jesus replied, "And you experts in the law, woe to you,
because you load people down with burdens they can hardly
carry, and you yourselves will not lift one finger to help them.
47"Woe to you, because you build tombs for the prophets, and
it was your forefathers who killed them. 48So you testify that you
approve of what your forefathers did; they killed the prophets, and
you build their tombs. 49Because of this, God in his wisdom said,
'I will send them prophets and apostles, some of whom they will
kill and others they will persecute.' 50Therefore this generation will
be held responsible for the blood of all the prophets that has been
shed since the beginning of the world, 51from the blood of Abel
to the blood of Zechariah, who was killed between the altar and
the sanctuary. Yes, I tell you, this generation will be held responsible for it all.
52"Woe to you experts in the law, because you have taken away
the key to knowledge. You yourselves have not entered, and you
have hindered those who were entering."
53When Jesus left there, the Pharisees and the teachers of the
law began to oppose him fiercely and to besiege him with questions, 54waiting to catch him in something he might say.

NIV [f] 41 Or *what you have*

## King James

12 IN THE mean time, when there were gathered together an innumerable multitude of people, insomuch that they trode one upon another, he began to say unto his disciples first of all, Beware ye of the leaven of the Pharisees, which is hypocrisy.

2For there is nothing covered, that shall not be revealed; neither hid, that shall not be known.

3Therefore whatsoever ye have spoken in darkness shall be heard in the light; and that which ye have spoken in the ear in closets shall be proclaimed upon the housetops.

4And I say unto you my friends, Be not afraid of them that kill the body, and after that have no more that they can do.

5But I will forewarn you whom ye shall fear: Fear him, which after he hath killed hath power to cast into hell; yea, I say unto you, Fear him.

6Are not five sparrows sold for two farthings, and not one of them is forgotten before God?

7But even the very hairs of your head are all numbered. Fear not therefore: ye are of more value than many sparrows.

8Also I say unto you, Whosoever shall confess me before men, him shall the Son of man also confess before the angels of God:

9But he that denieth me before men shall be denied before the angels of God.

10And whosoever shall speak a word against the Son of man, it shall be forgiven him: but unto him that blasphemeth against the Holy Ghost it shall not be forgiven.

11And when they bring you unto the synagogues, and *unto* magistrates, and powers, take ye no thought how or what thing ye shall answer, or what ye shall say:

12For the Holy Ghost shall teach you in the same hour what ye ought to say.

13¶ And one of the company said unto him, Master, speak to my brother, that he divide the inheritance with me.

14And he said unto him, Man, who made me a judge or a divider over you?

15And he said unto them, Take heed, and beware of covetousness: for a man's life consisteth not in the abundance of the things which he possesseth.

16And he spake a parable unto them, saying, The ground of a certain rich man brought forth plentifully:

17And he thought within himself, saying, What shall I do, because I have no room where to bestow my fruits?

18And he said, This will I do: I will pull down my barns, and build greater; and there will I bestow all my fruits and my goods.

19And I will say to my soul, Soul, thou hast much goods laid up for many years; take thine ease, eat, drink, *and* be merry.

20But God said unto him, *Thou* fool, this night thy soul shall be required of thee: then whose shall those things be, which thou hast provided?

21So *is* he that layeth up treasure for himself, and is not rich toward God.

22¶ And he said unto his disciples, Therefore I say unto you, Take no thought for your life, what ye shall eat; neither for the body, what ye shall put on.

## Amplified

12 IN THE meanwhile, when so many thousands of the people had gathered that they were trampling on one another, Jesus commenced by saying, primarily to His disciples, Be on your guard against the leaven (ferment) of the Pharisees which is hypocrisy [producing unrest and violent agitation].

2Nothing is [so closely] covered up that it will not be revealed, or hidden that will not be known.

3Whatever you have spoken in the darkness shall be heard *and* listened to in the light, and what you have whispered in [people's] ears and behind closed doors, will be proclaimed upon the housetops.

4I tell you, My friends, do not dread *and* be afraid of those who kill the body, and after that have nothing more that they can do.

5But I will warn you whom you should fear: fear Him Who, after killing, has power to hurl into hell (Gehenna); yes, I say to you, fear Him!

6Are not five sparrows sold for two pennies? And [yet] not one of them is forgotten *or* uncared for in the presence of God.

7But [even] the very hairs of your head are all numbered. Do not be struck with fear *or* seized with alarm; you are of greater worth than many [flocks] of sparrows.

8And I tell you: Whoever declares openly—speaking out freely— *and* confesses that he is My worshipper *and* acknowledges Me before men, the Son of man also will declare *and* confess *and* acknowledge him before the angels of God.

9But he who disowns *and* denies *and* rejects *and* refuses to acknowledge Me before men will be disowned *and* denied *and* rejected *and* refused acknowledgement in the presence of the angels of God.

10And everyone who makes a statement *or* speaks a word against the Son of man, it will be forgiven him; but he who blasphemes against the Holy Spirit [that is, whoever [a]intentionally comes short of the reverence due the Holy Spirit], it will not be forgiven him—for him there is no forgiveness.

11And when they bring you before the synagogues and the magistrates and the authorities, do not be anxious [beforehand] how you shall reply in defense or what you are to say.

12For the Holy Spirit will teach you in that every hour *and* [b]moment what [you] ought to say.

13Someone from the crowd said to Him, Master, order my brother to divide the inheritance *and* share it with me.

14But He told him, Man, who has appointed Me a judge or umpire *and* divider over you?

15And He said to them, Guard yourselves and keep free from all covetousness—the immoderate desire for wealth, the greedy longing to have more; for a man's life does not consist *and* is not derived from possessing [c]overflowing abundance, *or* that which is [d]over and above his needs.

16Then He told them a parable, saying, The land of a rich man was fertile *and* yielded plentifully;

17And he considered *and* debated within himself, What shall I do? I have no place to gather together my harvest.

18And he said, I will do this: I will pull down my storehouses and build larger ones; and there I will store all [e]my grain (produce) and my goods.

19And I will say to my soul, Soul, you have many good things laid up, [enough] for many years; take your ease, eat, drink *and* enjoy yourself merrily.

20But God said to him, You fool! This very night [f]they [that is, the messengers of God] demand your soul of you; and all the things that you have prepared, whose will they be? [Jer. 17:11; Job 27:8.]

21So it is with him who continues to lay up *and* hoard possessions for himself, and is not rich [in his relation] to God—this is how he fares.

22And [Jesus] said to His disciples, Therefore I tell you, do not be anxious *and* troubled [with cares] about your life, as to what you will [have to] eat, or about your body, as to what you will [have to] wear;

**AMP** [a] Thayer. [b] Moulton and Milligan. [c] Souter. [d] Abbott-Smith. [e] Some ancient texts read "grain." [f] Vincent: "The indefiniteness is impressive."

## New American Standard

*God Knows and Cares*

**12** UNDER THESE circumstances, after so many thousands
of the multitude had gathered together that they were
stepping on one another, He began saying to His disciples first *of*
*all,* "Beware of the leaven of the Pharisees, which is hypocrisy.
2"But there is nothing covered up that will not be revealed, and
hidden that will not be known.
3"Accordingly, whatever you have said in the dark shall be
heard in the light, and what you have whispered in the inner
rooms shall be proclaimed upon the housetops.
4"And I say to you, My friends, do not be afraid of those who
kill the body, and after that have no more that they can do.
5"But I will warn you whom to fear: fear the One who after He
has killed has authority to cast into hell; yes, I tell you, fear Him!
6"Are not five sparrows sold for two cents? And *yet* not one
of them is forgotten before God.
7"Indeed, the very hairs of your head are all numbered. Do not
fear; you are of more value than many sparrows.
8"And I say to you, everyone who confesses Me before men,
the Son of Man shall confess him also before the angels of God;
9but he who denies Me before men shall be denied before the
angels of God.
10"And everyone who will speak a word against the Son of
Man, it shall be forgiven him; but he who blasphemes against the
Holy Spirit, it shall not be forgiven him.
11"And when they bring you before the synagogues and the
rulers and the authorities, do not become anxious about how or
what you should speak in your defense, or what you should say;
12for the Holy Spirit will teach you in that very hour what you
ought to say."

*Covetousness Denounced*

13¶ And someone in the crowd said to Him, "Teacher, tell my
brother to divide the *family* inheritance with me."
14But He said to him, "Man, who appointed Me a judge or
arbiter over you?"
15And He said to them, "Beware, and be on your guard against
every form of greed; for not *even* when one has an abundance does
his life consist of his possessions."
16And He told them a parable, saying, "The land of a certain
rich man was very productive.
17"And he began reasoning to himself, saying, 'What shall I do,
since I have no place to store my crops?'
18"And he said, 'This is what I will do: I will tear down my barns
and build larger ones, and there I will store all my grain and my
goods.
19'And I will say to my soul, "Soul, you have many goods laid
up for many years *to come;* take your ease, eat, drink *and* be merry."'
20"But God said to him, 'You fool! This *very* night your soul is
required of you; and *now* who will own what you have prepared?'
21"So is the man who lays up treasure for himself, and is not
rich toward God."
22¶ And He said to His disciples, "For this reason I say to you,
do not be anxious for *your* life, *as to* what you shall eat; nor for your
body, *as to* what you shall put on.

## New International

*Warnings and Encouragements*

**12** MEANWHILE, WHEN a crowd of many thousands had
gathered, so that they were trampling on one another,
Jesus began to speak first to his disciples, saying: "Be on your
guard against the yeast of the Pharisees, which is hypocrisy.
2There is nothing concealed that will not be disclosed, or hidden
that will not be made known. 3What you have said in the dark will
be heard in the daylight, and what you have whispered in the ear
in the inner rooms will be proclaimed from the roofs.
4"I tell you, my friends, do not be afraid of those who kill the
body and after that can do no more. 5But I will show you whom
you should fear: Fear him who, after the killing of the body, has
power to throw you into hell. Yes, I tell you, fear him. 6Are not
five sparrows sold for two pennies[g] ? Yet not one of them is forgotten by God. 7Indeed, the very hairs of your head are all numbered.
Don't be afraid; you are worth more than many sparrows.
8"I tell you, whoever acknowledges me before men, the Son of
Man will also acknowledge him before the angels of God. 9But he
who disowns me before men will be disowned before the angels
of God. 10And everyone who speaks a word against the Son of
Man will be forgiven, but anyone who blasphemes against the
Holy Spirit will not be forgiven.
11"When you are brought before synagogues, rulers and authorities, do not worry about how you will defend yourselves or
what you will say, 12for the Holy Spirit will teach you at that time
what you should say."

*The Parable of the Rich Fool*

13Someone in the crowd said to him, "Teacher, tell my brother
to divide the inheritance with me."
14Jesus replied, "Man, who appointed me a judge or an arbiter
between you?" 15Then he said to them, "Watch out! Be on your
guard against all kinds of greed; a man's life does not consist in
the abundance of his possessions."
16And he told them this parable: "The ground of a certain rich
man produced a good crop. 17He thought to himself, 'What shall
I do? I have no place to store my crops.'
18"Then he said, 'This is what I'll do. I will tear down my barns
and build bigger ones, and there I will store all my grain and my
goods. 19And I'll say to myself, "You have plenty of good things
laid up for many years. Take life easy; eat, drink and be merry."'
20"But God said to him, 'You fool! This very night your life will
be demanded from you. Then who will get what you have prepared for yourself?'
21"This is how it will be with anyone who stores up things for
himself but is not rich toward God."

*Do Not Worry*

22Then Jesus said to his disciples: "Therefore I tell you, do not
worry about your life, what you will eat; or about your body, what
you will wear. 23Life is more than food, and the body more than

NIV [g] 6 Greek *two assaria*

## King James

23 The life is more than meat, and the body *is more* than raiment.

24 Consider the ravens: for they neither sow nor reap; which neither have storehouse nor barn; and God feedeth them: how much more are ye better than the fowls?

25 And which of you with taking thought can add to his stature one cubit?

26 If ye then be not able to do that thing which is least, why take ye thought for the rest?

27 Consider the lilies how they grow: they toil not, they spin not; and yet I say unto you, that Solomon in all his glory was not arrayed like one of these.

28 If then God so clothe the grass, which is today in the field, and tomorrow is cast into the oven; how much more *will he clothe* you, O ye of little faith?

29 And seek not ye what ye shall eat, or what ye shall drink, neither be ye of doubtful mind.

30 For all these things do the nations of the world seek after: and your Father knoweth that ye have need of these things.

31 ¶ But rather seek ye the kingdom of God; and all these things shall be added unto you.

32 Fear not, little flock; for it is your Father's good pleasure to give you the kingdom.

33 Sell that ye have, and give alms; provide yourselves bags which wax not old, a treasure in the heavens that faileth not, where no thief approacheth, neither moth corrupteth.

34 For where your treasure is, there will your heart be also.

35 Let your loins be girded about, and *your* lights burning;

36 And ye yourselves like unto men that wait for their lord, when he will return from the wedding; that when he cometh and knocketh, they may open unto him immediately.

37 Blessed *are* those servants, whom the lord when he cometh shall find watching: verily I say unto you, that he shall gird himself, and make them to sit down to meat, and will come forth and serve them.

38 And if he shall come in the second watch, or come in the third watch, and find *them* so, blessed are those servants.

39 And this know, that if the goodman of the house had known what hour the thief would come, he would have watched, and not have suffered his house to be broken through.

40 Be ye therefore ready also: for the Son of man cometh at an hour when ye think not.

41 ¶ Then Peter said unto him, Lord, speakest thou this parable unto us, or even to all?

42 And the Lord said, Who then is that faithful and wise steward, whom *his* lord shall make ruler over his household, to give *them their* portion of meat in due season?

43 Blessed *is* that servant, whom his lord when he cometh shall find so doing.

44 Of a truth I say unto you, that he will make him ruler over all that he hath.

45 But and if that servant say in his heart, My lord delayeth his coming; and shall begin to beat the menservants and maidens, and to eat and drink, and to be drunken;

46 The lord of that servant will come in a day when he looketh not for *him*, and at an hour when he is not aware, and will cut him in sunder, and will appoint him his portion with the unbelievers.

47 And that servant, which knew his lord's will, and prepared not *himself*, neither did according to his will, shall be beaten with many *stripes*.

## Amplified

23 For life is more than food, and the body [more] than clothes.

24 Observe *and* consider the ravens, for they neither sow nor reap, they have neither storehouse nor barns, and [yet] God feeds them. Of how much more worth are you than the birds!

25 And which of you by being over-anxious *and* troubled with cares can add a [a]cubit to his stature, *or* a moment [unit] of time to his [b]age—the length of his life?

26 If then you are not able to do such a little thing as that, why are you anxious *and* troubled with cares about the rest?

27 Consider the lilies, how they grow; they neither [wearily] toil nor spin *nor* [c]*weave*; yet I tell you, even Solomon in all his glory—his splendor and magnificence—was not arrayed like one of these. [I Kings 10:4-7.]

28 But if God so clothes the grass in the field, which is alive today and tomorrow is thrown into the furnace, how much more will He clothe you, O you [people] of little faith?

29 And you, do not seek [by meditating and reasoning to inquire into] what you are to eat and what you are to drink, nor be of anxious (troubled) mind—[d]unsettled, excited, worried and [e]in suspense;

30 For all the pagan world is [greedily] seeking after these things, and your Father knows that you need them.

31 Only aim at *and* strive for *and* seek after His kingdom, and all these things shall be supplied to you also.

32 Do not be seized with alarm *and* struck with fear, little flock, for it is your Father's good pleasure to give you the kingdom!

33 Sell what you possess and give donations to the poor; provide yourselves with purses *and* handbags that do not grow old, an unfailing *and* inexhaustible treasure in the heavens, where no thief comes near and no moth destroys.

34 For where your treasure is, there will your heart be also.

35 Keep your loins girded and your lamps burning,

36 And be yourselves like men who are waiting for their master to return home from the marriage feast, so that when he shall return from the wedding and comes and knocks, they may open to him immediately.

37 Blessed—happy, fortunate and [f]to be envied—are those servants whom the master finds awake *and* alert *and* watching when he comes. Truly, I say to you, he will gird himself and have them recline at table and will come and serve them!

38 If he comes in the second watch (before midnight), or the third watch (after midnight), and finds them so, blessed—happy, fortunate and [g]to be envied—are those servants!

39 But of this be assured, that if the householder had known at what time the burglar was coming, he would have been awake *and* alert *and* watching, and would not have permitted his house to be dug through *and* broken open.

40 You also must be ready, for the Son of man is coming at an hour *and* a [h]moment when you do not anticipate it.

41 Peter said, Lord, are You telling this parable for us, or for all alike?

42 And the Lord said, Who then is that faithful steward, the wise man whom his master will set over those in his household service, to supply them their allowance of food at the appointed time?

43 Blessed—happy, and [i]to be envied—is that servant whom his master finds so doing when he arrives.

44 Truly, I tell you, he will set him in charge over all his possessions.

45 But if that servant says in his heart, My master is late in coming, and begins to strike the menservants and the maids, and to eat and drink and get drunk,

46 The master of that servant will come on a day when he does not expect him and at an hour of which he does not know, and will punish him *and* [j]cut him off and assign his lot with [k]the unfaithful.

47 And that servant who knew his master's will, but did not get ready or act as he would wish him to act, shall be beaten with many [lashes].

**AMP** [a] Abbott-Smith: "A stage of growth whether measured by age or stature." [b] Abbott-Smith: "A stage of growth whether measured by age or stature." [c] Some ancient authorities read "weave." [d] Vincent. [e] Abbott-Smith. [f] Souter. [g] Souter. [h] Moulton and Milligan. [i] Souter. [j] Alternate reading. [k] Wycliffe.

## New American Standard

23"For life is more than food, and the body than clothing.
24"Consider the ravens, for they neither sow nor reap; and they
have no storeroom nor barn; and *yet* God feeds them; how much
more valuable you are than the birds!
25"And which of you by being anxious can add a *single* [l]cubit
to his [m]life's span?
26"If then you cannot do even a very little thing, why are you
anxious about other matters?
27"Consider the lilies, how they grow; they neither toil nor spin;
but I tell you, even Solomon in all his glory did not clothe himself
like one of these.
28"But if God so arrays the grass in the field, which is *alive* today
and tomorrow is thrown into the furnace, how much more *will He*
*clothe* you, O men of little faith!
29"And do not seek what you shall eat, and what you shall
drink, and do not keep worrying.
30"For all these things the nations of the world eagerly seek; but
your Father knows that you need these things.
31"But seek for His kingdom, and these things shall be added
to you.
32"Do not be afraid, little flock, for your Father has chosen
gladly to give you the kingdom.
33"Sell your possessions and give to charity; make yourselves
purses which do not wear out, an unfailing treasure in heaven,
where no thief comes near, nor moth destroys.
34"For where your treasure is, there will your heart be also.

*Be in Readiness*

35¶ "Be dressed in readiness, and *keep* your lamps alight.
36"And be like men who are waiting for their master when he
returns from the wedding feast, so that they may immediately
open *the door* to him when he comes and knocks.
37"Blessed are those slaves whom the master shall find on the
alert when he comes; truly I say to you, that he will gird himself
*to serve,* and have them recline *at the table,* and will come up and
wait on them.
38"Whether he comes in the [n]second watch, or even in the
[o]third, and finds *them* so, blessed are those *slaves.*
39"And be sure of this, that if the head of the house had known
at what hour the thief was coming, he would not have allowed his
house to be broken into.
40"You too, be ready; for the Son of Man is coming at an hour
that you do not expect."
41¶ And Peter said, "Lord, are You addressing this parable to
us, or to everyone *else* as well?"
42And the Lord said, "Who then is the faithful and sensible
steward, whom his master will put in charge of his servants, to
give them their rations at the proper time?
43"Blessed is that slave whom his master finds so doing when
he comes.
44"Truly I say to you, that he will put him in charge of all his
possessions.
45"But if that slave says in his heart, 'My master will be a long
time in coming,' and begins to beat the slaves, *both* men and
women, and to eat and drink and get drunk;
46the master of that slave will come on a day when he does not
expect *him,* and at an hour he does not know, and will cut him in
pieces, and assign him a place with the unbelievers.
47"And that slave who knew his master's will and did not get
ready or act in accord with his will, shall receive many lashes,

NAS [l] I.e., One cubit equals approx. 18 in. [m]Or, *height* [n] I.e., 9 p.m. to midnight [o] I.e., midnight to 3 a.m.

## New International

clothes. 24Consider the ravens: They do not sow or reap, they have
no storeroom or barn; yet God feeds them. And how much more
valuable you are than birds! 25Who of you by worrying can add a
single hour to his life[p]? 26Since you cannot do this very little thing,
why do you worry about the rest?
27"Consider how the lilies grow. They do not labor or spin. Yet
I tell you, not even Solomon in all his splendor was dressed like
one of these. 28If that is how God clothes the grass of the field,
which is here today, and tomorrow is thrown into the fire, how
much more will he clothe you, O you of little faith! 29And do not
set your heart on what you will eat or drink; do not worry about
it. 30For the pagan world runs after all such things, and your Father
knows that you need them. 31But seek his kingdom, and these
things will be given to you as well.
32"Do not be afraid, little flock, for your Father has been pleased
to give you the kingdom. 33Sell your possessions and give to the
poor. Provide purses for yourselves that will not wear out, a treasure in heaven that will not be exhausted, where no thief comes
near and no moth destroys. 34For where your treasure is, there
your heart will be also.

*Watchfulness*

35"Be dressed ready for service and keep your lamps burning,
36like men waiting for their master to return from a wedding
banquet, so that when he comes and knocks they can immediately
open the door for him. 37It will be good for those servants whose
master finds them watching when he comes. I tell you the truth,
he will dress himself to serve, will have them recline at the table
and will come and wait on them. 38It will be good for those servants whose master finds them ready, even if he comes in the
second or third watch of the night. 39But understand this: If the
owner of the house had known at what hour the thief was coming,
he would not have let his house be broken into. 40You also must
be ready, because the Son of Man will come at an hour when you
do not expect him."
41Peter asked, "Lord, are you telling this parable to us, or to
everyone?"
42The Lord answered, "Who then is the faithful and wise manager, whom the master puts in charge of his servants to give them
their food allowance at the proper time? 43It will be good for that
servant whom the master finds doing so when he returns. 44I tell
you the truth, he will put him in charge of all his possessions. 45But
suppose the servant says to himself, 'My master is taking a long
time in coming,' and he then begins to beat the menservants and
maidservants and to eat and drink and get drunk. 46The master of
that servant will come on a day when he does not expect him and
at an hour he is not aware of. He will cut him to pieces and assign
him a place with the unbelievers.
47"That servant who knows his master's will and does not get
ready or does not do what his master wants will be beaten with
many blows. 48But the one who does not know and does things

NIV [p] 25 Or *single cubit to his height*

## King James

48But he that knew not, and did commit things worthy of stripes, shall be beaten with few *stripes*. For unto whomsoever much is given, of him shall be much required: and to whom men have committed much, of him they will ask the more.

49¶ I am come to send fire on the earth; and what will I, if it be already kindled?

50But I have a baptism to be baptized with; and how am I straitened till it be accomplished!

51Suppose ye that I am come to give peace on earth? I tell you, Nay; but rather division:

52For from henceforth there shall be five in one house divided, three against two, and two against three.

53The father shall be divided against the son, and the son against the father; the mother against the daughter, and the daughter against the mother; the mother-in-law against her daughter-in-law, and the daughter-in-law against her mother-in-law.

54¶ And he said also to the people, When ye see a cloud rise out of the west, straightway ye say, There cometh a shower; and so it is.

55And when *ye see* the south wind blow, ye say, There will be heat; and it cometh to pass.

56*Ye* hypocrites, ye can discern the face of the sky and of the earth; but how is it that ye do not discern this time?

57Yea, and why even of yourselves judge ye not what is right?

58¶ When thou goest with thine adversary to the magistrate, *as thou art* in the way, give diligence that thou mayest be delivered from him; lest he hale thee to the judge, and the judge deliver thee to the officer, and the officer cast thee into prison.

59I tell thee, thou shalt not depart thence, till thou hast paid the very last mite.

**13** THERE WERE present at that season some that told him of the Galilaeans, whose blood Pilate had mingled with their sacrifices.

2And Jesus answering said unto them, Suppose ye that these Galilaeans were sinners above all the Galilaeans, because they suffered such things?

3I tell you, Nay: but, except ye repent, ye shall all likewise perish.

4Or those eighteen, upon whom the tower in Siloam fell, and slew them, think ye that they were sinners above all men that dwelt in Jerusalem?

5I tell you, Nay: but, except ye repent, ye shall all likewise perish.

6¶ He spake also this parable; A certain *man* had a fig tree planted in his vineyard; and he came and sought fruit thereon, and found none.

7Then said he unto the dresser of his vineyard, Behold, these three years I come seeking fruit on this fig tree, and find none: cut it down; why cumbereth it the ground?

8And he answering said unto him, Lord, let it alone this year also, till I shall dig about it, and dung *it:*

9And if it bear fruit, *well:* and if not, *then* after that thou shalt cut it down.

10And he was teaching in one of the synagogues on the sabbath.

## Amplified

48But he who did not know and did things worthy of a beating shall be beaten with few [lashes]. For every one to whom much is given, of him shall be much required; and of him to whom men entrust much they will require *and* demand the more. [Deut. 25:2, 3; Num. 15:29, 30.]

49I have come to cast fire upon the earth, and how I wish that it were already kindled!

50I have a baptism with which to be baptized, and how greatly *and* sorely I am urged—impelled, [a]constrained—until it is accomplished!

51Do you suppose that I have come to give peace upon earth? No, I say to you, but rather division;

52For from now on in one house there will be five divided [among themselves], three against two and two against three.

53They will be divided, father against son and son against father, mother against daughter and daughter against mother, mother-in-law against her daughter-in-law and daughter-in-law against her mother-in-law. [Mic. 7:6.]

54He also said to the crowds of people, When you see a cloud rising in the west, at once you say, It is going to rain! And so it does.

55And when [you see that] a south wind is blowing, you say, There will be severe heat! And it occurs.

56You play actors—hypocrites! You know how [intelligently] to discern *and* interpret *and* [b]prove the looks of the earth and sky, but how is it you do not know how to discern *and* interpret *and* apply the proof to the present time?

57And why do you not judge what is just, *and* personally decide what is right?

58Then, as you go with your accuser before a magistrate, on the way make diligent effort to settle *and* be quit of him, lest he drag you to the judge, and the judge turn you over to the officer, and the officer put you in prison.

59I tell you, you will never get out until you have paid the very last (fraction of a) cent.

**13** JUST AT that time there [arrived] some people who informed Jesus about the Galileans whose blood Pilate mixed with their sacrifices.

2And He replied by saying to them, Do you think that those Galileans were greater sinners than all the other Galileans, because they have suffered in this way?

3I tell you, No; but unless you repent—[that is,] [c]change your mind for the better and heartily amend your ways with abhorrence of your past sins—you will all likewise perish *and* be lost [[d]eternally].

4Or those eighteen on whom the tower in Siloam fell and killed them, do you think that they were more guilty offenders (debtors) than all the others who dwelt in Jerusalem?

5I tell you, No; but unless you repent—[that is,] [e]change your mind for the better and heartily amend your ways with abhorrence of your past sins—you will all likewise perish *and* be lost [[f]eternally].

6And He told them this parable: A certain man had a fig tree planted in his vineyard, and he came looking for fruit on it, but did not find [any].

7So he said to the vinedresser, See here! For these three years I have come looking for fruit on this fig tree and I find none. Cut it down; why should it continue also to use up the ground—that is, to [g]deplete the soil, intercept the sun and take up room?

8But he replied to him, Leave it alone, sir, [just] this one more year, till I dig around it and put manure [on the soil];

9Then perhaps it will bear fruit after this, but if not, you can cut it down *and* out.

10Now Jesus was teaching in one of the synagogues on the Sabbath.

**AMP** [a] Wycliffe. [b] Wycliffe. [c] Thayer. [d] Jamieson, Fausett and Brown; George W. Clark; Matthew Henry, etc. [e] Thayer. [f] Jamieson, Fausett and Brown; George W. Clark; Matthew Henry, etc. [g] Bengel's "Gnomon Novi Testamenti." (-Vincent)

## New American Standard

48but the one who did not know *it,* and committed deeds
worthy of a flogging, will receive but few. And from everyone who
has been given much shall much be required; and to whom they
entrusted much, of him they will ask all the more.

*Christ Divides Men*

49¶ "I have come to cast fire upon the earth; and how I wish it
were already kindled!

50"But I have a baptism to undergo, and how distressed I am
until it is accomplished!

51"Do you suppose that I came to grant peace on earth? I tell
you, no, but rather division;

52for from now on five *members* in one household will be divided, three against two, and two against three.

53"They will be divided, father against son, and son against
father; mother against daughter, and daughter against mother;
mother-in-law against daughter-in-law, and daughter-in-law
against mother-in-law."

54¶ And He was also saying to the multitudes, "When you see
a cloud rising in the west, immediately you say, 'A shower is
coming,' and so it turns out.

55"And when *you see* a south wind blowing, you say, 'It will be
a hot day,' and it turns out *that way.*

56"You hypocrites! You know how to analyze the appearance
of the earth and the sky, but why do you not analyze this present
time?

57"And why do you not even on your own initiative judge what
is right?

58"For while you are going with your opponent to appear before
the magistrate, on *your* way *there* make an effort to settle with him,
in order that he may not drag you before the judge, and the judge
turn you over to the constable, and the constable throw you into
prison.

59"I say to you, you shall not get out of there until you have paid
the very last cent."

*Call to Repent*

**13** NOW ON the same occasion there were some present
who reported to Him about the Galileans, whose blood
Pilate had mingled with their sacrifices.

2And He answered and said to them, "Do you suppose that
these Galileans were *greater* sinners than all *other* Galileans, because they suffered this *fate?*

3"I tell you, no, but, unless you repent, you will all likewise
perish.

4"Or do you suppose that those eighteen on whom the tower
in Siloam fell and killed them, were *worse* culprits than all the men
who live in Jerusalem?

5"I tell you, no, but unless you repent, you will all likewise
perish."

6¶ And He *began* telling this parable: "A certain man had a fig
tree which had been planted in his vineyard; and he came looking
for fruit on it, and did not find any.

7"And he said to the vineyard-keeper, 'Behold, for three years
I have come looking for fruit on this fig tree without finding any.
Cut it down! Why does it even use up the ground?'

8"And he answered and said to him, 'Let it alone, sir, for this
year too, until I dig around it and put in fertilizer;

9and if it bears fruit next year, *fine;* but if not, cut it down.' "

*Healing on the Sabbath*

10¶ And He was teaching in one of the synagogues on the
Sabbath.

## New International

deserving punishment will be beaten with few blows. From everyone who has been given much, much will be demanded; and from
the one who has been entrusted with much, much more will be
asked.

*Not Peace but Division*

49"I have come to bring fire on the earth, and how I wish it were
already kindled! 50But I have a baptism to undergo, and how
distressed I am until it is completed! 51Do you think I came to bring
peace on earth? No, I tell you, but division. 52From now on there
will be five in one family divided against each other, three against
two and two against three. 53They will be divided, father against
son and son against father, mother against daughter and daughter
against mother, mother-in-law against daughter-in-law and
daughter-in-law against mother-in-law."

*Interpreting the Times*

54He said to the crowd: "When you see a cloud rising in the
west, immediately you say, 'It's going to rain,' and it does. 55And
when the south wind blows, you say, 'It's going to be hot,' and
it is. 56Hypocrites! You know how to interpret the appearance of
the earth and the sky. How is it that you don't know how to
interpret this present time?

57"Why don't you judge for yourselves what is right? 58As you
are going with your adversary to the magistrate, try hard to be
reconciled to him on the way, or he may drag you off to the judge,
and the judge turn you over to the officer, and the officer throw
you into prison. 59I tell you, you will not get out until you have
paid the last penny.[h]"

*Repent or Perish*

**13** NOW THERE were some present at that time who told
Jesus about the Galileans whose blood Pilate had mixed
with their sacrifices. 2Jesus answered, "Do you think that these
Galileans were worse sinners than all the other Galileans because
they suffered this way? 3I tell you, no! But unless you repent, you
too will all perish. 4Or those eighteen who died when the tower
in Siloam fell on them—do you think they were more guilty than
all the others living in Jerusalem? 5I tell you, no! But unless you
repent, you too will all perish."

6Then he told this parable: "A man had a fig tree, planted in his
vineyard, and he went to look for fruit on it, but did not find any.
7So he said to the man who took care of the vineyard, 'For three
years now I've been coming to look for fruit on this fig tree and
haven't found any. Cut it down! Why should it use up the soil?'

8" 'Sir,' the man replied, 'leave it alone for one more year, and
I'll dig around it and fertilize it. 9If it bears fruit next year, fine! If
not, then cut it down.' "

*A Crippled Woman Healed on the Sabbath*

10On a Sabbath Jesus was teaching in one of the synagogues,

**NIV** [h] 59 Greek *lepton*

## King James

11¶ And, behold, there was a woman which had a spirit of infirmity eighteen years, and was bowed together, and could in no wise lift up *herself*.

12And when Jesus saw her, he called *her to him*, and said unto her, Woman, thou art loosed from thine infirmity.

13And he laid *his* hands on her: and immediately she was made straight, and glorified God.

14And the ruler of the synagogue answered with indignation, because that Jesus had healed on the sabbath day, and said unto the people, There are six days in which men ought to work: in them therefore come and be healed, and not on the sabbath day.

15The Lord then answered him, and said, *Thou* hypocrite, doth not each one of you on the sabbath loose his ox or *his* ass from the stall, and lead *him* away to watering?

16And ought not this woman, being a daughter of Abraham, whom Satan hath bound, lo, these eighteen years, be loosed from this bond on the sabbath day?

17And when he had said these things, all his adversaries were ashamed: and all the people rejoiced for all the glorious things that were done by him.

18¶ Then said he, Unto what is the kingdom of God like? and whereunto shall I resemble it?

19It is like a grain of mustard seed, which a man took, and cast into his garden; and it grew, and waxed a great tree; and the fowls of the air lodged in the branches of it.

20And again he said, Whereunto shall I liken the kingdom of God?

21It is like leaven, which a woman took and hid in three measures of meal, till the whole was leavened.

22And he went through the cities and villages, teaching, and journeying toward Jerusalem.

23Then said one unto him, Lord, are there few that be saved? And he said unto them,

24¶ Strive to enter in at the strait gate: for many, I say unto you, will seek to enter in, and shall not be able.

25When once the master of the house is risen up, and hath shut to the door, and ye begin to stand without, and to knock at the door, saying, Lord, Lord, open unto us; and he shall answer and say unto you, I know you not whence ye are:

26Then shall ye begin to say, We have eaten and drunk in thy presence, and thou hast taught in our streets.

27But he shall say, I tell you, I know you not whence ye are; depart from me, all *ye* workers of iniquity.

28There shall be weeping and gnashing of teeth, when ye shall see Abraham, and Isaac, and Jacob, and all the prophets, in the kingdom of God, and you *yourselves* thrust out.

29And they shall come from the east, and *from* the west, and from the north, and *from* the south, and shall sit down in the kingdom of God.

30And, behold, there are last which shall be first, and there are first which shall be last.

31¶ The same day there came certain of the Pharisees, saying unto him, Get thee out, and depart hence: for Herod will kill thee.

32And he said unto them, Go ye, and tell that fox, Behold, I cast out devils, and I do cures today and tomorrow, and the third *day* I shall be perfected.

33Nevertheless I must walk today, and tomorrow, and the *day* following: for it cannot be that a prophet perish out of Jerusalem.

34O Jerusalem, Jerusalem, which killest the prophets, and stonest them that are sent unto thee; how often would I have gathered thy children together, as a hen *doth gather* her brood under *her* wings, and ye would not!

## Amplified

11And there was a woman there who for eighteen years had had an [a]infirmity caused by a spirit [ [b]a demon of sickness]. She was [c]bent completely forward and utterly unable to straighten herself *or* to [d]look upward.

12And when Jesus saw her, He called [her to Him] and said to her, Woman, you are released from your infirmity!

13Then He laid [His] hands on her and instantly she was made straight, and she [e]recognized *and* thanked *and* praised God.

14But the [f]leader of the synagogue, indignant because Jesus had healed on the Sabbath, said to the crowd, There are six days on which work ought to be done, so come on those days and be cured, and not on the Sabbath day. [Exod. 20:9, 10.]

15But the Lord replied to him, saying, You play actors—hypocrites! Does not each one of you on the Sabbath loose his ox or his donkey from the stall, and lead it out to water it?

16And ought not this woman, a daughter of Abraham whom Satan has kept bound for eighteen years, be loosed from this bond on the Sabbath day?

17Even as He said this, all His opponents were put to shame, and all the people were rejoicing over all the glorious things that were being done by Him.

18This led Him to say, What is the kingdom of God like? And to what shall I compare it?

19It is like a grain of mustard seed which a man took and planted in his own garden; and it grew and became a tree, and the wild birds [g]found shelter *and* roosted *and* nested in its branches.

20And again He said, To what shall I liken the kingdom of God?

21It is like leaven which a woman took and hid in three measures of wheat flour *or* meal, until it was all leavened (fermented).

22[Jesus] journeyed on through towns and villages, teaching, and making His way toward Jerusalem.

23And one asked Him, Lord, will only a few be saved [that is, rescued, delivered from the penalties of the last judgment, and made partakers of the salvation by Christ]? And He said to them,

24Strive to enter by the narrow door—force yourselves through it—for many, I tell you, will try to enter and will not be able.

25When once the Master of the house gets up and closes the door, and you begin to stand outside and to knock at the door (again and again) saying, Lord, open to us! He will answer you, I do not know where [ [h]what household, certainly not Mine] you come from.

26Then you will begin to say, We ate and drank in Your presence, and You taught in our streets.

27But He will say, I tell you, I do not know where [ [i]what household—certainly not Mine] you come from; depart from Me, all you wrongdoers!

28There will be weeping and grinding of teeth, when you see Abraham and Isaac and Jacob and all the prophets in the kingdom of God, but you yourselves being cast forth—banished, driven away.

29And [people] will come from east and west, and from north and south, and sit down [feast at table] in the kingdom of God.

30And behold, there are some [now] last who will be first [then], and there are some [now] first who will be last [then].

31At that very hour some Pharisees came up and said to Him, Go away from here, for Herod is determined to kill You.

32And He said to them, Go and tell that fox [sly and crafty, skulking and cowardly], Behold, I drive out demons and perform healings today and tomorrow, and on the third day I finish (complete) My course.

33Nevertheless I must continue on My way today and tomorrow and the day after that, for it will never do for a prophet to be destroyed away from Jerusalem!

34O Jerusalem, Jerusalem, you who continue to kill the prophets and to stone those who are sent to you! How often I have desired *and* yearned to gather your children together [around Me], as a hen [gathers] her young under her wings, but you would not!

**AMP** [a] Vincent. [b] Cremer. [c] Thayer. [d] Souter. [e] Bengel's "Gnomon Novi Testamenti." (-Vincent) [f] Souter. [g] Moulton and Milligan. [h] Vincent. [i] Vincent.

## New American Standard

11And behold, there was a woman who for eighteen years had had a sickness caused by a spirit; and she was bent double, and could not straighten up at all.

12And when Jesus saw her, He called her over and said to her, "Woman, you are freed from your sickness."

13And He laid His hands upon her; and immediately she was made erect again, and *began* glorifying God.

14And the synagogue official, indignant because Jesus had healed on the Sabbath, *began* saying to the multitude in response, "There are six days in which work should be done; therefore come during them and get healed, and not on the Sabbath day."

15But the Lord answered him and said, "You hypocrites, does not each of you on the Sabbath untie his ox or his donkey from the stall, and lead him away to water *him?*

16"And this woman, a daughter of Abraham as she is, whom Satan has bound for eighteen long years, should she not have been released from this bond on the Sabbath day?"

17And as He said this, all His opponents were being humiliated; and the entire multitude was rejoicing over all the glorious things being done by Him.

*Parables of Mustard Seed and Leaven*

**18**¶ Therefore He was saying, "What is the kingdom of God like, and to what shall I compare it?

19"It is like a mustard seed, which a man took and threw into his own garden; and it grew and became a tree; and THE BIRDS OF THE AIR NESTED IN ITS BRANCHES."

**20**¶ And again He said, "To what shall I compare the kingdom of God?

21"It is like leaven, which a woman took and hid in three pecks of meal, until it was all leavened."

*Teaching in the Villages*

**22**¶ And He was passing through from one city and village to another, teaching, and proceeding on His way to Jerusalem.

23And someone said to Him, "Lord, are there *just* a few who are being saved?" And He said to them,

24"Strive to enter by the narrow door; for many, I tell you, will seek to enter and will not be able.

25"Once the head of the house gets up and shuts the door, and you begin to stand outside and knock on the door, saying, 'Lord, open up to us!' then He will answer and say to you, 'I do not know where you are from.'

26"Then you will begin to say, 'We ate and drank in Your presence, and You taught in our streets';

27and He will say, 'I tell you, I do not know where you are from; DEPART FROM ME, ALL YOU EVILDOERS.'

28"There will be weeping and gnashing of teeth there when you see Abraham and Isaac and Jacob and all the prophets in the kingdom of God, but yourselves being cast out.

29"And they will come from east and west, and from north and south, and will recline *at the table* in the kingdom of God.

30"And behold, *some* are last who will be first and *some* are first who will be last."

**31**¶ Just at that time some Pharisees came up, saying to Him, "Go away and depart from here, for Herod wants to kill You."

32And He said to them, "Go and tell that fox, 'Behold, I cast out demons and perform cures today and tomorrow, and the third *day* I reach My goal.'

33"Nevertheless I must journey on today and tomorrow and the next *day;* for it cannot be that a prophet should perish outside of Jerusalem.

34"O Jerusalem, Jerusalem, *the city* that kills the prophets and stones those sent to her! How often I wanted to gather your children together, just as a hen *gathers* her brood under her wings, and you would not *have it!*

## New International

11and a woman was there who had been crippled by a spirit for
eighteen years. She was bent over and could not straighten up at
all. 12When Jesus saw her, he called her forward and said to her,
"Woman, you are set free from your infirmity." 13Then he put his
hands on her, and immediately she straightened up and praised
God.

14Indignant because Jesus had healed on the Sabbath, the synagogue ruler said to the people, "There are six days for work. So come and be healed on those days, not on the Sabbath."

15The Lord answered him, "You hypocrites! Doesn't each of
you on the Sabbath untie his ox or donkey from the stall and lead
it out to give it water? 16Then should not this woman, a daughter
of Abraham, whom Satan has kept bound for eighteen long years,
be set free on the Sabbath day from what bound her?"

17When he said this, all his opponents were humiliated, but the people were delighted with all the wonderful things he was doing.

*The Parables of the Mustard Seed and the Yeast*

18Then Jesus asked, "What is the kingdom of God like? What
shall I compare it to? 19It is like a mustard seed, which a man took
and planted in his garden. It grew and became a tree, and the birds
of the air perched in its branches."

20Again he asked, "What shall I compare the kingdom of God
to? 21It is like yeast that a woman took and mixed into a large
amount[j] of flour until it worked all through the dough."

*The Narrow Door*

22Then Jesus went through the towns and villages, teaching as
he made his way to Jerusalem. 23Someone asked him, "Lord, are
only a few people going to be saved?"

He said to them, 24"Make every effort to enter through the
narrow door, because many, I tell you, will try to enter and will
not be able to. 25Once the owner of the house gets up and closes
the door, you will stand outside knocking and pleading, 'Sir, open
the door for us.'

"But he will answer, 'I don't know you or where you come from.'

26"Then you will say, 'We ate and drank with you, and you taught in our streets.'

27"But he will reply, 'I don't know you or where you come from. Away from me, all you evildoers!'

28"There will be weeping there, and gnashing of teeth, when
you see Abraham, Isaac and Jacob and all the prophets in the
kingdom of God, but you yourselves thrown out. 29People will
come from east and west and north and south, and will take their
places at the feast in the kingdom of God. 30Indeed there are those
who are last who will be first, and first who will be last."

*Jesus' Sorrow for Jerusalem*

31At that time some Pharisees came to Jesus and said to him, "Leave this place and go somewhere else. Herod wants to kill you."

32He replied, "Go tell that fox, 'I will drive out demons and heal
people today and tomorrow, and on the third day I will reach my
goal.' 33In any case, I must keep going today and tomorrow and
the next day—for surely no prophet can die outside Jerusalem!

34"O Jerusalem, Jerusalem, you who kill the prophets and stone
those sent to you, how often I have longed to gather your children
together, as a hen gathers her chicks under her wings, but you
were not willing! 35Look, your house is left to you desolate. I tell

**NIV** j 21 Greek *three satas* (probably about 1/2 bushel or 22 liters)

## King James

35Behold, your house is left unto you desolate: and verily I say unto you, Ye shall not see me, until *the time* come when ye shall say, Blessed *is* he that cometh in the name of the Lord.

**14** AND IT came to pass, as he went into the house of one of the chief Pharisees to eat bread on the sabbath day, that they watched him.

2And, behold, there was a certain man before him which had the dropsy.

3And Jesus answering spake unto the lawyers and Pharisees, saying, Is it lawful to heal on the sabbath day?

4And they held their peace. And he took *him*, and healed him, and let him go;

5And answered them, saying, Which of you shall have an ass or an ox fallen into a pit, and will not straightway pull him out on the sabbath day?

6And they could not answer him again to these things.

7¶ And he put forth a parable to those which were bidden, when he marked how they chose out the chief rooms; saying unto them,

8When thou art bidden of any *man* to a wedding, sit not down in the highest room; lest a more honourable man than thou be bidden of him;

9And he that bade thee and him come and say to thee, Give this man place; and thou begin with shame to take the lowest room.

10But when thou art bidden, go and sit down in the lowest room; that when he that bade thee cometh, he may say unto thee, Friend, go up higher: then shalt thou have worship in the presence of them that sit at meat with thee.

11For whosoever exalteth himself shall be abased; and he that humbleth himself shall be exalted.

12¶ Then said he also to him that bade him, When thou makest a dinner or a supper, call not thy friends, nor thy brethren, neither thy kinsmen, nor *thy* rich neighbours; lest they also bid thee again, and a recompence be made thee.

13But when thou makest a feast, call the poor, the maimed, the lame, the blind:

14And thou shalt be blessed; for they cannot recompense thee: for thou shalt be recompensed at the resurrection of the just.

15¶ And when one of them that sat at meat with him heard these things, he said unto him, Blessed *is* he that shall eat bread in the kingdom of God.

16Then said he unto him, A certain man made a great supper, and bade many:

17And sent his servant at supper time to say to them that were bidden, Come; for all things are now ready.

18And they all with one *consent* began to make excuse. The first said unto him, I have bought a piece of ground, and I must needs go and see it: I pray thee have me excused.

19And another said, I have bought five yoke of oxen, and I go to prove them: I pray thee have me excused.

20And another said, I have married a wife, and therefore I cannot come.

21So that servant came, and showed his lord these things. Then the master of the house being angry said to his servant, Go out quickly into the streets and lanes of the city, and bring in hither the poor, and the maimed, and the halt, and the blind.

22And the servant said, Lord, it is done as thou hast commanded, and yet there is room.

## Amplified

35Behold, your house is forsaken—abandoned, left to you destitute [of God's help]! And I tell you, you will not see Me again until the time comes when you shall say, Blessed (to be celebrated with praises) is He Who comes in the name of the Lord! [Jer. 22:5; Ps. 118:26.]

**14** IT OCCURRED one Sabbath, when [Jesus] went for a meal at the house of one of the ruling Pharisees, that they were (engaged in) watching Him (closely).

2And behold, [just] in front of Him there was a man who had dropsy.

3And Jesus asked the lawyers and the Pharisees, Is it lawful *and* right to cure on the Sabbath, or not?

4But they kept silent. Then He took hold [of the man and] cured him and [a]sent him away.

5And He said to them, Which of you, having [b]a son *or* a donkey or an ox that has fallen into a well, will not at once pull him out on the Sabbath day?

6And they were unable to reply to this.

7Now He told a parable to those who were invited, [when] He noticed how they were selecting the places of honor, saying to them,

8When you are invited by any one to a marriage feast, do not recline on the chief seat—in the place of honor—lest a more distinguished person than you has been invited by him; [Prov. 25:6, 7.]

9And he who invited both of you will come to you and say, Let this man have the place [you have taken]. Then with humiliation *and* a guilty sense of impropriety you will begin to take the lowest place.

10But when you are invited, go and recline in the lowest place, so that when your host comes in he may say to you, Friend, go up higher! Then you will be honored in the presence of all who sit [at table] with you.

11For every one who exalts himself will be humbled [that is, ranked below others who are honored or rewarded], and he who humbles himself [that is, keeps a modest opinion of himself and behaves accordingly] will be exalted—elevated in rank.

12Jesus also said to the man who had invited Him, When you give a dinner or a supper, do not invite your friends or your brothers or your relatives or your wealthy neighbors, lest perhaps they also invite you in return and you be paid back.

13But when you give a banquet *or* a reception, invite the poor, the disabled, the lame, and the blind.

14Then you will be blessed—happy, fortunate and [c]to be envied—because they have no way of repaying you, and you will be recompensed at the resurrection of the just (upright).

15When one of those who reclined [at the table] with [Him] heard this, he said to Him, Blessed—happy, fortunate and [d]to be envied—is he who shall eat bread in the kingdom of God!

16But Jesus said to him, A man was once giving a great supper and invited many;

17And at the hour for the supper he sent his servant to say to those who had been invited, Come, for all is now ready.

18But they all alike began to make excuses *and* to beg off. The first said to him, I have bought a piece of land, and I have to go out and see it; I beg you, have me excused.

19And another said, I have bought five yoke of oxen, and I am going to examine *and* [e]put my approval on them; I beg you, have me excused.

20And another said, I have married a wife, and because of this I am unable to come. [Deut. 24:5.]

21So the servant came and reported these [answers] to his master. Then the master of the house said in wrath to his servant, Go quickly to the [f]great streets and the small streets of the city, and bring in here the poor and the disabled and the blind and the lame.

22And the servant [returning] said, Sir, what you have commanded me to do has been done, and yet there is room.

**AMP** [a] Thayer. [b] Many ancient authorities so read. [c] Souter. [d] Souter. [e] Wuest's "Treasures from the Greek New Testament." [f] Wycliffe.

## New American Standard

35"Behold, your house is left to you *desolate;* and I say to you,
you shall not see Me until *the time* comes when you say, 'BLESSED
IS HE WHO COMES IN THE NAME OF THE LORD!' "

*Jesus Heals on the Sabbath*

**14** AND IT came about when He went into the house of one
of the leaders of the Pharisees on *the* Sabbath to eat bread,
that they were watching Him closely.
2And there, in front of Him was a certain man suffering from
dropsy.
3And Jesus answered and spoke to the lawyers and Pharisees,
saying, "Is it lawful to heal on the Sabbath, or not?"
4But they kept silent. And He took hold of him, and healed
him, and sent him away.
5And He said to them, "Which one of you shall have a son or
an ox fall into a well, and will not immediately pull him out on a
Sabbath day?"
6And they could make no reply to this.

*Parable of the Guests*

7¶ And He *began* speaking a parable to the invited guests when
He noticed how they had been picking out the places of honor *at
the table;* saying to them,
8"When you are invited by someone to a wedding feast, do not
take the place of honor, lest someone more distinguished than you
may have been invited by him,
9and he who invited you both shall come and say to you, 'Give
place to this man,' and then in disgrace you proceed to occupy the
last place.
10"But when you are invited, go and recline at the last place,
so that when the one who has invited you comes, he may say to
you, 'Friend, move up higher'; then you will have honor in the
sight of all who are at the table with you.
11"For everyone who exalts himself shall be humbled, and he
who humbles himself shall be exalted."
12¶ And He also went on to say to the one who had invited Him,
"When you give a luncheon or a dinner, do not invite your friends
or your brothers or your relatives or rich neighbors, lest they also
invite you in return, and repayment come to you.
13"But when you give a reception, invite *the* poor, *the* crippled,
*the* lame, *the* blind,
14and you will be blessed, since they do not have *the means* to
repay you; for you will be repaid at the resurrection of the righteous."
15¶ And when one of those who were reclining *at the table* with
Him heard this, he said to Him, "Blessed is everyone who shall eat
bread in the kingdom of God!"

*Parable of the Dinner*

16But He said to him, "A certain man was giving a big dinner,
and he invited many;
17and at the dinner hour he sent his slave to say to those who
had been invited, 'Come; for everything is ready now.'
18"But they all alike began to make excuses. The first one said
to him, 'I have bought a piece of land and I need to go out and look
at it; please consider me excused.'
19"And another one said, 'I have bought five yoke of oxen, and
I am going to try them out; please consider me excused.'
20"And another one said, 'I have married a wife, and for that
reason I cannot come.'
21"And the slave came *back* and reported this to his master.
Then the head of the household became angry and said to his
slave, 'Go out at once into the streets and lanes of the city and bring
in here the poor and crippled and blind and lame.'
22"And the slave said, 'Master, what you commanded has been
done, and still there is room.'

## New International

you, you will not see me again until you say, 'Blessed is he who
comes in the name of the Lord.'[g]"

*Jesus at a Pharisee's House*

**14** ONE SABBATH, when Jesus went to eat in the house of
a prominent Pharisee, he was being carefully watched.
2There in front of him was a man suffering from dropsy. 3Jesus
asked the Pharisees and experts in the law, "Is it lawful to heal on
the Sabbath or not?" 4But they remained silent. So taking hold of
the man, he healed him and sent him away.
5Then he asked them, "If one of you has a son[h] or an ox that
falls into a well on the Sabbath day, will you not immediately pull
him out?" 6And they had nothing to say.
7When he noticed how the guests picked the places of honor at
the table, he told them this parable: 8"When someone invites you
to a wedding feast, do not take the place of honor, for a person
more distinguished than you may have been invited. 9If so, the
host who invited both of you will come and say to you, 'Give this
man your seat.' Then, humiliated, you will have to take the least
important place. 10But when you are invited, take the lowest place,
so that when your host comes, he will say to you, 'Friend, move
up to a better place.' Then you will be honored in the presence of
all your fellow guests. 11For everyone who exalts himself will be
humbled, and he who humbles himself will be exalted."
12Then Jesus said to his host, "When you give a luncheon or
dinner, do not invite your friends, your brothers or relatives, or
your rich neighbors; if you do, they may invite you back and so
you will be repaid. 13But when you give a banquet, invite the poor,
the crippled, the lame, the blind, 14and you will be blessed. Although they cannot repay you, you will be repaid at the resurrection of the righteous."

*The Parable of the Great Banquet*

15When one of those at the table with him heard this, he said
to Jesus, "Blessed is the man who will eat at the feast in the
kingdom of God."
16Jesus replied: "A certain man was preparing a great banquet
and invited many guests. 17At the time of the banquet he sent his
servant to tell those who had been invited, 'Come, for everything
is now ready.'
18"But they all alike began to make excuses. The first said, 'I
have just bought a field, and I must go and see it. Please excuse
me.'
19"Another said, 'I have just bought five yoke of oxen, and I'm
on my way to try them out. Please excuse me.'
20"Still another said, 'I just got married, so I can't come.'
21"The servant came back and reported this to his master. Then
the owner of the house became angry and ordered his servant, 'Go
out quickly into the streets and alleys of the town and bring in the
poor, the crippled, the blind and the lame.'
22" 'Sir,' the servant said, 'what you ordered has been done, but
there is still room.'

NIV [g] 35 Psalm 118:26 [h] 5 Some manuscripts *donkey*

## King James

23And the lord said unto the servant, Go out into the highways
and hedges, and compel *them* to come in, that my house may be
filled.
24For I say unto you, That none of those men which were
bidden shall taste of my supper.
25¶ And there went great multitudes with him: and he turned,
and said unto them,
26If any *man* come to me, and hate not his father, and mother,
and wife, and children, and brethren, and sisters, yea, and his own
life also, he cannot be my disciple.
27And whosoever doth not bear his cross, and come after me,
cannot be my disciple.
28For which of you, intending to build a tower, sitteth not down
first, and counteth the cost, whether he have *sufficient* to finish *it?*
29Lest haply, after he hath laid the foundation, and is not able
to finish *it,* all that behold *it* begin to mock him,
30Saying, This man began to build, and was not able to finish.
31Or what king, going to make war against another king, sitteth
not down first, and consulteth whether he be able with ten thousand to meet him that cometh against him with twenty thousand?
32Or else, while the other is yet a great way off, he sendeth an
ambassage, and desireth conditions of peace.
33So likewise, whosoever he be of you that forsaketh not all that
he hath, he cannot be my disciple.
34¶ Salt *is* good: but if the salt have lost his savour, wherewith
shall it be seasoned?
35It is neither fit for the land, nor yet for the dunghill; *but* men
cast it out. He that hath ears to hear, let him hear.

**15** THEN DREW near unto him all the publicans and sinners
for to hear him.
2And the Pharisees and scribes murmured, saying, This man
receiveth sinners, and eateth with them.
3¶ And he spake this parable unto them, saying,
4What man of you, having an hundred sheep, if he lose one of
them, doth not leave the ninety and nine in the wilderness, and
go after that which is lost, until he find it?
5And when he hath found *it,* he layeth *it* on his shoulders,
rejoicing.
6And when he cometh home, he calleth together *his* friends and
neighbours, saying unto them, Rejoice with me; for I have found
my sheep which was lost.
7I say unto you, that likewise joy shall be in heaven over one
sinner that repenteth, more than over ninety and nine just persons, which need no repentance.
8¶ Either what woman having ten pieces of silver, if she lose one
piece, doth not light a candle, and sweep the house, and seek
diligently till she find *it?*
9And when she hath found *it,* she calleth *her* friends and *her*
neighbours together, saying, Rejoice with me; for I have found the
piece which I had lost.

## Amplified

23Then the master said to the servant, Go out into the highways
and hedges and urge *and* constrain [them] to yield *and* come in, so
that my house may be filled;
24For I tell you, that no one of those who were invited shall taste
my supper.
25Now huge crowds were going along with [Jesus]; and He
turned and said to them,
26If any one comes to Me and does not hate his [own] father and
mother [that is, [a]in the sense of indifference to or relative disregard for them in comparison with his attitude toward God] and
[likewise] his wife and children and brothers and sisters, [yes] and
even his own life also, he cannot be My disciple.
27Whoever does not persevere *and* carry his own cross and come
after (follow) Me, cannot be My disciple.
28For which of you, wishing to build a [b]farm-building, does not
first sit down and calculate the cost, whether he has sufficient
means to finish it?
29Otherwise, when he has laid the foundation and is unable to
complete [the building], all who see it begin to mock *and* jeer at
him,
30Saying, This man began to build, and was not able ([c]worth
enough) to finish.
31Or what king going to engage in conflict with another king,
will not first sit down and consider *and* take counsel whether he
is able with ten thousand to meet him who comes against him with
twenty thousand?
32And if he cannot [do so], when the other king is still a great
way off, he sends an envoy and asks the [terms] of peace.
33So then, whoever of you does not forsake—renounce, surrender claim to, give up, [d]say goodbye to—all that he has cannot be
My disciple.
34Salt is good—an excellent thing; but if salt has lost its strength
*and* has become saltless (insipid, flat), how shall its saltness be
restored?
35It is fit neither for the land nor for the manure heap; men
throw it away. He who has ears to hear, let him listen *and* consider
*and* comprehend by hearing!

**15** NOW THE tax collectors and (notorious and [e]especially
wicked) sinners were all coming near to [Jesus] to listen to
Him.
2And the Pharisees and the scribes kept muttering *and* indignantly complaining, saying, This man accepts *and* receives *and*
welcomes ([f]pre-eminently wicked) sinners and eats with them.
3So He told them this parable:
4What man of you, if he has a hundred sheep and should lose
one of them, does not leave the ninety-nine in the wilderness
(desert), and go after the one that is lost, until he finds it?
5And when he has found it, he lays it on his [own] shoulders
rejoicing.
6And when he gets home, he summons together [his] friends
and [his] neighbors, saying to them, Rejoice with me, because I
have found my sheep which was lost.
7Thus, I tell you, there will be more joy in heaven over one
([g]especially) wicked person who repents—[that is,] [h]changes his
mind, abhorring his errors and misdeeds, and determines to enter
upon a better course of life—than over ninety-nine righteous persons who have no need of repentance.
8Or what woman, having ten (silver) drachmas [each one equal
to a day's wages], if she loses one coin, does not light a lamp and
sweep the house and look carefully *and* diligently until she finds
it?
9And when she has found it, she summons her (women)
friends and neighbors, saying, Rejoice with me, for I have found
the silver coin which I had lost.

**AMP** [a] Abbott-Smith. [b] Moulton and Milligan. [c] Vincent. [d] Vincent.
[e] Thayer. [f] Thayer. [g] Thayer. [h] Thayer.

## New American Standard

23"And the master said to the slave, 'Go out into the highways
and along the hedges, and compel *them* to come in, that my house
may be filled.
24'For I tell you, none of those men who were invited shall taste
of my dinner.' "

*Discipleship Tested*

25¶ Now great multitudes were going along with Him; and He
turned and said to them,
26"If anyone comes to Me, and does not [i]hate his own father
and mother and wife and children and brothers and sisters, yes,
and even his own life, he cannot be My disciple.
27"Whoever does not carry his own cross and come after Me
cannot be My disciple.
28"For which one of you, when he wants to build a tower, does
not first sit down and calculate the cost, to see if he has enough
to complete it?
29"Otherwise, when he has laid a foundation, and is not able
to finish, all who observe it begin to ridicule him,
30saying, 'This man began to build and was not able to finish.'
31"Or what king, when he sets out to meet another king in
battle, will not first sit down and take counsel whether he is strong
enough with ten thousand *men* to encounter the one coming
against him with twenty thousand?
32"Or else, while the other is still far away, he sends a delegation and asks terms of peace.
33"So therefore, no one of you can be My disciple who does not
give up all his own possessions.
34"Therefore, salt is good; but if even salt has become tasteless,
with what will it be seasoned?
35"It is useless either for the soil or for the manure pile; it is
thrown out. He who has ears to hear, let him hear."

*The Lost Sheep*

15 NOW ALL the tax-gatherers and the sinners were coming
near Him to listen to Him.
2And both the Pharisees and the scribes *began* to grumble,
saying, "This man receives sinners and eats with them."
3¶ And He told them this parable, saying,
4"What man among you, if he has a hundred sheep and has
lost one of them, does not leave the ninety-nine in the open pasture, and go after the one which is lost, until he finds it?
5"And when he has found it, he lays it on his shoulders,
rejoicing.
6"And when he comes home, he calls together his friends and
his neighbors, saying to them, 'Rejoice with me, for I have found
my sheep which was lost!'
7"I tell you that in the same way, there will be *more* joy in
heaven over one sinner who repents, than over ninety-nine righteous persons who need no repentance.

*The Lost Coin*

8¶ "Or what woman, if she has ten silver coins and loses one
coin, does not light a lamp and sweep the house and search carefully until she finds it?
9"And when she has found it, she calls together her friends
and neighbors, saying, 'Rejoice with me, for I have found the coin
which I had lost!'

NAS [i] I.e., by comparison of his love for Me

## New International

23"Then the master told his servant, 'Go out to the roads and
country lanes and make them come in, so that my house will be
full. 24I tell you, not one of those men who were invited will get
a taste of my banquet.' "

*The Cost of Being a Disciple*

25Large crowds were traveling with Jesus, and turning to them
he said: 26"If anyone comes to me and does not hate his father and
mother, his wife and children, his brothers and sisters—yes, even
his own life—he cannot be my disciple. 27And anyone who does
not carry his cross and follow me cannot be my disciple.
28"Suppose one of you wants to build a tower. Will he not first
sit down and estimate the cost to see if he has enough money to
complete it? 29For if he lays the foundation and is not able to finish
it, everyone who sees it will ridicule him, 30saying, 'This fellow
began to build and was not able to finish.'
31"Or suppose a king is about to go to war against another king.
Will he not first sit down and consider whether he is able with ten
thousand men to oppose the one coming against him with twenty
thousand? 32If he is not able, he will send a delegation while the
other is still a long way off and will ask for terms of peace. 33In the
same way, any of you who does not give up everything he has
cannot be my disciple.
34"Salt is good, but if it loses its saltiness, how can it be made
salty again? 35It is fit neither for the soil nor for the manure pile;
it is thrown out.
"He who has ears to hear, let him hear."

*The Parable of the Lost Sheep*

15 NOW THE tax collectors and "sinners" were all gathering
around to hear him. 2But the Pharisees and the teachers
of the law muttered, "This man welcomes sinners and eats with
them."
3Then Jesus told them this parable: 4"Suppose one of you has
a hundred sheep and loses one of them. Does he not leave the
ninety-nine in the open country and go after the lost sheep until
he finds it? 5And when he finds it, he joyfully puts it on his
shoulders 6and goes home. Then he calls his friends and neighbors
together and says, 'Rejoice with me; I have found my lost sheep.'
7I tell you that in the same way there will be more rejoicing in
heaven over one sinner who repents than over ninety-nine righteous persons who do not need to repent.

*The Parable of the Lost Coin*

8"Or suppose a woman has ten silver coins[j] and loses one.
Does she not light a lamp, sweep the house and search carefully
until she finds it? 9And when she finds it, she calls her friends and
neighbors together and says, 'Rejoice with me; I have found my
lost coin.' 10In the same way, I tell you, there is rejoicing in the

NIV [j] 8 Greek *ten drachmas,* each worth about a day's wages

## King James

10Likewise, I say unto you, there is joy in the presence of the angels of God over one sinner that repenteth.

11¶ And he said, A certain man had two sons:

12And the younger of them said to *his* father, Father, give me the portion of goods that falleth *to me*. And he divided unto them *his* living.

13And not many days after the younger son gathered all together, and took his journey into a far country, and there wasted his substance with riotous living.

14And when he had spent all, there arose a mighty famine in that land; and he began to be in want.

15And he went and joined himself to a citizen of that country; and he sent him into his fields to feed swine.

16And he would fain have filled his belly with the husks that the swine did eat: and no man gave unto him.

17And when he came to himself, he said, How many hired servants of my father's have bread enough and to spare, and I perish with hunger!

18I will arise and go to my father, and will say unto him, Father, I have sinned against heaven, and before thee,

19And am no more worthy to be called thy son: make me as one of thy hired servants.

20And he arose, and came to his father. But when he was yet a great way off, his father saw him, and had compassion, and ran, and fell on his neck, and kissed him.

21And the son said unto him, Father, I have sinned against heaven, and in thy sight, and am no more worthy to be called thy son.

22But the father said to his servants, Bring forth the best robe, and put *it* on him; and put a ring on his hand, and shoes on *his* feet:

23And bring hither the fatted calf, and kill *it;* and let us eat, and be merry:

24For this my son was dead, and is alive again; he was lost, and is found. And they began to be merry.

25Now his elder son was in the field: and as he came and drew nigh to the house, he heard music and dancing.

26And he called one of the servants, and asked what these things meant.

27And he said unto him, Thy brother is come; and thy father hath killed the fatted calf, because he hath received him safe and sound.

28And he was angry, and would not go in: therefore came his father out, and entreated him.

29And he answering said to *his* father, Lo, these many years do I serve thee, neither transgressed I at any time thy commandment: and yet thou never gavest me a kid, that I might make merry with my friends:

30But as soon as this thy son was come, which hath devoured thy living with harlots, thou hast killed for him the fatted calf.

31And he said unto him, Son, thou art ever with me, and all that I have is thine.

32It was meet that we should make merry, and be glad: for this thy brother was dead, and is alive again; and was lost, and is found.

## Amplified

10Even so, I tell you, there is joy among *and* in the presence of the angels of God over one ([a]especially) wicked person who repents— [b]changes his mind for the better, heartily amending his ways with abhorrence for his past sins.

11And He said, There was a certain man who had two sons;

12And the younger of them said to his father, Father, give me the part of the property that falls [to me]. And he divided the livelihood [between] them. [Deut. 21:15-17.]

13And not many days after that the younger son gathered up all that he had and journeyed into a distant country, and there he wasted his fortune in reckless *and* loose-from-restraint living.

14And when he had spent all he had, a [c]mighty famine came upon that country, and he began to fall behind *and* be in want.

15So he went and forced (glued) himself upon one of the citizens of that country, who sent him into his fields to feed hogs.

16And he would gladly have fed on (and [d]filled his belly with) the [e]carob pods that the hogs were eating, but [they could not satisfy his hunger and] nobody gave him anything [better]. [Jer. 30:14.]

17Then when he came to himself, he said, How many hired servants of my father have enough food and to spare, but I am perishing (dying) here of hunger!

18I will get up and go to my father, and I will say to him, Father, I have sinned against heaven and in your sight;

19I am no longer worthy to be called your son; [just] make me as one of your hired servants.

20So he got up and came to his [own] father. But while he was still a long way off, his father saw him and was moved with pity *and* tenderness [for him], and he ran and embraced him and kissed him— [f]fervently.

21And the son said to him, Father, I have sinned against heaven and in your sight; I am no longer worthy to be called your son—I no longer deserve to be recognized as a son of yours!

22But the father said to his bond servants, Bring quickly the best robe—the festive, honor robe—and put it on him, and give him a ring for his hand and sandals for his feet; [Gen. 41:42; Zech. 3:4.]

23And bring out [g]that [wheat-] fattened calf and kill it, and let us [h]revel *and* feast *and* be happy *and* merry;

24Because this my son was dead, and is alive again; he was lost, and is found! And they began to [i]revel *and* feast *and* make merry.

25But his older son was in the field, and as he returned and came near to the house, he heard music and dancing.

26And having called one of the servant (boys) to him, he began to ask what this meant.

27And he said to him, Your brother has come, and your father has killed [j]that [wheat-]fattened calf, because he has received him safe and well.

28But [the elder brother] was angry—with deep-seated wrath—and resolved not to go in. Then his father came out [and] began to plead with him,

29But he answered his father, Lo, these many years I have served you, and I have never disobeyed your command; yet you never gave me [so much as] a (little) kid, that I might [k]revel *and* feast *and* be happy *and* make merry with my friends;

30But when this son of yours arrived, who has devoured your living with immoral women, you have killed for him [l]that [wheat-] fattened calf!

31And the father said to him, Son, you are always with me, and all that is mine is yours.

32But it was fitting to make merry, to [m]revel *and* feast and rejoice, for this brother of yours was dead, and is alive again! He was lost and is found!

**AMP** [a] Thayer. [b] Thayer. [c] Abbott-Smith. [d] Many ancient authorities so read. [e] Abbott-Smith. [f] Abbott-Smith. [g] Tyndale. [h] Souter. [i] Souter. [j] Tyndale. [k] Souter. [l] Tyndale. [m] Souter.

## New American Standard

10"In the same way, I tell you, there is joy in the presence of the angels of God over one sinner who repents."

*The Prodigal Son*

11¶ And He said, "A certain man had two sons;
12and the younger of them said to his father, 'Father, give me the share of the estate that falls to me.' And he divided his wealth between them.
13"And not many days later, the younger son gathered everything together and went on a journey into a distant country, and there he squandered his estate with loose living.
14"Now when he had spent everything, a severe famine occurred in that country, and he began to be in need.
15"And he went and attached himself to one of the citizens of that country, and he sent him into his fields to feed swine.
16"And he was longing to fill his stomach with the pods that the swine were eating, and no one was giving *anything* to him.
17"But when he came to his senses, he said, 'How many of my father's hired men have more than enough bread, but I am dying here with hunger!
18'I will get up and go to my father, and will say to him, "Father, I have sinned against heaven, and in your sight;
19I am no longer worthy to be called your son; make me as one of your hired men."'
20"And he got up and came to his father. But while he was still a long way off, his father saw him, and felt compassion *for him*, and ran and embraced him, and kissed him.
21"And the son said to him, 'Father, I have sinned against heaven and in your sight; I am no longer worthy to be called your son.'
22"But the father said to his slaves, 'Quickly bring out the best robe and put it on him, and put a ring on his hand and sandals on his feet;
23and bring the fattened calf, kill it, and let us eat and be merry;
24for this son of mine was dead, and has come to life again; he was lost, and has been found.' And they began to be merry.
25"Now his older son was in the field, and when he came and approached the house, he heard music and dancing.
26"And he summoned one of the servants and *began* inquiring what these things might be.
27"And he said to him, 'Your brother has come, and your father has killed the fattened calf, because he has received him back safe and sound.'
28"But he became angry, and was not willing to go in; and his father came out and *began* entreating him.
29"But he answered and said to his father, 'Look! For so many years I have been serving you, and I have never neglected a command of yours; and *yet* you have never given me a kid, that I might be merry with my friends;
30but when this son of yours came, who has devoured your wealth with harlots, you killed the fattened calf for him.'
31"And he said to him, '*My* child, you have always been with me, and all that is mine is yours.
32'But we had to be merry and rejoice, for this brother of yours was dead and *has begun* to live, and *was* lost and has been found.'"

## New International

presence of the angels of God over one sinner who repents."

*The Parable of the Lost Son*

11Jesus continued: "There was a man who had two sons. 12The
younger one said to his father, 'Father, give me my share of the
estate.' So he divided his property between them.
13"Not long after that, the younger son got together all he had,
set off for a distant country and there squandered his wealth in
wild living. 14After he had spent everything, there was a severe
famine in that whole country, and he began to be in need. 15So he
went and hired himself out to a citizen of that country, who sent
him to his fields to feed pigs. 16He longed to fill his stomach with
the pods that the pigs were eating, but no one gave him anything.
17"When he came to his senses, he said, 'How many of my
father's hired men have food to spare, and here I am starving to
death! 18I will set out and go back to my father and say to him:
Father, I have sinned against heaven and against you. 19I am no
longer worthy to be called your son; make me like one of your
hired men.' 20So he got up and went to his father.
"But while he was still a long way off, his father saw him and
was filled with compassion for him; he ran to his son, threw his
arms around him and kissed him.
21"The son said to him, 'Father, I have sinned against heaven
and against you. I am no longer worthy to be called your son.[n]'
22"But the father said to his servants, 'Quick! Bring the best robe
and put it on him. Put a ring on his finger and sandals on his feet.
23Bring the fattened calf and kill it. Let's have a feast and celebrate.
24For this son of mine was dead and is alive again; he was lost and
is found.' So they began to celebrate.
25"Meanwhile, the older son was in the field. When he came
near the house, he heard music and dancing. 26So he called one
of the servants and asked him what was going on. 27'Your brother
has come,' he replied, 'and your father has killed the fattened calf
because he has him back safe and sound.'
28"The older brother became angry and refused to go in. So his
father went out and pleaded with him. 29But he answered his
father, 'Look! All these years I've been slaving for you and never
disobeyed your orders. Yet you never gave me even a young goat
so I could celebrate with my friends. 30But when this son of yours
who has squandered your property with prostitutes comes home,
you kill the fattened calf for him!'
31" 'My son,' the father said, 'you are always with me, and
everything I have is yours. 32But we had to celebrate and be glad,
because this brother of yours was dead and is alive again; he was
lost and is found.' "

**NIV** [n] *21* Some early manuscripts *son. Make me like one of your hired men.*

## King James

**16** AND HE said also unto his disciples, There was a certain rich man, which had a steward; and the same was accused unto him that he had wasted his goods.

2And he called him, and said unto him, How is it that I hear this of thee? give an account of thy stewardship; for thou mayest be no longer steward.

3Then the steward said within himself, What shall I do? for my lord taketh away from me the stewardship: I cannot dig; to beg I am ashamed.

4I am resolved what to do, that, when I am put out of the stewardship, they may receive me into their houses.

5So he called every one of his lord's debtors *unto him,* and said unto the first, How much owest thou unto my lord?

6And he said, An hundred measures of oil. And he said unto him, Take thy bill, and sit down quickly, and write fifty.

7Then said he to another, And how much owest thou? And he said, An hundred measures of wheat. And he said unto him, Take thy bill, and write fourscore.

8And the lord commended the unjust steward, because he had done wisely: for the children of this world are in their generation wiser than the children of light.

9And I say unto you, Make to yourselves friends of the mammon of unrighteousness; that, when ye fail, they may receive you into everlasting habitations.

10He that is faithful in that which is least is faithful also in much: and he that is unjust in the least is unjust also in much.

11If therefore ye have not been faithful in the unrighteous mammon, who will commit to your trust the true *riches*?

12And if ye have not been faithful in that which is another man's, who shall give you that which is your own?

13¶ No servant can serve two masters: for either he will hate the one, and love the other; or else he will hold to the one, and despise the other. Ye cannot serve God and mammon.

14And the Pharisees also, who were covetous, heard all these things: and they derided him.

15And he said unto them, Ye are they which justify yourselves before men; but God knoweth your hearts: for that which is highly esteemed among men is abomination in the sight of God.

16The law and the prophets *were* until John: since that time the kingdom of God is preached, and every man presseth into it.

17And it is easier for heaven and earth to pass, than one tittle of the law to fail.

18Whosoever putteth away his wife, and marrieth another, committeth adultery: and whosoever marrieth her that is put away from *her* husband committeth adultery.

19¶ There was a certain rich man, which was clothed in purple and fine linen, and fared sumptuously every day:

20And there was a certain beggar named Lazarus, which was laid at his gate, full of sores,

## Amplified

**16** ALSO [JESUS] said to the disciples, There was a certain rich man who had a [a]manager of his estate, and accusations [against this man were brought] to him, that he was squandering his [master's] possessions.

2And he called him and said to him, What is this that I hear about you? Turn in the account of your management [of my affairs], for you can be [my] manager no longer.

3And the manager of the estate said to himself, What shall I do, seeing that my master is taking the management away from me? I am not able to dig, and I am ashamed to beg.

4I have come to know what I will do, so that they [my master's debtors] may accept *and* welcome me into their houses when I am put out of the management.

5So he summoned his master's debtors one by one, and he said to the first, How much do you owe my master?

6He said, A hundred measures [about nine hundred gallons] of oil. And he said to him, Take back your written acknowledgement of [b]obligation, and sit down quickly and write fifty [about four hundred fifty gallons].

7After that he said to another, And how much do you owe? He said, A hundred measures [about nine hundred bushels] of wheat. He said to him, Take back your written acknowledgement of [c]obligation, and write eighty [about seven hundred bushels].

8And [his] master praised the dishonest (unjust) manager for acting [d]shrewdly *and* [e]prudently; for the sons of this age are shrewder *and* more prudent *and* wiser in [ [f]relation to] their own generation—that is, to their own age and [g]kind—than are the sons of light.

9And I tell you, make friends for yourselves by means of unrighteous mammon [that is, [h]deceitful riches, money, possessions], so that when it fails, they [those you have favored] may receive *and* welcome you into the everlasting habitations (dwellings).

10He who is faithful in a very little [thing], is faithful also in much; and he who is dishonest *and* unjust in a very little [thing], is dishonest *and* unjust also in much.

11Therefore, if you have not been faithful in the [case of] the unrighteous mammon—the [i]deceitful riches, money, possessions—who will entrust to you the true riches?

12And if you have not proved faithful in that which belongs to another [whether God or man], who will give you that which is your own [that is, [j]the true riches]?

13No servant is able to serve two masters; for either he will hate the one and love the other, or he will stand by *and* be devoted to the one and despise the other. You cannot serve God and mammon—riches, that is, or [k]anything in which you trust and on which you rely.

14Now the Pharisees, who were covetous *and* lovers of money, heard all these things (taken together), and they began to sneer *and* ridicule *and* scoff at Him.

15But He said to them, You are they who declare yourselves just *and* upright before men, but God knows your hearts. For what is exalted *and* highly thought of among men is detestable *and* abhorrent (an abomination) in the sight of God. [I Sam. 16:7; Prov. 21:2.]

16Until John came, there were the Law and the prophets; since then the good news (the Gospel) of the kingdom of God is being preached, and every one strives violently to go in—would force his [ [l]own way, rather than God's] way into it.

17Yet it is easier for heaven and earth to pass away, than for one dot of the Law to become void *and* fail.

18Whoever (dismisses, repudiates and) divorces his wife and marries another commits adultery, and he who marries a woman who is divorced from her husband commits adultery.

19There was a certain rich man, who (habitually clothed himself in purple and fine linen, and [m]reveled *and* feasted *and* made merry in splendor every day.

20And at his gate there [n]was (carelessly) dropped down *and* left a certain [o]utterly destitute man, named Lazarus, (reduced to begging alms) and covered with ( [p]ulcerated) sores.

**AMP** [a] Moulton and Milligan. [b] Wycliffe. [c] Wycliffe. [d] Vincent. [e] Wycliffe. [f] Vincent. [g] Tyndale. [h] Souter. [i] Souter. [j] Vincent. [k] Thayer. [l] Berkeley Version. [m] Souter. [n] Vincent. [o] Vincent. [p] Vincent.

## New American Standard

*The Unrighteous Steward*

**16** NOW HE was also saying to the disciples, "There was a
certain rich man who had a steward, and this *steward* was
reported to him as squandering his possessions.
2 "And he called him and said to him, 'What is this I hear about
you? Give an account of your stewardship, for you can no longer
be steward.'
3 "And the steward said to himself, 'What shall I do, since my
master is taking the stewardship away from me? I am not strong
enough to dig; I am ashamed to beg.
4 'I know what I shall do, so that when I am removed from the
stewardship, they will receive me into their homes.'
5 "And he summoned each one of his master's debtors, and he
*began* saying to the first, 'How much do you owe my master?'
6 "And he said, 'A hundred measures of oil.' And he said to
him, 'Take your bill, and sit down quickly and write fifty.'
7 "Then he said to another, 'And how much do you owe?' And
he said, 'A hundred measures of wheat.' He *said to him, 'Take
your bill, and write eighty.'
8 "And his master praised the unrighteous steward because he
had acted shrewdly; for the sons of this age are more shrewd in
relation to their own kind than the sons of light.
9 "And I say to you, make friends for yourselves by means of
the [q]mammon of unrighteousness; that when it fails, they may
receive you into the eternal dwellings.
10 "He who is faithful in a very little thing is faithful also in
much; and he who is unrighteous in a very little thing is unrighteous also in much.
11 "If therefore you have not been faithful in the *use of* unrighteous mammon, who will entrust the true *riches* to you?
12 "And if you have not been faithful in *the use of* that which is
another's, who will give you that which is your own?
13 "No servant can serve two masters; for either he will hate the
one, and love the other, or else he will hold to one, and despise
the other. You cannot serve God and mammon."
14 ¶ Now the Pharisees, who were lovers of money, were listening to all these things, and they were scoffing at Him.
15 And He said to them, "You are those who justify yourselves
in the sight of men, but God knows your hearts; for that which is
highly esteemed among men is detestable in the sight of God.
16 "The Law and the Prophets *were proclaimed* until John; since
then the gospel of the kingdom of God is preached, and everyone
is forcing his way into it.
17 "But it is easier for heaven and earth to pass away than for
one stroke of a letter of the Law to fail.
18 "Everyone who divorces his wife and marries another commits adultery; and he who marries one who is divorced from a
husband commits adultery.

*The Rich Man and Lazarus*

19 ¶ "Now there was a certain rich man, and he habitually
dressed in purple and fine linen, gaily living in splendor every day.
20 "And a certain poor man named Lazarus was laid at his gate,
covered with sores,

NAS [q] Or, *riches*

## New International

*The Parable of the Shrewd Manager*

**16** JESUS TOLD his disciples: "There was a rich man whose
manager was accused of wasting his possessions. 2 So he
called him in and asked him, 'What is this I hear about you? Give
an account of your management, because you cannot be manager
any longer.'
3 "The manager said to himself, 'What shall I do now? My
master is taking away my job. I'm not strong enough to dig, and
I'm ashamed to beg— 4 I know what I'll do so that, when I lose my
job here, people will welcome me into their houses.'
5 "So he called in each one of his master's debtors. He asked the
first, 'How much do you owe my master?'
6 " 'Eight hundred gallons[r] of olive oil,' he replied.
"The manager told him, 'Take your bill, sit down quickly, and
make it four hundred.'
7 "Then he asked the second, 'And how much do you owe?'
" 'A thousand bushels[s] of wheat,' he replied.
"He told him, 'Take your bill and make it eight hundred.'
8 "The master commended the dishonest manager because he
had acted shrewdly. For the people of this world are more shrewd
in dealing with their own kind than are the people of the light. 9 I
tell you, use worldly wealth to gain friends for yourselves, so that
when it is gone, you will be welcomed into eternal dwellings.
10 "Whoever can be trusted with very little can also be trusted
with much, and whoever is dishonest with very little will also be
dishonest with much. 11 So if you have not been trustworthy in
handling worldly wealth, who will trust you with true riches?
12 And if you have not been trustworthy with someone else's property, who will give you property of your own?
13 "No servant can serve two masters. Either he will hate the one
and love the other, or he will be devoted to the one and despise
the other. You cannot serve both God and Money."
14 The Pharisees, who loved money, heard all this and were
sneering at Jesus. 15 He said to them, "You are the ones who justify
yourselves in the eyes of men, but God knows your hearts. What
is highly valued among men is detestable in God's sight.

*Additional Teachings*

16 "The Law and the Prophets were proclaimed until John. Since
that time, the good news of the kingdom of God is being preached,
and everyone is forcing his way into it. 17 It is easier for heaven and
earth to disappear than for the least stroke of a pen to drop out of
the Law.
18 "Anyone who divorces his wife and marries another woman
commits adultery, and the man who marries a divorced woman
commits adultery.

*The Rich Man and Lazarus*

19 "There was a rich man who was dressed in purple and fine
linen and lived in luxury every day. 20 At his gate was laid a beggar
named Lazarus, covered with sores 21 and longing to eat what fell

NIV [r] 6 Greek *one hundred batous* (probably about 3 kiloliters) [s] 7 Greek *one hundred korous* (probably about 35 kiloliters)

## King James

21 And desiring to be fed with the crumbs which fell from the rich man's table: moreover the dogs came and licked his sores.

22 And it came to pass, that the beggar died, and was carried by the angels into Abraham's bosom: the rich man also died, and was buried;

23 And in hell he lift up his eyes, being in torments, and seeth Abraham afar off, and Lazarus in his bosom.

24 And he cried and said, Father Abraham, have mercy on me, and send Lazarus, that he may dip the tip of his finger in water, and cool my tongue; for I am tormented in this flame.

25 But Abraham said, Son, remember that thou in thy lifetime receivedst thy good things, and likewise Lazarus evil things: but now he is comforted, and thou art tormented.

26 And beside all this, between us and you there is a great gulf fixed: so that they which would pass from hence to you cannot; neither can they pass to us, that *would come* from thence.

27 Then he said, I pray thee therefore, father, that thou wouldest send him to my father's house:

28 For I have five brethren; that he may testify unto them, lest they also come into this place of torment.

29 Abraham saith unto him, They have Moses and the prophets; let them hear them.

30 And he said, Nay, father Abraham: but if one went unto them from the dead, they will repent.

31 And he said unto him, If they hear not Moses and the prophets, neither will they be persuaded, though one rose from the dead.

**17** THEN SAID he unto the disciples, It is impossible but that offences will come: but woe *unto him,* through whom they come!

2 It were better for him that a millstone were hanged about his neck, and he cast into the sea, than that he should offend one of these little ones.

3 ¶ Take heed to yourselves: If thy brother trespass against thee, rebuke him; and if he repent, forgive him.

4 And if he trespass against thee seven times in a day, and seven times in a day turn again to thee, saying, I repent; thou shalt forgive him.

5 And the apostles said unto the Lord, Increase our faith.

6 And the Lord said, If ye had faith as a grain of mustard seed, ye might say unto this sycamine tree, Be thou plucked up by the root, and be thou planted in the sea; and it should obey you.

7 But which of you, having a servant plowing or feeding cattle, will say unto him by and by, when he is come from the field, Go and sit down to meat?

8 And will not rather say unto him, Make ready wherewith I may sup, and gird thyself, and serve me, till I have eaten and drunken; and afterward thou shalt eat and drink?

9 Doth he thank that servant because he did the things that were commanded him? I trow not.

10 So likewise ye, when ye shall have done all those things which are commanded you, say, We are unprofitable servants: we have done that which was our duty to do.

11 ¶ And it came to pass, as he went to Jerusalem, that he passed through the midst of Samaria and Galilee.

## Amplified

21 He [eagerly] desired to be satisfied with what fell from the rich man's table; moreover the dogs even came and licked his sores.

22 And it occurred that the man (reduced to) begging died, and was carried by the angels to Abraham's bosom. The rich man also died and was buried.

23 And in Hades [the realm of the dead], being in torment, he lifted up his eyes and saw Abraham far away and Lazarus in his bosom.

24 And he cried out and said, Father Abraham, have pity *and* mercy upon me, and send Lazarus to dip the tip of his finger in water and cool my tongue; for I am in anguish in this flame.

25 But Abraham said, Child, remember that you in your lifetime fully received (what is due you) in comforts *and* delights, and Lazarus in like manner the discomforts *and* distresses; but now he is comforted here, and you are in anguish.

26 And besides all this, between us and you there is a great chasm fixed, in order that those who want to pass from this [place] to you may not be able, and no one may pass from there to us.

27 And [the man] said, Then, father, I beseech you to send him to my father's house,

28 For I have five brothers, so that he may give (solemn) testimony *and* warn them, lest they too come into his place of torment.

29 But Abraham said, They have Moses and the prophets; let them hear *and* listen to them.

30 But he answered, No, father Abraham; but if some one from the dead goes to them, they will repent ( [a]change their minds for the better and heartily amend their ways with abhorrence of their past sins).

31 He said to him, If they do not hear *and* listen to Moses and the prophets, neither will they be persuaded *and* convinced *and* believe if some one should rise from the dead.

**17** AND [JESUS] said to His disciples, Temptations [that is, snares, traps set to entice to sin] are sure to come; but woe to him by *or* through whom they come!

2 It would be more profitable for him if a millstone were hung around his neck and he were hurled into the sea, than that he should cause to sin *or* be a snare to one of these little ones [ [b]lowly in rank or influence].

3 [c]Pay attention *and* always be on your guard—looking out for one another; if your brother sins (misses the mark), solemnly tell him so *and* reprove him, and if he repents (feels sorry for having sinned), forgive him.

4 And even if he sins against you seven times in a day, and turns to you seven times and says, I repent (I am sorry), you must forgive him—[that is,] give up resentment and consider the offense as recalled and annulled.

5 The apostles said to the Lord, Increase our faith—that trust and confidence that springs from our belief in God.

6 And the Lord answered, If you had faith (trust and confidence in God) even as a grain of mustard seed, you could say to this mulberry tree, Be pulled up by the roots, and be planted in the sea, and it would obey you.

7 Will any man of you, who has a servant plowing or tending sheep, say to him when he has come in from the field, Come at once and take your place at the table?

8 Will he not instead tell him, Get my supper ready, and gird yourself and serve me till I eat and drink; then afterward you yourself shall eat and drink?

9 Is he grateful *and* does he praise the servant because he did what he was ordered to do?

10 Even so on your part, when you have done everything that was assigned *and* commanded you, say, We are unworthy servants—possessing no merit, for we have not gone beyond our obligation; we have [merely] done what was our duty to do.

11 As He went His way to Jerusalem, it occurred that [Jesus] was passing [along the border] between Samaria and Galilee.

**AMP** [a] Thayer. [b] Abbott-Smith. [c] Moulton and Milligan.

# New American Standard

21and longing to be fed with the *crumbs* which were falling from
the rich man's table; besides, even the dogs were coming and
licking his sores.
22"Now it came about that the poor man died and he was
carried away by the angels to Abraham's bosom; and the rich man
also died and was buried.
23"And in Hades he lifted up his eyes, being in torment, and
*saw Abraham far away, and Lazarus in his bosom.
24"And he cried out and said, 'Father Abraham, have mercy on
me, and send Lazarus, that he may dip the tip of his finger in water
and cool off my tongue; for I am in agony in this flame.'
25"But Abraham said, 'Child, remember that during your life
you received your good things, and likewise Lazarus bad things;
but now he is being comforted here, and you are in agony.
26'And besides all this, between us and you there is a great
chasm fixed, in order that those who wish to come over from here
to you may not be able, and *that* none may cross over from there
to us.'
27"And he said, 'Then I beg you, Father, that you send him to
my father's house—
28for I have five brothers—that he may warn them, lest they also
come to this place of torment.'
29"But Abraham *said, 'They have Moses and the Prophets; let
them hear them.'
30"But he said, 'No, Father Abraham, but if someone goes to
them from the dead, they will repent!'
31"But he said to him, 'If they do not listen to Moses and the
Prophets, neither will they be persuaded if someone rises from the
dead.' "

*Instructions*

17 AND HE said to His disciples, "It is inevitable that stumbling blocks should come, but woe to him through whom
they come!
2"It would be better for him if a millstone were hung around
his neck and he were thrown into the sea, than that he should
cause one of these little ones to stumble.
3"Be on your guard! If your brother sins, rebuke him; and if
he repents, forgive him.
4"And if he sins against you seven times a day, and returns to
you seven times, saying, 'I repent,' forgive him."
5¶ And the apostles said to the Lord, "Increase our faith!"
6And the Lord said, "If you had faith like a mustard seed, you
would say to this mulberry tree, 'Be uprooted and be planted in
the sea'; and it would obey you.
7"But which of you, having a slave plowing or tending sheep,
will say to him when he has come in from the field, 'Come immediately and sit down to eat'?
8"But will he not say to him, 'Prepare something for me to eat,
and *properly* clothe yourself and serve me until I have eaten and
drunk; and afterward you will eat and drink'?
9"He does not thank the slave because he did the things which
were commanded, does he?
10"So you too, when you do all the things which are commanded you, say, 'We are unworthy slaves; we have done *only*
that which we ought to have done.' "

*Ten Lepers Cleansed*

11¶ And it came about while He was on the way to Jerusalem,
that He was passing between Samaria and Galilee.

# New International

from the rich man's table. Even the dogs came and licked his sores.
22"The time came when the beggar died and the angels carried
him to Abraham's side. The rich man also died and was buried.
23In hell,[d] where he was in torment, he looked up and saw Abraham far away, with Lazarus by his side. 24So he called to him,
'Father Abraham, have pity on me and send Lazarus to dip the tip
of his finger in water and cool my tongue, because I am in agony
in this fire.'
25"But Abraham replied, 'Son, remember that in your lifetime
you received your good things, while Lazarus received bad things,
but now he is comforted here and you are in agony. 26And besides
all this, between us and you a great chasm has been fixed, so that
those who want to go from here to you cannot, nor can anyone
cross over from there to us.'
27"He answered, 'Then I beg you, father, send Lazarus to my
father's house, 28for I have five brothers. Let him warn them, so
that they will not also come to this place of torment.'
29"Abraham replied, 'They have Moses and the Prophets; let
them listen to them.'
30" 'No, father Abraham,' he said, 'but if someone from the
dead goes to them, they will repent.'
31"He said to him, 'If they do not listen to Moses and the
Prophets, they will not be convinced even if someone rises from
the dead.' "

*Sin, Faith, Duty*

17 JESUS SAID to his disciples: "Things that cause people to
sin are bound to come, but woe to that person through
whom they come. 2It would be better for him to be thrown into the
sea with a millstone tied around his neck than for him to cause one
of these little ones to sin. 3So watch yourselves.
"If your brother sins, rebuke him, and if he repents, forgive
him. 4If he sins against you seven times in a day, and seven times
comes back to you and says, 'I repent,' forgive him."
5The apostles said to the Lord, "Increase our faith!"
6He replied, "If you have faith as small as a mustard seed, you
can say to this mulberry tree, 'Be uprooted and planted in the sea,'
and it will obey you.
7"Suppose one of you had a servant plowing or looking after
the sheep. Would he say to the servant when he comes in from the
field, 'Come along now and sit down to eat'? 8Would he not rather
say, 'Prepare my supper, get yourself ready and wait on me while
I eat and drink; after that you may eat and drink'? 9Would he thank
the servant because he did what he was told to do? 10So you also,
when you have done everything you were told to do, should say,
'We are unworthy servants; we have only done our duty.' "

*Ten Healed of Leprosy*

11Now on his way to Jerusalem, Jesus traveled along the border
between Samaria and Galilee. 12As he was going into a village, ten

NIV [d] 23 Greek *Hades*

## King James

12And as he entered into a certain village, there met him ten men that were lepers, which stood afar off:
13And they lifted up *their* voices, and said, Jesus, Master, have mercy on us.
14And when he saw *them,* he said unto them, Go show yourselves unto the priests. And it came to pass, that, as they went, they were cleansed.
15And one of them, when he saw that he was healed, turned back, and with a loud voice glorified God,
16And fell down on *his* face at his feet, giving him thanks: and he was a Samaritan.
17And Jesus answering said, Were there not ten cleansed? but where *are* the nine?
18There are not found that returned to give glory to God, save this stranger.
19And he said unto him, Arise, go thy way: thy faith hath made thee whole.
20¶ And when he was demanded of the Pharisees, when the kingdom of God should come, he answered them and said, The kingdom of God cometh not with observation:
21Neither shall they say, Lo here! or, lo there! for, behold, the kingdom of God is within you.
22And he said unto the disciples, The days will come, when ye shall desire to see one of the days of the Son of man, and ye shall not see *it.*
23And they shall say to you, See here; or, see there: go not after *them,* nor follow *them.*
24For as the lightning, that lighteneth out of the one *part* under heaven, shineth unto the other *part* under heaven; so shall also the Son of man be in his day.
25But first must he suffer many things, and be rejected of this generation.
26And as it was in the days of Noe, so shall it be also in the days of the Son of man.
27They did eat, they drank, they married wives, they were given in marriage, until the day that Noe entered into the ark, and the flood came, and destroyed them all.
28Likewise also as it was in the days of Lot; they did eat, they drank, they bought, they sold, they planted, they builded;
29But the same day that Lot went out of Sodom it rained fire and brimstone from heaven, and destroyed *them* all.
30Even thus shall it be in the day when the Son of man is revealed.
31In that day, he which shall be upon the housetop, and his stuff in the house, let him not come down to take it away: and he that is in the field, let him likewise not return back.
32Remember Lot's wife.
33Whosoever shall seek to save his life shall lose it; and whosoever shall lose his life shall preserve it.
34I tell you, in that night there shall be two *men* in one bed; the one shall be taken, and the other shall be left.
35Two *women* shall be grinding together; the one shall be taken, and the other left.
36Two *men* shall be in the field; the one shall be taken, and the other left.
37And they answered and said unto him, Where, Lord? And he said unto them, Wheresoever the body *is,* thither will the eagles be gathered together.

## Amplified

12And as He was going into one village, He was met by ten lepers, who stood at a distance.
13And they raised up their voices and called, Jesus, Master, take pity *and* have mercy on us!
14And when He saw them He said to them, Go (at once) and show yourselves to the priests. And as they went they were cured *and* made clean. [Lev. 14:2-32.]
15Then one of them, upon seeing that he was cured, turned back, [a]recognizing *and* thanking *and* praising God with a loud voice;
16And he fell prostrate at Jesus' feet, thanking Him (over and over). And he was a Samaritan.
17Then Jesus asked, Were not ten cleansed? Where are the nine?
18Was there no one found to return and to [b]recognize *and* give thanks *and* praise to God except this alien?
19And He said to him, Get up and go on your way. Your faith [that is, your trust and confidence that spring from your belief in God] has restored you to health.
20Asked by the Pharisees when the kingdom of God would come, He replied to them by saying, The kingdom of God does not come with signs to be observed *or* with visible display.
21Nor will people say, Look! Here [it is]! or, See, [it is] there! For behold, the kingdom of God is within you (in your hearts) *and* among you (surrounding you).
22And He said to the disciples, The time is coming when you will long to see [even] one of the days of the Son of man, and you will not see [it].
23And they will say to you, Lo, [He is] there! or, Lo, [He is] here! But do not go out or follow [them].
24For as the lightning that flashes and lights up the sky from [one end] to the [other], so will the Son of man be in His [own] day.
25But first He must suffer many things and be disapproved *and* repudiated *and* rejected by this age *and* generation.
26And [just] as it was in the days of Noah, so will it be in the time of the Son of man.
27[People] ate, they drank, they married, they were given in marriage, right up to the day when Noah went into the ark, and the flood came and destroyed them all. [Gen. 6:5-8; 7:6-24.]
28So also as it was in the days of Lot: [people] ate, they drank, they bought, they sold, they planted, they built;
29But on the [very] day that Lot went out of Sodom, it rained fire and brimstone from heaven and destroyed [them] all.
30That is the way it will be on the day that the Son of man is revealed. [Gen. 18:20-33; 19:24, 25.]
31On that day, let him that is on the housetop and his belongings in the house, not come down [and go inside] to carry them away; and likewise let him who is in the field not turn back.
32Remember Lot's wife! [Gen. 19:26.]
33Whoever tries to preserve his life will lose it, but whoever loses his life will preserve and [c]quicken it.
34I tell you, in that night there will be two men in one bed; one will be taken and the other will be left.
35There will be two women grinding together; one will be taken and the other will be left.
36 *Two men will be in the field; one will be taken and the other will be left.*
37Then they asked Him, Where, Lord? He said to them, Wherever the dead body is, there will the vultures ([d]or eagles) be gathered together.

AMP [a] Cremer. [b] Cremer. [c] Wycliffe. [d] Alternate reading.

## New American Standard

12And as He entered a certain village, ten leprous men who
stood at a distance met Him;
13and they raised their voices, saying, "Jesus, Master, have
mercy on us!"
14And when He saw them, He said to them, "Go and show
yourselves to the priests." And it came about that as they were
going, they were cleansed.
15Now one of them, when he saw that he had been healed,
turned back, glorifying God with a loud voice,
16and he fell on his face at His feet, giving thanks to Him. And
he was a Samaritan.
17And Jesus answered and said, "Were there not ten cleansed?
But the nine—where are they?
18"Was no one found who turned back to give glory to God,
except this foreigner?"
19And He said to him, "Rise, and go your way; your faith [e]has
made you well."
**20**¶ Now having been questioned by the Pharisees as to when
the kingdom of God was coming, He answered them and said,
"The kingdom of God is not coming with signs to be observed;
21nor will they say, 'Look, here *it is!*' or, 'There *it is!*' For behold,
the kingdom of God is in your midst."

*Second Coming Foretold*

**22**¶ And He said to the disciples, "The days shall come when
you will long to see one of the days of the Son of Man, and you
will not see it.
23"And they will say to you, 'Look there! Look here!' Do not go
away, and do not run after *them.*
24"For just as the lightning, when it flashes out of one part of
the sky, shines to the other part of the sky, so will the Son of Man
be in His day.
25"But first He must suffer many things and be rejected by this
generation.
26"And just as it happened in the days of Noah, so it shall be
also in the days of the Son of Man:
27they were eating, they were drinking, they were marrying,
they were being given in marriage, until the day that Noah entered
the ark, and the flood came and destroyed them all.
28"It was the same as happened in the days of Lot: they were
eating, they were drinking, they were buying, they were selling,
they were planting, they were building;
29but on the day that Lot went out from Sodom it rained fire and
brimstone from heaven and destroyed them all.
30"It will be just the same on the day that the Son of Man is
revealed.
31"On that day, let not the one who is on the housetop and
whose goods are in the house go down to take them away; and
likewise let not the one who is in the field turn back.
32"Remember Lot's wife.
33"Whoever seeks to keep his life shall lose it, and whoever
loses *his life* shall preserve it.
34"I tell you, on that night there will be two men in one bed;
one will be taken, and the other will be left.
35"There will be two women grinding at the same place; one
will be taken, and the other will be left.
36["[f]Two men will be in the field; one will be taken and the other
will be left."]
37And answering they *said to Him, "Where, Lord?" And He
said to them, "Where the body *is,* there also will the vultures be
gathered."

NAS [e] Or, *has saved you* [f] Many mss. do not contain this verse

## New International

men who had leprosy[g] met him. They stood at a distance 13and
called out in a loud voice, "Jesus, Master, have pity on us!"
14When he saw them, he said, "Go, show yourselves to the
priests." And as they went, they were cleansed.
15One of them, when he saw he was healed, came back, praising God in a loud voice. 16He threw himself at Jesus' feet and
thanked him—and he was a Samaritan.
17Jesus asked, "Were not all ten cleansed? Where are the other
nine? 18Was no one found to return and give praise to God except
this foreigner?" 19Then he said to him, "Rise and go; your faith has
made you well."

*The Coming of the Kingdom of God*

20Once, having been asked by the Pharisees when the kingdom
of God would come, Jesus replied, "The kingdom of God does not
come with your careful observation, 21nor will people say, 'Here
it is,' or 'There it is,' because the kingdom of God is within[h] you."
22Then he said to his disciples, "The time is coming when you
will long to see one of the days of the Son of Man, but you will
not see it. 23Men will tell you, 'There he is!' or 'Here he is!' Do not
go running off after them. 24For the Son of Man in his day[i] will
be like the lightning, which flashes and lights up the sky from one
end to the other. 25But first he must suffer many things and be
rejected by this generation.
26"Just as it was in the days of Noah, so also will it be in the
days of the Son of Man. 27People were eating, drinking, marrying
and being given in marriage up to the day Noah entered the ark.
Then the flood came and destroyed them all.
28"It was the same in the days of Lot. People were eating and
drinking, buying and selling, planting and building. 29But the day
Lot left Sodom, fire and sulfur rained down from heaven and
destroyed them all.
30"It will be just like this on the day the Son of Man is revealed.
31On that day no one who is on the roof of his house, with his
goods inside, should go down to get them. Likewise, no one in the
field should go back for anything. 32Remember Lot's wife! 33Who-
ever tries to keep his life will lose it, and whoever loses his life will
preserve it. 34I tell you, on that night two people will be in one bed;
one will be taken and the other left. 35Two women will be grinding
grain together; one will be taken and the other left.[j] "
37"Where, Lord?" they asked.
He replied, "Where there is a dead body, there the vultures will
gather."

NIV [g] *12* The Greek word was used for various diseases affecting the skin—not necessarily leprosy. [h] *21* Or *among* [i] *24* Some manuscripts do not have *in his day.* [j] *35* Some manuscripts *left.* *36Two men will be in the field; one will be taken and the other left.*

## King James

**18** AND HE spake a parable unto them *to this end*, that men ought always to pray, and not to faint;

2 Saying, There was in a city a judge, which feared not God, neither regarded man:

3 And there was a widow in that city; and she came unto him, saying, Avenge me of mine adversary.

4 And he would not for a while: but afterward he said within himself, Though I fear not God, nor regard man;

5 Yet because this widow troubleth me, I will avenge her, lest by her continual coming she weary me.

6 And the Lord said, Hear what the unjust judge saith.

7 And shall not God avenge his own elect, which cry day and night unto him, though he bear long with them?

8 I tell you that he will avenge them speedily. Nevertheless when the Son of man cometh, shall he find faith on the earth?

9 And he spake this parable unto certain which trusted in themselves that they were righteous, and despised others:

10 Two men went up into the temple to pray; the one a Pharisee, and the other a publican.

11 The Pharisee stood and prayed thus with himself, God, I thank thee, that I am not as other men *are*, extortioners, unjust, adulterers, or even as this publican.

12 I fast twice in the week, I give tithes of all that I possess.

13 And the publican, standing afar off, would not lift up so much as *his* eyes unto heaven, but smote upon his breast, saying, God be merciful to me a sinner.

14 I tell you, this man went down to his house justified *rather* than the other: for every one that exalteth himself shall be abased; and he that humbleth himself shall be exalted.

15 And they brought unto him also infants, that he would touch them: but when *his* disciples saw *it*, they rebuked them.

16 But Jesus called them *unto him*, and said, Suffer little children to come unto me, and forbid them not: for of such is the kingdom of God.

17 Verily I say unto you, Whosoever shall not receive the kingdom of God as a little child shall in no wise enter therein.

18 And a certain ruler asked him, saying, Good Master, what shall I do to inherit eternal life?

19 And Jesus said unto him, Why callest thou me good? none *is* good, save one, *that is*, God.

20 Thou knowest the commandments, Do not commit adultery, Do not kill, Do not steal, Do not bear false witness, Honour thy father and thy mother.

21 And he said, All these have I kept from my youth up.

22 Now when Jesus heard these things, he said unto him, Yet lackest thou one thing: sell all that thou hast, and distribute unto the poor, and thou shalt have treasure in heaven: and come, follow me.

23 And when he heard this, he was very sorrowful: for he was very rich.

## Amplified

**18** ALSO [JESUS] told them a parable, to the effect that they ought always to pray and not to [a]turn coward—faint, lose heart and give up.

2 He said, In a certain city there was a judge who neither reverenced *and* feared God nor respected *or* considered man.

3 And there was a widow in that city who kept coming to him and saying, Protect *and* defend *and* give me justice against my adversary.

4 And for a time he would not; but later he said to himself, Though I have neither reverence *or* fear for God nor respect *or* consideration for man,

5 Yet because this widow continues to bother me, I will defend *and* protect *and* avenge her; lest she give me [b]intolerable annoyance *and* wear me out by her continual coming, *or* [c]at the last she come and rail on me, *or* [d]assault me, *or* [e]strangle me.

6 Then the Lord said, Listen to what the unjust judge says!

7 And will not [our just] God defend *and* protect *and* avenge His elect (His chosen ones) who cry to Him day and night? Will He [f]defer them *and* [g]delay help on their behalf?

8 I tell you, He will defend *and* protect *and* avenge them speedily. However, when the Son of man comes will He find ([h]persistence in) the faith on the earth?

9 He also told this parable to some people who trusted in themselves *and* were confident that they were righteous [that is, that they were upright and in right standing with God], and scorned *and* made nothing of all the rest of men:

10 Two men went up into the temple ([i]enclosure) to pray, the one a Pharisee and the other a tax collector.

11 The Pharisee [j]took his stand ostentatiously, and began to pray thus before *and* with himself: God, I thank You that I am not as the rest of men, extortioners (robbers), swindlers—unrighteous in heart and life—adulterers, or even like this tax collector here.

12 I fast twice a week; I give tithes of all that I gain.

13 But the tax collector, [merely] standing at a distance, would not even lift up his eyes to heaven; but kept striking his breast, saying, O God, be favorable (be gracious, be merciful) to me, the [k]especially wicked sinner that I am!

14 I tell you, this man went down to his home justified—forgiven and made upright and in right standing with God—rather than the other man; for every one who exalts himself will be humbled, but he who humbles himself will be exalted.

15 Now they were also bringing even babies to Him that He might touch them, and when the disciples noticed it, they reproved them.

16 But Jesus called them [ [l]the parents] to Him, saying, Allow the little children to come to Me, and do not hinder them, for to such [as these] belongs the kingdom of God.

17 Truly, I say to you, whoever does not accept *and* receive *and* welcome the kingdom of God as a little child [does], shall not in any way enter it (at all).

18 And a certain ruler asked Him, Good Teacher, (You who are [m]essentially and perfectly [n]morally good), what shall I do to inherit eternal life [that is, to partake of eternal salvation in the Messiah's kingdom]?

19 Jesus said to him, Why do you call Me ([o]essentially and perfectly [p]morally) good? No one (is [q]essentially and perfectly [r]morally) good except God only.

20 You know the commandments: Do not commit adultery; do not kill; do not steal; do not witness falsely; honor your father and your mother. [Exod. 20:12-16; Deut. 5:16-20.]

21 And he replied, All these I have kept from my youth.

22 And when Jesus heard it, He said to him, One thing you still lack. Sell everything that you have and [s]divide [the money] among the poor, and you will have rich treasure in heaven; and come back [and] follow Me—become My disciple, join My party and accompany Me.

23 But when he heard this, he became distressed *and* very sorrowful, for he was rich, exceedingly so.

**AMP** [a] Vincent. [b] Thayer. [c] Tyndale. [d] Vincent. [e] Wycliffe. [f] Tyndale. [g] Vincent. [h] Vincent. [i] Trench. [j] Vincent. [k] Thayer. [l] Henry. [m] Thayer. [n] Cremer. [o] Thayer. [p] Cremer. [q] Thayer. [r] Cremer. [s] Thayer.

## New American Standard

*Parables on Prayer*

**18** NOW HE was telling them a parable to show that at all
times they ought to pray and not to lose heart,
2saying, "There was in a certain city a judge who did not fear
God, and did not respect man.
3"And there was a widow in that city, and she kept coming to
him, saying, 'Give me legal protection from my opponent.'
4"And for a while he was unwilling; but afterward he said to
himself, 'Even though I do not fear God nor respect man,
5yet because this widow bothers me, I will give her legal protection, lest by continually coming she wear me out.'"
6And the Lord said, "Hear what the unrighteous judge *said;
7now shall not God bring about justice for His elect, who cry
to Him day and night, and will He delay long over them?
8"I tell you that He will bring about justice for them speedily.
However, when the Son of Man comes, will He find faith on the
earth?"

*The Pharisee and the Publican*

9¶ And He also told this parable to certain ones who trusted
in themselves that they were righteous, and viewed others with
contempt:
10"Two men went up into the temple to pray, one a Pharisee,
and the other a tax-gatherer.
11"The Pharisee stood and was praying thus to himself, 'God,
I thank Thee that I am not like other people: swindlers, unjust,
adulterers, or even like this tax-gatherer.
12'I fast twice a week; I pay tithes of all that I get.'
13"But the tax-gatherer, standing some distance away, was
even unwilling to lift up his eyes to heaven, but was beating his
breast, saying, 'God, be merciful to me, the sinner!'
14"I tell you, this man went down to his house justified rather
than the other; for everyone who exalts himself shall be humbled,
but he who humbles himself shall be exalted."
15¶ And they were bringing even their babies to Him so that He
might touch them, but when the disciples saw it, they *began* rebuking them.
16But Jesus called for them, saying, "Permit the children to
come to Me, and do not hinder them, for the kingdom of God
belongs to such as these.
17"Truly I say to you, whoever does not receive the kingdom
of God like a child shall not enter it *at all*."

*The Rich Young Ruler*

18¶ And a certain ruler questioned Him, saying, "Good Teacher,
what shall I do to inherit eternal life?"
19And Jesus said to him, "Why do you call Me good? No one
is good except God alone.
20"You know the commandments, 'Do NOT COMMIT ADULTERY,
Do NOT MURDER, Do NOT STEAL, Do NOT BEAR FALSE WITNESS,
HONOR YOUR FATHER AND MOTHER.'"
21And he said, "All these things I have kept from *my* youth."
22And when Jesus heard *this*, He said to him, "One thing you
still lack; sell all that you possess, and distribute it to the poor, and
you shall have treasure in heaven; and come, follow Me."
23But when he had heard these things, he became very sad; for
he was extremely rich.

## New International

*The Parable of the Persistent Widow*

**18** THEN JESUS told his disciples a parable to show them
that they should always pray and not give up. 2He said:
"In a certain town there was a judge who neither feared God nor
cared about men. 3And there was a widow in that town who kept
coming to him with the plea, 'Grant me justice against my adversary.'
4"For some time he refused. But finally he said to himself, 'Even
though I don't fear God or care about men, 5yet because this
widow keeps bothering me, I will see that she gets justice, so that
she won't eventually wear me out with her coming!'"
6And the Lord said, "Listen to what the unjust judge says.
7And will not God bring about justice for his chosen ones, who cry
out to him day and night? Will he keep putting them off? 8I tell
you, he will see that they get justice, and quickly. However, when
the Son of Man comes, will he find faith on the earth?"

*The Parable of the Pharisee and the Tax Collector*

9To some who were confident of their own righteousness and
looked down on everybody else, Jesus told this parable: 10"Two
men went up to the temple to pray, one a Pharisee and the other
a tax collector. 11The Pharisee stood up and prayed about[t] himself:
'God, I thank you that I am not like other men—robbers, evildoers,
adulterers—or even like this tax collector. 12I fast twice a week and
give a tenth of all I get.'
13"But the tax collector stood at a distance. He would not even
look up to heaven, but beat his breast and said, 'God, have mercy
on me, a sinner.'
14"I tell you that this man, rather than the other, went home
justified before God. For everyone who exalts himself will be humbled, and he who humbles himself will be exalted."

*The Little Children and Jesus*

15People were also bringing babies to Jesus to have him touch
them. When the disciples saw this, they rebuked them. 16But Jesus
called the children to him and said, "Let the little children come
to me, and do not hinder them, for the kingdom of God belongs
to such as these. 17I tell you the truth, anyone who will not receive
the kingdom of God like a little child will never enter it."

*The Rich Ruler*

18A certain ruler asked him, "Good teacher, what must I do to
inherit eternal life?"
19"Why do you call me good?" Jesus answered. "No one is
good—except God alone. 20You know the commandments: 'Do
not commit adultery, do not murder, do not steal, do not give false
testimony, honor your father and mother.'[u]"
21"All these I have kept since I was a boy," he said.
22When Jesus heard this, he said to him, "You still lack one
thing. Sell everything you have and give to the poor, and you will
have treasure in heaven. Then come, follow me."
23When he heard this, he became very sad, because he was a
man of great wealth. 24Jesus looked at him and said, "How hard

NIV [t] *11* Or *to* [u] *20* Exodus 20:12-16; Deut. 5:16-20

## King James

24And when Jesus saw that he was very sorrowful, he said,
How hardly shall they that have riches enter into the kingdom of
God!
25For it is easier for a camel to go through a needle's eye, than
for a rich man to enter into the kingdom of God.
26And they that heard *it* said, Who then can be saved?
27And he said, The things which are impossible with men are
possible with God.
28Then Peter said, Lo, we have left all, and followed thee.
29And he said unto them, Verily I say unto you, There is no man
that hath left house, or parents, or brethren, or wife, or children,
for the kingdom of God's sake,
30Who shall not receive manifold more in this present time, and
in the world to come life everlasting.
31¶ Then he took *unto him* the twelve, and said unto them,
Behold, we go up to Jerusalem, and all things that are written by
the prophets concerning the Son of man shall be accomplished.
32For he shall be delivered unto the Gentiles, and shall be
mocked, and spitefully entreated, and spitted on:
33And they shall scourge *him,* and put him to death: and the
third day he shall rise again.
34And they understood none of these things: and this saying
was hid from them, neither knew they the things which were
spoken.
35¶ And it came to pass, that as he was come nigh unto Jericho,
a certain blind man sat by the way side begging:
36And hearing the multitude pass by, he asked what it meant.
37And they told him, that Jesus of Nazareth passeth by.
38And he cried, saying, Jesus, *thou* son of David, have mercy
on me.
39And they which went before rebuked him, that he should
hold his peace: but he cried so much the more, *Thou* son of David,
have mercy on me.
40And Jesus stood, and commanded him to be brought unto
him: and when he was come near, he asked him,
41Saying, What wilt thou that I shall do unto thee? And he said,
Lord, that I may receive my sight.
42And Jesus said unto him, Receive thy sight: thy faith hath
saved thee.
43And immediately he received his sight, and followed him,
glorifying God: and all the people, when they saw *it,* gave praise
unto God.

**19** AND *JESUS* entered and passed through Jericho.
2And, behold, *there was* a man named Zacchaeus, which
was the chief among the publicans, and he was rich.
3And he sought to see Jesus who he was; and could not for the
press, because he was little of stature.
4And he ran before, and climbed up into a sycamore tree to see
him: for he was to pass that *way.*
5And when Jesus came to the place, he looked up, and saw him,
and said unto him, Zacchaeus, make haste, and come down; for
today I must abide at thy house.
6And he made haste, and came down, and received him joyfully.
7And when they saw *it,* they all murmured, saying, That he was
gone to be guest with a man that is a sinner.

## Amplified

24Jesus observing him said, How difficult it is for those who
have wealth to enter into the kingdom of God!
25For it is easier for a camel to enter in through a needle's eye
than [for] a rich man to enter into the kingdom of God.
26And those who heard it said, Then who can be saved?
27But He said, What is impossible with men is possible with
God. [Gen. 18:14; Jer. 32:17.]
28And Peter said, See, we have left our own [things]—home,
family and business—and have followed You.
29And He said to them, I say to you, truly there is no one who
has left house or wife or brothers or parents or children for the sake
of the kingdom of God,
30Who will not receive in return many times more in this world,
and in the coming age eternal life.
31Then taking the twelve (apostles) aside, He said to them,
Listen! We are going up to Jerusalem, and all things that are
written about the Son of man through *and* by the prophets will be
fulfilled. [Isa. 53:1-12.]
32For He will be handed over to the Gentiles, and will be made
sport of *and* scoffed *and* jeered at and insulted and spit upon; [Isa.
50:6.]
33They will flog Him and kill Him, and on the third day He will
rise again. [Ps. 16:10.]
34But they understood nothing of these things; His words were
a mystery *and* hidden from them, and they did not comprehend
what He was telling them.
35As He came near to Jericho, it occurred that a blind man was
sitting by the roadside begging;
36And hearing a crowd going by, he asked what it meant.
37They told him, Jesus of Nazareth is passing by.
38And he shouted, saying, Jesus, Son of David, take pity *and*
have mercy on me!
39But those who were in front reproved him, [telling him] to
keep quiet; yet he [a]screamed *and* shrieked so much the more, Son
of David, take pity *and* have mercy on me!
40Then Jesus stood still, and ordered that he be led to Him; and
when he came near, Jesus asked him,
41What do you want Me to do for you? He said, Lord, let me
receive my sight!
42And Jesus said to him, Receive your sight! Your faith [that is,
[b]your trust and confidence springing from your faith in God] has
healed you.
43And instantly he received his sight and began to follow
Jesus— [c]recognizing, praising and honoring God; and all the
people, when they saw it, praised God.

**19** AND [JESUS] entered Jericho and was passing on through
it,
2And there was a man called Zacchaeus, a chief tax collector and
rich.
3And he was trying to see Jesus, which [one] He was; but he
could not on account of the crowd, because he was small in stature.
4So he ran on ahead, and climbed up in a sycamore tree in order
to see Him, for He was about to pass that way.
5And when Jesus reached the place, He looked up and said to
him, Zacchaeus, hurry and come down; for I must stay at your
house today.
6So he hurried and came down, and he received *and* welcomed
Him joyfully.
7And when the people saw it, they all [d]muttered among themselves *and* indignantly complained, He has gone in to be the guest
of *and* lodge with a man who is devoted to sin *and* pre-eminently
a sinner.

AMP [a] Vincent. [b] Thayer. [c] Cremer. [d] Abbott-Smith.

## New American Standard

24And Jesus looked at him and said, "How hard it is for those
who are wealthy to enter the kingdom of God!
25"For it is easier for a camel to go through the eye of a needle,
than for a rich man to enter the kingdom of God."
26And they who heard it said, "Then who can be saved?"
27But He said, "The things impossible with men are possible
with God."
28And Peter said, "Behold, we have left our own *homes*, and
followed You."
29And He said to them, "Truly I say to you, there is no one who
has left house or wife or brothers or parents or children, for the
sake of the kingdom of God,
30who shall not receive many times as much at this time and in
the age to come, eternal life."
31¶ And He took the twelve aside and said to them, "Behold,
we are going up to Jerusalem, and all things which are written
through the prophets about the Son of Man will be accomplished.
32"For He will be delivered to the Gentiles, and will be mocked
and mistreated and spit upon,
33and after they have scourged Him, they will kill Him; and the
third day He will rise again."
34And they understood none of these things, and this saying
was hidden from them, and they did not comprehend the things
that were said.

*Bartimaeus Receives Sight*

35¶ And it came about that as He was approaching Jericho, a
certain blind man was sitting by the road, begging.
36Now hearing a multitude going by, he *began* to inquire what
this might be.
37And they told him that Jesus of Nazareth was passing by.
38And he called out, saying, "Jesus, Son of David, have mercy
on me!"
39And those who led the way were sternly telling him to be
quiet; but he kept crying out all the more, "Son of David, have
mercy on me!"
40And Jesus stopped and commanded that he be brought to
Him; and when he had come near, He questioned him,
41"What do you want Me to do for you?" And he said, "Lord,
*I want* to regain my sight!"
42And Jesus said to him, "Receive your sight; your faith has
made you well."
43And immediately he regained his sight, and *began* following
Him, glorifying God; and when all the people saw it, they gave
praise to God.

*Zaccheus Converted*

**19** AND HE entered and was passing through Jericho.
2And behold, there was a man called by the name of Zaccheus; he was a chief tax-gatherer, and he was rich.
3And he was trying to see who Jesus was, and he was unable
because of the crowd, for he was small in stature.
4And he ran on ahead and climbed up into a sycamore tree in
order to see Him, for He was about to pass through that way.
5And when Jesus came to the place, He looked up and said to
him, "Zaccheus, hurry and come down, for today I must stay at
your house."
6And he hurried and came down, and received Him gladly.
7And when they saw it, they all *began* to grumble, saying, "He
has gone to be the guest of a man who is a sinner."

## New International

it is for the rich to enter the kingdom of God! 25Indeed, it is easier
for a camel to go through the eye of a needle than for a rich man
to enter the kingdom of God."
26Those who heard this asked, "Who then can be saved?"
27Jesus replied, "What is impossible with men is possible with
God."
28Peter said to him, "We have left all we had to follow you!"
29"I tell you the truth," Jesus said to them, "no one who has
left home or wife or brothers or parents or children for the sake of
the kingdom of God 30will fail to receive many times as much in
this age and, in the age to come, eternal life."

*Jesus Again Predicts His Death*

31Jesus took the Twelve aside and told them, "We are going up
to Jerusalem, and everything that is written by the prophets about
the Son of Man will be fulfilled. 32He will be handed over to the
Gentiles. They will mock him, insult him, spit on him, flog him
and kill him. 33On the third day he will rise again."
34The disciples did not understand any of this. Its meaning was
hidden from them, and they did not know what he was talking
about.

*A Blind Beggar Receives His Sight*

35As Jesus approached Jericho, a blind man was sitting by the
roadside begging. 36When he heard the crowd going by, he asked
what was happening. 37They told him, "Jesus of Nazareth is passing by."
38He called out, "Jesus, Son of David, have mercy on me!"
39Those who led the way rebuked him and told him to be quiet,
but he shouted all the more, "Son of David, have mercy on me!"
40Jesus stopped and ordered the man to be brought to him.
When he came near, Jesus asked him, 41"What do you want me
to do for you?"
"Lord, I want to see," he replied.
42Jesus said to him, "Receive your sight; your faith has healed
you." 43Immediately he received his sight and followed Jesus,
praising God. When all the people saw it, they also praised God.

*Zacchaeus the Tax Collector*

**19** JESUS ENTERED Jericho and was passing through. 2A
man was there by the name of Zacchaeus; he was a chief
tax collector and was wealthy. 3He wanted to see who Jesus was,
but being a short man he could not, because of the crowd. 4So he
ran ahead and climbed a sycamore-fig tree to see him, since Jesus
was coming that way.
5When Jesus reached the spot, he looked up and said to him,
"Zacchaeus, come down immediately. I must stay at your house
today." 6So he came down at once and welcomed him gladly.
7All the people saw this and began to mutter, "He has gone to
be the guest of a 'sinner.' "

## King James

8And Zacchaeus stood, and said unto the Lord; Behold, Lord, the half of my goods I give to the poor; and if I have taken any thing from any man by false accusation, I restore *him* fourfold.

9And Jesus said unto him, This day is salvation come to this house, forsomuch as he also is a son of Abraham.

10For the Son of man is come to seek and to save that which was lost.

11And as they heard these things, he added and spake a parable, because he was nigh to Jerusalem, and because they thought that the kingdom of God should immediately appear.

12He said therefore, A certain nobleman went into a far country to receive for himself a kingdom, and to return.

13And he called his ten servants, and delivered them ten pounds, and said unto them, Occupy till I come.

14But his citizens hated him, and sent a message after him, saying, We will not have this *man* to reign over us.

15And it came to pass, that when he was returned, having received the kingdom, then he commanded these servants to be called unto him, to whom he had given the money, that he might know how much every man had gained by trading.

16Then came the first, saying, Lord, thy pound hath gained ten pounds.

17And he said unto him, Well, thou good servant: because thou hast been faithful in a very little, have thou authority over ten cities.

18And the second came, saying, Lord, thy pound hath gained five pounds.

19And he said likewise to him, Be thou also over five cities.

20And another came, saying, Lord, behold, *here is* thy pound, which I have kept laid up in a napkin:

21For I feared thee, because thou art an austere man: thou takest up that thou layedst not down, and reapest that thou didst not sow.

22And he saith unto him, Out of thine own mouth will I judge thee, *thou* wicked servant. Thou knewest that I was an austere man, taking up that I laid not down, and reaping that I did not sow:

23Wherefore then gavest not thou my money into the bank, that at my coming I might have required mine own with usury?

24And he said unto them that stood by, Take from him the pound, and give *it* to him that hath ten pounds.

25(And they said unto him, Lord, he hath ten pounds.)

26For I say unto you, That unto every one which hath shall be given; and from him that hath not, even that he hath shall be taken away from him.

27But those mine enemies, which would not that I should reign over them, bring hither, and slay *them* before me.

28¶ And when he had thus spoken, he went before, ascending up to Jerusalem.

29And it came to pass, when he was come nigh to Bethphage and Bethany, at the mount called *the mount* of Olives, he sent two of his disciples,

30Saying, Go ye into the village over against *you;* in the which at your entering ye shall find a colt tied, whereon yet never man sat: loose him, and bring *him hither*.

31And if any man ask you, Why do ye loose *him?* thus shall ye say unto him, Because the Lord hath need of him.

32And they that were sent went their way, and found even as he had said unto them.

33And as they were loosing the colt, the owners thereof said unto them, Why loose ye the colt?

34And they said, The Lord hath need of him.

## Amplified

8So then Zacchaeus stood up and solemnly declared to the Lord, See, Lord, the half of my goods I [now] give [by way of restoration] to the poor; and if I have cheated any one out of anything, I [now] restore four times as much. [Exod. 22:1; Lev. 6:5; Num. 5:6, 7.]

9And Jesus said to him, Today is ([a]Messianic and spiritual) salvation come to [all the members of] this household, since Zacchaeus too is a [real spiritual] son of Abraham;

10For the Son of man came to seek and to save that which was lost.

11Now as they were listening to these things, He proceeded to tell a parable, because He was approaching Jerusalem, and because they thought that the kingdom of God was going to be brought to light *and* shown forth immediately.

12He therefore said, A certain nobleman went into a distant country to obtain for himself a kingdom and then return.

13Calling ten of his [own] bond servants, he gave them ten minas [each equal to about one hundred days' wages or nearly twenty dollars], and said to them, [b]Buy *and* sell with these [c]while I go *and* return.

14But his citizens detested him, and sent an embassy after him to say, We do not want this man to become ruler over us.

15When he returned, having received the kingdom, he ordered these bond servants to whom he had given the money to be called to him, that he might know how much each one had made by [d]buying *and* selling.

16The first one came before him, and he said, Lord, your mina has made ten [additional] minas.

17And he said to him, Well done, excellent bond servant! Because you have been faithful *and* trustworthy in a very little, you shall have authority over ten cities.

18The second one also came, and said, Lord, your mina has made five more minas.

19And he said also to him, And you will have charge over five cities.

20Then another came and said, Lord, here is your mina, which I have kept laid up in a [e]handkerchief.

21For I was constantly afraid of you, because you are a stern (hard, severe) man; you pick up what you did not lay down, and you reap what you did not sow.

22He said to the servant, I will judge *and* condemn you out of your own mouth, you wicked slave! You knew [did you], that I was a stern (hard, severe) man, picking up what I did not lay down, and reaping what I did not sow?

23Then why did you not put my money in a bank, so that on my return I might have collected it with interest?

24And he said to the bystanders, Take the mina away from him, and give it to him who has the ten minas.

25And they said to him, Lord, he has ten minas [already]!

26And [said Jesus,] I tell you, that to every one who gets *and* has, will more be given; but from the man who does not get, *and* does not have, will be taken away even what he has.

27[The indignant king ended by saying,] But as for these enemies of mine, who did not want me to reign over them, bring them here and [f]slaughter them in my presence!

28And after saying these things, Jesus went on ahead of them, going up to Jerusalem.

29When He came near Bethphage and Bethany, at the mount called Olives, He sent two of His disciples,

30Telling [them], Go into the village yonder; there as you go in you will find a donkey's colt tied, on which no man has ever yet sat; loose it and bring [it here].

31If anybody asks you, Why are you untying [it]? you shall say this, Because the Lord has need of it.

32So those who were sent went away, and found it as He had told them.

33And as they were loosening the colt, its owners said to them, Why are you untying the colt?

34And they said, The Lord has need of it.

**AMP** [a] Moulton and Milligan. [b] Tyndale. [c] Vincent. [d] Tyndale. [e] Moulton and Milligan. [f] Vincent.

## New American Standard

8 And Zaccheus stopped and said to the Lord, "Behold, Lord,
half of my possessions I will give to the poor, and if I have defrauded anyone of anything, I will give back four times as much."
9 And Jesus said to him, "Today salvation has come to this
house, because he, too, is a son of Abraham.
10 "For the Son of Man has come to seek and to save that which
was lost."

*Parable of Money Usage*

11 ¶ And while they were listening to these things, He went on
to tell a parable, because He was near Jerusalem, and they supposed that the kingdom of God was going to appear immediately.
12 He said therefore, "A certain nobleman went to a distant
country to receive a kingdom for himself, and *then* return.
13 "And he called ten of his slaves, and gave them ten [g]minas,
and said to them, 'Do business *with this* until I come *back*.'
14 "But his citizens hated him, and sent a delegation after him,
saying, 'We do not want this man to reign over us.'
15 "And it came about that when he returned, after receiving the
kingdom, he ordered that these slaves, to whom he had given the
money, be called to him in order that he might know what
business they had done.
16 "And the first appeared, saying, 'Master, your mina has made
ten minas more.'
17 "And he said to him, 'Well done, good slave, because you
have been faithful in a very little thing, be in authority over ten
cities.'
18 "And the second came, saying, 'Your mina, master, has made
five minas.'
19 "And he said to him also, 'And you are to be over five cities.'
20 "And another came, saying, 'Master, behold your mina,
which I kept put away in a handkerchief;
21 for I was afraid of you, because you are an exacting man; you
take up what you did not lay down, and reap what you did not
sow.'
22 "He *said to him, 'By your own words I will judge you, you
worthless slave. Did you know that I am an exacting man, taking
up what I did not lay down, and reaping what I did not sow?
23 'Then why did you not put the money in the bank, and having
come, I would have collected it with interest?'
24 "And he said to the bystanders, 'Take the mina away from
him, and give it to the one who has the ten minas.'
25 "And they said to him, 'Master, he has ten minas *already*.'
26 "I tell you, that to everyone who has shall *more* be given, but
from the one who does not have, even what he does have shall be
taken away.
27 "But these enemies of mine, who did not want me to reign
over them, bring them here and slay them in my presence."

*Triumphal Entry*

28 ¶ And after He had said these things, He was going on ahead,
ascending to Jerusalem.
29 ¶ And it came about that when He approached Bethphage and
Bethany, near the mount that is called Olivet, He sent two of the
disciples,
30 saying, "Go into the village opposite *you*, in which as you
enter you will find a colt tied, on which no one yet has ever sat;
untie it, and bring it *here*.
31 "And if anyone asks you, 'Why are you untying it?' thus shall
you speak, 'The Lord has need of it.' "
32 And those who were sent went away and found it just as He
had told them.
33 And as they were untying the colt, its owners said to them,
"Why are you untying the colt?"
34 And they said, "The Lord has need of it."

NAS [g] A mina is equal to about 100 days' wages or nearly $20

## New International

8 But Zacchaeus stood up and said to the Lord, "Look, Lord!
Here and now I give half of my possessions to the poor, and if I
have cheated anybody out of anything, I will pay back four times
the amount."
9 Jesus said to him, "Today salvation has come to this house,
because this man, too, is a son of Abraham. 10 For the Son of Man
came to seek and to save what was lost."

*The Parable of the Ten Minas*

11 While they were listening to this, he went on to tell them a
parable, because he was near Jerusalem and the people thought
that the kingdom of God was going to appear at once. 12 He said:
"A man of noble birth went to a distant country to have himself
appointed king and then to return. 13 So he called ten of his servants and gave them ten minas.[h] 'Put this money to work,' he
said, 'until I come back.'
14 "But his subjects hated him and sent a delegation after him
to say, 'We don't want this man to be our king.'
15 "He was made king, however, and returned home. Then he
sent for the servants to whom he had given the money, in order
to find out what they had gained with it.
16 "The first one came and said, 'Sir, your mina has earned ten
more.'
17 " 'Well done, my good servant!' his master replied. 'Because
you have been trustworthy in a very small matter, take charge of
ten cities.'
18 "The second came and said, 'Sir, your mina has earned five
more.'
19 "His master answered, 'You take charge of five cities.'
20 "Then another servant came and said, 'Sir, here is your mina;
I have kept it laid away in a piece of cloth. 21 I was afraid of you,
because you are a hard man. You take out what you did not put
in and reap what you did not sow.'
22 "His master replied, 'I will judge you by your own words, you
wicked servant! You knew, did you, that I am a hard man, taking
out what I did not put in, and reaping what I did not sow? 23 Why
then didn't you put my money on deposit, so that when I came
back, I could have collected it with interest?'
24 "Then he said to those standing by, 'Take his mina away from
him and give it to the one who has ten minas.'
25 " 'Sir,' they said, 'he already has ten!'
26 "He replied, 'I tell you that to everyone who has, more will
be given, but as for the one who has nothing, even what he has
will be taken away. 27 But those enemies of mine who did not want
me to be king over them—bring them here and kill them in front
of me.' "

*The Triumphal Entry*

28 After Jesus had said this, he went on ahead, going up to
Jerusalem. 29 As he approached Bethphage and Bethany at the hill
called the Mount of Olives, he sent two of his disciples, saying to
them, 30 "Go to the village ahead of you, and as you enter it, you
will find a colt tied there, which no one has ever ridden. Untie it
and bring it here. 31 If anyone asks you, 'Why are you untying it?'
tell him, 'The Lord needs it.' "
32 Those who were sent ahead went and found it just as he had
told them. 33 As they were untying the colt, its owners asked them,
"Why are you untying the colt?"
34 They replied, "The Lord needs it."

NIV [h] 13 A mina was about three months' wages.

## King James

35 And they brought him to Jesus: and they cast their garments upon the colt, and they set Jesus thereon.

36 And as he went, they spread their clothes in the way.

37 And when he was come nigh, even now at the descent of the mount of Olives, the whole multitude of the disciples began to rejoice and praise God with a loud voice for all the mighty works that they had seen;

38 Saying, Blessed *be* the King that cometh in the name of the Lord: peace in heaven, and glory in the highest.

39 And some of the Pharisees from among the multitude said unto him, Master, rebuke thy disciples.

40 And he answered and said unto them, I tell you that, if these should hold their peace, the stones would immediately cry out.

41 ¶ And when he was come near, he beheld the city, and wept over it,

42 Saying, If thou hadst known, even thou, at least in this thy day, the things *which belong* unto thy peace! but now they are hid from thine eyes.

43 For the days shall come upon thee, that thine enemies shall cast a trench about thee, and compass thee round, and keep thee in on every side,

44 And shall lay thee even with the ground, and thy children within thee; and they shall not leave in thee one stone upon another; because thou knewest not the time of thy visitation.

45 And he went into the temple, and began to cast out them that sold therein, and them that bought;

46 Saying unto them, It is written, My house is the house of prayer: but ye have made it a den of thieves.

47 And he taught daily in the temple. But the chief priests and the scribes and the chief of the people sought to destroy him,

48 And could not find what they might do: for all the people were very attentive to hear him.

**20** AND IT came to pass, *that* on one of those days, as he taught the people in the temple, and preached the gospel, the chief priests and the scribes came upon *him* with the elders,

2 And spake unto him, saying, Tell us, by what authority doest thou these things? or who is he that gave thee this authority?

3 And he answered and said unto them, I will also ask you one thing; and answer me:

4 The baptism of John, was it from heaven, or of men?

5 And they reasoned with themselves, saying, If we shall say, From heaven; he will say, Why then believed ye him not?

6 But and if we say, Of men; all the people will stone us: for they be persuaded that John was a prophet.

7 And they answered, that they could not tell whence *it was.*

8 And Jesus said unto them, Neither tell I you by what authority I do these things.

## Amplified

35 And they brought it to Jesus; then they threw their garments over the colt, and set Jesus upon it, [Zech. 9:9.]

36 And as He rode along, the people kept spreading their garments on the road. [II Kings 9:13.]

37 As He was approaching [the city], at the descent of the Mount of Olives, the whole crowd of the disciples began to rejoice and to praise God, (extolling Him exultantly and) loudly for all the mighty miracles *and* works of power that they had witnessed,

38 Crying, Blessed—celebrated with praises—be the King Who comes in the name of the Lord! Peace in heaven—[that is,] [a]freedom [there] from all the distresses that are experienced as the result of sin; and glory (majesty and splendor) in the highest [heaven]! [Ps. 118:26.]

39 And some of the Pharisees from the throng said to Jesus, Teacher, reprove Your disciples!

40 He replied, I tell you that if these kept silent, the very stones would cry out. [Hab. 2:11.]

41 And when as He approached He saw the city, He wept ([b]audibly) over it,

42 Exclaiming, Would that you had known personally, even at least in this your day, the things that make for peace (for [c]freedom from all the distresses that are experienced as the result of sin and upon which your peace, that is, your [d]security, safety, prosperity and happiness depends)! But now they are hidden from your eyes.

43 For a time is coming upon you when your enemies will throw up a [e]bank (with pointed stakes) about you, and surround you, and shut you in on every side. [Isa. 29:3; Jer. 6:6; Ezek. 4:2.]

44 And they will dash you down to the ground, you [Jerusalem] and your children within you, and they will not leave in you one stone upon another; [all] because you did not come progressively to recognize *and* know *and* understand [from observation and experience] the time of your visitation [that is, when God was visiting you, the time [f]in which God showed Himself gracious toward you and offered you salvation through Christ].

45 Then He went into the temple ([g]enclosure) and began to drive out those who were selling,

46 Telling them, It is written, My house shall be a house of prayer, but you have made it a [h]cave of robbers. [Isa. 56:7; Jer. 7:11.]

47 And He continued to teach day after day in the temple ([i]porches and courts). The chief priests and scribes and the leading men of the people were seeking to put Him to death,

48 But they did not discover anything they could do, for all the people hung upon His words *and* [j]stuck by Him.

**20** ONE DAY as Jesus was instructing the people in the temple [[k]porches] and preaching the good news (the Gospel), the chief priests and the scribes came up with the elders [members of the Sanhedrin]

2 And said to Him, Tell us by what (sort of) authority You are doing these things? Or who is it who gave You this authority?

3 He replied to them, I will also ask you a question. Now answer Me:

4 Was the baptism of John from heaven or from men?

5 And they argued *and* discussed [it] *and* reasoned together [l]with themselves, saying, If we reply, From heaven, He will say, Why then did you not believe him?

6 But if we answer, From men, all the people will stone us [m]to death; for they are [n]long since firmly convinced that John was a prophet.

7 So they replied that they did not know from where it came.

8 Then Jesus said to them, Neither do I tell you by what authority I do these things.

**AMP** [a] Cremer. [b] Vincent. [c] Cremer. [d] Thayer. [e] Vincent. [f] Thayer. [g] Trench's "Synonyms of the New Testament." [h] Moulton and Milligan. [i] Trench's "Synonyms of the New Testament." [j] Tyndale. [k] Trench's "Synonyms of the New Testament." [l] Vincent. [m] Vincent. [n] Vincent.

## New American Standard

35And they brought it to Jesus, and they threw their garments
on the colt, and put Jesus *on it.*
36And as He was going, they were spreading their garments in
the road.
37And as He was now approaching, near the descent of the
Mount of Olives, the whole multitude of the disciples began to
praise God joyfully with a loud voice for all the miracles which they
had seen,
38saying,

"BLESSED IS THE King WHO COMES IN THE NAME OF THE
LORD;
Peace in heaven and glory in the highest!"

39And some of the Pharisees in the multitude said to Him,
"Teacher, rebuke Your disciples."
40And He answered and said, "I tell you, if these become silent,
the stones will cry out!"
41¶ And when He approached, He saw the city and wept over
it,
42saying, "If you had known in this day, even you, the things
which make for peace! But now they have been hidden from your
eyes.
43"For the days shall come upon you when your enemies will
throw up a bank before you, and surround you, and hem you in
on every side,
44and will level you to the ground and your children within
you, and they will not leave in you one stone upon another,
because you did not recognize the time of your visitation."

*Traders Driven from the Temple*

45¶ And He entered the temple and began to cast out those who
were selling,
46saying to them, "It is written, 'AND MY HOUSE SHALL BE A
HOUSE OF PRAYER,' but you have made it a ROBBERS' DEN."
47¶ And He was teaching daily in the temple; but the chief
priests and the scribes and the leading men among the people were
trying to destroy Him,
48and they could not find anything that they might do, for all
the people were hanging upon His words.

*Jesus' Authority Questioned*

**20** AND IT came about on one of the days while He was
teaching the people in the temple and preaching the gospel, that the chief priests and the scribes with the elders confronted
*Him,*
2and they spoke, saying to Him, "Tell us by what authority
You are doing these things, or who is the one who gave You this
authority?"
3And He answered and said to them, "I shall also ask you a
question, and you tell Me:
4"Was the baptism of John from heaven or from men?"
5And they reasoned among themselves, saying, "If we say,
'From heaven,' He will say, 'Why did you not believe him?'
6"But if we say, 'From men,' all the people will stone us to
death, for they are convinced that John was a prophet."
7And they answered that they did not know where *it came*
from.
8And Jesus said to them, "Neither will I tell you by what
authority I do these things."

## New International

35They brought it to Jesus, threw their cloaks on the colt and put
Jesus on it. 36As he went along, people spread their cloaks on the
road.
37When he came near the place where the road goes down the
Mount of Olives, the whole crowd of disciples began joyfully to
praise God in loud voices for all the miracles they had seen:

38"Blessed is the king who comes in the name of the
Lord!"[o]
"Peace in heaven and glory in the highest!"

39Some of the Pharisees in the crowd said to Jesus, "Teacher,
rebuke your disciples!"
40"I tell you," he replied, "if they keep quiet, the stones will cry
out."
41As he approached Jerusalem and saw the city, he wept over
it 42and said, "If you, even you, had only known on this day what
would bring you peace—but now it is hidden from your eyes.
43The days will come upon you when your enemies will build an
embankment against you and encircle you and hem you in on
every side. 44They will dash you to the ground, you and the
children within your walls. They will not leave one stone on another, because you did not recognize the time of God's coming to
you."

*Jesus at the Temple*

45Then he entered the temple area and began driving out those
who were selling. 46"It is written," he said to them, " 'My house
will be a house of prayer'[p]; but you have made it 'a den of robbers.'[q]"
47Every day he was teaching at the temple. But the chief priests,
the teachers of the law and the leaders among the people were
trying to kill him. 48Yet they could not find any way to do it,
because all the people hung on his words.

*The Authority of Jesus Questioned*

**20** ONE DAY as he was teaching the people in the temple
courts and preaching the gospel, the chief priests and the
teachers of the law, together with the elders, came up to him.
2"Tell us by what authority you are doing these things," they said.
"Who gave you this authority?"
3He replied, "I will also ask you a question. Tell me, 4John's
baptism—was it from heaven, or from men?"
5They discussed it among themselves and said, "If we say,
'From heaven,' he will ask, 'Why didn't you believe him?' 6But if
we say, 'From men,' all the people will stone us, because they are
persuaded that John was a prophet."
7So they answered, "We don't know where it was from."
8Jesus said, "Neither will I tell you by what authority I am doing
these things."

NIV [o] *38* Psalm 118:26 [p] *46* Isaiah 56:7 [q] *46* Jer. 7:11

## King James

9Then began he to speak to the people this parable; A certain man planted a vineyard, and let it forth to husbandmen, and went into a far country for a long time.
10And at the season he sent a servant to the husbandmen, that they should give him of the fruit of the vineyard: but the husbandmen beat him, and sent *him* away empty.
11And again he sent another servant: and they beat him also, and entreated *him* shamefully, and sent *him* away empty.
12And again he sent a third: and they wounded him also, and cast *him* out.
13Then said the lord of the vineyard, What shall I do? I will send my beloved son: it may be they will reverence *him* when they see him.
14But when the husbandmen saw him, they reasoned among themselves, saying, This is the heir: come, let us kill him, that the inheritance may be ours.
15So they cast him out of the vineyard, and killed *him*. What therefore shall the lord of the vineyard do unto them?
16He shall come and destroy these husbandmen, and shall give the vineyard to others. And when they heard *it*, they said, God forbid.
17And he beheld them, and said, What is this then that is written, The stone which the builders rejected, the same is become the head of the corner?
18Whosoever shall fall upon that stone shall be broken; but on whomsoever it shall fall, it will grind him to powder.
19¶ And the chief priests and the scribes the same hour sought to lay hands on him; and they feared the people: for they perceived that he had spoken this parable against them.
20And they watched *him*, and sent forth spies, which should feign themselves just men, that they might take hold of his words, that so they might deliver him unto the power and authority of the governor.
21And they asked him, saying, Master, we know that thou sayest and teachest rightly, neither acceptest thou the person *of any*, but teachest the way of God truly:
22Is it lawful for us to give tribute unto Caesar, or no?
23But he perceived their craftiness, and said unto them, Why tempt ye me?
24Show me a penny. Whose image and superscription hath it? They answered and said, Caesar's.
25And he said unto them, Render therefore unto Caesar the things which be Caesar's, and unto God the things which be God's.
26And they could not take hold of his words before the people: and they marvelled at his answer, and held their peace.
27¶ Then came to *him* certain of the Sadducees, which deny that there is any resurrection; and they asked him,
28Saying, Master, Moses wrote unto us, If any man's brother die, having a wife, and he die without children, that his brother should take his wife, and raise up seed unto his brother.
29There were therefore seven brethren: and the first took a wife, and died without children.
30And the second took her to wife, and he died childless.
31And the third took her; and in like manner the seven also: and they left no children, and died.
32Last of all the woman died also.
33Therefore in the resurrection whose wife of them is she? for seven had her to wife.
34And Jesus answering said unto them, The children of this world marry, and are given in marriage:

## Amplified

9Then He began to relate to the people this parable— [a]this story to figuratively portray what He had to say: A man planted a vineyard, and leased it to some vinedressers and went into another country for a long stay. [Isa. 5:1-7.]
10When the [right] season came, he sent a bond servant to the tenants, that they might give him [his part] of the fruit of the vineyard; but the tenants beat ( [b]thrashed) him and sent him away empty-handed.
11And he sent still another servant; him they also beat ( [c]thrashed) and dishonored, *and* insulted him [d]disgracefully, and sent him away empty-handed.
12And he sent yet a third; this one they wounded and threw out [of the vineyard].
13Then the owner of the vineyard said, What shall I do? I will send my beloved son; it is [e]probable that they will respect him.
14But when the tenants saw him, they argued with themselves, saying, This is the heir; let us kill him, so that the inheritance may be ours.
15So they drove him out of the vineyard [and] killed him. What then will the owner of the vineyard do to them?
16He will come and ( [f]utterly) put an end to those tenants, and will give the vineyard to others. When they [the chief priests and the scribes and the elders] heard this, they said, May it never be!
17But [Jesus] looked at them and said, What then is [the meaning of] this that is written: The [very] Stone which the builders rejected has become the chief Stone of the corner? [Ps. 118:22, 23.]
18Every one who falls on that Stone will be broken [in pieces]; but upon whomever It falls, It will crush him—winnow him and [g]scatter him as dust. [Isa. 8:14, 15; Dan. 2:34, 35.]
19The scribes and the chief priests desired *and* tried to find a way to arrest Him at that very hour, but they were afraid of the people; for they discerned that He had related this parable against themselves.
20So they watched (for an opportunity to ensnare) Him, and sent spies who pretended to be upright (honest and sincere), that they might lay hold of something He might say, so as to turn Him over to the control and authority of the governor.
21They asked Him, Teacher, we know that You speak and teach what is right, and show no partiality to any one, but teach the way of God honestly *and* in truth.
22Is it lawful for us to give tribute to Caesar, or not?
23But He recognized *and* understood their cunning *and* [h]unscrupulousness, and said to them,
24Show Me (a coin,) a denarius! Whose image and inscription has it? They answered, Caesar's.
25He said to them, Then render to Caesar the things that are Caesar's, [i]and to God the things that are God's.
26So they could not in the presence of the people take hold of anything He said to turn it against Him, but marveling at His reply they were silent.
27Also there came to Him some Sadducees, those who say that there is no resurrection.
28And they asked Him a question, saying, Teacher, Moses wrote for us a law that if a man's brother dies, leaving a wife and no children, the man shall take the woman and raise up offspring for his brother. [Deut. 25:5, 6.]
29Now there were seven brothers, and the first took a wife and died without [having any] children,
30And the second,
31Then the third took her, and in like manner all seven, and they died leaving no children.
32Last of all the woman died also.
33Now in the resurrection, whose wife will the woman be? For the seven married her.
34And Jesus said to them, The people of this world *and* present age marry and are given in marriage;

**AMP** [a] Thayer. [b] Thayer. [c] Thayer. [d] Souter. [e] Vincent. [f] Thayer. [g] Moulton and Milligan. [h] Vincent. [i] A protest against Emperor-worship.

## New American Standard

*Parable of the Vine-growers*

9¶ And He began to tell the people this parable: "A man
planted a vineyard and rented it out to vine-growers, and went on
a journey for a long time.
10"And at the *harvest* time he sent a slave to the vine-growers,
in order that they might give him *some* of the produce of the
vineyard; but the vine-growers beat him and sent him away empty-handed.
11"And he proceeded to send another slave; and they beat him
also and treated him shamefully, and sent him away empty-handed.
12"And he proceeded to send a third; and this one also they
wounded and cast out.
13"And the owner of the vineyard said, 'What shall I do? I will
send my beloved son; perhaps they will respect him.'
14"But when the vine-growers saw him, they reasoned with one
another, saying, 'This is the heir; let us kill him that the inheritance
may be ours.'
15"And they threw him out of the vineyard and killed him.
What, therefore, will the owner of the vineyard do to them?
16"He will come and destroy these vine-growers and will give
the vineyard to others." And when they heard it, they said, "May
it never be!"
17But He looked at them and said, "What then is this that is
written,
'THE STONE WHICH THE BUILDERS REJECTED,
THIS BECAME THE CHIEF CORNER *stone*'?
18"Everyone who falls on that stone will be broken to pieces; but
on whomever it falls, it will scatter him like dust."

*Tribute to Caesar*

19¶ And the scribes and the chief priests tried to lay hands on
Him that very hour, and they feared the people; for they understood that He spoke this parable against them.
20And they watched Him, and sent spies who pretended to be
righteous, in order that they might catch Him in some statement,
so as to deliver Him up to the rule and the authority of the governor.
21And they questioned Him, saying, "Teacher, we know that
You speak and teach correctly, and You are not partial to any, but
teach the way of God in truth.
22"Is it lawful for us to pay taxes to Caesar, or not?"
23But He detected their trickery and said to them,
24"Show Me a [j]denarius. Whose likeness and inscription does
it have?" And they said, "Caesar's."
25And He said to them, "Then render to Caesar the things that
are Caesar's, and to God the things that are God's."
26And they were unable to catch Him in a saying in the presence
of the people; and marveling at His answer, they became silent.

*Is There a Resurrection?*

27¶ Now there came to Him some of the Sadducees (who say
that there is no resurrection),
28and they questioned Him, saying, "Teacher, Moses wrote for
us that IF A MAN'S BROTHER DIES, having a wife, AND HE IS CHILD-
LESS, HIS BROTHER SHOULD TAKE THE WIFE AND RAISE UP OFFSPRING
TO HIS BROTHER.
29"Now there were seven brothers; and the first took a wife,
and died childless;
30and the second
31and the third took her; and in the same way all seven died,
leaving no children.
32"Finally the woman died also.
33"In the resurrection therefore, which one's wife will she be?
For all seven had her as wife."
34And Jesus said to them, "The sons of this age marry and are
given in marriage,

NAS [j] The denarius was equivalent to one day's wage

## New International

*The Parable of the Tenants*

9He went on to tell the people this parable: "A man planted a
vineyard, rented it to some farmers and went away for a long time.
10At harvest time he sent a servant to the tenants so they would
give him some of the fruit of the vineyard. But the tenants beat him
and sent him away empty-handed. 11He sent another servant, but
that one also they beat and treated shamefully and sent away
empty-handed. 12He sent still a third, and they wounded him and
threw him out.
13"Then the owner of the vineyard said, 'What shall I do? I will
send my son, whom I love; perhaps they will respect him.'
14"But when the tenants saw him, they talked the matter over.
'This is the heir,' they said. 'Let's kill him, and the inheritance will
be ours.' 15So they threw him out of the vineyard and killed him.
"What then will the owner of the vineyard do to them? 16He will
come and kill those tenants and give the vineyard to others."
When the people heard this, they said, "May this never be!"
17Jesus looked directly at them and asked, "Then what is the
meaning of that which is written:
" 'The stone the builders rejected
has become the capstone[k]' [l]?
18Everyone who falls on that stone will be broken to pieces, but he
on whom it falls will be crushed."
19The teachers of the law and the chief priests looked for a way
to arrest him immediately, because they knew he had spoken this
parable against them. But they were afraid of the people.

*Paying Taxes to Caesar*

20Keeping a close watch on him, they sent spies, who pretended to be honest. They hoped to catch Jesus in something he said
so that they might hand him over to the power and authority of
the governor. 21So the spies questioned him: "Teacher, we know
that you speak and teach what is right, and that you do not show
partiality but teach the way of God in accordance with the truth.
22Is it right for us to pay taxes to Caesar or not?"
23He saw through their duplicity and said to them, 24"Show me
a denarius. Whose portrait and inscription are on it?"
25"Caesar's," they replied.
He said to them, "Then give to Caesar what is Caesar's, and to
God what is God's."
26They were unable to trap him in what he had said there in
public. And astonished by his answer, they became silent.

*The Resurrection and Marriage*

27Some of the Sadducees, who say there is no resurrection,
came to Jesus with a question. 28"Teacher," they said, "Moses
wrote for us that if a man's brother dies and leaves a wife but no
children, the man must marry the widow and have children for his
brother. 29Now there were seven brothers. The first one married
a woman and died childless. 30The second 31and then the third
married her, and in the same way the seven died, leaving no
children. 32Finally, the woman died too. 33Now then, at the resurrection whose wife will she be, since the seven were married to
her?"
34Jesus replied, "The people of this age marry and are given in
marriage. 35But those who are considered worthy of taking part in

NIV [k] 17 Or *cornerstone* [l] 17 Psalm 118:22

# King James

35But they which shall be accounted worthy to obtain that world, and the resurrection from the dead, neither marry, nor are given in marriage:

36Neither can they die any more: for they are equal unto the angels; and are the children of God, being the children of the resurrection.

37Now that the dead are raised, even Moses showed at the bush, when he calleth the Lord the God of Abraham, and the God of Isaac, and the God of Jacob.

38For he is not a God of the dead, but of the living: for all live unto him.

39¶ Then certain of the scribes answering said, Master, thou hast well said.

40And after that they durst not ask him any *question at all.*

41And he said unto them, How say they that Christ is David's son?

42And David himself saith in the book of Psalms, The Lord said unto my Lord, Sit thou on my right hand,

43Till I make thine enemies thy footstool.

44David therefore calleth him Lord, how is he then his son?

45¶ Then in the audience of all the people he said unto his disciples,

46Beware of the scribes, which desire to walk in long robes, and love greetings in the markets, and the highest seats in the synagogues, and the chief rooms at feasts;

47Which devour widows' houses, and for a show make long prayers: the same shall receive greater damnation.

**21** AND HE looked up, and saw the rich men casting their gifts into the treasury.

2And he saw also a certain poor widow casting in thither two mites.

3And he said, Of a truth I say unto you, that this poor widow hath cast in more than they all:

4For all these have of their abundance cast in unto the offerings of God: but she of her penury hath cast in all the living that she had.

5¶ And as some spake of the temple, how it was adorned with goodly stones and gifts, he said,

6 *As for* these things which ye behold, the days will come, in the which there shall not be left one stone upon another, that shall not be thrown down.

7And they asked him, saying, Master, but when shall these things be? and what sign *will there be* when these things shall come to pass?

8And he said, Take heed that ye be not deceived: for many shall come in my name, saying, I am *Christ;* and the time draweth near: go ye not therefore after them.

9But when ye shall hear of wars and commotions, be not terrified: for these things must first come to pass; but the end *is* not by and by.

10Then said he unto them, Nation shall rise against nation, and kingdom against kingdom:

11And great earthquakes shall be in divers places, and famines, and pestilences; and fearful sights and great signs shall there be from heaven.

# Amplified

35But those who are considered worthy to gain that other world *and* that future age and to attain to the resurrection from the dead neither marry nor are given in marriage.

36For they cannot die again, but they are [a]angel-like *and* [b]equal to angels; and being sons of [that is, [c]sharers in] the resurrection, they are sons of God.

37But that the dead are raised [ [d]from death], even Moses made known *and* showed in the passage concerning the [burning] bush, where he calls the Lord, The God of Abraham, the God of Isaac, and the God of Jacob. [Exod. 3:6.]

38Now He is not the God of the dead, but of the living; for, to Him, all men are alive [whether in the body or out of it]; *and* they are alive [not dead] unto Him [in definite relationship to Him].

39And some of the scribes replied, Teacher, you have spoken well *and* expertly— [e]so that there is no room for blame.

40For they did not dare to question Him more.

41But He asked them, How can people say that the Christ, the Messiah, the Anointed One, is David's Son?

42For David himself says in [the] Book of Psalms, The Lord said to my Lord, Sit at My right hand

43Till I make Your enemies a footstool for Your feet. [Ps. 110:1.]

44So David calls Him Lord; how then is He his Son?

45And with all the people listening, He said to His disciples,

46Beware of the scribes, who like to walk about in long robes, and love to be saluted (with honor) in places where people congregate, and love the front *and* best seats in the synagogues, and places of distinction at feasts,

47Who make away with *and* devour widows' houses, and (to cover it up) with pretense make long prayers. They will receive the greater condemnation—the heavier sentence, the severer punishment.

**21** LOOKING UP [Jesus] saw the rich people putting their gifts into the treasury,

2And He saw also a poor widow putting in two mites [copper coins].

3And He said, Truly I say to you, this poor widow has put in more than all of them;

4For they all gave out of their abundance—their surplus—but she has contributed out of her lack *and* her want, putting in all that she had on which to live.

5And as some were saying of the temple that it was decorated with handsome (shapely and magnificent) stones and consecrated offerings ( [f]laid up to be kept), He said,

6As for all this that you (thoughtfully) behold, the time will come when there shall not be left here one stone upon another that will not be thrown down.

7And they asked Him, Teacher, when will this happen, and what sign will there be when this is about to occur?

8And He said, Be on your guard *and* be careful that you are not led astray; for many will come in My name ( [g]appropriating to themselves the name [Messiah] which belongs to Me), saying, I am He! and, The time is at hand! Do not go out after them.

9And when you hear of wars and insurrections—disturbances, disorder and confusion—do not become alarmed *and* panic-stricken *and* terrified; for all this must take place first, but the end will not [come] immediately.

10Then He told them, Nation will rise against nation, and kingdom against kingdom. [II Chron. 15:6; Isa. 19:2.]

11There will be mighty *and* violent earthquakes, and in various places famines and pestilences (plagues, [h]malignant and contagious or infectious epidemic diseases, deadly and devastating). And there will be sights of terror and great signs from heaven.

**AMP**   a Cremer.      b Abbott-Smith.      c Thayer.      d Thayer.      e Thayer.
f Thayer.   g Thayer.   h Webster's definition of "plague" and "pestilence."

## New American Standard

35but those who are considered worthy to attain to that age and
the resurrection from the dead, neither marry, nor are given in
marriage;
36for neither can they die anymore, for they are like angels, and
are sons of God, being sons of the resurrection.
37"But that the dead are raised, even Moses showed, in the
*passage about the burning* bush, where he calls the Lord THE GOD OF
ABRAHAM, AND THE GOD OF ISAAC, AND THE GOD OF JACOB.
38"Now He is not the God of the dead, but of the living; for all
live to Him."
39And some of the scribes answered and said, "Teacher, You
have spoken well."
40For they did not have courage to question Him any longer
about anything.
41¶ And He said to them, "How *is it that* they say [i]the Christ
is David's son?
42"For David himself says in the book of Psalms,
'THE LORD SAID TO MY LORD,
"SIT AT MY RIGHT HAND,
43 UNTIL I MAKE THINE ENEMIES A FOOTSTOOL FOR THY
FEET." '
44"David therefore calls Him 'Lord,' and how is He his son?"
45¶ And while all the people were listening, He said to the
disciples,
46"Beware of the scribes, who like to walk around in long robes,
and love respectful greetings in the market places, and chief seats
in the synagogues, and places of honor at banquets,
47who devour widows' houses, and for appearance's sake offer
long prayers; these will receive greater condemnation."

### *The Widow's Gift*

**21** AND HE looked up and saw the rich putting their gifts
into the treasury.
2And He saw a certain poor widow putting in two small copper
coins.
3And He said, "Truly I say to you, this poor widow put in more
than all *of them;*
4for they all out of their surplus put into the offering; but she
out of her poverty put in all that she had to live on."
5¶ And while some were talking about the temple, that it was
adorned with beautiful stones and votive gifts, He said,
6" *As for* these things which you are looking at, the days will
come in which there will not be left one stone upon another which
will not be torn down."
7And they questioned Him, saying, "Teacher, when therefore
will these things be? And what *will be* the sign when these things
are about to take place?"
8And He said, "See to it that you be not misled; for many will
come in My name, saying, 'I am *He,*' and, 'The time is at hand';
do not go after them.
9"And when you hear of wars and disturbances, do not be
terrified; for these things must take place first, but the end *does* not
*follow* immediately."

### *Things to Come*

10¶ Then He continued by saying to them, "Nation will rise
against nation, and kingdom against kingdom,
11and there will be great earthquakes, and in various places
plagues and famines; and there will be terrors and great signs from
heaven.

NAS [i] I.e., the Messiah

## New International

that age and in the resurrection from the dead will neither marry
nor be given in marriage, 36and they can no longer die; for they
are like the angels. They are God's children, since they are children
of the resurrection. 37But in the account of the bush, even Moses
showed that the dead rise, for he calls the Lord 'the God of Abraham, and the God of Isaac, and the God of Jacob.'[j] 38He is not the
God of the dead, but of the living, for to him all are alive."
39Some of the teachers of the law responded, "Well said,
teacher!" 40And no one dared to ask him any more questions.

### *Whose Son Is the Christ?*

41Then Jesus said to them, "How is it that they say the Christ[k]
is the Son of David? 42David himself declares in the Book of
Psalms:

" 'The Lord said to my Lord:
"Sit at my right hand
43until I make your enemies
a footstool for your feet." '[l]

44David calls him 'Lord.' How then can he be his son?"
45While all the people were listening, Jesus said to his disciples,
46"Beware of the teachers of the law. They like to walk around in
flowing robes and love to be greeted in the marketplaces and have
the most important seats in the synagogues and the places of
honor at banquets. 47They devour widows' houses and for a show
make lengthy prayers. Such men will be punished most severely."

### *The Widow's Offering*

**21** AS HE looked up, Jesus saw the rich putting their gifts
into the temple treasury. 2He also saw a poor widow put
in two very small copper coins.[m] 3"I tell you the truth," he said,
"this poor widow has put in more than all the others. 4All these
people gave their gifts out of their wealth; but she out of her
poverty put in all she had to live on."

### *Signs of the End of the Age*

5Some of his disciples were remarking about how the temple
was adorned with beautiful stones and with gifts dedicated to
God. But Jesus said, 6"As for what you see here, the time will come
when not one stone will be left on another; every one of them will
be thrown down."
7"Teacher," they asked, "when will these things happen? And
what will be the sign that they are about to take place?"
8He replied: "Watch out that you are not deceived. For many
will come in my name, claiming, 'I am he,' and, 'The time is near.'
Do not follow them. 9When you hear of wars and revolutions, do
not be frightened. These things must happen first, but the end will
not come right away."
10Then he said to them: "Nation will rise against nation, and
kingdom against kingdom. 11There will be great earthquakes, famines and pestilences in various places, and fearful events and great
signs from heaven.

NIV [j] 37 Exodus 3:6 [k] 41 Or *Messiah* [l] 43 Psalm 110:1 [m] 2 Greek *two lepta*

## King James

12But before all these, they shall lay their hands on you, and persecute *you*, delivering *you* up to the synagogues, and into prisons, being brought before kings and rulers for my name's sake.

13And it shall turn to you for a testimony.

14Settle *it* therefore in your hearts, not to meditate before what ye shall answer:

15For I will give you a mouth and wisdom, which all your adversaries shall not be able to gainsay nor resist.

16And ye shall be betrayed both by parents, and brethren, and kinsfolks, and friends; and *some* of you shall they cause to be put to death.

17And ye shall be hated of all *men* for my name's sake.

18But there shall not an hair of your head perish.

19In your patience possess ye your souls.

20And when ye shall see Jerusalem compassed with armies, then know that the desolation thereof is nigh.

21Then let them which are in Judaea flee to the mountains; and let them which are in the midst of it depart out; and let not them that are in the countries enter thereinto.

22For these be the days of vengeance, that all things which are written may be fulfilled.

23But woe unto them that are with child, and to them that give suck, in those days! for there shall be great distress in the land, and wrath upon this people.

24And they shall fall by the edge of the sword, and shall be led away captive into all nations: and Jerusalem shall be trodden down of the Gentiles, until the times of the Gentiles be fulfilled.

25¶ And there shall be signs in the sun, and in the moon, and in the stars; and upon the earth distress of nations, with perplexity; the sea and the waves roaring;

26Men's hearts failing them for fear, and for looking after those things which are coming on the earth: for the powers of heaven shall be shaken.

27And then shall they see the Son of man coming in a cloud with power and great glory.

28And when these things begin to come to pass, then look up, and lift up your heads; for your redemption draweth nigh.

29And he spake to them a parable; Behold the fig tree, and all the trees;

30When they now shoot forth, ye see and know of your own selves that summer is now nigh at hand.

31So likewise ye, when ye see these things come to pass, know ye that the kingdom of God is nigh at hand.

32Verily I say unto you, This generation shall not pass away, till all be fulfilled.

33Heaven and earth shall pass away: but my words shall not pass away.

34¶ And take heed to yourselves, lest at any time your hearts be overcharged with surfeiting, and drunkenness, and cares of this life, and *so* that day come upon you unawares.

## Amplified

12But previous to all this they will lay their hands on you and persecute you, turning you over to the synagogues and prisons, and you will be led away before kings and governors for My name's sake.

13This will be a time (an opportunity) for you to bear testimony.

14Resolve *and* settle it in your minds, not to meditate *and* prepare beforehand how you are to make your defense *and* how you will answer;

15For I [Myself] will give you a mouth *and* such utterance and wisdom as all of your foes combined will be unable to stand against or refute.

16You will be delivered up *and* betrayed even by parents and brothers and relatives and friends, and [some] of you they will put to death.

17And you will be hated (despised) by everyone because [you bear] My name *and* for its sake.

18But not a hair of your head shall perish. [I Sam. 14:45.]

19By your steadfastness *and* patient endurance you [a]shall win the [b]true life of your souls.

20But when you see Jerusalem surrounded by armies, then know *and* understand that its desolation has come near.

21Then let those who are in Judea flee to the mountains, and let those who are inside [the city] get out of it, and let not those who are out in the country come into it;

22For those are days of vengeance (that is, of rendering full justice or satisfaction), that all things that are written may be fulfilled.

23Alas for those who are pregnant and for those who have babies which they are nursing in those days! For great misery *and* anguish *and* distress shall be upon the land, and indignation *and* punishment *and* retribution upon this people.

24They will fall by [c]the mouth *and* the edge of the sword, and be led away as captives to *and* among all nations, and Jerusalem will be trodden down by the Gentiles until the times of the Gentiles are fulfilled—completed. [Isa. 63:18; Dan. 8:13.]

25And there will be signs in the sun and moon and stars, and upon the earth distress (trouble and anguish) of nations in bewilderment *and* perplexity (that is, [d]without resources, left wanting, embarrassed, in doubt, not knowing which way to turn) at ([e]the echo) the roaring of the tossing of the sea; [Isa. 13:10; Joel 2:10; Zeph. 1:15.]

26Men swooning away *or* expiring with fear *and* dread *and* apprehension and expectation of the things that are coming on the world; for the [very] powers of the heavens will be shaken *and* [f]caused to totter.

27And then they will see the Son of man coming in a cloud with great (transcendent and overwhelming) power and [all His kingly] glory (majesty and splendor). [Dan. 7:13, 14.]

28Now when these things begin to occur, look up and lift up your heads, because your redemption (deliverance) is drawing near.

29And He told them a parable: Look at the fig tree, and all the trees;

30When they put forth their buds *and* come out in leaf, you see for yourselves and perceive *and* know that the summer is already near.

31Even so, when you see these things taking place, understand *and* know that the kingdom of God is at hand.

32Truly, I tell you, this generation (that is, [g]those living at that definite period of time), will not perish *and* pass away until all has taken place.

33The [h]sky and the earth (that is, [i]the universe, the world) will pass away; but My words will not pass away.

34But take heed to yourselves *and* be on your guard lest your hearts be overburdened *and* depressed—weighed down—with the [j]giddiness *and* headache *and* [k]nausea of self-indulgence, drunkenness, and worldly worries *and* cares pertaining to (the [l]business of) this life, and that day come upon you suddenly like a trap *or* a noose;

**AMP** [a] Vincent. [b] Thayer. [c] Wycliffe. [d] Thayer. [e] Vincent. [f] Thayer. [g] Cremer. [h] Moulton and Milligan. [i] Thayer. [j] Thayer. [k] Abbott-Smith. [l] Wycliffe.

## New American Standard

12"But before all these things, they will lay their hands on you
and will persecute you, delivering you to the synagogues and
prisons, bringing you before kings and governors for My name's
sake.
13"It will lead to an opportunity for your testimony.
14"So make up your minds not to prepare beforehand to defend
yourselves;
15for I will give you utterance and wisdom which none of your
opponents will be able to resist or refute.
16"But you will be delivered up even by parents and brothers
and relatives and friends, and they will put *some* of you to death,
17and you will be hated by all on account of My name.
18"Yet not a hair of your head will perish.
19"By your endurance you will gain your lives.
**20**¶ "But when you see Jerusalem surrounded by armies, then
recognize that her desolation is at hand.
21"Then let those who are in Judea flee to the mountains, and
let those who are in the midst of the city depart, and let not those
who are in the country enter the city;
22because these are days of vengeance, in order that all things
which are written may be fulfilled.
23"Woe to those who are with child and to those who nurse
babes in those days; for there will be great distress upon the land,
and wrath to this people,
24and they will fall by the edge of the sword, and will be led
captive into all the nations; and Jerusalem will be trampled under
foot by the Gentiles until the times of the Gentiles be fulfilled.

*The Return of Christ*

**25**¶ "And there will be signs in sun and moon and stars, and
upon the earth dismay among nations, in perplexity at the roaring
of the sea and the waves,
26men fainting from fear and the expectation of the things
which are coming upon the world; for the powers of the heavens
will be shaken.
27"And then they will see THE SON OF MAN COMING IN A CLOUD
with power and great glory.
28"But when these things begin to take place, straighten up and
lift up your heads, because your redemption is drawing near."
**29**¶ And He told them a parable: "Behold the fig tree and all the
trees;
30as soon as they put forth *leaves,* you see it and know for
yourselves that summer is now near.
31"Even so you, too, when you see these things happening,
recognize that the kingdom of God is near.
32"Truly I say to you, this generation will not pass away until
all things take place.
33"Heaven and earth will pass away, but My words will not
pass away.
**34**¶ "Be on guard, that your hearts may not be weighted down
with dissipation and drunkenness and the worries of life, and that
day come on you suddenly like a trap;

## New International

12"But before all this, they will lay hands on you and persecute
you. They will deliver you to synagogues and prisons, and you will
be brought before kings and governors, and all on account of my
name. 13This will result in your being witnesses to them. 14But
make up your mind not to worry beforehand how you will defend
yourselves. 15For I will give you words and wisdom that none of
your adversaries will be able to resist or contradict. 16You will be
betrayed even by parents, brothers, relatives and friends, and they
will put some of you to death. 17All men will hate you because of
me. 18But not a hair of your head will perish. 19By standing firm
you will gain life.
20"When you see Jerusalem being surrounded by armies, you
will know that its desolation is near. 21Then let those who are in
Judea flee to the mountains, let those in the city get out, and let
those in the country not enter the city. 22For this is the time of
punishment in fulfillment of all that has been written. 23How
dreadful it will be in those days for pregnant women and nursing
mothers! There will be great distress in the land and wrath against
this people. 24They will fall by the sword and will be taken as
prisoners to all the nations. Jerusalem will be trampled on by the
Gentiles until the times of the Gentiles are fulfilled.
25"There will be signs in the sun, moon and stars. On the earth,
nations will be in anguish and perplexity at the roaring and tossing
of the sea. 26Men will faint from terror, apprehensive of what is
coming on the world, for the heavenly bodies will be shaken. 27At
that time they will see the Son of Man coming in a cloud with
power and great glory. 28When these things begin to take place,
stand up and lift up your heads, because your redemption is
drawing near."
29He told them this parable: "Look at the fig tree and all the
trees. 30When they sprout leaves, you can see for yourselves and
know that summer is near. 31Even so, when you see these things
happening, you know that the kingdom of God is near.
32"I tell you the truth, this generation[m] will certainly not pass
away until all these things have happened. 33Heaven and earth
will pass away, but my words will never pass away.
34"Be careful, or your hearts will be weighed down with dissipation, drunkenness and the anxieties of life, and that day will
close on you unexpectedly like a trap. 35For it will come upon all

NIV [m]32 Or *race*

## King James

35For as a snare shall it come on all them that dwell on the face of the whole earth.

36Watch ye therefore, and pray always, that ye may be accounted worthy to escape all these things that shall come to pass, and to stand before the Son of man.

37And in the day time he was teaching in the temple; and at night he went out, and abode in the mount that is called *the mount* of Olives.

38And all the people came early in the morning to him in the temple, for to hear him.

**22** NOW THE feast of unleavened bread drew nigh, which is called the Passover.

2And the chief priests and scribes sought how they might kill him; for they feared the people.

3¶ Then entered Satan into Judas surnamed Iscariot, being of the number of the twelve.

4And he went his way, and communed with the chief priests and captains, how he might betray him unto them.

5And they were glad, and covenanted to give him money.
6And he promised, and sought opportunity to betray him unto them in the absence of the multitude.

7¶ Then came the day of unleavened bread, when the passover must be killed.

8And he sent Peter and John, saying, Go and prepare us the passover, that we may eat.

9And they said unto him, Where wilt thou that we prepare?

10And he said unto them, Behold, when ye are entered into the city, there shall a man meet you, bearing a pitcher of water; follow him into the house where he entereth in.

11And ye shall say unto the goodman of the house, The Master saith unto thee, Where is the guestchamber, where I shall eat the passover with my disciples?

12And he shall show you a large upper room furnished: there make ready.

13And they went, and found as he had said unto them: and they made ready the passover.

14And when the hour was come, he sat down, and the twelve apostles with him.

15And he said unto them, With desire I have desired to eat this passover with you before I suffer:

16For I say unto you, I will not any more eat thereof, until it be fulfilled in the kingdom of God.

17And he took the cup, and gave thanks, and said, Take this, and divide *it* among yourselves:

18For I say unto you, I will not drink of the fruit of the vine, until the kingdom of God shall come.

19¶ And he took bread, and gave thanks, and brake *it*, and gave unto them, saying, This is my body which is given for you: this do in remembrance of me.

20Likewise also the cup after supper, saying, This cup *is* the new testament in my blood, which is shed for you.

21¶ But, behold, the hand of him that betrayeth me *is* with me on the table.

22And truly the Son of man goeth, as it was determined: but woe unto that man by whom he is betrayed!

23And they began to inquire among themselves, which of them it was that should do this thing.

## Amplified

35For it will come upon all who live upon the face of the entire earth.

36Keep awake then *and* watch at all times (that is, be discreet, attentive and ready); praying that you may have the full strength *and* ability *and* be accounted worthy to escape all these things [taken together] that will take place, and to stand in the presence of the Son of man.

37Now in the daytime Jesus was teaching in ( [a]the porches and courts of) the temple, but at night He would go out and stay on the mount called Olivet.

38And early in the morning all the people came to Him in the temple ( [b]porches *or* courts) to listen to Him.

**22** NOW THE festival of Unleavened Bread was drawing near, which is called the Passover.

2And the chief priests and the scribes were seeking how to make away with [Jesus], for they feared the people.

3But [then] Satan entered into Judas called Iscariot, who was one of the twelve [apostles];

4And he went away and discussed with the chief priests and captains how he might betray Him *and* deliver Him up to them.

5And they were delighted, and pledged [themselves] to give him money.

6So he agreed [to this] and sought for an opportunity to betray Him to them [without an uprising] in the absence of the throng.

7Then the day of Unleavened Bread came, on which the passover [lamb] had to be slain. [Exod. 12:18-20; Deut. 16:5-8.]

8So Jesus sent Peter and John, saying, Go and prepare for us the passover meal, that we may eat it.

9They said to Him, Where do You want us to prepare [it]?

10He said to them, Behold, when you have gone into the city, a man carrying an earthen jug *or* pitcher of water will meet you; follow him into the house which he enters,

11And say to the master of the house, The Teacher asks you, Where is the guest room, where I may eat the passover [meal] with My disciples?

12And he will show you a large room upstairs, furnished [that is, with carpets and with couches properly spread]; there make [your] preparations.

13And they went and found it as He had said to them, and they made ready the passover [supper].

14And when the hour came, [Jesus] reclined at table, and the apostles with Him.

15And He said to them, I have earnestly *and* intensely desired to eat this passover with you before I suffer;

16For I say to you, I shall eat it no more until it is fulfilled in the kingdom of God.

17And He took a cup, and when He had given thanks He said, Take this, and divide *and* distribute it among yourselves;

18For I say to you that from now on I shall not drink of the fruit of the vine at all until the kingdom of God comes.

19Then He took a loaf [of bread], and when He had given thanks He broke [it] and gave it to them saying, This is My body which is given for you. Do this in remembrance of Me.

20And in like manner He took the cup after supper saying, This cup is the new testament *or* covenant [ratified] in My blood, which is shed (poured out) for you.

21But, lo, the hand of him who [c]is now engaged in betraying Me is with Me on the table. [Ps. 41:9.]

22For the Son of man goes as it has been determined *and* appointed, but woe to that man by whom He is betrayed *and* delivered up!

23And they began to inquire among themselves, which of them it was who was about to do this. [Ps. 41:9.]

**AMP** [a] Trench. [b] Trench. [c] Vincent.

## New American Standard

35for it will come upon all those who dwell on the face of all the
earth.
36"But keep on the alert at all times, praying in order that you
may have strength to escape all these things that are about to take
place, and to stand before the Son of Man."
37¶ Now during the day He was teaching in the temple, but at
evening He would go out and spend the night on the mount that
is called Olivet.
38And all the people would get up early in the morning *to come*
to Him in the temple to listen to Him.

*Preparing the Passover*

**22** NOW THE Feast of Unleavened Bread, which is called the
Passover, was approaching.
2And the chief priests and the scribes were seeking how they
might put Him to death; for they were afraid of the people.
3¶ And Satan entered into Judas who was called Iscariot, belonging to the number of the twelve.
4And he went away and discussed with the chief priests and
officers how he might betray Him to them.
5And they were glad, and agreed to give him money.
6And he consented, and *began* seeking a good opportunity to
betray Him to them apart from the multitude.
7¶ Then came the *first* day of Unleavened Bread on which the
Passover *lamb* had to be sacrificed.
8And He sent Peter and John, saying, "Go and prepare the
Passover for us, that we may eat it."
9And they said to Him, "Where do You want us to prepare it?"
10And He said to them, "Behold, when you have entered the
city, a man will meet you carrying a pitcher of water; follow him
into the house that he enters.
11"And you shall say to the owner of the house, 'The Teacher
says to you, "Where is the guest room in which I may eat the
Passover with My disciples?"'
12"And he will show you a large, furnished, upper room; prepare it there."
13And they departed and found *everything* just as He had told
them; and they prepared the Passover.

*The Lord's Supper*

14¶ And when the hour had come He reclined *at the table,* and
the apostles with Him.
15And He said to them, "I have earnestly desired to eat this
Passover with you before I suffer;
16for I say to you, I shall never again eat it until it is fulfilled in
the kingdom of God."
17And when He had taken a cup *and* given thanks, He said,
"Take this and share it among yourselves;
18for I say to you, I will not drink of the fruit of the vine from
now on until the kingdom of God comes."
19And when He had taken *some* bread *and* given thanks, He
broke *it,* and gave *it* to them, saying, "This is My body [d]which is
given for you; do this in remembrance of Me."
20And in the same way *He took* the cup after they had eaten,
saying, "This cup which is poured out for you is the new covenant
in My blood.
21"But behold, the hand of the one betraying Me is with Me on
the table.
22"For indeed, the Son of Man is going as it has been determined; but woe to that man by whom He is betrayed!"
23And they began to discuss among themselves which one of
them it might be who was going to do this thing.

NAS [d] Some ancient mss. do not contain the remainder of v. 19 nor any of v. 20

## New International

those who live on the face of the whole earth. 36Be always on the
watch, and pray that you may be able to escape all that is about
to happen, and that you may be able to stand before the Son of
Man."
37Each day Jesus was teaching at the temple, and each evening
he went out to spend the night on the hill called the Mount of
Olives, 38and all the people came early in the morning to hear him
at the temple.

*Judas Agrees to Betray Jesus*

**22** NOW THE Feast of Unleavened Bread, called the Passover, was approaching, 2and the chief priests and the
teachers of the law were looking for some way to get rid of Jesus,
for they were afraid of the people. 3Then Satan entered Judas,
called Iscariot, one of the Twelve. 4And Judas went to the chief
priests and the officers of the temple guard and discussed with
them how he might betray Jesus. 5They were delighted and agreed
to give him money. 6He consented, and watched for an opportunity to hand Jesus over to them when no crowd was present.

*The Last Supper*

7Then came the day of Unleavened Bread on which the Passover lamb had to be sacrificed. 8Jesus sent Peter and John, saying,
"Go and make preparations for us to eat the Passover."
9"Where do you want us to prepare for it?" they asked.
10He replied, "As you enter the city, a man carrying a jar of
water will meet you. Follow him to the house that he enters, 11and
say to the owner of the house, 'The Teacher asks: Where is the
guest room, where I may eat the Passover with my disciples?' 12He
will show you a large upper room, all furnished. Make preparations there."
13They left and found things just as Jesus had told them. So they
prepared the Passover.
14When the hour came, Jesus and his apostles reclined at the
table. 15And he said to them, "I have eagerly desired to eat this
Passover with you before I suffer. 16For I tell you, I will not eat it
again until it finds fulfillment in the kingdom of God."
17After taking the cup, he gave thanks and said, "Take this and
divide it among you. 18For I tell you I will not drink again of the
fruit of the vine until the kingdom of God comes."
19And he took bread, gave thanks and broke it, and gave it to
them, saying, "This is my body given for you; do this in remembrance of me."
20In the same way, after the supper he took the cup, saying,
"This cup is the new covenant in my blood, which is poured out
for you. 21But the hand of him who is going to betray me is with
mine on the table. 22The Son of Man will go as it has been decreed,
but woe to that man who betrays him." 23They began to question
among themselves which of them it might be who would do this.

## King James

24¶ And there was also a strife among them, which of them should be accounted the greatest.
25And he said unto them, The kings of the Gentiles exercise lordship over them; and they that exercise authority upon them are called benefactors.
26But ye *shall* not *be* so: but he that is greatest among you, let him be as the younger; and he that is chief, as he that doth serve.
27For whether *is* greater, he that sitteth at meat, or he that serveth? *is* not he that sitteth at meat? but I am among you as he that serveth.
28Ye are they which have continued with me in my temptations.
29And I appoint unto you a kingdom, as my Father hath appointed unto me;
30That ye may eat and drink at my table in my kingdom, and sit on thrones judging the twelve tribes of Israel.
31¶ And the Lord said, Simon, Simon, behold, Satan hath desired *to have* you, that he may sift *you* as wheat:
32But I have prayed for thee, that thy faith fail not: and when thou art converted, strengthen thy brethren.
33And he said unto him, Lord, I am ready to go with thee, both into prison, and to death.
34And he said, I tell thee, Peter, the cock shall not crow this day, before that thou shalt thrice deny that thou knowest me.
35And he said unto them, When I sent you without purse, and scrip, and shoes, lacked ye any thing? And they said, Nothing.
36Then said he unto them, But now, he that hath a purse, let him take *it*, and likewise *his* scrip: and he that hath no sword, let him sell his garment, and buy one.
37For I say unto you, that this that is written must yet be accomplished in me, And he was reckoned among the transgressors: for the things concerning me have an end.
38And they said, Lord, behold, here *are* two swords. And he said unto them, It is enough.
39¶ And he came out, and went, as he was wont, to the mount of Olives; and his disciples also followed him.
40And when he was at the place, he said unto them, Pray that ye enter not into temptation.
41And he was withdrawn from them about a stone's cast, and kneeled down, and prayed,
42Saying, Father, if thou be willing, remove this cup from me: nevertheless not my will, but thine, be done.
43And there appeared an angel unto him from heaven, strengthening him.
44And being in an agony he prayed more earnestly: and his sweat was as it were great drops of blood falling down to the ground.
45And when he rose up from prayer, and was come to his disciples, he found them sleeping for sorrow,
46And said unto them, Why sleep ye? rise and pray, lest ye enter into temptation.
47¶ And while he yet spake, behold a multitude, and he that was called Judas, one of the twelve, went before them, and drew near unto Jesus to kiss him.
48But Jesus said unto him, Judas, betrayest thou the Son of man with a kiss?
49When they which were about him saw what would follow, they said unto him, Lord, shall we smite with the sword?
50¶ And one of them smote the servant of the high priest, and cut off his right ear.
51And Jesus answered and said, Suffer ye thus far. And he touched his ear, and healed him.

## Amplified

24Now [a]an eager contention arose among them, which of them was considered *and* reputed to be the greatest.
25But Jesus said to them, The kings of the Gentiles [b]are deified by them *and* exercise lordship [ [c]ruling as emperor-gods] over them; and those in authority over them are called benefactors *and* well-doers.
26But this is not to be so with you; on the contrary let him who is the greatest among you become as the youngest, and him who is the chief *and* leader as one who serves.
27For which is the greater, he who reclines at table (the master), or he who serves? Is it not he who reclines at table? But I am in your midst as one who serves.
28And you are those who have remained (throughout) *and* persevered with Me in My trials;
29And as My Father has appointed a kingdom *and* conferred it on Me, so do I confer on you [the privilege and decree]
30That you may eat and drink at My table in My kingdom, and sit on thrones, judging the twelve tribes of Israel.
31Simon, Simon (Peter), listen! Satan [d]has asked excessively that (all of) you be given up to him—out of the power and keeping of God—that he might sift (all of) you like grain, [Job 1:6-12; Amos 9:9.]
32But I have prayed especially for you [Peter] that your [own] faith may not fail; and when you yourself have turned again, strengthen *and* establish your brethren.
33And [Simon Peter] said to Him, Lord, I am ready to go with You both to prison and to death.
34But Jesus said, I tell you, Peter, before a [single] cock shall crow this day, you will three times [utterly] deny that you know Me.
35And He said to them, When I sent you out with no purse or (provision) bag or sandals, did you lack anything? They answered, Nothing!
36Then He said to them, But now let him who has a purse take it, and also (his provision) bag; and let him who has no sword sell his mantle and buy a sword.
37For I tell you that this Scripture must yet be fulfilled in Me, And He was counted *and* classed among the wicked (the outlaws, the criminals); for what is written about Me has its fulfillment—has reached its end, and is finally settled. [Isa. 53:12.]
38And they said, Look, Lord! Here are two swords. And He said to them, It is enough.
39And He came out, and went, as was His habit, to the Mount of Olives; and the disciples also followed Him.
40And when [He] came to the place He said to them, Pray that you may not [at all] enter into temptation.
41And He withdrew from them about a stone's throw, and knelt down and prayed,
42Saying, Father, if You are willing, remove this cup from Me; yet not My will, but ( [e]always) Yours, be done.
43And there appeared to Him an angel from heaven, strengthening Him in spirit.
44And being in an agony [of mind] He prayed [the] more earnestly *and* intently; and His sweat became like great [f]clots of blood dropping down upon the ground.
45And when He got up from prayer, He came to the disciples and found them sleeping for grief,
46And He said to them, Why do you sleep? Get up and pray that you may not enter [at all] into temptation.
47And while He was still speaking, behold, there came a crowd, and the man called Judas, one of the twelve [apostles], was going before [leading] them. He drew near to Jesus to kiss Him;
48But Jesus said to him, Judas! Would you betray *and* deliver up the Son of man with a kiss?
49And when those who were around Him saw what was about to happen, they said, Lord, shall we strike with the sword?
50And one of them struck the bond servant of the high priest and cut off his ear, the right one.
51But Jesus said, Permit [g]them to go so far [as to seize Me]. And He touched the [h]little [insignificant] ear and healed him.

**AMP** [a] Vincent. [b] Wuest's "Bypaths in the Greek New Testament." [c] Wuest's "Bypaths in the Greek New Testament." [d] Thayer. [e] Williams: "in the present imperative." [f] Vincent. [g] Vincent. [h] Wycliffe.

## New American Standard

*Who Is Greatest*

**24**¶ And there arose also a dispute among them *as to* which one
of them was regarded to be greatest.
25And He said to them, "The kings of the Gentiles lord it over
them; and those who have authority over them are called 'Benefactors.'
26"But not so with you, but let him who is the greatest among
you become as the youngest, and the leader as the servant.
27"For who is greater, the one who reclines *at the table,* or the
one who serves? Is it not the one who reclines *at the table*? But I am
among you as the one who serves.
28"And you are those who have stood by Me in My trials;
29and just as My Father has granted Me a kingdom, I grant you
30that you may eat and drink at My table in My kingdom, and
you will sit on thrones judging the twelve tribes of Israel.
**31**¶ "Simon, Simon, behold, Satan has demanded *permission* to
sift you like wheat;
32but I have prayed for you, that your faith may not fail; and
you, when once you have turned again, strengthen your brothers."
33And he said to Him, "Lord, with You I am ready to go both
to prison and to death!"
34And He said, "I say to you, Peter, the cock will not crow today
until you have denied three times that you know Me."
**35**¶ And He said to them, "When I sent you out without purse
and bag and sandals, you did not lack anything, did you?" And
they said, "*No,* nothing."
36And He said to them, "But now, let him who has a purse take
it along, likewise also a bag, and let him who has no sword sell his
robe and buy one.
37"For I tell you, that this which is written must be fulfilled in
Me, 'AND HE WAS NUMBERED WITH TRANSGRESSORS'; for that which
refers to Me has *its* fulfillment."
38And they said, "Lord, look, here are two swords." And He
said to them, "It is enough."

*The Garden of Gethsemane*

**39**¶ And He came out and proceeded as was His custom to the
Mount of Olives; and the disciples also followed Him.
40And when He arrived at the place, He said to them, "Pray that
you may not enter into temptation."
41And He withdrew from them about a stone's throw, and He
knelt down and *began* to pray,
42saying, "Father, if Thou art willing, remove this cup from Me;
yet not My will, but Thine be done."
43Now an angel from heaven appeared to Him, strengthening
Him.
44And being in agony He was praying very fervently; and His
sweat became like drops of blood, falling down upon the ground.
45And when He rose from prayer, He came to the disciples and
found them sleeping from sorrow,
46and said to them, "Why are you sleeping? Rise and pray that
you may not enter into temptation."

*Jesus Betrayed by Judas*

**47**¶ While He was still speaking, behold, a multitude *came,* and
the one called Judas, one of the twelve, was preceding them; and
he approached Jesus to kiss Him.
48But Jesus said to him, "Judas, are you betraying the Son of
Man with a kiss?"
49And when those who were around Him saw what was going
to happen, they said, "Lord, shall we strike with the sword?"
50And a certain one of them struck the slave of the high priest
and cut off his right ear.
51But Jesus answered and said, "Stop! No more of this." And
He touched his ear and healed him.

## New International

24Also a dispute arose among them as to which of them was
considered to be greatest. 25Jesus said to them, "The kings of the
Gentiles lord it over them; and those who exercise authority over
them call themselves Benefactors. 26But you are not to be like that.
Instead, the greatest among you should be like the youngest, and
the one who rules like the one who serves. 27For who is greater,
the one who is at the table or the one who serves? Is it not the one
who is at the table? But I am among you as one who serves. 28You
are those who have stood by me in my trials. 29And I confer on you
a kingdom, just as my Father conferred one on me, 30so that you
may eat and drink at my table in my kingdom and sit on thrones,
judging the twelve tribes of Israel.
31"Simon, Simon, Satan has asked to sift you[i] as wheat. 32But
I have prayed for you, Simon, that your faith may not fail. And
when you have turned back, strengthen your brothers."
33But he replied, "Lord, I am ready to go with you to prison and
to death."
34Jesus answered, "I tell you, Peter, before the rooster crows
today, you will deny three times that you know me."
35Then Jesus asked them, "When I sent you without purse, bag
or sandals, did you lack anything?"
"Nothing," they answered.
36He said to them, "But now if you have a purse, take it, and
also a bag; and if you don't have a sword, sell your cloak and buy
one. 37It is written: 'And he was numbered with the transgressors'[j] ; and I tell you that this must be fulfilled in me. Yes, what
is written about me is reaching its fulfillment."
38The disciples said, "See, Lord, here are two swords."
"That is enough," he replied.

*Jesus Prays on the Mount of Olives*

39Jesus went out as usual to the Mount of Olives, and his
disciples followed him. 40On reaching the place, he said to them,
"Pray that you will not fall into temptation." 41He withdrew about
a stone's throw beyond them, knelt down and prayed, 42"Father,
if you are willing, take this cup from me; yet not my will, but yours
be done." 43An angel from heaven appeared to him and strengthened him. 44And being in anguish, he prayed more earnestly, and
his sweat was like drops of blood falling to the ground.[k]
45When he rose from prayer and went back to the disciples, he
found them asleep, exhausted from sorrow. 46"Why are you sleeping?" he asked them. "Get up and pray so that you will not fall
into temptation."

*Jesus Arrested*

47While he was still speaking a crowd came up, and the man
who was called Judas, one of the Twelve, was leading them. He
approached Jesus to kiss him, 48but Jesus asked him, "Judas, are
you betraying the Son of Man with a kiss?"
49When Jesus' followers saw what was going to happen, they
said, "Lord, should we strike with our swords?" 50And one of
them struck the servant of the high priest, cutting off his right ear.
51But Jesus answered, "No more of this!" And he touched the
man's ear and healed him.

**NIV** [i] *31* The Greek is plural. [j] *37* Isaiah 53:12 [k] *44* Some early manuscripts do not have verses 43 and 44.

## King James

52Then Jesus said unto the chief priests, and captains of the temple, and the elders, which were come to him, Be ye come out, as against a thief, with swords and staves?
53When I was daily with you in the temple, ye stretched forth no hands against me: but this is your hour, and the power of darkness.
54¶ Then took they him, and led *him*, and brought him into the high priest's house. And Peter followed afar off.
55And when they had kindled a fire in the midst of the hall, and were set down together, Peter sat down among them.
56But a certain maid beheld him as he sat by the fire, and earnestly looked upon him, and said, This man was also with him.
57And he denied him, saying, Woman, I know him not.
58And after a little while another saw him, and said, Thou art also of them. And Peter said, Man, I am not.
59And about the space of one hour after another confidently affirmed, saying, Of a truth this *fellow* also was with him: for he is a Galilaean.
60And Peter said, Man, I know not what thou sayest. And immediately, while he yet spake, the cock crew.
61And the Lord turned, and looked upon Peter. And Peter remembered the word of the Lord, how he had said unto him, Before the cock crow, thou shalt deny me thrice.
62And Peter went out, and wept bitterly.
63¶ And the men that held Jesus mocked him, and smote *him*.
64And when they had blindfolded him, they struck him on the face, and asked him, saying, Prophesy, who is it that smote thee?
65And many other things blasphemously spake they against him.
66¶ And as soon as it was day, the elders of the people and the chief priests and the scribes came together, and led him into their council, saying,
67Art thou the Christ? tell us. And he said unto them, If I tell you, ye will not believe:
68And if I also ask *you*, ye will not answer me, nor let *me* go.
69Hereafter shall the Son of man sit on the right hand of the power of God.
70Then said they all, Art thou then the Son of God? And he said unto them, Ye say that I am.
71And they said, What need we any further witness? for we ourselves have heard of his own mouth.

**23** AND THE whole multitude of them arose, and led him unto Pilate.
2And they began to accuse him, saying, We found this *fellow* perverting the nation, and forbidding to give tribute to Caesar, saying that he himself is Christ a King.
3And Pilate asked him, saying, Art thou the King of the Jews? And he answered him and said, Thou sayest *it*.
4Then said Pilate to the chief priests and *to* the people, I find no fault in this man.
5And they were the more fierce, saying, He stirreth up the people, teaching throughout all Jewry, beginning from Galilee to this place.
6When Pilate heard of Galilee, he asked whether the man were a Galilaean.

## Amplified

52Then Jesus said to those who had come out against Him, the chief priests and captains of the temple and elders [of the Sanhedrin], Have you come out with swords and clubs as against a robber?
53When I was with you day after day in the temple ( [a]enclosure), you did not stretch forth [your] hands against Me. But this is your hour, and the power [which] darkness [gives you has its way].
54Then they seized Him and led Him away, bringing Him into the house of the high priest. Peter was following at a distance.
55And when they had kindled a fire in the middle of the courtyard and were seated together, Peter sat among them.
56Then a servant girl, seeing him as he sat in the firelight and gazing (intently) at him said, This man too was with [b]Him.
57But he denied it and said, Woman, I do not know Him!
58And a little later someone else saw him and said, You are one of them also. But Peter said, Man, I am not!
59And when about an hour more had elapsed still another emphatically insisted, It is the truth that this man also was with Him, for he too is a Galilean!
60But Peter said, Man, I do not know what you are talking about. And instantly, while he was still speaking, the cock crowed.
61And the Lord turned and looked at Peter. And Peter recalled the Lord's words, how He had told him, Before the cock crows today, you will deny Me thrice.
62And he went out, and wept bitterly [that is, with painfully moving grief].
63Now the men who had Jesus in custody treated Him with contempt *and* scoffed at *and* ridiculed Him and beat Him;
64They blindfolded Him also, and asked Him, Prophesy! Who is it that struck [c]You?
65And they said many other evil *and* slanderous *and* insulting words against Him, reviling Him.
66As soon as it was day, the assembly of the elders of the people gathered together, both chief priests and scribes; and they led Him into their council [the Sanhedrin], and they said,
67If You are the Christ, the Messiah, tell us. But He said to them, If I tell you, you will not believe—trust in, cleave to and rely on what I say;
68And if I question you, you will not answer.
69But hereafter (from this time on) the Son of man shall be seated at the right hand of the power of God. [Ps. 110:1.]
70And they all said, You are the Son of God, then? And He said to them, [d]It is just as you say; I am.
71And they said, What further evidence do we need? For we have heard [it] ourselves from His own mouth!

**23** THEN THE whole assembly of them got up, and conducted [Jesus] before Pilate.
2And they began to accuse Him, asserting, We found this [e]Man perverting (misleading, corrupting and turning away) our nation, and forbidding to pay tribute to Caesar, saying that He Himself is Christ, the Messiah, the Anointed One, a King!
3So Pilate asked Him, Are You the King of the Jews? And He answered him, [ [f]It is just as] you say; [I am.]
4And Pilate said to the chief priests and the throngs, I find no guilt *or* crime in this Man.
5But they were urgent *and* emphatic, saying, He stirs up *and* excites the people, teaching throughout all Judea, from Galilee where He began, even to this place.
6Upon hearing this, Pilate asked whether the Man was a Galilean.

**AMP** [a] Trench. [b] Capitalized because of what He is, the spotless Son of God, not what the speaker may have thought He was. [c] Capitalized because of what He is, the spotless Son of God, not what the speaker may have thought He was. [d] Thayer. [e] Capitalized because of what He is, the spotless Son of God, not what the speaker may have thought He was. [f] Thayer.

## New American Standard

52And Jesus said to the chief priests and officers of the temple and elders who had come against Him, "Have you come out with swords and clubs as against a robber?

53"While I was with you daily in the temple, you did not lay hands on Me; but this hour and the power of darkness are yours."

*Jesus' Arrest*

54¶ And having arrested Him, they led Him *away,* and brought Him to the house of the high priest; but Peter was following at a distance.

55And after they had kindled a fire in the middle of the courtyard and had sat down together, Peter was sitting among them.

56And a certain servant-girl, seeing him as he sat in the firelight, and looking intently at him, said, "This man was with Him too."

57But he denied *it,* saying, "Woman, I do not know Him."

58And a little later, another saw him and said, "You are *one* of them too!" But Peter said, "Man, I am not!"

59And after about an hour had passed, another man *began* to insist, saying, "Certainly this man also was with Him, for he is a Galilean too."

60But Peter said, "Man, I do not know what you are talking about." And immediately, while he was still speaking, a cock crowed.

61And the Lord turned and looked at Peter. And Peter remembered the word of the Lord, how He had told him, "Before a cock crows today, you will deny Me three times."

62And he went out and wept bitterly.

63¶ And the men who were holding Jesus in custody were mocking Him, and beating Him,

64and they blindfolded Him and were asking Him, saying, "Prophesy, who is the one who hit You?"

65And they were saying many other things against Him, blaspheming.

*Jesus before the Sanhedrin*

66¶ And when it was day, the [g]Council of elders of the people assembled, both chief priests and scribes, and they led Him away to their council *chamber,* saying,

67"If You are the Christ, tell us." But He said to them, "If I tell you, you will not believe;

68and if I ask a question, you will not answer.

69"But from now on THE SON OF MAN WILL BE SEATED AT THE RIGHT HAND of the power OF GOD."

70And they all said, "Are You the Son of God, then?" And He said to them, "Yes, I am."

71And they said, "What further need do we have of testimony? For we have heard it ourselves from His own mouth."

*Jesus before Pilate*

**23** THEN THE whole body of them arose and brought Him before Pilate.

2And they began to accuse Him, saying, "We found this man misleading our nation and forbidding to pay taxes to Caesar, and saying that He Himself is Christ, a King."

3And Pilate asked Him, saying, "Are You the King of the Jews?" And He answered him and said, "*It is as* you say."

4And Pilate said to the chief priests and the multitudes, "I find no guilt in this man."

5But they kept on insisting, saying, "He stirs up the people, teaching all over Judea, starting from Galilee, even as far as this place."

6But when Pilate heard it, he asked whether the man was a Galilean.

NAS [g] Or, *Sanhedrin*

## New International

52Then Jesus said to the chief priests, the officers of the temple
guard, and the elders, who had come for him, "Am I leading a
rebellion, that you have come with swords and clubs? 53Every day
I was with you in the temple courts, and you did not lay a hand
on me. But this is your hour—when darkness reigns."

*Peter Disowns Jesus*

54Then seizing him, they led him away and took him into the
house of the high priest. Peter followed at a distance. 55But when
they had kindled a fire in the middle of the courtyard and had sat
down together, Peter sat down with them. 56A servant girl saw
him seated there in the firelight. She looked closely at him and
said, "This man was with him."

57But he denied it. "Woman, I don't know him," he said.

58A little later someone else saw him and said, "You also are one
of them."

"Man, I am not!" Peter replied.

59About an hour later another asserted, "Certainly this fellow
was with him, for he is a Galilean."

60Peter replied, "Man, I don't know what you're talking about!"
Just as he was speaking, the rooster crowed. 61The Lord turned
and looked straight at Peter. Then Peter remembered the word the
Lord had spoken to him: "Before the rooster crows today, you will
disown me three times." 62And he went outside and wept bitterly.

*The Soldiers Mock Jesus*

63The men who were guarding Jesus began mocking and beating him. 64They blindfolded him and demanded, "Prophesy! Who
hit you?" 65And they said many other insulting things to him.

*Jesus Before Pilate and Herod*

66At daybreak the council of the elders of the people, both the
chief priests and teachers of the law, met together, and Jesus was
led before them. 67"If you are the Christ,[h]" they said, "tell us."

Jesus answered, "If I tell you, you will not believe me, 68and if
I asked you, you would not answer. 69But from now on, the Son
of Man will be seated at the right hand of the mighty God."

70They all asked, "Are you then the Son of God?"

He replied, "You are right in saying I am."

71Then they said, "Why do we need any more testimony? We
have heard it from his own lips."

**23** THEN THE whole assembly rose and led him off to Pilate.
2And they began to accuse him, saying, "We have found
this man subverting our nation. He opposes payment of taxes to
Caesar and claims to be Christ,[i] a king."

3So Pilate asked Jesus, "Are you the king of the Jews?"

"Yes, it is as you say," Jesus replied.

4Then Pilate announced to the chief priests and the crowd, "I
find no basis for a charge against this man."

5But they insisted, "He stirs up the people all over Judea[j] by
his teaching. He started in Galilee and has come all the way here."

6On hearing this, Pilate asked if the man was a Galilean. 7When

NIV [h] 67 Or *Messiah* [i] 2 Or *Messiah;* also in verses 35 and 39 [j] 5 Or *over the land of the Jews*

## King James

7And as soon as he knew that he belonged unto Herod's jurisdiction, he sent him to Herod, who himself also was at Jerusalem at that time.

8¶ And when Herod saw Jesus, he was exceeding glad: for he was desirous to see him of a long *season,* because he had heard many things of him; and he hoped to have seen some miracle done by him.

9Then he questioned with him in many words; but he answered him nothing.

10And the chief priests and scribes stood and vehemently accused him.

11And Herod with his men of war set him at nought, and mocked *him,* and arrayed him in a gorgeous robe, and sent him again to Pilate.

12¶ And the same day Pilate and Herod were made friends together: for before they were at enmity between themselves.

13¶ And Pilate, when he had called together the chief priests and the rulers and the people,

14Said unto them, Ye have brought this man unto me, as one that perverteth the people: and, behold, I, having examined *him* before you, have found no fault in this man touching those things whereof ye accuse him:

15No, nor yet Herod: for I sent you to him; and, lo, nothing worthy of death is done unto him.

16I will therefore chastise him, and release *him.*

17(For of necessity he must release one unto them at the feast.)

18And they cried out all at once, saying, Away with this *man,* and release unto us Barabbas:

19(Who for a certain sedition made in the city, and for murder, was cast into prison.)

20Pilate therefore, willing to release Jesus, spake again to them.

21But they cried, saying, Crucify *him,* crucify him.

22And he said unto them the third time, Why, what evil hath he done? I have found no cause of death in him: I will therefore chastise him, and let *him* go.

23And they were instant with loud voices, requiring that he might be crucified. And the voices of them and of the chief priests prevailed.

24And Pilate gave sentence that it should be as they required.

25And he released unto them him that for sedition and murder was cast into prison, whom they had desired; but he delivered Jesus to their will.

26And as they led him away, they laid hold upon one Simon, a Cyrenian, coming out of the country, and on him they laid the cross, that he might bear *it* after Jesus.

27¶ And there followed him a great company of people, and of women, which also bewailed and lamented him.

28But Jesus turning unto them said, Daughters of Jerusalem, weep not for me, but weep for yourselves, and for your children.

29For, behold, the days are coming, in the which they shall say, Blessed *are* the barren, and the wombs that never bare, and the paps which never gave suck.

30Then shall they begin to say to the mountains, Fall on us; and to the hills, Cover us.

31For if they do these things in a green tree, what shall be done in the dry?

32And there were also two other, malefactors, led with him to be put to death.

## Amplified

7And when he found out certainly that He belonged to Herod's jurisdiction, he sent Him up to Herod, [a higher authority,] who was also in Jerusalem in those days.

8Now when Herod saw Jesus, he was exceedingly glad, for he had eagerly desired to see Him for a long time, because of what he had heard concerning Him, and he was hoping to witness some sign—some striking evidence or spectacular performance—done by Him.

9So he asked Him many questions, but He made no reply. [Isa. 53:7.]

10Meanwhile the chief priests and the scribes stood by, continuing vehemently *and* violently to accuse Him.

11And Herod with his soldiers treated Him with contempt, and scoffed at *and* ridiculed Him; then, dressing Him up in bright *and* gorgeous apparel, he sent Him back to Pilate. [Isa. 53:8.]

12And that very day Herod and Pilate became friends with each other, [though] they had been at enmity before this.

13Pilate then called together the chief priests and the rulers and the people,

14And said to them, You brought this Man before me as one Who was perverting *and* misleading *and* [a]turning away *and* corrupting the people; and behold, after examining Him before you, I have not found any offense, (crime or guilt) in this Man in regard to your accusations against Him;

15No, nor indeed did Herod, for he sent Him back to us. Behold, He has done nothing deserving of death.

16I will therefore chastise Him *and* [b]deliver Him amended (reformed, taught His lesson) and release Him.

17 *For it was necessary for him to release to them one prisoner at the feast.*

18But they all together raised a deep cry (from the depths of their throats), saying, Away with this Man! Release to us Barabbas!

19He was a man who had been thrown into prison for raising a riot in the city and for murder.

20Once more Pilate called to them, wishing to release Jesus;

21But they kept shouting out, Crucify, crucify Him!

22A third time he said to them, Why, what wrong has He done? I have found (no offense *or* crime *or* guilt) in Him, nothing deserving of death; I will therefore chastise Him ( [c]in order to teach Him better) and release Him.

23But they were insistent *and* urgent, demanding with loud cries that He should be crucified. And their voices prevailed—accomplished their purpose.

24And Pilate gave sentence that what they asked should be done.

25So he released the man who had been thrown into prison for riot and murder, for whom they continued to ask, but Jesus he delivered up to be done with as they willed.

26And as they led Him away, they seized one Simon of Cyrene, who was coming in from the country, and laid on him the cross and made him carry it behind Jesus.

27And there accompanied [Jesus] a great multitude of the people, [including] women who bewailed and lamented Him.

28But Jesus turning toward them said, Daughters of Jerusalem, do not weep for Me, but weep for yourselves and for your children.

29For behold, the days are coming during which they will say, Blessed—happy, fortunate and [d]to be envied—[are] the barren, and the wombs that have not borne, and the breasts that have never nursed [babies]!

30Then they will begin to say to the mountains, Fall on us; and to the hills, cover (conceal, hide) us!

31For if they do these things when the timber is green, what will happen when it is dry?

32Two others also, who were criminals, were led away to be executed with Him. [Isa. 53:12.]

**AMP** [a] Wycliffe. [b] Wycliffe. [c] Vincent. [d] Souter.

## New American Standard

7And when he learned that He belonged to Herod's jurisdiction, he sent Him to Herod, who himself also was in Jerusalem at that time.

*Jesus before Herod*

8¶ Now Herod was very glad when he saw Jesus; for he had wanted to see Him for a long time, because he had been hearing about Him and was hoping to see some sign performed by Him.

9And he questioned Him at some length; but He answered him nothing.

10And the chief priests and the scribes were standing there, accusing Him vehemently.

11And Herod with his soldiers, after treating Him with contempt and mocking Him, dressed Him in a gorgeous robe and sent Him back to Pilate.

12Now Herod and Pilate became friends with one another that very day; for before they had been at enmity with each other.

*Pilate Seeks Jesus' Release*

13¶ And Pilate summoned the chief priests and the rulers and the people,

14and said to them, "You brought this man to me as one who incites the people to rebellion, and behold, having examined Him before you, I have found no guilt in this man regarding the charges which you make against Him.

15"No, nor has Herod, for he sent Him back to us; and behold, nothing deserving death has been done by Him.

16"I will therefore punish Him and release Him."

17[ [e]Now he was obliged to release to them at the feast one prisoner.]

18But they cried out all together, saying, "Away with this man, and release for us Barabbas!"

19(He was one who had been thrown into prison for a certain insurrection made in the city, and for murder.)

20And Pilate, wanting to release Jesus, addressed them again,

21but they kept on calling out, saying, "Crucify, crucify Him!"

22And he said to them the third time, "Why, what evil has this man done? I have found in Him no guilt *demanding* death; I will therefore punish Him and release Him."

23But they were insistent, with loud voices asking that He be crucified. And their voices *began* to prevail.

24And Pilate pronounced sentence that their demand should be granted.

25And he released the man they were asking for who had been thrown into prison for insurrection and murder, but he delivered Jesus to their will.

*Simon Bears the Cross*

26¶ And when they led Him away, they laid hold of one Simon of Cyrene, coming in from the country, and placed on him the cross to carry behind Jesus.

27¶ And there were following Him a great multitude of the people, and of women who were mourning and lamenting Him.

28But Jesus turning to them said, "Daughters of Jerusalem, stop weeping for Me, but weep for yourselves and for your children.

29"For behold, the days are coming when they will say, 'Blessed are the barren, and the wombs that never bore, and the breasts that never nursed.'

30"Then they will begin TO SAY TO THE MOUNTAINS, 'FALL ON US,' AND TO THE HILLS, 'COVER US.'

31"For if they do these things in the green tree, what will happen in the dry?"

32¶ And two others also, who were criminals, were being led away to be put to death with Him.

NAS [e] Many mss. do not contain this verse

## New International

he learned that Jesus was under Herod's jurisdiction, he sent him
to Herod, who was also in Jerusalem at that time.
8When Herod saw Jesus, he was greatly pleased, because for a
long time he had been wanting to see him. From what he had
heard about him, he hoped to see him perform some miracle. 9He
plied him with many questions, but Jesus gave him no answer.
10The chief priests and the teachers of the law were standing there,
vehemently accusing him. 11Then Herod and his soldiers ridiculed
and mocked him. Dressing him in an elegant robe, they sent him
back to Pilate. 12That day Herod and Pilate became friends—before
this they had been enemies.

13Pilate called together the chief priests, the rulers and the
people, 14and said to them, "You brought me this man as one who
was inciting the people to rebellion. I have examined him in your
presence and have found no basis for your charges against him.
15Neither has Herod, for he sent him back to us; as you can see,
he has done nothing to deserve death. 16Therefore, I will punish
him and then release him.[f] "

18With one voice they cried out, "Away with this man! Release
Barabbas to us!" 19(Barabbas had been thrown into prison for an
insurrection in the city, and for murder.)

20Wanting to release Jesus, Pilate appealed to them again. 21But
they kept shouting, "Crucify him! Crucify him!"

22For the third time he spoke to them: "Why? What crime has
this man committed? I have found in him no grounds for the death
penalty. Therefore I will have him punished and then release
him."

23But with loud shouts they insistently demanded that he be
crucified, and their shouts prevailed. 24So Pilate decided to grant
their demand. 25He released the man who had been thrown into
prison for insurrection and murder, the one they asked for, and
surrendered Jesus to their will.

*The Crucifixion*

26As they led him away, they seized Simon from Cyrene, who
was on his way in from the country, and put the cross on him and
made him carry it behind Jesus. 27A large number of people followed him, including women who mourned and wailed for him.
28Jesus turned and said to them, "Daughters of Jerusalem, do not
weep for me; weep for yourselves and for your children. 29For the
time will come when you will say, 'Blessed are the barren women,
the wombs that never bore and the breasts that never nursed!'
30Then

" 'they will say to the mountains, "Fall on us!"
and to the hills, "Cover us!" '[g]

31For if men do these things when the tree is green, what will
happen when it is dry?"

32Two other men, both criminals, were also led out with him to
be executed. 33When they came to the place called the Skull, there

NIV [f] 16 Some manuscripts *him." 17Now he was obliged to release one man to them at the Feast.* [g] 30 Hosea 10:8

## King James

33And when they were come to the place, which is called Calvary, there they crucified him, and the malefactors, one on the right hand, and the other on the left.

34¶ Then said Jesus, Father, forgive them; for they know not what they do. And they parted his raiment, and cast lots.

35And the people stood beholding. And the rulers also with them derided *him,* saying, He saved others; let him save himself, if he be Christ, the chosen of God.

36And the soldiers also mocked him, coming to him, and offering him vinegar,

37And saying, If thou be the king of the Jews, save thyself.

38And a superscription also was written over him in letters of Greek, and Latin, and Hebrew, THIS IS THE KING OF THE JEWS.

39¶ And one of the malefactors which were hanged railed on him, saying, If thou be Christ, save thyself and us.

40But the other answering rebuked him, saying, Dost not thou fear God, seeing thou art in the same condemnation?

41And we indeed justly; for we receive the due reward of our deeds: but this man hath done nothing amiss.

42And he said unto Jesus, Lord, remember me when thou comest into thy kingdom.

43And Jesus said unto him, Verily I say unto thee, Today shalt thou be with me in paradise.

44And it was about the sixth hour, and there was a darkness over all the earth until the ninth hour.

45And the sun was darkened, and the veil of the temple was rent in the midst.

46¶ And when Jesus had cried with a loud voice, he said, Father, into thy hands I commend my spirit: and having said thus, he gave up the ghost.

47Now when the centurion saw what was done, he glorified God, saying, Certainly this was a righteous man.

48And all the people that came together to that sight, beholding the things which were done, smote their breasts, and returned.

49And all his acquaintance, and the women that followed him from Galilee, stood afar off, beholding these things.

50¶ And, behold, *there was* a man named Joseph, a counsellor; *and he was* a good man, and a just:

51(The same had not consented to the counsel and deed of them;) *he was* of Arimathaea, a city of the Jews: who also himself waited for the kingdom of God.

52This *man* went unto Pilate, and begged the body of Jesus.

53And he took it down, and wrapped it in linen, and laid it in a sepulchre that was hewn in stone, wherein never man before was laid.

54And that day was the preparation, and the sabbath drew on.

55And the women also, which came with him from Galilee, followed after, and beheld the sepulchre, and how his body was laid.

56And they returned, and prepared spices and ointments: and rested the sabbath day according to the commandment.

## Amplified

33And when they came to the place which is called The Skull [Calvary, from the Latin; Golgotha, the Hebrew equivalent], there they crucified Him [along with] the criminals, one on the right and one on the left.

34And Jesus prayed, Father, forgive them, for they know not what they do. And they divided His garments *and* distributed them by casting lots for them. [Ps. 22:18.]

35Now the people stood by, ([a]calmly and leisurely) watching; but the rulers scoffed *and* sneered ([b]turned up their noses) at Him, saying, He rescued others ([c]from death), let Him now rescue Himself, if He is the Christ, the Messiah of God, His Chosen One!

36The soldiers also ridiculed *and* made sport of Him, coming up and offering Him vinegar [a sour wine mixed with water], [Ps. 69:21.]

37And saying, If you are the King of the Jews, save (rescue) Yourself ([d]from death).

38For there was also an inscription above Him *in letters of Greek and Latin and Hebrew,* This is the King of the Jews.

39One of the criminals who were suspended kept up a railing at Him, saying, Are You not the Christ, the Messiah? Rescue Yourself and us ([e]from death)!

40But the other one reproved him, saying, Do you not even fear God, seeing you yourself are under the same sentence of condemnation *and* suffering the same penalty?

41And we indeed suffer it justly, receiving the due reward of our actions; but this Man has done nothing out of the way—nothing [f]strange or eccentric or perverse or unreasonable.

42Then he said *to* Jesus, *Lord,* remember me when You come [g]in Your kingly glory!

43And He answered him, Truly, I tell you, today you shall be with Me in Paradise.

44It was now about the sixth hour [midday], and darkness enveloped the whole land *and* earth until the ninth hour [about three o'clock in the afternoon],

45While the sun's light faded—[h]was darkened; and the curtain [of the Holy of Holies] of the temple was torn in two. [Exod. 26:31-35.]

46And Jesus, crying out with a loud voice, said, Father, into Your hands I commit My spirit! And with these words He expired. [Ps. 31:5.]

47Now the centurion, having seen what had taken place, [i]recognized God *and* thanked *and* praised Him, and said, Indeed, without question, this Man was upright—just and innocent!

48And all the throngs that had gathered to see this spectacle, when they saw what had taken place, returned to their homes beating their breasts.

49And all the acquaintances of [Jesus] and the women who had followed Him from Galilee stood at a distance and watched these things.

50Now notice, there was a man named Joseph from the Jewish town of Arimathea. He was a member of the council [the Sanhedrin], and a good (upright, [j]advantageous) man and righteous—in right standing with God and man,

51Who had not agreed with *or* assented to the purpose and action of the others, and he was expecting *and* waiting for the kingdom of God.

52This man went to Pilate and asked for the body of Jesus.

53Then he took it down and [k]rolled it up in a linen cloth [l]for swathing dead bodies, and laid Him in a rock-hewn tomb, where no one had ever yet been laid.

54It was the day of preparation [for the Sabbath], and the Sabbath was dawning (approaching).

55The women who had come with [Jesus] from Galilee followed closely, and saw the tomb, and how His body was laid;

56Then they went back, and made ready spices and ointments (perfumes). On the Sabbath day they rested in accordance with the commandment. [Exod. 12:16; 20:10.]

**AMP** [a] Vincent. [b] Literal meaning. [c] Cremer. [d] Cremer. [e] Cremer. [f] Vincent. [g] Vincent. [h] Many ancient manuscripts so read. [i] Cremer. [j] Cremer. [k] Young's Concordance. [l] Moulton and Milligan.

## New American Standard

*The Crucifixion*

33¶ And when they came to the place called The Skull, there
they crucified Him and the criminals, one on the right and the
other on the left.

34But Jesus was saying, "Father, forgive them; for they do not
know what they are doing." And they cast lots, dividing up His
garments among themselves.

35And the people stood by, looking on. And even the rulers
were sneering at Him, saying, "He saved others; let Him save
Himself if this is the Christ of God, His Chosen One."

36And the soldiers also mocked Him, coming up to Him, offering Him sour wine,

37and saying, "If You are the King of the Jews, save Yourself!"

38Now there was also an inscription above Him, "THIS IS THE
KING OF THE JEWS."

39¶ And one of the criminals who were hanged *there* was hurling
abuse at Him, saying, "Are You not the Christ? Save Yourself and
us!"

40But the other answered, and rebuking him said, "Do you not
even fear God, since you are under the same sentence of condemnation?

41"And we indeed justly, for we are receiving what we deserve
for our deeds; but this man has done nothing wrong."

42And he was saying, "Jesus, remember me when You come in
Your kingdom!"

43And He said to him, "Truly I say to you, today you shall be
with Me in Paradise."

44¶ And it was now about [m]the sixth hour, and darkness fell
over the whole land until [n]the ninth hour,

45the sun being obscured; and the veil of the temple was torn
in two.

46And Jesus, crying out with a loud voice, said, "Father, INTO
THY HANDS I COMMIT MY SPIRIT." And having said this, He
breathed His last.

47Now when the centurion saw what had happened, he *began*
praising God, saying, "Certainly this man was innocent."

48And all the multitudes who came together for this spectacle,
when they observed what had happened, *began* to return, beating
their breasts.

49And all His acquaintances and the women who accompanied
Him from Galilee, were standing at a distance, seeing these things.

*Jesus Is Buried*

50¶ And behold, a man named Joseph, who was a member of
the Council, a good and righteous man

51(he had not consented to their plan and action), *a man* from
Arimathea, a city of the Jews, who was waiting for the kingdom
of God;

52this man went to Pilate and asked for the body of Jesus.

53And he took it down and wrapped it in a linen cloth, and laid
Him in a tomb cut into the rock, where no one had ever lain.

54And it was the preparation day, and the Sabbath was about
to begin.

55Now the women who had come with Him out of Galilee
followed after, and saw the tomb and how His body was laid.

56And they returned and prepared spices and perfumes.

And on the Sabbath they rested according to the commandment.

NAS [m]I.e., 12 noon [n]I.e., 3 p.m.

## New International

they crucified him, along with the criminals—one on his right, the
other on his left. 34Jesus said, "Father, forgive them, for they do
not know what they are doing."[o] And they divided up his clothes
by casting lots.

35The people stood watching, and the rulers even sneered at
him. They said, "He saved others; let him save himself if he is the
Christ of God, the Chosen One."

36The soldiers also came up and mocked him. They offered him
wine vinegar 37and said, "If you are the king of the Jews, save
yourself."

38There was a written notice above him, which read: THIS IS THE
KING OF THE JEWS.

39One of the criminals who hung there hurled insults at him:
"Aren't you the Christ? Save yourself and us!"

40But the other criminal rebuked him. "Don't you fear God," he
said, "since you are under the same sentence? 41We are punished
justly, for we are getting what our deeds deserve. But this man has
done nothing wrong."

42Then he said, "Jesus, remember me when you come into your
kingdom.[p]"

43Jesus answered him, "I tell you the truth, today you will be
with me in paradise."

*Jesus' Death*

44It was now about the sixth hour, and darkness came over the
whole land until the ninth hour, 45for the sun stopped shining.
And the curtain of the temple was torn in two. 46Jesus called out
with a loud voice, "Father, into your hands I commit my spirit."
When he had said this, he breathed his last.

47The centurion, seeing what had happened, praised God and
said, "Surely this was a righteous man." 48When all the people
who had gathered to witness this sight saw what took place, they
beat their breasts and went away. 49But all those who knew him,
including the women who had followed him from Galilee, stood
at a distance, watching these things.

*Jesus' Burial*

50Now there was a man named Joseph, a member of the Council, a good and upright man, 51who had not consented to their
decision and action. He came from the Judean town of Arimathea
and he was waiting for the kingdom of God. 52Going to Pilate, he
asked for Jesus' body. 53Then he took it down, wrapped it in linen
cloth and placed it in a tomb cut in the rock, one in which no one
had yet been laid. 54It was Preparation Day, and the Sabbath was
about to begin.

55The women who had come with Jesus from Galilee followed
Joseph and saw the tomb and how his body was laid in it. 56Then
they went home and prepared spices and perfumes. But they
rested on the Sabbath in obedience to the commandment.

NIV [o]34 Some early manuscripts do not have this sentence. [p]42 Some
manuscripts *come with your kingly power*

## King James

**24** NOW UPON the first *day* of the week, very early in the morning, they came unto the sepulchre, bringing the spices which they had prepared, and certain *others* with them.

2And they found the stone rolled away from the sepulchre.

3And they entered in, and found not the body of the Lord Jesus.

4And it came to pass, as they were much perplexed thereabout, behold, two men stood by them in shining garments:

5And as they were afraid, and bowed down *their* faces to the earth, they said unto them, Why seek ye the living among the dead?

6He is not here, but is risen: remember how he spake unto you when he was yet in Galilee,

7Saying, The Son of man must be delivered into the hands of sinful men, and be crucified, and the third day rise again.

8And they remembered his words,

9And returned from the sepulchre, and told all these things unto the eleven, and to all the rest.

10It was Mary Magdalene, and Joanna, and Mary *the mother* of James, and other *women that were* with them, which told these things unto the apostles.

11And their words seemed to them as idle tales, and they believed them not.

12Then arose Peter, and ran unto the sepulchre; and stooping down, he beheld the linen clothes laid by themselves, and departed, wondering in himself at that which was come to pass.

13¶ And, behold, two of them went that same day to a village called Emmaus, which was from Jerusalem *about* threescore furlongs.

14And they talked together of all these things which had happened.

15And it came to pass, that, while they communed *together* and reasoned, Jesus himself drew near, and went with them.

16But their eyes were holden that they should not know him.

17And he said unto them, What manner of communications *are* these that ye have one to another, as ye walk, and are sad?

18And the one of them, whose name was Cleopas, answering said unto him, Art thou only a stranger in Jerusalem, and hast not known the things which are come to pass there in these days?

19And he said unto them, What things? And they said unto him, Concerning Jesus of Nazareth, which was a prophet mighty in deed and word before God and all the people:

20And how the chief priests and our rulers delivered him to be condemned to death, and have crucified him.

21But we trusted that it had been he which should have redeemed Israel: and beside all this, today is the third day since these things were done.

22Yea, and certain women also of our company made us astonished, which were early at the sepulchre;

23And when they found not his body, they came, saying, that they had also seen a vision of angels, which said that he was alive.

24And certain of them which were with us went to the sepulchre, and found *it* even so as the women had said: but him they saw not.

25Then he said unto them, O fools, and slow of heart to believe all that the prophets have spoken:

26Ought not Christ to have suffered these things, and to enter into his glory?

## Amplified

**24** BUT ON the first day of the week at early dawn [the women] went to the tomb, taking the spices which they had made ready.

2And they found the stone rolled back from the tomb,

3But when they went inside they did not find the body of the Lord Jesus.

4And while they were perplexed *and* wondering what to do about this, behold, two men in dazzling raiment suddenly stood beside them.

5And as [the women] were frightened and were bowing their faces to the ground, the men said to them, Why do you look for the living among [those who are] dead?

6He is not here, but has risen! Remember how He told you while He was still in Galilee,

7That the Son of man must be given over into the hands of sinful men [that is, men [a]whose way or nature is to act in opposition to God], and be crucified, and on the third day rise ( [b]from death). [Ps. 16:10.]

8And they remembered His words,

9And having returned from the tomb they reported all these things (taken together) to the eleven apostles and to all the rest.

10Now it was Mary Magdalene and Joanna and Mary the mother of James, and the other women with them who reported these things to the apostles;

11But these reports seemed to the men an idle tale— [c]madness, [d]feigned things, [e]nonsense—and they did not believe the women.

12But Peter got up and ran to the tomb, and stooping down and looking in, he saw the linen cloths alone by themselves, and he went away wondering about *and* marveling at what had happened.

13And behold, that very day two of [the disciples] were going to a village called Emmaus, [which is] about seven miles from Jerusalem,

14And they were talking with each other about all these things that had occurred.

15And while they were conversing and discussing together, Jesus Himself caught up with them and was already accompanying them.

16But their eyes were held, so that they did not recognize Him.

17And He said to them, What is this discussion that you are exchanging ( [f]throwing back and forth) between you as you walk along? And they stood still, looking sad *and* downcast.

18Then one of them named Cleopas answered Him, Do you alone dwell as a stranger in Jerusalem and not know the things that have occurred there in these days?

19And He said to them, What (kind of) things? And they said to Him, About Jesus of Nazareth, Who was a Prophet mighty in work and word before God and all the people,

20And how our chief priests and rulers gave Him up to be sentenced to death and crucified Him.

21But we were hoping that it was He Who would redeem *and* set Israel free. [Yes] and besides all this, it is now the third day since these things occurred.

22And moreover, some women of our company astounded us *and* [g]drove us out of our senses. They were at the tomb early [in the morning],

23But did not find His body; and they returned saying that they had [even] seen a vision of angels who said that He was alive!

24So some of those [who were] with us went to the tomb, and they found it just as the women had said; but Him they did not see.

25And [Jesus] said to them, O foolish ones (sluggish in mind, dull of perception) and slow of heart to believe—to adhere to and trust in and rely on—everything that the prophets have spoken!

26Was it not necessary *and* [h]essentially fitting that the Christ, the Messiah, should suffer all these things before entering into His glory (His majesty and splendor)?

**AMP** [a] Cremer. [b] Cremer. [c] Wycliffe. [d] Tyndale. [e] Moulton and Milligan. [f] Literal meaning. [g] Literal meaning. [h] Vincent.

## New American Standard

*The Resurrection*

24 BUT ON the first day of the week, at early dawn, they came to the tomb, bringing the spices which they had prepared.

2And they found the stone rolled away from the tomb,

3but when they entered, they did not find the body of the Lord Jesus.

4And it happened that while they were perplexed about this, behold, two men suddenly stood near them in dazzling apparel;

5and as *the women* were terrified and bowed their faces to the ground, *the men* said to them, "Why do you seek the living One among the dead?

6"He is not here, but He has risen. Remember how He spoke to you while He was still in Galilee,

7saying that the Son of Man must be delivered into the hands of sinful men, and be crucified, and the third day rise again."

8And they remembered His words,

9and returned from the tomb and reported all these things to the eleven and to all the rest.

10Now they were Mary Magdalene and Joanna and Mary the *mother* of James; also the other women with them were telling these things to the apostles.

11And these words appeared to them as nonsense, and they would not believe them.

12[ [i]But Peter arose and ran to the tomb; stooping and looking in, he *saw the linen wrappings only; and he went away to his home, marveling at that which had happened.]

*The Road to Emmaus*

13¶ And behold, two of them were going that very day to a village named Emmaus, which was [j]about seven miles from Jerusalem.

14And they were conversing with each other about all these things which had taken place.

15And it came about that while they were conversing and discussing, Jesus Himself approached, and *began* traveling with them.

16But their eyes were prevented from recognizing Him.

17And He said to them, "What are these words that you are exchanging with one another as you are walking?" And they stood still, looking sad.

18And one of them, named Cleopas, answered and said to Him, "Are You the only one visiting Jerusalem and unaware of the things which have happened here in these days?"

19And He said to them, "What things?" And they said to Him, "The things about Jesus the Nazarene, who was a prophet mighty in deed and word in the sight of God and all the people,

20and how the chief priests and our rulers delivered Him up to the sentence of death, and crucified Him.

21"But we were hoping that it was He who was going to redeem Israel. Indeed, besides all this, it is the third day since these things happened.

22"But also some women among us amazed us. When they were at the tomb early in the morning,

23and did not find His body, they came, saying that they had also seen a vision of angels, who said that He was alive.

24"And some of those who were with us went to the tomb and found it just exactly as the women also had said; but Him they did not see."

25And He said to them, "O foolish men and slow of heart to believe in all that the prophets have spoken!

26"Was it not necessary for the Christ to suffer these things and to enter into His glory?"

**NAS** [i] Some ancient mss. do not contain v. 12 [j] I.e., 60 stadia, one stadion was about 600 feet

## New International

*The Resurrection*

24 ON THE first day of the week, very early in the morning,
the women took the spices they had prepared and went
to the tomb. 2They found the stone rolled away from the tomb,
3but when they entered, they did not find the body of the Lord
Jesus. 4While they were wondering about this, suddenly two men
in clothes that gleamed like lightning stood beside them. 5In their
fright the women bowed down with their faces to the ground, but
the men said to them, "Why do you look for the living among the
dead? 6He is not here; he has risen! Remember how he told you,
while he was still with you in Galilee: 7'The Son of Man must be
delivered into the hands of sinful men, be crucified and on the
third day be raised again.' " 8Then they remembered his words.
9When they came back from the tomb, they told all these things
to the Eleven and to all the others. 10It was Mary Magdalene,
Joanna, Mary the mother of James, and the others with them who
told this to the apostles. 11But they did not believe the women,
because their words seemed to them like nonsense. 12Peter, however, got up and ran to the tomb. Bending over, he saw the strips
of linen lying by themselves, and he went away, wondering to
himself what had happened.

*On the Road to Emmaus*

13Now that same day two of them were going to a village called
Emmaus, about seven miles[k] from Jerusalem. 14They were talking
with each other about everything that had happened. 15As they
talked and discussed these things with each other, Jesus himself
came up and walked along with them; 16but they were kept from
recognizing him.
17He asked them, "What are you discussing together as you
walk along?"
They stood still, their faces downcast. 18One of them, named
Cleopas, asked him, "Are you only a visitor to Jerusalem and do
not know the things that have happened there in these days?"
19"What things?" he asked.
"About Jesus of Nazareth," they replied. "He was a prophet,
powerful in word and deed before God and all the people. 20The
chief priests and our rulers handed him over to be sentenced to
death, and they crucified him; 21but we had hoped that he was the
one who was going to redeem Israel. And what is more, it is the
third day since all this took place. 22In addition, some of our
women amazed us. They went to the tomb early this morning
23but didn't find his body. They came and told us that they had
seen a vision of angels, who said he was alive. 24Then some of our
companions went to the tomb and found it just as the women had
said, but him they did not see."
25He said to them, "How foolish you are, and how slow of heart
to believe all that the prophets have spoken! 26Did not the Christ[l]
have to suffer these things and then enter his glory?" 27And begin-

**NIV** [k] *13* Greek *sixty stadia* (about 11 kilometers) [l] *26* Or *Messiah;* also in verse 46

# King James

27And beginning at Moses and all the prophets, he expounded
unto them in all the scriptures the things concerning himself.
28And they drew nigh unto the village, whither they went: and
he made as though he would have gone further.
29But they constrained him, saying, Abide with us: for it is
toward evening, and the day is far spent. And he went in to tarry
with them.
30And it came to pass, as he sat at meat with them, he took
bread, and blessed *it*, and brake, and gave to them.
31And their eyes were opened, and they knew him; and he
vanished out of their sight.
32And they said one to another, Did not our heart burn within
us, while he talked with us by the way, and while he opened to
us the scriptures?
33And they rose up the same hour, and returned to Jerusalem,
and found the eleven gathered together, and them that were with
them,
34Saying, The Lord is risen indeed, and hath appeared to Simon.
35And they told what things *were done* in the way, and how he
was known of them in breaking of bread.
36¶ And as they thus spake, Jesus himself stood in the midst of
them, and saith unto them, Peace *be* unto you.
37But they were terrified and affrighted, and supposed that they
had seen a spirit.
38And he said unto them, Why are ye troubled? and why do
thoughts arise in your hearts?
39Behold my hands and my feet, that it is I myself: handle me,
and see; for a spirit hath not flesh and bones, as ye see me have.
40And when he had thus spoken, he showed them *his* hands
and *his* feet.
41And while they yet believed not for joy, and wondered, he
said unto them, Have ye here any meat?
42And they gave him a piece of a broiled fish, and of an honeycomb.
43And he took *it*, and did eat before them.
44And he said unto them, These *are* the words which I spake
unto you, while I was yet with you, that all things must be fulfilled,
which were written in the law of Moses, and *in* the prophets, and
*in* the psalms, concerning me.
45Then opened he their understanding, that they might understand the scriptures,
46And said unto them, Thus it is written, and thus it behooved
Christ to suffer, and to rise from the dead the third day:
47And that repentance and remission of sins should be
preached in his name among all nations, beginning at Jerusalem.
48And ye are witnesses of these things.
49¶ And, behold, I send the promise of my Father upon you: but
tarry ye in the city of Jerusalem, until ye be endued with power
from on high.
50¶ And he led them out as far as to Bethany, and he lifted up
his hands, and blessed them.
51And it came to pass, while he blessed them, he was parted
from them, and carried up into heaven.
52And they worshipped him, and returned to Jerusalem with
great joy:
53And were continually in the temple, praising and blessing
God. Amen.

# Amplified

27Then beginning with Moses and (throughout) all the prophets, He went on explaining *and* interpreting to them in all the
Scriptures the things concerning *and* referring to Himself.
28Then they drew near to the village to which they were going;
and He acted as if He would go further,
29But they urged *and* insisted, saying to Him, Remain with us,
for it is toward evening and the day is now far spent. So He went
in to stay with them.
30And it occurred that as He reclined at table with them, He
took [a loaf of] bread and praised [God] *and* gave thanks *and* asked
a blessing, then broke it and was giving it to them,
31When their eyes were [instantly] opened and they (clearly)
recognized Him; and He vanished ( [a]departed invisibly).
32And they said to one another, Was not our heart greatly
moved *and* burning within us while He was talking with us on the
road [and] as He opened *and* explained to us [the sense of] the
Scriptures?
33And rising up that very hour they went back to Jerusalem,
where they found the eleven [apostles] gathered together and
those who were with them,
34Who said, The Lord really is risen, and has appeared to Simon
[Peter]!
35Then they [themselves] [b]related in full what had happened
on the road, and how He was known *and* recognized by them in
the breaking of bread.
36Now while they were talking about this, Jesus Himself took
His stand among them and said to them, Peace [that is, [c]freedom
from all the distresses that are experienced as the result of sin] be
to you!
37But they were so startled and terrified that they thought they
saw a spirit.
38And He said to them, Why are you disturbed *and* troubled,
and why do such doubts *and* questionings arise in your hearts?
39See My hands and My feet, that it is I Myself; feel of *and*
handle Me and see, for a spirit does not have flesh and bones as
you see that I have.
40And when He had said this, He showed them His hands and
His feet.
41And while [since] they still could not believe it for sheer joy,
and marveled, He said to them, Have you anything here to eat?
42They gave Him a piece of broiled fish,
43And He took [it] and ate [it] before them.
44Then He said to them, This is what I told you while I was still
with you, that everything which is written concerning Me in the
Law of Moses and the prophets and the Psalms must be fulfilled.
45Then He (thoroughly) opened up their minds to understand
the Scriptures,
46And said to them, Thus it is written, that the Christ, the
Messiah, should suffer and on the third day rise from ( [d]among)
the dead, [Hos. 6:2.]
47And that repentance [with a view to and as the condition of]
forgiveness of sins should be preached in His name to all nations,
beginning from Jerusalem.
48You are witnesses of these things.
49And behold, I will send forth upon you what My Father has
promised; but remain in the city [Jerusalem] until you are clothed
with power from on high.
50Then He conducted them out as far as Bethany, and lifting up
His hands He invoked a blessing on them.
51And it occurred that while He was blessing them, He parted
from them and was taken up into heaven.
52And they worshipping Him went back to Jerusalem with great
joy,
53And they were continually in the temple *celebrating with praises*
*and* blessing *and* extolling God. *Amen.—So be it.*

**AMP** [a] Vincent. [b] Vincent. [c] Cremer. [d] Berry's "New Testament."

## New American Standard

27And beginning with Moses and with all the prophets, He explained to them the things concerning Himself in all the Scriptures.
28And they approached the village where they were going, and He acted as though He would go farther.
29And they urged Him, saying, "Stay with us, for it is *getting* toward evening, and the day is now nearly over." And He went in to stay with them.
30And it came about that when He had reclined *at the table* with them, He took the bread and blessed *it*, and breaking *it*, He *began* giving *it* to them.
31And their eyes were opened and they recognized Him; and He vanished from their sight.
32And they said to one another, "Were not our hearts burning within us while He was speaking to us on the road, while He was explaining the Scriptures to us?"
33And they arose that very hour and returned to Jerusalem, and found gathered together the eleven and those who were with them,
34saying, "The Lord has really risen, and has appeared to Simon."
35And they *began* to relate their experiences on the road and how He was recognized by them in the breaking of the bread.

*Other Appearances*

**36**¶ And while they were telling these things, He Himself stood in their midst.[e]
37But they were startled and frightened and thought that they were seeing a spirit.
38And He said to them, "Why are you troubled, and why do doubts arise in your hearts?
39"See My hands and My feet, that it is I Myself; touch Me and see, for a spirit does not have flesh and bones as you see that I have."
40[ [f]And when He had said this, He showed them His hands and His feet.]
41And while they still could not believe *it* for joy and were marveling, He said to them, "Have you anything here to eat?"
42And they gave Him a piece of a broiled fish;
43and He took it and ate *it* before them.
**44**¶ Now He said to them, "These are My words which I spoke to you while I was still with you, that all things which are written about Me in the Law of Moses and the Prophets and the Psalms must be fulfilled."
45Then He opened their minds to understand the Scriptures,
46and He said to them, "Thus it is written, that the Christ should suffer and rise again from the dead the third day;
47and that repentance for forgiveness of sins should be proclaimed in His name to all the nations, beginning from Jerusalem.
48"You are witnesses of these things.
49"And behold, I am sending forth the promise of My Father upon you; but you are to stay in the city until you are clothed with power from on high."

*The Ascension*

**50**¶ And He led them out as far as Bethany, and He lifted up His hands and blessed them.
51And it came about that while He was blessing them, He parted from them.[g]
52And they[h] returned to Jerusalem with great joy,
53and were continually in the temple, praising God.

NAS [e] Some ancient mss. insert *And He says to them, "Peace be to you."* [f] Many mss. do not contain this verse [g] Some mss. add *and was carried up into heaven* [h] Some mss. insert *worshiped Him, and*

## New International

ning with Moses and all the Prophets, he explained to them what was said in all the Scriptures concerning himself.
28As they approached the village to which they were going,
Jesus acted as if he were going farther. 29But they urged him
strongly, "Stay with us, for it is nearly evening; the day is almost
over." So he went in to stay with them.
30When he was at the table with them, he took bread, gave
thanks, broke it and began to give it to them. 31Then their eyes
were opened and they recognized him, and he disappeared from
their sight. 32They asked each other, "Were not our hearts burning
within us while he talked with us on the road and opened the
Scriptures to us?"
33They got up and returned at once to Jerusalem. There they
found the Eleven and those with them, assembled together 34and
saying, "It is true! The Lord has risen and has appeared to Simon."
35Then the two told what had happened on the way, and how
Jesus was recognized by them when he broke the bread.

*Jesus Appears to the Disciples*

36While they were still talking about this, Jesus himself stood
among them and said to them, "Peace be with you."
37They were startled and frightened, thinking they saw a ghost.
38He said to them, "Why are you troubled, and why do doubts rise
in your minds? 39Look at my hands and my feet. It is I myself!
Touch me and see; a ghost does not have flesh and bones, as you
see I have."
40When he had said this, he showed them his hands and feet.
41And while they still did not believe it because of joy and amazement, he asked them, "Do you have anything here to eat?" 42They
gave him a piece of broiled fish, 43and he took it and ate it in their
presence.
44He said to them, "This is what I told you while I was still with
you: Everything must be fulfilled that is written about me in the
Law of Moses, the Prophets and the Psalms."
45Then he opened their minds so they could understand the
Scriptures. 46He told them, "This is what is written: The Christ will
suffer and rise from the dead on the third day, 47and repentance
and forgiveness of sins will be preached in his name to all nations,
beginning at Jerusalem. 48You are witnesses of these things. 49I am
going to send you what my Father has promised; but stay in the
city until you have been clothed with power from on high."

*The Ascension*

50When he had led them out to the vicinity of Bethany, he lifted
up his hands and blessed them. 51While he was blessing them, he
left them and was taken up into heaven. 52Then they worshiped
him and returned to Jerusalem with great joy. 53And they stayed
continually at the temple, praising God.

## King James

THE GOSPEL

ACCORDING TO

# St. John

1 IN THE beginning was the Word, and the Word was with God, and the Word was God.

2The same was in the beginning with God.

3All things were made by him; and without him was not any thing made that was made.

4In him was life; and the life was the light of men.

5And the light shineth in darkness; and the darkness comprehended it not.

6¶ There was a man sent from God, whose name *was* John.

7The same came for a witness, to bear witness of the Light, that all *men* through him might believe.

8He was not that Light, but *was sent* to bear witness of that Light.

9 *That* was the true Light, which lighteth every man that cometh into the world.

10He was in the world, and the world was made by him, and the world knew him not.

11He came unto his own, and his own received him not.

12But as many as received him, to them gave he power to become the sons of God, *even* to them that believe on his name:

13Which were born, not of blood, nor of the will of the flesh, nor of the will of man, but of God.

14And the Word was made flesh, and dwelt among us, (and we beheld his glory, the glory as of the only begotten of the Father,) full of grace and truth.

15¶ John bare witness of him, and cried, saying, This was he of whom I spake, He that cometh after me is preferred before me: for he was before me.

16And of his fulness have all we received, and grace for grace.

17For the law was given by Moses, *but* grace and truth came by Jesus Christ.

**AMP** [a] Rev. 19:13, 16, "His name is called The Word of God . . . and Lord of Lords." [b] "God," emphatic, so "God Himself." (Williams' N.T.) [c] Literal translation. [d] Trench's "Synonyms of the New Testament."

## Amplified

THE GOSPEL

ACCORDING TO

# John

1 IN THE beginning [before all time] was the Word [ [a]Christ], and the Word was with God, and the Word was God [b]Himself. [Isa. 9:6.]

2He was present originally with God.

3All things were made *and* came into existence through Him; and without Him was not even one thing made that has come into being.

4In Him was Life and the Life was the Light of men.

5And the Light shines on in the darkness, for the darkness has never overpowered it—put it out, or has not absorbed it, has not appropriated it, and is unreceptive to it.

6There came a man, sent from God, whose name was John. [Mal. 3:1.]

7This man came to witness, that he might testify of the Light, that all men might believe in it—adhere to it, trust it and rely upon it—through him.

8He was not the Light himself, but came that he might bear witness regarding the Light.

9There it was; the true Light [was then] coming into the world—the genuine, perfect, steadfast Light—that illumines every person. [Isa. 49:6.]

10He came into the world, and though the world was made through Him, the world did not recognize Him—did not know Him.

11He came to that which belonged to Him—to His own [domain, creation, things, world]—and they who were His own did not receive Him *and* did not welcome Him.

12But to as many as did receive *and* welcome Him, He gave the authority [power, privilege, right] to become the children of God, that is, to those who believe in—adhere to, trust in and rely on—His name; [Isa. 56:5.]

13Who owe their birth neither to [c]bloods, nor to the will of the flesh [that of physical impulse], nor to the will of man [that of a natural father], but to God.—They are born of God!

14And the Word [Christ] became flesh (human, incarnate) and tabernacled—fixed His tent of flesh, lived awhile—among us; and we [actually] saw His glory—His honor, His majesty; such glory as an only begotten son receives from his father, full of grace (favor, loving-kindness) and truth. [Isa. 40:5.]

15John testified about Him and cried out, This is He of Whom I said, He that comes after me has priority over me, for He was before me—He takes rank above me, for He existed before I did. [He has advanced before me, because He is my Chief.]

16For out of His fullness (abundance) we all received—all had a share and we were all supplied with—one grace after another *and* spiritual blessing upon spiritual blessing, *and* even favor upon favor *and* gift [heaped] upon gift.

17For while the Law was given through Moses, grace—[d]unearned, undeserved favor and spiritual blessing—and truth came through Jesus Christ. [Exod. 20:1.]

## New American Standard

# John

*The Deity of Jesus Christ*

**1** IN THE beginning was the Word, and the Word was with
God, and the Word was God.
2He was in the beginning with God.
3All things came into being by Him, and apart from Him nothing came into being that has come into being.
4In Him was life, and the life was the light of men.
5And the light shines in the darkness, and the darkness did not [e]comprehend it.

*The Witness of John*

6¶ There [f]came a man, sent from God, whose name was John.
7He came for a witness, that he might bear witness of the light, that all might believe through him.
8He was not the light, but *came* that he might bear witness of the light.
9¶ There was the true light [g]which, coming into the world, enlightens every man.
10He was in the world, and the world was made through Him, and the world did not know Him.
11He came to His [h]own, and those who were His own did not receive Him.
12But as many as received Him, to them He gave the right to become children of God, *even* to those who believe in His name,
13who were born not of blood, nor of the will of the flesh, nor of the will of man, but of God.

*The Word Made Flesh*

14¶ And the Word became flesh, and dwelt among us, and we beheld His glory, glory as of the only begotten from the Father, full of grace and truth.
15John *bore witness of Him, and cried out, saying, "This was He of whom I said, 'He who comes after me has a higher rank than I, for He existed before me.' "
16For of His fulness we have all received, and grace upon grace.
17For the Law was given through Moses; grace and truth were realized through Jesus Christ.

**NAS** [e] Or, *overpower* [f] Or, *came into being* [g] Or, *which enlightens every man coming into the world* [h] Or, *own things, possessions, domain*

## New International

# John

*The Word Became Flesh*

**1** IN THE beginning was the Word, and the Word was with
God, and the Word was God. 2He was with God in the
beginning.
3Through him all things were made; without him nothing was
made that has been made. 4In him was life, and that life was the
light of men. 5The light shines in the darkness, but the darkness
has not understood[i] it.
6There came a man who was sent from God; his name was John.
7He came as a witness to testify concerning that light, so that
through him all men might believe. 8He himself was not the light;
he came only as a witness to the light. 9The true light that gives
light to every man was coming into the world.[j]
10He was in the world, and though the world was made
through him, the world did not recognize him. 11He came to that
which was his own, but his own did not receive him. 12Yet to all
who received him, to those who believed in his name, he gave the
right to become children of God— 13children born not of natural
descent,[k] nor of human decision or a husband's will, but born of
God.
14The Word became flesh and made his dwelling among us. We
have seen his glory, the glory of the One and Only,[l] who came
from the Father, full of grace and truth.
15John testifies concerning him. He cries out, saying, "This was
he of whom I said, 'He who comes after me has surpassed me
because he was before me.' " 16From the fullness of his grace we
have all received one blessing after another. 17For the law was
given through Moses; grace and truth came through Jesus Christ.

**NIV** [i] 5 Or *darkness, and the darkness has not overcome* [j] 9 Or *This was the true light that gives light to every man who comes into the world* [k] 13 Greek *of bloods* [l] 14 Or *the Only Begotten*

## King James

18 No man hath seen God at any time; the only begotten Son, which is in the bosom of the Father, he hath declared *him.*

19 ¶ And this is the record of John, when the Jews sent priests and Levites from Jerusalem to ask him, Who art thou?

20 And he confessed, and denied not; but confessed, I am not the Christ.

21 And they asked him, What then? Art thou Elias? And he saith, I am not. Art thou that prophet? And he answered, No.

22 Then said they unto him, Who art thou? that we may give an answer to them that sent us. What sayest thou of thyself?

23 He said, I *am* the voice of one crying in the wilderness, Make straight the way of the Lord, as said the prophet Esaias.

24 And they which were sent were of the Pharisees.

25 And they asked him, and said unto him, Why baptizest thou then, if thou be not that Christ, nor Elias, neither that prophet?

26 John answered them, saying, I baptize with water: but there standeth one among you, whom ye know not;

27 He it is, who coming after me is preferred before me, whose shoe's latchet I am not worthy to unloose.

28 These things were done in Bethabara beyond Jordan, where John was baptizing.

29 ¶ The next day John seeth Jesus coming unto him, and saith, Behold the Lamb of God, which taketh away the sin of the world.

30 This is he of whom I said, After me cometh a man which is preferred before me: for he was before me.

31 And I knew him not: but that he should be made manifest to Israel, therefore am I come baptizing with water.

32 And John bare record, saying, I saw the Spirit descending from heaven like a dove, and it abode upon him.

33 And I knew him not: but he that sent me to baptize with water, the same said unto me, Upon whom thou shalt see the Spirit descending, and remaining on him, the same is he which baptizeth with the Holy Ghost.

34 And I saw, and bare record that this is the Son of God.

35 ¶ Again the next day after John stood, and two of his disciples;

36 And looking upon Jesus as he walked, he saith, Behold the Lamb of God!

37 And the two disciples heard him speak, and they followed Jesus.

38 Then Jesus turned, and saw them following, and saith unto them, What seek ye? They said unto him, Rabbi, (which is to say, being interpreted, Master,) where dwellest thou?

39 He saith unto them, Come and see. They came and saw where he dwelt, and abode with him that day: for it was about the tenth hour.

40 One of the two which heard John *speak,* and followed him, was Andrew, Simon Peter's brother.

41 He first findeth his own brother Simon, and saith unto him, We have found the Messias, which is, being interpreted, the Christ.

42 And he brought him to Jesus. And when Jesus beheld him, he said, Thou art Simon the son of Jona: thou shalt be called Cephas, which is by interpretation, A stone.

## Amplified

18 No man has ever seen God at any time; the only [a]unique Son, [b]the only-begotten God, Who is in the bosom [that is, in the intimate presence] of the Father, He has declared Him—He has revealed Him, brought Him out where He can be seen; He has interpreted Him, *and* He has made Him known. [Prov. 8:30.]

19 And this is the testimony of John, when the Jews sent priests and Levites to him from Jerusalem to ask him, Who are you?

20 He confessed—admitted the truth—and did not try to conceal it, but acknowledged, I am not the Christ!

21 They asked him, What then? Are you Elijah? And he said, I am not! Are you the prophet? And he answered, No! [Mal. 4:5.]

22 Then they said to him, Who are you? Tell us, so that we may give an answer to them that sent us. What do you say about yourself?

23 He said, I am the voice of one crying aloud in the wilderness—the voice of one shouting in the desert—Prepare the way of the Lord (level, straighten out, the path of the Lord), as the prophet Isaiah said. [Isa. 40:3.]

24 The messengers had been sent from the Pharisees.

25 And they asked him, Why then are you baptizing, if you are not the Christ, nor Elijah, nor the prophet?

26 John answered them, I [only] baptize [c]in (with) water. Among you there stands One Whom you do not recognize *and* with Whom you are not acquainted *and* of Whom you know nothing. [Mal. 3:1.]

27 It is He Who coming after me is preferred before me, the string of Whose sandal I am not worthy to unloose.

28 These things occurred in Bethany (Bethabara) across the Jordan [[d]at the Jordan crossing] where John was then baptizing.

29 The next day John saw Jesus coming to him and said, Look! There is the Lamb of God, Who takes away the sin of the world! [Exod. 12:3; Isa. 53:7.]

30 This is He of Whom I said, After me comes a Man Who has priority over me—Who takes rank above me—because He was before me *and* existed before I did.

31 And I did not know Him *and* did not recognize Him [myself]; but it is in order that He should be made manifest *and* be revealed to Israel—be brought out where we can see Him—that I came baptizing [e]in (with) water.

32 John gave further evidence, saying, I have seen the Spirit descending as a dove out of heaven; and it dwelt on Him—not to depart.

33 And I did not know Him *nor* recognize Him; but He Who sent me to baptize [f]in (with) water said to me, Upon Whom you shall see the Spirit descend and remain, that One is He Who baptizes with the Holy Spirit.

34 And I have seen [that happen]—I actually did see it—and my testimony is that this is the Son of God!

35 Again the next day John was standing with two of his disciples,

36 And he looked at Jesus as He walked along and said, Look! There is the Lamb of God!

37 The two disciples heard him say this, and followed Him.

38 But Jesus turned and as He saw them following Him He said to them, What are you looking for? *And* what is it you wish? And they answered Him, Rabbi, which translated is Teacher, where do You stay?

39 He said to them, Come and see. So they went and saw where He was staying, and they remained with Him [g]that day. It was then about the tenth hour—about four o'clock in the afternoon.

40 One of the two who heard what John said and followed Jesus was Andrew, Simon Peter's brother.

41 He first sought out *and* found his own brother Simon and said to him, We have found (discovered) the Messiah! which translated is the Christ, the Anointed One.

42 Andrew then led (brought) Simon to Jesus. Jesus looked at him and said, You are Simon the son of John. You shall be called Cephas, which translated is Peter—meaning Stone.

**AMP** [a] Moulton and Milligan's "Vocabulary of the Greek Testament." [b] Supported by "a great mass of ancient evidence" (Vincent). [c] King James Version gives preference to "with," the American "Revised" Version to "in." Other versions are about equally divided in use of the two words. [d] Lamsa's "Modern New Testament." [e] King James Version gives preference to "with," the American "Revised" Version to "in." Other versions are about equally divided in use of the two words. [f] King James Version gives preference to "with," the American "Revised" Version to "in." Other versions are about equally divided in use of the two words. [g] In accordance with Oriental hospitality, the guests would be invited to remain that night also. (Lamsa's "Gospel Light.")

## New American Standard

18 No man has seen God at any time; the only begotten [h]God,
who is in the bosom of the Father, He has explained *Him*.

*The Testimony of John*

19 ¶ And this is the witness of John, when the Jews sent to him
priests and Levites from Jerusalem to ask him, "Who are you?"
20 And he confessed, and did not deny, and he confessed, "I am
not the Christ."
21 And they asked him, "What then? Are you Elijah?" And he
*said, "I am not." "Are you the Prophet?" And he answered,
"No."
22 They said then to him, "Who are you, so that we may give
an answer to those who sent us? What do you say about yourself?"
23 He said, "I am A VOICE OF ONE CRYING IN THE WILDERNESS,
'MAKE STRAIGHT THE WAY OF THE LORD,' as Isaiah the prophet
said."
24 Now they had been sent from the Pharisees.
25 And they asked him, and said to him, "Why then are you
baptizing, if you are not the Christ, nor Elijah, nor the Prophet?"
26 John answered them saying, "I baptize [i]in water, *but* among
you stands One whom you do not know.
27 "*It is* He who comes after me, the thong of whose sandal I
am not worthy to untie."
28 These things took place in Bethany beyond the Jordan, where
John was baptizing.
29 ¶ The next day he *saw Jesus coming to him, and *said,
"Behold, the Lamb of God who takes away the sin of the world!
30 "This is He on behalf of whom I said, 'After me comes a Man
who has a higher rank than I, for He existed before me.'
31 "And I did not recognize Him, but in order that He might be
manifested to Israel, I came baptizing [j]in water."
32 And John bore witness saying, "I have beheld the Spirit descending as a dove out of heaven, and He remained upon Him.
33 "And I did not recognize Him, but He who sent me to baptize
[k]in water said to me, 'He upon whom you see the Spirit descending and remaining upon Him, this is the one who baptizes in the
Holy Spirit.'
34 "And I have seen, and have borne witness that this is the Son
of God."

*Jesus' Public Ministry, First Converts*

35 ¶ Again the next day John was standing with two of his
disciples,
36 and he looked upon Jesus as He walked, and *said, "Behold,
the Lamb of God!"
37 And the two disciples heard him speak, and they followed
Jesus.
38 And Jesus turned, and beheld them following, and *said to
them, "What do you seek?" And they said to Him, "Rabbi (which
translated means Teacher), where are You staying?"
39 He *said to them, "Come, and you will see." They came
therefore and saw where He was staying; and they stayed with
Him that day, for it was about the [l]tenth hour.
40 One of the two who heard John *speak,* and followed Him, was
Andrew, Simon Peter's brother.
41 He *found first his own brother Simon, and *said to him, "We
have found the Messiah" (which translated means Christ).
42 He brought him to Jesus. Jesus looked at him, and said, "You
are Simon the son of John; you shall be called Cephas" (which is
translated Peter).

**NAS** [h] Some later mss. read *Son* [i] The Gr. here can be translated *in, with* or *by* [j] The Gr. here can be translated *in, with* or *by* [k] The Gr. here can be translated *in, with* or *by* [l] Perhaps 10 a.m. (Roman time)

## New International

18 No one has ever seen God, but God the One and Only,[m,n] who
is at the Father's side, has made him known.

*John the Baptist Denies Being the Christ*

19 Now this was John's testimony when the Jews of Jerusalem
sent priests and Levites to ask him who he was. 20 He did not fail
to confess, but confessed freely, "I am not the Christ.[o]"
21 They asked him, "Then who are you? Are you Elijah?"
He said, "I am not."
"Are you the Prophet?"
He answered, "No."
22 Finally they said, "Who are you? Give us an answer to take
back to those who sent us. What do you say about yourself?"
23 John replied in the words of Isaiah the prophet, "I am the
voice of one calling in the desert, 'Make straight the way for the
Lord.'"[p]
24 Now some Pharisees who had been sent 25 questioned him,
"Why then do you baptize if you are not the Christ, nor Elijah, nor
the Prophet?"
26 "I baptize with[q] water," John replied, "but among you stands
one you do not know. 27 He is the one who comes after me, the
thongs of whose sandals I am not worthy to untie."
28 This all happened at Bethany on the other side of the Jordan,
where John was baptizing.

*Jesus the Lamb of God*

29 The next day John saw Jesus coming toward him and said,
"Look, the Lamb of God, who takes away the sin of the world!
30 This is the one I meant when I said, 'A man who comes after me
has surpassed me because he was before me.' 31 I myself did not
know him, but the reason I came baptizing with water was that he
might be revealed to Israel."
32 Then John gave this testimony: "I saw the Spirit come down
from heaven as a dove and remain on him. 33 I would not have
known him, except that the one who sent me to baptize with water
told me, 'The man on whom you see the Spirit come down and
remain is he who will baptize with the Holy Spirit.' 34 I have seen
and I testify that this is the Son of God."

*Jesus' First Disciples*

35 The next day John was there again with two of his disciples.
36 When he saw Jesus passing by, he said, "Look, the Lamb of
God!"
37 When the two disciples heard him say this, they followed
Jesus. 38 Turning around, Jesus saw them following and asked,
"What do you want?"
They said, "Rabbi" (which means Teacher), "where are you
staying?"
39 "Come," he replied, "and you will see."
So they went and saw where he was staying, and spent that day
with him. It was about the tenth hour.
40 Andrew, Simon Peter's brother, was one of the two who
heard what John had said and who had followed Jesus. 41 The first
thing Andrew did was to find his brother Simon and tell him, "We
have found the Messiah" (that is, the Christ). 42 And he brought
him to Jesus.
Jesus looked at him and said, "You are Simon son of John. You
will be called Cephas" (which, when translated, is Peter[r]).

**NIV** [m] *18* Or *the Only Begotten* [n] *18* Some manuscripts *but the only* (or *only begotten*) *Son* [o] *20* Or *Messiah.* "The Christ" (Greek) and "the Messiah" (Hebrew) both mean "the Anointed One"; also in verse 25. [p] *23* Isaiah 40:3 [q] *26* Or *in;* also in verses 31 and 33 [r] *42* Both *Cephas* (Aramaic) and *Peter* (Greek) mean *rock.*

## King James

43¶ The day following Jesus would go forth into Galilee, and findeth Philip, and saith unto him, Follow me.
44Now Philip was of Bethsaida, the city of Andrew and Peter.
45Philip findeth Nathanael, and saith unto him, We have found him, of whom Moses in the law, and the prophets, did write, Jesus of Nazareth, the son of Joseph.
46And Nathanael said unto him, Can there any good thing come out of Nazareth? Philip saith unto him, Come and see.
47Jesus saw Nathanael coming to him, and saith of him, Behold an Israelite indeed, in whom is no guile!
48Nathanael saith unto him, Whence knowest thou me? Jesus answered and said unto him, Before that Philip called thee, when thou wast under the fig tree, I saw thee.
49Nathanael answered and saith unto him, Rabbi, thou art the Son of God; thou art the King of Israel.
50Jesus answered and said unto him, Because I said unto thee, I saw thee under the fig tree, believest thou? thou shalt see greater things than these.
51And he saith unto him, Verily, verily, I say unto you, Hereafter ye shall see heaven open, and the angels of God ascending and descending upon the Son of man.

2 AND THE third day there was a marriage in Cana of Galilee; and the mother of Jesus was there:
2And both Jesus was called, and his disciples, to the marriage.
3And when they wanted wine, the mother of Jesus saith unto him, They have no wine.
4Jesus saith unto her, Woman, what have I to do with thee? mine hour is not yet come.
5His mother saith unto the servants, Whatsoever he saith unto you, do *it*.
6And there were set there six waterpots of stone, after the manner of the purifying of the Jews, containing two or three firkins apiece.
7Jesus saith unto them, Fill the waterpots with water. And they filled them up to the brim.
8And he saith unto them, Draw out now, and bear unto the governor of the feast. And they bare *it*.
9When the ruler of the feast had tasted the water that was made wine, and knew not whence it was: (but the servants which drew the water knew;) the governor of the feast called the bridegroom,
10And saith unto him, Every man at the beginning doth set forth good wine; and when men have well drunk, then that which is worse: *but* thou hast kept the good wine until now.
11This beginning of miracles did Jesus in Cana of Galilee, and manifested forth his glory; and his disciples believed on him.
12¶ After this he went down to Capernaum, he, and his mother, and his brethren, and his disciples: and they continued there not many days.
13¶ And the Jews' passover was at hand, and Jesus went up to Jerusalem,
14And found in the temple those that sold oxen and sheep and doves, and the changers of money sitting:
15And when he had made a scourge of small cords, he drove them all out of the temple, and the sheep, and the oxen; and poured out the changers' money, and overthrew the tables;

## Amplified

43The next day Jesus desired *and* decided to go into Galilee; and He found Philip and said to him, Join Me as My attendant *and* follow Me.
44Now Philip was from Bethsaida, of the same city as Andrew and Peter.
45Philip sought for *and* found Nathanael and told him, We have found (discovered) the One Moses in the Law and also the prophets wrote about, Jesus from Nazareth, the [legal] son of Joseph!
46Nathanael answered him, [Nazareth!] Can any thing good come out of Nazareth? Philip replied, Come and see!
47Jesus saw Nathanael coming toward Him and said concerning him, See! Here is an Israelite indeed—a true descendant of Jacob—in whom there is no guile *nor* deceit *nor* falsehood *nor* duplicity!
48Nathanael said to Jesus, How do You know me?—How is it that You know these things about me?—Jesus answered him, Before ever Philip called you, when you were still under the fig tree, I saw you.
49Nathanael answered, Teacher, You are the Son of God! You are the King of Israel!
50Jesus replied, Because I said to you, I saw you beneath the fig tree, do you believe in *and* rely on *and* trust in Me? You shall see greater things than this!
51Then He said to him, I assure you, most solemnly I tell you all, you shall see Heaven opened up, and the angels of God ascending and descending upon the Son of man! [Gen. 28:12; Dan. 7:13.]

2 ON THE third day there was a wedding at Cana of Galilee, and the mother of Jesus was there.
2Jesus also was invited with His disciples to the wedding.
3And when the wine was all gone, the mother of Jesus said to Him, They have no more wine!
4Jesus said to her, ([a]Dear) woman, what is that to you and to Me? [What have we in common? Leave it to Me.] My time (hour to act) is not come yet. [Eccl. 3:1.]
5His mother said to the servants, Whatever He says to you, do it.
6Now there were six waterpots of stone standing there, as the Jewish custom of purification (ceremonial washing) demanded, holding twenty to thirty gallons apiece.
7Jesus said to them, Fill the waterpots with water. So they filled them up to the brim.
8Then He said to them, Draw some out now and take it to the manager of the feast—to the one presiding, the superintendent of the banquet. So they took him some.
9And when the manager tasted the water just now turned into wine, not knowing where it came from, though the servants that had drawn the water knew, he called the bridegroom,
10And said to him, Everyone else serves his best wine first, and when people have drunk freely, then he serves that which is not so good; but you have kept back the good wine until now!
11This first of His signs (miracles, wonderworks) Jesus performed in Cana of Galilee and manifested His glory—by it He displayed His greatness *and* His power openly; and His disciples believed in Him—adhered to, trusted in and relied on Him. [Deut. 5:24; Ps. 72:19.]
12After that He went down to Capernaum with His mother and brothers and disciples and they stayed there only a few days.
13Now the Passover of the Jews was approaching, so Jesus went up to Jerusalem.
14There He found in the temple [b]enclosure those who were selling oxen and sheep and doves, and the money changers sitting there [too at their stands].
15And having made a lash (a whip) of cords, He drove them all out of the temple [c]enclosure, both the sheep and the oxen; spilling *and* scattering the brokers' money and upsetting *and* tossing around their trays—their stands.

**AMP** [a] Abbott-Smith: "a term of respect and endearment." [b] Trench's "Synonyms of the New Testament." [c] Trench's "Synonyms of the New Testament."

## New American Standard

43¶ The next day He purposed to go forth into Galilee, and He
*found Philip. And Jesus *said to him, "Follow Me."
44Now Philip was from Bethsaida, of the city of Andrew and
Peter.
45Philip *found Nathanael and *said to him, "We have found
Him of whom Moses in the Law and *also* the Prophets wrote, Jesus
of Nazareth, the son of Joseph."
46And Nathanael *said to him, "Can any good thing come out
of Nazareth?" Philip *said to him, "Come and see."
47Jesus saw Nathanael coming to Him, and *said of him, "Behold, an Israelite indeed, in whom is no guile!"
48Nathanael *said to Him, "How do You know me?" Jesus
answered and said to him, "Before Philip called you, when you
were under the fig tree, I saw you."
49Nathanael answered Him, "Rabbi, You are the Son of God;
You are the King of Israel."
50Jesus answered and said to him, "Because I said to you that
I saw you under the fig tree, do you believe? You shall see greater
things than these."
51And He *said to him, "Truly, truly, I say to you, you shall see
the heavens opened, and the angels of God ascending and descending on the Son of Man."

*Miracle at Cana*

2 AND ON the third day there was a wedding in Cana of
Galilee, and the mother of Jesus was there;
2and Jesus also was invited, and His disciples, to the wedding.
3And when the wine gave out, the mother of Jesus *said to
Him, "They have no wine."
4And Jesus *said to her, "Woman, what do I have to do with
you? My hour has not yet come."
5His mother *said to the servants, "Whatever He says to you,
do it."
6Now there were six stone waterpots set there for the Jewish
custom of purification, containing twenty or thirty gallons each.
7Jesus *said to them, "Fill the waterpots with water." And they
filled them up to the brim.
8And He *said to them, "Draw *some* out now, and take it to the
[d]headwaiter." And they took it *to him*.
9And when the headwaiter tasted the water which had become
wine, and did not know where it came from (but the servants who
had drawn the water knew), the headwaiter *called the bridegroom,
10and *said to him, "Every man serves the good wine first, and
when *men* have drunk freely, *then* that which is poorer; you have
kept the good wine until now."
11This beginning of *His* signs Jesus did in Cana of Galilee, and
manifested His glory, and His disciples believed in Him.
12¶ After this He went down to Capernaum, He and His
mother, and *His* brothers, and His disciples; and there they stayed
a few days.

*First Passover—Cleansing the Temple*

13¶ And the Passover of the Jews was at hand, and Jesus went
up to Jerusalem.
14And He found in the temple those who were selling oxen and
sheep and doves, and the moneychangers seated.
15And He made a scourge of cords, and drove *them* all out of
the temple, with the sheep and the oxen; and He poured out the
coins of the moneychangers, and overturned their tables;

NAS [d] Or, *steward*

## New International

*Jesus Calls Philip and Nathanael*

43The next day Jesus decided to leave for Galilee. Finding
Philip, he said to him, "Follow me."
44Philip, like Andrew and Peter, was from the town of Bethsaida. 45Philip found Nathanael and told him, "We have found the
one Moses wrote about in the Law, and about whom the prophets
also wrote—Jesus of Nazareth, the son of Joseph."
46"Nazareth! Can anything good come from there?" Nathanael
asked.
"Come and see," said Philip.
47When Jesus saw Nathanael approaching, he said of him,
"Here is a true Israelite, in whom there is nothing false."
48"How do you know me?" Nathanael asked.
Jesus answered, "I saw you while you were still under the fig
tree before Philip called you."
49Then Nathanael declared, "Rabbi, you are the Son of God;
you are the King of Israel."
50Jesus said, "You believe[e] because I told you I saw you under
the fig tree. You shall see greater things than that." 51He then
added, "I tell you[f] the truth, you[g] shall see heaven open, and the
angels of God ascending and descending on the Son of Man."

*Jesus Changes Water to Wine*

2 ON THE third day a wedding took place at Cana in Galilee.
Jesus' mother was there, 2and Jesus and his disciples had also
been invited to the wedding. 3When the wine was gone, Jesus'
mother said to him, "They have no more wine."
4"Dear woman, why do you involve me?" Jesus replied, "My
time has not yet come."
5His mother said to the servants, "Do whatever he tells you."
6Nearby stood six stone water jars, the kind used by the Jews
for ceremonial washing, each holding from twenty to thirty gallons.[h]
7Jesus said to the servants, "Fill the jars with water"; so they
filled them to the brim.
8Then he told them, "Now draw some out and take it to the
master of the banquet."
They did so, 9and the master of the banquet tasted the water
that had been turned into wine. He did not realize where it had
come from, though the servants who had drawn the water knew.
Then he called the bridegroom aside 10and said, "Everyone brings
out the choice wine first and then the cheaper wine after the guests
have had too much to drink; but you have saved the best till now."
11This, the first of his miraculous signs, Jesus performed in
Cana of Galilee. He thus revealed his glory, and his disciples put
their faith in him.

*Jesus Clears the Temple*

12After this he went down to Capernaum with his mother and
brothers and his disciples. There they stayed for a few days.
13When it was almost time for the Jewish Passover, Jesus went
up to Jerusalem. 14In the temple courts he found men selling cattle,
sheep and doves, and others sitting at tables exchanging money.
15So he made a whip out of cords, and drove all from the temple
area, both sheep and cattle; he scattered the coins of the money
changers and overturned their tables. 16To those who sold doves

NIV [e] 50 Or *Do you believe . . . ?* [f] 51 The Greek is plural. [g] 51 The Greek is plural. [h] 6 Greek *two to three metretes* (probably about 75 to 115 liters)

## King James

16 And said unto them that sold doves, Take these things hence; make not my Father's house an house of merchandise.

17 And his disciples remembered that it was written, The zeal of thine house hath eaten me up.

18¶ Then answered the Jews and said unto him, What sign showest thou unto us, seeing that thou doest these things?

19 Jesus answered and said unto them, Destroy this temple, and in three days I will raise it up.

20 Then said the Jews, Forty and six years was this temple in building, and wilt thou rear it up in three days?

21 But he spake of the temple of his body.

22 When therefore he was risen from the dead, his disciples remembered that he had said this unto them; and they believed the scripture, and the word which Jesus had said.

23¶ Now when he was in Jerusalem at the passover, in the feast *day,* many believed in his name, when they saw the miracles which he did.

24 But Jesus did not commit himself unto them, because he knew all *men,*

25 And needed not that any should testify of man: for he knew what was in man.

**3** THERE WAS a man of the Pharisees, named Nicodemus, a ruler of the Jews:

2 The same came to Jesus by night, and said unto him, Rabbi, we know that thou art a teacher come from God: for no man can do these miracles that thou doest, except God be with him.

3 Jesus answered and said unto him, Verily, verily, I say unto thee, Except a man be born again, he cannot see the kingdom of God.

4 Nicodemus saith unto him, How can a man be born when he is old? can he enter the second time into his mother's womb, and be born?

5 Jesus answered, Verily, verily, I say unto thee, Except a man be born of water and *of* the Spirit, he cannot enter into the kingdom of God.

6 That which is born of the flesh is flesh; and that which is born of the Spirit is spirit.

7 Marvel not that I said unto thee, Ye must be born again.

8 The wind bloweth where it listeth, and thou hearest the sound thereof, but canst not tell whence it cometh, and whither it goeth: so is every one that is born of the Spirit.

9 Nicodemus answered and said unto him, How can these things be?

10 Jesus answered and said unto him, Art thou a master of Israel, and knowest not these things?

11 Verily, verily, I say unto thee, We speak that we do know, and testify that we have seen; and ye receive not our witness.

12 If I have told you earthly things, and ye believe not, how shall ye believe, if I tell you *of* heavenly things?

13 And no man hath ascended up to heaven, but he that came down from heaven, *even* the Son of man which is in heaven.

## Amplified

16 Then to them that sold the doves He said, Take these things away—out of here! Make not My Father's house a house of merchandise—a market place, a sales shop! [Ps. 93:5.]

17 And His disciples remembered that it is written [in the Holy Scriptures], The zeal—the fervor of love—for Your house will eat Me up.—I will be consumed with jealousy for the honor of Your house. [Ps. 69:9.]

18 Then the Jews retorted, What sign can [a]You show us, seeing You do these things?—What sign, miracle, token, indication can You give us as evidence that You have authority *and* are commissioned to act in this way?

19 Jesus answered them, Destroy (undo) this temple and in three days I will raise it up again.

20 Then the Jews replied, It took forty-six years to build this temple (sanctuary), and will You raise it up in three days?

21 But He spoke of the temple which was His body.

22 When therefore He had risen from the dead, His disciples remembered that He said this: and so they believed *and* trusted in *and* relied on the Scripture and the word (message) Jesus had spoken. [Ps. 16:10.]

23 But when He was in Jerusalem during the Passover Feast, many believed on His name [identified themselves with His party] after seeing His signs (wonders, miracles) which He was doing.

24 But Jesus [for His part] did not trust Himself to them, because He knew all [men];

25 And He did not need that any one should witness concerning man—needed no evidence from any one about men; for He Himself knew what was in human nature. [He could read men's hearts.] [I Sam. 16:7.]

**3** NOW THERE was a certain man among the Pharisees named Nicodemus, a ruler—a leader, an authority—among the Jews;

2 Who came to Jesus at night and said to Him, Rabbi, we know *and* are certain that You are come from God [as] a Teacher; for no one can do these signs—these wonderworks, these miracles, and produce the proofs—that You do, unless God is with him.

3 Jesus answered him, I assure you, most solemnly I tell you, that unless a person is born again (anew, from above), he cannot ever see—know, be acquainted with [and experience]—the kingdom of God.

4 Nicodemus said to Him, How can a man be born when he is old? Can he enter his mother's womb again, and be born?

5 Jesus answered, I assure you, most solemnly I tell you, except a man be born of water and ([b]even) the Spirit, he cannot [ever] enter the kingdom of God. [Ezek. 36:25-27.]

6 What is born of [from] the flesh is flesh—of the physical is physical; and what is born of the Spirit is spirit.

7 Marvel not—do not be surprised, astonished—at My telling you, You must all be born anew (from above).

8 The wind blows (breathes) where it will; and though you hear its sound, yet you neither know where it comes from nor where it goes. So it is with every one who is born of the Spirit.

9 Nicodemus answered by asking, How can all this be possible?

10 Jesus replied, Are you the teacher of Israel and yet do not know *nor* understand these things? [Are they strange to you?]

11 I assure you, most solemnly I tell you, We speak only of what we know—we know absolutely what we are talking about; we have actually seen what we are testifying to—were eyewitnesses of it. And still you do not receive our testimony—you reject, refuse our evidence [that of Myself and of all those who are born of the Spirit].

12 If I have told you of things that happen right here on the earth, and yet none of you believes Me, how can you believe—trust Me, adhere to Me, rely on Me—if I tell you of heavenly things?

13 And yet no one has ever gone up to heaven; but there is One Who has come down from heaven, the Son of man [Himself], *Who is—dwells, Whose home is—in heaven.*

**AMP** [a] Capitalized because of what He is, the spotless Son of God, not what the speaker may have thought He was. [b] "Kai" may be rendered "even."

## New American Standard

16and to those who were selling the doves He said, "Take these things away; stop making My Father's house a house of merchandise."

17His disciples remembered that it was written, "ZEAL FOR THY HOUSE WILL CONSUME ME."

18The Jews therefore answered and said to Him, "What sign do You show to us, seeing that You do these things?"

19Jesus answered and said to them, "Destroy this temple, and in three days I will raise it up."

20The Jews therefore said, "It took forty-six years to build this temple, and will You raise it up in three days?"

21But He was speaking of the temple of His body.

22When therefore He was raised from the dead, His disciples remembered that He said this; and they believed the Scripture, and the word which Jesus had spoken.

23¶ Now when He was in Jerusalem at the Passover, during the feast, many believed in His name, beholding His signs which He was doing.

24But Jesus, on His part, was not entrusting Himself to them, for He knew all men,

25and because He did not need anyone to bear witness concerning man for He Himself knew what was in man.

*The New Birth*

3 NOW THERE was a man of the Pharisees, named Nicodemus, a ruler of the Jews;

2this man came to Him by night, and said to Him, "Rabbi, we know that You have come from God *as* a teacher; for no one can do these signs that You do unless God is with him."

3Jesus answered and said to him, "Truly, truly, I say to you, unless one is born again, he cannot see the kingdom of God."

4Nicodemus *said to Him, "How can a man be born when he is old? He cannot enter a second time into his mother's womb and be born, can he?"

5Jesus answered, "Truly, truly, I say to you, unless one is born of water and the Spirit, he cannot enter into the kingdom of God.

6"That which is born of the flesh is flesh, and that which is born of the Spirit is spirit.

7"Do not marvel that I said to you, 'You must be born again.'

8"The wind blows where it wishes and you hear the sound of it, but do not know where it comes from and where it is going; so is everyone who is born of the Spirit."

9Nicodemus answered and said to Him, "How can these things be?"

10Jesus answered and said to him, "Are you the teacher of Israel, and do not understand these things?

11"Truly, truly, I say to you, we speak that which we know, and bear witness of that which we have seen; and you do not receive our witness.

12"If I told you earthly things and you do not believe, how shall you believe if I tell you heavenly things?

13"And no one has ascended into heaven, but He who descended from heaven, *even* the Son of Man.

## New International

he said, "Get these out of here! How dare you turn my Father's house into a market!"

17His disciples remembered that it is written: "Zeal for your house will consume me."[c]

18Then the Jews demanded of him, "What miraculous sign can you show us to prove your authority to do all this?"

19Jesus answered them, "Destroy this temple, and I will raise it again in three days."

20The Jews replied, "It has taken forty-six years to build this temple, and you are going to raise it in three days?" 21But the temple he had spoken of was his body. 22After he was raised from the dead, his disciples recalled what he had said. Then they believed the Scripture and the words that Jesus had spoken.

23Now while he was in Jerusalem at the Passover Feast, many people saw the miraculous signs he was doing and believed in his name.[d] 24But Jesus would not entrust himself to them, for he knew all men. 25He did not need man's testimony about man, for he knew what was in a man.

*Jesus Teaches Nicodemus*

3 NOW THERE was a man of the Pharisees named Nicodemus, a member of the Jewish ruling council. 2He came to Jesus at night and said, "Rabbi, we know you are a teacher who has come from God. For no one could perform the miraculous signs you are doing if God were not with him."

3In reply Jesus declared, "I tell you the truth, no one can see the kingdom of God unless he is born again.[e]"

4"How can a man be born when he is old?" Nicodemus asked. "Surely he cannot enter a second time into his mother's womb to be born!"

5Jesus answered, "I tell you the truth, no one can enter the kingdom of God unless he is born of water and the Spirit. 6Flesh gives birth to flesh, but the Spirit[f] gives birth to spirit. 7You should not be surprised at my saying, 'You[g] must be born again.' 8The wind blows wherever it pleases. You hear its sound, but you cannot tell where it comes from or where it is going. So it is with everyone born of the Spirit."

9"How can this be?" Nicodemus asked.

10"You are Israel's teacher," said Jesus, "and do you not understand these things? 11I tell you the truth, we speak of what we know, and we testify to what we have seen, but still you people do not accept our testimony. 12I have spoken to you of earthly things and you do not believe; how then will you believe if I speak of heavenly things? 13No one has ever gone into heaven except the one who came from heaven—the Son of Man.[h] 14Just as Moses

NIV [c] 17 Psalm 69:9 [d] 23 Or *and believed in him* [e] 3 Or *born from above;* also in verse 7 [f] 6 Or *but spirit* [g] 7 The Greek is plural. [h] 13 Some manuscripts *Man, who is in heaven*

## King James

14¶ And as Moses lifted up the serpent in the wilderness, even
so must the Son of man be lifted up:
15That whosoever believeth in him should not perish, but have
eternal life.
16¶ For God so loved the world, that he gave his only begotten
Son, that whosoever believeth in him should not perish, but have
everlasting life.
17For God sent not his Son into the world to condemn the
world; but that the world through him might be saved.
18¶ He that believeth on him is not condemned: but he that
believeth not is condemned already, because he hath not believed
in the name of the only begotton Son of God.
19And this is the condemnation, that light is come into the
world, and men loved darkness rather than light, because their
deeds were evil.
20For every one that doeth evil hateth the light, neither cometh
to the light, lest his deeds should be reproved.
21But he that doeth truth cometh to the light, that his deeds may
be made manifest, that they are wrought in God.
22¶ After these things came Jesus and his disciples into the land
of Judaea; and there he tarried with them, and baptized.
23¶ And John also was baptizing in Aenon near to Salim, because there was much water there: and they came, and were
baptized.
24For John was not yet cast into prison.
25¶ Then there arose a question between *some* of John's disciples
and the Jews about purifying.
26And they came unto John, and said unto him, Rabbi, he that
was with thee beyond Jordan, to whom thou barest witness, behold, the same baptizeth, and all *men* come to him.
27John answered and said, A man can receive nothing, except
it be given him from heaven.
28Ye yourselves bear me witness, that I said, I am not the Christ,
but that I am sent before him.
29He that hath the bride is the bridegroom: but the friend of the
bridegroom, which standeth and heareth him, rejoiceth greatly
because of the bridegroom's voice: this my joy therefore is fulfilled.
30He must increase, but I *must* decrease.
31He that cometh from above is above all: he that is of the earth
is earthly, and speaketh of the earth: he that cometh from heaven
is above all.

## Amplified

14And just as Moses lifted up the serpent in the desert [on a
pole], so must—so it is necessary that—the Son of man be lifted
up [on the cross]; [Num. 21:9.]
15In order that every one who believes in Him—who cleaves to
Him, trusts Him and relies on Him—may *not perish, but* have
eternal life *and* [actually] live forever!
16For God so greatly loved *and* dearly prized the world that He
[even] gave up His only-begotten ( [a]unique) Son, so that whoever
believes in (trusts, clings to, relies on) Him shall not perish—come
to destruction, be lost—but have eternal (everlasting) life.
17For God did not send the Son into the world in order to
judge—to reject, to condemn, to pass sentence on—the world; but
that the world might find salvation *and* be made safe *and* sound
through Him.
18He who believes on Him—who clings to, trusts in, relies on
Him—is not judged (he who trusts in Him never comes up for
judgment; for him there is no rejection, no condemnation; he
incurs no damnation). But he who does not believe (not cleave to,
rely on, trust in Him) is judged already; (he has already been
convicted; has already received his sentence) because he has not
believed on *and* trusted in the name of the only begotten Son of
God.—He is condemned for refusing to let his trust rest in Christ's
name.
19The [basis of the] judgment (indictment, the test by which
men are judged, the ground for the sentence) lies in this: that the
Light is come into the world, and people have loved the darkness
rather than *and* more than the Light, for their works (deeds) were
evil. [Isa. 5:20.]
20For every wrongdoer hates (loathes, detests) the light and will
not come out into the light, *but* shrinks from it, lest his works—his
deeds, his activities, his conduct—be exposed *and* reproved.
21But he who practices truth—who does what is right—comes
out into the light; so that his works may be plainly shown to be
what they are, wrought with God—divinely prompted, done with
God's help, in dependence upon Him.
22After this, Jesus and His disciples went into the land (the
countryside) of Judea, where He remained with them and baptized.
23But John also was baptizing at Aenon near Salim, for there
was an abundance of water there; and the people kept coming and
being baptized.
24For John had not yet been thrown into prison.
25Therefore there arose a controversy between some of John's
disciples and a Jew in regard to purification.
26So they came to John and reported to him, Rabbi, the Man
Who was with you on the other side of the Jordan [ [b]at the Jordan
crossing], and to Whom you yourself have borne testimony, notice, here He is baptizing too, and everybody is flocking to Him!
27John answered, A man can receive nothing—he can claim
nothing, he can [c]take unto himself nothing—except as it has been
granted to him from heaven. [A man must be content to receive
the gift which is given him from heaven; there is no other source.]
28You yourselves are my witnesses—you personally bear me
out—that I stated, I am not the Christ, the Anointed One, the
Messiah; but I have [only] been sent before Him—in advance of
Him, as His appointed forerunner, His messenger, His announcer.
[Mal. 3:1.]
29He who has the bride is the bridegroom; but the groomsman,
who stands by and listens to him, rejoices greatly *and* heartily on
account of the bridegroom's voice. This then is my pleasure *and*
joy, and it is now complete. [S. of Sol. 5:1.]
30He must increase, but I must decrease—He must grow more
prominent, I must grow less so. [Isa. 9:7.]
31He Who comes from above (heaven) is [far] above all [others].
He who comes from the earth belongs to the earth, and talks the
language of earth—his words are from an earthly standpoint. He
Who comes from heaven is [far] above all others—far superior to
all others in prominence and in excellence.

AMP [a] Moulton and Milligan. [b] Lamsa's New Testament. [c] Thayer.

## New American Standard

14"And as Moses lifted up the serpent in the wilderness, even so must the Son of Man be lifted up;

15that whoever [d]believes may in Him have eternal life.

**16**¶ "For God so loved the world, that He gave His only begotten Son, that whoever believes in Him should not perish, but have eternal life.

17"For God did not send the Son into the world to judge the world, but that the world should be saved through Him.

18"He who believes in Him is not judged; he who does not believe has been judged already, because he has not believed in the name of the only begotten Son of God.

19"And this is the judgment, that the light is come into the world, and men loved the darkness rather than the light; for their deeds were evil.

20"For everyone who does evil hates the light, and does not come to the light, lest his deeds should be exposed.

21"But he who practices the truth comes to the light, that his deeds may be manifested as having been wrought in God."

*John's Last Testimony*

**22**¶ After these things Jesus and His disciples came into the land of Judea, and there He was spending time with them and baptizing.

23And John also was baptizing in Aenon near Salim, because there was much water there; and they were coming and were being baptized.

24For John had not yet been thrown into prison.

25There arose therefore a discussion on the part of John's disciples with a Jew about purification.

26And they came to John and said to him, "Rabbi, He who was with you beyond the Jordan, to whom you have borne witness, behold, He is baptizing, and all are coming to Him."

27John answered and said, "A man can receive nothing, unless it has been given him from heaven.

28"You yourselves bear me witness, that I said, 'I am not the Christ,' but, 'I have been sent before Him.'

29"He who has the bride is the bridegroom; but the friend of the bridegroom, who stands and hears him, rejoices greatly because of the bridegroom's voice. And so this joy of mine has been made full.

30"He must increase, but I must decrease.

**31**¶ "He who comes from above is above all, he who is of the earth is from the earth and speaks of the earth. He who comes from heaven is above all.

NAS [d] Some mss. read *believes in Him may have eternal life*

## New International

lifted up the snake in the desert, so the Son of Man must be lifted
up, 15that everyone who believes in him may have eternal life.[e]
16"For God so loved the world that he gave his one and only
Son,[f] that whoever believes in him shall not perish but have
eternal life. 17For God did not send his Son into the world to
condemn the world, but to save the world through him. 18Who-
ever believes in him is not condemned, but whoever does not
believe stands condemned already because he has not believed in
the name of God's one and only Son.[g] 19This is the verdict: Light
has come into the world, but men loved darkness instead of light
because their deeds were evil. 20Everyone who does evil hates the
light, and will not come into the light for fear that his deeds will
be exposed. 21But whoever lives by the truth comes into the light,
so that it may be seen plainly that what he has done has been done
through God."[h]

*John the Baptist's Testimony About Jesus*

22After this, Jesus and his disciples went out into the Judean
countryside, where he spent some time with them, and baptized.
23Now John also was baptizing at Aenon near Salim, because there
was plenty of water, and people were constantly coming to be
baptized. 24(This was before John was put in prison.) 25An argument developed between some of John's disciples and a certain
Jew[i] over the matter of ceremonial washing. 26They came to John
and said to him, "Rabbi, that man who was with you on the other
side of the Jordan—the one you testified about—well, he is baptizing, and everyone is going to him."
27To this John replied, "A man can receive only what is given
him from heaven. 28You yourselves can testify that I said, 'I am not
the Christ[j] but am sent ahead of him.' 29The bride belongs to the
bridegroom. The friend who attends the bridegroom waits and
listens for him, and is full of joy when he hears the bridegroom's
voice. That joy is mine, and it is now complete. 30He must become
greater; I must become less.
31"The one who comes from above is above all; the one who is
from the earth belongs to the earth, and speaks as one from the
earth. The one who comes from heaven is above all. 32He testifies

NIV [e] 15 Or *believes may have eternal life in him* [f] 16 Or *his only begotten Son* [g] 18 Or *God's only begotten Son* [h] 21 Some interpreters end the quotation after verse 15. [i] 25 Some manuscripts *and certain Jews* [j] 28 Or *Messiah*

## King James

32And what he hath seen and heard, that he testifieth; and no man receiveth his testimony.

33He that hath received his testimony hath set to his seal that God is true.

34For he whom God hath sent speaketh the words of God: for God giveth not the Spirit by measure *unto him.*

35The Father loveth the Son, and hath given all things into his hand.

36He that believeth on the Son hath everlasting life: and he that believeth not the Son shall not see life; but the wrath of God abideth on him.

**4** WHEN THEREFORE the Lord knew how the Pharisees had heard that Jesus made and baptized more disciples than John,

2(Though Jesus himself baptized not, but his disciples,)

3He left Judaea, and departed again into Galilee.

4And he must needs go through Samaria.

5Then cometh he to a city of Samaria, which is called Sychar, near to the parcel of ground that Jacob gave to his son Joseph.

6Now Jacob's well was there. Jesus therefore, being wearied with *his* journey, sat thus on the well: *and* it was about the sixth hour.

7There cometh a woman of Samaria to draw water: Jesus saith unto her, Give me to drink.

8(For his disciples were gone away unto the city to buy meat.)

9Then saith the woman of Samaria unto him, How is it that thou, being a Jew, askest drink of me, which am a woman of Samaria? for the Jews have no dealings with the Samaritans.

10Jesus answered and said unto her, If thou knewest the gift of God, and who it is that saith to thee, Give me to drink; thou wouldest have asked of him, and he would have given thee living water.

11The woman saith unto him, Sir, thou hast nothing to draw with, and the well is deep: from whence then hast thou that living water?

12Art thou greater than our father Jacob, which gave us the well, and drank thereof himself, and his children, and his cattle?

13Jesus answered and said unto her, Whosoever drinketh of this water shall thirst again:

14But whosoever drinketh of the water that I shall give him shall never thirst; but the water that I shall give him shall be in him a well of water springing up into everlasting life.

15The woman saith unto him, Sir, give me this water, that I thirst not, neither come hither to draw.

16Jesus saith unto her, Go, call thy husband, and come hither.

17The woman answered and said, I have no husband. Jesus said unto her, Thou hast well said, I have no husband:

18For thou hast had five husbands; and he whom thou now hast is not thy husband: in that saidst thou truly.

19The woman saith unto him, Sir, I perceive that thou art a prophet.

20Our fathers worshipped in this mountain; and ye say, that in Jerusalem is the place where men ought to worship.

## Amplified

32It is to what He has [actually] seen and heard that He bears testimony; and yet no one accepts His testimony—no one receives His evidence as true.

33Whoever receives His testimony has set his seal of approval to this: that God is true—has definitely certified, acknowledged, declared once for all, is himself assured that it is divine truth, that God cannot lie.

34For since He Whom God has sent speaks the words of God—proclaims God's own message—God does not give Him His Spirit sparingly *or* by measure, *but* boundless is the gift God makes of His Spirit! [Deut. 18:18.]

35The Father loves the Son, and has given—entrusted, committed—everything into His hand. [Dan. 7:14.]

36And he who believes on—has faith in, clings to, relies on—the Son has (now possesses) eternal life. But whoever disobeys—is unbelieving toward, refuses to trust in, disregards, is not subject to—the Son will never see (experience) life. But instead the wrath of God abides on him—God's displeasure remains on him; His indignation hangs over him continually. [Hab. 2:4.]

**4** NOW WHEN the Lord knew (learned, was aware) that the Pharisees had been told that Jesus was winning and baptizing more disciples than John,

2Though Jesus Himself did not baptize, but His disciples,

3He left Judea and returned to Galilee.

4It was necessary for Him to go through Samaria.

5And in doing so He arrived at a Samaritan town called Sychar, near the tract of land that Jacob gave to his son Joseph.

6And Jacob's well was there. So Jesus, tired as He was from His journey, sat down [to rest] by the well. It was then about the sixth hour (about noon).

7Presently when a woman of Samaria came along to draw water, Jesus said to her, Give Me a drink.

8For His disciples had gone off into the town to buy food.

9The Samaritan woman said to Him, How is it that [a]You being a Jew ask me, a Samaritan [and a] woman, for a drink? For the Jews have nothing to do with the Samaritans.

10Jesus answered her, If you had only known *and* had recognized God's gift, and Who this is that is saying to you, Give Me a drink, you would have asked Him instead and He would have given you living water.

11She said to Him, Sir, [b]You have nothing to draw with (no draw-bucket) and the well is deep; how then can You provide living water?—Where do You get Your living water?

12Are You greater than *and* superior to our ancestor Jacob, who gave us this well, and who used to drink from it himself, and his sons and his cattle also?

13Jesus answered her, All who drink of this water will be thirsty again.

14But whoever takes a drink of the water that I will give him shall never, no never, be thirsty any more. But the water that I will give him shall become a spring of water welling up (flowing, bubbling) continually within him unto (into, for) eternal life.

15The woman said to Him, Sir, give me this water, so that I may never get thirsty, nor have to come [continually all the way] here to draw.

16At this Jesus said to her, Go, call your husband and come back here.

17The woman answered, I have no husband. Jesus said to her, You have spoken truly in saying, I have no husband.

18For you have had five husbands; but the man you are now living with is not your husband. In this you have spoken truly.

19The woman said to Him, Sir, I see *and* understand that You are a prophet.

20Our forefathers worshipped on this mountain, but you [Jews] say that Jerusalem is the place where it is necessary *and* proper to worship.

**AMP** [a] Capitalized because of what He is, the spotless Son of God, not what the speaker may have thought He was. [b] Capitalized because of what He is, the spotless Son of God, not what the speaker may have thought He was.

## New American Standard

32"What He has seen and heard, of that He bears witness; and
no man receives His witness.
33"He who has received His witness has set his seal to *this,* that
God is true.
34"For He whom God has sent speaks the words of God; for He
gives the Spirit without measure.
35"The Father loves the Son, and has given all things into His
hand.
36"He who believes in the Son has eternal life; but he who does
not obey the Son shall not see life, but the wrath of God abides on
him."

*Jesus Goes to Galilee*

4 WHEN THEREFORE the Lord knew that the Pharisees had
heard that Jesus was making and baptizing more disciples
than John
2(although Jesus Himself was not baptizing, but His disciples
were),
3He left Judea, and departed again into Galilee.
4And He had to pass through Samaria.
5So He *came to a city of Samaria, called Sychar, near the parcel
of ground that Jacob gave to his son Joseph;
6and Jacob's well was there. Jesus therefore, being wearied
from His journey, was sitting thus by the well. It was about [c]the
sixth hour.

*The Woman of Samaria*

7There *came a woman of Samaria to draw water. Jesus *said
to her, "Give Me a drink."
8For His disciples had gone away into the city to buy food.
9The Samaritan woman therefore *said to Him, "How is it that
You, being a Jew, ask me for a drink since I am a Samaritan
woman?" (For Jews have no dealings with Samaritans.)
10Jesus answered and said to her, "If you knew the gift of God,
and who it is who says to you, 'Give Me a drink,' you would have
asked Him, and He would have given you living water."
11She *said to Him, "Sir, You have nothing to draw with and
the well is deep; where then do You get that living water?
12"You are not greater than our father Jacob, are You, who gave
us the well, and drank of it himself, and his sons, and his cattle?"
13Jesus answered and said to her, "Everyone who drinks of this
water shall thirst again;
14but whoever drinks of the water that I shall give him shall
never thirst; but the water that I shall give him shall become in him
a well of water springing up to eternal life."
15The woman *said to Him, "Sir, give me this water, so I will
not be thirsty, nor come all the way here to draw."
16He *said to her, "Go, call your husband, and come here."
17The woman answered and said, "I have no husband." Jesus
*said to her, "You have well said, 'I have no husband';
18for you have had five husbands, and the one whom you now
have is not your husband; this you have said truly."
19The woman *said to Him, "Sir, I perceive that You are a
prophet.
20"Our fathers worshiped in this mountain, and you *people* say
that in Jerusalem is the place where men ought to worship."

NAS [c] Perhaps 6 p.m. (Roman time)

## New International

to what he has seen and heard, but no one accepts his testimony.
33The man who has accepted it has certified that God is truthful.
34For the one whom God has sent speaks the words of God, for
God[d] gives the Spirit without limit. 35The Father loves the Son and
has placed everything in his hands. 36Whoever believes in the Son
has eternal life, but whoever rejects the Son will not see life, for
God's wrath remains on him."[e]

*Jesus Talks With a Samaritan Woman*

4 THE PHARISEES heard that Jesus was gaining and baptizing
more disciples than John, 2although in fact it was not Jesus
who baptized, but his disciples. 3When the Lord learned of this,
he left Judea and went back once more to Galilee.
4Now he had to go through Samaria. 5So he came to a town in
Samaria called Sychar, near the plot of ground Jacob had given to
his son Joseph. 6Jacob's well was there, and Jesus, tired as he was
from the journey, sat down by the well. It was about the sixth
hour.
7When a Samaritan woman came to draw water, Jesus said to
her, "Will you give me a drink?" 8(His disciples had gone into the
town to buy food.)
9The Samaritan woman said to him, "You are a Jew and I am
a Samaritan woman. How can you ask me for a drink?" (For Jews
do not associate with Samaritans.[f])
10Jesus answered her, "If you knew the gift of God and who it
is that asks you for a drink, you would have asked him and he
would have given you living water."
11"Sir," the woman said, "you have nothing to draw with and
the well is deep. Where can you get this living water? 12Are you
greater than our father Jacob, who gave us the well and drank from
it himself, as did also his sons and his flocks and herds?"
13Jesus answered, "Everyone who drinks this water will be
thirsty again, 14but whoever drinks the water I give him will never
thirst. Indeed, the water I give him will become in him a spring
of water welling up to eternal life."
15The woman said to him, "Sir, give me this water so that I
won't get thirsty and have to keep coming here to draw water."
16He told her, "Go, call your husband and come back."
17"I have no husband," she replied.
Jesus said to her, "You are right when you say you have no
husband. 18The fact is, you have had five husbands, and the man
you now have is not your husband. What you have just said is
quite true."
19"Sir," the woman said, "I can see that you are a prophet.
20Our fathers worshiped on this mountain, but you Jews claim that
the place where we must worship is in Jerusalem."

NIV [d] 34 Greek *he* [e] 36 Some interpreters end the quotation after verse 30.
[f] 9 Or *do not use dishes Samaritans have used*

## King James

21 Jesus saith unto her, Woman, believe me, the hour cometh, when ye shall neither in this mountain, nor yet at Jerusalem, worship the Father.

22 Ye worship ye know not what: we know what we worship: for salvation is of the Jews.

23 But the hour cometh, and now is, when the true worshippers shall worship the Father in spirit and in truth: for the Father seeketh such to worship him.

24 God *is* a Spirit: and they that worship him must worship *him* in spirit and in truth.

25 The woman saith unto him, I know that Messias cometh, which is called Christ: when he is come, he will tell us all things.

26 Jesus saith unto her, I that speak unto thee am *he*.

27 ¶ And upon this came his disciples, and marvelled that he talked with the woman: yet no man said, What seekest thou? or, Why talkest thou with her?

28 The woman then left her waterpot, and went her way into the city, and saith to the men,

29 Come, see a man, which told me all things that ever I did: is not this the Christ?

30 Then they went out of the city, and came unto him.

31 ¶ In the mean while his disciples prayed him, saying, Master, eat.

32 But he said unto them, I have meat to eat that ye know not of.

33 Therefore said the disciples one to another, Hath any man brought him *aught* to eat?

34 Jesus saith unto them, My meat is to do the will of him that sent me, and to finish his work.

35 Say not ye, There are yet four months, and *then* cometh harvest? behold, I say unto you, Lift up your eyes, and look on the fields; for they are white already to harvest.

36 And he that reapeth receiveth wages, and gathereth fruit unto life eternal: that both he that soweth and he that reapeth may rejoice together.

37 And herein is that saying true, One soweth, and another reapeth.

38 I sent you to reap that whereon ye bestowed no labour: other men laboured, and ye are entered into their labours.

39 ¶ And many of the Samaritans of that city believed on him for the saying of the woman, which testified, He told me all that ever I did.

40 So when the Samaritans were come unto him, they besought him that he would tarry with them: and he abode there two days.

41 And many more believed because of his own word;

42 And said unto the woman, Now we believe, not because of thy saying: for we have heard *him* ourselves, and know that this is indeed the Christ, the Saviour of the world.

43 ¶ Now after two days he departed thence, and went into Galilee.

44 For Jesus himself testified, that a prophet hath no honour in his own country.

45 Then when he was come into Galilee, the Galilaeans received him, having seen all the things that he did at Jerusalem at the feast: for they also went unto the feast.

46 So Jesus came again into Cana of Galilee, where he made the water wine. And there was a certain nobleman, whose son was sick at Capernaum.

47 When he heard that Jesus was come out of Judaea into Galilee, he went unto him, and besought him that he would come down, and heal his son: for he was at the point of death.

## Amplified

21 Jesus said to her, Woman, believe Me, a time is coming when you will worship the Father neither [merely] in this mountain nor [merely] in Jerusalem.

22 You [Samaritans] do not know what you are worshipping—you worship what you do not comprehend. We do know what we are worshipping—we worship what we have knowledge of and understand; for [after all] salvation comes from [among] the Jews.

23 A time will come, however, indeed it is already here, when the true (genuine) worshippers will worship the Father in spirit and in truth (reality); for the Father is seeking just such people as these as His worshippers.

24 God is a Spirit (a spiritual Being) and those who worship Him must worship *Him* in spirit and in truth (reality).

25 The woman said to Him, I know that Messiah is coming, He Who is called the Christ, the Anointed One, and when He arrives He will tell us everything we need to know *and* make it clear to us.

26 Jesus said to her, I Who am now speaking with you am He.

27 Just then His disciples came and they wondered (were surprised, astonished) to find Him talking with a woman [a married woman]. However, not one of them asked Him, What are You inquiring? *or* What do You want? or, Why do You speak with her?

28 Then the woman left her water jar and went away to the town. And she began telling the people,

29 Come, see a Man Who has told me everything that I ever did! Can this be (is not this) the Christ?—Must not this be the Messiah, the Anointed One?

30 So the people left the town and set out to go to Him.

31 Meanwhile the disciples urged Him saying, Rabbi, eat something.

32 But He assured them, I have food (nourishment) to eat of which you know nothing *and* have no idea.

33 So the disciples said one to another, Has someone brought Him something to eat?

34 Jesus said to them, My food (nourishment) is to do the will (pleasure) of Him Who sent Me and to accomplish *and* completely finish His work.

35 Do you not say, It is still four months until harvest time comes? Look! I tell you, raise your eyes and observe the fields *and* see how they are already white for harvesting.

36 Already the reaper is getting his wages—he who does the cutting now has his reward—for he is gathering fruit (crop) unto life eternal. So that he who does the planting and he who does the reaping may rejoice together.

37 For in this the saying holds true, One sows and another reaps.

38 I sent you to reap a crop on which you have not toiled. Other men have labored and you step in to reap the results of their work.

39 Now numerous Samaritans from that town believed on *and* trusted in Him because of what the woman said when she declared *and* testified, He told me everything that I ever did.

40 So when the Samaritans arrived, they asked Him to remain with them, and He did stay there two days.

41 Then many more believed *and* adhered to *and* relied on Him because of His personal message—what He Himself said.

42 And they told the woman, Now we no longer believe (trust, have faith) just because of what you said; for we have heard Him ourselves—personally; and we know that He truly is the Savior of the world, *the Christ*.

43 But after these two days Jesus went on from there into Galilee,

44 Although He Himself declared that a prophet has no honor in his own country.

45 However, when He came into Galilee, the Galileans also welcomed Him *and* took Him to their hearts eagerly; for they had seen everything that He did in Jerusalem during the feast, for they too had attended the feast.

46 So Jesus came again to Cana of Galilee where He had turned the water into wine. And there was a certain royal official, whose son was lying ill in Capernaum.

47 Having heard that Jesus had come back from Judea into Galilee, he went away to meet Him and began to beg Him to come down and cure his son, for he was lying at the point of death.

## New American Standard

21Jesus *said to her, "Woman, believe Me, an hour is coming when neither in this mountain, nor in Jerusalem, shall you worship the Father.

22"You worship that which you do not know; we worship that which we know, for salvation is from the Jews.

23"But an hour is coming, and now is, when the true worshipers shall worship the Father in spirit and truth; for such people the Father seeks to be His worshipers.

24"God is spirit, and those who worship Him must worship in spirit and truth."

25The woman *said to Him, "I know that Messiah is coming (He who is called Christ); when that One comes, He will declare all things to us."

26Jesus *said to her, "I who speak to you am *He.*"

**27**¶ And at this point His disciples came, and they marveled that He had been speaking with a woman; yet no one said, "What do You seek?" or, "Why do You speak with her?"

28So the woman left her waterpot, and went into the city, and *said to the men,

29"Come, see a man who told me all the things that I *have* done; this is not the Christ, is it?"

30They went out of the city, and were coming to Him.

31In the meanwhile the disciples were requesting Him, saying, "Rabbi, eat."

32But He said to them, "I have food to eat that you do not know about."

33The disciples therefore were saying to one another, "No one brought Him *anything* to eat, did he?"

34Jesus *said to them, "My food is to do the will of Him who sent Me, and to accomplish His work.

35"Do you not say, 'There are yet four months, and *then* comes the harvest'? Behold, I say to you, lift up your eyes, and look on the fields, that they are white for harvest.

36"Already he who reaps is receiving wages, and is gathering fruit for life eternal; that he who sows and he who reaps may rejoice together.

37"For in this *case* the saying is true, 'One sows, and another reaps.'

38"I sent you to reap that for which you have not labored; others have labored, and you have entered into their labor."

*The Samaritans*

**39**¶ And from that city many of the Samaritans believed in Him because of the word of the woman who testified, "He told me all the things that I *have* done."

40So when the Samaritans came to Him, they were asking Him to stay with them; and He stayed there two days.

41And many more believed because of His word;

42and they were saying to the woman, "It is no longer because of what you said that we believe, for we have heard for ourselves and know that this One is indeed the Savior of the world."

**43**¶ And after the two days He went forth from there into Galilee.

44For Jesus Himself testified that a prophet has no honor in his own country.

45So when He came to Galilee, the Galileans received Him, having seen all the things that He did in Jerusalem at the feast; for they themselves also went to the feast.

*Healing a Nobleman's Son*

**46**¶ He came therefore again to Cana of Galilee where He had made the water wine. And there was a certain royal official, whose son was sick at Capernaum.

47When he heard that Jesus had come out of Judea into Galilee, he went to Him, and was requesting *Him* to come down and heal his son; for he was at the point of death.

## New International

21Jesus declared, "Believe me, woman, a time is coming when
you will worship the Father neither on this mountain nor in Jerusalem. 22You Samaritans worship what you do not know; we worship what we do know, for salvation is from the Jews. 23Yet a time
is coming and has now come when the true worshipers will worship the Father in spirit and truth, for they are the kind of worshipers the Father seeks. 24God is spirit, and his worshipers must
worship in spirit and in truth."

25The woman said, "I know that Messiah" (called Christ) "is
coming. When he comes, he will explain everything to us."

26Then Jesus declared, "I who speak to you am he."

*The Disciples Rejoin Jesus*

27Just then his disciples returned and were surprised to find
him talking with a woman. But no one asked, "What do you
want?" or "Why are you talking with her?"

28Then, leaving her water jar, the woman went back to the town
and said to the people, 29"Come, see a man who told me everything I ever did. Could this be the Christ[a] ?" 30They came out of
the town and made their way toward him.

31Meanwhile his disciples urged him, "Rabbi, eat something."

32But he said to them, "I have food to eat that you know nothing
about."

33Then his disciples said to each other, "Could someone have
brought him food?"

34"My food," said Jesus, "is to do the will of him who sent me
and to finish his work. 35Do you not say, 'Four months more and
then the harvest'? I tell you, open your eyes and look at the fields!
They are ripe for harvest. 36Even now the reaper draws his wages,
even now he harvests the crop for eternal life, so that the sower
and the reaper may be glad together. 37Thus the saying 'One sows
and another reaps' is true. 38I sent you to reap what you have not
worked for. Others have done the hard work, and you have reaped
the benefits of their labor."

*Many Samaritans Believe*

39Many of the Samaritans from that town believed in him because of the woman's testimony, "He told me everything I ever
did." 40So when the Samaritans came to him, they urged him to
stay with them, and he stayed two days. 41And because of his
words many more became believers.

42They said to the woman, "We no longer believe just because
of what you said; now we have heard for ourselves, and we know
that this man really is the Savior of the world."

*Jesus Heals the Official's Son*

43After the two days he left for Galilee. 44(Now Jesus himself
had pointed out that a prophet has no honor in his own country.)
45When he arrived in Galilee, the Galileans welcomed him. They
had seen all that he had done in Jerusalem at the Passover Feast,
for they also had been there.

46Once more he visited Cana in Galilee, where he had turned
the water into wine. And there was a certain royal official whose
son lay sick at Capernaum. 47When this man heard that Jesus had
arrived in Galilee from Judea, he went to him and begged him to
come and heal his son, who was close to death.

**NIV** [a] 29 Or *Messiah*

## King James

48 Then said Jesus unto him, Except ye see signs and wonders, ye will not believe.

49 The nobleman saith unto him, Sir, come down ere my child die.

50 Jesus saith unto him, Go thy way; thy son liveth. And the man believed the word that Jesus had spoken unto him, and he went his way.

51 And as he was now going down, his servants met him, and told *him*, saying, Thy son liveth.

52 Then inquired he of them the hour when he began to amend. And they said unto him, Yesterday at the seventh hour the fever left him.

53 So the father knew that *it was* at the same hour, in the which Jesus said unto him, Thy son liveth: and himself believed, and his whole house.

54 This *is* again the second miracle *that* Jesus did, when he was come out of Judaea into Galilee.

**5** AFTER THIS there was a feast of the Jews; and Jesus went up to Jerusalem.

2 Now there is at Jerusalem by the sheep *market* a pool, which is called in the Hebrew tongue Bethesda, having five porches.

3 In these lay a great multitude of impotent folk, of blind, halt, withered, waiting for the moving of the water.

4 For an angel went down at a certain season into the pool, and troubled the water: whosoever then first after the troubling of the water stepped in was made whole of whatsoever disease he had.

5 And a certain man was there, which had an infirmity thirty and eight years.

6 When Jesus saw him lie, and knew that he had been now a long time *in that case,* he saith unto him, Wilt thou be made whole?

7 The impotent man answered him, Sir, I have no man, when the water is troubled, to put me into the pool: but while I am coming, another steppeth down before me.

8 Jesus saith unto him, Rise, take up thy bed, and walk.

9 And immediately the man was made whole, and took up his bed, and walked: and on the same day was the sabbath.

10 ¶ The Jews therefore said unto him that was cured, It is the sabbath day: it is not lawful for thee to carry *thy* bed.

11 He answered them, He that made me whole, the same said unto me, Take up thy bed, and walk.

12 Then asked they him, What man is that which said unto thee, Take up thy bed, and walk?

13 And he that was healed wist not who it was: for Jesus had conveyed himself away, a multitude being in *that* place.

14 Afterward Jesus findeth him in the temple, and said unto him, Behold, thou art made whole: sin no more, lest a worse thing come unto thee.

15 The man departed, and told the Jews that it was Jesus, which had made him whole.

16 And therefore did the Jews persecute Jesus, and sought to slay him, because he had done these things on the sabbath day.

17 ¶ But Jesus answered them, My Father worketh hitherto, and I work.

18 Therefore the Jews sought the more to kill him, because he not only had broken the sabbath, but said also that God was his Father, making himself equal with God.

## Amplified

48 Then Jesus said to him, Unless you see signs and miracles happen, you [people] never will believe (trust, have faith) at all.

49 The king's officer pleaded with Him, Sir, do come down at once before my little child is dead!

50 Jesus answered him, Go in peace; your son will live! And the man put his trust in what Jesus said and started home.

51 But even as he was on the road going down, his servants met him and reported, saying, Your son lives!

52 So he asked them at what time he had begun to get better. They said, Yesterday during the seventh hour [about one o'clock in the afternoon] the fever left him.

53 Then the father knew that it was at that very hour when Jesus had said to him, Your son lives. And he and his entire household believed—they adhered to, trusted in and relied on Jesus.

54 This is the second sign (wonderwork, miracle) that Jesus performed after He had come out of Judea into Galilee.

**5** LATER ON there was a Jewish festival (feast), for which Jesus went up to Jerusalem.

2 Now there is in Jerusalem a pool near the Sheep Gate. This pool in the Hebrew is called Bethesda, having five porches (alcoves, colonnades, doorways).

3 In these lay a great number of sick folk, some blind, some crippled and some paralyzed (shriveled up), *waiting for the bubbling up of the water.* [a]

5 There was a certain man there who had suffered with a deep-seated *and* lingering disorder for thirty-eight years.

6 When Jesus noticed him lying there helpless, knowing that he had already been a long time in that condition, He said to him, Do you want to become well? [Are you really in earnest about getting well?]

7 The invalid answered, Sir, I have nobody when the water is moving to put me into the pool; but while I am trying to come myself, somebody else steps down ahead of me.

8 Jesus said to him, Get up; pick up your bed (sleeping pad) and walk!

9 Instantly the man became well *and* recovered his strength and picked up his bed and walked. But that happened on the Sabbath.

10 So the Jews kept saying to the man that had been healed, It is the Sabbath and you have no right to pick up your bed—it is not lawful.

11 He answered them, The [b]Man Who healed me *and* gave me back my strength, He Himself said to me, Pick up your bed and walk!

12 They asked him, Who is the Man Who told you, Pick up your bed and walk?

13 Now the invalid who had been healed did not know Who it was, for Jesus had quietly gone away (had passed on unnoticed), since there was a crowd in the place.

14 Afterward when Jesus found him in the temple, He said to him, See, you are well! Stop sinning, or something worse may happen to you.

15 The man went away and told the Jews that it was Jesus Who had made him well.

16 For this reason the Jews began to persecute (annoy, torment) Jesus, *and sought to kill Him,* because He was doing these things on the Sabbath.

17 But Jesus answered them, My Father has worked [even] until now.—He has never ceased working, He is still working—and I too must be at [divine] work.

18 This made the Jews more determined than ever to kill Him—to make away with Him; because He not only broke (weakened, violated) the Sabbath, but He actually spoke of God as being [in a special sense] His own Father, making Himself equal (putting Himself on a level) with God.

**AMP** [a] The best manuscripts omit verse 4, as does the American "Revised" Version (ASV). [b] Capitalized because of what He is, the spotless Son of God, not what the speaker may have thought He was.

## New American Standard

48Jesus therefore said to him, "Unless you *people* see signs and wonders, you *simply* will not believe."

49The royal official *said to Him, "Sir, come down before my child dies."

50Jesus *said to him, "Go your way; your son lives." The man believed the word that Jesus spoke to him, and he started off.

51And as he was now going down, *his* slaves met him, saying that his son was living.

52So he inquired of them the hour when he began to get better. They said therefore to him, "Yesterday at the [c]seventh hour the fever left him."

53So the father knew that *it was* at that hour in which Jesus said to him, "Your son lives"; and he himself believed, and his whole household.

54This is again a second sign that Jesus performed, when He had come out of Judea into Galilee.

*The Healing at Bethesda*

5 AFTER THESE things there was [d]a feast of the Jews, and Jesus went up to Jerusalem.

2Now there is in Jerusalem by the sheep *gate* a pool, which is called in Hebrew Bethesda, having five porticoes.

3In these lay a multitude of those who were sick, blind, lame, and withered, [ [e]waiting for the moving of the waters;

4for an angel of the Lord went down at certain seasons into the pool, and stirred up the water; whoever then first, after the stirring up of the water, stepped in was made well from whatever disease with which he was afflicted.]

5And a certain man was there, who had been thirty-eight years in his sickness.

6When Jesus saw him lying there, and knew that he had already been a long time *in that condition,* He *said to him, "Do you wish to get well?"

7The sick man answered Him, "Sir, I have no man to put me into the pool when the water is stirred up, but while I am coming, another steps down before me."

8Jesus *said to him, "Arise, take up your pallet, and walk."

9And immediately the man became well, and took up his pallet and *began* to walk.

¶ Now it was the Sabbath on that day.

10Therefore the Jews were saying to him who was cured, "It is the Sabbath, and it is not permissible for you to carry your pallet."

11But he answered them, "He who made me well was the one who said to me, 'Take up your pallet and walk.'"

12They asked him, "Who is the man who said to you, 'Take up *your pallet,* and walk'?"

13But he who was healed did not know who it was; for Jesus had slipped away while there was a crowd in *that* place.

14Afterward Jesus *found him in the temple, and said to him, "Behold, you have become well; do not sin anymore, so that nothing worse may befall you."

15The man went away, and told the Jews that it was Jesus who had made him well.

16And for this reason the Jews were persecuting Jesus, because He was doing these things on the Sabbath.

17But He answered them, "My Father is working until now, and I Myself am working."

*Jesus' Equality with God*

18For this cause therefore the Jews were seeking all the more to kill Him, because He not only was breaking the Sabbath, but also was calling God His own Father, making Himself equal with God.

**NAS** [c] Perhaps 7 p.m. (Roman time) [d] Many mss. read *the feast,* i.e., the Passover [e] Many mss. do not contain the remainder of v. 3 nor v. 4

## New International

48"Unless you people see miraculous signs and wonders," Jesus told him, "you will never believe."

49The royal official said, "Sir, come down before my child dies."

50Jesus replied, "You may go. Your son will live."

The man took Jesus at his word and departed. 51While he was still on the way, his servants met him with the news that his boy was living. 52When he inquired as to the time when his son got better, they said to him, "The fever left him yesterday at the seventh hour."

53Then the father realized that this was the exact time at which Jesus had said to him, "Your son will live." So he and all his household believed.

54This was the second miraculous sign that Jesus performed, having come from Judea to Galilee.

*The Healing at the Pool*

5 SOME TIME later, Jesus went up to Jerusalem for a feast of the Jews. 2Now there is in Jerusalem near the Sheep Gate a pool, which in Aramaic is called Bethesda[f] and which is surrounded by five covered colonnades. 3Here a great number of disabled people used to lie—the blind, the lame, the paralyzed.[g] 5One who was there had been an invalid for thirty-eight years. 6When Jesus saw him lying there and learned that he had been in this condition for a long time, he asked him, "Do you want to get well?"

7"Sir," the invalid replied, "I have no one to help me into the pool when the water is stirred. While I am trying to get in, someone else goes down ahead of me."

8Then Jesus said to him, "Get up! Pick up your mat and walk." 9At once the man was cured; he picked up his mat and walked.

The day on which this took place was a Sabbath, 10and so the Jews said to the man who had been healed, "It is the Sabbath; the law forbids you to carry your mat."

11But he replied, "The man who made me well said to me, 'Pick up your mat and walk.'"

12So they asked him, "Who is this fellow who told you to pick it up and walk?"

13The man who was healed had no idea who it was, for Jesus had slipped away into the crowd that was there.

14Later Jesus found him at the temple and said to him, "See, you are well again. Stop sinning or something worse may happen to you." 15The man went away and told the Jews that it was Jesus who had made him well.

*Life Through the Son*

16So, because Jesus was doing these things on the Sabbath, the Jews persecuted him. 17Jesus said to them, "My Father is always at his work to this very day, and I, too, am working." 18For this reason the Jews tried all the harder to kill him; not only was he breaking the Sabbath, but he was even calling God his own Father, making himself equal with God.

**NIV** [f] 2 Some manuscripts *Bethzatha;* other manuscripts *Bethsaida* [g] 3 Some less important manuscripts *paralyzed—and they waited for the moving of the waters. 4From time to time an angel of the Lord would come down and stir up the waters. The first one into the pool after each such disturbance would be cured of whatever disease he had.*

## King James

19 Then answered Jesus and said unto them, Verily, verily, I say unto you, The Son can do nothing of himself, but what he seeth the Father do: for what things soever he doeth, these also doeth the Son likewise.

20 For the Father loveth the Son, and showeth him all things that himself doeth: and he will show him greater works than these, that ye may marvel.

21 For as the Father raiseth up the dead, and quickeneth *them;* even so the Son quickeneth whom he will.

22 For the Father judgeth no man, but hath committed all judgment unto the Son:

23 That all *men* should honour the Son, even as they honour the Father. He that honoureth not the Son honoureth not the Father which hath sent him.

24 Verily, verily, I say unto you, He that heareth my word, and believeth on him that sent me, hath everlasting life, and shall not come into condemnation; but is passed from death unto life.

25 Verily, verily, I say unto you, The hour is coming, and now is, when the dead shall hear the voice of the Son of God: and they that hear shall live.

26 For as the Father hath life in himself; so hath he given to the Son to have life in himself;

27 And hath given him authority to execute judgment also, because he is the Son of man.

28 Marvel not at this: for the hour is coming, in the which all that are in the graves shall hear his voice,

29 And shall come forth; they that have done good, unto the resurrection of life; and they that have done evil, unto the resurrection of damnation.

30 I can of mine own self do nothing: as I hear, I judge: and my judgment is just; because I seek not mine own will, but the will of the Father which hath sent me.

31 If I bear witness of myself, my witness is not true.

32 ¶ There is another that beareth witness of me; and I know that the witness which he witnesseth of me is true.

33 Ye sent unto John, and he bare witness unto the truth.

34 But I receive not testimony from man: but these things I say, that ye might be saved.

35 He was a burning and a shining light: and ye were willing for a season to rejoice in his light.

36 ¶ But I have greater witness than *that* of John: for the works which the Father hath given me to finish, the same works that I do, bear witness of me, that the Father hath sent me.

37 And the Father himself, which hath sent me, hath borne witness of me. Ye have neither heard his voice at any time, nor seen his shape.

## Amplified

19 So Jesus answered them by saying, I assure you, most solemnly I tell you, the Son is able to do nothing from Himself—of His own accord; but He is able to do only what He sees the Father doing. For whatever the Father does is what the Son does in the same way [in His turn].

20 The Father dearly loves the Son and discloses (shows) to Him everything that He Himself does. And He will disclose to Him—let Him see—greater things yet than these, so that you may marvel *and* be full of wonder *and* astonishment.

21 Just as the Father raises up the dead and gives them life—makes them live on—so the Son also gives life to whomever He wills *and* is pleased to give it.

22 Even the Father judges no one; for He has given all judgment—the last judgment and the whole business of judging—entirely into the hands of the Son;

23 So that all men may give honor (reverence, homage) to the Son, just as they give honor to the Father. [In fact] whoever does not honor the Son, does not honor the Father Who has sent Him.

24 I assure you, most solemnly I tell you, the person whose ears are open to My words—who listens to My message—and believes *and* trusts in *and* clings to *and* relies on Him Who sent Me has (possesses now) eternal life. And he does not come into judgment—does not incur sentence of judgment, will not come under condemnation—but he has already passed over out of death into life.

25 Believe Me when I assure you, most solemnly I tell you, The time is coming and is here now when the dead shall hear the voice of the Son of God, and those who hear it shall live.

26 For even as the Father has life in Himself *and* is self-existent, so He has given to the Son to have life in Himself *and* be self-existent.

27 And He has given Him authority *and* granted Him power to execute (exercise, practice) judgment, because He is [a]a Son of man [very man].

28 Do not be surprised *and* wonder at this; for the time is coming when all those who are in the tombs shall hear His voice,

29 And they shall come out; those who have practiced doing good [will come out] to the resurrection of [new] life; and those who have done evil will be raised for judgment—raised to meet their sentence. [Dan. 12:2.]

30 I am able to do nothing from Myself—independently, of My own accord—but as I am taught by God *and* as I get His orders. [I decide as I am bidden to decide. As the voice comes to Me, so I give a decision.] Even as I hear, I judge and My judgment is right (just, righteous), because I do not seek *or* consult My own will—I have no desire to do what is pleasing to Myself, My own aim, My own purpose—but only the will *and* pleasure of the Father Who sent Me.

31 If I alone testify in My behalf, My testimony is not valid *and* can not be worth anything.

32 There is Another Who testifies concerning Me and I know *and* am certain that His evidence on My behalf is true and valid.

33 You yourselves have sent an inquiry to John and he has been a witness to the truth.

34 But I do not receive [a mere] human witness—the evidence which I accept on My behalf is not from man. But I simply mention all these things in order that you may be saved (made *and* kept safe *and* sound).

35 John was the lamp that kept on burning and shining [to show you the way], and you were willing for a while to delight (sun) yourselves in his light.

36 But I have as My witness something greater (weightier, higher, better) than that of John; for the works that the Father has appointed Me to accomplish *and* finish, the very same works that I am now doing, are a witness *and* proof that the Father has sent Me.

37 And the Father Who sent Me has Himself testified concerning Me. Not one of you has ever given ears to His voice, or seen His form (His face, what He is like).—You have always been deaf to His voice and blind to the vision of Him.

**AMP** [a] Vincent's "Word Studies in The New Testament."

## New American Standard

19¶ Jesus therefore answered and was saying to them, "Truly, truly, I say to you, the Son can do nothing of Himself, unless *it is* something He sees the Father doing; for whatever *the Father* does, these things the Son also does in like manner.

20"For the Father loves the Son, and shows Him all things that He Himself is doing; and greater works than these will He show Him, that you may marvel.

21"For just as the Father raises the dead and gives them life, even so the Son also gives life to whom He wishes.

22"For not even the Father judges anyone, but He has given all judgment to the Son,

23in order that all may honor the Son, even as they honor the Father. He who does not honor the Son does not honor the Father who sent Him.

24"Truly, truly, I say to you, he who hears My word, and believes Him who sent Me, has eternal life, and does not come into judgment, but has passed out of death into life.

*Two Resurrections*

25"Truly, truly, I say to you, an hour is coming and now is, when the dead shall hear the voice of the Son of God; and those who hear shall live.

26"For just as the Father has life in Himself, even so He gave to the Son also to have life in Himself;

27and He gave Him authority to execute judgment, because He is *the* Son of Man.

28"Do not marvel at this; for an hour is coming, in which all who are in the tombs shall hear His voice,

29and shall come forth; those who did the good *deeds* to a resurrection of life, those who committed the evil *deeds* to a resurrection of judgment.

30¶ "I can do nothing on My own initiative. As I hear, I judge; and My judgment is just, because I do not seek My own will, but the will of Him who sent Me.

31"If I *alone* bear witness of Myself, My testimony is not true.

32"There is another who bears witness of Me, and I know that the testimony which He bears of Me is true.

*Witness of John*

33"You have sent to John, and he has borne witness to the truth.

34"But the witness which I receive is not from man, but I say these things that you may be saved.

35"He was the lamp that was burning and was shining and you were willing to rejoice for a while in his light.

*Witness of Works*

36"But the witness which I have is greater than *that of* John; for the works which the Father has given Me to accomplish, the very works that I do, bear witness of Me, that the Father has sent Me.

*Witness of the Father*

37"And the Father who sent Me, He has borne witness of Me. You have neither heard His voice at any time, nor seen His form.

## New International

19Jesus gave them this answer: "I tell you the truth, the Son can
do nothing by himself; he can do only what he sees his Father
doing, because whatever the Father does the Son also does. 20For
the Father loves the Son and shows him all he does. Yes, to your
amazement he will show him even greater things than these. 21For
just as the Father raises the dead and gives them life, even so the
Son gives life to whom he is pleased to give it. 22Moreover, the
Father judges no one, but has entrusted all judgment to the Son,
23that all may honor the Son just as they honor the Father. He who
does not honor the Son does not honor the Father, who sent him.

24"I tell you the truth, whoever hears my word and believes him
who sent me has eternal life and will not be condemned; he has
crossed over from death to life. 25I tell you the truth, a time is
coming and has now come when the dead will hear the voice of
the Son of God and those who hear will live. 26For as the Father
has life in himself, so he has granted the Son to have life in himself.
27And he has given him authority to judge because he is the Son
of Man.

28"Do not be amazed at this, for a time is coming when all who
are in their graves will hear his voice 29and come out—those who
have done good will rise to live, and those who have done evil will
rise to be condemned. 30By myself I can do nothing; I judge only
as I hear, and my judgment is just, for I seek not to please myself
but him who sent me.

*Testimonies About Jesus*

31"If I testify about myself, my testimony is not valid. 32There
is another who testifies in my favor, and I know that his testimony
about me is valid.

33"You have sent to John and he has testified to the truth. 34Not
that I accept human testimony; but I mention it that you may be
saved. 35John was a lamp that burned and gave light, and you
chose for a time to enjoy his light.

36"I have testimony weightier than that of John. For the very
work that the Father has given me to finish, and which I am doing,
testifies that the Father has sent me. 37And the Father who sent
me has himself testified concerning me. You have never heard his
voice nor seen his form, 38nor does his word dwell in you, for you

## King James

38And ye have not his word abiding in you: for whom he hath sent, him ye believe not.

39¶ Search the scriptures; for in them ye think ye have eternal life: and they are they which testify of me.

40And ye will not come to me, that ye might have life.

41I receive not honour from men.

42But I know you, that ye have not the love of God in you.

43I am come in my Father's name, and ye receive me not: if another shall come in his own name, him ye will receive.

44How can ye believe, which receive honour one of another, and seek not the honour that *cometh* from God only?

45Do not think that I will accuse you to the Father: there is *one* that accuseth you, *even* Moses, in whom ye trust.

46For had ye believed Moses, ye would have believed me: for he wrote of me.

47But if ye believe not his writings, how shall ye believe my words?

6 AFTER THESE things Jesus went over the sea of Galilee, which is *the sea* of Tiberias.

2And a great multitude followed him, because they saw his miracles which he did on them that were diseased.

3And Jesus went up into a mountain, and there he sat with his disciples.

4And the passover, a feast of the Jews, was nigh.

5¶ When Jesus then lifted up *his* eyes, and saw a great company come unto him, he saith unto Philip, Whence shall we buy bread, that these may eat?

6And this he said to prove him: for he himself knew what he would do.

7Philip answered him, Two hundred pennyworth of bread is not sufficient for them, that every one of them may take a little.

8One of his disciples, Andrew, Simon Peter's brother, saith unto him,

9There is a lad here, which hath five barley loaves, and two small fishes: but what are they among so many?

10And Jesus said, Make the men sit down. Now there was much grass in the place. So the men sat down, in number about five thousand.

11And Jesus took the loaves; and when he had given thanks, he distributed to the disciples, and the disciples to them that were set down; and likewise of the fishes as much as they would.

12When they were filled, he said unto his disciples, Gather up the fragments that remain, that nothing be lost.

13Therefore they gathered *them* together, and filled twelve baskets with the fragments of the five barley loaves, which remained over and above unto them that had eaten.

## Amplified

38And you have not His word (His thought) living in your hearts, because you do not believe *and* adhere to, *and* trust in, *and* rely on Him Whom He has sent.—That is why you do not keep His message living in you, because you do not believe in the Messenger Whom He has sent.

39You search *and* investigate *and* pore over the Scriptures diligently, because you suppose *and* trust that you have eternal life through them. And these [very Scriptures] testify about Me!

40And still you are not willing (but refuse) to come to Me, so that you might have life.

41I receive not glory from men—I crave no human honor, I look for no mortal fame.

42But I know you *and* recognize *and* understand that you have not the love of God in you.

43I have come in My Father's name *and* with His power and you do not receive Me—your hearts are not open to Me, you give Me no welcome. But if another comes in his own name *and* his own power *and* with no other authority but himself, you will receive him *and* give him your approval.

44How is it possible for you to believe—how can you learn to believe—who [are content to seek for and] receive praise *and* honor *and* glory from one another, and do not seek the praise *and* honor *and* glory which come from Him Who alone is God?

45Put out of your minds the thought *and* do not suppose [as some of you are supposing] that I will accuse you to the Father. There is one who accuses you; it is Moses, the very one on whom you have built your hopes—in whom you trust.

46For if you believed in *and* relied on Moses, you would believe in *and* rely on Me, for he wrote about Me [personally].

47But if you do not believe *and* trust his writings, how then will you believe *and* trust My teachings—how shall you cleave to *and* rely on My words?

6 AFTER THIS Jesus went to the farther side of the Sea of Galilee, that is, the Sea of Tiberias.

2And a great crowd was following Him because they had seen the signs (miracles) which He [continually] performed upon those who were sick.

3And Jesus walked up the mountain side and sat down there with His disciples.

4Now the Passover, the feast of the Jews, was approaching.

5Jesus looked up, then, and seeing that a vast multitude was coming toward Him, He said to Philip, Where are we to buy bread, so that all these people may eat?

6But He said this to prove (test) him, for He well knew what He was about to do.

7Philip answered Him, Two hundred pennies' [forty dollars'] worth of bread is not enough that every one may receive even a little.

8Another of His disciples, Andrew, Simon Peter's brother, said to Him,

9There is a little boy here, who has [with him] five barley loaves and two small fish; but what are they among so many people?

10Jesus said, Make all the people recline (sit down). Now the ground [a pasture] was covered with thick grass at the spot, so the men threw themselves down, about five thousand in number.

11Jesus took the loaves and when He had given thanks He distributed *to the disciples and the disciples* to the reclining people; so also with the small fish, as much as they wanted.

12When they all had enough, He said to His disciples, Gather up now the fragments—the broken pieces that are left over—so that nothing may be lost *and* wasted.

13So accordingly they gathered them up, and they filled twelve [a]hand baskets with fragments left over by those who had eaten from the five barley loaves.

AMP [a] Abbott-Smith.

## New American Standard

38"And you do not have His word abiding in you, for you do
not believe Him whom He sent.

*Witness of the Scripture*

39"[b]You search the Scriptures, because you think that in them
you have eternal life; and it is these that bear witness of Me;
40and you are unwilling to come to Me, that you may have life.
41"I do not receive glory from men;
42but I know you, that you do not have the love of God in
yourselves.
43"I have come in My Father's name, and you do not receive
Me; if another shall come in his own name, you will receive him.
44"How can you believe, when you receive glory from one
another, and you do not seek the glory that is from the *one and* only
God?
45"Do not think that I will accuse you before the Father; the one
who accuses you is Moses, in whom you have set your hope.
46"For if you believed Moses, you would believe Me; for he
wrote of Me.
47"But if you do not believe his writings, how will you believe
My words?"

*Five Thousand Fed*

6 AFTER THESE things Jesus went away to the other side of the
Sea of Galilee (or Tiberias).
2And a great multitude was following Him, because they were
seeing the signs which He was performing on those who were sick.
3And Jesus went up on the mountain, and there He sat with
His disciples.
4Now the Passover, the feast of the Jews, was at hand.
5Jesus therefore lifting up His eyes, and seeing that a great
multitude was coming to Him, *said to Philip, "Where are we to
buy bread, that these may eat?"
6And this He was saying to test him; for He Himself knew what
He was intending to do.
7Philip answered Him, "Two hundred [c]denarii worth of bread
is not sufficient for them, for everyone to receive a little."
8One of His disciples, Andrew, Simon Peter's brother, *said to
Him,
9"There is a lad here who has five barley loaves and two fish,
but what are these for so many people?"
10Jesus said, "Have the people sit down." Now there was much
grass in the place. So the men sat down, in number about five
thousand.
11Jesus therefore took the loaves; and having given thanks, He
distributed to those who were seated; likewise also of the fish as
much as they wanted.
12And when they were filled, He *said to His disciples, "Gather
up the leftover fragments that nothing may be lost."
13And so they gathered them up, and filled twelve baskets with
fragments from the five barley loaves, which were left over by
those who had eaten.

NAS [b] Or, (a command) *Search the Scriptures!* [c] The denarius was equivalent
to one day's wage

## New International

do not believe the one he sent. 39You diligently study[d] the Scriptures because you think that by them you possess eternal life.
These are the Scriptures that testify about me, 40yet you refuse to
come to me to have life.
41"I do not accept praise from men, 42but I know you. I know
that you do not have the love of God in your hearts. 43I have come
in my Father's name, and you do not accept me; but if someone
else comes in his own name, you will accept him. 44How can you
believe if you accept praise from one another, yet make no effort
to obtain the praise that comes from the only God[e]?
45"But do not think I will accuse you before the Father. Your
accuser is Moses, on whom your hopes are set. 46If you believed
Moses, you would believe me, for he wrote about me. 47But since
you do not believe what he wrote, how are you going to believe
what I say?"

*Jesus Feeds the Five Thousand*

6 SOME TIME after this, Jesus crossed to the far shore of the
Sea of Galilee (that is, the Sea of Tiberias), 2and a great crowd
of people followed him because they saw the miraculous signs he
had performed on the sick. 3Then Jesus went up on a mountainside and sat down with his disciples. 4The Jewish Passover Feast
was near.
5When Jesus looked up and saw a great crowd coming toward
him, he said to Philip, "Where shall we buy bread for these people
to eat?" 6He asked this only to test him, for he already had in mind
what he was going to do.
7Philip answered him, "Eight months' wages[f] would not buy
enough bread for each one to have a bite!"
8Another of his disciples, Andrew, Simon Peter's brother,
spoke up, 9"Here is a boy with five small barley loaves and two
small fish, but how far will they go among so many?"
10Jesus said, "Have the people sit down." There was plenty of
grass in that place, and the men sat down, about five thousand of
them. 11Jesus then took the loaves, gave thanks, and distributed
to those who were seated as much as they wanted. He did the
same with the fish.
12When they had all had enough to eat, he said to his disciples,
"Gather the pieces that are left over. Let nothing be wasted." 13So
they gathered them and filled twelve baskets with the pieces of the
five barley loaves left over by those who had eaten.

NIV [d] 39 Or *Study diligently* (the imperative) [e] 44 Some early manuscripts
*the Only One* [f] 7 Greek *two hundred denarii*

# King James

14 Then those men, when they had seen the miracle that Jesus did, said, This is of a truth that prophet that should come into the world.

15 ¶ When Jesus therefore perceived that they would come and take him by force, to make him a king, he departed again into a mountain himself alone.

16 And when even was *now* come, his disciples went down unto the sea,

17 And entered into a ship, and went over the sea toward Capernaum. And it was now dark, and Jesus was not come to them.

18 And the sea arose by reason of a great wind that blew.

19 So when they had rowed about five and twenty or thirty furlongs, they see Jesus walking on the sea, and drawing nigh unto the ship: and they were afraid.

20 But he saith unto them, It is I; be not afraid.

21 Then they willingly received him into the ship: and immediately the ship was at the land whither they went.

22 ¶ The day following, when the people which stood on the other side of the sea saw that there was none other boat there, save that one whereinto his disciples were entered, and that Jesus went not with his disciples into the boat, but *that* his disciples were gone away alone;

23 (Howbeit there came other boats from Tiberias nigh unto the place where they did eat bread, after that the Lord had given thanks:)

24 When the people therefore saw that Jesus was not there, neither his disciples, they also took shipping, and came to Capernaum, seeking for Jesus.

25 And when they had found him on the other side of the sea, they said unto him, Rabbi, when camest thou hither?

26 Jesus answered them and said, Verily, verily, I say unto you, Ye seek me, not because ye saw the miracles, but because ye did eat of the loaves, and were filled.

27 Labour not for the meat which perisheth, but for that meat which endureth unto everlasting life, which the Son of man shall give unto you: for him hath God the Father sealed.

28 Then said they unto him, What shall we do, that we might work the works of God?

29 Jesus answered and said unto them, This is the work of God, that ye believe on him whom he hath sent.

30 They said therefore unto him, What sign showest thou then, that we may see, and believe thee? what dost thou work?

31 Our fathers did eat manna in the desert; as it is written, He gave them bread from heaven to eat.

32 Then Jesus said unto them, Verily, verily, I say unto you, Moses gave you not that bread from heaven; but my Father giveth you the true bread from heaven.

33 For the bread of God is he which cometh down from heaven, and giveth life unto the world.

34 Then said they unto him, Lord, evermore give us this bread.

35 And Jesus said unto them, I am the bread of life: he that cometh to me shall never hunger; and he that believeth on me shall never thirst.

36 But I said unto you, That ye also have seen me, and believe not.

# Amplified

14 When the people saw the sign (miracle) that Jesus had performed, they began saying, Surely *and* beyond a doubt this is the prophet who is to come into the world! [Deut. 18:18.]

15 Then Jesus, knowing that they meant to come and seize Him that they might make Him king, withdrew again to the hillside, Himself alone.

16 When evening came, His disciples went down to the sea.

17 And they took a boat and were going across the sea to Capernaum. It was now dark, and still Jesus had not [yet] come back to them.

18 Meanwhile the sea was getting rough *and* rising high because of a great *and* violent wind that was blowing.

19 [However,] when they had rowed three or four miles they saw Jesus walking on the sea and approaching the boat. And they were afraid—terrified.

20 But Jesus said to them, It is I; be not afraid!—I AM; stop being frightened! [Exod. 3:14.]

21 Then they were quite willing *and* glad for Him to come into the boat. And now the boat went at once to the land they steered for—and immediately they reached the shore toward which they had been [slowly] making.

22 The next day the crowd [that still remained] standing on the other side of the sea, realized that there had been only one small boat there, and that Jesus had not gone into it with His disciples, but that His disciples had gone away by themselves.

23 But now some other boats from Tiberias had come in near the place where they ate the bread after the Lord had given thanks.

24 So the people, finding that neither Jesus nor His disciples were there, themselves got into the small boats and came to Capernaum looking for Jesus.

25 And when they found Him on the other side of the lake, they said to Him, Rabbi! When did You come here?

26 Jesus answered them, I assure you, most solemnly I tell you, you have been searching for Me not because you saw the miracles *and* signs, but because you were fed with the loaves and were filled *and* satisfied.

27 Stop toiling *and* doing *and* producing for the food that perishes *and* decomposes in the using; but strive *and* work *and* produce rather for the lasting food which endures continually unto life eternal. The Son of man will give (furnish) you that, for God the Father has authorized *and* certified Him *and* put His seal of endorsement upon Him.

28 They then said, What are we to do that we may [habitually] be working the works of God?—What are we to do to carry out what God requires?

29 Jesus replied, This is the work (service) that God asks of you, that you believe in the One Whom He has sent—that you cleave to, trust, rely on and have faith in His Messenger.

30 Therefore they said to Him, What sign (miracle, wonderwork) will [a]You perform then, so that we may see it and believe *and* rely on *and* adhere to You?—What [supernatural] work have You to show what You can do?

31 Our forefathers ate the manna in the wilderness. As the Scripture says, He gave them bread out of heaven to eat. [Exod. 16:15; Ps. 78:24.]

32 Jesus then said to them, I assure you, I most solemnly tell you, Moses did not give you the bread from heaven—what Moses gave you was not the Bread from heaven—but it is My Father Who gives you the true, heavenly Bread.

33 For the Bread of God is He Who comes down out of heaven and gives life to the world.

34 Then they said to Him, Lord, give us this bread always—all the time!

35 Jesus replied, I am the Bread of Life. He who comes to Me will never be hungry and he who believes on *and* cleaves to *and* trusts in *and* relies on Me will never thirst any more—at any time.

36 But [as] I told you, Although you have seen *Me,* still you do not believe *and* trust *and* have faith.

**AMP** [a] Capitalized because of what He is, the spotless Son of God, not what the speaker may have thought He was.

## New American Standard

14When therefore the people saw the sign which He had performed, they said, "This is of a truth the Prophet who is to come into the world."

*Jesus Walks on the Water*

15¶ Jesus therefore perceiving that they were intending to come and take Him by force, to make Him king, withdrew again to the mountain by Himself alone.

16¶ Now when evening came, His disciples went down to the sea,

17and after getting into a boat, they *started to* cross the sea to Capernaum. And it had already become dark, and Jesus had not yet come to them.

18And the sea *began* to be stirred up because a strong wind was blowing.

19When therefore they had rowed about three or four miles, they *beheld Jesus walking on the sea and drawing near to the boat; and they were frightened.

20But He *said to them, "It is I; do not be afraid."

21They were willing therefore to receive Him into the boat; and immediately the boat was at the land to which they were going.

22¶ The next day the multitude that stood on the other side of the sea saw that there was no other small boat there, except one, and that Jesus had not entered with His disciples into the boat, but *that* His disciples had gone away alone.

23There came other small boats from Tiberias near to the place where they ate the bread after the Lord had given thanks.

24When the multitude therefore saw that Jesus was not there, nor His disciples, they themselves got into the small boats, and came to Capernaum, seeking Jesus.

25And when they found Him on the other side of the sea, they said to Him, "Rabbi, when did You get here?"

*Words to the People*

26Jesus answered them and said, "Truly, truly, I say to you, you seek Me, not because you saw signs, but because you ate of the loaves, and were filled.

27"Do not work for the food which perishes, but for the food which endures to eternal life, which the Son of Man shall give to you, for on Him the Father, *even* God, has set His seal."

28They said therefore to Him, "What shall we do, that we may work the works of God?"

29Jesus answered and said to them, "This is the work of God, that you believe in Him whom He has sent."

30They said therefore to Him, "What then do You do for a sign, that we may see, and believe You? What work do You perform?

31"Our fathers ate the manna in the wilderness; as it is written, 'HE GAVE THEM BREAD OUT OF HEAVEN TO EAT.' "

32Jesus therefore said to them, "Truly, truly, I say to you, it is not Moses who has given you the bread out of heaven, but it is My Father who gives you the true bread out of heaven.

33"For the bread of God is [b]that which comes down out of heaven, and gives life to the world."

34They said therefore to Him, "Lord, evermore give us this bread."

35Jesus said to them, "I am the bread of life; he who comes to Me shall not hunger, and he who believes in Me shall never thirst.

36"But I said to you, that you have seen Me, and yet do not believe.

NAS [b] Or, *He who comes*

## New International

14After the people saw the miraculous sign that Jesus did, they
began to say, "Surely this is the Prophet who is to come into the
world." 15Jesus, knowing that they intended to come and make
him king by force, withdrew again to a mountain by himself.

*Jesus Walks on the Water*

16When evening came, his disciples went down to the lake,
17where they got into a boat and set off across the lake for Capernaum. By now it was dark, and Jesus had not yet joined them. 18A
strong wind was blowing and the waters grew rough. 19When they
had rowed three or three and a half miles,[c] they saw Jesus approaching the boat, walking on the water; and they were terrified.
20But he said to them, "It is I; don't be afraid." 21Then they were
willing to take him into the boat, and immediately the boat reached
the shore where they were heading.
22The next day the crowd that had stayed on the opposite shore
of the lake realized that only one boat had been there, and that
Jesus had not entered it with his disciples, but that they had gone
away alone. 23Then some boats from Tiberias landed near the place
where the people had eaten the bread after the Lord had given
thanks. 24Once the crowd realized that neither Jesus nor his disciples were there, they got into the boats and went to Capernaum
in search of Jesus.

*Jesus the Bread of Life*

25When they found him on the other side of the lake, they asked
him, "Rabbi, when did you get here?"
26Jesus answered, "I tell you the truth, you are looking for me,
not because you saw miraculous signs but because you ate the
loaves and had your fill. 27Do not work for food that spoils, but
for food that endures to eternal life, which the Son of Man will give
you. On him God the Father has placed his seal of approval."
28Then they asked him, "What must we do to do the works God
requires?"
29Jesus answered, "The work of God is this: to believe in the one
he has sent."
30So they asked him, "What miraculous sign then will you give
that we may see it and believe you? What will you do? 31Our
forefathers ate the manna in the desert; as it is written: 'He gave
them bread from heaven to eat.'[d]"
32Jesus said to them, "I tell you the truth, it is not Moses who
has given you the bread from heaven, but it is my Father who gives
you the true bread from heaven. 33For the bread of God is he who
comes down from heaven and gives life to the world."
34"Sir," they said, "from now on give us this bread."
35Then Jesus declared, "I am the bread of life. He who comes
to me will never go hungry, and he who believes in me will never
be thirsty. 36But as I told you, you have seen me and still you do
not believe. 37All that the Father gives me will come to me, and

NIV [c] *19* Greek *rowed twenty-five or thirty stadia* (about 5 or 6 kilometers)
[d] *31* Exodus 16:4; Neh. 9:15; Psalm 78:24,25

## King James

37 All that the Father giveth me shall come to me; and him that cometh to me I will in no wise cast out.

38 For I came down from heaven, not to do mine own will, but the will of him that sent me.

39 And this is the Father's will which hath sent me, that of all which he hath given me I should lose nothing, but should raise it up again at the last day.

40 And this is the will of him that sent me, that every one which seeth the Son, and believeth on him, may have everlasting life: and I will raise him up at the last day.

41 The Jews then murmured at him, because he said, I am the bread which came down from heaven.

42 And they said, Is not this Jesus, the son of Joseph, whose father and mother we know? how is it then that he saith, I came down from heaven?

43 Jesus therefore answered and said unto them, Murmur not among yourselves.

44 No man can come to me, except the Father which hath sent me draw him: and I will raise him up at the last day.

45 It is written in the prophets, And they shall be all taught of God. Every man therefore that hath heard, and hath learned of the Father, cometh unto me.

46 Not that any man hath seen the Father, save he which is of God, he hath seen the Father.

47 Verily, verily, I say unto you, He that believeth on me hath everlasting life.

48 I am that bread of life.

49 Your fathers did eat manna in the wilderness, and are dead.

50 This is the bread which cometh down from heaven, that a man may eat thereof, and not die.

51 I am the living bread which came down from heaven: if any man eat of this bread, he shall live for ever: and the bread that I will give is my flesh, which I will give for the life of the world.

52 The Jews therefore strove among themselves, saying, How can this man give us *his* flesh to eat?

53 Then Jesus said unto them, Verily, verily, I say unto you, Except ye eat the flesh of the Son of man, and drink his blood, ye have no life in you.

54 Whoso eateth my flesh, and drinketh my blood, hath eternal life; and I will raise him up at the last day.

55 For my flesh is meat indeed, and my blood is drink indeed.

56 He that eateth my flesh, and drinketh my blood, dwelleth in me, and I in him.

57 As the living Father hath sent me, and I live by the Father: so he that eateth me, even he shall live by me.

58 This is that bread which came down from heaven: not as your fathers did eat manna, and are dead: he that eateth of this bread shall live for ever.

59 These things said he in the synagogue, as he taught in Capernaum.

60 Many therefore of his disciples, when they had heard *this,* said, This is an hard saying; who can hear it?

## Amplified

37 All whom My Father has given (entrusted) to Me will come to Me; and him who comes to Me I will most certainly not cast out—I will never, no never reject one of them who comes to Me.

38 For I have come down from heaven, not to do My own will *and* purpose; but to do the will *and* purpose of Him Who sent Me.

39 And this is the will of Him Who sent Me, that I should not lose any of all that He has given Me; but that I should give new life *and* raise [them all] up at the last day.

40 For this is My Father's will *and* His purpose, that every one who sees the Son and believes *and* cleaves to *and* trusts *and* relies on Him should have eternal life, and I will raise him up [from the dead] at the last day.

41 Now the Jews murmured *and* found fault *and* grumbled about Jesus because He said, I am [Myself] the Bread which came down from heaven.

42 They kept asking, Is not this Jesus, the [a]Son of Joseph, Whose father and mother we know? How then can He say, I have come down from heaven?

43 So Jesus answered them, Stop grumbling *and* saying things against Me to one another.

44 No one is able to come to Me unless the Father Who sent Me attracts *and* draws him *and* gives him the desire to come to Me; and [then] I will raise him [from the dead] at the last day.

45 It is written in the book of the prophets, And they shall all be taught of God—have Him in person for their teacher. Every one, who has listened and learned from the Father, comes to Me. [Isa. 54:13.]

46 Which does not imply that any one has seen the Father—not that any one has ever seen Him—except He [Who was with the Father] Who comes from God. He [alone] has seen the Father.

47 I assure you, I most solemnly tell you, he who believes *in Me*—who adheres to, trusts in, relies on and has faith in Me—has (now possesses) eternal life.

48 I am the Bread of life—that gives life, the Living Bread.

49 Your forefathers ate the manna in the wilderness, and [yet] they died.

50 [But] this is the Bread that comes down from heaven, so that (any) one may eat of it and never die.

51 I [Myself] am this Living Bread which came down from heaven. If any one eats of this Bread, he will live forever; and also the Bread that I shall give for the life of the world is My flesh (body).

52 Then the Jews angrily contended with one another saying, How is He able to give us His flesh to eat?

53 And Jesus said to them, I assure you, most solemnly I tell you, you cannot have any life in yourselves unless you eat the flesh of the Son of man and drink His blood—unless you appropriate His life and [the saving merit of] His blood.

54 He who feeds on My flesh and drinks My blood has (possesses now) eternal life; and I will raise him up [from the dead] on the last day.

55 For My flesh is true *and* genuine food; and My blood is true *and* genuine drink.

56 He who feeds on My flesh and drinks My blood dwells continually in Me, and I [in like manner dwell continually] in him.

57 Just as the living Father sent Me, and I live by (through, because of) the Father, even so whoever continues to feed on Me—who takes Me for his food *and* is nourished by Me—shall [in his turn] live through *and* because of Me.

58 This is the Bread which came down from heaven. It is not like the manna which our forefathers ate and yet died. He who takes this Bread for his food shall live forever.

59 He said these things in a synagogue while He was teaching at Capernaum.

60 When His disciples heard this, many of them said, This is a hard *and* difficult *and* strange saying—an offensive and unbearable message. Who can stand to hear it?—Who can be expected to listen to such teaching?

**AMP** [a] Capitalized because of what He is, the spotless Son of God, not what the speaker may have thought He was.

## New American Standard

37"All that the Father gives Me shall come to Me, and the one who comes to Me I will certainly not cast out.

38"For I have come down from heaven, not to do My own will, but the will of Him who sent Me.

39"And this is the will of Him who sent Me, that of all that He has given Me I lose nothing, but raise it up on the last day.

40"For this is the will of My Father, that everyone who beholds the Son and believes in Him, may have eternal life; and I Myself will raise him up on the last day."

*Words to the Jews*

41¶ The Jews therefore were grumbling about Him, because He said, "I am the bread that came down out of heaven."

42And they were saying, "Is not this Jesus, the son of Joseph, whose father and mother we know? How does He now say, 'I have come down out of heaven'?"

43Jesus answered and said to them, "Do not grumble among yourselves.

44"No one can come to Me, unless the Father who sent Me draws him; and I will raise him up on the last day.

45"It is written in the prophets, 'AND THEY SHALL ALL BE TAUGHT OF GOD.' Everyone who has heard and learned from the Father, comes to Me.

46"Not that any man has seen the Father, except the One who is from God; He has seen the Father.

47"Truly, truly, I say to you, he who believes has eternal life.

48"I am the bread of life.

49"Your fathers ate the manna in the wilderness, and they died.

50"This is the bread which comes down out of heaven, so that one may eat of it and not die.

51"I am the living bread that came down out of heaven; if anyone eats of this bread, he shall live forever; and the bread also which I shall give for the life of the world is My flesh."

52¶ The Jews therefore *began* to argue with one another, saying, "How can this man give us *His* flesh to eat?"

53Jesus therefore said to them, "Truly, truly, I say to you, unless you eat the flesh of the Son of Man and drink His blood, you have no life in yourselves.

54"He who eats My flesh and drinks My blood has eternal life, and I will raise him up on the last day.

55"For My flesh is true food, and My blood is true drink.

56"He who eats My flesh and drinks My blood abides in Me, and I in him.

57"As the living Father sent Me, and I live because of the Father, so he who eats Me, he also shall live because of Me.

58"This is the bread which came down out of heaven; not as the fathers ate, and died, he who eats this bread shall live forever."

*Words to the Disciples*

59These things He said in the synagogue, as He taught in Capernaum.

60¶ Many therefore of His disciples, when they heard *this* said, "This is a difficult statement; who can listen to it?"

## New International

whoever comes to me I will never drive away.
38For I have come down from heaven not to do my will but to do the will of him who sent me.
39And this is the will of him who sent me, that I shall lose none of all that he has given me, but raise them up at the last day.
40For my Father's will is that everyone who looks to the Son and believes in him shall have eternal life, and I will raise him up at the last day."

41At this the Jews began to grumble about him because he said, "I am the bread that came down from heaven."
42They said, "Is this not Jesus, the son of Joseph, whose father and mother we know? How can he now say, 'I came down from heaven'?"

43"Stop grumbling among yourselves," Jesus answered.
44"No one can come to me unless the Father who sent me draws him, and I will raise him up at the last day.
45It is written in the Prophets: 'They will all be taught by God.'[b] Everyone who listens to the Father and learns from him comes to me.
46No one has seen the Father except the one who is from God; only he has seen the Father.
47I tell you the truth, he who believes has everlasting life.
48I am the bread of life.
49Your forefathers ate the manna in the desert, yet they died.
50But here is the bread that comes down from heaven, which a man may eat and not die.
51I am the living bread that came down from heaven. If anyone eats of this bread, he will live forever. This bread is my flesh, which I will give for the life of the world."

52Then the Jews began to argue sharply among themselves, "How can this man give us his flesh to eat?"

53Jesus said to them, "I tell you the truth, unless you eat the flesh of the Son of Man and drink his blood, you have no life in you.
54Whoever eats my flesh and drinks my blood has eternal life, and I will raise him up at the last day.
55For my flesh is real food and my blood is real drink.
56Whoever eats my flesh and drinks my blood remains in me, and I in him.
57Just as the living Father sent me and I live because of the Father, so the one who feeds on me will live because of me.
58This is the bread that came down from heaven. Your forefathers ate manna and died, but he who feeds on this bread will live forever."
59He said this while teaching in the synagogue in Capernaum.

*Many Disciples Desert Jesus*

60On hearing it, many of his disciples said, "This is a hard teaching. Who can accept it?"

NIV [b] *45* Isaiah 54:13

## King James

61When Jesus knew in himself that his disciples murmured at it, he said unto them, Doth this offend you?
62 *What* and if ye shall see the Son of man ascend up where he was before?
63It is the spirit that quickeneth; the flesh profiteth nothing: the words that I speak unto you, *they* are spirit, and *they* are life.
64But there are some of you that believe not. For Jesus knew from the beginning who they were that believed not, and who should betray him.
65And he said, Therefore said I unto you, that no man can come unto me, except it were given unto him of my Father.
66¶ From that *time* many of his disciples went back, and walked no more with him.
67Then said Jesus unto the twelve, Will ye also go away?
68Then Simon Peter answered him, Lord, to whom shall we go? thou hast the words of eternal life.
69And we believe and are sure that thou art that Christ, the Son of the living God.
70Jesus answered them, Have not I chosen you twelve, and one of you is a devil?
71He spake of Judas Iscariot *the son* of Simon: for he it was that should betray him, being one of the twelve.

**7** AFTER THESE things Jesus walked in Galilee: for he would not walk in Jewry, because the Jews sought to kill him.
2Now the Jews' feast of tabernacles was at hand.
3His brethren therefore said unto him, Depart hence, and go into Judaea, that thy disciples also may see the works that thou doest.
4For *there is* no man *that* doeth any thing in secret, and he himself seeketh to be known openly. If thou do these things, show thyself to the world.
5For neither did his brethren believe in him.
6Then Jesus said unto them, My time is not yet come: but your time is always ready.
7The world cannot hate you; but me it hateth, because I testify of it, that the works thereof are evil.
8Go ye up unto this feast: I go not up yet unto this feast; for my time is not yet full come.
9When he had said these words unto them, he abode *still* in Galilee.
10¶ But when his brethren were gone up, then went he also up unto the feast, not openly, but as it were in secret.
11Then the Jews sought him at the feast, and said, Where is he?
12And there was much murmuring among the people concerning him: for some said, He is a good man: others said, Nay; but he deceiveth the people.
13Howbeit no man spake openly of him for fear of the Jews.
14¶ Now about the midst of the feast Jesus went up into the temple, and taught.

## Amplified

61But Jesus, knowing in Himself that His disciples were complaining *and* protesting *and* grumbling about it, said to them: Is this a stumbling block *and* an offense to you?—Does this upset and displease and shock and scandalize you?
62What then [will be your reaction] if you should see the Son of man ascending to the place where He was before?
63It is the Spirit that gives life—He is the Life-giver; the flesh conveys no benefit whatever—there is no profit in it. The words (truths) that I have been speaking to you are spirit and life.
64But [still] some of you fail to believe *and* trust *and* have faith. For Jesus knew from the first who did not believe *and* had no faith, and who would betray Him *and* be false to Him.
65And He said, This is why I told you that no one can come to Me unless it is granted him—unless he is enabled to do so—by the Father.
66After this many of His disciples drew back—returned to their old associations—and no longer accompanied Him.
67Jesus said to the twelve, Will you also go away? *And* do you too desire to leave Me?
68Simon Peter answered, Lord, to whom shall we go? You have the words (the message) of eternal life.
69And we have learned to believe *and* trust; and [more,] we have come to know [surely] that You are the Christ, the Anointed One, the Son of the living God.
70Jesus answered them, Did I not choose you, the twelve? And [even] of you one is a devil—of the evil one and a false accuser.
71He was speaking of Judas, the son of Simon Iscariot, for he was about to betray Him, [although] he was one of the twelve.

**7** AFTER THIS Jesus went from place to place in Galilee; for He would not travel in Judea, because the Jews sought to kill Him.
2Now the Jewish Feast of Tabernacles was drawing near.
3So His brothers said to Him, Leave here and go into Judea, so that [a]Your disciples [there] may also see the works that You do. [This is no place for You.]
4For no one does anything in secret, when he wishes to be conspicuous *and* secure publicity. If You [must] do these things—if [b]You must act like this—show Yourself openly *and* make Yourself known to the world!
5For His brothers did not believe in *or* adhere to *or* trust in *or* rely on Him either.
6Whereupon Jesus said to them, My time (opportunity) has not come yet; but any time is suitable for you *and* your opportunity is ready any time—is always here.
7The world cannot [be expected to] hate you, but it does hate Me, because I denounce it for its wicked works *and* reveal that its doings are evil.
8Go to the feast yourselves. I am not [yet] going up to the festival, because My time is not ripe—My term is not yet completed, it is not time for Me to go.
9Having said these things to them, He stayed behind in Galilee.
10But afterward, when His brothers had gone up to the feast, He went up also; not publicly, [not with a caravan] but by Himself quietly *and* as if He did not wish to be observed.
11Therefore the Jews kept looking for Him at the feast and asking, Where can He be?—Where is that Fellow?
12And there was among the mass of the people much whispered discussion *and* hot disputing about Him. Some were saying, He is good!—He is a good man! Others said, No, He misleads *and* deceives the people—gives them false ideas!
13But no one dared speak out boldly about Him for fear of [the leaders of] the Jews.
14When the feast was already half over, Jesus went up into the temple [c]court and began to teach.

**AMP** [a] Capitalized because of what He is, the spotless Son of God, not what the speaker may have thought He was. [b] Capitalized because of what He is, the spotless Son of God, not what the speaker may have thought He was. [c] Trench.

## New American Standard

61But Jesus, conscious that His disciples grumbled at this, said
to them, "Does this cause you to stumble?
62 "*What* then if you should behold the Son of Man ascending
where He was before?
63"It is the Spirit who gives life; the flesh profits nothing; the
words that I have spoken to you are spirit and are life.
64"But there are some of you who do not believe." For Jesus
knew from the beginning who they were who did not believe, and
who it was that would betray Him.
65And He was saying, "For this reason I have said to you, that
no one can come to Me, unless it has been granted him from the
Father."

*Peter's Confession of Faith*

66¶ As a result of this many of His disciples withdrew, and were
not walking with Him anymore.
67Jesus said therefore to the twelve, "You do not want to go
away also, do you?"
68Simon Peter answered Him, "Lord, to whom shall we go? You
have words of eternal life.
69"And we have believed and have come to know that You are
the Holy One of God."
70Jesus answered them, "Did I Myself not choose you, the
twelve, and *yet* one of you is a devil?"
71Now He meant Judas *the son* of Simon Iscariot, for he, one of
the twelve, was going to betray Him.

*Jesus Teaches at the Feast*

7 AND AFTER these things Jesus was walking in Galilee; for He
was unwilling to walk in Judea, because the Jews were seeking to kill Him.
2Now the feast of the Jews, the Feast of Booths, was at hand.
3His brothers therefore said to Him, "Depart from here, and
go into Judea, that Your disciples also may behold Your works
which You are doing.
4"For no one does anything in secret, when he himself seeks
to be *known* publicly. If You do these things, show Yourself to the
world."
5For not even His brothers were believing in Him.
6Jesus therefore *said to them, "My time is not yet at hand, but
your time is always opportune.
7"The world cannot hate you; but it hates Me because I testify
of it, that its deeds are evil.
8"Go up to the feast yourselves; I do not go up to this feast
because My time has not yet fully come."
9And having said these things to them, He stayed in Galilee.
10¶ But when His brothers had gone up to the feast, then He
Himself also went up, not publicly, but as it were, in secret.
11The Jews therefore were seeking Him at the feast, and were
saying, "Where is He?"
12And there was much grumbling among the multitudes concerning Him; some were saying, "He is a good man"; others were
saying, "No, on the contrary, He leads the multitude astray."
13Yet no one was speaking openly of Him for fear of the Jews.
14¶ But when it was now the midst of the feast Jesus went up
into the temple, and *began to* teach.

## New International

61Aware that his disciples were grumbling about this, Jesus said
to them, "Does this offend you? 62What if you see the Son of Man
ascend to where he was before! 63The Spirit gives life; the flesh
counts for nothing. The words I have spoken to you are spirit[d] and
they are life. 64Yet there are some of you who do not believe." For
Jesus had known from the beginning which of them did not believe
and who would betray him. 65He went on to say, "This is why I
told you that no one can come to me unless the Father has enabled
him."
66From this time many of his disciples turned back and no
longer followed him.
67"You do not want to leave too, do you?" Jesus asked the
Twelve.
68Simon Peter answered him, "Lord, to whom shall we go? You
have the words of eternal life. 69We believe and know that you are
the Holy One of God."
70Then Jesus replied, "Have I not chosen you, the Twelve? Yet
one of you is a devil!" 71(He meant Judas, the son of Simon Iscariot,
who, though one of the Twelve, was later to betray him.)

*Jesus Goes to the Feast of Tabernacles*

7 AFTER THIS, Jesus went around in Galilee, purposely staying away from Judea because the Jews there were waiting to
take his life. 2But when the Jewish Feast of Tabernacles was near,
3Jesus' brothers said to him, "You ought to leave here and go to
Judea, so that your disciples may see the miracles you do. 4No one
who wants to become a public figure acts in secret. Since you are
doing these things, show yourself to the world." 5For even his
own brothers did not believe in him.
6Therefore Jesus told them, "The right time for me has not yet
come; for you any time is right. 7The world cannot hate you, but
it hates me because I testify that what it does is evil. 8You go to
the Feast. I am not yet[e] going up to this Feast, because for me the
right time has not yet come." 9Having said this, he stayed in
Galilee.
10However, after his brothers had left for the Feast, he went
also, not publicly, but in secret. 11Now at the Feast the Jews were
watching for him and asking, "Where is that man?"
12Among the crowds there was widespread whispering about
him. Some said, "He is a good man."
Others replied, "No, he deceives the people." 13But no one
would say anything publicly about him for fear of the Jews.

*Jesus Teaches at the Feast*

14Not until halfway through the Feast did Jesus go up to the
temple courts and begin to teach. 15The Jews were amazed and

NIV [d] 63 Or *Spirit* [e] 8 Some early manuscripts do not have *yet.*

## King James

15 And the Jews marvelled, saying, How knoweth this man letters, having never learned?

16 Jesus answered them, and said, My doctrine is not mine, but his that sent me.

17 If any man will do his will, he shall know of the doctrine, whether it be of God, or *whether* I speak of myself.

18 He that speaketh of himself seeketh his own glory: but he that seeketh his glory that sent him, the same is true, and no unrighteousness is in him.

19 Did not Moses give you the law, and *yet* none of you keepeth the law? Why go ye about to kill me?

20 The people answered and said, Thou hast a devil: who goeth about to kill thee?

21 Jesus answered and said unto them, I have done one work, and ye all marvel.

22 Moses therefore gave unto you circumcision; (not because it is of Moses, but of the fathers;) and ye on the sabbath day circumcise a man.

23 If a man on the sabbath day receive circumcision, that the law of Moses should not be broken; are ye angry at me, because I have made a man every whit whole on the sabbath day?

24 Judge not according to the appearance, but judge righteous judgment.

25 Then said some of them of Jerusalem, Is not this he, whom they seek to kill?

26 But, lo, he speaketh boldly, and they say nothing unto him. Do the rulers know indeed that this is the very Christ?

27 Howbeit we know this man whence he is: but when Christ cometh, no man knoweth whence he is.

28 Then cried Jesus in the temple as he taught, saying, Ye both know me, and ye know whence I am: and I am not come of myself, but he that sent me is true, whom ye know not.

29 But I know him: for I am from him, and he hath sent me.

30 Then they sought to take him: but no man laid hands on him, because his hour was not yet come.

31 And many of the people believed on him, and said, When Christ cometh, will he do more miracles than these which this *man* hath done?

32 ¶ The Pharisees heard that the people murmured such things concerning him; and the Pharisees and the chief priests sent officers to take him.

33 Then said Jesus unto them, Yet a little while am I with you, and *then* I go unto him that sent me.

34 Ye shall seek me, and shall not find *me:* and where I am, *thither* ye cannot come.

35 Then said the Jews among themselves, Whither will he go, that we shall not find him? will he go unto the dispersed among the Gentiles, and teach the Gentiles?

36 What *manner of* saying is this that he said, Ye shall seek me, and shall not find *me:* and where I am, *thither* ye cannot come?

37 In the last day, that great *day* of the feast, Jesus stood and cried, saying, If any man thirst, let him come unto me, and drink.

## Amplified

15 The Jews were astonished. They said, How is it that this Man has learning—is so versed in the sacred Scriptures and in theology—when He has never studied?

16 Jesus answered them by saying, My teaching is not My own, but His Who sent Me.

17 If any man desires to do His will (God's pleasure), he will know—have the needed illumination to recognize, can tell for himself—whether the teaching is from God, or whether I am speaking from Myself *and* of My own accord *and* on My own authority.

18 He who speaks on his own authority seeks to win honor for himself—he whose teaching originates with himself seeks his own glory. But he who seeks the glory *and* is eager for the honor of him who sent him, he is true; and there is no unrighteousness *or* falsehood *or* deception in him.

19 Did not Moses give you the Law? And yet not one of you keeps the Law. [If that is the truth,] why do you seek to kill Me [for not keeping it]?

20 The crowd answered Him, You are possessed of a demon!—You are raving! Who seeks to kill You?

21 Jesus answered them, I did one work and you all were astounded. [John 5:1-9.]

22 Now, Moses established circumcision among you, though it did not originate with Moses but with previous patriarchs, and you circumcise a person [even] on the Sabbath day.

23 If to avoid breaking the Law of Moses a person undergoes circumcision on the Sabbath day, have you any cause to be angry with (indignant with, bitter against) Me for making a man's whole body well on the Sabbath?

24 Be honest in your judgment *and* do not decide at a glance—superficially *and* by appearances; but judge fairly *and* righteously.

25 Then some of the Jerusalem people said, Is not this the Man they seek to kill?

26 And here He is speaking openly, and they say nothing to Him! Can it be possible that the rulers have discovered *and* know that this is *truly* the Christ?

27 No, we know where this Man comes from; when the Christ arrives, no one is to know from what place He comes.

28 Whereupon Jesus called out as He taught in the temple [a]porches, Do you know Me, and do you know where I am from? I have not come on My own authority *and* of My own accord *and* self-appointed, but the One Who sent Me is true (real, genuine, steadfast) and Him you do not know!

29 I know Him [Myself], because I come from His [very] presence, and it was He [personally] Who sent Me.

30 Therefore they were eager to arrest Him; but no one laid a hand on Him, for His hour (time) had not yet come.

31 And besides, many of the multitude believed in Him—adhered to Him, trusted Him, relied on Him. And they kept saying, When the Christ comes, will He do—can He be expected to do—more miracles *and* produce more proofs *and* signs than what this Man has done?

32 The Pharisees learned how the people said these things about Him under their breath, and the chief priests and Pharisees sent (attendants, guards) to arrest Him.

33 Therefore Jesus said, For a little while I am [still] with you, and then I go back to Him Who sent Me.

34 You will look for Me, but you will not be able to find Me; where I am you cannot come.

35 Then the Jews said among themselves, Where can this Man intend to go, that we shall not find Him? Will He go to the Jews that are scattered in the Dispersion among the Greeks and teach the Greeks?

36 What does this statement of His mean, You will look for Me and not be able to find Me, and, Where I am you cannot come?

37 Now on the final and most important day of the feast, Jesus stood forth and He cried in a loud voice, If any man is thirsty, let him come to Me and drink!

AMP [a] Trench.

## New American Standard

15 The Jews therefore were marveling, saying, "How has this man become learned, having never been educated?"

16 Jesus therefore answered them, and said, "My teaching is not Mine, but His who sent Me.

17 "If any man is willing to do His will, he shall know of the teaching, whether it is of God, or *whether* I speak from Myself.

18 "He who speaks from himself seeks his own glory; but He who is seeking the glory of the one who sent Him, He is true, and there is no unrighteousness in Him.

19 "Did not Moses give you the Law, and *yet* none of you carries out the Law? Why do you seek to kill Me?"

20 The multitude answered, "You have a demon! Who seeks to kill You?"

21 Jesus answered and said to them, "I did one deed, and you all marvel.

22 "On this account Moses has given you circumcision (not because it is from Moses, but from the fathers), and on *the* Sabbath you circumcise a man.

23 "If a man receives circumcision on *the* Sabbath that the Law of Moses may not be broken, are you angry with Me because I made an entire man well on *the* Sabbath?

24 "Do not judge according to appearance, but judge with righteous judgment."

25 ¶ Therefore some of the people of Jerusalem were saying, "Is this not the man whom they are seeking to kill?

26 "And look, He is speaking publicly, and they are saying nothing to Him. The rulers do not really know that this is the Christ, do they?

27 "However, we know where this man is from; but whenever the Christ may come, no one knows where He is from."

28 Jesus therefore cried out in the temple, teaching and saying, "You both know Me and know where I am from; and I have not come of Myself, but He who sent Me is true, whom you do not know.

29 "I know Him; because I am from Him, and He sent Me."

30 They were seeking therefore to seize Him; and no man laid his hand on Him, because His hour had not yet come.

31 But many of the multitude believed in Him; and they were saying, "When the Christ shall come, He will not perform more signs than those which this man has, will He?"

32 The Pharisees heard the multitude muttering these things about Him; and the chief priests and the Pharisees sent officers to seize Him.

33 Jesus therefore said, "For a little while longer I am with you, then I go to Him who sent Me.

34 "You shall seek Me, and shall not find Me; and where I am, you cannot come."

35 The Jews therefore said to one another, "Where does this man intend to go that we shall not find Him? He is not intending to go to the Dispersion among the Greeks, and teach the Greeks, is He?

36 "What is this statement that He said, 'You will seek Me, and will not find Me; and where I am, you cannot come'?"

37 ¶ Now on the last day, the great *day* of the feast, Jesus stood and cried out, saying, "If any man is thirsty, let him come to Me and drink.

## New International

asked, "How did this man get such learning without having studied?"
16 Jesus answered, "My teaching is not my own. It comes from
him who sent me. 17 If anyone chooses to do God's will, he will find
out whether my teaching comes from God or whether I speak on
my own. 18 He who speaks on his own does so to gain honor for
himself, but he who works for the honor of the one who sent him
is a man of truth; there is nothing false about him. 19 Has not Moses
given you the law? Yet not one of you keeps the law. Why are you
trying to kill me?"
20 "You are demon-possessed," the crowd answered. "Who is
trying to kill you?"
21 Jesus said to them, "I did one miracle, and you are all astonished. 22 Yet, because Moses gave you circumcision (though actually it did not come from Moses, but from the patriarchs), you
circumcise a child on the Sabbath. 23 Now if a child can be circumcised on the Sabbath so that the law of Moses may not be broken,
why are you angry with me for healing the whole man on the
Sabbath? 24 Stop judging by mere appearances, and make a right
judgment."

*Is Jesus the Christ?*

25 At that point some of the people of Jerusalem began to ask,
"Isn't this the man they are trying to kill? 26 Here he is, speaking
publicly, and they are not saying a word to him. Have the authorities really concluded that he is the Christ[b] ? 27 But we know where
this man is from; when the Christ comes, no one will know where
he is from."
28 Then Jesus, still teaching in the temple courts, cried out, "Yes,
you know me, and you know where I am from. I am not here on
my own, but he who sent me is true. You do not know him, 29 but
I know him because I am from him and he sent me."
30 At this they tried to seize him, but no one laid a hand on him,
because his time had not yet come. 31 Still, many in the crowd put
their faith in him. They said, "When the Christ comes, will he do
more miraculous signs than this man?"
32 The Pharisees heard the crowd whispering such things about
him. Then the chief priests and the Pharisees sent temple guards
to arrest him.
33 Jesus said, "I am with you for only a short time, and then I
go to the one who sent me. 34 You will look for me, but you will
not find me; and where I am, you cannot come."
35 The Jews said to one another, "Where does this man intend
to go that we cannot find him? Will he go where our people live
scattered among the Greeks, and teach the Greeks? 36 What did he
mean when he said, 'You will look for me, but you will not find
me,' and 'Where I am, you cannot come'?"
37 On the last and greatest day of the Feast, Jesus stood and said
in a loud voice, "If anyone is thirsty, let him come to me and drink.

NIV [b] 26 Or *Messiah;* also in verses 27, 31, 41 and 42

## King James

38 He that believeth on me, as the scripture hath said, out of his belly shall flow rivers of living water.

39 (But this spake he of the Spirit, which they that believe on him should receive: for the Holy Ghost was not yet *given;* because that Jesus was not yet glorified.)

40 ¶ Many of the people therefore, when they heard this saying, said, Of a truth this is the Prophet.

41 Others said, This is the Christ. But some said, Shall Christ come out of Galilee?

42 Hath not the scripture said, That Christ cometh of the seed of David, and out of the town of Bethlehem, where David was?

43 So there was a division among the people because of him.

44 And some of them would have taken him; but no man laid hands on him.

45 ¶ Then came the officers to the chief priests and Pharisees; and they said unto them, Why have ye not brought him?

46 The officers answered, Never man spake like this man.

47 Then answered them the Pharisees, Are ye also deceived?

48 Have any of the rulers or of the Pharisees believed on him?

49 But this people who knoweth not the law are cursed.

50 Nicodemus saith unto them, (he that came to Jesus by night, being one of them,)

51 Doth our law judge *any* man, before it hear him, and know what he doeth?

52 They answered and said unto him, Art thou also of Galilee? Search, and look: for out of Galilee ariseth no prophet.

53 And every man went unto his own house.

8 JESUS WENT unto the mount of Olives.

2 And early in the morning he came again into the temple, and all the people came unto him; and he sat down, and taught them.

3 And the scribes and Pharisees brought unto him a woman taken in adultery; and when they had set her in the midst,

4 They say unto him, Master, this woman was taken in adultery, in the very act.

5 Now Moses in the law commanded us, that such should be stoned: but what sayest thou?

6 This they said, tempting him, that they might have to accuse him. But Jesus stooped down, and with *his* finger wrote on the ground, *as though he heard them not.*

7 So when they continued asking him, he lifted up himself, and said unto them, He that is without sin among you, let him first cast a stone at her.

8 And again he stooped down, and wrote on the ground.

9 And they which heard *it,* being convicted by *their own* conscience, went out one by one, beginning at the eldest, *even* unto the last: and Jesus was left alone, and the woman standing in the midst.

10 When Jesus had lifted up himself, and saw none but the woman, he said unto her, Woman, where are those thine accusers? hath no man condemned thee?

11 She said, No man, Lord. And Jesus said unto her, Neither do I condemn thee: go, and sin no more.

**AMP** [a] John 7:53 to 8:11 is not found in the older manuscripts, but it sounds so like Christ that we accept it as authentic, and feel that to omit it would be most unfortunate. [b] Trench.

## Amplified

38 He who believes in Me—who cleaves to *and* trusts in *and* relies on Me—as the Scripture has said, Out from his innermost being springs *and* rivers of living water shall flow (continuously).

39 But He was speaking here of the Spirit, Whom those who believed—trusted, had faith—in Him were afterward to receive. For the (Holy) Spirit had not yet been given; because Jesus was not yet glorified (raised to honor).

40 Listening to those words, some of the multitude said, This is certainly *and* beyond doubt the prophet! [Deut. 18:18.]

41 Others said, This is the Christ, the Anointed One! But some said, What? Does the Christ come out of Galilee?

42 Does not the Scripture tell us that the Christ is to come from the offspring of David, and from Bethlehem, the village where David lived? [Ps. 89:3, 4; Mic. 5:2.]

43 So there arose a division *and* dissension among the people concerning Him.

44 Some of them wanted to arrest Him, but no one [ventured and] laid hands on Him.

45 Meanwhile the attendants (guards) had gone back to the chief priests and Pharisees, who asked them, Why have you not brought Him here with you?

46 The attendants replied, Never has a man talked as this Man talks!—No mere man has ever spoken as He speaks!

47 The Pharisees said to them, Are you also deluded *and* led astray?—Are you also swept off your feet?

48 Have any of the authorities or of the Pharisees believed in Him?

49 As for this multitude (rabble) that does not know the Law, they are contemptible *and* doomed *and* accursed!

50 Then Nicodemus, who came to Jesus before at night and was one of them, asked,

51 Does our Law convict a man without giving him a hearing and finding out what he has done?

52 They answered him, Are you too from Galilee? Search [the Scriptures yourself] and you will see that no prophet comes—will rise to prominence—from Galilee.

53 [a]And they went [back], each to his own house.

8 BUT JESUS went to the Mount of Olives.

2 Early in the morning (at dawn), He came back into the temple [b]court and the people came to Him in crowds. He sat down and was teaching them,

3 When the scribes and Pharisees brought a woman who had been caught in adultery. They made her stand in the middle of the court and put the case before Him.

4 Teacher, they said, this woman has been caught in the very act of adultery.

5 Now Moses in the Law commanded us that such [women, offenders] shall be stoned to death. But what do You say [to do with her]?—What is Your sentence? [Deut. 22:22-24.]

6 This they said to try (test) Him, hoping they might find a charge for which to accuse Him. But Jesus stooped down and wrote on the ground with His finger.

7 However, when they persisted with their question, He raised Himself up and said, Let him who is without sin among you be the first to throw a stone at her.

8 Then He bent down and went on writing on the ground with His finger.

9 They listened to Him and then they began going out conscience-stricken one by one, from the oldest down to the last one of them, till Jesus was left alone with the woman standing there before Him in the center of the court.

10 When Jesus raised up He said to her, Woman, where are your accusers? Has no man condemned you?

11 She answered, No one, Lord! And Jesus said, I do not condemn you either. Go on your way, and from now on sin no more.

## New American Standard

38"He who believes in Me, as the Scripture said, 'From his
innermost being shall flow rivers of living water.'"
39But this He spoke of the Spirit, whom those who believed in
Him were to receive; for the Spirit was not yet *given*, because Jesus
was not yet glorified.

*Division of People over Jesus*

40 *Some* of the multitude therefore, when they heard these
words, were saying, "This certainly is the Prophet."
41Others were saying, "This is the Christ." Still others were
saying, "Surely the Christ is not going to come from Galilee, is He?
42"Has not the Scripture said that the Christ comes from the
offspring of David, and from Bethlehem, the village where David
was?"
43So there arose a division in the multitude because of Him.
44And some of them wanted to seize Him, but no one laid hands
on Him.
45¶ The officers therefore came to the chief priests and Pharisees, and they said to them, "Why did you not bring Him?"
46The officers answered, "Never did a man speak the way this
man speaks."
47The Pharisees therefore answered them, "You have not also
been led astray, have you?
48"No one of the rulers or Pharisees has believed in Him, has
he?
49"But this multitude which does not know the Law is accursed."
50Nicodemus *said to them (he who came to Him before, being
one of them),
51"Our Law does not judge a man, unless it first hears from him
and knows what he is doing, does it?"
52They answered and said to him, "You are not also from Galilee, are you? Search, and see that no prophet arises out of Galilee."
53[ [c]And everyone went to his home.

*The Adulterous Woman*

8 BUT JESUS went to the Mount of Olives.
2And early in the morning He came again into the temple,
and all the people were coming to Him; and He sat down and *began*
to teach them.
3And the scribes and the Pharisees *brought a woman caught
in adultery, and having set her in the midst,
4they *said to Him, "Teacher, this woman has been caught in
adultery, in the very act.
5"Now in the Law Moses commanded us to stone such
women; what then do You say?"
6And they were saying this, testing Him, in order that they
might have grounds for accusing Him. But Jesus stooped down,
and with His finger wrote on the ground.
7But when they persisted in asking Him, He straightened up,
and said to them, "He who is without sin among you, let him *be
the* first to throw a stone at her."
8And again He stooped down, and wrote on the ground.
9And when they heard it, they *began* to go out one by one,
beginning with the older ones, and He was left alone, and the
woman, where she was, in the midst.
10And straightening up, Jesus said to her, "Woman, where are
they? Did no one condemn you?"
11And she said, "No one, Lord." And Jesus said, "Neither do
I condemn you; go your way. From now on sin no more."]

NAS [c] John 7:53–8:11 is not found in most of the old mss.

## New International

38Whoever believes in me, as[d] the Scripture has said, streams of
living water will flow from within him." 39By this he meant the
Spirit, whom those who believed in him were later to receive. Up
to that time the Spirit had not been given, since Jesus had not yet
been glorified.
40On hearing his words, some of the people said, "Surely this
man is the Prophet."
41Others said, "He is the Christ."
Still others asked, "How can the Christ come from Galilee?
42Does not the Scripture say that the Christ will come from David's
family[e] and from Bethlehem, the town where David lived?"
43Thus the people were divided because of Jesus. 44Some wanted
to seize him, but no one laid a hand on him.

*Unbelief of the Jewish Leaders*

45Finally the temple guards went back to the chief priests and
Pharisees, who asked them, "Why didn't you bring him in?"
46"No one ever spoke the way this man does," the guards
declared.
47"You mean he has deceived you also?" the Pharisees retorted.
48"Has any of the rulers or of the Pharisees believed in him? 49No!
But this mob that knows nothing of the law—there is a curse on
them."
50Nicodemus, who had gone to Jesus earlier and who was one
of their own number, asked, 51"Does our law condemn anyone
without first hearing him to find out what he is doing?"
52They replied, "Are you from Galilee, too? Look into it, and
you will find that a prophet[f] does not come out of Galilee."

[The earliest and most reliable manuscripts and other ancient witnesses do not have John 7:53–8:11.]

53Then each went to his own home.

8 BUT JESUS went to the Mount of Olives. 2At dawn he appeared again in the temple courts, where all the people gathered around him, and he sat down to teach them. 3The teachers
of the law and the Pharisees brought in a woman caught in adultery. They made her stand before the group 4and said to Jesus,
"Teacher, this woman was caught in the act of adultery. 5In the
Law Moses commanded us to stone such women. Now what do
you say?" 6They were using this question as a trap, in order to have
a basis for accusing him.
But Jesus bent down and started to write on the ground with
his finger. 7When they kept on questioning him, he straightened
up and said to them, "If any one of you is without sin, let him be
the first to throw a stone at her." 8Again he stooped down and
wrote on the ground.
9At this, those who heard began to go away one at a time, the
older ones first, until only Jesus was left, with the woman still
standing there. 10Jesus straightened up and asked her, "Woman,
where are they? Has no one condemned you?"
11"No one, sir," she said.
"Then neither do I condemn you," Jesus declared. "Go now
and leave your life of sin."

NIV [d] 37,38 Or / *If anyone is thirsty, let him come to me. / And let him drink,* 38*who believes in me. / As* [e] 42 Greek *seed* [f] 52 Two early manuscripts *the Prophet*

## King James

12¶ Then spake Jesus again unto them, saying, I am the light of the world: he that followeth me shall not walk in darkness, but shall have the light of life.

13The Pharisees therefore said unto him, Thou bearest record of thyself; thy record is not true.

14Jesus answered and said unto them, Though I bear record of myself, *yet* my record is true: for I know whence I came, and whither I go; but ye cannot tell whence I come, and whither I go.

15Ye judge after the flesh; I judge no man.

16And yet if I judge, my judgment is true: for I am not alone, but I and the Father that sent me.

17It is also written in your law, that the testimony of two men is true.

18I am one that bear witness of myself, and the Father that sent me beareth witness of me.

19Then said they unto him, Where is thy Father? Jesus answered, Ye neither know me, nor my Father: if ye had known me, ye should have known my Father also.

20These words spake Jesus in the treasury, as he taught in the temple: and no man laid hands on him; for his hour was not yet come.

21Then said Jesus again unto them, I go my way, and ye shall seek me, and shall die in your sins: whither I go, ye cannot come.

22Then said the Jews, Will he kill himself? because he saith, Whither I go, ye cannot come.

23And he said unto them, Ye are from beneath; I am from above: ye are of this world; I am not of this world.

24I said therefore unto you, that ye shall die in your sins: for if ye believe not that I am *he*, ye shall die in your sins.

25Then said they unto him, Who art thou? And Jesus saith unto them, Even *the same* that I said unto you from the beginning.

26I have many things to say and to judge of you: but he that sent me is true; and I speak to the world those things which I have heard of him.

27They understood not that he spake to them of the Father.

28Then said Jesus unto them, When ye have lifted up the Son of man, then shall ye know that I am *he*, and *that* I do nothing of myself; but as my Father hath taught me, I speak these things.

29And he that sent me is with me: the Father hath not left me alone; for I do always those things that please him.

30As he spake these words, many believed on him.

31Then said Jesus to those Jews which believed on him, If ye continue in my word, *then* are ye my disciples indeed;

32And ye shall know the truth, and the truth shall make you free.

33¶ They answered him, We be Abraham's seed, and were never in bondage to any man: how sayest thou, Ye shall be made free?

34Jesus answered them, Verily, verily, I say unto you, Whosoever committeth sin is the servant of sin.

35And the servant abideth not in the house for ever: *but* the Son abideth ever.

36If the Son therefore shall make you free, ye shall be free indeed.

37I know that ye are Abraham's seed; but ye seek to kill me, because my word hath no place in you.

## Amplified

12Once more Jesus addressed the crowd. He said, I am the Light of the world. He who follows Me will not be walking in the dark, but will have the Light which is Life.

13Whereupon the Pharisees told Him, You are testifying on Your own behalf; Your testimony is not valid *and* is worthless.

14Jesus answered, Even if I do testify on My own behalf, My testimony is true *and* reliable *and* valid; for I know where I came from and where I am going; but you do not know where I came from or where I am going.

15You [set yourselves up to] judge according to the flesh—by what you see; you condemn by external, human standards. I do not [set Myself up to] judge *or* condemn *or* sentence anyone.

16Yet even if I do judge, My judgment is true—My decision is right; for I am not alone [in making it], but [there are two of Us], I and the Father Who sent Me.

17In your [own] Law it is written that the testimony (evidence) of two persons is reliable *and* valid. [Deut. 19:15.]

18I am one [of the Two] bearing testimony concerning Myself, and My Father Who sent Me, He also testifies about Me.

19Then they said to Him, Where is this [a]Father of Yours? Jesus answered, You know My Father as little as you know Me. If you knew Me, you would know My Father also.

20Jesus said these things in the treasury, while He was teaching in the temple [b]court; but no one ventured to arrest Him, because His hour had not yet come.

21Therefore He said again to them, I am going away, and you will be looking for Me, but you will die in [under the curse of] your sin. Where I am going, it is not possible for you to come.

22At this the Jews began to ask among themselves, Will He kill Himself? Is that why He says, Where I am going it is not possible for you to come?

23He said to them, You are from below; I am from above. You are of this world—of this earthly order. I am not of this world.

24That is why I told you that you will die in [under the curse of] your sins. For if you do not believe that I am He [Who I claim to be]—if you do not adhere to, trust in and rely on Me—you will die in your sins.

25Then they said to Him, Who are You anyway? Jesus replied, Why do I even speak to you! I am exactly what I have been telling you from the first.

26I have much to say about you and to judge *and* condemn. But He Who sent Me is true, and I tell the world [only] the things that I have heard from Him.

27They did not perceive (know, understand) that He was speaking to them of the Father.

28So Jesus added, When you have lifted up the Son of man [on the cross], you will realize (know, understand) that I am He [for Whom you look]; and that I do nothing from Myself—of My own accord, or on My own authority—but I say [exactly] what My Father has taught Me.

29And He Who sent Me is ever with Me; My Father has not left Me alone, for I always do what pleases Him.

30As He said these things, many believed on Him—trusted, relied on and adhered to Him.

31So Jesus said to those Jews who had believed in Him, If you abide in My Word—hold fast to My teachings *and* live in accordance with them—you are truly My disciples.

32And you will know the truth, and the truth will set you free.

33They answered Him, We are Abraham's offspring (descendants) and have never been in bondage to anybody. What do You mean by saying, You will be set free?

34Jesus answered them, I assure you, most solemnly I tell you, Whoever commits *and* practices sin is the slave of sin.

35Now a slave does not remain in a household permanently (forever); the son [of the house] does remain forever.

36So if the Son liberates you—makes you free men—then you are really *and* unquestionably free.

37[Yes] I know that you are Abraham's offspring; yet you plan to kill Me, because My word has no entrance—makes no progress, does not find any place—in you.

**AMP** [a] Capitalized because of what He is, the spotless Son of God, not what the speaker may have thought He was. [b] Trench.

## New American Standard

*Jesus Is the Light of the World*

12¶ Again therefore Jesus spoke to them, saying, "I am the light
of the world; he who follows Me shall not walk in the darkness,
but shall have the light of life."
13The Pharisees therefore said to Him, "You are bearing witness
of Yourself; Your witness is not true."
14Jesus answered and said to them, "Even if I bear witness of
Myself, My witness is true; for I know where I came from, and
where I am going; but you do not know where I come from, or
where I am going.
15"You people judge according to the flesh; I am not judging
anyone.
16"But even if I do judge, My judgment is true; for I am not
alone *in it*, but I and [c]He who sent Me.
17"Even in your law it has been written, that the testimony of
two men is true.
18"I am He who bears witness of Myself, and the Father who
sent Me bears witness of Me."
19And so they were saying to Him, "Where is Your Father?"
Jesus answered, "You know neither Me, nor My Father; if you
knew Me, you would know My Father also."
20These words He spoke in the treasury, as He taught in the
temple; and no one seized Him, because His hour had not yet
come.
21¶ He said therefore again to them, "I go away, and you shall
seek Me, and shall die in your sin; where I am going, you cannot
come."
22Therefore the Jews were saying, "Surely He will not kill Himself, will He, since He says, 'Where I am going, you cannot
come'?"
23And He was saying to them, "You are from below, I am from
above; you are of this world, I am not of this world.
24"I said therefore to you, that you shall die in your sins; for
unless you believe that I am *He,* you shall die in your sins."
25And so they were saying to Him, "Who are You?" Jesus said
to them, "What have I been saying to you *from* the beginning?
26"I have many things to speak and to judge concerning you,
but He who sent Me is true; and the things which I heard from
Him, these I speak to the world."
27They did not realize that He had been speaking to them about
the Father.
28Jesus therefore said, "When you lift up the Son of Man, then
you will know that I am *He,* and I do nothing on My own initiative,
but I speak these things as the Father taught Me.
29"And He who sent Me is with Me; He has not left Me alone,
for I always do the things that are pleasing to Him."
30As He spoke these things, many came to believe in Him.

*The Truth Shall Make You Free*

31¶ Jesus therefore was saying to those Jews who had believed
Him, "If you abide in My word, *then* you are truly disciples of
Mine;
32and you shall know the truth, and the truth shall make you
free."
33They answered Him, "We are Abraham's offspring, and have
never yet been enslaved to anyone; how is it that You say, 'You
shall become free'?"
34Jesus answered them, "Truly, truly, I say to you, everyone
who commits sin is the slave of sin.
35"And the slave does not remain in the house forever; the son
does remain forever.
36"If therefore the Son shall make you free, you shall be free
indeed.
37"I know that you are Abraham's offspring; yet you seek to kill
Me, because My word has no place in you.

NAS [c] Many ancient mss. read *the Father who sent Me*

## New International

*The Validity of Jesus' Testimony*

12When Jesus spoke again to the people, he said, "I am the light
of the world. Whoever follows me will never walk in darkness, but
will have the light of life."
13The Pharisees challenged him, "Here you are, appearing as
your own witness; your testimony is not valid."
14Jesus answered, "Even if I testify on my own behalf, my
testimony is valid, for I know where I came from and where I am
going. But you have no idea where I come from or where I am
going. 15You judge by human standards; I pass judgment on no
one. 16But if I do judge, my decisions are right, because I am not
alone. I stand with the Father, who sent me. 17In your own Law
it is written that the testimony of two men is valid. 18I am one who
testifies for myself; my other witness is the Father, who sent me."
19Then they asked him, "Where is your father?"
"You do not know me or my Father," Jesus replied. "If you
knew me, you would know my Father also." 20He spoke these
words while teaching in the temple area near the place where the
offerings were put. Yet no one seized him, because his time had
not yet come.
21Once more Jesus said to them, "I am going away, and you will
look for me, and you will die in your sin. Where I go, you cannot
come."
22This made the Jews ask, "Will he kill himself? Is that why he
says, 'Where I go, you cannot come'?"
23But he continued, "You are from below; I am from above. You
are of this world; I am not of this world. 24I told you that you would
die in your sins; if you do not believe that I am ˪the one I claim to
be˩,[d] you will indeed die in your sins."
25"Who are you?" they asked.
"Just what I have been claiming all along," Jesus replied. 26"I
have much to say in judgment of you. But he who sent me is
reliable, and what I have heard from him I tell the world."
27They did not understand that he was telling them about his
Father. 28So Jesus said, "When you have lifted up the Son of Man,
then you will know that I am ˪the one I claim to be˩ and that I do
nothing on my own but speak just what the Father has taught me.
29The one who sent me is with me; he has not left me alone, for
I always do what pleases him." 30Even as he spoke, many put their
faith in him.

*The Children of Abraham*

31To the Jews who had believed him, Jesus said, "If you hold
to my teaching, you are really my disciples. 32Then you will know
the truth, and the truth will set you free."
33They answered him, "We are Abraham's descendants[e] and
have never been slaves of anyone. How can you say that we shall
be set free?"
34Jesus replied, "I tell you the truth, everyone who sins is a
slave to sin. 35Now a slave has no permanent place in the family,
but a son belongs to it forever. 36So if the Son sets you free, you
will be free indeed. 37I know you are Abraham's descendants. Yet
you are ready to kill me, because you have no room for my word.

NIV [d] 24 Or *I am he;* also in verse 28 [e] 33 Greek *seed;* also in verse 37

## King James

38 I speak that which I have seen with my Father: and ye do that which ye have seen with your father.

39 They answered and said unto him, Abraham is our father. Jesus saith unto them, If ye were Abraham's children, ye would do the works of Abraham.

40 But now ye seek to kill me, a man that hath told you the truth, which I have heard of God: this did not Abraham.

41 Ye do the deeds of your father. Then said they to him, We be not born of fornication; we have one Father, *even* God.

42 Jesus said unto them, If God were your Father, ye would love me: for I proceeded forth and came from God; neither came I of myself, but he sent me.

43 Why do ye not understand my speech? *even* because ye cannot hear my word.

44 Ye are of *your* father the devil, and the lusts of your father ye will do. He was a murderer from the beginning, and abode not in the truth, because there is no truth in him. When he speaketh a lie, he speaketh of his own: for he is a liar, and the father of it.

45 And because I tell *you* the truth, ye believe me not.

46 Which of you convinceth me of sin? And if I say the truth, why do ye not believe me?

47 He that is of God heareth God's words: ye therefore hear *them* not, because ye are not of God.

48 Then answered the Jews, and said unto him, Say we not well that thou art a Samaritan, and hast a devil?

49 Jesus answered, I have not a devil; but I honour my Father, and ye do dishonour me.

50 And I seek not mine own glory: there is one that seeketh and judgeth.

51 Verily, verily, I say unto you, If a man keep my saying, he shall never see death.

52 Then said the Jews unto him, Now we know that thou hast a devil. Abraham is dead, and the prophets; and thou sayest, If a man keep my saying, he shall never taste of death.

53 Art thou greater than our father Abraham, which is dead? and the prophets are dead: whom makest thou thyself?

54 Jesus answered, If I honour myself, my honour is nothing: it is my Father that honoureth me; of whom ye say, that he is your God:

55 Yet ye have not known him; but I know him: and if I should say, I know him not, I shall be a liar like unto you: but I know him, and keep his saying.

56 Your father Abraham rejoiced to see my day: and he saw *it*, and was glad.

57 Then said the Jews unto him, Thou art not yet fifty years old, and hast thou seen Abraham?

58 Jesus said unto them, Verily, verily, I say unto you, Before Abraham was, I am.

## Amplified

38 I tell the things which I have seen *and* learned at My Father's side, and your actions also reflect what you have heard *and* learned from your father.

39 They retorted, Abraham is our father. Jesus said, If you were truly Abraham's children, then you would do the works of Abraham—you would follow his example, do as Abraham did.

40 But now [instead] you are wanting *and* seeking to kill Me, a Man Who has told you the truth which I have heard from God. This is not the way Abraham did.

41 You do the works of your father. They said to Him, We are not illegitimate children *and* born of fornication; we have one Father, even God.

42 Jesus said to them, If God were your Father, you would love Me *and* respect Me *and* welcome Me gladly; for I proceeded (came forth) from God—out of His very persence. I did not even come on My own authority *or* of My own accord (self-appointed), but He sent Me.

43 Why do you misunderstand what I say? It is because you are unable to hear what I am saying—you cannot bear to listen to My message, your ears are shut to My teaching.

44 You are of your father the devil; and it is your will to practice the lusts *and* gratify the desires [which are characteristic] of your father. He was a murderer from the beginning, and does not stand in the truth, because there is no truth in him. When he speaks a falsehood, he speaks what is natural to him; for he is a liar [himself] and the father of lies *and* of all that is false.

45 But because I speak the truth, you do not believe Me—do not trust Me, do not rely on Me or adhere to Me.

46 Who of you convicts Me of wrongdoing *or* finds Me guilty of sin? Then if I speak truth, why do you not believe Me—trust Me, rely on and adhere to Me?

47 Whoever is of God listens to God.—Those who belong to God hear the words of God. This is the reason that you do not listen [to them, to Me], because you do not belong to *and* are not of God *or* in harmony with God.

48 The Jews answered Him, Are we not right when we say You are a Samaritan, and that You have a demon—that You are under the power of an evil spirit?

49 Jesus answered, I am not possessed by a demon. On the other hand, I honor *and* reverence My Father, and you dishonor—despise, vilify and scorn—Me.

50 However, I am not in search of honor for Myself—I do not seek and am not aiming for My own glory. There is One Who [looks after that; He] seeks [My glory] and He is the Judge.

51 I assure you, most solemnly I tell you, if any one observes My teaching—lives in accordance with My message, keeps My word—he will by no means ever see *and* experience death.

52 The Jews said to Him, Now we know that [a]You are under the power of a demon ([b]insane). Abraham died and also the prophets; yet You say, If a man keeps My word he will never taste of death to all eternity.

53 Are You greater than our father Abraham? He died and all the prophets died! Who do You make Yourself out to be?

54 Jesus answered, If I were to glorify Myself (magnify, praise and honor Myself) I should have no real glory, for My glory would be nothing *and* worthless.—My honor must come to Me from My Father. It is My Father Who glorifies Me—Who extols Me, magnifies and praises Me—of Whom you say that He is your God.

55 Yet you do not know Him *nor* recognize Him *and* are not acquainted with Him, but I know Him. If I should say that I do not know Him, I would be a liar like you. But I know Him and keep His word—obey His teachings, am faithful to His message.

56 Your forefather Abraham was extremely happy at the hope *and* prospect of seeing My day [My incarnation]. And he did see it and was delighted. [Heb. 11:13.]

57 Then the Jews said to Him, You are not yet fifty years old, and have You seen Abraham?

58 Jesus replied, I assure you, I most solemnly tell you, before Abraham was born, I AM. [Exod. 3:14.]

**AMP** [a] Capitalized because of what He is, the spotless Son of God, not what the speaker may have thought He was. [b] Thayer.

## New American Standard

38"I speak the things which I have seen with *My* Father; therefore you also do the things which you heard from *your* father."
39They answered and said to Him, "Abraham is our father."
Jesus *said to them, "If you are Abraham's children, do the deeds
of Abraham.
40"But as it is, you are seeking to kill Me, a man who has told
you the truth, which I heard from God; this Abraham did not do.
41"You are doing the deeds of your father." They said to Him,
"We were not born of fornication; we have one Father, *even* God."
42Jesus said to them, "If God were your Father, you would love
Me; for I proceeded forth and have come from God, for I have not
even come on My own initiative, but He sent Me.
43"Why do you not understand what I am saying? *It is* because
you cannot hear My word.
44"You are of *your* father the devil, and you want to do the
desires of your father. He was a murderer from the beginning, and
does not stand in the truth, because there is no truth in him.
Whenever he speaks a lie, he speaks from his own *nature;* for he
is a liar, and the father of lies.
45"But because I speak the truth, you do not believe Me.
46"Which one of you convicts Me of sin? If I speak truth, why
do you not believe Me?
47"He who is of God hears the words of God; for this reason you
do not hear *them,* because you are not of God."
48¶ The Jews answered and said to Him, "Do we not say rightly
that You are a Samaritan and have a demon?"
49Jesus answered, "I do not have a demon; but I honor My
Father, and you dishonor Me.
50"But I do not seek My glory; there is One who seeks and
judges.
51"Truly, truly, I say to you, if anyone keeps My word he shall
never see death."
52The Jews said to Him, "Now we know that You have a demon. Abraham died, and the prophets *also;* and You say, 'If anyone keeps My word, he shall never taste of death.'
53"Surely You are not greater than our father Abraham, who
died? The prophets died too; whom do You make Yourself out *to
be?"*
54Jesus answered, "If I glorify Myself, My glory is nothing; it is
My Father who glorifies Me, of whom you say, 'He is our God';
55and you have not come to know Him, but I know Him; and
if I say that I do not know Him, I shall be a liar like you, but I do
know Him, and keep His word.
56"Your father Abraham rejoiced to see My day, and he saw *it*
and was glad."
57The Jews therefore said to Him, "You are not yet fifty years
old, and have You seen Abraham?"
58Jesus said to them, "Truly, truly, I say to you, before Abraham
was born, I am."

## New International

38I am telling you what I have seen in the Father's presence, and
you do what you have heard from your father.[c] "
39"Abraham is our father," they answered.
"If you were Abraham's children," said Jesus, "then you
would[d] do the things Abraham did. 40As it is, you are determined
to kill me, a man who has told you the truth that I heard from God.
Abraham did not do such things. 41You are doing the things your
own father does."
"We are not illegitimate children," they protested. "The only
Father we have is God himself."

*The Children of the Devil*

42Jesus said to them, "If God were your Father, you would love
me, for I came from God and now am here. I have not come on
my own; but he sent me. 43Why is my language not clear to you?
Because you are unable to hear what I say. 44You belong to your
father, the devil, and you want to carry out your father's desire.
He was a murderer from the beginning, not holding to the truth,
for there is no truth in him. When he lies, he speaks his native
language, for he is a liar and the father of lies. 45Yet because I tell
the truth, you do not believe me! 46Can any of you prove me guilty
of sin? If I am telling the truth, why don't you believe me? 47He
who belongs to God hears what God says. The reason you do not
hear is that you do not belong to God."

*The Claims of Jesus About Himself*

48The Jews answered him, "Aren't we right in saying that you
are a Samaritan and demon-possessed?"
49"I am not possessed by a demon," said Jesus, "but I honor
my Father and you dishonor me. 50I am not seeking glory for
myself; but there is one who seeks it, and he is the judge. 51I tell
you the truth, if anyone keeps my word, he will never see death."
52At this the Jews exclaimed, "Now we know that you are
demon-possessed! Abraham died and so did the prophets, yet you
say that if anyone keeps your word, he will never taste death.
53Are you greater than our father Abraham? He died, and so did
the prophets. Who do you think you are?"
54Jesus replied, "If I glorify myself, my glory means nothing.
My Father, whom you claim as your God, is the one who glorifies
me. 55Though you do not know him, I know him. If I said I did
not, I would be a liar like you, but I do know him and keep his
word. 56Your father Abraham rejoiced at the thought of seeing my
day; he saw it and was glad."
57"You are not yet fifty years old," the Jews said to him, "and
you have seen Abraham!"
58"I tell you the truth," Jesus answered, "before Abraham was

**NIV** [c] 38 Or *presence. Therefore do what you have heard from the Father.*
[d] 39 Some early manuscripts *"If you are Abraham's children," said Jesus, "then*

# King James

59 Then took they up stones to cast at him: but Jesus hid himself, and went out of the temple, going through the midst of them, and so passed by.

**9** AND AS *Jesus* passed by, he saw a man which was blind from *his* birth.

2 And his disciples asked him, saying, Master, who did sin, this man, or his parents, that he was born blind?

3 Jesus answered, Neither hath this man sinned, nor his parents: but that the works of God should be made manifest in him.

4 I must work the works of him that sent me, while it is day: the night cometh, when no man can work.

5 As long as I am in the world, I am the light of the world.

6 When he had thus spoken, he spat on the ground, and made clay of the spittle, and he anointed the eyes of the blind man with the clay,

7 And said unto him, Go, wash in the pool of Siloam, (which is by interpretation, Sent.) He went his way therefore, and washed, and came seeing.

8 ¶ The neighbours therefore, and they which before had seen him that he was blind, said, Is not this he that sat and begged?

9 Some said, This is he: others *said*, He is like him: *but* he said, I am *he*.

10 Therefore said they unto him, How were thine eyes opened?

11 He answered and said, A man that is called Jesus made clay, and anointed mine eyes, and said unto me, Go to the pool of Siloam, and wash: and I went and washed, and I received sight.

12 Then said they unto him, Where is he? He said, I know not.

13 ¶ They brought to the Pharisees him that aforetime was blind.

14 And it was the sabbath day when Jesus made the clay, and opened his eyes.

15 Then again the Pharisees also asked him how he had received his sight. He said unto them, He put clay upon mine eyes, and I washed, and do see.

16 Therefore said some of the Pharisees, This man is not of God, because he keepeth not the sabbath day. Others said, How can a man that is a sinner do such miracles? And there was a division among them.

17 They say unto the blind man again, What sayest thou of him, that he hath opened thine eyes? He said, He is a prophet.

18 But the Jews did not believe concerning him, that he had been blind, and received his sight, until they called the parents of him that had received his sight.

19 And they asked them, saying, Is this your son, who ye say was born blind? how then doth he now see?

20 His parents answered them and said, We know that this is our son, and that he was born blind:

21 But by what means he now seeth, we know not; or who hath opened his eyes, we know not: he is of age; ask him: he shall speak for himself.

22 These *words* spake his parents, because they feared the Jews: for the Jews had agreed already, that if any man did confess that he was Christ, he should be put out of the synagogue.

23 Therefore said his parents, He is of age; ask him.

24 Then again called they the man that was blind, and said unto him, Give God the praise: we know that this man is a sinner.

25 He answered and said, Whether he be a sinner *or no*, I know not: one thing I know, that, whereas I was blind, now I see.

26 Then said they to him again, What did he to thee? how opened he thine eyes?

# Amplified

59 So they took up stones to throw at Him, but Jesus by mixing with the crowd concealed Himself and went out of the temple [a]enclosure.

**9** AS HE passed along, He noticed a man blind from his birth.

2 His disciples asked Him, Rabbi, who sinned, this man or his parents, that he should be born blind?

3 Jesus answered, It was not that this man or his parents sinned; but he was born blind in order that the workings of God should be manifested—displayed and illustrated—in him.

4 We must work the works of Him Who sent Me, *and* be busy with His business while it is daylight; night is coming on when no man can work.

5 As long as I am in the world, I am the world's Light.

6 When He had said this, He spat on the ground and made clay (mud) with His saliva, and He spread it [as ointment] on the man's eyes.

7 And He said to him, Go, wash in the pool of Siloam, which means Sent. So he went and washed and came back seeing.

8 When the neighbors and those who used to know him by sight as a beggar saw him, they said, Is not this the man who used to sit and beg?

9 Some said, It is he. Others said, No, but he looks very much like him. But he said, Yes, I am the man.

10 So they said to him, How were your eyes opened?

11 He replied, The Man called Jesus made mud and smeared it on my eyes and said to me, Go to Siloam and wash. So I went and washed, and I obtained my sight!

12 They asked him, Where is He? He said, I do not know.

13 Then they conducted the man who had formerly been blind to the Pharisees.

14 Now it was on the Sabbath day that Jesus mixed the mud and opened the man's eyes.

15 So now again the Pharisees asked him how he received his sight. And he said to them, He smeared mud on my eyes and I washed and now I see.

16 Then some of the Pharisees said, This Man [Jesus] is not from God, because He does not observe the Sabbath. But others said, How can a man who is a sinner—a bad man—do such signs *and* miracles? So there was a difference of opinion among them.

17 Accordingly they said to the blind man again, What do you say about Him, seeing that He opened your eyes? And he said, He is—He must be—a prophet!

18 However the Jews did not believe that he had really been blind and that he had received his sight until they called (summoned) the parents of the man.

19 They asked them, Is this your son, whom you reported as having been born blind? How then does he see now?

20 His parents answered, We know that this is our son, and that he was born blind.

21 But as to how he can now see, we do not know; or who has opened his eyes we do not know. He is of age, ask him; let him speak for himself *and* give his own account of it.

22 His parents said this because they feared [the leaders of] the Jews. For the Jews had already agreed that if any one should acknowledge Jesus to be the Christ, he should be expelled *and* excluded from the synagogue.

23 On that account his parents said, He is of age, ask him.

24 So the second time they summoned the man who had been born blind, and said to him, Now give God the glory (praise). This [b]Fellow we know is only a sinner—a wicked person.

25 Then he answered, I do not know whether He is a sinner *and* wicked or not. But one thing I know, that whereas I was blind before, now I see.

26 So they said to him, What did He [actually] do to you? How did He open your eyes?

**AMP** [a] Trench. [b] Capitalized because of what He is, the spotless Son of God, not what the speaker may have thought He was.

## New American Standard

59Therefore they picked up stones to throw at Him; but Jesus
hid Himself, and went out of the temple.

*Healing the Man Born Blind*

9 AND AS He passed by, He saw a man blind from birth.
2And His disciples asked Him, saying, "Rabbi, who sinned,
this man or his parents, that he should be born blind?"
3Jesus answered, "*It was* neither *that* this man sinned, nor his
parents; but *it was* in order that the works of God might be displayed in him.
4"We must work the works of Him who sent Me, as long as
it is day; night is coming, when no man can work.
5"While I am in the world, I am the light of the world."
6When He had said this, He spat on the ground, and made clay
of the spittle, and applied the clay to his eyes,
7and said to him, "Go, wash in the pool of Siloam" (which is
translated, Sent). And so he went away and washed, and came
*back* seeing.
8The neighbors therefore, and those who previously saw him
as a beggar, were saying, "Is not this the one who used to sit and
beg?"
9Others were saying, "This is he," *still* others were saying,
"No, but he is like him." He kept saying, "I am the one."
10Therefore they were saying to him, "How then were your
eyes opened?"
11He answered, "The man who is called Jesus made clay, and
anointed my eyes, and said to me, 'Go to Siloam, and wash'; so
I went away and washed, and I received sight."
12And they said to him, "Where is He?" He *said, "I do not
know."

*Controversy over the Man*

13¶ They *brought to the Pharisees him who was formerly blind.
14Now it was a Sabbath on the day when Jesus made the clay,
and opened his eyes.
15Again, therefore, the Pharisees also were asking him how he
received his sight. And he said to them, "He applied clay to my
eyes, and I washed, and I see."
16Therefore some of the Pharisees were saying, "This man is not
from God, because He does not keep the Sabbath." But others
were saying, "How can a man who is a sinner perform such
signs?" And there was a division among them.
17They *said therefore to the blind man again, "What do you
say about Him, since He opened your eyes?" And he said, "He is
a prophet."
18The Jews therefore did not believe *it* of him, that he had been
blind, and had received sight, until they called the parents of the
very one who had received his sight,
19and questioned them, saying, "Is this your son, who you say
was born blind? Then how does he now see?"
20His parents answered them and said, "We know that this is
our son, and that he was born blind;
21but how he now sees, we do not know; or who opened his
eyes, we do not know. Ask him; he is of age, he shall speak for
himself."
22His parents said this because they were afraid of the Jews; for
the Jews had already agreed, that if anyone should confess Him
to be Christ, he should be put out of the synagogue.
23For this reason his parents said, "He is of age; ask him."
24¶ So a second time they called the man who had been blind,
and said to him, "Give glory to God; we know that this man is a
sinner."
25He therefore answered, "Whether He is a sinner, I do not
know; one thing I do know, that, whereas I was blind, now I see."
26They said therefore to him, "What did He do to you? How did
He open your eyes?"

## New International

born, I am!" 59At this, they picked up stones to stone him, but
Jesus hid himself, slipping away from the temple grounds.

*Jesus Heals a Man Born Blind*

9 AS HE went along, he saw a man blind from birth. 2His
disciples asked him, "Rabbi, who sinned, this man or his
parents, that he was born blind?"
3"Neither this man nor his parents sinned," said Jesus, "but
this happened so that the work of God might be displayed in his
life. 4As long as it is day, we must do the work of him who sent
me. Night is coming, when no one can work. 5While I am in the
world, I am the light of the world."
6Having said this, he spit on the ground, made some mud with
the saliva, and put it on the man's eyes. 7"Go," he told him, "wash
in the Pool of Siloam" (this word means Sent). So the man went
and washed, and came home seeing.
8His neighbors and those who had formerly seen him begging
asked, "Isn't this the same man who used to sit and beg?" 9Some
claimed that he was.
Others said, "No, he only looks like him."
But he himself insisted, "I am the man."
10"How then were your eyes opened?" they demanded.
11He replied, "The man they call Jesus made some mud and put
it on my eyes. He told me to go to Siloam and wash. So I went and
washed, and then I could see."
12"Where is this man?" they asked him.
"I don't know," he said.

*The Pharisees Investigate the Healing*

13They brought to the Pharisees the man who had been blind.
14Now the day on which Jesus had made the mud and opened the
man's eyes was a Sabbath. 15Therefore the Pharisees also asked
him how he had received his sight. "He put mud on my eyes," the
man replied, "and I washed, and now I see."
16Some of the Pharisees said, "This man is not from God, for
he does not keep the Sabbath."
But others asked, "How can a sinner do such miraculous
signs?" So they were divided.
17Finally they turned again to the blind man, "What have you
to say about him? It was your eyes he opened."
The man replied, "He is a prophet."
18The Jews still did not believe that he had been blind and had
received his sight until they sent for the man's parents. 19"Is this
your son?" they asked. "Is this the one you say was born blind?
How is it that now he can see?"
20"We know he is our son," the parents answered, "and we
know he was born blind. 21But how he can see now, or who
opened his eyes, we don't know. Ask him. He is of age; he will
speak for himself." 22His parents said this because they were afraid
of the Jews, for already the Jews had decided that anyone who
acknowledged that Jesus was the Christ[c] would be put out of the
synagogue. 23That was why his parents said, "He is of age; ask
him."
24A second time they summoned the man who had been blind.
"Give glory to God,[d]" they said. "We know this man is a sinner."
25He replied, "Whether he is a sinner or not, I don't know. One
thing I do know. I was blind but now I see!"
26Then they asked him, "What did he do to you? How did he
open your eyes?"

NIV [c]22 Or *Messiah* [d]24 A solemn charge to tell the truth (see Joshua 7:19)

## King James

27 He answered them, I have told you already, and ye did not
hear: wherefore would ye hear *it* again? will ye also be his disciples?
28 Then they reviled him, and said, Thou art his disciple; but we
are Moses' disciples.
29 We know that God spake unto Moses: *as for* this *fellow,* we
know not from whence he is.
30 The man answered and said unto them, Why herein is a
marvellous thing, that ye know not from whence he is, and *yet* he
hath opened mine eyes.
31 Now we know that God heareth not sinners: but if any man
be a worshipper of God, and doeth his will, him he heareth.
32 Since the world began was it not heard that any man opened
the eyes of one that was born blind.
33 If this man were not of God, he could do nothing.
34 They answered and said unto him, Thou wast altogether born
in sins, and dost thou teach us? And they cast him out.
35 Jesus heard that they had cast him out; and when he had
found him, he said unto him, Dost thou believe on the Son of God?
36 He answered and said, Who is he, Lord, that I might believe
on him?
37 And Jesus said unto him, Thou hast both seen him, and it is
he that talketh with thee.
38 And he said, Lord, I believe. And he worshipped him.
39 ¶ And Jesus said, For judgment I am come into this world, that
they which see not might see; and that they which see might be
made blind.
40 And *some* of the Pharisees which were with him heard these
words, and said unto him, Are we blind also?
41 Jesus said unto them, If ye were blind, ye should have no sin:
but now ye say, We see; therefore your sin remaineth.

**10** VERILY, VERILY, I say unto you, He that entereth not by
the door into the sheepfold, but climbeth up some other
way, the same is a thief and a robber.
2 But he that entereth in by the door is the shepherd of the
sheep.
3 To him the porter openeth; and the sheep hear his voice: and
he calleth his own sheep by name, and leadeth them out.
4 And when he putteth forth his own sheep, he goeth before
them, and the sheep follow him: for they know his voice.
5 And a stranger will they not follow, but will flee from him: for
they know not the voice of strangers.
6 This parable spake Jesus unto them: but they understood not
what things they were which he spake unto them.
7 Then said Jesus unto them again, Verily, verily, I say unto you,
I am the door of the sheep.
8 All that ever came before me are thieves and robbers: but the
sheep did not hear them.
9 I am the door: by me if any man enter in, he shall be saved,
and shall go in and out, and find pasture.
10 The thief cometh not, but for to steal, and to kill, and to
destroy: I am come that they might have life, and that they might
have *it* more abundantly.

AMP [a] Many ancient authorities read "the Son of God." [b] Vincent.
[c] Vincent. [d] Souter's "Pocket Lexicon to the Greek New Testament."

## Amplified

27 He answered, I already told you, and you would not listen.
Why do you want to hear it again? Can it be that you wish to
become His disciples also?
28 And they stormed at him—they jeered, they sneered, they
reviled him—and retorted, You are His disciple yourself, but we
are the disciples of Moses.
29 We know for certain that God spoke with Moses, but as for
this Fellow, we know nothing about where He hails from.
30 The man replied, Well, this is astonishing! Here a Man has
opened my eyes, and yet you do not know where He comes
from—that is amazing!
31 We know that God does not listen to sinners; but if any one
is God-fearing *and* a worshipper of Him and does His will, He
listens to him.
32 Since the beginning of time it was never heard of that any one
opened the eyes of a man born blind.
33 If that Man were not from God, He would not be able to do
anything like this.
34 They retorted, You were wholly born in sin—from head to
foot—and do you [presume to] teach us? So they cast him out—
threw him clear outside the synagogue.
35 Jesus heard that they had put him out, and meeting him He
said, Do you believe in *and* adhere to the Son of man— [a]the Son
of God?
36 He answered, Who is He, Sir? Tell me, that I may believe in
*and* adhere to Him.
37 Jesus said to him, You have seen Him; [in fact] He is talking
to you right now.
38 He called out, Lord, I believe—I rely on, I trust, I cleave to
You! And he worshipped Him.
39 Then Jesus said, I came into this world for judgment—as a
Separator, in order that there may be [b]separation [between those
who believe on Me and those who reject Me]—to make the sightless see, and that those who see may become blind.
40 Some Pharisees who were near, hearing this remark said to
Him, Are we also blind?
41 Jesus said to them, If you were blind, you would have no sin;
but because you now claim to have sight, your sin remains.—If you
were blind, you would not be guilty of sin; but because you insist,
We do see [clearly], you are unable to escape your guilt.

**10** I ASSURE you, most solemnly I tell you, he who does not
enter in by the door into the sheepfold, but climbs up
some other way (elsewhere, from some other quarter) is a thief and
a robber.
2 But he who enters by the door is the shepherd of the sheep.
3 The watchman opens the door for this man, and the sheep
listen to his voice *and* heed it, and he calls his own sheep by name
and brings (leads) them out.
4 When he has brought his own sheep outside, he walks on
before them, and the sheep follow him, because they know his
voice.
5 They will never [on any account] follow a stranger, but will run
away from him, because they do not know the voice of strangers
*or* recognize their call.
6 Jesus used this parable (illustration) with them, but they did
not understand what He was talking about.
7 So Jesus said again, I assure you, most solemnly I tell you, that
I Myself am the Door [c]for the sheep.
8 All others who came [as such] before Me are thieves and robbers; but the [true] sheep did not listen *and* obey them.
9 I am the Door. Any one who enters in through Me will be
saved—will live; he will come in and he will go out [freely], and
will find pasture.
10 The thief comes only in order that he may steal and may kill
and may destroy. I came that they may have *and* enjoy life, and
have it in abundance—to the full, till it [d]overflows.

## New American Standard

27He answered them, "I told you already, and you did not
listen; why do you want to hear *it* again? You do not want to
become His disciples too, do you?"
28And they reviled him, and said, "You are His disciple, but we
are disciples of Moses.
29"We know that God has spoken to Moses; but as for this man,
we do not know where He is from."
30The man answered and said to them, "Well, here is an amazing thing, that you do not know where He is from, and *yet* He
opened my eyes.
31"We know that God does not hear sinners; but if anyone is
God-fearing, and does His will, He hears him.
32"Since the beginning of time it has never been heard that
anyone opened the eyes of a person born blind.
33"If this man were not from God, He could do nothing."
34They answered and said to him, "You were born entirely in
sins, and are you teaching us?" And they put him out.

*Jesus Affirms His Deity*

35¶ Jesus heard that they had put him out; and finding him, He
said, "Do you believe in the Son of Man?"
36He answered and said, "And who is He, Lord, that I may
believe in Him?"
37Jesus said to him, "You have both seen Him, and He is the
one who is talking with you."
38And he said, "Lord, I believe." And he worshiped Him.
39And Jesus said, "For judgment I came into this world, that
those who do not see may see; and that those who see may become
blind."
40Those of the Pharisees who were with Him heard these
things, and said to Him, "We are not blind too, are we?"
41Jesus said to them, "If you were blind, you would have no sin;
but since you say, 'We see,' your sin remains.

*Parable of the Good Shepherd*

10 "TRULY, TRULY, I say to you, he who does not enter by
the door into the fold of the sheep, but climbs up some
other way, he is a thief and a robber.
2"But he who enters by the door is a shepherd of the sheep.
3"To him the doorkeeper opens, and the sheep hear his voice,
and he calls his own sheep by name, and leads them out.
4"When he puts forth all his own, he goes before them, and
the sheep follow him because they know his voice.
5"And a stranger they simply will not follow, but will flee from
him, because they do not know the voice of strangers."
6This figure of speech Jesus spoke to them, but they did not
understand what those things were which He had been saying to
them.
7¶ Jesus therefore said to them again, "Truly, truly, I say to
you, I am the door of the sheep.
8"All who came before Me are thieves and robbers, but the
sheep did not hear them.
9"I am the door; if anyone enters through Me, he shall be
saved, and shall go in and out, and find pasture.
10"The thief comes only to steal, and kill, and destroy; I came
that they might have life, and might have *it* abundantly.

## New International

27He answered, "I have told you already and you did not listen.
Why do you want to hear it again? Do you want to become his
disciples, too?"
28Then they hurled insults at him and said, "You are this fellow's disciple! We are disciples of Moses! 29We know that God
spoke to Moses, but as for this fellow, we don't even know where
he comes from."
30The man answered, "Now that is remarkable! You don't
know where he comes from, yet he opened my eyes. 31We know
that God does not listen to sinners. He listens to the godly man
who does his will. 32Nobody has ever heard of opening the eyes
of a man born blind. 33If this man were not from God, he could
do nothing."
34To this they replied, "You were steeped in sin at birth; how
dare you lecture us!" And they threw him out.

*Spiritual Blindness*

35Jesus heard that they had thrown him out, and when he
found him, he said, "Do you believe in the Son of Man?"
36"Who is he, sir?" the man asked. "Tell me so that I may
believe in him."
37Jesus said, "You have now seen him; in fact, he is the one
speaking with you."
38Then the man said, "Lord, I believe," and he worshiped him.
39Jesus said, "For judgment I have come into this world, so that
the blind will see and those who see will become blind."
40Some Pharisees who were with him heard him say this and
asked, "What? Are we blind too?"
41Jesus said, "If you were blind, you would not be guilty of sin;
but now that you claim you can see, your guilt remains.

*The Shepherd and His Flock*

10 "I TELL you the truth, the man who does not enter the
sheep pen by the gate, but climbs in by some other way,
is a thief and a robber. 2The man who enters by the gate is the
shepherd of his sheep. 3The watchman opens the gate for him, and
the sheep listen to his voice. He calls his own sheep by name and
leads them out. 4When he has brought out all his own, he goes on
ahead of them, and his sheep follow him because they know his
voice. 5But they will never follow a stranger; in fact, they will run
away from him because they do not recognize a stranger's voice."
6Jesus used this figure of speech, but they did not understand
what he was telling them.
7Therefore Jesus said again, "I tell you the truth, I am the gate
for the sheep. 8All who ever came before me were thieves and
robbers, but the sheep did not listen to them. 9I am the gate;
whoever enters through me will be saved.[e] He will come in and
go out, and find pasture. 10The thief comes only to steal and kill
and destroy; I have come that they may have life, and have it to
the full.

NIV [e] 9 Or *kept safe*

## King James

11 I am the good shepherd: the good shepherd giveth his life for the sheep.

12 But he that is an hireling, and not the shepherd, whose own the sheep are not, seeth the wolf coming, and leaveth the sheep, and fleeth: and the wolf catcheth them, and scattereth the sheep.

13 The hireling fleeth, because he is an hireling, and careth not for the sheep.

14 I am the good shepherd, and know my *sheep*, and am known of mine.

15 As the Father knoweth me, even so know I the Father: and I lay down my life for the sheep.

16 And other sheep I have, which are not of this fold: them also I must bring, and they shall hear my voice; and there shall be one fold, *and* one shepherd.

17 Therefore doth my Father love me, because I lay down my life, that I might take it again.

18 No man taketh it from me, but I lay it down of myself. I have power to lay it down, and I have power to take it again. This commandment have I received of my Father.

19 ¶ There was a division therefore again among the Jews for these sayings.

20 And many of them said, He hath a devil, and is mad; why hear ye him?

21 Others said, These are not the words of him that hath a devil. Can a devil open the eyes of the blind?

22 ¶ And it was at Jerusalem the feast of the dedication, and it was winter.

23 And Jesus walked in the temple in Solomon's porch.

24 Then came the Jews round about him, and said unto him, How long dost thou make us to doubt? If thou be the Christ, tell us plainly.

25 Jesus answered them, I told you, and ye believed not: the works that I do in my Father's name, they bear witness of me.

26 But ye believe not, because ye are not of my sheep, as I said unto you.

27 My sheep hear my voice, and I know them, and they follow me:

28 And I give unto them eternal life; and they shall never perish, neither shall any *man* pluck them out of my hand.

29 My Father, which gave *them* me, is greater than all; and no *man* is able to pluck *them* out of my Father's hand.

30 I and *my* Father are one.

31 Then the Jews took up stones again to stone him.

32 Jesus answered them, Many good works have I shown you from my Father; for which of those works do ye stone me?

33 The Jews answered him, saying, For a good work we stone thee not; but for blasphemy; and because that thou, being a man, makest thyself God.

34 Jesus answered them, Is it not written in your law, I said, Ye are gods?

35 If he called them gods, unto whom the word of God came, and the scripture cannot be broken;

36 Say ye of him, whom the Father hath sanctified, and sent into the world, Thou blasphemest; because I said, I am the Son of God?

## Amplified

11 I am the Good Shepherd. The good shepherd risks *and* lays down his [own] life for the sheep. [Ps. 23.]

12 But the hired servant—he who merely serves for wages—who is neither the shepherd nor the owner of the sheep, when he sees the wolf coming deserts the flock and runs away. And the wolf chases *and* snatches them and scatters [the flock].

13 Now *the hireling flees* because he merely serves for wages and is not himself concerned about the sheep—cares nothing for them.

14 I am the Good Shepherd and I know *and* recognize My own, and My own know *and* recognize Me,

15 Even as [truly as] the Father knows Me I also know the Father; and I am giving My [very own] life *and* laying it down in behalf of the sheep.

16 And I have other sheep [beside these], that are not of this fold. I must bring *and* [a]impel those also, and they will listen to My voice *and* heed My call, and so there will be (they will become) one flock under one Shepherd. [Ezek. 34:23.]

17 For this the Father loves Me, because I lay down My [own] life to take it back again.

18 No one takes it away from Me. On the contrary, I lay it down voluntarily—I put it from Myself. I am authorized *and* have power to lay it down—to resign it; and I am authorized *and* have power to take it back again. These are the instructions (orders) which I have received [as My charge] from My Father.

19 Then a fresh division of opinion arose among the Jews because of His saying these things.

20 And many of them said, He has a demon and He is mad—insane, He raves, He rambles. Why do you listen to Him?

21 Others argued, These are not the thoughts *and* the language of one possessed. Can a demon-possessed person open blind eyes?

22 After this the Feast of Dedication [of the reconsecration of the temple] was taking place at Jerusalem.

23 It was winter, and Jesus was walking in Solomon's porch in the temple area.

24 So the Jews surrounded Him and began asking Him, How long are You going to keep us in doubt *and* suspense? If You are really Christ, tell us so plainly *and* openly.

25 Jesus answered them, I have told you so, yet you do not believe Me—you do not trust Me *and* rely on Me. The very works that I do by the power of My Father *and* in My Father's name bear witness concerning Me—they are My credentials and evidence in support of Me.

26 But you do not believe *and* trust *and* rely on Me, because you do not belong to My fold—you are no sheep of Mine.

27 The sheep that are My own hear *and* are listening to My voice, and I know them and they follow Me,

28 And I give them eternal life, and they shall never lose it *or* perish throughout the ages—to all eternity they shall never by any means be destroyed. And no one is able to snatch them out of My hand.

29 My Father, Who has given them to Me, is greater *and* mightier than all else; and no one is able to snatch [them] out of the Father's hand.

30 I and the Father are One.

31 Again the Jews [b]brought up stones to stone Him.

32 Jesus said to them, My Father has enabled Me to do many good deeds—I have shown many acts of mercy in your presence. For which of these do you mean to stone Me?

33 The Jews replied, We are not going to stone You for a good act, but for blasphemy; because You, a mere man, make Yourself [out to be] God.

34 Jesus answered, Is it not written in your Law, I said, Ye are gods? [Ps. 82:6.]

35 So men are called gods—by the Law—men to whom God's message came, and the Scripture cannot be set aside *or* cancelled *or* broken *or* annulled. [If that is true] do you say [to Me],

36 The One Whom the Father consecrated *and* dedicated *and* set apart for Himself and sent into the world, You are blaspheming, because I said, I am the Son of God?

**AMP** [a] Abbott-Smith. [b] Vincent.

## New American Standard

11"I am the good shepherd; the good shepherd lays down His
life for the sheep.
12"He who is a hireling, and not a shepherd, who is not the
owner of the sheep, beholds the wolf coming, and leaves the
sheep, and flees, and the wolf snatches them, and scatters *them.*
13 *"He flees* because he is a hireling, and is not concerned about
the sheep.
14"I am the good shepherd; and I know My own, and My own
know Me,
15even as the Father knows Me and I know the Father; and I lay
down My life for the sheep.
16"And I have other sheep, which are not of this fold; I must
bring them also, and they shall hear My voice; and they shall
become one flock *with* one shepherd.
17"For this reason the Father loves Me, because I lay down My
life that I may take it again.
18"No one [c]has taken it away from Me, but I lay it down on My
own initiative. I have authority to lay it down, and I have authority
to take it up again. This commandment I received from My Father."

19¶ There arose a division again among the Jews because of
these words.
20And many of them were saying, "He has a demon and is
insane. Why do you listen to Him?"
21Others were saying, "These are not the sayings of one demon-possessed. A demon cannot open the eyes of the blind, can he?"

*Jesus Asserts His Deity*

22¶ At that time the Feast of the Dedication took place at Jerusalem;
23it was winter, and Jesus was walking in the temple in the
portico of Solomon.
24The Jews therefore gathered around Him, and were saying to
Him, "How long will You keep us in suspense? If You are the
Christ, tell us plainly."
25Jesus answered them, "I told you, and you do not believe; the
works that I do in My Father's name, these bear witness of Me.
26"But you do not believe, because you are not of My sheep.
27"My sheep hear My voice, and I know them, and they follow
Me;
28and I give eternal life to them, and they shall never perish; and
no one shall snatch them out of My hand.
29" [d]My Father, who has given *them* to Me, is greater than all;
and no one is able to snatch *them* out of the Father's hand.
30"I and the Father are one."
31¶ The Jews took up stones again to stone Him.
32Jesus answered them, "I showed you many good works from
the Father; for which of them are you stoning Me?"
33The Jews answered Him, "For a good work we do not stone
You, but for blasphemy; and because You, being a man, make
Yourself out *to be* God."
34Jesus answered them, "Has it not been written in your Law,
'I SAID, YOU ARE GODS'?
35"If he called them gods, to whom the word of God came (and
the Scripture cannot be broken),
36do you say of Him, whom the Father sanctified and sent into
the world, 'You are blaspheming,' because I said, 'I am the Son of
God'?

**NAS** [c] Many Gr. mss. read *takes* [d] Some early mss. read *What My Father has given Me is greater than all*

## New International

11"I am the good shepherd. The good shepherd lays down his
life for the sheep. 12The hired hand is not the shepherd who owns
the sheep. So when he sees the wolf coming, he abandons the
sheep and runs away. Then the wolf attacks the flock and scatters
it. 13The man runs away because he is a hired hand and cares
nothing for the sheep.
14"I am the good shepherd; I know my sheep and my sheep
know me— 15just as the Father knows me and I know the Father—
and I lay down my life for the sheep. 16I have other sheep that are
not of this sheep pen. I must bring them also. They too will listen
to my voice, and there shall be one flock and one shepherd. 17The
reason my Father loves me is that I lay down my life—only to take
it up again. 18No one takes it from me, but I lay it down of my own
accord. I have authority to lay it down and authority to take it up
again. This command I received from my Father."
19At these words the Jews were again divided. 20Many of them
said, "He is demon-possessed and raving mad. Why listen to
him?"
21But others said, "These are not the sayings of a man possessed by a demon. Can a demon open the eyes of the blind?"

*The Unbelief of the Jews*

22Then came the Feast of Dedication[e] at Jerusalem. It was winter, 23and Jesus was in the temple area walking in Solomon's
Colonnade. 24The Jews gathered around him, saying, "How long
will you keep us in suspense? If you are the Christ,[f] tell us plainly."
25Jesus answered, "I did tell you, but you do not believe. The
miracles I do in my Father's name speak for me, 26but you do not
believe because you are not my sheep. 27My sheep listen to my
voice; I know them, and they follow me. 28I give them eternal life,
and they shall never perish; no one can snatch them out of my
hand. 29My Father, who has given them to me, is greater than all[g];
no one can snatch them out of my Father's hand. 30I and the Father
are one."
31Again the Jews picked up stones to stone him, 32but Jesus said
to them, "I have shown you many great miracles from the Father.
For which of these do you stone me?"
33"We are not stoning you for any of these," replied the Jews,
"but for blasphemy, because you, a mere man, claim to be God."
34Jesus answered them, "Is it not written in your Law, 'I have
said you are gods'[h]? 35If he called them 'gods,' to whom the word
of God came—and the Scripture cannot be broken—36what about
the one whom the Father set apart as his very own and sent into
the world? Why then do you accuse me of blasphemy because I
said, 'I am God's Son'? 37Do not believe me unless I do what my

**NIV** [e] 22 That is, Hanukkah [f] 24 Or *Messiah* [g] 29 Many early manuscripts *What my Father has given me is greater than all* [h] 34 Psalm 82:6

## King James

37 If I do not the works of my Father, believe me not.

38 But if I do, though ye believe not me, believe the works: that ye may know, and believe, that the Father *is* in me, and I in him.

39 Therefore they sought again to take him: but he escaped out of their hand,

40 And went away again beyond Jordan into the place where John at first baptized; and there he abode.

41 And many resorted unto him, and said, John did no miracle: but all things that John spake of this man were true.

42 And many believed on him there.

**11** NOW A certain *man* was sick, *named* Lazarus, of Bethany, the town of Mary and her sister Martha.

2 (It was *that* Mary which anointed the Lord with ointment, and wiped his feet with her hair, whose brother Lazarus was sick.)

3 Therefore his sisters sent unto him, saying, Lord, behold, he whom thou lovest is sick.

4 When Jesus heard *that*, he said, This sickness is not unto death, but for the glory of God, that the Son of God might be glorified thereby.

5 Now Jesus loved Martha, and her sister, and Lazarus.

6 When he had heard therefore that he was sick, he abode two days still in the same place where he was.

7 Then after that saith he to *his* disciples, Let us go into Judaea again.

8 *His* disciples say unto him, Master, the Jews of late sought to stone thee; and goest thou thither again?

9 Jesus answered, Are there not twelve hours in the day? If any man walk in the day, he stumbleth not, because he seeth the light of this world.

10 But if a man walk in the night, he stumbleth, because there is no light in him.

11 These things said he: and after that he saith unto them, Our friend Lazarus sleepeth; but I go, that I may awake him out of sleep.

12 Then said his disciples, Lord, if he sleep, he shall do well.

13 Howbeit Jesus spake of his death: but they thought that he had spoken of taking of rest in sleep.

14 Then said Jesus unto them plainly, Lazarus is dead.

15 And I am glad for your sakes that I was not there, to the intent ye may believe; nevertheless let us go unto him.

16 Then said Thomas, which is called Didymus, unto his fellowdisciples, Let us also go, that we may die with him.

17 Then when Jesus came, he found that he had *lain* in the grave four days already.

18 Now Bethany was nigh unto Jerusalem, about fifteen furlongs off:

19 And many of the Jews came to Martha and Mary, to comfort them concerning their brother.

20 Then Martha, as soon as she heard that Jesus was coming, went and met him: but Mary sat *still* in the house.

21 Then said Martha unto Jesus, Lord, if thou hadst been here, my brother had not died.

22 But I know, that even now, whatsoever thou wilt ask of God, God will give *it* thee.

23 Jesus saith unto her, Thy brother shall rise again.

## Amplified

37 If I am not doing the works (performing the deeds) of My Father, then do not believe Me—do not adhere to Me and trust in and rely on Me.

38 But if I do them, even though you do not believe Me *nor* have faith in Me, [at least] believe the works *and* have faith in what I do, in order that you may know and understand [clearly] that the Father is in Me and I am in the Father—One with Him.

39 They sought again to arrest Him, but He escaped from their hands.

40 He went back again across the Jordan to the locality where John was when he first baptized, and there He remained.

41 And many came to Him, and they kept saying, John did not perform a [single] sign *or* miracle, but everything John said of this Man was true.

42 And many [people] there became believers on Him—they adhered to *and* trusted in *and* relied on Him.

**11** NOW A certain man named Lazarus was ill. He was of Bethany, the village where Mary and her sister Martha lived.

2 This Mary was the one who anointed the Lord with perfume and wiped His feet with her hair. It was her brother Lazarus who was [now] sick.

3 So the sisters sent to Him saying, Lord, he whom You love [so well] is sick.

4 When Jesus received the message He said, This sickness is not to end in death; but [on the contrary] it is to honor God *and* to promote His glory, that the Son of God may be glorified through (by) it.

5 Now Jesus loved Martha and her sister and Lazarus; [they were His dear friends and He held them in loving esteem].

6 Therefore, [even] when He heard that Lazarus was sick, He still stayed two days longer in the same place where He was.

7 Then, after that interval He said to His disciples, Let us go back again to Judea.

8 The disciples said to Him, Rabbi, the Jews only recently were intending *and* trying to stone You, and are You [thinking of] going back there again?

9 Jesus answered, Are there not twelve hours in the day? Any one who walks about in the daytime does not stumble, because he sees the light of this world.

10 But if any one walks about in the night, he does stumble, because there is no light in him—the light is lacking to him.

11 He said these things and then added, Our friend Lazarus is at rest *and* sleeping, but I am going there that I may awaken him out of his sleep.

12 The disciples answered, Lord, if he is sleeping, he will recover.

13 However, Jesus had spoken of his death, but they thought that He referred to falling into a refreshing *and* natural sleep.

14 So then Jesus told them plainly, Lazarus is dead;

15 And for your sake I am glad that I was not there; it will help you to believe—to trust and rely on Me. However, let us go to him.

16 Then Thomas, who was called the Twin, said to his fellow disciples, Let us go too, that we may die [be killed] along with Him.

17 So when Jesus arrived, He found that he [Lazarus] had already been in the tomb four days.

18 Bethany was near Jerusalem, only about two miles away.

19 And a considerable number of the Jews had gone out to see Martha and Mary to console them concerning their brother.

20 When Martha heard that Jesus was coming, she went to meet Him, while Mary remained sitting in the house.

21 Martha then said to Jesus, Master, if You had been here, my brother would not have died.

22 And even now I know that whatever You ask from God He will grant it to You.

23 Jesus said to her, Your brother shall rise again.

## New American Standard

37"If I do not do the works of My Father, do not believe Me;
38but if I do them, though you do not believe Me, believe the
works, that you may know and understand that the Father is in
Me, and I in the Father."
39Therefore they were seeking again to seize Him, and He
eluded their grasp.
40¶ And He went away again beyond the Jordan to the place
where John was first baptizing, and He was staying there.
41And many came to Him and were saying, "While John performed no sign, yet everything John said about this man was
true."
42And many believed in Him there.

*The Death and Resurrection of Lazarus*

11 NOW A certain man was sick, Lazarus of Bethany, the
village of Mary and her sister Martha.
2And it was the Mary who anointed the Lord with ointment,
and wiped His feet with her hair, whose brother Lazarus was sick.
3The sisters therefore sent to Him, saying, "Lord, behold, he
whom You love is sick."
4But when Jesus heard it, He said, "This sickness is not unto
death, but for the glory of God, that the Son of God may be
glorified by it."
5Now Jesus loved Martha, and her sister, and Lazarus.
6When therefore He heard that he was sick, He stayed then
two days *longer* in the place where He was.
7Then after this He *said to the disciples, "Let us go to Judea
again."
8The disciples *said to Him, "Rabbi, the Jews were just now
seeking to stone You, and are You going there again?"
9Jesus answered, "Are there not twelve hours in the day? If
anyone walks in the day, he does not stumble, because he sees the
light of this world.
10"But if anyone walks in the night, he stumbles, because the
light is not in him."
11This He said, and after that He *said to them, "Our friend
Lazarus has fallen asleep; but I go, that I may awaken him out of
sleep."
12The disciples therefore said to Him, "Lord, if he has fallen
asleep, he will recover."
13Now Jesus had spoken of his death, but they thought that He
was speaking of literal sleep.
14Then Jesus therefore said to them plainly, "Lazarus is dead,
15and I am glad for your sakes that I was not there, so that you
may believe; but let us go to him."
16Thomas therefore, who is called Didymus, said to *his* fellow
disciples, "Let us also go, that we may die with Him."
17¶ So when Jesus came, He found that he had already been in
the tomb four days.
18Now Bethany was near Jerusalem, about two miles off;
19and many of the Jews had come to Martha and Mary, to
console them concerning *their* brother.
20Martha therefore, when she heard that Jesus was coming,
went to meet Him; but Mary still sat in the house.
21Martha therefore said to Jesus, "Lord, if You had been here,
my brother would not have died.
22"Even now I know that whatever You ask of God, God will
give You."
23Jesus *said to her, "Your brother shall rise again."

## New International

Father does. 38But if I do it, even though you do not believe me,
believe the miracles, that you may know and understand that the
Father is in me, and I in the Father." 39Again they tried to seize
him, but he escaped their grasp.
40Then Jesus went back across the Jordan to the place where
John had been baptizing in the early days. Here he stayed 41and
many people came to him. They said, "Though John never performed a miraculous sign, all that John said about this man was
true." 42And in that place many believed in Jesus.

*The Death of Lazarus*

11 NOW A man named Lazarus was sick. He was from Bethany, the village of Mary and her sister Martha. 2This Mary,
whose brother Lazarus now lay sick, was the same one who
poured perfume on the Lord and wiped his feet with her hair. 3So
the sisters sent word to Jesus, "Lord, the one you love is sick."
4When he heard this, Jesus said, "This sickness will not end in
death. No, it is for God's glory so that God's Son may be glorified
through it." 5Jesus loved Martha and her sister and Lazarus. 6Yet
when he heard that Lazarus was sick, he stayed where he was two
more days.
7Then he said to his disciples, "Let us go back to Judea."
8"But Rabbi," they said, "a short while ago the Jews tried to
stone you, and yet you are going back there?"
9Jesus answered, "Are there not twelve hours of daylight? A
man who walks by day will not stumble, for he sees by this world's
light. 10It is when he walks by night that he stumbles, for he has
no light."
11After he had said this, he went on to tell them, "Our friend
Lazarus has fallen asleep; but I am going there to wake him up."
12His disciples replied, "Lord, if he sleeps, he will get better."
13Jesus had been speaking of his death, but his disciples thought
he meant natural sleep.
14So then he told them plainly, "Lazarus is dead, 15and for your
sake I am glad I was not there, so that you may believe. But let us
go to him."
16Then Thomas (called Didymus) said to the rest of the disciples, "Let us also go, that we may die with him."

*Jesus Comforts the Sisters*

17On his arrival, Jesus found that Lazarus had already been in
the tomb for four days. 18Bethany was less than two miles[a] from
Jerusalem, 19and many Jews had come to Martha and Mary to
comfort them in the loss of their brother. 20When Martha heard
that Jesus was coming, she went out to meet him, but Mary stayed
at home.
21"Lord," Martha said to Jesus, "if you had been here, my
brother would not have died. 22But I know that even now God will
give you whatever you ask."
23Jesus said to her, "Your brother will rise again."

**NIV** [a] *18* Greek *fifteen stadia* (about 3 kilometers)

## King James

24 Martha saith unto him, I know that he shall rise again in the resurrection at the last day.

25 Jesus said unto her, I am the resurrection, and the life: he that believeth in me, though he were dead, yet shall he live:

26 And whosoever liveth and believeth in me shall never die. Believest thou this?

27 She saith unto him, Yea, Lord: I believe that thou art the Christ, the Son of God, which should come into the world.

28 And when she had so said, she went her way, and called Mary her sister secretly, saying, The Master is come, and calleth for thee.

29 As soon as she heard *that,* she arose quickly, and came unto him.

30 Now Jesus was not yet come into the town, but was in that place where Martha met him.

31 The Jews then which were with her in the house, and comforted her, when they saw Mary, that she rose up hastily and went out, followed her, saying, She goeth unto the grave to weep there.

32 Then when Mary was come where Jesus was, and saw him, she fell down at his feet, saying unto him, Lord, if thou hadst been here, my brother had not died.

33 When Jesus therefore saw her weeping, and the Jews also weeping which came with her, he groaned in the spirit, and was troubled,

34 And said, Where have ye laid him? They said unto him, Lord, come and see.

35 Jesus wept.

36 Then said the Jews, Behold how he loved him!

37 And some of them said, Could not this man, which opened the eyes of the blind, have caused that even this man should not have died?

38 Jesus therefore again groaning in himself cometh to the grave. It was a cave, and a stone lay upon it.

39 Jesus said, Take ye away the stone. Martha, the sister of him that was dead, saith unto him, Lord, by this time he stinketh: for he hath been *dead* four days.

40 Jesus saith unto her, Said I not unto thee, that, if thou wouldest believe, thou shouldest see the glory of God?

41 Then they took away the stone *from the place* where the dead was laid. And Jesus lifted up *his* eyes, and said, Father, I thank thee that thou hast heard me.

42 And I knew that thou hearest me always: but because of the people which stand by I said *it,* that they may believe that thou hast sent me.

43 And when he thus had spoken, he cried with a loud voice, Lazarus, come forth.

44 And he that was dead came forth, bound hand and foot with graveclothes: and his face was bound about with a napkin. Jesus saith unto them, Loose him, and let him go.

45 Then many of the Jews which came to Mary, and had seen the things which Jesus did, believed on him.

46 But some of them went their ways to the Pharisees, and told them what things Jesus had done.

47 ¶ Then gathered the chief priests and the Pharisees a council, and said, What do we? for this man doeth many miracles.

48 If we let him thus alone, all *men* will believe on him: and the Romans shall come and take away both our place and nation.

49 And one of them, *named* Caiaphas, being the high priest that same year, said unto them, Ye know nothing at all,

## Amplified

24 Martha replied, I know that he will rise again at the resurrection in the last day.

25 Jesus said to her, I am [Myself] the Resurrection and the Life. Whoever believes in—adheres to, trusts in and relies on—Me, although he may die, yet he shall live.

26 And whoever continues to live and believes—has faith in, cleaves to and relies—on Me shall never [actually] die at all. Do you believe this?

27 She said to Him, Yes, Lord, I have believed—I do believe—that You are the Messiah, the Anointed One, the Son of God, [even He] Who was to come into the world. [It is for Your coming that the world has waited.]

28 After she had said this, she went back and called her sister Mary, privately whispering to her, The Teacher is close at hand and is asking for you.

29 When she heard this she sprang up quickly and went to Him.

30 Now Jesus had not yet entered the village, but was still at the same spot where Martha had met Him.

31 When the Jews who were sitting with her in the house and consoling her saw how hastily Mary had arisen and gone out, they followed her, supposing that she was going to the tomb to pour out her grief there.

32 When Mary came to the place where Jesus was and saw Him, she dropped down at His feet, saying to Him, Lord, if You had been here my brother would not have died.

33 When Jesus saw her sobbing, and the Jews who came with her [also] sobbing, He was deeply moved in spirit and troubled—He chafed in spirit, and sighed and was disturbed.

34 And He said, Where have you laid him? They said to Him, Lord, come and see.

35 Jesus wept.

36 The Jews said, See how tenderly He loved him!

37 But some of them said, Could not He, Who opened a blind man's eyes, have prevented this man from dying?

38 Now Jesus again sighing repeatedly *and* deeply disquieted, approached the tomb. It was a cave—a hole in the rock—and a boulder lay against [the entrance to close] it.

39 Jesus said, Take away the stone. Martha, the sister of the dead man, exclaimed, But Lord, by this time he [is decaying and] throws off an offensive odor, for he has been dead four days!

40 Jesus said to her, Did I not tell you *and* [a]promise you that if you would believe *and* rely on Me, you should see the glory of God?

41 So they took away the stone. And Jesus lifted up His eyes and said, Father, I thank You that You have heard Me.

42 Yes, I know You always hear *and* listen to Me; but I have said this on account of *and* for the benefit of the people standing around, so that they may believe You did send Me—that You have made Me Your Messenger.

43 When He had said this, He shouted with a loud voice, Lazarus, come out!

44 And out walked the man who had been dead, his hands and feet wrapped in burial cloths (linen strips), and with a [burial] napkin bound around his face. Jesus said to them, Free him of the burial wrappings and let him go.

45 Upon seeing what Jesus had done, many of the Jews who had come with Mary believed on Him—they trusted in Him and adhered to Him and relied on Him.

46 But some of them went back to the Pharisees and told them what Jesus had done.

47 So the chief priests and Pharisees called a meeting of the council [the Sanhedrin] and said, What are we to do? For this Man performs many signs (evidences, miracles).

48 If we let Him alone to go on like this, everyone will believe in Him *and* adhere to Him, and the Romans will come and suppress *and* destroy *and* take away our [holy] place and our nation [ [b]our temple and city, and our civil organization].

49 But one of them, Caiaphas, who was the high priest that year, declared, You know nothing at all.

**AMP** [a] Williams. [b] Vincent: "Word Studies in the New Testament."

## New American Standard

24Martha *said to Him, "I know that he will rise again in the
resurrection on the last day."
25Jesus said to her, "I am the resurrection and the life; he who
believes in Me shall live even if he dies,
26and everyone who lives and believes in Me shall never die.
Do you believe this?"
27She *said to Him, "Yes, Lord; I have believed that You are the
Christ, the Son of God, *even* He who comes into the world."
28And when she had said this, she went away, and called Mary
her sister, saying secretly, "The Teacher is here, and is calling for
you."
29And when she heard it, she *arose quickly, and was coming
to Him.
30¶ Now Jesus had not yet come into the village, but was still
in the place where Martha met Him.
31The Jews then who were with her in the house, and consoling
her, when they saw that Mary rose up quickly and went out,
followed her, supposing that she was going to the tomb to weep
there.
32Therefore, when Mary came where Jesus was, she saw Him,
and fell at His feet, saying to Him, "Lord, if You had been here,
my brother would not have died."
33When Jesus therefore saw her weeping, and the Jews who
came with her, *also* weeping, He was deeply moved in spirit, and
was troubled,
34and said, "Where have you laid him?" They *said to Him,
"Lord, come and see."
35Jesus wept.
36And so the Jews were saying, "Behold how He loved him!"
37But some of them said, "Could not this man, who opened the
eyes of him who was blind, have kept this man also from dying?"
38¶ Jesus therefore again being deeply moved within, *came to
the tomb. Now it was a cave, and a stone was lying against it.
39Jesus *said, "Remove the stone." Martha, the sister of the
deceased, *said to Him, "Lord, by this time there will be a stench,
for he has been *dead* four days."
40Jesus *said to her, "Did I not say to you, if you believe, you
will see the glory of God?"
41And so they removed the stone. And Jesus raised His eyes,
and said, "Father, I thank Thee that Thou heardest Me.
42"And I knew that Thou hearest Me always; but because of the
people standing around I said it, that they may believe that Thou
didst send Me."
43And when He had said these things, He cried out with a loud
voice, "Lazarus, come forth."
44He who had died came forth, bound hand and foot with
wrappings; and his face was wrapped around with a cloth. Jesus
*said to them, "Unbind him, and let him go."
45¶ Many therefore of the Jews, who had come to Mary and
beheld what He had done, believed in Him.
46But some of them went away to the Pharisees, and told them
the things which Jesus had done.

*Conspiracy to Kill Jesus*

47¶ Therefore the chief priests and the Pharisees convened a
council, and were saying, "What are we doing? For this man is
performing many signs.
48"If we let Him *go on* like this, all men will believe in Him, and
the Romans will come and take away both our place and our
nation."
49But a certain one of them, Caiaphas, who was high priest that
year, said to them, "You know nothing at all,

## New International

24Martha answered, "I know he will rise again in the resurrection at the last day."
25Jesus said to her, "I am the resurrection and the life. He who
believes in me will live, even though he dies; 26and whoever lives
and believes in me will never die. Do you believe this?"
27"Yes, Lord," she told him, "I believe that you are the Christ,[c]
the Son of God, who was to come into the world."
28And after she had said this, she went back and called her
sister Mary aside. "The Teacher is here," she said, "and is asking
for you." 29When Mary heard this, she got up quickly and went
to him. 30Now Jesus had not yet entered the village, but was still
at the place where Martha had met him. 31When the Jews who had
been with Mary in the house, comforting her, noticed how quickly
she got up and went out, they followed her, supposing she was
going to the tomb to mourn there.
32When Mary reached the place where Jesus was and saw him,
she fell at his feet and said, "Lord, if you had been here, my
brother would not have died."
33When Jesus saw her weeping, and the Jews who had come
along with her also weeping, he was deeply moved in spirit and
troubled. 34"Where have you laid him?" he asked.
"Come and see, Lord," they replied.
35Jesus wept.
36Then the Jews said, "See how he loved him!"
37But some of them said, "Could not he who opened the eyes
of the blind man have kept this man from dying?"

*Jesus Raises Lazarus From the Dead*

38Jesus, once more deeply moved, came to the tomb. It was a
cave with a stone laid across the entrance. 39"Take away the
stone," he said.
"But, Lord," said Martha, the sister of the dead man, "by this
time there is a bad odor, for he has been there four days."
40Then Jesus said, "Did I not tell you that if you believed, you
would see the glory of God?"
41So they took away the stone. Then Jesus looked up and said,
"Father, I thank you that you have heard me. 42I knew that you
always hear me, but I said this for the benefit of the people standing here, that they may believe that you sent me."
43When he had said this, Jesus called in a loud voice, "Lazarus,
come out!" 44The dead man came out, his hands and feet wrapped
with strips of linen, and a cloth around his face.
Jesus said to them, "Take off the grave clothes and let him go."

*The Plot to Kill Jesus*

45Therefore many of the Jews who had come to visit Mary, and
had seen what Jesus did, put their faith in him. 46But some of them
went to the Pharisees and told them what Jesus had done. 47Then
the chief priests and the Pharisees called a meeting of the Sanhedrin.
"What are we accomplishing?" they asked. "Here is this man
performing many miraculous signs. 48If we let him go on like this,
everyone will believe in him, and then the Romans will come and
take away both our place[d] and our nation."
49Then one of them, named Caiaphas, who was high priest that
year, spoke up, "You know nothing at all! 50You do not realize that

NIV [c] 27 Or *Messiah* [d] 48 Or *temple*

## King James

50 Nor consider that it is expedient for us, that one man should die for the people, and that the whole nation perish not.

51 And this spake he not of himself: but being high priest that year, he prophesied that Jesus should die for that nation;

52 And not for that nation only, but that also he should gather together in one the children of God that were scattered abroad.

53 Then from that day forth they took counsel together for to put him to death.

54 Jesus therefore walked no more openly among the Jews; but went thence unto a country near to the wilderness, into a city called Ephraim, and there continued with his disciples.

55 ¶ And the Jews' passover was nigh at hand: and many went out of the country up to Jerusalem before the passover, to purify themselves.

56 Then sought they for Jesus, and spake among themselves, as they stood in the temple, What think ye, that he will not come to the feast?

57 Now both the chief priests and the Pharisees had given a commandment, that, if any man knew where he were, he should show *it,* that they might take him.

**12** THEN JESUS six days before the passover came to Bethany, where Lazarus was which had been dead, whom he raised from the dead.

2 There they made him a supper; and Martha served: but Lazarus was one of them that sat at the table with him.

3 Then took Mary a pound of ointment of spikenard, very costly, and anointed the feet of Jesus, and wiped his feet with her hair: and the house was filled with the odour of the ointment.

4 Then saith one of his disciples, Judas Iscariot, Simon's *son,* which should betray him,

5 Why was not this ointment sold for three hundred pence, and given to the poor?

6 This he said, not that he cared for the poor; but because he was a thief, and had the bag, and bare what was put therein.

7 Then said Jesus, Let her alone: against the day of my burying hath she kept this.

8 For the poor always ye have with you; but me ye have not always.

9 Much people of the Jews therefore knew that he was there: and they came not for Jesus' sake only, but that they might see Lazarus also, whom he had raised from the dead.

10 ¶ But the chief priests consulted that they might put Lazarus also to death;

11 Because that by reason of him many of the Jews went away, and believed on Jesus.

12 ¶ On the next day much people that were come to the feast, when they heard that Jesus was coming to Jerusalem,

13 Took branches of palm trees, and went forth to meet him, and cried, Hosanna: Blessed *is* the King of Israel that cometh in the name of the Lord.

14 And Jesus, when he had found a young ass, sat thereon; as it is written,

15 Fear not, daughter of Sion: behold, thy King cometh, sitting on an ass's colt.

## Amplified

50 Nor do you understand *or* reason out that it is expedient *and* better for your own welfare that one man should die on behalf of the people than that the whole nation should perish (be destroyed, ruined).

51 Now he did not say this simply of his own accord—he was not self-moved; but being the high priest that year, he prophesied that Jesus was to die for the nation; [Isa. 53:8.]

52 And not only for the nation, but also for the purpose of uniting into one body the children of God who have been scattered far and wide. [Isa. 49:6.]

53 So from that day on they took counsel *and* plotted together how they might put Him to death.

54 For that reason Jesus no longer appeared publicly among the Jews, but left there and retired to the district that borders on the wilderness (the desert), to a village called Ephraim, and there He stayed with the disciples.

55 Now the Jewish Passover was at hand, and many from the country went up to Jerusalem in order that they might purify *and* consecrate themselves before the Passover.

56 So they kept looking for Jesus and questioned among themselves as they were standing about in the temple [a]area, What do you think? Will He not come to the feast at all?

57 Now the chief priests and Pharisees had given orders that if any one knew where He was, he should report it to them, so that they might arrest Him.

**12** SO SIX days before the Passover Feast Jesus came to Bethany where Lazarus was, who had died and whom He had raised from the dead.

2 So they made Him a supper, and Martha served, but Lazarus was one of those at the table with Him.

3 Mary took a pound of ointment of pure liquid nard [a rare perfume] that was very expensive, and she poured it on Jesus' feet and wiped them with her hair. And the whole house was filled with the fragrance of the perfume.

4 But Judas Iscariot, the one of His disciples who was about to betray Him, said,

5 Why was this perfume not sold for [b]three hundred denarii, and that given to the poor—the destitute?

6 Now he did not say this because he cared for the poor, but because he was a thief and having the bag [the money box, the purse of the twelve], he took for himself what was put into it—pilfering the collections.

7 But Jesus said, Let her alone. It was that she might keep it for the time of My preparation for burial—she has kept it that she might have it for the time of My [c]embalming.

8 You always have the poor with you, but you do not always have Me.

9 Now a great crowd of the Jews heard that He was at Bethany, and they came there, not only because of Jesus, but that they also might see Lazarus whom He had raised from the dead.

10 So the chief priests planned to put Lazarus to death also,

11 Because on account of him many of the Jews were going away—were withdrawing *and* leaving [the Judeans]—and believing in *and* adhering to Jesus.

12 The next day a vast crowd of those who had come to the Passover Feast heard that Jesus was coming to Jerusalem.

13 So they took branches of palm trees and went out to meet Him. And as they went they kept shouting, Hosanna! Blessed is He *and* praise to Him Who comes in the name of the Lord, even the King of Israel! [Ps. 118:26.]

14 And Jesus, having found a young donkey, rode upon it, [just] as it is written in the Scriptures,

15 Do not fear, O daughter of Zion! Look! Your King is coming, sitting on a donkey's colt! [Zech. 9:9.]

**AMP** [a] Trench. [b] The wages of an ordinary workman for a whole year. [c] Vincent.

# New American Standard

50nor do you take into account that it is expedient for you that
one man should die for the people, and that the whole nation
should not perish."
51Now this he did not say on his own initiative; but being high
priest that year, he prophesied that Jesus was going to die for the
nation,
52and not for the nation only, but that He might also gather
together into one the children of God who are scattered abroad.
53So from that day on they planned together to kill Him.
54¶ Jesus therefore no longer continued to walk publicly among
the Jews, but went away from there to the country near the wilderness, into a city called Ephraim; and there He stayed with the
disciples.
55Now the Passover of the Jews was at hand, and many went
up to Jerusalem out of the country before the Passover, to purify
themselves.
56Therefore they were seeking for Jesus, and were saying to one
another, as they stood in the temple, "What do you think; that He
will not come to the feast at all?"
57Now the chief priests and the Pharisees had given orders that
if anyone knew where He was, he should report it, that they might
seize Him.

*Mary Anoints Jesus*

**12** JESUS, THEREFORE, six days before the Passover, came
to Bethany where Lazarus was, whom Jesus had raised
from the dead.
2So they made Him a supper there, and Martha was serving;
but Lazarus was one of those reclining *at the table* with Him.
3Mary therefore took a pound of very costly perfume of pure
nard, and anointed the feet of Jesus, and wiped His feet with her
hair; and the house was filled with the fragrance of the perfume.
4But Judas Iscariot, one of His disciples, who was intending to
betray Him, *said,
5"Why was this perfume not sold for [d]three hundred denarii,
and given to poor *people?*"
6Now he said this, not because he was concerned about the
poor, but because he was a thief, and as he had the money box,
he used to pilfer what was put into it.
7Jesus therefore said, "Let her alone, in order that she may
keep [e]it for the day of My burial.
8"For the poor you always have with you, but you do not
always have Me."
9¶ The great multitude therefore of the Jews learned that He
was there; and they came, not for Jesus' sake only, but that they
might also see Lazarus, whom He raised from the dead.
10But the chief priests took counsel that they might put Lazarus
to death also;
11because on account of him many of the Jews were going away,
and were believing in Jesus.

*Jesus Enters Jerusalem*

12¶ On the next day the great multitude who had come to the
feast, when they heard that Jesus was coming to Jerusalem,
13took the branches of the palm trees, and went out to meet
Him, and *began* to cry out, "Hosanna! BLESSED IS HE WHO COMES
IN THE NAME OF THE LORD, even the King of Israel."
14And Jesus, finding a young donkey, sat on it; as it is written,
15"FEAR NOT, DAUGHTER OF ZION; BEHOLD, YOUR KING IS COM-
ING, SEATED ON A DONKEY'S COLT."

**NAS** [d] Equivalent to 11 months' wages [e] I.e., The custom of anointing for burial

# New International

it is better for you that one man die for the people than that the
whole nation perish."
51He did not say this on his own, but as high priest that year
he prophesied that Jesus would die for the Jewish nation, 52and
not only for that nation but also for the scattered children of God,
to bring them together and make them one. 53So from that day on
they plotted to take his life.
54Therefore Jesus no longer moved about publicly among the
Jews. Instead he withdrew to a region near the desert, to a village
called Ephraim, where he stayed with his disciples.
55When it was almost time for the Jewish Passover, many went
up from the country to Jerusalem for their ceremonial cleansing
before the Passover. 56They kept looking for Jesus, and as they
stood in the temple area they asked one another, "What do you
think? Isn't he coming to the Feast at all?" 57But the chief priests
and Pharisees had given orders that if anyone found out where
Jesus was, he should report it so that they might arrest him.

*Jesus Anointed at Bethany*

**12** SIX DAYS before the Passover, Jesus arrived at Bethany,
where Lazarus lived, whom Jesus had raised from the
dead. 2Here a dinner was given in Jesus' honor. Martha served,
while Lazarus was among those reclining at the table with him.
3Then Mary took about a pint[f] of pure nard, an expensive perfume; she poured it on Jesus' feet and wiped his feet with her hair.
And the house was filled with the fragrance of the perfume.
4But one of his disciples, Judas Iscariot, who was later to betray
him, objected, 5"Why wasn't this perfume sold and the money
given to the poor? It was worth a year's wages.[g]" 6He did not say
this because he cared about the poor but because he was a thief;
as keeper of the money bag, he used to help himself to what was
put into it.
7"Leave her alone," Jesus replied. "It was intended that she
should save this perfume for the day of my burial. 8You will always
have the poor among you, but you will not always have me."
9Meanwhile a large crowd of Jews found out that Jesus was
there and came, not only because of him but also to see Lazarus,
whom he had raised from the dead. 10So the chief priests made
plans to kill Lazarus as well, 11for on account of him many of the
Jews were going over to Jesus and putting their faith in him.

*The Triumphal Entry*

12The next day the great crowd that had come for the Feast
heard that Jesus was on his way to Jerusalem. 13They took palm
branches and went out to meet him, shouting,

"Hosanna![h]"

"Blessed is he who comes in the name of the Lord!"[i]

"Blessed is the King of Israel!"

14Jesus found a young donkey and sat upon it, as it is written,

15"Do not be afraid, O Daughter of Zion;
see, your king is coming,
seated on a donkey's colt."[j]

**NIV** [f] 3 Greek *a litra* (probably about 0.5 liter) [g] 5 Greek *three hundred denarii* [h] 13 A Hebrew expression meaning "Save!" which became an exclamation of praise [i] 13 Psalm 118:25, 26 [j] 15 Zech. 9:9

## King James

16These things understood not his disciples at the first: but when Jesus was glorified, then remembered they that these things were written of him, and *that* they had done these things unto him.

17The people therefore that was with him when he called Lazarus out of his grave, and raised him from the dead, bare record.

18For this cause the people also met him, for that they heard that he had done this miracle.

19The Pharisees therefore said among themselves, Perceive ye how ye prevail nothing? behold, the world is gone after him.

20¶ And there were certain Greeks among them that came up to worship at the feast:

21The same came therefore to Philip, which was of Bethsaida of Galilee, and desired him, saying, Sir, we would see Jesus.

22Philip cometh and telleth Andrew: and again Andrew and Philip tell Jesus.

23¶ And Jesus answered them, saying, The hour is come, that the Son of man should be glorified.

24Verily, verily, I say unto you, Except a corn of wheat fall into the ground and die, it abideth alone: but if it die, it bringeth forth much fruit.

25He that loveth his life shall lose it; and he that hateth his life in this world shall keep it unto life eternal.

26If any man serve me, let him follow me; and where I am, there shall also my servant be: if any man serve me, him will *my* Father honour.

27Now is my soul troubled; and what shall I say? Father, save me from this hour: but for this cause came I unto this hour.

28Father, glorify thy name. Then came there a voice from heaven, *saying*, I have both glorified *it*, and will glorify *it* again.

29The people therefore, that stood by, and heard *it*, said that it thundered: others said, An angel spake to him.

30Jesus answered and said, This voice came not because of me, but for your sakes.

31Now is the judgment of this world: now shall the prince of this world be cast out.

32And I, if I be lifted up from the earth, will draw all *men* unto me.

33This he said, signifying what death he should die.

34The people answered him, We have heard out of the law that Christ abideth for ever: and how sayest thou, The Son of man must be lifted up? who is this Son of man?

35Then Jesus said unto them, Yet a little while is the light with you. Walk while ye have the light, lest darkness come upon you: for he that walketh in darkness knoweth not whither he goeth.

36While ye have light, believe in the light, that ye may be the children of light. These things spake Jesus, and departed, and did hide himself from them.

37¶ But though he had done so many miracles before them, yet they believed not on him:

## Amplified

16His disciples did not understand *and* could not comprehend the meaning of these things at first, but when Jesus was glorified *and* exalted, they remembered that these things had been written about Him and had been done to Him.

17The group that had been with Jesus when He called Lazarus out of the tomb and raised him from among the dead, kept telling it to others—bearing witness.

18It was for this reason that the crowd went out to meet Him, because they had heard that He had performed this sign (proof, miracle).

19Then the Pharisees said among themselves, You see how futile your efforts are *and* how you accomplish nothing. See! The whole world is running after Him!

20Now among those who went up to worship at the feast were some Greeks.

21These came to Philip, who was from Bethsaida in Galilee, and they made this request, Sir, we desire to see Jesus.

22Philip came and told Andrew. Then Andrew and Philip together [went] and told Jesus.

23And Jesus answered them, The time has come for the Son of man to be glorified *and* exalted.

24I assure you, most solemnly I tell you, Unless a grain of wheat falls into the earth and dies, it remains [just one grain; never becomes more but lives] by itself alone. But if it dies, it produces many others *and* yields a rich harvest.

25Any one who loves his life loses it. But any one who hates his life in this world will keep it to life eternal.—Whoever has no love for, no concern for, no regard for his life here on the earth, but despises it, preserves his life forever and ever.

26If any one would serve Me, he must continue to follow Me— [a]to cleave steadfastly to Me, conform wholly to My example, in living and if need be in dying—and wherever I am, there will My servant be also. If any one serves Me, the Father will honor him.

27Now My soul is troubled *and* distressed, and what shall I say? Father, save Me from this hour [of trial and agony]? But it was for this very purpose that I have come to this hour [that I might undergo it].

28[Rather, I will say,] Father, glorify—honor and extol—Your own name! Then there came a voice out of heaven saying, I have already glorified it, and I will glorify it again.

29The crowd of bystanders heard the sound and said that it had thundered. Others said, An angel has spoken to Him!

30Jesus answered, This voice has not come for My sake, but for your sake.

31Now the judgment (crisis) of this world is [coming on]—sentence is now being passed on this world. Now the ruler (evil genius, prince) of this world shall be cast out—expelled.

32And I, if *and* when I am lifted up from the earth [on the cross], will draw *and* attract all men [Gentile as well as Jew] to Myself.

33He said this to signify in what manner He would die.

34At this the people answered Him, We have learned from the Law that the Christ is to remain forever. How then can You say, The Son of man must be lifted up [on the cross]? Who is this Son of man? [Ps. 110:4.]

35So Jesus said to them, You will have the Light only a little while longer. Walk while you have the Light—keep on living by it—so that darkness may not overtake *and* overcome you. He who walks about in the dark does not know where he goes—he is drifting.

36While you have the Light, believe in the Light—have faith in it, hold to it, rely on it—that you may become sons of the Light *and* be filled with light. Jesus said these things and then He went away and hid Himself from them—was lost to their view.

37Even though He had done so many miracles before them—right before their eyes—yet they still did not trust in Him *and* failed to believe on Him.

**AMP** [a] Thayer.

## New American Standard

16These things His disciples did not understand at the first; but
when Jesus was glorified, then they remembered that these things
were written of Him, and that they had done these things to Him.
17And so the multitude who were with Him when He called
Lazarus out of the tomb, and raised him from the dead, were
bearing Him witness.
18For this cause also the multitude went and met Him, because
they heard that He had performed this sign.
19The Pharisees therefore said to one another, "You see that
you are not doing any good; look, the world has gone after Him."

*Greeks Seek Jesus*

20¶ Now there were certain Greeks among those who were
going up to worship at the feast;
21these therefore came to Philip, who was from Bethsaida of
Galilee, and *began to* ask him, saying, "Sir, we wish to see Jesus."
22Philip *came and *told Andrew; Andrew and Philip *came,
and they *told Jesus.
23And Jesus *answered them, saying, "The hour has come for
the Son of Man to be glorified.
24"Truly, truly, I say to you, unless a grain of wheat falls into
the earth and dies, it remains by itself alone; but if it dies, it bears
much fruit.
25"He who loves his life loses it; and he who hates his life in this
world shall keep it to life eternal.
26"If anyone serves Me, let him follow Me; and where I am,
there shall My servant also be; if anyone serves Me, the Father will
honor him.

*Jesus Foretells His Death*

27¶ "Now My soul has become troubled; and what shall I say,
'Father, save Me from this hour'? But for this purpose I came to
this hour.
28"Father, glorify Thy name." There came therefore a voice out
of heaven: "I have both glorified it, and will glorify it again."
29The multitude therefore, who stood by and heard it, were
saying that it had thundered; others were saying, "An angel has
spoken to Him."
30Jesus answered and said, "This voice has not come for My
sake, but for your sakes.
31"Now judgment is upon this world; now the ruler of this
world shall be cast out.
32"And I, if I be lifted up from the earth, will draw all men to
Myself."
33But He was saying this to indicate the kind of death by which
He was to die.
34The multitude therefore answered Him, "We have heard out
of the Law that the Christ is to remain forever; and how can You
say, 'The Son of Man must be lifted up'? Who is this Son of Man?"
35Jesus therefore said to them, "For a little while longer the light
is among you. Walk while you have the light, that darkness may
not overtake you; he who walks in the darkness does not know
where he goes.
36"While you have the light, believe in the light, in order that
you may become sons of light."
¶ These things Jesus spoke, and He departed and hid Himself
from them.
37But though He had performed so many signs before them, *yet*
they were not believing in Him;

## New International

16At first his disciples did not understand all this. Only after
Jesus was glorified did they realize that these things had been
written about him and that they had done these things to him.
17Now the crowd that was with him when he called Lazarus
from the tomb and raised him from the dead continued to spread
the word. 18Many people, because they had heard that he had
given this miraculous sign, went out to meet him. 19So the Pharisees said to one another, "See, this is getting us nowhere. Look
how the whole world has gone after him!"

*Jesus Predicts His Death*

20Now there were some Greeks among those who went up to
worship at the Feast. 21They came to Philip, who was from Bethsaida in Galilee, with a request. "Sir," they said, "we would like
to see Jesus." 22Philip went to tell Andrew; Andrew and Philip in
turn told Jesus.
23Jesus replied, "The hour has come for the Son of Man to be
glorified. 24I tell you the truth, unless a kernel of wheat falls to the
ground and dies, it remains only a single seed. But if it dies, it
produces many seeds. 25The man who loves his life will lose it,
while the man who hates his life in this world will keep it for
eternal life. 26Whoever serves me must follow me; and where I am,
my servant also will be. My Father will honor the one who serves
me.
27"Now my heart is troubled, and what shall I say? 'Father, save
me from this hour'? No, it was for this very reason I came to this
hour. 28Father, glorify your name!"
Then a voice came from heaven, "I have glorified it, and will
glorify it again." 29The crowd that was there and heard it said it
had thundered; others said an angel had spoken to him.
30Jesus said, "This voice was for your benefit, not mine. 31Now
is the time for judgment on this world; now the prince of this world
will be driven out. 32But I, when I am lifted up from the earth, will
draw all men to myself." 33He said this to show the kind of death
he was going to die.
34The crowd spoke up, "We have heard from the Law that the
Christ[b] will remain forever, so how can you say, 'The Son of Man
must be lifted up'? Who is this 'Son of Man'?"
35Then Jesus told them, "You are going to have the light just
a little while longer. Walk while you have the light, before darkness overtakes you. The man who walks in the dark does not know
where he is going. 36Put your trust in the light while you have it,
so that you may become sons of light." When he had finished
speaking, Jesus left and hid himself from them.

*The Jews Continue in Their Unbelief*

37Even after Jesus had done all these miraculous signs in their

NIV [b] 34 Or *Messiah*

## King James

38 That the saying of Esaias the prophet might be fulfilled, which he spake, Lord, who hath believed our report? and to whom hath the arm of the Lord been revealed?

39 Therefore they could not believe, because that Esaias said again,

40 He hath blinded their eyes, and hardened their heart; that they should not see with *their* eyes, nor understand with *their* heart, and be converted, and I should heal them.

41 These things said Esaias, when he saw his glory, and spake of him.

42 ¶ Nevertheless among the chief rulers also many believed on him; but because of the Pharisees they did not confess *him*, lest they should be put out of the synagogue:

43 For they loved the praise of men more than the praise of God.

44 ¶ Jesus cried and said, He that believeth on me, believeth not on me, but on him that sent me.

45 And he that seeth me seeth him that sent me.

46 I am come a light into the world, that whosoever believeth on me should not abide in darkness.

47 And if any man hear my words, and believe not, I judge him not: for I came not to judge the world, but to save the world.

48 He that rejecteth me, and receiveth not my words, hath one that judgeth him: the word that I have spoken, the same shall judge him in the last day.

49 For I have not spoken of myself; but the Father which sent me, he gave me a commandment, what I should say, and what I should speak.

50 And I know that his commandment is life everlasting: whatsoever I speak therefore, even as the Father said unto me, so I speak.

**13** NOW BEFORE the feast of the passover, when Jesus knew that his hour was come that he should depart out of this world unto the Father, having loved his own which were in the world, he loved them unto the end.

2 And supper being ended, the devil having now put into the heart of Judas Iscariot, Simon's *son*, to betray him;

3 Jesus knowing that the Father had given all things into his hands, and that he was come from God, and went to God;

4 He riseth from supper, and laid aside his garments; and took a towel, and girded himself.

5 After that he poureth water into a basin, and began to wash the disciples' feet, and to wipe *them* with the towel wherewith he was girded.

6 Then cometh he to Simon Peter: and Peter saith unto him, Lord, dost thou wash my feet?

7 Jesus answered and said unto him, What I do thou knowest not now; but thou shalt know hereafter.

8 Peter saith unto him, Thou shalt never wash my feet. Jesus answered him, If I wash thee not, thou hast no part with me.

## Amplified

38 So that what Isaiah the prophet said was fulfilled, Lord, who has believed our report *and* our message? And to whom has the arm (the power) of the Lord been shown—unveiled and revealed? [Isa. 53:1.]

39 Therefore, they could not believe—they were unable to believe. For Isaiah has also said,

40 He has blinded their eyes, and hardened *and* benumbed their [callous, degenerated] heart—He has made their minds dull—to keep them from seeing with their eyes and understanding with their heart *and* mind and repenting *and* turning to Me to heal them.

41 Isaiah said this because he saw His glory and spoke of Him. [Isa. 6:9, 10.]

42 And yet [in spite of all this] many even of the leading men—of the authorities and the nobles—believed *and* trusted in Him. But because of the Pharisees they did not confess it, for fear [that if they should acknowledge Him] they would be expelled from the synagogue.

43 For they loved the approval *and* the praise *and* the glory that come from men [instead of and] more than the glory that comes from God.—They valued their credit with men more than their credit with God.

44 But Jesus loudly declared, The one who believes on Me, does not [only] believe on *and* trust in *and* rely on Me, but [in believing on Me he believes] on Him Who sent Me.

45 And whoever sees Me sees Him Who sent Me.

46 I have come a light into the world, so that whoever believes on Me—who cleaves to *and* trusts in *and* relies on Me—may not continue to live in darkness.

47 If any one hears My teachings and fails to observe them—does not keep them, but disregards them—it is not I who judges him. For I have not come to judge *and* to condemn *and* to pass sentence *and* to inflict penalty on the world, but to save the world.

48 Any one who rejects Me *and* persistently sets Me at naught, refusing to accept My teachings, has his judge [however]; for the [very] message that I have spoken will itself judge *and* convict him on the last day.

49 This is because I have never spoken on My own authority *or* of My own accord *or* self-appointed, but the Father Who has sent Me has Himself given Me orders what to say and what to tell. [Deut. 18:18, 19.]

50 And I know that His commandment is (means,) eternal life. So whatever I speak, I am saying [exactly] what My Father has told Me to say *and* in accordance with His instructions.

**13** [NOW] BEFORE the Passover Feast began, Jesus knew (was fully aware) that the time had come for Him to leave this world *and* return to the Father. And as He had loved those who were His own in the world, He loved them to the last *and* [a]to the highest degree.

2 So during supper, Satan having already put the thought of betraying Jesus in the heart of Judas Iscariot, Simon's son,

3 Jesus, knowing (fully aware) that the Father had put everything into His hands, and that He had come from God and was [now] returning to God,

4 Got up from supper, took off His garments and taking a [servant's] towel, He fastened it around His waist.

5 Then He poured water into the washbasin and began to wash the disciples' feet and to wipe them with the [servant's] towel with which He was girded.

6 When He came to Simon Peter, [Peter] said to Him, Lord, are my feet to be washed by You?—Is it for You to wash my feet?

7 Jesus said to him, You do not understand now what I am doing, but you will understand later on.

8 Peter said to Him, You shall never wash my feet! Jesus answered him, Unless I wash you, you have no part with [ [b]in] Me—no share in companionship with Me.

**AMP** [a] Chrysostom. [b] Origen; Adam Clarke, and others. cf. John 15:3-7, noticing "in Me . . . in Me . . . in Me . . .," concerning the same subject, the same evening.

## New American Standard

38 that the word of Isaiah the prophet might be fulfilled, which
he spoke, "LORD, WHO HAS BELIEVED OUR REPORT? AND TO WHOM
HAS THE ARM OF THE LORD BEEN REVEALED?"
39 For this cause they could not believe, for Isaiah said again,
40 "HE HAS BLINDED THEIR EYES, AND HE HARDENED THEIR HEART;
LEST THEY SEE WITH THEIR EYES, AND PERCEIVE WITH THEIR HEART,
AND BE CONVERTED, AND I HEAL THEM."
41 These things Isaiah said, because he saw His glory, and he
spoke of Him.
42 Nevertheless many even of the rulers believed in Him, but
because of the Pharisees they were not confessing *Him*, lest they
should be put out of the synagogue;
43 for they loved the approval of men rather than the approval
of God.
44 ¶ And Jesus cried out and said, "He who believes in Me does
not believe in Me, but in Him who sent Me.
45 "And he who beholds Me beholds the One who sent Me.
46 "I have come *as* light into the world, that everyone who
believes in Me may not remain in darkness.
47 "And if anyone hears My sayings, and does not keep them,
I do not judge him; for I did not come to judge the world, but to
save the world.
48 "He who rejects Me, and does not receive My sayings, has
one who judges him; the word I spoke is what will judge him at
the last day.
49 "For I did not speak on My own initiative, but the Father
Himself who sent Me has given Me commandment, what to say,
and what to speak.
50 "And I know that His commandment is eternal life; therefore
the things I speak, I speak just as the Father has told Me."

*The Lord's Supper*

13 NOW BEFORE the Feast of the Passover, Jesus knowing
that His hour had come that He should depart out of this
world to the Father, having loved His own who were in the world,
He loved them to the end.
2 And during supper, the devil having already put into the
heart of Judas Iscariot, *the son* of Simon, to betray Him,
3 *Jesus*, knowing that the Father had given all things into His
hands, and that He had come forth from God, and was going back
to God,
4 *rose from supper, and *laid aside His garments; and taking
a towel, He girded Himself about.

*Jesus Washes the Disciples' Feet*

5 Then He *poured water into the basin, and began to wash the
disciples' feet, and to wipe them with the towel with which He was
girded.
6 And so He *came to Simon Peter. He *said to Him, "Lord, do
You wash my feet?"
7 Jesus answered and said to him, "What I do you do not realize
now, but you shall understand hereafter."
8 Peter *said to Him, "Never shall You wash my feet!" Jesus
answered him, "If I do not wash you, you have no part with Me."

## New International

presence, they still would not believe in him. 38 This was to fulfill
the word of Isaiah the prophet:

"Lord, who has believed our message
and to whom has the arm of the Lord been revealed?"[c]

39 For this reason they could not believe, because, as Isaiah says
elsewhere:

40 "He has blinded their eyes
and deadened their hearts,
so they can neither see with their eyes,
nor understand with their hearts,
nor turn—and I would heal them."[d]

41 Isaiah said this because he saw Jesus' glory and spoke about him.
42 Yet at the same time many even among the leaders believed
in him. But because of the Pharisees they would not confess their
faith for fear they would be put out of the synagogue; 43 for they
loved praise from men more than praise from God.
44 Then Jesus cried out, "When a man believes in me, he does
not believe in me only, but in the one who sent me. 45 When he
looks at me, he sees the one who sent me. 46 I have come into the
world as a light, so that no one who believes in me should stay in
darkness.
47 "As for the person who hears my words but does not keep
them, I do not judge him. For I did not come to judge the world,
but to save it. 48 There is a judge for the one who rejects me and
does not accept my words; that very word which I spoke will
condemn him at the last day. 49 For I did not speak of my own
accord, but the Father who sent me commanded me what to say
and how to say it. 50 I know that his command leads to eternal life.
So whatever I say is just what the Father has told me to say."

*Jesus Washes His Disciples' Feet*

13 IT WAS just before the Passover Feast. Jesus knew that the
time had come for him to leave this world and go to the
Father. Having loved his own who were in the world, he now
showed them the full extent of his love.[e]
2 The evening meal was being served, and the devil had already
prompted Judas Iscariot, son of Simon, to betray Jesus. 3 Jesus
knew that the Father had put all things under his power, and that
he had come from God and was returning to God; 4 so he got up
from the meal, took off his outer clothing, and wrapped a towel
around his waist. 5 After that, he poured water into a basin and
began to wash his disciples' feet, drying them with the towel that
was wrapped around him.
6 He came to Simon Peter, who said to him, "Lord, are you
going to wash my feet?"
7 Jesus replied, "You do not realize now what I am doing, but
later you will understand."
8 "No," said Peter, "you shall never wash my feet."
Jesus answered, "Unless I wash you, you have no part with
me."

NIV [c] *38* Isaiah 53:1 [d] *40* Isaiah 6:10 [e] *1* Or *he loved them to the last*

## King James

9 Simon Peter saith unto him, Lord, not my feet only, but also *my* hands and *my* head.

10 Jesus saith to him, He that is washed needeth not save to wash *his* feet, but is clean every whit: and ye are clean, but not all.

11 For he knew who should betray him; therefore said he, Ye are not all clean.

12 So after he had washed their feet, and had taken his garments, and was set down again, he said unto them, Know ye what I have done to you?

13 Ye call me Master and Lord: and ye say well; for *so* I am.

14 If I then, *your* Lord and Master, have washed your feet; ye also ought to wash one another's feet.

15 For I have given you an example, that ye should do as I have done to you.

16 Verily, verily, I say unto you, The servant is not greater than his lord; neither he that is sent greater than he that sent him.

17 If ye know these things, happy are ye if ye do them.

18 ¶ I speak not of you all: I know whom I have chosen: but that the scripture may be fulfilled, He that eateth bread with me hath lifted up his heel against me.

19 Now I tell you before it come, that, when it is come to pass, ye may believe that I am *he*.

20 Verily, verily, I say unto you, He that receiveth whomsoever I send receiveth me; and he that receiveth me receiveth him that sent me.

21 When Jesus had thus said, he was troubled in spirit, and testified, and said, Verily, verily, I say unto you, that one of you shall betray me.

22 Then the disciples looked one on another, doubting of whom he spake.

23 Now there was leaning on Jesus' bosom one of his disciples, whom Jesus loved.

24 Simon Peter therefore beckoned to him, that he should ask who it should be of whom he spake.

25 He then lying on Jesus' breast saith unto him, Lord, who is it?

26 Jesus answered, He it is, to whom I shall give a sop, when I have dipped *it*. And when he had dipped the sop, he gave *it* to Judas Iscariot, *the son* of Simon.

27 And after the sop Satan entered into him. Then said Jesus unto him, That thou doest, do quickly.

28 Now no man at the table knew for what intent he spake this unto him.

29 For some *of them* thought, because Judas had the bag, that Jesus had said unto him, Buy *those things* that we have need of against the feast; or, that he should give something to the poor.

30 He then having received the sop went immediately out: and it was night.

31 ¶ Therefore, when he was gone out, Jesus said, Now is the Son of man glorified, and God is glorified in him.

32 If God be glorified in him, God shall also glorify him in himself, and shall straightway glorify him.

33 Little children, yet a little while I am with you. Ye shall seek me: and as I said unto the Jews, Whither I go, ye cannot come; so now I say to you.

## Amplified

9 Simon Peter said to Him, Lord, [wash] not only my feet, but my hands and my head, too!

10 Jesus said to him, Any one who is bathed needs not to wash *except his feet,* but is clean all over. And you [My disciples] are clean, but not all of you.

11 For He knew who was going to betray Him; that was the reason He said, You are not all of you clean.

12 So when He had finished washing their feet and had put on His garments and had sat down again, He said to them, Do you understand what I have done to you?

13 You call Me the Teacher (Master) and the Lord, and you are right in doing so, for that is what I am.

14 If I then, your Lord and Teacher (Master), have washed your feet, you ought—it is your duty, you are under obligation, you owe it—to wash one another's feet.

15 For I have given you this as an example, so that you should do [in your turn] what I have done to you.

16 I assure you, most solemnly I tell you, A servant is not greater than his master, and no one who is sent is superior to the one who sent him.

17 If you know these things, blessed *and* happy *and* [a]to be envied are you if you practice them—if you act accordingly and really do them.

18 I am not speaking of *and* I do not mean all of you. I know whom I have chosen; but it is that the Scripture may be fulfilled, He who eats [ [b]his] bread with Me has raised up his heel against Me. [Ps. 41:9.]

19 I tell you this now before it occurs, so that when it does take place you may be persuaded *and* believe that I am He—what I say I am, the Christ, the Anointed One, the Messiah.

20 I assure you, most solemnly I tell you, he who receives *and* welcomes *and* takes into his heart any messenger of Mine, receives Me [in just that way]; and he who receives *and* welcomes *and* takes Me into his heart, receives Him Who sent Me [in that same way].

21 After Jesus had said these things, He was troubled (disturbed, agitated) in spirit, and said, I assure you, most solemnly I tell you that one of you will deliver Me up—be false to Me and betray Me!

22 The disciples kept looking at one another, puzzled as to whom He could mean.

23 One of His disciples whom Jesus loved—whom He esteemed and delighted in—was reclining [next to Him] on Jesus' bosom.

24 So Simon Peter motioned to him to ask of whom He was speaking.

25 Then leaning back against Jesus' breast, he asked Him, Lord, who is it?

26 Jesus answered, It is the one to whom I am going to give this morsel (bit) of food after I have dipped it. So when He had dipped the morsel of bread [into the dish], He gave it to Judas, Simon Iscariot's son.

27 Then, after [he had taken] the bit of food, Satan entered into *and* took possession of [Judas]. Jesus said to him, What you are going to do, do [ [c]more swiftly than you seem to intend] *and* [d]make quick work of it.

28 But nobody reclining at the table knew why He spoke to him, *or* what He meant by telling him this.

29 Some thought that since Judas had the money box (the purse), Jesus was telling him, Buy what we need for the festival, or that he should give something to the poor.

30 So, after receiving the bit of bread, he went out immediately. And it was night.

31 When he had left, Jesus said, Now is the Son of man glorified!—Now He has achieved His glory, His honor, His exaltation; and God has been glorified through *and* in Him.

32 And if God is glorified through *and* in Him, God will also glorify Him in Himself; and He will glorify Him at once *and* not delay.

33 [Dear] little children, I am to be with you only a little longer. You will look for Me and, as I told the Jews so I tell you now, you are not able to come where I am going.

**AMP** [a] Souter's "Pocket Lexicon of the Greek New Testament." [b] Many ancient authorities read *"his bread with Me."* [c] Thayer: "Greek-English Lexicon of the New Testament—Grimm." [d] Williams: "New Testament in the Language of the People."

## New American Standard

9Simon Peter *said to Him, "Lord, not my feet only, but also
my hands and my head."
10Jesus *said to him, "He who has bathed needs only to wash
his feet, but is completely clean; and you are clean, but not all *of*
*you.*"
11For He knew the one who was betraying Him; for this reason
He said, "Not all of you are clean."
12¶ And so when He had washed their feet, and taken His
garments, and reclined *at the table* again, He said to them, "Do you
know what I have done to you?
13"You call Me Teacher and Lord; and you are right, for *so* I am.
14"If I then, the Lord and the Teacher, washed your feet, you
also ought to wash one another's feet.
15"For I gave you an example that you also should do as I did
to you.
16"Truly, truly, I say to you, a slave is not greater than his
master; neither *is* one who is sent greater than the one who sent
him.
17"If you know these things, you are blessed if you do them.
18"I do not speak of all of you. I know the ones I have chosen;
but *it is* that the Scripture may be fulfilled, 'He who eats My bread
has lifted up his heel against Me.'
19"From now on I am telling you before *it* comes to pass, so that
when it does occur, you may believe that I am *He.*
20"Truly, truly, I say to you, he who receives whomever I send
receives Me; and he who receives Me receives Him who sent Me."

*Jesus Predicts His Betrayal*

21¶ When Jesus had said this, He became troubled in spirit, and
testified, and said, "Truly, truly, I say to you, that one of you will
betray Me."
22The disciples *began* looking at one another, at a loss *to know*
of which one He was speaking.
23There was reclining on Jesus' breast one of His disciples,
whom Jesus loved.
24Simon Peter therefore *gestured to him, and *said to him,
"Tell *us* who it is of whom He is speaking."
25He, leaning back thus on Jesus' breast, *said to Him, "Lord,
who is it?"
26Jesus therefore *answered, "That is the one for whom I shall
dip the morsel and give it to him." So when He had dipped the
morsel, He *took and *gave it to Judas, *the son* of Simon Iscariot.
27And after the morsel, Satan then entered into him. Jesus
therefore *said to him, "What you do, do quickly."
28Now no one of those reclining *at the table* knew for what
purpose He had said this to him.
29For some were supposing, because Judas had the money box,
that Jesus was saying to him, "Buy the things we have need of for
the feast"; or else, that he should give something to the poor.
30And so after receiving the morsel he went out immediately;
and it was night.
31¶ When therefore he had gone out, Jesus *said, "Now is the
Son of Man glorified, and God is glorified in Him;
32if God is glorified in Him, God will also glorify Him in Himself, and will glorify Him immediately.
33"Little children, I am with you a little while longer. You shall
seek Me; and as I said to the Jews, I now say to you also, 'Where
I am going, you cannot come.'

## New International

9"Then, Lord," Simon Peter replied, "not just my feet but my
hands and my head as well!"
10Jesus answered, "A person who has had a bath needs only to
wash his feet; his whole body is clean. And you are clean, though
not every one of you." 11For he knew who was going to betray
him, and that was why he said not every one was clean.
12When he had finished washing their feet, he put on his
clothes and returned to his place. "Do you understand what I have
done for you?" he asked them. 13"You call me 'Teacher' and
'Lord,' and rightly so, for that is what I am. 14Now that I, your Lord
and Teacher, have washed your feet, you also should wash one
another's feet. 15I have set you an example that you should do as
I have done for you. 16I tell you the truth, no servant is greater than
his master, nor is a messenger greater than the one who sent him.
17Now that you know these things, you will be blessed if you do
them.

*Jesus Predicts His Betrayal*

18"I am not referring to all of you; I know those I have chosen.
But this is to fulfill the scripture: 'He who shares my bread has
lifted up his heel against me.'[e]
19"I am telling you now before it happens, so that when it does
happen you will believe that I am He. 20I tell you the truth, whoever accepts anyone I send accepts me; and whoever accepts me
accepts the one who sent me."
21After he had said this, Jesus was troubled in spirit and testified, "I tell you the truth, one of you is going to betray me."
22His disciples stared at one another, at a loss to know which
of them he meant. 23One of them, the disciple whom Jesus loved,
was reclining next to him. 24Simon Peter motioned to this disciple
and said, "Ask him which one he means."
25Leaning back against Jesus, he asked him, "Lord, who is it?"
26Jesus answered, "It is the one to whom I will give this piece
of bread when I have dipped it in the dish." Then, dipping the
piece of bread, he gave it to Judas Iscariot, son of Simon. 27As soon
as Judas took the bread, Satan entered into him.
"What you are about to do, do quickly," Jesus told him, 28but
no one at the meal understood why Jesus said this to him. 29Since
Judas had charge of the money, some thought Jesus was telling
him to buy what was needed for the Feast, or to give something
to the poor. 30As soon as Judas had taken the bread, he went out.
And it was night.

*Jesus Predicts Peter's Denial*

31When he was gone, Jesus said, "Now is the Son of Man
glorified and God is glorified in him. 32If God is glorified in him,[f]
God will glorify the Son in himself, and will glorify him at once.
33"My children, I will be with you only a little longer. You will
look for me, and just as I told the Jews, so I tell you now: Where
I am going, you cannot come.

NIV [e] *18* Psalm 41:9 [f] 32 Many early manuscripts do not have *If God is glorified in him.*

## King James

34A new commandment I give unto you, That ye love one another; as I have loved you, that ye also love one another.

35By this shall all *men* know that ye are my disciples, if ye have love one to another.

36¶ Simon Peter said unto him, Lord, whither goest thou? Jesus answered him, Whither I go, thou canst not follow me now; but thou shalt follow me afterwards.

37Peter said unto him, Lord, why cannot I follow thee now? I will lay down my life for thy sake.

38Jesus answered him, Wilt thou lay down thy life for my sake? Verily, verily, I say unto thee, The cock shall not crow, till thou hast denied me thrice.

**14** LET NOT your heart be troubled: ye believe in God, believe also in me.

2In my Father's house are many mansions: if *it were* not *so,* I would have told you. I go to prepare a place for you.

3And if I go and prepare a place for you, I will come again, and receive you unto myself; that where I am, *there* ye may be also.

4And whither I go ye know, and the way ye know.

5Thomas saith unto him, Lord, we know not whither thou goest; and how can we know the way?

6Jesus saith unto him, I am the way, the truth, and the life: no man cometh unto the Father, but by me.

7If ye had known me, ye should have known my Father also: and from henceforth ye know him, and have seen him.

8Philip saith unto him, Lord, show us the Father, and it sufficeth us.

9Jesus saith unto him, Have I been so long time with you, and yet hast thou not known me, Philip? he that hath seen me hath seen the Father; and how sayest thou *then,* Show us the Father?

10Believest thou not that I am in the Father, and the Father in me? the words that I speak unto you I speak not of myself: but the Father that dwelleth in me, he doeth the works.

11Believe me that I *am* in the Father, and the Father in me: or else believe me for the very works' sake.

12Verily, verily, I say unto you, He that believeth on me, the works that I do shall he do also; and greater *works* than these shall he do; because I go unto my Father.

13And whatsoever ye shall ask in my name, that will I do, that the Father may be glorified in the Son.

14If ye shall ask any thing in my name, I will do *it.*

15¶ If ye love me, keep my commandments.

16And I will pray the Father, and he shall give you another Comforter, that he may abide with you for ever;

17 *Even* the Spirit of truth; whom the world cannot receive, because it seeth him not, neither knoweth him: but ye know him; for he dwelleth with you, and shall be in you.

18I will not leave you comfortless: I will come to you.

19Yet a little while, and the world seeth me no more; but ye see me: because I live, ye shall live also.

## Amplified

34I give you a new commandment, that you should love one another; just as I have loved you, so you too should love one another.

35By this shall all [men] know that you are My disciples, if you love one another—if you keep on showing love among yourselves.

36Simon Peter said to Him, Lord, where are You going? Jesus answered, You are not able to follow Me now where I am going; but you shall follow Me afterwards.

37Peter said to Him, Lord, why cannot I follow You now? I will lay down my life for You.

38Jesus answered, Will you lay down your life for Me? I assure you, most solemnly I tell you, Before a rooster crows you will deny Me—completely disown Me—three times.

**14** DO NOT let your hearts be troubled (distressed, agitated). You believe in *and* adhere to *and* trust in *and* rely on God, believe in *and* adhere to *and* trust in *and* rely also on Me.

2In My Father's house there are many dwelling places (homes). If it were not so, I would have told you, for I am going away to prepare a place for you.

3And when (if) I go and make ready a place for you, I will come back again and will take you to Myself, that where I am you may be also.

4And [to the place] where I am going you know the way.

5Thomas said to Him, Lord, we do not know where You are going, so how can we know the way?

6Jesus said to him, I am the Way and the Truth and the Life; no one comes to the Father except by (through) Me.

7If you had known Me—had learned to recognize Me—you would also have known My Father. From now on you know Him and have seen Him.

8Philip said to Him, Lord, show us the Father—cause us to see the Father, that is all we ask; then we shall be satisfied.

9Jesus replied, Have I been with all of you for so long a time and do you not recognize *and* know Me yet, Philip? Any one who has seen Me has seen the Father. How can you say then, Show us the Father?

10Do you not believe that I am in the Father and that the Father is in Me? What I am telling you I do not say on My own authority *and* of My own accord, but the Father Who lives continually in Me does the works— [a]His miracles, His own deeds of power.

11Believe Me that I am in the Father and the Father in Me; or else believe Me for the sake of the [very] works themselves.—If you cannot trust Me, at least let these works that I do in My Father's name convince you.

12I assure you, most solemnly I tell you, if any one steadfastly believes in Me, he will himself be able to do the things that I do; and he will do even greater things than these, because I go to the Father.

13And I will do—I Myself will grant—whatever you may ask in My name [ [b]presenting all I AM] so that the Father may be glorified *and* extolled in [through] the Son. [Exod. 3:14.]

14[Yes] I will grant—will do for you—whatever you shall ask in My name [ [c]presenting all I AM].

15If you [really] love Me you will keep (obey) My commands.

16And I will ask the Father, and He will give you another Comforter (Counselor, Helper, Intercessor, Advocate, Strengthener and Standby) that He may remain with you forever,

17The Spirit of Truth, Whom the world cannot receive (welcome, take to its heart), because it does not see Him, nor know *and* recognize Him. But you know *and* recognize Him, for He lives with you [constantly] and will be in you.

18I will not leave you orphans—comfortless, desolate, bereaved, forlorn, helpless—I will come [back] to you.

19Just a little while now and the world will not see Me any more, but you will see Me; because I live, you will live also.

**AMP** [a] Several ancient authorities read "His works." [b] Cremer. [c] Cremer.

## New American Standard

34"A new commandment I give to you, that you love one another, even as I have loved you, that you also love one another.
35"By this all men will know that you are My disciples, if you
have love for one another."
36¶ Simon Peter *said to Him, "Lord, where are You going?"
Jesus answered, "Where I go, you cannot follow Me now; but you
shall follow later."
37Peter *said to Him, "Lord, why can I not follow You right
now? I will lay down my life for You."
38Jesus *answered, "Will you lay down your life for Me? Truly,
truly, I say to you, a cock shall not crow, until you deny Me three
times.

*Jesus Comforts His Disciples*

**14** "LET NOT your heart be troubled; [d]believe in God, believe also in Me.
2"In My Father's house are many dwelling places; if it were not
so, I would have told you; for I go to prepare a place for you.
3"And if I go and prepare a place for you, I will come again,
and receive you to Myself; that where I am, *there* you may be also.
4" [e]And you know the way where I am going."
5Thomas *said to Him, "Lord, we do not know where You are
going, how do we know the way?"
6Jesus *said to him, "I am the way, and the truth, and the life;
no one comes to the Father, but through Me.

*Oneness with the Father*

7"If you had known Me, you would have known My Father
also; from now on you know Him, and have seen Him."
8Philip *said to Him, "Lord, show us the Father, and it is
enough for us."
9Jesus *said to him, "Have I been so long with you, and *yet* you
have not come to know Me, Philip? He who has seen Me has seen
the Father; how do you say, 'Show us the Father'?
10"Do you not believe that I am in the Father, and the Father
is in Me? The words that I say to you I do not speak on My own
initiative, but the Father abiding in Me does His works.
11"Believe Me that I am in the Father, and the Father in Me;
otherwise believe on account of the works themselves.
12"Truly, truly, I say to you, he who believes in Me, the works
that I do shall he do also; and greater *works* than these shall he do;
because I go to the Father.
13"And whatever you ask in My name, that will I do, that the
Father may be glorified in the Son.
14"If you ask Me anything in My name, I will do *it*.
15"If you love Me, you will keep My commandments.

*Role of the Spirit*

16"And I will ask the Father, and He will give you another
Helper, that He may be with you forever;
17 *that is* the Spirit of truth, whom the world cannot receive,
because it does not behold Him or know Him, *but* you know Him
because He abides with you, and will be in you.
18"I will not leave you as orphans; I will come to you.
19"After a little while the world will behold Me no more; but you
*will* behold Me; because I live, you shall live also.

**NAS** [d] Or, *you believe in God* [e] Many ancient authorities read *And where I go you know, and the way you know*

## New International

34"A new command I give you: Love one another. As I have
loved you, so you must love one another. 35By this all men will
know that you are my disciples, if you love one another."
36Simon Peter asked him, "Lord, where are you going?"
Jesus replied, "Where I am going, you cannot follow now, but
you will follow later."
37Peter asked, "Lord, why can't I follow you now? I will lay
down my life for you."
38Then Jesus answered, "Will you really lay down your life for
me? I tell you the truth, before the rooster crows, you will disown
me three times!

*Jesus Comforts His Disciples*

**14** "DO NOT let your hearts be troubled. Trust in God[f]; trust
also in me. 2In my Father's house are many rooms; if it
were not so, I would have told you. I am going there to prepare
a place for you. 3And if I go and prepare a place for you, I will come
back and take you to be with me that you also may be where I am.
4You know the way to the place where I am going."

*Jesus the Way to the Father*

5Thomas said to him, "Lord, we don't know where you are
going, so how can we know the way?"
6Jesus answered, "I am the way and the truth and the life. No
one comes to the Father except through me. 7If you really knew
me, you would know[g] my Father as well. From now on, you do
know him and have seen him."
8Philip said, "Lord, show us the Father and that will be enough
for us."
9Jesus answered: "Don't you know me, Philip, even after I have
been among you such a long time? Anyone who has seen me has
seen the Father. How can you say, 'Show us the Father'? 10Don't
you believe that I am in the Father, and that the Father is in me?
The words I say to you are not just my own. Rather, it is the Father,
living in me, who is doing his work. 11Believe me when I say that
I am in the Father and the Father is in me; or at least believe on
the evidence of the miracles themselves. 12I tell you the truth,
anyone who has faith in me will do what I have been doing. He
will do even greater things than these, because I am going to the
Father. 13And I will do whatever you ask in my name, so that the
Son may bring glory to the Father. 14You may ask me for anything
in my name, and I will do it.

*Jesus Promises the Holy Spirit*

15"If you love me, you will obey what I command. 16And I will
ask the Father, and he will give you another Counselor to be with
you forever— 17the Spirit of truth. The world cannot accept him,
because it neither sees him nor knows him. But you know him, for
he lives with you and will be[h] in you. 18I will not leave you as
orphans; I will come to you. 19Before long, the world will not see
me anymore, but you will see me. Because I live, you also will live.

**NIV** [f] 1 Or *You trust in God* [g] 7 Some early manuscripts *If you really have known me, you will know* [h] 17 Some early manuscripts *and is*

## King James

20 At that day ye shall know that I *am* in my Father, and ye in
me, and I in you.
21 He that hath my commandments, and keepeth them, he it is
that loveth me: and he that loveth me shall be loved of my Father,
and I will love him, and will manifest myself to him.
22 Judas saith unto him, not Iscariot, Lord, how is it that thou
wilt manifest thyself unto us, and not unto the world?
23 Jesus answered and said unto him, If a man love me, he will
keep my words: and my Father will love him, and we will come
unto him, and make our abode with him.
24 He that loveth me not keepeth not my sayings: and the word
which ye hear is not mine, but the Father's which sent me.
25 These things have I spoken unto you, being *yet* present with
you.
26 But the Comforter, *which is* the Holy Ghost, whom the Father
will send in my name, he shall teach you all things, and bring all
things to your remembrance, whatsoever I have said unto you.
27 Peace I leave with you, my peace I give unto you: not as the
world giveth, give I unto you. Let not your heart be troubled,
neither let it be afraid.
28 Ye have heard how I said unto you, I go away, and come *again*
unto you. If ye loved me, ye would rejoice, because I said, I go unto
the Father: for my Father is greater than I.
29 And now I have told you before it come to pass, that, when
it is come to pass, ye might believe.
30 Hereafter I will not talk much with you: for the prince of this
world cometh, and hath nothing in me.
31 But that the world may know that I love the Father; and as the
Father gave me commandment, even so I do. Arise, let us go
hence.

**15** I AM the true vine, and my Father is the husbandman.
2 Every branch in me that beareth not fruit he taketh away:
and every *branch* that beareth fruit, he purgeth it, that it may bring
forth more fruit.
3 Now ye are clean through the word which I have spoken unto
you.
4 Abide in me, and I in you. As the branch cannot bear fruit of
itself, except it abide in the vine; no more can ye, except ye abide
in me.
5 I am the vine, ye *are* the branches: He that abideth in me, and
I in him, the same bringeth forth much fruit: for without me ye can
do nothing.
6 If a man abide not in me, he is cast forth as a branch, and is
withered; and men gather them, and cast *them* into the fire, and
they are burned.
7 If ye abide in me, and my words abide in you, ye shall ask what
ye will, and it shall be done unto you.

## Amplified

20 At that time—when that day comes—you will know [for your-
selves] that I am in My Father, and you [are] in Me, and I [am] in
you.
21 The person who has My commands and keeps them is the one
who [really] loves Me, and whoever [really] loves Me will be loved
by My Father. And I [too] will love him and will show (reveal,
manifest) Myself to him—I will let Myself be clearly seen by him
*and* make Myself real to him.
22 Judas, not Iscariot, asked Him, Lord, how is it that You will
reveal Yourself—make Yourself real—to us and not to the world?
23 Jesus answered, If a person [really] loves Me, he will keep My
word—obey My teaching; and My Father will love him, and We
will come to him and make Our home (abode, special dwelling
place) with him.
24 Any one who does not [really] love Me does not observe *and*
obey My teaching. And the teaching which you hear *and* heed is
not Mine, but [comes] from the Father Who sent Me.
25 I have told you these things while I am still with you.
26 But the Comforter (Counselor, Helper, Intercessor, Advocate,
Strengthener, Standby), the Holy Spirit, Whom the Father will
send in My name [in My place, to represent Me and act on My
behalf], He will teach you all things. And He will cause you to
recall—will remind you of, bring to your remembrance—everything I have told you.
27 Peace I leave with you; My [own] peace I now give *and* bequeath to you. Not as the world gives do I give to you. Do not let
your heart be troubled, neither let it be afraid—stop allowing
yourselves to be agitated and disturbed; and do not permit yourselves to be fearful *and* intimidated *and* cowardly *and* unsettled.
28 You heard Me tell you, I am going away, and I am coming
[back] to you. If you [really] loved Me, you would have been glad
because I am going to the Father; for the Father is greater *and*
mightier than I am.
29 And now I have told you [this] before it occurs, so that when
it does take place you may believe *and* have faith in *and* rely on Me.
30 I will not talk with you much more, for the prince (evil genius,
ruler) of the world is coming. And he has no claim on Me—he has
nothing in common with Me, there is nothing in Me that belongs
to him, he has no power over Me.
31 But [ [a]Satan is coming and] I do as the Father has commanded
Me, so that the world may know (be convinced) that I love the
Father, and that I do only what the Father has instructed Me to
do.—I act in full agreement with His orders. Rise, let us go away
from here.

**15** I AM the True Vine and My Father is the Vinedresser.
2 Any branch in Me that does not bear fruit—that stops
bearing—He cuts away (trims off, takes away). And He cleanses
*and* repeatedly prunes every branch that continues to bear fruit, to
make it bear more *and* richer *and* more excellent fruit.
3 You are cleansed *and* pruned already, because of the Word
which I have given you—the teachings I have discussed with you.
4 Dwell in Me and I will dwell in you.—Live in Me and I will live
in you. Just as no branch can bear fruit of itself without abiding in
(vitally united to) the vine, neither can you bear fruit unless you
abide in Me.
5 I am the Vine, you are the branches. Whoever lives in Me and
I in him bears much (abundant) fruit. However, apart from Me—
cut off from vital union with Me—you can do nothing.
6 If a person does not dwell in Me, he is thrown out as a [broken-
off] branch and withers. Such branches are gathered up and
thrown into the fire and they are burned.
7 If you live in Me—abide vitally united to Me—and My words
remain in you *and* continue to live in your hearts, ask whatever you
will and it shall be done for you.

AMP [a] Vincent.

## New American Standard

20"In that day you shall know that I am in My Father, and you
in Me, and I in you.
21"He who has My commandments and keeps them, he it is
who loves Me; and he who loves Me shall be loved by My Father,
and I will love him, and will disclose Myself to him."
22Judas (not Iscariot) *said to Him, "Lord, what then has happened that You are going to disclose Yourself to us, and not to the
world?"
23Jesus answered and said to him, "If anyone loves Me, he will
keep My word; and My Father will love him, and We will come
to him, and make Our abode with him.
24"He who does not love Me does not keep My words; and the
word which you hear is not Mine, but the Father's who sent Me.
25¶ "These things I have spoken to you, while abiding with you.
26"But the Helper, the Holy Spirit, whom the Father will send
in My name, He will teach you all things, and bring to your
remembrance all that I said to you.
27"Peace I leave with you; My peace I give to you; not as the
world gives, do I give to you. Let not your heart be troubled, nor
let it be fearful.
28"You heard that I said to you, 'I go away, and I will come to
you.' If you loved Me, you would have rejoiced, because I go to
the Father; for the Father is greater than I.
29"And now I have told you before it comes to pass, that when
it comes to pass, you may believe.
30"I will not speak much more with you, for the ruler of the
world is coming, and he has nothing in Me;
31but that the world may know that I love the Father, and as the
Father gave Me commandment, even so I do. Arise, let us go from
here.

*Jesus Is the Vine—Followers Are Branches*

**15** "I AM the true vine, and My Father is the vinedresser.
2"Every branch in Me that does not bear fruit, He takes
away; and every *branch* that bears fruit, He [b]prunes it, that it may
bear more fruit.
3"You are already clean because of the word which I have
spoken to you.
4"Abide in Me, and I in you. As the branch cannot bear fruit
of itself, unless it abides in the vine, so neither *can* you, unless you
abide in Me.
5"I am the vine, you are the branches; he who abides in Me,
and I in him, he bears much fruit; for apart from Me you can do
nothing.
6"If anyone does not abide in Me, he is thrown away as a
branch, and dries up; and they gather them, and cast them into the
fire, and they are burned.
7"If you abide in Me, and My words abide in you, ask whatever
you wish, and it shall be done for you.

NAS [b] Lit., *cleanses*

## New International

20On that day you will realize that I am in my Father, and you are
in me, and I am in you. 21Whoever has my commands and obeys
them, he is the one who loves me. He who loves me will be loved
by my Father, and I too will love him and show myself to him."
22Then Judas (not Judas Iscariot) said, "But, Lord, why do you
intend to show yourself to us and not to the world?"
23Jesus replied, "If anyone loves me, he will obey my teaching.
My Father will love him, and we will come to him and make our
home with him. 24He who does not love me will not obey my
teaching. These words you hear are not my own; they belong to
the Father who sent me.
25"All this I have spoken while still with you. 26But the Counsel-
or, the Holy Spirit, whom the Father will send in my name, will
teach you all things and will remind you of everything I have said
to you. 27Peace I leave with you; my peace I give you. I do not give
to you as the world gives. Do not let your hearts be troubled and
do not be afraid.
28"You heard me say, 'I am going away and I am coming back
to you.' If you loved me, you would be glad that I am going to the
Father, for the Father is greater than I. 29I have told you now before
it happens, so that when it does happen you will believe. 30I will
not speak with you much longer, for the prince of this world is
coming. He has no hold on me, 31but the world must learn that
I love the Father and that I do exactly what my Father has commanded me.
"Come now; let us leave.

*The Vine and the Branches*

**15** "I AM the true vine, and my Father is the gardener. 2He
cuts off every branch in me that bears no fruit, while every
branch that does bear fruit he prunes[c] so that it will be even more
fruitful. 3You are already clean because of the word I have spoken
to you. 4Remain in me, and I will remain in you. No branch can
bear fruit by itself; it must remain in the vine. Neither can you bear
fruit unless you remain in me.
5"I am the vine; you are the branches. If a man remains in me
and I in him, he will bear much fruit; apart from me you can do
nothing. 6If anyone does not remain in me, he is like a branch that
is thrown away and withers; such branches are picked up, thrown
into the fire and burned. 7If you remain in me and my words
remain in you, ask whatever you wish, and it will be given you.

NIV [c] 2 The Greek for *prunes* also means *cleans.*

## King James

8 Herein is my Father glorified, that ye bear much fruit; so shall ye be my disciples.

9 As the Father hath loved me, so have I loved you: continue ye in my love.

10 If ye keep my commandments, ye shall abide in my love; even as I have kept my Father's commandments, and abide in his love.

11 These things have I spoken unto you, that my joy might remain in you, and *that* your joy might be full.

12 This is my commandment, That ye love one another, as I have loved you.

13 Greater love hath no man than this, that a man lay down his life for his friends.

14 Ye are my friends, if ye do whatsoever I command you.

15 Henceforth I call you not servants; for the servant knoweth not what his lord doeth: but I have called you friends; for all things that I have heard of my Father I have made known unto you.

16 Ye have not chosen me, but I have chosen you, and ordained you, that ye should go and bring forth fruit, and *that* your fruit should remain: that whatsoever ye shall ask of the Father in my name, he may give it you.

17 These things I command you, that ye love one another.

18 If the world hate you, ye know that it hated me before *it hated* you.

19 If ye were of the world, the world would love his own: but because ye are not of the world, but I have chosen you out of the world, therefore the world hateth you.

20 Remember the word that I said unto you, The servant is not greater than his lord. If they have persecuted me, they will also persecute you; if they have kept my saying, they will keep yours also.

21 But all these things will they do unto you for my name's sake, because they know not him that sent me.

22 If I had not come and spoken unto them, they had not had sin: but now they have no cloak for their sin.

23 He that hateth me hateth my Father also.

24 If I had not done among them the works which none other man did, they had not had sin: but now have they both seen and hated both me and my Father.

25 But *this cometh to pass*, that the word might be fulfilled that is written in their law, They hated me without a cause.

26 But when the Comforter is come, whom I will send unto you from the Father, *even* the Spirit of truth, which proceedeth from the Father, he shall testify of me:

27 And ye also shall bear witness, because ye have been with me from the beginning.

**16** THESE THINGS have I spoken unto you, that ye should not be offended.

2 They shall put you out of the synagogues: yea, the time cometh, that whosoever killeth you will think that he doeth God service.

3 And these things will they do unto you, because they have not known the Father, nor me.

## Amplified

8 When you bear (produce) much fruit, My Father is honored *and* glorified; and you show *and* prove yourselves to be true followers of Mine.

9 I have loved you [just] as the Father has loved Me; abide in My love—[a]continue in His love with Me.

10 If you keep My commandments—if you continue to obey My instructions—you will abide in My love *and* live on in it; just as I have obeyed My Father's commandments and live on in His love.

11 I have told you these things that My joy *and* delight may be in you, and that your joy *and* gladness may be full measure *and* complete *and* overflowing.

12 This is My commandment, that you love one another [just] as I have loved you.

13 No one has greater love—no one has shown stronger affection—than to lay down (give up) his own life for his friends.

14 You are My friends, if you keep on doing the things which I command you to do.

15 I do not call you servants (slaves) any longer, for the servant does not know what his master is doing (working out). But I have called you My friends, because I have made known to you everything that I have heard from My Father—I have revealed to you everything that I have learned from Him.

16 You have not chosen Me, but I have chosen you—I have appointed you, I have planted you—that you might go and bear fruit *and* keep on bearing; that your fruit may be lasting (that it may remain, abide); so that whatever you ask the Father in My name [as [b]presenting all that I AM] He may give it to you.

17 This is what I command you, that you love one another.

18 If the world hates you, know that it hated Me before it hated you.

19 If you belonged to the world, the world would treat you with affection *and* would love you as its own. But because you are not of the world—are no longer one with it—but I have chosen (selected) you out of the world, the world hates (detests) you.

20 Remember that I told you, A servant is not greater than his master—is not superior to him. If they persecuted Me, they will also persecute you; if they kept My word *and* obeyed My teachings, they will also keep *and* obey yours.

21 But they will do all this to you—inflict all this suffering on you—because of [your bearing] My name, *and* on My account, for they do not know *or* understand the One Who sent Me.

22 If I had not come and spoken to them, they would not be guilty of sin; but now they have no excuse for their sin.

23 Whoever hates Me also hates My Father.

24 If I had not done (accomplished) among them the works which no one else ever did, they would not be guilty of sin—would be blameless. But [the fact is] now they have both seen [these works] and have hated both Me and My Father.

25 But [this is so] that the word written in their Law might be fulfilled, They hated Me without a cause. [Ps. 35:19; 69:4.]

26 But when the Comforter (Counselor, Helper, Advocate, Intercessor, Strengthener) comes Whom I will send to you from the Father, the Spirit of Truth Who comes (proceeds) from the Father, He [Himself] will testify regarding Me.

27 But you also will testify *and* be My witnesses, because you have been with Me from the beginning.

**16** I HAVE told you all these things so that you should not be offended—taken unawares and falter, or be caused to stumble and fall away, *and* to keep you from being scandalized and repelled.

2 They will put you out of the synagogues—expel you. But an hour is coming when whoever kills you will think *and* claim that he has offered service to God.

3 And they will do this because they have not known the Father nor Me.

AMP [a] Cremer's "Biblico-Theological Lexicon." [b] Cremer.

## New American Standard

8"By this is My Father glorified, that you bear much fruit, and *so* prove to be My disciples.

9"Just as the Father has loved Me, I have also loved you; abide in My love.

10"If you keep My commandments, you will abide in My love; just as I have kept My Father's commandments, and abide in His love.

11"These things I have spoken to you, that My joy may be in you, and *that* your joy may be made full.

*Disciples' Relation to Each Other*

12"This is My commandment, that you love one another, just as I have loved you.

13"Greater love has no one than this, that one lay down his life for his friends.

14"You are My friends, if you do what I command you.

15"No longer do I call you slaves, for the slave does not know what his master is doing; but I have called you friends, for all things that I have heard from My Father I have made known to you.

16"You did not choose Me, but I chose you, and appointed you, that you should go and bear fruit, and *that* your fruit should remain, that whatever you ask of the Father in My name, He may give to you.

17"This I command you, that you love one another.

*Disciples' Relation to the World*

18"If the world hates you, you know that it has hated Me before *it hated* you.

19"If you were of the world, the world would love its own; but because you are not of the world, but I chose you out of the world, therefore the world hates you.

20"Remember the word that I said to you, 'A slave is not greater than his master.' If they persecuted Me, they will also persecute you; if they kept My word, they will keep yours also.

21"But all these things they will do to you for My name's sake, because they do not know the One who sent Me.

22"If I had not come and spoken to them, they would not have sin, but now they have no excuse for their sin.

23"He who hates Me hates My Father also.

24"If I had not done among them the works which no one else did, they would not have sin; but now they have both seen and hated Me and My Father as well.

25"But *they have done this* in order that the word may be fulfilled that is written in their Law, 'THEY HATED ME WITHOUT A CAUSE.'

26"When the Helper comes, whom I will send to you from the Father, *that is* the Spirit of truth, who proceeds from the Father, He will bear witness of Me,

27and you *will* bear witness also, because you have been with Me from the beginning.

*Jesus' Warning*

**16** "THESE THINGS I have spoken to you, that you may be kept from stumbling.

2"They will make you outcasts from the synagogue, but an hour is coming for everyone who kills you to think that he is offering service to God.

3"And these things they will do, because they have not known the Father, or Me.

## New International

8This is to my Father's glory, that you bear much fruit, showing
yourselves to be my disciples.
9"As the Father has loved me, so have I loved you. Now remain
in my love. 10If you obey my commands, you will remain in my
love, just as I have obeyed my Father's commands and remain in
his love. 11I have told you this so that my joy may be in you and
that your joy may be complete. 12My command is this: Love each
other as I have loved you. 13Greater love has no one than this, that
he lay down his life for his friends. 14You are my friends if you do
what I command. 15I no longer call you servants, because a servant
does not know his master's business. Instead, I have called you
friends, for everything that I learned from my Father I have made
known to you. 16You did not choose me, but I chose you and
appointed you to go and bear fruit—fruit that will last. Then the
Father will give you whatever you ask in my name. 17This is my
command: Love each other.

*The World Hates the Disciples*

18"If the world hates you, keep in mind that it hated me first.
19If you belonged to the world, it would love you as its own. As
it is, you do not belong to the world, but I have chosen you out
of the world. That is why the world hates you. 20Remember the
words I spoke to you: 'No servant is greater than his master.'[c] If
they persecuted me, they will persecute you also. If they obeyed
my teaching, they will obey yours also. 21They will treat you this
way because of my name, for they do not know the One who sent
me. 22If I had not come and spoken to them, they would not be
guilty of sin. Now, however, they have no excuse for their sin.
23He who hates me hates my Father as well. 24If I had not done
among them what no one else did, they would not be guilty of sin.
But now they have seen these miracles, and yet they have hated
both me and my Father. 25But this is to fulfill what is written in
their Law: 'They hated me without reason.'[d]
26"When the Counselor comes, whom I will send to you from
the Father, the Spirit of truth who goes out from the Father, he will
testify about me. 27And you also must testify, for you have been
with me from the beginning.

**16** "ALL THIS I have told you so that you will not go astray.
2They will put you out of the synagogue; in fact, a time is
coming when anyone who kills you will think he is offering a
service to God. 3They will do such things because they have not
known the Father or me. 4I have told you this, so that when the

NIV [c] *20* John 13:16 [d] *25* Psalms 35:19; 69:4

## King James

4 But these things have I told you, that when the time shall come, ye may remember that I told you of them. And these things I said not unto you at the beginning, because I was with you.

5 But now I go my way to him that sent me; and none of you asketh me, Whither goest thou?

6 But because I have said these things unto you, sorrow hath filled your heart.

7 Nevertheless I tell you the truth; It is expedient for you that I go away: for if I go not away, the Comforter will not come unto you; but if I depart, I will send him unto you.

8 And when he is come, he will reprove the world of sin, and of righteousness, and of judgment:

9 Of sin, because they believe not on me;

10 Of righteousness, because I go to my Father, and ye see me no more;

11 Of judgment, because the prince of this world is judged.

12 I have yet many things to say unto you, but ye cannot bear them now.

13 Howbeit when he, the Spirit of truth, is come, he will guide you into all truth: for he shall not speak of himself; but whatsoever he shall hear, *that* shall he speak: and he will show you things to come.

14 He shall glorify me: for he shall receive of mine, and shall show *it* unto you.

15 All things that the Father hath are mine: therefore said I, that he shall take of mine, and shall show *it* unto you.

16 A little while, and ye shall not see me: and again, a little while, and ye shall see me, because I go to the Father.

17 Then said *some* of his disciples among themselves, What is this that he saith unto us, A little while, and ye shall not see me: and again, a little while, and ye shall see me: and, Because I go to the Father?

18 They said therefore, What is this that he saith, A little while? we cannot tell what he saith.

19 Now Jesus knew that they were desirous to ask him, and said unto them, Do ye inquire among yourselves of that I said, A little while, and ye shall not see me: and again, a little while, and ye shall see me?

20 Verily, verily, I say unto you, That ye shall weep and lament, but the world shall rejoice: and ye shall be sorrowful, but your sorrow shall be turned into joy.

21 A woman when she is in travail hath sorrow, because her hour is come: but as soon as she is delivered of the child, she remembereth no more the anguish, for joy that a man is born into the world.

22 And ye now therefore have sorrow: but I will see you again, and your heart shall rejoice, and your joy no man taketh from you.

23 And in that day ye shall ask me nothing. Verily, verily, I say unto you, Whatsoever ye shall ask the Father in my name, he will give *it* you.

## Amplified

4 But I have told you these things now so that when they occur you will remember that I told you of them. I did not say these things to you from the beginning, because I was with you.

5 But now I am going to Him Who sent Me; yet none of you asks Me, Where are You going?

6 But because I have said these things to you sorrow has filled your hearts—taken complete possession of them.

7 However, I am telling you nothing but the truth when I say, it is profitable—good, expedient, advantageous—for you that I go away. Because if I do not go away, the Comforter (Counselor, Helper, Advocate, Intercessor, Strengthener, Standby) will not come to you—into close fellowship with you. But if I go away, I will send Him to you—to be in close fellowship with you.

8 And when He comes, He will convict *and* convince the world *and* bring demonstration to it about sin and about righteousness—uprightness of heart and right standing with God—and about judgment.

9 About sin, because they do not believe on Me—trust in, rely on and adhere to Me.

10 About righteousness—uprightness of heart and right standing with God—because I go to My Father and you will see Me no longer.

11 About judgment, because the ruler (prince) of this world [Satan] is judged *and* condemned *and* sentence already is passed upon him.

12 I have still many things to say to you, but you are not able to bear them *nor* to take them upon you *nor* to grasp them now.

13 But when He, the Spirit of Truth (the truth-giving Spirit) comes, He will guide you into all the truth—the whole, full truth. For He will not speak His own message—on His own authority—but He will tell whatever He hears [from the Father, He will give the message that has been given to Him] and He will announce *and* declare to you the things that are to come—that will happen in the future.

14 He will honor *and* glorify Me, because He will take of (receive, draw upon) what is Mine and will reveal (declare, disclose, transmit) it to you.

15 Everything that the Father has is Mine. That is what I meant when I said that He will take the things that are Mine and will reveal (declare, disclose, transmit) them to you.

16 In a little while you will no longer see Me, and again after a short while you will see Me.

17 So some of His disciples questioned among themselves, What does He mean when He tells us, A little while and you will no longer see Me, and again after a short while you will see Me, and, Because I go to My Father?

18 What does He mean by a little while? We do not know *nor* understand what He is talking about.

19 Jesus knew that they wanted to ask Him, so He said to them, Are you wondering *and* inquiring among yourselves what I meant when I said, In a little while you will see Me no longer, and again after a short while you will see Me?

20 I assure you, most solemnly I tell you, that you shall weep and grieve, but the world will rejoice. You will be sorrowful, but your sorrow will be turned into joy.

21 A woman, when she gives birth to a child has grief (anguish, agony), because her time has come. But when she is delivered of the child, she no longer remembers her pain (trouble, anguish), because she is so glad that a man (a child, a human being) has been born into the world.

22 So for the present you are also in sorrow—in distress and depressed. But I will see you again and [then] your hearts will rejoice, and no one can take from you your joy (gladness, delight).

23 And when that time comes, you will ask nothing of Me—you will need to ask Me no questions. I assure you, most solemnly I tell you, that My Father will grant you whatever you ask in My name [ [a]presenting all I AM]. [Exod. 3:14.]

AMP [a] Cremer.

## New American Standard

4"But these things I have spoken to you, that when their hour
comes, you may remember that I told you of them. And these
things I did not say to you at the beginning, because I was with
you.

*The Holy Spirit Promised*

5"But now I am going to Him who sent Me; and none of you
asks Me, 'Where are You going?'
6"But because I have said these things to you, sorrow has filled
your heart.
7"But I tell you the truth, it is to your advantage that I go away;
for if I do not go away, the Helper shall not come to you; but if I
go, I will send Him to you.
8"And He, when He comes, will convict the world concerning
sin, and righteousness, and judgment;
9concerning sin, because they do not believe in Me;
10and concerning righteousness, because I go to the Father, and
you no longer behold Me;
11and concerning judgment, because the ruler of this world has
been judged.
12"I have many more things to say to you, but you cannot bear
*them* now.
13"But when He, the Spirit of truth, comes, He will guide you
into all the truth; for He will not speak on His own initiative, but
whatever He hears, He will speak; and He will disclose to you
what is to come.
14"He shall glorify Me; for He shall take of Mine, and shall
disclose *it* to you.
15"All things that the Father has are Mine; therefore I said, that
He takes of Mine, and will disclose *it* to you.

*Jesus' Death and Resurrection Foretold*

16"A little while, and you will no longer behold Me; and again
a little while, and you will see Me."
17 *Some* of His disciples therefore said to one another, "What is
this thing He is telling us, 'A little while, and you will not behold
Me; and again a little while, and you will see Me'; and, 'because
I go to the Father'?"
18And so they were saying, "What is this that He says, 'A little
while'? We do not know what He is talking about."
19Jesus knew that they wished to question Him, and He said to
them, "Are you deliberating together about this, that I said, 'A
little while, and you will not behold Me, and again a little while,
and you will see Me'?
20"Truly, truly, I say to you, that you will weep and lament, but
the world will rejoice; you will be sorrowful, but your sorrow will
be turned to joy.
21"Whenever a woman is in travail she has sorrow, because her
hour has come; but when she gives birth to the child, she remembers the anguish no more, for joy that a child has been born into
the world.
22"Therefore you too now have sorrow; but I will see you again,
and your heart will rejoice, and no one takes your joy away from
you.

*Prayer Promises*

23"And in that day you will ask Me no question. Truly, truly,
I say to you, if you shall ask the Father for anything, He will give
it to you in My name.

## New International

time comes you will remember that I warned you. I did not tell you
this at first because I was with you.

*The Work of the Holy Spirit*

5"Now I am going to him who sent me, yet none of you asks
me, 'Where are you going?' 6Because I have said these things, you
are filled with grief. 7But I tell you the truth: It is for your good that
I am going away. Unless I go away, the Counselor will not come
to you; but if I go, I will send him to you. 8When he comes, he will
convict the world of guilt[b] in regard to sin and righteousness and
judgment: 9in regard to sin, because men do not believe in me; 10in
regard to righteousness, because I am going to the Father, where
you can see me no longer; 11and in regard to judgment, because
the prince of this world now stands condemned.
12"I have much more to say to you, more than you can now
bear. 13But when he, the Spirit of truth, comes, he will guide you
into all truth. He will not speak on his own; he will speak only what
he hears, and he will tell you what is yet to come. 14He will bring
glory to me by taking from what is mine and making it known to
you. 15All that belongs to the Father is mine. That is why I said the
Spirit will take from what is mine and make it known to you.
16"In a little while you will see me no more, and then after a
little while you will see me."

*The Disciples' Grief Will Turn to Joy*

17Some of his disciples said to one another, "What does he
mean by saying, 'In a little while you will see me no more, and then
after a little while you will see me,' and 'Because I am going to the
Father'?" 18They kept asking, "What does he mean by 'a little
while'? We don't understand what he is saying."
19Jesus saw that they wanted to ask him about this, so he said
to them, "Are you asking one another what I meant when I said,
'In a little while you will see me no more, and then after a little
while you will see me'? 20I tell you the truth, you will weep and
mourn while the world rejoices. You will grieve, but your grief will
turn to joy. 21A woman giving birth to a child has pain because her
time has come; but when her baby is born she forgets the anguish
because of her joy that a child is born into the world. 22So with you:
Now is your time of grief, but I will see you again and you will
rejoice, and no one will take away your joy. 23In that day you will
no longer ask me anything. I tell you the truth, my Father will give
you whatever you ask in my name. 24Until now you have not

NIV [b] 8 Or *will expose the guilt of the world*

## King James

24 Hitherto have ye asked nothing in my name: ask, and ye shall receive, that your joy may be full.

25 These things have I spoken unto you in proverbs: but the time cometh, when I shall no more speak unto you in proverbs, but I shall show you plainly of the Father.

26 At that day ye shall ask in my name: and I say not unto you, that I will pray the Father for you:

27 For the Father himself loveth you, because ye have loved me, and have believed that I came out from God.

28 I came forth from the Father, and am come into the world: again, I leave the world, and go to the Father.

29 His disciples said unto him, Lo, now speakest thou plainly, and speakest no proverb.

30 Now are we sure that thou knowest all things, and needest not that any man should ask thee: by this we believe that thou camest forth from God.

31 Jesus answered them, Do ye now believe?

32 Behold, the hour cometh, yea, is now come, that ye shall be scattered, every man to his own, and shall leave me alone: and yet I am not alone, because the Father is with me.

33 These things I have spoken unto you, that in me ye might have peace. In the world ye shall have tribulation: but be of good cheer; I have overcome the world.

**17** THESE WORDS spake Jesus, and lifted up his eyes to heaven, and said, Father, the hour is come; glorify thy Son, that thy Son also may glorify thee:

2 As thou hast given him power over all flesh, that he should give eternal life to as many as thou hast given him.

3 And this is life eternal, that they might know thee the only true God, and Jesus Christ, whom thou hast sent.

4 I have glorified thee on the earth: I have finished the work which thou gavest me to do.

5 And now, O Father, glorify thou me with thine own self with the glory which I had with thee before the world was.

6 I have manifested thy name unto the men which thou gavest me out of the world: thine they were, and thou gavest them me; and they have kept thy word.

7 Now they have known that all things whatsoever thou hast given me are of thee.

8 For I have given unto them the words which thou gavest me; and they have received *them,* and have known surely that I came out from thee, and they have believed that thou didst send me.

9 I pray for them: I pray not for the world, but for them which thou hast given me; for they are thine.

10 And all mine are thine, and thine are mine; and I am glorified in them.

## Amplified

24 Up to this time, you have not asked a [single] thing in My name [that is, [a]presenting all I AM] *but now* ask *and* keep on asking and you will receive, so that your joy (gladness, delight) may be full *and* complete.

25 I have told you these things in parables (veiled language, allegories, dark sayings). The hour is now coming when I shall no longer speak to you in figures of speech, but I shall tell you about the Father in plain words *and* openly—without reserve.

26 At that time you will ask (pray) in My name, and I am not saying that I will ask the Father on your behalf [for it will be unnecessary].

27 For the Father Himself tenderly loves you, because you have loved Me, and have believed that I came out from the Father.

28 I came out from the Father and have come into the world; again, I am leaving the world and going to the Father.

29 His disciples said, Ah, now You are speaking plainly to us, and not in parables—not in veiled language and figures of speech!

30 Now we know that You are acquainted with everything and have no need to be asked questions. Because of this, we believe that you [really] came from God.

31 Jesus answered them, Do you now believe—do you believe it at last?

32 But take notice, the hour is coming and it has arrived, when you will all be dispersed *and* scattered every man to his own home, leaving Me alone. Yet I am not alone, because the Father is with Me.

33 I have told you these things so that in Me you may have perfect peace *and* confidence. In the world you have tribulation *and* trials *and* distress *and* frustration; but be of good cheer—take courage, be confident, certain, undaunted—for I have overcome the world.—I have deprived it of power to harm, have conquered it [for you].

**17** WHEN JESUS had spoken these things, He lifted up His eyes to heaven and said, Father, the hour is come. Glorify *and* exalt *and* honor *and* magnify Your Son, so that Your Son may glorify *and* extol *and* honor *and* magnify You.

2 Just as You have granted Him power *and* authority over all flesh (all human kind), *now glorify Him,* so that He may give eternal life to all whom You have given Him.

3 And this is eternal life: [it means] to know (to perceive, recognize, become acquainted with and understand) You, the only true *and* real God, and [likewise] to know Him, Jesus [as the] Christ, the Anointed One, the Messiah, Whom You have sent.

4 I have glorified You down here on the earth by completing the work that You gave Me to do.

5 And now, Father, glorify Me along with Yourself *and* restore Me to such majesty *and* honor in Your presence as I had with You before the world existed.

6 I have manifested Your name—I have revealed Your very Self, Your real Self—to the people whom You have given Me out of the world. They were Yours, and You gave them to Me, and they have obeyed *and* kept Your Word.

7 Now [at last] they know *and* understand that all You have given Me belongs to You—is really and truly Yours.

8 For the uttered words that You gave Me I have given them. And they have received *and* accepted [them], and have come to know positively *and* in reality—to believe with absolute assurance—that I came forth from Your presence. And they have believed *and* are convinced that You did send Me.

9 I am praying for them. I am not praying (requesting) for the world; but for those You have given Me, for they belong to You.

10 All Mine are Yours, and all that are Yours belong to Me; and I am glorified in (through) them—they have done Me honor, in them My glory is achieved.

AMP [a] Cremer.

## New American Standard

24"Until now you have asked for nothing in My name; ask, and
you will receive, that your joy may be made full.
25¶ "These things I have spoken to you in figurative language;
an hour is coming when I will speak no more to you in figurative
language, but will tell you plainly of the Father.
26"In that day you will ask in My name, and I do not say to you
that I will request the Father on your behalf;
27for the Father Himself loves you, because you have loved Me,
and have believed that I came forth from the Father.
28"I came forth from the Father, and have come into the world;
I am leaving the world again, and going to the Father."
29His disciples *said, "Lo, now You are speaking plainly, and
are not using a figure of speech.
30"Now we know that You know all things, and have no need
for anyone to question You; by this we believe that You came from
God."
31Jesus answered them, "Do you now believe?
32"Behold, an hour is coming, and has *already* come, for you to
be scattered, each to his own *home*, and to leave Me alone; and *yet*
I am not alone, because the Father is with Me.
33"These things I have spoken to you, that in Me you may have
peace. In the world you have tribulation, but take courage; I have
overcome the world."

*The High Priestly Prayer*

17 THESE THINGS Jesus spoke; and lifting up His eyes to
heaven, He said, "Father, the hour has come; glorify Thy
Son, that the Son may glorify Thee,
2even as Thou gavest Him authority over all mankind, that to
all whom Thou hast given Him, He may give eternal life.
3"And this is eternal life, that they may know Thee, the only
true God, and Jesus Christ whom Thou hast sent.
4"I glorified Thee on the earth, having accomplished the work
which Thou hast given Me to do.
5"And now, glorify Thou Me together with Thyself, Father,
with the glory which I had with Thee before the world was.
6"I manifested Thy name to the men whom Thou gavest Me
out of the world; Thine they were, and Thou gavest them to Me,
and they have kept Thy word.
7"Now they have come to know that everything Thou hast
given Me is from Thee;
8for the words which Thou gavest Me I have given to them;
and they received *them*, and truly understood that I came forth
from Thee, and they believed that Thou didst send Me.
9"I ask on their behalf; I do not ask on behalf of the world, but
of those whom Thou hast given Me; for they are Thine;
10and all things that are Mine are Thine, and Thine are Mine;
and I have been glorified in them.

## New International

asked for anything in my name. Ask and you will receive, and your
joy will be complete.
25"Though I have been speaking figuratively, a time is coming
when I will no longer use this kind of language but will tell you
plainly about my Father. 26In that day you will ask in my name.
I am not saying that I will ask the Father on your behalf. 27No, the
Father himself loves you because you have loved me and have
believed that I came from God. 28I came from the Father and
entered the world; now I am leaving the world and going back to
the Father."
29Then Jesus' disciples said, "Now you are speaking clearly and
without figures of speech. 30Now we can see that you know all
things and that you do not even need to have anyone ask you
questions. This makes us believe that you came from God."
31"You believe at last!"[b] Jesus answered. 32"But a time is coming, and has come, when you will be scattered, each to his own
home. You will leave me all alone. Yet I am not alone, for my
Father is with me.
33"I have told you these things, so that in me you may have
peace. In this world you will have trouble. But take heart! I have
overcome the world."

*Jesus Prays for Himself*

17 AFTER JESUS said this, he looked toward heaven and
prayed:

"Father, the time has come. Glorify your Son, that your
Son may glorify you. 2For you granted him authority over all
people that he might give eternal life to all those you have
given him. 3Now this is eternal life: that they may know you,
the only true God, and Jesus Christ, whom you have sent. 4I
have brought you glory on earth by completing the work you
gave me to do. 5And now, Father, glorify me in your presence
with the glory I had with you before the world began.

*Jesus Prays for His Disciples*

6"I have revealed you[c] to those whom you gave me out of
the world. They were yours; you gave them to me and they
have obeyed your word. 7Now they know that everything
you have given me comes from you. 8For I gave them the
words you gave me and they accepted them. They knew with
certainty that I came from you, and they believed that you
sent me. 9I pray for them. I am not praying for the world, but
for those you have given me, for they are yours. 10All I have
is yours, and all you have is mine. And glory has come to me
through them. 11I will remain in the world no longer, but they

**NIV** [b] 31 Or *"Do you now believe?"* [c] 6 Greek *your name;* also in verse 26

## King James

11And now I am no more in the world, but these are in the world, and I come to thee. Holy Father, keep through thine own name those whom thou hast given me, that they may be one, as we *are*.

12While I was with them in the world, I kept them in thy name: those that thou gavest me I have kept, and none of them is lost, but the son of perdition; that the scripture might be fulfilled.

13And now come I to thee; and these things I speak in the world, that they might have my joy fulfilled in themselves.

14I have given them thy word; and the world hath hated them, because they are not of the world, even as I am not of the world.

15I pray not that thou shouldest take them out of the world, but that thou shouldest keep them from the evil.

16They are not of the world, even as I am not of the world.

17Sanctify them through thy truth: thy word is truth.

18As thou hast sent me into the world, even so have I also sent them into the world.

19And for their sakes I sanctify myself, that they also might be sanctified through the truth.

20Neither pray I for these alone, but for them also which shall believe on me through their word;

21That they all may be one; as thou, Father, *art* in me, and I in thee, that they also may be one in us: that the world may believe that thou hast sent me.

22And the glory which thou gavest me I have given them; that they may be one, even as we are one:

23I in them, and thou in me, that they may be made perfect in one; and that the world may know that thou hast sent me, and hast loved them, as thou hast loved me.

24Father, I will that they also, whom thou hast given me, be with me where I am; that they may behold my glory, which thou hast given me: for thou lovedst me before the foundation of the world.

25O righteous Father, the world hath not known thee: but I have known thee, and these have known that thou hast sent me.

26And I have declared unto them thy name, and will declare *it*: that the love wherewith thou hast loved me may be in them, and I in them.

**18** WHEN JESUS had spoken these words, he went forth with his disciples over the brook Cedron, where was a garden, into the which he entered, and his disciples.

2And Judas also, which betrayed him, knew the place: for Jesus ofttimes resorted thither with his disciples.

3Judas then, having received a band *of men* and officers from the chief priests and Pharisees, cometh thither with lanterns and torches and weapons.

## Amplified

11And [now] I am no more in the world, but these are in the world and I am coming to You. Holy Father, keep in Your name [ [a]in the knowledge of Yourself] them whom You have given Me, that they may be one, as We [are one].

12While I was with them, I kept *and* preserved them in Your name [ [b]in the knowledge and worship of You]. Those You have given Me I guarded *and* protected, and not one of them has perished *or* is lost except the son of perdition [Judas Iscariot]—the one who is now doomed to destruction, destined to be lost—that the Scripture might be fulfilled. [Ps. 41:9; John 6:70.]

13And now I am coming to You. I say these things while I am still in the world, so that My joy may be made full *and* complete *and* perfect in them—that they may experience My delight fulfilled in them, that My enjoyment may be perfected in their own souls, that they may have My gladness within them filling their hearts.

14I have given *and* delivered to them Your Word (message); and the world has hated them, because they are not of the world—do not belong to the world—[just] as I am not of the world.

15I do not ask that You will take them out of the world, but that You will keep *and* protect them from the evil [one].

16They are not of the world (worldly, belonging to the world), [just] as I am not of the world.

17Sanctify them—purify, consecrate, separate them for Yourself, make them holy—by the Truth. Your Word is Truth.

18Just as You sent Me into the world, I also have sent them into the world.

19And so for their sake *and* on their behalf I sanctify (dedicate, consecrate) Myself, that they also may be sanctified (dedicated, consecrated, made holy) in the Truth.

20Neither for these alone do I pray—it is not for their sake only that I make this request—but also for all those who will ever come to believe in (trust, cling to, rely on) Me through their word *and* teaching;

21So that they all may be one [just] as You, Father, are in Me and I in You, that they also may be one in Us, so that the world may believe *and* be convinced that You have sent Me.

22I have given to them the glory *and* honor which You have given Me, that they may be one, [even] as We are one:

23I in them and You in Me, in order that they may become one *and* perfectly united, that the world may know *and* [definitely] recognize that You sent Me, and that You have loved them [even] as You have loved Me.

24Father, I desire that they also whom You have entrusted to Me [Your gift to Me,] may be with Me where I am, so that they may see My glory, which You have given Me—Your love gift to Me—for You loved Me before the foundation of the world.

25O just *and* righteous Father, although the world has not known You *and* has failed to recognize You *and* has never acknowledged You, I have known You continually. And these men understand *and* know that You have sent Me.

26I made Your name known to them *and* revealed Your character *and* Your very [c]Self, and I will continue to make [You] known, that the love which You have bestowed upon Me may be in them—felt in their hearts—and that I [Myself] may be in them.

**18** HAVING SAID these things, Jesus went out with His disciples beyond (across) the winter torrent of the Kidron (in the Ravine of the Cedars). There was a garden there, which He and His disciples entered.

2And Judas, who was betraying Him *and* delivering Him up, also knew the place, because Jesus had often retired there with His disciples.

3So Judas, obtaining *and* taking charge of the band of soldiers and some guards (attendants) of the high priests and Pharisees, came there with lanterns and torches and weapons.

**AMP** [a] Barnes' "Notes on Luke and John." [b] Barnes' "Notes on Luke and John." [c] Thayer.

## New American Standard

11"And I am no more in the world; and *yet* they themselves are
in the world, and I come to Thee. Holy Father, keep them in Thy
name, *the name* which Thou hast given Me, that they may be one,
even as We *are.*
12"While I was with them, I was keeping them in Thy name
which Thou hast given Me; and I guarded them, and not one of
them perished but the son of perdition, that the Scripture might
be fulfilled.

*The Disciples in the World*

13"But now I come to Thee; and these things I speak in the
world, that they may have My joy made full in themselves.
14"I have given them Thy word; and the world has hated them,
because they are not of the world, even as I am not of the world.
15"I do not ask Thee to take them out of the world, but to keep
them from the evil *one.*
16"They are not of the world, even as I am not of the world.
17"Sanctify them in the truth; Thy word is truth.
18"As Thou didst send Me into the world, I also have sent them
into the world.
19"And for their sakes I sanctify Myself, that they themselves
also may be sanctified in truth.
20"I do not ask in behalf of these alone, but for those also who
believe in Me through their word;
21that they may all be one; even as Thou, Father, *art* in Me, and
I in Thee, that they also may be in Us; that the world may believe
that Thou didst send Me.

*Their Future Glory*

22"And the glory which Thou hast given Me I have given to
them; that they may be one, just as We are one;
23I in them, and Thou in Me, that they may be perfected in
unity, that the world may know that Thou didst send Me, and
didst love them, even as Thou didst love Me.
24"Father, I desire that they also, whom Thou hast given Me,
be with Me where I am, in order that they may behold My glory,
which Thou hast given Me; for Thou didst love Me before the
foundation of the world.
25"O righteous Father, although the world has not known
Thee, yet I have known Thee; and these have known that Thou
didst send Me;
26and I have made Thy name known to them, and will make it
known; that the love wherewith Thou didst love Me may be in
them, and I in them."

*Judas Betrays Jesus*

**18** WHEN JESUS had spoken these words, He went forth
with His disciples over the ravine of the Kidron, where
there was a garden, into which He Himself entered, and His
disciples.
2Now Judas also, who was betraying Him, knew the place; for
Jesus had often met there with His disciples.
3Judas then, having received the *Roman* cohort, and officers
from the chief priests and the Pharisees, *came there with lanterns
and torches and weapons.

## New International

are still in the world, and I am coming to you. Holy Father,
protect them by the power of your name—the name you gave
me—so that they may be one as we are one. 12While I was
with them, I protected them and kept them safe by that name
you gave me. None has been lost except the one doomed to
destruction so that Scripture would be fulfilled.
13"I am coming to you now, but I say these things while
I am still in the world, so that they may have the full measure
of my joy within them. 14I have given them your word and
the world has hated them, for they are not of the world any
more than I am of the world. 15My prayer is not that you take
them out of the world but that you protect them from the evil
one. 16They are not of the world, even as I am not of it.
17Sanctify[d] them by the truth; your word is truth. 18As you
sent me into the world, I have sent them into the world. 19For
them I sanctify myself, that they too may be truly sanctified.

*Jesus Prays for All Believers*

20"My prayer is not for them alone. I pray also for those
who will believe in me through their message, 21that all of
them may be one, Father, just as you are in me and I am in
you. May they also be in us so that the world may believe that
you have sent me. 22I have given them the glory that you gave
me, that they may be one as we are one: 23I in them and you
in me. May they be brought to complete unity to let the world
know that you sent me and have loved them even as you have
loved me.
24"Father, I want those you have given me to be with me
where I am, and to see my glory, the glory you have given me
because you loved me before the creation of the world.
25"Righteous Father, though the world does not know
you, I know you, and they know that you have sent me. 26I
have made you known to them, and will continue to make
you known in order that the love you have for me may be in
them and that I myself may be in them."

*Jesus Arrested*

**18** WHEN HE had finished praying, Jesus left with his disciples and crossed the Kidron Valley. On the other side
there was an olive grove, and he and his disciples went into it.
2Now Judas, who betrayed him, knew the place, because Jesus
had often met there with his disciples. 3So Judas came to the grove,
guiding a detachment of soldiers and some officials from the chief
priests and Pharisees. They were carrying torches, lanterns and
weapons.

NIV d 17 Greek *hagiazo (set apart for sacred use* or *make holy);* also in verse 19

## King James

4Jesus therefore, knowing all things that should come upon him, went forth, and said unto them, Whom seek ye?

5They answered him, Jesus of Nazareth. Jesus saith unto them, I am *he.* And Judas also, which betrayed him, stood with them.

6As soon then as he had said unto them, I am *he,* they went backward, and fell to the ground.

7Then asked he them again, Whom seek ye? And they said, Jesus of Nazareth.

8Jesus answered, I have told you that I am *he:* if therefore ye seek me, let these go their way:

9That the saying might be fulfilled, which he spake, Of them which thou gavest me have I lost none.

10Then Simon Peter having a sword drew it, and smote the high priest's servant, and cut off his right ear. The servant's name was Malchus.

11Then said Jesus unto Peter, Put up thy sword into the sheath: the cup which my Father hath given me, shall I not drink it?

12Then the band and the captain and officers of the Jews took Jesus, and bound him,

13And led him away to Annas first; for he was father-in-law to Caiaphas, which was the high priest that same year.

14Now Caiaphas was he, which gave counsel to the Jews, that it was expedient that one man should die for the people.

15¶ And Simon Peter followed Jesus, and *so did* another disciple: that disciple was known unto the high priest, and went in with Jesus into the palace of the high priest.

16But Peter stood at the door without. Then went out that other disciple, which was known unto the high priest, and spake unto her that kept the door, and brought in Peter.

17Then saith the damsel that kept the door unto Peter, Art not thou also *one* of this man's disciples? He saith, I am not.

18And the servants and officers stood there, who had made a fire of coals; for it was cold: and they warmed themselves: and Peter stood with them, and warmed himself.

19¶ The high priest then asked Jesus of his disciples, and of his doctrine.

20Jesus answered him, I spake openly to the world; I ever taught in the synagogue, and in the temple, whither the Jews always resort; and in secret have I said nothing.

21Why askest thou me? ask them which heard me, what I have said unto them: behold, they know what I said.

22And when he had thus spoken, one of the officers which stood by struck Jesus with the palm of his hand, saying, Answerest thou the high priest so?

23Jesus answered him, If I have spoken evil, bear witness of the evil: but if well, why smitest thou me?

24Now Annas had sent him bound unto Caiaphas the high priest.

25And Simon Peter stood and warmed himself. They said therefore unto him, Art not thou also *one* of his disciples? He denied *it,* and said, I am not.

26One of the servants of the high priest, being *his* kinsman whose ear Peter cut off, saith, Did not I see thee in the garden with him?

27Peter then denied again: and immediately the cock crew.

28¶ Then led they Jesus from Caiaphas unto the hall of judgment: and it was early; and they themselves went not into the judgment hall, lest they should be defiled; but that they might eat the passover.

## Amplified

4Then Jesus, knowing all that was about to befall Him, went out to them and said, Whom are you seeking—Whom do you want?

5They answered Him, Jesus the Nazarene. Jesus said to them, I am He. Judas, who was betraying Him, was also standing with them.

6When Jesus said to them, I am He, they went backwards—drew back, lurched backward—and fell to the ground.

7Then again He asked them, Whom are you seeking? And they said, Jesus the Nazarene.

8Jesus answered, I told you that I am He. So, if you want Me—if it is only I for Whom you are looking—let these men go their way.

9Thus what He had said was fulfilled *and* verified, Of those whom You have given Me, I have not lost even one. [John 17:12.]

10Then Simon Peter, who had a sword, drew it and struck the high priest's servant and cut off his right ear. The servant's name was Malchus.

11Therefore, Jesus said to Peter, Put the sword [back] into the sheath! The cup which My Father has given Me, shall I not drink it?

12So the troops and their captain and the guards (attendants) of the Jews seized Jesus and bound Him.

13And they brought Him first to Annas, for he was the father-in-law of Caiaphas, who was the high priest that year.

14It was Caiaphas who had counselled the Jews that it was expedient *and* for their welfare that one man should die for (instead of, in behalf of) the people.

15Now Simon Peter and another disciple followed Jesus. And that disciple was known to the high priest, so he entered along with Jesus into the court of the palace of the high priest.

16But Peter was standing outside at the door. So the other disciple, who was known to the high priest, went out and spoke to the maid who kept the door and brought Peter inside.

17Then the maid who was in charge at the door said to Peter, You are not also one of the disciples of this [a]Man, are you? He said, I am not!

18Now the servants and the guards (the attendants) had made a fire of coals, for it was cold, and they were standing and warming themselves. And Peter was with them, standing and warming himself.

19Then the high priest questioned Jesus about His disciples and about His teaching.

20Jesus answered him, I have spoken openly to the world; I have always taught in a synagogue and in the temple area, where the Jews habitually congregate (assemble), and I have spoken nothing secretly.

21Why do you ask Me? Ask those who have heard [Me] what I said to them. See! They know what I said.

22But when He said this, one of the attendants who stood by struck Jesus, saying, Is that how [b]You answer the high priest?

23Jesus replied, If I have said anything wrong—have spoken abusively, if there was evil in what I said—tell what was wrong with it. But if I spoke rightly *and* properly, why do you strike Me?

24Then Annas sent Him bound to Caiaphas the high priest.

25But Simon Peter [still] was standing and was warming himself. They said to him, You are not also one of His disciples, are you? He denied and said, I am not!

26One of the high priest's servants, a relative of the man whose ear Peter cut off, said, Did I not see you in the garden with Him?

27And again Peter denied it. And immediately a rooster crowed.

28Then they brought Jesus from Caiaphas into the praetorium (judgment hall, governor's palace). And it was early. They themselves did not enter the praetorium, that they might not be defiled (become ceremonially unclean), but might be fit to eat the Passover [supper].

**AMP** [a] Capitalized because of what He is, the spotless Son of God, not what the speaker may have thought He was. [b] Capitalized because of what He is, the spotless Son of God, not what the speaker may have thought He was.

## New American Standard

4 Jesus therefore, knowing all the things that were coming
upon Him, went forth, and *said to them, "Whom do you seek?"
5 They answered Him, "Jesus the Nazarene." He *said to them,
"I am *He*." And Judas also who was betraying Him, was standing
with them.
6 When therefore He said to them, "I am *He*," they drew back,
and fell to the ground.
7 Again therefore He asked them, "Whom do you seek?" And
they said, "Jesus the Nazarene."
8 Jesus answered, "I told you that I am *He*; if therefore you seek
Me, let these go their way,"
9 that the word might be fulfilled which He spoke, "Of those
whom Thou hast given Me I lost not one."
10 Simon Peter therefore having a sword, drew it, and struck the
high priest's slave, and cut off his right ear; and the slave's name
was Malchus.
11 Jesus therefore said to Peter, "Put the sword into the sheath;
the cup which the Father has given Me, shall I not drink it?"

*Jesus before the Priests*

12¶ So the *Roman* cohort and the commander, and the officers
of the Jews, arrested Jesus and bound Him,
13 and led Him to Annas first; for he was father-in-law of Caiaphas, who was high priest that year.
14 Now Caiaphas was the one who had advised the Jews that it
was expedient for one man to die on behalf of the people.
15¶ And Simon Peter was following Jesus, and *so was* another
disciple. Now that disciple was known to the high priest, and
entered with Jesus into the court of the high priest,
16 but Peter was standing at the door outside. So the other
disciple, who was known to the high priest, went out and spoke
to the doorkeeper, and brought in Peter.
17 The slave-girl therefore who kept the door *said to Peter,
"You are not also *one* of this man's disciples, are you?" He *said,
"I am not."
18 Now the slaves and the officers were standing *there*, having
made a charcoal fire, for it was cold and they were warming
themselves; and Peter also was with them, standing and warming
himself.
19¶ The high priest therefore questioned Jesus about His disciples, and about His teaching.
20 Jesus answered him, "I have spoken openly to the world; I
always taught in synagogues, and in the temple, where all the Jews
come together; and I spoke nothing in secret.
21 "Why do you question Me? Question those who have heard
what I spoke to them; behold, these know what I said."
22 And when He had said this, one of the officers standing by
gave Jesus a blow, saying, "Is that the way You answer the high
priest?"
23 Jesus answered him, "If I have spoken wrongly, bear witness
of the wrong; but if rightly, why do you strike Me?"
24 Annas therefore sent Him bound to Caiaphas the high priest.

*Peter's Denial of Jesus*

25¶ Now Simon Peter was standing and warming himself. They
said therefore to him, "You are not also *one* of His disciples, are
you?" He denied *it*, and said, "I am not."
26 One of the slaves of the high priest, being a relative of the one
whose ear Peter cut off, *said, "Did I not see you in the garden with
Him?"
27 Peter therefore denied *it* again; and immediately a cock
crowed.

*Jesus before Pilate*

28¶ They *led Jesus therefore from Caiaphas into the
[c]Praetorium, and it was early; and they themselves did not enter
into the Praetorium in order that they might not be defiled, but
might eat the Passover.

NAS [c] I.e., governor's official residence

## New International

4 Jesus, knowing all that was going to happen to him, went out
and asked them, "Who is it you want?"
5 "Jesus of Nazareth," they replied.
"I am he," Jesus said. (And Judas the traitor was standing there
with them.) 6 When Jesus said, "I am he," they drew back and fell
to the ground.
7 Again he asked them, "Who is it you want?"
And they said, "Jesus of Nazareth."
8 "I told you that I am he," Jesus answered. "If you are looking
for me, then let these men go." 9 This happened so that the words
he had spoken would be fulfilled: "I have not lost one of those you
gave me."[d]
10 Then Simon Peter, who had a sword, drew it and struck the
high priest's servant, cutting off his right ear. (The servant's name
was Malchus.)
11 Jesus commanded Peter, "Put your sword away! Shall I not
drink the cup the Father has given me?"

*Jesus Taken to Annas*

12 Then the detachment of soldiers with its commander and the
Jewish officials arrested Jesus. They bound him 13 and brought him
first to Annas, who was the father-in-law of Caiaphas, the high
priest that year. 14 Caiaphas was the one who had advised the Jews
that it would be good if one man died for the people.

*Peter's First Denial*

15 Simon Peter and another disciple were following Jesus. Because this disciple was known to the high priest, he went with
Jesus into the high priest's courtyard, 16 but Peter had to wait
outside at the door. The other disciple, who was known to the high
priest, came back, spoke to the girl on duty there and brought
Peter in.
17 "You are not one of his disciples, are you?" the girl at the door
asked Peter.
He replied, "I am not."
18 It was cold, and the servants and officials stood around a fire
they had made to keep warm. Peter also was standing with them,
warming himself.

*The High Priest Questions Jesus*

19 Meanwhile, the high priest questioned Jesus about his disciples and his teaching.
20 "I have spoken openly to the world," Jesus replied. "I always
taught in synagogues or at the temple, where all the Jews come
together. I said nothing in secret. 21 Why question me? Ask those
who heard me. Surely they know what I said."
22 When Jesus said this, one of the officials nearby struck him
in the face. "Is this the way you answer the high priest?" he
demanded.
23 "If I said something wrong," Jesus replied, "testify as to what
is wrong. But if I spoke the truth, why did you strike me?" 24 Then
Annas sent him, still bound, to Caiaphas the high priest.[e]

*Peter's Second and Third Denials*

25 As Simon Peter stood warming himself, he was asked, "You
are not one of his disciples, are you?"
He denied it, saying, "I am not."
26 One of the high priest's servants, a relative of the man whose
ear Peter had cut off, challenged him, "Didn't I see you with him
in the olive grove?" 27 Again Peter denied it, and at that moment
a rooster began to crow.

*Jesus Before Pilate*

28 Then the Jews led Jesus from Caiaphas to the palace of the
Roman governor. By now it was early morning, and to avoid
ceremonial uncleanness the Jews did not enter the palace; they
wanted to be able to eat the Passover. 29 So Pilate came out to them

NIV [d] 9 John 6:39 [e] 24 Or (*Now Annas had sent him, still bound, to Caiaphas the high priest.*)

## King James

29Pilate then went out unto them, and said, What accusation bring ye against this man?

30They answered and said unto him, If he were not a malefactor, we would not have delivered him up unto thee.

31Then said Pilate unto them, Take ye him, and judge him according to your law. The Jews therefore said unto him, It is not lawful for us to put any man to death:

32That the saying of Jesus might be fulfilled, which he spake, signifying what death he should die.

33Then Pilate entered into the judgment hall again, and called Jesus, and said unto him, Art thou the King of the Jews?

34Jesus answered him, Sayest thou this thing of thyself, or did others tell it thee of me?

35Pilate answered, Am I a Jew? Thine own nation and the chief priests have delivered thee unto me: what hast thou done?

36Jesus answered, My kingdom is not of this world: if my kingdom were of this world, then would my servants fight, that I should not be delivered to the Jews: but now is my kingdom not from hence.

37Pilate therefore said unto him, Art thou a king then? Jesus answered, Thou sayest that I am a king. To this end was I born, and for this cause came I into the world, that I should bear witness unto the truth. Every one that is of the truth heareth my voice.

38Pilate saith unto him, What is truth? And when he had said this, he went out again unto the Jews, and saith unto them, I find in him no fault *at all*.

39But ye have a custom, that I should release unto you one at the passover: will ye therefore that I release unto you the King of the Jews?

40Then cried they all again, saying, Not this man, but Barabbas. Now Barabbas was a robber.

**19** THEN PILATE therefore took Jesus, and scourged *him*.

2And the soldiers plaited a crown of thorns, and put *it* on his head, and they put on him a purple robe,

3And said, Hail, King of the Jews! and they smote him with their hands.

4Pilate therefore went forth again, and saith unto them, Behold, I bring him forth to you, that ye may know that I find no fault in him.

5Then came Jesus forth, wearing the crown of thorns, and the purple robe. And *Pilate* saith unto them, Behold the man!

6When the chief priests therefore and officers saw him, they cried out, saying, Crucify *him*, crucify *him*. Pilate saith unto them, Take ye him, and crucify *him*: for I find no fault in him.

7The Jews answered him, We have a law, and by our law he ought to die, because he made himself the Son of God.

8¶ When Pilate therefore heard that saying, he was the more afraid;

9And went again into the judgment hall, and saith unto Jesus, Whence art thou? But Jesus gave him no answer.

10Then saith Pilate unto him, Speakest thou not unto me? knowest thou not that I have power to crucify thee, and have power to release thee?

11Jesus answered, Thou couldest have no power *at all* against me, except it were given thee from above: therefore he that delivered me unto thee hath the greater sin.

## Amplified

29So Pilate went out to them and said, What accusation do you bring against this [a]Man?

30They retorted, If He were not an evildoer (criminal) we would not have handed Him over to you.

31Pilate said to them, Take Him yourselves and judge *and* sentence *and* punish Him according to your [own] law. The Jews answered, It is not lawful for us to put any one to death.

32This was to fulfill the word which Jesus had spoken to show (indicate, predict) by what manner of death He was to die.

33So Pilate went back again into the judgment hall and called Jesus and asked Him, Are You the King of the Jews?

34Jesus replied, Are you saying this of yourself—on your own initiative—or have others told it to you about Me?

35Pilate answered, Am I a Jew? Your [own] people *and* nation and their chief priests have delivered You to me. What have You done?

36Jesus answered, My kingdom (kingship, royal power) belongs not to this world. If My kingdom were of this world, My followers would have been fighting to keep Me from being handed over to the Jews. But as it is, My kingdom is not from [this world]—has no such origin *or* source.

37Pilate said to Him, Then You are a King? Jesus answered, You say it! (You speak correctly,) for I am a King.—Certainly I am a King! This is why I was born, and for this I have come into the world, to bear witness to the Truth. Everyone who is of the Truth (who is a friend of the Truth, who belongs to the Truth) hears *and* listens to My voice.

38Pilate said to Him, What is truth? On saying this he went out to the Jews again and told them, I find no fault in [b]Him.

39But it is your custom that I release one [prisoner] for you at the Passover. So shall I release for you the King of the Jews?

40Then they all shouted back again, Not Him—not this Man—but Barabbas! Now Barabbas was a robber.

**19** SO THEN Pilate took Jesus and scourged (flogged, whipped) Him.

2And the soldiers, having twisted a crown of thorns, put it on His head and threw a purple cloak around Him.

3And they kept coming to Him and saying, Hail, King of the Jews! (Good health to you! Peace to you! Long life to you, King of the Jews!) And they struck Him with the palms of their hands. [Isa. 53:3, 5, 7.]

4Then Pilate went out again and said to them, See, I bring Him out to you so that you may know I find no fault (crime, cause for accusation) in Him.

5So Jesus came out, wearing the thorny crown and purple cloak, and Pilate said to them, See, [here is] the [c]Man!

6When the chief priests and attendants (guards) saw Him, they cried out, Crucify Him! Crucify Him! Pilate said to them, Take Him yourselves and crucify Him, for I find no fault (crime) in Him.

7The Jews answered him, We have a Law, and according to that Law He should die, because He has claimed *and* made Himself out to be the Son of God.

8So, when Pilate heard this said, he was more alarmed *and* awe-stricken *and* afraid than before.

9He went into the judgment hall again and said to Jesus, Where are You from?—To what world do You belong? But Jesus did not answer him.

10So Pilate said to Him, Will You not speak [even] to me? Do You not know that I have power (authority) to release You and I have power to crucify You?

11Jesus answered, You would not have any power *or* authority whatever against (over) Me, if it were not given you from above. For this reason the sin *and* guilt of the one who delivered Me over to you is greater.

**AMP** [a] Capitalized because of what He is, the spotless Son of God, not what the speaker may have thought He was. [b] Capitalized because of what He is, the spotless Son of God, not what the speaker may have thought He was. [c] Capitalized because of what He is, the spotless Son of God, not what the speaker may have thought He was.

## New American Standard

29Pilate therefore went out to them, and *said, "What accusation do you bring against this Man?"
30They answered and said to him, "If this Man were not an
evildoer, we would not have delivered Him up to you."
31Pilate therefore said to them, "Take Him yourselves, and
judge Him according to your law." The Jews said to him, "We are
not permitted to put anyone to death,"
32that the word of Jesus might be fulfilled, which He spoke,
signifying by what kind of death He was about to die.
33¶ Pilate therefore entered again into the [d]Praetorium, and
summoned Jesus, and said to Him, "Are You the King of the
Jews?"
34Jesus answered, "Are you saying this on your own initiative,
or did others tell you about Me?"
35Pilate answered, "I am not a Jew, am I? Your own nation and
the chief priests delivered You up to me; what have You done?"
36Jesus answered, "My kingdom is not of this world. If My
kingdom were of this world, then My servants would be fighting,
that I might not be delivered up to the Jews; but as it is, My
kingdom is not [e]of this realm."
37Pilate therefore said to Him, "So You are a king?" Jesus answered, "You say *correctly* that I am a king. For this I have been
born, and for this I have come into the world, to bear witness to
the truth. Everyone who is of the truth hears My voice."
38Pilate *said to Him, "What is truth?"
¶ And when he had said this, he went out again to the Jews,
and said to them, "I find no guilt in Him.
39"But you have a custom, that I should release someone for
you at the Passover; do you wish then that I release for you the
King of the Jews?"
40Therefore they cried out again, saying, "Not this Man, but
Barabbas." Now Barabbas was a robber.

*The Crown of Thorns*

**19** THEN PILATE therefore took Jesus, and scourged Him.
2And the soldiers wove a crown of thorns and put it on
His head, and arrayed Him in a purple robe;
3and they *began* to come up to Him, and say, "Hail, King of the
Jews!" and to give Him blows *in the face*.
4And Pilate came out again, and *said to them, "Behold, I am
bringing Him out to you, that you may know that I find no guilt
in Him."
5Jesus therefore came out, wearing the crown of thorns and the
purple robe. And *Pilate* *said to them, "Behold, the Man!"
6When therefore the chief priests and the officers saw Him,
they cried out, saying, "Crucify, crucify!" Pilate *said to them,
"Take Him yourselves, and crucify Him, for I find no guilt in
Him."
7The Jews answered him, "We have a law, and by that law He
ought to die because He made Himself out *to be* the Son of God."
8When Pilate therefore heard this statement, he was the more
afraid;
9and he entered into the [f]Praetorium again, and *said to Jesus,
"Where are You from?" But Jesus gave him no answer.
10Pilate therefore *said to Him, "You do not speak to me? Do
You not know that I have authority to release You, and I have
authority to crucify You?"
11Jesus answered, "You would have no authority over Me,
unless it had been given you from above; for this reason he who
delivered Me up to you has *the* greater sin."

**NAS** [d] I.e., governor's official residence [e] Lit., *from here* [f] I.e., governor's official residence

## New International

and asked, "What charges are you bringing against this man?"
30"If he were not a criminal," they replied, "we would not have
handed him over to you."
31Pilate said, "Take him yourselves and judge him by your own
law."
"But we have no right to execute anyone," the Jews objected.
32This happened so that the words Jesus had spoken indicating the
kind of death he was going to die would be fulfilled.
33Pilate then went back inside the palace, summoned Jesus and
asked him, "Are you the king of the Jews?"
34"Is that your own idea," Jesus asked, "or did others talk to
you about me?"
35"Am I a Jew?" Pilate replied. "It was your people and your
chief priests who handed you over to me. What is it you have
done?"
36Jesus said, "My kingdom is not of this world. If it were, my
servants would fight to prevent my arrest by the Jews. But now my
kingdom is from another place."
37"You are a king, then!" said Pilate.
Jesus answered, "You are right in saying I am a king. In fact,
for this reason I was born, and for this I came into the world, to
testify to the truth. Everyone on the side of truth listens to me."
38"What is truth?" Pilate asked. With this he went out again to
the Jews and said, "I find no basis for a charge against him. 39But
it is your custom for me to release to you one prisoner at the time
of the Passover. Do you want me to release 'the king of the Jews'?"
40They shouted back, "No, not him! Give us Barabbas!" Now
Barabbas had taken part in a rebellion.

*Jesus Sentenced to be Crucified*

**19** THEN PILATE took Jesus and had him flogged. 2The
soldiers twisted together a crown of thorns and put it on
his head. They clothed him in a purple robe 3and went up to him
again and again, saying, "Hail, king of the Jews!" And they struck
him in the face.
4Once more Pilate came out and said to the Jews, "Look, I am
bringing him out to you to let you know that I find no basis for a
charge against him." 5When Jesus came out wearing the crown of
thorns and the purple robe, Pilate said to them, "Here is the man!"
6As soon as the chief priests and their officials saw him, they
shouted, "Crucify! Crucify!"
But Pilate answered, "You take him and crucify him. As for me,
I find no basis for a charge against him."
7The Jews insisted, "We have a law, and according to that law
he must die, because he claimed to be the Son of God."
8When Pilate heard this, he was even more afraid, 9and he went
back inside the palace. "Where do you come from?" he asked
Jesus, but Jesus gave him no answer. 10"Do you refuse to speak
to me?" Pilate said. "Don't you realize I have power either to free
you or to crucify you?"
11Jesus answered, "You would have no power over me if it were
not given to you from above. Therefore the one who handed me
over to you is guilty of a greater sin."

## King James

12And from thenceforth Pilate sought to release him: but the Jews cried out, saying, If thou let this man go, thou art not Caesar's friend: whosoever maketh himself a king speaketh against Caesar.

13¶ When Pilate therefore heard that saying, he brought Jesus forth, and sat down in the judgment seat in a place that is called the Pavement, but in the Hebrew, Gabbatha.

14And it was the preparation of the passover, and about the sixth hour: and he saith unto the Jews, Behold your King!

15But they cried out, Away with *him*, away with *him*, crucify him. Pilate saith unto them, Shall I crucify your King? The chief priests answered, We have no king but Caesar.

16Then delivered he him therefore unto them to be crucified. And they took Jesus, and led *him* away.

17And he bearing his cross went forth into a place called *the place* of a skull, which is called in the Hebrew Golgotha:

18Where they crucified him, and two other with him, on either side one, and Jesus in the midst.

19¶ And Pilate wrote a title, and put *it* on the cross. And the writing was, JESUS OF NAZARETH THE KING OF THE JEWS.

20This title then read many of the Jews: for the place where Jesus was crucified was nigh to the city: and it was written in Hebrew, *and* Greek, *and* Latin.

21Then said the chief priests of the Jews to Pilate, Write not, The King of the Jews; but that he said, I am King of the Jews.

22Pilate answered, What I have written I have written.

23¶ Then the soldiers, when they had crucified Jesus, took his garments, and made four parts, to every soldier a part; and also *his* coat: now the coat was without seam, woven from the top throughout.

24They said therefore among themselves, Let us not rend it, but cast lots for it, whose it shall be: that the scripture might be fulfilled, which saith, They parted my raiment among them, and for my vesture they did cast lots. These things therefore the soldiers did.

25¶ Now there stood by the cross of Jesus his mother, and his mother's sister, Mary the *wife* of Cleophas, and Mary Magdalene.

26When Jesus therefore saw his mother, and the disciple standing by, whom he loved, he saith unto his mother, Woman, behold thy son!

27Then saith he to the disciple, Behold thy mother! And from that hour that disciple took her unto his own *home*.

28¶ After this, Jesus knowing that all things were now accomplished, that the scripture might be fulfilled, saith, I thirst.

29Now there was set a vessel full of vinegar: and they filled a sponge with vinegar, and put *it* upon hyssop, and put *it* to his mouth.

30When Jesus therefore had received the vinegar, he said, It is finished: and he bowed his head, and gave up the ghost.

31The Jews therefore, because it was the preparation, that the bodies should not remain upon the cross on the sabbath day, (for that sabbath day was an high day,) besought Pilate that their legs might be broken, and *that* they might be taken away.

32Then came the soldiers, and brake the legs of the first, and of the other which was crucified with him.

33But when they came to Jesus, and saw that he was dead already, they brake not his legs:

34But one of the soldiers with a spear pierced his side, and forthwith came there out blood and water.

## Amplified

12Upon this Pilate wanted (sought, was anxious) to release Him, but the Jews kept shrieking, If you release this Man, you are no friend of Caesar's! Anybody who makes himself a king sets himself up against Caesar—is a rebel against the emperor!

13Hearing this, Pilate brought Jesus out and sat down on the judgment seat at a place called the Pavement—the Mosaic Pavement, the Stone Platform; but in Hebrew, Gabbatha.

14Now it was the day of Preparation for the Passover, and it was about the sixth hour—about twelve o'clock noon. He said to the Jews, See, [here is] your King!

15But they shouted, Away with Him! Away with Him! Crucify Him! Pilate said to them, Crucify your King? The chief priests answered, We have no king but Caesar!

16Then he delivered Him over to them to be crucified.

17And they took Jesus *and* led [Him] away; so He went out, bearing His own cross, to the spot called [Place of a] Skull; in Hebrew it is called Golgotha.

18There they crucified Him, and with Him two others, one on either side and Jesus between them. [Isa. 53:12.]

19And Pilate also wrote a title [an inscription on a placard] and put it on the cross. And the writing was, Jesus the Nazarene, the King of the Jews.

20So many of the Jews read this title, for the place where Jesus was crucified was near the city, and it was written in Hebrew, in Latin [and] in Greek.

21Then the chief priests of the Jews said to Pilate, Do not write, The King of the Jews, but, He said, I am King of the Jews.

22Pilate replied, What I have written, I have written.

23Then the soldiers when they had crucified Jesus took His garments and made four parts, one share for each soldier, and also the tunic [the long shirt-like undergarment]. But the tunic was seamless, woven from the top throughout.

24So they said to one another, Let us not tear it, but let us cast lots to decide whose it shall be. This was to fulfill the Scripture, They parted My garments among them, and for My clothing they cast lots. So the soldiers did these things. [Ps. 22:18.]

25But by the cross of Jesus stood His mother, and His mother's sister, Mary the [wife] of Clopas, and Mary Magdalene.

26So Jesus, seeing His mother, and the disciple whom He loved standing near, said to His mother, [ [a]Dear] lady, behold (see) your son!

27Then He said to the disciple, Behold your mother! And from that hour the disciple took her to his own [keeping, own home].

28After this, Jesus, knowing that all was now finished (ended), said in fulfillment of the Scripture, I thirst. [Ps. 69:21.]

29A vessel (bowl) full of vinegar (a sour wine) was placed there. So they put a sponge soaked in the vinegar on [a stalk, reed of] hyssop and held it to [His] mouth.

30When Jesus had received the vinegar, He said, It is finished! and He bowed His head and gave up His spirit.

31Since it was the day of Preparation, in order to prevent the bodies from hanging on the cross on the Sabbath, for that Sabbath was a very solemn *and* important one, the Jews requested Pilate to have the legs broken and the bodies taken away.

32So the soldiers came and broke the legs of the first one and of the other who had been crucified with Him.

33But when they came to Jesus, and they saw that He was already dead, they did not break His legs.

34But one of the soldiers pierced His side with a spear, and immediately blood and water came (flowed) out.

**AMP** [a] Abbott-Smith: "A term of respect and endearment."

## New American Standard

12 As a result of this Pilate made efforts to release Him, but the
Jews cried out, saying, "If you release this Man, you are no friend
of Caesar; everyone who makes himself out *to be* a king opposes
Caesar."

13 When Pilate therefore heard these words, he brought Jesus
out, and sat down on the judgment seat at a place called The
Pavement, but in Hebrew, Gabbatha.

14 Now it was the day of preparation for the Passover; it was
about the [b]sixth hour. And he *said to the Jews, "Behold, your
King!"

15 They therefore cried out, "Away with *Him,* away with *Him,*
crucify Him!" Pilate *said to them, "Shall I crucify your King?" The
chief priests answered, "We have no king but Caesar."

*The Crucifixion*

16 So he then delivered Him to them to be crucified.

**17**¶ They took Jesus therefore, and He went out, bearing His
own cross, to the place called the Place of a Skull, which is called
in Hebrew, Golgotha.

18 There they crucified Him, and with Him two other men, one
on either side, and Jesus in between.

19 And Pilate wrote an inscription also, and put it on the cross.
And it was written, "JESUS THE NAZARENE, THE KING OF THE
JEWS."

20 Therefore this inscription many of the Jews read, for the place
where Jesus was crucified was near the city; and it was written in
Hebrew, Latin, *and* in Greek.

21 And so the chief priests of the Jews were saying to Pilate, "Do
not write, 'The King of the Jews'; but that He said, 'I am King of
the Jews.' "

22 Pilate answered, "What I have written I have written."

**23**¶ The soldiers therefore, when they had crucified Jesus, took
His outer garments and made four parts, a part to every soldier
and *also* the [c]tunic; now the tunic was seamless, woven in one
piece.

24 They said therefore to one another, "Let us not tear it, but cast
lots for it, *to decide* whose it shall be"; that the Scripture might be
fulfilled, "THEY DIVIDED MY OUTER GARMENTS AMONG THEM, AND
FOR MY CLOTHING THEY CAST LOTS."

25 Therefore the soldiers did these things. But there were standing by the cross of Jesus His mother, and His mother's sister, Mary
the *wife* of Clopas, and Mary Magdalene.

26 When Jesus therefore saw His mother, and the disciple whom
He loved standing nearby, He *said to His mother, "Woman,
behold, your son!"

27 Then He *said to the disciple, "Behold, your mother!" And
from that hour the disciple took her into his own *household.*

**28**¶ After this, Jesus, knowing that all things had already been
accomplished, in order that the Scripture might be fulfilled, *said,
"I am thirsty."

29 A jar full of sour wine was standing there; so they put a
sponge full of the sour wine upon *a branch of* hyssop, and brought
it up to His mouth.

30 When Jesus therefore had received the sour wine, He said, "It
is finished!" And He bowed His head, and gave up His spirit.

*Care of the Body of Jesus*

**31**¶ The Jews therefore, because it was the day of preparation,
so that the bodies should not remain on the cross on the Sabbath
(for that Sabbath was a high *day*), asked Pilate that their legs might
be broken, and *that* they might be taken away.

32 The soldiers therefore came, and broke the legs of the first
man, and of the other man who was crucified with Him;

33 but coming to Jesus, when they saw that He was already
dead, they did not break His legs;

34 but one of the soldiers pierced His side with a spear, and
immediately there came out blood and water.

NAS [b] Perhaps 6 a.m. (Roman time) [c] Gr., *khiton,* the garment worn next to the skin

## New International

12 From then on, Pilate tried to set Jesus free, but the Jews kept
shouting, "If you let this man go, you are no friend of Caesar.
Anyone who claims to be a king opposes Caesar."

13 When Pilate heard this, he brought Jesus out and sat down
on the judge's seat at a place known as the Stone Pavement (which
in Aramaic is Gabbatha). 14 It was the day of Preparation of Passover Week, about the sixth hour.

"Here is your king," Pilate said to the Jews.

15 But they shouted, "Take him away! Take him away! Crucify
him!"

"Shall I crucify your king?" Pilate asked.

"We have no king but Caesar," the chief priests answered.

16 Finally Pilate handed him over to them to be crucified.

*The Crucifixion*

So the soldiers took charge of Jesus. 17 Carrying his own cross,
he went out to the place of the Skull (which in Aramaic is called
Golgotha). 18 Here they crucified him, and with him two others—
one on each side and Jesus in the middle.

19 Pilate had a notice prepared and fastened to the cross. It read:
JESUS OF NAZARETH, THE KING OF THE JEWS. 20 Many of the Jews read
this sign, for the place where Jesus was crucified was near the city,
and the sign was written in Aramaic, Latin and Greek. 21 The chief
priests of the Jews protested to Pilate, "Do not write 'The King of
the Jews,' but that this man claimed to be king of the Jews."

22 Pilate answered, "What I have written, I have written."

23 When the soldiers crucified Jesus, they took his clothes, dividing them into four shares, one for each of them, with the undergarment remaining. This garment was seamless, woven in one piece
from top to bottom.

24 "Let's not tear it," they said to one another. "Let's decide by
lot who will get it."

This happened that the scripture might be fulfilled which said,

> "They divided my garments among them
> and cast lots for my clothing."[d]

So this is what the soldiers did.

25 Near the cross of Jesus stood his mother, his mother's sister,
Mary the wife of Clopas, and Mary Magdalene. 26 When Jesus saw
his mother there, and the disciple whom he loved standing nearby, he said to his mother, "Dear woman, here is your son," 27 and
to the disciple, "Here is your mother." From that time on, this
disciple took her into his home.

*The Death of Jesus*

28 Later, knowing that all was now completed, and so that the
Scripture would be fulfilled, Jesus said, "I am thirsty." 29 A jar of
wine vinegar was there, so they soaked a sponge in it, put the
sponge on a stalk of the hyssop plant, and lifted it to Jesus' lips.
30 When he had received the drink, Jesus said, "It is finished."
With that, he bowed his head and gave up his spirit.

31 Now it was the day of Preparation, and the next day was to
be a special Sabbath. Because the Jews did not want the bodies left
on the crosses during the Sabbath, they asked Pilate to have the
legs broken and the bodies taken down. 32 The soldiers therefore
came and broke the legs of the first man who had been crucified
with Jesus, and then those of the other. 33 But when they came to
Jesus and found that he was already dead, they did not break his
legs. 34 Instead, one of the soldiers pierced Jesus' side with a spear,
bringing a sudden flow of blood and water. 35 The man who saw

NIV [d] *24* Psalm 22:18

## King James

35And he that saw *it* bare record, and his record is true: and he
knoweth that he saith true, that ye might believe.
36For these things were done, that the scripture should be fulfilled, A bone of him shall not be broken.
37And again another scripture saith, They shall look on him
whom they pierced.
38¶ And after this Joseph of Arimathaea, being a disciple of
Jesus, but secretly for fear of the Jews, besought Pilate that he
might take away the body of Jesus: and Pilate gave *him* leave. He
came therefore, and took the body of Jesus.
39And there came also Nicodemus, which at the first came to
Jesus by night, and brought a mixture of myrrh and aloes, about
an hundred pound *weight*.
40Then took they the body of Jesus, and wound it in linen
clothes with the spices, as the manner of the Jews is to bury.
41Now in the place where he was crucified there was a garden;
and in the garden a new sepulchre, wherein was never man yet
laid.
42There laid they Jesus therefore because of the Jews' preparation *day*; for the sepulchre was nigh at hand.

**20** THE FIRST *day* of the week cometh Mary Magdalene early, when it was yet dark, unto the sepulchre, and seeth the
stone taken away from the sepulchre.
2Then she runneth, and cometh to Simon Peter, and to the
other disciple, whom Jesus loved, and saith unto them, They have
taken away the Lord out of the sepulchre, and we know not where
they have laid him.
3Peter therefore went forth, and that other disciple, and came
to the sepulchre.
4So they ran both together: and the other disciple did outrun
Peter, and came first to the sepulchre.
5And he stooping down, *and looking in*, saw the linen clothes
lying; yet went he not in.
6Then cometh Simon Peter following him, and went into the
sepulchre, and seeth the linen clothes lie,
7And the napkin, that was about his head, not lying with the
linen clothes, but wrapped together in a place by itself.
8Then went in also that other disciple, which came first to the
sepulchre, and he saw, and believed.
9For as yet they knew not the scripture, that he must rise again
from the dead.
10Then the disciples went away again unto their own home.
11¶ But Mary stood without at the sepulchre weeping: and as
she wept, she stooped down, *and looked* into the sepulchre,
12And seeth two angels in white sitting, the one at the head,
and the other at the feet, where the body of Jesus had lain.
13And they say unto her, Woman, why weepest thou? She saith
unto them, Because they have taken away my Lord, and I know
not where they have laid him.
14And when she had thus said, she turned herself back, and
saw Jesus standing, and knew not that it was Jesus.
15Jesus saith unto her, Woman, why weepest thou? whom
seekest thou? She, supposing him to be the gardener, saith unto
him, Sir, if thou have borne him hence, tell me where thou hast
laid him, and I will take him away.
16Jesus saith unto her, Mary. She turned herself, and saith unto
him, Rabboni; which is to say, Master.
17Jesus saith unto her, Touch me not; for I am not yet ascended
to my Father: but go to my brethren, and say unto them, I ascend
unto my Father, and your Father; and *to* my God, and your God.

## Amplified

35And he who saw it—the eyewitness—gives this evidence and
his testimony is true, and he knows that he tells the truth, that you
may believe also.
36For these things took place that the Scripture might be fulfilled
(verified, carried out), Not one of His bones shall be broken. [Exod.
12:46; Num. 9:12; Ps. 34:20.]
37And again another Scripture says, They shall look on Him
Whom they have pierced. [Zech. 12:10.]
38And after this Joseph of Arimathea, a disciple of Jesus, but
secretly for fear of the Jews, asked Pilate to let him take away the
body of Jesus. And Pilate granted him permission. So he came and
took away His body.
39And Nicodemus also, who at first had come to Jesus by night,
came bringing a mixture of myrrh and aloes, [weighing] about a
hundred pounds.
40So they took Jesus' body, and bound it in linen cloths with the
spices (aromatics), as is the Jews' customary way to prepare for
burial.
41Now there was a garden in the place where He was crucified
and in the garden a new tomb, in which no one had ever [yet] been
laid.
42So there, because of the Jewish day of Preparation [and] as the
tomb was near by, they laid Jesus.

**20** NOW ON the first day of the week Mary Magdalene came
to the tomb early, while it was still dark, and saw the stone
had been removed from—lifted out of [the groove across the entrance of]—the tomb.
2So she ran and went to Simon Peter and the other disciple
whom Jesus tenderly loved, and said to them, They have taken
away the Lord out of the tomb, and we do not know where they
have laid Him!
3Upon this Peter and the other disciple came out and they went
toward the tomb.
4And they came running together, but the other disciple outran
Peter and arrived at the tomb first.
5And stooping down he saw the linen cloths lying there, but he
did not enter.
6Then Simon Peter came up, following him, and went into the
tomb, and saw the linen cloths lying there.
7But the burial napkin (or kerchief) which had been around
Jesus' head, was not lying with the other linen cloths, but was
[still] [a]rolled up—wrapped round and round—in a place by itself.
8Then the other disciple, who reached the tomb first, went in
too, and he saw and was convinced *and* believed.
9For as yet they did not know (understand) the statement of
Scripture that He must rise again from the dead. [Ps. 16:10.]
10Then the disciples went back again to their [lodging places].
11But Mary remained standing outside the tomb sobbing. As
she wept, she stooped down [and looked] into the tomb.
12And she saw two angels in white sitting there, one at the head
and one at the feet, where the body of Jesus had lain.
13And they said to her, Woman, why are you sobbing? She told
them, Because they have taken away my Lord and I do not know
where they have laid Him.
14On saying this, she turned around and saw Jesus standing
[there], but she did not know (recognize) that it was Jesus.
15Jesus said to her, Woman, why are you crying [so]? For whom
are you looking? Supposing that it was the gardener, she replied,
Sir, if you carried Him from here, tell me where you put Him and
I will take Him away.
16Jesus said to her, Mary! Turning around she said to Him in
Hebrew, Rabboni! which means Teacher *or* Master.
17Jesus said to her, Do not cling to Me [do not hold Me] for I
have not yet ascended to the Father. But go to My brethren and
tell them, I am ascending to My Father and your Father, and to My
God and your God.

**AMP** [a] ASV, Vincent, Thayer, etc.

## New American Standard

35And he who has seen has borne witness, and his witness is
true; and he knows that he is telling the truth, so that you also may
believe.
36For these things came to pass, that the Scripture might be
fulfilled, "NOT A BONE OF HIM SHALL BE BROKEN."
37And again another Scripture says, "THEY SHALL LOOK ON HIM
WHOM THEY PIERCED."
38¶ And after these things Joseph of Arimathea, being a disciple
of Jesus, but a secret *one*, for fear of the Jews, asked Pilate that he
might take away the body of Jesus; and Pilate granted permission.
He came therefore, and took away His body.
39And Nicodemus came also, who had first come to Him by
night; bringing a mixture of myrrh and aloes, about a hundred
pounds *weight*.
40And so they took the body of Jesus, and bound it in linen
wrappings with the spices, as is the burial custom of the Jews.
41Now in the place where He was crucified there was a garden;
and in the garden a new tomb, in which no one had yet been laid.
42Therefore on account of the Jewish day of preparation, because the tomb was nearby, they laid Jesus there.

*The Empty Tomb*

**20** NOW ON the first *day* of the week Mary Magdalene *came
early to the tomb, while it *was still dark, and *saw the
stone *already* taken away from the tomb.
2And so she *ran and *came to Simon Peter, and to the other
disciple whom Jesus loved, and *said to them, "They have taken
away the Lord out of the tomb, and we do not know where they
have laid Him."
3Peter therefore went forth, and the other disciple, and they
were going to the tomb.
4And the two were running together; and the other disciple ran
ahead faster than Peter, and came to the tomb first;
5and stooping and looking in, he *saw the linen wrappings
lying *there;* but he did not go in.
6Simon Peter therefore also *came, following him, and entered
the tomb; and he *beheld the linen wrappings lying *there,*
7and the face-cloth, which had been on His head, not lying
with the linen wrappings, but rolled up in a place by itself.
8So the other disciple who had first come to the tomb entered
then also, and he saw and believed.
9For as yet they did not understand the Scripture, that He must
rise again from the dead.
10So the disciples went away again to their own homes.
11¶ But Mary was standing outside the tomb weeping; and so,
as she wept, she stooped and looked into the tomb;
12and she *beheld two angels in white sitting, one at the head,
and one at the feet, where the body of Jesus had been lying.
13And they *said to her, "Woman, why are you weeping?" She
*said to them, "Because they have taken away my Lord, and I do
not know where they have laid Him."
14When she had said this, she turned around, and *beheld Jesus
standing *there,* and did not know that it was Jesus.
15Jesus *said to her, "Woman, why are you weeping? Whom are
you seeking?" Supposing Him to be the gardener, she *said to
Him, "Sir, if you have carried Him away, tell me where you have
laid Him, and I will take Him away."
16Jesus *said to her, "Mary!" She *turned and *said to Him in
Hebrew, "Rabboni!" (which means, Teacher).
17Jesus *said to her, "Stop clinging to Me, for I have not yet
ascended to the Father; but go to My brethren, and say to them,
'I ascend to My Father and your Father, and My God and your
God.' "

## New International

it has given testimony, and his testimony is true. He knows that
he tells the truth, and he testifies so that you also may believe.
36These things happened so that the scripture would be fulfilled:
"Not one of his bones will be broken,"[b] 37and, as another scripture
says, "They will look on the one they have pierced."[c]

*The Burial of Jesus*

38Later, Joseph of Arimathea asked Pilate for the body of Jesus.
Now Joseph was a disciple of Jesus, but secretly because he feared
the Jews. With Pilate's permission, he came and took the body
away. 39He was accompanied by Nicodemus, the man who earlier
had visited Jesus at night. Nicodemus brought a mixture of myrrh
and aloes, about seventy-five pounds.[d] 40Taking Jesus' body, the
two of them wrapped it, with the spices, in strips of linen. This was
in accordance with Jewish burial customs. 41At the place where
Jesus was crucified, there was a garden, and in the garden a new
tomb, in which no one had ever been laid. 42Because it was the
Jewish day of Preparation and since the tomb was nearby, they laid
Jesus there.

*The Empty Tomb*

**20** EARLY ON the first day of the week, while it was still
dark, Mary Magdalene went to the tomb and saw that the
stone had been removed from the entrance. 2So she came running
to Simon Peter and the other disciple, the one Jesus loved, and
said, "They have taken the Lord out of the tomb, and we don't
know where they have put him!"
3So Peter and the other disciple started for the tomb. 4Both were
running, but the other disciple outran Peter and reached the tomb
first. 5He bent over and looked in at the strips of linen lying there
but did not go in. 6Then Simon Peter, who was behind him,
arrived and went into the tomb. He saw the strips of linen lying
there, 7as well as the burial cloth that had been around Jesus' head.
The cloth was folded up by itself, separate from the linen. 8Finally
the other disciple, who had reached the tomb first, also went
inside. He saw and believed. 9(They still did not understand from
Scripture that Jesus had to rise from the dead.)

*Jesus Appears to Mary Magdalene*

10Then the disciples went back to their homes, 11but Mary stood
outside the tomb crying. As she wept, she bent over to look into
the tomb 12and saw two angels in white, seated where Jesus' body
had been, one at the head and the other at the foot.
13They asked her, "Woman, why are you crying?"
"They have taken my Lord away," she said, "and I don't know
where they have put him." 14At this, she turned around and saw
Jesus standing there, but she did not realize that it was Jesus.
15"Woman," he said, "why are you crying? Who is it you are
looking for?"
Thinking he was the gardener, she said, "Sir, if you have carried him away, tell me where you have put him, and I will get
him."
16Jesus said to her, "Mary."
She turned toward him and cried out in Aramaic, "Rabboni!"
(which means Teacher).
17Jesus said, "Do not hold on to me, for I have not yet returned
to the Father. Go instead to my brothers and tell them, 'I am
returning to my Father and your Father, to my God and your
God.' "

**NIV** [b] 36 Exodus 12:46; Num. 9:12; Psalm 34:20 [c] 37 Zech. 12:10
[d] 39 Greek *a hundred litrai* (about 34 kilograms)

## King James

18Mary Magdalene came and told the disciples that she had seen the Lord, and *that* he had spoken these things unto her.

19¶ Then the same day at evening, being the first *day* of the week, when the doors were shut where the disciples were assembled for fear of the Jews, came Jesus and stood in the midst, and saith unto them, Peace *be* unto you.

20And when he had so said, he showed unto them *his* hands and his side. Then were the disciples glad, when they saw the Lord.

21Then said Jesus to them again, Peace *be* unto you: as *my* Father hath sent me, even so send I you.

22And when he had said this, he breathed on *them*, and saith unto them, Receive ye the Holy Ghost:

23Whosesoever sins ye remit, they are remitted unto them; *and* whosesoever *sins* ye retain, they are retained.

24¶ But Thomas, one of the twelve, called Didymus, was not with them when Jesus came.

25The other disciples therefore said unto him, We have seen the Lord. But he said unto them, Except I shall see in his hands the print of the nails, and put my finger into the print of the nails, and thrust my hand into his side, I will not believe.

26¶ And after eight days again his disciples were within, and Thomas with them: *then* came Jesus, the doors being shut, and stood in the midst, and said, Peace *be* unto you.

27Then saith he to Thomas, Reach hither thy finger, and behold my hands; and reach hither thy hand, and thrust *it* into my side: and be not faithless, but believing.

28And Thomas answered and said unto him, My Lord and my God.

29Jesus saith unto him, Thomas, because thou hast seen me, thou hast believed: blessed *are* they that have not seen, and *yet* have believed.

30¶ And many other signs truly did Jesus in the presence of his disciples, which are not written in this book:

31But these are written, that ye might believe that Jesus is the Christ, the Son of God; and that believing ye might have life through his name.

**21** AFTER THESE things Jesus showed himself again to the disciples at the sea of Tiberias; and on this wise showed he *himself*.

2There were together Simon Peter, and Thomas called Didymus, and Nathanael of Cana in Galilee, and the *sons* of Zebedee, and two other of his disciples.

3Simon Peter saith unto them, I go a-fishing. They say unto him, We also go with thee. They went forth, and entered into a ship immediately; and that night they caught nothing.

4But when the morning was now come, Jesus stood on the shore: but the disciples knew not that it was Jesus.

5Then Jesus saith unto them, Children, have ye any meat? They answered him, No.

6And he said unto them, Cast the net on the right side of the ship, and ye shall find. They cast therefore, and now they were not able to draw it for the multitude of fishes.

7Therefore that disciple whom Jesus loved saith unto Peter, It is the Lord. Now when Simon Peter heard that it was the Lord, he girt *his* fisher's coat *unto him*, (for he was naked,) and did cast himself into the sea.

## Amplified

18Away came Mary Magdalene, bringing the disciples news (word) that she had seen the Lord and that He had said these things to her.

19Then that same first day of the week, when it was evening, though the disciples were behind closed doors for fear of the Jews, Jesus came and stood among them, and said, Peace to You!

20So saying, He showed them His hands and His side. And when the disciples saw the Lord they were filled with joy (delight, exultation, ecstasy, rapture).

21Then Jesus said to them again, Peace to you! [Just] as the Father has sent Me forth, so I am sending you.

22And having said this, He breathed on [them] and said to them, Receive (admit) the Holy Spirit!

23[Now, having received the Holy Spirit, and being [a]led and directed by Him] if you forgive the sins of any one they are forgiven; if you retain the sins of any one, they are retained.

24But Thomas, one of the twelve, called the Twin, was not with them when Jesus came.

25So the other disciples kept telling him, We have seen the Lord. But he said to them, Unless I see in His hands the mark made by the nails, and put my finger into the nail prints, and put my hand into His side, I will never believe [it].

26Eight days later His disciples were again in the house, and Thomas was with them. Jesus came, though they were behind closed doors, and stood among them and said, Peace to you!

27Then He said to Thomas, Reach out your finger here and see My hands; and put out your hand and place [it] in My side. Do not be faithless *and* incredulous, but [stop your unbelief and] believe!

28Thomas answered Him, My Lord and my God!

29Jesus said to him, Because you have seen Me, *Thomas,* do you now believe (trust, have faith)? Blessed *and* happy *and* [b]to be envied are those who have never seen Me, and yet have believed *and* adhered to *and* trusted in *and* relied on Me.

30There are also many other signs *and* miracles, which Jesus performed in the presence of the disciples, which are not written in this book.

31But these are written (recorded) in order that you may believe that Jesus is the Christ, the Anointed One, the Son of God, and that through believing *and* cleaving to *and* trusting in *and* relying upon Him you may have life through (in) His name [that is, [c]through what He is]. [Ps. 2:7, 12.]

**21** AFTER THIS Jesus let Himself be seen *and* revealed [Himself] again to the disciples at the Sea of Tiberias. And He did it in this way:

2There were together Simon Peter, and Thomas, called the Twin, and Nathanael from Cana of Galilee, also the sons of Zebedee and two others of His disciples.

3Simon Peter said to them, I am going fishing! They said to him, And we are coming with you! So they went out and got into the boat, and throughout that night they caught nothing.

4Morning was already breaking when Jesus came to the beach and stood there. However, the disciples did not know that it was Jesus.

5So Jesus said to them, [d]Boys (children) [have you caught anything to eat with bread?] You do not have any meat (fish) do you? They answered Him, No!

6But He said to them, Cast the net on the right side of the boat and you will find [some]. So they cast the net, and now they were not able to haul it in for such a big catch (mass, quantity) of fish [was in it].

7Then the disciple whom Jesus loved said to Peter, It is the Lord! Simon Peter, hearing him say that it was the Lord, put (girded) on his upper garment—his fisherman's coat, his outer tunic—for he was stripped [for work], and sprang into the sea.

**AMP** [a] Matthew Henry's Commentary. [b] Souter. [c] Cremer: "Biblico-Theological Lexicon of New Testament Greek." [d] Souter.

## New American Standard

18Mary Magdalene *came, announcing to the disciples, "I have
seen the Lord," and *that* He had said these things to her.

*Jesus among His Disciples*

19¶ When therefore it was evening, on that day, the first *day* of
the week, and when the doors were shut where the disciples were,
for fear of the Jews, Jesus came and stood in their midst, and *said
to them, "Peace *be* with you."
20And when He had said this, He showed them both His hands
and His side. The disciples therefore rejoiced when they saw the
Lord.
21Jesus therefore said to them again, "Peace *be* with you; as the
Father has sent Me, I also send you."
22And when He had said this, He breathed on them, and *said
to them, "Receive the Holy Spirit.
23"If you forgive the sins of any, *their sins* have been forgiven
them; if you retain the *sins* of any, they have been retained."
24¶ But Thomas, one of the twelve, called Didymus, was not
with them when Jesus came.
25The other disciples therefore were saying to him, "We have
seen the Lord!" But he said to them, "Unless I shall see in His
hands the imprint of the nails, and put my finger into the place of
the nails, and put my hand into His side, I will not believe."
26¶ And after eight days again His disciples were inside, and
Thomas with them. Jesus *came, the doors having been shut, and
stood in their midst, and said, "Peace *be* with you."
27Then He *said to Thomas, "Reach here your finger, and see
My hands; and reach here your hand, and put it into My side; and
be not unbelieving, but believing."
28Thomas answered and said to Him, "My Lord and my God!"
29Jesus *said to him, "Because you have seen Me, have you
believed? Blessed *are* they who did not see, and *yet* believed."

*Why This Gospel Was Written*

30¶ Many other signs therefore Jesus also performed in the
presence of the disciples, which are not written in this book;
31but these have been written that you may believe that Jesus
is the Christ, the Son of God; and that believing you may have life
in His name.

*Jesus Appears at the Sea of Galilee*

21 AFTER THESE things Jesus manifested Himself again to
the disciples at the Sea of Tiberias, and He manifested
*Himself* in this way.
2There were together Simon Peter, and Thomas called Didymus, and Nathanael of Cana in Galilee, and the *sons* of Zebedee,
and two others of His disciples.
3Simon Peter *said to them, "I am going fishing." They *said
to him, "We will also come with you." They went out, and got into
the boat; and that night they caught nothing.
4But when the day was now breaking, Jesus stood on the
beach; yet the disciples did not know that it was Jesus.
5Jesus therefore *said to them, "Children, you do not have any
fish, do you?" They answered Him, "No."
6And He said to them, "Cast the net on the right-hand side of
the boat, and you will find *a catch*." They cast therefore, and then
they were not able to haul it in because of the great number of fish.
7That disciple therefore whom Jesus loved *said to Peter, "It
is the Lord." And so when Simon Peter heard that it was the Lord,
he put his outer garment on (for he was stripped *for work*), and
threw himself into the sea.

## New International

18Mary Magdalene went to the disciples with the news: "I have
seen the Lord!" And she told them that he had said these things
to her.

*Jesus Appears to His Disciples*

19On the evening of that first day of the week, when the disciples were together, with the doors locked for fear of the Jews, Jesus
came and stood among them and said, "Peace be with you!"
20After he said this, he showed them his hands and side. The
disciples were overjoyed when they saw the Lord.
21Again Jesus said, "Peace be with you! As the Father has sent
me, I am sending you." 22And with that he breathed on them and
said, "Receive the Holy Spirit. 23If you forgive anyone his sins,
they are forgiven; if you do not forgive them, they are not forgiven."

*Jesus Appears to Thomas*

24Now Thomas (called Didymus), one of the Twelve, was not
with the disciples when Jesus came. 25So the other disciples told
him, "We have seen the Lord!"
But he said to them, "Unless I see the nail marks in his hands
and put my finger where the nails were, and put my hand into his
side, I will not believe it."
26A week later his disciples were in the house again, and Thomas was with them. Though the doors were locked, Jesus came and
stood among them and said, "Peace be with you!" 27Then he said
to Thomas, "Put your finger here; see my hands. Reach out your
hand and put it into my side. Stop doubting and believe."
28Thomas said to him, "My Lord and my God!"
29Then Jesus told him, "Because you have seen me, you have
believed; blessed are those who have not seen and yet have believed."
30Jesus did many other miraculous signs in the presence of his
disciples, which are not recorded in this book. 31But these are
written that you may[e] believe that Jesus is the Christ, the Son of
God, and that by believing you may have life in his name.

*Jesus and the Miraculous Catch of Fish*

21 AFTERWARD JESUS appeared again to his disciples, by
the Sea of Tiberias.[f] It happened this way: 2Simon Peter,
Thomas (called Didymus), Nathanael from Cana in Galilee, the
sons of Zebedee, and two other disciples were together. 3"I'm
going out to fish," Simon Peter told them, and they said, "We'll
go with you." So they went out and got into the boat, but that night
they caught nothing.
4Early in the morning, Jesus stood on the shore, but the disciples did not realize that it was Jesus.
5He called out to them, "Friends, haven't you any fish?"
"No," they answered.
6He said, "Throw your net on the right side of the boat and you
will find some." When they did, they were unable to haul the net
in because of the large number of fish.
7Then the disciple whom Jesus loved said to Peter, "It is the
Lord!" As soon as Simon Peter heard him say, "It is the Lord," he
wrapped his outer garment around him (for he had taken it off)
and jumped into the water. 8The other disciples followed in the

NIV e *31* Some manuscripts *may continue to* f *1* That is, Sea of Galilee

## King James

8 And the other disciples came in a little ship; (for they were not far from land, but as it were two hundred cubits,) dragging the net with fishes.

9 As soon then as they were come to land, they saw a fire of coals there, and fish laid thereon, and bread.

10 Jesus saith unto them, Bring of the fish which ye have now caught.

11 Simon Peter went up, and drew the net to land full of great fishes, an hundred and fifty and three: and for all there were so many, yet was not the net broken.

12 Jesus saith unto them, Come *and* dine. And none of the disciples durst ask him, Who art thou? knowing that it was the Lord.

13 Jesus then cometh, and taketh bread, and giveth them, and fish likewise.

14 This is now the third time that Jesus showed himself to his disciples, after that he was risen from the dead.

15 ¶ So when they had dined, Jesus saith to Simon Peter, Simon, *son* of Jonas, lovest thou me more than these? He saith unto him, Yea, Lord; thou knowest that I love thee. He saith unto him, Feed my lambs.

16 He saith to him again the second time, Simon, *son* of Jonas, lovest thou me? He saith unto him, Yea, Lord; thou knowest that I love thee. He saith unto him, Feed my sheep.

17 He saith unto him the third time, Simon, *son* of Jonas, lovest thou me? Peter was grieved because he said unto him the third time, Lovest thou me? And he said unto him, Lord, thou knowest all things; thou knowest that I love thee. Jesus saith unto him, Feed my sheep.

18 Verily, verily, I say unto thee, When thou wast young, thou girdedst thyself, and walkedst whither thou wouldest: but when thou shalt be old, thou shalt stretch forth thy hands, and another shall gird thee, and carry *thee* whither thou wouldest not.

19 This spake he, signifying by what death he should glorify God. And when he had spoken this, he saith unto him, Follow me.

20 Then Peter, turning about, seeth the disciple whom Jesus loved following; which also leaned on his breast at supper, and said, Lord, which is he that betrayeth thee?

21 Peter seeing him saith to Jesus, Lord, and what *shall* this man *do?*

22 Jesus saith unto him, If I will that he tarry till I come, what *is that* to thee? follow thou me.

23 Then went this saying abroad among the brethren, that that disciple should not die: yet Jesus said not unto him, He shall not die; but, If I will that he tarry till I come, what *is that* to thee?

24 This is the disciple which testifieth of these things, and wrote these things: and we know that his testimony is true.

25 And there are also many other things which Jesus did, the which, if they should be written every one, I suppose that even the world itself could not contain the books that should be written. Amen.

## Amplified

8 And the other disciples came in the small boat, for they were not far from shore, only some hundred yards away, dragging the net full of fish.

9 When they got out on land (the beach), they saw a fire of coals there and fish lying on it [cooking], and bread.

10 Jesus said to them, Bring some of the fish which you have just caught.

11 So Simon Peter went aboard and hauled the net to land, full of large fish, a hundred [and] fifty-three of them. And [though] there were so many of them, the net was not torn.

12 Jesus said to them, Come [and] have breakfast. But none of the disciples ventured *or* dared to ask Him, Who are You? Because they [well] knew that it was the Lord.

13 Jesus came and took the bread and gave it to them, and also the fish.

14 This was now the third time that Jesus revealed Himself (appeared, was manifest) to the disciples after He had risen from the dead.

15 When they had eaten, Jesus said to Simon Peter, Simon, son of John, do you love Me more than these [others do]—with reasoning, intentional, spiritual devotion, as one loves the Father? He said to Him, Yes, Lord; You know that I love You—that I have deep, instinctive, personal affection for You, as for a close friend. He said to him, Feed My lambs.

16 Again He said to him the second time, Simon, son of John, do you love Me—with reasoning, intentional, spiritual devotion, as one loves the Father? He said to Him, Yes, Lord, You know that I love You—that I have a deep, instinctive, personal affection for You, as for a close friend. He said to him, Shepherd (tend) My sheep.

17 He said to him the third time, Simon, son of John, do you love Me—with a deep, instinctive, personal affection for Me, as for a close friend? Peter was grieved—took it ill—that He should ask him the third time, Do you love Me? And he said to Him, Lord, You know everything; You know that I love You—that I have a deep, instinctive, personal affection for You, as for a close friend. Jesus said to him, Feed My sheep.

18 I assure you, most solemnly I tell you, when you were young, you girded yourself—put on your own belt (girdle)—and you walked about wherever you pleased to go. But when you grow old you will stretch out your hands and someone else will put a girdle around you, and carry you where you do not wish to go.

19 He said this to indicate by what kind of death Peter would glorify God. And after this He said to him, Follow Me!

20 But Peter had turned and saw the disciple whom Jesus loved, following, who also had leaned back on His breast at the supper and had said, Lord, who is it that is going to betray You?

21 When Peter saw him, he said to Jesus, Lord, what about this man?

22 Jesus said to him, If I will have him to stay (survive, live) till I come, what is that to you?—What concern is it of yours? You follow Me!

23 So word went out among the brethren that this disciple was not to die; yet Jesus did not say to him that he was not to die, but, If I want him to stay (survive, live) till I come, what is that to you?

24 It is this same disciple who is bearing witness to these things, and who has recorded (written) them; and we [well] know that his testimony is true.

25 And there are also many other things which Jesus did. If they should be all recorded one by one [in detail], I suppose that even the world itself could not contain (have room for) the books that would be written.

## New American Standard

8But the other disciples came in the little boat, for they were
not far from the land, but about one hundred yards away, dragging the net *full* of fish.
9And so when they got out upon the land, they *saw a charcoal
fire *already* laid, and fish placed on it, and bread.
10Jesus *said to them, "Bring some of the fish which you have
now caught."
11Simon Peter went up, and drew the net to land, full of large
fish, a hundred and fifty-three; and although there were so many,
the net was not torn.

*Jesus Provides*

12Jesus *said to them, "Come *and* have breakfast." None of the
disciples ventured to question Him, "Who are You?" knowing that
it was the Lord.
13Jesus *came and *took the bread, and *gave them, and the fish
likewise.
14This is now the third time that Jesus was manifested to the
disciples, after He was raised from the dead.

*The Love Motivation*

15¶ So when they had finished breakfast, Jesus *said to Simon
Peter, "Simon, *son* of John, do you love Me more than these?" He
*said to Him, "Yes, Lord; You know that I love You." He *said to
him, "Tend My lambs."
16He *said to him again a second time, "Simon, *son* of John, do
you love Me?" He *said to Him, "Yes, Lord; You know that I love
You." He *said to him, "Shepherd My sheep."
17He *said to him the third time, "Simon, *son* of John, do you
love Me?" Peter was grieved because He said to him the third time,
"Do you love Me?" And he said to Him, "Lord, You know all
things; You know that I love You." Jesus *said to him, "Tend My
sheep.

*Our Times Are in His Hand*

18"Truly, truly, I say to you, when you were younger, you used
to gird yourself, and walk wherever you wished; but when you
grow old, you will stretch out your hands, and someone else will
gird you, and bring you where you do not wish to *go*."
19Now this He said, signifying by what kind of death he would
glorify God. And when He had spoken this, He *said to him,
"Follow Me!"
20Peter, turning around, *saw the disciple whom Jesus loved
following *them;* the one who also had leaned back on His breast at
the supper, and said, "Lord, who is the one who betrays You?"
21Peter therefore seeing him *said to Jesus, "Lord, and what
about this man?"
22Jesus *said to him, "If I want him to remain until I come, what
*is that* to you? You follow Me!"
23This saying therefore went out among the brethren that that
disciple would not die; yet Jesus did not say to him that he would
not die, but *only*, "If I want him to remain until I come, what *is that*
to you?"
24¶ This is the disciple who bears witness of these things, and
wrote these things; and we know that his witness is true.
25¶ And there are also many other things which Jesus did,
which if they *were written in detail, I suppose that even the world
itself *would not contain the books which *were written.

## New International

boat, towing the net full of fish, for they were not far from shore,
about a hundred yards.[a] 9When they landed, they saw a fire of
burning coals there with fish on it, and some bread.
10Jesus said to them, "Bring some of the fish you have just
caught."
11Simon Peter climbed aboard and dragged the net ashore. It
was full of large fish, 153, but even with so many the net was not
torn. 12Jesus said to them, "Come and have breakfast." None of
the disciples dared ask him, "Who are you?" They knew it was the
Lord. 13Jesus came, took the bread and gave it to them, and did
the same with the fish. 14This was now the third time Jesus appeared to his disciples after he was raised from the dead.

*Jesus Reinstates Peter*

15When they had finished eating, Jesus said to Simon Peter,
"Simon son of John, do you truly love me more than these?"
"Yes, Lord," he said, "you know that I love you."
Jesus said, "Feed my lambs."
16Again Jesus said, "Simon son of John, do you truly love me?"
He answered, "Yes, Lord, you know that I love you."
Jesus said, "Take care of my sheep."
17The third time he said to him, "Simon son of John, do you love
me?"
Peter was hurt because Jesus asked him the third time, "Do you
love me?" He said, "Lord, you know all things; you know that I
love you."
Jesus said, "Feed my sheep. 18I tell you the truth, when you
were younger you dressed yourself and went where you wanted;
but when you are old you will stretch out your hands, and someone else will dress you and lead you where you do not want to go."
19Jesus said this to indicate the kind of death by which Peter would
glorify God. Then he said to him, "Follow me!"
20Peter turned and saw that the disciple whom Jesus loved was
following them. (This was the one who had leaned back against
Jesus at the supper and had said, "Lord, who is going to betray
you?") 21When Peter saw him, he asked, "Lord, what about him?"
22Jesus answered, "If I want him to remain alive until I return,
what is that to you? You must follow me." 23Because of this, the
rumor spread among the brothers that this disciple would not die.
But Jesus did not say that he would not die; he only said, "If I want
him to remain alive until I return, what is that to you?"
24This is the disciple who testifies to these things and who
wrote them down. We know that his testimony is true.
25Jesus did many other things as well. If every one of them were
written down, I suppose that even the whole world would not
have room for the books that would be written.

NIV [a] *8* Greek *about two hundred cubits* (about 90 meters)

## King James

THE

# Acts

OF THE APOSTLES

1 THE FORMER treatise have I made, O Theophilus, of all that Jesus began both to do and teach,

2 Until the day in which he was taken up, after that he through the Holy Ghost had given commandments unto the apostles whom he had chosen:

3 To whom also he showed himself alive after his passion by many infallible proofs, being seen of them forty days, and speaking of the things pertaining to the kingdom of God:

4 And, being assembled together with *them*, commanded them that they should not depart from Jerusalem, but wait for the promise of the Father, which, *saith he*, ye have heard of me.

5 For John truly baptized with water; but ye shall be baptized with the Holy Ghost not many days hence.

6 When they therefore were come together, they asked of him, saying, Lord, wilt thou at this time restore again the kingdom to Israel?

7 And he said unto them, It is not for you to know the times or the seasons, which the Father hath put in his own power.

8 But ye shall receive power, after that the Holy Ghost is come upon you: and ye shall be witnesses unto me both in Jerusalem, and in all Judaea, and in Samaria, and unto the uttermost part of the earth.

9 And when he had spoken these things, while they beheld, he was taken up; and a cloud received him out of their sight.

10 And while they looked stedfastly toward heaven as he went up, behold, two men stood by them in white apparel;

11 Which also said, Ye men of Galilee, why stand ye gazing up into heaven? this same Jesus, which is taken up from you into heaven, shall so come in like manner as ye have seen him go into heaven.

12 Then returned they unto Jerusalem from the mount called Olivet, which is from Jerusalem a sabbath day's journey.

13 And when they were come in, they went up into an upper room, where abode both Peter, and James, and John, and Andrew, Philip, and Thomas, Bartholomew, and Matthew, James *the son* of Alphaeus, and Simon Zelotes, and Judas *the brother* of James.

14 These all continued with one accord in prayer and supplication, with the women, and Mary the mother of Jesus, and with his brethren.

## Amplified

THE

# Acts

OF THE APOSTLES

1 [IN] THE former [account which I prepared] O Theophilus, I made a continuous report dealing with all the things which Jesus began to do and to teach,

2 Until the day when He ascended, after He through the Holy Spirit had instructed *and* commanded the apostles (special messengers) whom He had chosen.

3 To them also He showed Himself alive after His passion (His suffering in the garden and on the cross), by [a series of] many convincing demonstrations—unquestionable evidence and infallible proofs—appearing to them during forty days, and talking [to them] about the things of the kingdom of God.

4 And while being in their company *and* eating at the table with them, He commanded them not to leave Jerusalem, but to wait for what the Father had promised, Of which, He said, you have heard Me speak.

5 For John baptized with water, but not many days from now you shall be baptized with— [a]placed in, introduced into—the Holy Spirit.

6 So when they were assembled they asked Him, Lord, is this the time when You will re-establish the kingdom *and* restore it to Israel?

7 He said to them, It is not for you to become acquainted with *and* know [b]what time brings—the things and events of time and their definite periods—fixed [c]years and seasons (their critical nick of time), which the Father has appointed (fixed and reserved) by His own choice *and* authority *and* personal power.

8 But you shall receive power—ability, efficiency and might—when the Holy Spirit has come upon you; and you shall be My witnesses in Jerusalem and all Judea and Samaria and to the ends—the very bounds—of the earth.

9 And when He had said this, even as they were looking [at Him], He was caught up, and a cloud received *and* carried Him away out of their sight.

10 And while they were gazing intently into heaven as He went, behold, two men [dressed] in white robes suddenly stood beside them,

11 Who said, Men of Galilee, why do you stand gazing into heaven? This same Jesus, Who was caught away *and* lifted up from among you into heaven, will return in [just] the same way in which you saw Him go into heaven.

12 Then [the disciples] went back to Jerusalem from the hill called Olivet, which is near Jerusalem, [only] a Sabbath day's journey [three-quarters of a mile] away.

13 And when they had entered [the city], they mounted to the upper room where they were [d]indefinitely staying—Peter and John and James and Andrew, Philip and Thomas, Bartholomew and Matthew, James the son of Alphaeus and Simon the Zealot and Judas the [son] of James.

14 All of these with their minds in full agreement devoted themselves steadfastly to prayer, [waiting together] with the women and Mary the mother of Jesus, and with His brothers.

**AMP** [a] Wuest's "Untranslatable Riches from the Greek New Testament." [b] Thayer's "Greek-English Lexicon of the New Testament—Grimm." [c] Trench's "Synonyms of Greek New Testament." [d] Moulton and Milligan.

## New American Standard

# Acts

*Introduction*

1 THE FIRST account I composed, Theophilus, about all that
Jesus began to do and teach,
2until the day when He was taken up, after He had by the Holy
Spirit given orders to the apostles whom He had chosen.
3To these He also presented Himself alive, after His suffering,
by many convincing proofs, appearing to them over *a period of* forty
days, and speaking of the things concerning the kingdom of God.
4And gathering them together, He commanded them not to
leave Jerusalem, but to wait for what the Father had promised,
"Which," *He said,* "you heard of from Me;
5for John baptized with water, but you shall be baptized with
the Holy Spirit not many days from now."
6¶ And so when they had come together, they were asking
Him, saying, "Lord, is it at this time You are restoring the kingdom
to Israel?"
7He said to them, "It is not for you to know times or epochs
which the Father has fixed by His own authority;
8but you shall receive power when the Holy Spirit has come
upon you; and you shall be My witnesses both in Jerusalem, and
in all Judea and Samaria, and even to the remotest part of the
earth."

*The Ascension*

9And after He had said these things, He was lifted up while
they were looking on, and a cloud received Him out of their sight.
10And as they were gazing intently into the sky while He was
departing, behold, two men in white clothing stood beside them;
11and they also said, "Men of Galilee, why do you stand looking
into the sky? This Jesus, who has been taken up from you into
heaven, will come in just the same way as you have watched Him
go into heaven."

*The Upper Room*

12¶ Then they returned to Jerusalem from the mount called
Olivet, which is near Jerusalem, a Sabbath day's journey away.
13And when they had entered, they went up to the upper room,
where they were staying; that is, Peter and John and James and
Andrew, Philip and Thomas, Bartholomew and Matthew, James
*the son* of Alphaeus, and Simon the Zealot, and Judas *the son* of
James.
14These all with one mind were continually devoting themselves to prayer, along with *the* women, and Mary the mother of
Jesus, and with His brothers.

## New International

# Acts

*Jesus Taken Up Into Heaven*

1 IN MY former book, Theophilus, I wrote about all that Jesus
began to do and to teach 2until the day he was taken up to
heaven, after giving instructions through the Holy Spirit to the
apostles he had chosen. 3After his suffering, he showed himself
to these men and gave many convincing proofs that he was alive.
He appeared to them over a period of forty days and spoke about
the kingdom of God. 4On one occasion, while he was eating with
them, he gave them this command: "Do not leave Jerusalem, but
wait for the gift my Father promised, which you have heard me
speak about. 5For John baptized with[e] water, but in a few days you
will be baptized with the Holy Spirit."
6So when they met together, they asked him, "Lord, are you
at this time going to restore the kingdom to Israel?"
7He said to them: "It is not for you to know the times or dates
the Father has set by his own authority. 8But you will receive
power when the Holy Spirit comes on you; and you will be my
witnesses in Jerusalem, and in all Judea and Samaria, and to the
ends of the earth."
9After he said this, he was taken up before their very eyes, and
a cloud hid him from their sight.
10They were looking intently up into the sky as he was going,
when suddenly two men dressed in white stood beside them.
11"Men of Galilee," they said, "why do you stand here looking
into the sky? This same Jesus, who has been taken from you into
heaven, will come back in the same way you have seen him go into
heaven."

*Matthias Chosen to Replace Judas*

12Then they returned to Jerusalem from the hill called the
Mount of Olives, a Sabbath day's walk[f] from the city. 13When they
arrived, they went upstairs to the room where they were staying.
Those present were Peter, John, James and Andrew; Philip and
Thomas, Bartholomew and Matthew; James son of Alphaeus and
Simon the Zealot, and Judas son of James. 14They all joined to-
gether constantly in prayer, along with the women and Mary the
mother of Jesus, and with his brothers.

**NIV** [e] 5 Or *in* [f] 12 That is, about 3/4 mile (about 1,100 meters)

## King James

15¶ And in those days Peter stood up in the midst of the disciples, and said, (the number of names together were about an hundred and twenty,)

16Men *and* brethren, this scripture must needs have been fulfilled, which the Holy Ghost by the mouth of David spake before concerning Judas, which was guide to them that took Jesus.

17For he was numbered with us, and had obtained part of this ministry.

18Now this man purchased a field with the reward of iniquity; and falling headlong, he burst asunder in the midst, and all his bowels gushed out.

19And it was known unto all the dwellers at Jerusalem; insomuch as that field is called in their proper tongue, Aceldama, that is to say, The field of blood.

20For it is written in the book of Psalms, Let his habitation be desolate, and let no man dwell therein: and his bishopric let another take.

21Wherefore of these men which have companied with us all the time that the Lord Jesus went in and out among us,

22Beginning from the baptism of John, unto that same day that he was taken up from us, must one be ordained to be a witness with us of his resurrection.

23And they appointed two, Joseph called Barsabas, who was surnamed Justus, and Matthias.

24And they prayed, and said, Thou, Lord, which knowest the hearts of all *men*, show whether of these two thou hast chosen,

25That he may take part of this ministry and apostleship, from which Judas by transgression fell, that he might go to his own place.

26And they gave forth their lots; and the lot fell upon Matthias; and he was numbered with the eleven apostles.

2 AND WHEN the day of Pentecost was fully come, they were all with one accord in one place.

2And suddenly there came a sound from heaven as of a rushing mighty wind, and it filled all the house where they were sitting.

3And there appeared unto them cloven tongues like as of fire, and it sat upon each of them.

4And they were all filled with the Holy Ghost, and began to speak with other tongues, as the Spirit gave them utterance.

5And there were dwelling at Jerusalem Jews, devout men, out of every nation under heaven.

6Now when this was noised abroad, the multitude came together, and were confounded, because that every man heard them speak in his own language.

7And they were all amazed and marvelled, saying one to another, Behold, are not all these which speak Galilaeans?

8And how hear we every man in our own tongue, wherein we were born?

9Parthians, and Medes, and Elamites, and the dwellers in Mesopotamia, and in Judaea, and Cappadocia, in Pontus, and Asia,

10Phrygia, and Pamphylia, in Egypt, and in the parts of Libya about Cyrene, and strangers of Rome, Jews and proselytes,

11Cretes and Arabians, we do hear them speak in our tongues the wonderful works of God.

## Amplified

15Now one of those days Peter arose among the brethren, the whole number of whom gathered together was about a hundred and twenty.

16Brethren, he said, it was necessary that the Scripture be fulfilled, which the Holy Spirit foretold by the lips of David, about Judas who acted as guide to those who arrested Jesus.

17For he was counted among us and received [by divine allotment] his portion of this ministry.

18Now this [man] obtained a piece of land with the [money paid him as a] reward for his treachery *and* wickedness, and falling headlong he burst open in the middle [of his body] and all his intestines poured forth.

19And all the residents of Jerusalem became acquainted with the facts, so that they called the piece of land in their own dialect, Akeldama, that is, Field of Blood.

20For in the book of Psalms it is written, Let his place of residence become deserted *and* gloomy, and let there be no one to live in it; and [again], Let another take his position *or* overseership. [Ps. 69:25; 109:8.]

21So one of the [other] men who have accompanied us [apostles] during all the time that the Lord Jesus went in and out among us,

22From the baptism of John at the outset until the day when He was taken up from among us, one of these men must join with us and become a witness to testify to His resurrection.

23And they accordingly proposed (nominated) two men, Joseph called Barsabbas, who was surnamed Justus, and Matthias.

24And they prayed and said, You, Lord, Who know all hearts [[a]their thoughts, passions, desires, appetites, purposes and endeavors], indicate to us which one of these two You have chosen

25To take the place in this ministry and receive the position of an apostle from which Judas fell away *and* went astray to go (where he belonged,) to his own (proper) place.

26And they drew lots [between the two], and the lot fell on Matthias; and he was added to *and* counted with the eleven apostles (special messengers).

2 AND WHEN the day of Pentecost had fully come, they were all assembled together in one place,

2When suddenly there came a sound from heaven like the rushing of a violent tempest blast, and it filled the whole house in which they were sitting.

3And there appeared to them tongues resembling fire, which were separated *and* distributed and that settled on each one of them.

4And they were all filled—diffused throughout their souls—with the Holy Spirit and began to speak in other (different, foreign) languages, as the Spirit [b]kept giving them clear *and* loud expression (in each tongue in appropriate words).

5Now there were then residing in Jerusalem Jews, devout *and* God-fearing men from every country under heaven.

6And when this sound was heard, the multitude came together and they were astonished *and* bewildered, because each one heard them speaking in his own (particular) dialect.

7And they were beside themselves with amazement, saying, Are not all these who are talking Galileans?

8Then how is it that we hear, each of us in our own (particular) dialect to which we were born?

9Parthians and Medes and Elamites and inhabitants of Mesopotamia, Judea and Cappadocia, Pontus and [the province of] Asia,

10Phrygia and Pamphylia, Egypt and the parts of Libya about Cyrene, and the transient residents from Rome, both Jews and the proselytes [to Judaism from other religions];

11Cretans and Arabians too—we all hear them speaking in our own native tongues [and telling of] the mighty works of God!

AMP [a] Thayer. [b] Vincent's "Word Studies in the New Testament."

## New American Standard

15¶ And at this time Peter stood up in the midst of the brethren (a gathering of about one hundred and twenty persons was there together), and said,

16"Brethren, the Scripture had to be fulfilled, which the Holy Spirit foretold by the mouth of David concerning Judas, who became a guide to those who arrested Jesus.

17"For he was counted among us, and received his portion in this ministry."

18(Now this man acquired a field with the price of his wickedness; and falling headlong, he burst open in the middle and all his bowels gushed out.

19And it became known to all who were living in Jerusalem; so that in their own language that field was called Hakeldama, that is, Field of Blood.)

20"For it is written in the book of Psalms,

'LET HIS HOMESTEAD BE MADE DESOLATE,
AND LET NO MAN DWELL IN IT';
and,
'HIS OFFICE LET ANOTHER MAN TAKE.'

21"It is therefore necessary that of the men who have accompanied us all the time that the Lord Jesus went in and out among us—

22beginning with the baptism of John, until the day that He was taken up from us—one of these should become a witness with us of His resurrection."

23And they put forward two men, Joseph called Barsabbas (who was also called Justus), and Matthias.

24And they prayed, and said, "Thou, Lord, who knowest the hearts of all men, show which one of these two Thou hast chosen

25to occupy this ministry and apostleship from which Judas turned aside to go to his own place."

26And they drew lots for them, and the lot fell to Matthias; and he was numbered with the eleven apostles.

*The Day of Pentecost*

**2** AND WHEN the day of Pentecost had come, they were all together in one place.

2And suddenly there came from heaven a noise like a violent, rushing wind, and it filled the whole house where they were sitting.

3And there appeared to them tongues as of fire distributing themselves, and they rested on each one of them.

4And they were all filled with the Holy Spirit and began to speak with other tongues, as the Spirit was giving them utterance.

5¶ Now there were Jews living in Jerusalem, devout men, from every nation under heaven.

6And when this sound occurred, the multitude came together, and were bewildered, because they were each one hearing them speak in his own language.

7And they were amazed and marveled, saying, "Why, are not all these who are speaking Galileans?

8"And how is it that we each hear *them* in our own language to which we were born?

9"Parthians and Medes and Elamites, and residents of Mesopotamia, Judea and Cappadocia, Pontus and Asia,

10Phrygia and Pamphylia, Egypt and the districts of Libya around Cyrene, and visitors from Rome, both Jews and [c]proselytes,

11Cretans and Arabs—we hear them in our *own* tongues speaking of the mighty deeds of God."

NAS [c] I.e., Gentile converts to Judaism

## New International

15In those days Peter stood up among the believers[d] (a group
numbering about a hundred and twenty) 16and said, "Brothers,
the Scripture had to be fulfilled which the Holy Spirit spoke long
ago through the mouth of David concerning Judas, who served as
guide for those who arrested Jesus— 17he was one of our number
and shared in this ministry."
18(With the reward he got for his wickedness, Judas bought a
field; there he fell headlong, his body burst open and all his intestines spilled out. 19Everyone in Jerusalem heard about this, so they
called that field in their language Akeldama, that is, Field of
Blood.)
20"For," said Peter, "it is written in the book of Psalms,

" 'May his place be deserted;
let there be no one to dwell in it,'[e]

and,

" 'May another take his place of leadership.'[f]

21Therefore it is necessary to choose one of the men who have been
with us the whole time the Lord Jesus went in and out among us,
22beginning from John's baptism to the time when Jesus was taken
up from us. For one of these must become a witness with us of his
resurrection."
23So they proposed two men: Joseph called Barsabbas (also
known as Justus) and Matthias. 24Then they prayed, "Lord, you
know everyone's heart. Show us which of these two you have
chosen 25to take over this apostolic ministry, which Judas left to
go where he belongs." 26Then they cast lots, and the lot fell to
Matthias; so he was added to the eleven apostles.

*The Holy Spirit Comes at Pentecost*

**2** WHEN THE day of Pentecost came, they were all together in
one place. 2Suddenly a sound like the blowing of a violent
wind came from heaven and filled the whole house where they
were sitting. 3They saw what seemed to be tongues of fire that
separated and came to rest on each of them. 4All of them were
filled with the Holy Spirit and began to speak in other tongues[g]
as the Spirit enabled them.
5Now there were staying in Jerusalem God-fearing Jews from
every nation under heaven. 6When they heard this sound, a crowd
came together in bewilderment, because each one heard them
speaking in his own language. 7Utterly amazed, they asked: "Are
not all these men who are speaking Galileans? 8Then how is it that
each of us hears them in his own native language? 9Parthians,
Medes and Elamites; residents of Mesopotamia, Judea and Cappadocia, Pontus and Asia, 10Phrygia and Pamphylia, Egypt and
the parts of Libya near Cyrene; visitors from Rome 11(both Jews
and converts to Judaism); Cretans and Arabs—we hear them de-

NIV [d] *15* Greek *brothers* [e] *20* Psalm 69:25 [f] *20* Psalm 109:8 [g] *4* Or *languages;* also in verse 11

## King James

12And they were all amazed, and were in doubt, saying one to another, What meaneth this?

13Others mocking said, These men are full of new wine.

14¶ But Peter, standing up with the eleven, lifted up his voice, and said unto them, Ye men of Judaea, and all *ye* that dwell at Jerusalem, be this known unto you, and hearken to my words:

15For these are not drunken, as ye suppose, seeing it is *but* the third hour of the day.

16But this is that which was spoken by the prophet Joel;

17And it shall come to pass in the last days, saith God, I will pour out of my Spirit upon all flesh: and your sons and your daughters shall prophesy, and your young men shall see visions, and your old men shall dream dreams:

18And on my servants and on my handmaidens I will pour out in those days of my Spirit; and they shall prophesy:

19And I will show wonders in heaven above, and signs in the earth beneath; blood, and fire, and vapour of smoke:

20The sun shall be turned into darkness, and the moon into blood, before that great and notable day of the Lord come:

21And it shall come to pass, *that* whosoever shall call on the name of the Lord shall be saved.

22Ye men of Israel, hear these words; Jesus of Nazareth, a man approved of God among you by miracles and wonders and signs, which God did by him in the midst of you, as ye yourselves also know:

23Him, being delivered by the determinate counsel and foreknowledge of God, ye have taken, and by wicked hands have crucified and slain:

24Whom God hath raised up, having loosed the pains of death: because it was not possible that he should be holden of it.

25For David speaketh concerning him, I foresaw the Lord always before my face, for he is on my right hand, that I should not be moved:

26Therefore did my heart rejoice, and my tongue was glad; moreover also my flesh shall rest in hope:

27Because thou wilt not leave my soul in hell, neither wilt thou suffer thine Holy One to see corruption.

28Thou hast made known to me the ways of life; thou shalt make me full of joy with thy countenance.

29Men *and* brethren, let me freely speak unto you of the patriarch David, that he is both dead and buried, and his sepulchre is with us unto this day.

30Therefore being a prophet, and knowing that God had sworn with an oath to him, that of the fruit of his loins, according to the flesh, he would raise up Christ to sit on his throne;

31He seeing this before spake of the resurrection of Christ, that his soul was not left in hell, neither his flesh did see corruption.

32This Jesus hath God raised up, whereof we all are witnesses.

## Amplified

12And all were beside themselves with amazement and were puzzled *and* bewildered, saying one to another, What can this mean?

13But others made a joke of it *and* derisively said, They are simply drunk *and* full of sweet [intoxicating] wine.

14But Peter, standing with the eleven, raised his voice and addressed them: You Jews and all you residents of Jerusalem, let this be [explained] to you so that you will know *and* understand; listen closely to what I have to say.

15For these men are not drunk, as you imagine, for it is [only] the third hour [about nine o'clock] of the day;

16But [instead,] this is [the beginning of] what was spoken through the prophet Joel:

17And it shall come to pass in the last days, God declares, that I will pour out of My Spirit upon all mankind, and your sons and your daughters shall prophesy—[a]telling forth the divine counsels—and your young men shall see visions (that is, [b]divinely granted appearances), and your old men shall dream [[c]divinely suggested] dreams.

18Yes, and on My menservants also and on My maidservants in those days I will pour out of My Spirit, and they shall prophesy—[d]telling forth the divine counsels and [e]predicting future events pertaining especially to God's kingdom.

19And I will show wonders in the sky above and signs on the earth beneath, blood and fire and smoking vapor;

20The sun shall be turned into darkness and the moon into blood, before the obvious day of the Lord comes, that great and notable *and* conspicuous and renowned [day].

21And it shall be that whosoever shall call upon the name of the Lord—that is, [f]invoking, adoring and worshipping the Lord (Christ)—shall be saved. [Joel 2:28-32.]

22You men of Israel, listen to what I have to say: Jesus of Nazareth, a Man accredited *and* pointed out *and* shown forth *and* commended *and* attested to you by God, by the mighty works and [the power of performing] wonders and signs which God worked through Him [right] in your midst, as you yourselves know,

23This Jesus, when delivered up according to the definite *and* fixed purpose *and* settled plan and foreknowledge of God, you crucified *and* put out of the way, [killing Him] by the hands of lawless *and* wicked men.

24[But] God raised Him up, liberating Him from the pangs of death, seeing that it was not possible for Him to continue to be controlled *or* retained by it.

25For David says in regard to Him, I saw the Lord constantly before me, for He is at my right hand that I may not be shaken *or* overthrown *or* cast down [from my secure and happy state].

26Therefore my heart rejoiced, and my tongue exulted exceedingly; moreover my flesh also will rest in hope—will encamp, pitch its tent and dwell on hope [in anticipation of the resurrection].

27For You will not abandon My soul, leaving it helpless in Hades [the state of departed spirits], nor let Your Holy One know decay *or* see destruction [of the body after death].

28You have made known to Me the ways of life; You will enrapture Me—diffusing My soul with joy—with *and* in Your presence. [Ps. 16:8-11.]

29Brethren, it is permitted me to tell you confidently *and* with freedom concerning the patriarch David that he both died and was buried, and his tomb is with us to this day.

30Being however a prophet, and knowing that God had sealed to him with an oath that He would set one of his descendants on his throne, [Ps. 132:11.]

31He foreseeing this, spoke (by foreknowledge) of the resurrection of the Christ, the Messiah, that He was not deserted [in death] *and* left in Hades [the state of departed spirits], nor did His body know decay *or* see destruction. [Ps. 16:10.]

32This Jesus God raised up, and of that all we [His disciples] are witnesses.

**AMP** [a] Abbott-Smith's "Manual Greek Lexicon of the New Testament." [b] Thayer. [c] Thayer. [d] Abbott-Smith's "Manual Greek Lexicon of the New Testament." [e] Thayer. [f] Thayer.

## New American Standard

12And they all continued in amazement and great perplexity,
saying to one another, "What does this mean?"
13But others were mocking and saying, "They are full of sweet
wine."

*Peter's Sermon*

14¶ But Peter, taking his stand with the eleven, raised his voice
and declared to them: "Men of Judea, and all you who live in
Jerusalem, let this be known to you, and give heed to my words.
15"For these men are not drunk, as you suppose, for it is *only*
the [g]third hour of the day;
16but this is what was spoken of through the prophet Joel:

17 'AND IT SHALL BE IN THE LAST DAYS,' God says,
'THAT I WILL POUR FORTH OF MY SPIRIT UPON ALL MANKIND;
AND YOUR SONS AND YOUR DAUGHTERS SHALL PROPHESY,
AND YOUR YOUNG MEN SHALL SEE VISIONS,
AND YOUR OLD MEN SHALL DREAM DREAMS;
18 EVEN UPON MY BONDSLAVES, BOTH MEN AND WOMEN,
I WILL IN THOSE DAYS POUR FORTH OF MY SPIRIT
And they shall prophesy.
19 'AND I WILL GRANT WONDERS IN THE SKY ABOVE,
AND SIGNS ON THE EARTH BENEATH,
BLOOD, AND FIRE, AND VAPOR OF SMOKE.
20 'THE SUN SHALL BE TURNED INTO DARKNESS,
AND THE MOON INTO BLOOD,
BEFORE THE GREAT AND GLORIOUS DAY OF THE LORD SHALL COME.
21 'AND IT SHALL BE, THAT EVERYONE WHO CALLS ON THE NAME OF THE LORD SHALL BE SAVED.'

22¶ "Men of Israel, listen to these words: Jesus the Nazarene,
a man attested to you by God with miracles and wonders and signs
which God performed through Him in your midst, just as you
yourselves know—
23this *Man*, delivered up by the predetermined plan and foreknowledge of God, you nailed to a cross by the hands of godless
men and put *Him* to death.
24"And God raised Him up again, putting an end to the agony
of death, since it was impossible for Him to be held in its power.
25"For David says of Him,

'I WAS ALWAYS BEHOLDING THE LORD IN MY PRESENCE;
FOR HE IS AT MY RIGHT HAND, THAT I MAY NOT BE SHAKEN.
26 'THEREFORE MY HEART WAS GLAD AND MY TONGUE EXULTED;
MOREOVER MY FLESH ALSO WILL ABIDE IN HOPE;
27 BECAUSE THOU WILT NOT ABANDON MY SOUL TO HADES,
NOR ALLOW THY HOLY ONE TO UNDERGO DECAY.
28 'THOU HAST MADE KNOWN TO ME THE WAYS OF LIFE;
THOU WILT MAKE ME FULL OF GLADNESS WITH THY PRESENCE.'

29"Brethren, I may confidently say to you regarding the patriarch David that he both died and was buried, and his tomb is
with us to this day.
30"And so, because he was a prophet, and knew that GOD HAD
SWORN TO HIM WITH AN OATH TO SEAT *one* OF HIS DESCENDANTS
UPON HIS THRONE,
31he looked ahead and spoke of the resurrection of [h]the Christ,
that HE WAS NEITHER ABANDONED TO HADES, NOR DID His flesh
SUFFER DECAY.
32"This Jesus God raised up again, to which we are all witnesses.

NAS [g] I.e., 9 a.m. [h] I.e., the Messiah

## New International

claring the wonders of God in our own tongues!" 12Amazed and
perplexed, they asked one another, "What does this mean?"
13Some, however, made fun of them and said, "They have had
too much wine.[i] "

*Peter Addresses the Crowd*

14Then Peter stood up with the Eleven, raised his voice and
addressed the crowd: "Fellow Jews and all of you who live in
Jerusalem, let me explain this to you; listen carefully to what I say.
15These men are not drunk, as you suppose. It's only nine in the
morning! 16No, this is what was spoken by the prophet Joel:

17" 'In the last days, God says,
I will pour out my Spirit on all people.
Your sons and daughters will prophesy,
your young men will see visions,
your old men will dream dreams.
18Even on my servants, both men and women,
I will pour out my Spirit in those days,
and they will prophesy.
19I will show wonders in the heaven above
and signs on the earth below,
blood and fire and billows of smoke.
20The sun will be turned to darkness
and the moon to blood
before the coming of the great and glorious day of the Lord.
21And everyone who calls
on the name of the Lord will be saved.[j]

22"Men of Israel, listen to this: Jesus of Nazareth was a man
accredited by God to you by miracles, wonders and signs, which
God did among you through him, as you yourselves know. 23This
man was handed over to you by God's set purpose and foreknowledge; and you, with the help of wicked men,[k] put him to death
by nailing him to the cross. 24But God raised him from the dead,
freeing him from the agony of death, because it was impossible for
death to keep its hold on him. 25David said about him:

" 'I saw the Lord always before me.
Because he is at my right hand,
I will not be shaken.
26Therefore my heart is glad and my tongue rejoices;
my body also will live in hope,
27because you will not abandon me to the grave,
nor will you let your Holy One see decay.
28You have made known to me the paths of life;
you will fill me with joy in your presence.'[l]

29"Brothers, I can tell you confidently that the patriarch David
died and was buried, and his tomb is here to this day. 30But he was
a prophet and knew that God had promised him on oath that he
would place one of his descendants on his throne. 31Seeing what
was ahead, he spoke of the resurrection of the Christ,[m] that he was
not abandoned to the grave, nor did his body see decay. 32God has
raised this Jesus to life, and we are all witnesses of the fact. 33Exalt-

NIV [i] 13 Or *sweet wine* [j] 21 Joel 2:28-32 [k] 23 Or *of those not having the law* (that is, Gentiles) [l] 28 Psalm 16:8-11 [m] 31 Or *Messiah.* "The Christ" (Greek) and "the Messiah" (Hebrew) both mean "the Anointed One"; also in verse 36.

## King James

33Therefore being by the right hand of God exalted, and having received of the Father the promise of the Holy Ghost, he hath shed forth this, which ye now see and hear.

34For David is not ascended into the heavens: but he saith himself, The LORD said unto my Lord, Sit thou on my right hand,

35Until I make thy foes thy footstool.

36Therefore let all the house of Israel know assuredly, that God hath made that same Jesus, whom ye have crucified, both Lord and Christ.

37¶ Now when they heard *this*, they were pricked in their heart, and said unto Peter and to the rest of the apostles, Men *and* brethren, what shall we do?

38Then Peter said unto them, Repent, and be baptized every one of you in the name of Jesus Christ for the remission of sins, and ye shall receive the gift of the Holy Ghost.

39For the promise is unto you, and to your children, and to all that are afar off, *even* as many as the Lord our God shall call.

40And with many other words did he testify and exhort, saying, Save yourselves from this untoward generation.

41¶ Then they that gladly received his word were baptized: and the same day there were added *unto them* about three thousand souls.

42And they continued stedfastly in the apostles' doctrine and fellowship, and in breaking of bread, and in prayers.

43And fear came upon every soul: and many wonders and signs were done by the apostles.

44And all that believed were together, and had all things common;

45And sold their possessions and goods, and parted them to all *men*, as every man had need.

46And they, continuing daily with one accord in the temple, and breaking bread from house to house, did eat their meat with gladness and singleness of heart,

47Praising God, and having favour with all the people. And the Lord added to the church daily such as should be saved.

**3** NOW PETER and John went up together into the temple at the hour of prayer, *being* the ninth *hour*.

2And a certain man lame from his mother's womb was carried, whom they laid daily at the gate of the temple which is called Beautiful, to ask alms of them that entered into the temple;

3Who seeing Peter and John about to go into the temple asked an alms.

4And Peter, fastening his eyes upon him with John, said, Look on us.

5And he gave heed unto them, expecting to receive something of them.

## Amplified

33Being therefore lifted high by the right hand of God, and having received from the Father [a]the promised [blessing which is the] Holy Spirit, He has made this outpouring which you yourselves both see and hear.

34For David did not ascend into the heavens; yet he himself says, The Lord said to my Lord, Sit at My right hand, *and* share My throne

35Till I make Your enemies a footstool for Your feet. [Ps. 110:1.]

36Therefore let the whole house of Israel recognize beyond all doubt *and* acknowledge assuredly that God has made Him both Lord and Christ, the Messiah, this Jesus Whom you crucified.

37Now when they heard this they were stung (cut) to the heart, and they said to Peter and the rest of the apostles (special messengers), Brethren, what shall we do?

38And Peter answered them, Repent—change your views, and purpose to accept the will of God in your inner selves instead of rejecting it—and be baptized every one of you in the name of Jesus Christ for the forgiveness of *and* release from your sins; and you shall receive the gift of the Holy Spirit.

39For the promise (of the Holy Spirit) is to *and* for you and your children, and to *and* for all that are far away, [even] to as many as the Lord our God invites *and* bids come to Himself. [Isa. 57:19; Joel 2:32.]

40And [Peter] [b]solemnly *and* earnestly witnessed (testified) and admonished (exhorted) with much more continuous speaking *and* warned (reproved, advised, encouraged) them, saying, Be saved from this crooked (perverse, wicked, unjust) generation.

41Therefore those who accepted *and* welcomed his message were baptized, and there were added that day about three thousand souls.

42And they steadfastly persevered, devoting themselves constantly to the instruction and fellowship of the apostles, to the breaking of bread [including [c]the Lord's Supper] and prayers.

43And a sense of awe (reverential fear) came upon every soul, and many wonders and signs were performed through the apostles—the special messengers.

44And all who believed—that is, who adhered to and trusted in and relied on Jesus Christ—were united, *and* together they had everything in common;

45And they sold their possessions [both their landed property and their movable goods] and distributed the price among all, according as any had need.

46And day after day they regularly assembled in the temple with united purpose, and in their homes they broke bread [including the Lord's Supper]. They partook of their food with gladness and simplicity *and* generous hearts,

47Constantly praising God and being in favor *and* goodwill with all the people, and the Lord kept adding [to their number] daily those who were being saved (from spiritual death).

**3** NOW PETER and John were going up to the temple at the hour of prayer, the ninth hour (three o'clock in the afternoon),

2[When] a certain man crippled from his birth was being carried along, who was laid each day at that gate of the temple [which is] called Beautiful, that he might beg for charitable gifts from those who entered the temple.

3So when he saw Peter and John about to go into the temple, he asked them to give him a gift.

4And Peter directed his gaze intently at him, and so did John, and said, Look at us!

5And [the man] paid attention to them, expecting that he was going to get something from them.

**AMP** [a] Thayer. [b] Vincent: The preposition *dia* gives this force. [c] Many authorities.

## New American Standard

33"Therefore having been exalted to the right hand of God, and having received from the Father the promise of the Holy Spirit, He has poured forth this which you both see and hear.
34"For it was not David who ascended into heaven, but he himself says:
'THE LORD SAID TO MY LORD,
"SIT AT MY RIGHT HAND,
35 UNTIL I MAKE THINE ENEMIES A FOOTSTOOL FOR THY FEET."'
36"Therefore let all the house of Israel know for certain that God has made Him both Lord and Christ—this Jesus whom you crucified."

*The Ingathering*

37¶ Now when they heard *this*, they were pierced to the heart, and said to Peter and the rest of the apostles, "Brethren, what shall we do?"
38And Peter *said* to them, "Repent, and let each of you be baptized in the name of Jesus Christ for the forgiveness of your sins; and you shall receive the gift of the Holy Spirit.
39"For the promise is for you and your children, and for all who are far off, as many as the Lord our God shall call to Himself."
40And with many other words he solemnly testified and kept on exhorting them, saying, "Be saved from this perverse generation!"
41So then, those who had received his word were baptized; and there were added that day about three thousand [d]souls.
42And they were continually devoting themselves to the apostles' teaching and to fellowship, to the breaking of bread and to prayer.
43¶ And everyone kept feeling a sense of awe; and many wonders and signs were taking place through the apostles [e].
44And all those who had believed [f]were together, and had all things in common;
45and they *began* selling their property and possessions, and were sharing them with all, as anyone might have need.
46And day by day continuing with one mind in the temple, and breaking bread from house to house, they were taking their meals together with gladness and sincerity of heart,
47praising God, and having favor with all the people. And the Lord was adding to their number day by day those who were being saved.

*Healing the Lame Beggar*

3 NOW PETER and John were going up to the temple at the [g]ninth *hour*, the hour of prayer.
2And a certain man who had been lame from his mother's womb was being carried along, whom they used to set down every day at the gate of the temple which is called Beautiful, in order to beg [h]alms of those who were entering the temple.
3And when he saw Peter and John about to go into the temple, he *began* asking to receive alms.
4And Peter, along with John, fixed his gaze upon him and said, "Look at us!"
5And he *began* to give them his attention, expecting to receive something from them.

NAS [d] I.e., persons [e] Some ancient mss. add *in Jerusalem; and great fear was upon all* [f] Some ancient mss. do not contain *were* [g] I.e., 3 p.m. [h] Or, *a gift of charity*

## New International

ed to the right hand of God, he has received from the Father the promised Holy Spirit and has poured out what you now see and hear. 34For David did not ascend to heaven, and yet he said,
"'The Lord said to my Lord:
"Sit at my right hand
35until I make your enemies
a footstool for your feet."'[i]
36"Therefore let all Israel be assured of this: God has made this Jesus, whom you crucified, both Lord and Christ."
37When the people heard this, they were cut to the heart and said to Peter and the other apostles, "Brothers, what shall we do?"
38Peter replied, "Repent and be baptized, every one of you, in the name of Jesus Christ for the forgiveness of your sins. And you will receive the gift of the Holy Spirit. 39The promise is for you and your children and for all who are far off—for all whom the Lord our God will call."
40With many other words he warned them; and he pleaded with them, "Save yourselves from this corrupt generation."
41Those who accepted his message were baptized, and about three thousand were added to their number that day.

*The Fellowship of the Believers*

42They devoted themselves to the apostles' teaching and to the fellowship, to the breaking of bread and to prayer. 43Everyone was filled with awe, and many wonders and miraculous signs were done by the apostles. 44All the believers were together and had everything in common. 45Selling their possessions and goods, they gave to anyone as he had need. 46Every day they continued to meet together in the temple courts. They broke bread in their homes and ate together with glad and sincere hearts, 47praising God and enjoying the favor of all the people. And the Lord added to their number daily those who were being saved.

*Peter Heals the Crippled Beggar*

3 ONE DAY Peter and John were going up to the temple at the time of prayer—at three in the afternoon. 2Now a man crippled from birth was being carried to the temple gate called Beautiful, where he was put every day to beg from those going into the temple courts. 3When he saw Peter and John about to enter, he asked them for money. 4Peter looked straight at him, as did John. Then Peter said, "Look at us!" 5So the man gave them his attention, expecting to get something from them.

NIV [i] 35 Psalm 110:1

## King James

6Then Peter said, Silver and gold have I none; but such as I have give I thee: In the name of Jesus Christ of Nazareth rise up and walk.

7And he took him by the right hand, and lifted *him* up: and immediately his feet and ankle bones received strength.

8And he leaping up stood, and walked, and entered with them into the temple, walking, and leaping, and praising God.

9And all the people saw him walking and praising God:

10And they knew that it was he which sat for alms at the Beautiful gate of the temple: and they were filled with wonder and amazement at that which had happened unto him.

11And as the lame man which was healed held Peter and John, all the people ran together unto them in the porch that is called Solomon's, greatly wondering.

12¶ And when Peter saw *it,* he answered unto the people, Ye men of Israel, why marvel ye at this? or why look ye so earnestly on us, as though by our own power or holiness we had made this man to walk?

13The God of Abraham, and of Isaac, and of Jacob, the God of our fathers, hath glorified his Son Jesus; whom ye delivered up, and denied him in the presence of Pilate, when he was determined to let *him* go.

14But ye denied the Holy One and the Just, and desired a murderer to be granted unto you;

15And killed the Prince of life, whom God hath raised from the dead; whereof we are witnesses.

16And his name through faith in his name hath made this man strong, whom ye see and know: yea, the faith which is by him hath given him this perfect soundness in the presence of you all.

17And now, brethren, I wot that through ignorance ye did *it,* as *did* also your rulers.

18But those things, which God before had shown by the mouth of all his prophets, that Christ should suffer, he hath so fulfilled.

19¶ Repent ye therefore, and be converted, that your sins may be blotted out, when the times of refreshing shall come from the presence of the Lord;

20And he shall send Jesus Christ, which before was preached unto you:

21Whom the heaven must receive until the times of restitution of all things, which God hath spoken by the mouth of all his holy prophets since the world began.

22For Moses truly said unto the fathers, A prophet shall the Lord your God raise up unto you of your brethren, like unto me; him shall ye hear in all things whatsoever he shall say unto you.

23And it shall come to pass, *that* every soul, which will not hear that prophet, shall be destroyed from among the people.

24Yea, and all the prophets from Samuel and those that follow after, as many as have spoken, have likewise foretold of these days.

25Ye are the children of the prophets, and of the covenant which God made with our fathers, saying unto Abraham, And in thy seed shall all the kindreds of the earth be blessed.

26Unto you first God, having raised up his Son Jesus, sent him to bless you, in turning away every one of you from his iniquities.

## Amplified

6But Peter said, Silver and gold [money], I have none; but what I do have, that I give to you: in (the [a]use of) the name of Jesus Christ of Nazareth, walk!

7Then he took hold of the man's right hand with a firm grip and raised him up. And at once his feet and ankle bones became strong *and* steady,

8And leaping forth he stood and [b]began to walk, and he went into the temple with them, walking and leaping and praising God.

9And all the people saw him walking about and praising God,

10And they recognized him as the man who usually sat [begging] for alms at the Beautiful Gate of the temple, and they were filled with wonder and amazement (bewilderment, consternation) over what had occurred to him.

11Now while he [still] firmly clung to Peter and John, all the people in utmost amazement ran together *and* crowded around them in the covered porch (walk) called Solomon's.

12And Peter seeing it, answered the people, You men, Israelites, why are you so surprised *and* wondering at this? Why do you keep staring at us, as though by our [own individual] power *or* [active] piety we had made [this man able] to walk?

13The God of Abraham and of Isaac and of Jacob, the God of our forefathers, has glorified His Servant and [c]Son Jesus—doing Him this honor—Whom you indeed delivered up and denied *and* rejected *and* disowned in the presence of Pilate, when he had determined to let Him go. [Exod. 3:6; Isa. 52:13.]

14But you denied *and* rejected *and* disowned the Pure *and* Holy, the Just *and* Blameless One, and demanded [the pardon of] a murderer to be granted to you.

15But you killed the very Source—the Author—of life, Whom God raised from the dead. To this we are witnesses.

16And His name, through *and* by faith in His name, has made this man whom you see and recognize well *and* strong. [Yes,] the faith which is through *and* by Him [Jesus] has given the man this perfect soundness [of body] before all of you.

17And now, brethren, I know that you acted in ignorance—not aware of what you were doing—as did your rulers also.

18Thus has God fulfilled what He foretold by the mouth of all the prophets, that His Christ, the Messiah, should undergo ill treatment *and* be afflicted *and* suffer.

19So repent—change your mind *and* purpose; turn around *and* return [to God], that your sins may be erased (blotted out, wiped clean), that times of refreshing—of recovering from the effects of heat, of [d]reviving with fresh air—may come from the presence of the Lord;

20And that He may send [to you] the Christ, the Messiah, Who before was designated *and* appointed for you, Jesus,

21Whom heaven must receive [and retain] until the time for the complete restoration of all that God spoke by the mouth of all His holy prophets for ages past—from the most ancient time in the memory of man.

22Thus Moses said *to the forefathers,* The Lord God will raise up for you a Prophet from among your brethren as [He raised up] me; Him you shall listen to *and* understand by hearing, *and* heed in all things whatever He tells you.

23And it shall be that every soul that does not listen to *and* understand by hearing *and* heed that Prophet shall be utterly [e]exterminated from among the people. [Deut. 18:15-19; Lev. 23:29.]

24Indeed, all the prophets from Samuel and those who came afterwards, as many as have spoken also promised *and* foretold *and* proclaimed these days.

25You are the descendants (sons) of the prophets and the heirs of the covenant which God made *and* gave to your forefathers, saying to Abraham, And in your Seed (Heir), shall all the families of the earth be blessed *and* benefited. [Gen. 22:18; cf. Gal. 3:16.]

26It was to you first that God sent His Servant *and* [f]Son *Jesus,* when He raised Him up ([g]provided, gave Him) to bless you in turning every one of you from your wickedness *and* evil ways.

**AMP** [a] Thayer. [b] Vincent. [c] Alternate reading. [d] Vincent. [e] Souter. [f] Alternate reading. [g] Jamieson, Fausett and Brown.

## New American Standard

6But Peter said, "I do not possess silver and gold, but what I do have I give to you: In the name of Jesus Christ the Nazarene—walk!"

7And seizing him by the right hand, he raised him up; and immediately his feet and his ankles were strengthened.

8And with a leap, he stood upright and *began* to walk; and he entered the temple with them, walking and leaping and praising God.

9And all the people saw him walking and praising God;

10and they were taking note of him as being the one who used to sit at the Beautiful Gate of the temple to *beg* alms, and they were filled with wonder and amazement at what had happened to him.

*Peter's Second Sermon*

11¶ And while he was clinging to Peter and John, all the people ran together to them at the so-called portico of Solomon, full of amazement.

12But when Peter saw *this*, he replied to the people, "Men of Israel, why do you marvel at this, or why do you gaze at us, as if by our own power or piety we had made him walk?

13"The God of Abraham, Isaac, and Jacob, the God of our fathers, has glorified His servant Jesus, *the one* whom you delivered up, and disowned in the presence of Pilate, when he had decided to release Him.

14"But you disowned the Holy and Righteous One, and asked for a murderer to be granted to you,

15but put to death the Prince of life, *the one* whom God raised from the dead, *a fact* to which we are witnesses.

16"And on the basis of faith in His name, *it is* the name of Jesus which has strengthened this man whom you see and know; and the faith which *comes* through Him has given him this perfect health in the presence of you all.

17"And now, brethren, I know that you acted in ignorance, just as your rulers did also.

18"But the things which God announced beforehand by the mouth of all the prophets, that His Christ should suffer, He has thus fulfilled.

19"Repent therefore and return, that your sins may be wiped away, in order that times of refreshing may come from the presence of the Lord;

20and that He may send Jesus, the Christ appointed for you,

21whom heaven must receive until *the* period of restoration of all things about which God spoke by the mouth of His holy prophets from ancient time.

22"Moses said, 'THE LORD GOD SHALL RAISE UP FOR YOU A PROPHET LIKE ME FROM YOUR BRETHREN; TO HIM YOU SHALL GIVE HEED in everything He says to you.

23'And it shall be that every soul that does not heed that prophet shall be utterly destroyed from among the people.'

24"And likewise, all the prophets who have spoken, from Samuel and *his* successors onward, also announced these days.

25"It is you who are the sons of the prophets, and of the covenant which God made with your fathers, saying to Abraham, 'AND IN YOUR SEED ALL THE FAMILIES OF THE EARTH SHALL BE BLESSED.'

26"For you first, God raised up His Servant, and sent Him to bless you by turning every one *of you* from your wicked ways."

## New International

6Then Peter said, "Silver or gold I do not have, but what I have
I give you. In the name of Jesus Christ of Nazareth, walk." 7Taking
him by the right hand, he helped him up, and instantly the man's
feet and ankles became strong. 8He jumped to his feet and began
to walk. Then he went with them into the temple courts, walking
and jumping, and praising God. 9When all the people saw him
walking and praising God, 10they recognized him as the same man
who used to sit begging at the temple gate called Beautiful, and
they were filled with wonder and amazement at what had happened to him.

*Peter Speaks to the Onlookers*

11While the beggar held on to Peter and John, all the people
were astonished and came running to them in the place called
Solomon's Colonnade. 12When Peter saw this, he said to them:
"Men of Israel, why does this surprise you? Why do you stare at
us as if by our own power or godliness we had made this man
walk? 13The God of Abraham, Isaac and Jacob, the God of our
fathers, has glorified his servant Jesus. You handed him over to be
killed, and you disowned him before Pilate, though he had decided to let him go. 14You disowned the Holy and Righteous One
and asked that a murderer be released to you. 15You killed the
author of life, but God raised him from the dead. We are witnesses
of this. 16By faith in the name of Jesus, this man whom you see and
know was made strong. It is Jesus' name and the faith that comes
through him that has given this complete healing to him, as you
can all see.

17"Now, brothers, I know that you acted in ignorance, as did
your leaders. 18But this is how God fulfilled what he had foretold
through all the prophets, saying that his Christ[h] would suffer.
19Repent, then, and turn to God, so that your sins may be wiped
out, that times of refreshing may come from the Lord, 20and that
he may send the Christ, who has been appointed for you—even
Jesus. 21He must remain in heaven until the time comes for God
to restore everything, as he promised long ago through his holy
prophets. 22For Moses said, 'The Lord your God will raise up for
you a prophet like me from among your own people; you must
listen to everything he tells you. 23Anyone who does not listen to
him will be completely cut off from among his people.'[i]

24"Indeed, all the prophets from Samuel on, as many as have
spoken, have foretold these days. 25And you are heirs of the
prophets and of the covenant God made with your fathers. He said
to Abraham, 'Through your offspring all peoples on earth will be
blessed.'[j] 26When God raised up his servant, he sent him first to
you to bless you by turning each of you from your wicked ways."

NIV [h] *18* Or *Messiah;* also in verse 20 [i] *23* Deut. 18:15,18,19 [j] *25* Gen. 22:18; 26:4

## King James

**4** AND AS they spake unto the people, the priests, and the captain of the temple, and the Sadducees, came upon them,

2 Being grieved that they taught the people, and preached through Jesus the resurrection from the dead.

3 And they laid hands on them, and put *them* in hold unto the next day: for it was now eventide.

4 Howbeit many of them which heard the word believed; and the number of the men was about five thousand.

5 ¶ And it came to pass on the morrow, that their rulers, and elders, and scribes,

6 And Annas the high priest, and Caiaphas, and John, and Alexander, and as many as were of the kindred of the high priest, were gathered together at Jerusalem.

7 And when they had set them in the midst, they asked, By what power, or by what name, have ye done this?

8 Then Peter, filled with the Holy Ghost, said unto them, Ye rulers of the people, and elders of Israel,

9 If we this day be examined of the good deed done to the impotent man, by what means he is made whole;

10 Be it known unto you all, and to all the people of Israel, that by the name of Jesus Christ of Nazareth, whom ye crucified, whom God raised from the dead, *even* by him doth this man stand here before you whole.

11 This is the stone which was set at nought of you builders, which is become the head of the corner.

12 Neither is there salvation in any other: for there is none other name under heaven given among men, whereby we must be saved.

13 ¶ Now when they saw the boldness of Peter and John, and perceived that they were unlearned and ignorant men, they marvelled; and they took knowledge of them, that they had been with Jesus.

14 And beholding the man which was healed standing with them, they could say nothing against it.

15 But when they had commanded them to go aside out of the council, they conferred among themselves,

16 Saying, What shall we do to these men? for that indeed a notable miracle hath been done by them *is* manifest to all them that dwell in Jerusalem; and we cannot deny *it*.

17 But that it spread no further among the people, let us straitly threaten them, that they speak henceforth to no man in this name.

18 And they called them, and commanded them not to speak at all nor teach in the name of Jesus.

19 But Peter and John answered and said unto them, Whether it be right in the sight of God to hearken unto you more than unto God, judge ye.

20 For we cannot but speak the things which we have seen and heard.

21 So when they had further threatened them, they let them go, finding nothing how they might punish them, because of the people: for all *men* glorified God for that which was done.

22 For the man was above forty years old, on whom this miracle of healing was shown.

23 ¶ And being let go, they went to their own company, and reported all that the chief priests and elders had said unto them.

## Amplified

**4** AND WHILE they [Peter and John] were talking to the people, the high priests and the military commander of the temple, and the Sadducees came upon them,

2 Being vexed *and* indignant through *and* through because they were teaching the people *and* proclaiming in [the case of] Jesus the resurrection from the dead.

3 So they laid hands on them (arrested them) and put them in prison until the following day, for it was already evening.

4 But many of those who heard the message believed—adhered to and trusted in and relied on [Jesus as the Christ]. And their number grew *and* came to about five thousand.

5 Then on the following day their magistrates and elders and scribes were assembled in Jerusalem,

6 Including Annas the high priest and Caiaphas and John and Alexander, and all others who belonged to the high priestly relationship.

7 And they set the men in the midst and repeatedly demanded, By what sort of power or by what kind of authority did [such people as] you do this [healing]?

8 Then Peter, [because he was] filled with [and controlled by] the Holy Spirit, said to them, Rulers of the people and members of the council,

9 If we are being put on trial [here] today *and* examined concerning a good deed done to benefit a feeble (helpless) cripple, by what means this man has been restored to health,

10 Let it be known *and* understood by you all, and by the whole house of Israel, that in the name and through the power *and* authority of Jesus Christ of Nazareth, Whom you crucified, [but] Whom God raised from the dead, in Him *and* by means [of Him] this man is standing here before you well *and* sound in body.

11 This [Jesus] is the Stone which was despised *and* rejected by you, the builders, but which has become the Head [the external angle] of the corner—the Cornerstone. [Ps. 118:22.]

12 And there is salvation in *and* through no one else, for there is no other name under heaven given among men by *and* in which we must be saved.

13 Now when they saw the boldness *and* unfettered eloquence of Peter and John, and perceived that they were unlearned *and* untrained in the schools—common men with no advantages—they marvelled; and they recognized that they had been with Jesus.

14 And since they saw the man who had been cured standing there beside them, they could not contradict the fact *or* say anything in opposition.

15 But, having ordered [the prisoners] to go aside out of the council [chamber], they conferred (debated) among themselves,

16 Saying, What are we to do with these men? For that an extraordinary miracle has been performed by (through) them is plain to all the residents of Jerusalem, and we cannot deny it.

17 But in order that it may not spread further among the people *and* the nation, let us warn *and* forbid them with a stern threat to speak any more to any one in this name—or about this Person.

18 [So] they summoned them and imperatively instructed them not to converse in any way *or* teach at all in *or* about the name of Jesus.

19 But Peter and John replied to them, Whether it is right in the sight of God to listen to you *and* obey you rather than God, you must decide (judge).

20 But we [ourselves] cannot help telling what we have seen and heard.

21 Then when [the rulers and council members] had further threatened them, they let them go, not seeing how they could secure a conviction against them, because of the people; for everybody was praising *and* glorifying God for what had occurred,

22 For the man on whom this sign (miracle) of healing was performed was more than forty years old.

23 After they were permitted to go, [the apostles] returned to their own [company] and told all that the chief priests and elders had said to them.

## New American Standard

*Peter and John Arrested*

4 AND AS they were speaking to the people, the priests and the captain of the temple *guard,* and the Saddducees, came upon them,

2being greatly disturbed because they were teaching the people and proclaiming in Jesus the resurrection from the dead.

3And they laid hands on them, and put them in jail until the next day, for it was already evening.

4But many of those who had heard the message believed; and the number of the men came to be about five thousand.

5¶ And it came about on the next day, that their rulers and elders and scribes were gathered together in Jerusalem;

6and Annas the high priest *was there,* and Caiaphas and John and Alexander, and all who were of high-priestly descent.

7And when they had placed them in the center, they *began to* inquire, "By what power, or in what name, have you done this?"

8Then Peter, filled with the Holy Spirit, said to them, "Rulers and elders of the people,

9if we are on trial today for a benefit done to a sick man, as to how this man has been made well,

10let it be known to all of you, and to all the people of Israel, that by the name of Jesus Christ the Nazarene, whom you crucified, whom God raised from the dead—by this *name* this man stands here before you in good health.

11"He is the STONE WHICH WAS REJECTED by you, THE BUILDERS, *but* WHICH BECAME THE VERY CORNER *stone.*

12"And there is salvation in no one else; for there is no other name under heaven that has been given among men, by which we must be saved."

*Threat and Release*

13¶ Now as they observed the confidence of Peter and John, and understood that they were uneducated and untrained men, they were marveling, and *began* to recognize them as having been with Jesus.

14And seeing the man who had been healed standing with them, they had nothing to say in reply.

15But when they had ordered them to go aside out of the Council, they *began* to confer with one another,

16saying, "What shall we do with these men? For the fact that a noteworthy miracle has taken place through them is apparent to all who live in Jerusalem, and we cannot deny it.

17"But in order that it may not spread any further among the people, let us warn them to speak no more to any man in this name."

18And when they had summoned them, they commanded them not to speak or teach at all in the name of Jesus.

19But Peter and John answered and said to them, "Whether it is right in the sight of God to give heed to you rather than to God, you be the judge;

20for we cannot stop speaking what we have seen and heard."

21And when they had threatened them further, they let them go (finding no basis on which they might punish them) on account of the people, because they were all glorifying God for what had happened;

22for the man was more than forty years old on whom this miracle of healing had been performed.

23¶ And when they had been released, they went to their own *companions,* and reported all that the chief priests and the elders had said to them.

## New International

*Peter and John Before the Sanhedrin*

4 THE PRIESTS and the captain of the temple guard and the Sadducees came up to Peter and John while they were speaking to the people. 2They were greatly disturbed because the apos-
tles were teaching the people and proclaiming in Jesus the resurrection of the dead. 3They seized Peter and John, and because it
was evening, they put them in jail until the next day. 4But many
who heard the message believed, and the number of men grew to
about five thousand.

5The next day the rulers, elders and teachers of the law met in
Jerusalem. 6Annas the high priest was there, and so were Caiaphas, John, Alexander and the other men of the high priest's
family. 7They had Peter and John brought before them and began
to question them: "By what power or what name did you do this?"
8Then Peter, filled with the Holy Spirit, said to them: "Rulers
and elders of the people! 9If we are being called to account today
for an act of kindness shown to a cripple and are asked how he was
healed, 10then know this, you and all the people of Israel: It is by
the name of Jesus Christ of Nazareth, whom you crucified but
whom God raised from the dead, that this man stands before you
healed. 11He is

"'the stone you builders rejected,
which has become the capstone.[a]' [b]

12Salvation is found in no one else, for there is no other name
under heaven given to men by which we must be saved."

13When they saw the courage of Peter and John and realized
that they were unschooled, ordinary men, they were astonished
and they took note that these men had been with Jesus. 14But since
they could see the man who had been healed standing there with
them, there was nothing they could say. 15So they ordered them
to withdraw from the Sanhedrin and then conferred together.
16"What are we going to do with these men?" they asked. "Everybody living in Jerusalem knows they have done an outstanding
miracle, and we cannot deny it. 17But to stop this thing from
spreading any further among the people, we must warn these men
to speak no longer to anyone in this name."

18Then they called them in again and commanded them not to
speak or teach at all in the name of Jesus. 19But Peter and John
replied, "Judge for yourselves whether it is right in God's sight to
obey you rather than God. 20For we cannot help speaking about
what we have seen and heard."

21After further threats they let them go. They could not decide
how to punish them, because all the people were praising God for
what had happened. 22For the man who was miraculously healed
was over forty years old.

*The Believers' Prayer*

23On their release, Peter and John went back to their own
people and reported all that the chief priests and elders had said
to them. 24When they heard this, they raised their voices together

NIV [a] *11* Or *cornerstone* [b] *11* Psalm 118:22

## King James

24And when they heard that, they lifted up their voice to God with one accord, and said, Lord, thou *art* God, which hast made heaven, and earth, and the sea, and all that in them is:
25Who by the mouth of thy servant David hast said, Why did the heathen rage, and the people imagine vain things?
26The kings of the earth stood up, and the rulers were gathered together against the Lord, and against his Christ.
27For of a truth against thy holy child Jesus, whom thou hast anointed, both Herod, and Pontius Pilate, with the Gentiles, and the people of Israel, were gathered together,
28For to do whatsoever thy hand and thy counsel determined before to be done.
29And now, Lord, behold their threatenings: and grant unto thy servants, that with all boldness they may speak thy word,
30By stretching forth thine hand to heal; and that signs and wonders may be done by the name of thy holy child Jesus.
31¶ And when they had prayed, the place was shaken where they were assembled together; and they were all filled with the Holy Ghost, and they spake the word of God with boldness.
32And the multitude of them that believed were of one heart and of one soul: neither said any *of them* that aught of the things which he possessed was his own; but they had all things common.
33And with great power gave the apostles witness of the resurrection of the Lord Jesus: and great grace was upon them all.
34Neither was there any among them that lacked: for as many as were possessors of lands or houses sold them, and brought the prices of the things that were sold,
35And laid *them* down at the apostles' feet: and distribution was made unto every man according as he had need.
36And Joses, who by the apostles was surnamed Barnabas, (which is, being interpreted, The son of consolation,) a Levite, *and* of the country of Cyprus,
37Having land, sold *it*, and brought the money, and laid *it* at the apostles' feet.

**5** BUT A certain man named Ananias, with Sapphira his wife, sold a possession,
2And kept back *part* of the price, his wife also being privy *to it*, and brought a certain part, and laid *it* at the apostles' feet.
3But Peter said, Ananias, why hath Satan filled thine heart to lie to the Holy Ghost, and to keep back *part* of the price of the land?
4Whiles it remained, was it not thine own? and after it was sold, was it not in thine own power? why hast thou conceived this thing in thine heart? thou hast not lied unto men, but unto God.
5And Ananias hearing these words fell down, and gave up the ghost: and great fear came on all them that heard these things.
6And the young men arose, wound him up, and carried *him* out, and buried *him*.

## Amplified

24And they, when they heard it, lifted their voices together with one united mind to God and said, O Sovereign Lord, You are He Who made the heaven and the earth and the sea and everything that is in them, [Exod. 20:11; Ps. 146:6.]
25Who by the mouth of our forefather David, Your servant *and* [a]child, said through the Holy Spirit, Why did the heathen [Gentiles] become wanton *and* insolent *and* rage, and the people imagine *and* study *and* plan vain (fruitless) things—that will not succeed?
26The kings of the earth took their stand in array [for attack], and the rulers were assembled *and* combined together against the Lord and against His Anointed, Christ, the Messiah. [Ps. 2:1, 2.]
27For in this city there actually met and plotted together against Your holy Child *and* [b]Servant Jesus, Whom You consecrated by anointing, both Herod and Pontius Pilate with the Gentiles and peoples of Israel, [Ps. 2:1, 2.]
28To carry out all that Your hand and Your will *and* purpose had predestined (predetermined) should occur.
29And now, Lord, observe their threats and grant to Your bond servants [full freedom] to declare Your message fearlessly,
30While You stretch out Your hand to cure and to perform signs *and* wonders through the authority *and* by the power of the name of Your holy Child *and* [c]Servant Jesus.
31And when they had prayed, the place in which they were assembled was shaken; and they were all filled with the Holy Spirit, and they continued to speak the Word of God with freedom *and* boldness *and* courage.
32Now the company of believers was of one heart and soul, and not one of them claimed that anything which he possessed was [exclusively] his own, but everything they had was in common *and* for the use of all.
33And with great strength *and* ability *and* power the apostles delivered their testimony to the resurrection of the Lord Jesus, and great grace—loving kindness and favor and goodwill—rested richly upon them all.
34Nor was there a destitute *or* needy person among them, for as many as were owners of lands or houses proceeded to sell them, and one by one they brought (gave back) the amount received from the sales
35And laid it at the feet of the apostles. Then distribution was made according as any one had need.
36Now Joseph, a Levite and native of Cyprus who was surnamed Barnabas by the apostles (special messengers), which interpreted means, Son of Encouragement,
37Sold a field which belonged to him, and brought the sum of money and laid it at the feet of the apostles.

**5** BUT A certain man named Ananias with his wife Sapphira sold a piece of property,
2And with his wife's knowledge *and* connivance he kept back *and* wrongfully appropriated some of the proceeds, bringing a part only and putting it at the feet of the apostles.
3But Peter said, Ananias, why has Satan filled your heart that you should lie to *and* attempt to deceive the Holy Spirit, and should [in violation of your promise] withdraw secretly *and* appropriate to your own use part of the price from the sale of the land?
4As long as it remained unsold, was it not still your own? And [even] after it was sold, was not [the money] at your disposal *and* under your control? Why then, is it that you have proposed *and* purposed in your heart to do this thing?—How could you have the heart to do such a deed? You have not (simply) lied to men—playing false and showing yourself utterly deceitful—but to God.
5Upon hearing these words, Ananias fell down and died. And great dread *and* terror took possession of all who heard of it.
6And the young men arose and wrapped up [the body] and carried it out [and] buried it.

AMP [a] Alternate reading. [b] Alternate reading. [c] Alternate reading.

## New American Standard

24And when they heard *this,* they lifted their voices to God with
one accord and said, "O Lord, it is Thou who DIDST MAKE THE
HEAVEN AND THE EARTH AND THE SEA, AND ALL THAT IS IN THEM,
25who by the Holy Spirit, *through* the mouth of our father David
Thy servant, didst say,
'WHY DID THE [d]GENTILES RAGE,
AND THE PEOPLES DEVISE FUTILE THINGS?
26 'THE KINGS OF THE EARTH TOOK THEIR STAND,
AND THE RULERS WERE GATHERED TOGETHER
AGAINST THE LORD, AND AGAINST HIS CHRIST.'
27"For truly in this city there were gathered together against
Thy holy servant Jesus, whom Thou didst anoint, both Herod and
Pontius Pilate, along with the Gentiles and the peoples of Israel,
28to do whatever Thy hand and Thy purpose predestined to
occur.
29"And now, Lord, take note of their threats, and grant that Thy
bond-servants may speak Thy word with all confidence,
30while Thou dost extend Thy hand to heal, and signs and
wonders take place through the name of Thy holy servant Jesus."
31And when they had prayed, the place where they had gathered together was shaken, and they were all filled with the Holy
Spirit, and *began* to speak the word of God with boldness.

*Sharing among Believers*

32¶ And the congregation of those who believed were of one
heart and soul; and not one *of them* claimed that anything belonging to him was his own; but all things were common property to
them.
33And with great power the apostles were giving witness to the
resurrection of the Lord Jesus, and abundant grace was upon them
all.
34For there was not a needy person among them, for all who
were owners of land or houses would sell them and bring the
proceeds of the sales,
35and lay them at the apostles' feet; and they would be distributed to each, as any had need.
36¶ And Joseph, a Levite of Cyprian birth, who was also called
Barnabas by the apostles (which translated means, Son of Encouragement),
37and who owned a tract of land, sold it and brought the money
and laid it at the apostles' feet.

*Fate of Ananias and Sapphira*

5 BUT A certain man named Ananias, with his wife Sapphira,
sold a piece of property,
2and kept back *some* of the price for himself, with his wife's full
knowledge, and bringing a portion of it, he laid it at the apostles'
feet.
3But Peter said, "Ananias, why has Satan filled your heart to
lie to the Holy Spirit, and to keep back *some* of the price of the land?
4"While it remained *unsold,* did it not remain your own? And
after it was sold, was it not under your control? Why is it that you
have conceived this deed in your heart? You have not lied to men,
but to God."
5And as he heard these words, Ananias fell down and
breathed his last; and great fear came upon all who heard of it.
6And the young men arose and covered him up, and after
carrying him out, they buried him.

NAS [d] Or, *nations*

## New International

in prayer to God. "Sovereign Lord," they said, "you made the
heaven and the earth and the sea, and everything in them. 25You
spoke by the Holy Spirit through the mouth of your servant, our
father David:

"Why do the nations rage
and the peoples plot in vain?
26The kings of the earth take their stand
and the rulers gather together
against the Lord
and against his Anointed One.[e][f]

27Indeed Herod and Pontius Pilate met together with the Gentiles
and the peoples[g] of Israel in this city to conspire against your holy
servant Jesus, whom you anointed. 28They did what your power
and will had decided beforehand should happen. 29Now, Lord,
consider their threats and enable your servants to speak your word
with great boldness. 30Stretch out your hand to heal and perform
miraculous signs and wonders through the name of your holy
servant Jesus."
31After they prayed, the place where they were meeting was
shaken. And they were all filled with the Holy Spirit and spoke the
word of God boldly.

*The Believers Share Their Possessions*

32All the believers were one in heart and mind. No one claimed
that any of his possessions was his own, but they shared everything they had. 33With great power the apostles continued to
testify to the resurrection of the Lord Jesus, and much grace was
upon them all. 34There were no needy persons among them. For
from time to time those who owned lands or houses sold them,
brought the money from the sales 35and put it at the apostles' feet,
and it was distributed to anyone as he had need.
36Joseph, a Levite from Cyprus, whom the apostles called Barnabas (which means Son of Encouragement), 37sold a field he
owned and brought the money and put it at the apostles' feet.

*Ananias and Sapphira*

5 NOW A man named Ananias, together with his wife Sapphira, also sold a piece of property. 2With his wife's full
knowledge he kept back part of the money for himself, but brought
the rest and put it at the apostles' feet.
3Then Peter said, "Ananias, how is it that Satan has so filled
your heart that you have lied to the Holy Spirit and have kept for
yourself some of the money you received for the land? 4Didn't it
belong to you before it was sold? And after it was sold, wasn't the
money at your disposal? What made you think of doing such a
thing? You have not lied to men but to God."
5When Ananias heard this, he fell down and died. And great
fear seized all who heard what had happened. 6Then the young
men came forward, wrapped up his body, and carried him out and
buried him.

NIV [e] *26* That is, Christ or Messiah [f] *26* Psalm 2:1,2 [g] *27* The Greek is plural.

## King James

7And it was about the space of three hours after, when his wife, not knowing what was done, came in.

8And Peter answered unto her, Tell me whether ye sold the land for so much? And she said, Yea, for so much.

9Then Peter said unto her, How is it that ye have agreed together to tempt the Spirit of the Lord? behold, the feet of them which have buried thy husband *are* at the door, and shall carry thee out.

10Then fell she down straightway at his feet, and yielded up the ghost: and the young men came in, and found her dead, and, carrying *her* forth, buried *her* by her husband.

11And great fear came upon all the church, and upon as many as heard these things.

12¶ And by the hands of the apostles were many signs and wonders wrought among the people; (and they were all with one accord in Solomon's porch.

13And of the rest durst no man join himself to them: but the people magnified them.

14And believers were the more added to the Lord, multitudes both of men and women.)

15Insomuch that they brought forth the sick into the streets, and laid *them* on beds and couches, that at the least the shadow of Peter passing by might overshadow some of them.

16There came also a multitude *out* of the cities round about unto Jerusalem, bringing sick folks, and them which were vexed with unclean spirits: and they were healed every one.

17¶ Then the high priest rose up, and all they that were with him, (which is the sect of the Sadducees,) and were filled with indignation,

18And laid their hands on the apostles, and put them in the common prison.

19But the angel of the Lord by night opened the prison doors, and brought them forth, and said,

20Go, stand and speak in the temple to the people all the words of this life.

21And when they heard *that*, they entered into the temple early in the morning, and taught. But the high priest came, and they that were with him, and called the council together, and all the senate of the children of Israel, and sent to the prison to have them brought.

22But when the officers came, and found them not in the prison, they returned, and told,

23Saying, The prison truly found we shut with all safety, and the keepers standing without before the doors: but when we had opened, we found no man within.

24Now when the high priest and the captain of the temple and the chief priests heard these things, they doubted of them whereunto this would grow.

25Then came one and told them, saying, Behold, the men whom ye put in prison are standing in the temple, and teaching the people.

26Then went the captain with the officers, and brought them without violence: for they feared the people, lest they should have been stoned.

27And when they had brought them, they set *them* before the council: and the high priest asked them,

28Saying, Did not we straitly command you that ye should not teach in this name? and, behold, ye have filled Jerusalem with your doctrine, and intend to bring this man's blood upon us.

29¶ Then Peter and the *other* apostles answered and said, We ought to obey God rather than men.

30The God of our fathers raised up Jesus, whom ye slew and hanged on a tree.

## Amplified

7Now after an interval of about three hours his wife came in, not having learned of what had happened.

8And Peter said to her, Tell me, did you sell the land for so much? Yes, she said, for so much.

9Then Peter said to her, How could you two have agreed *and* conspired together to try to deceive the Spirit of the Lord? Listen! The feet of those who have buried your husband are at the door, and they will carry you out [also].

10And instantly she fell down at his feet and died, and the young men entering found her dead, and they carried her out and buried her beside her husband.

11And the whole church was appalled—great awe and strange terror and dread seized them—and all others who heard of these things.

12Now by the hands of the apostles (special messengers) numerous *and* startling signs *and* wonders were being performed among the people. And by common consent they all met together [at the temple] in the porch *or* covered walk called Solomon's.

13And none of those who were not of their number dared to join *and* associate with them, but the people held them in high regard *and* praised *and* made much of them.

14More *and* more there were being added to the Lord those who believed—[that is,] those who acknowledged Jesus as their Savior and devoted themselves to Him, joined and gathered with them—crowds both of men and of women.

15So that they [even] kept carrying out the sick into the streets and placing them on couches and sleeping pads, [in the hope] that as Peter passed by at least his shadow might fall on some of them.

16And the people gathered also from the towns *and* hamlets around Jerusalem, bringing the sick and those troubled with foul spirits, and they were all cured.

17But the high priest rose up and all who were his supporters, that is, the party of the Sadducees, and being filled with [a]jealousy *and* indignation *and* rage

18They seized and arrested the apostles (special messengers) and put them in the public jail.

19But during the night an angel of the Lord opened the prison doors and leading them out said,

20Go, take your stand in the temple courts and declare to the people the whole doctrine concerning this Life [the eternal life which Christ revealed].

21And when they heard this, they accordingly went into the temple about daybreak and began to teach. Now the high priest and his supporters who were with him arrived and called together the council (Sanhedrin) and [even] all the senate of the Jews, and they sent to the prison to have [the apostles] brought.

22But when the attendants arrived there they failed to find them in the jail; so they came back and reported,

23We found the prison quite safely locked up and the guards were on duty outside the doors, but when we opened [it] we found no one on the inside.

24Now when the military leader of the temple area and the chief priests heard these facts, they were much perplexed *and* thoroughly at a loss about them, wondering into what this might grow.

25But some man came and reported to them, saying, Listen! The men whom you put in jail are standing [right here] in the temple and teaching the people!

26Then the military leader went with the attendants and brought [the prisoners], but without violence for they dreaded the people lest they be stoned by them.

27So they brought them [and] set them before the council (Sanhedrin). And the high priest examined them by questioning,

28Saying, We definitely commanded *and* strictly charged you not to teach in *or* about this Name; yet here you have flooded Jerusalem with your doctrine and you intend to bring this [b]Man's blood upon us.

29Then Peter and the apostles replied, We must obey God rather than men.

30The God of our forefathers raised up Jesus Whom you killed by hanging Him on a tree (cross). [Deut. 21:22, 23.]

**AMP** [a] Abbott-Smith. [b] Capitalized because of what He is, the spotless Son of God, not what the speakers may have thought Him to be.

## New American Standard

7¶ Now there elapsed an interval of about three hours, and his wife came in, not knowing what had happened.

8And Peter responded to her, "Tell me whether you sold the land for such and such a price?" And she said, "Yes, that was the price."

9Then Peter *said* to her, "Why is it that you have agreed together to put the Spirit of the Lord to the test? Behold, the feet of those who have buried your husband are at the door, and they shall carry you out *as well*."

10And she fell immediately at his feet, and breathed her last; and the young men came in and found her dead, and they carried her out and buried her beside her husband.

11And great fear came upon the whole church, and upon all who heard of these things.

12¶ And at the hands of the apostles many signs and wonders were taking place among the people; and they were all with one accord in Solomon's portico.

13But none of the rest dared to associate with them; however, the people held them in high esteem.

14And all the more believers in the Lord, multitudes of men and women, were constantly added to *their number;*

15to such an extent that they even carried the sick out into the streets, and laid them on cots and pallets, so that when Peter came by, at least his shadow might fall on any one of them.

16And also the people from the cities in the vicinity of Jerusalem were coming together, bringing people who were sick [c]or afflicted with unclean spirits; and they were all being healed.

*Imprisonment and Release*

17¶ But the high priest rose up, along with all his associates (that is the sect of the Sadducees), and they were filled with jealousy;

18and they laid hands on the apostles, and put them in a public jail.

19But an angel of the Lord during the night opened the gates of the prison, and taking them out he said,

20"Go your way, stand and speak to the people in the temple the whole message of this Life."

21And upon hearing *this,* they entered into the temple about daybreak, and *began* to teach. Now when the high priest and his associates had come, they called the Council together, even all the Senate of the sons of Israel, and sent *orders* to the prison house for them to be brought.

22But the officers who came did not find them in the prison; and they returned, and reported back,

23saying, "We found the prison house locked quite securely and the guards standing at the doors; but when we had opened up, we found no one inside."

24Now when the captain of the temple *guard* and the chief priests heard these words, they were greatly perplexed about them as to what would come of this.

25But someone came and reported to them, "Behold, the men whom you put in prison are standing in the temple and teaching the people!"

26Then the captain went along with the officers and *proceeded* to bring them *back* without violence (for they were afraid of the people, lest they should be stoned).

27And when they had brought them, they stood them before the Council. And the high priest questioned them,

28saying, "We gave you strict orders not to continue teaching in this name, and behold, you have filled Jerusalem with your teaching, and intend to bring this man's blood upon us."

29But Peter and the apostles answered and said, "We must obey God rather than men.

30"The God of our fathers raised up Jesus, whom you had put to death by hanging Him on a cross.

NAS c Lit., *and*

## New International

7About three hours later his wife came in, not knowing what
had happened. 8Peter asked her, "Tell me, is this the price you and
Ananias got for the land?"

"Yes," she said, "that is the price."

9Peter said to her, "How could you agree to test the Spirit of the
Lord? Look! The feet of the men who buried your husband are at
the door, and they will carry you out also."

10At that moment she fell down at his feet and died. Then the
young men came in and, finding her dead, carried her out and
buried her beside her husband. 11Great fear seized the whole
church and all who heard about these events.

*The Apostles Heal Many*

12The apostles performed many miraculous signs and wonders
among the people. And all the believers used to meet together in
Solomon's Colonnade. 13No one else dared join them, even
though they were highly regarded by the people. 14Nevertheless,
more and more men and women believed in the Lord and were
added to their number. 15As a result, people brought the sick into
the streets and laid them on beds and mats so that at least Peter's
shadow might fall on some of them as he passed by. 16Crowds
gathered also from the towns around Jerusalem, bringing their sick
and those tormented by evil[d] spirits, and all of them were healed.

*The Apostles Persecuted*

17Then the high priest and all his associates, who were members of the party of the Sadducees, were filled with jealousy.
18They arrested the apostles and put them in the public jail. 19But
during the night an angel of the Lord opened the doors of the jail
and brought them out. 20"Go, stand in the temple courts," he said,
"and tell the people the full message of this new life."

21At daybreak they entered the temple courts, as they had been
told, and began to teach the people.

When the high priest and his associates arrived, they called
together the Sanhedrin—the full assembly of the elders of Israel—
and sent to the jail for the apostles. 22But on arriving at the jail, the
officers did not find them there. So they went back and reported,
23"We found the jail securely locked, with the guards standing at
the doors; but when we opened them, we found no one inside."
24On hearing this report, the captain of the temple guard and the
chief priests were puzzled, wondering what would come of this.

25Then someone came and said, "Look! The men you put in jail
are standing in the temple courts teaching the people." 26At that,
the captain went with his officers and brought the apostles. They
did not use force, because they feared that the people would stone
them.

27Having brought the apostles, they made them appear before
the Sanhedrin to be questioned by the high priest. 28"We gave you
strict orders not to teach in this name," he said. "Yet you have
filled Jerusalem with your teaching and are determined to make us
guilty of this man's blood."

29Peter and the other apostles replied: "We must obey God
rather than men! 30The God of our fathers raised Jesus from the
dead—whom you had killed by hanging him on a tree. 31God

NIV d 16 Greek *unclean*

## King James

31Him hath God exalted with his right hand *to be* a Prince and a Saviour, for to give repentance to Israel, and forgiveness of sins.

32And we are his witnesses of these things; and *so is* also the Holy Ghost, whom God hath given to them that obey him.

33¶ When they heard *that,* they were cut *to the heart,* and took counsel to slay them.

34Then stood there up one in the council, a Pharisee, named Gamaliel, a doctor of the law, had in reputation among all the people, and commanded to put the apostles forth a little space;

35And said unto them, Ye men of Israel, take heed to yourselves what ye intend to do as touching these men.

36For before these days rose up Theudas, boasting himself to be somebody; to whom a number of men, about four hundred, joined themselves: who was slain; and all, as many as obeyed him, were scattered, and brought to nought.

37After this man rose up Judas of Galilee in the days of the taxing, and drew away much people after him: he also perished; and all, *even* as many as obeyed him, were dispersed.

38And now I say unto you, Refrain from these men, and let them alone: for if this counsel or this work be of men, it will come to nought:

39But if it be of God, ye cannot overthrow it; lest haply ye be found even to fight against God.

40And to him they agreed: and when they had called the apostles, and beaten *them,* they commanded that they should not speak in the name of Jesus, and let them go.

41¶ And they departed from the presence of the council, rejoicing that they were counted worthy to suffer shame for his name.

42And daily in the temple, and in every house, they ceased not to teach and preach Jesus Christ.

6 AND IN those days, when the number of the disciples was multiplied, there arose a murmuring of the Grecians against the Hebrews, because their widows were neglected in the daily ministration.

2Then the twelve called the multitude of the disciples *unto them,* and said, It is not reason that we should leave the word of God, and serve tables.

3Wherefore, brethren, look ye out among you seven men of honest report, full of the Holy Ghost and wisdom, whom we may appoint over this business.

4But we will give ourselves continually to prayer, and to the ministry of the word.

5¶ And the saying pleased the whole multitude: and they chose Stephen, a man full of faith and of the Holy Ghost, and Philip, and Prochorus, and Nicanor, and Timon, and Parmenas, and Nicolas a proselyte of Antioch:

6Whom they set before the apostles: and when they had prayed, they laid *their* hands on them.

## Amplified

31God exalted Him to His right hand to be Prince *and* Leader and Savior *and* Deliverer *and* Preserver, in order to grant repentance to Israel and to bestow forgiveness *and* release from sins.

32And we are witnesses of these things, and the Holy Spirit is also, Whom God has bestowed on those who obey Him.

33Now when they heard this they were cut to the heart *and* infuriated and wanted to kill the disciples.

34But a certain Pharisee in the council (Sanhedrin) named Gamaliel, a teacher of the Law, highly esteemed by all the people, standing up, ordered that the apostles be taken outside for a little while.

35Then he [addressed the council] saying, Men of Israel, take care in regard to what you propose to do concerning these men.

36For before our time there arose Theudas, asserting himself to be a person of importance, with whom a number of men allied themselves, about four hundred; but he was killed and all who had listened to *and* adhered to him were scattered and brought to nothing.

37And after this one, rose up Judas the Galilean, [who led an uprising] during the time of the census and drew away a popular following after him; he also perished and all his adherents were scattered.

38Now in the present case let me say to you, stand off (withdraw) from these men and let them alone. For if this doctrine *or* purpose or undertaking *or* movement is of human origin, it will fail—be overthrown and come to nothing;

39But if it is of God, you will not be able to stop *or* overthrow or destroy them; you might even be found fighting against God!

40So, convinced by him they took his advice, and summoning the apostles they flogged them and sternly forbade them to speak in *or* about the name of Jesus, and allowed them to go.

41So they went out from the presence of the council (Sanhedrin), rejoicing that they were being counted worthy—dignified by the indignity—to suffer shame *and* be exposed to disgrace for [the sake of] His name.

42Yet [in spite of the threats] they never ceased for a single day both in the temple area and at home to teach *and* to proclaim the good news (Gospel) of Jesus [as] the Christ, the Messiah.

6 NOW ABOUT this time, when the number of the disciples was greatly increasing, complaint was made by the Hellenists (the Greek-speaking Jews), against the [native] Hebrews because their widows were being overlooked *and* neglected in the daily ministration—distribution [of relief].

2So the twelve (apostles) convened the multitude of the disciples and said, It is not seemly *or* desirable *or* right that we should have to give up *or* neglect [preaching] the Word of God in order to attend to serving at tables *and* superintending the distribution of food.

3Therefore select out from among yourselves, brethren, seven men of good *and* attested character *and* repute, full of the (Holy) Spirit and wisdom, whom we may assign to look after this business *and* duty.

4But we will continue to devote ourselves steadfastly to prayer and the ministry of the Word.

5And the suggestion pleased the whole assembly, and they selected Stephen, a man full of faith [that is, of a strong and welcome belief that Jesus is the Messiah], and full of *and* controlled by the Holy Spirit; and Philip, and Prochorus, and Nicanor, and Timon, and Parmenas, and Nicolaus, a proselyte [convert] from Antioch.

6These they presented to the apostles, who after prayer laid their hands on them.

## New American Standard

31"He is the one whom God exalted to His right hand as a Prince and a Savior, to grant repentance to Israel, and forgiveness of sins.

32"And we are witnesses [a] of these things; and *so is* the Holy Spirit, whom God has given to those who obey Him."

*Gamaliel's Counsel*

33¶ But when they heard this, they were cut to the quick and were intending to slay them.

34But a certain Pharisee named Gamaliel, a teacher of the Law, respected by all the people, stood up in the Council and gave orders to put the men outside for a short time.

35And he said to them, "Men of Israel, take care what you propose to do with these men.

36"For some time ago Theudas rose up, claiming to be somebody; and a group of about four hundred men joined up with him. And he was slain; and all who followed him were dispersed and came to nothing.

37"After this man Judas of Galilee rose up in the days of the census, and drew away *some* people after him, he too perished, and all those who followed him were scattered.

38"And so in the present case, I say to you, stay away from these men and let them alone, for if this plan or action should be of men, it will be overthrown;

39but if it is of God, you will not be able to overthrow them; or else you may even be found fighting against God."

40And they took his advice; and after calling the apostles in, they flogged them and ordered them to speak no more in the name of Jesus, and *then* released them.

41So they went on their way from the presence of the Council, rejoicing that they had been considered worthy to suffer shame for *His* name.

42And every day, in the temple and from house to house, they kept right on teaching and preaching Jesus *as* the Christ.

*Choosing of the Seven*

**6** NOW AT this time while the disciples were increasing *in number,* a complaint arose on the part of the [b]Hellenistic *Jews* against the *native* Hebrews, because their widows were being overlooked in the daily serving *of food.*

2And the twelve summoned the congregation of the disciples and said, "It is not desirable for us to neglect the word of God in order to serve tables.

3"But select from among you, brethren, seven men of good reputation, full of the Spirit and of wisdom, whom we may put in charge of this task.

4"But we will devote ourselves to prayer, and to the ministry of the word."

5And the statement found approval with the whole congregation; and they chose Stephen, a man full of faith and of the Holy Spirit, and Philip, Prochorus, Nicanor, Timon, Parmenas and Nicolas, a [c]proselyte from Antioch.

6And these they brought before the apostles; and after praying, they laid their hands on them.

NAS [a] Some mss. add *in Him,* or, *of Him* [b] I.e., non-Palestinian Jews who normally spoke Greek [c] I.e., a Gentile convert to Judaism

## New International

exalted him to his own right hand as Prince and Savior that he
might give repentance and forgiveness of sins to Israel. 32We are
witnesses of these things, and so is the Holy Spirit, whom God has
given to those who obey him."
33When they heard this, they were furious and wanted to put
them to death. 34But a Pharisee named Gamaliel, a teacher of the
law, who was honored by all the people, stood up in the Sanhedrin
and ordered that the men be put outside for a little while. 35Then
he addressed them: "Men of Israel, consider carefully what you
intend to do to these men. 36Some time ago Theudas appeared,
claiming to be somebody, and about four hundred men rallied to
him. He was killed, all his followers were dispersed, and it all came
to nothing. 37After him, Judas the Galilean appeared in the days
of the census and led a band of people in revolt. He too was killed,
and all his followers were scattered. 38Therefore, in the present
case I advise you: Leave these men alone! Let them go! For if their
purpose or activity is of human origin, it will fail. 39But if it is from
God, you will not be able to stop these men; you will only find
yourselves fighting against God."
40His speech persuaded them. They called the apostles in and
had them flogged. Then they ordered them not to speak in the
name of Jesus, and let them go.
41The apostles left the Sanhedrin, rejoicing because they had
been counted worthy of suffering disgrace for the Name. 42Day
after day, in the temple courts and from house to house, they
never stopped teaching and proclaiming the good news that Jesus
is the Christ.[d]

*The Choosing of the Seven*

**6** IN THOSE days when the number of disciples was increasing, the Grecian Jews among them complained against the
Hebraic Jews because their widows were being overlooked in the
daily distribution of food. 2So the Twelve gathered all the disciples
together and said, "It would not be right for us to neglect the
ministry of the word of God in order to wait on tables. 3Brothers,
choose seven men from among you who are known to be full of
the Spirit and wisdom. We will turn this responsibility over to
them 4and will give our attention to prayer and the ministry of the
word."
5This proposal pleased the whole group. They chose Stephen,
a man full of faith and of the Holy Spirit; also Philip, Procorus,
Nicanor, Timon, Parmenas, and Nicolas from Antioch, a convert
to Judaism. 6They presented these men to the apostles, who
prayed and laid their hands on them.

NIV [d] 42 Or *Messiah*

## King James

7 And the word of God increased; and the number of the disciples multiplied in Jerusalem greatly; and a great company of the priests were obedient to the faith.

8 And Stephen, full of faith and power, did great wonders and miracles among the people.

9 ¶ Then there arose certain of the synagogue, which is called *the synagogue* of the Libertines, and Cyrenians, and Alexandrians, and of them of Cilicia and of Asia, disputing with Stephen.

10 And they were not able to resist the wisdom and the spirit by which he spake.

11 Then they suborned men, which said, We have heard him speak blasphemous words against Moses, and *against* God.

12 And they stirred up the people, and the elders, and the scribes, and came upon *him*, and caught him, and brought *him* to the council,

13 And set up false witnesses, which said, This man ceaseth not to speak blasphemous words against this holy place, and the law:

14 For we have heard him say, that this Jesus of Nazareth shall destroy this place, and shall change the customs which Moses delivered us.

15 And all that sat in the council, looking stedfastly on him, saw his face as it had been the face of an angel.

**7** THEN SAID the high priest, Are these things so?

2 And he said, Men, brethren, and fathers, hearken; The God of glory appeared unto our father Abraham, when he was in Mesopotamia, before he dwelt in Charran,

3 And said unto him, Get thee out of thy country, and from thy kindred, and come into the land which I shall show thee.

4 Then came he out of the land of the Chaldaeans, and dwelt in Charran: and from thence, when his father was dead, he removed him into this land, wherein ye now dwell.

5 And he gave him none inheritance in it, no, not *so much as* to set his foot on: yet he promised that he would give it to him for a possession, and to his seed after him, when *as yet* he had no child.

6 And God spake on this wise, That his seed should sojourn in a strange land; and that they should bring them into bondage, and entreat *them* evil four hundred years.

7 And the nation to whom they shall be in bondage will I judge, said God: and after that shall they come forth, and serve me in this place.

8 And he gave him the covenant of circumcision: and so *Abraham* begat Isaac, and circumcised him the eighth day; and Isaac *begat* Jacob; and Jacob *begat* the twelve patriarchs.

9 And the patriarchs, moved with envy, sold Joseph into Egypt: but God was with him,

## Amplified

7 And the message of God kept on spreading, and the number of disciples multiplied greatly in Jerusalem; and [besides] a large number of the priests were obedient to the faith [in Jesus as the Messiah, through Whom is obtained eternal salvation in the kingdom of God].

8 Now Stephen, full of grace—divine blessing and favor—and power—strength and ability—worked great wonders and signs (miracles) among the people.

9 However, some of those who belonged to the synagogue of the Freedmen [freed Jewish slaves], as it was called, and [of the synagogues] of the Cyrenians, and of the Alexandrians, and of those from Cilicia and [the province of] Asia, arose [and undertook] to debate *and* dispute with Stephen.

10 But they were not able to resist the intelligence *and* the wisdom and [the inspiration of] the Spirit with which he spoke.

11 So they [secretly] instigated *and* instructed men to say, We have heard this man speak, using slanderous *and* abusive *and* blasphemous language against Moses and God.

12 [Thus] they incited the people as well as the elders and the scribes, and they came upon Stephen and arrested him and took him before the council (Sanhedrin).

13 And they brought forward false witnesses who asserted, This man never stops making statements against this sacred place and the Law [of Moses];

14 For we have heard him say that this Jesus the Nazarene will tear down *and* destroy this place, and will alter the institutions *and* usages which Moses transmitted to us.

15 Then all who sat in the council (Sanhedrin), as they gazed intently at Stephen, saw that his face [had the appearance of] the face of an angel.

**7** AND THE high priest asked [Stephen], Are these charges true?

2 And he answered, Brethren and fathers, listen to me. The God of glory appeared to our forefather Abraham, when he was still in Mesopotamia, before he [went to] live in Haran, [Ps. 29:3; Gen. 11:31; 15:7.]

3 And He said to him, Leave your own country and your relatives and come into the land (region) that I will point out to you. [Gen. 12:1.]

4 So then he went forth from the land of the Chaldeans and settled in Haran. And from there, after his father died [God] transferred him to this country in which you are now dwelling. [Gen. 11:31; 15:7; 12:5.]

5 Yet He gave him no inheritable property in it, [no] not even enough ground to set his foot on; but He promised that He would give it to Him for a [a]permanent possession and to his descendants after him, [even though as yet] he had no child. [Deut. 2:5; Gen. 12:7; 17:8.]

6 And this is [in effect] what God told him: That his descendants would be aliens (sojourners) in a land belonging to other people, who would bring them into bondage and ill-treat them four hundred years.

7 But I will judge the nation to whom they shall be slaves, said God, and after that they shall escape *and* come forth and worship Me in this [very] place. [Gen. 15:13, 14; Exod. 3:12.]

8 And [God] made with Abraham a covenant—an agreement to be religiously observed— [b]of which circumcision was the seal. And under these circumstances [Abraham] became the father of Isaac, and circumcised him on the eighth day; and Isaac [did so] when he became the father of Jacob, and Jacob [when each of his sons was born], the twelve patriarchs. [Gen. 17:10-14; 21:2-4; 25:26; 29:31-35; 30:1-24; 35:16-26.]

9 And the patriarchs [Jacob's sons] boiling with envy *and* hatred *and* anger, sold Joseph into slavery in Egypt; but God was with him, [Gen. 37:11, 28; 45:4.]

**AMP** [a] Vincent. [b] Vincent.

## New American Standard

7¶ And the word of God kept on spreading; and the number
of the disciples continued to increase greatly in Jerusalem, and a
great many of the priests were becoming obedient to the faith.
8¶ And Stephen, full of grace and power, was performing great
wonders and signs among the people.
9But some men from what was called the Synagogue of the
Freedmen, *including* both Cyrenians and Alexandrians, and some
from Cilicia and Asia, rose up and argued with Stephen.
10And *yet* they were unable to cope with the wisdom and the
Spirit with which he was speaking.
11Then they secretly induced men to say, "We have heard him
speak blasphemous words against Moses and *against* God."
12And they stirred up the people, the elders and the scribes,
and they came upon him and dragged him away, and brought him
before the Council.
13And they put forward false witnesses who said, "This man
incessantly speaks against this holy place, and the Law;
14for we have heard him say that this Nazarene, Jesus, will
destroy this place and alter the customs which Moses handed
down to us."
15And fixing their gaze on him, all who were sitting in the
Council saw his face like the face of an angel.

*Stephen's Defense*

7 AND THE high priest said, "Are these things so?"
2¶ And he said, "Hear me, brethren and fathers! The God of
glory appeared to our father Abraham when he was in Mesopotamia, before he lived in Haran,
3and said to him, 'DEPART FROM YOUR COUNTRY AND YOUR
RELATIVES, AND COME INTO THE LAND THAT I WILL SHOW YOU.'
4"Then he departed from the land of the Chaldeans, and settled in Haran. And from there, after his father died, *God* removed
him into this country in which you are now living.
5"And He gave him no inheritance in it, not even a foot of
ground; and *yet*, even when he had no child, He promised that HE
WOULD GIVE IT TO HIM AS A POSSESSION, AND TO HIS OFFSPRING
AFTER HIM.
6"But God spoke to this effect, that his OFFSPRING WOULD BE
ALIENS IN A FOREIGN LAND, AND THAT THEY WOULD BE ENSLAVED
AND MISTREATED FOR FOUR HUNDRED YEARS.
7" 'AND WHATEVER NATION TO WHICH THEY SHALL BE IN BOND-
AGE I MYSELF WILL JUDGE,' said God, 'AND AFTER THAT THEY WILL
COME OUT AND [c]SERVE ME IN THIS PLACE.'
8"And He gave him the covenant of circumcision; and so *Abraham* became the father of Isaac, and circumcised him on the eighth
day; and Isaac *became the father of* Jacob, and Jacob *of* the twelve
patriarchs.
9"And the patriarchs became jealous of Joseph and sold him
into Egypt. And *yet* God was with him,

NAS [c] Or, *worship*

## New International

7So the word of God spread. The number of disciples in Jerusalem increased rapidly, and a large number of priests became obedient to the faith.

*Stephen Seized*

8Now Stephen, a man full of God's grace and power, did great
wonders and miraculous signs among the people. 9Opposition
arose, however, from members of the Synagogue of the Freedmen
(as it was called)—Jews of Cyrene and Alexandria as well as the
provinces of Cilicia and Asia. These men began to argue with
Stephen, 10but they could not stand up against his wisdom or the
Spirit by whom he spoke.
11Then they secretly persuaded some men to say, "We have
heard Stephen speak words of blasphemy against Moses and
against God."
12So they stirred up the people and the elders and the teachers
of the law. They seized Stephen and brought him before the Sanhedrin. 13They produced false witnesses, who testified, "This fellow never stops speaking against this holy place and against the
law. 14For we have heard him say that this Jesus of Nazareth will
destroy this place and change the customs Moses handed down
to us."
15All who were sitting in the Sanhedrin looked intently at Stephen, and they saw that his face was like the face of an angel.

*Stephen's Speech to the Sanhedrin*

7 THEN THE high priest asked him, "Are these charges true?"
2To this he replied: "Brothers and fathers, listen to me! The
God of glory appeared to our father Abraham while he was still in
Mesopotamia, before he lived in Haran. 3'Leave your country and
your people,' God said, 'and go to the land I will show you.'[d]
4"So he left the land of the Chaldeans and settled in Haran.
After the death of his father, God sent him to this land where you
are now living. 5He gave him no inheritance here, not even a foot
of ground. But God promised him that he and his descendants
after him would possess the land, even though at that time Abraham had no child. 6God spoke to him in this way: 'Your descendants will be strangers in a country not their own, and they will be
enslaved and mistreated four hundred years. 7But I will punish the
nation they serve as slaves,' God said, 'and afterward they will
come out of that country and worship me in this place.'[e] 8Then he
gave Abraham the covenant of circumcision. And Abraham
became the father of Isaac and circumcised him eight days after his
birth. Later Isaac became the father of Jacob, and Jacob became the
father of the twelve patriarchs.
9"Because the patriarchs were jealous of Joseph, they sold him
as a slave into Egypt. But God was with him 10and rescued him

NIV [d] 3 Gen. 12:1 [e] 7 Gen. 15:13,14

## King James

10 And delivered him out of all his afflictions, and gave him favour and wisdom in the sight of Pharaoh king of Egypt; and he made him governor over Egypt and all his house.

11 Now there came a dearth over all the land of Egypt and Chanaan, and great affliction: and our fathers found no sustenance.

12 But when Jacob heard that there was corn in Egypt, he sent out our fathers first.

13 And at the second *time* Joseph was made known to his brethren; and Joseph's kindred was made known unto Pharaoh.

14 Then sent Joseph, and called his father Jacob to *him*, and all his kindred, threescore and fifteen souls.

15 So Jacob went down into Egypt, and died, he, and our fathers,

16 And were carried over into Sychem, and laid in the sepulchre that Abraham bought for a sum of money of the sons of Emmor *the father* of Sychem.

17 But when the time of the promise drew nigh, which God had sworn to Abraham, the people grew and multiplied in Egypt,

18 Till another king arose, which knew not Joseph.

19 The same dealt subtly with our kindred, and evil entreated our fathers, so that they cast out their young children, to the end they might not live.

20 In which time Moses was born, and was exceeding fair, and nourished up in his father's house three months:

21 And when he was cast out, Pharaoh's daughter took him up, and nourished him for her own son.

22 And Moses was learned in all the wisdom of the Egyptians, and was mighty in words and in deeds.

23 And when he was full forty years old, it came into his heart to visit his brethren the children of Israel.

24 And seeing one *of them* suffer wrong, he defended *him*, and avenged him that was oppressed, and smote the Egyptian:

25 For he supposed his brethren would have understood how that God by his hand would deliver them: but they understood not.

26 And the next day he showed himself unto them as they strove, and would have set them at one again, saying, Sirs, ye are brethren; why do ye wrong one to another?

27 But he that did his neighbour wrong thrust him away, saying, Who made thee a ruler and a judge over us?

28 Wilt thou kill me, as thou diddest the Egyptian yesterday?

29 Then fled Moses at this saying, and was a stranger in the land of Madian, where he begat two sons.

30 And when forty years were expired, there appeared to him in the wilderness of mount Sina an angel of the Lord in a flame of fire in a bush.

31 When Moses saw *it*, he wondered at the sight: and as he drew near to behold *it*, the voice of the Lord came unto him,

32 *Saying*, I *am* the God of thy fathers, the God of Abraham, and the God of Isaac, and the God of Jacob. Then Moses trembled, and durst not behold.

33 Then said the Lord to him, Put off thy shoes from thy feet: for the place where thou standest is holy ground.

## Amplified

10 And delivered him from all his distressing afflictions, and won him goodwill *and* favor and wisdom *and* understanding in the sight of Pharaoh, king of Egypt, who made him governor over Egypt and all his house. [Gen. 39:2, 3, 21; 41:40-46; Ps. 105:21.]

11 Then there came a famine over all of Egypt and Canaan, with great distress, and our forefathers could find no fodder [for the cattle] *or* vegetable sustenance [for their households]. [Gen. 41:54, 55; 42:5.]

12 But when Jacob heard that there was grain in Egypt, he sent forth our forefathers [to go there on their] first trip. [Gen. 42:2.]

13 And on their second visit Joseph revealed [himself] to his brothers, and the family of Joseph became known to Pharaoh, *and* his origin *and* race. [Gen. 45:1-4.]

14 And Joseph sent an invitation calling to himself Jacob his father and all his kindred, seventy-five persons in all. [Gen. 45:9, 10.]

15 And Jacob went down into Egypt, where he himself died, as did [also] our forefathers; [Deut. 10:22.]

16 And their bodies were taken back to Shechem and laid in the tomb which Abraham had purchased for a sum of silver money from the sons of Hamor in Shechem. [Josh. 24:32; Gen. 50:13.]

17 But [in proportion] as the time for the fulfillment of the promise drew near, which God had made to Abraham, the [Hebrew] people increased and multiplied in Egypt,

18 Until [the time when] there arose over Egypt another *and* a different king who did not know Joseph—his history and services, and did not recognize his merits. [Exod. 1:7, 8.]

19 He dealt treacherously with *and* defrauded our race; he abused *and* oppressed our forefathers, forcing them to expose their babies so that they might not be kept alive. [Exod. 1:7-11, 15-22.]

20 At this juncture Moses was born, and was exceedingly beautiful in God's sight; for three months he was nurtured in his father's house; [Exod. 2:2.]

21 Then when he was exposed [to perish], the daughter of Pharaoh rescued him and took him *and* reared him as her own son. [Exod. 2:5, 6, 10.]

22 So Moses was educated in all the wisdom *and* culture of the Egyptians, and he was mighty (powerful) in his speech and deeds.

23 And when he was in his fortieth year, it came into his heart to visit his kinsmen the children of Israel [a]with help and to care for them.

24 And on seeing one of them being unjustly treated, he defended the oppressed man and avenged him by striking down the Egyptian *and* slaying [him].

25 He expected his brethren to understand that God was granting them deliverance by his hand—taking it for granted that they would accept him; but they did not understand.

26 Then on the next day he [b]suddenly appeared to some who were quarreling *and* fighting among themselves, and he urged them to make peace *and* become reconciled, saying, Men, you are brethren; why do you abuse *and* wrong one another?

27 Whereupon the man who was abusing his neighbor pushed [Moses] aside, saying, Who appointed you a ruler (umpire) and a judge over us?

28 Do you intend to slay me as you slew the Egyptian yesterday?

29 At that reply Moses sought safety by flight, and he was an exile *and* an alien in the country of Midian, where he became the father of two sons. [Exod. 2:11-15, 22; 18:3, 4.]

30 And when forty years had gone by, there appeared to him in the wilderness (desert) of Mount Sinai an angel, in the flame of a burning bramble-bush.

31 When Moses saw it he was astonished *and* marvelled at the sight; but when he went close to investigate, there came to him the voice of the Lord, saying,

32 I am the God of your forefathers, the God of Abraham and of Isaac and of Jacob. And Moses trembled *and* was so terrified that he did not venture to look.

33 Then the Lord said to him, Remove the sandals from your feet, for the place where you are standing is holy ground *and* worthy of veneration.

**AMP** [a] Abbott-Smith. [b] Vincent.

## New American Standard

10and rescued him from all his afflictions, and granted him favor
and wisdom in the sight of Pharaoh, king of Egypt; and he made
him governor over Egypt and all his household.
11"Now a famine came over all Egypt and Canaan, and great
affliction *with it;* and our fathers could find no food.
12"But when Jacob heard that there was grain in Egypt, he sent
our fathers *there* the first time.
13"And on the second *visit* Joseph made himself known to his
brothers, and Joseph's family was disclosed to Pharaoh.
14"And Joseph sent *word* and invited Jacob his father and all his
relatives to come to him, seventy-five persons *in all.*
15"And Jacob went down to Egypt and *there* passed away, he
and our fathers.
16"And *from there* they were removed to Shechem, and laid in
the tomb which Abraham had purchased for a sum of money from
the sons of Hamor in Shechem.
17"But as the time of the promise was approaching which God
had assured to Abraham, the people increased and multiplied in
Egypt,
18until THERE AROSE ANOTHER KING OVER EGYPT WHO KNEW
NOTHING ABOUT JOSEPH.
19"It was he who took shrewd advantage of our race, and
mistreated our fathers so that they would expose their infants and
they would not survive.
20"And it was at this time that Moses was born; and he was
lovely in the sight of God; and he was nurtured three months in
his father's home.
21"And after he had been exposed, Pharaoh's daughter took
him away, and nurtured him as her own son.
22"And Moses was educated in all the learning of the Egyptians,
and he was a man of power in words and deeds.
23"But when he was approaching the age of forty, it entered his
mind to visit his brethren, the sons of Israel.
24"And when he saw one *of them* being treated unjustly, he
defended him and took vengeance for the oppressed by striking
down the Egyptian.
25"And he supposed that his brethren understood that God was
granting them deliverance through him; but they did not understand.
26"And on the following day he appeared to them as they were
fighting together, and he tried to reconcile them in peace, saying,
'Men, you are brethren, why do you injure one another?'
27"But the one who was injuring his neighbor pushed him
away, saying, 'WHO MADE YOU A RULER AND JUDGE OVER US?
28'YOU DO NOT MEAN TO KILL ME AS YOU KILLED THE EGYPTIAN
YESTERDAY, DO YOU?'
29"And at this remark MOSES FLED, AND BECAME AN ALIEN IN
THE LAND OF MIDIAN, where he became the father of two sons.
30"And after forty years had passed, AN ANGEL APPEARED TO
HIM IN THE WILDERNESS OF MOUNT Sinai, IN THE FLAME OF A BURN-
ING THORN BUSH.
31"And when Moses saw it, he *began* to marvel at the sight; and
as he approached to look *more* closely, there came the voice of the
Lord:
32'I AM THE GOD OF YOUR FATHERS, THE GOD OF ABRAHAM AND
ISAAC AND JACOB.' And Moses shook with fear and would not
venture to look.
33"BUT THE LORD SAID TO HIM, 'TAKE OFF THE SANDALS FROM
YOUR FEET, FOR THE PLACE ON WHICH YOU ARE STANDING IS HOLY
GROUND.

## New International

from all his troubles. He gave Joseph wisdom and enabled him to
gain the goodwill of Pharaoh king of Egypt; so he made him ruler
over Egypt and all his palace.
11"Then a famine struck all Egypt and Canaan, bringing great
suffering, and our fathers could not find food. 12When Jacob heard
that there was grain in Egypt, he sent our fathers on their first visit.
13On their second visit, Joseph told his brothers who he was, and
Pharaoh learned about Joseph's family. 14After this, Joseph sent
for his father Jacob and his whole family, seventy-five in all.
15Then Jacob went down to Egypt, where he and our fathers died.
16Their bodies were brought back to Shechem and placed in the
tomb that Abraham had bought from the sons of Hamor at Shechem for a certain sum of money.
17"As the time drew near for God to fulfill his promise to Abraham, the number of our people in Egypt greatly increased. 18Then
another king, who knew nothing about Joseph, became ruler of
Egypt. 19He dealt treacherously with our people and oppressed
our forefathers by forcing them to throw out their newborn babies
so that they would die.
20"At that time Moses was born, and he was no ordinary child.[c]
For three months he was cared for in his father's house. 21When
he was placed outside, Pharaoh's daughter took him and brought
him up as her own son. 22Moses was educated in all the wisdom
of the Egyptians and was powerful in speech and action.
23"When Moses was forty years old, he decided to visit his
fellow Israelites. 24He saw one of them being mistreated by an
Egyptian, so he went to his defense and avenged him by killing
the Egyptian. 25Moses thought that his own people would realize
that God was using him to rescue them, but they did not. 26The
next day Moses came upon two Israelites who were fighting. He
tried to reconcile them by saying, 'Men, you are brothers; why do
you want to hurt each other?'
27"But the man who was mistreating the other pushed Moses
aside and said, 'Who made you ruler and judge over us? 28Do you
want to kill me as you killed the Egyptian yesterday?'[d] 29When
Moses heard this, he fled to Midian, where he settled as a foreigner
and had two sons.
30"After forty years had passed, an angel appeared to Moses in
the flames of a burning bush in the desert near Mount Sinai.
31When he saw this, he was amazed at the sight. As he went over
to look more closely, he heard the Lord's voice: 32'I am the God
of your fathers, the God of Abraham, Isaac and Jacob.'[e] Moses
trembled with fear and did not dare to look.
33"Then the Lord said to him, 'Take off your sandals; the place
where you are standing is holy ground. 34I have indeed seen the

NIV [c] 20 Or *was fair in the sight of God* [d] 28 Exodus 2:14 [e] 32 Exodus 3:6

## King James

34 I have seen, I have seen the affliction of my people which is in Egypt, and I have heard their groaning, and am come down to deliver them. And now come, I will send thee into Egypt.

35 This Moses whom they refused, saying, Who made thee a ruler and a judge? the same did God send *to be* a ruler and a deliverer by the hand of the angel which appeared to him in the bush.

36 He brought them out, after that he had shown wonders and signs in the land of Egypt, and in the Red sea, and in the wilderness forty years.

37 ¶ This is that Moses, which said unto the children of Israel, A prophet shall the Lord your God raise up unto you of your brethren, like unto me; him shall ye hear.

38 This is he, that was in the church in the wilderness with the angel which spake to him in the mount Sina, and *with* our fathers: who received the lively oracles to give unto us:

39 To whom our fathers would not obey, but thrust *him* from them, and in their hearts turned back again into Egypt,

40 Saying unto Aaron, Make us gods to go before us: for *as for* this Moses, which brought us out of the land of Egypt, we wot not what is become of him.

41 And they made a calf in those days, and offered sacrifice unto the idol, and rejoiced in the works of their own hands.

42 Then God turned, and gave them up to worship the host of heaven; as it is written in the book of the prophets, O ye house of Israel, have ye offered to me slain beasts and sacrifices *by the space of* forty years in the wilderness?

43 Yea, ye took up the tabernacle of Moloch, and the star of your god Remphan, figures which ye made to worship them: and I will carry you away beyond Babylon.

44 Our fathers had the tabernacle of witness in the wilderness, as he had appointed, speaking unto Moses, that he should make it according to the fashion that he had seen.

45 Which also our fathers that came after brought in with Jesus into the possession of the Gentiles, whom God drave out before the face of our fathers, unto the days of David;

46 Who found favour before God, and desired to find a tabernacle for the God of Jacob.

47 But Solomon built him an house.

48 Howbeit the most High dwelleth not in temples made with hands; as saith the prophet,

49 Heaven *is* my throne, and earth *is* my footstool: what house will ye build me? saith the Lord: or what *is* the place of my rest?

50 Hath not my hand made all these things?

51 ¶ Ye stiffnecked and uncircumcised in heart and ears, ye do always resist the Holy Ghost: as your fathers *did,* so *do* ye.

52 Which of the prophets have not your fathers persecuted? and they have slain them which showed before of the coming of the Just One; of whom ye have been now the betrayers and murderers:

53 Who have received the law by the disposition of angels, and have not kept *it.*

## Amplified

34 Because I have most assuredly seen the abuse *and* oppression of My people in Egypt, and have heard their sighing *and* groaning, I have come down to rescue them. So, now come! I will send you back to Egypt [as My messenger]. [Exod. 3:1-10.]

35 It was this very Moses whom they had denied—disowned and rejected—saying, Who made you our ruler (referee) and judge? whom God sent to be a ruler and deliverer *and* redeemer, by *and* with the [protecting and helping] hand of the Angel that appeared to him in the bramble-bush. [Exod. 2:14.]

36 He it was who led them forth, having worked wonders and signs in Egypt and at the Red Sea, and during the forty years in the wilderness (desert). [Exod. 7:3; 14:21; Num. 14:33.]

37 It was this [very] Moses who said to the children of Israel, God will raise up for you a Prophet from among your brethren as He raised me up. [Deut. 18:15, 18.]

38 This is he who in the assembly in the wilderness (desert) was the go-between for the Angel who spoke to him on Mount Sinai, and our forefathers; and he received to be handed down to us living oracles—words that still live. [Exod. 19.]

39 [And yet] our forefathers determined not to be subject to him—refusing to listen to *or* obey him; but thrusting him aside they rejected him, and in their hearts yearned for and turned back to Egypt. [Num. 14:3, 4.]

40 And they said to Aaron, Make us gods who shall [be our leaders and] go before us; as for this Moses who led us forth from the land of Egypt, we have no knowledge of what has happened to him. [Exod. 32:1, 23.]

41 And they [even] made a calf in those days, and offered sacrifice to the idol and made merry *and* exulted in the work of their [own] hands. [Exod. 32:4, 6.]

42 But God turned [away from them] and delivered them up to worship *and* serve the host (stars) of heaven, as it is written in the book of the prophets: Did you [really] offer to Me slain beasts and sacrifices for forty years in the wilderness (desert), O house of Israel? [Jer. 19:13.]

43 [No!] You took up the tent—the portable temple—of Moloch *and* carried it [with you], and the star-idol of the god Rephan, the images which you [yourselves] made that you might worship them; and I will remove you—carrying you away [into exile]—beyond Babylon. [Amos 5:25-27.]

44 Our forefathers had the tent (tabernacle) of witness in the wilderness, even as He Who directed Moses to make it had ordered, according to the pattern *and* model he had seen. [Exod. 25:9-40.]

45 Our forefathers in turn brought [this tent of witness into the land with them when] with Joshua they dispossessed the nations which God drove out before the face of our forefathers. [So it remained there] until the time of David, [Josh. 3:14-17; Deut. 32:49.]

46 Who found grace (favor and spiritual blessing) in the sight of God and prayed that he might be allowed to find a dwelling place for the God of Jacob. [II Sam. 7:8-16; Ps. 132:1-5.]

47 But it was Solomon who built a house for Him. [I Kings 6.]

48 However the Most High does not dwell in houses *and* temples made with hands; as the prophet says, [Isa. 66:1, 2.]

49 Heaven [is] My throne, and earth the footstool for My feet. What [kind of] house can you build for Me, says the Lord, or what is the place in which I can rest?

50 Was it not My hand that made all these things? [Isa. 66:1, 2.]

51 You stubborn *and* stiff-necked people, still heathenish *and* uncircumcised in heart and ears, you are always [a]actively resisting the Holy Spirit. As your forefathers [were], so you [are and so you do]! [Exod. 33:3, 5; Jer. 9:26; 6:10; Num. 27:14; Isa. 63:10.]

52 Which of the prophets did your forefathers not persecute? And they slew those who proclaimed beforehand the coming of the Righteous One, Whom you now have betrayed and murdered,

53 You who received the Law as it was ordained *and* set in order *and* delivered by angels, and [yet] you did not obey it!

**AMP** [a] Vincent.

## New American Standard

34'I HAVE CERTAINLY SEEN THE OPPRESSION OF MY PEOPLE IN
EGYPT, AND HAVE HEARD THEIR GROANS, AND I HAVE COME DOWN
TO DELIVER THEM; COME NOW, AND I WILL SEND YOU TO EGYPT.'
35"This Moses whom they disowned, saying, 'WHO MADE YOU
A RULER AND A JUDGE?' is the one whom God sent *to be* both a ruler
and a deliverer with the help of the angel who appeared to him
in the thorn bush.
36"This man led them out, performing wonders and signs in the
land of Egypt and in the Red Sea and in the wilderness for forty
years.
37"This is the Moses who said to the sons of Israel, 'GOD SHALL
RAISE UP FOR YOU A PROPHET LIKE ME FROM YOUR BRETHREN.'
38"This is the one who was in the congregation in the wilderness together with the angel who was speaking to him on Mount
Sinai, and *who was* with our fathers; and he received living oracles
to pass on to you.
39"And our fathers were unwilling to be obedient to him, but
repudiated him and in their hearts turned back to Egypt,
40SAYING TO AARON, 'MAKE FOR US GODS WHO WILL GO BEFORE
US; FOR THIS MOSES WHO LED US OUT OF THE LAND OF EGYPT—WE
DO NOT KNOW WHAT HAPPENED TO HIM.'
41"And at that time they made a calf and brought a sacrifice to
the idol, and were rejoicing in the works of their hands.
42"But God turned away and delivered them up to serve the
host of heaven; as it is written in the book of the prophets, 'IT WAS
NOT TO ME THAT YOU OFFERED VICTIMS AND SACRIFICES FORTY YEARS
IN THE WILDERNESS, WAS IT, O HOUSE OF ISRAEL?
43'YOU ALSO TOOK ALONG THE TABERNACLE OF MOLOCH AND THE
STAR OF THE GOD ROMPHA, THE IMAGES WHICH YOU MADE TO WOR-
SHIP THEM. I ALSO WILL REMOVE YOU BEYOND BABYLON.'
44"Our fathers had the tabernacle of testimony in the wilderness, just as He who spoke to Moses directed *him* to make it
according to the pattern which he had seen.
45"And having received it in their turn, our fathers brought it
in with Joshua upon dispossessing the nations whom God drove
out before our fathers, until the time of David.
46"And *David* found favor in God's sight, and asked that he
might find a dwelling place for the [b]God of Jacob.
47"But it was Solomon who built a house for Him.
48"However, the Most High does not dwell in *houses* made by
*human* hands; as the prophet says:

49 'HEAVEN IS MY THRONE,
AND EARTH IS THE FOOTSTOOL OF MY FEET;
WHAT KIND OF HOUSE WILL YOU BUILD FOR ME?' says the
Lord;
'OR WHAT PLACE IS THERE FOR MY REPOSE?
50 'WAS IT NOT MY HAND WHICH MADE ALL THESE THINGS?'

51¶ "You men who are stiff-necked and uncircumcised in heart
and ears are always resisting the Holy Spirit; you are doing just as
your fathers did.
52"Which one of the prophets did your fathers not persecute?
And they killed those who had previously announced the coming
of the Righteous One, whose betrayers and murderers you have
now become;
53you who received the law as ordained by angels, and *yet* did
not keep it."

NAS [b] The earliest mss. read *house* instead of *God;* the Septuagint reads *God*

## New International

oppression of my people in Egypt. I have heard their groaning and
have come down to set them free. Now come, I will send you back
to Egypt.'[c]
35"This is the same Moses whom they had rejected with the
words, 'Who made you ruler and judge?' He was sent to be their
ruler and deliverer by God himself, through the angel who appeared to him in the bush. 36He led them out of Egypt and did
wonders and miraculous signs in Egypt, at the Red Sea[d] and for
forty years in the desert.
37"This is that Moses who told the Israelites, 'God will send you
a prophet like me from your own people.'[e] 38He was in the assembly in the desert, with the angel who spoke to him on Mount Sinai,
and with our fathers; and he received living words to pass on to
us.
39"But our fathers refused to obey him. Instead, they rejected
him and in their hearts turned back to Egypt. 40They told Aaron,
'Make us gods who will go before us. As for this fellow Moses who
led us out of Egypt—we don't know what has happened to him!'[f]
41That was the time they made an idol in the form of a calf. They
brought sacrifices to it and held a celebration in honor of what their
hands had made. 42But God turned away and gave them over to
the worship of the heavenly bodies. This agrees with what is
written in the book of the prophets:

" 'Did you bring me sacrifices and offerings
forty years in the desert, O house of Israel?
43You have lifted up the shrine of Molech
and the star of your god Rephan,
the idols you made to worship.
Therefore I will send you into exile'[g] beyond Babylon.

44"Our forefathers had the tabernacle of the Testimony with
them in the desert. It had been made as God directed Moses,
according to the pattern he had seen. 45Having received the tabernacle, our fathers under Joshua brought it with them when they
took the land from the nations God drove out before them. It
remained in the land until the time of David, 46who enjoyed God's
favor and asked that he might provide a dwelling place for the God
of Jacob.[h] 47But it was Solomon who built the house for him.
48"However, the Most High does not live in houses made by
men. As the prophet says:

49" 'Heaven is my throne,
and the earth is my footstool.
What kind of house will you build for me?
says the Lord.
Or where will my resting place be?
50Has not my hand made all these things?'[i]

51"You stiff-necked people, with uncircumcised hearts and
ears! You are just like your fathers: You always resist the Holy
Spirit! 52Was there ever a prophet your fathers did not persecute?
They even killed those who predicted the coming of the Righteous
One. And now you have betrayed and murdered him— 53you who
have received the law that was put into effect through angels but
have not obeyed it."

NIV [c] *34* Exodus 3:5,7,8,10 [d] *36* That is, Sea of Reeds [e] *37* Deut. 18:15
[f] *40* Exodus 32:1 [g] *43* Amos 5:25-27 [h] *46* Some early manuscripts *the house of Jacob* [i] *50* Isaiah 66:1,2

## King James

54¶ When they heard these things, they were cut to the heart, and they gnashed on him with *their* teeth.

55But he, being full of the Holy Ghost, looked up stedfastly into heaven, and saw the glory of God, and Jesus standing on the right hand of God,

56And said, Behold, I see the heavens opened, and the Son of man standing on the right hand of God.

57Then they cried out with a loud voice, and stopped their ears, and ran upon him with one accord,

58And cast *him* out of the city, and stoned *him:* and the witnesses laid down their clothes at a young man's feet, whose name was Saul.

59And they stoned Stephen, calling upon *God,* and saying, Lord Jesus, receive my spirit.

60And he kneeled down, and cried with a loud voice, Lord, lay not this sin to their charge. And when he had said this, he fell asleep.

**8** AND SAUL was consenting unto his death. And at that time there was a great persecution against the church which was at Jerusalem; and they were all scattered abroad throughout the regions of Judaea and Samaria, except the apostles.

2And devout men carried Stephen *to his burial,* and made great lamentation over him.

3As for Saul, he made havock of the church, entering into every house, and haling men and women committed *them* to prison.

4Therefore they that were scattered abroad went every where preaching the word.

5Then Philip went down to the city of Samaria, and preached Christ unto them.

6And the people with one accord gave heed unto those things which Philip spake, hearing and seeing the miracles which he did.

7For unclean spirits, crying with loud voice, came out of many that were possessed *with them:* and many taken with palsies, and that were lame, were healed.

8And there was great joy in that city.

9But there was a certain man, called Simon, which beforetime in the same city used sorcery, and bewitched the people of Samaria, giving out that himself was some great one:

10To whom they all gave heed, from the least to the greatest, saying, This man is the great power of God.

11And to him they had regard, because that of long time he had bewitched them with sorceries.

12But when they believed Philip preaching the things concerning the kingdom of God, and the name of Jesus Christ, they were baptized, both men and women.

13Then Simon himself believed also: and when he was baptized, he continued with Philip, and wondered, beholding the miracles and signs which were done.

14Now when the apostles which were at Jerusalem heard that Samaria had received the word of God, they sent unto them Peter and John:

## Amplified

54Now upon hearing these things, they [the Jews] were cut to the heart *and* infuriated, and they ground their teeth against [Stephen].

55But he, full of the Holy Spirit *and* controlled by [Him], gazed into heaven and saw the glory—the splendor and majesty—of God, and Jesus standing at God's right hand;

56And he said, Look! I see the heavens opened, and the Son of man standing at God's right hand!

57But they raised a great shout and put their hands over their ears and rushed together upon him.

58Then they dragged him out of the city and began to stone him, and the witnesses placed their garments at the feet of a young man named Saul.

59And while they were stoning Stephen, he prayed, Lord Jesus, receive *and* accept *and* welcome my spirit!

60And falling on his knees, he cried out loudly, Lord, [a]fix not this sin upon them—lay it not to their charge! And when he had said this, he fell asleep [b][in death].

**8** AND SAUL was [not only] consenting to [Stephen's] death—[he was] [c]pleased and [d]entirely approving. On that day a great *and* severe persecution broke out against the church which was in Jerusalem; and they were all scattered throughout the regions of Judea and Samaria, except the apostles—the special messengers.

2[A party of] devout men [e]with others helped to carry out *and* bury Stephen, and made great lamentation over him.

3But Saul shamefully treated *and* laid waste the church continuously,—with cruelty *and* violence; and entering house after house, he dragged out men and women and committed them to prison.

4Now those who were scattered abroad went about through [the land from place to place] preaching the glad tidings, the Word [that is, [f]the doctrine concerning the attainment through Christ of salvation in the kingdom of God].

5Philip [the deacon, not the apostle] went down to the city of Samaria, and proclaimed the Christ, the Messiah, to them [the people]; [Acts 6:5.]

6And great crowds of people with one accord listened to *and* heeded what was said by Philip, as they heard him *and* watched the miracles *and* wonders which he kept performing [from time to time].

7For foul spirits came out of many who were possessed by them, screaming *and* shouting with a loud voice, and many who were suffering from palsy or were crippled were restored to health.

8And there was great rejoicing in that city.

9But there was a man named Simon who had formerly practiced magic arts in the city to the utter amazement of the Samaritan nation, claiming that he himself was an extraordinary *and* distinguished person.

10They all paid earnest attention to him, from the least to the greatest, saying, This man is that exhibition of the power of God which is called Great (intense).

11And they were attentive *and* made much of him, because for a long time he had amazed *and* bewildered *and* dazzled them with his skill in magic arts.

12But when they believed the good news (the Gospel) about the kingdom of God and the name of Jesus Christ, the Messiah, as Philip preached it, they were baptized, both men and women.

13Even Simon himself believed—[that is,] he adhered to, trusted in and relied on the teaching of Philip—and after being baptized devoted himself constantly to him. And seeing signs *and* miracles of great power which were being performed, he was utterly amazed.

14Now when the apostles (special messengers) at Jerusalem heard that [the country of] Samaria had accepted *and* welcomed the Word of God, they sent Peter and John to them,

**AMP** [a] Literal translation. [b] Cremer. [c] Thayer. [d] Souter. [e] Thayer. [f] Thayer.

## New American Standard

*Stephen Put to Death*

54¶ Now when they heard this, they were cut to the quick, and they *began* gnashing their teeth at him.

55But being full of the Holy Spirit, he gazed intently into heaven and saw the glory of God, and Jesus standing at the right hand of God;

56and he said, "Behold, I see the heavens opened up and the Son of Man standing at the right hand of God."

57But they cried out with a loud voice, and covered their ears, and they rushed upon him with one impulse.

58And when they had driven him out of the city, they *began* stoning *him*, and the witnesses laid aside their robes at the feet of a young man named Saul.

59And they went on stoning Stephen as he called upon *the Lord* and said, "Lord Jesus, receive my spirit!"

60And falling on his knees, he cried out with a loud voice, "Lord, do not hold this sin against them!" And having said this, he fell asleep.

*Saul Persecutes the Church*

**8** AND SAUL was in hearty agreement with putting him to death.

¶And on that day a great persecution arose against the church in Jerusalem; and they were all scattered throughout the regions of Judea and Samaria, except the apostles.

2And *some* devout men buried Stephen, and made loud lamentation over him.

3But Saul *began* ravaging the church, entering house after house; and dragging off men and women, he would put them in prison.

*Philip in Samaria*

4¶ Therefore, those who had been scattered went about preaching the word.

5And Philip went down to the city of Samaria and *began* proclaiming Christ to them.

6And the multitudes with one accord were giving attention to what was said by Philip, as they heard and saw the signs which he was performing.

7For *in the case of* many who had unclean spirits, they were coming out *of them* shouting with a loud voice; and many who had been paralyzed and lame were healed.

8And there was much rejoicing in that city.

9¶ Now there was a certain man named Simon, who formerly was practicing magic in the city, and astonishing the people of Samaria, claiming to be someone great;

10and they all, from smallest to greatest, were giving attention to him, saying, "This man is what is called the Great Power of God."

11And they were giving him attention because he had for a long time astonished them with his magic arts.

12But when they believed Philip preaching the good news about the kingdom of God and the name of Jesus Christ, they were being baptized, men and women alike.

13And even Simon himself believed; and after being baptized, he continued on with Philip; and as he observed signs and great miracles taking place, he was constantly amazed.

14¶ Now when the apostles in Jerusalem heard that Samaria had received the word of God, they sent them Peter and John,

## New International

*The Stoning of Stephen*

54When they heard this, they were furious and gnashed their
teeth at him. 55But Stephen, full of the Holy Spirit, looked up to
heaven and saw the glory of God, and Jesus standing at the right
hand of God. 56"Look," he said, "I see heaven open and the Son
of Man standing at the right hand of God."
57At this they covered their ears and, yelling at the top of their
voices, they all rushed at him, 58dragged him out of the city and
began to stone him. Meanwhile, the witnesses laid their clothes at
the feet of a young man named Saul.
59While they were stoning him, Stephen prayed, "Lord Jesus,
receive my spirit." 60Then he fell on his knees and cried out,
"Lord, do not hold this sin against them." When he had said this,
he fell asleep.

**8** AND SAUL was there, giving approval to his death.

*The Church Persecuted and Scattered*

On that day a great persecution broke out against the church
at Jerusalem, and all except the apostles were scattered throughout
Judea and Samaria. 2Godly men buried Stephen and mourned
deeply for him. 3But Saul began to destroy the church. Going from
house to house, he dragged off men and women and put them in
prison.

*Philip in Samaria*

4Those who had been scattered preached the word wherever
they went. 5Philip went down to a city in Samaria and proclaimed
the Christ[g] there. 6When the crowds heard Philip and saw the
miraculous signs he did, they all paid close attention to what he
said. 7With shrieks, evil[h] spirits came out of many, and many
paralytics and cripples were healed. 8So there was great joy in that
city.

*Simon the Sorcerer*

9Now for some time a man named Simon had practiced sorcery
in the city and amazed all the people of Samaria. He boasted that
he was someone great, 10and all the people, both high and low,
gave him their attention and exclaimed, "This man is the divine
power known as the Great Power." 11They followed him because
he had amazed them for a long time with his magic. 12But when
they believed Philip as he preached the good news of the kingdom
of God and the name of Jesus Christ, they were baptized, both men
and women. 13Simon himself believed and was baptized. And he
followed Philip everywhere, astonished by the great signs and
miracles he saw.
14When the apostles in Jerusalem heard that Samaria had accepted the word of God, they sent Peter and John to them. 15When

NIV g 5 Or *Messiah* h 7 Greek *unclean*

## King James

15Who, when they were come down, prayed for them, that they might receive the Holy Ghost:

16(For as yet he was fallen upon none of them: only they were baptized in the name of the Lord Jesus.)

17Then laid they *their* hands on them, and they received the Holy Ghost.

18And when Simon saw that through laying on of the apostles' hands the Holy Ghost was given, he offered them money,

19Saying, Give me also this power, that on whomsoever I lay hands, he may receive the Holy Ghost.

20But Peter said unto him, Thy money perish with thee, because thou hast thought that the gift of God may be purchased with money.

21Thou hast neither part nor lot in this matter: for thy heart is not right in the sight of God.

22Repent therefore of this thy wickedness, and pray God, if perhaps the thought of thine heart may be forgiven thee.

23For I perceive that thou art in the gall of bitterness, and *in* the bond of iniquity.

24Then answered Simon, and said, Pray ye to the Lord for me, that none of these things which ye have spoken come upon me.

25And they, when they had testified and preached the word of the Lord, returned to Jerusalem, and preached the gospel in many villages of the Samaritans.

26And the angel of the Lord spake unto Philip, saying, Arise, and go toward the south unto the way that goeth down from Jerusalem unto Gaza, which is desert.

27And he arose and went: and, behold, a man of Ethiopia, an eunuch of great authority under Candace queen of the Ethiopians, who had the charge of all her treasure, and had come to Jerusalem for to worship,

28Was returning, and sitting in his chariot read Esaias the prophet.

29Then the Spirit said unto Philip, Go near, and join thyself to this chariot.

30And Philip ran thither to *him,* and heard him read the prophet Esaias, and said, Understandest thou what thou readest?

31And he said, How can I, except some man should guide me? And he desired Philip that he would come up and sit with him.

32The place of the scripture which he read was this, He was led as a sheep to the slaughter; and like a lamb dumb before his shearer, so opened he not his mouth:

33In his humiliation his judgment was taken away: and who shall declare his generation? for his life is taken from the earth.

34And the eunuch answered Philip, and said, I pray thee, of whom speaketh the prophet this? of himself, or of some other man?

35Then Philip opened his mouth, and began at the same scripture, and preached unto him Jesus.

36And as they went on *their* way, they came unto a certain water: and the eunuch said, See, *here is* water; what doth hinder me to be baptized?

37And Philip said, If thou believest with all thine heart, thou mayest. And he answered and said, I believe that Jesus Christ is the Son of God.

38And he commanded the chariot to stand still: and they went down both into the water, both Philip and the eunuch; and he baptized him.

**AMP** [a] Vincent. [b] Thayer. [c] Alternate reading. [d] Vincent. [e] Clarke quoting others. [f] Vincent. [g] Thayer. [h] Thayer.

## Amplified

15And they came down and prayed for them that the Samaritans might receive the Holy Spirit;

16For He had not yet fallen upon any of them, but they had only been baptized into the name of the Lord Jesus.

17Then [the apostles] laid their hands on them one by one and they received the Holy Spirit.

18However, when Simon saw that the (Holy) Spirit was imparted through the laying on of the apostles' hands, he brought money *and* offered it to them,

19Saying, Grant me also this power *and* authority, in order that any one on whom I place my hands may receive the Holy Spirit.

20But Peter said to him, Destruction overtake your money and you, because you imagined you could obtain the [free] gift of God with money!

21You have neither part nor lot in this matter, for your heart is all wrong in God's sight—[it is] not straightforward *or* right *or* true before God. [Ps. 78:37.]

22So repent of this depravity *and* wickedness of yours, and pray to the Lord that, if possible, this [a]contriving thought *and* purpose of your heart may be removed *and* disregarded *and* forgiven you.

23For I see that you are in the gall of bitterness and [b]a bond forged by iniquity [to fetter souls]. [Isa. 58:6.]

24And Simon answered, Pray for me!—Beseech the Lord, both of you—that nothing of what you have said may befall me!

25Now when [the apostles] had borne their testimony and preached the message of the Lord, they went back to Jerusalem, proclaiming the glad tidings (Gospel) to many villages of the Samaritans [on the way].

26But an angel of the Lord said to Philip, Rise and proceed southward [c]at midday on the road that runs from Jerusalem down to Gaza. This is the desert [[d]route].

27So he got up and went. And, behold, an Ethiopian, a eunuch, of great authority under Candace the queen of the Ethiopians, who was in charge of all her treasure, had come to Jerusalem to worship.

28And he was [now] returning, and sitting in his chariot he was reading the book of the prophet Isaiah.

29Then the (Holy) Spirit said to Philip, Go forward and join yourself to this chariot.

30Accordingly Philip, running up to him, heard [the man] reading the prophet Isaiah, and asked, Do you really understand what you are reading?

31And he said, How is it possible for me to do so, unless some one explains it to me *and* guides me [in the right way]? And he earnestly requested Philip to come up and sit beside him.

32Now this was the passage of Scripture which he was reading: Like a sheep He was led to the slaughter, and as a lamb before its shearer is dumb, so He opens not His mouth.

33In His humiliation [e]He was taken away by distressing *and* oppressive judgment, *and* justice was denied Him (caused to cease). Who can describe *or* relate in full [f]the wickedness of His contemporaries (generation)? For His life is taken from the earth *and* [g]a bloody death inflicted upon Him. [Isa. 53:7, 8.]

34And the eunuch said to Philip, I beg of you, tell me about whom does the prophet say this, about himself or about someone else?

35Then Philip opened his mouth, and beginning with this portion of Scripture he announced to him the glad tidings (Gospel) of Jesus *and* about [Him].

36And as they continued along on the way, they came to some water, and the eunuch exclaimed, See, [here is] water! What is to hinder my being baptized?

37 *And Philip said, If you believe with all your heart ⌊that is, if you have [h]a conviction, full of joyful trust, that Jesus is the Messiah, and accept Him as the Author of your salvation in the kingdom of God, giving Him your obedience, then⌋ you may. And he replied, I do believe that Jesus Christ is the Son of God,*

38And he ordered that the chariot be stopped, and both Philip and the eunuch went down into the water, and [Philip] baptized him.

## New American Standard

15who came down and prayed for them, that they might receive
the Holy Spirit.
16For He had not yet fallen upon any of them; they had simply
been baptized in the name of the Lord Jesus.
17Then they *began* laying their hands on them, and they were
receiving the Holy Spirit.
18Now when Simon saw that the Spirit was bestowed through
the laying on of the apostles' hands, he offered them money,
19saying, "Give this authority to me as well, so that everyone
on whom I lay my hands may receive the Holy Spirit."
20But Peter said to him, "May your silver perish with you,
because you thought you could obtain the gift of God with money!
21"You have no part or portion in this matter, for your heart is
not right before God.
22"Therefore repent of this wickedness of yours, and pray the
Lord that if possible, the intention of your heart may be forgiven
you.
23"For I see that you are in the gall of bitterness and in the
bondage of iniquity."
24But Simon answered and said, "Pray to the Lord for me
yourselves, so that nothing of what you have said may come upon
me."

*An Ethiopian Receives Christ*

25¶ And so, when they had solemnly testified and spoken the
word of the Lord, they started back to Jerusalem, and were preaching the gospel to many villages of the Samaritans.
26¶ But an angel of the Lord spoke to Philip saying, "Arise and
go south to the road that descends from Jerusalem to Gaza." (This
is a desert *road*.)
27And he arose and went; and behold, there was an Ethiopian
eunuch, a court official of Candace, queen of the Ethiopians, who
was in charge of all her treasure; and he had come to Jerusalem to
worship.
28And he was returning and sitting in his chariot, and was
reading the prophet Isaiah.
29And the Spirit said to Philip, "Go up and join this chariot."
30And when Philip had run up, he heard him reading Isaiah the
prophet, and said, "Do you understand what you are reading?"
31And he said, "Well, how could I, unless someone guides
me?" And he invited Philip to come up and sit with him.
32Now the passage of Scripture which he was reading was this:
"HE WAS LED AS A SHEEP TO SLAUGHTER;
AND AS A LAMB BEFORE ITS SHEARER IS SILENT,
SO HE DOES NOT OPEN HIS MOUTH.
33 "IN HUMILIATION HIS JUDGMENT WAS TAKEN AWAY;
WHO SHALL RELATE HIS GENERATION?
FOR HIS LIFE IS REMOVED FROM THE EARTH."
34And the eunuch answered Philip and said, "Please *tell me*, of
whom does the prophet say this? Of himself, or of someone else?"
35And Philip opened his mouth, and beginning from this Scripture he preached Jesus to him.
36And as they went along the road they came to some water;
and the eunuch *said, "Look! Water! What prevents me from being
baptized?"
37[ [i]And Philip said, "If you believe with all your heart, you
may." And he answered and said, "I believe that Jesus Christ is
the Son of God."]
38And he ordered the chariot to stop; and they both went down
into the water, Philip as well as the eunuch; and he baptized him.

NAS [i] Many mss. do not contain this verse

## New International

they arrived, they prayed for them that they might receive the
Holy Spirit, 16because the Holy Spirit had not yet come upon any
of them; they had simply been baptized into[j] the name of the Lord
Jesus. 17Then Peter and John placed their hands on them, and they
received the Holy Spirit.
18When Simon saw that the Spirit was given at the laying on of
the apostles' hands, he offered them money 19and said, "Give me
also this ability so that everyone on whom I lay my hands may
receive the Holy Spirit."
20Peter answered: "May your money perish with you, because
you thought you could buy the gift of God with money! 21You have
no part or share in this ministry, because your heart is not right
before God. 22Repent of this wickedness and pray to the Lord.
Perhaps he will forgive you for having such a thought in your
heart. 23For I see that you are full of bitterness and captive to sin."
24Then Simon answered, "Pray to the Lord for me so that
nothing you have said may happen to me."
25When they had testified and proclaimed the word of the Lord,
Peter and John returned to Jerusalem, preaching the gospel in
many Samaritan villages.

*Philip and the Ethiopian*

26Now an angel of the Lord said to Philip, "Go south to the
road—the desert road—that goes down from Jerusalem to Gaza."
27So he started out, and on his way he met an Ethiopian[k] eunuch,
an important official in charge of all the treasury of Candace, queen
of the Ethiopians. This man had gone to Jerusalem to worship,
28and on his way home was sitting in his chariot reading the book
of Isaiah the prophet. 29The Spirit told Philip, "Go to that chariot
and stay near it."
30Then Philip ran up to the chariot and heard the man reading
Isaiah the prophet. "Do you understand what you are reading?"
Philip asked.
31"How can I," he said, "unless someone explains it to me?" So
he invited Philip to come up and sit with him.
32The eunuch was reading this passage of Scripture:
"He was led like a sheep to the slaughter,
and as a lamb before the shearer is silent,
so he did not open his mouth.
33In his humiliation he was deprived of justice.
Who can speak of his descendants?
For his life was taken from the earth."[l]
34The eunuch asked Philip, "Tell me, please, who is the prophet
talking about, himself or someone else?" 35Then Philip began with
that very passage of Scripture and told him the good news about
Jesus.
36As they traveled along the road, they came to some water and
the eunuch said, "Look, here is water. Why shouldn't I be baptized?"[m] 38And he gave orders to stop the chariot. Then both Philip
and the eunuch went down into the water and Philip baptized
him. 39When they came up out of the water, the Spirit of the Lord

NIV [j] *16* Or *in* [k] *27* That is, from the upper Nile region [l] *33* Isaiah 53:7,8
[m] *36* Some late manuscripts *baptized?" 37Philip said, "If you believe with all your heart, you may." The eunuch answered, "I believe that Jesus Christ is the Son of God."*

## King James

39And when they were come up out of the water, the Spirit of the Lord caught away Philip, that the eunuch saw him no more: and he went on his way rejoicing.

40But Philip was found at Azotus: and passing through he preached in all the cities, till he came to Caesarea.

**9** AND SAUL, yet breathing out threatenings and slaughter against the disciples of the Lord, went unto the high priest,

2And desired of him letters to Damascus to the synagogues, that if he found any of this way, whether they were men or women, he might bring them bound unto Jerusalem.

3And as he journeyed, he came near Damascus: and suddenly there shined round about him a light from heaven:

4And he fell to the earth, and heard a voice saying unto him, Saul, Saul, why persecutest thou me?

5And he said, Who art thou, Lord? And the Lord said, I am Jesus whom thou persecutest: *it is* hard for thee to kick against the pricks.

6And he trembling and astonished said, Lord, what wilt thou have me to do? And the Lord *said* unto him, Arise, and go into the city, and it shall be told thee what thou must do.

7And the men which journeyed with him stood speechless, hearing a voice, but seeing no man.

8And Saul arose from the earth; and when his eyes were opened, he saw no man: but they led him by the hand, and brought *him* into Damascus.

9And he was three days without sight, and neither did eat nor drink.

10¶ And there was a certain disciple at Damascus, named Ananias; and to him said the Lord in a vision, Ananias. And he said, Behold, I *am here*, Lord.

11And the Lord *said* unto him, Arise, and go into the street which is called Straight, and inquire in the house of Judas for *one* called Saul, of Tarsus: for, behold, he prayeth,

12And hath seen in a vision a man named Ananias coming in, and putting *his* hand on him, that he might receive his sight.

13Then Ananias answered, Lord, I have heard by many of this man, how much evil he hath done to thy saints at Jerusalem:

14And here he hath authority from the chief priests to bind all that call on thy name.

15But the Lord said unto him, Go thy way: for he is a chosen vessel unto me, to bear my name before the Gentiles, and kings, and the children of Israel:

16For I will show him how great things he must suffer for my name's sake.

17And Ananias went his way, and entered into the house; and putting his hands on him said, Brother Saul, the Lord, *even* Jesus, that appeared unto thee in the way as thou camest, hath sent me, that thou mightest receive thy sight, and be filled with the Holy Ghost.

18And immediately there fell from his eyes as it had been scales: and he received sight forthwith, and arose, and was baptized.

19And when he had received meat, he was strengthened. Then was Saul certain days with the disciples which were at Damascus.

20And straightway he preached Christ in the synagogues, that he is the Son of God.

21But all that heard *him* were amazed, and said; Is not this he that destroyed them which called on this name in Jerusalem, and came hither for that intent, that he might bring them bound unto the chief priests?

## Amplified

39And when they came up out of the water, the Spirit of the Lord [ [a]suddenly] caught away Philip; and the eunuch saw him no more, and he went on his way rejoicing.

40But Philip was found at Azotus, and passing on he preached the good news (Gospel) to all the towns until he reached Caesarea.

**9** MEANWHILE SAUL, [b]still drawing his breath hard from threatening and murderous desire against the disciples of the Lord, went to the high priest

2And requested of him letters to the synagogues at Damascus [authorizing him], so that if he found any men or women belonging to the Way [of life as determined by faith in Jesus Christ], he might bring them bound [with chains] to Jerusalem.

3Now as he traveled on, he came near to Damascus, and suddenly a light from heaven flashed around him,

4And he fell to the ground. Then he heard a voice saying to him, Saul, Saul, why are you persecuting Me—harassing, troubling and molesting Me?

5And Saul said, Who are You, Lord? And He said, I am Jesus, Whom you are persecuting. *It is dangerous and it turns out badly for you to keep kicking against the goad—that is, to offer vain and perilous resistance.*

6 *Trembling and astonished he asked, Lord, what do You desire me to do? The Lord said to him,* But arise and go into the city and you will be told what you must do.

7The men who were accompanying him were unable to speak [for terror], hearing the voice but seeing no one.

8Then Saul got up from the ground, but though his eyes were opened, he could see nothing; so they led him by the hand and brought him into Damascus.

9And he was unable to see for three days, and he neither ate nor drank [anything].

10Now there was in Damascus a disciple named Ananias. The Lord said to him in a vision, Ananias. And he answered, [Here am] I, Lord.

11And the Lord said to him, Get up and go to the street called Straight, and ask at the house of Judas for a man of Tarsus named Saul, for behold, he is praying [there].

12And he has seen *in a vision* a man named Ananias enter and lay his hands on him so that he might regain his sight.

13But Ananias answered, Lord, I have heard many people tell about this man, especially how much evil *and* what great suffering he has brought on Your saints at Jerusalem;

14Now he is here and has authority from the high priests to put in chains all who call upon Your name.

15But the Lord said to him, Go, for this man is a chosen instrument of Mine to bear My name before the Gentiles and kings and the descendants of Israel;

16For I will make clear to him how much he will be afflicted *and* must endure *and* suffer for My name's sake.

17So Ananias left and went into the house. And he laid his hands on Saul and said, Brother Saul, the Lord Jesus Who appeared to you along the way by which you came here, has sent me that you may recover your sight and be filled with the Holy Spirit.

18And instantly something like scales fell from [Saul's] eyes, and he recovered his sight. Then he arose and was baptized,

19And after he took some food he was strengthened. For several days [afterward] he remained with the disciples at Damascus.

20And immediately in the synagogues he proclaimed Jesus, saying, He is the Son of God!

21And all who heard him were amazed, and said, Is not this the very man who harassed *and* overthrew *and* destroyed in Jerusalem those who called upon this Name? And he has come here for the express purpose of arresting them *and* bringing them in chains before the chief priests.

AMP [a] Vincent. [b] Vincent.

## New American Standard

39And when they came up out of the water, the Spirit of the Lord snatched Philip away; and the eunuch saw him no more, but went on his way rejoicing.

40But Philip found himself at Azotus; and as he passed through he kept preaching the gospel to all the cities, until he came to Caesarea.

*The Conversion of Saul*

9 NOW SAUL, still breathing threats and murder against the disciples of the Lord, went to the high priest,

2and asked for letters from him to the synagogues at Damascus, so that if he found any belonging to the Way, both men and women, he might bring them bound to Jerusalem.

3And it came about that as he journeyed, he was approaching Damascus, and suddenly a light from heaven flashed around him;

4and he fell to the ground, and heard a voice saying to him, "Saul, Saul, why are you persecuting Me?"

5And he said, "Who art Thou, Lord?" And He *said,* "I am Jesus whom you are persecuting,

6but rise, and enter the city, and it shall be told you what you must do."

7And the men who traveled with him stood speechless, hearing the voice, but seeing no one.

8And Saul got up from the ground, and though his eyes were open, he could see nothing; and leading him by the hand, they brought him into Damascus.

9And he was three days without sight, and neither ate nor drank.

10¶ Now there was a certain disciple at Damascus, named Ananias; and the Lord said to him in a vision, "Ananias." And he said, "Behold, *here am* I, Lord."

11And the Lord *said* to him, "Arise and go to the street called Straight, and inquire at the house of Judas for a man from Tarsus named Saul, for behold, he is praying,

12and he has seen [c]in a vision a man named Ananias come in and lay his hands on him, so that he might regain his sight."

13But Ananias answered, "Lord, I have heard from many about this man, how much harm he did to Thy saints at Jerusalem;

14and here he has authority from the chief priests to bind all who call upon Thy name."

15But the Lord said to him, "Go, for he is a chosen [d]instrument of Mine, to bear My name before the Gentiles and kings and the sons of Israel;

16for I will show him how much he must suffer for My name's sake."

17And Ananias departed and entered the house, and after laying his hands on him said, "Brother Saul, the Lord Jesus, who appeared to you on the road by which you were coming, has sent me so that you may regain your sight, and be filled with the Holy Spirit."

18And immediately there fell from his eyes something like scales, and he regained his sight, and he arose and was baptized;

19and he took food and was strengthened.

*Saul Begins to Preach Christ*

¶ Now for several days he was with the disciples who were at Damascus,

20and immediately he *began* to proclaim Jesus in the synagogues, saying, "He is the Son of God."

21And all those hearing him continued to be amazed, and were saying, "Is this not he who in Jerusalem destroyed those who called on this name, and *who* had come here for the purpose of bringing them bound before the chief priests?"

**NAS** [c] Some mss. do not contain *in a vision* [d] Or, *vessel*

## New International

suddenly took Philip away, and the eunuch did not see him again,
but went on his way rejoicing.
40Philip, however, appeared at
Azotus and traveled about, preaching the gospel in all the towns
until he reached Caesarea.

*Saul's Conversion*

9 MEANWHILE, SAUL was still breathing out murderous
threats against the Lord's disciples. He went to the high priest
2and asked him for letters to the synagogues in Damascus, so that
if he found any there who belonged to the Way, whether men or
women, he might take them as prisoners to Jerusalem.
3As he
neared Damascus on his journey, suddenly a light from heaven
flashed around him.
4He fell to the ground and heard a voice say
to him, "Saul, Saul, why do you persecute me?"
5"Who are you, Lord?" Saul asked.
"I am Jesus, whom you are persecuting," he replied.
6"Now get
up and go into the city, and you will be told what you must do."
7The men traveling with Saul stood there speechless; they
heard the sound but did not see anyone.
8Saul got up from the
ground, but when he opened his eyes he could see nothing. So
they led him by the hand into Damascus.
9For three days he was
blind, and did not eat or drink anything.
10In Damascus there was a disciple named Ananias. The Lord
called to him in a vision, "Ananias!"
"Yes, Lord," he answered.
11The Lord told him, "Go to the house of Judas on Straight
Street and ask for a man from Tarsus named Saul, for he is praying.
12In a vision he has seen a man named Ananias come and place
his hands on him to restore his sight."
13"Lord," Ananias answered, "I have heard many reports
about this man and all the harm he has done to your saints in
Jerusalem.
14And he has come here with authority from the chief
priests to arrest all who call on your name."
15But the Lord said to Ananias, "Go! This man is my chosen
instrument to carry my name before the Gentiles and their kings
and before the people of Israel.
16I will show him how much he
must suffer for my name."
17Then Ananias went to the house and entered it. Placing his
hands on Saul, he said, "Brother Saul, the Lord—Jesus, who appeared to you on the road as you were coming here—has sent me
so that you may see again and be filled with the Holy Spirit."
18Immediately, something like scales fell from Saul's eyes, and he
could see again. He got up and was baptized,
19and after taking
some food, he regained his strength.

*Saul in Damascus and Jerusalem*

Saul spent several days with the disciples in Damascus.
20At
once he began to preach in the synagogues that Jesus is the Son
of God.
21All those who heard him were astonished and asked,
"Isn't he the man who raised havoc in Jerusalem among those who
call on this name? And hasn't he come here to take them as
prisoners to the chief priests?"
22Yet Saul grew more and more

## King James

22 But Saul increased the more in strength, and confounded the Jews which dwelt at Damascus, proving that this is very Christ.

23 ¶ And after that many days were fulfilled, the Jews took counsel to kill him:

24 But their laying await was known of Saul. And they watched the gates day and night to kill him.

25 Then the disciples took him by night, and let *him* down by the wall in a basket.

26 And when Saul was come to Jerusalem, he assayed to join himself to the disciples: but they were all afraid of him, and believed not that he was a disciple.

27 But Barnabas took him, and brought *him* to the apostles, and declared unto them how he had seen the Lord in the way, and that he had spoken to him, and how he had preached boldly at Damascus in the name of Jesus.

28 And he was with them coming in and going out at Jerusalem.

29 And he spake boldly in the name of the Lord Jesus, and disputed against the Grecians: but they went about to slay him.

30 *Which* when the brethren knew, they brought him down to Caesarea, and sent him forth to Tarsus.

31 Then had the churches rest throughout all Judaea and Galilee and Samaria, and were edified; and walking in the fear of the Lord, and in the comfort of the Holy Ghost, were multiplied.

32 ¶ And it came to pass, as Peter passed throughout all *quarters*, he came down also to the saints which dwelt at Lydda.

33 And there he found a certain man named Aeneas, which had kept his bed eight years, and was sick of the palsy.

34 And Peter said unto him, Aeneas, Jesus Christ maketh thee whole: arise, and make thy bed. And he arose immediately.

35 And all that dwelt at Lydda and Saron saw him, and turned to the Lord.

36 ¶ Now there was at Joppa a certain disciple named Tabitha, which by interpretation is called Dorcas: this woman was full of good works and almsdeeds which she did.

37 And it came to pass in those days, that she was sick, and died: whom when they had washed, they laid *her* in an upper chamber.

38 And forasmuch as Lydda was nigh to Joppa, and the disciples had heard that Peter was there, they sent unto him two men, desiring *him* that he would not delay to come to them.

39 Then Peter arose and went with them. When he was come, they brought him into the upper chamber: and all the widows stood by him weeping, and showing the coats and garments which Dorcas made, while she was with them.

40 But Peter put them all forth, and kneeled down, and prayed; and turning *him* to the body said, Tabitha, arise. And she opened her eyes: and when she saw Peter, she sat up.

41 And he gave her *his* hand, and lifted her up, and when he had called the saints and widows, presented her alive.

42 And it was known throughout all Joppa; and many believed in the Lord.

43 And it came to pass, that he tarried many days in Joppa with one Simon a tanner.

**10** THERE WAS a certain man in Caesarea called Cornelius, a centurion of the band called the Italian *band*,

## Amplified

22 But Saul increased all the more in strength, and continued to confound *and* put to confusion the Jews who lived in Damascus by comparing *and* examining evidence *and* proving that Jesus is the Christ, the Messiah.

23 After considerable time had elapsed, the Jews conspired to put Saul out of the way by slaying him,

24 But [the knowledge of] their plot was made known to Saul. They were guarding the [city's] gates day and night to kill him,

25 But his disciples took him at night and let him down through the [city's] wall, lowering him in a basket *or* hamper.

26 And when he had arrived in Jerusalem he tried to associate himself with the disciples, but they were all afraid of him, for they did not believe he really was a disciple.

27 However, Barnabas took him and brought him to the apostles, and he explained to them how along the way he had seen the Lord, Who spoke to him, and how at Damascus he had preached freely *and* confidently *and* courageously in the name of Jesus.

28 So he went in and out [as one] among them at Jerusalem,

29 Preaching freely *and* confidently *and* boldly in the name of the Lord. And he spoke and discussed with *and* disputed against the Hellenists [the Grecian Jews], but they were seeking to slay him.

30 And when the brethren found it out, they brought him down to Caesarea, and sent him off to Tarsus [his home town].

31 So the church throughout the whole of Judea and Galilee and Samaria had peace and was edified—growing in wisdom, virtue and piety—and walking in the respect *and* reverential fear of the Lord and in the consolation *and* exhortation of the Holy Spirit, continued to increase *and* was multiplied.

32 Now as Peter went here and there among them all, he went down also to the saints who lived at Lydda.

33 There he found a man named Aeneas, who had been bedfast for eight years and was paralyzed.

34 And Peter said to him, Aeneas, Jesus Christ, the Messiah, [now] makes you whole. Get up and make your bed! And immediately [Aeneas] stood up.

35 Then all the inhabitants of Lydda and the plain of Sharon saw [what had happened to] him and they turned to the Lord.

36 Now there was at Joppa [a woman], a disciple named [in Aramaic] Tabitha, which [in Greek] means Dorcas or [in English] Gazelle. She was abounding in good deeds and acts of charity.

37 About that time she fell sick and died, and when they had cleansed her, they laid [her] in an upper room.

38 Since Lydda was near Joppa [however], the disciples hearing that Peter was there, sent two men to him begging him, Do come on to us without delay.

39 So Peter [immediately] rose and accompanied them. And when he had arrived, they took him to the upper room. All the widows stood around him crying, and displaying under-shirts (tunics) and [other] garments such as Dorcas was accustomed to make while she was with them.

40 But Peter put them all out [of the room] and knelt down and prayed; then turning to the body he said, Tabitha, get up! And she opened her eyes, and when she saw Peter she raised herself *and* sat upright.

41 And he gave her his hand and lifted her up. Then calling in God's people and the widows he presented her to them alive.

42 And this became known throughout all Joppa, and many came to believe on the Lord—that is, to adhere to and trust in and rely on Him as the Christ and as their Savior.

43 And Peter remained in Joppa for considerable time with one Simon, a tanner.

**10** NOW [LIVING] at Caesarea there was a man whose name was Cornelius, a centurion of what was known as the Italian Regiment,

## New American Standard

22But Saul kept increasing in strength and confounding the
Jews who lived at Damascus by proving that this *Jesus* is the Christ.
23¶ And when many days had elapsed, the Jews plotted together to do away with him,
24but their plot became known to Saul. And they were also
watching the gates day and night so that they might put him to
death;
25but his disciples took him by night, and let him down through
*an opening in* the wall, lowering him in a large basket.
26¶ And when he had come to Jerusalem, he was trying to
associate with the disciples; and they were all afraid of him, not
believing that he was a disciple.
27But Barnabas took hold of him and brought him to the apostles and described to them how he had seen the Lord on the road,
and that He had talked to him, and how at Damascus he had
spoken out boldly in the name of Jesus.
28And he was with them moving about freely in Jerusalem,
speaking out boldly in the name of the Lord.
29And he was talking and arguing with the Hellenistic *Jews;* but
they were attempting to put him to death.
30But when the brethren learned *of it,* they brought him down
to Caesarea and sent him away to Tarsus.
31¶ So the church throughout all Judea and Galilee and Samaria
enjoyed peace, being built up; and, going on in the fear of the Lord
and in the comfort of the Holy Spirit, it continued to increase.

*Peter's Ministry*

32¶ Now it came about that as Peter was traveling through all
*those parts,* he came down also to the saints who lived at Lydda.
33And there he found a certain man named Aeneas, who had
been bedridden eight years, for he was paralyzed.
34And Peter said to him, "Aeneas, Jesus Christ heals you; arise,
and make your bed." And immediately he arose.
35And all who lived at Lydda and Sharon saw him, and they
turned to the Lord.
36¶ Now in Joppa there was a certain disciple named Tabitha
(which translated *in Greek* is called Dorcas); this woman was
abounding with deeds of kindness and charity, which she continually did.
37And it came about at that time that she fell sick and died; and
when they had washed her body, they laid it in an upper room.
38And since Lydda was near Joppa, the disciples, having heard
that Peter was there, sent two men to him, entreating him, "Do
not delay to come to us."
39And Peter arose and went with them. And when he had
come, they brought him into the upper room; and all the widows
stood beside him weeping, and showing all the [a]tunics and garments that Dorcas used to make while she was with them.
40But Peter sent them all out and knelt down and prayed, and
turning to the body, he said, "Tabitha, arise." And she opened her
eyes, and when she saw Peter, she sat up.
41And he gave her his hand and raised her up; and calling the
saints and widows, he presented her alive.
42And it became known all over Joppa, and many believed in
the Lord.
43And it came about that he stayed many days in Joppa with a
certain tanner, Simon.

*Cornelius' Vision*

**10** NOW *THERE was* a certain man at Caesarea named Cornelius, a centurion of what was called the Italian [b]cohort,

NAS [a] Or, *inner garments* [b] Or, *battalion*

## New International

powerful and baffled the Jews living in Damascus by proving that
Jesus is the Christ.[c]
23After many days had gone by, the Jews conspired to kill him,
24but Saul learned of their plan. Day and night they kept close
watch on the city gates in order to kill him. 25But his followers took
him by night and lowered him in a basket through an opening in
the wall.
26When he came to Jerusalem, he tried to join the disciples, but
they were all afraid of him, not believing that he really was a
disciple. 27But Barnabas took him and brought him to the apostles.
He told them how Saul on his journey had seen the Lord and that
the Lord had spoken to him, and how in Damascus he had
preached fearlessly in the name of Jesus. 28So Saul stayed with
them and moved about freely in Jerusalem, speaking boldly in the
name of the Lord. 29He talked and debated with the Grecian Jews,
but they tried to kill him. 30When the brothers learned of this, they
took him down to Caesarea and sent him off to Tarsus.
31Then the church throughout Judea, Galilee and Samaria enjoyed a time of peace. It was strengthened; and encouraged by the
Holy Spirit, it grew in numbers, living in the fear of the Lord.

*Aeneas and Dorcas*

32As Peter traveled about the country, he went to visit the saints
in Lydda. 33There he found a man named Aeneas, a paralytic who
had been bedridden for eight years. 34"Aeneas," Peter said to him,
"Jesus Christ heals you. Get up and take care of your mat."
Immediately Aeneas got up. 35All those who lived in Lydda and
Sharon saw him and turned to the Lord.
36In Joppa there was a disciple named Tabitha (which, when
translated, is Dorcas[d]), who was always doing good and helping
the poor. 37About that time she became sick and died, and her
body was washed and placed in an upstairs room. 38Lydda was
near Joppa; so when the disciples heard that Peter was in Lydda,
they sent two men to him and urged him, "Please come at once!"
39Peter went with them, and when he arrived he was taken
upstairs to the room. All the widows stood around him, crying and
showing him the robes and other clothing that Dorcas had made
while she was still with them.
40Peter sent them all out of the room; then he got down on his
knees and prayed. Turning toward the dead woman, he said,
"Tabitha, get up." She opened her eyes, and seeing Peter she sat
up. 41He took her by the hand and helped her to her feet. Then
he called the believers and the widows and presented her to them
alive. 42This became known all over Joppa, and many people believed in the Lord. 43Peter stayed in Joppa for some time with a
tanner named Simon.

*Cornelius Calls for Peter*

**10** AT CAESAREA there was a man named Cornelius, a
centurion in what was known as the Italian Regiment. 2He

NIV [c] 22 Or *Messiah* [d] 36 Both *Tabitha* (Aramaic) and *Dorcas* (Greek) mean *gazelle.*

## King James

2 *A* devout *man,* and one that feared God with all his house, which gave much alms to the people, and prayed to God always.

3 He saw in a vision evidently about the ninth hour of the day an angel of God coming in to him, and saying unto him, Cornelius.

4 And when he looked on him, he was afraid, and said, What is it, Lord? And he said unto him, Thy prayers and thine alms are come up for a memorial before God.

5 And now send men to Joppa, and call for *one* Simon, whose surname is Peter:

6 He lodgeth with one Simon a tanner, whose house is by the sea side: he shall tell thee what thou oughtest to do.

7 And when the angel which spake unto Cornelius was departed, he called two of his household servants, and a devout soldier of them that waited on him continually;

8 And when he had declared all *these* things unto them, he sent them to Joppa.

9 ¶ On the morrow, as they went on their journey, and drew nigh unto the city, Peter went up upon the housetop to pray about the sixth hour:

10 And he became very hungry, and would have eaten: but while they made ready, he fell into a trance,

11 And saw heaven opened, and a certain vessel descending unto him, as it had been a great sheet knit at the four corners, and let down to the earth:

12 Wherein were all manner of fourfooted beasts of the earth, and wild beasts, and creeping things, and fowls of the air.

13 And there came a voice to him, Rise, Peter; kill, and eat.

14 But Peter said, Not so, Lord; for I have never eaten any thing that is common or unclean.

15 And the voice *spake* unto him again the second time, What God hath cleansed, *that* call not thou common.

16 This was done thrice: and the vessel was received up again into heaven.

17 Now while Peter doubted in himself what this vision which he had seen should mean, behold, the men which were sent from Cornelius had made inquiry for Simon's house, and stood before the gate,

18 And called, and asked whether Simon, which was surnamed Peter, were lodged there.

19 ¶ While Peter thought on the vision, the Spirit said unto him, Behold, three men seek thee.

20 Arise therefore, and get thee down, and go with them, doubting nothing: for I have sent them.

21 Then Peter went down to the men which were sent unto him from Cornelius; and said, Behold, I am he whom ye seek: what *is* the cause wherefore ye are come?

22 And they said, Cornelius the centurion, a just man, and one that feareth God, and of good report among all the nation of the Jews, was warned from God by an holy angel to send for thee into his house, and to hear words of thee.

23 Then called he them in, and lodged *them.* And on the morrow Peter went away with them, and certain brethren from Joppa accompanied him.

24 And the morrow after they entered into Caesarea. And Cornelius waited for them, and had called together his kinsmen and near friends.

25 And as Peter was coming in, Cornelius met him, and fell down at his feet, and worshipped *him.*

26 But Peter took him up, saying, Stand up; I myself also am a man.

27 And as he talked with him, he went in, and found many that were come together.

## Amplified

2 A devout man who venerated God *and* treated Him with reverential obedience, as did all his household, and he gave much alms to the people, and prayed continually to God.

3 About the ninth hour (three o'clock) of the day he saw clearly in a vision an angel of God entering and saying to him, Cornelius!

4 And he gazing intently at him became frightened, and said, What is it, Lord? And the angel said to him, Your prayers and your [generous] gifts to the poor have come up [as a sacrifice] to God *and* have been remembered by Him.

5 And now send men to Joppa, and have them call for *and* invite here one Simon whose surname is Peter;

6 He is lodging with Simon a tanner, whose house is by the seaside.

7 When the angel who spoke to him had left, Cornelius called two of his servants and a God-fearing soldier from among his own personal attendants.

8 And having rehearsed everything to them, he sent them to Joppa.

9 The next day as they were still on their way and were approaching the town, Peter went up to the roof of the house to pray, about the sixth hour (noon).

10 But he became very hungry, and wanted something to eat; and while the meal was being prepared a trance came over him,

11 And he saw the sky opened and something like a great sheet lowered by the four corners, descending to the earth.

12 It contained all kinds of quadrupeds *and wild beasts* and creeping things of the earth and birds of the air.

13 And there came a voice to him saying, Rise up, Peter, kill and eat.

14 But Peter said, No, by no means, Lord; for I have never eaten anything that is common *and* unhallowed or [ceremonially] unclean.

15 And the voice came to him again a second time, What God has cleansed *and* pronounced clean, do not you defile *and* profane by regarding *and* calling common *and* unhallowed or unclean.

16 This occurred three times, then immediately the sheet was taken up to heaven.

17 Now Peter was still inwardly perplexed *and* doubted as to what the vision which he had seen could mean, when [just then] behold the messengers that were sent by Cornelius, who had made inquiry for Simon's house, stopped *and* stood before the gate.

18 And they called out to inquire whether Simon who was surnamed Peter was staying there.

19 And while Peter was [a]earnestly revolving the vision in his mind *and* meditating on it, the (Holy) Spirit said to him, Behold, three men are looking for you!

20 Get up and go below and accompany them without any doubt [about its legality] *or* any discrimination *or* hesitation, for I have sent them.

21 Then Peter went down to the men and said, I am the man you seek; what is the purpose of your coming?

22 And they said, Cornelius, a centurion (captain) who is just *and* upright *and* in right standing with God, being God-fearing *and* obedient, and well spoken of by the whole Jewish nation, has been instructed by a holy angel to send for you to come to his house; and he [b]has received in answer [to prayer] a warning to listen to *and* act upon what you have to say.

23 So Peter invited them in to be his guests [for the night]. The next day he arose and went away with them, and some of the brethren from Joppa accompanied him.

24 And on the following day they entered Caesarea. Cornelius was waiting for *and* expecting them, and he had invited together his relatives and his intimate friends.

25 As Peter arrived, Cornelius met him, and falling down at his feet he made obeisance *and* paid worshipful reverence to him.

26 But Peter raised him up, saying, Get up; I myself am also a man.

27 And as [Peter] spoke with him, he entered the house and found a large group of persons assembled;

**AMP** [a] Vincent. [b] Vincent.

## New American Standard

2 a devout man, and one who feared God with all his household, and gave many [c]alms to the *Jewish* people, and prayed to God continually.

3 About the [d]ninth hour of the day he clearly saw in a vision an angel of God who had *just* come in to him, and said to him, "Cornelius!"

4 And fixing his gaze upon him and being much alarmed, he said, "What is it, Lord?" And he said to him, "Your prayers and [e]alms have ascended as a memorial before God.

5 "And now dispatch *some* men to Joppa, and send for a man *named* Simon, who is also called Peter;

6 he is staying with a certain tanner *named* Simon, whose house is by the sea."

7 And when the angel who was speaking to him had departed, he summoned two of his servants and a devout soldier of those who were in constant attendance upon him,

8 and after he had explained everything to them, he sent them to Joppa.

9 ¶ And on the next day, as they were on their way, and approaching the city, Peter went up on the housetop about the [f]sixth hour to pray.

10 And he became hungry, and was desiring to eat; but while they were making preparations, he fell into a trance;

11 and he *beheld the sky opened up, and a certain [g]object like a great sheet coming down, lowered by four corners to the ground,

12 and there were in it all *kinds of* four-footed animals and [h]crawling creatures of the earth and birds of the air.

13 And a voice came to him, "Arise, Peter, kill and eat!"

14 But Peter said, "By no means, Lord, for I have never eaten anything unholy and unclean."

15 And again a voice *came* to him a second time, "What God has cleansed, no *longer* consider unholy."

16 And this happened three times; and immediately the object was taken up into the sky.

17 ¶ Now while Peter was greatly perplexed in mind as to what the vision which he had seen might be, behold, the men who had been sent by Cornelius, having asked directions for Simon's house, appeared at the gate;

18 and calling out, they were asking whether Simon, who was also called Peter, was staying there.

19 And while Peter was reflecting on the vision, the Spirit said to him, "Behold, three men are looking for you.

20 "But arise, go downstairs, and accompany them without misgivings; for I have sent them Myself."

21 And Peter went down to the men and said, "Behold, I am the one you are looking for; what is the reason for which you have come?"

22 And they said, "Cornelius, a centurion, a righteous and God-fearing man well spoken of by the entire nation of the Jews, was *divinely* directed by a holy angel to send for you *to come* to his house and hear a message from you."

23 And so he invited them in and gave them lodging.

*Peter at Caesarea*

¶ And on the next day he arose and went away with them, and some of the brethren from Joppa accompanied him.

24 And on the following day he entered Caesarea. Now Cornelius was waiting for them, and had called together his relatives and close friends.

25 And when it came about that Peter entered, Cornelius met him, and fell at his feet and worshiped *him.*

26 But Peter raised him up, saying, "Stand up; I too am *just* a man."

27 And as he talked with him, he entered, and found many people assembled.

NAS [c] Or, *gifts of charity* [d] I.e., 3 p.m. [e] Or, *deeds of charity* [f] I.e., noon [g] Or, *vessel* [h] Or possibly, *reptiles*

## New International

and all his family were devout and God-fearing; he gave generously to those in need and prayed to God regularly.
3 One day at about
three in the afternoon he had a vision. He distinctly saw an angel
of God, who came to him and said, "Cornelius!"
4 Cornelius stared at him in fear. "What is it, Lord?" he asked.
The angel answered, "Your prayers and gifts to the poor have
come up as a memorial offering before God.
5 Now send men to
Joppa to bring back a man named Simon who is called Peter.
6 He
is staying with Simon the tanner, whose house is by the sea."
7 When the angel who spoke to him had gone, Cornelius called
two of his servants and a devout soldier who was one of his
attendants.
8 He told them everything that had happened and sent
them to Joppa.

*Peter's Vision*

9 About noon the following day as they were on their journey
and approaching the city, Peter went up on the roof to pray.
10 He
became hungry and wanted something to eat, and while the meal
was being prepared, he fell into a trance.
11 He saw heaven opened
and something like a large sheet being let down to earth by its four
corners.
12 It contained all kinds of four-footed animals, as well as
reptiles of the earth and birds of the air.
13 Then a voice told him,
"Get up, Peter. Kill and eat."
14 "Surely not, Lord!" Peter replied. "I have never eaten anything impure or unclean."
15 The voice spoke to him a second time, "Do not call anything
impure that God has made clean."
16 This happened three times, and immediately the sheet was
taken back to heaven.
17 While Peter was wondering about the meaning of the vision,
the men sent by Cornelius found out where Simon's house was
and stopped at the gate.
18 They called out, asking if Simon who
was known as Peter was staying there.
19 While Peter was still thinking about the vision, the Spirit said
to him, "Simon, three[i] men are looking for you.
20 So get up and
go downstairs. Do not hesitate to go with them, for I have sent
them."
21 Peter went down and said to the men, "I'm the one you're
looking for. Why have you come?"
22 The men replied, "We have come from Cornelius the centurion. He is a righteous and God-fearing man, who is respected by
all the Jewish people. A holy angel told him to have you come to
his house so that he could hear what you have to say."
23 Then
Peter invited the men into the house to be his guests.

*Peter at Cornelius' House*

The next day Peter started out with them, and some of the
brothers from Joppa went along.
24 The following day he arrived
in Caesarea. Cornelius was expecting them and had called together his relatives and close friends.
25 As Peter entered the house,
Cornelius met him and fell at his feet in reverence.
26 But Peter
made him get up. "Stand up," he said, "I am only a man myself."
27 Talking with him, Peter went inside and found a large gathering of people.
28 He said to them: "You are well aware that it is

NIV [i] *19* One early manuscript *two;* other manuscripts do not have the number.

## King James

28And he said unto them, Ye know how that it is an unlawful thing for a man that is a Jew to keep company, or come unto one of another nation; but God hath shown me that I should not call any man common or unclean.

29Therefore came I *unto you* without gainsaying, as soon as I was sent for: I ask therefore for what intent ye have sent for me?

30And Cornelius said, Four days ago I was fasting until this hour; and at the ninth hour I prayed in my house, and, behold, a man stood before me in bright clothing,

31And said, Cornelius, thy prayer is heard, and thine alms are had in remembrance in the sight of God.

32Send therefore to Joppa, and call hither Simon, whose surname is Peter; he is lodged in the house of *one* Simon a tanner by the sea side: who, when he cometh, shall speak unto thee.

33Immediately therefore I sent to thee; and thou hast well done that thou art come. Now therefore are we all here present before God, to hear all things that are commanded thee of God.

34¶ Then Peter opened *his* mouth, and said, Of a truth I perceive that God is no respecter of persons:

35But in every nation he that feareth him, and worketh righteousness, is accepted with him.

36The word which *God* sent unto the children of Israel, preaching peace by Jesus Christ: (he is Lord of all:)

37That word, *I say*, ye know, which was published throughout all Judaea, and began from Galilee, after the baptism which John preached;

38How God anointed Jesus of Nazareth with the Holy Ghost and with power: who went about doing good, and healing all that were oppressed of the devil; for God was with him.

39And we are witnesses of all things which he did both in the land of the Jews, and in Jerusalem; whom they slew and hanged on a tree:

40Him God raised up the third day, and showed him openly;

41Not to all the people, but unto witnesses chosen before of God, *even* to us, who did eat and drink with him after he rose from the dead.

42And he commanded us to preach unto the people, and to testify that it is he which was ordained of God *to be* the Judge of quick and dead.

43To him give all the prophets witness, that through his name whosoever believeth in him shall receive remission of sins.

44¶ While Peter yet spake these words, the Holy Ghost fell on all them which heard the word.

45And they of the circumcision which believed were astonished, as many as came with Peter, because that on the Gentiles also was poured out the gift of the Holy Ghost.

46For they heard them speak with tongues, and magnify God. Then answered Peter,

47Can any man forbid water, that these should not be baptized, which have received the Holy Ghost as well as we?

48And he commanded them to be baptized in the name of the Lord. Then prayed they him to tarry certain days.

## Amplified

28And he said to them, You yourselves are aware how it is not lawful *or* permissible for a Jew to keep company with *or* to visit *or* [even] to come near *or* to speak first to any one of another nationality, but God has shown *and* taught me by words that I should not call any human being common *or* unhallowed or (ceremonially) unclean.

29Therefore when I was sent for, I came without hesitation *or* objection *or* misgivings. So now I ask for what reason you sent for me.

30And Cornelius said, This is now the fourth day since about this time I was observing the ninth hour [three o'clock in the afternoon] of prayer in my lodging place, when [suddenly] a man stood before me in dazzling apparel;

31And he said, Cornelius, your prayer has been heard *and* harkened to, and your donations to the poor have been known *and* [a]preserved before God—so that He heeds and is about to help you.

32Send therefore to Joppa and ask for Simon who is surnamed Peter; he is staying in the house of Simon the tanner, by the seaside.

33So at once I sent for you, and you [being a Jew] have done a kind *and* [b]courteous *and* handsome thing in coming. Now then, we are all present in the sight of God to listen to all that you have been instructed by the Lord to say.

34And Peter opened his mouth and said: Most certainly *and* thoroughly I now perceive *and* understand that God shows no partiality *and* is no respecter of persons,

35But in every nation he who venerates *and* has a reverential fear for God, treating Him with worshipful obedience and living uprightly, is acceptable to Him, *and* [c]sure of being received and welcomed [by Him].

36You know the contents of the message which He sent to Israel, announcing the good news (Gospel) of peace by Jesus Christ, Who is Lord of all,

37The [same] message which was proclaimed throughout all Judea, starting from Galilee after the baptism preached by John:

38How God anointed *and* consecrated Jesus of Nazareth with the (Holy) Spirit and with strength *and* ability *and* power; how He went about doing good and [d]in particular curing all that were harassed *and* oppressed by [the power of] the devil, for God was with Him.

39And we are [eye and ear] witnesses of everything that He did both in the land of the Jews and in Jerusalem. And [yet] they put Him out of the way—murdered Him—by hanging Him on a tree;

40But God raised Him to life on the third day and caused Him to be manifest—to be plainly seen—

41Not by all the people but to us who were chosen (designated) beforehand by God as witnesses, who ate and drank with Him after He arose from the dead.

42And He charged us to preach to the people, and to bear solemn testimony that He is the God-appointed *and* God-ordained Judge of the living and the dead.

43To Him all the prophets testify (bear witness) that every one who believes in Him—who adheres to, trusts in and relies on Him, giving himself up to Him—receives forgiveness of sins through His name.

44While Peter was still speaking these words, the Holy Spirit fell on all who were listening to the message.

45And the believers from among the circumcised [the Jews] who came with Peter were surprised *and* amazed, because the free gift of the Holy Spirit had been bestowed *and* poured out largely even on the Gentiles.

46For they heard them talking in [unknown] languages and extolling *and* magnifying God. Then Peter asked,

47Can any one forbid *or* refuse water for baptizing these people, seeing that they have received the Holy Spirit just as we have?

48And he ordered that they be baptized in the name of Jesus Christ, the Messiah. Then they begged him to stay on there for some days.

**AMP** [a] Thayer. [b] Vincent. [c] Webster's definition of "acceptable." [d] Vincent

## New American Standard

28And he said to them, "You yourselves know how unlawful
it is for a man who is a Jew to associate with a foreigner or to visit
him; and *yet* God has shown me that I should not call any man
unholy or unclean.
29"That is why I came without even raising any objection when
I was sent for. And so I ask for what reason you have sent for me."
30And Cornelius said, "Four days ago to this hour, I was praying in my house during the [e]ninth hour; and behold, a man stood
before me in shining garments,
31and he *said, 'Cornelius, your prayer has been heard and your
alms have been remembered before God.
32'Send therefore to Joppa and invite Simon, who is also called
Peter, to come to you; he is staying at the house of Simon *the* tanner
by the sea.'
33"And so I sent to you immediately, and you have been kind
enough to come. Now then, we are all here present before God to
hear all that you have been commanded by the Lord."

*Gentiles Hear Good News*

34And opening his mouth, Peter said:
¶ "I most certainly understand *now* that God is not one to show
partiality,
35but in every nation the man who fears Him and does what is
right, is welcome to Him.
36"The word which He sent to the sons of Israel, preaching
peace through Jesus Christ (He is Lord of all)—
37you yourselves know the thing which took place throughout
all Judea, starting from Galilee, after the baptism which John proclaimed.
38" *You know of* Jesus of Nazareth, how God anointed Him with
the Holy Spirit and with power, and *how* He went about doing
good, and healing all who were oppressed by the devil; for God
was with Him.
39"And we are witnesses of all the things He did both in the
land of the Jews and in Jerusalem. And they also put Him to death
by hanging Him on a cross.
40"God raised Him up on the third day, and granted that He
should become visible,
41not to all the people, but to witnesses who were chosen
beforehand by God, *that is,* to us, who ate and drank with Him
after He arose from the dead.
42"And He ordered us to preach to the people, and solemnly
to testify that this is the One who has been appointed by God as
Judge of the living and the dead.
43"Of Him all the prophets bear witness that through His name
everyone who believes in Him receives forgiveness of sins."
44¶ While Peter was still speaking these words, the Holy Spirit
fell upon all those who were listening to the message.
45And all the circumcised believers who had come with Peter
were amazed, because the gift of the Holy Spirit had been poured
out upon the Gentiles also.
46For they were hearing them speaking with tongues and exalting God. Then Peter answered,
47"Surely no one can refuse the water for these to be baptized
who have received the Holy Spirit just as we *did,* can he?"
48And he ordered them to be baptized in the name of Jesus
Christ. Then they asked him to stay on for a few days.

NAS [e] I.e., 3 to 4 p.m.

## New International

against our law for a Jew to associate with a Gentile or visit him.
But God has shown me that I should not call any man impure or
unclean. 29So when I was sent for, I came without raising any
objection. May I ask why you sent for me?"
30Cornelius answered: "Four days ago I was in my house praying at this hour, at three in the afternoon. Suddenly a man in
shining clothes stood before me 31and said, 'Cornelius, God has
heard your prayer and remembered your gifts to the poor. 32Send
to Joppa for Simon who is called Peter. He is a guest in the home
of Simon the tanner, who lives by the sea.' 33So I sent for you
immediately, and it was good of you to come. Now we are all here
in the presence of God to listen to everything the Lord has commanded you to tell us."
34Then Peter began to speak: "I now realize how true it is that
God does not show favoritism 35but accepts men from every nation
who fear him and do what is right. 36You know the message God
sent to the people of Israel, telling the good news of peace through
Jesus Christ, who is Lord of all. 37You know what has happened
throughout Judea, beginning in Galilee after the baptism that John
preached— 38how God anointed Jesus of Nazareth with the Holy
Spirit and power, and how he went around doing good and healing all who were under the power of the devil, because God was
with him.
39"We are witnesses of everything he did in the country of the
Jews and in Jerusalem. They killed him by hanging him on a tree,
40but God raised him from the dead on the third day and caused
him to be seen. 41He was not seen by all the people, but by
witnesses whom God had already chosen—by us who ate and
drank with him after he rose from the dead. 42He commanded us
to preach to the people and to testify that he is the one whom God
appointed as judge of the living and the dead. 43All the prophets
testify about him that everyone who believes in him receives forgiveness of sins through his name."
44While Peter was still speaking these words, the Holy Spirit
came on all who heard the message. 45The circumcised believers
who had come with Peter were astonished that the gift of the Holy
Spirit had been poured out even on the Gentiles. 46For they heard
them speaking in tongues[f] and praising God.
Then Peter said, 47"Can anyone keep these people from being
baptized with water? They have received the Holy Spirit just as we
have." 48So he ordered that they be baptized in the name of Jesus
Christ. Then they asked Peter to stay with them for a few days.

NIV [f] 46 Or *other languages*

## King James

11 AND THE apostles and brethren that were in Judaea heard that the Gentiles had also received the word of God.

2And when Peter was come up to Jerusalem, they that were of the circumcision contended with him,

3Saying, Thou wentest in to men uncircumcised, and didst eat with them.

4But Peter rehearsed *the matter* from the beginning, and expounded *it* by order unto them, saying,

5I was in the city of Joppa praying: and in a trance I saw a vision, A certain vessel descend, as it had been a great sheet, let down from heaven by four corners; and it came even to me:

6Upon the which when I had fastened mine eyes, I considered, and saw fourfooted beasts of the earth, and wild beasts, and creeping things, and fowls of the air.

7And I heard a voice saying unto me, Arise, Peter; slay and eat.

8But I said, Not so, Lord: for nothing common or unclean hath at any time entered into my mouth.

9But the voice answered me again from heaven, What God hath cleansed, *that* call not thou common.

10And this was done three times: and all were drawn up again into heaven.

11And, behold, immediately there were three men already come unto the house where I was, sent from Caesarea unto me.

12And the Spirit bade me go with them, nothing doubting. Moreover these six brethren accompanied me, and we entered into the man's house:

13And he showed us how he had seen an angel in his house, which stood and said unto him, Send men to Joppa, and call for Simon, whose surname is Peter;

14Who shall tell thee words, whereby thou and all thy house shall be saved.

15And as I began to speak, the Holy Ghost fell on them, as on us at the beginning.

16Then remembered I the word of the Lord, how that he said, John indeed baptized with water; but ye shall be baptized with the Holy Ghost.

17Forasmuch then as God gave them the like gift as *he did* unto us, who believed on the Lord Jesus Christ; what was I, that I could withstand God?

18When they heard these things, they held their peace, and glorified God, saying, Then hath God also to the Gentiles granted repentance unto life.

19¶ Now they which were scattered abroad upon the persecution that arose about Stephen travelled as far as Phenice, and Cyprus, and Antioch, preaching the word to none but unto the Jews only.

20And some of them were men of Cyprus and Cyrene, which, when they were come to Antioch, spake unto the Grecians, preaching the Lord Jesus.

21And the hand of the Lord was with them: and a great number believed, and turned unto the Lord.

22¶ Then tidings of these things came unto the ears of the church which was in Jerusalem: and they sent forth Barnabas, that he should go as far as Antioch.

## Amplified

11 NOW THE apostles (special messengers) and the brethren who were throughout Judea heard [with astonishment] that the Gentiles (heathen) also had received *and* accepted *and* welcomed the Word of God—that is, the doctrine concerning the attainment through Christ of salvation in the kingdom of God.

2So when Peter went up to Jerusalem, the circumcision party [the Jewish Christians] found fault with him—separating themselves from him in a hostile spirit, opposing and disputing and contending with him—

3Saying, Why do you go to uncircumcised men and [even] eat with them?

4But Peter began [at the beginning] and narrated *and* explained to them step by step [the whole list of events]. He said:

5I was in the town of Joppa praying, and [falling] in a trance I saw a vision, of something coming down from heaven, like a huge sheet lowered by the four corners; and it descended until it came to me.

6Gazing intently *and* closely at it I observed in it [a variety] of four-footed animals and wild beasts and reptiles of the earth and birds of the air,

7And I heard a voice saying to me, Get up, Peter; kill and eat.

8But I said, [No] by no means, Lord; for nothing common *or* unhallowed or (ceremonially) unclean has ever entered my mouth.

9But the voice answered a second time from heaven, What God has cleansed *and* pronounced clean, do not you defile *and* profane by regarding *or* calling it common *or* unhallowed or unclean.

10This occurred three times, and then all was drawn up again into heaven.

11And right then the three men sent to me from Caesarea arrived at the house in which we were.

12And the (Holy) Spirit instructed me to accompany them without [the least] hesitation *or* misgivings *or* discrimination. So these six brethren accompanied me also and we went into the man's house.

13And he related to us how he had seen the angel in his house which stood and said to him, Send men to Joppa and bring Simon who is surnamed Peter;

14He will give *and* explain to you a message by means of which you and all your household [as well] will be saved [ [a]from eternal death].

15When I began to speak, the Holy Spirit fell on them just as on us at the beginning.

16Then I recalled the declaration of the Lord, how He said, John indeed baptized with water, but you shall be baptized with— [b]be placed in, introduced into—the Holy Spirit.

17If then God gave to them the same Gift [equally] as He gave to us when we believed—adhering to, trusting in and relying on—the Lord Jesus Christ, who was I *and* what power *or* authority had I to interfere *or* hinder *or* forbid *or* withstand God?

18When they heard this they were quieted *and* made no further objection. And they glorified God, saying, Then God has also granted to the Gentiles repentance [c]unto [real] life [after resurrection].

19Meanwhile those who were scattered because of the persecution that arose in connection with Stephen had traveled as far away as Phoenicia and Cyprus and Antioch, without delivering the message [concerning [d]the attainment through Christ of salvation in the kingdom of God] to any one except Jews.

20But there were some of them, men of Cyprus and Cyrene, who on returning to Antioch spoke to the Greeks also, proclaiming [to them] the good news, the Lord Jesus.

21And the presence of the Lord was with them with power, so that a great number [learned] to believe—to adhere to and trust in and rely on the Lord—and turned *and* surrendered themselves to Him.

22The rumors of this came to the ears of the church (assembly) in Jerusalem, and they sent Barnabas to Antioch.

**AMP** [a] Cremer. [b] Wuest's "Untranslatable Riches from the Greek New Testament." [c] Thayer. [d] Cremer's "Biblico-Theological Lexicon in New Testament Greek."

## New American Standard

*Peter Reports at Jerusalem*

**11** NOW THE apostles and the brethren who were throughout Judea heard that the Gentiles also had received the word of God.

2And when Peter came up to Jerusalem, those who were circumcised took issue with him,

3saying, "You went to uncircumcised men and ate with them."

4But Peter began *speaking* and *proceeded* to explain to them in orderly sequence, saying,

5"I was in the city of Joppa praying; and in a trance I saw a vision, a certain object coming down like a great sheet lowered by four corners from the sky; and it came right down to me,

6and when I had fixed my gaze upon it and was observing it I saw the four-footed animals of the earth and the wild beasts and the [e]crawling creatures and the birds of the air.

7"And I also heard a voice saying to me, 'Arise, Peter; kill and eat.'

8"But I said, 'By no means, Lord, for nothing unholy or unclean has ever entered my mouth.'

9"But a voice from heaven answered a second time, 'What God has cleansed, no longer consider unholy.'

10"And this happened three times, and everything was drawn back up into the sky.

11"And behold, at that moment three men appeared before the house in which we were *staying,* having been sent to me from Caesarea.

12"And the Spirit told me to go with them without misgivings. And these six brethren also went with me, and we entered the man's house.

13"And he reported to us how he had seen the angel standing in his house, and saying, 'Send to Joppa, and have Simon, who is also called Peter, brought here;

14and he shall speak words to you by which you will be saved, you and all your household.'

15"And as I began to speak, the Holy Spirit fell upon them, just as *He did* upon us at the beginning.

16"And I remembered the word of the Lord, how He used to say, 'John baptized with water, but you shall be baptized with the Holy Spirit.'

17"If God therefore gave to them the same gift as *He gave* to us also after believing in the Lord Jesus Christ, who was I that I could stand in God's way?"

18And when they heard this, they quieted down, and glorified God, saying, "Well then, God has granted to the Gentiles also the repentance *that leads* to life."

*The Church at Antioch*

19¶ So then those who were scattered because of the persecution that arose in connection with Stephen made their way to Phoenicia and Cyprus and Antioch, speaking the word to no one except to Jews alone.

20But there were some of them, men of Cyprus and Cyrene, who came to Antioch and *began* speaking to the [f]Greeks also, preaching the Lord Jesus.

21And the hand of the Lord was with them, and a large number who believed turned to the Lord.

22And the news about them reached the ears of the church at Jerusalem, and they sent Barnabas off to Antioch.

NAS [e] Or possibly, *reptiles* [f] Some mss. read *Greek-speaking Jews*

## New International

*Peter Explains His Actions*

**11** THE APOSTLES and the brothers throughout Judea heard
that the Gentiles also had received the word of God. 2So
when Peter went up to Jerusalem, the circumcised believers criticized him 3and said, "You went into the house of uncircumcised
men and ate with them."

4Peter began and explained everything to them precisely as it
had happened: 5"I was in the city of Joppa praying, and in a trance
I saw a vision. I saw something like a large sheet being let down
from heaven by its four corners, and it came down to where I was.
6I looked into it and saw four-footed animals of the earth, wild
beasts, reptiles, and birds of the air. 7Then I heard a voice telling
me, 'Get up, Peter. Kill and eat.'

8"I replied, 'Surely not, Lord! Nothing impure or unclean has
ever entered my mouth.'

9"The voice spoke from heaven a second time, 'Do not call
anything impure that God has made clean.' 10This happened three
times, and then it was all pulled up to heaven again.

11"Right then three men who had been sent to me from Caesarea stopped at the house where I was staying. 12The Spirit told me
to have no hesitation about going with them. These six brothers
also went with me, and we entered the man's house. 13He told us
how he had seen an angel appear in his house and say, 'Send to
Joppa for Simon who is called Peter. 14He will bring you a message
through which you and all your household will be saved.'

15"As I began to speak, the Holy Spirit came on them as he had
come on us at the beginning. 16Then I remembered what the Lord
had said: 'John baptized with[g] water, but you will be baptized with
the Holy Spirit.' 17So if God gave them the same gift as he gave
us, who believed in the Lord Jesus Christ, who was I to think that
I could oppose God?"

18When they heard this, they had no further objections and
praised God, saying, "So then, God has granted even the Gentiles
repentance unto life."

*The Church in Antioch*

19Now those who had been scattered by the persecution in
connection with Stephen traveled as far as Phoenicia, Cyprus and
Antioch, telling the message only to Jews. 20Some of them, however, men from Cyprus and Cyrene, went to Antioch and began
to speak to Greeks also, telling them the good news about the Lord
Jesus. 21The Lord's hand was with them, and a great number of
people believed and turned to the Lord.

22News of this reached the ears of the church at Jerusalem, and
they sent Barnabas to Antioch. 23When he arrived and saw the

NIV [g] *16* Or *in*

## King James

23 Who, when he came, and had seen the grace of God, was
glad, and exhorted them all, that with purpose of heart they would
cleave unto the Lord.
24 For he was a good man, and full of the Holy Ghost and of
faith: and much people was added unto the Lord.
25 Then departed Barnabas to Tarsus, for to seek Saul:
26 And when he had found him, he brought him unto Antioch.
And it came to pass, that a whole year they assembled themselves
with the church, and taught much people. And the disciples were
called Christians first in Antioch.
27 ¶ And in these days came prophets from Jerusalem unto
Antioch.
28 And there stood up one of them named Agabus, and signified
by the Spirit that there should be great dearth throughout all the
world: which came to pass in the days of Claudius Caesar.
29 Then the disciples, every man according to his ability, determined to send relief unto the brethren which dwelt in Judaea:
30 Which also they did, and sent it to the elders by the hands of
Barnabas and Saul.

**12** NOW ABOUT that time Herod the king stretched forth *his*
hands to vex certain of the church.
2 And he killed James the brother of John with the sword.
3 And because he saw it pleased the Jews, he proceeded further
to take Peter also. (Then were the days of unleavened bread.)
4 And when he had apprehended him, he put *him* in prison, and
delivered *him* to four quaternions of soldiers to keep him; intending after Easter to bring him forth to the people.
5 Peter therefore was kept in prison: but prayer was made without ceasing of the church unto God for him.
6 And when Herod would have brought him forth, the same
night Peter was sleeping between two soldiers, bound with two
chains: and the keepers before the door kept the prison.
7 And, behold, the angel of the Lord came upon *him*, and a light
shined in the prison: and he smote Peter on the side, and raised
him up, saying, Arise up quickly. And his chains fell off from *his*
hands.
8 And the angel said unto him, Gird thyself, and bind on thy
sandals. And so he did. And he saith unto him, Cast thy garment
about thee, and follow me.
9 And he went out, and followed him; and wist not that it was
true which was done by the angel; but thought he saw a vision.
10 When they were past the first and the second ward, they came
unto the iron gate that leadeth unto the city; which opened to them
of his own accord: and they went out, and passed on through one
street; and forthwith the angel departed from him.
11 And when Peter was come to himself, he said, Now I know
of a surety, that the Lord hath sent his angel, and hath delivered
me out of the hand of Herod, and *from* all the expectation of the
people of the Jews.
12 And when he had considered *the thing*, he came to the house
of Mary the mother of John, whose surname was Mark; where
many were gathered together praying.
13 And as Peter knocked at the door of the gate, a damsel came
to hearken, named Rhoda.

## Amplified

23 When he arrived and saw what grace (favor) God was bestowing upon them, he was full of joy; and he continuously exhorted—
warned, urged and encouraged—them all to cleave unto *and* remain faithful *and* devoted to the Lord with [resolute and steady]
purpose of heart.
24 For he was a good man [ [a]good in himself and also at once for
the good and the advantage of other people], full of *and* controlled
by the Holy Spirit and full of faith [that is, of his [b]belief that Jesus
is the Messiah, through Whom we obtain eternal salvation]. And
a large company was added to the Lord.
25 [Barnabas] went on to Tarsus to hunt for Saul.
26 And when he had found him, he brought him back to Antioch. For a whole year they assembled together with *and* [c]were
guests of the church, and instructed a large number of people; and
in Antioch the disciples were first called Christians.
27 And during these days prophets—inspired teachers and interpreters of the divine will and purpose—came down from Jerusalem to Antioch.
28 And one of them named Agabus stood up and prophesied
through the (Holy) Spirit that there would be a great *and* severe
famine come upon the whole world. And this did occur during the
reign of Claudius.
29 So the disciples resolved to send relief, every one according
to his individual ability—in proportion as he had prospered—to
the brethren who lived in Judea.
30 And so they did, sending [their contributions] to the elders by
the hand of Barnabas and Saul.

**12** ABOUT THAT time Herod the king stretched forth his
hands to afflict *and* oppress *and* torment some who belonged to the church (assembly).
2 And he killed James the brother of John with a sword;
3 And when he saw that it was pleasing to the Jews, he proceeded further and arrested Peter also. This was during the days
of Unleavened Bread (the Passover week).
4 And when he had seized [Peter], he put him in prison and
delivered him to four squads of soldiers of four each to guard him,
purposing after the Passover to bring him forth to the people.
5 So Peter was kept in prison; but fervent prayer for him was
persistently made to God by the church (assembly).
6 The very night before Herod was about to bring him forth,
Peter was sleeping between two soldiers, fastened with two
chains, and sentries before the door were guarding the prison.
7 And suddenly an angel of the Lord appeared, standing beside
him, and a light shone in the place where he was. And the angel
gently smote Peter on the side and awakened him, saying, Get up
quickly! And the chains fell off his hands.
8 And the angel said to him, Tighten your girdle and bind on
your sandals. And he did so. And he said to him, Wrap your outer
garment around you and follow me.
9 And [Peter] went out [along] following him, and he was not
conscious that what was apparently being done by the angel was
real, but thought he was seeing a vision.
10 When they had passed through the first guard and the second, they came to the iron gate which leads into the city. Of its own
accord [the gate] swung open, and they went out and passed on
through one street; and at once the angel left him.
11 Then Peter came to himself, and said, Now I really know *and*
am sure that the Lord has sent His angel and delivered me out of
the hand of Herod and from all that the Jewish people were expecting to do to me.
12 When he at a glance became aware of this— [d]comprehending
[all the elements of the case]—he went to the house of Mary, the
mother of John whose surname was Mark, where a large number
were assembled together and were praying.
13 And when he knocked at the gate of the porch, a maid named
Rhoda [Rose, in English] came to answer.

**AMP** [a] Cremer's "Biblico-Theological Lexicon in New Testament Greek."
[b] Thayer. [c] Alternate reading. [d] Vincent.

## New American Standard

23Then when he had come and witnessed the grace of God, he
rejoiced and *began* to encourage them all with resolute heart to
remain *true* to the Lord;
24for he was a good man, and full of the Holy Spirit and of faith.
And considerable numbers were brought to the Lord.
25And he left for Tarsus to look for Saul;
26and when he had found him, he brought him to Antioch. And
it came about that for an entire year they met with the church, and
taught considerable numbers; and the disciples were first called
Christians in Antioch.
27¶ Now at this time some prophets came down from Jerusalem
to Antioch.
28And one of them named Agabus stood up and *began* to indicate by the Spirit that there would certainly be a great famine all
over the world. And this took place in the *reign* of Claudius.
29And in the proportion that any of the disciples had means,
each of them determined to send *a contribution* for the relief of the
brethren living in Judea.
30And this they did, sending it in charge of Barnabas and Saul
to the elders.

*Peter's Arrest and Deliverance*

**12** NOW ABOUT that time Herod the king laid hands on
some who belonged to the church, in order to mistreat
them.
2And he had James the brother of John put to death with a
sword.
3And when he saw that it pleased the Jews, he proceeded to
arrest Peter also. Now it was during the days of Unleavened Bread.
4And when he had seized him, he put him in prison, delivering him to four squads of soldiers to guard him, intending after the
Passover to bring him out before the people.
5So Peter was kept in the prison, but prayer for him was being
made fervently by the church to God.
6And on the very night when Herod was about to bring him
forward, Peter was sleeping between two soldiers, bound with
two chains; and guards in front of the door were watching over the
prison.
7And behold, an angel of the Lord suddenly appeared, and a
light shone in the cell; and he struck Peter's side and roused him,
saying, "Get up quickly." And his chains fell off his hands.
8And the angel said to him, "Gird yourself and put on your
sandals." And he did so. And he *said to him, "Wrap your cloak
around you and follow me."
9And he went out and continued to follow, and he did not
know that what was being done by the angel was real, but thought
he was seeing a vision.
10And when they had passed the first and second guard, they
came to the iron gate that leads into the city, which opened for
them by itself; and they went out and went along one street; and
immediately the angel departed from him.
11And when Peter came to himself, he said, "Now I know for
sure that the Lord has sent forth His angel and rescued me from
the hand of Herod and from all that the Jewish people were expecting."
12And when he realized *this*, he went to the house of Mary, the
mother of John who was also called Mark, where many were
gathered together and were praying.
13And when he knocked at the door of the gate, a servant-girl
named Rhoda came to answer.

## New International

evidence of the grace of God, he was glad and encouraged them
all to remain true to the Lord with all their hearts. 24He was a good
man, full of the Holy Spirit and faith, and a great number of people
were brought to the Lord.
25Then Barnabas went to Tarsus to look for Saul, 26and when
he found him, he brought him to Antioch. So for a whole year
Barnabas and Saul met with the church and taught great numbers
of people. The disciples were called Christians first at Antioch.
27During this time some prophets came down from Jerusalem
to Antioch. 28One of them, named Agabus, stood up and through
the Spirit predicted that a severe famine would spread over the
entire Roman world. (This happened during the reign of Claudius.) 29The disciples, each according to his ability, decided to provide help for the brothers living in Judea. 30This they did, sending
their gift to the elders by Barnabas and Saul.

*Peter's Miraculous Escape From Prison*

**12** IT WAS about this time that King Herod arrested some
who belonged to the church, intending to persecute them.
2He had James, the brother of John, put to death with the sword.
3When he saw that this pleased the Jews, he proceeded to seize
Peter also. This happened during the Feast of Unleavened Bread.
4After arresting him, he put him in prison, handing him over to
be guarded by four squads of four soldiers each. Herod intended
to bring him out for public trial after the Passover.
5So Peter was kept in prison, but the church was earnestly
praying to God for him.
6The night before Herod was to bring him to trial, Peter was
sleeping between two soldiers, bound with two chains, and sentries stood guard at the entrance. 7Suddenly an angel of the Lord
appeared and a light shone in the cell. He struck Peter on the side
and woke him up. "Quick, get up!" he said, and the chains fell off
Peter's wrists.
8Then the angel said to him, "Put on your clothes and sandals."
And Peter did so. "Wrap your cloak around you and follow me,"
the angel told him. 9Peter followed him out of the prison, but he
had no idea that what the angel was doing was really happening;
he thought he was seeing a vision. 10They passed the first and
second guards and came to the iron gate leading to the city. It
opened for them by itself, and they went through it. When they
had walked the length of one street, suddenly the angel left him.
11Then Peter came to himself and said, "Now I know without
a doubt that the Lord sent his angel and rescued me from Herod's
clutches and from everything the Jewish people were anticipat-
ing."
12When this had dawned on him, he went to the house of Mary
the mother of John, also called Mark, where many people had
gathered and were praying. 13Peter knocked at the outer entrance,
and a servant girl named Rhoda came to answer the door. 14When

## King James

14And when she knew Peter's voice, she opened not the gate for gladness, but ran in, and told how Peter stood before the gate.

15And they said unto her, Thou art mad. But she constantly affirmed that it was even so. Then said they, It is his angel.

16But Peter continued knocking: and when they had opened *the door,* and saw him, they were astonished.

17But he, beckoning unto them with the hand to hold their peace, declared unto them how the Lord had brought him out of the prison. And he said, Go show these things unto James, and to the brethren. And he departed, and went into another place.

18Now as soon as it was day, there was no small stir among the soldiers, what was become of Peter.

19And when Herod had sought for him, and found him not, he examined the keepers, and commanded that *they* should be put to death. And he went down from Judaea to Caesarea, and *there* abode.

20¶ And Herod was highly displeased with them of Tyre and Sidon: but they came with one accord to him, and, having made Blastus the king's chamberlain their friend, desired peace; because their country was nourished by the king's *country.*

21And upon a set day Herod, arrayed in royal apparel, sat upon his throne, and made an oration unto them.

22And the people gave a shout, *saying, It is* the voice of a god, and not of a man.

23And immediately the angel of the Lord smote him, because he gave not God the glory: and he was eaten of worms, and gave up the ghost.

24¶ But the word of God grew and multiplied.

25And Barnabas and Saul returned from Jerusalem, when they had fulfilled *their* ministry, and took with them John, whose surname was Mark.

**13** NOW THERE were in the church that was at Antioch certain prophets and teachers; as Barnabas, and Simeon that was called Niger, and Lucius of Cyrene, and Manaen, which had been brought up with Herod the tetrarch, and Saul.

2As they ministered to the Lord, and fasted, the Holy Ghost said, Separate me Barnabas and Saul for the work whereunto I have called them.

3And when they had fasted and prayed, and laid *their* hands on them, they sent *them* away.

4¶ So they, being sent forth by the Holy Ghost, departed unto Seleucia; and from thence they sailed to Cyprus.

5And when they were at Salamis, they preached the word of God in the synagogues of the Jews: and they had also John to *their* minister.

6And when they had gone through the isle unto Paphos, they found a certain sorcerer, a false prophet, a Jew, whose name *was* Bar-jesus:

7Which was with the deputy of the country, Sergius Paulus, a prudent man; who called for Barnabas and Saul, and desired to hear the word of God.

8But Elymas the sorcerer (for so is his name by interpretation) withstood them, seeking to turn away the deputy from the faith.

## Amplified

14And recognizing Peter's voice, in her joy she failed to open the gate, but ran in and told the people that Peter was standing before the porch gate.

15They said to her, You are crazy! But she persistently *and* strongly *and* confidently affirmed that it was the truth. They said, It is his angel!

16But meanwhile Peter continued knocking, and when they opened the gate and saw him, they were amazed.

17But motioning to them with his hand to keep quiet *and* listen, he related to them how the Lord had delivered him out of the prison. And he said, Report all this to James [the less] and to the brethren. Then he left and went to some other place.

18Now as soon as it was day, there was no small disturbance among the soldiers over what had become of Peter.

19And when Herod had looked for him and could not find him, he placed the guards on trial and commanded that they should be led away [to execution]. Then [Herod] went down from Judea to Caesarea, and stayed on there.

20Now [Herod] cherished bitter animosity *and* hostility for the people of Tyre and Sidon; and [their deputies] came to him in a united body, and having made Blastus the king's chamberlain their friend, they asked for peace, because their country was nourished by *and* depended on the king's [country] for food.

21On an appointed day Herod arrayed himself in his royal robes, took his seat upon [his] throne, and addressed an oration to them.

22And the assembled people shouted, It is the voice of a god, and not of a man!

23And at once an angel of the Lord smote him *and* cut him down, because he did not give God the glory—that is, the pre-eminence and kingly majesty that belong to Him as the supreme Ruler; and he was eaten by worms and died.

24But the Word of the Lord [concerning the attainment through Christ of salvation in the kingdom of God] continued to grow and spread.

25And Barnabas and Saul came back from Jerusalem when they had completed their mission, bringing with them John whose surname was Mark.

**13** NOW IN the church (assembly) at Antioch there were prophets—inspired interpreters of the will and purposes of God—and teachers, Barnabas, Symeon who was called Niger [black], Lucius of Cyrene, Manaen a member of the court of Herod the tetrarch, and Saul.

2While they were worshipping the Lord and fasting, the Holy Spirit said, Separate now for Me Barnabas and Saul for the work to which I have called them.

3Then after fasting and praying they put their hands on them and sent them away.

4So then, being sent out by the Holy Spirit, they went down to Seleucia, and from [that port] they sailed away to Cyprus.

5When they arrived at Salamis they preached the Word of God [concerning the attainment through Christ of salvation in the kingdom of God] in the synagogues of the Jews. And they had John [Mark] as an attendant to assist them.

6When they had passed through the entire island of Cyprus as far as Paphos, they came upon a certain Jewish wizard *or* sorcerer, a false prophet named Bar-Jesus.

7He was closely associated with the proconsul, Sergius Paulus, who was an intelligent *and* sensible man of sound understanding; he summoned to him Barnabas and Saul and sought to hear the Word of God [concerning salvation in the kingdom of God attained through Christ].

8But Elymas [a]the wise man, for that is the translation of his name [ [b]which he had given himself], opposed them, seeking to keep the proconsul from accepting the faith.

**AMP** [a] Abbott-Smith. [b] Alford's "The Greek Testament, with Notes."

## New American Standard

14And when she recognized Peter's voice, because of her joy
she did not open the gate, but ran in and announced that Peter was
standing in front of the gate.
15And they said to her, "You are out of your mind!" But she
kept insisting that it was so. And they kept saying, "It is his
angel."
16But Peter continued knocking; and when they had opened *the
door*, they saw him and were amazed.
17But motioning to them with his hand to be silent, he described
to them how the Lord had led him out of the prison. And he said,
"Report these things to James and the brethren." And he departed
and went to another place.
**18**¶ Now when day came, there was no small disturbance
among the soldiers *as to* what could have become of Peter.
19And when Herod had searched for him and had not found
him, he examined the guards and ordered that they be led away
*to execution.* And he went down from Judea to Caesarea and was
spending time there.

*Death of Herod*

**20**¶ Now he was very angry with the people of Tyre and Sidon;
and with one accord they came to him, and having won over
Blastus the king's chamberlain, they were asking for peace, because their country was fed by the king's country.
21And on an appointed day Herod, having put on his royal
apparel, took his seat on the rostrum and *began* delivering an
address to them.
22And the people kept crying out, "The voice of a god and not
of a man!"
23And immediately an angel of the Lord struck him because he
did not give God the glory, and he was eaten by worms and died.
**24**¶ But the word of the Lord continued to grow and to be
multiplied.
**25**¶ And Barnabas and Saul returned from Jerusalem when they
had fulfilled their mission, taking along with *them* John, who was
also called Mark.

*First Missionary Journey*

**13** NOW THERE were at Antioch, in the church that was
*there,* prophets and teachers: Barnabas, and Simeon who
was called Niger, and Lucius of Cyrene, and Manaen who had
been brought up with Herod the tetrarch, and Saul.
2And while they were ministering to the Lord and fasting, the
Holy Spirit said, "Set apart for Me Barnabas and Saul for the work
to which I have called them."
3Then, when they had fasted and prayed and laid their hands
on them, they sent them away.
**4**¶ So, being sent out by the Holy Spirit, they went down to
Seleucia and from there they sailed to Cyprus.
5And when they reached Salamis, they *began* to proclaim the
word of God in the synagogues of the Jews; and they also had John
as their helper.
6And when they had gone through the whole island as far as
Paphos, they found a certain magician, a Jewish false prophet
whose name was Bar-Jesus,
7who was with the proconsul, Sergius Paulus, a man of intelligence. This man summoned Barnabas and Saul and sought to hear
the word of God.
8But Elymas the magician (for thus his name is translated) was
opposing them, seeking to turn the proconsul away from the faith.

## New International

she recognized Peter's voice, she was so overjoyed she ran back
without opening it and exclaimed, "Peter is at the door!"
15"You're out of your mind," they told her. When she kept
insisting that it was so, they said, "It must be his angel."
16But Peter kept on knocking, and when they opened the door
and saw him, they were astonished. 17Peter motioned with his
hand for them to be quiet and described how the Lord had brought
him out of prison. "Tell James and the brothers about this," he
said, and then he left for another place.
18In the morning, there was no small commotion among the
soldiers as to what had become of Peter. 19After Herod had a
thorough search made for him and did not find him, he cross-
examined the guards and ordered that they be executed.

*Herod's Death*

Then Herod went from Judea to Caesarea and stayed there a
while. 20He had been quarreling with the people of Tyre and
Sidon; they now joined together and sought an audience with him.
Having secured the support of Blastus, a trusted personal servant
of the king, they asked for peace, because they depended on the
king's country for their food supply.
21On the appointed day Herod, wearing his royal robes, sat on
his throne and delivered a public address to the people. 22They
shouted, "This is the voice of a god, not of a man." 23Immediately,
because Herod did not give praise to God, an angel of the Lord
struck him down, and he was eaten by worms and died.
24But the word of God continued to increase and spread.
25When Barnabas and Saul had finished their mission, they
returned from[c] Jerusalem, taking with them John, also called
Mark.

*Barnabas and Saul Sent Off*

**13** IN THE church at Antioch there were prophets and teachers: Barnabas, Simeon called Niger, Lucius of Cyrene,
Manaen (who had been brought up with Herod the tetrarch) and
Saul. 2While they were worshiping the Lord and fasting, the Holy
Spirit said, "Set apart for me Barnabas and Saul for the work to
which I have called them." 3So after they had fasted and prayed,
they placed their hands on them and sent them off.

*On Cyprus*

4The two of them, sent on their way by the Holy Spirit, went
down to Seleucia and sailed from there to Cyprus. 5When they
arrived at Salamis, they proclaimed the word of God in the Jewish
synagogues. John was with them as their helper.
6They traveled through the whole island until they came to
Paphos. There they met a Jewish sorcerer and false prophet named
Bar-Jesus, 7who was an attendant of the proconsul, Sergius
Paulus. The proconsul, an intelligent man, sent for Barnabas and
Saul because he wanted to hear the word of God. 8But Elymas the
sorcerer (for that is what his name means) opposed them and tried
to turn the proconsul from the faith. 9Then Saul, who was also

**NIV** [c] 25 Some manuscripts *to*

## King James

9Then Saul, (who also *is called* Paul,) filled with the Holy Ghost, set his eyes on him,

10And said, O full of all subtlety and all mischief, *thou* child of the devil, *thou* enemy of all righteousness, wilt thou not cease to pervert the right ways of the Lord?

11And now, behold, the hand of the Lord *is* upon thee, and thou shalt be blind, not seeing the sun for a season. And immediately there fell on him a mist and a darkness; and he went about seeking some to lead him by the hand.

12Then the deputy, when he saw what was done, believed, being astonished at the doctrine of the Lord.

13Now when Paul and his company loosed from Paphos, they came to Perga in Pamphylia: and John departing from them returned to Jerusalem.

14¶ But when they departed from Perga, they came to Antioch in Pisidia, and went into the synagogue on the sabbath day, and sat down.

15And after the reading of the law and the prophets the rulers of the synagogue sent unto them, saying, *Ye* men *and* brethren, if ye have any word of exhortation for the people, say on.

16Then Paul stood up, and beckoning with *his* hand said, Men of Israel, and ye that fear God, give audience.

17The God of this people of Israel chose our fathers, and exalted the people when they dwelt as strangers in the land of Egypt, and with an high arm brought he them out of it.

18And about the time of forty years suffered he their manners in the wilderness.

19And when he had destroyed seven nations in the land of Chanaan, he divided their land to them by lot.

20And after that he gave *unto them* judges about the space of four hundred and fifty years, until Samuel the prophet.

21And afterward they desired a king: and God gave unto them Saul the son of Cis, a man of the tribe of Benjamin, by the space of forty years.

22And when he had removed him, he raised up unto them David to be their king; to whom also he gave testimony, and said, I have found David the *son* of Jesse, a man after mine own heart, which shall fulfil all my will.

23Of this man's seed hath God according to *his* promise raised unto Israel a Saviour, Jesus:

24When John had first preached before his coming the baptism of repentance to all the people of Israel.

25And as John fulfilled his course, he said, Whom think ye that I am? I am not *he.* But, behold, there cometh one after me, whose shoes of *his* feet I am not worthy to loose.

26Men *and* brethren, children of the stock of Abraham, and whosoever among you feareth God, to you is the word of this salvation sent.

27For they that dwell at Jerusalem, and their rulers, because they knew him not, nor yet the voices of the prophets which are read every sabbath day, they have fulfilled *them* in condemning *him.*

28And though they found no cause of death *in him,* yet desired they Pilate that he should be slain.

29And when they had fulfilled all that was written of him, they took *him* down from the tree, and laid *him* in a sepulchre.

30But God raised him from the dead:

31And he was seen many days of them which came up with him from Galilee to Jerusalem, who are his witnesses unto the people.

## Amplified

9But Saul, who is also called Paul, filled with *and* controlled by the Holy Spirit, looked steadily at [Elymas]

10And said, You master in every form of deception *and* recklessness, unscrupulousness *and* wickedness, you son of the devil, you enemy of everything that is upright *and* good, will you never stop perverting *and* making crooked the straight paths of the Lord *and* plotting against His saving purposes? [Hos. 14:9.]

11And now, lo, the hand of the Lord is upon you, and you shall be blind, [so blind that you will be] unable to see the sun for a time. Instantly there fell upon him a mist and a darkness, and he groped about seeking persons who would lead him by the hand.

12Then the proconsul believed—became a Christian—when he saw what had occurred, for he was astonished *and* deeply touched at the teaching concerning the Lord *and* from [Him].

13Now Paul and his companions sailed from Paphos, and came to Perga in Pamphylia. And John [Mark] separated himself from them and went back to Jerusalem;

14But they [themselves] came on from Perga and arrived at Antioch in Pisidia. And on the Sabbath day they went into the synagogue there and sat down.

15After the reading of the Law and the prophets, the leaders [of the worship] of the synagogue sent to them saying, Brethren, if you have any word of exhortation *or* consolation *or* encouragement for the people, say it.

16So Paul arose, and motioning with his hand said, Men of Israel, and you who reverence *and* fear God, listen!

17The God of this people Israel selected our forefathers and made this people great *and* important during their stay in the land of Egypt, and then with uplifted arm He led them out from there. [Exod. 6:1, 6.]

18And for about forty years [ [a]as a nursing-father] He cared for them in the wilderness, *and* endured their behavior. [Deut. 1:31.]

19When He had destroyed seven nations in the land of Canaan, He gave them [the Hebrews] their land as an inheritance—distributing it to them by lot; [all of which took] about four hundred and fifty years. [Deut. 7:1; Josh. 14:1.]

20After that He gave them judges until the prophet Samuel.

21Then they asked for a king; and God gave them Saul the son of Kish, a man of the tribe of Benjamin, for forty years.

22And when He had deposed him, He raised up David to be their king; of him He bore witness and said, I have found David the son of Jesse a man after My own heart, who will do all My will *and* carry out My program fully. [Ps. 89:20; I Sam. 13:14; Isa. 44:28.]

23Of this man's descendants God has brought to Israel a Savior [in the person of Jesus], according to His promise.

24Before His coming John had (already) preached baptism of repentance to all the people of Israel.

25And as John was ending his course, he asked, What do you secretly think that I am? I am not He [the Christ. No], but note that after me One is coming, the sandals of Whose feet I am not worthy to untie!

26Brethren, sons of the race of Abraham, and all those others among you who reverence *and* fear God, to us has been sent the message of this salvation—the salvation obtained through Jesus Christ. [Ps. 107:20.]

27For those who dwell in Jerusalem and their rulers, because they did not know *or* recognize Him or understand the utterances of the prophets which are read every Sabbath, by condemning *and* sentencing [Him] have actually fulfilled these very predictions.

28And although they could find no cause deserving death with which to charge Him, yet they asked Pilate to have Him executed *and* put out of the way.

29And when they had finished *and* fulfilled everything that was written about Him, they took Him down from the tree and laid Him in a tomb.

30But God raised Him from the dead.

31And for many days He appeared to those who came up with Him from Galilee to Jerusalem, and they are His witnesses to the people.

**AMP** [a] Some ancient authorities so read.

## New American Standard

9But Saul, who was also *known as* Paul, filled with the Holy Spirit, fixed his gaze upon him,

10and said, "You who are full of all deceit and fraud, you son of the devil, you enemy of all righteousness, will you not cease to make crooked the straight ways of the Lord?

11"And now, behold, the hand of the Lord is upon you, and you will be blind and not see the sun for a time." And immediately a mist and a darkness fell upon him, and he went about seeking those who would lead him by the hand.

12Then the proconsul believed when he saw what had happened, being amazed at the teaching of the Lord.

13¶ Now Paul and his companions put out to sea from Paphos and came to Perga in Pamphylia; and John left them and returned to Jerusalem.

14But going on from Perga, they arrived at Pisidian Antioch, and on the Sabbath day they went into the synagogue and sat down.

15And after the reading of the Law and the Prophets the synagogue officials sent to them, saying, "Brethren, if you have any word of exhortation for the people, say it."

16And Paul stood up, and motioning with his hand, he said,
¶"Men of Israel, and you who fear God, listen:

17"The God of this people Israel chose our fathers, and made the people great during their stay in the land of Egypt, and with an uplifted arm He led them out from it.

18"And for a period of about forty years He put up with them in the wilderness.

19"And when He had destroyed seven nations in the land of Canaan, He distributed their land as an inheritance— *all of which took* about four hundred and fifty years.

20"And after these things He gave *them* judges until Samuel the prophet.

21"And then they asked for a king, and God gave them Saul the son of Kish, a man of the tribe of Benjamin, for forty years.

22"And after He had removed him, He raised up David to be their king, concerning whom He also testified and said, 'I HAVE FOUND DAVID the son of Jesse, A MAN AFTER MY HEART, who will do all My will.'

23"From the offspring of this man, according to promise, God has brought to Israel a Savior, Jesus,

24after John had proclaimed before His coming a baptism of repentance to all the people of Israel.

25"And while John was completing his course, he kept saying, 'What do you suppose that I am? I am not *He*. But behold, one is coming after me the sandals of whose feet I am not worthy to untie.'

26"Brethren, sons of Abraham's family, and those among you who fear God, to us the word of this salvation is sent out.

27"For those who live in Jerusalem, and their rulers, recognizing neither Him nor the utterances of the prophets which are read every Sabbath, fulfilled *these* by condemning *Him*.

28"And though they found no ground for *putting Him to* death, they asked Pilate that He be executed.

29"And when they had carried out all that was written concerning Him, they took Him down from the cross and laid Him in a tomb.

30"But God raised Him from the dead;

31and for many days He appeared to those who came up with Him from Galilee to Jerusalem, the very ones who are now His witnesses to the people.

## New International

called Paul, filled with the Holy Spirit, looked straight at Elymas
and said, 10"You are a child of the devil and an enemy of everything that is right! You are full of all kinds of deceit and trickery.
Will you never stop perverting the right ways of the Lord? 11Now
the hand of the Lord is against you. You are going to be blind, and
for a time you will be unable to see the light of the sun."
Immediately mist and darkness came over him, and he groped
about, seeking someone to lead him by the hand. 12When the
proconsul saw what had happened, he believed, for he was
amazed at the teaching about the Lord.

*In Pisidian Antioch*

13From Paphos, Paul and his companions sailed to Perga in
Pamphylia, where John left them to return to Jerusalem. 14From
Perga they went on to Pisidian Antioch. On the Sabbath they
entered the synagogue and sat down. 15After the reading from the
Law and the Prophets, the synagogue rulers sent word to them,
saying, "Brothers, if you have a message of encouragement for the
people, please speak."
16Standing up, Paul motioned with his hand and said: "Men of
Israel and you Gentiles who worship God, listen to me! 17The God
of the people of Israel chose our fathers; he made the people
prosper during their stay in Egypt, with mighty power he led them
out of that country, 18he endured their conduct[b] for about forty
years in the desert, 19he overthrew seven nations in Canaan and
gave their land to his people as their inheritance. 20All this took
about 450 years.
"After this, God gave them judges until the time of Samuel the
prophet. 21Then the people asked for a king, and he gave them
Saul son of Kish, of the tribe of Benjamin, who ruled forty years.
22After removing Saul, he made David their king. He testified
concerning him: 'I have found David son of Jesse a man after my
own heart; he will do everything I want him to do.'
23"From this man's descendants God has brought to Israel the
Savior Jesus, as he promised. 24Before the coming of Jesus, John
preached repentance and baptism to all the people of Israel. 25As
John was completing his work, he said: 'Who do you think I am?
I am not that one. No, but he is coming after me, whose sandals
I am not worthy to untie.'
26"Brothers, children of Abraham, and you God-fearing Gentiles, it is to us that this message of salvation has been sent. 27The
people of Jerusalem and their rulers did not recognize Jesus, yet
in condemning him they fulfilled the words of the prophets that
are read every Sabbath. 28Though they found no proper ground
for a death sentence, they asked Pilate to have him executed.
29When they had carried out all that was written about him, they
took him down from the tree and laid him in a tomb. 30But God
raised him from the dead, 31and for many days he was seen by
those who had traveled with him from Galilee to Jerusalem. They
are now his witnesses to our people.

NIV [b] *18* Some manuscripts *and cared for them*

## King James

32And we declare unto you glad tidings, how that the promise which was made unto the fathers,

33God hath fulfilled the same unto us their children, in that he hath raised up Jesus again; as it is also written in the second psalm, Thou art my Son, this day have I begotten thee.

34And as concerning that he raised him up from the dead, *now* no more to return to corruption, he said on this wise, I will give you the sure mercies of David.

35Wherefore he saith also in another *psalm*, Thou shalt not suffer thine Holy One to see corruption.

36For David, after he had served his own generation by the will of God, fell on sleep, and was laid unto his fathers, and saw corruption:

37But he, whom God raised again, saw no corruption.

38¶ Be it known unto you therefore, men *and* brethren, that through this man is preached unto you the forgiveness of sins:

39And by him all that believe are justified from all things, from which ye could not be justified by the law of Moses.

40Beware therefore, lest that come upon you, which is spoken of in the prophets;

41Behold, ye despisers, and wonder, and perish: for I work a work in your days, a work which ye shall in no wise believe, though a man declare it unto you.

42And when the Jews were gone out of the synagogue, the Gentiles besought that these words might be preached to them the next sabbath.

43Now when the congregation was broken up, many of the Jews and religious proselytes followed Paul and Barnabas: who, speaking to them, persuaded them to continue in the grace of God.

44¶ And the next sabbath day came almost the whole city together to hear the word of God.

45But when the Jews saw the multitudes, they were filled with envy, and spake against those things which were spoken by Paul, contradicting and blaspheming.

46Then Paul and Barnabas waxed bold, and said, It was necessary that the word of God should first have been spoken to you: but seeing ye put it from you, and judge yourselves unworthy of everlasting life, lo, we turn to the Gentiles.

47For so hath the Lord commanded us, *saying*, I have set thee to be a light of the Gentiles, that thou shouldest be for salvation unto the ends of the earth.

48And when the Gentiles heard this, they were glad, and glorified the word of the Lord: and as many as were ordained to eternal life believed.

49And the word of the Lord was published throughout all the region.

50But the Jews stirred up the devout and honourable women, and the chief men of the city, and raised persecution against Paul and Barnabas, and expelled them out of their coasts.

## Amplified

32So now we are bringing you the good news that what God promised to our forefathers,

33This He has [a]completely fulfilled to us their children by raising up Jesus, as it is written in the second Psalm, You are My Son; today I have begotten You—[b]caused You to arise, to be born, [[c]formally shown You to be the Messiah by the resurrection]. [Ps. 2:7.]

34And as to His having raised Him from among the dead, now no more to return to [undergo] putrefaction *and* dissolution [of the grave], He spoke in this way, I will fulfill *and* give to you the holy and sure mercies *and* blessings [that were promised and assured] to David. [Isa. 55:3.]

35For this reason He says also in another Psalm, You will not allow Your Holy One to see corruption—to undergo putrefaction and dissolution [of the grave]. [Ps. 16:10.]

36For David, after he had served God's will *and* purpose *and* counsel in his own generation, fell asleep [[d]in death], and was buried among his forefathers, and he did see corruption *and* undergo putrefaction *and* dissolution [of the grave].

37But He Whom God raised up [to life] saw no corruption—did not experience putrefaction and dissolution [of the grave].

38So let it be clearly known *and* understood by you, brethren, that through this Man forgiveness *and* removal of sins is now proclaimed to you;

39And that through Him every one who believes, [that is, who [e]acknowledges Jesus as his Savior and devotes himself to Him] is absolved (cleared and freed) from every charge from which you could not be justified *and* freed by the Law of Moses, *and* given right standing with God.

40Take care, therefore, lest there come upon you what is spoken in the prophets:

41Look, you scoffers *and* scorners, and marvel, and perish, *and* vanish away; for I am doing a deed in your days, a deed which you will never have confidence in *or* believe, [even] if some one—[f]clearly describing it in detail—declares it to you. [Hab. 1:5.]

42As they [Paul and Barnabas] went out [of the synagogue], the people earnestly begged that these things might be told to them [further] the next Sabbath.

43And when the congregation of the synagogue dispersed, many of the Jews and the devout converts to Judaism followed Paul and Barnabas, who talked to them and urged them to continue [to trust themselves to and stand fast] in the grace—that is, the unmerited favor and blessing—of God.

44The next Sabbath almost the entire city gathered together to hear the Word of God—concerning [g]the attainment through Christ of salvation in the kingdom of God.

45But when the Jews saw the crowds, filled with envy *and* jealousy they contradicted what was said by Paul, and talked abusively—reviling and slandering him.

46And Paul and Barnabas spoke out plainly *and* boldly, saying, It was necessary that God's message (concerning [h]salvation through Christ) should be spoken to you first. But since you thrust it from you, you pass this judgment on yourselves that you are unworthy of eternal life, *and* out of your own mouth you shall be judged. [Now] behold, we turn to the Gentiles—the heathen.

47For so the Lord has charged us, saying, I have set you to be a light for the Gentiles—the heathen—that you may bring (eternal) salvation to the uttermost parts of the earth. [Isa. 49:6.]

48And when the Gentiles heard this, they rejoiced and glorified (praised and gave thanks for) the Word of God; and as many as were destined (appointed and ordained) to eternal life believed—adhered to, trusted in and relied on Jesus as the Christ and their Savior.

49And so the Word of the Lord (concerning eternal salvation through Christ) scattered *and* spread throughout the whole region.

50But the Jews stirred up the devout women of high rank and the outstanding men of the town, and instigated persecution against Paul and Barnabas, and drove them out of their boundaries.

**AMP** [a] Vincent. [b] Thayer. [c] Thayer. [d] Cremer. [e] Thayer. [f] Vincent. [g] Thayer. [h] Thayer.

## New American Standard

32"And we preach to you the good news of the promise made to the fathers,
33that God has fulfilled this *promise* to our children in that He raised up Jesus, as it is also written in the second Psalm, 'THOU ART MY SON; TODAY I HAVE BEGOTTEN THEE.'
34" *And as for the fact* that He raised Him up from the dead, no more to return to decay, He has spoken in this way: 'I WILL GIVE YOU THE HOLY *and* SURE *blessings* OF DAVID.'
35"Therefore He also says in another *Psalm*, 'THOU WILT NOT ALLOW THY HOLY ONE TO UNDERGO DECAY.'
36"For David, after he had served the purpose of God in his own generation, fell asleep, and was laid among his fathers, and underwent decay;
37but He whom God raised did not undergo decay.
38"Therefore let it be known to you, brethren, that through Him forgiveness of sins is proclaimed to you,
39and through Him everyone who believes is freed from all things, from which you could not be freed through the Law of Moses.
40"Take heed therefore, so that the thing spoken of in the Prophets may not come upon *you*:

41 'BEHOLD, YOU SCOFFERS, AND MARVEL, AND PERISH;
FOR I AM ACCOMPLISHING A WORK IN YOUR DAYS,
A WORK WHICH YOU WILL NEVER BELIEVE, THOUGH
SOMEONE SHOULD DESCRIBE IT TO YOU.' "

42¶ And as Paul and Barnabas were going out, the people kept begging that these things might be spoken to them the next Sabbath.
43Now when *the meeting of* the synagogue had broken up, many of the Jews and of the God-fearing proselytes followed Paul and Barnabas, who, speaking to them, were urging them to continue in the grace of God.

*Paul Turns to the Gentiles*

44¶ And the next Sabbath nearly the whole city assembled to hear the word of God.
45But when the Jews saw the crowds, they were filled with jealousy, and *began* contradicting the things spoken by Paul, and were blaspheming.
46And Paul and Barnabas spoke out boldly and said, "It was necessary that the word of God should be spoken to you first; since you repudiate it, and judge yourselves unworthy of eternal life, behold, we are turning to the Gentiles.
47"For thus the Lord has commanded us,

'I HAVE PLACED YOU AS A LIGHT FOR THE GENTILES,
THAT YOU SHOULD BRING SALVATION TO THE END OF THE EARTH.' "

48And when the Gentiles heard this, they *began* rejoicing and glorifying the word of the Lord; and as many as had been appointed to eternal life believed.
49And the word of the Lord was being spread through the whole region.
50But the Jews aroused the devout women of prominence and the leading men of the city, and instigated a persecution against Paul and Barnabas, and drove them out of their district.

## New International

32"We tell you the good news: What God promised our fathers
33he has fulfilled for us, their children, by raising up Jesus. As it
is written in the second Psalm:

" 'You are my Son;
today I have become your Father.[i]'[j]

34The fact that God raised him from the dead, never to decay, is
stated in these words:

" 'I will give you the holy and sure blessings promised to David.'[k]

35So it is stated elsewhere:

" 'You will not let your Holy One see decay.'[l]

36"For when David had served God's purpose in his own generation, he fell asleep; he was buried with his fathers and his body
decayed. 37But the one whom God raised from the dead did not
see decay.
38"Therefore, my brothers, I want you to know that through
Jesus the forgiveness of sins is proclaimed to you. 39Through him
everyone who believes is justified from everything you could not
be justified from by the law of Moses. 40Take care that what the
prophets have said does not happen to you:

41" 'Look, you scoffers,
wonder and perish,
for I am going to do something in your days
that you would never believe,
even if someone told you.'[m]"

42As Paul and Barnabas were leaving the synagogue, the people
invited them to speak further about these things on the next Sabbath. 43When the congregation was dismissed, many of the Jews
and devout converts to Judaism followed Paul and Barnabas, who
talked with them and urged them to continue in the grace of God.
44On the next Sabbath almost the whole city gathered to hear
the word of the Lord. 45When the Jews saw the crowds, they were
filled with jealousy and talked abusively against what Paul was
saying.
46Then Paul and Barnabas answered them boldly: "We had to
speak the word of God to you first. Since you reject it and do not
consider yourselves worthy of eternal life, we now turn to the
Gentiles. 47For this is what the Lord has commanded us:

" 'I have made you[n] a light for the Gentiles,
that you[o] may bring salvation to the ends of the earth.'[p]"

48When the Gentiles heard this, they were glad and honored
the word of the Lord; and all who were appointed for eternal life
believed.
49The word of the Lord spread through the whole region. 50But
the Jews incited the God-fearing women of high standing and the
leading men of the city. They stirred up persecution against Paul
and Barnabas, and expelled them from their region. 51So they

NIV [i] 33 Or *have begotten you* [j] 33 Psalm 2:7 [k] 34 Isaiah 55:3 [l] 35 Psalm 16:10 [m] 41 Hab. 1:5 [n] 47 The Greek is singular. [o] 47 The Greek is singular. [p] 47 Isaiah 49:6

## King James

51But they shook off the dust of their feet against them, and came unto Iconium.

52And the disciples were filled with joy, and with the Holy Ghost.

**14** AND IT came to pass in Iconium, that they went both together into the synagogue of the Jews, and so spake, that a great multitude both of the Jews and also of the Greeks believed.

2But the unbelieving Jews stirred up the Gentiles, and made their minds evil affected against the brethren.

3Long time therefore abode they speaking boldly in the Lord, which gave testimony unto the word of his grace, and granted signs and wonders to be done by their hands.

4But the multitude of the city was divided: and part held with the Jews, and part with the apostles.

5And when there was an assault made both of the Gentiles, and also of the Jews with their rulers, to use *them* despitefully, and to stone them,

6They were ware of *it,* and fled unto Lystra and Derbe, cities of Lycaonia, and unto the region that lieth round about:

7And there they preached the gospel.

8¶ And there sat a certain man at Lystra, impotent in his feet, being a cripple from his mother's womb, who never had walked:

9The same heard Paul speak: who stedfastly beholding him, and perceiving that he had faith to be healed,

10Said with a loud voice, Stand upright on thy feet. And he leaped and walked.

11And when the people saw what Paul had done, they lifted up their voices, saying in the speech of Lycaonia, The gods are come down to us in the likeness of men.

12And they called Barnabas, Jupiter; and Paul, Mercurius, because he was the chief speaker.

13Then the priest of Jupiter, which was before their city, brought oxen and garlands unto the gates, and would have done sacrifice with the people.

14 *Which* when the apostles, Barnabas and Paul, heard *of,* they rent their clothes, and ran in among the people, crying out,

15And saying, Sirs, why do ye these things? We also are men of like passions with you, and preach unto you that ye should turn from these vanities unto the living God, which made heaven, and earth, and the sea, and all things that are therein:

16Who in times past suffered all nations to walk in their own ways.

17Nevertheless he left not himself without witness, in that he did good, and gave us rain from heaven, and fruitful seasons, filling our hearts with food and gladness.

18And with these sayings scarce restrained they the people, that they had not done sacrifice unto them.

19¶ And there came thither *certain* Jews from Antioch and Iconium, who persuaded the people, and, having stoned Paul, drew *him* out of the city, supposing he had been dead.

20Howbeit, as the disciples stood round about him, he rose up, and came into the city: and the next day he departed with Barnabas to Derbe.

21And when they had preached the gospel to that city, and had taught many, they returned again to Lystra, and *to* Iconium, and Antioch,

22Confirming the souls of the disciples, *and* exhorting them to continue in the faith, and that we must through much tribulation enter into the kingdom of God.

## Amplified

51But [the apostles] shook off the dust from their feet against them, and went to Iconium.

52And the disciples were continually diffused [throughout their souls] with joy and the Holy Spirit.

**14** NOW AT Iconium [also Paul and Barnabas] went into the Jewish synagogue together and spoke with such power that a great number both of Jews and of Greeks believed—became Christians;

2But the unbelieving Jews (who rejected their message) aroused the Gentiles and embittered their minds against the brethren.

3So [Paul and Barnabas] stayed on there for a long time, speaking freely *and* fearlessly *and* boldly in the Lord, Who continued to bear testimony to the Word of His grace, granting signs and wonders to be performed by their hands.

4But the residents of the town were divided, some siding with the Jews and some with the apostles.

5When there was an attempt both on the part of the Gentiles and the Jews together with their rulers, to insult *and* abuse *and* molest [Paul and Barnabas] and to stone them,

6They, aware of the situation, made their escape to Lystra and Derbe, cities of Lycaonia, and the neighboring districts;

7And there they continued to preach the glad tidings (Gospel).

8Now at Lystra a man sat whose feet it was impossible for him to use, for he was a cripple from birth and had never walked.

9He was listening to Paul as he talked, and [Paul] gazing intently at him and observing that he had faith to be healed,

10Shouted at him, saying, Stand erect on your feet! And he leaped up and walked.

11And the crowds, when they saw what Paul had done, lifted up their voices, shouting in the Lycaonian language, The gods have come down to us in human form!

12They called Barnabas Zeus, and they called Paul, because he led in the discourse, Hermes [god of speech].

13And the priest of Zeus, whose [temple] was at the entrance of the town, brought bulls and garlands to the [city's] gates and wanted to join the people in offering sacrifice.

14But when the apostles Barnabas and Paul heard of it, they tore their clothing and dashed out among the crowd, shouting,

15Men, why are you doing this? We also are [only] human beings, of nature like your own, and we bring you the good news that you should turn away from these foolish *and* vain things to the living God, Who made the heaven and the earth and the sea and everything that they contain. [Exod. 20:11; Ps. 146:6.]

16In generations past He permitted all the nations to walk in their own ways;

17Yet He did not neglect to leave some witness of Himself, for He did you good *and* kindnesses, and gave you rains from heaven and fruitful seasons, satisfying your hearts with nourishment and happiness.

18Even in [the light of] these words they with difficulty prevented the people from offering sacrifice to them.

19But some Jews arrived there from Antioch and Iconium; and having persuaded the people *and* won them over, they stoned Paul and [ [a]afterward] dragged him out of the town, thinking that he was dead.

20But the disciples formed a circle about him, and he got up and went back into the town; and on the morrow he went on with Barnabas to Derbe.

21When they had preached the Gospel to that town and made disciples of many of the people, they went back to Lystra and Iconium and Antioch,

22Establishing *and* strengthening the souls *and* the hearts of the disciples, urging *and* warning *and* encouraging them to stand firm in the faith, and telling them that it is through many hardships *and* tribulations we must enter the kingdom of God.

**AMP** [a] Alford.

## New American Standard

51But they shook off the dust of their feet *in protest* against them and went to Iconium.

52And the disciples were continually filled with joy and with the Holy Spirit.

*Acceptance and Opposition*

**14** AND IT came about that in Iconium they entered the synagogue of the Jews together, and spoke in such a manner that a great multitude believed, both of Jews and of Greeks.

2But the Jews who disbelieved stirred up the minds of the Gentiles, and embittered them against the brethren.

3Therefore they spent a long time *there* speaking boldly *with reliance* upon the Lord, who was bearing witness to the word of His grace, granting that signs and wonders be done by their hands.

4But the multitude of the city was divided; and some sided with the Jews, and some with the apostles.

5And when an attempt was made by both the Gentiles and the Jews with their rulers, to mistreat and to stone them,

6they became aware of it and fled to the cities of Lycaonia, Lystra and Derbe, and the surrounding region;

7and there they continued to preach the gospel.

8¶ And at Lystra there was sitting a certain man, without strength in his feet, lame from his mother's womb, who had never walked.

9This man was listening to Paul as he spoke, who, when he had fixed his gaze upon him, and had seen that he had faith to be made well,

10said with a loud voice, "Stand upright on your feet." And he leaped up and *began* to walk.

11And when the multitudes saw what Paul had done, they raised their voice, saying in the Lycaonian language, "The gods have become like men and have come down to us."

12And they *began* calling Barnabas, Zeus, and Paul, Hermes, because he was the chief speaker.

13And the priest of Zeus, whose *temple* was just outside the city, brought oxen and garlands to the gates, and wanted to offer sacrifice with the crowds.

14But when the apostles, Barnabas and Paul, heard of it, they tore their robes and rushed out into the crowd, crying out

15and saying, "Men, why are you doing these things? We are also men of the same nature as you, and preach the gospel to you in order that you should turn from these [b]vain things to a living God, WHO MADE THE HEAVEN AND THE EARTH AND THE SEA, AND ALL THAT IS IN THEM.

16"And in the generations gone by He permitted all the nations to go their own ways;

17and yet He did not leave Himself without witness, in that He did good and gave you rains from heaven and fruitful seasons, satisfying your hearts with food and gladness."

18And *even* saying these things, they with difficulty restrained the crowds from offering sacrifice to them.

19¶ But Jews came from Antioch and Iconium, and having won over the multitudes, they stoned Paul and dragged him out of the city, supposing him to be dead.

20But while the disciples stood around him, he arose and entered the city. And the next day he went away with Barnabas to Derbe.

21And after they had preached the gospel to that city and had made many disciples, they returned to Lystra and to Iconium and to Antioch,

22strengthening the souls of the disciples, encouraging them to continue in the faith, and *saying*, "Through many tribulations we must enter the kingdom of God."

NAS [b] I.e., idols

## New International

shook the dust from their feet in protest against them and went to Iconium. 52And the disciples were filled with joy and with the Holy Spirit.

*In Iconium*

**14** AT ICONIUM Paul and Barnabas went as usual into the Jewish synagogue. There they spoke so effectively that a great number of Jews and Gentiles believed. 2But the Jews who refused to believe stirred up the Gentiles and poisoned their minds against the brothers. 3So Paul and Barnabas spent considerable time there, speaking boldly for the Lord, who confirmed the message of his grace by enabling them to do miraculous signs and wonders. 4The people of the city were divided; some sided with the Jews, others with the apostles. 5There was a plot afoot among the Gentiles and Jews, together with their leaders, to mistreat them and stone them. 6But they found out about it and fled to the Lycaonian cities of Lystra and Derbe and to the surrounding country, 7where they continued to preach the good news.

*In Lystra and Derbe*

8In Lystra there sat a man crippled in his feet, who was lame from birth and had never walked. 9He listened to Paul as he was speaking. Paul looked directly at him, saw that he had faith to be healed 10and called out, "Stand up on your feet!" At that, the man jumped up and began to walk.

11When the crowd saw what Paul had done, they shouted in the Lycaonian language, "The gods have come down to us in human form!" 12Barnabas they called Zeus, and Paul they called Hermes because he was the chief speaker. 13The priest of Zeus, whose temple was just outside the city, brought bulls and wreaths to the city gates because he and the crowd wanted to offer sacrifices to them.

14But when the apostles Barnabas and Paul heard of this, they tore their clothes and rushed out into the crowd, shouting: 15"Men, why are you doing this? We too are only men, human like you. We are bringing you good news, telling you to turn from these worthless things to the living God, who made heaven and earth and sea and everything in them. 16In the past, he let all nations go their own way. 17Yet he has not left himself without testimony: He has shown kindness by giving you rain from heaven and crops in their seasons; he provides you with plenty of food and fills your hearts with joy." 18Even with these words, they had difficulty keeping the crowd from sacrificing to them.

19Then some Jews came from Antioch and Iconium and won the crowd over. They stoned Paul and dragged him outside the city, thinking he was dead. 20But after the disciples had gathered around him, he got up and went back into the city. The next day he and Barnabas left for Derbe.

*The Return to Antioch in Syria*

21They preached the good news in that city and won a large number of disciples. Then they returned to Lystra, Iconium and Antioch, 22strengthening the disciples and encouraging them to remain true to the faith. "We must go through many hardships to enter the kingdom of God," they said. 23Paul and Barnabas ap-

## King James

23And when they had ordained them elders in every church,
and had prayed with fasting, they commended them to the Lord,
on whom they believed.
24And after they had passed throughout Pisidia, they came to
Pamphylia.
25And when they had preached the word in Perga, they went
down into Attalia:
26And thence sailed to Antioch, from whence they had been
recommended to the grace of God for the work which they fulfilled.
27And when they were come, and had gathered the church
together, they rehearsed all that God had done with them, and
how he had opened the door of faith unto the Gentiles.
28And there they abode long time with the disciples.

15 AND CERTAIN men which came down from Judaea
taught the brethren, *and said,* Except ye be circumcised
after the manner of Moses, ye cannot be saved.
2When therefore Paul and Barnabas had no small dissension
and disputation with them, they determined that Paul and Barnabas,
and certain other of them, should go up to Jerusalem unto
the apostles and elders about this question.
3And being brought on their way by the church, they passed
through Phenice and Samaria, declaring the conversion of the
Gentiles: and they caused great joy unto all the brethren.
4And when they were come to Jerusalem, they were received
of the church, and *of* the apostles and elders, and they declared all
things that God had done with them.
5But there rose up certain of the sect of the Pharisees which
believed, saying, That it was needful to circumcise them, and to
command *them* to keep the law of Moses.
6¶ And the apostles and elders came together for to consider of
this matter.
7And when there had been much disputing, Peter rose up, and
said unto them, Men *and* brethren, ye know how that a good while
ago God made choice among us, that the Gentiles by my mouth
should hear the word of the gospel, and believe.
8And God, which knoweth the hearts, bare them witness, giving
them the Holy Ghost, even as *he did* unto us;
9And put no difference between us and them, purifying their
hearts by faith.
10Now therefore why tempt ye God, to put a yoke upon the
neck of the disciples, which neither our fathers nor we were able
to bear?
11But we believe that through the grace of the Lord Jesus Christ
we shall be saved, even as they.
12¶ Then all the multitude kept silence, and gave audience to
Barnabas and Paul, declaring what miracles and wonders God had
wrought among the Gentiles by them.
13¶ And after they had held their peace, James answered, saying,
Men *and* brethren, hearken unto me:
14Simeon hath declared how God at the first did visit the Gentiles,
to take out of them a people for his name.
15And to this agree the words of the prophets; as it is written,

## Amplified

23And when they had appointed *and* ordained elders for them
in each church, with prayer and fasting, they committed them to
the Lord in Whom they had come to believe [being full of joyful
trust that He is the Christ, the Messiah].
24Then they went through Pisidia and arrived at Pamphylia.
25And when they had spoken the Word in Perga, [that is, the
doctrine concerning the attainment through Christ of salvation in
the kingdom of God], they went down to Attalia;
26And from there they sailed back to Antioch, where they had
[first] been commended to the grace of God for the work which
they had [now] completed.
27Arriving there, they gathered the church together and declared
all that God had accomplished with them, and how He had
opened to the Gentiles a door of faith [in Jesus as the Messiah,
through Whom we obtain salvation in the kingdom of God].
28And there they stayed no little time with the disciples.

15 BUT SOME men came down from Judea and were instructing
the brethren, Unless you are circumcised in
accordance with the Mosaic custom, you cannot be saved.
2And when Paul and Barnabas had no small disagreement and
discussion with them, it was decided that Paul and Barnabas and
some of the others of their number should go up to Jerusalem [and
confer] with the apostles (special messengers) and the elders about
this matter.
3So, being [a]fitted out *and* sent on their way by the church, they
went through both Phoenicia and Samaria telling of the conversion
of the Gentiles, and they caused great rejoicing among all the
brethren.
4When they arrived in Jerusalem, they were heartily welcomed
by the church and the apostles and the elders, and they told them
all that God had accomplished through them.
5But some who believed [that is, who [b]acknowledged Jesus as
their Savior and devoted themselves to Him] belonged to the sect
of the Pharisees, and they rose up and said, It is necessary to
circumcise [the Gentile converts], and to charge them to obey the
Law of Moses.
6The apostles and the elders were assembled together to look
into *and* consider this matter.
7And after there had been a long debate, Peter got up and said
to them, Brethren, you know that quite a while ago God made a
selection from among you, that by my mouth the Gentiles should
hear the message of the Gospel [concerning the [c]attainment
through Christ of salvation in the kingdom of God] and believe—
that is, credit *and* place their confidence in it.
8And God, Who is acquainted with *and* understands the heart,
bore witness to them, giving them the Holy Spirit as also He did
to us;
9And He made no difference between us and them, but
cleansed their hearts by faith [that is, [d]by a strong and welcome
conviction that Jesus is the Messiah, through Whom we obtain
eternal salvation in the kingdom of God].
10Now then, why do you try to test God by putting a yoke on
the necks of the disciples, such as neither our forefathers nor we
[ourselves] were able to endure?
11But we believe that we are saved through the grace [the undeserved
favor and mercy] of the Lord Jesus, just as they [are].
12Then the whole assembly remained silent, and they listened
[attentively] as Barnabas and Paul rehearsed what signs and wonders
God had performed through them among the Gentiles.
13When they had finished talking, James replied, Brethren,
listen to me.
14Symeon [Peter] has rehearsed how God first visited the Gentiles,
to take out of them a people [to bear and honor] His name.
15And with this the predictions of the prophets agree, as it is
written,

**AMP** [a] Thayer. [b] Thayer. [c] Thayer. [d] Thayer.

## New American Standard

23And when they had appointed elders for them in every
church, having prayed with fasting, they commended them to the
Lord in whom they had believed.
24And they passed through Pisidia and came into Pamphylia.
25And when they had spoken the word in Perga, they went
down to Attalia;
26and from there they sailed to Antioch, from which they had
been commended to the grace of God for the work that they had
accomplished.
27And when they had arrived and gathered the church together, they *began* to report all things that God had done with them
and how He had opened a door of faith to the Gentiles.
28And they spent a long time with the disciples.

*The Council at Jerusalem*

15 AND SOME men came down from Judea and *began* teaching the brethren, "Unless you are circumcised according
to the custom of Moses, you cannot be saved."
2And when Paul and Barnabas had great dissension and debate with them, *the brethren* determined that Paul and Barnabas
and certain others of them should go up to Jerusalem to the apostles and elders concerning this issue.
3Therefore, being sent on their way by the church, they were
passing through both Phoenicia and Samaria, describing in detail
the conversion of the Gentiles, and were bringing great joy to all
the brethren.
4And when they arrived at Jerusalem, they were received by
the church and the apostles and the elders, and they reported all
that God had done with them.
5But certain ones of the sect of the Pharisees who had believed,
stood up, saying, "It is necessary to circumcise them, and to direct
them to observe the Law of Moses."
6¶ And the apostles and the elders came together to look into
this matter.
7And after there had been much debate, Peter stood up and
said to them, "Brethren, you know that in the early days God
made a choice among you, that by my mouth the Gentiles should
hear the word of the gospel and believe.
8"And God, who knows the heart, bore witness to them, giving them the Holy Spirit, just as He also did to us;
9and He made no distinction between us and them, cleansing
their hearts by faith.
10"Now therefore why do you put God to the test by placing
upon the neck of the disciples a yoke which neither our fathers nor
we have been able to bear?
11"But we believe that we are saved through the grace of the
Lord Jesus, in the same way as they also are."
12¶ And all the multitude kept silent, and they were listening
to Barnabas and Paul as they were relating what signs and wonders God had done through them among the Gentiles.

*James' Judgment*

13And after they had stopped speaking, James answered, saying, "Brethren, listen to me.
14"Simeon has related how God first concerned Himself about
taking from among the Gentiles a people for His name.
15"And with this the words of the Prophets agree, just as it is
written,

## New International

pointed elders[e] for them in each church and, with prayer and
fasting, committed them to the Lord, in whom they had put their
trust. 24After going through Pisidia, they came into Pamphylia,
25and when they had preached the word in Perga, they went down
to Attalia.
26From Attalia they sailed back to Antioch, where they had been
committed to the grace of God for the work they had now completed. 27On arriving there, they gathered the church together and
reported all that God had done through them and how he had
opened the door of faith to the Gentiles. 28And they stayed there
a long time with the disciples.

*The Council at Jerusalem*

15 SOME MEN came down from Judea to Antioch and were
teaching the brothers: "Unless you are circumcised, according to the custom taught by Moses, you cannot be saved."
2This brought Paul and Barnabas into sharp dispute and debate
with them. So Paul and Barnabas were appointed, along with
some other believers, to go up to Jerusalem to see the apostles and
elders about this question. 3The church sent them on their way,
and as they traveled through Phoenicia and Samaria, they told
how the Gentiles had been converted. This news made all the
brothers very glad. 4When they came to Jerusalem, they were
welcomed by the church and the apostles and elders, to whom
they reported everything God had done through them.
5Then some of the believers who belonged to the party of the
Pharisees stood up and said, "The Gentiles must be circumcised
and required to obey the law of Moses."
6The apostles and elders met to consider this question. 7After
much discussion, Peter got up and addressed them: "Brothers,
you know that some time ago God made a choice among you that
the Gentiles might hear from my lips the message of the gospel and
believe. 8God, who knows the heart, showed that he accepted
them by giving the Holy Spirit to them, just as he did to us. 9He
made no distinction between us and them, for he purified their
hearts by faith. 10Now then, why do you try to test God by putting
on the necks of the disciples a yoke that neither we nor our fathers
have been able to bear? 11No! We believe it is through the grace
of our Lord Jesus that we are saved, just as they are."
12The whole assembly became silent as they listened to Barnabas and Paul telling about the miraculous signs and wonders
God had done among the Gentiles through them. 13When they
finished, James spoke up: "Brothers, listen to me. 14Simon[f] has
described to us how God at first showed his concern by taking
from the Gentiles a people for himself. 15The words of the prophets are in agreement with this, as it is written:

**NIV** [e] 23 Or *Barnabas ordained elders;* or *Barnabas had elders elected* [f] 14 Greek *Simeon,* a variant of *Simon;* that is, Peter

## King James

16After this I will return, and will build again the tabernacle of David, which is fallen down; and I will build again the ruins thereof, and I will set it up:

17That the residue of men might seek after the Lord, and all the Gentiles, upon whom my name is called, saith the Lord, who doeth all these things.

18Known unto God are all his works from the beginning of the world.

19Wherefore my sentence is, that we trouble not them, which from among the Gentiles are turned to God:

20But that we write unto them, that they abstain from pollutions of idols, and *from* fornication, and *from* things strangled, and *from* blood.

21For Moses of old time hath in every city them that preach him, being read in the synagogues every sabbath day.

22Then pleased it the apostles and elders, with the whole church, to send chosen men of their own company to Antioch with Paul and Barnabas; *namely,* Judas surnamed Barsabas, and Silas, chief men among the brethren:

23And they wrote *letters* by them after this manner; The apostles and elders and brethren *send* greeting unto the brethren which are of the Gentiles in Antioch and Syria and Cilicia:

24Forasmuch as we have heard, that certain which went out from us have troubled you with words, subverting your souls, saying, *Ye must* be circumcised, and keep the law: to whom we gave no *such* commandment:

25It seemed good unto us, being assembled with one accord, to send chosen men unto you with our beloved Barnabas and Paul,

26Men that have hazarded their lives for the name of our Lord Jesus Christ.

27We have sent therefore Judas and Silas, who shall also tell *you* the same things by mouth.

28For it seemed good to the Holy Ghost, and to us, to lay upon you no greater burden than these necessary things;

29That ye abstain from meats offered to idols, and from blood, and from things strangled, and from fornication: from which if ye keep yourselves, ye shall do well. Fare ye well.

30So when they were dismissed, they came to Antioch: and when they had gathered the multitude together, they delivered the epistle:

31 *Which* when they had read, they rejoiced for the consolation.

32And Judas and Silas, being prophets also themselves, exhorted the brethren with many words, and confirmed *them.*

33And after they had tarried *there* a space, they were let go in peace from the brethren unto the apostles.

34Notwithstanding it pleased Silas to abide there still.

35Paul also and Barnabas continued in Antioch, teaching and preaching the word of the Lord, with many others also.

36¶ And some days after Paul said unto Barnabas, Let us go again and visit our brethren in every city where we have preached the word of the Lord, *and see* how they do.

37And Barnabas determined to take with them John, whose surname was Mark.

38But Paul thought not good to take him with them, who departed from them from Pamphylia, and went not with them to the work.

## Amplified

16After this I will come back, and will rebuild the house of David, which has fallen; I will rebuild its [very] ruins, and I will set it up again,

17So that the rest of men may seek the Lord, and all the Gentiles upon whom My name has been invoked,

18Says the Lord Who has been making [a]these things known from the beginning of the world. [Amos 9:11, 12; Jer. 12:15; Isa. 45:21.]

19Therefore it is my opinion that we should not put obstacles in the way *and* annoy *and* disturb those of the Gentiles who turn to God,

20But we should send word to them in writing to abstain from *and* avoid anything that has been polluted by being offered to idols, and all sexual impurity, and [meat of animals] that have been strangled, and [tasting] of blood.

21For from ancient generations Moses has had in every town his preachers, for he is read [aloud] every Sabbath in the synagogues.

22Then the apostles and the elders, together with the whole church, resolved to select men from among their number and send them to Antioch with Paul and Barnabas. They chose Judas called Barsabbas, and Silas, [both] leading men among the brethren, *and* sent them.

23With [them they sent] the following letter: The brethren, both the apostles and the elders, to the brethren who are of the Gentiles in Antioch and Syria and Cilicia, greeting:

24As we have heard that some persons from our number have disturbed you with their teaching, unsettling your minds *and* [b]throwing you into confusion, although we gave them no express orders *or* instructions [on the points in question],

25It has been resolved by us in assembly to select men and send them [as messengers] to you with our beloved Barnabas and Paul,

26Men who have hazarded their lives for the sake of our Lord Jesus Christ.

27So we have sent Judas and Silas, who themselves will bring you the same message by word of mouth.

28For it has seemed good to the Holy Spirit and to us not to lay upon you any greater burden than these indispensable requirements:

29That you abstain from what has been sacrificed to idols and from [tasting] blood and from [eating the meat of animals] that have been strangled and from sexual impurity. If you keep yourselves from these things, you will do well. Farewell—be strong!

30So when [the messengers] were sent off, they went down to Antioch; and having assembled the congregation, they delivered the letter.

31And when they read it, the people rejoiced at the consolation *and* encouragement [it brought them].

32And Judas and Silas, who were themselves prophets (inspired interpreters of the will and purposes of God) urged *and* warned *and* consoled *and* encouraged the brethren with many words and strengthened them.

33And after spending some time there, they were sent back by the brethren with [the greeting] Peace, to those who had sent them.

34 *Though Silas decided to stay on there.*

35But Paul and Barnabas remained in Antioch and with many others also continued teaching and proclaiming the Word of the Lord [concerning the [c]attainment through Christ of eternal salvation in God's kingdom].

36And after some time Paul said to Barnabas, Come, let us go back and again visit *and* help *and* minister to the brethren in every town where we made known the message of the Lord, and see how they are getting along.

37Now Barnabas wanted to take with them John called Mark [his near relative].

38But Paul did not think it best to have along with them the one who had quit *and* deserted them in Pamphylia, and had not gone on with them to the work.

**AMP** [a] Vincent. [b] Vincent. [c] Thayer.

## New American Standard

16 'AFTER THESE THINGS I will return,
AND I WILL REBUILD THE TABERNACLE OF DAVID WHICH HAS FALLEN,
AND I WILL REBUILD ITS RUINS,
AND I WILL RESTORE IT,
17 IN ORDER THAT THE REST OF MANKIND MAY SEEK THE LORD,
AND ALL THE GENTILES WHO ARE CALLED BY MY NAME,'
18 SAYS THE LORD, WHO MAKES THESE THINGS KNOWN FROM OF OLD.

19 "Therefore it is my judgment that we do not trouble those
who are turning to God from among the Gentiles,

20 but that we write to them that they abstain from things contaminated by idols and from fornication and from what is strangled and from blood.

21 "For Moses from ancient generations has in every city those who preach him, since he is read in the synagogues every Sabbath."

22 ¶ Then it seemed good to the apostles and the elders, with the whole church, to choose men from among them to send to Antioch with Paul and Barnabas—Judas called Barsabbas, and Silas, leading men among the brethren,

23 and they sent this letter by them,
"The apostles and the brethren who are elders, to the brethren in Antioch and Syria and Cilicia who are from the Gentiles, greetings.
24 "Since we have heard that some of our number to whom we gave no instruction have disturbed you with *their* words, unsettling your souls,
25 it seemed good to us, having become of one mind, to select men to send to you with our beloved Barnabas and Paul,
26 men who have risked their lives for the name of our Lord Jesus Christ.
27 "Therefore we have sent Judas and Silas, who themselves will also report the same things by word *of mouth*.
28 "For it seemed good to the Holy Spirit and to us to lay upon you no greater burden than these essentials:
29 that you abstain from things sacrificed to idols and from blood and from things strangled and from fornication; if you keep yourselves free from such things, you will do well. Farewell."

30 ¶ So, when they were sent away, they went down to Antioch; and having gathered the congregation together, they delivered the letter.

31 And when they had read it, they rejoiced because of its encouragement.

32 And Judas and Silas, also being prophets themselves, encouraged and strengthened the brethren with a lengthy message.

33 And after they had spent time *there*, they were sent away from the brethren in peace to those who had sent them out.

34 [ [d]But it seemed good to Silas to remain there.]

35 But Paul and Barnabas stayed in Antioch, teaching and preaching, with many others also, the word of the Lord.

*Second Missionary Journey*

36 ¶ And after some days Paul said to Barnabas, "Let us return and visit the brethren in every city in which we proclaimed the word of the Lord, *and see* how they are."

37 And Barnabas was desirous of taking John, called Mark, along with them also.

38 But Paul kept insisting that they should not take him along who had deserted them in Pamphylia and had not gone with them to the work.

NAS [d] Many mss. do not contain this verse

## New International

16 " 'After this I will return
and rebuild David's fallen tent.
Its ruins I will rebuild,
and I will restore it,
17 that the remnant of men may seek the Lord,
and all the Gentiles who bear my name,
says the Lord, who does these things'[e]
18 that have been known for ages.[f]

19 "It is my judgment, therefore, that we should not make it
difficult for the Gentiles who are turning to God.
20 Instead we
should write to them, telling them to abstain from food polluted
by idols, from sexual immorality, from the meat of strangled animals and from blood.
21 For Moses has been preached in every city
from the earliest times and is read in the synagogues on every
Sabbath."

*The Council's Letter to Gentile Believers*

22 Then the apostles and elders, with the whole church, decided
to choose some of their own men and send them to Antioch with
Paul and Barnabas. They chose Judas (called Barsabbas) and Silas,
two men who were leaders among the brothers.
23 With them they
sent the following letter:

The apostles and elders, your brothers,

To the Gentile believers in Antioch, Syria and Cilicia:

Greetings.

24 We have heard that some went out from us without our
authorization and disturbed you, troubling your minds by
what they said.
25 So we all agreed to choose some men and
send them to you with our dear friends Barnabas and Paul—
26 men who have risked their lives for the name of our Lord
Jesus Christ.
27 Therefore we are sending Judas and Silas to
confirm by word of mouth what we are writing.
28 It seemed
good to the Holy Spirit and to us not to burden you with
anything beyond the following requirements:
29 You are to
abstain from food sacrificed to idols, from blood, from the
meat of strangled animals and from sexual immorality. You
will do well to avoid these things.
Farewell.

30 The men were sent off and went down to Antioch, where they
gathered the church together and delivered the letter.
31 The
people read it and were glad for its encouraging message.
32 Judas
and Silas, who themselves were prophets, said much to encourage
and strengthen the brothers.
33 After spending some time there,
they were sent off by the brothers with the blessing of peace to
return to those who had sent them.[g]
35 But Paul and Barnabas
remained in Antioch, where they and many others taught and
preached the word of the Lord.

*Disagreement Between Paul and Barnabas*

36 Some time later Paul said to Barnabas, "Let us go back and
visit the brothers in all the towns where we preached the word of
the Lord and see how they are doing."
37 Barnabas wanted to take
John, also called Mark, with them,
38 but Paul did not think it wise
to take him, because he had deserted them in Pamphylia and had
not continued with them in the work.
39 They had such a sharp

NIV [e] 17 Amos 9:11,12 [f] 17,18 Some manuscripts *things'— / 18known to the Lord for ages is his work* [g] 33 Some manuscripts *them, 34but Silas decided to remain there*

## King James

39And the contention was so sharp between them, that they departed asunder one from the other: and so Barnabas took Mark, and sailed unto Cyprus;

40And Paul chose Silas, and departed, being recommended by the brethren unto the grace of God.

41And he went through Syria and Cilicia, confirming the churches.

**16** THEN CAME he to Derbe and Lystra: and, behold, a certain disciple was there, named Timotheus, the son of a certain woman, which was a Jewess, and believed; but his father *was* a Greek:

2Which was well reported of by the brethren that were at Lystra and Iconium.

3Him would Paul have to go forth with him; and took and circumcised him because of the Jews which were in those quarters: for they knew all that his father was a Greek.

4And as they went through the cities, they delivered them the decrees for to keep, that were ordained of the apostles and elders which were at Jerusalem.

5And so were the churches established in the faith, and increased in number daily.

6Now when they had gone throughout Phrygia and the region of Galatia, and were forbidden of the Holy Ghost to preach the word in Asia,

7After they were come to Mysia, they assayed to go into Bithynia: but the Spirit suffered them not.

8And they passing by Mysia came down to Troas.

9And a vision appeared to Paul in the night; There stood a man of Macedonia, and prayed him, saying, Come over into Macedonia, and help us.

10And after he had seen the vision, immediately we endeavoured to go into Macedonia, assuredly gathering that the Lord had called us for to preach the gospel unto them.

11Therefore loosing from Troas, we came with a straight course to Samothracia, and the next *day* to Neapolis;

12And from thence to Philippi, which is the chief city of that part of Macedonia, *and* a colony: and we were in that city abiding certain days.

13And on the sabbath we went out of the city by a river side, where prayer was wont to be made; and we sat down, and spake unto the women which resorted *thither*.

14¶ And a certain woman named Lydia, a seller of purple, of the city of Thyatira, which worshipped God, heard *us:* whose heart the Lord opened, that she attended unto the things which were spoken of Paul.

15And when she was baptized, and her household, she besought *us*, saying, If ye have judged me to be faithful to the Lord, come into my house, and abide *there*. And she constrained us.

16¶ And it came to pass, as we went to prayer, a certain damsel possessed with a spirit of divination met us, which brought her masters much gain by soothsaying:

17The same followed Paul and us, and cried, saying, These men are the servants of the most high God, which show unto us the way of salvation.

18And this did she many days. But Paul, being grieved, turned and said to the spirit, I command thee in the name of Jesus Christ to come out of her. And he came out the same hour.

19¶ And when her masters saw that the hope of their gains was gone, they caught Paul and Silas, and drew *them* into the marketplace unto the rulers,

## Amplified

39And there followed a sharp disagreement between them, so that they separated from each other, and Barnabas took Mark with him and sailed away to Cyprus.

40But Paul selected Silas and set out, being commended by the brethren to the grace—the favor and mercy—of the Lord.

41And he passed through Syria and Cilicia, establishing *and* strengthening the churches.

**16** AND [PAUL] went down to Derbe and also to Lystra. A disciple named Timothy was there, the son of a Jewish woman who was a believer—that is, she had become [a]convinced that Jesus is the Messiah, and the Author of eternal salvation, and yielded obedience to Him; but [Timothy's] father was a Greek.

2He [Timothy] had a good reputation among the brethren at Lystra and Iconium.

3Paul desired Timothy to go with him [[b]as a missionary]; and he took him and circumcised him, because of the Jews that were in those places, all of whom knew that his father was a Greek.

4As they went on their way from town to town, they delivered over to the assemblies for their observance the regulations decided upon by the apostles and elders who were at Jerusalem.

5So the churches were strengthened *and* made firm in the faith, and they increased in number day after day.

6And Paul and Silas passed through the territory of Phrygia and Galatia, having been forbidden by the Holy Spirit to proclaim the Word in [the province of] Asia.

7And when they had come opposite Mysia, they tried to go into Bithynia, but the Spirit of Jesus did not permit them.

8So passing by Mysia, they went down to Troas.

9[There] a vision appeared to Paul in the night: a man from Macedonia stood pleading with him and saying, Come over to Macedonia and help us!

10And when he had seen the vision, we at once endeavored to go on into Macedonia, confidently inferring that God had called us to proclaim the glad tidings (Gospel) to them.

11Therefore, setting sail from Troas, we came in a direct course to Samothrace, and the next day went on to Neapolis.

12And from there [we came] to Philippi, which is the chief city of the district of Macedonia, and a [Roman] colony. We stayed on in this place some days;

13And on the Sabbath day we went outside the [city's] gate to the bank of the river, where we supposed there was [an accustomed] place of prayer, and we sat down and addressed the women who had assembled there.

14One of those who listened to us was a woman named Lydia, from the city of Thyatira, a dealer in fabrics dyed in purple. She was [already] a worshipper of God, and the Lord opened her heart to pay attention to what was said by Paul.

15And when she was baptized along with her household, she earnestly entreated us, saying, If in your opinion I am one really convinced [that Jesus is the Messiah and the Author of salvation], *and* that I will be faithful to the Lord, come to my house and stay. And she induced us [to do it].

16As we were on our way to the place of prayer, we were met by a slave girl who was possessed by a spirit of divination—claiming to foretell future events and to discover hidden knowledge—and she brought her owners much gain by her fortunetelling.

17She kept following Paul and [the rest of] us, shouting loudly, These men are the servants of the Most High God! They announce to you the way of salvation!

18And she did this for many days. Then Paul, being sorely annoyed *and* worn out, turned and said to the spirit within her, I charge you in the name of Jesus Christ to come out of her! And it came out that very [c]moment.

19But when her owners discovered that their hope of profit was gone, they caught hold of Paul and Silas and dragged them before the authorities in the forum—market place [where trials are held].

**AMP** [a] Thayer. [b] Vincent. [c] Moulton and Milligan's "The Vocabulary of the Greek Testament."

## New American Standard

39And there arose such a sharp disagreement that they separated from one another, and Barnabas took Mark with him and sailed away to Cyprus.

40But Paul chose Silas and departed, being committed by the brethren to the grace of the Lord.

41And he was traveling through Syria and Cilicia, strengthening the churches.

*The Macedonian Vision*

16 AND HE came also to Derbe and to Lystra. And behold, a certain disciple was there, named Timothy, the son of a Jewish woman who was a believer, but his father was a Greek,

2and he was well spoken of by the brethren who were in Lystra and Iconium.

3Paul wanted this man to go with him; and he took him and circumcised him because of the Jews who were in those parts, for they all knew that his father was a Greek.

4Now while they were passing through the cities, they were delivering the decrees, which had been decided upon by the apostles and elders who were in Jerusalem, for them to observe.

5So the churches were being strengthened in the faith, and were increasing in number daily.

6¶ And they passed through the Phrygian and Galatian region, having been forbidden by the Holy Spirit to speak the word in Asia;

7and when they had come to Mysia, they were trying to go into Bithynia, and the Spirit of Jesus did not permit them;

8and passing by Mysia, they came down to Troas.

9And a vision appeared to Paul in the night: a certain man of Macedonia was standing and appealing to him, and saying, "Come over to Macedonia and help us."

10And when he had seen the vision, immediately we sought to go into Macedonia, concluding that God had called us to preach the gospel to them.

11¶ Therefore putting out to sea from Troas, we ran a straight course to Samothrace, and on the day following to Neapolis;

12and from there to Philippi, which is a leading city of the district of Macedonia, a *Roman* colony; and we were staying in this city for some days.

13And on the Sabbath day we went outside the gate to a riverside, where we were supposing that there would be a place of prayer; and we sat down and began speaking to the women who had assembled.

*First Convert in Europe*

14And a certain woman named Lydia, from the city of Thyatira, a seller of purple fabrics, a worshiper of God, was listening; and the Lord opened her heart to respond to the things spoken by Paul.

15And when she and her household had been baptized, she urged us, saying, "If you have judged me to be faithful to the Lord, come into my house and stay." And she prevailed upon us.

16¶ And it happened that as we were going to the place of prayer, a certain slave-girl having a spirit of divination met us, who was bringing her masters much profit by fortunetelling.

17Following after Paul and us, she kept crying out, saying, "These men are bond-servants of the Most High God, who are proclaiming to you the way of salvation."

18And she continued doing this for many days. But Paul was greatly annoyed, and turned and said to the spirit, "I command you in the name of Jesus Christ to come out of her!" And it came out at that very moment.

19¶ But when her masters saw that their hope of profit was gone, they seized Paul and Silas and dragged them into the market place before the authorities,

## New International

disagreement that they parted company. Barnabas took Mark and
sailed for Cyprus, 40but Paul chose Silas and left, commended by
the brothers to the grace of the Lord. 41He went through Syria and
Cilicia, strengthening the churches.

*Timothy Joins Paul and Silas*

16 HE CAME to Derbe and then to Lystra, where a disciple
named Timothy lived, whose mother was a Jewess and a
believer, but whose father was a Greek. 2The brothers at Lystra
and Iconium spoke well of him. 3Paul wanted to take him along
on the journey, so he circumcised him because of the Jews who
lived in that area, for they all knew that his father was a Greek.
4As they traveled from town to town, they delivered the decisions
reached by the apostles and elders in Jerusalem for the people to
obey. 5So the churches were strengthened in the faith and grew
daily in numbers.

*Paul's Vision of the Man of Macedonia*

6Paul and his companions traveled throughout the region of
Phrygia and Galatia, having been kept by the Holy Spirit from
preaching the word in the province of Asia. 7When they came to
the border of Mysia, they tried to enter Bithynia, but the Spirit of
Jesus would not allow them to. 8So they passed by Mysia and went
down to Troas. 9During the night Paul had a vision of a man of
Macedonia standing and begging him, "Come over to Macedonia
and help us." 10After Paul had seen the vision, we got ready at
once to leave for Macedonia, concluding that God had called us to
preach the gospel to them.

*Lydia's Conversion in Philippi*

11From Troas we put out to sea and sailed straight for Samothrace, and the next day on to Neapolis. 12From there we traveled
to Philippi, a Roman colony and the leading city of that district of
Macedonia. And we stayed there several days.
13On the Sabbath we went outside the city gate to the river,
where we expected to find a place of prayer. We sat down and
began to speak to the women who had gathered there. 14One of
those listening was a woman named Lydia, a dealer in purple cloth
from the city of Thyatira, who was a worshiper of God. The Lord
opened her heart to respond to Paul's message. 15When she and
the members of her household were baptized, she invited us to her
home. "If you consider me a believer in the Lord," she said, "come
and stay at my house." And she persuaded us.

*Paul and Silas in Prison*

16Once when we were going to the place of prayer, we were met
by a slave girl who had a spirit by which she predicted the future.
She earned a great deal of money for her owners by fortune-telling.
17This girl followed Paul and the rest of us, shouting, "These men
are servants of the Most High God, who are telling you the way
to be saved." 18She kept this up for many days. Finally Paul
became so troubled that he turned around and said to the spirit,
"In the name of Jesus Christ I command you to come out of her!"
At that moment the spirit left her.
19When the owners of the slave girl realized that their hope of
making money was gone, they seized Paul and Silas and dragged
them into the marketplace to face the authorities. 20They brought

## King James

20And brought them to the magistrates, saying, These men, being Jews, do exceedingly trouble our city,

21And teach customs, which are not lawful for us to receive, neither to observe, being Romans.

22And the multitude rose up together against them: and the magistrates rent off their clothes, and commanded to beat *them.*

23And when they had laid many stripes upon them, they cast *them* into prison, charging the jailer to keep them safely:

24Who, having received such a charge, thrust them into the inner prison, and made their feet fast in the stocks.

25¶ And at midnight Paul and Silas prayed, and sang praises unto God: and the prisoners heard them.

26And suddenly there was a great earthquake, so that the foundations of the prison were shaken: and immediately all the doors were opened, and every one's bands were loosed.

27And the keeper of the prison awaking out of his sleep, and seeing the prison doors open, he drew out his sword, and would have killed himself, supposing that the prisoners had been fled.

28But Paul cried with a loud voice, saying, Do thyself no harm: for we are all here.

29Then he called for a light, and sprang in, and came trembling, and fell down before Paul and Silas,

30And brought them out, and said, Sirs, what must I do to be saved?

31And they said, Believe on the Lord Jesus Christ, and thou shalt be saved, and thy house.

32And they spake unto him the word of the Lord, and to all that were in his house.

33And he took them the same hour of the night, and washed *their* stripes; and was baptized, he and all his, straightway.

34And when he had brought them into his house, he set meat before them, and rejoiced, believing in God with all his house.

35And when it was day, the magistrates sent the sergeants, saying, Let those men go.

36And the keeper of the prison told this saying to Paul, The magistrates have sent to let you go: now therefore depart, and go in peace.

37But Paul said unto them, They have beaten us openly uncondemned, being Romans, and have cast *us* into prison; and now do they thrust us out privily? nay verily; but let them come themselves and fetch us out.

38And the sergeants told these words unto the magistrates: and they feared, when they heard that they were Romans.

39And they came and besought them, and brought *them* out, and desired *them* to depart out of the city.

40And they went out of the prison, and entered into *the house of* Lydia: and when they had seen the brethren, they comforted them, and departed.

## Amplified

20And when they had brought them before the magistrates, they declared, These fellows are Jews and they are throwing our city into great confusion.

21They encourage the practice of customs which it is unlawful for us Romans to accept or observe!

22The crowd [also] joined in the attack upon them, and the rulers tore the clothes off of them and commanded that they be beaten with rods.

23And when they had struck them with many blows, they threw them into prison, charging the jailer to keep them safely.

24He, having received [so strict a] charge, put them into the inner prison [the dungeon] and fastened their feet in the stocks.

25But about midnight, as Paul and Silas were praying and singing hymns of praise to God, and the [other] prisoners were listening to them,

26Suddenly there was a great earthquake, so that the very foundations of the prison were shaken; and at once all the doors were opened and every one's shackles were unfastened.

27When the jailer, startled out of his sleep, saw that the prison doors were open, he drew his sword and was on the point of killing himself, because he supposed that the prisoners had escaped.

28But Paul shouted, Do not harm yourself, for we are all here!

29Then [the jailer] called for lights and rushed in, and trembling *and* terrified he fell down before Paul and Silas.

30And he brought them out [of the dungeon] and said, Men, what is it necessary for me to do that I may be saved?

31And they answered, Believe in *and* on the Lord Jesus *Christ*—that is, [a]give yourself up to Him, [b]take yourself out of your own keeping and entrust yourself into His keeping, and you will be saved; [and this applies both to] you and your household as well.

32And they declared the Word of the Lord [that is, the doctrine concerning the [c]attainment through Christ of eternal salvation in the kingdom of God] to him and to all who were in his house.

33And he took them the same hour of the night and [d]bathed [them because of their bloody] wounds, and he was baptized immediately and all [the members] of his [household].

34Then he took them up into his house and set food before them; and he [e]leaped much for joy *and* exulted with all his family that he believed in God [accepting and joyously welcoming what He had made known through Christ].

35But when it was day, the magistrates sent policemen, saying, Release those fellows *and* let them go.

36And the jailer repeated the words to Paul, saying, The magistrates have sent to release you *and* let you go; now therefore come out and go in peace.

37But Paul answered them, They have beaten us openly *and* publicly, without a trial *and* uncondemned, men who are Roman citizens, and have thrown us into prison; and do they now thrust us out secretly? No, indeed! Let them come here themselves and conduct us out!

38The police reported this message to the magistrates, and they were frightened when they heard that the prisoners were Roman citizens;

39So they came themselves and—striving to appease them by entreaty—apologized to them. And they brought them out and asked them to leave the city.

40So [Paul and Silas] left the prison, and went to Lydia's house; and when they had seen the brethren, they warned *and* urged *and* consoled *and* encouraged them and departed.

**AMP** [a] Thayer. [b] Wuest's "Golden Nuggets from the Greek New Testament." [c] Thayer. [d] Vincent's "Word Studies in the New Testament." [e] Young's Concordance.

## New American Standard

20and when they had brought them to the chief magistrates,
they said, "These men are throwing our city into confusion, being
Jews,
21and are proclaiming customs which it is not lawful for us to
accept or to observe, being Romans."

*Paul and Silas Imprisoned*

22And the crowd rose up together against them, and the chief
magistrates tore their robes off them, and proceeded to order *them*
to be beaten with rods.
23And when they had inflicted many blows upon them, they
threw them into prison, commanding the jailer to guard them
securely;
24and he, having received such a command, threw them into
the inner prison, and fastened their feet in the stocks.
25But about midnight Paul and Silas were praying and singing
hymns of praise to God, and the prisoners were listening to them;
26and suddenly there came a great earthquake, so that the
foundations of the prison house were shaken; and immediately all
the doors were opened, and everyone's chains were unfastened.
27And when the jailer had been roused out of sleep and had
seen the prison doors opened, he drew his sword and was about
to kill himself, supposing that the prisoners had escaped.
28But Paul cried out with a loud voice, saying, "Do yourself no
harm, for we are all here!"
29And he called for lights and rushed in and, trembling with
fear, he fell down before Paul and Silas,
30and after he brought them out, he said, "Sirs, what must I do
to be saved?"

*The Jailer Converted*

31And they said, "Believe in the Lord Jesus, and you shall be
saved, you and your household."
32And they spoke the word of the Lord to him together with all
who were in his house.
33And he took them that *very* hour of the night and washed their
wounds, and immediately he was baptized, he and all his *household*.
34And he brought them into his house and set food before
them, and rejoiced greatly, having believed in God with his whole
household.
35¶ Now when day came, the chief magistrates sent their policemen, saying, "Release those men."
36And the jailer reported these words to Paul, *saying*, "The chief
magistrates have sent to release you. Now therefore, come out and
go in peace."
37But Paul said to them, "They have beaten us in public without
trial, men who are Romans, and have thrown us into prison; and
now are they sending us away secretly? No indeed! But let them
come themselves and bring us out."
38And the policemen reported these words to the chief magistrates. And they were afraid when they heard that they were
Romans,
39and they came and appealed to them, and when they had
brought them out, they kept begging them to leave the city.
40And they went out of the prison and entered *the house of*
Lydia, and when they saw the brethren, they encouraged them
and departed.

## New International

them before the magistrates and said, "These men are Jews, and
are throwing our city into an uproar 21by advocating customs
unlawful for us Romans to accept or practice."
22The crowd joined in the attack against Paul and Silas, and the
magistrates ordered them to be stripped and beaten. 23After they
had been severely flogged, they were thrown into prison, and the
jailer was commanded to guard them carefully. 24Upon receiving
such orders, he put them in the inner cell and fastened their feet
in the stocks.
25About midnight Paul and Silas were praying and singing
hymns to God, and the other prisoners were listening to them.
26Suddenly there was such a violent earthquake that the foundations of the prison were shaken. At once all the prison doors flew
open, and everybody's chains came loose. 27The jailer woke up,
and when he saw the prison doors open, he drew his sword and
was about to kill himself because he thought the prisoners had
escaped. 28But Paul shouted, "Don't harm yourself! We are all
here!"
29The jailer called for lights, rushed in and fell trembling before
Paul and Silas. 30He then brought them out and asked, "Sirs, what
must I do to be saved?"
31They replied, "Believe in the Lord Jesus, and you will be
saved—you and your household." 32Then they spoke the word of
the Lord to him and to all the others in his house. 33At that hour
of the night the jailer took them and washed their wounds; then
immediately he and all his family were baptized. 34The jailer
brought them into his house and set a meal before them; he was
filled with joy because he had come to believe in God—he and his
whole family.
35When it was daylight, the magistrates sent their officers to the
jailer with the order: "Release those men." 36The jailer told Paul,
"The magistrates have ordered that you and Silas be released.
Now you can leave. Go in peace."
37But Paul said to the officers: "They beat us publicly without
a trial, even though we are Roman citizens, and threw us into
prison. And now do they want to get rid of us quietly? No! Let
them come themselves and escort us out."
38The officers reported this to the magistrates, and when they
heard that Paul and Silas were Roman citizens, they were alarmed.
39They came to appease them and escorted them from the prison,
requesting them to leave the city. 40After Paul and Silas came out
of the prison, they went to Lydia's house, where they met with the
brothers and encouraged them. Then they left.

## King James

17 NOW WHEN they had passed through Amphipolis and Apollonia, they came to Thessalonica, where was a synagogue of the Jews:

2And Paul, as his manner was, went in unto them, and three sabbath days reasoned with them out of the scriptures,

3Opening and alleging, that Christ must needs have suffered, and risen again from the dead; and that this Jesus, whom I preach unto you, is Christ.

4And some of them believed, and consorted with Paul and Silas; and of the devout Greeks a great multitude, and of the chief women not a few.

5¶ But the Jews which believed not, moved with envy, took unto them certain lewd fellows of the baser sort, and gathered a company, and set all the city on an uproar, and assaulted the house of Jason, and sought to bring them out to the people.

6And when they found them not, they drew Jason and certain brethren unto the rulers of the city, crying, These that have turned the world upside down are come hither also;

7Whom Jason hath received: and these all do contrary to the decrees of Caesar, saying that there is another king, *one* Jesus.

8And they troubled the people and the rulers of the city, when they heard these things.

9And when they had taken security of Jason, and of the other, they let them go.

10¶ And the brethren immediately sent away Paul and Silas by night unto Berea: who coming *thither* went into the synagogue of the Jews.

11These were more noble than those in Thessalonica, in that they received the word with all readiness of mind, and searched the scriptures daily, whether those things were so.

12Therefore many of them believed; also of honourable women which were Greeks, and of men, not a few.

13But when the Jews of Thessalonica had knowledge that the word of God was preached of Paul at Berea, they came thither also, and stirred up the people.

14And then immediately the brethren sent away Paul to go as it were to the sea: but Silas and Timotheus abode there still.

15And they that conducted Paul brought him unto Athens: and receiving a commandment unto Silas and Timotheus for to come to him with all speed, they departed.

16¶ Now while Paul waited for them at Athens, his spirit was stirred in him, when he saw the city wholly given to idolatry.

17Therefore disputed he in the synagogue with the Jews, and with the devout persons, and in the market daily with them that met with him.

18Then certain philosophers of the Epicureans, and of the Stoics, encountered him. And some said, What will this babbler say? other some, He seemeth to be a setter forth of strange gods: because he preached unto them Jesus, and the resurrection.

19And they took him, and brought him unto Areopagus, saying, May we know what this new doctrine, whereof thou speakest, *is?*

20For thou bringest certain strange things to our ears: we would know therefore what these things mean.

21(For all the Athenians and strangers which were there spent their time in nothing else, but either to tell, or to hear some new thing.)

## Amplified

17 NOW AFTER [Paul and Silas] had passed through Amphipolis and Apollonia, they came to Thessalonica, where there was a synagogue of the Jews.

2And Paul entered, as he usually did, and for three Sabbaths he reasoned *and* argued with them from the Scriptures,

3Explaining [them] *and* [quoting passages] setting forth *and* proving that it was necessary for Christ to suffer and to rise from the dead, and saying, This Jesus, Whom I proclaim to you, is the Christ, the Messiah.

4And some of them [accordingly] were induced to believe, and associated themselves with Paul and Silas, as did a great number of the devout Greeks and not a few of the leading women.

5But the unbelieving Jews were aroused to jealousy, and getting hold of some loungers in the market place—ruffians *and* rascals—they gathered together a mob, set the town in an uproar, and attacked the house of Jason, seeking to bring [Paul and Silas] out to the people.

6But when they failed to find them, they dragged Jason and some of the brethren before the city authorities, crying, These men who have turned the world upside down have come here also,

7And Jason has received them to his house *and* privately protected them! And they are all ignoring *and* acting contrary to the decrees of Caesar, [actually] asserting that there is another king, one Jesus!

8And both the crowd and the city authorities on hearing this were irritated—stirred up and troubled.

9And when they had taken security [bail] from Jason and the others, they let them go.

10Now the brethren at once sent Paul and Silas away by night to Beroea, and when they arrived they entered the synagogue of the Jews.

11Now these [Jews] were better disposed *and* more noble than those in Thessalonica, for they were entirely ready and accepted *and* welcomed the message [ [a]concerning the attainment through Christ of eternal salvation in the kingdom of God], with inclination of mind *and* eagerness, searching *and* examining the Scriptures daily to see if these things were so.

12Many of them therefore became believers, together with not a few prominent Greeks, women as well as men;

13But when the Jews of Thessalonica learned that the Word of God [ [b]concerning the attainment through Christ of eternal salvation in the kingdom of God] was preached at Beroea also by Paul, they came there too, disturbing *and* inciting the masses.

14At once the brethren sent Paul off on his way to the sea, but Silas and Timothy remained behind.

15Those who escorted Paul brought him as far as Athens; and receiving instructions for Silas and Timothy that they should come to him as soon as possible, they departed.

16Now while Paul was awaiting them at Athens, his spirit was grieved *and* roused to anger as he saw that the city was full of idols.

17So he reasoned *and* argued in the synagogue with the Jews and those who worshipped there, and in the market place [where assemblies are held], day after day with any who chanced to be there.

18And some also of the Epicurean and Stoic philosophers encountered him *and* began to engage in discussion. And some said, What is this blabber with his scrap-picked learning trying to say? Others said, He seems to be an announcer of foreign deities, because he preached Jesus and the resurrection.

19And they took hold of him and brought him to the Areopagus [Mars Hill auditorium] saying, May we know what this novel—unheard of and unprecedented—teaching is which you are openly declaring?

20For you set forth some startling things, foreign *and* strange to our ears; we wish to know therefore just what these things mean.

21For the Athenians, all of them, and the foreign residents *and* visitors among them spent all their leisure time in nothing except telling or hearing something newer than the last.

**AMP** [a] Thayer. [b] Thayer.

## New American Standard

*Paul at Thessalonica*

17 NOW WHEN they had traveled through Amphipolis and Apollonia, they came to Thessalonica, where there was a synagogue of the Jews.
2And according to Paul's custom, he went to them, and for three Sabbaths reasoned with them from the Scriptures,
3explaining and giving evidence that the Christ had to suffer and rise again from the dead, and *saying,* "This Jesus whom I am proclaiming to you is the Christ."
4And some of them were persuaded and joined Paul and Silas, along with a great multitude of the God-fearing Greeks and a number of the leading women.
5But the Jews, becoming jealous and taking along some wicked men from the market place, formed a mob and set the city in an uproar; and coming upon the house of Jason, they were seeking to bring them out to the people.
6And when they did not find them, they *began* dragging Jason and some brethren before the city authorities, shouting, "These men who have upset [c]the world have come here also;
7and Jason has welcomed them, and they all act contrary to the decrees of Caesar, saying that there is another king, Jesus."
8And they stirred up the crowd and the city authorities who heard these things.
9And when they had received a pledge from Jason and the others, they released them.

*Paul at Berea*

10¶ And the brethren immediately sent Paul and Silas away by night to Berea; and when they arrived, they went into the synagogue of the Jews.
11Now these were more noble-minded than those in Thessalonica, for they received the word with great eagerness, examining the Scriptures daily, *to see* whether these things were so.
12Many of them therefore believed, along with a number of prominent Greek women and men.
13But when the Jews of Thessalonica found out that the word of God had been proclaimed by Paul in Berea also, they came there likewise, agitating and stirring up the crowds.
14And then immediately the brethren sent Paul out to go as far as the sea; and Silas and Timothy remained there.
15Now those who conducted Paul brought him as far as Athens; and receiving a command for Silas and Timothy to come to him as soon as possible, they departed.

*Paul at Athens*

16¶ Now while Paul was waiting for them at Athens, his spirit was being provoked within him as he was beholding the city full of idols.
17So he was reasoning in the synagogue with the Jews and the God-fearing *Gentiles,* and in the market place every day with those who happened to be present.
18And also some of the Epicurean and Stoic philosophers were conversing with him. And some were saying, "What would this idle babbler wish to say?" Others, "He seems to be a proclaimer of strange deities,"—because he was preaching Jesus and the resurrection.
19And they took him and brought him to the Areopagus, saying, "May we know what this new teaching is which you are proclaiming?
20"For you are bringing some strange things to our ears; we want to know therefore what these things mean."
21(Now all the Athenians and the strangers visiting there used to spend their time in nothing other than telling or hearing something new.)

NAS [c] Lit., *the inhabited earth*

## New International

*In Thessalonica*

17 WHEN THEY had passed through Amphipolis and Apollonia, they came to Thessalonica, where there was a
Jewish synagogue. 2As his custom was, Paul went into the synagogue, and on three Sabbath days he reasoned with them from the
Scriptures, 3explaining and proving that the Christ[d] had to suffer
and rise from the dead. "This Jesus I am proclaiming to you is the
Christ,[e]" he said. 4Some of the Jews were persuaded and joined
Paul and Silas, as did a large number of God-fearing Greeks and
not a few prominent women.
5But the Jews were jealous; so they rounded up some bad
characters from the marketplace, formed a mob and started a riot
in the city. They rushed to Jason's house in search of Paul and Silas
in order to bring them out to the crowd.[f] 6But when they did not
find them, they dragged Jason and some other brothers before the
city officials, shouting: "These men who have caused trouble all
over the world have now come here, 7and Jason has welcomed
them into his house. They are all defying Caesar's decrees, saying
that there is another king, one called Jesus." 8When they heard
this, the crowd and the city officials were thrown into turmoil.
9Then they made Jason and the others post bond and let them go.

*In Berea*

10As soon as it was night, the brothers sent Paul and Silas away
to Berea. On arriving there, they went to the Jewish synagogue.
11Now the Bereans were of more noble character than the Thessalonians, for they received the message with great eagerness and
examined the Scriptures every day to see if what Paul said was
true. 12Many of the Jews believed, as did also a number of prominent Greek women and many Greek men.
13When the Jews in Thessalonica learned that Paul was preaching the word of God at Berea, they went there too, agitating the
crowds and stirring them up. 14The brothers immediately sent
Paul to the coast, but Silas and Timothy stayed at Berea. 15The men
who escorted Paul brought him to Athens and then left with
instructions for Silas and Timothy to join him as soon as possible.

*In Athens*

16While Paul was waiting for them in Athens, he was greatly
distressed to see that the city was full of idols. 17So he reasoned
in the synagogue with the Jews and the God-fearing Greeks, as
well as in the marketplace day by day with those who happened
to be there. 18A group of Epicurean and Stoic philosophers began
to dispute with him. Some of them asked, "What is this babbler
trying to say?" Others remarked, "He seems to be advocating
foreign gods." They said this because Paul was preaching the good
news about Jesus and the resurrection. 19Then they took him and
brought him to a meeting of the Areopagus, where they said to
him, "May we know what this new teaching is that you are presenting? 20You are bringing some strange ideas to our ears, and we
want to know what they mean." 21(All the Athenians and the
foreigners who lived there spent their time doing nothing but
talking about and listening to the latest ideas.)

NIV [d] 3 Or *Messiah* [e] 3 Or *Messiah* [f] 5 Or *the assembly of the people*

## King James

22¶ Then Paul stood in the midst of Mars' hill, and said, *Ye* men of Athens, I perceive that in all things ye are too superstitious.

23For as I passed by, and beheld your devotions, I found an altar with this inscription, TO THE UNKNOWN GOD. Whom therefore ye ignorantly worship, him declare I unto you.

24God that made the world and all things therein, seeing that he is Lord of heaven and earth, dwelleth not in temples made with hands;

25Neither is worshipped with men's hands, as though he needed any thing, seeing he giveth to all life, and breath, and all things;

26And hath made of one blood all nations of men for to dwell on all the face of the earth, and hath determined the times before appointed, and the bounds of their habitation;

27That they should seek the Lord, if haply they might feel after him, and find him, though he be not far from every one of us:

28For in him we live, and move, and have our being; as certain also of your own poets have said, For we are also his offspring.

29Forasmuch then as we are the offspring of God, we ought not to think that the Godhead is like unto gold, or silver, or stone, graven by art and man's device.

30And the times of this ignorance God winked at; but now commandeth all men every where to repent:

31Because he hath appointed a day, in the which he will judge the world in righteousness by *that* man whom he hath ordained; *whereof* he hath given assurance unto all *men,* in that he hath raised him from the dead.

32¶ And when they heard of the resurrection of the dead, some mocked: and others said, We will hear thee again of this *matter.*

33So Paul departed from among them.

34Howbeit certain men clave unto him, and believed: among the which *was* Dionysius the Areopagite, and a woman named Damaris, and others with them.

**18** AFTER THESE things Paul departed from Athens, and came to Corinth:

2And found a certain Jew named Aquila, born in Pontus, lately come from Italy, with his wife Priscilla; (because that Claudius had commanded all Jews to depart from Rome:) and came unto them.

3And because he was of the same craft, he abode with them, and wrought: for by their occupation they were tentmakers.

4And he reasoned in the synagogue every sabbath, and persuaded the Jews and the Greeks.

5And when Silas and Timotheus were come from Macedonia, Paul was pressed in the spirit, and testified to the Jews *that* Jesus *was* Christ.

6And when they opposed themselves, and blasphemed, he shook *his* raiment, and said unto them, Your blood *be* upon your own heads; I *am* clean: from henceforth I will go unto the Gentiles.

## Amplified

22So Paul, standing in the center of the Areopagus [Mars Hill auditorium] said: Men of Athens, I perceive in every way—on every hand and with every turn I make—that you are most religious (very reverent to demons).

23For as I passed along and carefully observed your objects of worship, I came also upon an altar with this inscription, To the unknown god. Now what you are already worshipping as unknown, this I set forth to you.

24The God Who produced *and* formed the world and all things in it, being Lord of heaven and earth, does not dwell in handmade shrines.

25Neither is He served by human hands, as though He lacked anything, for it is He Himself Who gives life and breath and all things to all [people]. [Isa. 42:5.]

26And He made from one [common origin, one source, one blood] all nations of men to settle on the face of the earth, having definitely determined [their] allotted periods of time and the fixed boundaries of their habitation—their settlements, lands and abodes;

27So that they should seek God, in the hope that they might feel after Him and find Him, although He is not far from each one of us.

28For in Him we live and move and have our being; as even some of your [own] poets have said, For we are also His offspring.

29Since then we are God's offspring, we ought not to suppose that Deity— [a]the Godhead—is like gold or silver or stone, [that is, of the nature of] a representation by human art and imagination, *or* anything constructed *or* invented.

30Such [former] ages of ignorance God, it is true, ignored *and* allowed to pass unnoticed; but now He charges all people everywhere to repent—[that is,] [b]to change their minds for the better and heartily to amend their ways, with abhorrence for their past sins.

31Because He has fixed a day when He will judge the world righteously (justly) by a Man Whom He has destined *and* appointed for that task, and He has made this credible *and* given conviction *and* assurance *and* evidence to everyone by raising Him from the dead. [Ps. 9:8; 96:13; 98:9.]

32Now when they had heard [that there had been] a resurrection from the dead, some scoffed; but others said, We will hear you again about this matter.

33So Paul went out from among them.

34But some men were on his side *and* joined him and believed (became Christians); among them were Dionysius, a judge of the Areopagus, and a woman named Damaris and some others with them.

**18** AFTER THIS [Paul] departed from Athens and went to Corinth.

2There he met a Jew named Aquila, a native of Pontus, recently arrived from Italy with Priscilla his wife, due to the fact that Claudius had issued an edict that all the Jews were to leave Rome. And [Paul] went to see them;

3And because he was of the same occupation he stayed with them, and they worked [together], for they were tentmakers by trade.

4But he discoursed *and* argued in the synagogue every Sabbath, and won over [both] Jews and Greeks.

5By the time Silas and Timothy arrived from Macedonia, Paul was completely engrossed with preaching, earnestly arguing *and* testifying to the Jews that Jesus [is] the Christ.

6But since they kept opposing *and* abusing *and* reviling him, he shook out his clothing [against them] and said to them, Your blood be upon your [own] heads! I am innocent [of it]. From now on I will go to the Gentiles.

AMP [a] King James Version. [b] Thayer.

## New American Standard

*Sermon on Mars Hill*

22And Paul stood in the midst of the Areopagus and said, "Men
of Athens, I observe that you are very religious in all respects.
23"For while I was passing through and examining the objects
of your worship, I also found an altar with this inscription, 'TO AN
UNKNOWN GOD.' What therefore you worship in ignorance,
this I proclaim to you.
24"The God who made the world and all things in it, since He
is Lord of heaven and earth, does not dwell in temples made with
hands;
25neither is He served by human hands, as though He needed
anything, since He Himself gives to all life and breath and all
things;
26and He made from [c]one, every nation of mankind to live on
all the face of the earth, having determined *their* appointed times,
and the boundaries of their habitation,
27that they should seek God, if perhaps they might grope for
Him and find Him, though He is not far from each one of us;
28for in Him we live and move and exist, as even some of your
own poets have said, 'For we also are His offspring.'
29"Being then the offspring of God, we ought not to think that
the Divine Nature is like gold or silver or stone, an image formed
by the art and thought of man.
30"Therefore having overlooked the times of ignorance, God is
now declaring to men that all everywhere should repent,
31because He has fixed a day in which He will judge the world
in righteousness through a Man whom He has appointed, having
furnished proof to all men by raising Him from the dead."
32¶ Now when they heard of the resurrection of the dead, some
*began* to sneer, but others said, "We shall hear you again concerning this."
33So Paul went out of their midst.
34But some men joined him and believed, among whom also
were Dionysius the Areopagite and a woman named Damaris and
others with them.

*Paul at Corinth*

18 AFTER THESE things he left Athens and went to Corinth.
2And he found a certain Jew named Aquila, a native of
Pontus, having recently come from Italy with his wife Priscilla,
because Claudius had commanded all the Jews to leave Rome. He
came to them,
3and because he was of the same trade, he stayed with them
and they were working; for by trade they were tent-makers.
4And he was reasoning in the synagogue every Sabbath and
trying to persuade Jews and Greeks.
5¶ But when Silas and Timothy came down from Macedonia,
Paul *began* devoting himself completely to the word, solemnly
testifying to the Jews that Jesus was the Christ.
6And when they resisted and blasphemed, he shook out his
garments and said to them, "Your blood *be* upon your own heads!
I am clean. From now on I shall go to the Gentiles."

NAS [c] Some later mss. read *one blood*

## New International

22Paul then stood up in the meeting of the Areopagus and said:
"Men of Athens! I see that in every way you are very religious.
23For as I walked around and looked carefully at your objects of
worship, I even found an altar with this inscription: TO AN UNKNOWN GOD. Now what you worship as something unknown I am
going to proclaim to you.
24"The God who made the world and everything in it is the
Lord of heaven and earth and does not live in temples built by
hands. 25And he is not served by human hands, as if he needed
anything, because he himself gives all men life and breath and
everything else. 26From one man he made every nation of men,
that they should inhabit the whole earth; and he determined the
times set for them and the exact places where they should live.
27God did this so that men would seek him and perhaps reach out
for him and find him, though he is not far from each one of us.
28'For in him we live and move and have our being.' As some of
your own poets have said, 'We are his offspring.'
29"Therefore since we are God's offspring, we should not think
that the divine being is like gold or silver or stone—an image made
by man's design and skill. 30In the past God overlooked such
ignorance, but now he commands all people everywhere to repent. 31For he has set a day when he will judge the world with
justice by the man he has appointed. He has given proof of this
to all men by raising him from the dead."
32When they heard about the resurrection of the dead, some of
them sneered, but others said, "We want to hear you again on this
subject." 33At that, Paul left the Council. 34A few men became
followers of Paul and believed. Among them was Dionysius, a
member of the Areopagus, also a woman named Damaris, and a
number of others.

*In Corinth*

18 AFTER THIS, Paul left Athens and went to Corinth.
2There he met a Jew named Aquila, a native of Pontus,
who had recently come from Italy with his wife Priscilla, because
Claudius had ordered all the Jews to leave Rome. Paul went to see
them, 3and because he was a tentmaker as they were, he stayed
and worked with them. 4Every Sabbath he reasoned in the synagogue, trying to persuade Jews and Greeks.
5When Silas and Timothy came from Macedonia, Paul devoted
himself exclusively to preaching, testifying to the Jews that Jesus
was the Christ.[d] 6But when the Jews opposed Paul and became
abusive, he shook out his clothes in protest and said to them,
"Your blood be on your own heads! I am clear of my responsibility.
From now on I will go to the Gentiles."

NIV [d] 5 Or *Messiah;* also in verse 28

## King James

7And he departed thence, and entered into a certain *man's* house, named Justus, *one* that worshipped God, whose house joined hard to the synagogue.

8And Crispus, the chief ruler of the synagogue, believed on the Lord with all his house; and many of the Corinthians hearing believed, and were baptized.

9Then spake the Lord to Paul in the night by a vision, Be not afraid, but speak, and hold not thy peace:

10For I am with thee, and no man shall set on thee to hurt thee: for I have much people in this city.

11And he continued *there* a year and six months, teaching the word of God among them.

12¶ And when Gallio was the deputy of Achaia, the Jews made insurrection with one accord against Paul, and brought him to the judgment seat,

13Saying, This *fellow* persuadeth men to worship God contrary to the law.

14And when Paul was now about to open *his* mouth, Gallio said unto the Jews, If it were a matter of wrong or wicked lewdness, O *ye* Jews, reason would that I should bear with you:

15But if it be a question of words and names, and *of* your law, look ye *to it;* for I will be no judge of such *matters*.

16And he drave them from the judgment seat.

17Then all the Greeks took Sosthenes, the chief ruler of the synagogue, and beat *him* before the judgment seat. And Gallio cared for none of those things.

18¶ And Paul *after this* tarried *there* yet a good while, and then took his leave of the brethren, and sailed thence into Syria, and with him Priscilla and Aquila; having shorn *his* head in Cenchrea: for he had a vow.

19And he came to Ephesus, and left them there: but he himself entered into the synagogue, and reasoned with the Jews.

20When they desired *him* to tarry longer time with them, he consented not;

21But bade them farewell, saying, I must by all means keep this feast that cometh in Jerusalem: but I will return again unto you, if God will. And he sailed from Ephesus.

22And when he had landed at Caesarea, and gone up, and saluted the church, he went down to Antioch.

23And after he had spent some time *there,* he departed, and went over *all* the country of Galatia and Phrygia in order, strengthening all the disciples.

24¶ And a certain Jew named Apollos, born at Alexandria, an eloquent man, *and* mighty in the scriptures, came to Ephesus.

25This man was instructed in the way of the Lord; and being fervent in the spirit, he spake and taught diligently the things of the Lord, knowing only the baptism of John.

26And he began to speak boldly in the synagogue: whom when Aquila and Priscilla had heard, they took him unto *them,* and expounded unto him the way of God more perfectly.

27And when he was disposed to pass into Achaia, the brethren wrote, exhorting the disciples to receive him: who, when he was come, helped them much which had believed through grace:

28For he mightily convinced the Jews, *and that* publicly, shewing by the scriptures that Jesus was Christ.

## Amplified

7He then left there and went to the house of a man named Titus Justus, who worshipped God, and whose house was next door to the synagogue.

8But Crispus, the leader of the synagogue, believed [that Jesus is the Messiah and acknowledged Him with joyful trust as Savior and Lord], together with his entire household; and many of the Corinthians who listened [to Paul also] believed and were baptized.

9And one night the Lord said to Paul in a vision, Have no fear, but speak and do not keep silent;

10For I am with you, and no man shall assault you to harm you; for I have many people in this city. [Isa. 43:5; Jer. 1:8.]

11So he settled down among them for a year and six months, teaching the Word of God [concerning the [a]attainment through Christ of eternal salvation in the kingdom of God].

12But when Gallio was proconsul of Achaia [most of Greece], the Jews unitedly made an attack upon Paul and brought him before the judge's seat,

13Declaring, This fellow is advising *and* inducing *and* inciting people to worship God in violation of the Law [of Moses].

14But when Paul was about to open his mouth to reply, Gallio said to the Jews, If it were a matter of some misdemeanor or villainy, O Jews, I should have cause to bear with you *and* listen;

15But since it is merely a question (of doctrine) about words and names and your own law, see to it yourselves; I decline to be a judge of such matters *and* I have no intention of trying such cases.

16And he drove them away from the judgment seat.

17Then they [the Greeks] all seized Sosthenes, the leader of the synagogue, and beat him right in front of the judgment seat. But Gallio paid no attention to any of this.

18Afterward Paul remained many days longer, and then told the brethren farewell and sailed for Syria, and he was accompanied by Priscilla and Aquila. At Cenchreae he [ [b]Paul] cut his hair, for he had made a vow.

19Then they arrived in Ephesus, and [Paul] left the others there; but he himself entered the synagogue and discoursed *and* argued with the Jews.

20When they asked him to remain for a longer time, he would not consent,

21But when he was leaving them he said, I will return to you if God is willing, and he set sail from Ephesus.

22When he landed at Caesarea, he went up and saluted the church [at Jerusalem], and then went down to Antioch.

23After staying there some time, he left and went from place to place in an orderly journey through the territory of Galatia and Phrygia, establishing the disciples *and* imparting new strength to them.

24Meanwhile there was a Jew named Apollos, a native of Alexandria, who came to Ephesus. He was a cultured *and* eloquent man, well versed *and* mighty in the Scriptures.

25He had been instructed in the way of the Lord, and burning with spiritual zeal, he spoke and taught diligently *and* accurately the things concerning Jesus, though he was acquainted only with the baptism of John.

26He began to speak freely—fearlessly and boldly—in the synagogue; but when Priscilla and Aquila heard him, they took him with them and expounded to him the way of God more definitely *and* accurately.

27And when [Apollos] wished to cross to Achaia [most of Greece], the brethren wrote to the disciples there, urging *and* encouraging them to accept *and* welcome him heartily. When he arrived, he proved a great help to those who through grace—God's unmerited favor and mercy—had believed (adhered to, trusted in and relied on [Christ as Lord and Savior]).

28For with great power he refuted the Jews in public [discussions], showing *and* proving by the Scriptures that Jesus is the Christ, the Messiah.

**AMP** [a] Thayer. [b] Vincent. Alford. Stanley. Others think Aquila is meant.

## New American Standard

7And he departed from there and went to the house of a certain man named Titius Justus, a worshiper of God, whose house was next to the synagogue.

8And Crispus, the leader of the synagogue, believed in the Lord with all his household, and many of the Corinthians when they heard were believing and being baptized.

9And the Lord said to Paul in the night by a vision, "Do not be afraid *any longer,* but go on speaking and do not be silent;

10for I am with you, and no man will attack you in order to harm you, for I have many people in this city."

11And he settled *there* a year and six months, teaching the word of God among them.

12¶ But while Gallio was proconsul of Achaia, the Jews with one accord rose up against Paul and brought him before the judgment seat,

13saying, "This man persuades men to worship God contrary to the law."

14But when Paul was about to open his mouth, Gallio said to the Jews, "If it were a matter of wrong or of vicious crime, O Jews, it would be reasonable for me to put up with you;

15but if there are questions about words and names and your own law, look after it yourselves; I am unwilling to be a judge of these matters."

16And he drove them away from the judgment seat.

17And they all took hold of Sosthenes, the leader of the synagogue, and *began* beating him in front of the judgment seat. And Gallio was not concerned about any of these things.

18¶ And Paul, having remained many days longer, took leave of the brethren and put out to sea for Syria, and with him were Priscilla and Aquila. In Cenchrea he had his hair cut, for he was keeping a vow.

19And they came to Ephesus, and he left them there. Now he himself entered the synagogue and reasoned with the Jews.

20And when they asked him to stay for a longer time, he did not consent,

21but taking leave of them and saying, "I will return to you again if God wills," he set sail from Ephesus.

22¶ And when he had landed at Caesarea, he went up and greeted the church, and went down to Antioch.

*Third Missionary Journey*

23And having spent some time *there,* he departed and passed successively through the Galatian region and Phrygia, strengthening all the disciples.

24¶ Now a certain Jew named Apollos, an Alexandrian by birth, an eloquent man, came to Ephesus; and he was mighty in the Scriptures.

25This man had been instructed in the way of the Lord; and being fervent in spirit, he was speaking and teaching accurately the things concerning Jesus, being acquainted only with the baptism of John;

26and he began to speak out boldly in the synagogue. But when Priscilla and Aquila heard him, they took him aside and explained to him the way of God more accurately.

27And when he wanted to go across to Achaia, the brethren encouraged him and wrote to the disciples to welcome him; and when he had arrived, he helped greatly those who had believed through grace;

28for he powerfully refuted the Jews in public, demonstrating by the Scriptures that Jesus was the Christ.

## New International

7Then Paul left the synagogue and went next door to the house
of Titius Justus, a worshiper of God. 8Crispus, the synagogue
ruler, and his entire household believed in the Lord; and many of
the Corinthians who heard him believed and were baptized.
9One night the Lord spoke to Paul in a vision: "Do not be afraid;
keep on speaking, do not be silent. 10For I am with you, and no
one is going to attack and harm you, because I have many people
in this city." 11So Paul stayed for a year and a half, teaching them
the word of God.
12While Gallio was proconsul of Achaia, the Jews made a united
attack on Paul and brought him into court. 13"This man," they
charged, "is persuading the people to worship God in ways contrary to the law."
14Just as Paul was about to speak, Gallio said to the Jews, "If
you Jews were making a complaint about some misdemeanor or
serious crime, it would be reasonable for me to listen to you. 15But
since it involves questions about words and names and your own
law—settle the matter yourselves. I will not be a judge of such
things." 16So he had them ejected from the court. 17Then they all
turned on Sosthenes the synagogue ruler and beat him in front of
the court. But Gallio showed no concern whatever.

*Priscilla, Aquila and Apollos*

18Paul stayed on in Corinth for some time. Then he left the
brothers and sailed for Syria, accompanied by Priscilla and Aquila.
Before he sailed, he had his hair cut off at Cenchrea because of a
vow he had taken. 19They arrived at Ephesus, where Paul left
Priscilla and Aquila. He himself went into the synagogue and
reasoned with the Jews. 20When they asked him to spend more
time with them, he declined. 21But as he left, he promised, "I will
come back if it is God's will." Then he set sail from Ephesus.
22When he landed at Caesarea, he went up and greeted the church
and then went down to Antioch.
23After spending some time in Antioch, Paul set out from there
and traveled from place to place throughout the region of Galatia
and Phrygia, strengthening all the disciples.
24Meanwhile a Jew named Apollos, a native of Alexandria,
came to Ephesus. He was a learned man, with a thorough knowledge of the Scriptures. 25He had been instructed in the way of the
Lord, and he spoke with great fervor[c] and taught about Jesus
accurately, though he knew only the baptism of John. 26He began
to speak boldly in the synagogue. When Priscilla and Aquila heard
him, they invited him to their home and explained to him the way
of God more adequately.
27When Apollos wanted to go to Achaia, the brothers encouraged him and wrote to the disciples there to welcome him. On
arriving, he was a great help to those who by grace had believed.
28For he vigorously refuted the Jews in public debate, proving from
the Scriptures that Jesus was the Christ.

NIV [c] 25 Or *with fervor in the Spirit*

## King James

**19** AND IT came to pass, that, while Apollos was at Corinth, Paul having passed through the upper coasts came to Ephesus: and finding certain disciples,

2He said unto them, Have ye received the Holy Ghost since ye believed? And they said unto him, We have not so much as heard whether there be any Holy Ghost.

3And he said unto them, Unto what then were ye baptized? And they said, Unto John's baptism.

4Then said Paul, John verily baptized with the baptism of repentance, saying unto the people, that they should believe on him which should come after him, that is, on Christ Jesus.

5When they heard *this,* they were baptized in the name of the Lord Jesus.

6And when Paul had laid *his* hands upon them, the Holy Ghost came on them; and they spake with tongues, and prophesied.

7And all the men were about twelve.

8And he went into the synagogue, and spake boldly for the space of three months, disputing and persuading the things concerning the kingdom of God.

9But when divers were hardened, and believed not, but spake evil of that way before the multitude, he departed from them, and separated the disciples, disputing daily in the school of one Tyrannus.

10And this continued by the space of two years; so that all they which dwelt in Asia heard the word of the Lord Jesus, both Jews and Greeks.

11And God wrought special miracles by the hands of Paul:

12So that from his body were brought unto the sick handkerchiefs or aprons, and the diseases departed from them, and the evil spirits went out of them.

13¶ Then certain of the vagabond Jews, exorcists, took upon them to call over them which had evil spirits the name of the Lord Jesus, saying, We adjure you by Jesus whom Paul preacheth.

14And there were seven sons of *one* Sceva, a Jew, *and* chief of the priests, which did so.

15And the evil spirit answered and said, Jesus I know, and Paul I know; but who are ye?

16And the man in whom the evil spirit was leaped on them, and overcame them, and prevailed against them, so that they fled out of that house naked and wounded.

17And this was known to all the Jews and Greeks also dwelling at Ephesus; and fear fell on them all, and the name of the Lord Jesus was magnified.

18And many that believed came, and confessed, and showed their deeds.

19Many of them also which used curious arts brought their books together, and burned them before all *men:* and they counted the price of them, and found *it* fifty thousand *pieces* of silver.

20So mightily grew the word of God and prevailed.

21¶ After these things were ended, Paul purposed in the spirit, when he had passed through Macedonia and Achaia, to go to Jerusalem, saying, After I have been there, I must also see Rome.

22So he sent into Macedonia two of them that ministered unto him, Timotheus and Erastus; but he himself stayed in Asia for a season.

**AMP** [a] Added by some ancient authorities. [b] Thayer. [c] A weaker verb. [d] The best texts read "both of them." [e] Vincent. [f] Vincent. [g] Vincent. [h] Thayer.

## Amplified

**19** WHILE APOLLOS was in Corinth, Paul went through the upper inland districts and came down to Ephesus. There he found some disciples.

2And he asked them, Did you receive the Holy Spirit when you believed [on Jesus as the Christ]? And they said, No, we have not even heard that there is a Holy Spirit.

3And he asked, Into what then were you baptized? They said, Into John's baptism.

4And Paul said, John baptized with the baptism of repentance, continually telling the people that they should believe in the One Who was to come after him, that is, in Jesus [having a conviction full of joyful trust that He is Christ, the Messiah, and being obedient to Him].

5On hearing this they were baptized [again, this time] in the name of the Lord Jesus.

6And as Paul laid his hands upon them, the Holy Spirit came on them; and they spoke in foreign languages and prophesied.

7There were about twelve of them in all.

8And he went into the synagogue and for three months spoke boldly, persuading *and* arguing and pleading about the kingdom of God.

9But when some became more and more stubborn (hardened and unbelieving), discrediting *and* reviling *and* speaking evil of the Way [of the Lord] before the congregation, he separated himself from them, taking the disciples with him, and went on holding daily discussions in the lecture room of Tyrannus [ [a]from about ten o'clock till three].

10This continued for two years, so that all the inhabitants of [the province of] Asia, Jews as well as Greeks, heard the Word of the Lord [concerning the [b]attainment through Christ of eternal salvation in the kingdom of God].

11And God did unusual *and* extraordinary miracles by the hands of Paul,

12So that handkerchiefs *or* towels or aprons which had touched his skin were carried away *and* put upon the sick, and their diseases left them, and the evil spirits came out of them.

13Then some of the traveling Jewish exorcists [men who adjure evil spirits] also undertook to call the name of the Lord Jesus over those who had evil spirits, saying, I solemnly implore *and* charge you by the Jesus Whom Paul preaches!

14Seven sons of a certain Jewish chief priest named Sceva were doing this.

15But [one] evil spirit retorted, Jesus I know, and Paul I know [c]about, but who are you?

16Then the man in whom the evil spirit dwelt, leaped upon them, mastering [d]two of them, and was so violent against them that they dashed out of that house [in fear], stripped naked and wounded.

17This became known to all who lived in Ephesus, both Jews and Greeks, and alarm *and* terror fell upon them all; and the name of the Lord Jesus was extolled *and* magnified.

18Many also of those who were now believers came making [e]full confession *and* thoroughly exposing their [former deceptive and evil] practices.

19And many of those who had practiced curious magical arts collected their books and (throwing them [f]book after book on the pile) burned them in the sight of everybody. When they counted the value of them, they found it amounted to fifty thousand pieces of silver ( [g]about $9,300).

20Thus the Word of the Lord [concerning the [h]attainment through Christ of eternal salvation in the kingdom of God] grew *and* spread *and* intensified, prevailing mightily.

21Now after these events Paul determined in the (Holy) Spirit that he would travel through Macedonia and Achaia [most of Greece], and go to Jerusalem, saying, After I have been there, I must visit Rome also.

22And having sent two of his assistants, Timothy and Erastus, into Macedonia, he himself stayed on in [the province of] Asia for a while.

## New American Standard

*Paul at Ephesus*

**19** AND IT came about that while Apollos was at Corinth, Paul having passed through the upper country came to Ephesus, and found some disciples,

2and he said to them, "Did you receive the Holy Spirit when you believed?" And they *said* to him, "No, we have not even heard whether there is a Holy Spirit."

3And he said, "Into what then were you baptized?" And they said, "Into John's baptism."

4And Paul said, "John baptized with the baptism of repentance, telling the people to believe in Him who was coming after him, that is, in Jesus."

5And when they heard this, they were baptized in the name of the Lord Jesus.

6And when Paul had laid his hands upon them, the Holy Spirit came on them, and they *began* speaking with tongues and prophesying.

7And there were in all about twelve men.

8¶ And he entered the synagogue and continued speaking out boldly for three months, reasoning and persuading *them* about the kingdom of God.

9But when some were becoming hardened and disobedient, speaking evil of the Way before the multitude, he withdrew from them and took away the disciples, reasoning daily in the school of Tyrannus.

10And this took place for two years, so that all who lived in Asia heard the word of the Lord, both Jews and Greeks.

*Miracles at Ephesus*

11And God was performing extraordinary miracles by the hands of Paul,

12so that handkerchiefs or aprons were even carried from his body to the sick, and the diseases left them and the evil spirits went out.

13But also some of the Jewish exorcists, who went from place to place, attempted to name over those who had the evil spirits the name of the Lord Jesus, saying, "I adjure you by Jesus whom Paul preaches."

14And seven sons of one Sceva, a Jewish chief priest, were doing this.

15And the evil spirit answered and said to them, "I recognize Jesus, and I know about Paul, but who are you?"

16And the man, in whom was the evil spirit, leaped on them and subdued all of them and overpowered them, so that they fled out of that house naked and wounded.

17And this became known to all, both Jews and Greeks, who lived in Ephesus; and fear fell upon them all and the name of the Lord Jesus was being magnified.

18Many also of those who had believed kept coming, confessing and disclosing their practices.

19And many of those who practiced magic brought their books together and *began* burning them in the sight of all; and they counted up the price of them and found it fifty thousand pieces of silver.

20So the word of the Lord was growing mightily and prevailing.

**21**¶ Now after these things were finished, Paul purposed in the spirit to go to Jerusalem after he had passed through Macedonia and Achaia, saying, "After I have been there, I must also see Rome."

22And having sent into Macedonia two of those who ministered to him, Timothy and Erastus, he himself stayed in Asia for a while.

## New International

*Paul in Ephesus*

**19** WHILE APOLLOS was at Corinth, Paul took the road
through the interior and arrived at Ephesus. There he
found some disciples 2and asked them, "Did you receive the Holy
Spirit when[i] you believed?"
They answered, "No, we have not even heard that there is a
Holy Spirit."
3So Paul asked, "Then what baptism did you receive?"
"John's baptism," they replied.
4Paul said, "John's baptism was a baptism of repentance. He
told the people to believe in the one coming after him, that is, in
Jesus." 5On hearing this, they were baptized into[j] the name of the
Lord Jesus. 6When Paul placed his hands on them, the Holy Spirit
came on them, and they spoke in tongues[k] and prophesied.
7There were about twelve men in all.
8Paul entered the synagogue and spoke boldly there for three
months, arguing persuasively about the kingdom of God. 9But
some of them became obstinate; they refused to believe and publicly maligned the Way. So Paul left them. He took the disciples with
him and had discussions daily in the lecture hall of Tyrannus.
10This went on for two years, so that all the Jews and Greeks who
lived in the province of Asia heard the word of the Lord.
11God did extraordinary miracles through Paul, 12so that even
handkerchiefs and aprons that had touched him were taken to the
sick, and their illnesses were cured and the evil spirits left them.
13Some Jews who went around driving out evil spirits tried to
invoke the name of the Lord Jesus over those who were demon-
possessed. They would say, "In the name of Jesus, whom Paul
preaches, I command you to come out." 14Seven sons of Sceva, a
Jewish chief priest, were doing this. 15⌞One day⌟ the evil spirit
answered them, "Jesus I know, and I know about Paul, but who
are you?" 16Then the man who had the evil spirit jumped on them
and overpowered them all. He gave them such a beating that they
ran out of the house naked and bleeding.
17When this became known to the Jews and Greeks living in
Ephesus, they were all seized with fear, and the name of the Lord
Jesus was held in high honor. 18Many of those who believed now
came and openly confessed their evil deeds. 19A number who had
practiced sorcery brought their scrolls together and burned them
publicly. When they calculated the value of the scrolls, the total
came to fifty thousand drachmas.[l] 20In this way the word of the
Lord spread widely and grew in power.
21After all this had happened, Paul decided to go to Jerusalem,
passing through Macedonia and Achaia. "After I have been
there," he said, "I must visit Rome also." 22He sent two of his
helpers, Timothy and Erastus, to Macedonia, while he stayed in
the province of Asia a little longer.

**NIV** [i] 2 Or *after* [j] 5 Or *in* [k] 6 Or *other languages* [l] 19 A drachma was a silver coin worth about a day's wages.

## King James

23 And the same time there arose no small stir about that way.

24 For a certain *man* named Demetrius, a silversmith, which made silver shrines for Diana, brought no small gain unto the craftsmen;

25 Whom he called together with the workmen of like occupation, and said, Sirs, ye know that by this craft we have our wealth.

26 Moreover ye see and hear, that not alone at Ephesus, but almost throughout all Asia, this Paul hath persuaded and turned away much people, saying that they be no gods, which are made with hands:

27 So that not only this our craft is in danger to be set at nought; but also that the temple of the great goddess Diana should be despised, and her magnificence should be destroyed, whom all Asia and the world worshippeth.

28 And when they heard *these sayings*, they were full of wrath, and cried out, saying, Great *is* Diana of the Ephesians.

29 And the whole city was filled with confusion: and having caught Gaius and Aristarchus, men of Macedonia, Paul's companions in travel, they rushed with one accord into the theatre.

30 And when Paul would have entered in unto the people, the disciples suffered him not.

31 And certain of the chief of Asia, which were his friends, sent unto him, desiring *him* that he would not adventure himself into the theatre.

32 Some therefore cried one thing, and some another: for the assembly was confused; and the more part knew not wherefore they were come together.

33 And they drew Alexander out of the multitude, the Jews putting him forward. And Alexander beckoned with the hand, and would have made his defence unto the people.

34 But when they knew that he was a Jew, all with one voice about the space of two hours cried out, Great *is* Diana of the Ephesians.

35 And when the townclerk had appeased the people, he said, *Ye* men of Ephesus, what man is there that knoweth not how that the city of the Ephesians is a worshipper of the great goddess Diana, and of the *image* which fell down from Jupiter?

36 Seeing then that these things cannot be spoken against, ye ought to be quiet, and to do nothing rashly.

37 For ye have brought hither these men, which are neither robbers of churches, nor yet blasphemers of your goddess.

38 Wherefore if Demetrius, and the craftsmen which are with him, have a matter against any man, the law is open, and there are deputies: let them implead one another.

39 But if ye inquire any thing concerning other matters, it shall be determined in a lawful assembly.

40 For we are in danger to be called in question for this day's uproar, there being no cause whereby we may give an account of this concourse.

41 And when he had thus spoken, he dismissed the assembly.

## Amplified

23 But as time went on there arose no little disturbance concerning the Way [of the Lord].

24 For a man named Demetrius, a silversmith, who made silver shrines of (the goddess) Artemis [not Diana], brought no small income to his craftsmen.

25 These he called together, along with the workmen of similar trades, and said, Men, you are acquainted with the facts *and* understand that from this business we derive our wealth *and* livelihood.

26 Now you notice and hear that not only at Ephesus but almost all over [the province of] Asia this Paul has persuaded *and* induced people to believe his teaching and has alienated a considerable company of them, saying that gods that are made with human hands are not really gods at all.

27 Now there is danger not merely that this trade of ours may be discredited, but also that the temple of the great goddess Artemis may come into disrepute *and* count for nothing, and that her glorious magnificence may be degraded and fall into contempt, she whom all Asia and the wide world worship.

28 As they listened to this they were filled with rage, and they continued to shout, Great is Artemis of the Ephesians!

29 Then the city was filled with confusion; and they rushed together into the amphitheater, dragging along with them Gaius and Aristarchus, Macedonians who were fellow travelers with Paul.

30 Paul wished to go in among the crowd, but the disciples would not permit him to do it.

31 Even some of the Asiarchs [presidents of athletic games in Asia] who were his friends, also sent to him and warned him not to risk venturing into the theater.

32 Now some shouted one thing and some another, for the gathering was in a tumult, and most of them did not know why they had come together.

33 Some of the crowd called upon Alexander [to speak], since the Jews had pushed *and* urged him forward. And Alexander motioned with his hand, wishing to make a defense *and* [was about] to apologize to the people.

34 But as soon as they saw him *and* recognized that he was a Jew, a shout went up from them as the voice of one man, as for about two hours they cried, Great is Artemis of the Ephesians!

35 And when the town clerk had calmed the crowd down, he said, Men of Ephesus, what man is there who does not know that the city of the Ephesians is guardian of the temple of the great Artemis, and of the sacred stone [image of her] that fell from the sky?

36 Seeing then that these things cannot be denied, you ought to (keep yourselves in check) be quiet and do nothing rashly.

37 For you have brought these men here, [who are guilty] neither of temple robberies nor of blasphemous speech about our goddess.

38 Now then, if Demetrius and his fellow tradesmen who are with him have a grievance against any one, the courts are open, and proconsuls are [available]; let them bring charges against one another [legally].

39 But if you require anything about this further *or* [a]about other matters, it must be decided *and* cleared up in the regular assembly.

40 For we are in danger of being called to render an account *and* of being accused of rioting because of [this commotion] today, there being no reason that we can offer to justify this disorder.

41 And when he had said these things, he dismissed the assembly.

## King James

**20** AND AFTER the uproar was ceased, Paul called unto *him* the disciples, and embraced *them*, and departed for to go into Macedonia.

2 And when he had gone over those parts, and had given them much exhortation, he came into Greece,

## Amplified

**20** AFTER THE uproar had ceased, Paul sent for the disciples and warned *and* consoled *and* urged *and* encouraged them; then he embraced them *and* told them farewell, and set forth on his journey to Macedonia.

2 Then after he had gone through those districts and had warned *and* consoled *and* urged *and* encouraged the brethren with much discourse, he came to Greece.

**AMP** [a] Alternate reading.

## New American Standard

23¶ And about that time there arose no small disturbance concerning the Way.

24For a certain man named Demetrius, a silversmith, who made silver shrines of Artemis, was bringing no little business to the craftsmen;

25these he gathered together with the workmen of similar *trades*, and said, "Men, you know that our prosperity depends upon this business.

26"And you see and hear that not only in Ephesus, but in almost all of Asia, this Paul has persuaded and turned away a considerable number of people, saying that gods made with hands are no gods *at all*.

27"And not only is there danger that this trade of ours fall into disrepute, but also that the temple of the great goddess Artemis be regarded as worthless and that she whom all of Asia and the world worship should even be dethroned from her magnificence."

28And when they heard *this* and were filled with rage, they *began* crying out, saying, "Great is Artemis of the Ephesians!"

29And the city was filled with the confusion, and they rushed with one accord into the theater, dragging along Gaius and Aristarchus, Paul's traveling companions from Macedonia.

30And when Paul wanted to go into the assembly, the disciples would not let him.

31And also some of the [b]Asiarchs who were friends of his sent to him and repeatedly urged him not to venture into the theater.

32So then, some were shouting one thing and some another, for the assembly was in confusion, and the majority did not know for what cause they had come together.

33And some of the crowd concluded *it was* Alexander, since the Jews had put him forward; and having motioned with his hand, Alexander was intending to make a defense to the assembly.

34But when they recognized that he was a Jew, a *single* outcry arose from them all as they shouted for about two hours, "Great is Artemis of the Ephesians!"

35And after quieting the multitude, the town clerk *said, "Men of Ephesus, what man is there after all who does not know that the city of the Ephesians is guardian of the temple of the great Artemis, and of the *image* which fell down from heaven?

36"Since then these are undeniable facts, you ought to keep calm and to do nothing rash.

37"For you have brought these men *here* who are neither robbers of temples nor blasphemers of our goddess.

38"So then, if Demetrius and the craftsmen who are with him have a complaint against any man, the courts are in session and proconsuls are *available*; let them bring charges against one another.

39"But if you want anything beyond this, it shall be settled in the lawful assembly.

40"For indeed we are in danger of being accused of a riot in connection with today's affair, since there is no *real* cause *for it*; and in this connection we shall be unable to account for this disorderly gathering."

41And after saying this he dismissed the assembly.

*Paul in Macedonia and Greece*

**20** AND AFTER the uproar had ceased, Paul sent for the disciples and when he had exhorted them and taken his leave of them, he departed to go to Macedonia.

2And when he had gone through those districts and had given them much exhortation, he came to Greece.

NAS [b] I.e., political or religious officials of the province of Asia

## New International

*The Riot in Ephesus*

23About that time there arose a great disturbance about the Way. 24A silversmith named Demetrius, who made silver shrines of Artemis, brought in no little business for the craftsmen. 25He called them together, along with the workmen in related trades, and said: "Men, you know we receive a good income from this business. 26And you see and hear how this fellow Paul has convinced and led astray large numbers of people here in Ephesus and in practically the whole province of Asia. He says that man-made gods are no gods at all. 27There is danger not only that our trade will lose its good name, but also that the temple of the great goddess Artemis will be discredited, and the goddess herself, who is worshiped throughout the province of Asia and the world, will be robbed of her divine majesty."

28When they heard this, they were furious and began shouting: "Great is Artemis of the Ephesians!" 29Soon the whole city was in an uproar. The people seized Gaius and Aristarchus, Paul's traveling companions from Macedonia, and rushed as one man into the theater. 30Paul wanted to appear before the crowd, but the disciples would not let him. 31Even some of the officials of the province, friends of Paul, sent him a message begging him not to venture into the theater.

32The assembly was in confusion: Some were shouting one thing, some another. Most of the people did not even know why they were there. 33The Jews pushed Alexander to the front, and some of the crowd shouted instructions to him. He motioned for silence in order to make a defense before the people. 34But when they realized he was a Jew, they all shouted in unison for about two hours: "Great is Artemis of the Ephesians!"

35The city clerk quieted the crowd and said: "Men of Ephesus, doesn't all the world know that the city of Ephesus is the guardian of the temple of the great Artemis and of her image, which fell from heaven? 36Therefore, since these facts are undeniable, you ought to be quiet and not do anything rash. 37You have brought these men here, though they have neither robbed temples nor blasphemed our goddess. 38If, then, Demetrius and his fellow craftsmen have a grievance against anybody, the courts are open and there are proconsuls. They can press charges. 39If there is anything further you want to bring up, it must be settled in a legal assembly. 40As it is, we are in danger of being charged with rioting because of today's events. In that case we would not be able to account for this commotion, since there is no reason for it." 41After he had said this, he dismissed the assembly.

*Through Macedonia and Greece*

**20** WHEN THE uproar had ended, Paul sent for the disciples and, after encouraging them, said good-by and set out for Macedonia. 2He traveled through that area, speaking many words of encouragement to the people, and finally arrived in Greece,

## King James

3And *there* abode three months. And when the Jews laid wait
for him, as he was about to sail into Syria, he purposed to return
through Macedonia.
4And there accompanied him into Asia Sopater of Berea; and of
the Thessalonians, Aristarchus and Secundus; and Gaius of Derbe,
and Timotheus; and of Asia, Tychicus and Trophimus.
5These going before tarried for us at Troas.
6And we sailed away from Philippi after the days of unleavened
bread, and came unto them to Troas in five days; where we abode
seven days.
7And upon the first *day* of the week, when the disciples came
together to break bread, Paul preached unto them, ready to depart
on the morrow; and continued his speech until midnight.
8And there were many lights in the upper chamber, where they
were gathered together.
9And there sat in a window a certain young man named Eutychus, being fallen into a deep sleep: and as Paul was long preaching, he sunk down with sleep, and fell down from the third loft,
and was taken up dead.
10And Paul went down, and fell on him, and embracing *him*
said, Trouble not yourselves; for his life is in him.
11When he therefore was come up again, and had broken bread,
and eaten, and talked a long while, even till break of day, so he
departed.
12And they brought the young man alive, and were not a little
comforted.
13¶ And we went before to ship, and sailed unto Assos, there
intending to take in Paul: for so had he appointed, minding himself
to go afoot.
14And when he met with us at Assos, we took him in, and came
to Mitylene.
15And we sailed thence, and came the next *day* over against
Chios; and the next *day* we arrived at Samos, and tarried at Trogyl-
lium; and the next *day* we came to Miletus.
16For Paul had determined to sail by Ephesus, because he
would not spend the time in Asia: for he hasted, if it were possible
for him, to be at Jerusalem the day of Pentecost.
17¶ And from Miletus he sent to Ephesus, and called the elders
of the church.
18And when they were come to him, he said unto them, Ye
know, from the first day that I came into Asia, after what manner
I have been with you at all seasons,
19Serving the Lord with all humility of mind, and with many
tears, and temptations, which befell me by the lying in wait of the
Jews:
20 *And* how I kept back nothing that was profitable *unto you*, but
have shown you, and have taught you publicly, and from house
to house,
21Testifying both to the Jews, and also to the Greeks, repentance toward God, and faith toward our Lord Jesus Christ.
22And now, behold, I go bound in the spirit unto Jerusalem, not
knowing the things that shall befall me there:
23Save that the Holy Ghost witnesseth in every city, saying that
bonds and afflictions abide me.
24But none of these things move me, neither count I my life dear
unto myself, so that I might finish my course with joy, and the
ministry, which I have received of the Lord Jesus, to testify the
gospel of the grace of God.
25And now, behold, I know that ye all, among whom I have
gone preaching the kingdom of God, shall see my face no more.

## Amplified

3Having spent three months there, when a plot was formed
against him by the Jews as he was about to set sail for Syria, he
resolved to go back through Macedonia.
4He was accompanied by Sopater, the son of Pyrrhus from
Beroea; and by the Thessalonians, Aristarchus and Secundus; and
Gaius of Derbe, and Timothy; and the Asians, Tychicus and
Trophimus.
5These went on ahead and were waiting for us [including Luke]
at Troas,
6But we [ourselves] sailed from Philippi after the days of Unleavened Bread [the Passover week], and in five days we joined
them at Troas, where we remained for seven days.
7And on the first day of the week, when we were assembled
together to break bread [ [a]the Lord's Supper], Paul discoursed with
them, intending to leave the next morning; and he kept on with
his message until midnight.
8Now there were numerous lights in the upper room where we
were assembled,
9And there was a young man named Eutychus sitting in the
window. He was borne down with deep sleep as Paul kept on
talking still longer, and [finally] completely overcome by sleep, he
fell down from the third story, and was picked up dead.
10But Paul went down and bent over him and embraced him,
saying, Make no ado; his life is within him.
11When Paul had gone back upstairs and had broken bread and
eaten [with them], and after he had (talked confidentially,) communing with them for considerable time, until daybreak [in fact],
he departed.
12They took the youth home alive, and were not a little comforted *and* cheered *and* refreshed *and* encouraged.
13But going on before to the ship, the rest of us set sail for Assos,
intending to take Paul aboard there, for that was what he had
directed, intending himself to go by land—on foot.
14So when he met us at Assos, we took him aboard and sailed
on to Mitylene.
15And sailing from there, we arrived the day after at a point
opposite Chios; the following day we struck across to Samos, and
the next day we arrived at Miletus.
16For Paul had determined to sail on past Ephesus, lest he might
have to spend time [unnecessarily] in [the province of] Asia; for he
was hastening on that he might reach Jerusalem, if at all possible,
by the day of Pentecost.
17However from Miletus he sent to Ephesus and summoned the
elders of the church [to come to him there].
18And when they arrived he said to them: You yourselves are
well acquainted with my manner of living among you from the first
day that I set foot in [the province of] Asia, and how I continued
afterward,
19Serving the Lord with all humility in tears and in the midst
of adversity (affliction) *and* trials which befell me, due to the plots
of the Jews [against me];
20How I did not shrink from telling you anything that was for
your benefit, and teaching you in public meetings and from house
to house,
21But constantly *and* earnestly I bore testimony both to Jews and
Greeks, urging them to turn in repentance [ [b]that is due] to God
and have the faith in our Lord Jesus Christ [ [c]that is due Him].
22And now, you see, I am going to Jerusalem, bound by the
(Holy) Spirit, *and* obligated *and* compelled by the [convictions of
my own] spirit, not knowing what will befall me there;
23Except that the Holy Spirit clearly *and* emphatically affirms to
me in city after city that imprisonment and suffering await me.
24But *none of these things move me;* neither do I esteem my life
dear to myself, if only I may finish my course *with joy*, and the
ministry which I have obtained of [entrusted to me by] the Lord
Jesus, faithfully to attest the good news (Gospel) of God's grace—
His unmerited favor, spiritual blessing and mercy.
25And now, observe, I perceive that all of you, among whom
I have gone in and out proclaiming the kingdom, will see my face
no more.

**AMP** [a] Thayer. [b] Vincent. [c] Vincent.

## New American Standard

3And *there* he spent three months, and when a plot was formed
against him by the Jews as he was about to set sail for Syria, he
determined to return through Macedonia.
4And he was accompanied by Sopater of Berea, *the son* of
Pyrrhus; and by Aristarchus and Secundus of the Thessalonians;
and Gaius of Derbe, and Timothy; and Tychicus and Trophimus
of Asia.
5But these had gone on ahead and were waiting for us at Troas.
6And we sailed from Philippi after the days of Unleavened
Bread, and came to them at Troas within five days; and there we
stayed seven days.
7¶ And on the first day of the week, when we were gathered
together to break bread, Paul *began* talking to them, intending to
depart the next day, and he prolonged his message until midnight.
8And there were many lamps in the upper room where we
were gathered together.
9And there was a certain young man named Eutychus sitting
on the window sill, sinking into a deep sleep; and as Paul kept on
talking, he was overcome by sleep and fell down from the third
floor, and was picked up dead.
10But Paul went down and fell upon him and after embracing
him, he said, "Do not be troubled, for his life is in him."
11And when he had gone *back* up, and had broken the bread and
eaten, he talked with them a long while, until daybreak, and so
departed.
12And they took away the boy alive, and were greatly comforted.

*Troas to Miletus*

13¶ But we, going ahead to the ship, set sail for Assos, intending
from there to take Paul on board; for thus he had arranged it,
intending himself to go by land.
14And when he met us at Assos, we took him on board and
came to Mitylene.
15And sailing from there, we arrived the following day opposite
Chios; and the next day we crossed over to Samos; and the day
following we came to Miletus.
16For Paul had decided to sail past Ephesus in order that he
might not have to spend time in Asia; for he was hurrying to be
in Jerusalem, if possible, on the day of Pentecost.

*Farewell to Ephesus*

17¶ And from Miletus he sent to Ephesus and called to him the
elders of the church.
18And when they had come to him, he said to them,
¶"You yourselves know, from the first day that I set foot in
Asia, how I was with you the whole time,
19serving the Lord with all humility and with tears and with
trials which came upon me through the plots of the Jews;
20how I did not shrink from declaring to you anything that was
profitable, and teaching you publicly and from house to house,
21solemnly testifying to both Jews and Greeks of repentance
toward God and faith in our Lord Jesus Christ.
22"And now, behold, bound in spirit, I am on my way to Jerusalem, not knowing what will happen to me there,
23except that the Holy Spirit solemnly testifies to me in every
city, saying that bonds and afflictions await me.
24"But I do not consider my life of any account as dear to myself,
in order that I may finish my course, and the ministry which I
received from the Lord Jesus, to testify solemnly of the gospel of
the grace of God.
25"And now, behold, I know that all of you, among whom I
went about preaching the kingdom, will see my face no more.

## New International

3where he stayed three months. Because the Jews made a plot
against him just as he was about to sail for Syria, he decided to go
back through Macedonia. 4He was accompanied by Sopater son of
Pyrrhus from Berea, Aristarchus and Secundus from Thessalonica,
Gaius from Derbe, Timothy also, and Tychicus and Trophimus
from the province of Asia. 5These men went on ahead and waited
for us at Troas. 6But we sailed from Philippi after the Feast of
Unleavened Bread, and five days later joined the others at Troas,
where we stayed seven days.

*Eutychus Raised From the Dead at Troas*

7On the first day of the week we came together to break bread.
Paul spoke to the people and, because he intended to leave the
next day, kept on talking until midnight. 8There were many lamps
in the upstairs room where we were meeting. 9Seated in a window
was a young man named Eutychus, who was sinking into a deep
sleep as Paul talked on and on. When he was sound asleep, he fell
to the ground from the third story and was picked up dead. 10Paul
went down, threw himself on the young man and put his arms
around him. "Don't be alarmed," he said. "He's alive!" 11Then he
went upstairs again and broke bread and ate. After talking until
daylight, he left. 12The people took the young man home alive and
were greatly comforted.

*Paul's Farewell to the Ephesian Elders*

13We went on ahead to the ship and sailed for Assos, where we
were going to take Paul aboard. He had made this arrangement
because he was going there on foot. 14When he met us at Assos,
we took him aboard and went on to Mitylene. 15The next day we
set sail from there and arrived off Kios. The day after that we
crossed over to Samos, and on the following day arrived at Miletus. 16Paul had decided to sail past Ephesus to avoid spending time
in the province of Asia, for he was in a hurry to reach Jerusalem,
if possible, by the day of Pentecost.
17From Miletus, Paul sent to Ephesus for the elders of the
church. 18When they arrived, he said to them: "You know how I
lived the whole time I was with you, from the first day I came into
the province of Asia. 19I served the Lord with great humility and
with tears, although I was severely tested by the plots of the Jews.
20You know that I have not hesitated to preach anything that
would be helpful to you but have taught you publicly and from
house to house. 21I have declared to both Jews and Greeks that
they must turn to God in repentance and have faith in our Lord
Jesus.
22"And now, compelled by the Spirit, I am going to Jerusalem,
not knowing what will happen to me there. 23I only know that in
every city the Holy Spirit warns me that prison and hardships are
facing me. 24However, I consider my life worth nothing to me, if
only I may finish the race and complete the task the Lord Jesus has
given me—the task of testifying to the gospel of God's grace.
25"Now I know that none of you among whom I have gone
about preaching the kingdom will ever see me again. 26Therefore,

# King James

26Wherefore I take you to record this day, that I *am* pure from the blood of all *men.*

27For I have not shunned to declare unto you all the counsel of God.

28¶ Take heed therefore unto yourselves, and to all the flock, over the which the Holy Ghost hath made you overseers, to feed the church of God, which he hath purchased with his own blood.

29For I know this, that after my departing shall grievous wolves enter in among you, not sparing the flock.

30Also of your own selves shall men arise, speaking perverse things, to draw away disciples after them.

31Therefore watch, and remember, that by the space of three years I ceased not to warn every one night and day with tears.

32And now, brethren, I commend you to God, and to the word of his grace, which is able to build you up, and to give you an inheritance among all them which are sanctified.

33I have coveted no man's silver, or gold, or apparel.

34Yea, ye yourselves know, that these hands have ministered unto my necessities, and to them that were with me.

35I have shown you all things, how that so labouring ye ought to support the weak, and to remember the words of the Lord Jesus, how he said, It is more blessed to give than to receive.

36¶ And when he had thus spoken, he kneeled down, and prayed with them all.

37And they all wept sore, and fell on Paul's neck, and kissed him,

38Sorrowing most of all for the words which he spake, that they should see his face no more. And they accompanied him unto the ship.

**21** AND IT came to pass, that after we were gotten from them, and had launched, we came with a straight course unto Coos, and the *day* following unto Rhodes, and from thence unto Patara:

2And finding a ship sailing over unto Phenicia, we went aboard, and set forth.

3Now when we had discovered Cyprus, we left it on the left hand, and sailed into Syria, and landed at Tyre: for there the ship was to unlade her burden.

4And finding disciples, we tarried there seven days: who said to Paul through the Spirit, that he should not go up to Jerusalem.

5And when we had accomplished those days, we departed and went our way; and they all brought us on our way, with wives and children, till *we were* out of the city: and we kneeled down on the shore, and prayed.

6And when we had taken our leave one of another, we took ship; and they returned home again.

7And when we had finished *our* course from Tyre, we came to Ptolemais, and saluted the brethren, and abode with them one day.

8And the next *day* we that were of Paul's company departed, and came unto Caesarea: and we entered into the house of Philip the evangelist, which was *one* of the seven; and abode with him.

9And the same man had four daughters, virgins, which did prophesy.

# Amplified

26Therefore I testify *and* protest to you on this [our parting] day that I am clean *and* innocent *and* not responsible for the blood of any of you.

27For I never shrank *or* kept back *or* fell short from declaring to you the whole purpose *and* plan *and* counsel of God.

28Take care *and* be on guard for yourselves and the whole flock over which the Holy Spirit has appointed you bishops and guardians, to shepherd the church (that is, tend and feed and guide the church) of the Lord a(God) which He obtained for Himself—buying it and saving it [for Himself]—with His own blood.

29I know that after I am gone ferocious wolves will get in among you, not sparing the flock;

30Even from among your own selves men will come to the front, who by saying perverse (distorted and corrupt) things will endeavor to draw away the disciples after them [to their own party].

31Therefore be always alert *and* on your guard, being mindful that for three years I never stopped night or day seriously to admonish *and* advise *and* exhort you one by one with tears.

32And now, *brethren,* I commit you to God—that is, I deposit you in His charge, entrusting you to His protection and care. And I commend you to the Word of His grace—to the commands and counsels and promises of His unmerited favor. It is able to build you up and to give you [your rightful] inheritance among all God's set-apart ones—those consecrated, purified *and* transformed of soul.

33I coveted no man's silver or gold or [costly] garments.

34You yourselves know personally that these hands ministered to my own needs and those [of the persons] who were with me.

35In everything I have pointed out to you [by example] that, by working diligently thus we ought to assist the weak, being mindful of the words of the Lord Jesus, how He Himself said, It is more blessed—makes one happier and more bto be envied—to give than to receive.

36Having spoken thus, he knelt down with them all and prayed.

37And they all wept freely and threw their arms around Paul's neck and kissed him fervently *and* repeatedly,

38Being especially distressed *and* sorrowful because he had stated that they were about to see his face no more. And they accompanied him to the ship.

**21** AND WHEN we had torn ourselves away from them *and* withdrawn, we set sail and made a straight run to Cos, and on the following [day came] to Rhodes, and from there to Patara.

2There we found a ship crossing over to Phoenicia, so we went aboard, and sailed away.

3After we had sighted Cyprus, leaving it on our left we sailed on to Syria and put in at Tyre, for there the ship was to unload her cargo.

4And having looked up the disciples there, we remained with them for seven days. Prompted by the (Holy) Spirit they kept telling Paul not to set foot in Jerusalem.

5But when our time there was ended, we left and proceeded on our journey; and all of them with their wives and children accompanied us on our way till we were outside the city. There we knelt down on the beach and prayed.

6Then when we had told one another farewell we went on board the ship, and they returned to their own homes.

7When we had completed the voyage from Tyre, we landed at Ptolemais, where we paid our respects to the brethren and remained with them for one day.

8On the morrow we left there and came to Caesarea; and we went into the house of Philip the evangelist, who was one of the seven [first deacons], and stayed with him. [Acts 6:5.]

9And he had four maiden daughters who had the gift of prophecy.

**AMP** a Many ancient authorities read "of God." b Souter.

## New American Standard

26"Therefore I testify to you this day, that I am innocent of the
blood of all men.
27"For I did not shrink from declaring to you the whole purpose
of God.
28"Be on guard for yourselves and for all the flock, among
which the Holy Spirit has made you overseers, to shepherd the
church of God which He purchased with His own blood.
29"I know that after my departure savage wolves will come in
among you, not sparing the flock;
30and from among your own selves men will arise, speaking
perverse things, to draw away the disciples after them.
31"Therefore be on the alert, remembering that night and day
for a period of three years I did not cease to admonish each one
with tears.
32"And now I commend you to God and to the word of His
grace, which is able to build *you* up and to give *you* the inheritance
among all those who are sanctified.
33"I have coveted no one's silver or gold or clothes.
34"You yourselves know that these hands ministered to my *own*
needs and to the men who were with me.
35"In everything I showed you that by working hard in this
manner you must help the weak and remember the words of the
Lord Jesus, that He Himself said, 'It is more blessed to give than
to receive.' "
36¶ And when he had said these things, he knelt down and
prayed with them all.
37And they *began* to weep aloud and embraced Paul, and repeatedly kissed him,
38grieving especially over the word which he had spoken, that
they should see his face no more. And they were accompanying
him to the ship.

*Paul Sails from Miletus*

**21** AND WHEN it came about that we had parted from them
and had set sail, we ran a straight course to Cos and the
next day to Rhodes and from there to Patara;
2and having found a ship crossing over to Phoenicia, we went
aboard and set sail.
3And when we had come in sight of Cyprus, leaving it on the
left, we kept sailing to Syria and landed at Tyre; for there the ship
was to unload its cargo.
4And after looking up the disciples, we stayed there seven
days; and they kept telling Paul through the Spirit not to set foot
in Jerusalem.
5And when it came about that our days there were ended, we
departed and started on our journey, while they all, with wives
and children, escorted us until *we were* out of the city. And after
kneeling down on the beach and praying, we said farewell to one
another.
6Then we went on board the ship, and they returned home
again.
7¶ And when we had finished the voyage from Tyre, we arrived at Ptolemais; and after greeting the brethren, we stayed with
them for a day.
8And on the next day we departed and came to Caesarea; and
entering the house of Philip the evangelist, who was one of the
seven, we stayed with him.
9Now this man had four virgin daughters who were proph-
etesses.

## New International

I declare to you today that I am innocent of the blood of all men.
27For I have not hesitated to proclaim to you the whole will of God.
28Keep watch over yourselves and all the flock of which the Holy
Spirit has made you overseers.[c] Be shepherds of the church of
God,[d] which he bought with his own blood. 29I know that after
I leave, savage wolves will come in among you and will not spare
the flock. 30Even from your own number men will arise and distort
the truth in order to draw away disciples after them. 31So be on
your guard! Remember that for three years I never stopped warning each of you night and day with tears.
32"Now I commit you to God and to the word of his grace,
which can build you up and give you an inheritance among all
those who are sanctified. 33I have not coveted anyone's silver or
gold or clothing. 34You yourselves know that these hands of mine
have supplied my own needs and the needs of my companions.
35In everything I did, I showed you that by this kind of hard work
we must help the weak, remembering the words the Lord Jesus
himself said: 'It is more blessed to give than to receive.' "
36When he had said this, he knelt down with all of them and
prayed. 37They all wept as they embraced him and kissed him.
38What grieved them most was his statement that they would
never see his face again. Then they accompanied him to the ship.

*On to Jerusalem*

**21** AFTER WE had torn ourselves away from them, we put
out to sea and sailed straight to Cos. The next day we went
to Rhodes and from there to Patara. 2We found a ship crossing over
to Phoenicia, went on board and set sail. 3After sighting Cyprus
and passing to the south of it, we sailed on to Syria. We landed
at Tyre, where our ship was to unload its cargo. 4Finding the
disciples there, we stayed with them seven days. Through the
Spirit they urged Paul not to go on to Jerusalem. 5But when our
time was up, we left and continued on our way. All the disciples
and their wives and children accompanied us out of the city, and
there on the beach we knelt to pray. 6After saying good-by to each
other, we went aboard the ship, and they returned home.
7We continued our voyage from Tyre and landed at Ptolemais,
where we greeted the brothers and stayed with them for a day.
8Leaving the next day, we reached Caesarea and stayed at the
house of Philip the evangelist, one of the Seven. 9He had four
unmarried daughters who prophesied.

NIV [c] 28 Traditionally *bishops* [d] 28 Many manuscripts *of the Lord*

## King James

10And as we tarried *there* many days, there came down from Judaea a certain prophet, named Agabus.

11And when he was come unto us, he took Paul's girdle, and bound his own hands and feet, and said, Thus saith the Holy Ghost, So shall the Jews at Jerusalem bind the man that owneth this girdle, and shall deliver *him* into the hands of the Gentiles.

12And when we heard these things, both we, and they of that place, besought him not to go up to Jerusalem.

13Then Paul answered, What mean ye to weep and to break mine heart? for I am ready not to be bound only, but also to die at Jerusalem for the name of the Lord Jesus.

14And when he would not be persuaded, we ceased, saying, The will of the Lord be done.

15And after those days we took up our carriages, and went up to Jerusalem.

16There went with us also *certain* of the disciples of Caesarea, and brought with them one Mnason of Cyprus, an old disciple, with whom we should lodge.

17And when we were come to Jerusalem, the brethren received us gladly.

18And the *day* following Paul went in with us unto James; and all the elders were present.

19And when he had saluted them, he declared particularly what things God had wrought among the Gentiles by his ministry.

20And when they heard *it*, they glorified the Lord, and said unto him, Thou seest, brother, how many thousands of Jews there are which believe; and they are all zealous of the law:

21And they are informed of thee, that thou teachest all the Jews which are among the Gentiles to forsake Moses, saying that they ought not to circumcise *their* children, neither to walk after the customs.

22What is it therefore? the multitude must needs come together: for they will hear that thou art come.

23Do therefore this that we say to thee: We have four men which have a vow on them;

24Them take, and purify thyself with them, and be at charges with them, that they may shave *their* heads: and all may know that those things, whereof they were informed concerning thee, are nothing; but *that* thou thyself also walkest orderly, and keepest the law.

25As touching the Gentiles which believe, we have written *and* concluded that they observe no such thing, save only that they keep themselves from *things* offered to idols, and from blood, and from strangled, and from fornication.

26Then Paul took the men, and the next day purifying himself with them entered into the temple, to signify the accomplishment of the days of purification, until that an offering should be offered for every one of them.

27And when the seven days were almost ended, the Jews which were of Asia, when they saw him in the temple, stirred up all the people, and laid hands on him,

28Crying out, Men of Israel, help: This is the man, that teacheth all *men* every where against the people, and the law, and this place: and further brought Greeks also into the temple, and hath polluted this holy place.

29(For they had seen before with him in the city Trophimus an Ephesian, whom they supposed that Paul had brought into the temple.)

30And all the city was moved, and the people ran together: and they took Paul, and drew him out of the temple: and forthwith the doors were shut.

## Amplified

10While we were remaining there for some time, a prophet named Agabus came down from Judea.

11And coming to [see] us, he took Paul's belt and with it bound his own feet and hands, and said, Thus says the Holy Spirit, The Jews at Jerusalem shall bind like this the man who owns this belt, and they shall deliver him into the hands of the Gentiles (heathen).

12When we heard this, both we and the residents of that place pleaded with him not to go up to Jerusalem.

13Then Paul replied, What do you mean by weeping and breaking my heart like this? For I hold myself in readiness not only to be arrested *and* bound *and* imprisoned at Jerusalem, but also [even] to die for the name of the Lord Jesus.

14And when he would not yield to [our] persuading, we stopped [urging and imploring him], saying, The Lord's will be done!

15After these days we packed our baggage and went up to Jerusalem.

16And some of the disciples from Caesarea came with us, conducting us to the house of Mnason, a man from Cyprus, one of the disciples of long standing, with whom we were to lodge.

17When we arrived in Jerusalem, the brethren received *and* welcomed us gladly.

18On the next day Paul went in with us to [see] James, and all the elders of the church were present [also].

19After saluting them, Paul gave a detailed account of the things God had done among the Gentiles through his ministry.

20And upon hearing it, they adored *and* exalted *and* praised *and* thanked God. And they said to [Paul], You see, brother, how many thousands of believers there are among the Jews, and all of them are enthusiastic upholders of the [Mosaic] Law.

21Now they have been informed about you that you continually teach all the Jews who live among the Gentiles to turn back from *and* forsake Moses, advising them not to circumcise their children or pay any attention to the observance of the [Mosaic] customs.

22What then [is it best] should be done? A multitude will come together, for they will surely hear that you have arrived.

23Therefore do just what we tell you. With us are four men who have taken a vow upon themselves.

24Take these men and purify yourself along with them, and pay their expenses [for the temple offering], so that they may have their heads shaved. Thus everybody will know that there is no truth in what they have been told about you, but that you yourself walk in observance of the Law.

25But with regard to the Gentiles who have believed—adhered to, trusted in and relied on Christ—we have sent them a letter with our decision that they should keep themselves free from anything that has been sacrificed to idols and from [tasting] blood and [the meat of animals] which have been strangled and from all impurity *and* sexual immorality.

26Then Paul took the [four] men with him and the following day [he went through the rites of] purifying himself along with them. And they entered the temple to give notice when the days of purification (the ending of each vow) would be fulfilled and the usual offering could be presented on behalf of each of them.

27When the seven days were drawing to a close, some of the Jews from [the province of] Asia, who had caught sight of Paul in the temple, incited all the rabble, and laid hands on him,

28Shouting, Men of Israel, help! [help!] This is the man who is teaching everybody everywhere against the people and the Law and this place! Moreover he has also [actually] brought Greeks into the temple; he has desecrated *and* polluted this holy place!

29For they had previously seen Trophimus the Ephesian in the city with Paul and they supposed that he had brought the man into the temple—[that is,] into the inner court [forbidden to Gentiles].

30Then the whole city was aroused *and* thrown into confusion, and the people rushed together; they laid hands on Paul and dragged him outside the temple, and immediately the gates were closed.

## New American Standard

10 And as we were staying there for some days, a certain prophet
named Agabus came down from Judea.
11 And coming to us, he took Paul's belt and bound his own feet
and hands, and said, "This is what the Holy Spirit says: 'In this
way the Jews at Jerusalem will bind the man who owns this belt
and deliver him into the hands of the Gentiles.'"
12 And when we had heard this, we as well as the local residents
*began* begging him not to go up to Jerusalem.
13 Then Paul answered, "What are you doing, weeping and
breaking my heart? For I am ready not only to be bound, but even
to die at Jerusalem for the name of the Lord Jesus."
14 And since he would not be persuaded, we fell silent, remarking, "The will of the Lord be done!"

*Paul at Jerusalem*

15 ¶ And after these days we got ready and started on our way
up to Jerusalem.
16 And *some* of the disciples from Caesarea also came with us,
taking us to Mnason of Cyprus, a disciple of long standing with
whom we were to lodge.
17 ¶ And when we had come to Jerusalem, the brethren received
us gladly.
18 And now the following day Paul went in with us to James,
and all the elders were present.
19 And after he had greeted them, he *began* to relate one by one
the things which God had done among the Gentiles through his
ministry.
20 And when they heard it they *began* glorifying God; and they
said to him, "You see, brother, how many thousands there are
among the Jews of those who have believed, and they are all
zealous for the Law;
21 and they have been told about you, that you are teaching all
the Jews who are among the Gentiles to forsake Moses, telling
them not to circumcise their children nor to walk according to the
customs.
22 "What, then, is *to be done*? They will certainly hear that you
have come.
23 "Therefore do this that we tell you. We have four men who
are under a vow;
24 take them and purify yourself along with them, and pay their
expenses in order that they may shave their heads; and all will
know that there is nothing to the things which they have been told
about you, but that you yourself also walk orderly, keeping the
Law.
25 "But concerning the Gentiles who have believed, we wrote,
having decided that they should abstain from meat sacrificed to
idols and from blood and from what is strangled and from fornication."
26 Then Paul took the men, and the next day, purifying himself
along with them, went into the temple, giving notice of the completion of the days of purification, until the sacrifice was offered
for each one of them.

*Paul Seized in the Temple*

27 ¶ And when the seven days were almost over, the Jews from
Asia, upon seeing him in the temple, *began* to stir up all the multitude and laid hands on him,
28 crying out, "Men of Israel, come to our aid! This is the man
who preaches to all men everywhere against our people, and the
Law, and this place; and besides he has even brought Greeks into
the temple and has defiled this holy place."
29 For they had previously seen Trophimus the Ephesian in the
city with him, and they supposed that Paul had brought him into
the temple.
30 And all the city was aroused, and the people rushed together;
and taking hold of Paul, they dragged him out of the temple; and
immediately the doors were shut.

## New International

10 After we had been there a number of days, a prophet named
Agabus came down from Judea. 11 Coming over to us, he took
Paul's belt, tied his own hands and feet with it and said, "The Holy
Spirit says, 'In this way the Jews of Jerusalem will bind the owner
of this belt and will hand him over to the Gentiles.'"
12 When we heard this, we and the people there pleaded with
Paul not to go up to Jerusalem. 13 Then Paul answered, "Why are
you weeping and breaking my heart? I am ready not only to be
bound, but also to die in Jerusalem for the name of the Lord Jesus."
14 When he would not be dissuaded, we gave up and said, "The
Lord's will be done."
15 After this, we got ready and went up to Jerusalem. 16 Some of
the disciples from Caesarea accompanied us and brought us to the
home of Mnason, where we were to stay. He was a man from
Cyprus and one of the early disciples.

*Paul's Arrival at Jerusalem*

17 When we arrived at Jerusalem, the brothers received us
warmly. 18 The next day Paul and the rest of us went to see James,
and all the elders were present. 19 Paul greeted them and reported
in detail what God had done among the Gentiles through his
ministry.
20 When they heard this, they praised God. Then they said to
Paul: "You see, brother, how many thousands of Jews have believed, and all of them are zealous for the law. 21 They have been
informed that you teach all the Jews who live among the Gentiles
to turn away from Moses, telling them not to circumcise their
children or live according to our customs. 22 What shall we do?
They will certainly hear that you have come, 23 so do what we tell
you. There are four men with us who have made a vow. 24 Take
these men, join in their purification rites and pay their expenses,
so that they can have their heads shaved. Then everybody will
know there is no truth in these reports about you, but that you
yourself are living in obedience to the law. 25 As for the Gentile
believers, we have written to them our decision that they should
abstain from food sacrificed to idols, from blood, from the meat of
strangled animals and from sexual immorality."
26 The next day Paul took the men and purified himself along
with them. Then he went to the temple to give notice of the date
when the days of purification would end and the offering would
be made for each of them.

*Paul Arrested*

27 When the seven days were nearly over, some Jews from the
province of Asia saw Paul at the temple. They stirred up the whole
crowd and seized him, 28 shouting, "Men of Israel, help us! This
is the man who teaches all men everywhere against our people and
our law and this place. And besides, he has brought Greeks into
the temple area and defiled this holy place." 29 (They had previously seen Trophimus the Ephesian in the city with Paul and assumed
that Paul had brought him into the temple area.)
30 The whole city was aroused, and the people came running
from all directions. Seizing Paul, they dragged him from the temple, and immediately the gates were shut. 31 While they were try-

## King James

31 And as they went about to kill him, tidings came unto the chief captain of the band, that all Jerusalem was in an uproar.

32 Who immediately took soldiers and centurions, and ran down unto them: and when they saw the chief captain and the soldiers, they left beating of Paul.

33 Then the chief captain came near, and took him, and commanded *him* to be bound with two chains; and demanded who he was, and what he had done.

34 And some cried one thing, some another, among the multitude: and when he could not know the certainty for the tumult, he commanded him to be carried into the castle.

35 And when he came upon the stairs, so it was, that he was borne of the soldiers for the violence of the people.

36 For the multitude of the people followed after, crying, Away with him.

37 And as Paul was to be led into the castle, he said unto the chief captain, May I speak unto thee? Who said, Canst thou speak Greek?

38 Art not thou that Egyptian, which before these days madest an uproar, and leddest out into the wilderness four thousand men that were murderers?

39 But Paul said, I am a man *which am* a Jew of Tarsus, *a city* in Cilicia, a citizen of no mean city: and, I beseech thee, suffer me to speak unto the people.

40 And when he had given him licence, Paul stood on the stairs, and beckoned with the hand unto the people. And when there was made a great silence, he spake unto *them* in the Hebrew tongue, saying,

**22** MEN, BRETHREN, and fathers, hear ye my defence *which I make* now unto you.

2 (And when they heard that he spake in the Hebrew tongue to them, they kept the more silence: and he saith,)

3 I am verily a man *which am* a Jew, born in Tarsus, *a city* in Cilicia, yet brought up in this city at the feet of Gamaliel, *and* taught according to the perfect manner of the law of the fathers, and was zealous toward God, as ye all are this day.

4 And I persecuted this way unto the death, binding and delivering into prisons both men and women.

5 As also the high priest doth bear me witness, and all the estate of the elders: from whom also I received letters unto the brethren, and went to Damascus, to bring them which were there bound unto Jerusalem, for to be punished.

6 And it came to pass, that, as I made my journey, and was come nigh unto Damascus about noon, suddenly there shone from heaven a great light round about me.

7 And I fell unto the ground, and heard a voice saying unto me, Saul, Saul, why persecutest thou me?

8 And I answered, Who art thou, Lord? And he said unto me, I am Jesus of Nazareth, whom thou persecutest.

9 And they that were with me saw indeed the light, and were afraid; but they heard not the voice of him that spake to me.

10 And I said, What shall I do, Lord? And the Lord said unto me, Arise, and go into Damascus; and there it shall be told thee of all things which are appointed for thee to do.

11 And when I could not see for the glory of that light, being led by the hand of them that were with me, I came into Damascus.

12 And one Ananias, a devout man according to the law, having a good report of all the Jews which dwelt *there*,

## Amplified

31 Now while they were trying to kill him, word came to the commandant of the regular Roman garrison that the whole of Jerusalem was in a state of ferment.

32 So immediately he took soldiers and centurions and hurried down among them; and when the people saw the commandant and the troops, they stopped beating Paul.

33 Then the commandant approached and arrested Paul, and ordered that he be secured with two chains. He then inquired who he was and what he had done.

34 Some in the crowd kept shouting back one thing and others something else, and since he could not ascertain the facts because of the furore, he ordered that Paul be removed to the barracks.

35 And when [Paul] came to mount the steps, he was actually being carried by the soldiers because of the violence of the mob;

36 For the mass of the people kept following them, shouting, Away with him!—Kill him!

37 Just as Paul was about to be taken into the barracks, he asked the commandant, May I say something to you? And the man replied, Can you speak Greek?

38 Are you not then [as I supposed] the Egyptian who not long ago stirred up a rebellion and led those four thousand men of the cutthroats out into the wilderness?

39 Paul answered, I am a Jew, from Tarsus in Cilicia, a citizen of no insignificant *or* undistinguished city. I beg you, allow me to address the people.

40 And when the man had granted him permission, Paul, standing on the steps, gestured with his hand to the people; and there was a great hush. Then he spoke to them in the Hebrew dialect, saying:

**22** BRETHREN AND fathers, listen to the defense which I now make in your presence.

2 And when they heard that he addressed them in the Hebrew tongue, they were all the more quiet. And he continued,

3 I am a Jew, born in Tarsus of Cilicia, but reared in this city. At the feet of Gamaliel I was educated according to the strictest care in the Law of our fathers, being ardent—even a zealot—for God, as all you are today.

4 [Yes,] I harassed (troubled, molested and persecuted) this Way [of the Lord] to the death, putting in chains and committing to prison both men and women,

5 As the high priest and whole council of elders [Sanhedrin] can testify; for from them indeed I received letters with which I was on my way to the brethren in Damascus in order to take also those [believers] who were there, and bring them in chains to Jerusalem that they might be punished.

6 But as I was on my journey and approached Damascus, about noon a great blaze of light flashed suddenly from heaven and shone about me.

7 And I fell to the ground and heard a voice saying to me, Saul, Saul, why do you persecute Me—harass and trouble and molest Me?

8 And I replied, Who are You, Lord? And He said to me, I am Jesus the Nazarene, Whom you are persecuting.

9 Now the men who were with me saw the light, but they did not hear [ [a]the sound of the uttered words of] the voice of the One Who was speaking to me—so that they could [b]understand it.

10 And I asked, What shall I do, Lord? And the Lord answered me, Get up and go into Damascus, and there it will be told you all that it is destined *and* appointed for you to do.

11 And since I could not see, because (of the dazzlingly glorious intensity) of the brightness of that light, I was led by the hand by those who were with me, and [thus] I arrived in Damascus.

12 And one Ananias, a devout man according to the Law, well spoken of by all the Jews who resided there,

**AMP** [a] Thayer. [b] Vincent.

## New American Standard

31 And while they were seeking to kill him, a report came up to the [c]commander of the *Roman* cohort that all Jerusalem was in confusion.

32 And at once he took along *some* soldiers and centurions, and ran down to them; and when they saw the commander and the soldiers, they stopped beating Paul.

33 Then the commander came up and took hold of him, and ordered him to be bound with two chains; and he *began* asking who he was and what he had done.

34 But among the crowd some were shouting one thing *and* some another, and when he could not find out the facts on account of the uproar, he ordered him to be brought into the barracks.

35 And when he got to the stairs, it so happened that he was carried by the soldiers because of the violence of the mob;

36 for the multitude of the people kept following behind, crying out, "Away with him!"

37 ¶ And as Paul was about to be brought into the barracks, he said to the commander, "May I say something to you?" And he *said, "Do you know Greek?

38 "Then you are not the Egyptian who some time ago stirred up a revolt and led the four thousand men of the Assassins out into the wilderness?"

39 But Paul said, "I am a Jew of Tarsus in Cilicia, a citizen of no insignificant city; and I beg you, allow me to speak to the people."

40 And when he had given him permission, Paul, standing on the stairs, motioned to the people with his hand; and when there was a great hush, he spoke to them in the Hebrew dialect, saying,

*Paul's Defense before the Jews*

**22** "BRETHREN AND fathers, hear my defense which I now *offer* to you."

2 ¶ And when they heard that he was addressing them in the Hebrew dialect, they became even more quiet; and he *said,

3 ¶ "I am a Jew, born in Tarsus of Cilicia, but brought up in this city, educated under Gamaliel, strictly according to the law of our fathers, being zealous for God, just as you all are today.

4 "And I persecuted this Way to the death, binding and putting both men and women into prisons,

5 as also the high priest and all the Council of the elders can testify. From them I also received letters to the brethren, and started off for Damascus in order to bring even those who were there to Jerusalem as prisoners to be punished.

6 "And it came about that as I was on my way, approaching Damascus about noontime, a very bright light suddenly flashed from heaven all around me,

7 and I fell to the ground and heard a voice saying to me, 'Saul, Saul, why are you persecuting Me?'

8 "And I answered, 'Who art Thou, Lord?' And He said to me, 'I am Jesus the Nazarene, whom you are persecuting.'

9 "And those who were with me beheld the light, to be sure, but did not understand the voice of the One who was speaking to me.

10 "And I said, 'What shall I do, Lord?' And the Lord said to me, 'Arise and go on into Damascus; and there you will be told of all that has been appointed for you to do.'

11 "But since I could not see because of the brightness of that light, I was led by the hand by those who were with me, and came into Damascus.

12 "And a certain Ananias, a man who was devout by the standard of the Law, *and* well spoken of by all the Jews who lived there,

NAS [c] I.e., chiliarch, in command of one thousand troops

## New International

ing to kill him, news reached the commander of the Roman troops
that the whole city of Jerusalem was in an uproar. 32 He at once took
some officers and soldiers and ran down to the crowd. When the
rioters saw the commander and his soldiers, they stopped beating
Paul.
33 The commander came up and arrested him and ordered him
to be bound with two chains. Then he asked who he was and what
he had done. 34 Some in the crowd shouted one thing and some
another, and since the commander could not get at the truth
because of the uproar, he ordered that Paul be taken into the
barracks. 35 When Paul reached the steps, the violence of the mob
was so great he had to be carried by the soldiers. 36 The crowd that
followed kept shouting, "Away with him!"

*Paul Speaks to the Crowd*

37 As the soldiers were about to take Paul into the barracks, he
asked the commander, "May I say something to you?"
"Do you speak Greek?" he replied. 38 "Aren't you the Egyptian
who started a revolt and led four thousand terrorists out into the
desert some time ago?"
39 Paul answered, "I am a Jew, from Tarsus in Cilicia, a citizen
of no ordinary city. Please let me speak to the people."
40 Having received the commander's permission, Paul stood on
the steps and motioned to the crowd. When they were all silent,
he said to them in Aramaic[d]:

**22** "BROTHERS AND fathers, listen now to my defense."
2 When they heard him speak to them in Aramaic, they
became very quiet.
Then Paul said: 3 "I am a Jew, born in Tarsus of Cilicia, but
brought up in this city. Under Gamaliel I was thoroughly trained
in the law of our fathers and was just as zealous for God as any
of you are today. 4 I persecuted the followers of this Way to their
death, arresting both men and women and throwing them into
prison, 5 as also the high priest and all the Council can testify. I
even obtained letters from them to their brothers in Damascus, and
went there to bring these people as prisoners to Jerusalem to be
punished.
6 "About noon as I came near Damascus, suddenly a bright light
from heaven flashed around me. 7 I fell to the ground and heard
a voice say to me, 'Saul! Saul! Why do you persecute me?'
8 " 'Who are you, Lord?' I asked.
" 'I am Jesus of Nazareth, whom you are persecuting,' he replied. 9 My companions saw the light, but they did not understand
the voice of him who was speaking to me.
10 " 'What shall I do, Lord?' I asked.
" 'Get up,' the Lord said, 'and go into Damascus. There you will
be told all that you have been assigned to do.' 11 My companions
led me by the hand into Damascus, because the brilliance of the
light had blinded me.
12 "A man named Ananias came to see me. He was a devout
observer of the law and highly respected by all the Jews living

NIV [d] 40 Or possibly *Hebrew;* also in 22:2

## King James

13 Came unto me, and stood, and said unto me, Brother Saul, receive thy sight. And the same hour I looked up upon him.

14 And he said, The God of our fathers hath chosen thee, that thou shouldest know his will, and see that Just One, and shouldest hear the voice of his mouth.

15 For thou shalt be his witness unto all men of what thou hast seen and heard.

16 And now why tarriest thou? arise, and be baptized, and wash away thy sins, calling on the name of the Lord.

17 And it came to pass, that, when I was come again to Jerusalem, even while I prayed in the temple, I was in a trance;

18 And saw him saying unto me, Make haste, and get thee quickly out of Jerusalem: for they will not receive thy testimony concerning me.

19 And I said, Lord, they know that I imprisoned and beat in every synagogue them that believed on thee:

20 And when the blood of thy martyr Stephen was shed, I also was standing by, and consenting unto his death, and kept the raiment of them that slew him.

21 And he said unto me, Depart: for I will send thee far hence unto the Gentiles.

22 And they gave him audience unto this word, and *then* lifted up their voices, and said, Away with such a *fellow* from the earth: for it is not fit that he should live.

23 And as they cried out, and cast off *their* clothes, and threw dust into the air,

24 The chief captain commanded him to be brought into the castle, and bade that he should be examined by scourging; that he might know wherefore they cried so against him.

25 And as they bound him with thongs, Paul said unto the centurion that stood by, Is it lawful for you to scourge a man that is a Roman, and uncondemned?

26 When the centurion heard *that,* he went and told the chief captain, saying, Take heed what thou doest: for this man is a Roman.

27 Then the chief captain came, and said unto him, Tell me, art thou a Roman? He said, Yea.

28 And the chief captain answered, With a great sum obtained I this freedom. And Paul said, But I was *free* born.

29 Then straightway they departed from him which should have examined him: and the chief captain also was afraid, after he knew that he was a Roman, and because he had bound him.

30 On the morrow, because he would have known the certainty wherefore he was accused of the Jews, he loosed him from *his* bands, and commanded the chief priests and all their council to appear, and brought Paul down, and set him before them.

**23** AND PAUL, earnestly beholding the council, said, Men *and* brethren, I have lived in all good conscience before God until this day.

2 And the high priest Ananias commanded them that stood by him to smite him on the mouth.

3 Then said Paul unto him, God shall smite thee, *thou* whited wall: for sittest thou to judge me after the law, and commandest me to be smitten contrary to the law?

4 And they that stood by said, Revilest thou God's high priest?

## Amplified

13 Came to see me, and standing by my side said to me, Brother Saul, [a]look up—and receive back your sight. And in that very [b]instant I [recovered my sight and] looking up saw him.

14 And he said, The God of our forefathers has destined *and* appointed you to come progressively to know His will—that is, to perceive, to recognize more strongly and clearly and to become better and more intimately acquainted with His will; and to see the Righteous One *Jesus Christ, the Messiah* and to hear a voice from His [own] mouth *and* a message from His [own] lips;

15 For you will be His witness unto all men of everything that you have seen and heard.

16 And now, why do you delay? Rise and be baptized, and [c]by calling upon His name wash away your sins.

17 Then when I had come back to Jerusalem and was praying in the temple [d]enclosure, I fell into a trance—an ecstasy;

18 And I saw Him as He said to me, Hurry, get quickly out of Jerusalem, because they will not receive your testimony about Me.

19 And I said, Lord, they themselves well know that throughout all the synagogues I cast into prison and flogged those who believed—who adhered to and trusted in and relied—on You.

20 And when the blood of Your (martyr) witness Stephen was shed, I also was personally standing by and consenting *and* approving, and guarding the garments of those who slew him.

21 And the Lord said to me, Go, for I will send you far away unto the Gentiles (nations).

22 Up to the moment that Paul made this last statement, the people listened to him; but now they raised their voices and shouted, Away with such a fellow from the earth! He is not fit to live!

23 And as they were shouting and tossing *and* waving their garments and throwing dust into the air,

24 The commandant ordered that Paul be brought into the barracks, and that he be examined by scourging, in order that [the commandant] might learn why the people cried out thus against him.

25 But when they had stretched him out with the thongs [leather straps], Paul asked the centurion who was standing by, Is it legal for you to flog a man who is a Roman citizen, and without a trial (uncondemned)?

26 When the centurion heard that, he went to the commandant and said to him, What are you about to do? This man is a Roman citizen!

27 So the commandant came and said to [Paul], Tell me, are you a Roman citizen? And he said, Yes [indeed]!

28 The commandant replied, I purchased this citizenship (as a capital investment) for a big price. Paul said, But I was [Roman] born!

29 Instantly those who were about to examine (and flog) him withdrew from him; and the commandant also was frightened, for he realized that [Paul] was a Roman citizen and he had put him in chains.

30 But the next day, desiring to know the real cause for which the Jews accused him, he unbound him and ordered the chief priests and all the council [Sanhedrin] to assemble, and he brought Paul down and placed him before them.

**23** THEN PAUL, gazing earnestly at the council [Sanhedrin], said, Brethren, I have lived before God, doing my duty with a perfectly good conscience until this very day— [e]as a citizen, a true and loyal Jew.

2 At this the high priest Ananias ordered those who stood near him to strike him on the mouth.

3 Then Paul said to him, God is about to strike you, you whitewashed wall! Do you sit as a judge to try me in accordance with the Law, and yet in defiance of the Law you order me to be struck?

4 Those who stood near exclaimed, Do you rail at *and* insult the high priest of God?

**AMP** [a] Thayer. [b] Moulton and Milligan. [c] Williams: Adverbial participle of means. [d] Trench. [e] Vincent.

## New American Standard

13came to me, and standing near said to me, 'Brother Saul,
receive your sight!' And at that very time I looked up at him.
14"And he said, 'The God of our fathers has appointed you to
know His will, and to see the Righteous One, and to hear an
utterance from His mouth.
15'For you will be a witness for Him to all men of what you have
seen and heard.
16'And now why do you delay? Arise, and be baptized, and
wash away your sins, calling on His name.'
17"And it came about when I returned to Jerusalem and was
praying in the temple, that I fell into a trance,
18and I saw Him saying to me, 'Make haste, and get out of
Jerusalem quickly, because they will not accept your testimony
about Me.'
19"And I said, 'Lord, they themselves understand that in one
synagogue after another I used to imprison and beat those who
believed in Thee.
20'And when the blood of Thy witness Stephen was being shed,
I also was standing by approving, and watching out for the cloaks
of those who were slaying him.'
21"And He said to me, 'Go! For I will send you far away to the
Gentiles.' "
22¶ And they listened to him up to this statement, and *then* they
raised their voices and said, "Away with such a fellow from the
earth, for he should not be allowed to live!"
23And as they were crying out and throwing off their cloaks and
tossing dust into the air,
24the [f]commander ordered him to be brought into the barracks,
stating that he should be examined by scourging so that he might
find out the reason why they were shouting against him that way.
25And when they stretched him out with thongs, Paul said to
the centurion who was standing by, "Is it lawful for you to scourge
a man who is a Roman and uncondemned?"
26And when the centurion heard *this*, he went to the commander and told him, saying, "What are you about to do? For this
man is a Roman."
27And the commander came and said to him, "Tell me, are you
a Roman?" And he said, "Yes."
28And the commander answered, "I acquired this citizenship
with a large sum of money." And Paul said, "But I was actually
born *a citizen*."
29Therefore those who were about to examine him immediately
let go of him; and the commander also was afraid when he found
out that he was a Roman, and because he had put him in chains.
30¶ But on the next day, wishing to know for certain why he had
been accused by the Jews, he released him and ordered the chief
priests and all the Council to assemble, and brought Paul down
and set him before them.

*Paul before the Council*

23 AND PAUL, looking intently at the Council, said, "Brethren, I have lived my life with a perfectly good conscience
before God up to this day."
2And the high priest Ananias commanded those standing beside him to strike him on the mouth.
3Then Paul said to him, "God is going to strike you, you
whitewashed wall! And do you sit to try me according to the Law,
and in violation of the Law order me to be struck?"
4But the bystanders said, "Do you revile God's high priest?"

NAS [f] I.e., chiliarch, in command of one thousand troops

## New International

there. 13He stood beside me and said, 'Brother Saul, receive your
sight!' And at that very moment I was able to see him.
14"Then he said: 'The God of our fathers has chosen you to
know his will and to see the Righteous One and to hear words from
his mouth. 15You will be his witness to all men of what you have
seen and heard. 16And now what are you waiting for? Get up, be
baptized and wash your sins away, calling on his name.'
17"When I returned to Jerusalem and was praying at the temple,
I fell into a trance 18and saw the Lord speaking. 'Quick!' he said
to me. 'Leave Jerusalem immediately, because they will not accept
your testimony about me.'
19" 'Lord,' I replied, 'these men know that I went from one
synagogue to another to imprison and beat those who believe in
you. 20And when the blood of your martyr[g] Stephen was shed, I
stood there giving my approval and guarding the clothes of those
who were killing him.'
21"Then the Lord said to me, 'Go; I will send you far away to
the Gentiles.' "

*Paul the Roman Citizen*

22The crowd listened to Paul until he said this. Then they raised
their voices and shouted, "Rid the earth of him! He's not fit to
live!"
23As they were shouting and throwing off their cloaks and
flinging dust into the air, 24the commander ordered Paul to be
taken into the barracks. He directed that he be flogged and questioned in order to find out why the people were shouting at him
like this. 25As they stretched him out to flog him, Paul said to the
centurion standing there, "Is it legal for you to flog a Roman citizen
who hasn't even been found guilty?"
26When the centurion heard this, he went to the commander
and reported it. "What are you going to do?" he asked. "This man
is a Roman citizen."
27The commander went to Paul and asked, "Tell me, are you
a Roman citizen?"
"Yes, I am," he answered.
28Then the commander said, "I had to pay a big price for my
citizenship."
"But I was born a citizen," Paul replied.
29Those who were about to question him withdrew immediately. The commander himself was alarmed when he realized that
he had put Paul, a Roman citizen, in chains.

*Before the Sanhedrin*

30The next day, since the commander wanted to find out exactly
why Paul was being accused by the Jews, he released him and
ordered the chief priests and all the Sanhedrin to assemble. Then
he brought Paul and had him stand before them.

23 PAUL LOOKED straight at the Sanhedrin and said, "My
brothers, I have fulfilled my duty to God in all good conscience to this day." 2At this the high priest Ananias ordered those
standing near Paul to strike him on the mouth. 3Then Paul said to
him, "God will strike you, you whitewashed wall! You sit there to
judge me according to the law, yet you yourself violate the law by
commanding that I be struck!"
4Those who were standing near Paul said, "You dare to insult
God's high priest?"

NIV [g] 20 Or *witness*

## King James

5Then said Paul, I wist not, brethren, that he was the high priest: for it is written, Thou shalt not speak evil of the ruler of thy people.

6But when Paul perceived that the one part were Sadducees, and the other Pharisees, he cried out in the council, Men *and* brethren, I am a Pharisee, the son of a Pharisee: of the hope and resurrection of the dead I am called in question.

7And when he had so said, there arose a dissension between the Pharisees and the Sadducees: and the multitude was divided.

8For the Sadducees say that there is no resurrection, neither angel, nor spirit: but the Pharisees confess both.

9And there arose a great cry: and the scribes *that were* of the Pharisees' part arose, and strove, saying, We find no evil in this man: but if a spirit or an angel hath spoken to him, let us not fight against God.

10And when there arose a great dissension, the chief captain, fearing lest Paul should have been pulled in pieces of them, commanded the soldiers to go down, and to take him by force from among them, and to bring *him* into the castle.

11And the night following the Lord stood by him, and said, Be of good cheer, Paul: for as thou hast testified of me in Jerusalem, so must thou bear witness also at Rome.

12And when it was day, certain of the Jews banded together, and bound themselves under a curse, saying that they would neither eat nor drink till they had killed Paul.

13And they were more than forty which had made this conspiracy.

14And they came to the chief priests and elders, and said, We have bound ourselves under a great curse, that we will eat nothing until we have slain Paul.

15Now therefore ye with the council signify to the chief captain that he bring him down unto you tomorrow, as though ye would inquire something more perfectly concerning him: and we, or ever he come near, are ready to kill him.

16And when Paul's sister's son heard of their lying in wait, he went and entered into the castle, and told Paul.

17Then Paul called one of the centurions unto *him*, and said, Bring this young man unto the chief captain: for he hath a certain thing to tell him.

18So he took him, and brought *him* to the chief captain, and said, Paul the prisoner called me unto *him*, and prayed me to bring this young man unto thee, who hath something to say unto thee.

19Then the chief captain took him by the hand, and went *with him* aside privately, and asked *him*, What is that thou hast to tell me?

20And he said, The Jews have agreed to desire thee that thou wouldest bring down Paul tomorrow into the council, as though they would inquire somewhat of him more perfectly.

21But do not thou yield unto them: for there lie in wait for him of them more than forty men, which have bound themselves with an oath, that they will neither eat nor drink till they have killed him: and now are they ready, looking for a promise from thee.

22So the chief captain *then* let the young man depart, and charged *him*, *See thou* tell no man that thou hast shown these things to me.

23And he called unto *him* two centurions, saying, Make ready two hundred soldiers to go to Caesarea, and horsemen threescore and ten, and spearmen two hundred, at the third hour of the night;

24And provide *them* beasts, that they may set Paul on, and bring *him* safe unto Felix the governor.

25And he wrote a letter after this manner:

26Claudius Lysias unto the most excellent governor Felix *sendeth* greeting.

## Amplified

5And Paul said, I was not conscious, brethren, that he is a high priest; for the Scripture says, You shall not speak ill of a ruler of your people. [Exod. 22:28.]

6But Paul, when he perceived that one part of them were Sadducees and the other part Pharisees, cried out to the council [Sanhedrin], Brethren, I am a Pharisee, a son of Pharisees; it is with regard to the hope and the resurrection of the dead that I am indicted *and* being judged.

7So when he had said this, an angry dispute arose between the Pharisees and the Sadducees; and the whole [crowded] assemblage was divided [into two factions].

8For the Sadducees hold that there is no resurrection, nor angel nor spirit; but the Pharisees declare openly *and* speak out freely, acknowledging [their faith in] them both.

9Then a great uproar ensued, and some of the scribes of the Pharisees' party stood up and thoroughly fought the case, (contending fiercely) and declaring, We find nothing evil *or* wrong in this man. But if a spirit or an angel [really] spoke to him—? *Let us not fight against God!*

10And when the strife became more and more tense *and* violent, the commandant, fearing that Paul would be torn in pieces by them, ordered the troops to go down and take him forcibly from among them and conduct him back into the barracks.

11And [that same] following night the Lord stood beside Paul and said, Take courage, *Paul*, for as you have borne faithful witness concerning Me at Jerusalem, so you must also bear witness at Rome.

12Now when daylight came, the Jews formed a plot and bound themselves by an oath *and* under a curse neither to eat nor drink till they had done away with Paul.

13There were more than forty [men of them], who formed this conspiracy—swearing together this oath and curse.

14And they went to the chief priests and elders saying, We have strictly bound ourselves by an oath *and* under a curse not to taste any food until we have slain Paul.

15So now, you along with the council [Sanhedrin] give notice to the commandant to bring [Paul] down to you, as if you were going to investigate his case more accurately. But we [ourselves] are ready to slay him before he comes near.

16But the son of Paul's sister heard of their intended attack, and he went and got into the barracks and told Paul.

17Then Paul, calling in one of the centurions, said, Take this young man to the commandant, for he has something to report to him.

18So he took him and conducted him to the commandant and said, Paul the prisoner called me to him and requested me to conduct this young man to you, for he has something to report to you.

19The commandant took him by the hand, and going aside with him asked privately, What is it that you have to report to me?

20And he replied, The Jews have agreed to ask you to bring Paul down to the council [Sanhedrin] tomorrow, as if [they were] intending to examine him more exactly.

21But do not yield to their persuasion, for more than forty of their men are lying in ambush waiting for him, having bound themselves by an oath *and* under a curse neither to eat nor drink till they have killed him; and even now they are all ready, [just] waiting for your promise.

22So the commandant sent the youth away, charging him, Do not disclose to any one that you have given me this information.

23Then summoning two of the centurions, he said, Have two hundred footmen ready by the third hour of tonight (about nine o'clock) to go as far as Caesarea, with seventy horsemen and two hundred spearmen.

24Also provide beasts for mounts for Paul to ride, and bring him in safety to Felix the governor.

25And he wrote a letter having this message:

26Claudius Lysias sends greetings to His Excellency Felix the governor.

## New American Standard

5And Paul said, "I was not aware, brethren, that he was high priest; for it is written, 'YOU SHALL NOT SPEAK EVIL OF A RULER OF YOUR PEOPLE.' "

6But perceiving that one part were Sadducees and the other Pharisees, Paul *began* crying out in the Council, "Brethren, I am a Pharisee, a son of Pharisees; I am on trial for the hope and resurrection of the dead!"

7And as he said this, there arose a dissension between the Pharisees and Sadducees; and the assembly was divided.

8For the Sadducees say that there is no resurrection, nor an angel, nor a spirit; but the Pharisees acknowledge them all.

9And there arose a great uproar; and some of the scribes of the Pharisaic party stood up and *began* to argue heatedly, saying, "We find nothing wrong with this man; suppose a spirit or an angel has spoken to him?"

10And as a great dissension was developing, the [a]commander was afraid Paul would be torn to pieces by them and ordered the troops to go down and take him away from them by force, and bring him into the barracks.

11¶ But on the night *immediately* following, the Lord stood at his side and said, "Take courage; for as you have solemnly witnessed to My cause at Jerusalem, so you must witness at Rome also."

*A Conspiracy to Kill Paul*

12¶ And when it was day, the Jews formed a conspiracy and bound themselves under an oath, saying that they would neither eat nor drink until they had killed Paul.

13And there were more than forty who formed this plot.

14And they came to the chief priests and the elders, and said, "We have bound ourselves under a solemn oath to taste nothing until we have killed Paul.

15"Now, therefore, you and the Council notify the commander to bring him down to you, as though you were going to determine his case by a more thorough investigation; and we for our part are ready to slay him before he comes near *the place.*"

16But the son of Paul's sister heard of their ambush, and he came and entered the barracks and told Paul.

17And Paul called one of the centurions to him and said, "Lead this young man to the commander, for he has something to report to him."

18So he took him and led him to the commander and *said, "Paul the prisoner called me to him and asked me to lead this young man to you since he has something to tell you."

19And the commander took him by the hand and stepping aside, *began* to inquire of him privately, "What is it that you have to report to me?"

20And he said, "The Jews have agreed to ask you to bring Paul down tomorrow to the Council, as though they were going to inquire somewhat more thoroughly about him.

21"So do not listen to them, for more than forty of them are lying in wait for him who have bound themselves under a curse not to eat or drink until they slay him; and now they are ready and waiting for the promise from you."

22Therefore the commander let the young man go, instructing him, "Tell no one that you have notified me of these things."

*Paul Moved to Caesarea*

23And he called to him two of the centurions, and said, "Get two hundred soldiers ready by [b]the third hour of the night to proceed to Caesarea, with seventy horsemen and two hundred spearmen."

24 *They were* also to provide mounts to put Paul on and bring him safely to Felix the governor.

25And he wrote a letter having this form:

26¶ "Claudius Lysias, to the most excellent governor
Felix, greetings.

NAS [a] I.e., chiliarch, in command of one thousand troops [b] I.e., 9 p.m.

## New International

5Paul replied, "Brothers, I did not realize that he was the high priest; for it is written: 'Do not speak evil about the ruler of your people.'[c] "

6Then Paul, knowing that some of them were Sadducees and the others Pharisees, called out in the Sanhedrin, "My brothers, I am a Pharisee, the son of a Pharisee. I stand on trial because of my hope in the resurrection of the dead." 7When he said this, a dispute broke out between the Pharisees and the Sadducees, and the assembly was divided. 8(The Sadducees say that there is no resurrection, and that there are neither angels nor spirits, but the Pharisees acknowledge them all.)

9There was a great uproar, and some of the teachers of the law who were Pharisees stood up and argued vigorously. "We find nothing wrong with this man," they said. "What if a spirit or an angel has spoken to him?" 10The dispute became so violent that the commander was afraid Paul would be torn to pieces by them. He ordered the troops to go down and take him away from them by force and bring him into the barracks.

11The following night the Lord stood near Paul and said, "Take courage! As you have testified about me in Jerusalem, so you must also testify in Rome."

*The Plot to Kill Paul*

12The next morning the Jews formed a conspiracy and bound themselves with an oath not to eat or drink until they had killed Paul. 13More than forty men were involved in this plot. 14They went to the chief priests and elders and said, "We have taken a solemn oath not to eat anything until we have killed Paul. 15Now then, you and the Sanhedrin petition the commander to bring him before you on the pretext of wanting more accurate information about his case. We are ready to kill him before he gets here."

16But when the son of Paul's sister heard of this plot, he went into the barracks and told Paul.

17Then Paul called one of the centurions and said, "Take this young man to the commander; he has something to tell him." 18So he took him to the commander.

The centurion said, "Paul, the prisoner, sent for me and asked me to bring this young man to you because he has something to tell you."

19The commander took the young man by the hand, drew him aside and asked, "What is it you want to tell me?"

20He said: "The Jews have agreed to ask you to bring Paul before the Sanhedrin tomorrow on the pretext of wanting more accurate information about him. 21Don't give in to them, because more than forty of them are waiting in ambush for him. They have taken an oath not to eat or drink until they have killed him. They are ready now, waiting for your consent to their request."

22The commander dismissed the young man and cautioned him, "Don't tell anyone that you have reported this to me."

*Paul Transferred to Caesarea*

23Then he called two of his centurions and ordered them, "Get ready a detachment of two hundred soldiers, seventy horsemen and two hundred spearmen[d] to go to Caesarea at nine tonight. 24Provide mounts for Paul so that he may be taken safely to Governor Felix."

25He wrote a letter as follows:

26Claudius Lysias,

To His Excellency, Governor Felix:

Greetings.

NIV [c] 5 Exodus 22:28 [d] 23 The meaning of the Greek for this word is uncertain.

## King James

27This man was taken of the Jews, and should have been killed of them: then came I with an army, and rescued him, having understood that he was a Roman.

28And when I would have known the cause wherefore they accused him, I brought him forth into their council:

29Whom I perceived to be accused of questions of their law, but to have nothing laid to his charge worthy of death or of bonds.

30And when it was told me how that the Jews laid wait for the man, I sent straightway to thee, and gave commandment to his accusers also to say before thee what *they had* against him. Farewell.

31Then the soldiers, as it was commanded them, took Paul, and brought *him* by night to Antipatris.

32On the morrow they left the horsemen to go with him, and returned to the castle:

33Who, when they came to Caesarea, and delivered the epistle to the governor, presented Paul also before him.

34And when the governor had read *the letter*, he asked of what province he was. And when he understood that *he was* of Cilicia;

35I will hear thee, said he, when thine accusers are also come. And he commanded him to be kept in Herod's judgment hall.

**24** AND AFTER five days Ananias the high priest descended with the elders, and *with* a certain orator *named* Tertullus, who informed the governor against Paul.

2And when he was called forth, Tertullus began to accuse *him*, saying, Seeing that by thee we enjoy great quietness, and that very worthy deeds are done unto this nation by thy providence,

3We accept *it* always, and in all places, most noble Felix, with all thankfulness.

4Notwithstanding, that I be not further tedious unto thee, I pray thee that thou wouldest hear us of thy clemency a few words.

5For we have found this man *a* pestilent *fellow*, and a mover of sedition among all the Jews throughout the world, and a ringleader of the sect of the Nazarenes:

6Who also hath gone about to profane the temple: whom we took, and would have judged according to our law.

7But the chief captain Lysias came *upon us*, and with great violence took *him* away out of our hands,

8Commanding his accusers to come unto thee: by examining of whom thyself mayest take knowledge of all these things, whereof we accuse him.

9And the Jews also assented, saying that these things were so.

10Then Paul, after that the governor had beckoned unto him to speak, answered, Forasmuch as I know that thou hast been of many years a judge unto this nation, I do the more cheerfully answer for myself:

11Because that thou mayest understand, that there are yet but twelve days since I went up to Jerusalem for to worship.

12And they neither found me in the temple disputing with any man, neither raising up the people, neither in the synagogues, nor in the city:

13Neither can they prove the things whereof they now accuse me.

## Amplified

27This man was seized [as prisoner] by the Jews, and was about to be killed by them, when I came upon them with the troops and rescued him, because I learned that he is a Roman citizen.

28And wishing to know the exact accusation which they were making against him, I brought him down before their council [Sanhedrin],

29[Where] I found that he was charged in regard to questions of their own law, but he was accused of nothing that would call for death or [even] for imprisonment.

30[However] when it was pointed out to me that there would be a conspiracy against the man, I sent him to you immediately, directing his accusers also to present before you their charge against him.

31So the soldiers, in compliance with their instructions, took Paul and conducted him during the night to Antipatris.

32And the next day they returned to the barracks, leaving the mounted men to proceed with him.

33When these came to Caesarea and gave the letter to the governor, they also presented Paul before him.

34Having read the letter, he asked to what kind of a province [Paul] belonged. When he discovered that he was from Cilicia [an imperial province],

35He said, I will hear your case [a]fully when your accusers also have come. And he ordered that an eye be kept on him in Herod's palace—the praetorium.

**24** FIVE DAYS later, the high priest Ananias came down [from Jerusalem to Caesarea] with some elders, and a certain forensic advocate Tertullus—acting as spokesman and counsel. They presented to the governor their evidence against Paul.

2And when he was called, Tertullus began the complaint [against him] by saying:

3Most Excellent Felix, since through you we obtain *and* enjoy much peace, and since by your foresight *and* provision wonderful reforms (amendments and improvements) are introduced *and* effected on behalf of this nation, in every way and in every place we accept *and* acknowledge this with deep appreciation *and* with all gratitude.

4But not to hinder *or* detain you too long, I beg you in your clemency *and* courtesy *and* kindness to grant us a brief *and* [b]concise hearing.

5For we have found this man a perfect pest—a real plague—an agitator *and* source of disturbance to all the Jews throughout the world, and a ringleader of the (heretical, [c]division-producing) sect of the Nazarenes.

6He also [even] tried to desecrate *and* defile the temple, but we laid hands on him

7 *And would have sentenced him by our Law, but the commandant Lysias came and took him from us with violence and force, and ordered his accusers to present themselves to you.*

8By examining *and* cross-questioning him yourself you will be able to ascertain the truth from him about all these things with which we charge him.

9The Jews also agreed *and* joined in the accusation, declaring that all these things were exactly so.

10And when the governor had beckoned to Paul to speak, he answered: Because I know that for many years you have been a judge over this nation, I find it easier to make my defense, *and* do it cheerfully *and* with good courage.

11As you can readily verify, it is not more than twelve days since I went up to Jerusalem to worship;

12And neither in the temple nor in the synagogues nor in the city did they find me disputing with anybody or bringing together a seditious crowd.

13Neither can they present argument *or* evidence to prove to you what they now bring against me.

**AMP** [a] Vincent. [b] Vincent. [c] Vincent.

## New American Standard

27 "When this man was arrested by the Jews and was
about to be slain by them, I came upon them with
the troops and rescued him, having learned that he
was a Roman.
28 "And wanting to ascertain the charge for which they
were accusing him, I brought him down to their
Council;
29 and I found him to be accused over questions about
their Law, but under no accusation deserving death
or imprisonment.
30 "And when I was informed that there would be a
plot against the man, I sent him to you at once, also
instructing his accusers to bring charges against
him before you."
31¶ So the soldiers, in accordance with their orders, took Paul
and brought him by night to Antipatris.
32But the next day, leaving the horsemen to go on with him,
they returned to the barracks.
33And when these had come to Caesarea and delivered the
letter to the governor, they also presented Paul to him.
34And when he had read it, he asked from what province he
was; and when he learned that he was from Cilicia,
35he said, "I will give you a hearing after your accusers arrive
also," giving orders for him to be kept in Herod's [d]Praetorium.

### *Paul before Felix*

**24** AND AFTER five days the high priest Ananias came down
with some elders, with a certain attorney *named* Tertullus;
and they brought charges to the governor against Paul.
2And after *Paul* had been summoned, Tertullus began to accuse him, saying *to the governor*,
¶"Since we have through you attained much peace, and since
by your providence reforms are being carried out for this nation,
3we acknowledge *this* in every way and everywhere, most
excellent Felix, with all thankfulness.
4"But, that I may not weary you any further, I beg you to grant
us, by your kindness, a brief hearing.
5"For we have found this man a real pest and a fellow who stirs
up dissension among all the Jews throughout [e]the world, and a
ringleader of the sect of the Nazarenes.
6"And he even tried to desecrate the temple; and then we
arrested him. [ [f]And we wanted to judge him according to our own
Law.
7"But Lysias the commander came along, and with much violence took him out of our hands,
8ordering his accusers to come before you.] And by examining
him yourself concerning all these matters, you will be able to
ascertain the things of which we accuse him."
9And the Jews also joined in the attack, asserting that these
things were so.
10¶ And when the governor had nodded for him to speak, Paul
responded:
¶"Knowing that for many years you have been a judge to this
nation, I cheerfully make my defense,
11since you can take note of the fact that no more than twelve
days ago I went up to Jerusalem to worship.
12"And neither in the temple, nor in the synagogues, nor in the
city *itself* did they find me carrying on a discussion with anyone
or causing a riot.
13"Nor can they prove to you *the charges* of which they now
accuse me.

NAS [d] I.e., governor's official residence [e] Lit., *the inhabited earth* [f] Many mss. do not contain the remainder of v. 6, v. 7, nor the first part of v. 8

## New International

27This man was seized by the Jews and they were about to
kill him, but I came with my troops and rescued him, for I had
learned that he is a Roman citizen. 28I wanted to know why
they were accusing him, so I brought him to their Sanhedrin.
29I found that the accusation had to do with questions about
their law, but there was no charge against him that deserved
death or imprisonment. 30When I was informed of a plot to
be carried out against the man, I sent him to you at once. I also
ordered his accusers to present to you their case against him.

31So the soldiers, carrying out their orders, took Paul with them
during the night and brought him as far as Antipatris. 32The next
day they let the cavalry go on with him, while they returned to the
barracks. 33When the cavalry arrived in Caesarea, they delivered
the letter to the governor and handed Paul over to him. 34The
governor read the letter and asked what province he was from.
Learning that he was from Cilicia, 35he said, "I will hear your case
when your accusers get here." Then he ordered that Paul be kept
under guard in Herod's palace.

### *The Trial Before Felix*

**24** FIVE DAYS later the high priest Ananias went down to
Caesarea with some of the elders and a lawyer named
Tertullus, and they brought their charges against Paul before the
governor. 2When Paul was called in, Tertullus presented his case
before Felix: "We have enjoyed a long period of peace under you,
and your foresight has brought about reforms in this nation.
3Everywhere and in every way, most excellent Felix, we acknowledge this with profound gratitude. 4But in order not to weary you
further, I would request that you be kind enough to hear us briefly.
5"We have found this man to be a troublemaker, stirring up
riots among the Jews all over the world. He is a ringleader of the
Nazarene sect 6and even tried to desecrate the temple; so we
seized him. 8By[g] examining him yourself you will be able to learn
the truth about all these charges we are bringing against him."
9The Jews joined in the accusation, asserting that these things
were true.
10When the governor motioned for him to speak, Paul replied:
"I know that for a number of years you have been a judge over this
nation; so I gladly make my defense. 11You can easily verify that
no more than twelve days ago I went up to Jerusalem to worship.
12My accusers did not find me arguing with anyone at the temple,
or stirring up a crowd in the synagogues or anywhere else in the
city. 13And they cannot prove to you the charges they are now
making against me. 14However, I admit that I worship the God of

NIV [g] 6-8 Some manuscripts *him and wanted to judge him according to our law.* [7]*But the commander, Lysias, came and with the use of much force snatched him from our hands* [8]*and ordered his accusers to come before you. By*

## King James

14But this I confess unto thee, that after the way which they call heresy, so worship I the God of my fathers, believing all things which are written in the law and in the prophets:
15And have hope toward God, which they themselves also allow, that there shall be a resurrection of the dead, both of the just and unjust.
16And herein do I exercise myself, to have always a conscience void of offence toward God, and *toward* men.
17Now after many years I came to bring alms to my nation, and offerings.
18Whereupon certain Jews from Asia found me purified in the temple, neither with multitude, nor with tumult.
19Who ought to have been here before thee, and object, if they had aught against me.
20Or else let these same *here* say, if they have found any evil doing in me, while I stood before the council,
21Except it be for this one voice, that I cried standing among them, Touching the resurrection of the dead I am called in question by you this day.
22And when Felix heard these things, having more perfect knowledge of *that* way, he deferred them, and said, When Lysias the chief captain shall come down, I will know the uttermost of your matter.
23And he commanded a centurion to keep Paul, and to let *him* have liberty, and that he should forbid none of his acquaintance to minister or come unto him.
24And after certain days, when Felix came with his wife Drusilla, which was a Jewess, he sent for Paul, and heard him concerning the faith in Christ.
25And as he reasoned of righteousness, temperance, and judgment to come, Felix trembled, and answered, Go thy way for this time; when I have a convenient season, I will call for thee.
26He hoped also that money should have been given him of Paul, that he might loose him: wherefore he sent for him the oftener, and communed with him.
27But after two years Porcius Festus came into Felix' room: and Felix, willing to show the Jews a pleasure, left Paul bound.

25 NOW WHEN Festus was come into the province, after three days he ascended from Caesarea to Jerusalem.
2Then the high priest and the chief of the Jews informed him against Paul, and besought him,
3And desired favour against him, that he would send for him to Jerusalem, laying wait in the way to kill him.
4But Festus answered, that Paul should be kept at Caesarea, and that he himself would depart shortly *thither*.
5Let them therefore, said he, which among you are able, go down with *me*, and accuse this man, if there be any wickedness in him.
6And when he had tarried among them more than ten days, he went down unto Caesarea; and the next day sitting on the judgment seat commanded Paul to be brought.

## Amplified

14But this I confess to you, however, that in accordance with the Way [of the Lord], which they call (an heretical, division-producing) sect, I worship (serve) the God of our fathers, still persuaded of the truth of *and* believing *and* placing full confidence in everything laid down in the Law [of Moses] *or* written in the prophets;
15Having [the same] hope in God which these themselves hold *and* look for, that there is to be a resurrection both of the righteous and the unrighteous—the just and the unjust.
16Therefore I always exercise *and* discipline myself—mortifying my body [deadening my carnal affections, bodily appetites and worldly desires], endeavoring in all respects—to have a clear (unshaken, blameless) conscience, void of offense toward God and toward men.
17Now after several years I came up to bring my race contributions of charity and offerings.
18While I was engaged in presenting these, they found me [occupied in the rites of purification] in the temple, without any crowd or uproar. But some Jews from [the province of] Asia [were there],
19Who ought to be here before you and to present their charges, if they have anything against me.
20Or else let these men themselves tell of what crime *or* wrongdoing they found me guilty when I appeared before the council [Sanhedrin],
21Unless it be this one sentence which I cried out as I stood among them, In regard to the resurrection of the dead I am indicted *and* on trial before you this day!
22But Felix, having a rather accurate understanding of the Way [of the Lord], put them off *and* adjourned the trial, saying, When Lysias the commandant comes down, I will determine your case more fully.
23Then he ordered the centurion to keep [Paul] in custody, but to treat him with indulgence—giving him some liberty—and not to hinder his friends from ministering to his needs *and* serving him.
24Some days later Felix came with his wife Drusilla, who was a Jewess; and he sent for Paul and listened to him [talk] about faith in Christ Jesus.
25But as he continued to argue about uprightness, purity of life—the control of the passions—and the judgment to come, Felix became alarmed *and* terrified and said, Go away for the present; when I have a convenient opportunity I will send for you.
26At the same time he hoped to get money from Paul, for which reason he continued to send for him, and was in his company *and* conversed with him often.
27But when two years had gone by, Felix was succeeded in office by Porcius Festus, and wishing to gain favor with the Jews, Felix left Paul still a prisoner in chains.

25 NOW WHEN Festus had entered into his own province, after three days he went up from Caesarea to Jerusalem.
2And [there] the chief priests and the principal men of the Jews laid charges before him against Paul, and they kept begging *and* urging him,
3Asking as a favor that he would have him brought to Jerusalem; [meanwhile] they were planning an ambush to slay him on the way.
4Festus answered that Paul was in custody in Caesarea and that he himself planned to leave for there soon.
5So, said he, let those who are in a position of authority *and* are influential among you go down with me, and if there is anything amiss *or* criminal about the man, let them so charge him.
6So when Festus had remained among them not more than eight or ten days, he went down to Caesarea, took his seat next day on the judgment bench and ordered Paul to be brought before him.

## New American Standard

14"But this I admit to you, that according to the Way which they call a sect I do serve the God of our fathers, believing everything that is in accordance with the Law, and that is written in the Prophets;

15having a hope in God, which these men cherish themselves, that there shall certainly be a resurrection of both the righteous and the wicked.

16"In view of this, I also do my best to maintain always a blameless conscience *both* before God and before men.

17"Now after several years I came to bring [a]alms to my nation and to present offerings;

18in which they found me *occupied* in the temple, having been purified, without *any* crowd or uproar. But *there were* certain Jews from Asia—

19who ought to have been present before you, and to make accusation, if they should have anything against me.

20"Or else let these men themselves tell what misdeed they found when I stood before the Council,

21other than for this one statement which I shouted out while standing among them, 'For the resurrection of the dead I am on trial before you today.'"

22¶ But Felix, having a more exact knowledge about the Way, put them off, saying, "When Lysias the [b]commander comes down, I will decide your case."

23And he gave orders to the centurion for him to be kept in custody and *yet* have *some* freedom, and not to prevent any of his friends from ministering to him.

24¶ But some days later, Felix arrived with Drusilla, his wife who was a Jewess, and sent for Paul, and heard him *speak* about faith in Christ Jesus.

25And as he was discussing righteousness, self-control and the judgment to come, Felix became frightened and said, "Go away for the present, and when I find time, I will summon you."

26At the same time too, he was hoping that money would be given him by Paul; therefore he also used to send for him quite often and converse with him.

27But after two years had passed, Felix was succeeded by Porcius Festus; and wishing to do the Jews a favor, Felix left Paul imprisoned.

*Paul before Festus*

**25** FESTUS THEREFORE, having arrived in the province, three days later went up to Jerusalem from Caesarea.

2And the chief priests and the leading men of the Jews brought charges against Paul; and they were urging him,

3requesting a concession against Paul, that he might have him brought to Jerusalem (*at the same time*, setting an ambush to kill him on the way).

4Festus then answered that Paul was being kept in custody at Caesarea and that he himself was about to leave shortly.

5"Therefore," he *said, "let the influential men among you go there with me, and if there is anything wrong about the man, let them prosecute him."

6¶ And after he had spent not more than eight or ten days among them, he went down to Caesarea; and on the next day he took his seat on the tribunal and ordered Paul to be brought.

NAS [a] Or, *gifts to charity* [b] I.e., chiliarch, in command of one thousand troops

## New International

our fathers as a follower of the Way, which they call a sect. I believe
everything that agrees with the Law and that is written in the
Prophets, 15and I have the same hope in God as these men, that
there will be a resurrection of both the righteous and the wicked.
16So I strive always to keep my conscience clear before God and
man.

17"After an absence of several years, I came to Jerusalem to
bring my people gifts for the poor and to present offerings. 18I was
ceremonially clean when they found me in the temple courts doing
this. There was no crowd with me, nor was I involved in any
disturbance. 19But there are some Jews from the province of Asia,
who ought to be here before you and bring charges if they have
anything against me. 20Or these who are here should state what
crime they found in me when I stood before the Sanhedrin—
21unless it was this one thing I shouted as I stood in their presence:
'It is concerning the resurrection of the dead that I am on trial
before you today.'"

22Then Felix, who was well acquainted with the Way, adjourned the proceedings. "When Lysias the commander comes,"
he said, "I will decide your case." 23He ordered the centurion to
keep Paul under guard but to give him some freedom and permit
his friends to take care of his needs.

24Several days later Felix came with his wife Drusilla, who was
a Jewess. He sent for Paul and listened to him as he spoke about
faith in Christ Jesus. 25As Paul discoursed on righteousness, self-control and the judgment to come, Felix was afraid and said,
"That's enough for now! You may leave. When I find it convenient, I will send for you." 26At the same time he was hoping that
Paul would offer him a bribe, so he sent for him frequently and
talked with him.

27When two years had passed, Felix was succeeded by Porcius
Festus, but because Felix wanted to grant a favor to the Jews, he
left Paul in prison.

*The Trial Before Festus*

**25** THREE DAYS after arriving in the province, Festus went
up from Caesarea to Jerusalem, 2where the chief priests
and Jewish leaders appeared before him and presented the charges
against Paul. 3They urgently requested Festus, as a favor to them,
to have Paul transferred to Jerusalem, for they were preparing an
ambush to kill him along the way. 4Festus answered, "Paul is
being held at Caesarea, and I myself am going there soon. 5Let
some of your leaders come with me and press charges against the
man there, if he has done anything wrong."

6After spending eight or ten days with them, he went down to
Caesarea, and the next day he convened the court and ordered that
Paul be brought before him. 7When Paul appeared, the Jews who

## King James

7And when he was come, the Jews which came down from Jerusalem stood round about, and laid many and grievous complaints against Paul, which they could not prove.

8While he answered for himself, Neither against the law of the Jews, neither against the temple, nor yet against Caesar, have I offended any thing at all.

9But Festus, willing to do the Jews a pleasure, answered Paul, and said, Wilt thou go up to Jerusalem, and there be judged of these things before me?

10Then said Paul, I stand at Caesar's judgment seat, where I ought to be judged: to the Jews have I done no wrong, as thou very well knowest.

11For if I be an offender, or have committed any thing worthy of death, I refuse not to die: but if there be none of these things whereof these accuse me, no man may deliver me unto them. I appeal unto Caesar.

12Then Festus, when he had conferred with the council, answered, Hast thou appealed unto Caesar? unto Caesar shalt thou go.

13And after certain days king Agrippa and Bernice came unto Caesarea to salute Festus.

14And when they had been there many days, Festus declared Paul's cause unto the king, saying, There is a certain man left in bonds by Felix:

15About whom, when I was at Jerusalem, the chief priests and the elders of the Jews informed *me,* desiring *to have* judgment against him.

16To whom I answered, It is not the manner of the Romans to deliver any man to die, before that he which is accused have the accusers face to face, and have licence to answer for himself concerning the crime laid against him.

17Therefore, when they were come hither, without any delay on the morrow I sat on the judgment seat, and commanded the man to be brought forth.

18Against whom when the accusers stood up, they brought none accusation of such things as I supposed:

19But had certain questions against him of their own superstition, and of one Jesus, which was dead, whom Paul affirmed to be alive.

20And because I doubted of such manner of questions, I asked *him* whether he would go to Jerusalem, and there be judged of these matters.

21But when Paul had appealed to be reserved unto the hearing of Augustus, I commanded him to be kept till I might send him to Caesar.

22Then Agrippa said unto Festus, I would also hear the man myself. Tomorrow, said he, thou shalt hear him.

23And on the morrow, when Agrippa was come, and Bernice, with great pomp, and was entered into the place of hearing, with the chief captains, and principal men of the city, at Festus' commandment Paul was brought forth.

24And Festus said, King Agrippa, and all men which are here present with us, ye see this man, about whom all the multitude of the Jews have dealt with me, both at Jerusalem, and *also* here, crying that he ought not to live any longer.

25But when I found that he had committed nothing worthy of death, and that he himself hath appealed to Augustus, I have determined to send him.

26Of whom I have no certain thing to write unto my lord. Wherefore I have brought him forth before you, and specially before thee, O king Agrippa, that, after examination had, I might have somewhat to write.

27For it seemeth to me unreasonable to send a prisoner, and not withal to signify the crimes *laid* against him.

## Amplified

7And when he arrived, the Jews who had come down from Jerusalem stood all around him, bringing many grave accusations against him which they were not able to prove.

8Paul declared in [his own] defense, Neither against the Law of the Jews, nor against the temple, nor against Caesar have I offended in any way.

9But Festus, wishing to ingratiate himself with the Jews, answered Paul, Are you willing to go up to Jerusalem, and there be put on trial [ [a]before the Jewish Sanhedrin] in my presence concerning these charges?

10But Paul replied, I am standing before Caesar's judgment seat, where I ought to be tried. To the Jews I have done no wrong, as you know [b]better [than your question implies].

11If then I am a wrongdoer *and* a criminal, and have committed anything for which I deserve to die, I do not beg off *and* seek to escape death; but if there is no ground for their accusations against me, no one can give me up *and* [c]make a present of me to them. I appeal to Caesar.

12Then Festus, when he had consulted with the [ [d]men who formed his] council, answered, You have appealed to Caesar; to Caesar you shall go.

13Now after an interval of some days, Agrippa the king and Bernice arrived at Caesarea to pay their respects to Festus—to welcome him and wish him well.

14And while they remained there for many days, Festus acquainted the king with Paul's case, telling him, There is a man left a prisoner in chains by Felix;

15And when I was at Jerusalem, the chief priests and the elders of the Jews informed me about him, petitioning for a judicial hearing *and* condemnation of him.

16But I replied to them that it was not the custom of the Romans to give up freely any man for punishment before the accused had met the accusers face to face, and had opportunity to defend himself concerning the charge brought against him.

17So when they came here together, I did not delay, but on the morrow took my place on the judgment seat and ordered that the man be brought before me.

18[But] when the accusers stood up, they brought forward no accusation [in his case] of any such misconduct as I was expecting.

19Instead they had some points of controversy with him about their own religion *or* superstition and concerning one Jesus, Who had died, but Whom Paul kept asserting [over and over] to be alive.

20And I, being puzzled to know how to make inquiries into such questions, asked whether he would be willing to go to Jerusalem and there be tried regarding them.

21But when Paul had appealed to have his case retained for examination *and* decision by the emperor, I ordered that he be detained until I could send him to Caesar.

22Then Agrippa said to Festus, I am also desiring to hear the man myself. Tomorrow, [Festus] replied, you shall hear him.

23So the next day Agrippa and Bernice approached with great display, and they went into the audience hall accompanied by the military commandants and the prominent citizens of the city. At the order of Festus Paul was brought in.

24Then Festus said, King Agrippa and all the men present with us, you see this man about whom the whole Jewish people came to me *and* complained, both at Jerusalem and here, insisting *and* shouting that he ought not to live any longer.

25But I found nothing that he had done deserving of death. Still, as he himself appealed to the emperor, I determined to send him to Rome.

26[However] I have nothing in particular *and* definite to write to my lord concerning him. So I have brought him before you all, and especially before you, King Agrippa, that, after [further] examination has been made, I may have something to put in writing.

27For it seems to me senseless *and* absurd to send a prisoner and not state the accusations against him.

**AMP** [a] Vincent. [b] Vincent. [c] Abbott-Smith: "bestow, give freely."
[d] Vincent.

## New American Standard

[7]And after he had arrived, the Jews who had come down from Jerusalem stood around him, bringing many and serious charges against him which they could not prove;

[8]while Paul said in his own defense, "I have committed no offense either against the Law of the Jews or against the temple or against Caesar."

[9]But Festus, wishing to do the Jews a favor, answered Paul and said, "Are you willing to go up to Jerusalem and stand trial before me on these *charges?*"

[10]But Paul said, "I am standing before Caesar's tribunal, where I ought to be tried. I have done no wrong to *the* Jews, as you also very well know.

[11]"If then I am a wrongdoer, and have committed anything worthy of death, I do not refuse to die; but if none of those things is *true* of which these men accuse me, no one can hand me over to them. I appeal to Caesar."

[12]Then when Festus had conferred with his council, he answered, "You have appealed to Caesar, to Caesar you shall go."

**13**¶ Now when several days had elapsed, King Agrippa and Bernice arrived at Caesarea, and paid their respects to Festus.

[14]And while they were spending many days there, Festus laid Paul's case before the king, saying, "There is a certain man left a prisoner by Felix;

[15]and when I was at Jerusalem, the chief priests and the elders of the Jews brought charges against him, asking for a sentence of condemnation upon him.

[16]"And I answered them that it is not the custom of the Romans to hand over any man before the accused meets his accusers face to face, and has an opportunity to make his defense against the charges.

[17]"And so after they had assembled here, I made no delay, but on the next day took my seat on the tribunal, and ordered the man to be brought.

[18]"And when the accusers stood up, they *began* bringing charges against him not of such crimes as I was expecting;

[19]but they *simply* had some points of disagreement with him about their own religion and about a certain dead man, Jesus, whom Paul asserted to be alive.

[20]"And being at a loss how to investigate such matters, I asked whether he was willing to go to Jerusalem and there stand trial on these matters.

[21]"But when Paul appealed to be held in custody for [e]the Emperor's decision, I ordered him to be kept in custody until I send him to Caesar."

[22]And Agrippa *said* to Festus, "I also would like to hear the man myself." "Tomorrow," he *said, "you shall hear him."

*Paul before Agrippa*

**23**¶ And so, on the next day when Agrippa had come together with Bernice, amid great pomp, and had entered the auditorium [f]accompanied by the commanders and the prominent men of the city, at the command of Festus, Paul was brought in.

[24]And Festus *said, "King Agrippa, and all you gentlemen here present with us, you behold this man about whom all the people of the Jews appealed to me, both at Jerusalem and here, loudly declaring that he ought not to live any longer.

[25]"But I found that he had committed nothing worthy of death; and since he himself appealed to the Emperor, I decided to send him.

[26]"Yet I have nothing definite about him to write to my lord. Therefore I have brought him before you *all* and especially before you, King Agrippa, so that after the investigation has taken place, I may have something to write.

[27]"For it seems absurd to me in sending a prisoner, not to indicate also the charges against him."

**NAS** [e] Lit., *the Augustus'* (in this case Nero) [f] Lit., *and with*

## New International

had come down from Jerusalem stood around him, bringing many serious charges against him, which they could not prove.

[8]Then Paul made his defense: "I have done nothing wrong against the law of the Jews or against the temple or against Caesar."

[9]Festus, wishing to do the Jews a favor, said to Paul, "Are you willing to go up to Jerusalem and stand trial before me there on these charges?"

[10]Paul answered: "I am now standing before Caesar's court, where I ought to be tried. I have not done any wrong to the Jews, as you yourself know very well. [11]If, however, I am guilty of doing anything deserving death, I do not refuse to die. But if the charges brought against me by these Jews are not true, no one has the right to hand me over to them. I appeal to Caesar!"

[12]After Festus had conferred with his council, he declared: "You have appealed to Caesar. To Caesar you will go!"

*Festus Consults King Agrippa*

[13]A few days later King Agrippa and Bernice arrived at Caesarea to pay their respects to Festus. [14]Since they were spending many days there, Festus discussed Paul's case with the king. He said: "There is a man here whom Felix left as a prisoner. [15]When I went to Jerusalem, the chief priests and elders of the Jews brought charges against him and asked that he be condemned.

[16]"I told them that it is not the Roman custom to hand over any man before he has faced his accusers and has had an opportunity to defend himself against their charges. [17]When they came here with me, I did not delay the case, but convened the court the next day and ordered the man to be brought in. [18]When his accusers got up to speak, they did not charge him with any of the crimes I had expected. [19]Instead, they had some points of dispute with him about their own religion and about a dead man named Jesus who Paul claimed was alive. [20]I was at a loss how to investigate such matters; so I asked if he would be willing to go to Jerusalem and stand trial there on these charges. [21]When Paul made his appeal to be held over for the Emperor's decision, I ordered him held until I could send him to Caesar."

[22]Then Agrippa said to Festus, "I would like to hear this man myself."

He replied, "Tomorrow you will hear him."

*Paul Before Agrippa*

[23]The next day Agrippa and Bernice came with great pomp and entered the audience room with the high ranking officers and the leading men of the city. At the command of Festus, Paul was brought in. [24]Festus said: "King Agrippa, and all who are present with us, you see this man! The whole Jewish community has petitioned me about him in Jerusalem and here in Caesarea, shouting that he ought not to live any longer. [25]I found he had done nothing deserving of death, but because he made his appeal to the Emperor I decided to send him to Rome. [26]But I have nothing definite to write to His Majesty about him. Therefore I have brought him before all of you, and especially before you, King Agrippa, so that as a result of this investigation I may have something to write. [27]For I think it is unreasonable to send on a prisoner without specifying the charges against him."

## King James

**26** THEN AGRIPPA said unto Paul, Thou art permitted to speak for thyself. Then Paul stretched forth the hand, and answered for himself:

2 I think myself happy, king Agrippa, because I shall answer for myself this day before thee touching all the things whereof I am accused of the Jews:

3 Especially *because I know* thee to be expert in all customs and questions which are among the Jews: wherefore I beseech thee to hear me patiently.

4 My manner of life from my youth, which was at the first among mine own nation at Jerusalem, know all the Jews;

5 Which knew me from the beginning, if they would testify, that after the most straitest sect of our religion I lived a Pharisee.

6 And now I stand and am judged for the hope of the promise made of God unto our fathers:

7 Unto which *promise* our twelve tribes, instantly serving *God* day and night, hope to come. For which hope's sake, king Agrippa, I am accused of the Jews.

8 Why should it be thought a thing incredible with you, that God should raise the dead?

9 I verily thought with myself, that I ought to do many things contrary to the name of Jesus of Nazareth.

10 Which thing I also did in Jerusalem: and many of the saints did I shut up in prison, having received authority from the chief priests; and when they were put to death, I gave my voice against *them*.

11 And I punished them oft in every synagogue, and compelled *them* to blaspheme; and being exceedingly mad against them, I persecuted *them* even unto strange cities.

12 Whereupon as I went to Damascus with authority and commission from the chief priests,

13 At midday, O king, I saw in the way a light from heaven, above the brightness of the sun, shining round about me and them which journeyed with me.

14 And when we were all fallen to the earth, I heard a voice speaking unto me, and saying in the Hebrew tongue, Saul, Saul, why persecutest thou me? *it is* hard for thee to kick against the pricks.

15 And I said, Who art thou, Lord? And he said, I am Jesus whom thou persecutest.

16 But rise, and stand upon thy feet: for I have appeared unto thee for this purpose, to make thee a minister and a witness both of these things which thou hast seen, and of those things in the which I will appear unto thee;

17 Delivering thee from the people, and *from* the Gentiles, unto whom now I send thee,

18 To open their eyes, *and* to turn *them* from darkness to light, and *from* the power of Satan unto God, that they may receive forgiveness of sins, and inheritance among them which are sanctified by faith that is in me.

19 Whereupon, O king Agrippa, I was not disobedient unto the heavenly vision:

20 But showed first unto them of Damascus, and at Jerusalem, and throughout all the coasts of Judaea, and *then* to the Gentiles, that they should repent and turn to God, and do works meet for repentance.

21 For these causes the Jews caught me in the temple, and went about to kill *me*.

## Amplified

**26** THEN AGRIPPA said to Paul, You are permitted to speak on your own behalf. At that Paul stretched forth his hand and made his defense [as follows]:

2 I consider myself fortunate, King Agrippa, that it is before you that I am to make my defense today in regard to all the charges brought against me by [the] Jews,

3 [Especially] because you are so fully *and* unusually conversant with all [the] Jewish customs and controversies; therefore, I beg you to hear me patiently.

4 My behavior *and* manner of living from my youth up is known by all the Jews; [they are aware] that from [its] commencement my youth was spent among my own race in Jerusalem.

5 They have had knowledge of me for a long time, if they are willing to testify to it, that in accordance with the [very] strictest sect of our religion I have lived as a Pharisee.

6 And now I stand here on trial (to be judged on the ground) of the hope of that promise made to our forefathers by God, [See Acts 13:32, 33.]

7 Which hope [of the Messiah and the resurrection] our twelve tribes confidently expect to realize, as they fervently worship (without ceasing) night and day. And for that hope, O king, I am accused by Jews *and* as a criminal!

8 Why is it thought incredible by any of you that God raises the dead?

9 I myself indeed was [once] persuaded that it was my duty to do many things contrary to *and* in defiance of the name of Jesus of Nazareth.

10 And that is what I did in Jerusalem; I [not only] shut up many of the faithful holy ones in prison by virtue of authority received from the chief priests, but when they were being condemned to death I cast my vote against them.

11 And frequently I punished them in all the synagogues to make them blaspheme; and in my bitter fury against them, I harassed (troubled, molested, persecuted) *and* pursued them even to foreign cities.

12 Thus engaged I proceeded to Damascus with the authority and orders of the chief priests,

13 When on the road at midday, O king, I saw a light from heaven surpassing the brightness of the sun, flashing about me and those who were traveling with me.

14 And when we had all fallen to the ground, I heard a voice in the Hebrew tongue saying to me, Saul, Saul, why do you continue to persecute Me—to harass and trouble and molest Me? It is dangerous *and* turns out badly for you to keep kicking against the goads—[that is,] to offer vain and perilous resistance.

15 And I said, Who are You, Lord? And the Lord said, I am Jesus Whom you are persecuting.

16 But arise and stand upon your feet; for I have appeared to you for this purpose, that I might appoint you to serve as [My] minister and to bear witness both to what you have seen of Me and to that in which I will appear to you,

17 [a]Choosing you out (selecting you for Myself) *and* [b]delivering you from among this [Jewish] people and the Gentiles to whom I am sending you, [Ezek. 2:1, 3.]

18 To open their eyes, that they may turn from darkness to light, and from the power of Satan to God, so that they may thus receive forgiveness *and* release from their sins and a place *and* portion among those who are consecrated *and* purified by faith in me. [Isa. 42:7, 16.]

19 Wherefore, O King Agrippa, I was not disobedient unto the heavenly vision,

20 But made known openly first of all to those at Damascus, then at Jerusalem and throughout the whole land of Judea, and also among the Gentiles, that they should repent and turn to God and do works *and* live lives consistent with *and* worthy of their repentance.

21 Because of these things the Jews seized me in the temple [c]enclosure and tried to do away with me.

**AMP** [a] Thayer. [b] Abbott-Smith. [c] Trench.

## New American Standard

*Paul's Defense before Agrippa*

**26** AND AGRIPPA said to Paul, "You are permitted to speak
for yourself." Then Paul stretched out his hand and *proceeded* to make his defense:
2¶ "In regard to all the things of which I am accused by the
Jews, I consider myself fortunate, King Agrippa, that I am about
to make my defense before you today;
3especially because you are an expert in all customs and questions among *the* Jews; therefore I beg you to listen to me patiently.
4"So then, all Jews know my manner of life from my youth up,
which from the beginning was spent among my *own* nation and
at Jerusalem;
5since they have known about me for a long time previously,
if they are willing to testify, that I lived *as* a Pharisee according to
the strictest sect of our religion.
6"And now I am standing trial for the hope of the promise
made by God to our fathers;
7 *the promise* to which our twelve tribes hope to attain, as they
earnestly serve *God* night and day. And for this hope, O King, I
am being accused by Jews.
8"Why is it considered incredible among you *people* if God does
raise the dead?
9"So then, I thought to myself that I had to do many things
hostile to the name of Jesus of Nazareth.
10"And this is just what I did in Jerusalem; not only did I lock
up many of the saints in prisons, having received authority from
the chief priests, but also when they were being put to death I cast
my vote against them.
11"And as I punished them often in all the synagogues, I tried
to force them to blaspheme; and being furiously enraged at them,
I kept pursuing them even to foreign cities.
12"While thus engaged as I was journeying to Damascus with
the authority and commission of the chief priests,
13at midday, O King, I saw on the way a light from heaven,
brighter than the sun, shining all around me and those who were
journeying with me.
14"And when we had all fallen to the ground, I heard a voice
saying to me in the Hebrew dialect, 'Saul, Saul, why are you
persecuting Me? It is hard for you to kick against the goads.'
15"And I said, 'Who art Thou, Lord?' And the Lord said, 'I am
Jesus whom you are persecuting.
16'But arise, and stand on your feet; for this purpose I have
appeared to you, to appoint you a minister and a witness not only
to the things which you have seen, but also to the things in which
I will appear to you;
17delivering you from the *Jewish* people and from the Gentiles,
to whom I am sending you,
18to open their eyes so that they may turn from darkness to light
and from the dominion of Satan to God, in order that they may
receive forgiveness of sins and an inheritance among those who
have been sanctified by faith in Me.'
19"Consequently, King Agrippa, I did not prove disobedient to
the heavenly vision,
20but *kept* declaring both to those of Damascus first, and *also* at
Jerusalem and *then* throughout all the region of Judea, and *even* to
the Gentiles, that they should repent and turn to God, performing
deeds appropriate to repentance.
21"For this reason *some* Jews seized me in the temple and tried
to put me to death.

## New International

**26** THEN AGRIPPA said to Paul, "You have permission to
speak for yourself."
So Paul motioned with his hand and began his defense: 2"King
Agrippa, I consider myself fortunate to stand before you today as
I make my defense against all the accusations of the Jews, 3and
especially so because you are well acquainted with all the Jewish
customs and controversies. Therefore, I beg you to listen to me
patiently.
4"The Jews all know the way I have lived ever since I was a
child, from the beginning of my life in my own country, and also
in Jerusalem. 5They have known me for a long time and can testify,
if they are willing, that according to the strictest sect of our religion, I lived as a Pharisee. 6And now it is because of my hope in
what God has promised our fathers that I am on trial today. 7This
is the promise our twelve tribes are hoping to see fulfilled as they
earnestly serve God day and night. O king, it is because of this
hope that the Jews are accusing me. 8Why should any of you
consider it incredible that God raises the dead?
9"I too was convinced that I ought to do all that was possible
to oppose the name of Jesus of Nazareth. 10And that is just what
I did in Jerusalem. On the authority of the chief priests I put many
of the saints in prison, and when they were put to death, I cast my
vote against them. 11Many a time I went from one synagogue to
another to have them punished, and I tried to force them to blaspheme. In my obsession against them, I even went to foreign cities
to persecute them.
12"On one of these journeys I was going to Damascus with the
authority and commission of the chief priests. 13About noon, O
king, as I was on the road, I saw a light from heaven, brighter than
the sun, blazing around me and my companions. 14We all fell to
the ground, and I heard a voice saying to me in Aramaic,[d] 'Saul,
Saul, why do you persecute me? It is hard for you to kick against
the goads.'
15"Then I asked, 'Who are you, Lord?'
"'I am Jesus, whom you are persecuting,' the Lord replied.
16'Now get up and stand on your feet. I have appeared to you to
appoint you as a servant and as a witness of what you have seen
of me and what I will show you. 17I will rescue you from your own
people and from the Gentiles. I am sending you to them 18to open
their eyes and turn them from darkness to light, and from the
power of Satan to God, so that they may receive forgiveness of sins
and a place among those who are sanctified by faith in me.'
19"So then, King Agrippa, I was not disobedient to the vision
from heaven. 20First to those in Damascus, then to those in Jerusalem and in all Judea, and to the Gentiles also, I preached that they
should repent and turn to God and prove their repentance by their
deeds. 21That is why the Jews seized me in the temple courts and
tried to kill me. 22But I have had God's help to this very day, and

NIV [d] 14 Or *Hebrew*

## King James

22Having therefore obtained help of God, I continue unto this day, witnessing both to small and great, saying none other things than those which the prophets and Moses did say should come:

23That Christ should suffer, *and* that he should be the first that should rise from the dead, and should show light unto the people, and to the Gentiles.

24And as he thus spake for himself, Festus said with a loud voice, Paul, thou art beside thyself; much learning doth make thee mad.

25But he said, I am not mad, most noble Festus; but speak forth the words of truth and soberness.

26For the king knoweth of these things, before whom also I speak freely: for I am persuaded that none of these things are hidden from him; for this thing was not done in a corner.

27King Agrippa, believest thou the prophets? I know that thou believest.

28Then Agrippa said unto Paul, Almost thou persuadest me to be a Christian.

29And Paul said, I would to God, that not only thou, but also all that hear me this day, were both almost, and altogether such as I am, except these bonds.

30And when he had thus spoken, the king rose up, and the governor, and Bernice, and they that sat with them:

31And when they were gone aside, they talked between themselves, saying, This man doeth nothing worthy of death or of bonds.

32Then said Agrippa unto Festus, This man might have been set at liberty, if he had not appealed unto Caesar.

**27** AND WHEN it was determined that we should sail into Italy, they delivered Paul and certain other prisoners unto *one* named Julius, a centurion of Augustus' band.

2And entering into a ship of Adramyttium, we launched, meaning to sail by the coasts of Asia; *one* Aristarchus, a Macedonian of Thessalonica, being with us.

3And the next *day* we touched at Sidon. And Julius courteously entreated Paul, and gave *him* liberty to go unto his friends to refresh himself.

4And when we had launched from thence, we sailed under Cyprus, because the winds were contrary.

5And when we had sailed over the sea of Cilicia and Pamphylia, we came to Myra, *a city* of Lycia.

6And there the centurion found a ship of Alexandria sailing into Italy; and he put us therein.

7And when we had sailed slowly many days, and scarce were come over against Cnidus, the wind not suffering us, we sailed under Crete, over against Salmone;

8And, hardly passing it, came unto a place which is called The fair havens; nigh whereunto was the city *of* Lasea.

9Now when much time was spent, and when sailing was now dangerous, because the fast was now already past, Paul admonished *them,*

10And said unto them, Sirs, I perceive that this voyage will be with hurt and much damage, not only of the lading and ship, but also of our lives.

11Nevertheless the centurion believed the master and the owner of the ship, more than those things which were spoken by Paul.

## Amplified

22[But] to this day I have had the help which comes from God (as my [a]ally), and so I stand here testifying to small and great alike, asserting nothing beyond what the prophets and Moses declared would come to pass;

23That the Christ, the Anointed One, must suffer; and that He, by being the first to rise from the dead, would declare *and* show light both to the [Jewish] people and to the Gentiles.

24And as he thus proceeded with his defense, Festus called out loudly, Paul, you are mad! Your great learning is driving you insane!

25But Paul replied, I am not mad, most noble Festus, but I am uttering the straight, sound truth.

26For the king understands about these things well enough, and [therefore] to him I speak with bold frankness *and* confidence. I am convinced that not one of these things has escaped his notice, for all this did not take place in a corner—in secret.

27King Agrippa, do you believe the prophets?—Do you give credence to God's messengers and their words? I perceive *and* know that you do believe.

28Then Agrippa said to Paul, You think it a small task to make a Christian of me—just off hand to induce me with little ado and persuasion, at very short notice.

29And Paul replied, Whether short or long, I would to God that not only you but also all who are listening to me today might become such as I am, except for these chains.

30Then the king arose, and the governor and Bernice and all those who were seated with them;

31And after they had gone out, they said to one another, This man is doing nothing deserving of death or [even] of imprisonment.

32And Agrippa said to Festus, This man could have been set at liberty, if he had not appealed to Caesar.

**27** NOW WHEN it was determined that we should sail for Italy, they turned Paul and some other prisoners over to a centurion of the imperial regiment, named Julius.

2And going aboard a ship of Adramyttium, which was about to sail for the ports along the coast of [the province of] Asia, we put out to sea, and Aristarchus, a Macedonian from Thessalonica, accompanied us.

3The following day we landed at Sidon, and Julius treated Paul in a man-loving way, with much consideration (kindness and care), permitting him to go to his friends [there] and be refreshed *and* be cared for.

4After putting to sea from there we passed to the leeward [south side] of Cyprus [for protection], for the winds were contrary to us.

5And when we had sailed over [the whole length] of sea which lies off Cilicia and Pamphylia, we reached Myra in Lycia.

6There the centurion found an Alexandrian ship bound for Italy, and he transferred us to it.

7For a number of days we made slow progress, and arrived with difficulty off Cnidus; then, as the wind did not permit us to proceed, we went under the lee (shelter) of Crete off Salmone,

8And coasting along it with difficulty, we arrived at a place called Fair Havens, near which is located the town of Lasea.

9But [as the season was well advanced], for much time had been lost and navigation was already dangerous, for the time for the Fast [the day of Atonement, about the middle of September] had already gone by, Paul warned *and* advised them,

10Saying, Sirs, I perceive [after careful observation] that this voyage will be attended with disaster and much heavy loss, not only of the cargo and the ship but of our lives also.

11However, the centurion paid greater attention to the pilot and to the owner of the ship than to what Paul said.

AMP [a] Cf. Abbott-Smith.

## New American Standard

22"And so, having obtained help from God, I stand to this day testifying both to small and great, stating nothing but what the Prophets and Moses said was going to take place;

23that the Christ was to suffer, *and* that by reason of *His* resurrection from the dead He should be the first to proclaim light both to the *Jewish* people and to the Gentiles."

24¶ And while *Paul* was saying this in his defense, Festus *said in a loud voice, "Paul, you are out of your mind! *Your* great learning is driving you mad."

25But Paul *said, "I am not out of my mind, most excellent Festus, but I utter words of sober truth.

26"For the king knows about these matters, and I speak to him also with confidence, since I am persuaded that none of these things escape his notice; for this has not been done in a corner.

27"King Agrippa, do you believe the Prophets? I know that you do."

28And Agrippa *replied* to Paul, "In a short time you will persuade me to become a Christian."

29And Paul *said,* "I would to God, that whether in a short or long time, not only you, but also all who hear me this day, might become such as I am, except for these chains."

30¶ And the king arose and the governor and Bernice, and those who were sitting with them,

31and when they had drawn aside, they *began* talking to one another, saying, "This man is not doing anything worthy of death or imprisonment."

32And Agrippa said to Festus, "This man might have been set free if he had not appealed to Caesar."

### *Paul Is Sent to Rome*

**27** AND WHEN it was decided that we should sail for Italy, they proceeded to deliver Paul and some other prisoners to a centurion of the Augustan [b]cohort named Julius.

2And embarking in an Adramyttian ship, which was about to sail to the regions along the coast of Asia, we put out to sea, accompanied by Aristarchus, a Macedonian of Thessalonica.

3And the next day we put in at Sidon; and Julius treated Paul with consideration and allowed him to go to his friends and receive care.

4And from there we put out to sea and sailed under the shelter of Cyprus because the winds were contrary.

5And when we had sailed through the sea along the coast of Cilicia and Pamphylia, we landed at Myra in Lycia.

6And there the centurion found an Alexandrian ship sailing for Italy, and he put us aboard it.

7And when we had sailed slowly for a good many days, and with difficulty had arrived off Cnidus, since the wind did not permit us *to go* farther, we sailed under the shelter of Crete, off Salmone;

8and with difficulty sailing past it we came to a certain place called Fair Havens, near which was the city of Lasea.

9¶ And when considerable time had passed and the voyage was now dangerous, since even the [c]fast was already over, Paul *began* to admonish them,

10and said to them, "Men, I perceive that the voyage will certainly be *attended* with damage and great loss, not only of the cargo and the ship, but also of our lives."

11But the centurion was more persuaded by the pilot and the captain of the ship, than by what was being said by Paul.

## New International

so I stand here and testify to small and great alike. I am saying nothing beyond what the prophets and Moses said would happen— 23that the Christ[d] would suffer and, as the first to rise from the dead, would proclaim light to his own people and to the Gentiles."

24At this point Festus interrupted Paul's defense. "You are out of your mind, Paul!" he shouted. "Your great learning is driving you insane."

25"I am not insane, most excellent Festus," Paul replied. "What I am saying is true and reasonable. 26The king is familiar with these things, and I can speak freely to him. I am convinced that none of this has escaped his notice, because it was not done in a corner. 27King Agrippa, do you believe the prophets? I know you do."

28Then Agrippa said to Paul, "Do you think that in such a short time you can persuade me to be a Christian?"

29Paul replied, "Short time or long—I pray God that not only you but all who are listening to me today may become what I am, except for these chains."

30The king rose, and with him the governor and Bernice and those sitting with them. 31They left the room, and while talking with one another, they said, "This man is not doing anything that deserves death or imprisonment."

32Agrippa said to Festus, "This man could have been set free if he had not appealed to Caesar."

### *Paul Sails for Rome*

**27** WHEN IT was decided that we would sail for Italy, Paul and some other prisoners were handed over to a centurion named Julius, who belonged to the Imperial Regiment. 2We boarded a ship from Adramyttium about to sail for ports along the coast of the province of Asia, and we put out to sea. Aristarchus, a Macedonian from Thessalonica, was with us.

3The next day we landed at Sidon; and Julius, in kindness to Paul, allowed him to go to his friends so they might provide for his needs. 4From there we put out to sea again and passed to the lee of Cyprus because the winds were against us. 5When we had sailed across the open sea off the coast of Cilicia and Pamphylia, we landed at Myra in Lycia. 6There the centurion found an Alexandrian ship sailing for Italy and put us on board. 7We made slow headway for many days and had difficulty arriving off Cnidus. When the wind did not allow us to hold our course, we sailed to the lee of Crete, opposite Salmone. 8We moved along the coast with difficulty and came to a place called Fair Havens, near the town of Lasea.

9Much time had been lost, and sailing had already become dangerous because by now it was after the Fast.[e] So Paul warned them, 10"Men, I can see that our voyage is going to be disastrous and bring great loss to ship and cargo, and to our own lives also." 11But the centurion, instead of listening to what Paul said, followed the advice of the pilot and of the owner of the ship. 12Since

NAS [b] Or, *battalion* [c] I.e., Day of Atonement in September or October

NIV [d] 23 Or *Messiah* [e] 9 That is, the Day of Atonement (Yom Kippur)

## King James

12 And because the haven was not commodious to winter in, the more part advised to depart thence also, if by any means they might attain to Phenice, *and there* to winter; *which is* an haven of Crete, and lieth toward the south west and north west.

13 And when the south wind blew softly, supposing that they had obtained *their* purpose, loosing *thence,* they sailed close by Crete.

14 But not long after there arose against it a tempestuous wind, called Euroclydon.

15 And when the ship was caught, and could not bear up into the wind, we let *her* drive.

16 And running under a certain island which is called Clauda, we had much work to come by the boat:

17 Which when they had taken up, they used helps, undergirding the ship; and, fearing lest they should fall into the quicksands, strake sail, and so were driven.

18 And we being exceedingly tossed with a tempest, the next *day* they lightened the ship;

19 And the third *day* we cast out with our own hands the tackling of the ship.

20 And when neither sun nor stars in many days appeared, and no small tempest lay on *us,* all hope that we should be saved was then taken away.

21 But after long abstinence Paul stood forth in the midst of them, and said, Sirs, ye should have hearkened unto me, and not have loosed from Crete, and to have gained this harm and loss.

22 And now I exhort you to be of good cheer: for there shall be no loss of *any man's* life among you, but of the ship.

23 For there stood by me this night the angel of God, whose I am, and whom I serve,

24 Saying, Fear not, Paul; thou must be brought before Caesar: and, lo, God hath given thee all them that sail with thee.

25 Wherefore, sirs, be of good cheer: for I believe God, that it shall be even as it was told me.

26 Howbeit we must be cast upon a certain island.

27 But when the fourteenth night was come, as we were driven up and down in Adria, about midnight the shipmen deemed that they drew near to some country;

28 And sounded, and found *it* twenty fathoms: and when they had gone a little further, they sounded again, and found *it* fifteen fathoms.

29 Then fearing lest we should have fallen upon rocks, they cast four anchors out of the stern, and wished for the day.

30 And as the shipmen were about to flee out of the ship, when they had let down the boat into the sea, under colour as though they would have cast anchors out of the foreship,

31 Paul said to the centurion and to the soldiers, Except these abide in the ship, ye cannot be saved.

32 Then the soldiers cut off the ropes of the boat, and let her fall off.

33 And while the day was coming on, Paul besought *them* all to take meat, saying, This day is the fourteenth day that ye have tarried and continued fasting, having taken nothing.

34 Wherefore I pray you to take *some* meat: for this is for your health: for there shall not an hair fall from the head of any of you.

35 And when he had thus spoken, he took bread, and gave thanks to God in presence of them all: and when he had broken *it,* he began to eat.

## Amplified

12 And as the harbor was not well situated *and* so unsuitable to winter in, the majority favored the plan of putting to sea again from there, hoping somehow to reach Phoenice, a harbor of Crete facing northeast and southeast, and winter there.

13 So when the south wind blew softly, supposing they were gaining their object, they weighed anchor and sailed along Crete, hugging the coast.

14 But soon afterward a violent wind [of the character of a typhoon] called a northeaster, came bursting down from the island.

15 And when the ship was caught and was unable to head against the wind, we gave up and letting her drift were borne along.

16 We ran under the shelter of a small island called Cauda, where we managed with [much] difficulty to draw the [ship's small] boat on deck *and* secure it.

17 After hoisting it on board, they used supports with ropes to undergird *and* brace the ship; then afraid that they would be driven into the Syrtis [quicksands off the north coast of Africa], they lowered the gear [sails and ropes], and so were driven along.

18 As we were being dangerously tossed about by the violence of the storm, the next day they began to throw the freight overboard;

19 And the third day they threw out with their own hands the ship's equipment—the tackle *and* the furniture.

20 And when neither sun nor stars were visible for many days, and no small tempest kept raging about us, all hope of our being saved was finally abandoned.

21 Then as they had eaten nothing for a long time, Paul came forward into their midst and said, Men, you should have listened to me, and should not have put to sea from Crete and brought on this disaster and harm *and* misery *and* loss.

22 But [even] now I beg you be in good spirits *and* take heart, for there will be no loss of life among you but only of the ship.

23 For this [very] night there stood by my side an angel of the God to Whom I belong and Whom I serve *and* worship,

24 And he said, Do not be frightened, Paul! It is necessary for you to stand before Caesar; and behold, God has given you all those who are sailing with you.

25 So keep up your courage, men, for I have faith—complete confidence—in God that it will be exactly as it was told me;

26 But we shall have to be stranded on some island.

27 The fourteenth night had come and we were drifting *and* being driven about in the Adriatic Sea, when about midnight the sailors began to suspect that they were drawing near to some land.

28 So they took soundings and found twenty fathoms, and a little farther on they sounded again and found fifteen fathoms.

29 Then fearing that we might fall off [our course] onto rocks, they dropped four anchors from the stern, and kept wishing for daybreak to come.

30 And, as the sailors were trying to escape [secretly] from the ship, and were lowering the small boat into the sea, pretending that they were going to lay out anchors from the bow,

31 Paul said to the centurion and the soldiers, Unless these men remain in the ship, you cannot be saved.

32 Then the soldiers cut away the ropes that held the small boat, and let it fall *and* drift away.

33 While they waited until it should become day, Paul entreated them all to take some food, saying, This is the fourteenth day that you have been continually in suspense *and* on the alert without food, having eaten nothing.

34 So I urge you to take some food for your safety—it will give you strength; for not a hair is to perish from the head of any one of you.

35 Having said these words, he took bread, and giving thanks to God before them all he broke it and began to eat.

## New American Standard

12And because the harbor was not suitable for wintering, the majority reached a decision to put out to sea from there, if somehow they could reach Phoenix, a harbor of Crete, facing southwest and northwest, and spend the winter *there.*

13And when a moderate south wind came up, supposing that they had gained their purpose, they weighed anchor and *began* sailing along Crete, close *inshore.*

*Shipwreck*

14But before very long there rushed down from the land a violent wind, called [a]Euraquilo;

15and when the ship was caught *in it,* and could not face the wind, we gave way *to it,* and let ourselves be driven along.

16And running under the shelter of a small island called Clauda, we were scarcely able to get the *ship's* boat under control.

17And after they had hoisted it up, they used supporting cables in undergirding the ship; and fearing that they might run aground on *the shallows* of Syrtis, they let down the sea anchor, and so let themselves be driven along.

18The next day as we were being violently storm-tossed, they began to jettison the cargo;

19and on the third day they threw the ship's tackle overboard with their own hands.

20And since neither sun nor stars appeared for many days, and no small storm was assailing *us,* from then on all hope of our being saved was gradually abandoned.

21And when they had gone a long time without food, then Paul stood up in their midst and said, "Men, you ought to have followed my advice and not to have set sail from Crete, and incurred this damage and loss.

22"And *yet* now I urge you to keep up your courage, for there shall be no loss of life among you, but *only* of the ship.

23"For this very night an angel of the God to whom I belong and whom I serve stood before me,

24saying, 'Do not be afraid, Paul; you must stand before Caesar; and behold, God has granted you all those who are sailing with you.'

25"Therefore, keep up your courage, men, for I believe God, that it will turn out exactly as I have been told.

26"But we must run aground on a certain island."

27¶ But when the fourteenth night had come, as we were being driven about in the Adriatic Sea, about midnight the sailors *began* to surmise that they were approaching some land.

28And they took soundings, and found *it to be* twenty fathoms; and a little farther on they took another sounding and found *it to be* fifteen fathoms.

29And fearing that we might run aground somewhere on the rocks, they cast four anchors from the stern and wished for daybreak.

30And as the sailors were trying to escape from the ship, and had let down the *ship's* boat into the sea, on the pretense of intending to lay out anchors from the bow,

31Paul said to the centurion and to the soldiers, "Unless these men remain in the ship, you yourselves cannot be saved."

32Then the soldiers cut away the ropes of the *ship's* boat, and let it fall away.

33And until the day was about to dawn, Paul was encouraging them all to take some food, saying, "Today is the fourteenth day that you have been constantly watching and going without eating, having taken nothing.

34"Therefore I encourage you to take some food, for this is for your preservation; for not a hair from the head of any of you shall perish."

35And having said this, he took bread and gave thanks to God in the presence of all; and he broke it and began to eat.

**NAS** [a] I.e., a northeaster

## New International

the harbor was unsuitable to winter in, the majority decided that
we should sail on, hoping to reach Phoenix and winter there. This
was a harbor in Crete, facing both southwest and northwest.

*The Storm*

13When a gentle south wind began to blow, they thought they
had obtained what they wanted; so they weighed anchor and
sailed along the shore of Crete.
14Before very long, a wind of
hurricane force, called the "northeaster," swept down from the
island.
15The ship was caught by the storm and could not head into
the wind; so we gave way to it and were driven along.
16As we
passed to the lee of a small island called Cauda, we were hardly
able to make the lifeboat secure.
17When the men had hoisted it
aboard, they passed ropes under the ship itself to hold it together.
Fearing that they would run aground on the sandbars of Syrtis,
they lowered the sea anchor and let the ship be driven along.
18We
took such a violent battering from the storm that the next day they
began to throw the cargo overboard.
19On the third day, they
threw the ship's tackle overboard with their own hands.
20When
neither sun nor stars appeared for many days and the storm continued raging, we finally gave up all hope of being saved.

21After the men had gone a long time without food, Paul stood
up before them and said: "Men, you should have taken my advice
not to sail from Crete; then you would have spared yourselves this
damage and loss.
22But now I urge you to keep up your courage,
because not one of you will be lost; only the ship will be destroyed.
23Last night an angel of the God whose I am and whom I serve
stood beside me
24and said, 'Do not be afraid, Paul. You must
stand trial before Caesar; and God has graciously given you the
lives of all who sail with you.'
25So keep up your courage, men,
for I have faith in God that it will happen just as he told me.
26Nevertheless, we must run aground on some island."

*The Shipwreck*

27On the fourteenth night we were still being driven across the
Adriatic[b] Sea, when about midnight the sailors sensed they were
approaching land.
28They took soundings and found that the
water was a hundred and twenty feet[c] deep. A short time later
they took soundings again and found it was ninety feet[d] deep.
29Fearing that we would be dashed against the rocks, they
dropped four anchors from the stern and prayed for daylight.
30In
an attempt to escape from the ship, the sailors let the lifeboat down
into the sea, pretending they were going to lower some anchors
from the bow.
31Then Paul said to the centurion and the soldiers,
"Unless these men stay with the ship, you cannot be saved."
32So
the soldiers cut the ropes that held the lifeboat and let it fall away.

33Just before dawn Paul urged them all to eat. "For the last
fourteen days," he said, "you have been in constant suspense and
have gone without food—you haven't eaten anything.
34Now I
urge you to take some food. You need it to survive. Not one of you
will lose a single hair from his head."
35After he said this, he took
some bread and gave thanks to God in front of them all. Then he
broke it and began to eat.
36They were all encouraged and ate some

**NIV** [b] *27* In ancient times the name referred to an area extending well south of Italy. [c] *28* Greek *twenty orguias* (about 37 meters) [d] *28* Greek *fifteen orguias* (about 27 meters)

## King James

36Then were they all of good cheer, and they also took *some*
meat.
37And we were in all in the ship two hundred threescore and
sixteen souls.
38And when they had eaten enough, they lightened the ship,
and cast out the wheat into the sea.
39And when it was day, they knew not the land: but they
discovered a certain creek with a shore, into the which they were
minded, if it were possible, to thrust in the ship.
40And when they had taken up the anchors, they committed
*themselves* unto the sea, and loosed the rudder bands, and hoisted
up the mainsail to the wind, and made toward shore.
41And falling into a place where two seas met, they ran the ship
aground; and the forepart stuck fast, and remained unmoveable,
but the hinderpart was broken with the violence of the waves.
42And the soldiers' counsel was to kill the prisoners, lest any of
them should swim out, and escape.
43But the centurion, willing to save Paul, kept them from *their*
purpose; and commanded that they which could swim should cast
*themselves* first *into the sea*, and get to land:
44And the rest, some on boards, and some on *broken pieces* of the
ship. And so it came to pass, that they escaped all safe to land.

**28** AND WHEN they were escaped, then they knew that the
island was called Melita.
2And the barbarous people showed us no little kindness: for
they kindled a fire, and received us every one, because of the
present rain, and because of the cold.
3And when Paul had gathered a bundle of sticks, and laid *them*
on the fire, there came a viper out of the heat, and fastened on his
hand.
4And when the barbarians saw the *venomous* beast hang on his
hand, they said among themselves, No doubt this man is a murderer, whom, though he hath escaped the sea, yet vengeance
suffereth not to live.
5And he shook off the beast into the fire, and felt no harm.
6Howbeit they looked when he should have swollen, or fallen
down dead suddenly: but after they had looked a great while, and
saw no harm come to him, they changed their minds, and said that
he was a god.
7In the same quarters were possessions of the chief man of the
island, whose name was Publius; who received us, and lodged us
three days courteously.
8And it came to pass, that the father of Publius lay sick of a fever
and of a bloody flux: to whom Paul entered in, and prayed, and
laid his hands on him, and healed him.
9So when this was done, others also, which had diseases in the
island, came, and were healed:
10Who also honoured us with many honours; and when we
departed, they laded *us* with such things as were necessary.
11And after three months we departed in a ship of Alexandria,
which had wintered in the isle, whose sign was Castor and Pollux.
12And landing at Syracuse, we tarried *there* three days.
13And from thence we fetched a compass, and came to Rhegium: and after one day the south wind blew, and we came the next
day to Puteoli:

## Amplified

36Then they all became more cheerful *and* were encouraged and
took food themselves.
37All told, there were [a]two hundred and seventy-six souls of us
in the ship.
38And after they had eaten sufficiently, [they proceeded] to
lighten the ship, throwing out the wheat into the sea.
39Now when it was day [and they saw] the land, they did not
recognize [it], but they noticed a bay with a beach on which they—
taking counsel—purposed to run the ship ashore if they possibly
could.
40So they cut the cables *and* severed the anchors and left them
in the sea; at the same time unlashing the ropes that held the
rudders, and hoisting the foresail to the wind they headed for the
beach.
41But striking a crosscurrent—a place open to two seas—they
ran the ship aground. The prow stuck fast and remained immovable, and the stern began to break up under the violent force of the
waves.
42It was the counsel of the soldiers to kill the prisoners, lest any
of them should swim to land and escape;
43But the centurion, wishing to save Paul, prevented their carrying out their purpose. He commanded those who could swim to
throw themselves overboard first and make for the shore,
44And the rest on heavy boards or pieces of the vessel. And so
it was that all escaped safely to land.

**28** AFTER WE were safe on the island, we knew *and* recognized that it was called Malta.
2And the natives showed us unusual *and* remarkable kindness,
for they kindled a fire and welcomed *and* received us all, since it
had begun to rain and was cold.
3Now Paul had gathered a bundle of sticks, and he was laying
them on the fire, when a viper crawled out because of the heat and
fastened itself on his hand.
4When the natives saw the little animal hanging from his hand,
they said to one another, Doubtless this man is a murderer, for
though he has been saved from the sea, Justice [ [b]the goddess],
avenging, has not permitted that he should live.
5Then [Paul simply] shook off the small creature into the fire
and suffered no evil effects.
6However, they were waiting, expecting him to swell up or
suddenly drop dead; but when they had watched him a long time
and saw nothing fatal *or* harmful come to him, they changed their
minds and kept saying over and over that he was a god.
7In the vicinity of that place there were estates belonging to the
head man of the island, named Publius, who accepted *and* welcomed *and* entertained us with hearty hospitality for three days.
8And it happened that the father of Publius was sick in bed with
recurring attacks of fever and dysentery; and Paul went to see him,
and after praying and laying his hands on him he healed him.
9After this had occurred, the other people on the island who
had diseases also kept coming and were cured.
10They showed us every respect, *and* presented many gifts to
us, honoring us with many honors; and when we sailed, they
provided *and* put on [board our ship] everything we needed.
11It was after three months' stay there that we set sail in a ship
which had wintered in the island, an Alexandrian ship, with the
Twin Brothers [Castor and Pollux] as its figurehead.
12We landed at Syracuse and remained there three days,
13And from there we made a circuit—following the coast—and
reached Rhegium, and one day later a south wind sprang up and
the next day we arrived at Puteoli.

AMP [a] Some ancient authorities read "seventy-six." [b] Souter, Thayer.

## New American Standard

36And all of them were encouraged, and they themselves also took food.

37And all of us in the ship were two hundred and seventy-six persons.

38And when they had eaten enough, they *began* to lighten the ship by throwing out the wheat into the sea.

39And when day came, they could not recognize the land; but they did observe a certain bay with a beach, and they resolved to [c]drive the ship onto it if they could.

40And casting off the anchors, they left them in the sea while at the same time they were loosening the ropes of the rudders, and hoisting the foresail to the wind, they were heading for the beach.

41But striking a reef where two seas met, they ran the vessel aground; and the prow stuck fast and remained immovable, but the stern *began* to be broken up by the force *of the waves.*

42And the soldiers' plan was to kill the prisoners, that none *of them* should swim away and escape;

43but the centurion, wanting to bring Paul safely through, kept them from their intention, and commanded that those who could swim should jump overboard first and get to land,

44and the rest *should follow,* some on planks, and others on various things from the ship. And thus it happened that they all were brought safely to land.

*Safe at Malta*

**28** AND WHEN they had been brought safely through, then we found out that the island was called Malta.

2And the natives showed us extraordinary kindness; for because of the rain that had set in and because of the cold, they kindled a fire and received us all.

3But when Paul had gathered a bundle of sticks and laid them on the fire, a viper came out because of the heat, and fastened on his hand.

4And when the natives saw the creature hanging from his hand, they *began* saying to one another, "Undoubtedly this man is a murderer, and though he has been saved from the sea, justice has not allowed him to live."

5However he shook the creature off into the fire and suffered no harm.

6But they were expecting that he was about to swell up or suddenly fall down dead. But after they had waited a long time and had seen nothing unusual happen to him, they changed their minds and *began* to say that he was a god.

7¶ Now in the neighborhood of that place were lands belonging to the leading man of the island, named Publius, who welcomed us and entertained us courteously three days.

8And it came about that the father of Publius was lying *in bed* afflicted with *recurrent* fever and dysentery; and Paul went in *to see* him and after he had prayed, he laid his hands on him and healed him.

9And after this had happened, the rest of the people on the island who had diseases were coming to him and getting cured.

10And they also honored us with many marks of respect; and when we were setting sail, they supplied *us* with all we needed.

*Paul Arrives at Rome*

**11**¶ And at the end of three months we set sail on an Alexandrian ship which had wintered at the island, and which had the Twin Brothers for its figurehead.

12And after we put in at Syracuse, we stayed there for three days.

13And from there we sailed around and arrived at Rhegium, and a day later a south wind sprang up, and on the second day we came to Puteoli.

**NAS** [c] Some ancient mss. read *bring the ship safely ashore*

## New International

food themselves. 37Altogether there were 276 of us on board. 38When they had eaten as much as they wanted, they lightened the ship by throwing the grain into the sea.

39When daylight came, they did not recognize the land, but they saw a bay with a sandy beach, where they decided to run the ship aground if they could. 40Cutting loose the anchors, they left them in the sea and at the same time untied the ropes that held the rudders. Then they hoisted the foresail to the wind and made for the beach. 41But the ship struck a sandbar and ran aground. The bow stuck fast and would not move, and the stern was broken to pieces by the pounding of the surf.

42The soldiers planned to kill the prisoners to prevent any of them from swimming away and escaping. 43But the centurion wanted to spare Paul's life and kept them from carrying out their plan. He ordered those who could swim to jump overboard first and get to land. 44The rest were to get there on planks or on pieces of the ship. In this way everyone reached land in safety.

*Ashore on Malta*

**28** ONCE SAFELY on shore, we found out that the island was called Malta. 2The islanders showed us unusual kindness. They built a fire and welcomed us all because it was raining and cold. 3Paul gathered a pile of brushwood and, as he put it on the fire, a viper, driven out by the heat, fastened itself on his hand. 4When the islanders saw the snake hanging from his hand, they said to each other, "This man must be a murderer; for though he escaped from the sea, Justice has not allowed him to live." 5But Paul shook the snake off into the fire and suffered no ill effects. 6The people expected him to swell up or suddenly fall dead, but after waiting a long time and seeing nothing unusual happen to him, they changed their minds and said he was a god.

7There was an estate nearby that belonged to Publius, the chief official of the island. He welcomed us to his home and for three days entertained us hospitably. 8His father was sick in bed, suffering from fever and dysentery. Paul went in to see him and, after prayer, placed his hands on him and healed him. 9When this had happened, the rest of the sick on the island came and were cured. 10They honored us in many ways and when we were ready to sail, they furnished us with the supplies we needed.

*Arrival at Rome*

11After three months we put out to sea in a ship that had wintered in the island. It was an Alexandrian ship with the figurehead of the twin gods Castor and Pollux. 12We put in at Syracuse and stayed there three days. 13From there we set sail and arrived at Rhegium. The next day the south wind came up, and on the following day we reached Puteoli. 14There we found some broth-

## King James

14Where we found brethren, and were desired to tarry with them seven days: and so we went toward Rome.

15And from thence, when the brethren heard of us, they came to meet us as far as Appiiforum, and The three taverns: whom when Paul saw, he thanked God, and took courage.

16And when we came to Rome, the centurion delivered the prisoners to the captain of the guard: but Paul was suffered to dwell by himself with a soldier that kept him.

17And it came to pass, that after three days Paul called the chief of the Jews together: and when they were come together, he said unto them, Men *and* brethren, though I have committed nothing against the people, or customs of our fathers, yet was I delivered prisoner from Jerusalem into the hands of the Romans.

18Who, when they had examined me, would have let *me* go, because there was no cause of death in me.

19But when the Jews spake against *it,* I was constrained to appeal unto Caesar; not that I had aught to accuse my nation of.

20For this cause therefore have I called for you, to see *you,* and to speak with *you:* because that for the hope of Israel I am bound with this chain.

21And they said unto him, We neither received letters out of Judaea concerning thee, neither any of the brethren that came showed or spake any harm of thee.

22But we desire to hear of thee what thou thinkest: for as concerning this sect, we know that every where it is spoken against.

23And when they had appointed him a day, there came many to him into *his* lodging; to whom he expounded and testified the kingdom of God, persuading them concerning Jesus, both out of the law of Moses, and *out of* the prophets, from morning till evening.

24And some believed the things which were spoken, and some believed not.

25And when they agreed not among themselves, they departed, after that Paul had spoken one word, Well spake the Holy Ghost by Esaias the prophet unto our fathers,

26Saying, Go unto this people, and say, Hearing ye shall hear, and shall not understand; and seeing ye shall see, and not perceive:

27For the heart of this people is waxed gross, and their ears are dull of hearing, and their eyes have they closed; lest they should see with *their* eyes, and hear with *their* ears, and understand with *their* heart, and should be converted, and I should heal them.

28Be it known therefore unto you, that the salvation of God is sent unto the Gentiles, and *that* they will hear it.

29And when he had said these words, the Jews departed, and had great reasoning among themselves.

30And Paul dwelt two whole years in his own hired house, and received all that came in unto him,

31Preaching the kingdom of God, and teaching those things which concern the Lord Jesus Christ, with all confidence, no man forbidding him.

## Amplified

14There we found some [Christian] brethren, and were entreated to stay with them for seven days. And so we came to Rome.

15And the [Christian] brethren there, having had news of us, came as far as the Forum of Appius and the Three Taverns to meet us. When Paul saw them, he thanked God and received new courage.

16When we arrived at Rome, *the centurion delivered the prisoners to the captain of the guard, but* Paul was permitted to live by himself with the soldier who guarded him.

17Three days after [our arrival], he called together the leading local Jews; and when they had gathered, he said to them, Brethren, though I have done nothing against the people or against the customs of our forefathers, yet I was turned over as a prisoner from Jerusalem into the hands of the Romans.

18After they had examined me, they were ready to release me, because I was innocent of any offense deserving the death penalty.

19But when the Jews protested, I was forced to appeal to Caesar, though it was not because I had any charge to make against my nation.

20This is the reason therefore why I have begged to see you and to talk with you, since it is because of the Hope of Israel [the Messiah] that I am bound with this chain.

21And they answered him, We have not received any letters about you from Judea, and none of the [Jewish] brethren coming here has reported or spoken anything evil about you.

22But we think it fitting *and* are eager to hear from you what it is that you have in mind, *and* believe, *and* what your opinion is, for with regard to this sect it is known to all of us that it is everywhere denounced.

23So when they had set a day with him, they came in large numbers to his lodging. And he fully set forth *and* explained the matter to them, from morning until night, testifying to the kingdom of God and trying to persuade them concerning Jesus both from the Law of Moses and from the prophets.

24And some were convinced *and* believed what he said, and others did not believe.

25And as they disagreed among themselves, they began to leave, [but not before] Paul had added one statement [more]: The Holy Spirit was right in saying through Isaiah the prophet to your forefathers:

26Go to this people, and say to them, You will indeed hear *and* hear with your ears, but will not understand; and you will indeed look *and* look with your eyes, but will not see—not perceive, have knowledge of or become acquainted with what you look at, at all.

27For the heart—the understanding, the soul—of this people has grown dull (stupid, hardened and calloused) and their ears are heavy *and* hard of hearing, and they have shut tight their eyes, so that they may not perceive *and* have knowledge *and* become acquainted with their eyes, and hear with their ears, and understand with their souls, and turn (to Me, be converted) that I may heal them. [Isa. 6:9, 10.]

28So let it be understood by you then that [this message of] the salvation of God has been sent to the Gentiles, and they will listen [to it]! [Ps. 67:2.]

29 *And when he had said these things, the Jews went away, arguing and disputing among themselves.*

30After this Paul lived there for two entire years at his own expense, in his own rented lodging, and he welcomed all who came to him,

31Preaching to them the kingdom of God and teaching them about the Lord Jesus Christ with boldness *and* quite openly, and without being molested *or* hindered. *Amen—so be it.*

## New American Standard

14There we found *some* brethren, and were invited to stay with them for seven days; and thus we came to Rome.

15And the brethren, when they heard about us, came from there as far as the Market of Appius and Three Inns to meet us; and when Paul saw them, he thanked God and took courage.

16¶ And when we entered Rome, Paul was allowed to stay by himself, with the soldier who was guarding him.

17¶ And it happened that after three days he called together those who were the leading men of the Jews, and when they had come together, he *began* saying to them, "Brethren, though I had done nothing against our people, or the customs of our fathers, yet I was delivered prisoner from Jerusalem into the hands of the Romans.

18"And when they had examined me, they were willing to release me because there was no ground for putting me to death.

19"But when the Jews objected, I was forced to appeal to Caesar; not that I had any accusation against my nation.

20"For this reason therefore, I requested to see you and to speak with you, for I am wearing this chain for the sake of the hope of Israel."

21And they said to him, "We have neither received letters from Judea concerning you, nor have any of the brethren come here and reported or spoken anything bad about you.

22"But we desire to hear from you what your views are; for concerning this sect, it is known to us that it is spoken against everywhere."

23¶ And when they had set a day for him, they came to him at his lodging in large numbers; and he was explaining to them by solemnly testifying about the kingdom of God, and trying to persuade them concerning Jesus, from both the Law of Moses and from the Prophets, from morning until evening.

24And some were being persuaded by the things spoken, but others would not believe.

25And when they did not agree with one another, they *began* leaving after Paul had spoken one *parting* word, "The Holy Spirit rightly spoke through Isaiah the prophet to your fathers,

26saying,
'GO TO THIS PEOPLE AND SAY,
"YOU WILL KEEP ON HEARING, BUT WILL NOT UNDERSTAND;
AND YOU WILL KEEP ON SEEING, BUT WILL NOT PERCEIVE;
27 FOR THE HEART OF THIS PEOPLE HAS BECOME DULL,
AND WITH THEIR EARS THEY SCARCELY HEAR,
AND THEY HAVE CLOSED THEIR EYES;
LEST THEY SHOULD SEE WITH THEIR EYES,
AND HEAR WITH THEIR EARS,
AND UNDERSTAND WITH THEIR HEART AND RETURN,
AND I SHOULD HEAL THEM."'

28"Let it be known to you therefore, that this salvation of God has been sent to the Gentiles; they will also listen."

29[ [a]And when he had spoken these words, the Jews departed, having a great dispute among themselves.]

30¶ And he stayed two full years in his own rented quarters, and was welcoming all who came to him,

31preaching the kingdom of God, and teaching concerning the Lord Jesus Christ with all openness, unhindered.

NAS [a] Many mss. do not contain this verse

## New International

ers who invited us to spend a week with them. And so we came
to Rome. 15The brothers there had heard that we were coming, and
they traveled as far as the Forum of Appius and the Three Taverns
to meet us. At the sight of these men Paul thanked God and was
encouraged. 16When we got to Rome, Paul was allowed to live by
himself, with a soldier to guard him.

*Paul Preaches at Rome Under Guard*

17Three days later he called together the leaders of the Jews.
When they had assembled, Paul said to them: "My brothers, although I have done nothing against our people or against the
customs of our ancestors, I was arrested in Jerusalem and handed
over to the Romans. 18They examined me and wanted to release
me, because I was not guilty of any crime deserving death. 19But
when the Jews objected, I was compelled to appeal to Caesar—not
that I had any charge to bring against my own people. 20For this
reason I have asked to see you and talk with you. It is because of
the hope of Israel that I am bound with this chain."

21They replied, "We have not received any letters from Judea
concerning you, and none of the brothers who have come from
there has reported or said anything bad about you. 22But we want
to hear what your views are, for we know that people everywhere
are talking against this sect."

23They arranged to meet Paul on a certain day, and came in
even larger numbers to the place where he was staying. From
morning till evening he explained and declared to them the kingdom of God and tried to convince them about Jesus from the Law
of Moses and from the Prophets. 24Some were convinced by what
he said, but others would not believe. 25They disagreed among
themselves and began to leave after Paul had made this final
statement: "The Holy Spirit spoke the truth to your forefathers
when he said through Isaiah the prophet:

26" 'Go to this people and say,
"You will be ever hearing but never understanding;
you will be ever seeing but never perceiving."
27For this people's heart has become calloused;
they hardly hear with their ears,
and they have closed their eyes.
Otherwise they might see with their eyes,
hear with their ears,
understand with their hearts
and turn, and I would heal them.'[b]

28"Therefore I want you to know that God's salvation has been
sent to the Gentiles, and they will listen!"[c]

30For two whole years Paul stayed there in his own rented
house and welcomed all who came to see him. 31Boldly and without hindrance he preached the kingdom of God and taught about
the Lord Jesus Christ.

NIV [b] 27 Isaiah 6:9,10 [c] 28 Some manuscripts *listen!" 29After he said this, the Jews left, arguing vigorously among themselves.*

## King James

THE EPISTLE OF PAUL

THE APOSTLE TO THE

# Romans

**1** PAUL, A servant of Jesus Christ, called *to be* an apostle, separated unto the gospel of God,

2(Which he had promised afore by his prophets in the holy scriptures,)

3Concerning his Son Jesus Christ our Lord, which was made of the seed of David according to the flesh;

4And declared *to be* the Son of God with power, according to the spirit of holiness, by the resurrection from the dead:

5By whom we have received grace and apostleship, for obedience to the faith among all nations, for his name:

6Among whom are ye also the called of Jesus Christ:

7To all that be in Rome, beloved of God, called *to be* saints: Grace to you and peace from God our Father, and the Lord Jesus Christ.

8First, I thank my God through Jesus Christ for you all, that your faith is spoken of throughout the whole world.

9For God is my witness, whom I serve with my spirit in the gospel of his Son, that without ceasing I make mention of you always in my prayers;

10Making request, if by any means now at length I might have a prosperous journey by the will of God to come unto you.

11For I long to see you, that I may impart unto you some spiritual gift, to the end ye may be established;

12That is, that I may be comforted together with you by the mutual faith both of you and me.

13Now I would not have you ignorant, brethren, that oftentimes I purposed to come unto you, (but was let hitherto,) that I might have some fruit among you also, even as among other Gentiles.

14I am debtor both to the Greeks, and to the Barbarians; both to the wise, and to the unwise.

15So, as much as in me is, I am ready to preach the gospel to you that are at Rome also.

16For I am not ashamed of the gospel of Christ: for it is the power of God unto salvation to every one that believeth; to the Jew first, and also to the Greek.

17For therein is the righteousness of God revealed from faith to faith: as it is written, The just shall live by faith.

## Amplified

THE LETTER OF PAUL

TO THE

# Romans

**1** FROM PAUL, a bond servant of Jesus Christ, the Messiah, called to be an apostle, a (special messenger) set apart to [preach] the Gospel (good news) of *and* from God,

2Which He promised in advance [long ago] through His prophets in the sacred Scriptures,

3[The Gospel] regarding His Son, Who as to the flesh (His human nature) was descended from David;

4And [as to His divine nature] according to the Spirit of holiness, was openly [a]designated the Son of God in power—in a striking, triumphant and miraculous manner—by His resurrection from the dead, even Jesus Christ our Lord, the Messiah, the Anointed One.

5It is through Him that we have received grace—God's unmerited favor—and [our] apostleship to promote obedience to the faith *and* make disciples for His name's sake among all the nations,

6And this includes yourselves, called of Jesus Christ *and* invited [as you are] to belong to Him.

7To [you then,] all God's beloved ones in Rome, called to be saints *and* designated for a consecrated life: Grace *and* spiritual blessing and peace be yours from God our Father and from the Lord Jesus Christ.

8First, I thank my God through Jesus Christ for all of you, because [the report of] your faith is made known to all the world *and* is [b]commended everywhere.

9For God is my witness, Whom I serve with [all] my spirit—rendering priestly and spiritual service—in [preaching] the Gospel *and* telling the good news of His Son, how incessantly I always mention you when at my prayers.

10I keep pleading that somehow by God's will I may now at last be prospered *and* come to you.

11For I am yearning to see you, that I may impart *and* share with you some spiritual gift to strengthen *and* establish you;

12That is, that we may be mutually strengthened *and* encouraged *and* comforted by each other's faith, both yours and mine.

13I want you to know, brethren, that many times I have planned *and* intended to come to you, though thus far I have been hindered *and* prevented, in order that I might have some fruit—some result of my labors—among you, as I have among the rest of the Gentiles.

14Both to Greeks and to barbarians (to the cultured and to the uncultured), both to the wise and the foolish I have an obligation to discharge *and* a duty to perform *and* a debt to pay.

15So, for my part, I am willing *and* eagerly ready to preach the Gospel to you also who are in Rome.

16For I am not ashamed of the Gospel (good news) *of Christ;* for it is God's power working unto salvation (for deliverance from eternal death) to every one who believes *with* a personal trust *and* a confident surrender *and* firm reliance, to the Jew first and also to the Greek,

17For in the Gospel a righteousness which God ascribes is revealed, both springing from faith and leading to faith—disclosed through the way of faith that arouses to more faith. As it is written, The man who through faith is just *and* upright shall live *and* [c]shall live by faith. [Hab. 2:4.]

**AMP** [a] Vincent. [b] Vincent. [c] Alternate reading.

## New American Standard

# Romans

*The Gospel Exalted*

**1** PAUL, A bond-servant of Christ Jesus, called *as* an apostle, set apart for the gospel of God,

2which He promised beforehand through His prophets in the holy Scriptures,

3concerning His Son, who was born of a descendant of David according to the flesh,

4who was declared the Son of God with power [d]by the resurrection from the dead, according to the spirit of holiness, Jesus Christ our Lord,

5through whom we have received grace and apostleship to bring about *the* obedience of faith among all the Gentiles, for His name's sake,

6among whom you also are the called of Jesus Christ;

7to all who are beloved of God in Rome, called *as* saints: Grace to you and peace from God our Father and the Lord Jesus Christ.

8¶ First, I thank my God through Jesus Christ for you all, because your faith is being proclaimed throughout the whole world.

9For God, whom I serve in my spirit in the *preaching of the* gospel of His Son, is my witness *as to* how unceasingly I make mention of you,

10always in my prayers making request, if perhaps now at last by the will of God I may succeed in coming to you.

11For I long to see you in order that I may impart some spiritual gift to you, that you may be established;

12that is, that I may be encouraged together with you *while* among you, each of us by the other's faith, both yours and mine.

13And I do not want you to be unaware, brethren, that often I have planned to come to you (and have been prevented thus far) in order that I might obtain some fruit among you also, even as among the rest of the Gentiles.

14I am [e]under obligation both to Greeks and to barbarians, both to the wise and to the foolish.

15Thus, for my part, I am eager to preach the gospel to you also who are in Rome.

16¶ For I am not ashamed of the gospel, for it is the power of God for salvation to everyone who believes, to the Jew first and also to the Greek.

17For in it *the* righteousness of God is revealed from faith to faith; as it is written, "BUT THE RIGHTEOUS *man* SHALL LIVE BY FAITH."

**NAS** [d] Or, *as a result of* [e] Lit., *debtor*

## New International

# Romans

**1** PAUL, A servant of Christ Jesus, called to be an apostle and
set apart for the gospel of God— 2the gospel he promised
beforehand through his prophets in the Holy Scriptures 3regard-
ing his Son, who as to his human nature was a descendant of
David, 4and who through the Spirit[f] of holiness was declared with
power to be the Son of God[g] by his resurrection from the dead:
Jesus Christ our Lord. 5Through him and for his name's sake, we
received grace and apostleship to call people from among all the
Gentiles to the obedience that comes from faith. 6And you also are
among those who are called to belong to Jesus Christ.

7To all in Rome who are loved by God and called to be saints:

Grace and peace to you from God our Father and from the Lord Jesus Christ.

*Paul's Longing to Visit Rome*

8First, I thank my God through Jesus Christ for all of you,
because your faith is being reported all over the world. 9God,
whom I serve with my whole heart in preaching the gospel of his
Son, is my witness how constantly I remember you 10in my prayers
at all times; and I pray that now at last by God's will the way may
be opened for me to come to you.

11I long to see you so that I may impart to you some spiritual
gift to make you strong— 12that is, that you and I may be mutually
encouraged by each other's faith. 13I do not want you to be unaware, brothers, that I planned many times to come to you (but
have been prevented from doing so until now) in order that I might
have a harvest among you, just as I have had among the other
Gentiles.

14I am obligated both to Greeks and non-Greeks, both to the
wise and the foolish. 15That is why I am so eager to preach the
gospel also to you who are at Rome.

16I am not ashamed of the gospel, because it is the power of God
for the salvation of everyone who believes: first for the Jew, then
for the Gentile. 17For in the gospel a righteousness from God is
revealed, a righteousness that is by faith from first to last,[h] just as
it is written: "The righteous will live by faith."[i]

**NIV** [f] 4 Or *who as to his spirit* [g] 4 Or *was appointed to be the Son of God with power* [h] 17 Or *is from faith to faith* [i] 17 Hab. 2:4

## King James

18 For the wrath of God is revealed from heaven against all ungodliness and unrighteousness of men, who hold the truth in unrighteousness;

19 Because that which may be known of God is manifest in them; for God hath shown *it* unto them.

20 For the invisible things of him from the creation of the world are clearly seen, being understood by the things that are made, *even* his eternal power and Godhead; so that they are without excuse:

21 Because that, when they knew God, they glorified *him* not as God, neither were thankful; but became vain in their imaginations, and their foolish heart was darkened.

22 Professing themselves to be wise, they became fools,

23 And changed the glory of the uncorruptible God into an image made like to corruptible man, and to birds, and fourfooted beasts, and creeping things.

24 Wherefore God also gave them up to uncleanness through the lusts of their own hearts, to dishonour their own bodies between themselves:

25 Who changed the truth of God into a lie, and worshipped and served the creature more than the Creator, who is blessed for ever. Amen.

26 For this cause God gave them up unto vile affections: for even their women did change the natural use into that which is against nature:

27 And likewise also the men, leaving the natural use of the woman, burned in their lust one toward another; men with men working that which is unseemly, and receiving in themselves that recompence of their error which was meet.

28 And even as they did not like to retain God in *their* knowledge, God gave them over to a reprobate mind, to do those things which are not convenient;

29 Being filled with all unrighteousness, fornication, wickedness, covetousness, maliciousness; full of envy, murder, debate, deceit, malignity; whisperers,

30 Backbiters, haters of God, despiteful, proud, boasters, inventors of evil things, disobedient to parents,

31 Without understanding, covenantbreakers, without natural affection, implacable, unmerciful:

32 Who knowing the judgment of God, that they which commit such things are worthy of death, not only do the same, but have pleasure in them that do them.

**2** THEREFORE THOU art inexcusable, O man, whosoever thou art that judgest: for wherein thou judgest another, thou condemnest thyself; for thou that judgest doest the same things.

2 But we are sure that the judgment of God is according to truth against them which commit such things.

## Amplified

18 For God's [holy] wrath *and* indignation are revealed from heaven against all ungodliness and unrighteousness of men, who in their wickedness repress *and* hinder the truth *and* make it inoperative.

19 For that which is known about God is evident to them *and* made plain in their inner consciousness, because God [Himself] has shown it to them.

20 For ever since the creation of the world His invisible nature *and* attributes, that is, His eternal power and divinity have been made intelligible *and* clearly discernible in *and* through the things that have been made—His handiworks. So [men] are without excuse—altogether without any defense or justification; [Ps. 19: 1-4.]

21 Because when they knew *and* recognized Him as the God, they did not honor *and* glorify Him as God, or give Him thanks. But instead they became futile *and* [a]godless in their thinking—with vain imaginings, foolish reasoning and stupid speculations—and their senseless minds were darkened.

22 Claiming to be wise, they became fools—professing to be smart, they made simpletons of themselves.

23 And by them the glory and majesty *and* excellence of the immortal God were exchanged for *and* represented by images, resembling mortal man and birds and beasts and reptiles.

24 Therefore God gave them up in the lusts of their [own] hearts to sexual impurity, to the dishonoring of their bodies among themselves, abandoning them to the degrading power of sin.

25 Because they exchanged the truth of God for a lie and worshipped and served the creature rather than the Creator, Who is blessed forever! Amen—so be it. [Jer. 2:11.]

26 For this reason God gave them over *and* abandoned them to vile affections *and* degrading passions. For their women exchanged their natural function for an unnatural *and* abnormal one;

27 And the men also turned from natural relations with women and were set ablaze (burned out, consumed) with lust for one another, men committing shameful acts with men and suffering in their own [b]bodies *and* personalities the inevitable consequences *and* penalty of their wrong doing *and* going astray, which was [their] fitting retribution.

28 And so, since they did not see fit to acknowledge God *or* approve of Him *or* consider Him worth the knowing, God gave them over to a base *and* condemned mind to do things not proper *or* decent *but* loathsome;

29 Until they were filled—permeated and saturated—with every kind of unrighteousness, iniquity, grasping *and* covetous greed, [and] malice. [They were] full of envy *and* jealousy, murder, strife, deceit *and* treachery, ill will *and* cruel ways. [They were] secret backbiters *and* gossipers,

30 Slanderers, hateful to *and* hating God, full of insolence, arrogance [and] boasting; inventors of new forms of evil, disobedient *and* undutiful to parents.

31 [They were] without understanding, conscienceless *and* faithless, heartless *and* loveless [and] merciless.

32 Though they are fully aware of God's righteous decree that those who do such things deserve to die, they not only do them themselves but approve *and* applaud others who practice them.

**2** THEREFORE YOU have no excuse *or* defense *or* justification, O man, whoever you are who judges *and* condemns another. For in posing as judge *and* passing sentence on another you condemn yourself, because you who judge are habitually practicing the very same things [that you censure and denounce].

2 [But] we know that the judgment (adverse verdict, sentence) of God falls justly *and* in accordance with truth upon those who practice such things.

AMP [a] Souter. [b] Webster, defining "selves."

## New American Standard

*Unbelief and Its Consequences*

18¶ For the wrath of God is revealed from heaven against all ungodliness and unrighteousness of men, who suppress the truth in unrighteousness,

19because that which is known about God is evident within them; for God made it evident to them.

20For since the creation of the world His invisible attributes, His eternal power and divine nature, have been clearly seen, being understood through what has been made, so that they are without excuse.

21For even though they knew God, they did not [c]honor Him as God, or give thanks; but they became futile in their speculations, and their foolish heart was darkened.

22Professing to be wise, they became fools,

23and exchanged the glory of the incorruptible God for an image in the form of corruptible man and of birds and four-footed animals and [d]crawling creatures.

24¶ Therefore God gave them over in the lusts of their hearts to impurity, that their bodies might be dishonored among them.

25For they exchanged the truth of God for a lie, and worshiped and served the creature rather than the Creator, who is blessed forever. Amen.

26¶ For this reason God gave them over to degrading passions; for their women exchanged the natural function for that which is unnatural,

27and in the same way also the men abandoned the natural function of the woman and burned in their desire toward one another, men with men committing indecent acts and receiving in their own persons the due penalty of their error.

28¶ And just as they did not see fit to acknowledge God any longer, God gave them over to a depraved mind, to do those things which are not proper,

29being filled with all unrighteousness, wickedness, greed, evil; full of envy, murder, strife, deceit, malice; *they are* gossips,

30slanderers, haters of God, insolent, arrogant, boastful, inventors of evil, disobedient to parents,

31without understanding, untrustworthy, unloving, unmerciful;

32and, although they know the ordinance of God, that those who practice such things are worthy of death, they not only do the same, but also give hearty approval to those who practice them.

*The Impartiality of God*

**2** THEREFORE YOU are without excuse, every man *of you* who passes judgment, for in that you judge another, you condemn yourself; for you who judge practice the same things.

2And we know that the judgment of God rightly falls upon those who practice such things.

NAS [c] Lit., *glorify* [d] Or possibly, *reptiles*

## New International

*God's Wrath Against Mankind*

18The wrath of God is being revealed from heaven against all
the godlessness and wickedness of men who suppress the truth
by their wickedness, 19since what may be known about God is
plain to them, because God has made it plain to them. 20For since
the creation of the world God's invisible qualities—his eternal
power and divine nature—have been clearly seen, being understood from what has been made, so that men are without excuse.
21For although they knew God, they neither glorified him as
God nor gave thanks to him, but their thinking became futile and
their foolish hearts were darkened. 22Although they claimed to be
wise, they became fools 23and exchanged the glory of the immortal
God for images made to look like mortal man and birds and animals and reptiles.
24Therefore God gave them over in the sinful desires of their
hearts to sexual impurity for the degrading of their bodies with one
another. 25They exchanged the truth of God for a lie, and worshiped and served created things rather than the Creator—who is
forever praised. Amen.
26Because of this, God gave them over to shameful lusts. Even
their women exchanged natural relations for unnatural ones. 27In
the same way the men also abandoned natural relations with
women and were inflamed with lust for one another. Men committed indecent acts with other men, and received in themselves the
due penalty for their perversion.
28Furthermore, since they did not think it worthwhile to retain
the knowledge of God, he gave them over to a depraved mind, to
do what ought not to be done. 29They have become filled with
every kind of wickedness, evil, greed and depravity. They are full
of envy, murder, strife, deceit and malice. They are gossips, 30slanderers, God-haters, insolent, arrogant and boastful; they invent
ways of doing evil; they disobey their parents; 31they are senseless,
faithless, heartless, ruthless. 32Although they know God's righteous decree that those who do such things deserve death, they not
only continue to do these very things but also approve of those
who practice them.

*God's Righteous Judgment*

**2** YOU, THEREFORE, have no excuse, you who pass judgment
on someone else, for at whatever point you judge the other,
you are condemning yourself, because you who pass judgment do
the same things. 2Now we know that God's judgment against
those who do such things is based on truth. 3So when you, a mere

## King James

3And thinkest thou this, O man, that judgest them which do such things, and doest the same, that thou shalt escape the judgment of God?

4Or despisest thou the riches of his goodness and forbearance and longsuffering; not knowing that the goodness of God leadeth thee to repentance?

5But after thy hardness and impenitent heart treasurest up unto thyself wrath against the day of wrath and revelation of the righteous judgment of God;

6Who will render to every man according to his deeds:

7To them who by patient continuance in well doing seek for glory and honour and immortality, eternal life:

8But unto them that are contentious, and do not obey the truth, but obey unrighteousness, indignation and wrath,

9Tribulation and anguish, upon every soul of man that doeth evil, of the Jew first, and also of the Gentile;

10But glory, honour, and peace, to every man that worketh good, to the Jew first, and also to the Gentile:

11For there is no respect of persons with God.

12For as many as have sinned without law shall also perish without law: and as many as have sinned in the law shall be judged by the law;

13(For not the hearers of the law *are* just before God, but the doers of the law shall be justified.

14For when the Gentiles, which have not the law, do by nature the things contained in the law, these, having not the law, are a law unto themselves:

15Which show the work of the law written in their hearts, their conscience also bearing witness, and *their* thoughts the mean while accusing or else excusing one another;)

16In the day when God shall judge the secrets of men by Jesus Christ according to my gospel.

17Behold, thou art called a Jew, and restest in the law, and makest thy boast of God,

18And knowest *his* will, and approvest the things that are more excellent, being instructed out of the law;

19And art confident that thou thyself art a guide of the blind, a light of them which are in darkness,

20An instructor of the foolish, a teacher of babes, which hast the form of knowledge and of the truth in the law.

21Thou therefore which teachest another, teachest thou not thyself? thou that preachest a man should not steal, dost thou steal?

22Thou that sayest a man should not commit adultery, dost thou commit adultery? thou that abhorrest idols, dost thou commit sacrilege?

23Thou that makest thy boast of the law, through breaking the law dishonourest thou God?

## Amplified

3And do you think *or* imagine, O man, when you judge *and* condemn those who practice such things and yet do them yourself, that you will escape God's judgment *and* elude His sentence *and* adverse verdict?

4Or are you [so blind as] to trifle with *and* presume upon *and* despise *and* underestimate the wealth of His kindness and forbearance and long-enduring patience? Are you unmindful *or* actually ignorant [of the fact] that God's kindness is intended to lead you to repent— [a]to change your mind and inner man to accept God's will?

5But by your callous stubbornness *and* impenitence of heart you are storing up wrath *and* indignation for yourself on the day of wrath *and* indignation, when God's righteous judgment (just doom) will be revealed.

6For He will render to every man according to his works—justly, as his deeds deserve: [Ps. 62:12.]

7To those who by patient persistence in welldoing [ [b]springing from piety] seek for [unseen but sure] glory and honor and [ [c]the eternal blessedness of] immortality, He will give eternal life.

8But for those who are self-seeking *and* self-willed *and* disobedient to the Truth but responsive to wickedness, there will be indignation and wrath.

9[And] there will be tribulation *and* anguish and calamity *and* constraint for every soul of man who (habitually) does evil, the Jew first and also the Greek.

10But glory and honor and heart-peace shall be awarded to every one who (habitually) does good, the Jew first and also [d]the Greek.

11For God shows no partiality ( [e]undue favor, or unfairness; with Him one man is not different from another). [Deut. 10:17; II Chron. 19:7.]

12All who have sinned without the Law will also perish without [regard to] the Law, and all who have sinned under the Law will be judged *and* condemned by the Law.

13For it is not merely hearing the Law [read] that makes one righteous before God, but it is the doers of the Law who will be held guiltless *and* acquitted *and* justified.

14When Gentiles who have not [the divine] Law do instinctively what the Law requires, they are a law to themselves, since they do not have the Law.

15They show that the essential requirements of the Law are written in their hearts *and* are operating there; with which their conscience (sense of right and wrong) also bears witness; and their [moral] [f]decisions—their arguments of reason, their condemning or approving [g]thoughts—will accuse or perhaps defend *and* excuse [them]

16On that day when, as my Gospel proclaims, God by Jesus Christ will judge men in regard to [h]the things which they conceal—their hidden thoughts. [Eccl. 12:14.]

17But if you bear the name of Jew and rely upon the Law and pride yourselves in God *and* your relationship to Him,

18And know *and* understand His will and discerningly approve the better things *and* have a sense of what is vital, because you are instructed by the Law;

19And if you are confident that you [yourself] are a guide to the blind, a light to those who are in darkness, and [that

20You are] a corrector of the foolish, a teacher of the childish, having in the Law the embodiment of knowledge and truth;

21Well then, you who teach others, do you not teach yourself? While you teach against stealing, do you steal—take what does not really belong to you?

22You who say not to commit adultery, do you commit adultery—are you unchaste in action or in thought? You who abhor *and* loathe idols, do you rob temples—appropriate to your own use what is consecrated to God, thus robbing the sanctuary and [i]doing sacrilege?

23You who boast in the Law, do you dishonor God by breaking the Law—by stealthily infringing upon or carelessly neglecting or openly breaking it?

**AMP** [a] Souter. [b] Thayer. [c] Thayer. [d] A Pauline term for Gentile. [e] Moulton and Milligan. [f] Thayer. [g] Alford, Vincent, AV, ASV, etc. [h] Alford, Vincent, AV, ASV, etc. [i] Moulton and Milligan.

## New American Standard

3And do you suppose this, O man, when you pass judgment
upon those who practice such things and do the same *yourself*, that
you will escape the judgment of God?
4Or do you think lightly of the riches of His kindness and
forbearance and patience, not knowing that the kindness of God
leads you to repentance?
5But because of your stubbornness and unrepentant heart you
are storing up wrath for yourself in the day of wrath and revelation
of the righteous judgment of God,
6who WILL RENDER TO EVERY MAN ACCORDING TO HIS DEEDS:
7to those who by perseverance in doing good seek for glory
and honor and immortality, eternal life;
8but to those who are selfishly ambitious and do not obey the
truth, but obey unrighteousness, wrath and indignation.
9 *There will be* tribulation and distress for every soul of man who
does evil, of the Jew first and also of the Greek,
10but glory and honor and peace to every man who does good,
to the Jew first and also to the Greek.
11For there is no partiality with God.
12For all who have sinned without the Law will also perish
without the Law; and all who have sinned under the Law will be
judged by the Law;
13for not the hearers of the Law are just before God, but the
doers of the Law will be justified.
14For when Gentiles who do not have the Law do instinctively
the things of the Law, these, not having the Law, are a law to
themselves,
15in that they show the work of the Law written in their hearts,
their conscience bearing witness, and their thoughts alternately
accusing or else defending them,
16on the day when, according to my gospel, God will judge the
secrets of men through Christ Jesus.

*The Jew Is Condemned by the Law*

17¶ But if you bear the name "Jew," and rely upon the Law, and
boast in God,
18and know *His* will, and approve the things that are essential,
being instructed out of the Law,
19and are confident that you yourself are a guide to the blind,
a light to those who are in darkness,
20a corrector of the foolish, a teacher of the immature, having
in the Law the embodiment of knowledge and of the truth,
21you, therefore, who teach another, do you not teach yourself? You who preach that one should not steal, do you steal?
22You who say that one should not commit adultery, do you
commit adultery? You who abhor idols, do you rob temples?
23You who boast in the Law, through your breaking the Law,
do you dishonor God?

## New International

man, pass judgment on them and yet do the same things, do you
think you will escape God's judgment? 4Or do you show contempt
for the riches of his kindness, tolerance and patience, not realizing
that God's kindness leads you toward repentance?
5But because of your stubbornness and your unrepentant heart,
you are storing up wrath against yourself for the day of God's
wrath, when his righteous judgment will be revealed. 6God "will
give to each person according to what he has done."[j] 7To those
who by persistence in doing good seek glory, honor and immortality, he will give eternal life. 8But for those who are self-seeking and
who reject the truth and follow evil, there will be wrath and anger.
9There will be trouble and distress for every human being who
does evil: first for the Jew, then for the Gentile; 10but glory, honor
and peace for everyone who does good: first for the Jew, then for
the Gentile. 11For God does not show favoritism.
12All who sin apart from the law will also perish apart from the
law, and all who sin under the law will be judged by the law. 13For
it is not those who hear the law who are righteous in God's sight,
but it is those who obey the law who will be declared righteous.
14(Indeed, when Gentiles, who do not have the law, do by nature
things required by the law, they are a law for themselves, even
though they do not have the law, 15since they show that the
requirements of the law are written on their hearts, their consciences also bearing witness, and their thoughts now accusing,
now even defending them.) 16This will take place on the day when
God will judge men's secrets through Jesus Christ, as my gospel
declares.

*The Jews and the Law*

17Now you, if you call yourself a Jew; if you rely on the law and
brag about your relationship to God; 18if you know his will and
approve of what is superior because you are instructed by the law;
19if you are convinced that you are a guide for the blind, a light for
those who are in the dark, 20an instructor of the foolish, a teacher
of infants, because you have in the law the embodiment of knowledge and truth— 21you, then, who teach others, do you not teach
yourself? You who preach against stealing, do you steal? 22You
who say that people should not commit adultery, do you commit
adultery? You who abhor idols, do you rob temples? 23You who
brag about the law, do you dishonor God by breaking the law?

NIV [j] 6 Psalm 62:12; Prov. 24:12

## King James

24 For the name of God is blasphemed among the Gentiles through you, as it is written.

25 For circumcision verily profiteth, if thou keep the law: but if thou be a breaker of the law, thy circumcision is made uncircumcision.

26 Therefore if the uncircumcision keep the righteousness of the law, shall not his uncircumcision be counted for circumcision?

27 And shall not uncircumcision which is by nature, if it fulfil the law, judge thee, who by the letter and circumcision dost transgress the law?

28 For he is not a Jew, which is one outwardly; neither *is that* circumcision, which is outward in the flesh:

29 But he *is* a Jew, which is one inwardly; and circumcision *is that* of the heart, in the spirit, *and* not in the letter; whose praise *is* not of men, but of God.

**3** WHAT ADVANTAGE then hath the Jew? or what profit *is there* of circumcision?

2 Much every way: chiefly, because that unto them were committed the oracles of God.

3 For what if some did not believe? shall their unbelief make the faith of God without effect?

4 God forbid: yea, let God be true, but every man a liar; as it is written, That thou mightest be justified in thy sayings, and mightest overcome when thou art judged.

5 But if our unrighteousness commend the righteousness of God, what shall we say? *Is* God unrighteous who taketh vengeance? (I speak as a man)

6 God forbid: for then how shall God judge the world?

7 For if the truth of God hath more abounded through my lie unto his glory; why yet am I also judged as a sinner?

8 And not *rather*, (as we be slanderously reported, and as some affirm that we say,) Let us do evil, that good may come? whose damnation is just.

9 What then? are we better *than they?* No, in no wise: for we have before proved both Jews and Gentiles, that they are all under sin;

10 As it is written, There is none righteous, no, not one:

11 There is none that understandeth, there is none that seeketh after God.

12 They are all gone out of the way, they are together become unprofitable; there is none that doeth good, no, not one.

13 Their throat *is* an open sepulchre; with their tongues they have used deceit; the poison of asps *is* under their lips:

14 Whose mouth *is* full of cursing and bitterness:

15 Their feet *are* swift to shed blood:

16 Destruction and misery *are* in their ways:

17 And the way of peace have they not known:

18 There is no fear of God before their eyes.

## Amplified

24 For, as it is written, The name of God is maligned *and* blasphemed among the Gentiles because of you!—The words to this effect are from [your own] Scriptures. [Isa. 52:5; Ezek. 36:20.]

25 Circumcision does indeed profit if you keep the Law; but if you habitually transgress the Law; your circumcision is made uncircumcision.

26 So, if a man who is uncircumcised keeps the requirements of the Law, will not his uncircumcision be credited to him [as equivalent to] circumcision?

27 Then those who are physically uncircumcised but keep the Law will condemn you who, although you have the code in writing and have circumcision, break the Law.

28 For he is not a [real] Jew who is only one outwardly *and* publicly, nor is [true] circumcision something external and physical.

29 But he is a Jew who is one inwardly, and [true] circumcision is of the heart, a spiritual and not a literal [matter]. His praise is not from men but from God.

**3** THEN WHAT advantage remains to the Jew?—How is he favored? Or what is the value *or* benefit of circumcision?

2 Much in every way. To begin with, to the Jews were entrusted the oracles (the brief communications, the intentions, the utterances) of God. [Ps. 147:19.]

3 What if some did not believe *and* were without faith? Does their lack of faith *and* their faithlessness nullify *and* make ineffective *and* void the faithfulness of God *and* His fidelity [to His Word]?

4 By no means! Let God be found true though every human being be false *and* a liar, as it is written, That You may be justified *and* shown to be upright in what You say, and prevail when You are judged [by sinful men]. [Ps. 51:4.]

5 But if our unrighteousness thus establishes *and* exhibits the righteousness of God, what shall we say? That God is unjust *and* wrong to inflict His wrath upon us [Jews]? I speak in a [purely] human way.

6 By no means! Otherwise, how could God judge the world?

7 But [you say,] if through my falsehood God's integrity is magnified *and* advertised *and* abounds to His glory, why am I still being judged as a sinner?

8 And why should we not do evil that good may come? as some slanderously charge us with teaching. Such [false teaching] is justly condemned by them.

9 Well then, are we [Jews] superior *and* better off than they? No, not at all. We have already charged that all men, both Jews and Greeks, are under sin—held down by and subject to its power and control.

10 As it is written, None is righteous, just *and* truthful *and* upright *and* conscientious, no, not one. [Ps. 14:3.]

11 No one understands—no one intelligently discerns *or* comprehends; no one seeks out God. [Ps. 14:2.]

12 All have turned aside; together they have gone wrong *and* have become unprofitable *and* worthless; no one does right, not even one!

13 Their throat is a yawning grave; they use their tongues to deceive—to mislead and to deal treacherously. The venom of asps is beneath their lips. [Ps. 5:9; 140:3.]

14 Their mouth is full of cursing and bitterness. [Ps. 10:7.]

15 Their feet are swift to shed blood.

16 Destruction (as it dashes them to pieces) and misery mark their ways.

17 And they have no experience of the way of peace—they know nothing about peace, for a peaceful way they do not even recognize. [Isa. 59:7, 8.]

18 There is no (reverential) fear of God before their eyes. [Ps. 36:1.]

## New American Standard

24For "THE NAME OF GOD IS BLASPHEMED AMONG THE GENTILES
BECAUSE OF YOU," just as it is written.
25For indeed circumcision is of value, if you practice the Law;
but if you are a transgressor of the Law, your circumcision has
become uncircumcision.
26If therefore the uncircumcised man keeps the requirements of
the Law, will not his uncircumcision be regarded as circumcision?
27And will not he who is physically uncircumcised, if he keeps
the Law, will he not judge you who though having the letter *of the*
*Law* and circumcision are a transgressor of the Law?
28For he is not a Jew who is one outwardly; neither is circumcision that which is outward in the flesh.
29But he is a Jew who is one inwardly; and circumcision is that
which is of the heart, by the Spirit, not by the letter; and his praise
is not from men, but from God.

*All the World Guilty*

3 THEN WHAT advantage has the Jew? Or what is the benefit
of circumcision?
2Great in every respect. First of all, that they were entrusted
with the oracles of God.
3What then? If some did not believe, their unbelief will not
nullify the faithfulness of God, will it?
4May it never be! Rather, let God be found true, though every
man *be found* a liar, as it is written,
"THAT THOU MIGHTEST BE JUSTIFIED IN THY WORDS,
AND MIGHTEST PREVAIL WHEN THOU ART JUDGED."
5But if our unrighteousness demonstrates the righteousness of
God, what shall we say? The God who inflicts wrath is not unrighteous, is He? (I am speaking in human terms.)
6May it never be! For otherwise how will God judge the world?
7But if through my lie the truth of God abounded to His glory,
why am I also still being judged as a sinner?
8And why not *say* (as we are slanderously reported and as
some affirm that we say), "Let us do evil that good may come"?
Their condemnation is just.
9¶ What then? Are we better than they? Not at all; for we have
already charged that both Jews and Greeks are all under sin;
10as it is written,
"THERE IS NONE RIGHTEOUS, NOT EVEN ONE;
11 THERE IS NONE WHO UNDERSTANDS,
THERE IS NONE WHO SEEKS FOR GOD;
12 ALL HAVE TURNED ASIDE, TOGETHER THEY HAVE BECOME
USELESS;
THERE IS NONE WHO DOES GOOD,
THERE IS NOT EVEN ONE."
13 "THEIR THROAT IS AN OPEN GRAVE,
WITH THEIR TONGUES THEY KEEP DECEIVING,"
"THE POISON OF ASPS IS UNDER THEIR LIPS";
14 "WHOSE MOUTH IS FULL OF CURSING AND BITTERNESS";
15 "THEIR FEET ARE SWIFT TO SHED BLOOD,
16 DESTRUCTION AND MISERY ARE IN THEIR PATHS,
17 AND THE PATH OF PEACE HAVE THEY NOT KNOWN."
18 "THERE IS NO FEAR OF GOD BEFORE THEIR EYES."

## New International

24As it is written: "God's name is blasphemed among the Gentiles
because of you."[a]
25Circumcision has value if you observe the law, but if you
break the law, you have become as though you had not been
circumcised. 26If those who are not circumcised keep the law's
requirements, will they not be regarded as though they were circumcised? 27The one who is not circumcised physically and yet
obeys the law will condemn you who, even though you have the[b]
written code and circumcision, are a lawbreaker.
28A man is not a Jew if he is only one outwardly, nor is circumcision merely outward and physical. 29No, a man is a Jew if he is one
inwardly; and circumcision is circumcision of the heart, by the
Spirit, not by the written code. Such a man's praise is not from
men, but from God.

*God's Faithfulness*

3 WHAT ADVANTAGE, then, is there in being a Jew, or what
value is there in circumcision? 2Much in every way! First of
all, they have been entrusted with the very words of God.
3What if some did not have faith? Will their lack of faith nullify
God's faithfulness? 4Not at all! Let God be true, and every man a
liar. As it is written:

"So that you may be proved right when you speak
and prevail when you judge."[c]

5But if our unrighteousness brings out God's righteousness
more clearly, what shall we say? That God is unjust in bringing his
wrath on us? (I am using a human argument.) 6Certainly not! If
that were so, how could God judge the world? 7Someone might
argue, "If my falsehood enhances God's truthfulness and so increases his glory, why am I still condemned as a sinner?" 8Why
not say—as we are being slanderously reported as saying and as
some claim that we say—"Let us do evil that good may result"?
Their condemnation is deserved.

*No One Is Righteous*

9What shall we conclude then? Are we any better[d]? Not at all!
We have already made the charge that Jews and Gentiles alike are
all under sin. 10As it is written:

"There is no one righteous, not even one;
11 there is no one who understands,
no one who seeks God.
12All have turned away,
they have together become worthless;
there is no one who does good,
not even one."[e]
13"Their throats are open graves;
their tongues practice deceit."[f]
"The poison of vipers is on their lips."[g]
14 "Their mouths are full of cursing and bitterness."[h]
15"Their feet are swift to shed blood;
16 ruin and misery mark their ways,
17and the way of peace they do not know."[i]
18 "There is no fear of God before their eyes."[j]

NIV [a] *24* Isaiah 52:5; Ezek. 36:22 [b] *27* Or *who, by means of a* [c] *4* Psalm 51:4 [d] *9* Or *worse* [e] *12* Psalms 14:1-3; 53:1-3; Eccles. 7:20 [f] *13* Psalm 5:9 [g] *13* Psalm 140:3 [h] *14* Psalm 10:7 [i] *17* Isaiah 59:7,8 [j] *18* Psalm 36:1

## King James

19Now we know that what things soever the law saith, it saith to them who are under the law: that every mouth may be stopped, and all the world may become guilty before God.

20Therefore by the deeds of the law there shall no flesh be justified in his sight: for by the law *is* the knowledge of sin.

21But now the righteousness of God without the law is manifested, being witnessed by the law and the prophets;

22Even the righteousness of God *which is* by faith of Jesus Christ unto all and upon all them that believe: for there is no difference:

23For all have sinned, and come short of the glory of God;

24Being justified freely by his grace through the redemption that is in Christ Jesus:

25Whom God hath set forth *to be* a propitiation through faith in his blood, to declare his righteousness for the remission of sins that are past, through the forbearance of God;

26To declare, *I say,* at this time his righteousness: that he might be just, and the justifier of him which believeth in Jesus.

27Where *is* boasting then? It is excluded. By what law? of works? Nay: but by the law of faith.

28Therefore we conclude that a man is justified by faith without the deeds of the law.

29 *Is he* the God of the Jews only? *is he* not also of the Gentiles? Yes, of the Gentiles also:

30Seeing *it is* one God, which shall justify the circumcision by faith, and uncircumcision through faith.

31Do we then make void the law through faith? God forbid: yea, we establish the law.

**4** WHAT SHALL we say then that Abraham our father, as pertaining to the flesh, hath found?

2For if Abraham were justified by works, he hath *whereof* to glory; but not before God.

3For what saith the scripture? Abraham believed God, and it was counted unto him for righteousness.

4Now to him that worketh is the reward not reckoned of grace, but of debt.

5But to him that worketh not, but believeth on him that justifieth the ungodly, his faith is counted for righteousness.

## Amplified

19Now we know that whatever the Law says it speaks to those who are under the Law, so that [the murmurs and excuses of] every mouth may be hushed, and all the world may be held accountable to God.

20For no person will be justified—made righteous, acquitted and judged acceptable—in His sight by observing the works prescribed by the Law. For [the real function of] the Law is to make men recognize *and* be conscious of sin [ [a]not mere perception, but an acquaintance with sin which works toward repentance, faith and holy character].

21But now the righteousness of God has been revealed independently *and* altogether apart from law, although actually it is attested by the Law and the prophets,

22Namely, the righteousness of God which comes by believing *with* personal trust *and* confident reliance on Jesus Christ, the Messiah. [And it is meant] for all who believe. For there is no distinction,

23Since all have sinned and are falling short of the honor *and* glory [b]which God bestows *and* receives.

24[All] are justified *and* made upright *and* in right standing with God, freely *and* gratuitously by His grace (His unmerited favor and mercy), through the redemption which is [provided] in Christ Jesus,

25Whom God put forward [ [c]before the eyes of all] as a mercy seat *and* propitiation by His blood—the cleansing and life-giving sacrifice of atonement and reconciliation—[to be received] through faith. This was to show God's righteousness, because in His divine forbearance He had passed over *and* ignored former sins without punishment.

26It was to demonstrate *and* prove at the present time ( [d]in the now season) that He Himself is righteous and that He justifies *and* accepts as righteous him who has [true] faith in Jesus.

27Then what becomes of [our] pride *and* [our] boasting? It is excluded—banished, ruled out entirely. On what principle? [On the principle] of doing good deeds? No, but on the principle of faith.

28For we hold that a man is justified *and* made upright by faith independent of *and* distinctly apart from good deeds (works of law).—The observance of the Law has nothing to do with justification.

29Or is God merely [the God] of Jews? Is He not the God of Gentiles also? Yes, of Gentiles also,

30Since it is one and the same God Who will justify the circumcised by faith [ [e]which germinated from Abraham] and the uncircumcised through their [newly acquired] faith.—[For] it is the same trusting faith in both cases, a firmly relying faith [in Jesus Christ].

31Do we then by [this] faith make the Law of no effect, overthrow it *or* make it a dead letter? Certainly not! On the contrary, we confirm *and* establish *and* uphold the Law.

**4** [BUT] IF so, what shall we say about Abraham, our forefather humanly speaking? (How does this affect his position, and what [f]was gained by him?)

2For if Abraham was justified (that is, [g]established as just by acquittal from guilt) by good works [that he did, then] he has grounds for boasting. But not before God!

3For what does the Scripture say? Abraham believed (trusted in) God, and it was credited to his account as righteousness—right living and right standing with God. [Gen. 15:6.]

4Now to a laborer, his wages are not counted as a favor *or* a gift, but as an obligation—something owed to him.

5But to one who not working [by Law] trusts (believes fully) in Him Who justifies the ungodly, his faith is credited to him as righteousness—the standing acceptable to God.

**AMP** [a] Vincent. [b] Vincent. [c] Bengel. [d] Literal translation. [e] Vincent. [f] Some ancient authorities so read. [g] Cremer.

## New American Standard

19¶ Now we know that whatever the Law says, it speaks to those who are under the Law, that every mouth may be closed, and all the world may become accountable to God;

20because by the works of the Law no flesh will be justified in His sight; for through the Law *comes* the knowledge of sin.

*Justification by Faith*

21¶ But now apart from the Law *the* righteousness of God has been manifested, being witnessed by the Law and the Prophets,

22even *the* righteousness of God through faith in Jesus Christ for all those who believe; for there is no distinction;

23for all have sinned and fall short of the glory of God,

24being justified as a gift by His grace through the redemption which is in Christ Jesus;

25whom God displayed publicly as a propitiation in His blood through faith. *This was* to demonstrate His righteousness, because in the forbearance of God He passed over the sins previously committed;

26for the demonstration, *I say*, of His righteousness at the present time, that He might be just and the justifier of the one who has faith in Jesus.

27Where then is boasting? It is excluded. By what kind of law? Of works? No, but by a law of faith.

28For we maintain that a man is justified by faith apart from works of the Law.

29Or is God *the God* of Jews only? Is He not *the God* of Gentiles also? Yes, of Gentiles also,

30since indeed God who will justify the circumcised by faith and the uncircumcised through faith is one.

31¶ Do we then nullify the Law through faith? May it never be! On the contrary, we establish the Law.

*Justification by Faith Evidenced in Old Testament*

4 WHAT THEN shall we say that Abraham, our forefather according to the flesh, has found?

2For if Abraham was justified by works, he has something to boast about; but not before God.

3For what does the Scripture say? "AND ABRAHAM BELIEVED GOD, AND IT WAS RECKONED TO HIM AS RIGHTEOUSNESS."

4Now to the one who works, his wage is not reckoned as a favor, but as what is due.

5But to the one who does not work, but believes in Him who justifies the ungodly, his faith is reckoned as righteousness,

## New International

19Now we know that whatever the law says, it says to those
who are under the law, so that every mouth may be silenced and
the whole world held accountable to God. 20Therefore no one will
be declared righteous in his sight by observing the law; rather,
through the law we become conscious of sin.

*Righteousness Through Faith*

21But now a righteousness from God, apart from law, has been
made known, to which the Law and the Prophets testify. 22This
righteousness from God comes through faith in Jesus Christ to all
who believe. There is no difference, 23for all have sinned and fall
short of the glory of God, 24and are justified freely by his grace
through the redemption that came by Christ Jesus. 25God
presented him as a sacrifice of atonement,[h] through faith in his
blood. He did this to demonstrate his justice, because in his forbearance he had left the sins committed beforehand unpunished — 26he did it to demonstrate his justice at the present time,
so as to be just and the one who justifies those who have faith in
Jesus.

27Where, then, is boasting? It is excluded. On what principle?
On that of observing the law? No, but on that of faith. 28For we
maintain that a man is justified by faith apart from observing the
law. 29Is God the God of Jews only? Is he not the God of Gentiles
too? Yes, of Gentiles too, 30since there is only one God, who will
justify the circumcised by faith and the uncircumcised through
that same faith. 31Do we, then, nullify the law by this faith? Not
at all! Rather, we uphold the law.

*Abraham Justified by Faith*

4 WHAT THEN shall we say that Abraham, our forefather,
discovered in this matter? 2If, in fact, Abraham was justified
by works, he had something to boast about—but not before God.
3What does the Scripture say? "Abraham believed God, and it was
credited to him as righteousness."[i]

4Now when a man works, his wages are not credited to him as
a gift, but as an obligation. 5However, to the man who does not
work but trusts God who justifies the wicked, his faith is credited
as righteousness. 6David says the same thing when he speaks of

**NIV** [h] 25 Or *as the one who would turn aside his wrath, taking away sin*
[i] 3 Gen. 15:6; also in verse 22

## King James

6Even as David also describeth the blessedness of the man, unto
whom God imputeth righteousness without works,
7 *Saying,* Blessed *are* they whose iniquities are forgiven, and
whose sins are covered.
8Blessed *is* the man to whom the Lord will not impute sin.
9 *Cometh* this blessedness then upon the circumcision *only,* or
upon the uncircumcision also? for we say that faith was reckoned
to Abraham for righteousness.
10How was it then reckoned? when he was in circumcision, or
in uncircumcision? Not in circumcision, but in uncircumcision.
11And he received the sign of circumcision, a seal of the righteousness of the faith which *he had yet* being uncircumcised: that he
might be the father of all them that believe, though they be not
circumcised; that righteousness might be imputed unto them also:
12And the father of circumcision to them who are not of the
circumcision only, but who also walk in the steps of that faith of
our father Abraham, which *he had* being *yet* uncircumcised.
13For the promise, that he should be the heir of the world, *was*
not to Abraham, or to his seed, through the law, but through the
righteousness of faith.
14For if they which are of the law *be* heirs, faith is made void,
and the promise made of none effect:
15Because the law worketh wrath: for where no law is, *there is*
no transgression.
16Therefore *it is* of faith, that *it might be* by grace; to the end the
promise might be sure to all the seed; not to that only which is of
the law, but to that also which is of the faith of Abraham; who is
the father of us all,
17(As it is written, I have made thee a father of many nations,)
before him whom he believed, *even* God, who quickeneth the
dead, and calleth those things which be not as though they were.
18Who against hope believed in hope, that he might become the
father of many nations, according to that which was spoken, So
shall thy seed be.
19And being not weak in faith, he considered not his own body
now dead, when he was about an hundred years old, neither yet
the deadness of Sarah's womb:
20He staggered not at the promise of God through unbelief; but
was strong in faith, giving glory to God;
21And being fully persuaded that, what he had promised, he
was able also to perform.
22And therefore it was imputed to him for righteousness.
23Now it was not written for his sake alone, that it was imputed
to him;
24But for us also, to whom it shall be imputed, if we believe on
him that raised up Jesus our Lord from the dead;
25Who was delivered for our offences, and was raised again for
our justification.

## Amplified

6Thus David [a]congratulates the man *and* pronounces a blessing
on him to whom God credits righteousness apart from the works
he does:
7Blessed *and* happy *and* [b]to be envied are those whose iniquities
are forgiven and whose sins are covered up *and* completely buried.
8Blessed *and* happy *and* [c]to be envied is the person of whose sin
the Lord will take no account *nor* reckon it against him. [Ps. 32:1,
2.]
9Is this blessing (this happiness) then meant only for the circumcised, or also for the uncircumcised? We say that faith was
credited to Abraham as righteousness.
10How then was it credited [to him]? Was it before or after he
had been circumcised? It was not after, but before he was circumcised.
11He received the mark of circumcision as a token *or* an evidence
or seal of the righteousness which he had by faith while he was
still uncircumcised, [faith] that he was to be made the father of all
who [truly] believe though without circumcision and who thus
have righteousness (right standing with God) imputed to them *and*
credited to their account,
12As well as to make him the father of those circumcised persons, who are not merely circumcised, but also walk in the way of
that faith which our father Abraham had before he was circumcised.
13For the promise to Abraham or his posterity, that he should
inherit the world, did not come through [observing the commands
of] the Law but through the righteousness of faith. [Gen. 17:4-6;
22:16-18.]
14If it is the adherents of the Law who are to be the heirs, then
faith is made futile *and* empty of all meaning, and the promise [of
God] is made void—is annulled and has no power.
15For the Law results in [divine] wrath, but where there is no
law there is no transgression [of it either].
16Therefore [inheriting] the promise is the outcome of faith *and*
depends [entirely] on faith, in order that it might be given as an
act of grace (unmerited favor), to make it stable *and* valid *and*
guaranteed to all his descendants; not only to the devotees *and*
adherents of the Law but also to those who share the faith of
Abraham, who is [thus] the father of us all,
17As it is written, I have made you the father of many nations.—He was appointed our father—in the sight of God in
Whom he believed, Who gives life to the dead and speaks of the
nonexistent things that [He has foretold and promised] as if they
[already] existed. [Gen. 17:5.]
18[For Abraham, human reason for] hope being gone, hoped on
in faith that he should become the father of many nations, as he
had been promised, So [numberless] shall your descendants be.
[Gen. 15:5.]
19He did not weaken in faith when he considered the [utter]
impotence of his own body, which was as good as dead because
he was about a hundred years old, or [when he considered] the
barrenness of Sarah's (deadened) womb. [Gen. 17:17; 18:11.]
20No unbelief *or* distrust made him waver *or* doubtingly question concerning the promise of God, but he grew strong *and* was
empowered by faith as he gave praise *and* glory to God,
21Fully satisfied *and* assured that God was able *and* mighty to
keep His word *and* to do what He had promised.
22That is why his faith was accredited to him as righteousness—
right standing with God.
23But [the words], It was accredited to him, were written not for
his sake alone,
24But [they were written] for our sakes too. [Righteousness,
standing acceptable to God] will be granted *and* accredited to us
also who believe—trust in, adhere to and rely on—God Who raised
Jesus our Lord from the dead,
25Who was betrayed and put to death because of our misdeeds
and was raised to secure our justification—our [d]acquittal, and to
make our account balance, absolving us from all guilt before God.

AMP [a] Souter. [b] Souter. [c] Souter. [d] Abbott-Smith.

## New American Standard

6just as David also speaks of the blessing upon the man to
whom God reckons righteousness apart from works:

7 "BLESSED ARE THOSE WHOSE LAWLESS DEEDS HAVE BEEN
FORGIVEN,
AND WHOSE SINS HAVE BEEN COVERED.
8 "BLESSED IS THE MAN WHOSE SIN THE LORD WILL NOT
TAKE INTO ACCOUNT."

9Is this blessing then upon the circumcised, or upon the uncircumcised also? For we say, "FAITH WAS RECKONED TO ABRAHAM AS
RIGHTEOUSNESS."
10How then was it reckoned? While he was circumcised, or
uncircumcised? Not while circumcised, but while uncircumcised;
11and he received the sign of circumcision, a seal of the righteousness of the faith which he had while uncircumcised, that he
might be the father of all who believe without being circumcised,
that righteousness might be reckoned to them,
12and the father of circumcision to those who not only are of the
circumcision, but who also follow in the steps of the faith of our
father Abraham which he had while uncircumcised.
13For the promise to Abraham or to his descendants that he
would be heir of the world was not through the Law, but through
the righteousness of faith.
14For if those who are of the Law are heirs, faith is made void
and the promise is nullified;
15for the Law brings about wrath, but where there is no law,
neither is there violation.
16For this reason *it is* by faith, that *it might be* in accordance with
grace, in order that the promise may be certain to all the descendants, not only to those who are of the Law, but also to those who
are of the faith of Abraham, who is the father of us all,
17(as it is written, "A FATHER OF MANY NATIONS HAVE I MADE
YOU") in the sight of Him whom he believed, *even* God, who gives
life to the dead and calls into being that which does not exist.
18In hope against hope he believed, in order that he might
become a father of many nations, according to that which had been
spoken, "SO SHALL YOUR DESCENDANTS BE."
19And without becoming weak in faith he contemplated his
own body, now as good as dead since he was about a hundred
years old, and the deadness of Sarah's womb;
20yet, with respect to the promise of God, he did not waver in
unbelief, but grew strong in faith, giving glory to God,
21and being fully assured that what He had promised, He was
able also to perform.
22Therefore also IT WAS RECKONED TO HIM AS RIGHTEOUSNESS.
23Now not for his sake only was it written, that it was reckoned
to him,
24but for our sake also, to whom it will be reckoned, as those
who believe in Him who raised Jesus our Lord from the dead,
25 *He* who was delivered up because of our transgressions, and
was raised because of our justification.

## New International

the blessedness of the man to whom God credits righteousness
apart from works:

7"Blessed are they
whose transgressions are forgiven,
whose sins are covered.
8Blessed is the man
whose sin the Lord will never count against him."[e]

9Is this blessedness only for the circumcised, or also for the
uncircumcised? We have been saying that Abraham's faith was
credited to him as righteousness. 10Under what circumstances was
it credited? Was it after he was circumcised, or before? It was not
after, but before! 11And he received the sign of circumcision, a seal
of the righteousness that he had by faith while he was still uncircumcised. So then, he is the father of all who believe but have not
been circumcised, in order that righteousness might be credited to
them. 12And he is also the father of the circumcised who not only
are circumcised but who also walk in the footsteps of the faith that
our father Abraham had before he was circumcised.
13It was not through law that Abraham and his offspring received the promise that he would be heir of the world, but through
the righteousness that comes by faith. 14For if those who live by
law are heirs, faith has no value and the promise is worthless,
15because law brings wrath. And where there is no law there is no
transgression.
16Therefore, the promise comes by faith, so that it may be by
grace and may be guaranteed to all Abraham's offspring—not only
to those who are of the law but also to those who are of the faith
of Abraham. He is the father of us all. 17As it is written: "I have
made you a father of many nations."[f] He is our father in the sight
of God, in whom he believed—the God who gives life to the dead
and calls things that are not as though they were.
18Against all hope, Abraham in hope believed and so became
the father of many nations, just as it had been said to him, "So shall
your offspring be."[g] 19Without weakening in his faith, he faced
the fact that his body was as good as dead—since he was about a
hundred years old—and that Sarah's womb was also dead. 20Yet
he did not waver through unbelief regarding the promise of God,
but was strengthened in his faith and gave glory to God, 21being
fully persuaded that God had power to do what he had promised.
22This is why "it was credited to him as righteousness." 23The
words "it was credited to him" were written not for him alone,
24but also for us, to whom God will credit righteousness—for us
who believe in him who raised Jesus our Lord from the dead. 25He
was delivered over to death for our sins and was raised to life for
our justification.

**NIV** [e] *8* Psalm 32:1,2 [f] *17* Gen. 17:5 [g] *18* Gen. 15:5

## King James

5 THEREFORE BEING justified by faith, we have peace with God through our Lord Jesus Christ:

2By whom also we have access by faith into this grace wherein we stand, and rejoice in hope of the glory of God.

3And not only *so*, but we glory in tribulations also: knowing that tribulation worketh patience;

4And patience, experience; and experience, hope:

5And hope maketh not ashamed; because the love of God is shed abroad in our hearts by the Holy Ghost which is given unto us.

6For when we were yet without strength, in due time Christ died for the ungodly.

7For scarcely for a righteous man will one die: yet peradventure for a good man some would even dare to die.

8But God commendeth his love toward us, in that, while we were yet sinners, Christ died for us.

9Much more then, being now justified by his blood, we shall be saved from wrath through him.

10For if, when we were enemies, we were reconciled to God by the death of his Son, much more, being reconciled, we shall be saved by his life.

11And not only *so*, but we also joy in God through our Lord Jesus Christ, by whom we have now received the atonement.

12Wherefore, as by one man sin entered into the world, and death by sin; and so death passed upon all men, for that all have sinned:

13(For until the law sin was in the world: but sin is not imputed when there is no law.

14Nevertheless death reigned from Adam to Moses, even over them that had not sinned after the similitude of Adam's transgression, who is the figure of him that was to come.

15But not as the offence, so also *is* the free gift. For if through the offence of one many be dead, much more the grace of God, and the gift by grace, *which is* by one man, Jesus Christ, hath abounded unto many.

16And not as *it was* by one that sinned, *so is* the gift: for the judgment *was* by one to condemnation, but the free gift *is* of many offences unto justification.

17For if by one man's offence death reigned by one; much more they which receive abundance of grace and of the gift of righteousness shall reign in life by one, Jesus Christ.)

## Amplified

5 THEREFORE, SINCE we are justified— [a]acquitted, declared righteous, and given a right standing with God—through faith, let us [grasp the fact that we] have [the peace of reconciliation] to hold *and* to [b]enjoy, peace with God through our Lord Jesus Christ, the Messiah, the Anointed One.

2Through Him also we have [our] access (entrance, introduction) by faith into this grace—state of God's favor—in which we [firmly and safely] stand. And [c]let us rejoice *and* exult in our hope of experiencing *and* enjoying the glory of God.

3Moreover—let us also be full of joy now! [d]Let us exult *and* triumph in our troubles *and* rejoice in our sufferings, knowing that pressure *and* affliction *and* hardship produce patient *and* unswerving endurance.

4And endurance (fortitude) develops maturity of [e]character—that is, approved faith and [f]tried integrity. And character [of this sort] produces [the habit of] [g]joyful and confident hope of eternal salvation.

5Such hope never disappoints *or* deludes *or* shames us, for God's love has been poured out in our hearts through the Holy Spirit Who has been given to us.

6While we were yet in weakness—powerless to help ourselves—at the fitting time Christ died for (in behalf of) the ungodly.

7Now it is an extraordinary thing for one to give his life even for an upright man, though perhaps for a noble *and* lovable *and* generous benefactor someone might even dare to die.

8But God shows *and* clearly proves His [own] love for us by the fact that while we were still sinners Christ, the Messiah, the Anointed One, died for us.

9Therefore, since we are now justified— [h]acquitted, made righteous and brought into right relationship with God—by Christ's blood, how much more [certain is it that] we shall be saved by Him from the indignation *and* wrath of God.

10For if while we were enemies we were reconciled to God through the death of His Son, it is much more [certain], now that we are reconciled, that we shall be saved [daily delivered from sin's dominion] through His [ [i]resurrection] life.

11Not only so, but we also rejoice *and* exultingly glory in God [His love and perfection] through our Lord Jesus Christ, through Whom we have now received *and* enjoy [our] reconciliation. [Jer. 9:24.]

12Therefore as sin came into the world through one man and death as the result of sin, so death spread to all men, [ [j]no one being able to stop it *or* to escape its power] because all men sinned.

13[To be sure,] sin was in the world before ever the Law was given, but sin is not charged to men's account where there is no law [to transgress].

14Yet death held sway from Adam to Moses [the Lawgiver], even over those who did not themselves transgress [a positive command] as Adam did. Adam was a type (prefigure) of the One Who was to come [in reverse, [k]the former destructive, the Latter saving]. [Gen. 5:5; 7:22; Deut. 34:5.]

15But God's free gift is not at all to be compared to the trespass—His grace is out of all proportion to the fall of man. For if many died through one man's falling away—his lapse, his offense—much more profusely did God's grace and the free gift [that comes] through the undeserved favor of the one Man Jesus Christ, abound *and* overflow to *and* for [the benefit of] many.

16Nor is the free gift at all to be compared to the effect of that one [man's] sin. For the sentence [following the trespass] of one [man] brought condemnation, whereas the free gift [following] many transgressions brings justification— [l]an act of righteousness.

17For if, because of one man's trespass (lapse, offense) death reigned through that one, much more surely will those who receive [God's] overflowing grace (unmerited favor) and the free gift of righteousness (putting them into right standing with Himself) reign as kings in life through the One, Jesus Christ, the Messiah, the Anointed One.

**AMP** [a] Abbott-Smith. [b] Literally, "have" or "hold," so "enjoy." [c] Alternate reading. [d] Alternate reading. [e] Souter. [f] Vincent. [g] Thayer. [h] Abbott-Smith. [i] Abbott-Smith. [j] Thayer. [k] Thayer. [l] Literal meaning.

## New American Standard

*Results of Justification*

5 THEREFORE HAVING been justified by faith, we have peace with God through our Lord Jesus Christ,

2through whom also we have obtained our introduction by faith into this grace in which we stand; and we exult in hope of the glory of God.

3And not only this, but we also exult in our tribulations, knowing that tribulation brings about perseverance;

4and perseverance, proven character; and proven character, hope;

5and hope does not disappoint, because the love of God has been poured out within our hearts through the Holy Spirit who was given to us.

6For while we were still helpless, at the right time Christ died for the ungodly.

7For one will hardly die for a righteous man; though perhaps for the good man someone would dare even to die.

8But God demonstrates His own love toward us, in that while we were yet sinners, Christ died for us.

9Much more then, having now been justified by His blood, we shall be saved from the wrath *of God* through Him.

10For if while we were enemies, we were reconciled to God through the death of His Son, much more, having been reconciled, we shall be saved by His life.

11And not only this, but we also exult in God through our Lord Jesus Christ, through whom we have now received the reconciliation.

12¶ Therefore, just as through one man sin entered into the world, and death through sin, and so death spread to all men, because all sinned—

13for until the Law sin was in the world; but sin is not imputed when there is no law.

14Nevertheless death reigned from Adam until Moses, even over those who had not sinned in the likeness of the offense of Adam, who is a [m]type of Him who was to come.

15But the free gift is not like the transgression. For if by the transgression of the one the many died, much more did the grace of God and the gift by the grace of the one Man, Jesus Christ, abound to the many.

16And the gift is not like *that which came* through the one who sinned; for on the one hand the judgment *arose* from one *transgression* resulting in condemnation, but on the other hand the free gift *arose* from many transgressions resulting in justification.

17For if by the transgression of the one, death reigned through the one, much more those who receive the abundance of grace and of the gift of righteousness will reign in life through the One, Jesus Christ.

NAS [m]Or, *foreshadowing*

## New International

*Peace and Joy*

5 THEREFORE, SINCE we have been justified through faith,
we[n] have peace with God through our Lord Jesus Christ,
2through whom we have gained access by faith into this grace in
which we now stand. And we[o] rejoice in the hope of the glory of
God. 3Not only so, but we[p] also rejoice in our sufferings, because
we know that suffering produces perseverance; 4perseverance,
character; and character, hope. 5And hope does not disappoint us,
because God has poured out his love into our hearts by the Holy
Spirit, whom he has given us.

6You see, at just the right time, when we were still powerless,
Christ died for the ungodly. 7Very rarely will anyone die for a
righteous man, though for a good man someone might possibly
dare to die. 8But God demonstrates his own love for us in this:
While we were still sinners, Christ died for us.

9Since we have now been justified by his blood, how much
more shall we be saved from God's wrath through him! 10For if,
when we were God's enemies, we were reconciled to him through
the death of his Son, how much more, having been reconciled,
shall we be saved through his life! 11Not only is this so, but we also
rejoice in God through our Lord Jesus Christ, through whom we
have now received reconciliation.

*Death Through Adam, Life Through Christ*

12Therefore, just as sin entered the world through one man, and
death through sin, and in this way death came to all men, because
all sinned— 13for before the law was given, sin was in the world.
But sin is not taken into account when there is no law. 14Neverthe-
less, death reigned from the time of Adam to the time of Moses,
even over those who did not sin by breaking a command, as did
Adam, who was a pattern of the one to come.

15But the gift is not like the trespass. For if the many died by
the trespass of the one man, how much more did God's grace and
the gift that came by the grace of the one man, Jesus Christ,
overflow to the many! 16Again, the gift of God is not like the result
of the one man's sin: The judgment followed one sin and brought
condemnation, but the gift followed many trespasses and brought
justification. 17For if, by the trespass of the one man, death reigned
through that one man, how much more will those who receive
God's abundant provision of grace and of the gift of righteousness
reign in life through the one man, Jesus Christ.

NIV [n]1 Or *let us* [o]2 Or *let us* [p]3 Or *let us*

## King James

18 Therefore as by the offence of one *judgment came* upon all men to condemnation; even so by the righteousness of one *the free gift came* upon all men unto justification of life.

19 For as by one man's disobedience many were made sinners, so by the obedience of one shall many be made righteous.

20 Moreover the law entered, that the offence might abound. But where sin abounded, grace did much more abound:

21 That as sin hath reigned unto death, even so might grace reign through righteousness unto eternal life by Jesus Christ our Lord.

**6** WHAT SHALL we say then? Shall we continue in sin, that grace may abound?

2 God forbid. How shall we, that are dead to sin, live any longer therein?

3 Know ye not, that so many of us as were baptized into Jesus Christ were baptized into his death?

4 Therefore we are buried with him by baptism into death: that like as Christ was raised up from the dead by the glory of the Father, even so we also should walk in newness of life.

5 For if we have been planted together in the likeness of his death, we shall be also *in the likeness* of *his* resurrection:

6 Knowing this, that our old man is crucified with *him,* that the body of sin might be destroyed, that henceforth we should not serve sin.

7 For he that is dead is freed from sin.

8 Now if we be dead with Christ, we believe that we shall also live with him:

9 Knowing that Christ being raised from the dead dieth no more; death hath no more dominion over him.

10 For in that he died, he died unto sin once: but in that he liveth, he liveth unto God.

11 Likewise reckon ye also yourselves to be dead indeed unto sin, but alive unto God through Jesus Christ our Lord.

12 Let not sin therefore reign in your mortal body, that ye should obey it in the lusts thereof.

13 Neither yield ye your members *as* instruments of unrighteousness unto sin: but yield yourselves unto God, as those that are alive from the dead, and your members *as* instruments of righteousness unto God.

14 For sin shall not have dominion over you: for ye are not under the law, but under grace.

15 What then? shall we sin, because we are not under the law, but under grace? God forbid.

16 Know ye not, that to whom ye yield yourselves servants to obey, his servants ye are to whom ye obey; whether of sin unto death, or of obedience unto righteousness?

## Amplified

18 Well then, as one man's trespass—one man's false step and falling away—[led] to condemnation for all men, so one Man's act of righteousness [leads] to acquittal *and* right standing with God, and life for all men.

19 For just as by one man's disobedience (failing to hear, [a]heedlessness and carelessness) the many were constituted sinners, so by one Man's obedience the many will be constituted righteous—made acceptable to God, brought into right standing with Him.

20 But then Law came in, [only] to expand *and* increase the trespass [making it more apparent and exciting opposition]. But where sin increased *and* abounded, grace (God's unmerited favor) has surpassed it *and* increased the more *and* superabounded.

21 So that, [just] as sin has reigned in death, so grace—His unearned and undeserved favor—might reign also through righteousness (right standing with God) which issues in eternal life through Jesus Christ, the Messiah, the Anointed One, our Lord.

**6** WHAT SHALL we say [to all this]? Are we to remain in sin in order that God's grace (favor and mercy) may multiply *and* overflow?

2 Certainly not! How can we who died to sin live in it any longer?

3 Are you ignorant of the fact that all of us who have been baptized into Christ Jesus were baptized into His death?

4 We were buried therefore with Him by the baptism into death, so that just as Christ was raised from the dead by the glorious [power] of the Father, so we too might habitually live *and* behave in newness of life.

5 For if we have become one with Him by sharing a death like His, we shall also be [one with Him in sharing] His resurrection [by a new life lived for God].

6 We know that our old (unrenewed) self was nailed to the cross with Him in order that [our] body, [which is the instrument] of sin, might be made ineffective *and* inactive for evil, that we might no longer be the slaves of sin.

7 For when a man dies he is freed—loosed, delivered—from [the power of] sin [among men].

8 Now if we have died with Christ, we believe that we shall also live with Him.

9 Because we know that Christ, the Anointed One, being once raised from the dead will never die again; death no longer has power over Him.

10 For by the death He died, He died to sin [ending His relation to it] once for all, and the life that He lives He is living to God—in unbroken fellowship with Him.

11 Even so consider yourselves also dead to sin *and* your relation to it broken, but [that you are] alive to God—living in unbroken fellowship with Him—in Christ Jesus.

12 Let not sin therefore rule as king in your mortal (short-lived, perishable) bodies, to make you yield to their cravings *and* be subject to their lusts *and* evil passions.

13 Do not continue offering or yielding your bodily members [and [b]faculties] to sin as instruments (tools) of wickedness. But offer *and* yield yourselves to God as though you have been raised from the dead to [perpetual] life, and your bodily members [and [c]faculties] to God, presenting them as implements of righteousness.

14 For sin shall not [any longer] exert dominion over you, since now you are not under Law [as slaves], but under grace—as subjects of God's favor and mercy.

15 What then [are we to conclude]? Shall we sin because we live not under Law but under God's favor *and* mercy? Certainly not!

16 Do you not know that if you continually surrender yourselves to any one to do his will, you are the slaves of him whom you obey, whether that be to sin, which leads to death, or to obedience which leads to righteousness—right doing and right standing with God?

**AMP** [a] Vincent, Bengel. [b] *Mele*—"Physical; though some include mental faculties."—Vincent's "Word Studies in The New Testament." [c] *Mele*—"Physical; though some include mental faculties."—Vincent's "Word Studies in The New Testament."

## New American Standard

18So then as through one transgression there resulted condemnation to all men, even so through one act of righteousness there resulted justification of life to all men.

19For as through the one man's disobedience the many were made sinners, even so through the obedience of the One the many will be made righteous.

20And the Law came in that the transgression might increase; but where sin increased, grace abounded all the more,

21that, as sin reigned in death, even so grace might reign through righteousness to eternal life through Jesus Christ our Lord.

*Believers Are Dead to Sin, Alive to God*

6 WHAT SHALL we say then? Are we to continue in sin that grace might increase?

2May it never be! How shall we who died to sin still live in it?

3Or do you not know that all of us who have been baptized into Christ Jesus have been baptized into His death?

4Therefore we have been buried with Him through baptism into death, in order that as Christ was raised from the dead through the glory of the Father, so we too might walk in newness of life.

5For if we have become united with *Him* in the likeness of His death, certainly we shall be also *in the likeness* of His resurrection,

6knowing this, that our old self was crucified with *Him*, that our body of sin might be done away with, that we should no longer be slaves to sin;

7for he who has died is freed from sin.

8Now if we have died with Christ, we believe that we shall also live with Him,

9knowing that Christ, having been raised from the dead, is never to die again; death no longer is master over Him.

10For the death that He died, He died to sin, once for all; but the life that He lives, He lives to God.

11Even so consider yourselves to be dead to sin, but alive to God in Christ Jesus.

12¶ Therefore do not let sin reign in your mortal body that you should obey its lusts,

13and do not go on presenting the members of your body to sin *as* instruments of unrighteousness; but present yourselves to God as those alive from the dead, and your members *as* instruments of righteousness to God.

14For sin shall not be master over you, for you are not under law, but under grace.

15¶ What then? Shall we sin because we are not under law but under grace? May it never be!

16Do you not know that when you present yourselves to someone *as* slaves for obedience, you are slaves of the one whom you obey, either of sin resulting in death, or of obedience resulting in righteousness?

## New International

18Consequently, just as the result of one trespass was condemnation for all men, so also the result of one act of righteousness was
justification that brings life for all men. 19For just as through the
disobedience of the one man the many were made sinners, so also
through the obedience of the one man the many will be made
righteous.
20The law was added so that the trespass might increase. But
where sin increased, grace increased all the more, 21so that, just
as sin reigned in death, so also grace might reign through righteousness to bring eternal life through Jesus Christ our Lord.

*Dead to Sin, Alive in Christ*

6 WHAT SHALL we say, then? Shall we go on sinning so that
grace may increase? 2By no means! We died to sin; how can
we live in it any longer? 3Or don't you know that all of us who were
baptized into Christ Jesus were baptized into his death? 4We were
therefore buried with him through baptism into death in order
that, just as Christ was raised from the dead through the glory of
the Father, we too may live a new life.
5If we have been united with him like this in his death, we will
certainly also be united with him in his resurrection. 6For we know
that our old self was crucified with him so that the body of sin
might be done away with,[d] that we should no longer be slaves to
sin— 7because anyone who has died has been freed from sin.
8Now if we died with Christ, we believe that we will also live
with him. 9For we know that since Christ was raised from the
dead, he cannot die again; death no longer has mastery over him.
10The death he died, he died to sin once for all; but the life he lives,
he lives to God.
11In the same way, count yourselves dead to sin but alive to God
in Christ Jesus. 12Therefore do not let sin reign in your mortal body
so that you obey its evil desires. 13Do not offer the parts of your
body to sin, as instruments of wickedness, but rather offer yourselves to God, as those who have been brought from death to life;
and offer the parts of your body to him as instruments of righteousness. 14For sin shall not be your master, because you are not
under law, but under grace.

*Slaves to Righteousness*

15What then? Shall we sin because we are not under law but
under grace? By no means! 16Don't you know that when you offer
yourselves to someone to obey him as slaves, you are slaves to the
one whom you obey—whether you are slaves to sin, which leads
to death, or to obedience, which leads to righteousness? 17But

NIV [d] 6 Or *be rendered powerless*

## King James

17 But God be thanked, that ye were the servants of sin, but ye have obeyed from the heart that form of doctrine which was delivered you.

18 Being then made free from sin, ye became the servants of righteousness.

19 I speak after the manner of men because of the infirmity of your flesh: for as ye have yielded your members servants to uncleanness and to iniquity unto iniquity; even so now yield your members servants to righteousness unto holiness.

20 For when ye were the servants of sin, ye were free from righteousness.

21 What fruit had ye then in those things whereof ye are now ashamed? for the end of those things *is* death.

22 But now being made free from sin, and become servants to God, ye have your fruit unto holiness, and the end everlasting life.

23 For the wages of sin *is* death; but the gift of God *is* eternal life through Jesus Christ our Lord.

7 KNOW YE not, brethren, (for I speak to them that know the law,) how that the law hath dominion over a man as long as he liveth?

2 For the woman which hath an husband is bound by the law to *her* husband so long as he liveth; but if the husband be dead, she is loosed from the law of *her* husband.

3 So then if, while *her* husband liveth, she be married to another man, she shall be called an adulteress: but if her husband be dead, she is free from that law; so that she is no adulteress, though she be married to another man.

4 Wherefore, my brethren, ye also are become dead to the law by the body of Christ; that ye should be married to another, *even* to him who is raised from the dead, that we should bring forth fruit unto God.

5 For when we were in the flesh, the motions of sins, which were by the law, did work in our members to bring forth fruit unto death.

6 But now we are delivered from the law, that being dead wherein we were held; that we should serve in newness of spirit, and not *in* the oldness of the letter.

7 What shall we say then? *Is* the law sin? God forbid. Nay, I had not known sin, but by the law: for I had not known lust, except the law had said, Thou shalt not covet.

8 But sin, taking occasion by the commandment, wrought in me all manner of concupiscence. For without the law sin *was* dead.

9 For I was alive without the law once: but when the commandment came, sin revived, and I died.

10 And the commandment, which *was ordained* to life, I found *to be* unto death.

## Amplified

17 But thank God, though you were once slaves of sin you have become obedient with all your heart to the standard of teaching in which you were instructed *and* to which you were committed.

18 And, having been set free from sin, you have become the servants of righteousness—of conformity to the divine will in thought, purpose and action.

19 I am speaking in familiar human terms, because of your natural limitations. For as you yielded your bodily members [and [a]faculties] as servants to impurity and ever increasing lawlessness, so now yield your bodily members [and [b]faculties] once for all as servants to righteousness—right being and doing—[which leads] to sanctification.

20 For when you were slaves of sin, you were free in regard to righteousness.

21 But then what benefit (return) did you get from the things of which you are now ashamed? [None,] for the end of those things is death.

22 But now since you have been set free from sin and have become the slaves of God, you have your present reward in holiness and its end is eternal life.

23 For the wages which sin pays is death; but the [bountiful] free gift of God is eternal life through (in union with) Jesus Christ our Lord.

7 DO YOU not know, brethren, for I am speaking to men who are acquainted with the Law, that legal claims have power over a person only for so long as he is alive?

2 For [instance] a married woman is bound by law to her husband as long as he lives; but if her husband dies she is loosed *and* discharged from the law concerning her husband.

3 Accordingly, she will be held an adulteress if she unites herself to another man while her husband lives. But if her husband dies, the marriage law no longer is binding on her—she is free from that law—and if she unites herself to another man she is not an adulteress.

4 Likewise, my brethren, you have undergone death as to the Law through the [crucified] body of Christ, so that now you may belong to Another, to Him Who was raised from the dead in order that we may bear fruit for God.

5 When we were living in the flesh (mere physical lives) the sinful passions that were awakened *and* aroused up by [what] the Law [makes sin] were constantly operating in our natural powers—in our bodily organs, [c]in the sensitive appetites and wills of the flesh—so that we bore fruit for death.

6 But now we are discharged from the Law *and* have terminated all intercourse with it, having died to what once restrained *and* held us captive. So now we serve not under [obedience to] the old code of written regulations, but [under obedience to the promptings] of the Spirit in newness [of life].

7 What then do we conclude? Is the Law identical with sin? Certainly not! Nevertheless, if it had not been for the Law, I should not have recognized sin *or* have known its meaning. [For instance] I would not have known about covetousness—would have had no consciousness of sin or sense of guilt—if the Law had not [repeatedly] said, You shall not covet *and* have an evil desire [for one thing and another]. [Exod. 20:17; Deut. 5:21.]

8 But sin, finding opportunity in the commandment [to express itself] got a hold on me *and* aroused *and* stimulated all kinds of forbidden desires (lust, covetousness). For without the Law sin is dead—the sense of it is inactive and a lifeless thing.

9 Once I was alive but quite apart from *and* unconscious of the Law. But when the commandment came, sin lived again, and I died—was sentenced by the Law to death. [Ps. 73:22.]

10 And the very legal ordinance which was designed *and* intended to bring life, actually proved [to mean to me] death. [Lev. 18:5.]

**AMP** [a] *Mele*—"Physical; though some include mental faculties."—Vincent's "Word Studies in The New Testament." [b] *Mele*—"Physical; though some include mental faculties."—Vincent's "Word Studies in The New Testament." [c] Matthew Henry's Commentary.

## New American Standard

17But thanks be to God that though you were slaves of sin, you
became obedient from the heart to that form of teaching to which
you were committed,
18and having been freed from sin, you became slaves of righteousness.
19I am speaking in human terms because of the weakness of
your flesh. For just as you presented your members *as* slaves to
impurity and to lawlessness, resulting in *further* lawlessness, so
now present your members *as* slaves to righteousness, resulting in
sanctification.
20For when you were slaves of sin, you were free in regard to
righteousness.
21Therefore what benefit were you then deriving from the
things of which you are now ashamed? For the outcome of those
things is death.
22But now having been freed from sin and enslaved to God, you
derive your benefit, resulting in sanctification, and the outcome,
eternal life.
23For the wages of sin is death, but the free gift of God is eternal
life in Christ Jesus our Lord.

*Believers United to Christ*

7 OR DO you not know, brethren (for I am speaking to those
who know the law), that the law has jurisdiction over a person as long as he lives?
2For the married woman is bound by law to her husband while
he is living; but if her husband dies, she is released from the law
concerning the husband.
3So then if, while her husband is living, she is joined to another
man, she shall be called an adulteress; but if her husband dies, she
is free from the law, so that she is not an adulteress, though she
is joined to another man.
4Therefore, my brethren, you also were made to die to the Law
through the body of Christ, that you might be joined to another,
to Him who was raised from the dead, that we might bear fruit for
God.
5For while we were in the flesh, the sinful passions, which
were *aroused* by the Law, were at work in the members of our body
to bear fruit for death.
6But now we have been released from the Law, having died to
that by which we were bound, so that we serve in newness of the
[d]Spirit and not in oldness of the letter.
7¶ What shall we say then? Is the Law sin? May it never be! On
the contrary, I would not have come to know sin except through
the Law; for I would not have known about coveting if the Law
had not said, "YOU SHALL NOT COVET."
8But sin, taking opportunity through the commandment, produced in me coveting of every kind; for apart from the Law sin *is*
dead.
9And I was once alive apart from the Law; but when the
commandment came, sin became alive, and I died;
10and this commandment, which was to result in life, proved
to result in death for me;

NAS [d] Or, *spirit*

## New International

thanks be to God that, though you used to be slaves to sin, you
wholeheartedly obeyed the form of teaching to which you were
entrusted. 18You have been set free from sin and have become
slaves to righteousness.
19I put this in human terms because you are weak in your
natural selves. Just as you used to offer the parts of your body in
slavery to impurity and to ever-increasing wickedness, so now
offer them in slavery to righteousness leading to holiness. 20When
you were slaves to sin, you were free from the control of righteousness. 21What benefit did you reap at that time from the things you
are now ashamed of? Those things result in death! 22But now that
you have been set free from sin and have become slaves to God,
the benefit you reap leads to holiness, and the result is eternal life.
23For the wages of sin is death, but the gift of God is eternal life
in[e] Christ Jesus our Lord.

*An Illustration From Marriage*

7 DO YOU not know, brothers—for I am speaking to men who
know the law—that the law has authority over a man only as
long as he lives? 2For example, by law a married woman is bound
to her husband as long as he is alive, but if her husband dies, she
is released from the law of marriage. 3So then, if she marries
another man while her husband is still alive, she is called an
adulteress. But if her husband dies, she is released from that law
and is not an adulteress, even though she marries another man.
4So, my brothers, you also died to the law through the body of
Christ, that you might belong to another, to him who was raised
from the dead, in order that we might bear fruit to God. 5For when
we were controlled by the sinful nature,[f] the sinful passions
aroused by the law were at work in our bodies, so that we bore fruit
for death. 6But now, by dying to what once bound us, we have
been released from the law so that we serve in the new way of the
Spirit, and not in the old way of the written code.

*Struggling With Sin*

7What shall we say, then? Is the law sin? Certainly not! Indeed
I would not have known what sin was except through the law. For
I would not have known what coveting really was if the law had
not said, "Do not covet."[g] 8But sin, seizing the opportunity afforded by the commandment, produced in me every kind of covetous
desire. For apart from law, sin is dead. 9Once I was alive apart from
law; but when the commandment came, sin sprang to life and I
died. 10I found that the very commandment that was intended to
bring life actually brought death. 11For sin, seizing the opportunity

NIV [e] 23 Or *through* [f] 5 Or *the flesh;* also in verse 25 [g] 7 Exodus 20:17;
Deut. 5:21

## King James

11For sin, taking occasion by the commandment, deceived me, and by it slew *me.*

12Wherefore the law *is* holy, and the commandment holy, and just, and good.

13Was then that which is good made death unto me? God forbid. But sin, that it might appear sin, working death in me by that which is good; that sin by the commandment might become exceeding sinful.

14For we know that the law is spiritual: but I am carnal, sold under sin.

15For that which I do I allow not: for what I would, that do I not; but what I hate, that do I.

16If then I do that which I would not, I consent unto the law that *it is* good.

17Now then it is no more I that do it, but sin that dwelleth in me.

18For I know that in me (that is, in my flesh,) dwelleth no good thing: for to will is present with me; but *how* to perform that which is good I find not.

19For the good that I would I do not: but the evil which I would not, that I do.

20Now if I do that I would not, it is no more I that do it, but sin that dwelleth in me.

21I find then a law, that, when I would do good, evil is present with me.

22For I delight in the law of God after the inward man:

23But I see another law in my members, warring against the law of my mind, and bringing me into captivity to the law of sin which is in my members.

24O wretched man that I am! who shall deliver me from the body of this death?

25I thank God through Jesus Christ our Lord. So then with the mind I myself serve the law of God; but with the flesh the law of sin.

**8** *THERE IS* therefore now no condemnation to them which are in Christ Jesus, who walk not after the flesh, but after the Spirit.

2For the law of the Spirit of life in Christ Jesus hath made me free from the law of sin and death.

3For what the law could not do, in that it was weak through the flesh, God sending his own Son in the likeness of sinful flesh, and for sin, condemned sin in the flesh:

4That the righteousness of the law might be fulfilled in us, who walk not after the flesh, but after the Spirit.

## Amplified

11For sin, seizing the opportunity *and* getting a hold on me [by taking its incentive] from the commandment, beguiled *and* entrapped *and* cheated me, and using it [as a weapon] killed me.

12The Law therefore is holy, and [each] commandment is holy and just and good.

13Did that which is good then prove fatal (bringing death) to me? Certainly not! It was sin, working death in me by using this good thing [as a weapon], in order that through the commandment sin might be shown up clearly to be sin, that the extreme malignity and immeasurable sinfulness of sin might plainly appear.

14We know that the Law is spiritual; but I am a creature of the flesh (carnal, unspiritual), having been sold into slavery under [the control of] sin.

15For I do not understand my own actions—I am baffled, bewildered. I do not practice *or* accomplish what I wish, but I do the very thing that I loathe [ [a]which my moral instinct condemns].

16Now if I do [habitually] what is contrary to my desire, [that means that] I acknowledge *and* agree that the Law is good (morally excellent) *and* that I take sides with it.

17However, it is no longer I who do the deed, but the sin [principle] which is at home in me *and* has possession of me.

18For I know that nothing good dwells within me, that is, in my flesh. I can will what is right, but I cannot perform it.—I have the intention and urge to do what is right, but no power to carry it out;

19For I fail to practice the good deeds I desire to do, but the evil deeds that I do not desire to do are what I am [ever] doing.

20Now if I do what I do not desire to do, it is no longer I doing it—it is not myself that acts—but the sin [principle] which dwells within me [ [b]fixed and operating in my soul].

21So I find it to be a law [of my being] that when I want to do what is right *and* good, evil is ever present with me *and* I am subject to its insistent demands.

22For I endorse *and* delight in the Law of God in my inmost self—with my new nature. [Ps. 1:2.]

23But I discern in my bodily members— [c]in the sensitive appetites and wills of the flesh—a different law (rule of action) at war against the law of my mind (my reason) and making me a prisoner to the law of sin that dwells in my bodily organs— [d]in the sensitive appetites and wills of the flesh.

24O unhappy *and* pitiable *and* wretched man that I am! Who will release *and* deliver me from [the shackles of] this body of death?

25O thank God!—He will! through Jesus Christ, the Anointed One, our Lord! So then indeed I of myself with the mind *and* heart serve the Law of God, but with the flesh the law of sin.

**8** THEREFORE [THERE is] now no condemnation—no adjudging guilty of wrong—for those who are in Christ Jesus, *who live not after the dictates of the flesh, but after the dictates of the Spirit.* [cf. John 3:18.]

2For the law of the Spirit of life [which is] in Christ Jesus [the law of our new being], has freed me from the law of sin and of death.

3For God has done what the Law could not do, [its power] being weakened by the flesh [that is, [e]the entire nature of man without the Holy Spirit]. Sending His own Son in the guise of sinful flesh and [f]as an offering for sin, [God] condemned sin in the flesh— [g]subdued, overcame, [h]deprived it of its power [over all who accept that sacrifice]. [Lev. 7:37.]

4So that the righteous *and* just requirement of the Law might be fully met in us, who live *and* move not in the ways of the flesh but in the ways of the Spirit—our lives governed not by the standards *and* according to the dictates of the flesh, but controlled by the (Holy) Spirit.

**AMP** [a] Godet (—Vincent). [b] Thayer. [c] Matthew Henry's Commentary. [d] Matthew Henry's Commentary. [e] Melanchthon (—Vincent). [f] Alternate reading. [g] Thayer. [h] Vincent.

## New American Standard

11for sin, taking opportunity through the commandment, deceived me, and through it killed me.
12So then, the Law is holy, and the commandment is holy and
righteous and good.
13Therefore did that which is good become *a cause of* death for
me? May it never be! Rather it was sin, in order that it might be
shown to be sin by effecting my death through that which is good,
that through the commandment sin might become utterly sinful.

*The Conflict of Two Natures*

14For we know that the Law is spiritual; but I am of flesh, sold
into bondage to sin.
15For that which I am doing, I do not understand; for I am not
practicing what I *would* like to *do,* but I am doing the very thing I
hate.
16But if I do the very thing I do not wish *to do,* I agree with the
Law, *confessing* that it is good.
17So now, no longer am I the one doing it, but sin which
indwells me.
18For I know that nothing good dwells in me, that is, in my
flesh; for the wishing is present in me, but the doing of the good
*is* not.
19For the good that I wish, I do not do; but I practice the very
evil that I do not wish.
20But if I am doing the very thing I do not wish, I am no longer
the one doing it, but sin which dwells in me.
21I find then the principle that evil is present in me, the one who
wishes to do good.
22For I joyfully concur with the law of God in the inner man,
23but I see a different law in the members of my body, waging
war against the law of my mind, and making me a prisoner of the
law of sin which is in my members.
24Wretched man that I am! Who will set me free from the body
of this death?
25Thanks be to God through Jesus Christ our Lord! So then, on
the one hand I myself with my mind am serving the law of God,
but on the other, with my flesh the law of sin.

*Deliverance from Bondage*

8 THERE IS therefore now no condemnation for those who are
in Christ Jesus.
2For the law of the Spirit of life in Christ Jesus has set [i]you free
from the law of sin and of death.
3For what the Law could not do, weak as it was through the
flesh, God *did:* sending His own Son in the likeness of sinful flesh
and *as an offering* for sin, He condemned sin in the flesh,
4in order that the requirement of the Law might be fulfilled in
us, who do not walk according to the flesh, but according to the
Spirit.

NAS [i] Some ancient mss. read *me*

## New International

afforded by the commandment, deceived me, and through the
commandment put me to death. 12So then, the law is holy, and the
commandment is holy, righteous and good.
13Did that which is good, then, become death to me? By no
means! But in order that sin might be recognized as sin, it produced death in me through what was good, so that through the
commandment sin might become utterly sinful.
14We know that the law is spiritual; but I am unspiritual, sold
as a slave to sin. 15I do not understand what I do. For what I want
to do I do not do, but what I hate I do. 16And if I do what I do not
want to do, I agree that the law is good. 17As it is, it is no longer
I myself who do it, but it is sin living in me. 18I know that nothing
good lives in me, that is, in my sinful nature.[j] For I have the desire
to do what is good, but I cannot carry it out. 19For what I do is not
the good I want to do; no, the evil I do not want to do—this I keep
on doing. 20Now if I do what I do not want to do, it is no longer
I who do it, but it is sin living in me that does it.
21So I find this law at work: When I want to do good, evil is right
there with me. 22For in my inner being I delight in God's law; 23but
I see another law at work in the members of my body, waging war
against the law of my mind and making me a prisoner of the law
of sin at work within my members. 24What a wretched man I am!
Who will rescue me from this body of death? 25Thanks be to
God—through Jesus Christ our Lord!
So then, I myself in my mind am a slave to God's law, but in
the sinful nature a slave to the law of sin.

*Life Through the Spirit*

8 THEREFORE, THERE is now no condemnation for those who
are in Christ Jesus,[k] 2because through Christ Jesus the law of
the Spirit of life set me free from the law of sin and death. 3For what
the law was powerless to do in that it was weakened by the sinful
nature,[l] God did by sending his own Son in the likeness of sinful
man to be a sin offering.[m] And so he condemned sin in sinful
man,[n] 4in order that the righteous requirements of the law might
be fully met in us, who do not live according to the sinful nature
but according to the Spirit.

NIV [j] *18* Or *my flesh* [k] *1* Some later manuscripts *Jesus, who do not live according to the sinful nature but according to the Spirit,* [l] *3* Or *the flesh;* also in verses 4, 5, 8, 9, 12 and 13 [m] *3* Or *man, for sin* [n] *3* Or *in the flesh*

## King James

5 For they that are after the flesh do mind the things of the flesh; but they that are after the Spirit the things of the Spirit.

6 For to be carnally minded *is* death; but to be spiritually minded *is* life and peace.

7 Because the carnal mind *is* enmity against God: for it is not subject to the law of God, neither indeed can be.

8 So then they that are in the flesh cannot please God.

9 But ye are not in the flesh, but in the Spirit, if so be that the Spirit of God dwell in you. Now if any man have not the Spirit of Christ, he is none of his.

10 And if Christ *be* in you, the body *is* dead because of sin; but the Spirit *is* life because of righteousness.

11 But if the Spirit of him that raised up Jesus from the dead dwell in you, he that raised up Christ from the dead shall also quicken your mortal bodies by his Spirit that dwelleth in you.

12 Therefore, brethren, we are debtors, not to the flesh, to live after the flesh.

13 For if ye live after the flesh, ye shall die: but if ye through the Spirit do mortify the deeds of the body, ye shall live.

14 For as many as are led by the Spirit of God, they are the sons of God.

15 For ye have not received the spirit of bondage again to fear; but ye have received the Spirit of adoption, whereby we cry, Abba, Father.

16 The Spirit itself beareth witness with our spirit, that we are the children of God:

17 And if children, then heirs; heirs of God, and joint-heirs with Christ; if so be that we suffer with *him,* that we may be also glorified together.

18 For I reckon that the sufferings of this present time *are* not worthy *to be compared* with the glory which shall be revealed in us.

19 For the earnest expectation of the creature waiteth for the manifestation of the sons of God.

20 For the creature was made subject to vanity, not willingly, but by reason of him who hath subjected *the same* in hope,

21 Because the creature itself also shall be delivered from the bondage of corruption into the glorious liberty of the children of God.

22 For we know that the whole creation groaneth and travaileth in pain together until now.

23 And not only *they,* but ourselves also, which have the firstfruits of the Spirit, even we ourselves groan within ourselves, waiting for the adoption, *to wit,* the redemption of our body.

24 For we are saved by hope: but hope that is seen is not hope: for what a man seeth, why doth he yet hope for?

## Amplified

5 For those who are according to the flesh *and* controlled by its unholy desires, set their minds on *and* [a]pursue those things which gratify the flesh. But those who are according to the Spirit *and* [controlled by the desires] of the Spirit, set their minds on *and* [b]seek those things which gratify the (Holy) Spirit.

6 Now the mind of the flesh [which is sense and reason without the Holy Spirit] is death—death that [c]comprises all the miseries arising from sin, both here and hereafter. But the mind of the (Holy) Spirit is life and soul-peace [both now and forever].

7 [That is] because the mind of the flesh—with its carnal thoughts and purposes—is hostile to God; for it does not submit itself to God's Law, indeed it cannot.

8 So then those who are living the life of the flesh—catering to the appetites and impulses of their carnal nature—cannot please *or* satisfy God, *or* be acceptable to Him.

9 But you are not living the life of the flesh, you are living the life of the Spirit, if the (Holy) Spirit of God [really] dwells within you—directs *and* controls you. But if any one does not possess the (Holy) Spirit of Christ, he is none of His—he does not belong to Christ [is not truly a child of God]. [v. 14.]

10 But if Christ lives in you, [then although your natural] body is dead by reason of sin *and* guilt, the spirit is alive because of [the] righteousness [that He imputes to you].

11 And if the Spirit of Him Who raised up Jesus from the dead dwells in you, [then] He Who raised up Christ *Jesus* from the dead will also restore to life your mortal (short-lived, perishable) bodies through His Spirit Who dwells in you.

12 So then, brethren, we are debtors, but not to the flesh—we are not obligated to our carnal nature—to live [a life ruled by the standards set up by the dictates] of the flesh.

13 For if you live according to [the dictates of] the flesh you will surely die. But if through the power of the (Holy) Spirit you are habitually putting to death—making extinct, deadening—the [evil] deeds prompted by the body, you shall (really and genuinely) live forever.

14 For all who are led by the Spirit of God are sons of God.

15 For [the Spirit which] you have now received [is] not a spirit of slavery to put you once more in bondage to fear, but you have received the Spirit of adoption—the Spirit producing sonship—in [the bliss of] which we cry, Abba! [That is,] Father!

16 The Spirit Himself [thus] testifies together with our own spirit, [assuring us] that we are children of God.

17 And if we are [His] children, then we are [His] heirs also: heirs of God and fellow heirs with Christ—sharing His inheritance with Him; only we must share His suffering if we are to share His glory.

18 [But what of that?] For I consider that the sufferings of this present time (this present life) are not worth being compared with the glory that is about to be revealed to us *and* in us *and* [d]for us, *and* [e]conferred on us!

19 For (even the whole) creation (all nature) waits expectantly *and* longs earnestly for God's sons to be made known—waits for the revealing, the disclosing of their sonship.

20 For the creation (nature) was subjected to [f]frailty—to futility, condemned to frustration—not because of some intentional fault on its part, but by the will of Him Who so subjected it. [Yet] with the hope [Eccl. 1:2.]

21 That nature (creation) itself will be set free from its bondage to decay *and* corruption [and gain an entrance] into the glorious freedom of God's children.

22 We know that the whole creation (of irrational creatures) has been moaning together in the pains of labor until now. [Jer. 12:4, 11.]

23 And not only the creation, but we ourselves too, who have *and* enjoy the first fruits of the (Holy) Spirit—a foretaste of the blissful things to come—groan inwardly as we wait for the redemption of our bodies [from sensuality and the grave, which will reveal] our adoption (our manifestation as God's sons).

24 For in [this] hope we were saved. But hope [the object of] which is seen is not hope. For how can one hope for what he already sees?

**AMP** [a] Thayer. [b] Thayer. [c] Thayer. [d] Williams' "The New Testament in the Language of the People." [e] Thayer. [f] Thayer.

## New American Standard

5For those who are according to the flesh set their minds on
the things of the flesh, but those who are according to the Spirit,
the things of the Spirit.
6For the mind set on the flesh is death, but the mind set on the
Spirit is life and peace,
7because the mind set on the flesh is hostile toward God; for
it does not subject itself to the law of God, for it is not even able
*to do so;*
8and those who are in the flesh cannot please God.
9However, you are not in the flesh but in the Spirit, if indeed
the Spirit of God dwells in you. But if anyone does not have the
Spirit of Christ, he does not belong to Him.
10And if Christ is in you, though the body is dead because of
sin, yet the spirit is alive because of righteousness.
11But if the Spirit of Him who raised Jesus from the dead dwells
in you, He who raised Christ Jesus from the dead will also give life
to your mortal bodies [g]through His Spirit who indwells you.
12¶ So then, brethren, we are under obligation, not to the flesh,
to live according to the flesh—
13for if you are living according to the flesh, you must die; but
if by the Spirit you are putting to death the deeds of the body, you
will live.
14For all who are being led by the Spirit of God, these are sons
of God.
15For you have not received a spirit of slavery leading to fear
again, but you have received a spirit of adoption as sons by which
we cry out, "Abba! Father!"
16The Spirit Himself bears witness with our spirit that we are
children of God,
17and if children, heirs also, heirs of God and fellow heirs with
Christ, if indeed we suffer with *Him* in order that we may also be
glorified with *Him.*
18¶ For I consider that the sufferings of this present time are not
worthy to be compared with the glory that is to be revealed to us.
19For the anxious longing of the creation waits eagerly for the
revealing of the sons of God.
20For the creation was subjected to futility, not of its own will,
but because of Him who subjected it, [h]in hope
21that the creation itself also will be set free from its slavery to
corruption into the freedom of the glory of the children of God.
22For we know that the whole creation groans and suffers the
pains of childbirth together until now.
23And not only this, but also we ourselves, having the first
fruits of the Spirit, even we ourselves groan within ourselves,
waiting eagerly for *our* adoption as sons, the redemption of our
body.
24For in hope we have been saved, but hope that is seen is not
hope; for [i]why does one also hope for what he sees?

## New International

5Those who live according to the sinful nature have their minds
set on what that nature desires; but those who live in accordance
with the Spirit have their minds set on what the Spirit desires. 6The
mind of sinful man[j] is death, but the mind controlled by the Spirit
is life and peace; 7the sinful mind[k] is hostile to God. It does not
submit to God's law, nor can it do so. 8Those controlled by the
sinful nature cannot please God.
9You, however, are controlled not by the sinful nature but by
the Spirit, if the Spirit of God lives in you. And if anyone does not
have the Spirit of Christ, he does not belong to Christ. 10But if
Christ is in you, your body is dead because of sin, yet your spirit
is alive because of righteousness. 11And if the Spirit of him who
raised Jesus from the dead is living in you, he who raised Christ
from the dead will also give life to your mortal bodies through his
Spirit, who lives in you.
12Therefore, brothers, we have an obligation—but it is not to the
sinful nature, to live according to it. 13For if you live according to
the sinful nature, you will die; but if by the Spirit you put to death
the misdeeds of the body, you will live, 14because those who are
led by the Spirit of God are sons of God. 15For you did not receive
a spirit that makes you a slave again to fear, but you received the
Spirit of sonship.[l] And by him we cry, "*Abba*,[m] Father." 16The
Spirit himself testifies with our spirit that we are God's children.
17Now if we are children, then we are heirs—heirs of God and
co-heirs with Christ, if indeed we share in his sufferings in order
that we may also share in his glory.

*Future Glory*

18I consider that our present sufferings are not worth comparing with the glory that will be revealed in us. 19The creation waits
in eager expectation for the sons of God to be revealed. 20For the
creation was subjected to frustration, not by its own choice, but by
the will of the one who subjected it, in hope 21that[n] the creation
itself will be liberated from its bondage to decay and brought into
the glorious freedom of the children of God.
22We know that the whole creation has been groaning as in the
pains of childbirth right up to the present time. 23Not only so, but
we ourselves, who have the firstfruits of the Spirit, groan inwardly
as we wait eagerly for our adoption as sons, the redemption of our
bodies. 24For in this hope we were saved. But hope that is seen is

**NAS** [g] Some ancient mss. read *because of* [h] Some ancient mss. read *in hope; because the creation* [i] Some ancient mss. read *who hopes for what he sees?*

**NIV** [j] 6 Or *mind set on the flesh* [k] 7 Or *the mind set on the flesh* [l] 15 Or *adoption* [m] 15 Aramaic for *Father* [n] 20,21 Or *subjected it in hope.* 21*For*

## King James

25 But if we hope for that we see not, *then* do we with patience
wait for *it.*
26 Likewise the Spirit also helpeth our infirmities: for we know
not what we should pray for as we ought: but the Spirit itself
maketh intercession for us with groanings which cannot be uttered.
27 And he that searcheth the hearts knoweth what *is* the mind
of the Spirit, because he maketh intercession for the saints according to *the will of* God.
28 And we know that all things work together for good to them
that love God, to them who are the called according to *his* purpose.
29 For whom he did foreknow, he also did predestinate *to be*
conformed to the image of his Son, that he might be the firstborn
among many brethren.
30 Moreover whom he did predestinate, them he also called: and
whom he called, them he also justified: and whom he justified,
them he also glorified.
31 What shall we then say to these things? If God *be* for us, who
*can be* against us?
32 He that spared not his own Son, but delivered him up for us
all, how shall he not with him also freely give us all things?
33 Who shall lay any thing to the charge of God's elect? *It is* God
that justifieth.
34 Who *is* he that condemneth? *It is* Christ that died, yea rather,
that is risen again, who is even at the right hand of God, who also
maketh intercession for us.
35 Who shall separate us from the love of Christ? *shall* tribulation, or distress, or persecution, or famine, or nakedness, or peril,
or sword?
36 As it is written, For thy sake we are killed all the day long; we
are accounted as sheep for the slaughter.
37 Nay, in all these things we are more than conquerors through
him that loved us.
38 For I am persuaded, that neither death, nor life, nor angels,
nor principalities, nor powers, nor things present, nor things to
come,
39 Nor height, nor depth, nor any other creature, shall be able
to separate us from the love of God, which is in Christ Jesus our
Lord.

**9** I SAY the truth in Christ, I lie not, my conscience also bearing
me witness in the Holy Ghost,
2 That I have great heaviness and continual sorrow in my heart.
3 For I could wish that myself were accursed from Christ for my
brethren, my kinsmen according to the flesh:
4 Who are Israelites; to whom *pertaineth* the adoption, and the
glory, and the covenants, and the giving of the law, and the service
*of God,* and the promises;

## Amplified

25 But if we hope for what is still unseen by us, we wait for it
with patience *and* composure.
26 So too the (Holy) Spirit comes to our aid *and* bears us up in
our weakness; for we do not know what prayer to offer *nor* how
to offer it worthily as we ought, but the Spirit Himself goes to meet
our supplication *and* pleads in our behalf with unspeakable yearn-
ings *and* groanings too deep for utterance.
27 And He Who searches the hearts of men knows what is in the
mind of the (Holy) Spirit—what His intent is—because the Spirit
intercedes *and* pleads [before God] in behalf of the saints according
to *and* in harmony with God's will. [Ps. 139:1, 2.]
28 We are assured *and* know that [ [a]God being a partner in their
labor], all things work together *and* are [fitting into a plan] for good
to those who love God and are called according to [His] design *and*
purpose.
29 For those whom He foreknew—of whom He was [b]aware and
[c]loved beforehand—He also destined from the beginning (foreor-
daining them) to be molded into the image of His Son [and share
inwardly His likeness], that He might become the first-born among
many brethren.
30 And those whom He thus foreordained He also called; and
those whom He called He also justified—acquitted, made righteous, putting them into right standing with Himself. And those
whom He justified He also glorified—raising them to a heavenly
dignity and condition [state of being].
31 What then shall we say to [all] this? If God be for us, who [can
be] against us?—Who can be our foe, if God is on our side? [Ps.
118:6.]
32 He who did not withhold *or* spare [even] His own Son but
gave Him up for us all, will He not also with Him freely *and*
graciously give us all [other] things?
33 Who shall bring any charge against God's elect [when it is]
God Who justifies—Who puts us in right relation to Himself? (Who
shall come forward and accuse or impeach those whom God has
chosen? Will God, Who acquits us?)
34 Who is there to condemn [us]? Will Christ Jesus, the Messiah,
Who died, or rather Who was raised from the dead, Who is at the
right hand of God actually pleading *as* He intercedes for us?
35 Who shall ever separate us from Christ's love? Shall suffering
*and* affliction *and* tribulation? Or calamity *and* distress? Or persecution, or hunger, or destitution, or peril, or sword?
36 Even as it is written, For Thy sake we are put to death all the
day long, we are regarded *and* counted as sheep for the slaughter.
[Ps. 44:22.]
37 Yet amid all these things we are more than conquerors [d] *and*
gain a surpassing victory through Him Who loved us.
38 For I am persuaded beyond doubt—am sure—that neither
death, nor life, nor angels, nor principalities, nor things
[e]impending *and* threatening, nor things to come, nor powers,
39 Nor height, nor depth, nor anything else in all creation will
be able to separate us from the love of God which is in Christ Jesus
our Lord.

**9** I AM speaking the truth in Christ. I am not lying; my conscience [enlightened and prompted] by the Holy Spirit, bearing witness with me
2 That I have bitter grief and incessant anguish in my heart.
3 For I could wish that I myself were accursed *and* cut off *and*
banished from Christ, for the sake of my brethren *and* instead of
them, my natural kinsmen *and* my fellow countrymen. [Exod.
32:32.]
4 For they are Israelites, and to them belong God's adoption [as
a nation] and the glorious (Shekinah) Presence. With them were
the special covenants made, to them was the Law given. To them
[the temple] worship was revealed and [God's own] promises
announced. [Exod. 4:22; Hos. 11:1.]

**AMP** [a] Some authorities read, "God worketh all things with them." [b] Meyer [—Vincent]. [c] John Murray's "The Sovereignty of God." [d] Thayer. [e] Vincent. Literal meaning, "standing in sight."

## New American Standard

25But if we hope for what we do not see, with perseverance we
wait eagerly for it.

*Our Victory in Christ*

26¶ And in the same way the Spirit also helps our weakness; for
we do not know how to pray as we should, but the Spirit Himself
intercedes for *us* with groanings too deep for words;
27and He who searches the hearts knows what the mind of the
Spirit is, because He intercedes for the saints according to *the will
of* God.
28And we know that [f]God causes all things to work together
for good to those who love God, to those who are called according
to *His* purpose.
29For whom He foreknew, He also predestined *to become* conformed to the image of His Son, that He might be the first-born
among many brethren;
30and whom He predestined, these He also called; and whom
He called, these He also justified; and whom He justified, these He
also glorified.
31¶ What then shall we say to these things? If God *is* for us, who
*is* against us?
32He who did not spare His own Son, but delivered Him up for
us all, how will He not also with Him freely give us all things?
33Who will bring a charge against God's elect? God is the one
who justifies;
34who is the one who condemns? Christ Jesus is He who died,
yes, rather who was [g]raised, who is at the right hand of God, who
also intercedes for us.
35Who shall separate us from the love of [h]Christ? Shall tribulation, or distress, or persecution, or famine, or nakedness, or peril,
or sword?
36Just as it is written,

"For Thy sake we are being put to death all day
long;
We were considered as sheep to be slaughtered."

37But in all these things we overwhelmingly conquer through
Him who loved us.
38For I am convinced that neither death, nor life, nor angels, nor
principalities, nor things present, nor things to come, nor powers,
39nor height, nor depth, nor any other created thing, shall be
able to separate us from the love of God, which is in Christ Jesus
our Lord.

*Solicitude for Israel*

9 I AM telling the truth in Christ, I am not lying, my conscience
bearing me witness in the Holy Spirit,
2that I have great sorrow and unceasing grief in my heart.
3For I could wish that I myself were accursed, *separated* from
Christ for the sake of my brethren, my kinsmen according to the
flesh,
4who are Israelites, to whom belongs the adoption as sons and
the glory and the covenants and the giving of the Law and the
*temple* service and the promises,

NAS [f] Some ancient mss. read *all things work together for good* [g] Some ancient mss. read *raised from the dead* [h] Some ancient mss. read *God*

## New International

no hope at all. Who hopes for what he already has? 25But if we
hope for what we do not yet have, we wait for it patiently.
26In the same way, the Spirit helps us in our weakness. We do
not know what we ought to pray for, but the Spirit himself intercedes for us with groans that words cannot express. 27And he who
searches our hearts knows the mind of the Spirit, because the Spirit
intercedes for the saints in accordance with God's will.

*More Than Conquerors*

28And we know that in all things God works for the good of
those who love him,[i] who[j] have been called according to his
purpose. 29For those God foreknew he also predestined to be
conformed to the likeness of his Son, that he might be the firstborn
among many brothers. 30And those he predestined, he also called;
those he called, he also justified; those he justified, he also glorified.
31What, then, shall we say in response to this? If God is for us,
who can be against us? 32He who did not spare his own Son, but
gave him up for us all—how will he not also, along with him,
graciously give us all things? 33Who will bring any charge against
those whom God has chosen? It is God who justifies. 34Who is he
that condemns? Christ Jesus, who died—more than that, who was
raised to life—is at the right hand of God and is also interceding
for us. 35Who shall separate us from the love of Christ? Shall
trouble or hardship or persecution or famine or nakedness or
danger or sword? 36As it is written:

"For your sake we face death all day long;
we are considered as sheep to be slaughtered."[k]

37No, in all these things we are more than conquerors through him
who loved us. 38For I am convinced that neither death nor life,
neither angels nor demons,[l] neither the present nor the future,
nor any powers, 39neither height nor depth, nor anything else in
all creation, will be able to separate us from the love of God that
is in Christ Jesus our Lord.

*God's Sovereign Choice*

9 I SPEAK the truth in Christ—I am not lying, my conscience
confirms it in the Holy Spirit— 2I have great sorrow and
unceasing anguish in my heart. 3For I could wish that I myself
were cursed and cut off from Christ for the sake of my brothers,
those of my own race, 4the people of Israel. Theirs is the adoption
as sons; theirs the divine glory, the covenants, the receiving of the
law, the temple worship and the promises. 5Theirs are the pa-

NIV [i] 28 Some manuscripts *And we know that all things work together for good to those who love God* [j] 28 *Or works together with those who love him to bring about what is good—with those who* [k] 36 Psalm 44:22 [l] 38 Or *nor heavenly rulers*

## King James

5Whose *are* the fathers, and of whom as concerning the flesh Christ *came,* who is over all, God blessed for ever. Amen.
6Not as though the word of God hath taken none effect. For they *are* not all Israel, which are of Israel:
7Neither, because they are the seed of Abraham, *are they* all children: but, In Isaac shall thy seed be called.
8That is, They which are the children of the flesh, these *are* not the children of God: but the children of the promise are counted for the seed.
9For this *is* the word of promise, At this time will I come, and Sarah shall have a son.
10And not only *this;* but when Rebecca also had conceived by one, *even* by our father Isaac;
11(For *the children* being not yet born, neither having done any good or evil, that the purpose of God according to election might stand, not of works, but of him that calleth;)
12It was said unto her, The elder shall serve the younger.
13As it is written, Jacob have I loved, but Esau have I hated.
14What shall we say then? *Is there* unrighteousness with God? God forbid.
15For he saith to Moses, I will have mercy on whom I will have mercy, and I will have compassion on whom I will have compassion.
16So then *it is* not of him that willeth, nor of him that runneth, but of God that showeth mercy.
17For the scripture saith unto Pharaoh, Even for this same purpose have I raised thee up, that I might show my power in thee, and that my name might be declared throughout all the earth.
18Therefore hath he mercy on whom he will *have mercy,* and whom he will he hardeneth.
19Thou wilt say then unto me, Why doth he yet find fault? For who hath resisted his will?
20Nay but, O man, who art thou that repliest against God? Shall the thing formed say to him that formed *it,* Why hast thou made me thus?
21Hath not the potter power over the clay, of the same lump to make one vessel unto honour, and another unto dishonour?
22 *What* if God, willing to show *his* wrath, and to make his power known, endured with much longsuffering the vessels of wrath fitted to destruction:
23And that he might make known the riches of his glory on the vessels of mercy, which he had afore prepared unto glory,
24Even us, whom he hath called, not of the Jews only, but also of the Gentiles?
25As he saith also in Osee, I will call them my people, which were not my people; and her beloved, which was not beloved.
26And it shall come to pass, *that* in the place where it was said unto them, Ye *are* not my people; there shall they be called the children of the living God.
27Esaias also crieth concerning Israel, Though the number of the children of Israel be as the sand of the sea, a remnant shall be saved:

## Amplified

5To them belong the patriarchs, and as far as His natural descent was concerned from them is the Christ, Who is exalted *and* supreme over all, God, blessed forever! Amen—so let it be.
6However, it is not as though God's Word had failed—coming to nothing. For it is not everybody who is a descendant of Jacob (Israel) who belongs to [the true] Israel.
7And they are not all the children of Abraham because they are by blood his descendants. [No, the promise was,] Your descendants will be called *and* counted through the line of Isaac [though Abraham had an older son]. [Gen. 21:9-12.]
8That is to say, it is not the children of the body [of Abraham] who are made God's children, but it is the offspring to whom the promise applies that shall be counted [as Abraham's true] descendants.
9For this is what the promise said, About this time [next year] will I return and Sarah shall have a son. [Gen. 18:10.]
10And not only that, but this too: Rebecca conceived [two sons under exactly the same circumstances] by our forefather Isaac.
11And the children were yet unborn and had so far done nothing either good or evil. Even so, in order further to carry out God's purpose of selection (election, choice), which depends not on works *or* what men can do, but on Him Who calls [them],
12It was said to her that the elder [son] should serve the younger [son]. [Gen. 25:21-23.]
13As it is written, Jacob have I loved, but Esau have I hated [held in [a]relative disregard in comparison with My feeling for Jacob]. [Mal. 1:2, 3.]
14What shall we conclude then? Is there injustice upon God's part? Certainly not!
15For He says to Moses, I will have mercy on whom I will have mercy and I will have compassion (pity) on whom I will have compassion. [Exod. 33:19.]
16So then [God's gift] is not a question of human will and human effort, but of God's mercy.—It depends not on one's own willingness nor on his strenuous exertion as in running a race, but on God's having mercy on him.
17For the Scripture says to Pharaoh, I have raised you up for this very purpose of displaying My power in [dealing with] you, so that My name may be proclaimed the whole world over.
18So then He has mercy on whomever He wills (chooses) and He hardens—makes stubborn and unyielding the heart of—whomever He wills.
19You will say to me, Why then does He still find fault *and* blame us [for sinning]? For who can resist *and* withstand His will?
20But who are you, a mere man, to criticize *and* contradict *and* answer back to God? Will what is formed say to him that formed it, Why have you made me thus? [Isa. 29:16; 45:9.]
21Has the potter no right over the clay, to make out of the same mass (lump) one vessel for beauty *and* distinction *and* honorable use, and another for menial *or* ignoble *and* dishonorable use?
22What if God, although fully intending to show (the awfulness of) His wrath and to make known His power *and* authority, has tolerated with much patience the vessels (objects) of [His] anger which are ripe for destruction? [Prov. 16:4.]
23And [what if] He thus purposes to make known *and* show the wealth of His glory in [dealing with] the vessels (objects) of His mercy which He has prepared beforehand for glory,
24Even including ourselves whom He has called, not only from among the Jews but also from among the Gentiles (heathen)?
25Just as He says in Hosea, Those who were not My people I will call My people, and her who was not beloved [I will call] My beloved. [Hos. 2:23.]
26And it shall be in the very place where it was said to them, You are not My people, they shall be called sons of the living God. [Hos. 1:10.]
27And Isaiah calls out (solemnly cries aloud) over Israel: Though the number of the sons of Israel be as the sand of the sea, only the remnant—a small part of them—will be saved [ [b]from perdition, condemnation, judgment]!

**AMP** [a] Abbott-Smith's "Manual Greek Lexicon of The New Testament."
[b] Cremer's "Biblico-Theological Lexicon of New Testament Greek."

## New American Standard

5whose are the fathers, and from whom is the Christ according
to the flesh, who is over all, God blessed forever. Amen.
6¶ But *it is* not as though the word of God has failed. For they
are not all Israel who are *descended* from Israel;
7neither are they all children because they are Abraham's descendants, but: "THROUGH ISAAC YOUR DESCENDANTS WILL BE
NAMED."
8That is, it is not the children of the flesh who are children of
God, but the children of the promise are regarded as descendants.
9For this is a word of promise: "AT THIS TIME I WILL COME, AND
SARAH SHALL HAVE A SON."
10And not only this, but there was Rebekah also, when she had
conceived *twins* by one man, our father Isaac;
11for though *the twins* were not yet born, and had not done
anything good or bad, in order that God's purpose according to *His*
choice might stand, not because of works, but because of Him who
calls,
12it was said to her, "THE OLDER WILL SERVE THE YOUNGER."
13Just as it is written, "JACOB I LOVED, BUT ESAU I HATED."
14¶ What shall we say then? There is no injustice with God, is
there? May it never be!
15For He says to Moses, "I WILL HAVE MERCY ON WHOM I HAVE
MERCY, AND I WILL HAVE COMPASSION ON WHOM I HAVE COMPAS-
SION."
16So then it *does* not *depend* on the man who wills or the man
who runs, but on God who has mercy.
17For the Scripture says to Pharaoh, "FOR THIS VERY PURPOSE I
RAISED YOU UP, TO DEMONSTRATE MY POWER IN YOU, AND THAT MY
NAME MIGHT BE PROCLAIMED THROUGHOUT THE WHOLE EARTH."
18So then He has mercy on whom He desires, and He hardens
whom He desires.
19¶ You will say to me then, "Why does He still find fault? For
who resists His will?"
20On the contrary, who are you, O man, who answers back to
God? The thing molded will not say to the molder, "Why did you
make me like this," will it?
21Or does not the potter have a right over the clay, to make from
the same lump one vessel for honorable use, and another for
common use?
22What if God, although willing to demonstrate His wrath and
to make His power known, endured with much patience vessels
of wrath prepared for destruction?
23And *He did so* in order that He might make known the riches
of His glory upon vessels of mercy, which He prepared beforehand
for glory,
24 *even* us, whom He also called, not from among Jews only, but
also from among Gentiles.
25As He says also in Hosea,
"I WILL CALL THOSE WHO WERE NOT MY PEOPLE, 'MY
PEOPLE,'
AND HER WHO WAS NOT BELOVED, 'BELOVED.' "
26 "AND IT SHALL BE THAT IN THE PLACE WHERE IT WAS SAID
TO THEM, 'YOU ARE NOT MY PEOPLE,'
THERE THEY SHALL BE CALLED SONS OF THE LIVING GOD."
27And Isaiah cries out concerning Israel, "THOUGH THE NUMBER
OF THE SONS OF ISRAEL BE AS THE SAND OF THE SEA, IT IS THE
REMNANT THAT WILL BE SAVED;

## New International

triarchs, and from them is traced the human ancestry of Christ,
who is God over all, forever praised![c] Amen.
6It is not as though God's word had failed. For not all who are
descended from Israel are Israel. 7Nor because they are his descendants are they all Abraham's children. On the contrary, "It is
through Isaac that your offspring will be reckoned."[d] 8In other
words, it is not the natural children who are God's children, but
it is the children of the promise who are regarded as Abraham's
offspring. 9For this was how the promise was stated: "At the
appointed time I will return, and Sarah will have a son."[e]
10Not only that, but Rebekah's children had one and the same
father, our father Isaac. 11Yet, before the twins were born or had
done anything good or bad—in order that God's purpose in election might stand: 12not by works but by him who calls—she was
told, "The older will serve the younger."[f] 13Just as it is written:
"Jacob I loved, but Esau I hated."[g]
14What then shall we say? Is God unjust? Not at all! 15For he
says to Moses,

"I will have mercy on whom I have mercy,
and I will have compassion on whom I have
compassion."[h]

16It does not, therefore, depend on man's desire or effort, but on
God's mercy. 17For the Scripture says to Pharaoh: "I raised you up
for this very purpose, that I might display my power in you and
that my name might be proclaimed in all the earth."[i] 18Therefore
God has mercy on whom he wants to have mercy, and he hardens
whom he wants to harden.
19One of you will say to me: "Then why does God still blame
us? For who resists his will?" 20But who are you, O man, to talk
back to God? "Shall what is formed say to him who formed it,
'Why did you make me like this?' "[j] 21Does not the potter have
the right to make out of the same lump of clay some pottery for
noble purposes and some for common use?
22What if God, choosing to show his wrath and make his power
known, bore with great patience the objects of his wrath—prepared for destruction? 23What if he did this to make the riches of
his glory known to the objects of his mercy, whom he prepared in
advance for glory— 24even us, whom he also called, not only from
the Jews but also from the Gentiles? 25As he says in Hosea:

"I will call them 'my people' who are not my people;
and I will call her 'my loved one' who is not my loved
one,"[k]

26and,

"It will happen that in the very place where it was said to
them,
'You are not my people,'
they will be called 'sons of the living God.' "[l]

27Isaiah cries out concerning Israel:

"Though the number of the Israelites be like the sand by
the sea,
only the remnant will be saved.

NIV [c] 5 Or *Christ, who is over all. God be forever praised!* Or *Christ. God who is over all be forever praised!* [d] *7* Gen. 21:12 [e] *9* Gen. 18:10,14 [f] *12* Gen. 25:23 [g] *13* Mal. 1:2,3 [h] *15* Exodus 33:19 [i] *17* Exodus 9:16 [j] *20* Isaiah 29:16; 45:9 [k] *25* Hosea 2:23 [l] *26* Hosea 1:10

## King James

28 For he will finish the work, and cut *it* short in righteousness: because a short work will the Lord make upon the earth.

29 And as Esaias said before, Except the Lord of Sabaoth had left us a seed, we had been as Sodoma, and been made like unto Gomorrha.

30 What shall we say then? That the Gentiles, which followed not after righteousness, have attained to righteousness, even the righteousness which is of faith.

31 But Israel, which followed after the law of righteousness, hath not attained to the law of righteousness.

32 Wherefore? Because *they sought it* not by faith, but as it were by the works of the law. For they stumbled at that stumblingstone;

33 As it is written, Behold, I lay in Sion a stumblingstone and rock of offence: and whosoever believeth on him shall not be ashamed.

**10** BRETHREN, MY heart's desire and prayer to God for Israel is, that they might be saved.

2 For I bear them record that they have a zeal of God, but not according to knowledge.

3 For they being ignorant of God's righteousness, and going about to establish their own righteousness, have not submitted themselves unto the righteousness of God.

4 For Christ *is* the end of the law for righteousness to every one that believeth.

5 For Moses describeth the righteousness which is of the law, That the man which doeth those things shall live by them.

6 But the righteousness which is of faith speaketh on this wise, Say not in thine heart, Who shall ascend into heaven? (that is, to bring Christ down *from above:*)

7 Or, Who shall descend into the deep? (that is, to bring up Christ again from the dead.)

8 But what saith it? The word is nigh thee, *even* in thy mouth, and in thy heart: that is, the word of faith, which we preach;

9 That if thou shalt confess with thy mouth the Lord Jesus, and shalt believe in thine heart that God hath raised him from the dead, thou shalt be saved.

10 For with the heart man believeth unto righteousness; and with the mouth confession is made unto salvation.

11 For the scripture saith, Whosoever believeth on him shall not be ashamed.

12 For there is no difference between the Jew and the Greek: for the same Lord over all is rich unto all that call upon him.

## Amplified

28 For the Lord will execute His sentence upon the earth—He will conclude, close, His account with men completely and without delay—rigorously cutting it short in His justice. [Isa. 10:22, 23.]

29 It is as Isaiah predicted, If the Lord of hosts had not left us a seed [from which to propagate descendants], we (Israel) would have fared like Sodom and have been made like Gomorrah. [Isa. 1:9.]

30 What shall we say then? That Gentiles who did not follow after righteousness—who did not seek salvation by right relationship to God—have attained it by faith (that is, righteousness imputed by God, based on and produced by faith).

31 Whereas Israel, though ever in pursuit of a law [for the securing] of righteousness (right standing with God), actually did not succeed in fulfilling the Law. [Isa. 51:1.]

32 For what reason? Because [they pursued it] not through faith—they did not depend on faith but on what they could do—relying on the merit of their works. They have stumbled over the Stumbling Stone. [Isa. 28:16; 8:14.]

33 As it is written, Behold I am laying in Zion a Stone that will make men stumble, a Rock that will make them fall; but he who believes in Him (who adheres to, trusts in and relies on Him) shall not be put to shame *nor* be disappointed in his expectations. [Isa. 28:16.]

**10** BRETHREN, [WITH all] my heart's desire *and* goodwill for (Israel) I long and pray to God that they may be saved.

2 I bear them witness that they have a [certain] zeal *and* enthusiasm for God, but it is not enlightened *and* according to [correct and vital] knowledge.

3 For being ignorant of the righteousness that God ascribes (which makes one acceptable to Him in word, thought and deed), and seeking to establish a *righteousness (a means of salvation)* of their own, they did not obey *or* submit themselves to God's righteousness.

4 For Christ is the end of the Law—the limit at which it ceases to be, for the Law leads up to Him Who is the fulfillment of its types, and in Him the purpose which it was designed to accomplish is fulfilled.—That is, the purpose of the Law is fulfilled in Him—as the means of righteousness (right relationship to God) for everyone who trusts in *and* adheres to *and* relies on Him.

5 For Moses writes that the man who [can] practice the righteousness (perfect conformity to God's will) which is based on the Law [with all its intricate demands] shall live by it. [Lev. 18:5.]

6 But the righteousness based on faith—imputed by God and bringing right relationship with Him—says, Do not say in your heart, Who will ascend into Heaven? that is, to bring Christ down,

7 Or who will descend into the abyss? that is, to bring Christ up from the dead [as if we could be saved by our own efforts], [Deut. 30:12, 13.]

8 But what does it say? The Word (God's message in Christ) is near you, on your lips and in your heart; that is, the Word—the message, the basis and object—of faith, which we preach. [Deut. 30:14.]

9 Because if you acknowledge *and* confess with your lips that Jesus is Lord and in your heart believe (adhere to, trust in and rely on the truth) that God raised Him from the dead, you will be saved.

10 For with the heart a person believes (adheres to, trusts in and relies on Christ) and so is justified (declared righteous, acceptable to God), and with the mouth he confesses—declares openly and speaks out freely his faith— *and* confirms [his] salvation.

11 The Scripture says, No man who believes in Him—who adheres to, relies on and trusts in Him—will [ever] be put to shame *or* be disappointed. [Isa. 28:16; 49:23; Jer. 17:7; Ps. 34:22.]

12 [No one,] for there is no distinction between Jew and Greek. The same Lord is Lord over all [of us] and He generously bestows His riches upon all who call upon Him [in faith].

## New American Standard

28FOR THE LORD WILL EXECUTE HIS WORD UPON THE EARTH, THOROUGHLY AND QUICKLY."
29And just as Isaiah foretold,
"EXCEPT THE LORD OF SABAOTH HAD LEFT TO US A POSTERITY,
WE WOULD HAVE BECOME AS SODOM, AND WOULD HAVE RESEMBLED GOMORRAH."
30¶ What shall we say then? That Gentiles, who did not pursue righteousness, attained righteousness, even the righteousness which is by faith;
31but Israel, pursuing a law of righteousness, did not arrive at *that* law.
32Why? Because *they did* not *pursue it* by faith, but as though *it were* by works. They stumbled over the stumbling stone,
33just as it is written,
"BEHOLD, I LAY IN ZION A STONE OF STUMBLING AND A ROCK OF OFFENSE,
AND HE WHO BELIEVES IN HIM WILL NOT BE DISAPPOINTED."

*The Word of Faith Brings Salvation*

10 BRETHREN, MY heart's desire and my prayer to God for them is for *their* salvation.
2For I bear them witness that they have a zeal for God, but not in accordance with knowledge.
3For not knowing about God's righteousness, and seeking to establish their own, they did not subject themselves to the righteousness of God.
4For Christ is the end of the law for righteousness to everyone who believes.
5For Moses writes that the man who practices the righteousness which is based on law shall live by that righteousness.
6But the righteousness based on faith speaks thus, "DO NOT SAY IN YOUR HEART, 'WHO WILL ASCEND INTO HEAVEN?' (that is, to bring Christ down),
7or 'WHO WILL DESCEND INTO THE ABYSS?' (that is, to bring Christ up from the dead)."
8But what does it say? "THE WORD IS NEAR YOU, IN YOUR MOUTH AND IN YOUR HEART"—that is, the word of faith which we are preaching,
9that if you confess with your mouth Jesus *as* Lord, and believe in your heart that God raised Him from the dead, you shall be saved;
10for with the heart man believes, resulting in righteousness, and with the mouth he confesses, resulting in salvation.
11For the Scripture says, "WHOEVER BELIEVES IN HIM WILL NOT BE DISAPPOINTED."
12For there is no distinction between Jew and Greek; for the same *Lord* is Lord of all, abounding in riches for all who call upon Him;

## New International

28For the Lord will carry out
his sentence on earth with speed and finality."[a]

29It is just as Isaiah said previously:
"Unless the Lord Almighty
had left us descendants,
we would have become like Sodom,
we would have been like Gomorrah."[b]

*Israel's Unbelief*

30What then shall we say? That the Gentiles, who did not pursue righteousness, have obtained it, a righteousness that is by faith; 31but Israel, who pursued a law of righteousness, has not attained it. 32Why not? Because they pursued it not by faith but as if it were by works. They stumbled over the "stumbling stone."
33As it is written:

"See, I lay in Zion a stone that causes men to stumble
and a rock that makes them fall,
and the one who trusts in him will never be put to
shame."[c]

10 BROTHERS, MY heart's desire and prayer to God for the Israelites is that they may be saved. 2For I can testify about them that they are zealous for God, but their zeal is not based on knowledge. 3Since they did not know the righteousness that comes from God and sought to establish their own, they did not submit to God's righteousness. 4Christ is the end of the law so that there may be righteousness for everyone who believes.
5Moses describes in this way the righteousness that is by the law: "The man who does these things will live by them."[d] 6But the righteousness that is by faith says: "Do not say in your heart, 'Who will ascend into heaven?'[e] " (that is, to bring Christ down) 7"or 'Who will descend into the deep?'[f] " (that is, to bring Christ up from the dead). 8But what does it say? "The word is near you; it is in your mouth and in your heart,"[g] that is, the word of faith we are proclaiming: 9That if you confess with your mouth, "Jesus is Lord," and believe in your heart that God raised him from the dead, you will be saved. 10For it is with your heart that you believe and are justified, and it is with your mouth that you confess and are saved. 11As the Scripture says, "Anyone who trusts in him will never be put to shame."[h] 12For there is no difference between Jew and Gentile—the same Lord is Lord of all and richly blesses all who

NIV [a] *28* Isaiah 10:22,23 [b] *29* Isaiah 1:9 [c] *33* Isaiah 8:14; 28:16 [d] *5* Lev. 18:5 [e] *6* Deut. 30:12 [f] *7* Deut. 30:13 [g] *8* Deut. 30:14 [h] *11* Isaiah 28:16

## King James

13For whosoever shall call upon the name of the Lord shall be saved.

14How then shall they call on him in whom they have not believed? and how shall they believe in him of whom they have not heard? and how shall they hear without a preacher?

15And how shall they preach, except they be sent? as it is written, How beautiful are the feet of them that preach the gospel of peace, and bring glad tidings of good things!

16But they have not all obeyed the gospel. For Esaias saith, Lord, who hath believed our report?

17So then faith *cometh* by hearing, and hearing by the word of God.

18But I say, Have they not heard? Yes verily, their sound went into all the earth, and their words unto the ends of the world.

19But I say, Did not Israel know? First Moses saith, I will provoke you to jealousy by *them that are* no people, *and* by a foolish nation I will anger you.

20But Esaias is very bold, and saith, I was found of them that sought me not; I was made manifest unto them that asked not after me.

21But to Israel he saith, All day long I have stretched forth my hands unto a disobedient and gainsaying people.

**11** I SAY then, Hath God cast away his people? God forbid. For I also am an Israelite, of the seed of Abraham, *of* the tribe of Benjamin.

2God hath not cast away his people which he foreknew. Wot ye not what the scripture saith of Elias? how he maketh intercession to God against Israel, saying,

3Lord, they have killed thy prophets, and digged down thine altars; and I am left alone, and they seek my life.

4But what saith the answer of God unto him? I have reserved to myself seven thousand men, who have not bowed the knee to *the image of* Baal.

5Even so then at this present time also there is a remnant according to the election of grace.

6And if by grace, then *is it* no more of works: otherwise grace is no more grace. But if *it be* of works, then is it no more grace: otherwise work is no more work.

7What then? Israel hath not obtained that which he seeketh for; but the election hath obtained it, and the rest were blinded

8(According as it is written, God hath given them the spirit of slumber, eyes that they should not see, and ears that they should not hear;) unto this day.

9And David saith, Let their table be made a snare, and a trap, and a stumblingblock, and a recompence unto them:

10Let their eyes be darkened, that they may not see, and bow down their back always.

## Amplified

13For every one who calls upon the name of the Lord [invoking Him as Lord] will be saved. [Joel 2:32.]

14But how are people to call upon Him Whom they have not believed—in Whom they have no faith, on Whom they have no reliance? And how are they to believe in Him—adhere to, trust in and rely upon Him—of Whom they have never heard? And how are they to hear without a preacher?

15And how can men [be expected to] preach unless they are sent? As it is written, How beautiful are the feet of those who bring glad tidings!—How welcome is the coming of those who preach the good news of His good things! [Isa. 52:7.]

16But they have not all heeded the Gospel; for Isaiah says, Lord, who has believed (had faith in) what he has heard from us? [Isa. 53:1.]

17So faith comes by hearing [what is told], and what is heard comes by the preaching [of the message that came from the lips] of Christ, the Messiah [Himself].

18But I ask, Have they not heard? Indeed they have; [for the Scripture says,] Their voice [that of nature bearing God's message] has gone out to all the earth, and their words to the far bounds of the world. [Ps. 19:4.]

19Again I ask, Did Israel not understand?—Did the Jews have no warning that the Gospel was to go forth to the Gentiles, to all the earth? First, there is Moses who says, I will make you jealous of those who are not a nation; with a foolish nation I will make you angry. [Deut. 32:21.]

20Then Isaiah is so bold as to say, I have been found by those who did not seek Me; I have shown (revealed) Myself to those who did not [consciously] ask for Me. [Isa. 65:1.]

21But of Israel he says, All day long I have stretched out My hands to a people unyielding *and* disobedient and self-willed—to a fault-finding, contrary and contradicting people. [Isa. 65:2.]

**11** I ASK then, has God totally rejected and disowned His people? Of course not! Why, I myself am an Israelite, a descendant of Abraham, a member of the tribe of Benjamin! [I Sam. 12:22; Jer. 31:37; 33:24-26.]

2No, God has not rejected *and* disowned His people [whose destiny] He had marked out *and* appointed *and* foreknown from the beginning. Do you not know what the Scripture says of Elijah, how he pleads with God against Israel? [Ps. 94:14; I Kings 19.]

3Lord, they have killed Your prophets, they have demolished Your altars, and I alone am left, and they seek my life.

4But what is God's reply to him? I have kept for Myself seven thousand men who have not bowed the knee to Baal! [I Kings 19:18.]

5So too at the present time there is a remnant (a small believing minority), selected (chosen) by grace—by God's unmerited favor and graciousness.

6But if it is by grace—His unmerited favor and graciousness—it is no longer conditioned on works or anything men have done. Otherwise, grace would no longer be grace—it would be meaningless.

7What then [shall we conclude]? Israel failed to obtain what it sought [God's favor by obedience to law]. Only the elect (those chosen few) obtained it; while the rest of them became callously indifferent—blinded, hardened and made insensible to it.

8As it is written, God gave them a spirit (an attitude) of stupor, eyes that should not see and ears that should not hear, [that has continued] down to this very day. [Isa. 29:10; Deut. 29:4.]

9And David says, Let their table (their feasting, banqueting) become a snare and a trap, a pitfall and a [a]just retribution—[b]rebounding as a boomerang upon them; [Ps. 69:22.]

10Let their eyes be darkened (dimmed) so that they cannot see, and make them bend their back [stooping beneath their burden] forever. [Ps. 69:23.]

**AMP** [a] Vincent. [b] Greek, literally, *a return, a recompense, etc.*

## New American Standard

13for "WHOEVER WILL CALL UPON THE NAME OF THE LORD WILL
BE SAVED."
14How then shall they call upon Him in whom they have not
believed? And how shall they believe in Him whom they have not
heard? And how shall they hear without a preacher?
15And how shall they preach unless they are sent? Just as it is
written, "HOW BEAUTIFUL ARE THE FEET OF THOSE WHO BRING GLAD
TIDINGS OF GOOD THINGS!"
16¶ However, they did not all heed the glad tidings; for Isaiah
says, "LORD, WHO HAS BELIEVED OUR REPORT?"
17So faith *comes* from hearing, and hearing by the word of
Christ.
18But I say, surely they have never heard, have they? Indeed
they have;

"THEIR VOICE HAS GONE OUT INTO ALL THE EARTH,
AND THEIR WORDS TO THE ENDS OF THE WORLD."

19But I say, surely Israel did not know, did they? At the first
Moses says,

"I WILL MAKE YOU JEALOUS BY THAT WHICH IS NOT A
NATION,
BY A NATION WITHOUT UNDERSTANDING WILL I ANGER
YOU."

20And Isaiah is very bold and says,

"I WAS FOUND BY THOSE WHO SOUGHT ME NOT,
I BECAME MANIFEST TO THOSE WHO DID NOT ASK FOR
ME."

21But as for Israel He says, "ALL THE DAY LONG I HAVE
STRETCHED OUT MY HANDS TO A DISOBEDIENT AND OBSTINATE
PEOPLE."

### *Israel Is Not Cast Away*

**11** I SAY then, God has not rejected His people, has He? May
it never be! For I too am an Israelite, a descendant of
Abraham, of the tribe of Benjamin.
2God has not rejected His people whom He foreknew. Or do
you not know what the Scripture says in *the passage about* Elijah,
how he pleads with God against Israel?
3"Lord, THEY HAVE KILLED THY PROPHETS, THEY HAVE TORN
DOWN THINE ALTARS, AND I ALONE AM LEFT, AND THEY ARE SEEKING
MY LIFE."
4But what is the divine response to him? "I HAVE KEPT for
Myself SEVEN THOUSAND MEN WHO HAVE NOT BOWED THE KNEE TO
BAAL."
5In the same way then, there has also come to be at the present
time a remnant according to *God's* gracious choice.
6But if it is by grace, it is no longer on the basis of works,
otherwise grace is no longer grace.
7What then? That which Israel is seeking for, it has not obtained, but those who were chosen obtained it, and the rest were
hardened;
8just as it is written,

"GOD GAVE THEM A SPIRIT OF STUPOR,
EYES TO SEE NOT AND EARS TO HEAR NOT,
DOWN TO THIS VERY DAY."

9And David says,

"LET THEIR TABLE BECOME A SNARE AND A TRAP,
AND A STUMBLING BLOCK AND A RETRIBUTION TO THEM.
10 "LET THEIR EYES BE DARKENED TO SEE NOT,
AND BEND THEIR BACKS FOREVER."

## New International

call on him, 13for, "Everyone who calls on the name of the Lord
will be saved."[c]
14How, then, can they call on the one they have not believed
in? And how can they believe in the one of whom they have not
heard? And how can they hear without someone preaching to
them? 15And how can they preach unless they are sent? As it is
written, "How beautiful are the feet of those who bring good
news!"[d]
16But not all the Israelites accepted the good news. For Isaiah
says, "Lord, who has believed our message?"[e] 17Consequently,
faith comes from hearing the message, and the message is heard
through the word of Christ. 18But I ask: Did they not hear? Of
course they did:

"Their voice has gone out into all the earth,
their words to the ends of the world."[f]

19Again I ask: Did Israel not understand? First, Moses says,

"I will make you envious by those who are not a nation;
I will make you angry by a nation that has no
understanding."[g]

20And Isaiah boldly says,

"I was found by those who did not seek me;
I revealed myself to those who did not ask for me."[h]

21But concerning Israel he says,

"All day long I have held out my hands
to a disobedient and obstinate people."[i]

### *The Remnant of Israel*

**11** I ASK then: Did God reject his people? By no means! I am
an Israelite myself, a descendant of Abraham, from the
tribe of Benjamin. 2God did not reject his people, whom he foreknew. Don't you know what the Scripture says in the passage
about Elijah—how he appealed to God against Israel: 3"Lord, they
have killed your prophets and torn down your altars; I am the only
one left, and they are trying to kill me"[j] ? 4And what was God's
answer to him? "I have reserved for myself seven thousand who
have not bowed the knee to Baal."[k] 5So too, at the present time
there is a remnant chosen by grace. 6And if by grace, then it is no
longer by works; if it were, grace would no longer be grace.[l]
7What then? What Israel sought so earnestly it did not obtain,
but the elect did. The others were hardened, 8as it is written:

"God gave them a spirit of stupor,
eyes so that they could not see
and ears so that they could not hear,
to this very day."[m]

9And David says,

"May their table become a snare and a trap,
a stumbling block and a retribution for them.
10May their eyes be darkened so they cannot see,
and their backs be bent forever."[n]

**NIV** [c] *13* Joel 2:32 [d] *15* Isaiah 52:7 [e] *16* Isaiah 53:1 [f] *18* Psalm 19:4
[g] *19* Deut. 32:21 [h] *20* Isaiah 65:1 [i] *21* Isaiah 65:2 [j] *3* 1 Kings 19:10,14
[k] *4* 1 Kings 19:18 [l] *6* Some manuscripts *by grace. But if by works, then it is no longer grace; if it were, work would no longer be work.* [m] *8* Deut. 29:4; Isaiah 29:10
[n] *10* Psalm 69:22,23

## King James

11 I say then, Have they stumbled that they should fall? God forbid: but *rather* through their fall salvation *is come* unto the Gentiles, for to provoke them to jealousy.

12 Now if the fall of them *be* the riches of the world, and the diminishing of them the riches of the Gentiles; how much more their fulness?

13 For I speak to you Gentiles, inasmuch as I am the apostle of the Gentiles, I magnify mine office:

14 If by any means I may provoke to emulation *them which are* my flesh, and might save some of them.

15 For if the casting away of them *be* the reconciling of the world, what *shall* the receiving *of them be*, but life from the dead?

16 For if the firstfruit *be* holy, the lump *is* also *holy*: and if the root *be* holy, so *are* the branches.

17 And if some of the branches be broken off, and thou, being a wild olive tree, wert grafted in among them, and with them partakest of the root and fatness of the olive tree;

18 Boast not against the branches. But if thou boast, thou bearest not the root, but the root thee.

19 Thou wilt say then, The branches were broken off, that I might be grafted in.

20 Well; because of unbelief they were broken off, and thou standest by faith. Be not highminded, but fear:

21 For if God spared not the natural branches, *take heed* lest he also spare not thee.

22 Behold therefore the goodness and severity of God: on them which fell, severity; but toward thee, goodness, if thou continue in *his* goodness: otherwise thou also shalt be cut off.

23 And they also, if they abide not still in unbelief, shall be grafted in: for God is able to graft them in again.

24 For if thou wert cut out of the olive tree which is wild by nature, and wert grafted contrary to nature into a good olive tree: how much more shall these, which be the natural *branches*, be grafted into their own olive tree?

25 For I would not, brethren, that ye should be ignorant of this mystery, lest ye should be wise in your own conceits; that blindness in part is happened to Israel, until the fulness of the Gentiles be come in.

26 And so all Israel shall be saved: as it is written, There shall come out of Sion the Deliverer, and shall turn away ungodliness from Jacob:

27 For this *is* my covenant unto them, when I shall take away their sins.

28 As concerning the gospel, *they are* enemies for your sakes: but as touching the election, *they are* beloved for the fathers' sakes.

29 For the gifts and calling of God *are* without repentance.

## Amplified

11 So I ask, Have they stumbled so as to fall—to their utter spiritual ruin, irretrievably? By no means! But through their false step *and* transgression salvation [has come] to the Gentiles, so as to arouse Israel [to see and feel what they forfeited] and so to make them jealous.

12 Now if their stumbling—their lapse, their transgression—has so enriched the world [at large], and if [Israel's] failure means such riches for the Gentiles, think what an enrichment *and* greater advantage will follow their full reinstatement!

13 But now I am speaking to you who are Gentiles. Inasmuch then as I am an apostle to the Gentiles, I lay great stress on my ministry *and* magnify my office,

14 In the hope of making my fellow Jews jealous—in order to stir them up to imitate, copy and appropriate—and thus managing to save some of them.

15 For if their rejection *and* exclusion from the benefits of salvation were [overruled] for the reconciliation of a world to God, what will their acceptance *and* admission mean? [It will be nothing short of] life from the dead!

16 Now if the first handful of dough offered as the first fruits [Abraham and the patriarchs] is consecrated (holy), so is the whole mass [the nation of Israel]; and if the root [Abraham] is consecrated (holy), so are the branches. [Num. 15:19-21.]

17 But if some of the branches were broken off, while you, a wild olive shoot, were grafted in among them to share the richness [of the root and sap] of the olive tree,

18 Do not boast over the branches *and* pride yourself at their expense. If you do boast *and* feel superior, remember it is not you that support the root, but the root [that supports] you.

19 You will say then, Branches were broken (pruned) off so that I might be grafted in!

20 That is true. But they were broken (pruned) off because of their unbelief—their lack of real faith, and you are established through faith—because you do believe. So do not become proud *and* conceited, but rather stand in awe *and* be reverently afraid.

21 For if God did not spare the natural branches [because of unbelief], neither will He spare you [if you are guilty of the same offense].

22 Then note *and* appreciate the gracious kindness and the severity of God; severity toward those who have fallen, but God's gracious kindness to you. [That is, to you] provided you continue in His grace *and* to abide in His kindness; otherwise you too will be cut off—pruned away.

23 And even those others (the fallen branches, Jews), if they do not persist in [clinging to] their unbelief, will be grafted in, for God has the power to graft them in again.

24 For if you have been cut from what is by nature a wild olive tree, and against nature grafted into a cultivated olive tree, how much easier will it be to graft these natural [branches] back on [the original parent stock of] their own olive tree.

25 Lest you be self-opinionated—wise in your own conceits—I do not want you to miss this hidden truth *and* mystery, brethren: a hardening (insensibility) has [temporarily] befallen a part of Israel [to last] until the [a]full number of the ingathering of the Gentiles has come in,

26 And so all Israel will be saved. As it is written, The Deliverer will come from Zion, He will banish ungodliness from Jacob. [Isa. 59:20, 21.]

27 And this will be My covenant—My agreement—with them when I shall take away their sins. [Jer. 31:33; Isa. 27:9.]

28 From the point of view of the Gospel (good news) they [the Jews, at present] are enemies [of God], which is for your advantage *and* benefit. But from the point of view of God's choice—of election, of divine selection—they are still the beloved [dear to Him] for the sake of their forefathers.

29 For God's gifts and His call are irrevocable—He never withdraws them when once they are given, and He does not change His mind about those to whom He gives His grace or to whom He sends His call.

**AMP** [a] Thayer.

# New American Standard

11¶ I say then, they did not stumble so as to fall, did they? May it never be! But by their transgression salvation *has come* to the Gentiles, to make them jealous.

12Now if their transgression be riches for the world and their failure be riches for the Gentiles, how much more will their fulfillment be!

13But I am speaking to you who are Gentiles. Inasmuch then as I am an apostle of Gentiles, I magnify my ministry,

14if somehow I might move to jealousy my fellow countrymen and save some of them.

15For if their rejection be the reconciliation of the world, what will *their* acceptance be but life from the dead?

16And if the first piece *of dough* be holy, the lump is also; and if the root be holy, the branches are too.

17But if some of the branches were broken off, and you, being a wild olive, were grafted in among them and became partaker with them of the rich root of the olive tree,

18do not be arrogant toward the branches; but if you are arrogant, *remember that* it is not you who supports the root, but the root *supports* you.

19You will say then, "Branches were broken off so that I might be grafted in."

20Quite right, they were broken off for their unbelief, but you stand by your faith. Do not be conceited, but fear;

21for if God did not spare the natural branches, neither will He spare you.

22Behold then the kindness and severity of God; to those who fell, severity, but to you, God's kindness, if you continue in His kindness; otherwise you also will be cut off.

23And they also, if they do not continue in their unbelief, will be grafted in; for God is able to graft them in again.

24For if you were cut off from what is by nature a wild olive tree, and were grafted contrary to nature into a cultivated olive tree, how much more shall these who are the natural *branches* be grafted into their own olive tree?

25¶ For I do not want you, brethren, to be uninformed of this mystery, lest you be wise in your own estimation, that a partial hardening has happened to Israel until the fulness of the Gentiles has come in;

26and thus all Israel will be saved; just as it is written,
"THE DELIVERER WILL COME FROM ZION,
HE WILL REMOVE UNGODLINESS FROM JACOB."
27 "AND THIS IS MY COVENANT WITH THEM,
WHEN I TAKE AWAY THEIR SINS."

28From the standpoint of the gospel they are enemies for your sake, but from the standpoint of *God's* choice they are beloved for the sake of the fathers;

29for the gifts and the calling of God are irrevocable.

# New International

*Ingrafted Branches*

11Again I ask: Did they stumble so as to fall beyond recovery?
Not at all! Rather, because of their transgression, salvation has
come to the Gentiles to make Israel envious.
12But if their transgression means riches for the world, and their loss means riches
for the Gentiles, how much greater riches will their fullness bring!
13I am talking to you Gentiles. Inasmuch as I am the apostle to
the Gentiles, I make much of my ministry
14in the hope that I may
somehow arouse my own people to envy and save some of them.
15For if their rejection is the reconciliation of the world, what will
their acceptance be but life from the dead?
16If the part of the
dough offered as firstfruits is holy, then the whole batch is holy;
if the root is holy, so are the branches.

17If some of the branches have been broken off, and you,
though a wild olive shoot, have been grafted in among the others
and now share in the nourishing sap from the olive root,
18do not
boast over those branches. If you do, consider this: You do not
support the root, but the root supports you.
19You will say then,
"Branches were broken off so that I could be grafted in."
20Granted. But they were broken off because of unbelief, and you
stand by faith. Do not be arrogant, but be afraid.
21For if God did
not spare the natural branches, he will not spare you either.

22Consider therefore the kindness and sternness of God: sternness to those who fell, but kindness to you, provided that you
continue in his kindness. Otherwise, you also will be cut off.
23And if they do not persist in unbelief, they will be grafted in, for
God is able to graft them in again.
24After all, if you were cut out
of an olive tree that is wild by nature, and contrary to nature were
grafted into a cultivated olive tree, how much more readily will
these, the natural branches, be grafted into their own olive tree!

*All Israel Will Be Saved*

25I do not want you to be ignorant of this mystery, brothers, so
that you may not be conceited: Israel has experienced a hardening
in part until the full number of the Gentiles has come in.
26And so
all Israel will be saved, as it is written:

"The deliverer will come from Zion;
he will turn godlessness away from Jacob.
27And this is[b] my covenant with them
when I take away their sins."[c]

28As far as the gospel is concerned, they are enemies on your
account; but as far as election is concerned, they are loved on
account of the patriarchs,
29for God's gifts and his call are irrevocable.
30Just as you who were at one time disobedient to God have

NIV [b] 27 Or *will be* [c] 27 Isaiah 59:20,21; 27:9; Jer. 31:33,34

## King James

30 For as ye in times past have not believed God, yet have now obtained mercy through their unbelief:

31 Even so have these also now not believed, that through your mercy they also may obtain mercy.

32 For God hath concluded them all in unbelief, that he might have mercy upon all.

33 O the depth of the riches both of the wisdom and knowledge of God! how unsearchable *are* his judgments, and his ways past finding out!

34 For who hath known the mind of the Lord? or who hath been his counsellor?

35 Or who hath first given to him, and it shall be recompensed unto him again?

36 For of him, and through him, and to him, *are* all things: to whom *be* glory for ever. Amen.

**12** I BESEECH you therefore, brethren, by the mercies of God, that ye present your bodies a living sacrifice, holy, acceptable unto God, *which is* your reasonable service.

2 And be not conformed to this world: but be ye transformed by the renewing of your mind, that ye may prove what *is* that good, and acceptable, and perfect, will of God.

3 For I say, through the grace given unto me, to every man that is among you, not to think *of himself* more highly than he ought to think; but to think soberly, according as God hath dealt to every man the measure of faith.

4 For as we have many members in one body, and all members have not the same office:

5 So we, *being* many, are one body in Christ, and every one members one of another.

6 Having then gifts differing according to the grace that is given to us, whether prophecy, *let us prophesy* according to the proportion of faith;

7 Or ministry, *let us wait* on *our* ministering: or he that teacheth, on teaching;

8 Or he that exhorteth, on exhortation: he that giveth, *let him do it* with simplicity; he that ruleth, with diligence; he that showeth mercy, with cheerfulness.

9 *Let* love be without dissimulation. Abhor that which is evil; cleave to that which is good.

10 *Be* kindly affectioned one to another with brotherly love; in honour preferring one another;

11 Not slothful in business; fervent in spirit; serving the Lord;

12 Rejoicing in hope; patient in tribulation; continuing instant in prayer;

## Amplified

30 Just as you were once disobedient *and* rebellious toward God but now have obtained [His] mercy, through their disobedience,

31 So they also now are being disobedient (when you are receiving mercy, that they in turn may one day share the mercy [through you as messengers of the Gospel to them] which has been shown to you). Thus through the mercy you are enjoying, they may *now* also receive mercy.

32 For God has consigned (penned up) all men to disobedience, only that He may have mercy on them all [alike].

33 O the depth of the riches and wisdom and knowledge of God! How unfathomable (inscrutable, unsearchable) are His judgments—His decisions! And how untraceable (mysterious, undiscoverable) are His ways—His methods, His paths!

34 For who has known the mind of the Lord *and* who has understood His thoughts, or who has [ever] been His counselor? [Isa. 40:13, 14.]

35 Or who has first given God anything that he might be paid back *or* that he could claim a recompense?

36 For from Him and through Him and to Him are all things.—For all things originate with Him and come from Him; all things live through Him, and all things center in and tend to consummate and to end in Him. To Him be glory forever! Amen—so be it.

**12** I APPEAL to you therefore, brethren, *and* beg of you in view of [all] the mercies of God, to make a decisive dedication of your bodies—presenting all your members and faculties—as a living sacrifice, holy (devoted, consecrated) and well pleasing to God, which is your reasonable (rational, intelligent) service *and* spiritual worship.

2 Do not be conformed to this world—this [a]age, fashioned after and adapted to its external, superficial customs. But be transformed (changed) by the [entire] renewal of your mind—by its new ideals and its new attitude—so that you may prove [for yourselves] what is the good and acceptable and perfect will of God, [b]*even* the thing which is good and acceptable and perfect [in His sight for you].

3 For by the grace (unmerited favor of God) given to me I warn every one among you not to estimate *and* think of himself more highly than he ought—not to have an exaggerated opinion of his own importance; but to rate his ability with sober judgment, each according to the degree of faith apportioned by God to him.

4 For as in one physical body we have many parts (organs, members) and all of these parts do not have the same function *or* use,

5 So we, numerous as we are, are one body in Christ, the Messiah, and individually we are parts one of another—mutually dependent on one another.

6 Having gifts (faculties, talents, qualities) that differ according to the grace given us, let us use them: [He whose gift is] prophecy, [let him prophesy] according to the proportion of his faith;

7 [He whose gift is] practical service, let him give himself to serving; he who teaches, to his teaching;

8 (He who exhorts, encourages), to his exhortation; he who contributes, let him do it in simplicity *and* liberality; he who gives aid *and* superintends, with zeal *and* singleness of mind; he who does acts of mercy, with genuine cheerfulness *and* joyful eagerness.

9 [Let your] love be sincere—a real thing; hate what is evil (loathe all ungodliness, turn in horror from wickedness), but hold fast to that which is good.

10 Love one another with brotherly affection—as members of one family—giving precedence *and* showing honor to one another.

11 Never lag in zeal *and* in earnest endeavor; be aglow *and* burning with the Spirit, serving the Lord.

12 Rejoice *and* exult in hope; be steadfast and patient in suffering *and* tribulation; be constant in prayer.

**AMP** [a] Alternate reading. [b] Alternate reading.

## New American Standard

30For just as you once were disobedient to God, but now have
been shown mercy because of their disobedience,
31so these also now have been disobedient, in order that because of the mercy shown to you they also may now be shown
mercy.
32For God has shut up all in disobedience that He might show
mercy to all.
33¶ Oh, the depth of the riches both of the wisdom and knowledge of God! How unsearchable are His judgments and unfathomable His ways!
34For WHO HAS KNOWN THE MIND OF THE LORD, OR WHO BECAME
HIS COUNSELOR?
35Or WHO HAS FIRST GIVEN TO HIM THAT IT MIGHT BE PAID BACK
TO HIM AGAIN?
36For from Him and through Him and to Him are all things. To
Him *be* the glory forever. Amen.

## New International

now received mercy as a result of their disobedience, 31so they too
have now become disobedient in order that they too may now[d]
receive mercy as a result of God's mercy to you. 32For God has
bound all men over to disobedience so that he may have mercy on
them all.

*Doxology*

33Oh, the depth of the riches of the wisdom and[e]
knowledge of God!
How unsearchable his judgments,
and his paths beyond tracing out!
34"Who has known the mind of the Lord?
Or who has been his counselor?"[f]
35"Who has ever given to God,
that God should repay him?"[g]
36For from him and through him and to him are all things.
To him be the glory forever! Amen.

*Dedicated Service*

**12** I URGE you therefore, brethren, by the mercies of God,
to present your bodies a living and holy sacrifice, acceptable to God, *which is* your spiritual service of worship.
2And do not be conformed to this world, but be transformed
by the renewing of your mind, that you may prove what the will
of God is, that which is good and acceptable and perfect.
3¶ For through the grace given to me I say to every man among
you not to think more highly of himself than he ought to think; but
to think so as to have sound judgment, as God has allotted to each
a measure of faith.
4For just as we have many members in one body and all the
members do not have the same function,
5so we, who are many, are one body in Christ, and individually members one of another.
6And since we have gifts that differ according to the grace
given to us, *let each exercise them accordingly:* if prophecy, according
to the proportion of his faith;
7if service, in his serving; or he who teaches, in his teaching;
8or he who exhorts, in his exhortation; he who gives, with
[c]liberality; he who leads, with diligence; he who shows mercy,
with cheerfulness.
9¶ Let love be without hypocrisy. Abhor what is evil; cling to
what is good.
10Be devoted to one another in brotherly love; give preference
to one another in honor;
11not lagging behind in diligence, fervent in spirit, serving the
Lord;
12rejoicing in hope, persevering in tribulation, devoted to
prayer,

*Living Sacrifices*

**12** THEREFORE, I urge you, brothers, in view of God's
mercy, to offer your bodies as living sacrifices, holy and
pleasing to God—this is your spiritual[h] act of worship. 2Do not
conform any longer to the pattern of this world, but be transformed by the renewing of your mind. Then you will be able to test
and approve what God's will is—his good, pleasing and perfect
will.
3For by the grace given me I say to every one of you: Do not
think of yourself more highly than you ought, but rather think of
yourself with sober judgment, in accordance with the measure of
faith God has given you. 4Just as each of us has one body with
many members, and these members do not all have the same
function, 5so in Christ we who are many form one body, and each
member belongs to all the others. 6We have different gifts, according to the grace given us. If a man's gift is prophesying, let him
use it in proportion to his[i] faith. 7If it is serving, let him serve; if
it is teaching, let him teach; 8if it is encouraging, let him encourage;
if it is contributing to the needs of others, let him give generously;
if it is leadership, let him govern diligently; if it is showing mercy,
let him do it cheerfully.

*Love*

9Love must be sincere. Hate what is evil; cling to what is good.
10Be devoted to one another in brotherly love. Honor one another
above yourselves. 11Never be lacking in zeal, but keep your spiritual fervor, serving the Lord. 12Be joyful in hope, patient in afflic-

NAS [c] Or, *simplicity*

NIV [d] *31* Some manuscripts do not have *now.* [e] *33* Or *riches and the wisdom and the* [f] *34* Isaiah 40:13 [g] *35* Job 41:11 [h] *1* Or *reasonable* [i] *6* Or *in agreement with the*

# King James

<sup>13</sup>Distributing to the necessity of saints; given to hospitality.

<sup>14</sup>Bless them which persecute you: bless, and curse not.

<sup>15</sup>Rejoice with them that do rejoice, and weep with them that weep.

<sup>16</sup> *Be* of the same mind one toward another. Mind not high things, but condescend to men of low estate. Be not wise in your own conceits.

<sup>17</sup>Recompense to no man evil for evil. Provide things honest in the sight of all men.

<sup>18</sup>If it be possible, as much as lieth in you, live peaceably with all men.

<sup>19</sup>Dearly beloved, avenge not yourselves, but *rather* give place unto wrath: for it is written, Vengeance *is* mine; I will repay, saith the Lord.

<sup>20</sup>Therefore if thine enemy hunger, feed him; if he thirst, give him drink: for in so doing thou shalt heap coals of fire on his head.

<sup>21</sup>Be not overcome of evil, but overcome evil with good.

**13** LET EVERY soul be subject unto the higher powers. For there is no power but of God: the powers that be are ordained of God.

<sup>2</sup>Whosoever therefore resisteth the power, resisteth the ordinance of God: and they that resist shall receive to themselves damnation.

<sup>3</sup>For rulers are not a terror to good works, but to the evil. Wilt thou then not be afraid of the power? do that which is good, and thou shalt have praise of the same:

<sup>4</sup>For he is the minister of God to thee for good. But if thou do that which is evil, be afraid; for he beareth not the sword in vain: for he is the minister of God, a revenger to *execute* wrath upon him that doeth evil.

<sup>5</sup>Wherefore *ye* must needs be subject, not only for wrath, but also for conscience sake.

<sup>6</sup>For for this cause pay ye tribute also: for they are God's ministers, attending continually upon this very thing.

<sup>7</sup>Render therefore to all their dues: tribute to whom tribute *is due;* custom to whom custom; fear to whom fear; honour to whom honour.

<sup>8</sup>Owe no man any thing, but to love one another: for he that loveth another hath fulfilled the law.

<sup>9</sup>For this, Thou shalt not commit adultery, Thou shalt not kill, Thou shalt not steal, Thou shalt not bear false witness, Thou shalt not covet; and if *there be* any other commandment, it is briefly comprehended in this saying, namely, Thou shalt love thy neighbour as thyself.

<sup>10</sup>Love worketh no ill to his neighbour: therefore love *is* the fulfilling of the law.

<sup>11</sup>And that, knowing the time, that now *it is* high time to awake out of sleep: for now *is* our salvation nearer than when we believed.

# Amplified

<sup>13</sup>Contribute to the needs of God's people—sharing in the necessities of the saints—pursuing the practice of hospitality.

<sup>14</sup>Bless those who persecute you—who are cruel in their attitude toward you; bless and do not curse them.

<sup>15</sup>[Share others' joy], rejoicing with those who rejoice; and [share others' grief], weeping with those who weep.

<sup>16</sup>Live in harmony with one another; do not be haughty (snobbish, high-minded, exclusive), but readily adjust yourself to [people, things] *and* give yourselves to humble tasks. Never overestimate yourself *or* be wise in your own conceits. [Prov. 3:7.]

<sup>17</sup>Repay no one evil for evil, but take thought for what is honest *and* proper *and* noble—aiming to be above reproach—in the sight of every one. [Prov. 20:22.]

<sup>18</sup>If possible, as far as it depends on you, live at peace with every one.

<sup>19</sup>Beloved, never avenge yourselves, but leave the way open for [God's] wrath; for it is written, Vengeance is Mine, I will repay (requite), says the Lord. [Deut. 32:35.]

<sup>20</sup>But, if your enemy is hungry, feed him; if he is thirsty, give him drink; for by so doing you will heap burning coals upon his head. [Prov. 25:21, 22.]

<sup>21</sup>Do not let yourself be overcome by evil, but overcome (master) evil with good.

**13** LET EVERY person be loyally subject to the governing (civil) authorities. For there is no authority except from God—by His permission, His sanction; and those that exist do so by God's appointment. [Prov. 8:15.]

<sup>2</sup>Therefore he who resists *and* sets himself up against the authorities resists what God has appointed *and* arranged—in divine order. And those who resist will bring down judgment upon themselves—receiving the penalty due them.

<sup>3</sup>For civil authorities are not a terror to [people of] good conduct, but to [those of] bad behavior. Would you have no dread of him who is in authority? Then do what is right and you will receive his approval *and* commendation.

<sup>4</sup>For he is God's servant for your good. But if you do wrong, [you should dread him and] be afraid, for he does not bear *and* wear the sword for nothing. He is God's servant to execute His wrath (His punishment, His vengeance) on the wrongdoer.

<sup>5</sup>Therefore one must be subject, not only to avoid God's wrath *and* escape punishment, but also as a matter of principle *and* for the sake of conscience.

<sup>6</sup>For this same reason you pay taxes, for [the civil authorities] are official servants under God, devoting themselves to attending to this very service.

<sup>7</sup>Render to all men their dues. [Pay] taxes to whom taxes are due, revenue to whom revenue is due, respect to whom respect is due, and honor to whom honor is due.

<sup>8</sup>Keep out of debt *and* owe no man anything, except to love one another; for he who loves his neighbor—who practices loving others—has fulfilled the Law [relating to one's fellowmen], meeting all its requirements.

<sup>9</sup>The commandments, You shall not commit adultery, You shall not kill, You shall not steal, You shall not covet (have an evil desire), and any other commandment, are summed up in the single command, You shall love your neighbor as yourself. [Exod. 20:13-17; Lev. 19:18.]

<sup>10</sup>Love does no wrong to one's neighbor—it never hurts anybody. Therefore love meets all the requirements *and* is the fulfilling of the Law.

<sup>11</sup>Besides this you know what [a critical] hour this is, how it is high time now for you to wake up out of your sleep—rouse to reality. For salvation (final deliverance) is nearer to us now than when we first believed—adhered to, trusted in and relied on Christ, the Messiah.

## New American Standard

13contributing to the needs of the saints, practicing hospitality.
14Bless those who persecute [a]you; bless and curse not.
15Rejoice with those who rejoice, and weep with those who
weep.
16Be of the same mind toward one another; do not be haughty
in mind, but associate with the lowly. Do not be wise in your own
estimation.
17Never pay back evil for evil to anyone. Respect what is right
in the sight of all men.
18If possible, so far as it depends on you, be at peace with all
men.
19Never take your own revenge, beloved, but leave room for the
wrath *of God,* for it is written, "VENGEANCE IS MINE, I WILL REPAY,"
says the Lord.
20"BUT IF YOUR ENEMY IS HUNGRY, FEED HIM, AND IF HE IS
THIRSTY, GIVE HIM A DRINK; FOR IN SO DOING YOU WILL HEAP BURN-
ING COALS UPON HIS HEAD."
21Do not be overcome by evil, but overcome evil with good.

*Be Subject to Government*

**13** LET EVERY person be in subjection to the governing authorities. For there is no authority except from God, and
those which exist are established by God.
2Therefore he who resists authority has opposed the ordinance
of God; and they who have opposed will receive condemnation
upon themselves.
3For rulers are not a cause of fear for good behavior, but for
evil. Do you want to have no fear of authority? Do what is good,
and you will have praise from the same;
4for it is a minister of God to you for good. But if you do what
is evil, be afraid; for it does not bear the sword for nothing; for it
is a minister of God, an avenger who brings wrath upon the one
who practices evil.
5Wherefore it is necessary to be in subjection, not only because
of wrath, but also for conscience' sake.
6For because of this you also pay taxes, for *rulers* are servants
of God, devoting themselves to this very thing.
7Render to all what is due them: tax to whom tax *is due;* custom
to whom custom; fear to whom fear; honor to whom honor.
8¶ Owe nothing to anyone except to love one another; for he
who loves his neighbor has fulfilled *the* law.
9For this, "YOU SHALL NOT COMMIT ADULTERY, YOU SHALL NOT
MURDER, YOU SHALL NOT STEAL, YOU SHALL NOT COVET," and if
there is any other commandment, it is summed up in this saying,
"YOU SHALL LOVE YOUR NEIGHBOR AS YOURSELF."
10Love does no wrong to a neighbor; love therefore is the fulfillment of *the* law.
11¶ And this *do,* knowing the time, that it is already the hour
for you to awaken from sleep; for now [b]salvation is nearer to us
than when we believed.

**NAS** [a] Some ancient mss. do not contain *you* [b] Or, *our salvation is nearer than when*

## New International

tion, faithful in prayer. 13Share with God's people who are in need.
Practice hospitality.
14Bless those who persecute you; bless and do not curse. 15Re-
joice with those who rejoice; mourn with those who mourn. 16Live
in harmony with one another. Do not be proud, but be willing to
associate with people of low position.[c] Do not be conceited.
17Do not repay anyone evil for evil. Be careful to do what is right
in the eyes of everybody. 18If it is possible, as far as it depends on
you, live at peace with everyone. 19Do not take revenge, my
friends, but leave room for God's wrath, for it is written: "It is mine
to avenge; I will repay,"[d] says the Lord. 20On the contrary:

"If your enemy is hungry, feed him;
if he is thirsty, give him something to drink.
In doing this, you will heap burning coals on his head."[e]

21Do not be overcome by evil, but overcome evil with good.

*Submission to the Authorities*

**13** EVERYONE MUST submit himself to the governing authorities, for there is no authority except that which God
has established. The authorities that exist have been established by
God. 2Consequently, he who rebels against the authority is rebelling against what God has instituted, and those who do so will
bring judgment on themselves. 3For rulers hold no terror for those
who do right, but for those who do wrong. Do you want to be free
from fear of the one in authority? Then do what is right and he will
commend you. 4For he is God's servant to do you good. But if you
do wrong, be afraid, for he does not bear the sword for nothing.
He is God's servant, an agent of wrath to bring punishment on the
wrongdoer. 5Therefore, it is necessary to submit to the authorities,
not only because of possible punishment but also because of conscience.
6This is also why you pay taxes, for the authorities are God's
servants, who give their full time to governing. 7Give everyone
what you owe him: If you owe taxes, pay taxes; if revenue, then
revenue; if respect, then respect; if honor, then honor.

*Love, for the Day Is Near*

8Let no debt remain outstanding, except the continuing debt to
love one another, for he who loves his fellowman has fulfilled the
law. 9The commandments, "Do not commit adultery," "Do not
murder," "Do not steal," "Do not covet,"[f] and whatever other
commandment there may be, are summed up in this one rule:
"Love your neighbor as yourself."[g] 10Love does no harm to its
neighbor. Therefore love is the fulfillment of the law.
11And do this, understanding the present time. The hour has
come for you to wake up from your slumber, because our salvation
is nearer now than when we first believed. 12The night is nearly

**NIV** [c] *16* Or *willing to do menial work* [d] *19* Deut. 32:35 [e] *20* Prov. 25:21,22
[f] *9* Exodus 20:13-15,17; Deut. 5:17-19,21 [g] *9* Lev. 19:18

## King James

12The night is far spent, the day is at hand: let us therefore cast
off the works of darkness, and let us put on the armour of light.
13Let us walk honestly, as in the day; not in rioting and drunkenness, not in chambering and wantonness, not in strife and envying.
14But put ye on the Lord Jesus Christ, and make not provision
for the flesh, to *fulfil* the lusts *thereof*.

**14** HIM THAT is weak in the faith receive ye, *but* not to
doubtful disputations.
2For one believeth that he may eat all things: another, who is
weak, eateth herbs.
3Let not him that eateth despise him that eateth not; and let not
him which eateth not judge him that eateth: for God hath received
him.
4Who art thou that judgest another man's servant? to his own
master he standeth or falleth. Yea, he shall be holden up: for God
is able to make him stand.
5One man esteemeth one day above another: another esteemeth every day *alike*. Let every man be fully persuaded in his
own mind.
6He that regardeth the day, regardeth *it* unto the Lord; and he
that regardeth not the day, to the Lord he doth not regard *it*. He
that eateth, eateth to the Lord, for he giveth God thanks; and he
that eateth not, to the Lord he eateth not, and giveth God thanks.
7For none of us liveth to himself, and no man dieth to himself.
8For whether we live, we live unto the Lord; and whether we
die, we die unto the Lord: whether we live therefore, or die, we
are the Lord's.
9For to this end Christ both died, and rose, and revived, that
he might be Lord both of the dead and living.
10But why dost thou judge thy brother? or why dost thou set
at nought thy brother? for we shall all stand before the judgment
seat of Christ.
11For it is written, *As* I live, saith the Lord, every knee shall bow
to me, and every tongue shall confess to God.
12So then every one of us shall give account of himself to God.
13Let us not therefore judge one another any more: but judge
this rather, that no man put a stumblingblock or an occasion to fall
in *his* brother's way.
14I know, and am persuaded by the Lord Jesus, that *there is*
nothing unclean of itself: but to him that esteemeth any thing to
be unclean, to him *it is* unclean.
15But if thy brother be grieved with *thy* meat, now walkest thou
not charitably. Destroy not him with thy meat, for whom Christ
died.
16Let not then your good be evil spoken of:
17For the kingdom of God is not meat and drink; but righteousness, and peace, and joy in the Holy Ghost.
18For he that in these things serveth Christ *is* acceptable to God,
and approved of men.

## Amplified

12The night is far gone [and] the day is almost here. Let us then
drop (fling away) the works *and* deeds of darkness and put on the
[full] armor of light.
13Let us live *and* conduct ourselves honorably *and* becomingly
as in the [open light of] day; not in reveling (carousing) and drunkenness, not in immorality and debauchery (sensuality and licentiousness), not in quarreling and jealousy.
14But clothe yourself with the Lord Jesus Christ, the Messiah,
and make no provision for [indulging] the flesh—put a stop to
thinking about the evil cravings of your physical nature—to [grati-
fy its] desires (lusts).

**14** AS FOR the man who is a weak believer, welcome him
[into your fellowship], but not to criticize his opinions *or*
pass judgment on his scruples *or* perplex him with discussions.
2One [man's faith permits him] to believe he may eat anything,
while a weaker one [limits his] eating to vegetables.
3Let not him who eats look down on *or* despise him who abstains, and let not him who abstains criticize *and* pass judgment on
him who eats; for God has accepted *and* welcomed him.
4Who are you to pass judgment on *and* censure another's household servant? It is before his own Master that he stands or falls.
And he shall stand *and* be upheld, for the Master—the Lord—is
mighty to support him *and* make him stand.
5One man esteems one day as better than another, while another man esteems all days alike [sacred]. Let every one be fully
convinced (satisfied) in his own mind.
6He who observes the day, observes it in honor of the Lord. He
also who eats, eats in honor of the Lord, since he gives thanks to
God; while he who abstains, abstains in honor of the Lord and
gives thanks to God.
7None of us lives to himself (but to the Lord), and none of us
dies to himself (but to the Lord, for)
8If we live, we live to the Lord, and if we die, we die to the Lord.
So then, whether we live or we die, we belong to the Lord.
9For Christ died and lived again for this very purpose, that He
might be Lord both of the dead and of the living.
10Why do you criticize *and* pass judgment on your brother? Or
you, why do you look down upon *or* despise your brother? For we
shall all stand before the judgment seat of God.
11For it is written, As I live, says the Lord, every knee shall bow
to Me, and every tongue shall confess to God—that is, acknowledge Him to His honor and to His praise. [Isa. 45:23.]
12And so each of us shall give an account of himself—give an
answer in reference to judgment—to God.
13Then let us no more criticize *and* blame *and* pass judgment on
one another, but rather decide *and* endeavor never to put a stumbling block *or* an obstacle or a hindrance in the way of a brother.
14I know and am convinced (persuaded) as one in the Lord
Jesus, that nothing is [forbidden as] essentially unclean—that is,
defiled and unholy in itself. But [none the less] it is unclean
(defiled and unholy) to any one who thinks it is unclean.
15But if your brother is being pained *or* his feelings hurt *or* if he
is being injured by what you eat, [then] you are no longer walking
in love.—That is, you have ceased to be living and conducting
yourself by the standard of love toward him. Do not let what you
eat hurt *or* cause the ruin of one for whom Christ died!
16Do not therefore let what seems good to you be considered
an evil thing [by someone else].—[In other words], do not give
occasion for others to criticize that which is justifiable for you.
17[After all,] the kingdom of God is not a matter of [getting the]
food and drink [one likes], but instead, it is righteousness—that
state which makes a person acceptable to God—and heartpeace
and joy in the Holy Spirit.
18He who serves Christ in this way is acceptable *and* pleasing
to God and is approved by men.

## New American Standard

12The night is almost gone, and the day is at hand. Let us therefore lay aside the deeds of darkness and put on the armor of light.

13Let us behave properly as in the day, not in carousing and drunkenness, not in sexual promiscuity and sensuality, not in strife and jealousy.

14But put on the Lord Jesus Christ, and make no provision for the flesh in regard to *its* lusts.

*Principles of Conscience*

**14** NOW ACCEPT the one who is weak in faith, *but* not for *the purpose of* passing judgment on his opinions.

2One man has faith that he may eat all things, but he who is weak eats vegetables *only*.

3Let not him who eats regard with contempt him who does not eat, and let not him who does not eat judge him who eats, for God has accepted him.

4Who are you to judge the servant of another? To his own master he stands or falls; and stand he will, for the Lord is able to make him stand.

5One man regards one day above another, another regards every day *alike*. Let each man be fully convinced in his own mind.

6He who observes the day, observes it for the Lord, and he who eats, does so for the Lord, for he gives thanks to God; and he who eats not, for the Lord he does not eat, and gives thanks to God.

7For not one of us lives for himself, and not one dies for himself;

8for if we live, we live for the Lord, or if we die, we die for the Lord; therefore whether we live or die, we are the Lord's.

9For to this end Christ died and lived *again*, that He might be Lord both of the dead and of the living.

10But you, why do you judge your brother? Or you again, why do you regard your brother with contempt? For we shall all stand before the judgment seat of God.

11For it is written,

"AS I LIVE, SAYS THE LORD, EVERY KNEE SHALL BOW TO ME,
AND EVERY TONGUE SHALL GIVE PRAISE TO GOD."

12So then each one of us shall give account of himself to God.

13¶ Therefore let us not judge one another anymore, but rather determine this—not to put an obstacle or a stumbling block in a brother's way.

14I know and am convinced in the Lord Jesus that nothing is unclean in itself; but to him who thinks anything to be unclean, to him it is unclean.

15For if because of food your brother is hurt, you are no longer walking according to love. Do not destroy with your food him for whom Christ died.

16Therefore do not let what is for you a good thing be spoken of as evil;

17for the kingdom of God is not eating and drinking, but righteousness and peace and joy in the Holy Spirit.

18For he who in this *way* serves Christ is acceptable to God and approved by men.

## New International

over; the day is almost here. So let us put aside the deeds of
darkness and put on the armor of light. 13Let us behave decently,
as in the daytime, not in orgies and drunkenness, not in sexual
immorality and debauchery, not in dissension and jealousy.
14Rather, clothe yourselves with the Lord Jesus Christ, and do not
think about how to gratify the desires of the sinful nature.[a]

*The Weak and the Strong*

**14** ACCEPT HIM whose faith is weak, without passing judgment on disputable matters. 2One man's faith allows him
to eat everything, but another man, whose faith is weak, eats only
vegetables. 3The man who eats everything must not look down on
him who does not, and the man who does not eat everything must
not condemn the man who does, for God has accepted him. 4Who
are you to judge someone else's servant? To his own master he
stands or falls. And he will stand, for the Lord is able to make him
stand.
5One man considers one day more sacred than another; another
man considers every day alike. Each one should be fully convinced
in his own mind. 6He who regards one day as special, does so to
the Lord. He who eats meat, eats to the Lord, for he gives thanks
to God; and he who abstains, does so to the Lord and gives thanks
to God. 7For none of us lives to himself alone and none of us dies
to himself alone. 8If we live, we live to the Lord; and if we die, we
die to the Lord. So, whether we live or die, we belong to the Lord.
9For this very reason, Christ died and returned to life so that
he might be the Lord of both the dead and the living. 10You, then,
why do you judge your brother? Or why do you look down on
your brother? For we will all stand before God's judgment seat. 11It
is written:

"'As surely as I live,' says the Lord,
'every knee will bow before me;
every tongue will confess to God.'"[b]

12So then, each of us will give an account of himself to God.
13Therefore let us stop passing judgment on one another. Instead, make up your mind not to put any stumbling block or
obstacle in your brother's way. 14As one who is in the Lord Jesus,
I am fully convinced that no food[c] is unclean in itself. But if anyone
regards something as unclean, then for him it is unclean. 15If your
brother is distressed because of what you eat, you are no longer
acting in love. Do not by your eating destroy your brother for
whom Christ died. 16Do not allow what you consider good to be
spoken of as evil. 17For the kingdom of God is not a matter of
eating and drinking, but of righteousness, peace and joy in the
Holy Spirit, 18because anyone who serves Christ in this way is
pleasing to God and approved by men.

NIV [a] 14 Or *the flesh* [b] 11 Isaiah 45:23 [c] 14 Or *that nothing*

## King James

19 Let us therefore follow after the things which make for peace,
and things wherewith one may edify another.
20 For meat destroy not the work of God. All things indeed *are*
pure; but *it is* evil for that man who eateth with offence.
21 *It is* good neither to eat flesh, nor to drink wine, nor *any thing*
whereby thy brother stumbleth, or is offended, or is made weak.
22 Hast thou faith? have *it* to thyself before God. Happy *is* he that
condemneth not himself in that thing which he alloweth.
23 And he that doubteth is damned if he eat, because *he eateth*
not of faith: for whatsoever *is* not of faith is sin.

**15** WE THEN that are strong ought to bear the infirmities of
the weak, and not to please ourselves.
2 Let every one of us please *his* neighbour for *his* good to edification.
3 For even Christ pleased not himself; but, as it is written, The
reproaches of them that reproached thee fell on me.
4 For whatsoever things were written aforetime were written for
our learning, that we through patience and comfort of the scriptures might have hope.
5 Now the God of patience and consolation grant you to be
likeminded one toward another according to Christ Jesus:
6 That ye may with one mind *and* one mouth glorify God, even
the Father of our Lord Jesus Christ.
7 Wherefore receive ye one another, as Christ also received us
to the glory of God.
8 Now I say that Jesus Christ was a minister of the circumcision
for the truth of God, to confirm the promises *made* unto the fathers:
9 And that the Gentiles might glorify God for *his* mercy; as it is
written, For this cause I will confess to thee among the Gentiles,
and sing unto thy name.
10 And again he saith, Rejoice, ye Gentiles, with his people.
11 And again, Praise the Lord, all ye Gentiles; and laud him all
ye people.
12 And again, Esaias saith, There shall be a root of Jesse, and he
that shall rise to reign over the Gentiles; in him shall the Gentiles
trust.
13 Now the God of hope fill you with all joy and peace in believing, that ye may abound in hope, through the power of the Holy
Ghost.

## Amplified

19 So let us then definitely aim for *and* eagerly pursue what
makes for harmony and for mutual upbuilding (edification and
development) of one another.
20 You must not, for the sake of food, undo *and* break down and
destroy the work of God! Everything is indeed (ceremonially) clean
*and* pure, but it is wrong for any one to hurt the conscience of
others *or* to make them fall by what he eats.
21 The right thing is to eat no meat or drink no wine [at all], or
[do anything else] if it [hurts your brother's conscience or] makes
him stumble, *or* offends or weakens him.
22 Your personal convictions [on such matters] exercise as in
God's presence, keeping them to yourself—striving only to know
the truth and obey His will. Blessed, happy, [a]to be envied is he
who has no reason to judge himself for what he approves—who
does not convict himself by what he chooses to do.
23 But the man who has doubts—misgivings, an uneasy conscience—about eating, and then eats [perhaps because of you],
stands condemned [before God], because he is not true to his
convictions *and* he does not act from faith. For whatever does not
originate *and* proceed from faith is sin—that is, whatever is done
without a conviction of its approval by God is sinful.

**15** WE WHO are strong [in our convictions and of robust
faith] ought to bear with the failings *and* the frailties *and*
the tender scruples of the weak.—We ought to help carry the
doubts and qualms of others—and not to please ourselves.
2 Let each one of us make it a practice to please (make happy)
his neighbor for his good *and* for his true welfare, to edify him—
that is, to strengthen him and build him up spiritually.
3 For Christ (gave no thought to His own interests) to please
Himself; but, as it is written, The reproaches *and* abuses of those
who reproached *and* abused you fell on Me. [Ps. 69:9.]
4 For whatever was thus written in former days was written for
our instruction, that by [our steadfast and patient] endurance and
the encouragement [drawn] from the Scriptures we might hold fast
*and* cherish hope.
5 Now may the God Who gives the power of patient endurance
(steadfastness) and Who supplies encouragement, grant you to
live in such mutual harmony *and* such full sympathy with one
another, in accord with Christ Jesus,
6 That together you may (unanimously) with united hearts *and*
one voice, praise and glorify the God and Father of our Lord Jesus
Christ, the Messiah.
7 Welcome *and* receive (to your hearts) one another, then, even
as Christ has welcomed *and* received you, for the glory of God.
8 For I tell you that Christ, the Messiah, became a servant *and*
a minister to the circumcised [the Jews] in order to show God's
truthfulness *and* honesty by confirming (verifying) the promises
[given to our] fathers,
9 And [also in order] that the Gentiles might glorify God for [His
uncovenanted] mercy to them. As it is written, Therefore I will
praise You among the Gentiles, and sing praises to Your name.
[Ps. 18:49.]
10 Again it is said, Rejoice (exult), O Gentiles, along with His
[own] people; [Deut. 32:43.]
11 And again, Praise the Lord, all you Gentiles (nations), and let
all the peoples praise Him! [Ps. 117:1.]
12 And further Isaiah says, There shall be a [b]Sprout from the
[c]Root of Jesse, He Who rises to rule over the Gentiles; in Him shall
the Gentiles hope. [Isa. 11:1, 10.]
13 May the God of your hope so fill you with all joy and peace
in believing—through the experience of your faith—that by the
power of the Holy Spirit you may abound *and* be overflowing
(bubbling over) with hope.

**AMP** [a] Souter. [b] Abbott-Smith. [c] Rev. 5:5; 22:16.

## New American Standard

19So then [d]let us pursue the things which make for peace and
the building up of one another.
20Do not tear down the work of God for the sake of food. All
things indeed are clean, but they are evil for the man who eats and
gives offense.
21It is good not to eat meat or to drink wine, or *to do anything*
by which your brother stumbles.
22The faith which you have, have as your own conviction before
God. Happy is he who does not condemn himself in what he
approves.
23But he who doubts is condemned if he eats, because *his eating*
*is* not from faith; and whatever is not from faith is sin.

*Self-denial on Behalf of Others*

**15** NOW WE who are strong ought to bear the weaknesses
of those without strength and not *just* please ourselves.
2Let each of us please his neighbor for his good, to his edification.
3For even Christ did not please Himself; but as it is written,
"THE REPROACHES OF THOSE WHO REPROACHED THEE FELL UPON
ME."
4For whatever was written in earlier times was written for our
instruction, that through perseverance and the encouragement of
the Scriptures we might have hope.
5Now may the God who gives perseverance and encouragement grant you to be of the same mind with one another according
to Christ Jesus;
6that with one accord you may with one voice glorify the God
and Father of our Lord Jesus Christ.
7¶ Wherefore, accept one another, just as Christ also accepted
us to the glory of God.
8For I say that Christ has become a servant to the circumcision
on behalf of the truth of God to confirm the promises *given* to the
fathers,
9and for the Gentiles to glorify God for His mercy; as it is
written,
"THEREFORE I WILL GIVE PRAISE TO THEE AMONG THE
GENTILES,
AND I WILL SING TO THY NAME."
10And again he says,
"REJOICE, O GENTILES, WITH HIS PEOPLE."
11And again,
"PRAISE THE LORD ALL YOU GENTILES,
AND LET ALL THE PEOPLES PRAISE HIM."
12And again Isaiah says,
"THERE SHALL COME THE ROOT OF JESSE,
AND HE WHO ARISES TO RULE OVER THE GENTILES,
IN HIM SHALL THE GENTILES HOPE."
13Now may the God of hope fill you with all joy and peace in
believing, that you may abound in hope by the power of the Holy
Spirit.

NAS [d] Many ancient mss. read *we pursue*

## New International

19Let us therefore make every effort to do what leads to peace
and to mutual edification.
20Do not destroy the work of God for
the sake of food. All food is clean, but it is wrong for a man to eat
anything that causes someone else to stumble.
21It is better not to
eat meat or drink wine or to do anything else that will cause your
brother to fall.
22So whatever you believe about these things keep between
yourself and God. Blessed is the man who does not condemn
himself by what he approves.
23But the man who has doubts is
condemned if he eats, because his eating is not from faith; and
everything that does not come from faith is sin.

**15** WE WHO are strong ought to bear with the failings of the
weak and not to please ourselves.
2Each of us should
please his neighbor for his good, to build him up.
3For even Christ
did not please himself but, as it is written: "The insults of those
who insult you have fallen on me."[e]
4For everything that was
written in the past was written to teach us, so that through endurance and the encouragement of the Scriptures we might have
hope.
5May the God who gives endurance and encouragement give
you a spirit of unity among yourselves as you follow Christ Jesus,
6so that with one heart and mouth you may glorify the God and
Father of our Lord Jesus Christ.
7Accept one another, then, just as Christ accepted you, in order
to bring praise to God.
8For I tell you that Christ has become a
servant of the Jews[f] on behalf of God's truth, to confirm the
promises made to the patriarchs
9so that the Gentiles may glorify
God for his mercy, as it is written:

"Therefore I will praise you among the Gentiles;
I will sing hymns to your name."[g]

10Again, it says,

"Rejoice, O Gentiles, with his people."[h]

11And again,

"Praise the Lord, all you Gentiles,
and sing praises to him, all you peoples."[i]

12And again, Isaiah says,

"The Root of Jesse will spring up,
one who will arise to rule over the nations;
the Gentiles will hope in him."[j]

13May the God of hope fill you with all joy and peace as you
trust in him, so that you may overflow with hope by the power of
the Holy Spirit.

NIV [e] *3* Psalm 69:9 [f] *8* Greek *circumcision* [g] *9* 2 Samuel 22:50; Psalm 18:49
[h] *10* Deut. 32:43 [i] *11* Psalm 117:1 [j] *12* Isaiah 11:10

## King James

14 And I myself also am persuaded of you, my brethren, that ye also are full of goodness, filled with all knowledge, able also to admonish one another.

15 Nevertheless, brethren, I have written the more boldly unto you in some sort, as putting you in mind, because of the grace that is given to me of God,

16 That I should be the minister of Jesus Christ to the Gentiles, ministering the gospel of God, that the offering up of the Gentiles might be acceptable, being sanctified by the Holy Ghost.

17 I have therefore whereof I may glory through Jesus Christ in those things which pertain to God.

18 For I will not dare to speak of any of those things which Christ hath not wrought by me, to make the Gentiles obedient, by word and deed,

19 Through mighty signs and wonders, by the power of the Spirit of God; so that from Jerusalem, and round about unto Illyricum, I have fully preached the gospel of Christ.

20 Yea, so have I strived to preach the gospel, not where Christ was named, lest I should build upon another man's foundation:

21 But as it is written, To whom he was not spoken of, they shall see: and they that have not heard shall understand.

22 For which cause also I have been much hindered from coming to you.

23 But now having no more place in these parts, and having a great desire these many years to come unto you;

24 Whensoever I take my journey into Spain, I will come to you: for I trust to see you in my journey, and to be brought on my way thitherward by you, if first I be somewhat filled with your *company*.

25 But now I go unto Jerusalem to minister unto the saints.

26 For it hath pleased them of Macedonia and Achaia to make a certain contribution for the poor saints which are at Jerusalem.

27 It hath pleased them verily; and their debtors they are. For if the Gentiles have been made partakers of their spiritual things, their duty is also to minister unto them in carnal things.

28 When therefore I have performed this, and have sealed to them this fruit, I will come by you into Spain.

29 And I am sure that, when I come unto you, I shall come in the fulness of the blessing of the gospel of Christ.

30 Now I beseech you, brethren, for the Lord Jesus Christ's sake, and for the love of the Spirit, that ye strive together with me in *your* prayers to God for me;

31 That I may be delivered from them that do not believe in Judaea; and that my service which *I have* for Jerusalem may be accepted of the saints;

32 That I may come unto you with joy by the will of God, and may with you be refreshed.

33 Now the God of peace *be* with you all. Amen.

**16** I COMMEND unto you Phebe our sister, which is a servant of the church which is at Cenchrea;

## Amplified

14 Personally I am satisfied about you, my brethren, that you yourselves are rich in goodness, amply filled with all [spiritual] knowledge and competent to admonish *and* counsel *and* instruct one another also.

15 Still on some points I have written to you the more boldly *and* unreservedly by way of reminder. [I have done so] because of the grace—the unmerited favor—bestowed on me by God

16 In making me a minister of Christ Jesus to the Gentiles. I act in the priestly service of the Gospel (the good news) of God, in order that the sacrificial offering of the Gentiles may be acceptable [to God], consecrated *and* made holy by the Holy Spirit.

17 In Christ Jesus, then, I have legitimate reason to glory (to exult) in my work for God—in what through Christ Jesus I have accomplished concerning the things of God.

18 For [of course] I will not venture (presume) to speak thus of any work except what Christ has actually done through me—as an instrument in His hands—to win obedience from the Gentiles, by word and deed,

19 [And as my preaching has been accompanied] with the power of signs and wonders, [and all of it] by the power of the Holy Spirit. So that starting from Jerusalem and as far round as Illyricum I have fully preached the Gospel—faithfully executing, accomplishing, carrying out to the full the good news—of Christ, the Messiah, in its entirety.

20 Thus my ambition has been to preach the Gospel, not where Christ's name has already been known, lest I build on another man's foundation;

21 But [instead I would act on the principle], as it is written, They shall see who have never been told of Him, and they shall understand who have never heard [of Him]. [Isa. 52:15.]

22 This [ambition] is the reason why I have so frequently been hindered from coming to visit you.

23 But now since I have no further opportunity for work in these regions, and since I have longed for [a]enough years to come to you,

24 I hope to see you in passing [through Rome] as I go [on my intended trip] to Spain, and to be aided on my journey there by you, after I have enjoyed your company for a little while.

25 For the present, however, I am going to Jerusalem to bring aid (relief) for the saints—God's people there.

26 For it has been the good pleasure of Macedonia and Achaia to make some contribution for the poor among the saints of Jerusalem.

27 They were pleased to do it, and surely they are in debt to them, for if these Gentiles have come to share in their [the Jerusalem Jews'] spiritual blessings, then they ought also to be of service to them in material blessings.

28 When therefore I have completed this mission, and have delivered to them [at Jerusalem] what has been raised, I shall go on by way of you to Spain.

29 And I know that when I do come to you I shall come in the abundant blessing *of the Gospel* of Christ.

30 I appeal to you—I entreat you—brethren, for the sake of our Lord Jesus Christ and by the love [given by] the Spirit, to unite with me in earnest wrestling in prayer to God in my behalf.

31 [Pray] that I may be delivered (rescued) from the unbelievers in Judea, and that my mission of relief to Jerusalem may be acceptable *and* graciously received by the saints—God's people there.

32 So that by God's will I may subsequently come to you with joy—with a happy heart—and be refreshed [by the interval of rest] in your company.

33 May [our] peace-giving God be with you all! Amen—so be it.

**16** NOW I introduce *and* commend to you our sister Phoebe, a deaconess of the church at Cenchreae,

AMP [a] Vincent.

## New American Standard

14¶ And concerning you, my brethren, I myself also am convinced that you yourselves are full of goodness, filled with all
knowledge, and able also to admonish one another.
15But I have written very boldly to you on some points, so as
to remind you again, because of the grace that was given me from
God,
16to be a minister of Christ Jesus to the Gentiles, ministering as
a priest the gospel of God, that *my* offering of the Gentiles might
become acceptable, sanctified by the Holy Spirit.
17Therefore in Christ Jesus I have found reason for boasting in
things pertaining to God.
18For I will not presume to speak of anything except what Christ
has accomplished through me, resulting in the obedience of the
Gentiles by word and deed,
19in the power of signs and wonders, in the power of the Spirit;
so that from Jerusalem and round about as far as Illyricum I have
fully preached the gospel of Christ.
20And thus I aspired to preach the gospel, not where Christ was
*already* named, that I might not build upon another man's foundation;
21but as it is written,

"THEY WHO HAD NO NEWS OF HIM SHALL SEE,
AND THEY WHO HAVE NOT HEARD SHALL UNDERSTAND."

22¶ For this reason I have often been hindered from coming to
you;
23but now, with no further place for me in these regions, and
since I have had for many years a longing to come to you
24whenever I go to Spain—for I hope to see you in passing, and
to be helped on my way there by you, when I have first enjoyed
your company for a while—
25but now, I am going to Jerusalem serving the saints.
26For Macedonia and Achaia have been pleased to make a contribution for the poor among the saints in Jerusalem.
27Yes, they were pleased *to do so*, and they are indebted to them.
For if the Gentiles have shared in their spiritual things, they are
indebted to minister to them also in material things.
28Therefore, when I have finished this, and have put my seal
on this fruit of theirs, I will go on by way of you to Spain.
29And I know that when I come to you, I will come in the fulness
of the blessing of Christ.
30¶ Now I urge you, brethren, by our Lord Jesus Christ and by
the love of the Spirit, to strive together with me in your prayers
to God for me,
31that I may be delivered from those who are disobedient in
Judea, and *that* my service for Jerusalem may prove acceptable to
the saints;
32so that I may come to you in joy by the will of God and find
*refreshing* rest in your company.
33Now the God of peace be with you all. Amen.

*Greetings and Love Expressed*

**16** I COMMEND to you our sister Phoebe, who is a servant
of the church which is at Cenchrea;

## New International

*Paul the Minister to the Gentiles*

14I myself am convinced, my brothers, that you yourselves are
full of goodness, complete in knowledge and competent to instruct
one another. 15I have written you quite boldly on some points, as
if to remind you of them again, because of the grace God gave me
16to be a minister of Christ Jesus to the Gentiles with the priestly
duty of proclaiming the gospel of God, so that the Gentiles might
become an offering acceptable to God, sanctified by the Holy
Spirit.
17Therefore I glory in Christ Jesus in my service to God. 18I will
not venture to speak of anything except what Christ has accomplished through me in leading the Gentiles to obey God by what
I have said and done— 19by the power of signs and miracles,
through the power of the Spirit. So from Jerusalem all the way
around to Illyricum, I have fully proclaimed the gospel of Christ.
20It has always been my ambition to preach the gospel where
Christ was not known, so that I would not be building on someone
else's foundation. 21Rather, as it is written:

"Those who were not told about him will see,
and those who have not heard will understand."[b]

22This is why I have often been hindered from coming to you.

*Paul's Plan to Visit Rome*

23But now that there is no more place for me to work in these
regions, and since I have been longing for many years to see you,
24I plan to do so when I go to Spain. I hope to visit you while
passing through and to have you assist me on my journey there,
after I have enjoyed your company for a while. 25Now, however,
I am on my way to Jerusalem in the service of the saints there. 26For
Macedonia and Achaia were pleased to make a contribution for the
poor among the saints in Jerusalem. 27They were pleased to do it,
and indeed they owe it to them. For if the Gentiles have shared
in the Jews' spiritual blessings, they owe it to the Jews to share
with them their material blessings. 28So after I have completed this
task and have made sure that they have received this fruit, I will
go to Spain and visit you on the way. 29I know that when I come
to you, I will come in the full measure of the blessing of Christ.
30I urge you, brothers, by our Lord Jesus Christ and by the love
of the Spirit, to join me in my struggle by praying to God for me.
31Pray that I may be rescued from the unbelievers in Judea and that
my service in Jerusalem may be acceptable to the saints there, 32so
that by God's will I may come to you with joy and together with
you be refreshed. 33The God of peace be with you all. Amen.

*Personal Greetings*

**16** I COMMEND to you our sister Phoebe, a servant[c] of the
church in Cenchrea. 2I ask you to receive her in the Lord

NIV [b] *21* Isaiah 52:15 [c] *1* Or *deaconess*

## King James

2 That ye receive her in the Lord, as becometh saints, and that ye assist her in whatsoever business she hath need of you: for she hath been a succourer of many, and of myself also.

3 Greet Priscilla and Aquila my helpers in Christ Jesus:

4 Who have for my life laid down their own necks: unto whom not only I give thanks, but also all the churches of the Gentiles.

5 Likewise *greet* the church that is in their house. Salute my wellbeloved Epaenetus, who is the firstfruits of Achaia unto Christ.

6 Greet Mary, who bestowed much labour on us.

7 Salute Andronicus and Junia, my kinsmen, and my fellowprisoners, who are of note among the apostles, who also were in Christ before me.

8 Greet Amplias my beloved in the Lord.

9 Salute Urbane, our helper in Christ, and Stachys my beloved.

10 Salute Apelles approved in Christ. Salute them which are of Aristobulus' *household.*

11 Salute Herodion my kinsman. Greet them that be of the *household* of Narcissus, which are in the Lord.

12 Salute Tryphena and Tryphosa, who labour in the Lord. Salute the beloved Persis, which laboured much in the Lord.

13 Salute Rufus chosen in the Lord, and his mother and mine.

14 Salute Asyncritus, Phlegon, Hermas, Patrobas, Hermes, and the brethren which are with them.

15 Salute Philologus, and Julia, Nereus, and his sister, and Olympas, and all the saints which are with them.

16 Salute one another with an holy kiss. The churches of Christ salute you.

17 Now I beseech you, brethren, mark them which cause divisions and offences contrary to the doctrine which ye have learned; and avoid them.

18 For they that are such serve not our Lord Jesus Christ, but their own belly; and by good words and fair speeches deceive the hearts of the simple.

19 For your obedience is come abroad unto all *men.* I am glad therefore on your behalf: but yet I would have you wise unto that which is good, and simple concerning evil.

20 And the God of peace shall bruise Satan under your feet shortly. The grace of our Lord Jesus Christ *be* with you. Amen.

21 Timotheus my workfellow, and Lucius, and Jason, and Sosipater, my kinsmen, salute you.

22 I Tertius, who wrote *this* epistle, salute you in the Lord.

23 Gaius mine host, and of the whole church, saluteth you. Erastus the chamberlain of the city saluteth you, and Quartus a brother.

24 The grace of our Lord Jesus Christ *be* with you all. Amen.

25 Now to him that is of power to stablish you according to my gospel, and the preaching of Jesus Christ, according to the revelation of the mystery, which was kept secret since the world began,

26 But now is made manifest, and by the scriptures of the prophets, according to the commandment of the everlasting God, made known to all nations for the obedience of faith:

27 To God only wise, *be* glory through Jesus Christ for ever. Amen.

## Amplified

2 That you may receive her in the Lord—with a Christian welcome—as saints (God's people) ought to receive one another. And help her in whatever matter she may require assistance from you, for she has been a helper of many including myself—shielding us from suffering.

3 Give my greetings to Prisca and Aquila, my fellow workers in Christ Jesus,

4 Who risked their lives—endangering their very necks—for my life. To them not only I but also all the churches among the Gentiles give thanks.

5 [Remember me] also to the church [that meets] in their house. Greet my beloved Epaenetus, who was a first fruit (convert) to Christ in Asia.

6 Greet Mary, who has worked so hard among you.

7 Remember me to Andronicus and Junias, my tribal kinsmen and once my fellow prisoners. They are men held in high esteem among the apostles, who also were in Christ before I was.

8 Remember me to Ampliatus, my beloved in the Lord.

9 Salute Urbanus, our fellow worker in Christ, and my dear Stachys.

10 Greet Apelles, that one tried *and* approved in Christ, the Messiah. Remember me to those who belong to the household of Aristobulus.

11 Greet my tribal kinsman Herodion, and those in the Lord who belong to the household of Narcissus.

12 Salute those workers in the Lord, Tryphaena and Tryphosa. Greet my dear Persis, who has worked so hard in the Lord.

13 Remember me to Rufus, eminent in the Lord, also to his mother [who has been] a mother to me also.

14 Greet Asyncritus, Phlegon, Hermes, Patrobas, Hermas, and the brethren who are with them.

15 Greet Philologus, Julia, Nereus and his sister, and Olympas, and all the saints who are with them.

16 Greet one another with a holy (consecrated) kiss. All the churches of Christ, the Messiah, wish to be remembered to you.

17 I appeal to you, brethren, to be on your guard concerning those who create dissensions and difficulties *and* cause divisions, in opposition to the doctrine—the teaching—which you have been taught. [I warn you to turn aside from them, to] avoid them.

18 For such persons do not serve our Lord Christ but their own appetites *and* base desires, and by ingratiating and flattering speech they beguile the hearts of the unsuspecting *and* simple-minded [people].

19 For while your loyalty *and* obedience is known to all, so that I rejoice over you, I would have you well-versed *and* wise as to what is good, and innocent *and* guileless as to what is evil.

20 And the God of peace will soon crush Satan under your feet. The grace of our Lord Jesus Christ, the Messiah, be with you.

21 Timothy, my fellow worker, wishes to be remembered to you, as do Lucius and Jason and Sosipater, my tribal kinsmen.

22 I Tertius, the writer of this letter, greet you in the Lord.

23 Gaius, who is host to me and to the whole church here, greets you. So do Erastus, the city treasurer, and our brother Quartus.

24 *The grace of our Lord Jesus Christ, the Messiah, be with you all. Amen—so be it.*

25 Now to Him Who is able to strengthen you in the faith which is in accordance with my Gospel and the preaching of (concerning) Jesus Christ, the Messiah, according to the revelation—the unveiling—of the mystery of the plan of redemption which was kept in silence *and* secret for long ages,

26 But is now disclosed and through the prophetic Scriptures is made known to all nations, according to the command of the eternal God, [to win them] to obedience to the faith,

27 To [the] only wise God be glory for evermore through Jesus Christ, the Anointed One! Amen—so be it.

## New American Standard

2that you receive her in the Lord in a manner worthy of the saints, and that you help her in whatever matter she may have need of you; for she herself has also been a helper of many, and of myself as well.
3¶ Greet Prisca and Aquila, my fellow workers in Christ Jesus,
4who for my life risked their own necks, to whom not only do I give thanks, but also all the churches of the Gentiles;
5also *greet* the church that is in their house. Greet Epaenetus, my beloved, who is the first convert to Christ from Asia.
6Greet Mary, who has worked hard for you.
7Greet Andronicus and Junias, my kinsmen, and my fellow prisoners, who are outstanding among the apostles, who also were in Christ before me.
8Greet Ampliatus, my beloved in the Lord.
9Greet Urbanus, our fellow worker in Christ, and Stachys my beloved.
10Greet Apelles, the approved in Christ. Greet those who are of the *household* of Aristobulus.
11Greet Herodion, my kinsman. Greet those of the *household* of Narcissus, who are in the Lord.
12Greet Tryphaena and Tryphosa, workers in the Lord. Greet Persis the beloved, who has worked hard in the Lord.
13Greet Rufus, a choice man in the Lord, also his mother and mine.
14Greet Asyncritus, Phlegon, Hermes, Patrobas, Hermas and the brethren with them.
15Greet Philologus and Julia, Nereus and his sister, and Olympas, and all the saints who are with them.
16Greet one another with a holy kiss. All the churches of Christ greet you.
17¶ Now I urge you, brethren, keep your eye on those who cause dissensions and hindrances contrary to the teaching which you learned, and turn away from them.
18For such men are slaves, not of our Lord Christ but of their own appetites; and by their smooth and flattering speech they deceive the hearts of the unsuspecting.
19For the report of your obedience has reached to all; therefore I am rejoicing over you, but I want you to be wise in what is good, and innocent in what is evil.
20And the God of peace will soon crush Satan under your feet.
¶ The grace of our Lord Jesus be with you.
21¶ Timothy my fellow worker greets you, and *so do* Lucius and Jason and Sosipater, my kinsmen.
22I, Tertius, who write this letter, greet you in the Lord.
23Gaius, host to me and to the whole church, greets you. Erastus, the city treasurer greets you, and Quartus, the brother.
24[ [a]The grace of our Lord Jesus Christ be with you all. Amen.]
25¶ Now to Him who is able to establish you according to my gospel and the preaching of Jesus Christ, according to the revelation of the mystery which has been kept secret for long ages past,
26but now is manifested, and by the Scriptures of the prophets, according to the commandment of the eternal God, has been made known to all the nations, *leading* to obedience of faith;
27to the only wise God, through Jesus Christ, be the glory forever. Amen.

NAS [a] Many mss. do not contain this verse

## New International

in a way worthy of the saints and to give her any help she may need from you, for she has been a great help to many people, including me.

3Greet Priscilla[b] and Aquila, my fellow workers in Christ Jesus.
4They risked their lives for me. Not only I but all the churches of the Gentiles are grateful to them.
5Greet also the church that meets at their house.
Greet my dear friend Epenetus, who was the first convert to Christ in the province of Asia.
6Greet Mary, who worked very hard for you.
7Greet Andronicus and Junias, my relatives who have been in prison with me. They are outstanding among the apostles, and they were in Christ before I was.
8Greet Ampliatus, whom I love in the Lord.
9Greet Urbanus, our fellow worker in Christ, and my dear friend Stachys.
10Greet Apelles, tested and approved in Christ.
Greet those who belong to the household of Aristobulus.
11Greet Herodion, my relative.
Greet those in the household of Narcissus who are in the Lord.
12Greet Tryphena and Tryphosa, those women who work hard in the Lord.
Greet my dear friend Persis, another woman who has worked very hard in the Lord.
13Greet Rufus, chosen in the Lord, and his mother, who has been a mother to me, too.
14Greet Asyncritus, Phlegon, Hermes, Patrobas, Hermas and the brothers with them.
15Greet Philologus, Julia, Nereus and his sister, and Olympas and all the saints with them.
16Greet one another with a holy kiss.
All the churches of Christ send greetings.

17I urge you, brothers, to watch out for those who cause divisions and put obstacles in your way that are contrary to the teaching you have learned. Keep away from them. 18For such people are not serving our Lord Christ, but their own appetites. By smooth talk and flattery they deceive the minds of naive people. 19Everyone has heard about your obedience, so I am full of joy over you; but I want you to be wise about what is good, and innocent about what is evil.
20The God of peace will soon crush Satan under your feet.
The grace of our Lord Jesus be with you.
21Timothy, my fellow worker, sends his greetings to you, as do Lucius, Jason and Sosipater, my relatives.
22I, Tertius, who wrote down this letter, greet you in the Lord.
23Gaius, whose hospitality I and the whole church here enjoy, sends you his greetings.
Erastus, who is the city's director of public works, and our brother Quartus send you their greetings.[c]
25Now to him who is able to establish you by my gospel and the proclamation of Jesus Christ, according to the revelation of the mystery hidden for long ages past, 26but now revealed and made known through the prophetic writings by the command of the eternal God, so that all nations might believe and obey him— 27to the only wise God be glory forever through Jesus Christ! Amen.

NIV [b] 3 Greek *Prisca,* a variant of *Priscilla* [c] 23 Some manuscripts *their greetings. 24May the grace of our Lord Jesus Christ be with all of you. Amen.*

## King James

THE FIRST EPISTLE OF

PAUL THE APOSTLE TO THE

# Corinthians

**1** PAUL, CALLED *to be* an apostle of Jesus Christ through the will of God, and Sosthenes *our* brother,

2 Unto the church of God which is at Corinth, to them that are sanctified in Christ Jesus, called *to be* saints, with all that in every place call upon the name of Jesus Christ our Lord, both theirs and ours:

3 Grace *be* unto you, and peace, from God our Father, and *from* the Lord Jesus Christ.

4 I thank my God always on your behalf, for the grace of God which is given you by Jesus Christ;

5 That in every thing ye are enriched by him, in all utterance, and *in* all knowledge;

6 Even as the testimony of Christ was confirmed in you:

7 So that ye come behind in no gift; waiting for the coming of our Lord Jesus Christ:

8 Who shall also confirm you unto the end, *that ye may be* blameless in the day of our Lord Jesus Christ.

9 God *is* faithful, by whom ye were called unto the fellowship of his Son Jesus Christ our Lord.

10 Now I beseech you, brethren, by the name of our Lord Jesus Christ, that ye all speak the same thing, and *that* there be no divisions among you; but *that* ye be perfectly joined together in the same mind and in the same judgment.

11 For it hath been declared unto me of you, my brethren, by them *which are of the house* of Chloe, that there are contentions among you.

12 Now this I say, that every one of you saith, I am of Paul; and I of Apollos; and I of Cephas; and I of Christ.

13 Is Christ divided? was Paul crucified for you? or were ye baptized in the name of Paul?

14 I thank God that I baptized none of you, but Crispus and Gaius;

15 Lest any should say that I had baptized in mine own name.

16 And I baptized also the household of Stephanas: besides, I know not whether I baptized any other.

## Amplified

THE FIRST LETTER OF

PAUL TO THE

# Corinthians

**1** PAUL, SUMMONED by the will *and* purpose of God to be an apostle (special messenger) of Christ Jesus, and our brother Sosthenes,

2 To the church (assembly) of God which is in Corinth, to those consecrated *and* purified *and* made holy in Christ Jesus, [who are] selected *and* called to be saints (God's people) together with all those who in any place call upon *and* give honor to the name of our Lord Jesus Christ, both their Lord and ours:

3 Grace (favor and spiritual blessing) be to you and (heart) peace from God our Father and the Lord Jesus Christ.

4 I thank my God at all times for you because of the grace (the favor and spiritual blessing) of God which was bestowed on you in Christ Jesus.

5 [So] that in Him in every respect you were enriched, in full power *and* readiness of speech (to speak of your faith), and complete knowledge *and* illumination (to give you full insight into its meaning).

6 In this way [our] witnessing concerning Christ, the Messiah, was so confirmed *and* established *and* made sure in you

7 That you are not (consciously) falling behind *or* lacking in any special spiritual endowment *or* Christian grace ( [a]the reception of which is due to the power of divine grace operating in your souls by the Holy Spirit), while you wait *and* watch (constantly living in hope) for the coming of our Lord Jesus Christ *and* [His] being made visible to all.

8 And He will establish you to the end—keep you steadfast, give you strength, and guarantee your vindication, that is, be your warrant against all accusation or indictment—[so that you will be] guiltless *and* irreproachable in the day of our Lord Jesus Christ, the Messiah.

9 God is faithful—reliable, trustworthy and [therefore] ever true to His promise, and He can be depended on; by Him you were called into companionship *and* participation with His Son, Jesus Christ our Lord.

10 But I urge *and* entreat you, brethren, by the name of our Lord Jesus Christ, that all of you be in perfect harmony, *and* full agreement in what you say, and that there be no dissensions *or* factions *or* divisions among you; but that you be perfectly united in your common understanding and in your opinions *and* judgments.

11 For it has been made clear to me, my brethren, by those of Chloe's household that there are contentions *and* wrangling *and* factions among you.

12 What I mean is this, that each one of you [either] says, I belong to Paul, or I belong to Apollos, or I belong to Cephas (Peter), or I belong to Christ.

13 Is Christ, the Messiah, divided into parts? Was Paul crucified on behalf of you? Or were you baptized into the name of Paul?

14 I thank God that I did not baptize any of you except Crispus and Gaius,

15 Lest any one should say that I baptized in my own name.

16 [Yes] I did baptize the household of Stephanas, also. More than these, I do not remember that I baptized any one.

AMP [a] Thayer's "Greek-English Lexicon of the New Testament—Grimm."

## New American Standard

# 1 Corinthians

*Appeal to Unity*

1 PAUL, CALLED *as* an apostle of Jesus Christ by the will of
God, and Sosthenes our brother,
2to the church of God which is at Corinth, to those who have
been sanctified in Christ Jesus, saints by calling, with all who in
every place call upon the name of our Lord Jesus Christ, their *Lord*
and ours:
3Grace to you and peace from God our Father and the Lord
Jesus Christ.
4¶ I thank [b]my God always concerning you, for the grace of
God which was given you in Christ Jesus,
5that in everything you were enriched in Him, in all speech
and all knowledge,
6even as the testimony concerning Christ was confirmed in
you,
7so that you are not lacking in any gift, awaiting eagerly the
revelation of our Lord Jesus Christ,
8who shall also confirm you to the end, blameless in the day
of our Lord Jesus Christ.
9God is faithful, through whom you were called into fellowship with His Son, Jesus Christ our Lord.
10¶ Now I exhort you, brethren, by the name of our Lord Jesus
Christ, that you all agree, and there be no divisions among you,
but you be made complete in the same mind and in the same
judgment.
11For I have been informed concerning you, my brethren, by
Chloe's *people,* that there are quarrels among you.
12Now I mean this, that each one of you is saying, "I am of
Paul," and "I of Apollos," and "I of Cephas," and "I of Christ."
13Has Christ been divided? Paul was not crucified for you, was
he? Or were you baptized in the name of Paul?
14 [c]I thank God that I baptized none of you except Crispus and
Gaius,
15that no man should say you were baptized in my name.
16Now I did baptize also the household of Stephanas; beyond
that, I do not know whether I baptized any other.

NAS [b] Some ancient mss. do not contain *my* [c] Some ancient mss. read *I give thanks that*

## New International

# 1 Corinthians

1 PAUL, CALLED to be an apostle of Christ Jesus by the will
of God, and our brother Sosthenes,
2To the church of God in Corinth, to those sanctified in Christ
Jesus and called to be holy, together with all those everywhere
who call on the name of our Lord Jesus Christ—their Lord and
ours:
3Grace and peace to you from God our Father and the Lord
Jesus Christ.

*Thanksgiving*

4I always thank God for you because of his grace given you in
Christ Jesus. 5For in him you have been enriched in every way—in
all your speaking and in all your knowledge— 6because our testimony about Christ was confirmed in you. 7Therefore you do not
lack any spiritual gift as you eagerly wait for our Lord Jesus Christ
to be revealed. 8He will keep you strong to the end, so that you
will be blameless on the day of our Lord Jesus Christ. 9God, who
has called you into fellowship with his Son Jesus Christ our Lord,
is faithful.

*Divisions in the Church*

10I appeal to you, brothers, in the name of our Lord Jesus
Christ, that all of you agree with one another so that there may be
no divisions among you and that you may be perfectly united in
mind and thought. 11My brothers, some from Chloe's household
have informed me that there are quarrels among you. 12What I
mean is this: One of you says, "I follow Paul"; another, "I follow
Apollos"; another, "I follow Cephas[d]"; still another, "I follow
Christ."
13Is Christ divided? Was Paul crucified for you? Were you baptized into[e] the name of Paul? 14I am thankful that I did not baptize
any of you except Crispus and Gaius, 15so no one can say that you
were baptized into my name. 16(Yes, I also baptized the household
of Stephanas; beyond that, I don't remember if I baptized anyone
else.) 17For Christ did not send me to baptize, but to preach the

NIV [d] *12* That is, Peter [e] *13* Or *in;* also in verse 15

## King James

17 For Christ sent me not to baptize, but to preach the gospel: not with wisdom of words, lest the cross of Christ should be made of none effect.

18 For the preaching of the cross is to them that perish foolishness; but unto us which are saved it is the power of God.

19 For it is written, I will destroy the wisdom of the wise, and will bring to nothing the understanding of the prudent.

20 Where *is* the wise? where *is* the scribe? where *is* the disputer of this world? hath not God made foolish the wisdom of this world?

21 For after that in the wisdom of God the world by wisdom knew not God, it pleased God by the foolishness of preaching to save them that believe.

22 For the Jews require a sign, and the Greeks seek after wisdom:

23 But we preach Christ crucified, unto the Jews a stumblingblock, and unto the Greeks foolishness;

24 But unto them which are called, both Jews and Greeks, Christ the power of God, and the wisdom of God.

25 Because the foolishness of God is wiser than men; and the weakness of God is stronger than men.

26 For ye see your calling, brethren, how that not many wise men after the flesh, not many mighty, not many noble, *are called:*

27 But God hath chosen the foolish things of the world to confound the wise; and God hath chosen the weak things of the world to confound the things which are mighty;

28 And base things of the world, and things which are despised, hath God chosen, *yea,* and things which are not, to bring to nought things that are:

29 That no flesh should glory in his presence.

30 But of him are ye in Christ Jesus, who of God is made unto us wisdom, and righteousness, and sanctification, and redemption:

31 That, according as it is written, He that glorieth, let him glory in the Lord.

**2** AND I, brethren, when I came to you, came not with excellency of speech or of wisdom, declaring unto you the testimony of God.

## Amplified

17 For Christ, the Messiah, sent me out not to baptize but (to evangelize by) preaching the glad tidings (the Gospel); and that not with verbal eloquence, lest the cross of Christ should be deprived of force *and* emptied of its power *and* rendered vain—fruitless, void of value and of no effect.

18 For the story *and* message of the cross is sheer absurdity *and* folly to those who are perishing *and* on their way to perdition, but to us who are being saved it is the [manifestation of] the power of God.

19 For it is written, I will baffle *and* render useless *and* destroy the learning of the learned *and* the philosophy of the philosophers and the cleverness of the clever *and* the discernment of the discerning, I will frustrate *and* nullify [them] *and* bring [them] to nothing. [Isa. 29:14.]

20 Where is the wise man—the philosopher? Where is the scribe—the scholar? Where is the investigator—the logician, the debater—of this present time *and* age? Has not God shown up the nonsense *and* the folly of this world's wisdom?

21 For when the world with all its earthly wisdom failed to perceive *and* recognize *and* know God by means of its own philosophy, God in His wisdom was pleased through the foolishness of preaching [of salvation, procured by Christ and to be had through Him], to save those who believed—who clung to and trusted in and relied on Him.

22 For while Jews (demandingly) ask for signs *and* miracles, and Greeks pursue philosophy *and wisdom,*

23 We preach Christ, the Messiah, crucified, which to the Jews is a scandal *and* an offensive stumbling block (that springs a snare-trap), and to the Gentiles it is absurd *and* utterly unphilosophical nonsense.

24 But to those who are called, whether Jew or Greek (Gentile), Christ [is] the power of God and the wisdom of God.

25 [This is] because the foolish thing [that has its source in] God is wiser than men, and the weak thing [that springs from] God is stronger than men.

26 For [simply] consider your own call, brethren; not many [of you were considered to be] wise, according to human estimates *and* standards; not many influential *and* powerful; not many of high *and* noble birth.

27 [No,] for God selected—deliberately chose—what in the world is foolish to put the wise to shame, and what the world calls weak to put the strong to shame.

28 And God also selected—deliberately chose—[what] in the world [is] lowborn *and* insignificant, and branded *and* treated with contempt, even the things that are nothing, that He might depose *and* bring to nothing the things that are;

29 So that no mortal man should (have pretense for glorying and) boast in the presence of God.

30 But it is from Him that you have your life in Christ Jesus, Whom God made our Wisdom from God, [that is, revealed to us a knowledge of the divine plan of salvation previously hidden, manifesting itself as] our Righteousness *and thus* making us upright and putting us in right standing with God; and our Consecration—making us pure and holy; and our Redemption—providing our ransom from eternal penalty for sin.

31 So then, as it is written, Let him who boasts *and* proudly rejoices *and* glories, boast *and* proudly rejoice *and* glory in the Lord. [Jer. 9:24.]

**2** AS FOR myself, brethren, when I came to you [I] did not come proclaiming to you the testimony *and* evidence *or* [a]mystery *or* secret of God [concerning what He has done through Christ for the salvation of men] in lofty words of eloquence or human philosophy *and* wisdom;

AMP [a] Many ancient authorities so read.

## New American Standard

17For Christ did not send me to baptize, but to preach the
gospel, not in cleverness of speech, that the cross of Christ should
not be made void.

*The Wisdom of God*

18¶ For the word of the cross is to those who are perishing
foolishness, but to us who are being saved it is the power of God.
19For it is written,
"I WILL DESTROY THE WISDOM OF THE WISE,
AND THE CLEVERNESS OF THE CLEVER I WILL SET ASIDE."
20Where is the wise man? Where is the scribe? Where is the
debater of this age? Has not God made foolish the wisdom of the
world?
21For since in the wisdom of God the world through its wisdom
did not *come to* know God, God was well-pleased through the
foolishness of the message preached to save those who believe.
22For indeed Jews ask for signs, and Greeks search for wisdom;
23but we preach [b]Christ crucified, to Jews a stumbling block,
and to Gentiles foolishness,
24but to those who are the called, both Jews and Greeks, Christ
the power of God and the wisdom of God.
25Because the foolishness of God is wiser than men, and the
weakness of God is stronger than men.
26¶ For consider your calling, brethren, that there were not
many wise according to the flesh, not many mighty, not many
noble;
27but God has chosen the foolish things of the world to shame
the wise, and God has chosen the weak things of the world to
shame the things which are strong,
28and the base things of the world and the despised, God has
chosen, the things that are not, that He might nullify the things
that are,
29that no man should boast before God.
30But by His doing you are in Christ Jesus, who became to us
wisdom from God, and righteousness and sanctification, and redemption,
31that, just as it is written, "LET HIM WHO BOASTS, BOAST IN THE
LORD."

*Paul's Reliance upon the Spirit*

**2** AND WHEN I came to you, brethren, I did not come with
superiority of speech or of wisdom, proclaiming to you the
[c]testimony of God.

NAS [b] I.e., Messiah [c] Some ancient mss. read *mystery*

## New International

gospel—not with words of human wisdom, lest the cross of Christ
be emptied of its power.

*Christ the Wisdom and Power of God*

18For the message of the cross is foolishness to those who are
perishing, but to us who are being saved it is the power of God.
19For it is written:

"I will destroy the wisdom of the wise;
the intelligence of the intelligent I will frustrate."[d]

20Where is the wise man? Where is the scholar? Where is the
philosopher of this age? Has not God made foolish the wisdom of
the world? 21For since in the wisdom of God the world through its
wisdom did not know him, God was pleased through the foolishness of what was preached to save those who believe. 22Jews
demand miraculous signs and Greeks look for wisdom, 23but we
preach Christ crucified: a stumbling block to Jews and foolishness
to Gentiles, 24but to those whom God has called, both Jews and
Greeks, Christ the power of God and the wisdom of God. 25For the
foolishness of God is wiser than man's wisdom, and the weakness
of God is stronger than man's strength.
26Brothers, think of what you were when you were called. Not
many of you were wise by human standards; not many were
influential; not many were of noble birth. 27But God chose the
foolish things of the world to shame the wise; God chose the weak
things of the world to shame the strong. 28He chose the lowly
things of this world and the despised things—and the things that
are not—to nullify the things that are, 29so that no one may boast
before him. 30It is because of him that you are in Christ Jesus, who
has become for us wisdom from God—that is, our righteousness,
holiness and redemption. 31Therefore, as it is written: "Let him
who boasts boast in the Lord."[e]

**2** WHEN I came to you, brothers, I did not come with eloquence or superior wisdom as I proclaimed to you the testimony about God.[f] 2For I resolved to know nothing while I was

NIV [d] 19 Isaiah 29:14 [e] 31 Jer. 9:24 [f] 1 Some manuscripts *as I proclaimed to you God's mystery*

## King James

2For I determined not to know any thing among you, save Jesus Christ, and him crucified.
3And I was with you in weakness, and in fear, and in much trembling.
4And my speech and my preaching *was* not with enticing words of man's wisdom, but in demonstration of the Spirit and of power:
5That your faith should not stand in the wisdom of men, but in the power of God.
6Howbeit we speak wisdom among them that are perfect: yet not the wisdom of this world, nor of the princes of this world, that come to nought:
7But we speak the wisdom of God in a mystery, *even* the hidden *wisdom*, which God ordained before the world unto our glory:
8Which none of the princes of this world knew: for had they known *it*, they would not have crucified the Lord of glory.
9But as it is written, Eye hath not seen, nor ear heard, neither have entered into the heart of man, the things which God hath prepared for them that love him.
10But God hath revealed *them* unto us by his Spirit: for the Spirit searcheth all things, yea, the deep things of God.
11For what man knoweth the things of a man, save the spirit of man which is in him? even so the things of God knoweth no man, but the Spirit of God.
12Now we have received, not the spirit of the world, but the spirit which is of God; that we might know the things that are freely given to us of God.
13Which things also we speak, not in the words which man's wisdom teacheth, but which the Holy Ghost teacheth; comparing spiritual things with spiritual.
14But the natural man receiveth not the things of the Spirit of God: for they are foolishness unto him: neither can he know *them*, because they are spiritually discerned.
15But he that is spiritual judgeth all things, yet he himself is judged of no man.
16For who hath known the mind of the Lord, that he may instruct him? But we have the mind of Christ.

## Amplified

2For I resolved to know nothing—to be acquainted with [nothing], to make a display of the knowledge of [nothing], and to be conscious of [nothing]—among you except Jesus Christ, the Messiah, and Him crucified.
3And I ([a]passed into a state of) weakness and was in fear (dread) and great trembling [[b]after I had come] among you.
4And my language and my message were not set forth in persuasive (enticing and plausible) words of wisdom, but they were in demonstration of the (Holy) Spirit and power [that is, [c]a proof by the Spirit and power of God, operating on me and stirring in the minds of my hearers the most holy emotions and thus persuading them],
5So that your faith might not rest in the wisdom of men (human philosophy), but in the power of God.
6Yet when we are among the full-grown—spiritually mature Christians who are ripe in understanding—we do impart a (higher) wisdom [that is, the knowledge of the divine plan previously hidden]; but it is indeed not a wisdom of this present age nor of this world *or* of the leaders *and* rulers of this age, who are being brought to nothing *and* are doomed to pass away.
7But rather what we are setting forth is a wisdom of God once hidden [from the human understanding] and now revealed to us by God; [that wisdom] which God devised *and* decreed before the ages for our glorification [that is, to lift us into the glory of His presence].
8None of the rulers of this age *or* world perceived *and* recognized *and* understood this; for if they had, they would never have crucified the Lord of glory.
9But, on the contrary, as the Scripture says, What eye has not seen, and ear has not heard, and has not entered into the heart of man, [all that,] God has prepared—made and keeps ready—for those who love Him [[d]that is, for those who hold Him in affectionate reverence, promptly obeying Him and gratefully recognizing the benefits He has bestowed]. [Isa. 64:4; 65:17.]
10Yet to us God has unveiled *and* revealed them by *and* through His Spirit, for the (Holy) Spirit searches diligently, exploring *and* examining everything, even sounding the profound and bottomless things of God—the [e]divine counsels and things hidden and beyond man's scrutiny.
11For what person perceives (knows and understands) what passes through a man's thoughts except the man's own spirit within him? Just so no one discerns (comes to know and comprehend) the thoughts of God except the Spirit of God.
12Now we have not received the spirit (that belongs to) the world, but the (Holy) Spirit Who is from God, [given to us] that we might realize *and* comprehend *and* appreciate the gifts (of divine favor and blessing so freely and lavishly) bestowed on us by God.
13And we are setting these truths forth in words not taught by human wisdom but taught by the (Holy) Spirit, combining *and* interpreting spiritual truths with spiritual language [to those who possess the (Holy) Spirit].
14But the natural, nonspiritual man does not accept *or* welcome *or* admit into his heart the gifts *and* teachings *and* revelations of the Spirit of God, for they are folly (meaningless nonsense) to him; and he is incapable of knowing them—of progressively recognizing, understanding and becoming better acquainted with them—because they are spiritually discerned *and* estimated *and* appreciated.
15But the spiritual man tries all things—[that is,] he [f]examines, investigates, inquires into, questions, and discerns all things; yet is himself to be put on trial and judged by no one.—He can read the meaning of everything, but no one can properly discern *or* appraise *or* get an insight into him.
16For who has known *or* understood the mind (the counsels and purposes) of the Lord so as to guide *and* instruct [Him] *and* give Him knowledge? But we have the mind of Christ, the Messiah, *and* do hold the thoughts (feelings and purposes) of His heart. [Isa. 40:13.]

AMP [a] Vincent. [b] Vincent. [c] Thayer's "Greek-English Lexicon of the New Testament—Grimm." [d] Thayer. [e] Thayer. [f] Lightfoot.

## New American Standard

2For I determined to know nothing among you except Jesus
Christ, and Him crucified.
3And I was with you in weakness and in fear and in much
trembling.
4And my message and my preaching were not in persuasive
words of wisdom, but in demonstration of the Spirit and of power,
5that your faith should not rest on the wisdom of men, but on
the power of God.
6¶ Yet we do speak wisdom among those who are mature; a
wisdom, however, not of this age, nor of the rulers of this age, who
are passing away;
7but we speak God's wisdom in a mystery, the hidden *wisdom*,
which God predestined before the ages to our glory;
8 *the wisdom* which none of the rulers of this age has understood; for if they had understood it, they would not have crucified
the Lord of glory;
9but just as it is written,

"THINGS WHICH EYE HAS NOT SEEN AND EAR HAS NOT
HEARD,
AND *which* HAVE NOT ENTERED THE HEART OF MAN,
ALL THAT GOD HAS PREPARED FOR THOSE WHO LOVE
HIM."

10 [g]For to us God revealed *them* through the Spirit; for the Spirit
searches all things, even the depths of God.
11For who among men knows the *thoughts* of a man except the
spirit of the man, which is in him? Even so the *thoughts* of God no
one knows except the Spirit of God.
12Now we have received, not the spirit of the world, but the
Spirit who is from God, that we might know the things freely given
to us by God,
13which things we also speak, not in words taught by human
wisdom, but in those taught by the Spirit, combining spiritual
*thoughts* with spiritual *words*.
14But a natural man does not accept the things of the Spirit of
God; for they are foolishness to him, and he cannot understand
them, because they are spiritually appraised.
15But he who is spiritual appraises all things, yet he himself is
appraised by no man.
16FOR WHO HAS KNOWN THE MIND OF THE LORD, THAT HE SHOULD
INSTRUCT HIM? But we have the mind of Christ.

NAS [g] Some ancient mss. use *But*

## New International

with you except Jesus Christ and him crucified. 3I came to you in
weakness and fear, and with much trembling. 4My message and
my preaching were not with wise and persuasive words, but with
a demonstration of the Spirit's power, 5so that your faith might not
rest on men's wisdom, but on God's power.

*Wisdom From the Spirit*

6We do, however, speak a message of wisdom among the mature, but not the wisdom of this age or of the rulers of this age, who
are coming to nothing. 7No, we speak of God's secret wisdom, a
wisdom that has been hidden and that God destined for our glory
before time began. 8None of the rulers of this age understood it,
for if they had, they would not have crucified the Lord of glory.
9However, as it is written:

"No eye has seen,
no ear has heard,
no mind has conceived
what God has prepared for those who love him"[h]—

10but God has revealed it to us by his Spirit.
The Spirit searches all things, even the deep things of God.
11For who among men knows the thoughts of a man except the
man's spirit within him? In the same way no one knows the
thoughts of God except the Spirit of God. 12We have not received
the spirit of the world but the Spirit who is from God, that we may
understand what God has freely given us. 13This is what we speak,
not in words taught us by human wisdom but in words taught by
the Spirit, expressing spiritual truths in spiritual words.[i] 14The
man without the Spirit does not accept the things that come from
the Spirit of God, for they are foolishness to him, and he cannot
understand them, because they are spiritually discerned. 15The
spiritual man makes judgments about all things, but he himself is
not subject to any man's judgment:

16"For who has known the mind of the Lord
that he may instruct him?"[j]

But we have the mind of Christ.

NIV [h] 9 Isaiah 64:4 [i] 13 Or *Spirit, interpreting spiritual truths to spiritual men*
[j] 16 Isaiah 40:13

## King James

# 3

AND I, brethren, could not speak unto you as unto spiritual,
but as unto carnal, *even* as unto babes in Christ.
2 I have fed you with milk, and not with meat: for hitherto ye
were not able *to bear it,* neither yet now are ye able.
3 For ye are yet carnal: for whereas *there is* among you envying,
and strife, and divisions, are ye not carnal, and walk as men?
4 For while one saith, I am of Paul; and another, I *am* of Apollos;
are ye not carnal?
5 Who then is Paul, and who *is* Apollos, but ministers by whom
ye believed, even as the Lord gave to every man?
6 I have planted, Apollos watered; but God gave the increase.
7 So then neither is he that planteth any thing, neither he that
watereth; but God that giveth the increase.
8 Now he that planteth and he that watereth are one: and every
man shall receive his own reward according to his own labour.
9 For we are labourers together with God: ye are God's husbandry, *ye are* God's building.
10 According to the grace of God which is given unto me, as a
wise masterbuilder, I have laid the foundation, and another
buildeth thereon. But let every man take heed how he buildeth
thereupon.
11 For other foundation can no man lay than that is laid, which
is Jesus Christ.
12 Now if any man build upon this foundation gold, silver,
precious stones, wood, hay, stubble;
13 Every man's work shall be made manifest: for the day shall
declare it, because it shall be revealed by fire; and the fire shall try
every man's work of what sort it is.
14 If any man's work abide which he hath built thereupon, he
shall receive a reward.
15 If any man's work shall be burned, he shall suffer loss: but he
himself shall be saved; yet so as by fire.
16 Know ye not that ye are the temple of God, and *that* the Spirit
of God dwelleth in you?
17 If any man defile the temple of God, him shall God destroy;
for the temple of God is holy, which *temple* ye are.
18 Let no man deceive himself. If any man among you seemeth
to be wise in this world, let him become a fool, that he may be wise.
19 For the wisdom of this world is foolishness with God. For it
is written, He taketh the wise in their own craftiness.
20 And again, The Lord knoweth the thoughts of the wise, that
they are vain.

## Amplified

# 3

HOWEVER BRETHREN, I could not talk to you as to spiritual
[men], but as to nonspiritual (men of the flesh, in whom the
carnal nature predominates), as to mere infants [in the new life]
in Christ—[a]unable to talk yet!
2 I fed you with milk, not solid food, for you were not yet strong
enough [to be ready for it]; but even yet you are not strong enough
[to be ready for it],
3 For you are still (unspiritual, having the nature) of the flesh—
under the control of ordinary impulses. For as long as [there are]
envying and jealousy *and* wrangling and factions among you, are
you not unspiritual *and* of the flesh, behaving yourselves after a
human standard *and* like mere (unchanged) men?
4 For when one says, I belong to Paul, and another, I belong to
Apollos, are you not [proving yourselves] ordinary (unchanged)
men?
5 What then is Apollos? What is Paul? Ministering servants [not
heads of parties], through whom you believed, even as the Lord
appointed to each his task:
6 I planted, Apollos watered, but God [all the while] was making
it grow, *and* [He] gave the increase.
7 So neither he who plants is anything nor he who waters, but
[only] God Who makes it grow *and* become greater.
8 He who plants and he who waters are equal—one in aim, of
the same importance and esteem—yet each shall receive his own
reward (wages), according to his own labor.
9 For we are fellow workmen—joint promoters, laborers together—with *and* for God; *you* are God's [b]garden *and* vineyard *and* field
under cultivation; [you are] God's building. [Isa. 61:3.]
10 According to the grace—the special endowment for my task—
of God bestowed on me, like a skillful architect *and* master builder
I laid [the] foundation, and now another [man] is building upon
it. But let each [man] be careful how he builds upon it,
11 For no other foundation can any one lay than that which is
[already] laid, which is Jesus Christ, the Messiah, the Anointed
One.
12 But if any one builds upon the Foundation, whether it be with
gold, silver, precious stones, wood, hay, straw,
13 The work of each [one] will become (plainly, openly)
known—shown for what it is; for the day (of Christ) will disclose
*and* declare it, because it will be revealed with fire, and the fire will
test *and* critically appraise the character *and* worth of the work each
person has done.
14 If the work which any person has built on this Foundation—
any product of his efforts whatever—survives (this test), he will
get his reward.
15 But if any person's work is burned up [under the test], he will
suffer the loss (of it all, losing his reward), though he himself will
be saved, but only as [one who has passed] through fire. [Job
23:10.]
16 Do you not discern *and* understand that you [the whole
church at Corinth] are God's temple (His sanctuary), and that
God's Spirit has His permanent dwelling in you—to be at home in
you [ [c]collectively as a church and also individually]?
17 If any one [d]does hurt to God's temple *or* corrupts [ [e]it with
false doctrines] *or* destroys it, God will [f]do hurt to him *and* bring
him to the corruption of death *and* destroy him. For the temple of
God is holy—sacred to Him—and that [temple] you [ [g]the believing
church and its individual believers] are.
18 Let no person deceive himself. If any one among you supposes that he is wise in this age—let him discard his [worldly]
discernment and recognize himself as dull, stupid and foolish,
without [true] learning and scholarship; let him become a fool that
he may become [really] wise. [Isa. 5:21.]
19 For this world's wisdom is foolishness—absurdity and stupidity—with God. For it is written, He lays hold of the wise in their
[own] craftiness; [Job 5:13.]
20 And again, The Lord knows the thoughts *and* reasonings of
the [humanly] wise *and* recognizes how futile they are. [Ps. 94:11.]

**AMP** [a] Literally, "non-speakers." [b] Bengel. [c] Matthew Henry and many others. [d] Cambridge Bible. [e] Matthew Henry and many others. [f] Cambridge Bible. [g] Matthew Henry and many others.

## New American Standard

*Foundations for Living*

3 AND I, brethren, could not speak to you as to spiritual men,
but as to men of flesh, as to babes in Christ.
2 I gave you milk to drink, not solid food; for you were not yet
able *to receive it.* Indeed, even now you are not yet able,
3 for you are still fleshly. For since there is jealousy and strife
among you, are you not fleshly, and are you not walking like mere
men?
4 For when one says, "I am of Paul," and another, "I am of
Apollos," are you not *mere* men?
5 What then is Apollos? And what is Paul? Servants through
whom you believed, even as the Lord gave *opportunity* to each one.
6 I planted, Apollos watered, but God was causing the growth.
7 So then neither the one who plants nor the one who waters
is anything, but God who causes the growth.
8 Now he who plants and he who waters are one; but each will
receive his own reward according to his own labor.
9 For we are God's fellow workers; you are God's field, God's
building.
10 ¶ According to the grace of God which was given to me, as
a wise master builder I laid a foundation, and another is building
upon it. But let each man be careful how he builds upon it.
11 For no man can lay a foundation other than the one which is
laid, which is Jesus Christ.
12 Now if any man builds upon the foundation with gold, silver,
precious stones, wood, hay, straw,
13 each man's work will become evident; for the day will show
it, because it is *to be* revealed with fire; and the fire itself will test
the quality of each man's work.
14 If any man's work which he has built upon it remains, he shall
receive a reward.
15 If any man's work is burned up, he shall suffer loss; but he
himself shall be saved, yet so as through fire.
16 ¶ Do you not know that you are a temple of God, and *that* the
Spirit of God dwells in you?
17 If any man destroys the temple of God, God will destroy him,
for the temple of God is holy, and that is what you are.
18 ¶ Let no man deceive himself. If any man among you thinks
that he is wise in this age, let him become foolish that he may
become wise.
19 For the wisdom of this world is foolishness before God. For
it is written, *"He is* THE ONE WHO CATCHES THE WISE IN THEIR
CRAFTINESS";
20 and again, "THE LORD KNOWS THE REASONINGS of the wise,
THAT THEY ARE USELESS."

## New International

*On Divisions in the Church*

3 BROTHERS, I could not address you as spiritual but as worldly—mere infants in Christ. 2 I gave you milk, not solid food,
for you were not yet ready for it. Indeed, you are still not ready.
3 You are still worldly. For since there is jealousy and quarreling
among you, are you not worldly? Are you not acting like mere
men? 4 For when one says, "I follow Paul," and another, "I follow
Apollos," are you not mere men?
5 What, after all, is Apollos? And what is Paul? Only servants,
through whom you came to believe—as the Lord has assigned to
each his task. 6 I planted the seed, Apollos watered it, but God
made it grow. 7 So neither he who plants nor he who waters is
anything, but only God, who makes things grow. 8 The man who
plants and the man who waters have one purpose, and each will
be rewarded according to his own labor. 9 For we are God's fellow
workers; you are God's field, God's building.
10 By the grace God has given me, I laid a foundation as an
expert builder, and someone else is building on it. But each one
should be careful how he builds. 11 For no one can lay any foundation other than the one already laid, which is Jesus Christ. 12 If any
man builds on this foundation using gold, silver, costly stones,
wood, hay or straw, 13 his work will be shown for what it is,
because the Day will bring it to light. It will be revealed with fire,
and the fire will test the quality of each man's work. 14 If what he
has built survives, he will receive his reward. 15 If it is burned up,
he will suffer loss; he himself will be saved, but only as one
escaping through the flames.
16 Don't you know that you yourselves are God's temple and
that God's Spirit lives in you? 17 If anyone destroys God's temple,
God will destroy him; for God's temple is sacred, and you are that
temple.
18 Do not deceive yourselves. If any one of you thinks he is wise
by the standards of this age, he should become a "fool" so that he
may become wise. 19 For the wisdom of this world is foolishness
in God's sight. As it is written: "He catches the wise in their
craftiness"[h]; 20 and again, "The Lord knows that the thoughts of
the wise are futile."[i] 21 So then, no more boasting about men! All

**NIV** [h] *19* Job 5:13 [i] *20* Psalm 94:11

## King James

21Therefore let no man glory in men. For all things are yours;

22Whether Paul, or Apollos, or Cephas, or the world, or life, or death, or things present, or things to come; all are yours;

23And ye are Christ's; and Christ *is* God's.

**4** LET A man so account of us, as of the ministers of Christ, and stewards of the mysteries of God.

2Moreover it is required in stewards, that a man be found faithful.

3But with me it is a very small thing that I should be judged of you, or of man's judgment: yea, I judge not mine own self.

4For I know nothing by myself; yet am I not hereby justified: but he that judgeth me is the Lord.

5Therefore judge nothing before the time, until the Lord come, who both will bring to light the hidden things of darkness, and will make manifest the counsels of the hearts: and then shall every man have praise of God.

6And these things, brethren, I have in a figure transferred to myself and *to* Apollos for your sakes; that ye might learn in us not to think *of men* above that which is written, that no one of you be puffed up for one against another.

7For who maketh thee to differ *from another?* and what hast thou that thou didst not receive? now if thou didst receive *it*, why dost thou glory, as if thou hadst not received *it?*

8Now ye are full, now ye are rich, ye have reigned as kings without us: and I would to God ye did reign, that we also might reign with you.

9For I think that God hath set forth us the apostles last, as it were appointed to death: for we are made a spectacle unto the world, and to angels, and to men.

10We *are* fools for Christ's sake, but ye *are* wise in Christ; we *are* weak, but ye *are* strong; ye *are* honourable, but we *are* despised.

11Even unto this present hour we both hunger, and thirst, and are naked, and are buffeted, and have no certain dwellingplace;

12And labour, working with our own hands: being reviled, we bless; being persecuted, we suffer it:

13Being defamed, we entreat: we are made as the filth of the world, *and are* the offscouring of all things unto this day.

14I write not these things to shame you, but as my beloved sons I warn *you*.

## Amplified

21So let no one exult proudly concerning men [boasting of having this or that man as a leader], for all things are yours,

22Whether Paul or Apollos or Cephas (Peter), or the universe or life or death, or the immediate *and* [a]threatening present or the [subsequent and uncertain] future; all are yours,

23And you are Christ's, and Christ is God's.

**4** SO THEN let us [apostles] be looked upon as ministering servants of Christ and stewards (trustees) of the mysteries—that is, the secret purposes—of God.

2Moreover, it is [essentially] required of stewards that a man should be found faithful—proving himself worthy of trust.

3But (as for me personally) it matters very little to me that I should be put on trial by you [on this point], *and* that you or any other human tribunal should investigate *and* question *and* cross-question me. I do not even put myself on trial *and* judge myself.

4I am not conscious of anything against myself, *and* I feel blameless; but I am not vindicated *and* acquitted before God on that account. It is the Lord [Himself] Who examines *and* judges me.

5So do not make any hasty *or* premature judgments before the time when the Lord comes [again], for He will both bring to light the secret things that are (now hidden) in darkness, and disclose *and* expose the (secret) aims (motives and purposes) of hearts. Then every man will receive his (due) commendation from God.

6Now I have applied all this [about parties and factions] to myself and Apollos for your sakes, brethren, so that from what I have said of us [as illustrations] you may learn [to think of men in accordance with Scripture and] not to go beyond that which is written; that none of you may be puffed up *and* inflated with pride *and* boast in favor of one [minister and teacher] against another.

7For who separates you from the others [as a faction leader]?—Who makes you superior and sets you apart from another, giving you the pre-eminence? What have you that was not given to you? If then you received it [from someone], why do you boast as if you had not received (but had gained it by your own efforts)?

8[ [b]You behave as if] you are already filled *and* think you have enough—you are full and content, feeling no need of anything more! Already you have become rich (in spiritual gifts and graces)! [Without any counsel or instruction from us, that is, in your conceit], you have ascended your thrones *and* come into your kingdom without including us! And would that it were true *and* that you did reign, so that we might be sharing the kingdom with you!

9For it seems to me that God has made an exhibit of us apostles, exposing us to view last [of all, like men in a triumphal procession who are] sentenced to death [and displayed at the end of the line]. For we have become a spectacle to the world—a show in the world's amphitheatre—with both men and angels (as spectators).

10We are [looked upon as] fools on account of Christ *and* for His sake, but you are [supposedly] so amazingly wise *and* prudent in Christ! We are weak, but you are [so very] strong! You are highly esteemed, but we are in disrepute *and* contempt!

11To this hour we have gone both hungry and thirsty; we [c]habitually wear but one undergarment [and shiver in the cold]; we are roughly knocked about and wander around homeless.

12And we still toil unto weariness [for our living], working hard with our own hands. When men revile us—that is, [d]wound us with an accursed sting—we bless them. When we are persecuted, we take it patiently *and* endure it.

13When we are slandered *and* defamed, we [try to] answer softly *and* bring comfort. We have been made and are now the rubbish *and* filth of the world—the offscouring of all things, the scum of the earth.

14I do not write this to shame you, but to warn *and* counsel you as my beloved children.

**AMP** [a] Vincent. [b] Alford. [c] Souter. [d] Wuest's "Byways in the Greek New Testament."

## New American Standard

21So then let no one boast in men. For all things belong to you,
22whether Paul or Apollos or Cephas or the world or life or
death or things present or things to come; all things belong to you,
23and you belong to Christ; and Christ belongs to God.

*Servants of Christ*

**4** LET A man regard us in this manner, as servants of Christ,
and stewards of the mysteries of God.
2In this case, moreover, it is required of stewards that one be
found trustworthy.
3But to me it is a very small thing that I should be examined
by you, or by *any* human court; in fact, I do not even examine
myself.
4For I am conscious of nothing against myself, yet I am not by
this acquitted; but the one who examines me is the Lord.
5Therefore do not go on passing judgment before [e]the time,
*but wait* until the Lord comes who will both bring to light the things
hidden in the darkness and disclose the motives of *men's* hearts;
and then each man's praise will come to him from God.
6¶ Now these things, brethren, I have figuratively applied to
myself and Apollos for your sakes, that in us you might learn not
to exceed what is written, in order that no one of you might
become arrogant in behalf of one against the other.
7For who regards you as superior? And what do you have that
you did not receive? But if you did receive it, why do you boast
as if you had not received it?
8You are already filled, you have already become rich, you
have become kings without us; and *I* would indeed that you had
become kings so that we also might reign with you.
9For, I think, God has exhibited us apostles last of all, as men
condemned to death; because we have become a spectacle to the
world, both to angels and to men.
10We are fools for Christ's sake, but you are prudent in Christ;
we are weak, but you are strong; you are distinguished, but we are
without honor.
11To this present hour we are both hungry and thirsty, and are
poorly clothed, and are roughly treated, and are homeless;
12and we toil, working with our own hands; when we are
reviled, we bless; when we are persecuted, we endure;
13when we are slandered, we try to conciliate; we have become
as the scum of the world, the dregs of all things, *even* until now.
14¶ I do not write these things to shame you, but to admonish
you as my beloved children.

NAS [e] I.e., the appointed time of judgment

## New International

things are yours, 22whether Paul or Apollos or Cephas[f] or the
world or life or death or the present or the future—all are yours,
23and you are of Christ, and Christ is of God.

*Apostles of Christ*

**4** SO THEN, men ought to regard us as servants of Christ and
as those entrusted with the secret things of God. 2Now it is
required that those who have been given a trust must prove faithful. 3I care very little if I am judged by you or by any human court;
indeed, I do not even judge myself. 4My conscience is clear, but
that does not make me innocent. It is the Lord who judges me.
5Therefore judge nothing before the appointed time; wait till the
Lord comes. He will bring to light what is hidden in darkness and
will expose the motives of men's hearts. At that time each will
receive his praise from God.
6Now, brothers, I have applied these things to myself and
Apollos for your benefit, so that you may learn from us the meaning of the saying, "Do not go beyond what is written." Then you
will not take pride in one man over against another. 7For who
makes you different from anyone else? What do you have that you
did not receive? And if you did receive it, why do you boast as
though you did not?
8Already you have all you want! Already you have become rich!
You have become kings—and that without us! How I wish that you
really had become kings so that we might be kings with you! 9For
it seems to me that God has put us apostles on display at the end
of the procession, like men condemned to die in the arena. We
have been made a spectacle to the whole universe, to angels as well
as to men. 10We are fools for Christ, but you are so wise in Christ!
We are weak, but you are strong! You are honored, we are dishonored! 11To this very hour we go hungry and thirsty, we are in rags,
we are brutally treated, we are homeless. 12We work hard with our
own hands. When we are cursed, we bless; when we are persecuted, we endure it; 13when we are slandered, we answer kindly.
Up to this moment we have become the scum of the earth, the
refuse of the world.
14I am not writing this to shame you, but to warn you, as my
dear children. 15Even though you have ten thousand guardians in

NIV [f] 22 That is, Peter

## King James

15For though ye have ten thousand instructors in Christ, yet *have ye* not many fathers: for in Christ Jesus I have begotten you through the gospel.

16Wherefore I beseech you, be ye followers of me.

17For this cause have I sent unto you Timotheus, who is my beloved son, and faithful in the Lord, who shall bring you into remembrance of my ways which be in Christ, as I teach every where in every church.

18Now some are puffed up, as though I would not come to you.

19But I will come to you shortly, if the Lord will, and will know, not the speech of them which are puffed up, but the power.

20For the kingdom of God *is* not in word, but in power.

21What will ye? shall I come unto you with a rod, or in love, and *in* the spirit of meekness?

**5** IT IS reported commonly *that there is* fornication among you, and such fornication as is not so much as named among the Gentiles, that one should have his father's wife.

2And ye are puffed up, and have not rather mourned, that he that hath done this deed might be taken away from among you.

3For I verily, as absent in body, but present in spirit, have judged already, as though I were present, *concerning* him that hath so done this deed,

4In the name of our Lord Jesus Christ, when ye are gathered together, and my spirit, with the power of our Lord Jesus Christ,

5To deliver such an one unto Satan for the destruction of the flesh, that the spirit may be saved in the day of the Lord Jesus.

6Your glorying *is* not good. Know ye not that a little leaven leaveneth the whole lump?

7Purge out therefore the old leaven, that ye may be a new lump, as ye are unleavened. For even Christ our passover is sacrificed for us:

8Therefore let us keep the feast, not with old leaven, neither with the leaven of malice and wickedness; but with the unleavened *bread* of sincerity and truth.

9I wrote unto you in an epistle not to company with fornicators:

10Yet not altogether with the fornicators of this world, or with the covetous, or extortioners, or with idolaters; for then must ye needs go out of the world.

11But now I have written unto you not to keep company, if any man that is called a brother be a fornicator, or covetous, or an idolater, or a railer, or a drunkard, or an extortioner; with such an one no not to eat.

12For what have I to do to judge them also that are without? do not ye judge them that are within?

## Amplified

15After all, though you should have ten thousand teachers (guides to direct you) in Christ, yet you do not have many fathers. For I became your father in Christ Jesus through the glad tidings (the Gospel).

16So I urge *and* implore you, be imitators of me.

17For this very cause I sent to you Timothy who is my beloved and trustworthy child in the Lord, who will recall to your minds my methods of proceeding *and* course of conduct *and* way of life in Christ, such as I teach everywhere in each of the churches.

18Some of you have become conceited *and* arrogant *and* pretentious, counting on my not coming to you.

19But I will come to you [and] shortly, if the Lord is willing, and then I will perceive *and* understand not what the talk of these puffed up *and* arrogant spirits amount to, but their force—that is, [a]the moral power and excellence of soul they really possess.

20For the kingdom of God consists of *and* is based on not talk but power— [b]moral power and excellence of soul.

21Now which do you prefer? Shall I come to you with a rod of correction, or with love and in a spirit of gentleness?

**5** IT IS actually reported that there is sexual immorality among you, impurity of a sort that is condemned *and* does not occur even among the heathen; for a man has [his own] father's wife. [Deut. 22:30; 27:20.]

2And you are proud *and* arrogant! And you ought rather to mourn—bow in sorrow and in shame—until the person who has done this (shameful) thing is removed from your fellowship *and* your midst!

3As for my attitude, though I am absent [from you] in body, I am present in spirit, and I have already decided *and* passed judgment, as if actually present,

4In the name of the Lord Jesus *Christ*, on the man who has committed such a deed. When you and my own spirit are met together with the power of our Lord Jesus,

5You are to deliver this man over to Satan [c]for physical discipline—to destroy carnal lusts [which prompted him to incest]—that [his] spirit may [yet] be saved in the day of the Lord Jesus.

6[About the condition of your church] your boasting is not good—indeed it is most unseemly and entirely out of place. Do you not know that [just] a little leaven will ferment the whole lump [of dough]?

7Purge (clean out) the old leaven that you may be fresh (new) dough, still uncontaminated (as you are), for Christ, our Passover [Lamb], has been sacrificed.

8Therefore, let us keep the feast, not with old leaven, nor with leaven of vice *and* malice and wickedness, but with the unleavened [bread] of purity (nobility, honor) *and* sincerity and (unadulterated) truth. [Exod. 12:19; 13:7; Deut. 16:3.]

9I wrote you in my [previous] letter not to associate (closely and habitually) with unchaste (impure) people;

10Not [meaning of course that you must] altogether shun the immoral people of this world, or the greedy graspers and cheats *and* thieves or idolaters, since otherwise you would need to get out of the world *and* human society altogether!

11But now I write to you not to associate with any one who bears the name of [Christian] brother, if he is known to be guilty of immorality or greed, or is an idolater—that is, whose soul is devoted to any object that usurps the place of God—or [is] a person with a foul tongue (railing, abusing, reviling, slandering), or is a drunkard, or a swindler *or* a robber. [No] you must not so much as eat with such a person.

12What [business] of mine is it *and* what right have I to judge outsiders? Is it not those inside [the church] upon whom you are to pass disciplinary judgment—passing censuring sentence on them [as the facts require]?

**AMP** [a] Thayer's "Greek-English Lexicon of the New Testament—Grimm."
[b] Thayer's "Greek-English Lexicon of the New Testament—Grimm."
[c] Abbott-Smith's "Manual Greek Lexicon of the New Testament."

## New American Standard

15For if you were to have countless tutors in Christ, yet *you*
*would* not *have* many fathers; for in Christ Jesus I became your
father through the gospel.
16I exhort you therefore, be imitators of me.
17For this reason I have sent to you Timothy, who is my beloved
and faithful child in the Lord, and he will remind you of my ways
which are in Christ, just as I teach everywhere in every church.
18Now some have become arrogant, as though I were not coming to you.
19But I will come to you soon, if the Lord wills, and I shall find
out, not the words of those who are arrogant, but their power.
20For the kingdom of God does not consist in words, but in
power.
21What do you desire? Shall I come to you with a rod or with
love and a spirit of gentleness?

*Immorality Rebuked*

**5** IT IS actually reported that there is immorality among you,
and immorality of such a kind as does not exist even among
the Gentiles, that someone has his father's wife.
2And you have become arrogant, and have not mourned instead, in order that the one who had done this deed might be
removed from your midst.
3For I, on my part, though absent in body but present in spirit,
have already judged him who has so committed this, as though I
were present.
4In the name of our Lord Jesus, when you are assembled, and
I with you in spirit, with the power of our Lord Jesus,
5 *I have decided* to deliver such a one to Satan for the destruction
of his flesh, that his spirit may be saved in the day of the Lord
[d]Jesus.
6Your boasting is not good. Do you not know that a little leaven
leavens the whole lump *of dough*?
7Clean out the old leaven, that you may be a new lump, just
as you are *in fact* unleavened. For Christ our Passover also has been
sacrificed.
8Let us therefore celebrate the feast, not with old leaven, nor
with the leaven of malice and wickedness, but with the unleavened bread of sincerity and truth.
9¶ I wrote you in my letter not to associate with immoral
people;
10I *did* not at all *mean* with the immoral people of this world, or
with the covetous and swindlers, or with idolaters; for then you
would have to go out of the world.
11But actually, I wrote to you not to associate with any so-called
brother if he should be an immoral person, or covetous, or an
idolater, or a reviler, or a drunkard, or a swindler—not even to eat
with such a one.
12For what have I to do with judging outsiders? Do you not
judge those who are within *the church*?

NAS [d] Some ancient mss. do not contain *Jesus*

## New International

Christ, you do not have many fathers, for in Christ Jesus I became
your father through the gospel. 16Therefore I urge you to imitate
me. 17For this reason I am sending to you Timothy, my son whom
I love, who is faithful in the Lord. He will remind you of my way
of life in Christ Jesus, which agrees with what I teach everywhere
in every church.
18Some of you have become arrogant, as if I were not coming
to you. 19But I will come to you very soon, if the Lord is willing,
and then I will find out not only how these arrogant people are
talking, but what power they have. 20For the kingdom of God is
not a matter of talk but of power. 21What do you prefer? Shall I
come to you with a whip, or in love and with a gentle spirit?

*Expel the Immoral Brother!*

**5** IT IS actually reported that there is sexual immorality among
you, and of a kind that does not occur even among pagans:
A man has his father's wife. 2And you are proud! Shouldn't you
rather have been filled with grief and have put out of your fellowship the man who did this? 3Even though I am not physically
present, I am with you in spirit. And I have already passed judgment on the one who did this, just as if I were present. 4When you
are assembled in the name of our Lord Jesus and I am with you
in spirit, and the power of our Lord Jesus is present, 5hand this
man over to Satan, so that the sinful nature[e] may be destroyed and
his spirit saved on the day of the Lord.
6Your boasting is not good. Don't you know that a little yeast
works through the whole batch of dough? 7Get rid of the old yeast
that you may be a new batch without yeast—as you really are. For
Christ, our Passover lamb, has been sacrificed. 8Therefore let us
keep the Festival, not with the old yeast, the yeast of malice and
wickedness, but with bread without yeast, the bread of sincerity
and truth.
9I have written you in my letter not to associate with sexually
immoral people— 10not at all meaning the people of this world
who are immoral, or the greedy and swindlers, or idolaters. In that
case you would have to leave this world. 11But now I am writing
you that you must not associate with anyone who calls himself a
brother but is sexually immoral or greedy, an idolater or a slanderer, a drunkard or a swindler. With such a man do not even eat.
12What business is it of mine to judge those outside the church?

NIV [e] 5 Or *that his body;* or *that the flesh*

## King James

13 But them that are without God judgeth. Therefore put away from among yourselves that wicked person.

**6** DARE ANY of you, having a matter against another, go to law before the unjust, and not before the saints?

2 Do ye not know that the saints shall judge the world? and if the world shall be judged by you, are ye unworthy to judge the smallest matters?

3 Know ye not that we shall judge angels? how much more things that pertain to this life?

4 If then ye have judgments of things pertaining to this life, set them to judge who are least esteemed in the church.

5 I speak to your shame. Is it so, that there is not a wise man among you? no, not one that shall be able to judge between his brethren?

6 But brother goeth to law with brother, and that before the unbelievers.

7 Now therefore there is utterly a fault among you, because ye go to law one with another. Why do ye not rather take wrong? why do ye not rather *suffer yourselves to* be defrauded?

8 Nay, ye do wrong, and defraud, and that *your* brethren.

9 Know ye not that the unrighteous shall not inherit the kingdom of God? Be not deceived: neither fornicators, nor idolaters, nor adulterers, nor effeminate, nor abusers of themselves with mankind,

10 Nor thieves, nor covetous, nor drunkards, nor revilers, nor extortioners, shall inherit the kingdom of God.

11 And such were some of you: but ye are washed, but ye are sanctified, but ye are justified in the name of the Lord Jesus, and by the Spirit of our God.

12 All things are lawful unto me, but all things are not expedient: all things are lawful for me, but I will not be brought under the power of any.

13 Meats for the belly, and the belly for meats: but God shall destroy both it and them. Now the body *is* not for fornication, but for the Lord; and the Lord for the body.

14 And God hath both raised up the Lord, and will also raise up us by his own power.

15 Know ye not that your bodies are the members of Christ? shall I then take the members of Christ, and make *them* the members of an harlot? God forbid.

16 What? know ye not that he which is joined to an harlot is one body? for two, saith he, shall be one flesh.

17 But he that is joined unto the Lord is one spirit.

## Amplified

13 God alone sits in judgment on those who are outside. Drive out that wicked one from among you—expel him from your church.

**6** DOES ANY of you dare, when he has a matter of complaint against another [brother], to go to law before unrighteous men—men neither upright nor right with God, laying it before them—instead of before the saints (the people of God)?

2 Do you not know that the saints [the Christians] will [one day] judge *and* govern the world? And if the world [itself] is to be judged *and* ruled by you, are you unworthy *and* incompetent to try [such petty matters] of the smallest courts of justice?

3 Do you not know also that we [Christians] are to judge the [very] angels *and* pronounce opinion between right and wrong [for them]? How much more then [as to] matters pertaining to this world *and* of this life only!

4 If then you do have such cases of everyday life to decide, why do you appoint [as judges to lay them before], those who [from the standpoint] of the church count for least *and* are without standing?

5 I say this to move you to shame. Can it be that there really is not one man among you who [in action is governed by piety and integrity and] is wise *and* competent enough to decide [the private grievances, disputes and quarrels] between members of the brotherhood,

6 But brother goes to law against brother, and that before [Gentile judges] who are unbelievers—without faith or trust in the Gospel of Christ?

7 Why, the very fact of your having lawsuits with one another at all is a defect—a defeat, an evidence of positive moral loss for you. Why not rather let yourselves suffer wrong *and* be deprived of what is your due? Why not rather be cheated—defrauded and robbed?

8 But [instead it is you] yourselves who wrong and defraud, and that even your own brethren [by so treating them]!

9 Do you not know that the unrighteous *and* the wrongdoers will not inherit *or* have any share in the kingdom of God? Do not be deceived (misled); neither the impure *and* immoral, nor idolaters, nor adulterers, nor those who participate in homosexuality,

10 Nor cheats—swindlers and thieves; nor greedy graspers, nor drunkards, nor foulmouthed revilers *and* slanderers, nor extortioners *and* robbers will inherit *or* have any share in the kingdom of God.

11 And such some of you were (once). But you were washed clean [purified by a complete atonement for sin and made free from the guilt of sin]; and you were consecrated (set apart, hallowed); and you were justified (pronounced righteous, by trust) in the name of the Lord Jesus Christ and in the (Holy) Spirit of our God.

12 Everything is permissible for me—allowable and lawful; but not all things are helpful—good for me to do, expedient and profitable when considered with other things. Everything is lawful for me, but I will not become the slave of anything *or* be brought under its power.

13 Food [is intended] for the stomach and the stomach for food, but God will finally end [the functions of] both *and* bring them to nothing. The body is not intended for sexual immorality, but [is intended] for the Lord, and the Lord [is intended] for the body [ [a]to save, sanctify and raise it again].

14 And God both raised the Lord to life and will also raise us up by His power.

15 Do you not see *and* know that your bodies are members (bodily parts) of Christ, the Messiah? Am I therefore to take the parts of Christ and make [them] parts of a prostitute? Never! Never!

16 Or do you not know *and* realize that when a man joins himself to a prostitute he becomes one body with her? The two, it is written, shall become one flesh. [Gen. 2:24.]

17 But the person who is united to the Lord becomes one spirit with Him.

**AMP** [a] Cambridge Bible. (See Rom. 8:11; I Cor. 15:35-54.)

## New American Standard

13But those who are outside, God judges. REMOVE THE WICKED
MAN FROM AMONG YOURSELVES.

*Lawsuits Discouraged*

6 DOES ANY one of you, when he has a case against his
neighbor, dare to go to law before the unrighteous, and not
before the saints?
2Or do you not know that the saints will judge the world? And
if the world is judged by you, are you not competent *to constitute*
the smallest law courts?
3Do you not know that we shall judge angels? How much
more, matters of this life?
4If then you have law courts dealing with matters of this life,
do you appoint them as judges who are of no account in the
church?
5I say *this* to your shame. *Is it* so, *that* there is not among you
one wise man who will be able to decide between his brethren,
6but brother goes to law with brother, and that before unbelievers?
7Actually, then, it is already a defeat for you, that you have
lawsuits with one another. Why not rather be wronged? Why not
rather be defrauded?
8On the contrary, you yourselves wrong and defraud, and that
*your* brethren.
9Or do you not know that the unrighteous shall not inherit the
kingdom of God? Do not be deceived; neither fornicators, nor
idolaters, nor adulterers, nor [b]effeminate, nor homosexuals,
10nor thieves, nor *the* covetous, nor drunkards, nor revilers, nor
swindlers, shall inherit the kingdom of God.
11And such were some of you; but you were washed, but you
were sanctified, but you were justified in the name of the Lord
Jesus Christ, and in the Spirit of our God.

*The Body Is the Lord's*

12¶ All things are lawful for me, but not all things are profitable.
All things are lawful for me, but I will not be mastered by anything.
13Food is for the stomach, and the stomach is for food; but God
will do away with both of them. Yet the body is not for immorality,
but for the Lord; and the Lord is for the body.
14Now God has not only raised the Lord, but will also raise us
up through His power.
15Do you not know that your bodies are members of Christ?
Shall I then take away the members of Christ and make them
members of a harlot? May it never be!
16Or do you not know that the one who joins himself to a harlot
is one body *with her*? For He says, "THE TWO WILL BECOME ONE
FLESH."
17But the one who joins himself to the Lord is one spirit *with
Him.*

NAS [b] I.e., effeminate by perversion

## New International

Are you not to judge those inside? 13God will judge those outside.
"Expel the wicked man from among you."[c]

*Lawsuits Among Believers*

6 IF ANY of you has a dispute with another, dare he take it
before the ungodly for judgment instead of before the saints?
2Do you not know that the saints will judge the world? And if you
are to judge the world, are you not competent to judge trivial
cases? 3Do you not know that we will judge angels? How much
more the things of this life! 4Therefore, if you have disputes about
such matters, appoint as judges even men of little account in the
church![d] 5I say this to shame you. Is it possible that there is nobody
among you wise enough to judge a dispute between believers?
6But instead, one brother goes to law against another—and this in
front of unbelievers!
7The very fact that you have lawsuits among you means you
have been completely defeated already. Why not rather be
wronged? Why not rather be cheated? 8Instead, you yourselves
cheat and do wrong, and you do this to your brothers.
9Do you not know that the wicked will not inherit the kingdom
of God? Do not be deceived: Neither the sexually immoral nor
idolaters nor adulterers nor male prostitutes nor homosexual offenders 10nor thieves nor the greedy nor drunkards nor slanderers
nor swindlers will inherit the kingdom of God. 11And that is what
some of you were. But you were washed, you were sanctified, you
were justified in the name of the Lord Jesus Christ and by the Spirit
of our God.

*Sexual Immorality*

12"Everything is permissible for me"—but not everything is
beneficial. "Everything is permissible for me"—but I will not be
mastered by anything. 13"Food for the stomach and the stomach
for food"—but God will destroy them both. The body is not meant
for sexual immorality, but for the Lord, and the Lord for the body.
14By his power God raised the Lord from the dead, and he will
raise us also. 15Do you not know that your bodies are members of
Christ himself? Shall I then take the members of Christ and unite
them with a prostitute? Never! 16Do you not know that he who
unites himself with a prostitute is one with her in body? For it is
said, "The two will become one flesh."[e] 17But he who unites
himself with the Lord is one with him in spirit.

NIV [c] 13 Deut. 17:7; 19:19; 21:21; 22:21,24; 24:7 [d] 4 Or *matters, do you appoint as judges men of little account in the church?* [e] 16 Gen. 2:24

## King James

18Flee fornication. Every sin that a man doeth is without the
body; but he that committeth fornication sinneth against his own
body.
19What? know ye not that your body is the temple of the Holy
Ghost *which is* in you, which ye have of God, and ye are not your
own?
20For ye are bought with a price: therefore glorify God in your
body, and in your spirit, which are God's.

7 NOW CONCERNING the things whereof ye wrote unto me:
*It is* good for a man not to touch a woman.
2Nevertheless, *to avoid* fornication, let every man have his own
wife, and let every woman have her own husband.
3Let the husband render unto the wife due benevolence: and
likewise also the wife unto the husband.
4The wife hath not power of her own body, but the husband:
and likewise also the husband hath not power of his own body,
but the wife.
5Defraud ye not one the other, except *it be* with consent for a
time, that ye may give yourselves to fasting and prayer; and come
together again, that Satan tempt you not for your incontinency.
6But I speak this by permission, *and* not of commandment.
7For I would that all men were even as I myself. But every man
hath his proper gift of God, one after this manner, and another
after that.
8I say therefore to the unmarried and widows, It is good for
them if they abide even as I.
9But if they cannot contain, let them marry: for it is better to
marry than to burn.
10And unto the married I command, *yet* not I, but the Lord, Let
not the wife depart from *her* husband:
11But and if she depart, let her remain unmarried, or be reconciled to *her* husband: and let not the husband put away *his* wife.
12But to the rest speak I, not the Lord: If any brother hath a wife
that believeth not, and she be pleased to dwell with him, let him
not put her away.
13And the woman which hath an husband that believeth not,
and if he be pleased to dwell with her, let her not leave him.
14For the unbelieving husband is sanctified by the wife, and the
unbelieving wife is sanctified by the husband: else were your
children unclean; but now are they holy.
15But if the unbelieving depart, let him depart. A brother or a
sister is not under bondage in such *cases:* but God hath called us
to peace.
16For what knowest thou, O wife, whether thou shalt save *thy*
husband? or how knowest thou, O man, whether thou shalt save
*thy* wife?

## Amplified

18Shun immorality *and* all sexual looseness—flee from impurity
[in thought, word or deed]. Any other sin which a man commits
is one outside the body, but he who commits sexual immorality
sins against his own body.
19Do you not know that your body is the temple—the very
sanctuary—of the Holy Spirit Who lives within you, Whom you
have received [as a Gift] from God? You are not your own,
20You were bought for a price—purchased with a
[a]preciousness and paid for, [b]made His own. So then, honor God
*and* bring glory to Him in your body.

7 NOW AS to the matters of which you wrote me. It is well—
[and by that I mean] advantageous, expedient, profitable and
wholesome—for a man not to touch a woman (to cohabit with her),
*but* to remain unmarried.
2But because of the temptation to impurity *and* to avoid immorality, let each [man] have his own wife and let each [woman] have
her own husband.
3The husband should give to his wife her conjugal rights—
goodwill, kindness and what is due her as his wife; and likewise
the wife to her husband.
4For the wife does not have [exclusive] authority *and* control
over her own body, but the husband [has his rights]; likewise also
the husband does not have [exclusive] authority *and* control over
his body, but the wife [has her rights].
5Do not refuse *and* deprive *and* defraud each other (of your due
marital rights), except perhaps by mutual consent for a time, that
you may devote yourselves unhindered to prayer. But afterwards
resume marital relations, lest Satan tempt you [to sin] through
your lack of restraint of sexual desire. [Exod. 19:15.]
6But I am saying this more as a matter of permission *and* concession, not as a command *or* regulation.
7I wish that all men were like I myself am [in this matter of
self-control]. But each has his own special gift from God, one of
this kind and one of another.
8But to the unmarried people and to the widows, I declare that
it is well—good, advantageous, expedient and wholesome—for
them to remain [single] even as I do.
9But if they have not self-control (restraint of their passions),
they should marry. For it is better to marry than to be aflame (with
passion and tortured continually with ungratified desire).
10But to the married [people] I give charge, not I but the Lord,
that the wife is not to separate from her husband.
11But if she does [separate from and divorce him], let her remain
single or else be reconciled to her husband. And [I charge] the
husband [also] that he should not put away *or* divorce his wife.
12To the rest I declare, I, not the Lord [for Jesus did not discuss
this], that if any brother has a wife who does not believe [on
Christ], and she consents to live with him, he should not leave *or*
divorce her.
13And if any woman has an unbelieving husband, and he consents to live with her, she should not leave *or* divorce him.
14For the unbelieving husband is set apart (separated, withdrawn from heathen contamination and affiliated with the Christian people) by union with his consecrated (set-apart) wife; and the
unbelieving wife is set apart *and* separated through union with her
consecrated husband. Otherwise your children would be unclean
[unblessed heathen, [c]outside the Christian covenant], but as it is
they are [d]prepared for God—pure and clean.
15But if the unbelieving partner [actually] leaves, let him do so;
in such [cases the remaining] brother or sister is not morally
bound. But God has called us to peace.
16For, wife, how can you be sure of converting *and* saving your
husband? Husband, how can you be sure of converting *and* saving
your wife?

**AMP** [a] Thayer. [b] Thayer. [c] Jamieson, Fausset and Brown. [d] Thayer.

## New American Standard

18 Flee immorality. Every *other* sin that a man commits is outside
the body, but the immoral man sins against his own body.
19 Or do you not know that your body is a temple of the Holy
Spirit who is in you, whom you have from God, and that you are
not your own?
20 For you have been bought with a price: therefore glorify God
in your body.

*Advice on Marriage*

**7** NOW CONCERNING the things about which you wrote, it
is good for a man not to touch a woman.
2 But because of immoralities, let each man have his own wife,
and let each woman have her own husband.
3 Let the husband fulfill his duty to his wife, and likewise also
the wife to her husband.
4 The wife does not have authority over her own body, but the
husband *does*; and likewise also the husband does not have authority over his own body, but the wife *does*.
5 Stop depriving one another, except by agreement for a time
that you may devote yourselves to prayer, and come together
again lest Satan tempt you because of your lack of self-control.
6 But this I say by way of concession, not of command.
7 [e]Yet I wish that all men were even as I myself am. However,
each man has his own gift from God, one in this manner, and
another in that.
8 ¶ But I say to the unmarried and to widows that it is good for
them if they remain even as I.
9 But if they do not have self-control, let them marry; for it is
better to marry than to burn.
10 But to the married I give instructions, not I, but the Lord, that
the wife should not leave her husband
11 (but if she does leave, let her remain unmarried, or else be
reconciled to her husband), and that the husband should not send
his wife away.
12 But to the rest I say, not the Lord, that if any brother has a
wife who is an unbeliever, and she consents to live with him, let
him not send her away.
13 And a woman who has an unbelieving husband, and he
consents to live with her, let her not send her husband away.
14 For the unbelieving husband is sanctified through his wife,
and the unbelieving wife is sanctified through her believing husband; for otherwise your children are unclean, but now they are
holy.
15 Yet if the unbelieving one leaves, let him leave; the brother or
the sister is not under bondage in such *cases*, but God has called
[f]us to peace.
16 For how do you know, O wife, whether you will save your
husband? Or how do you know, O husband, whether you will
save your wife?

NAS [e] Some ancient mss. read *For* [f] Some ancient mss. read *you*

## New International

18 Flee from sexual immorality. All other sins a man commits are
outside his body, but he who sins sexually sins against his own
body.
19 Do you not know that your body is a temple of the Holy
Spirit, who is in you, whom you have received from God? You are
not your own;
20 you were bought at a price. Therefore honor God
with your body.

*Marriage*

**7** NOW FOR the matters you wrote about: It is good for a man
not to marry.[g]
2 But since there is so much immorality, each
man should have his own wife, and each woman her own husband.
3 The husband should fulfill his marital duty to his wife, and
likewise the wife to her husband.
4 The wife's body does not belong
to her alone but also to her husband. In the same way, the husband's body does not belong to him alone but also to his wife.
5 Do
not deprive each other except by mutual consent and for a time,
so that you may devote yourselves to prayer. Then come together
again so that Satan will not tempt you because of your lack of
self-control.
6 I say this as a concession, not as a command.
7 I wish
that all men were as I am. But each man has his own gift from God;
one has this gift, another has that.
8 Now to the unmarried and the widows I say: It is good for them
to stay unmarried, as I am.
9 But if they cannot control themselves,
they should marry, for it is better to marry than to burn with
passion.
10 To the married I give this command (not I, but the Lord): A
wife must not separate from her husband.
11 But if she does, she
must remain unmarried or else be reconciled to her husband. And
a husband must not divorce his wife.
12 To the rest I say this (I, not the Lord): If any brother has a wife
who is not a believer and she is willing to live with him, he must
not divorce her.
13 And if a woman has a husband who is not a
believer and he is willing to live with her, she must not divorce
him.
14 For the unbelieving husband has been sanctified through
his wife, and the unbelieving wife has been sanctified through her
believing husband. Otherwise your children would be unclean,
but as it is, they are holy.
15 But if the unbeliever leaves, let him do so. A believing man
or woman is not bound in such circumstances; God has called us
to live in peace.
16 How do you know, wife, whether you will save
your husband? Or, how do you know, husband, whether you will
save your wife?

NIV [g] 1 Or *"It is good for a man not to have sexual relations with a woman."*

## King James

17 But as God hath distributed to every man, as the Lord hath called every one, so let him walk. And so ordain I in all churches.

18 Is any man called being circumcised? let him not become uncircumcised. Is any called in uncircumcision? let him not be circumcised.

19 Circumcision is nothing, and uncircumcision is nothing, but the keeping of the commandments of God.

20 Let every man abide in the same calling wherein he was called.

21 Art thou called *being* a servant? care not for it: but if thou mayest be made free, use *it* rather.

22 For he that is called in the Lord, *being* a servant, is the Lord's freeman: likewise also he that is called, *being* free, is Christ's servant.

23 Ye are bought with a price; be not ye the servants of men.

24 Brethren, let every man, wherein he is called, therein abide with God.

25 Now concerning virgins I have no commandment of the Lord: yet I give my judgment, as one that hath obtained mercy of the Lord to be faithful.

26 I suppose therefore that this is good for the present distress, *I say,* that *it is* good for a man so to be.

27 Art thou bound unto a wife? seek not to be loosed. Art thou loosed from a wife? seek not a wife.

28 But and if thou marry, thou hast not sinned; and if a virgin marry, she hath not sinned. Nevertheless such shall have trouble in the flesh: but I spare you.

29 But this I say, brethren, the time *is* short: it remaineth, that both they that have wives be as though they had none;

30 And they that weep, as though they wept not; and they that rejoice, as though they rejoiced not; and they that buy, as though they possessed not;

31 And they that use this world, as not abusing *it:* for the fashion of this world passeth away.

32 But I would have you without carefulness. He that is unmarried careth for the things that belong to the Lord, how he may please the Lord:

33 But he that is married careth for the things that are of the world, how he may please *his* wife.

34 There is difference *also* between a wife and a virgin. The unmarried woman careth for the things of the Lord, that she may be holy both in body and in spirit: but she that is married careth for the things of the world, how she may please *her* husband.

35 And this I speak for your own profit; not that I may cast a snare upon you, but for that which is comely, and that ye may attend upon the Lord without distraction.

36 But if any man think that he behaveth himself uncomely toward his virgin, if she pass the flower of *her* age, and need so require, let him do what he will, he sinneth not: let them marry.

## Amplified

17 Only, let each one (seek to conduct himself and regulate his affairs so as to) lead the life which the Lord has allotted *and* imparted to him, *and* to which God has invited *and* summoned him. This is my order in all the churches.

18 Was any one at the time of his summons [from God] already circumcised? Let him not seek to remove the evidence of circumcision. Was any one at the time [God] called him, uncircumcised? Let him not be circumcised.

19 For circumcision is nothing *and* counts for nothing, neither does uncircumcision, but [what counts is] keeping the commandments of God.

20 Every one should remain after God calls him in the station *or* condition of life in which the summons found him.

21 Were you a slave when you were called? Do not let that trouble you. But if you are able to gain your freedom, avail yourself of the opportunity.

22 For he who as a slave was summoned in [to union with] the Lord is a freedman of the Lord; just so he who was free when he was called is a bond servant of Christ, the Messiah.

23 You were bought with a price—purchased with a preciousness and paid for [by Christ]; then do not yield yourselves up to become [in your own estimation] slaves to men, [but consider yourselves slaves to Christ].

24 So, brethren, in whatever station *or* state *or* condition of life each one was when he was called, let him continue there, with *and* close to God.

25 Now concerning the virgins—the marriageable [a]maidens—I have no command of the Lord, but I give my opinion *and* advice as one who by the Lord's mercy is rendered trustworthy *and* faithful.

26 I think then, because of the impending distress (that is even now setting in), it is well—expedient, profitable and wholesome—for a person to remain as he *or* she is.

27 Are you bound to a wife? Do not seek to be free. Are you free from a wife? Do not seek a wife.

28 But if you do marry, you do not sin [in doing so], and if a virgin marries, she does not sin [in doing so]. Yet those who marry will have physical *and* earthly troubles, and I would like to spare you that.

29 I mean, brethren, the appointed time has been [b]winding up *and* it has grown very short. From now on, let even those who have wives be as if they had none,

30 And those who weep *and* mourn as though they were not weeping *and* mourning, and those who rejoice as though they were not rejoicing, and those who buy as though they did not possess anything,

31 And those who deal with this world— [c]over-using the enjoyments of this life—let them live as though they were not absorbed by it, *and* as if they had no dealings with it. For the outward form of this world—the present world order—is passing away.

32 My desire is to have you free from all anxiety *and* distressing care. The unmarried [man] is anxious about the things of the Lord, how he may please the Lord;

33 But the married man is anxious about worldly matters, how he may please his wife.

34 And he is drawn in diverging directions—his interests are divided, *and* he is distracted [from his devotion to God]. And the unmarried woman or girl is concerned *and* anxious about the matters of the Lord, how to be wholly separated *and* set apart in body and spirit; but the married woman has her cares [centered] in earthly affairs, how she may please her husband.

35 Now I say this for your own welfare *and* profit, not to put (a halter of) restraint upon you, but to promote what is seemly *and* good order and to secure your undistracted *and* undivided devotion to the Lord.

36 But if any man thinks that he is not acting properly toward *and* in regard to his virgin, [that he is preparing disgrace for her or incurring reproach] in case she is passing the bloom of her youth, and if there is need for it, let him do what to him seems right; he does not sin; let them marry.

**AMP** [a] Vincent. [b] Vincent. [c] Vincent.

## New American Standard

17¶ Only, as the Lord has assigned to each one, as God has
called each, in this manner let him walk. And thus I direct in all
the churches.
18Was any man called *already* circumcised? Let him not become
uncircumcised. Has anyone been called in uncircumcision? Let
him not be circumcised.
19Circumcision is nothing, and uncircumcision is nothing, but
*what matters is* the keeping of the commandments of God.
20Let each man remain in that condition in which he was called.
21Were you called while a slave? Do not worry about it; but if
you are able also to become free, rather do that.
22For he who was called in the Lord while a slave, is the Lord's
freedman; likewise he who was called while free, is Christ's slave.
23You were bought with a price; do not become slaves of men.
24Brethren, let each man remain with God in that *condition* in
which he was called.
25¶ Now concerning virgins I have no command of the Lord, but
I give an opinion as one who by the mercy of the Lord is trustworthy.
26I think then that this is good in view of the present distress,
that it is good for a man to remain as he is.
27Are you bound to a wife? Do not seek to be released. Are you
released from a wife? Do not seek a wife.
28But if you should marry, you have not sinned; and if a virgin
should marry, she has not sinned. Yet such will have trouble in
this life, and I am trying to spare you.
29But this I say, brethren, the time has been shortened, so that
from now on those who have wives should be as though they had
none;
30and those who weep, as though they did not weep; and those
who rejoice, as though they did not rejoice; and those who buy,
as though they did not possess;
31and those who use the world, as though they did not make
full use of it; for the form of this world is passing away.
32But I want you to be free from concern. One who is unmarried
is concerned about the things of the Lord, how he may please the
Lord;
33but one who is married is concerned about the things of the
world, how he may please his [d]wife,
34and *his interests* are divided. And the woman who is unmarried, and the virgin, is concerned about the things of the Lord, that
she may be holy both in body and spirit; but one who is married
is concerned about the things of the world, how she may please
her husband.
35And this I say for your own benefit; not to put a restraint upon
you, but to promote what is seemly, and *to secure* undistracted
devotion to the Lord.
36¶ But if any man thinks that he is acting unbecomingly toward
his virgin *daughter*, if she should be of full age, and if it must be
so, let him do what he wishes, he does not sin; let her marry.

**NAS** [d] Some mss. read *wife. And there is a difference also between the wife and the virgin. One who is unmarried is concerned . . .*

## New International

17Nevertheless, each one should retain the place in life that the
Lord assigned to him and to which God has called him. This is the
rule I lay down in all the churches. 18Was a man already circumcised when he was called? He should not become uncircumcised.
Was a man uncircumcised when he was called? He should not be
circumcised. 19Circumcision is nothing and uncircumcision is
nothing. Keeping God's commands is what counts. 20Each one
should remain in the situation which he was in when God called
him. 21Were you a slave when you were called? Don't let it trouble
you—although if you can gain your freedom, do so. 22For he who
was a slave when he was called by the Lord is the Lord's freedman;
similarly, he who was a free man when he was called is Christ's
slave. 23You were bought at a price; do not become slaves of men.
24Brothers, each man, as responsible to God, should remain in the
situation God called him to.
25Now about virgins: I have no command from the Lord, but I
give a judgment as one who by the Lord's mercy is trustworthy.
26Because of the present crisis, I think that it is good for you to
remain as you are. 27Are you married? Do not seek a divorce. Are
you unmarried? Do not look for a wife. 28But if you do marry, you
have not sinned; and if a virgin marries, she has not sinned. But
those who marry will face many troubles in this life, and I want
to spare you this.
29What I mean, brothers, is that the time is short. From now on
those who have wives should live as if they had none; 30those who
mourn, as if they did not; those who are happy, as if they were
not; those who buy something, as if it were not theirs to keep;
31those who use the things of the world, as if not engrossed in
them. For this world in its present form is passing away.
32I would like you to be free from concern. An unmarried man
is concerned about the Lord's affairs—how he can please the Lord.
33But a married man is concerned about the affairs of this world—
how he can please his wife— 34and his interests are divided. An
unmarried woman or virgin is concerned about the Lord's affairs:
Her aim is to be devoted to the Lord in both body and spirit. But
a married woman is concerned about the affairs of this world—
how she can please her husband. 35I am saying this for your own
good, not to restrict you, but that you may live in a right way in
undivided devotion to the Lord.
36If anyone thinks he is acting improperly toward the virgin he
is engaged to, and if she is getting along in years and he feels he
ought to marry, he should do as he wants. He is not sinning. They
should get married. 37But the man who has settled the matter in

## King James

37Nevertheless he that standeth stedfast in his heart, having no necessity, but hath power over his own will, and hath so decreed in his heart that he will keep his virgin, doeth well.

38So then he that giveth *her* in marriage doeth well; but he that giveth *her* not in marriage doeth better.

39The wife is bound by the law as long as her husband liveth; but if her husband be dead, she is at liberty to be married to whom she will; only in the Lord.

40But she is happier if she so abide, after my judgment: and I think also that I have the Spirit of God.

**8** NOW AS touching things offered unto idols, we know that we all have knowledge. Knowledge puffeth up, but charity edifieth.

2And if any man think that he knoweth any thing, he knoweth nothing yet as he ought to know.

3But if any man love God, the same is known of him.

4As concerning therefore the eating of those things that are offered in sacrifice unto idols, we know that an idol *is* nothing in the world, and that *there is* none other God but one.

5For though there be that are called gods, whether in heaven or in earth, (as there be gods many, and lords many,)

6But to us *there is but* one God, the Father, of whom *are* all things, and we in him; and one Lord Jesus Christ, by whom *are* all things, and we by him.

7Howbeit *there is* not in every man that knowledge: for some with conscience of the idol unto this hour eat *it* as a thing offered unto an idol; and their conscience being weak is defiled.

8But meat commendeth us not to God: for neither, if we eat, are we the better; neither, if we eat not, are we the worse.

9But take heed lest by any means this liberty of yours become a stumblingblock to them that are weak.

10For if any man see thee which hast knowledge sit at meat in the idol's temple, shall not the conscience of him which is weak be emboldened to eat those things which are offered to idols;

11And through thy knowledge shall the weak brother perish, for whom Christ died?

12But when ye sin so against the brethren, and wound their weak conscience, ye sin against Christ.

13Wherefore, if meat make my brother to offend, I will eat no flesh while the world standeth, lest I make my brother to offend.

## Amplified

37But whoever is firmly established in his heart—strong in mind and purpose—not being forced by necessity but having control over his own will *and* desire, and has resolved this in his heart, to keep his own virginity, he is doing well.

38So also then, he [the father] who gives [his daughter, virgin] in marriage does well; and he [the father] who does not give [her] in marriage does better.

39A wife is bound to her husband by the law as long as he lives. If the husband dies, she is free to be married to whom she will, only [provided that he too is] in the Lord.

40But in my opinion [a widow] is happier (more blessed and [a]to be envied) if she does not remarry. And also I think I have the Spirit of God.

**8** NOW ABOUT food offered to idols: of course we know that all of us possess knowledge [concerning these matters. Yet mere] knowledge causes people to be puffed up—to bear themselves loftily and be proud; but love, [that is,] affection *and* goodwill *and* benevolence, edifies *and* builds up *and* encourages one to grow [to his full stature].

2If any one imagines that he has come to know *and* understand much [of divine things, without love], he does not yet perceive *and* recognize *and* understand as strongly *and* clearly, *nor* has he become as intimately acquainted with anything as he ought *or* as is necessary.

3But if one loves God truly—[b]with affectionate reverence, prompt obedience and grateful recognition of His blessing—he is known by God [that is, [c]recognized as worthy of His intimacy and love, and he is owned by Him].

4In this matter, then, of the eating of food offered to idols, we know that an idol is nothing—has no real existence—and that there is no God but One. [Deut. 6:4.]

5For although there may be so-called gods, whether in heaven or on earth, as indeed there are many of them, both of gods and of lords *and* masters,

6Yet for us there is [only] one God, the Father, Who is the Source of all things, and for Whom we [have life], and one Lord, Jesus Christ, through *and* by Whom are all things and through *and* by Whom we [ourselves exist]. [Mal. 2:10.]

7Nevertheless, not all [believers] possess this knowledge. But some, through being all their lives until now accustomed to [thinking of] idols [as real and living], still consider the food [offered to an idol] as that sacrificed to an [actual] god; and their weak conscience becomes defiled *and* injured [if they] eat [it].

8Now food [itself] will not cause our acceptance by God *nor* commend us to Him. Eating [food offered to idols] gives us no advantage, neither do we come short *or* become any the worse if we do not eat [it].

9Only be careful that this power of choice—this permission and liberty to do as you please—which is yours, does not [somehow] become a hindrance (cause of stumbling) to the weak *or* overscrupulous [giving them an impulse to sin].

10For suppose any one sees you, a man having knowledge [of God, with an intelligent view of this subject] reclining at table in an idol's temple; might he not be encouraged *and* emboldened [to violate his own conscientious scruples], if he is weak *and* uncertain, and eat what [to him] is for the purpose of idol worship?

11And so by your enlightenment (your knowledge of spiritual things), this weak man is ruined—is lost and perishes—the brother for whom Christ, the Messiah, died!

12And when you sin against your brethren in this way, wounding *and* damaging their weak conscience, you sin against Christ.

13Therefore, if [my eating a] food is a cause of my brother's falling *or* of hindering [his spiritual advancement], I will not eat [such] flesh forever, lest I cause my brother to be tripped up *and* fall *and* to offend.

**AMP** [a] Souter's "Pocket Lexicon to the Greek New Testament." [b] Thayer's "Greek-English Lexicon of the New Testament—Grimm." [c] Souter's "Pocket Lexicon to the Greek New Testament."

## New American Standard

37But he who stands firm in his heart, being under no constraint, but has authority over his own will, and has decided this in his own heart, to keep his own virgin *daughter*, he will do well.

38So then both he who gives his own virgin *daughter* in marriage does well, and he who does not give her in marriage will do better.

39¶ A wife is bound as long as her husband lives; but if her husband is dead, she is free to be married to whom she wishes, only in the Lord.

40But in my opinion she is happier if she remains as she is; and I think that I also have the Spirit of God.

*Take Care with Your Liberty*

**8** NOW CONCERNING things sacrificed to idols, we know that we all have knowledge. Knowledge makes arrogant, but love edifies.

2If anyone supposes that he knows anything, he has not yet known as he ought to know;

3but if anyone loves God, he is known by Him.

4Therefore concerning the eating of things sacrificed to idols, we know that [d]there is no such thing as an idol in the world, and that there is no God but one.

5For even if there are so-called gods whether in heaven or on earth, as indeed there are many gods and many lords,

6yet for us there is *but* one God, the Father, from whom are all things, and we *exist* for Him; and one Lord, Jesus Christ, by whom are all things, and we *exist* through Him.

7¶ However not all men have this knowledge; but some, being accustomed to the idol until now, eat *food* as if it were sacrificed to an idol; and their conscience being weak is defiled.

8But food will not commend us to God; we are neither the worse if we do not eat, nor the better if we do eat.

9But take care lest this liberty of yours somehow become a stumbling block to the weak.

10For if someone sees you, who have knowledge, dining in an idol's temple, will not his conscience, if he is weak, be strengthened to eat things sacrificed to idols?

11For through your knowledge he who is weak is ruined, the brother for whose sake Christ died.

12And thus, by sinning against the brethren and wounding their conscience when it is weak, you sin against Christ.

13Therefore, if food causes my brother to stumble, I will never eat meat again, that I might not cause my brother to stumble.

NAS [d] I.e., has no real existence

## New International

his own mind, who is under no compulsion but has control over his own will, and who has made up his mind not to marry the virgin—this man also does the right thing. 38So then, he who marries the virgin does right, but he who does not marry her does even better.[e]

39A woman is bound to her husband as long as he lives. But if her husband dies, she is free to marry anyone she wishes, but he must belong to the Lord. 40In my judgment, she is happier if she stays as she is—and I think that I too have the Spirit of God.

*Food Sacrificed to Idols*

**8** NOW ABOUT food sacrificed to idols: We know that we all possess knowledge.[f] Knowledge puffs up, but love builds up. 2The man who thinks he knows something does not yet know as he ought to know. 3But the man who loves God is known by God.

4So then, about eating food sacrificed to idols: We know that an idol is nothing at all in the world and that there is no God but one. 5For even if there are so-called gods, whether in heaven or on earth (as indeed there are many "gods" and many "lords"), 6yet for us there is but one God, the Father, from whom all things came and for whom we live; and there is but one Lord, Jesus Christ, through whom all things came and through whom we live.

7But not everyone knows this. Some people are still so accustomed to idols that when they eat such food they think of it as having been sacrificed to an idol, and since their conscience is weak, it is defiled. 8But food does not bring us near to God; we are no worse if we do not eat, and no better if we do.

9Be careful, however, that the exercise of your freedom does not become a stumbling block to the weak. 10For if anyone with a weak conscience sees you who have this knowledge eating in an idol's temple, won't he be emboldened to eat what has been sacrificed to idols? 11So this weak brother, for whom Christ died, is destroyed by your knowledge. 12When you sin against your brothers in this way and wound their weak conscience, you sin against Christ. 13Therefore, if what I eat causes my brother to fall into sin, I will never eat meat again, so that I will not cause him to fall.

NIV [e] 36-38 Or *36If anyone thinks he is not treating his daughter properly, and if she is getting along in years, and he feels she ought to marry, he should do as he wants. He is not sinning. He should let her get married. 37But the man who has settled the matter in his own mind, who is under no compulsion but has control over his own will, and who has made up his mind to keep the virgin unmarried—this man also does the right thing. 38So then, he who gives his virgin in marriage does right, but he who does not give her in marriage does even better.* [f] 1 Or *"We all possess knowledge," as you say*

## King James

9 AM I not an apostle? am I not free? have I not seen Jesus Christ our Lord? are not ye my work in the Lord?

2 If I be not an apostle unto others, yet doubtless I am to you: for the seal of mine apostleship are ye in the Lord.

3 Mine answer to them that do examine me is this,

4 Have we not power to eat and to drink?

5 Have we not power to lead about a sister, a wife, as well as other apostles, and *as* the brethren of the Lord, and Cephas?

6 Or I only and Barnabas, have not we power to forbear working?

7 Who goeth a warfare any time at his own charges? who planteth a vineyard, and eateth not of the fruit thereof? or who feedeth a flock, and eateth not of the milk of the flock?

8 Say I these things as a man? or saith not the law the same also?

9 For it is written in the law of Moses, Thou shalt not muzzle the mouth of the ox that treadeth out the corn. Doth God take care for oxen?

10 Or saith he *it* altogether for our sakes? For our sakes, no doubt, *this* is written: that he that ploweth should plow in hope; and that he that thresheth in hope should be partaker of his hope.

11 If we have sown unto you spiritual things, *is it* a great thing if we shall reap your carnal things?

12 If others be partakers of *this* power over you, *are* not we rather? Nevertheless we have not used this power; but suffer all things, lest we should hinder the gospel of Christ.

13 Do ye not know that they which minister about holy things live *of the things* of the temple? and they which wait at the altar are partakers with the altar?

14 Even so hath the Lord ordained that they which preach the gospel should live of the gospel.

15 But I have used none of these things: neither have I written these things, that it should be so done unto me: for *it were* better for me to die, than that any man should make my glorying void.

16 For though I preach the gospel, I have nothing to glory of: for necessity is laid upon me; yea, woe is unto me, if I preach not the gospel!

17 For if I do this thing willingly, I have a reward: but if against my will, a dispensation *of the gospel* is committed unto me.

18 What is my reward then? *Verily* that, when I preach the gospel, I may make the gospel of Christ without charge, that I abuse not my power in the gospel.

19 For though I be free from all *men*, yet have I made myself servant unto all, that I might gain the more.

20 And unto the Jews I became as a Jew, that I might gain the Jews; to them that are under the law, as under the law, that I might gain them that are under the law;

## Amplified

9 AM I not an apostle (a special messenger)? Am I not free—unrestrained and exempt from any obligation? Have I not seen Jesus our Lord? Are you [yourselves] not (the product and proof of) my workmanship in the Lord?

2 Even if I am not considered an apostle (a special messenger) by others, at least I am one to you; for you are the seal (the certificate, the living evidence) of my apostleship in the Lord—confirming and authenticating it.

3 This is my [real ground of] defense—my vindication of myself—to those who would put me on trial *and* cross-examine me.

4 Have we not the right to our food and drink [at the expense of the churches]?

5 Have we not the right also to take along with us a Christian sister as wife, as do the other apostles and the Lord's brothers and Cephas (Peter)?

6 Or is it only Barnabas and I who have no right to refrain from doing manual labor for a livelihood [in order to go about the work of the ministry]?

7 [Consider this:] What soldier at any time serves at his own expense? Who plants a vineyard and does not eat any of the fruit of it? Who tends a flock and does not partake of the milk of the flock?

8 Do I say this only on human authority *and* as a man reasons? Does not the Law endorse the same principle?

9 For in the Law of Moses it is written, You shall not muzzle an ox when it is treading out the corn. Is it [only] for oxen that God is having a care? [Deut. 25:4.]

10 Or does He speak certainly *and* entirely for our sakes? [Assuredly] it is written for our sakes, because the plowman ought to plow in hope, and the thresher ought to thresh in expectation of partaking of the harvest.

11 If we have sown [the seed of] spiritual good among you, [is it too] much if we reap from your material benefits?

12 If others share in this rightful claim upon you, do not we [have a still better and greater claim]? However, we have never exercised this right, but we endure everything rather than put a hindrance in the way [of the spread] of the good news (the Gospel) of Christ.

13 Do you not know that those men who are employed in the services of the temple get their food from the temple? And that those who tend the altar share with the altar [in the offerings brought]? [Deut. 18:1.]

14 (On the same principle) the Lord directed that those who publish the good news (the Gospel) should live (get their maintenance) by the Gospel.

15 But I have not made use of any of these privileges, nor am I writing this [to suggest] that any such provision be made for me [now]. For it would be better for me to die than to have any one make void *and* deprive me of my [ground for] glorifying [in this matter].

16 For if I [merely] preach the Gospel, that gives me no reason to boast, for I feel compelled of necessity to do it. Woe is me if I do not preach the glad tidings (the Gospel)!

17 For if I do this work of my own free will, then I have my pay—my reward; but if it is not of my own will, but is done reluctantly *and* under compulsion, I am [still] entrusted with a [sacred] trusteeship *and* commission.

18 What then is the [actual] reward that I get? Just this: that in my preaching the good news (the Gospel), I may offer it [absolutely] free of expense [to anybody], not taking advantage of my rights *and* privileges [as a preacher of] the Gospel.

19 For although I am free in every way from any one's control, I have made myself a bond servant to everyone, so that I might gain the more [for Christ].

20 To the Jews I became as a Jew, that I might win Jews; to men under the Law, [I became] as one under the Law, though not myself being under the Law, that I might win those under the Law.

## New American Standard

*Paul's Use of Liberty*

9 AM I not free? Am I not an apostle? Have I not seen Jesus our Lord? Are you not my work in the Lord?

2If to others I am not an apostle, at least I am to you; for you are the seal of my apostleship in the Lord.

3¶ My defense to those who examine me is this:

4Do we not have a right to eat and drink?

5Do we not have a right to take along a believing wife, even as the rest of the apostles, and the brothers of the Lord, and Cephas?

6Or do only Barnabas and I not have a right to refrain from working?

7Who at any time serves as a soldier at his own expense? Who plants a vineyard, and does not eat the fruit of it? Or who tends a flock and does not use the milk of the flock?

8I am not speaking these things according to human judgment, am I? Or does not the Law also say these things?

9For it is written in the Law of Moses, "YOU SHALL NOT MUZZLE THE OX WHILE HE IS THRESHING." God is not concerned about oxen, is He?

10Or is He speaking altogether for our sake? Yes, for our sake it was written, because the plowman ought to plow in hope, and the thresher *to thresh* in hope of sharing *the crops.*

11If we sowed spiritual things in you, is it too much if we should reap material things from you?

12If others share the right over you, do we not more? Nevertheless, we did not use this right, but we endure all things, that we may cause no hindrance to the gospel of Christ.

13Do you not know that those who perform sacred services eat the *food* of the temple, *and* those who attend regularly to the altar have their share with the altar?

14So also the Lord directed those who proclaim the gospel to get their living from the gospel.

15But I have used none of these things. And I am not writing these things that it may be done so in my case; for it would be better for me to die than have any man make my boast an empty one.

16For if I preach the gospel, I have nothing to boast of, for I am under compulsion; for woe is me if I do not preach the gospel.

17For if I do this voluntarily, I have a reward; but if against my will, I have a stewardship entrusted to me.

18What then is my reward? That, when I preach the gospel, I may offer the gospel without charge, so as not to make full use of my right in the gospel.

19¶ For though I am free from all *men,* I have made myself a slave to all, that I might win the more.

20And to the Jews I became as a Jew, that I might win Jews; to those who are under the Law, as under the Law, though not being myself under the Law, that I might win those who are under the Law;

## New International

*The Rights of an Apostle*

9 AM I not free? Am I not an apostle? Have I not seen Jesus our
Lord? Are you not the result of my work in the Lord? 2Even
though I may not be an apostle to others, surely I am to you! For
you are the seal of my apostleship in the Lord.
3This is my defense to those who sit in judgment on me. 4Don't
we have the right to food and drink? 5Don't we have the right to
take a believing wife along with us, as do the other apostles and
the Lord's brothers and Cephas[a]? 6Or is it only I and Barnabas
who must work for a living?
7Who serves as a soldier at his own expense? Who plants a
vineyard and does not eat of its grapes? Who tends a flock and
does not drink of the milk? 8Do I say this merely from a human
point of view? Doesn't the Law say the same thing? 9For it is
written in the Law of Moses: "Do not muzzle an ox while it is
treading out the grain."[b] Is it about oxen that God is concerned?
10Surely he says this for us, doesn't he? Yes, this was written for
us, because when the plowman plows and the thresher threshes,
they ought to do so in the hope of sharing in the harvest. 11If we
have sown spiritual seed among you, is it too much if we reap a
material harvest from you? 12If others have this right of support
from you, shouldn't we have it all the more?
But we did not use this right. On the contrary, we put up with
anything rather than hinder the gospel of Christ. 13Don't you
know that those who work in the temple get their food from the
temple, and those who serve at the altar share in what is offered
on the altar? 14In the same way, the Lord has commanded that
those who preach the gospel should receive their living from the
gospel.
15But I have not used any of these rights. And I am not writing
this in the hope that you will do such things for me. I would rather
die than have anyone deprive me of this boast. 16Yet when I preach
the gospel, I cannot boast, for I am compelled to preach. Woe to
me if I do not preach the gospel! 17If I preach voluntarily, I have
a reward; if not voluntarily, I am simply discharging the trust
committed to me. 18What then is my reward? Just this: that in
preaching the gospel I may offer it free of charge, and so not make
use of my rights in preaching it.
19Though I am free and belong to no man, I make myself a slave
to everyone, to win as many as possible. 20To the Jews I became
like a Jew, to win the Jews. To those under the law I became like
one under the law (though I myself am not under the law), so as
to win those under the law. 21To those not having the law I became

NIV [a] 5 That is, Peter [b] 9 Deut. 25:4

## King James

21To them that are without law, as without law, (being not without law to God, but under the law to Christ,) that I might gain them that are without law.
22To the weak became I as weak, that I might gain the weak: I am made all things to all *men*, that I might by all means save some.
23And this I do for the gospel's sake, that I might be partaker thereof with *you*.
24Know ye not that they which run in a race run all, but one receiveth the prize? So run, that ye may obtain.
25And every man that striveth for the mastery is temperate in all things. Now they *do it* to obtain a corruptible crown; but we an incorruptible.
26I therefore so run, not as uncertainly; so fight I, not as one that beateth the air:
27But I keep under my body, and bring *it* into subjection: lest that by any means, when I have preached to others, I myself should be a castaway.

**10** MOREOVER, BRETHREN, I would not that ye should be ignorant, how that all our fathers were under the cloud, and all passed through the sea;
2And were all baptized unto Moses in the cloud and in the sea;
3And did all eat the same spiritual meat;
4And did all drink the same spiritual drink: for they drank of that spiritual Rock that followed them: and that Rock was Christ.
5But with many of them God was not well pleased: for they were overthrown in the wilderness.
6Now these things were our examples, to the intent we should not lust after evil things, as they also lusted.
7Neither be ye idolaters, as *were* some of them; as it is written, The people sat down to eat and drink, and rose up to play.
8Neither let us commit fornication, as some of them committed, and fell in one day three and twenty thousand.
9Neither let us tempt Christ, as some of them also tempted, and were destroyed of serpents.
10Neither murmur ye, as some of them also murmured, and were destroyed of the destroyer.
11Now all these things happened unto them for examples: and they are written for our admonition, upon whom the ends of the world are come.

## Amplified

21To those without law I became as one without law, not that I am without the law of God *and* lawless toward Him, but that I am [especially keeping] within *and* committed to the law of Christ, that I might win those who are without (outside) law.
22To the weak (wanting in discernment) I have become weak (wanting in discernment) that I might win the weak *and* overscrupulous. I have [in short] become all things to all men, that I might by all means—at all costs and in any and every way—save some [by winning them to faith in Jesus Christ].
23And I do this for the sake of the good news (the Gospel), in order that I may become a participator in it *and* share it its [blessings along with you].
24Do you not know that in a race all the runners compete, but [only] one receives the prize? So run [your race] that you may lay hold [of the prize] *and* make it yours.
25Now every athlete who goes into training conducts himself temperately *and* restricts himself in all things. They do it to win a wreath that will soon wither, but we [do it to receive a crown of eternal blessedness] that cannot wither.
26Therefore I do not run uncertainly—without definite aim. I do not box as one beating the air *and* striking without an adversary.
27But [like a boxer] I buffet my body—handle it roughly, discipline it by hardships—and subdue it, for fear that after proclaiming to others the Gospel *and* things pertaining to it, I myself should become unfit—not stand the test and be unapproved— *and* rejected [as a counterfeit].

**10** FOR I do not want you to be ignorant, brethren, that our forefathers were every one of them under *and* protected by the cloud [in which God's Presence went before them], and every one of them passed safely through the (Red) sea, [Exod. 13:21; 14:22, 29.]
2And every one of them (allowed himself too) to be baptized into Moses in the cloud and in the sea, [that is, they were thus brought under obligation to the Law, to Moses and to the covenant, consecrated and set apart to the service of God];
3And all [of them] ate the same spiritual (supernaturally given) food, [Exod. 16:4, 35.]
4And they all drank the same supernaturally given drink. For they drank from a spiritual Rock which followed them—produced by the sole power of God Himself without natural instrumentality—and the Rock was Christ. [Exod. 17:6; Num. 20:11.]
5Nevertheless God was not pleased with the great majority of them, for they were overthrown *and* strewn down along [the ground] in the wilderness. [Num. 14:29, 30.]
6Now these things are examples (warnings and admonitions) for us not to desire *or* crave *or* covet *or* lust after evil *and* carnal things as they did. [Num. 11:4, 34.]
7Do not be worshippers of false gods as some of them were, as it is written, The people sat down to eat and drink [the sacrifices offered to the golden calf at Horeb] and rose to sport—to dance and give way to jesting and hilarity. [Exod. 32:4, 6.]
8We must not gratify evil desire *and* indulge in immorality as some of them did, and twenty-three thousand [suddenly] fell *dead* in a single day! [Num. 25:1-18.]
9We should not tempt the Lord—try His patience, become a trial to Him, critically appraise Him and exploit His goodness—as some of them did and were killed by poisonous serpents; [Num. 21:5, 6.]
10Nor discontentedly complain as some of them did and were [a]put out of the way entirely by the destroyer [death]. [Num. 16:41, 49.]
11Now these things befell them by way of a figure—as an example and warning [to us]; they were written to admonish *and* fit us for right action by good instruction, we in whose days the ages have reached their climax—their consummation and concluding period.

AMP [a] Thayer.

## New American Standard

21to those who are without law, as without law, though not
being without the law of God but under the law of Christ, that I
might win those who are without law.
22To the weak I became weak, that I might win the weak; I have
become all things to all men, that I may by all means save some.
23And I do all things for the sake of the gospel, that I may
become a fellow partaker of it.
24¶ Do you not know that those who run in a race all run, but
*only* one receives the prize? Run in such a way that you may win.
25And everyone who competes in the games exercises self-control in all things. They then *do it* to receive a perishable wreath, but
we an imperishable.
26Therefore I run in such a way, as not without aim; I box in
such a way, as not beating the air;
27but I buffet my body and make it my slave, lest possibly, after
I have preached to others, I myself should be disqualified.

*Avoid Israel's Mistakes*

10 FOR I do not want you to be unaware, brethren, that our
fathers were all under the cloud, and all passed through
the sea;
2and all [b]were baptized into Moses in the cloud and in the sea;
3and all ate the same spiritual food;
4and all drank the same spiritual drink, for they were drinking
from a spiritual rock which followed them; and the rock was
Christ.
5Nevertheless, with most of them God was not well-pleased;
for they were laid low in the wilderness.
6Now these things happened as examples for us, that we
should not crave evil things, as they also craved.
7And do not be idolaters, as some of them were; as it is written,
"THE PEOPLE SAT DOWN TO EAT AND DRINK, AND STOOD UP TO PLAY."
8Nor let us act immorally, as some of them did, and twenty-
three thousand fell in one day.
9Nor let us try the Lord, as some of them did, and were
destroyed by the serpents.
10Nor grumble, as some of them did, and were destroyed by the
destroyer.
11Now these things happened to them as an example, and they
were written for our instruction, upon whom the ends of the ages
have come.

NAS [b] Some ancient mss. read *received baptism*

## New International

like one not having the law (though I am not free from God's law
but am under Christ's law), so as to win those not having the law.
22To the weak I became weak, to win the weak. I have become all
things to all men so that by all possible means I might save some.
23I do all this for the sake of the gospel, that I may share in its
blessings.
24Do you not know that in a race all the runners run, but only
one gets the prize? Run in such a way as to get the prize. 25Every-
one who competes in the games goes into strict training. They do
it to get a crown that will not last; but we do it to get a crown that
will last forever. 26Therefore I do not run like a man running
aimlessly; I do not fight like a man beating the air. 27No, I beat my
body and make it my slave so that after I have preached to others,
I myself will not be disqualified for the prize.

*Warnings From Israel's History*

10 FOR I do not want you to be ignorant of the fact, brothers,
that our forefathers were all under the cloud and that they
all passed through the sea. 2They were all baptized into Moses in
the cloud and in the sea. 3They all ate the same spiritual food 4and
drank the same spiritual drink; for they drank from the spiritual
rock that accompanied them, and that rock was Christ. 5Neverthe-
less, God was not pleased with most of them; their bodies were
scattered over the desert.
6Now these things occurred as examples[c] to keep us from
setting our hearts on evil things as they did. 7Do not be idolaters,
as some of them were; as it is written: "The people sat down to eat
and drink and got up to indulge in pagan revelry."[d] 8We should
not commit sexual immorality, as some of them did—and in one
day twenty-three thousand of them died. 9We should not test the
Lord, as some of them did—and were killed by snakes. 10And do
not grumble, as some of them did—and were killed by the destroying angel.
11These things happened to them as examples and were written
down as warnings for us, on whom the fulfillment of the ages has
come. 12So, if you think you are standing firm, be careful that you

NIV [c] 6 Or *types;* also in verse 11 [d] 7 Exodus 32:6

## King James

12Wherefore let him that thinketh he standeth take heed lest he fall.

13There hath no temptation taken you but such as is common to man: but God *is* faithful, who will not suffer you to be tempted above that ye are able; but will with the temptation also make a way to escape, that ye may be able to bear *it*.

14Wherefore, my dearly beloved, flee from idolatry.

15I speak as to wise men; judge ye what I say.

16The cup of blessing which we bless, is it not the communion of the blood of Christ? The bread which we break, is it not the communion of the body of Christ?

17For we *being* many are one bread, *and* one body: for we are all partakers of that one bread.

18Behold Israel after the flesh: are not they which eat of the sacrifices partakers of the altar?

19What say I then? that the idol is any thing, or that which is offered in sacrifice to idols is any thing?

20But *I say*, that the things which the Gentiles sacrifice, they sacrifice to devils, and not to God: and I would not that ye should have fellowship with devils.

21Ye cannot drink the cup of the Lord, and the cup of devils: ye cannot be partakers of the Lord's table, and of the table of devils.

22Do we provoke the Lord to jealousy? are we stronger than he?

23All things are lawful for me, but all things are not expedient: all things are lawful for me, but all things edify not.

24Let no man seek his own, but every man another's *wealth*.

25Whatsoever is sold in the shambles, *that* eat, asking no question for conscience sake:

26For the earth *is* the Lord's, and the fulness thereof.

27If any of them that believe not bid you *to a feast*, and ye be disposed to go; whatsoever is set before you, eat, asking no question for conscience sake.

28But if any man say unto you, This is offered in sacrifice unto idols, eat not for his sake that showed it, and for conscience sake: for the earth *is* the Lord's, and the fulness thereof:

29Conscience, I say, not thine own, but of the other: for why is my liberty judged of another *man's* conscience?

30For if I by grace be a partaker, why am I evil spoken of for that for which I give thanks?

31Whether therefore ye eat, or drink, or whatsoever ye do, do all to the glory of God.

## Amplified

12Therefore let any one who thinks he stands—who feels sure that he has a steadfast mind and is standing firm—take heed lest he fall [into sin].

13For no temptation—no trial regarded as enticing to sin [no matter how it comes or where it leads]—has overtaken you *and* laid hold on you that is not common to man—that is, no temptation or trial has come to you that is beyond human resistance and that is not [a]adjusted and [b]adapted and belonging to human experience, and such as man can bear. But God is faithful [to His Word and to His compassionate nature], and He [can be trusted] not to let you be tempted *and* tried *and* assayed beyond your ability *and* strength of resistance *and* power to endure, but with the temptation He will [always] also provide the way out—the means of escape to [c]a landing place—that you may be capable *and* strong *and* powerful patiently to bear up under it.

14Therefore, my dearly beloved, shun—keep clear away from, avoid by flight if need be—any sort of idolatry (of loving or venerating anything more than God).

15I am speaking as to intelligent (sensible) men. Think over *and* make up your minds [for yourselves] about what I say.—I appeal to your reason and your discernment in these matters.

16The cup of blessing [of wine at the Lord's Supper] upon which we ask [God's] blessing, does it not mean [that in drinking it] we participate in *and* share a fellowship (a communion) in the blood of Christ, the Messiah? The bread which we break, does it not mean [that in eating it] we participate in *and* share a fellowship (a communion) in the body of Christ?

17For we [no matter how] numerous we are, are one body, because we all partake of the one Bread [the One Whom the communion bread represents].

18Consider those [physically] people of Israel. Are not those who eat the sacrifices partners of the altar—united in their worship of the same God? [Lev. 7:6.]

19What do I imply then? That food offered to idols is [intrinsically changed by the fact and amounts to] anything *or* that an idol itself is a [living] thing?

20No, I am suggesting that what the pagans sacrifice they offer [in effect] to demons—to evil spiritual powers—and not to God [at all]. I do not want you to fellowship *and* be partners with diabolical spirits [by eating at their feasts]. [Deut. 32:17.]

21You cannot drink the Lord's cup and the demons' cup. You cannot partake of the Lord's table and the demons' table.

22Shall we thus provoke the Lord to jealousy *and* anger *and* indignation? Are we stronger than He [that we should defy Him]? [Deut. 32:21; Eccl. 6:10; Isa. 45:9.]

23All things are legitimate—permissible, and we are free to do anything we please; but not all things are helpful (expedient, profitable and wholesome). All things are legitimate, but not all things are constructive [to character] *and* edifying [to spiritual life].

24Let not one then seek his own good *and* advantage *and* profit, but [rather let him seek the welfare of his neighbor] each one of the other.

25[As to meat offered to idols] eat anything that is sold in the meat market without raising any question *or* investigating on the grounds of conscientious scruples,

26For the (whole) earth is the Lord's and everything that is in it. [Ps. 24:1; 50:12.]

27In case one of the unbelievers invites you to a meal and you want to go, eat whatever is served to you without examining into its source because of conscientious scruples.

28But if some one tells you, This has been offered in sacrifice to an idol, do not eat it, out of consideration for the person who informed you, and for conscience's sake; [that is,]

29I mean for the sake of his conscience, not yours, [do not eat it]. For why should another man's scruples apply to me, *and* my liberty of action be determined by his conscience?

30If I partake [of my food] with thankfulness, why am I accused *and* evil spoken of because of that for which I give thanks?

31So then, whether you eat or drink, or whatever you may do, do all for the honor *and* glory of God.

**AMP** [a] Thayer. [b] Alford. [c] Vincent.

## New American Standard

12 Therefore let him who thinks he stands take heed lest he fall.
13 No temptation has overtaken you but such as is common to
man; and God is faithful, who will not allow you to be tempted
beyond what you are able, but with the temptation will provide the
way of escape also, that you may be able to endure it.
14 ¶ Therefore, my beloved, flee from idolatry.
15 I speak as to wise men; you judge what I say.
16 Is not the cup of blessing which we bless a sharing in the blood
of Christ? Is not the bread which we break a sharing in the body
of Christ?
17 Since there is one bread, we who are many are one body; for
we all partake of the one bread.
18 Look at the nation Israel; are not those who eat the sacrifices
sharers in the altar?
19 What do I mean then? That a thing sacrificed to idols is anything, or that an idol is anything?
20 *No*, but *I say* that the things which the Gentiles sacrifice, they
sacrifice to demons, and not to God; and I do not want you to
become sharers in demons.
21 You cannot drink the cup of the Lord and the cup of demons;
you cannot partake of the table of the Lord and the table of demons.
22 Or do we provoke the Lord to jealousy? We are not stronger
than He, are we?
23 ¶ All things are lawful, but not all things are profitable. All
things are lawful, but not all things edify.
24 Let no one seek his own *good*, but that of his neighbor.
25 Eat anything that is sold in the meat market, without asking
questions for conscience' sake;
26 FOR THE EARTH IS THE LORD'S, AND ALL IT CONTAINS.
27 If one of the unbelievers invites you, and you wish to go, eat
anything that is set before you, without asking questions for conscience' sake.
28 But if anyone should say to you, "This is meat sacrificed to
idols," do not eat *it*, for the sake of the one who informed *you*, and
for conscience' sake;
29 I mean not your own conscience, but the other *man's*; for why
is my freedom judged by another's conscience?
30 If I partake with thankfulness, why am I slandered concerning
that for which I give thanks?
31 Whether, then, you eat or drink or whatever you do, do all
to the glory of God.

## New International

don't fall! 13 No temptation has seized you except what is common
to man. And God is faithful; he will not let you be tempted beyond
what you can bear. But when you are tempted, he will also provide
a way out so that you can stand up under it.

*Idol Feasts and the Lord's Supper*

14 Therefore, my dear friends, flee from idolatry. 15 I speak to
sensible people; judge for yourselves what I say. 16 Is not the cup
of thanksgiving for which we give thanks a participation in the
blood of Christ? And is not the bread that we break a participation
in the body of Christ? 17 Because there is one loaf, we, who are
many, are one body, for we all partake of the one loaf.
18 Consider the people of Israel: Do not those who eat the sacrifices participate in the altar? 19 Do I mean then that a sacrifice
offered to an idol is anything, or that an idol is anything? 20 No, but
the sacrifices of pagans are offered to demons, not to God, and I
do not want you to be participants with demons. 21 You cannot
drink the cup of the Lord and the cup of demons too; you cannot
have a part in both the Lord's table and the table of demons. 22 Are
we trying to arouse the Lord's jealousy? Are we stronger than he?

*The Believer's Freedom*

23 "Everything is permissible"—but not everything is beneficial.
"Everything is permissible"—but not everything is constructive.
24 Nobody should seek his own good, but the good of others.
25 Eat anything sold in the meat market without raising questions of conscience, 26 for, "The earth is the Lord's, and everything
in it."[d]
27 If some unbeliever invites you to a meal and you want to go,
eat whatever is put before you without raising questions of conscience. 28 But if anyone says to you, "This has been offered in
sacrifice," then do not eat it, both for the sake of the man who told
you and for conscience' sake[e] — 29 the other man's conscience, I
mean, not yours. For why should my freedom be judged by another's conscience? 30 If I take part in the meal with thankfulness,
why am I denounced because of something I thank God for?
31 So whether you eat or drink or whatever you do, do it all for
the glory of God. 32 Do not cause anyone to stumble, whether Jews,

NIV [d] 26 Psalm 24:1 [e] 28 Some manuscripts *conscience' sake, for "the earth is the Lord's and everything in it"*

## King James

32Give none offence, neither to the Jews, nor to the Gentiles,
nor to the church of God:
33Even as I please all *men* in all *things*, not seeking mine own
profit, but the *profit* of many, that they may be saved.

**11** BE YE followers of me, even as I also *am* of Christ.
2Now I praise you, brethren, that ye remember me in all
things, and keep the ordinances, as I delivered *them* to you.
3But I would have you know, that the head of every man is
Christ; and the head of the woman *is* the man; and the head of
Christ *is* God.
4Every man praying or prophesying, having *his* head covered,
dishonoureth his head.
5But every woman that prayeth or prophesieth with *her* head
uncovered dishonoureth her head: for that is even all one as if she
were shaven.
6For if the woman be not covered, let her also be shorn: but if
it be a shame for a woman to be shorn or shaven, let her be
covered.
7For a man indeed ought not to cover *his* head, forasmuch as
he is the image and glory of God: but the woman is the glory of
the man.
8For the man is not of the woman; but the woman of the man.
9Neither was the man created for the woman; but the woman
for the man.
10For this cause ought the woman to have power on *her* head
because of the angels.
11Nevertheless neither is the man without the woman, neither
the woman without the man, in the Lord.
12For as the woman *is* of the man, even so *is* the man also by
the woman; but all things of God.
13Judge in yourselves: is it comely that a woman pray unto God
uncovered?
14Doth not even nature itself teach you, that, if a man have long
hair, it is a shame unto him?
15But if a woman have long hair, it is a glory to her: for *her* hair
is given her for a covering.
16But if any man seem to be contentious, we have no such
custom, neither the churches of God.
17Now in this that I declare *unto you* I praise *you* not, that ye
come together not for the better, but for the worse.
18For first of all, when ye come together in the church, I hear
that there be divisions among you; and I partly believe it.

## Amplified

32Do not let yourselves be [hindrances by giving] offense to the
Jews or to the Greeks or to the church of God— [a]do not lead others
into sin by your mode of life;
33Just as I myself strive to please—to accommodate myself to
the opinions, desires and interests of others—[adapting myself to]
all men in everything I do; not aiming at *or* considering my own
profit *and* advantage, but that of the many in order that they may
be saved.

**11** PATTERN AFTER me, follow my example, as I imitate *and*
follow Christ, the Messiah.
2I appreciate *and* commend you because you always remember
me in everything and keep firm possession of the traditions (the
substance of my instructions), just as I have (verbally) passed them
on to you.
3But I want you to know *and* realize that Christ is the head of
every man, the head of a woman is her husband, and the Head
of Christ is God.
4Any man who prays or prophesies—that is, teaches, refutes,
reproves, admonishes and comforts—with his head covered dishonors his Head (Christ).
5And any woman who [publicly] prays or prophesies (teaches,
refutes, reproves, admonishes or comforts) when she is barehead-
ed dishonors her head (her husband); it is the same as [if her head
were] shaved.
6For if a woman will not wear [a head] covering, then she
should cut off her hair too; but if it is disgraceful for a woman to
have her head shorn or shaven, let her cover [her head].
7For a man ought not to wear anything on his head [in church],
for he is the image and [reflected] glory of God, [that is, [b]his
function of government reflects the majesty of the divine Rule]; but
woman is [the expression of] man's glory (majesty, pre-eminence).
[Gen. 1:26.]
8For man was not [created] from woman, but woman from man;
[Gen. 2:21-23.]
9Neither was man created on account of *or* for the benefit of
woman, but woman on account of *and* for the benefit of man. [Gen.
2:18.]
10 [c]Therefore she should [be subject to his authority and should]
have a covering on her head [as a token, a symbol, of her submis-
sion] to authority, [ [d]that she may show reverence as do] the angels
*and* not displease them.
11Nevertheless, in [the plan of] the Lord *and* from His point of
view woman is not apart from *and* independent of man, nor is man
aloof from *and* independent of woman;
12For as woman was made from man, even so man is also born
of woman. And all [whether male or female go forth] from God (as
their Author).
13Consider for yourselves; is it proper *and* decent [according to
your customs] for a woman to offer prayer to God [publicly] with
her head uncovered?
14Does not (experience, common sense, reason and) [e]the native
sense of propriety itself teach you that for a man to wear long hair
is a dishonor (humiliating and degrading) to him,
15But if a woman has long hair, it is her ornament *and* glory? For
her hair is given to her for a covering.
16Now if any one is disposed to be argumentative *and* contentious about this, we hold to *and* recognize no other custom [in
worship] than this, nor do the churches of God generally.
17But in what I instruct [you] next I do not commend [you],
because when you meet together it is not for the better but for the
worse.
18For, in the first place, when you assemble as a congregation,
I hear that there are cliques (divisions and factions) among you;
and I in part believe it,

**AMP** [a] Thayer. [b] Thayer. [c] Kypke, quoted in Clarke's Commentary.
[d] Thayer. [e] Thayer.

## New American Standard

32Give no offense either to Jews or to Greeks or to the church of God;
33just as I also please all men in all things, not seeking my own profit, but the *profit* of the many, that they may be saved.

*Christian Order*

11 BE IMITATORS of me, just as I also am of Christ.
2¶ Now I praise you because you remember me in everything, and hold firmly to the traditions, just as I delivered them to you.
3But I want you to understand that Christ is the head of every man, and the man is the head of a woman, and God is the head of Christ.
4Every man who has *something* on his head while praying or prophesying, disgraces his head.
5But every woman who has her head uncovered while praying or prophesying, disgraces her head; for she is one and the same with her whose head is shaved.
6For if a woman does not cover her head, let her also have her hair cut off; but if it is disgraceful for a woman to have her hair cut off or her head shaved, let her cover her head.
7For a man ought not to have his head covered, since he is the image and glory of God; but the woman is the glory of man.
8For man does not originate from woman, but woman from man;
9for indeed man was not created for the woman's sake, but woman for the man's sake.
10Therefore the woman ought to have *a symbol of* authority on her head, because of the angels.
11However, in the Lord, neither is woman independent of man, nor is man independent of woman.
12For as the woman originates from the man, so also the man *has his birth* through the woman; and all things originate from God.
13Judge for yourselves: is it proper for a woman to pray to God *with head* uncovered?
14Does not even nature itself teach you that if a man has long hair, it is a dishonor to him,
15but if a woman has long hair, it is a glory to her? For her hair is given to her for a covering.
16But if one is inclined to be contentious, we have no other practice, nor have the churches of God.
17¶ But in giving this instruction, I do not praise you, because you come together not for the better but for the worse.
18For, in the first place, when you come together as a church, I hear that divisions exist among you; and in part, I believe it.

## New International

Greeks or the church of God— 33even as I try to please everybody
in every way. For I am not seeking my own good but the good of
many, so that they may be saved.

11 FOLLOW MY example, as I follow the example of Christ.

*Propriety in Worship*

2I praise you for remembering me in everything and for holding
to the teachings,[f] just as I passed them on to you.
3Now I want you to realize that the head of every man is Christ,
and the head of the woman is man, and the head of Christ is God.
4Every man who prays or prophesies with his head covered dishonors his head. 5And every woman who prays or prophesies
with her head uncovered dishonors her head—it is just as though
her head were shaved. 6If a woman does not cover her head, she
should have her hair cut off; and if it is a disgrace for a woman to
have her hair cut or shaved off, she should cover her head. 7A man
ought not to cover his head,[g] since he is the image and glory of
God; but the woman is the glory of man. 8For man did not come
from woman, but woman from man; 9neither was man created for
woman, but woman for man. 10For this reason, and because of the
angels, the woman ought to have a sign of authority on her head.
11In the Lord, however, woman is not independent of man, nor
is man independent of woman. 12For as woman came from man,
so also man is born of woman. But everything comes from God.
13Judge for yourselves: Is it proper for a woman to pray to God
with her head uncovered? 14Does not the very nature of things
teach you that if a man has long hair, it is a disgrace to him, 15but
that if a woman has long hair, it is her glory? For long hair is given
to her as a covering. 16If anyone wants to be contentious about this,
we have no other practice—nor do the churches of God.

*The Lord's Supper*

17In the following directives I have no praise for you, for your
meetings do more harm than good. 18In the first place, I hear that
when you come together as a church, there are divisions among
you, and to some extent I believe it. 19No doubt there have to be

**NIV** [f] 2 Or *traditions* [g] 4-7 Or 4*Every man who prays or prophesies with long hair dishonors his head.* 5*And every woman who prays or prophesies with no covering ⌊of hair⌋ on her head dishonors her head—she is just like one of the "shorn women."* 6*If a woman has no covering, let her be for now with short hair, but since it is a disgrace for a woman to have her hair shorn or shaved, she should grow it again.* 7*A man ought not to have long hair*

## King James

19 For there must be also heresies among you, that they which are approved may be made manifest among you.

20 When ye come together therefore into one place, *this* is not to eat the Lord's supper.

21 For in eating every one taketh before *other* his own supper: and one is hungry, and another is drunken.

22 What? have ye not houses to eat and to drink in? or despise ye the church of God, and shame them that have not? What shall I say to you? shall I praise you in this? I praise *you* not.

23 For I have received of the Lord that which also I delivered unto you, That the Lord Jesus the *same* night in which he was betrayed took bread:

24 And when he had given thanks, he brake *it*, and said, Take, eat: this is my body, which is broken for you: this do in remembrance of me.

25 After the same manner also *he took* the cup, when he had supped, saying, This cup is the new testament in my blood: this do ye, as oft as ye drink *it*, in remembrance of me.

26 For as often as ye eat this bread, and drink this cup, ye do show the Lord's death till he come.

27 Wherefore whosoever shall eat this bread, and drink *this* cup of the Lord, unworthily, shall be guilty of the body and blood of the Lord.

28 But let a man examine himself, and so let him eat of *that* bread, and drink of *that* cup.

29 For he that eateth and drinketh unworthily, eateth and drinketh damnation to himself, not discerning the Lord's body.

30 For this cause many *are* weak and sickly among you, and many sleep.

31 For if we would judge ourselves, we should not be judged.

32 But when we are judged, we are chastened of the Lord, that we should not be condemned with the world.

33 Wherefore, my brethren, when ye come together to eat, tarry one for another.

34 And if any man hunger, let him eat at home; that ye come not together unto condemnation. And the rest will I set in order when I come.

**12** NOW CONCERNING spiritual *gifts*, brethren, I would not have you ignorant.

2 Ye know that ye were Gentiles, carried away unto these dumb idols, even as ye were led.

3 Wherefore I give you to understand, that no man speaking by the Spirit of God calleth Jesus accursed: and *that* no man can say that Jesus is the Lord, but by the Holy Ghost.

4 Now there are diversities of gifts, but the same Spirit.

5 And there are differences of administrations, but the same Lord.

## Amplified

19 For doubtless there have to be factions *or* parties among you in order that they who are genuine *and* of approved fitness may become evident *and* plainly recognized among you.

20 So when you gather for your meetings, it is not the Supper instituted by the Lord that you eat,

21 For in eating each one [hurries] to get his own supper first [not waiting for the poor], and one goes hungry while another gets drunk.

22 What! Do you have no houses in which to eat and drink? Or do you despise the church of God *and* mean to show contempt for it, while you humiliate those who are poor—have no homes and have brought no food? What shall I say to you? Shall I commend you in this? No, [most certainly] I will not!

23 For I received from the Lord Himself that which I passed on to you—it was given to me personally; that the Lord Jesus on the night when He was treacherously delivered up *and* while His betrayal was in progress took bread,

24 And when He had given thanks, He broke [it], and said, *Take, eat.* This is My body which is broken for you. Do this to call Me [affectionately] to remembrance.

25 Similarly when supper was ended, He took the cup also, saying, This cup is the new covenant [ratified and established] in My blood. Do this, as often as you drink [it], to call Me [affectionately] to remembrance.

26 For every time you eat this bread and drink this cup, you are representing *and* signifying *and* proclaiming the fact of the Lord's death until He comes [again].

27 So then whoever eats the bread or drinks the cup of the Lord in a way that is unworthy [of Him] will be guilty of (profaning and sinning against) the body and blood of the Lord.

28 Let a man [thoroughly] examine himself, and [only] when he has done so should he eat of the bread and drink of the cup.

29 For any one who eats and drinks without discriminating *and* recognizing with due appreciation that [it is Christ's] body, eats and drinks a sentence—a verdict of judgment—upon himself.

30 That [careless and unworthy participation] is the reason many of you are weak and sickly, and quite enough of you are fallen into the sleep of death.

31 For if we searchingly examined ourselves—detecting our shortcomings and recognizing our own condition—we should not be judged *and* penalty decreed [by the divine judgment].

32 But when we [fall short and] are judged by the Lord, we are disciplined *and* chastened so that we may not (finally) be condemned (to eternal punishment along) with the world.

33 So then, my brothers, when you gather together to eat [the Lord's Supper], wait for one another.

34 If any one is hungry, let him eat at home, lest you come together to bring judgment [on yourselves]. About the other matters, I will give you directions (personally) when I come.

**12** NOW ABOUT the spiritual gifts (the special endowments of supernatural energy), brethren, I do not want you to be misinformed.

2 You know that [when] you were heathen, you were led off after idols that could not speak—habitually—as impulse directed *and* whenever the occasion might arise.

3 Therefore I want you to understand that no one speaking under the power *and* influence of the (Holy) Spirit of God [ever] can say, Jesus be cursed! And no one can [really] say, Jesus is [my] Lord, except by *and* under the power *and* influence of the Holy Spirit.

4 Now there are distinctive varieties *and* distributions of endowments [ [a]extraordinary powers distinguishing certain Christians, due to the power of divine grace operating in their souls by the Holy Spirit] and they vary, but the (Holy) Spirit remains the same.

5 And there are distinctive varieties of service *and* ministration, but it is the same Lord [Who is served].

**AMP** [a] Thayer.

## New American Standard

19For there must also be factions among you, in order that those who are approved may have become evident among you.
20Therefore when you meet together, it is not to eat the Lord's Supper,
21for in your eating each one takes his own supper first; and one is hungry and another is drunk.
22What! Do you not have houses in which to eat and drink? Or do you despise the church of God, and shame those who have nothing? What shall I say to you? Shall I praise you? In this I will not praise you.

*The Lord's Supper*

23For I received from the Lord that which I also delivered to you, that the Lord Jesus in the night in which He was betrayed took bread;
24and when He had given thanks, He broke it, and said, "This is My body, which [b]is for you; do this in remembrance of Me."
25In the same way *He took* the cup also, after supper, saying, "This cup is the new covenant in My blood; do this, as often as you drink *it*, in remembrance of Me."
26For as often as you eat this bread and drink the cup, you proclaim the Lord's death until He comes.
27Therefore whoever eats the bread or drinks the cup of the Lord in an unworthy manner, shall be guilty of the body and the blood of the Lord.
28But let a man examine himself, and so let him eat of the bread and drink of the cup.
29For he who eats and drinks, eats and drinks judgment to himself, if he does not judge the body rightly.
30For this reason many among you are weak and sick, and a number sleep.
31But if we judged ourselves rightly, we should not be judged.
32But when we are judged, we are disciplined by the Lord in order that we may not be condemned along with the world.
33So then, my brethren, when you come together to eat, wait for one another.
34If anyone is hungry, let him eat at home, so that you may not come together for judgment. And the remaining matters I shall arrange when I come.

*The Use of Spiritual Gifts*

12 NOW CONCERNING spiritual *gifts*, brethren, I do not want you to be unaware.
2You know that when you were pagans, *you were* led astray to the dumb idols, however you were led.
3Therefore I make known to you, that no one speaking by the Spirit of God says, "Jesus is accursed"; and no one can say, "Jesus is Lord," except by the Holy Spirit.
4¶ Now there are varieties of gifts, but the same Spirit.
5And there are varieties of ministries, and the same Lord.

NAS [b] Some ancient mss. read *is broken*

## New International

differences among you to show which of you have God's approval.
20When you come together, it is not the Lord's Supper you eat,
21for as you eat, each of you goes ahead without waiting for anybody else. One remains hungry, another gets drunk. 22Don't you
have homes to eat and drink in? Or do you despise the church of
God and humiliate those who have nothing? What shall I say to
you? Shall I praise you for this? Certainly not!
23For I received from the Lord what I also passed on to you: The
Lord Jesus, on the night he was betrayed, took bread, 24and when
he had given thanks, he broke it and said, "This is my body, which
is for you; do this in remembrance of me." 25In the same way, after
supper he took the cup, saying, "This cup is the new covenant in
my blood; do this, whenever you drink it, in remembrance of me."
26For whenever you eat this bread and drink this cup, you proclaim the Lord's death until he comes.
27Therefore, whoever eats the bread or drinks the cup of the
Lord in an unworthy manner will be guilty of sinning against the
body and blood of the Lord. 28A man ought to examine himself
before he eats of the bread and drinks of the cup. 29For anyone who
eats and drinks without recognizing the body of the Lord eats and
drinks judgment on himself. 30That is why many among you are
weak and sick, and a number of you have fallen asleep. 31But if we
judged ourselves, we would not come under judgment. 32When
we are judged by the Lord, we are being disciplined so that we will
not be condemned with the world.
33So then, my brothers, when you come together to eat, wait
for each other. 34If anyone is hungry, he should eat at home, so
that when you meet together it may not result in judgment.
And when I come I will give further directions.

*Spiritual Gifts*

12 NOW ABOUT spiritual gifts, brothers, I do not want you
to be ignorant. 2You know that when you were pagans,
somehow or other you were influenced and led astray to mute
idols. 3Therefore I tell you that no one who is speaking by the Spirit
of God says, "Jesus be cursed," and no one can say, "Jesus is
Lord," except by the Holy Spirit.
4There are different kinds of gifts, but the same Spirit. 5There
are different kinds of service, but the same Lord. 6There are differ-

## King James

6 And there are diversities of operations, but it is the same God which worketh all in all.

7 But the manifestation of the Spirit is given to every man to profit withal.

8 For to one is given by the Spirit the word of wisdom; to another the word of knowledge by the same Spirit;

9 To another faith by the same Spirit; to another the gifts of healing by the same Spirit;

10 To another the working of miracles; to another prophecy; to another discerning of spirits; to another *divers* kinds of tongues; to another the interpretation of tongues:

11 But all these worketh that one and the selfsame Spirit, dividing to every man severally as he will.

12 For as the body is one, and hath many members, and all the members of that one body, being many, are one body: so also *is* Christ.

13 For by one Spirit are we all baptized into one body, whether *we be* Jews or Gentiles, whether *we be* bond or free; and have been all made to drink into one Spirit.

14 For the body is not one member, but many.

15 If the foot shall say, Because I am not the hand, I am not of the body; is it therefore not of the body?

16 And if the ear shall say, Because I am not the eye, I am not of the body; is it therefore not of the body?

17 If the whole body *were* an eye, where *were* the hearing? If the whole *were* hearing, where *were* the smelling?

18 But now hath God set the members every one of them in the body, as it hath pleased him.

19 And if they were all one member, where *were* the body?

20 But now *are they* many members, yet but one body.

21 And the eye cannot say unto the hand, I have no need of thee: nor again the head to the feet, I have no need of you.

22 Nay, much more those members of the body, which seem to be more feeble, are necessary:

23 And those *members* of the body, which we think to be less honourable, upon these we bestow more abundant honour; and our uncomely *parts* have more abundant comeliness.

24 For our comely *parts* have no need: but God hath tempered the body together, having given more abundant honour to that *part* which lacked:

25 That there should be no schism in the body; but *that* the members should have the same care one for another.

26 And whether one member suffer, all the members suffer with it; or one member be honoured, all the members rejoice with it.

27 Now ye are the body of Christ, and members in particular.

28 And God hath set some in the church, first apostles, secondarily prophets, thirdly teachers, after that miracles, then gifts of healings, helps, governments, diversities of tongues.

**AMP** [a] Vincent. [b] Abbott-Smith. [c] Wuest's "Untranslatable Riches from the Greek New Testament." [d] Thayer. [e] Vincent.

## Amplified

6 And there are distinctive varieties of operation—of working to accomplish things—but it is the same God Who inspires *and* energizes them all in all.

7 But to each one is given the manifestation of the (Holy) Spirit—that is, the evidence, the spiritual illumination of the Spirit—for good *and* profit.

8 To one is given in *and* through the (Holy) Spirit [the power to speak] a message of wisdom, and to another [the power to express] a word of knowledge *and* understanding according to the same (Holy) Spirit;

9 To another ([a]wonder-working) faith by the same (Holy) Spirit, to another the extraordinary powers of healing by the one Spirit;

10 To another the working of miracles, to another prophetic insight—that is, [b]the gift of interpreting the divine will and purpose; to another the ability to discern *and* distinguish between [the utterances of true] spirits [and false ones], to another various kinds of [unknown] tongues, to another the ability to interpret [such] tongues.

11 All these [achievements and abilities] are inspired *and* brought to pass by one and the same (Holy) Spirit, Who apportions to each person individually [exactly] as He chooses.

12 For just as the body is a unity and yet has many parts, and all the parts, though many, form [only] one body, so it is with Christ, the Messiah, the Anointed One.

13 For by ([c]means of the personal agency of) one (Holy) Spirit we were all, whether Jews or Greeks, slaves or free, baptized [and [d]by baptism united together] into one body, and all made to drink of one (Holy) Spirit.

14 For the body does not consist of one limb *or* organ but of many.

15 If the foot should say, Because I am not the hand, I do not belong to the body, would it be therefore not [a part] of the body?

16 If the ear should say, Because I am not the eye, I do not belong to the body, would it be therefore not [a part] of the body?

17 If the whole body were an eye, where [would be the sense of] hearing? If the whole body were an ear, where [would be the sense of] smell?

18 But as it is, God has placed *and* arranged the limbs *and* organs in the body, each (particular one) of them, just as He wished *and* saw fit *and* with the best adaptation.

19 But if [the whole] were all a single organ, where would the body be?

20 And now there are [certainly] many limbs *and* organs, but a single body.

21 And the eye is not able to say to the hand, I have no need of you, nor again the head to the feet, I have no need of you.

22 But instead, there is [absolute] necessity for the parts of the body that are considered the more weak.

23 And those [parts] of the body which we consider rather ignoble are [the very parts] which we invest with additional honor; and our unseemly parts *and* those unsuitable for exposure are treated with seemliness (modesty and decorum),

24 Which our more presentable parts do not require. But God has so adjusted (mingled, harmonized and subtly proportioned the parts of the whole) body, giving the greater honor *and* richer endowment to the inferior parts which lack [apparent importance],

25 So that there is no division *or* discord *or* lack of adaptation (of the parts of the body to each other), but the members all alike have a mutual interest in *and* care for one another.

26 And if one member suffers, all the parts [share] the suffering; if one member is honored, all the members [share in] the enjoyment of it.

27 Now you (collectively) are Christ's body and (individually) you are members of it, each part severally *and* distinct—each with his own place and function.

28 So God has appointed some in the church ([e]for His own use): first apostles (special messengers); second prophets (inspired preachers and expounders); third teachers, then wonder-workers, then those with ability to heal the sick, helpers, administrators, [speakers in] different [unknown] tongues.

## New American Standard

6And there are varieties of effects, but the same God who
works all things in all *persons.*
7But to each one is given the manifestation of the Spirit for the
common good.
8For to one is given the word of wisdom through the Spirit, and
to another the word of knowledge according to the same Spirit;
9to another faith by the same Spirit, and to another gifts of
healing by the one Spirit,
10and to another the effecting of miracles, and to another prophecy, and to another the distinguishing of spirits, to another *various*
kinds of tongues, and to another the interpretation of tongues.
11But one and the same Spirit works all these things, distributing to each one individually just as He wills.
12¶ For even as the body is one and *yet* has many members, and
all the members of the body, though they are many, are one body,
so also is Christ.
13For by one Spirit we were all baptized into one body, whether
Jews or Greeks, whether slaves or free, and we were all made to
drink of one Spirit.
14For the body is not one member, but many.
15If the foot should say, "Because I am not a hand, I am not *a*
*part* of the body," it is not for this reason any the less *a part* of the
body.
16And if the ear should say, "Because I am not an eye, I am not
*a part* of the body," it is not for this reason any the less *a part* of
the body.
17If the whole body were an eye, where would the hearing be?
If the whole were hearing, where would the sense of smell be?
18But now God has placed the members, each one of them, in
the body, just as He desired.
19And if they were all one member, where would the body be?
20But now there are many members, but one body.
21And the eye cannot say to the hand, "I have no need of you";
or again the head to the feet, "I have no need of you."
22On the contrary, it is much truer that the members of the body
which seem to be weaker are necessary;
23and those *members* of the body, which we deem less honorable, on these we bestow more abundant honor, and our unseemly
*members come to* have more abundant seemliness,
24whereas our seemly *members* have no need *of it.* But God has
*so* composed the body, giving more abundant honor to that *member*
which lacked,
25that there should be no division in the body, but *that* the
members should have the same care for one another.
26And if one member suffers, all the members suffer with it; if
*one* member is honored, all the members rejoice with it.
27Now you are Christ's body, and individually members of it.
28And God has appointed in the church, first apostles, second
prophets, third teachers, then miracles, then gifts of healings,
helps, administrations, *various* kinds of tongues.

## New International

ent kinds of working, but the same God works all of them in all
men.
7Now to each one the manifestation of the Spirit is given for the
common good. 8To one there is given through the Spirit the message of wisdom, to another the message of knowledge by means
of the same Spirit, 9to another faith by the same Spirit, to another
gifts of healing by that one Spirit, 10to another miraculous powers,
to another prophecy, to another distinguishing between spirits, to
another speaking in different kinds of tongues,[f] and to still another the interpretation of tongues.[g] 11All these are the work of
one and the same Spirit, and he gives them to each one, just as he
determines.

*One Body, Many Parts*

12The body is a unit, though it is made up of many parts; and
though all its parts are many, they form one body. So it is with
Christ. 13For we were all baptized by[h] one Spirit into one body—
whether Jews or Greeks, slave or free—and we were all given the
one Spirit to drink.
14Now the body is not made up of one part but of many. 15If
the foot should say, "Because I am not a hand, I do not belong to
the body," it would not for that reason cease to be part of the body.
16And if the ear should say, "Because I am not an eye, I do not
belong to the body," it would not for that reason cease to be part
of the body. 17If the whole body were an eye, where would the
sense of hearing be? If the whole body were an ear, where would
the sense of smell be? 18But in fact God has arranged the parts in
the body, every one of them, just as he wanted them to be. 19If they
were all one part, where would the body be? 20As it is, there are
many parts, but one body.
21The eye cannot say to the hand, "I don't need you!" And the
head cannot say to the feet, "I don't need you!" 22On the contrary,
those parts of the body that seem to be weaker are indispensable,
23and the parts that we think are less honorable we treat with
special honor. And the parts that are unpresentable are treated
with special modesty, 24while our presentable parts need no
special treatment. But God has combined the members of the body
and has given greater honor to the parts that lacked it, 25so that
there should be no division in the body, but that its parts should
have equal concern for each other. 26If one part suffers, every part
suffers with it; if one part is honored, every part rejoices with it.
27Now you are the body of Christ, and each one of you is a part
of it. 28And in the church God has appointed first of all apostles,
second prophets, third teachers, then workers of miracles, also
those having gifts of healing, those able to help others, those with
gifts of administration, and those speaking in different kinds of
tongues. 29Are all apostles? Are all prophets? Are all teachers? Do

NIV [f] 10 Or *languages;* also in verse 28 [g] 10 Or *languages;* also in verse 28
[h] 13 Or *with;* or *in*

## King James

29 *Are* all apostles? *are* all prophets? *are* all teachers? *are* all
workers of miracles?
30 Have all the gifts of healing? do all speak with tongues? do
all interpret?
31 But covet earnestly the best gifts: and yet show I unto you a
more excellent way.

13 THOUGH I speak with the tongues of men and of angels,
and have not charity, I am become *as* sounding brass, or
a tinkling cymbal.
2 And though I have *the gift of* prophecy, and understand all
mysteries, and all knowledge; and though I have all faith, so that
I could remove mountains, and have not charity, I am nothing.
3 And though I bestow all my goods to feed *the poor,* and though
I give my body to be burned, and have not charity, it profiteth me
nothing.
4 Charity suffereth long, *and* is kind; charity envieth not; charity
vaunteth not itself, is not puffed up,
5 Doth not behave itself unseemly, seeketh not her own, is not
easily provoked, thinketh no evil;
6 Rejoiceth not in iniquity, but rejoiceth in the truth;
7 Beareth all things, believeth all things, hopeth all things, endureth all things.
8 Charity never faileth: but whether *there be* prophecies, they
shall fail; whether *there be* tongues, they shall cease; whether *there*
*be* knowledge, it shall vanish away.
9 For we know in part, and we prophesy in part.
10 But when that which is perfect is come, then that which is in
part shall be done away.
11 When I was a child, I spake as a child, I understood as a child,
I thought as a child: but when I became a man, I put away childish
things.
12 For now we see through a glass, darkly; but then face to face:
now I know in part; but then shall I know even as also I am known.
13 And now abideth faith, hope, charity, these three; but the
greatest of these *is* charity.

## Amplified

29 Are all apostles, (special messengers)? Are all prophets—
inspired interpreters of the will and purposes of God? Are all
teachers? Do all have the power of performing miracles?
30 Do all possess extraordinary powers of healing? Do all speak
with tongues? Do all interpret?
31 But earnestly desire *and* zealously cultivate the greatest *and*
best—the higher [gifts] and the choicest [graces]. And yet I will
show you a still more excellent way—one that is better by far and
the highest of them all, [love].

13 IF I [can] speak in the tongues of men and [even] of angels,
but have not love [that reasoning, intentional, spiritual
devotion such [a]as is inspired by God's love for and in us], I am
only a noisy gong *or* a clanging cymbal.
2 And if I have prophetic powers—that is, [b]the gift of interpreting the divine will and purpose; and understand all the secret
truths *and* mysteries and possess all knowledge, and if I have
(sufficient) faith so that I can remove mountains, but have not love
[God's love in me] I am nothing—a useless nobody.
3 Even if I dole out all that I have [to the poor in providing] food,
and if I surrender my body to be burned [or [c]in order that I may
glory], but have not love [God's love in me], I gain nothing.
4 Love endures long *and* is patient and kind; love never is envious *nor* boils over with jealousy; is not boastful *or* vainglorious,
does not display itself haughtily.
5 It is not conceited—arrogant and inflated with pride; it is not
rude (unmannerly), *and* does not act unbecomingly. Love [God's
love in us] does not insist on its own rights *or* its own way, *for* it
is not self-seeking; it is not touchy *or* fretful *or* resentful; it takes
no account of the evil done to it—pays no attention to a suffered
wrong.
6 It does not rejoice at injustice *and* unrighteousness, but rejoices
when right *and* truth prevail.
7 Love bears up under anything *and* everything that comes, is
ever ready to believe the best of every person, its hopes are fade-
less under all circumstances and it endures everything [without
weakening].
8 Love never fails—never fades out or becomes obsolete or
comes to an end. As for prophecy [that is, [d]the gift of interpreting
the divine will and purpose], it will be fulfilled *and* pass away; as
for tongues, they will be destroyed *and* cease; as for knowledge,
it will pass away [that is, it will lose its value and be superseded
by truth].
9 For our knowledge is fragmentary (incomplete and imperfect),
and our prophecy (our teaching) is fragmentary (incomplete and
imperfect).
10 But when the complete *and* perfect [total] comes, the incomplete *and* imperfect will vanish away—become antiquated, void
and superseded.
11 When I was a child, I talked like a child, I thought like a child,
I reasoned like a child; now that I have become a man, I am done
with childish ways *and* have put them aside.
12 For now we are looking in a mirror that gives only a dim
(blurred) reflection [of reality as [e]in a riddle or enigma], but then
[when perfection comes] we shall see in reality *and* face to face!
Now I know in part (imperfectly); but then I shall know *and* understand [f]fully *and* clearly, even in the same manner as I have been
[g]fully *and* clearly known *and* understood [[h]by God].
13 And so faith, hope, love abide; [faith, conviction and belief
respecting man's relation to God and divine things; hope, joyful
and confident expectation of eternal salvation; love, true affection
for God and man, growing out of God's love for and in us], these
three, but the greatest of these is love.

**AMP** [a] Souter. [b] Abbott-Smith. [c] Some ancient authorities so read. [d] Abbott-Smith's "Manual Greek Lexicon of the New Testament." [e] Vincent's "Word Studies in the New Testament." [f] Vincent's "Word Studies in the New Testament." [g] Vincent's "Word Studies in the New Testament." [h] Matthew Henry and others.

## New American Standard

29All are not apostles, are they? All are not prophets, are they? All are not teachers, are they? All are not *workers of* miracles, are they?
30All do not have gifts of healings, do they? All do not speak with tongues, do they? All do not interpret, do they?
31But earnestly desire the greater gifts.
¶And I show you a still more excellent way.

*The Excellence of Love*

**13** IF I speak with the tongues of men and of angels, but do not have love, I have become a noisy gong or a clanging cymbal.
2And if I have *the gift of* prophecy, and know all mysteries and all knowledge; and if I have all faith, so as to remove mountains, but do not have love, I am nothing.
3And if I give all my possessions to feed *the poor,* and if I deliver my body [i]to be burned, but do not have love, it profits me nothing.
4Love is patient, love is kind, *and* is not jealous; love does not brag *and* is not arrogant,
5does not act unbecomingly; it does not seek its own, is not provoked, does not take into account a wrong *suffered,*
6does not rejoice in unrighteousness, but rejoices with the truth;
7bears all things, believes all things, hopes all things, endures all things.
8Love never fails; but if *there are gifts of* prophecy, they will be done away; if *there are* tongues, they will cease; if *there is* knowledge, it will be done away.
9For we know in part, and we prophesy in part;
10but when the perfect comes, the partial will be done away.
11When I was a child, I used to speak as a child, think as a child, reason as a child; when I became a man, I did away with childish things.
12For now we see in a mirror dimly, but then face to face; now I know in part, but then I shall know fully just as I also have been fully known.
13But now abide faith, hope, love, these three; but the greatest of these is love.

**NAS** [i] Some ancient mss. read *that I may boast*

## New International

all work miracles? 30Do all have gifts of healing? Do all speak in tongues[j]? Do all interpret? 31But eagerly desire[k] the greater gifts.

*Love*

And now I will show you the most excellent way.

**13** IF I speak in the tongues[l] of men and of angels, but have not love, I am only a resounding gong or a clanging cymbal. 2If I have the gift of prophecy and can fathom all mysteries and all knowledge, and if I have a faith that can move mountains, but have not love, I am nothing. 3If I give all I possess to the poor and surrender my body to the flames,[m] but have not love, I gain nothing.
4Love is patient, love is kind. It does not envy, it does not boast, it is not proud. 5It is not rude, it is not self-seeking, it is not easily angered, it keeps no record of wrongs. 6Love does not delight in evil but rejoices with the truth. 7It always protects, always trusts, always hopes, always perseveres.
8Love never fails. But where there are prophecies, they will cease; where there are tongues, they will be stilled; where there is knowledge, it will pass away. 9For we know in part and we prophesy in part, 10but when perfection comes, the imperfect disappears. 11When I was a child, I talked like a child, I thought like a child, I reasoned like a child. When I became a man, I put childish ways behind me. 12Now we see but a poor reflection as in a mirror; then we shall see face to face. Now I know in part; then I shall know fully, even as I am fully known.
13And now these three remain: faith, hope and love. But the greatest of these is love.

**NIV** [j] 30 Or *other languages* [k] 31 Or *But you are eagerly desiring* [l] 1 Or *languages* [m] 3 Some early manuscripts *body that I may boast*

# King James

**14** FOLLOW AFTER charity, and desire spiritual *gifts,* but rather that ye may prophesy.

2For he that speaketh in an *unknown* tongue speaketh not unto men, but unto God: for no man understandeth *him;* howbeit in the spirit he speaketh mysteries.

3But he that prophesieth speaketh unto men *to* edification, and exhortation, and comfort.

4He that speaketh in an *unknown* tongue edifieth himself; but he that prophesieth edifieth the church.

5I would that ye all spake with tongues, but rather that ye prophesied: for greater *is* he that prophesieth than he that speaketh with tongues, except he interpret, that the church may receive edifying.

6Now, brethren, if I come unto you speaking with tongues, what shall I profit you, except I shall speak to you either by revelation, or by knowledge, or by prophesying, or by doctrine?

7And even things without life giving sound, whether pipe or harp, except they give a distinction in the sounds, how shall it be known what is piped or harped?

8For if the trumpet give an uncertain sound, who shall prepare himself to the battle?

9So likewise ye, except ye utter by the tongue words easy to be understood, how shall it be known what is spoken? for ye shall speak into the air.

10There are, it may be, so many kinds of voices in the world, and none of them *is* without signification.

11Therefore if I know not the meaning of the voice, I shall be unto him that speaketh a barbarian, and he that speaketh *shall be* a barbarian unto me.

12Even so ye, forasmuch as ye are zealous of spiritual *gifts,* seek that ye may excel to the edifying of the church.

13Wherefore let him that speaketh in an *unknown* tongue pray that he may interpret.

14For if I pray in an *unknown* tongue, my spirit prayeth, but my understanding is unfruitful.

15What is it then? I will pray with the spirit, and I will pray with the understanding also: I will sing with the spirit, and I will sing with the understanding also.

16Else when thou shalt bless with the spirit, how shall he that occupieth the room of the unlearned say Amen at thy giving of thanks, seeing he understandeth not what thou sayest?

17For thou verily givest thanks well, but the other is not edified.

18I thank my God, I speak with tongues more than ye all:

# Amplified

**14** EAGERLY PURSUE *and* seek to acquire [this] love—make it your aim, your great quest; and earnestly desire *and* cultivate the spiritual endowments, especially that you may prophesy—that is, [a]interpret the divine will and purpose in inspired preaching and teaching.

2For one who speaks in an [unknown] tongue speaks not to men but to God, for no one understands *or* catches his meaning, because in the (Holy) Spirit he utters secret truths *and* hidden things [not obvious to the understanding].

3But [on the other hand], the one who prophesies—who [b]interprets the divine will and purpose in inspired preaching and teaching—speaks to men for their upbuilding *and* constructive spiritual progress and encouragement and consolation.

4He who speaks in a [strange] tongue edifies *and* improves himself, but he who prophesies— [c]interpreting the divine will and purpose and teaching with inspiration—edifies *and* improves the church *and* promotes growth [in Christian wisdom, piety, holiness and happiness].

5Now I wish that you might all speak in [unknown] tongues, but more especially [I want you] to prophesy—to be inspired to preach and interpret the divine will and purpose. He who prophesies—who is inspired to preach and teach—is greater (more useful and more important) than he who speaks in [unknown] tongues, unless he should interpret [what he says], so that the church may be edified *and* get good out of it.

6Now, brethren, if I come to you speaking in [unknown] tongues, how shall I make it to your advantage unless I speak to you either in revelation—disclosure of God's will to man—in knowledge or in prophecy or in instruction?

7If even inanimate musical instruments, such as the flute or the harp, do not give distinct notes, how will any one [listening] know *or* understand what is played?

8And if the war bugle gives an uncertain (indistinct) call, who will prepare for battle?

9Just so it is with you; if you in the [unknown] tongue speak words that are not intelligible, how will any one understand what you are saying? For you will be talking into empty space!

10There are, I suppose, all these many [to us unknown] tongues in the world [somewhere], and none is destitute of [its own power of] expression *and* meaning.

11But if I do not know the force *and* significance of the speech (language), I shall seem to be a foreigner to the one who speaks [to me], and the speaker who addresses [me] will seem a foreigner to me.

12So it is with yourselves; since you are so eager *and* ambitious to possess spiritual endowments *and* manifestations of the (Holy) Spirit, [concentrate on] striving to excel *and* to abound [in them] in ways that will build up the church.

13Therefore, the person who speaks in an [unknown] tongue should pray [for the power] to interpret *and* explain what he says.

14For if I pray in an [unknown] tongue, my spirit [by the [d]Holy Spirit within me] prays, but my mind is unproductive—bears no fruit and helps nobody.

15Then what am I to do? I will pray with my spirit—by the [e]Holy Spirit that is within me; but I will also pray intelligently—with my mind and understanding; I will sing with my spirit—by the Holy Spirit that is within me; but I will sing (intelligently) with my mind *and* understanding also.

16Otherwise, if you bless *and* render thanks with [your] spirit [ [f]thoroughly aroused by the Holy Spirit], how can any one in the position of an outsider, or [g]he who is not gifted with [interpreting of unknown] tongues, say the Amen to your thanksgiving, since he does not know what you are saying? [I Chron. 16:36; Ps. 106:48.]

17To be sure, you may give thanks well (nobly), but the bystander is not edified—it does him no good.

18I thank God that I speak in [strange] languages more than any of you *or* all of you put together;

**AMP** [a] Abbott-Smith. [b] Abbott-Smith. [c] Abbott-Smith. [d] Vincent. [e] Vincent. [f] Thayer. [g] Alternate reading.

## New American Standard

*Prophecy a Superior Gift*

**14** PURSUE LOVE, yet desire earnestly spiritual *gifts*, but especially that you may prophesy.

2For one who speaks in a tongue does not speak to men, but to God; for no one understands, but in *his* spirit he speaks mysteries.

3But one who prophesies speaks to men for edification and exhortation and consolation.

4One who speaks in a tongue edifies himself; but one who prophesies edifies the church.

5Now I wish that you all spoke in tongues, but *even* more that you would prophesy; and greater is one who prophesies than one who speaks in tongues, unless he interprets, so that the church may receive edifying.

6But now, brethren, if I come to you speaking in tongues, what shall I profit you, unless I speak to you either by way of revelation or of knowledge or of prophecy or of teaching?

7Yet *even* lifeless things, either flute or harp, in producing a sound, if they do not produce a distinction in the tones, how will it be known what is played on the flute or on the harp?

8For if the bugle produces an indistinct sound, who will prepare himself for battle?

9So also you, unless you utter by the tongue speech that is clear, how will it be known what is spoken? For you will be speaking into the air.

10There are, perhaps, a great many kinds of languages in the world, and no *kind* is without meaning.

11If then I do not know the meaning of the language, I shall be to the one who speaks a barbarian, and the one who speaks will be a barbarian to me.

12So also you, since you are zealous of spiritual *gifts*, seek to abound for the edification of the church.

13Therefore let one who speaks in a tongue pray that he may interpret.

14For if I pray in a tongue, my spirit prays, but my mind is unfruitful.

15What is *the outcome* then? I shall pray with the spirit and I shall pray with the mind also; I shall sing with the spirit and I shall sing with the mind also.

16Otherwise if you bless in the spirit *only*, how will the one who fills the place of the ungifted say the "Amen" at your giving of thanks, since he does not know what you are saying?

17For you are giving thanks well enough, but the other man is not edified.

18I thank God, I speak in tongues more than you all;

## New International

*Gifts of Prophecy and Tongues*

**14** FOLLOW THE way of love and eagerly desire spiritual
gifts, especially the gift of prophecy. 2For anyone who
speaks in a tongue[h] does not speak to men but to God. Indeed,
no one understands him; he utters mysteries with his spirit.[i] 3But
everyone who prophesies speaks to men for their strengthening,
encouragement and comfort. 4He who speaks in a tongue edifies
himself, but he who prophesies edifies the church. 5I would like
every one of you to speak in tongues,[j] but I would rather have you
prophesy. He who prophesies is greater than one who speaks in
tongues,[k] unless he interprets, so that the church may be edified.
6Now, brothers, if I come to you and speak in tongues, what
good will I be to you, unless I bring you some revelation or knowledge or prophecy or word of instruction? 7Even in the case of
lifeless things that make sounds, such as the flute or harp, how will
anyone know what tune is being played unless there is a distinction in the notes? 8Again, if the trumpet does not sound a clear call,
who will get ready for battle? 9So it is with you. Unless you speak
intelligible words with your tongue, how will anyone know what
you are saying? You will just be speaking into the air. 10Undoubt-
edly there are all sorts of languages in the world, yet none of them
is without meaning. 11If then I do not grasp the meaning of what
someone is saying, I am a foreigner to the speaker, and he is a
foreigner to me. 12So it is with you. Since you are eager to have
spiritual gifts, try to excel in gifts that build up the church.
13For this reason anyone who speaks in a tongue should pray
that he may interpret what he says. 14For if I pray in a tongue, my
spirit prays, but my mind is unfruitful. 15So what shall I do? I will
pray with my spirit, but I will also pray with my mind; I will sing
with my spirit, but I will also sing with my mind. 16If you are
praising God with your spirit, how can one who finds himself
among those who do not understand[l] say "Amen" to your
thanksgiving, since he does not know what you are saying? 17You
may be giving thanks well enough, but the other man is not
edified.
18I thank God that I speak in tongues more than all of you. 19But

**NIV** [h] 2 Or *another language;* also in verses 4, 13, 14, 19, 26 and 27 [i] 2 Or *by the Spirit* [j] 5 Or *other languages;* also in verses 6, 18, 22, 23 and 39 [k] 5 Or *other languages;* also in verses 6, 18, 22, 23 and 39 [l] 16 Or *among the inquirers*

## King James

19 Yet in the church I had rather speak five words with my understanding, that *by my voice* I might teach others also, than ten thousand words in an *unknown* tongue.

20 Brethren, be not children in understanding: howbeit in malice be ye children, but in understanding be men.

21 In the law it is written, With *men of* other tongues and other lips will I speak unto this people; and yet for all that will they not hear me, saith the Lord.

22 Wherefore tongues are for a sign, not to them that believe, but to them that believe not: but prophesying *serveth* not for them that believe not, but for them which believe.

23 If therefore the whole church be come together into one place, and all speak with tongues, and there come in *those that are* unlearned, or unbelievers, will they not say that ye are mad?

24 But if all prophesy, and there come in one that believeth not, or *one* unlearned, he is convinced of all, he is judged of all:

25 And thus are the secrets of his heart made manifest; and so falling down on *his* face he will worship God, and report that God is in you of a truth.

26 How is it then, brethren? when ye come together, every one of you hath a psalm, hath a doctrine, hath a tongue, hath a revelation, hath an interpretation. Let all things be done unto edifying.

27 If any man speak in an *unknown* tongue, *let it be* by two, or at the most *by* three, and *that* by course; and let one interpret.

28 But if there be no interpreter, let him keep silence in the church; and let him speak to himself, and to God.

29 Let the prophets speak two or three, and let the other judge.

30 If *any thing* be revealed to another that sitteth by, let the first hold his peace.

31 For ye may all prophesy one by one, that all may learn, and all may be comforted.

32 And the spirits of the prophets are subject to the prophets.

33 For God is not *the author* of confusion, but of peace, as in all churches of the saints.

34 Let your women keep silence in the churches: for it is not permitted unto them to speak; but *they are commanded* to be under obedience, as also saith the law.

35 And if they will learn any thing, let them ask their husbands at home: for it is a shame for women to speak in the church.

36 What? came the word of God out from you? or came it unto you only?

37 If any man think himself to be a prophet, or spiritual, let him acknowledge that the things that I write unto you are the commandments of the Lord.

38 But if any man be ignorant, let him be ignorant.

## Amplified

19 Nevertheless, in public worship, I would rather say five words with my understanding, *and* intelligently in order to instruct others, than ten thousand words in a [strange] language.

20 Brethren, do not be children (immature) in your thinking; continue to be babes in [matters of] evil, but in your minds be mature [men].

21 It is written in the Law, By men of strange languages *and* by the lips of foreigners will I speak to this people, and not even then will they listen to Me, says the Lord. [Isa. 28:11, 12.]

22 Thus [unknown] tongues are meant for a (supernatural) sign, not for believers but for unbelievers [on the point of believing], while prophecy (inspired preaching and teaching, interpreting the divine will and purpose) is not for unbelievers [on the point of believing] but for believers.

23 Therefore, if the whole church assembles and all of you speak in [unknown] tongues, and the ungifted *and* uninitiated or unbelievers come in, will they not say that you are demented?

24 But if all prophesy—giving inspired testimony and interpreting the divine will and purpose—and an unbeliever or untaught outsider comes in, he is told of his sin *and* reproved *and* convicted *and* convinced by all, and his defects *and* needs are examined (estimated, determined), *and* he is called to account by all,

25 The secrets of his heart are laid bare; and so, falling on [his] face, he will worship God, declaring that God is among you in very truth.

26 What then, brethren, is [the right course]? When you meet together, each one has a hymn, a teaching, a disclosure of special knowledge *or* information, an utterance in a [strange] tongue or an interpretation of it. [But] let everything be constructive *and* edifying *and* for the good of all.

27 If some speak in a [strange] tongue, let the number be limited to two or at the most three, and each one [taking his] turn, and let one interpret *and* explain [what is said].

28 But if there is no one to do the interpreting, let each of them keep still in church and talk to himself and to God.

29 So, let two or three prophets speak—those inspired to preach or teach—while the rest pay attention *and* weigh *and* discern what is said.

30 But if an inspired revelation comes to another who is sitting by, then let the first one be silent.

31 For in this way you can give testimony—prophesying and thus interpreting the divine will and purpose—one by one, so that all may be instructed and all may be stimulated *and* encouraged;

32 For the spirits of the prophets [the speakers in tongues] are under the speaker's control [and subject to being silenced as may be necessary],

33 For He [Who is the source of their prophesying] is not a God of confusion *and* disorder but of peace *and* order. As [is the practice] in all the churches of the saints (God's people),

34 The women should keep quiet in the churches, for they are not authorized to speak, but should take a secondary *and* subordinate place, just as the Law also says. [Gen. 3:16.]

35 But if there is anything they want to learn, they should ask their own husbands at home, for it is disgraceful for a woman to talk in church [that is, [a]for her to usurp and exercise authority over men in the church].

36 What! Did the Word of the Lord originate with you [Corinthians], or has it reached only you?

37 If any one thinks *and* claims that he is a prophet—filled with and governed by the Holy Spirit of God and inspired to interpret the divine will and purpose in preaching or teaching—or [to have any other] spiritual endowment, let him understand (recognize and acknowledge) that what I am writing to you is a command of the Lord.

38 But if any one disregards *or* does not recognize [ [b]that it is a command of the Lord], he is disregarded *and* not recognized—he is [c]one whom God knows not.

**AMP** [a] "Expositor's Greek Testament." [b] Thayer. [c] Vincent. Some authorities read "he is not known."

## New American Standard

19however, in the church I desire to speak five words with my mind, that I may instruct others also, rather than ten thousand words in a tongue.

*Instruction for the Church*

**20**¶ Brethren, do not be children in your thinking; yet in evil be babes, but in your thinking be mature.

21In the Law it is written, "BY MEN OF STRANGE TONGUES AND BY THE LIPS OF STRANGERS I WILL SPEAK TO THIS PEOPLE, AND EVEN SO THEY WILL NOT LISTEN TO ME," says the Lord.

22So then tongues are for a sign, not to those who believe, but to unbelievers; but prophecy *is for a sign,* not to unbelievers, but to those who believe.

23If therefore the whole church should assemble together and all speak in tongues, and ungifted men or unbelievers enter, will they not say that you are mad?

24But if all prophesy, and an unbeliever or an ungifted man enters, he is convicted by all, he is called to account by all;

25the secrets of his heart are disclosed; and so he will fall on his face and worship God, declaring that God is certainly among you.

**26**¶ What is *the outcome* then, brethren? When you assemble, each one has a psalm, has a teaching, has a revelation, has a tongue, has an interpretation. Let all things be done for edification.

27If anyone speaks in a tongue, *it should be* by two or at the most three, and *each* in turn, and let one interpret;

28but if there is no interpreter, let him keep silent in the church; and let him speak to himself and to God.

29And let two or three prophets speak, and let the others pass judgment.

30But if a revelation is made to another who is seated, let the first keep silent.

31For you can all prophesy one by one, so that all may learn and all may be exhorted;

32and the spirits of prophets are subject to prophets;

33for God is not *a God* of confusion but of peace, as in all the churches of the saints.

**34**¶ Let the women keep silent in the churches; for they are not permitted to speak, but let them subject themselves, just as the Law also says.

35And if they desire to learn anything, let them ask their own husbands at home; for it is improper for a woman to speak in church.

36Was it from you that the word of God *first* went forth? Or has it come to you only?

**37**¶ If anyone thinks he is a prophet or spiritual, let him recognize that the things which I write to you are the Lord's commandment.

38But if anyone [d]does not recognize *this,* he is not recognized.

NAS [d] Some ancient mss. read *is ignorant, let him be ignorant*

## New International

in the church I would rather speak five intelligible words to instruct others than ten thousand words in a tongue.

20Brothers, stop thinking like children. In regard to evil be infants, but in your thinking be adults. 21In the Law it is written:

"Through men of strange tongues
and through the lips of foreigners
I will speak to this people,
but even then they will not listen to me,"[e]
says the Lord.

22Tongues, then, are a sign, not for believers but for unbelievers; prophecy, however, is for believers, not for unbelievers. 23So if the whole church comes together and everyone speaks in tongues, and some who do not understand[f] or some unbelievers come in, will they not say that you are out of your mind? 24But if an unbeliever or someone who does not understand[g] comes in while everybody is prophesying, he will be convinced by all that he is a sinner and will be judged by all, 25and the secrets of his heart will be laid bare. So he will fall down and worship God, exclaiming, "God is really among you!"

*Orderly Worship*

26What then shall we say, brothers? When you come together, everyone has a hymn, or a word of instruction, a revelation, a tongue or an interpretation. All of these must be done for the strengthening of the church. 27If anyone speaks in a tongue, two—or at the most three—should speak, one at a time, and someone must interpret. 28If there is no interpreter, the speaker should keep quiet in the church and speak to himself and God.

29Two or three prophets should speak, and the others should weigh carefully what is said. 30And if a revelation comes to someone who is sitting down, the first speaker should stop. 31For you can all prophesy in turn so that everyone may be instructed and encouraged. 32The spirits of prophets are subject to the control of prophets. 33For God is not a God of disorder but of peace.

As in all the congregations of the saints, 34women should remain silent in the churches. They are not allowed to speak, but must be in submission, as the Law says. 35If they want to inquire about something, they should ask their own husbands at home; for it is disgraceful for a woman to speak in the church.

36Did the word of God originate with you? Or are you the only people it has reached? 37If anybody thinks he is a prophet or spiritually gifted, let him acknowledge that what I am writing to you is the Lord's command. 38If he ignores this, he himself will be ignored.[h]

NIV [e] *21* Isaiah 28:11,12 [f] *23* Or *some inquirers* [g] *24* Or *or some inquirer* [h] *38* Some manuscripts *If he is ignorant of this, let him be ignorant*

## King James

39Wherefore, brethren, covet to prophesy, and forbid not to speak with tongues.
40Let all things be done decently and in order.

15 MOREOVER, BRETHREN, I declare unto you the gospel which I preached unto you, which also ye have received, and wherein ye stand;
2By which also ye are saved, if ye keep in memory what I preached unto you, unless ye have believed in vain.
3For I delivered unto you first of all that which I also received, how that Christ died for our sins according to the scriptures;
4And that he was buried, and that he rose again the third day according to the scriptures:
5And that he was seen of Cephas, then of the twelve:
6After that, he was seen of above five hundred brethren at once; of whom the greater part remain unto this present, but some are fallen asleep.
7After that, he was seen of James; then of all the apostles.
8And last of all he was seen of me also, as of one born out of due time.
9For I am the least of the apostles, that am not meet to be called an apostle, because I persecuted the church of God.
10But by the grace of God I am what I am: and his grace which *was bestowed* upon me was not in vain; but I laboured more abundantly than they all: yet not I, but the grace of God which was with me.
11Therefore whether *it were* I or they, so we preach, and so ye believed.
12Now if Christ be preached that he rose from the dead, how say some among you that there is no resurrection of the dead?
13But if there be no resurrection of the dead, then is Christ not risen:
14And if Christ be not risen, then *is* our preaching vain, and your faith *is* also vain.
15Yea, and we are found false witnesses of God; because we have testified of God that he raised up Christ: whom he raised not up, if so be that the dead rise not.
16For if the dead rise not, then is not Christ raised:
17And if Christ be not raised, your faith *is* vain; ye are yet in your sins.
18Then they also which are fallen asleep in Christ are perished.
19If in this life only we have hope in Christ, we are of all men most miserable.
20But now is Christ risen from the dead, *and* become the firstfruits of them that slept.

## Amplified

39So [to conclude], my brethren, earnestly desire *and* set your hearts on prophesying—on being inspired to preach and teach and to interpret God's will and purpose—and do not forbid *or* hinder speaking in [unknown] tongues.
40But all things should be done with regard to decency *and* propriety *and* in an orderly fashion.

15 AND NOW let me remind you [since it seems to have escaped you], brethren, of the Gospel—the glad tidings of salvation—which I proclaimed to you, which you welcomed *and* accepted and upon which your faith rests;
2And by which you are saved, if you hold fast *and* keep firmly what I preached to you, unless you believed at first without effect *and* all for nothing.
3For I passed on to you first of all what I also had received, that Christ, the Messiah, the Anointed One, died for our sins in accordance with [what] the Scriptures [foretold], [Isa. 53:5-12.]
4That He was buried, that He arose on the third day as the Scriptures foretold, [Ps. 16:9, 10.]
5And [also] that He appeared to Cephas [Peter], then to the twelve.
6Then later He showed Himself to more than five hundred brethren at one time, the majority of whom are still alive, but some have fallen asleep [in death].
7Afterward He was seen by James, then by all the apostles (the special messengers),
8And last of all He appeared to me also, as to one prematurely *and* dead born [ [a]no better than an unperfected fetus among living men].
9For I am least [worthy] of the apostles, who am not fit *or* deserving to be called an apostle, because I once wronged *and* pursued *and* molested the church of God—oppressing it with cruelty and violence.
10But by the grace (the unmerited favor and blessing) of God, I am what I am, and His grace toward me was not [found to be] for nothing—fruitless and without effect. In fact, I worked harder than all of them [the apostles], though it was not really I, but the grace (the unmerited favor and blessing) of God which was with me.
11So, whether then it was I or they, this is what we preach and this is what you believed—what you adhered to, trusted in and relied on.
12But now if Christ, the Messiah, is preached as raised from the dead, how is it that some of you say that there is no resurrection of the dead?
13But if there is no resurrection of the dead, then Christ has not risen;
14And if Christ has not risen, then our preaching is in vain (amounts to nothing) and your faith is devoid of truth *and* is fruitless—without effect, empty, imaginary and unfounded.
15We are even discovered to be misrepresenting God, for we testified of Him that He raised Christ Whom He did not raise, in case it is true that the dead are not raised.
16For if the dead are not raised, then Christ has not been raised;
17And if Christ has not been raised, your faith is mere delusion (futile, fruitless), and you are still in your sins—that is, under the control and penalty of sin;
18And further, those who have died in ( [b]spiritual fellowship and union with) Christ have perished—are lost!
19If we who are [abiding] in Christ have hope only in this life *and* that is all, then we are of all people most miserable *and* to be pitied.
20But the fact is that Christ, the Messiah, has been raised from the dead, *and He became* the first fruits of those who have fallen asleep [in death].

AMP [a] Vincent's "Word Studies in the New Testament." [b] Thayer.

## New American Standard

39¶ Therefore, my brethren, desire earnestly to prophesy, and do not forbid to speak in tongues.
40But let all things be done properly and in an orderly manner.

*The Fact of Christ's Resurrection*

**15** NOW I make known to you, brethren, the gospel which I preached to you, which also you received, in which also you stand,
2by which also you are saved, if you hold fast the word which I preached to you, unless you believed in vain.
3For I delivered to you as of first importance what I also received, that Christ died for our sins according to the Scriptures,
4and that He was buried, and that He was raised on the third day according to the Scriptures,
5and that He appeared to Cephas, then to the twelve.
6After that He appeared to more than five hundred brethren at one time, most of whom remain until now, but some have fallen asleep;
7then He appeared to James, then to all the apostles;
8and last of all, as it were to one untimely born, He appeared to me also.
9For I am the least of the apostles, who am not fit to be called an apostle, because I persecuted the church of God.
10But by the grace of God I am what I am, and His grace toward me did not prove vain; but I labored even more than all of them, yet not I, but the grace of God with me.
11Whether then *it was* I or they, so we preach and so you believed.
12¶ Now if Christ is preached, that He has been raised from the dead, how do some among you say that there is no resurrection of the dead?
13But if there is no resurrection of the dead, not even Christ has been raised;
14and if Christ has not been raised, then our preaching is vain, your faith also is vain.
15Moreover we are even found *to be* false witnesses of God, because we witnessed against God that He raised [c]Christ, whom He did not raise, if in fact the dead are not raised.
16For if the dead are not raised, not even Christ has been raised;
17and if Christ has not been raised, your faith is worthless; you are still in your sins.
18Then those also who have fallen asleep in Christ have perished.
19If we have hoped in Christ in this life only, we are of all men most to be pitied.

*The Order of Resurrection*

20¶ But now Christ has been raised from the dead, the first fruits of those who are asleep.

NAS [c] I.e., the Messiah

## New International

39Therefore, my brothers, be eager to prophesy, and do not
forbid speaking in tongues. 40But everything should be done in a
fitting and orderly way.

*The Resurrection of Christ*

**15** NOW, BROTHERS, I want to remind you of the gospel I
preached to you, which you received and on which you
have taken your stand. 2By this gospel you are saved, if you hold
firmly to the word I preached to you. Otherwise, you have believed in vain.
3For what I received I passed on to you as of first importance[d]:
that Christ died for our sins according to the Scriptures, 4that he
was buried, that he was raised on the third day according to the
Scriptures, 5and that he appeared to Peter,[e] and then to the
Twelve. 6After that, he appeared to more than five hundred of the
brothers at the same time, most of whom are still living, though
some have fallen asleep. 7Then he appeared to James, then to all
the apostles, 8and last of all he appeared to me also, as to one
abnormally born.
9For I am the least of the apostles and do not even deserve to
be called an apostle, because I persecuted the church of God. 10But
by the grace of God I am what I am, and his grace to me was not
without effect. No, I worked harder than all of them—yet not I, but
the grace of God that was with me. 11Whether, then, it was I or
they, this is what we preach, and this is what you believed.

*The Resurrection of the Dead*

12But if it is preached that Christ has been raised from the dead,
how can some of you say that there is no resurrection of the dead?
13If there is no resurrection of the dead, then not even Christ has
been raised. 14And if Christ has not been raised, our preaching is
useless and so is your faith. 15More than that, we are then found
to be false witnesses about God, for we have testified about God
that he raised Christ from the dead. But he did not raise him if in
fact the dead are not raised. 16For if the dead are not raised, then
Christ has not been raised either. 17And if Christ has not been
raised, your faith is futile; you are still in your sins. 18Then those
also who have fallen asleep in Christ are lost. 19If only for this life
we have hope in Christ, we are to be pitied more than all men.
20But Christ has indeed been raised from the dead, the firstfruits of those who have fallen asleep. 21For since death came

NIV [d] 3 Or *you at the first* [e] 5 Greek *Cephas*

## King James

21 For since by man *came* death, by man *came* also the resurrection of the dead.

22 For as in Adam all die, even so in Christ shall all be made alive.

23 But every man in his own order: Christ the firstfruits; afterward they that are Christ's at his coming.

24 Then *cometh* the end, when he shall have delivered up the kingdom to God, even the Father; when he shall have put down all rule and all authority and power.

25 For he must reign, till he hath put all enemies under his feet.

26 The last enemy *that* shall be destroyed *is* death.

27 For he hath put all things under his feet. But when he saith all things are put under *him, it is* manifest that he is excepted, which did put all things under him.

28 And when all things shall be subdued unto him, then shall the Son also himself be subject unto him that put all things under him, that God may be all in all.

29 Else what shall they do which are baptized for the dead, if the dead rise not at all? why are they then baptized for the dead?

30 And why stand we in jeopardy every hour?

31 I protest by your rejoicing which I have in Christ Jesus our Lord, I die daily.

32 If after the manner of men I have fought with beasts at Ephesus, what advantageth it me, if the dead rise not? let us eat and drink; for tomorrow we die.

33 Be not deceived: evil communications corrupt good manners.

34 Awake to righteousness, and sin not; for some have not the knowledge of God: I speak *this* to your shame.

35 But some *man* will say, How are the dead raised up? and with what body do they come?

36 *Thou* fool, that which thou sowest is not quickened, except it die:

37 And that which thou sowest, thou sowest not that body that shall be, but bare grain, it may chance of wheat, or of some other *grain:*

38 But God giveth it a body as it hath pleased him, and to every seed his own body.

39 All flesh *is* not the same flesh: but *there is* one *kind of* flesh of men, another flesh of beasts, another of fishes, *and* another of birds.

40 *There are* also celestial bodies, and bodies terrestrial: but the glory of the celestial *is* one, and the *glory* of the terrestrial *is* another.

41 *There is* one glory of the sun, and another glory of the moon, and another glory of the stars: for *one* star differeth from *another* star in glory.

42 So also *is* the resurrection of the dead. It is sown in corruption; it is raised in incorruption:

43 It is sown in dishonour; it is raised in glory: it is sown in weakness; it is raised in power:

## Amplified

21 For since [it was] through a man that death [came into the world, it is] also through a Man that the resurrection of the dead [has come].

22 For just as [because of [a]union of nature] in Adam all people die, so also [by virtue of their [b]union of nature] shall all in Christ be made alive.

23 But each in his own rank *and* turn: Christ, the Messiah, [is] the first fruits, then those who are Christ's [own will be resurrected] at His coming.

24 After that comes the end (the completion), when He delivers over the kingdom to God the Father after rendering inoperative *and* abolishing every [other] rule and every authority and power.

25 For [Christ] must be King *and* reign until He has put all [His] enemies under His feet. [Ps. 110:1.]

26 The last enemy to be subdued *and* abolished is death.

27 For He [the Father] has put all things in subjection under His [Christ's] feet. But when it says, All things are put in subjection [under Him], it is evident that He [Himself] is excepted Who does the subjecting of all things to Him. [Ps. 8:6.]

28 However, when everything is subjected to Him, then the Son Himself will also subject Himself to [the Father] Who put all things under Him, so that God may be all in all—that is, be everything to everyone, supreme, the indwelling and controlling factor of life.

29 Otherwise, what do people mean by being [themselves] baptized in behalf of the dead? If the dead are not raised at all, why are people baptized for them?

30 [For that matter], why do I live [dangerously as I do, running such risks that I am] in peril every hour?

31 [I assure you] by the pride which I have in you in (your [c]fellowship and union with) Christ Jesus our Lord, that I die daily—that is, that I face death every day and die to self.

32 What do I gain if, merely from the human point of view, I fought with [wild] beasts at Ephesus? If the dead are not raised [at all], let us eat and drink, for tomorrow we will be dead. [Isa. 22:13.]

33 Do not be so deceived *and* misled! Evil companionships, (communion, associations) corrupt *and* deprave good manners *and* morals *and* character.

34 Awake ([d]from your drunken stupor and return) to sober sense *and* your right minds, and sin no more. For some of you have not the knowledge of God—you are utterly and wilfully and disgracefully ignorant, and continue to be so, lacking the sense of God's presence and all true knowledge of Him. I say this to your shame.

35 But some one will say, How can the dead be raised? With what [kind of] body will they come forth?

36 You foolish man! Every time you plant seed you sow something that does not come to life (germinating, springing up and growing) unless it dies first.

37 Nor is the seed you sow, then in the body which it is going to have [later], but it is a naked kernel, perhaps of wheat or some of the rest of the grains.

38 But God gives to it the body that He plans *and* sees fit, and to each kind of seed a body of its own. [Gen. 1:11.]

39 For all flesh is not the same, but there is one kind for humans, another for beasts, another for birds, and another for fish.

40 There are heavenly bodies [sun, moon and stars] and there are earthly bodies [of men, animals and plants], but the beauty *and* glory of the heavenly bodies is of one kind, while the beauty *and* glory of earthly bodies is a different kind.

41 The sun is glorious in one way, and the moon is glorious in another way, and the stars are glorious in their own (distinctive) way; for one star differs from *and* surpasses another in its beauty *and* brilliance.

42 So it is with the resurrection of the dead. [The body] that is sown is perishable *and* decays, but [the body] that is resurrected is imperishable—immune to decay, immortal. [Dan. 12:3.]

43 It is sown in dishonor *and* humiliation; it is raised in honor *and* glory. It is sown in infirmity *and* weakness; it is resurrected in strength *and* endued with power.

**AMP** [a] Jamieson, Fausset and Brown. [b] Jamieson, Fausset and Brown. [c] Thayer. [d] Vincent.

## New American Standard

21 For since by a man *came* death, by a man also *came* the resurrection of the dead.
22 For as in Adam all die, so also in Christ all shall be made alive.
23 But each in his own order: Christ the first fruits, after that
those who are Christ's at His coming,
24 then *comes* the end, when He delivers up the kingdom to the
God and Father, when He has abolished all rule and all authority
and power.
25 For He must reign until He has put all His enemies under His
feet.
26 The last enemy that will be abolished is death.
27 For HE HAS PUT ALL THINGS IN SUBJECTION UNDER HIS FEET. But
when He says, "All things are put in subjection," it is evident that
He is excepted who put all things in subjection to Him.
28 And when all things are subjected to Him, then the Son
Himself also will be subjected to the One who subjected all things
to Him, that God may be all in all.
**29**¶ Otherwise, what will those do who are baptized for the
dead? If the dead are not raised at all, why then are they baptized
for them?
30 Why are we also in danger every hour?
31 I protest, brethren, by the boasting in you, which I have in
Christ Jesus our Lord, I die daily.
32 If from human motives I fought with wild beasts at Ephesus,
what does it profit me? If the dead are not raised, LET US EAT AND
DRINK, FOR TOMORROW WE DIE.
33 Do not be deceived: "Bad company corrupts good morals."
34 Become sober-minded as you ought, and stop sinning; for
some have no knowledge of God. I speak *this* to your shame.
**35**¶ But someone will say, "How are the dead raised? And with
what kind of body do they come?"
36 You fool! That which you sow does not come to life unless it
dies;
37 and that which you sow, you do not sow the body which is
to be, but a bare grain, perhaps of wheat or of something else.
38 But God gives it a body just as He wished, and to each of the
seeds a body of its own.
39 All flesh is not the same flesh, but there is one *flesh* of men,
and another flesh of beasts, and another flesh of birds, and another
of fish.
40 There are also heavenly bodies and earthly bodies, but the
glory of the heavenly is one, and the *glory* of the earthly is another.
41 There is one glory of the sun, and another glory of the moon,
and another glory of the stars; for star differs from star in glory.
42 So also is the resurrection of the dead. It is sown a perishable
*body*, it is raised an imperishable *body*;
43 it is sown in dishonor, it is raised in glory; it is sown in
weakness, it is raised in power;

## New International

through a man, the resurrection of the dead comes also through
a man. 22 For as in Adam all die, so in Christ all will be made alive.
23 But each in his own turn: Christ, the firstfruits; then, when he
comes, those who belong to him. 24 Then the end will come, when
he hands over the kingdom to God the Father after he has destroyed all dominion, authority and power. 25 For he must reign
until he has put all his enemies under his feet. 26 The last enemy
to be destroyed is death. 27 For he "has put everything under his
feet."[e] Now when it says that "everything" has been put under
him, it is clear that this does not include God himself, who put
everything under Christ. 28 When he has done this, then the Son
himself will be made subject to him who put everything under
him, so that God may be all in all.
29 Now if there is no resurrection, what will those do who are
baptized for the dead? If the dead are not raised at all, why are
people baptized for them? 30 And as for us, why do we endanger
ourselves every hour? 31 I die every day—I mean that, brothers—
just as surely as I glory over you in Christ Jesus our Lord. 32 If I
fought wild beasts in Ephesus for merely human reasons, what
have I gained? If the dead are not raised,

"Let us eat and drink,
for tomorrow we die."[f]

33 Do not be misled: "Bad company corrupts good character."
34 Come back to your senses as you ought, and stop sinning; for
there are some who are ignorant of God—I say this to your shame.

*The Resurrection Body*

35 But someone may ask, "How are the dead raised? With what
kind of body will they come?" 36 How foolish! What you sow does
not come to life unless it dies. 37 When you sow, you do not plant
the body that will be, but just a seed, perhaps of wheat or of
something else. 38 But God gives it a body as he has determined,
and to each kind of seed he gives its own body. 39 All flesh is not
the same: Men have one kind of flesh, animals have another, birds
another and fish another. 40 There are also heavenly bodies and
there are earthly bodies; but the splendor of the heavenly bodies
is one kind, and the splendor of the earthly bodies is another.
41 The sun has one kind of splendor, the moon another and the
stars another; and star differs from star in splendor.
42 So will it be with the resurrection of the dead. The body that
is sown is perishable, it is raised imperishable; 43 it is sown in
dishonor, it is raised in glory; it is sown in weakness, it is raised
in power; 44 it is sown a natural body, it is raised a spiritual body.

NIV [e] 27 Psalm 8:6 [f] 32 Isaiah 22:13

## King James

44It is sown a natural body; it is raised a spiritual body. There
is a natural body, and there is a spiritual body.
45And so it is written, The first man Adam was made a living
soul; the last Adam *was made* a quickening spirit.
46Howbeit that *was* not first which is spiritual, but that which
is natural; and afterward that which is spiritual.
47The first man *is* of the earth, earthy: the second man *is* the
Lord from heaven.
48As *is* the earthy, such *are* they also that are earthy: and as *is*
the heavenly, such *are* they also that are heavenly.
49And as we have borne the image of the earthy, we shall also
bear the image of the heavenly.
50Now this I say, brethren, that flesh and blood cannot inherit
the kingdom of God; neither doth corruption inherit incorruption.
51Behold, I show you a mystery; We shall not all sleep, but we
shall all be changed,
52In a moment, in the twinkling of an eye, at the last trump: for
the trumpet shall sound, and the dead shall be raised incorruptible, and we shall be changed.
53For this corruptible must put on incorruption, and this mortal
*must* put on immortality.
54So when this corruptible shall have put on incorruption, and
this mortal shall have put on immortality, then shall be brought to
pass the saying that is written, Death is swallowed up in victory.
55O death, where *is* thy sting? O grave, where *is* thy victory?
56The sting of death *is* sin; and the strength of sin *is* the law.
57But thanks *be* to God, which giveth us the victory through our
Lord Jesus Christ.
58Therefore, my beloved brethren, be ye stedfast, unmoveable,
always abounding in the work of the Lord, forasmuch as ye know
that your labour is not in vain in the Lord.

16 NOW CONCERNING the collection for the saints, as I
have given order to the churches of Galatia, even so do ye.
2Upon the first *day* of the week let every one of you lay by him
in store, as *God* hath prospered him, that there be no gatherings
when I come.
3And when I come, whomsoever ye shall approve by *your* letters, them will I send to bring your liberality unto Jerusalem.
4And if it be meet that I go also, they shall go with me.
5Now I will come unto you, when I shall pass through Macedonia: for I do pass through Macedonia.
6And it may be that I will abide, yea, and winter with you, that
ye may bring me on my journey whithersoever I go.
7For I will not see you now by the way; but I trust to tarry a while
with you, if the Lord permit.
8But I will tarry at Ephesus until Pentecost.

## Amplified

44It is sown a natural (physical) body; it is raised a supernatural
(a spiritual) body. [As surely as] there is a physical body, there is
also a spiritual body.
45Thus it is written, The first man Adam became a living being—an individual personality; the last Adam (Christ) became a
life-giving Spirit—restoring the dead to life.
46But [it is] not the spiritual life which came first, but the physical and then the spiritual.
47The first man [was] from out of earth, made of dust—earth-
minded; the second Man [is] *the Lord* from out of heaven. [Gen.
2:7.]
48Now those who are made of the dust are like him who was
first made of the dust—earth-minded; and as is [the Man] from
heaven, so also [are those] who are of heaven—heaven-minded.
49And just as we have borne the image of the [man] of dust, so
shall we *and* so [a]let us also bear the image of the [Man] of heaven.
50But I tell you this, brethren, flesh and blood cannot (become
partakers of eternal salvation and) inherit *or* share in the kingdom
of God; nor does the perishable—that which is decaying—inherit
*or* share in the imperishable (the immortal).
51Take notice! I tell you a mystery—a secret truth, an event
decreed by the hidden purpose or counsel of God. We shall not all
fall asleep [in death], but we shall all be changed (transformed)
52In a moment, in the twinkling of an eye, at the (sound of the)
last trumpet call. For a trumpet will sound, and the dead [in Christ]
will be raised imperishable—free and immune from decay—and
we shall be changed (transformed).
53For this perishable [part of us] must put on the imperishable
[nature], and this mortal [part of us]—this nature that is capable
of dying—must put on immortality (freedom from death).
54And when this perishable puts on the imperishable and this
[that was] capable of dying puts on freedom from death, then shall
be fulfilled the Scripture that says, Death is swallowed up (utterly
vanquished, [b]forever) in *and* unto victory. [Isa. 25:8.]
55O death, where is your victory? O death, where is your sting?
[Hos. 13:14.]
56Now sin is the sting of death, and sin exercises its power
[c][upon the soul] through [d][the abuse of] the Law.
57But thanks be to God, Who gives us the victory—making us
conquerors—through our Lord Jesus Christ.
58Therefore, my beloved brethren, be firm (steadfast), immovable, always abounding in the work of the Lord—that is, always
being superior (excelling, doing more than enough) in the service
of the Lord, knowing *and* being continually aware that your labor
in the Lord is not futile—never wasted or to no purpose.

16 NOW CONCERNING the money contributed for [the relief of] the saints (God's people): you are to do the same
as I directed the churches of Galatia to do.
2On the first [day] of each week, let everyone of you (personally) put aside something and save it up as he has prospered—in
proportion to what he is given—so that no collections will need to
be taken after I come.
3And when I arrive, I will send on those whom you approve *and*
authorize with credentials to carry your gift (of charity) to Jerusalem.
4If it seems worthwhile that I should go too, they will accompany me.
5After passing through Macedonia, I will visit you, for I intend
[only] to pass through Macedonia;
6But it may be that I will stay with you [for a while], perhaps
even spend the winter, so that you may bring me forward [on my
journey] to wherever I may go.
7For I am unwilling to see you right now [just] in passing, but
I hope later to remain for some time with you, if the Lord permits.
8I will remain in Ephesus [however] until Pentecost,

**AMP** [a] Many ancient authorities read "let us." [b] Vincent's "Word Studies in the New Testament." [c] Thayer. [d] Thayer.

## New American Standard

44it is sown a natural body, it is raised a spiritual body. If there is a natural body, there is also a spiritual *body*.

45So also it is written, "The first MAN, Adam, BECAME A LIVING SOUL." The last Adam *became* a life-giving spirit.

46However, the spiritual is not first, but the natural; then the spiritual.

47The first man is from the earth, earthy; the second man is from heaven.

48As is the earthy, so also are those who are earthy; and as is the heavenly, so also are those who are heavenly.

49And just as we have borne the image of the earthy, [e]we shall also bear the image of the heavenly.

*The Mystery of Resurrection*

50¶ Now I say this, brethren, that flesh and blood cannot inherit the kingdom of God; nor does the perishable inherit the imperishable.

51Behold, I tell you a mystery; we shall not all sleep, but we shall all be changed,

52in a moment, in the twinkling of an eye, at the last trumpet; for the trumpet will sound, and the dead will be raised imperishable, and we shall be changed.

53For this perishable must put on the imperishable, and this mortal must put on immortality.

54But when this perishable will have put on the imperishable, and this mortal will have put on immortality, then will come about the saying that is written, "DEATH IS SWALLOWED UP in victory.

55"O DEATH, WHERE IS YOUR VICTORY? O DEATH, WHERE IS YOUR STING?"

56The sting of death is sin, and the power of sin is the law;

57but thanks be to God, who gives us the victory through our Lord Jesus Christ.

58Therefore, my beloved brethren, be steadfast, immovable, always abounding in the work of the Lord, knowing that your toil is not *in* vain in the Lord.

## New International

If there is a natural body, there is also a spiritual body. 45So it
is written: "The first man Adam became a living being"[f]; the last
Adam, a life-giving spirit. 46The spiritual did not come first, but the
natural, and after that the spiritual. 47The first man was of the dust
of the earth, the second man from heaven. 48As was the earthly
man, so are those who are of the earth; and as is the man from
heaven, so also are those who are of heaven. 49And just as we have
borne the likeness of the earthly man, so shall we[g] bear the likeness of the man from heaven.

50I declare to you, brothers, that flesh and blood cannot inherit
the kingdom of God, nor does the perishable inherit the imperishable. 51Listen, I tell you a mystery: We will not all sleep, but we
will all be changed— 52in a flash, in the twinkling of an eye, at the
last trumpet. For the trumpet will sound, the dead will be raised
imperishable, and we will be changed. 53For the perishable must
clothe itself with the imperishable, and the mortal with immortality. 54When the perishable has been clothed with the imperishable,
and the mortal with immortality, then the saying that is written
will come true: "Death has been swallowed up in victory."[h]

> 55"Where, O death, is your victory?
> Where, O death, is your sting?"[i]

56The sting of death is sin, and the power of sin is the law. 57But
thanks be to God! He gives us the victory through our Lord Jesus
Christ.

58Therefore, my dear brothers, stand firm. Let nothing move
you. Always give yourselves fully to the work of the Lord, because
you know that your labor in the Lord is not in vain.

*Instructions and Greetings*

**16** NOW CONCERNING the collection for the saints, as I directed the churches of Galatia, so do you also.

2On the first day of every week let each one of you put aside and save, as he may prosper, that no collections be made when I come.

3And when I arrive, whomever you may approve, I shall send them with letters to carry your gift to Jerusalem;

4and if it is fitting for me to go also, they will go with me.

5But I shall come to you after I go through Macedonia, for I am going through Macedonia;

6and perhaps I shall stay with you, or even spend the winter, that you may send me on my way wherever I may go.

7For I do not wish to see you now *just* in passing; for I hope to remain with you for some time, if the Lord permits.

8But I shall remain in Ephesus until Pentecost;

*The Collection for God's People*

**16** NOW ABOUT the collection for God's people: Do what I
told the Galatian churches to do. 2On the first day of every
week, each one of you should set aside a sum of money in keeping
with his income, saving it up, so that when I come no collections
will have to be made. 3Then, when I arrive, I will give letters of
introduction to the men you approve and send them with your gift
to Jerusalem. 4If it seems advisable for me to go also, they will
accompany me.

*Personal Requests*

5After I go through Macedonia, I will come to you—for I will
be going through Macedonia. 6Perhaps I will stay with you awhile,
or even spend the winter, so that you can help me on my journey,
wherever I go. 7I do not want to see you now and make only a
passing visit; I hope to spend some time with you, if the Lord
permits. 8But I will stay on at Ephesus until Pentecost, 9because

NAS [e] Some ancient mss. read *let us also*

NIV [f] 45 Gen. 2:7 [g] 49 Some early manuscripts *so let us* [h] 54 Isaiah 25:8
[i] 55 Hosea 13:14

## King James

9 For a great door and effectual is opened unto me, and *there are* many adversaries.

10 Now if Timotheus come, see that he may be with you without fear: for he worketh the work of the Lord, as I also *do*.

11 Let no man therefore despise him: but conduct him forth in peace, that he may come unto me: for I look for him with the brethren.

12 As touching *our* brother Apollos, I greatly desired him to come unto you with the brethren: but his will was not at all to come at this time; but he will come when he shall have convenient time.

13 Watch ye, stand fast in the faith, quit you like men, be strong.

14 Let all your things be done with charity.

15 I beseech you, brethren, (ye know the house of Stephanas, that it is the firstfruits of Achaia, and *that* they have addicted themselves to the ministry of the saints,)

16 That ye submit yourselves unto such, and to every one that helpeth with *us*, and laboureth.

17 I am glad of the coming of Stephanas and Fortunatus and Achaicus: for that which was lacking on your part they have supplied.

18 For they have refreshed my spirit and yours: therefore acknowledge ye them that are such.

19 The churches of Asia salute you. Aquila and Priscilla salute you much in the Lord, with the church that is in their house.

20 All the brethren greet you. Greet ye one another with an holy kiss.

21 The salutation of *me* Paul with mine own hand.

22 If any man love not the Lord Jesus Christ, let him be Anathema Maranatha.

23 The grace of our Lord Jesus Christ *be* with you.

24 My love *be* with you all in Christ Jesus. Amen.

## Amplified

9 For a wide door of opportunity for effectual [service] has opened to me [there]—one great and promising—and many adversaries.

10 When Timothy arrives, look to it that [you put him at ease, so that] he may be fearless among you, for he is [devotedly] doing the Lord's work, just as I am.

11 [So see to it that] no one despises him, *or* treats him as if he were of no account *or* slights him. But send him off (cordially, speed him on his way) in peace that he may come to me, for I am expecting him [to come along] with the other brethren.

12 As for our brother Apollos, I have urgently encouraged him to visit you with the other brethren, but it was not at all (his will, or) [a]God's will that he should go now. He will come when he has opportunity.

13 Be alert *and* on your guard; stand firm in your faith [that is, in [b]your conviction respecting man's relationship to God and divine things, keeping the trust and holy fervor born of faith and a part of it]. Act like men *and* be courageous; grow in strength! [Ps. 31:24.]

14 Let everything you do be done in love [true love to God and man as inspired by God's love for us].

15 Now, brethren, you know that the household of Stephanas were the first converts *and* our first fruits in Achaia [most of Greece], and how they have consecrated *and* devoted themselves to the service of the saints (God's people).

16 I urge you to pay all deference to such leaders *and* to enlist under them *and* be subject to them, as well as to every one who joins *and* co-operates [with you] *and* labors earnestly.

17 I am happy because Stephanas and Fortunatus and Achaicus have come [to me], for they have made up for your absence.

18 For they gave me [c]respite from labor *and* rested me *and* refreshed my spirit as well as yours. Deeply appreciate *and* thoroughly know *and* fully recognize such men.

19 The churches of Asia send greetings *and* best wishes. Aquila and Prisca, together with the church [that meets] in their house, send you their hearty greetings in the Lord.

20 All the brethren wish to be remembered to you *and* wish you well. Greet one another with a holy kiss.

21 I, Paul, [add this final] greeting with my own hand.

22 If any one does not love the Lord—does not have a friendly affection for Him and is not kindly disposed toward Him—he shall be accursed! Our Lord will come! (Maranatha!)

23 The grace (favor and spiritual blessing) of our Lord Jesus *Christ* be with you.

24 My love [that true love growing out of sincere devotion to God] be with you all in Christ Jesus. *Amen—so be it.*

**AMP** [a] "His" may refer to Apollos, but probably means "God's." [b] Thayer. [c] Abbott-Smith.

## New American Standard

9for a wide door for effective *service* has opened to me, and
there are many adversaries.
10¶ Now if Timothy comes, see that he is with you without cause
to be afraid; for he is doing the Lord's work, as I also am.
11Let no one therefore despise him. But send him on his way
in peace, so that he may come to me; for I expect him with the
brethren.
12But concerning Apollos our brother, I encouraged him greatly
to come to you with the brethren; and it was not at all *his* desire
to come now, but he will come when he has opportunity.
13¶ Be on the alert, stand firm in the faith, act like men, be
strong.
14Let all that you do be done in love.
15¶ Now I urge you, brethren (you know the household of
Stephanas, that they were the first fruits of Achaia, and that they
have devoted themselves for ministry to the saints),
16that you also be in subjection to such men and to everyone
who helps in the work and labors.
17And I rejoice over the coming of Stephanas and Fortunatus
and Achaicus; because they have supplied what was lacking on
your part.
18For they have refreshed my spirit and yours. Therefore acknowledge such men.
19¶ The churches of Asia greet you. Aquila and Prisca greet you
heartily in the Lord, with the church that is in their house.
20All the brethren greet you. Greet one another with a holy kiss.
21¶ The greeting is in my own hand—Paul.
22If anyone does not love the Lord, let him be accursed.
Maranatha.
23The grace of the Lord Jesus be with you.
24My love be with you all in Christ Jesus. Amen.

## New International

a great door for effective work has opened to me, and there are
many who oppose me.
10If Timothy comes, see to it that he has nothing to fear while
he is with you, for he is carrying on the work of the Lord, just as
I am. 11No one, then, should refuse to accept him. Send him on
his way in peace so that he may return to me. I am expecting him
along with the brothers.
12Now about our brother Apollos: I strongly urged him to go to
you with the brothers. He was quite unwilling to go now, but he
will go when he has the opportunity.
13Be on your guard; stand firm in the faith; be men of courage;
be strong. 14Do everything in love.
15You know that the household of Stephanas were the first
converts in Achaia, and they have devoted themselves to the
service of the saints. I urge you, brothers, 16to submit to such as
these and to everyone who joins in the work, and labors at it. 17I
was glad when Stephanas, Fortunatus and Achaicus arrived, because they have supplied what was lacking from you. 18For they
refreshed my spirit and yours also. Such men deserve recognition.

*Final Greetings*

19The churches in the province of Asia send you greetings.
Aquila and Priscilla[d] greet you warmly in the Lord, and so does
the church that meets at their house. 20All the brothers here send
you greetings. Greet one another with a holy kiss.
21I, Paul, write this greeting in my own hand.
22If anyone does not love the Lord—a curse be on him. Come,
O Lord[e] !
23The grace of the Lord Jesus be with you.
24My love to all of you in Christ Jesus. Amen.[f]

**NIV** [d] 19 Greek *Prisca,* a variant of *Priscilla* [e] 22 In Aramaic the expression *Come, O Lord* is *Marana tha.* [f] 24 Some manuscripts do not have *Amen.*

## King James

THE SECOND EPISTLE OF
PAUL THE APOSTLE TO THE

# Corinthians

**1** PAUL, AN apostle of Jesus Christ by the will of God, and Timothy *our* brother, unto the church of God which is at Corinth, with all the saints which are in all Achaia:

2Grace *be* to you and peace from God our Father, and *from* the Lord Jesus Christ.

3Blessed *be* God, even the Father of our Lord Jesus Christ, the Father of mercies, and the God of all comfort;

4Who comforteth us in all our tribulation, that we may be able to comfort them which are in any trouble, by the comfort wherewith we ourselves are comforted of God.

5For as the sufferings of Christ abound in us, so our consolation also aboundeth by Christ.

6And whether we be afflicted, *it is* for your consolation and salvation, which is effectual in the enduring of the same sufferings which we also suffer: or whether we be comforted, *it is* for your consolation and salvation.

7And our hope of you *is* stedfast, knowing, that as ye are partakers of the sufferings, so *shall ye be* also of the consolation.

8For we would not, brethren, have you ignorant of our trouble which came to us in Asia, that we were pressed out of measure, above strength, insomuch that we despaired even of life:

9But we had the sentence of death in ourselves, that we should not trust in ourselves, but in God which raiseth the dead:

10Who delivered us from so great a death, and doth deliver: in whom we trust that he will yet deliver *us;*

11Ye also helping together by prayer for us, that for the gift *bestowed* upon us by the means of many persons thanks may be given by many on our behalf.

## Amplified

THE SECOND LETTER OF
PAUL TO THE

# Corinthians

**1** PAUL, AN apostle (a special messenger) of Christ Jesus by the will of God, and Timothy [our] brother, to the church (assembly) of God which is at Corinth, and to all the saints (the people of God) throughout Achaia [most of Greece]:

2Grace (favor and spiritual blessing) to you and (heart) peace from God our Father and the Lord Jesus Christ, the Messiah, the Anointed One.

3Blessed [be] the God and Father of our Lord Jesus Christ, the Father of sympathy (pity and mercies) and the God [Who is the Source] of every consolation *and* comfort *and* encouragement;

4Who consoles *and* comforts *and* encourages us in every trouble (calamity and affliction), so that we may also be able to console (comfort and encourage) those who are in any kind of trouble *or* distress, with the consolation (comfort and encouragement) with which we ourselves are consoled *and* comforted *and* encouraged by God.

5For just as Christ's ( [a]own) sufferings fall to our lot [b][as they overflow upon His disciples, and we share and experience them] abundantly, so through Christ comfort *and* consolation *and* encouragement are also [shared and experienced] abundantly by us.

6But if we are troubled (afflicted and distressed), it is for your comfort (consolation and encouragement) and [for your] salvation; and if we are comforted (consoled and encouraged), it is for your comfort *and* consolation *and* encouragement, which work [in you when you] patiently endure the same evils (misfortunes and calamities) that we also suffer *and* undergo.

7And our hope for you—that is, our joyful and confident expectation of good for you—is ever unwavering, (assured and unshaken); for we know that just as you share *and* are partners in [our] sufferings *and* calamities, you also share *and* are partners in [our] comfort (consolation and encouragement).

8For we do not want you to be uninformed, brethren, about the affliction *and* oppressing distress which befell us in [the province of] Asia, how we were so utterly and unbearably weighed down *and* crushed that we despaired even of life [itself].

9Indeed, we felt within ourselves that we had received the [very] sentence of death; but that was to keep us from trusting *and* depending on ourselves instead of on God Who raises the dead.

10[For it is He] Who rescued *and* saved us from such a perilous death, and He will still rescue *and* save us; in *and* on Him we have set our hope (our joyful and confident expectation) that He will again deliver us from danger *and* destruction *and* [c]draw [us] to Himself,

11While you also co-operate by your prayers for us—helping *and* laboring together with us. Thus the lips of many persons Godward turned will [eventually] give thanks on our behalf for the grace (the blessing of deliverance) granted us at the request of the many who have prayed.

**AMP** [a] Vincent's "Word Studies in the New Testament." [b] Vincent's "Word Studies in the New Testament." [c] Primary meaning, "to draw to one's self." (Thayer.)

## New American Standard

# 2 Corinthians

*Introduction*

1 PAUL, AN apostle of Christ Jesus by the will of God, and
Timothy *our* brother, to the church of God which is at Corinth
with all the saints who are throughout Achaia:
2Grace to you and peace from God our Father and the Lord
Jesus Christ.
3¶ Blessed *be* the God and Father of our Lord Jesus Christ, the
Father of mercies and God of all comfort;
4who comforts us in all our affliction so that we may be able
to comfort those who are in any affliction with the comfort with
which we ourselves are comforted by God.
5For just as the sufferings of Christ are ours in abundance, so
also our comfort is abundant through Christ.
6But if we are afflicted, it is for your comfort and salvation; or
if we are comforted, it is for your comfort, which is effective in the
patient enduring of the same sufferings which we also suffer;
7and our hope for you is firmly grounded, knowing that as you
are sharers of our sufferings, so also you are *sharers* of our comfort.
8For we do not want you to be unaware, brethren, of our
affliction which came *to us* in Asia, that we were burdened excessively, beyond our strength, so that we despaired even of life;
9indeed, we had the sentence of death within ourselves in
order that we should not trust in ourselves, but in God who raises
the dead;
10who delivered us from so great a *peril of* death, and will deliver
*us,* He on whom we have set our hope. And He will yet deliver
us,
11you also joining in helping us through your prayers, that
thanks may be given by many persons on our behalf for the favor
bestowed upon us through *the prayers of* many.

## New International

# 2 Corinthians

1 PAUL, AN apostle of Christ Jesus by the will of God, and
Timothy our brother,

To the church of God in Corinth, together with all the saints
throughout Achaia:

2Grace and peace to you from God our Father and the Lord
Jesus Christ.

*The God of All Comfort*

3Praise be to the God and Father of our Lord Jesus Christ, the
Father of compassion and the God of all comfort, 4who comforts
us in all our troubles, so that we can comfort those in any trouble
with the comfort we ourselves have received from God. 5For just
as the sufferings of Christ flow over into our lives, so also through
Christ our comfort overflows. 6If we are distressed, it is for your
comfort and salvation; if we are comforted, it is for your comfort,
which produces in you patient endurance of the same sufferings
we suffer. 7And our hope for you is firm, because we know that
just as you share in our sufferings, so also you share in our comfort.

8We do not want you to be uninformed, brothers, about the
hardships we suffered in the province of Asia. We were under
great pressure, far beyond our ability to endure, so that we despaired even of life. 9Indeed, in our hearts we felt the sentence of
death. But this happened that we might not rely on ourselves but
on God, who raises the dead. 10He has delivered us from such a
deadly peril, and he will deliver us. On him we have set our hope
that he will continue to deliver us, 11as you help us by your
prayers. Then many will give thanks on our[d] behalf for the gracious favor granted us in answer to the prayers of many.

NIV [d] *11* Many manuscripts *your*

## King James

12For our rejoicing is this, the testimony of our conscience, that in simplicity and godly sincerity, not with fleshly wisdom, but by the grace of God, we have had our conversation in the world, and more abundantly to you-ward.

13For we write none other things unto you, than what ye read or acknowledge; and I trust ye shall acknowledge even to the end;

14As also ye have acknowledged us in part, that we are your rejoicing, even as ye also *are* ours in the day of the Lord Jesus.

15And in this confidence I was minded to come unto you before, that ye might have a second benefit;

16And to pass by you into Macedonia, and to come again out of Macedonia unto you, and of you to be brought on my way toward Judaea.

17When I therefore was thus minded, did I use lightness? or the things that I purpose, do I purpose according to the flesh, that with me there should be yea yea, and nay nay?

18But *as* God *is* true, our word toward you was not yea and nay.

19For the Son of God, Jesus Christ, who was preached among you by us, *even* by me and Silvanus and Timotheus, was not yea and nay, but in him was yea.

20For all the promises of God in him *are* yea, and in him Amen, unto the glory of God by us.

21Now he which stablisheth us with you in Christ, and hath anointed us, *is* God;

22Who hath also sealed us, and given the earnest of the Spirit in our hearts.

23Moreover I call God for a record upon my soul, that to spare you I came not as yet unto Corinth.

24Not for that we have dominion over your faith, but are helpers of your joy: for by faith ye stand.

**2** BUT I determined this with myself, that I would not come again to you in heaviness.

2For if I make you sorry, who is he then that maketh me glad, but the same which is made sorry by me?

3And I wrote this same unto you, lest, when I came, I should have sorrow from them of whom I ought to rejoice; having confidence in you all, that my joy is *the joy* of you all.

4For out of much affliction and anguish of heart I wrote unto you with many tears; not that ye should be grieved, but that ye might know the love which I have more abundantly unto you.

## Amplified

12It is a reason for pride *and* exultation to which our conscience testifies, that we have conducted ourselves in the world [generally] and more especially toward you, with devout *and* pure motives and godly sincerity, not in fleshly wisdom but by the grace of God—the unmerited favor and [a]merciful kindness [by which God exerting His holy influence upon souls, turns them to Christ, and keeps, strengthens and increases them in Christian virtues].

13For we write you nothing else but simply what you can read and understand—that is, there is no double meaning to what we say—and I hope that you will become thoroughly acquainted [with [b]divine things] *and* know *and* understand [them] accurately *and* well to the end,

14[Just] as you have (already) partially known *and* understood *and* acknowledged us *and* recognized that you can [honestly] be proud of us, even as we [can be proud] of you on the day of our Lord Jesus.

15It was with assurance of this that I wanted *and* planned to visit you first [of all], so that you might have a double *favor and* token of grace (good will).

16[I wanted] to visit you on my way to Macedonia, and [then] to come again to you [on my return trip] from Macedonia and have you send me forward on my way to Judea.

17Now because I changed my original plan was I being unstable *and* capricious? Or what I plan do I plan according to the flesh—like a worldly man—ready to say Yes, yes, [when it may mean] No, no?

18As surely as God is trustworthy *and* faithful *and* means what He says, our speech *and* message to you have not been Yes [that might mean] No.

19For the Son of God, Christ Jesus, the Messiah, Who has been preached among you by us, by myself, Silvanus and Timothy, was not Yes and No; but in Him it is [always the divine] Yes.

20For as many as are the promises of God, they all find their Yes (answer) in Him (Christ). For this reason we also utter the Amen (so be it) to God through Him—that is, in His Person and by His agency—to the glory of God.

21But it is God Who confirms *and* makes us steadfast *and* establishes us (in joint fellowship) with you in Christ, and has consecrated *and* anointed us— [c]enduing us with the gifts of the Holy Spirit.

22[He has also appropriated and acknowledged us as His], putting His seal upon us and giving us His (Holy) Spirit in our hearts as the security deposit *and* guarantee [of the fulfillment of His promise].

23But I call upon God as my soul's witness, it was to avoid hurting you that I refrained from coming to Corinth;

24Not that we have dominion [over you] *and* lord it over your faith, but (rather that we work with you as) fellow laborers [to promote] your joy, for in [your] faith [that is, [d]in your strong and welcome conviction or belief that Jesus is the Messiah, through Whom we obtain eternal salvation in the kingdom of God] you stand firm.

**2** BUT I definitely made up my mind not to grieve you with another painful *and* distressing visit.

2For if I cause you pain [with merited rebuke], who is there to provide me enjoyment but the [very] one whom I have grieved *and* made sad?

3And I wrote the same to you so that when I came I might not be myself pained by those who are the [very] ones who ought to make me glad, for I trusted in you all *and* felt confident that my joy would be shared by all of you.

4For I wrote you out of great sorrow and deep distress (with mental torture and anxiety) of heart, [yes, and] with many tears, not to cause you pain but in order to make you realize the overflowing love that I continue increasingly to have for you.

**AMP** [a] Thayer's "Greek-English Lexicon of the New Testament—Grimm." [b] Thayer's "Greek-English Lexicon of the New Testament—Grimm." [c] Thayer. [d] Cf. Westcott on I John 2:20.

## New American Standard

*Paul's Integrity*

12¶ For our proud confidence is this, the testimony of our conscience, that in holiness and godly sincerity, not in fleshly wisdom but in the grace of God, we have conducted ourselves in the world, and especially toward you.

13For we write nothing else to you than what you read and understand, and I hope you will understand until the end;

14just as you also partially did understand us, that we are your reason to be proud as you also are ours, in the day of our Lord Jesus.

15¶ And in this confidence I intended at first to come to you, that you might twice receive a blessing;

16that is, to pass your way into Macedonia, and again from Macedonia to come to you, and by you to be helped on my journey to Judea.

17Therefore, I was not vacillating when I intended to do this, was I? Or that which I purpose, do I purpose according to the flesh, that with me there should be yes, yes and no, no *at the same time*?

18But as God is faithful, our word to you is not yes and no.

19For the Son of God, Christ Jesus, who was preached among you by us—by me and Silvanus and Timothy—was not yes and no, but is yes in Him.

20For as many as may be the promises of God, in Him they are yes; wherefore also by Him is our Amen to the glory of God through us.

21Now He who establishes us with you in Christ and anointed us is God,

22who also sealed us and gave *us* the Spirit in our hearts as a pledge.

23¶ But I call God as witness to my soul, that to spare you I came no more to Corinth.

24Not that we lord it over your faith, but are workers with you for your joy; for in your faith you are standing firm.

*Reaffirm Your Love*

**2** BUT I determined this for my own sake, that I would not come to you in sorrow again.

2For if I cause you sorrow, who then makes me glad but the one whom I made sorrowful?

3And this is the very thing I wrote you, lest, when I came, I should have sorrow from those who ought to make me rejoice; having confidence in you all, that my joy would be *the joy* of you all.

4For out of much affliction and anguish of heart I wrote to you with many tears; not that you should be made sorrowful, but that you might know the love which I have especially for you.

## New International

*Paul's Change of Plans*

12Now this is our boast: Our conscience testifies that we have
conducted ourselves in the world, and especially in our relations
with you, in the holiness and sincerity that are from God. We have
done so not according to worldly wisdom but according to God's
grace. 13For we do not write you anything you cannot read or
understand. And I hope that, 14as you have understood us in part,
you will come to understand fully that you can boast of us just as
we will boast of you in the day of the Lord Jesus.
15Because I was confident of this, I planned to visit you first so
that you might benefit twice. 16I planned to visit you on my way
to Macedonia and to come back to you from Macedonia, and then
to have you send me on my way to Judea. 17When I planned this,
did I do it lightly? Or do I make my plans in a worldly manner so
that in the same breath I say, "Yes, yes" and "No, no"?
18But as surely as God is faithful, our message to you is not
"Yes" and "No." 19For the Son of God, Jesus Christ, who was
preached among you by me and Silas[e] and Timothy, was not
"Yes" and "No," but in him it has always been "Yes." 20For no
matter how many promises God has made, they are "Yes" in
Christ. And so through him the "Amen" is spoken by us to the
glory of God. 21Now it is God who makes both us and you stand
firm in Christ. He anointed us, 22set his seal of ownership on us,
and put his Spirit in our hearts as a deposit, guaranteeing what is
to come.
23I call God as my witness that it was in order to spare you that
I did not return to Corinth. 24Not that we lord it over your faith,
but we work with you for your joy, because it is by faith you stand
firm.

**2** SO I made up my mind that I would not make another painful
visit to you. 2For if I grieve you, who is left to make me glad
but you whom I have grieved? 3I wrote as I did so that when I came
I should not be distressed by those who ought to make me rejoice.
I had confidence in all of you, that you would all share my joy. 4For
I wrote you out of great distress and anguish of heart and with
many tears, not to grieve you but to let you know the depth of my
love for you.

NIV [e] 19 Greek *Silvanus*, a variant of *Silas*

## King James

5 But if any have caused grief, he hath not grieved me, but in part: that I may not overcharge you all.

6 Sufficient to such a man *is* this punishment, which *was inflicted* of many.

7 So that contrariwise ye *ought* rather to forgive *him*, and comfort *him*, lest perhaps such a one should be swallowed up with overmuch sorrow.

8 Wherefore I beseech you that ye would confirm *your* love toward him.

9 For to this end also did I write, that I might know the proof of you, whether ye be obedient in all things.

10 To whom ye forgive any thing, I *forgive* also: for if I forgave any thing, to whom I forgave *it*, for your sakes *forgave I it* in the person of Christ;

11 Lest Satan should get an advantage of us: for we are not ignorant of his devices.

12 Furthermore, when I came to Troas to *preach* Christ's gospel, and a door was opened unto me of the Lord,

13 I had no rest in my spirit, because I found not Titus my brother: but taking my leave of them, I went from thence into Macedonia.

14 Now thanks *be* unto God, which always causeth us to triumph in Christ, and maketh manifest the savour of his knowledge by us in every place.

15 For we are unto God a sweet savour of Christ, in them that are saved, and in them that perish:

16 To the one *we are* the savour of death unto death; and to the other the savour of life unto life. And who *is* sufficient for these things?

17 For we are not as many, which corrupt the word of God: but as of sincerity, but as of God, in the sight of God speak we in Christ.

## Amplified

5 But if some one [the one among you who committed incest] has caused [all this] grief *and* pain, he has caused it not to me, but in some measure, not to put it too severely, [he has distressed] all of you.

6 For such a one this censure by the majority [which he has received is] sufficient [punishment].

7 So [instead of further rebuke, now] you should rather turn *and* (graciously) forgive and comfort *and* encourage [him], to keep him from being overwhelmed by excessive sorrow *and* despair.

8 I therefore beg you to reinstate him in your affections *and* assure him by your love for him;

9 For this is my purpose in writing you, to test your attitude *and* see if you would stand the test, whether you are obedient *and* altogether agreeable [to following my orders] in everything.

10 If you forgive any one anything, I too forgive that one; and what I have forgiven, if I have forgiven anything, has been for your sakes in the presence [and with the approval] of Christ, the Messiah,

11 To keep Satan from getting the advantage over us; for we are not ignorant of his wiles *and* intentions.

12 Now when I arrived at Troas [to preach] the good news (the Gospel) of Christ, a door of opportunity was opened for me in the Lord,

13 Yet my spirit could not rest (relax, get relief) because I did not find my brother Titus there. So I took leave from them *and* departed for Macedonia.

14 But thanks be to God, Who in Christ always leads us in triumph—as trophies of Christ's victory—and through us spreads *and* makes evident the fragrance of the knowledge of God everywhere,

15 For we are the sweet fragrance of Christ [which exhales] unto God, [discernible alike] among those who are being saved *and* among those who are perishing:

16 To the latter it is an aroma [wafted] from death to death—a fatal odor, the smell of doom; to the former it is an aroma from life to life—a vital fragrance, living and fresh. And who is qualified (fit and sufficient) for these things?—Who is able for such a ministry? [We?]

17 For we are not, like so many (as hucksters, tavern keepers, making a trade of) peddling God's Word—short-measuring and adulterating the divine message; but as [men] of sincerity *and* the purest motive, commissioned *and* sent by God, we speak [His message] in Christ, the Messiah, in the [very] sight *and* presence of God.

## King James

**3** DO WE begin again to commend ourselves? or need we, as some *others*, epistles of commendation to you, or *letters* of commendation from you?

2 Ye are our epistle written in our hearts, known and read of all men:

3 *Forasmuch as ye are* manifestly declared to be the epistle of Christ ministered by us, written not with ink, but with the Spirit of the living God; not in tables of stone, but in fleshy tables of the heart.

4 And such trust have we through Christ to God-ward:

5 Not that we are sufficient of ourselves to think any thing as of ourselves; but our sufficiency *is* of God;

6 Who also hath made us able ministers of the new testament; not of the letter, but of the spirit: for the letter killeth, but the spirit giveth life.

## Amplified

**3** ARE WE starting to commend ourselves again? Or we do not, as some [false teachers], need written credentials *or* letters of recommendation to you or from you, [do we]?

2 [No, you] yourselves are our letter of recommendation (our credentials), written in [a]your hearts, to be (perceived, recognized,) known and read by everybody.

3 You show *and* make obvious that you are a letter from Christ delivered by us, not written with ink but with [the] Spirit of [the] living God, not on tablets of stone but on tablets of human hearts. [Exod. 24:12; 31:18; 32:15, 16; Jer. 31:33.]

4 Such is the reliance *and* confidence that we have through Christ toward *and* with reference to God.

5 Not that we are fit (qualified and sufficient in ability) of ourselves to form personal judgments *or* to claim *or* count anything as coming from us; but our power *and* ability *and* sufficiency are from God.

6 [It is He] Who has qualified us (making us to be fit and worthy and sufficient) as ministers *and* dispensers of a new covenant [of salvation through Christ], not [ministers] of the letter—that is, of legally written code—but of the Spirit; for the code [of the Law] kills, but the (Holy) Spirit makes alive. [Jer. 31:31.]

**AMP** [a] Many ancient authorities read "our."

## New American Standard

5¶ But if any has caused sorrow, he has caused sorrow not to me, but in some degree—in order not to say too much—to all of you.

6Sufficient for such a one is this punishment which was *inflicted by* the majority,

7so that on the contrary you should rather forgive and comfort *him,* lest somehow such a one be overwhelmed by excessive sorrow.

8Wherefore I urge you to reaffirm *your* love for him.

9For to this end also I wrote that I might put you to the test, whether you are obedient in all things.

10But whom you forgive anything, I *forgive* also; for indeed what I have forgiven, if I have forgiven anything, *I did it* for your sakes in the presence of Christ,

11in order that no advantage be taken of us by Satan; for we are not ignorant of his schemes.

12¶ Now when I came to Troas for the gospel of Christ and when a door was opened for me in the Lord,

13I had no rest for my spirit, not finding Titus my brother; but taking my leave of them, I went on to Macedonia.

14¶ But thanks be to God, who always leads us in His triumph in Christ, and manifests through us the sweet aroma of the knowledge of Him in every place.

15For we are a fragrance of Christ to God among those who are being saved and among those who are perishing;

16to the one an aroma from death to death, to the other an aroma from life to life. And who is adequate for these things?

17For we are not like many, [b]peddling the word of God, but as from sincerity, but as from God, we speak in Christ in the sight of God.

*Ministers of a New Covenant*

3 ARE WE beginning to commend ourselves again? Or do we need, as some, letters of commendation to you or from you?

2You are our letter, written in our hearts, known and read by all men;

3being manifested that you are a letter of Christ, cared for by us, written not with ink, but with the Spirit of the living God, not on tablets of stone, but on tablets of human hearts.

4And such confidence we have through Christ toward God.

5Not that we are adequate in ourselves to consider anything as *coming* from ourselves, but our adequacy is from God,

6who also made us adequate *as* servants of a new covenant, not of the letter, but of the Spirit; for the letter kills, but the Spirit gives life.

**NAS** [b] Or, *corrupting*

## New International

*Forgiveness for the Sinner*

5If anyone has caused grief, he has not so much grieved me as
he has grieved all of you, to some extent—not to put it too severely.
6The punishment inflicted on him by the majority is sufficient for
him. 7Now instead, you ought to forgive and comfort him, so that
he will not be overwhelmed by excessive sorrow. 8I urge you,
therefore, to reaffirm your love for him. 9The reason I wrote you
was to see if you would stand the test and be obedient in everything. 10If you forgive anyone, I also forgive him. And what I have
forgiven—if there was anything to forgive—I have forgiven in the
sight of Christ for your sake, 11in order that Satan might not outwit
us. For we are not unaware of his schemes.

*Ministers of the New Covenant*

12Now when I went to Troas to preach the gospel of Christ and
found that the Lord had opened a door for me, 13I still had no
peace of mind, because I did not find my brother Titus there. So
I said good-by to them and went on to Macedonia.

14But thanks be to God, who always leads us in triumphal
procession in Christ and through us spreads everywhere the fragrance of the knowledge of him. 15For we are to God the aroma
of Christ among those who are being saved and those who are
perishing. 16To the one we are the smell of death; to the other, the
fragrance of life. And who is equal to such a task? 17Unlike so
many, we do not peddle the word of God for profit. On the
contrary, in Christ we speak before God with sincerity, like men
sent from God.

3 ARE WE beginning to commend ourselves again? Or do we
need, like some people, letters of recommendation to you or
from you? 2You yourselves are our letter, written on our hearts,
known and read by everybody. 3You show that you are a letter
from Christ, the result of our ministry, written not with ink but
with the Spirit of the living God, not on tablets of stone but on
tablets of human hearts.

4Such confidence as this is ours through Christ before God.
5Not that we are competent in ourselves to claim anything for
ourselves, but our competence comes from God. 6He has made us
competent as ministers of a new covenant—not of the letter but of
the Spirit; for the letter kills, but the Spirit gives life.

## King James

7 But if the ministration of death, written *and* engraven in stones,
was glorious, so that the children of Israel could not stedfastly
behold the face of Moses for the glory of his countenance; which
*glory* was to be done away:
8 How shall not the ministration of the spirit be rather glorious?
9 For if the ministration of condemnation *be* glory, much more
doth the ministration of righteousness exceed in glory.
10 For even that which was made glorious had no glory in this
respect, by reason of the glory that excelleth.
11 For if that which is done away *was* glorious, much more that
which remaineth *is* glorious.
12 Seeing then that we have such hope, we use great plainness
of speech:
13 And not as Moses, *which* put a veil over his face, that the
children of Israel could not stedfastly look to the end of that which
is abolished:
14 But their minds were blinded: for until this day remaineth the
same veil untaken away in the reading of the old testament; which
*veil* is done away in Christ.
15 But even unto this day, when Moses is read, the veil is upon
their heart.
16 Nevertheless when it shall turn to the Lord, the veil shall be
taken away.
17 Now the Lord is that Spirit: and where the Spirit of the Lord
*is*, there *is* liberty.
18 But we all, with open face beholding as in a glass the glory
of the Lord, are changed into the same image from glory to glory,
*even* as by the Spirit of the Lord.

**4** THEREFORE SEEING we have this ministry, as we have
received mercy, we faint not;
2 But have renounced the hidden things of dishonesty, not
walking in craftiness, nor handling the word of God deceitfully;
but by manifestation of the truth commending ourselves to every
man's conscience in the sight of God.
3 But if our gospel be hid, it is hid to them that are lost:
4 In whom the god of this world hath blinded the minds of them
which believe not, lest the light of the glorious gospel of Christ,
who is the image of God, should shine unto them.
5 For we preach not ourselves, but Christ Jesus the Lord; and
ourselves your servants for Jesus' sake.

## Amplified

7 Now if (the ministration of the Law,) the dispensation of death
engraved in letters on stone, was inaugurated with such glory *and*
splendor that the Israelities were not able to look steadily at the
face of Moses because of its brilliance, (a glory) that was to fade
*and* pass away, [Exod. 34:29-35.]
8 Why should not the dispensation of the Spirit [that is, this
spiritual [a]ministry whose task it is to cause men to obtain and be
governed by the Holy Spirit] be attended with much greater *and*
more splendid glory?
9 For if the service that condemns, (the ministration of doom,)
had glory, how infinitely more abounding in splendor *and* glory
must be the service that makes righteous—the ministry that produces and fosters righteous living and right standing with God!
10 Indeed, in view of this fact, what once had splendor [ [b]the
glory of the Law in the face of Moses] has come to have no splendor
at all, because of the overwhelming glory that exceeds *and* excels
it, [ [c]the glory of the Gospel in the face of Jesus Christ].
11 For if that which was but passing *and* fading away came with
splendor, how much more must that abide in glory *and* splendor
which remains *and* is permanent!
12 Since we have such [glorious] hope—such [joyful and confi-
dent] expectation—we speak very freely *and* openly *and* fearlessly.
13 Nor [do we act] like Moses, who put a veil over his face so that
the Israelites might not gaze upon the finish of the vanishing
[splendor which had been upon it].
14 In fact, their minds were grown hard *and* calloused—they had
become dull and had lost the power of understanding; for until this
present day, when the Old Testament [the old covenant] is being
read, that same veil still lies [on their hearts], not being lifted [to
reveal] that in Christ it is made void *and* done away.
15 Yes, down to this [very] day whenever Moses is read a veil
lies upon their minds *and* hearts.
16 But whenever a person turns (in repentance) to the Lord the
veil is stripped off *and* taken away.
17 Now the Lord is the Spirit, and where the Spirit of the Lord
is, there is liberty—emancipation from bondage, freedom. [Isa.
61:1, 2.]
18 And all of us, as with unveiled face, [because we] continued
to behold [in the Word of God] as in a mirror the glory of the Lord,
are constantly being transfigured into His *very own* image in ever
increasing splendor *and* from one degree of glory to another; [for
this comes] from the Lord [Who is] the Spirit.

**4** THEREFORE, SINCE we do hold *and* engage in this ministry
by the mercy of God [granting us favor, benefits, opportu-
nities and especially salvation], we do not get discouraged—spiritless and despondent with fear, or become faint with weariness and
exhaustion.
2 We have renounced disgraceful ways—secret thoughts, feelings, desires and underhandedness, methods and arts that men
hide through shame; we refuse to deal craftily (to practice trickery
and cunning) or to adulterate *or* handle dishonestly the Word of
God; but we state the truth openly—clearly and candidly. And so
we commend ourselves in the sight *and* presence of God to every
man's conscience.
3 But even if our Gospel (the glad tidings) also be hid—obscured
and covered up with a veil [that hinders the knowledge of God]—it
is hid [only] to those who are perishing, *and* obscured [only] to
those who are spiritually dying, *and* veiled [only] to those who are
lost.
4 For the god of this world has blinded the unbelievers' minds
(that they should not discern the truth), preventing them from
seeing the illuminating light of the Gospel of the glory of Christ,
the Messiah, Who is the image *and* likeness of God.
5 For what we preach is not ourselves, but Jesus Christ as Lord,
and ourselves [merely] as your servants (slaves) for Jesus' sake.

**AMP** [a] Thayer. [b] Vincent's "Word Studies in the New Testament."
[c] Vincent's "Word Studies in the New Testament."

## New American Standard

7But if the ministry of death, in letters engraved on stones, came with glory, so that the sons of Israel could not look intently at the face of Moses because of the glory of his face, fading *as* it was,

8how shall the ministry of the Spirit fail to be even more with glory?

9For if the ministry of condemnation has glory, much more does the ministry of righteousness abound in glory.

10For indeed what had glory, in this case has no glory on account of the glory that surpasses *it*.

11For if that which fades away *was* with glory, much more that which remains *is* in glory.

12¶ Having therefore such a hope, we use great boldness in *our* speech,

13and *are* not as Moses, *who* used to put a veil over his face that the sons of Israel might not look intently at the end of what was fading away.

14But their minds were hardened; for until this very day at the reading of the old covenant the same veil remains unlifted, because it is removed in Christ.

15But to this day whenever Moses is read, a veil lies over their heart;

16but whenever a man turns to the Lord, the veil is taken away.

17Now the Lord is the Spirit; and where the Spirit of the Lord is, *there* is liberty.

18But we all, with unveiled face beholding as in a mirror the glory of the Lord, are being transformed into the same image from glory to glory, just as from the Lord, the Spirit.

*Paul's Apostolic Ministry*

**4** THEREFORE, SINCE we have this ministry, as we received mercy, we do not lose heart,

2but we have renounced the things hidden because of shame, not walking in craftiness or adulterating the word of God, but by the manifestation of truth commending ourselves to every man's conscience in the sight of God.

3And even if our gospel is veiled, it is veiled to those who are perishing,

4in whose case the god of this world has blinded the minds of the unbelieving, that they might not see the light of the gospel of the glory of Christ, who is the image of God.

5For we do not preach ourselves but Christ Jesus as Lord, and ourselves as your bond-servants for Jesus' sake.

## New International

*The Glory of the New Covenant*

7Now if the ministry that brought death, which was engraved
in letters on stone, came with glory, so that the Israelites could not
look steadily at the face of Moses because of its glory, fading
though it was, 8will not the ministry of the Spirit be even more
glorious? 9If the ministry that condemns men is glorious, how
much more glorious is the ministry that brings righteousness!
10For what was glorious has no glory now in comparison with the
surpassing glory. 11And if what was fading away came with glory,
how much greater is the glory of that which lasts!

12Therefore, since we have such a hope, we are very bold. 13We
are not like Moses, who would put a veil over his face to keep the
Israelites from gazing at it while the radiance was fading away.
14But their minds were made dull, for to this day the same veil
remains when the old covenant is read. It has not been removed,
because only in Christ is it taken away. 15Even to this day when
Moses is read, a veil covers their hearts. 16But whenever anyone
turns to the Lord, the veil is taken away. 17Now the Lord is the
Spirit, and where the Spirit of the Lord is, there is freedom. 18And
we, who with unveiled faces all reflect[d] the Lord's glory, are being
transformed into his likeness with ever-increasing glory, which
comes from the Lord, who is the Spirit.

*Treasures in Jars of Clay*

**4** THEREFORE, SINCE through God's mercy we have this ministry, we do not lose heart. 2Rather, we have renounced secret
and shameful ways; we do not use deception, nor do we distort
the word of God. On the contrary, by setting forth the truth plainly
we commend ourselves to every man's conscience in the sight of
God. 3And even if our gospel is veiled, it is veiled to those who
are perishing. 4The god of this age has blinded the minds of
unbelievers, so that they cannot see the light of the gospel of the
glory of Christ, who is the image of God. 5For we do not preach
ourselves, but Jesus Christ as Lord, and ourselves as your servants
for Jesus' sake. 6For God, who said, "Let light shine out of dark-

NIV [d] 18 Or *contemplate*

## King James

6For God, who commanded the light to shine out of darkness, hath shined in our hearts, to *give* the light of the knowledge of the glory of God in the face of Jesus Christ.

7But we have this treasure in earthen vessels, that the excellency of the power may be of God, and not of us.

8 *We are* troubled on every side, yet not distressed; *we are* perplexed, but not in despair;

9Persecuted, but not forsaken; cast down, but not destroyed;

10Always bearing about in the body the dying of the Lord Jesus, that the life also of Jesus might be made manifest in our body.

11For we which live are always delivered unto death for Jesus' sake, that the life also of Jesus might be made manifest in our mortal flesh.

12So then death worketh in us, but life in you.

13We having the same spirit of faith, according as it is written, I believed, and therefore have I spoken; we also believe, and therefore speak;

14Knowing that he which raised up the Lord Jesus shall raise up us also by Jesus, and shall present *us* with you.

15For all things *are* for your sakes, that the abundant grace might through the thanksgiving of many redound to the glory of God.

16For which cause we faint not; but though our outward man perish, yet the inward *man* is renewed day by day.

17For our light affliction, which is but for a moment, worketh for us a far more exceeding *and* eternal weight of glory;

18While we look not at the things which are seen, but at the things which are not seen: for the things which are seen *are* temporal; but the things which are not seen *are* eternal.

5 FOR WE know that if our earthly house of *this* tabernacle were dissolved, we have a building of God, an house not made with hands, eternal in the heavens.

2For in this we groan, earnestly desiring to be clothed upon with our house which is from heaven:

3If so be that being clothed we shall not be found naked.

4For we that are in *this* tabernacle do groan, being burdened: not for that we would be unclothed, but clothed upon, that mortality might be swallowed up of life.

5Now he that hath wrought us for the selfsame thing *is* God, who also hath given unto us the earnest of the Spirit.

## Amplified

6For God Who said, Let light shine out of darkness, has shone in our hearts so as [to beam forth] the Light for the illumination of the knowledge of the majesty *and* glory of God [as it is manifest in the Person and is revealed] in the face of *Jesus* Christ, the Messiah. [Gen. 1:3.]

7However, we possess this precious treasure [the divine Light of the Gospel] in [frail, human] vessels of earth, that the grandeur *and* exceeding greatness of the power may be shown to be of God and not from ourselves.

8We are hedged in (pressed) on every side—troubled and oppressed in every way; but not cramped *or* crushed; we suffer embarrassments *and* are perplexed *and* unable to find a way out, but not driven to despair;

9We are (persecuted and hard driven,) pursued, but not deserted—to stand alone; we are struck down to the ground, but never struck out *and* destroyed;

10Always carrying about in the body the liability *and* exposure to the same putting to death that *the Lord* Jesus suffered, so that the [ [a]resurrection-] life of Jesus also may be shown forth by *and* in our bodies.

11For we who live are constantly [experiencing] being handed over to death for Jesus' sake, that the [ [b]resurrection-] life of Jesus also may be evidenced through our flesh which is liable to death.

12Thus death is actively at work in us, but [it is in order that [c]our] life [may be actively at work] in you.

13Yet we have the same spirit of faith as he had who wrote, I have believed, and therefore have I spoken. We too believe, and therefore we speak. [Ps. 116:10.]

14Assured that He Who raised up the Lord Jesus will raise us up also with Jesus and bring us [along] with you into His presence.

15For all [these] things are [taking place] for your sake, so that the more the grace (divine favor and spiritual blessing) extends to more and more people *and* multiplies through the many, the more the thanksgiving may increase [and redound] to the glory of God.

16Therefore we do not become discouraged—utterly spiritless, exhausted, and wearied out through fear. Though our outer man is (progressively) decaying *and* wasting away, yet our inner self is being (progressively) renewed day after day.

17For our light, momentary affliction (this slight distress of the passing hour) is ever more and more abundantly preparing *and* producing *and* achieving for us an everlasting weight of glory—beyond all measure, excessively surpassing all comparisons and all calculations, a vast and transcendent glory and blessedness never to cease!

18Since we consider *and* look not to the things that are seen but to the things that are unseen; for the things that are visible are temporal (brief and fleeting), but the things that are invisible are deathless *and* everlasting.

5 FOR WE know that if the tent which is our earthly home is destroyed (dissolved), we have from God a building, a house not made with hands, eternal in the heavens.

2Here indeed, in this (present abode, body), we sigh *and* groan inwardly, because we yearn to be clothed over—to put on our celestial body like a garment, to be fitted out—with our heavenly dwelling;

3So that by putting it on we may not be found naked—without a body.

4For while we are still in this tent, we groan under the burden *and* sigh deeply—weighed down, depressed, oppressed; not that we want to put off the body (the clothing of the spirit), but rather that we would be further clothed, so that what is mortal (our dying body) may be swallowed up by life [ [d]after the resurrection].

5Now He Who has fashioned us (preparing and making us fit) for this very thing is God, Who also has given us the (Holy) Spirit as a guarantee [of the fulfillment of His promise].

**AMP** [a] Vincent. [b] Vincent. [c] Thayer. [d] Thayer.

## New American Standard

6For God, who said, "Light shall shine out of darkness," is the
One who has shone in our hearts to give the light of the knowledge
of the glory of God in the face of Christ.

7¶ But we have this treasure in earthen vessels, that the surpassing greatness of the power may be of God and not from
ourselves;

8 *we are* afflicted in every way, but not crushed; perplexed, but
not despairing;

9persecuted, but not forsaken; struck down, but not destroyed;

10always carrying about in the body the dying of Jesus, that the
life of Jesus also may be manifested in our body.

11For we who live are constantly being delivered over to death
for Jesus' sake, that the life of Jesus also may be manifested in our
mortal flesh.

12So death works in us, but life in you.

13But having the same spirit of faith, according to what is written, "I BELIEVED, THEREFORE I SPOKE," we also believe, therefore
also we speak;

14knowing that He who raised the Lord Jesus will raise us also
with Jesus and will present us with you.

15For all things *are* for your sakes, that the grace which is
spreading to more and more people may cause the giving of thanks
to abound to the glory of God.

**16**¶ Therefore we do not lose heart, but though our outer man
is decaying, yet our inner man is being renewed day by day.

17For momentary, light affliction is producing for us an eternal
weight of glory far beyond all comparison,

18while we look not at the things which are seen, but at the
things which are not seen; for the things which are seen are temporal, but the things which are not seen are eternal.

*The Temporal and Eternal*

**5** FOR WE know that if the earthly tent which is our house is
torn down, we have a building from God, a house not made
with hands, eternal in the heavens.

2For indeed in this *house* we groan, longing to be clothed with
our dwelling from heaven;

3inasmuch as we, having put it on, shall not be found naked.

4For indeed while we are in this tent, we groan, being burdened, because we do not want to be unclothed, but to be clothed,
in order that what is mortal may be swallowed up by life.

5Now He who prepared us for this very purpose is God, who
gave to us the Spirit as a pledge.

## New International

ness,"[e] made his light shine in our hearts to give us the light of
the knowledge of the glory of God in the face of Christ.
7But we have this treasure in jars of clay to show that this
all-surpassing power is from God and not from us. 8We are hard
pressed on every side, but not crushed; perplexed, but not in
despair; 9persecuted, but not abandoned; struck down, but not
destroyed. 10We always carry around in our body the death of
Jesus, so that the life of Jesus may also be revealed in our body.
11For we who are alive are always being given over to death for
Jesus' sake, so that his life may be revealed in our mortal body. 12So
then, death is at work in us, but life is at work in you.
13It is written: "I believed; therefore I have spoken."[f] With that
same spirit of faith we also believe and therefore speak, 14because
we know that the one who raised the Lord Jesus from the dead will
also raise us with Jesus and present us with you in his presence.
15All this is for your benefit, so that the grace that is reaching more
and more people may cause thanksgiving to overflow to the glory
of God.
16Therefore we do not lose heart. Though outwardly we are
wasting away, yet inwardly we are being renewed day by day.
17For our light and momentary troubles are achieving for us an
eternal glory that far outweighs them all. 18So we fix our eyes not
on what is seen, but on what is unseen. For what is seen is
temporary, but what is unseen is eternal.

*Our Heavenly Dwelling*

**5** NOW WE know that if the earthly tent we live in is destroyed,
we have a building from God, an eternal house in heaven, not
built by human hands. 2Meanwhile we groan, longing to be
clothed with our heavenly dwelling, 3because when we are
clothed, we will not be found naked. 4For while we are in this tent,
we groan and are burdened, because we do not wish to be unclothed but to be clothed with our heavenly dwelling, so that what
is mortal may be swallowed up by life. 5Now it is God who has
made us for this very purpose and has given us the Spirit as a
deposit, guaranteeing what is to come.

**NIV** e *6* Gen. 1:3 f *13* Psalm 116:10

## King James

6Therefore *we are* always confident, knowing that, whilst we are at home in the body, we are absent from the Lord:

7(For we walk by faith, not by sight:)

8We are confident, *I say*, and willing rather to be absent from the body, and to be present with the Lord.

9Wherefore we labour, that, whether present or absent, we may be accepted of him.

10For we must all appear before the judgment seat of Christ; that every one may receive the things *done* in *his* body, according to that he hath done, whether *it be* good or bad.

11Knowing therefore the terror of the Lord, we persuade men; but we are made manifest unto God; and I trust also are made manifest in your consciences.

12For we commend not ourselves again unto you, but give you occasion to glory on our behalf, that ye may have somewhat to *answer* them which glory in appearance, and not in heart.

13For whether we be beside ourselves, *it is* to God: or whether we be sober, *it is* for your cause.

14For the love of Christ constraineth us; because we thus judge, that if one died for all, then were all dead:

15And *that* he died for all, that they which live should not henceforth live unto themselves, but unto him which died for them, and rose again.

16Wherefore henceforth know we no man after the flesh: yea, though we have known Christ after the flesh, yet now henceforth know we *him* no more.

17Therefore if any man *be* in Christ, *he is* a new creature: old things are passed away; behold, all things are become new.

18And all things *are* of God, who hath reconciled us to himself by Jesus Christ, and hath given to us the ministry of reconciliation;

19To wit, that God was in Christ, reconciling the world unto himself, not imputing their trespasses unto them; and hath committed unto us the word of reconciliation.

20Now then we are ambassadors for Christ, as though God did beseech *you* by us: we pray *you* in Christ's stead, be ye reconciled to God.

21For he hath made him *to be* sin for us, who knew no sin; that we might be made the righteousness of God in him.

## Amplified

6So then, we are always full of good *and* hopeful *and* confident courage; we know that while we are at home in the body we are abroad from the home with the Lord [that is promised us].

7For we walk by faith [that is, we [a]regulate our lives and conduct ourselves by our conviction or belief respecting man's relationship to God and divine things, with trust and holy fervor; thus we walk] not by sight *or* appearance.

8[Yes] we have confident *and* hopeful courage, and are well-pleased rather to be away from home out of the body and be at home with the Lord.

9Therefore, whether we are at home [on earth away from Him], or away from home [and with Him], we are constantly ambitious *and* strive earnestly to be well-pleasing to Him.

10For we must all appear *and* be revealed as we are before the judgment seat of Christ, so that each one may receive [his pay] according to what he has done in the body, whether good or evil, [considering [b]what his purpose and motive have been, and what he has [c]achieved, been busy with and given himself and his attention to accomplishing].

11Therefore, being conscious of fearing the Lord with respect *and* reverence, we seek to win people over—to persuade them. But [d]what sort of persons we are is plainly recognized *and* thoroughly understood by God, and I hope that it is plainly recognized *and* thoroughly understood also by your consciences—that is, by your inborn discernment.

12We are not commending ourselves to you again, but we are providing you with an occasion *and* incentive to be [rightfully] proud of us, so that you may have a reply for those who pride themselves on surface appearances— [e]on the virtues they only appear to have—although their heart is devoid of them.

13For if we are beside ourselves [mad, as some say], it is for God *and* concerns Him; if we are in our right mind, it is for your benefit,

14For the love of Christ controls *and* urges *and* impels us, because we are of the opinion *and* conviction that [if] One died for all, then all died;

15And He died for all, so that all those who live might live no longer to *and* for themselves, but to *and* for Him Who died and was raised again for their sake.

16Consequently, from now on we estimate *and* regard no one from a [purely] human point of view—in terms of natural standards of value. [No] even though we once did estimate Christ from a human viewpoint *and* as a man, yet now [we have such knowledge of Him that] we know Him no longer [in terms of the flesh].

17Therefore if any person is (ingrafted) in Christ, the Messiah, he is (a new creature altogether,) a new creation; the old (previous moral and spiritual condition) has passed away. Behold, the fresh *and* new has come!

18But all things are from God, Who through *Jesus* Christ reconciled us to Himself (received us into favor, brought us into harmony with Himself) and gave to us the ministry of reconciliation—that by word and deed we might aim to bring others into harmony with Him.

19It was God (personally present) in Christ, reconciling *and* restoring the world to favor with Himself, not counting up *and* holding against [men] their trespasses [but cancelling them]; and committing to us the message of reconciliation—of the restoration to favor.

20So we are Christ's ambassadors, God making His appeal as it were through us. We [as Christ's personal representatives] beg you for His sake to lay hold of the divine favor [now offered you] *and* be reconciled to God.

21For our sake He made Christ [virtually] to be sin Who knew no sin, so that in *and* through Him we might become [ [f]endued with, viewed as in and examples of] the righteousness of God—what we ought to be, approved and acceptable and in right relationship with Him, by His goodness.

**AMP** [a] Thayer. [b] Souter's "Pocket Lexicon to the Greek New Testament." [c] Thayer. [d] Thayer. [e] Thayer. [f] Alford.

## New American Standard

6Therefore, being always of good courage, and knowing that
while we are at home in the body we are absent from the Lord—
7for we walk by faith, not by sight—
8we are of good courage, I say, and prefer rather to be absent
from the body and to be at home with the Lord.
9Therefore also we have as our ambition, whether at home or
absent, to be pleasing to Him.
10For we must all appear before the judgment seat of Christ,
that each one may be recompensed for his deeds in the body,
according to what he has done, whether good or bad.
11¶ Therefore knowing the fear of the Lord, we persuade men,
but we are made manifest to God; and I hope that we are made
manifest also in your consciences.
12We are not again commending ourselves to you but *are* giving
you an occasion to be proud of us, that you may have *an answer*
for those who take pride in appearance, and not in heart.
13For if we are beside ourselves, it is for God; if we are of sound
mind, it is for you.
14For the love of Christ controls us, having concluded this, that
one died for all, therefore all died;
15and He died for all, that they who live should no longer live
for themselves, but for Him who died and rose again on their
behalf.
16Therefore from now on we recognize no man according to the
flesh; even though we have known Christ according to the flesh,
yet now we know *Him thus* no longer.
17Therefore if any man is in Christ, *he is* a new creature; the old
things passed away; behold, new things have come.
18Now all *these* things are from God, who reconciled us to
Himself through Christ, and gave us the ministry of reconciliation,
19namely, that God was in Christ reconciling the world to Himself, not counting their trespasses against them, and He has committed to us the word of reconciliation.
20¶ Therefore, we are ambassadors for Christ, as though God
were entreating through us; we beg you on behalf of Christ, be
reconciled to God.
21He made Him who knew no sin *to be* sin on our behalf, that
we might become the righteousness of God in Him.

## New International

6Therefore we are always confident and know that as long as
we are at home in the body we are away from the Lord. 7We live
by faith, not by sight. 8We are confident, I say, and would prefer
to be away from the body and at home with the Lord. 9So we make
it our goal to please him, whether we are at home in the body or
away from it. 10For we must all appear before the judgment seat
of Christ, that each one may receive what is due him for the things
done while in the body, whether good or bad.

*The Ministry of Reconciliation*

11Since, then, we know what it is to fear the Lord, we try to
persuade men. What we are is plain to God, and I hope it is also
plain to your conscience. 12We are not trying to commend ourselves to you again, but are giving you an opportunity to take pride
in us, so that you can answer those who take pride in what is seen
rather than in what is in the heart. 13If we are out of our mind, it
is for the sake of God; if we are in our right mind, it is for you. 14For
Christ's love compels us, because we are convinced that one died
for all, and therefore all died. 15And he died for all, that those who
live should no longer live for themselves but for him who died for
them and was raised again.
16So from now on we regard no one from a worldly point of
view. Though we once regarded Christ in this way, we do so no
longer. 17Therefore, if anyone is in Christ, he is a new creation; the
old has gone, the new has come! 18All this is from God, who
reconciled us to himself through Christ and gave us the ministry
of reconciliation: 19that God was reconciling the world to himself
in Christ, not counting men's sins against them. And he has committed to us the message of reconciliation. 20We are therefore
Christ's ambassadors, as though God were making his appeal
through us. We implore you on Christ's behalf: Be reconciled to
God. 21God made him who had no sin to be sin[g] for us, so that
in him we might become the righteousness of God.

**NIV** [g] 21 Or *be a sin offering*

## King James

6 WE THEN, *as* workers together *with him*, beseech *you* also that ye receive not the grace of God in vain.

2(For he saith, I have heard thee in a time accepted, and in the day of salvation have I succoured thee: behold, now *is* the accepted time; behold, now *is* the day of salvation.)

3Giving no offence in any thing, that the ministry be not blamed:

4But in all *things* approving ourselves as the ministers of God, in much patience, in afflictions, in necessities, in distresses,

5In stripes, in imprisonments, in tumults, in labours, in watchings, in fastings;

6By pureness, by knowledge, by longsuffering, by kindness, by the Holy Ghost, by love unfeigned,

7By the word of truth, by the power of God, by the armour of righteousness on the right hand and on the left,

8By honour and dishonour, by evil report and good report: as deceivers, and *yet* true;

9As unknown, and *yet* well known; as dying, and, behold, we live; as chastened, and not killed;

10As sorrowful, yet always rejoicing; as poor, yet making many rich; as having nothing, and *yet* possessing all things.

11O *ye* Corinthians, our mouth is open unto you, our heart is enlarged.

12Ye are not straitened in us, but ye are straitened in your own bowels.

13Now for a recompence in the same, (I speak as unto *my* children,) be ye also enlarged.

14Be ye not unequally yoked together with unbelievers: for what fellowship hath righteousness with unrighteousness? and what communion hath light with darkness?

15And what concord hath Christ with Belial? or what part hath he that believeth with an infidel?

16And what agreement hath the temple of God with idols? for ye are the temple of the living God; as God hath said, I will dwell in them, and walk in *them;* and I will be their God, and they shall be my people.

17Wherefore come out from among them, and be ye separate, saith the Lord, and touch not the unclean *thing;* and I will receive you,

18And will be a Father unto you, and ye shall be my sons and daughters, saith the Lord Almighty.

## Amplified

6 (AS GOD'S fellow workers) laboring together with Him then, we beg of you not to receive the grace of God in vain—that [a]merciful kindness by which God exerts His holy influence on souls and turns them to Christ, keeping and strengthening them, do not receive it to no purpose.

2For He says, In the time of favor (of an assured welcome) I have listened to *and* heeded your call, and I have helped you on the day of deliverance—the day of salvation. Behold, now is truly the time for a gracious welcome *and* acceptance [of you from God]; behold, now is the day of salvation! [Isa. 49:8.]

3We (give no offense in anything,) put no obstruction in anybody's way, so that no fault may be found *and* [our] ministry blamed *and* discredited.

4But we commend ourselves in every way as [true] servants of God: through great endurance, in tribulation *and* suffering, in hardships *and* privations, in sore straits *and* calamities,

5In beatings, imprisonments, riots, labors, sleepless watching, hunger;

6By innocence *and* purity, knowledge *and* spiritual insight, longsuffering *and* patience, kindness, in the Holy Spirit, in unfeigned love;

7By [speaking] the word of truth, in the power of God, with the weapons of righteousness for the right hand [to attack] and for the left hand [to defend];

8Amid honor and dishonor; in defaming *and* evil report and in praise *and* good report. [We are branded] as deceivers (impostors), and [yet vindicated as] truthful *and* honest.

9[We are treated] as unknown *and* ignored [by the world], and [yet we are] well-known *and* recognized [by God and His people]; as dying, and yet here we are alive; as chastened by suffering and [yet] not killed;

10As grieved *and* mourning, yet [we are] always rejoicing; as poor [ourselves, yet] bestowing riches on many; as having nothing, and [yet in reality] possessing all things.

11Our mouth is open to you, Corinthians—we are hiding nothing, keeping nothing back; and our heart is expanded wide [for you]! [Ezek. 33:22; Isa. 60:5.]

12There is no lack of room for you in [our hearts], but you lack room in your own affections [for us].

13By way of return then, do this for me—I speak as to children—open wide your hearts also [to us].

14Do not be unequally yoked up with unbelievers—do not make mismated alliances with them, or come under a different yoke with them [inconsistent with your faith]. For what partnership have right living *and* right standing with God with iniquity *and* lawlessness? Or how can light fellowship with darkness?

15What harmony can there be between Christ and Belial [the devil]? Or what has a believer in common with an unbeliever?

16What agreement [can there be between] a temple of God and idols? For we are the temple of the living God; even as God said, I will dwell in *and* with *and* among them and will walk in *and* with *and* among them, and I will be their God, and they shall be My people. [Exod. 25:8; 29:45; Lev. 26:12; Ezek. 37:27; Jer. 31:1.]

17So, come out from among (unbelievers), and separate (sever) yourselves from them, says the Lord, and touch not [any] unclean thing; then I will receive you kindly *and* treat you with favor, [Isa. 52:11.]

18And I will be a Father to you, and you shall be My sons and daughters, says the Lord Almighty. [Hos. 1:10; Isa. 43:6.]

**AMP** [a] Thayer.

## New American Standard

*Their Ministry Commended*

6 AND WORKING together *with Him,* we also urge you not to
receive the grace of God in vain—
2for He says,

"AT THE ACCEPTABLE TIME I LISTENED TO YOU,
AND ON THE DAY OF SALVATION I HELPED YOU";

behold, now is "THE ACCEPTABLE TIME," behold, now is "THE DAY
OF SALVATION"—
3giving no cause for offense in anything, in order that the
ministry be not discredited,
4but in everything commending ourselves as servants of God,
in much endurance, in afflictions, in hardships, in distresses,
5in beatings, in imprisonments, in tumults, in labors, in sleep-
lessness, in hunger,
6in purity, in knowledge, in patience, in kindness, in the Holy
Spirit, in genuine love,
7in the word of truth, in the power of God; by the weapons of
righteousness for the right hand and the left,
8by glory and dishonor, by evil report and good report; *regarded*
as deceivers and yet true;
9as unknown yet well-known, as dying yet behold, we live; as
punished yet not put to death,
10as sorrowful yet always rejoicing, as poor yet making many
rich, as having nothing yet possessing all things.
11¶ Our mouth has spoken freely to you, O Corinthians, our
heart is opened wide.
12You are not restrained by us, but you are restrained in your
own affections.
13Now in a like exchange—I speak as to children—open wide
*to us* also.
14¶ Do not be bound together with unbelievers; for what partnership have righteousness and lawlessness, or what fellowship
has light with darkness?
15Or what harmony has Christ with Belial, or what has a believer in common with an unbeliever?
16Or what agreement has the temple of God with idols? For we
are the temple of the living God; just as God said,

"I WILL DWELL IN THEM AND WALK AMONG THEM;
AND I WILL BE THEIR GOD, AND THEY SHALL BE MY
PEOPLE.
17 "Therefore, COME OUT FROM THEIR MIDST AND BE
SEPARATE," says the Lord.
"AND DO NOT TOUCH WHAT IS UNCLEAN;
And I will welcome you.
18 "And I will be a father to you,
And you shall be sons and daughters to Me,"
Says the Lord Almighty.

## New International

6 AS GOD'S fellow workers we urge you not to receive God's
grace in vain. 2For he says,

"In the time of my favor I heard you,
and in the day of salvation I helped you."[b]

I tell you, now is the time of God's favor, now is the day of
salvation.

*Paul's Hardships*

3We put no stumbling block in anyone's path, so that our ministry will not be discredited. 4Rather, as servants of God we commend ourselves in every way: in great endurance; in troubles,
hardships and distresses; 5in beatings, imprisonments and riots; in
hard work, sleepless nights and hunger; 6in purity, understanding, patience and kindness; in the Holy Spirit and in sincere love;
7in truthful speech and in the power of God; with weapons of
righteousness in the right hand and in the left; 8through glory and
dishonor, bad report and good report; genuine, yet regarded as
impostors; 9known, yet regarded as unknown; dying, and yet we
live on; beaten, and yet not killed; 10sorrowful, yet always rejoicing; poor, yet making many rich; having nothing, and yet possessing everything.
11We have spoken freely to you, Corinthians, and opened wide
our hearts to you. 12We are not withholding our affection from
you, but you are withholding yours from us. 13As a fair exchange—I speak as to my children—open wide your hearts also.

*Do Not Be Yoked With Unbelievers*

14Do not be yoked together with unbelievers. For what do
righteousness and wickedness have in common? Or what fellowship can light have with darkness? 15What harmony is there between Christ and Belial[c]? What does a believer have in common
with an unbeliever? 16What agreement is there between the temple
of God and idols? For we are the temple of the living God. As God
has said: "I will live with them and walk among them, and I will
be their God, and they will be my people."[d]

17"Therefore come out from them
and be separate,
says the Lord.
Touch no unclean thing,
and I will receive you."[e]
18"I will be a Father to you,
and you will be my sons and daughters,
says the Lord Almighty."[f]

NIV [b] 2 Isaiah 49:8 [c] 15 Greek *Beliar,* a variant of *Belial* [d] 16 Lev. 26:12; Jer. 32:38; Ezek. 37:27 [e] 17 Isaiah 52:11; Ezek. 20:34,41 [f] 18 2 Samuel 7:14; 7:8

## King James

7 HAVING THEREFORE these promises, dearly beloved, let us cleanse ourselves from all filthiness of the flesh and spirit, perfecting holiness in the fear of God.

2 Receive us; we have wronged no man, we have corrupted no man, we have defrauded no man.

3 I speak not *this* to condemn *you:* for I have said before, that ye are in our hearts to die and live with *you.*

4 Great *is* my boldness of speech toward you, great *is* my glorying of you: I am filled with comfort, I am exceeding joyful in all our tribulation.

5 For, when we were come into Macedonia, our flesh had no rest, but we were troubled on every side; without *were* fightings, within *were* fears.

6 Nevertheless God, that comforteth those that are cast down, comforted us by the coming of Titus;

7 And not by his coming only, but by the consolation wherewith he was comforted in you, when he told us your earnest desire, your mourning, your fervent mind toward me; so that I rejoiced the more.

8 For though I made you sorry with a letter, I do not repent, though I did repent: for I perceive that the same epistle hath made you sorry, though *it were* but for a season.

9 Now I rejoice, not that ye were made sorry, but that ye sorrowed to repentance: for ye were made sorry after a godly manner, that ye might receive damage by us in nothing.

10 For godly sorrow worketh repentance to salvation not to be repented of: but the sorrow of the world worketh death.

11 For behold this selfsame thing, that ye sorrowed after a godly sort, what carefulness it wrought in you, yea, *what* clearing of yourselves, yea, *what* indignation, yea, *what* fear, yea, *what* vehement desire, yea, *what* zeal, yea, *what* revenge! In all *things* ye have approved yourselves to be clear in this matter.

12 Wherefore, though I wrote unto you, *I did it* not for his cause that had done the wrong, nor for his cause that suffered wrong, but that our care for you in the sight of God might appear unto you.

13 Therefore we were comforted in your comfort: yea, and exceedingly the more joyed we for the joy of Titus, because his spirit was refreshed by you all.

14 For if I have boasted any thing to him of you, I am not ashamed; but as we spake all things to you in truth, even so our boasting, which *I made* before Titus, is found a truth.

15 And his inward affection is more abundant toward you, whilst he remembereth the obedience of you all, how with fear and trembling ye received him.

16 I rejoice therefore that I have confidence in you in all *things.*

## Amplified

7 THEREFORE, SINCE these [great] promises are ours, beloved, let us cleanse ourselves from everything that contaminates *and* defiles body and spirit, and bring [our] consecration to completeness in the (reverential) fear of God.

2 Do open your hearts to us again—enlarge them to take us in. We have wronged no one; we have betrayed *or* corrupted no one; we have cheated *or* taken advantage of no one.

3 I do not say this to reproach *or* condemn [you], for I have said before that you are (nested) in our hearts, [and you will remain there] whether we die or live, it will be together.

4 I have great boldness *and* free *and* fearless confidence *and* cheerful courage toward you; my pride in you is great; I am filled brimful with the comfort [of it]. With all our tribulation *and* in spite of it, I am filled with comfort, I am overflowing with joy.

5 For even when we arrived in Macedonia, our bodies had no ease *or* rest, but we were oppressed in every way *and* afflicted at every turn—fighting *and* contentions without, dread *and* fears within [us];

6 But God, Who comforts *and* encourages *and* refreshes *and* cheers the depressed *and* the sinking, comforted *and* encouraged *and* refreshed *and* cheered us by the arrival of Titus.

7 [Yes] and not only by his coming but also by [his account of] the comfort with which he was encouraged *and* refreshed *and* cheered as to you, while he told us of your yearning affection, of how sorry you were [for me] and how eagerly you took my part, so that I rejoiced still more.

8 For even though I did grieve you with my letter, I do not regret [it now], though I did regret it, for I see that that letter did pain you, though only for a little while;

9 Yet I am glad now, not because you were pained, but because you were pained into repentance (that turned you to God); for you felt a grief such as God meant you to feel, so that in nothing you might suffer loss through us *or* harm for what we did.

10 For godly grief *and* the pain God is permitted to direct, produce a repentance that leads *and* contributes to salvation *and* deliverance from evil, and it never brings regret; but worldly grief [the hopeless sorrow that is characteristic of the pagan world] is deadly—breeding *and* ending in death.

11 For [you can look back now and] observe what this same godly sorrow has done for you *and* has produced in you: what eagerness *and* earnest care to explain *and* clear yourselves [of all [a]complicity in the condoning of incest], what indignation [at the sin], what alarm, what yearning, what zeal [to do justice to all concerned], what readiness to mete out punishment [ [b]to the offender]! At every point you have proved yourselves cleared *and* guiltless in the matter. [I Cor. 5.]

12 So although I did write to you [as I did], it was not for the sake *and* because of the one who did [the] wrong, nor on account of the one who suffered [the] wrong, but in order that you might realize before God [that your readiness to accept our authority revealed] how zealously you do care for us.

13 Therefore we are relieved *and* comforted *and* encouraged [at the result]. And in addition to our own (personal) consolation, we were especially delighted at the joy of Titus, because you have all set his mind at rest, soothing *and* refreshing his spirit.

14 For if I had boasted to him at all concerning you, I was not disappointed *or* put to shame, but just as everything we ever said to you was true, so our boasting [about you] to Titus has proved true also.

15 And his heart goes out to you more abundantly than ever as he recalls how submissive [to his guidance] you all were, and the reverence *and* anxiety [to meet all requirements] with which you accepted *and* welcomed him.

16 I am very happy because I now am of good courage *and* have perfect confidence in you in all things.

**AMP** [a] Vincent. [b] Vincent.

## New American Standard

*Paul Reveals His Heart*

7 THEREFORE, HAVING these promises, beloved, let us cleanse ourselves from all defilement of flesh and spirit, perfecting holiness in the fear of God.

2¶ Make room for us *in your hearts;* we wronged no one, we corrupted no one, we took advantage of no one.

3I do not speak to condemn you; for I have said before that you are in our hearts to die together and to live together.

4Great is my confidence in you, great is my boasting on your behalf; I am filled with comfort. I am overflowing with joy in all our affliction.

5¶ For even when we came into Macedonia our flesh had no rest, but we were afflicted on every side: conflicts without, fears within.

6But God, who comforts the depressed, comforted us by the coming of Titus;

7and not only by his coming, but also by the comfort with which he was comforted in you, as he reported to us your longing, your mourning, your zeal for me; so that I rejoiced even more.

8For though I caused you sorrow by my letter, I do not regret it; though I did regret it— *for* I see that that letter caused you sorrow, though only for a while—

9I now rejoice, not that you were made sorrowful, but that you were made sorrowful to *the point of* repentance; for you were made sorrowful according to *the will of* God, in order that you might not suffer loss in anything through us.

10For the sorrow that is according to *the will of* God produces a repentance without regret, *leading* to salvation; but the sorrow of the world produces death.

11For behold what earnestness this very thing, this godly sorrow, has produced in you: what vindication of yourselves, what indignation, what fear, what longing, what zeal, what avenging of wrong! In everything you demonstrated yourselves to be innocent in the matter.

12So although I wrote to you *it was* not for the sake of the offender, nor for the sake of the one offended, but that your earnestness on our behalf might be made known to you in the sight of God.

13For this reason we have been comforted.

¶ And besides our comfort, we rejoiced even much more for the joy of Titus, because his spirit has been refreshed by you all.

14For if in anything I have boasted to him about you, I was not put to shame; but as we spoke all things to you in truth, so also our boasting before Titus proved to be *the* truth.

15And his affection abounds all the more toward you, as he remembers the obedience of you all, how you received him with fear and trembling.

16I rejoice that in everything I have confidence in you.

## New International

7 SINCE WE have these promises, dear friends, let us purify ourselves from everything that contaminates body and spirit, perfecting holiness out of reverence for God.

*Paul's Joy*

2Make room for us in your hearts. We have wronged no one,
we have corrupted no one, we have exploited no one. 3I do not say
this to condemn you; I have said before that you have such a place
in our hearts that we would live or die with you. 4I have great
confidence in you; I take great pride in you. I am greatly encouraged; in all our troubles my joy knows no bounds.

5For when we came into Macedonia, this body of ours had no
rest, but we were harassed at every turn—conflicts on the outside,
fears within. 6But God, who comforts the downcast, comforted us
by the coming of Titus, 7and not only by his coming but also by
the comfort you had given him. He told us about your longing for
me, your deep sorrow, your ardent concern for me, so that my joy
was greater than ever.

8Even if I caused you sorrow by my letter, I do not regret it.
Though I did regret it—I see that my letter hurt you, but only for
a little while— 9yet now I am happy, not because you were made
sorry, but because your sorrow led you to repentance. For you
became sorrowful as God intended and so were not harmed in any
way by us. 10Godly sorrow brings repentance that leads to salvation and leaves no regret, but worldly sorrow brings death. 11See
what this godly sorrow has produced in you: what earnestness,
what eagerness to clear yourselves, what indignation, what alarm,
what longing, what concern, what readiness to see justice done.
At every point you have proved yourselves to be innocent in this
matter. 12So even though I wrote to you, it was not on account of
the one who did the wrong or of the injured party, but rather that
before God you could see for yourselves how devoted to us you
are. 13By all this we are encouraged.

In addition to our own encouragement, we were especially
delighted to see how happy Titus was, because his spirit has been
refreshed by all of you. 14I had boasted to him about you, and you
have not embarrassed me. But just as everything we said to you
was true, so our boasting about you to Titus has proved to be true
as well. 15And his affection for you is all the greater when he
remembers that you were all obedient, receiving him with fear and
trembling. 16I am glad I can have complete confidence in you.

## King James

8 MOREOVER, BRETHREN, we do you to wit of the grace of
God bestowed on the churches of Macedonia;
2How that in a great trial of affliction the abundance of their joy
and their deep poverty abounded unto the riches of their liberality.
3For to *their* power, I bear record, yea, and beyond *their* power
*they were* willing of themselves;
4Praying us with much entreaty that we would receive the gift,
and *take upon us* the fellowship of the ministering to the saints.
5And *this they did,* not as we hoped, but first gave their own
selves to the Lord, and unto us by the will of God.
6Insomuch that we desired Titus, that as he had begun, so he
would also finish in you the same grace also.
7Therefore, as ye abound in every *thing, in* faith, and utterance,
and knowledge, and *in* all diligence, and *in* your love to us, *see* that
ye abound in this grace also.
8I speak not by commandment, but by occasion of the forwardness of others, and to prove the sincerity of your love.
9For ye know the grace of our Lord Jesus Christ, that, though
he was rich, yet for your sakes he became poor, that ye through
his poverty might be rich.
10And herein I give *my* advice: for this is expedient for you, who
have begun before, not only to do, but also to be forward a year
ago.
11Now therefore perform the doing *of it;* that as *there was* a
readiness to will, so *there may be* a performance also out of that
which ye have.
12For if there be first a willing mind, *it is* accepted according to
that a man hath, *and* not according to that he hath not.
13For *I mean* not that other men be eased, and ye burdened:
14But by an equality, *that* now at this time your abundance *may
be a supply* for their want, that their abundance also may be *a supply*
for your want: that there may be equality:
15As it is written, He that *had gathered* much had nothing over;
and he that *had gathered* little had no lack.
16But thanks *be* to God, which put the same earnest care into
the heart of Titus for you.
17For indeed he accepted the exhortation; but being more forward, of his own accord he went unto you.
18And we have sent with him the brother, whose praise *is* in the
gospel throughout all the churches;
19And not *that* only, but who was also chosen of the churches
to travel with us with this grace, which is administered by us to
the glory of the same Lord, and *declaration of* your ready mind:
20Avoiding this, that no man should blame us in this abundance
which is administered by us:

AMP [a] Thayer.

## Amplified

8 WE WANT to tell you further, brethren, about the grace (the
favor and spiritual blessing) of God which has been evident
in the churches of Macedonia [arousing in them the desire to give
alms];
2For in the midst of an ordeal of severe tribulation, their abundance of joy and their depth of poverty [together] have overflowed
in wealth of lavish generosity on their part.
3For, as I can bear witness, [they gave] according to their ability,
yes, and beyond their ability; and [they did it] voluntarily,
4Begging us most insistently for the favor *and* the fellowship of
contributing in this ministration for [the relief and support of] the
saints [in Jerusalem].
5Nor [was this gift of theirs merely the contribution] that we
expected, but first they gave themselves to the Lord and to us [as
His agents] by the will of God—that is, [a]entirely disregarding their
personal interests, they gave as much as they possibly could,
having put themselves at our disposal to be directed by the will of
God.
6So much so that we have urged Titus that as he began it, he
should also complete this beneficent *and* gracious contribution
among you, [the church at Corinth].
7Now as you abound *and* excel *and* are at the front in everything,
in faith, in expressing yourselves, in knowledge, in all zeal, and
in your love for us, [see to it that you come to the front now and]
abound *and* excel in this gracious work [of almsgiving] also.
8I give this not as an order—to dictate to you—but to prove by
[pointing out] the zeal of others the sincerity of your [own] love
also.
9For you are coming progressively to be acquainted with *and* to
recognize more strongly *and* clearly the grace of our Lord Jesus
Christ—His kindness, His gracious generosity, His undeserved
favor and spiritual blessing; [in] that though He was [so very] rich,
yet for your sakes He became [so very] poor, in order that by His
poverty you might become enriched—abundantly supplied.
10[It is then] my counsel *and* my opinion in this matter that I give
[you, when I say], it is profitable *and* fitting for you [now to complete the enterprise], which more than a year ago you not only
began, but were the first to wish to do anything [about contributions for the relief of the saints at Jerusalem].
11So now finish doing it, that your (enthusiastic) readiness in
desiring it may be equalled by your completion of it according to
your ability *and* means.
12For if the (eager) readiness to give is there, then it is acceptable
*and* welcomed in proportion to what a person has, not according
to what he does not have.
13For it is not [intended] that other people be eased *and* relieved
(of their responsibility) and you be burdened *and* suffer (unfairly),
14But to have equality—share and share alike; your surplus over
necessity at the present time going to meet their want *and* to
equalize the difference created by it, so that [at some other time]
their surplus in turn may be given to supply your want. Thus there
may be equality.
15As it is written, He who gathered much had nothing over, and
he who gathered little did not lack. [Exod. 16:18.]
16But thanks be to God Who planted the same earnest zeal *and*
care for you in the heart of Titus.
17For he not only welcomed *and* responded to our appeal, but
was himself so keen in his enthusiasm *and* interest in you that he
is going to you of his own accord.
18But we are sending along with him that brother [Luke?]
whose praise in the Gospel ministry [is spread] throughout all the
churches;
19And more than that, he has been appointed by the churches
to travel as our companion in regard to this bountiful contribution
which we are administering for the glory of the Lord Himself, and
[to show] our eager readiness [as Christians to help one another].
20[For] we are on our guard, intending that no one should find
anything for which to blame us in regard to our administration of
this large contribution.

## New American Standard

*Great Generosity*

8 NOW, BRETHREN, we *wish to* make known to you the grace
of God which has been given in the churches of Macedonia,
2that in a great ordeal of affliction their abundance of joy and
their deep poverty overflowed in the wealth of their liberality.
3For I testify that according to their ability, and beyond their
ability *they gave* of their own accord,
4begging us with much entreaty for the favor of participation
in the support of the saints,
5and *this,* not as we had expected, but they first gave themselves to the Lord and to us by the will of God.
6Consequently we urged Titus that as he had previously made
a beginning, so he would also complete in you this gracious work
as well.
7But just as you abound in everything, in faith and utterance
and knowledge and in all earnestness and in the [b]love we inspired
in you, *see* that you abound in this gracious work also.
8I am not speaking *this* as a command, but as proving through
the earnestness of others the sincerity of your love also.
9For you know the grace of our Lord Jesus Christ, that though
He was rich, yet for your sake He became poor, that you through
His poverty might become rich.
10And I give *my* opinion in this matter, for this is to your
advantage, who were the first to begin a year ago not only to do
*this,* but also to desire *to do it.*
11But now finish doing it also; that just as *there was* the readiness
to desire it, so *there may be* also the completion of it by your ability.
12For if the readiness is present, it is acceptable according to
what *a man* has, not according to what he does not have.
13For *this* is not for the ease of others *and* for your affliction, but
by way of equality—
14at this present time your abundance *being a supply* for their
want, that their abundance also may become *a supply* for your
want, that there may be equality;
15as it is written, "HE WHO *gathered* MUCH DID NOT HAVE TOO
MUCH, AND HE WHO *gathered* LITTLE HAD NO LACK."
16¶ But thanks be to God, who puts the same earnestness on
your behalf in the heart of Titus.
17For he not only accepted our appeal, but being himself very
earnest, he has gone to you of his own accord.
18And we have sent along with him the brother whose fame in
*the things of* the gospel *has spread* through all the churches;
19and not only *this,* but he has also been appointed by the
churches to travel with us in this gracious work, which is being
administered by us for the glory of the Lord Himself, and *to show*
our readiness,
20taking precaution that no one should discredit us in our administration of this generous gift;

NAS [b] Lit., *love from us in you;* some ancient mss. read *your love for us*

## New International

*Generosity Encouraged*

8 AND NOW, brothers, we want you to know about the grace
that God has given the Macedonian churches. 2Out of the
most severe trial, their overflowing joy and their extreme poverty
welled up in rich generosity. 3For I testify that they gave as much
as they were able, and even beyond their ability. Entirely on their
own, 4they urgently pleaded with us for the privilege of sharing
in this service to the saints. 5And they did not do as we expected,
but they gave themselves first to the Lord and then to us in keeping
with God's will. 6So we urged Titus, since he had earlier made a
beginning, to bring also to completion this act of grace on your
part. 7But just as you excel in everything—in faith, in speech, in
knowledge, in complete earnestness and in your love for us[c] —see
that you also excel in this grace of giving.
8I am not commanding you, but I want to test the sincerity of
your love by comparing it with the earnestness of others. 9For you
know the grace of our Lord Jesus Christ, that though he was rich,
yet for your sakes he became poor, so that you through his poverty
might become rich.
10And here is my advice about what is best for you in this
matter: Last year you were the first not only to give but also to have
the desire to do so. 11Now finish the work, so that your eager
willingness to do it may be matched by your completion of it,
according to your means. 12For if the willingness is there, the gift
is acceptable according to what one has, not according to what he
does not have.
13Our desire is not that others might be relieved while you are
hard pressed, but that there might be equality. 14At the present
time your plenty will supply what they need, so that in turn their
plenty will supply what you need. Then there will be equality, 15as
it is written: "He who gathered much did not have too much, and
he who gathered little did not have too little."[d]

*Titus Sent to Corinth*

16I thank God, who put into the heart of Titus the same concern
I have for you. 17For Titus not only welcomed our appeal, but he
is coming to you with much enthusiasm and on his own initiative.
18And we are sending along with him the brother who is praised
by all the churches for his service to the gospel. 19What is more,
he was chosen by the churches to accompany us as we carry the
offering, which we administer in order to honor the Lord himself
and to show our eagerness to help. 20We want to avoid any criticism of the way we administer this liberal gift. 21For we are taking

NIV [c] 7 Some manuscripts *in our love for you* [d] 15 Exodus 16:18

## King James

21Providing for honest things, not only in the sight of the Lord,
but also in the sight of men.
22And we have sent with them our brother, whom we have
oftentimes proved diligent in many things, but now much more
diligent, upon the great confidence which *I have* in you.
23Whether *any do inquire* of Titus, *he is* my partner and fellow-
helper concerning you: or our brethren *be inquired of, they are* the
messengers of the churches, *and* the glory of Christ.
24Wherefore show ye to them, and before the churches, the
proof of your love, and of our boasting on your behalf.

9 FOR AS touching the ministering to the saints, it is superfluous for me to write to you:
2For I know the forwardness of your mind, for which I boast of
you to them of Macedonia, that Achaia was ready a year ago; and
your zeal hath provoked very many.
3Yet have I sent the brethren, lest our boasting of you should
be in vain in this behalf; that, as I said, ye may be ready:
4Lest haply if they of Macedonia come with me, and find you
unprepared, we (that we say not, ye) should be ashamed in this
same confident boasting.
5Therefore I thought it necessary to exhort the brethren, that
they would go before unto you, and make up beforehand your
bounty, whereof ye had notice before, that the same might be
ready, as *a matter of* bounty, and not as *of* covetousness.
6But this *I say,* He which soweth sparingly shall reap also sparingly; and he which soweth bountifully shall reap also bountifully.
7Every man according as he purposeth in his heart, *so let him
give;* not grudgingly, or of necessity: for God loveth a cheerful
giver.
8And God *is* able to make all grace abound toward you; that ye,
always having all sufficiency in all *things,* may abound to every
good work:
9(As it is written, He hath dispersed abroad; he hath given to
the poor: his righteousness remaineth for ever.
10Now he that ministereth seed to the sower both minister
bread for *your* food, and multiply your seed sown, and increase the
fruits of your righteousness;)
11Being enriched in every thing to all bountifulness, which
causeth through us thanksgiving to God.
12For the administration of this service not only supplieth the
want of the saints, but is abundant also by many thanksgivings
unto God;

## Amplified

21For we take thought beforehand *and* aim to be honest *and*
absolutely above suspicion not only in the sight of the Lord but
also in the sight of men.
22Moreover along with them we are sending our brother, whom
we have often put to the test and have found him zealous (devoted
and earnest) in many matters, but who is now more (eagerly)
earnest than ever because of [his] absolute confidence in you.
23As for Titus, he is my colleague and shares my work in your
service; and as for the [other two] brethren, they are the (special)
messengers of the churches, a credit *and* glory to Christ, the Messiah.
24Show to these men, therefore, in the sight of the churches, the
reality *and* plain truth of your love—your affection, goodwill and
benevolence—and what [good reasons] I had for boasting about
*and* being proud of you.

9 NOW ABOUT the offering that is [to be made] for the saints—
God's people [in Jerusalem]—it is quite superfluous that I
should write you;
2For I am well acquainted with your willingness—your readiness and your eagerness to promote it—and I have proudly told
about you to the people of Macedonia, saying that Achaia [most
of Greece] has been prepared since last year for this contribution;
and [consequently] your enthusiasm has stimulated the majority
of them.
3Still, I am sending the brethren [on to you], lest our pride in
you should be made an empty boast in this particular case, and so
that you may be all ready, as I told them you would be;
4Lest, if [any] Macedonians should come with me and find you
unprepared [for this generosity], we, to say nothing of yourselves,
be humiliated for our being so confident.
5That is why I thought it necessary to urge these brethren to go
to you before I do, and make arrangements in advance for this
bountiful, promised gift of yours; so that it may be ready, not as
an extortion—wrung out of you—but as a generous *and* willing
gift.
6[Remember] this: he who sows sparingly *and* grudgingly will
also reap sparingly *and* grudgingly, and he who sows generously
*and* [a]that blessings may come to someone, will also reap generously *and* with blessings.
7Let each one [give] as he has made up his own mind *and*
purposed in his heart, not reluctantly *or* sorrowfully or under
compulsion, for God loves (that is, He [b]takes pleasure in, prizes
above other things, and is unwilling to abandon or to do without)
a cheerful (joyous, prompt-to-do-it) giver—whose heart is in his
giving. [Prov. 22:9.]
8And God is able to make all grace (every favor and [c]earthly
blessing) come to you in abundance, so that you may always *and*
under all circumstances *and* whatever the need, [d]be self-sufficient—possessing enough to require no aid or support and furnished in abundance for every good work and charitable donation.
9As it is written, He [the benevolent person] scatters abroad, He
gives to the poor; His deeds of justice *and* goodness *and* kindness
*and* benevolence will go on *and* endure forever! [Ps. 112:9.]
10And [God] Who provides seed for the sower and bread for
eating will also provide and multiply your [resources for] sowing,
and increase the fruits of your righteousness [ [e]which manifests
itself in active goodness, kindness and charity]. [Isa. 55:10; Hos.
10:12.]
11Thus you will be enriched in all things *and* in every way, so
that you can be generous, [and your generosity as it is] administered by us will bring forth thanksgiving to God.
12For the service the ministering of this fund renders does not
only fully supply what is lacking to the saints (God's people), but
it also overflows in many [cries of] thanksgiving to God.

AMP [a] Thayer. [b] Thayer. [c] Thayer. [d] Vincent. [e] Thayer.

## New American Standard

21for we have regard for what is honorable, not only in the sight
of the Lord, but also in the sight of men.
22And we have sent with them our brother, whom we have
often tested and found diligent in many things, but now even more
diligent, because of *his* great confidence in you.
23As for Titus, *he is* my partner and fellow worker among you;
as for our brethren, *they are* messengers of the churches, a glory
to Christ.
24Therefore openly before the churches show them the proof of
your love and of our reason for boasting about you.

*God Gives Most*

9 FOR IT is superfluous for me to write to you about this
ministry to the saints;
2for I know your readiness, of which I boast about you to the
Macedonians, *namely,* that Achaia has been prepared since last
year, and your zeal has stirred up most of them.
3But I have sent the brethren, that our boasting about you may
not be made empty in this case, that, as I was saying, you may be
prepared;
4lest if any Macedonians come with me and find you unprepared, we (not to speak of you) should be put to shame by this
confidence.
5So I thought it necessary to urge the brethren that they would
go on ahead to you and arrange beforehand your previously promised bountiful gift, that the same might be ready as a bountiful gift,
and not affected by covetousness.
6¶ Now this *I say,* he who sows sparingly shall also reap sparingly; and he who sows bountifully shall also reap bountifully.
7Let each one *do* just as he has purposed in his heart; not
grudgingly or under compulsion; for God loves a cheerful giver.
8And God is able to make all grace abound to you, that always
having all sufficiency in everything, you may have an abundance
for every good deed;
9as it is written,

"HE SCATTERED ABROAD, HE GAVE TO THE POOR,
HIS RIGHTEOUSNESS ABIDES FOREVER."

10Now He who supplies seed to the sower and bread for food,
will supply and multiply your seed for sowing and increase the
harvest of your righteousness;
11you will be enriched in everything for all liberality, which
through us is producing thanksgiving to God.
12For the ministry of this service is not only fully supplying the
needs of the saints, but is also overflowing through many thanksgivings to God.

## New International

pains to do what is right, not only in the eyes of the Lord but also
in the eyes of men.
22In addition, we are sending with them our brother who has
often proved to us in many ways that he is zealous, and now even
more so because of his great confidence in you. 23As for Titus, he
is my partner and fellow worker among you; as for our brothers,
they are representatives of the churches and an honor to Christ.
24Therefore show these men the proof of your love and the reason
for our pride in you, so that the churches can see it.

9 THERE IS no need for me to write to you about this service
to the saints. 2For I know your eagerness to help, and I have
been boasting about it to the Macedonians, telling them that since
last year you in Achaia were ready to give; and your enthusiasm
has stirred most of them to action. 3But I am sending the brothers
in order that our boasting about you in this matter should not
prove hollow, but that you may be ready, as I said you would be.
4For if any Macedonians come with me and find you unprepared,
we—not to say anything about you—would be ashamed of having
been so confident. 5So I thought it necessary to urge the brothers
to visit you in advance and finish the arrangements for the generous gift you had promised. Then it will be ready as a generous gift,
not as one grudgingly given.

*Sowing Generously*

6Remember this: Whoever sows sparingly will also reap sparingly, and whoever sows generously will also reap generously.
7Each man should give what he has decided in his heart to give,
not reluctantly or under compulsion, for God loves a cheerful
giver. 8And God is able to make all grace abound to you, so that
in all things at all times, having all that you need, you will abound
in every good work. 9As it is written:

"He has scattered abroad his gifts to the poor;
his righteousness endures forever."[f]

10Now he who supplies seed to the sower and bread for food will
also supply and increase your store of seed and will enlarge the
harvest of your righteousness. 11You will be made rich in every
way so that you can be generous on every occasion, and through
us your generosity will result in thanksgiving to God.
12This service that you perform is not only supplying the needs
of God's people but is also overflowing in many expressions of
thanks to God. 13Because of the service by which you have proved

NIV [f] 9 Psalm 112:9

## King James

13 Whiles by the experiment of this ministration they glorify God for your professed subjection unto the gospel of Christ, and for *your* liberal distribution unto them, and unto all *men;*

14 And by their prayer for you, which long after you for the exceeding grace of God in you.

15 Thanks *be* unto God for his unspeakable gift.

**10** NOW I Paul myself beseech you by the meekness and gentleness of Christ, who in presence *am* base among you, but being absent am bold toward you:

2 But I beseech *you,* that I may not be bold when I am present with that confidence, wherewith I think to be bold against some, which think of us as if we walked according to the flesh.

3 For though we walk in the flesh, we do not war after the flesh:

4 (For the weapons of our warfare *are* not carnal, but mighty through God to the pulling down of strong holds;)

5 Casting down imaginations, and every high thing that exalteth itself against the knowledge of God, and bringing into captivity every thought to the obedience of Christ;

6 And having in a readiness to revenge all disobedience, when your obedience is fulfilled.

7 Do ye look on things after the outward appearance? If any man trust to himself that he is Christ's, let him of himself think this again, that, as he *is* Christ's, even so *are* we Christ's.

8 For though I should boast somewhat more of our authority, which the Lord hath given us for edification, and not for your destruction, I should not be ashamed:

9 That I may not seem as if I would terrify you by letters.

10 For *his* letters, say they, *are* weighty and powerful; but *his* bodily presence *is* weak, and *his* speech contemptible.

11 Let such an one think this, that, such as we are in word by letters when we are absent, such *will we be* also in deed when we are present.

12 For we dare not make ourselves of the number, or compare ourselves with some that commend themselves: but they measuring themselves by themselves, and comparing themselves among themselves, are not wise.

13 But we will not boast of things without *our* measure, but according to the measure of the rule which God hath distributed to us, a measure to reach even unto you.

14 For we stretch not ourselves beyond *our measure,* as though we reached not unto you: for we are come as far as to you also in *preaching* the gospel of Christ:

15 Not boasting of things without *our* measure, *that is,* of other men's labours; but having hope, when your faith is increased, that we shall be enlarged by you according to our rule abundantly,

16 To preach the gospel in the *regions* beyond you, *and* not to boast in another man's line of things made ready to our hand.

## Amplified

13 Because at [your] standing of the test of this ministry, they will glorify God at your loyalty *and* obedience to the Gospel of Christ which you confess, as well as for your generous-hearted liberality to them and to all [the other needy ones].

14 And they yearn for you while they pray for you, because of the surpassing measure of God's grace (His favor and mercy and spiritual blessing which is shown forth) in you.

15 Now thanks be to God for His Gift, [precious] beyond telling—His indescribable, inexpressible, free Gift!

**10** NOW I myself, Paul, beseech you, by the gentleness and consideration of Christ [Himself; I] who [am] lowly enough [so they say] when among you face to face, but bold (fearless and outspoken to you when I am) absent from you!

2 I entreat you when I do come [to you] that I may not [be driven to such] boldness as I intend to show toward those few who suspect us of acting according to the flesh—on the low level of worldly motives and as if invested with only human powers.

3 For though we walk [live] in the flesh, we are not carrying on our warfare according to the flesh *and* using mere human weapons.

4 For the weapons of our warfare are not physical (weapons of flesh and blood), but they are mighty before God for the overthrow *and* destruction of strongholds,

5 [Inasmuch as we] refute arguments *and* theories *and* reasonings and every proud *and* lofty thing that sets itself up against the (true) knowledge of God; and we lead every thought *and* purpose away captive into the obedience of Christ, the Messiah, the Anointed One,

6 Being in readiness to punish every [insubordinate for his] disobedience, when your own submission *and* obedience [as a church] are fully secured *and* complete.

7 Look at [this obvious fact] which is before your eyes. If any one is confident that he is Christ's, let him reflect *and* remind himself that even as he is Christ's, so too are we.

8 For even though I boast rather freely about our power *and* authority, which the Lord gave for your upbuilding and not for demolishing you, yet I shall not be put to shame [for exceeding the truth],

9 Neither would I seem to be overawing *or* frightening you with my letters;

10 For they say, His letters are weighty *and* impressive and forceful *and* telling, but his personality *and* bodily presence are weak, and his speech *and* delivery are utterly contemptible—of no account.

11 Let such people realize that what we say by letters when we are absent, [we put] also into deeds when we are present.

12 Not that we [have the audacity to] venture to class or [even to] compare ourselves with some who exalt *and* furnish testimonials for themselves! However, when they measure themselves with themselves and compare themselves with one another, they are without understanding *and* behave unwisely.

13 We, on the other hand, will not boast beyond our legitimate province *and* proper limit, but will keep within the limits [of our commission which] God has allotted us as our measuring line, and which reaches *and* includes even you.

14 For we are not overstepping the limits of our province *and* stretching beyond our ability to reach, as though we (had no legitimate mission to) you, for we were [the very first] to come even as far as to you with the good news (the Gospel) of Christ.

15 We do not boast therefore beyond our proper limit, over other men's labors, but we have the hope *and* confident expectation that as your faith continues to grow our field among you may be greatly enlarged, still within the limits of our commission,

16 So that [we may even] preach the Gospel in lands [lying] beyond you, without making a boast of work already done in another [man's] sphere of activity [before we came on the scene].

## New American Standard

13Because of the proof given by this ministry they will glorify
God for *your* obedience to your confession of the gospel of Christ,
and for the liberality of your contribution to them and to all,
14while they also, by prayer on your behalf, yearn for you
because of the surpassing grace of God in you.
15Thanks be to God for His indescribable gift!

*Paul Describes Himself*

**10** NOW I, Paul, myself urge you by the meekness and gentleness of Christ—I who am meek when face to face with you, but bold toward you when absent!

2I ask that when I am present I may not be bold with the confidence with which I propose to be courageous against some, who regard us as if we walked according to the flesh.

3For though we walk in the flesh, we do not war according to the flesh,

4for the weapons of our warfare are not of the flesh, but divinely powerful for the destruction of fortresses.

5 *We are* destroying speculations and every lofty thing raised up against the knowledge of God, and *we are* taking every thought captive to the obedience of Christ,

6and we are ready to punish all disobedience, whenever your obedience is complete.

7You are looking at things as they are outwardly. If anyone is confident in himself that he is Christ's, let him consider this again within himself, that just as he is Christ's, so also are we.

8For even if I should boast somewhat further about our authority, which the Lord gave for building you up and not for destroying you, I shall not be put to shame,

9for I do not wish to seem as if I would terrify you by my letters.

10For they say, "His letters are weighty and strong, but his personal presence is unimpressive, and his speech contemptible."

11Let such a person consider this, that what we are in word by letters when absent, such persons *we are* also in deed when present.

12For we are not bold to class or compare ourselves with some of those who commend themselves; but when they measure themselves by themselves, and compare themselves with themselves, they are without understanding.

13But we will not boast beyond *our* measure, but within the measure of the sphere which God apportioned to us as a measure, to reach even as far as you.

14For we are not overextending ourselves, as if we did not reach to you, for we were the first to come even as far as you in the gospel of Christ;

15not boasting beyond *our* measure, *that is,* in other men's labors, but with the hope that as your faith grows, we shall be, within our sphere, enlarged even more by you,

16so as to preach the gospel even to the regions beyond you, *and* not to boast in what has been accomplished in the sphere of another.

## New International

yourselves, men will praise God for the obedience that accompanies your confession of the gospel of Christ, and for your generosity in sharing with them and with everyone else.
14And in their prayers for you their hearts will go out to you, because of the surpassing grace God has given you.
15Thanks be to God for his indescribable gift!

*Paul's Defense of His Ministry*

**10** BY THE meekness and gentleness of Christ, I appeal to you—I, Paul, who am "timid" when face to face with you, but "bold" when away!
2I beg you that when I come I may not have to be as bold as I expect to be toward some people who think that we live by the standards of this world.
3For though we live in the world, we do not wage war as the world does.
4The weapons we fight with are not the weapons of the world. On the contrary, they have divine power to demolish strongholds.
5We demolish arguments and every pretension that sets itself up against the knowledge of God, and we take captive every thought to make it obedient to Christ.
6And we will be ready to punish every act of disobedience, once your obedience is complete.
7You are looking only on the surface of things.[a] If anyone is confident that he belongs to Christ, he should consider again that we belong to Christ just as much as he.
8For even if I boast somewhat freely about the authority the Lord gave us for building you up rather than pulling you down, I will not be ashamed of it.
9I do not want to seem to be trying to frighten you with my letters.
10For some say, "His letters are weighty and forceful, but in person he is unimpressive and his speaking amounts to nothing."
11Such people should realize that what we are in our letters when we are absent, we will be in our actions when we are present.
12We do not dare to classify or compare ourselves with some who commend themselves. When they measure themselves by themselves and compare themselves with themselves, they are not wise.
13We, however, will not boast beyond proper limits, but will confine our boasting to the field God has assigned to us, a field that reaches even to you.
14We are not going too far in our boasting, as would be the case if we had not come to you, for we did get as far as you with the gospel of Christ.
15Neither do we go beyond our limits by boasting of work done by others.[b] Our hope is that, as your faith continues to grow, our area of activity among you will greatly expand,
16so that we can preach the gospel in the regions beyond you. For we do not want to boast about work already done in another man's territory.
17But, "Let him who boasts boast in the

**NIV** [a] 7 Or *Look at the obvious facts* [b] 13-15 Or *13We, however, will not boast about things that cannot be measured, but we will boast according to the standard of measurement that the God of measure has assigned us—a measurement that relates even to you. 14 . . . . 15Neither do we boast about things that cannot be measured in regard to the work done by others.*

## King James

17But he that glorieth, let him glory in the Lord.

18For not he that commendeth himself is approved, but whom the Lord commendeth.

# 11

WOULD TO God ye could bear with me a little in *my* folly: and indeed bear with me.

2For I am jealous over you with godly jealousy: for I have espoused you to one husband, that I may present *you as* a chaste virgin to Christ.

3But I fear, lest by any means, as the serpent beguiled Eve through his subtlety, so your minds should be corrupted from the simplicity that is in Christ.

4For if he that cometh preacheth another Jesus, whom we have not preached, or *if* ye receive another spirit, which ye have not received, or another gospel, which ye have not accepted, ye might well bear with *him.*

5For I suppose I was not a whit behind the very chiefest apostles.

6But though *I be* rude in speech, yet not in knowledge; but we have been thoroughly made manifest among you in all things.

7Have I committed an offence in abasing myself that ye might be exalted, because I have preached to you the gospel of God freely?

8I robbed other churches, taking wages *of them,* to do you service.

9And when I was present with you, and wanted, I was chargeable to no man: for that which was lacking to me the brethren which came from Macedonia supplied: and in all *things* I have kept myself from being burdensome unto you, and *so* will I keep *myself.*

10As the truth of Christ is in me, no man shall stop me of this boasting in the regions of Achaia.

11Wherefore? because I love you not? God knoweth.

12But what I do, that I will do, that I may cut off occasion from them which desire occasion; that wherein they glory, they may be found even as we.

13For such *are* false apostles, deceitful workers, transforming themselves into the apostles of Christ.

14And no marvel; for Satan himself is transformed into an angel of light.

15Therefore *it is* no great thing if his ministers also be transformed as the ministers of righteousness; whose end shall be according to their works.

16I say again, Let no man think me a fool; if otherwise, yet as a fool receive me, that I may boast myself a little.

17That which I speak, I speak *it* not after the Lord, but as it were foolishly, in this confidence of boasting.

18Seeing that many glory after the flesh, I will glory also.

19For ye suffer fools gladly, seeing ye *yourselves* are wise.

## Amplified

17However, let him who boasts *and* glories, boast *and* glory in the Lord. [Jer. 9:24.]

18For [it is] not [the man] who praises *and* commends himself who is approved *and* accepted, but [it is the person] whom the Lord accredits *and* commends.

# 11

I WISH you would bear with me while I indulge in a little [so-called] foolishness. Do bear with me!

2For I am [a]zealous for you with a godly eagerness *and* a divine jealousy, for I have betrothed you to one Husband, to present you a chaste virgin to Christ. [Hos. 2:19, 20.]

3But [now] I am fearful lest that even as the serpent beguiled Eve by his cunning, so your minds may be corrupted *and* seduced from wholehearted *and* sincere *and* pure devotion to Christ. [Gen. 3:4.]

4For [you seem readily to endure it] if a man comes and preaches another Jesus than the One we preached, or if you receive a different spirit from the [Spirit] you [once] received, or a different gospel from the one you [then] received *and* welcomed. You tolerate [all that] well enough!

5Yet I consider myself as in no way inferior to these (precious) [b]extra-super [false] apostles.

6But even if [I am] unskilled in speaking, yet [I am] not [unskilled] in knowledge—I know what I am talking about; we have made this evident to you in all things.

7But did I perhaps make a mistake *and* do you a wrong in debasing *and* cheapening myself so that you might be exalted *and* enriched in dignity *and* honor *and* happiness, by preaching God's Gospel without expense to you?

8Other churches I have robbed by accepting [more than their share of] support for my ministry [from them in order] to serve you.

9And when I was with you and ran short financially, I did not burden any [of you], for what I lacked was abundantly made up by the brethren who came from Macedonia. So I kept myself from being burdensome to you in any way, and will continue to keep [myself from being so].

10As the truth of Christ is in me, this my boast [of independence] shall not be debarred (silenced or checked) in the regions of Achaia [most of Greece].

11And why? Because I do not love you—do not have a preference for you, wish you well and regard your welfare? God perceives *and* knows that I do!

12But what I do I will continue to do, [for I am determined to maintain this independence] in order to cut off the claim of those who would like [to find an occasion and incentive] to claim that in their boasted [mission] they work on the same terms that we do.

13For such men are false apostles—spurious, counterfeits—deceitful workmen, masquerading as apostles (special messengers) of Christ, the Messiah.

14And it is no wonder, for Satan himself masquerades as an angel of light,

15So it is not surprising if his servants also masquerade as ministers of righteousness. [But] their end will correspond with their deeds.

16I repeat then, let no one think I have lost my wits; but even if you do, then bear with a witless man, so that I too may boast a little.

17What I say by way of this confident boasting, I say not with the Lord's authority (by inspiration) but as it were in pure witlessness.

18[For], since many boast of worldly things *and* according to the flesh, I will glory (boast) also.

19For you readily *and* gladly bear with the foolish, since you are so smart *and* wise yourselves!

**AMP** [a] Abbott-Smith, Thayer, Berry, etc. [b] Farrar's "Life and Work of Saint Paul."

## New American Standard

17But HE WHO BOASTS, LET HIM BOAST IN THE LORD.
18For not he who commends himself is approved, but whom the Lord commends.

*Paul Defends His Apostleship*

**11** I WISH that you would bear with me in a little foolishness; but indeed you are bearing with me.
2For I am jealous for you with a godly jealousy; for I betrothed you to one husband, that to Christ I might present you *as* a pure virgin.
3But I am afraid, lest as the serpent deceived Eve by his craftiness, your minds should be led astray from the simplicity and purity *of devotion* to Christ.
4For if one comes and preaches another Jesus whom we have not preached, or you receive a different spirit which you have not received, or a different gospel which you have not accepted, you bear *this* beautifully.
5For I consider myself not in the least inferior to the most eminent apostles.
6But even if I am unskilled in speech, yet I am not *so* in knowledge; in fact, in every way we have made *this* evident to you in all things.
7Or did I commit a sin in humbling myself that you might be exalted, because I preached the gospel of God to you without charge?
8I robbed other churches, taking wages *from them* to serve you;
9and when I was present with you and was in need, I was not a burden to anyone; for when the brethren came from Macedonia, they fully supplied my need, and in everything I kept myself from being a burden to you, and will continue to do so.
10As the truth of Christ is in me, this boasting of mine will not be stopped in the regions of Achaia.
11Why? Because I do not love you? God knows *I do!*
12But what I am doing, I will continue to do, that I may cut off opportunity from those who desire an opportunity to be regarded just as we are in the matter about which they are boasting.
13For such men are false apostles, deceitful workers, disguising themselves as apostles of Christ.
14And no wonder, for even Satan disguises himself as an angel of light.
15Therefore it is not surprising if his servants also disguise themselves as servants of righteousness; whose end shall be according to their deeds.
16¶ Again I say, let no one think me foolish; but if *you do,* receive me even as foolish, that I also may boast a little.
17That which I am speaking, I am not speaking as the Lord would, but as in foolishness, in this confidence of boasting.
18Since many boast according to the flesh, I will boast also.
19For you, being *so* wise, bear with the foolish gladly.

## New International

Lord."[c] 18For it is not the one who commends himself who is approved, but the one whom the Lord commends.

*Paul and the False Apostles*

**11** I HOPE you will put up with a little of my foolishness; but you are already doing that. 2I am jealous for you with a godly jealousy. I promised you to one husband, to Christ, so that I might present you as a pure virgin to him. 3But I am afraid that just as Eve was deceived by the serpent's cunning, your minds may somehow be led astray from your sincere and pure devotion to Christ. 4For if someone comes to you and preaches a Jesus other than the Jesus we preached, or if you receive a different spirit from the one you received, or a different gospel from the one you accepted, you put up with it easily enough. 5But I do not think I am in the least inferior to those "super-apostles." 6I may not be a trained speaker, but I do have knowledge. We have made this perfectly clear to you in every way.

7Was it a sin for me to lower myself in order to elevate you by preaching the gospel of God to you free of charge? 8I robbed other churches by receiving support from them so as to serve you. 9And when I was with you and needed something, I was not a burden to anyone, for the brothers who came from Macedonia supplied what I needed. I have kept myself from being a burden to you in any way, and will continue to do so. 10As surely as the truth of Christ is in me, nobody in the regions of Achaia will stop this boasting of mine. 11Why? Because I do not love you? God knows I do! 12And I will keep on doing what I am doing in order to cut the ground from under those who want an opportunity to be considered equal with us in the things they boast about.

13For such men are false apostles, deceitful workmen, masquerading as apostles of Christ. 14And no wonder, for Satan himself masquerades as an angel of light. 15It is not surprising, then, if his servants masquerade as servants of righteousness. Their end will be what their actions deserve.

*Paul Boasts About His Sufferings*

16I repeat: Let no one take me for a fool. But if you do, then receive me just as you would a fool, so that I may do a little boasting. 17In this self-confident boasting I am not talking as the Lord would, but as a fool. 18Since many are boasting in the way the world does, I too will boast. 19You gladly put up with fools since you are so wise! 20In fact, you even put up with anyone who

NIV [c] *17* Jer. 9:24

## King James

20For ye suffer, if a man bring you into bondage, if a man devour *you*, if a man take *of you*, if a man exalt himself, if a man smite you on the face.

21I speak as concerning reproach, as though we had been weak. Howbeit whereinsoever any is bold, (I speak foolishly,) I am bold also.

22Are they Hebrews? so *am* I. Are they Israelites? so *am* I. Are they the seed of Abraham? so *am* I.

23Are they ministers of Christ? (I speak as a fool) I *am* more; in labours more abundant, in stripes above measure, in prisons more frequent, in deaths oft.

24Of the Jews five times received I forty *stripes* save one.

25Thrice was I beaten with rods, once was I stoned, thrice I suffered shipwreck, a night and a day I have been in the deep;

26 *In* journeyings often, *in* perils of waters, *in* perils of robbers, *in* perils by *mine own* countrymen, *in* perils by the heathen, *in* perils in the city, *in* perils in the wilderness, *in* perils in the sea, *in* perils among false brethren;

27In weariness and painfulness, in watchings often, in hunger and thirst, in fastings often, in cold and nakedness.

28Beside those things that are without, that which cometh upon me daily, the care of all the churches.

29Who is weak, and I am not weak? who is offended, and I burn not?

30If I must needs glory, I will glory of the things which concern mine infirmities.

31The God and Father of our Lord Jesus Christ, which is blessed for evermore, knoweth that I lie not.

32In Damascus the governor under Aretas the king kept the city of the Damascenes with a garrison, desirous to apprehend me:

33And through a window in a basket was I let down by the wall, and escaped his hands.

**12** IT IS not expedient for me doubtless to glory. I will come to visions and revelations of the Lord.

2I knew a man in Christ above fourteen years ago, (whether in the body, I cannot tell; or whether out of the body, I cannot tell: God knoweth;) such an one caught up to the third heaven.

3And I knew such a man, (whether in the body, or out of the body, I cannot tell: God knoweth;)

4How that he was caught up into paradise, and heard unspeakable words, which it is not lawful for a man to utter.

5Of such an one will I glory: yet of myself I will not glory, but in mine infirmities.

6For though I would desire to glory, I shall not be a fool; for I will say the truth: but *now* I forbear, lest any man should think of me above that which he seeth me *to be*, or *that* he heareth of me.

## Amplified

20For you endure it if a man assumes control of your souls *and* makes slaves of you, or devours (your substance, spends your money) *and* preys upon you, or deceives *and* takes advantage of you, or is arrogant *and* puts on airs, or strikes you in the face.

21To my discredit, I must say, we have shown ourselves too weak [for you to show such tolerance of us; for us to do strong, courageous things like that to you]! But in whatever any person is bold *and* dares [to boast], mind I am speaking in this foolish (witless) way, I also am bold *and* dare [to boast].

22They are Hebrews? So am I! They are Israelites? So am I! They are descendants of Abraham? So am I!

23Are they (ministering) servants of Christ, the Messiah? I am talking like one beside himself, [but] I am more, with far more extensive *and* abundant labors, with far more imprisonments, [beaten] with countless stripes, and frequently [at the point of] death.

24Five times I received from [the hands of] the Jews forty [lashes all] but one; [Deut. 25:3.]

25Three times I have been beaten with rods; once I was stoned. Three times I have been aboard a ship wrecked at sea; a [whole] night and a day I have spent (adrift) on the deep;

26Many times on journeys, [exposed to] perils from rivers, perils from bandits, perils from [my own] nation, perils from the Gentiles, perils in the city, perils in the desert places, perils in the sea, perils from those posing as believers—but destitute of Christian knowledge and piety;

27In toil and hardship, watching often (through sleepless nights), in hunger and thirst, frequently driven to fasting by want, in cold and exposure *and* lack of clothing.

28And besides those things that are without, there is the daily [inescapable pressure] of my care *and* anxiety for all the churches!

29Who is weak, and I do not feel [his] weakness? Who is made to stumble *and* fall *and* have his faith hurt, and I am not on fire [with sorrow or indignation]?

30If I must boast, I will boast of the things that [show] my infirmity—of the things by which I am made weak and contemptible [in the eyes of my opponents].

31The God and Father of the Lord Jesus *Christ* knows, He Who is blessed *and* to be praised forevermore, that I do not lie.

32In Damascus, the city governor acting under King Aretas guarded the city of Damascus [on purpose] to arrest me,

33And I was [actually] let down in a (rope) basket *or* hamper, through a window [a small door] in the wall, and I escaped through his fingers.

**12** TRUE, THERE is nothing to be gained by it, but [as I am obliged] to boast I will go on to visions and revelations of the Lord.

2I know a man in Christ who fourteen years ago, whether in the body or out of the body I do not know, God knows, was caught up to the third heaven.

3And I know that this man was caught up into Paradise, whether in the body or away from the body I do not know, God knows.

4And he heard utterances beyond the power of man to put into words, which man is not permitted to utter.

5Of this same [man's experiences] I will boast, but of myself (personally) I will not boast, except as regards my infirmities—my weaknesses.

6Should I desire to boast, I shall not be a witless braggart, for I shall be speaking the truth. But I abstain [from it] so that no one may form a higher estimate of me than [is justified by] what he sees in me or hears from me.

## New American Standard

20For you bear with anyone if he enslaves you, if he devours you, if he takes advantage of you, if he exalts himself, if he hits you in the face.

21To *my* shame I *must* say that we have been weak *by comparison.* But in whatever respect anyone *else* is bold (I speak in foolishness), I am just as bold myself.

22Are they Hebrews? So am I. Are they Israelites? So am I. Are they descendants of Abraham? So am I.

23Are they servants of Christ? (I speak as if insane) I more so; in far more labors, in far more imprisonments, beaten times without number, often in danger of death.

24Five times I received from the Jews thirty-nine *lashes.*

25Three times I was beaten with rods, once I was stoned, three times I was shipwrecked, a night and a day I have spent in the deep.

26 *I have been* on frequent journeys, in dangers from rivers, dangers from robbers, dangers from *my* countrymen, dangers from the Gentiles, dangers in the city, dangers in the wilderness, dangers on the sea, dangers among false brethren;

27 *I have been* in labor and hardship, through many sleepless nights, in hunger and thirst, often without food, in cold and exposure.

28Apart from *such* external things, there is the daily pressure upon me *of* concern for all the churches.

29Who is weak without my being weak? Who is led into sin without my intense concern?

30If I have to boast, I will boast of what pertains to my weakness.

31The God and Father of the Lord Jesus, He who is blessed forever, knows that I am not lying.

32In Damascus the ethnarch under Aretas the king was guarding the city of the Damascenes in order to seize me,

33and I was let down in a basket through a window in the wall, and *so* escaped his hands.

*Paul's Vision*

**12** BOASTING IS necessary, though it is not profitable; but I will go on to visions and revelations of the Lord.

2I know a man in Christ who fourteen years ago—whether in the body I do not know, or out of the body I do not know, God knows—such a man was caught up to the third heaven.

3And I know how such a man—whether in the body or apart from the body I do not know, God knows—

4was caught up into Paradise, and heard inexpressible words, which a man is not permitted to speak.

5On behalf of such a man will I boast; but on my own behalf I will not boast, except in regard to *my* weaknesses.

6For if I do wish to boast I shall not be foolish, for I shall be speaking the truth; but I refrain *from this,* so that no one may credit me with more than he sees *in* me or hears from me.

## New International

enslaves you or exploits you or takes advantage of you or pushes
himself forward or slaps you in the face. 21To my shame I admit
that we were too weak for that!

What anyone else dares to boast about—I am speaking as a
fool—I also dare to boast about. 22Are they Hebrews? So am I. Are
they Israelites? So am I. Are they Abraham's descendants? So am
I. 23Are they servants of Christ? (I am out of my mind to talk like
this.) I am more. I have worked much harder, been in prison more
frequently, been flogged more severely, and been exposed to
death again and again. 24Five times I received from the Jews the
forty lashes minus one. 25Three times I was beaten with rods, once
I was stoned, three times I was shipwrecked, I spent a night and
a day in the open sea, 26I have been constantly on the move. I have
been in danger from rivers, in danger from bandits, in danger from
my own countrymen, in danger from Gentiles; in danger in the
city, in danger in the country, in danger at sea; and in danger from
false brothers. 27I have labored and toiled and have often gone
without sleep; I have known hunger and thirst and have often
gone without food; I have been cold and naked. 28Besides everything else, I face daily the pressure of my concern for all the
churches. 29Who is weak, and I do not feel weak? Who is led into
sin, and I do not inwardly burn?

30If I must boast, I will boast of the things that show my weakness. 31The God and Father of the Lord Jesus, who is to be praised
forever, knows that I am not lying. 32In Damascus the governor
under King Aretas had the city of the Damascenes guarded in
order to arrest me. 33But I was lowered in a basket from a window
in the wall and slipped through his hands.

*Paul's Vision and His Thorn*

**12** I MUST go on boasting. Although there is nothing to be
gained, I will go on to visions and revelations from the
Lord. 2I know a man in Christ who fourteen years ago was caught
up to the third heaven. Whether it was in the body or out of the
body I do not know—God knows. 3And I know that this man—
whether in the body or apart from the body I do not know, but God
knows— 4was caught up to paradise. He heard inexpressible
things, things that man is not permitted to tell. 5I will boast about
a man like that, but I will not boast about myself, except about my
weaknesses. 6Even if I should choose to boast, I would not be a
fool, because I would be speaking the truth. But I refrain, so no
one will think more of me than is warranted by what I do or say.

## King James

7And lest I should be exalted above measure through the abundance of the revelations, there was given to me a thorn in the flesh, the messenger of Satan to buffet me, lest I should be exalted above measure.

8For this thing I besought the Lord thrice, that it might depart from me.

9And he said unto me, My grace is sufficient for thee: for my strength is made perfect in weakness. Most gladly therefore will I rather glory in my infirmities, that the power of Christ may rest upon me.

10Therefore I take pleasure in infirmities, in reproaches, in necessities, in persecutions, in distresses for Christ's sake: for when I am weak, then am I strong.

11I am become a fool in glorying; ye have compelled me: for I ought to have been commended of you: for in nothing am I behind the very chiefest apostles, though I be nothing.

12Truly the signs of an apostle were wrought among you in all patience, in signs, and wonders, and mighty deeds.

13For what is it wherein ye were inferior to other churches, except *it be* that I myself was not burdensome to you? forgive me this wrong.

14Behold, the third time I am ready to come to you; and I will not be burdensome to you: for I seek not yours, but you: for the children ought not to lay up for the parents, but the parents for the children.

15And I will very gladly spend and be spent for you, though the more abundantly I love you, the less I be loved.

16But be it so, I did not burden you: nevertheless, being crafty, I caught you with guile.

17Did I make a gain of you by any of them whom I sent unto you?

18I desired Titus, and with *him* I sent a brother. Did Titus make a gain of you? walked we not in the same spirit? *walked we* not in the same steps?

19Again, think ye that we excuse ourselves unto you? we speak before God in Christ: but *we do* all things, dearly beloved, for your edifying.

20For I fear, lest, when I come, I shall not find you such as I would, and *that* I shall be found unto you such as ye would not: lest *there be* debates, envyings, wraths, strifes, backbitings, whisperings, swellings, tumults:

21 *And* lest, when I come again, my God will humble me among you, and *that* I shall bewail many which have sinned already, and have not repented of the uncleanness and fornication and lasciviousness which they have committed.

## Amplified

7And to keep me from being puffed up *and* too much elated by the exceeding greatness (pre-eminence) of these revelations, there was given me a thorn ([a]a splinter) in the flesh, a messenger of Satan, to rack *and* buffet *and* harass me, to keep me from being excessively exalted. [Job. 2:6.]

8Three times I called upon the Lord *and* besought [Him] about this *and* begged that it might depart from me;

9But He said to me, My grace—My favor and loving-kindness and mercy—are enough for you, [that is, sufficient against any danger and to enable you to bear the trouble manfully]; for *My* strength *and* power are made perfect—fulfilled and completed *and* [b]*show themselves most effective*—in [your] weakness. Therefore, I will all the more gladly glory in my weaknesses *and* infirmities, that the strength *and* power of Christ, the Messiah, may rest—yes, may [c]pitch a tent [over] and dwell—upon me!

10So for the sake of Christ, I am well pleased *and* take pleasure in infirmities, insults, hardships, persecutions, perplexities *and* distresses; for when I am weak ([d]in human strength), then am I [truly] strong—able, powerful [e]in divine strength.

11Now I have been [speaking like] a fool! But you forced me to it, for I ought to have been [[f]saved the necessity and] commended by you. For I have not fallen short one bit *or* proved myself at all inferior to those superlative [false] apostles [of yours], even if I am nothing—a nobody.

12Indeed, the signs that indicate [a genuine] apostle were performed among you fully *and* most patiently in miracles and wonders and mighty works.

13For in what respect were you put to a disadvantage in comparison with the rest of the churches, unless [it was for the fact] that I myself did not burden you [with my financial support]? Pardon me [for doing you] this injustice!

14Now for the third time I am ready to come to [visit] you. And I will not burden you [financially], for it is not yours that I want but you; for children are not duty bound to lay up store for their parents, but parents for their children.

15But I will most gladly spend and be utterly spent [myself] for your souls. If I love you exceedingly, am I to be loved [by you] the less?

16But though granting that I did not burden you [with my support, some say] I was crafty, *and* that I cheated *and* got the better of you with my trickery.

17Did I [then] take advantage of you *or* make any money out of you through any of those [messengers] whom I sent to you?

18[Actually] I urged Titus [to go], and I sent the brother with [him]. Did Titus overreach *or* take advantage of you [in anything]? Did he *and* I not act in the same spirit? Did we not [take the] same steps?

19Have you been supposing [all this time] that we have been defending ourselves *and* apologizing to you? [It is] in the sight *and* the [very] presence of God [and as one] in Christ, the Messiah, that we have been speaking, dearly beloved, and all in order to build you up [spiritually].

20For I am fearful lest somehow or other I may come and find you not what I desire to find you, and that you may find me too not what you want to find me; lest perhaps there may be factions (quarreling), jealousy, temper (wrath, intrigues, rivalry, divided loyalties), selfishness, whispering, gossip, arrogance (self-assertion) and disorder among you.

21[I am fearful] that when I come again my God may humiliate *and* humble me in your regard, and that I may have to sorrow over many of those who sinned before and have not repented of the impurity, sexual vice and sensuality which they formerly practiced.

**AMP** [a] Moulton and Milligan's "The Vocabulary of the Greek Testament." [b] Two Greek texts so read. [c] Vincent. [d] Thayer. [e] Thayer. [f] Vincent.

## New American Standard

*A Thorn in the Flesh*

7And because of the surpassing greatness of the revelations,
for this reason, to keep me from exalting myself, there was given
me a thorn in the flesh, a messenger of Satan to buffet me—to keep
me from exalting myself!
8Concerning this I entreated the Lord three times that it might
depart from me.
9And He has said to me, "My grace is sufficient for you, for
[g]power is perfected in weakness." Most gladly, therefore, I will
rather boast about my weaknesses, that the power of Christ may
dwell in me.
10Therefore I am well content with weaknesses, with insults,
with distresses, with persecutions, with difficulties, for Christ's
sake; for when I am weak, then I am strong.
11¶ I have become foolish; you yourselves compelled me. Actually I should have been commended by you, for in no respect was
I inferior to the most eminent apostles, even though I am a nobody.
12The signs of a true apostle were performed among you with
all perseverance, by signs and wonders and miracles.
13For in what respect were you treated as inferior to the rest of
the churches, except that I myself did not become a burden to you?
Forgive me this wrong!
14¶ Here for this third time I am ready to come to you, and I will
not be a burden to you; for I do not seek what is yours, but you;
for children are not responsible to save up for *their* parents, but
parents for *their* children.
15And I will most gladly spend and be expended for your souls.
If I love you the more, am I to be loved the less?
16But be that as it may, I did not burden you myself; nevertheless, crafty fellow that I am, I took you in by deceit.
17*Certainly* I have not taken advantage of you through any of
those whom I have sent to you, have I?
18I urged Titus *to go,* and sent the brother with him. Titus did
not take any advantage of you, did he? Did we not conduct ourselves in the same spirit *and walk* in the same steps?
19¶ All this time you have been thinking that we are defending
ourselves to you. *Actually,* it is in the sight of God that we have
been speaking in Christ; and all for your upbuilding, beloved.
20For I am afraid that perhaps when I come I may find you to
be not what I wish and may be found by you to be not what you
wish; that perhaps *there may be* strife, jealousy, angry tempers,
disputes, slanders, gossip, arrogance, disturbances;
21I am afraid that when I come again my God may humiliate me
before you, and I may mourn over many of those who have sinned
in the past and not repented of the impurity, immorality and
sensuality which they have practiced.

NAS g Later mss. read *My power*

## New International

7To keep me from becoming conceited because of these surpass-
ingly great revelations, there was given me a thorn in my flesh, a
messenger of Satan, to torment me. 8Three times I pleaded with
the Lord to take it away from me. 9But he said to me, "My grace
is sufficient for you, for my power is made perfect in weakness."
Therefore I will boast all the more gladly about my weaknesses, so
that Christ's power may rest on me. 10That is why, for Christ's
sake, I delight in weaknesses, in insults, in hardships, in persecutions, in difficulties. For when I am weak, then I am strong.

*Paul's Concern for the Corinthians*

11I have made a fool of myself, but you drove me to it. I ought
to have been commended by you, for I am not in the least inferior
to the "super-apostles," even though I am nothing. 12The things
that mark an apostle—signs, wonders and miracles—were done
among you with great perseverance. 13How were you inferior to
the other churches, except that I was never a burden to you?
Forgive me this wrong!
14Now I am ready to visit you for the third time, and I will not
be a burden to you, because what I want is not your possessions
but you. After all, children should not have to save up for their
parents, but parents for their children. 15So I will very gladly spend
for you everything I have and expend myself as well. If I love you
more, will you love me less? 16Be that as it may, I have not been
a burden to you. Yet, crafty fellow that I am, I caught you by
trickery! 17Did I exploit you through any of the men I sent you? 18I
urged Titus to go to you and I sent our brother with him. Titus did
not exploit you, did he? Did we not act in the same spirit and follow
the same course?
19Have you been thinking all along that we have been defending ourselves to you? We have been speaking in the sight of God
as those in Christ; and everything we do, dear friends, is for your
strengthening. 20For I am afraid that when I come I may not find
you as I want you to be, and you may not find me as you want
me to be. I fear that there may be quarreling, jealousy, outbursts
of anger, factions, slander, gossip, arrogance and disorder. 21I am
afraid that when I come again my God will humble me before you,
and I will be grieved over many who have sinned earlier and have
not repented of the impurity, sexual sin and debauchery in which
they have indulged.

## King James

13 THIS *IS* the third *time* I am coming to you. In the mouth
of two or three witnesses shall every word be established.
2I told you before, and foretell you, as if I were present, the second time; and being absent now I write to them which heretofore have sinned, and to all other, that, if I come again, I will not spare:
3Since ye seek a proof of Christ speaking in me, which to you-ward is not weak, but is mighty in you.
4For though he was crucified through weakness, yet he liveth by the power of God. For we also are weak in him, but we shall live with him by the power of God toward you.
5Examine yourselves, whether ye be in the faith; prove your own selves. Know ye not your own selves, how that Jesus Christ is in you, except ye be reprobates?
6But I trust that ye shall know that we are not reprobates.
7Now I pray to God that ye do no evil; not that we should appear approved, but that ye should do that which is honest, though we be as reprobates.
8For we can do nothing against the truth, but for the truth.
9For we are glad, when we are weak, and ye are strong: and this also we wish, *even* your perfection.
10Therefore I write these things being absent, lest being present I should use sharpness, according to the power which the Lord hath given me to edification, and not to destruction.
11Finally, brethren, farewell. Be perfect, be of good comfort, be of one mind, live in peace; and the God of love and peace shall be with you.
12Greet one another with an holy kiss.
13All the saints salute you.
14The grace of the Lord Jesus Christ, and the love of God, and the communion of the Holy Ghost, *be* with you all. Amen.

## Amplified

13 THIS IS the third time that I am coming to you. By the
testimony of two or three witnesses must any charge *and* every accusing statement be sustained *and* confirmed. [Deut. 19:15.]
2I have already warned those who sinned formerly and all the rest also, and I warn them now again while I am absent, as I did when present on my second visit, that if I come back I will not spare [them],
3Since you desire *and* seek (perceptible) proof of the Christ Who speaks in *and* through me. [For He] is not weak *and* feeble in dealing with you, but is a mighty power within you;
4For though He was crucified in weakness, yet He goes on living by the power of God. And though we too are weak in Him [as He was humanly weak], yet in dealing with you [we shall show ourselves] alive *and* strong in (fellowship with) Him by the power of God.
5Examine *and* test *and* evaluate your own selves, to see whether you are holding to your faith *and* showing the proper fruits of it. Test *and* prove yourselves, [ [a]not Christ]. Do you not yourselves realize *and* know (thoroughly by an ever-increasing experience) that Jesus Christ is in you? unless you are [counterfeits] disapproved on trial *and* rejected!
6But I hope you will recognize *and* know that we are not disapproved on trial and rejected.
7But I pray to God that you may do nothing wrong, not in order that we [ [b]our teaching] may appear to be approved, but that you may continue doing right, [though] we may seem to have failed *and* be unapproved.
8For we can do nothing against the Truth [ [c]not serve any party or personal interest], but only for the Truth [ [d]which is the Gospel].
9For we are glad when we are weak ( [e]unapproved) and you are really strong. And this we also pray for, your all round strengthening *and* perfecting of soul.
10So I write these things while I am absent from you, that when I come to you I may not have to deal sharply in my use of the authority which the Lord has given me, [to be employed, however] for building [you] up and not for tearing [you] down.
11Finally, brethren, farewell—rejoice! Be strengthened—perfected, completed, made what you ought to be; be encouraged *and* consoled *and* comforted; be of the same (agreeable) mind one with another; live in peace, and [then] the God of love [Who is the Source]—of affection, goodwill, love and benevolence toward men—and the Author *and* Promoter of peace will be with you.
12Greet one another with a consecrated kiss.
13All the saints (the people of God here) salute you.
14The grace (favor and spiritual blessing) of the Lord Jesus Christ and the love of God and the presence *and* fellowship (the communion and sharing together, and participation) in the Holy Spirit be with you all. *Amen—so be it.*

**AMP** [a] Vincent. [b] Vincent. [c] Gray and Adams' Commentary. [d] Thayer. [e] Vincent.

## New American Standard

*Examine Yourselves*

**13** THIS IS the third time I am coming to you. EVERY FACT IS TO BE CONFIRMED BY THE TESTIMONY OF TWO OR THREE WITNESSES.

2I have previously said when present the second time, and though now absent I say in advance to those who have sinned in the past and to all the rest as well, that if I come again, I will not spare *anyone*,

3since you are seeking for proof of the Christ who speaks in me, and who is not weak toward you, but mighty in you.

4For indeed He was crucified because of weakness, yet He lives because of the power of God. For we also are weak [f]in Him, yet we shall live with Him because of the power of God *directed* toward you.

5Test yourselves *to see* if you are in the faith; examine yourselves! Or do you not recognize this about yourselves, that Jesus Christ is in you—unless indeed you fail the test?

6But I trust that you will realize that we ourselves do not fail the test.

7Now we pray to God that you do no wrong; not that we ourselves may appear approved, but that you may do what is right, even though we should appear unapproved.

8For we can do nothing against the truth, but *only* for the truth.

9For we rejoice when we ourselves are weak but you are strong; this we also pray for, that you be made complete.

10For this reason I am writing these things while absent, in order that when present I may not use severity, in accordance with the authority which the Lord gave me, for building up and not for tearing down.

11¶ Finally, brethren, rejoice, be made complete, be comforted, be like-minded, live in peace; and the God of love and peace shall be with you.

12Greet one another with a holy kiss.

13All the saints greet you.

14¶ The grace of the Lord Jesus Christ, and the love of God, and the fellowship of the Holy Spirit, be with you all.

NAS [f] Some early mss. read *with Him*

## New International

*Final Warnings*

**13** THIS WILL be my third visit to you. "Every matter must be established by the testimony of two or three witnesses."[g] 2I already gave you a warning when I was with you the second time. I now repeat it while absent: On my return I will not spare those who sinned earlier or any of the others, 3since you are demanding proof that Christ is speaking through me. He is not weak in dealing with you, but is powerful among you. 4For to be sure, he was crucified in weakness, yet he lives by God's power. Likewise, we are weak in him, yet by God's power we will live with him to serve you.

5Examine yourselves to see whether you are in the faith; test yourselves. Do you not realize that Christ Jesus is in you—unless, of course, you fail the test? 6And I trust that you will discover that we have not failed the test. 7Now we pray to God that you will not do anything wrong. Not that people will see that we have stood the test but that you will do what is right even though we may seem to have failed. 8For we cannot do anything against the truth, but only for the truth. 9We are glad whenever we are weak but you are strong; and our prayer is for your perfection. 10This is why I write these things when I am absent, that when I come I may not have to be harsh in my use of authority—the authority the Lord gave me for building you up, not for tearing you down.

*Final Greetings*

11Finally, brothers, good-by. Aim for perfection, listen to my appeal, be of one mind, live in peace. And the God of love and peace will be with you.

12Greet one another with a holy kiss. 13All the saints send their greetings.

14May the grace of the Lord Jesus Christ, and the love of God, and the fellowship of the Holy Spirit be with you all.

NIV [g] *1* Deut. 19:15

## King James

THE EPISTLE OF
PAUL THE APOSTLE TO THE

# Galatians

1 PAUL, AN apostle, (not of men, neither by man, but by Jesus Christ, and God the Father, who raised him from the dead;)

2 And all the brethren which are with me, unto the churches of Galatia:

3 Grace *be* to you and peace from God the Father, and *from* our Lord Jesus Christ,

4 Who gave himself for our sins, that he might deliver us from this present evil world, according to the will of God and our Father:

5 To whom *be* glory for ever and ever. Amen.

6 I marvel that ye are so soon removed from him that called you into the grace of Christ unto another gospel:

7 Which is not another; but there be some that trouble you, and would pervert the gospel of Christ.

8 But though we, or an angel from heaven, preach any other gospel unto you than that which we have preached unto you, let him be accursed.

9 As we said before, so say I now again, If any *man* preach any other gospel unto you than that ye have received, let him be accursed.

10 For do I now persuade men, or God? or do I seek to please men? for if I yet pleased men, I should not be the servant of Christ.

11 But I certify you, brethren, that the gospel which was preached of me is not after man.

12 For I neither received it of man, neither was I taught *it*, but by the revelation of Jesus Christ.

13 For ye have heard of my conversation in time past in the Jews' religion, how that beyond measure I persecuted the church of God, and wasted it:

14 And profited in the Jews' religion above many my equals in mine own nation, being more exceedingly zealous of the traditions of my fathers.

15 But when it pleased God, who separated me from my mother's womb, and called *me* by his grace,

## Amplified

THE LETTER OF PAUL
TO THE

# Galatians

1 PAUL, AN apostle—special messenger appointed and commissioned and sent out—not from [any body of] men nor by *or* through [a]any man, but by *and* through Jesus Christ, the Messiah, and God the Father Who raised Him from among the dead;

2 And all the brethren who are with me, to the churches of Galatia:

3 Grace *and* spiritual blessing be to you and soul peace from God the Father and our Lord Jesus Christ, the Messiah,

4 Who gave (yielded) Himself up [ [b]to atone] for our sins (and [c]to save and sanctify us), in order to rescue *and* deliver us from this present wicked age *and* world order, in accordance with the will *and* purpose *and* plan of our God and Father.

5 To Him [be ascribed all] the glory through all the ages of the ages *and* the eternities of the eternities! Amen—so be it.

6 I am surprised *and* astonished that you are so quickly [d]turning renegade *and* deserting Him Who invited *and* called you [e]by the grace (unmerited favor) of Christ, the Messiah, [and that you are transferring your allegiance] to a different, *even* an opposition gospel.

7 Not that there is [or could be] any other [genuine Gospel], but there are [obviously] some who are troubling *and* disturbing *and* bewildering you ( [f]with a different kind of teaching which they offer as a gospel) and want to pervert *and* distort the Gospel of Christ, the Messiah [into something which it absolutely is not].

8 But even if we or an angel from heaven should preach to you a gospel contrary to *and* different from that which we preached to you, let him be accursed—anathema, devoted to destruction, doomed to eternal punishment!

9 As we said before, so I now say again, If any one is preaching to you a gospel different from *or* contrary to that which you received [from us], let him be accursed—anathema, devoted to destruction, doomed to eternal punishment!

10 Now, am I trying to win the favor of men, or of God? Do I seek to be a man-pleaser? If I were still seeking popularity with men, I should not be a bondservant of Christ, the Messiah.

11 For I want you to know, brethren, that the Gospel which was proclaimed *and* made known by me is not man's gospel—a human invention, according to or patterned after any human standard.

12 For indeed I did not receive it from man, nor was I taught it; [it came to me] through a [direct] revelation [given] by Jesus Christ, the Messiah.

13 You have heard of my earlier career *and* former manner of life in the Jewish religion (Judaism), how I persecuted *and* abused the church of God furiously *and* extensively, and [with fanatical zeal did my best] to make havoc of it *and* destroy it.

14 And [have heard how] I outstripped many of the men of my own generation among the people of my race, in [my advancement in study and observance of the laws of] Judaism, so extremely enthusiastic *and* zealous I was for the traditions of my ancestors.

15 But when He Who had chosen *and* set me apart [even] before I was born, and had called me by His grace (His undeserved favor and blessing), [Isa. 49:1; Jer. 1:5.]

**AMP** [a] Vincent. [b] Vincent. [c] Vincent. [d] Lightfoot. [e] Vincent. [f] Vincent.

## New American Standard

# Galatians

*Introduction*

1 PAUL, AN apostle (not *sent* from men, nor through the
agency of man, but through Jesus Christ, and God the Father,
who raised Him from the dead),
2and all the brethren who are with me, to the churches of
Galatia:
3Grace to you and peace from God our Father, and the Lord
Jesus Christ,
4who gave Himself for our sins, that He might deliver us out
of this present evil age, according to the will of our God and Father,
5to whom *be* the glory forevermore. Amen.

*Perversion of the Gospel*

6¶ I am amazed that you are so quickly deserting Him who
called you by the grace of Christ, for a different gospel;
7which is *really* not another; only there are some who are
disturbing you, and want to distort the gospel of Christ.
8But even though we, or an angel from heaven, should preach
to you a gospel contrary to that which we have preached to you,
let him be accursed.
9As we have said before, so I say again now, if any man is
preaching to you a gospel contrary to that which you received, let
him be accursed.
10For am I now seeking the favor of men, or of God? Or am I
striving to please men? If I were still trying to please men, I would
not be a bond-servant of Christ.

*Paul Defends His Ministry*

11¶ For I would have you know, brethren, that the gospel which
was preached by me is not according to man.
12For I neither received it from man, nor was I taught it, but *I
received it* through a revelation of Jesus Christ.
13For you have heard of my former manner of life in Judaism,
how I used to persecute the church of God beyond measure, and
tried to destroy it;
14and I was advancing in Judaism beyond many of my contemporaries among my countrymen, being more extremely zealous for
my ancestral traditions.
15But when He who had set me apart, *even* from my mother's
womb, and called me through His grace, was pleased

## New International

# Galatians

1 PAUL, AN apostle—sent not from men nor by man, but by
Jesus Christ and God the Father, who raised him from the
dead— 2and all the brothers with me,

To the churches in Galatia:

3Grace and peace to you from God our Father and the Lord
Jesus Christ, 4who gave himself for our sins to rescue us from the
present evil age, according to the will of our God and Father, 5to
whom be glory for ever and ever. Amen.

*No Other Gospel*

6I am astonished that you are so quickly deserting the one who
called you by the grace of Christ and are turning to a different
gospel— 7which is really no gospel at all. Evidently some people
are throwing you into confusion and are trying to pervert the
gospel of Christ. 8But even if we or an angel from heaven should
preach a gospel other than the one we preached to you, let him
be eternally condemned! 9As we have already said, so now I say
again: If anybody is preaching to you a gospel other than what you
accepted, let him be eternally condemned!
10Am I now trying to win the approval of men, or of God? Or
am I trying to please men? If I were still trying to please men, I
would not be a servant of Christ.

*Paul Called by God*

11I want you to know, brothers, that the gospel I preached is
not something that man made up. 12I did not receive it from any
man, nor was I taught it; rather, I received it by revelation from
Jesus Christ.
13For you have heard of my previous way of life in Judaism,
how intensely I persecuted the church of God and tried to destroy
it. 14I was advancing in Judaism beyond many Jews of my own age
and was extremely zealous for the traditions of my fathers. 15But
when God, who set me apart from birth[g] and called me by his
grace, was pleased 16to reveal his Son in me so that I might preach

NIV [g] 15 Or *from my mother's womb*

## King James

16 To reveal his Son in me, that I might preach him among the heathen; immediately I conferred not with flesh and blood:

17 Neither went I up to Jerusalem to them which were apostles before me; but I went into Arabia, and returned again unto Damascus.

18 Then after three years I went up to Jerusalem to see Peter, and abode with him fifteen days.

19 But other of the apostles saw I none, save James the Lord's brother.

20 Now the things which I write unto you, behold, before God, I lie not.

21 Afterwards I came into the regions of Syria, and Cilicia;

22 And was unknown by face unto the churches of Judaea which were in Christ:

23 But they had heard only, That he which persecuted us in times past now preacheth the faith which once he destroyed.

24 And they glorified God in me.

**2** THEN FOURTEEN years after I went up again to Jerusalem with Barnabas, and took Titus with *me* also.

2 And I went up by revelation, and communicated unto them that gospel which I preach among the Gentiles, but privately to them which were of reputation, lest by any means I should run, or had run, in vain.

3 But neither Titus, who was with me, being a Greek, was compelled to be circumcised:

4 And that because of false brethren unawares brought in, who came in privily to spy out our liberty which we have in Christ Jesus, that they might bring us into bondage:

5 To whom we gave place by subjection, no, not for an hour; that the truth of the gospel might continue with you.

6 But of these who seemed to be somewhat, (whatsoever they were, it maketh no matter to me: God accepteth no man's person:) for they who seemed *to be somewhat* in conference added nothing to me:

7 But contrariwise, when they saw that the gospel of the uncircumcision was committed unto me, as *the gospel* of the circumcision *was* unto Peter;

8 (For he that wrought effectually in Peter to the apostleship of the circumcision, the same was mighty in me toward the Gentiles:)

## Amplified

16 Saw fit *and* was pleased to reveal (unveil, disclose) His Son within me so that I might proclaim Him among the Gentiles [the non-Jewish world] as the glad tidings, immediately I did not confer with flesh and blood—did not consult or counsel with any frail human being or communicate with any one.

17 Nor did I [even] go up to Jerusalem to those who were apostles—special messengers of Christ—before I was; but I went away *and* retired into Arabia, and afterward I came back again to Damascus.

18 Then three years later, I did go up to Jerusalem to become (personally) acquainted with Cephas (Peter), and remained with him for fifteen days.

19 But I did not see any of the other apostles—the special messengers of Christ—except James the brother of our Lord.

20 Now—[note carefully] what I am telling you, [for] it is the truth; I write it as if I were standing before the bar of God; I do not lie.

21 Then I went into the districts (countries, regions) of Syria and Cilicia.

22 And so far I was still unknown by sight to the churches of Christ in Judea [the country surrounding Jerusalem].

23 They were only hearing it said, He who used to persecute us is now proclaiming the very faith he once reviled *and* which he set out to ruin *and* tried [with all his might] to destroy.

24 And they glorified God [as the Author and Source of what had taken place] in me.

**2** THEN AFTER (an interval) of fourteen years I again went up to Jerusalem. [This time I went] with Barnabas, taking Titus along with [me] also.

2 I went because it was specially *and* divinely revealed to me that I should go, and I put before them the Gospel, [declaring to them that] which I preach among the Gentiles. However, [I presented the matter] privately before those of repute, [for I wanted to make certain, by thus at first confining my communication to this private conference] that I was not running or had not run in vain—guarding against being discredited either in what I was planning to do or had already done.

3 But [all went well]; even Titus, who was with me, was not compelled [as some had anticipated] to be circumcised, although he was a Greek.

4 [My precaution was] because of [some men who were Christians in name only], false brethren who had been secretly smuggled in [to the Christian brotherhood]; they had slipped in to spy on our liberty *and* the freedom which we have in Christ Jesus, that they might again bring us into bondage [under the Law of Moses].

5 To them we did not yield submission even for a moment, that the truth of the Gospel might continue to be [preserved] for you [in its purity].

6 Moreover, [no new requirements were made] by those who were reputed to be something, though what was their individual position *and* whether they really were of importance or not makes no difference to me; God is not impressed with the positions that men hold *and* He is not partial *and* recognizes no external distinctions. Those [I say] who were of repute imposed no new requirements upon me—had nothing to add to my Gospel and from them I received no new suggestions. [Deut. 10:17.]

7 But on the contrary, when they [really] saw that I had been entrusted [to carry] the Gospel to the uncircumcised [Gentiles, just as definitely] as Peter had been entrusted [to proclaim] the Gospel to the circumcised [Jews, they were agreeable];

8 For He Who motivated *and* fitted Peter *and* worked effectively through him for the mission to the circumcised, motivated *and* fitted me *and* worked through me also for [the mission to] the Gentiles.

## New American Standard

16to reveal His Son in me, that I might preach Him among the
Gentiles, I did not immediately consult with flesh and blood,
17nor did I go up to Jerusalem to those who were apostles before
me; but I went away to Arabia, and returned once more to Damascus.
18¶ Then three years later I went up to Jerusalem to become
acquainted with Cephas, and stayed with him fifteen days.
19But I did not see any other of the apostles except James, the
Lord's brother.
20(Now in what I am writing to you, I assure you before God
that I am not lying.)
21Then I went into the regions of Syria and Cilicia.
22And I was *still* unknown by sight to the churches of Judea
which were in Christ;
23but only, they kept hearing, "He who once persecuted us is
now preaching the faith which he once tried to destroy."
24And they were glorifying God because of me.

*The Council at Jerusalem*

**2** THEN AFTER an interval of fourteen years I went up again
to Jerusalem with Barnabas, taking Titus along also.
2And it was because of a revelation that I went up; and I
submitted to them the gospel which I preach among the Gentiles,
but *I did so* in private to those who were of reputation, for fear that
I might be running, or had run, in vain.
3But not even Titus who was with me, though he was a Greek,
was compelled to be circumcised.
4But *it was* because of the false brethren who had sneaked in
to spy out our liberty which we have in Christ Jesus, in order to
bring us into bondage.
5But we did not yield in subjection to them for even an hour,
so that the truth of the gospel might remain with you.
6But from those who were of high reputation (what they were
makes no difference to me; God shows no partiality)—well, those
who were of reputation contributed nothing to me.
7But on the contrary, seeing that I had been entrusted with the
gospel to the uncircumcised, just as Peter *had been* to the circumcised
8(for He who effectually worked for Peter in *his* apostleship to
the circumcised effectually worked for me also to the Gentiles),

## New International

him among the Gentiles, I did not consult any man, 17nor did I go
up to Jerusalem to see those who were apostles before I was, but
I went immediately into Arabia and later returned to Damascus.
18Then after three years, I went up to Jerusalem to get acquainted with Peter[a] and stayed with him fifteen days. 19I saw
none of the other apostles—only James, the Lord's brother. 20I
assure you before God that what I am writing you is no lie. 21Later
I went to Syria and Cilicia. 22I was personally unknown to the
churches of Judea that are in Christ. 23They only heard the report:
"The man who formerly persecuted us is now preaching the faith
he once tried to destroy." 24And they praised God because of me.

*Paul Accepted by the Apostles*

**2** FOURTEEN YEARS later I went up again to Jerusalem, this
time with Barnabas. I took Titus along also. 2I went in response to a revelation and set before them the gospel that I preach
among the Gentiles. But I did this privately to those who seemed
to be leaders, for fear that I was running or had run my race in vain.
3Yet not even Titus, who was with me, was compelled to be
circumcised, even though he was a Greek. 4⌊This matter arose⌋
because some false brothers had infiltrated our ranks to spy on the
freedom we have in Christ Jesus and to make us slaves. 5We did
not give in to them for a moment, so that the truth of the gospel
might remain with you.
6As for those who seemed to be important—whatever they
were makes no difference to me; God does not judge by external
appearance—those men added nothing to my message. 7On the
contrary, they saw that I had been entrusted with the task of
preaching the gospel to the Gentiles,[b] just as Peter had been to the
Jews.[c] 8For God, who was at work in the ministry of Peter as an
apostle to the Jews, was also at work in my ministry as an apostle
to the Gentiles. 9James, Peter[d] and John, those reputed to be

**NIV** [a] *18* Greek *Cephas* [b] *7* Greek *uncircumcised* [c] *7* Greek *circumcised;* also in verses 8 and 9 [d] *9* Greek *Cephas;* also in verses 11 and 14

## King James

9And when James, Cephas, and John, who seemed to be pillars, perceived the grace that was given unto me, they gave to me and Barnabas the right hands of fellowship; that we *should go* unto the heathen, and they unto the circumcision.

10Only *they would* that we should remember the poor; the same which I also was forward to do.

11But when Peter was come to Antioch, I withstood him to the face, because he was to be blamed.

12For before that certain came from James, he did eat with the Gentiles: but when they were come, he withdrew and separated himself, fearing them which were of the circumcision.

13And the other Jews dissembled likewise with him; insomuch that Barnabas also was carried away with their dissimulation.

14But when I saw that they walked not uprightly according to the truth of the gospel, I said unto Peter before *them* all, If thou, being a Jew, livest after the manner of Gentiles, and not as do the Jews, why compellest thou the Gentiles to live as do the Jews?

15We *who are* Jews by nature, and not sinners of the Gentiles,

16Knowing that a man is not justified by the works of the law, but by the faith of Jesus Christ, even we have believed in Jesus Christ, that we might be justified by the faith of Christ, and not by the works of the law: for by the works of the law shall no flesh be justified.

17But if, while we seek to be justified by Christ, we ourselves also are found sinners, *is* therefore Christ the minister of sin? God forbid.

18For if I build again the things which I destroyed, I make myself a transgressor.

19For I through the law am dead to the law, that I might live unto God.

20I am crucified with Christ: nevertheless I live; yet not I, but Christ liveth in me: and the life which I now live in the flesh I live by the faith of the Son of God, who loved me, and gave himself for me.

21I do not frustrate the grace of God: for if righteousness *come* by the law, then Christ is dead in vain.

## Amplified

9And when they knew (perceived, recognized, understood and acknowledged) the grace (God's unmerited favor and spiritual blessing) that had been bestowed upon me, James and Cephas (Peter) and John, who were reputed to be pillars of the Jerusalem church, gave to me and Barnabas the right hand of fellowship, with the understanding that we should go to the Gentiles and they to the circumcised (Jews).

10They only [made one stipulation], that we were to remember the poor, which very thing I was also eager to do.

11But when Cephas (Peter) came to Antioch I protested *and* opposed him to his face [concerning his conduct there], for he was blameable *and* stood condemned.

12For up to the time that certain persons came from James, he ate his meals with the Gentile [converts]; but when the men [from Jerusalem] arrived he withdrew *and* held himself aloof from the Gentiles and [ate] separately for fear of those of the circumcision [party].

13And the rest of the Jews along with him also concealed their true convictions *and* acted insincerely, with the result that even Barnabas was carried away by their hypocrisy—that is, by their example of insincerity and pretense.

14But as soon as I saw that they were not straightforward *and* were not living up to the truth of the Gospel, I said to Cephas (Peter) before everybody present, If you, though born a Jew, can live [as you have been living] like a Gentile and not as a Jew, how do you dare now to urge *and* practically force the Gentiles to [comply with the ritual of Judaism and] live like Jews?

15[I went on to say], Although we ourselves—you and I—are Jews by birth and not Gentile (heathen) sinners,

16Yet we know that a man is justified *or* reckoned righteous *and* in right standing with God, not by works of law but [only] through faith *and* [absolute] reliance on *and* adherence to *and* trust in Jesus Christ, the Messiah, the Anointed One. [Therefore] even we [ourselves] have believed on Christ Jesus, in order to be justified by faith in Christ and not by works of the Law—for we cannot be justified by any observance of [the ritual of] the Law [given by Moses]; because by keeping legal rituals *and* by works no human being can ever be justified—declared righteous and put in right standing with God. [Ps. 143:2.]

17But if, in our desire *and* endeavor to be justified in Christ—to be declared righteous and put in right standing with God wholly and solely through Christ—we have shown ourselves sinners also *and* convicted of sin, does that make Christ a minister (a party and contributor) to our sin? Banish the thought!—Of course not!

18For if I [or any other]—who have taught that the observance of the Law of Moses is not essential to being justified by God, should now by word or practice teach or intimate that it is essential—building up again what I tore down, I prove myself a transgressor.

19For I through the Law—under the operation [of the curse] of the Law—have [in Christ's death for me] myself died to the Law *and* all the Law's demands upon me, so that I may [henceforth] live to *and* for God.

20I have been crucified with Christ—[in Him] I have shared His crucifixion; it is no longer I who live, but Christ, the Messiah, lives in me; and the life I now live in the body I live by faith—by adherence to *and* reliance on *and* [complete] trust—in the Son of God, Who loved me and gave Himself up for me.

21[Therefore, I do not treat God's gracious gift as something of minor importance and defeat its very purpose]; I do not set aside *and* invalidate *and* frustrate *and* nullify the grace (unmerited favor) of God. For if justification (righteousness, acquittal from guilt) comes through [observing the ritual of] the Law, then Christ, the Messiah, died groundlessly *and* to no purpose *and* in vain.—His death was then wholly superfluous.

## New American Standard

9and recognizing the grace that had been given to me, James
and Cephas and John, who were reputed to be pillars, gave to me
and Barnabas the right hand of fellowship, that we *might go* to the
Gentiles, and they to the circumcised.
10 *They* only *asked* us to remember the poor—the very thing I
also was eager to do.

*Peter (Cephas) Opposed by Paul*

11¶ But when Cephas came to Antioch, I opposed him to his
face, because he stood condemned.
12For prior to the coming of certain men from James, he used
to eat with the Gentiles; but when they came, he *began* to withdraw
and hold himself aloof, fearing the party of the circumcision.
13And the rest of the Jews joined him in hypocrisy, with the
result that even Barnabas was carried away by their hypocrisy.
14But when I saw that they were not straightforward about the
truth of the gospel, I said to Cephas in the presence of all, "If you,
being a Jew, live like the Gentiles and not like the Jews, how *is it
that* you compel the Gentiles to live like Jews?
15"We *are* Jews by nature, and not sinners from among the
Gentiles;
16nevertheless knowing that a man is not justified by the works
of the Law but through faith in Christ Jesus, even we have believed
in Christ Jesus, that we may be justified by faith in Christ, and not
by the works of the Law; since by the works of the Law shall no
flesh be justified.
17"But if, while seeking to be justified in Christ, we ourselves
have also been found sinners, is Christ then a minister of sin? May
it never be!
18"For if I rebuild what I have *once* destroyed, I prove myself to
be a transgressor.
19"For through the Law I died to the Law, that I might live to
God.
20"I have been crucified with Christ; and it is no longer I who
live, but Christ lives in me; and the *life* which I now live in the flesh
I live by faith in the Son of God, who loved me, and delivered
Himself up for me.
21"I do not nullify the grace of God; for if righteousness *comes*
through the Law, then Christ died needlessly."

## New International

pillars, gave me and Barnabas the right hand of fellowship when
they recognized the grace given to me. They agreed that we should
go to the Gentiles, and they to the Jews. 10All they asked was that
we should continue to remember the poor, the very thing I was
eager to do.

*Paul Opposes Peter*

11When Peter came to Antioch, I opposed him to his face,
because he was clearly in the wrong. 12Before certain men came
from James, he used to eat with the Gentiles. But when they
arrived, he began to draw back and separate himself from the
Gentiles because he was afraid of those who belonged to the
circumcision group. 13The other Jews joined him in his hypocrisy,
so that by their hypocrisy even Barnabas was led astray.
14When I saw that they were not acting in line with the truth
of the gospel, I said to Peter in front of them all, "You are a Jew,
yet you live like a Gentile and not like a Jew. How is it, then, that
you force Gentiles to follow Jewish customs?
15"We who are Jews by birth and not 'Gentile sinners' 16know
that a man is not justified by observing the law, but by faith in Jesus
Christ. So we, too, have put our faith in Christ Jesus that we may
be justified by faith in Christ and not by observing the law, because
by observing the law no one will be justified.
17"If, while we seek to be justified in Christ, it becomes evident
that we ourselves are sinners, does that mean that Christ promotes
sin? Absolutely not! 18If I rebuild what I destroyed, I prove that I
am a lawbreaker. 19For through the law I died to the law so that
I might live for God. 20I have been crucified with Christ and I no
longer live, but Christ lives in me. The life I live in the body, I live
by faith in the Son of God, who loved me and gave himself for me.
21I do not set aside the grace of God, for if righteousness could be
gained through the law, Christ died for nothing!"[a]

NIV [a] *21* Some interpreters end the quotation after verse 14.

## King James

**3** O FOOLISH Galatians, who hath bewitched you, that ye should not obey the truth, before whose eyes Jesus Christ hath been evidently set forth, crucified among you?

2This only would I learn of you, Received ye the Spirit by the works of the law, or by the hearing of faith?

3Are ye so foolish? having begun in the Spirit, are ye now made perfect by the flesh?

4Have ye suffered so many things in vain? if *it be* yet in vain.

5He therefore that ministereth to you the Spirit, and worketh miracles among you, *doeth he it* by the works of the law, or by the hearing of faith?

6Even as Abraham believed God, and it was accounted to him for righteousness.

7Know ye therefore that they which are of faith, the same are the children of Abraham.

8And the scripture, foreseeing that God would justify the heathen through faith, preached before the gospel unto Abraham, *saying,* In thee shall all nations be blessed.

9So then they which be of faith are blessed with faithful Abraham.

10For as many as are of the works of the law are under the curse: for it is written, Cursed *is* every one that continueth not in all things which are written in the book of the law to do them.

11But that no man is justified by the law in the sight of God, *it is* evident: for, The just shall live by faith.

12And the law is not of faith: but, The man that doeth them shall live in them.

13Christ hath redeemed us from the curse of the law, being made a curse for us: for it is written, Cursed *is* every one that hangeth on a tree:

14That the blessing of Abraham might come on the Gentiles through Jesus Christ; that we might receive the promise of the Spirit through faith.

15Brethren, I speak after the manner of men; Though *it be* but a man's covenant, yet *if it be* confirmed, no man disannulleth, or addeth thereto.

## Amplified

**3** O YOU poor *and* silly *and* thoughtless *and* unreflecting *and* senseless Galatians! Who has fascinated *or* bewitched *or* cast a spell over you, unto whom—right before your very eyes—Jesus Christ, the Messiah, was openly *and* graphically set forth *and* portrayed as crucified?

2Let me ask you this one question: Did you receive the (Holy) Spirit as the result of obeying the Law *and* doing its works, or was it by hearing [the message of the Gospel] and believing [it]?—Was it from observing a law of rituals or from a message of faith?

3Are you so foolish *and* so senseless *and* so silly? Having begun [your new life spiritually] with the (Holy) Spirit, are you now reaching perfection [by dependence] on the flesh?

4Have you suffered so many things *and* experienced so much all for nothing—to no purpose? if it really is to no purpose *and* in vain,

5Then does He Who supplies you with His marvelous (Holy) Spirit, and works powerfully *and* miraculously among you, [do so on the grounds of your doing] what the Law demands, or because of your believing *and* adhering to *and* trusting in *and* relying on the message that you heard?

6Thus Abraham believed *and* adhered to *and* trusted in *and* relied on God, and it was reckoned *and* placed to his account *and* accredited as righteousness—as conformity to the divine will in purpose, thought and action. [Gen. 15:6.]

7Know *and* understand that it is [really] the people [who live] by faith who are [the true] sons of Abraham.

8And the Scripture, foreseeing that God would justify—declare righteous, put in right standing with Himself—the Gentiles in consequence of faith, proclaimed the Gospel [foretelling the glad tidings of a Savior long beforehand] to Abraham in the promise, saying, In you shall all the nations [of the earth] be blessed. [Gen. 12:3.]

9So then, those who are people of faith are blessed *and* made happy *and* favored by God [as partners in fellowship] with the believing *and* trusting Abraham.

10And all who depend on the Law—who are seeking to be justified by obedience to the Law of rituals—are under a curse *and* doomed to disappointment *and* destruction; for it is written in the Scriptures, Cursed (accursed, devoted to destruction, doomed to eternal punishment) be everyone who does not continue to abide (live and remain) by all the precepts *and* commands written in the book of the Law, and practice them. [Deut. 27:26.]

11Now it is evident that no person is justified—declared righteous and brought into right standing with God—through the Law; for the Scripture says, The man in right standing with God (the just, the righteous) shall live by *and* out of faith, *and* he who through *and* by faith is declared righteous *and* in right standing with God shall live. [Hab. 2:4.]

12But the Law does not rest on faith—does not require faith, has nothing to do with faith—for it itself says, He who does them (the things prescribed by the Law) shall live by them, [not by faith]. [Lev. 18:5.]

13Christ purchased our freedom (redeeming us) from the curse (doom) of the Law's (condemnation), by [Himself] becoming a curse for us, for it is written [in the Scriptures], Cursed is everyone who hangs on a tree (is crucified); [Deut. 21:23.]

14To the end that through [their receiving] Christ Jesus, the blessing [promised] to Abraham might come upon the Gentiles, so that we through faith might [all] receive [the realization of] the promise of the (Holy) Spirit.

15To speak in terms of human relations, brethren, [if] even a man makes a last will and testament [a merely human covenant], no one sets it aside *or* makes it void *or* adds to it, when once it has been drawn up *and* signed (ratified, confirmed).

## New American Standard

*Faith Brings Righteousness*

**3** YOU FOOLISH Galatians, who has bewitched you, before whose eyes Jesus Christ was publicly portrayed *as* crucified?

2This is the only thing I want to find out from you: did you receive the Spirit by the works of the Law, or by hearing with faith?

3Are you so foolish? Having begun by the Spirit, are you now being perfected by the flesh?

4Did you suffer so many things in vain—if indeed it was in vain?

5Does He then, who provides you with the Spirit and works miracles among you, do it by the works of the Law, or by hearing with faith?

6Even so Abraham BELIEVED GOD, AND IT WAS RECKONED TO HIM AS RIGHTEOUSNESS.

7Therefore, be sure that it is those who are of faith who are sons of Abraham.

8And the Scripture, foreseeing that God would justify the Gentiles by faith, preached the gospel beforehand to Abraham, *saying,* "ALL THE NATIONS SHALL BE BLESSED IN YOU."

9So then those who are of faith are blessed with Abraham, the believer.

10For as many as are of the works of the Law are under a curse; for it is written, "CURSED IS EVERYONE WHO DOES NOT ABIDE BY ALL THINGS WRITTEN IN THE BOOK OF THE LAW, TO PERFORM THEM."

11Now that no one is justified by the Law before God is evident; for, "THE RIGHTEOUS MAN SHALL LIVE BY FAITH."

12However, the Law is not of faith; on the contrary, "HE WHO PRACTICES THEM SHALL LIVE BY THEM."

13Christ redeemed us from the curse of the Law, having become a curse for us—for it is written, "CURSED IS EVERYONE WHO HANGS ON A TREE"—

14in order that in Christ Jesus the blessing of Abraham might come to the Gentiles, so that we might receive the promise of the Spirit through faith.

*Intent of the Law*

15¶ Brethren, I speak in terms of human relations: even though it is *only* a man's covenant, yet when it has been ratified, no one sets it aside or adds conditions to it.

## New International

*Faith or Observance of the Law*

**3** YOU FOOLISH Galatians! Who has bewitched you? Before your very eyes Jesus Christ was clearly portrayed as crucified. 2I would like to learn just one thing from you: Did you receive the Spirit by observing the law, or by believing what you heard? 3Are you so foolish? After beginning with the Spirit, are you now trying to attain your goal by human effort? 4Have you suffered so much for nothing—if it really was for nothing? 5Does God give you his Spirit and work miracles among you because you observe the law, or because you believe what you heard?

6Consider Abraham: "He believed God, and it was credited to him as righteousness."[a] 7Understand, then, that those who believe are children of Abraham. 8The Scripture foresaw that God would justify the Gentiles by faith, and announced the gospel in advance to Abraham: "All nations will be blessed through you."[b] 9So those who have faith are blessed along with Abraham, the man of faith.

10All who rely on observing the law are under a curse, for it is written: "Cursed is everyone who does not continue to do everything written in the Book of the Law."[c] 11Clearly no one is justified before God by the law, because, "The righteous will live by faith."[d] 12The law is not based on faith; on the contrary, "The man who does these things will live by them."[e] 13Christ redeemed us from the curse of the law by becoming a curse for us, for it is written: "Cursed is everyone who is hung on a tree."[f] 14He redeemed us in order that the blessing given to Abraham might come to the Gentiles through Christ Jesus, so that by faith we might receive the promise of the Spirit.

*The Law and the Promise*

15Brothers, let me take an example from everyday life. Just as no one can set aside or add to a human covenant that has been duly established, so it is in this case. 16The promises were spoken to

**NIV** [a] *6* Gen. 15:6 [b] *8* Gen. 12:3; 18:18; 22:18 [c] *10* Deut. 27:26 [d] *11* Hab. 2:4 [e] *12* Lev. 18:5 [f] *13* Deut. 21:23

## King James

16 Now to Abraham and his seed were the promises made. He saith not, And to seeds, as of many; but as of one, And to thy seed, which is Christ.

17 And this I say, *that* the covenant, that was confirmed before of God in Christ, the law, which was four hundred and thirty years after, cannot disannul, that it should make the promise of none effect.

18 For if the inheritance *be* of the law, *it is* no more of promise: but God gave *it* to Abraham by promise.

19 Wherefore then *serveth* the law? It was added because of transgressions, till the seed should come to whom the promise was made; *and it was* ordained by angels in the hand of a mediator.

20 Now a mediator is not *a mediator* of one, but God is one.

21 *Is* the law then against the promises of God? God forbid: for if there had been a law given which could have given life, verily righteousness should have been by the law.

22 But the scripture hath concluded all under sin, that the promise by faith of Jesus Christ might be given to them that believe.

23 But before faith came, we were kept under the law, shut up unto the faith which should afterwards be revealed.

24 Wherefore the law was our schoolmaster *to bring us* unto Christ, that we might be justified by faith.

25 But after that faith is come, we are no longer under a schoolmaster.

26 For ye are all the children of God by faith in Christ Jesus.

27 For as many of you as have been baptized into Christ have put on Christ.

28 There is neither Jew nor Greek, there is neither bond nor free, there is neither male nor female: for ye are all one in Christ Jesus.

29 And if ye *be* Christ's, then are ye Abraham's seed, and heirs according to the promise.

## Amplified

16 Now the promises (covenants, agreements) were decreed *and* made to Abraham and his Seed (his Offspring, his Heir). He (God) does not say, And to seeds (descendants, heirs), as if referring to many persons; but, And to your Seed (your Descendant, your Heir), obviously referring to one individual, Who is [none other than] Christ, the Messiah. [Gen. 13:15; 17:8.]

17 This is my argument: The Law, which began four hundred and thirty years after the covenant [concerning the coming Messiah], does not *and* can not annul the covenant previously established (ratified) by God, so as to abolish the promise *and* make it void. [Exod. 12:40.]

18 For if the inheritance [of the promise depends on observing] the Law [as these false teachers would like you to believe], it no longer [depends] on the promise; however, God gave it to Abraham [as a free gift solely] by virtue of His promise.

19 What then was the purpose of the Law? It was added—later on, after the promise, to disclose and expose to men their guilt—because of transgressions *and* [to make men more conscious of the sinfulness] of sin; and it was intended to be in effect until the Seed (the Descendant, the Heir) should come, to *and* concerning Whom the promise had been made. And it (the Law) was arranged *and* ordained *and* appointed through the instrumentality of angels [and was given] by the hand (in the person) of a go-between—an intermediary person (Moses) between God and man.

20 Now a go-between (intermediary) has to do with *and* implies more than one party—there can be no mediator with just one person. Yet God is [only] one person—and He was the sole party [in giving that promise to Abraham. But the Law was a contract between two, God and Israel; its validity was dependent on both].

21 Is the Law then contrary *and* opposed to the promises of God? Of course not! For if a Law had been given which could confer [spiritual] life, then righteousness *and* right standing with God would certainly have come by Law.

22 But the Scripture [pictures all mankind as sinners] shut up *and* imprisoned by sin, so that [the inheritance, blessing] which was promised through faith in Jesus Christ, the Messiah, might be given (released, delivered and committed) to [all] those who believe—who adhere to and trust in and rely on Him.

23 Now before the faith came we were perpetually guarded under the Law, kept in custody in preparation for the faith that was destined to be revealed (unveiled, disclosed).

24 So that the Law served [a][to us Jews] as our trainer—our guardian, our guide to Christ, to lead us—until Christ [came], that we might be justified (declared righteous, put in right standing with God) by *and* through faith.

25 But now that the faith has come, we are no longer under a trainer—the guardian of our childhood.

26 For in Christ Jesus you are all sons of God through faith.

27 For as many [of you] as were baptized into Christ—into a spiritual union and communion with Christ, the Anointed One, the Messiah—have put on (clothed yourselves with) Christ.

28 There is [now no distinction], neither Jew nor Greek, there is neither slave nor free, there is not male [b]and female; for you are all one in Christ Jesus.

29 And if you belong to Christ (are in Him, Who is Abraham's Seed), then you are Abraham's offspring and (spiritual) heirs according to promise.

## King James

4 NOW I say, *That* the heir, as long as he is a child, differeth nothing from a servant, though he be lord of all;

2 But is under tutors and governors until the time appointed of the father.

3 Even so we, when we were children, were in bondage under the elements of the world:

## Amplified

4 NOW WHAT I mean is that as long as the inheritor (heir) is a child and under age, he does not differ from a slave, although he is the master of all the estate;

2 But he is under guardians and administrators *or* trustees until the date fixed by his father.

3 So we [Jewish Christians] also, when we were minors were kept like slaves under (the rules of the Hebrew ritual and subject to) the elementary teachings of a system of external observations *and* regulations.

AMP [a] Vincent. [b] Literal translation.

## New American Standard

16 Now the promises were spoken to Abraham and to his seed.
He does not say, "And to seeds," as *referring* to many, but *rather*
to one, "And to your seed," that is, Christ.
17 What I am saying is this: the Law, which came four hundred
and thirty years later, does not invalidate a covenant previously
ratified by God, so as to nullify the promise.
18 For if the inheritance is based on law, it is no longer based on
a promise; but God has granted it to Abraham by means of a
promise.
19 Why the Law then? It was added because of transgressions,
having been ordained through angels by the agency of a mediator,
until the seed should come to whom the promise had been made.
20 Now a mediator is not for one *party only*; whereas God is *only*
one.
21 Is the Law then contrary to the promises of God? May it never
be! For if a law had been given which was able to impart life, then
righteousness would indeed have been based on law.
22 But the Scripture has shut up all men under sin, that the
promise by faith in Jesus Christ might be given to those who
believe.
23 ¶ But before faith came, we were kept in custody under the
law, being shut up to the faith which was later to be revealed.
24 Therefore the Law has become our tutor *to lead us* to Christ,
that we may be justified by faith.
25 But now that faith has come, we are no longer under a tutor.
26 For you are all sons of God through faith in Christ Jesus.
27 For all of you who were baptized into Christ have clothed
yourselves with Christ.
28 There is neither Jew nor Greek, there is neither slave nor free
man, there is neither male nor female; for you are all one in Christ
Jesus.
29 And if you belong to Christ, then you are Abraham's offspring, heirs according to promise.

*Sonship in Christ*

4 NOW I say, as long as the heir is a child, he does not differ
at all from a slave although he is owner of everything,
2 but he is under guardians and managers until the date set by
the father.
3 So also we, while we were children, were held in bondage
under the elemental things of the world.

## New International

Abraham and to his seed. The Scripture does not say "and to
seeds," meaning many people, but "and to your seed,"[c] meaning
one person, who is Christ. 17 What I mean is this: The law, introduced 430 years later, does not set aside the covenant previously
established by God and thus do away with the promise. 18 For if
the inheritance depends on the law, then it no longer depends on
a promise; but God in his grace gave it to Abraham through a
promise.
19 What, then, was the purpose of the law? It was added because
of transgressions until the Seed to whom the promise referred had
come. The law was put into effect through angels by a mediator.
20 A mediator, however, does not represent just one party; but God
is one.
21 Is the law, therefore, opposed to the promises of God? Absolutely not! For if a law had been given that could impart life, then
righteousness would certainly have come by the law. 22 But the
Scripture declares that the whole world is a prisoner of sin, so that
what was promised, being given through faith in Jesus Christ,
might be given to those who believe.
23 Before this faith came, we were held prisoners by the law,
locked up until faith should be revealed. 24 So the law was put in
charge to lead us to Christ[d] that we might be justified by faith.
25 Now that faith has come, we are no longer under the supervision
of the law.

*Sons of God*

26 You are all sons of God through faith in Christ Jesus, 27 for all
of you who were baptized into Christ have clothed yourselves with
Christ. 28 There is neither Jew nor Greek, slave nor free, male nor
female, for you are all one in Christ Jesus. 29 If you belong to Christ,
then you are Abraham's seed, and heirs according to the promise.

4 WHAT I am saying is that as long as the heir is a child, he is
no different from a slave, although he owns the whole estate.
2 He is subject to guardians and trustees until the time set by his
father. 3 So also, when we were children, we were in slavery under
the basic principles of the world. 4 But when the time had fully

NIV [c] 16 Gen. 12:7; 13:15; 24:7 [d] 24 Or *charge until Christ came*

## King James

4But when the fulness of the time was come, God sent forth his Son, made of a woman, made under the law,

5To redeem them that were under the law, that we might receive the adoption of sons.

6And because ye are sons, God hath sent forth the Spirit of his Son into your hearts, crying, Abba, Father.

7Wherefore thou art no more a servant, but a son; and if a son, then an heir of God through Christ.

8Howbeit then, when ye knew not God, ye did service unto them which by nature are no gods.

9But now, after that ye have known God, or rather are known of God, how turn ye again to the weak and beggarly elements, whereunto ye desire again to be in bondage?

10Ye observe days, and months, and times, and years.

11I am afraid of you, lest I have bestowed upon you labour in vain.

12Brethren, I beseech you, be as I *am;* for I *am* as ye *are:* ye have not injured me at all.

13Ye know how through infirmity of the flesh I preached the gospel unto you at the first.

14And my temptation which was in my flesh ye despised not, nor rejected; but received me as an angel of God, *even* as Christ Jesus.

15Where is then the blessedness ye spake of? for I bear you record, that, if *it had been* possible, ye would have plucked out your own eyes, and have given them to me.

16Am I therefore become your enemy, because I tell you the truth?

17They zealously affect you, *but* not well; yea, they would exclude you, that ye might affect them.

18But *it is* good to be zealously affected always in *a* good *thing,* and not only when I am present with you.

19My little children, of whom I travail in birth again until Christ be formed in you,

20I desire to be present with you now, and to change my voice; for I stand in doubt of you.

21Tell me, ye that desire to be under the law, do ye not hear the law?

22For it is written, that Abraham had two sons, the one by a bondmaid, the other by a freewoman.

23But he *who was* of the bondwoman was born after the flesh; but he of the freewoman *was* by promise.

24Which things are an allegory: for these are the two covenants; the one from the mount Sinai, which gendereth to bondage, which is Agar.

## Amplified

4But when the proper time had fully come, God sent His Son, born of a woman, born subject to [the regulations of] the Law,

5To purchase the freedom of (to ransom, to redeem, to [a]atone for) those who were subject to the Law, that we might be adopted *and* have sonship conferred upon us—be recognized as [God's] sons.

6And because you [really] are (His) sons, God has sent the ([b]Holy) Spirit of His Son into our hearts, crying, Abba (Father)! Father!

7Therefore, you are no longer a slave (bond servant) but a son; and if a son, then [it follows that you are] an heir [c]by the aid of God, *through Christ.*

8But at that previous time, when you had not come to be acquainted with *and* understand *and* know the true God, you [Gentiles] were in bondage to gods that by their very nature could not be gods at all—gods that really did not exist.

9Now however that you have come to be acquainted with *and* understand *and* know [the true] God, or rather to be understood *and* known by God, how can you turn back again to the weak and beggarly *and* worthless elementary things [[d]of all religions before Christ came] whose slaves you once more want to become?

10You observe [particular] days, and months, and seasons and years!

11I am alarmed [about you] lest I have labored among *and* over you to no purpose *and* in vain.

12Brethren, I beg of you, become as I am [free from the bondage of Jewish ritualism and ordinances]; for I also have become as you are [[e]a Gentile]. You did me no wrong [[f]in those days, do not do it now].

13On the contrary, you know that it was on account of a bodily ailment that [I remained and] preached the Gospel to you the first time.

14And [yet], although my physical condition was [such] a trial to you, you did not regard it with contempt, or scorn *and* loathe *and* reject me; but you received me as an angel of God, [even] as Christ Jesus [Himself]!

15What has become of that blessed enjoyment *and* satisfaction *and* self-congratulation that once was yours [in what I taught you and in your regard for me]? For I bear you witness that you would have torn out your own eyes and have given them to me [to replace mine], if that were possible.

16Have I then become your enemy by telling the truth to you *and* dealing sincerely with you?

17These men [the Judaizing teachers] are zealously trying to dazzle you—paying court to you, making much of you; but their purpose is not honorable *or* worthy *or* for any good. What they want to do is to isolate you [from us who oppose them], so that they may win you over to their side *and* get you to court their favor.

18It is always a fine thing [of course] to be zealously sought after [as you are, provided that it is] for a good purpose *and* done [g]by reason of purity of heart and life, and not just when I am present with you!

19My little children, for whom I am again suffering birth pangs until Christ is completely *and* permanently formed (molded) within you!

20Would that I were with you now and could coax you vocally, for I am fearful *and* perplexed about you.

21Tell me, you who are bent on being under law, will you listen to what the Law [really] says?

22For it is written that Abraham had two sons, one by the bondmaid and one by the free [woman]. [Gen. 16:15; 21:2, 9.]

23But whereas the child of the slave woman was born according to the flesh *and* had an ordinary birth, the son of the free [woman] was born in fulfillment of the promise.

24Now all this is an allegory; these [two women] represent two covenants. One covenant originated from Mount Sinai [where the Law was given], and bears [children destined] for slavery; this is Hagar.

**AMP** [a] Webster, defining "redeem." [b] Vincent. [c] Thayer. [d] Thayer. [e] Vincent. [f] Vincent. [g] Thayer.

## New American Standard

4But when the fulness of the time came, God sent forth His Son, born of a woman, born under the Law,

5in order that He might redeem those who were under the Law, that we might receive the adoption as sons.

6And because you are sons, God has sent forth the Spirit of His Son into our hearts, crying, "Abba! Father!"

7Therefore you are no longer a slave, but a son; and if a son, then an heir through God.

8¶ However at that time, when you did not know God, you were slaves to those which by nature are no gods.

9But now that you have come to know God, or rather to be known by God, how is it that you turn back again to the weak and worthless elemental things, to which you desire to be enslaved all over again?

10You observe days and months and seasons and years.

11I fear for you, that perhaps I have labored over you in vain.

12¶ I beg of you, brethren, become as I *am*, for I also *have become* as you *are*. You have done me no wrong;

13but you know that it was because of a bodily illness that I preached the gospel to you the first time;

14and that which was a trial to you in my bodily condition you did not despise or loathe, but you received me as an angel of God, as Christ Jesus *Himself*.

15Where then is that sense of blessing you had? For I bear you witness, that if possible, you would have plucked out your eyes and given them to me.

16Have I therefore become your enemy by telling you the truth?

17They eagerly seek you, not commendably, but they wish to shut you out, in order that you may seek them.

18But it is good always to be eagerly sought in a commendable manner, and not only when I am present with you.

19My children, with whom I am again in labor until Christ is formed in you—

20but I could wish to be present with you now and to change my tone, for I am perplexed about you.

*Bond and Free*

21¶ Tell me, you who want to be under law, do you not listen to the law?

22For it is written that Abraham had two sons, one by the bondwoman and one by the free woman.

23But the son by the bondwoman was born according to the flesh, and the son by the free woman through the promise.

24This is allegorically speaking: for these *women* are two covenants, one *proceeding* from Mount Sinai bearing children who are to be slaves; she is Hagar.

## New International

come, God sent his Son, born of a woman, born under law, 5to redeem those under law, that we might receive the full rights of sons. 6Because you are sons, God sent the Spirit of his Son into our hearts, the Spirit who calls out, "*Abba*,[h] Father." 7So you are no longer a slave, but a son; and since you are a son, God has made you also an heir.

*Paul's Concern for the Galatians*

8Formerly, when you did not know God, you were slaves to those who by nature are not gods. 9But now that you know God—or rather are known by God—how is it that you are turning back to those weak and miserable principles? Do you wish to be enslaved by them all over again? 10You are observing special days and months and seasons and years! 11I fear for you, that somehow I have wasted my efforts on you.

12I plead with you, brothers, become like me, for I became like you. You have done me no wrong. 13As you know, it was because of an illness that I first preached the gospel to you. 14Even though my illness was a trial to you, you did not treat me with contempt or scorn. Instead, you welcomed me as if I were an angel of God, as if I were Christ Jesus himself. 15What has happened to all your joy? I can testify that, if you could have done so, you would have torn out your eyes and given them to me. 16Have I now become your enemy by telling you the truth?

17Those people are zealous to win you over, but for no good. What they want is to alienate you ⌊from us⌋, so that you may be zealous for them. 18It is fine to be zealous, provided the purpose is good, and to be so always and not just when I am with you. 19My dear children, for whom I am again in the pains of childbirth until Christ is formed in you, 20how I wish I could be with you now and change my tone, because I am perplexed about you!

*Hagar and Sarah*

21Tell me, you who want to be under the law, are you not aware of what the law says? 22For it is written that Abraham had two sons, one by the slave woman and the other by the free woman. 23His son by the slave woman was born in the ordinary way; but his son by the free woman was born as the result of a promise.

24These things may be taken figuratively, for the women represent two covenants. One covenant is from Mount Sinai and bears children who are to be slaves: This is Hagar. 25Now Hagar stands

NIV [h] 6 Aramaic for *Father*

## King James

25For this Agar is mount Sinai in Arabia, and answereth to Jerusalem which now is, and is in bondage with her children.

26But Jerusalem which is above is free, which is the mother of us all.

27For it is written, Rejoice, *thou* barren that bearest not; break forth and cry, thou that travailest not: for the desolate hath many more children than she which hath an husband.

28Now we, brethren, as Isaac was, are the children of promise.

29But as then he that was born after the flesh persecuted him *that was born* after the Spirit, even so *it is* now.

30Nevertheless what saith the scripture? Cast out the bondwoman and her son: for the son of the bondwoman shall not be heir with the son of the freewoman.

31So then, brethren, we are not children of the bondwoman, but of the free.

**5** STAND FAST therefore in the liberty wherewith Christ hath made us free, and be not entangled again with the yoke of bondage.

2Behold, I Paul say unto you, that if ye be circumcised, Christ shall profit you nothing.

3For I testify again to every man that is circumcised, that he is a debtor to do the whole law.

4Christ is become of no effect unto you, whosoever of you are justified by the law; ye are fallen from grace.

5For we through the Spirit wait for the hope of righteousness by faith.

6For in Jesus Christ neither circumcision availeth any thing, nor uncircumcision; but faith which worketh by love.

7Ye did run well; who did hinder you that ye should not obey the truth?

8This persuasion *cometh* not of him that calleth you.

9A little leaven leaveneth the whole lump.

10I have confidence in you through the Lord, that ye will be none otherwise minded: but he that troubleth you shall bear his judgment, whosoever he be.

11And I, brethren, if I yet preach circumcision, why do I yet suffer persecution? then is the offence of the cross ceased.

12I would they were even cut off which trouble you.

13For, brethren, ye have been called unto liberty; only *use* not liberty for an occasion to the flesh, but by love serve one another.

## Amplified

25Now Hagar is (stands for) Mount Sinai in Arabia and she corresponds to *and* belongs in the same category with the present Jerusalem, for she is in bondage together with her children.

26But the Jerusalem above, [ [a]the Messianic kingdom of Christ], is free and she is our mother.

27For it is written in the Scriptures, Rejoice, O barren woman who has not given birth to children; break forth into a joyful shout, you who are not feeling birth pangs, for the desolate woman has many more children than she who has a husband. [Isa. 54:1.]

28But we, brethren, are children [ [b]not by physical descent, as was Ishmael, but] like Isaac born [c]in virtue of promise.

29Yet [just] as at that time the child (of ordinary birth,) born according to the flesh, despised *and* persecuted him [who was born remarkably,] according to [the promise and the working of] the (Holy) Spirit, so it is now also. [Gen. 21:9.]

30But what does the Scripture say? Cast out *and* send away the slave woman and her son, for never shall the son of the slave woman be heir *and* share the inheritance with the son of the free [woman]. [Gen. 21:10.]

31So, brethren, we [who are born again] are not children of a slave woman [ [d]the natural], but of the free [ [e]the supernatural].

**5** IN [THIS] freedom Christ has made us free—completely liberated us; stand fast then, and do not be hampered *and* held ensnared *and* submit again to a yoke of slavery—which you have once put off.

2Notice, it is I, Paul, who tells you that if you receive circumcision, Christ will be of no profit (advantage, avail) to you, [ [f]for if you distrust Him, you can gain nothing from Him].

3I once more protest *and* testify to every man who receives circumcision that he is under obligation *and* bound to practice the whole of the Law *and* its ordinances.

4If you seek to be justified *and* declared righteous *and* to be given a right standing with God through the Law, you are brought to nothing *and* so separated (severed) from Christ. You have fallen away from grace—from God's gracious favor and unmerited blessing.

5For we [not relying on the Law], through the (Holy) Spirit's [help] by faith anticipate *and* wait for the blessing *and* good for which our righteousness *and* right standing with God—our [g]conformity to His will in purpose, thought and action—[causes us] to hope.

6For [if we are] in Christ Jesus, neither circumcision nor uncircumcision counts for anything, but only faith activated *and* energized *and* expressed *and* working through love.

7You were running the race nobly. Who has interfered (hindered and stopped you) from heeding *and* following the Truth?

8This [evil] persuasion is not from Him Who called you—Who invited you to freedom in Christ.

9A little leaven [a slight inclination to error, or a few false teachers] leavens the whole lump [perverts the whole conception of faith, or misleads the whole church].

10[For my part] I have confidence [toward you] in the Lord that you will take no contrary view of the matter *but* will come to think with me. But he who is unsettling you, whoever he is, will have to bear the penalty.

11But, brethren, if I still preach circumcision [as some accuse me of doing, as necessary to salvation], why am I still suffering persecution? In that case the cross has ceased to be a stumbling block *and* is made meaningless—done away.

12I wish those who unsettle *and* confuse you would [ [h]go all the way and] cut themselves off!

13For you, brethren, were [indeed] called to freedom; only [do not let your] freedom be an incentive to your flesh *and* an opportunity *or* excuse [for [i]selfishness], but through love you should serve one another.

**AMP** [a] Vincent. [b] Vincent. [c] Vincent. [d] The Biblical Illustrator. [e] The Biblical Illustrator. [f] Chrysostom. [g] Abbott-Smith. [h] Vincent. [i] Vincent.

## New American Standard

25Now this Hagar is Mount Sinai in Arabia, and corresponds to the present Jerusalem, for she is in slavery with her children.

26But the Jerusalem above is free; she is our mother.

27For it is written,

"REJOICE, BARREN WOMAN WHO DOES NOT BEAR;
BREAK FORTH AND SHOUT, YOU WHO ARE NOT IN LABOR;
FOR MORE ARE THE CHILDREN OF THE DESOLATE
THAN OF THE ONE WHO HAS A HUSBAND."

28And you brethren, like Isaac, are children of promise.

29But as at that time he who was born according to the flesh persecuted him *who was born* according to the Spirit, so it is now also.

30But what does the Scripture say?

"CAST OUT THE BONDWOMAN AND HER SON,
FOR THE SON OF THE BONDWOMAN SHALL NOT BE AN HEIR WITH THE SON OF THE FREE WOMAN."

31So then, brethren, we are not children of a bondwoman, but of the free woman.

*Walk by the Spirit*

**5** IT WAS for freedom that Christ set us free; therefore keep standing firm and do not be subject again to a yoke of slavery.

2¶ Behold I, Paul, say to you that if you receive circumcision, Christ will be of no benefit to you.

3And I testify again to every man who receives circumcision, that he is under obligation to keep the whole Law.

4You have been severed from Christ, you who are seeking to be justified by law; you have fallen from grace.

5For we through the Spirit, by faith, are waiting for the hope of righteousness.

6For in Christ Jesus neither circumcision nor uncircumcision means anything, but faith working through love.

7You were running well; who hindered you from obeying the truth?

8This persuasion *did* not *come* from Him who calls you.

9A little leaven leavens the whole lump *of dough.*

10I have confidence in you in the Lord, that you will adopt no other view; but the one who is disturbing you shall bear his judgment, whoever he is.

11But I, brethren, if I still preach circumcision, why am I still persecuted? Then the stumbling block of the cross has been abolished.

12Would that those who are troubling you would even mutilate themselves.

13¶ For you were called to freedom, brethren; only *do* not *turn* your freedom into an opportunity for the flesh, but through love serve one another.

## New International

for Mount Sinai in Arabia and corresponds to the present city of
Jerusalem, because she is in slavery with her children. 26But the
Jerusalem that is above is free, and she is our mother. 27For it is
written:

"Be glad, O barren woman,
who bears no children;
break forth and cry aloud,
you who have no labor pains;
because more are the children of the desolate woman
than of her who has a husband."[j]

28Now you, brothers, like Isaac, are children of promise. 29At
that time the son born in the ordinary way persecuted the son born
by the power of the Spirit. It is the same now. 30But what does the
Scripture say? "Get rid of the slave woman and her son, for the
slave woman's son will never share in the inheritance with the free
woman's son."[k] 31Therefore, brothers, we are not children of the
slave woman, but of the free woman.

*Freedom in Christ*

**5** IT IS for freedom that Christ has set us free. Stand firm, then,
and do not let yourselves be burdened again by a yoke of
slavery.

2Mark my words! I, Paul, tell you that if you let yourselves be
circumcised, Christ will be of no value to you at all. 3Again I declare
to every man who lets himself be circumcised that he is obligated
to obey the whole law. 4You who are trying to be justified by law
have been alienated from Christ; you have fallen away from grace.
5But by faith we eagerly await through the Spirit the righteousness
for which we hope. 6For in Christ Jesus neither circumcision nor
uncircumcision has any value. The only thing that counts is faith
expressing itself through love.

7You were running a good race. Who cut in on you and kept
you from obeying the truth? 8That kind of persuasion does not
come from the one who calls you. 9"A little yeast works through
the whole batch of dough." 10I am confident in the Lord that you
will take no other view. The one who is throwing you into confusion will pay the penalty, whoever he may be. 11Brothers, if I am
still preaching circumcision, why am I still being persecuted? In
that case the offense of the cross has been abolished. 12As for those
agitators, I wish they would go the whole way and emasculate
themselves!

13You, my brothers, were called to be free. But do not use your
freedom to indulge the sinful nature[l] ; rather, serve one another
in love. 14The entire law is summed up in a single command: "Love

NIV [j] 27 Isaiah 54:1 [k] 30 Gen. 21:10 [l] 13 Or *the flesh;* also in verses 16, 17, 19 and 24

## King James

14For all the law is fulfilled in one word, *even* in this; Thou shalt love thy neighbour as thyself.

15But if ye bite and devour one another, take heed that ye be not consumed one of another.

16 *This* I say then, Walk in the Spirit, and ye shall not fulfil the lust of the flesh.

17For the flesh lusteth against the Spirit, and the Spirit against the flesh: and these are contrary the one to the other: so that ye cannot do the things that ye would.

18But if ye be led of the Spirit, ye are not under the law.

19Now the works of the flesh are manifest, which are *these;* Adultery, fornication, uncleanness, lasciviousness,

20Idolatry, witchcraft, hatred, variance, emulations, wrath, strife, seditions, heresies,

21Envyings, murders, drunkenness, revellings, and such like: of the which I tell you before, as I have also told *you* in time past, that they which do such things shall not inherit the kingdom of God.

22But the fruit of the Spirit is love, joy, peace, longsuffering, gentleness, goodness, faith,

23Meekness, temperance: against such there is no law.

24And they that are Christ's have crucified the flesh with the affections and lusts.

25If we live in the Spirit, let us also walk in the Spirit.

26Let us not be desirous of vain glory, provoking one another, envying one another.

6 BRETHREN, IF a man be overtaken in a fault, ye which are spiritual, restore such an one in the spirit of meekness; considering thyself, lest thou also be tempted.

2Bear ye one another's burdens, and so fulfil the law of Christ.

3For if a man think himself to be something, when he is nothing, he deceiveth himself.

4But let every man prove his own work, and then shall he have rejoicing in himself alone, and not in another.

5For every man shall bear his own burden.

6Let him that is taught in the word communicate unto him that teacheth in all good things.

## Amplified

14For the whole Law [concerning human relationships] is [a]complied with in the one precept, You shall love your neighbor as yourself. [Lev. 19:18.]

15But if you bite and devour one another [in partisan strife], be careful that you [and your whole fellowship] are not consumed by one another.

16But I say, walk *and* live habitually in the (Holy) Spirit—responsive to *and* controlled *and* guided by the Spirit; then you will certainly not gratify the cravings *and* desires of the flesh—of human nature without God.

17For the desires of the flesh are opposed to the (Holy) Spirit, and the [desires of the] Spirit are opposed to the flesh (Godless human nature); for these are antagonistic to each other—continually withstanding and in conflict with each other—so that you are not free *but* are prevented from doing what you desire to do.

18But if you are guided (led) by the (Holy) Spirit you are not subject to the Law.

19Now the doings (practices) of the flesh are clear—obvious: they are immorality, impurity, indecency;

20Idolatry, sorcery, enmity, strife, jealousy, anger (ill temper), selfishness, divisions (dissensions), party spirit (factions, sects with peculiar opinions, heresies);

21Envy, drunkenness, carousing, and the like. I warn you beforehand, just as I did previously, that those who do such things shall not inherit the kingdom of God.

22But the fruit of the (Holy) Spirit, [the work which His presence within accomplishes]—is love, joy (gladness), peace, patience (an even temper, forbearance), kindness, goodness (benevolence), faithfulness;

23(Meekness, humility) gentleness, self-control (self-restraint, continence). Against such things there is no law [ [b]that can bring a charge].

24And those who belong to Christ Jesus, the Messiah, have crucified the flesh—the Godless human nature—with its passions and appetites *and* desires.

25If we live by the (Holy) Spirit, let us also walk by the Spirit.—If by the (Holy) Spirit [c]we have our life [in God], let us go forward [d]walking in line, our conduct controlled by the Spirit.

26Let us not become vainglorious *and* self-conceited, competitive *and* challenging *and* provoking *and* irritating to one another, envying *and* being jealous of one another.

6 BRETHREN, IF any person is overtaken in misconduct *or* sin of any sort, you who are spiritual—who are responsive to and controlled by the Spirit—should set him right *and* restore *and* reinstate him, without any sense of superiority *and* with all gentleness, keeping an attentive eye on yourself, lest you should be tempted also.

2Bear (endure, carry) one another's burdens *and* [e]troublesome moral faults, and in this way fulfill *and* observe perfectly the law of Christ, the Messiah, *and* complete [f]what is lacking [in your obedience to it].

3For if any person thinks himself to be somebody [too important to condescend to shoulder another's load], when he is nobody [of superiority except in his own estimation], he deceives *and* deludes *and* cheats himself.

4But let every person carefully scrutinize *and* examine *and* test his own conduct *and* his own work. He can then have the personal satisfaction *and* joy of doing something commendable [ [g]in itself alone] without [resorting to] boastful comparison with his neighbor.

5For every person will have to bear [h][be equal to understanding and calmly receive] his own ( [i]little) load [j][of oppressive faults].

6Let him who receives instruction in the Word [of God] share all good things with his teacher—contributing to his support.

**AMP** [a] Vincent. [b] Vincent. [c] Adam Clarke. [d] Vincent. [e] Thayer. [f] Vincent. [g] Vincent. [h] Thayer. [i] Diminutive form of the Greek word. [j] Thayer.

## New American Standard

14For the whole Law is fulfilled in one word, in the *statement*,
"YOU SHALL LOVE YOUR NEIGHBOR AS YOURSELF."
15But if you bite and devour one another, take care lest you be
consumed by one another.
16¶ But I say, walk by the Spirit, and you will not carry out the
desire of the flesh.
17For the flesh sets its desire against the Spirit, and the Spirit
against the flesh; for these are in opposition to one another, so that
you may not do the things that you please.
18But if you are led by the Spirit, you are not under the Law.
19Now the deeds of the flesh are evident, which are: immorality, impurity, sensuality,
20idolatry, sorcery, enmities, strife, jealousy, outbursts of anger, disputes, dissensions, factions,
21envying, drunkenness, carousing, and things like these, of
which I forewarn you just as I have forewarned you that those who
practice such things shall not inherit the kingdom of God.
22But the fruit of the Spirit is love, joy, peace, patience, kindness, goodness, faithfulness,
23gentleness, self-control; against such things there is no law.
24Now those who belong to Christ Jesus have crucified the flesh
with its passions and desires.
25¶ If we live by the Spirit, let us also walk by the Spirit.
26Let us not become boastful, challenging one another, envying
one another.

*Bear One Another's Burdens*

6 BRETHREN, EVEN if a man is caught in any trespass, you
who are spiritual, restore such a one in a spirit of gentleness;
*each one* looking to yourself, lest you too be tempted.
2Bear one another's burdens, and thus fulfill the law of Christ.
3For if anyone thinks he is something when he is nothing, he
deceives himself.
4But let each one examine his own work, and then he will have
*reason for* boasting in regard to himself alone, and not in regard to
another.
5For each one shall bear his own load.
6¶ And let the one who is taught the word share all good things
with him who teaches.

## New International

your neighbor as yourself."[k] 15If you keep on biting and devouring each other, watch out or you will be destroyed by each
other.

*Life by the Spirit*

16So I say, live by the Spirit, and you will not gratify the desires
of the sinful nature. 17For the sinful nature desires what is contrary
to the Spirit, and the Spirit what is contrary to the sinful nature.
They are in conflict with each other, so that you do not do what
you want. 18But if you are led by the Spirit, you are not under law.
19The acts of the sinful nature are obvious: sexual immorality,
impurity and debauchery; 20idolatry and witchcraft; hatred, discord, jealousy, fits of rage, selfish ambition, dissensions, factions
21and envy; drunkenness, orgies, and the like. I warn you, as I did
before, that those who live like this will not inherit the kingdom
of God.
22But the fruit of the Spirit is love, joy, peace, patience, kindness, goodness, faithfulness, 23gentleness and self-control.
Against such things there is no law. 24Those who belong to Christ
Jesus have crucified the sinful nature with its passions and desires.
25Since we live by the Spirit, let us keep in step with the Spirit.
26Let us not become conceited, provoking and envying each other.

*Doing Good to All*

6 BROTHERS, IF someone is caught in a sin, you who are
spiritual should restore him gently. But watch yourself, or
you also may be tempted. 2Carry each other's burdens, and in this
way you will fulfill the law of Christ. 3If anyone thinks he is
something when he is nothing, he deceives himself. 4Each one
should test his own actions. Then he can take pride in himself,
without comparing himself to somebody else, 5for each one should
carry his own load.
6Anyone who receives instruction in the word must share all
good things with his instructor.

NIV [k] *14* Lev. 19:18

## King James

7Be not deceived; God is not mocked: for whatsoever a man soweth, that shall he also reap.

8For he that soweth to his flesh shall of the flesh reap corruption; but he that soweth to the Spirit shall of the Spirit reap life everlasting.

9And let us not be weary in well doing: for in due season we shall reap, if we faint not.

10As we have therefore opportunity, let us do good unto all *men*, especially unto them who are of the household of faith.

11Ye see how large a letter I have written unto you with mine own hand.

12As many as desire to make a fair show in the flesh, they constrain you to be circumcised; only lest they should suffer persecution for the cross of Christ.

13For neither they themselves who are circumcised keep the law; but desire to have you circumcised, that they may glory in your flesh.

14But God forbid that I should glory, save in the cross of our Lord Jesus Christ, by whom the world is crucified unto me, and I unto the world.

15For in Christ Jesus neither circumcision availeth any thing, nor uncircumcision, but a new creature.

16And as many as walk according to this rule, peace *be* on them, and mercy, and upon the Israel of God.

17From henceforth let no man trouble me: for I bear in my body the marks of the Lord Jesus.

18Brethren, the grace of our Lord Jesus Christ *be* with your spirit. Amen.

## Amplified

7Do not be deceived *and* deluded *and* misled; God will not allow Himself to be sneered at—scorned, disdained or mocked [ [a]by mere pretensions or professions, or His precepts being set aside].—He inevitably deludes himself who attempts to delude God. For whatever a man sows, that *and* [b]that only is what he will reap.

8For he who sows to his own flesh (lower nature, sensuality) will from the flesh reap decay *and* ruin *and* destruction; but he who sows to the Spirit will from the Spirit reap life eternal.

9And let us not lose heart *and* grow weary *and* faint in acting nobly *and* doing right, for in due time *and* at the appointed season we shall reap, if we do not loosen *and* relax our courage *and* faint.

10So then, as occasion *and* opportunity open to us, let us do good ( [c]morally) to all people [not only [d]being useful or profitable to them, but also doing what is for their spiritual good and advantage]. Be mindful to be a blessing, especially to those of the household of faith—those who belong to God's family with you, the believers.

11[ [e]Mark carefully these closing words of mine.] See with what large letters I am writing them with my own hand.

12Those who want to make a good impression *and* a fine show in the flesh, would try to compel you to receive circumcision simply so that they may escape being persecuted for allegiance to the cross of Christ, the Messiah, the Anointed One.

13For even the circumcised [Jews] themselves do not [really] keep the Law, but they want to have you circumcised in order that they may glory in your flesh—your subjection to external rites.

14But far be it from me to glory [in anything or any one] except in the cross of our Lord Jesus Christ, the Messiah, through Whom the world has been crucified to me, and I to the world!

15For neither is circumcision [now] of any importance, nor uncircumcision, but [only] a new creation [the result of a new birth and a new nature in Christ Jesus, the Messiah].

16Peace and mercy be upon all who walk by this rule—who discipline themselves and regulate their lives by this principle—even upon the [true] Israel of God! [Ps. 125:5.]

17From now on let no person trouble me [by [f]making it necessary for me to vindicate my apostolic authority and the divine truth of my Gospel]; for I bear on my body the brand marks of the Lord Jesus, [the wounds, scars and other outward evidence of persecutions].—These testify to His ownership of me!

18The grace (spiritual favor, blessing) of our Lord Jesus Christ, the Anointed One, the Messiah, be with your spirit, brethren. Amen—so be it.

**AMP** [a] Matthew Henry. [b] Vincent. [c] Vincent. [d] Vincent. [e] Vincent. [f] Vincent.

## New American Standard

7Do not be deceived, God is not mocked; for whatever a man
sows, this he will also reap.
8For the one who sows to his own flesh shall from the flesh
reap corruption, but the one who sows to the Spirit shall from the
Spirit reap eternal life.
9And let us not lose heart in doing good, for in due time we
shall reap if we do not grow weary.
10So then, while we have opportunity, let us do good to all men,
and especially to those who are of the household of the faith.
11¶ See with what large letters I am writing to you with my own
hand.
12Those who desire to make a good showing in the flesh try to
compel you to be circumcised, simply that they may not be persecuted for the cross of Christ.
13For those who [g]are circumcised do not even keep the Law
themselves, but they desire to have you circumcised, that they
may boast in your flesh.
14But may it never be that I should boast, except in the cross of
our Lord Jesus Christ, through which the world has been crucified
to me, and I to the world.
15For neither is circumcision anything, nor uncircumcision, but
a new creation.
16And those who will walk by this rule, peace and mercy *be*
upon them, and upon the Israel of God.
17¶ From now on let no one cause trouble for me, for I bear on
my body the brand-marks of Jesus.
18¶ The grace of our Lord Jesus Christ be with your spirit,
brethren. Amen.

NAS [g] Some ancient mss. read *have been*

## New International

7Do not be deceived: God cannot be mocked. A man reaps what
he sows. 8The one who sows to please his sinful nature, from that
nature[h] will reap destruction; the one who sows to please the
Spirit, from the Spirit will reap eternal life. 9Let us not become
weary in doing good, for at the proper time we will reap a harvest
if we do not give up. 10Therefore, as we have opportunity, let us
do good to all people, especially to those who belong to the family
of believers.

*Not Circumcision but a New Creation*

11See what large letters I use as I write to you with my own
hand!
12Those who want to make a good impression outwardly are
trying to compel you to be circumcised. The only reason they do
this is to avoid being persecuted for the cross of Christ. 13Not even
those who are circumcised obey the law, yet they want you to be
circumcised that they may boast about your flesh. 14May I never
boast except in the cross of our Lord Jesus Christ, through which[i]
the world has been crucified to me, and I to the world. 15Neither
circumcision nor uncircumcision means anything; what counts is
a new creation. 16Peace and mercy to all who follow this rule, even
to the Israel of God.
17Finally, let no one cause me trouble, for I bear on my body the
marks of Jesus.
18The grace of our Lord Jesus Christ be with your spirit, brothers. Amen.

NIV [h] 8 Or *his flesh, from the flesh* [i] 14 Or *whom*

## King James

THE EPISTLE OF

PAUL THE APOSTLE TO THE

# Ephesians

1 PAUL, AN apostle of Jesus Christ by the will of God, to the saints which are at Ephesus, and to the faithful in Christ Jesus:

2 Grace *be* to you, and peace, from God our Father, and *from* the Lord Jesus Christ.

3 Blessed *be* the God and Father of our Lord Jesus Christ, who hath blessed us with all spiritual blessings in heavenly *places* in Christ:

4 According as he hath chosen us in him before the foundation of the world, that we should be holy and without blame before him in love:

5 Having predestinated us unto the adoption of children by Jesus Christ to himself, according to the good pleasure of his will,

6 To the praise of the glory of his grace, wherein he hath made us accepted in the beloved.

7 In whom we have redemption through his blood, the forgiveness of sins, according to the riches of his grace;

8 Wherein he hath abounded toward us in all wisdom and prudence;

9 Having made known unto us the mystery of his will, according to his good pleasure which he hath purposed in himself:

10 That in the dispensation of the fulness of times he might gather together in one all things in Christ, both which are in heaven, and which are on earth; *even* in him:

11 In whom also we have obtained an inheritance, being predestinated according to the purpose of him who worketh all things after the counsel of his own will:

12 That we should be to the praise of his glory, who first trusted in Christ.

13 In whom ye also *trusted,* after that ye heard the word of truth, the gospel of your salvation: in whom also after that ye believed, ye were sealed with that holy Spirit of promise,

14 Which is the earnest of our inheritance until the redemption of the purchased possession, unto the praise of his glory.

**AMP** [a] Many ancient authorities so read. [b] Many ancient authorities so read. [c] Vincent. [d] Some interpret "in Him" to mean "in Himself"; others, "in Christ." [e] Alternate reading.

## Amplified

THE LETTER OF

PAUL TO THE

# Ephesians

1 PAUL, AN apostle (special messenger) of Christ Jesus, the Messiah, by the divine will—the purpose and the choice of God—to the saints (the consecrated, set-apart ones) [a]at Ephesus who are also faithful *and* loyal *and* steadfast in Christ Jesus:

2 May grace (which is God's unmerited favor) and spiritual peace (which means peace with God and harmony, unity and undisturbedness) be yours from God our Father and from the Lord Jesus Christ.

3 Blessing (praise, laudation and eulogy) be to the God and Father of our Lord Jesus Christ, the Messiah, Who has blessed us *in Christ* with every spiritual (Holy Spirit given) blessing in the heavenly realm!

4 Even as [ [b]in His love] He chose us—actually picked us out for Himself as His own—in Christ before the foundation of the world; that we should be holy (consecrated and set apart for Him) and blameless in His sight, *even* above reproach, before Him in love.

5 For He foreordained us (destined us, planned in love for us) to be adopted [revealed] as His own children through Jesus Christ, in accordance with the purpose of His will— [c]because it pleased Him and was His kind intent;

6 [So that we might be] to the praise *and* the commendation of His glorious grace—favor and mercy—which He so freely bestowed on us in the Beloved.

7 In Him we have redemption (deliverance and salvation) through His blood, the remission (forgiveness) of our offenses (shortcomings and trespasses), in accordance with the riches *and* the generosity of His gracious favor,

8 Which He lavished upon us in every kind of wisdom and understanding (practical insight and prudence),

9 Making known to us the mystery (secret) of His will—of His plan, of His purpose. [And it is this:] In accordance with His good pleasure (His merciful intention) which He had previously purposed *and* set forth in [d]Him,

10 [He planned] for the maturity of the times *and* the climax of the ages to unify all things *and* head them up *and* consummate them in Christ, [both] things in heaven and things on the earth.

11 In Him we also were made [God's] heritage (portion) *and* [e]we obtained an inheritance; for we had been foreordained (chosen and appointed beforehand) in accordance with His purpose, Who works out everything in agreement with the counsel *and* design of His [own] will.

12 So that we who first hoped in Christ—who first put our confidence in Him—[have been destined and appointed] to live for the praise of His glory!

13 In Him you also who have heard the Word of Truth, the glad tidings (Gospel) of your salvation, and have believed in *and* have adhered to *and* have relied on Him, were stamped with the seal of the long-promised Holy Spirit.

14 That [Spirit] is the guarantee of our inheritance—the first fruit, the pledge and foretaste, the down payment on our heritage—in anticipation of its full redemption *and* our acquiring [complete] possession of it, to the praise of His glory.

## New American Standard

# Ephesians

*The Blessings of Redemption*

1 PAUL, AN apostle of Christ Jesus by the will of God, to the
saints who are [f]at Ephesus, and *who are* faithful in Christ
Jesus:
2Grace to you and peace from God our Father and the Lord
Jesus Christ.
3¶ Blessed *be* the God and Father of our Lord Jesus Christ, who
has blessed us with every spiritual blessing in the heavenly *places*
in Christ,
4just as He chose us in Him before the foundation of the world,
that we should be holy and blameless before [g]Him. In love
5He predestined us to adoption as sons through Jesus Christ
to Himself, according to the kind intention of His will,
6to the praise of the glory of His grace, which He freely bestowed on us in the Beloved.
7In Him we have redemption through His blood, the forgiveness of our trespasses, according to the riches of His grace,
8which He lavished upon us. In all wisdom and insight
9He made known to us the mystery of His will, according to
His kind intention which He purposed in Him
10with a view to an administration suitable to the fulness of the
times, *that is,* the summing up of all things in Christ, things in the
heavens and things upon the earth. In Him
11also we have obtained an inheritance, having been predestined according to His purpose who works all things after the
counsel of His will,
12to the end that we who were the first to hope in [h]Christ
should be to the praise of His glory.
13In Him, you also, after listening to the message of truth, the
gospel of your salvation—having also believed, you were sealed in
Him with the Holy Spirit of promise,
14who is given as a pledge of our inheritance, with a view to the
redemption of *God's own* possession, to the praise of His glory.

NAS [f] Some ancient mss. do not contain *at Ephesus* [g] Or, *Him, in love.*
[h] I.e., the Messiah

## New International

# Ephesians

1 PAUL, AN apostle of Christ Jesus by the will of God,
To the saints in Ephesus,[i] the faithful[j] in Christ Jesus:
2Grace and peace to you from God our Father and the Lord
Jesus Christ.

*Spiritual Blessings in Christ*

3Praise be to the God and Father of our Lord Jesus Christ, who
has blessed us in the heavenly realms with every spiritual blessing
in Christ. 4For he chose us in him before the creation of the world
to be holy and blameless in his sight. In love 5he[k] predestined us
to be adopted as his sons through Jesus Christ, in accordance with
his pleasure and will— 6to the praise of his glorious grace, which
he has freely given us in the One he loves. 7In him we have
redemption through his blood, the forgiveness of sins, in accordance with the riches of God's grace 8that he lavished on us with
all wisdom and understanding. 9And he[l] made known to us the
mystery of his will according to his good pleasure, which he purposed in Christ, 10to be put into effect when the times will have
reached their fulfillment—to bring all things in heaven and on
earth together under one head, even Christ.
11In him we were also chosen,[m] having been predestined according to the plan of him who works out everything in conformity
with the purpose of his will, 12in order that we, who were the first
to hope in Christ, might be for the praise of his glory. 13And you
also were included in Christ when you heard the word of truth,
the gospel of your salvation. Having believed, you were marked
in him with a seal, the promised Holy Spirit, 14who is a deposit
guaranteeing our inheritance until the redemption of those who
are God's possession—to the praise of his glory.

NIV [i] *1* Some early manuscripts do not have *in Ephesus.* [j] *1* Or *believers who are* [k] *4,5* Or *sight in love. 5He* [l] *8,9* Or *us. With all wisdom and understanding, 9he* [m]*11* Or *were made heirs*

## King James

15Wherefore I also, after I heard of your faith in the Lord Jesus,
and love unto all the saints,
16Cease not to give thanks for you, making mention of you in
my prayers;
17That the God of our Lord Jesus Christ, the Father of glory,
may give unto you the spirit of wisdom and revelation in the
knowledge of him:
18The eyes of your understanding being enlightened; that ye
may know what is the hope of his calling, and what the riches of
the glory of his inheritance in the saints,
19And what *is* the exceeding greatness of his power to us-ward
who believe, according to the working of his mighty power,
20Which he wrought in Christ, when he raised him from the
dead, and set *him* at his own right hand in the heavenly *places,*
21Far above all principality, and power, and might, and dominion, and every name that is named, not only in this world, but also
in that which is to come:
22And hath put all *things* under his feet, and gave him *to be* the
head over all *things* to the church,
23Which is his body, the fulness of him that filleth all in all.

2 AND YOU *hath he quickened,* who were dead in trespasses and
sins;
2Wherein in time past ye walked according to the course of this
world, according to the prince of the power of the air, the spirit
that now worketh in the children of disobedience:
3Among whom also we all had our conversation in times past
in the lusts of our flesh, fulfilling the desires of the flesh and of the
mind; and were by nature the children of wrath, even as others.
4But God, who is rich in mercy, for his great love wherewith he
loved us,
5Even when we were dead in sins, hath quickened us together
with Christ, (by grace ye are saved;)
6And hath raised *us* up together, and made *us* sit together in
heavenly *places* in Christ Jesus:
7That in the ages to come he might show the exceeding riches
of his grace in *his* kindness toward us through Christ Jesus.

## Amplified

15For this reason, because I have heard of your faith in the Lord
Jesus and your love toward all the saints (the people of God),
16I do not cease to give thanks for you, making mention of you
in my prayers.
17[For I always pray] the God of our Lord Jesus Christ, the
Father of Glory, that He may grant you a spirit of wisdom and
revelation—of insight into mysteries and secrets—in the [deep and
intimate] knowledge of Him,
18By having the eyes of your heart flooded with light, so that
you can know *and* understand the hope to which He has called you
and how rich is His glorious inheritance in the saints—His set-
apart ones.
19And [so that you can know and understand] what is the
immeasurable *and* unlimited *and* surpassing greatness of His
power in *and* for us who believe, as demonstrated in the working
of His mighty strength,
20Which He exerted in Christ when He raised Him from the
dead and seated Him at His [own] right hand in the heavenly
[places],
21Far above all rule and authority and power and dominion, and
every name that is named—above every title that can be conferred—not only in this age *and* in this world, but also in the age
*and* the world which are to come.
22And He has put all things under His feet and has appointed
Him the universal and supreme Head of the church (a headship
exercised throughout the church), [Ps. 8:6.]
23Which is His body, the fullness of Him Who fills all in all—for
in that body lives the full measure of Him Who makes everything
complete, and Who fills everything everywhere [with Himself].

2 AND YOU [He made alive], when you were dead [slain] by
[your] trespasses and sins
2In which at one time you walked habitually. You were following the course *and* fashion of this world—were under the sway of
the tendency of this present age—following the prince of the
power of the air. (You were obedient to him and were under his
control,) the [demon] spirit that still constantly works in the sons
of disobedience—the careless, the rebellious and the unbelieving,
who go against the purposes of God.
3Among these we as well as you once lived *and* conducted
ourselves in the passions of our flesh—our behavior governed by
our corrupt and sensual nature; obeying the impulses of the flesh
and the thoughts of the mind—our cravings dictated by our senses
and our dark imaginings. We were then by nature children of
[God's] wrath *and* heirs of [His] indignation, like the rest of mankind.
4But God! So rich is He in His mercy! Because of *and* in order
to satisfy the great *and* wonderful *and* intense love with which He
loved us,
5Even when we were dead [slain] by [our own] shortcomings
*and* trespasses, He made us alive together in fellowship *and* in
union with Christ.—He gave us the very life of Christ Himself, the
same new life with which He quickened Him. [For] it is by grace—
by His favor and mercy which you did not deserve—that you are
saved ( [a]delivered from judgment *and* made partakers of Christ's
salvation).
6And He raised us up together with Him and made us sit down
together—giving us [b]joint seating with Him—in the heavenly
sphere [by virtue of our being] in Christ Jesus, the Messiah, the
Anointed One.
7He did this that He might clearly demonstrate through the ages
to come the immeasurable (limitless, surpassing) riches of His free
grace (His unmerited favor) in kindness *and* goodness of heart
toward us in Christ Jesus.

AMP [a] Thayer. [b] Meyer's Commentary.

## New American Standard

15¶ For this reason I too, having heard of the faith in the Lord
Jesus which *exists* among you, and [c]your love for all the saints,
16do not cease giving thanks for you, while making mention *of*
*you* in my prayers;
17that the God of our Lord Jesus Christ, the Father of glory, may
give to you a spirit of wisdom and of revelation in the knowledge
of Him.
18 *I pray that* the eyes of your heart may be enlightened, so that
you may know what is the hope of His calling, what are the riches
of the glory of His inheritance in the saints,
19and what is the surpassing greatness of His power toward us
who believe. *These are* in accordance with the working of the
strength of His might
20which He brought about in Christ, when He raised Him from
the dead, and seated Him at His right hand in the heavenly *places,*
21far above all rule and authority and power and dominion, and
every name that is named, not only in this age, but also in the one
to come.
22And He put all things in subjection under His feet, and gave
Him as head over all things to the church,
23which is His body, the fulness of Him who fills all in all.

*Made Alive in Christ*

**2** AND YOU were dead in your trespasses and sins,
2in which you formerly walked according to the course of this
world, according to the prince of the power of the air, of the spirit
that is now working in the sons of disobedience.
3Among them we too all formerly lived in the lusts of our flesh,
indulging the desires of the flesh and of the mind, and were by
nature children of wrath, even as the rest.
4But God, being rich in mercy, because of His great love with
which He loved us,
5even when we were dead in our transgressions, made us alive
together [d]with Christ (by grace you have been saved),
6and raised us up with Him, and seated us with Him in the
heavenly *places,* in Christ Jesus,
7in order that in the ages to come He might show the surpassing riches of His grace in kindness toward us in Christ Jesus.

NAS [c] Many ancient mss. do not contain *your love* [d] Some ancient mss. read *in Christ*

## New International

*Thanksgiving and Prayer*

15For this reason, ever since I heard about your faith in the Lord
Jesus and your love for all the saints, 16I have not stopped giving
thanks for you, remembering you in my prayers. 17I keep asking
that the God of our Lord Jesus Christ, the glorious Father, may
give you the Spirit[e] of wisdom and revelation, so that you may
know him better. 18I pray also that the eyes of your heart may be
enlightened in order that you may know the hope to which he has
called you, the riches of his glorious inheritance in the saints, 19and
his incomparably great power for us who believe. That power is
like the working of his mighty strength, 20which he exerted in
Christ when he raised him from the dead and seated him at his
right hand in the heavenly realms, 21far above all rule and authority, power and dominion, and every title that can be given, not
only in the present age but also in the one to come. 22And God
placed all things under his feet and appointed him to be head over
everything for the church, 23which is his body, the fullness of him
who fills everything in every way.

*Made Alive in Christ*

**2** AS FOR you, you were dead in your transgressions and sins,
2in which you used to live when you followed the ways of this
world and of the ruler of the kingdom of the air, the spirit who is
now at work in those who are disobedient. 3All of us also lived
among them at one time, gratifying the cravings of our sinful
nature[f] and following its desires and thoughts. Like the rest, we
were by nature objects of wrath. 4But because of his great love for
us, God, who is rich in mercy, 5made us alive with Christ even
when we were dead in transgressions—it is by grace you have
been saved. 6And God raised us up with Christ and seated us with
him in the heavenly realms in Christ Jesus, 7in order that in the
coming ages he might show the incomparable riches of his grace,
expressed in his kindness to us in Christ Jesus. 8For it is by grace

NIV [e] *17 Or a spirit* [f] 3 Or *our flesh*

## King James

8 For by grace are ye saved through faith; and that not of yourselves: *it is* the gift of God:

9 Not of works, lest any man should boast.

10 For we are his workmanship, created in Christ Jesus unto good works, which God hath before ordained that we should walk in them.

11 Wherefore remember, that ye *being* in time past Gentiles in the flesh, who are called Uncircumcision by that which is called the Circumcision in the flesh made by hands;

12 That at that time ye were without Christ, being aliens from the commonwealth of Israel, and strangers from the covenants of promise, having no hope, and without God in the world:

13 But now in Christ Jesus ye who sometimes were far off are made nigh by the blood of Christ.

14 For he is our peace, who hath made both one, and hath broken down the middle wall of partition *between us;*

15 Having abolished in his flesh the enmity, *even* the law of commandments *contained* in ordinances; for to make in himself of twain one new man, *so* making peace;

16 And that he might reconcile both unto God in one body by the cross, having slain the enmity thereby:

17 And came and preached peace to you which were afar off, and to them that were nigh.

18 For through him we both have access by one Spirit unto the Father.

19 Now therefore ye are no more strangers and foreigners, but fellowcitizens with the saints, and of the household of God;

20 And are built upon the foundation of the apostles and prophets, Jesus Christ himself being the chief corner *stone;*

21 In whom all the building fitly framed together groweth unto an holy temple in the Lord:

22 In whom ye also are builded together for an habitation of God through the Spirit.

## Amplified

8 For it is by free grace (God's unmerited favor) that you are saved ([a]delivered from judgment *and* made partakers of Christ's salvation) through [your] faith. And this [salvation] is not of yourselves—of your own doing, it came not through your own striving—but it is the gift of God;

9 Not because of works [not the fulfillment of the Law's demands], lest any man should boast.—It is not the result of what any one can possibly do, so no one can pride himself in it or take glory to himself.

10 For we are God's [own] handiwork (His workmanship), [b]recreated in Christ Jesus, [born anew] that we may do those good works which God predestined (planned beforehand) for us, (taking paths which He prepared ahead of time) that we should walk in them—living the good life which He prearranged and made ready for us to live.

11 Therefore remember that at one time you were Gentiles [heathen] in the flesh; called Uncircumcision by those who called themselves Circumcision, [itself a [c]mere mark] in the flesh made by human hands.

12 Remember that you were at that time separated (living apart) from Christ—excluded from all part in Him; utterly estranged *and* outlawed from the rights of Israel as a nation, and strangers with no share in the sacred compacts of the [Messianic] promise—with no knowledge of or right in God's agreements, His covenants. And you had no hope—no promise; you were in the world without God.

13 But now in Christ Jesus, you who once were [so] far away, through (by, in) the blood of Christ have been brought near.

14 For He is [Himself] our peace—our bond of unity and harmony. He has made us both [Jew and Gentile] one (body), and has broken down (destroyed, abolished) the hostile dividing wall between us,

15 By abolishing in His [own crucified] flesh the enmity [caused by] the Law with its decrees and ordinances—which He annulled; that He from the two might create in Himself one new man—one new quality of humanity out of the two—so making peace.

16 And [He designed] to reconcile to God both [Jew and Gentile, united] in a single body by means of His cross; thereby killing the mutual enmity *and* bringing the feud to an end.

17 And He came and preached the glad tidings of peace to you who were afar off and [peace] to those who were near. [Isa. 57:19.]

18 For it is through Him that we both [whether far off or near] now have an introduction (access) by one (Holy) Spirit to the Father—so that we are able to approach Him.

19 Therefore you are no longer outsiders—exiles, migrants and aliens, excluded from the rights of citizens; but you now share citizenship with the saints—God's own people, consecrated and set apart for Himself; and you belong to God's [own] household.

20 You are built upon the foundation of the apostles and prophets with Christ Jesus Himself the chief Cornerstone.

21 In Him the whole structure is joined (bound, welded) together harmoniously; and it continues to rise (grow, increase) into a holy temple in the Lord—a sanctuary dedicated, consecrated and sacred to the presence of the Lord.

22 In Him—and in fellowship with one another—you yourselves also are being built up [into this structure] with the rest, to form a fixed abode (dwelling place) of God in (by, through) the Spirit.

## King James

**3** FOR THIS cause I Paul, the prisoner of Jesus Christ for you Gentiles,

## Amplified

**3** FOR THIS reason [[d]because I preached that you are thus builded together], I, Paul, am the prisoner of Jesus the Christ [e]for the sake *and* on behalf of you Gentiles.

**AMP** [a] Thayer. [b] Arthur S. Way: "The Letters of St. Paul and Hebrews." [c] Arthur S. Way: "The Letters of St. Paul and Hebrews." [d] The Jews persecuted and imprisoned Paul because he was an apostle to the Gentiles and preached the gospel to them.—Matthew Henry. [e] The Jews persecuted and imprisoned Paul because he was an apostle to the Gentiles and preached the gospel to them.—Matthew Henry.

## New American Standard

8For by grace you have been saved through faith; and that not
of yourselves, *it is* the gift of God;

9not as a result of works, that no one should boast.

10For we are His workmanship, created in Christ Jesus for good
works, which God prepared beforehand, that we should walk in
them.

11¶ Therefore remember, that formerly you, the Gentiles in the
flesh, who are called "Uncircumcision" by the so-called "Circumcision," *which is* performed in the flesh by human hands—

12 *remember* that you were at that time separate from Christ,
excluded from the commonwealth of Israel, and strangers to the
covenants of promise, having no hope and without God in the
world.

13But now in Christ Jesus you who formerly were far off have
been brought near by the blood of Christ.

14For He Himself is our peace, who made both *groups into* one,
and broke down the barrier of the dividing wall,

15by abolishing in His flesh the enmity, *which is* the Law of
commandments *contained* in ordinances, that in Himself He might
make the two into one new man, *thus* establishing peace,

16and might reconcile them both in one body to God through
the cross, by it having put to death the enmity.

17AND HE CAME AND PREACHED PEACE TO YOU WHO WERE FAR
AWAY, AND PEACE TO THOSE WHO WERE NEAR;

18for through Him we both have our access in one Spirit to the
Father.

19So then you are no longer strangers and aliens, but you are
fellow citizens with the saints, and are of God's household,

20having been built upon the foundation of the apostles and
prophets, Christ Jesus Himself being the corner *stone,*

21in whom the whole building, being fitted together is growing
into a holy temple in the Lord;

22in whom you also are being built together into a dwelling of
God in the Spirit.

*Paul's Stewardship*

**3** FOR THIS reason I, Paul, the prisoner of Christ Jesus for the
sake of you Gentiles—

## New International

you have been saved, through faith—and this not from yourselves, it is the gift of God— 9not by works, so that no one can
boast. 10For we are God's workmanship, created in Christ Jesus to
do good works, which God prepared in advance for us to do.

*One in Christ*

11Therefore, remember that formerly you who are Gentiles by
birth and called "uncircumcised" by those who call themselves
"the circumcision" (that done in the body by the hands of men)—
12remember that at that time you were separate from Christ, excluded from citizenship in Israel and foreigners to the covenants
of the promise, without hope and without God in the world. 13But
now in Christ Jesus you who once were far away have been
brought near through the blood of Christ.

14For he himself is our peace, who has made the two one and
has destroyed the barrier, the dividing wall of hostility, 15by abolishing in his flesh the law with its commandments and regulations.
His purpose was to create in himself one new man out of the two,
thus making peace, 16and in this one body to reconcile both of
them to God through the cross, by which he put to death their
hostility. 17He came and preached peace to you who were far away
and peace to those who were near. 18For through him we both
have access to the Father by one Spirit.

19Consequently, you are no longer foreigners and aliens, but
fellow citizens with God's people and members of God's household, 20built on the foundation of the apostles and prophets, with
Christ Jesus himself as the chief cornerstone. 21In him the whole
building is joined together and rises to become a holy temple in the
Lord. 22And in him you too are being built together to become a
dwelling in which God lives by his Spirit.

*Paul the Preacher to the Gentiles*

**3** FOR THIS reason I, Paul, the prisoner of Christ Jesus for the
sake of you Gentiles—

## King James

2 If ye have heard of the dispensation of the grace of God which is given me to you-ward:

3 How that by revelation he made known unto me the mystery; (as I wrote afore in few words,

4 Whereby, when ye read, ye may understand my knowledge in the mystery of Christ)

5 Which in other ages was not made known unto the sons of men, as it is now revealed unto his holy apostles and prophets by the Spirit;

6 That the Gentiles should be fellowheirs, and of the same body, and partakers of his promise in Christ by the gospel:

7 Whereof I was made a minister, according to the gift of the grace of God given unto me by the effectual working of his power.

8 Unto me, who am less than the least of all saints, is this grace given, that I should preach among the Gentiles the unsearchable riches of Christ;

9 And to make all *men* see what *is* the fellowship of the mystery, which from the beginning of the world hath been hid in God, who created all things by Jesus Christ:

10 To the intent that now unto the principalities and powers in heavenly *places* might be known by the church the manifold wisdom of God,

11 According to the eternal purpose which he purposed in Christ Jesus our Lord:

12 In whom we have boldness and access with confidence by the faith of him.

13 Wherefore I desire that ye faint not at my tribulations for you, which is your glory.

14 For this cause I bow my knees unto the Father of our Lord Jesus Christ,

15 Of whom the whole family in heaven and earth is named,

16 That he would grant you, according to the riches of his glory, to be strengthened with might by his Spirit in the inner man;

17 That Christ may dwell in your hearts by faith; that ye, being rooted and grounded in love,

18 May be able to comprehend with all saints what *is* the breadth, and length, and depth, and height;

19 And to know the love of Christ, which passeth knowledge, that ye might be filled with all the fulness of God.

20 Now unto him that is able to do exceeding abundantly above all that we ask or think, according to the power that worketh in us,

## Amplified

2 Assuming that you have heard of the stewardship of God's grace (His unmerited favor) that was entrusted to me [to dispense to you] for your benefit;

3 And how the mystery (secret) was made known to me *and* I was allowed to comprehend it by direct revelation, as I already briefly wrote you,

4 When you read this you can understand my insight into the mystery of Christ.

5 [This mystery] was never disclosed to human beings in past generations as it has now been revealed to His holy apostles [consecrated messengers] and prophets by the (Holy) Spirit.

6 [It is this:] that the Gentiles are now to be fellow heirs [with the Jews], members of the same body, and joint partakers (sharing) in the same divine promise in Christ through [their acceptance of] the glad tidings (the Gospel).

7 Of this [Gospel] I was made a minister according to the gift of God's free grace (undeserved favor), which was bestowed on me by the exercise—the working in all its effectiveness—of His power.

8 To me, though I am the very least of all the saints (God's consecrated people), this grace (favor, privilege) was granted *and* graciously entrusted: to proclaim to the Gentiles the unending (boundless, fathomless, incalculable and exhaustless) riches of Christ—wealth which no human being could have searched out.

9 Also to enlighten all men *and* make plain to them what is the plan [regarding the Gentiles and providing for the salvation of all men,] of the mystery kept hidden through the ages *and* concealed until now in [the mind of] God Who created all things *by Christ Jesus.*

10 [The purpose is] that through the church the [a]complicated, many-sided wisdom of God in all its infinite variety *and* innumerable aspects might now be made known to the angelic rulers and authorities (principalities and powers) in the heavenly sphere.

11 This is in accordance with the terms of the eternal *and* timeless purpose which He has realized *and* carried into effect, in [the person of] Christ Jesus our Lord;

12 In Whom, because of our faith in Him, we dare to have the boldness (courage and confidence) of free access—an unreserved approach to God with freedom and without fear.

13 So I ask you not to lose heart—not to faint or become despondent through fear—at what I am suffering in your behalf. [Rather glory in it] for it is an honor to you.

14 For this reason [ [b]seeing the greatness of this plan by which you are built together in Christ], I bow my knees before the Father *of our Lord Jesus Christ,*

15 For Whom every family in heaven and on earth is named—[that Father] from Whom all [c]fatherhood takes its title and derives its name.

16 May He grant you out of the rich treasury of His glory to be strengthened *and* reinforced with mighty power in the inner man by the (Holy) Spirit [Himself]—indwelling your innermost being and personality.

17 May Christ through your faith [actually] dwell—settle down, abide, make His permanent home—in your hearts! May you be rooted deep in love *and* founded securely on love,

18 That you may have the power *and* be strong to apprehend *and* grasp with all the saints (God's devoted people, the experience of that love) what is the breadth and length and height and depth [of it];

19 [That you may really come] to know—practically, [d]through experience for yourselves—the love of Christ, which far surpasses [e]mere knowledge (without experience); that you may be filled (through all your being) [f]unto all the fullness of God—[that is] may have the richest measure of the divine Presence, and [g]become a body wholly filled and flooded with God Himself!

20 Now to Him Who, by (in consequence of) the [action of His] power that is at work within us, is able to [carry out His purpose and] do superabundantly, far over *and* above all that we [dare] ask or think—infinitely beyond our highest prayers, desires, thoughts, hopes or dreams—

**AMP** [a] Webster in defining "manifold" (the King James rendering of "polupoikilos"). [b] Many authorities consider that Paul here resumes the thread of verse. [c] Alternate reading. [d] Vincent's Word Studies. [e] Vincent's Word Studies. [f] Vincent's Word Studies. [g] Thayer.

## New American Standard

2if indeed you have heard of the stewardship of God's grace which was given to me for you;

3that by revelation there was made known to me the mystery, as I wrote before in brief.

4And by referring to this, when you read you can understand my insight into the mystery of Christ,

5which in other generations was not made known to the sons of men, as it has now been revealed to His holy apostles and prophets in the Spirit;

6 *to be specific,* that the Gentiles are fellow heirs and fellow members of the body, and fellow partakers of the promise in Christ Jesus through the gospel,

7of which I was made a minister, according to the gift of God's grace which was given to me according to the working of His power.

8To me, the very least of all saints, this grace was given, to preach to the Gentiles the unfathomable riches of Christ,

9and to bring to light what is the administration of the mystery which for ages has been hidden in God, who created all things;

10in order that the manifold wisdom of God might now be made known through the church to the rulers and the authorities in the heavenly *places.*

11 *This was* in accordance with the eternal purpose which He carried out in Christ Jesus our Lord,

12in whom we have boldness and confident access through faith in Him.

13Therefore I ask you not to lose heart at my tribulations on your behalf, for they are your glory.

**14**¶ For this reason, I bow my knees before the Father,

15from whom every family in heaven and on earth derives its name,

16that He would grant you, according to the riches of His glory, to be strengthened with power through His Spirit in the inner man;

17so that Christ may dwell in your hearts through faith; *and* that you, being rooted and grounded in love,

18may be able to comprehend with all the saints what is the breadth and length and height and depth,

19and to know the love of Christ which surpasses knowledge, that you may be filled up to all the fulness of God.

**20**¶ Now to Him who is able to do exceeding abundantly beyond all that we ask or think, according to the power that works within us,

## New International

2Surely you have heard about the administration of God's grace
that was given to me for you, 3that is, the mystery made known
to me by revelation, as I have already written briefly. 4In reading
this, then, you will be able to understand my insight into the
mystery of Christ, 5which was not made known to men in other
generations as it has now been revealed by the Spirit to God's holy
apostles and prophets. 6This mystery is that through the gospel
the Gentiles are heirs together with Israel, members together of
one body, and sharers together in the promise in Christ Jesus.
7I became a servant of this gospel by the gift of God's grace
given me through the working of his power. 8Although I am less
than the least of all God's people, this grace was given me: to
preach to the Gentiles the unsearchable riches of Christ, 9and to
make plain to everyone the administration of this mystery, which
for ages past was kept hidden in God, who created all things. 10His
intent was that now, through the church, the manifold wisdom of
God should be made known to the rulers and authorities in the
heavenly realms, 11according to his eternal purpose which he accomplished in Christ Jesus our Lord. 12In him and through faith
in him we may approach God with freedom and confidence. 13I ask
you, therefore, not to be discouraged because of my sufferings for
you, which are your glory.

*A Prayer for the Ephesians*

14For this reason I kneel before the Father, 15from whom his
whole family[h] in heaven and on earth derives its name. 16I pray
that out of his glorious riches he may strengthen you with power
through his Spirit in your inner being, 17so that Christ may dwell
in your hearts through faith. And I pray that you, being rooted and
established in love, 18may have power, together with all the saints,
to grasp how wide and long and high and deep is the love of
Christ, 19and to know this love that surpasses knowledge—that
you may be filled to the measure of all the fullness of God.
20Now to him who is able to do immeasurably more than all we
ask or imagine, according to his power that is at work within us,

**NIV** [h] 15 Or *whom all fatherhood*

## King James

21 Unto him *be* glory in the church by Christ Jesus throughout all ages, world without end. Amen.

# 4

I THEREFORE, the prisoner of the Lord, beseech you that ye walk worthy of the vocation wherewith ye are called,

2 With all lowliness and meekness, with longsuffering, forbearing one another in love;

3 Endeavouring to keep the unity of the Spirit in the bond of peace.

4 *There is* one body, and one Spirit, even as ye are called in one hope of your calling;

5 One Lord, one faith, one baptism,

6 One God and Father of all, who *is* above all, and through all, and in you all.

7 But unto every one of us is given grace according to the measure of the gift of Christ.

8 Wherefore he saith, When he ascended up on high, he led captivity captive, and gave gifts unto men.

9 (Now that he ascended, what is it but that he also descended first into the lower parts of the earth?

10 He that descended is the same also that ascended up far above all heavens, that he might fill all things.)

11 And he gave some, apostles; and some, prophets; and some, evangelists; and some, pastors and teachers;

12 For the perfecting of the saints, for the work of the ministry, for the edifying of the body of Christ:

13 Till we all come in the unity of the faith, and of the knowledge of the Son of God, unto a perfect man, unto the measure of the stature of the fulness of Christ:

14 That we *henceforth* be no more children, tossed to and fro, and carried about with every wind of doctrine, by the sleight of men, *and* cunning craftiness, whereby they lie in wait to deceive;

15 But speaking the truth in love, may grow up into him in all things, which is the head, *even* Christ:

16 From whom the whole body fitly joined together and compacted by that which every joint supplieth, according to the effectual working in the measure of every part, maketh increase of the body unto the edifying of itself in love.

17 This I say therefore, and testify in the Lord, that ye henceforth walk not as other Gentiles walk, in the vanity of their mind,

## Amplified

21 To Him be glory in the church and in Christ Jesus throughout all generations, for ever and ever. Amen—so be it.

# 4

I THEREFORE, the prisoner for the Lord, appeal to *and* beg you to walk (lead a life) worthy of the [divine] calling to which you have been called—with behavior that is a credit to the summons to God's service,

2 Living as becomes you—with complete lowliness of mind (humility) and meekness (unselfishness, gentleness, mildness), with patience, bearing with one another *and* making allowances because you love one another.

3 Be eager *and* strive earnestly to guard *and* keep the harmony *and* oneness of [produced by] the Spirit in the binding power of peace.

4 [There is] one body and one Spirit, just as there is also one hope [that belongs] to the calling you received.

5 [There is] one Lord, one faith, one baptism,

6 One God and Father of [us] all, Who is above all (Sovereign over all), pervading all and [living] in [us] all.

7 Yet grace (God's unmerited favor) was given to each of us individually—not indiscriminately, but in different ways—in proportion to the measure of Christ's [rich and bounteous] gift.

8 Therefore it is said, When He ascended on high, He led captivity captive—He led a train of [a]vanquished foes—and He bestowed gifts on men. [Ps. 68:18.]

9 [But He ascended?] Now what can this, He ascended, mean but that He had previously descended from the height of heaven into [the depth], the lower parts of the earth?

10 He Who descended is the [very] same as He Who also has ascended high above all the heavens, that He [His presence] might fill all things—the whole universe, from the lowest to the highest.

11 And His gifts were [varied; He Himself appointed and gave men to us,] some to be apostles (special messengers), some prophets (inspired preachers and expounders), some evangelists (preachers of the Gospel, traveling missionaries), some pastors (shepherds of His flock) and teachers.

12 His intention was the perfecting *and* the full equipping of the saints (His consecrated people), [that they should do] the work of ministering toward building up Christ's body (the church),

13 [That it might develop] until we all attain oneness in the faith and in the comprehension of the [b]full and accurate knowledge of the Son of God; that [we might arrive] at really mature manhood—the completeness of personality which is nothing less than the standard height of Christ's own perfection—the measure of the stature of the fullness of the Christ, *and* the completeness found in Him.

14 So then, we may no longer be children, tossed [like ships] to and fro between chance gusts of teaching, *and* wavering with every changing wind of doctrine, [the prey of] the cunning *and* cleverness of [c]unscrupulous men, (gamblers engaged) in every shifting form of trickery in inventing errors to mislead.

15 Rather, let our lives lovingly [d]express truth in all things—speaking truly, dealing truly, living truly. Enfolded in love, let us grow up in every way *and* in all things into Him, Who is the Head, [even] Christ, the Messiah, the Anointed One.

16 For because of Him the whole body (the church, in all its various parts closely) joined and firmly knit together by the joints *and* ligaments with which it is supplied, when each part [with power adapted to its need] is working properly (in all its functions), grows to full maturity, building itself up in love.

17 So this I say and solemnly testify in [the name of] the Lord [as in His Presence], that you must no longer live as the heathen (the Gentiles) do in their perverseness—in the folly, vanity and emptiness of their souls and the futility—of their minds.

**AMP** [a] "He conquered those who had conquered us; such as sin, the devil and death."—Matthew Henry. [b] Vincent. [c] Literally, *dice-playing*. [d] Vincent.

## New American Standard

21to Him *be* the glory in the church and in Christ Jesus to all generations forever and ever. Amen.

*Unity of the Spirit*

**4** I, THEREFORE, the prisoner of the Lord, entreat you to walk in a manner worthy of the calling with which you have been called,

2with all humility and gentleness, with patience, showing forbearance to one another in love,

3being diligent to preserve the unity of the Spirit in the bond of peace.

4 *There is* one body and one Spirit, just as also you were called in one hope of your calling;

5one Lord, one faith, one baptism,

6one God and Father of all who is over all and through all and in all.

7But to each one of us grace was given according to the measure of Christ's gift.

8 Therefore it says,

"When He ascended on high,
He led captive a host of captives,
And He gave gifts to men."

9(Now this *expression,* "He ascended," what does it mean except that He also had descended into the lower parts of the earth?

10He who descended is Himself also He who ascended far above all the heavens, that He might fill all things.)

11And He gave some *as* apostles, and some *as* prophets, and some *as* evangelists, and some *as* pastors and teachers,

12for the equipping of the saints for the work of service, to the building up of the body of Christ;

13until we all attain to the unity of the faith, and of the knowledge of the Son of God, to a mature man, to the measure of the stature which belongs to the fulness of Christ.

14As a result, we are no longer to be children, tossed here and there by waves, and carried about by every wind of doctrine, by the trickery of men, by craftiness in deceitful scheming;

15but speaking the truth in love, we are to grow up in all *aspects* into Him, who is the head, *even* Christ,

16from whom the whole body, being fitted and held together by that which every joint supplies, according to the proper working of each individual part, causes the growth of the body for the building up of itself in love.

*The Christian's Walk*

17¶ This I say therefore, and affirm together with the Lord, that you walk no longer just as the Gentiles also walk, in the futility of their mind,

## New International

21to him be glory in the church and in Christ Jesus throughout all generations, for ever and ever! Amen.

*Unity in the Body of Christ*

**4** AS A prisoner for the Lord, then, I urge you to live a life worthy of the calling you have received. 2Be completely humble and gentle; be patient, bearing with one another in love. 3Make every effort to keep the unity of the Spirit through the bond of peace. 4There is one body and one Spirit— just as you were called to one hope when you were called— 5one Lord, one faith, one baptism; 6one God and Father of all, who is over all and through all and in all.

7But to each one of us grace has been given as Christ apportioned it. 8This is why it[e] says:

"When he ascended on high,
he led captives in his train
and gave gifts to men."[f]

9(What does "he ascended" mean except that he also descended to the lower, earthly regions[g]? 10He who descended is the very one who ascended higher than all the heavens, in order to fill the whole universe.) 11It was he who gave some to be apostles, some to be prophets, some to be evangelists, and some to be pastors and teachers, 12to prepare God's people for works of service, so that the body of Christ may be built up 13until we all reach unity in the faith and in the knowledge of the Son of God and become mature, attaining to the whole measure of the fullness of Christ.

14Then we will no longer be infants, tossed back and forth by the waves, and blown here and there by every wind of teaching and by the cunning and craftiness of men in their deceitful scheming. 15Instead, speaking the truth in love, we will in all things grow up into him who is the Head, that is, Christ. 16From him the whole body, joined and held together by every supporting ligament, grows and builds itself up in love, as each part does its work.

*Living as Children of Light*

17So I tell you this, and insist on it in the Lord, that you must no longer live as the Gentiles do, in the futility of their thinking.

NIV [e] 8 Or *God* [f] 8 Psalm 68:18 [g] 9 Or *the depths of the earth*

## King James

18Having the understanding darkened, being alienated from the life of God through the ignorance that is in them, because of the blindness of their heart:
19Who being past feeling have given themselves over unto lasciviousness, to work all uncleanness with greediness.
20But ye have not so learned Christ;
21If so be that ye have heard him, and have been taught by him, as the truth is in Jesus:
22That ye put off concerning the former conversation the old man, which is corrupt according to the deceitful lusts;
23And be renewed in the spirit of your mind;
24And that ye put on the new man, which after God is created in righteousness and true holiness.
25Wherefore putting away lying, speak every man truth with his neighbour: for we are members one of another.
26Be ye angry, and sin not: let not the sun go down upon your wrath:
27Neither give place to the devil.
28Let him that stole steal no more: but rather let him labour, working with *his* hands the thing which is good, that he may have to give to him that needeth.
29Let no corrupt communication proceed out of your mouth, but that which is good to the use of edifying, that it may minister grace unto the hearers.
30And grieve not the holy Spirit of God, whereby ye are sealed unto the day of redemption.
31Let all bitterness, and wrath, and anger, and clamour, and evil speaking, be put away from you, with all malice:
32And be ye kind one to another, tenderhearted, forgiving one another, even as God for Christ's sake hath forgiven you.

5 BE YE therefore followers of God, as dear children;
2And walk in love, as Christ also hath loved us, and hath given himself for us an offering and a sacrifice to God for a sweetsmelling savour.
3But fornication, and all uncleanness, or covetousness, let it not be once named among you, as becometh saints;
4Neither filthiness, nor foolish talking, nor jesting, which are not convenient: but rather giving of thanks.

## Amplified

18Their [a]moral understanding is darkened *and* their reasoning is beclouded. [They are] alienated (estranged, self-banished) from the life of God—with no share in it. [This is] because of the ignorance—the want of knowledge and perception, the willful blindness—that is [b]deep-seated in them, due to their hardness of heart (to the insensitiveness of their moral nature).
19In their spiritual apathy they have become callous *and* past feeling *and* reckless, and have abandoned themselves [a prey] to unbridled sensuality, eager *and* greedy to indulge in every form of impurity [that their depraved desires may suggest and demand].
20But you did not so learn Christ!
21Assuming that you have really heard Him *and* been taught by Him, as [all] Truth is in Jesus—embodied and personified in Him:
22Strip yourselves of your former nature—put off and discard your old unrenewed self—which characterized your previous manner of life and becomes corrupt through lusts *and* desires that spring from delusion;
23And be constantly renewed in the spirit of your mind—having a fresh mental and spiritual attitude;
24And put on the new nature (the regenerate self) created in God's image, (Godlike) in true righteousness and holiness.
25Therefore, rejecting all falsity *and* done now with it, let every one express the truth with his neighbor, for we are all parts of one body *and* members one of another. [Zech. 8:16.]
26When angry, do not sin; do not ever let your wrath—your exasperation, your fury or indignation—last until the sun goes down.
27Leave no [such] room *or* foothold for the devil—give no opportunity to him.
28Let the thief steal no more, but rather let him be industrious, making an honest living with his own hands, so that he may be able to give to those in need.
29Let no foul *or* polluting language, *nor* evil word, *nor* unwholesome *or* worthless talk [ever] come out of your mouth; but only such [speech] as is good *and* beneficial to the spiritual progress of others, as is fitting to the need *and* the occasion, that it may be a blessing *and* give grace (God's favor) to those who hear it.
30And do not grieve the Holy Spirit of God, (do not offend, or vex, or sadden Him) by Whom you were sealed (marked, branded as God's own, secured) for the day of redemption—of final deliverance through Christ from evil and the consequences of sin.
31Let all bitterness and indignation *and* wrath (passion, rage, bad temper) and resentment (anger, animosity) and quarreling (brawling, clamor, contention) and slander (evilspeaking, abusive or blasphemous language) be banished from you, with all malice (spite, ill will or baseness of any kind).
32And become useful *and* helpful *and* kind to one another, tenderhearted (compassionate, understanding, loving-hearted), forgiving one another [readily and freely], as God in Christ forgave you.

5 THEREFORE BE imitators of God—copy Him *and* follow His example—as well-beloved children [imitate their father].
2And walk in love—esteeming and delighting in one another—as Christ loved us and gave Himself up for us, a [c]slain offering and sacrifice to God [for you, so that it became] a sweet fragrance. [Ezek. 20:41.]
3But immorality (sexual vice) and all impurity [ [d]of lustful, rich, wasteful living] or greediness must not even be named among you, as is fitting *and* proper among saints (God's consecrated people).
4Let there be no filthiness (obscenity, indecency) nor foolish *and* sinful (silly and corrupt) talk, nor coarse jesting, which are not fitting *or* becoming; but instead voice your thankfulness [to God].

AMP [a] Vincent. [b] Vincent. [c] Vincent. [d] Thayer.

## New American Standard

18being darkened in their understanding, excluded from the life of God, because of the ignorance that is in them, because of the hardness of their heart;
19and they, having become callous, have given themselves over to sensuality, for the practice of every kind of impurity with greediness.
20But you did not learn Christ in this way,
21if indeed you have heard Him and have been taught in Him, just as truth is in Jesus,
22that, in reference to your former manner of life, you lay aside the old self, which is being corrupted in accordance with the lusts of deceit,
23and that you be renewed in the spirit of your mind,
24and put on the new self, which in *the likeness of* God has been created in righteousness and holiness of the truth.
25¶ Therefore, laying aside falsehood, SPEAK TRUTH, EACH ONE *of you*, WITH HIS NEIGHBOR, for we are members of one another.
26BE ANGRY, AND *yet* DO NOT SIN; do not let the sun go down on your anger,
27and do not give the devil an opportunity.
28Let him who steals steal no longer; but rather let him labor, performing with his own hands what is good, in order that he may have *something* to share with him who has need.
29Let no unwholesome word proceed from your mouth, but only such *a word* as is good for edification according to the need *of the moment*, that it may give grace to those who hear.
30And do not grieve the Holy Spirit of God, by whom you were sealed for the day of redemption.
31Let all bitterness and wrath and anger and clamor and slander be put away from you, along with all malice.
32And be kind to one another, tender-hearted, forgiving each other, just as God in Christ also has forgiven [e]you.

*Be Imitators of God*

**5** THEREFORE BE imitators of God, as beloved children;
2and walk in love, just as Christ also loved [f]you, and gave Himself up for us, an offering and a sacrifice to God as a fragrant aroma.
3¶ But do not let immorality or any impurity or greed even be named among you, as is proper among saints;
4and *there must be no* filthiness and silly talk, or coarse jesting, which are not fitting, but rather giving of thanks.

NAS [e] Some ancient mss. read *us* [f] Some ancient mss. read *us*

## New International

18They are darkened in their understanding and separated from
the life of God because of the ignorance that is in them due to the
hardening of their hearts. 19Having lost all sensitivity, they have
given themselves over to sensuality so as to indulge in every kind
of impurity, with a continual lust for more.
20You, however, did not come to know Christ that way. 21Sure-
ly you heard of him and were taught in him in accordance with the
truth that is in Jesus. 22You were taught, with regard to your
former way of life, to put off your old self, which is being corrupted
by its deceitful desires; 23to be made new in the attitude of your
minds; 24and to put on the new self, created to be like God in true
righteousness and holiness.
25Therefore each of you must put off falsehood and speak truthfully to his neighbor, for we are all members of one body. 26"In
your anger do not sin"[g]: Do not let the sun go down while you
are still angry, 27and do not give the devil a foothold. 28He who
has been stealing must steal no longer, but must work, doing
something useful with his own hands, that he may have something to share with those in need.
29Do not let any unwholesome talk come out of your mouths,
but only what is helpful for building others up according to their
needs, that it may benefit those who listen. 30And do not grieve
the Holy Spirit of God, with whom you were sealed for the day
of redemption. 31Get rid of all bitterness, rage and anger, brawling
and slander, along with every form of malice. 32Be kind and compassionate to one another, forgiving each other, just as in Christ
God forgave you.

**5** BE IMITATORS of God, therefore, as dearly loved children
2and live a life of love, just as Christ loved us and gave himself
up for us as a fragrant offering and sacrifice to God.
3But among you there must not be even a hint of sexual immorality, or of any kind of impurity, or of greed, because these are
improper for God's holy people. 4Nor should there be obscenity,
foolish talk or coarse joking, which are out of place, but rather
thanksgiving. 5For of this you can be sure: No immoral, impure or

NIV [g] 26 Psalm 4:4

## King James

5For this ye know, that no whoremonger, nor unclean person, nor covetous man, who is an idolater, hath any inheritance in the kingdom of Christ and of God.

6Let no man deceive you with vain words: for because of these things cometh the wrath of God upon the children of disobedience.

7Be not ye therefore partakers with them.

8For ye were sometimes darkness, but now *are ye* light in the Lord: walk as children of light:

9(For the fruit of the Spirit *is* in all goodness and righteousness and truth;)

10Proving what is acceptable unto the Lord.

11And have no fellowship with the unfruitful works of darkness, but rather reprove *them*.

12For it is a shame even to speak of those things which are done of them in secret.

13But all things that are reproved are made manifest by the light: for whatsoever doth make manifest is light.

14Wherefore he saith, Awake thou that sleepest, and arise from the dead, and Christ shall give thee light.

15See then that ye walk circumspectly, not as fools, but as wise,

16Redeeming the time, because the days are evil.

17Wherefore be ye not unwise, but understanding what the will of the Lord *is*.

18And be not drunk with wine, wherein is excess; but be filled with the Spirit;

19Speaking to yourselves in psalms and hymns and spiritual songs, singing and making melody in your heart to the Lord;

20Giving thanks always for all things unto God and the Father in the name of our Lord Jesus Christ;

21Submitting yourselves one to another in the fear of God.

22Wives, submit yourselves unto your own husbands, as unto the Lord.

23For the husband is the head of the wife, even as Christ is the head of the church: and he is the saviour of the body.

24Therefore as the church is subject unto Christ, so *let* the wives *be* to their own husbands in every thing.

25Husbands, love your wives, even as Christ also loved the church, and gave himself for it;

26That he might sanctify and cleanse it with the washing of water by the word,

27That he might present it to himself a glorious church, not having spot, or wrinkle, or any such thing; but that it should be holy and without blemish.

28So ought men to love their wives as their own bodies. He that loveth his wife loveth himself.

29For no man ever yet hated his own flesh; but nourisheth and cherisheth it, even as the Lord the church:

30For we are members of his body, of his flesh, and of his bones.

31For this cause shall a man leave his father and mother, and shall be joined unto his wife, and they two shall be one flesh.

32This is a great mystery: but I speak concerning Christ and the church.

## Amplified

5For be sure of this, that no person practicing sexual vice or impurity in thought or in life, or one who is covetous—that is, who has lustful desire for the property of others and is greedy for gain—[for] that [in effect] is an idolater, has any inheritance in the kingdom of Christ and of God.

6Let no one delude *and* deceive you with empty excuses *and* groundless arguments [for these sins], for through these things the wrath of God comes upon the sons of rebellion *and* disobedience.

7So do not associate *or* be sharers with them.

8For once you were darkness, but now you are light in the Lord; walk as children of light—lead the lives of those native-born to the Light.

9For the fruit—the effect, the product—of the Light, [a]the Spirit, [consists] in every form of kindly goodness, uprightness of heart and trueness of life.

10And try to learn [in your experience] what is pleasing to the Lord;—[let your lives be constant] proofs of what is most acceptable to Him.

11Take no part in *and* have no fellowship with the fruitless deeds *and* enterprises of darkness, but instead [let your lives be so in contrast as to] [b]expose *and* reprove *and* convict them.

12For it is a shame even to speak of *or* mention the things that [such people] practice in secret.

13But when anything is exposed *and* reproved by the light, it is made visible *and* clear; and where everything is visible *and* clear there is light.

14Therefore He says, Awake, O sleeper, and arise from the dead, and Christ shall shine [make day dawn] upon you *and* give you light. [Isa. 60:1, 2 with 26:19.]

15Look carefully then how you walk! Live purposefully *and* worthily *and* accurately, not as the unwise *and* witless, but as wise—sensible, intelligent people;

16Making the very most of the time— [c]buying up each opportunity—because the days are evil.

17Therefore do not be vague *and* thoughtless *and* foolish, but understanding *and* firmly grasping what the will of the Lord is.

18And do not get drunk with wine, for that is debauchery; but ever be filled *and* stimulated with the (Holy) Spirit. [Prov. 23:20.]

19Speak out to one another in psalms and hymns and spiritual songs, offering praise with voices [ [d]and instruments], and making melody with all your heart to the Lord,

20At all times and for everything giving thanks in the name of our Lord Jesus Christ to God the Father.

21Be subject to one another out of reverence for Christ, the Messiah, the Anointed One.

22Wives, be subject—be submissive and adapt yourselves—to your own husbands as [a service] to the Lord.

23For the husband is head of the wife as Christ is the Head of the church, Himself the Savior of [His] body.

24As the church is subject to Christ, so let wives also be subject in everything to their husbands.

25Husbands, love your wives, as Christ loved the church and gave Himself up for her,

26So that He might sanctify her, having cleansed her by the washing of water with the Word,

27That He might present the church to Himself in glorious splendor, without spot or wrinkle or any such things—that she might be holy and faultless.

28Even so husbands should love their wives as [being in a sense] their own bodies. He who loves his own wife loves himself.

29For no man ever hated his own flesh, but nourishes *and* carefully protects and cherishes it, as Christ does the church,

30Because we are members (parts) of His body.

31For this reason a man shall leave his father and his mother and shall be joined to his wife, and the two shall become one flesh. [Gen. 2:24.]

32This mystery is very great, but I speak concerning [the relation of] Christ and the church.

**AMP** [a] Some ancient authorities so read. [b] Thayer. [c] Alternate reading. [d] Berry's "Greek-English New Testament Lexicon."

## New American Standard

5For this you know with certainty, that no immoral or impure
person or covetous man, who is an idolater, has an inheritance in
the kingdom of Christ and God.
6Let no one deceive you with empty words, for because of
these things the wrath of God comes upon the sons of disobedience.
7Therefore do not be partakers with them;
8for you were formerly darkness, but now you are light in the
Lord; walk as children of light
9(for the fruit of the light *consists* in all goodness and righteousness and truth),
10trying to learn what is pleasing to the Lord.
11And do not participate in the unfruitful deeds of darkness, but
instead even expose them;
12for it is disgraceful even to speak of the things which are done
by them in secret.
13But all things become visible when they are exposed by the
light, for everything that becomes visible is light.
14For this reason it says,

"Awake, sleeper,
And arise from the dead,
And Christ will shine on you."

15¶ Therefore be careful how you walk, not as unwise men, but
as wise,
16making the most of your time, because the days are evil.
17So then do not be foolish, but understand what the will of the
Lord is.
18And do not get drunk with wine, for that is dissipation, but
be filled with the Spirit,
19speaking to one another in psalms and hymns and spiritual
songs, singing and making melody with your heart to the Lord;
20always giving thanks for all things in the name of our Lord
Jesus Christ to God, even the Father;
21and be subject to one another in the fear of Christ.

*Marriage Like Christ and the Church*

22¶ Wives, *be subject* to your own husbands, as to the Lord.
23For the husband is the head of the wife, as Christ also is the
head of the church, He Himself *being* the Savior of the body.
24But as the church is subject to Christ, so also the wives *ought
to be* to their husbands in everything.
25Husbands, love your wives, just as Christ also loved the
church and gave Himself up for her;
26that He might sanctify her, having cleansed her by the washing of water with the word,
27that He might present to Himself the church in all her glory,
having no spot or wrinkle or any such thing; but that she should
be holy and blameless.
28So husbands ought also to love their own wives as their own
bodies. He who loves his own wife loves himself;
29for no one ever hated his own flesh, but nourishes and
cherishes it, just as Christ also *does* the church,
30because we are members of His body.
31FOR THIS CAUSE A MAN SHALL LEAVE HIS FATHER AND MOTHER,
AND SHALL CLEAVE TO HIS WIFE; AND THE TWO SHALL BECOME ONE
FLESH.
32This mystery is great; but I am speaking with reference to
Christ and the church.

## New International

greedy person—such a man is an idolater—has any inheritance in
the kingdom of Christ and of God.[e] 6Let no one deceive you with
empty words, for because of such things God's wrath comes on
those who are disobedient. 7Therefore do not be partners with
them.
8For you were once darkness, but now you are light in the Lord.
Live as children of light 9(for the fruit of the light consists in all
goodness, righteousness and truth) 10and find out what pleases
the Lord. 11Have nothing to do with the fruitless deeds of darkness, but rather expose them. 12For it is shameful even to mention
what the disobedient do in secret. 13But everything exposed by the
light becomes visible, 14for it is light that makes everything visible.
This is why it is said:

"Wake up, O sleeper,
rise from the dead,
and Christ will shine on you."

15Be very careful, then, how you live—not as unwise but as
wise, 16making the most of every opportunity, because the days
are evil. 17Therefore do not be foolish, but understand what the
Lord's will is. 18Do not get drunk on wine, which leads to debauchery. Instead, be filled with the Spirit. 19Speak to one another with
psalms, hymns and spiritual songs. Sing and make music in your
heart to the Lord, 20always giving thanks to God the Father for
everything, in the name of our Lord Jesus Christ.
21Submit to one another out of reverence for Christ.

*Wives and Husbands*

22Wives, submit to your husbands as to the Lord. 23For the
husband is the head of the wife as Christ is the head of the church,
his body, of which he is the Savior. 24Now as the church submits
to Christ, so also wives should submit to their husbands in everything.
25Husbands, love your wives, just as Christ loved the church
and gave himself up for her 26to make her holy, cleansing[f] her by
the washing with water through the word, 27and to present her to
himself as a radiant church, without stain or wrinkle or any other
blemish, but holy and blameless. 28In this same way, husbands
ought to love their wives as their own bodies. He who loves his
wife loves himself. 29After all, no one ever hated his own body,
but he feeds and cares for it, just as Christ does the church— 30for
we are members of his body. 31"For this reason a man will leave
his father and mother and be united to his wife, and the two will
become one flesh."[g] 32This is a profound mystery—but I am talking about Christ and the church. 33However, each one of you also

NIV [e] 5 Or *kingdom of the Christ and God* [f] 26 Or *having cleansed* [g] 31 Gen. 2:24

## King James

33 Nevertheless let every one of you in particular so love his wife even as himself; and the wife *see* that she reverence *her* husband.

6 CHILDREN, OBEY your parents in the Lord: for this is right.
2 Honour thy father and mother; which is the first commandment with promise;
3 That it may be well with thee, and thou mayest live long on the earth.
4 And, ye fathers, provoke not your children to wrath: but bring them up in the nurture and admonition of the Lord.
5 Servants, be obedient to them that are *your* masters according to the flesh, with fear and trembling, in singleness of your heart, as unto Christ;
6 Not with eyeservice, as menpleasers; but as the servants of Christ, doing the will of God from the heart;
7 With good will doing service, as to the Lord, and not to men:
8 Knowing that whatsoever good thing any man doeth, the same shall he receive of the Lord, whether *he be* bond or free.
9 And, ye masters, do the same things unto them, forbearing threatening: knowing that your Master also is in heaven; neither is there respect of persons with him.
10 Finally, my brethren, be strong in the Lord, and in the power of his might.
11 Put on the whole armour of God, that ye may be able to stand against the wiles of the devil.
12 For we wrestle not against flesh and blood, but against principalities, against powers, against the rulers of the darkness of this world, against spiritual wickedness in high *places*.
13 Wherefore take unto you the whole armour of God, that ye may be able to withstand in the evil day, and having done all, to stand.
14 Stand therefore, having your loins girt about with truth, and having on the breastplate of righteousness;
15 And your feet shod with the preparation of the gospel of peace;
16 Above all, taking the shield of faith, wherewith ye shall be able to quench all the fiery darts of the wicked.
17 And take the helmet of salvation, and the sword of the Spirit, which is the word of God:
18 Praying always with all prayer and supplication in the Spirit, and watching thereunto with all perseverance and supplication for all saints;
19 And for me, that utterance may be given unto me, that I may open my mouth boldly, to make known the mystery of the gospel,

## Amplified

33 However, let each man of you (without exception) love his wife as [being in a sense] his very own self; and let the wife see that she respects *and* reverences her husband—[a]that she notices him, regards him, honors him, prefers him, venerates and esteems him; and [b]that she defers to him, praises him, and loves and admires him exceedingly.

6 CHILDREN, OBEY your parents in the Lord [as His representatives], for this is just and right.
2 Honor (esteem and value as precious) your father and your mother; this is the first commandment with a promise: [Exod. 20:12.]
3 That all may be well with you and that you may live long on the earth.
4 Fathers, do not irritate *and* provoke your children to anger—do not exasperate them to resentment—but rear them [tenderly] in the training *and* discipline and the counsel *and* admonition of the Lord.
5 Servants (slaves), be obedient to those who are your physical masters, having respect for them and eager concern to please them, in singleness of motive *and* with all your heart, as [service] to Christ [Himself.]
6 Not in the way of eyeservice—as if they were watching you—and only to please men; but as servants (slaves) of Christ, doing the will of God heartily *and* with your whole soul;
7 Rendering service readily with goodwill, as to the Lord and not to men,
8 Knowing that for whatever good any one does, he will receive his reward from the Lord, whether he is slave or free.
9 You masters, act on the same [principle] toward them, and give up threatening *and* using violent *and* abusive words, knowing that He Who is both their Master and yours is in heaven, and that there is no respect of persons—no partiality—with Him.
10 In conclusion, be strong in the Lord—be empowered through your union with Him; draw your strength from Him—that strength which His [boundless] might provides.
11 Put on God's whole armor—the armor of a heavy-armed soldier, which God supplies—that you may be able successfully to stand up against [all] the strategies *and* the deceits of the devil.
12 For we are not wrestling with flesh and blood—contending only with physical opponents—but against the despotisms, against the powers, against [the master spirits who are] the world rulers of this present darkness, against the spirit forces of wickedness in the heavenly (supernatural) sphere.
13 Therefore put on God's complete armor, that you may be able to resist *and* stand your ground on the evil day [of danger], and having done all [the crisis demands], to stand [firmly in your place].
14 Stand therefore—hold your ground—having tightened the belt of truth around your loins, and having put on the breastplate of integrity *and* of moral rectitude *and* right standing with God;
15 And having shod your feet in preparation [to face the enemy with the [c]firm-footed stability, the promptness and the readiness [d]produced by the good news] of the Gospel of peace. [Isa. 52:7.]
16 Lift up over all the (covering) shield of [e]saving faith, upon which you can quench all the flaming missiles of the wicked [one].
17 And take the helmet of salvation and the sword the Spirit [f]wields, which is the Word of God.
18 Pray at all times—on every occasion, in every season—in the Spirit, with all [manner of] prayer and entreaty. To that end keep alert and watch with strong purpose *and* perseverance, interceding in behalf of all the saints (God's consecrated people).
19 And also for me, that [freedom of] utterance may be given me, that I may open my mouth to proclaim boldly the mystery of the good news [of the Gospel],

**AMP** [a] Webster's list of English words with the same or nearly the same essential meaning as "respect" and "reverence." The latter includes the word "adore" in the sense not applied to Deity. [b] Webster's list of English words with the same or nearly the same essential meaning as "respect" and "reverence." The latter includes the word "adore" in the sense not applied to Deity. [c] Vincent. [d] Thayer. [e] Vincent. [f] Williams: Subjective genitive.

## New American Standard

33Nevertheless let each individual among you also love his own
wife even as himself; and *let* the wife *see to it* that she respect her
husband.

*Family Relationships*

6 CHILDREN, OBEY your parents in the Lord, for this is right.
2HONOR YOUR FATHER AND MOTHER (which is the first commandment with a promise),
3THAT IT MAY BE WELL WITH YOU, AND THAT YOU MAY LIVE LONG
ON THE EARTH.
4And, fathers, do not provoke your children to anger; but bring
them up in the discipline and instruction of the Lord.
5¶ Slaves, be obedient to those who are your masters according
to the flesh, with fear and trembling, in the sincerity of your heart,
as to Christ;
6not by way of eyeservice, as men-pleasers, but as slaves of
Christ, doing the will of God from the heart.
7With good will render service, as to the Lord, and not to men,
8knowing that whatever good thing each one does, this he will
receive back from the Lord, whether slave or free.
9And, masters, do the same things to them, and give up threatening, knowing that both their Master and yours is in heaven, and
there is no partiality with Him.

*The Armor of God*

10¶ Finally, be strong in the Lord, and in the strength of His
might.
11Put on the full armor of God, that you may be able to stand
firm against the schemes of the devil.
12For our struggle is not against flesh and blood, but against the
rulers, against the powers, against the world forces of this darkness, against the spiritual *forces* of wickedness in the heavenly
*places*.
13Therefore, take up the full armor of God, that you may be able
to resist in the evil day, and having done everything, to stand firm.
14Stand firm therefore, HAVING GIRDED YOUR LOINS WITH TRUTH,
and HAVING PUT ON THE BREASTPLATE OF RIGHTEOUSNESS,
15and having shod YOUR FEET WITH THE PREPARATION OF THE
GOSPEL OF PEACE;
16in addition to all, taking up the shield of faith with which you
will be able to extinguish all the flaming missiles of the evil *one*.
17And take THE HELMET OF SALVATION, and the sword of the
Spirit, which is the word of God.
18With all prayer and petition pray at all times in the Spirit, and
with this in view, be on the alert with all perseverance and petition
for all the saints,
19and *pray* on my behalf, that utterance may be given to me in
the opening of my mouth, to make known with boldness the
mystery of the gospel,

## New International

must love his wife as he loves himself, and the wife must respect
her husband.

*Children and Parents*

6 CHILDREN, OBEY your parents in the Lord, for this is right.
2"Honor your father and mother"—which is the first commandment with a promise— 3"that it may go well with you and
that you may enjoy long life on the earth."[g]
4Fathers, do not exasperate your children; instead, bring them
up in the training and instruction of the Lord.

*Slaves and Masters*

5Slaves, obey your earthly masters with respect and fear, and
with sincerity of heart, just as you would obey Christ. 6Obey them
not only to win their favor when their eye is on you, but like slaves
of Christ, doing the will of God from your heart. 7Serve wholeheartedly, as if you were serving the Lord, not men, 8because you
know that the Lord will reward everyone for whatever good he
does, whether he is slave or free.
9And masters, treat your slaves in the same way. Do not threaten them, since you know that he who is both their Master and
yours is in heaven, and there is no favoritism with him.

*The Armor of God*

10Finally, be strong in the Lord and in his mighty power. 11Put
on the full armor of God so that you can take your stand against
the devil's schemes. 12For our struggle is not against flesh and
blood, but against the rulers, against the authorities, against the
powers of this dark world and against the spiritual forces of evil
in the heavenly realms. 13Therefore put on the full armor of God,
so that when the day of evil comes, you may be able to stand your
ground, and after you have done everything, to stand. 14Stand
firm then, with the belt of truth buckled around your waist, with
the breastplate of righteousness in place, 15and with your feet
fitted with the readiness that comes from the gospel of peace. 16In
addition to all this, take up the shield of faith, with which you can
extinguish all the flaming arrows of the evil one. 17Take the helmet
of salvation and the sword of the Spirit, which is the word of God.
18And pray in the Spirit on all occasions with all kinds of prayers
and requests. With this in mind, be alert and always keep on
praying for all the saints.
19Pray also for me, that whenever I open my mouth, words may
be given me so that I will fearlessly make known the mystery of

NIV g 3 Deut. 5:16

## King James

20For which I am an ambassador in bonds: that therein I may
speak boldly, as I ought to speak.
21But that ye also may know my affairs, *and* how I do, Tychicus,
a beloved brother and faithful minister in the Lord, shall make
known to you all things:
22Whom I have sent unto you for the same purpose, that ye
might know our affairs, and *that* he might comfort your hearts.
23Peace *be* to the brethren, and love with faith, from God the
Father and the Lord Jesus Christ.
24Grace *be* with all them that love our Lord Jesus Christ in
sincerity. Amen.

## Amplified

20For which I am an ambassador in a coupling chain [in prison.
Pray] that I may declare it boldly *and* courageously as I ought to
do.
21Now that you may know how I am and what I am doing,
Tychicus the beloved brother and faithful minister in the Lord [and
His service] will tell you everything.
22I have sent him to you for this very purpose, that you may
know how we are and that he may [a]console *and* cheer *and* encourage
*and* strengthen your hearts.
23Peace be to the brethren, and love joined with faith, from God
the Father and the Lord Jesus Christ, the Messiah, the Anointed
One.
24Grace (God's undeserved favor) be with all who love our Lord
Jesus Christ with undying *and* incorruptible [love]. *Amen—so let it
be.*

**AMP** [a] Thayer.

## New American Standard

20for which I am an ambassador in chains; that [b]in *proclaiming*
it I may speak boldly, as I ought to speak.
21¶ But that you also may know about my circumstances, how
I am doing, Tychicus, the beloved brother and faithful minister in
the Lord, will make everything known to you.
22And I have sent him to you for this very purpose, so that you
may know about us, and that he may comfort your hearts.
23¶ Peace be to the brethren, and love with faith, from God the
Father and the Lord Jesus Christ.
24Grace be with all those who love our Lord Jesus Christ with
*a love* incorruptible.

## New International

the gospel, 20for which I am an ambassador in chains. Pray that
I may declare it fearlessly, as I should.

*Final Greetings*

21Tychicus, the dear brother and faithful servant in the Lord,
will tell you everything, so that you also may know how I am and
what I am doing. 22I am sending him to you for this very purpose,
that you may know how we are, and that he may encourage you.
23Peace to the brothers, and love with faith from God the Father
and the Lord Jesus Christ. 24Grace to all who love our Lord Jesus
Christ with an undying love.

**NAS** [b] Some ancient mss. read *I may speak it boldly*

**King James**

THE EPISTLE OF

PAUL THE APOSTLE TO THE

# Philippians

1 PAUL AND Timotheus, the servants of Jesus Christ, to all the
saints in Christ Jesus which are at Philippi, with the bishops
and deacons:
2Grace *be* unto you, and peace, from God our Father, and *from*
the Lord Jesus Christ.
3I thank my God upon every remembrance of you,
4Always in every prayer of mine for you all making request with
joy,
5For your fellowship in the gospel from the first day until now;
6Being confident of this very thing, that he which hath begun
a good work in you will perform *it* until the day of Jesus Christ:
7Even as it is meet for me to think this of you all, because I have
you in my heart; inasmuch as both in my bonds, and in the defence
and confirmation of the gospel, ye all are partakers of my grace.
8For God is my record, how greatly I long after you all in the
bowels of Jesus Christ.
9And this I pray, that your love may abound yet more and more
in knowledge and *in* all judgment;
10That ye may approve things that are excellent; that ye may be
sincere and without offence till the day of Christ;
11Being filled with the fruits of righteousness, which are by
Jesus Christ, unto the glory and praise of God.
12But I would ye should understand, brethren, that the things
*which happened* unto me have fallen out rather unto the furtherance
of the gospel;
13So that my bonds in Christ are manifest in all the palace, and
in all other *places;*
14And many of the brethren in the Lord, waxing confident by
my bonds, are much more bold to speak the word without fear.

**Amplified**

THE LETTER OF

PAUL TO THE

# Philippians

1 PAUL AND Timothy, bondservants of Christ Jesus, the Messiah, to all the saints (God's consecrated people) in Christ
Jesus who are at Philippi, with the bishops [overseers] and deacons [assistants]:
2Grace (favor and blessing) to you and heart peace from God
our Father and the Lord Jesus Christ, the Messiah.
3I thank my God in all my remembrance of you.
4In every prayer of mine I always make my entreaty *and* petition
for you all with joy (delight).
5[I thank my God] for your fellowship—your [a]sympathetic co-
operation and contributions and partnership—in advancing the
good news (the Gospel) from the first day [you heard it] until now.
6And I am convinced *and* sure of this very thing, that He Who
began a good work in you will continue until the day of Jesus
Christ—right up to the time of His return—developing [that good
work] *and* perfecting *and* bringing it to full completion in you.
7It is right *and* appropriate for me to have this confidence *and*
feel this way about you all, because even as [b]you do me, I hold
you in my heart as partakers *and* sharers, one *and* all with me, of
grace (God's unmerited favor and spiritual blessing). [This is true]
both when I am shut up in prison and when I am out in the defense
and confirmation of the good news (the Gospel).
8For God is my witness how I long for *and* [c]pursue you all with
love, in the tender mercies of Christ Jesus [Himself]!
9And this I pray, that your love may abound yet more and more
*and* extend to its fullest development in knowledge and all keen
insight—that is, that your love may [ [d]display itself in] greater
depth of acquaintance and more comprehensive discernment;
10So that you may surely learn to sense what is vital, *and* approve *and* prize what is excellent *and* of real value—recognizing the
highest and the best, and [e]distinguishing the moral differences;
and that you may be untainted *and* pure and unerring *and* blameless, that—with hearts sincere and certain and unsullied—you
may [approach] the day of Christ, not stumbling *nor* causing others
to stumble.
11May you abound in *and* be filled with the fruits of righteousness (of right standing with God and right doing) which come
through Jesus Christ, the Anointed One, to the honor and praise
of God— [f]that His glory may be both manifested and recognized.
12Now I want you to know *and* continue to rest assured, brethren, that what [has happened] to me [this imprisonment,] has
actually only served to advance *and* give a renewed impetus to the
[spreading of the] good news—of the Gospel.
13So much is this a fact that throughout the whole imperial
guard and to all the rest [here], my imprisonment has become
generally known to be in Christ—in that I am a prisoner in His
service and for Him.
14And [also] most of the brethren have derived fresh confidence
in the Lord because of my chains, and are much more bold to speak
*and* publish fearlessly the Word of God—acting with more freedom
and indifference to the consequences.

**AMP** [a] Vincent. [b] Alternate reading, "you have me in your heart." [c] Thayer. [d] Vincent. [e] Alternate reading, "distinguish the things that differ." [f] Vincent.

## New American Standard

# Philippians

*Thanksgiving*

1 PAUL AND Timothy, bond-servants of Christ Jesus, to all the saints in Christ Jesus who are in Philippi, including the overseers and deacons:

2 Grace to you and peace from God our Father and the Lord Jesus Christ.

3 ¶ I thank my God in all my remembrance of you,

4 always offering prayer with joy in my every prayer for you all,

5 in view of your participation in the gospel from the first day until now.

6 *For I am* confident of this very thing, that He who began a good work in you will perfect it until the day of Christ Jesus.

7 For it is only right for me to feel this way about you all, because I have you in my heart, since both in my imprisonment and in the defense and confirmation of the gospel, you all are partakers of grace with me.

8 For God is my witness, how I long for you all with the affection of Christ Jesus.

9 And this I pray, that your love may abound still more and more in real knowledge and all discernment,

10 so that you may approve the things that are excellent, in order to be sincere and blameless until the day of Christ;

11 having been filled with the fruit of righteousness which *comes* through Jesus Christ, to the glory and praise of God.

*The Gospel Is Preached*

12 ¶ Now I want you to know, brethren, that my circumstances have turned out for the greater progress of the gospel,

13 so that my imprisonment in *the cause of* Christ has become well known throughout the whole [g]praetorian guard and to everyone else,

14 and that most of the brethren, trusting in the Lord because of my imprisonment, have far more courage to speak the word of God without fear.

NAS [g] Or, *governor's palace*

## New International

# Philippians

1 PAUL AND Timothy, servants of Christ Jesus,
To all the saints in Christ Jesus at Philippi, together with the overseers[h] and deacons:
2 Grace and peace to you from God our Father and the Lord Jesus Christ.

*Thanksgiving and Prayer*

3 I thank my God every time I remember you. 4 In all my prayers
for all of you, I always pray with joy 5 because of your partnership
in the gospel from the first day until now, 6 being confident of this,
that he who began a good work in you will carry it on to completion
until the day of Christ Jesus.
7 It is right for me to feel this way about all of you, since I have
you in my heart; for whether I am in chains or defending and
confirming the gospel, all of you share in God's grace with me.
8 God can testify how I long for all of you with the affection of
Christ Jesus.
9 And this is my prayer: that your love may abound more and
more in knowledge and depth of insight, 10 so that you may be able
to discern what is best and may be pure and blameless until the
day of Christ, 11 filled with the fruit of righteousness that comes
through Jesus Christ—to the glory and praise of God.

*Paul's Chains Advance the Gospel*

12 Now I want you to know, brothers, that what has happened
to me has really served to advance the gospel. 13 As a result, it has
become clear throughout the whole palace guard[i] and to everyone
else that I am in chains for Christ. 14 Because of my chains, most
of the brothers in the Lord have been encouraged to speak the
word of God more courageously and fearlessly.

NIV [h] 1 Traditionally *bishops* [i] 13 Or *whole palace*

## King James

15 Some indeed preach Christ even of envy and strife; and some
also of good will:
16 The one preach Christ of contention, not sincerely, supposing
to add affliction to my bonds:
17 But the other of love, knowing that I am set for the defence
of the gospel.
18 What then? notwithstanding, every way, whether in pretence, or in truth, Christ is preached; and I therein do rejoice, yea,
and will rejoice.
19 For I know that this shall turn to my salvation through your
prayer, and the supply of the Spirit of Jesus Christ,
20 According to my earnest expectation and *my* hope, that in
nothing I shall be ashamed, but *that* with all boldness, as always,
*so* now also Christ shall be magnified in my body, whether *it be* by
life, or by death.
21 For to me to live *is* Christ, and to die *is* gain.
22 But if I live in the flesh, this *is* the fruit of my labour: yet what
I shall choose I wot not.
23 For I am in a strait betwixt two, having a desire to depart, and
to be with Christ; which is far better:
24 Nevertheless to abide in the flesh *is* more needful for you.
25 And having this confidence, I know that I shall abide and
continue with you all for your furtherance and joy of faith;
26 That your rejoicing may be more abundant in Jesus Christ for
me by my coming to you again.
27 Only let your conversation be as it becometh the gospel of
Christ: that whether I come and see you, or else be absent, I may
hear of your affairs, that ye stand fast in one spirit, with one mind
striving together for the faith of the gospel;
28 And in nothing terrified by your adversaries: which is to them
an evident token of perdition, but to you of salvation, and that of
God.
29 For unto you it is given in the behalf of Christ, not only to
believe on him, but also to suffer for his sake;
30 Having the same conflict which ye saw in me, and now hear
*to be* in me.

**2** IF *THERE be* therefore any consolation in Christ, if any comfort of love, if any fellowship of the Spirit, if any bowels and
mercies,
2 Fulfil ye my joy, that ye be likeminded, having the same love,
*being* of one accord, of one mind.

## Amplified

15 Some, it is true, [actually] preach Christ, the Messiah, [for no
better reason than] out of envy and rivalry (party spirit); but others
are doing so out of a loyal spirit *and* goodwill.
16 [a]The latter [proclaim Christ] out of love, because they recognize *and* know that I am (providentially) put here for the defense
of the good news (the Gospel).
17 [b]But the former preach Christ out of a party spirit, insincerely—out of no pure motive, but thinking to annoy me—supposing
they are making my bondage more bitter *and* my chains more
galling.
18 But what does it matter, so long as either way, whether in
pretense [for personal ends] or in all honesty [for the furtherance
of the Truth], Christ is being proclaimed? And in that I [now]
rejoice,
19 Yes, and I shall rejoice [hereafter] also. For I am well assured
*and* indeed know that through your prayers and a [c]bountiful
supply of the Spirit of Jesus Christ, the Messiah, this will turn out
for my preservation [for the spiritual health and [d]welfare of my
own soul and avail toward the saving work of the Gospel].
20 This is in keeping with my own eager desire *and* persistent
expectation *and* hope, that I shall not disgrace myself *nor* be put to
shame in anything; but that with the utmost freedom of speech *and*
unfailing courage, now as always heretofore, Christ, the Messiah,
will be magnified *and* get glory *and* praise in this body of mine *and*
be boldly exalted in my person, whether through (by) life or
through (by) death.
21 For me, to live is Christ—His life in me; and to die is gain—
[the gain of the glory of eternity].
22 If, however, it is to be life in the flesh *and* I am to live on here,
that means fruitful service for me; so I can say nothing as to my
personal preference—I cannot choose,
23 But I am hard pressed between the two. My yearning desire
is to depart—to be free of this world, to set forth—and be with
Christ, for that is far, far better;
24 But to remain in my body is more needful *and* essential for
your sake.
25 Since I am convinced of this, I know that I shall remain and
stay by you all, to promote your progress and joy in believing.
26 So that in me you may have abundant cause for exultation *and*
glorying in Christ Jesus, through my coming to you again.
27 Only be sure as citizens so to conduct yourselves *that* your
manner of life will be worthy of the good news (the Gospel) of
Christ, so that whether I [do] come and see you or am absent, I
may hear this of you: that you are standing firm in united spirit
*and* purpose, striving side by side *and* contending with a single
mind for the faith of the glad tidings (the Gospel).
28 And do not [for a moment] be frightened *or* intimidated in
anything by your opponents *and* adversaries, for such [constancy
and fearlessness] will be a clear sign (proof and seal) to them of
[their impending] destruction; but [a sure token and evidence] of
your deliverance *and* salvation, and that from God.
29 For you have been granted [the privilege] for Christ's sake not
only to believe—adhere to, rely on and trust—in Him but also to
suffer in His behalf.
30 So you are engaged in the same conflict which you saw me
[wage] and which you now hear to be mine [still].

**2** SO BY whatever [appeal to you there is in our mutual dwelling in Christ, by whatever] strengthening *and* consoling *and*
encouraging [our relationship] in Him [affords], by whatever persuasive [e]incentive there is in love, by whatever participation in the
(Holy) Spirit [we share] and by whatever depth of affection and
compassionate sympathy,
2 Fill up *and* complete my joy by living in harmony *and* being of
the same mind *and* one in purpose, having the same love, being
in full accord and of one harmonious mind *and* intention.

**AMP** [a] The order of verses 16 and 17 has been reversed for the sake of clarity in almost all versions since the King James. [b] The order of verses 16 and 17 has been reversed for the sake of clarity in almost all versions since the King James. [c] Vincent. [d] Vincent. [e] Vincent.

## New American Standard

15Some, to be sure, are preaching Christ even from envy and strife, but some also from good will;

16 [f]the latter *do it* out of love, knowing that I am appointed for the defense of the gospel;

17the former proclaim Christ out of selfish ambition, rather than from pure motives, thinking to cause me distress in my imprisonment.

18What then? Only that in every way, whether in pretense or in truth, Christ is proclaimed; and in this I rejoice, yes, and I will rejoice.

19For I know that this shall turn out for my deliverance through your prayers and the provision of the Spirit of Jesus Christ,

20according to my earnest expectation and hope, that I shall not be put to shame in anything, but *that* with all boldness, Christ shall even now, as always, be exalted in my body, whether by life or by death.

*To Live Is Christ*

21For to me, to live is Christ, and to die is gain.

22But if *I am* to live *on* in the flesh, this *will mean* fruitful labor for me; and I do not know which to choose.

23But I am hard-pressed from both *directions*, having the desire to depart and be with Christ, for *that* is very much better;

24yet to remain on in the flesh is more necessary for your sake.

25And convinced of this, I know that I shall remain and continue with you all for your progress and joy in the faith,

26so that your proud confidence in me may abound in Christ Jesus through my coming to you again.

27¶ Only conduct yourselves in a manner worthy of the gospel of Christ; so that whether I come and see you or remain absent, I may hear of you that you are standing firm in one spirit, with one mind striving together for the faith of the gospel;

28in no way alarmed by *your* opponents—which is a sign of destruction for them, but of salvation for you, and that *too*, from God.

29For to you it has been granted for Christ's sake, not only to believe in Him, but also to suffer for His sake,

30experiencing the same conflict which you saw in me, and now hear *to be* in me.

*Be Like Christ*

2 IF THEREFORE there is any encouragement in Christ, if there is any consolation of love, if there is any fellowship of the Spirit, if any affection and compassion,

2make my joy complete by being of the same mind, maintaining the same love, united in spirit, intent on one purpose.

NAS [f] Some later mss. reverse the order of vv. 16 and 17

## New International

15It is true that some preach Christ out of envy and rivalry, but
others out of goodwill. 16The latter do so in love, knowing that
I am put here for the defense of the gospel. 17The former preach
Christ out of selfish ambition, not sincerely, supposing that they
can stir up trouble for me while I am in chains.[g] 18But what does
it matter? The important thing is that in every way, whether from
false motives or true, Christ is preached. And because of this I
rejoice.
Yes, and I will continue to rejoice, 19for I know that through
your prayers and the help given by the Spirit of Jesus Christ, what
has happened to me will turn out for my deliverance.[h] 20I eagerly
expect and hope that I will in no way be ashamed, but will have
sufficient courage so that now as always Christ will be exalted in
my body, whether by life or by death. 21For to me, to live is Christ
and to die is gain. 22If I am to go on living in the body, this will
mean fruitful labor for me. Yet what shall I choose? I do not know!
23I am torn between the two: I desire to depart and be with Christ,
which is better by far; 24but it is more necessary for you that I
remain in the body. 25Convinced of this, I know that I will remain,
and I will continue with all of you for your progress and joy in the
faith, 26so that through my being with you again your joy in Christ
Jesus will overflow on account of me.
27Whatever happens, conduct yourselves in a manner worthy
of the gospel of Christ. Then, whether I come and see you or only
hear about you in my absence, I will know that you stand firm in
one spirit, contending as one man for the faith of the gospel
28without being frightened in any way by those who oppose you.
This is a sign to them that they will be destroyed, but that you will
be saved—and that by God. 29For it has been granted to you on
behalf of Christ not only to believe on him, but also to suffer for
him, 30since you are going through the same struggle you saw I
had, and now hear that I still have.

*Imitating Christ's Humility*

2 IF YOU have any encouragement from being united with
Christ, if any comfort from his love, if any fellowship with the
Spirit, if any tenderness and compassion, 2then make my joy
complete by being like-minded, having the same love, being one
in spirit and purpose. 3Do nothing out of selfish ambition or vain

NIV [g] *16,17* Some late manuscripts have verses 16 and 17 in reverse order.
[h] *19* Or *salvation*

## King James

3 *Let* nothing *be done* through strife or vainglory; but in lowliness of mind let each esteem other better than themselves.
4Look not every man on his own things, but every man also on the things of others.
5Let this mind be in you, which was also in Christ Jesus:
6Who, being in the form of God, thought it not robbery to be equal with God:
7But made himself of no reputation, and took upon him the form of a servant, and was made in the likeness of men:
8And being found in fashion as a man, he humbled himself, and became obedient unto death, even the death of the cross.
9Wherefore God also hath highly exalted him, and given him a name which is above every name:
10That at the name of Jesus every knee should bow, of *things* in heaven, and *things* in earth, and *things* under the earth;
11And *that* every tongue should confess that Jesus Christ *is* Lord, to the glory of God the Father.
12Wherefore, my beloved, as ye have always obeyed, not as in my presence only, but now much more in my absence, work out your own salvation with fear and trembling.
13For it is God which worketh in you both to will and to do of *his* good pleasure.
14Do all things without murmurings and disputings:
15That ye may be blameless and harmless, the sons of God, without rebuke, in the midst of a crooked and perverse nation, among whom ye shine as lights in the world;
16Holding forth the word of life; that I may rejoice in the day of Christ, that I have not run in vain, neither laboured in vain.
17Yea, and if I be offered upon the sacrifice and service of your faith, I joy, and rejoice with you all.
18For the same cause also do ye joy, and rejoice with me.
19But I trust in the Lord Jesus to send Timotheus shortly unto you, that I also may be of good comfort, when I know your state.
20For I have no man likeminded, who will naturally care for your state.
21For all seek their own, not the things which are Jesus Christ's.
22But ye know the proof of him, that, as a son with the father, he hath served with me in the gospel.

**AMP** [a] Warfield's "Biblical Doctrines." [b] Thayer. [c] Thayer. [d] Berry. [e] Vincent. [f] "Should" is past tense of "shall," implying authority or compulsion. [g] Vincent. [h] Vincent. [i] Vincent. [j] Souter. [k] Vincent. [l] Vincent. [m] Lightfoot: "St. Paul's Epistle to the Philippians"; Moulton and Milligan: "The Vocabulary of the Greek Testament." [n] Lightfoot: "St. Paul's Epistle to the Philippians"; Moulton and Milligan: "The Vocabulary of the Greek Testament."

## Amplified

3Do nothing from factional motives—through contentiousness, strife, selfishness or for unworthy ends—or prompted by conceit *and* empty arrogance. Instead, in the true spirit of humility (lowliness of mind) let each regard the others as better than *and* superior to himself—thinking more highly of one another than you do of yourselves.
4Let each of you esteem *and* look upon *and* be concerned for not [merely] his own interests, but also each for the interests of others.
5Let this same attitude *and* purpose *and* [humble] mind be in you which was in Christ Jesus.—Let Him be your example in humility—
6Who, although being essentially one with God *and* in the form of God [ [a]possessing the fullness of the attributes which make God God], did not [b]think this equality with God was a thing to be eagerly grasped [c]or retained;
7But stripped Himself [of all privileges and [d]rightful dignity] so as to assume the guise of a servant (slave), in that He became like men *and* was born a human being.
8And after He had appeared in human form He abased *and* humbled Himself [still further] and carried His obedience to the extreme of death, even the death of [the] cross!
9Therefore [because He stooped so low], God has highly exalted Him and has [e]freely bestowed on Him the name that is above every name,
10That in (at) the name of Jesus every knee [f]should (must) bow, in heaven and on earth and under the earth,
11And every tongue [ [g]frankly and openly] confess *and* acknowledge that Jesus Christ is Lord, to the glory of God the Father.
12Therefore, my dear ones, as you have always obeyed [my suggestions], so now, not only [with the enthusiasm you would show] in my presence but much more because I am absent, work out—cultivate, carry out to the goal and fully complete—your own salvation with reverence *and* awe and trembling [self-distrust, that is, [h]with serious caution, tenderness of conscience, watchfulness against temptation; timidly shrinking from whatever might offend God and discredit the name of Christ].
13[Not in your own strength] for it is God Who is all the while [i]effectually at work in you—energizing and creating in you the power and desire—both to will and to work for His good pleasure *and* satisfaction *and* [j]delight.
14Do all things without grumbling *and* faultfinding *and* complaining [ [k]against God] and [l]questioning *and* doubting [among yourselves],
15That you may show yourselves to be blameless *and* guileless, innocent *and* uncontaminated, children of God without blemish (faultless, unrebukable) in the midst of a crooked *and* wicked generation—[spiritually] perverted and perverse. Among whom you are seen as bright lights—stars or beacons shining out clearly—in the [dark] world;
16Holding out [to it] *and* offering [to all men] the Word of Life, so that in the day of Christ I may have something of which exultantly to rejoice *and* glory in that I did not run my race in vain or spend my labor to no purpose.
17Even if [my lifeblood] must be poured out as a libation on the sacrificial offering of your faith [to God], still I am glad [to do it] and [m]congratulate you all on [your share in] it;
18And you also in like manner be glad and [n]congratulate me on [my share in] it.
19But I hope *and* trust in the Lord Jesus soon to send Timothy to you, so that I may also be encouraged *and* cheered by learning news of you.
20For I have no one like him—no one of so kindred a spirit—who will be so genuinely interested in your welfare *and* devoted to your interests.
21For the others all seek [to advance] their own interests, not those of Jesus Christ, the Messiah.
22But Timothy's tested worth you know, how as a son with his father he has toiled with me zealously [serving and helping to advance] the good news (the Gospel).

## New American Standard

3Do nothing from selfishness or empty conceit, but with
humility of mind let each of you regard one another as more
important than himself;
4do not *merely* look out for your own personal interests, but
also for the interests of others.
5Have this attitude in yourselves which was also in Christ
Jesus,
6who, although He existed in the form of God, did not regard
equality with God a thing to be grasped,
7but [o]emptied Himself, taking the form of a bond-servant, *and*
being made in the likeness of men.
8And being found in appearance as a man, He humbled Himself by becoming obedient to the point of death, even death on a
cross.
9Therefore also God highly exalted Him, and bestowed on Him
the name which is above every name,
10that at the name of Jesus EVERY KNEE SHOULD BOW, of those
who are in heaven, and on earth, and under the earth,
11and that every tongue should confess that Jesus Christ is
Lord, to the glory of God the Father.
12¶ So then, my beloved, just as you have always obeyed, not
as in my presence only, but now much more in my absence, work
out your salvation with fear and trembling;
13for it is God who is at work in you, both to will and to work
for *His* good pleasure.
14Do all things without grumbling or disputing;
15that you may prove yourselves to be blameless and innocent,
children of God above reproach in the midst of a crooked and
perverse generation, among whom you appear as lights in the
world,
16holding fast the word of life, so that in the day of Christ I may
have cause to glory because I did not run in vain nor toil in vain.
17But even if I am being poured out as a drink offering upon the
sacrifice and service of your faith, I rejoice and share my joy with
you all.
18And you too, *I urge you,* rejoice in the same way and share
your joy with me.

*Timothy and Epaphroditus*

19¶ But I hope in the Lord Jesus to send Timothy to you shortly,
so that I also may be encouraged when I learn of your condition.
20For I have no one *else* of kindred spirit who will genuinely be
concerned for your welfare.
21For they all seek after their own interests, not those of Christ
Jesus.
22But you know of his proven worth that he served with me in
the furtherance of the gospel like a child *serving* his father.

NAS [o] I.e., laid aside His privileges

## New International

conceit, but in humility consider others better than yourselves.
4Each of you should look not only to your own interests, but also
to the interests of others.
5Your attitude should be the same as that of Christ Jesus:

6Who, being in very nature[p] God,
did not consider equality with God something to be grasped,
7but made himself nothing,
taking the very nature[q] of a servant,
being made in human likeness.
8And being found in appearance as a man,
he humbled himself
and became obedient to death—
even death on a cross!
9Therefore God exalted him to the highest place
and gave him the name that is above every name,
10that at the name of Jesus every knee should bow,
in heaven and on earth and under the earth,
11and every tongue confess that Jesus Christ is Lord,
to the glory of God the Father.

*Shining as Stars*

12Therefore, my dear friends, as you have always obeyed—not
only in my presence, but now much more in my absence—continue to work out your salvation with fear and trembling, 13for it is
God who works in you to will and to act according to his good
purpose.
14Do everything without complaining or arguing, 15so that you
may become blameless and pure, children of God without fault in
a crooked and depraved generation, in which you shine like stars
in the universe 16as you hold out[r] the word of life—in order that
I may boast on the day of Christ that I did not run or labor for
nothing. 17But even if I am being poured out like a drink offering
on the sacrifice and service coming from your faith, I am glad and
rejoice with all of you. 18So you too should be glad and rejoice with
me.

*Timothy and Epaphroditus*

19I hope in the Lord Jesus to send Timothy to you soon, that I
also may be cheered when I receive news about you. 20I have no
one else like him, who takes a genuine interest in your welfare.
21For everyone looks out for his own interests, not those of Jesus
Christ. 22But you know that Timothy has proved himself, because
as a son with his father he has served with me in the work of the
gospel. 23I hope, therefore, to send him as soon as I see how things

NIV [p] 6 Or *in the form of* [q] 7 Or *the form* [r] 16 Or *hold on to*

## King James

23 Him therefore I hope to send presently, so soon as I shall see how it will go with me.

24 But I trust in the Lord that I also myself shall come shortly.

25 Yet I supposed it necessary to send to you Epaphroditus, my brother, and companion in labour, and fellowsoldier, but your messenger, and he that ministered to my wants.

26 For he longed after you all, and was full of heaviness, because that ye had heard that he had been sick.

27 For indeed he was sick nigh unto death: but God had mercy on him; and not on him only, but on me also, lest I should have sorrow upon sorrow.

28 I sent him therefore the more carefully, that, when ye see him again, ye may rejoice, and that I may be the less sorrowful.

29 Receive him therefore in the Lord with all gladness; and hold such in reputation:

30 Because for the work of Christ he was nigh unto death, not regarding his life, to supply your lack of service toward me.

**3** FINALLY, MY brethren, rejoice in the Lord. To write the same things to you, to me indeed *is* not grievous, but for you *it is* safe.

2 Beware of dogs, beware of evil workers, beware of the concision.

3 For we are the circumcision, which worship God in the spirit, and rejoice in Christ Jesus, and have no confidence in the flesh.

4 Though I might also have confidence in the flesh. If any other man thinketh that he hath whereof he might trust in the flesh, I more:

5 Circumcised the eighth day, of the stock of Israel, *of* the tribe of Benjamin, an Hebrew of the Hebrews; as touching the law, a Pharisee;

6 Concerning zeal, persecuting the church; touching the righteousness which is in the law, blameless.

7 But what things were gain to me, those I counted loss for Christ.

8 Yea doubtless, and I count all things *but* loss for the excellency of the knowledge of Christ Jesus my Lord: for whom I have suffered the loss of all things, and do count them *but* dung, that I may win Christ,

9 And be found in him, not having mine own righteousness, which is of the law, but that which is through the faith of Christ, the righteousness which is of God by faith:

## Amplified

23 I hope therefore to send him promptly, just as soon as I know how my case is going to turn out.

24 But [really] I am confident *and* fully trusting in the Lord that shortly I myself shall come to you also.

25 However, I thought it necessary to send Epaphroditus [back] to you. [He has been] my brother and companion in labor and my fellow soldier, as well as [having come as] your special messenger (apostle) and minister to my need.

26 For he has been (homesick,) longing for you all and has been distressed because you had heard that he was ill.

27 He certainly was ill [too], near to death. But God had compassion on him, and not only on him but also on me, lest I should have sorrow [over him] [a]coming upon sorrow.

28 So I have sent him the more willingly *and* eagerly, that you may be gladdened at seeing him again, and that I may be the less disquieted.

29 Welcome him [home] then in the Lord with all joy, and honor *and* highly appreciate men like him,

30 For it was through working for Christ that he came so near death, risking his [very] life to complete the deficiencies in your service to me [which distance prevented you yourselves from rendering].

**3** FOR THE rest, my brethren, delight yourselves in the Lord *and* continue to rejoice that you are in Him. To keep writing to you [over and over] of the same things is not irksome to me, and it is [a precaution] for your safety.

2 Look out for those dogs [the Judaizers], look out for those mischief-workers, look out for those who mutilate the flesh.

3 For we [Christians] are the true circumcision, who worship God [b]in spirit *and* by the Spirit of God, and exult *and* glory *and* pride ourselves in Jesus Christ, and put no confidence *or* dependence [on what we are] in the flesh *and* on outward privileges *and* physical advantages and external appearances.

4 Though for myself I have [at least grounds] to rely on the flesh. If any other man considers that he has *or* seems to have reason to rely on the flesh *and* his physical *and* outward advantages, still more have I!

5 Circumcised when I was eight days old, of the race of Israel, of the tribe of Benjamin, a Hebrew [and the son] of Hebrews; as to the observance of the Law I was of [the party of] the Pharisees,

6 As to my zeal I was a persecutor of the church, and by the Law's standard of righteousness—[supposed] justice, uprightness and right standing with God—I was proven to be blameless *and* no fault was found with me.

7 But whatever former things I had that might have been gains to me, I have come to consider as ( [c]one combined) loss for Christ's sake.

8 Yes, furthermore I count everything as loss compared to the possession of the priceless privilege—the overwhelming preciousness, the surpassing worth and supreme advantage—of knowing Christ Jesus my Lord, *and* of progressively becoming more deeply *and* intimately acquainted with Him, of perceiving *and* recognizing *and* understanding Him more fully *and* clearly. For His sake I have lost everything and consider it all to be mere rubbish (refuse, dregs), in order that I may win (gain) Christ, the Anointed One,

9 And that I may [actually] be found *and* known as in Him, not having any (self-achieved) righteousness that can be called my own, based on my obedience to the Law's demands—ritualistic uprightness and [supposed] right standing with God thus acquired—but possessing that [genuine righteousness] which comes through faith in Christ, the Anointed One, the [truly] right standing with God, which comes from God by (saving) faith.

**AMP** [a] Vincent. [b] Alternate reading. [c] His "gains" are plural, but they are all counted as one "loss," singular. (-Vincent.)

# New American Standard

23Therefore I hope to send him immediately, as soon as I see how things *go* with me;

24and I trust in the Lord that I myself also shall be coming shortly.

25But I thought it necessary to send to you Epaphroditus, my brother and fellow worker and fellow soldier, who is also your messenger and minister to my need;

26because he was longing [d]for you all and was distressed because you had heard that he was sick.

27For indeed he was sick to the point of death, but God had mercy on him, and not on him only but also on me, lest I should have sorrow upon sorrow.

28Therefore I have sent him all the more eagerly in order that when you see him again you may rejoice and I may be less concerned *about you.*

29Therefore receive him in the Lord with all joy, and hold men like him in high regard;

30because he came close to death for the work of Christ, risking his life to complete what was deficient in your service to me.

*The Goal of Life*

**3** FINALLY, MY brethren, rejoice in the Lord. To write the same things *again* is no trouble to me, and it is a safeguard for you.

2Beware of the dogs, beware of the evil workers, beware of the false circumcision;

3for we are the *true* circumcision, who worship in the Spirit of God and glory in Christ Jesus and put no confidence in the flesh,

4although I myself might have confidence even in the flesh. If anyone else has a mind to put confidence in the flesh, I far more:

5circumcised the eighth day, of the nation of Israel, of the tribe of Benjamin, a Hebrew of Hebrews; as to the Law, a Pharisee;

6as to zeal, a persecutor of the church; as to the righteousness which is in the Law, found blameless.

7But whatever things were gain to me, those things I have counted as loss for the sake of Christ.

8More than that, I count all things to be loss in view of the surpassing value of knowing Christ Jesus my Lord, for whom I have suffered the loss of all things, and count them but rubbish in order that I may gain Christ,

9and may be found in Him, not having a righteousness of my own derived from *the* Law, but that which is through faith in Christ, the righteousness which *comes* from God on the basis of faith,

NAS [d] Some ancient mss. read *to see you all*

# New International

go with me. 24And I am confident in the Lord that I myself will come soon.

25But I think it is necessary to send back to you Epaphroditus, my brother, fellow worker and fellow soldier, who is also your messenger, whom you sent to take care of my needs. 26For he longs for all of you and is distressed because you heard he was ill. 27Indeed he was ill, and almost died. But God had mercy on him, and not on him only but also on me, to spare me sorrow upon sorrow. 28Therefore I am all the more eager to send him, so that when you see him again you may be glad and I may have less anxiety. 29Welcome him in the Lord with great joy, and honor men like him, 30because he almost died for the work of Christ, risking his life to make up for the help you could not give me.

*No Confidence in the Flesh*

**3** FINALLY, MY brothers, rejoice in the Lord! It is no trouble for me to write the same things to you again, and it is a safeguard for you.

2Watch out for those dogs, those men who do evil, those mutilators of the flesh. 3For it is we who are the circumcision, we who worship by the Spirit of God, who glory in Christ Jesus, and who put no confidence in the flesh— 4though I myself have reasons for such confidence.

If anyone else thinks he has reasons to put confidence in the flesh, I have more: 5circumcised on the eighth day, of the people of Israel, of the tribe of Benjamin, a Hebrew of Hebrews; in regard to the law, a Pharisee; 6as for zeal, persecuting the church; as for legalistic righteousness, faultless.

7But whatever was to my profit I now consider loss for the sake of Christ. 8What is more, I consider everything a loss compared to the surpassing greatness of knowing Christ Jesus my Lord, for whose sake I have lost all things. I consider them rubbish, that I may gain Christ 9and be found in him, not having a righteousness of my own that comes from the law, but that which is through faith in Christ—the righteousness that comes from God and is by faith.

## King James

10 That I may know him, and the power of his resurrection, and
the fellowship of his sufferings, being made conformable unto his
death;
11 If by any means I might attain unto the resurrection of the
dead.
12 Not as though I had already attained, either were already
perfect: but I follow after, if that I may apprehend that for which
also I am apprehended of Christ Jesus.
13 Brethren, I count not myself to have apprehended: but *this*
one thing *I do*, forgetting those things which are behind, and
reaching forth unto those things which are before,
14 I press toward the mark for the prize of the high calling of God
in Christ Jesus.
15 Let us therefore, as many as be perfect, be thus minded: and
if in any thing ye be otherwise minded, God shall reveal even this
unto you.
16 Nevertheless, whereto we have already attained, let us walk
by the same rule, let us mind the same thing.
17 Brethren, be followers together of me, and mark them which
walk so as ye have us for an example.
18 (For many walk, of whom I have told you often, and now tell
you even weeping, *that they are* the enemies of the cross of Christ:
19 Whose end *is* destruction, whose God *is their* belly, and *whose*
glory *is* in their shame, who mind earthly things.)
20 For our conversation is in heaven; from whence also we look
for the Saviour, the Lord Jesus Christ:
21 Who shall change our vile body, that it may be fashioned like
unto his glorious body, according to the working whereby he is
able even to subdue all things unto himself.

**4** THEREFORE, MY brethren dearly beloved and longed for,
my joy and crown, so stand fast in the Lord, *my* dearly beloved.
2 I beseech Euodias, and beseech Syntyche, that they be of the
same mind in the Lord.
3 And I entreat thee also, true yokefellow, help those women
which laboured with me in the gospel, with Clement also, and *with*
other my fellowlabourers, whose names *are* in the book of life.
4 Rejoice in the Lord always: *and* again I say, Rejoice.
5 Let your moderation be known unto all men. The Lord *is* at
hand.
6 Be careful for nothing; but in every thing by prayer and supplication with thanksgiving let your requests be made known unto
God.

## Amplified

10 [For my determined purpose is] that I may know Him—that
I may progressively become more deeply and intimately acquainted with Him, perceiving and recognizing and understanding [the wonders of His Person] more strongly and more clearly.
And that I may in that same way come to know the power outflow-
ing from His resurrection [ [a]which it exerts over believers]; and that
I may so share His sufferings as to be continually transformed [in
spirit into His likeness even] to His death, [in the hope]
11 That if possible I may attain to the [ [b]spiritual and moral]
resurrection [that lifts me] out from among the dead [even while
in the body].
12 Not that I have now attained [this ideal] or am already made
perfect, but I press on to lay hold of (grasp) *and* make my own, that
for which Christ Jesus, the Messiah, has laid hold of me *and* made
me His own.
13 I do not consider, brethren, that I have captured *and* made it
my own [yet]; but one thing I do—it is my one aspiration: forgetting what lies behind and straining forward to what lies ahead,
14 I press on toward the goal to win the [supreme and heavenly]
prize to which God in Christ Jesus is calling us upward.
15 So let those [of us] who are spiritually mature *and* full-grown
have this mind *and* hold these convictions, and if in any respect
you have a different attitude of mind, God will make that clear to
you also.
16 Only let us hold true to what we have already attained *and*
walk *and* order our lives by that.
17 Brethren, together follow my example and observe those who
live after the pattern we have set you.
18 For there are many, of whom I have often told you and now
tell you even with tears, who walk (live) as enemies of the cross
of Christ, the Anointed One.
19 They are doomed *and* their [c]fate [is] eternal misery (perdition); their god is their stomach (their appetites, their sensuality)
and they glory in their shame, [d]siding with earthly things *and*
being of their party.
20 But we are citizens of the state (commonwealth, homeland)
which is in heaven, and from it also we [e]earnestly *and* patiently
await [the coming of] the Lord Jesus Christ, the Messiah, [as]
Savior,
21 Who will [f]transform *and* fashion anew the body of our
humiliation to conform to *and* be like the body of His glory *and*
majesty, by exerting that power which enables Him even to subject
everything to Himself.

**4** THEREFORE, MY brethren, whom I love and yearn to see,
my delight and crown (wreath of victory), thus stand firm in
the Lord, my beloved.
2 I entreat *and* advise Euodia and I entreat *and* advise Syntyche
to agree *and* to work in harmony in the Lord.
3 And I exhort you too, [my] genuine yokefellow, help these
[two women to keep on co-operating], for they have toiled along
with me in [the spreading of] the good news (the Gospel), as have
Clement and the rest of my fellow workers whose names are in the
Book of Life.
4 Rejoice in the Lord always—delight, gladden yourselves in
Him; again I say, Rejoice! [Ps. 37:4.]
5 Let all men know *and* perceive *and* recognize your unselfishness—your considerateness, your forbearing spirit. The Lord is
near—He is [g]coming soon.
6 Do not fret *or* have any anxiety about anything, but in every
circumstance *and* in everything by prayer and petition [ [h]definite
requests] with thanksgiving continue to make your wants known
to God.

**AMP** [a] Vincent. [b] Williams: Double compound "non," meaning a spiritual, moral resurrection, not the final, physical one, which will be the climax. [c] Thayer. [d] Thayer. [e] Vincent. [f] Vincent. [g] Thayer. [h] Thayer.

## New American Standard

10that I may know Him, and the power of His resurrection and
the fellowship of His sufferings, being conformed to His death;
11in order that I may attain to the resurrection from the dead.
12Not that I have already obtained *it*, or have already become
perfect, but I press on in order that I may lay hold of that for which
also I was laid hold of by Christ Jesus.
13Brethren, I do not regard myself as having laid hold of *it* yet;
but one thing *I do:* forgetting what *lies* behind and reaching forward
to what *lies* ahead,
14I press on toward the goal for the prize of the upward call of
God in Christ Jesus.
15Let us therefore, as many as are perfect, have this attitude;
and if in anything you have a different attitude, God will reveal
that also to you;
16however, let us keep living by that same *standard* to which we
have attained.
17¶ Brethren, join in following my example, and observe those
who walk according to the pattern you have in us.
18For many walk, of whom I often told you, and now tell you
even weeping, *that they are* enemies of the cross of Christ,
19whose end is destruction, whose god is *their* appetite, and
*whose* glory is in their shame, who set their minds on earthly
things.
20For our citizenship is in heaven, from which also we eagerly
wait for a Savior, the Lord Jesus Christ;
21who will transform the body of our humble state into conformity with the body of His glory, by the exertion of the power
that He has even to subject all things to Himself.

*Think of Excellence*

**4** THEREFORE, MY beloved brethren whom I long *to see,* my
joy and crown, so stand firm in the Lord, my beloved.
2¶ I urge Euodia and I urge Syntyche to live in harmony in the
Lord.
3Indeed, true comrade, I ask you also to help these women
who have shared my struggle in *the cause of* the gospel, together
with Clement also, and the rest of my fellow workers, whose
names are in the book of life.
4¶ Rejoice in the Lord always; again I will say, rejoice!
5Let your forbearing *spirit* be known to all men. The Lord is
near.
6Be anxious for nothing, but in everything by prayer and supplication with thanksgiving let your requests be made known to
God.

## New International

10I want to know Christ and the power of his resurrection and the
fellowship of sharing in his sufferings, becoming like him in his
death, 11and so, somehow, to attain to the resurrection from the
dead.

*Pressing on Toward the Goal*

12Not that I have already obtained all this, or have already been
made perfect, but I press on to take hold of that for which Christ
Jesus took hold of me. 13Brothers, I do not consider myself yet to
have taken hold of it. But one thing I do: Forgetting what is behind
and straining toward what is ahead, 14I press on toward the goal
to win the prize for which God has called me heavenward in Christ
Jesus.
15All of us who are mature should take such a view of things.
And if on some point you think differently, that too God will make
clear to you. 16Only let us live up to what we have already attained.
17Join with others in following my example, brothers, and take
note of those who live according to the pattern we gave you. 18For,
as I have often told you before and now say again even with tears,
many live as enemies of the cross of Christ. 19Their destiny is
destruction, their god is their stomach, and their glory is in their
shame. Their mind is on earthly things. 20But our citizenship is in
heaven. And we eagerly await a Savior from there, the Lord Jesus
Christ, 21who, by the power that enables him to bring everything
under his control, will transform our lowly bodies so that they will
be like his glorious body.

**4** THEREFORE, MY brothers, you whom I love and long for,
my joy and crown, that is how you should stand firm in the
Lord, dear friends!

*Exhortations*

2I plead with Euodia and I plead with Syntyche to agree with
each other in the Lord. 3Yes, and I ask you, loyal yokefellow,[i] help
these women who have contended at my side in the cause of the
gospel, along with Clement and the rest of my fellow workers,
whose names are in the book of life.
4Rejoice in the Lord always. I will say it again: Rejoice! 5Let your
gentleness be evident to all. The Lord is near. 6Do not be anxious
about anything, but in everything, by prayer and petition, with
thanksgiving, present your requests to God. 7And the peace of

NIV [i] 3 Or *loyal Syzygus*

## King James

7And the peace of God, which passeth all understanding, shall keep your hearts and minds through Christ Jesus.

8Finally, brethren, whatsoever things are true, whatsoever things *are* honest, whatsoever things *are* just, whatsoever things *are* pure, whatsoever things *are* lovely, whatsoever things *are* of good report; if *there be* any virtue, and if *there be* any praise, think on these things.

9Those things, which ye have both learned, and received, and heard, and seen in me, do: and the God of peace shall be with you.

10But I rejoiced in the Lord greatly, that now at the last your care of me hath flourished again; wherein ye were also careful, but ye lacked opportunity.

11Not that I speak in respect of want: for I have learned, in whatsoever state I am, *therewith* to be content.

12I know both how to be abased, and I know how to abound: every where and in all things I am instructed both to be full and to be hungry, both to abound and to suffer need.

13I can do all things through Christ which strengtheneth me.

14Notwithstanding ye have well done, that ye did communicate with my affliction.

15Now ye Philippians know also, that in the beginning of the gospel, when I departed from Macedonia, no church communicated with me as concerning giving and receiving, but ye only.

16For even in Thessalonica ye sent once and again unto my necessity.

17Not because I desire a gift: but I desire fruit that may abound to your account.

18But I have all, and abound: I am full, having received of Epaphroditus the things *which were sent* from you, an odour of a sweet smell, a sacrifice acceptable, wellpleasing to God.

19But my God shall supply all your need according to his riches in glory by Christ Jesus.

20Now unto God and our Father *be* glory for ever and ever. Amen.

21Salute every saint in Christ Jesus. The brethren which are with me greet you.

22All the saints salute you, chiefly they that are of Caesar's household.

23The grace of our Lord Jesus Christ *be* with you all. Amen.

## Amplified

7And God's peace [be yours, that [a]tranquil state of a soul assured of its salvation through Christ, and so fearing nothing from God and content with its earthly lot of whatever sort that is, that peace] which transcends all understanding, shall [b]garrison *and* mount guard over your hearts and minds in Christ Jesus.

8For the rest, brethren, whatever is true, whatever is worthy of reverence *and* is honorable *and* seemly, whatever is just, whatever is pure, whatever is lovely *and* lovable, whatever is kind *and* winsome *and* gracious, if there is any virtue *and* excellence, if there is anything worthy of praise, think on *and* weigh *and* take account of these things—fix your minds on them.

9Practice what you have learned and received and heard and seen in me, *and* model your way of living on it, and the God of peace—of [c]untroubled, undisturbed well-being—will be with you.

10I was made very happy in the Lord that now you have revived your interest in my welfare after so long a time; you were indeed thinking of me, but you had no opportunity to show it.

11Not that I am implying that I was in any personal want, for I have learned how to be content (satisfied to the point where I am not disturbed or disquieted) in whatever state I am.

12I know how to be abased *and* live humbly in straitened circumstances, and I know also how to enjoy plenty *and* live in abundance. I have learned in any and all circumstances, the secret of facing every situation, whether well-fed or going hungry, having a sufficiency *and* to spare or going without *and* being in want.

13I have strength for all things in Christ Who empowers me—I am ready for anything and equal to anything through Him Who [d]infuses inner strength into me, [that is, I am [e]self-sufficient in Christ's sufficiency].

14But it was right *and* commendable *and* noble of you to contribute for my needs *and* to share my difficulties with me.

15And you Philippians yourselves well know that in the early days of the Gospel ministry, when I left Macedonia, no church (assembly) entered into partnership with me *and* opened up [a debit and credit] account in giving and receiving except you only.

16For even in Thessalonica you sent [me contributions] for my needs, not only once but a second time.

17Not that I seek *or* am eager for [your] gift, but I do seek *and* am eager for the fruit which increases to your credit—the harvest of blessing that is accumulating to your account.

18But I have [your full payment] and more; I have everything I need *and* am amply supplied, now that I have received from Epaphroditus the gifts you sent me. [They are the] fragrant odor [of] an offering *and* sacrifice which God welcomes *and* in which He delights.

19And my God will liberally supply ( [f]fill to the full) your every need according to His riches in glory in Christ Jesus.

20To our God and Father be glory forever and ever—through the endless eternities of the eternities. *Amen, so be it.*

21Remember me to every saint (every born-again believer) in Christ Jesus. The brethren (my [g]associates) who are with me greet you.

22All the saints—God's consecrated ones here—wish to be remembered to you, especially those of Caesar's household.

23The grace (spiritual favor and blessing) of the Lord Jesus Christ, the Anointed One, be with your spirit. *Amen—so be it.*

**AMP** [a] Thayer. [b] Gurnall (-Vincent.) [c] Cremer. [d] Vincent. [e] "Content" (v.11) literally means "self-sufficient." [f] Thayer. [g] Souter's "Pocket Lexicon to the Greek New Testament."

## New American Standard

7And the peace of God, which surpasses all comprehension, shall guard your hearts and your minds in Christ Jesus.

8¶ Finally, brethren, whatever is true, whatever is honorable, whatever is right, whatever is pure, whatever is lovely, whatever is of good repute, if there is any excellence and if anything worthy of praise, let your mind dwell on these things.

9The things you have learned and received and heard and seen in me, practice these things; and the God of peace shall be with you.

*God's Provisions*

10¶ But I rejoiced in the Lord greatly, that now at last you have revived your concern for me; indeed, you were concerned *before,* but you lacked opportunity.

11Not that I speak from want; for I have learned to be content in whatever circumstances I am.

12I know how to get along with humble means, and I also know how to live in prosperity; in any and every circumstance I have learned the secret of being filled and going hungry, both of having abundance and suffering need.

13I can do all things through Him who strengthens me.

14Nevertheless, you have done well to share *with me* in my affliction.

15And you yourselves also know, Philippians, that at the first preaching of the gospel, after I departed from Macedonia, no church shared with me in the matter of giving and receiving but you alone;

16for even in Thessalonica you sent *a gift* more than once for my needs.

17Not that I seek the gift itself, but I seek for the profit which increases to your account.

18But I have received everything in full, and have an abundance; I am amply supplied, having received from Epaphroditus what you have sent, a fragrant aroma, an acceptable sacrifice, well-pleasing to God.

19And my God shall supply all your needs according to His riches in glory in Christ Jesus.

20Now to our God and Father *be* the glory forever and ever. Amen.

21¶ Greet every saint in Christ Jesus. The brethren who are with me greet you.

22All the saints greet you, especially those of Caesar's household.

23¶ The grace of the Lord Jesus Christ be with your spirit.

## New International

God, which transcends all understanding, will guard your hearts
and your minds in Christ Jesus.
8Finally, brothers, whatever is true, whatever is noble, whatever is right, whatever is pure, whatever is lovely, whatever is
admirable—if anything is excellent or praiseworthy—think about
such things. 9Whatever you have learned or received or heard
from me, or seen in me—put it into practice. And the God of peace
will be with you.

*Thanks for Their Gifts*

10I rejoice greatly in the Lord that at last you have renewed your
concern for me. Indeed, you have been concerned, but you had no
opportunity to show it. 11I am not saying this because I am in need,
for I have learned to be content whatever the circumstances. 12I
know what it is to be in need, and I know what it is to have plenty.
I have learned the secret of being content in any and every situation, whether well fed or hungry, whether living in plenty or in
want. 13I can do everything through him who gives me strength.
14Yet it was good of you to share in my troubles. 15Moreover,
as you Philippians know, in the early days of your acquaintance
with the gospel, when I set out from Macedonia, not one church
shared with me in the matter of giving and receiving, except you
only; 16for even when I was in Thessalonica, you sent me aid again
and again when I was in need. 17Not that I am looking for a gift,
but I am looking for what may be credited to your account. 18I have
received full payment and even more; I am amply supplied, now
that I have received from Epaphroditus the gifts you sent. They are
a fragrant offering, an acceptable sacrifice, pleasing to God. 19And
my God will meet all your needs according to his glorious riches
in Christ Jesus.
20To our God and Father be glory for ever and ever. Amen.

*Final Greetings*

21Greet all the saints in Christ Jesus. The brothers who are with
me send greetings. 22All the saints send you greetings, especially
those who belong to Caesar's household.
23The grace of the Lord Jesus Christ be with your spirit. Amen.[h]

NIV [h] 23 Some manuscripts do not have *Amen.*

## King James

THE EPISTLE OF

PAUL THE APOSTLE TO THE

# Colossians

1 PAUL, AN apostle of Jesus Christ by the will of God, and
Timotheus *our* brother,
2To the saints and faithful brethren in Christ which are at Colosse: Grace *be* unto you, and peace, from God our Father and the
Lord Jesus Christ.
3We give thanks to God and the Father of our Lord Jesus Christ,
praying always for you,
4Since we heard of your faith in Christ Jesus, and of the love
*which ye have* to all the saints,
5For the hope which is laid up for you in heaven, whereof ye
heard before in the word of the truth of the gospel;
6Which is come unto you, as *it is* in all the world; and bringeth
forth fruit, as *it doth* also in you, since the day ye heard *of it*, and
knew the grace of God in truth:
7As ye also learned of Epaphras our dear fellowservant, who is
for you a faithful minister of Christ;
8Who also declared unto us your love in the Spirit.
9For this cause we also, since the day we heard *it*, do not cease
to pray for you, and to desire that ye might be filled with the
knowledge of his will in all wisdom and spiritual understanding;
10That ye might walk worthy of the Lord unto all pleasing,
being fruitful in every good work, and increasing in the knowledge
of God;
11Strengthened with all might, according to his glorious power,
unto all patience and longsuffering with joyfulness;
12Giving thanks unto the Father, which hath made us meet to
be partakers of the inheritance of the saints in light:
13Who hath delivered us from the power of darkness, and hath
translated *us* into the kingdom of his dear Son:
14In whom we have redemption through his blood, *even* the
forgiveness of sins:
15Who is the image of the invisible God, the firstborn of every
creature:

## Amplified

THE LETTER OF

PAUL TO THE

# Colossians

1 PAUL, AN apostle (special messenger) of Christ Jesus, the
Messiah, by the will of God, and Timothy [our] brother,
2To the saints (the consecrated people of God) and [a]believing
*and* faithful brethren in Christ, who are at Colossae: Grace (spiritual favor and blessing) to you and heart peace from God our
Father.
3We [b]continually give thanks to God the Father of our Lord
Jesus Christ, the Messiah, as we are praying for you,
4For we have heard of your faith in Christ Jesus [ [c]the leaning
of your entire human personality on Him in absolute trust and
confidence in His power, wisdom and goodness] and of the love
which you [have and show] for all the saints (God's consecrated
ones),
5Because of the hope [of experiencing what is] laid
up—[d]reserved and waiting—for you in heaven. Of this [hope] you
heard in the past in the message of the truth of the Gospel,
6Which has come to you. Indeed in the whole world [that
Gospel] is bearing fruit *and* still is growing [e][by its own inherent
power], even as it has done among yourselves ever since the day
you first heard and came to know *and* understand the grace of God
in truth.—[That is,] you came to know the grace (undeserved
favor) of God in reality, deeply and clearly and thoroughly, becoming accurately and intimately acquainted with it.
7You so learned it from Epaphras our beloved fellow servant.
He is a faithful minister of Christ in our stead *and* as our representative, *and* [f]yours.
8Also he has informed us of your love in the (Holy) Spirit.
9For this reason we also, from the day we heard of it, have not
ceased to pray *and* make [ [g]special] request for you, [asking] that
you may be filled with the [h]full (deep and clear) knowledge of His
will in all spiritual wisdom [that is, [i]in comprehensive insight into
the ways and purposes of God] and in understanding *and* discernment of spiritual things;
10That you may walk (live and conduct yourselves) in a manner
worthy of the Lord, fully pleasing to Him *and* [j]desiring to please
Him in all things, bearing fruit in every good work and steadily
growing *and* increasing in (and [k]by) the knowledge of God—with
fuller, deeper and clearer insight, [l]acquaintance and recognition.
11[We pray] that you may be invigorated *and* strengthened with
all power, according to the might of His glory, [to exercise] every
kind of endurance and patience (perseverance and forbearance)
with joy,
12Giving thanks to the Father, Who has qualified *and* made us
fit to share the [m]portion which is the inheritance of the saints
(God's holy people) in the Light.
13[The Father] has delivered *and* [n]drawn us to Himself out of
the control *and* the dominion of darkness and has transferred us
into the kingdom of the Son [o]of His love,
14In Whom we have our redemption *through His blood,* [which
means] the forgiveness of our sins.
15[Now] He is the [p]exact likeness of the unseen God—the visible representation of the invisible; He is the First-born—of all
creation.

**AMP** [a] Vincent. [b] *Always;* belongs with *give thanks,* not elsewhere (-Vincent.) [c] Souter's "Pocket Lexicon to the Greek New Testament." [d] Vincent. [e] Souter's "Pocket Lexicon to the Greek New Testament." [f] Many ancient authorities read "your." [g] Vincent. [h] Vincent. [i] Souter. [j] Thayer. [k] The best texts read "by." [l] Abbott-Smith. [m] Vincent. [n] Thayer. [o] Literal meaning. [p] Williams: "Strong terms; so *exact likeness.*"

## New American Standard

# Colossians

*Thankfulness for Spiritual Attainments*

**1** PAUL, AN apostle of Jesus Christ by the will of God, and Timothy our brother,

2to the saints and faithful brethren in Christ *who are* at Colossae: Grace to you and peace from God our Father.

3¶ We give thanks to God, the Father of our Lord Jesus Christ, praying always for you,

4since we heard of your faith in Christ Jesus and the love which you have for all the saints;

5because of the hope laid up for you in heaven, of which you previously heard in the word of truth, the gospel,

6which has come to you, just as in all the world also it is constantly bearing fruit and increasing, even as *it has been doing* in you also since the day you heard *of it* and understood the grace of God in truth;

7just as you learned *it* from Epaphras, our beloved fellow bond-servant, who is a faithful servant of Christ on [q]our behalf,

8and he also informed us of your love in the Spirit.

9¶ For this reason also, since the day we heard *of it,* we have not ceased to pray for you and to ask that you may be filled with the knowledge of His will in all spiritual wisdom and understanding,

10so that you may walk in a manner worthy of the Lord, to please *Him* in all respects, bearing fruit in every good work and increasing in the knowledge of God;

11strengthened with all power, according to His glorious might, for the attaining of all steadfastness and patience; joyously

12giving thanks to the Father, who has qualified us to share in the inheritance of the saints in light.

*The Incomparable Christ*

13For He delivered us from the domain of darkness, and transferred us to the kingdom of His beloved Son,

14in whom we have redemption, the forgiveness of sins.

15And He is the image of the invisible God, the first-born of all creation.

**NAS** [q] Some later mss. read *your*

## New International

# Colossians

**1** PAUL, AN apostle of Christ Jesus by the will of God, and Timothy our brother,

2To the holy and faithful[r] brothers in Christ at Colosse:

Grace and peace to you from God our Father.[s]

*Thanksgiving and Prayer*

3We always thank God, the Father of our Lord Jesus Christ, when we pray for you, 4because we have heard of your faith in Christ Jesus and of the love you have for all the saints— 5the faith and love that spring from the hope that is stored up for you in heaven and that you have already heard about in the word of truth, the gospel 6that has come to you. All over the world this gospel is bearing fruit and growing, just as it has been doing among you since the day you heard it and understood God's grace in all its truth. 7You learned it from Epaphras, our dear fellow servant, who is a faithful minister of Christ on our[t] behalf, 8and who also told us of your love in the Spirit.

9For this reason, since the day we heard about you, we have not stopped praying for you and asking God to fill you with the knowledge of his will through all spiritual wisdom and understanding. 10And we pray this in order that you may live a life worthy of the Lord and may please him in every way: bearing fruit in every good work, growing in the knowledge of God, 11being strengthened with all power according to his glorious might so that you may have great endurance and patience, and joyfully 12giving thanks to the Father, who has qualified you[u] to share in the inheritance of the saints in the kingdom of light. 13For he has rescued us from the dominion of darkness and brought us into the kingdom of the Son he loves, 14in whom we have redemption,[v] the forgiveness of sins.

*The Supremacy of Christ*

15He is the image of the invisible God, the firstborn over all creation. 16For by him all things were created: things in heaven and

**NIV** [r] 2 Or *believing* [s] 2 Some manuscripts *Father and the Lord Jesus Christ* [t] 7 Some manuscripts *your* [u] 12 Some manuscripts *us* [v] 14 A few late manuscripts *redemption through his blood*

## King James

16 For by him were all things created, that are in heaven, and that are in earth, visible and invisible, whether *they be* thrones, or dominions, or principalities, or powers: all things were created by him, and for him:

17 And he is before all things, and by him all things consist.

18 And he is the head of the body, the church: who is the beginning, the firstborn from the dead; that in all *things* he might have the preeminence.

19 For it pleased *the Father* that in him should all fulness dwell;

20 And, having made peace through the blood of his cross, by him to reconcile all things unto himself; by him, *I say*, whether *they be* things in earth, or things in heaven.

21 And you, that were sometime alienated and enemies in *your* mind by wicked works, yet now hath he reconciled

22 In the body of his flesh through death, to present you holy and unblameable and unreproveable in his sight:

23 If ye continue in the faith grounded and settled, and *be* not moved away from the hope of the gospel, which ye have heard, *and* which was preached to every creature which is under heaven; whereof I Paul am made a minister;

24 Who now rejoice in my sufferings for you, and fill up that which is behind of the afflictions of Christ in my flesh for his body's sake, which is the church:

25 Whereof I am made a minister, according to the dispensation of God which is given to me for you, to fulfil the word of God;

26 *Even* the mystery which hath been hid from ages and from generations, but now is made manifest to his saints:

27 To whom God would make known what *is* the riches of the glory of this mystery among the Gentiles; which is Christ in you, the hope of glory:

28 Whom we preach, warning every man, and teaching every man in all wisdom; that we may present every man perfect in Christ Jesus:

29 Whereunto I also labour, striving according to his working, which worketh in me mightily.

**2** FOR I would that ye knew what great conflict I have for you, and *for* them at Laodicea, and *for* as many as have not seen my face in the flesh;

2 That their hearts might be comforted, being knit together in love, and unto all riches of the full assurance of understanding, to the acknowledgement of the mystery of God, and of the Father, and of Christ;

3 In whom are hid all the treasures of wisdom and knowledge.

## Amplified

16 For it was in Him that all things were created, in heaven and on earth, things seen and things unseen, whether thrones, dominions, rulers or authorities; all things were created *and* exist through Him (by His service, intervention) *and* in and for Him.

17 And He Himself existed before all things and in Him all things consist—cohere, are held together. [Prov. 8:22-31.]

18 He also is the Head of [His] body, the church; seeing He is the Beginning, the First-born from among the dead, so that He alone in everything *and* in every respect might occupy the chief place—stand first and be pre-eminent.

19 For it has pleased [the Father] that all the divine fullness—the sum total of the divine perfection, powers and attributes—should dwell in Him [a]permanently.

20 And God purposed that through—[b]by the service, the intervention of—Him (the Son) all things should be completely reconciled [c]back to Himself, whether on earth or in heaven, as through Him [the Father] made peace by means of the blood of His cross.

21 And although you at one time were estranged *and* alienated from Him and of hostile attitude of mind in your wicked activities,

22 Yet now has [Christ, the Messiah,] reconciled [you to God] in the body of His flesh through death, in order to present you holy and faultless and irreproachable in His [the Father's] presence.

23 [And this He will do] provided that you continue to [d]stay with *and* in the faith [in Christ], well-grounded and settled *and* steadfast, not shifting *or* moving away from the hope [which rests on and is inspired by] the glad tidings (the Gospel), which you heard and which has been preached [e][as being designed for and offered without restrictions] to every person under heaven, and of which [Gospel] I, Paul, became a minister.

24 [Even] now I rejoice in [f]the midst of my sufferings on your behalf. And in my own person I am making up whatever is still lacking *and* remains to be completed [[g]on our part] of Christ's afflictions, for the sake of His body, which is the Church.

25 In it I became a minister in accordance with the divine [h]stewardship which was entrusted to me for you—as its object and for your benefit—to make the Word of God fully known [among you].

26 The mystery of which was hidden for ages and generations ([i]from angels and men), but is now revealed to His holy people (the saints),

27 To whom God was pleased to make known how great for the Gentiles are the riches of the glory of this mystery, which is, Christ within *and* among you the hope of [realizing] the glory.

28 Him we preach *and* proclaim, warning *and* admonishing every one and instructing every one in all wisdom, [[j]in comprehensive insight into the ways and purposes of God], that we may present every person mature—full-grown, fully initiated, complete and perfect—in Christ, the Anointed One.

29 For this I labor [[k]unto weariness], striving with all the [l]superhuman energy which He so mightily enkindles *and* works within me.

**2** FOR I want you to know how great is my solicitude for you—in how severe an inward struggle I am engaged for you—and for those [believers] at Laodicea, and for all who ([m]like yourselves) have never seen my face *and* known me personally.

2 [For my concern is] that their hearts may be [n]braced (comforted, cheered and encouraged) as they are knit together in love, that they may come to have all the abounding wealth *and* blessings of assured conviction of understanding, and that they may become progressively [o]more intimately acquainted with, *and* may know more definitely *and* accurately *and* thoroughly, that mystic secret of God [which is] Christ, the Anointed One.

3 In Him all the treasures of [divine] wisdom, [of [p]comprehensive insight into the ways and purposes of God], and [all the riches of spiritual] knowledge *and* enlightenment are stored up *and* lie hidden.

**AMP** [a] Vincent. [b] Thayer. [c] Vincent. [d] Vincent. [e] Clarke's Commentary, and others. [f] Vincent. [g] Vincent. [h] Vincent. [i] Bengel. Alford (Jamieson, Fausset and Brown). [j] Souter. [k] Vincent. [l] Vincent. [m] Vincent. [n] Vincent. [o] Trench. [p] Souter.

## New American Standard

16For by Him all things were created, *both* in the heavens and
on earth, visible and invisible, whether thrones or dominions or
rulers or authorities—all things have been created by Him and for
Him.
17And He is before all things, and in Him all things hold together.
18He is also head of the body, the church; and He is the beginning, the first-born from the dead; so that He Himself might come
to have first place in everything.
19For it was the *Father's* good pleasure for all the fulness to dwell
in Him,
20and through Him to reconcile all things to Himself, having
made peace through the blood of His cross; through Him, *I say*,
whether things on earth or things in heaven.
21And although you were formerly alienated and hostile in
mind, *engaged* in evil deeds,
22yet He has now reconciled you in His fleshly body through
death, in order to present you before Him holy and blameless and
beyond reproach—
23if indeed you continue in the faith firmly established and
steadfast, and not moved away from the hope of the gospel that
you have heard, which was proclaimed in all creation under
heaven, and of which I, Paul, was made a minister.
24¶ Now I rejoice in my sufferings for your sake, and in my flesh
I do my share on behalf of His body (which is the church) in filling
up that which is lacking in Christ's afflictions.
25Of *this church* I was made a minister according to the stewardship from God bestowed on me for your benefit, that I might fully
carry out the *preaching of* the word of God,
26 *that is*, the mystery which has been hidden from the *past* ages
and generations; but has now been manifested to His saints,
27to whom God willed to make known what is the riches of the
glory of this mystery among the Gentiles, which is Christ in you,
the hope of glory.
28And we proclaim Him, admonishing every man and teaching
every man with all wisdom, that we may present every man complete in Christ.
29And for this purpose also I labor, striving according to His
power, which mightily works within me.

*You Are Built Up in Christ*

**2** FOR I want you to know how great a struggle I have on your
behalf, and for those who are at Laodicea, and for all those
who have not personally seen my face,
2that their hearts may be encouraged, having been knit together in love, and *attaining* to all the wealth that comes from the
full assurance of understanding, *resulting* in a true knowledge of
God's mystery, *that is*, Christ *Himself*,
3in whom are hidden all the treasures of wisdom and knowledge.

## New International

on earth, visible and invisible, whether thrones or powers or rulers
or authorities; all things were created by him and for him. 17He is
before all things, and in him all things hold together. 18And he is
the head of the body, the church; he is the beginning and the
firstborn from among the dead, so that in everything he might
have the supremacy. 19For God was pleased to have all his fullness
dwell in him, 20and through him to reconcile to himself all things,
whether things on earth or things in heaven, by making peace
through his blood, shed on the cross.
21Once you were alienated from God and were enemies in your
minds because of[q] your evil behavior. 22But now he has reconciled
you by Christ's physical body through death to present you holy
in his sight, without blemish and free from accusation— 23if you
continue in your faith, established and firm, not moved from the
hope held out in the gospel. This is the gospel that you heard and
that has been proclaimed to every creature under heaven, and of
which I, Paul, have become a servant.

*Paul's Labor for the Church*

24Now I rejoice in what was suffered for you, and I fill up in my
flesh what is still lacking in regard to Christ's afflictions, for the
sake of his body, which is the church. 25I have become its servant
by the commission God gave me to present to you the word of God
in its fullness— 26the mystery that has been kept hidden for ages
and generations, but is now disclosed to the saints. 27To them God
has chosen to make known among the Gentiles the glorious riches
of this mystery, which is Christ in you, the hope of glory.
28We proclaim him, admonishing and teaching everyone with
all wisdom, so that we may present everyone perfect in Christ.
29To this end I labor, struggling with all his energy, which so
powerfully works in me.

**2** I WANT you to know how much I am struggling for you and
for those at Laodicea, and for all who have not met me personally. 2My purpose is that they may be encouraged in heart and
united in love, so that they may have the full riches of complete
understanding, in order that they may know the mystery of God,
namely, Christ, 3in whom are hidden all the treasures of wisdom
and knowledge. 4I tell you this so that no one may deceive you by

NIV q 21 Or *minds, as shown by*

## King James

4And this I say, lest any man should beguile you with enticing words.

5For though I be absent in the flesh, yet am I with you in the spirit, joying and beholding your order, and the stedfastness of your faith in Christ.

6As ye have therefore received Christ Jesus the Lord, *so* walk ye in him:

7Rooted and built up in him, and stablished in the faith, as ye have been taught, abounding therein with thanksgiving.

8Beware lest any man spoil you through philosophy and vain deceit, after the tradition of men, after the rudiments of the world, and not after Christ.

9For in him dwelleth all the fulness of the Godhead bodily.

10And ye are complete in him, which is the head of all principality and power:

11In whom also ye are circumcised with the circumcision made without hands, in putting off the body of the sins of the flesh by the circumcision of Christ:

12Buried with him in baptism, wherein also ye are risen with *him* through the faith of the operation of God, who hath raised him from the dead.

13And you, being dead in your sins and the uncircumcision of your flesh, hath he quickened together with him, having forgiven you all trespasses;

14Blotting out the handwriting of ordinances that was against us, which was contrary to us, and took it out of the way, nailing it to his cross;

15 *And* having spoiled principalities and powers, he made a show of them openly, triumphing over them in it.

16Let no man therefore judge you in meat, or in drink, or in respect of an holyday, or of the new moon, or of the sabbath *days:*

17Which are a shadow of things to come; but the body *is* of Christ.

18Let no man beguile you of your reward in a voluntary humility and worshipping of angels, intruding into those things which he hath not seen, vainly puffed up by his fleshly mind,

19And not holding the Head, from which all the body by joints and bands having nourishment ministered, and knit together, increaseth with the increase of God.

## Amplified

4I say this in order that no one may mislead *and* delude you by plausible *and* persuasive *and* attractive arguments *and* beguiling speech.

5For though I am away from you in body, yet I am with you in spirit, delighted at the sight of your [standing shoulder to shoulder in such] orderly array and the firmness *and* the solid front *and* steadfastness of your faith in Christ, [that [a]leaning of the entire human personality on Him in absolute trust and confidence in His power, wisdom and goodness].

6As you have therefore received the Christ, [even] Jesus the Lord, [so] walk—regulate your lives *and* conduct yourselves—in union with *and* conformity to Him.

7Have the roots [of your being] firmly *and* deeply planted [in Him]—fixed and founded in Him—being continually built up in Him, becoming increasingly more confirmed *and* established in the faith, just as you were taught, and abounding *and* overflowing in it with thanksgiving.

8See to it that no one carries you off as spoil *or* makes you yourselves captive by his so-called philosophy *and* intellectualism, and vain deceit (idle fancies and plain nonsense), following human tradition—men's ideas of the material [rather than the spiritual] world—just crude notions following the rudimentary *and* elemental teachings of the universe, and disregarding [the teachings of] Christ, the Messiah.

9For in Him the whole fullness of Deity (the Godhead), continues to dwell in bodily form—giving complete expression of the divine nature.

10And you [b]are in Him, made full *and* have come to fullness of life—in Christ you too are filled with the Godhead: Father, Son and Holy Spirit, and reach full spiritual stature. And He is the Head of all rule and authority—of every angelic principality and power.

11In Him also you were circumcised with a circumcision not made with hands, but in a [spiritual] circumcision [performed by] Christ by stripping off the body of the flesh [the whole corrupt, carnal nature with its passions and lusts].

12[Thus [c]you were circumcised when] you were buried with Him in [your] baptism, in which you were also raised with Him [ [d]to a new life] through [your] faith in the working of God [ [e]as displayed] when He raised Him up from the dead.

13And you, who were dead in trespasses and in the uncircumcision of your flesh—your sensuality, your sinful carnal nature—[God] brought to life together with [Christ], having (freely) forgiven us all our transgressions;

14Having cancelled *and* blotted out *and* wiped away the handwriting of the note (or bond) with its legal decrees *and* demands, which was in force *and* stood against us—hostile to us. This [note with its regulations, decrees and demands] He set aside *and* cleared [f]completely out of our way by nailing it to [His] cross.

15[God] disarmed the principalities and powers ranged against us and made a bold display *and* public example of them, in triumphing over them in Him *and* [g]in it [the cross].

16Therefore let no one sit in judgment on you in matters of food and drink, or with regard to a feast day or a new moon or a Sabbath.

17Such [things] are only the shadow of things that are to come, *and* they have only a symbolic value. But the reality—the substance, the solid fact of what is foreshadowed, the body of it—belongs to Christ.

18Let no one defraud you by acting as an umpire *and* declaring you unworthy *and* disqualifying you for the prize, insisting on self-abasement and worship of angels, taking his stand on visions [he claims] he has seen, vainly puffed up by his sensuous notions *and* inflated by his unspiritual thoughts *and* fleshly conceit,

19And not holding fast to the Head, from Whom the entire body, supplied and knit together by means of its joints and ligaments, grows with a growth that is from God.

**AMP** [a] Souter's "Pocket Lexicon to the New Testament." [b] Vincent's "Word Studies in the New Testament." [c] "The aorist tense puts the burial as contemporaneous with the circumcision" (Vincent). [d] Vincent's "Word Studies in the New Testament." [e] Vincent's "Word Studies in the New Testament." [f] Vincent's "Word Studies in the New Testament." [g] Alternate reading, "in it [the cross]."

## New American Standard

4 I say this in order that no one may delude you with persuasive argument.

5 For even though I am absent in body, nevertheless I am with you in spirit, rejoicing to see your good discipline and the stability of your faith in Christ.

6 ¶ As you therefore have received Christ Jesus the Lord, *so* walk in Him,

7 having been firmly rooted *and now* being built up in Him and established [h]in your faith, just as you were instructed, *and* overflowing with gratitude.

8 ¶ See to it that no one takes you captive through philosophy and empty deception, according to the tradition of men, according to the elementary principles of the world, rather than according to Christ.

9 For in Him all the fulness of Deity dwells in bodily form,

10 and in Him you have been made complete, and He is the head over all rule and authority;

11 and in Him you were also circumcised with a circumcision made without hands, in the removal of the body of the flesh by the circumcision of Christ;

12 having been buried with Him in baptism, in which you were also raised up with Him through faith in the working of God, who raised Him from the dead.

13 And when you were dead in your transgressions and the uncircumcision of your flesh, He made you alive together with Him, having forgiven us all our transgressions,

14 having canceled out the certificate of debt consisting of decrees against us *and* which was hostile to us; and He has taken it out of the way, having nailed it to the cross.

15 When He had disarmed the rulers and authorities, He made a public display of them, having triumphed over them through Him.

16 ¶ Therefore let no one act as your judge in regard to food or drink or in respect to a festival or a new moon or a Sabbath day—

17 things which are a *mere* shadow of what is to come; but the substance belongs to Christ.

18 Let no one keep defrauding you of your prize by delighting in self-abasement and the worship of the angels, taking his stand on *visions* he has seen, inflated without cause by his fleshly mind,

19 and not holding fast to the head, from whom the entire body, being supplied and held together by the joints and ligaments, grows with a growth which is from God.

NAS [h] Or, *by*

## New International

fine-sounding arguments. 5 For though I am absent from you in
body, I am present with you in spirit and delight to see how
orderly you are and how firm your faith in Christ is.

*Freedom From Human Regulations Through Life With Christ*

6 So then, just as you received Christ Jesus as Lord, continue to
live in him, 7 rooted and built up in him, strengthened in the faith
as you were taught, and overflowing with thankfulness.
8 See to it that no one takes you captive through hollow and
deceptive philosophy, which depends on human tradition and the
basic principles of this world rather than on Christ.
9 For in Christ all the fullness of the Deity lives in bodily form,
10 and you have been given fullness in Christ, who is the head over
every power and authority. 11 In him you were also circumcised,
in the putting off of the sinful nature,[i] not with a circumcision
done by the hands of men but with the circumcision done by
Christ, 12 having been buried with him in baptism and raised with
him through your faith in the power of God, who raised him from
the dead.
13 When you were dead in your sins and in the uncircumcision
of your sinful nature,[j] God made you[k] alive with Christ. He
forgave us all our sins, 14 having canceled the written code, with
its regulations, that was against us and that stood opposed to us;
he took it away, nailing it to the cross. 15 And having disarmed the
powers and authorities, he made a public spectacle of them, triumphing over them by the cross.[l]
16 Therefore do not let anyone judge you by what you eat or
drink, or with regard to a religious festival, a New Moon celebration or a Sabbath day. 17 These are a shadow of the things that were
to come; the reality, however, is found in Christ. 18 Do not let
anyone who delights in false humility and the worship of angels
disqualify you for the prize. Such a person goes into great detail
about what he has seen, and his unspiritual mind puffs him up
with idle notions. 19 He has lost connection with the Head, from
whom the whole body, supported and held together by its ligaments and sinews, grows as God causes it to grow.

NIV [i] 11 Or *the flesh* [j] 13 Or *your flesh* [k] 13 Some manuscripts *us*
[l] 15 Or *them in him*

## King James

20 Wherefore if ye be dead with Christ from the rudiments of the world, why, as though living in the world, are ye subject to ordinances,
21 (Touch not; taste not; handle not;
22 Which all are to perish with the using;) after the commandments and doctrines of men?
23 Which things have indeed a show of wisdom in will-worship, and humility, and neglecting of the body; not in any honour to the satisfying of the flesh.

**3** IF YE then be risen with Christ, seek those things which are above, where Christ sitteth on the right hand of God.
2 Set your affection on things above, not on things on the earth.
3 For ye are dead, and your life is hid with Christ in God.
4 When Christ, *who is* our life, shall appear, then shall ye also appear with him in glory.
5 Mortify therefore your members which are upon the earth; fornication, uncleanness, inordinate affection, evil concupiscence, and covetousness, which is idolatry:
6 For which things' sake the wrath of God cometh on the children of disobedience:
7 In the which ye also walked some time, when ye lived in them.
8 But now ye also put off all these; anger, wrath, malice, blasphemy, filthy communication out of your mouth.
9 Lie not one to another, seeing that ye have put off the old man with his deeds;
10 And have put on the new *man*, which is renewed in knowledge after the image of him that created him:
11 Where there is neither Greek nor Jew, circumcision nor uncircumcision, Barbarian, Scythian, bond *nor* free: but Christ *is* all, and in all.
12 Put on therefore, as the elect of God, holy and beloved, bowels of mercies, kindness, humbleness of mind, meekness, longsuffering;
13 Forbearing one another, and forgiving one another, if any man have a quarrel against any: even as Christ forgave you, so also *do* ye.
14 And above all these things *put on* charity, which is the bond of perfectness.

## Amplified

20 If then you have died with Christ to material ways of looking at things *and* have escaped from the world's crude *and* elemental notions *and* teachings of externalism, why do you live as if you still belong to the world?—Why do you submit to rules *and* regulations? [such as],
21 Do not handle [this], Do not taste [that], Do not even touch [them],
22 Referring to things all of which perish with being used. To do this is to follow human precepts and doctrines. [Isa. 29:13.]
23 Such [practices] have indeed the outward appearance [that popularly passes] for wisdom, in promoting self-imposed rigor of devotion *and* delight in self-humiliation *and* severity of discipline of the body, but they are of no value in checking the indulgence of the flesh—the lower nature. [Instead, they do not honor God] but [a]serve only to indulge the flesh.

**3** IF THEN you have been raised with Christ [to a new life, thus sharing His resurrection from the dead], aim at *and* seek the [rich, eternal treasures] that are above, where Christ is, seated at the right hand of God. [Ps. 110:1.]
2 And set your minds *and* keep them set on what is above—the higher things—not on the things that are on the earth.
3 For [as far as this world is concerned] you have died, and your [new, real] life is hid with Christ in God.
4 When Christ Who is our life appears, then you also will appear with Him in (the splendor of His) glory.
5 So kill (deaden, [b]deprive of power) the evil desire lurking in your members—those animal impulses and all that is earthly in you that is employed in sin: sexual vice, impurity, sensual appetites, unholy desires, and all greed *and* covetousness, for that is idolatry [the deifying of self and other created things instead of God].
6 It is on account of these [very sins] that the [holy] anger of God is ever coming upon (those who are obstinately opposed to the divine will) the sons of disobedience,
7 Among whom you also once walked, when you were living in *and* addicted to [such practices].
8 But now put away *and* rid yourselves [completely] of all these things: anger, rage, bad feeling toward others, curses *and* slander and foulmouthed abuse *and* shameful utterances from your lips!
9 Do not lie to one another, for you have stripped off the old (unregenerate) self with its evil practices,
10 And have clothed yourselves with the new [spiritual self], which is (ever in the process of being) renewed *and* remoulded into (fuller and more perfect [c]knowledge upon) knowledge, after the image (the likeness) of Him Who created it. [Gen. 1:26.]
11 [In this new creation all distinctions vanish]; there [d]is no room for *and* there can be neither Greek nor Jew, circumcised nor uncircumcised, [nor difference between nations whether alien] barbarians or Scythians [ [e]who are the most savage of all], nor slave or free man; but Christ is all and in all— [f]everything and everywhere, to all men, without distinction of person.
12 Clothe yourselves therefore, as (God's own picked representatives,) His own chosen ones, [who are] purified *and* holy and well-beloved [by God Himself, by putting on behavior marked by] tenderhearted pity *and* mercy, kind feeling, a lowly opinion of yourselves, gentle ways, [and] patience—which is tireless, longsuffering and has the power to endure whatever comes, with good temper.
13 Be gentle *and* forbearing with one another and, if one has a difference (a grievance or complaint) against another, readily pardoning each other; even as the Lord has freely forgiven you, so must you also [forgive.]
14 And above all these [put on] love *and* enfold yourselves with the bond of perfectness—which binds everything together completely in ideal harmony.

**AMP** [a] Alternate reading. [b] Thayer. [c] Literal translation. [d] Vincent. [e] Vincent. [f] Gray and Adams' Commentary.

## New American Standard

20¶ If you have died with Christ to the elementary principles of
the world, why, as if you were living in the world, do you submit
yourself to decrees, such as,
21"Do not handle, do not taste, do not touch!"
22(which all *refer to* things destined to perish with the using)—in
accordance with the commandments and teachings of men?
23These are matters which have, to be sure, the appearance of
wisdom in self-made religion and self-abasement and severe treatment of the body, *but are* of no value against fleshly indulgence.

*Put On the New Self*

3 IF THEN you have been raised up with Christ, keep seeking
the things above, where Christ is, seated at the right hand of
God.
2Set your mind on the things above, not on the things that are
on earth.
3For you have died and your life is hidden with Christ in God.
4When Christ, who is our life, is revealed, then you also will
be revealed with Him in glory.
5¶ Therefore consider the members of your earthly body as
dead to immorality, impurity, passion, evil desire, and greed,
which amounts to idolatry.
6For it is on account of these things that the wrath of God will
come [g],
7and in them you also once walked, when you were living in
them.
8But now you also, put them all aside: anger, wrath, malice,
slander, *and* abusive speech from your mouth.
9Do not lie to one another, since you laid aside the old self with
its *evil* practices,
10and have put on the new self who is being renewed to a true
knowledge according to the image of the One who created him
11— *a renewal* in which there is no *distinction between* Greek and
Jew, circumcised and uncircumcised, barbarian, Scythian, slave
and freeman, but Christ is all, and in all.
12¶ And so, as those who have been chosen of God, holy and
beloved, put on a heart of compassion, kindness, humility, gentleness and patience;
13bearing with one another, and forgiving each other, whoever
has a complaint against anyone; just as the Lord forgave you, so
also should you.
14And beyond all these things *put on* love, which is the perfect
bond of unity.

NAS [g] Some early mss. add *upon the sons of disobedience*

## New International

20Since you died with Christ to the basic principles of this
world, why, as though you still belonged to it, do you submit to
its rules: 21"Do not handle! Do not taste! Do not touch!"? 22These
are all destined to perish with use, because they are based on
human commands and teachings. 23Such regulations indeed have
an appearance of wisdom, with their self-imposed worship, their
false humility and their harsh treatment of the body, but they lack
any value in restraining sensual indulgence.

*Rules for Holy Living*

3 SINCE, THEN, you have been raised with Christ, set your
hearts on things above, where Christ is seated at the right
hand of God. 2Set your minds on things above, not on earthly
things. 3For you died, and your life is now hidden with Christ in
God. 4When Christ, who is your[h] life, appears, then you also will
appear with him in glory.
5Put to death, therefore, whatever belongs to your earthly nature: sexual immorality, impurity, lust, evil desires and greed,
which is idolatry. 6Because of these, the wrath of God is coming.[i]
7You used to walk in these ways, in the life you once lived. 8But
now you must rid yourselves of all such things as these: anger,
rage, malice, slander, and filthy language from your lips. 9Do not
lie to each other, since you have taken off your old self with its
practices 10and have put on the new self, which is being renewed
in knowledge in the image of its Creator. 11Here there is no Greek
or Jew, circumcised or uncircumcised, barbarian, Scythian, slave
or free, but Christ is all, and is in all.
12Therefore, as God's chosen people, holy and dearly loved,
clothe yourselves with compassion, kindness, humility, gentleness and patience. 13Bear with each other and forgive whatever
grievances you may have against one another. Forgive as the Lord
forgave you. 14And over all these virtues put on love, which binds
them all together in perfect unity.

NIV [h] 4 Some manuscripts *our* [i] 6 Some early manuscripts *coming on those who are disobedient*

# King James

15And let the peace of God rule in your hearts, to the which also ye are called in one body; and be ye thankful.

16Let the word of Christ dwell in you richly in all wisdom; teaching and admonishing one another in psalms and hymns and spiritual songs, singing with grace in your hearts to the Lord.

17And whatsoever ye do in word or deed, *do* all in the name of the Lord Jesus, giving thanks to God and the Father by him.

18Wives, submit yourselves unto your own husbands, as it is fit in the Lord.

19Husbands, love *your* wives, and be not bitter against them.

20Children, obey *your* parents in all things: for this is well-pleasing unto the Lord.

21Fathers, provoke not your children *to anger,* lest they be discouraged.

22Servants, obey in all things *your* masters according to the flesh; not with eyeservice, as menpleasers; but in singleness of heart, fearing God:

23And whatsoever ye do, do *it* heartily, as to the Lord, and not unto men;

24Knowing that of the Lord ye shall receive the reward of the inheritance: for ye serve the Lord Christ.

25But he that doeth wrong shall receive for the wrong which he hath done: and there is no respect of persons.

**4** MASTERS, GIVE unto *your* servants that which is just and equal; knowing that ye also have a Master in heaven.

2Continue in prayer, and watch in the same with thanksgiving;

3Withal praying also for us, that God would open unto us a door of utterance, to speak the mystery of Christ, for which I am also in bonds:

4That I may make it manifest, as I ought to speak.

5Walk in wisdom toward them that are without, redeeming the time.

6Let your speech *be* always with grace, seasoned with salt, that ye may know how ye ought to answer every man.

7All my state shall Tychicus declare unto you, *who is* a beloved brother, and a faithful minister and fellowservant in the Lord:

8Whom I have sent unto you for the same purpose, that he might know your estate, and comfort your hearts;

# Amplified

15And let the peace (soul harmony which comes) from the Christ rule (act as umpire continually) in your hearts—deciding and settling with finality all questions that arise in your minds—[in that peaceful state] to which [as members of Christ's] one body you were also called [to live]. And be thankful—appreciative, giving praise to God always.

16Let the word [spoken by] the Christ, the Messiah, have its home (in your hearts and minds) *and* dwell in you in [all its] richness, as you teach and admonish *and* train one another in all insight *and* intelligence *and* wisdom [in spiritual things, and sing] psalms and hymns and spiritual songs, making melody to God with [His] grace in your hearts.

17And whatever you do—no matter what it is—in word or deed, do everything in the name of the Lord Jesus *and* in [dependence upon] His Person, giving praise to God the Father through Him.

18Wives, be subject to your husbands—subordinate and adapt yourselves to them—as is right *and* fitting *and* your proper duty in the Lord.

19Husbands, love your wives—be affectionate and sympathetic with them—and do not be harsh *or* bitter *or* resentful toward them.

20Children, obey your parents in everything, for this is well-pleasing to the Lord.

21Fathers, do not provoke *or* irritate *or* fret your children—do not be hard on them or harass them; lest they become discouraged *and* sullen *and* morose *and* feel inferior *and* frustrated; do not break their spirit.

22Servants, obey in everything those who are your earthly masters, not only when their eyes are on you, as pleasers of men, but in simplicity of purpose (with all your heart) because of your reverence for the Lord *and* as a sincere expression of your devotion to Him.

23Whatever may be your task, work at it heartily (from the soul), as [something done] for the Lord and not for men,

24Knowing (with all certainty) that it is from the Lord [and not from men] that you will receive the inheritance which is your (real) reward. [The One Whom] you are actually serving [is] the Lord Christ, the Messiah.

25For he who deals wrongfully will [reap the fruit of his folly and] be punished for his wrongdoing. And [with God] there is no partiality [no matter what a person's position may be, whether he is the slave or the master].

**4** MASTERS, [ON your part] deal with your slaves justly and fairly, knowing that also you have a Master in heaven. [Lev. 25:43, 53.]

2Be earnest *and* unwearied *and* steadfast in your prayer [life], being [both] alert *and* intent in [your praying] with thanksgiving.

3And at the same time pray for us also, that God may open a door to us for the Word (the Gospel), to proclaim the mystery concerning Christ, the Messiah, on account of which I am in prison;

4That I may (speak boldly and unfold that mystery,) proclaim it fully *and* make it clear, as is my duty.

5Behave yourselves wisely—living prudently and with discretion—in your relations with those of the outside world (the non-Christians), making the very most of the time *and* seizing (buying up) the opportunity.

6Let your speech at all times be gracious (pleasant and winsome), seasoned [as it were] with salt, [so that you may never be at a loss] to know how you ought to answer any one [who puts a question to you].

7Tychicus will give you full information about my affairs; [he is] a much-loved brother and faithful ministering assistant and fellow servant [with us] in the Lord.

8I have sent him to you for this very purpose, that you may know how we are faring and that he may comfort *and* cheer *and* encourage your hearts.

## New American Standard

15And let the peace of Christ rule in your hearts, to which
indeed you were called in one body; and be thankful.
16Let the word of [a]Christ richly dwell within you, with all
wisdom teaching and admonishing one another with psalms *and*
hymns *and* spiritual songs, singing with thankfulness in your
hearts to God.
17And whatever you do in word or deed, *do* all in the name of
the Lord Jesus, giving thanks through Him to God the Father.

*Family Relations*

**18**¶ Wives, be subject to your husbands, as is fitting in the Lord.
19Husbands, love your wives, and do not be embittered against
them.
20Children, be obedient to your parents in all things, for this is
well-pleasing to the Lord.
21Fathers, do not [b]exasperate your children, that they may not
lose heart.
22Slaves, in all things obey those who are your masters on earth,
not with external service, as those who *merely* please men, but with
sincerity of heart, fearing the Lord.
23Whatever you do, do your work heartily, as for the Lord
rather than for men;
24knowing that from the Lord you will receive the reward of the
inheritance. It is the Lord Christ whom you serve.
25For he who does wrong will receive the consequences of the
wrong which he has done, and that without partiality.

## New International

15Let the peace of Christ rule in your hearts, since as members
of one body you were called to peace. And be thankful. 16Let the
word of Christ dwell in you richly as you teach and admonish one
another with all wisdom, and as you sing psalms, hymns and
spiritual songs with gratitude in your hearts to God. 17And whatever you do, whether in word or deed, do it all in the name of the
Lord Jesus, giving thanks to God the Father through him.

*Rules for Christian Households*

18Wives, submit to your husbands, as is fitting in the Lord.
19Husbands, love your wives and do not be harsh with them.
20Children, obey your parents in everything, for this pleases the
Lord.
21Fathers, do not embitter your children, or they will become
discouraged.
22Slaves, obey your earthly masters in everything; and do it, not
only when their eye is on you and to win their favor, but with
sincerity of heart and reverence for the Lord. 23Whatever you do,
work at it with all your heart, as working for the Lord, not for men,
24since you know that you will receive an inheritance from the
Lord as a reward. It is the Lord Christ you are serving. 25Anyone
who does wrong will be repaid for his wrong, and there is no
favoritism.

*Fellow Workers*

**4** MASTERS, GRANT to your slaves justice and fairness, knowing that you too have a Master in heaven.
**2**¶ Devote yourselves to prayer, keeping alert in it with *an
attitude of* thanksgiving;
3praying at the same time for us as well, that God may open
up to us a door for the word, so that we may speak forth the
mystery of Christ, for which I have also been imprisoned;
4in order that I may make it clear in the way I ought to speak.
5Conduct yourselves with wisdom toward outsiders, making
the most of the opportunity.
6Let your speech always be with grace, seasoned, *as it were,*
with salt, so that you may know how you should respond to each
person.
**7**¶ As to all my affairs, Tychicus, *our* beloved brother and
faithful servant and fellow bond-servant in the Lord, will bring you
information.
8For I have sent him to you for this very purpose, that you may
know *about* our circumstances and that he may encourage your
hearts;

**4** MASTERS, PROVIDE your slaves with what is right and fair,
because you know that you also have a Master in heaven.

*Further Instructions*

2Devote yourselves to prayer, being watchful and thankful.
3And pray for us, too, that God may open a door for our message,
so that we may proclaim the mystery of Christ, for which I am in
chains. 4Pray that I may proclaim it clearly, as I should. 5Be wise
in the way you act toward outsiders; make the most of every
opportunity. 6Let your conversation be always full of grace, seasoned with salt, so that you may know how to answer everyone.

*Final Greetings*

7Tychicus will tell you all the news about me. He is a dear
brother, a faithful minister and fellow servant in the Lord. 8I am
sending him to you for the express purpose that you may know
about our[c] circumstances and that he may encourage your hearts.

**NAS** [a] Some mss. read *the Lord;* others read *God* [b] Some early mss. read *provoke to anger*

**NIV** [c] 8 Some manuscripts *that he may know about your*

## King James

9With Onesimus, a faithful and beloved brother, who is *one* of you. They shall make known unto you all things which *are done* here.
10Aristarchus my fellowprisoner saluteth you, and Marcus, sister's son to Barnabas, (touching whom ye received commandments: if he come unto you, receive him;)
11And Jesus, which is called Justus, who are of the circumcision. These only *are my* fellowworkers unto the kingdom of God, which have been a comfort unto me.
12Epaphras, who is *one* of you, a servant of Christ, saluteth you, always labouring fervently for you in prayers, that ye may stand perfect and complete in all the will of God.
13For I bear him record, that he hath a great zeal for you, and them *that are* in Laodicea, and them in Hierapolis.
14Luke, the beloved physician, and Demas, greet you.
15Salute the brethren which are in Laodicea, and Nymphas, and the church which is in his house.
16And when this epistle is read among you, cause that it be read also in the church of the Laodiceans; and that ye likewise read the *epistle* from Laodicea.
17And say to Archippus, Take heed to the ministry which thou hast received in the Lord, that thou fulfil it.
18The salutation by the hand of me Paul. Remember my bonds. Grace *be* with you. Amen.

## Amplified

9And with [him is] Onesimus, [our] faithful and beloved brother, who is [one] of yourselves. They will let you know everything that has taken place here [in Rome].
10Aristarchus my fellow prisoner wishes to be remembered to you, as does Mark the relative of Barnabas. You received instructions concerning him; if he comes to you give him a ( [a]hearty) welcome.
11And [greetings also from] Jesus who is called Justus. These [Hebrew Christians] alone of the circumcision are among my fellow workers for [the extension of] God's kingdom, and they have proved a relief *and* a comfort to me.
12Epaphras, who is one of yourselves, a servant of Christ Jesus, sends you greetings. [He is] always striving for you earnestly in his prayers, [pleading] that you may—as persons of ripe character and clear conviction—stand firm *and* mature (in spiritual growth), convinced *and* fully assured in [b]everything willed by God.
13For I bear him testimony that he has labored hard in your behalf and for [the believers] in Laodicea and those in Hierapolis.
14Luke the beloved physician and Demas salute you.
15Give my greetings to the brethren at Laodicea, and to Nympha and the assembly [the church] which meets in her house.
16And when this epistle has been read before you, [see] that it is read also in the assembly [the church] of the Laodiceans; and also [see] that you yourselves in turn read the [letter that comes to you] from Laodicea.
17And say to Archippus, See that you discharge carefully [the duties of] the ministry *and* fulfill the stewardship which you have received in the Lord.
18I, Paul, [add this final] greeting, writing with my own hand. Remember I am still in prison *and* in chains. May grace (God's unmerited favor and blessing) be with you! *Amen, so be it.*

**AMP** [a] Williams: "A very strong verb, so *give him a hearty welcome.*"
[b] Vincent.

## New American Standard

9and with him Onesimus, *our* faithful and beloved brother,
who is one of your *number*. They will inform you about the whole
situation here.
10¶ Aristarchus, my fellow prisoner, sends you his greetings;
and *also* Barnabas' cousin Mark (about whom you received instructions: if he comes to you, welcome him);
11and *also* Jesus who is called Justus; these are the only fellow
workers for the kingdom of God who are from the circumcision;
and they have proved to be an encouragement to me.
12Epaphras, who is one of your number, a bondslave of Jesus
Christ, sends you his greetings, always laboring earnestly for you
in his prayers, that you may stand perfect and fully assured in all
the will of God.
13For I bear him witness that he has a deep concern for you and
for those who are in Laodicea and Hierapolis.
14Luke, the beloved physician, sends you his greetings, and *also*
Demas.
15Greet the brethren who are in Laodicea and also [c]Nympha
and the church that is in her house.
16And when this letter is read among you, have it also read in
the church of the Laodiceans; and you, for your part read my letter
*that is coming* from Laodicea.
17And say to Archippus, "Take heed to the ministry which you
have received in the Lord, that you may fulfill it."
18¶ I, Paul, write this greeting with my own hand. Remember
my imprisonment. Grace be with you.

NAS [c] Or, *Nymphas* (masc.)

## New International

9He is coming with Onesimus, our faithful and dear brother, who
is one of you. They will tell you everything that is happening here.
10My fellow prisoner Aristarchus sends you his greetings, as
does Mark, the cousin of Barnabas. (You have received instructions about him; if he comes to you, welcome him.) 11Jesus, who
is called Justus, also sends greetings. These are the only Jews
among my fellow workers for the kingdom of God, and they have
proved a comfort to me. 12Epaphras, who is one of you and a
servant of Christ Jesus, sends greetings. He is always wrestling in
prayer for you, that you may stand firm in all the will of God,
mature and fully assured. 13I vouch for him that he is working hard
for you and for those at Laodicea and Hierapolis. 14Our dear friend
Luke, the doctor, and Demas send greetings. 15Give my greetings
to the brothers at Laodicea, and to Nympha and the church in her
house.
16After this letter has been read to you, see that it is also read
in the church of the Laodiceans and that you in turn read the letter
from Laodicea.
17Tell Archippus: "See to it that you complete the work you
have received in the Lord."
18I, Paul, write this greeting in my own hand. Remember my
chains. Grace be with you.

## King James

THE FIRST EPISTLE OF

PAUL THE APOSTLE TO THE

# Thessalonians

**1** PAUL, AND Silvanus, and Timotheus, unto the church of the Thessalonians *which is* in God the Father and *in* the Lord Jesus Christ: Grace *be* unto you, and peace, from God our Father, and the Lord Jesus Christ.

2 We give thanks to God always for you all, making mention of you in our prayers;

3 Remembering without ceasing your work of faith, and labour of love, and patience of hope in our Lord Jesus Christ, in the sight of God and our Father;

4 Knowing, brethren beloved, your election of God.

5 For our gospel came not unto you in word only, but also in power, and in the Holy Ghost, and in much assurance; as ye know what manner of men we were among you for your sake.

6 And ye became followers of us, and of the Lord, having received the word in much affliction, with joy of the Holy Ghost:

7 So that ye were examples to all that believe in Macedonia and Achaia.

8 For from you sounded out the word of the Lord not only in Macedonia and Achaia, but also in every place your faith to God-ward is spread abroad; so that we need not to speak any thing.

9 For they themselves show of us what manner of entering in we had unto you, and how ye turned to God from idols to serve the living and true God;

10 And to wait for his Son from heaven, whom he raised from the dead, *even* Jesus, which delivered us from the wrath to come.

**2** FOR YOURSELVES, brethren, know our entrance in unto you, that it was not in vain:

2 But even after that we had suffered before, and were shamefully entreated, as ye know, at Philippi, we were bold in our God to speak unto you the gospel of God with much contention.

3 For our exhortation *was* not of deceit, nor of uncleanness, nor in guile:

## Amplified

THE FIRST LETTER OF

PAUL TO THE

# Thessalonians

**1** PAUL, SILVANUS (Silas) and Timothy to the assembly (church) of the Thessalonians in God the Father and the Lord Jesus Christ, the Messiah: Grace (spiritual blessing and divine favor) to you and heart peace.

2 We are ever giving thanks to God for all of you, continually mentioning [you when engaged] in our prayers,

3 Recalling unceasingly before our God and Father your work energized by faith and service motivated by love, and unwavering hope in (the return of) our Lord Jesus Christ, the Messiah. [1:10.]

4 [O] brethren beloved by God, we recognize *and* know that He has selected (chosen) you;

5 For our [preaching of the] glad tidings (the Gospel) came to you not only in word, but also in (its own inherent) power and in the Holy Spirit, and with great conviction *and* absolute certainty (on our part). You know what kind of men we proved [ourselves] to be among you for your good.

6 And you [set yourselves to] become imitators of us and [through us] of the Lord Himself, for you welcomed our message in [spite of the] much persecution, with joy [inspired] of the Holy Spirit;

7 So that you [thus] became a pattern to all the believers—those who adhere to, trust in and rely on Christ Jesus—in Macedonia and Achaia [most of Greece].

8 For not only has the Word concerning *and* from the Lord resounded forth from you unmistakably in Macedonia and Achaia, but everywhere the report has gone forth of your faith in God—of your [a]leaning of your whole personality on Him in complete trust and confidence in His power, wisdom and goodness. So we [find that we] never need to tell people anything [further about it].

9 For they themselves volunteer testimony concerning us, telling what an entrance we had among you, and how you turned to God from [your] idols to serve a God Who is alive and true *and* genuine;

10 And [how you] look forward to *and* await the coming of His Son from heaven, Whom He raised from the dead, Jesus Who personally rescues *and* delivers us out of *and* from the wrath (bringing punishment) which is coming [upon the impenitent] *and* [b]draws us to Himself [that is, [c]invests us with all the privileges and rewards of the new life in Christ, the Messiah].

**2** FOR YOU yourselves know, brethren, that our coming among you was not useless *and* fruitless.

2 But though we had already suffered and been outrageously treated at Philippi, as you know, yet in [the strength of] our God we summoned courage to proclaim to you unfalteringly the good news (the Gospel) with earnest contention, much conflict *and* great opposition.

3 For our appeal [in preaching] does not [originate] from delusion *or* error or impure purpose *or* motive, nor in fraud *or* deceit.

AMP [a] Souter. [b] Literal meaning of the verb "to deliver." [c] Vincent.

## New American Standard

# 1 Thessalonians

*Thanksgiving for These Believers*

**1** PAUL AND Silvanus and Timothy to the church of the Thessalonians in God the Father and the Lord Jesus Christ: Grace
to you and peace.

2¶ We give thanks to God always for all of you, making mention *of you* in our prayers;

3constantly bearing in mind your work of faith and labor of
love and steadfastness of hope in our Lord Jesus Christ in the
presence of our God and Father,

4knowing, brethren beloved by God, *His* choice of you;

5for our gospel did not come to you in word only, but also in
power and in the Holy Spirit and with full conviction; just as you
know what kind of men we proved to be among you for your sake.

6You also became imitators of us and of the Lord, having
received the word in much tribulation with the joy of the Holy
Spirit,

7so that you became an example to all the believers in Macedonia and in Achaia.

8For the word of the Lord has sounded forth from you, not
only in Macedonia and Achaia, but also in every place your faith
toward God has gone forth, so that we have no need to say anything.

9For they themselves report about us what kind of a reception
we had with you, and how you turned to God from idols to serve
a living and true God,

10and to wait for His Son from heaven, whom He raised from
the dead, *that is* Jesus, who delivers us from the wrath to come.

*Paul's Ministry*

**2** FOR YOU yourselves know, brethren, that our coming to you
was not in vain,

2but after we had already suffered and been mistreated in
Philippi, as you know, we had the boldness in our God to speak
to you the gospel of God amid much opposition.

3For our exhortation does not *come* from error or impurity or
by way of deceit;

## New International

# 1 Thessalonians

**1** PAUL, SILAS[d] and Timothy,

To the church of the Thessalonians in God the Father and the
Lord Jesus Christ:

Grace and peace to you.[e]

*Thanksgiving for the Thessalonians' Faith*

2We always thank God for all of you, mentioning you in our
prayers. 3We continually remember before our God and Father
your work produced by faith, your labor prompted by love, and
your endurance inspired by hope in our Lord Jesus Christ.

4For we know, brothers loved by God, that he has chosen you,
5because our gospel came to you not simply with words, but also
with power, with the Holy Spirit and with deep conviction. You
know how we lived among you for your sake. 6You became imitators of us and of the Lord; in spite of severe suffering, you welcomed the message with the joy given by the Holy Spirit. 7And so
you became a model to all the believers in Macedonia and Achaia.
8The Lord's message rang out from you not only in Macedonia and
Achaia—your faith in God has become known everywhere. Therefore we do not need to say anything about it, 9for they themselves
report what kind of reception you gave us. They tell how you
turned to God from idols to serve the living and true God, 10and
to wait for his Son from heaven, whom he raised from the dead—
Jesus, who rescues us from the coming wrath.

*Paul's Ministry in Thessalonica*

**2** YOU KNOW, brothers, that our visit to you was not a failure.
2We had previously suffered and been insulted in Philippi, as
you know, but with the help of our God we dared to tell you his
gospel in spite of strong opposition. 3For the appeal we make does
not spring from error or impure motives, nor are we trying to trick
you. 4On the contrary, we speak as men approved by God to be

NIV [d] *1 Greek Silvanus, a variant of Silas* [e] *1* Some early manuscripts *you from God our Father and the Lord Jesus Christ*

## King James

4But as we were allowed of God to be put in trust with the gospel, even so we speak; not as pleasing men, but God, which trieth our hearts.

5For neither at any time used we flattering words, as ye know, nor a cloak of covetousness; God *is* witness:

6Nor of men sought we glory, neither of you, nor *yet* of others, when we might have been burdensome, as the apostles of Christ.

7But we were gentle among you, even as a nurse cherisheth her children:

8So being affectionately desirous of you, we were willing to have imparted unto you, not the gospel of God only, but also our own souls, because ye were dear unto us.

9For ye remember, brethren, our labour and travail: for labouring night and day, because we would not be chargeable unto any of you, we preached unto you the gospel of God.

10Ye *are* witnesses, and God *also*, how holily and justly and unblameably we behaved ourselves among you that believe:

11As ye know how we exhorted and comforted and charged every one of you, as a father *doth* his children,

12That ye would walk worthy of God, who hath called you unto his kingdom and glory.

13For this cause also thank we God without ceasing, because, when ye received the word of God which ye heard of us, ye received *it* not *as* the word of men, but as it is in truth, the word of God, which effectually worketh also in you that believe.

14For ye, brethren, became followers of the churches of God which in Judaea are in Christ Jesus: for ye also have suffered like things of your own countrymen, even as they *have* of the Jews:

15Who both killed the Lord Jesus, and their own prophets, and have persecuted us; and they please not God, and are contrary to all men:

16Forbidding us to speak to the Gentiles that they might be saved, to fill up their sins always: for the wrath is come upon them to the uttermost.

17But we, brethren, being taken from you for a short time in presence, not in heart, endeavoured the more abundantly to see your face with great desire.

18Wherefore we would have come unto you, even I Paul, once and again; but Satan hindered us.

19For what *is* our hope, or joy, or crown of rejoicing? *Are* not even ye in the presence of our Lord Jesus Christ at his coming?

20For ye are our glory and joy.

3 WHEREFORE WHEN we could no longer forbear, we thought it good to be left at Athens alone;

2And sent Timotheus, our brother, and minister of God, and our fellowlabourer in the gospel of Christ, to establish you, and to comfort you concerning your faith:

## Amplified

4But just as we have been approved by God to be entrusted with the glad tidings (the Gospel), so we speak not to please men, but to please God, Who tests our hearts ( [a]expecting them to be approved).

5For, as you well know, we never resorted either to words of flattery or to any cloak to conceal greedy motives *or* pretexts for gain, [as] God is our witness.

6Nor did we seek to extract praise *and* honor *and* glory from men, either from you or from any one else, though we might have asserted our authority (stood on our dignity and claimed honor) as apostles (special missionaries) of Christ, the Messiah.

7But we behaved gently when we were among you, like a devoted mother nursing *and* cherishing her own children.

8So, being thus tenderly *and* affectionately desirous of you, we continued to share with you not only God's good news (the Gospel) but also our own lives as well, for you had become so very dear to us.

9For you recall our hard toil and struggles, brethren. We worked night and day [and plied our trade] in order not to be a burden to any of you [for our support] while we proclaimed the glad tidings (the Gospel) of God to you.

10You are witnesses, [yes] and God [also], how unworldly and upright and blameless was our behavior toward you believers—who adhered to and trusted in and relied on our Lord Jesus Christ.

11For you know how, like a father [dealing with] his children, we used to exhort each of you personally, stimulating *and* encouraging and charging you

12To live lives worthy of God, Who calls you into His own kingdom and the glorious blessedness [ [b]into which true believers will enter after Christ's return].

13And we also [especially] thank God continually for this, that when you received the message of God [which you heard] from us, you welcomed it not as the word of [mere] men but as what it truly is, the Word of God, which is effectually at work in you who believe— [c]exercising its [superhuman] power in those who adhere to and trust in and rely on it.

14For you, brethren, became imitators of the assemblies (churches) of God in Christ Jesus which are in Judea, for you too have suffered the same kind of treatment from your own fellow countrymen as they did [who were persecuted at the hands] of the Jews,

15Who killed both the Lord Jesus and the prophets, and harassed *and* drove us out; and continue to make themselves hateful *and* offensive to God and to show themselves foes of all men,

16Forbidding *and* hindering us from speaking to the Gentiles [the nations] that they may be saved. So as always they fill up (to the brim the measure of) their sins. But God's wrath has come upon them at last—completely and forever! [Gen. 15:16.]

17But since we were bereft of you, brethren, for a little while in person, [of course] not in heart, we endeavored the more eagerly and with great longing to see you face to face,

18Because it was our will to come to you. [I mean that] I, Paul, again and again [wanted to come], but Satan hindered *and* impeded us.

19For what is our hope or happiness or our victor's wreath of exultant triumph when we stand in the presence of our Lord Jesus at His coming? Are not you?

20For you are [indeed] our glory and our joy!

3 THEREFORE WHEN [the suspense of separation and our yearning for some personal communication from you] became intolerable, we consented to being left behind alone at Athens.

2And we sent Timothy, our brother and God's servant in [spreading] the good news (the Gospel) of Christ, to strengthen *and* establish, exhort *and* comfort *and* encourage you in your faith,

**AMP** [a] Abbott-Smith. [b] Thayer. [c] Vincent.

## New American Standard

4but just as we have been approved by God to be entrusted
with the gospel, so we speak, not as pleasing men but God, who
examines our hearts.
5For we never came with flattering speech, as you know, nor
with a pretext for greed—God is witness—
6nor did we seek glory from men, either from you or from
others, even though as apostles of Christ we might have asserted
our authority.
7But we proved to be [d]gentle among you, as a nursing *mother*
tenderly cares for her own children.
8Having thus a fond affection for you, we were well-pleased
to impart to you not only the gospel of God but also our own lives,
because you had become very dear to us.
9For you recall, brethren, our labor and hardship, *how* working
night and day so as not to be a burden to any of you, we proclaimed to you the gospel of God.
10You are witnesses, and *so is* God, how devoutly and uprightly
and blamelessly we behaved toward you believers;
11just as you know how we *were* exhorting and encouraging and
imploring each one of you as a father *would* his own children,
12so that you may walk in a manner worthy of the God who calls
you into His own kingdom and glory.
13¶ And for this reason we also constantly thank God that when
you received from us the word of God's message, you accepted *it*
not *as* the word of men, but *for* what it really is, the word of God,
which also performs its work in you who believe.
14For you, brethren, became imitators of the churches of God
in Christ Jesus that are in Judea, for you also endured the same
sufferings at the hands of your own countrymen, even as they *did*
from the Jews,
15who both killed the Lord Jesus and the prophets, and drove
us out. They are not pleasing to God, but hostile to all men,
16hindering us from speaking to the Gentiles that they might be
saved; with the result that they always fill up the measure of their
sins. But wrath has come upon them [e]to the utmost.
17¶ But we, brethren, having been bereft of you for a short
while—in person, not in spirit—were all the more eager with great
desire to see your face.
18For we wanted to come to you—I, Paul, more than once—and
*yet* Satan thwarted us.
19For who is our hope or joy or crown of exultation? Is it not
even you, in the presence of our Lord Jesus at His coming?
20For you are our glory and joy.

*Encouragement of Timothy's Visit*

**3** THEREFORE WHEN we could endure *it* no longer, we
thought it best to be left behind at Athens alone;
2and we sent Timothy, our brother and God's fellow worker
in the gospel of Christ, to strengthen and encourage you as to your
faith,

NAS [d] Some ancient mss. read *babes* [e] Or, *forever;* or, *altogether*

## New International

entrusted with the gospel. We are not trying to please men but
God, who tests our hearts. 5You know we never used flattery, nor
did we put on a mask to cover up greed—God is our witness. 6We
were not looking for praise from men, not from you or anyone else.
As apostles of Christ we could have been a burden to you, 7but
we were gentle among you, like a mother caring for her little
children. 8We loved you so much that we were delighted to share
with you not only the gospel of God but our lives as well, because
you had become so dear to us. 9Surely you remember, brothers,
our toil and hardship; we worked night and day in order not to be
a burden to anyone while we preached the gospel of God to you.
10You are witnesses, and so is God, of how holy, righteous and
blameless we were among you who believed. 11For you know that
we dealt with each of you as a father deals with his own children,
12encouraging, comforting and urging you to live lives worthy of
God, who calls you into his kingdom and glory.
13And we also thank God continually because, when you received the word of God, which you heard from us, you accepted
it not as the word of men, but as it actually is, the word of God,
which is at work in you who believe. 14For you, brothers, became
imitators of God's churches in Judea, which are in Christ Jesus:
You suffered from your own countrymen the same things those
churches suffered from the Jews, 15who killed the Lord Jesus and
the prophets and also drove us out. They displease God and are
hostile to all men 16in their effort to keep us from speaking to the
Gentiles so that they may be saved. In this way they always heap
up their sins to the limit. The wrath of God has come upon them
at last.[f]

*Paul's Longing to See the Thessalonians*

17But, brothers, when we were torn away from you for a short
time (in person, not in thought), out of our intense longing we
made every effort to see you. 18For we wanted to come to you—
certainly I, Paul, did, again and again—but Satan stopped us. 19For
what is our hope, our joy, or the crown in which we will glory in
the presence of our Lord Jesus when he comes? Is it not you?
20Indeed, you are our glory and joy.

**3** SO WHEN we could stand it no longer, we thought it best to
be left by ourselves in Athens. 2We sent Timothy, who is our
brother and God's fellow worker[g] in spreading the gospel of
Christ, to strengthen and encourage you in your faith, 3so that no

NIV [f] 16 Or *them fully* [g] 2 Some manuscripts *brother and fellow worker;* other manuscripts *brother and God's servant*

## King James

3That no man should be moved by these afflictions: for yourselves know that we are appointed thereunto.

4For verily, when we were with you, we told you before that we should suffer tribulation; even as it came to pass, and ye know.

5For this cause, when I could no longer forbear, I sent to know your faith, lest by some means the tempter have tempted you, and our labour be in vain.

6But now when Timotheus came from you unto us, and brought us good tidings of your faith and charity, and that ye have good remembrance of us always, desiring greatly to see us, as we also *to see* you:

7Therefore, brethren, we were comforted over you in all our affliction and distress by your faith:

8For now we live, if ye stand fast in the Lord.

9For what thanks can we render to God again for you, for all the joy wherewith we joy for your sakes before our God;

10Night and day praying exceedingly that we might see your face, and might perfect that which is lacking in your faith?

11Now God himself and our Father, and our Lord Jesus Christ, direct our way unto you.

12And the Lord make you to increase and abound in love one toward another, and toward all *men*, even as we *do* toward you:

13To the end he may stablish your hearts unblameable in holiness before God, even our Father, at the coming of our Lord Jesus Christ with all his saints.

4 FURTHERMORE THEN we beseech you, brethren, and exhort *you* by the Lord Jesus, that as ye have received of us how ye ought to walk and to please God, *so* ye would abound more and more.

2For ye know what commandments we gave you by the Lord Jesus.

3For this is the will of God, *even* your sanctification, that ye should abstain from fornication:

4That every one of you should know how to possess his vessel in sanctification and honour;

5Not in the lust of concupiscence, even as the Gentiles which know not God:

6That no *man* go beyond and defraud his brother in *any* matter: because that the Lord *is* the avenger of all such, as we also have forewarned you and testified.

7For God hath not called us unto uncleanness, but unto holiness.

8He therefore that despiseth, despiseth not man, but God, who hath also given unto us his holy Spirit.

## Amplified

3That no one [of you] should be disturbed *and* beguiled *and* led astray by these afflictions *and* difficulties [to which I have referred]. For you yourselves know that this is [unavoidable in our position, and must be recognized as] our appointed lot.

4For even when we were with you [you know] we warned you plainly beforehand that we were to be pressed with difficulties *and* made to suffer affliction, just as to your own knowledge has [since] happened.

5That is the reason that, when I could bear [the suspense] no longer, I sent that I might learn [how you were standing the strain, and the endurance of] your faith, [for I was fearful] lest somehow the tempter had tempted you and our toil [among you should prove to] be fruitless *and* to no purpose.

6But now that Timothy has just come back to us from [his visit to] you, and has brought us the good news of [the steadfastness of] your faith and [the warmth of your] love, and [reported] how kindly you cherish a constant *and* affectionate remembrance of us, [and that you are] longing to see us as we [are to see] you,

7Brethren, for this reason, in [spite of all] our stress and crushing difficulties we have been filled with comfort *and* cheer about you [because of] your faith— [a]the leaning of your whole personality on God in complete trust and confidence.

8Because now we [really] live, if you stand [firm] in the Lord.

9For what [adequate] thanksgiving can we render to God for you, for all the gladness *and* delight which we enjoy for your sakes before our God?

10[And we] continue to pray especially *and* with most intense earnestness night and day that we may see you face to face and mend *and* make good whatever may be imperfect *and* lacking in your faith.

11Now may our God and Father Himself, and our Lord Jesus *Christ, the Messiah*, guide our steps to you.

12And may the Lord make you to increase and excel *and* overflow in love for one another and for all people, just as we also do for you.

13So that He may strengthen *and* confirm *and* establish your hearts faultlessly pure *and* unblamable in holiness in the sight of our God and Father, at the coming of our Lord Jesus *Christ, the Messiah*, with all His saints—the [b]holy and glorified people of God! *Amen, so be it!*

4 FURTHERMORE, [c]BRETHREN, we beg and admonish you in [virture of our union with] the Lord Jesus, that [you follow the instructions which] you learned from us about how you ought to walk so as to please *and* gratify God, as indeed you are doing; that you do so even more and more abundantly—attaining yet greater perfection in living this life.

2For you know what charges *and* precepts we gave you [ [d]on the authority and by the inspiration of] the Lord Jesus.

3For this is the will of God, that you should be consecrated—separated and set apart for pure and holy living: that you should abstain *and* shrink from all sexual vice;

4That each one of you should know how to [e]possess [control, manage] his own [f]body (in purity, separated from things profane, and) in consecration and honor,

5Not [to be used] in the passion of lust, like the heathen who are ignorant of the true God *and* have no knowledge of His will,

6That no man transgress, and overreach his brother *and* defraud him in this matter *or* defraud his brother in business. For the Lord is an avenger in all these things, as we have already warned you solemnly *and* [g]told you plainly.

7For God has not called us to impurity, but to consecration [to dedicate ourselves to the most thorough purity].

8Therefore whoever disregards—sets aside and rejects this—disregards not man but God, Whose [very] Spirit [Whom] He gives to you [is] holy—chaste, pure.

**AMP** [a] Souter. [b] Vincent. [c] Vincent. [d] Abbott-Smith. [e] ASV and others. [f] Moulton and Milligan: "'body' rather than 'wife'." Allowed by lexicons generally. Supported by Knox, Phillips, Way, etc. Early versions say "vessel." [g] Abbott-Smith.

## New American Standard

3so that no man may be disturbed by these afflictions; for you yourselves know that we have been destined for this.

4For indeed when we were with you, we *kept* telling you in advance that we were going to suffer affliction; and so it came to pass, as you know.

5For this reason, when I could endure *it* no longer, I also sent to find out about your faith, for fear that the tempter might have tempted you, and our labor should be in vain.

6But now that Timothy has come to us from you, and has brought us good news of your faith and love, and that you always think kindly of us, longing to see us just as we also long to see you,

7for this reason, brethren, in all our distress and affliction we were comforted about you through your faith;

8for now we *really* live, if you stand firm in the Lord.

9For what thanks can we render to God for you in return for all the joy with which we rejoice before our God on your account,

10as we night and day keep praying most earnestly that we may see your face, and may complete what is lacking in your faith?

11¶ Now may our God and Father Himself and Jesus our Lord direct our way to you;

12and may the Lord cause you to increase and abound in love for one another, and for all men, just as we also *do* for you; 13so that He may establish your hearts unblamable in holiness before our God and Father at the coming of our Lord Jesus with all His saints.

*Sanctification and Love*

4 FINALLY THEN, brethren, we request and exhort you in the Lord Jesus, that, as you received from us *instruction* as to how you ought to walk and please God (just as you actually do [h]walk), that you may excel still more.

2For you know what commandments we gave you [i]by *the authority of* the Lord Jesus.

3For this is the will of God, your sanctification; *that is,* that you abstain from sexual immorality;

4that each of you know how to possess his own [j]vessel in sanctification and honor,

5not in lustful passion, like the Gentiles who do not know God;

6 *and* that no man transgress and defraud his brother in the matter because the Lord is *the* avenger in all these things, just as we also told you before and solemnly warned *you.*

7For God has not called us for the purpose of impurity, but in sanctification.

8Consequently, he who rejects *this* is not rejecting man but the God who gives His Holy Spirit to you.

NAS [h] Or, *conduct yourselves* [i] Lit., *through the Lord* [j] I.e., body; or possibly, wife

## New International

one would be unsettled by these trials. You know quite well that we were destined for them. 4In fact, when we were with you, we kept telling you that we would be persecuted. And it turned out that way, as you well know. 5For this reason, when I could stand it no longer, I sent to find out about your faith. I was afraid that in some way the tempter might have tempted you and our efforts might have been useless.

*Timothy's Encouraging Report*

6But Timothy has just now come to us from you and has brought good news about your faith and love. He has told us that you always have pleasant memories of us and that you long to see us, just as we also long to see you. 7Therefore, brothers, in all our distress and persecution we were encouraged about you because of your faith. 8For now we really live, since you are standing firm in the Lord. 9How can we thank God enough for you in return for all the joy we have in the presence of our God because of you? 10Night and day we pray most earnestly that we may see you again and supply what is lacking in your faith.

11Now may our God and Father himself and our Lord Jesus clear the way for us to come to you. 12May the Lord make your love increase and overflow for each other and for everyone else, just as ours does for you. 13May he strengthen your hearts so that you will be blameless and holy in the presence of our God and Father when our Lord Jesus comes with all his holy ones.

*Living to Please God*

4 FINALLY, BROTHERS, we instructed you how to live in order to please God, as in fact you are living. Now we ask you and urge you in the Lord Jesus to do this more and more. 2For you know what instructions we gave you by the authority of the Lord Jesus.

3It is God's will that you should be sanctified: that you should avoid sexual immorality; 4that each of you should learn to control his own body[k] in a way that is holy and honorable, 5not in passionate lust like the heathen, who do not know God; 6and that in this matter no one should wrong his brother or take advantage of him. The Lord will punish men for all such sins, as we have already told you and warned you. 7For God did not call us to be impure, but to live a holy life. 8Therefore, he who rejects this instruction does not reject man but God, who gives you his Holy Spirit.

NIV [k] 4 Or *learn to live with his own wife;* or *learn to acquire a wife*

# King James

9But as touching brotherly love ye need not that I write unto you: for ye yourselves are taught of God to love one another.

10And indeed ye do it toward all the brethren which are in all Macedonia: but we beseech you, brethren, that ye increase more and more;

11And that ye study to be quiet, and to do your own business, and to work with your own hands, as we commanded you;

12That ye may walk honestly toward them that are without, and *that* ye may have lack of nothing.

13But I would not have you to be ignorant, brethren, concerning them which are asleep, that ye sorrow not, even as others which have no hope.

14For if we believe that Jesus died and rose again, even so them also which sleep in Jesus will God bring with him.

15For this we say unto you by the word of the Lord, that we which are alive *and* remain unto the coming of the Lord shall not prevent them which are asleep.

16For the Lord himself shall descend from heaven with a shout, with the voice of the archangel, and with the trump of God: and the dead in Christ shall rise first:

17Then we which are alive *and* remain shall be caught up together with them in the clouds, to meet the Lord in the air: and so shall we ever be with the Lord.

18Wherefore comfort one another with these words.

**5** BUT OF the times and the seasons, brethren, ye have no need that I write unto you.

2For yourselves know perfectly that the day of the Lord so cometh as a thief in the night.

3For when they shall say, Peace and safety; then sudden destruction cometh upon them, as travail upon a woman with child; and they shall not escape.

4But ye, brethren, are not in darkness, that that day should overtake you as a thief.

5Ye are all the children of light, and the children of the day: we are not of the night, nor of darkness.

6Therefore let us not sleep, as *do* others; but let us watch and be sober.

7For they that sleep sleep in the night; and they that be drunken are drunken in the night.

8But let us, who are of the day, be sober, putting on the breastplate of faith and love; and for an helmet, the hope of salvation.

9For God hath not appointed us to wrath, but to obtain salvation by our Lord Jesus Christ,

10Who died for us, that, whether we wake or sleep, we should live together with him.

11Wherefore comfort yourselves together, and edify one another, even as also ye do.

# Amplified

9But concerning brotherly love [for all other Christians], you have no need to have any one write you, for you yourselves have been (personally) taught of God to love one another.

10And indeed you already are [extending and displaying your love] to all the brethren throughout Macedonia. But we beseech *and* earnestly exhort you, brethren, that you [a]excel [in this matter] more and more;

11To make it your ambition *and* definitely endeavor to live quietly *and* peacefully, to mind your own affairs, and to work with your hands, as we charged you;

12So that you may bear yourselves becomingly, be correct *and* honorable *and* command the respect of the outside world, being (self-supporting,) dependent on nobody *and* having need of nothing.

13Now also we would not have you ignorant, brethren, about those who fall asleep [in death], that you may not grieve [for them], as the rest do who have no hope [beyond the grave].

14For since we believe that Jesus died and rose again, even so God will also bring with Him through Jesus those who have fallen asleep [ [b]in death].

15For this we declare to you by the Lord's [own] word, that we who are alive and remain until the coming of the Lord, shall in no way precede [into His presence] *or* have any advantage at all over those who have previously fallen asleep [in Him [c]in death].

16For the Lord Himself will descend from heaven with a loud cry of summons, with the shout of an archangel, and with the blast of the trumpet of God. And those who have departed this life in Christ will rise first.

17Then we, the still living who remain [on the earth], shall simultaneously be caught up along with (the resurrected dead) in the clouds to meet the Lord in the air; and so always—through the eternity of the eternities—we shall be with the Lord!

18Therefore comfort *and* encourage one another with these words.

**5** BUT AS to the suitable times and the precise seasons *and* dates, brethren, you have no necessity for anything being written to you.

2For you yourselves know perfectly well that the day of the Lord['s return] will come [as unexpectedly and suddenly] as a thief in the night.

3When people are saying, All is well and secure, *and,* There is peace and safety, then in a moment unforeseen destruction (ruin and death) will come upon them as suddenly as labor pains come upon a woman with child; and they shall by no means escape, *for* there will be no escape.

4But you are not in [given up to the power of] darkness, brethren, for that day to overtake you by surprise like a thief.

5For you are all sons of light and sons of the day; we do not belong either to the night or to darkness.

6Accordingly then, let us not sleep, as the rest do, but let us keep wide awake (alert, watchful, cautious and on our guard and let us be sober (calm, collected and circumspect).

7For those who sleep sleep at night, and those who are drunk get drunk at night.

8But we belong to the day, therefore let us be sober, and put on the breastplate (corslet) of faith and love and for a helmet the hope of salvation.

9For God has not appointed us to [incur His] wrath—He did not select us to condemn us—but [that we might] obtain [His] salvation through our Lord Jesus Christ, the Messiah,

10Who died for us so that whether we are still alive or are dead [at Christ's appearing] we might live together with Him *and* share His life.

11Therefore encourage (admonish, exhort) one another and edify—strengthen and build up—one another, just as you are doing.

**AMP**   [a] Abbott-Smith.   [b] Cremer.   [c] Cremer.

## New American Standard

9¶ Now as to the love of the brethren, you have no need for
*anyone* to write to you, for you yourselves are taught by God to love
one another;
10for indeed you do practice it toward all the brethren who are
in all Macedonia. But we urge you, brethren, to excel still more,
11and to make it your ambition to lead a quiet life and attend
to your own business and work with your hands, just as we
commanded you;
12so that you may behave properly toward outsiders and not be
in any need.

*Those Who Died in Christ*

13¶ But we do not want you to be uninformed, brethren, about
those who are asleep, that you may not grieve, as do the rest who
have no hope.
14For if we believe that Jesus died and rose again, even so God
will bring with Him those who have fallen asleep in Jesus.
15For this we say to you by the word of the Lord, that we who
are alive, and remain until the coming of the Lord, shall not precede those who have fallen asleep.
16For the Lord Himself will descend from heaven with a shout,
with the voice of *the* archangel, and with the trumpet of God; and
the dead in Christ shall rise first.
17Then we who are alive and remain shall be caught up together
with them in the clouds to meet the Lord in the air, and thus we
shall always be with the Lord.
18Therefore comfort one another with these words.

*The Day of the Lord*

5 NOW AS to the times and the epochs, brethren, you have no
need of anything to be written to you.
2For you yourselves know full well that the day of the Lord will
come just like a thief in the night.
3While they are saying, "Peace and safety!" then destruction
will come upon them suddenly like birth pangs upon a woman
with child; and they shall not escape.
4But you, brethren, are not in darkness, that the day should
overtake you like a thief;
5for you are all sons of light and sons of day. We are not of
night nor of darkness;
6so then let us not sleep as others do, but let us be alert and
[d]sober.
7For those who sleep do their sleeping at night, and those who
get drunk get drunk at night.
8But since we are of *the* day, let us be [e]sober, having put on
the breastplate of faith and love, and as a helmet, the hope of
salvation.
9For God has not destined us for wrath, but for obtaining
salvation through our Lord Jesus Christ,
10who died for us, that whether we are awake or asleep, we may
live together with Him.
11Therefore encourage one another, and build up one another,
just as you also are doing.

NAS [d] Or, *self-controlled* [e] Or, *self-controlled*

## New International

9Now about brotherly love we do not need to write to you, for
you yourselves have been taught by God to love each other. 10And
in fact, you do love all the brothers throughout Macedonia. Yet we
urge you, brothers, to do so more and more.
11Make it your ambition to lead a quiet life, to mind your own
business and to work with your hands, just as we told you, 12so
that your daily life may win the respect of outsiders and so that
you will not be dependent on anybody.

*The Coming of the Lord*

13Brothers, we do not want you to be ignorant about those who
fall asleep, or to grieve like the rest of men, who have no hope.
14We believe that Jesus died and rose again and so we believe that
God will bring with Jesus those who have fallen asleep in him.
15According to the Lord's own word, we tell you that we who are
still alive, who are left till the coming of the Lord, will certainly not
precede those who have fallen asleep. 16For the Lord himself will
come down from heaven, with a loud command, with the voice of
the archangel and with the trumpet call of God, and the dead in
Christ will rise first. 17After that, we who are still alive and are left
will be caught up together with them in the clouds to meet the Lord
in the air. And so we will be with the Lord forever. 18Therefore
encourage each other with these words.

5 NOW, BROTHERS, about times and dates we do not need to
write to you, 2for you know very well that the day of the Lord
will come like a thief in the night. 3While people are saying, "Peace
and safety," destruction will come on them suddenly, as labor
pains on a pregnant woman, and they will not escape.
4But you, brothers, are not in darkness so that this day should
surprise you like a thief. 5You are all sons of the light and sons of
the day. We do not belong to the night or to the darkness. 6So then,
let us not be like others, who are asleep, but let us be alert and
self-controlled. 7For those who sleep, sleep at night, and those
who get drunk, get drunk at night. 8But since we belong to the day,
let us be self-controlled, putting on faith and love as a breastplate,
and the hope of salvation as a helmet. 9For God did not appoint
us to suffer wrath but to receive salvation through our Lord Jesus
Christ. 10He died for us so that, whether we are awake or asleep,
we may live together with him. 11Therefore encourage one another
and build each other up, just as in fact you are doing.

## King James

12And we beseech you, brethren, to know them which labour among you, and are over you in the Lord, and admonish you;
13And to esteem them very highly in love for their work's sake. *And* be at peace among yourselves.
14Now we exhort you, brethren, warn them that are unruly, comfort the feebleminded, support the weak, be patient toward all *men*.
15See that none render evil for evil unto any *man*; but ever follow that which is good, both among yourselves, and to all *men*.
16Rejoice evermore.
17Pray without ceasing.
18In every thing give thanks: for this is the will of God in Christ Jesus concerning you.
19Quench not the Spirit.
20Despise not prophesyings.
21Prove all things; hold fast that which is good.
22Abstain from all appearance of evil.
23And the very God of peace sanctify you wholly; and *I pray God* your whole spirit and soul and body be preserved blameless unto the coming of our Lord Jesus Christ.
24Faithful *is* he that calleth you, who also will do *it*.
25Brethren, pray for us.
26Greet all the brethren with an holy kiss.
27I charge you by the Lord that this epistle be read unto all the holy brethren.
28The grace of our Lord Jesus Christ *be* with you. Amen.

## Amplified

12Now also we beseech you, brethren, get to know those who labor among you—recognize them for what they are, acknowledge and appreciate and respect them all—your leaders who are over you in the Lord, and those who warn *and* kindly reprove *and* exhort you.

13And hold them in very high and most affectionate esteem in [intelligent and sympathetic] appreciation of their work. Be at peace among yourselves.

14And we earnestly beseech you, brethren, admonish (warn and seriously advise) those who are out of line—the loafers, the disorderly and the unruly; encourage the timid *and* fainthearted, help *and* give your support to the weak souls [and] be very patient with everybody—always keeping your temper. [Isa. 35:4.]

15See that none of you repays another with evil for evil, but always aim to show kindness *and* seek to do good to one another and to everybody.

16Be happy [in your faith] *and* rejoice *and* be glad-hearted continually—always.

17Be unceasing in prayer—praying perseveringly;

18Thank [God] in everything—no matter what the circumstances may be, be thankful and give thanks; for this is the will of God for you [who are] in Christ Jesus [the Revealer and Mediator of that will].

19Do not quench (suppress or subdue) the (Holy) Spirit.

20Do not spurn the gifts *and* utterances of the prophets—do not depreciate prophetic revelations nor despise inspired instruction or exhortation or warning.

21But test *and* prove all things [until you can recognize] what is good; [to that] hold fast.

22Abstain from evil—shrink from it and keep aloof from it—in whatever form *or* whatever kind it may be.

23And may the God of peace Himself sanctify you through and through—that is, separate you from profane things, make you pure and wholly consecrated to God—and may your spirit and soul and body be preserved sound *and* complete [and found] blameless at the coming of our Lord Jesus Christ, the Messiah.

24Faithful is He Who is calling you [to Himself] *and* utterly trustworthy, and He will also do it [that is, fulfill His call by hallowing and keeping you].

25Brethren, pray for us.

26Greet all the brethren with a sacred kiss.

27I solemnly charge you [in the name of] the Lord to have this letter read before all the brethren.

28The grace (the unmerited favor and blessings) of our Lord Jesus Christ, the Messiah, be with you all. *Amen, so be it.*

## New American Standard

*Christian Conduct*

12¶ But we request of you, brethren, that you appreciate those who diligently labor among you, and have charge over you in the Lord and give you instruction,

13and that you esteem them very highly in love because of their work. Live in peace with one another.

14And we urge you, brethren, admonish the unruly, encourage the fainthearted, help the weak, be patient with all men.

15See that no one repays another with evil for evil, but always seek after that which is good for one another and for all men.

16Rejoice always;

17pray without ceasing;

18in everything give thanks; for this is God's will for you in Christ Jesus.

19Do not quench the Spirit;

20do not despise prophetic [a]utterances.

21But examine everything *carefully;* hold fast to that which is good;

22abstain from every [b]form of evil.

23¶ Now may the God of peace Himself sanctify you entirely; and may your spirit and soul and body be preserved complete, without blame at the coming of our Lord Jesus Christ.

24Faithful is He who calls you, and He also will bring it to pass.

25¶ Brethren, pray for us [c].

26¶ Greet all the brethren with a holy kiss.

27I adjure you by the Lord to have this letter read to all the brethren.

28¶ The grace of our Lord Jesus Christ be with you.

NAS [a] Or, *gifts* [b] Or, *appearance* [c] Some mss. add *also*

## New International

*Final Instructions*

12Now we ask you, brothers, to respect those who work hard
among you, who are over you in the Lord and who admonish you.
13Hold them in the highest regard in love because of their work.
Live in peace with each other. 14And we urge you, brothers, warn
those who are idle, encourage the timid, help the weak, be patient
with everyone. 15Make sure that nobody pays back wrong for
wrong, but always try to be kind to each other and to everyone
else.

16Be joyful always; 17pray continually; 18give thanks in all circumstances, for this is God's will for you in Christ Jesus.

19Do not put out the Spirit's fire; 20do not treat prophecies with
contempt. 21Test everything. Hold on to the good. 22Avoid every
kind of evil.

23May God himself, the God of peace, sanctify you through and
through. May your whole spirit, soul and body be kept blameless
at the coming of our Lord Jesus Christ. 24The one who calls you
is faithful and he will do it.

25Brothers, pray for us. 26Greet all the brothers with a holy kiss.
27I charge you before the Lord to have this letter read to all the
brothers.

28The grace of our Lord Jesus Christ be with you.

## King James

THE SECOND EPISTLE OF

PAUL THE APOSTLE TO THE

# Thessalonians

**1** PAUL, AND Silvanus, and Timotheus, unto the church of the Thessalonians in God our Father and the Lord Jesus Christ:

2Grace unto you, and peace, from God our Father and the Lord Jesus Christ.

3We are bound to thank God always for you, brethren, as it is meet, because that your faith groweth exceedingly, and the charity of every one of you all toward each other aboundeth;

4So that we ourselves glory in you in the churches of God for your patience and faith in all your persecutions and tribulations that ye endure:

5 *Which is* a manifest token of the righteous judgment of God, that ye may be counted worthy of the kingdom of God, for which ye also suffer:

6Seeing *it is* a righteous thing with God to recompense tribulation to them that trouble you;

7And to you who are troubled rest with us, when the Lord Jesus shall be revealed from heaven with his mighty angels,

8In flaming fire taking vengeance on them that know not God, and that obey not the gospel of our Lord Jesus Christ:

9Who shall be punished with everlasting destruction from the presence of the Lord, and from the glory of his power;

10When he shall come to be glorified in his saints, and to be admired in all them that believe (because our testimony among you was believed) in that day.

11Wherefore also we pray always for you, that our God would count you worthy of *this* calling, and fulfil all the good pleasure of *his* goodness, and the work of faith with power:

12That the name of our Lord Jesus Christ may be glorified in you, and ye in him, according to the grace of our God and the Lord Jesus Christ.

## Amplified

THE SECOND LETTER OF

PAUL TO THE

# Thessalonians

**1** PAUL, SILVANUS (Silas) and Timothy to the church (assembly) of the Thessalonians in God our Father and the Lord Jesus Christ, the Messiah, the Anointed One:

2Grace (unmerited favor) be to you and heart peace from God the Father and the Lord Jesus Christ, the Messiah, the Anointed One.

3We ought *and* indeed are obligated [as those in debt] to give thanks always to God for you, brethren, as is fitting, because your faith is growing exceedingly, and the love of every one of you each toward the others is increasing *and* abounds.

4And this is a cause of our mentioning you with pride among the churches (assemblies) of God for your steadfastness—your unflinching endurance and patience—and your firm faith in the midst of all the persecutions and crushing distresses *and* afflictions under which you are holding up.

5This is positive proof of the just *and* right judgment of God to the end that you may be deemed deserving of His kingdom—a plain token of His fair verdict [which designs] that you should be made *and* counted worthy of the kingdom of God—for the sake of which you are also suffering.

6[It is a fair decision] since it is a righteous thing with God to repay with distress *and* affliction those who distress *and* afflict you,

7And to [ [a]recompense] you who are so distressed *and* afflicted [by granting you] relief *and* rest along with us—your fellow sufferers—when the Lord Jesus is revealed from heaven with His mighty angels in a flame of fire;

8To deal out retribution—chastisement and vengeance—upon those who do not know *or* perceive *or* become acquainted with God, and [upon those] who ignore *and* refuse to obey the Gospel of our Lord Jesus *Christ.*

9Such people will pay the penalty *and* suffer the punishment of everlasting ruin (destruction and perdition) and [eternal exclusion and banishment] from the presence of the Lord and from the glory of His power,

10When He comes to be glorified in His saints. (That is, on that day He will be made more glorious in His consecrated people) and [He will] be marveled at *and* admired [in His glory reflected] in all who have believed—who have adhered to, trusted in and relied on Him—because our witnessing among you was confidently accepted *and* believed [and confirmed in your lives].

11With this in view we constantly pray for you, that our God may deem *and* count you worthy of [your] calling and [His] every gracious purpose of goodness, and with power complete in every particular [your] work of faith [faith which is that [b]leaning of the whole human personality on God in absolute trust and confidence in His power, wisdom and goodness].

12Thus may the name of our Lord Jesus *Christ* be glorified *and* become more glorious through *and* in you, and may you [also be glorified] in Him according to the grace (favor and blessing) of our God and the Lord Jesus Christ, the Messiah, the Anointed One.

**AMP** [a] Jamieson, Fausset and Brown. [b] Souter's "Pocket Lexicon to the Greek New Testament."

## New American Standard

# 2 Thessalonians

*Thanksgiving for Faith and Perseverance*

**1** PAUL AND Silvanus and Timothy to the church of the Thessalonians in God our Father and the Lord Jesus Christ:

2 Grace to you and peace from God the Father and the Lord Jesus Christ.

3 ¶ We ought always to give thanks to God for you, brethren, as is *only* fitting, because your faith is greatly enlarged, and the love of each one of you toward one another grows *ever* greater;

4 therefore, we ourselves speak proudly of you among the churches of God for your perseverance and faith in the midst of all your persecutions and afflictions which you endure.

5 *This is* a plain indication of God's righteous judgment so that you may be considered worthy of the kingdom of God, for which indeed you are suffering.

6 For after all it is *only* just for God to repay with affliction those who afflict you,

7 and *to give* relief to you who are afflicted and to us as well when the Lord Jesus shall be revealed from heaven with His mighty angels in flaming fire,

8 dealing out retribution to those who do not know God and to those who do not obey the gospel of our Lord Jesus.

9 And these will pay the penalty of eternal destruction, away from the presence of the Lord and from the glory of His power,

10 when He comes to be glorified in His saints on that day, and to be marveled at among all who have believed—for our testimony to you was believed.

11 To this end also we pray for you always that our God may count you worthy of your calling, and fulfill every desire for goodness and the work of faith with power;

12 in order that the name of our Lord Jesus may be glorified in you, and you in Him, according to the grace of our God and the Lord Jesus Christ.

## New International

# 2 Thessalonians

**1** PAUL, SILAS[c] and Timothy,

To the church of the Thessalonians in God our Father and the Lord Jesus Christ:

2 Grace and peace to you from God the Father and the Lord Jesus Christ.

*Thanksgiving and Prayer*

3 We ought always to thank God for you, brothers, and rightly so, because your faith is growing more and more, and the love every one of you has for each other is increasing. 4 Therefore, among God's churches we boast about your perseverance and faith in all the persecutions and trials you are enduring.

5 All this is evidence that God's judgment is right, and as a result you will be counted worthy of the kingdom of God, for which you are suffering. 6 God is just: He will pay back trouble to those who trouble you 7 and give relief to you who are troubled, and to us as well. This will happen when the Lord Jesus is revealed from heaven in blazing fire with his powerful angels. 8 He will punish those who do not know God and do not obey the gospel of our Lord Jesus. 9 They will be punished with everlasting destruction and shut out from the presence of the Lord and from the majesty of his power 10 on the day he comes to be glorified in his holy people and to be marveled at among all those who have believed. This includes you, because you believed our testimony to you.

11 With this in mind, we constantly pray for you, that our God may count you worthy of his calling, and that by his power he may fulfill every good purpose of yours and every act prompted by your faith. 12 We pray this so that the name of our Lord Jesus may be glorified in you, and you in him, according to the grace of our God and the Lord Jesus Christ.[d]

**NIV** [c] *1* Greek *Silvanus,* a variant of *Silas* [d] *12* Or *God and Lord, Jesus Christ*

## King James

**2** NOW WE beseech you, brethren, by the coming of our Lord
Jesus Christ, and *by* our gathering together unto him,
2That ye be not soon shaken in mind, or be troubled, neither
by spirit, nor by word, nor by letter as from us, as that the day of
Christ is at hand.
3Let no man deceive you by any means: for *that day shall not*
*come,* except there come a falling away first, and that man of sin
be revealed, the son of perdition;
4Who opposeth and exalteth himself above all that is called
God, or that is worshipped; so that he as God sitteth in the temple
of God, showing himself that he is God.
5Remember ye not, that, when I was yet with you, I told you
these things?
6And now ye know what withholdeth that he might be revealed
in his time.
7For the mystery of iniquity doth already work: only he who
now letteth *will let,* until he be taken out of the way.
8And then shall that Wicked be revealed, whom the Lord shall
consume with the spirit of his mouth, and shall destroy with the
brightness of his coming:
9 *Even him,* whose coming is after the working of Satan with all
power and signs and lying wonders,
10And with all deceivableness of unrighteousness in them that
perish; because they received not the love of the truth, that they
might be saved.
11And for this cause God shall send them strong delusion, that
they should believe a lie:
12That they all might be damned who believed not the truth, but
had pleasure in unrighteousness.
13But we are bound to give thanks always to God for you,
brethren beloved of the Lord, because God hath from the beginning chosen you to salvation through sanctification of the Spirit
and belief of the truth:
14Whereunto he called you by our gospel, to the obtaining of
the glory of our Lord Jesus Christ.
15Therefore, brethren, stand fast, and hold the traditions which
ye have been taught, whether by word, or our epistle.
16Now our Lord Jesus Christ himself, and God, even our Father, which hath loved us, and hath given *us* everlasting consolation and good hope through grace,
17Comfort your hearts, and stablish you in every good word
and work.

## Amplified

**2** BUT RELATIVE to the coming of our Lord Jesus Christ, the
Messiah, and our gathering together to [meet] Him, we beg
you, brethren,
2Not to allow your minds to be quickly unsettled *or* disturbed
or kept excited *or* alarmed, whether it be by some [pretended]
revelation of [the] Spirit or by word or by letter [alleged to be] from
us, to the effect that the day of the Lord has [already] arrived *and*
is here.
3Let no one deceive *or* beguile you in any way, for that day will
not come except the [a]apostasy comes first—that is, unless the
[predicted] great [b]falling away of those who have professed to be
Christians has come—and the man of lawlessness (sin) is revealed,
who is the son of doom (of perdition), [I Tim. 4:1; Dan. 7:25; 8:25.]
4Who opposes and exalts himself so proudly *and* insolently
against *and* over all that is called God or that is worshiped, [even
to his actually] taking his seat in the temple of God, proclaiming
that he himself is God. [Dan. 11:36, 37; Ezek. 28:2.]
5Do you not recollect that when I was still with you I told you
these things?
6And now you know what is restraining him [from being revealed at this time]; it is so that he may be manifested (revealed)
in his own [appointed] time.
7For the mystery of lawlessness—that hidden principle of rebellion against constituted authority—is already at work in the world,
[but it is] restrained only until [c]he who restrains is taken out of the
way.
8And then the lawless one (the Antichrist) will be revealed and
the Lord Jesus will slay him with the breath of His mouth and bring
him to an end by His appearing *at* His coming. [Isa. 11:4.]
9The coming [of the lawless one, the Antichrist] is through the
activity *and* working of Satan, and will be attended by great power
and with all sorts of [pretended] miracles and signs *and* delusive
marvels—[all of them] lying wonders—
10And by unlimited seduction to evil *and* with all wicked deception for those who are (going to perdition,) perishing because they
did not welcome the Truth *but* refused to love it that they might
be saved.
11Therefore God sends upon them a misleading influence, a
working of error *and* a strong delusion to make them believe what
is false,
12In order that all may be judged *and* condemned who did not
believe—who refused to adhere to, trust in and rely on—the Truth,
but [instead] took pleasure in unrighteousness.
13But we, brethren beloved by the Lord, ought *and* are obligated
[as those who are in debt] to give thanks always to God for you,
because God chose you from the beginning [ [d]to be the first con-
verts] for salvation through the sanctifying work of the (Holy)
Spirit and [your] belief in—adherence to, trust in and reliance
on—the Truth.
14[It was] to this end that He called you through our Gospel, so
that you may obtain *and* share in the glory of our Lord Jesus Christ,
the Messiah.
15So then, brethren, stand firm and hold fast to the traditions
*and* instructions which you were taught by us, whether by our
word of mouth or by letter.
16Now may our Lord Jesus Christ Himself, and God our Father,
Who loved us and gave us everlasting consolation *and* encouragement and well-founded hope through [His] grace (unmerited favor),
17Comfort and encourage your hearts and strengthen them—
make them steadfast and keep them unswerving—in every good
work and word.

**AMP** [a] A possible rendering of apostasia is "departure [of the church]." [b] A possible rendering of apostasia is "departure [of the church]." [c] Many believe this one who restrains the Antichrist to be the Holy Spirit, Who lives in all believers and will be removed with them at Christ's coming. A majority think it refers to the Roman Empire. [d] Many ancient authorities so read.

## New American Standard

*Man of Lawlessness*

2 NOW WE request you, brethren, with regard to the coming of our Lord Jesus Christ, and our gathering together to Him,
2that you may not be quickly shaken from your composure or be disturbed either by a spirit or a message or a letter as if from us, to the effect that the day of the Lord has come.
3Let no one in any way deceive you, for *it will not come* unless the [e]apostasy comes first, and the man of lawlessness is revealed, the son of destruction,
4who opposes and exalts himself above every so-called god or object of worship, so that he takes his seat in the temple of God, displaying himself as being God.
5Do you not remember that while I was still with you, I was telling you these things?
6And you know what restrains him now, so that in his time he may be revealed.
7For the mystery of lawlessness is already at work; only he who now restrains *will do so* until he is taken out of the way.
8And then that lawless one will be revealed whom the Lord will slay with the breath of His mouth and bring to an end by the appearance of His coming;
9 *that is,* the one whose coming is in accord with the activity of Satan, with all power and signs and false wonders,
10and with all the deception of wickedness for those who perish, because they did not receive the love of the truth so as to be saved.
11And for this reason God will send upon them a deluding influence so that they might believe what is false,
12in order that they all may be judged who did not believe the truth, but took pleasure in wickedness.
13¶ But we should always give thanks to God for you, brethren beloved by the Lord, because God has chosen you [f]from the beginning for salvation through sanctification by the Spirit and faith in the truth.
14And it was for this He called you through our gospel, that you may gain the glory of our Lord Jesus Christ.
15So then, brethren, stand firm and hold to the traditions which you were taught, whether by word *of mouth* or by letter from us.
16¶ Now may our Lord Jesus Christ Himself and God our Father, who has loved us and given us eternal comfort and good hope by grace,
17comfort and strengthen your hearts in every good work and word.

NAS [e] Or, *falling away* from the faith [f] Some ancient mss. read *first fruits*

## New International

*The Man of Lawlessness*

2 CONCERNING THE coming of our Lord Jesus Christ and our
being gathered to him, we ask you, brothers, 2not to become
easily unsettled or alarmed by some prophecy, report or letter supposed to have come from us, saying that the day of the Lord
has already come. 3Don't let anyone deceive you in any way, for
⌊that day will not come⌋ until the rebellion occurs and the man of
lawlessness[g] is revealed, the man doomed to destruction. 4He will
oppose and will exalt himself over everything that is called God or is worshiped, so that he sets himself up in God's temple, proclaiming himself to be God.
5Don't you remember that when I was with you I used to tell
you these things? 6And now you know what is holding him back,
so that he may be revealed at the proper time. 7For the secret
power of lawlessness is already at work; but the one who now holds it back will continue to do so till he is taken out of the way.
8And then the lawless one will be revealed, whom the Lord Jesus will overthrow with the breath of his mouth and destroy by the
splendor of his coming. 9The coming of the lawless one will be in
accordance with the work of Satan displayed in all kinds of counterfeit miracles, signs and wonders, 10and in every sort of evil that
deceives those who are perishing. They perish because they refused to love the truth and so be saved. 11For this reason God
sends them a powerful delusion so that they will believe the lie
12and so that all will be condemned who have not believed the truth but have delighted in wickedness.

*Stand Firm*

13But we ought always to thank God for you, brothers loved by the Lord, because from the beginning God chose you[h] to be saved through the sanctifying work of the Spirit and through belief in the
truth. 14He called you to this through our gospel, that you might
share in the glory of our Lord Jesus Christ. 15So then, brothers,
stand firm and hold to the teachings[i] we passed on to you, whether by word of mouth or by letter.
16May our Lord Jesus Christ himself and God our Father, who loved us and by his grace gave us eternal encouragement and good
hope, 17encourage your hearts and strengthen you in every good deed and word.

NIV [g] 3 Some manuscripts *sin* [h] 13 Some manuscripts *because God chose you as his firstfruits* [i] 15 Or *traditions*

## King James

**3** FINALLY, BRETHREN, pray for us, that the word of the Lord
may have *free* course, and be glorified, even as *it is* with you:
2 And that we may be delivered from unreasonable and wicked
men: for all *men* have not faith.
3 But the Lord is faithful, who shall stablish you, and keep *you*
from evil.
4 And we have confidence in the Lord touching you, that ye
both do and will do the things which we command you.
5 And the Lord direct your hearts into the love of God, and into
the patient waiting for Christ.
6 Now we command you, brethren, in the name of our Lord
Jesus Christ, that ye withdraw yourselves from every brother that
walketh disorderly, and not after the tradition which he received
of us.
7 For yourselves know how ye ought to follow us: for we
behaved not ourselves disorderly among you;
8 Neither did we eat any man's bread for nought; but wrought
with labour and travail night and day, that we might not be chargeable to any of you:
9 Not because we have not power, but to make ourselves an
example unto you to follow us.
10 For even when we were with you, this we commanded you,
that if any would not work, neither should he eat.
11 For we hear that there are some which walk among you
disorderly, working not at all, but are busybodies.
12 Now them that are such we command and exhort by our Lord
Jesus Christ, that with quietness they work, and eat their own
bread.
13 But ye, brethren, be not weary in well doing.
14 And if any man obey not our word by this epistle, note that
man, and have no company with him, that he may be ashamed.
15 Yet count *him* not as an enemy, but admonish *him* as a brother.
16 Now the Lord of peace himself give you peace always by all
means. The Lord *be* with you all.
17 The salutation of Paul with mine own hand, which is the
token in every epistle: so I write.
18 The grace of our Lord Jesus Christ *be* with you all. Amen.

## Amplified

**3** FURTHERMORE, BRETHREN, do pray for us, that the Word
of the Lord may speed on (spread rapidly and run its course)
and be glorified (extolled) *and* triumph, even as [it has done] with
you.
2 And that we may be delivered from perverse (improper, unrighteous) and wicked (actively malicious) men, for not everybody
has faith *and* is held by it.
3 Yet the Lord is faithful and He will strengthen [you] *and* set you
on a firm foundation and guard you from the evil [one].
4 And we have confidence in the Lord concerning you, that you
are doing and will continue to do the things which we suggest *and*
with which we charge you.
5 May the Lord direct your hearts into [realizing and showing]
the love of God, and into the steadfastness *and* patience of Christ
*in* [a]waiting for His return.
6 Now we charge you, brethren, in the name *and* on the authority of our Lord Jesus Christ, the Messiah, that you withdraw *and*
keep away from every brother (fellow believer) who is slack in the
performance of duty *and* is disorderly, living as a shirker *and* not
walking in accord with the traditions *and* instructions that you
have received from us.
7 For you yourselves know how it is necessary to imitate our
example, for we were not disorderly *or* shirking of duty when we
were with you—we were not idle.
8 Nor did we eat any one's bread without paying for it, but with
toil and struggle we worked night and day, that we might not be
a burden *or* impose on any of you [for our support].
9 [It was] not because we do not have a right [to such support],
but [we wished] to make ourselves an example for you to follow.
10 For while we were yet with you we gave you this rule *and*
charge: If any one will not work, neither let him eat.
11 Indeed, we hear that some among you are disorderly—that
they are passing their lives in idleness, neglectful of duty—being
busy with other people's affairs instead of their own and doing no
work.
12 Now we charge and exhort such persons [as [b]ministers in
Him exhorting those] in the Lord Jesus Christ, the Messiah, that
they work in quietness and earn their own food *and* other necessities.
13 And as for you, brethren, do not be weary *or* lose heart in
doing right [but continue in well-doing without weakening].
14 But if any one [in the church] refuses to obey what we say in
this letter, take note of that person, and do not associate with him,
that he may be ashamed.
15 Do not regard him as an enemy, but simply admonish and
warn him as [being still] a brother.
16 Now may the Lord of peace Himself grant you His peace [the
peace of His kingdom] at all times and in all ways—under all
circumstances and conditions, whatever comes. The Lord [be]
with you all.
17 I, Paul, write you this final greeting with my own hand. This
is the mark *and* sign [that it is not a forgery] in every letter of mine.
It is the way I write—my handwriting and signature.
18 The grace (spiritual blessing and favor) of our Lord Jesus
Christ, the Messiah, be with you all. *Amen, so be it.*

**AMP** [a] Alternate translation. (Thayer.) [b] Jamieson, Fausset and Brown.

## New American Standard

*Exhortation*

**3** FINALLY, BRETHREN, pray for us that the word of the Lord may spread rapidly and be glorified, just as *it did* also with you;

2and that we may be delivered from perverse and evil men; for not all have faith.

3But the Lord is faithful, and He will strengthen and protect you from the evil *one.*

4And we have confidence in the Lord concerning you, that you are doing and will *continue to* do what we command.

5And may the Lord direct your hearts into the love of God and into the steadfastness of Christ.

6¶ Now we command you, brethren, in the name of our Lord Jesus Christ, that you keep aloof from every brother who leads an unruly life and not according to the tradition which you received from us.

7For you yourselves know how you ought to follow our example, because we did not act in an undisciplined manner among you,

8nor did we eat anyone's bread without paying for it, but with labor and hardship we *kept* working night and day so that we might not be a burden to any of you;

9not because we do not have the right *to this,* but in order to offer ourselves as a model for you, that you might follow our example.

10For even when we were with you, we used to give you this order: if anyone will not work, neither let him eat.

11For we hear that some among you are leading an undisciplined life, doing no work at all, but acting like busybodies.

12Now such persons we command and exhort in the Lord Jesus Christ to work in quiet fashion and eat their own bread.

13But as for you, brethren, do not grow weary of doing good.

14And if anyone does not obey our instruction in this letter, take special note of that man and do not associate with him, so that he may be put to shame.

15And *yet* do not regard him as an enemy, but admonish him as a brother.

16¶ Now may the Lord of peace Himself continually grant you peace in every circumstance. The Lord be with you all!

17¶ I, Paul, write this greeting with my own hand, and this is a distinguishing mark in every letter; this is the way I write.

18The grace of our Lord Jesus Christ be with you all.

## New International

*Request for Prayer*

**3** FINALLY, BROTHERS, pray for us that the message of the
Lord may spread rapidly and be honored, just as it was with
you. 2And pray that we may be delivered from wicked and evil
men, for not everyone has faith. 3But the Lord is faithful, and he
will strengthen and protect you from the evil one. 4We have confidence in the Lord that you are doing and will continue to do the
things we command. 5May the Lord direct your hearts into God's
love and Christ's perseverance.

*Warning Against Idleness*

6In the name of the Lord Jesus Christ, we command you, brothers, to keep away from every brother who is idle and does not live
according to the teaching[c] you received from us. 7For you yourselves know how you ought to follow our example. We were not
idle when we were with you, 8nor did we eat anyone's food
without paying for it. On the contrary, we worked night and day,
laboring and toiling so that we would not be a burden to any of
you. 9We did this, not because we do not have the right to such
help, but in order to make ourselves a model for you to follow.
10For even when we were with you, we gave you this rule: "If a
man will not work, he shall not eat."

11We hear that some among you are idle. They are not busy;
they are busybodies. 12Such people we command and urge in the
Lord Jesus Christ to settle down and earn the bread they eat. 13And
as for you, brothers, never tire of doing what is right.

14If anyone does not obey our instruction in this letter, take
special note of him. Do not associate with him, in order that he
may feel ashamed. 15Yet do not regard him as an enemy, but warn
him as a brother.

*Final Greetings*

16Now may the Lord of peace himself give you peace at all times
and in every way. The Lord be with all of you.

17I, Paul, write this greeting in my own hand, which is the
distinguishing mark in all my letters. This is how I write.

18The grace of our Lord Jesus Christ be with you all.

**NIV** c 6 Or *tradition*

## King James

THE FIRST EPISTLE OF

PAUL THE APOSTLE TO

# Timothy

1 PAUL, AN apostle of Jesus Christ by the commandment of God our Saviour, and Lord Jesus Christ, *which is* our hope;

2 Unto Timothy, *my* own son in the faith: Grace, mercy, *and* peace, from God our Father and Jesus Christ our Lord.

3 As I besought thee to abide still at Ephesus, when I went into Macedonia, that thou mightest charge some that they teach no other doctrine,

4 Neither give heed to fables and endless genealogies, which minister questions, rather than godly edifying which is in faith: *so do*.

5 Now the end of the commandment is charity out of a pure heart, and *of* a good conscience, and *of* faith unfeigned:

6 From which some having swerved have turned aside unto vain jangling;

7 Desiring to be teachers of the law; understanding neither what they say, nor whereof they affirm.

8 But we know that the law *is* good, if a man use it lawfully;

9 Knowing this, that the law is not made for a righteous man, but for the lawless and disobedient, for the ungodly and for sinners, for unholy and profane, for murderers of fathers and murderers of mothers, for manslayers,

10 For whoremongers, for them that defile themselves with mankind, for menstealers, for liars, for perjured persons, and if there be any other thing that is contrary to sound doctrine;

11 According to the glorious gospel of the blessed God, which was committed to my trust.

12 And I thank Christ Jesus our Lord, who hath enabled me, for that he counted me faithful, putting me into the ministry;

13 Who was before a blasphemer, and a persecutor, and injurious: but I obtained mercy, because I did *it* ignorantly in unbelief.

14 And the grace of our Lord was exceeding abundant with faith and love which is in Christ Jesus.

## Amplified

THE FIRST LETTER OF

PAUL TO

# Timothy

1 PAUL, AN apostle (special messenger) of Christ Jesus by appointment *and* command of God our Savior and of Christ Jesus, the Messiah, our Hope,

2 To Timothy, my true son in the faith: Grace (spiritual blessing and favor), mercy and heart peace [be yours] from God the Father and Christ Jesus our Lord.

3 As I urged you when I was on my way to Macedonia, stay on where you are at Ephesus in order that you may warn *and* admonish *and* charge certain individuals not to teach any different doctrine,

4 Nor to give importance to *or* occupy themselves with legends (fables, myths) and endless genealogies which foster *and* promote useless speculations *and* questionings, rather than acceptance in faith of God's administration *and* the divine training that is in faith, [ [a]in that leaning of the entire human personality on God in absolute trust and confidence];

5 Whereas the object *and* purpose of our instruction *and* charge is love which springs from a pure heart and a good (clear) conscience and sincere (unfeigned) faith.

6 But certain individuals have missed the mark on this very matter [and] have wandered away into vain arguments *and* discussions *and* purposeless talk.

7 They are ambitious to be doctors of the Law—teachers of the Mosaic ritual—but they have no understanding either of the words *and* terms they use or of the subjects about which they make [such] dogmatic assertions.

8 Now we recognize *and* know that the Law is good, if any one uses it lawfully—for the purpose for which it was designed;

9 Knowing *and* understanding this: that the Law is not enacted for the righteous—the upright and just, who are in right standing with God; but for the lawless and unruly, for the ungodly and sinful, for the irreverent and profane, for those who strike *and* beat *and* [even] murder fathers and strike *and* beat *and* [even] murder mothers; for manslayers,

10 [For] impure *and* immoral persons, those who abuse themselves with men, kidnapers, liars, perjurers and whatever else is opposed to wholesome teaching *and* sound doctrine,

11 As laid down by the glorious Gospel of the blessed God, with which I have been entrusted.

12 I give thanks to Him Who has granted me (the needed) strength *and* made me able [for this], Christ Jesus our Lord, because He has judged *and* counted me faithful *and* trustworthy, appointing me to [this stewardship of] the ministry.

13 Though I formerly blasphemed and persecuted and was shamefully *and* outrageously *and* aggressively insulting [to Him], nevertheless I obtained mercy because I had acted out of ignorance in unbelief.

14 And the grace (unmerited favor and blessing) of our Lord [actually] flowed out superabundantly *and* beyond measure for me, accompanied by faith and love that are [to be realized] in Christ Jesus.

**AMP** [a] Souter's "Pocket Lexicon to the Greek New Testament."

## New American Standard

# 1 Timothy

*Misleadings in Doctrine and Living*

**1** PAUL, AN apostle of Christ Jesus according to the commandment of God our Savior, and of Christ Jesus, *who is* our hope;
2to Timothy, *my* true child in *the* faith: Grace, mercy *and* peace from God the Father and Christ Jesus our Lord.
3¶ As I urged you upon my departure for Macedonia, remain on at Ephesus, in order that you may instruct certain men not to teach strange doctrines,
4nor to pay attention to myths and endless genealogies, which give rise to mere speculation rather than *furthering* the administration of God which is by faith.
5But the goal of our instruction is love from a pure heart and a good conscience and a sincere faith.
6For some men, straying from these things, have turned aside to fruitless discussion,
7wanting to be teachers of the Law, even though they do not understand either what they are saying or the matters about which they make confident assertions.
8But we know that the Law is good, if one uses it lawfully,
9realizing the fact that law is not made for a righteous man, but for those who are lawless and rebellious, for the ungodly and sinners, for the unholy and profane, for those who kill their fathers or mothers, for murderers
10and immoral men and homosexuals and kidnappers and liars and perjurers, and whatever else is contrary to sound teaching,
11according to the glorious gospel of the blessed God, with which I have been entrusted.
12¶ I thank Christ Jesus our Lord, who has strengthened me, because He considered me faithful, putting me into service;
13even though I was formerly a blasphemer and a persecutor and a violent aggressor. And yet I was shown mercy, because I acted ignorantly in unbelief;
14and the grace of our Lord was more than abundant, with the faith and love which are *found* in Christ Jesus.

## New International

# 1 Timothy

**1** PAUL, AN apostle of Christ Jesus by the command of God our Savior and of Christ Jesus our hope,

2To Timothy my true son in the faith:

Grace, mercy and peace from God the Father and Christ Jesus our Lord.

*Warning Against False Teachers of the Law*

3As I urged you when I went into Macedonia, stay there in
Ephesus so that you may command certain men not to teach false
doctrines any longer 4nor to devote themselves to myths and
endless genealogies. These promote controversies rather than
God's work—which is by faith. 5The goal of this command is love,
which comes from a pure heart and a good conscience and a
sincere faith. 6Some have wandered away from these and turned
to meaningless talk. 7They want to be teachers of the law, but they
do not know what they are talking about or what they so confidently affirm.

8We know that the law is good if one uses it properly. 9We also
know that law[b] is made not for the righteous but for lawbreakers
and rebels, the ungodly and sinful, the unholy and irreligious; for
those who kill their fathers or mothers, for murderers, 10for adulterers and perverts, for slave traders and liars and perjurers—and
for whatever else is contrary to the sound doctrine 11that conforms
to the glorious gospel of the blessed God, which he entrusted to
me.

*The Lord's Grace to Paul*

12I thank Christ Jesus our Lord, who has given me strength,
that he considered me faithful, appointing me to his service.
13Even though I was once a blasphemer and a persecutor and a
violent man, I was shown mercy because I acted in ignorance and
unbelief. 14The grace of our Lord was poured out on me abundantly, along with the faith and love that are in Christ Jesus.

NIV [b] 9 Or *that the law*

## King James

[15]This *is* a faithful saying, and worthy of all acceptation, that Christ Jesus came into the world to save sinners; of whom I am chief.
[16]Howbeit for this cause I obtained mercy, that in me first Jesus Christ might show forth all longsuffering, for a pattern to them which should hereafter believe on him to life everlasting.
[17]Now unto the King eternal, immortal, invisible, the only wise God, *be* honour and glory for ever and ever. Amen.
[18]This charge I commit unto thee, son Timothy, according to the prophecies which went before on thee, that thou by them mightest war a good warfare;
[19]Holding faith, and a good conscience; which some having put away concerning faith have made shipwreck:
[20]Of whom is Hymenaeus and Alexander; whom I have delivered unto Satan, that they may learn not to blaspheme.

**2** I EXHORT therefore, that, first of all, supplications, prayers, intercessions, *and* giving of thanks, be made for all men;
[2]For kings, and *for* all that are in authority; that we may lead a quiet and peaceable life in all godliness and honesty.
[3]For this *is* good and acceptable in the sight of God our Saviour;
[4]Who will have all men to be saved, and to come unto the knowledge of the truth.
[5]For *there is* one God, and one mediator between God and men, the man Christ Jesus;
[6]Who gave himself a ransom for all, to be testified in due time.
[7]Whereunto I am ordained a preacher, and an apostle, (I speak the truth in Christ, *and* lie not;) a teacher of the Gentiles in faith and verity.
[8]I will therefore that men pray every where, lifting up holy hands, without wrath and doubting.
[9]In like manner also, that women adorn themselves in modest apparel, with shamefacedness and sobriety; not with braided hair, or gold, or pearls, or costly array;
[10]But (which becometh women professing godliness) with good works.
[11]Let the woman learn in silence with all subjection.
[12]But I suffer not a woman to teach, nor to usurp authority over the man, but to be in silence.
[13]For Adam was first formed, then Eve.
[14]And Adam was not deceived, but the woman being deceived was in the transgression.
[15]Notwithstanding she shall be saved in childbearing, if they continue in faith and charity and holiness with sobriety.

## Amplified

[15]The saying is sure *and* true and worthy of full *and* universal acceptance, that Christ Jesus, the Messiah, came into the world to save sinners, of whom I am foremost.
[16]But I obtained mercy for the reason that in me, as the foremost [of sinners], Jesus Christ might show forth *and* display all His perfect long-suffering *and* patience for an example to [encourage] those who would thereafter believe on Him for [the gaining of] eternal life.
[17]Now to the King of eternity, incorruptible *and* immortal, invisible, the only God, be honor and glory forever and ever—to the ages of ages. Amen—so be it.
[18]This charge *and* admonition I commit in trust to you, Timothy, my son, [a]in accordance with prophetic intimations which I formerly received concerning you, that inspired *and* aided by them you may wage the good warfare,
[19]Keeping fast hold on faith [ [b]that leaning of the entire human personality on God in absolute trust and confidence] and a good (clear) conscience. By rejecting *and* thrusting from them [their conscience], some individuals have made shipwreck of their faith.
[20]Among them are Hymenaeus and Alexander, whom I have delivered to Satan in order that they may be disciplined [by punishment and learn] not to blaspheme.

**2** FIRST OF all, then, I admonish *and* urge that petitions, prayers, intercessions and thanksgivings be offered on behalf of all men,
[2]For kings and all who are in positions of authority *or* high responsibility, that [outwardly] we may pass a quiet *and* undisturbed life [and inwardly] a peaceable one in all godliness *and* reverence and seriousness in every way.
[3]For such [praying] is good *and* right, and [it is] pleasing *and* acceptable to God our Savior,
[4]Who wishes all men to be saved and increasingly to perceive *and* recognize *and* discern *and* know precisely *and* correctly the [divine] Truth:
[5]That there [is only] one God, and [only] one mediator between God and men, the Man Christ Jesus,
[6]Who gave Himself a ransom for all [people, a fact that was] attested to at the right *and* proper time.
[7]And of this matter I was appointed a preacher and an apostle (special messenger); I am speaking the truth *in Christ*, I do not falsify [when I say this], a teacher of the Gentiles in [the realm of] faith and truth.
[8]I desire therefore that in every place men should pray, without anger *or* quarreling *or* resentment or doubt [in their minds], lifting up holy hands.
[9]Also [I desire] that women should adorn themselves modestly *and* appropriately and sensibly in seemly apparel, not with [elaborate] hair arrangement or gold or pearls or expensive clothing,
[10]But by doing good deeds—that is, deeds in themselves good, and for the good and advantage of those contacted by them—as befits women who profess reverential fear for *and* devotion to God.
[11]Let a woman learn in quietness in entire submissiveness.
[12]I allow no woman to teach or to have authority over men; she is to remain in quietness *and* keep silence [in religious assemblies].
[13]For Adam was first formed, then Eve; [Gen. 2:7, 21, 22.]
[14]And it was not Adam who was deceived, but [the] woman who was deceived *and* deluded and fell into transgression. [Gen. 3:1-6.]
[15]Nevertheless (the sentence put upon women [of pain in motherhood] does not hinder their [souls'] salvation), and they will be saved [eternally] if they continue in faith and love and holiness, with self-control; [saved indeed] [c]through the Childbearing, that is, [d]by the birth of the [divine] Child.

**AMP** [a] Vincent's "Word Studies in the New Testament." [b] Souter's "Pocket Lexicon to the Greek New Testament." [c] Vincent. Doddridge. Macknight. Clark. ASV margin, and others. Cf. Gal. 4:4. [d] Alternate reading.

## New American Standard

15It is a trustworthy statement, deserving full acceptance, that Christ Jesus came into the world to save sinners, among whom I am foremost *of all.*
16And yet for this reason I found mercy, in order that in me as the foremost, Jesus Christ might demonstrate His perfect patience, as an example for those who would believe in Him for eternal life.
17Now to the King eternal, immortal, invisible, the only God, *be* honor and glory forever and ever. Amen.
18¶ This command I entrust to you, Timothy, my son, in accordance with the prophecies previously made concerning you, that by them you may fight the good fight,
19keeping faith and a good conscience, which some have rejected and suffered shipwreck in regard to their faith.
20Among these are Hymenaeus and Alexander, whom I have delivered over to Satan, so that they may be taught not to blaspheme.

*A Call to Prayer*

**2** FIRST OF all, then, I urge that entreaties *and* prayers, petitions *and* thanksgivings, be made on behalf of all men,
2for kings and all who are in authority, in order that we may lead a tranquil and quiet life in all godliness and dignity.
3This is good and acceptable in the sight of God our Savior,
4who desires all men to be saved and to come to the knowledge of the truth.
5For there is one God, *and* one mediator also between God and men, *the* man Christ Jesus,
6who gave Himself as a ransom for all, the testimony *borne* at the proper time.
7And for this I was appointed a preacher and an apostle (I am telling the truth, I am not lying) as a teacher of the Gentiles in faith and truth.
8¶ Therefore I want the men in every place to pray, lifting up holy hands, without wrath and dissension.

*Women Instructed*

9Likewise, *I want* women to adorn themselves with proper clothing, modestly and discreetly, not with braided hair and gold or pearls or costly garments;
10but rather by means of good works, as befits women making a claim to godliness.
11Let a woman quietly receive instruction with entire submissiveness.
12But I do not allow a woman to teach or exercise authority over a man, but to remain quiet.
13For it was Adam who was first created, *and* then Eve.
14And *it was* not Adam *who* was deceived, but the woman being quite deceived, fell into transgression.
15But *women* shall be preserved through the bearing of children if they continue in faith and love and sanctity with self-restraint.

## New International

15Here is a trustworthy saying that deserves full acceptance:
Christ Jesus came into the world to save sinners—of whom I am
the worst. 16But for that very reason I was shown mercy so that
in me, the worst of sinners, Christ Jesus might display his unlimited patience as an example for those who would believe on him
and receive eternal life. 17Now to the King eternal, immortal,
invisible, the only God, be honor and glory for ever and ever.
Amen.
18Timothy, my son, I give you this instruction in keeping with
the prophecies once made about you, so that by following them
you may fight the good fight, 19holding on to faith and a good
conscience. Some have rejected these and so have shipwrecked
their faith. 20Among them are Hymenaeus and Alexander, whom
I have handed over to Satan to be taught not to blaspheme.

*Instructions on Worship*

**2** I URGE, then, first of all, that requests, prayers, intercession
and thanksgiving be made for everyone— 2for kings and all
those in authority, that we may live peaceful and quiet lives in all
godliness and holiness. 3This is good, and pleases God our Savior,
4who wants all men to be saved and to come to a knowledge of the
truth. 5For there is one God and one mediator between God and
men, the man Christ Jesus, 6who gave himself as a ransom for all
men—the testimony given in its proper time. 7And for this purpose I was appointed a herald and an apostle—I am telling the
truth, I am not lying—and a teacher of the true faith to the Gentiles.
8I want men everywhere to lift up holy hands in prayer, without
anger or disputing.
9I also want women to dress modestly, with decency and propriety, not with braided hair or gold or pearls or expensive clothes,
10but with good deeds, appropriate for women who profess to
worship God.
11A woman should learn in quietness and full submission. 12I
do not permit a woman to teach or to have authority over a man;
she must be silent. 13For Adam was formed first, then Eve. 14And
Adam was not the one deceived; it was the woman who was
deceived and became a sinner. 15But women[e] will be saved[f]
through childbearing—if they continue in faith, love and holiness
with propriety.

NIV [e] 15 Greek *she* [f] 15 Or *restored*

## King James

**3** THIS *IS* a true saying, If a man desire the office of a bishop, he desireth a good work.

2A bishop then must be blameless, the husband of one wife, vigilant, sober, of good behaviour, given to hospitality, apt to teach;

3Not given to wine, no striker, not greedy of filthy lucre; but patient, not a brawler, not covetous;

4One that ruleth well his own house, having his children in subjection with all gravity;

5(For if a man know not how to rule his own house, how shall he take care of the church of God?)

6Not a novice, lest being lifted up with pride he fall into the condemnation of the devil.

7Moreover he must have a good report of them which are without; lest he fall into reproach and the snare of the devil.

8Likewise *must* the deacons *be* grave, not doubletongued, not given to much wine, not greedy of filthy lucre;

9Holding the mystery of the faith in a pure conscience.

10And let these also first be proved; then let them use the office of a deacon, being *found* blameless.

11Even so *must their* wives *be* grave, not slanderers, sober, faithful in all things.

12Let the deacons be the husbands of one wife, ruling their children and their own houses well.

13For they that have used the office of a deacon well purchase to themselves a good degree, and great boldness in the faith which is in Christ Jesus.

14These things write I unto thee, hoping to come unto thee shortly:

15But if I tarry long, that thou mayest know how thou oughtest to behave thyself in the house of God, which is the church of the living God, the pillar and ground of the truth.

16And without controversy great is the mystery of godliness: God was manifest in the flesh, justified in the Spirit, seen of angels, preached unto the Gentiles, believed on in the world, received up into glory.

## Amplified

**3** THE SAYING is true *and* irrefutable: If any man [eagerly] seeks the office of bishop (superintendent, overseer), he desires an excellent task (work).

2Now a bishop (superintendent, overseer) must give no grounds for accusation *but* must be above reproach, the husband of one wife, circumspect *and* temperate *and* self-controlled; [he must be] sensible *and* well behaved *and* dignified and lead an orderly (disciplined) life; [he must be] hospitable—showing love for and being a friend to the believers, especially strangers or foreigners—[and] be a capable *and* qualified teacher,

3Not given to wine, not combative but gentle *and* considerate, not quarrelsome *but* forbearing *and* peaceable, and not a lover of money—insatiable for wealth and ready to obtain it by questionable means.

4He must rule his own household well, keeping his children under control, with true dignity, commanding their respect in every way *and* keeping them respectful.

5For if a man does not know how to rule his own household, how is he to take care of the church of God?

6He must not be a new convert, or he may [develop a beclouded and stupid state of mind] as the result of pride, [be blinded by] conceit, and fall into the condemnation that the devil [once] did. [Isa. 14:12-14.]

7Furthermore he must have a good reputation *and* be well thought of by those outside [the church], lest he become involved in slander *and* incur reproach and fall into the devil's trap.

8In like manner the deacons [must be] worthy of respect, not shifty *and* double talkers *but* sincere in what they say, not given to much wine, not greedy for base gain—craving wealth and resorting to ignoble and dishonest methods of getting it.

9They must possess the mystic secret of the faith [Christian truth as hidden from ungodly men,] with a clear conscience.

10And let them also be tried *and* investigated *and* proved first; then, [if they turn out to be] above reproach, let them serve [as deacons].

11 [a][The] women likewise must be worthy of respect *and* serious, not gossipers, but temperate *and* self-controlled, [thoroughly] trustworthy in all things.

12Let deacons be the husbands of but one wife, and let them manage [their] children and their own households well;

13For those who perform well as deacons acquire a good standing for themselves and also gain much confidence *and* freedom *and* boldness in the faith which is [founded on and centers] in Christ Jesus.

14Although I hope to come to you before long, I am writing these instructions to you so that,

15If I am detained, you may know how people ought to conduct themselves in the household of God, which is the church of the living God, the pillar and stay—the prop and support—of the Truth.

16And great *and* important *and* weighty, we confess, is the hidden truth—the mystic secret—of godliness. He [b](God) was made visible in human flesh, justified *and* vindicated in the (Holy) Spirit, was seen by angels, preached among the nations, believed on in the world [and] taken up in glory.

## King James

**4** NOW THE Spirit speaketh expressly, that in the latter times some shall depart from the faith, giving heed to seducing spirits, and doctrines of devils;

2Speaking lies in hypocrisy; having their conscience seared with a hot iron;

## Amplified

**4** BUT THE (Holy) Spirit distinctly *and* expressly declares that in latter times some will turn away from the faith, giving attention to deluding *and* seducing spirits and doctrines that demons teach

2Through the hypocrisy *and* pretensions of liars whose consciences are seared (cauterized),

**AMP** [a] Either their wives or the deaconesses, or both. [b] Some authorities read "God."

## New American Standard

*Overseers and Deacons*

**3** IT IS a trustworthy statement: if any man aspires to the office of overseer, it is a fine work he desires *to do.*

2An overseer, then, must be above reproach, the husband of one wife, temperate, prudent, respectable, hospitable, able to teach,

3not addicted to wine or pugnacious, but gentle, uncontentious, free from the love of money.

4 *He must be* one who manages his own household well, keeping his children under control with all dignity

5(but if a man does not know how to manage his own household, how will he take care of the church of God?);

6 *and* not a new convert, lest he become conceited and fall into the condemnation incurred by the devil.

7And he must have a good reputation with those outside *the church,* so that he may not fall into reproach and the snare of the devil.

8Deacons likewise *must be* men of dignity, not double-tongued, or addicted to much wine or fond of sordid gain,

9 *but* holding to the mystery of the faith with a clear conscience.

10And let these also first be tested; then let them serve as deacons if they are beyond reproach.

11Women *must* likewise *be* dignified, not malicious gossips, but temperate, faithful in all things.

12Let deacons be husbands of *only* one wife, *and* good managers of *their* children and their own households.

13For those who have served well as deacons obtain for themselves a high standing and great confidence in the faith that is in Christ Jesus.

14¶ I am writing these things to you, hoping to come to you before long;

15but in case I am delayed, *I write* so that you may know how one ought to conduct himself in the household of God, which is the church of the living God, the pillar and support of the truth.

16And by common confession great is the mystery of godliness:

[c]He who was revealed in the flesh,
Was vindicated in the Spirit,
Beheld by angels,
Proclaimed among the nations,
Believed on in the world,
Taken up in glory.

*Apostasy*

**4** BUT THE Spirit explicitly says that in later times some will fall away from the faith, paying attention to deceitful spirits and doctrines of demons,

2by means of the hypocrisy of liars seared in their own conscience as with a branding iron,

NAS [c] Some later mss. read *God*

## New International

*Overseers and Deacons*

**3** HERE IS a trustworthy saying: If anyone sets his heart on
being an overseer,[d] he desires a noble task. 2Now the overseer must be above reproach, the husband of but one wife, temperate, self-controlled, respectable, hospitable, able to teach, 3not
given to drunkenness, not violent but gentle, not quarrelsome, not
a lover of money. 4He must manage his own family well and see
that his children obey him with proper respect. 5(If anyone does
not know how to manage his own family, how can he take care
of God's church?) 6He must not be a recent convert, or he may
become conceited and fall under the same judgment as the devil.
7He must also have a good reputation with outsiders, so that he
will not fall into disgrace and into the devil's trap.

8Deacons, likewise, are to be men worthy of respect, sincere,
not indulging in much wine, and not pursuing dishonest gain.
9They must keep hold of the deep truths of the faith with a clear
conscience. 10They must first be tested; and then if there is nothing
against them, let them serve as deacons.

11In the same way, their wives[e] are to be women worthy of
respect, not malicious talkers but temperate and trustworthy in
everything.

12A deacon must be the husband of but one wife and must
manage his children and his household well. 13Those who have
served well gain an excellent standing and great assurance in their
faith in Christ Jesus.

14Although I hope to come to you soon, I am writing you these
instructions so that, 15if I am delayed, you will know how people
ought to conduct themselves in God's household, which is the
church of the living God, the pillar and foundation of the truth.
16Beyond all question, the mystery of godliness is great:

He[f] appeared in a body,[g]
was vindicated by the Spirit,
was seen by angels,
was preached among the nations,
was believed on in the world,
was taken up in glory.

*Instructions to Timothy*

**4** THE SPIRIT clearly says that in later times some will abandon
the faith and follow deceiving spirits and things taught by
demons. 2Such teachings come through hypocritical liars, whose
consciences have been seared as with a hot iron. 3They forbid

NIV [d] *1* Traditionally *bishop;* also in verse 2 [e] *11* Or *way, deaconesses* [f] *16* Some manuscripts *God* [g] *16* Or *in the flesh*

## King James

3 Forbidding to marry, *and commanding* to abstain from meats,
which God hath created to be received with thanksgiving of them
which believe and know the truth.
4 For every creature of God *is* good, and nothing to be refused,
if it be received with thanksgiving:
5 For it is sanctified by the word of God and prayer.
6 If thou put the brethren in remembrance of these things, thou
shalt be a good minister of Jesus Christ, nourished up in the words
of faith and of good doctrine, whereunto thou hast attained.
7 But refuse profane and old wives' fables, and exercise thyself
*rather* unto godliness.
8 For bodily exercise profiteth little: but godliness is profitable
unto all things, having promise of the life that now is, and of that
which is to come.
9 This *is* a faithful saying and worthy of all acceptation.
10 For therefore we both labour and suffer reproach, because we
trust in the living God, who is the Saviour of all men, specially of
those that believe.
11 These things command and teach.
12 Let no man despise thy youth; but be thou an example of the
believers, in word, in conversation, in charity, in spirit, in faith,
in purity.
13 Till I come, give attendance to reading, to exhortation, to
doctrine.
14 Neglect not the gift that is in thee, which was given thee by
prophecy, with the laying on of the hands of the presbytery.
15 Meditate upon these things; give thyself wholly to them; that
thy profiting may appear to all.
16 Take heed unto thyself, and unto the doctrine; continue in
them: for in doing this thou shalt both save thyself, and them that
hear thee.

## Amplified

3 Who forbid people to marry and [teach them] to abstain from
[certain kinds of] foods which God created to be received with
thanksgiving by those who believe *and* have (an increasingly clear)
knowledge of the truth.
4 For everything God has created is good, and nothing is to be
thrown away *or* refused if it is received with thanksgiving.
5 For it is hallowed *and* consecrated by the Word of God and by
prayer.
6 If you lay all these instructions before the brethren, you will
be a worthy steward *and* a good minister of Christ Jesus, ever
nourishing your own self on the truths of the faith and of the good
[Christian] instruction which you have closely followed.
7 But refuse *and* avoid irreverent legends—profane and impure
and godless fictions, mere grandmothers' tales—and silly myths,
*and* express your disapproval of them. Train yourself toward godliness (piety)—keeping yourself spiritually fit.
8 For physical training is of some value—useful for a little; but
godliness [spiritual training] is useful *and* of value in everything
*and* in every way, for it holds promise for the present life and also
for the life which is to come.
9 This saying is reliable *and* worthy of complete acceptance by
everybody.
10 With a view to this we toil *and* strive, [yes] and [a]suffer reproach, because we have [fixed our] hope on the living God, Who
is the Savior (Preserver, Maintainer, Deliverer) of all men, especially of those who believe—trust in, rely on and adhere to Him.
11 Continue to command these things and to teach them.
12 Let no one despise *or* think less of you because of your youth,
but be an example (pattern) for the believers, in speech, in conduct, in love, in faith and in purity.
13 Till I come, devote yourself to [public and private] reading, to
exhortation—preaching and personal appeals—and to teaching
*and* instilling doctrine.
14 Do not neglect the gift which is in you, [that special inward
endowment] which was directly imparted to you [by the Holy
Spirit] by prophetic utterance when the elders laid their hands
upon you [at your ordination].
15 Practice *and* cultivate *and* meditate upon these duties, throw
yourself wholly into them [your ministry], so that your progress
may be evident to everybody.
16 Look well to yourself (to your own personality) and to [your]
teaching; persevere in these things—hold to them; for by so doing
you will save both yourself and those who hear you.

**5** REBUKE NOT an elder, but entreat *him* as a father; *and* the
younger men as brethren;
2 The elder women as mothers; the younger as sisters, with all
purity.
3 Honour widows that are widows indeed.
4 But if any widow have children or nephews, let them learn first
to show piety at home, and to requite their parents: for that is good
and acceptable before God.
5 Now she that is a widow indeed, and desolate, trusteth in
God, and continueth in supplications and prayers night and day.
6 But she that liveth in pleasure is dead while she liveth.
7 And these things give in charge, that they may be blameless.

**5** DO NOT sharply censure *or* rebuke an older man, but entreat
*and* plead with him as [you would with] a father; treat younger men like brothers.
2 [Treat] older women like mothers [and] younger women like
sisters, in all purity.
3 [Always] treat with great consideration *and* give aid to those
who are truly widowed—solitary and without support.
4 But if a widow has children or grandchildren, see to it that
these are first made to understand that it is their religious duty (to
defray their natural obligation to those) at home, and make return
to their parents *or* grandparents [for all their care by contributing
to their maintenance], for this is acceptable in the sight of God.
5 Now [a woman] who is a real widow, and is left entirely alone
*and* desolate, has fixed her hope on God and perseveres in supplications and prayers night and day;
6 Whereas she who lives in pleasure *and* self-gratification—giving herself up to luxury and self-indulgence—is dead even while
she [still] lives.
7 Charge [the people] thus, so that they may be without reproach *and* blameless.

**AMP** [a] Alternate reading.

## New American Standard

3 *men* who forbid marriage *and advocate* abstaining from foods, which God has created to be gratefully shared in by those who believe and know the truth.

4For everything created by God is good, and nothing is to be rejected, if it is received with gratitude;

5for it is sanctified by means of the word of God and prayer.

*A Good Minister's Discipline*

6¶ In pointing out these things to the brethren, you will be a good servant of Christ Jesus, *constantly* nourished on the words of the faith and of the sound doctrine which you have been following.

7But have nothing to do with worldly fables fit only for old women. On the other hand, discipline yourself for the purpose of godliness;

8for bodily discipline is only of little profit, but godliness is profitable for all things, since it holds promise for the present life and *also* for the *life* to come.

9It is a trustworthy statement deserving full acceptance.

10For it is for this we labor and strive, because we have fixed our hope on the living God, who is the Savior of all men, especially of believers.

11Prescribe and teach these things.

12Let no one look down on your youthfulness, but *rather* in speech, conduct, love, faith *and* purity, show yourself an example of those who believe.

13Until I come, give attention to the *public* reading *of Scripture,* to exhortation and teaching.

14Do not neglect the spiritual gift within you, which was bestowed upon you through prophetic utterance with the laying on of hands by the presbytery.

15Take pains with these things; be *absorbed* in them, so that your progress may be evident to all.

16Pay close attention to yourself and to your teaching; persevere in these things; for as you do this you will insure salvation both for yourself and for those who hear you.

*Honor Widows*

5 DO NOT sharply rebuke an older man, but *rather* appeal to *him* as a father, *to* the younger men as brothers,

2the older women as mothers, *and* the younger women as sisters, in all purity.

3Honor widows who are widows indeed;

4but if any widow has children or grandchildren, let them first learn to practice piety in regard to their own family, and to make some return to their parents; for this is acceptable in the sight of God.

5Now she who is a widow indeed, and who has been left alone has fixed her hope on God, and continues in entreaties and prayers night and day.

6But she who gives herself to wanton pleasure is dead even while she lives.

7Prescribe these things as well, so that they may be above reproach.

## New International

people to marry and order them to abstain from certain foods,
which God created to be received with thanksgiving by those who
believe and who know the truth. 4For everything God created is
good, and nothing is to be rejected if it is received with thanksgiving, 5because it is consecrated by the word of God and prayer.
6If you point these things out to the brothers, you will be a good
minister of Christ Jesus, brought up in the truths of the faith and
of the good teaching that you have followed. 7Have nothing to do
with godless myths and old wives' tales; rather, train yourself to
be godly. 8For physical training is of some value, but godliness has
value for all things, holding promise for both the present life and
the life to come.
9This is a trustworthy saying that deserves full acceptance
10(and for this we labor and strive), that we have put our hope in
the living God, who is the Savior of all men, and especially of those
who believe.
11Command and teach these things. 12Don't let anyone look
down on you because you are young, but set an example for the
believers in speech, in life, in love, in faith and in purity. 13Until
I come, devote yourself to the public reading of Scripture, to
preaching and to teaching. 14Do not neglect your gift, which was
given you through a prophetic message when the body of elders
laid their hands on you.
15Be diligent in these matters; give yourself wholly to them, so
that everyone may see your progress. 16Watch your life and doctrine closely. Persevere in them, because if you do, you will save
both yourself and your hearers.

*Advice About Widows, Elders and Slaves*

5 DO NOT rebuke an older man harshly, but exhort him as if
he were your father. Treat younger men as brothers, 2older
women as mothers, and younger women as sisters, with absolute
purity.
3Give proper recognition to those widows who are really in
need. 4But if a widow has children or grandchildren, these should
learn first of all to put their religion into practice by caring for their
own family and so repaying their parents and grandparents, for
this is pleasing to God. 5The widow who is really in need and left
all alone puts her hope in God and continues night and day to pray
and to ask God for help. 6But the widow who lives for pleasure is
dead even while she lives. 7Give the people these instructions, too,
so that no one may be open to blame. 8If anyone does not provide

## King James

8But if any provide not for his own, and specially for those of his own house, he hath denied the faith, and is worse than an infidel.

9Let not a widow be taken into the number under threescore years old, having been the wife of one man,

10Well reported of for good works; if she have brought up children, if she have lodged strangers, if she have washed the saints' feet, if she have relieved the afflicted, if she have diligently followed every good work.

11But the younger widows refuse: for when they have begun to wax wanton against Christ, they will marry;

12Having damnation, because they have cast off their first faith.

13And withal they learn *to be* idle, wandering about from house to house; and not only idle, but tattlers also and busybodies, speaking things which they ought not.

14I will therefore that the younger women marry, bear children, guide the house, give none occasion to the adversary to speak reproachfully.

15For some are already turned aside after Satan.

16If any man or woman that believeth have widows, let them relieve them, and let not the church be charged; that it may relieve them that are widows indeed.

17Let the elders that rule well be counted worthy of double honour, especially they who labour in the word and doctrine.

18For the scripture saith, Thou shalt not muzzle the ox that treadeth out the corn. And, The labourer *is* worthy of his reward.

19Against an elder receive not an accusation, but before two or three witnesses.

20Them that sin rebuke before all, that others also may fear.

21I charge *thee* before God, and the Lord Jesus Christ, and the elect angels, that thou observe these things without preferring one before another, doing nothing by partiality.

22Lay hands suddenly on no man, neither be partaker of other men's sins: keep thyself pure.

23Drink no longer water, but use a little wine for thy stomach's sake and thine often infirmities.

24Some men's sins are open beforehand, going before to judgment; and some *men* they follow after.

25Likewise also the good works *of some* are manifest beforehand; and they that are otherwise cannot be hid.

**6** LET AS many servants as are under the yoke count their own masters worthy of all honour, that the name of God and *his* doctrine be not blasphemed.

## Amplified

8If any one fails to provide for his relatives, and especially for those of his own family, he has disowned the faith [by failing to accompany it with fruits], and is worse than an unbeliever [who performs his obligation in these matters].

9Let no one be put on the roll of widows [who are to receive church support] who is under sixty years of age, or who has been the wife of more than one man;

10And she must have a reputation for good deeds, as one who has brought up children, who has practiced hospitality to strangers [of the brotherhood], washed the feet of the saints, helped to relieve the distressed, [and] devoted herself diligently to doing good in every way.

11But refuse [to enroll on this list the] younger widows, for when they become restive *and* their natural desires grow strong, they withdraw themselves against Christ [and] wish to marry [again].

12And so they incur condemnation for having set aside *and* slighted their previous pledge.

13Moreover, as they go about from house to house they learn to be idlers, and not only idlers but gossips and busybodies, saying what they should not say *and* talking of things they should not mention.

14So I would have younger [widows] marry, bear children, guide the household, [and] not give opponents of the faith occasion for slander or reproach.

15For already some [widows] have turned aside after Satan.

16If any believing [a] *man or* woman has [relatives or persons in the household who are] widows, let him relieve them; let the church not be burdened [with them]; so that it may [be free to] assist those who are truly widows—those who are all alone and are dependent.

17Let the elders who perform the duties of their office well be considered doubly worthy of honor [and of adequate [b]financial support], especially those who labor faithfully in preaching and teaching.

18For the Scripture says, You shall not muzzle an ox when it is treading out the grain, and again, The laborer is worthy of his hire. [Deut. 25:4.]

19Listen to no accusation preferred [before a judge] against an elder except it be confirmed by the testimony of two or three witnesses. [Deut. 19:15.]

20As for those who are guilty *and* persist in sin, rebuke *and* admonish them in the presence of all, so that the rest may be warned *and* stand in wholesome awe *and* fear.

21I solemnly charge you in the presence of God and of Christ Jesus and of the chosen angels, that you guard *and* keep [these rules] without personal prejudice *or* favor, doing nothing from partiality.

22Do not be in a hurry in the laying on of hands—giving the sanction of the church too hastily [in reinstating expelled offenders or in ordination in questionable cases]—nor share *or* participate in another man's sins; keep yourself pure.

23Drink water no longer exclusively, but use a little wine for the sake of your stomach and your frequent illnesses.

24The sins of some men are conspicuous—openly evident to all eyes—going before them to the judgment [seat] *and* proclaiming their sentence in advance; but the sins of others appear later—following the offender to the bar of judgment and coming into view there.

25So also good deeds are evident *and* conspicuous, and even when they are not, they cannot remain hidden [indefinitely].

**6** LET ALL who are under the yoke as bond servants esteem their own [personal] masters worthy of honor *and* fullest respect, so that the name of God and the teaching may not be brought into disrepute *and* blasphemed.

**AMP** [a] Some ancient authorities so read. [b] Vincent.

## New American Standard

8But if anyone does not provide for his own, and especially for
those of his household, he has denied the faith, and is worse than
an unbeliever.
9Let a widow be put on the list only if she is not less than sixty
years old, *having been* the wife of one man,
10having a reputation for good works; *and* if she has brought up
children, if she has shown hospitality to strangers, if she has
washed the saints' feet, if she has assisted those in distress, *and* if
she has devoted herself to every good work.
11But refuse *to put* younger widows *on the list*, for when they feel
sensual desires in disregard of Christ, they want to get married,
12 *thus* incurring condemnation, because they have set aside
their previous pledge.
13And at the same time they also learn *to be* idle, as they go
around from house to house; and not merely idle, but also gossips
and busybodies, talking about things not proper *to mention*.
14Therefore, I want younger *widows* to get married, bear children, keep house, *and* give the enemy no occasion for reproach;
15for some have already turned aside to follow Satan.
16If any woman who is a believer has *dependent* widows, let her
assist them, and let not the church be burdened, so that it may
assist those who are widows indeed.

*Concerning Elders*

17¶ Let the elders who rule well be considered worthy of double
honor, especially those who work hard at preaching and teaching.
18For the Scripture says, "YOU SHALL NOT MUZZLE THE OX WHILE
HE IS THRESHING," and "The laborer is worthy of his wages."
19Do not receive an accusation against an elder except on the
basis of two or three witnesses.
20Those who continue in sin, rebuke in the presence of all, so
that the rest also may be fearful *of sinning*.
21I solemnly charge you in the presence of God and of Christ
Jesus and of *His* chosen angels, to maintain these *principles* without
bias, doing nothing in a *spirit of* partiality.
22Do not lay hands upon anyone *too* hastily and thus share
*responsibility for* the sins of others; keep yourself free from sin.
23No longer drink water *exclusively*, but use a little wine for the
sake of your stomach and your frequent ailments.
24The sins of some men are quite evident, going before them to
judgment; for others, their *sins* follow after.
25Likewise also, deeds that are good are quite evident, and
those which are otherwise cannot be concealed.

*Instructions to Those Who Minister*

6 LET ALL who are under the yoke as slaves regard their own
masters as worthy of all honor so that the name of God and
*our* doctrine may not be spoken against.

## New International

for his relatives, and especially for his immediate family, he has
denied the faith and is worse than an unbeliever.
9No widow may be put on the list of widows unless she is over
sixty, has been faithful to her husband,[c] 10and is well known for
her good deeds, such as bringing up children, showing hospitality, washing the feet of the saints, helping those in trouble and
devoting herself to all kinds of good deeds.
11As for younger widows, do not put them on such a list. For
when their sensual desires overcome their dedication to Christ,
they want to marry. 12Thus they bring judgment on themselves,
because they have broken their first pledge. 13Besides, they get
into the habit of being idle and going about from house to house.
And not only do they become idlers, but also gossips and busybodies, saying things they ought not to. 14So I counsel younger
widows to marry, to have children, to manage their homes and to
give the enemy no opportunity for slander. 15Some have in fact
already turned away to follow Satan.
16If any woman who is a believer has widows in her family, she
should help them and not let the church be burdened with them,
so that the church can help those widows who are really in need.
17The elders who direct the affairs of the church well are worthy
of double honor, especially those whose work is preaching and
teaching. 18For the Scripture says, "Do not muzzle the ox while it
is treading out the grain,"[d] and "The worker deserves his
wages."[e] 19Do not entertain an accusation against an elder unless
it is brought by two or three witnesses. 20Those who sin are to be
rebuked publicly, so that the others may take warning.
21I charge you, in the sight of God and Christ Jesus and the elect
angels, to keep these instructions without partiality, and to do
nothing out of favoritism.
22Do not be hasty in the laying on of hands, and do not share
in the sins of others. Keep yourself pure.
23Stop drinking only water, and use a little wine because of your
stomach and your frequent illnesses.
24The sins of some men are obvious, reaching the place of
judgment ahead of them; the sins of others trail behind them. 25In
the same way, good deeds are obvious, and even those that are not
cannot be hidden.

6 ALL WHO are under the yoke of slavery should consider
their masters worthy of full respect, so that God's name and
our teaching may not be slandered. 2Those who have believing

NIV [c] 9 Or *has had but one husband* [d] 18 Deut. 25:4 [e] 18 Luke 10:7

## King James

2And they that have believing masters, let them not despise
*them,* because they are brethren; but rather do *them* service, because they are faithful and beloved, partakers of the benefit. These
things teach and exhort.
3If any man teach otherwise, and consent not to wholesome
words, *even* the words of our Lord Jesus Christ, and to the doctrine
which is according to godliness;
4He is proud, knowing nothing, but doting about questions and
strifes of words, whereof cometh envy, strife, railings, evil surmis-
ings,
5Perverse disputings of men of corrupt minds, and destitute of
the truth, supposing that gain is godliness: from such withdraw
thyself.
6But godliness with contentment is great gain.
7For we brought nothing into *this* world, *and it is* certain we can
carry nothing out.
8And having food and raiment let us be therewith content.
9But they that will be rich fall into temptation and a snare, and
*into* many foolish and hurtful lusts, which drown men in destruction and perdition.
10For the love of money is the root of all evil: which while some
coveted after, they have erred from the faith, and pierced themselves through with many sorrows.
11But thou, O man of God, flee these things; and follow after
righteousness, godliness, faith, love, patience, meekness.
12Fight the good fight of faith, lay hold on eternal life, whereunto thou art also called, and hast professed a good profession
before many witnesses.
13I give thee charge in the sight of God, who quickeneth all
things, and *before* Christ Jesus, who before Pontius Pilate witnessed a good confession;
14That thou keep *this* commandment without spot, unrebuke-
able, until the appearing of our Lord Jesus Christ:
15Which in his times he shall show, *who is* the blessed and only
Potentate, the King of kings, and Lord of lords;
16Who only hath immortality, dwelling in the light which no
man can approach unto; whom no man hath seen, nor can see: to
whom *be* honour and power everlasting. Amen.
17Charge them that are rich in this world, that they be not
highminded, nor trust in uncertain riches, but in the living God,
who giveth us richly all things to enjoy;
18That they do good, that they be rich in good works, ready to
distribute, willing to communicate;
19Laying up in store for themselves a good foundation against
the time to come, that they may lay hold on eternal life.
20O Timothy, keep that which is committed to thy trust, avoiding profane *and* vain babblings, and oppositions of science falsely
so called:
21Which some professing have erred concerning the faith.
Grace *be* with thee. Amen.

## Amplified

2Let those who have believing masters not be disrespectful *or*
scornful [to them] on the grounds that they are brothers [in Christ];
rather, they should serve [them all the better] because those who
benefit by their kindly service are believers and beloved. Teach and
urge these duties.
3But if any one teaches otherwise and does not [a]assent to the
sound *and* wholesome messages of our Lord Jesus Christ, the
Messiah, and the teaching which is in agreement with godliness—
piety toward God—
4He is puffed up with pride *and* stupefied with conceit, [al-
though he is] woefully ignorant. He has a [b]morbid fondness for
controversy and disputes *and* strife about words, which result in
(producing) envy *and* jealousy, quarrels *and* dissension, abuse *and*
insults *and* slander, and base suspicions,
5And protracted wrangling *and* wearing discussion *and* perpetual friction among men who are corrupted in mind and bereft of the
truth, who imagine that godliness *or* righteousness is a [c]source of
profit—a money-making business, a means of livelihood. *From
such withdraw.*
6[And it is, indeed, a source of immense profit, for] godliness
accompanied with contentment—that contentment which is a
sense of [d]inward sufficiency—is great *and* abundant gain.
7For we brought nothing into the world, and *obviously* we cannot take anything out of the world;
8But if we have food and clothing, with these we shall be
content (satisfied).
9But those who crave to be rich fall into temptation and a snare,
and into many foolish (useless, godless) and hurtful desires that
plunge men into ruin *and* destruction and miserable perishing.
10For the love of money is a root of all evils; it is through this
craving that some have been led astray, *and* have wandered from
the faith and pierced themselves through with many [e]acute [men-
tal] pangs.
11But as for you, O man of God, flee from all these things; aim
at *and* pursue righteousness—that is, right standing with God and
true goodness; godliness (which is the loving fear of God and
Christlikeness), faith, love, steadfastness (patience) and gentle-
heartedness.
12Fight the good fight of the faith; lay hold of the eternal life to
which you were summoned, and confessed the good confession
[of faith] before many witnesses.
13In the presence of God Who preserves alive all living things,
and Christ Jesus Who in His testimony before Pontius Pilate made
the good confession,
14I [solemnly] charge you to keep all His precepts unsullied *and*
flawless, irreproachable until the appearing of our Lord Jesus
Christ, the Anointed One.
15Which will be shown forth in His own proper time by the
blessed, only Sovereign, the King of kings and the Lord of lords;
16Who alone has immortality [in the sense of exemption from
every kind of death] and lives in unapproachable light, Whom no
man has ever seen or can see. Unto Him be honor and everlasting
power *and* dominion. Amen—so be it.
17As for the rich in this world, charge them not to be proud *and*
arrogant *and* contemptuous of others, nor to set their hopes on
uncertain riches but on God, Who richly *and* ceaselessly provides
us with everything for [our] enjoyment;
18[Charge them] to do good, to be rich in good works, to be
liberal *and* generous-hearted, ready to share [with others],
19In this way laying up for themselves [the riches that endure
forever] a good foundation for the future, so that they may grasp
that which is life indeed.
20O Timothy, guard *and* keep the deposit entrusted [to you]!
Turn away from the irreverent babble *and* godless chatter, *with* the
vain *and* empty *and* worldly phrases, and the subtleties *and* the
contradictions in what is falsely called knowledge *and* spiritual
illumination.
21[For] by making such profession some have erred—missed
the mark—as regards the faith. Grace (divine favor and blessing)
be with you all! *Amen—so be it.*

**AMP** [a] Vincent. [b] Thayer. [c] Vincent. [d] Vincent. [e] Souter.

## New American Standard

2And let those who have believers as their masters not be disrespectful to them because they are brethren, but let them serve them all the more, because those who partake of the benefit are believers and beloved. Teach and preach these *principles.*

3¶ If anyone advocates a different doctrine, and does not agree with sound words, those of our Lord Jesus Christ, and with the doctrine conforming to godliness,

4he is conceited *and* understands nothing; but he has a morbid interest in controversial questions and disputes about words, out of which arise envy, strife, abusive language, evil suspicions,

5and constant friction between men of depraved mind and deprived of the truth, who suppose that godliness is a means of gain.

6But godliness *actually* is a means of great gain, when accompanied by contentment.

7For we have brought nothing into the world, [f]so we cannot take anything out of it either.

8And if we have food and covering, with these we shall be content.

9But those who want to get rich fall into temptation and a snare and many foolish and harmful desires which plunge men into ruin and destruction.

10For the love of money is a root of all sorts of evil, and some by longing for it have wandered away from the faith, and pierced themselves with many a pang.

11¶ But flee from these things, you man of God; and pursue righteousness, godliness, faith, love, perseverance *and* gentleness.

12Fight the good fight of faith; take hold of the eternal life to which you were called, and you made the good confession in the presence of many witnesses.

13I charge you in the presence of God, who gives life to all things, and of Christ Jesus, who testified the good confession before Pontius Pilate,

14that you keep the commandment without stain or reproach until the appearing of our Lord Jesus Christ,

15which He will bring about at the proper time—He who is the blessed and only Sovereign, the King of kings and Lord of lords;

16who alone possesses immortality and dwells in unapproachable light; whom no man has seen or can see. To Him *be* honor and eternal dominion! Amen.

17¶ Instruct those who are rich in this present world not to be conceited or to fix their hope on the uncertainty of riches, but on God, who richly supplies us with all things to enjoy.

18 *Instruct them* to do good, to be rich in good works, to be generous and ready to share,

19storing up for themselves the treasure of a good foundation for the future, so that they may take hold of that which is life indeed.

20¶ O Timothy, guard what has been entrusted to you, avoiding worldly *and* empty chatter *and* the opposing arguments of what is falsely called "knowledge"—

21which some have professed and thus gone astray from the faith.

¶ Grace be with you.

NAS [f] Later mss. read *it is clear that*

## New International

masters are not to show less respect for them because they are brothers. Instead, they are to serve them even better, because those who benefit from their service are believers, and dear to them. These are the things you are to teach and urge on them.

*Love of Money*

3If anyone teaches false doctrines and does not agree to the sound instruction of our Lord Jesus Christ and to godly teaching,
4he is conceited and understands nothing. He has an unhealthy interest in controversies and quarrels about words that result in envy, strife, malicious talk, evil suspicions
5and constant friction between men of corrupt mind, who have been robbed of the truth and who think that godliness is a means to financial gain.
6But godliness with contentment is great gain.
7For we brought nothing into the world, and we can take nothing out of it.
8But if we have food and clothing, we will be content with that.
9People who want to get rich fall into temptation and a trap and into many foolish and harmful desires that plunge men into ruin and destruction.
10For the love of money is a root of all kinds of evil. Some people, eager for money, have wandered from the faith and pierced themselves with many griefs.

*Paul's Charge to Timothy*

11But you, man of God, flee from all this, and pursue righteousness, godliness, faith, love, endurance and gentleness.
12Fight the good fight of the faith. Take hold of the eternal life to which you were called when you made your good confession in the presence of many witnesses.
13In the sight of God, who gives life to everything, and of Christ Jesus, who while testifying before Pontius Pilate made the good confession, I charge you
14to keep this command without spot or blame until the appearing of our Lord Jesus Christ,
15which God will bring about in his own time—God, the blessed and only Ruler, the King of kings and Lord of lords,
16who alone is immortal and who lives in unapproachable light, whom no one has seen or can see. To him be honor and might forever. Amen.

17Command those who are rich in this present world not to be arrogant nor to put their hope in wealth, which is so uncertain, but to put their hope in God, who richly provides us with everything for our enjoyment.
18Command them to do good, to be rich in good deeds, and to be generous and willing to share.
19In this way they will lay up treasure for themselves as a firm foundation for the coming age, so that they may take hold of the life that is truly life.

20Timothy, guard what has been entrusted to your care. Turn away from godless chatter and the opposing ideas of what is falsely called knowledge,
21which some have professed and in so doing have wandered from the faith.

Grace be with you.

## King James

THE SECOND EPISTLE OF

PAUL THE APOSTLE TO

# Timothy

1 PAUL, AN apostle of Jesus Christ by the will of God, according to the promise of life which is in Christ Jesus,

2To Timothy, *my* dearly beloved son: Grace, mercy, *and* peace, from God the Father and Christ Jesus our Lord.

3I thank God, whom I serve from *my* forefathers with pure conscience, that without ceasing I have remembrance of thee in my prayers night and day;

4Greatly desiring to see thee, being mindful of thy tears, that I may be filled with joy;

5When I call to remembrance the unfeigned faith that is in thee, which dwelt first in thy grandmother Lois, and thy mother Eunice; and I am persuaded that in thee also.

6Wherefore I put thee in remembrance that thou stir up the gift of God, which is in thee by the putting on of my hands.

7For God hath not given us the spirit of fear; but of power, and of love, and of a sound mind.

8Be not thou therefore ashamed of the testimony of our Lord, nor of me his prisoner: but be thou partaker of the afflictions of the gospel according to the power of God;

9Who hath saved us, and called *us* with an holy calling, not according to our works, but according to his own purpose and grace, which was given us in Christ Jesus before the world began,

10But is now made manifest by the appearing of our Saviour Jesus Christ, who hath abolished death, and hath brought life and immortality to light through the gospel:

11Whereunto I am appointed a preacher, and an apostle, and a teacher of the Gentiles.

12For the which cause I also suffer these things: nevertheless I am not ashamed: for I know whom I have believed, and am persuaded that he is able to keep that which I have committed unto him against that day.

13Hold fast the form of sound words, which thou hast heard of me, in faith and love which is in Christ Jesus.

## Amplified

THE SECOND LETTER OF

PAUL TO

# Timothy

1 PAUL, AN apostle (special messenger) of Christ Jesus by the will of God according to the promise of life that is in Christ Jesus,

2To Timothy, [my] beloved child: Grace (favor and spiritual blessing), mercy and (heart) peace from God the Father and Christ Jesus our Lord!

3I thank God Whom I worship with a pure conscience, [ [a]in the spirit of] my fathers, when without ceasing I remember you night and day in my prayers,

4And when as I recall your tears, I yearn to see you, that I may be filled with joy.

5I am calling up memories of your sincere *and* unqualified faith [the [b]leaning of your entire personality on God in Christ in absolute trust and confidence in His power, wisdom and goodness, a faith] that first lived permanently in (the heart of) your grandmother Lois and your mother Eunice and now, I am [fully] persuaded, (dwells) in you also.

6That is why I would remind you to stir up—rekindle the embers, fan the flame and keep burning—the [gracious] gift of God, [the inner fire] that is in you by means of the laying on of my hands [ [c]with those of the elders at your ordination].

7For God did not give us a spirit of timidity—of cowardice, of craven and cringing and fawning fear—but [He has given us a spirit] of power and of love and of calm *and* well-balanced mind *and* discipline *and* self-control.

8Do not blush *or* be ashamed then to testify to *and* for our Lord, nor of me, a prisoner for His sake, but [ [d]with me] take your share of the suffering [to which the preaching] of the Gospel [may expose you, and do it] in the power of God.

9[For it is He] Who delivered *and* saved us and called us with a calling in itself holy *and* leading to holiness—that is, to a life of consecration, a vocation of holiness; [He did it] not because of anything of merit that we have done, but because of *and* to further His own purpose and grace (unmerited favor) which was given us in Christ Jesus before the world began—eternal ages ago.

10[It is that purpose and grace] which He now has made known *and* has fully disclosed *and* made real [to us] through the appearing of our Savior Christ Jesus Who annulled death *and* made it of no effect, and brought life and immortality—that is, immunity from eternal death—to light through the Gospel.

11For [the proclaiming of] this [Gospel], I was appointed a herald (preacher) and an apostle (special messenger) and a teacher *of the Gentiles*.

12And this is why I am suffering as I do. Still I am not ashamed, for I know—I perceive, have knowledge of and am acquainted with—Him Whom I have believed (adhered to and trusted in and relied on), and I am [positively] persuaded that He is able to guard *and* keep that which has been entrusted to me *and* which [e]I have committed [to Him], until that day.

13Hold fast *and* follow the pattern of wholesome *and* sound teaching which you have heard from me, in [all] the faith and love which are [for us] in Christ Jesus.

**AMP** [a] Vincent. [b] Souter. [c] Vincent. [d] Vincent. [e] Alternate reading.

## New American Standard

# 2 Timothy

*Timothy Charged to Guard His Trust*

1 PAUL, AN apostle of Christ Jesus by the will of God, according to the promise of life in Christ Jesus,
2to Timothy, my beloved son: Grace, mercy *and* peace from God the Father and Christ Jesus our Lord.
3¶ I thank God, whom I serve with a clear conscience the way my forefathers did, as I constantly remember you in my prayers night and day,
4longing to see you, even as I recall your tears, so that I may be filled with joy.
5For I am mindful of the sincere faith within you, which first dwelt in your grandmother Lois, and your mother Eunice, and I am sure that *it is* in you as well.
6And for this reason I remind you to kindle afresh the gift of God which is in you through the laying on of my hands.
7For God has not given us a spirit of timidity, but of power and love and discipline.
8Therefore do not be ashamed of the testimony of our Lord, or of me His prisoner; but join with *me* in suffering for the gospel according to the power of God,
9who has saved us, and called us with a holy calling, not according to our works, but according to His own purpose and grace which was granted us in Christ Jesus from all eternity,
10but now has been revealed by the appearing of our Savior Christ Jesus, who abolished death, and brought life and immortality to light through the gospel,
11for which I was appointed a preacher and an apostle and a teacher.
12For this reason I also suffer these things, but I am not ashamed; for I know whom I have believed and I am convinced that He is able to guard what I have entrusted to Him until that day.
13Retain the standard of sound words which you have heard from me, in the faith and love which are in Christ Jesus.

## New International

# 2 Timothy

1 PAUL, AN apostle of Christ Jesus by the will of God, according to the promise of life that is in Christ Jesus,
2To Timothy, my dear son:
Grace, mercy and peace from God the Father and Christ Jesus our Lord.

*Encouragement to Be Faithful*

3I thank God, whom I serve, as my forefathers did, with a clear
conscience, as night and day I constantly remember you in my
prayers. 4Recalling your tears, I long to see you, so that I may be
filled with joy. 5I have been reminded of your sincere faith, which
first lived in your grandmother Lois and in your mother Eunice
and, I am persuaded, now lives in you also. 6For this reason I
remind you to fan into flame the gift of God, which is in you
through the laying on of my hands. 7For God did not give us a
spirit of timidity, but a spirit of power, of love and of self-discipline.
8So do not be ashamed to testify about our Lord, or ashamed
of me his prisoner. But join with me in suffering for the gospel,
by the power of God, 9who has saved us and called us to a holy
life—not because of anything we have done but because of his own
purpose and grace. This grace was given us in Christ Jesus before
the beginning of time, 10but it has now been revealed through the
appearing of our Savior, Christ Jesus, who has destroyed death
and has brought life and immortality to light through the gospel.
11And of this gospel I was appointed a herald and an apostle and
a teacher. 12That is why I am suffering as I am. Yet I am not
ashamed, because I know whom I have believed, and am convinced that he is able to guard what I have entrusted to him for
that day.
13What you heard from me, keep as the pattern of sound teaching, with faith and love in Christ Jesus. 14Guard the good deposit

# King James

14That good thing which was committed unto thee keep by the
Holy Ghost which dwelleth in us.
15This thou knowest, that all they which are in Asia be turned
away from me; of whom are Phygellus and Hermogenes.
16The Lord give mercy unto the house of Onesiphorus; for he
oft refreshed me, and was not ashamed of my chain:
17But, when he was in Rome, he sought me out very diligently,
and found *me.*
18The Lord grant unto him that he may find mercy of the Lord
in that day: and in how many things he ministered unto me at
Ephesus, thou knowest very well.

**2** THOU THEREFORE, my son, be strong in the grace that is
in Christ Jesus.
2And the things that thou hast heard of me among many witnesses, the same commit thou to faithful men, who shall be able
to teach others also.
3Thou therefore endure hardness, as a good soldier of Jesus
Christ.
4No man that warreth entangleth himself with the affairs of *this*
life; that he may please him who hath chosen him to be a soldier.
5And if a man also strive for masteries, *yet* is he not crowned,
except he strive lawfully.
6The husbandman that laboureth must be first partaker of the
fruits.
7Consider what I say; and the Lord give thee understanding in
all things.
8Remember that Jesus Christ of the seed of David was raised
from the dead according to my gospel:
9Wherein I suffer trouble, as an evildoer, *even* unto bonds; but
the word of God is not bound.
10Therefore I endure all things for the elect's sakes, that they
may also obtain the salvation which is in Christ Jesus with eternal
glory.
11 *It is* a faithful saying: For if we be dead with *him,* we shall also
live with *him:*
12If we suffer, we shall also reign with *him:* if we deny *him,* he
also will deny us:
13If we believe not, *yet* he abideth faithful: he cannot deny
himself.
14Of these things put *them* in remembrance, charging *them* before the Lord that they strive not about words to no profit, *but* to
the subverting of the hearers.
15Study to show thyself approved unto God, a workman that
needeth not to be ashamed, rightly dividing the word of truth.
16But shun profane *and* vain babblings: for they will increase
unto more ungodliness.
17And their word will eat as doth a canker: of whom is Hymenaeus and Philetus;

# Amplified

14Guard *and* keep [with the greatest care] the precious *and* excellently adapted [Truth] which has been entrusted [to you], by the
[help of the] Holy Spirit Who makes His home in us.
15You already know that all who are in Asia turned away *and*
forsook me, Phygelus and Hermogenes among them.
16May the Lord grant [His] mercy to the family of Onesiphorus,
for he often showed me kindness *and* ministered to my needs—
comforting and reviving and bracing me like fresh air! He was not
ashamed of my chains *and* imprisonment [for Christ's sake].
17No, rather when he reached Rome he searched diligently *and*
eagerly for me and found [me].
18May the Lord grant to him that he may find mercy from the
Lord on that [great] day! And you know how many things he did
for me *and* what a help he was at Ephesus better [than I can tell
you].

**2** SO YOU, my son, be strong—strengthened inwardly—in the
grace (spiritual blessing) that is [to be found only] in Christ
Jesus.
2And the [instructions] which you have heard from me, along
with many witnesses, transmit *and* entrust (as a deposit) to reliable
*and* faithful men who will be competent *and* qualified to teach
others also.
3Take [with me] your share of the hardships *and* suffering
[which you are called to endure] as a good (first class) soldier of
Christ Jesus.
4No soldier when in service gets entangled in the enterprises of
[civilian] life; his aim is to satisfy *and* please the one who enlisted
him.
5And if any one enters competitive games, he is not crowned
unless he competes lawfully—fairly, according to the rules laid
down.
6[It is] the hard-working farmer (who labors to produce) who
must be the first partaker of the fruits.
7Think over these things I am saying—understand them and
grasp their application—for the Lord will grant you full insight *and*
understanding in everything.
8Constantly keep in mind Jesus Christ, the Messiah, [as] risen
from the dead, [as the prophesied King] descended from David,
according to the good news (the Gospel) that I preach. [Ps. 16:10.]
9For that [Gospel] I am suffering affliction *and* even wearing
chains, like a criminal. But the Word of God is not chained *or*
imprisoned!
10Therefore I [am ready to] persevere *and* stand my ground with
patience *and* endure everything for the sake of the elect [God's
chosen], so that they too may obtain [the] salvation which is in
Christ Jesus with [the reward of] eternal glory.
11The saying is worthy of confidence *and* sure: If we have died
with Him, we shall also live with Him.
12If we endure, we shall also reign with Him. If we deny *and*
disown *and* reject Him, He will also deny *and* disown *and* reject us.
13If we are faithless (do not believe and are untrue to Him), He
remains true [faithful to His Word and His righteous character], for
He cannot deny Himself.
14Remind [the people] of these facts, and [solemnly] charge
them in the presence of the Lord to avoid petty controversy over
words, which does no good, but upsets *and* undermines the faith
of the hearers.
15Study *and* be eager *and* do your utmost to present yourself to
God approved (tested by trial), a workman who has no cause to
be ashamed, correctly analyzing *and* accurately dividing—rightly
handling and skillfully teaching—the Word of Truth.
16But avoid all empty (vain, useless, idle) talk, for it will lead
people into more *and* more ungodliness.
17And their teaching [will devour; it] will eat its way like cancer
*or* spread like gangrene. So it is with Hymenaeus and Philetus,

## New American Standard

[14]Guard, through the Holy Spirit who dwells in us, the treasure which has been entrusted to *you.*

[15]¶ You are aware of the fact that all who are in Asia turned away from me, among whom are Phygelus and Hermogenes.

[16]The Lord grant mercy to the house of Onesiphorus for he often refreshed me, and was not ashamed of my chains;

[17]but when he was in Rome, he eagerly searched for me, and found me—

[18]the Lord grant to him to find mercy from the Lord on that day—and you know very well what services he rendered at Ephesus.

*Be Strong*

**2** YOU THEREFORE, my son, be strong in the grace that is in Christ Jesus.

[2]And the things which you have heard from me in the presence of many witnesses, these entrust to faithful men, who will be able to teach others also.

[3]Suffer hardship with *me,* as a good soldier of Christ Jesus.

[4]No soldier in active service entangles himself in the affairs of everyday life, so that he may please the one who enlisted him as a soldier.

[5]And also if anyone competes as an athlete, he does not win the prize unless he competes according to the rules.

[6]The hard-working farmer ought to be the first to receive his share of the crops.

[7]Consider what I say, for the Lord will give you understanding in everything.

[8]Remember Jesus Christ, risen from the dead, descendant of David, according to my gospel,

[9]for which I suffer hardship even to imprisonment as a criminal; but the word of God is not imprisoned.

[10]For this reason I endure all things for the sake of those who are chosen, that they also may obtain the salvation which is in Christ Jesus *and* with *it* eternal glory.

[11]It is a trustworthy statement:

For if we died with Him, we shall also live with Him;<br>
12 If we endure, we shall also reign with Him;<br>
If we deny Him, He also will deny us;<br>
13 If we are faithless, He remains faithful; for He cannot deny Himself.

*An Unashamed Workman*

[14]¶ Remind *them* of these things, and solemnly charge *them* in the presence of God not to wrangle about words, which is useless, *and leads* to the ruin of the hearers.

[15]Be diligent to present yourself approved to God as a workman who does not need to be ashamed, handling accurately the word of truth.

[16]But avoid worldly *and* empty chatter, for it will lead to further ungodliness,

[17]and their talk will spread like [a]gangrene. Among them are Hymenaeus and Philetus,

NAS [a] Or, *cancer*

## New International

that was entrusted to you—guard it with the help of the Holy Spirit
who lives in us.
[15]You know that everyone in the province of Asia has deserted
me, including Phygelus and Hermogenes.
[16]May the Lord show mercy to the household of Onesiphorus,
because he often refreshed me and was not ashamed of my chains.
[17]On the contrary, when he was in Rome, he searched hard for me
until he found me. [18]May the Lord grant that he will find mercy
from the Lord on that day! You know very well in how many ways
he helped me in Ephesus.

**2** YOU THEN, my son, be strong in the grace that is in Christ
Jesus. [2]And the things you have heard me say in the presence
of many witnesses entrust to reliable men who will also be qualified to teach others. [3]Endure hardship with us like a good soldier
of Christ Jesus. [4]No one serving as a soldier gets involved in
civilian affairs—he wants to please his commanding officer. [5]Simi-
larly, if anyone competes as an athlete, he does not receive the
victor's crown unless he competes according to the rules. [6]The
hardworking farmer should be the first to receive a share of the
crops. [7]Reflect on what I am saying, for the Lord will give you
insight into all this.
[8]Remember Jesus Christ, raised from the dead, descended from
David. This is my gospel, [9]for which I am suffering even to the
point of being chained like a criminal. But God's word is not
chained. [10]Therefore I endure everything for the sake of the elect,
that they too may obtain the salvation that is in Christ Jesus, with
eternal glory.
[11]Here is a trustworthy saying:

If we died with him,<br>
we will also live with him;<br>
[12]if we endure,<br>
we will also reign with him.<br>
If we disown him,<br>
he will also disown us;<br>
[13]if we are faithless,<br>
he will remain faithful,<br>
for he cannot disown himself.

*A Workman Approved by God*

[14]Keep reminding them of these things. Warn them before God
against quarreling about words; it is of no value, and only ruins
those who listen. [15]Do your best to present yourself to God as one
approved, a workman who does not need to be ashamed and who
correctly handles the word of truth. [16]Avoid godless chatter, because those who indulge in it will become more and more ungodly.
[17]Their teaching will spread like gangrene. Among them are Hymenaeus and Philetus, [18]who have wandered away from the truth.

# King James

18Who concerning the truth have erred, saying that the resurrection is past already; and overthrow the faith of some.

19Nevertheless the foundation of God standeth sure, having this seal, The Lord knoweth them that are his. And, Let every one that nameth the name of Christ depart from iniquity.

20But in a great house there are not only vessels of gold and of silver, but also of wood and of earth; and some to honour, and some to dishonour.

21If a man therefore purge himself from these, he shall be a vessel unto honour, sanctified, and meet for the master's use, *and* prepared unto every good work.

22Flee also youthful lusts: but follow righteousness, faith, charity, peace, with them that call on the Lord out of a pure heart.

23But foolish and unlearned questions avoid, knowing that they do gender strifes.

24And the servant of the Lord must not strive; but be gentle unto all *men,* apt to teach, patient,

25In meekness instructing those that oppose themselves; if God peradventure will give them repentance to the acknowledging of the truth;

26And *that* they may recover themselves out of the snare of the devil, who are taken captive by him at his will.

**3** THIS KNOW also, that in the last days perilous times shall come.

2For men shall be lovers of their own selves, covetous, boasters, proud, blasphemers, disobedient to parents, unthankful, unholy,

3Without natural affection, trucebreakers, false accusers, incontinent, fierce, despisers of those that are good,

4Traitors, heady, highminded, lovers of pleasures more than lovers of God;

5Having a form of godliness, but denying the power thereof: from such turn away.

6For of this sort are they which creep into houses, and lead captive silly women laden with sins, led away with divers lusts,

7Ever learning, and never able to come to the knowledge of the truth.

# Amplified

18Who have missed the mark *and* swerved from the truth by arguing that the resurrection has already taken place. They are undermining the faith of some.

19But the firm foundation [laid by] God stands, sure *and* unshaken, bearing this seal (inscription): The Lord knows those who are His, and, Let every one who names [himself by] the name of the Lord give up all iniquity *and* stand aloof from it. [Num. 16:5; Isa. 26:13.]

20But in a great house there are not only vessels of gold and silver but also [utensils] of wood and earthenware, and some for honorable *and* noble [use] and some for menial *and* ignoble [use].

21So whoever cleanses himself [from what is ignoble *and* unclean]—who separates himself from contact with contaminating and corrupting influences—will [then himself] be a vessel set apart *and* useful for honorable *and* noble purposes, consecrated and profitable to the Master, fit *and* ready for any good work.

22Shun youthful lusts *and* flee from them, and aim at *and* pursue righteousness—all that is virtuous and good, right living, conformity to the will of God in thought, word and deed. [And aim at and pursue] faith, love, [and] peace—which is harmony and concord with others—in fellowship with all [Christians], who call upon the Lord out of a pure heart.

23But refuse—shut your mind against, have nothing to do with—trifling (ill-informed, unedifying, stupid) controversies over ignorant questionings, for you know that they foster strife *and* breed quarrels.

24And the servant of the Lord must not be quarrelsome—fighting and contending. Instead he must be kindly to every one *and* mild-tempered—preserving the bond of peace; he must be a skilled *and* suitable teacher, patient *and* forbearing *and* willing to suffer wrong.

25He must correct his opponents with courtesy *and* gentleness, in the hope that God may grant that they will repent and come to know the Truth—that is, that they will perceive and recognize and become accurately acquainted with and acknowledge it,

26And that they may come to their senses [and] escape out of the snare of the devil, having been held captive by him, [henceforth] to do His [God's] will.

**3** BUT UNDERSTAND this, that in the last days there will set in perilous times of great stress *and* trouble—hard to deal with and hard to bear.

2For people will be lovers of self *and* [utterly] self-centered, lovers of money *and* aroused by an inordinate (greedy) desire for wealth, proud *and* arrogant *and* contemptuous boasters. They will be abusive (blasphemous, scoffers), disobedient to parents, ungrateful, unholy *and* profane.

3[They will be] without natural (human) affection (callous and inhuman), relentless—admitting of no truce *or* appeasement. [They will be] slanderers—false accusers, trouble makers; intemperate *and* loose in morals *and* conduct, uncontrolled *and* fierce, haters of good.

4[They will be] treacherous (betrayers), rash [and] inflated with self-conceit. [They will be] lovers of sensual pleasures *and* vain amusements more than *and* rather than lovers of God.

5For [although] they hold a form of piety (true religion), they deny *and* reject *and* are strangers to the power of it—their conduct belies the genuineness of their profession. Avoid [all] such people—turn away from them.

6For among them are those who worm their way into homes and captivate silly *and* weak-natured *and* spiritually dwarfed women, loaded down with [the burden of their] sins, [and easily] swayed *and* led away by various evil desires *and* seductive impulses.

7[These weak women will listen to anybody who will teach them]; they are forever inquiring *and* getting information, but are never able to arrive at a recognition *and* knowledge of the Truth.

## New American Standard

18 *men* who have gone astray from the truth saying that the
resurrection has already taken place, and thus they upset the faith
of some.
19Nevertheless, the firm foundation of God stands, having this
seal, "The Lord knows those who are His," and, "Let everyone
who names the name of the Lord abstain from wickedness."
20Now in a large house there are not only gold and silver vessels, but also vessels of wood and of earthenware, and some to
honor and some to dishonor.
21Therefore, if a man cleanses himself from these *things*, he will
be a vessel for honor, sanctified, useful to the Master, prepared for
every good work.
22Now flee from youthful lusts, and pursue righteousness,
faith, love *and* peace, with those who call on the Lord from a pure
heart.
23But refuse foolish and ignorant speculations, knowing that
they produce quarrels.
24And the Lord's bond-servant must not be quarrelsome, but be
kind to all, able to teach, patient when wronged,
25with gentleness correcting those who are in opposition, if
perhaps God may grant them repentance leading to the knowledge of the truth,
26and they may come to their senses *and escape* from the snare
of the devil, having been held captive by him to do his will.

## New International

They say that the resurrection has already taken place, and they
destroy the faith of some. 19Nevertheless, God's solid foundation
stands firm, sealed with this inscription: "The Lord knows those
who are his,"[a] and, "Everyone who confesses the name of the
Lord must turn away from wickedness."
20In a large house there are articles not only of gold and silver,
but also of wood and clay; some are for noble purposes and some
for ignoble. 21If a man cleanses himself from the latter, he will be
an instrument for noble purposes, made holy, useful to the Master
and prepared to do any good work.
22Flee the evil desires of youth, and pursue righteousness,
faith, love and peace, along with those who call on the Lord out
of a pure heart. 23Don't have anything to do with foolish and
stupid arguments, because you know they produce quarrels.
24And the Lord's servant must not quarrel; instead, he must be
kind to everyone, able to teach, not resentful. 25Those who oppose
him he must gently instruct, in the hope that God will grant them
repentance leading them to a knowledge of the truth, 26and that
they will come to their senses and escape from the trap of the devil,
who has taken them captive to do his will.

### New American Standard

*"Difficult Times Will Come"*

**3** BUT REALIZE this, that in the last days difficult times will
come.
2For men will be lovers of self, lovers of money, boastful,
arrogant, revilers, disobedient to parents, ungrateful, unholy,
3unloving, irreconcilable, malicious gossips, without self-control, brutal, haters of good,
4treacherous, reckless, conceited, lovers of pleasure rather
than lovers of God;
5holding to a form of godliness, although they have denied its
power; and avoid such men as these.
6For among them are those who enter into households and
captivate weak women weighed down with sins, led on by various
impulses,
7always learning and never able to come to the knowledge of
the truth.

### New International

*Godlessness in the Last Days*

**3** BUT MARK this: There will be terrible times in the last days.
2People will be lovers of themselves, lovers of money, boastful, proud, abusive, disobedient to their parents, ungrateful, unholy, 3without love, unforgiving, slanderous, without self-control,
brutal, not lovers of the good, 4treacherous, rash, conceited, lovers
of pleasure rather than lovers of God— 5having a form of godliness
but denying its power. Have nothing to do with them.
6They are the kind who worm their way into homes and gain
control over weak-willed women, who are loaded down with sins
and are swayed by all kinds of evil desires, 7always learning but
never able to acknowledge the truth. 8Just as Jannes and Jambres

NIV [a] *19* Num. 16:5 (see Septuagint)

# King James

8Now as Jannes and Jambres withstood Moses, so do these also resist the truth: men of corrupt minds, reprobate concerning the faith.

9But they shall proceed no further: for their folly shall be manifest unto all *men*, as theirs also was.

10But thou hast fully known my doctrine, manner of life, purpose, faith, longsuffering, charity, patience,

11Persecutions, afflictions, which came unto me at Antioch, at Iconium, at Lystra; what persecutions I endured: but out of *them* all the Lord delivered me.

12Yea, and all that will live godly in Christ Jesus shall suffer persecution.

13But evil men and seducers shall wax worse and worse, deceiving, and being deceived.

14But continue thou in the things which thou hast learned and hast been assured of, knowing of whom thou hast learned *them;*

15And that from a child thou hast known the holy scriptures, which are able to make thee wise unto salvation through faith which is in Christ Jesus.

16All scripture *is* given by inspiration of God, and *is* profitable for doctrine, for reproof, for correction, for instruction in righteousness:

17That the man of God may be perfect, thoroughly furnished unto all good works.

**4** I CHARGE *thee* therefore before God, and the Lord Jesus Christ, who shall judge the quick and the dead at his appearing and his kingdom;

2Preach the word; be instant in season, out of season; reprove, rebuke, exhort with all longsuffering and doctrine.

3For the time will come when they will not endure sound doctrine; but after their own lusts shall they heap to themselves teachers, having itching ears;

4And they shall turn away *their* ears from the truth, and shall be turned unto fables.

5But watch thou in all things, endure afflictions, do the work of an evangelist, make full proof of thy ministry.

6For I am now ready to be offered, and the time of my departure is at hand.

7I have fought a good fight, I have finished *my* course, I have kept the faith:

8Henceforth there is laid up for me a crown of righteousness, which the Lord, the righteous judge, shall give me at that day: and not to me only, but unto all them also that love his appearing.

# Amplified

8Now just as Jannes and Jambres were hostile to *and* resisted Moses, so these men also are hostile to *and* oppose the Truth. They have depraved *and* distorted minds, and are reprobate *and* counterfeit *and* to be rejected as far as the faith is concerned. [Exod. 7:11.]

9But they will not get very far, for their rash folly will become obvious to everybody, as was that of those [magicians mentioned].

10Now you have closely observed *and* diligently followed my teaching, conduct, purpose in life, faith, patience, love, steadfastness,

11Persecutions, sufferings, such as occurred to me at Antioch, at Iconium, and at Lystra, persecutions I endured, but out of them all the Lord delivered me.

12Indeed all who delight in piety *and* are determined to live a devoted *and* godly life in Christ Jesus will meet with persecution—that is, will be made to suffer because of their religious stand.

13But wicked men and imposters will go on from bad to worse, deceiving *and* leading astray others and being deceived *and* led astray themselves.

14But as for you, continue to hold to the things that you have learned and of which you are convinced, knowing from whom you learned [them],

15And how from your childhood you have had a knowledge of *and* been acquainted with the sacred writings which are able to instruct you *and* give you the understanding for salvation which comes through faith in Christ Jesus [that is, through the ᵃleaning of the entire human personality on God in Christ Jesus in absolute trust and confidence in His power, wisdom and goodness].

16Every Scripture *is* God-breathed—given by His inspiration—and profitable for instruction, for reproof *and* conviction of sin, for correction of error *and* discipline in obedience, *and* for training in righteousness [that is, in holy living, in conformity to God's will in thought, purpose and action],

17So that the man of God may be complete *and* proficient, well-fitted *and* thoroughly equipped for every good work.

**4** I CHARGE [you] in the presence of God and of Christ Jesus Who is to judge the living and the dead, and by (in the light of) His coming and His kingdom:

2Herald *and* preach the Word! Keep your sense of urgency (stand by, be at hand and ready, whether the opportunity seems to be favorable or unfavorable, whether it is convenient or inconvenient, whether it be welcome or unwelcome, you as preacher of the Word are to show people in what way their lives are wrong) *and* convince them, rebuking *and* correcting, warning *and* urging *and* encouraging them, being unflagging *and* inexhaustible in patience and teaching.

3For the time is coming when [people] will not tolerate (endure) sound *and* wholesome instruction, but having ears itching [for something pleasing and gratifying], they will gather to themselves one teacher after another to a considerable number, chosen to satisfy their own liking *and* to foster the errors they hold,

4And will turn aside from hearing the truth and wander off into myths *and* man-made fictions.

5As for you, be calm *and* cool *and* steady, accept *and* suffer unflinchingly every hardship, do the work of an evangelist; fully perform all the duties of your ministry.

6For I am already about to be sacrificed—my life is about to be poured out [as a drink offering]; the time of my [spirit's] release [from the body] is at hand *and* I will soon go free.

7I have fought the good (worthy, honorable and noble) fight; I have finished the race; I have kept (firmly held) the faith.

8(As to what remains,) henceforth there is laid up for me the [victor's] crown of righteousness—for being right with God and doing right—which the Lord, the righteous Judge, will award to me *and* recompense me on that [great] day; and not to me only but also to all those who have loved *and* yearned for *and* welcomed His appearing [His return].

## New American Standard

8And just as Jannes and Jambres opposed Moses, so these *men* also oppose the truth, men of depraved mind, rejected as regards the faith.
9But they will not make further progress; for their folly will be obvious to all, as also that of those *two* came to be.
10But you followed my teaching, conduct, purpose, faith, patience, love, perseverance,
11persecutions, *and* sufferings, such as happened to me at Antioch, at Iconium *and* at Lystra; what persecutions I endured, and out of them all the Lord delivered me!
12And indeed, all who desire to live godly in Christ Jesus will be persecuted.
13But evil men and impostors will proceed *from bad* to worse, deceiving and being deceived.
14You, however, continue in the things you have learned and become convinced of, knowing from whom you have learned *them;*
15and that from childhood you have known the sacred writings which are able to give you the wisdom that leads to salvation through faith which is in Christ Jesus.
16 [b]All Scripture is inspired by God and profitable for teaching, for reproof, for correction, for training in righteousness;
17that the man of God may be adequate, equipped for every good work.

## New International

opposed Moses, so also these men oppose the truth—men of
depraved minds, who, as far as the faith is concerned, are rejected.
9But they will not get very far because, as in the case of those men,
their folly will be clear to everyone.

*Paul's Charge to Timothy*

10You, however, know all about my teaching, my way of life,
my purpose, faith, patience, love, endurance, 11persecutions, sufferings—what kinds of things happened to me in Antioch, Iconium and Lystra, the persecutions I endured. Yet the Lord rescued
me from all of them. 12In fact, everyone who wants to live a godly
life in Christ Jesus will be persecuted, 13while evil men and impostors will go from bad to worse, deceiving and being deceived. 14But
as for you, continue in what you have learned and have become
convinced of, because you know those from whom you learned it,
15and how from infancy you have known the holy Scriptures,
which are able to make you wise for salvation through faith in
Christ Jesus. 16All Scripture is God-breathed and is useful for
teaching, rebuking, correcting and training in righteousness, 17so
that the man of God may be thoroughly equipped for every good
work.

*"Preach the Word"*

**4** I SOLEMNLY charge *you* in the presence of God and of Christ Jesus, who is to judge the living and the dead, and by His appearing and His kingdom:
2preach the word; be ready in season *and* out of season; reprove, rebuke, exhort, with great patience and instruction.
3For the time will come when they will not endure sound doctrine; but *wanting* to have their ears tickled, they will accumulate for themselves teachers in accordance to their own desires;
4and will turn away their ears from the truth, and will turn aside to myths.
5But you, be sober in all things, endure hardship, do the work of an evangelist, fulfill your ministry.
6For I am already being poured out as a drink offering, and the time of my departure has come.
7I have fought the good fight, I have finished the course, I have kept the faith;
8in the future there is laid up for me the crown of righteousness, which the Lord, the righteous Judge, will award to me on that day; and not only to me, but also to all who have loved His appearing.

**4** IN THE presence of God and of Christ Jesus, who will judge
the living and the dead, and in view of his appearing and his
kingdom, I give you this charge: 2Preach the Word; be prepared
in season and out of season; correct, rebuke and encourage—with
great patience and careful instruction. 3For the time will come
when men will not put up with sound doctrine. Instead, to suit
their own desires, they will gather around them a great number
of teachers to say what their itching ears want to hear. 4They will
turn their ears away from the truth and turn aside to myths. 5But
you, keep your head in all situations, endure hardship, do the
work of an evangelist, discharge all the duties of your ministry.
6For I am already being poured out like a drink offering, and
the time has come for my departure. 7I have fought the good fight,
I have finished the race, I have kept the faith. 8Now there is in store
for me the crown of righteousness, which the Lord, the righteous
Judge, will award to me on that day—and not only to me, but also
to all who have longed for his appearing.

**NAS** [b] Or possibly, *Every Scripture inspired by God is also profitable*

## King James

9 Do thy diligence to come shortly unto me:

10 For Demas hath forsaken me, having loved this present world, and is departed unto Thessalonica; Crescens to Galatia, Titus unto Dalmatia.

11 Only Luke is with me. Take Mark, and bring him with thee: for he is profitable to me for the ministry.

12 And Tychicus have I sent to Ephesus.

13 The cloak that I left at Troas with Carpus, when thou comest, bring *with thee*, and the books, *but* especially the parchments.

14 Alexander the coppersmith did me much evil: the Lord reward him according to his works:

15 Of whom be thou ware also; for he hath greatly withstood our words.

16 At my first answer no man stood with me, but all *men* forsook me: *I pray God* that it may not be laid to their charge.

17 Notwithstanding the Lord stood with me, and strengthened me; that by me the preaching might be fully known, and *that* all the Gentiles might hear: and I was delivered out of the mouth of the lion.

18 And the Lord shall deliver me from every evil work, and will preserve *me* unto his heavenly kingdom: to whom *be* glory for ever and ever. Amen.

19 Salute Prisca and Aquila, and the household of Onesiphorus.

20 Erastus abode at Corinth: but Trophimus have I left at Miletum sick.

21 Do thy diligence to come before winter. Eubulus greeteth thee, and Pudens, and Linus, and Claudia, and all the brethren.

22 The Lord Jesus Christ *be* with thy spirit. Grace *be* with you. Amen.

## Amplified

9 Make every effort to come to me soon.

10 For Demas has deserted me for love of this present world and has gone to Thessalonica; Crescens [has gone] to Galatia, Titus to Dalmatia.

11 Luke alone is with me. Get Mark and bring him with you, for he is very helpful to me for the ministry.

12 Tychicus I have sent to Ephesus.

13 [When] you come, bring the cloak that I left at Troas with Carpus; also the books, especially the parchments.

14 Alexander the coppersmith did me great wrongs. The Lord will pay him back for his actions.

15 Beware of him yourself, for he opposed *and* resisted our message very strongly *and* exceedingly.

16 At my first trial no one acted in my defense (as my advocate) *or* took my part *or* [even] stood with me, but all forsook me. May it not be charged against them!

17 But the Lord stood by me and strengthened me, so that through me the (Gospel) message might be fully proclaimed and all the Gentiles might hear it. So I was delivered out of the jaws of the lion.

18 [And indeed] the Lord will certainly deliver *and* [a]draw me to Himself from every assault of evil. He will preserve *and* bring [me] safe unto His heavenly kingdom. To Him be the glory forever and ever. Amen—so be it.

19 Give my greetings to Prisca and Aquila, and to the household of Onesiphorus.

20 Erastus stayed on at Corinth, but Trophimus I left ill at Miletus.

21 Do hasten *and* try your best to come to me before winter. Eubulus wishes to be remembered to you, as do Pudens and Linus and Claudia and all the brethren.

22 The Lord *Jesus Christ* be with your spirit. Grace (God's favor and blessing) be with you. *Amen.*

**AMP** [a] Primary meaning of the Greek: "draw to one's self." Thayer; Abbott-Smith.

## New American Standard

*Personal Concerns*

9¶ Make every effort to come to me soon;

10for Demas, having loved this present world, has deserted me and gone to Thessalonica; Crescens *has gone* to Galatia, Titus to Dalmatia.

11Only Luke is with me. Pick up Mark and bring him with you, for he is useful to me for service.

12But Tychicus I have sent to Ephesus.

13When you come bring the cloak which I left at Troas with Carpus, and the books, especially the parchments.

14Alexander the coppersmith did me much harm; the Lord will repay him according to his deeds.

15Be on guard against him yourself, for he vigorously opposed our teaching.

16At my first defense no one supported me, but all deserted me; may it not be counted against them.

17But the Lord stood with me, and strengthened me, in order that through me the proclamation might be fully accomplished, and that all the Gentiles might hear; and I was delivered out of the lion's mouth.

18The Lord will deliver me from every evil deed, and will bring me safely to His heavenly kingdom; to Him *be* the glory forever and ever. Amen.

19¶ Greet Prisca and Aquila, and the household of Onesiphorus.

20Erastus remained at Corinth, but Trophimus I left sick at Miletus.

21Make every effort to come before winter. Eubulus greets you, also Pudens and Linus and Claudia and all the brethren.

22¶ The Lord be with your spirit. Grace be with you.

## New International

*Personal Remarks*

9Do your best to come to me quickly, 10for Demas, because he
loved this world, has deserted me and has gone to Thessalonica.
Crescens has gone to Galatia, and Titus to Dalmatia. 11Only Luke
is with me. Get Mark and bring him with you, because he is helpful
to me in my ministry. 12I sent Tychicus to Ephesus. 13When you
come, bring the cloak that I left with Carpus at Troas, and my
scrolls, especially the parchments.
14Alexander the metalworker did me a great deal of harm. The
Lord will repay him for what he has done. 15You too should be on
your guard against him, because he strongly opposed our message.

16At my first defense, no one came to my support, but everyone
deserted me. May it not be held against them. 17But the Lord stood
at my side and gave me strength, so that through me the message
might be fully proclaimed and all the Gentiles might hear it. And
I was delivered from the lion's mouth. 18The Lord will rescue me
from every evil attack and will bring me safely to his heavenly
kingdom. To him be glory for ever and ever. Amen.

*Final Greetings*

19Greet Priscilla[b] and Aquila and the household of Onesiphorus.
20Erastus stayed in Corinth, and I left Trophimus sick in
Miletus. 21Do your best to get here before winter. Eubulus greets
you, and so do Pudens, Linus, Claudia and all the brothers.
22The Lord be with your spirit. Grace be with you.

**NIV** [b] 19 Greek *Prisca*, a variant of *Priscilla*

## King James

THE EPISTLE OF

PAUL TO

# Titus

**1** PAUL, A servant of God, and an apostle of Jesus Christ, according to the faith of God's elect, and the acknowledging of the truth which is after godliness;

2In hope of eternal life, which God, that cannot lie, promised before the world began;

3But hath in due times manifested his word through preaching, which is committed unto me according to the commandment of God our Saviour;

4To Titus, *mine* own son after the common faith: Grace, mercy, *and* peace, from God the Father and the Lord Jesus Christ our Saviour.

5For this cause left I thee in Crete, that thou shouldest set in order the things that are wanting, and ordain elders in every city, as I had appointed thee:

6If any be blameless, the husband of one wife, having faithful children not accused of riot or unruly.

7For a bishop must be blameless, as the steward of God; not self-willed, not soon angry, not given to wine, no striker, not given to filthy lucre;

8But a lover of hospitality, a lover of good men, sober, just, holy, temperate;

9Holding fast the faithful word as he hath been taught, that he may be able by sound doctrine both to exhort and to convince the gainsayers.

10For there are many unruly and vain talkers and deceivers, specially they of the circumcision:

11Whose mouths must be stopped, who subvert whole houses, teaching things which they ought not, for filthy lucre's sake.

12One of themselves, *even* a prophet of their own, said, The Cretians *are* always liars, evil beasts, slow bellies.

13This witness is true. Wherefore rebuke them sharply, that they may be sound in the faith;

## Amplified

THE LETTER OF

PAUL TO

# Titus

**1** PAUL, A bond servant of God and an apostle (a special messenger) of Jesus Christ, the Messiah, to stimulate *and* promote the faith of God's chosen ones and lead them on to accurate discernment *and* recognition of *and* acquaintance with the Truth which belongs to *and* harmonizes with *and* tends to godliness,

2(Resting) in the hope of eternal life, [life] which the ever-truthful God Who cannot deceive, promised before the world *or* the ages of time began.

3And [now] in His own appointed time He has made manifest (made known) His Word *and* revealed it as His message through the preaching entrusted to me by command of God our Savior;

4To Titus, my true child according to a common (general) faith: Grace (favor and spiritual blessing) and heart-peace from God the Father and *the Lord* Christ Jesus our Savior.

5For this reason I left you [behind] in Crete, that you might set right what was defective *and* finish what was left undone, and that you might appoint elders *and* set them over the churches (assemblies) in every city as I directed you.

6[These elders should be] men who are of unquestionable integrity *and* are irreproachable, the husband of [but] one wife, whose children are [well-trained and are] believers, not open to the accusation of being loose in morals *and* conduct or unruly *and* disorderly.

7For the bishop *as* an overseer and God's steward must be blameless; not self-willed *or* arrogant *or* presumptuous; he must not be quick-tempered *or* given to drink or pugnacious (brawling, violent); he must not be grasping *and* greedy for filthy lucre (financial gain);

8But he must be hospitable—loving and a friend to believers, especially to the strangers and foreigners. [He must be] a lover of goodness—of good people and good things; sober-minded (sensible, discreet); upright *and* fair-minded, a devout man *and* religiously right, temperate *and* keeping himself in hand.

9He must hold fast to the sure *and* trustworthy Word of God as he was taught it, so that he may be able both to give stimulating instruction *and* encouragement in sound (wholesome) doctrine, and to refute *and* convict those who contradict *and* oppose it—showing the wayward their error.

10For there are many disorderly *and* unruly men who are idle (vain, empty) *and* misleading talkers and self-deceivers, *as well as* deceiving others. [This is true] especially of those [who have come over from Judaism] of the circumcision party.

11Their mouths must be stopped, for they are mentally distressing *and* subverting whole families by teaching what they ought not to teach, for the purpose of getting base advantage *and* disreputable gain.

12One of their [very] number, a prophet of their own, said, Cretans are always liars, hurtful beasts, idle *and* lazy gluttons.

13And this account of them is [really] true. Because it is [true], rebuke them sharply—deal sternly, [even] severely with them—so that they may be sound in the faith *and* free from error,

## New American Standard

# Titus

*Salutation*

1 PAUL, A bond-servant of God, and an apostle of Jesus Christ,
for the faith of those chosen of God and the knowledge of the
truth which is according to godliness,
2in the hope of eternal life, which God, who cannot lie, promised long ages ago,
3but at the proper time manifested, *even* His word, in the
proclamation with which I was entrusted according to the commandment of God our Savior;
4to Titus, my true child in a common faith: Grace and peace
from God the Father and Christ Jesus our Savior.

*Qualifications of Elders*

5¶ For this reason I left you in Crete, that you might set in order
what remains, and appoint elders in every city as I directed you,
6 *namely*, if any man be above reproach, the husband of one
wife, having children who believe, not accused of dissipation or
rebellion.
7For the overseer must be above reproach as God's steward,
not self-willed, not quick-tempered, not addicted to wine, not
pugnacious, not fond of sordid gain,
8but hospitable, loving what is good, sensible, just, devout,
self-controlled,
9holding fast the faithful word which is in accordance with the
teaching, that he may be able both to exhort in sound doctrine and
to refute those who contradict.
10¶ For there are many rebellious men, empty talkers and deceivers, especially those of the circumcision,
11who must be silenced because they are upsetting whole families, teaching things they should not *teach*, for the sake of sordid
gain.
12One of themselves, a prophet of their own, said, "Cretans are
always liars, evil beasts, lazy gluttons."
13This testimony is true. For this cause reprove them severely
that they may be sound in the faith,

## New International

# Titus

1 PAUL, A servant of God and an apostle of Jesus Christ for the
faith of God's elect and the knowledge of the truth that leads
to godliness— 2a faith and knowledge resting on the hope of
eternal life, which God, who does not lie, promised before the
beginning of time, 3and at his appointed season he brought his
word to light through the preaching entrusted to me by the command of God our Savior,

4To Titus, my true son in our common faith:

Grace and peace from God the Father and Christ Jesus our
Savior.

*Titus' Task on Crete*

5The reason I left you in Crete was that you might straighten
out what was left unfinished and appoint[a] elders in every town,
as I directed you. 6An elder must be blameless, the husband of but
one wife, a man whose children believe and are not open to the
charge of being wild and disobedient. 7Since an overseer[b] is entrusted with God's work, he must be blameless—not overbearing,
not quick-tempered, not given to drunkenness, not violent, not
pursuing dishonest gain. 8Rather he must be hospitable, one who
loves what is good, who is self-controlled, upright, holy and disciplined. 9He must hold firmly to the trustworthy message as it has
been taught, so that he can encourage others by sound doctrine
and refute those who oppose it.
10For there are many rebellious people, mere talkers and deceivers, especially those of the circumcision group. 11They must be
silenced, because they are ruining whole households by teaching
things they ought not to teach—and that for the sake of dishonest
gain. 12Even one of their own prophets has said, "Cretans are
always liars, evil brutes, lazy gluttons." 13This testimony is true.
Therefore, rebuke them sharply, so that they will be sound in the
faith 14and will pay no attention to Jewish myths or to the com-

NIV [a] 5 Or *ordain* [b] 7 Traditionally *bishop*

## King James

14Not giving heed to Jewish fables, and commandments of
men, that turn from the truth.

15Unto the pure all things *are* pure: but unto them that are
defiled and unbelieving *is* nothing pure; but even their mind and
conscience is defiled.

16They profess that they know God; but in works they deny
*him*, being abominable, and disobedient, and unto every good
work reprobate.

**2** BUT SPEAK thou the things which become sound doctrine:
2That the aged men be sober, grave, temperate, sound in
faith, in charity, in patience.

3The aged women likewise, that *they be* in behaviour as
becometh holiness, not false accusers, not given to much wine,
teachers of good things;

4That they may teach the young women to be sober, to love
their husbands, to love their children,

5 *To be* discreet, chaste, keepers at home, good, obedient to their
own husbands, that the word of God be not blasphemed.

6Young men likewise exhort to be sober minded.

7In all things showing thyself a pattern of good works: in doctrine *showing* uncorruptness, gravity, sincerity,

8Sound speech, that cannot be condemned; that he that is of the
contrary part may be ashamed, having no evil thing to say of you.

9 *Exhort* servants to be obedient unto their own masters, *and* to
please *them* well in all *things;* not answering again;

10Not purloining, but showing all good fidelity; that they may
adorn the doctrine of God our Saviour in all things.

11For the grace of God that bringeth salvation hath appeared to
all men,

12Teaching us that, denying ungodliness and worldly lusts, we
should live soberly, righteously, and godly, in this present world;

13Looking for that blessed hope, and the glorious appearing of
the great God and our Saviour Jesus Christ;

14Who gave himself for us, that he might redeem us from all
iniquity, and purify unto himself a peculiar people, zealous of
good works.

15These things speak, and exhort, and rebuke with all authority. Let no man despise thee.

## Amplified

14[And may show their soundness by] ceasing to give attention
to Jewish myths *and* fables or to rules [laid down] by [mere] men
who reject *and* turn their backs on the Truth.

15To the pure [in heart and conscience] all things are pure, but
to the defiled *and* corrupt and unbelieving nothing is pure; their
very mind and conscience are defiled *and* polluted.

16They profess to know God—to recognize, perceive and be
acquainted with Him—but deny *and* disown *and* renounce Him by
what they do; they are detestable *and* loathsome, unbelieving *and*
disobedient *and* disloyal *and* rebellious, and [they are] unfit *and*
worthless for good work (deed or enterprise) of any kind.

**2** BUT [AS for] you, teach what is fitting *and* becoming to sound
(wholesome) doctrine—the character and right living that
identify true Christians.

2Urge the older men to be temperate, venerable (serious), sensible, self-controlled; sound in the faith, in the love, and in the
steadfastness *and* patience [of Christ].

3Bid the older women similarly to be reverent *and* devout in
their deportment, as becomes those engaged in sacred service, not
slanderers or slaves to drink. They are to give good counsel *and* be
teachers of what is right *and* noble,

4So that they will wisely train the young women to be [a]sane and
sober-minded—temperate, disciplined—and to love their husbands and their children;

5To be self-controlled, chaste, homemakers, good-natured
(kindhearted), adapting *and* subordinating themselves to their
husbands, that the word of God may not be exposed to reproach—
blasphemed or discredited.

6In a similar way urge the younger men to be self-restrained *and*
to behave prudently—taking life seriously.

7And show your own self in all respects to be a pattern *and* a
model of good deeds *and* works, teaching what is unadulterated,
showing gravity—[that is,] having the strictest regard for truth and
purity of motive, with dignity and seriousness.

8And let your instruction be sound *and* fit *and* wise *and* wholesome, vigorous and [b]irrefutable *and* above censure, so that the
opponent may be put to shame, finding nothing discrediting *or* evil
to say about us.

9[Tell] bond servants to be submissive to their masters, to be
pleasing *and* give satisfaction in every way. [Warn them] not to talk
back *or* contradict,

10Nor to steal by taking things of small value, but to prove
themselves truly loyal *and* entirely reliable *and* faithful throughout,
so that in everything they may be an ornament *and* do credit to the
teaching [which is [c]from and about] God our Savior.

11For the grace of God—His unmerited favor and blessing—has
come forward (appeared) for the deliverance from sin *and* the
eternal salvation for all mankind.

12It has trained us to reject *and* renounce all ungodliness (irreli-
gion) and worldly (passionate) desires, to live discreet (temperate,
self-controlled), upright, devout (spiritually-whole) lives in this
present world,

13Awaiting *and* looking for the [fulfillment, the realization of
our] blessed hope, even the glorious appearing of our great God
and Savior Christ Jesus, the Messiah, the Anointed One,

14Who gave Himself on our behalf that He might redeem us
(purchase our freedom) from all iniquity and purify for Himself a
people—to be peculiarly His own—[people who are] eager *and*
enthusiastic about [living a life that is good and filled with] beneficial deeds. [Ps. 130:8; Ezek. 37:23; Deut. 14:2.]

15Tell [them all] these things. Urge (advise, encourage, warn)
and rebuke with full authority. Let no one despise *or* disregard *or*
think little of you—conduct yourself and your teaching so as to
command respect.

**AMP** [a] The Greek verb here for "train" means to make sane, sober-minded; to
moderate, to discipline. (-Vincent.) [b] Way. [c] Greek, "of."

## New American Standard

14not paying attention to Jewish myths and commandments of men who turn away from the truth.

15To the pure, all things are pure; but to those who are defiled and unbelieving, nothing is pure, but both their mind and their conscience are defiled.

16They profess to know God, but by *their* deeds they deny *Him*, being detestable and disobedient, and worthless for any good deed.

*Duties of the Older and Younger*

**2** BUT AS for you, speak the things which are fitting for sound doctrine.

2Older men are to be temperate, dignified, sensible, sound in faith, in love, in perseverance.

3Older women likewise are to be reverent in their behavior, not malicious gossips, nor enslaved to much wine, teaching what is good,

4that they may encourage the young women to love their husbands, to love their children,

5 *to be* sensible, pure, workers at home, kind, being subject to their own husbands, that the word of God may not be dishonored.

6Likewise urge the young men to be sensible;

7in all things show yourself to be an example of good deeds, *with* purity in doctrine, dignified,

8sound *in* speech which is beyond reproach, in order that the opponent may be put to shame, having nothing bad to say about us.

9 *Urge* bondslaves to be subject to their own masters in everything, to be well-pleasing, not argumentative,

10not pilfering, but showing all good faith that they may adorn the doctrine of God our Savior in every respect.

11For the grace of God has appeared, bringing salvation to all men,

12instructing us to deny ungodliness and worldly desires and to live sensibly, righteously and godly in the present age,

13looking for the blessed hope and the appearing of the glory of our great God and Savior, Christ Jesus;

14who gave Himself for us, that He might redeem us from every lawless deed and purify for Himself a people for His own possession, zealous for good deeds.

15¶ These things speak and exhort and reprove with all authority. Let no one disregard you.

## New International

mands of those who reject the truth. 15To the pure, all things are
pure, but to those who are corrupted and do not believe, nothing
is pure. In fact, both their minds and consciences are corrupted.
16They claim to know God, but by their actions they deny him.
They are detestable, disobedient and unfit for doing anything
good.

*What Must Be Taught to Various Groups*

**2** YOU MUST teach what is in accord with sound doctrine.
2Teach the older men to be temperate, worthy of respect,
self-controlled, and sound in faith, in love and in endurance.
3Likewise, teach the older women to be reverent in the way
they live, not to be slanderers or addicted to much wine, but to
teach what is good. 4Then they can train the younger women to
love their husbands and children, 5to be self-controlled and pure,
to be busy at home, to be kind, and to be subject to their husbands,
so that no one will malign the word of God.
6Similarly, encourage the young men to be self-controlled. 7In
everything set them an example by doing what is good. In your
teaching show integrity, seriousness 8and soundness of speech
that cannot be condemned, so that those who oppose you may be
ashamed because they have nothing bad to say about us.
9Teach slaves to be subject to their masters in everything, to try
to please them, not to talk back to them, 10and not to steal from
them, but to show that they can be fully trusted, so that in every
way they will make the teaching about God our Savior attractive.
11For the grace of God that brings salvation has appeared to all
men. 12It teaches us to say "No" to ungodliness and worldly
passions, and to live self-controlled, upright and godly lives in this
present age, 13while we wait for the blessed hope—the glorious
appearing of our great God and Savior, Jesus Christ, 14who gave
himself for us to redeem us from all wickedness and to purify for
himself a people that are his very own, eager to do what is good.
15These, then, are the things you should teach. Encourage and
rebuke with all authority. Do not let anyone despise you.

## King James

3 PUT THEM in mind to be subject to principalities and powers, to obey magistrates, to be ready to every good work,

2To speak evil of no man, to be no brawlers, *but* gentle, showing all meekness unto all men.

3For we ourselves also were sometimes foolish, disobedient, deceived, serving divers lusts and pleasures, living in malice and envy, hateful, *and* hating one another.

4But after that the kindness and love of God our Saviour toward man appeared,

5Not by works of righteousness which we have done, but according to his mercy he saved us, by the washing of regeneration, and renewing of the Holy Ghost;

6Which he shed on us abundantly through Jesus Christ our Saviour;

7That being justified by his grace, we should be made heirs according to the hope of eternal life.

8 *This is* a faithful saying, and these things I will that thou affirm constantly, that they which have believed in God might be careful to maintain good works. These things are good and profitable unto men.

9But avoid foolish questions, and genealogies, and contentions, and strivings about the law; for they are unprofitable and vain.

10A man that is an heretic after the first and second admonition reject;

11Knowing that he that is such is subverted, and sinneth, being condemned of himself.

12When I shall send Artemas unto thee, or Tychicus, be diligent to come unto me to Nicopolis: for I have determined there to winter.

13Bring Zenas the lawyer and Apollos on their journey diligently, that nothing be wanting unto them.

14And let ours also learn to maintain good works for necessary uses, that they be not unfruitful.

15All that are with me salute thee. Greet them that love us in the faith. Grace *be* with you all. Amen.

## Amplified

3 REMIND PEOPLE to be submissive to [their] magistrates and authorities, to be obedient, to be prepared *and* willing to do any upright *and* honorable work;

2To slander *or* abuse *or* speak evil of no one, to avoid being contentious, to be forbearing—yielding, gentle and conciliatory—and to show unqualified courtesy toward everybody.

3For we also were once thoughtless *and* senseless, obstinate *and* disobedient, deluded *and* misled; [we too were once] slaves to all sorts of cravings *and* pleasures, wasting our days in malice and jealousy *and* envy, hateful (hated, detestable) and hating one another.

4But when the goodness and loving kindness of God our Savior to man [as man] appeared,

5He saved us, not because of any works of righteousness that we had done, but because of His own pity *and* mercy, by [the] cleansing (bath) of the new birth (regeneration) and renewing of the Holy Spirit,

6Which He poured out [so] richly upon us through Jesus Christ our Savior.

7[And He did it in order] that we might be justified by His grace—by His favor, wholly undeserved, that is, that we might be acknowledged and counted as conformed to the Divine will in purpose, thought and action; and that we might become heirs of eternal life according to [our] hope.

8This message is most trustworthy, and concerning these things I want you to insist steadfastly, so that those who have believed in (trusted, relied on) God may be careful to apply themselves to honorable occupations *and* to doing good, for such things are [not only] excellent *and* right [in themselves], but [they are] good *and* profitable for the people.

9But avoid stupid *and* foolish controversies and genealogies and dissensions and wrangling about the Law, for they are unprofitable and futile.

10[As for] a man who is factious—a heretical sectarian and cause of divisions—after admonishing him a first and second time reject (him from your fellowship and have nothing more to do with him),

11Well aware that such a person has utterly changed—is perverted and corrupted; he goes on sinning [though] he is convicted of guilt *and* self-condemned.

12When I send Artemas or [perhaps] Tychicus to you, lose no time *but* make every effort to come to me at Nicopolis, for I have decided to spend the winter there.

13Do your utmost to speed Zenas the lawyer and Apollos on their way; see that they want for nothing.

14And let our [own people really] learn to apply themselves to good deeds—to honest labor and honorable employment—so that they may be able to meet necessary demands [a]whenever the occasion may require and not be living idle *and* uncultivated *and* unfruitful lives.

15All who are with me wish to be remembered to you. Greet those who love us in the faith. Grace (God's favor and blessing) be with you all. *Amen, so be it.*

**AMP** [a] Vincent.

## New American Standard

*Godly Living*

**3** REMIND THEM to be subject to rulers, to authorities, to be
obedient, to be ready for every good deed,
2 to malign no one, to be uncontentious, gentle, showing every
consideration for all men.
3 For we also once were foolish ourselves, disobedient, deceived, enslaved to various lusts and pleasures, spending our life
in malice and envy, hateful, hating one another.
4 But when the kindness of God our Savior and *His* love for
mankind appeared,
5 He saved us, not on the basis of deeds which we have done
in righteousness, but according to His mercy, by the washing of
regeneration and renewing by the Holy Spirit,
6 whom He poured out upon us richly through Jesus Christ our
Savior,
7 that being justified by His grace we might be made heirs
according to *the* hope of eternal life.
8 This is a trustworthy statement; and concerning these things
I want you to speak confidently, so that those who have believed
God may be careful to engage in good deeds. These things are
good and profitable for men.
9 But shun foolish controversies and genealogies and strife and
disputes about the Law; for they are unprofitable and worthless.
10 Reject a factious man after a first and second warning,
11 knowing that such a man is perverted and is sinning, being
self-condemned.

*Personal Concerns*

12 ¶ When I send Artemas or Tychicus to you, make every effort
to come to me at Nicopolis, for I have decided to spend the winter
there.
13 Diligently help Zenas the lawyer and Apollos on their way so
that nothing is lacking for them.
14 And let our *people* also learn to engage in good deeds to meet
pressing needs, that they may not be unfruitful.
15 ¶ All who are with me greet you. Greet those who love us in
*the* faith.
¶ Grace be with you all.

## New International

*Doing What Is Good*

**3** REMIND THE people to be subject to rulers and authorities,
to be obedient, to be ready to do whatever is good, 2 to slander
no one, to be peaceable and considerate, and to show true humility
toward all men.
3 At one time we too were foolish, disobedient, deceived and
enslaved by all kinds of passions and pleasures. We lived in malice
and envy, being hated and hating one another. 4 But when the
kindness and love of God our Savior appeared, 5 he saved us, not
because of righteous things we had done, but because of his
mercy. He saved us through the washing of rebirth and renewal
by the Holy Spirit, 6 whom he poured out on us generously
through Jesus Christ our Savior, 7 so that, having been justified by
his grace, we might become heirs having the hope of eternal life.
8 This is a trustworthy saying. And I want you to stress these
things, so that those who have trusted in God may be careful to
devote themselves to doing what is good. These things are excellent and profitable for everyone.
9 But avoid foolish controversies and genealogies and arguments and quarrels about the law, because these are unprofitable
and useless. 10 Warn a divisive person once, and then warn him a
second time. After that, have nothing to do with him. 11 You may
be sure that such a man is warped and sinful; he is self-condemned.

*Final Remarks*

12 As soon as I send Artemas or Tychicus to you, do your best
to come to me at Nicopolis, because I have decided to winter there.
13 Do everything you can to help Zenas the lawyer and Apollos on
their way and see that they have everything they need. 14 Our
people must learn to devote themselves to doing what is good, in
order that they may provide for daily necessities and not live
unproductive lives.
15 Everyone with me sends you greetings. Greet those who love
us in the faith.
Grace be with you all.

## King James

THE EPISTLE OF PAUL TO

# Philemon

1PAUL, A prisoner of Jesus Christ, and Timothy *our* brother,
unto Philemon our dearly beloved, and fellowlabourer,
2And to *our* beloved Apphia, and Archippus our fellowsoldier,
and to the church in thy house:
3Grace to you, and peace, from God our Father and the Lord
Jesus Christ.
4I thank my God, making mention of thee always in my
prayers,
5Hearing of thy love and faith, which thou hast toward the Lord
Jesus, and toward all saints;
6That the communication of thy faith may become effectual by
the acknowledging of every good thing which is in you in Christ
Jesus.
7For we have great joy and consolation in thy love, because the
bowels of the saints are refreshed by thee, brother.
8Wherefore, though I might be much bold in Christ to enjoin
thee that which is convenient,
9Yet for love's sake I rather beseech *thee,* being such an one as
Paul the aged, and now also a prisoner of Jesus Christ.
10I beseech thee for my son Onesimus, whom I have begotten
in my bonds:
11Which in time past was to thee unprofitable, but now profitable to thee and to me:
12Whom I have sent again: thou therefore receive him, that is,
mine own bowels:
13Whom I would have retained with me, that in thy stead he
might have ministered unto me in the bonds of the gospel:
14But without thy mind would I do nothing; that thy benefit
should not be as it were of necessity, but willingly.
15For perhaps he therefore departed for a season, that thou
shouldest receive him for ever;
16Not now as a servant, but above a servant, a brother beloved,
specially to me, but how much more unto thee, both in the flesh,
and in the Lord?
17If thou count me therefore a partner, receive him as myself.
18If he hath wronged thee, or oweth *thee* aught, put that on
mine account;

## Amplified

THE LETTER OF
PAUL TO

# Philemon

1PAUL, A prisoner [for the sake] of Christ Jesus, the Messiah,
and our brother Timothy, to Philemon our dearly loved sharer
with us in our work,
2And to Apphia our sister and Archippus our fellow soldier [in
the Christian warfare], and to the church (assembly that meets) in
your house:
3Grace (spiritual blessing and favor) be to you all and heart-peace from God our Father and the Lord Jesus Christ, the Messiah.
4I give thanks to my God for you always when I mention you
in my prayers,
5Because I continue to hear of your love and of your loyal faith
which you have toward the Lord Jesus and [which you show]
toward all the saints—God's consecrated people.
6[And I pray] that the participation in *and* sharing of your faith
may produce *and* promote full recognition *and* appreciation *and*
understanding *and* precise knowledge of every good [thing] that
is ours in [our identification with] Christ *Jesus—and* unto [His
glory].
7For I have derived great joy and comfort *and* encouragement
from your love, because the hearts of the saints [who are your
fellow Christians] have been cheered *and* refreshed through you,
[my] brother.
8Therefore, though I have abundant boldness in Christ to
charge you to do what is fitting *and* required *and* your duty to do,
9Yet for love's sake I prefer to appeal to you just for what I am:
I, Paul, an ambassador [of Christ Jesus] *and* an old man and now
a prisoner for His sake also.
10I appeal to you for my [own spiritual] child, Onesimus [meaning profitable], whom I have begotten [in the faith] while a captive
in these chains.
11Once he was unprofitable to you, but now he is indeed profitable to you as well as to me.
12I am sending him back to you in [a]his own person (and it is
like sending) my very heart.
13I would have chosen to keep him with me, in order that he
might minister to my needs in your stead during my imprisonment
for the Gospel's sake.
14But it has been my wish to do nothing about it without first
consulting you *and* getting your consent, in order that your
benevolence might not seem to be the result of compulsion *or* of
pressure but might be voluntary [on your part].
15Perhaps it was for this reason that he was separated [from
you] for a while, that you might have him back as yours forever,
16Not as a slave any longer but as [something] more than a
slave, as a brother [Christian], especially dear to me but how much
more to you, both in the flesh [as a servant] and in the Lord [as
a fellow believer].
17If then you consider me a partner *and* a [b]comrade in fellowship, welcome *and* receive him as you would [welcome and receive] me.
18And if he has done you any wrong in any way, or owes
anything [to you], charge that to my account.

**AMP** [a] Vincent. [b] Vincent.

## New American Standard

# Philemon

*Salutation*

1 PAUL, A prisoner of Christ Jesus, and Timothy our brother, to Philemon our beloved *brother* and fellow worker,

2 and to Apphia our sister, and to Archippus our fellow soldier, and to the church in your house:

3 Grace to you and peace from God our Father and the Lord Jesus Christ.

*Philemon's Love and Faith*

**4**¶ I thank my God always, making mention of you in my prayers,

5 because I hear of your love, and of the faith which you have toward the Lord Jesus, and toward all the saints;

6 *and I pray* that the fellowship of your faith may become effective [c]through the knowledge of every good thing which is in [d]you for Christ's sake.

7 For I have come to have much joy and comfort in your love, because the hearts of the saints have been refreshed through you, brother.

**8**¶ Therefore, though I have enough confidence in Christ to order you *to do* that which is proper,

9 yet for love's sake I rather appeal *to you*—since I am such a person as Paul, the aged, and now also a prisoner of Christ Jesus—

*Plea for Onesimus, a Free Man*

10 I appeal to you for my child, whom I have begotten in my imprisonment, [e]Onesimus,

11 who formerly was useless to you, but now is useful both to you and to me.

12 And I have sent him back to you in person, that is, *sending* my very heart,

13 whom I wished to keep with me, that in your behalf he might minister to me in my imprisonment for the gospel;

14 but without your consent I did not want to do anything, that your goodness should not be as it were by compulsion, but of your own free will.

15 For perhaps he was for this reason parted *from you* for a while, that you should have him back forever,

16 no longer as a slave, but more than a slave, a beloved brother, especially to me, but how much more to you, both in the flesh and in the Lord.

17 If then you regard me a partner, accept him as *you would* me.

18 But if he has wronged you in any way, or owes you anything, charge that to my account;

**NAS** [c] Or, *in* [d] Some ancient mss. read *us* [e] I.e., useful

## New International

# Philemon

1 PAUL, A prisoner of Christ Jesus, and Timothy our brother,

To Philemon our dear friend and fellow worker, 2 to Apphia our
sister, to Archippus our fellow soldier and to the church that meets
in your home:

3 Grace to you and peace from God our Father and the Lord
Jesus Christ.

*Thanksgiving and Prayer*

4 I always thank my God as I remember you in my prayers,
5 because I hear about your faith in the Lord Jesus and your love
for all the saints. 6 I pray that you may be active in sharing your
faith, so that you will have a full understanding of every good
thing we have in Christ. 7 Your love has given me great joy and
encouragement, because you, brother, have refreshed the hearts
of the saints.

*Paul's Plea for Onesimus*

8 Therefore, although in Christ I could be bold and order you to
do what you ought to do, 9 yet I appeal to you on the basis of love.
I then, as Paul—an old man and now also a prisoner of Christ
Jesus— 10 I appeal to you for my son Onesimus,[f] who became my
son while I was in chains. 11 Formerly he was useless to you, but
now he has become useful both to you and to me.

12 I am sending him—who is my very heart—back to you. 13 I
would have liked to keep him with me so that he could take your
place in helping me while I am in chains for the gospel. 14 But I did
not want to do anything without your consent, so that any favor
you do will be spontaneous and not forced. 15 Perhaps the reason
he was separated from you for a little while was that you might
have him back for good— 16 no longer as a slave, but better than
a slave, as a dear brother. He is very dear to me but even dearer
to you, both as a man and as a brother in the Lord.

17 So if you consider me a partner, welcome him as you would
welcome me. 18 If he has done you any wrong or owes you anything, charge it to me. 19 I, Paul, am writing this with my own

**NIV** [f] *10 Onesimus* means *useful.*

## King James

19I Paul have written *it* with mine own hand, I will repay *it:* albeit I do not say to thee how thou owest unto me even thine own self besides.
20Yea, brother, let me have joy of thee in the Lord: refresh my bowels in the Lord.
21Having confidence in thy obedience I wrote unto thee, knowing that thou wilt also do more than I say.
22But withal prepare me also a lodging: for I trust that through your prayers I shall be given unto you.
23There salute thee Epaphras, my fellowprisoner in Christ Jesus;
24Marcus, Aristarchus, Demas, Lucas, my fellowlabourers.
25The grace of our Lord Jesus Christ *be* with your spirit. Amen.

## Amplified

19I, Paul, write it with my own hand, I promise to repay it [in full]—and that is to say nothing [of the fact] that you owe me your very self!
20Yes, brother, let me have some profit from you in the Lord. Cheer *and* refresh my heart in Christ.
21I write to you [perfectly] confident of your obedient compliance, knowing that you will do even more than I ask.
22At the same time prepare a guest room [in expectation of extending your hospitality to] me, for I am hoping through your prayers to be granted [the gracious privilege of coming] to you.
23Greetings to you from Epaphras my fellow prisoner here in [the cause of] Christ Jesus, the Messiah,
24And [from] Mark, Aristarchus, Demas and Luke, my fellow workers.
25The grace (blessing and favor) of the Lord Jesus Christ, the Messiah, be with your spirit. *Amen, so be it.*

## New American Standard

19I, Paul, am writing this with my own hand, I will repay it (lest
I should mention to you that you owe to me even your own self
as well).
20Yes, brother, let me benefit from you in the Lord; refresh my
heart in Christ.
21¶ Having confidence in your obedience, I write to you, since
I know that you will do even more than what I say.
22And at the same time also prepare me a lodging; for I hope
that through your prayers I shall be given to you.
23¶ Epaphras, my fellow prisoner in Christ Jesus, greets you,
24 *as do* Mark, Aristarchus, Demas, Luke, my fellow workers.
25¶ The grace of the Lord Jesus Christ be with your spirit. [a]

## New International

hand. I will pay it back—not to mention that you owe me your very
self. 20I do wish, brother, that I may have some benefit from you
in the Lord; refresh my heart in Christ. 21Confident of your obedience, I write to you, knowing that you will do even more than I
ask.
22And one thing more: Prepare a guest room for me, because
I hope to be restored to you in answer to your prayers.

23Epaphras, my fellow prisoner in Christ Jesus, sends you
greetings. 24And so do Mark, Aristarchus, Demas and Luke, my
fellow workers.
25The grace of the Lord Jesus Christ be with your spirit.

**NAS** [a] Some ancient mss. add *Amen*

## King James

THE EPISTLE OF

PAUL THE APOSTLE TO THE

# Hebrews

1 GOD, WHO at sundry times and in divers manners spake in time past unto the fathers by the prophets,

2Hath in these last days spoken unto us by *his* Son, whom he hath appointed heir of all things, by whom also he made the worlds;

3Who being the brightness of *his* glory, and the express image of his person, and upholding all things by the word of his power, when he had by himself purged our sins, sat down on the right hand of the Majesty on high;

4Being made so much better than the angels, as he hath by inheritance obtained a more excellent name than they.

5For unto which of the angels said he at any time, Thou art my Son, this day have I begotten thee? And again, I will be to him a Father, and he shall be to me a Son?

6And again, when he bringeth in the first begotten into the world, he saith, And let all the angels of God worship him.

7And of the angels he saith, Who maketh his angels spirits, and his ministers a flame of fire.

8But unto the Son *he saith,* Thy throne, O God, *is* for ever and ever: a sceptre of righteousness *is* the sceptre of thy kingdom.

9Thou hast loved righteousness, and hated iniquity; therefore God, *even* thy God, hath anointed thee with the oil of gladness above thy fellows.

10And, Thou, Lord, in the beginning hast laid the foundation of the earth; and the heavens are the works of thine hands:

11They shall perish; but thou remainest; and they all shall wax old as doth a garment;

12And as a vesture shalt thou fold them up, and they shall be changed: but thou art the same, and thy years shall not fail.

13But to which of the angels said he at any time, Sit on my right hand, until I make thine enemies thy footstool?

## Amplified

THE LETTER

TO THE

# Hebrews

1 IN MANY separate revelations— [a]each of which set forth a portion of the Truth—and in different ways God spoke of old to [our] forefathers in *and* by the prophets.

2[But] in [b]the last of these days He has spoken to us in [the person of a] Son, Whom He appointed Heir *and* lawful Owner of all things, also by *and* through Whom He created the worlds [c] *and* the reaches of space *and* the ages of time—[that is,] He made, produced, built, operated and arranged them in order.

3He is the sole expression of the glory of God—the Light-being, the [d]out-raying of the divine—and He is the perfect imprint *and* very image of [God's] nature, upholding *and* maintaining *and* guiding *and* propelling the universe by His mighty word of power. When He had by offering Himself accomplished *our* cleansing of sins *and* riddance of guilt, He sat down at the right hand of the divine Majesty on high,

4[Taking a place and rank by which] He Himself became as much superior to angels as the glorious Name (title) which He has inherited is different from *and* more excellent than theirs.

5For to which of the angels did (God) ever say, You are My Son, today I have begotten You [that is, established You in an official Sonship relation, with kingly dignity]? And again, I will be to Him a Father, and He will be to Me a Son? [Ps. 2:7; II Sam. 7:14.]

6Moreover, when He brings the first-born Son [e]again into the habitable world, He says, Let all the angels of God worship Him.

7Referring to the angels He says, (God) Who makes His angels [f]winds, and His ministering servants flames of fire; [Ps. 104:4.]

8But as to the Son, He says to Him, Your throne, O God, is forever and ever (to the ages of the ages), and the scepter of Your kingdom is a scepter of absolute righteousness—of justice and straightforwardness.

9You have loved righteousness—You have delighted in integrity, virtue and uprightness in purpose, thought and action—and You have hated lawlessness (injustice and iniquity). Therefore God, [even] Your God ( [g]God-head), has anointed You with the oil of exultant joy *and* gladness above *and* beyond Your companions. [Ps. 45:6, 7.]

10And [further], You, Lord, did lay the foundation of the earth in the beginning, and the heavens are the works of Your hands.

11They will perish, but You remain *and* continue permanently; they will all grow old *and* wear out like a garment.

12Like a mantle [thrown about one's self] You will roll them up, and they will be changed *and* replaced by others. But You remain the same and Your years will never end *nor* come to failure. [Ps. 102:25-27.]

13Besides, to which of the angels has He ever said, Sit at My right hand—associated with Me in My royal dignity—till I make your enemies a stool for your feet? [Ps. 110:1.]

**AMP** [a] Vincent. [b] Alford's "Greek Testament." [c] Literal translation. [d] Literal translation. [e] Alford. Expositors. Vincent. Wuest's "Hebrews." [f] Many authorities. [g] Way's "The Letters of Saint Paul and Hebrews."

## New American Standard

# Hebrews

*God's Final Word in His Son*

1 GOD, AFTER He spoke long ago to the fathers in the prophets in many portions and in many ways,
2in these last days has spoken to us in *His* Son, whom He appointed heir of all things, through whom also He made the world.
3And He is the radiance of His glory and the exact representation of His nature, and upholds all things by the word of His power. When He had made purification of sins, He sat down at the right hand of the Majesty on high;
4having become as much better than the angels, as He has inherited a more excellent name than they.
5For to which of the angels did He ever say,

"THOU ART MY SON,
TODAY I HAVE BEGOTTEN THEE"?

And again,

"I WILL BE A FATHER TO HIM,
AND HE SHALL BE A SON TO ME"?

6And when He again brings the first-born into the world, He says,

"AND LET ALL THE ANGELS OF GOD WORSHIP HIM."

7And of the angels He says,

"WHO MAKES HIS ANGELS WINDS,
AND HIS MINISTERS A FLAME OF FIRE."

8But of the Son *He says,*

"THY THRONE, O GOD, IS FOREVER AND EVER,
AND THE RIGHTEOUS SCEPTER IS THE SCEPTER OF [h]HIS KINGDOM.
9 "THOU HAST LOVED RIGHTEOUSNESS AND HATED LAWLESSNESS;
THEREFORE GOD, THY GOD, HATH ANOINTED THEE
WITH THE OIL OF GLADNESS ABOVE THY COMPANIONS."

10And,

"THOU, LORD, IN THE BEGINNING DIDST LAY THE FOUNDATION OF THE EARTH,
AND THE HEAVENS ARE THE WORKS OF THY HANDS;
11 THEY WILL PERISH, BUT THOU REMAINEST;
AND THEY ALL WILL BECOME OLD AS A GARMENT,
12 AND AS A MANTLE THOU WILT ROLL THEM UP;
AS A GARMENT THEY WILL ALSO BE CHANGED.
BUT THOU ART THE SAME,
AND THY YEARS WILL NOT COME TO AN END."

13But to which of the angels has He ever said,

"SIT AT MY RIGHT HAND,
UNTIL I MAKE THINE ENEMIES
A FOOTSTOOL FOR THY FEET"?

NAS [h] Some mss. read *Thy*

## New International

# Hebrews

*The Son Superior to Angels*

1 IN THE past God spoke to our forefathers through the prophets at many times and in various ways, 2but in these last days
he has spoken to us by his Son, whom he appointed heir of all things, and through whom he made the universe. 3The Son is the radiance of God's glory and the exact representation of his being, sustaining all things by his powerful word. After he had provided purification for sins, he sat down at the right hand of the Majesty in heaven. 4So he became as much superior to the angels as the name he has inherited is superior to theirs.
5For to which of the angels did God ever say,

"You are my Son;
today I have become your Father[i]"[j]?

Or again,

"I will be his Father,
and he will be my Son"[k]?

6And again, when God brings his firstborn into the world, he says,

"Let all God's angels worship him."[l]

7In speaking of the angels he says,

"He makes his angels winds,
his servants flames of fire."[m]

8But about the Son he says,

"Your throne, O God, will last for ever and ever,
and righteousness will be the scepter of your kingdom.
9You have loved righteousness and hated wickedness;
therefore God, your God, has set you above your companions
by anointing you with the oil of joy."[n]

10He also says,

"In the beginning, O Lord, you laid the foundations of the earth,
and the heavens are the work of your hands.
11They will perish, but you remain;
they will all wear out like a garment.
12You will roll them up like a robe;
like a garment they will be changed.
But you remain the same,
and your years will never end."[o]

13To which of the angels did God ever say,

"Sit at my right hand
until I make your enemies
a footstool for your feet"[p]?

NIV [i] *5* Or *have begotten you* [j] *5* Psalm 2:7 [k] *5* 2 Samuel 7:14; 1 Chron. 17:13 [l] *6* Deut. 32:43 (see Dead Sea Scrolls and Septuagint) [m] *7* Psalm 104:4 [n] *9* Psalm 45:6,7 [o] *12* Psalm 102:25-27 [p] *13* Psalm 110:1

## King James

14 Are they not all ministering spirits, sent forth to minister for them who shall be heirs of salvation?

**2** THEREFORE WE ought to give the more earnest heed to the things which we have heard, lest at any time we should let *them* slip.

2 For if the word spoken by angels was stedfast, and every transgression and disobedience received a just recompence of reward;

3 How shall we escape, if we neglect so great salvation; which at the first began to be spoken by the Lord, and was confirmed unto us by them that heard *him;*

4 God also bearing *them* witness, both with signs and wonders, and with divers miracles, and gifts of the Holy Ghost, according to his own will?

5 For unto the angels hath he not put in subjection the world to come, whereof we speak.

6 But one in a certain place testified, saying, What is man, that thou art mindful of him? or the son of man, that thou visitest him?

7 Thou madest him a little lower than the angels; thou crownedst him with glory and honour, and didst set him over the works of thy hands:

8 Thou hast put all things in subjection under his feet. For in that he put all in subjection under him, he left nothing *that is* not put under him. But now we see not yet all things put under him.

9 But we see Jesus, who was made a little lower than the angels for the suffering of death, crowned with glory and honour; that he by the grace of God should taste death for every man.

10 For it became him, for whom *are* all things, and by whom *are* all things, in bringing many sons unto glory, to make the captain of their salvation perfect through sufferings.

11 For both he that sanctifieth and they who are sanctified *are* all of one: for which cause he is not ashamed to call them brethren,

12 Saying, I will declare thy name unto my brethren, in the midst of the church will I sing praise unto thee.

13 And again, I will put my trust in him. And again, Behold I and the children which God hath given me.

14 Forasmuch then as the children are partakers of flesh and blood, he also himself likewise took part of the same; that through death he might destroy him that had the power of death, that is, the devil;

15 And deliver them who through fear of death were all their lifetime subject to bondage.

16 For verily he took not on *him the nature of* angels; but he took on *him* the seed of Abraham.

## Amplified

14 Are not the angels all (servants) ministering spirits, sent out in the service [of God for the assistance] of those who are to inherit salvation?

**2** SINCE ALL this is true, we ought to pay much closer attention than ever to the truths that we have heard, lest in any way we drift past [them] *and* slip away.

2 For if the message given through angels [that is, the Law spoken by them to Moses] was authentic *and* proved sure, and every violation and disobedience received an appropriate (just and adequate) penalty,

3 How shall we escape [appropriate retribution] if we neglect *and* refuse to pay attention to such a great salvation [as is now offered to us, letting it drift past us forever]? For it was declared at first by the Lord [Himself], and it was confirmed to us *and* proved to be real *and* genuine by those who personally heard [Him speak].

4 [Besides these evidences] it was also established *and* plainly endorsed by God, Who showed His approval of it by signs and wonders and various miraculous manifestations of [His] power and by imparting the gifts of the Holy Spirit [to the believers] according to His own will.

5 For it was not to angels that God subjected the habitable world of the future, of which we are speaking.

6 It has been solemnly *and* earnestly said in a certain place, What is man that You are mindful of him, or the son of man that You graciously *and* helpfully care for *and* visit *and* look after him?

7 For some little time You have ranked him lower than *and* inferior to the angels, You have crowned him with glory and honor, *and set him over the works of Your hands,* [Ps. 8:4-6.]

8 For You have put everything in subjection under his feet. Now in putting everything in subjection to man, He left nothing outside [of man's] control. But at present we do not yet see all things subjected to him [man].

9 But we are able to see Jesus, Who was ranked lower than the angels for a little while, crowned with glory and honor because of His having suffered death, in order that by the grace (unmerited favor) of God [to us sinners] He might experience death for every individual person.

10 For it was an act worthy [of God] *and* fitting [to the divine nature] that He, for Whose sake and by Whom all things have their existence, in bringing many sons into glory, should make the Pioneer of their salvation perfect [that is, should bring to maturity the human experience necessary for a perfect equipment for His office as High Priest], through suffering.

11 For both He Who sanctifies—making men holy—and those who are sanctified all have one [Father]. For this reason He is not ashamed to call them brethren,

12 For He says, I will declare Your [the Father's] name to My brethren; in the midst of the (worshipping) congregation I will sing hymns of praise to You. [Ps. 22:22.]

13 And again He says, My trust *and* assured reliance *and* confident hope shall be fixed in Him. And yet again, Here I am, I and the children whom God has given Me. [Isa. 8:17, 18.]

14 Since, therefore, [these His] children share in flesh and blood—that is, in the physical nature of human beings—He [Himself] in a similar manner partook of the same [nature], that by [going through] death He might bring to nought *and* make of no effect him who had the power of death, that is, the devil;

15 And also that He might deliver *and* completely set free all those who through the (haunting) fear of death were held in bondage throughout the whole course of their lives.

16 For, as we all know, He (Christ) did not take hold of angels [ [a]the fallen angels]—to give them a helping and delivering hand; but He did take hold of [ [b]the fallen] descendants of Abraham—to reach them a helping and delivering hand. [Isa. 41:8, 9.]

**AMP** [a] Matthew Henry's Commentary, and others. [b] Matthew Henry's Commentary, and others.

## New American Standard

14Are they not all ministering spirits, sent out to render service for the sake of those who will inherit salvation?

*Give Heed*

**2** FOR THIS reason we must pay much closer attention to what we have heard, lest we drift away *from it.*

2For if the word spoken through angels proved unalterable, and every transgression and disobedience received a just recompense,

3how shall we escape if we neglect so great a salvation? After it was at the first spoken through the Lord, it was confirmed to us by those who heard,

4God also bearing witness with them, both by signs and wonders and by various miracles and by gifts of the Holy Spirit according to His own will.

*Earth Subject to Man*

5¶ For He did not subject to angels the world to come, concerning which we are speaking.

6But one has testified somewhere, saying,

"What is man, that Thou rememberest him?
Or the son of man, that Thou art concerned about him?
7 "Thou hast made him for a little while lower than the angels;
Thou hast crowned him with glory and honor,
[c]And hast appointed him over the works of Thy hands;
8 Thou hast put all things in subjection under his feet."

For in subjecting all things to him, He left nothing that is not subject to him. But now we do not yet see all things subjected to him.

*Jesus Briefly Humbled*

9But we do see Him who has been made for a little while lower than the angels, *namely,* Jesus, because of the suffering of death crowned with glory and honor, that by the grace of God He might taste death for everyone.

10For it was fitting for Him, for whom are all things, and through whom are all things, in bringing many sons to glory, to perfect the author of their salvation through sufferings.

11For both He who sanctifies and those who are sanctified are all from one *Father;* for which reason He is not ashamed to call them brethren,

12saying,

"I will proclaim Thy name to My brethren,
In the midst of the congregation I will sing Thy praise."

13And again,

"I will put My trust in Him."

And again,

"Behold, I and the children whom God has given Me."

14Since then the children share in flesh and blood, He Himself likewise also partook of the same, that through death He might render powerless him who had the power of death, that is, the devil;

15and might deliver those who through fear of death were subject to slavery all their lives.

16For assuredly He does not give help to angels, but He gives help to the descendant of Abraham.

NAS [c] Some ancient mss. do not contain *And . . . hands*

## New International

14Are not all angels ministering spirits sent to serve those who will inherit salvation?

*Warning to Pay Attention*

**2** WE MUST pay more careful attention, therefore, to what we have heard, so that we do not drift away. 2For if the message
spoken by angels was binding, and every violation and disobedience received its just punishment, 3how shall we escape if we
ignore such a great salvation? This salvation, which was first announced by the Lord, was confirmed to us by those who heard
him. 4God also testified to it by signs, wonders and various miracles, and gifts of the Holy Spirit distributed according to his will.

*Jesus Made Like His Brothers*

5It is not to angels that he has subjected the world to come,
about which we are speaking. 6But there is a place where someone
has testified:

"What is man that you are mindful of him,
the son of man that you care for him?
7You made him a little[d] lower than the angels;
you crowned him with glory and honor
8 and put everything under his feet."[e]

In putting everything under him, God left nothing that is not subject to him. Yet at present we do not see everything subject to
him. 9But we see Jesus, who was made a little lower than the angels, now crowned with glory and honor because he suffered death, so that by the grace of God he might taste death for everyone.

10In bringing many sons to glory, it was fitting that God, for whom and through whom everything exists, should make the author of their salvation perfect through suffering. 11Both the one
who makes men holy and those who are made holy are of the same family. So Jesus is not ashamed to call them brothers. 12He says,

"I will declare your name to my brothers;
in the presence of the congregation I will sing your praises."[f]

13And again,

"I will put my trust in him."[g]

And again he says,

"Here am I, and the children God has given me."[h]

14Since the children have flesh and blood, he too shared in their humanity so that by his death he might destroy him who holds the power of death—that is, the devil— 15and free those who all their
lives were held in slavery by their fear of death. 16For surely it is
not angels he helps, but Abraham's descendants. 17For this reason

NIV [d] 7 Or *him for a little while;* also in verse 9 [e] *8* Psalm 8:4-6 [f] *12* Psalm 22:22 [g] *13* Isaiah 8:17 [h] *13* Isaiah 8:18

## King James

17Wherefore in all things it behooved him to be made like unto *his* brethren, that he might be a merciful and faithful high priest in things *pertaining* to God, to make reconciliation for the sins of the people.
18For in that he himself hath suffered being tempted, he is able to succour them that are tempted.

**3** WHEREFORE, HOLY brethren, partakers of the heavenly calling, consider the Apostle and High Priest of our profession, Christ Jesus;
2Who was faithful to him that appointed him, as also Moses *was faithful* in all his house.
3For this *man* was counted worthy of more glory than Moses, inasmuch as he who hath builded the house hath more honour than the house.
4For every house is builded by some *man;* but he that built all things *is* God.
5And Moses verily *was* faithful in all his house, as a servant, for a testimony of those things which were to be spoken after;
6But Christ as a son over his own house; whose house are we, if we hold fast the confidence and the rejoicing of the hope firm unto the end.
7Wherefore (as the Holy Ghost saith, Today if ye will hear his voice,
8Harden not your hearts, as in the provocation, in the day of temptation in the wilderness:
9When your fathers tempted me, proved me, and saw my works forty years.
10Wherefore I was grieved with that generation, and said, They do always err in *their* heart; and they have not known my ways.
11So I sware in my wrath, They shall not enter into my rest.)
12Take heed, brethren, lest there be in any of you an evil heart of unbelief, in departing from the living God.
13But exhort one another daily, while it is called Today; lest any of you be hardened through the deceitfulness of sin.
14For we are made partakers of Christ, if we hold the beginning of our confidence stedfast unto the end;
15While it is said, Today if ye will hear his voice, harden not your hearts, as in the provocation.
16For some, when they had heard, did provoke: howbeit not all that came out of Egypt by Moses.

## Amplified

17So it is evident that it was essential that He be made like His brethren in every respect, in order that He might become a merciful (sympathetic) and faithful High Priest in the things related to God, to make atonement *and* propitiation for the people's sins.
18For because He Himself [in His humanity] has suffered in being tempted (tested and tried), He is able (immediately) [a]to run to the cry of (assist, relieve) those who are being tempted *and* tested *and* tried [and who therefore are being exposed to suffering].

**3** SO THEN, brethren, consecrated *and* set apart for God, who share in the heavenly calling, thoughtfully *and* attentively consider Jesus, the Apostle and High Priest Whom we confessed as ours [when we embraced the Christian faith].
2[See how] faithful He was to Him Who appointed Him [Apostle and High Priest], as Moses was also faithful in the whole household [of God]. [Num. 12:7.]
3Yet Jesus has been considered worthy of as much greater honor *and* glory than Moses as the builder of a house has more honor than the house [itself].
4For, [of course,] every house is built *and* furnished by someone, but the Builder of all things *and* the Furnisher [of the entire equipment of all things] is God.
5And Moses certainly was faithful in the administration of all God's house, [but it was only] as a ministering servant. [In his entire ministry he was but] a testimony to the things which were to be spoken—the revelations to be given afterward [in Christ]. [Num. 12:7.]
6But Christ, the Messiah, was faithful over His [own Father's] house as a Son [and Master of it]. And it is we who are [now members of] this house, if we hold fast *and firm to the end* our joyful *and* exultant confidence and sense of triumph in our hope [in Christ].
7Therefore, as the Holy Spirit says, Today, if you will hear His voice,
8Do not harden your hearts, as [happened] in the rebellion [of Israel] *and* their provocation *and* [b]embitterment [of Me] in the day of testing in the wilderness,
9Where your fathers tried [My patience] *and* tested [My forbearance] and [c]found I stood their test, and they saw My works for forty years.
10And so I was provoked (displeased and sorely grieved) with that generation, and said, They always err *and* are led astray in their hearts, and they have not perceived *or* recognized My ways *and* become progressively better *and* more experimentally *and* intimately acquainted with them.
11Accordingly I swore in My wrath *and* indignation, They shall not enter into My rest. [Ps. 95:7-11.]
12[Therefore beware,] brethren; take care lest there be in any one of you a wicked, unbelieving heart—which refuses to cleave to, trust in and rely on Him—leading you to turn away *and* desert *or* stand aloof from the living God.
13But instead warn (admonish, urge and encourage) one another every day, as long as it is called Today, that none of you may be hardened [into settled rebellion] by the deceitfulness of sin—[that is,] by the fraudulence, the stratagem, the trickery which the delusive glamor of his sin may play on him.
14For we [d]have become fellows with Christ, the Messiah, *and* share in all He has for us, if only we hold our first newborn confidence *and* original assured expectation [in virtue of which we are believers] firm *and* unshaken to the end.
15Then while it is [still] called Today, if you would hear His voice, *and* when you hear it, do not harden your hearts as in the rebellion [in the desert, when the people provoked and irritated and embittered God against them]. [Ps. 95:7, 8.]
16For who were they that heard *and* yet were rebellious *and* provoked [Him]? Was it not all those who came out of Egypt led by Moses?

**AMP** [a] Wuest's "Hebrews." [b] Souter. [c] Williams. [d] Vincent.

## New American Standard

17Therefore, He had to be made like His brethren in all things,
that He might become a merciful and faithful high priest in things
pertaining to God, to make propitiation for the sins of the people.
18For since He Himself was tempted in that which He has
suffered, He is able to come to the aid of those who are tempted.

*Jesus Our High Priest*

3 THEREFORE, HOLY brethren, partakers of a heavenly calling, consider Jesus, the Apostle and High Priest of our confession.

2He was faithful to Him who appointed Him, as Moses also
was in all His house.
3For He has been counted worthy of more glory than Moses,
by just so much as the builder of the house has more honor than
the house.
4For every house is built by someone, but the builder of all
things is God.
5Now Moses was faithful in all His house as a servant, for a
testimony of those things which were to be spoken later;
6but Christ *was faithful* as a Son over His house whose house
we are, if we hold fast our confidence and the boast of our hope
firm until the end.
7Therefore, just as the Holy Spirit says,
"TODAY IF YOU HEAR HIS VOICE,
8 DO NOT HARDEN YOUR HEARTS AS WHEN THEY PROVOKED ME,
AS IN THE DAY OF TRIAL IN THE WILDERNESS,
9 WHERE YOUR FATHERS TRIED *ME* BY TESTING *ME*,
AND SAW MY WORKS FOR FORTY YEARS.
10 "THEREFORE I WAS ANGRY WITH THIS GENERATION,
AND SAID, 'THEY ALWAYS GO ASTRAY IN THEIR HEART;
AND THEY DID NOT KNOW MY WAYS';
11 AS I SWORE IN MY WRATH,
'THEY SHALL NOT ENTER MY REST.' "

*The Peril of Unbelief*

12Take care, brethren, lest there should be in any one of you an
evil, unbelieving heart, in falling away from the living God.
13But encourage one another day after day, as long as it is *still*
called "Today," lest any one of you be hardened by the deceitfulness of sin.
14For we have become partakers of Christ, if we hold fast the
beginning of our assurance firm until the end;
15while it is said,
"TODAY IF YOU HEAR HIS VOICE,
DO NOT HARDEN YOUR HEARTS, AS WHEN THEY PROVOKED ME."
16For who provoked *Him* when they had heard? Indeed, did not
all those who came out of Egypt *led* by Moses?

## New International

he had to be made like his brothers in every way, in order that he
might become a merciful and faithful high priest in service to God,
and that he might make atonement for[e] the sins of the people.
18Because he himself suffered when he was tempted, he is able to
help those who are being tempted.

*Jesus Greater Than Moses*

3 THEREFORE, HOLY brothers, who share in the heavenly
calling, fix your thoughts on Jesus, the apostle and high priest
whom we confess. 2He was faithful to the one who appointed him,
just as Moses was faithful in all God's house. 3Jesus has been
found worthy of greater honor than Moses, just as the builder of
a house has greater honor than the house itself. 4For every house
is built by someone, but God is the builder of everything. 5Moses
was faithful as a servant in all God's house, testifying to what
would be said in the future. 6But Christ is faithful as a son over
God's house. And we are his house, if we hold on to our courage
and the hope of which we boast.

*Warning Against Unbelief*

7So, as the Holy Spirit says:

"Today, if you hear his voice,
8 do not harden your hearts
as you did in the rebellion,
during the time of testing in the desert,
9where your fathers tested and tried me
and for forty years saw what I did.
10That is why I was angry with that generation,
and I said, 'Their hearts are always going astray,
and they have not known my ways.'
11So I declared on oath in my anger,
'They shall never enter my rest.' "[f]

12See to it, brothers, that none of you has a sinful, unbelieving
heart that turns away from the living God. 13But encourage one
another daily, as long as it is called Today, so that none of you may
be hardened by sin's deceitfulness. 14We have come to share in
Christ if we hold firmly till the end the confidence we had at first.
15As has just been said:

"Today, if you hear his voice,
do not harden your hearts
as you did in the rebellion."[g]

16Who were they who heard and rebelled? Were they not all
those Moses led out of Egypt? 17And with whom was he angry for

**NIV** [e] 17 *Or and that he might turn aside God's wrath, taking away* [f] 11 Psalm 95:7-11 [g] 15 Psalm 95:7,8

## King James

17 But with whom was he grieved forty years? *was it* not with them that had sinned, whose carcases fell in the wilderness?

18 And to whom sware he that they should not enter into his rest, but to them that believed not?

19 So we see that they could not enter in because of unbelief.

**4** LET US therefore fear, lest, a promise being left *us* of entering into his rest, any of you should seem to come short of it.

2 For unto us was the gospel preached, as well as unto them: but the word preached did not profit them, not being mixed with faith in them that heard *it*.

3 For we which have believed do enter into rest, as he said, As I have sworn in my wrath, if they shall enter into my rest: although the works were finished from the foundation of the world.

4 For he spake in a certain place of the seventh *day* on this wise, And God did rest the seventh day from all his works.

5 And in this *place* again, If they shall enter into my rest.

6 Seeing therefore it remaineth that some must enter therein, and they to whom it was first preached entered not in because of unbelief:

7 Again, he limiteth a certain day, saying in David, Today, after so long a time; as it is said, Today if ye will hear his voice, harden not your hearts.

8 For if Jesus had given them rest, then would he not afterward have spoken of another day.

9 There remaineth therefore a rest to the people of God.

10 For he that is entered into his rest, he also hath ceased from his own works, as God *did* from his.

11 Let us labour therefore to enter into that rest, lest any man fall after the same example of unbelief.

12 For the word of God *is* quick, and powerful, and sharper than any twoedged sword, piercing even to the dividing asunder of soul and spirit, and of the joints and marrow, and *is* a discerner of the thoughts and intents of the heart.

13 Neither is there any creature that is not manifest in his sight: but all things *are* naked and opened unto the eyes of him with whom we have to do.

## Amplified

17 And with whom was He irritated *and* provoked *and* grieved for forty years? Was it not with those who sinned, whose [a]dismembered bodies were strewn *and* left in the desert?

18 And to whom did He swear that they should not enter His rest, but to those who disobeyed—who had not listened to His word, and who refused to be compliant or be persuaded?

19 So we see that they were not able to enter [into His rest] because of their unwillingness to adhere to *and* trust *and* rely on God—unbelief had shut them out. [Num. 14:1-35.]

**4** THEREFORE, WHILE the promise of entering His rest still holds *and* is offered [today], let us be afraid [ [b]to distrust it], lest any of you should [c]think he has come too late *and* has come short of [reaching] it.

2 For indeed we have had the glad tidings [of God] proclaimed to us just as truly as they [the Israelites of old did when the good news of deliverance from bondage came to them]; but the message they heard did not benefit them, because it was not mixed with faith [that is, with [d]the leaning of the entire personality on God in absolute trust and confidence in His power, wisdom and goodness] by those who heard it; *neither* were they [e]united in faith with [Joshua and Caleb] the ones who heard [did believe].

3 For we who have believed—who have adhered to and trusted and relied on God—do enter into that rest, [f]in accordance with His declaration that those [who did not believe] should not enter when He said, As I swore in My wrath, They shall not enter into My rest; and this He said although [His] works had been completed *and* prepared [and waiting for all who would believe] from the foundation of the world. [Ps. 95:11.]

4 For in a certain place He has said this about the seventh day: And God rested on the seventh day from all His works. [Gen. 2:2.]

5 And [they forfeited their part in it, for] in this [passage] He said, They shall not enter into My rest. [Ps. 95:11.]

6 Seeing then that the promise remains over [from past times] for some to enter that rest, and that those who formerly were given the good news about it *and* the opportunity, failed to appropriate it *and* did not enter because of disobedience,

7 Again He sets a definite day, [a new] Today, [and gives another opportunity of securing that rest,] saying through David after so long a time, in the words already quoted, Today, if you would hear His voice, *and* when you hear it, do not harden your hearts. [Ps. 95:7, 8.]

8 [This mention of a rest was not a reference to their entering into Canaan], for if Joshua had given them rest, He (God) would not speak afterward about another day.

9 So then, there is still awaiting a full *and* complete Sabbath rest reserved for the [true] people of God;

10 For he who has once entered into [God's] rest also has ceased from [the weariness and pain] of human labors, just as God rested from those labors [g]peculiarly His own. [Gen. 2:2.]

11 Let us therefore be zealous *and* exert ourselves *and* strive diligently to enter into that rest [of God]—to know and experience it for ourselves—that no one may fall *or* perish by the same kind of unbelief *and* disobedience [into which those in the wilderness fell].

12 For the Word that God speaks is alive and full of power—making it active, operative, energizing and effective; it is sharper than any two-edged sword, penetrating to the dividing line of the [h]breath of life (soul) and [the immortal] spirit, and of joints and marrow [that is, of the deepest parts of our nature] exposing *and* sifting *and* analyzing *and* judging the very thoughts and purposes of the heart.

13 And not a creature exists that is concealed from His sight, but all things are open *and* exposed, naked *and* defenseless to the eyes of Him with Whom we have to do.

**AMP** [a] Vincent. [b] Vincent. [c] Vincent. [d] Souter. [e] Many manuscripts so read. [f] Vincent. [g] Vincent's "Word Studies in the New Testament." [h] Thayer.

## New American Standard

17And with whom was He angry for forty years? Was it not with
those who sinned, whose bodies fell in the wilderness?
18And to whom did He swear that they should not enter His
rest, but to those who were disobedient?
19And *so* we see that they were not able to enter because of
unbelief.

*The Believer's Rest*

4 THEREFORE, LET us fear lest, while a promise remains of
entering His rest, any one of you should seem to have come
short of it.
2For indeed we have had good news preached to us, just as
they also; but the word they heard did not profit them, because it
was not united by faith in those who heard.
3 [i]For we who have believed enter that rest, just as He has said,
"AS I SWORE IN MY WRATH,
THEY SHALL NOT ENTER MY REST,"
although His works were finished from the foundation of the
world.
4For He has thus said somewhere concerning the seventh *day,*
"AND GOD RESTED ON THE SEVENTH DAY FROM ALL HIS WORKS";
5and again in this *passage,* "THEY SHALL NOT ENTER MY REST."
6Since therefore it remains for some to enter it, and those who
formerly had good news preached to them failed to enter because
of disobedience,
7He again fixes a certain day, "Today," saying through David
after so long a time just as has been said before,
"TODAY IF YOU HEAR HIS VOICE,
DO NOT HARDEN YOUR HEARTS."
8For if Joshua had given them rest, He would not have spoken
of another day after that.
9There remains therefore a Sabbath rest for the people of God.
10For the one who has entered His rest has himself also rested
from his works, as God did from His.
11Let us therefore be diligent to enter that rest, lest anyone fall
through *following* the same example of disobedience.
12For the word of God is living and active and sharper than any
two-edged sword, and piercing as far as the division of soul and
spirit, of both joints and marrow, and able to judge the thoughts
and intentions of the heart.
13And there is no creature hidden from His sight, but all things
are open and laid bare to the eyes of Him with whom we have to
do.

NAS [i] Some ancient mss. read *Therefore*

## New International

forty years? Was it not with those who sinned, whose bodies fell
in the desert? 18And to whom did God swear that they would
never enter his rest if not to those who disobeyed[j] ? 19So we see
that they were not able to enter, because of their unbelief.

*A Sabbath-Rest for the People of God*

4 THEREFORE, SINCE the promise of entering his rest still
stands, let us be careful that none of you be found to have
fallen short of it. 2For we also have had the gospel preached to us,
just as they did; but the message they heard was of no value to
them, because those who heard did not combine it with faith.[k]
3Now we who have believed enter that rest, just as God has said,

"So I declared on oath in my anger,
'They shall never enter my rest.' "[l]

And yet his work has been finished since the creation of the world.
4For somewhere he has spoken about the seventh day in these
words: "And on the seventh day God rested from all his work."[m]
5And again in the passage above he says, "They shall never enter
my rest."
6It still remains that some will enter that rest, and those who
formerly had the gospel preached to them did not go in, because
of their disobedience. 7Therefore God again set a certain day,
calling it Today, when a long time later he spoke through David,
as was said before:

"Today, if you hear his voice,
do not harden your hearts."[n]

8For if Joshua had given them rest, God would not have spoken
later about another day. 9There remains, then, a Sabbath-rest for
the people of God; 10for anyone who enters God's rest also rests
from his own work, just as God did from his. 11Let us, therefore,
make every effort to enter that rest, so that no one will fall by
following their example of disobedience.
12For the word of God is living and active. Sharper than any
double-edged sword, it penetrates even to dividing soul and spirit,
joints and marrow; it judges the thoughts and attitudes of the
heart. 13Nothing in all creation is hidden from God's sight Everything is uncovered and laid bare before the eyes of him to whom
we must give account.

NIV [j] 18 Or *disbelieved* [k] 2 Many manuscripts *because they did not share in the faith of those who obeyed* [l] 3 Psalm 95:11; also in verse 5 [m] 4 Gen. 2:2 [n] 7 Psalm 95:7,8

## King James

14Seeing then that we have a great high priest, that is passed into the heavens, Jesus the Son of God, let us hold fast *our* profession.

15For we have not an high priest which cannot be touched with the feeling of our infirmities; but was in all points tempted like as *we are, yet* without sin.

16Let us therefore come boldly unto the throne of grace, that we may obtain mercy, and find grace to help in time of need.

5 FOR EVERY high priest taken from among men is ordained for men in things *pertaining* to God, that he may offer both gifts and sacrifices for sins:

2Who can have compassion on the ignorant, and on them that are out of the way; for that he himself also is compassed with infirmity.

3And by reason hereof he ought, as for the people, so also for himself, to offer for sins.

4And no man taketh this honour unto himself, but he that is called of God, as *was* Aaron.

5So also Christ glorified not himself to be made an high priest; but he that said unto him, Thou art my Son, today have I begotten thee.

6As he saith also in another *place,* Thou *art* a priest for ever after the order of Melchisedec.

7Who in the days of his flesh, when he had offered up prayers and supplications with strong crying and tears unto him that was able to save him from death, and was heard in that he feared;

8Though he were a Son, yet learned he obedience by the things which he suffered;

9And being made perfect, he became the author of eternal salvation unto all them that obey him;

10Called of God an high priest after the order of Melchisedec.

11Of whom we have many things to say, and hard to be uttered, seeing ye are dull of hearing.

12For when for the time ye ought to be teachers, ye have need that one teach you again which *be* the first principles of the oracles of God; and are become such as have need of milk, and not of strong meat.

13For every one that useth milk *is* unskilful in the word of righteousness: for he is a babe.

14But strong meat belongeth to them that are of full age, *even* those who by reason of use have their senses exercised to discern both good and evil.

## Amplified

14Inasmuch then as we have a great High Priest Who has [already] ascended *and* passed through the heavens, Jesus the Son of God, let us hold fast our confession [of faith in Him],

15For we do not have a High Priest Who is unable to understand *and* sympathize *and* have a fellow feeling with our weaknesses *and* infirmities *and* liability to the assaults of temptation, but One Who has been tempted in every respect as we are, yet without sinning.

16Let us then fearlessly *and* confidently *and* boldly draw near to the throne of grace—the throne of God's unmerited favor [to us sinners]; that we may receive mercy [for our failures] and find grace to help in good time for every need—appropriate help and well-timed help, coming just when we need it.

5 FOR EVERY high priest chosen from among men is appointed to act in behalf of men in things relating to God, to offer both gifts and sacrifices for sins.

2He is able to exercise gentleness *and* forbearance toward the ignorant and erring, since he himself also is liable to moral weakness *and* physical infirmity.

3And because of this he is obliged to offer sacrifice for his own sins as well as for those of the people.

4Besides, one does not appropriate for himself the honor [of being high priest], but he is called by God *and* receives it of Him, just as Aaron did.

5So too Christ, the Messiah, did not exalt Himself to be made a high priest, but was appointed *and* exalted by Him Who said to Him, You are My Son, today I have begotten You; [Ps. 2:7.]

6As He says also in another place, You are a Priest [appointed] forever after the order (rank) of Melchizedek. [Ps. 110:4.]

7In the days of His flesh [Jesus] offered up definite, special petitions [for that which He not only wanted [a]but needed], and supplications, with strong crying and tears, to Him Who was [always] able to save Him (out) from death, and He was heard because of His reverence toward God—His godly fear, His piety [ [b]that is, in that He shrank from the horrors of separation from the bright presence of the Father].

8Although He was a Son, He learned [active, special] obedience through what He suffered;

9And [His completed experience] making Him perfect [in equipment], He became the Author *and* Source of eternal salvation to all those who give heed *and* obey Him, [Isa. 45:17.]

10Being [c]designated *and* recognized *and* saluted by God as High Priest after the order [with [d]the rank] of Melchizedek. [Ps. 110:4.]

11Concerning this we have much to say which is hard to explain, since you have become dull in your [spiritual] hearing *and* sluggish, *even* [e]slothful [in achieving spiritual insight].

12For even though by this time you ought to be teaching others, you actually need some one to teach you over again the very first principles of God's Word. You have come to need milk, not solid food.

13For every one who continues to feed on milk is obviously inexperienced *and* unskilled in the doctrine of righteousness, [that is, of conformity to the divine will in purpose, thought and action,] for he is a mere infant—not able to talk yet!

14But solid food is for full-grown men, for those whose senses *and* mental faculties are trained by practice to discriminate *and* distinguish between what is morally good *and* noble and what is evil *and* contrary either to divine or human law.

**AMP** [a] Abbott-Smith. [b] Jamieson, Fausset and Brown's "Commentary on the Old and New Testaments." [c] Souter. [d] Thayer. [e] Abbott-Smith.

## New American Standard

14¶ Since then we have a great high priest who has passed through the heavens, Jesus the Son of God, let us hold fast our confession.

15For we do not have a high priest who cannot sympathize with our weaknesses, but one who has been tempted in all things as *we are, yet* without sin.

16Let us therefore draw near with confidence to the throne of grace, that we may receive mercy and may find grace to help in time of need.

*The Perfect High Priest*

**5** FOR EVERY high priest taken from among men is appointed on behalf of men in things pertaining to God, in order to offer both gifts and sacrifices for sins;

2he can deal gently with the ignorant and misguided, since he himself also is beset with weakness;

3and because of it he is obligated to offer *sacrifices* for sins, as for the people, so also for himself.

4And no one takes the honor to himself, but *receives it* when he is called by God, even as Aaron was.

5So also Christ did not glorify Himself so as to become a high priest, but He who said to Him,

"THOU ART MY SON,
TODAY I HAVE BEGOTTEN THEE";

6just as He says also in another *passage,*

"THOU ART A PRIEST FOREVER
ACCORDING TO THE ORDER OF MELCHIZEDEK."

7In the days of His flesh, He offered up both prayers and supplications with loud crying and tears to the One able to save Him from death, and He was heard because of His piety.

8Although He was a Son, He learned obedience from the things which He suffered.

9And having been made perfect, He became to all those who obey Him the source of eternal salvation,

10being designated by God as a high priest according to the order of Melchizedek.

11¶ Concerning [f]him we have much to say, and *it is* hard to explain, since you have become dull of hearing.

12For though by this time you ought to be teachers, you have need again for someone to teach you the elementary principles of the oracles of God, and you have come to need milk and not solid food.

13For everyone who partakes *only* of milk is not accustomed to the word of righteousness, for he is a babe.

14But solid food is for the mature, who because of practice have their senses trained to discern good and evil.

NAS [f] Or, *Him;* or, *this*

## New International

*Jesus the Great High Priest*

14Therefore, since we have a great high priest who has gone
through the heavens,[g] Jesus the Son of God, let us hold firmly to
the faith we profess. 15For we do not have a high priest who is
unable to sympathize with our weaknesses, but we have one who
has been tempted in every way, just as we are—yet was without
sin. 16Let us then approach the throne of grace with confidence,
so that we may receive mercy and find grace to help us in our time
of need.

**5** EVERY HIGH priest is selected from among men and is appointed to represent them in matters related to God, to offer
gifts and sacrifices for sins. 2He is able to deal gently with those
who are ignorant and are going astray, since he himself is subject
to weakness. 3This is why he has to offer sacrifices for his own sins,
as well as for the sins of the people.
4No one takes this honor upon himself; he must be called by
God, just as Aaron was. 5So Christ also did not take upon himself
the glory of becoming a high priest. But God said to him,

"You are my Son;
today I have become your Father."[h][i]

6And he says in another place,

"You are a priest forever,
in the order of Melchizedek."[j]

7During the days of Jesus' life on earth, he offered up prayers
and petitions with loud cries and tears to the one who could save
him from death, and he was heard because of his reverent submission. 8Although he was a son, he learned obedience from what he
suffered 9and, once made perfect, he became the source of eternal
salvation for all who obey him 10and was designated by God to be
high priest in the order of Melchizedek.

*Warning Against Falling Away*

11We have much to say about this, but it is hard to explain
because you are slow to learn. 12In fact, though by this time you
ought to be teachers, you need someone to teach you the elementary truths of God's word all over again. You need milk, not solid
food! 13Anyone who lives on milk, being still an infant, is not
acquainted with the teaching about righteousness. 14But solid food
is for the mature, who by constant use have trained themselves to
distinguish good from evil.

NIV [g] 14 Or *gone into heaven* [h] 5 Or *have begotten you* [i] 5 Psalm 2:7
[j] 6 Psalm 110:4

## King James

6 THEREFORE LEAVING the principles of the doctrine of Christ, let us go on unto perfection; not laying again the foundation of repentance from dead works, and of faith toward God,

2 Of the doctrine of baptisms, and of laying on of hands, and of resurrection of the dead, and of eternal judgment.

3 And this will we do, if God permit.

4 For *it is* impossible for those who were once enlightened, and have tasted of the heavenly gift, and were made partakers of the Holy Ghost,

5 And have tasted the good word of God, and the powers of the world to come,

6 If they shall fall away, to renew them again unto repentance; seeing they crucify to themselves the Son of God afresh, and put *him* to an open shame.

7 For the earth which drinketh in the rain that cometh oft upon it, and bringeth forth herbs meet for them by whom it is dressed, receiveth blessing from God:

8 But that which beareth thorns and briers *is* rejected, and *is* nigh unto cursing; whose end *is* to be burned.

9 But, beloved, we are persuaded better things of you, and things that accompany salvation, though we thus speak.

10 For God *is* not unrighteous to forget your work and labour of love, which ye have shown toward his name, in that ye have ministered to the saints, and do minister.

11 And we desire that every one of you do show the same diligence to the full assurance of hope unto the end:

12 That ye be not slothful, but followers of them who through faith and patience inherit the promises.

13 For when God made promise to Abraham, because he could swear by no greater, he sware by himself,

14 Saying, Surely blessing I will bless thee, and multiplying I will multiply thee.

15 And so, after he had patiently endured, he obtained the promise.

16 For men verily swear by the greater: and an oath for confirmation *is* to them an end of all strife.

17 Wherein God, willing more abundantly to show unto the heirs of promise the immutability of his counsel, confirmed *it* by an oath:

18 That by two immutable things, in which *it was* impossible for God to lie, we might have a strong consolation, who have fled for refuge to lay hold upon the hope set before us:

19 Which *hope* we have as an anchor of the soul, both sure and stedfast, and which entereth into that within the veil;

## Amplified

6 THEREFORE LET us go on and get past the elementary stage in the teachings *and* doctrine of Christ, the Messiah, advancing steadily toward the completeness *and* perfection that belongs to spiritual maturity. Let us not again be laying the foundation of repentance *and* abandonment of dead works [dead formalism], and of the faith [by which you turned] to God,

2 With teachings about purifying, the laying on of hands, the resurrection from the dead, and eternal judgment *and* punishment. [These are all matters of which you should have been fully aware long, long ago.]

3 If indeed God permits we will [now] proceed [to advanced teaching].

4 For it is impossible [to restore *and* bring again to repentance] those who have been once for all enlightened, who have consciously tasted the heavenly gift, and have become sharers of the Holy Spirit,

5 And have felt how good the Word of God is and the mighty powers of the age *and* world to come,

6 If they then deviate from the faith *and* turn away from their allegiance; [it is impossible] to bring them back to repentance, for (because, [a]while, as long as) they nail up on the cross the Son of God afresh, as far as they are concerned, and are holding [Him] up to contempt *and* shame *and* public disgrace.

7 For the soil which has drunk the rain that repeatedly falls upon it, and produces vegetation useful to those for whose benefit it is cultivated, partakes of a blessing from God.

8 But if [that same soil] persistently bears thorns and thistles, it is considered worthless and near to being cursed, whose end is to be burned. [Gen. 3:17, 18.]

9 Even though we speak this way, yet in your case, beloved, we are now firmly convinced of better things that are near to salvation *and* accompany it.

10 For God is not unrighteous to forget *or* overlook your labor and the love which you have shown for His name's sake in ministering to the needs of the saints—His own consecrated people—as you still do.

11 But we do [ [b]strongly and earnestly] desire for each of you to show the same diligence *and* sincerity [all the way through] in realizing *and* enjoying the full assurance *and* development of [your] hope until the end,

12 In order that you may not grow disinterested *and* become [spiritual] sluggards but imitators, behaving as do those who through faith [that is, [c]by their leaning of the entire personality on God in Christ in absolute trust and confidence in His power, wisdom and goodness], and by practice of patient endurance *and* waiting are [now] inheriting the promises.

13 For when God made [His] promise to Abraham, He swore by Himself, since He had no one greater by whom to swear,

14 Saying, Blessing I certainly will bless you and multiplying I will multiply you. [Gen. 22:16, 17.]

15 And so it was that he [Abraham] having waited long *and* endured patiently, realized *and* obtained [in the birth of Isaac as a pledge of what was to come] what God had promised him.

16 Men indeed swear by a greater [than themselves], and with them in all disputes the oath taken for confirmation is final—ending strife.

17 Accordingly God also, in His desire to show more convincingly *and* beyond doubt, to those who were to inherit the promise, the unchangeableness of His purpose *and* plan, intervened (mediated) with an oath.

18 This was so that by two unchangeable things [His promise and His oath], in which it is impossible for God ever to prove false *or* deceive us, we who have fled [to Him] for refuge might have mighty indwelling strength *and* strong encouragement to grasp *and* hold fast the hope appointed for us *and* set before [us].

19 [Now] we have this [hope] as a sure and steadfast anchor of the soul—it cannot slip and it cannot [d]break down under whoever steps out upon it—[a hope] that reaches [e]farther *and* enters into [the very certainty of the Presence] within the veil, [Lev. 16:2.]

AMP [a] Alternate reading. [b] Vincent. [c] Souter. [d] Vincent. [e] Vincent.

## New American Standard

*The Peril of Falling Away*

6 THEREFORE LEAVING the elementary teaching about the
Christ, let us press on to maturity, not laying again a foundation of repentance from dead works and of faith toward God,
2of instruction about washings, and laying on of hands, and
the resurrection of the dead, and eternal judgment.
3And this we shall do, if God permits.
4For in the case of those who have once been enlightened and
have tasted of the heavenly gift and have been made partakers of
the Holy Spirit,
5and have tasted the good word of God and the powers of the
age to come,
6and *then* have fallen away, it is impossible to renew them
again to repentance, since they again crucify to themselves the Son
of God, and put Him to open shame.
7For ground that drinks the rain which often falls upon it and
brings forth vegetation useful to those for whose sake it is also
tilled, receives a blessing from God;
8but if it yields thorns and thistles, it is worthless and close to
being cursed, and it ends up being burned.

*Better Things for You*

9¶ But, beloved, we are convinced of better things concerning
you, and things that accompany salvation, though we are speaking in this way.
10For God is not unjust so as to forget your work and the love
which you have shown toward His name, in having ministered
and in still ministering to the saints.
11And we desire that each one of you show the same diligence
so as to realize the full assurance of hope until the end,
12that you may not be sluggish, but imitators of those who
through faith and patience inherit the promises.
13¶ For when God made the promise to Abraham, since He
could swear by no one greater, He swore by Himself,
14saying, "I WILL SURELY BLESS YOU, AND I WILL SURELY MULTIPLY
YOU."
15And thus, having patiently waited, he obtained the promise.
16For men swear by one greater *than themselves*, and with them
an oath *given* as confirmation is an end of every dispute.
17In the same way God, desiring even more to show to the heirs
of the promise the unchangeableness of His purpose, interposed
with an oath,
18in order that by two unchangeable things, in which it is impossible for God to lie, we may have strong encouragement, we
who have fled for refuge in laying hold of the hope set before us.
19This hope we have as an anchor of the soul, a *hope* both sure
and steadfast and one which enters within the veil,

## New International

6 THEREFORE LET us leave the elementary teachings about
Christ and go on to maturity, not laying again the foundation
of repentance from acts that lead to death,[f] and of faith in God,
2instruction about baptisms, the laying on of hands, the resurrection of the dead, and eternal judgment. 3And God permitting, we
will do so.
4It is impossible for those who have once been enlightened,
who have tasted the heavenly gift, who have shared in the Holy
Spirit, 5who have tasted the goodness of the word of God and the
powers of the coming age, 6if they fall away, to be brought back
to repentance, because[g] to their loss they are crucifying the Son
of God all over again and subjecting him to public disgrace.
7Land that drinks in the rain often falling on it and that produces a crop useful to those for whom it is farmed receives the
blessing of God. 8But land that produces thorns and thistles is
worthless and is in danger of being cursed. In the end it will be
burned.
9Even though we speak like this, dear friends, we are confident
of better things in your case—things that accompany salvation.
10God is not unjust; he will not forget your work and the love you
have shown him as you have helped his people and continue to
help them. 11We want each of you to show this same diligence to
the very end, in order to make your hope sure. 12We do not want
you to become lazy, but to imitate those who through faith and
patience inherit what has been promised.

*The Certainty of God's Promise*

13When God made his promise to Abraham, since there was no
one greater for him to swear by, he swore by himself, 14saying, "I
will surely bless you and give you many descendants."[h] 15And so
after waiting patiently, Abraham received what was promised.
16Men swear by someone greater than themselves, and the oath
confirms what is said and puts an end to all argument. 17Because
God wanted to make the unchanging nature of his purpose very
clear to the heirs of what was promised, he confirmed it with an
oath. 18God did this so that, by two unchangeable things in which
it is impossible for God to lie, we who have fled to take hold of the
hope offered to us may be greatly encouraged. 19We have this
hope as an anchor for the soul, firm and secure. It enters the inner
sanctuary behind the curtain, 20where Jesus, who went before us,

NIV [f] 1 Or *from useless rituals* [g] 6 Or *repentance while* [h] 14 Gen. 22:17

## King James

20Whither the forerunner is for us entered, *even* Jesus, made an high priest for ever after the order of Melchisedec.

**7** FOR THIS Melchisedec, king of Salem, priest of the most high God, who met Abraham returning from the slaughter of the kings, and blessed him;

2To whom also Abraham gave a tenth part of all; first being by interpretation King of righteousness, and after that also King of Salem, which is, King of peace;

3Without father, without mother, without descent, having neither beginning of days, nor end of life; but made like unto the Son of God; abideth a priest continually.

4Now consider how great this man *was,* unto whom even the patriarch Abraham gave the tenth of the spoils.

5And verily they that are of the sons of Levi, who receive the office of the priesthood, have a commandment to take tithes of the people according to the law, that is, of their brethren, though they come out of the loins of Abraham:

6But he whose descent is not counted from them received tithes of Abraham, and blessed him that had the promises.

7And without all contradiction the less is blessed of the better.

8And here men that die receive tithes; but there he *receiveth them,* of whom it is witnessed that he liveth.

9And as I may so say, Levi also, who receiveth tithes, paid tithes in Abraham.

10For he was yet in the loins of his father, when Melchisedec met him.

11If therefore perfection were by the Levitical priesthood, (for under it the people received the law,) what further need *was there* that another priest should rise after the order of Melchisedec, and not be called after the order of Aaron?

12For the priesthood being changed, there is made of necessity a change also of the law.

13For he of whom these things are spoken pertaineth to another tribe, of which no man gave attendance at the altar.

14For *it is* evident that our Lord sprang out of Judah; of which tribe Moses spake nothing concerning priesthood.

15And it is yet far more evident: for that after the similitude of Melchisedec there ariseth another priest,

16Who is made, not after the law of a carnal commandment, but after the power of an endless life.

17For he testifieth, Thou *art* a priest for ever after the order of Melchisedec.

18For there is verily a disannulling of the commandment going before for the weakness and unprofitableness thereof.

19For the law made nothing perfect, but the bringing in of a better hope *did;* by the which we draw nigh unto God.

20And inasmuch as not without an oath *he was made priest:*

## Amplified

20Where Jesus has entered in for us [in advance], a Forerunner having become a High Priest forever after the order [with [a]the rank] of Melchizedek. [Ps. 110:4.]

**7** FOR THIS Melchizedek, king of Salem [and] priest of the Most High God, met Abraham as he returned from the slaughter of the kings and blessed him;

2And Abraham gave to him a tenth portion of all [the spoil]. He is primarily, as his name when translated indicates, king of righteousness, and then he is also king of Salem, which means king of peace.

3Without [record of] father or mother or ancestral line, nor with beginning of days or ending of life, but resembling the Son of God he continues to be a priest without interruption *and* without successor.

4Now observe *and* consider how great [a personage] this was to whom even Abraham the patriarch gave a tenth—the topmost [the pick] of the heap—of the spoils.

5And it is true that those descendants of Levi who are charged with the priestly office are commanded in the Law to take tithes from the people, which means from their brethren, though these have descended from Abraham.

6But this person who has not their Levitical ancestry received tithes from Abraham [himself] and blessed him who possessed the promises [of God].

7Yet it is beyond all contradiction that it is the lesser person who is blessed by the greater one.

8Furthermore, here [in the Levitical priesthood] tithes are received by men who are subject to death; while there [in the case of Melchizedek], they are received by one of whom it is testified that he lives [perpetually].

9A person might even say that through Abraham, Levi [the father of the priestly tribe] himself, who received tithes, paid tithes through Abraham.

10For he was still in the loins of his forefather [Abraham] when Melchizedek met him [Abraham].

11Now if perfection [that is, a perfect fellowship between God and the worshipper,] had been attainable by the Levitical priesthood, for under it the people were given the Law, why was it further necessary that there should arise another *and* different kind of Priest, one after the order of Melchizedek, rather than one appointed after the order *and* rank of Aaron?

12For when there is a change in the priesthood, there is of necessity an alteration of the law [concerning the priesthood] as well.

13For the One of Whom these things are said belonged [not to the priestly line but] to another tribe, no member of which has officiated at the altar.

14For it is obvious that our Lord sprang from the tribe of Judah, and Moses mentioned nothing about priests in connection with that tribe.

15And this becomes more plainly evident when another Priest arises Who bears the likeness of Melchizedek, [Ps. 110:4.]

16Who has been constituted a Priest, not on the basis of a bodily legal requirement—an externally imposed command concerning His physical ancestry—but on the basis of the power of an endless *and* indestructible Life.

17For it is witnessed of Him, You are a Priest forever after the order [rank] of Melchizedek. [Ps. 110:4.]

18So, a previous physical regulation *and* command is cancelled because of its weakness *and* ineffectiveness and uselessness,

19For the Law never made anything perfect, but instead a better hope is introduced through which we [now] come close to God.

20And it was not without the taking of an oath [that Christ was made Priest],

**AMP** [a] Thayer.

## New American Standard

20 where Jesus has entered as a forerunner for us, having become a high priest forever according to the order of Melchizedek.

*Melchizedek's Priesthood Like Christ's*

**7** FOR THIS Melchizedek, king of Salem, priest of the Most High God, who met Abraham as he was returning from the slaughter of the kings and blessed him,

2 to whom also Abraham apportioned a tenth part of all *the spoils,* was first of all, by the translation *of his name,* king of righteousness, and then also king of Salem, which is king of peace.

3 Without father, without mother, without genealogy, having neither beginning of days nor end of life, but made like the Son of God, he abides a priest perpetually.

4 ¶ Now observe how great this man was to whom Abraham, the patriarch, gave a tenth of the choicest spoils.

5 And those indeed of the sons of Levi who receive the priest's office have commandment in the Law to collect a tenth from the people, that is, from their brethren, although these are descended from Abraham.

6 But the one whose genealogy is not traced from them collected a tenth from Abraham, and blessed the one who had the promises.

7 But without any dispute the lesser is blessed by the greater.

8 And in this case mortal men receive tithes, but in that case one *receives them,* of whom it is witnessed that he lives on.

9 And, so to speak, through Abraham even Levi, who received tithes, paid tithes,

10 for he was still in the loins of his father when Melchizedek met him.

11 ¶ Now if perfection was through the Levitical priesthood (for on the basis of it the people received the Law), what further need *was there* for another priest to arise according to the order of Melchizedek, and not be designated according to the order of Aaron?

12 For when the priesthood is changed, of necessity there takes place a change of law also.

13 For the one concerning whom these things are spoken belongs to another tribe, from which no one has officiated at the altar.

14 For it is evident that our Lord was descended from Judah, a tribe with reference to which Moses spoke nothing concerning priests.

15 And this is clearer still, if another priest arises according to the likeness of Melchizedek,

16 who has become *such* not on the basis of a law of physical requirement, but according to the power of an indestructible life.

17 For it is witnessed *of Him,*

"THOU ART A PRIEST FOREVER
ACCORDING TO THE ORDER OF MELCHIZEDEK."

18 For, on the one hand, there is a setting aside of a former commandment because of its weakness and uselessness

19 (for the Law made nothing perfect), and on the other hand there is a bringing in of a better hope, through which we draw near to God.

20 And inasmuch as *it was* not without an oath

## New International

has entered on our behalf. He has become a high priest forever, in the order of Melchizedek.

*Melchizedek the Priest*

**7** THIS MELCHIZEDEK was king of Salem and priest of God
Most High. He met Abraham returning from the defeat of the
kings and blessed him,
2 and Abraham gave him a tenth of everything. First, his name means "king of righteousness"; then also, "king of Salem" means "king of peace."
3 Without father or
mother, without genealogy, without beginning of days or end of
life, like the Son of God he remains a priest forever.
4 Just think how great he was: Even the patriarch Abraham gave
him a tenth of the plunder!
5 Now the law requires the descendants
of Levi who become priests to collect a tenth from the people—that
is, their brothers—even though their brothers are descended from
Abraham.
6 This man, however, did not trace his descent from
Levi, yet he collected a tenth from Abraham and blessed him who
had the promises.
7 And without doubt the lesser person is blessed
by the greater.
8 In the one case, the tenth is collected by men who
die; but in the other case, by him who is declared to be living.
9 One
might even say that Levi, who collects the tenth, paid the tenth
through Abraham,
10 because when Melchizedek met Abraham,
Levi was still in the body of his ancestor.

*Jesus Like Melchizedek*

11 If perfection could have been attained through the Levitical
priesthood (for on the basis of it the law was given to the people),
why was there still need for another priest to come—one in the
order of Melchizedek, not in the order of Aaron?
12 For when there
is a change of the priesthood, there must also be a change of the
law.
13 He of whom these things are said belonged to a different
tribe, and no one from that tribe has ever served at the altar.
14 For
it is clear that our Lord descended from Judah, and in regard to
that tribe Moses said nothing about priests.
15 And what we have
said is even more clear if another priest like Melchizedek appears,
16 one who has become a priest not on the basis of a regulation as
to his ancestry but on the basis of the power of an indestructible
life.
17 For it is declared:

"You are a priest forever,
in the order of Melchizedek."[b]

18 The former regulation is set aside because it was weak and
useless
19 (for the law made nothing perfect), and a better hope is
introduced, by which we draw near to God.
20 And it was not without an oath! Others became priests with-

NIV [b] *17* Psalm 110:4

## King James

21(For those priests were made without an oath; but this with an oath by him that said unto him, The Lord sware and will not repent, Thou *art* a priest for ever after the order of Melchisedec:)

22By so much was Jesus made a surety of a better testament.

23And they truly were many priests, because they were not suffered to continue by reason of death:

24But this *man*, because he continueth ever, hath an unchangeable priesthood.

25Wherefore he is able also to save them to the uttermost that come unto God by him, seeing he ever liveth to make intercession for them.

26For such an high priest became us, *who is* holy, harmless, undefiled, separate from sinners, and made higher than the heavens;

27Who needeth not daily, as those high priests, to offer up sacrifice, first for his own sins, and then for the people's: for this he did once, when he offered up himself.

28For the law maketh men high priests which have infirmity; but the word of the oath, which was since the law, *maketh* the Son, who is consecrated for evermore.

**8** NOW OF the things which we have spoken *this is* the sum: We have such an high priest, who is set on the right hand of the throne of the Majesty in the heavens;

2A minister of the sanctuary, and of the true tabernacle, which the Lord pitched, and not man.

3For every high priest is ordained to offer gifts and sacrifices: wherefore *it is* of necessity that this man have somewhat also to offer.

4For if he were on earth, he should not be a priest, seeing that there are priests that offer gifts according to the law:

5Who serve unto the example and shadow of heavenly things, as Moses was admonished of God when he was about to make the tabernacle: for, See, saith he, *that* thou make all things according to the pattern shown to thee in the mount.

6But now hath he obtained a more excellent ministry, by how much also he is the mediator of a better covenant, which was established upon better promises.

7For if that first *covenant* had been faultless, then should no place have been sought for the second.

8For finding fault with them, he saith, Behold, the days come, saith the Lord, when I will make a new covenant with the house of Israel and with the house of Judah:

9Not according to the covenant that I made with their fathers in the day when I took them by the hand to lead them out of the land of Egypt; because they continued not in my covenant, and I regarded them not, saith the Lord.

## Amplified

21For those who formerly became priests received their office without its being confirmed by the taking of an oath by God, but this One was designated *and* addressed *and* saluted with an oath, The Lord has sworn and will not regret it *or* change His mind, You are a Priest forever *according to the order of Melchizedek.* [Ps. 110:4.]

22In keeping with [the oath's greater strength and force], Jesus has become the Guarantee of a better (stronger) agreement—a more excellent and more advantageous covenant.

23[Again, the former successive line of priests] was made up of many, because they were each prevented by death from continuing [perpetually in office];

24But He holds His priesthood unchangeably because He lives on forever.

25Therefore He is able also to save to the uttermost—completely, perfectly, finally and for all time and eternity—those who come to God through Him, since He is always living to make petition to God *and* intercede with Him *and* intervene for them.

26[Here is] the High Priest [perfectly adapted] to our needs, as was fitting, holy, blameless, unstained by sin, separated from sinners and exalted higher than the heavens.

27He has no day by day necessity, as [do each of these other] high priests, to offer sacrifice first of all for his own [personal] sins and then for those of the people; because He [met all the requirements] once for all when He brought Himself [as a sacrifice] which He offered up.

28For the Law sets up men in their weakness [frail, sinful, dying human beings] as high priests, but the word of [God's] oath, which [was spoken later], after the institution of the Law, [chooses *and* appoints as priest One Whose appointment is complete and permanent], a Son Who has been made perfect forever. [Ps. 110:4.]

**8** NOW THE main point of what we have to say is this: We have such a High Priest, One Who is seated at the right hand of the majestic [God] in heaven, [Ps. 110:1.]

2As officiating Priest, a Minister in the holy places *and* in the true tabernacle which is erected not by man but by the Lord.

3For every high priest is appointed to offer up gifts and sacrifices; so it is essential for this [High Priest] to have some offering to make also.

4If then He were still living on earth, He would not be a priest at all, for there are [already priests] who offer the gifts in accordance with the Law.

5[But these offer service merely as] a pattern and as a foreshadowing of [what has its true existence and reality in] the heavenly sanctuary. For when Moses was about to erect the tabernacle, he was warned by God, saying, See to it that you make it all [exactly] according to the copy (the model) which was shown to you on the mountain. [Exod. 25:40.]

6But as it now is, He [Christ] has acquired a [priestly] ministry which is as much superior *and* more excellent [than the old] as the covenant—the agreement—of which He is the Mediator (the Arbiter, Agent) is superior *and* more excellent; [because] it is enacted *and* rests upon more important (sublimer, higher and nobler) promises.

7For if that first covenant had been without defect, there would have been no room for another one *or* an attempt to institute another one.

8However He finds fault with them, [showing its inadequacy], when He says, Behold, the days will come, says the Lord, when I will make *and* ratify a new covenant *or* agreement with the house of Israel and with the house of Judah.

9It will not be like the covenant that I made with their forefathers on the day when I grasped them by the hand to help *and* relieve them *and* to lead them out from the land of Egypt, for they did not abide in My agreement with them, and so I withdrew My favor *and* disregarded them, says the Lord.

## New American Standard

21(for they indeed became priests without an oath, but He with
an oath through the One who said to Him,
"THE LORD HAS SWORN
AND WILL NOT CHANGE HIS MIND,
'THOU ART A PRIEST FOREVER'");
22so much the more also Jesus has become the guarantee of a
better covenant.
23And the *former* priests, on the one hand, existed in greater
numbers, because they were prevented by death from continuing,
24but He, on the other hand, because He abides forever, holds
His priesthood permanently.
25Hence, also, He is able to save forever those who draw near
to God through Him, since He always lives to make intercession
for them.
26¶ For it was fitting that we should have such a high priest,
holy, innocent, undefiled, separated from sinners and exalted
above the heavens;
27who does not need daily, like those high priests, to offer up
sacrifices, first for His own sins, and then for the *sins* of the people,
because this He did once for all when He offered up Himself.
28For the Law appoints men as high priests who are weak, but
the word of the oath, which came after the Law, *appoints* a Son,
made perfect forever.

*A Better Ministry*

8 NOW THE main point in what has been said *is this*: we have
such a high priest, who has taken His seat at the right hand
of the throne of the Majesty in the heavens,
2a minister in the sanctuary, and in the true tabernacle, which
the Lord pitched, not man.
3For every high priest is appointed to offer both gifts and
sacrifices; hence it is necessary that this *high priest* also have something to offer.
4Now if He were on earth, He would not be a priest at all, since
there are those who offer the gifts according to the Law;
5who serve a copy and shadow of the heavenly things, just as
Moses was warned *by God* when he was about to erect the tabernacle; for, "SEE," He says, "THAT YOU MAKE all things ACCORDING
TO THE PATTERN WHICH WAS SHOWN YOU ON THE MOUNTAIN."
6But now He has obtained a more excellent ministry, by as
much as He is also the mediator of a better covenant, which has
been enacted on better promises.

*A New Covenant*

7For if that first *covenant* had been faultless, there would have
been no occasion sought for a second.
8For finding fault with them, He says,
"BEHOLD, DAYS ARE COMING, SAYS THE LORD,
WHEN I WILL EFFECT A NEW COVENANT
WITH THE HOUSE OF ISRAEL AND WITH THE HOUSE OF
JUDAH;
9 NOT LIKE THE COVENANT WHICH I MADE WITH THEIR
FATHERS
ON THE DAY WHEN I TOOK THEM BY THE HAND
TO LEAD THEM OUT OF THE LAND OF EGYPT;
FOR THEY DID NOT CONTINUE IN MY COVENANT,
AND I DID NOT CARE FOR THEM, SAYS THE LORD.

## New International

out any oath, 21but he became a priest with an oath when God said
to him:
"The Lord has sworn
and will not change his mind:
'You are a priest forever.' "[a]
22Because of this oath, Jesus has become the guarantee of a better
covenant.
23Now there have been many of those priests, since death prevented them from continuing in office; 24but because Jesus lives
forever, he has a permanent priesthood. 25Therefore he is able to
save completely[b] those who come to God through him, because
he always lives to intercede for them.
26Such a high priest meets our need—one who is holy, blameless, pure, set apart from sinners, exalted above the heavens.
27Unlike the other high priests, he does not need to offer sacrifices
day after day, first for his own sins, and then for the sins of the
people. He sacrificed for their sins once for all when he offered
himself. 28For the law appoints as high priests men who are weak;
but the oath, which came after the law, appointed the Son, who
has been made perfect forever.

*The High Priest of a New Covenant*

8 THE POINT of what we are saying is this: We do have such
a high priest, who sat down at the right hand of the throne
of the Majesty in heaven, 2and who serves in the sanctuary, the
true tabernacle set up by the Lord, not by man.
3Every high priest is appointed to offer both gifts and sacrifices,
and so it was necessary for this one also to have something to offer.
4If he were on earth, he would not be a priest, for there are already
men who offer the gifts prescribed by the law. 5They serve at a
sanctuary that is a copy and shadow of what is in heaven. This is
why Moses was warned when he was about to build the tabernacle: "See to it that you make everything according to the pattern
shown you on the mountain."[c] 6But the ministry Jesus has received is as superior to theirs as the covenant of which he is
mediator is superior to the old one, and it is founded on better
promises.
7For if there had been nothing wrong with that first covenant,
no place would have been sought for another. 8But God found
fault with the people and said[d]:
"The time is coming, declares the Lord,
when I will make a new covenant
with the house of Israel
and with the house of Judah.
9It will not be like the covenant
I made with their forefathers
when I took them by the hand
to lead them out of Egypt,
because they did not remain faithful to my covenant,
and I turned away from them,
declares the Lord.

NIV [a] *21* Psalm 110:4 [b] *25* Or *forever* [c] *5* Exodus 25:40 [d] *8* Some manuscripts may be translated *fault and said to the people.*

## King James

10For this *is* the covenant that I will make with the house of Israel after those days, saith the Lord; I will put my laws into their mind, and write them in their hearts: and I will be to them a God, and they shall be to me a people:

11And they shall not teach every man his neighbour, and every man his brother, saying, Know the Lord: for all shall know me, from the least to the greatest.

12For I will be merciful to their unrighteousness, and their sins and their iniquities will I remember no more.

13In that he saith, A new *covenant*, he hath made the first old. Now that which decayeth and waxeth old *is* ready to vanish away.

9 THEN VERILY the first *covenant* had also ordinances of divine service, and a worldly sanctuary.

2For there was a tabernacle made; the first, wherein *was* the candlestick, and the table, and the showbread; which is called the sanctuary.

3And after the second veil, the tabernacle which is called the Holiest of all;

4Which had the golden censer, and the ark of the covenant overlaid round about with gold, wherein *was* the golden pot that had manna, and Aaron's rod that budded, and the tables of the covenant;

5And over it the cherubims of glory shadowing the mercyseat; of which we cannot now speak particularly.

6Now when these things were thus ordained, the priests went always into the first tabernacle, accomplishing the service *of God.*

7But into the second *went* the high priest alone once every year, not without blood, which he offered for himself, and *for* the errors of the people:

8The Holy Ghost this signifying, that the way into the holiest of all was not yet made manifest, while as the first tabernacle was yet standing:

9Which *was* a figure for the time then present, in which were offered both gifts and sacrifices, that could not make him that did the service perfect, as pertaining to the conscience;

10 *Which stood* only in meats and drinks, and divers washings, and carnal ordinances, imposed *on them* until the time of reformation.

11But Christ being come an high priest of good things to come, by a greater and more perfect tabernacle, not made with hands, that is to say, not of this building;

## Amplified

10For this is the covenant that I will make with the house of Israel after those days, says the Lord: I will imprint My laws upon their minds, even upon their innermost thoughts *and* understanding, and engrave them upon their hearts, and I will be their God, and they shall be My people.

11And it will nevermore be necessary for every one to teach his neighbor and his fellow citizen or every one his brother, saying, Know—[that is,] perceive, have knowledge of and get acquainted by experience with—the Lord; for all will know Me, from the smallest to the greatest of them.

12For I will be merciful *and* gracious toward their sins and I will remember their deeds of unrighteousness no more. [Jer. 31:31-34.]

13When God speaks of a new [covenant or agreement], He makes the first one obsolete—out of use. And what is obsolete—out of use *and* annulled because of age—is ripe for disappearance *and* to be dispensed with altogether.

9 NOW EVEN the first covenant had its own rules *and* regulations for divine worship, and it had a sanctuary, [but one] of this world. [Exod. 25:10-40.]

2For a tabernacle (tent) was erected, in the outer division *or* compartment of which were the lampstand and the table with [its loaves of] the showbread set forth. [This portion] is called the Holy [Place]. [Lev. 24:5, 6.]

3But [inside], beyond the second curtain *or* veil, [there stood another] tabernacle [division] known as the Holy of Holies. [Exod. 26:31-33.]

4It had the golden [a]altar of incense and the ark (chest) of the covenant, covered over with wrought gold. This [ark] contained a golden jar which held the manna, and the rod of Aaron that sprouted, and the [two stone] slabs of the covenant, [bearing the Ten Commandments]. [Exod. 30:1-6; 16:32-34; Num. 17:8-10.]

5Above [the ark] and overshadowing the mercy seat were the representations of the cherubim [winged creatures which were the symbols] of glory. We cannot now go into detail about these things.

6These arrangements having thus been made, the priests enter habitually into the outer division of the tabernacle, in performance of their ritual acts of worship.

7But into the second [division of the tabernacle] none but the high priest goes, and he only once a year, and never without taking a sacrifice of blood with him, which he offers for himself and for the errors *and* sins of ignorance *and* thoughtlessness which the people have committed. [Lev. 16:15.]

8By this the Holy Spirit points out that the way into the [true Holy of] Holies is not yet thrown open as long as the former [the outer portion of the] tabernacle remains a recognized institution *and* is still standing,

9Seeing that that first [outer portion of the] tabernacle was a parable—a visible symbol or type or picture of the present age. In it gifts and sacrifices are offered, and yet are incapable of perfecting the conscience *or* of cleansing *and* renewing the inner man of the worshipper.

10For [the ceremonies] deal only with clean and unclean meats and drinks and different washings, [mere] external rules *and* regulations for the body imposed to tide the worshippers over until the time of setting things straight—of reformation, [of the complete new order when Christ, the Messiah, shall establish the reality of what these things foreshadow, a better covenant].

11But [that appointed time came] when Christ, the Messiah, appeared as a High Priest of the better things that have come *and* [b]are to come. [Then] through the greater and more perfect tabernacle, not made with [human] hands, that is, not a part of this material creation,

**AMP** [a] Not kept permanently in the Holy of Holies, but taken in on the Day of Atonement, as the Mischna explains.—Alford. Cited by Wuest in "Hebrews."
[b] Alternate reading.

## New American Standard

10 "FOR THIS IS THE COVENANT THAT I WILL MAKE WITH THE
HOUSE OF ISRAEL
AFTER THOSE DAYS, SAYS THE LORD:
I WILL PUT MY LAWS INTO THEIR MINDS,
AND I WILL WRITE THEM UPON THEIR HEARTS.
AND I WILL BE THEIR GOD,
AND THEY SHALL BE MY PEOPLE.
11 "AND THEY SHALL NOT TEACH EVERYONE HIS FELLOW
CITIZEN,
AND EVERYONE HIS BROTHER, SAYING, 'KNOW THE LORD,'
FOR ALL SHALL KNOW ME,
FROM THE LEAST TO THE GREATEST OF THEM.
12 "FOR I WILL BE MERCIFUL TO THEIR INIQUITIES,
AND I WILL REMEMBER THEIR SINS NO MORE."

13When He said, "A new *covenant*," He has made the first obsolete. But whatever is becoming obsolete and growing old is ready to disappear.

*The Old and the New*

**9** NOW EVEN the first *covenant* had regulations of divine worship and the earthly sanctuary.

2For there was a tabernacle prepared, the outer one, in which *were* the lampstand and the table and the sacred bread; this is called the holy place.

3And behind the second veil, there was a tabernacle which is called the Holy of Holies,

4having a golden altar of incense and the ark of the covenant covered on all sides with gold, in which *was* a golden jar holding the manna, and Aaron's rod which budded, and the tables of the covenant.

5And above it *were* the cherubim of glory overshadowing the mercy seat; but of these things we cannot now speak in detail.

6Now when these things have been thus prepared, the priests are continually entering the outer tabernacle, performing the divine worship,

7but into the second only the high priest *enters*, once a year, not without *taking* blood, which he offers for himself and for the sins of the people committed in ignorance.

8The Holy Spirit *is* signifying this, that the way into the holy place has not yet been disclosed, while the outer tabernacle is still standing,

9which *is* a symbol for the present time. Accordingly both gifts and sacrifices are offered which cannot make the worshiper perfect in conscience,

10since they *relate* only to food and drink and various washings, regulations for the body imposed until a time of reformation.

11¶ But when Christ appeared *as* a high priest of the good things [c]to come, *He entered* through the greater and more perfect tabernacle, not made with hands, that is to say, not of this creation;

## New International

10This is the covenant I will make with the house of Israel
after that time, declares the Lord.
I will put my laws in their minds
and write them on their hearts.
I will be their God,
and they will be my people.
11No longer will a man teach his neighbor,
or a man his brother, saying, 'Know the Lord,'
because they will all know me,
from the least of them to the greatest.
12For I will forgive their wickedness
and will remember their sins no more."[d]

13By calling this covenant "new," he has made the first one obsolete; and what is obsolete and aging will soon disappear.

*Worship in the Earthly Tabernacle*

**9** NOW THE first covenant had regulations for worship and
also an earthly sanctuary. 2A tabernacle was set up. In its first
room were the lampstand, the table and the consecrated bread;
this was called the Holy Place. 3Behind the second curtain was a
room called the Most Holy Place, 4which had the golden altar of
incense and the gold-covered ark of the covenant. This ark contained the gold jar of manna, Aaron's staff that had budded, and
the stone tablets of the covenant. 5Above the ark were the cherubim of the Glory, overshadowing the atonement cover.[e] But we
cannot discuss these things in detail now.
6When everything had been arranged like this, the priests entered regularly into the outer room to carry on their ministry. 7But
only the high priest entered the inner room, and that only once a
year, and never without blood, which he offered for himself and
for the sins the people had committed in ignorance. 8The Holy
Spirit was showing by this that the way into the Most Holy Place
had not yet been disclosed as long as the first tabernacle was still
standing. 9This is an illustration for the present time, indicating
that the gifts and sacrifices being offered were not able to clear the
conscience of the worshiper. 10They are only a matter of food and
drink and various ceremonial washings—external regulations applying until the time of the new order.

*The Blood of Christ*

11When Christ came as high priest of the good things that are
already here,[f] he went through the greater and more perfect
tabernacle that is not man-made, that is to say, not a part of this
creation. 12He did not enter by means of the blood of goats and

NAS [c] Some ancient mss. read *that have come*

NIV [d] 12 Jer. 31:31-34 [e] 5 Traditionally *the mercy seat* [f] 11 Some early manuscripts *are to come*

## King James

12 Neither by the blood of goats and calves, but by his own blood he entered in once into the holy place, having obtained eternal redemption *for us*.

13 For if the blood of bulls and of goats, and the ashes of an heifer sprinkling the unclean, sanctifieth to the purifying of the flesh:

14 How much more shall the blood of Christ, who through the eternal Spirit offered himself without spot to God, purge your conscience from dead works to serve the living God?

15 And for this cause he is the mediator of the new testament, that by means of death, for the redemption of the transgressions *that were* under the first testament, they which are called might receive the promise of eternal inheritance.

16 For where a testament *is*, there must also of necessity be the death of the testator.

17 For a testament *is* of force after men are dead: otherwise it is of no strength at all while the testator liveth.

18 Whereupon neither the first *testament* was dedicated without blood.

19 For when Moses had spoken every precept to all the people according to the law, he took the blood of calves and of goats, with water, and scarlet wool, and hyssop, and sprinkled both the book, and all the people,

20 Saying, This *is* the blood of the testament which God hath enjoined unto you.

21 Moreover he sprinkled with blood both the tabernacle, and all the vessels of the ministry.

22 And almost all things are by the law purged with blood; and without shedding of blood is no remission.

23 *It was* therefore necessary that the patterns of things in the heavens should be purified with these; but the heavenly things themselves with better sacrifices than these.

24 For Christ is not entered into the holy places made with hands, *which are* the figures of the true; but into heaven itself, now to appear in the presence of God for us:

25 Nor yet that he should offer himself often, as the high priest entereth into the holy place every year with blood of others;

26 For then must he often have suffered since the foundation of the world: but now once in the end of the world hath he appeared to put away sin by the sacrifice of himself.

27 And as it is appointed unto men once to die, but after this the judgment:

28 So Christ was once offered to bear the sins of many; and unto them that look for him shall he appear the second time without sin unto salvation.

## Amplified

12 He went once for all into the [Holy of] Holies [of heaven], not by virtue of the blood of goats and calves [by which to make reconciliation between God and man], but His own blood, having found *and* secured a complete redemption—an everlasting release [for us].

13 For if [the mere] sprinkling of unholy *and* defiled persons with blood of goats and bulls and with the ashes of a burnt heifer is sufficient for the purification of the body, [Lev. 16:6, 16; Num. 19:9, 17, 18.]

14 How much more surely shall the blood of Christ, Who [a]by virtue of [ [b]His] eternal Spirit [ [c]His own pre-existent [d]divine personality] has offered Himself an unblemished sacrifice to God, purify our consciences from dead works *and* lifeless observances to serve the [ever-] living God?

15 [Christ, the Messiah] is therefore the Negotiator *and* Mediator of an [entirely] new agreement (testament, covenant), so that those who are called *and* offered it, may receive the fulfillment of the promised everlasting inheritance, since a death has taken place which rescues *and* delivers *and* redeems them from the transgressions committed under the [old], first agreement.

16 For where there is a [last] will *and* testament involved, the death of the one who made it must be established,

17 For a will *and* testament is valid and takes effect only at death, since it has no force *or* legal power as long as the one who made it is alive.

18 So even the (old) first covenant [God's will] was not inaugurated *and* ratified *and* put in force without the shedding of blood.

19 For when every command of the Law had been read out by Moses to all the people, he took the blood of slain calves and goats, together with water and scarlet wool, and with a bunch of hyssop sprinkled both the Book [the roll of the Law and covenant] itself, and all the people,

20 Saying these words: This is the blood that seals *and* ratifies the agreement (the testament, the covenant) which God commanded [me to deliver to] you [Exod. 24:6-8.]

21 And in the same way he sprinkled with the blood both the tabernacle and all the [sacred] vessels *and* appliances used in [divine] worship.

22 [In fact], under the Law almost everything is purified by means of blood, and without the shedding of blood there is neither release from sin *and* its guilt *nor* the remission of the due *and* merited punishment for sins.

23 By such means therefore it was necessary for the [earthly] copies of the heavenly things to be purified, but the actual heavenly things themselves [required far] better *and* nobler sacrifices than these.

24 For Christ, the Messiah, has not entered into a sanctuary made with [human] hands, only a copy *and* pattern *and* type of the true one, but [He has entered] into heaven itself, now to appear in the [very] presence of God on our behalf.

25 Nor did He [enter into the heavenly sanctuary to] offer Himself regularly again and again, as the high priest enters the [Holy of] Holies every year with blood not his own;

26 For then would He often have had to suffer, [over and over again] since the foundation of the world. But as it now is, He has once for all at the consummation *and* close of the ages appeared to put away *and* abolish sin by His sacrifice [of Himself].

27 And just as it is appointed for [all] men once to die and after that the [certain] judgment,

28 Even so it is that Christ having been offered to take upon Himself *and* bear as a burden the sins of many once *and* [e]once for all, will appear a second time, not carrying any burden of sin *nor* to deal with sin, but to bring to full salvation those who are (eagerly, constantly and patiently) waiting for *and* expecting Him.

**AMP** [a] Vincent. [b] Many authorities. [c] Many authorities. [d] Alford, cited by Wuest. [e] Abbott-Smith.

## New American Standard

12and not through the blood of goats and calves, but through His own blood, He entered the holy place once for all, having obtained eternal redemption.

13For if the blood of goats and bulls and the ashes of a heifer sprinkling those who have been defiled, sanctify for the cleansing of the flesh,

14how much more will the blood of Christ, who through the eternal Spirit offered Himself without blemish to God, cleanse your conscience from dead works to serve the living God?

15And for this reason He is the mediator of a new covenant, in order that since a death has taken place for the redemption of the transgressions that were *committed* under the first covenant, those who have been called may receive the promise of the eternal inheritance.

16For where a covenant is, there must of necessity be the death of the one who made it.

17For a covenant is valid *only* when men are dead, [f]for it is never in force while the one who made it lives.

18Therefore even the first *covenant* was not inaugurated without blood.

19For when every commandment had been spoken by Moses to all the people according to the Law, he took the blood of the calves and the goats, with water and scarlet wool and hyssop, and sprinkled both the book itself and all the people,

20saying, "THIS IS THE BLOOD OF THE COVENANT WHICH GOD COMMANDED YOU."

21And in the same way he sprinkled both the tabernacle and all the vessels of the ministry with the blood.

22And according to the Law, *one may* almost *say*, all things are cleansed with blood, and without shedding of blood there is no forgiveness.

23¶ Therefore it was necessary for the copies of the things in the heavens to be cleansed with these, but the heavenly things themselves with better sacrifices than these.

24For Christ did not enter a holy place made with hands, a *mere* copy of the true one, but into heaven itself, now to appear in the presence of God for us;

25nor was it that He should offer Himself often, as the high priest enters the holy place year by year with blood not his own.

26Otherwise, He would have needed to suffer often since the foundation of the world; but now once at the consummation of the ages He has been manifested to put away sin by the sacrifice of Himself.

27And inasmuch as it is appointed for men to die once and after this *comes* judgment,

28so Christ also, having been offered once to bear the sins of many, shall appear a second time for salvation without *reference to* sin, to those who eagerly await Him.

NAS [f] Some ancient mss. read *for is it then . . . lives?*

## New International

calves; but he entered the Most Holy Place once for all by his own
blood, having obtained eternal redemption. 13The blood of goats
and bulls and the ashes of a heifer sprinkled on those who are
ceremonially unclean sanctify them so that they are outwardly
clean. 14How much more, then, will the blood of Christ, who
through the eternal Spirit offered himself unblemished to God,
cleanse our consciences from acts that lead to death,[g] so that we
may serve the living God!

15For this reason Christ is the mediator of a new covenant, that
those who are called may receive the promised eternal inheritance—now that he has died as a ransom to set them free from the
sins committed under the first covenant.

16In the case of a will,[h] it is necessary to prove the death of the
one who made it, 17because a will is in force only when somebody
has died; it never takes effect while the one who made it is living.
18This is why even the first covenant was not put into effect without blood. 19When Moses had proclaimed every commandment of
the law to all the people, he took the blood of calves, together with
water, scarlet wool and branches of hyssop, and sprinkled the
scroll and all the people. 20He said, "This is the blood of the
covenant, which God has commanded you to keep."[i] 21In the
same way, he sprinkled with the blood both the tabernacle and
everything used in its ceremonies. 22In fact, the law requires that
nearly everything be cleansed with blood, and without the shedding of blood there is no forgiveness.

23It was necessary, then, for the copies of the heavenly things
to be purified with these sacrifices, but the heavenly things themselves with better sacrifices than these. 24For Christ did not enter
a man-made sanctuary that was only a copy of the true one; he
entered heaven itself, now to appear for us in God's presence.
25Nor did he enter heaven to offer himself again and again, the
way the high priest enters the Most Holy Place every year with
blood that is not his own. 26Then Christ would have had to suffer
many times since the creation of the world. But now he has appeared once for all at the end of the ages to do away with sin by
the sacrifice of himself. 27Just as man is destined to die once, and
after that to face judgment, 28so Christ was sacrificed once to take
away the sins of many people; and he will appear a second time,
not to bear sin, but to bring salvation to those who are waiting for
him.

NIV [g] *14* Or *from useless rituals* [h] *16* Same Greek word as *covenant;* also in verse 17 [i] *20* Exodus 24:8

## King James

**10** FOR THE law having a shadow of good things to come, *and* not the very image of the things, can never with those sacrifices which they offered year by year continually make the comers thereunto perfect.

2 For then would they not have ceased to be offered? because that the worshippers once purged should have had no more conscience of sins.

3 But in those *sacrifices there is* a remembrance again *made* of sins every year.

4 For *it is* not possible that the blood of bulls and of goats should take away sins.

5 Wherefore when he cometh into the world, he saith, Sacrifice and offering thou wouldest not, but a body hast thou prepared me:

6 In burnt offerings and *sacrifices* for sin thou hast had no pleasure.

7 Then said I, Lo, I come (in the volume of the book it is written of me,) to do thy will, O God.

8 Above when he said, Sacrifice and offering and burnt offerings and *offering* for sin thou wouldest not, neither hadst pleasure *therein;* which are offered by the law;

9 Then said he, Lo, I come to do thy will, O God. He taketh away the first, that he may establish the second.

10 By the which will we are sanctified through the offering of the body of Jesus Christ once *for all.*

11 And every priest standeth daily ministering and offering oftentimes the same sacrifices, which can never take away sins:

12 But this man, after he had offered one sacrifice for sins for ever, sat down on the right hand of God;

13 From henceforth expecting till his enemies be made his footstool.

14 For by one offering he hath perfected for ever them that are sanctified.

15 *Whereof* the Holy Ghost also is a witness to us: for after that he had said before,

16 This *is* the covenant that I will make with them after those days, saith the Lord, I will put my laws into their hearts, and in their minds will I write them;

17 And their sins and iniquities will I remember no more.

18 Now where remission of these *is, there is* no more offering for sin.

19 Having therefore, brethren, boldness to enter into the holiest by the blood of Jesus,

20 By a new and living way, which he hath consecrated for us, through the veil, that is to say, his flesh;

21 And *having* an high priest over the house of God;

22 Let us draw near with a true heart in full assurance of faith, having our hearts sprinkled from an evil conscience, and our bodies washed with pure water.

23 Let us hold fast the profession of *our* faith without wavering; (for he *is* faithful that promised;)

## Amplified

**10** FOR SINCE the Law has merely a rude outline (foreshadowing) of the good things to come, instead of fully expressing those things, it can never by offering the same sacrifices continually year after year make perfect those who approach [its altars].

2 For were it otherwise, would [these sacrifices] not have stopped being offered? Since the worshippers had [a]once for all been cleansed, they would no longer have any guilt *or* consciousness of sin.

3 But [as it is], these sacrifices annually bring a fresh remembrance of sins [to be atoned for],

4 Because the blood of bulls and goats is powerless to take sins away.

5 Hence, when He (Christ) entered into the world, He said, Sacrifices and offerings You have not desired, but instead You have made ready a body for Me [to offer];

6 In burnt offerings and sin offerings You have taken no delight.

7 Then I said, Lo, here I am, come to do Your will, O God; [to fulfill] what is written of Me in the volume of the Book. [Ps. 40:6-8.]

8 When He said just before, You have neither desired nor have You taken delight in sacrifices and offerings and burnt offerings and sin offerings, all of which are offered according to the Law,

9 He then went on to say, Lo [here] I am, come to do Your will. Thus He does away with *and* annuls the first (former) order [as a means of expiating sin] so that He might inaugurate *and* establish the second (latter) order. [Ps. 40:6-8.]

10 And in accordance with this will [of God] we have been made holy (consecrated and sanctified) through the offering made once for all of the body of Jesus Christ, the Anointed One.

11 Furthermore, every [human] priest stands [at his altar of service] ministering daily, offering the same sacrifices over and over again, which never are able to strip (from every side of us) the sins [that envelop us], *and* take them away.

12 Whereas this One (Christ), after He had offered a single Sacrifice for our sins [that shall avail] for all time, sat down at the right hand of God,

13 Then to wait until His enemies should be made a stool beneath His feet. [Ps. 110:1.]

14 For by a single offering He has forever completely cleansed *and* perfected those who are consecrated *and* made holy.

15 And also the Holy Spirit adds His testimony to us [in confirmation of this]. For having said,

16 This is the agreement (testament, covenant) that I will set up *and* conclude with them after those days, says the Lord: I will imprint My laws upon their hearts, and I will inscribe them on their minds—on their inmost thoughts and understanding,

17 He then goes on to say, And their sins and their lawbreakings I will remember no more. [Jer. 31:33, 34.]

18 Now where there is absolute remission—forgiveness and cancellation of the penalty—of these [sins and lawbreakings] there is no longer any offering made to atone for sin.

19 Therefore, brethren, since we have full freedom *and* confidence to enter into the [Holy of] Holies [by the power and virtue] in the blood of Jesus,

20 By this fresh (new) and living way which He initiated *and* dedicated *and* opened for us through the separating curtain [veil of the Holy of Holies], that is, through His flesh;

21 And since we have [such] a great *and* wonderful *and* noble Priest [Who rules] over the house of God,

22 Let us all come forward *and* draw near with true (honest and sincere) hearts in unqualified assurance *and* absolute conviction engendered by faith, [that is, by [b]that leaning of the entire human personality on God in absolute trust and confidence in His power, wisdom and goodness,] having our hearts sprinkled *and* purified from a guilty (evil) conscience and with our bodies cleansed with pure water.

23 So let us seize *and* hold fast *and* retain without wavering the [c]hope we cherish *and* confess, *and* our acknowledgement of it, for He Who promised is reliable (sure) *and* faithful to His word.

**AMP** [a] Abbott-Smith. [b] Souter. [c] Tyndale, Coverdale, and many early Bibles.

## New American Standard

*One Sacrifice of Christ Is Sufficient*

**10** FOR THE Law, since it has *only* a shadow of the good
things to come *and* not the very form of things, [d]can never
by the same sacrifices year by year, which they offer continually,
make perfect those who draw near.
2Otherwise, would they not have ceased to be offered, because
the worshipers, having once been cleansed, would no longer have
had consciousness of sins?
3But in those *sacrifices* there is a reminder of sins year by year.
4For it is impossible for the blood of bulls and goats to take
away sins.
5Therefore, when He comes into the world, He says,

"SACRIFICE AND OFFERING THOU HAST NOT DESIRED,
BUT A BODY THOU HAST PREPARED FOR ME;
6 IN WHOLE BURNT OFFERINGS AND *sacrifices* FOR SIN THOU
HAST TAKEN NO PLEASURE.
7 "THEN I SAID, 'BEHOLD, I HAVE COME
(IN THE ROLL OF THE BOOK IT IS WRITTEN OF ME)
TO DO THY WILL, O GOD.' "

8After saying above, "SACRIFICES AND OFFERINGS AND WHOLE
BURNT OFFERINGS AND *sacrifices* FOR SIN THOU HAST NOT DESIRED,
NOR HAST THOU TAKEN PLEASURE *in them*" (which are offered according to the Law),
9then He said, "BEHOLD, I HAVE COME TO DO THY WILL." He
takes away the first in order to establish the second.
10By this will we have been sanctified through the offering of
the body of Jesus Christ once for all.
11And every priest stands daily ministering and offering time
after time the same sacrifices, which can never take away sins;
12but He, having offered one sacrifice for sins for all time, SAT
DOWN AT THE RIGHT HAND OF GOD,
13waiting from that time onward UNTIL HIS ENEMIES BE MADE A
FOOTSTOOL FOR HIS FEET.
14For by one offering He has perfected for all time those who
are sanctified.
15And the Holy Spirit also bears witness to us; for after saying,

16 "THIS IS THE COVENANT THAT I WILL MAKE WITH THEM
AFTER THOSE DAYS, SAYS THE LORD:
I WILL PUT MY LAWS UPON THEIR HEART,
AND UPON THEIR MIND I WILL WRITE THEM,"

*He then says,*

17 "AND THEIR SINS AND THEIR LAWLESS DEEDS
I WILL REMEMBER NO MORE."

18Now where there is forgiveness of these things, there is no
longer *any* offering for sin.

*A New and Living Way*

19¶ Since therefore, brethren, we have confidence to enter the
holy place by the blood of Jesus,
20by a new and living way which He inaugurated for us through
the veil, that is, His flesh,
21and since *we have* a great priest over the house of God,
22let us draw near with a sincere heart in full assurance of faith,
having our hearts sprinkled *clean* from an evil conscience and our
bodies washed with pure water.
23Let us hold fast the confession of our hope without wavering,
for He who promised is faithful;

NAS [d] Some ancient mss. read *they can*

## New International

*Christ's Sacrifice Once for All*

**10** THE LAW is only a shadow of the good things that are
coming—not the realities themselves. For this reason it
can never, by the same sacrifices repeated endlessly year after
year, make perfect those who draw near to worship. 2If it could,
would they not have stopped being offered? For the worshipers
would have been cleansed once for all, and would no longer have
felt guilty for their sins. 3But those sacrifices are an annual reminder of sins, 4because it is impossible for the blood of bulls and goats
to take away sins.
5Therefore, when Christ came into the world, he said:

"Sacrifice and offering you did not desire,
but a body you prepared for me;
6with burnt offerings and sin offerings
you were not pleased.
7Then I said, 'Here I am—it is written about me in the
scroll—
I have come to do your will, O God.' "[e]

8First he said, "Sacrifices and offerings, burnt offerings and sin
offerings you did not desire, nor were you pleased with them"
(although the law required them to be made). 9Then he said, "Here
I am, I have come to do your will." He sets aside the first to
establish the second. 10And by that will, we have been made holy
through the sacrifice of the body of Jesus Christ once for all.
11Day after day every priest stands and performs his religious
duties; again and again he offers the same sacrifices, which can
never take away sins. 12But when this priest had offered for all time
one sacrifice for sins, he sat down at the right hand of God. 13Since
that time he waits for his enemies to be made his footstool, 14be-
cause by one sacrifice he has made perfect forever those who are
being made holy.
15The Holy Spirit also testifies to us about this. First he says:

16"This is the covenant I will make with them
after that time, says the Lord.
I will put my laws in their hearts,
and I will write them on their minds."[f]

17Then he adds:

"Their sins and lawless acts
I will remember no more."[g]

18And where these have been forgiven, there is no longer any
sacrifice for sin.

*A Call to Persevere*

19Therefore, brothers, since we have confidence to enter the
Most Holy Place by the blood of Jesus, 20by a new and living way
opened for us through the curtain, that is, his body, 21and since
we have a great priest over the house of God, 22let us draw near
to God with a sincere heart in full assurance of faith, having our
hearts sprinkled to cleanse us from a guilty conscience and having
our bodies washed with pure water. 23Let us hold unswervingly
to the hope we profess, for he who promised is faithful. 24And let

NIV [e] *7* Psalm 40:6-8 (see Septuagint) [f] *16* Jer. 31:33 [g] *17* Jer. 31:34

## King James

24And let us consider one another to provoke unto love and to good works:
25Not forsaking the assembling of ourselves together, as the manner of some *is;* but exhorting *one another:* and so much the more, as ye see the day approaching.
26For if we sin wilfully after that we have received the knowledge of the truth, there remaineth no more sacrifice for sins,
27But a certain fearful looking for of judgment and fiery indignation, which shall devour the adversaries.
28He that despised Moses' law died without mercy under two or three witnesses:
29Of how much sorer punishment, suppose ye, shall he be thought worthy, who hath trodden under foot the Son of God, and hath counted the blood of the covenant, wherewith he was sanctified, an unholy thing, and hath done despite unto the Spirit of grace?
30For we know him that hath said, Vengeance *belongeth* unto me, I will recompense, saith the Lord. And again, The Lord shall judge his people.
31 *It is* a fearful thing to fall into the hands of the living God.
32But call to remembrance the former days, in which, after ye were illuminated, ye endured a great fight of afflictions;
33Partly, whilst ye were made a gazingstock both by reproaches and afflictions; and partly, whilst ye became companions of them that were so used.
34For ye had compassion of me in my bonds, and took joyfully the spoiling of your goods, knowing in yourselves that ye have in heaven a better and an enduring substance.
35Cast not away therefore your confidence, which hath great recompence of reward.
36For ye have need of patience, that, after ye have done the will of God, ye might receive the promise.
37For yet a little while, and he that shall come will come, and will not tarry.
38Now the just shall live by faith: but if *any man* draw back, my soul shall have no pleasure in him.
39But we are not of them who draw back unto perdition; but of them that believe to the saving of the soul.

**11** NOW FAITH is the substance of things hoped for, the evidence of things not seen.

## Amplified

24And let us consider *and* give [a]attentive, continuous care to watching over one another, studying how we may stir up (stimulate and incite) to love *and* helpful deeds *and* noble activities;
25Not forsaking *or* neglecting to assemble together [as believers], as is the habit of some people, but admonishing—warning, urging and encouraging—one another, and all the more faithfully as you see the day approaching.
26For if we go on deliberately *and* willingly sinning after once acquiring the knowledge of the Truth, there is no longer any sacrifice left to atone for [our] sins—no further offering to which to look forward.
27[There is nothing left for us then] but a kind of awful *and* fearful prospect *and* expectation of divine judgment and the fury of burning wrath *and* indignation which will consume those who put themselves in opposition [to God]. [Isa. 26:11.]
28Any person who has violated *and* [thus] rejected *and* set at naught the Law of Moses is put to death without pity *or* mercy on the evidence of two or three witnesses. [Deut. 17:2-6.]
29How much worse (sterner and heavier) punishment do you suppose he will be judged to deserve who has spurned *and* [thus] trampled under foot the Son of God, and who has considered the covenant blood by which he was consecrated common *and* unhallowed, thus profaning it *and* insulting *and* outraging the (Holy) Spirit [Who imparts] grace—the unmerited favor and blessing of God? [Exod. 24:8.]
30For we know Him Who said, Vengeance is Mine—retribution and the meting out of full justice rest with Me; I will repay—I will exact the compensation, *says the Lord.* And again, The Lord will judge *and* determine *and* solve *and* settle the cause *and* the cases of His people. [Deut. 32:35, 36.]
31It is a fearful (formidable and terrible) thing to incur the divine penalties *and* be cast into the hands of the living God!
32But be ever mindful of the days gone by in which, after you were first spiritually enlightened, you endured a great *and* painful struggle,
33Sometimes being yourselves a gazingstock, publicly exposed to insults *and* abuse and distress, and sometimes claiming fellowship *and* making common cause with others who were so treated.
34For you did sympathize *and* suffer along with those who were imprisoned, and you bore cheerfully the plundering of your belongings *and* the confiscation of your property, in the knowledge *and* consciousness that you yourselves had a better and lasting possession.
35Do not, therefore, fling away your fearless confidence, for it carries a great *and* glorious compensation of reward.
36For you have need of steadfast patience *and* endurance, so that you may perform *and* fully accomplish the will of God, and thus receive *and* [b]carry away [and enjoy to the full] what is promised.
37For still a little while—a very little while—and the Coming One will come and He will not delay.
38But the just shall live by faith [that is, My righteous servant shall live [c]by his conviction respecting man's relationship to God and divine things, and holy fervor born of faith and conjoined with it]; and if he draws back *and* shrinks in fear, My soul has no delight *or* pleasure in him. [Hab. 2:3, 4.]
39But our way is not that of those who draw back to eternal misery (perdition) and are utterly destroyed, but we are of those who believe—who cleave to and trust in and rely on God through Jesus Christ, the Messiah— *and* by faith preserve the soul.

**11** NOW FAITH is the assurance (the confirmation, [d]the title-deed) of the things [we] hope for, being the proof of things [we] do not see *and* the conviction of their reality—faith perceiving as real fact what is not revealed to the senses.

**AMP** [a] Vincent. [b] Vincent. [c] Thayer's "Greek-English Lexicon of the New Testament." [d] Moulton and Milligan.

## New American Standard

24and let us consider how to stimulate one another to love and
good deeds,
25not forsaking our own assembling together, as is the habit of
some, but encouraging *one another;* and all the more, as you see the
day drawing near.

*Christ or Judgment*

26¶ For if we go on sinning willfully after receiving the knowledge of the truth, there no longer remains a sacrifice for sins,
27but a certain terrifying expectation of judgment, and THE FURY
OF A FIRE WHICH WILL CONSUME THE ADVERSARIES.
28Anyone who has set aside the Law of Moses dies without
mercy on *the testimony of* two or three witnesses.
29How much severer punishment do you think he will deserve
who has trampled under foot the Son of God, and has regarded
as unclean the blood of the covenant by which he was sanctified,
and has insulted the Spirit of grace?
30For we know Him who said, "VENGEANCE IS MINE, I WILL
REPAY." And again, "THE LORD WILL JUDGE HIS PEOPLE."
31It is a terrifying thing to fall into the hands of the living God.
32¶ But remember the former days, when, after being enlightened, you endured a great conflict of sufferings,
33partly, by being made a public spectacle through reproaches
and tribulations, and partly by becoming sharers with those who
were so treated.
34For you showed sympathy to the prisoners, and accepted
joyfully the seizure of your property, knowing that you have for
yourselves a better possession and an abiding one.
35Therefore, do not throw away your confidence, which has a
great reward.
36For you have need of endurance, so that when you have done
the will of God, you may receive what was promised.

37 FOR YET IN A VERY LITTLE WHILE,
HE WHO IS COMING WILL COME, AND WILL NOT DELAY.
38 BUT MY RIGHTEOUS ONE SHALL LIVE BY FAITH;
AND IF HE SHRINKS BACK, MY SOUL HAS NO PLEASURE IN
HIM.

39But we are not of those who shrink back to destruction, but
of those who have faith to the preserving of the soul.

*The Triumphs of Faith*

**11** NOW FAITH is the assurance of *things* hoped for, the
conviction of things not seen.

## New International

us consider how we may spur one another on toward love and
good deeds. 25Let us not give up meeting together, as some are in
the habit of doing, but let us encourage one another—and all the
more as you see the Day approaching.
26If we deliberately keep on sinning after we have received the
knowledge of the truth, no sacrifice for sins is left, 27but only a
fearful expectation of judgment and of raging fire that will consume the enemies of God. 28Anyone who rejected the law of
Moses died without mercy on the testimony of two or three witnesses. 29How much more severely do you think a man deserves
to be punished who has trampled the Son of God under foot, who
has treated as an unholy thing the blood of the covenant that
sanctified him, and who has insulted the Spirit of grace? 30For we
know him who said, "It is mine to avenge; I will repay,"[e] and
again, "The Lord will judge his people."[f] 31It is a dreadful thing
to fall into the hands of the living God.
32Remember those earlier days after you had received the light,
when you stood your ground in a great contest in the face of
suffering. 33Sometimes you were publicly exposed to insult and
persecution; at other times you stood side by side with those who
were so treated. 34You sympathized with those in prison and
joyfully accepted the confiscation of your property, because you
knew that you yourselves had better and lasting possessions.
35So do not throw away your confidence; it will be richly rewarded. 36You need to persevere so that when you have done the
will of God, you will receive what he has promised. 37For in just
a very little while,

"He who is coming will come and will not delay.
38 But my righteous one[g] will live by faith.
And if he shrinks back,
I will not be pleased with him."[h]

39But we are not of those who shrink back and are destroyed, but
of those who believe and are saved.

*By Faith*

**11** NOW FAITH is being sure of what we hope for and certain
of what we do not see. 2This is what the ancients were
commended for.

NIV [e] *30* Deut. 32:35 [f] *30* Deut. 32:36; Psalm 135:14 [g] *38* One early manuscript *But the righteous* [h] *38* Hab. 2:3,4

## King James

2 For by it the elders obtained a good report.

3 Through faith we understand that the worlds were framed by the word of God, so that things which are seen were not made of things which do appear.

4 By faith Abel offered unto God a more excellent sacrifice than Cain, by which he obtained witness that he was righteous, God testifying of his gifts: and by it he being dead yet speaketh.

5 By faith Enoch was translated that he should not see death; and was not found, because God had translated him: for before his translation he had this testimony, that he pleased God.

6 But without faith *it is* impossible to please *him:* for he that cometh to God must believe that he is, and *that* he is a rewarder of them that diligently seek him.

7 By faith Noah, being warned of God of things not seen as yet, moved with fear, prepared an ark to the saving of his house; by the which he condemned the world, and became heir of the righteousness which is by faith.

8 By faith Abraham, when he was called to go out into a place which he should after receive for an inheritance, obeyed; and he went out, not knowing whither he went.

9 By faith he sojourned in the land of promise, as *in* a strange country, dwelling in tabernacles with Isaac and Jacob, the heirs with him of the same promise:

10 For he looked for a city which hath foundations, whose builder and maker *is* God.

11 Through faith also Sarah herself received strength to conceive seed, and was delivered of a child when she was past age, because she judged him faithful who had promised.

12 Therefore sprang there even of one, and him as good as dead, *so many* as the stars of the sky in multitude, and as the sand which is by the sea shore innumerable.

13 These all died in faith, not having received the promises, but having seen them afar off, and were persuaded of *them,* and embraced *them,* and confessed that they were strangers and pilgrims on the earth.

14 For they that say such things declare plainly that they seek a country.

15 And truly, if they had been mindful of that *country* from whence they came out, they might have had opportunity to have returned.

16 But now they desire a better *country,* that is, an heavenly: wherefore God is not ashamed to be called their God: for he hath prepared for them a city.

## Amplified

2 For by [faith], *and* [a]trust *and* holy fervor born of faith, the men of old had divine testimony borne to them *and* obtained a good report.

3 By faith we understand that the worlds [during the successive ages] were framed—fashioned, put in order and equipped for their intended purpose—by the word of God, so that what we see was not made out of things which are visible.

4 [Prompted, actuated] by faith Abel brought God a better and more acceptable sacrifice than Cain, because of which it was testified of him that he was righteous—[that is,] that he was upright and in right standing with God—and God bore witness by accepting *and* acknowledging his gifts. And though he died, yet through [the incident] he is still speaking. [Gen. 4:3-10.]

5 Because of faith Enoch was caught up *and* transferred to heaven, so that he did not have a glimpse of death; and he was not found, because God had translated him. For even before he was taken to heaven he received testimony [still on record] that he had pleased *and* been satisfactory to God. [Gen. 5:21-24.]

6 But without faith it is impossible to please *and* be satisfactory to Him. For whoever would come near to God must (necessarily) believe that God exists and that He is the Rewarder of those who earnestly *and* diligently seek Him (out).

7 [Prompted] by faith Noah, being forewarned of God concerning events of which as yet there was no visible sign, took heed *and* diligently *and* reverently constructed *and* prepared an ark for the deliverance of his own family. By this [his faith which relied on God] he passed judgment *and* sentence on the world's unbelief and became an heir *and* possessor of righteousness, [ [b]that relation of being right into which God puts the person who has faith]. [Gen. 6.13-22.]

8 [Urged on] by faith Abraham when he was called, obeyed and went forth to a place which he was destined to receive as an inheritance; and he went, although he did not know *or* trouble his mind about where he was to go.

9 [Prompted] by faith he dwelt as a temporary resident in the land which was designated in the promise [of God, though he was as a stranger] in a strange country, living in tents with Isaac and Jacob, fellow heirs with him of the same promise. [Gen. 12:1-8.]

10 For he was waiting expectantly *and* confidently, looking forward to the city which has fixed *and* firm foundations, whose Architect *and* Builder is God.

11 Because of faith also Sarah herself received physical power to conceive a child, even when she was long past the age for it, because she considered [God] Who had given her the promise, reliable *and* trustworthy *and* true to His word. [Gen. 17:19; 18:11-14; 21:2.]

12 So from one man, though he was physically as good as dead, there have sprung descendants whose number is as the stars of heaven, and as countless as the innumerable sands on the seashore. [Gen. 15:5, 6; 22:17; 32:12.]

13 These people all died controlled *and* sustained by their faith, but not having received the tangible fulfillment of [God's] promises, only having seen it *and* greeted it from a great distance by faith, and all the while acknowledging *and* confessing that they were strangers *and* temporary residents *and* exiles upon the earth. [Ps. 39:12; Gen. 23:4.]

14 Now those people who talk as they did show plainly that they are in search of a fatherland—their own country.

15 If they had been thinking with [homesick] remembrance of that country from which they were emigrants, they would have found constant opportunity to return to it;

16 But the truth is that they were yearning for *and* aspiring to a better *and* more desirable country, that is, a heavenly [one]. For that reason God is not ashamed to be called their God—even to be surnamed their God [the God of Abraham, Isaac and Jacob]; for He has prepared a city for them. [Exod. 3:6, 15; 4:5.]

**AMP** [a] Thayer. [b] Thayer.

## New American Standard

2For by it the men of old gained approval.
3By faith we understand that the worlds were prepared by the
word of God, so that what is seen was not made out of things
which are visible.
4By faith Abel offered to God a better sacrifice than Cain,
through which he obtained the testimony that he was righteous,
God testifying about his gifts, and through faith, though he is
dead, he still speaks.
5By faith Enoch was taken up so that he should not see death;
AND HE WAS NOT FOUND BECAUSE GOD TOOK HIM UP; for he obtained
the witness that before his being taken up he was pleasing to God.
6And without faith it is impossible to please *Him*, for he who
comes to God must believe that He is, and *that* He is a rewarder
of those who seek Him.
7By faith Noah, being warned *by God* about things not yet seen,
in reverence prepared an ark for the salvation of his household, by
which he condemned the world, and became an heir of the righteousness which is according to faith.
8By faith Abraham, when he was called, obeyed by going out
to a place which he was to receive for an inheritance; and he went
out, not knowing where he was going.
9By faith he lived as an alien in the land of promise, as in a
foreign *land*, dwelling in tents with Isaac and Jacob, fellow heirs
of the same promise;
10for he was looking for the city which has foundations, whose
architect and builder is God.
11By faith even Sarah herself received ability to conceive, even
beyond the proper time of life, since she considered Him faithful
who had promised;
12therefore, also, there was born of one man, and him as good
as dead at that, *as many descendants* AS THE STARS OF HEAVEN IN
NUMBER, AND INNUMERABLE AS THE SAND WHICH IS BY THE SEA-
SHORE.
13¶ All these died in faith, without receiving the promises, but
having seen them and having welcomed them from a distance, and
having confessed that they were strangers and exiles on the earth.
14For those who say such things make it clear that they are
seeking a country of their own.
15And indeed if they had been thinking of that *country* from
which they went out, they would have had opportunity to return.
16But as it is, they desire a better *country*, that is a heavenly one.
Therefore God is not ashamed to be called their God; for He has
prepared a city for them.

## New International

3By faith we understand that the universe was formed at God's
command, so that what is seen was not made out of what was
visible.
4By faith Abel offered God a better sacrifice than Cain did. By
faith he was commended as a righteous man, when God spoke
well of his offerings. And by faith he still speaks, even though he
is dead.
5By faith Enoch was taken from this life, so that he did not
experience death; he could not be found, because God had taken
him away. For before he was taken, he was commended as one
who pleased God. 6And without faith it is impossible to please
God, because anyone who comes to him must believe that he exists
and that he rewards those who earnestly seek him.
7By faith Noah, when warned about things not yet seen, in holy
fear built an ark to save his family. By his faith he condemned the
world and became heir of the righteousness that comes by faith.
8By faith Abraham, when called to go to a place he would later
receive as his inheritance, obeyed and went, even though he did
not know where he was going. 9By faith he made his home in the
promised land like a stranger in a foreign country; he lived in tents,
as did Isaac and Jacob, who were heirs with him of the same
promise. 10For he was looking forward to the city with foundations, whose architect and builder is God.
11By faith Abraham, even though he was past age—and Sarah
herself was barren—was enabled to become a father because he[c]
considered him faithful who had made the promise. 12And so from
this one man, and he as good as dead, came descendants as
numerous as the stars in the sky and as countless as the sand on
the seashore.
13All these people were still living by faith when they died.
They did not receive the things promised; they only saw them and
welcomed them from a distance. And they admitted that they were
aliens and strangers on earth. 14People who say such things show
that they are looking for a country of their own. 15If they had been
thinking of the country they had left, they would have had opportunity to return. 16Instead, they were longing for a better country—a heavenly one. Therefore God is not ashamed to be called
their God, for he has prepared a city for them.

NIV [c] 11 Or *By faith even Sarah, who was past age, was enabled to bear children because she*

## King James

17By faith Abraham, when he was tried, offered up Isaac: and he that had received the promises offered up his only begotten *son*,
18Of whom it was said, That in Isaac shall thy seed be called:
19Accounting that God *was* able to raise *him* up, even from the dead; from whence also he received him in a figure.
20By faith Isaac blessed Jacob and Esau concerning things to come.
21By faith Jacob, when he was a-dying, blessed both the sons of Joseph; and worshipped, *leaning* upon the top of his staff.
22By faith Joseph, when he died, made mention of the departing of the children of Israel; and gave commandment concerning his bones.
23By faith Moses, when he was born, was hid three months of his parents, because they saw *he was* a proper child; and they were not afraid of the king's commandment.
24By faith Moses, when he was come to years, refused to be called the son of Pharaoh's daughter;
25Choosing rather to suffer affliction with the people of God, than to enjoy the pleasures of sin for a season;
26Esteeming the reproach of Christ greater riches than the treasures in Egypt: for he had respect unto the recompence of the reward.
27By faith he forsook Egypt, not fearing the wrath of the king: for he endured, as seeing him who is invisible.
28Through faith he kept the passover, and the sprinkling of blood, lest he that destroyed the firstborn should touch them.
29By faith they passed through the Red sea as by dry *land:* which the Egyptians assaying to do were drowned.
30By faith the walls of Jericho fell down, after they were compassed about seven days.
31By faith the harlot Rahab perished not with them that believed not, when she had received the spies with peace.
32And what shall I more say? for the time would fail me to tell of Gedeon, and *of* Barak, and *of* Samson, and *of* Jephthae; *of* David also, and Samuel, and *of* the prophets:
33Who through faith subdued kingdoms, wrought righteousness, obtained promises, stopped the mouths of lions,
34Quenched the violence of fire, escaped the edge of the sword, out of weakness were made strong, waxed valiant in fight, turned to flight the armies of the aliens.
35Women received their dead raised to life again: and others were tortured, not accepting deliverance; that they might obtain a better resurrection:
36And others had trial of *cruel* mockings and scourgings, yea, moreover of bonds and imprisonment:

## Amplified

17By faith Abraham, when he was put to the test—that is, while the testing of his faith was [a]still in progress—[b]had already brought Isaac for an offering; he who had [c]gladly received *and* welcomed [God's] promises was ready to sacrifice his only son, [Gen. 22:1-10.]
18Of whom it was said, Through Isaac shall your descendants be reckoned. [Gen. 21:12.]
19For he reasoned that God was able to raise [him] up even from among the dead. Indeed in the sense that Isaac was figuratively dead (potentially sacrificed), he did [actually] receive him back from the dead.
20[With eyes of] faith Isaac, looking far into the future, invoked blessings upon Jacob and Esau. [Gen. 27:27-29, 39, 40.]
21[Prompted] by faith Jacob, when he was dying, blessed each of Joseph's sons, and bowed in prayer over the top of his staff. [Gen. 48.]
22[Actuated] by faith Joseph, when nearing the end of his life, referred to [the promise of God for] the departure of the Israelites out of Egypt, and gave instructions concerning the burial of his own bones. [Gen. 50:24, 25; Exod. 13:19.]
23[Prompted] by faith Moses after his birth was kept concealed for three months by his parents, because they saw how comely the child was; and they were not overawed *and* terrified by the king's decree. [Exod. 2:2; 1:22.]
24[Aroused] by faith Moses, when he had grown to maturity *and* [d]become great, refused to be called the son of Pharaoh's daughter, [Exod. 2:10, 15.]
25Because he preferred rather to share the oppression (suffer the hardships) *and* bear the shame of the people of God than to have the fleeting enjoyment of a sinful life.
26He considered the contempt *and* abuse *and* shame [borne for] the Christ, the Messiah [Who was to come], to be greater wealth than all the treasures of Egypt, for he looked forward *and* away to the reward (recompense).
27[Motivated] by faith he left Egypt behind him, being unawed *and* undismayed by the wrath of the king; for he never flinched *but* held staunchly to his purpose *and* endured steadfastly as one who gazed on Him Who is invisible. [Exod. 2:15.]
28By faith (simple trust and confidence in God) he instituted *and* carried out the Passover and the sprinkling of the blood [on the doorposts], so that [the angel], the destroyer of the first-born, might not touch those [of the children of Israel]. [Exod. 12:21-30.]
29[Urged on] by faith the people crossed the Red Sea as though on dry land, but when the Egyptians tried to do the same thing they were swallowed up [by the sea]. [Exod. 14:21-31.]
30Because of faith the walls of Jericho fell down after they had been encompassed for seven days [by the Israelites]. [Josh. 6:12-21.]
31[Prompted] by faith Rahab the prostitute was not destroyed along with those who refused to believe *and* obey, because she had received the spies in peace (without enmity). [Josh. 2:1-21; 6:22-25.]
32And what shall I say further? For time would fail me to tell of Gideon, Barak, Samson, Jephthah, of David and Samuel and the prophets, [Judg. 6:1-8, 35; 4:1-5, 31; 13:1-16, 31; 11:1-12, 15; I Sam. 1-30; II Sam. 1-24; I Kings 1-2; Acts 3:24.]
33Who by [the help of] faith subdued kingdoms, administered justice, obtained promised blessings, closed the mouths of lions, [Dan. 6.]
34Extinguished the power of raging fire, escaped the devourings of the sword, out of frailty *and* weakness won strength *and* became stalwart, even mighty *and* resistless in battle, routing alien hosts. [Dan. 3.]
35[Some] women received again their dead by a resurrection. Others were tortured [e]to death with clubs, refusing to accept release [offered on the terms of denying their faith], that they might be resurrected to a better life. [I Kings 17:17-24; II Kings 4:25-37.]
36Others had to suffer the trial of mocking and scourging, and even chains and imprisonment.

**AMP** [a] Vincent. [b] Vincent. [c] American Standard Version. [d] Literal translation. [e] Vincent.

## New American Standard

17¶ By faith Abraham, when he was tested, offered up Isaac; and he who had received the promises was offering up his only begotten *son;*

18 *it was he* to whom it was said, "IN ISAAC YOUR DESCENDANTS SHALL BE CALLED."

19He considered that God is able to raise *men* even from the dead; from which he also received him back as a type.

20By faith Isaac blessed Jacob and Esau, even regarding things to come.

21By faith Jacob, as he was dying, blessed each of the sons of Joseph, and worshiped, *leaning* on the top of his staff.

22By faith Joseph, when he was dying, made mention of the exodus of the sons of Israel, and gave orders concerning his bones.

23By faith Moses, when he was born, was hidden for three months by his parents, because they saw he was a beautiful child; and they were not afraid of the king's edict.

24By faith Moses, when he had grown up, refused to be called the son of Pharaoh's daughter;

25choosing rather to endure ill-treatment with the people of God, than to enjoy the passing pleasures of sin;

26considering the reproach of Christ greater riches than the treasures of Egypt; for he was looking to the reward.

27By faith he left Egypt, not fearing the wrath of the king; for he endured, as seeing Him who is unseen.

28By faith he kept the Passover and the sprinkling of the blood, so that he who destroyed the first-born might not touch them.

29By faith they passed through the Red Sea as though *they were passing* through dry land; and the Egyptians, when they attempted it, were drowned.

30By faith the walls of Jericho fell down, after they had been encircled for seven days.

31By faith Rahab the harlot did not perish along with those who were disobedient, after she had welcomed the spies in peace.

32¶ And what more shall I say? For time will fail me if I tell of Gideon, Barak, Samson, Jephthah, of David and Samuel and the prophets,

33who by faith conquered kingdoms, performed *acts of* righteousness, obtained promises, shut the mouths of lions,

34quenched the power of fire, escaped the edge of the sword, from weakness were made strong, became mighty in war, put foreign armies to flight.

35Women received *back* their dead by resurrection; and others were tortured, not accepting their release, in order that they might obtain a better resurrection;

36and others experienced mockings and scourgings, yes, also chains and imprisonment.

## New International

17By faith Abraham, when God tested him, offered Isaac as a sacrifice. He who had received the promises was about to sacrifice his one and only son, 18even though God had said to him, "It is through Isaac that your offspring[f] will be reckoned."[g] 19Abraham reasoned that God could raise the dead, and figuratively speaking, he did receive Isaac back from death.

20By faith Isaac blessed Jacob and Esau in regard to their future.

21By faith Jacob, when he was dying, blessed each of Joseph's sons, and worshiped as he leaned on the top of his staff.

22By faith Joseph, when his end was near, spoke about the exodus of the Israelites from Egypt and gave instructions about his bones.

23By faith Moses' parents hid him for three months after he was born, because they saw he was no ordinary child, and they were not afraid of the king's edict.

24By faith Moses, when he had grown up, refused to be known as the son of Pharaoh's daughter. 25He chose to be mistreated along with the people of God rather than to enjoy the pleasures of sin for a short time. 26He regarded disgrace for the sake of Christ as of greater value than the treasures of Egypt, because he was looking ahead to his reward. 27By faith he left Egypt, not fearing the king's anger; he persevered because he saw him who is invisible. 28By faith he kept the Passover and the sprinkling of blood, so that the destroyer of the firstborn would not touch the firstborn of Israel.

29By faith the people passed through the Red Sea[h] as on dry land; but when the Egyptians tried to do so, they were drowned.

30By faith the walls of Jericho fell, after the people had marched around them for seven days.

31By faith the prostitute Rahab, because she welcomed the spies, was not killed with those who were disobedient.[i]

32And what more shall I say? I do not have time to tell about Gideon, Barak, Samson, Jephthah, David, Samuel and the prophets, 33who through faith conquered kingdoms, administered justice, and gained what was promised; who shut the mouths of lions, 34quenched the fury of the flames, and escaped the edge of the sword; whose weakness was turned to strength; and who became powerful in battle and routed foreign armies. 35Women received back their dead, raised to life again. Others were tortured and refused to be released, so that they might gain a better resurrection. 36Some faced jeers and flogging, while still others were chained and put in prison. 37They were stoned[j]; they were sawed

**NIV** [f] 18 Greek *seed* [g] 18 Gen. 21:12 [h] 29 That is, Sea of Reeds [i] 31 Or *unbelieving* [j] 37 Some early manuscripts *stoned; they were put to the test;*

## King James

37They were stoned, they were sawn asunder, were tempted, were slain with the sword: they wandered about in sheepskins and goatskins; being destitute, afflicted, tormented;

38(Of whom the world was not worthy:) they wandered in deserts, and *in* mountains, and *in* dens and caves of the earth.

39And these all, having obtained a good report through faith, received not the promise:

40God having provided some better thing for us, that they without us should not be made perfect.

**12** WHEREFORE SEEING we also are compassed about with so great a cloud of witnesses, let us lay aside every weight, and the sin which doth so easily beset *us,* and let us run with patience the race that is set before us,

2Looking unto Jesus the author and finisher of *our* faith; who for the joy that was set before him endured the cross, despising the shame, and is set down at the right hand of the throne of God.

3For consider him that endured such contradiction of sinners against himself, lest ye be wearied and faint in your minds.

4Ye have not yet resisted unto blood, striving against sin.

5And ye have forgotten the exhortation which speaketh unto you as unto children, My son, despise not thou the chastening of the Lord, nor faint when thou art rebuked of him:

6For whom the Lord loveth he chasteneth, and scourgeth every son whom he receiveth.

7If ye endure chastening, God dealeth with you as with sons; for what son is he whom the father chasteneth not?

8But if ye be without chastisement, whereof all are partakers, then are ye bastards, and not sons.

9Furthermore we have had fathers of our flesh which corrected *us,* and we gave *them* reverence: shall we not much rather be in subjection unto the Father of spirits, and live?

10For they verily for a few days chastened *us* after their own pleasure; but he for *our* profit, that *we* might be partakers of his holiness.

11Now no chastening for the present seemeth to be joyous, but grievous: nevertheless afterward it yieldeth the peaceable fruit of righteousness unto them which are exercised thereby.

## Amplified

37They were stoned to death; they were lured with tempting offers [to renounce their faith]; they were sawn asunder; they were slaughtered by the sword; [while they were alive] they had to go about wrapped in the skins of sheep and goats, utterly destitute, oppressed, cruelly treated,

38[Men] of whom the world was not worthy, roaming over the desolate places and the mountains, and [living] in caves *and* caverns and holes of the earth.

39And all of these, though they won divine approval by [means of] their faith, did not receive the fulfillment of what was promised,

40Because God had us in mind *and* had something better *and* greater in view for us, so that they [these heroes and heroines of faith] should not come to perfection apart from us, [that is, before we could join them].

**12** THEREFORE THEN, since we are surrounded by so great a cloud of witnesses [who have borne testimony of the Truth], let us strip off *and* throw aside every encumbrance—unnecessary weight—and that sin which so readily (deftly and cleverly) clings to *and* entangles us, and let us run with patient endurance *and* steady *and* active persistence the appointed course of the race that is set before us,

2Looking away [from all that will distract] to Jesus, Who is the Leader *and* the Source of *our* faith [giving the first incentive for our belief] and is also its Finisher, [bringing it to maturity and perfection]. He, for the joy [of obtaining the prize] that was set before Him, endured the cross, despising *and* ignoring the shame, and is now seated at the right hand of the throne of God. [Ps. 110:1.]

3Just think of Him Who endured from sinners such grievous opposition *and* bitter hostility against Himself—reckon up and consider it all in comparison with your trials—so that you may not grow weary *or* exhausted, losing heart *and* relaxing *and* fainting in your minds.

4You have not yet struggled *and* fought agonizingly against sin, *nor* have you yet resisted *and* withstood to the point of pouring out your [own] blood.

5And have you [completely] forgotten the divine word of appeal *and* encouragement in which you are reasoned with *and* addressed as sons? My son, do not think lightly *or* scorn to submit to the correction *and* discipline of the Lord, nor lose courage *and* give up *and* faint when you are reproved *or* corrected by Him;

6For the Lord corrects *and* disciplines every one whom He loves, and He punishes, even scourges, every son whom He accepts *and* welcomes to His heart *and* cherishes.

7You must submit to *and* endure [correction] for discipline. God is dealing with you as with sons; for what son is there whom his father does not [thus] train *and* correct *and* discipline?

8Now if you are exempt from correction *and* left without discipline in which all [of God's children] share, then you are illegitimate offspring *and* not true sons [at all]. [Prov. 3:11, 12.]

9Moreover, we have had earthly fathers who disciplined us and we yielded [to them] *and* respected [them for training us]. Shall we not much more cheerfully submit to the Father of spirits and so [truly] live?

10For [our earthly fathers] disciplined us for only a short period of time *and* chastised us as seemed proper *and* good to them, but He disciplines us for our certain good, that we may become sharers in His own holiness.

11For the time being no discipline brings joy but seems grievous *and* painful, but afterwards it yields peaceable fruit of righteousness to those who have been trained by it—a harvest of fruit which consists in righteousness, [that is, in conformity to God's will in purpose, thought and action, resulting in right living and right standing with God].

## New American Standard

37They were stoned, they were sawn in two, [a]they were tempted, they were put to death with the sword; they went about in sheepskins, in goatskins, being destitute, afflicted, ill-treated
38( *men* of whom the world was not worthy), wandering in deserts and mountains and caves and holes in the ground.
39And all these, having gained approval through their faith, did not receive what was promised,
40because God had provided something better for us, so that apart from us they should not be made perfect.

*Jesus, the Example*

**12** THEREFORE, SINCE we have so great a cloud of witnesses surrounding us, let us also lay aside every encumbrance, and the sin which so easily entangles us, and let us run with endurance the race that is set before us,
2fixing our eyes on Jesus, the author and perfecter of faith, who for the joy set before Him endured the cross, despising the shame, and has sat down at the right hand of the throne of God.
3For consider Him who has endured such hostility by sinners against Himself, so that you may not grow weary and lose heart.

*A Father's Discipline*

4You have not yet resisted to the point of shedding blood in your striving against sin;
5and you have forgotten the exhortation which is addressed to you as sons,

"My son, do not regard lightly the discipline of the Lord,
Nor faint when you are reproved by Him;
6 For those whom the Lord loves He disciplines,
And He scourges every son whom He receives."

7It is for discipline that you endure; God deals with you as with sons; for what son is there whom *his* father does not discipline?
8But if you are without discipline, of which all have become partakers, then you are illegitimate children and not sons.
9Furthermore, we had earthly fathers to discipline us, and we respected them; shall we not much rather be subject to the Father of spirits, and live?
10For they disciplined us for a short time as seemed best to them, but He *disciplines us* for *our* good, that we may share His holiness.
11All discipline for the moment seems not to be joyful, but sorrowful; yet to those who have been trained by it, afterwards it yields the peaceful fruit of righteousness.

NAS [a] Some mss. do not contain *they were tempted*

## New International

in two; they were put to death by the sword. They went about in sheepskins and goatskins, destitute, persecuted and mistreated—
38the world was not worthy of them. They wandered in deserts and mountains, and in caves and holes in the ground.
39These were all commended for their faith, yet none of them received what had been promised. 40God had planned something better for us so that only together with us would they be made perfect.

*God Disciplines His Sons*

**12** THEREFORE, SINCE we are surrounded by such a great cloud of witnesses, let us throw off everything that hinders and the sin that so easily entangles, and let us run with perseverance the race marked out for us.
2Let us fix our eyes on Jesus, the author and perfecter of our faith, who for the joy set before him endured the cross, scorning its shame, and sat down at the right hand of the throne of God.
3Consider him who endured such opposition from sinful men, so that you will not grow weary and lose heart.
4In your struggle against sin, you have not yet resisted to the point of shedding your blood.
5And you have forgotten that word of encouragement that addresses you as sons:

"My son, do not make light of the Lord's discipline,
and do not lose heart when he rebukes you,
6because the Lord disciplines those he loves,
and he punishes everyone he accepts as a son."[b]

7Endure hardship as discipline; God is treating you as sons. For what son is not disciplined by his father?
8If you are not disciplined (and everyone undergoes discipline), then you are illegitimate children and not true sons.
9Moreover, we have all had human fathers who disciplined us and we respected them for it. How much more should we submit to the Father of our spirits and live!
10Our fathers disciplined us for a little while as they thought best; but God disciplines us for our good, that we may share in his holiness.
11No discipline seems pleasant at the time, but painful. Later on, however, it produces a harvest of righteousness and peace for those who have been trained by it.

NIV [b] 6 Prov. 3:11,12

## King James

12 Wherefore lift up the hands which hang down, and the feeble knees;

13 And make straight paths for your feet, lest that which is lame be turned out of the way; but let it rather be healed.

14 Follow peace with all *men,* and holiness, without which no man shall see the Lord:

15 Looking diligently lest any man fail of the grace of God; lest any root of bitterness springing up trouble *you,* and thereby many be defiled;

16 Lest there *be* any fornicator, or profane person, as Esau, who for one morsel of meat sold his birthright.

17 For ye know how that afterward, when he would have inherited the blessing, he was rejected: for he found no place of repentance, though he sought it carefully with tears.

18 For ye are not come unto the mount that might be touched, and that burned with fire, nor unto blackness, and darkness, and tempest,

19 And the sound of a trumpet, and the voice of words; which *voice* they that heard entreated that the word should not be spoken to them any more:

20 (For they could not endure that which was commanded, And if so much as a beast touch the mountain, it shall be stoned, or thrust through with a dart:

21 And so terrible was the sight, *that* Moses said, I exceedingly fear and quake:)

22 But ye are come unto mount Sion, and unto the city of the living God, the heavenly Jerusalem, and to an innumerable company of angels,

23 To the general assembly and church of the firstborn, which are written in heaven, and to God the Judge of all, and to the spirits of just men made perfect,

24 And to Jesus the mediator of the new covenant, and to the blood of sprinkling, that speaketh better things than *that of* Abel.

25 See that ye refuse not him that speaketh. For if they escaped not who refused him that spake on earth, much more *shall not* we *escape,* if we turn away from him that *speaketh* from heaven:

26 Whose voice then shook the earth: but now he hath promised, saying, Yet once more I shake not the earth only, but also heaven.

27 And this *word,* Yet once more, signifieth the removing of those things that are shaken, as of things that are made, that those things which cannot be shaken may remain.

28 Wherefore we receiving a kingdom which cannot be moved, let us have grace, whereby we may serve God acceptably with reverence and godly fear:

29 For our God *is* a consuming fire.

## Amplified

12 So then, brace up *and* reinvigorate *and* set right your slackened *and* weakened *and* drooping hands, and strengthen your feeble *and* palsied *and* tottering knees, [Isa. 35:3.]

13 And cut through *and* make firm *and* plain *and* smooth, straight paths for your feet—[yes, make them] safe and upright and happy paths that go in the right direction—so that the lame *and* halting [limbs] may not be put out of joint, but rather may be cured.

14 Strive to live in peace with everybody, and pursue that consecration *and* holiness without which no one will [ever] see the Lord.

15 Exercise foresight *and* be on the watch to look [after one another], to see that no one falls back from *and* fails to secure God's grace (His unmerited favor and spiritual blessing), in order that no root of resentment (rancor, bitterness or hatred) shoot forth and cause trouble *and* bitter torment, and the many become contaminated *and* defiled by it;

16 That no one may become guilty of sexual vice, or become a profane (godless and sacrilegious) person as Esau did, who sold his own birthright for a single meal. [Gen. 25:29-34.]

17 For you understand that later on, when he wanted [to regain title to] his inheritance of the blessing, he was rejected (disqualified and set aside), for he could find no opportunity to repair by repentance [what he had done]—that is, no chance to recall the choice he had made—although he sought for it carefully with [bitter] tears. [Gen. 27:30-40.]

18 For you have not come [as did the Israelites in the wilderness] to a [material] mountain that can be touched, [a mountain] that is ablaze with fire, and to gloom and darkness and a raging storm,

19 And the blast of a trumpet, and a voice whose words make the listeners beg that nothing more be said to them. [Exod. 19:12-22; 20:18-21; Deut. 4:11, 12; 5:22-27.]

20 For they could not bear the command that was given, If even a wild animal touches the mountain, it shall be stoned to death. [Exod. 19:12, 13.]

21 In fact, so awful *and* terrifying was the (phenomenal) sight that Moses said, I am terrified—aghast and trembling with fear. [Deut. 9:19.]

22 But rather, you have approached unto Mount Zion, even to the city of the living God, the heavenly Jerusalem, and to countless multitudes of angels in festal gathering,

23 And to the church (assembly) of the First-born who are registered [as citizens] in heaven, and to the Judge Who is God of all, and to the spirits of the righteous [the redeemed in heaven] who have been made perfect;

24 And to Jesus, the Mediator—Go-between, Agent—of a new covenant, and to the sprinkled blood which speaks [of mercy,] a better *and* nobler *and* more gracious message than the blood of Abel [which cried out for vengeance]. [Gen. 4:10.]

25 So see to it that you do not reject Him *or* refuse to listen to *and* heed Him Who is speaking [to you now]. For if they [the Israelites] did not escape when they refused to listen *and* heed Him Who warned *and* divinely instructed them [here] on earth—revealing with heavenly warnings His will—how much less shall we escape if we reject *and* turn our backs on Him Who cautions *and* admonishes [us] from heaven?

26 Then [at Mount Sinai] His voice shook the earth; but now He has given a promise, Yet once more I will shake *and* make tremble not only the earth but also the (starry) heavens. [Hag. 2:6.]

27 Now this expression, Yet once more, indicates the final removal *and* transformation of all [that can be] shaken, that is, of that which has been created, in order that what cannot be shaken may remain *and* continue. [Ps. 102:26.]

28 Let us therefore, receiving a kingdom that is firm *and* stable *and* cannot be shaken, offer to God pleasing service *and* acceptable worship, with modesty *and* pious care and godly fear *and* awe;

29 For our God [is indeed] a consuming fire. [Deut. 4:24.]

## New American Standard

12Therefore, strengthen the hands that are weak and the knees that are feeble,

13and make straight paths for your feet, so that *the limb* which is lame may not be put out of joint, but rather be healed.

14¶ Pursue peace with all men, and the sanctification without which no one will see the Lord.

15See to it that no one comes short of the grace of God; that no root of bitterness springing up causes trouble, and by it many be defiled;

16that *there be* no immoral or godless person like Esau, who sold his own birthright for a *single* meal.

17For you know that even afterwards, when he desired to inherit the blessing, he was rejected, for he found no place for repentance, though he sought for it with tears.

*Contrast of Sinai and Zion*

18¶ For you have not come to *a mountain* that may be touched and to a blazing fire, and to darkness and gloom and whirlwind,

19and to the blast of a trumpet and the sound of words which *sound was such that* those who heard begged that no further word should be spoken to them.

20For they could not bear the command, "IF EVEN A BEAST TOUCHES THE MOUNTAIN, IT WILL BE STONED."

21And so terrible was the sight, *that* Moses said, "I AM FULL OF FEAR and trembling."

22But you have come to Mount Zion and to the city of the living God, the heavenly Jerusalem, and to myriads of angels,

23to the general assembly and church of the first-born who are enrolled in heaven, and to God, the Judge of all, and to the spirits of righteous men made perfect,

24and to Jesus, the mediator of a new covenant, and to the sprinkled blood, which speaks better than *the blood* of Abel.

*The Unshaken Kingdom*

25See to it that you do not refuse Him who is speaking. For if those did not escape when they refused him who warned *them* on earth, much less *shall* we *escape* who turn away from Him who *warns* from heaven.

26And His voice shook the earth then, but now He has promised, saying, "YET ONCE MORE I WILL SHAKE NOT ONLY THE EARTH, BUT ALSO THE HEAVEN."

27And this *expression*, "Yet once more," denotes the removing of those things which can be shaken, as of created things, in order that those things which cannot be shaken may remain.

28Therefore, since we receive a kingdom which cannot be shaken, let us show gratitude, by which we may offer to God an acceptable service with reverence and awe;

29for our God is a consuming fire.

## New International

12Therefore, strengthen your feeble arms and weak knees.
13"Make level paths for your feet,"[a] so that the lame may not be
disabled, but rather healed.

*Warning Against Refusing God*

14Make every effort to live in peace with all men and to be holy;
without holiness no one will see the Lord. 15See to it that no one
misses the grace of God and that no bitter root grows up to cause
trouble and defile many. 16See that no one is sexually immoral, or
is godless like Esau, who for a single meal sold his inheritance
rights as the oldest son. 17Afterward, as you know, when he
wanted to inherit this blessing, he was rejected. He could bring
about no change of mind, though he sought the blessing with
tears.

18You have not come to a mountain that can be touched and that
is burning with fire; to darkness, gloom and storm; 19to a trumpet
blast or to such a voice speaking words that those who heard it
begged that no further word be spoken to them, 20because they
could not bear what was commanded: "If even an animal touches
the mountain, it must be stoned."[b] 21The sight was so terrifying
that Moses said, "I am trembling with fear."[c]

22But you have come to Mount Zion, to the heavenly Jerusalem,
the city of the living God. You have come to thousands upon
thousands of angels in joyful assembly, 23to the church of the
firstborn, whose names are written in heaven. You have come to
God, the judge of all men, to the spirits of righteous men made
perfect, 24to Jesus the mediator of a new covenant, and to the
sprinkled blood that speaks a better word than the blood of Abel.

25See to it that you do not refuse him who speaks. If they did
not escape when they refused him who warned them on earth,
how much less will we, if we turn away from him who warns us
from heaven? 26At that time his voice shook the earth, but now he
has promised, "Once more I will shake not only the earth but also
the heavens."[d] 27The words "once more" indicate the removing
of what can be shaken—that is, created things—so that what cannot be shaken may remain.

28Therefore, since we are receiving a kingdom that cannot be
shaken, let us be thankful, and so worship God acceptably with
reverence and awe, 29for our "God is a consuming fire."[e]

NIV [a] *13* Prov. 4:26 [b] *20* Exodus 19:12,13 [c] *21* Deut. 9:19 [d] *26* Haggai 2:6 [e] *29* Deut.4:24

## King James

**13** LET BROTHERLY love continue.

2 Be not forgetful to entertain strangers: for thereby some have entertained angels unawares.

3 Remember them that are in bonds, as bound with them; *and* them which suffer adversity, as being yourselves also in the body.

4 Marriage *is* honourable in all, and the bed undefiled: but whoremongers and adulterers God will judge.

5 *Let your* conversation *be* without covetousness; *and be* content with such things as ye have: for he hath said, I will never leave thee, nor forsake thee.

6 So that we may boldly say, The Lord *is* my helper, and I will not fear what man shall do unto me.

7 Remember them which have the rule over you, who have spoken unto you the word of God: whose faith follow, considering the end of *their* conversation.

8 Jesus Christ the same yesterday, and today, and for ever.

9 Be not carried about with divers and strange doctrines. For *it is* a good thing that the heart be established with grace; not with meats, which have not profited them that have been occupied therein.

10 We have an altar, whereof they have no right to eat which serve the tabernacle.

11 For the bodies of those beasts, whose blood is brought into the sanctuary by the high priest for sin, are burned without the camp.

12 Wherefore Jesus also, that he might sanctify the people with his own blood, suffered without the gate.

13 Let us go forth therefore unto him without the camp, bearing his reproach.

14 For here have we no continuing city, but we seek one to come.

15 By him therefore let us offer the sacrifice of praise to God continually, that is, the fruit of *our* lips giving thanks to his name.

16 But to do good and to communicate forget not: for with such sacrifices God is well pleased.

## Amplified

**13** LET LOVE for your fellow believers continue *and* be a fixed practice with you—never let it fail.

2 Do not forget *or* neglect *or* refuse to extend hospitality to strangers [in the brotherhood]—being friendly, cordial and gracious, sharing the comforts of your home and doing your part generously—for through it some have entertained angels without knowing it. [Gen. 18:1-8; 19:1-3.]

3 Remember those who are in prison, as if you were their fellow prisoner; and those who are ill-treated, since you also are liable to bodily sufferings.

4 Let marriage be held in honor—esteemed worthy, precious, [that is,] of great price and especially dear—in all things. And thus let the marriage bed be (kept undishonored,) undefiled; for God will judge *and* punish the unchaste (all guilty of sexual vice) and adulterous.

5 Let your [a]character *or* moral disposition be free from love of money—[including] greed, avarice, lust and craving for earthly possessions—and be satisfied with your present [circumstances and with what you have]; for He (God) [b]Himself has said, I will not in any way fail you *nor* [c]give you up *nor* leave you without support. [I will] not, [d][I will] not, [I will] not in any degree leave you helpless, *nor* forsake *nor* [e]let [you] down, [ [f]relax My hold on you].—[g]Assuredly not! [Josh. 1:5.]

6 So we take comfort *and* are encouraged *and* confidently *and* boldly say, The Lord is my Helper, I will not be seized with alarm—I will not fear or dread or be terrified. What can man do to me? [Ps. 118:6; 27:1.]

7 Remember your leaders *and* superiors in authority, [for it was they] who brought to you the Word of God. Observe attentively *and* consider their manner of living—the outcome of their well-spent lives—and imitate their faith [that is, [h]their conviction that God exists and is the Creator and Ruler of all things, the Provider and Bestower of eternal salvation through Christ; and their [i]leaning of the entire human personality on God in absolute trust and confidence in His power, wisdom and goodness].

8 Jesus Christ, the Messiah, [is always] the same, yesterday, today, [yes,] and forever—to the ages.

9 Do not be carried about by different *and* varied and alien teachings; for it is good for the heart to be established *and* ennobled *and* strengthened by means of grace (God's favor and spiritual blessing) and not [to be devoted to] foods (rules of diet and ritualistic meals) which bring no [spiritual] benefit *or* profit to those who observe them.

10 We have an altar from which those who serve *and* [j]worship in the tabernacle have no right to eat.

11 For when the blood of animals is brought into the sanctuary by the high priest as a sacrifice for sin, the victims' bodies are burned outside the limits of the camp. [Lev. 16:27.]

12 Therefore Jesus also suffered *and* died outside the [city's] gate in order that He might purify *and* consecrate the people through [the shedding of] His own blood, *and* set them apart as holy—for God.

13 Let us then go forth [from all that would prevent us] to Him outside the camp, [at Calvary,] bearing the contempt *and* abuse *and* shame [with] Him. [Lev. 16:27.]

14 For here we have no permanent city, but we are looking for the one which is to come.

15 Through Him therefore let us constantly *and* at all times offer up to God a sacrifice of praise, which is the fruit of lips that thankfully acknowledge *and* confess *and* glorify His name. [Lev. 7:12; Isa. 57:19; Hos. 14:2.]

16 Do not forget *or* neglect to do kindness *and* good, to be generous *and* distribute *and* contribute to the needy [of the church [k]as embodiment and proof of fellowship], for such sacrifices are well-pleasing to God.

**AMP** [a] Vincent. [b] Vincent. [c] Vincent. [d] Wuest. Three negatives precede the verb. [e] Wuest. Three negatives precede the verb. [f] Vincent. [g] Souter. [h] Thayer. [i] Souter. [j] Vincent. [k] Thayer.

## New American Standard

*The Changeless Christ*

**13** LET LOVE of the brethren continue.
2Do not neglect to show hospitality to strangers, for by this
some have entertained angels without knowing it.
3Remember the prisoners, as though in prison with them, and
those who are ill-treated, since you yourselves also are in the body.
4 *Let* marriage *be held* in honor among all, and let the *marriage*
bed *be* undefiled; for fornicators and adulterers God will judge.
5Let your character be free from the love of money, being
content with what you have; for He Himself has said, "I WILL
NEVER DESERT YOU, NOR WILL I EVER FORSAKE YOU,"
6so that we confidently say,

"THE LORD IS MY HELPER, I WILL NOT BE AFRAID.
WHAT SHALL MAN DO TO ME?"

7¶ Remember those who led you, who spoke the word of God
to you; and considering the result of their conduct, imitate their
faith.
8Jesus Christ *is* the same yesterday and today, *yes* and forever.
9Do not be carried away by varied and strange teachings; for
it is good for the heart to be strengthened by grace, not by foods,
through which those who were thus occupied were not benefited.
10We have an altar, from which those who serve the tabernacle
have no right to eat.
11For the bodies of those animals whose blood is brought into
the holy place by the high priest *as an offering* for sin, are burned
outside the camp.
12Therefore Jesus also, that He might sanctify the people
through His own blood, suffered outside the gate.
13Hence, let us go out to Him outside the camp, bearing His
reproach.
14For here we do not have a lasting city, but we are seeking *the*
*city* which is to come.

*God-pleasing Sacrifices*

15Through Him then, let us continually offer up a sacrifice of
praise to God, that is, the fruit of lips that give thanks to His name.
16And do not neglect doing good and sharing; for with such
sacrifices God is pleased.

## New International

*Concluding Exhortations*

**13** KEEP ON loving each other as brothers. 2Do not forget to
entertain strangers, for by so doing some people have
entertained angels without knowing it. 3Remember those in prison
as if you were their fellow prisoners, and those who are mistreated
as if you yourselves were suffering.
4Marriage should be honored by all, and the marriage bed kept
pure, for God will judge the adulterer and all the sexually immoral.
5Keep your lives free from the love of money and be content with
what you have, because God has said,

"Never will I leave you;
never will I forsake you."[l]

6So we say with confidence,

"The Lord is my helper; I will not be afraid.
What can man do to me?"[m]

7Remember your leaders, who spoke the word of God to you.
Consider the outcome of their way of life and imitate their faith.
8Jesus Christ is the same yesterday and today and forever.
9Do not be carried away by all kinds of strange teachings. It is
good for our hearts to be strengthened by grace, not by ceremonial
foods, which are of no value to those who eat them. 10We have an
altar from which those who minister at the tabernacle have no right
to eat.
11The high priest carries the blood of animals into the Most Holy
Place as a sin offering, but the bodies are burned outside the camp.
12And so Jesus also suffered outside the city gate to make the
people holy through his own blood. 13Let us, then, go to him
outside the camp, bearing the disgrace he bore. 14For here we do
not have an enduring city, but we are looking for the city that is
to come.
15Through Jesus, therefore, let us continually offer to God a
sacrifice of praise—the fruit of lips that confess his name. 16And
do not forget to do good and to share with others, for with such
sacrifices God is pleased.

NIV [l] 5 Deut. 31:6 [m] 6 Psalm 118:6,7

## King James

17 Obey them that have the rule over you, and submit yourselves: for they watch for your souls, as they that must give account, that they may do it with joy, and not with grief: for that *is*
unprofitable for you.
18 Pray for us: for we trust we have a good conscience, in all
things willing to live honestly.
19 But I beseech *you* the rather to do this, that I may be restored
to you the sooner.
20 Now the God of peace, that brought again from the dead our
Lord Jesus, that great shepherd of the sheep, through the blood
of the everlasting covenant,
21 Make you perfect in every good work to do his will, working
in you that which is wellpleasing in his sight, through Jesus Christ;
to whom *be* glory for ever and ever. Amen.
22 And I beseech you, brethren, suffer the word of exhortation:
for I have written a letter unto you in few words.
23 Know ye that *our* brother Timothy is set at liberty; with whom,
if he come shortly, I will see you.
24 Salute all them that have the rule over you, and all the saints.
They of Italy salute you.
25 Grace *be* with you all. Amen.

## Amplified

17 Obey your spiritual leaders and submit to them—continually
recognizing their authority over you; for they are constantly keeping watch over your souls *and* guarding your spiritual welfare, as
men who will have to render an account [of their trust]. [Do your
part to] let them do this with gladness, and not with sighing *and*
groaning, for that would not be profitable to you [either].
18 Keep praying for us, for we are convinced that we have a good
(clear) conscience, that we want to walk uprightly *and* to live a
noble life, acting honorably *and* in complete honesty in all things.
19 And I beg of you [to pray for us] the more earnestly in order
that I may be restored to you the sooner.
20 Now may the God of peace—[Who is] the Author and the
Giver of peace—and Who brought again from among the dead our
Lord Jesus, that great Shepherd of the sheep, by the blood [that
sealed, ratified] the everlasting agreement [covenant, testament],
[Isa. 63:11; Zech. 9:11; Isa. 55:3; Ezek. 37:26.]
21 Strengthen (complete, perfect) *and* make you what you ought
to be, *and* equip you with everything good that you may carry out
His will; [while He Himself] works in you *and* accomplishes that
which is pleasing in His sight, through Jesus Christ, the Messiah;
to Whom be the glory forever and ever—to the ages of the ages.
Amen—so be it.
22 I call on you, brethren, to listen patiently *and* bear with this
message of exhortation *and* admonition *and* encouragement, for I
have written to you briefly.
23 Notice that our brother Timothy has been released [from pris-
on]. If he comes here soon, I will see you along with him.
24 Give our greetings to all of your spiritual leaders and to all of
(God's consecrated believers, your fellow) saints. The Italian
Christians send you their greetings [also].
25 Grace (God's favor and spiritual blessing) be with you all.
Amen— *so be it.*

## New American Standard

17Obey your leaders, and submit *to them;* for they keep watch over your souls, as those who will give an account. Let them do this with joy and not with grief, for this would be unprofitable for you.

18¶ Pray for us, for we are sure that we have a good conscience, desiring to conduct ourselves honorably in all things.

19And I urge *you* all the more to do this, that I may be restored to you the sooner.

*Benediction*

20¶ Now the God of peace, who brought up from the dead the great Shepherd of the sheep through the blood of the eternal covenant, *even* Jesus our Lord,

21equip you in every good thing to do His will, working in us that which is pleasing in His sight, through Jesus Christ, to whom *be* the glory forever and ever. Amen.

22¶ But I urge you, brethren, bear with this word of exhortation, for I have written to you briefly.

23Take notice that our brother Timothy has been released, with whom, if he comes soon, I shall see you.

24Greet all of your leaders and all the saints. Those from Italy greet you.

25¶ Grace be with you all.

## New International

17Obey your leaders and submit to their authority. They keep watch over you as men who must give an account. Obey them so that their work will be a joy, not a burden, for that would be of no advantage to you.

18Pray for us. We are sure that we have a clear conscience and desire to live honorably in every way. 19I particularly urge you to pray so that I may be restored to you soon.

20May the God of peace, who through the blood of the eternal covenant brought back from the dead our Lord Jesus, that great Shepherd of the sheep, 21equip you with everything good for doing his will, and may he work in us what is pleasing to him, through Jesus Christ, to whom be glory for ever and ever. Amen.

22Brothers, I urge you to bear with my word of exhortation, for I have written you only a short letter.

23I want you to know that our brother Timothy has been released. If he arrives soon, I will come with him to see you.

24Greet all your leaders and all God's people. Those from Italy send you their greetings.

25Grace be with you all.

## King James

THE GENERAL EPISTLE OF

# James

**1** JAMES, A servant of God and of the Lord Jesus Christ, to the twelve tribes which are scattered abroad, greeting.

2My brethren, count it all joy when ye fall into divers temptations;

3Knowing *this,* that the trying of your faith worketh patience.

4But let patience have *her* perfect work, that ye may be perfect and entire, wanting nothing.

5If any of you lack wisdom, let him ask of God, that giveth to all *men* liberally, and upbraideth not; and it shall be given him.

6But let him ask in faith, nothing wavering. For he that wavereth is like a wave of the sea driven with the wind and tossed.

7For let not that man think that he shall receive any thing of the Lord.

8A double minded man *is* unstable in all his ways.

9Let the brother of low degree rejoice in that he is exalted:

10But the rich, in that he is made low: because as the flower of the grass he shall pass away.

11For the sun is no sooner risen with a burning heat, but it withereth the grass, and the flower thereof falleth, and the grace of the fashion of it perisheth: so also shall the rich man fade away in his ways.

12Blessed *is* the man that endureth temptation: for when he is tried, he shall receive the crown of life, which the Lord hath promised to them that love him.

13Let no man say when he is tempted, I am tempted of God: for God cannot be tempted with evil, neither tempteth he any man:

14But every man is tempted, when he is drawn away of his own lust, and enticed.

15Then when lust hath conceived, it bringeth forth sin: and sin, when it is finished, bringeth forth death.

16Do not err, my beloved brethren.

17Every good gift and every perfect gift is from above, and cometh down from the Father of lights, with whom is no variableness, neither shadow of turning.

18Of his own will begat he us with the word of truth, that we should be a kind of firstfruits of his creatures.

## Amplified

THE LETTER OF

# James

**1** JAMES, A servant of God and of the Lord Jesus Christ, to the twelve tribes scattered abroad (among the Gentiles, in the dispersion): Greeting—[a] rejoice!

2Consider it wholly joyful, my brethren, whenever you are enveloped in *or* encounter trials of any sort, *or* fall into various temptations.

3Be assured *and* understand that the trial *and* proving of your faith bring out endurance *and* steadfastness *and* patience.

4But let endurance *and* steadfastness *and* patience have full play *and* do a thorough work, so that you may be [people] perfectly and fully developed (with no defects), lacking in nothing.

5If any of you is deficient in wisdom, let him ask of [b]the giving God [Who gives] to every one liberally *and* ungrudgingly, without reproaching *or* faultfinding, and it will be given him.

6Only it must be in faith that he asks, with no wavering—no hesitating, no doubting. For the one who wavers (hesitates, doubts) is like the billowing surge out at sea, that is blown hither *and* thither and tossed by the wind.

7For truly, let not such a person imagine that he will receive anything [he asks for] from the Lord,

8[For being as he is] a man of two minds—hesitating, dubious, irresolute—[he is] unstable *and* unreliable *and* uncertain about everything (he thinks, feels, decides).

9Let the brother in humble circumstances glory in his elevation [as a Christian, called to the true riches and to be an heir of God];

10And the rich [person ought to glory] in being humbled [by being shown his human frailty], because like the flower of the grass he will pass away.

11For the sun comes up with a scorching heat and parches the grass; its flower falls off and its beauty fades away. Even so will the rich man wither *and* die in the midst of his pursuits. [Isa. 40:6, 7.]

12Blessed, happy, [c]to be envied is the man who is patient under trial *and* stands up under temptation, for when he has stood the test *and* been approved he will receive [the victor's] crown of life which God has promised to those who love Him.

13Let no one say when he is tempted, I am tempted from God; for God is incapable of being tempted by [what is] evil and He Himself tempts no one.

14But every person is tempted when he is drawn away, enticed *and* baited by his own evil desire (lust, passions).

15Then the evil desire when it has conceived gives birth to sin, and sin when it is fully matured brings forth death.

16Do not be misled, my beloved brethren.

17Every good gift and every perfect ([d]free, large, full) gift is from above; it comes down from the Father of all [that gives] light, in [the shining of] Whom there can be no variation [rising or setting] or shadow cast by His turning [as in an eclipse].

18And it was of His own [free] will that He gave us birth (as sons) by [His] Word of Truth, so that we should be a kind of first fruits of His creatures—[a sample] of what He created to be consecrated to Himself.

**AMP** [a] Literal meaning. [b] Literal meaning. [c] Souter. [d] Vincent.

## New American Standard

# James

*Testing Your Faith*

1 JAMES, A bond-servant of God and of the Lord Jesus Christ,
to the twelve tribes who are dispersed abroad, greetings.
2¶ Consider it all joy, my brethren, when you encounter various trials,
3knowing that the testing of your faith produces endurance.
4And let endurance have *its* perfect result, that you may be
perfect and complete, lacking in nothing.
5¶ But if any of you lacks wisdom, let him ask of God, who
gives to all men generously and without reproach, and it will be
given to him.
6But let him ask in faith without any doubting, for the one who
doubts is like the surf of the sea driven and tossed by the wind.
7For let not that man expect that he will receive anything from
the Lord,
8 *being* a double-minded man, unstable in all his ways.
9¶ But let the brother of humble circumstances glory in his high
position;
10and *let* the rich man *glory* in his humiliation, because like
flowering grass he will pass away.
11For the sun rises with a scorching wind, and withers the grass;
and its flower falls off, and the beauty of its appearance is destroyed; so too the rich man in the midst of his pursuits will fade
away.
12¶ Blessed is a man who perseveres under trial; for once he has
been approved, he will receive the crown of life, which *the Lord* has
promised to those who love Him.
13Let no one say when he is tempted, "I am being tempted by
God"; for God cannot be tempted by evil, and He Himself does not
tempt anyone.
14But each one is tempted when he is carried away and enticed
by his own lust.
15Then when lust has conceived, it gives birth to sin; and when
sin is accomplished, it brings forth death.
16Do not be deceived, my beloved brethren.
17Every good thing bestowed and every perfect gift is from
above, coming down from the Father of lights, with whom there
is no variation, or shifting shadow.
18In the exercise of His will He brought us forth by the word of
truth, so that we might be, as it were, the first fruits among His
creatures.

## New International

# James

1 JAMES, A servant of God and of the Lord Jesus Christ,

To the twelve tribes scattered among the nations:

Greetings.

*Trials and Temptations*

2Consider it pure joy, my brothers, whenever you face trials of
many kinds, 3because you know that the testing of your faith
develops perseverance. 4Perseverance must finish its work so that
you may be mature and complete, not lacking anything. 5If any of
you lacks wisdom, he should ask God, who gives generously to
all without finding fault, and it will be given to him. 6But when he
asks, he must believe and not doubt, because he who doubts is like
a wave of the sea, blown and tossed by the wind. 7That man
should not think he will receive anything from the Lord; 8he is a
double-minded man, unstable in all he does.
9The brother in humble circumstances ought to take pride in his
high position. 10But the one who is rich should take pride in his
low position, because he will pass away like a wild flower. 11For
the sun rises with scorching heat and withers the plant; its blossom
falls and its beauty is destroyed. In the same way, the rich man will
fade away even while he goes about his business.
12Blessed is the man who perseveres under trial, because when
he has stood the test, he will receive the crown of life that God has
promised to those who love him.
13When tempted, no one should say, "God is tempting me."
For God cannot be tempted by evil, nor does he tempt anyone;
14but each one is tempted when, by his own evil desire, he is
dragged away and enticed. 15Then, after desire has conceived, it
gives birth to sin; and sin, when it is full-grown, gives birth to
death.
16Don't be deceived, my dear brothers. 17Every good and perfect gift is from above, coming down from the Father of the heavenly lights, who does not change like shifting shadows. 18He chose
to give us birth through the word of truth, that we might be a kind
of firstfruits of all he created.

# King James

19Wherefore, my beloved brethren, let every man be swift to hear, slow to speak, slow to wrath:

20For the wrath of man worketh not the righteousness of God.

21Wherefore lay apart all filthiness and superfluity of naughtiness, and receive with meekness the engrafted word, which is able to save your souls.

22But be ye doers of the word, and not hearers only, deceiving your own selves.

23For if any be a hearer of the word, and not a doer, he is like unto a man beholding his natural face in a glass:

24For he beholdeth himself, and goeth his way, and straightway forgetteth what manner of man he was.

25But whoso looketh into the perfect law of liberty, and continueth *therein*, he being not a forgetful hearer, but a doer of the work, this man shall be blessed in his deed.

26If any man among you seem to be religious, and bridleth not his tongue, but deceiveth his own heart, this man's religion *is* vain.

27Pure religion and undefiled before God and the Father is this, To visit the fatherless and widows in their affliction, *and* to keep himself unspotted from the world.

**2** MY BRETHREN, have not the faith of our Lord Jesus Christ, *the Lord* of glory, with respect of persons.

2For if there come unto your assembly a man with a gold ring, in goodly apparel, and there come in also a poor man in vile raiment;

3And ye have respect to him that weareth the gay clothing, and say unto him, Sit thou here in a good place; and say to the poor, Stand thou there, or sit here under my footstool:

4Are ye not then partial in yourselves, and are become judges of evil thoughts?

5Hearken, my beloved brethren, Hath not God chosen the poor of this world rich in faith, and heirs of the kingdom which he hath promised to them that love him?

6But ye have despised the poor. Do not rich men oppress you, and draw you before the judgment seats?

7Do not they blaspheme that worthy name by the which ye are called?

8If ye fulfil the royal law according to the scripture, Thou shalt love thy neighbour as thyself, ye do well:

9But if ye have respect to persons, ye commit sin, and are convinced of the law as transgressors.

10For whosoever shall keep the whole law, and yet offend in one *point*, he is guilty of all.

# Amplified

19Understand [this], my beloved brethren. Let every man be quick to hear, (a ready listener,) slow to speak, slow to take offense *and* to get angry.

20For man's anger does not promote the righteousness God [wishes and requires].

21So get rid of all uncleanness and the rampant outgrowth of wickedness, and in a humble (gentle, modest) spirit receive *and* welcome the Word which implanted *and* rooted [in your hearts] contains the power to save your souls.

22But—obey the message; be doers of the Word, and not merely listeners to it, betraying yourselves [into deception by reasoning contrary to the Truth].

23For if any one only listens to the Word without obeying it *and* being a doer of it, he is like a man who looks carefully at his [own] natural face in a mirror;

24For he thoughtfully observes himself, then goes off and promptly forgets what he was like.

25But he who looks carefully into the faultless law, the [law] of liberty, and is faithful to it *and* perseveres in looking into it, being not a heedless listener who forgets, but an active doer [who obeys], he shall be blessed in his doing—in his life of obedience.

26If any one thinks himself to be religious—piously observant of the external duties of his faith—and does not bridle his tongue, but deludes his own heart, this person's religious service is worthless (futile, barren).

27External ªreligious worship (ᵇreligion as it is expressed in outward acts) that is pure and unblemished in the sight of God the Father is this: to visit *and* help *and* care for the orphans and widows in their affliction *and* need, and to keep oneself unspotted *and* uncontaminated from the world.

**2** MY BRETHREN, pay no servile regard to people—show no prejudice, no partiality. Do not [attempt to] hold *and* practice the faith of our Lord Jesus Christ [the Lord] of glory together with—snobbery!

2For if a person comes into your congregation whose hands are adorned with gold rings and who is wearing splendid apparel, and also a poor [man] in shabby clothes comes in,

3And you pay special attention to the one who wears the splendid clothes and say to him, Sit here in this preferable seat! while you tell the poor [man], Stand there! or, Sit there on the floor at my feet!

4Are you not discriminating among your own, and becoming critics *and* judges with wrong motives?

5Listen, my beloved brethren. Has not God chosen those who are poor in the eyes of the world to be rich in faith *and* in their position as believers, and to inherit the kingdom which He has promised to those who love Him?

6But you [in contrast] have insulted—humiliated, dishonored and shown your contempt for—the poor. Is it not the rich who domineer over you? Is it not they who drag you into the law courts?

7Is it not they who slander *and* blaspheme that precious name by which you are distinguished *and* called [the name of Christ invoked in baptism]?

8If indeed you [really] fulfill the royal Law, in accordance with the Scripture, You shall love your neighbor as [you love] yourself, you do well. [Lev. 19:18.]

9But if you show servile regard (prejudice, favoritism) for people, you commit sin and are rebuked *and* convicted by the Law as violators *and* offenders.

10For whosoever keeps the Law [as a] whole, but stumbles *and* offends in one [single instance] has become guilty of [breaking] all of it.

---

**AMP** ª "Religion in its rise interests us about *ourselves*; in its progress, about our *fellow-creatures*; in its highest stage, about the honor of *God*." (—Jamieson, Fausset and Brown). ᵇ Abbott-Smith; Moulton and Milligan; Vincent, etc.

## New American Standard

19¶ [c] *This* you know, my beloved brethren. But let everyone be quick to hear, slow to speak *and* slow to anger;
20for the anger of man does not achieve the righteousness of God.
21Therefore putting aside all filthiness and *all* that remains of wickedness, in humility receive the word implanted, which is able to save your souls.
22But prove yourselves doers of the word, and not merely hearers who delude themselves.
23For if anyone is a hearer of the word and not a doer, he is like a man who looks at his natural face in a mirror;
24for *once* he has looked at himself and gone away, he has immediately forgotten what kind of person he was.
25But one who looks intently at the perfect law, the *law* of liberty, and abides by it, not having become a forgetful hearer but an effectual doer, this man shall be blessed in what he does.
26If anyone thinks himself to be religious, and yet does not bridle his tongue but deceives his *own* heart, this man's religion is worthless.
27This is pure and undefiled religion in the sight of *our* God and Father, to visit orphans and widows in their distress, *and* to keep oneself unstained by the world.

*The Sin of Partiality*

2 MY BRETHREN, do not hold your faith in our glorious Lord Jesus Christ with *an attitude of* personal favoritism.
2For if a man comes into your assembly with a gold ring and dressed in fine clothes, and there also comes in a poor man in dirty clothes,
3and you pay special attention to the one who is wearing the fine clothes, and say, "You sit here in a good place," and you say to the poor man, "You stand over there, or sit down by my footstool,"
4have you not made distinctions among yourselves, and become judges with evil motives?
5Listen, my beloved brethren: did not God choose the poor of this world *to be* rich in faith and heirs of the kingdom which He promised to those who love Him?
6But you have dishonored the poor man. Is it not the rich who oppress you and personally drag you into court?
7Do they not blaspheme the fair name by which you have been called?
8If, however, you are fulfilling the royal law, according to the Scripture, "YOU SHALL LOVE YOUR NEIGHBOR AS YOURSELF," you are doing well.
9But if you show partiality, you are committing sin *and* are convicted by the law as transgressors.
10For whoever keeps the whole law and yet stumbles in one *point*, he has become guilty of all.

NAS [c] Or, *Know* this

## New International

*Listening and Doing*

19My dear brothers, take note of this: Everyone should be quick
to listen, slow to speak and slow to become angry, 20for man's
anger does not bring about the righteous life that God desires.
21Therefore, get rid of all moral filth and the evil that is so prevalent
and humbly accept the word planted in you, which can save you.
22Do not merely listen to the word, and so deceive yourselves.
Do what it says. 23Anyone who listens to the word but does not
do what it says is like a man who looks at his face in a mirror 24and,
after looking at himself, goes away and immediately forgets what
he looks like. 25But the man who looks intently into the perfect law
that gives freedom, and continues to do this, not forgetting what
he has heard, but doing it—he will be blessed in what he does.
26If anyone considers himself religious and yet does not keep
a tight rein on his tongue, he deceives himself and his religion is
worthless. 27Religion that God our Father accepts as pure and
faultless is this: to look after orphans and widows in their distress
and to keep oneself from being polluted by the world.

*Favoritism Forbidden*

2 MY BROTHERS, as believers in our glorious Lord Jesus
Christ, don't show favoritism. 2Suppose a man comes into
your meeting wearing a gold ring and fine clothes, and a poor man
in shabby clothes also comes in. 3If you show special attention to
the man wearing fine clothes and say, "Here's a good seat for
you," but say to the poor man, "You stand there" or "Sit on the
floor by my feet," 4have you not discriminated among yourselves
and become judges with evil thoughts?
5Listen, my dear brothers: Has not God chosen those who are
poor in the eyes of the world to be rich in faith and to inherit the
kingdom he promised those who love him? 6But you have insulted
the poor. Is it not the rich who are exploiting you? Are they not
the ones who are dragging you into court? 7Are they not the ones
who are slandering the noble name of him to whom you belong?
8If you really keep the royal law found in Scripture, "Love your
neighbor as yourself,"[d] you are doing right. 9But if you show
favoritism, you sin and are convicted by the law as lawbreakers.
10For whoever keeps the whole law and yet stumbles at just one
point is guilty of breaking all of it. 11For he who said, "Do not

NIV [d] *8* Lev. 19:18

## King James

11For he that said, Do not commit adultery, said also, Do not kill. Now if thou commit no adultery, yet if thou kill, thou art become a transgressor of the law.

12So speak ye, and so do, as they that shall be judged by the law of liberty.

13For he shall have judgment without mercy, that hath shown no mercy; and mercy rejoiceth against judgment.

14What *doth it* profit, my brethren, though a man say he hath faith, and have not works? can faith save him?

15If a brother or sister be naked, and destitute of daily food,

16And one of you say unto them, Depart in peace, be *ye* warmed and filled; notwithstanding ye give them not those things which are needful to the body; what *doth it* profit?

17Even so faith, if it hath not works, is dead, being alone.

18Yea, a man may say, Thou hast faith, and I have works: show me thy faith without thy works, and I will show thee my faith by my works.

19Thou believest that there is one God; thou doest well: the devils also believe, and tremble.

20But wilt thou know, O vain man, that faith without works is dead?

21Was not Abraham our father justified by works, when he had offered Isaac his son upon the altar?

22Seest thou how faith wrought with his works, and by works was faith made perfect?

23And the scripture was fulfilled which saith, Abraham believed God, and it was imputed unto him for righteousness: and he was called the Friend of God.

24Ye see then how that by works a man is justified, and not by faith only.

25Likewise also was not Rahab the harlot justified by works, when she had received the messengers, and had sent *them* out another way?

26For as the body without the spirit is dead, so faith without works is dead also.

**3** MY BRETHREN, be not many masters, knowing that we shall receive the greater condemnation.

2For in many things we offend all. If any man offend not in word, the same *is* a perfect man, *and* able also to bridle the whole body.

3Behold, we put bits in the horses' mouths, that they may obey us; and we turn about their whole body.

4Behold also the ships, which though *they be* so great, and *are* driven of fierce winds, yet are they turned about with a very small helm, whithersoever the governor listeth.

## Amplified

11For He Who said, You shall not commit adultery, also said, You shall not kill. If you do not commit adultery but do kill, you have become guilty of transgressing the [whole] Law. [Exod. 20:13, 14; Deut. 5:17, 18.]

12So speak and so act as [people should] who are to be judged under the law of liberty [the moral instruction given by Christ, especially about love].

13For to him who has shown no mercy the judgment [will be] merciless; but mercy [full of glad confidence] exults victoriously over judgment.

14What is the use (profit), my brethren, for any one to profess to have faith if he has no [good] works [to show for it]? Can [such] faith save [his soul]?

15If a brother or sister is poorly clad and lacks food for each day,

16And one of you says to him, Goodbye! Keep [yourself] warm and well fed, without giving him the necessities for the body, what good does that do?

17So also faith if it does not have works (deeds and actions of obedience to back it up), by itself is destitute of power—inoperative, dead.

18But some one will say [to you then], You [say you] have faith and I have [good] works. Now you show me your [alleged] faith apart from any [good] works [if you can], and I by [good] works [of obedience] will show you my faith.

19You believe that God is one; you do well. So do the demons believe, and shudder [in terror and horror such as [a]make a man's hair stand on end and contract the surface of his skin]!

20Are you willing to be shown [proof], you foolish, unproductive, spiritually-deficient fellow, that faith apart from [good] works is inactive *and* ineffective *and* worthless?

21Was not our forefather Abraham [shown to be] justified—made acceptable to God—by [his] works when he brought to the altar as an offering his [own] son Isaac? [Gen. 22:1-14.]

22You see that [his] faith was co-operating with his works, and [his] faith was completed *and* reached its supreme expression [when he implemented it] by [good] works.

23And [so] the Scripture was fulfilled that says, Abraham believed—adhered to, trusted in and relied on—God, and this was accounted to him as righteousness [as conformity to God's will in thought and deed], and he was called God's friend. [Gen. 15:6; Isa. 41:8; II Chron. 20:7.]

24You see that a man is justified (pronounced righteous before God) through what he does and not alone through faith—through works of obedience as well as by what he believes.

25So also with Rahab the harlot. Was she not shown to be justified (pronounced righteous before God) by [good] deeds when she took in the scouts (spies) and got them away by a different route? [Josh. 2:1-21.]

26For as the human body apart from the spirit is lifeless, so faith apart from [its] works of obedience is also dead.

**3** NOT MANY [of you] should become teachers [[b]self-constituted censors and reprovers of others], my brethren, for you know that we [teachers] will be judged by a higher standard *and* with greater severity [than other people].—Thus we assume the greater accountability and the more condemnation.

2For we all often stumble *and* fall *and* offend in many things. And if any one does not offend in speech—never says the wrong things—he is a fully developed character *and* a perfect man, able to control his whole body *and* to curb his entire nature.

3If we set bits in the horses' mouths to make them obey us, we can turn their whole bodies about.

4Likewise look at the ships, though they are so great and are driven by rough winds, they are steered by a very small rudder wherever the impulse of the helmsman determines.

**AMP** [a] Vincent's "Word Studies in the New Testament." [b] John Calvin, quoted by Jamieson, Fausset and Brown in "A Commentary on the Old and New Testaments."

## New American Standard

11 For He who said, "Do NOT COMMIT ADULTERY," also said, "Do
NOT COMMIT MURDER." Now if you do not commit adultery, but do
commit murder, you have become a transgressor of the law.
12 So speak and so act, as those who are to be judged by *the* law
of liberty.
13 For judgment *will be* merciless to one who has shown no
mercy; mercy triumphs over judgment.

*Faith and Works*

14 ¶ What use is it, my brethren, if a man says he has faith, but
he has no works? Can that faith save him?
15 If a brother or sister is without clothing and in need of daily
food,
16 and one of you says to them, "Go in peace, be warmed and
be filled," and yet you do not give them what is necessary for *their*
body, what use is that?
17 Even so faith, if it has no works, is dead, *being* by itself.
18 But someone may *well* say, "You have faith, and I have works;
show me your faith without the works, and I will show you my
faith by my works."
19 You believe that [c]God is one. You do well; the demons also
believe, and shudder.
20 But are you willing to recognize, you foolish fellow, that faith
without works is useless?
21 Was not Abraham our father justified by works, when he
offered up Isaac his son on the altar?
22 You see that faith was working with his works, and as a result
of the works, faith was perfected;
23 and the Scripture was fulfilled which says, "AND ABRAHAM
BELIEVED GOD, AND IT WAS RECKONED TO HIM AS RIGHTEOUSNESS,"
and he was called the friend of God.
24 You see that a man is justified by works, and not by faith
alone.
25 And in the same way was not Rahab the harlot also justified
by works, when she received the messengers and sent them out
by another way?
26 For just as the body without *the* spirit is dead, so also faith
without works is dead.

*The Tongue Is a Fire*

3 LET NOT many *of you* become teachers, my brethren, knowing that as such we shall incur a stricter judgment.
2 For we all stumble in many *ways.* If anyone does not stumble
in what he says, he is a perfect man, able to bridle the whole body
as well.
3 Now if we put the bits into the horses' mouths so that they
may obey us, we direct their entire body as well.
4 Behold, the ships also, though they are so great and are
driven by strong winds, are still directed by a very small rudder,
wherever the inclination of the pilot desires.

NAS [c] Or, *there is one God*

## New International

commit adultery,"[d] also said, "Do not murder."[e] If you do not
commit adultery but do commit murder, you have become a lawbreaker.
12 Speak and act as those who are going to be judged by the law
that gives freedom, 13 because judgment without mercy will be
shown to anyone who has not been merciful. Mercy triumphs over
judgment!

*Faith and Deeds*

14 What good is it, my brothers, if a man claims to have faith but
has no deeds? Can such faith save him? 15 Suppose a brother or
sister is without clothes and daily food. 16 If one of you says to him,
"Go, I wish you well; keep warm and well fed," but does nothing
about his physical needs, what good is it? 17 In the same way, faith
by itself, if it is not accompanied by action, is dead.
18 But someone will say, "You have faith; I have deeds."
Show me your faith without deeds, and I will show you my
faith by what I do. 19 You believe that there is one God. Good! Even
the demons believe that—and shudder.
20 You foolish man, do you want evidence that faith without
deeds is useless[f]? 21 Was not our ancestor Abraham considered
righteous for what he did when he offered his son Isaac on the
altar? 22 You see that his faith and his actions were working together, and his faith was made complete by what he did. 23 And
the scripture was fulfilled that says, "Abraham believed God, and
it was credited to him as righteousness,"[g] and he was called God's
friend. 24 You see that a person is justified by what he does and not
by faith alone.
25 In the same way, was not even Rahab the prostitute considered righteous for what she did when she gave lodging to the
spies and sent them off in a different direction? 26 As the body
without the spirit is dead, so faith without deeds is dead.

*Taming the Tongue*

3 NOT MANY of you should presume to be teachers, my brothers, because you know that we who teach will be judged more
strictly. 2 We all stumble in many ways. If anyone is never at fault
in what he says, he is a perfect man, able to keep his whole body
in check.
3 When we put bits into the mouths of horses to make them obey
us, we can turn the whole animal. 4 Or take ships as an example.
Although they are so large and are driven by strong winds, they
are steered by a very small rudder wherever the pilot wants to go.

NIV [d] *11* Exodus 20:14; Deut. 5:18 [e] *11* Exodus 20:13; Deut. 5:17
[f] *20* Some early manuscripts *dead* [g] *23* Gen. 15:6

## King James

5Even so the tongue is a little member, and boasteth great
things. Behold, how great a matter a little fire kindleth!
6And the tongue *is* a fire, a world of iniquity: so is the tongue
among our members, that it defileth the whole body, and setteth
on fire the course of nature; and it is set on fire of hell.
7For every kind of beasts, and of birds, and of serpents, and of
things in the sea, is tamed, and hath been tamed of mankind:
8But the tongue can no man tame; *it is* an unruly evil, full of
deadly poison.
9Therewith bless we God, even the Father; and therewith curse
we men, which are made after the similitude of God.
10Out of the same mouth proceedeth blessing and cursing. My
brethren, these things ought not so to be.
11Doth a fountain send forth at the same place sweet *water* and
bitter?
12Can the fig tree, my brethren, bear olive berries? either a vine,
figs? so *can* no fountain both yield salt water and fresh.
13Who *is* a wise man and endued with knowledge among you?
let him show out of a good conversation his works with meekness
of wisdom.
14But if ye have bitter envying and strife in your hearts, glory
not, and lie not against the truth.
15This wisdom descendeth not from above, but *is* earthly, sensual, devilish.
16For where envying and strife *is*, there *is* confusion and every
evil work.
17But the wisdom that is from above is first pure, then peaceable, gentle, *and* easy to be entreated, full of mercy and good fruits,
without partiality, and without hypocrisy.
18And the fruit of righteousness is sown in peace of them that
make peace.

4 FROM WHENCE *come* wars and fightings among you? *come*
*they* not hence, *even* of your lusts that war in your members?
2Ye lust, and have not: ye kill, and desire to have, and cannot
obtain: ye fight and war, yet ye have not, because ye ask not.
3Ye ask, and receive not, because ye ask amiss, that ye may
consume *it* upon your lusts.
4Ye adulterers and adulteresses, know ye not that the friendship of the world is enmity with God? whosoever therefore will be
a friend of the world is the enemy of God.

## Amplified

5Even so the tongue is a little member, and it can boast of great
things. See how much wood *or* how great a forest a tiny spark can
set ablaze!
6And the tongue [is] a fire. [The tongue is a] world of wickedness set among our members, contaminating *and* depraving the
whole body and setting on fire the wheel of birth—the cycle of
man's nature—being itself ignited by hell (Gehenna).
7For every kind of beast and bird, of reptile and sea animal, can
be tamed and has been tamed by human genius (nature).
8But the human tongue can be tamed by no man. It is (an
undisciplined, irreconcilable) restless evil, full of death-bringing
poison.
9With it we bless the Lord and Father, and with it we curse men
who were made in God's likeness!
10Out of the same mouth come forth blessing and cursing.
These things, my brethren, ought not to be so.
11Does a fountain send forth [simultaneously] from the same
opening fresh water and bitter?
12Can a fig tree, my brethren, bear olives, or a grapevine figs?
Neither can a salt spring furnish fresh water.
13Who is there among you who is wise and intelligent? Then let
him by his noble living show forth his [good] works with the
(unobtrusive) humility [which is the proper attribute] of true wisdom.
14But if you have bitter jealousy (envy) and contention (rivalry,
selfish ambition) in your hearts, do not pride yourselves on it and
thus be in defiance of *and* false to the Truth.
15This [superficial] wisdom is not such as comes down from
above, but is earthly, unspiritual (animal), even devilish (demonia-
cal).
16For wherever there is jealousy (envy) and contention (rivalry
and selfish ambition) there will also be confusion (unrest, dishar-
mony, rebellion) and all sorts of evil *and* vile practices.
17But the wisdom from above is first of all pure (undefiled); then
it is peace-loving, courteous (considerate, gentle). [It is willing to]
yield to reason, full of compassion and good fruits; it is wholehearted *and* straightforward, impartial *and* unfeigned—free from
doubts, wavering and insincerity.
18And the harvest of righteousness (of conformity to God's will
in thought and deed) is [the fruit of the seed] sown in peace by
those who work for *and* make peace—in themselves and in others,
[that is,] that peace which means concord (agreement, harmony)
between individuals, with undisturbedness, in a peaceful mind
free from fears and agitating passions and moral conflicts.

4 WHAT LEADS to strife (discord and feuds) *and* how do conflicts (quarrels and fightings) originate among you? Do they
not arise from your sensual desires that are ever warring in your
bodily members?
2You are jealous *and* covet [what others have] and your desires
go unfulfilled; [so] you become murderers. [ [a]To hate is to murder
as far as your hearts are concerned.] You burn with envy *and* anger
and are not able to obtain [the gratification, the contentment and
the happiness that you seek], so you fight and war. You do not
have because you do not ask.
3[Or] you do ask [God for them] and yet fail to receive, because
you ask with wrong purpose and evil, selfish motives. Your intention is, [when you get what you desire] to spend it in sensual
pleasures.
4You [are like] unfaithful wives [having illicit love affairs with
the world] *and* [b]breaking your marriage vow to God! Do you not
know that being the world's friend is being God's enemy? So
whoever chooses to be a friend of the world takes his stand as an
enemy of God.

AMP [a] I John 3:15. [b] Alternate reading.

## New American Standard

5So also the tongue is a small part of the body, and *yet* it boasts
of great things. Behold, how great a forest is set aflame by such
a small fire!
6And the tongue is a fire, the *very* world of iniquity; the tongue
is set among our members as that which defiles the entire body,
and sets on fire the course of *our* life, and is set on fire by hell.
7For every species of beasts and birds, of reptiles and creatures
of the sea, is tamed, and has been tamed by the human race.
8But no one can tame the tongue; *it is* a restless evil *and* full of
deadly poison.
9With it we bless *our* Lord and Father; and with it we curse
men, who have been made in the likeness of God;
10from the same mouth come *both* blessing and cursing. My
brethren, these things ought not to be this way.
11Does a fountain send out from the same opening *both* fresh
and bitter *water*?
12Can a fig tree, my brethren, produce olives, or a vine produce
figs? Neither *can* salt water produce fresh.

*Wisdom from Above*

13¶ Who among you is wise and understanding? Let him show
by his good behavior his deeds in the gentleness of wisdom.
14But if you have bitter jealousy and selfish ambition in your
heart, do not be arrogant and *so* lie against the truth.
15This wisdom is not that which comes down from above, but
is earthly, natural, demonic.
16For where jealousy and selfish ambition exist, there is disorder and every evil thing.
17But the wisdom from above is first pure, then peaceable,
gentle, reasonable, full of mercy and good fruits, unwavering,
without hypocrisy.
18And the seed whose fruit is righteousness is sown in peace
by those who make peace.

*Things to Avoid*

4 WHAT IS the source of quarrels and conflicts among you? Is
not the source your pleasures that wage war in your members?
2You lust and do not have; *so* you commit murder. And you
are envious and cannot obtain; *so* you fight and quarrel. You do
not have because you do not ask.
3You ask and do not receive, because you ask with wrong
motives, so that you may spend *it* on your pleasures.
4You adulteresses, do you not know that friendship with the
world is hostility toward God? Therefore whoever wishes to be a
friend of the world makes himself an enemy of God.

## New International

5Likewise the tongue is a small part of the body, but it makes great
boasts. Consider what a great forest is set on fire by a small spark.
6The tongue also is a fire, a world of evil among the parts of the
body. It corrupts the whole person, sets the whole course of his
life on fire, and is itself set on fire by hell.
7All kinds of animals, birds, reptiles and creatures of the sea are
being tamed and have been tamed by man, 8but no man can tame
the tongue. It is a restless evil, full of deadly poison.
9With the tongue we praise our Lord and Father, and with it we
curse men, who have been made in God's likeness. 10Out of the
same mouth come praise and cursing. My brothers, this should not
be. 11Can both fresh water and salt[c] water flow from the same
spring? 12My brothers, can a fig tree bear olives, or a grapevine
bear figs? Neither can a salt spring produce fresh water.

*Two Kinds of Wisdom*

13Who is wise and understanding among you? Let him show it
by his good life, by deeds done in the humility that comes from
wisdom. 14But if you harbor bitter envy and selfish ambition in
your hearts, do not boast about it or deny the truth. 15Such "wisdom" does not come down from heaven but is earthly, unspiritual,
of the devil. 16For where you have envy and selfish ambition, there
you find disorder and every evil practice.
17But the wisdom that comes from heaven is first of all pure;
then peace-loving, considerate, submissive, full of mercy and good
fruit, impartial and sincere. 18Peacemakers who sow in peace raise
a harvest of righteousness.

*Submit Yourselves to God*

4 WHAT CAUSES fights and quarrels among you? Don't they
come from your desires that battle within you? 2You want
something but don't get it. You kill and covet, but you cannot have
what you want. You quarrel and fight. You do not have, because
you do not ask God. 3When you ask, you do not receive, because
you ask with wrong motives, that you may spend what you get on
your pleasures.
4You adulterous people, don't you know that friendship with
the world is hatred toward God? Anyone who chooses to be a
friend of the world becomes an enemy of God. 5Or do you think

NIV [c] 11 Greek *bitter* (see also verse 14)

# King James

5Do ye think that the scripture saith in vain, The spirit that
dwelleth in us lusteth to envy?
6But he giveth more grace. Wherefore he saith, God resisteth
the proud, but giveth grace unto the humble.
7Submit yourselves therefore to God. Resist the devil, and he
will flee from you.
8Draw nigh to God, and he will draw nigh to you. Cleanse *your*
hands, *ye* sinners; and purify *your* hearts, *ye* double minded.
9Be afflicted, and mourn, and weep: let your laughter be turned
to mourning, and *your* joy to heaviness.
10Humble yourselves in the sight of the Lord, and he shall lift
you up.
11Speak not evil one of another, brethren. He that speaketh evil
of *his* brother, and judgeth his brother, speaketh evil of the law,
and judgeth the law: but if thou judge the law, thou art not a doer
of the law, but a judge.
12There is one lawgiver, who is able to save and to destroy: who
art thou that judgest another?
13Go to now, ye that say, Today or tomorrow we will go into
such a city, and continue there a year, and buy and sell, and get
gain:
14Whereas ye know not what *shall be* on the morrow. For what
*is* your life? It is even a vapour, that appeareth for a little time, and
then vanisheth away.
15For that ye *ought* to say, If the Lord will, we shall live, and do
this, or that.
16But now ye rejoice in your boastings: all such rejoicing is evil.
17Therefore to him that knoweth to do good, and doeth *it* not,
to him it is sin.

5 GO TO now, *ye* rich men, weep and howl for your miseries
that shall come upon *you.*
2Your riches are corrupted, and your garments are motheaten.
3Your gold and silver is cankered; and the rust of them shall be
a witness against you, and shall eat your flesh as it were fire. Ye
have heaped treasure together for the last days.
4Behold, the hire of the labourers who have reaped down your
fields, which is of you kept back by fraud, crieth: and the cries of
them which have reaped are entered into the ears of the Lord of
sabaoth.
5Ye have lived in pleasure on the earth, and been wanton; ye
have nourished your hearts, as in a day of slaughter.
6Ye have condemned *and* killed the just; *and* he doth not resist
you.
7Be patient therefore, brethren, unto the coming of the Lord.
Behold, the husbandman waiteth for the precious fruit of the
earth, and hath long patience for it, until he receive the early and
latter rain.

# Amplified

5Or do you suppose that the Scripture is speaking to no purpose
that says, The Spirit Whom He has caused to dwell in us yearns
over us—and [a]He yearns for the Spirit [to be welcome]—with a
jealous love? [Jer. 3:14; Hos. 2:19f.]
6But He gives us more and more grace [ [b]power of the Holy
Spirit, to meet this evil tendency and all others fully]. That is why
He says, God sets Himself against the proud and haughty, but
gives grace [continually] to the lowly—those who are humble-
minded [enough to receive it]. [Prov. 3:34.]
7So be subject to God.—Stand firm against the devil; resist him
and he will flee from you.
8Come close to God and He will come close to you. [Recognize
that you are] sinners, get your soiled hands clean; [realize that you
have been disloyal] wavering individuals with divided interests,
and purify your hearts [of your spiritual adultery].
9[As you draw near to God] be deeply penitent and grieve, even
weep [over your disloyalty]. Let your laughter be turned to grief
and your mirth to dejection *and* heartfelt shame [for your sins].
10Humble yourselves—feeling very insignificant—in the presence of the Lord, and He will exalt you.—He will lift you up and
make your lives significant.
11[My] brethren, do not speak evil about or accuse one another.
He that maligns a brother or judges his brother is maligning *and*
criticizing the Law *and* judging the Law. But if you judge the Law,
you are not a practicer of the Law but a censor *and* judge [of it].
12One only is the Lawgiver *and* Judge—[the One] Who has the
absolute power of life and death—Who is able to save and to
destroy. [But you], who are you that [you presume to] pass judgment on your neighbor?
13Come now, you who say, Today or tomorrow we will go into
such *and* such a city and spend a year there and carry on our
business and make money.
14Yet you do not know [the least thing] about what may happen
tomorrow. What is the nature of your life? You are [really] but a
wisp of vapor—a puff of smoke, a mist—that is visible for a little
while and then disappears [into thin air].
15You ought instead to say, If the Lord is willing, we shall live
and we shall do this or that [thing].
16But as it is, you boast [falsely] in your presumption *and* your
self-conceit. All such boasting is wrong.
17So any person who knows what is right to do but does not do
it, to him it is sin.

5 COME NOW, you rich [people], weep aloud and lament over
the miseries—the woes—that are surely coming upon you.
2Your abundant wealth has rotted *and* is ruined and your
[many] garments have become moth-eaten.
3Your gold and silver are completely rusted through, and their
rust will be testimony against you and it will devour your flesh as
if it were fire. You have heaped together treasure for the last days.
4[But] look! [Here are] the wages that you have withheld by
fraud from the laborers who have reaped your fields, crying out
(for vengeance), and the cries of the harvesters have come to the
ears of the Lord of hosts.
5[Here] on earth you have abandoned yourselves to soft (prodigal) living and to [the pleasures of] self-indulgence *and* self-gratification. You have fattened your hearts in a day of slaughter.
6You have condemned, you have murdered the (innocent)
righteous [man, while] he offers no resistance to you.
7So be patient, brethren, [as you wait] till the coming of the
Lord. See how the farmer waits expectantly for the precious harvest from the land. [See how] he keeps up his patient [vigil] over
it until it receives the early and late rains.

**AMP** [a] Alternate reading. [b] Adam Clarke.

## New American Standard

5Or do you think that the Scripture speaks to no purpose:
"[c]He jealously desires the Spirit which He has made to dwell in
us"?
6But He gives a greater grace. Therefore *it* says, "GOD IS OP-
POSED TO THE PROUD, BUT GIVES GRACE TO THE HUMBLE."
7Submit therefore to God. Resist the devil and he will flee from
you.
8Draw near to God and He will draw near to you. Cleanse your
hands, you sinners; and purify your hearts, you double-minded.
9Be miserable and mourn and weep; let your laughter be
turned into mourning, and your joy to gloom.
10Humble yourselves in the presence of the Lord, and He will
exalt you.
11¶ Do not speak against one another, brethren. He who speaks
against a brother, or judges his brother, speaks against the law,
and judges the law; but if you judge the law, you are not a doer
of the law, but a judge *of it*.
12There is *only* one Lawgiver and Judge, the One who is able
to save and to destroy; but who are you who judge your neighbor?
13¶ Come now, you who say, "Today or tomorrow, we shall go
to such and such a city, and spend a year there and engage in
business and make a profit."
14Yet you do not know what your life will be like tomorrow. You
are *just* a vapor that appears for a little while and then vanishes
away.
15Instead, *you ought* to say, "If the Lord wills, we shall live and
also do this or that."
16But as it is, you boast in your arrogance; all such boasting is
evil.
17Therefore, to one who knows *the* right thing to do, and does
not do it, to him it is sin.

*Misuse of Riches*

5 COME NOW, you rich, weep and howl for your miseries
which are coming upon you.
2Your riches have rotted and your garments have become
moth-eaten.
3Your gold and your silver have rusted; and their rust will be
a witness against you and will consume your flesh like fire. It is
in the last days that you have stored up your treasure!
4Behold, the pay of the laborers who mowed your fields, *and*
which has been withheld by you, cries out *against you*; and the
outcry of those who did the harvesting has reached the ears of the
Lord of Sabaoth.
5You have lived luxuriously on the earth and led a life of
wanton pleasure; you have fattened your hearts in a day of slaughter.
6You have condemned and put to death the righteous *man*; he
does not resist you.

*Exhortation*

7¶ Be patient, therefore, brethren, until the coming of the Lord.
Behold, the farmer waits for the precious produce of the soil, being
patient about it, until it gets the early and late rains.

NAS [c] Or, *The Spirit which He has made to dwell in us jealously desires us*

## New International

Scripture says without reason that the spirit he caused to live in
us envies intensely?[d] 6But he gives us more grace. That is why
Scripture says:

"God opposes the proud
but gives grace to the humble."[e]

7Submit yourselves, then, to God. Resist the devil, and he will
flee from you. 8Come near to God and he will come near to you.
Wash your hands, you sinners, and purify your hearts, you double-minded. 9Grieve, mourn and wail. Change your laughter to
mourning and your joy to gloom. 10Humble yourselves before the
Lord, and he will lift you up.
11Brothers, do not slander one another. Anyone who speaks
against his brother or judges him speaks against the law and
judges it. When you judge the law, you are not keeping it, but
sitting in judgment on it. 12There is only one Lawgiver and Judge,
the one who is able to save and destroy. But you—who are you
to judge your neighbor?

*Boasting About Tomorrow*

13Now listen, you who say, "Today or tomorrow we will go to
this or that city, spend a year there, carry on business and make
money." 14Why, you do not even know what will happen tomorrow. What is your life? You are a mist that appears for a little while
and then vanishes. 15Instead, you ought to say, "If it is the Lord's
will, we will live and do this or that." 16As it is, you boast and brag.
All such boasting is evil. 17Anyone, then, who knows the good he
ought to do and doesn't do it, sins.

*Warning to Rich Oppressors*

5 NOW LISTEN, you rich people, weep and wail because of the
misery that is coming upon you. 2Your wealth has rotted, and
moths have eaten your clothes. 3Your gold and silver are corroded.
Their corrosion will testify against you and eat your flesh like fire.
You have hoarded wealth in the last days. 4Look! The wages you
failed to pay the workmen who mowed your fields are crying out
against you. The cries of the harvesters have reached the ears of
the Lord Almighty. 5You have lived on earth in luxury and self-
indulgence. You have fattened yourselves in the day of slaughter.[f]
6You have condemned and murdered innocent men, who were
not opposing you.

*Patience in Suffering*

7Be patient, then, brothers, until the Lord's coming. See how
the farmer waits for the land to yield its valuable crop and how
patient he is for the autumn and spring rains. 8You too, be patient

NIV [d] 5 *Or that God jealously longs for the spirit that he made to live in us; or that the Spirit he caused to live in us longs jealously* [e] 6 Prov. 3:34 [f] 5 *Or yourselves as in a day of feasting*

## King James

8 Be ye also patient; stablish your hearts: for the coming of the Lord draweth nigh.

9 Grudge not one against another, brethren, lest ye be condemned: behold, the judge standeth before the door.

10 Take, my brethren, the prophets, who have spoken in the name of the Lord, for an example of suffering affliction, and of patience.

11 Behold, we count them happy which endure. Ye have heard of the patience of Job, and have seen the end of the Lord; that the Lord is very pitiful, and of tender mercy.

12 But above all things, my brethren, swear not, neither by heaven, neither by the earth, neither by any other oath: but let your yea be yea; and *your* nay, nay; lest ye fall into condemnation.

13 Is any among you afflicted? let him pray. Is any merry? let him sing psalms.

14 Is any sick among you? let him call for the elders of the church; and let them pray over him, anointing him with oil in the name of the Lord:

15 And the prayer of faith shall save the sick, and the Lord shall raise him up; and if he have committed sins, they shall be forgiven him.

16 Confess *your* faults one to another, and pray one for another, that ye may be healed. The effectual fervent prayer of a righteous man availeth much.

17 Elias was a man subject to like passions as we are, and he prayed earnestly that it might not rain: and it rained not on the earth by the space of three years and six months.

18 And he prayed again, and the heaven gave rain, and the earth brought forth her fruit.

19 Brethren, if any of you do err from the truth, and one convert him;

20 Let him know, that he which converteth the sinner from the error of his way shall save a soul from death, and shall hide a multitude of sins.

## Amplified

8 So you also must be patient. Establish your hearts—strengthen and confirm them in the final certainty—for the coming of the Lord is very near.

9 Do not complain, brethren, against one another, so that you [yourselves] may not be judged. Look! The Judge is [already] standing at the very door.

10 [As] an example of suffering and ill-treatment together with patience, brethren, take the prophets who spoke in the name of the Lord—as His messengers.

11 You know how we call those blessed (happy) who were steadfast—who endured. You have heard of the endurance of Job; and you have seen the Lord's [purpose and how He richly blessed him in the] end, in as much as the Lord is full of pity *and* compassion *and* tenderness and mercy. [Job 1:21, 22; 42:10; Ps. 111:4.]

12 But above all [things], my brethren, do not swear, either by heaven or by earth or by any other oath; but let your yes be [a simple] yes and your no be [a simple] no, so that you may not sin *and* fall under condemnation.

13 Is any one among you afflicted—ill-treated, suffering evil? He should pray. Is any one glad at heart? He should sing praise [to God].

14 Is any one among you sick? He should call in the church elders—the spiritual guides. And they should pray over him, anointing him with oil in the Lord's name.

15 And the prayer [that is] of faith will save him that is sick, and the Lord will restore him; and if he has committed sins, he will be forgiven.

16 Confess to one another therefore your faults—your slips, your false steps, your offenses, your sins; and pray [also] for one another, that you may be healed *and* restored—to a spiritual tone of mind and heart. The earnest (heartfelt, continued) prayer of a righteous man makes tremendous power available—dynamic in its working.

17 Elijah was a human being with a nature such as we have—with feelings, affections and constitution as ourselves; and he prayed earnestly for it not to rain, and no rain fell on the earth for three years and six months. [I Kings 17:1.]

18 And [then] he prayed again and the heavens supplied rain and the land produced its crops [as usual]. [I Kings 18:42-45.]

19 [My] brethren, if any one among you strays from the Truth *and* falls into error, and another [person] brings him back [to God],

20 Let the [latter] one be sure that whoever turns a sinner from his evil course will save [that one's] soul from death and will cover a multitude of sins [that is, [a]procure the pardon of the many sins committed by the convert].

**AMP** [a] Adam Clarke; Jamieson, Fausset and Brown; Matthew Henry, and many other translators.

## New American Standard

8You too be patient; strengthen your hearts, for the coming of
the Lord is at hand.
9Do not complain, brethren, against one another, that you
yourselves may not be judged; behold, the Judge is standing right
at the door.
10As an example, brethren, of suffering and patience, take the
prophets who spoke in the name of the Lord.
11Behold, we count those blessed who endured. You have
heard of the endurance of Job and have seen the outcome of the
Lord's dealings, that the Lord is full of compassion and *is* merciful.
12¶ But above all, my brethren, do not swear, either by heaven
or by earth or with any other oath; but let your yes be yes, and your
no, no; so that you may not fall under judgment.
13¶ Is anyone among you suffering? Let him pray. Is anyone
cheerful? Let him sing praises.
14Is anyone among you sick? Let him call for the elders of the
church, and let them pray over him, anointing him with oil in the
name of the Lord;
15and the prayer offered in faith will [b]restore the one who is
sick, and the Lord will raise him up, and if he has committed sins,
they will be forgiven him.
16Therefore, confess your sins to one another, and pray for one
another, so that you may be healed. The effective prayer of a
righteous man can accomplish much.
17Elijah was a man with a nature like ours, and he prayed
earnestly that it might not rain; and it did not rain on the earth for
three years and six months.
18And he prayed again, and the sky poured rain, and the earth
produced its fruit.
19¶ My brethren, if any among you strays from the truth, and
one turns him back,
20let him know that he who turns a sinner from the error of his
way will save his soul from death, and will cover a multitude of
sins.

NAS [b] Or, *save*

## New International

and stand firm, because the Lord's coming is near. 9Don't grumble
against each other, brothers, or you will be judged. The Judge is
standing at the door!
10Brothers, as an example of patience in the face of suffering,
take the prophets who spoke in the name of the Lord. 11As you
know, we consider blessed those who have persevered. You have
heard of Job's perseverance and have seen what the Lord finally
brought about. The Lord is full of compassion and mercy.
12Above all, my brothers, do not swear—not by heaven or by
earth or by anything else. Let your "Yes" be yes, and your "No,"
no, or you will be condemned.

*The Prayer of Faith*

13Is any one of you in trouble? He should pray. Is anyone
happy? Let him sing songs of praise. 14Is any one of you sick? He
should call the elders of the church to pray over him and anoint
him with oil in the name of the Lord. 15And the prayer offered in
faith will make the sick person well; the Lord will raise him up. If
he has sinned, he will be forgiven. 16Therefore confess your sins
to each other and pray for each other so that you may be healed.
The prayer of a righteous man is powerful and effective.
17Elijah was a man just like us. He prayed earnestly that it
would not rain, and it did not rain on the land for three and a half
years. 18Again he prayed, and the heavens gave rain, and the earth
produced its crops.
19My brothers, if one of you should wander from the truth and
someone should bring him back, 20remember this: Whoever turns
a sinner from the error of his way will save him from death and
cover over a multitude of sins.

## King James

THE FIRST

EPISTLE GENERAL OF

# Peter

1 PETER, AN apostle of Jesus Christ, to the strangers scattered throughout Pontus, Galatia, Cappadocia, Asia, and Bithynia,

2 Elect according to the foreknowledge of God the Father, through sanctification of the Spirit, unto obedience and sprinkling of the blood of Jesus Christ: Grace unto you, and peace, be multiplied.

3 Blessed *be* the God and Father of our Lord Jesus Christ, which according to his abundant mercy hath begotten us again unto a lively hope by the resurrection of Jesus Christ from the dead,

4 To an inheritance incorruptible, and undefiled, and that fadeth not away, reserved in heaven for you,

5 Who are kept by the power of God through faith unto salvation ready to be revealed in the last time.

6 Wherein ye greatly rejoice, though now for a season, if need be, ye are in heaviness through manifold temptations:

7 That the trial of your faith, being much more precious than of gold that perisheth, though it be tried with fire, might be found unto praise and honour and glory at the appearing of Jesus Christ:

8 Whom having not seen, ye love; in whom, though now ye see *him* not, yet believing, ye rejoice with joy unspeakable and full of glory:

9 Receiving the end of your faith, *even* the salvation of *your* souls.

10 Of which salvation the prophets have inquired and searched diligently, who prophesied of the grace *that should come* unto you:

11 Searching what, or what manner of time the Spirit of Christ which was in them did signify, when it testified beforehand the sufferings of Christ, and the glory that should follow.

12 Unto whom it was revealed, that not unto themselves, but unto us they did minister the things, which are now reported unto you by them that have preached the gospel unto you with the Holy Ghost sent down from heaven; which things the angels desire to look into.

13 Wherefore gird up the loins of your mind, be sober, and hope to the end for the grace that is to be brought unto you at the revelation of Jesus Christ;

14 As obedient children, not fashioning yourselves according to the former lusts in your ignorance:

**AMP** [a] Cremer. [b] Webster, in definition of "peace" in this sense. [c] Williams.

## Amplified

THE FIRST LETTER OF

# Peter

1 PETER, AN apostle (a special messenger) of Jesus Christ, [writing] to the elect exiles of the dispersion scattered (sowed) abroad in Pontus, Galatia, Cappadocia, Asia and Bithynia,

2 Who were chosen *and* foreknown by God the Father and consecrated (sanctified, made holy) by the Spirit to be obedient to Jesus Christ, the Messiah, and to be sprinkled with [His] blood: May grace (spiritual blessing) and peace be given you in increasing abundance—that spiritual peace to be [a]realized in and through Christ, [b]freedom from fears, agitating passions and moral conflicts.

3 Praised (honored, blessed be) the God and Father of our Lord Jesus Christ, the Messiah! By His boundless mercy we have been born again to an ever living hope through the resurrection of Jesus Christ from the dead;

4 [Born anew] into an inheritance which is beyond the reach of change *and* decay (imperishable), unsullied, and unfading, reserved in heaven for you,

5 Who are being guarded (garrisoned) by God's power through [your] faith [till you fully inherit that [c]final] salvation that is ready to be revealed [for you] in the last time.

6 [You should] be exceedingly glad on this account, though now for a little while you may be distressed by trials *and* suffer temptations,

7 So that [the genuineness] of your faith may be tested, [your faith] which is infinitely more precious than the perishable gold which is tested *and* purified by fire. [This proving of your faith is intended] to redound to [your] praise and glory and honor when Jesus Christ, the Messiah, the Anointed One, is revealed.

8 Without having seen Him you love Him; though you do not [even] now see Him you believe in Him, and exult *and* thrill with inexpressible and glorious (triumphant, heavenly) joy.

9 [At the same time] you receive the result (outcome, consummation) of your faith, the salvation of your souls.

10 The prophets who prophesied of the grace [divine blessing] which was intended for you, searched and inquired earnestly about this salvation.

11 They sought [to find out] to whom or when this was to come which the Spirit of Christ working within them indicated when He predicted the sufferings of Christ and the glories that should follow [them].

12 It was then disclosed to them that the services they were rendering were not meant for themselves *and* their period of time, but for you. [It is these very] things which have now already been made known plainly to you by those who preached the good news (the Gospel) to you by the [same] Holy Spirit sent from heaven. Into these things [the very] angels long to look!

13 So brace up your minds; be sober—circumspect [morally alert]; set your hope wholly *and* unchangeably on the grace (divine favor) that is coming to you when Jesus Christ, the Messiah, is revealed.

14 [Live] as children of obedience [to God]; do not conform yourselves to the evil desires [that governed you] in your former ignorance [when you did not know the requirements of the Gospel].

## New American Standard

# 1 Peter

*A Living Hope, and a Sure Salvation*

**1** PETER, AN apostle of Jesus Christ, to those who reside as aliens, scattered throughout Pontus, Galatia, Cappadocia, Asia, and Bithynia, who are chosen

2according to the foreknowledge of God the Father, by the sanctifying work of the Spirit, that you may obey Jesus Christ and be sprinkled with His blood: May grace and peace be yours in fullest measure.

3¶ Blessed be the God and Father of our Lord Jesus Christ, who according to His great mercy has caused us to be born again to a living hope through the resurrection of Jesus Christ from the dead,

4to *obtain* an inheritance *which is* imperishable and undefiled and will not fade away, reserved in heaven for you,

5who are protected by the power of God through faith for a salvation ready to be revealed in the last time.

6In this you greatly rejoice, even though now for a little while, if necessary, you have been distressed by various trials,

7that the proof of your faith, *being* more precious than gold which is perishable, even though tested by fire, may be found to result in praise and glory and honor at the revelation of Jesus Christ;

8and though you have not seen Him, you love Him, and though you do not see Him now, but believe in Him, you greatly rejoice with joy inexpressible and full of glory,

9obtaining as the outcome of your faith the salvation of [d]your souls.

10As to this salvation, the prophets who prophesied of the grace that *would come* to you made careful search and inquiry,

11seeking to know what person or time the Spirit of Christ within them was indicating as He predicted the sufferings of Christ and the glories to follow.

12It was revealed to them that they were not serving themselves, but you, in these things which now have been announced to you through those who preached the gospel to you by the Holy Spirit sent from heaven—things into which angels long to look.

13¶ Therefore, gird your minds for action, keep sober *in spirit,* fix your hope completely on the grace to be brought to you at the revelation of Jesus Christ.

14As obedient children, do not be conformed to the former lusts *which were yours* in your ignorance,

NAS [d] Some ancient mss. do not contain *your*

## New International

# 1 Peter

**1** PETER, AN apostle of Jesus Christ,

To God's elect, strangers in the world, scattered throughout
Pontus, Galatia, Cappadocia, Asia and Bithynia, 2who have been
chosen according to the foreknowledge of God the Father, through
the sanctifying work of the Spirit, for obedience to Jesus Christ and
sprinkling by his blood:

Grace and peace be yours in abundance.

*Praise to God for a Living Hope*

3Praise be to the God and Father of our Lord Jesus Christ! In his
great mercy he has given us new birth into a living hope through
the resurrection of Jesus Christ from the dead, 4and into an inheritance that can never perish, spoil or fade—kept in heaven for you,
5who through faith are shielded by God's power until the coming
of the salvation that is ready to be revealed in the last time. 6In this
you greatly rejoice, though now for a little while you may have had
to suffer grief in all kinds of trials. 7These have come so that your
faith—of greater worth than gold, which perishes even though
refined by fire—may be proved genuine and may result in praise,
glory and honor when Jesus Christ is revealed. 8Though you have
not seen him, you love him; and even though you do not see him
now, you believe in him and are filled with an inexpressible and
glorious joy, 9for you are receiving the goal of your faith, the
salvation of your souls.

10Concerning this salvation, the prophets, who spoke of the
grace that was to come to you, searched intently and with the
greatest care, 11trying to find out the time and circumstances to
which the Spirit of Christ in them was pointing when he predicted
the sufferings of Christ and the glories that would follow. 12It was
revealed to them that they were not serving themselves but you,
when they spoke of the things that have now been told you by
those who have preached the gospel to you by the Holy Spirit sent
from heaven. Even angels long to look into these things.

*Be Holy*

13Therefore, prepare your minds for action; be self-controlled;
set your hope fully on the grace to be given you when Jesus Christ
is revealed. 14As obedient children, do not conform to the evil
desires you had when you lived in ignorance. 15But just as he who

## King James

15 But as he which hath called you is holy, so be ye holy in all manner of conversation;

16 Because it is written, Be ye holy; for I am holy.

17 And if ye call on the Father, who without respect of persons judgeth according to every man's work, pass the time of your sojourning *here* in fear:

18 Forasmuch as ye know that ye were not redeemed with corruptible things, *as* silver and gold, from your vain conversation *received* by tradition from your fathers;

19 But with the precious blood of Christ, as of a lamb without blemish and without spot:

20 Who verily was foreordained before the foundation of the world, but was manifest in these last times for you,

21 Who by him do believe in God, that raised him up from the dead, and gave him glory; that your faith and hope might be in God.

22 Seeing ye have purified your souls in obeying the truth through the Spirit unto unfeigned love of the brethren, *see that ye* love one another with a pure heart fervently:

23 Being born again, not of corruptible seed, but of incorruptible, by the word of God, which liveth and abideth for ever.

24 For all flesh *is* as grass, and all the glory of man as the flower of grass. The grass withereth, and the flower thereof falleth away:

25 But the word of the Lord endureth for ever. And this is the word which by the gospel is preached unto you.

**2** WHEREFORE LAYING aside all malice, and all guile, and hypocrisies, and envies, and all evil speakings,

2 As newborn babes, desire the sincere milk of the word, that ye may grow thereby:

3 If so be ye have tasted that the Lord *is* gracious.

4 To whom coming, *as unto* a living stone, disallowed indeed of men, but chosen of God, *and* precious,

5 Ye also, as lively stones, are built up a spiritual house, an holy priesthood, to offer up spiritual sacrifices, acceptable to God by Jesus Christ.

6 Wherefore also it is contained in the scripture, Behold, I lay in Sion a chief corner stone, elect, precious: and he that believeth on him shall not be confounded.

7 Unto you therefore which believe *he is* precious: but unto them which be disobedient, the stone which the builders disallowed, the same is made the head of the corner,

8 And a stone of stumbling, and a rock of offence, *even to them* which stumble at the word, being disobedient: whereunto also they were appointed.

## Amplified

15 But as the One Who called you is holy, you yourselves also be holy in all your conduct *and* manner of living.

16 For it is written, You shall be holy, for I am holy. [Lev. 11:44, 45.]

17 And if you call upon Him as [your] Father Who judges each one impartially according to what he does, [then] you should conduct yourselves with true reverence throughout the time of your temporary residence [on the earth, whether long or short].

18 You must know (recognize) that you were redeemed (ransomed) from the useless (fruitless) way of living inherited by tradition from [your] forefathers, not with corruptible things [such as] silver and gold,

19 But [you were purchased] with the precious blood of Christ, the Messiah, like that of a [sacrificial] lamb without blemish or spot.

20 It is true that He was chosen *and* foreordained (destined and foreknown for it) before the foundation of the world, but He was brought out to public view (made manifest) in these last days—at the end of the times—for the sake of you.

21 Through Him you believe—adhere to, rely on—God, Who raised Him up from the dead and gave Him honor *and* glory, so that your faith and hope are [centered and rest] in God.

22 Since by your obedience to the Truth *through the* [ *Holy*] *Spirit* you have purified your hearts for the sincere affection of the brethren, [see that you] love one another fervently from a *pure* heart.

23 You have been regenerated—born again—not from a mortal [a]origin ( [b]seed, sperm) but from one that is immortal by the *ever* living and lasting Word of God.

24 Because all flesh [mankind] is like grass and all its glory (honor) like [the] flower of grass. The grass withers, and the flower drops off,

25 But the Word of the Lord [ [c]divine instruction, the Gospel] endures forever. And this Word is the good news which was preached to you. [Isa. 40:6-9.]

**2** SO BE done with every trace of wickedness (depravity, malignity) and all deceit and insincerity (pretense, hypocrisy) and grudges (envy, jealousy) and slander *and* evil speaking of every kind.

2 Like newborn babies you should crave—thirst for, earnestly desire—the pure (unadulterated) spiritual milk, that by it you may be nurtured *and* grow unto [completed] salvation;

3 Since you have [already] tasted the goodness *and* kindness of the Lord. [Ps. 34:8.]

4 Come to Him [then, to that] Living Stone which men [d]tried *and* threw away, but which is chosen [and] precious in God's sight. [Ps. 118:22; Isa. 28:16.]

5 [Come] and as living stones be yourselves built [into] a spiritual house, for a holy (dedicated, consecrated) priesthood, to offer up [those] spiritual sacrifices [that are] acceptable *and* well-pleasing to God through Jesus Christ.

6 For thus it stands in Scripture: Behold, I am laying in Zion a chosen, ( [e]honored,) precious chief Cornerstone; and he who believes in Him—who adheres to, trusts in and relies on Him—shall never be [f]disappointed *or* put to shame. [Isa. 28:16.]

7 To you then who believe—who adhere to, trust in and rely on Him—is the preciousness; but for those who disbelieve [it is true], The [very] Stone which the builders rejected has become the main Cornerstone, [Ps. 118:22.]

8 And a Stone that will cause stumbling and a Rock that will give [men] offense; they stumble because they disobey *and* disbelieve [God's] Word, as those [who reject Him] were destined (appointed) to do.

**AMP** [a] Thayer. [b] Abbott-Smith. cf. Moulton and Milligan. [c] Thayer. [d] Vincent. [e] Vincent. [f] Thayer.

## New American Standard

15but like the Holy One who called you, be holy yourselves also
in all *your* behavior;
16because it is written, "YOU SHALL BE HOLY, FOR I AM HOLY."
17And if you address as Father the One who impartially judges
according to each man's work, conduct yourselves in fear during
the time of your stay *upon earth;*
18knowing that you were not redeemed with perishable things
like silver or gold from your futile way of life inherited from your
forefathers,
19but with precious blood, as of a lamb unblemished and spotless, *the blood* of Christ.
20For He was foreknown before the foundation of the world,
but has appeared in these last times for the sake of you
21who through Him are believers in God, who raised Him from
the dead and gave Him glory, so that your faith and hope are in
God.
22¶ Since you have in obedience to the truth purified your souls
for a sincere love of the brethren, fervently love one another from
[g]the heart,
23for you have been born again not of seed which is perishable
but imperishable, *that is,* through the living and abiding word of
God.
24For,
"ALL FLESH IS LIKE GRASS,
AND ALL ITS GLORY LIKE THE FLOWER OF GRASS.
THE GRASS WITHERS,
AND THE FLOWER FALLS OFF,
25 BUT THE WORD OF THE LORD ABIDES FOREVER."
And this is the word which was preached to you.

*As Newborn Babes*

**2** THEREFORE, PUTTING aside all malice and all guile and
hypocrisy and envy and all slander,
2like newborn babes, long for the pure milk of the word, that
by it you may grow in respect to salvation,
3if you have tasted the kindness of the Lord.

*As Living Stones*

4And coming to Him as to a living stone, rejected by men, but
choice and precious in the sight of God,
5you also, as living stones, are being built up as a spiritual
house for a holy priesthood, to offer up spiritual sacrifices acceptable to God through Jesus Christ.
6For *this* is contained in Scripture:
"BEHOLD I LAY IN ZION A CHOICE STONE, A PRECIOUS
CORNER *stone,*
AND HE WHO BELIEVES IN HIM SHALL NOT BE
DISAPPOINTED."
7This precious value, then, is for you who believe. But for
those who disbelieve,
"THE STONE WHICH THE BUILDERS REJECTED,
THIS BECAME THE VERY CORNER *stone,*"
8and,
"A STONE OF STUMBLING AND A ROCK OF OFFENSE";
for they stumble because they are disobedient to the word, and to
this *doom* they were also appointed.

NAS [g] Some mss. read *a clean heart*

## New International

called you is holy, so be holy in all you do; 16for it is written: "Be
holy, because I am holy."[h]
17Since you call on a Father who judges each man's work impartially, live your lives as strangers here in reverent fear. 18For you
know that it was not with perishable things such as silver or gold
that you were redeemed from the empty way of life handed down
to you from your forefathers, 19but with the precious blood of
Christ, a lamb without blemish or defect. 20He was chosen before
the creation of the world, but was revealed in these last times for
your sake. 21Through him you believe in God, who raised him
from the dead and glorified him, and so your faith and hope are
in God.
22Now that you have purified yourselves by obeying the truth
so that you have sincere love for your brothers, love one another
deeply, from the heart.[i] 23For you have been born again, not of
perishable seed, but of imperishable, through the living and enduring word of God. 24For,

"All men are like grass,
and all their glory is like the flowers of the field;
the grass withers and the flowers fall,
25 but the word of the Lord stands forever."[j]

And this is the word that was preached to you.

**2** THEREFORE, RID yourselves of all malice and all deceit,
hypocrisy, envy, and slander of every kind. 2Like newborn
babies, crave pure spiritual milk, so that by it you may grow up
in your salvation, 3now that you have tasted that the Lord is good.

*The Living Stone and a Chosen People*

4As you come to him, the living Stone—rejected by men but
chosen by God and precious to him— 5you also, like living stones,
are being built into a spiritual house to be a holy priesthood,
offering spiritual sacrifices acceptable to God through Jesus Christ.
6For in Scripture it says:

"See, I lay a stone in Zion,
a chosen and precious cornerstone,
and the one who trusts in him
will never be put to shame."[k]

7Now to you who believe, this stone is precious. But to those who
do not believe,

"The stone the builders rejected
has become the capstone,[l]"[m]

8and,

"A stone that causes men to stumble
and a rock that makes them fall."[n]

They stumble because they disobey the message—which is also
what they were destined for.

NIV [h] *16* Lev. 11:44,45; 19:2; 20:7 [i] 22 Some early manuscripts *from a pure heart* [j] *25* Isaiah 40:6-8 [k] *6* Isaiah 28:16 [l] *7* Or *cornerstone* [m] *7* Psalm 118:22 [n] *8* Isaiah 8:14

## King James

9But ye *are* a chosen generation, a royal priesthood, an holy nation, a peculiar people; that ye should show forth the praises of him who hath called you out of darkness into his marvellous light:

10Which in time past *were* not a people, but *are* now the people of God: which had not obtained mercy, but now have obtained mercy.

11Dearly beloved, I beseech *you* as strangers and pilgrims, abstain from fleshly lusts, which war against the soul;

12Having your conversation honest among the Gentiles: that, whereas they speak against you as evildoers, they may by *your* good works, which they shall behold, glorify God in the day of visitation.

13Submit yourselves to every ordinance of man for the Lord's sake: whether it be to the king, as supreme;

14Or unto governors, as unto them that are sent by him for the punishment of evildoers, and for the praise of them that do well.

15For so is the will of God, that with well doing ye may put to silence the ignorance of foolish men:

16As free, and not using *your* liberty for a cloak of maliciousness, but as the servants of God.

17Honour all *men*. Love the brotherhood. Fear God. Honour the king.

18Servants, *be* subject to *your* masters with all fear; not only to the good and gentle, but also to the froward.

19For this *is* thankworthy, if a man for conscience toward God endure grief, suffering wrongfully.

20For what glory *is it*, if, when ye be buffeted for your faults, ye shall take it patiently? but if, when ye do well, and suffer *for it*, ye take it patiently, this *is* acceptable with God.

21For even hereunto were ye called: because Christ also suffered for us, leaving us an example, that ye should follow his steps:

22Who did no sin, neither was guile found in his mouth:

23Who, when he was reviled, reviled not again; when he suffered, he threatened not; but committed *himself* to him that judgeth righteously:

24Who his own self bare our sins in his own body on the tree, that we, being dead to sins, should live unto righteousness: by whose stripes ye were healed.

25For ye were as sheep going astray; but are now returned unto the Shepherd and Bishop of your souls.

**3** LIKEWISE, YE wives, *be* in subjection to your own husbands; that, if any obey not the word, they also may without the word be won by the conversation of the wives;

## Amplified

9But you are a chosen race, a royal priesthood, a dedicated nation, [ [a]God's] own [b]purchased, special people, that you may set forth the wonderful deeds *and* display the virtues *and* perfections of Him Who called you out of darkness into His marvelous light. [Exod. 19:5, 6.]

10Once you were not a people [at all], but now you are God's people; once you were unpitied, but now you are pitied *and* have received mercy. [Hos. 2:23.]

11Beloved, I implore you as sojourners, strangers *and* exiles [in this world] to abstain from the sensual urges—the evil desires, the passions of the flesh [your lower nature]—that wage war against the soul.

12Conduct yourselves properly (honorably, righteously) among the Gentiles, so that although they may slander you as evildoers, [yet] they may by witnessing your good deeds [come to] glorify God in the day of inspection [ [c]when God shall look upon (you) wanderers, as a pastor (shepherd) over his flock].

13Be submissive to every human institution *and* authority for the sake of the Lord, whether it be to the emperor as supreme,

14Or to governors as sent by him to bring vengeance (punishment, justice) to those who do wrong, and to encourage those who do good service.

15For it is God's will *and* intention that by doing right [your] good *and* honest lives should silence (muzzle, gag) the ignorant charges *and* ill-informed criticisms of foolish persons.

16[Live] as free people, [yet] without employing your freedom as a pretext for wickedness; but [live at all times] as servants of God.

17Show respect for all men—treat them honorably. Love the brotherhood [the Christian fraternity of which Christ is the Head]. Reverence God. Honor the emperor.

18[You who are] household servants, be submissive to your masters with all (proper) respect, not only to those who are kind, considerate *and* reasonable but also to those who are surly—overbearing, unjust and crooked.

19For one is regarded favorably (is approved, acceptable and thankworthy) if, as in the sight of God, he endures the pain of unjust suffering.

20[After all] what [d]kind of glory [is there in it] if when you do wrong and are punished for it you take it patiently? But if you bear patiently with suffering [which results] when you do right *and* that is undeserved, it is acceptable *and* well-pleasing to God.

21For even to this were you called—it is inseparable from your vocation. For Christ also suffered for you, leaving you [His personal] example, so that you should follow on in His footsteps.

22He was guilty of no sin; neither was deceit (guile) ever found on His lips. [Isa. 53:9.]

23When He was reviled *and* insulted, He did not revile *or* offer insult in return; [when] He was abused *and* suffered, He made no threats [of vengeance]; but he trusted [Himself and everything] to Him Who judges fairly.

24He personally bore our sins in His [own] body to the tree [e][as to an altar and offered Himself on it], that we might die (cease to exist) to sin and live to righteousness. By His wounds you have been healed.

25For you were going astray like [so many] sheep, but now you have come back to the Shepherd and Guardian (the Bishop) of your souls. [Isa. 53:5, 6.]

**3** IN LIKE manner you married women, be submissive to your own husbands—subordinate yourselves as being secondary to and dependent on them, and adapt yourselves to them. So that even if any do not obey the Word [of God], they may be won over not by discussion but by the [godly] lives of their wives,

**AMP** [a] ASV. [b] Wycliffe. [c] J. Rawson Lumby in "Speaker's Commentary." [d] Literal meaning. [e] Vincent.

## New American Standard

9But you are A CHOSEN RACE, A royal PRIESTHOOD, A HOLY NATION, A PEOPLE FOR *God's* OWN POSSESSION, that you may proclaim the excellencies of Him who has called you out of darkness into His marvelous light;
10for you once were NOT A PEOPLE, but now you are THE PEOPLE OF GOD; you had NOT RECEIVED MERCY, but now you have RECEIVED MERCY.
11¶ Beloved, I urge you as aliens and strangers to abstain from fleshly lusts, which wage war against the soul.
12Keep your behavior excellent among the Gentiles, so that in the thing in which they slander you as evildoers, they may on account of your good deeds, as they observe *them*, glorify God in the day of [f]visitation.

*Honor Authority*

13¶ Submit yourselves for the Lord's sake to every human institution, whether to a king as the one in authority,
14or to governors as sent by him for the punishment of evildoers and the praise of those who do right.
15For such is the will of God that by doing right you may silence the ignorance of foolish men.
16 *Act* as free men, and do not use your freedom as a covering for evil, but *use it* as bondslaves of God.
17Honor all men; love the brotherhood, fear God, honor the king.
18¶ Servants, be submissive to your masters with all respect, not only to those who are good and gentle, but also to those who are unreasonable.
19For this *finds* favor, if for the sake of conscience toward God a man bears up under sorrows when suffering unjustly.
20For what credit is there if, when you sin and are harshly treated, you endure it with patience? But if when you do what is right and suffer *for it* you patiently endure it, this *finds* favor with God.

*Christ Is Our Example*

21For you have been called for this purpose, since Christ also suffered for you, leaving you an example for you to follow in His steps,
22WHO COMMITTED NO SIN, NOR WAS ANY DECEIT FOUND IN HIS MOUTH;
23and while being reviled, He did not revile in return; while suffering, He uttered no threats, but kept entrusting *Himself* to Him who judges righteously;
24and He Himself bore our sins in His body on the cross, that we might die to sin and live to righteousness; for by His wounds you were healed.
25For you were continually straying like sheep, but now you have returned to the Shepherd and Guardian of your souls.

*Godly Living*

**3** IN THE same way, you wives, be submissive to your own husbands so that even if any *of them* are disobedient to the word, they may be won without a word by the behavior of their wives,

NAS [f] I.e., Christ's coming again in judgment

## New International

9But you are a chosen people, a royal priesthood, a holy nation,
a people belonging to God, that you may declare the praises of him
who called you out of darkness into his wonderful light. 10Once
you were not a people, but now you are the people of God; once
you had not received mercy, but now you have received mercy.
11Dear friends, I urge you, as aliens and strangers in the world,
to abstain from sinful desires, which war against your soul. 12Live
such good lives among the pagans that, though they accuse you
of doing wrong, they may see your good deeds and glorify God
on the day he visits us.

*Submission to Rulers and Masters*

13Submit yourselves for the Lord's sake to every authority instituted among men: whether to the king, as the supreme authority, 14or to governors, who are sent by him to punish those who
do wrong and to commend those who do right. 15For it is God's
will that by doing good you should silence the ignorant talk of
foolish men. 16Live as free men, but do not use your freedom as
a cover-up for evil; live as servants of God. 17Show proper respect
to everyone: Love the brotherhood of believers, fear God, honor
the king.
18Slaves, submit yourselves to your masters with all respect, not
only to those who are good and considerate, but also to those who
are harsh. 19For it is commendable if a man bears up under the pain
of unjust suffering because he is conscious of God. 20But how is
it to your credit if you receive a beating for doing wrong and
endure it? But if you suffer for doing good and you endure it, this
is commendable before God. 21To this you were called, because
Christ suffered for you, leaving you an example, that you should
follow in his steps.

22"He committed no sin,
and no deceit was found in his mouth."[g]

23When they hurled their insults at him, he did not retaliate; when
he suffered, he made no threats. Instead, he entrusted himself to
him who judges justly. 24He himself bore our sins in his body on
the tree, so that we might die to sins and live for righteousness;
by his wounds you have been healed. 25For you were like sheep
going astray, but now you have returned to the Shepherd and
Overseer of your souls.

*Wives and Husbands*

**3** WIVES, IN the same way be submissive to your husbands so that, if any of them do not believe the word, they may be won over without words by the behavior of their wives, 2when they see

NIV [g] 22 Isaiah 53:9

## King James

2 While they behold your chaste conversation *coupled* with fear.

3 Whose adorning let it not be that outward *adorning* of plaiting the hair, and of wearing of gold, or of putting on of apparel;

4 But *let it be* the hidden man of the heart, in that which is not corruptible, *even the ornament* of a meek and quiet spirit, which is in the sight of God of great price.

5 For after this manner in the old time the holy women also, who trusted in God, adorned themselves, being in subjection unto their own husbands:

6 Even as Sarah obeyed Abraham, calling him lord: whose daughters ye are, as long as ye do well, and are not afraid with any amazement.

7 Likewise, ye husbands, dwell with *them* according to knowledge, giving honour unto the wife, as unto the weaker vessel, and as being heirs together of the grace of life; that your prayers be not hindered.

8 Finally, *be ye* all of one mind, having compassion one of another, love as brethren, *be* pitiful, *be* courteous:

9 Not rendering evil for evil, or railing for railing: but contrariwise blessing; knowing that ye are thereunto called, that ye should inherit a blessing.

10 For he that will love life, and see good days, let him refrain his tongue from evil, and his lips that they speak no guile:

11 Let him eschew evil, and do good; let him seek peace, and ensue it.

12 For the eyes of the Lord *are* over the righteous, and his ears *are open* unto their prayers: but the face of the Lord *is* against them that do evil.

13 And who *is* he that will harm you, if ye be followers of that which is good?

14 But and if ye suffer for righteousness' sake, happy *are ye:* and be not afraid of their terror, neither be troubled;

15 But sanctify the Lord God in your hearts: and *be* ready always to *give* an answer to every man that asketh you a reason of the hope that is in you with meekness and fear:

16 Having a good conscience; that, whereas they speak evil of you, as of evildoers, they may be ashamed that falsely accuse your good conversation in Christ.

17 For *it is* better, if the will of God be so, that ye suffer for well doing, than for evil doing.

## Amplified

2 When they observe the pure *and* modest way in which you conduct yourselves, together with your [a]reverence [for your husband. That is, you are to feel for him all that reverence includes]— [b]to respect, defer to, revere him; [revere means] [c]to honor, esteem (appreciate, prize), and [in the human sense] adore him; [and adore means] [d]to admire, praise, be devoted to, deeply love and [e]enjoy [your husband].

3 Let not yours be the [merely] external adorning with [elaborate] [f]interweaving *and* knotting of the hair, the wearing of jewelry, or changes of clothes;

4 But let it be the inward adorning *and* beauty of the hidden person of the heart, with the incorruptible *and* unfading charm of a gentle and peaceful spirit, which (is not anxious or wrought up, but) is very precious in the sight of God.

5 For it was thus that the pious women of old who hoped in God were (accustomed) to beautify themselves, and were submissive to their husbands—adapting themselves to them as themselves secondary and dependent upon them.

6 It was thus that Sarah obeyed Abraham (following his guidance and acknowledging his headship over her by) calling him lord—master, leader, authority. And you are now her true daughters if you do right and let nothing terrify you—not giving way to hysterical fears or letting anxieties unnerve you.

7 In the same way you married men should live considerately with [your wives], with an [g]intelligent recognition [of the marriage relation], honoring the woman as [physically] the weaker, but [realizing that you] are joint heirs of the grace (God's unmerited favor) of life, in order that your prayers may not be hindered *and* cut off.—Otherwise you cannot pray effectively.

8 Finally, all [of you] should be of one *and* the same mind (united in spirit), sympathizing [with one another], loving [each the others] as brethren (of one household), compassionate *and* courteous—tenderhearted and humble-minded.

9 Never return evil for evil or insult for insult—scolding, tongue-lashing, berating; but on the contrary blessing—praying for their welfare, happiness and protection, and truly pitying and loving them. For *know that* to this you have been called, that you may yourselves inherit a blessing [from God]—obtain a blessing as heirs, bringing welfare and happiness and protection.

10 For let him who wants to enjoy life and see good days (good whether apparent or not), keep his tongue free from evil, and his lips from guile (treachery, deceit).

11 Let him turn away from wickedness *and* shun it; and let him do right. Let him search for peace—harmony, undisturbedness from fears, agitating passions and moral conflicts—and seek it eagerly.—Do not merely desire peaceful relations [with God, with your fellowmen, and with yourself], but pursue, go after them!

12 For the eyes of the Lord are upon the righteous—those who are upright and in right standing with God—and His ears are attentive to their prayer. But the face of the Lord is against those who practice evil—to oppose them, to frustrate and defeat them. [Ps. 34:12-16.]

13 Now who is there to hurt you if you are [h]zealous followers of that which is good?

14 But even in case you should suffer for the sake of righteousness, [you are] blessed—happy, to be envied. Do not dread *or* be afraid of their threats, nor be disturbed [by their opposition].

15 But in your hearts set Christ apart as holy [and acknowledge Him] as Lord. Always be ready to give a logical defense to any one who asks you to account for the hope that is in you, but do it courteously and respectfully. [Isa. 8:12, 13.]

16 [And see to it that] your conscience is [i]entirely clear, so that, when you are falsely accused as evildoers, those who threaten you abusively *and* revile your right behavior in Christ may come to be ashamed [of slandering your good lives].

17 For [it is] better to suffer [unjustly] for doing right, if that should be God's will, than to suffer [justly] for doing wrong.

**AMP** [a] Thayer. [b] English synonyms of the preceding to-be-defined word. [c] English synonyms of the preceding to-be-defined word. [d] English synonyms of the preceding to-be-defined word. [e] English synonyms of the preceding to-be-defined word. [f] Thayer. [g] Vincent. [h] Best authorities read "zealous." [i] Vincent: "unimpaired."

## New American Standard

2as they observe your chaste and respectful behavior.
3And let not your adornment be *merely* external—braiding the
hair, and wearing gold jewelry, or putting on dresses;
4but *let it be* the hidden person of the heart, with the imperishable quality of a gentle and quiet spirit, which is precious in the
sight of God.
5For in this way in former times the holy women also, who
hoped in God, used to adorn themselves, being submissive to their
own husbands.
6Thus Sarah obeyed Abraham, calling him lord, and you have
become her children if you do what is right without being frightened by any fear.
7¶ You husbands likewise, live with *your wives* in an understanding way, as with a weaker vessel, since she is a woman; and
grant her honor as a fellow heir of the grace of life, so that your
prayers may not be hindered.
8¶ To sum up, let all be harmonious, sympathetic, brotherly,
kindhearted, and humble in spirit;
9not returning evil for evil, or insult for insult, but giving a
blessing instead; for you were called for the very purpose that you
might inherit a blessing.
10For,

"LET HIM WHO MEANS TO LOVE LIFE AND SEE GOOD DAYS
REFRAIN HIS TONGUE FROM EVIL AND HIS LIPS FROM
SPEAKING GUILE.
11 "AND LET HIM TURN AWAY FROM EVIL AND DO GOOD;
LET HIM SEEK PEACE AND PURSUE IT.
12 "FOR THE EYES OF THE LORD ARE UPON THE RIGHTEOUS,
AND HIS EARS ATTEND TO THEIR PRAYER,
BUT THE FACE OF THE LORD IS AGAINST THOSE WHO DO
EVIL."

13¶ And who is there to harm you if you prove zealous for what
is good?
14But even if you should suffer for the sake of righteousness,
*you are* blessed. AND DO NOT FEAR THEIR INTIMIDATION, AND DO
NOT BE TROUBLED,
15but [j]sanctify Christ as Lord in your hearts, always *being* ready
to make a defense to everyone who asks you to give an account
for the hope that is in you, yet with gentleness and reverence;
16and keep a good conscience so that in the thing in which you
are slandered, those who revile your good behavior in Christ may
be put to shame.
17For it is better, if God should will it so, that you suffer for
doing what is right rather than for doing what is wrong.

NAS [j] I.e., set apart

## New International

the purity and reverence of your lives. 3Your beauty should not
come from outward adornment, such as braided hair and the
wearing of gold jewelry and fine clothes. 4Instead, it should be that
of your inner self, the unfading beauty of a gentle and quiet spirit,
which is of great worth in God's sight. 5For this is the way the holy
women of the past who put their hope in God used to make
themselves beautiful. They were submissive to their own husbands, 6like Sarah, who obeyed Abraham and called him her master. You are her daughters if you do what is right and do not give
way to fear.
7Husbands, in the same way be considerate as you live with
your wives, and treat them with respect as the weaker partner and
as heirs with you of the gracious gift of life, so that nothing will
hinder your prayers.

*Suffering for Doing Good*

8Finally, all of you, live in harmony with one another; be sympathetic, love as brothers, be compassionate and humble. 9Do not
repay evil with evil or insult with insult, but with blessing, because
to this you were called so that you may inherit a blessing. 10For,

"Whoever would love life
and see good days
must keep his tongue from evil
and his lips from deceitful speech.
11He must turn from evil and do good;
he must seek peace and pursue it.
12For the eyes of the Lord are on the righteous
and his ears are attentive to their prayer,
but the face of the Lord is against those who do evil."[k]

13Who is going to harm you if you are eager to do good? 14But
even if you should suffer for what is right, you are blessed. "Do
not fear what they fear[l]; do not be frightened."[m] 15But in your
hearts set apart Christ as Lord. Always be prepared to give an
answer to everyone who asks you to give the reason for the hope
that you have. But do this with gentleness and respect, 16keeping
a clear conscience, so that those who speak maliciously against
your good behavior in Christ may be ashamed of their slander. 17It
is better, if it is God's will, to suffer for doing good than for doing
evil. 18For Christ died for sins once for all, the righteous for the

NIV [k] *12* Psalm 34:12-16 [l] *14* Or *not fear their threats* [m] *14* Isaiah 8:12

## King James

18For Christ also hath once suffered for sins, the just for the
unjust, that he might bring us to God, being put to death in the
flesh, but quickened by the Spirit:
19By which also he went and preached unto the spirits in prison;
20Which sometime were disobedient, when once the longsuffering of God waited in the days of Noah, while the ark was
a-preparing, wherein few, that is, eight souls were saved by water.
21The like figure whereunto *even* baptism doth also now save us
(not the putting away of the filth of the flesh, but the answer of
a good conscience toward God,) by the resurrection of Jesus Christ:
22Who is gone into heaven, and is on the right hand of God;
angels and authorities and powers being made subject unto him.

4 FORASMUCH THEN as Christ hath suffered for us in the
flesh, arm yourselves likewise with the same mind: for he that
hath suffered in the flesh hath ceased from sin;
2That he no longer should live the rest of *his* time in the flesh
to the lusts of men, but to the will of God.
3For the time past of *our* life may suffice us to have wrought the
will of the Gentiles, when we walked in lasciviousness, lusts,
excess of wine, revellings, banquetings, and abominable idolatries:
4Wherein they think it strange that ye run not with *them* to the
same excess of riot, speaking evil of *you:*
5Who shall give account to him that is ready to judge the quick
and the dead.
6For for this cause was the gospel preached also to them that
are dead, that they might be judged according to men in the flesh,
but live according to God in the spirit.
7But the end of all things is at hand: be ye therefore sober, and
watch unto prayer.
8And above all things have fervent charity among yourselves:
for charity shall cover the multitude of sins.
9Use hospitality one to another without grudging.
10As every man hath received the gift, *even so* minister the same
one to another, as good stewards of the manifold grace of God.
11If any man speak, *let him speak* as the oracles of God; if any
man minister, *let him do it* as of the ability which God giveth: that
God in all things may be glorified through Jesus Christ, to whom
be praise and dominion for ever and ever. Amen.

## Amplified

18For Christ, the Messiah, [Himself] died for sins once [a]for all,
the Righteous for the unrighteous—the Just for the unjust, the
Innocent for the guilty—that He might bring us to God. In His
human body He was put to death but He was made alive in the
spirit,
19In which He went and preached to the spirits in prison,
20[The souls of those] who long before in the days of Noah had
been disobedient, when God's patience waited during the building
of the ark in which a few [people], actually eight in number, were
saved through water. [Gen. 6-8.]
21And baptism, which is a figure [of their deliverance], does
now also save you [from inward questionings and fears], not by
the removing of outward body filth (bathing), but by [providing
you with] the answer of a good and clear conscience [inward
cleanness and peace] before God, [because you are demonstrating
what you believe to be yours] through the resurrection of Jesus
Christ.
22[And He] has now entered into heaven and is at the right
hand of God, with [all] angels and authorities and powers made
subservient to Him.

4 SO, SINCE Christ suffered in the flesh [ [b]for us, for you], arm
yourselves with the same thought *and* [c]purpose [patiently to
suffer rather than fail to please God]. For whoever has suffered in
the flesh [having [d]the mind of Christ] has done with [intentional]
sin—has stopped pleasing himself and the world, and pleases
God.
2So that he can no longer spend the rest of his natural life living
by [his] human appetites *and* desires, but [he lives] for what God
wills.
3For the time that is past already suffices for doing what the
Gentiles like to do, living (as you have done) in shameless, insolent
wantonness, in lustful desires, drunkenness, reveling, drinking
bouts *and* abominable, lawless idolatries.
4They are astonished *and* think it very queer that you do not
now run hand in hand with them in the same excesses of dissipation, and they abuse [you].
5But they will have to give an account to Him Who is ready to
judge *and* pass sentence on the living and the dead.
6For this is why the good news (the Gospel) was preached [ [e]in
their lifetime] even to the dead, that though judged in fleshly
bodies as men are, they might live in the spirit as God does.
7But the end *and* culmination of all things has now come near;
keep sound-minded *and* self-restrained and alert therefore for [the
practice of] prayer.
8Above all things have intense *and* unfailing love for one another, for love covers a multitude of sins—forgives and
[f]disregards the offenses of others. [Prov. 10:12.]
9Practice hospitality to one another—that is, those of the household of faith. (Be hospitable, that is, be a lover of strangers, with
brotherly affection for the unknown guests, the foreigners, the
poor and all others who come your way who are of Christ's body.)
And [in each instance] do it ungrudgingly—cordially and graciously without complaining [but as representing Him].
10As each of you has received a gift (a particular spiritual talent,
a gracious divine endowment), employ it for one another as [befits]
good trustees of God's many-sided grace—faithful stewards of the
[g]extremely diverse [powers and gifts granted to Christians by]
unmerited favor.
11Whoever speaks, [let him do it as one who utters] oracles of
God; whoever renders service, [let him do it] as with the strength
which God furnishes [h]abundantly; so that in all things God may
be glorified through Jesus Christ, the Messiah. To Him be the glory
and dominion for ever and ever—through endless ages. Amen—
so be it.

**AMP** [a] Thayer. [b] Some ancient authorities read "for us," some "for you." [c] Abbott-Smith. [d] Cambridge Bible (—Gray and Adams). [e] Many commentators. [f] Thayer. [g] Thayer. [h] Thayer.

## New American Standard

18For Christ also died for sins once for all, *the* just for *the* unjust, in order that He might bring us to God, having been put to death in the flesh, but made alive in the spirit;

19in which also He went and made proclamation to the spirits *now* in prison,

20who once were disobedient, when the patience of God kept waiting in the days of Noah, during the construction of the ark, in which a few, that is, eight persons, were brought safely through *the* water.

21And corresponding to that, baptism now saves you—not the removal of dirt from the flesh, but an appeal to God for a good conscience—through the resurrection of Jesus Christ,

22who is at the right hand of God, having gone into heaven, after angels and authorities and powers had been subjected to Him.

*Keep Fervent in Your Love*

4 THEREFORE, SINCE Christ has [i]suffered in the flesh, arm yourselves also with the same purpose, because he who has suffered in the flesh has ceased from sin,

2so as to live the rest of the time in the flesh no longer for the lusts of men, but for the will of God.

3For the time already past is sufficient *for you* to have carried out the desire of the Gentiles, having pursued a course of sensuality, lusts, drunkenness, carousals, drinking parties and abominable idolatries.

4And in *all* this, they are surprised that you do not run with *them* into the same excess of dissipation, and they malign *you;*

5but they shall give account to Him who is ready to judge the living and the dead.

6For the gospel has for this purpose been preached even to those who are dead, that though they are judged in the flesh as men, they may live in the spirit according to *the will of* God.

7¶ The end of all things is at hand; therefore, be of sound judgment and sober *spirit* for the purpose of prayer.

8Above all, keep fervent in your love for one another, because love covers a multitude of sins.

9Be hospitable to one another without complaint.

10As each one has received a *special* gift, employ it in serving one another, as good stewards of the manifold grace of God.

11Whoever speaks, *let him speak,* as it were, the utterances of God; whoever serves, *let him do so* as by the strength which God supplies; so that in all things God may be glorified through Jesus Christ, to whom belongs the glory and dominion forever and ever. Amen.

NAS [i] I.e., suffered death

## New International

unrighteous, to bring you to God. He was put to death in the body
but made alive by the Spirit, 19through whom[j] also he went and
preached to the spirits in prison 20who disobeyed long ago when
God waited patiently in the days of Noah while the ark was being
built. In it only a few people, eight in all, were saved through
water, 21and this water symbolizes baptism that now saves you
also—not the removal of dirt from the body but the pledge[k] of a
good conscience toward God. It saves you by the resurrection of
Jesus Christ, 22who has gone into heaven and is at God's right
hand—with angels, authorities and powers in submission to him.

*Living for God*

4 THEREFORE, SINCE Christ suffered in his body, arm yourselves also with the same attitude, because he who has suffered in his body is done with sin. 2As a result, he does not live
the rest of his earthly life for evil human desires, but rather for the
will of God. 3For you have spent enough time in the past doing
what pagans choose to do—living in debauchery, lust, drunkenness, orgies, carousing and detestable idolatry. 4They think it
strange that you do not plunge with them into the same flood of
dissipation, and they heap abuse on you. 5But they will have to
give account to him who is ready to judge the living and the dead.
6For this is the reason the gospel was preached even to those who
are now dead, so that they might be judged according to men in
regard to the body, but live according to God in regard to the spirit.
7The end of all things is near. Therefore be clear minded and
self-controlled so that you can pray. 8Above all, love each other
deeply, because love covers over a multitude of sins. 9Offer hospitality to one another without grumbling. 10Each one should use
whatever gift he has received to serve others, faithfully administering God's grace in its various forms. 11If anyone speaks, he should
do it as one speaking the very words of God. If anyone serves, he
should do it with the strength God provides, so that in all things
God may be praised through Jesus Christ. To him be the glory and
the power for ever and ever. Amen.

NIV [j] 18,19 Or *alive in the spirit, 19through which* [k] 21 Or *response*

## King James

12Beloved, think it not strange concerning the fiery trial which is to try you, as though some strange thing happened unto you:

13But rejoice, inasmuch as ye are partakers of Christ's sufferings; that, when his glory shall be revealed, ye may be glad also with exceeding joy.

14If ye be reproached for the name of Christ, happy *are ye;* for the spirit of glory and of God resteth upon you: on their part he is evil spoken of, but on your part he is glorified.

15But let none of you suffer as a murderer, or *as* a thief, or *as* an evildoer, or as a busybody in other men's matters.

16Yet if *any man suffer* as a Christian, let him not be ashamed; but let him glorify God on this behalf.

17For the time *is come* that judgment must begin at the house of God: and if *it* first *begin* at us, what shall the end *be* of them that obey not the gospel of God?

18And if the righteous scarcely be saved, where shall the ungodly and the sinner appear?

19Wherefore let them that suffer according to the will of God commit the keeping of their souls *to him* in well doing, as unto a faithful Creator.

**5** THE ELDERS which are among you I exhort, who am also an elder, and a witness of the sufferings of Christ, and also a partaker of the glory that shall be revealed:

2Feed the flock of God which is among you, taking the oversight *thereof,* not by constraint, but willingly; not for filthy lucre, but of a ready mind;

3Neither as being lords over *God's* heritage, but being examples to the flock.

4And when the chief Shepherd shall appear, ye shall receive a crown of glory that fadeth not away.

5Likewise, ye younger, submit yourselves unto the elder. Yea, all *of you* be subject one to another, and be clothed with humility: for God resisteth the proud, and giveth grace to the humble.

6Humble yourselves therefore under the mighty hand of God, that he may exalt you in due time:

7Casting all your care upon him; for he careth for you.

8Be sober, be vigilant; because your adversary the devil, as a roaring lion, walketh about, seeking whom he may devour:

## Amplified

12Beloved, do not be amazed *and* bewildered at the fiery ordeal which is taking place to test your quality, as though something strange—unusual and alien to you and your position—were befalling you.

13But in so far as you are sharing Christ's sufferings, rejoice, so that when His glory (full of radiance and splendor) is revealed you may also rejoice with triumph—exultantly.

14If you are censured *and* suffer abuse [because you bear] the name of Christ, blessed [are you]—happy, fortunate, [a]to be envied, [b]with life-joy and satisfaction in God's favor and salvation, regardless of your outward condition—because the Spirit of glory, the Spirit of God, is resting upon you. *On their part He is blasphemed, but on your part He is glorified.* [Isa. 11:2.]

15But let none of you suffer as a murderer, or a thief, or any sort of criminal; or as a mischief-maker (a meddler) in the affairs of others—infringing on their rights.

16But if [one is ill-treated and suffers] as a Christian [which he is contemptuously called], let him not be ashamed, but give glory to God that he is [deemed worthy] to suffer in this name.

17For the time [has arrived] for judgment to begin with the household of God; and if it begins with us, what will [be] the end of those who do not respect *or* believe *or* obey the good news (the Gospel) of God?

18And if the righteous are barely saved, what will become of the godless and wicked? [Prov. 11:31.]

19Therefore, those who are ill-treated *and* suffer in accordance with God's will must do right, and commit their souls (in charge as a deposit) to the One Who created them *and* will never fail [them].

**5** I WARN *and* counsel the elders among you—the pastors and spiritual guides of the church—as a fellow elder and as an eyewitness [called to testify] of the sufferings of Christ, as well as a sharer in the glory (the honor and splendor) that is to be revealed (disclosed, unfolded):

2Tend—nurture, guard, guide and fold—the flock of God that is [your responsibility], not by coercion *or* constraint but willingly; not dishonorably motivated by the advantages *and* profits [belonging to the office] but eagerly *and* cheerfully.

3Not (as arrogant, dictatorial and overbearing persons) domineering over those in your charge, but being examples—patterns and models of Christian living—to the flock (the congregation).

4And [then] when the Chief Shepherd is revealed you will win the [c]conqueror's crown of glory.

5Likewise you that are younger *and* of lesser rank be subject to the elders—the ministers and spiritual guides of the church, giving them due respect and yielding to their counsel. Clothe (apron) yourselves, all of you, with humility—as the garb of a servant, [d]so that its covering cannot possibly be stripped from you, with freedom from pride and arrogance—toward one another. For God sets Himself against the proud—the insolent, the overbearing, the disdainful, the presumptuous, the boastful, and opposes, frustrates and defeats them—but gives grace (favor, blessing) to the humble. [Prov. 3:34.]

6Therefore humble yourselves (demote, lower yourselves in your own estimation) under the mighty hand of God, that in due time He may exalt you.

7Casting the [e]whole of your care—all your anxieties, all your worries, all your concerns, [f]once and for all—on Him; for He cares for you affectionately, *and* cares about you [g]watchfully. [Ps. 55:22.]

8Be well-balanced—temperate, sober-minded; be vigilant *and* cautious at all times, for that enemy of yours, the devil, roams around like a lion roaring [ [h]in fierce hunger], seeking someone to seize upon *and* devour.

**AMP** [a] Souter. [b] Cremer. [c] Vincent: "In Paul . . . always the *conqueror's* crown." [d] Bengel. [e] Vincent. [f] Vincent. [g] Vincent. [h] Vincent.

## New American Standard

*Share the Sufferings of Christ*

12 ¶ Beloved, do not be surprised at the fiery ordeal among you, which comes upon you for your testing, as though some strange thing were happening to you;

13 but to the degree that you share the sufferings of Christ, keep on rejoicing; so that also at the revelation of His glory, you may rejoice with exultation.

14 If you are reviled for the name of Christ, you are blessed, because the Spirit of glory and of God rests upon you.

15 By no means let any of you suffer as a murderer, or thief, or evildoer, or a troublesome meddler;

16 but if *anyone suffers* as a Christian, let him not feel ashamed, but in that name let him glorify God.

17 For *it is* time for judgment to begin with the household of God; and if *it begins* with us first, what *will be* the outcome for those who do not obey the gospel of God?

18 AND IF IT IS WITH DIFFICULTY THAT THE RIGHTEOUS IS SAVED, WHAT WILL BECOME OF THE GODLESS MAN AND THE SINNER?

19 Therefore, let those also who suffer according to the will of God entrust their souls to a faithful Creator in doing what is right.

## New International

*Suffering for Being a Christian*

12 Dear friends, do not be surprised at the painful trial you are
suffering, as though something strange were happening to you.
13 But rejoice that you participate in the sufferings of Christ, so that
you may be overjoyed when his glory is revealed. 14 If you are
insulted because of the name of Christ, you are blessed, for the
Spirit of glory and of God rests on you. 15 If you suffer, it should
not be as a murderer or thief or any other kind of criminal, or even
as a meddler. 16 However, if you suffer as a Christian, do not be
ashamed, but praise God that you bear that name. 17 For it is time
for judgment to begin with the family of God; and if it begins with
us, what will the outcome be for those who do not obey the gospel
of God? 18 And,

"If it is hard for the righteous to be saved,
what will become of the ungodly and the sinner?"[i]

19 So then, those who suffer according to God's will should commit themselves to their faithful Creator and continue to do good.

## New American Standard

*Serve God Willingly*

5 THEREFORE, I exhort the elders among you, as *your* fellow elder and witness of the sufferings of Christ, and a partaker also of the glory that is to be revealed,

2 shepherd the flock of God among you, exercising oversight not under compulsion, but voluntarily, according to *the will of* God; and not for sordid gain, but with eagerness;

3 nor yet as lording it over those allotted to your charge, but proving to be examples to the flock.

4 And when the Chief Shepherd appears, you will receive the unfading crown of glory.

5 You younger men, likewise, be subject to your elders; and all of you, clothe yourselves with humility toward one another, for GOD IS OPPOSED TO THE PROUD, BUT GIVES GRACE TO THE HUMBLE.

6 ¶ Humble yourselves, therefore, under the mighty hand of God, that He may exalt you at the proper time,

7 casting all your anxiety upon Him, because He cares for you.

8 Be of sober *spirit*, be on the alert. Your adversary, the devil, prowls about like a roaring lion, seeking someone to devour.

## New International

*To Elders and Young Men*

5 TO THE elders among you, I appeal as a fellow elder, a
witness of Christ's sufferings and one who also will share in
the glory to be revealed: 2 Be shepherds of God's flock that is under
your care, serving as overseers—not because you must, but because you are willing, as God wants you to be; not greedy for
money, but eager to serve; 3 not lording it over those entrusted to
you, but being examples to the flock. 4 And when the Chief Shepherd appears, you will receive the crown of glory that will never
fade away.

5 Young men, in the same way be submissive to those who are older. All of you, clothe yourselves with humility toward one another, because,

"God opposes the proud
but gives grace to the humble."[j]

6 Humble yourselves, therefore, under God's mighty hand, that he
may lift you up in due time. 7 Cast all your anxiety on him because
he cares for you.

8 Be self-controlled and alert. Your enemy the devil prowls
around like a roaring lion looking for someone to devour. 9 Resist

NIV [i] *18* Prov. 11:31 [j] *5* Prov. 3:34

## King James

9Whom resist stedfast in the faith, knowing that the same afflictions are accomplished in your brethren that are in the world.
10But the God of all grace, who hath called us unto his eternal
glory by Christ Jesus, after that ye have suffered a while, make you
perfect, stablish, strengthen, settle *you.*
11To him *be* glory and dominion for ever and ever. Amen.
12By Silvanus, a faithful brother unto you, as I suppose, I have
written briefly, exhorting, and testifying that this is the true grace
of God wherein ye stand.
13The *church that is* at Babylon, elected together with *you,* saluteth you; and *so doth* Marcus my son.
14Greet ye one another with a kiss of charity. Peace *be* with you
all that are in Christ Jesus. Amen.

## Amplified

9Withstand him; be firm in faith [against his onset],—rooted, established, strong, immovable and determined—knowing that the same ( [a]identical) sufferings are appointed to your brotherhood (the whole body of Christians) throughout the world.
10And after you have suffered a little while, the God of all grace—Who imparts all blessing and favor—Who has called you to His [own] eternal glory in Christ *Jesus,* will Himself complete *and* make you what you ought to be, establish *and* ground you securely, *and* strengthen (and [b]settle) you.
11To Him be the dominion—power, authority, rule—forever and ever. Amen—so be it.
12By Silvanus, a true (loyal, consistent, incorruptible) brother, as I consider him, I have written briefly to you, to counsel *and* urge *and* stimulate [you] and to declare [to you] that this is the true [account of the] grace (the undeserved favor) of God. Be steadfast *and* persevere in it.
13She [your sister-church(?) here] in Babylon, [who is] elect (chosen) with [yourselves], sends you greetings, and [so does] my son (disciple) Mark.
14Salute one another with a kiss of love—the symbol of mutual affection. To all of you that are in Christ *Jesus,* the Messiah, may there be peace— [c]every kind of peace (blessing), especially peace with God, and [d]freedom from fears, agitating passions and moral conflicts. *Amen—so be it.*

**AMP** [a] Vincent. [b] Many ancient authorities so read. [c] Thayer. [d] Webster, in definition of "peace" in this sense.

## New American Standard

9But resist him, firm in *your* faith, knowing that the same experiences of suffering are being accomplished by your brethren who are in the world.

10And after you have suffered for a little while, the God of all grace, who called you to His eternal glory in Christ, will Himself perfect, confirm, strengthen *and* establish you.

11To Him *be* dominion forever and ever. Amen.

12¶ Through Silvanus, our faithful brother (for so I regard *him*), I have written to you briefly, exhorting and testifying that this is the true grace of God. Stand firm in it!

13 [e]She who is in Babylon, chosen together with you, sends you greetings, and *so does* my son, Mark.

14Greet one another with a kiss of love.

¶Peace be to you all who are in Christ.

NAS [e] Some mss. read *The church which*

## New International

him, standing firm in the faith, because you know that your brothers throughout the world are undergoing the same kind of sufferings.

10And the God of all grace, who called you to his eternal glory in Christ, after you have suffered a little while, will himself restore you and make you strong, firm and steadfast. 11To him be the power for ever and ever. Amen.

*Final Greetings*

12With the help of Silas,[f] whom I regard as a faithful brother, I have written to you briefly, encouraging you and testifying that this is the true grace of God. Stand fast in it.

13She who is in Babylon, chosen together with you, sends you her greetings, and so does my son Mark. 14Greet one another with a kiss of love.

Peace to all of you who are in Christ.

NIV [f] 12 Greek *Silvanus,* a variant of *Silas*

## King James

THE SECOND

EPISTLE GENERAL OF

# Peter

1 SIMON PETER, a servant and an apostle of Jesus Christ, to
them that have obtained like precious faith with us through
the righteousness of God and our Saviour Jesus Christ:
2Grace and peace be multiplied unto you through the knowledge of God, and of Jesus our Lord,
3According as his divine power hath given unto us all things
that *pertain* unto life and godliness, through the knowledge of him
that hath called us to glory and virtue:
4Whereby are given unto us exceeding great and precious
promises: that by these ye might be partakers of the divine nature,
having escaped the corruption that is in the world through lust.
5And beside this, giving all diligence, add to your faith virtue;
and to virtue knowledge;
6And to knowledge temperance; and to temperance patience;
and to patience godliness;
7And to godliness brotherly kindness; and to brotherly kindness charity.
8For if these things be in you, and abound, they make *you that
ye shall* neither *be* barren nor unfruitful in the knowledge of our
Lord Jesus Christ.
9But he that lacketh these things is blind, and cannot see afar
off, and hath forgotten that he was purged from his old sins.
10Wherefore the rather, brethren, give diligence to make your
calling and election sure: for if ye do these things, ye shall never
fall:
11For so an entrance shall be ministered unto you abundantly
into the everlasting kingdom of our Lord and Saviour Jesus Christ.
12Wherefore I will not be negligent to put you always in remembrance of these things, though ye know *them,* and be established
in the present truth.
13Yea, I think it meet, as long as I am in this tabernacle, to stir
you up by putting *you* in remembrance;
14Knowing that shortly I must put off *this* my tabernacle, even
as our Lord Jesus Christ hath shown me.
15Moreover I will endeavour that ye may be able after my decease to have these things always in remembrance.

## Amplified

THE SECOND LETTER OF

# Peter

1 SIMON PETER, a servant and apostle (special messenger) of
Jesus Christ, to those who have received (obtained an equal
privilege of) like precious faith with ourselves in *and* through the
righteousness of our God and Savior Jesus Christ:
2May grace (God's favor) and peace, (which is [a]perfect well-
being, all necessary good, all spiritual prosperity and [b]freedom
from fears and agitating passions and moral conflicts) be multiplied to you in (the full, personal, [c]precise and correct) knowledge
of God and of Jesus our Lord.
3For His divine power has bestowed upon us all things that [are
requisite and suited] to life and godliness, through the ([d]full,
personal) knowledge of Him Who called us by *and* to His own glory
and excellence (virtue).
4By means of these He has bestowed on us His precious and
exceedingly great promises, so that through them you may escape
(by flight) from the moral decay (rottenness and corruption) that
is in the world because of covetousness (lust and greed), and
become sharers (partakers) of the divine nature.
5For this very reason, [e]adding your diligence [to the divine
promises], employ every effort in [f]exercising your faith to develop
virtue (excellence, resolution, Christian energy); and in [exercis-
ing] virtue [develop] knowledge (intelligence),
6And in [exercising] knowledge [develop] self-control; and in
[exercising] self-control [develop] steadfastness (patience, endurance), and in [exercising] steadfastness [develop] godliness
(piety),
7And in [exercising] godliness [develop] brotherly affection,
and in [exercising] brotherly affection [develop] Christian love.
8For as these qualities are yours and increasingly abound in
you, they will keep [you] from being idle or unfruitful unto the
([g]full personal) knowledge of our Lord Jesus Christ, the Messiah,
the Anointed One.
9For whoever lacks these qualities is blind, [[h]spiritually] short-
sighted, [i]seeing only what is near to him; and has become oblivious [of the fact] that he was cleansed from his old sins.
10Because of this, brethren, be all the more solicitous *and* eager
to make sure (to ratify, to strengthen, to make steadfast) your
calling and election; for if you do this you will never stumble *or* fall.
11Thus there will be richly *and* abundantly provided for you
entry into the eternal kingdom of our Lord and Savior Jesus Christ.
12So I intend always to remind you about these things, although
indeed you know them and are firm in the truth that [you] now
[hold].
13I think it right, as long as I am in this tabernacle (tent, body),
to stir you up by way of remembrance;
14Since I know that the laying aside of this body of mine will
come speedily, as our Lord Jesus Christ made clear to me.
15Moreover, I will diligently endeavor [to see to it] that [even]
after my departure (decease) you may be able at all times to call
these things to mind.

**AMP** [a] Matthew Henry. [b] Webster, defining "peace" in this sense. [c] Thayer. [d] Vincent. [e] Vincent. [f] Vincent. [g] Vincent. [h] Vincent. [i] Rotherham's "Emphasized Bible."

## New American Standard

# 2 Peter

*Growth in Christian Virtue*

**1** [j]SIMON PETER, a bond-servant and apostle of Jesus Christ,
to those who have received a faith of the same kind as ours,
by the righteousness of our God and Savior, Jesus Christ:
2Grace and peace be multiplied to you in the knowledge of God
and of Jesus our Lord;
3seeing that His divine power has granted to us everything
pertaining to life and godliness, through the true knowledge of
Him who called us by His own glory and excellence.
4For by these He has granted to us His precious and magnificent promises, in order that by them you might become partakers
of *the* divine nature, having escaped the corruption that is in the
world by lust.
5Now for this very reason also, applying all diligence, in your
faith supply moral excellence, and in *your* moral excellence, knowledge;
6and in *your* knowledge, self-control, and in *your* self-control,
perseverance, and in *your* perseverance, godliness;
7and in *your* godliness, brotherly kindness, and in *your* brotherly kindness, love.
8For if these *qualities* are yours and are increasing, they render
you neither useless nor unfruitful in the true knowledge of our
Lord Jesus Christ.
9For he who lacks these *qualities* is blind *or* short-sighted, having forgotten *his* purification from his former sins.
10Therefore, brethren, be all the more diligent to make certain
about His calling and choosing you; for as long as you practice
these things, you will never stumble;
11for in this way the entrance into the eternal kingdom of our
Lord and Savior Jesus Christ will be abundantly supplied to you.
12¶ Therefore, I shall always be ready to remind you of these
things, even though you *already* know *them*, and have been established in the truth which is present with *you*.
13And I consider it right, as long as I am in this *earthly* dwelling,
to stir you up by way of reminder,
14knowing that the laying aside of my *earthly* dwelling is imminent, as also our Lord Jesus Christ has made clear to me.
15And I will also be diligent that at any time after my departure
you may be able to call these things to mind.

NAS [j] Most early mss. read *Simeon*

## New International

# 2 Peter

**1** SIMON PETER, a servant and apostle of Jesus Christ,
To those who through the righteousness of our God and
Savior Jesus Christ have received a faith as precious as ours:
2Grace and peace be yours in abundance through the knowledge of God and of Jesus our Lord.

*Making One's Calling and Election Sure*

3His divine power has given us everything we need for life and
godliness through our knowledge of him who called us by his own
glory and goodness. 4Through these he has given us his very great
and precious promises, so that through them you may participate
in the divine nature and escape the corruption in the world caused
by evil desires.
5For this very reason, make every effort to add to your faith
goodness; and to goodness, knowledge; 6and to knowledge, self-
control; and to self-control, perseverance; and to perseverance,
godliness; 7and to godliness, brotherly kindness; and to brotherly
kindness, love. 8For if you possess these qualities in increasing
measure, they will keep you from being ineffective and unproductive in your knowledge of our Lord Jesus Christ. 9But if anyone
does not have them, he is nearsighted and blind, and has forgotten
that he has been cleansed from his past sins.
10Therefore, my brothers, be all the more eager to make your
calling and election sure. For if you do these things, you will never
fall, 11and you will receive a rich welcome into the eternal kingdom
of our Lord and Savior Jesus Christ.

*Prophecy of Scripture*

12So I will always remind you of these things, even though you
know them and are firmly established in the truth you now have.
13I think it is right to refresh your memory as long as I live in the
tent of this body, 14because I know that I will soon put it aside, as
our Lord Jesus Christ has made clear to me. 15And I will make
every effort to see that after my departure you will always be able
to remember these things.

## King James

16For we have not followed cunningly devised fables, when we made known unto you the power and coming of our Lord Jesus Christ, but were eyewitnesses of his majesty.

17For he received from God the Father honour and glory, when there came such a voice to him from the excellent glory, This is my beloved Son, in whom I am well pleased.

18And this voice which came from heaven we heard, when we were with him in the holy mount.

19We have also a more sure word of prophecy; whereunto ye do well that ye take heed, as unto a light that shineth in a dark place, until the day dawn, and the day star arise in your hearts:

20Knowing this first, that no prophecy of the scripture is of any private interpretation.

21For the prophecy came not in old time by the will of man: but holy men of God spake *as they were* moved by the Holy Ghost.

**2** BUT THERE were false prophets also among the people, even as there shall be false teachers among you, who privily shall bring in damnable heresies, even denying the Lord that bought them, and bring upon themselves swift destruction.

2And many shall follow their pernicious ways; by reason of whom the way of truth shall be evil spoken of.

3And through covetousness shall they with feigned words make merchandise of you: whose judgment now of a long time lingereth not, and their damnation slumbereth not.

4For if God spared not the angels that sinned, but cast *them* down to hell, and delivered *them* into chains of darkness, to be reserved unto judgment;

5And spared not the old world, but saved Noah the eighth *person,* a preacher of righteousness, bringing in the flood upon the world of the ungodly;

6And turning the cities of Sodom and Gomorrha into ashes condemned *them* with an overthrow, making *them* an example unto those that after should live ungodly;

7And delivered just Lot, vexed with the filthy conversation of the wicked:

8(For that righteous man dwelling among them, in seeing and hearing, vexed *his* righteous soul from day to day with *their* unlawful deeds;)

9The Lord knoweth how to deliver the godly out of temptations, and to reserve the unjust unto the day of judgment to be punished:

10But chiefly them that walk after the flesh in the lust of uncleanness, and despise government. Presumptuous *are they,* self-willed, they are not afraid to speak evil of dignities.

11Whereas angels, which are greater in power and might, bring not railing accusation against them before the Lord.

12But these, as natural brute beasts, made to be taken and destroyed, speak evil of the things that they understand not; and shall utterly perish in their own corruption;

## Amplified

16For we were not following out cleverly devised stories when we made known to you the power and coming of our Lord Jesus Christ, the Messiah, but we were eyewitnesses of His majesty—grandeur, authority of sovereign power.

17For when He was invested with honor and glory from God the Father and a voice was borne to Him by the (splendid) Majestic Glory [in the bright cloud that overshadowed Him, saying], This is My beloved Son in Whom I am well pleased *and* delight,

18We [actually] heard this voice borne out of heaven, for we were together with Him on the holy mountain.

19And we have the prophetic word [made] firmer still. You will do well to pay close attention to it as to a lamp shining in a dismal (squalid and dark) place, until the day breaks through [the gloom] and the Morning Star rises ( [a]comes into being) in your hearts.

20[Yet] first [you must] understand this, that no prophecy of Scripture is [a matter] of any personal *or* private *or* special interpretation (loosening, solving).

21For no prophecy ever originated because some man willed it [to do so]—it never came by human impulse—but as men spoke from God who were borne along (moved and impelled) by the Holy Spirit.

**2** BUT ALSO [in those days] there arose false prophets among the people, just as there will be false teachers among yourselves, who will subtly *and* stealthily introduce heretical doctrines—destructive heresies—even denying *and* disowning the Master Who bought them, bringing upon themselves swift destruction.

2And many will follow their immoral ways *and* lascivious doings; because of them the true Way will be maligned *and* defamed.

3And in their covetousness (lust, greed) they will exploit you with (cunning) false arguments. From of old the sentence [of condemnation] for them has not been idle; their destruction (eternal misery) has not been asleep.

4For God [even] spared not angels that sinned, but cast them into hell, delivering them to be kept there in pits of gloom till the judgment *and* their doom.

5And He spared not the ancient world, but preserved Noah, a preacher of righteousness, with seven other persons, when He brought a flood upon the world of ungodly [people]. [Gen. 8:18; 6-8.]

6And He condemned to ruin *and* extinction the cities of Sodom and Gomorrah, reducing them to ashes [and thus] set them forth as an example to those who would be ungodly. [Gen. 19:24.]

7And He rescued righteous Lot, greatly worn out *and* distressed by the wanton ways of the ungodly *and* lawless. [Gen. 19:16, 29.]

8For that just man, living [there] among them, tortured his righteous soul every day with what he saw and heard of [their] unlawful and wicked deeds.

9Now if [all these things be true, then be sure] the Lord knows how to rescue the godly out of temptations *and* trials, and how to keep the ungodly under chastisement until the day of judgment *and* doom;

10And particularly those who walk after the flesh and indulge in the lust of polluting passion, and scorn *and* despise authority. Presumptuous *and* daring—self-willed *and* self-loving [creatures]! They scoff at *and* revile dignitaries (glorious ones) without trembling,

11Whereas [even] angels, though superior in might and power, do not bring a defaming charge against them before the Lord.

12But these [people]! Like unreasoning beasts, mere creatures of instinct, born [only] to be captured and destroyed, railing at things of which they are ignorant, they shall utterly perish in their [own] corruption—in their destroying they shall surely be destroyed,

**AMP** [a] Abbott-Smith.

## New American Standard

*Eyewitnesses*

16For we did not follow cleverly devised tales when we made known to you the power and coming of our Lord Jesus Christ, but we were eyewitnesses of His majesty.

17For when He received honor and glory from God the Father, such an utterance as this was made to Him by the Majestic Glory, "This is My beloved Son with whom I am well-pleased"—

18and we ourselves heard this utterance made from heaven when we were with Him on the holy mountain.

19And *so* we have the prophetic word *made* more sure, to which you do well to pay attention as to a lamp shining in a dark place, until the day dawns and the morning star arises in your hearts.

20But know this first of all, that no prophecy of Scripture is *a matter* of one's own interpretation,

21for no prophecy was ever made by an act of human will, but men moved by the Holy Spirit spoke from God.

*The Rise of False Prophets*

**2** BUT FALSE prophets also arose among the people, just as there will also be false teachers among you, who will secretly introduce destructive heresies, even denying the Master who bought them, bringing swift destruction upon themselves.

2And many will follow their sensuality, and because of them the way of the truth will be maligned;

3and in *their* greed they will exploit you with false words; their judgment from long ago is not idle, and their destruction is not asleep.

4For if God did not spare angels when they sinned, but cast them into hell and committed them to pits of darkness, reserved for judgment;

5and did not spare the ancient world, but preserved Noah, a preacher of righteousness, with seven others, when He brought a flood upon the world of the ungodly;

6and *if* He condemned the cities of Sodom and Gomorrah to destruction by reducing *them* to ashes, having made them an example to those who would live ungodly thereafter;

7and *if* He rescued righteous Lot, oppressed by the sensual conduct of unprincipled men

8(for by what he saw and heard *that* righteous man, while living among them, felt *his* righteous soul tormented day after day with *their* lawless deeds),

9 *then* the Lord knows how to rescue the godly from temptation, and to keep the unrighteous under punishment for the day of judgment,

10and especially those who indulge the flesh in *its* corrupt desires and despise authority. Daring, self-willed, they do not tremble when they revile angelic majesties,

11whereas angels who are greater in might and power do not bring a reviling judgment against them before the Lord.

12But these, like unreasoning animals, born as creatures of instinct to be captured and killed, reviling where they have no knowledge, will in the destruction of those creatures also be destroyed,

## New International

16We did not follow cleverly invented stories when we told you
about the power and coming of our Lord Jesus Christ, but we were
eyewitnesses of his majesty. 17For he received honor and glory
from God the Father when the voice came to him from the Majestic
Glory, saying, "This is my Son, whom I love; with him I am well
pleased."[b] 18We ourselves heard this voice that came from heaven
when we were with him on the sacred mountain.
19And we have the word of the prophets made more certain,
and you will do well to pay attention to it, as to a light shining in
a dark place, until the day dawns and the morning star rises in
your hearts. 20Above all, you must understand that no prophecy
of Scripture came about by the prophet's own interpretation. 21For
prophecy never had its origin in the will of man, but men spoke
from God as they were carried along by the Holy Spirit.

*False Teachers and Their Destruction*

**2** BUT THERE were also false prophets among the people, just
as there will be false teachers among you. They will secretly
introduce destructive heresies, even denying the sovereign Lord
who bought them—bringing swift destruction on themselves.
2Many will follow their shameful ways and will bring the way of
truth into disrepute. 3In their greed these teachers will exploit you
with stories they have made up. Their condemnation has long
been hanging over them, and their destruction has not been sleeping.
4For if God did not spare angels when they sinned, but sent
them to hell,[c] putting them into gloomy dungeons[d] to be held for
judgment; 5if he did not spare the ancient world when he brought
the flood on its ungodly people, but protected Noah, a preacher
of righteousness, and seven others; 6if he condemned the cities of
Sodom and Gomorrah by burning them to ashes, and made them
an example of what is going to happen to the ungodly; 7and if he
rescued Lot, a righteous man, who was distressed by the filthy
lives of lawless men 8(for that righteous man, living among them
day after day, was tormented in his righteous soul by the lawless
deeds he saw and heard)— 9if this is so, then the Lord knows how
to rescue godly men from trials and to hold the unrighteous for the
day of judgment, while continuing their punishment.[e] 10This is
especially true of those who follow the corrupt desire of the sinful
nature[f] and despise authority.
Bold and arrogant, these men are not afraid to slander celestial
beings; 11yet even angels, although they are stronger and more
powerful, do not bring slanderous accusations against such beings
in the presence of the Lord. 12But these men blaspheme in matters
they do not understand. They are like brute beasts, creatures of
instinct, born only to be caught and destroyed, and like beasts they
too will perish.

NIV [b] 17 Matt. 17:5; Mark 9:7; Luke 9:35 [c] 4 Greek *Tartarus* [d] 4 Some manuscripts *into chains of darkness* [e] 9 Or *unrighteous for punishment until the day of judgment* [f] 10 Or *the flesh*

# King James

13And shall receive the reward of unrighteousness, *as* they that count it pleasure to riot in the day time. Spots *they are* and blemishes, sporting themselves with their own deceivings while they feast with you;

14Having eyes full of adultery, and that cannot cease from sin; beguiling unstable souls: an heart they have exercised with covetous practices; cursed children:

15Which have forsaken the right way, and are gone astray, following the way of Balaam *the son* of Bosor, who loved the wages of unrighteousness;

16But was rebuked for his iniquity: the dumb ass speaking with man's voice forbad the madness of the prophet.

17These are wells without water, clouds that are carried with a tempest; to whom the mist of darkness is reserved for ever.

18For when they speak great swelling *words* of vanity, they allure through the lusts of the flesh, *through much* wantonness, those that were clean escaped from them who live in error.

19While they promise them liberty, they themselves are the servants of corruption: for of whom a man is overcome, of the same is he brought in bondage.

20For if after they have escaped the pollutions of the world through the knowledge of the Lord and Saviour Jesus Christ, they are again entangled therein, and overcome, the latter end is worse with them than the beginning.

21For it had been better for them not to have known the way of rightousness, than, after they have known *it,* to turn from the holy commandment delivered unto them.

22But it is happened unto them according to the true proverb, The dog *is* turned to his own vomit again; and the sow that was washed to her wallowing in the mire.

**3** THIS SECOND epistle, beloved, I now write unto you; in *both* which I stir up your pure minds by way of remembrance:

2That ye may be mindful of the words which were spoken before by the holy prophets, and of the commandment of us the apostles of the Lord and Saviour:

3Knowing this first, that there shall come in the last days scoffers, walking after their own lusts,

4And saying, Where is the promise of his coming? for since the fathers fell asleep, all things continue as *they were* from the beginning of the creation.

5For this they willingly are ignorant of, that by the word of God the heavens were of old, and the earth standing out of the water and in the water:

6Whereby the world that then was, being overflowed with water, perished:

7But the heavens and the earth, which are now, by the same word are kept in store, reserved unto fire against the day of judgment and perdition of ungodly men.

8But, beloved, be not ignorant of this one thing, that one day *is* with the Lord as a thousand years, and a thousand years as one day.

9The Lord is not slack concerning his promise, as some men count slackness; but is longsuffering to us-ward, not willing that any should perish, but that all should come to repentance.

# Amplified

13Being destined to receive [punishment as] the reward of [their] unrighteousness—suffering wrong as the hire for [their] wrongdoing. They count it a delight to revel in the daytime—living luxuriously and delicately. They are blots and blemishes, revelling in their [a]deceptions (at love feasts) *and* carousing together [even] as they feast with you.

14They have eyes full of harlotry, insatiable for sin. They beguile *and* bait *and* lure away unstable souls. Their hearts are trained in covetousness—lust, greed. [They are [b]exposed to cursing,] children of a curse!

15Forsaking the straight road they have gone astray; they have followed the way of Balaam, [the son] of Beor, who loved the reward of wickedness. [Num. 22:5, 7.]

16But he was rebuked for his own transgression when a dumb beast of burden spoke with human voice and checked the prophet's madness. [Num. 22:21-31.]

17These are springs without water and mists driven along before a tempest, for whom is reserved *forever* the gloom of darkness.

18For uttering loud boasts of folly, they beguile *and* lure with lustful desires of the flesh those who are barely escaping from them who are wrongdoers.

19They promise them liberty, when they themselves are the slaves of depravity *and* defilement, for by whatever anyone is made inferior *or* overcome *or* worsted, to that [person or thing] he is enslaved.

20For if, after they have escaped the pollutions of the world through (the full, personal) knowledge of our Lord and Savior Jesus Christ, they again become entangled in them and are overcome, their last condition is worse [for them] than the first.

21For never to have obtained a (full, personal) knowledge of the Way of righteousness would have been better for them than, having obtained [such knowledge], to turn back from the holy commandment which was (verbally) delivered to them.

22There has befallen them the thing spoken of in the true proverb, The dog turns back to his own vomit, and the sow is washed only to wallow again in the mire. [Prov. 26:11.]

**3** BELOVED, I am now writing you this second letter. In [both of] them I have stirred up your unsullied (sincere) mind by way of remembrance;

2That you should recall the predictions of the holy (consecrated, dedicated) prophets and the commandment of the Lord and Savior [given] through your apostles, [His] special messengers.

3To begin with, you must know *and* understand this, that scoffers (mockers) will come in the last days with scoffing; [people who] walk after their own fleshly desires

4And saying, Where is the promise of His coming? For since the forefathers fell asleep, all things have continued exactly as they did from beginning of creation.

5For they wilfully overlook *and* forget this [fact], that heavens [came into] existence long ago by the word of God, and an earth also which was formed out of water and by means of water,

6Through which the world that then [existed] was deluged with water and perished. [Gen. 1:6-8; 7:11.]

7But by the same word the present heavens and earth have been stored up (reserved) for fire, being kept until the day of judgment and destruction of the ungodly people.

8Nevertheless do not let this one fact escape you, beloved, that with the Lord one day is as a thousand years, and a thousand years as one day. [Ps. 90:4.]

9The Lord does not delay *and* be tardy *or* slow about what He promises, according to some people's conception of slowness, but He is long-suffering (extraordinarily patient) toward you, not desiring that any should perish, but that all should turn to repentance.

**AMP** [a] Some ancient authorities read "love feasts." [b] Thayer.

## New American Standard

13 suffering wrong as the wages of doing wrong. They count it a pleasure to revel in the daytime. They are stains and blemishes, reveling in their [c]deceptions, as they carouse with you,

14 having eyes full of adultery and that never cease from sin, enticing unstable souls, having a heart trained in greed, accursed children;

15 forsaking the right way they have gone astray, having followed the way of Balaam, the *son* of Beor, who loved the wages of unrighteousness,

16 but he received a rebuke for his own transgression; *for* a dumb donkey, speaking with a voice of a man, restrained the madness of the prophet.

17 These are springs without water, and mists driven by a storm, for whom the black darkness has been reserved.

18 For speaking out arrogant *words* of vanity they entice by fleshly desires, by sensuality, those who barely escape from the ones who live in error,

19 promising them freedom while they themselves are slaves of corruption; for by what a man is overcome, by this he is enslaved.

20 For if after they have escaped the defilements of the world by the knowledge of the Lord and Savior Jesus Christ, they are again entangled in them and are overcome, the last state has become worse for them than the first.

21 For it would be better for them not to have known the way of righteousness, than having known it, to turn away from the holy commandment delivered to them.

22 It has happened to them according to the true proverb, "A DOG RETURNS TO ITS OWN VOMIT," and, "A sow, after washing, *returns* to wallowing in the mire."

*Purpose of This Letter*

3 THIS IS now, beloved, the second letter I am writing to you in which I am stirring up your sincere mind by way of reminder,

2 that you should remember the words spoken beforehand by the holy prophets and the commandment of the Lord and Savior *spoken* by your apostles.

*The Coming Day of the Lord*

3 Know this first of all, that in the last days mockers will come with *their* mocking, following after their own lusts,

4 and saying, "Where is the promise of His coming? For *ever* since the fathers fell asleep, all continues just as it was from the beginning of creation."

5 For when they maintain this, it escapes their notice that by the word of God *the* heavens existed long ago and *the* earth was formed out of water and by water,

6 through which the world at that time was destroyed, being flooded with water.

7 But the present heavens and earth by His word are being reserved for fire, kept for the day of judgment and destruction of ungodly men.

8 ¶ But do not let this one *fact* escape your notice, beloved, that with the Lord one day is as a thousand years, and a thousand years as one day.

9 The Lord is not slow about His promise, as some count slowness, but is patient toward you, not wishing for any to perish but for all to come to repentance.

NAS [c] Some ancient mss. read *love feasts,* (cf. Jude 12)

## New International

13 They will be paid back with harm for the harm they have
done. Their idea of pleasure is to carouse in broad daylight. They
are blots and blemishes, reveling in their pleasures while they feast
with you.[d] 14 With eyes full of adultery, they never stop sinning;
they seduce the unstable; they are experts in greed—an accursed
brood! 15 They have left the straight way and wandered off to
follow the way of Balaam son of Beor, who loved the wages of
wickedness. 16 But he was rebuked for his wrongdoing by a donkey—a beast without speech—who spoke with a man's voice and
restrained the prophet's madness.

17 These men are springs without water and mists driven by a
storm. Blackest darkness is reserved for them. 18 For they mouth
empty, boastful words and, by appealing to the lustful desires of
sinful human nature, they entice people who are just escaping
from those who live in error. 19 They promise them freedom, while
they themselves are slaves of depravity—for a man is a slave to
whatever has mastered him. 20 If they have escaped the corruption
of the world by knowing our Lord and Savior Jesus Christ and are
again entangled in it and overcome, they are worse off at the end
than they were at the beginning. 21 It would have been better for
them not to have known the way of righteousness, than to have
known it and then to turn their backs on the sacred command that
was passed on to them. 22 Of them the proverbs are true: "A dog
returns to its vomit,"[e] and, "A sow that is washed goes back to
her wallowing in the mud."

*The Day of the Lord*

3 DEAR FRIENDS, this is now my second letter to you. I have
written both of them as reminders to stimulate you to wholesome thinking. 2 I want you to recall the words spoken in the past
by the holy prophets and the command given by our Lord and
Savior through your apostles.

3 First of all, you must understand that in the last days scoffers
will come, scoffing and following their own evil desires. 4 They will
say, "Where is this 'coming' he promised? Ever since our fathers
died, everything goes on as it has since the beginning of creation."
5 But they deliberately forget that long ago by God's word the
heavens existed and the earth was formed out of water and by
water. 6 By these waters also the world of that time was deluged
and destroyed. 7 By the same word the present heavens and earth
are reserved for fire, being kept for the day of judgment and
destruction of ungodly men.

8 But do not forget this one thing, dear friends: With the Lord
a day is like a thousand years, and a thousand years are like a day.
9 The Lord is not slow in keeping his promise, as some understand
slowness. He is patient with you, not wanting anyone to perish,
but everyone to come to repentance.

NIV [d] *13* Some manuscripts *in their love feasts* [e] *22* Prov. 26:11

## King James

10But the day of the Lord will come as a thief in the night; in the which the heavens shall pass away with a great noise, and the elements shall melt with fervent heat, the earth also and the works that are therein shall be burned up.

11 *Seeing* then *that* all these things shall be dissolved, what manner *of persons* ought ye to be in *all* holy conversation and godliness,

12Looking for and hasting unto the coming of the day of God, wherein the heavens being on fire shall be dissolved, and the elements shall melt with fervent heat?

13Nevertheless we, according to his promise, look for new heavens and a new earth, wherein dwelleth righteousness.

14Wherefore, beloved, seeing that ye look for such things, be diligent that ye may be found of him in peace, without spot, and blameless.

15And account *that* the longsuffering of our Lord *is* salvation; even as our beloved brother Paul also according to the wisdom given unto him hath written unto you;

16As also in all *his* epistles, speaking in them of these things; in which are some things hard to be understood, which they that are unlearned and unstable wrest, as *they do* also the other scriptures, unto their own destruction.

17Ye therefore, beloved, seeing ye know *these things* before, beware lest ye also, being led away with the error of the wicked, fall from your own stedfastness.

18But grow in grace, and *in* the knowledge of our Lord and Saviour Jesus Christ. To him *be* glory both now and for ever. Amen.

## Amplified

10But the day of the Lord will come as a thief, and then the heavens will vanish (pass away) with a thunderous crash, and the [ [a]material] elements [of the universe] will be dissolved with fire, and the earth and the works that are upon it will be burned up.

11Since all these things are thus [b]in the process of being dissolved, what kind of person ought [each of] you to be [in the meanwhile] in consecrated *and* holy behavior and devout *and* godly qualities?

12While you wait and earnestly long for—expecting and [c]hastening—the coming of the day of God by reason of which the flaming heavens will be dissolved, and the [ [d]material] elements [of the universe] will flare *and* melt with fire. [Isa. 34:4.]

13But we look for new heavens and a new earth according to His promise, in which righteousness (uprightness, freedom from sin, and right standing with God) is to abide. [Isa. 65:17; 66:22.]

14So, beloved, since you are expecting these things, be eager to be found by Him [at His coming] without spot or blemish, and at peace—in serene confidence, free from fears and agitating passions and moral conflicts.

15And consider that the long-suffering of our Lord [ [e]His slowness in avenging wrongs and judging the world] is salvation, [ [f]that which conduces to the soul's safety]; even as our beloved brother Paul also wrote to you according to the spiritual insight given him,

16Speaking of this as he does in all of his letters. There are some things in those [epistles of Paul] that are difficult to understand, which the ignorant and unstable twist *and* misconstrue to their own [g]utter destruction, just as [they distort and misinterpret] the rest of the Scriptures.

17Let me warn you therefore, beloved, that knowing these things beforehand, you should be on your guard lest you be carried away by the error of lawless *and* wicked [persons and] fall from your own [present] firm condition—your own steadfastness [of mind].

18But grow in grace (undeserved favor, spiritual strength) and [h]recognition *and* knowledge *and* understanding of our Lord and Savior Jesus Christ, the Messiah. To Him [be] glory (honor, majesty and splendor) both now and to the day of eternity. Amen—so be it!

**AMP** [a] Abbott-Smith. [b] Vincent. [c] Alternate reading. [d] Abbott-Smith. [e] Thayer. [f] Thayer. [g] Thayer. [h] Cremer.

## New American Standard

*A New Heaven and Earth*

10But the day of the Lord will come like a thief, in which the
heavens will pass away with a roar and the elements will be
destroyed with intense heat, and the earth and its works will be
[i]burned up.
11Since all these things are to be destroyed in this way, what
sort of people ought you to be in holy conduct and godliness,
12looking for and hastening the coming of the day of God, on
account of which the heavens will be destroyed by burning, and
the elements will melt with intense heat!
13But according to His promise we are looking for new heavens
and a new earth, in which righteousness dwells.
14¶ Therefore, beloved, since you look for these things, be diligent
to be found by Him in peace, spotless and blameless,
15and regard the patience of our Lord *to be* salvation; just as also
our beloved brother Paul, according to the wisdom given him,
wrote to you,
16as also in all *his* letters, speaking in them of these things, in
which are some things hard to understand, which the untaught
and unstable distort, as *they do* also the rest of the Scriptures, to
their own destruction.
17You therefore, beloved, knowing this beforehand, be on your
guard lest, being carried away by the error of unprincipled men,
you fall from your own steadfastness,
18but grow in the grace and knowledge of our Lord and Savior
Jesus Christ. To Him *be* the glory, both now and to the day of
eternity. Amen.

**NAS** [i] Some ancient mss. read *discovered*

## New International

10But the day of the Lord will come like a thief. The heavens will
disappear with a roar; the elements will be destroyed by fire, and
the earth and everything in it will be laid bare.[j]
11Since everything will be destroyed in this way, what kind of
people ought you to be? You ought to live holy and godly lives 12as
you look forward to the day of God and speed its coming.[k] That
day will bring about the destruction of the heavens by fire, and the
elements will melt in the heat. 13But in keeping with his promise
we are looking forward to a new heaven and a new earth, the home
of righteousness.
14So then, dear friends, since you are looking forward to this,
make every effort to be found spotless, blameless and at peace with
him. 15Bear in mind that our Lord's patience means salvation, just
as our dear brother Paul also wrote you with the wisdom that God
gave him. 16He writes the same way in all his letters, speaking in
them of these matters. His letters contain some things that are hard
to understand, which ignorant and unstable people distort, as they
do the other Scriptures, to their own destruction.
17Therefore, dear friends, since you already know this, be on
your guard so that you may not be carried away by the error of
lawless men and fall from your secure position. 18But grow in the
grace and knowledge of our Lord and Savior Jesus Christ. To him
be glory both now and forever! Amen.

**NIV** [j] *10* Some manuscripts *be burned up* [k] *12* Or *as you wait eagerly for the day of God to come*

## King James

THE FIRST EPISTLE

OF

# John

1 THAT WHICH was from the beginning, which we have heard, which we have seen with our eyes, which we have looked upon, and our hands have handled, of the Word of life;

2(For the life was manifested, and we have seen *it*, and bear witness, and show unto you that eternal life, which was with the Father, and was manifested unto us;)

3That which we have seen and heard declare we unto you, that ye also may have fellowship with us: and truly our fellowship *is* with the Father, and with his Son Jesus Christ.

4And these things write we unto you, that your joy may be full.

5This then is the message which we have heard of him, and declare unto you, that God is light, and in him is no darkness at all.

6If we say that we have fellowship with him, and walk in darkness, we lie, and do not the truth:

7But if we walk in the light, as he is in the light, we have fellowship one with another, and the blood of Jesus Christ his Son cleanseth us from all sin.

8If we say that we have no sin, we deceive ourselves, and the truth is not in us.

9If we confess our sins, he is faithful and just to forgive us *our* sins, and to cleanse us from all unrighteousness.

10If we say that we have not sinned, we make him a liar, and his word is not in us.

2 MY LITTLE children, these things write I unto you, that ye sin not. And if any man sin, we have an advocate with the Father, Jesus Christ the righteous:

2And he is the propitiation for our sins: and not for ours only, but also for *the sins of* the whole world.

## Amplified

THE FIRST LETTER OF

# John

1 [WE ARE writing] about the Word of Life [ [a]in] Him Who existed from the beginning, Whom we have heard, Whom we have seen with our [own] eyes, Whom we have gazed upon [for ourselves] and have touched with our [own] hands.

2And the Life [ [b]an aspect of His being] was revealed (made manifest, demonstrated), and we saw (as eyewitnesses) and are testifying to and declare to you the Life, the eternal Life [ [c]in Him] Who already existed with the Father and Who [actually] was made visible—was revealed—to us [His followers].

3What we have seen and [ourselves] heard we are also telling you, so that you too may [d]realize *and* enjoy fellowship as partners *and* partakers with us. And [this] fellowship that we have (which is a [e]distinguishing mark of Christians) is with the Father and with His Son Jesus Christ, the Messiah.

4And we are now writing these things to you so that our joy [in seeing you included] may be full—and [f]your joy may be complete.

5And this is the message—the message of [g]promise—which we have heard from Him and now are reporting to you: God is Light and there is no darkness in Him at all—[h]no, not in any way.

6[So] if we say we are partakers together *and* enjoy fellowship with Him when we live *and* move *and* are walking about in darkness, we are [both] speaking falsely and do not live *and* practice the Truth [of the Gospel].

7But if we [really] are living *and* walking in the Light as He [Himself] is in the Light, we have [true, unbroken] fellowship with one another, and the blood of Jesus *Christ* His Son cleanses (removes) us from all sin *and* guilt—keeps us cleansed from sin in all its forms *and* manifestations.

8If we say we have no sin—refusing to admit that we are sinners—we delude *and* lead ourselves astray, and the Truth [which the Gospel presents] is not in us—does not dwell in our hearts.

9If we [freely] admit that we have sinned *and* confess our sins, He is faithful and just [true to His own nature and promises] and will forgive our sins (dismiss our lawlessness) and continuously cleanse us from all unrighteousness—everything not in conformity to His will in purpose, thought and action.

10If we say (claim) we have not sinned, we contradict His Word *and* make Him out to be false *and* a liar, and His Word is not in us—the divine message of the Gospel is not in our hearts.

2 MY LITTLE children, I write you these things so that you may not violate God's law *and* sin; but if any one should sin, we have an Advocate (One Who will intercede for us) with the Father; [it is] Jesus Christ [the all] righteous—upright, just, Who conforms to the Father's will in every purpose, thought and action.

2And He— [i]that same Jesus Himself—is the propitiation (the atoning sacrifice) for our sins, and not for ours alone but also for [the sins of] the whole world.

**AMP** [a] Vincent. [b] Vincent. [c] Vincent. [d] Vincent. [e] Vincent. [f] Many ancient texts read "your joy." [g] Vincent. [h] Literal meaning. [i] Vincent.

## New American Standard

# 1 John

*Introduction*

*The Incarnate Word*

**1** WHAT WAS from the beginning, what we have heard, what we have seen with our eyes, what we beheld and our hands handled, concerning the Word of Life—

2and the life was manifested, and we have seen and bear witness and proclaim to you the eternal life, which was with the Father and was manifested to us—

3what we have seen and heard we proclaim to you also, that you also may have fellowship with us; and indeed our fellowship is with the Father, and with His Son Jesus Christ.

4And these things we write, so that our joy may be made complete.

*God Is Light*

5¶ And this is the message we have heard from Him and announce to you, that God is light, and in Him there is no darkness at all.

6If we say that we have fellowship with Him and *yet* walk in the darkness, we lie and do not practice the truth;

7but if we walk in the light as He Himself is in the light, we have fellowship with one another, and the blood of Jesus His Son cleanses us from all sin.

8If we say that we have no sin, we are deceiving ourselves, and the truth is not in us.

9If we confess our sins, He is faithful and righteous to forgive us our sins and to cleanse us from all unrighteousness.

10If we say that we have not sinned, we make Him a liar, and His word is not in us.

*Christ Is Our Advocate*

**2** MY LITTLE children, I am writing these things to you that you may not sin. And if anyone sins, we have an [j]Advocate with the Father, Jesus Christ the righteous;

2and He Himself is the propitiation for our sins; and not for ours only, but also for *those of* the whole world.

**NAS** [j] Gr., *Paracletos*, one called alongside to help

## New International

# 1 John

*The Word of Life*

**1** THAT WHICH was from the beginning, which we have heard, which we have seen with our eyes, which we have looked at and our hands have touched—this we proclaim concern-
ing the Word of life. 2The life appeared; we have seen it and testify to it, and we proclaim to you the eternal life, which was with the Father and has appeared to us. 3We proclaim to you what we have seen and heard, so that you also may have fellowship with us. And our fellowship is with the Father and with his Son, Jesus Christ.
4We write this to make our[k] joy complete.

*Walking in the Light*

5This is the message we have heard from him and declare to
you: God is light; in him there is no darkness at all. 6If we claim
to have fellowship with him yet walk in the darkness, we lie and
do not live by the truth. 7But if we walk in the light, as he is in the light, we have fellowship with one another, and the blood of Jesus, his Son, purifies us from all[l] sin.
8If we claim to be without sin, we deceive ourselves and the
truth is not in us. 9If we confess our sins, he is faithful and just and will forgive us our sins and purify us from all unrighteousness.
10If we claim we have not sinned, we make him out to be a liar and his word has no place in our lives.

**2** MY DEAR children, I write this to you so that you will not sin. But if anybody does sin, we have one who speaks to the
Father in our defense—Jesus Christ, the Righteous One. 2He is the atoning sacrifice for our sins, and not only for ours but also for[m] the sins of the whole world.

**NIV** [k]4 Some manuscripts *your* [l]7 Or *every* [m]2 Or *He is the one who turns aside God's wrath, taking away our sins, and not only ours but also*

## King James

3 And hereby we do know that we know him, if we keep his commandments.

4 He that saith, I know him, and keepeth not his commandments, is a liar, and the truth is not in him.

5 But whoso keepeth his word, in him verily is the love of God perfected: hereby know we that we are in him.

6 He that saith he abideth in him ought himself also so to walk, even as he walked.

7 Brethren, I write no new commandment unto you, but an old commandment which ye had from the beginning. The old commandment is the word which ye have heard from the beginning.

8 Again, a new commandment I write unto you, which thing is true in him and in you: because the darkness is past, and the true light now shineth.

9 He that saith he is in the light, and hateth his brother, is in darkness even until now.

10 He that loveth his brother abideth in the light, and there is none occasion of stumbling in him.

11 But he that hateth his brother is in darkness, and walketh in darkness, and knoweth not whither he goeth, because that darkness hath blinded his eyes.

12 I write unto you, little children, because your sins are forgiven you for his name's sake.

13 I write unto you, fathers, because ye have known him *that is* from the beginning. I write unto you, young men, because ye have overcome the wicked one. I write unto you, little children, because ye have known the Father.

14 I have written unto you, fathers, because ye have known him *that is* from the beginning. I have written unto you, young men, because ye are strong, and the word of God abideth in you, and ye have overcome the wicked one.

15 Love not the world, neither the things *that are* in the world. If any man love the world, the love of the Father is not in him.

16 For all that *is* in the world, the lust of the flesh, and the lust of the eyes, and the pride of life, is not of the Father, but is of the world.

17 And the world passeth away, and the lust thereof: but he that doeth the will of God abideth for ever.

18 Little children, it is the last time: and as ye have heard that antichrist shall come, even now are there many antichrists; whereby we know that it is the last time.

19 They went out from us, but they were not of us; for if they had been of us, they would *no doubt* have continued with us: but *they went out,* that they might be made manifest that they were not all of us.

## Amplified

3 And this is how we may discern [ [a]daily by experience] that we are coming to know Him—to perceive, recognize, understand and become better acquainted with Him: if we keep (bear in mind, observe, practice) His teachings (precepts, commandments).

4 Whoever says, I know Him—I perceive, recognize, understand and am acquainted with Him—but fails to keep *and* obey His commandments (teachings) is a liar, and the Truth [ [b]of the Gospel] is not in him.

5 But he who keeps [treasures] His Word—who bears in mind His precepts, who observes His message in its entirety—truly in him has the love of *and* for God been perfected (completed, reached maturity). By this we may perceive *and* know *and* recognize *and* be sure that we are in Him:

6 Whoever says he abides in Him ought—as [c]a personal debt—to walk *and* conduct himself in the same way in which He walked *and* conducted Himself.

7 Beloved, I am writing you no new commandment, but an old commandment which you have had *from the beginning;* the old commandment is the message which you have heard—the [d]doctrine [of salvation through Christ].

8 Yet I am writing you a new commandment, which is true—is realized—in Him and in you, because the darkness ( [e]moral blindness) is clearing away and the true Light [ [f]the revelation of God in Christ] is already shining.

9 Whoever says he is in the Light and [yet] hates his brother [Christian, [g]born-again child of God his own Father] is in darkness even until now.

10 Whoever loves his brother [believer] abides (lives) in the Light, and in It *or* in [h]him there is no occasion for stumbling *or* cause for error *or* sin.

11 But he who hates (detests, despises) his brother [ [i]in Christ] is in darkness and walking (living) in the dark; he is straying *and* does not perceive *or* know where he is going, because the darkness has blinded his eyes.

12 I am writing to you, little children, because for His name's sake your sins are forgiven—pardoned through His name and on account of confessing His name.

13 I am writing to you, fathers, because you have come to know (recognize, be aware of and understand) Him Who [has existed] from the beginning. I am writing to you, young men, because you have been victorious over the wicked [one]. I write to you, [j]boys (lads), because you have come to know *and* recognize *and* be aware of the Father.

14 I write to you, fathers, because you have come to know (recognize, be conscious of and understand) Him Who [has existed] from the beginning. I write to you, young men, because you are strong *and* vigorous, and the Word of God is (always in your hearts) abiding in you, and you have been victorious over the wicked one.

15 Do not love *or* cherish the world or the things that are in the world. If any one loves the world, love for the Father is not in him.

16 For all that is in the world, the lust of the flesh [craving for sensual gratification], and the lust of the eyes [greedy longings of the mind] and the pride of life [assurance in one's own resources *or* in the stability of earthly things]—these do not come from the Father but are from the world [itself].

17 And the world passes away *and* disappears, and with it the forbidden cravings (the passionate desires, the lust) of it; but he who does the will of God and carries out His purposes in his life, abides (remains) forever.

18 [k]Boys (lads), it is the last time—hour [the end of this age]. And as you have heard that Antichrist [he who will oppose Christ in the guise of Christ] is coming, even now many antichrists have arisen, which confirms our belief that it is the final (the end) time.

19 They went out from our number, but they did not [really] belong to us; for if they had been of us, they would have remained with us. But [they withdrew] that it might be plain that they all are not of us.

**AMP** [a] Vincent. [b] Thayer. [c] Vincent. [d] Thayer. [e] Vincent. [f] Vincent. [g] Thayer. [h] Alternate reading, "it" or "him." [i] Thayer. [j] Abbott-Smith. [k] Abbott-Smith.

## New American Standard

3 And by this we know that we have come to know Him, if we keep His commandments.

4 The one who says, "I have come to know Him," and does not keep His commandments, is a liar, and the truth is not in him; 5 but whoever keeps His word, in him the love of God has truly been perfected. By this we know that we are in Him:

6 the one who says he abides in Him ought himself to walk in the same manner as He walked.

7¶ Beloved, I am not writing a new commandment to you, but an old commandment which you have had from the beginning; the old commandment is the word which you have heard.

8 On the other hand, I am writing a new commandment to you, which is true in Him and in you, because the darkness is passing away, and the true light is already shining.

9 The one who says he is in the light and *yet* hates his brother is in the darkness until now.

10 The one who loves his brother abides in the light and there is no cause for stumbling in him.

11 But the one who hates his brother is in the darkness and walks in the darkness, and does not know where he is going because the darkness has blinded his eyes.

12¶ I am writing to you, little children, because your sins are forgiven you for His name's sake.

13 I am writing to you, fathers, because you know Him who has been from the beginning. I am writing to you, young men, because you have overcome the evil one. I have written to you, children, because you know the Father.

14 I have written to you, fathers, because you know Him who has been from the beginning. I have written to you, young men, because you are strong, and the word of God abides in you, and you have overcome the evil one.

*Do Not Love the World*

15 Do not love the world, nor the things in the world. If anyone loves the world, the love of the Father is not in him.

16 For all that is in the world, the lust of the flesh and the lust of the eyes and the boastful pride of life, is not from the Father, but is from the world.

17 And the world is passing away, and *also* its lusts; but the one who does the will of God abides forever.

18¶ Children, it is the last hour; and just as you heard that antichrist is coming, even now many antichrists have arisen; from this we know that it is the last hour.

19 They went out from us, but they were not *really* of us; for if they had been of us, they would have remained with us; but *they went out,* in order that it might be shown that they all are not of us.

## New International

3 We know that we have come to know him if we obey his commands. 4 The man who says, "I know him," but does not do what he commands is a liar, and the truth is not in him. 5 But if anyone obeys his word, God's love[l] is truly made complete in him. This is how we know we are in him: 6 Whoever claims to live in him must walk as Jesus did.

7 Dear friends, I am not writing you a new command but an old one, which you have had since the beginning. This old command is the message you have heard. 8 Yet I am writing you a new command; its truth is seen in him and you, because the darkness is passing and the true light is already shining.

9 Anyone who claims to be in the light but hates his brother is still in the darkness. 10 Whoever loves his brother lives in the light, and there is nothing in him[m] to make him stumble. 11 But whoever hates his brother is in the darkness and walks around in the darkness; he does not know where he is going, because the darkness has blinded him.

12 I write to you, dear children,
because your sins have been forgiven on account of his name.
13 I write to you, fathers,
because you have known him who is from the beginning.
I write to you, young men,
because you have overcome the evil one.
I write to you, dear children,
because you have known the Father.
14 I write to you, fathers,
because you have known him who is from the beginning.
I write to you, young men,
because you are strong,
and the word of God lives in you,
and you have overcome the evil one.

*Do Not Love the World*

15 Do not love the world or anything in the world. If anyone loves the world, the love of the Father is not in him. 16 For everything in the world—the cravings of sinful man, the lust of his eyes and the boasting of what he has and does—comes not from the Father but from the world. 17 The world and its desires pass away, but the man who does the will of God lives forever.

*Warning Against Antichrists*

18 Dear children, this is the last hour; and as you have heard that the antichrist is coming, even now many antichrists have come. This is how we know it is the last hour. 19 They went out from us, but they did not really belong to us. For if they had belonged to us, they would have remained with us; but their going showed that none of them belonged to us.

**NIV** [l] 5 Or *word, love for God* [m] 10 Or *it*

## King James

20But ye have an unction from the Holy One, and ye know all things.

21I have not written unto you because ye know not the truth, but because ye know it, and that no lie is of the truth.

22Who is a liar but he that denieth that Jesus is the Christ? He is antichrist, that denieth the Father and the Son.

23Whosoever denieth the Son, the same hath not the Father: *but] he that acknowledgeth the Son hath the Father also.*

24Let that therefore abide in you, which ye have heard from the beginning. If that which ye have heard from the beginning shall remain in you, ye also shall continue in the Son, and in the Father.

25And this is the promise that he hath promised us, *even* eternal life.

26These *things* have I written unto you concerning them that seduce you.

27But the anointing which ye have received of him abideth in you, and ye need not that any man teach you: but as the same anointing teacheth you of all things, and is truth, and is no lie, and even as it hath taught you, ye shall abide in him.

28And now, little children, abide in him; that, when he shall appear, we may have confidence, and not be ashamed before him at his coming.

29If ye know that he is righteous, ye know that every one that doeth righteousness is born of him.

**3** BEHOLD, WHAT manner of love the Father hath bestowed upon us, that we should be called the sons of God: therefore the world knoweth us not, because it knew him not.

2Beloved, now are we the sons of God, and it doth not yet appear what we shall be: but we know that, when he shall appear, we shall be like him; for we shall see him as he is.

3And every man that hath this hope in him purifieth himself, even as he is pure.

4Whosoever committeth sin transgresseth also the law: for sin is the transgression of the law.

5And ye know that he was manifested to take away our sins; and in him is no sin.

6Whosoever abideth in him sinneth not: whosoever sinneth hath not seen him, neither known him.

## Amplified

20But—you hold a sacred appointment, you have been given an unction—you have been anointed by the Holy One, and you all know [the Truth].

21I write to you, not because you are ignorant *and* do not perceive *and* know the Truth, but because you do perceive *and* know it, and [know positively] that nothing false—no deception, no lie—is of the Truth.

22Who is [such a] liar as he who denies that Jesus is the Christ, the Messiah? He is antichrist, (the antagonist of Christ), who [a]habitually denies *and* refuses to acknowledge the Father and the Son.

23No one who [b]habitually denies (disowns) the Son [c]even has the Father. *Whoever confesses (acknowledges and has) the Son has the Father also.*

24As for you, keep in your hearts what you have heard from the beginning. If what you heard from the first dwells *and* remains in you, then you will dwell in the Son and in the Father (always).

25And this is what He Himself has promised us, the life, the eternal [life].

26I write this to you with reference to those who would deceive you—seduce and lead you astray;

27But as for you, (the sacred appointment, the unction) the anointing which you received from Him, abides ([d]permanently) in you; [so] then you have no need that any one should instruct you. But just as His anointing teaches you concerning everything, and is true, and is no falsehood, so you must abide—live, never to depart [[e]rooted in Him, knit to Him] just as [His anointing] has taught you [to do].

28And now, little children, abide (live, remain [f]permanently) in Him, so that when He is made visible, we may have *and* enjoy perfect confidence (boldness, assurance) and not be ashamed *and* shrink from Him at His coming.

29If you know (perceive and are sure) that He [Christ] is absolutely righteous (conforming to the Father's will in purpose, thought and action), you may also know (be sure) that every one who does righteously [and is therefore in like manner conformed to the divine will] is born (begotten) of Him [[g]God].

**3** SEE WHAT [[h]an incredible] quality of love the Father has given (shown, bestowed on) us, that we should [be permitted to] be named *and* called *and* counted the children of God! And so we are! The reason that the world does not know (recognize, acknowledge) us, is that it does not know (recognize, acknowledge) Him.

2Beloved, we are [even here and] now God's children; it is not yet disclosed (made clear) what we shall be [hereafter], but we know that when He comes *and* is manifested we shall [[i]as God's children] resemble *and* be like Him, for we shall see Him [j]just as He [really] is.

3And every one who has this hope [resting] on Him cleanses (purifies) himself just as He is pure—chaste, undefiled, guiltless.

4Every one who commits (practices) sin is guilty of lawlessness; for [that is what] sin is, lawlessness [the breaking, violating of God's law by transgression or neglect; being unrestrained and unregulated by His commands and His will].

5You know that He appeared in visible form *and* became Man to take away [upon Himself] sins, and in Him there is no sin—[k]essentially and forever.

6No one who abides in Him—who lives and remains [l]in communion with and in obedience to Him, [deliberately and knowingly] [m]habitually commits (practices) sin. No one who habitually sins has either seen *or* known Him—recognized, perceived or understood Him, or has had an experimental acquaintance with Him.

**AMP** [a] Vincent. [b] Vincent. [c] Vincent. [d] Thayer. [e] Thayer. [f] Thayer. [g] Westcott: When John thinks of God in relation to men he never thinks of Him apart from Christ. [h] Vincent. [i] Jamieson, Fausset and Brown. [j] Vincent. [k] Vincent. [l] Vincent. [m] Vincent.

## New American Standard

20But you have an anointing from the Holy One, and you all
know.
21I have not written to you because you do not know the truth,
but because you do know it, and because no lie is of the truth.
22Who is the liar but the one who denies that Jesus is the Christ?
This is the antichrist, the one who denies the Father and the Son.
23Whoever denies the Son does not have the Father; the one
who confesses the Son has the Father also.
24As for you, let that abide in you which you heard from the
beginning. If what you heard from the beginning abides in you,
you also will abide in the Son and in the Father.

*The Promise Is Eternal Life*

25And this is the promise which He Himself made to us: eternal
life.
26These things I have written to you concerning those who are
trying to deceive you.
27And as for you, the anointing which you received from Him
abides in you, and you have no need for anyone to teach you; but
as His anointing teaches you about all things, and is true and is
not a lie, and just as it has taught you, you abide in Him.
28And now, little children, abide in Him, so that when He
appears, we may have confidence and not shrink away from Him
in shame at His coming.
29If you know that He is righteous, you know that everyone also
who practices righteousness is born of Him.

*Children of God Love One Another*

**3** SEE HOW great a love the Father has bestowed upon us, that
we should be called children of God; and *such* we are. For this
reason the world does not know us, because it did not know Him.
2Beloved, now we are children of God, and it has not appeared
as yet what we shall be. We know that, when He appears, we shall
be like Him, because we shall see Him just as He is.
3And everyone who has this hope *fixed* on Him purifies himself, just as He is pure.
4Everyone who practices sin also practices lawlessness; and sin
is lawlessness.
5And you know that He appeared in order to take away sins;
and in Him there is no sin.
6No one who abides in Him sins; no one who sins has seen
Him or knows Him.

## New International

20But you have an anointing from the Holy One, and all of you
know the truth.[n] 21I do not write to you because you do not know
the truth, but because you do know it and because no lie comes
from the truth. 22Who is the liar? It is the man who denies that
Jesus is the Christ. Such a man is the antichrist—he denies the
Father and the Son. 23No one who denies the Son has the Father;
whoever acknowledges the Son has the Father also.
24See that what you have heard from the beginning remains in
you. If it does, you also will remain in the Son and in the Father.
25And this is what he promised us—even eternal life.
26I am writing these things to you about those who are trying
to lead you astray. 27As for you, the anointing you received from
him remains in you, and you do not need anyone to teach you. But
as his anointing teaches you about all things and as that anointing
is real, not counterfeit—just as it has taught you, remain in him.

*Children of God*

28And now, dear children, continue in him, so that when he
appears we may be confident and unashamed before him at his
coming.
29If you know that he is righteous, you know that everyone who
does what is right has been born of him.

**3** HOW GREAT is the love the Father has lavished on us, that
we should be called children of God! And that is what we are!
The reason the world does not know us is that it did not know him.
2Dear friends, now we are children of God, and what we will be
has not yet been made known. But we know that when he appears,[o] we shall be like him, for we shall see him as he is. 3Every-
one who has this hope in him purifies himself, just as he is pure.
4Everyone who sins breaks the law; in fact, sin is lawlessness.
5But you know that he appeared so that he might take away our
sins. And in him is no sin. 6No one who lives in him keeps on
sinning. No one who continues to sin has either seen him or
known him.

**NIV** [n] 20 Some manuscripts *and you know all things* [o] 2 Or *when it is made known*

## King James

7 Little children, let no man deceive you: he that doeth righteousness is righteous, even as he is righteous.

8 He that committeth sin is of the devil; for the devil sinneth from the beginning. For this purpose the Son of God was manifested, that he might destroy the works of the devil.

9 Whosoever is born of God doth not commit sin; for his seed remaineth in him: and he cannot sin, because he is born of God.

10 In this the children of God are manifest, and the children of the devil: whosoever doeth not righteousness is not of God, neither he that loveth not his brother.

11 For this is the message that ye heard from the beginning, that we should love one another.

12 Not as Cain, *who* was of that wicked one, and slew his brother. And wherefore slew he him? Because his own works were evil, and his brother's righteous.

13 Marvel not, my brethren, if the world hate you.

14 We know that we have passed from death unto life, because we love the brethren. He that loveth not *his* brother abideth in death.

15 Whosoever hateth his brother is a murderer: and ye know that no murderer hath eternal life abiding in him.

16 Hereby perceive we the love *of God*, because he laid down his life for us: and we ought to lay down *our* lives for the brethren.

17 But whoso hath this world's good, and seeth his brother have need, and shutteth up his bowels *of compassion* from him, how dwelleth the love of God in him?

18 My little children, let us not love in word, neither in tongue; but in deed and in truth.

19 And hereby we know that we are of the truth, and shall assure our hearts before him.

20 For if our heart condemn us, God is greater than our heart, and knoweth all things.

21 Beloved, if our heart condemn us not, *then* have we confidence toward God.

22 And whatsoever we ask, we receive of him, because we keep his commandments, and do those things that are pleasing in his sight.

23 And this is his commandment, That we should believe on the name of his Son Jesus Christ, and love one another, as he gave us commandment.

24 And he that keepeth his commandments dwelleth in him, and he in him. And hereby we know that he abideth in us, by the Spirit which he hath given us.

## Amplified

7 [a]Boys (lads), let no one deceive *and* lead you astray. He who practices righteousness—who is upright, conforming to the divine will in purpose, thought and action, living a consistently conscientious life—is righteous, even as He is righteous.

8 [But] he who commits sin (who practices evil doing) is of the devil—takes his character from the evil one; for the devil has sinned (has violated the divine law) from the beginning. The reason the Son of God was made manifest (visible) was to undo (destroy, loosen and dissolve) the works the devil [has done].

9 No one born (begotten) of God [deliberately and knowingly] [b]habitually practices sin, for God's nature abides in him—His principle of life, the divine sperm, remains permanently within him—and he cannot practice sinning because he is born (begotten) of God.

10 By this it is made clear who take their nature from God *and* are His children, and who take their nature from the devil *and* are his children: no one who does not practice righteousness—who does not conform to God's will in purpose, thought and action—is of God; neither is any one who does not love his brother [his fellow [c]believer in Christ].

11 Because this is the message—the announcement—which you have heard from the first, that we should love one another,

12 [And] not be like Cain who [took his nature and got his motivation] from the evil one and slew his brother. And why did he slay him? Because his deeds (activities, works) were wicked *and* malicious and his brother's were righteous—virtuous.

13 Do not be surprised *and* wonder, brethren, that the world detests *and* pursues you with hatred.

14 We know that we have passed over out of the death into the Life by the fact that we love the brethren, [our fellow Christians]. He who does not love abides—remains, is [d]held and kept continually—in [spiritual] death.

15 Any one who (abominates, detests) hates his brother [in Christ] is [at heart] a murderer, and you know that no murderer has eternal life abiding ( [e]persevering) within him.

16 By this we come to know—progressively to recognize, to perceive, to understand the [essential] love: that He laid down His [own] life for us; and we ought to lay [our] lives down for [those who are our] brothers [ [f]in Him].

17 But if any one has this world's goods—resources for sustaining life—and sees his brother *and* [g]fellow believer in need, yet closes his heart of compassion against him, how can the love of God live *and* remain in him?

18 Little children, let us not love [merely] in theory *or* in speech but in deed and in truth—in practice and in sincerity.

19 By this we shall come to know—perceive and recognize and understand—that we are of the Truth, and can reassure (quiet, conciliate and pacify) our hearts in His presence.

20 In whatever our hearts in [ [h]tormenting] self-accusation make us feel guilty *and* condemn us. For [ [i]we are in God's hands]; He is above *and* greater than our consciences (our hearts), and He knows (perceives and understands) everything—nothing is hidden from Him.

21 And, beloved, if our consciences (our hearts) do not accuse us—if they do not make us feel guilty and condemn us—we have confidence (complete assurance and boldness) before God;

22 And we receive from Him whatever we ask for, because we ( [j]watchfully) obey His orders—observe His suggestions and injunctions, follow His plan for us— *and* ( [k]habitually) practice what is pleasing to Him.

23 And this is His order (His command, His injunction), that we should believe—put our faith and trust in and adhere to and rely—on the name of His Son Jesus Christ, the Messiah, and that we should love one another, just as He has commanded us.

24 All who keep His commandments (who obey His orders and follow His plan, live and continue to live, to stay and) abide in Him, and He in them.— [l]They let Christ be a home to them and they are the home of Christ. And by this we know *and* understand *and* have the proof that He [really] lives *and* makes His home in us, by the (Holy) Spirit Whom He has given us.

**AMP** [a] Abbott-Smith. [b] Vincent. [c] Thayer. [d] Thayer. [e] Thayer. [f] Thayer. [g] Thayer. [h] Vincent. [i] Vincent. [j] Vincent. [k] Vincent. [l] After Bede.

## New American Standard

7 Little children, let no one deceive you; the one who practices righteousness is righteous, just as He is righteous;

8 the one who practices sin is of the devil; for the devil has sinned from the beginning. The Son of God appeared for this purpose, that He might destroy the works of the devil.

9 No one who is born of God practices sin, because His seed abides in him; and he cannot sin, because he is born of God.

10 By this the children of God and the children of the devil are obvious: anyone who does not practice righteousness is not of God, nor the one who does not love his brother.

11 For this is the message which you have heard from the beginning, that we should love one another;

12 not as Cain, *who* was of the evil one, and slew his brother. And for what reason did he slay him? Because his deeds were evil, and his brother's were righteous.

13 ¶ Do not marvel, brethren, if the world hates you.

14 We know that we have passed out of death into life, because we love the brethren. He who does not love abides in death.

15 Everyone who hates his brother is a murderer; and you know that no murderer has eternal life abiding in him.

16 We know love by this, that He laid down His life for us; and we ought to lay down our lives for the brethren.

17 But whoever has the world's goods, and beholds his brother in need and closes his heart against him, how does the love of God abide in him?

18 Little children, let us not love with word or with tongue, but in deed and truth.

19 We shall know by this that we are of the truth, and shall assure our heart before Him,

20 in whatever our heart condemns us; for God is greater than our heart, and knows all things.

21 Beloved, if our heart does not condemn us, we have confidence before God;

22 and whatever we ask we receive from Him, because we keep His commandments and do the things that are pleasing in His sight.

23 And this is His commandment, that we believe in the name of His Son Jesus Christ, and love one another, just as He commanded us.

24 And the one who keeps His commandments abides in Him, and He in him. And we know by this that He abides in us, by the Spirit whom He has given us.

## New International

7 Dear children, do not let anyone lead you astray. He who does what is right is righteous, just as he is righteous. 8 He who does what is sinful is of the devil, because the devil has been sinning from the beginning. The reason the Son of God appeared was to destroy the devil's work. 9 No one who is born of God will continue to sin, because God's seed remains in him; he cannot go on sinning, because he has been born of God. 10 This is how we know who the children of God are and who the children of the devil are: Anyone who does not do what is right is not a child of God; nor is anyone who does not love his brother.

*Love One Another*

11 This is the message you heard from the beginning: We should love one another. 12 Do not be like Cain, who belonged to the evil one and murdered his brother. And why did he murder him? Because his own actions were evil and his brother's were righteous. 13 Do not be surprised, my brothers, if the world hates you. 14 We know that we have passed from death to life, because we love our brothers. Anyone who does not love remains in death. 15 Anyone who hates his brother is a murderer, and you know that no murderer has eternal life in him.

16 This is how we know what love is: Jesus Christ laid down his life for us. And we ought to lay down our lives for our brothers. 17 If anyone has material possessions and sees his brother in need but has no pity on him, how can the love of God be in him? 18 Dear children, let us not love with words or tongue but with actions and in truth. 19 This then is how we know that we belong to the truth, and how we set our hearts at rest in his presence 20 whenever our hearts condemn us. For God is greater than our hearts, and he knows everything.

21 Dear friends, if our hearts do not condemn us, we have confidence before God 22 and receive from him anything we ask, because we obey his commands and do what pleases him. 23 And this is his command: to believe in the name of his Son, Jesus Christ, and to love one another as he commanded us. 24 Those who obey his commands live in him, and he in them. And this is how we know that he lives in us: We know it by the Spirit he gave us.

## King James

4 BELOVED, BELIEVE not every spirit, but try the spirits
whether they are of God: because many false prophets are
gone out into the world.
2Hereby know ye the Spirit of God: Every spirit that confesseth
that Jesus Christ is come in the flesh is of God:
3And every spirit that confesseth not that Jesus Christ is come
in the flesh is not of God: and this is that *spirit* of antichrist,
whereof ye have heard that it should come; and even now already
is it in the world.
4Ye are of God, little children, and have overcome them: because greater is he that is in you, than he that is in the world.
5They are of the world: therefore speak they of the world, and
the world heareth them.
6We are of God: he that knoweth God heareth us; he that is not
of God heareth not us. Hereby know we the spirit of truth, and
the spirit of error.
7Beloved, let us love one another: for love is of God; and every
one that loveth is born of God, and knoweth God.
8He that loveth not knoweth not God; for God is love.
9In this was manifested the love of God toward us, because that
God sent his only begotten Son into the world, that we might live
through him.
10Herein is love, not that we loved God, but that he loved us,
and sent his Son *to be* the propitiation for our sins.
11Beloved, if God so loved us, we ought also to love one another.
12No man hath seen God at any time. If we love one another,
God dwelleth in us, and his love is perfected in us.
13Hereby know we that we dwell in him, and he in us, because
he hath given us of his Spirit.
14And we have seen and do testify that the Father sent the Son
*to be* the Saviour of the world.
15Whosoever shall confess that Jesus is the Son of God, God
dwelleth in him, and he in God.
16And we have known and believed the love that God hath to
us. God is love; and he that dwelleth in love dwelleth in God, and
God in him.
17Herein is our love made perfect, that we may have boldness
in the day of judgment: because as he is, so are we in this world.
18There is no fear in love; but perfect love casteth out fear:
because fear hath torment. He that feareth is not made perfect in
love.
19We love him, because he first loved us.

## Amplified

4 BELOVED, DO not put faith in every spirit, but prove (test)
the spirits to discover whether they proceed from God; for
many false prophets have gone forth into the world.
2By this you may know (perceive and recognize) the Spirit of
God: every spirit which acknowledges *and* confesses [the fact] that
Jesus Christ, the Messiah, [actually] has become man *and* has come
in the flesh is of God—has God for its source.
3And every spirit which does not acknowledge *and* confess *that*
Jesus *Christ has come in the flesh* [but would [a]annul, destroy,
[b]sever, disunite Him] is not of God—does not proceed from Him.
This [ [c]non-confession] is the [spirit] of antichrist, [of] which you
heard that it was coming, and now it is already in the world.
4Little children, you are of God—you belong to Him—and have
[already] defeated *and* overcome them [the agents of antichrist],
because He Who lives in you is greater (mightier) than he who is
in the world.
5They proceed from the world *and* are of the world, therefore
it is out of the world [its [d]whole economy morally considered] that
they speak, and the world listens (pays attention) to them.
6We are [children] of God. Whoever is learning to know God—
progressively to perceive, recognize and understand God [by observation and experience] and to [e]get an ever clearer knowledge
of Him—listens to us; and he who is not of God does not listen *or*
pay attention to us. By this we know (recognize) the Spirit of Truth
and the spirit of error.
7Beloved, let us love one another; for love [springs] from God,
and he who loves [his fellow men] is begotten (born) of God and
is coming (progressively) to know *and* understand God—to perceive and recognize and get a better and clearer knowledge of Him.
8He who does not love has not become acquainted with God—
does not *and* never did know Him; for God is love.
9In this the love of God was made manifest (displayed), where
we are concerned, in that God sent His Son, the only begotten *or*
[f]unique [Son], into the world so that we might live through Him.
10In this is love, not that we loved God, but that He loved us
and sent His Son to be the propitiation (the atoning sacrifice) for
our sins.
11Beloved, if God loved us so [very much], we also ought to love
one another.
12No man has at any time [yet] seen God. But if we love one
another, God abides (lives and remains) in us and His love [that
love which is essentially His] is brought to completion—to its full
maturity, runs its full course, is perfected—in us!
13By this we come to know (perceive, recognize and understand) that we abide (live and remain) in Him and He in us:
because He has given (imparted) to us of His (Holy) Spirit.
14And [besides] we ourselves have seen [have deliberately and
steadfastly contemplated], and bear witness that the Father has
sent the Son [as the] Savior of the world.
15Any one who confesses (acknowledges, owns) that Jesus is
the Son of God, God abides (lives, makes His home) in him, and
he (abides, lives, makes his home) in God.
16And we know (understand, recognize, are conscious of, by
observation and by experience), and believe (adhere to and put
faith in and rely on) the love God cherishes for us. God is love, and
he who dwells *and* continues in love dwells *and* continues in God,
and God dwells *and* continues in him.
17In this [union and communion with Him] love is brought to
completion *and* attains perfection with us, that we may have confidence for the day of judgment—with assurance and boldness to
face Him—because as He is, so are we in this world.
18There is no fear in love—dread does not exist; but full-grown
(complete, perfect) love [g]turns fear out of doors *and* expels every
trace of terror! For fear [h]brings with it the thought of punishment,
and [so] he who is afraid has not reached the full maturity of
love—is not yet grown into love's complete perfection.
19We love *Him,* because He first loved us.

**AMP** [a] An ancient reading. [b] The Vulgate translation. [c] Vincent. [d] Vincent. [e] Vincent. [f] Moulton and Milligan. [g] Vincent. [h] Thayer.

## New American Standard

*Testing the Spirits*

4 BELOVED, DO not believe every spirit, but test the spirits to
see whether they are from God; because many false prophets
have gone out into the world.
2By this you know the Spirit of God: every spirit that confesses
that Jesus Christ has come in the flesh is from God;
3and every spirit that does not confess Jesus is not from God;
and this is the *spirit* of the antichrist, of which you have heard that
it is coming, and now it is already in the world.
4You are from God, little children, and have overcome them;
because greater is He who is in you than he who is in the world.
5They are from the world; therefore they speak *as* from the
world, and the world listens to them.
6We are from God; he who knows God listens to us; he who
is not from God does not listen to us. By this we know the spirit
of truth and the spirit of error.

*God Is Love*

7¶ Beloved, let us love one another, for love is from God; and
everyone who loves is born of God and knows God.
8The one who does not love does not know God, for God is
love.
9By this the love of God was manifested in us, that God has
sent His only begotten Son into the world so that we might live
through Him.
10In this is love, not that we loved God, but that He loved us
and sent His Son *to be* the propitiation for our sins.
11Beloved, if God so loved us, we also ought to love one another.
12No one has beheld God at any time; if we love one another,
God abides in us, and His love is perfected in us.
13By this we know that we abide in Him and He in us, because
He has given us of His Spirit.
14And we have beheld and bear witness that the Father has sent
the Son *to be* the Savior of the world.
15Whoever confesses that Jesus is the Son of God, God abides
in him, and he in God.
16And we have come to know and have believed the love which
God has for us. God is love, and the one who abides in love abides
in God, and God abides in him.
17By this, love is perfected with us, that we may have confidence in the day of judgment; because as He is, so also are we in
this world.
18There is no fear in love; but perfect love casts out fear, because
fear involves punishment, and the one who fears is not perfected
in love.
19We love, because He first loved us.

## New International

*Test the Spirits*

4 DEAR FRIENDS, do not believe every spirit, but test the
spirits to see whether they are from God, because many false
prophets have gone out into the world. 2This is how you can
recognize the Spirit of God: Every spirit that acknowledges that
Jesus Christ has come in the flesh is from God, 3but every spirit
that does not acknowledge Jesus is not from God. This is the spirit
of the antichrist, which you have heard is coming and even now
is already in the world.
4You, dear children, are from God and have overcome them,
because the one who is in you is greater than the one who is in the
world. 5They are from the world and therefore speak from the
viewpoint of the world, and the world listens to them. 6We are
from God, and whoever knows God listens to us; but whoever is
not from God does not listen to us. This is how we recognize the
Spirit[i] of truth and the spirit of falsehood.

*God's Love and Ours*

7Dear friends, let us love one another, for love comes from God.
Everyone who loves has been born of God and knows God. 8Who-
ever does not love does not know God, because God is love. 9This
is how God showed his love among us: He sent his one and only
Son[j] into the world that we might live through him. 10This is love:
not that we loved God, but that he loved us and sent his Son as
an atoning sacrifice for[k] our sins. 11Dear friends, since God so
loved us, we also ought to love one another. 12No one has ever
seen God; but if we love one another, God lives in us and his love
is made complete in us.
13We know that we live in him and he in us, because he has
given us of his Spirit. 14And we have seen and testify that the
Father has sent his Son to be the Savior of the world. 15If anyone
acknowledges that Jesus is the Son of God, God lives in him and
he in God. 16And so we know and rely on the love God has for
us.
God is love. Whoever lives in love lives in God, and God in him.
17In this way, love is made complete among us so that we will have
confidence on the day of judgment, because in this world we are
like him. 18There is no fear in love. But perfect love drives out fear,
because fear has to do with punishment. The one who fears is not
made perfect in love.
19We love because he first loved us. 20If anyone says, "I love

**NIV** [i] 6 Or *spirit* [j] 9 Or *his only begotten Son* [k] 10 Or *as the one who would turn aside his wrath, taking away*

## King James

20If a man say, I love God, and hateth his brother, he is a liar: for he that loveth not his brother whom he hath seen, how can he love God whom he hath not seen?

21And this commandment have we from him, That he who loveth God love his brother also.

**5** WHOSOEVER BELIEVETH that Jesus is the Christ is born of God: and every one that loveth him that begat loveth him also that is begotten of him.

2By this we know that we love the children of God, when we love God, and keep his commandments.

3For this is the love of God, that we keep his commandments: and his commandments are not grievous.

4For whatsoever is born of God overcometh the world: and this is the victory that overcometh the world, *even* our faith.

5Who is he that overcometh the world, but he that believeth that Jesus is the Son of God?

6This is he that came by water and blood, *even* Jesus Christ; not by water only, but by water and blood. And it is the Spirit that beareth witness, because the Spirit is truth.

7For there are three that bear record in heaven, the Father, the Word, and the Holy Ghost: and these three are one.

8And there are three that bear witness in earth, the spirit, and the water, and the blood: and these three agree in one.

9If we receive the witness of men, the witness of God is greater: for this is the witness of God which he hath testified of his Son.

10He that believeth on the Son of God hath the witness in himself: he that believeth not God hath made him a liar; because he believeth not the record that God gave of his Son.

11And this is the record, that God hath given to us eternal life, and this life is in his Son.

12He that hath the Son hath life; *and* he that hath not the Son of God hath not life.

13These things have I written unto you that believe on the name of the Son of God; that ye may know that ye have eternal life, and that ye may believe on the name of the Son of God.

14And this is the confidence that we have in him, that, if we ask any thing according to his will, he heareth us:

15And if we know that he hear us, whatsoever we ask, we know that we have the petitions that we desired of him.

16If any man see his brother sin a sin *which is* not unto death, he shall ask, and he shall give him life for them that sin not unto death. There is a sin unto death: I do not say that he shall pray for it.

## Amplified

20If any one says, I love God, and (detests, abominates) hates his brother [ [a]in Christ], he is a liar; for he who does not love his brother whom he has seen, cannot love God Whom he has not seen.

21And this command (charge, order, injunction) we have from Him, that he who loves God shall love his brother [ [b]believer] also.

**5** EVERY ONE who believes—adheres to, trusts in and relies [on the fact]—that Jesus is the Christ, the Messiah, is a born-again child of God; and every one who loves the Father also loves the one born of Him—His offspring.

2By this we come to know (recognize and understand) that we love the children of God: when we love God and obey His commands—orders, charges; when we keep His ordinances and are mindful of His precepts and His teaching.

3For the [true] love of God is this, that we do His commands—keep His ordinances and are mindful of His precepts and teaching. And these orders of His are not irksome—burdensome, oppressive or grievous.

4For whatever is born of God is victorious over the world; and this is the victory that conquers the world, even our faith.

5Who is it that is victorious over (that conquers) the world but he who believes that Jesus is the Son of God—who adheres to, trusts in and relies [on that fact]?

6This is He Who came by (with) water and blood [ [c]His baptism and His death], Jesus Christ, the Messiah; not by (in) the water only but by (in) the water and the blood.

7And it is the (Holy) Spirit Who bears witness, because the (Holy) Spirit is the Truth.

8So there are three witnesses *in heaven, the Father, the Word and the Holy Spirit, and these three are One; and there are three witnesses on the earth*, the Spirit, the water and the blood; and these three agree—are in unison, their testimony coincides.

9If we accept [as we do] the testimony of men (if we are willing to take human authority), the testimony of God is greater (stronger authority), for this is the testimony of God; even the witness which He has borne regarding His Son.

10He who believes in the Son of God—who adheres to and trusts in and relies on Him, possesses this divine attestation—has the testimony within himself. He who does not believe God (in this way) has made Him out to be *and* represented Him as a liar, because he has not believed—put his faith in and adhered to and relied on the testimony—the evidence that God has borne regarding His Son.

11And this is that testimony—that evidence: God gave us eternal life, and this life is in His Son.

12He who possesses the Son has that life; he who does not possess the Son of God does not have that life.

13I write this to you who believe in (adhere to, trust in and rely on) the name of the Son of God—that is, in [d]the peculiar services and blessings conferred by Him on men—so that you may know (with settled and absolute knowledge) that you [already] have life, [e]yes, eternal life.

14And this is the confidence—the assurance, the [privilege of] boldness—which we have in Him: [we are sure] that if we ask anything (make any request) according to His will (in agreement with His own plan) He listens to *and* hears us.

15And if (since) we [positively] know that He listens to us in whatever we ask, we also know [with settled and absolute knowledge] that we have [granted us as our present possessions] the requests made of Him.

16If any one sees his brother [believer] committing a sin that does not [lead to] death [the extinguishing of life], he will pray and (God) will give him life—yes, He will grant life to all those whose sin is not [one leading] to death. There is a sin [that leads] to death; I do not say that one should pray for that.

**AMP** [a] Thayer. [b] Thayer. [c] Vincent. [d] Thayer. [e] Westcott in Speaker's Commentary.

## New American Standard

20If someone says, "I love God," and hates his brother, he is a liar; for the one who does not love his brother whom he has seen, cannot love God whom he has not seen.

21And this commandment we have from Him, that the one who loves God should love his brother also.

*Overcoming the World*

**5** WHOEVER BELIEVES that Jesus is the [f]Christ is born of God; and whoever loves the Father loves the *child* born of Him.

2By this we know that we love the children of God, when we love God and observe His commandments.

3For this is the love of God, that we keep His commandments; and His commandments are not burdensome.

4For whatever is born of God overcomes the world; and this is the victory that has overcome the world—our faith.

5And who is the one who overcomes the world, but he who believes that Jesus is the Son of God?

6This is the one who came by water and blood, Jesus Christ; not with the water only, but with the water and with the blood.

7And it is the Spirit who bears witness, because the Spirit is the truth.

8For there are three that bear witness, [g]the Spirit and the water and the blood; and the three are in agreement.

9If we receive the witness of men, the witness of God is greater; for the witness of God is this, that He has borne witness concerning His Son.

10The one who believes in the Son of God has the witness in himself; the one who does not believe God has made Him a liar, because he has not believed in the witness that God has borne concerning His Son.

11And the witness is this, that God has given us eternal life, and this life is in His Son.

12He who has the Son has the life; he who does not have the Son of God does not have the life.

*This Is Written That You May Know*

**13**¶ These things I have written to you who believe in the name of the Son of God, in order that you may know that you have eternal life.

14And this is the confidence which we have before Him, that, if we ask anything according to His will, He hears us.

15And if we know that He hears us *in* whatever we ask, we know that we have the requests which we have asked from Him.

16If anyone sees his brother committing a sin not *leading* to death, he shall ask and *God* will for him give life to those who commit sin not *leading* to death. There is a sin *leading* to death; I do not say that he should make request for this.

NAS [f] I.e., Messiah [g] A few late mss. read *in heaven, the Father, the Word, and the Holy Spirit, and these three are one. And there are three that bear witness on earth, the Spirit*

## New International

God," yet hates his brother, he is a liar. For anyone who does not
love his brother, whom he has seen, cannot love God, whom he
has not seen. 21And he has given us this command: Whoever loves
God must also love his brother.

*Faith in the Son of God*

**5** EVERYONE WHO believes that Jesus is the Christ is born of
God, and everyone who loves the father loves his child as
well. 2This is how we know that we love the children of God: by
loving God and carrying out his commands. 3This is love for God:
to obey his commands. And his commands are not burdensome,
4for everyone born of God overcomes the world. This is the victory
that has overcome the world, even our faith. 5Who is it that overcomes the world? Only he who believes that Jesus is the Son of
God.
6This is the one who came by water and blood—Jesus Christ.
He did not come by water only, but by water and blood. And it
is the Spirit who testifies, because the Spirit is the truth. 7For there
are three that testify: 8the[h] Spirit, the water and the blood; and the
three are in agreement. 9We accept man's testimony, but God's
testimony is greater because it is the testimony of God, which he
has given about his Son. 10Anyone who believes in the Son of God
has this testimony in his heart. Anyone who does not believe God
has made him out to be a liar, because he has not believed the
testimony God has given about his Son. 11And this is the testimony: God has given us eternal life, and this life is in his Son. 12He
who has the Son has life; he who does not have the Son of God
does not have life.

*Concluding Remarks*

13I write these things to you who believe in the name of the Son
of God so that you may know that you have eternal life. 14This is
the confidence we have in approaching God: that if we ask anything according to his will, he hears us. 15And if we know that he
hears us—whatever we ask—we know that we have what we
asked of him.
16If anyone sees his brother commit a sin that does not lead to
death, he should pray and God will give him life. I refer to those
whose sin does not lead to death. There is a sin that leads to death.

NIV [h] *7,8* Late manuscripts of the Vulgate *testify in heaven: the Father, the Word and the Holy Spirit, and these three are one. 8And there are three that testify on earth: the* (not found in any Greek manuscript before the sixteenth century)

## King James

17 All unrighteousness is sin: and there is a sin not unto death.

18 We know that whosoever is born of God sinneth not; but he that is begotten of God keepeth himself, and that wicked one toucheth him not.

19 *And* we know that we are of God, and the whole world lieth in wickedness.

20 And we know that the Son of God is come, and hath given us an understanding, that we may know him that is true, and we are in him that is true, *even* in his Son Jesus Christ. This is the true God, and eternal life.

21 Little children, keep yourselves from idols. Amen.

## Amplified

17 All wrongdoing is sin, and there is sin which does not [involve] death—that may be repented of and forgiven.

18 We know [absolutely] that any one born of God does not [deliberately and knowingly] practice committing sin, but the One Who was begotten of God carefully watches over *and* protects him—Christ's divine presence within him preserves him against the evil—and the wicked one does not lay hold (get a grip) on him *or* touch [him].

19 We know [positively] that we are of God, and the whole world [around us] is under the power of the evil one.

20 And we [have seen and] know [positively] that the Son of God has [actually] come to this world and has given us understanding *and* insight progressively to perceive (recognize) *and* come to know better *and* more clearly Him Who is true; and we are in Him Who is true, in His Son Jesus Christ, the Messiah. This is the true God and Life eternal.

21 Little children, keep yourselves from idols—false gods, [from anything and everything that would occupy the place in your heart due to God, from any sort of substitute for Him that would take first place in your life]. *Amen. So let it be.*

## New American Standard

17All unrighteousness is sin, and there is a sin not *leading* to death.
18¶ We know that no one who is born of God sins; but He who was born of God keeps him and the evil one does not touch him.
19We know that we are of God, and the whole world lies in *the power of* the evil one.
20And we know that the Son of God has come, and has given us understanding, in order that we might know Him who is true, and we are in Him who is true, in His Son Jesus Christ. This is the true God and eternal life.
21Little children, guard yourselves from idols.

## New International

I am not saying that he should pray about that. 17All wrongdoing
is sin, and there is sin that does not lead to death.
18We know that anyone born of God does not continue to sin;
the one who was born of God keeps him safe, and the evil one
cannot harm him. 19We know that we are children of God, and that
the whole world is under the control of the evil one. 20We know
also that the Son of God has come and has given us understanding,
so that we may know him who is true. And we are in him who is
true—even in his Son Jesus Christ. He is the true God and eternal
life.
21Dear children, keep yourselves from idols.

## King James

THE SECOND EPISTLE

OF

# John

1THE ELDER unto the elect lady and her children, whom I love
in the truth; and not I only, but also all they that have known the
truth;
2For the truth's sake, which dwelleth in us, and shall be with
us for ever.
3Grace be with you, mercy, *and* peace, from God the Father, and
from the Lord Jesus Christ, the Son of the Father, in truth and love.
4I rejoiced greatly that I found of thy children walking in truth,
as we have received a commandment from the Father.
5And now I beseech thee, lady, not as though I wrote a new
commandment unto thee, but that which we had from the beginning, that we love one another.
6And this is love, that we walk after his commandments. This
is the commandment, That, as ye have heard from the beginning,
ye should walk in it.
7For many deceivers are entered into the world, who confess
not that Jesus Christ is come in the flesh. This is a deceiver and an
antichrist.
8Look to yourselves, that we lose not those things which we
have wrought, but that we receive a full reward.
9Whosoever transgresseth, and abideth not in the doctrine of
Christ, hath not God. He that abideth in the doctrine of Christ, he
hath both the Father and the Son.
10If there come any unto you, and bring not this doctrine,
receive him not into *your* house, neither bid him God speed:
11For he that biddeth him God speed is partaker of his evil
deeds.
12Having many things to write unto you, I would not *write* with
paper and ink: but I trust to come unto you, and speak face to face,
that our joy may be full.
13The children of thy elect sister greet thee. Amen.

## Amplified

THE SECOND LETTER OF

# John

1THE ELDERLY elder [of the church addresses this letter] to the
elect (chosen) lady (Cyria) and her children, whom I truly love, and
not only I but also all who are progressively learning to recognize
*and* know *and* understand the Truth,
2Because of the Truth which lives *and* stays on in our hearts and
will be with us forever:
3Grace (spiritual blessing), mercy and soul-peace will be with
us, from God the Father and from Jesus Christ, the Messiah, the
Father's Son, in all sincerity (truth) and love.
4I was greatly delighted to find some of your children walking
(living) in [the] Truth, just as we have been commanded by the
Father [Himself].
5And now I beg you, lady (Cyria), not as if I were issuing a new
charge (injunction or command), but [simply recalling to your
mind] the one we have had from the beginning, that we love one
another.
6And what this love consists in is this, that we live *and* walk in
accordance with *and* guided by His commandments—His orders,
ordinances, precepts, teaching. This is the commandment, as you
have heard from the beginning, that you continue to walk in
love—guided by it and following it.
7For many imposters—seducers, deceivers and false leaders—
have gone out into the world, men who will not acknowledge
(confess, admit) the coming of Jesus Christ, the Messiah, in bodily
form; such a one is the imposter—the seducer, the deceiver, the
false leader, the antagonist of Christ—and the Antichrist.
8—Take care; look to yourselves that you may not lose (throw
away or destroy) all that we *and* you have labored for, but that you
may [persevere until you] win *and* receive back a perfect reward—
in full.
9Any one who runs on ahead [of God] and does not abide in
the doctrine of Christ—who is not content with what He taught—
does not have God; but he who continues to live in the doctrine
(teaching) of Christ—does have God; he has both the Father and
the Son.
10If any one comes to you and does not bring this doctrine (is
disloyal to what Jesus Christ taught), do not receive him—do not
accept him, do not welcome *or* admit him—into [your] house or bid
him Godspeed *or* give him any encouragement.
11For he who wishes him success—who encourages him, wishing him Godspeed—is a partaker in his evil doings.
12Although I have many things to write to you, I prefer not to
do so with paper and ink, but I hope to come to see you and talk
with you by word of mouth, so that our joy may be complete.
13The children of your elect (chosen) sister wish to be remembered to you. *Amen. So be it.*

## New American Standard

# 2 John

*Walk According to His Commandments*

1THE ELDER to the chosen lady and her children, whom I love
in truth; and not only I, but also all who know the truth,
2for the sake of the truth which abides in us and will be with
us forever:

3Grace, mercy *and* peace will be with us, from God the Father
and from Jesus Christ, the Son of the Father, in truth and love.

**4**¶ I was very glad to find *some* of your children walking in
truth, just as we have received commandment *to do* from the
Father.

5And now I ask you, lady, not as writing to you a new commandment, but the one which we have had from the beginning,
that we love one another.

6And this is love, that we walk according to His commandments. This is the commandment, just as you have heard from the
beginning, that you should walk in it.

7For many deceivers have gone out into the world, those who
do not acknowledge Jesus Christ *as* coming in the flesh. This is the
deceiver and the antichrist.

8Watch yourselves, that you might not lose what we have
accomplished, but that you may receive a full reward.

9Anyone who goes too far and does not abide in the teaching
of Christ, does not have God; the one who abides in the teaching,
he has both the Father and the Son.

10If anyone comes to you and does not bring this teaching, do
not receive him into *your* house, and do not give him a greeting;
11for the one who gives him a greeting participates in his evil
deeds.

**12**¶ Having many things to write to you, I do not want to *do so*
with paper and ink; but I hope to come to you and speak face to
face, that your joy may be made full.

13The children of your chosen sister greet you.

## New International

# 2 John

1THE ELDER,

To the chosen lady and her children, whom I love in the truth—
and not I only, but also all who know the truth— 2because of the
truth, which lives in us and will be with us forever:

3Grace, mercy and peace from God the Father and from Jesus
Christ, the Father's Son, will be with us in truth and love.

4It has given me great joy to find some of your children walking
in the truth, just as the Father commanded us. 5And now, dear
lady, I am not writing you a new command but one we have had
from the beginning. I ask that we love one another. 6And this is
love: that we walk in obedience to his commands. As you have
heard from the beginning, his command is that you walk in love.

7Many deceivers, who do not acknowledge Jesus Christ as coming in the flesh, have gone out into the world. Any such person
is the deceiver and the antichrist. 8Watch out that you do not lose
what you have worked for, but that you may be rewarded fully.
9Anyone who runs ahead and does not continue in the teaching
of Christ does not have God; whoever continues in the teaching
has both the Father and the Son. 10If anyone comes to you and
does not bring this teaching, do not take him into your house or
welcome him. 11Anyone who welcomes him shares in his wicked
work.

12I have much to write to you, but I do not want to use paper
and ink. Instead, I hope to visit you and talk with you face to face,
so that our joy may be complete.

13The children of your chosen sister send their greetings.

## King James

THE THIRD EPISTLE

OF

# John

1THE ELDER unto the wellbeloved Gaius, whom I love in the truth.

2Beloved, I wish above all things that thou mayest prosper and be in health, even as thy soul prospereth.

3For I rejoiced greatly, when the brethren came and testified of the truth that is in thee, even as thou walkest in the truth.

4I have no greater joy than to hear that my children walk in truth.

5Beloved, thou doest faithfully whatsoever thou doest to the brethren, and to strangers;

6Which have borne witness of thy charity before the church: whom if thou bring forward on their journey after a godly sort, thou shalt do well:

7Because that for his name's sake they went forth, taking nothing of the Gentiles.

8We therefore ought to receive such, that we might be fellowhelpers to the truth.

9I wrote unto the church: but Diotrephes, who loveth to have the preeminence among them, receiveth us not.

10Wherefore, if I come, I will remember his deeds which he doeth, prating against us with malicious words: and not content therewith, neither doth he himself receive the brethren, and forbiddeth them that would, and casteth *them* out of the church.

11Beloved, follow not that which is evil, but that which is good. He that doeth good is of God: but he that doeth evil hath not seen God.

12Demetrius hath good report of all *men,* and of the truth itself: yea, and we *also* bear record; and ye know that our record is true.

13I had many things to write, but I will not with ink and pen write unto thee:

14But I trust I shall shortly see thee, and we shall speak face to face. Peace *be* to thee. *Our* friends salute thee. Greet the friends by name.

## Amplified

THE THIRD LETTER OF

# John

1THE ELDERLY elder [of the church addresses this letter] to the (esteemed) beloved Gaius, whom I truly love.

2Beloved, I pray that you may prosper in every way and [that your body] may keep well, even as [I know] your soul keeps well *and* prospers.

3In fact, I greatly rejoiced [when some of] the brethren from time to time arrived and spoke [so highly] of the sincerity *and* fidelity of your life, as indeed you do live in the Truth [the whole Gospel presents].

4I have no greater joy than this, to hear that my [spiritual] children are living their lives in the Truth.

5Beloved, it is a fine *and* faithful work that you are doing when you give any service to the [Christian] brethren, and [especially when they are] strangers.

6They have testified before the church of your love *and* friendship. You will do well to forward them on their journey, [and you will please do so] in a way worthy of God's [service].

7For these [traveling missionaries] have gone out for the Name's sake—for His sake—and are accepting nothing from the heathen (the Gentiles, the non-Israelites).

8So we ourselves ought to support such people—to welcome and provide for them—in order that we may be fellow workers in the Truth (the whole Gospel) *and* co-operate with its teachers.

9I have written briefly to the church; but Diotrephes, who likes to take the lead among them *and* put himself first, does not acknowledge my authority *and* refuses to accept my suggestions *or* to listen to me.

10So when I arrive, I will call attention to what he is doing, his boiling over *and* casting malicious reflections upon us with insinuating language. And not satisfied with that, he refuses to receive *and* welcome the [missionary] brethren himself, and also interferes with *and* forbids those who would welcome them, and tries to expel (excommunicate) them from the church.

11Beloved, do not imitate evil, but imitate good. He who does good is of God; he who does evil has not seen (discerned or experienced) God—has enjoyed no vision of Him and does not know Him at all.

12Demetrius has warm commendation from everyone, and from the Truth itself; we add our testimony also, and you know that our testimony is true.

13I had much [to say to you when I began] to write, but I prefer not to put it down with pen (a reed) and ink;

14I hope to see you soon, and we will talk together by word of mouth.

15[Goodbye!] Peace be to you! The friends here send you greetings. Remember me to the friends there, (to every one of them personally) by name.

## New American Standard

# 3 John

*You Walk in the Truth*

1 THE ELDER to the beloved Gaius, whom I love in truth.
2 ¶ Beloved, I pray that in all respects you may prosper and be
in good health, just as your soul prospers.
3 For I was very glad when brethren came and bore witness to
your truth, *that is*, how you are walking in truth.
4 I have no greater joy than this, to hear of my children walking
in the truth.
5 ¶ Beloved, you are acting faithfully in whatever you accomplish for the brethren, and especially *when they are* strangers;
6 and they bear witness to your love before the church; and you
will do well to send them on their way in a manner worthy of God.
7 For they went out for the sake of the Name, accepting nothing
from the Gentiles.
8 Therefore we ought to support such men, that we may be
fellow workers with the truth.
9 ¶ I wrote something to the church; but Diotrephes, who loves
to be first among them, does not accept what we say.
10 For this reason, if I come, I will call attention to his deeds
which he does, unjustly accusing us with wicked words; and not
satisfied with this, neither does he himself receive the brethren,
and he forbids those who desire *to do so*, and puts *them* out of the
church.
11 Beloved, do not imitate what is evil, but what is good. The one
who does good is of God; the one who does evil has not seen God.
12 Demetrius has received a *good* testimony from everyone, and
from the truth itself; and we also bear witness, and you know that
our witness is true.
13 ¶ I had many things to write to you, but I am not willing to
write *them* to you with pen and ink;
14 but I hope to see you shortly, and we shall speak face to face.
Peace *be* to you. The friends greet you. Greet the friends by name.

## New International

# 3 John

1 THE ELDER,

To my dear friend Gaius, whom I love in the truth.

2 Dear friend, I pray that you may enjoy good health and that
all may go well with you, even as your soul is getting along well.
3 It gave me great joy to have some brothers come and tell about
your faithfulness to the truth and how you continue to walk in the
truth. 4 I have no greater joy than to hear that my children are
walking in the truth.
5 Dear friend, you are faithful in what you are doing for the
brothers, even though they are strangers to you. 6 They have told
the church about your love. You will do well to send them on their
way in a manner worthy of God. 7 It was for the sake of the Name
that they went out, receiving no help from the pagans. 8 We ought
therefore to show hospitality to such men so that we may work
together for the truth.
9 I wrote to the church, but Diotrephes, who loves to be first, will
have nothing to do with us. 10 So if I come, I will call attention to
what he is doing, gossiping maliciously about us. Not satisfied
with that, he refuses to welcome the brothers. He also stops those
who want to do so and puts them out of the church.
11 Dear friend, do not imitate what is evil but what is good.
Anyone who does what is good is from God. Anyone who does
what is evil has not seen God. 12 Demetrius is well spoken of by
everyone—and even by the truth itself. We also speak well of him,
and you know that our testimony is true.
13 I have much to write you, but I do not want to do so with pen
and ink. 14 I hope to see you soon, and we will talk face to face.

Peace to you. The friends here send their greetings. Greet the
friends there by name.

## King James

THE GENERAL EPISTLE OF

# Jude

1JUDE, THE servant of Jesus Christ, and brother of James, to them that are sanctified by God the Father, and preserved in Jesus Christ, *and* called:

2Mercy unto you, and peace, and love, be multiplied.

3Beloved, when I gave all diligence to write unto you of the common salvation, it was needful for me to write unto you, and exhort *you* that ye should earnestly contend for the faith which was once delivered unto the saints.

4For there are certain men crept in unawares, who were before of old ordained to this condemnation, ungodly men, turning the grace of our God into lasciviousness, and denying the only Lord God, and our Lord Jesus Christ.

5I will therefore put you in remembrance, though ye once knew this, how that the Lord, having saved the people out of the land of Egypt, afterward destroyed them that believed not.

6And the angels which kept not their first estate, but left their own habitation, he hath reserved in everlasting chains under darkness unto the judgment of the great day.

7Even as Sodom and Gomorrha, and the cities about them in like manner, giving themselves over to fornication, and going after strange flesh, are set forth for an example, suffering the vengeance of eternal fire.

8Likewise also these *filthy* dreamers defile the flesh, despise dominion, and speak evil of dignities.

9Yet Michael the archangel, when contending with the devil he disputed about the body of Moses, durst not bring against him a railing accusation, but said, The Lord rebuke thee.

10But these speak evil of those things which they know not: but what they know naturally, as brute beasts, in those things they corrupt themselves.

11Woe unto them! for they have gone in the way of Cain, and ran greedily after the error of Balaam for reward, and perished in the gainsaying of Core.

## Amplified

THE LETTER OF

# Jude

1JUDE, A servant of Jesus Christ, the Messiah, and brother of James, [writes this letter] to those who are called (chosen), dearly loved by God the Father ( [a]and separated, set apart), and kept for Jesus Christ:

2May mercy, soul-peace and love be multiplied to you.

3Beloved, my whole concern was to write to you in regard to our common salvation. [But] I found it necessary *and* was impelled to write you and urgently appeal to *and* exhort [you] to contend for the faith which was once for all [b]handed down to the saints—the faith [which is that sum of Christian belief] which was delivered [c]verbally to the holy people of God.

4For certain men have crept in stealthily— [d]gaining entrance secretly by a side [door]. Their doom was predicted long ago, (impious, profane) ungodly persons who pervert the grace (the spiritual blessing and favor) of our God into lawlessness *and* wantonness *and* immorality, and disown *and* deny our sole Master and Lord, Jesus Christ, the Messiah, the Anointed One.

5Now I want to remind you, though you were fully informed once for all, that though the Lord [at one time] delivered a people out of the land of Egypt, He subsequently destroyed those [of them] who did not believe—who [refused] to adhere to, trust in and rely upon Him.

6And angels that did not keep (care for, guard and hold to) their own first place of power but abandoned their proper dwelling place, He has reserved in custody in eternal chains (bonds) under the thick gloom of utter darkness until the judgment *and* doom of the great day.

7Just as Sodom and Gomorrah and the adjacent towns, which likewise gave themselves over to impurity and indulged in unnatural vice *and* sensual perversity, are laid out [in plain sight] as an exhibit of perpetual punishment [to warn] of everlasting fire [the wicked are sentenced to suffer]. [Gen. 19.]

8Nevertheless in like manner these dreamers also corrupt the body, scorn *and* reject authority *and* government, and revile *and* libel *and* scoff at [heavenly] glories (the glorious ones).

9But when [even] the archangel Michael, contending with the devil, judicially argued (disputed) about the body of Moses, he dared not (presume to) bring an abusive condemnation against him, but [simply] said, The Lord rebuke you! [Zech. 3:2.]

10But these men revile (scoff and sneer at) anything they do not happen to be acquainted with *and* do not understand; and whatever they do understand physically, [that which they know by mere instinct] like irrational beasts, by these they corrupt themselves *and* are destroyed (perish).

11Woe to them! For they have run riotously in the way of Cain, and have abandoned themselves for the sake of gain [it offers them] to the error of Balaam, and have perished in rebellion [like that] of Korah! [Gen. 4:3-8; Num. 22-24; 16.]

**AMP** [a] Some texts so read. [b] Abbott-Smith. [c] Abbott-Smith. [d] Meaning of the verb.

## New American Standard

# Jude

*The Warnings of History to the Ungodly*

1 JUDE, A bond-servant of Jesus Christ, and brother of James,
to those who are the called, beloved in God the Father, and kept
for Jesus Christ:
2 May mercy and peace and love be multiplied to you.
3 ¶ Beloved, while I was making every effort to write you about
our common salvation, I felt the necessity to write to you appealing
that you contend earnestly for the faith which was once for all
delivered to the saints.
4 For certain persons have crept in unnoticed, those who were
long beforehand marked out for this condemnation, ungodly persons who turn the grace of our God into licentiousness and deny
our only Master and Lord, Jesus Christ.
5 ¶ Now I desire to remind you, though you know all things
once for all, that [e]the Lord, after saving a people out of the land
of Egypt, subsequently destroyed those who did not believe.
6 And angels who did not keep their own domain, but abandoned their proper abode, He has kept in eternal bonds under
darkness for the judgment of the great day.
7 Just as Sodom and Gomorrah and the cities around them,
since they in the same way as these indulged in gross immorality
and went after strange flesh, are exhibited as an example, in undergoing the punishment of eternal fire.
8 Yet in the same manner these men, also by dreaming, defile
the flesh, and reject authority, and revile angelic majesties.
9 But Michael the archangel, when he disputed with the devil
and argued about the body of Moses, did not dare pronounce
against him a railing judgment, but said, "The Lord rebuke you."
10 But these men revile the things which they do not understand; and the things which they know by instinct, like unreasoning animals, by these things they are destroyed.
11 Woe to them! For they have gone the way of Cain, and for pay
they have rushed headlong into the error of Balaam, and perished
in the rebellion of Korah.

**NAS** [e] Some ancient mss. read *Jesus*

## New International

# Jude

1 JUDE, A servant of Jesus Christ and a brother of James,

To those who have been called, who are loved by God the
Father and kept by[f] Jesus Christ:

2 Mercy, peace and love be yours in abundance.

*The Sin and Doom of Godless Men*

3 Dear friends, although I was very eager to write to you about
the salvation we share, I felt I had to write and urge you to contend
for the faith that was once for all entrusted to the saints. 4 For
certain men whose condemnation was written about[g] long ago
have secretly slipped in among you. They are godless men, who
change the grace of our God into a license for immorality and deny
Jesus Christ our only Sovereign and Lord.
5 Though you already know all this, I want to remind you that
the Lord[h] delivered his people out of Egypt, but later destroyed
those who did not believe. 6 And the angels who did not keep their
positions of authority but abandoned their own home—these he
has kept in darkness, bound with everlasting chains for judgment
on the great Day. 7 In a similar way, Sodom and Gomorrah and the
surrounding towns gave themselves up to sexual immorality and
perversion. They serve as an example of those who suffer the
punishment of eternal fire.
8 In the very same way, these dreamers pollute their own bodies, reject authority and slander celestial beings. 9 But even the
archangel Michael, when he was disputing with the devil about
the body of Moses, did not dare to bring a slanderous accusation
against him, but said, "The Lord rebuke you!" 10 Yet these men
speak abusively against whatever they do not understand; and
what things they do understand by instinct, like unreasoning animals—these are the very things that destroy them.
11 Woe to them! They have taken the way of Cain; they have
rushed for profit into Balaam's error; they have been destroyed in
Korah's rebellion.

**NIV** [f] 1 Or *for;* or *in* [g] 4 Or *men who were marked out for condemnation*
[h] 5 Some early manuscripts *Jesus*

## King James

12 These are spots in your feasts of charity, when they feast with you, feeding themselves without fear: clouds *they are* without water, carried about of winds; trees whose fruit withereth, without fruit, twice dead, plucked up by the roots;

13 Raging waves of the sea, foaming out their own shame; wandering stars, to whom is reserved the blackness of darkness for ever.

14 And Enoch also, the seventh from Adam, prophesied of these, saying, Behold, the Lord cometh with ten thousands of his saints,

15 To execute judgment upon all, and to convince all that are ungodly among them of all their ungodly deeds which they have ungodly committed, and of all their hard *speeches* which ungodly sinners have spoken against him.

16 These are murmurers, complainers, walking after their own lusts; and their mouth speaketh great swelling *words,* having men's persons in admiration because of advantage.

17 But, beloved, remember ye the words which were spoken before of the apostles of our Lord Jesus Christ;

18 How that they told you there should be mockers in the last time, who should walk after their own ungodly lusts.

19 These be they who separate themselves, sensual, having not the Spirit.

20 But ye, beloved, building up yourselves on your most holy faith, praying in the Holy Ghost,

21 Keep yourselves in the love of God, looking for the mercy of our Lord Jesus Christ unto eternal life.

22 And of some have compassion, making a difference:

23 And others save with fear, pulling *them* out of the fire; hating even the garment spotted by the flesh.

24 Now unto him that is able to keep you from falling, and to present *you* faultless before the presence of his glory with exceeding joy,

25 To the only wise God our Saviour, *be* glory and majesty, dominion and power, both now and ever. Amen.

## Amplified

12 These are (elements of danger,) hidden reefs in your love feasts, where they boldly feast sumptuously—carousing together [in your midst]—without scruple providing for themselves [alone]. They are clouds without water, swept along by the winds, trees without fruit at the late autumn gathering time, twice (doubly) dead, [lifeless and] plucked up by the roots;

13 Wild waves of the sea, flinging up the foam of their own shame *and* disgrace; wandering stars for whom the gloom of eternal darkness has been reserved forever.

14 It was of these people moreover that Enoch in the seventh [generation] from Adam prophesied when he said, Behold, the Lord comes with His myriads of holy ones—ten thousands of His saints;

15 To execute judgment upon all, and to convict all the impious (unholy ones) of all their ungodly deeds which they have committed [in such an] ungodly [way], and of all the severe—abusive, soul-jarring—things which ungodly sinners have spoken against Him.

16 These are inveterate murmurers (grumblers), that complain [of their lot in life], going after their own desires—controlled by their passions; their talk is boastful *and* arrogant, [and they claim to] admire men's persons *and* pay people flattering compliments to gain advantage.

17 But you must remember, beloved, the predictions which were made by the apostles (the special messengers) of our Lord Jesus Christ, the Messiah, the Anointed One.

18 They told you beforehand, In the last days (in the end time) there will be scoffers—who seek to gratify their own unholy desires—following after their own ungodly passions.

19 It is these who are (agitators) setting up distinctions *and* causing divisions; merely sensual [creatures]—carnal, worldly-minded people—devoid of the (Holy) Spirit *and* destitute of any higher spiritual life.

20 But you, beloved, build yourselves up [founded] on your most holy faith— [a]make progress, rise like an edifice higher and higher—praying in the Holy Spirit;

21 Guard *and* keep yourselves in the love of God; expect *and* patiently wait for the mercy of our Lord Jesus Christ, the Messiah, [which will bring you] unto life eternal.

22 And ( [b]refute [so as to] convict some who dispute with you, *and*) on some have mercy who waver *and* doubt.

23 [Strive to] save others, snatching [them] out of [the] fire; on others take pity [but] with fear, loathing even the garment spotted by the flesh *and* polluted by their sensuality. [Zech. 3:2-4.]

24 Now to Him Who is able to keep you without stumbling, *or* slipping, *or* falling and to present [you] unblemished (blameless and faultless) before the presence of His glory—with unspeakable, ecstatic delight—in triumphant joy *and* exultation,

25 To the one only God, our Savior through Jesus Christ our Lord, be glory (splendor), majesty, might *and* dominion, and power *and* authority, before all time and now and forever—unto all the ages of eternity. Amen—so be it.

**AMP** [a] Quoted by Thayer. [b] Some ancient authorities so read.

## New American Standard

12These men are those who are hidden reefs in your love feasts when they feast with you without fear, caring for themselves; clouds without water, carried along by winds; autumn trees without fruit, doubly dead, uprooted;
13wild waves of the sea, casting up their own shame like foam; wandering stars, for whom the black darkness has been reserved forever.
14And about these also Enoch, *in* the seventh *generation* from Adam, prophesied, saying, "Behold, the Lord came with many thousands of His holy ones,
15to execute judgment upon all, and to convict all the ungodly of all their ungodly deeds which they have done in an ungodly way, and of all the harsh things which ungodly sinners have spoken against Him."
16These are grumblers, finding fault, following after their *own* lusts; they speak arrogantly, flattering people for the sake of *gaining an* advantage.

*Keep Yourselves in the Love of God*

17¶ But you, beloved, ought to remember the words that were spoken beforehand by the apostles of our Lord Jesus Christ,
18that they were saying to you, "In the last time there shall be mockers, following after their own ungodly lusts."
19These are the ones who cause divisions, worldly-minded, devoid of the Spirit.
20But you, beloved, building yourselves up on your most holy faith; praying in the Holy Spirit;
21keep yourselves in the love of God, waiting anxiously for the mercy of our Lord Jesus Christ to eternal life.
22And have mercy on some, who are doubting;
23save others, snatching them out of the fire; and on some have mercy with fear, hating even the garment polluted by the flesh.
24¶ Now to Him who is able to keep you from stumbling, and to make you stand in the presence of His glory blameless with great joy,
25to the only God our Savior, through Jesus Christ our Lord, *be* glory, majesty, dominion and authority, before all time and now and forever. Amen.

## New International

12These men are blemishes at your love feasts, eating with you without the slightest qualm—shepherds who feed only themselves. They are clouds without rain, blown along by the wind; autumn trees, without fruit and uprooted—twice dead.
13They are wild waves of the sea, foaming up their shame; wandering stars, for whom blackest darkness has been reserved forever.
14Enoch, the seventh from Adam, prophesied about these men: "See, the Lord is coming with thousands upon thousands of his holy ones
15to judge everyone, and to convict all the ungodly of all the ungodly acts they have done in the ungodly way, and of all the harsh words ungodly sinners have spoken against him."
16These men are grumblers and faultfinders; they follow their own evil desires; they boast about themselves and flatter others for their own advantage.

*A Call to Persevere*

17But, dear friends, remember what the apostles of our Lord Jesus Christ foretold.
18They said to you, "In the last times there will be scoffers who will follow their own ungodly desires."
19These are the men who divide you, who follow mere natural instincts and do not have the Spirit.
20But you, dear friends, build yourselves up in your most holy faith and pray in the Holy Spirit.
21Keep yourselves in God's love as you wait for the mercy of our Lord Jesus Christ to bring you to eternal life.
22Be merciful to those who doubt;
23snatch others from the fire and save them; to others show mercy, mixed with fear—hating even the clothing stained by corrupted flesh.

*Doxology*

24To him who is able to keep you from falling and to present you before his glorious presence without fault and with great joy—
25to the only God our Savior be glory, majesty, power and authority, through Jesus Christ our Lord, before all ages, now and forevermore! Amen.

## King James

THE

# Revelation

OF ST. JOHN THE DIVINE

**1** THE REVELATION of Jesus Christ, which God gave unto him, to show unto his servants things which must shortly come to pass; and he sent and signified *it* by his angel unto his servant John:

2 Who bare record of the word of God, and of the testimony of Jesus Christ, and of all things that he saw.

3 Blessed *is* he that readeth, and they that hear the words of this prophecy, and keep those things which are written therein: for the time *is* at hand.

4 John to the seven churches which are in Asia: Grace *be* unto you, and peace, from him which is, and which was, and which is to come; and from the seven Spirits which are before his throne;

5 And from Jesus Christ, *who is* the faithful witness, *and* the first begotten of the dead, and the prince of the kings of the earth. Unto him that loved us, and washed us from our sins in his own blood,

6 And hath made us kings and priests unto God and his Father; to him *be* glory and dominion for ever and ever. Amen.

7 Behold, he cometh with clouds; and every eye shall see him, and they *also* which pierced him: and all kindreds of the earth shall wail because of him. Even so, Amen.

8 I am Alpha and Omega, the beginning and the ending, saith the Lord, which is, and which was, and which is to come, the Almighty.

9 I John, who also am your brother, and companion in tribulation, and in the kingdom and patience of Jesus Christ, was in the isle that is called Patmos, for the word of God, and for the testimony of Jesus Christ.

10 I was in the Spirit on the Lord's day, and heard behind me a great voice, as of a trumpet,

11 Saying, I am Alpha and Omega, the first and the last: and, What thou seest, write in a book, and send *it* unto the seven churches which are in Asia; unto Ephesus, and unto Smyrna, and unto Pergamos, and unto Thyatira, and unto Sardis, and unto Philadelphia, and unto Laodicea.

12 And I turned to see the voice that spake with me. And being turned, I saw seven golden candlesticks;

13 And in the midst of the seven candlesticks *one* like unto the Son of man, clothed with a garment down to the foot, and girt about the paps with a golden girdle.

14 His head and *his* hairs *were* white like wool, as white as snow; and his eyes *were* as a flame of fire;

**AMP** [a] Vincent. [b] Vincent. [c] Souter. [d] Souter. [e] Abbott-Smith, "Manual Greek Lexicon of the New Testament." [f] Trench and many others. [g] Williams: "ever" and "once" found in the tenses. [h] Williams: "ever" and "once" found in the tenses. [i] Vincent.

## Amplified

THE

# Revelation

TO JOHN

**1** [THIS IS] the revelation of Jesus Christ—His unveiling of the divine mysteries. God gave it to Him to disclose *and* make known to His bond servants certain things which must shortly *and* speedily come to pass [a]in their entirety. And He sent and communicated it through His angel (messenger) to His bond servant John,

2 Who has testified to *and* vouched for all that he saw [ [b]in his visions], the Word of God and the testimony of Jesus Christ.

3 Blessed (happy, [c]to be envied) is the man who reads aloud [in the assemblies] the word of this prophecy; and blessed (happy, [d]to be envied) are those who hear [it read] and who keep themselves true to the things which are written in it—heeding them and laying them to heart—for the time [for them to be fulfilled] is near.

4 John to the seven assemblies (churches) that are in Asia: May grace (God's unmerited favor) be granted to you and spiritual peace [ [e]the peace of Christ's kingdom] from Him Who is and Who was and Who is to come. And from the seven Spirits—that is, [f]the sevenfold Holy Spirit—before His throne. [Isa. 11:2.]

5 And from Jesus Christ the faithful *and* trustworthy Witness, the First-born of the dead [that is, first to be brought back to life] and the Prince (Ruler) of the kings of the earth. To Him Who [g]ever loves us and has [h]once [for all] loosed *and* freed us from our sins by His own blood, [Ps. 89:27.]

6 And formed us into a kingdom [a royal race], priests to His God and Father, to Him be the glory and the power *and* the majesty and the dominion throughout the ages *and* forever and ever. Amen, so be it. [Exod. 19:6; Isa. 61:6.]

7 Lo, He is coming with the clouds, and every eye will see Him, even those who pierced Him; and all the tribes of the earth shall gaze upon Him *and* beat their breasts *and* mourn *and* lament over Him. Even so [must it be]. Amen—so be it. [Dan. 7:13; Zech. 12:10.]

8 I am the Alpha and the Omega *the Beginning and the End,* says the Lord God, He Who is and Who was and Who is to come, the Almighty—the Ruler of all. [Isa. 9:6.]

9 I, John, your brother *and* companion—sharer and participator—with you in the tribulation and kingdom and patient endurance [which are] in Jesus *Christ,* was on the isle called Patmos, [banished] on account of [my witnessing to] the Word of God and the testimony—the proof, the evidence—for Jesus *Christ.*

10 I was in the Spirit—rapt in His power—on the Lord's day, and I heard behind me a great voice like the calling of a [i]war trumpet,

11 Saying, *I am the Alpha and the Omega, the First and the Last.* Write promptly what you see (your vision) in a book and send it to the seven churches *which are in Asia*—to Ephesus and to Smyrna and to Pergamum and to Thyatira and to Sardis and to Philadelphia and to Laodicea.

12 Then I turned to see [whose was] the voice that was speaking to me, and on turning I saw seven golden lampstands,

13 And in the midst of the lampstands [One] like a Son of man, clothed with a robe which reached to His feet and with a girdle of gold about His breast. [Dan. 7:13; 10:5.]

14 His head and His hair were white like white wool, [as white] as snow, and His eyes [flashed] like a flame of fire. [Dan. 7:9.]

## New American Standard

# Revelation

*The Revelation of Jesus Christ*

**1** THE REVELATION of Jesus Christ, which God gave Him to show to His bond-servants, the things which must shortly take place; and He sent and communicated *it* by His angel to His bond-servant John,

2who bore witness to the word of God and to the testimony of Jesus Christ, *even* to all that he saw.

3Blessed is he who reads and those who hear the words of the prophecy, and heed the things which are written in it; for the time is near.

*Message to the Seven Churches*

4¶ John to the seven churches that are in Asia: Grace to you and peace, from Him who is and who was and who is to come; and from the seven Spirits who are before His throne;

5and from Jesus Christ, the faithful witness, the first-born of the dead, and the ruler of the kings of the earth. To Him who loves us, and released us from our sins by His blood,

6and He has made us *to be* a kingdom, priests to His God and Father; to Him *be* the glory and the dominion forever and ever. Amen.

7BEHOLD, HE IS COMING WITH THE CLOUDS, and every eye will see Him, even those who pierced Him; and all the tribes of the earth will mourn over Him. Even so. Amen.

8¶ "I am the Alpha and the Omega," says the Lord God, "who is and who was and who is to come, the Almighty."

*The Patmos Vision*

9¶ I, John, your brother and fellow partaker in the tribulation and kingdom and perseverance *which are* in Jesus, was on the island called Patmos, because of the word of God and the testimony of Jesus.

10I was [j]in the Spirit on the Lord's day, and I heard behind me a loud voice like *the sound* of a trumpet,

11saying, "Write in a book what you see, and send *it* to the seven churches: to Ephesus and to Smyrna and to Pergamum and to Thyatira and to Sardis and to Philadelphia and to Laodicea."

12And I turned to see the voice that was speaking with me. And having turned I saw seven golden lampstands;

13and in the middle of the lampstands one like [k]a son of man, clothed in a robe reaching to the feet, and girded across His breast with a golden girdle.

14And His head and His hair were white like white wool, like snow; and His eyes were like a flame of fire;

NAS [j] Or, *in spirit* [k] Or, *the Son of Man*

## New International

# Revelation

*Prologue*

**1** THE REVELATION of Jesus Christ, which God gave him to show his servants what must soon take place. He made it known by sending his angel to his servant John, 2who testifies to everything he saw—that is, the word of God and the testimony of Jesus Christ. 3Blessed is the one who reads the words of this prophecy, and blessed are those who hear it and take to heart what is written in it, because the time is near.

*Greetings and Doxology*

4John,

To the seven churches in the province of Asia:

Grace and peace to you from him who is, and who was, and who is to come, and from the seven spirits[l] before his throne, 5and from Jesus Christ, who is the faithful witness, the firstborn from the dead, and the ruler of the kings of the earth.

To him who loves us and has freed us from our sins by his blood, 6and has made us to be a kingdom and priests to serve his God and Father—to him be glory and power for ever and ever! Amen.

7Look, he is coming with the clouds,  
and every eye will see him,  
even those who pierced him;  
and all the peoples of the earth will mourn because of him.  
So shall it be! Amen.

8"I am the Alpha and the Omega," says the Lord God, "who is, and who was, and who is to come, the Almighty."

*One Like a Son of Man*

9I, John, your brother and companion in the suffering and kingdom and patient endurance that are ours in Jesus, was on the island of Patmos because of the word of God and the testimony of Jesus. 10On the Lord's Day I was in the Spirit, and I heard behind me a loud voice like a trumpet, 11which said: "Write on a scroll what you see and send it to the seven churches: to Ephesus, Smyrna, Pergamum, Thyatira, Sardis, Philadelphia and Laodicea."

12I turned around to see the voice that was speaking to me. And when I turned I saw seven golden lampstands, 13and among the lampstands was someone "like a son of man,"[m] dressed in a robe reaching down to his feet and with a golden sash around his chest. 14His head and hair were white like wool, as white as snow, and his eyes were like blazing fire. 15His feet were like bronze glowing

NIV [l] 4 Or *the sevenfold Spirit* [m] 13 Daniel 7:13

## King James

15 And his feet like unto fine brass, as if they burned in a furnace; and his voice as the sound of many waters.

16 And he had in his right hand seven stars: and out of his mouth went a sharp twoedged sword: and his countenance *was* as the sun shineth in his strength.

17 And when I saw him, I fell at his feet as dead. And he laid his right hand upon me, saying unto me, Fear not; I am the first and the last:

18 *I am* he that liveth, and was dead; and, behold, I am alive for evermore, Amen; and have the keys of hell and of death.

19 Write the things which thou hast seen, and the things which are, and the things which shall be hereafter;

20 The mystery of the seven stars which thou sawest in my right hand, and the seven golden candlesticks. The seven stars are the angels of the seven churches: and the seven candlesticks which thou sawest are the seven churches.

**2** UNTO THE angel of the church of Ephesus write; These things saith he that holdeth the seven stars in his right hand, who walketh in the midst of the seven golden candlesticks;

2 I know thy works, and thy labour, and thy patience, and how thou canst not bear them which are evil: and thou hast tried them which say they are apostles, and are not, and hast found them liars:

3 And hast borne, and hast patience, and for my name's sake hast laboured, and hast not fainted.

4 Nevertheless I have *somewhat* against thee, because thou hast left thy first love.

5 Remember therefore from whence thou art fallen, and repent, and do the first works; or else I will come unto thee quickly, and will remove thy candlestick out of his place, except thou repent.

6 But this thou hast, that thou hatest the deeds of the Nicolaitans, which I also hate.

7 He that hath an ear, let him hear what the Spirit saith unto the churches; To him that overcometh will I give to eat of the tree of life, which is in the midst of the paradise of God.

8 And unto the angel of the church in Smyrna write; These things saith the first and the last, which was dead, and is alive;

9 I know thy works, and tribulation, and poverty, (but thou art rich) and *I know* the blasphemy of them which say they are Jews, and are not, but *are* the synagogue of Satan.

10 Fear none of those things which thou shalt suffer: behold, the devil shall cast *some* of you into prison, that ye may be tried; and ye shall have tribulation ten days: be thou faithful unto death, and I will give thee a crown of life.

11 He that hath an ear, let him hear what the Spirit saith unto the churches; He that overcometh shall not be hurt of the second death.

12 And to the angel of the church in Pergamos write; These things saith he which hath the sharp sword with two edges;

## Amplified

15 His feet glowed like (bright,) burnished bronze as it is refined in a furnace, and His voice was like the sound of many waters. [Dan. 10:6.]

16 In His right hand He held seven stars, and from His mouth there came forth a sharp two-edged sword, and His face was like the sun shining in full power at midday. [Exod. 34:29.]

17 When I saw Him I fell at His feet as if dead. But He laid His right hand on me and said, Do not be afraid! I am the First and the Last, [Isa. 44:6.]

18 And the Ever-living One—I am living in the eternity of the eternities. I died, but see, I am alive for evermore; and I possess the keys of Death and Hades [the realm of the dead].

19 Write therefore the things you see, what they are [and signify], and what is to take place hereafter.

20 As to the hidden meaning (the mystery) of the seven stars which you saw on My right hand and the seven lampstands of gold, the seven stars are the seven angels (messengers) of the seven churches (assemblies) and the seven lampstands are the seven churches.

**2** TO THE angel (messenger) of the assembly (church) in Ephesus write: These are the words of Him Who holds the seven stars [which are the messengers of the seven churches] in His right hand, Who goes about among the seven golden lampstands [which are the seven churches].

2 I know your industry *and* activities, laborious toil *and* trouble, and your patient endurance, and how you cannot tolerate wicked [men] and have tested *and* critically appraised those who call [themselves] apostles (special messengers [of Christ]) and yet are not, and have found them to be impostors *and* liars.

3 I know you are enduring patiently and are bearing up for My name's sake, and you have not fainted *or* become exhausted *or* grown weary.

4 But I have this [one charge to make] against you, that you have left (abandoned) the love that you had at first—you have deserted [Me], your first love.

5 Remember then from what heights you have fallen. Repent—change the inner man to meet God's will—and do the works you did previously [when first you knew the Lord]. Or else I will visit you and remove your lampstand from its place, unless you change your mind *and* repent.

6 Yet you have this—in your favor and to your credit—you hate the works of the Nicolaitans [what they are doing as corrupters of the people], which I Myself also detest.

7 He who is able to hear, let him listen to *and* give heed to what the Spirit says to the assemblies (the churches). To him who overcomes (is victorious) I will grant to eat [of the fruit] of the tree of life, which is in the paradise of God. [Gen. 2:9; 3:24.]

8 And to the angel (messenger) of the assembly (church) in Smyrna write, These are the words of the First and the Last, Who died and came to life again: [Isa. 44:6.]

9 I know your affliction *and* distress *and* pressing trouble, and your poverty; but you are rich! and how you are abused *and* reviled *and* slandered by those who say they are Jews and are not, but are a synagogue of Satan.

10 Fear nothing that you are about to suffer.—Dismiss your dread and your fears! Behold, the devil is indeed about to throw some of you into prison, that you may be tested *and* proved *and* critically appraised; and for ten days you will have affliction. Be loyally faithful unto death—[that is,] even if you must die for it—and I will give you the crown of life. [Rev. 3:10, 11.]

11 He who is able to hear, let him listen to *and* heed what the Spirit says to the assemblies (the churches). He who overcomes (is victorious) shall in no way be injured by the second death.

12 Then to the angel (messenger) of the assembly (church) in Pergamum write: These are the words of Him Who has *and* wields the sharp two-edged sword.

## New American Standard

15 and His feet *were* like burnished bronze, when it has been caused to glow in a furnace, and His voice *was* like the sound of many waters.

16 And in His right hand He held seven stars; and out of His mouth came a sharp two-edged sword; and His face was like the sun shining in its strength.

17 And when I saw Him, I fell at His feet as a dead man. And He laid His right hand upon me, saying, "Do not be afraid; I am the first and the last,

18 and the living One; and I was dead, and behold, I am alive forevermore, and I have the keys of death and of Hades.

19 "Write therefore the things which you have seen, and the things which are, and the things which shall take place after these things.

20 "As for the mystery of the seven stars which you saw in My right hand, and the seven golden lampstands: the seven stars are the angels of the seven churches, and the seven lampstands are the seven churches.

*Message to Ephesus*

**2** "TO THE angel of the church in Ephesus write:

¶ The One who holds the seven stars in His right hand, the One who walks among the seven golden lampstands, says this:

2 'I know your deeds and your toil and perseverance, and that you cannot endure evil men, and you put to the test those who call themselves apostles, and they are not, and you found them *to be* false;

3 and you have perseverance and have endured for My name's sake, and have not grown weary.

4 'But I have *this* against you, that you have left your first love.

5 'Remember therefore from where you have fallen, and repent and do the deeds you did at first; or else I am coming to you, and will remove your lampstand out of its place—unless you repent.

6 'Yet this you do have, that you hate the deeds of the Nicolaitans, which I also hate.

7 'He who has an ear, let him hear what the Spirit says to the churches. To him who overcomes, I will grant to eat of the tree of life, which is in the Paradise of God.'

*Message to Smyrna*

8 ¶ "And to the angel of the church in Smyrna write:

¶ The first and the last, who was dead, and has come to life, says this:

9 'I know your tribulation and your poverty (but you are rich), and the blasphemy by those who say they are Jews and are not, but are a synagogue of Satan.

10 'Do not fear what you are about to suffer. Behold, the devil is about to cast some of you into prison, that you may be tested, and you will have tribulation ten days. Be faithful until death, and I will give you the crown of life.

11 'He who has an ear, let him hear what the Spirit says to the churches. He who overcomes shall not be hurt by the second death.'

*Message to Pergamum*

12 ¶ "And to the angel of the church in Pergamum write:

¶ The One who has the sharp two-edged sword says this:

## New International

in a furnace, and his voice was like the sound of rushing waters. 16 In his right hand he held seven stars, and out of his mouth came a sharp double-edged sword. His face was like the sun shining in all its brilliance.

17 When I saw him, I fell at his feet as though dead. Then he placed his right hand on me and said: "Do not be afraid. I am the First and the Last. 18 I am the Living One; I was dead, and behold I am alive for ever and ever! And I hold the keys of death and Hades.

19 "Write, therefore, what you have seen, what is now and what will take place later. 20 The mystery of the seven stars that you saw in my right hand and of the seven golden lampstands is this: The seven stars are the angels[a] of the seven churches, and the seven lampstands are the seven churches.

*To the Church in Ephesus*

**2** "TO THE angel[b] of the church in Ephesus write:

These are the words of him who holds the seven stars in his right hand and walks among the seven golden lampstands: 2 I know your deeds, your hard work and your perseverance. I know that you cannot tolerate wicked men, that you have tested those who claim to be apostles but are not, and have found them false. 3 You have persevered and have endured hardships for my name, and have not grown weary.

4 Yet I hold this against you: You have forsaken your first love. 5 Remember the height from which you have fallen! Repent and do the things you did at first. If you do not repent, I will come to you and remove your lampstand from its place. 6 But you have this in your favor: You hate the practices of the Nicolaitans, which I also hate.

7 He who has an ear, let him hear what the Spirit says to the churches. To him who overcomes, I will give the right to eat from the tree of life, which is in the paradise of God.

*To the Church in Smyrna*

8 "To the angel of the church in Smyrna write:

These are the words of him who is the First and the Last, who died and came to life again. 9 I know your afflictions and your poverty—yet you are rich! I know the slander of those who say they are Jews and are not, but are a synagogue of Satan. 10 Do not be afraid of what you are about to suffer. I tell you, the devil will put some of you in prison to test you, and you will suffer persecution for ten days. Be faithful, even to the point of death, and I will give you the crown of life.

11 He who has an ear, let him hear what the Spirit says to the churches. He who overcomes will not be hurt at all by the second death.

*To the Church in Pergamum*

12 "To the angel of the church in Pergamum write:

These are the words of him who has the sharp, double-edged sword. 13 I know where you live—where Satan has his

NIV [a] *20* Or *messengers* [b] *1* Or *messenger;* also in verses 8, 12 and 18

## King James

13I know thy works, and where thou dwellest, *even* where Satan's seat *is:* and thou holdest fast my name, and hast not denied my faith, even in those days wherein Antipas *was* my faithful martyr, who was slain among you, where Satan dwelleth.

14But I have a few things against thee, because thou hast there them that hold the doctrine of Balaam, who taught Balac to cast a stumblingblock before the children of Israel, to eat things sacrificed unto idols, and to commit fornication.

15So hast thou also them that hold the doctrine of the Nicolaitans, which thing I hate.

16Repent; or else I will come unto thee quickly, and will fight against them with the sword of my mouth.

17He that hath an ear, let him hear what the Spirit saith unto the churches; To him that overcometh will I give to eat of the hidden manna, and will give him a white stone, and in the stone a new name written, which no man knoweth saving he that receiveth *it*.

18And unto the angel of the church in Thyatira write; These things saith the Son of God, who hath his eyes like unto a flame of fire, and his feet *are* like fine brass;

19I know thy works, and charity, and service, and faith, and thy patience, and thy works; and the last *to be* more than the first.

20Notwithstanding I have a few things against thee, because thou sufferest that woman Jezebel, which calleth herself a prophetess, to teach and to seduce my servants to commit fornication, and to eat things sacrificed unto idols.

21And I gave her space to repent of her fornication; and she repented not.

22Behold, I will cast her into a bed, and them that commit adultery with her into great tribulation, except they repent of their deeds.

23And I will kill her children with death; and all the churches shall know that I am he which searcheth the reins and hearts: and I will give unto every one of you according to your works.

24But unto you I say, and unto the rest in Thyatira, as many as have not this doctrine, and which have not known the depths of Satan, as they speak; I will put upon you none other burden.

25But that which ye have *already* hold fast till I come.

26And he that overcometh, and keepeth my works unto the end, to him will I give power over the nations:

27And he shall rule them with a rod of iron; as the vessels of a potter shall they be broken to shivers: even as I received of my Father.

28And I will give him the morning star.

29He that hath an ear, let him hear what the Spirit saith unto the churches.

## Amplified

13I know where you live, a place where Satan sits enthroned. [Yet] you are clinging to *and* holding fast My name and you did not deny My faith even in the days of Antipas My witness, My faithful one, who was killed, [martyred] in your midst where Satan dwells.

14Nevertheless I have a few things against you: you have some people there who are clinging to the teaching of Balaam, who taught Balak to set a trap *and* a stumbling block before the sons of Israel, [to entice them] to eat food that had been sacrificed to idols and to practice lewdness—giving themselves up to sexual vice. [Num. 31:16; 25:1, 2.]

15You also have some who in a similar way are clinging to the teaching of the Nicolaitans [those corrupters of the people], which thing I hate.

16Repent [then]! Or else I will come to you quickly and fight against them with the sword of My mouth.

17He who is able to hear, let him listen to *and* heed what the Spirit says to the assemblies (the churches). To him who overcomes (who conquers) I will give to eat of the manna that is hidden, and I will give him a white stone, with a new name engraved on the stone which no one knows *or* understands except he who receives it. [Ps. 78:24; Isa. 62:2.]

18And to the angel (the messenger) of the assembly (church) in Thyatira write: These are the words of the Son of God, Who has eyes that flash like a flame of fire, and Whose feet glow like bright *and* burnished *and* white-hot bronze. [Dan. 10:6.]

19I know your record *and* what you are doing, your love and faith and service and patient endurance, and that your recent works are more numerous *and* greater than your first ones.

20But I have this against you, that you tolerate the woman Jezebel, who calls herself a prophetess (claiming to be inspired), and who is teaching and leading astray my servants *and* beguiling them into practicing sexual vice and eating food sacrificed to idols. [I Kings 16:31; II Kings 9:22, 30.]

21I gave her time to repent, but she has no desire to repent ([a]out) of her immorality [symbolic of idolatry] *and* refuses to do so.

22Take note: I will throw her on a bed [[b]of anguish], and those [her paramours] who commit adultery with her I will bring down to [c]pressing distress *and* severe affliction, unless they turn away their minds from conduct [such as] hers *and* repent of ([d]their) doings.

23And I will strike her children [her proper followers] dead—thoroughly exterminating them. And all the assemblies (the churches) shall recognize *and* understand that I am He Who searches minds—the thoughts, feelings and purposes—and the [inmost] hearts, and I will give to each of you [the reward for what you have done] as your work deserves. [Jer. 17:10; Ps. 62:12.]

24But to the rest of you in Thyatira, who do not hold this teaching, who have not explored *and* known the depths of Satan, as they say, I tell you that I do not lay upon you any other (fresh) burden;

25Only hold fast to what you have until I come.

26And he who overcomes (is victorious) and who obeys My commands to the [very] end—doing the works [that please Me]—I will give him authority *and* power over the nations;

27And he shall rule them with a sceptre (rod) of iron, as when earthen pots are broken in pieces, and [his power over them shall be] like that which I Myself have received from My Father; [Ps. 2:8, 9.]

28And I will give him the Morning Star.

29He who is able to hear, let him listen to *and* heed what the (Holy) Spirit says to the assemblies (the churches).

**AMP** [a] Literal meaning. [b] Vincent. [c] Literal meaning. [d] Many ancient authorities so read.

## New American Standard

13'I know where you dwell, where Satan's throne is; and you
hold fast My name, and did not deny My faith, even in the days
of Antipas, My witness, My faithful one, who was killed among
you, where Satan dwells.
14'But I have a few things against you, because you have there
some who hold the teaching of Balaam, who kept teaching Balak
to put a stumbling block before the sons of Israel, to eat things
sacrificed to idols, and to commit *acts of* immorality.
15'Thus you also have some who in the same way hold the
teaching of the Nicolaitans.
16'Repent therefore; or else I am coming to you quickly, and I
will make war against them with the sword of My mouth.
17'He who has an ear, let him hear what the Spirit says to the
churches. To him who overcomes, to him I will give *some* of the
hidden manna, and I will give him a white stone, and a new name
written on the stone which no one knows but he who receives it.'

*Message to Thyatira*

18¶ "And to the angel of the church in Thyatira write:
¶ The Son of God, who has eyes like a flame of fire, and His feet
are like burnished bronze, says this:
19'I know your deeds, and your love and faith and service and
perseverance, and that your deeds of late are greater than at first.
20'But I have *this* against you, that you tolerate the woman
Jezebel, who calls herself a prophetess, and she teaches and leads
My bond-servants astray, so that they commit *acts of* immorality
and eat things sacrificed to idols.
21'And I gave her time to repent; and she does not want to
repent of her immorality.
22'Behold, I will cast her upon a bed *of sickness*, and those who
commit adultery with her into great tribulation, unless they repent
of [e]her deeds.
23'And I will kill her children with pestilence; and all the
churches will know that I am He who searches the minds and
hearts; and I will give to each one of you according to your deeds.
24'But I say to you, the rest who are in Thyatira, who do not hold
this teaching, who have not known the deep things of Satan, as
they call them—I place no other burden on you.
25'Nevertheless what you have, hold fast until I come.
26'And he who overcomes, and he who keeps My deeds until
the end, TO HIM I WILL GIVE AUTHORITY OVER THE NATIONS;
27AND HE SHALL RULE THEM WITH A ROD OF IRON, AS THE VESSELS
OF THE POTTER ARE BROKEN TO PIECES, as I also have received
*authority* from My Father;
28and I will give him the morning star.
29'He who has an ear, let him hear what the Spirit says to the
churches.'

NAS [e] Some mss. read *their*

## New International

throne. Yet you remain true to my name. You did not renounce your faith in me, even in the days of Antipas, my
faithful witness, who was put to death in your city—where
Satan lives.
14Nevertheless, I have a few things against you: You have
people there who hold to the teaching of Balaam, who taught
Balak to entice the Israelites to sin by eating food sacrificed to
idols and by committing sexual immorality. 15Likewise you
also have those who hold to the teaching of the Nicolaitans.
16Repent therefore! Otherwise, I will soon come to you and
will fight against them with the sword of my mouth.
17He who has an ear, let him hear what the Spirit says to
the churches. To him who overcomes, I will give some of the
hidden manna. I will also give him a white stone with a new
name written on it, known only to him who receives it.

*To the Church in Thyatira*

18"To the angel of the church in Thyatira write:

These are the words of the Son of God, whose eyes are like
blazing fire and whose feet are like burnished bronze. 19I
know your deeds, your love and faith, your service and perseverance, and that you are now doing more than you did at
first.
20Nevertheless, I have this against you: You tolerate that
woman Jezebel, who calls herself a prophetess. By her teaching she misleads my servants into sexual immorality and the
eating of food sacrificed to idols. 21I have given her time to
repent of her immorality, but she is unwilling. 22So I will cast
her on a bed of suffering, and I will make those who commit
adultery with her suffer intensely, unless they repent of her
ways. 23I will strike her children dead. Then all the churches
will know that I am he who searches hearts and minds, and
I will repay each of you according to your deeds. 24Now I say
to the rest of you in Thyatira, to you who do not hold to her
teaching and have not learned Satan's so-called deep secrets
(I will not impose any other burden on you): 25Only hold on
to what you have until I come.
26To him who overcomes and does my will to the end, I will
give authority over the nations—

27'He will rule them with an iron scepter;
he will dash them to pieces like pottery'[f] —

just as I have received authority from my Father. 28I will also
give him the morning star. 29He who has an ear, let him hear
what the Spirit says to the churches.

NIV [f] 27 Psalm 2:9

## King James

3 AND UNTO the angel of the church in Sardis write; These things saith he that hath the seven Spirits of God, and the seven stars; I know thy works, that thou hast a name that thou livest, and art dead.

2 Be watchful, and strengthen the things which remain, that are ready to die: for I have not found thy works perfect before God.

3 Remember therefore how thou hast received and heard, and hold fast, and repent. If therefore thou shalt not watch, I will come on thee as a thief, and thou shalt not know what hour I will come upon thee.

4 Thou hast a few names even in Sardis which have not defiled their garments; and they shall walk with me in white: for they are worthy.

5 He that overcometh, the same shall be clothed in white raiment; and I will not blot out his name out of the book of life, but I will confess his name before my Father, and before his angels.

6 He that hath an ear, let him hear what the Spirit saith unto the churches.

7 And to the angel of the church in Philadelphia write; These things saith he that is holy, he that is true, he that hath the key of David, he that openeth, and no man shutteth; and shutteth, and no man openeth;

8 I know thy works: behold, I have set before thee an open door, and no man can shut it: for thou hast a little strength, and hast kept my word, and hast not denied my name.

9 Behold, I will make them of the synagogue of Satan, which say they are Jews, and are not, but do lie; behold, I will make them to come and worship before thy feet, and to know that I have loved thee.

10 Because thou hast kept the word of my patience, I also will keep thee from the hour of temptation, which shall come upon all the world, to try them that dwell upon the earth.

11 Behold, I come quickly: hold that fast which thou hast, that no man take thy crown.

12 Him that overcometh will I make a pillar in the temple of my God, and he shall go no more out: and I will write upon him the name of my God, and the name of the city of my God, *which is* new Jerusalem, which cometh down out of heaven from my God: and *I will write upon him* my new name.

13 He that hath an ear, let him hear what the Spirit saith unto the churches.

14 And unto the angel of the church of the Laodiceans write; These things saith the Amen, the faithful and true witness, the beginning of the creation of God;

15 I know thy works, that thou art neither cold nor hot: I would thou wert cold or hot.

16 So then because thou art lukewarm, and neither cold nor hot, I will spew thee out of my mouth.

17 Because thou sayest, I am rich, and increased with goods, and have need of nothing; and knowest not that thou art wretched, and miserable, and poor, and blind, and naked:

18 I counsel thee to buy of me gold tried in the fire, that thou mayest be rich; and white raiment, that thou mayest be clothed, and *that* the shame of thy nakedness do not appear; and anoint thine eyes with eyesalve, that thou mayest see.

## Amplified

3 AND TO the angel (the messenger) of the assembly (the church) in Sardis write: These are the words of Him Who has the seven Spirits of God [that is, [a]the sevenfold Holy Spirit] and the seven stars: I know your record *and* what you are doing; you are supposed to be alive, but [in reality] you are dead.

2 Rouse yourselves *and* keep awake, and strengthen *and* invigorate what remains and is on the point of dying; for I have not found a thing that you have done—any work of yours—meeting the requirements of My God *or* perfect in His sight.

3 So call to mind the lessons you received and heard; continually lay them to heart *and* obey them, and repent. In case you will not rouse yourselves *and* keep awake *and watch* I will come upon you like a thief, and you will not know *or* suspect at what hour I will come.

4 Yet you still have a few [persons'] names in Sardis who have not soiled their clothes, and they shall walk with Me in white, because they are worthy *and* deserving.

5 Thus shall he who conquers (is victorious) be clad in white garments, and I will not erase *or* blot out his name from the Book of Life; I will acknowledge him [as Mine], *and* I will confess his name openly before My Father and before His angels. [Ps. 69:28; Dan. 12:1.]

6 He who is able to hear, let him listen to *and* heed what the (Holy) Spirit says to the assemblies (the churches).

7 And to the angel (the messenger) of the assembly (the church) in Philadelphia write: These are the words of the Holy One, the True One, He Who has the key of David, Who opens and no one shall shut, Who shuts and no one shall open. [Isa. 22:22.]

8 I know your [record of] works *and* what you are doing. See! I have set before you a door wide open, which no one is able to shut; I know that you have but little power, and yet you have kept My Word *and* guarded My message, and have not renounced *or* denied My name.

9 Take note! I will make those of the synagogue of Satan who say they are Jews and are not, but lie, behold, I will make them come and bow down before your feet, and learn *and* acknowledge that I have loved you. [Isa. 60:14; 49:23; 43:4.]

10 Because you have guarded *and* kept My word of patient endurance—have held fast the [b]lesson of My patience with the [c]expectant endurance that I give you—I also will keep you (safe) from the hour of trial (testing) which is coming on the whole world, to try those who dwell upon the earth.

11 I am coming quickly; hold fast what you have, so that no one may rob you *and* deprive you of your crown.

12 He who overcomes (is victorious), I will make him a pillar in the sanctuary of My God; he shall never be put out of it *or* go out of it, and I will write on him the name of My God, and the name of the city of My God, the new Jerusalem which descends from My God out of heaven, and My own new name. [Isa. 62:2; Ezek. 48:35.]

13 He who can hear, let him listen to *and* heed what the Spirit says to the assemblies (the churches).

14 And to the angel (messenger) of the assembly (the church) in Laodicea write: These are the words of the Amen, the trusty *and* faithful and true Witness, the Origin *and* Beginning *and* Author of God's creation. [Isa. 55:4; Prov. 8:22.]

15 I know your [record of] works *and* what you are doing; you are neither cold nor hot. Would that you were cold or hot!

16 So, because you are lukewarm, and neither cold nor hot, I will spew you out of My mouth!

17 For you say, I am rich, I have prospered *and* grown wealthy, and I am in need of nothing; and do not realize *and* understand that you are wretched, pitiable, poor, blind and naked. [Hos. 12:8.]

18 Therefore I counsel you to purchase from Me gold refined *and* tested by fire, that you may be [truly] wealthy, and white clothes to clothe you and to keep the shame of your nudity from being seen, and salve to put on your eyes that you may see.

**AMP** [a] Trench. [b] Greek, "of my endurance"; "a patient, steadfast waiting for" (Thayer). [c] Greek, "of my endurance"; "a patient, steadfast waiting for" (Thayer).

## New American Standard

*Message to Sardis*

3 "AND TO the angel of the church in Sardis write:
¶ **He** who has the seven Spirits of God, and the seven stars,
says this: 'I know your deeds, that you have a name that you are
alive, but you are dead.
2 'Wake up, and strengthen the things that remain, which were
about to die; for I have not found your deeds completed in the sight
of My God.
3 'Remember therefore what you have received and heard; and
keep *it*, and repent. If therefore you will not wake up, I will come
like a thief, and you will not know at what hour I will come upon
you.
4 'But you have a few people in Sardis who have not soiled their
garments; and they will walk with Me in white; for they are
worthy.
5 'He who overcomes shall thus be clothed in white garments;
and I will not erase his name from the book of life, and I will
confess his name before My Father, and before His angels.
6 'He who has an ear, let him hear what the Spirit says to the
churches.'

*Message to Philadelphia*

7 ¶ "And to the angel of the church in Philadelphia write:
¶ **He** who is holy, who is true, who has the key of David, who
opens and no one will shut, and who shuts and no one opens, says
this:
8 'I know your [d]deeds. Behold, I have put before you an open
door which no one can shut, because you have a little power, and
have kept My word, and have not denied My name.
9 'Behold, I will cause *those* of the synagogue of Satan, who say
that they are Jews, and are not, but lie—behold, I will make them
to come and bow down at your feet, and to know that I have loved
you.
10 'Because you have kept the word of My perseverance, I also
will keep you from the hour of testing, that *hour* which is about
to come upon the whole world, to test those who dwell upon the
earth.
11 'I am coming quickly; hold fast what you have, in order that
no one take your crown.
12 'He who overcomes, I will make him a pillar in the temple of
My God, and he will not go out from it anymore; and I will write
upon him the name of My God, and the name of the city of My
God, the new Jerusalem, which comes down out of heaven from
My God, and My new name.
13 'He who has an ear, let him hear what the Spirit says to the
churches.'

*Message to Laodicea*

14 ¶ "And to the angel of the church in Laodicea write:
¶ The Amen, the faithful and true Witness, the [e]Beginning of
the creation of God, says this:
15 'I know your deeds, that you are neither cold nor hot; I would
that you were cold or hot.
16 'So because you are lukewarm, and neither hot nor cold, I will
spit you out of My mouth.
17 'Because you say, "I am rich, and have become wealthy, and
have need of nothing," and you do not know that you are
wretched and miserable and poor and blind and naked,
18 I advise you to buy from Me gold refined by fire, that you may
become rich, and white garments, that you may clothe yourself,
and *that* the shame of your nakedness may not be revealed; and
eye salve to anoint your eyes, that you may see.

NAS [d] Or, *deeds (behold . . . shut), that you* [e] I.e., origin or source

## New International

*To the Church in Sardis*

3 "TO THE angel[f] of the church in Sardis write:
These are the words of him who holds the seven spirits[g]
of God and the seven stars. I know your deeds; you have a
reputation of being alive, but you are dead. 2 Wake up!
Strengthen what remains and is about to die, for I have not
found your deeds complete in the sight of my God. 3 Remember, therefore, what you have received and heard; obey it, and
repent. But if you do not wake up, I will come like a thief, and
you will not know at what time I will come to you.
4 Yet you have a few people in Sardis who have not soiled
their clothes. They will walk with me, dressed in white, for
they are worthy. 5 He who overcomes will, like them, be
dressed in white. I will never blot out his name from the book
of life, but will acknowledge his name before my Father and
his angels. 6 He who has an ear, let him hear what the Spirit
says to the churches.

*To the Church in Philadelphia*

7 "To the angel of the church in Philadelphia write:
These are the words of him who is holy and true, who
holds the key of David. What he opens no one can shut, and
what he shuts no one can open. 8 I know your deeds. See, I
have placed before you an open door that no one can shut.
I know that you have little strength, yet you have kept my
word and have not denied my name. 9 I will make those who
are of the synagogue of Satan, who claim to be Jews though
they are not, but are liars—I will make them come and fall
down at your feet and acknowledge that I have loved you.
10 Since you have kept my command to endure patiently, I will
also keep you from the hour of trial that is going to come upon
the whole world to test those who live on the earth.
11 I am coming soon. Hold on to what you have, so that no
one will take your crown. 12 Him who overcomes I will make
a pillar in the temple of my God. Never again will he leave it.
I will write on him the name of my God and the name of the
city of my God, the new Jerusalem, which is coming down out
of heaven from my God; and I will also write on him my new
name. 13 He who has an ear, let him hear what the Spirit says
to the churches.

*To the Church in Laodicea*

14 "To the angel of the church in Laodicea write:
These are the words of the Amen, the faithful and true
witness, the ruler of God's creation. 15 I know your deeds, that
you are neither cold nor hot. I wish you were either one or
the other! 16 So, because you are lukewarm—neither hot nor
cold—I am about to spit you out of my mouth. 17 You say, 'I
am rich; I have acquired wealth and do not need a thing.' But
you do not realize that you are wretched, pitiful, poor, blind
and naked. 18 I counsel you to buy from me gold refined in the
fire, so you can become rich; and white clothes to wear, so you
can cover your shameful nakedness; and salve to put on your
eyes, so you can see.

NIV [f] *1* Or *messenger;* also in verses 7 and 14 [g] *1* Or *the sevenfold Spirit*

## King James

19As many as I love, I rebuke and chasten: be zealous therefore, and repent.

20Behold, I stand at the door, and knock: if any man hear my voice, and open the door, I will come in to him, and will sup with him, and he with me.

21To him that overcometh will I grant to sit with me in my throne, even as I also overcame, and am set down with my Father in his throne.

22He that hath an ear, let him hear what the Spirit saith unto the churches.

**4** AFTER THIS I looked, and, behold, a door *was* opened in heaven: and the first voice which I heard *was* as it were of a trumpet talking with me; which said, Come up hither, and I will show thee things which must be hereafter.

2And immediately I was in the spirit: and, behold, a throne was set in heaven, and *one* sat on the throne.

3And he that sat was to look upon like a jasper and a sardine stone: and *there was* a rainbow round about the throne, in sight like unto an emerald.

4And round about the throne *were* four and twenty seats: and upon the seats I saw four and twenty elders sitting, clothed in white raiment; and they had on their heads crowns of gold.

5And out of the throne proceeded lightnings and thunderings and voices: and *there were* seven lamps of fire burning before the throne, which are the seven Spirits of God.

6And before the throne *there was* a sea of glass like unto crystal: and in the midst of the throne, and round about the throne, *were* four beasts full of eyes before and behind.

7And the first beast *was* like a lion, and the second beast like a calf, and the third beast had a face as a man, and the fourth beast *was* like a flying eagle.

8And the four beasts had each of them six wings about *him;* and *they were* full of eyes within: and they rest not day and night, saying, Holy, holy, holy, Lord God Almighty, which was, and is, and is to come.

9And when those beasts give glory and honour and thanks to him that sat on the throne, who liveth for ever and ever,

10The four and twenty elders fall down before him that sat on the throne, and worship him that liveth for ever and ever, and cast their crowns before the throne, saying,

11Thou art worthy, O Lord, to receive glory and honour and power: for thou hast created all things, and for thy pleasure they are and were created.

**5** AND I saw in the right hand of him that sat on the throne a book written within and on the backside, sealed with seven seals.

## Amplified

19Those whom I [dearly and tenderly] love, I tell their faults and convict *and* convince *and* reprove and chasten—[that is,] I discipline and instruct them. So be enthusiastic *and* in earnest *and* burning with zeal, and repent—changing your mind and attitude. [Prov. 3:12.]

20Behold, I stand at the door and knock; if any one hears *and* listens to *and* heeds My voice and opens the door, I will come in to him and will eat with him, and he [shall eat] with Me.

21He who overcomes (is victorious), I will grant him to sit beside Me on My throne, as I Myself overcame (was victorious) and sat down beside My Father on His throne.

22He who is able to hear, let him listen to *and* heed what the (Holy) Spirit says to the assemblies (the churches).

**4** AFTER THIS I looked, and lo, a door standing open in heaven! And the first voice, which I had heard addressed to me like [the calling of] a [a]war trumpet, said, Come up here, and I will show you what must take place in the future.

2At once I came under the (Holy) Spirit's power, and lo, a throne stood in heaven, with One seated on the throne! [Ezek. 1:26.]

3And He Who sat there appeared like [the crystalline brightness of] jasper and [the fiery] sardius, and encircling the throne there was a halo that looked like [a rainbow of] emerald. [Ezek. 1:28.]

4Twenty-four other thrones surrounded the throne and seated on these thrones were twenty-four elders, [ [b]the members of the heavenly Sanhedrin], arrayed in white clothing, with crowns of gold upon their heads.

5Out from the throne came flashes of lightning and rumblings and peals of thunder, and in front of the throne seven blazing torches burned, which are the seven Spirits of God [ [c]the sevenfold (Holy) Spirit];

6And in front of the throne there is also what looks like a transparent glassy sea, as if of crystal. And around the throne, in the center at each side of the throne, are four living creatures (ones, or beings) that are full of eyes in front and behind [with intelligence as to what is before and at the rear of them]. [Ezek. 1:5, 18.]

7The first living creature (one, or being) was like a lion, the second living creature like an ox, the third living creature had the face of a man, and the fourth living creature [was] like a flying eagle. [Ezek. 1:10.]

8And the four living creatures, individually having six wings, are full of eyes all over and within [underneath their wings]; and day and night they never stop saying, Holy, holy, holy is the Lord God Almighty (Omnipotent), Who was and Who is and Who is to come. [Isa. 6:1-3.]

9And whenever the living creatures offer glory and honor and thanksgiving to Him Who sits on the throne, Who lives forever and ever—through the eternities of the eternities—[Ps. 47:8.]

10The twenty-four elders [ [d]the members of the heavenly Sanhedrin] fall prostrate before Him Who is sitting on the throne and they worship Him Who lives forever and ever; and they throw down their crowns before the throne, crying out,

11Worthy are You, our Lord and God, to receive the glory and the honor and dominion, for You created all things; by Your will they were [brought into being] and were created. [Ps. 19:1.]

**5** AND I saw lying on the [e]open hand of Him Who was seated on the throne a (book) scroll written within and on the back, closed *and* sealed with seven seals; [Ezek. 2:9, 10; Isa. 29:11; Dan. 12:4.]

**AMP** [a] Vincent. [b] Berry's "Greek-English Lexicon to the New Testament," and others. [c] Richard of St. Victor, cited by Trench. [d] Berry. [e] Vincent.

## New American Standard

19'Those whom I love, I reprove and discipline; be zealous therefore, and repent.

20'Behold, I stand at the door and knock; if anyone hears My voice and opens the door, I will come in to him, and will dine with him, and he with Me.

21'He who overcomes, I will grant to him to sit down with Me on My throne, as I also overcame and sat down with My Father on His throne.

22'He who has an ear, let him hear what the Spirit says to the churches.' "

*Scene in Heaven*

**4** AFTER THESE things I looked, and behold, a door *standing* open in heaven, and the first voice which I had heard, like *the sound* of a trumpet speaking with me, said, "Come up here, and I will show you what must take place after these things."

2Immediately I was [f]in the Spirit; and behold, a throne was standing in heaven, and One sitting on the throne.

3And He who was sitting *was* like a jasper stone and a sardius in appearance; and *there was* a rainbow around the throne, like an emerald in appearance.

4And around the throne *were* twenty-four thrones; and upon the thrones *I saw* twenty-four elders sitting, clothed in white garments, and golden crowns on their heads.

*The Throne and Worship of the Creator*

5And from the throne proceed flashes of lightning and sounds and peals of thunder. And *there were* seven lamps of fire burning before the throne, which are the seven Spirits of God;

6and before the throne *there was,* as it were, a sea of glass like crystal; and in the center and around the throne, four living creatures full of eyes in front and behind.

7And the first creature *was* like a lion, and the second creature like a calf, and the third creature had a face like that of a man, and the fourth creature *was* like a flying eagle.

8And the four living creatures, each one of them having six wings, are full of eyes around and within; and day and night they do not cease to say,

"HOLY, HOLY, HOLY, *is* THE LORD GOD, THE ALMIGHTY,
who was and who is and who is to come."

9And when the living creatures give glory and honor and thanks to Him who sits on the throne, to Him who lives forever and ever,

10the twenty-four elders will fall down before Him who sits on the throne, and will worship Him who lives forever and ever, and will cast their crowns before the throne, saying,

11 "Worthy art Thou, our Lord and our God, to receive glory and honor and power; for Thou didst create all things, and because of Thy will they existed, and were created."

*The Book with Seven Seals*

**5** AND I saw in the right hand of Him who sat on the throne a book written inside and on the back, sealed up with seven seals.

NAS [f] Or, *in spirit*

## New International

19Those whom I love I rebuke and discipline. So be earnest,
and repent. 20Here I am! I stand at the door and knock. If
anyone hears my voice and opens the door, I will come in and
eat with him, and he with me.
21To him who overcomes, I will give the right to sit with
me on my throne, just as I overcame and sat down with my
Father on his throne. 22He who has an ear, let him hear what
the Spirit says to the churches."

*The Throne in Heaven*

**4** AFTER THIS I looked, and there before me was a door standing open in heaven. And the voice I had first heard speaking
to me like a trumpet said, "Come up here, and I will show you
what must take place after this." 2At once I was in the Spirit, and
there before me was a throne in heaven with someone sitting on
it. 3And the one who sat there had the appearance of jasper and
carnelian. A rainbow, resembling an emerald, encircled the
throne. 4Surrounding the throne were twenty-four other thrones,
and seated on them were twenty-four elders. They were dressed
in white and had crowns of gold on their heads. 5From the throne
came flashes of lightning, rumblings and peals of thunder. Before
the throne, seven lamps were blazing. These are the seven spirits[g]
of God. 6Also before the throne there was what looked like a sea
of glass, clear as crystal.
In the center, around the throne, were four living creatures, and
they were covered with eyes, in front and in back. 7The first living
creature was like a lion, the second was like an ox, the third had
a face like a man, the fourth was like a flying eagle. 8Each of the
four living creatures had six wings and was covered with eyes all
around, even under his wings. Day and night they never stop
saying:

"Holy, holy, holy
is the Lord God Almighty,
who was, and is, and is to come."

9Whenever the living creatures give glory, honor and thanks to
him who sits on the throne and who lives for ever and ever, 10the
twenty-four elders fall down before him who sits on the throne,
and worship him who lives for ever and ever. They lay their
crowns before the throne and say:

11"You are worthy, our Lord and God,
to receive glory and honor and power,
for you created all things,
and by your will they were created
and have their being."

*The Scroll and the Lamb*

**5** THEN I saw in the right hand of him who sat on the throne
a scroll with writing on both sides and sealed with seven
seals. 2And I saw a mighty angel proclaiming in a loud voice,

NIV [g] 5 Or *the sevenfold Spirit*

## King James

2 And I saw a strong angel proclaiming with a loud voice, Who is worthy to open the book, and to loose the seals thereof?

3 And no man in heaven, nor in earth, neither under the earth, was able to open the book, neither to look thereon.

4 And I wept much, because no man was found worthy to open and to read the book, neither to look thereon.

5 And one of the elders saith unto me, Weep not: behold, the Lion of the tribe of Judah, the Root of David, hath prevailed to open the book, and to loose the seven seals thereof.

6 And I beheld, and, lo, in the midst of the throne and of the four beasts, and in the midst of the elders, stood a Lamb as it had been slain, having seven horns and seven eyes, which are the seven Spirits of God sent forth into all the earth.

7 And he came and took the book out of the right hand of him that sat upon the throne.

8 And when he had taken the book, the four beasts and four *and* twenty elders fell down before the Lamb, having every one of them harps, and golden vials full of odours, which are the prayers of saints.

9 And they sung a new song, saying, Thou art worthy to take the book, and to open the seals thereof: for thou wast slain, and hast redeemed us to God by thy blood out of every kindred, and tongue, and people, and nation;

10 And hast made us unto our God kings and priests: and we shall reign on the earth.

11 And I beheld, and I heard the voice of many angels round about the throne and the beasts and the elders: and the number of them was ten thousand times ten thousand, and thousands of thousands;

12 Saying with a loud voice, Worthy is the Lamb that was slain to receive power, and riches, and wisdom, and strength, and honour, and glory, and blessing.

13 And every creature which is in heaven, and on the earth, and under the earth, and such as are in the sea, and all that are in them, heard I saying, Blessing, and honour, and glory, and power, *be* unto him that sitteth upon the throne, and unto the Lamb for ever and ever.

14 And the four beasts said, Amen. And the four *and* twenty elders fell down and worshipped him that liveth for ever and ever.

**6** AND I saw when the Lamb opened one of the seals, and I heard, as it were the noise of thunder, one of the four beasts saying, Come and see.

2 And I saw, and behold a white horse: and he that sat on him had a bow; and a crown was given unto him: and he went forth conquering, and to conquer.

3 And when he had opened the second seal, I heard the second beast say, Come and see.

## Amplified

2 And I saw a strong angel announcing in a loud voice, Who is worthy to open the scroll? And—who is entitled and deserves and is morally fit—to break its seals?

3 And no one in heaven or on earth or under the earth [in the realm of the dead, Hades] was able to open the scroll or to take a [single] look at its contents.

4 And I wept audibly *and* bitterly because no one was found fit to open the scroll or to inspect it.

5 Then one of the elders [ [a]of the heavenly Sanhedrin] said to me, Stop weeping! See, the Lion of the tribe of Judah, the [b]Root (Source) of David, has won—has overcome *and* conquered! He can open the scroll and break its seven seals! [Gen. 49:9, 10; Isa. 11:1, 10.]

6 And there between the throne and the four living creatures (ones, or beings) and among the elders [ [c]of the heavenly Sanhedrin], I saw a Lamb standing, as though it had been slain, with seven horns and with seven eyes, which are the seven Spirits of God [that is, [d]the sevenfold Holy Spirit] Who have been sent [on duty far and wide] into all the earth. [Isa. 53:7; Zech. 4:10; 3:8, 9.]

7 He then went and took the scroll from the right hand of Him Who sat on the throne.

8 And when He had taken the scroll (book), the four living creatures and the twenty-four elders [ [e]of the heavenly Sanhedrin] prostrated themselves before the Lamb. Each was holding a harp [lute or guitar], and they had golden bowls full of incense [fragrant spices and gums for burning], which are the prayers of God's people—the saints.

9 And [now] they sing a new song, saying, You are worthy to take the scroll and to break the seals that are on it, for You were slain (sacrificed) and with Your blood You purchased men unto God from every tribe and language and people and nation. [Ps. 33:3.]

10 And You have made them a kingdom [royal race] and priests to our God, and they shall reign [as kings] over the earth! [Exod. 19:6; Isa. 61:6.]

11 Then I looked, and I heard the voices of many angels on every side of the throne, and of the living creatures and the elders [ [f]of the heavenly Sanhedrin], and they numbered ten thousand times ten thousand and thousands of thousands, [Dan. 7:10.]

12 Saying in a loud voice, Deserving is the Lamb that was sacrificed, to receive all the power and riches and wisdom and might and honor and majesty (glory, splendor) and blessing!

13 And I heard every created thing in heaven and on earth and under the earth [in Hades, the place of departed spirits] and on the sea and all that is in it, crying out together, To Him Who is seated on the throne and to the Lamb be ascribed the blessing and the honor and the majesty (glory, splendor) and the power (might and dominion) forever and ever—through the eternities of the eternities! [Dan. 7:13, 14.]

14 Then the four living creatures (ones, or beings) said, Amen—so be it! and the elders [ [g]of the heavenly Sanhedrin] prostrated themselves and worshipped *Him Who lives forever and ever.*

**6** THEN I saw as the Lamb broke open one of the seven seals, and as if in a voice of thunder I heard one of the four living creatures call out, Come!

2 And I looked, and saw there a white horse whose rider carried a bow. And a crown was given him, and he rode forth conquering and to conquer. [Zech. 1:8; 6:1-3; Ps. 45:4, 5.]

3 And when He broke the second seal, I heard the second living creature call out, Come!

**AMP** [a] Berry's "Greek-English Lexicon to the New Testament," and others. [b] Rev. 22:16. [c] Berry's "Greek-English Lexicon to the New Testament," and others. [d] Vincent. [e] Berry's "Greek-English Lexicon to the New Testament," and others. [f] Berry's "Greek-English Lexicon to the New Testament," and others. [g] Berry's "Greek-English Lexicon to the New Testament," and others.

## New American Standard

2And I saw a strong angel proclaiming with a loud voice, "Who is worthy to open the book and to break its seals?"

3And no one in heaven, or on the earth, or under the earth, was able to open the book, or to look into it.

4And I *began* to weep greatly, because no one was found worthy to open the book, or to look into it;

5and one of the elders *said to me, "Stop weeping; behold, the Lion that is from the tribe of Judah, the Root of David, has overcome so as to open the book and its seven seals."

6And I saw [h]between the throne (with the four living creatures) and the elders a Lamb standing, as if slain, having seven horns and seven eyes, which are the seven Spirits of God, sent out into all the earth.

7And He came, and He took *it* out of the right hand of Him who sat on the throne.

8And when He had taken the book, the four living creatures and the twenty-four elders fell down before the Lamb, having each one a harp, and golden bowls full of incense, which are the prayers of the saints.

9And they *sang a new song, saying,

"Worthy art Thou to take the book, and to break its seals; for Thou wast slain, and didst purchase for God with Thy blood *men* from every tribe and tongue and people and nation.

10 "And Thou hast made them *to be* a kingdom and priests to our God; and they will reign upon the earth."

*Angels Exalt the Lamb*

11And I looked, and I heard the voice of many angels around the throne and the living creatures and the elders; and the number of them was myriads of myriads, and thousands of thousands,

12saying with a loud voice,

"Worthy is the Lamb that was slain to receive power and riches and wisdom and might and honor and glory and blessing."

13And every created thing which is in heaven and on the earth and under the earth and on the sea, and all things in them, I heard saying,

"To Him who sits on the throne, and to the Lamb, *be* blessing and honor and glory and dominion forever and ever."

14And the four living creatures kept saying, "Amen." And the elders fell down and worshiped.

*The Book Opened*

*The First Seal—False Christ*

6 AND I saw when the Lamb broke one of the seven seals, and I heard one of the four living creatures saying as with a voice of thunder, "Come."

2And I looked, and behold, a white horse, and he who sat on it had a bow; and a crown was given to him; and he went out conquering, and to conquer.

*The Second Seal—War*

3¶ And when He broke the second seal, I heard the second living creature saying, "Come."

NAS [h] Lit., *in the middle of the throne and of the four living creatures, and in the middle of the elders*

## New International

"Who is worthy to break the seals and open the scroll?" 3But no one in heaven or on earth or under the earth could open the scroll or even look inside it. 4I wept and wept because no one was found who was worthy to open the scroll or look inside. 5Then one of the elders said to me, "Do not weep! See, the Lion of the tribe of Judah, the Root of David, has triumphed. He is able to open the scroll and its seven seals."

6Then I saw a Lamb, looking as if it had been slain, standing in the center of the throne, encircled by the four living creatures and the elders. He had seven horns and seven eyes, which are the seven spirits[i] of God sent out into all the earth. 7He came and took the scroll from the right hand of him who sat on the throne. 8And when he had taken it, the four living creatures and the twenty-four elders fell down before the Lamb. Each one had a harp and they were holding golden bowls full of incense, which are the prayers of the saints. 9And they sang a new song:

"You are worthy to take the scroll
and to open its seals,
because you were slain,
and with your blood you purchased men for God
from every tribe and language and people and nation.
10You have made them to be a kingdom and priests to
serve our God,
and they will reign on the earth."

11Then I looked and heard the voice of many angels, numbering thousands upon thousands, and ten thousand times ten thousand. They encircled the throne and the living creatures and the elders. 12In a loud voice they sang:

"Worthy is the Lamb, who was slain,
to receive power and wealth and wisdom and strength
and honor and glory and praise!"

13Then I heard every creature in heaven and on earth and under the earth and on the sea, and all that is in them, singing:

"To him who sits on the throne and to the Lamb
be praise and honor and glory and power,
for ever and ever!"

14The four living creatures said, "Amen," and the elders fell down and worshiped.

*The Seals*

6 I WATCHED as the Lamb opened the first of the seven seals. Then I heard one of the four living creatures say in a voice like thunder, "Come!" 2I looked, and there before me was a white horse! Its rider held a bow, and he was given a crown, and he rode out as a conqueror bent on conquest.

3When the Lamb opened the second seal, I heard the second living creature say, "Come!" 4Then another horse came out, a fiery

NIV [i] 6 Or *the sevenfold Spirit*

## King James

4And there went out another horse *that was* red: and *power* was
given to him that sat thereon to take peace from the earth, and that
they should kill one another: and there was given unto him a great
sword.
5And when he had opened the third seal, I heard the third beast
say, Come and see. And I beheld, and lo a black horse; and he that
sat on him had a pair of balances in his hand.
6And I heard a voice in the midst of the four beasts say, A
measure of wheat for a penny, and three measures of barley for
a penny; and *see* thou hurt not the oil and the wine.
7And when he had opened the fourth seal, I heard the voice of
the fourth beast say, Come and see.
8And I looked, and behold a pale horse: and his name that sat
on him was Death, and Hell followed with him. And power was
given unto them over the fourth part of the earth, to kill with
sword, and with hunger, and with death, and with the beasts of
the earth.
9And when he had opened the fifth seal, I saw under the altar
the souls of them that were slain for the word of God, and for the
testimony which they held:
10And they cried with a loud voice, saying, How long, O Lord,
holy and true, dost thou not judge and avenge our blood on them
that dwell on the earth?
11And white robes were given unto every one of them; and it
was said unto them, that they should rest yet for a little season,
until their fellowservants also and their brethren, that should be
killed as they *were*, should be fulfilled.
12And I beheld when he had opened the sixth seal, and, lo,
there was a great earthquake; and the sun became black as sackcloth of hair, and the moon became as blood;
13And the stars of heaven fell unto the earth, even as a fig tree
casteth her untimely figs, when she is shaken of a mighty wind.
14And the heaven departed as a scroll when it is rolled together;
and every mountain and island were moved out of their places.
15And the kings of the earth, and the great men, and the rich
men, and the chief captains, and the mighty men, and every
bondman, and every free man, hid themselves in the dens and in
the rocks of the mountains;
16And said to the mountains and rocks, Fall on us, and hide us
from the face of him that sitteth on the throne, and from the wrath
of the Lamb:
17For the great day of his wrath is come; and who shall be able
to stand?

7 AND AFTER these things I saw four angels standing on the
four corners of the earth, holding the four winds of the earth,
that the wind should not blow on the earth, nor on the sea, nor
on any tree.
2And I saw another angel ascending from the east, having the
seal of the living God: and he cried with a loud voice to the four
angels, to whom it was given to hurt the earth and the sea,
3Saying, Hurt not the earth, neither the sea, nor the trees, till
we have sealed the servants of our God in their foreheads.

## Amplified

4And another horse came out, flaming red. And its rider was
empowered to take the peace from the earth, so that men slaughtered one another; and he was given a huge sword.
5When He broke open the third seal, I heard the third living
creature call out, Come *and look*! And I saw, and behold, a black
horse, and in his hand the rider had a pair of scales (a balance).
6And I heard what seemed to be a voice from the midst of the
four living creatures saying, A quart of wheat for a denarius [a
whole day's wages], and three quarts of barley for a denarius; but
do not harm the oil and the wine! [II Kings 6:25.]
7When the Lamb broke open the fourth seal, I heard the fourth
living creature call out, Come!
8So I looked, and behold, an ashy pale horse [ [a]black and blue
as if made so by bruising], and its rider's name was Death, and
Hades [the realm of the dead] followed him closely; and they were
given authority *and* power over a fourth part of the earth, to kill
with the sword and with famine and with plague (pestilence,
disease) and with wild beasts of the earth. [Hos. 13:14; Ezek. 5:12.]
9When the Lamb broke open the fifth seal, I saw at the foot of
the altar the souls of those whose lives had been sacrificed for
[adhering to] the Word of God and for the testimony they had
borne.
10They cried in a loud voice, O (Sovereign) Lord, holy and true,
how long now before You will sit in judgment and avenge our
blood upon those who dwell on the earth? [Zech. 1:12; Ps. 79:5;
Gen. 4:10.]
11Then they were each given a [b]long *and* flowing *and* festive
white robe and told to rest *and* wait patiently a little while longer,
until the number should be complete of their fellow servants and
their brethren, who were to be killed as they themselves had been.
12When He [the Lamb] broke open the sixth seal, I looked, and
there was a great earthquake; and the sun grew black as sackcloth
of hair, (the full disc of) the moon became like blood. [Joel 2:10, 31.]
13And the stars of the sky dropped to the earth like a fig tree
shedding its unripe fruit out of season when shaken by a strong
wind. [Isa. 34:4.]
14And the [c]sky rolled up like a scroll *and* vanished, and every
mountain and island was dislodged from its place.
15Then the kings of the earth and their noblemen and their
magnates and their military chiefs and the wealthy and the strong
and [everyone, whether] slave or free, hid themselves in the caves
and among the rocks of the mountains, [Isa. 2:10.]
16And they called to the mountains and the rocks, Fall on (before) us and hide us from the face of Him Who sits on the throne,
and from the [d]deep-seated indignation *and* wrath of the Lamb.
[Hos. 10:8; Isa. 2:19-21.]
17For the great day of His wrath (vengeance, retribution, indignation) has come, and who is able to stand before it? [Joel 2:11; Mal.
3:2.]

7 AFTER THIS I saw four angels stationed at the four corners
of the earth, [e]firmly holding back the four winds of the earth,
so that no wind should blow on the earth or sea or upon any tree.
[Zech. 6:5.]
2Then I saw a second angel coming up from the east (the rising
of the sun), and carrying the seal of the living God. And with a
loud voice he called out to the four angels who had been given
authority *and* power to injure earth and sea,
3Saying, Harm neither the earth nor the sea nor the trees, until
we have sealed the bond servants of our God upon their foreheads.
[Ezek. 9:4.]

**AMP** [a] Definition of "livid," symbolizing death and pestilence. [b] Vincent. [c] Moulton and Milligan. [d] Vincent. [e] Vincent.

## New American Standard

4And another, a red horse, went out; and to him who sat on
it, it was granted to take peace from the earth, and that *men* should
slay one another; and a great sword was given to him.

*The Third Seal—Famine*

5¶ And when He broke the third seal, I heard the third living
creature saying, "Come." And I looked, and behold, a black horse;
and he who sat on it had a pair of scales in his hand.
6And I heard as it were a voice in the center of the four living
creatures saying, "A [f]quart of wheat for a [g]denarius, and three
quarts of barley for a denarius; and do not harm the oil and the
wine."

*The Fourth Seal—Death*

7¶ And when He broke the fourth seal, I heard the voice of the
fourth living creature saying, "Come."
8And I looked, and behold, an ashen horse; and he who sat on
it had the name Death; and Hades was following with him. And
authority was given to them over a fourth of the earth, to kill with
sword and with famine and with pestilence and by the wild beasts
of the earth.

*The Fifth Seal—Martyrs*

9¶ And when He broke the fifth seal, I saw underneath the altar
the souls of those who had been slain because of the word of God,
and because of the testimony which they had maintained;
10and they cried out with a loud voice, saying, "How long, O
Lord, holy and true, wilt Thou refrain from judging and avenging
our blood on those who dwell on the earth?"
11And there was given to each of them a white robe; and they
were told that they should rest for a little while longer, until *the
number of* their fellow servants and their brethren who were to be
killed even as they had been, should be completed also.

*The Sixth Seal—Terror*

12¶ And I looked when He broke the sixth seal, and there was
a great earthquake; and the sun became black as sackcloth *made* of
hair, and the whole moon became like blood;
13and the stars of the sky fell to the earth, as a fig tree casts its
unripe figs when shaken by a great wind.
14And the sky was split apart like a scroll when it is rolled up;
and every mountain and island were moved out of their places.
15And the kings of the earth and the great men and the
[h]commanders and the rich and the strong and every slave and free
man, hid themselves in the caves and among the rocks of the
mountains;
16and they *said to the mountains and to the rocks, "Fall on us
and hide us from the presence of Him who sits on the throne, and
from the wrath of the Lamb;
17for the great day of their wrath has come; and who is able to
stand?"

## New International

red one. Its rider was given power to take peace from the earth and
to make men slay each other. To him was given a large sword.
5When the Lamb opened the third seal, I heard the third living
creature say, "Come!" I looked, and there before me was a black
horse! Its rider was holding a pair of scales in his hand. 6Then I
heard what sounded like a voice among the four living creatures,
saying, "A quart[i] of wheat for a day's wages,[j] and three quarts
of barley for a day's wages,[k] and do not damage the oil and the
wine!"
7When the Lamb opened the fourth seal, I heard the voice of
the fourth living creature say, "Come!" 8I looked, and there before
me was a pale horse! Its rider was named Death, and Hades was
following close behind him. They were given power over a fourth
of the earth to kill by sword, famine and plague, and by the wild
beasts of the earth.
9When he opened the fifth seal, I saw under the altar the souls
of those who had been slain because of the word of God and the
testimony they had maintained. 10They called out in a loud voice,
"How long, Sovereign Lord, holy and true, until you judge the
inhabitants of the earth and avenge our blood?" 11Then each of
them was given a white robe, and they were told to wait a little
longer, until the number of their fellow servants and brothers who
were to be killed as they had been was completed.
12I watched as he opened the sixth seal. There was a great
earthquake. The sun turned black like sackcloth made of goat hair,
the whole moon turned blood red, 13and the stars in the sky fell
to earth, as late figs drop from a fig tree when shaken by a strong
wind. 14The sky receded like a scroll, rolling up, and every mountain and island was removed from its place.
15Then the kings of the earth, the princes, the generals, the rich,
the mighty, and every slave and every free man hid in caves and
among the rocks of the mountains. 16They called to the mountains
and the rocks, "Fall on us and hide us from the face of him who
sits on the throne and from the wrath of the Lamb! 17For the great
day of their wrath has come, and who can stand?"

### New American Standard

*An Interlude*

7 AFTER THIS I saw four angels standing at the four corners
of the earth, holding back the four winds of the earth, so that
no wind should blow on the earth or on the sea or on any tree.
2And I saw another angel ascending from the rising of the sun,
having the seal of the living God; and he cried out with a loud voice
to the four angels to whom it was granted to harm the earth and
the sea,
3saying, "Do not harm the earth or the sea or the trees, until
we have sealed the bond-servants of our God on their foreheads."

### New International

*144,000 Sealed*

7 AFTER THIS I saw four angels standing at the four corners
of the earth, holding back the four winds of the earth to
prevent any wind from blowing on the land or on the sea or on
any tree. 2Then I saw another angel coming up from the east,
having the seal of the living God. He called out in a loud voice to
the four angels who had been given power to harm the land and
the sea: 3"Do not harm the land or the sea or the trees until we put
a seal on the foreheads of the servants of our God." 4Then I heard

NAS [f] Gr., *choenix;* i.e., a dry measure almost equal to a quart [g] The denarius was equivalent to one day's wage [h] I.e., chiliarchs, in command of one thousand troops

NIV [i] 6 Greek *a choinix* (probably about a liter) [j] 6 Greek *a denarius* [k] 6 Greek *a denarius*

## King James

4 And I heard the number of them which were sealed: *and there were* sealed an hundred *and* forty *and* four thousand of all the tribes of the children of Israel.

5 Of the tribe of Judah *were* sealed twelve thousand. Of the tribe of Reuben *were* sealed twelve thousand. Of the tribe of Gad *were* sealed twelve thousand.

6 Of the tribe of Aser *were* sealed twelve thousand. Of the tribe of Nepthalim *were* sealed twelve thousand. Of the tribe of Manasses *were* sealed twelve thousand.

7 Of the tribe of Simeon *were* sealed twelve thousand. Of the tribe of Levi *were* sealed twelve thousand. Of the tribe of Issachar *were* sealed twelve thousand.

8 Of the tribe of Zabulon *were* sealed twelve thousand. Of the tribe of Joseph *were* sealed twelve thousand. Of the tribe of Benjamin *were* sealed twelve thousand.

9 After this I beheld, and, lo, a great multitude, which no man could number, of all nations, and kindreds, and people, and tongues, stood before the throne, and before the Lamb, clothed with white robes, and palms in their hands;

10 And cried with a loud voice, saying, Salvation to our God which sitteth upon the throne, and unto the Lamb.

11 And all the angels stood round about the throne, and *about* the elders and the four beasts, and fell before the throne on their faces, and worshipped God,

12 Saying, Amen: Blessing, and glory, and wisdom, and thanksgiving, and honour, and power, and might, *be* unto our God for ever and ever. Amen.

13 And one of the elders answered, saying unto me, What are these which are arrayed in white robes? and whence came they?

14 And I said unto him, Sir, thou knowest. And he said to me, These are they which came out of great tribulation, and have washed their robes, and made them white in the blood of the Lamb.

15 Therefore are they before the throne of God, and serve him day and night in his temple: and he that sitteth on the throne shall dwell among them.

16 They shall hunger no more, neither thirst any more; neither shall the sun light on them, nor any heat.

17 For the Lamb which is in the midst of the throne shall feed them, and shall lead them unto living fountains of waters: and God shall wipe away all tears from their eyes.

**8** AND WHEN he had opened the seventh seal, there was silence in heaven about the space of half an hour.

2 And I saw the seven angels which stood before God; and to them were given seven trumpets.

3 And another angel came and stood at the altar, having a golden censer; and there was given unto him much incense, that he should offer *it* with the prayers of all saints upon the golden altar which was before the throne.

## Amplified

4 And [then] I heard how many were sealed (marked) out of every tribe of the sons of Israel; there were a hundred and forty-four thousand sealed.

5 Twelve thousand were sealed (marked) out of the tribe of Judah, twelve thousand of the tribe of Reuben, twelve thousand of the tribe of Gad,

6 Twelve thousand of the tribe of Asher, twelve thousand of the tribe of Naphtali, twelve thousand of the tribe of Manasseh,

7 Twelve thousand of the tribe of Simeon, twelve thousand of the tribe of Levi, twelve thousand of the tribe of Issachar,

8 Twelve thousand of the tribe of Zebulun, twelve thousand of the tribe of Joseph, twelve thousand of the tribe of Benjamin.

9 After this I looked and a vast host appeared which no one could count, [gathered out] of every nation, from all tribes and peoples and languages. These stood before the throne and before the Lamb; they were attired in white robes, with palm branches in their hands.

10 In loud voice they cried, saying, [Our] salvation is due to our God Who is seated on the throne, and to the Lamb—to Them [we owe our] deliverance!

11 And all the angels were standing round the throne and round the elders [ [a]of the heavenly Sanhedrin] and the four living creatures, and they fell prostrate before the throne and worshipped God.

12 Amen! (So be it!) they cried. Blessing and glory *and* majesty *and* splendor and wisdom and thanks and honor and power and might [be ascribed] to our God to the ages and ages—forever and ever, throughout the eternities of the eternities! Amen! (So be it!)

13 Then, addressing me, one of the elders [ [b]of the heavenly Sanhedrin] said, Who are these [people] clothed in the long white robes? And from where have they come?

14 I replied, Sir, you know. And he said to me, These are they who have come out of the great tribulation (persecution), and have washed their robes and made them white in the blood of the Lamb. [Dan. 12:1; Gen. 49:11.]

15 For this reason they are [now] before the [very] throne of God, and serve Him day and night in His (temple) sanctuary; and He Who is sitting upon the throne will protect *and* spread His tabernacle over *and* shelter them with His presence.

16 They shall hunger no more, neither thirst any more, neither shall the sun smite them, nor any [c]scorching heat. [Isa. 49:10; Ps. 121:6.]

17 For the Lamb Who is in the midst of the throne will be their Shepherd, and He will guide them to the springs of the waters of Life; and God will wipe every tear away from their eyes. [Ezek. 34:23; Ps. 23:2; Isa. 25:8.]

**8** WHEN HE [the Lamb] broke open the seventh seal, there was silence for about half an hour in heaven.

2 Then I saw the seven angels who stand before God, and to them were given seven trumpets.

3 And another angel came and stood over the altar. He had a golden censer, and he was given very much incense [fragrant spices and gums which exhale perfume when burned], that he might mingle it with the prayers of all the people of God (the saints) upon the altar of gold before the throne. [Ps. 141:2.]

**AMP** [a] Souter: "A Pocket Lexicon to the Greek New Testament," and others.
[b] Souter: "A Pocket Lexicon to the Greek New Testament," and others.
[c] Berry: "Greek-English Lexicon to the New Testament," and others.

## New American Standard

*A Remnant of Israel—144,000*

4And I heard the number of those who were sealed, one hundred and forty-four thousand sealed from every tribe of the sons of Israel:

5from the tribe of Judah, twelve thousand *were* sealed, from the tribe of Reuben twelve thousand, from the tribe of Gad twelve thousand,

6from the tribe of Asher twelve thousand, from the tribe of Naphtali twelve thousand, from the tribe of Manasseh twelve thousand,

7from the tribe of Simeon twelve thousand, from the tribe of Levi twelve thousand, from the tribe of Issachar twelve thousand,

8from the tribe of Zebulun twelve thousand, from the tribe of Joseph twelve thousand, from the tribe of Benjamin, twelve thousand *were* sealed.

*A Multitude from the Tribulation*

9¶ After these things I looked, and behold, a great multitude, which no one could count, from every nation and *all* tribes and peoples and tongues, standing before the throne and before the Lamb, clothed in white robes, and palm branches *were* in their hands;

10and they cry out with a loud voice, saying,

¶ "Salvation to our God who sits on the throne, and to the Lamb."

11And all the angels were standing around the throne and *around* the elders and the four living creatures; and they fell on their faces before the throne and worshiped God,

12saying,

¶ "Amen, blessing and glory and wisdom and thanksgiving and honor and power and might, *be* to our God forever and ever. Amen."

13And one of the elders answered, saying to me, "These who are clothed in the white robes, who are they, and from where have they come?"

14And I said to him, "My lord, you know." And he said to me, "These are the ones who come out of the great tribulation, and they have washed their robes and made them white in the blood of the Lamb.

15"For this reason, they are before the throne of God; and they serve Him day and night in His temple; and He who sits on the throne shall spread His tabernacle over them.

16"They shall hunger no more, neither thirst anymore; neither shall the sun beat down on them, nor any heat;

17for the Lamb in the center of the throne shall be their shepherd, and shall guide them to springs of the water of life; and God shall wipe every tear from their eyes."

*The Seventh Seal—the Trumpets*

**8** AND WHEN He broke the seventh seal, there was silence in heaven for about half an hour.

2And I saw the seven angels who stand before God; and seven trumpets were given to them.

3¶ And another angel came and stood at the altar, holding a golden censer; and much incense was given to him, that he might add it to the prayers of all the saints upon the golden altar which was before the throne.

## New International

the number of those who were sealed: 144,000 from all the tribes of Israel.

5From the tribe of Judah 12,000 were sealed,
from the tribe of Reuben 12,000,
from the tribe of Gad 12,000,
6from the tribe of Asher 12,000,
from the tribe of Naphtali 12,000,
from the tribe of Manasseh 12,000,
7from the tribe of Simeon 12,000,
from the tribe of Levi 12,000,
from the tribe of Issachar 12,000,
8from the tribe of Zebulun 12,000,
from the tribe of Joseph 12,000,
from the tribe of Benjamin 12,000.

*The Great Multitude in White Robes*

9After this I looked and there before me was a great multitude that no one could count, from every nation, tribe, people and language, standing before the throne and in front of the Lamb. They were wearing white robes and were holding palm branches in their hands. 10And they cried out in a loud voice:

"Salvation belongs to our God,
who sits on the throne,
and to the Lamb."

11All the angels were standing around the throne and around the elders and the four living creatures. They fell down on their faces before the throne and worshiped God, 12saying:

"Amen!
Praise and glory
and wisdom and thanks and honor
and power and strength
be to our God for ever and ever.
Amen!"

13Then one of the elders asked me, "These in white robes—who are they, and where did they come from?"

14I answered, "Sir, you know."

And he said, "These are they who have come out of the great tribulation; they have washed their robes and made them white in the blood of the Lamb. 15Therefore,

"they are before the throne of God
and serve him day and night in his temple;
and he who sits on the throne will spread his tent over them.
16Never again will they hunger;
never again will they thirst.
The sun will not beat upon them,
nor any scorching heat.
17For the Lamb at the center of the throne will be their shepherd;
he will lead them to springs of living water.
And God will wipe away every tear from their eyes."

*The Seventh Seal and the Golden Censer*

**8** WHEN HE opened the seventh seal, there was silence in heaven for about half an hour.

2And I saw the seven angels who stand before God, and to them were given seven trumpets.

3Another angel, who had a golden censer, came and stood at the altar. He was given much incense to offer, with the prayers of all the saints, on the golden altar before the throne. 4The smoke

## King James

4And the smoke of the incense, *which came* with the prayers of the saints, ascended up before God out of the angel's hand.

5And the angel took the censer, and filled it with fire of the altar, and cast *it* into the earth: and there were voices, and thunderings, and lightnings, and an earthquake.

6And the seven angels which had the seven trumpets prepared themselves to sound.

7The first angel sounded, and there followed hail and fire mingled with blood, and they were cast upon the earth: and the third part of trees was burnt up, and all green grass was burnt up.

8And the second angel sounded, and as it were a great mountain burning with fire was cast into the sea: and the third part of the sea became blood;

9And the third part of the creatures which were in the sea, and had life, died; and the third part of the ships were destroyed.

10And the third angel sounded, and there fell a great star from heaven, burning as it were a lamp, and it fell upon the third part of the rivers, and upon the fountains of waters;

11And the name of the star is called Wormwood: and the third part of the waters became wormwood; and many men died of the waters, because they were made bitter.

12And the fourth angel sounded, and the third part of the sun was smitten, and the third part of the moon, and the third part of the stars; so as the third part of them was darkened, and the day shone not for a third part of it, and the night likewise.

13And I beheld, and heard an angel flying through the midst of heaven, saying with a loud voice, Woe, woe, woe, to the inhabiters of the earth by reason of the other voices of the trumpet of the three angels, which are yet to sound!

9 AND THE fifth angel sounded, and I saw a star fall from heaven unto the earth: and to him was given the key of the bottomless pit.

2And he opened the bottomless pit; and there arose a smoke out of the pit, as the smoke of a great furnace; and the sun and the air were darkened by reason of the smoke of the pit.

3And there came out of the smoke locusts upon the earth: and unto them was given power, as the scorpions of the earth have power.

4And it was commanded them that they should not hurt the grass of the earth, neither any green thing, neither any tree; but only those men which have not the seal of God in their foreheads.

5And to them it was given that they should not kill them, but that they should be tormented five months: and their torment *was* as the torment of a scorpion, when he striketh a man.

6And in those days shall men seek death, and shall not find it; and shall desire to die, and death shall flee from them.

7And the shapes of the locusts *were* like unto horses prepared unto battle; and on their heads *were* as it were crowns like gold, and their faces *were* as the faces of men.

8And they had hair as the hair of women, and their teeth were as *the teeth* of lions.

9And they had breastplates, as it were breastplates of iron; and the sound of their wings *was* as the sound of chariots of many horses running to battle.

10And they had tails like unto scorpions, and there were stings in their tails: and their power *was* to hurt men five months.

## Amplified

4And the smoke of the incense (the perfume) arose in the presence of God with the prayers of the people of God (the saints) from the hand of the angel.

5So the angel took the censer and filled it with fire from the altar and cast it upon the earth. Then there followed thunder peals *and* loud rumblings *and* blasts *and* noises, and lightning flashes, and an earthquake. [Lev. 16:12; Ezek. 10:2.]

6Then the seven angels who had the seven trumpets prepared to sound them.

7The first angel blew [his] trumpet, and there was a storm of hail and fire mingled with blood, cast upon the earth. And a third part of the earth was burned up, and a third of the trees was burned up and all the green grass was burned up. [Exod. 9:23-25.]

8The second angel blew his trumpet, and something resembling a great mountain, blazing with fire, was hurled into the sea. [Jer. 51:25.]

9And a third of the sea was turned to blood, a third of the living creatures in the sea perished, and a third of the ships were destroyed.

10The third angel blew [his] trumpet, and a huge star fell from heaven, burning like a torch, and it dropped on a third of the rivers and on the springs of water.

11And the name of the star is Wormwood. A third part of the waters was changed into wormwood, and many people died from using the water, because it had become bitter.

12Then the fourth angel blew [his] trumpet, and a third of the sun was smitten, and a third of the moon, and a third of the stars, so that [the light of] a third of them was darkened, and a third of the daylight [itself] was withdrawn and likewise a third [of the light] of the night was kept from shining.

13Then I [looked and I] saw a solitary eagle flying in midheaven, and as it flew I heard it crying with a loud voice, Woe, woe, woe to those who dwell on the earth, because of the rest of the trumpet blasts which the three angels are about to sound!

9 THEN THE fifth angel blew [his] trumpet, and I saw a star that had fallen from the sky to the earth, and to the angel was given the key [a]of the shaft of the abyss—the bottomless pit.

2He opened the [b]long shaft of the abyss—the bottomless pit—and smoke like the smoke of a huge furnace puffed out of the [c]long shaft, so that the sun and the atmosphere were darkened by the smoke from the long shaft. [Gen. 19:28; Exod. 19:18; Joel 2:10.]

3Then out of the smoke locusts came forth on the earth, and such power was granted them as the power the earth's scorpions have. [Exod. 10: 12-15.]

4They were told not to injure the herbage of the earth nor any green thing nor any tree, but only [to attack] such human beings as do not have the seal (mark) of God on their foreheads. [Ezek. 9:4.]

5They were not permitted to kill them, but to torment (distress, vex) them for five months, and the pain caused them was like the torture of a scorpion when it stings a person.

6And in those days people will seek death and will not find it, and they will yearn to die, but death evades *and* flees from them. [Job 3:21.]

7The locusts resembled horses equipped for battle. On their heads was something like golden crowns. Their faces resembled the faces of people. [Joel 2:4.]

8They had hair like the hair of women, and their teeth were like lions' teeth. [Joel 1:6.]

9Their breastplates [scales] resembled breastplates made of iron, and the [whirring] noise made by their wings was like the roar of a vast number of horse-drawn chariots going at full speed into battle. [Joel 2:5.]

10They have tails like scorpions, and they have stings, and in their tails lies their ability to hurt men for (the) five months.

AMP [a] Vincent. [b] Vincent. [c] Vincent.

## New American Standard

4And the smoke of the incense, with the prayers of the saints,
went up before God out of the angel's hand.
5And the angel took the censer; and he filled it with the fire of
the altar and threw it to the earth; and there followed peals of
thunder and sounds and flashes of lightning and an earthquake.
6¶ And the seven angels who had the seven trumpets prepared
themselves to sound them.
7¶ And the first sounded, and there came hail and fire, mixed
with blood, and they were thrown to the earth; and a third of the
earth was burned up, and a third of the trees were burned up, and
all the green grass was burned up.
8¶ And the second angel sounded, and *something* like a great
mountain burning with fire was thrown into the sea; and a third
of the sea became blood;
9and a third of the creatures, which were in the sea and had
life, died; and a third of the ships were destroyed.
10¶ And the third angel sounded, and a great star fell from
heaven, burning like a torch, and it fell on a third of the rivers and
on the springs of waters;
11and the name of the star is called Wormwood; and a third of
the waters became wormwood; and many men died from the
waters, because they were made bitter.
12¶ And the fourth angel sounded, and a third of the sun and
a third of the moon and a third of the stars were smitten, so that
a third of them might be darkened and the day might not shine
for a third of it, and the night in the same way.
13¶ And I looked, and I heard an eagle flying in midheaven,
saying with a loud voice, "Woe, woe, woe, to those who dwell on
the earth, because of the remaining blasts of the trumpet of the
three angels who are about to sound!"

## New International

of the incense, together with the prayers of the saints, went up
before God from the angel's hand. 5Then the angel took the censer,
filled it with fire from the altar, and hurled it on the earth; and there
came peals of thunder, rumblings, flashes of lightning and an
earthquake.

*The Trumpets*

6Then the seven angels who had the seven trumpets prepared
to sound them.
7The first angel sounded his trumpet, and there came hail and
fire mixed with blood, and it was hurled down upon the earth. A
third of the earth was burned up, a third of the trees were burned
up, and all the green grass was burned up.
8The second angel sounded his trumpet, and something like a
huge mountain, all ablaze, was thrown into the sea. A third of the
sea turned into blood, 9a third of the living creatures in the sea
died, and a third of the ships were destroyed.
10The third angel sounded his trumpet, and a great star, blazing
like a torch, fell from the sky on a third of the rivers and on the
springs of water— 11the name of the star is Wormwood.[d] A third
of the waters turned bitter, and many people died from the waters
that had become bitter.
12The fourth angel sounded his trumpet, and a third of the sun
was struck, a third of the moon, and a third of the stars, so that
a third of them turned dark. A third of the day was without light,
and also a third of the night.
13As I watched, I heard an eagle that was flying in midair call
out in a loud voice: "Woe! Woe! Woe to the inhabitants of the
earth, because of the trumpet blasts about to be sounded by the
other three angels!"

*The Fifth Trumpet—the Bottomless Pit*

9 AND THE fifth angel sounded, and I saw a star from heaven
which had fallen to the earth; and the key of the bottomless
pit was given to him.
2And he opened the bottomless pit; and smoke went up out
of the pit, like the smoke of a great furnace; and the sun and the
air were darkened by the smoke of the pit.
3And out of the smoke came forth locusts upon the earth; and
power was given them, as the scorpions of the earth have power.
4And they were told that they should not hurt the grass of the
earth, nor any green thing, nor any tree, but only the men who
do not have the seal of God on their foreheads.
5And they were not permitted to kill anyone, but to torment
for five months; and their torment was like the torment of a scorpion when it stings a man.
6And in those days men will seek death and will not find it;
and they will long to die and death flees from them.
7And the appearance of the locusts was like horses prepared
for battle; and on their heads, as it were, crowns like gold, and
their faces were like the faces of men.
8And they had hair like the hair of women, and their teeth
were like *the teeth* of lions.
9And they had breastplates like breastplates of iron; and the
sound of their wings was like the sound of chariots, of many
horses rushing to battle.
10And they have tails like scorpions, and stings; and in their
tails is their power to hurt men for five months.

9 THE FIFTH angel sounded his trumpet, and I saw a star that
had fallen from the sky to the earth. The star was given the
key to the shaft of the Abyss. 2When he opened the Abyss, smoke
rose from it like the smoke from a gigantic furnace. The sun and
sky were darkened by the smoke from the Abyss. 3And out of the
smoke locusts came down upon the earth and were given power
like that of scorpions of the earth. 4They were told not to harm the
grass of the earth or any plant or tree, but only those people who
did not have the seal of God on their foreheads. 5They were not
given power to kill them, but only to torture them for five months.
And the agony they suffered was like that of the sting of a scorpion
when it strikes a man. 6During those days men will seek death, but
will not find it; they will long to die, but death will elude them.
7The locusts looked like horses prepared for battle. On their
heads they wore something like crowns of gold, and their faces
resembled human faces. 8Their hair was like women's hair, and
their teeth were like lions' teeth. 9They had breastplates like breastplates of iron, and the sound of their wings was like the thundering of many horses and chariots rushing into battle. 10They had
tails and stings like scorpions, and in their tails they had power to
torment people for five months. 11They had as king over them the

NIV [d] *11* That is, Bitterness

## King James

11 And they had a king over them, *which is* the angel of the
bottomless pit, whose name in the Hebrew tongue *is* Abaddon, but
in the Greek tongue hath *his* name Apollyon.
12 One woe is past; *and,* behold, there come two woes more
hereafter.
13 And the sixth angel sounded, and I heard a voice from the
four horns of the golden altar which is before God,
14 Saying to the sixth angel which had the trumpet, Loose the
four angels which are bound in the great river Euphrates.
15 And the four angels were loosed, which were prepared for an
hour, and a day, and a month, and a year, for to slay the third part
of men.
16 And the number of the army of the horsemen *were* two hundred thousand thousand: and I heard the number of them.
17 And thus I saw the horses in the vision, and them that sat on
them, having breastplates of fire, and of jacinth, and brimstone:
and the heads of the horses *were* as the heads of lions; and out of
their mouths issued fire and smoke and brimstone.
18 By these three was the third part of men killed, by the fire,
and by the smoke, and by the brimstone, which issued out of their
mouths.
19 For their power is in their mouth, and in their tails: for their
tails *were* like unto serpents, and had heads, and with them they
do hurt.
20 And the rest of the men which were not killed by these
plagues yet repented not of the works of their hands, that they
should not worship devils, and idols of gold, and silver, and brass,
and stone, and of wood: which neither can see, nor hear, nor walk:
21 Neither repented they of their murders, nor of their sorceries,
nor of their fornication, nor of their thefts.

## Amplified

11 Over them as king they have the angel of the abyss—of the
bottomless pit. In Hebrew his name is Abaddon [destruction], but
in Greek he is called Apollyon [destroyer].
12 The first woe (calamity) has passed; lo, two others are yet to
follow.
13 Then the sixth angel blew [his] trumpet, and from the four
horns of the altar of gold which stands before God I heard a solitary
voice,
14 Saying to the sixth angel who had the trumpet, Liberate the
four angels who are bound at the great river Euphrates.
15 So the four angels, who had been in readiness for that hour
in the appointed day, month and year, were liberated to destroy
a third of mankind.
16 The number of their troops of cavalry was twice ten thousand
times ten thousand (200,000,000); I heard what their number was.
17 And in [my] vision the horses and their riders appeared to me
like this: the riders wore breastplates the color of fiery red and
sapphire blue and sulphur (brimstone) yellow. The heads of the
horses looked like lions' heads, and from their mouths there
poured fire and smoke and sulphur (brimstone).
18 A third of mankind was killed by these three plagues, by the
fire and the smoke and the sulphur (brimstone) that poured from
the mouths of the horses.
19 For the power of the horses to do harm is in their mouths and
also in their tails. Their tails are like serpents, for they have heads,
and it is by means of them that they wound people.
20 And the rest of humanity, who were not killed by these
plagues, even then did not repent (out) of [the worship of] the
works of their [own] hands, so as to cease paying homage to the
demons and idols of gold and silver and bronze and stone and
wood, which can neither see nor hear nor move. [Isa. 17:8; Ps.
115:4-7; 135:15-17.]
21 And they did not repent (out) of their murders or their practice of magic (sorceries) or their sexual vice or their thefts.

**10** AND I saw another mighty angel come down from
heaven, clothed with a cloud: and a rainbow *was* upon his
head, and his face *was* as it were the sun, and his feet as pillars of
fire:
2 And he had in his hand a little book open: and he set his right
foot upon the sea, and *his* left *foot* on the earth,
3 And cried with a loud voice, as *when* a lion roareth: and when
he had cried, seven thunders uttered their voices.
4 And when the seven thunders had uttered their voices, I was
about to write: and I heard a voice from heaven saying unto me,
Seal up those things which the seven thunders uttered, and write
them not.
5 And the angel which I saw stand upon the sea and upon the
earth lifted up his hand to heaven,
6 And sware by him that liveth for ever and ever, who created
heaven, and the things that therein are, and the earth, and the
things that therein are, and the sea, and the things which are
therein, that there should be time no longer:
7 But in the days of the voice of the seventh angel, when he shall
begin to sound, the mystery of God should be finished, as he hath
declared to his servants the prophets.
8 And the voice which I heard from heaven spake unto me
again, and said, Go *and* take the little book which is open in the
hand of the angel which standeth upon the sea and upon the earth.
9 And I went unto the angel, and said unto him, Give me the
little book. And he said unto me, Take *it,* and eat it up; and it shall
make thy belly bitter, but it shall be in thy mouth sweet as honey.

**10** THEN I saw another mighty angel coming down from
heaven, robed in a cloud, with a [halo like a] rainbow over
his head; his face was like the sun, and his feet [legs] were like
columns of fire.
2 He had a little book (scroll) open in his hand. He set his right
foot on the sea and his left foot on the land,
3 And he shouted with a loud voice like the roaring of a lion; and
when he had shouted, the seven thunders gave voice *and* uttered
their message in distinct words.
4 And when the seven thunders had spoken (sounded), I was
going to write [it down], but I heard a voice from heaven saying,
Seal up what the seven thunders have said! Do not write it down!
5 Then the [mighty] angel whom I had seen stationed on sea and
land raised his right hand to heaven (the [a]sky), [Deut. 32:40; Dan.
12:6, 7.]
6 And swore in the name of (by) Him Who lives forever and
ever, Who created the heavens ([b]sky) and all they contain, and the
earth and all that it contains, and the sea and all that it contains.
[He swore] that no more time should intervene *and* there should
be no more waiting *or* delay,
7 But that when the days come that the trumpet call of the
seventh angel is about to be sounded, then God's mystery—His
secret design, His hidden purpose—as He had announced the glad
tidings to His servants the prophets, should be fulfilled (accomplished, completed). [Dan. 12:6, 7.]
8 Then the voice that I heard from heaven spoke again to me,
saying, Go and take the little book (scroll) which is open on the
hand of the angel who is standing on the sea and on the land.
9 So I went up to the angel and asked him to give me the little
book. And he said to me, Take it and eat it. It will embitter your
stomach, though in your mouth it will be sweet as honey. [Ezek.
2:8, 9; 3:1-3.]

**AMP** [a] Abbott-Smith. [b] Abbott-Smith.

## New American Standard

11They have as king over them, the angel of the abyss; his name in Hebrew is [c]Abaddon, and in the Greek he has the name Apollyon.

12¶ The first woe is past; behold, two woes are still coming after these things.

*The Sixth Trumpet—Army from the East*

13¶ And the sixth angel sounded, and I heard a voice from the [d]four horns of the golden altar which is before God,

14one saying to the sixth angel who had the trumpet, "Release the four angels who are bound at the great river Euphrates."

15And the four angels, who had been prepared for the hour and day and month and year, were released, so that they might kill a third of mankind.

16And the number of the armies of the horsemen was two hundred million; I heard the number of them.

17And this is how I saw in the vision the horses and those who sat on them: *the riders* had breastplates *the color* of fire and of hyacinth and of brimstone; and the heads of the horses are like the heads of lions; and out of their mouths proceed fire and smoke and brimstone.

18A third of mankind was killed by these three plagues, by the fire and the smoke and the brimstone, which proceeded out of their mouths.

19For the power of the horses is in their mouths and in their tails; for their tails are like serpents and have heads; and with them they do harm.

20And the rest of mankind, who were not killed by these plagues, did not repent of the works of their hands, so as not to worship demons, and the idols of gold and of silver and of brass and of stone and of wood, which can neither see nor hear nor walk;

21and they did not repent of their murders nor of their sorceries nor of their immorality nor of their thefts.

*The Angel and the Little Book*

10 AND I saw another strong angel coming down out of heaven, clothed with a cloud; and the rainbow was upon his head, and his face was like the sun, and his feet like pillars of fire;

2and he had in his hand a little book which was open. And he placed his right foot on the sea and his left on the land;

3and he cried out with a loud voice, as when a lion roars; and when he had cried out, the seven peals of thunder uttered their voices.

4And when the seven peals of thunder had spoken, I was about to write; and I heard a voice from heaven saying, "Seal up the things which the seven peals of thunder have spoken, and do not write them."

5And the angel whom I saw standing on the sea and on the land lifted up his right hand to heaven,

6and swore by Him who lives forever and ever, WHO CREATED HEAVEN AND THE THINGS IN IT, AND THE EARTH AND THE THINGS IN IT, AND THE SEA AND THE THINGS IN IT, that there shall be delay no longer,

7but in the days of the voice of the seventh angel, when he is about to sound, then the mystery of God is finished, as He preached to His servants the prophets.

8And the voice which I heard from heaven, *I heard* again speaking with me, and saying, "Go, take the book which is open in the hand of the angel who stands on the sea and on the land."

9And I went to the angel, telling him to give me the little book. And he *said to me, "Take it, and eat it; and it will make your stomach bitter, but in your mouth it will be sweet as honey."

NAS [c] I.e., destruction [d] Some ancient mss. do not contain *four*

## New International

angel of the Abyss, whose name in Hebrew is Abaddon, and in
Greek, Apollyon.[e]
12The first woe is past; two other woes are yet to come.
13The sixth angel sounded his trumpet, and I heard a voice
coming from the horns[f] of the golden altar that is before God. 14It
said to the sixth angel who had the trumpet, "Release the four
angels who are bound at the great river Euphrates." 15And the four
angels who had been kept ready for this very hour and day and
month and year were released to kill a third of mankind. 16The
number of the mounted troops was two hundred million. I heard
their number.
17The horses and riders I saw in my vision looked like this: Their
breastplates were fiery red, dark blue, and yellow as sulfur. The
heads of the horses resembled the heads of lions, and out of their
mouths came fire, smoke and sulfur. 18A third of mankind was
killed by the three plagues of fire, smoke and sulfur that came out
of their mouths. 19The power of the horses was in their mouths
and in their tails; for their tails were like snakes, having heads with
which they inflict injury.
20The rest of mankind that were not killed by these plagues still
did not repent of the work of their hands; they did not stop
worshiping demons, and idols of gold, silver, bronze, stone and
wood—idols that cannot see or hear or walk. 21Nor did they repent
of their murders, their magic arts, their sexual immorality or their
thefts.

*The Angel and the Little Scroll*

10 THEN I saw another mighty angel coming down from
heaven. He was robed in a cloud, with a rainbow above
his head; his face was like the sun, and his legs were like fiery
pillars. 2He was holding a little scroll, which lay open in his hand.
He planted his right foot on the sea and his left foot on the land,
3and he gave a loud shout like the roar of a lion. When he shouted,
the voices of the seven thunders spoke. 4And when the seven
thunders spoke, I was about to write; but I heard a voice from
heaven say, "Seal up what the seven thunders have said and do
not write it down."
5Then the angel I had seen standing on the sea and on the land
raised his right hand to heaven. 6And he swore by him who lives
for ever and ever, who created the heavens and all that is in them,
the earth and all that is in it, and the sea and all that is in it, and
said, "There will be no more delay! 7But in the days when the
seventh angel is about to sound his trumpet, the mystery of God
will be accomplished, just as he announced to his servants the
prophets."
8Then the voice that I had heard from heaven spoke to me once
more: "Go, take the scroll that lies open in the hand of the angel
who is standing on the sea and on the land."
9So I went to the angel and asked him to give me the little scroll.
He said to me, "Take it and eat it. It will turn your stomach sour,
but in your mouth it will be as sweet as honey." 10I took the little

NIV [e] *11 Abaddon* and *Apollyon* mean *Destroyer.* [f] 13 That is, projections

## King James

10And I took the little book out of the angel's hand, and ate it up; and it was in my mouth sweet as honey: and as soon as I had eaten it, my belly was bitter.

11And he said unto me, Thou must prophesy again before many peoples, and nations, and tongues, and kings.

**11** AND THERE was given me a reed like unto a rod: and the angel stood, saying, Rise, and measure the temple of God, and the altar, and them that worship therein.

2But the court which is without the temple leave out, and measure it not; for it is given unto the Gentiles: and the holy city shall they tread under foot forty *and* two months.

3And I will give *power* unto my two witnesses, and they shall prophesy a thousand two hundred *and* threescore days, clothed in sackcloth.

4These are the two olive trees, and the two candlesticks standing before the God of the earth.

5And if any man will hurt them, fire proceedeth out of their mouth, and devoureth their enemies: and if any man will hurt them, he must in this manner be killed.

6These have power to shut heaven, that it rain not in the days of their prophecy: and have power over waters to turn them to blood, and to smite the earth with all plagues, as often as they will.

7And when they shall have finished their testimony, the beast that ascendeth out of the bottomless pit shall make war against them, and shall overcome them, and kill them.

8And their dead bodies *shall lie* in the street of the great city, which spiritually is called Sodom and Egypt, where also our Lord was crucified.

9And they of the people and kindreds and tongues and nations shall see their dead bodies three days and an half, and shall not suffer their dead bodies to be put in graves.

10And they that dwell upon the earth shall rejoice over them, and make merry, and shall send gifts one to another; because these two prophets tormented them that dwelt on the earth.

11And after three days and an half the Spirit of life from God entered into them, and they stood upon their feet; and great fear fell upon them which saw them.

12And they heard a great voice from heaven saying unto them, Come up hither. And they ascended up to heaven in a cloud; and their enemies beheld them.

13And the same hour was there a great earthquake, and the tenth part of the city fell, and in the earthquake were slain of men seven thousand: and the remnant were affrighted, and gave glory to the God of heaven.

14The second woe is past; *and,* behold, the third woe cometh quickly.

15And the seventh angel sounded; and there were great voices in heaven, saying, The kingdoms of this world are become *the kingdoms* of our Lord, and of his Christ; and he shall reign for ever and ever.

16And the four and twenty elders, which sat before God on their seats, fell upon their faces, and worshipped God,

## Amplified

10So I took the little book from the angel's hand and ate *and* swallowed it; it was sweet as honey in my mouth, but once I had swallowed it my stomach was embittered.

11Then they said to me, You are to make a fresh prophecy concerning many peoples *and* races and nations and languages and kings. [Jer. 1:10.]

**11** A REED [as a measuring rod] was then given to me, [shaped] like a staff, and I was told: Rise up and measure the sanctuary of God and the altar [of incense], and [number] those who worship there; [Ezek. 40:3.]

2But leave out of your measuring the court outside the sanctuary of God; omit that, for it is given over to the Gentiles (the nations), and they will trample the holy city under foot for forty-two months [three and one-half years]. [Zech. 12:3; Isa. 63:18.]

3And I will grant the power of prophecy to My two witnesses for twelve hundred and sixty days [forty-two months; three and one-half years], dressed in sackcloth.

4These [witnesses] are the two olive trees and the two lampstands which stand before the Lord of the earth. [Zech. 4:3, 11-14.]

5And if any one attempts to injure them, fire pours from their mouth and consumes their enemies; if any one should attempt to harm them, thus he is doomed to be slain. [II Kings 1:10; Jer. 5:14.]

6These [two witnesses] have power to shut up the sky, so that no rain may fall during the days of their prophesying [their [a]prediction of events relating to Christ's kingdom and its speedy triumph] and they also have power to turn the waters into blood, and to smite *and* scourge the earth with all manner of plagues, as often as they choose. [I Kings 17:1; Exod. 7:17, 19.]

7But when they have finished their testimony *and* their evidence is all in, the beast (monster) that comes up out of the abyss (bottomless pit) will wage war on them and conquer them and kill them. [Dan. 7:3, 7, 21.]

8And their dead bodies [will lie exposed] in the open street ([b]a public square) of the great city which is in a spiritual sense called by the mystical *and* allegorical names of Sodom and Egypt, where also their Lord was crucified. [Isa. 1:9.]

9For three and a half days men from the races and tribes and languages and nations will gaze at their dead bodies and will not allow them to be put in a tomb.

10And those who dwell on the earth will gloat *and* exult over them *and* rejoice exceedingly, taking their ease and sending presents (in congratulation) to one another, because these two prophets had been such a vexation *and* trouble *and* torment to all the dwellers on the earth.

11But after three and a half days, by God's gift the breath of life again entered into them, and they rose up on their feet and great dread and terror fell on those who watched them. [Ezek. 37:5, 10.]

12Then [the two witnesses] heard a strong voice from heaven calling to them, Come up here! And before the very eyes of their enemies they ascended into heaven in a cloud. [II Kings 2:11.]

13And at that [very] hour there was a tremendous earthquake and one tenth of the city was destroyed (fell); seven thousand people perished in the earthquake, and those who remained were filled with dread *and* terror *and* were awe-struck, and they glorified the God of heaven.

14The second woe (calamity) has passed; now the third woe is speedily to come.

15The seventh angel then blew his trumpet and there were mighty voices in heaven, shouting, The dominion (kingdom, sovereignty, rule) of the world has now come into the possession and become the kingdom of our Lord and of His Christ, the Messiah, and He shall reign forever and ever—for the eternities of the eternities! [Ps. 22:28; Dan. 7:13, 14, 27.]

16Then the twenty-four elders [of [c]the heavenly Sanhedrin] who sit on their thrones before God prostrated themselves before Him and worshipped,

**AMP** [a] Thayer. [b] Souter. [c] Souter, and others.

## New American Standard

10And I took the little book out of the angel's hand and ate it, and it was in my mouth sweet as honey; and when I had eaten it, my stomach was made bitter.

11And they *said to me, "You must prophesy again concerning many peoples and nations and tongues and kings."

*The Two Witnesses*

**11** AND THERE was given me a measuring rod like a staff; and someone said, "Rise and measure the temple of God, and the altar, and those who worship in it.

2"And leave out the court which is outside the temple, and do not measure it, for it has been given to the nations; and they will tread under foot the holy city for forty-two months.

3"And I will grant *authority* to my two witnesses, and they will prophesy for twelve hundred and sixty days, clothed in sackcloth."

4These are the two olive trees and the two lampstands that stand before the Lord of the earth.

5And if anyone desires to harm them, fire proceeds out of their mouth and devours their enemies; and if anyone would desire to harm them, in this manner he must be killed.

6These have the power to shut up the sky, in order that rain may not fall during the days of their prophesying; and they have power over the waters to turn them into blood, and to smite the earth with every plague, as often as they desire.

7And when they have finished their testimony, the beast that comes up out of the abyss will make war with them, and overcome them and kill them.

8And their dead [d]bodies *will lie* in the street of the great city which [e]mystically is called Sodom and Egypt, where also their Lord was crucified.

9And those from the peoples and tribes and tongues and nations *will* look at their dead [f]bodies for three and a half days, and will not permit their dead bodies to be laid in a tomb.

10And those who dwell on the earth *will* rejoice over them and make merry; and they will send gifts to one another, because these two prophets tormented those who dwell on the earth.

11And after the three and a half days the breath of life from God came into them, and they stood on their feet; and great fear fell upon those who were beholding them.

12And they heard a loud voice from heaven saying to them, "Come up here." And they went up into heaven in the cloud, and their enemies beheld them.

13And in that hour there was a great earthquake, and a tenth of the city fell; and seven thousand people were killed in the earthquake, and the rest were terrified and gave glory to the God of heaven.

14¶ The second woe is past; behold, the third woe is coming quickly.

*The Seventh Trumpet—Christ's Reign Foreseen*

15¶ And the seventh angel sounded; and there arose loud voices in heaven, saying,

¶ "The kingdom of the world has become *the kingdom* of our Lord, and of His [g]Christ; and He will reign forever and ever."

16And the twenty-four elders, who sit on their thrones before God, fell on their faces and worshiped God,

NAS [d] Some ancient mss. read *body* [e] Lit., *spiritually* [f] Some ancient mss. read *body* [g] I.e., Messiah

## New International

scroll from the angel's hand and ate it. It tasted as sweet as honey in my mouth, but when I had eaten it, my stomach turned sour. 11Then I was told, "You must prophesy again about many peoples, nations, languages and kings."

*The Two Witnesses*

**11** I WAS given a reed like a measuring rod and was told, "Go and measure the temple of God and the altar, and count the worshipers there. 2But exclude the outer court; do not measure it, because it has been given to the Gentiles. They will trample on the holy city for 42 months. 3And I will give power to my two witnesses, and they will prophesy for 1,260 days, clothed in sackcloth." 4These are the two olive trees and the two lampstands that stand before the Lord of the earth. 5If anyone tries to harm them, fire comes from their mouths and devours their enemies. This is how anyone who wants to harm them must die. 6These men have power to shut up the sky so that it will not rain during the time they are prophesying; and they have power to turn the waters into blood and to strike the earth with every kind of plague as often as they want.

7Now when they have finished their testimony, the beast that comes up from the Abyss will attack them, and overpower and kill them. 8Their bodies will lie in the street of the great city, which is figuratively called Sodom and Egypt, where also their Lord was crucified. 9For three and a half days men from every people, tribe, language and nation will gaze on their bodies and refuse them burial. 10The inhabitants of the earth will gloat over them and will celebrate by sending each other gifts, because these two prophets had tormented those who live on the earth.

11But after the three and a half days a breath of life from God entered them, and they stood on their feet, and terror struck those who saw them. 12Then they heard a loud voice from heaven saying to them, "Come up here." And they went up to heaven in a cloud, while their enemies looked on.

13At that very hour there was a severe earthquake and a tenth of the city collapsed. Seven thousand people were killed in the earthquake, and the survivors were terrified and gave glory to the God of heaven.

14The second woe has passed; the third woe is coming soon.

*The Seventh Trumpet*

15The seventh angel sounded his trumpet, and there were loud voices in heaven, which said:

"The kingdom of the world has become the kingdom of
our Lord and of his Christ,
and he will reign for ever and ever."

16And the twenty-four elders, who were seated on their thrones before God, fell on their faces and worshiped God, 17saying:

## King James

17Saying, We give thee thanks, O Lord God Almighty, which art, and wast, and art to come; because thou hast taken to thee thy great power, and hast reigned.

18And the nations were angry, and thy wrath is come, and the time of the dead, that they should be judged, and that thou shouldest give reward unto thy servants the prophets, and to the saints, and them that fear thy name, small and great; and shouldest destroy them which destroy the earth.

19And the temple of God was opened in heaven, and there was seen in his temple the ark of his testament: and there were lightnings, and voices, and thunderings, and an earthquake, and great hail.

**12** AND THERE appeared a great wonder in heaven; a woman clothed with the sun, and the moon under her feet, and upon her head a crown of twelve stars:

2And she being with child cried, travailing in birth, and pained to be delivered.

3And there appeared another wonder in heaven; and behold a great red dragon, having seven heads and ten horns, and seven crowns upon his heads.

4And his tail drew the third part of the stars of heaven, and did cast them to the earth: and the dragon stood before the woman which was ready to be delivered, for to devour her child as soon as it was born.

5And she brought forth a man child, who was to rule all nations with a rod of iron: and her child was caught up unto God, and *to* his throne.

6And the woman fled into the wilderness, where she hath a place prepared of God, that they should feed her there a thousand two hundred *and* threescore days.

7And there was war in heaven: Michael and his angels fought against the dragon; and the dragon fought and his angels,

8And prevailed not; neither was their place found any more in heaven.

9And the great dragon was cast out, that old serpent, called the Devil, and Satan, which deceiveth the whole world: he was cast out into the earth, and his angels were cast out with him.

10And I heard a loud voice saying in heaven, Now is come salvation, and strength, and the kingdom of our God, and the power of his Christ: for the accuser of our brethren is cast down, which accused them before our God day and night.

11And they overcame him by the blood of the Lamb, and by the word of their testimony; and they loved not their lives unto the death.

12Therefore rejoice, *ye* heavens, and ye that dwell in them. Woe to the inhabiters of the earth and of the sea! for the devil is come down unto you, having great wrath, because he knoweth that he hath but a short time.

13And when the dragon saw that he was cast unto the earth, he persecuted the woman which brought forth the man *child.*

## Amplified

17Exclaiming, To You we give thanks, Lord God Omnipotent, Who are and [ever] were, for assuming the high sovereignty *and* the great power that are Yours and beginning to reign.

18And the heathen (the nations) raged, but Your wrath (retribution, indignation) came, the time when the dead will be judged and to reward Your servants, the prophets and saints, and those who revere (fear) Your name, both low and high *and* small and great; and [the time] for destroying the corrupters of the earth. [Ps. 2:1.]

19Then the sanctuary of God in heaven was thrown open, and the ark of His covenant was seen standing inside in His sanctuary; and there were lightning flashes, loud rumblings (blasts, mutterings), peals of thunder, an earthquake, and a terrific hailstorm. [I Kings 8:1-6.]

**12** AND A great sign [wonder warning of future events of ominous significance] appeared in heaven, a woman clothed with the sun, with the moon under her feet, and with a crownlike garland (tiara) of twelve stars on her head.

2She was pregnant and she cried out in her birth pangs, in the anguish of her delivery.

3Then another ominous sign (wonder) was seen in heaven. Behold, a huge, fiery-red dragon, with seven heads and ten horns, and seven kingly crowns (diadems) upon his heads. [Dan. 7:7.]

4His tail swept [across the sky] *and* dragged down a third of the stars, and flung them to the earth. And the dragon stationed himself in front of the woman who was about to be delivered, so that he might devour her child as soon as she brought it forth. [Dan. 8:10.]

5And she brought forth a male Child, One Who is destined to shepherd (rule) all the nations with an iron staff (scepter), and her Child was caught up to God and to His throne. [Ps. 2:8, 9; 110:1, 2.]

6And the woman [herself] fled into the desert (wilderness), where she has a retreat prepared [for her] by God, in which she is to be fed *and* kept safe for one thousand two hundred and sixty days [forty-two months; three and one-half years].

7Then war broke out in heaven, Michael and his angels going forth to battle with the dragon; and the dragon and his angels fought,

8But they were defeated and there was no room found for them in heaven any longer.

9And the huge dragon was cast down *and* out, that ages-old serpent, who is called the Devil and Satan, he who is the seducer (deceiver) of all humanity the world over; he was forced out *and* down to the earth, and his angels were flung out along with him. [Gen. 3:1, 14, 15; Zech. 3:1.]

10Then I heard a strong voice in heaven, saying, Now it has come, the salvation and the power and the kingdom (the dominion, the reign) of our God and the power (the sovereignty, the authority) of His Christ, the Messiah; for the accuser of our brethren, he who keeps bringing before our God charges against them day and night, has been cast out! [Job 1:9-11.]

11And they have overcome (conquered) him by means of the blood of the Lamb and by the utterance of their testimony, for they did not love *and* cling to life even when faced with death—holding their lives cheap till they had to die [for their witnessing].

12Therefore be glad (exult), O heavens and you that dwell in them! But woe to you, O earth and sea, for the devil has come down to you in fierce anger (fury), because he knows that he has [only] a short time [left]! [Isa. 44:23; 49:13.]

13And when the dragon saw that he was cast down to the earth, he went in pursuit of the woman who had given birth to the male Child.

## New American Standard

17saying,
¶ "We give Thee thanks, O Lord God, the Almighty, who art and who wast, because Thou hast taken Thy great power and hast begun to reign.

18"And the nations were enraged, and Thy wrath came, and the time *came* for the dead to be judged, and *the time* to give their reward to Thy bond-servants the prophets and to the saints and to those who fear Thy name, the small and the great, and to destroy those who destroy the earth."

19¶ And the temple of God which is in heaven was opened; and the ark of His covenant appeared in His temple, and there were flashes of lightning and sounds and peals of thunder and an earthquake and a great hailstorm.

*The Woman, Israel*

**12** AND A great sign appeared in heaven: a woman clothed with the sun, and the moon under her feet, and on her head a crown of twelve stars;

2and she was with child; and she *cried out, being in labor and in pain to give birth.

*The Red Dragon, Satan*

3And another sign appeared in heaven: and behold, a great red dragon having seven heads and ten horns, and on his heads *were* seven diadems.

4And his tail *swept away a third of the stars of heaven, and threw them to the earth. And the dragon stood before the woman who was about to give birth, so that when she gave birth he might devour her child.

*The Male Child, Christ*

5And she gave birth to a son, a male *child*, who is to rule all the nations with a rod of iron; and her child was caught up to God and to His throne.

6And the woman fled into the wilderness where she *had a place prepared by God, so that there she might be nourished for one thousand two hundred and sixty days.

*The Angel, Michael*

7¶ And there was war in heaven, Michael and his angels waging war with the dragon. And the dragon and his angels waged war,

8and they were not strong enough, and there was no longer a place found for them in heaven.

9And the great dragon was thrown down, the serpent of old who is called the devil and Satan, who deceives the whole world; he was thrown down to the earth, and his angels were thrown down with him.

10And I heard a loud voice in heaven, saying,
¶ " Now the salvation, and the power, and the kingdom of our God and the authority of His Christ have come, for the accuser of our brethren has been thrown down, who accuses them before our God day and night.

11"And they overcame him because of the blood of the Lamb and because of the word of their testimony, and they did not love their life even to death.

12"For this reason, rejoice, O heavens and you who dwell in them. Woe to the earth and the sea, because the devil has come down to you, having great wrath, knowing that he has *only* a short time."

13¶ And when the dragon saw that he was thrown down to the earth, he persecuted the woman who gave birth to the male *child*.

## New International

"We give thanks to you, Lord God Almighty,
the One who is and who was,
because you have taken your great power
and have begun to reign.
18The nations were angry;
and your wrath has come.
The time has come for judging the dead,
and for rewarding your servants the prophets
and your saints and those who reverence your name,
both small and great—
and for destroying those who destroy the earth."

19Then God's temple in heaven was opened, and within his temple was seen the ark of his covenant. And there came flashes of lightning, rumblings, peals of thunder, an earthquake and a great hailstorm.

*The Woman and the Dragon*

**12** A GREAT and wondrous sign appeared in heaven: a
woman clothed with the sun, with the moon under her
feet and a crown of twelve stars on her head. 2She was pregnant
and cried out in pain as she was about to give birth. 3Then another
sign appeared in heaven: an enormous red dragon with seven
heads and ten horns and seven crowns on his heads. 4His tail
swept a third of the stars out of the sky and flung them to the earth.
The dragon stood in front of the woman who was about to give
birth, so that he might devour her child the moment it was born.
5She gave birth to a son, a male child, who will rule all the nations
with an iron scepter. And her child was snatched up to God and
to his throne. 6The woman fled into the desert to a place prepared
for her by God, where she might be taken care of for 1,260 days.
7And there was war in heaven. Michael and his angels fought
against the dragon, and the dragon and his angels fought back.
8But he was not strong enough, and they lost their place in heaven.
9The great dragon was hurled down—that ancient serpent called
the devil, or Satan, who leads the whole world astray. He was
hurled to the earth, and his angels with him.
10Then I heard a loud voice in heaven say:

"Now have come the salvation and the power and the
kingdom of our God,
and the authority of his Christ.
For the accuser of our brothers,
who accuses them before our God day and night,
has been hurled down.
11They overcame him
by the blood of the Lamb
and by the word of their testimony;
they did not love their lives so much
as to shrink from death.
12Therefore rejoice, you heavens
and you who dwell in them!
But woe to the earth and the sea,
because the devil has gone down to you!
He is filled with fury,
because he knows that his time is short."

13When the dragon saw that he had been hurled to the earth, he pursued the woman who had given birth to the male child.

## King James

14 And to the woman were given two wings of a great eagle, that she might fly into the wilderness, into her place, where she is nourished for a time, and times, and half a time, from the face of the serpent.

15 And the serpent cast out of his mouth water as a flood after the woman, that he might cause her to be carried away of the flood.

16 And the earth helped the woman, and the earth opened her mouth, and swallowed up the flood which the dragon cast out of his mouth.

17 And the dragon was wroth with the woman, and went to make war with the remnant of her seed, which keep the commandments of God, and have the testimony of Jesus Christ.

## Amplified

14 But the woman was supplied with the two wings of a giant eagle, so that she might fly from the presence of the serpent into the desert (wilderness, to the retreat) where she is to be kept safe *and* fed for a time, and times, and half a time [three and one-half years, or twelve hundred sixty days]. [Dan. 7:25; 12:7.]

15 Then out of his mouth the serpent spouted forth water like a flood after the woman, that she might be carried off with the torrent.

16 But the earth came to the rescue of the woman, and the ground opened its mouth and swallowed up the stream of water which the dragon had spouted from his mouth.

17 So then the dragon was furious (enraged) at the woman, and he went away to wage war on the remainder of her descendants, [on those] who obey God's commandments and who have the testimony of Jesus *Christ*—and adhere to it and [a]bear witness to Him.

## King James

**13** AND I stood upon the sand of the sea, and saw a beast rise up out of the sea, having seven heads and ten horns, and upon his horns ten crowns, and upon his heads the name of blasphemy.

2 And the beast which I saw was like unto a leopard, and his feet were as *the feet* of a bear, and his mouth as the mouth of a lion: and the dragon gave him his power, and his seat, and great authority.

3 And I saw one of his heads as it were wounded to death; and his deadly wound was healed: and all the world wondered after the beast.

4 And they worshipped the dragon which gave power unto the beast: and they worshipped the beast, saying, Who *is* like unto the beast? who is able to make war with him?

5 And there was given unto him a mouth speaking great things and blasphemies; and power was given unto him to continue forty *and* two months.

6 And he opened his mouth in blasphemy against God, to blaspheme his name, and his tabernacle, and them that dwell in heaven.

7 And it was given unto him to make war with the saints, and to overcome them: and power was given him over all kindreds, and tongues, and nations.

8 And all that dwell upon the earth shall worship him, whose names are not written in the book of life of the Lamb slain from the foundation of the world.

9 If any man have an ear, let him hear.

10 He that leadeth into captivity shall go into captivity: he that killeth with the sword must be killed with the sword. Here is the patience and the faith of the saints.

11 And I beheld another beast coming up out of the earth; and he had two horns like a lamb, and he spake as a dragon.

12 And he exerciseth all the power of the first beast before him, and causeth the earth and them which dwell therein to worship the first beast, whose deadly wound was healed.

13 And he doeth great wonders, so that he maketh fire come down from heaven on the earth in the sight of men,

14 And deceiveth them that dwell on the earth by *the means of* those miracles which he had power to do in the sight of the beast; saying to them that dwell on the earth, that they should make an image to the beast, which had the wound by a sword, and did live.

## Amplified

**13** [AS] [b]I stood on the sandy beach, I saw a beast coming up out of the sea with ten horns and seven heads. On his horns he had ten royal crowns (diadems) and blasphemous titles (names) on his heads.

2 And the beast that I saw resembled a leopard, his feet were like those of a bear, and his mouth was like that of a lion. And to him the dragon gave his [own] might *and* power, and his [own] throne and great dominion.

3 And one of his heads seemed to have a deadly wound. But his death stroke was healed, and the whole earth went after the beast in amazement *and* admiration.

4 They fell down *and* did homage to the dragon, because he had bestowed on the beast all his dominion *and* authority; they also praised *and* worshipped the beast, exclaiming, Who is a match for the beast, and who can make war against him?

5 And the beast was given the power of speech, uttering boastful and blasphemous words, and he was given freedom to exert his authority *and* to exercise his will during forty-two months [three and a half years]. [Dan. 7:8.]

6 And he opened his mouth to speak slanders against God, blaspheming His name and His abode, [even vilifying] those who live in heaven.

7 He was further permitted to wage war on God's holy people (the saints) and to overcome them. And power was given him to extend his authority over every tribe and people and tongue and nation, [Dan. 7:21, 25.]

8 And all the inhabitants of the earth will fall down in adoration *and* pay him homage, every one whose name has not been recorded from the foundation of the world in the Book of Life of the Lamb that was slain [in sacrifice] [c]from the foundation of the world.

9 If any one is able to hear, let him listen:

10 Whoever leads into captivity will himself go into captivity; if any one slays with the sword, with the sword must he be slain. Herein is [the call for] the patience and the faith *and* fidelity of the saints (God's people). [Jer. 15:2.]

11 Then I saw another beast rising up out of the land [itself]; he had two horns like a lamb and he spoke (roared) like a dragon.

12 He exerts all the power *and* right of control of the former beast in his presence, and causes the earth and those who dwell upon it to exalt *and* deify the first beast, whose deadly wound was healed, *and* worship him.

13 He performs great signs—startling miracles—even making fire fall from the sky to the earth in men's sight.

14 And because of the signs (miracles) which he is allowed to perform in the presence of the [first] beast, he deceives those who inhabit the earth, commanding them to erect a statue (an image) in the likeness of the beast which was wounded by the (small) sword and still lived. [Deut. 13:1-5.]

**AMP** [a] Williams. [b] Many ancient authorities read "he." [c] Alternate reading: construing these words with *slain* or with *recorded*.

## New American Standard

14And the two wings of the great eagle were given to the
woman, in order that she might fly into the wilderness to her
place, where she *was nourished for a time and times and half a
time, from the presence of the serpent.
15And the serpent poured water like a river out of his mouth
after the woman, so that he might cause her to be swept away with
the flood.
16And the earth helped the woman, and the earth opened its
mouth and drank up the river which the dragon poured out of his
mouth.
17And the dragon was enraged with the woman, and went off
to make war with the rest of her offspring, who keep the commandments of God and hold to the testimony of Jesus.

*The Beast from the Sea*

13 AND HE stood on the sand of the seashore.
And I saw a beast coming up out of the sea, having ten
horns and seven heads, and on his horns *were* ten diadems, and
on his heads *were* blasphemous names.
2And the beast which I saw was like a leopard, and his feet
were *like those* of a bear, and his mouth like the mouth of a lion.
And the dragon gave him his power and his throne and great
authority.
3And *I saw* one of his heads as if it had been slain, and his fatal
wound was healed. And the whole earth was amazed *and followed*
after the beast;
4and they worshiped the dragon, because he gave his authority to the beast; and they worshiped the beast, saying, "Who is like
the beast, and who is able to wage war with him?"
5And there was given to him a mouth speaking arrogant words
and blasphemies; and authority to act for forty-two months was
given to him.
6And he opened his mouth in blasphemies against God, to
blaspheme His name and His tabernacle, *that is,* those who dwell
in heaven.
7And it was given to him to make war with the saints and to
overcome them; and authority over every tribe and people and
tongue and nation was given to him.
8And all who dwell on the earth will worship him, *everyone*
whose name has not been [d]written from the foundation of the
world in the book of life of the Lamb who has been slain.
9If anyone has an ear, let him hear.
10If anyone [e]*is destined* for captivity, to captivity he goes; if
anyone kills with the sword, with the sword he must be killed.
Here is the perseverance and the faith of the saints.

*The Beast from the Earth*

11¶ And I saw another beast coming up out of the earth; and he
had two horns like a lamb, and he spoke as a dragon.
12And he exercises all the authority of the first beast in his
presence. And he makes the earth and those who dwell in it to
worship the first beast, whose fatal wound was healed.
13And he performs great signs, so that he even makes fire come
down out of heaven to the earth in the presence of men.
14And he deceives those who dwell on the earth because of the
signs which it was given him to perform in the presence of the
beast, telling those who dwell on the earth to make an image to
the beast who *had the wound of the sword and has come to life.

NAS [d] Or, *written in the book . . . slain from the foundation of the world* [e] Or, leads *into captivity*

## New International

14The woman was given the two wings of a great eagle, so that she
might fly to the place prepared for her in the desert, where she
would be taken care of for a time, times and half a time, out of the
serpent's reach. 15Then from his mouth the serpent spewed water
like a river, to overtake the woman and sweep her away with the
torrent. 16But the earth helped the woman by opening its mouth
and swallowing the river that the dragon had spewed out of his
mouth. 17Then the dragon was enraged at the woman and went
off to make war against the rest of her offspring—those who obey
God's commandments and hold to the testimony of Jesus.

13 AND THE dragon[f] stood on the shore of the sea.

*The Beast out of the Sea*

And I saw a beast coming out of the sea. He had ten horns and
seven heads, with ten crowns on his horns, and on each head a
blasphemous name. 2The beast I saw resembled a leopard, but had
feet like those of a bear and a mouth like that of a lion. The dragon
gave the beast his power and his throne and great authority. 3One
of the heads of the beast seemed to have had a fatal wound, but
the fatal wound had been healed. The whole world was astonished
and followed the beast. 4Men worshiped the dragon because he
had given authority to the beast, and they also worshiped the beast
and asked, "Who is like the beast? Who can make war against
him?"
5The beast was given a mouth to utter proud words and blasphemies and to exercise his authority for forty-two months. 6He
opened his mouth to blaspheme God, and to slander his name and
his dwelling place and those who live in heaven. 7He was given
power to make war against the saints and to conquer them. And
he was given authority over every tribe, people, language and
nation. 8All inhabitants of the earth will worship the beast—all
whose names have not been written in the book of life belonging
to the Lamb that was slain from the creation of the world.[g]
9He who has an ear, let him hear.

10If anyone is to go into captivity,
  into captivity he will go.
If anyone is to be killed[h] with the sword,
  with the sword he will be killed.

This calls for patient endurance and faithfulness on the part of the
saints.

*The Beast out of the Earth*

11Then I saw another beast, coming out of the earth. He had two
horns like a lamb, but he spoke like a dragon. 12He exercised all
the authority of the first beast on his behalf, and made the earth
and its inhabitants worship the first beast, whose fatal wound had
been healed. 13And he performed great and miraculous signs,
even causing fire to come down from heaven to earth in full view
of men. 14Because of the signs he was given power to do on behalf
of the first beast, he deceived the inhabitants of the earth. He
ordered them to set up an image in honor of the beast who was
wounded by the sword and yet lived. 15He was given power to

NIV [f] 1 Some late manuscripts *And I* [g] 8 Or *written from the creation of the world in the book of life belonging to the Lamb that was slain* [h] 10 Some manuscripts *anyone kills*

## King James

15And he had power to give life unto the image of the beast, that the image of the beast should both speak, and cause that as many as would not worship the image of the beast should be killed.

16And he causeth all, both small and great, rich and poor, free and bond, to receive a mark in their right hand, or in their foreheads:

17And that no man might buy or sell, save he that had the mark, or the name of the beast, or the number of his name.

18Here is wisdom. Let him that hath understanding count the number of the beast: for it is the number of a man; and his number *is* Six hundred threescore *and* six.

**14** AND I looked, and, lo, a Lamb stood on the mount Sion, and with him an hundred forty *and* four thousand, having his Father's name written in their foreheads.

2And I heard a voice from heaven, as the voice of many waters, and as the voice of a great thunder: and I heard the voice of harpers harping with their harps:

3And they sung as it were a new song before the throne, and before the four beasts, and the elders: and no man could learn that song but the hundred *and* forty *and* four thousand, which were redeemed from the earth.

4These are they which were not defiled with women; for they are virgins. These are they which follow the Lamb whithersoever he goeth. These were redeemed from among men, *being* the firstfruits unto God and to the Lamb.

5And in their mouth was found no guile: for they are without fault before the throne of God.

6And I saw another angel fly in the midst of heaven, having the everlasting gospel to preach unto them that dwell on the earth, and to every nation, and kindred, and tongue, and people,

7Saying with a loud voice, Fear God, and give glory to him; for the hour of his judgment is come: and worship him that made heaven, and earth, and the sea, and the fountains of waters.

8And there followed another angel, saying, Babylon is fallen, is fallen, that great city, because she made all nations drink of the wine of the wrath of her fornication.

9And the third angel followed them, saying with a loud voice, If any man worship the beast and his image, and receive *his* mark in his forehead, or in his hand,

10The same shall drink of the wine of the wrath of God, which is poured out without mixture into the cup of his indignation; and he shall be tormented with fire and brimstone in the presence of the holy angels, and in the presence of the Lamb:

11And the smoke of their torment ascendeth up for ever and ever: and they have no rest day nor night, who worship the beast and his image, and whosoever receiveth the mark of his name.

12Here is the patience of the saints: here *are* they that keep the commandments of God, and the faith of Jesus.

## Amplified

15And he was permitted [also] to impart the breath of life into the beast's image so that the statue of the beast could actually talk, and to cause to be put to death those who would not bow down *and* worship the image of the beast. [Dan. 3:5.]

16Also he compels all [alike], both small and great, both the rich and the poor, both free and slave to be marked with an inscription ([a]stamped) on their right hands or on their foreheads.

17So that no one will have power to buy or sell unless he bears the stamp (mark, inscription), [that is,] the name of the beast or the number of his name.

18Here is [room for] discernment—a call for the wisdom [[b]of interpretation]; let any one who has intelligence (penetration and insight enough) calculate the number of the beast, for it is a human number—the number of a certain man; his number is six hundred and sixty-six.

**14** THEN I looked and lo, the Lamb stood on Mount Zion, and with Him a hundred and forty-four thousand [men] who had His name and His Father's name inscribed on their foreheads.

2And I heard a voice from heaven like the sound of great waters and like the rumbling of mighty thunder; the voice I heard [seemed like the music] of harpists [c]accompanying themselves on their harps.

3And they sing a new song before the throne [of God] and before the four living creatures and before the elders [of [d]the heavenly Sanhedrin]. No one could learn [to sing] that song except the hundred and forty-four thousand who had been ransomed (purchased, redeemed) from the earth.

4These are they who have not defiled themselves by relations with women, for they are [[e]pure as] virgins. These are they who follow the Lamb wherever He goes. These are they who have been ransomed (purchased, redeemed) from among men as the first fruits for God and the Lamb.

5No lie was found to be upon their lips, for they are blameless—spotless, untainted, without blemish— *before the throne of God.*

6Then I saw another angel flying in mid-air, with an eternal Gospel (good news) to tell to the inhabitants of the earth, to every race and tribe and language and people.

7And he cried with a mighty voice, Revere God and give Him glory (honor and praise in worship), for the hour of His judgment has arrived. Fall down before Him; pay Him homage *and* adoration *and* worship Him Who created heaven and earth, the sea and the springs (fountains) of water.

8Then another angel, a second, followed, declaring, Fallen, fallen is Babylon the great! She who made all nations drink of the [maddening] wine of her passionate unchastity [[f]idolatry]. [Isa. 21:9.]

9Then another angel, a third, followed them, saying with a mighty voice, Whoever pays homage to the beast and his statue and permits the [beast's] stamp (mark, inscription) to be put on his forehead or on his hand,

10He too shall [have to] drink of the wine of God's indignation *and* wrath, poured undiluted into the cup of His anger, and he shall be tormented with fire and brimstone in the presence of the holy angels and in the presence of the Lamb. [Gen. 19:24.]

11And the smoke of their torment ascends forever and ever, and they have no respite—no pause, no intermission, no rest, no peace—day or night, these who pay homage to the beast and to his image, and whoever receives the stamp of his name upon him. [Isa. 34:10.]

12Here [comes in a call for] the steadfastness of the saints—the patience, the endurance of the people of God—those who (habitually) keep God's commandments and [their] faith in Jesus.

**AMP** [a] Thayer. [b] Thayer. [c] Vincent. [d] Souter, and others. [e] Williams. [f] Thayer.

## New American Standard

15And there was given to him to give breath to the image of the beast, that the image of the beast might even [g]speak and cause as many as do not worship the image of the beast to be killed.

16And he causes all, the small and the great, and the rich and the poor, and the free men and the slaves, to be given a mark on their right hand, or on their forehead,

17and *he provides* that no one should be able to buy or to sell, except the one who has the mark, *either* the name of the beast or the number of his name.

18Here is wisdom. Let him who has understanding calculate the number of the beast, for the number is that of a man; and his number is [h]six hundred and sixty-six.

*The Lamb and the 144,000 on Mount Zion*

**14** AND I looked, and behold, the Lamb *was* standing on Mount Zion, and with Him one hundred and forty-four thousand, having His name and the name of His Father written on their foreheads.

2And I heard a voice from heaven, like the sound of many waters and like the sound of loud thunder, and the voice which I heard *was* like *the sound* of harpists playing on their harps.

3And they *sang a new song before the throne and before the four living creatures and the elders; and no one could learn the song except the one hundred and forty-four thousand who had been purchased from the earth.

4These are the ones who have not been defiled with women, for they [i]have kept themselves chaste. These *are* the ones who follow the Lamb wherever He goes. These have been purchased from among men as first fruits to God and to the Lamb.

5And no lie was found in their mouth; they are blameless.

*Vision of the Angel with the Gospel*

6¶ And I saw another angel flying in midheaven, having an eternal gospel to preach to those who live on the earth, and to every nation and tribe and tongue and people;

7and he said with a loud voice, "Fear God, and give Him glory, because the hour of His judgment has come; and worship Him who made the heaven and the earth and sea and springs of waters."

8¶ And another angel, a second one, followed, saying, "Fallen, fallen is Babylon the great, she who has made all the nations drink of the wine of the passion of her immorality."

*Doom for Worshipers of the Beast*

9¶ And another angel, a third one, followed them, saying with a loud voice, "If anyone worships the beast and his image, and receives a mark on his forehead or upon his hand,

10he also will drink of the wine of the wrath of God, which is mixed in full strength in the cup of His anger; and he will be tormented with fire and brimstone in the presence of the holy angels and in the presence of the Lamb.

11"And the smoke of their torment goes up forever and ever; and they have no rest day and night, those who worship the beast and his image, and whoever receives the mark of his name."

12Here is the perseverance of the saints who keep the commandments of God and their faith in Jesus.

NAS [g] Some ancient mss. read *speak, and he will cause* [h] Some mss. read 616
[i] Lit., *are chaste men*

## New International

give breath to the image of the first beast, so that it could speak
and cause all who refused to worship the image to be killed. 16He
also forced everyone, small and great, rich and poor, free and
slave, to receive a mark on his right hand or on his forehead, 17so
that no one could buy or sell unless he had the mark, which is the
name of the beast or the number of his name.

18This calls for wisdom. If anyone has insight, let him calculate
the number of the beast, for it is man's number. His number is 666.

*The Lamb and the 144,000*

**14** THEN I looked, and there before me was the Lamb, standing on Mount Zion, and with him 144,000 who had his
name and his Father's name written on their foreheads. 2And I
heard a sound from heaven like the roar of rushing waters and like
a loud peal of thunder. The sound I heard was like that of harpists
playing their harps. 3And they sang a new song before the throne
and before the four living creatures and the elders. No one could
learn the song except the 144,000 who had been redeemed from
the earth. 4These are those who did not defile themselves with
women, for they kept themselves pure. They follow the Lamb
wherever he goes. They were purchased from among men and
offered as firstfruits to God and the Lamb. 5No lie was found in
their mouths; they are blameless.

*The Three Angels*

6Then I saw another angel flying in midair, and he had the
eternal gospel to proclaim to those who live on the earth—to every
nation, tribe, language and people. 7He said in a loud voice, "Fear
God and give him glory, because the hour of his judgment has
come. Worship him who made the heavens, the earth, the sea and
the springs of water."

8A second angel followed and said, "Fallen! Fallen is Babylon
the Great, which made all the nations drink the maddening wine
of her adulteries."

9A third angel followed them and said in a loud voice: "If
anyone worships the beast and his image and receives his mark on
the forehead or on the hand, 10he, too, will drink of the wine of
God's fury, which has been poured full strength into the cup of his
wrath. He will be tormented with burning sulfur in the presence
of the holy angels and of the Lamb. 11And the smoke of their
torment rises for ever and ever. There is no rest day or night for
those who worship the beast and his image, or for anyone who
receives the mark of his name." 12This calls for patient endurance
on the part of the saints who obey God's commandments and
remain faithful to Jesus.

## King James

13 And I heard a voice from heaven saying unto me, Write, Blessed *are* the dead which die in the Lord from henceforth: Yea, saith the Spirit, that they may rest from their labours; and their works do follow them.

14 And I looked, and behold a white cloud, and upon the cloud *one* sat like unto the Son of man, having on his head a golden crown, and in his hand a sharp sickle.

15 And another angel came out of the temple, crying with a loud voice to him that sat on the cloud, Thrust in thy sickle, and reap: for the time is come for thee to reap; for the harvest of the earth is ripe.

16 And he that sat on the cloud thrust in his sickle on the earth; and the earth was reaped.

17 And another angel came out of the temple which is in heaven, he also having a sharp sickle.

18 And another angel came out from the altar, which had power over fire; and cried with a loud cry to him that had the sharp sickle, saying, Thrust in thy sharp sickle, and gather the clusters of the vine of the earth; for her grapes are fully ripe.

19 And the angel thrust in his sickle into the earth, and gathered the vine of the earth, and cast *it* into the great winepress of the wrath of God.

20 And the winepress was trodden without the city, and blood came out of the winepress, even unto the horse bridles, by the space of a thousand *and* six hundred furlongs.

**15** AND I saw another sign in heaven, great and marvellous, seven angels having the seven last plagues; for in them is filled up the wrath of God.

2 And I saw as it were a sea of glass mingled with fire: and them that had gotten the victory over the beast, and over his image, and over his mark, *and* over the number of his name, stand on the sea of glass, having the harps of God.

3 And they sing the song of Moses the servant of God, and the song of the Lamb, saying, Great and marvellous *are* thy works, Lord God Almighty; just and true *are* thy ways, thou King of saints.

4 Who shall not fear thee, O Lord, and glorify thy name? for *thou* only *art* holy: for all nations shall come and worship before thee; for thy judgments are made manifest.

5 And after that I looked, and, behold, the temple of the tabernacle of the testimony in heaven was opened:

6 And the seven angels came out of the temple, having the seven plagues, clothed in pure and white linen, and having their breasts girded with golden girdles.

7 And one of the four beasts gave unto the seven angels seven golden vials full of the wrath of God, who liveth for ever and ever.

8 And the temple was filled with smoke from the glory of God, and from his power; and no man was able to enter into the temple, till the seven plagues of the seven angels were fulfilled.

## Amplified

13 Then I heard further, [ [a]perceiving the distinct words of] a voice from heaven saying, Write this: Blessed—happy, [b]to be envied—are the dead from now on who die in the Lord! Yes, blessed—happy, [c]to be envied indeed—says the Spirit, [in] that they may rest from their labors, for their works (deeds) do follow (attend, accompany) them!

14 Again I looked, and lo, [I saw] a white cloud, and sitting on the cloud [d] *One* resembling a [e] *Son* of man, with a crown of gold on *H*is head, and a sharp scythe (sickle) in *H*is hand. [Dan. 7:13.]

15 And another angel came out of the temple sanctuary, calling with a mighty voice to [f] *Him Who* was sitting upon the cloud, Put in *Y*our scythe and reap, for the hour has arrived to gather the harvest, for the earth's crop is fully ripened. [Joel 3:13.]

16 So [g] *He Who* was sitting upon the cloud swung *H*is scythe (sickle) on the earth and the earth's crop was harvested.

17 Then another angel came out of the temple sanctuary in heaven, and he also carried a sharp scythe (sickle).

18 And another angel came forth from the altar, [the angel] who has authority *and* power over fire, and he called with a loud cry to him who had the sharp scythe (sickle), Put forth your scythe and reap the fruitage of the vine of the earth, for its grapes are entirely ripe.

19 So the angel swung his scythe on the earth and stripped the grapes *and* gathered the vintage from the vines of the earth, and cast it into the huge wine press of God's indignation *and* wrath.

20 And [the grapes in] the wine press were trodden outside the city, and blood poured from the wine press, [reaching] as high as horses' bridles, for a distance of one thousand and six hundred stadia [about two hundred miles]. [Joel 3:13.]

**15** THEN I saw another wonder (sign, token, symbol) in heaven, great and marvelous [warning of events of ominous significance]. There were seven angels bringing seven plagues (afflictions, calamities), which are the last, for with them God's wrath (indignation) is completely expressed—reaches its climax and is ended. [Lev. 26:21.]

2 Then I saw what seemed to be a glassy sea blended with fire, and those who had come off victorious from the beast, and from his statue and from the number corresponding to his name, were standing beside the glassy sea with harps of God in their hands.

3 And they sing the song of Moses, the servant of God, and the song of the Lamb, saying, Mighty and marvelous are Your works, O Lord God the Omnipotent! Righteous (just) and true are Your ways, O Sovereign of the ages—King of the [h]nations! [Exod. 15:1; Ps. 145:17.]

4 Who shall not reverence and glorify Your name, O Lord—giving You honor and praise in worship? For You only are holy. All the nations shall come and pay homage *and* adoration to You, for Your just judgments—Your righteous sentences and deeds—have been made known *and* displayed. [Jer. 10:7; Ps. 86:9, 10.]

5 After this I looked and the sanctuary of the tent of the testimony in heaven was thrown open

6 And there came out of the temple sanctuary the seven angels bringing the seven plagues (afflictions, calamities). They were arrayed in pure gleaming linen, and around their breasts they wore girdles of gold.

7 And one of the four living creatures [then] gave the seven angels seven bowls of gold full of the wrath *and* indignation of God Who lives forever and ever—in the eternities of the eternities.

8 And the sanctuary was filled with smoke from the glory (the radiance, the splendor) of God and from His might *and* power, and no one was able to go into the sanctuary until the seven plagues (afflictions, calamities) of the seven angels were ended. [I Kings 8:10; Isa. 6:4; Ezek. 44:4.]

**AMP** [a] Thayer. [b] Souter. [c] Souter. [d] Capitals suppositional. Many question whether this refers to Christ. [e] Capitals suppositional. Many question whether this refers to Christ. [f] Capitals suppositional. Many question whether this refers to Christ. [g] Capitals suppositional. Many question whether this refers to Christ. [h] Many authorities read "nations."

## New American Standard

13¶ And I heard a voice from heaven, saying, "Write, 'Blessed are the dead who die in the Lord from now on!' " "Yes," says the Spirit, "that they may rest from their labors, for their deeds follow with them."

*The Reapers*

14¶ And I looked, and behold, a white cloud, and sitting on the cloud *was* one like [i]a son of man, having a golden crown on His head, and a sharp sickle in His hand.

15And another angel came out of the temple, crying out with a loud voice to Him who sat on the cloud, "Put in your sickle and reap, because the hour to reap has come, because the harvest of the earth is ripe."

16And He who sat on the cloud swung His sickle over the earth; and the earth was reaped.

17¶ And another angel came out of the temple which is in heaven, and he also had a sharp sickle.

18And another angel, the one who has power over fire, came out from the altar; and he called with a loud voice to him who had the sharp sickle, saying, "Put in your sharp sickle, and gather the clusters from the vine of the earth, because her grapes are ripe."

19And the angel swung his sickle to the earth, and gathered *the clusters from* the vine of the earth, and threw them into the great wine press of the wrath of God.

20And the wine press was trodden outside the city, and blood came out from the wine press, up to the horses' bridles, for a distance of [j]two hundred miles.

*A Scene of Heaven*

**15** AND I saw another sign in heaven, great and marvelous, seven angels who had seven plagues, *which are* the last, because in them the wrath of God is finished.

2¶ And I saw, as it were, a sea of glass mixed with fire, and those who had come off victorious from the beast and from his image and from the number of his name, standing on the sea of glass, holding harps of God.

3And they *sang the song of Moses the bond-servant of God and the song of the Lamb, saying,

¶ "Great and marvelous are Thy works,
O Lord God, the Almighty;
Righteous and true are Thy ways,
Thou King of the [k]nations.
4 "Who will not fear, O Lord, and glorify Thy name?
For Thou alone art holy;
FOR ALL THE NATIONS WILL COME AND WORSHIP BEFORE THEE,
For Thy righteous acts have been revealed."

5¶ After these things I looked, and the temple of the tabernacle of testimony in heaven was opened,

6and the seven angels who had the seven plagues came out of the temple, clothed in [l]linen, clean *and* bright, and girded around their breasts with golden girdles.

7And one of the four living creatures gave to the seven angels seven golden bowls full of the wrath of God, who lives forever and ever.

8And the temple was filled with smoke from the glory of God and from His power; and no one was able to enter the temple until the seven plagues of the seven angels were finished.

NAS [i] Or, *the Son of Man* [j] Lit., *sixteen hundred stadia.* A stadion was about six hundred feet. [k] Some ancient mss. read *ages* [l] Some mss. read *stone*

## New International

13Then I heard a voice from heaven say, "Write: Blessed are the dead who die in the Lord from now on."

"Yes," says the Spirit, "they will rest from their labor, for their deeds will follow them."

*The Harvest of the Earth*

14I looked, and there before me was a white cloud, and seated on the cloud was one "like a son of man"[m] with a crown of gold on his head and a sharp sickle in his hand.
15Then another angel came out of the temple and called in a loud voice to him who was sitting on the cloud, "Take your sickle and reap, because the time to reap has come, for the harvest of the earth is ripe."
16So he who was seated on the cloud swung his sickle over the earth, and the earth was harvested.

17Another angel came out of the temple in heaven, and he too had a sharp sickle.
18Still another angel, who had charge of the fire, came from the altar and called in a loud voice to him who had the sharp sickle, "Take your sharp sickle and gather the clusters of grapes from the earth's vine, because its grapes are ripe."
19The angel swung his sickle on the earth, gathered its grapes and threw them into the great winepress of God's wrath.
20They were trampled in the winepress outside the city, and blood flowed out of the press, rising as high as the horses' bridles for a distance of 1,600 stadia.[n]

*Seven Angels With Seven Plagues*

**15** I SAW in heaven another great and marvelous sign: seven angels with the seven last plagues—last, because with them God's wrath is completed.
2And I saw what looked like a sea of glass mixed with fire and, standing beside the sea, those who had been victorious over the beast and his image and over the number of his name. They held harps given them by God
3and sang the song of Moses the servant of God and the song of the Lamb:

"Great and marvelous are your deeds,
Lord God Almighty.
Just and true are your ways,
King of the ages.
4Who will not fear you, O Lord,
and bring glory to your name?
For you alone are holy.
All nations will come
and worship before you,
for your righteous acts have been revealed."

5After this I looked and in heaven the temple, that is, the tabernacle of the Testimony, was opened.
6Out of the temple came the seven angels with the seven plagues. They were dressed in clean, shining linen and wore golden sashes around their chests.
7Then one of the four living creatures gave to the seven angels seven golden bowls filled with the wrath of God, who lives for ever and ever.
8And the temple was filled with smoke from the glory of God and from his power, and no one could enter the temple until the seven plagues of the seven angels were completed.

NIV [m] *14* Daniel 7:13 [n] *20* That is, about 180 miles (about 300 kilometers)

## King James

**16** AND I heard a great voice out of the temple saying to the seven angels, Go your ways, and pour out the vials of the wrath of God upon the earth.

2 And the first went, and poured out his vial upon the earth; and there fell a noisome and grievous sore upon the men which had the mark of the beast, and *upon* them which worshipped his image.

3 And the second angel poured out his vial upon the sea; and it became as the blood of a dead *man:* and every living soul died in the sea.

4 And the third angel poured out his vial upon the rivers and fountains of waters; and they became blood.

5 And I heard the angel of the waters say, Thou art righteous, O Lord, which art, and wast, and shalt be, because thou hast judged thus.

6 For they have shed the blood of saints and prophets, and thou hast given them blood to drink; for they are worthy.

7 And I heard another out of the altar say, Even so, Lord God Almighty, true and righteous *are* thy judgments.

8 And the fourth angel poured out his vial upon the sun; and power was given unto him to scorch men with fire.

9 And men were scorched with great heat, and blasphemed the name of God, which hath power over these plagues: and they repented not to give him glory.

10 And the fifth angel poured out his vial upon the seat of the beast; and his kingdom was full of darkness; and they gnawed their tongues for pain,

11 And blasphemed the God of heaven because of their pains and their sores, and repented not of their deeds.

12 And the sixth angel poured out his vial upon the great river Euphrates; and the water thereof was dried up, that the way of the kings of the east might be prepared.

13 And I saw three unclean spirits like frogs *come* out of the mouth of the dragon, and out of the mouth of the beast, and out of the mouth of the false prophet.

14 For they are the spirits of devils, working miracles, *which* go forth unto the kings of the earth and of the whole world, to gather them to the battle of that great day of God Almighty.

15 Behold, I come as a thief. Blessed *is* he that watcheth, and keepeth his garments, lest he walk naked, and they see his shame.

16 And he gathered them together into a place called in the Hebrew tongue Armageddon.

17 And the seventh angel poured out his vial into the air; and there came a great voice out of the temple of heaven, from the throne, saying, It is done.

18 And there were voices, and thunders, and lightnings; and there was a great earthquake, such as was not since men were upon the earth, so mighty an earthquake, *and* so great.

19 And the great city was divided into three parts, and the cities of the nations fell: and great Babylon came in remembrance before God, to give unto her the cup of the wine of the fierceness of his wrath.

20 And every island fled away, and the mountains were not found.

## Amplified

**16** THEN I heard a mighty voice from the temple sanctuary saying to the seven angels, Go and empty out on the earth the seven bowls of God's wrath *and* indignation. [Isa. 66:6; Ps. 69:24.]

2 So the first [angel] went and emptied his bowl on the earth, and foul and painful ulcers (sores) came on the people who were marked with the stamp of the beast and who did homage to his image. [Exod. 9:10, 11; Deut. 28:35.]

3 The second *angel* emptied his bowl into the sea, and it turned into blood like that of a corpse [thick, corrupt, ill-smelling and disgusting], and every living thing that was in the sea perished.

4 Then the third *angel* emptied out his bowl into the rivers and the springs of water, and they turned into (became) blood. [Exod. 7:17-21.]

5 And I also heard the angel of the waters say, Righteous (just) are You in these Your decisions *and* judgments, You Who are and were, O Holy One!

6 Because they have poured out the blood of (the saints) Your people and the prophets, and You have given them blood to drink. Such is their due—they deserve it! [Ps. 79:3.]

7 And [from] the altar I heard [the] cry, Yes, Lord God the Omnipotent, Your judgments (sentences, decisions) are true and just *and* righteous! [Ps. 119:137.]

8 Then the fourth *angel* emptied out his bowl upon the sun, and it was permitted to burn (scorch) humanity with [fierce, glowing] heat (fire).

9 People were severely burned (scorched) by the fiery heat, and they reviled *and* blasphemed the name of God Who has control of these plagues, and they did not repent of their sins—felt no regret, contrition and compunction for their waywardness, refusing to amend their ways—to give Him glory.

10 Then the fifth *angel* emptied his bowl on the throne of the beast, and his kingdom was [plunged] in darkness, and people gnawed their tongues for the torment—of their excruciating distress and severe pain—[Exod. 10:21.]

11 And blasphemed the God of heaven because of their anguish and their ulcers (sores), and they did not deplore their wicked deeds *or* repent—for what they had done.

12 Then the sixth *angel* emptied his bowl on the mighty river Euphrates, and its water was dried up to make ready a road for [the coming of] the kings of the east (from the rising sun). [Isa. 11:15, 16.]

13 And I saw three loathsome spirits like frogs, [leaping] from the mouth of the dragon and from the mouth of the beast and from the mouth of the false prophet. [I Kings 22:21-23; Exod. 8:3.]

14 For really they are the spirits of demons that perform signs (wonders, miracles). And they go forth to the rulers *and* leaders all over the world, to gather them together for war on the great day of God the Almighty.

15 Lo, I am going to come like a thief! Blessed—happy, [a]to be envied—is he who stays awake (alert) and who guards his clothes so that he may not be naked and [have the shame of being] seen exposed!

16 And they gathered them together at the place which in Hebrew is called Armageddon. [II Kings 9:27.]

17 Then the seventh *angel* emptied out his bowl into the air, and a mighty voice came out of the sanctuary *of heaven* from the throne [of God], saying, It is done! (It is all over, it is all accomplished, it has come!) [Isa. 66:6.]

18 And there followed lightning flashes, loud rumblings, peals of thunder, and a tremendous earthquake; nothing like it has ever occurred since men dwelt on the earth, so severe *and* far reaching was that earthquake. [Exod. 19:16; Dan. 12:1.]

19 The mighty city was broken into three parts, and the cities of the nations fell. And God kept in mind mighty Babylon, to make her drain the cup of His furious wrath *and* indignation.

20 And every island fled and no mountains could be found.

AMP [a] Souter.

## New American Standard

*Six Bowls of Wrath*

**16** AND I heard a loud voice from the temple, saying to the
seven angels, "Go and pour out the seven bowls of the
wrath of God into the earth."
2¶ And the first *angel* went and poured out his bowl into the
earth; and it became a loathsome and malignant sore upon the men
who had the mark of the beast and who worshiped his image.
3¶ And the second *angel* poured out his bowl into the sea, and
it became blood like *that* of a dead man; and every living [b]thing
in the sea died.
4¶ And the third *angel* poured out his bowl into the rivers and
the springs of waters; and [c]they became blood.
5And I heard the angel of the waters saying, "Righteous art
Thou, who art and who wast, O Holy One, because Thou didst
judge these things;
6for they poured out the blood of saints and prophets, and
Thou hast given them blood to drink. They deserve it."
7And I heard the altar saying, "Yes, O Lord God, the Almighty, true and righteous are Thy judgments."
8¶ And the fourth *angel* poured out his bowl upon the sun; and
it was given to it to scorch men with fire.
9And men were scorched with fierce heat; and they blasphemed the name of God who has the power over these plagues;
and they did not repent, so as to give Him glory.
10¶ And the fifth *angel* poured out his bowl upon the throne of
the beast; and his kingdom became darkened; and they gnawed
their tongues because of pain,
11and they blasphemed the God of heaven because of their
pains and their sores; and they did not repent of their deeds.
12¶ And the sixth *angel* poured out his bowl upon the great river,
the Euphrates; and its water was dried up, that the way might be
prepared for the kings from the east.

*Armageddon*

13And I saw *coming* out of the mouth of the dragon and out of
the mouth of the beast and out of the mouth of the false prophet,
three unclean spirits like frogs;
14for they are spirits of demons, performing signs, which go out
to the kings of the whole world, to gather them together for the
war of the great day of God, the Almighty.
15("Behold, I am coming like a thief. Blessed is the one who
stays awake and keeps his garments, lest he walk about naked and
men see his shame.")
16And they gathered them together to the place which in Hebrew is called [d]Har-Magedon.

*Seventh Bowl of Wrath*

17¶ And the seventh *angel* poured out his bowl upon the air; and
a loud voice came out of the temple from the throne, saying, "It
is done."
18And there were flashes of lightning and sounds and peals of
thunder; and there was a great earthquake, such as there had not
been since man came to be upon the earth, so great an earthquake
*was it, and* so mighty.
19And the great city was split into three parts, and the cities of
the nations fell. And Babylon the great was remembered before
God, to give her the cup of the wine of His fierce wrath.
20And every island fled away, and the mountains were not
found.

**NAS** [b] Lit., *soul.* Some ancient mss. read *thing, the things in the sea.* [c] Some ancient mss. read *it became* [d] Some authorities read *Armageddon*

## New International

*The Seven Bowls of God's Wrath*

**16** THEN I heard a loud voice from the temple saying to the
seven angels, "Go, pour out the seven bowls of God's
wrath on the earth."
2The first angel went and poured out his bowl on the land, and
ugly and painful sores broke out on the people who had the mark
of the beast and worshiped his image.
3The second angel poured out his bowl on the sea, and it turned
into blood like that of a dead man, and every living thing in the
sea died.
4The third angel poured out his bowl on the rivers and springs
of water, and they became blood. 5Then I heard the angel in charge
of the waters say:

"You are just in these judgments,
you who are and who were, the Holy One,
because you have so judged;
6for they have shed the blood of your saints and prophets,
and you have given them blood to drink as they
deserve."

7And I heard the altar respond:

"Yes, Lord God Almighty,
true and just are your judgments."

8The fourth angel poured out his bowl on the sun, and the sun
was given power to scorch people with fire. 9They were seared by
the intense heat and they cursed the name of God, who had
control over these plagues, but they refused to repent and glorify
him.
10The fifth angel poured out his bowl on the throne of the beast,
and his kingdom was plunged into darkness. Men gnawed their
tongues in agony 11and cursed the God of heaven because of their
pains and their sores, but they refused to repent of what they had
done.
12The sixth angel poured out his bowl on the great river Euphrates, and its water was dried up to prepare the way for the kings
from the East. 13Then I saw three evil[e] spirits that looked like
frogs; they came out of the mouth of the dragon, out of the mouth
of the beast and out of the mouth of the false prophet. 14They are
spirits of demons performing miraculous signs, and they go out to
the kings of the whole world, to gather them for the battle on the
great day of God Almighty.
15"Behold, I come like a thief! Blessed is he who stays awake
and keeps his clothes with him, so that he may not go naked and
be shamefully exposed."
16Then they gathered the kings together to the place that in
Hebrew is called Armageddon.
17The seventh angel poured out his bowl into the air, and out
of the temple came a loud voice from the throne, saying, "It is
done!" 18Then there came flashes of lightning, rumblings, peals of
thunder and a severe earthquake. No earthquake like it has ever
occurred since man has been on earth, so tremendous was the
quake. 19The great city split into three parts, and the cities of the
nations collapsed. God remembered Babylon the Great and gave
her the cup filled with the wine of the fury of his wrath. 20Every
island fled away and the mountains could not be found. 21From

**NIV** [e] *13* Greek *unclean*

## King James

21 And there fell upon men a great hail out of heaven, *every stone* about the weight of a talent: and men blasphemed God because of the plague of the hail; for the plague thereof was exceeding great.

**17** AND THERE came one of the seven angels which had the seven vials, and talked with me, saying unto me, Come hither; I will show unto thee the judgment of the great whore that sitteth upon many waters:

2 With whom the kings of the earth have committed fornication, and the inhabitants of the earth have been made drunk with the wine of her fornication.

3 So he carried me away in the spirit into the wilderness: and I saw a woman sit upon a scarlet coloured beast, full of names of blasphemy, having seven heads and ten horns.

4 And the woman was arrayed in purple and scarlet colour, and decked with gold and precious stones and pearls, having a golden cup in her hand full of abominations and filthiness of her fornication:

5 And upon her forehead *was* a name written, MYSTERY, BABYLON THE GREAT, THE MOTHER OF HARLOTS AND ABOMINATIONS OF THE EARTH.

6 And I saw the woman drunken with the blood of the saints, and with the blood of the martyrs of Jesus: and when I saw her, I wondered with great admiration.

7 And the angel said unto me, Wherefore didst thou marvel? I will tell thee the mystery of the woman, and of the beast that carrieth her, which hath the seven heads and ten horns.

8 The beast that thou sawest was, and is not; and shall ascend out of the bottomless pit, and go into perdition: and they that dwell on the earth shall wonder, whose names were not written in the book of life from the foundation of the world, when they behold the beast that was, and is not, and yet is.

9 And here *is* the mind which hath wisdom. The seven heads are seven mountains, on which the woman sitteth.

10 And there are seven kings: five are fallen, and one is, *and* the other is not yet come; and when he cometh, he must continue a short space.

11 And the beast that was, and is not, even he is the eighth, and is of the seven, and goeth into perdition.

12 And the ten horns which thou sawest are ten kings, which have received no kingdom as yet; but receive power as kings one hour with the beast.

13 These have one mind, and shall give their power and strength unto the beast.

14 These shall make war with the Lamb, and the Lamb shall overcome them: for he is Lord of lords, and King of kings: and they that are with him *are* called, and chosen, and faithful.

15 And he saith unto me, The waters which thou sawest, where the whore sitteth, are peoples, and multitudes, and nations, and tongues.

## Amplified

21 And great—excessively oppressive—hailstones, as heavy as a talent [between fifty and sixty pounds], of immense size, fell from the sky on the people, and men blasphemed God for the plague of the hail, so very great was [the torture] of that plague. [Exod. 9:23.]

**17** ONE OF the seven angels who had the seven bowls then came and spoke to me, saying, Come with me! I will show you the doom (sentence, judgment) of the great harlot [idolatress] who is seated on many waters, [Jer. 51:13.]

2 [She] with whom the rulers of the earth have joined in prostitution [idolatry], and with the wine of whose immorality [idolatry] the inhabitants of the earth have become intoxicated. [Jer. 25:15, 16.]

3 And [the angel] bore me away [rapt] in the Spirit into a desert (wilderness), and I saw a woman seated on a scarlet beast that was all covered with blasphemous titles (names), and he had seven heads and ten horns.

4 The woman was robed in purple and scarlet, and bedecked with gold, precious stones and pearls [and she was] holding in her hand a cup of gold full of the accursed offenses and the filth of her lewdness *and* vice. [Jer. 51:7.]

5 And on her forehead there was inscribed a name of mystery—with a secret symbolic meaning: Babylon the great, the mother of prostitutes [idolatresses] and of the filth *and* atrocities *and* abominations of the earth.

6 I also saw that the woman was drunk, [drunk] with the blood of the saints (God's people), and the blood of the martyrs [who witnessed] for Jesus. And when I saw her I was utterly amazed *and* wondered greatly.

7 But the angel said to me, Why do you wonder? I will explain to you the [secret symbolic meaning of the] mystery of the woman, as well as of the beast having the seven heads and ten horns that carries her.

8 The beast that you saw [once] was, but [now] is no more, and he is going to come up out of the abyss (the bottomless pit) and proceed to go to perdition; and the inhabitants of the earth whose names have not been recorded in the Book of Life from the foundation of the world, will be astonished when they look at the beast, because he [once] was, but [now] is no more, and he is [yet] to come. [Dan. 7:3.]

9 This calls for a mind [to consider that is packed] with wisdom *and* intelligence—it is something for a particular mode of thinking and judging of thoughts, feelings and purposes. The seven heads are seven hills upon which the woman is sitting;

10 And they are also seven kings, five of whom have fallen, one still exists—and is reigning; the other [the seventh] has not yet appeared, and when he does arrive he must stay [but] a brief time.

11 And as for the beast that [once] was, but now is no more, he [himself] is an eighth ruler (king, head), but he is of the seven *and* belongs to them, and he goes to perdition.

12 Also the ten horns that you observed are ten rulers (kings) who have as yet received no royal dominion, but together they are to receive power *and* authority as rulers for a single hour, along with the beast. [Dan. 7:20-24.]

13 These have one common policy (opinion, purpose), and they deliver their power and authority to the beast.

14 They will wage war against the Lamb, and the Lamb will triumph over them; for He is Lord of lords and King of kings, and those with Him *and* on His side are chosen and called [elected] and loyal *and* faithful followers. [Dan. 2:47.]

15 And [the angel further] said to me, The waters that you observed, where the harlot is seated, are races and multitudes and nations and dialects (languages).

## New American Standard

21And huge hailstones, about [a]one hundred pounds each, *came down from heaven upon men; and men blasphemed God because of the plague of the hail, because its plague *was extremely severe.

*The Doom of Babylon*

17 AND ONE of the seven angels who had the seven bowls came and spoke with me, saying, "Come here, I shall show you the judgment of the great harlot who sits on many waters,

2with whom the kings of the earth committed *acts of* immorality, and those who dwell on the earth were made drunk with the wine of her immorality."

3And he carried me away [b]in the Spirit into a wilderness; and I saw a woman sitting on a scarlet beast, full of blasphemous names, having seven heads and ten horns.

4And the woman was clothed in purple and scarlet, and adorned with gold and precious stones and pearls, having in her hand a gold cup full of abominations and of the unclean things of her immorality,

5and upon her forehead a name *was* written, a mystery, "BABYLON THE GREAT, THE MOTHER OF HARLOTS AND OF THE ABOMINATIONS OF THE EARTH."

6And I saw the woman drunk with the blood of the saints, and with the blood of the witnesses of Jesus. And when I saw her, I wondered greatly.

7And the angel said to me, "Why do you wonder? I shall tell you the mystery of the woman and of the beast that carries her, which has the seven heads and the ten horns.

8"The beast that you saw was and is not, and is about to come up out of the abyss and [c]to go to destruction. And those who dwell on the earth will wonder, whose name has not been written in the book of life from the foundation of the world, when they see the beast, that he was and is not and will come.

9"Here is the mind which has wisdom. The seven heads are seven mountains on which the woman sits,

10and they are seven kings; five have fallen, one is, the other has not yet come; and when he comes, he must remain a little while.

11"And the beast which was and is not, is himself also an eighth, and is *one* of the seven, and he goes to destruction.

12"And the ten horns which you saw are ten kings, who have not yet received a kingdom, but they receive authority as kings with the beast for one hour.

13"These have one purpose and they give their power and authority to the beast.

*Victory for the Lamb*

14"These will wage war against the Lamb, and the Lamb will overcome them, because He is Lord of lords and King of kings, and those who are with Him *are the* called and chosen and faithful."

15And he *said to me, "The waters which you saw where the harlot sits, are peoples and multitudes and nations and tongues.

NAS [a] Lit., *the weight of a talent* [b] Or, *in spirit* [c] Some ancient mss. read *he goes*

## New International

the sky huge hailstones of about a hundred pounds each fell upon men. And they cursed God on account of the plague of hail, because the plague was so terrible.

*The Woman on the Beast*

17 ONE OF the seven angels who had the seven bowls came and said to me, "Come, I will show you the punishment of the great prostitute, who sits on many waters. 2With her the kings of the earth committed adultery and the inhabitants of the earth were intoxicated with the wine of her adulteries."

3Then the angel carried me away in the Spirit into a desert. There I saw a woman sitting on a scarlet beast that was covered with blasphemous names and had seven heads and ten horns. 4The woman was dressed in purple and scarlet, and was glittering with gold, precious stones and pearls. She held a golden cup in her hand, filled with abominable things and the filth of her adulteries. 5This title was written on her forehead:

MYSTERY
BABYLON THE GREAT
THE MOTHER OF PROSTITUTES
AND OF THE ABOMINATIONS OF THE EARTH.

6I saw that the woman was drunk with the blood of the saints, the blood of those who bore testimony to Jesus.

When I saw her, I was greatly astonished. 7Then the angel said to me: "Why are you astonished? I will explain to you the mystery of the woman and of the beast she rides, which has the seven heads and ten horns. 8The beast, which you saw, once was, now is not, and will come up out of the Abyss and go to his destruction. The inhabitants of the earth whose names have not been written in the book of life from the creation of the world will be astonished when they see the beast, because he once was, now is not, and yet will come.

9"This calls for a mind with wisdom. The seven heads are seven hills on which the woman sits. 10They are also seven kings. Five have fallen, one is, the other has not yet come; but when he does come, he must remain for a little while. 11The beast who once was, and now is not, is an eighth king. He belongs to the seven and is going to his destruction.

12"The ten horns you saw are ten kings who have not yet received a kingdom, but who for one hour will receive authority as kings along with the beast. 13They have one purpose and will give their power and authority to the beast. 14They will make war against the Lamb, but the Lamb will overcome them because he is Lord of lords and King of kings—and with him will be his called, chosen and faithful followers."

15Then the angel said to me, "The waters you saw, where the prostitute sits, are peoples, multitudes, nations and languages.

## King James

16 And the ten horns which thou sawest upon the beast, these shall hate the whore, and shall make her desolate and naked, and shall eat her flesh, and burn her with fire.

17 For God hath put in their hearts to fulfil his will, and to agree, and give their kingdom unto the beast, until the words of God shall be fulfilled.

18 And the woman which thou sawest is that great city, which reigneth over the kings of the earth.

**18** AND AFTER these things I saw another angel come down from heaven, having great power; and the earth was lightened with his glory.

2 And he cried mightily with a strong voice, saying, Babylon the great is fallen, is fallen, and is become the habitation of devils, and the hold of every foul spirit, and a cage of every unclean and hateful bird.

3 For all nations have drunk of the wine of the wrath of her fornication, and the kings of the earth have committed fornication with her, and the merchants of the earth are waxed rich through the abundance of her delicacies.

4 And I heard another voice from heaven, saying, Come out of her, my people, that ye be not partakers of her sins, and that ye receive not of her plagues.

5 For her sins have reached unto heaven, and God hath remembered her iniquities.

6 Reward her even as she rewarded you, and double unto her double according to her works: in the cup which she hath filled fill to her double.

7 How much she hath glorified herself, and lived deliciously, so much torment and sorrow give her: for she saith in her heart, I sit a queen, and am no widow, and shall see no sorrow.

8 Therefore shall her plagues come in one day, death, and mourning, and famine; and she shall be utterly burned with fire: for strong *is* the Lord God who judgeth her.

9 And the kings of the earth, who have committed fornication and lived deliciously with her, shall bewail her, and lament for her, when they shall see the smoke of her burning,

10 Standing afar off for the fear of her torment, saying, Alas, alas, that great city Babylon, that mighty city! for in one hour is thy judgment come.

11 And the merchants of the earth shall weep and mourn over her; for no man buyeth their merchandise any more:

12 The merchandise of gold, and silver, and precious stones, and of pearls, and fine linen, and purple, and silk, and scarlet, and all thyine wood, and all manner vessels of ivory, and all manner vessels of most precious wood, and of brass, and iron, and marble,

13 And cinnamon, and odours, and ointments, and frankincense, and wine, and oil, and fine flour, and wheat, and beasts, and sheep, and horses, and chariots, and slaves, and souls of men.

14 And the fruits that thy soul lusted after are departed from thee, and all things which were dainty and goodly are departed from thee, and thou shalt find them no more at all.

15 The merchants of these things, which were made rich by her, shall stand afar off for the fear of her torment, weeping and wailing,

## Amplified

16 And the ten horns that you saw, they and the beast will [be the very ones to] hate the harlot [the idolatrous woman]; they will make her cheerless (bereaved, desolate) and they will strip her, and eat up her flesh and utterly consume her with fire.

17 For God has put it into their hearts to carry out His own purpose by acting in harmony in surrendering their royal power *and* authority to the beast, until the prophetic words—intentions and promises—of God shall be fulfilled.

18 And the woman that you saw is herself the great city which dominates *and* controls the rulers *and* the leaders of the earth.

**18** THEN I saw another angel descending from heaven, possessing great authority, and the earth was illuminated with his radiance *and* splendor.

2 And he shouted with a mighty voice, She is fallen! Mighty Babylon is fallen! She has become a resort *and* dwelling place for demons, a dungeon haunted by every loathsome spirit, an abode for every filthy and detestable bird;

3 Because all nations have drunk the wine of her passionate unchastity, and the rulers *and* leaders of the earth have joined with her in committing fornication [idolatry], and the businessmen of the earth have become rich with the wealth of her excessive luxury *and* wantonness. [Jer. 25:15, 27.]

4 I then heard another voice from heaven saying, Come out from her, my people, so that you may not share in her sins, neither participate in her plagues. [Isa. 48:20; Jer. 50:8.]

5 For her iniquities—her crimes and transgressions—are piled up as high as heaven, and God has remembered her wickedness *and* [her] crimes—and calls them up for settlement. [Jer. 51:9.]

6 Repay to her what she herself has paid [to others] and double [her doom] in accordance with what she has done. Mix a double portion for her in the cup she mixed [for others]. [Ps. 137:8.]

7 To the degree that she glorified herself and reveled in her wantonness—living deliciously and luxuriously—to that measure impose on her torment *and* anguish and tears *and* mourning. Since in her heart she boasts, I am not a widow; as a queen [on a throne] I sit, and I shall never see suffering *or* experience sorrow, [Isa. 47:8, 9.]

8 So shall her plagues (afflictions, calamities) come thick upon her in a single day, pestilence and anguish *and* sorrow and famine, and she shall be utterly consumed—burned up with fire; for mighty is the Lord God Who judges her.

9 And the rulers *and* leaders of the earth, who joined her in her immorality [idolatry] and luxuriated with her, will weep *and* beat their breasts and lament over her when they see the smoke of her conflagration. [Ezek. 26:16, 17.]

10 They will stand a long way off, in terror of her torment, and they will cry, Woe *and* alas! the great city! the mighty city, Babylon! In one single hour how your doom (judgment) has overtaken you!

11 And earth's businessmen weep and grieve over her, because no one buys their freight (cargo) any more. [Ezek. 27:36.]

12 Their merchandise is of gold, silver, precious stones and pearls; of fine linen, purple, silk and scarlet [stuffs]; all kinds of scented wood, all sorts of articles of ivory, all varieties of objects of costly woods, bronze, iron and marble; [Ezek. 27:12, 13, 22.]

13 Of cinnamon, spices, incense, ointment *and* perfume, and frankincense; of wine and olive oil, fine flour and wheat; of cattle and sheep, horses and conveyances; and of slaves, [that is,] the bodies, and souls of men!

14 The ripe fruits *and* delicacies for which your soul longed have gone from you, and all your luxuries *and* dainties, your elegance *and* splendor are lost to you, never again to be recovered *or* experienced!

15 The dealers who handled these articles, who grew wealthy through their business with her, will stand a long way off, in terror of her doom *and* torment, weeping and grieving aloud, and saying,

## New American Standard

16"And the ten horns which you saw, and the beast, these will
hate the harlot and will make her desolate and naked, and will eat
her flesh and will burn her up with fire.
17"For God has put it in their hearts to execute His purpose by
having a common purpose, and by giving their kingdom to the
beast, until the words of God should be fulfilled.
18"And the woman whom you saw is the great city, which
reigns over the kings of the earth."

*Babylon Is Fallen*

**18** AFTER THESE things I saw another angel coming down
from heaven, having great authority, and the earth was
illumined with his glory.
2And he cried out with a mighty voice, saying, "Fallen, fallen
is Babylon the great! And she has become a dwelling place of
demons and a prison of every unclean spirit, and a prison of every
unclean and hateful bird.
3"For all the nations [a]have drunk of the wine of the passion
of her immorality, and the kings of the earth have committed *acts
of* immorality with her, and the merchants of the earth have
become rich by the wealth of her sensuality."
4¶ And I heard another voice from heaven, saying, "Come out
of her, my people, that you may not participate in her sins and that
you may not receive of her plagues;
5for her sins have piled up as high as heaven, and God has
remembered her iniquities.
6"Pay her back even as she has paid, and give back *to her*
double according to her deeds; in the cup which she has mixed,
mix twice as much for her.
7"To the degree that she glorified herself and lived sensuously,
to the same degree give her torment and mourning; for she says
in her heart, 'I SIT *as* A QUEEN AND I AM NOT A WIDOW, and will
never see mourning.'
8"For this reason in one day her plagues will come, pestilence
and mourning and famine, and she will be burned up with fire; for
the Lord God who judges her is strong.

*Lament for Babylon*

9"And the kings of the earth, who committed *acts of* immorality
and lived sensuously with her, will weep and lament over her
when they see the smoke of her burning,
10standing at a distance because of the fear of her torment,
saying, 'Woe, woe, the great city, Babylon, the strong city! For in
one hour your judgment has come.'
11"And the merchants of the earth weep and mourn over her,
because no one buys their cargoes any more;
12cargoes of gold and silver and precious stones and pearls and
fine linen and purple and silk and scarlet, and every *kind of* citron
wood and every article of ivory and every article *made* from very
costly wood and bronze and iron and marble,
13and cinnamon and spice and incense and perfume and frankincense and wine and olive oil and fine flour and wheat and cattle
and sheep, and *cargoes* of horses and chariots and slaves and
human lives.
14"And the fruit you long for has gone from you, and all things
that were luxurious and splendid have passed away from you and
*men* will no longer find them.
15"The merchants of these things, who became rich from her,
will stand at a distance because of the fear of her torment, weeping
and mourning,

**NAS** [a] Many ancient mss. read *have fallen by*

## New International

16The beast and the ten horns you saw will hate the prostitute.
They will bring her to ruin and leave her naked; they will eat her
flesh and burn her with fire. 17For God has put it into their hearts
to accomplish his purpose by agreeing to give the beast their power
to rule, until God's words are fulfilled. 18The woman you saw is
the great city that rules over the kings of the earth."

*The Fall of Babylon*

**18** AFTER THIS I saw another angel coming down from
heaven. He had great authority, and the earth was illuminated by his splendor. 2With a mighty voice he shouted:

"Fallen! Fallen is Babylon the Great!
She has become a home for demons
and a haunt for every evil[b] spirit,
a haunt for every unclean and detestable bird.
3For all the nations have drunk
the maddening wine of her adulteries.
The kings of the earth committed adultery with her,
and the merchants of the earth grew rich from her
excessive luxuries."

4Then I heard another voice from heaven say:

"Come out of her, my people,
so that you will not share in her sins,
so that you will not receive any of her plagues;
5for her sins are piled up to heaven,
and God has remembered her crimes.
6Give back to her as she has given;
pay her back double for what she has done.
Mix her a double portion from her own cup.
7Give her as much torture and grief
as the glory and luxury she gave herself.
In her heart she boasts,
'I sit as queen; I am not a widow,
and I will never mourn.'
8Therefore in one day her plagues will overtake her:
death, mourning and famine.
She will be consumed by fire,
for mighty is the Lord God who judges her.

9"When the kings of the earth who committed adultery with her
and shared her luxury see the smoke of her burning, they will
weep and mourn over her. 10Terrified at her torment, they will
stand far off and cry:

" 'Woe! Woe, O great city,
O Babylon, city of power!
In one hour your doom has come!'

11"The merchants of the earth will weep and mourn over her
because no one buys their cargoes any more— 12cargoes of gold,
silver, precious stones and pearls; fine linen, purple, silk and
scarlet cloth; every sort of citron wood, and articles of every kind
made of ivory, costly wood, bronze, iron and marble; 13cargoes of
cinnamon and spice, of incense, myrrh and frankincense, of wine
and olive oil, of fine flour and wheat; cattle and sheep; horses and
carriages; and bodies and souls of men.
14"They will say, 'The fruit you longed for is gone from you. All
your riches and splendor have vanished, never to be recovered.'
15The merchants who sold these things and gained their wealth
from her will stand far off, terrified at her torment. They will weep
and mourn 16and cry out:

**NIV** [b] 2 Greek *unclean*

## King James

16 And saying, Alas, alas, that great city, that was clothed in fine linen, and purple, and scarlet, and decked with gold, and precious stones, and pearls!

17 For in one hour so great riches is come to nought. And every shipmaster, and all the company in ships, and sailors, and as many as trade by sea, stood afar off,

18 And cried when they saw the smoke of her burning, saying, What *city is* like unto this great city!

19 And they cast dust on their heads, and cried, weeping and wailing, saying, Alas, alas, that great city, wherein were made rich all that had ships in the sea by reason of her costliness! for in one hour is she made desolate.

20 Rejoice over her, *thou* heaven, and *ye* holy apostles and prophets; for God hath avenged you on her.

21 And a mighty angel took up a stone like a great millstone, and cast *it* into the sea, saying, Thus with violence shall that great city Babylon be thrown down, and shall be found no more at all.

22 And the voice of harpers, and musicians, and of pipers, and trumpeters, shall be heard no more at all in thee; and no craftsman, of whatsoever craft *he be*, shall be found any more in thee; and the sound of a millstone shall be heard no more at all in thee;

23 And the light of a candle shall shine no more at all in thee; and the voice of the bridegroom and of the bride shall be heard no more at all in thee: for thy merchants were the great men of the earth; for by thy sorceries were all nations deceived.

24 And in her was found the blood of prophets, and of saints, and of all that were slain upon the earth.

**19** AND AFTER these things I heard a great voice of much people in heaven, saying, Alleluia; Salvation, and glory, and honour, and power, unto the Lord our God:

2 For true and righteous *are* his judgments: for he hath judged the great whore, which did corrupt the earth with her fornication, and hath avenged the blood of his servants at her hand.

3 And again they said, Alleluia. And her smoke rose up for ever and ever.

4 And the four and twenty elders and the four beasts fell down and worshipped God that sat on the throne, saying, Amen; Alleluia.

5 And a voice came out of the throne, saying, Praise our God, all ye his servants, and ye that fear him, both small and great.

6 And I heard as it were the voice of a great multitude, and as the voice of many waters, and as the voice of mighty thunderings, saying, Alleluia: for the Lord God omnipotent reigneth.

## Amplified

16 Alas, alas for the great city that was robed in fine linen, in purple and scarlet, bedecked *and* glittering with gold, with precious stones, and with pearls! [Ezek. 27:36, 31.]

17 Because in one [single] hour all the vast wealth has been destroyed—wiped out. And all ship captains *and* pilots, navigators and all who live by seafaring, the crews and all who ply their trade on the sea, stood a long way off, [Isa. 23:14; Ezek. 27:26-30.]

18 And exclaimed as they watched the smoke of her burning, What city could be compared to the great city!

19 And they threw dust on their heads, as they wept and grieved, exclaiming, Woe *and* alas, for the great city where all who had ships on the sea grew rich [through her extravagance] from her great wealth! In one single hour she has been destroyed *and* has become a desert! [Ezek. 27:30-34.]

20 Rejoice (celebrate) over her, O heaven! O saints (people of God) and apostles and prophets, because God has executed vengeance for you upon her! [Isa. 44:23; Jer. 51:48.]

21 Then a single powerful angel took up a boulder like a great millstone and flung it into the sea, crying, With such violence shall Babylon the great city be hurled down to destruction and shall never again be found. [Jer. 51:63, 64; Ezek. 26:21.]

22 And the sound of harpists and minstrels and flute players and trumpeters shall never again be heard in you, and no skilled artisan of any craft shall ever again be found in you, and the sound of the millstone shall never again be heard in you. [Isa. 24:8; Ezek. 26:13.]

23 And never again shall the light of a lamp shine in you, and the voice of bridegroom and bride shall never be heard in you again; for your businessmen were the great *and* prominent men of the earth, and by your magic spells *and* poisonous charm all nations were led astray—seduced and deluded.

24 And in her was found the blood of prophets and of saints, and of all those who have been slain (slaughtered) on earth. [Jer. 51:49.]

**19** AFTER THIS I heard what sounded like a mighty shout of a great crowd in heaven, exclaiming, Hallelujah—praise the Lord! Salvation and glory (splendor and majesty) and power (dominion and authority [belong]) to our God!

2 Because His judgments—His condemnation and punishment, His sentences of doom—are true *and* sound just *and* upright. He has judged—convicted, pronounced sentence and doomed the great *and* notorious harlot [idolatress] who corrupted *and* demoralized *and* poisoned the earth with her lewdness *and* adultery [idolatry]. And He has avenged—visited on her the penalty for—the blood of His servants at her hand. [Deut. 32:43.]

3 And again they shouted, Hallelujah—praise the Lord! The smoke of her [burning] shall continue to ascend forever and ever—through the eternities of the eternities. [Isa. 34:10.]

4 Then the tweny-four elders [of [a]the heavenly Sanhedrin] and the four living creatures fell prostrate and worshipped (paying divine honors to) God Who sits on the throne, saying, Amen! Hallelujah—praise the Lord!

5 Then from the throne there came a voice saying, Praise our God, all you servants of His, you who reverence Him, both small and great! [Ps. 115:13.]

6 After that I heard what sounded like the shout of a vast throng, like the boom of many pounding waves and like the roar of terrific *and* mighty thunderpeals, exclaiming, Hallelujah—praise the Lord! For now the Lord our God the Omnipotent—the All-Ruler—reigns!

**AMP** [a] Berry, and others.

## New American Standard

16saying, 'Woe, woe, the great city, she who was clothed in fine
linen and purple and scarlet, and adorned with gold and precious
stones and pearls;
17for in one hour such great wealth has been laid waste!' And
every shipmaster and every passenger and sailor, and as many as
make their living by the sea, stood at a distance,
18and were crying out as they saw the smoke of her burning,
saying, 'What *city* is like the great city?'
19"And they threw dust on their heads and were crying out,
weeping and mourning, saying, 'Woe, woe, the great city, in
which all who had ships at sea became rich by her wealth, for in
one hour she has been laid waste!'
20"Rejoice over her, O heaven, and you saints and apostles and
prophets, because God has pronounced judgment for you against
her."
21¶ And a strong angel took up a stone like a great millstone and
threw it into the sea, saying, "Thus will Babylon, the great city, be
thrown down with violence, and will not be found any longer.
22"And the sound of harpists and musicians and flute-players
and trumpeters will not be heard in you any longer; and no craftsman of any craft will be found in you any longer; and the sound
of a mill will not be heard in you any longer;
23and the light of a lamp will not shine in you any longer; and
the voice of the bridegroom and bride will not be heard in you any
longer; for your merchants were the great men of the earth, because all the nations were deceived by your sorcery.
24"And in her was found the blood of prophets and of saints
and of all who have been slain on the earth."

*The Fourfold Hallelujah*

**19** AFTER THESE things I heard, as it were, a loud voice of
a great multitude in heaven, saying,
¶ "Hallelujah! Salvation and glory and power belong to our
God;
2BECAUSE HIS JUDGMENTS ARE TRUE AND RIGHTEOUS; for He has
judged the great harlot who was corrupting the earth with her
immorality, and HE HAS AVENGED THE BLOOD OF HIS BOND-SER-
VANTS ON HER."
3And a second time they said, "Hallelujah! HER SMOKE RISES
UP FOREVER AND EVER."
4And the twenty-four elders and the four living creatures fell
down and worshiped God who sits on the throne saying, "Amen.
Hallelujah!"
5And a voice came from the throne, saying,
¶ "Give praise to our God, all you His bond-servants, you who
fear Him, the small and the great."
6And I heard, as it were, the voice of a great multitude and as
the sound of many waters and as the sound of mighty peals of
thunder, saying,
¶ "Hallelujah! For the Lord our God, the Almighty, reigns.

## New International

" 'Woe! Woe, O great city,
dressed in fine linen, purple and scarlet,
and glittering with gold, precious stones and pearls!
17In one hour such great wealth has been brought to ruin!'

"Every sea captain, and all who travel by ship, the sailors, and
all who earn their living from the sea, will stand far off. 18When
they see the smoke of her burning, they will exclaim, 'Was there
ever a city like this great city?' 19They will throw dust on their
heads, and with weeping and mourning cry out:

" 'Woe! Woe, O great city,
where all who had ships on the sea
became rich through her wealth!
In one hour she has been brought to ruin!
20Rejoice over her, O heaven!
Rejoice, saints and apostles and prophets!
God has judged her for the way she treated you.' "

21Then a mighty angel picked up a boulder the size of a large
millstone and threw it into the sea, and said:

"With such violence
the great city of Babylon will be thrown down,
never to be found again.
22The music of harpists and musicians, flute players and
trumpeters,
will never be heard in you again.
No workman of any trade
will ever be found in you again.
The sound of a millstone
will never be heard in you again.
23The light of a lamp
will never shine in you again.
The voice of bridegroom and bride
will never be heard in you again.
Your merchants were the world's great men.
By your magic spell all the nations were led astray.
24In her was found the blood of prophets and of the saints,
and of all who have been killed on the earth."

*Hallelujah!*

**19** AFTER THIS I heard what sounded like the roar of a great
multitude in heaven shouting:

"Hallelujah!
Salvation and glory and power belong to our God,
2 for true and just are his judgments.
He has condemned the great prostitute
who corrupted the earth by her adulteries.
He has avenged on her the blood of his servants."

3And again they shouted:

"Hallelujah!
The smoke from her goes up for ever and ever."

4The twenty-four elders and the four living creatures fell down
and worshiped God, who was seated on the throne. And they
cried:

"Amen, Hallelujah!"

5Then a voice came from the throne, saying:

"Praise our God,
all you his servants,
you who fear him,
both small and great!"

6Then I heard what sounded like a great multitude, like the roar
of rushing waters and like loud peals of thunder, shouting:

"Hallelujah!
For our Lord God Almighty reigns.

## King James

7Let us be glad and rejoice, and give honour to him: for the marriage of the Lamb is come, and his wife hath made herself ready.

8And to her was granted that she should be arrayed in fine linen, clean and white: for the fine linen is the righteousness of saints.

9And he saith unto me, Write, Blessed *are* they which are called unto the marriage supper of the Lamb. And he saith unto me, These are the true sayings of God.

10And I fell at his feet to worship him. And he said unto me, See *thou do it* not: I am thy fellowservant, and of thy brethren that have the testimony of Jesus: worship God: for the testimony of Jesus is the spirit of prophecy.

11And I saw heaven opened, and behold a white horse; and he that sat upon him *was* called Faithful and True, and in righteousness he doth judge and make war.

12His eyes *were* as a flame of fire, and on his head *were* many crowns; and he had a name written, that no man knew, but he himself.

13And he *was* clothed with a vesture dipped in blood: and his name is called The Word of God.

14And the armies *which were* in heaven followed him upon white horses, clothed in fine linen, white and clean.

15And out of his mouth goeth a sharp sword, that with it he should smite the nations: and he shall rule them with a rod of iron: and he treadeth the winepress of the fierceness and wrath of Almighty God.

16And he hath on *his* vesture and on his thigh a name written, KING OF KINGS, AND LORD OF LORDS.

17And I saw an angel standing in the sun; and he cried with a loud voice, saying to all the fowls that fly in the midst of heaven, Come and gather yourselves together unto the supper of the great God;

18That ye may eat the flesh of kings, and the flesh of captains, and the flesh of mighty men, and the flesh of horses, and of them that sit on them, and the flesh of all *men, both* free and bond, both small and great.

19And I saw the beast, and the kings of the earth, and their armies, gathered together to make war against him that sat on the horse, and against his army.

20And the beast was taken, and with him the false prophet that wrought miracles before him, with which he deceived them that had received the mark of the beast, and them that worshipped his image. These both were cast alive into a lake of fire burning with brimstone.

21And the remnant were slain with the sword of him that sat upon the horse, which *sword* proceeded out of his mouth: and all the fowls were filled with their flesh.

## Amplified

7Let us rejoice—and shout for joy—exulting *and* triumphant! Let us celebrate *and* ascribe to Him glory *and* honor, for the marriage of the Lamb [at last] has come and His bride has prepared herself. [Ps. 118:24.]

8She has been permitted to dress in fine (radiant) linen—dazzling and white, for the fine linen is (signifies, represents) the righteousness—the upright, just and godly living [deeds, conduct] and right standing with God—of the saints (God's holy people).

9Then [the angel] said to me, Write this down: Blessed—happy, [a]to be envied—are those who are summoned (invited, called) to the marriage supper of the Lamb. And he said to me [further], These are the true words—the genuine *and* exact declarations—of God.

10Then I fell prostrate at his feet to worship—to pay divine honors—to him, but he [restrained me] and said, Refrain!—You must not do that! I am [only] another servant with you and your brethren who have [accepted and hold] the testimony borne by Jesus. Worship God! For the substance (essence) of the truth revealed by Jesus is the spirit of all prophecy—the vital breath, the inspiration of all inspired preaching and interpretation of the divine will and purpose [including both mine and yours].

11After that I saw heaven opened, and behold, a white horse [appeared]! The One Who was riding it is called Faithful (trustworthy, loyal, incorruptible, steady) and True, and He passes judgment and wages war in righteousness—holiness, justice and uprightness. [Ezek. 1:1.]

12His eyes [blaze] like a flame of fire, and on His head are many kingly crowns (diadems); and He has a title (name) inscribed which He alone knows *or* can understand. [Dan. 10:6.]

13He is dressed in a robe dyed by [b]dipping in blood, and the title by which He is called is The Word of God.

14And the troops of heaven, clothed in fine linen, dazzling and clean, followed Him on white horses.

15From His mouth goes forth a sharp sword with which He can smite (afflict, strike) the nations, and He will shepherd *and* control them with a staff (scepter, rod) of iron. He will tread the wine press of the fierceness of the wrath *and* indignation of God the All-Ruler—the Almighty, the Omnipotent. [Ps. 2:9.]

16And on His garment (robe) and on His thigh He has a name (title) inscribed, KING OF KINGS AND LORD OF LORDS. [Deut. 10:17; Dan. 2:47.]

17Then I saw a single angel stationed in the sun's [c]light, and with a mighty voice he shouted to all the birds that fly across the sky, Come, gather yourselves together for the great supper of God, [Ezek. 39:4, 17-20.]

18That you may feast on the flesh of rulers, the flesh of generals *and* captains, the flesh of powerful *and* mighty men, the flesh of horses and their riders, and the flesh of all humanity, both free and slave, both small and great!

19Then I saw the beast and the rulers *and* leaders of the earth with their troops mustered to go into battle *and* make war against Him Who is mounted on the horse and against His troops.

20And the beast was seized *and* overpowered, and with him the false prophet who in his presence had worked wonders *and* performed miracles by which he led astray those who had accepted *or* permitted to be placed upon them the stamp (mark) of the beast, and those who paid homage *and* gave divine honors to his statue. Both of the two were hurled alive into the fiery lake that burns *and* blazes with brimstone.

21And the rest were killed with the sword that issues from the mouth of Him Who is mounted on the horse, and all the birds fed ravenously *and* glutted themselves with their flesh.

**AMP** [a] Souter. [b] Some ancient authorities read "sprinkled with blood." [c] Thayer, Berry, etc.

## New American Standard

*Marriage of the Lamb*

7"Let us rejoice and be glad and give the glory to Him, for the marriage of the Lamb has come and His bride has made herself ready."

8And it was given to her to clothe herself in fine linen, bright *and* clean; for the fine linen is the righteous acts of the saints.

9And he *said to me, "Write, 'Blessed are those who are invited to the marriage supper of the Lamb.' " And he *said to me, "These are true words of God."

10And I fell at his feet to worship him. And he *said to me, "Do not do that; I am a fellow servant of yours and your brethren who hold the testimony of Jesus; worship God. For the testimony of Jesus is the spirit of prophecy."

*The Coming of Christ*

11¶ And I saw heaven opened; and behold, a white horse, and He who sat upon it *is* called Faithful and True; and in righteousness He judges and wages war.

12And His eyes *are* a flame of fire, and upon His head *are* many diadems; and He has a name written *upon Him* which no one knows except Himself.

13And *He is* clothed with a robe dipped in blood; and His name is called The Word of God.

14And the armies which are in heaven, clothed in fine linen, white *and* clean, were following Him on white horses.

15And from His mouth comes a sharp sword, so that with it He may smite the nations; and He will rule them with a rod of iron; and He treads the wine press of the fierce wrath of God, the Almighty.

16And on His robe and on His thigh He has a name written, "KING OF KINGS, AND LORD OF LORDS."

17¶ And I saw an angel standing in the sun; and he cried out with a loud voice, saying to all the birds which fly in midheaven, "Come, assemble for the great supper of God;

18in order that you may eat the flesh of kings and the flesh of [d]commanders and the flesh of mighty men and the flesh of horses and of those who sit on them and the flesh of all men, both free men and slaves, and small and great."

19¶ And I saw the beast and the kings of the earth and their armies, assembled to make war against Him who sat upon the horse, and against His army.

*Doom of the Beast and False Prophet*

20And the beast was seized, and with him the false prophet who performed the signs in his presence, by which he deceived those who had received the mark of the beast and those who worshiped his image; these two were thrown alive into the lake of fire which burns with brimstone.

21And the rest were killed with the sword which came from the mouth of Him who sat upon the horse, and all the birds were filled with their flesh.

NAS [d] I.e., chiliarchs, in command of one thousand troops

## New International

7Let us rejoice and be glad
and give him glory!
For the wedding of the Lamb has come,
and his bride has made herself ready.
8Fine linen, bright and clean,
was given her to wear."
(Fine linen stands for the righteous acts of the saints.)

9Then the angel said to me, "Write: 'Blessed are those who are invited to the wedding supper of the Lamb!' " And he added, "These are the true words of God."

10At this I fell at his feet to worship him. But he said to me, "Do not do it! I am a fellow servant with you and with your brothers who hold to the testimony of Jesus. Worship God! For the testimony of Jesus is the spirit of prophecy."

*The Rider on the White Horse*

11I saw heaven standing open and there before me was a white horse, whose rider is called Faithful and True. With justice he judges and makes war.
12His eyes are like blazing fire, and on his head are many crowns. He has a name written on him that no one knows but he himself.
13He is dressed in a robe dipped in blood, and his name is the Word of God.
14The armies of heaven were following him, riding on white horses and dressed in fine linen, white and clean.
15Out of his mouth comes a sharp sword with which to strike down the nations. "He will rule them with an iron scepter."[e] He treads the winepress of the fury of the wrath of God Almighty.
16On his robe and on his thigh he has this name written:

KING OF KINGS AND LORD OF LORDS.

17And I saw an angel standing in the sun, who cried in a loud voice to all the birds flying in midair, "Come, gather together for the great supper of God,
18so that you may eat the flesh of kings, generals, and mighty men, of horses and their riders, and the flesh of all people, free and slave, small and great."

19Then I saw the beast and the kings of the earth and their armies gathered together to make war against the rider on the horse and his army.
20But the beast was captured, and with him the false prophet who had performed the miraculous signs on his behalf. With these signs he had deluded those who had received the mark of the beast and worshiped his image. The two of them were thrown alive into the fiery lake of burning sulfur.
21The rest of them were killed with the sword that came out of the mouth of the rider on the horse, and all the birds gorged themselves on their flesh.

NIV [e] *15* Psalm 2:9

## King James

**20** AND I saw an angel come down from heaven, having the key of the bottomless pit and a great chain in his hand.

2 And he laid hold on the dragon, that old serpent, which is the Devil, and Satan, and bound him a thousand years,

3 And cast him into the bottomless pit, and shut him up, and set a seal upon him, that he should deceive the nations no more, till the thousand years should be fulfilled: and after that he must be loosed a little season.

4 And I saw thrones, and they sat upon them, and judgment was given unto them: and *I saw* the souls of them that were beheaded for the witness of Jesus, and for the word of God, and which had not worshipped the beast, neither his image, neither had received *his* mark upon their foreheads, or in their hands; and they lived and reigned with Christ a thousand years.

5 But the rest of the dead lived not again until the thousand years were finished. This *is* the first resurrection.

6 Blessed and holy *is* he that hath part in the first resurrection: on such the second death hath no power, but they shall be priests of God and of Christ, and shall reign with him a thousand years.

7 And when the thousand years are expired, Satan shall be loosed out of his prison,

8 And shall go out to deceive the nations which are in the four quarters of the earth, Gog and Magog, to gather them together to battle: the number of whom *is* as the sand of the sea.

9 And they went up on the breadth of the earth, and compassed the camp of the saints about, and the beloved city: and fire came down from God out of heaven, and devoured them.

10 And the devil that deceived them was cast into the lake of fire and brimstone, where the beast and the false prophet *are*, and shall be tormented day and night for ever and ever.

11 And I saw a great white throne, and him that sat on it, from whose face the earth and the heaven fled away; and there was found no place for them.

12 And I saw the dead, small and great, stand before God; and the books were opened: and another book was opened, which is *the book* of life: and the dead were judged out of those things which were written in the books, according to their works.

13 And the sea gave up the dead which were in it; and death and hell delivered up the dead which were in them: and they were judged every man according to their works.

14 And death and hell were cast into the lake of fire. This is the second death.

15 And whosoever was not found written in the book of life was cast into the lake of fire.

## Amplified

**20** THEN I saw an angel descending from heaven; he was holding the key of the abyss—the bottomless pit—and a great chain was in his hand.

2 And he gripped *and* overpowered the dragon, that old serpent of primeval times, who is the devil and Satan, and [securely] bound him for a thousand years.

3 Then he hurled him into the abyss—the bottomless pit—and closed it and sealed it above him, so that he should no longer lead astray *and* deceive *and* seduce the nations until the thousand years were at an end. After that he must be liberated for a short time.

4 Then I saw thrones, and sitting on them were those to whom authority to act as judges *and* pass sentence was entrusted. Also I saw the souls of those who had been slain with axes (beheaded) for their witnessing to Jesus and [for preaching and testifying] for the Word of God, and who had refused to pay homage to the beast or his statue and had not accepted his mark *or* permitted it to be stamped on their foreheads or on their hands. And they lived again, and ruled with Christ, the Messiah, a thousand years. [Dan. 7:9, 22, 27.]

5 The remainder of the dead were not restored to life again until the thousand years were completed. This is the first resurrection.

6 Blessed (happy, [a]to be envied) and holy—spiritually whole, of unimpaired innocence and proved virtue—is the person who takes part (shares) in the first resurrection! Over them the second death exerts no power *or* authority, but they shall be ministers of God and of Christ, the Messiah, and they shall rule along with Him a thousand years.

7 And when the thousand years are completed, Satan will be released from his place of confinement,

8 And he will go forth to deceive *and* seduce *and* lead astray the nations which are in the four quarters of the earth, that is, Gog and Magog, to muster them for war; their number is as the sand of the sea. [Ezek. 38:2, 9, 15, 22.]

9 And they swarmed up over the broad plain of the earth and encircled the fortress (camp) of God's people (the saints) and the beloved city; but fire descended from heaven and consumed them. [II Kings 1:10-12; Ezek. 38:2, 22.]

10 Then the devil who had led them astray—deceiving and seducing them—was hurled into the fiery lake of burning brimstone where the beast and false prophet were; and they will be tormented day and night forever and ever—through the ages of the ages.

11 Then I saw a great white throne and the One Who was seated upon it, from Whose presence *and* from the sight of Whose face earth and sky fled away and no place was found for them.

12 I [also] saw the dead, great and small; they stood before the throne, and books were opened. Then another book was opened, which is [the Book] of Life. And the dead were judged (sentenced) by what they had done [ [b]their whole way of feeling and acting, their aims and endeavors] in accordance with what was recorded in the books.

13 And the sea delivered up the dead who were in it, Death and Hades [ [c]the state of death or disembodied existence] surrendered the dead in them; and all were tried *and* their cases determined by what they had done—according to their motives, aims and works.

14 Then death and Hades [ [d]the state of death or disembodied existence] were thrown into the lake of fire. This is the second death, the lake of fire.

15 And if any one's [name] was not found recorded in the Book of Life, he was hurled into the lake of fire.

## King James

**21** AND I saw a new heaven and a new earth: for the first heaven and the first earth were passed away; and there was no more sea.

## Amplified

**21** THEN I saw a new [e]sky (heaven) and a new earth; for the former [f]sky and the former earth had passed away (vanished), and there no longer existed any sea. [Isa. 65:17; 66:22.]

**AMP** [a] Souter. [b] Thayer. [c] "The International Bible Encyclopedia." [d] "The International Bible Encyclopedia." [e] Thayer. [f] Thayer.

## New American Standard

*Satan Bound*

**20** AND I saw an angel coming down from heaven, having
the key of the abyss and a great chain in his hand.
2And he laid hold of the dragon, the serpent of old, who is the
devil and Satan, and bound him for a thousand years,
3and threw him into the abyss, and shut *it* and sealed *it* over
him, so that he should not deceive the nations any longer, until
the thousand years were completed; after these things he must be
released for a short time.
4¶ And I saw thrones, and they sat upon them, and judgment
was given to them. And I *saw* the souls of those who had been
beheaded because of the testimony of Jesus and because of the
word of God, and those who had not worshiped the beast or his
image, and had not received the mark upon their forehead and
upon their hand; and they came to life and reigned with Christ for
a thousand years.
5The rest of the dead did not come to life until the thousand
years were completed. This is the first resurrection.
6Blessed and holy is the one who has a part in the first resurrection;
over these the second death has no power, but they will be
priests of God and of Christ and will reign with Him for a thousand
years.

*Satan Freed, Doomed*

7¶ And when the thousand years are completed, Satan will be
released from his prison,
8and will come out to deceive the nations which are in the four
corners of the earth, Gog and Magog, to gather them together for
the war; the number of them is like the sand of the seashore.
9And they came up on the broad plain of the earth and surrounded
the camp of the saints and the beloved city, and fire came
down from heaven and devoured them.
10And the devil who deceived them was thrown into the lake
of fire and brimstone, where the beast and the false prophet are
also; and they will be tormented day and night forever and ever.

*Judgment at the Throne of God*

11¶ And I saw a great white throne and Him who sat upon it,
from whose presence earth and heaven fled away, and no place
was found for them.
12And I saw the dead, the great and the small, standing before
the throne, and books were opened; and another book was
opened, which is *the book* of life; and the dead were judged from
the things which were written in the books, according to their
deeds.
13And the sea gave up the dead which were in it, and death and
Hades gave up the dead which were in them; and they were
judged, every one *of them* according to their deeds.
14And death and Hades were thrown into the lake of fire. This
is the second death, the lake of fire.
15And if anyone's name was not found written in the book of
life, he was thrown into the lake of fire.

*The New Heaven and Earth*

**21** AND I saw a new heaven and a new earth; for the first
heaven and the first earth passed away, and there is no
longer *any* sea.

## New International

*The Thousand Years*

**20** AND I saw an angel coming down out of heaven, having
the key to the Abyss and holding in his hand a great chain.
2He seized the dragon, that ancient serpent, who is the devil, or
Satan, and bound him for a thousand years. 3He threw him into
the Abyss, and locked and sealed it over him, to keep him from
deceiving the nations anymore until the thousand years were
ended. After that, he must be set free for a short time.
4I saw thrones on which were seated those who had been given
authority to judge. And I saw the souls of those who had been
beheaded because of their testimony for Jesus and because of the
word of God. They had not worshiped the beast or his image and
had not received his mark on their foreheads or their hands. They
came to life and reigned with Christ a thousand years. 5(The rest
of the dead did not come to life until the thousand years were
ended.) This is the first resurrection. 6Blessed and holy are those
who have part in the first resurrection. The second death has no
power over them, but they will be priests of God and of Christ and
will reign with him for a thousand years.

*Satan's Doom*

7When the thousand years are over, Satan will be released from
his prison 8and will go out to deceive the nations in the four
corners of the earth—Gog and Magog—to gather them for battle.
In number they are like the sand on the seashore. 9They marched
across the breadth of the earth and surrounded the camp of God's
people, the city he loves. But fire came down from heaven and
devoured them. 10And the devil, who deceived them, was thrown
into the lake of burning sulfur, where the beast and the false
prophet had been thrown. They will be tormented day and night
for ever and ever.

*The Dead Are Judged*

11Then I saw a great white throne and him who was seated on
it. Earth and sky fled from his presence, and there was no place
for them. 12And I saw the dead, great and small, standing before
the throne, and books were opened. Another book was opened,
which is the book of life. The dead were judged according to what
they had done as recorded in the books. 13The sea gave up the
dead that were in it, and death and Hades gave up the dead that
were in them, and each person was judged according to what he
had done. 14Then death and Hades were thrown into the lake of
fire. The lake of fire is the second death. 15If anyone's name was
not found written in the book of life, he was thrown into the lake
of fire.

*The New Jerusalem*

**21** THEN I saw a new heaven and a new earth, for the first
heaven and the first earth had passed away, and there was
no longer any sea. 2I saw the Holy City, the new Jerusalem, com-

## King James

2And I John saw the holy city, new Jerusalem, coming down from God out of heaven, prepared as a bride adorned for her husband.
3And I heard a great voice out of heaven saying, Behold, the tabernacle of God *is* with men, and he will dwell with them, and they shall be his people, and God himself shall be with them, *and be* their God.
4And God shall wipe away all tears from their eyes; and there shall be no more death, neither sorrow, nor crying, neither shall there be any more pain: for the former things are passed away.
5And he that sat upon the throne said, Behold, I make all things new. And he said unto me, Write: for these words are true and faithful.
6And he said unto me, It is done. I am Alpha and Omega, the beginning and the end. I will give unto him that is athirst of the fountain of the water of life freely.
7He that overcometh shall inherit all things; and I will be his God, and he shall be my son.
8But the fearful, and unbelieving, and the abominable, and murderers, and whoremongers, and sorcerers, and idolaters, and all liars, shall have their part in the lake which burneth with fire and brimstone: which is the second death.
9And there came unto me one of the seven angels which had the seven vials full of the seven last plagues, and talked with me, saying, Come hither, I will show thee the bride, the Lamb's wife.
10And he carried me away in the spirit to a great and high mountain, and showed me that great city, the holy Jerusalem, descending out of heaven from God,
11Having the glory of God: and her light *was* like unto a stone most precious, even like a jasper stone, clear as crystal;
12And had a wall great and high, *and* had twelve gates, and at the gates twelve angels, and names written thereon, which are *the names* of the twelve tribes of the children of Israel:
13On the east three gates; on the north three gates; on the south three gates; and on the west three gates.
14And the wall of the city had twelve foundations, and in them the names of the twelve apostles of the Lamb.
15And he that talked with me had a golden reed to measure the city, and the gates thereof, and the wall thereof.
16And the city lieth foursquare, and the length is as large as the breadth: and he measured the city with the reed, twelve thousand furlongs. The length and the breadth and the height of it are equal.
17And he measured the wall thereof, an hundred *and* forty *and* four cubits, *according to* the measure of a man, that is, of the angel.
18And the building of the wall of it was *of* jasper: and the city *was* pure gold, like unto clear glass.
19And the foundations of the wall of the city *were* garnished with all manner of precious stones. The first foundation *was* jasper; the second, sapphire; the third, a chalcedony; the fourth, an emerald;
20The fifth, sardonyx; the sixth, sardius; the seventh, chrysolite; the eighth, beryl; the ninth, a topaz; the tenth, a chrysoprasus; the eleventh, a jacinth; the twelfth, an amethyst.

## Amplified

2And I saw the holy city, the new Jerusalem, descending out of heaven from God, all arrayed like a bride beautified *and* adorned for her husband;
3Then I heard a mighty voice from the throne *and* I perceived its distinct words, saying, See! The abode of God is with men, and He will live (encamp, tent) among them, and they shall be His people and God shall personally be with them and be their God. [Ezek. 37:27.]
4God will wipe away every tear from their eyes, and death shall be no more, neither shall there be anguish—sorrow and mourning—nor grief nor pain any more; for the old conditions *and* the former order of things have passed away. [Isa. 25:8; 35:10.]
5And He Who is seated on the throne said, See! I make all things new. Also He said, Record this, for these sayings are faithful—accurate, incorruptible and trustworthy—and true (genuine). [Isa. 43:19.]
6And He [further] said to me, It is done! I am the Alpha and the Omega, the Beginning and the End. To the thirsty I [Myself] will give water without price from the fountain (springs) of the water of Life. [Isa. 55:1.]
7He who is victorious shall inherit all these things, and I will be God to him and he shall be My son.
8But as for the cowards *and* the ignoble *and* the contemptible *and* the cravenly lacking in courage *and* the cowardly submissive; and as for the unbelieving and faithless; and as for the depraved and defiled with abominations; and as for murderers and the lewd and adulterous and the practicers of magic arts and the idolaters [those who give supreme devotion to any one or anything other than God] and all liars [those who knowingly convey untruth by word or deed, all of these shall have] their part in the lake that blazes with fire and brimstone. This is the second death. [Isa. 30:33.]
9Then one of the seven angels who had the seven bowls filled with the seven final plagues (afflictions, calamities) came and spoke to me. He said, Come with me! I will show you the bride, the Lamb's wife.
10Then in the Spirit He conveyed me away to a vast and lofty mountain, and exhibited to me the holy (hallowed, consecrated) city of Jerusalem descending out of heaven from God, [Ezek. 40:2.]
11Clothed in God's glory—in all its splendor and radiance. The luster of it resembled a rare *and* most precious jewel, like jasper, shining clear as crystal.
12It had a massive and high wall with twelve [large] gates, and at the gates [there were stationed] twelve angels, and [on the gates] the names of the twelve tribes of the sons of Israel were written; [Ezek. 48:30-35; Exod. 28:21.]
13On the east side three gates, on the north side three gates, on the south side three gates, and on the west side three gates.
14And the wall of the city had twelve foundation [stones], and on them the twelve names of the twelve apostles of the Lamb.
15And he who spoke to me had a golden measuring reed (rod) to measure the city and its gates and its wall. [Ezek. 40:5.]
16The city lies in a square, its length being the same as its width. And he measured the city with his reed, twelve thousand stadia [about fifteen hundred miles]; its length and width and height are the same.
17He measured its wall also, one hundred and forty-four cubits (about seventy-two yards) by a man's measure [ [a]of a cubit from his elbow to his third finger tip] which is [the measure] of the angel.
18The wall was built of jasper, while the city [itself was of] pure gold, clear and transparent like glass.
19The foundation [stones] of the wall of the city were ornamented with all of the precious stones. The first foundation [stone] was jasper, the second sapphire, the third chalcedony (or white agate), the fourth emerald, [Isa. 54:11, 12.]
20The fifth onyx, the sixth sardius, the seventh chrysolite, the eighth beryl, the ninth topaz, the tenth chrysoprase, the eleventh jacinth, the twelfth amethyst.

**AMP** [a] Clarke's Commentary.

## New American Standard

2And I saw the holy city, new Jerusalem, coming down out of heaven from God, made ready as a bride adorned for her husband.

3And I heard a loud voice from the throne, saying, "Behold, the tabernacle of God is among men, and He shall dwell among them, and they shall be His people, and God Himself shall be among them,[b]

4and He shall wipe away every tear from their eyes; and there shall no longer be *any* death; there shall no longer be *any* mourning, or crying, or pain; the first things have passed away."

5And He who sits on the throne said, "Behold, I am making all things new." And He *said, "Write, for these words are faithful and true."

6And He said to me, "It is done. I am the Alpha and the Omega, the beginning and the end. I will give to the one who thirsts from the spring of the water of life without cost.

7"He who overcomes shall inherit these things, and I will be his God and he will be My son.

8"But for the cowardly and unbelieving and abominable and murderers and immoral persons and sorcerers and idolaters and all liars, their part *will be* in the lake that burns with fire and brimstone, which is the second death."

9¶ And one of the seven angels who had the seven bowls full of the seven last plagues, came and spoke with me, saying, "Come here, I shall show you the bride, the wife of the Lamb."

*The New Jerusalem*

10And he carried me away [c]in the Spirit to a great and high mountain, and showed me the holy city, Jerusalem, coming down out of heaven from God,

11having the glory of God. Her brilliance was like a very costly stone, as a stone of crystal-clear jasper.

12It had a great and high wall, with twelve gates, and at the gates twelve angels; and names *were* written on them, which are *those* of the twelve tribes of the sons of Israel.

13 *There were* three gates on the east and three gates on the north and three gates on the south and three gates on the west.

14And the wall of the city had twelve foundation stones, and on them *were* the twelve names of the twelve apostles of the Lamb.

15And the one who spoke with me had a gold measuring rod to measure the city, and its gates and its wall.

16And the city is laid out as a square, and its length is as great as the width; and he measured the city with the rod, [d]fifteen hundred miles; its length and width and height are equal.

17And he measured its wall, [e]seventy-two yards, *according to* human measurements, which are *also* angelic *measurements.*

18And the material of the wall was jasper; and the city was pure gold, like clear glass.

19The foundation stones of the city wall were adorned with every kind of precious stone. The first foundation stone was jasper; the second, sapphire; the third, chalcedony; the fourth, emerald;

20the fifth, sardonyx; the sixth, sardius; the seventh, chrysolite; the eighth, beryl; the ninth, topaz; the tenth, chrysoprase; the eleventh, jacinth; the twelfth, amethyst.

**NAS** [b] Some ancient mss. add, and be *their God* [c] Or, *in spirit* [d] Lit., *twelve thousand stadia;* a stadion was about 600 ft. [e] Lit., *one hundred forty-four cubits*

## New International

ing down out of heaven from God, prepared as a bride beautifully dressed for her husband. 3And I heard a loud voice from the throne saying, "Now the dwelling of God is with men, and he will live with them. They will be his people, and God himself will be with them and be their God. 4He will wipe every tear from their eyes. There will be no more death or mourning or crying or pain, for the old order of things has passed away."

5He who was seated on the throne said, "I am making everything new!" Then he said, "Write this down, for these words are trustworthy and true."

6He said to me: "It is done. I am the Alpha and the Omega, the Beginning and the End. To him who is thirsty I will give to drink without cost from the spring of the water of life. 7He who overcomes will inherit all this, and I will be his God and he will be my son. 8But the cowardly, the unbelieving, the vile, the murderers, the sexually immoral, those who practice magic arts, the idolaters and all liars—their place will be in the fiery lake of burning sulfur. This is the second death."

9One of the seven angels who had the seven bowls full of the seven last plagues came and said to me, "Come, I will show you the bride, the wife of the Lamb." 10And he carried me away in the Spirit to a mountain great and high, and showed me the Holy City, Jerusalem, coming down out of heaven from God. 11It shone with the glory of God, and its brilliance was like that of a very precious jewel, like a jasper, clear as crystal. 12It had a great, high wall with twelve gates, and with twelve angels at the gates. On the gates were written the names of the twelve tribes of Israel. 13There were three gates on the east, three on the north, three on the south and three on the west. 14The wall of the city had twelve foundations, and on them were the names of the twelve apostles of the Lamb.

15The angel who talked with me had a measuring rod of gold to measure the city, its gates and its walls. 16The city was laid out like a square, as long as it was wide. He measured the city with the rod and found it to be 12,000 stadia[f] in length, and as wide and high as it is long. 17He measured its wall and it was 144 cubits[g] thick,[h] by man's measurement, which the angel was using. 18The wall was made of jasper, and the city of pure gold, as pure as glass. 19The foundations of the city walls were decorated with every kind of precious stone. The first foundation was jasper, the second sapphire, the third chalcedony, the fourth emerald, 20the fifth sardonyx, the sixth carnelian, the seventh chrysolite, the eighth beryl, the ninth topaz, the tenth chrysoprase, the eleventh jacinth, and the twelfth amethyst.[i] 21The twelve gates were twelve pearls,

**NIV** [f] *16* That is, about 1,400 miles (about 2,200 kilometers) [g] *17* That is, about 200 feet (about 65 meters) [h] *17* Or *high* [i] *20* The precise identification of some of these precious stones is uncertain.

## King James

21 And the twelve gates *were* twelve pearls; every several gate was of one pearl: and the street of the city *was* pure gold, as it were transparent glass.

22 And I saw no temple therein: for the Lord God Almighty and the Lamb are the temple of it.

23 And the city had no need of the sun, neither of the moon, to shine in it: for the glory of God did lighten it, and the Lamb *is* the light thereof.

24 And the nations of them which are saved shall walk in the light of it: and the kings of the earth do bring their glory and honour into it.

25 And the gates of it shall not be shut at all by day: for there shall be no night there.

26 And they shall bring the glory and honour of the nations into it.

27 And there shall in no wise enter into it any thing that defileth, neither *whatsoever* worketh abomination, or *maketh* a lie: but they which are written in the Lamb's book of life.

**22** AND HE showed me a pure river of water of life, clear as crystal, proceeding out of the throne of God and of the Lamb.

2 In the midst of the street of it, and on either side of the river, *was there* the tree of life, which bare twelve *manner of* fruits, *and* yielded her fruit every month: and the leaves of the tree *were* for the healing of the nations.

3 And there shall be no more curse: but the throne of God and of the Lamb shall be in it; and his servants shall serve him:

4 And they shall see his face; and his name *shall be* in their foreheads.

5 And there shall be no night there; and they need no candle, neither light of the sun; for the Lord God giveth them light: and they shall reign for ever and ever.

6 And he said unto me, These sayings *are* faithful and true: and the Lord God of the holy prophets sent his angel to show unto his servants the things which must shortly be done.

7 Behold, I come quickly: blessed *is* he that keepeth the sayings of the prophecy of this book.

8 And I John saw these things, and heard *them.* And when I had heard and seen, I fell down to worship before the feet of the angel which showed me these things.

9 Then saith he unto me, See *thou do it* not: for I am thy fellowservant, and of thy brethren the prophets, and of them which keep the sayings of this book: worship God.

10 And he saith unto me, Seal not the sayings of the prophecy of this book: for the time is at hand.

11 He that is unjust, let him be unjust still: and he which is filthy, let him be filthy still: and he that is righteous, let him be righteous still: and he that is holy, let him be holy still.

12 And, behold, I come quickly; and my reward *is* with me, to give every man according as his work shall be.

13 I am Alpha and Omega, the beginning and the end, the first and the last.

## Amplified

21 And the twelve gates were twelve pearls, each separate gate being built of one solid pearl. And the main street (the broadway) of the city was of gold as pure *and* translucent as glass.

22 I saw no temple in the city, for the Lord God Omnipotent [Himself] and the Lamb [Himself] are its temple.

23 And the city has no need of the sun nor of the moon to give light to it, for the splendor *and* radiance (glory) of God illuminate it, and the Lamb is its lamp. [Isa. 24:23; 60:1, 19.]

24 The nations shall walk by its light and the rulers *and* leaders of the earth shall bring into it their glory.

25 And its gates shall never be closed by day, and there shall be no night there. [Isa. 60:11.]

26 They shall bring the glory—the splendor and majesty—and the honor of the nations into it.

27 But nothing that defiles *or* profanes *or* is [a]unwashed shall ever enter it, nor any one who commits abominations—that is, unclean, detestable, morally repugnant things—or practices falsehood, but only those whose names are recorded in the Lamb's Book of Life.

**22** THEN HE showed me the river whose waters give life, sparkling like crystal, flowing out from the throne of God and of the Lamb

2 Through the middle of the broad way of the city; also, on either side of the river, the tree of life with its twelve varieties of fruit, yielding each month its fresh crop; and the leaves of the tree were for the healing *and* the restoration of the nations. [Gen. 2:9.]

3 There shall no longer exist there anything that is accursed—detestable, foul, offensive, impure, hateful or horrible. But the throne of God and of the Lamb shall be in it, and His servants shall worship Him—pay divine honors to Him and do Him holy service. [Zech. 14:21.]

4 They shall see His face, and His name shall be on their foreheads. [Ps. 17:15.]

5 And there shall be no more night; they have no need for lamplight or sunlight, for the Lord God will illuminate them *and* be their light, and they shall reign (as kings) forever and ever—through the eternities of the eternities.

6 And he [of the seven angels further] said to me, These statements are reliable—worthy of confidence—and genuine (true). And the Lord, the God of the spirits of the prophets, has sent His messenger (angel) to make known *and* exhibit to His servants what must soon come to pass.

7 And behold, I am coming speedily. Blessed (happy and [b]to be envied) is he who observes *and* lays to heart *and* keeps the truths of the prophecy—the predictions, consolations and warnings—contained in this little book.

8 And I John am he who heard and witnessed these things. And when I heard and saw them, I fell prostrate before the feet of the messenger (angel) who showed them to me, to worship him.

9 But he said to me, Refrain!—You must not do that! I am [only] a fellow servant along with yourself and of your brethren the prophets, and of those who are mindful *and* practice [the truths contained in] the messages of this book. Worship God!

10 And he [further] told me, Do not seal up the words of the prophecy of this book *and* make no secret of them; for the time [c]when things are brought to a crisis *and* the period of their fulfillment is near.

11 He who is unrighteous (unjust, wicked) let him be unrighteous still, and he that is filthy (vile, impure) let him be filthy still, and he that is righteous (just, upright, in right standing with God) let him do right still, and he who is holy let him be holy still. [Dan. 12:10.]

12 Behold, I am coming soon, and I shall bring My wages *and* rewards with Me, to repay *and* render to each one just what his own actions *and* his own work merit. [Isa. 40:10; Jer. 17:10.]

13 I am the Alpha and the Omega, the First and the Last (the Before all and at the End of all). [Isa. 44:6; 48:12.]

**AMP** [a] Souter. [b] Souter. [c] Thayer.

## New American Standard

21And the twelve gates were twelve pearls; each one of the gates
was a single pearl. And the street of the city was pure gold, like
transparent glass.
22And I saw no temple in it, for the Lord God, the Almighty,
and the Lamb, are its temple.
23And the city has no need of the sun or of the moon to shine
upon it, for the glory of God has illumined it, and its lamp *is* the
Lamb.
24And the nations shall walk by its light, and the kings of the
earth shall bring their glory into it.
25And in the daytime (for there shall be no night there) its gates
shall never be closed;
26and they shall bring the glory and the honor of the nations
into it;
27and nothing unclean and no one who practices abomination
and lying, shall ever come into it, but only those whose names are
written in the Lamb's book of life.

*The River and the Tree of Life*

**22** AND HE showed me a river of the water of life, clear as
crystal, coming from the throne of God and of [d]the Lamb,
2in the middle of its street. And on either side of the river was
the tree of life, bearing twelve [e] *kinds of* fruit, yielding its fruit every
month; and the leaves of the tree were for the healing of the
nations.
3And there shall no longer be any curse; and the throne of God
and of the Lamb shall be in it, and His bond-servants shall serve
Him;
4and they shall see His face, and His name *shall be* on their
foreheads.
5And there shall no longer be *any* night; and they shall not have
need of the light of a lamp nor the light of the sun, because the
Lord God shall illumine them; and they shall reign forever and
ever.
6¶ And he said to me, "These words are faithful and true"; and
the Lord, the God of the spirits of the prophets, sent His angel to
show to His bond-servants the things which must shortly take
place.
7"And behold, I am coming quickly. Blessed is he who heeds
the words of the prophecy of this book."
8¶ And I, John, am the one who heard and saw these things.
And when I heard and saw, I fell down to worship at the feet of
the angel who showed me these things.
9And he *said to me, "Do not do that; I am a fellow servant of
yours and of your brethren the prophets and of those who heed
the words of this book; worship God."

*The Final Message*

**10**¶ And he *said to me, "Do not seal up the words of the
prophecy of this book, for the time is near.
11"Let the one who does wrong, still do wrong; and let the one
who is filthy, still be filthy; and let the one who is righteous, still
practice righteousness; and let the one who is holy, still keep
himself holy."
12"Behold, I am coming quickly, and My reward *is* with Me, to
render to every man according to what he has done.
13"I am the Alpha and the Omega, the first and the last, the
beginning and the end."

**NAS** [d] Or, *the Lamb. In the middle of its street, and on either side of the river, was*
[e] Or, crops of *fruit*

## New International

each gate made of a single pearl. The great street of the city was
of pure gold, like transparent glass.
22I did not see a temple in the city, because the Lord God
Almighty and the Lamb are its temple.
23The city does not need
the sun or the moon to shine on it, for the glory of God gives it
light, and the Lamb is its lamp.
24The nations will walk by its light,
and the kings of the earth will bring their splendor into it.
25On
no day will its gates ever be shut, for there will be no night there.
26The glory and honor of the nations will be brought into it.
27Nothing impure will ever enter it, nor will anyone who does
what is shameful or deceitful, but only those whose names are
written in the Lamb's book of life.

*The River of Life*

**22** THEN THE angel showed me the river of the water of life,
as clear as crystal, flowing from the throne of God and of
the Lamb
2down the middle of the great street of the city. On each
side of the river stood the tree of life, bearing twelve crops of fruit,
yielding its fruit every month. And the leaves of the tree are for
the healing of the nations.
3No longer will there be any curse. The
throne of God and of the Lamb will be in the city, and his servants
will serve him.
4They will see his face, and his name will be on their
foreheads.
5There will be no more night. They will not need the
light of a lamp or the light of the sun, for the Lord God will give
them light. And they will reign for ever and ever.
6The angel said to me, "These words are trustworthy and true.
The Lord, the God of the spirits of the prophets, sent his angel to
show his servants the things that must soon take place."

*Jesus Is Coming*

7"Behold, I am coming soon! Blessed is he who keeps the words
of the prophecy in this book."

8I, John, am the one who heard and saw these things. And
when I had heard and seen them, I fell down to worship at the feet
of the angel who had been showing them to me.
9But he said to
me, "Do not do it! I am a fellow servant with you and with your
brothers the prophets and of all who keep the words of this book.
Worship God!"
10Then he told me, "Do not seal up the words of the prophecy
of this book, because the time is near.
11Let him who does wrong
continue to do wrong; let him who is vile continue to be vile; let
him who does right continue to do right; and let him who is holy
continue to be holy."

12"Behold, I am coming soon! My reward is with me, and I will
give to everyone according to what he has done.
13I am the Alpha
and the Omega, the First and the Last, the Beginning and the End.

# King James

14Blessed *are* they that do his commandments, that they may
have right to the tree of life, and may enter in through the gates
into the city.
15For without *are* dogs, and sorcerers, and whoremongers, and
murderers, and idolaters, and whosoever loveth and maketh a lie.
16I Jesus have sent mine angel to testify unto you these things
in the churches. I am the root and the offspring of David, *and* the
bright and morning star.
17And the Spirit and the bride say, Come. And let him that
heareth say, Come. And let him that is athirst come. And whosoever will, let him take the water of life freely.
18For I testify unto every man that heareth the words of the
prophecy of this book, If any man shall add unto these things, God
shall add unto him the plagues that are written in this book:
19And if any man shall take away from the words of the book
of this prophecy, God shall take away his part out of the book of
life, and out of the holy city, and *from* the things which are written
in this book.
20He which testifieth these things saith, Surely I come quickly.
Amen. Even so, come, Lord Jesus.
21The grace of our Lord Jesus Christ *be* with you all. Amen.

# Amplified

14Blessed (happy and [a]to be envied) are those who cleanse their garments that they may have the authority *and* right to [approach] the tree of life and to enter in through the gates to the city. [Gen. 2:9; 3:22, 24.]
15[But] without are the dogs and those who practice sorceries (magic arts) and impurity (the lewd, adulterers) and the murderers and idolaters and every one who loves and deals in falsehood—untruth, error, deception, cheating.
16I, Jesus, have sent My messenger (angel) to you to witness *and* to give you assurance of these things for the churches (assemblies). I am [both] the Root (the Source) and the Offspring of David, the radiant *and* brilliant Morning Star. [Isa. 11:1, 10.]
17The (Holy) Spirit and the bride [the church, the true Christians] say, Come! And let him who is listening say, Come! And let every one come who is thirsty [who is painfully conscious of his need [b]of those things by which the soul is refreshed, supported and strengthened]; and whoever [earnestly] desires to do it, let him come and take *and* appropriate (drink) the Water of Life without cost. [Isa. 55:1.]
18I [personally solemnly] warn every one who listens to the statements of the prophecy [the [c]predictions and the consolations and admonitions pertaining to them] in this book: if any one shall add anything to them, God will add *and* lay upon him the plagues—the afflictions and the calamities—that are recorded *and* described in this book.
19And if any one cancels *or* takes away from the statements of the book of this prophecy—these [d]predictions relating to Christ's kingdom and its speedy triumph, together with the consolations and admonitions (warnings) pertaining to them—God will cancel *and* take away from him his share in the tree of life and in the city of holiness (pure and hallowed) which are described *and* promised in this book.
20He Who gives this warning *and* affirms *and* testifies to these things, says, Yes—it is true. [Surely] I am coming quickly—swiftly, speedily. Amen—so let it be! Yes, come, Lord Jesus!
21The grace (blessing and favor) of the Lord Jesus *Christ, the Messiah* be [e]with all the saints—God's holy people [ [f]those set apart for God, to be, as it were, exclusively His]. Amen—so let it be!

AMP [a] Souter. [b] Thayer. [c] Thayer. [d] Thayer. [e] Some authorities omit either "all" or "the saints." [f] Thayer.

## New American Standard

14Blessed are those who wash their robes, that they may have the right to the tree of life, and may enter by the gates into the city.
15Outside are the dogs and the sorcerers and the immoral persons and the murderers and the idolaters, and everyone who loves and practices lying.
**16**¶ "I, Jesus, have sent My angel to testify to you these things for the churches. I am the root and the offspring of David, the bright morning star."
**17**¶ And the Spirit and the bride say, "Come." And let the one who hears say, "Come." And let the one who is thirsty come; let the one who wishes take the water of life without cost.
**18**¶ I testify to everyone who hears the words of the prophecy of this book: if anyone adds to them, God shall add to him the plagues which are written in this book;
19and if anyone takes away from the words of the book of this prophecy, God shall take away his part from the tree of life and from the holy city, which are written in this book.
**20**¶ He who testifies to these things says, "Yes, I am coming quickly." Amen. Come, Lord Jesus.
**21**¶ The grace of the Lord Jesus be with [g]all. Amen.

## New International

14"Blessed are those who wash their robes, that they may have
the right to the tree of life and may go through the gates into the
city. 15Outside are the dogs, those who practice magic arts, the
sexually immoral, the murderers, the idolaters and everyone who
loves and practices falsehood.
16"I, Jesus, have sent my angel to give you[h] this testimony for the churches. I am the Root and the Offspring of David, and the bright Morning Star."

17The Spirit and the bride say, "Come!" And let him who hears say, "Come!" Whoever is thirsty, let him come; and whoever wishes, let him take the free gift of the water of life.

18I warn everyone who hears the words of the prophecy of this
book: If anyone adds anything to them, God will add to him the
plagues described in this book. 19And if anyone takes words away
from this book of prophecy, God will take away from him his share
in the tree of life and in the holy city, which are described in this
book.
20He who testifies to these things says, "Yes, I am coming soon."
Amen. Come, Lord Jesus.
21The grace of the Lord Jesus be with God's people. Amen.

NAS [g] Some ancient mss. read *the saints*

NIV [h] *16* The Greek is plural.